T0398832

UNITED STATES   OF AMERICA

Congressional Record

PROCEEDINGS AND DEBATES OF THE 114th CONGRESS

SECOND SESSION

VOLUME 162—PART 11

NOVEMBER 18, 2016 TO DECEMBER 5, 2016

(PAGES 14569 TO 15770)

UNITED STATES GOVERNMENT PUBLISHING OFFICE, WASHINGTON, 2016

Congressional Record

United States
of America

PROCEEDINGS AND DEBATES OF THE *114*th CONGRESS, SECOND SESSION

SENATE—*Friday, November 18, 2016*

The Senate met at 9:32 and 1 second a.m. and was called to order by the Honorable DAN SULLIVAN, a Senator from the State of Alaska.

APPOINTMENT OF ACTING PRESIDENT PRO TEMPORE

The PRESIDING OFFICER. The clerk will please read a communication to the Senate from the President pro tempore (Mr. HATCH).

The senior assistant legislative clerk read the following letter:

U.S. SENATE,
PRESIDENT PRO TEMPORE,
Washington, DC, November 18, 2016.
To the Senate:

Under the provisions of rule I, paragraph 3, of the Standing Rules of the Senate, I hereby appoint the Honorable DAN SULLIVAN, a Senator from the State of Alaska, to perform the duties of the Chair.

ORRIN G. HATCH,
President pro tempore.

Mr. SULLIVAN thereupon assumed the Chair as Acting President pro tempore.

ADJOURNMENT UNTIL TUESDAY, NOVEMBER 22, 2016, AT 11 A.M.

The ACTING PRESIDENT pro tempore. Under the previous order, the Senate stands adjourned until 11 a.m. on Tuesday, November 22, 2016.

Thereupon, the Senate, at 9:32 and 30 seconds a.m., adjourned until Tuesday, November 22, 2016, at 11 a.m.

● This "bullet" symbol identifies statements or insertions which are not spoken by a member of the Senate on the floor.

HOUSE OF REPRESENTATIVES—*Friday, November 18, 2016*

The House met at 3 p.m. and was called to order by the Speaker pro tempore (Mr. MESSER).

DESIGNATION OF THE SPEAKER PRO TEMPORE

The SPEAKER pro tempore laid before the House the following communication from the Speaker:

WASHINGTON, DC,
November 18, 2016.

I hereby appoint the Honorable LUKE MESSER to act as Speaker pro tempore on this day.

PAUL D. RYAN,
Speaker of the House of Representatives.

PRAYER

Reverend Vincent DeRosa, St. Joseph's Catholic Church, Washington, D.C., offered the following prayer:

Gracious God from whom all truth, rights, and authority descend, grant this House wisdom to perceive the common good, strong resolve to carry it out in the service of our citizens, prudence to do so justly, and love to do so with compassion and empathy for those most in need. We ask this in Your most holy name.

Amen.

THE JOURNAL

The SPEAKER pro tempore. Pursuant to section 3(a) of House Resolution 921, the Journal of the last day's proceedings is approved.

PLEDGE OF ALLEGIANCE

The SPEAKER pro tempore. The Chair will lead the House in the Pledge of Allegiance.

The SPEAKER pro tempore led the Pledge of Allegiance as follows:

I pledge allegiance to the Flag of the United States of America, and to the Republic for which it stands, one nation under God, indivisible, with liberty and justice for all.

ANNOUNCEMENT BY THE SPEAKER PRO TEMPORE

The SPEAKER pro tempore. Pursuant to clause 4 of rule I, the following enrolled bills were signed by the Speaker on Thursday, November 17, 2016:

H.R. 845, to direct the Secretary of Agriculture to publish in the Federal Register a strategy to significantly increase the role of volunteers and partners in National Forest System trail maintenance, and for other purposes;

H.R. 5392, to direct the Secretary of Veterans Affairs to improve the Veterans Crisis Line;

H.R. 6007, to amend title 49, United States Code, to include consideration of certain impacts on commercial space launch and reentry activities in a navigable airspace analysis, and for other purposes.

COMMUNICATION FROM THE CLERK OF THE HOUSE

The SPEAKER pro tempore laid before the House the following communication from the Clerk of the House of Representatives:

OFFICE OF THE CLERK,
HOUSE OF REPRESENTATIVES,
Washington, DC, November 18, 2016.
Hon. PAUL D. RYAN,
The Speaker, House of Representatives,
Washington, DC.

DEAR MR. SPEAKER: Pursuant to the permission granted in clause 2(h) of rule II of the Rules of the U.S. House of Representatives, the Clerk received the following message from the Secretary of the Senate on November 18, 2016 at 10:52 a.m.:

That the Senate concur in House amendments to text and title of the bill S. 2754.

That the Senate passed S. 3395.

That the Senate passed S. 434.

That the Senate passed without amendment H.R. 5873.

That the Senate passed without amendment H.R. 4902.

That the Senate passed with an amendment H.R. 3471.

With best wishes, I am

Sincerely,

KAREN L. HAAS.

SENATE BILLS REFERRED

Bills of the Senate of the following titles were taken from the Speaker's table and, under the rule, referred as follows:

S. 434. An act to strengthen the accountability of individuals involved in misconduct affecting the integrity of background investigations, to update guidelines for security clearances, to prevent conflicts of interest relating to contractors providing background investigation fieldwork services and investigative support services, and for other purposes; to the Committee on Oversight and Government Reform.

S. 3395. An act to require limitations on prescribing burns; to the Committee on Agriculture; in addition, to the Committee on Natural Resources for a period to be subsequently determined by the Speaker, in each case for consideration of such provisions as fall within the jurisdiction of the committee concerned.

ENROLLED BILLS SIGNED

Karen L. Haas, Clerk of the House, reported and found truly enrolled bills of the House of the following titles, which were thereupon signed by the Speaker:

H.R. 845. An act to direct the Secretary of Agriculture to publish in the Federal Register a strategy to significantly increase the role of volunteers and partners in National Forest System trail maintenance, and for other purposes.

H.R. 4902. An act to amend title 5, United States Code, to expand law enforcement availability pay to employees of U.S. Customs and Border Protection's Air and Marine Operations.

H.R. 5392. An act to direct the Secretary of Veterans Affairs to improve the Veterans Crisis Line.

H.R. 5873. An act to designate the Federal building and United States courthouse located at 511 East San Antonio Avenue in El Paso, Texas, as the "R.E. Thomason Federal Building and United States Courthouse".

H.R. 6007. An act to amend title 49, United States Code, to include consideration of certain impacts on commercial space launch and reentry activities in a navigable airspace analysis, and for other purposes.

SENATE ENROLLED BILL SIGNED

The Speaker announced his signature to an enrolled bill of the Senate of the following title:

S. 2754. An act to designate the Federal building and United States courthouse located at 300 Fannin Street in Shreveport, Louisiana, as the "Tom Stagg United States Court House."

BILLS PRESENTED TO THE PRESIDENT

Karen L. Haas, Clerk of the House, reported that on November 17, 2016, she presented to the President of the United States, for his approval, the following bill:

H.R. 4511. To amend the Veterans' Oral History Project Act to allow the collection of video and audio recordings of biographical histories by immediate family members of members of the Armed Forces who died as a result of their service during a period of war.

Karen L. Haas, Clerk of the House, further reported that on November 18, 2016, she presented to the President of the United States, for his approval, the following bills:

H.R. 845. To direct the Secretary of Agriculture to publish in the Federal Register a strategy to significantly increase the role of volunteers and partners in National Forest System trail maintenance, and for other purposes.

H.R. 5392. To direct the Secretary of Veterans Affairs to improve the Veterans Crisis Line.

H.R. 6007. To amend title 49, United States Code, to include consideration of certain impacts on commercial space launch and reentry activities in a navigable airspace analysis, and for other purposes.

☐ This symbol represents the time of day during the House proceedings, e.g., ☐1407 is 2:07 p.m.

Matter set in this typeface indicates words inserted or appended, rather than spoken, by a Member of the House on the floor.

ADJOURNMENT

The SPEAKER pro tempore. Pursuant to section 3(b) of House Resolution 921, the House stands adjourned until 2:30 p.m. on Tuesday, November 22, 2016.

Thereupon (at 3 o'clock and 3 minutes p.m.), under its previous order, the House adjourned until Tuesday, November 22, 2016, at 2:30 p.m.

OATH FOR ACCESS TO CLASSIFIED INFORMATION

Under clause 13 of rule XXIII, the following Members executed the oath for access to classified information:

Ralph Lee Abraham, Alma S. Adams, Robert B. Aderholt, Pete Aguilar, Rick W. Allen, Justin Amash, Mark E. Amodei, Brad Ashford, Brian Babin, Lou Barletta, Andy Barr, Joe Barton, Karen Bass, Joyce Beatty, Xavier Becerra, Dan Benishek, Ami Bera, Donald S. Beyer, Jr., Gus M. Bilirakis, Mike Bishop, Rob Bishop, Sanford D. Bishop, Jr., Diane Black, Marsha Blackburn, Rod Blum, Earl Blumenauer, John A. Boehner*, Suzanne Bonamici, Madeleine Z. Bordallo, Mike Bost, Charles W. Boustany, Jr., Brendan F. Boyle, Kevin Brady, Robert A. Brady, Dave Brat, Jim Bridenstine, Mo Brooks, Susan W. Brooks, Corrine Brown, Julia Brownley, Vern Buchanan, Ken Buck, Larry Bucshon, Michael C. Burgess, Cheri Bustos, G. K. Butterfield, Bradley Byrne, Ken Calvert, Lois Capps, Michael E. Capuano, Tony Cárdenas, John C. Carney, Jr., André Carson, Earl L. "Buddy" Carter, John R. Carter, Matt Cartwright, Kathy Castor, Joaquin Castro, Steve Chabot, Jason Chaffetz, Judy Chu, David N. Cicilline, Katherine M. Clark, Yvette D. Clarke, Curt Clawson, Wm. Lacy Clay, Emanuel Cleaver, James E. Clyburn, Mike Coffman, Steve Cohen, Tom Cole, Chris Collins, Doug Collins, James Comer, Barbara Comstock, K. Michael Conaway, Gerald E. Connolly, John Conyers, Jr., Paul Cook, Jim Cooper, Jim Costa, Ryan A. Costello, Joe Courtney, Kevin Cramer, Eric A. "Rick" Crawford, Ander Crenshaw, Joseph Crowley, Henry Cuellar, John Abney Culberson, Elijah E. Cummings, Carlos Curbelo, Warren Davidson, Danny K. Davis, Rodney Davis, Susan A. Davis, Peter A. DeFazio, Diana DeGette, John K. Delaney, Rosa L. DeLauro, Suzan K. DelBene, Jeff Denham, Charles W. Dent, Ron DeSantis, Mark DeSaulnier, Scott DesJarlais, Theodore E. Deutch, Mario Diaz-Balart, Debbie Dingell, Lloyd Doggett, Robert J. Dold, Daniel M. Donovan, Jr., Michael F. Doyle, Tammy Duckworth, Sean P. Duffy, Jeff Duncan, John J. Duncan, Jr.

Donna F. Edwards, Keith Ellison, Renee L. Ellmers, Tom Emmer, Eliot L. Engel, Anna G. Eshoo, Elizabeth H. Esty, Dwight Evans, Blake Farenthold, Sam Farr, Chaka Fattah*, Stephen Lee Fincher, Michael G. Fitzpatrick, Charles J. "Chuck" Fleischmann, John Fleming, Bill Flores, J. Randy Forbes, Jeff Fortenberry, Bill Foster, Virginia Foxx, Lois Frankel, Trent Franks, Rodney P. Frelinghuysen, Marcia L. Fudge, Tulsi Gabbard, Ruben Gallego, John Garamendi, Scott Garrett, Bob Gibbs, Christopher P. Gibson, Louie Gohmert, Bob Goodlatte, Paul A. Gosar, Trey Gowdy, Gwen Graham, Kay Granger, Garret Graves, Sam Graves, Tom Graves, Alan Grayson, Al Green, Gene Green, H. Morgan Griffith, Raúl M. Grijalva, Glenn Grothman, Frank C.

Guinta, Brett Guthrie, Luis V. Gutiérrez, Janice Hahn, Colleen Hanabusa, Richard L. Hanna, Cresent Hardy, Gregg Harper, Andy Harris, Vicky Hartzler, Alcee L. Hastings, Denny Heck, Joseph J. Heck, Jeb Hensarling, Jaime Herrera Beutler, Jody B. Hice, Brian Higgins, J. French Hill, James A. Himes, Rubén Hinojosa, George Holding, Michael M. Honda, Steny H. Hoyer, Richard Hudson, Tim Huelskamp, Jared Huffman, Bill Huizenga, Randy Hultgren, Duncan Hunter, Will Hurd, Robert Hurt, Steve Israel, Darrell E. Issa, Sheila Jackson Lee, Hakeem S. Jeffries, Evan H. Jenkins, Lynn Jenkins, Bill Johnson, Eddie Bernice Johnson, Henry C. "Hank" Johnson, Jr., Sam Johnson, David W. Jolly, Walter B. Jones, Jim Jordan, David P. Joyce, Marcy Kaptur, John Katko, William R. Keating, Mike Kelly, Robin L. Kelly, Trent Kelly, Joseph P. Kennedy III, Daniel T. Kildee, Derek Kilmer, Ron Kind, Peter T. King, Steve King, Adam Kinzinger, Ann Kirkpatrick, John Kline, Stephen Knight, Ann M. Kuster.

Raúl R. Labrador, Darin LaHood, Doug LaMalfa, Doug Lamborn, Leonard Lance, James R. Langevin, Rick Larsen, John B. Larson, Robert E. Latta, Brenda L. Lawrence, Barbara Lee, Sander M. Levin, John Lewis, Ted Lieu, Daniel Lipinski, Frank A. LoBiondo, David Loebsack, Zoe Lofgren, Billy Long, Barry Loudermilk, Mia B. Love, Alan S. Lowenthal, Nita M. Lowey, Frank D. Lucas, Blaine Luetkemeyer, Ben Ray Luján, Michelle Lujan Grisham, Cynthia M. Lummis, Stephen F. Lynch, Thomas MacArthur, Carolyn B. Maloney, Sean Patrick Maloney, Kenny Marchant, Tom Marino, Thomas Massie, Doris O. Matsui, Kevin McCarthy, Michael T. McCaul, Tom McClintock, Betty McCollum, James P. McGovern, Patrick T. McHenry, David B. McKinley, Cathy McMorris Rodgers, Jerry McNerney, Martha McSally, Mark Meadows, Patrick Meehan, Gregory W. Meeks, Grace Meng, Luke Messer, John L. Mica, Candice S. Miller, Jeff Miller, John R. Moolenaar, Alexander X. Mooney, Gwen Moore, Seth Moulton, Markwayne Mullin, Mick Mulvaney, Patrick Murphy, Tim Murphy, Jerrold Nadler, Grace F. Napolitano, Richard E. Neal, Randy Neugebauer, Dan Newhouse, Kristi L. Noem, Richard M. Nolan, Donald Norcross, Eleanor Holmes Norton, Richard B. Nugent, Devin Nunes, Alan Nunnelee*, Pete Olson, Beto O'Rourke, Steven M. Palazzo, Frank Pallone, Jr., Gary J. Palmer, Bill Pascrell, Jr., Erik Paulsen, Donald M. Payne, Jr., Stevan Pearce, Nancy Pelosi, Ed Perlmutter, Scott Perry, Scott H. Peters, Collin C. Peterson, Pedro R. Pierluisi, Chellie Pingree, Robert Pittenger, Joseph R. Pitts, Stacey E. Plaskett, Mark Pocan, Ted Poe, Bruce Poliquin, Jared Polis, Mike Pompeo, Bill Posey, David E. Price, Tom Price.

Mike Quigley, Amata Coleman Radewagen, Charles B. Rangel, John Ratcliffe, Tom Reed, David G. Reichert, James B. Renacci, Reid J. Ribble, Kathleen M. Rice, Tom Rice, Cedric L. Richmond, E. Scott Rigell, Martha Roby, David P. Roe, Harold Rogers, Mike Rogers, Dana Rohrabacher, Todd Rokita, Thomas J. Rooney, Peter J. Roskam, Ileana Ros-Lehtinen, Dennis A. Ross, Keith J. Rothfus, David Rouzer, Lucille Roybal-Allard, Edward R. Royce, Raul Ruiz, C. A. Dutch Ruppersberger, Bobby L. Rush, Steve Russell, Paul Ryan, Tim Ryan, Gregorio Kilili Camacho Sablan, Matt Salmon, Linda T. Sánchez, Loretta Sanchez, Mark Sanford, John P. Sarbanes, Steve Scalise, Janice D. Schakowsky, Adam B. Schiff, Aaron Schock*, Kurt Schrader, David Schweikert, Austin Scott, David Scott, Robert C. "Bobby" Scott, F. James

Sensenbrenner, Jr., José E. Serrano, Pete Sessions, Terri A. Sewell, Brad Sherman, John Shimkus, Bill Shuster, Michael K. Simpson, Kyrsten Sinema, Albio Sires, Louise McIntosh Slaughter, Adam Smith, Adrian Smith, Christopher H. Smith, Jason Smith, Lamar Smith, Jackie Speier, Elise M. Stefanik, Chris Stewart, Steve Stivers, Marlin A. Stutzman, Eric Swalwell.

Mark Takai*, Mark Takano, Bennie G. Thompson, Glenn Thompson, Mike Thompson, Mac Thornberry, Patrick J. Tiberi, Scott R. Tipton, Dina Titus, Paul Tonko, Norma J. Torres, David A. Trott, Niki Tsongas, Michael R. Turner, Fred Upton, David G. Valadao, Chris Van Hollen, Juan Vargas, Marc A. Veasey, Filemon Vela, Nydia M. Velázquez, Peter J. Visclosky, Ann Wagner, Tim Walberg, Greg Walden, Mark Walker, Jackie Walorski, Mimi Walters, Timothy J. Walz, Debbie Wasserman Schultz, Maxine Waters, Bonnie Watson Coleman, Randy K. Weber, Sr., Daniel Webster, Peter Welch, Brad R. Wenstrup, Bruce Westerman, Lynn A. Westmoreland, Ed Whitfield*, Roger Williams, Frederica S. Wilson, Joe Wilson, Robert J. Wittman, Steve Womack, Rob Woodall, John A. Yarmuth, Kevin Yoder, Ted S. Yoho, David Young, Don Young, Todd C. Young, Lee M. Zeldin, Ryan K. Zinke.

EXECUTIVE COMMUNICATIONS, ETC.

Under clause 2 of rule XIV, executive communications were taken from the Speaker's table and referred as follows:

7513. A letter from the Assistant General Counsel for Legislation, Regulation and Energy Efficiency, Office of Energy Efficiency and Renewable Energy, Department of Energy, transmitting the Department's final rule — Energy Conservation Program for Consumer Products and Certain Commercial and Industrial Equipment: Final Determination of Compressors as Covered Equipment [Docket No.: EERE-2012-BT-DET-0033] (RIN: 1904-AC83) received November 15, 2016, pursuant to 5 U.S.C. 801(a)(1)(A); Public Law 104-121, Sec. 251; (110 Stat. 868); to the Committee on Energy and Commerce.

7514. A letter from the Director, Regulatory Management Division, Environmental Protection Agency, transmitting the Agency's final rule — Trifloxystrobin; Pesticide Tolerances [EPA-HQ-OPP-2015-0745; FRL-9954-04] received November 9, 2016, pursuant to 5 U.S.C. 801(a)(1)(A); Public Law 104-121, Sec. 251; (110 Stat. 868); to the Committee on Energy and Commerce.

7515. A letter from the Director, Regulatory Management Division, Environmental Protection Agency, transmitting the Agency's direct final rule — Significant New Use Rules on Certain Chemical Substances [EPA-HQ-OPPT-2016-0207; FRL-9953-41] (RIN: 2070-AB27) received November 9, 2016, pursuant to 5 U.S.C. 801(a)(1)(A); Public Law 104-121, Sec. 251; (110 Stat. 868); to the Committee on Energy and Commerce.

7516. A letter from the Director, Regulatory Management Division, Environmental Protection Agency, transmitting the Agency's final rule — Promulgation of Air Quality Implementation Plans; Arizona; Regional Haze Federal Implementation Plan; Reconsideration [EPA-R09-OAR-2015-0846; FRL-9955-17-Region 9] received November 9, 2016, pursuant to 5 U.S.C. 801(a)(1)(A); Public Law 104-121, Sec. 251; (110 Stat. 868); to the Committee on Energy and Commerce.

7517. A letter from the Director, Regulatory Management Division, Environmental

Protection Agency, transmitting the Agency's final rule — Prothioconazole; Pesticide Tolerances [EPA-HQ-OPP-2015-0722; FRL-9953-71) received November 9, 2016, pursuant to 5 U.S.C. 801(a)(1)(A); Public Law 104-121, Sec. 251; (110 Stat. 868); to the Committee on Energy and Commerce.

7518. A letter from the Director, Regulatory Management Division, Environmental Protection Agency, transmitting the Agency's final rule — Iron oxide yellow; Exemption from the Requirement of a Tolerance [EPA-HQ-OPP-2016-0159; FRL-9953-21] received November 9, 2016, pursuant to 5 U.S.C. 801(a)(1)(A); Public Law 104-121, Sec. 251; (110 Stat. 868); to the Committee on Energy and Commerce.

7519. A letter from the Director, Regulatory Management Division, Environmental Protection Agency, transmitting the Agency's final rule — Di-n-butyl Adipate; Exemption from the Requirement of a Tolerance [EPA-HQ-OPP-2015-0631; FRL-9954-58] received November 9, 2016, pursuant to 5 U.S.C. 801(a)(1)(A); Public Law 104-121, Sec. 251; (110 Stat. 868); to the Committee on Energy and Commerce.

7520. A letter from the Director, Regulatory Management Division, Environmental Protection Agency, transmitting the Agency's final rule — Clomazone; Pesticide Tolerances [EPA-HQ-OPP-2015-0712; FRL-9953-88] received November 9, 2016, pursuant to 5 U.S.C. 801(a)(1)(A); Public Law 104-121, Sec. 251; (110 Stat. 868); to the Committee on Energy and Commerce.

7521. A letter from the Director, Regulatory Management Division, Environmental Protection Agency, transmitting the Agency's final rule — Approval and Promulgation of Implementation Plans: Texas; Approval of Substitution for Transportation Control Measures [EPA-R06-OAR-2016-0329; FRL-9954-36-Region 6] received November 9, 2016, pursuant to 5 U.S.C. 801(a)(1)(A); Public Law 104-121, Sec. 251; (110 Stat. 868); to the Committee on Energy and Commerce.

7522. A letter from the Director, Regulatory Management Division, Environmental Protection Agency, transmitting the Agency's final rule — 2-Pyrrolidinone, 1-butyl-; Exemption from the Requirement of a Tolerance [EPA-HQ-OPP-2015-0655; FRL-9953-82] received November 9, 2016, pursuant to 5 U.S.C. 801(a)(1)(A); Public Law 104-121, Sec. 251; (110 Stat. 868); to the Committee on Energy and Commerce.

7523. A letter from the Deputy Bureau Chief, Public Safety and Homeland Security Bureau, Federal Communications Commission, transmitting the Commission's final rule — Wireless Emergency Alerts [PS Docket No.: 15-91]; Amendments to Part 11 of the Commission's Rules Regarding the Emergency Alert System [PS Docket No.: 15-94] received November 15, 2016, pursuant to 5 U.S.C. 801(a)(1)(A); Public Law 104-121, Sec. 251; (110 Stat. 868); to the Committee on Energy and Commerce.

7524. A letter from the Assistant Secretary for Export Administration, Bureau of Industry and Security, Department of Commerce, transmitting the Department's final rule — Amendments to the Export Administration Regulations: Update of Arms Embargoes on Cote d'Ivoire, Liberia, Sri Lanka and Vietnam, and Recognition of India as Member of the Missile Technology Control Regime [Docket No.: 160810723-6723-01] (RIN: 0694-AH07) received November 15, 2016, pursuant to 5 U.S.C. 801(a)(1)(A); Public Law 104-121, Sec. 251; (110 Stat. 868); to the Committee on Foreign Affairs.

7525. A letter from the Assistant Secretary, Legislative Affairs, Department of State,

transmitting the Department's final rule — Amendment to the International Traffic in Arms Regulations: Revision of U.S. Munitions List Categories VIII and XIX [Public Notice: 9604] (RIN: 1400-AD89) received November 15, 2016, pursuant to 5 U.S.C. 801(a)(1)(A); Public Law 104-121, Sec. 251; (110 Stat. 868); to the Committee on Foreign Affairs.

7526. A letter from the Acting Chief, Unified Listing Team, Fish and Wildlife Service, Department of the Interior, transmitting the Department's final rule — Endangered and Threatened Wildlife and Plants; Adding Ten Species and Updating Five Species on the List of Endangered and Threatened Wildlife [Docket No.: FWS-HQ-ES-2016-0109; 4500030113] (RIN: 1018-BB82) received November 15, 2016, pursuant to 5 U.S.C. 801(a)(1)(A); Public Law 104-121, Sec. 251; (110 Stat. 868); to the Committee on Natural Resources.

7527. A letter from the Chief, Branch of Recovery and State Grants, Fish and Wildlife Service, Department of the Interior, transmitting the Department's final rule — Endangered and Threatened Wildlife and Plants; Removal of Solidago albopilosa (White-haired Goldenrod) From the Federal List of Endangered and Threatened Plants [Docket No. FWS-R4-ES-2014-0054; FXES11130900000 167 FF09E42000] (RIN: 1018-BA46) received November 15, 2016, pursuant to 5 U.S.C. 801(a)(1)(A); Public Law 104-121, Sec. 251; (110 Stat. 868); to the Committee on Natural Resources.

7528. A letter from the Chief, Branch of Recovery and State Grants, Fish and Wildlife Service, Department of the Interior, transmitting the Department's final rule — Endangered and Threatened Wildlife and Plants; Reclassifying the Columbia River District Population Segment of the Columbian White-Tailed Deer as Threatened With a Rule Under Section 4(d) of the Act [Docket No.: FWS-R1-ES-2014-0045; FXES11130900000C6-167-FF09E42000] (RIN: 1018-BA30) received November 15, 2016, pursuant to 5 U.S.C. 801(a)(1)(A); Public Law 104-121, Sec. 251; (110 Stat. 868); to the Committee on Natural Resources.

7529. A letter from the Conservation Policy Specialist, Fish and Wildlife Service, Department of the Interior, transmitting the Department's final rule — Management of Non-Federal Oil and Gas Rights [Docket No.: FWS-HQ-NWRS-2012-0086; FXRS12610900000-156-FF09R24000] (RIN: 1018-AX36) received November 15, 2016, pursuant to 5 U.S.C. 801(a)(1)(A); Public Law 104-121, Sec. 251; (110 Stat. 868); to the Committee on Natural Resources.

7530. A letter from the Acting Director, Office of Sustainable Fisheries, NMFS, GAR, National Oceanic and Atmospheric Administration, transmitting the Administration's temporary rule — Fisheries of the Northeastern United States; Atlantic Bluefish Fishery; Quota Transfer [Docket No.: 151130999-6225-01] (RIN: 0648-XE895) received November 16, 2016, pursuant to 5 U.S.C. 801(a)(1)(A); Public Law 104-121, Sec. 251; (110 Stat. 868); to the Committee on Natural Resources.

7531. A letter from the Acting Director, Office of Sustainable Fisheries, NMFS, GARFO, National Oceanic and Atmospheric Administration, transmitting the Administration's temporary rule — Fisheries of the Northeastern United States; Northeast Multispecies Fishery; Gulf of Maine Cod Trimester Total Allowable Catch Area Closure for the Common Pool Fishery [Docket No.: 151211999-6343-02] (RIN: 0648-XE811) received November 16, 2016, pursuant to 5 U.S.C.

801(a)(1)(A); Public Law 104-121, Sec. 251; (110 Stat. 868); to the Committee on Natural Resources.

7532. A letter from the Director, Office of Sustainable Fisheries, NMFS, National Oceanic and Atmospheric Administration, transmitting the Administration's temporary rule — Fisheries of the Exclusive Economic Zone Off Alaska; Deep-Water Species Fishery by Vessels Using Trawl Gear in the Gulf of Alaska [Docket No.: 150818742-6210-02] (RIN: 0648-XE822) received November 16, 2016, pursuant to 5 U.S.C. 801(a)(1)(A); Public Law 104-121, Sec. 251; (110 Stat. 868); to the Committee on Natural Resources.

7533. A letter from the Director, Office of Sustainable Fisheries, NMFS, National Oceanic and Atmospheric Administration, transmitting the Administration's temporary rule — Fisheries of the Exclusive Economic Zone Off Alaska; Pacific Cod in the Bering Sea and Aleutian Islands Management Area [Docket No.: 150916863-6211-02] (RIN: 0648-XE828) received November 16, 2016, pursuant to 5 U.S.C. 801(a)(1)(A); Public Law 104-121, Sec. 251; (110 Stat. 868); to the Committee on Natural Resources.

7534. A letter from the Acting Director, Office of Sustainable Fisheries, NMFS, National Oceanic and Atmospheric Administration, transmitting the Administration's temporary rule — Fisheries of the Exclusive Economic Zone Off Alaska; Exchange of Flatfish in the Bering Sea and Aleutian Islands Management Area [Docket No.: 150916863-6211-02] (RIN: 0648-XE745) received November 16, 2016, pursuant to 5 U.S.C. 801(a)(1)(A); Public Law 104-121, Sec. 251; (110 Stat. 868); to the Committee on Natural Resources.

7535. A letter from the Director, Office of Sustainable Fisheries, NMFS, National Oceanic and Atmospheric Administration, transmitting the Administration's temporary rule — Fisheries of the Exclusive Economic Zone Off Alaska; Reallocation of Pacific Cod in the Bering Sea and Aleutian Islands Management Area [Docket No.: 150916863-6211-02] (RIN: 0648-XE827) received November 16, 2016, pursuant to 5 U.S.C. 801(a)(1)(A); Public Law 104-121, Sec. 251; (110 Stat. 868); to the Committee on Natural Resources.

7536. A letter from the Acting Director, Office of Sustainable Fisheries, NMFS, National Oceanic and Atmospheric Administration, transmitting the Administration's temporary rule — Atlantic Highly Migratory Species; Atlantic Bluefin Tuna Fisheries [Docket No.: 150121066-5717-02] (RIN: 0648-XE820) received November 16, 2016, pursuant to 5 U.S.C. 801(a)(1)(A); Public Law 104-121, Sec. 251; (110 Stat. 868); to the Committee on Natural Resources.

7537. A letter from the Acting Director, Office of Sustainable Fisheries, NMFS, National Oceanic and Atmospheric Administration, transmitting the Administration's temporary rule — Fisheries of the Economic Exclusive Zone Off Alaska; Deep-Water Species Fishery by Vessels Using Trawl Gear in the Gulf of Alaska [Docket No.: 150818742-6210-02] (RIN: 0648-XE835) received November 16, 2016, pursuant to 5 U.S.C. 801(a)(1)(A); Public Law 104-121, Sec. 251; (110 Stat. 868); to the Committee on Natural Resources.

7538. A letter from the Acting Director, Office of Sustainable Fisheries, NMFS, National Oceanic and Atmospheric Administration, transmitting the Administration's temporary rule — Snapper-Grouper Fishery of the South Atlantic; 2016 Recreational Accountability Measure and Closure for the South Atlantic Other Porgies Complex [Docket No.: 120815345-3525-02] (RIN: 0648-XE831) received November 16, 2016, pursuant to 5 U.S.C. 801(a)(1)(A); Public Law 104-121, Sec. 251; (110 Stat. 868); to the Committee on Natural Resources.

7539. A letter from the Acting Director, Office of Sustainable Fisheries, NMFS, National Oceanic and Atmospheric Administration, transmitting the Administration's temporary rule — Atlantic Highly Migratory Species; Atlantic Bluefin Tuna Fisheries [Docket No.: 150121066-5717-02] (RIN: 0648-XE963) received November 16, 2016, pursuant to 5 U.S.C. 801(a)(1)(A); Public Law 104-121, Sec. 251; (110 Stat. 868); to the Committee on Natural Resources.

7540. A letter from the Acting Director, Office of Sustainable Fisheries, NMFS, National Oceanic and Atmospheric Administration, transmitting the Administration's temporary rule — Fisheries of the Exclusive Economic Zone Off Alaska; Pacific Ocean Perch in the Central Regulatory Area of the Gulf of Alaska [Docket No.: 150818742-6210-02] (RIN: 0648-XE966) received November 16, 2016, pursuant to 5 U.S.C. 801(a)(1)(A); Public Law 104-121, Sec. 251; (110 Stat. 868); to the Committee on Natural Resources.

7541. A letter from the Acting Director, Office of Sustainable Fisheries, NMFS, National Oceanic and Atmospheric Administration, transmitting the Administration's temporary rule — Fisheries of the Exclusive Economic Zone Off Alaska; Reallocation of Pacific Cod in the Bering Sea and Aleutian Islands Management Area [Docket No.: 150916863-6211-02] (RIN: 0648-XE924) received November 16, 2016, pursuant to 5 U.S.C. 801(a)(1)(A); Public Law 104-121, Sec. 251; (110 Stat. 868); to the Committee on Natural Resources.

7542. A letter from the Acting Director, Office of Sustainable Fisheries, NMFS, National Oceanic and Atmospheric Administration, transmitting the Administration's temporary rule — Fisheries of the Caribbean, Gulf of Mexico, and South Atlantic; 2016 Commercial Accountability Measures and Closure for Blueline Tilefish in the South Atlantic Region [Docket No.: 140501394-5279-02] (RIN: 0648-XE830) received November 16, 2016, pursuant to 5 U.S.C. 801(a)(1)(A); Public Law 104-121, Sec. 251; (110 Stat. 868); to the Committee on Natural Resources.

7543. A letter from the Acting Director, Office of Sustainable Fisheries, NMFS, National Oceanic and Atmospheric Administration, transmitting the Administration's temporary rule — Fisheries of the Exclusive Economic Zone Off Alaska; Pacific Cod by Pot Catcher/Processors in the Bering Sea and Aleutian Islands Management Area [Docket No.: 150916863-6211-02] (RIN: 0648-XE879) received November 16, 2016, pursuant to 5 U.S.C. 801(a)(1)(A); Public Law 104-121, Sec. 251; (110 Stat. 868); to the Committee on Natural Resources.

7544. A letter from the Acting Director, Office of Sustainable Fisheries, NMFS, National Oceanic and Atmospheric Administration, transmitting the Administration's final rule — Magnuson-Stevens Act Provisions; Fisheries Off West Coast States; Pacific Coast Groundfish Fishery; 2015-2016 Biennial Specifications and Management Measures; Inseason Adjustments [Docket No.: 140904754-5188-02] (RIN: 0648-BG27) received November 16, 2016, pursuant to 5 U.S.C. 801(a)(1)(A); Public Law 104-121, Sec. 251; (110 Stat. 868); to the Committee on Natural Resources.

7545. A letter from the Acting Director, Office of Sustainable Fisheries, NMFS, National Oceanic and Atmospheric Administration, transmitting the Administration's temporary rule — Fisheries of the Exclusive Economic Zone Off Alaska; Inseason Adjustment

to the 2016 Gulf of Alaska Pollock Seasonal Apportionments [Docket No.: 150818742-6210-02] (RIN: 0648-XE837) received November 16, 2016, pursuant to 5 U.S.C. 801(a)(1)(A); Public Law 104-121, Sec. 251; (110 Stat. 868); to the Committee on Natural Resources.

7546. A letter from the Acting Director, Office of Sustainable Fisheries, NMFS, National Oceanic and Atmospheric Administration, transmitting the Administration's temporary rule — Fisheries of the Exclusive Economic Zone Off Alaska; Reallocation of Pacific Cod in the Bering Sea and Aleutian Islands Management Area [Docket No.: 150916863-6211-02] (RIN: 0648-XE851) received November 16, 2016, pursuant to 5 U.S.C. 801(a)(1)(A); Public Law 104-121, Sec. 251; (110 Stat. 868); to the Committee on Natural Resources.

7547. A letter from the Acting Director, Office of Sustainable Fisheries, NMFS, SERO, National Oceanic and Atmospheric Administration, transmitting the Administration's temporary rule — Coastal Migratory Pelagic Resources of the Gulf of Mexico and South Atlantic; 2016-2017 Commercial Accountability Measures and Closure for King Mackerel in Western Zone of the Gulf of Mexico [Docket No.: 101206604-1758-02] (RIN: 0648-XE959) received November 16, 2016, pursuant to 5 U.S.C. 801(a)(1)(A); Public Law 104-121, Sec. 251; (110 Stat. 868); to the Committee on Natural Resources.

PUBLIC BILLS AND RESOLUTIONS

Under clause 2 of rule XII, public bills and resolutions of the following titles were introduced and severally referred, as follows:

By Mr. HURD of Texas:

H.R. 6380. A bill to amend the Omnibus Crime Control and Safe Streets Act of 1968 to authorize COPS grantees to use grant funds to hire veterans as career law enforcement officers, and for other purposes; to the Committee on the Judiciary.

By Mr. McCAUL:

H.R. 6381. A bill to provide for certain homeland security improvements, and for other purposes; to the Committee on Homeland Security, and in addition to the Committees on Foreign Affairs, the Judiciary, Transportation and Infrastructure, Energy and Commerce, Agriculture, Oversight and Government Reform, Ways and Means, Science, Space, and Technology, and Financial Services, for a period to be subsequently determined by the Speaker, in each case for consideration of such provisions as fall within the jurisdiction of the committee concerned.

By Ms. DELBENE (for herself, Ms. JUDY CHU of California, Ms. MATSUI, Mr. COHEN, Ms. WASSERMAN SCHULTZ, Mr. CONYERS, Mr. CARSON of Indiana, Mr. ELLISON, and Mr. LEWIS):

H.R. 6382. A bill to prohibit the collection of information and the establishment or utilization of a registry for the purposes of classifying certain United States persons and other individuals on the basis of religious affiliation, and for other purposes; to the Committee on the Judiciary.

By Mr. GRAYSON:

H.R. 6383. A bill to amend the Internal Revenue Code of 1986 to extend for two years the credit for qualified microturbine property; to the Committee on Ways and Means.

By Mr. GRAYSON:

H.R. 6384. A bill to amend the Internal Revenue Code of 1986 to extend for one year the credit for qualified microturbine property; to the Committee on Ways and Means.

By Mr. GRAYSON:

H.R. 6385. A bill to amend the Internal Revenue Code of 1986 to extend for two years the credit for qualified fuel cell property; to the Committee on Ways and Means.

By Mr. GRAYSON:

H.R. 6386. A bill to amend the Internal Revenue Code of 1986 to extend for one year the credit for qualified fuel cell property; to the Committee on Ways and Means.

By Mr. GRAYSON:

H.R. 6387. A bill to amend the Internal Revenue Code of 1986 to extend for one year the credit for mortgage insurance premiums treated as interest; to the Committee on Ways and Means.

By Mr. GRAYSON:

H.R. 6388. A bill to amend the Internal Revenue Code of 1986 to extend for two years the credit for mortgage insurance premiums treated as interest; to the Committee on Ways and Means.

By Mr. LAMBORN:

H.R. 6389. A bill to condition assistance to the West Bank and Gaza on steps by the Palestinian Authority to end violence and terrorism against Israeli citizens; to the Committee on Foreign Affairs.

By Mr. LUETKEMEYER:

H.R. 6390. A bill to amend the Dodd-Frank Wall Street Reform and Consumer Protection Act to specify when bank holding companies may be subject to certain enhanced supervision, and for other purposes; to the Committee on Financial Services.

By Mr. LUETKEMEYER:

H.R. 6391. A bill to amend the Dodd-Frank Wall Street Reform and Consumer Protection Act to specify when bank holding companies may be subject to certain enhanced supervision, and for other purposes; to the Committee on Financial Services.

MEMORIALS

Under clause 3 of rule XII, memorials were presented and referred as follows:

308. The SPEAKER presented a memorial of the Senate of the State of Michigan, relative to Senate Resolution No. 214, urging the President of the United States to direct the U.S. Department of Education to stop its federal overreach as it relates to the "supplement not supplant" provisions of the Every Student Succeeds Act; and to memorialize Congress to enact legislation that clarifies the Department of Education's role and authority as it pertains to "supplement not supplant" provisions; to the Committee on Education and the Workforce.

309. Also, a memorial of the Senate of the State of Michigan, relative to Senate Resolution No. 204, urging the U.S. Congress to pass the Americans with Disabilities Act Education and Reform Act of 2015; to the Committee on the Judiciary.

CONSTITUTIONAL AUTHORITY STATEMENT

Pursuant to clause 7 of rule XII of the Rules of the House of Representatives, the following statements are submitted regarding the specific powers granted to Congress in the Constitution to enact the accompanying bill or joint resolution.

By Mr. HURD of Texas:

H.R. 6380.

Congress has the power to enact this legislation pursuant to the following:

Article I, Section 8, Clause 1
By Mr. McCAUL:
H.R. 6381.
Congress has the power to enact this legislation pursuant to the following:
Article I, Section 8, Clause 18—"To make all Laws which shall be necessary and proper for carrying into Execution the foregoing Powers, and all other Powers vested by this Constitution in the Government of the United States, or in any Department or Officer thereof."
By Ms. DELBENE:
H.R. 6382.
Congress has the power to enact this legislation pursuant to the following:
Article I, Section 8 of the United States Constitution.
By Mr. GRAYSON:
H.R. 6383.
Congress has the power to enact this legislation pursuant to the following:
Article I, Section 8, of the United States Constitution.
By Mr. GRAYSON:
H.R. 6384.
Congress has the power to enact this legislation pursuant to the following:
Article I, Section 8, of the United States Constitution.
By Mr. GRAYSON:
H.R. 6385.
Congress has the power to enact this legislation pursuant to the following:
Article I, Section 8, of the United States Constitution.
By Mr. GRAYSON:
H.R. 6386.
Congress has the power to enact this legislation pursuant to the following:
Article I, Section 8, of the United States Constitution.
By Mr. GRAYSON:
H.R. 6387.

Congress has the power to enact this legislation pursuant to the following:
Article I, Section 8, of the United States Constitution.
By Mr. GRAYSON:
H.R. 6388.
Congress has the power to enact this legislation pursuant to the following:
Article I, Section 8, of the United States Constitution.
By Mr. LAMBORN:
H.R. 6389.
Congress has the power to enact this legislation pursuant to the following:
Article I, Section 9, Clause 7
By Mr. LUETKEMEYER:
H.R. 6390.
Congress has the power to enact this legislation pursuant to the following:
The constitutional authority on which this bill rests lies in Article 1, Section 7, Clause 2 of the Constitution, which allows for every bill passed by the House of Representatives and the Senate and signed by the President to be codified into law; and therefore implicitly allows Congress to repeal any bill that has been passed by both chambers and signed into law by the President.
Additionally, the Constitution grants to Congress the explicit power to regulate commerce in and among the states, as enumerate in Article 1, Section 8, Clause 3, the Commerce Clause.
By Mr. LUETKEMEYER:
H.R. 6391.
Congress has the power to enact this legislation pursuant to the following:
The constitutional authority on which this bill rests lies in Article 1, Section 7, Clause 2 of the Constitution, which allows for every bill passed by the House of Representatives and the Senate and signed by the President to be codified into law; and therefore implicitly allows Congress to repeal any bill that

has been passed by both chambers and signed into law by the President.
Additionally, the Constitution grants to Congress the explicit power to regulate commerce in and among the states, as enumerate in Article 1, Section 8, Clause 3, the Commerce Clause.

ADDITIONAL SPONSORS

Under clause 7 of rule XII, sponsors were added to public bills and resolutions, as follows:

H.R. 213: Ms. BASS, Mr. THOMPSON of California, and Mr. VAN HOLLEN.
H.R. 759: Ms. PINGREE.
H.R. 1453: Ms. BONAMICI.
H.R. 2224: Mr. DESAULNIER.
H.R. 2368: Mr. GRAYSON.
H.R. 2858: Mr. YODER, Mr. SCHRADER, and Mr. BUTTERFIELD.
H.R. 4535: Mr. THOMPSON of California.
H.R. 4818: Mr. WEBSTER of Florida.
H.R. 4927: Mr. CARTWRIGHT.
H.R. 5432: Ms. STEFANIK.
H.R. 5624: Mr. PAULSEN.
H.R. 5797: Mr. BLUMENAUER.
H.R. 5858: Mr. LIPINSKI.
H.R. 5900: Mr. McGOVERN.
H.R. 6176: Mr. KIND.
H.R. 6306: Mr. LOWENTHAL.
H.R. 6346: Mrs. CAROLYN B. MALONEY of New York, Mr. GRIJALVA, and Mr. McGOVERN.
H. Con. Res. 159: Mr. YOUNG of Alaska and Mr. GARAMENDI.
H. Con. Res. 171: Ms. ROYBAL-ALLARD and Mr. LOWENTHAL.
H. Res. 922: Mr. GRIJALVA and Mrs. DINGELL.

EXTENSIONS OF REMARKS

IN RECOGNITION OF CHIEF RANDY M. SOBEL

HON. FRANK C. GUINTA
OF NEW HAMPSHIRE
IN THE HOUSE OF REPRESENTATIVES
Friday, November 18, 2016

Mr. GUINTA. Mr. Speaker, I rise to recognize the public service of Chief Randy M. Sobel of the Middleton Police Department. Chief Sobel retired on October 31, 2016 after twenty-seven years of law enforcement service to the people of Strafford County in New Hampshire.

Chief Sobel began his law enforcement career in 1989 with the Milton Police Department and followed that with four years' service with the Farmington Police Department. However, it is his twenty-two-year career in Middleton that is most noteworthy, having served as Chief of the Middleton Police Department since 2002. Throughout his career, he performed his duties without great public recognition yet he was always a well-respected and admired member of the communities he represented. On behalf of the people of the First Congressional District, I thank him for his career dedicated to public safety and wish him a long and happy retirement.

HONORING THE 10TH ANNIVERSARY OF THE AMERICAN CANYON FAMILY RESOURCE CENTER

HON. MIKE THOMPSON
OF CALIFORNIA
IN THE HOUSE OF REPRESENTATIVES
Friday, November 18, 2016

Mr. THOMPSON of California. Mr. Speaker, I rise today to honor the American Canyon Family Resource Center which is celebrating its 10th Anniversary of offering support and resources to the families, children, and seniors of our community.

The American Canyon Family Resource Center opened in April 2006 with the mission to strengthen our community, embrace diversity, and promote and provide local services. The Center has made childcare, housing, legal aid, tax assistance, education, and immigration resources available to every resident of American Canyon, California.

The American Canyon Family Resource Center provides families with tools to help themselves. The Center looks at the strengths of the people they serve and helps them to build upon those strengths to create better and healthier situations for their families. The Center acts as an integrated service system to connect families with nonprofit organizations and government agencies to establish a support system which secures our community's families.

In addition to connecting families to outside community resources, the Center hosts workshops and classes with topics on establishing credit, buying a home, and securing employment, giving community members confidence, knowledge, and training to provide for their families. The American Canyon Resource Center's financial coaching service focuses on helping our community members increase income, manage credit, and build assets by providing training and job placement, helping individuals create a budget and manage credit, and introducing them to matched savings accounts and first-time home buyer programs. The Center helps families get back on their feet and take control of their own futures.

Mr. Speaker, for a decade this institution has been instrumental in shaping the families in our community and promoting a sense of belonging and safety for children, families, and seniors. Therefore, it is fitting and proper that we honor the American Canyon Family Resource Center here today.

HONORING THE LIFE OF MR. CHARLES R. NEWMAN

HON. CHRIS COLLINS
OF NEW YORK
IN THE HOUSE OF REPRESENTATIVES
Friday, November 18, 2016

Mr. COLLINS of New York. Mr. Speaker, I rise today to recognize and honor the memory of a distinguished member of New York's 27th District. Mr. Charles R. Newman of Arcade, New York, passed away November 12, 2016.

Charles was born in Buffalo, New York on October 6, 1925. He attended St. Bonaventure University with a major in Accounting and Pre-Law while also participating in the Army Reserves. He served in the United States Army as a First Lieutenant from 1943 to 1946 during World War II, and for his bravery and patriotism Charles was awarded the WWII Victory Medal, the Army Occupation Medal, and the Army Commendation Ribbon. After his years of service, Charles returned to Western New York to graduate from Buffalo Law School in 1950. Charles went on to practice law in Arcade for twenty-seven years before serving as Arcade Village Justice, Town of Arcade Justice, Wyoming County Attorney, and eventually Wyoming County Court Judge for many years.

Charles was a community leader and was dedicated to helping the young men and women of our community. He was a Boy Scout leader and sat on the Board of Directors for the Genesee County Boy Scouts, an organization vital in helping many young men reach their full potential. Charles also served as Clerk to the Arcade Central and Pioneer Central School boards.

Charles also contributed to the Arcade community by serving as board member of the AJ Odell Medical Foundation, a member of the Arcade Chamber of Commerce, President of the New York State Magistrates Association, Member of the Free-Masons for over 63 years, and Member of the American legion for over 68 years. Charles was an important and loved member of the town of Arcade that left a deep impression on everyone he met.

I had the privilege to meet and honor Charles as New York 27th's Congressional District Veteran of the Month—fittingly this Veterans Day. Dozens of members of the Veterans of Foreign Wars and American Legion attended the ceremony, and I was despondent to hear of his passing the following day. After many years of service to his community, I would like to again recognize this American patriot.

RECOGNIZING THE 100TH ANNIVERSARY OF GLENBARD TOWNSHIP HIGH SCHOOLS

HON. PETER J. ROSKAM
OF ILLINOIS
IN THE HOUSE OF REPRESENTATIVES
Friday, November 18, 2016

Mr. ROSKAM. Mr. Speaker, today I commemorate the 100th Anniversary of Glenbard Township High School District 87. On November 26th, District 87 will celebrate its centennial, representing 100 years of dedication to academic excellence and student success.

Glenbard Township High School District 87 was first established in 1916 in the second floor of the DuPage bank building. At that time, the school consisted of 120 students and 5 facility members. Fast forward one hundred years and District 87 is still based in Glen Ellyn but now consists of Glenbard South, Glenbard North, Glenbard East, and Glenbard West high schools. It is now the third largest school district in the state and is known for its fantastic academic achievement.

I applaud District 87's commitment to its excellent teachers, who have consistently challenged their students to achieve high standards and follow their dreams. District 87 schools have helped students consistently succeed at rigorous academic levels while instilling the values of community, kindness, respect, hard work, and love of learning.

On this special occasion, we recognize District 87's rich history of academic excellence. We thank the District for its partnership with parents, who strive to educate the current generation that will become our nation's future leaders. For well over a century, Glenbard Township High Schools have contributed toward this brighter future.

Mr. Speaker and Distinguished Colleagues, please join me in honoring the legacy of Glenbard Township High School District 87, and in wishing them continued success.

TRIBUTE TO JACK H. BROWN

HON. PETE AGUILAR
OF CALIFORNIA
IN THE HOUSE OF REPRESENTATIVES
Friday, November 18, 2016

Mr. AGUILAR. Mr. Speaker, I rise on behalf of both myself and Representative KEN CALVERT from Riverside County to honor and pay tribute to the remarkable Jack H. Brown who passed away on Sunday, November 13, 2016. Jack was a pillar of the community in the Inland Empire, California, and he will be deeply missed.

A native of San Bernardino, California, Jack began his career in the grocery business as a box boy at Berk's Market Spot in San Bernardino when he was just thirteen years old. In 1981, Jack was hired by Stater Bros. Markets, where he would serve as President and Chief Executive Officer for over thirty-five years and as Chairman for over thirty years. Jack's leadership and wisdom allowed Stater Bros. Markets to become Southern California's largest privately-owned supermarket chain, and as of 2015, the Inland Empire's largest private employer.

During the Vietnam War era, Jack proudly served his nation in the Navy and as a sailor in the Pacific Fleet. In the years after his military service, Jack would become a strong supporter of our armed forces and our nation's veterans. In recognition of his support and the many contributions of Stater Bros., Jack received the "Friend of the Veteran Award" from the Riverside National Cemetery's Veterans' Advisory Committee as well as the Congressional Medal of Honor Society's highest honor, the "Patriot Award." He was also a recipient of the prestigious Horatio Alger Award in honor of his efforts to fulfill the "American Dream" and for his contributions to our nation. Jack is survived by his wife Debbie, three beloved daughters: J. Kathleen Smith (Michael Smith), Cara Hoffman (Scott Hoffman) and Melissa Koss (Pete Koss). He had seven grandchildren, Kaitlyn, Colleen, Caden, Dylan, Julianna, Jack Ryan and Emma.

Jack's life serves as an inspiration to all of us, reminding us that a strong work ethic and a dedication to serving others can lead to a lifetime of happiness and fulfillment. His commitment to our country and community, as well as his love for his family and work, has cemented his legacy as a true leader in our region. We are honored to have been able to call Jack a friend, and we will always miss him. Our hearts go out to Jack's friends and family as they navigate this loss, but we know they may take comfort in the fact that the positive impacts he made on our community will be felt by generations to come.

PERSONAL EXPLANATION

HON. RYAN A. COSTELLO
OF PENNSYLVANIA
IN THE HOUSE OF REPRESENTATIVES
Friday, November 18, 2016

Mr. COSTELLO of Pennsylvania. Mr. Speaker, unfortunately, on November 17, 2016, I missed three recorded votes on the House floor due to a family event. I ask that the RECORD reflect that had I been present, I would have voted Nay on Roll Call 581, Nay on Roll Call 582, and Nay on Roll Call 583.

TRIBUTE TO THE HONOR FLIGHT OF OREGON

HON. GREG WALDEN
OF OREGON
IN THE HOUSE OF REPRESENTATIVES
Friday, November 18, 2016

Mr. WALDEN. Mr. Speaker, I rise to recognize the seven World War II veterans and six Korean War veterans from Oregon who visited their memorial on the National Mall on Saturday, October 8, 2016 through Honor Flight of Oregon. Every time I have the chance to meet one of these heroes from the "Greatest Generation," I am reminded of the poignant words of General Dwight D. Eisenhower. In a message to Allied troops just before D–Day, he said, "The eyes of the world are upon you. The hopes and prayers of liberty loving people everywhere march with you."

He was right then, of course, Mr. Speaker. But over 70 years later, liberty loving people everywhere continue to owe these heroes for their extraordinary service and their incredible stories of sacrifice and bravery on behalf of our country. That's why it is my privilege to enter their names into the CONGRESSIONAL RECORD today.

The veterans on this Honor Flight from Oregon are as follows: Shirley Boehmer, Army; Arnold Ebert, Army; Gordon Nelson, Army; John Hull, Marine Corps; Clarence Kelm, Marine Corps; Albert Pule, Marine Corps; Bruce Pence, Marine Corps; James Estep, Navy; William Isely, Navy; Johnny Johnson, Navy; Wilma Norris, Navy; Marvin Stuber, Navy; and Helen Watson, Navy.

These 13 heroes join the over 150,000 veterans who have been honored through the Honor Flight Network of volunteers nationwide since 2005.

I would also like to recognize the three guardians traveling on this trip who have also served our country: Jeffrey Hull, Army; Rosemary Agee, Navy; and Terry Haines, Navy. Terry served Oregon's Second District for many years as our veterans outreach liaison, and has always been a strong advocate for the men and women who have worn the uniform.

I also want to thank and recognize Janet Yakopatz and Rita "Sam" Boyd, the group leaders on this flight, as well as the dedicated Board Members of Honor Flight of Oregon, who worked so hard to make this trip happen.

And, of course, none of this would be possible without Gail Yakopatz, the longtime President of Honor Flight of Southern Oregon. Gail is one of a kind. For many years, she has been a tireless advocate for Oregon's veterans, and I am proud to call her my friend.

Mr. Speaker, at the height of the Civil War in 1863, President Abraham Lincoln wrote, "Honor to the Soldier, and Sailor everywhere, who bravely bears his country's cause." Each of us in this Chamber and in this nation should be humbled by the courage of these brave veterans who put themselves in harm's way for our country and way of life. As a nation, we can never fully repay the debt of gratitude owed to them for their honor, commitment, and sacrifice in defense of the freedoms we have today.

My colleagues, please join me in thanking these veterans and the volunteers of Honor Flight of Oregon for their exemplary dedication and service to this great country.

PERSONAL EXPLANATION

HON. EARL BLUMENAUER
OF OREGON
IN THE HOUSE OF REPRESENTATIVES
Friday, November 18, 2016

Mr. BLUMENAUER. Mr. Speaker, had I been present for today's votes on the amendments to H.R. 5982, I would have voted "yea" on the Conyers Amendment (Roll no. 581), "yea" on the Jackson-Lee Amendment (Roll no. 582), and "yea" on the Connolly En Bloc Amendment (Roll no. 583). I would have also voted "yea" on the Democratic Motion to Recommit (Roll no. 584), which would add an exemption to the underlying bill for any rule that pertains to improving employment, job retention, or the quality of the workforce.

I would have voted "nay" on the final passage of H.R. 5982 (Roll no. 585). Should it become law, H.R. 5982 would amend the Congressional Review Act (CRA) to allow for the en bloc disapproval of all regulations finalized near the end of presidential terms, jeopardizing important public protections affecting public health, safety, and the environment.

Had I been present for the vote on the Democratic Motion to Recommit H.R. 5711 (Roll no. 586), which would have prohibited the Secretary of the Treasury from authorizing a transaction by any U.S. financial institution engaged in business with a foreign entity that has been found to have engaged in or authorized cyber-attacks targeting any election held in the United States, I would have voted "yea".

Additionally, had I been present for the vote on Final Passage of H.R. 5711 (Roll no. 587), a bill to prohibit the Secretary of the Treasury from authorizing certain transactions by a U.S. financial institution in connection with the export or re-export of a commercial passenger aircraft to the Islamic Republic of Iran, I would have voted "nay." I oppose H.R. 5711, which would undermine the Joint Comprehensive Plan of Action, the agreement reached between Iran, the United States and five other countries designed to force Iran to back away from the nuclear threshold. I celebrate the agreement—that Iran is complying, that the U.S. can benefit, and that we have an opportunity to strengthen ties with a former enemy.

IN HONOR OF BILL STANFILL

HON. SANFORD D. BISHOP, JR.
OF GEORGIA
IN THE HOUSE OF REPRESENTATIVES
Friday, November 18, 2016

Mr. BISHOP of Georgia. Mr. Speaker, it is with a heavy heart and solemn remembrance that I pay tribute to an outstanding athlete, businessman, and citizen, William Thomas "Bill" Stanfill, Sr. Sadly, Bill passed away on Thursday, November 10, 2016. A memorial service was held on Monday, November 14, 2016 at Albany First United Methodist Church in Albany, Georgia.

A Georgia man through and through, Bill Stanfill was born in Cairo, Georgia. According to him, growing up on a farm doing farm work helped prepare him to play football. While at Cairo High School, Bill was selected as the Class Double-A Lineman of the Year. He also led the basketball team to the state championship and was named MVP of the state tournament. As if that were not enough, Bill excelled in track and field, earning three state Double-A discus championships and a shot put title.

After high school, Bill attended the University of Georgia on a football scholarship. He was in the first recruiting class of legendary UGA football coach, Vince Dooley. As a defensive tackle for the Georgia Bulldogs, he played on two SEC championship teams in 1966 and 1968. In 1968, he was elected permanent team captain, was a consensus All-American, and became Georgia's first and only winner of the Outland Trophy, which is awarded annually to the best college football interior lineman in the country.

Bill was drafted in the first round with the eleventh overall pick by the Miami Dolphins in the 1969 draft. That year, he was named AFL Rookie of the Year runner up. In 1972, he was the leader of the "No-Name Defense" on the undefeated Miami Dolphins team that went on to win the Super Bowl. He was also the starting defensive end on the Dolphins' 1973 Super Bowl team. That year, he recorded 18½ sacks, a single season Dolphins record that still stands today. His career sack total stands at 67½, which places him among the greatest Dolphins pass rushers of all time. He was a four-time Pro Bowler in his eight-year career with Miami.

After suffering numerous injuries, Bill retired from football but unfortunately, those injuries followed him for the rest of his life. Nevertheless, Bill always remained close to the sport and his former teammates. He was inducted into the Miami Dolphins' Honor Roll, the Georgia Sports Hall of Fame, and the UGA Circle of Honor.

Bill followed his NFL career with a successful business career with Dozier-Stanfill Real Estate Company in Albany, Georgia. He was a member of the First United Methodist Church of Albany and served as the Secretary/Treasurer of the Monk Thompson Sunday School Class.

Bill is survived by his wife, Gail; four children, Stan, Jake, Kristin, and Scott; five grandchildren, Cole, Jack, Samuel, Grace, and Luke; two sisters, Beth and Tommie; and numerous nieces and nephews.

Mr. Speaker, my wife Vivian and I, along with the more than 730,000 residents of the Second Congressional District of Georgia, salute Bill Stanfill for his drive, perseverance, and dedication, which contributed to the long list of accomplishments still remembered and admired by many today. I ask my colleagues in the House of Representatives to join us in extending our deepest condolences to Bill Stanfill's family and friends during this difficult time. We pray that they will be consoled and comforted by an abiding faith and the Holy Spirit in the days, weeks and months ahead.

SENATE—*Tuesday, November 22, 2016*

The Senate met at 11 and 8 seconds a.m. and was called to order by the Honorable DANIEL COATS, a Senator from the State of Indiana.

APPOINTMENT OF ACTING PRESIDENT PRO TEMPORE

The PRESIDING OFFICER. The clerk will please read a communication to the Senate from the President pro tempore (Mr. HATCH).

The legislative clerk read the following letter:

U.S. SENATE,
PRESIDENT PRO TEMPORE,
Washington, DC, November 22, 2016.

To the Senate:

Under the provisions of rule I, paragraph 3, of the Standing Rules of the Senate, I hereby appoint the Honorable DANIEL COATS, a Senator from the State of Indiana, to perform the duties of the Chair.

ORRIN G. HATCH,
President pro tempore.

Mr. COATS thereupon assumed the Chair as Acting President pro tempore.

ADJOURNMENT UNTIL FRIDAY, NOVEMBER 25, 2016, AT 11 A.M.

The ACTING PRESIDENT pro tempore. Under the previous order, the Senate stands adjourned until 11 a.m. on Friday, November 25, 2016.

Thereupon, the Senate, at 11 and 43 seconds a.m., adjourned until Friday, November 25, 2016, at 11 a.m.

HOUSE OF REPRESENTATIVES—*Tuesday, November 22, 2016*

The House met at 2:30 p.m. and was called to order by the Speaker pro tempore (Mr. ROONEY of Florida).

DESIGNATION OF THE SPEAKER PRO TEMPORE

The SPEAKER pro tempore laid before the House the following communication from the Speaker:

WASHINGTON, DC,
November 22, 2016.

I hereby appoint the Honorable THOMAS J. ROONEY to act as Speaker pro tempore on this day.

PAUL D. RYAN,
Speaker of the House of Representatives.

PRAYER

Reverend John Hopkins, LC, Our Lady of Bethesda Retreat Center, Bethesda, Maryland, offered the following prayer:

Heavenly Father, we ask You to help us to start anew in our quest to build up our country and truly do what is best for our people.

Help us to put aside all struggles for power and learn how to come together for the common good.

Let us put aside all demagoguery and self-importance and cling to what is good and right.

Keep this country safe, and help us always to strive towards a true peace and authentic justice.

Give us the courage to defend and promote the values and principles that have made our country great, and free our lawmakers from all egotism, hate, or cowardice.

Inspire them to think outside the box in finding solutions and to look to You for their inspiration.

We ask this through Christ our Lord. Amen.

THE JOURNAL

The SPEAKER pro tempore. Pursuant to section 3(a) of House Resolution 921, the Journal of the last day's proceedings is approved.

PLEDGE OF ALLEGIANCE

The SPEAKER pro tempore. The Chair will lead the House in the Pledge of Allegiance.

The SPEAKER pro tempore led the Pledge of Allegiance as follows:

I pledge allegiance to the Flag of the United States of America, and to the Republic for which it stands, one nation under God, indivisible, with liberty and justice for all.

ADJOURNMENT

The SPEAKER pro tempore. Pursuant to section 3(b) of House Resolution 921, the House stands adjourned until 9:30 a.m. on Friday, November 25, 2016.

Thereupon (at 2 o'clock and 32 minutes p.m.), under its previous order, the House adjourned until Friday, November 25, 2016, at 9:30 a.m.

EXECUTIVE COMMUNICATIONS, ETC.

Under clause 2 of rule XIV, executive communications were taken from the Speaker's table and referred as follows:

7548. A letter from the Assistant Secretary for Legislation, Department of Health and Human Services, transmitting the Department's annual report titled "2016 Report to Congress on Health IT Progress: Examining the HITECH Era and the Future of Health IT", pursuant to Sec. 13113(a) of the American Recovery and Reinvestment Act of 2009, Public Law 111-5; to the Committee on Energy and Commerce.

7549. A letter from the Regulations Coordinator, Centers for Medicare and Medicaid Services, Department of Health and Human Services, transmitting the Department's Major notice — Medicaid Program; Final FY 2014 and Preliminary FY 2016 Disproportionate Share Hospital Allotments, and Final FY 2014 and Preliminary FY 2016 Institutions for Mental Diseases Disproportionate Share Hospital Limits [CMS-2401-N] (RIN: 0938-ZB30) received November 16, 2016, pursuant to 5 U.S.C. 801(a)(1)(A); Public Law 104-121, Sec. 251; (110 Stat. 868); to the Committee on Energy and Commerce.

7550. A letter from the Deputy Director, Regulations Policy and Management Staff, FDA, Department of Health and Human Services, transmitting the Department's final rule — Revision of Organization and Conforming Changes to Regulation [Docket No.: FDA-2012-N-0222] received November 17, 2016, pursuant to 5 U.S.C. 801(a)(1)(A); Public Law 104-121, Sec. 251; (110 Stat. 868); to the Committee on Energy and Commerce.

7551. A letter from the Director, Regulatory Management Division, Environmental Protection Agency, transmitting the Agency's direct final rule — State of Nebraska; Authorization of State Hazardous Waste Management Program [EPA-R07-RCRA-2016-067; FRL-9955-25-Region 7] received November 15, 2016, pursuant to 5 U.S.C. 801(a)(1)(A); Public Law 104-121, Sec. 251; (110 Stat. 868); to the Committee on Energy and Commerce.

7552. A letter from the Director, Regulatory Management Division, Environmental Protection Agency, transmitting the Agency's direct final rule — Revisions to Procedure 2 — Quality Assurance Requirements for Particulate Matter Continuous Emission Monitoring Systems at Stationary Sources [EPA-HQ-OAR-2016-0382; FRL-9955-20-OAR] (RIN: 2060-AT15) received November 15, 2016, pursuant to 5 U.S.C. 801(a)(1)(A); Public Law 104-121, Sec. 251; (110 Stat. 868); to the Committee on Energy and Commerce.

7553. A letter from the Director, Regulatory Management Division, Environmental Protection Agency, transmitting the Agency's final rule — Air Quality Plan; Georgia; Infrastructure Requirements for the 2012 PM2.5 NAAQS [EPA-R04-OAR-2014-0425; FRL-9955-32-Region 4] received November 15, 2016, pursuant to 5 U.S.C. 801(a)(1)(A); Public Law 104-121, Sec. 251; (110 Stat. 868); to the Committee on Energy and Commerce.

7554. A letter from the Director, Regulatory Management Division, Environmental Protection Agency, transmitting the Agency's final rule — Revisions to the California State Implementation Plan; South Coast Air Quality Management District; Control of Oxides of Nitrogen Emissions from Off-Road Diesel Vehicles [EPA-R09-OAR-2015-0819; FRL-9954-78-Region 9] received November 15, 2016, pursuant to 5 U.S.C. 801(a)(1)(A); Public Law 104-121, Sec. 251; (110 Stat. 868); to the Committee on Energy and Commerce.

7555. A letter from the Director, Regulatory Management Division, Environmental Protection Agency, transmitting the Agency's final rule — Hazardous Waste Generator Improvements Rule [EPA-HQ-RCRA-2012-0121; FRL-9947-26-OLEM] (RIN: 2050-AG70) received November 15, 2016, pursuant to 5 U.S.C. 801(a)(1)(A); Public Law 104-121, Sec. 251; (110 Stat. 868); to the Committee on Energy and Commerce.

7556. A letter from the Director, Regulatory Management Division, Environmental Protection Agency, transmitting the Agency's final rule — Hazardous Waste Export-Import Revisions [EPA-HQ-RCRA-2015-0147; FRL-9947-74-OLEM] (RIN: 2050-AG77) received November 15, 2016, pursuant to 5 U.S.C. 801(a)(1)(A); Public Law 104-121, Sec. 251; (110 Stat. 868); to the Committee on Energy and Commerce.

7557. A letter from the Director, Regulatory Management Division, Environmental Protection Agency, transmitting the Agency's final rule — Approval and Promulgation of Implementation Plans; State of Arizona; Revised Format for Materials Incorporated By Reference [AZ-127-NBK; FRL-9948-55-Region 9] received November 15, 2016, pursuant to 5 U.S.C. 801(a)(1)(A); Public Law 104-121, Sec. 251; (110 Stat. 868); to the Committee on Energy and Commerce.

7558. A letter from the Director, Regulatory Management Division, Environmental Protection Agency, transmitting the Agency's final rule — Air Plan Approval; KY Infrastructure Requirements for the 2010 1-hour NO2 NAAQS [EPA-R04-OAR-2014-0767; FRL-9955-19-Region 4] received November 15, 2016, pursuant to 5 U.S.C. 801(a)(1)(A); Public Law 104-121, Sec. 251; (110 Stat. 868); to the Committee on Energy and Commerce.

7559. A letter from the Secretary, Department of Commerce, transmitting the Periodic Report on the National Emergency Caused by the Lapse of the Export Administration Act of 1979 for February 26, 2016, to August 25, 2016, pursuant to 50 U.S.C. 1641(c); Public Law 94-412, Sec. 401(c); (90 Stat. 1257) and 50 U.S.C. 1703(c); Public Law 95-223, Sec 204(c); (91 Stat. 1627); to the Committee on Foreign Affairs.

7560. A letter from the Secretary, Department of the Treasury, transmitting a six-

---

☐ This symbol represents the time of day during the House proceedings, e.g., ☐ 1407 is 2:07 p.m.

Matter set in this typeface indicates words inserted or appended, rather than spoken, by a Member of the House on the floor.

month periodic report on the national emergency with respect to the Central African Republic that was declared in Executive Order 13667 of May 12, 2014, pursuant to 50 U.S.C. 1641(c); Public Law 94-412, Sec. 401(c); (90 Stat. 1257) and 50 U.S.C. 1703(c); Public Law 95-223, Sec 204(c); (91 Stat. 1627); to the Committee on Foreign Affairs.

7561. A letter from the Secretary, Department of the Treasury, transmitting a six-month periodic report on the national emergency with respect to Syria that was declared in Executive Order 13338 of May 11, 2004, pursuant to 50 U.S.C. 1641(c); Public Law 94-412, Sec. 401(c); (90 Stat. 1257) and 50 U.S.C. 1703(c); Public Law 95-223, Sec 204(c); (91 Stat. 1627); to the Committee on Foreign Affairs.

7562. A letter from the Director, Defense Security Cooperation Agency, Department of Defense, transmitting a proposed Letter of Offer and Acceptance to the Republic of Korea, Transmittal No. 16-43, pursuant to Sec. 36(b)(1) of the Arms Export Control Act, as amended; to the Committee on Foreign Affairs.

7563. A letter from the Director, Defense Security Cooperation Agency, Department of Defense, transmitting a proposed Letter of Offer and Acceptance to the United Kingdom, Transmittal No. 16-53, pursuant to Sec. 36(b)(1) of the Arms Export Control Act, as amended; to the Committee on Foreign Affairs.

7564. A letter from the Assistant Secretary, Legislative Affairs, Department of State, transmitting the Department's Human Rights Report for International Military Education and Training Recipients for CY 2015, in accordance with Sec. 549 of the Foreign Assistance Act of 1961, as amended; to the Committee on Foreign Affairs.

7565. A letter from the Administrator and Chief Executive Officer, Bonneville Power Administration, Department of Energy, transmitting the Bonneville Power Administration's 2016 Annual Report, in accordance with requirements of the Third Powerplant at Grand Coulee Dam Act, Public Law 89-448, and the Chief Financial Officers Act, Public Law 101-576; to the Committee on Oversight and Government Reform.

7566. A letter from the Deputy Under Secretary for Management and Chief Financial Officer, Department of Homeland Security, transmitting the Department's FY 2016 Agency Financial Report, pursuant to 31 U.S.C. 3515(a)(1); Public Law 101-576, Sec. 303(a)(1) (as amended by Public Law 107-289, Sec. 2(a)); (116 Stat. 2049); to the Committee on Oversight and Government Reform.

7567. A letter from the Assistant Secretary, Legislative Affairs, Department of State, transmitting a letter with information on accessing the Department's FY 2016 Agency Financial Report electronically, pursuant to 31 U.S.C. 3515(a)(1); Public Law 101-576, Sec. 303(a)(1) (as amended by Public Law 107-289, Sec. 2(a)); (116 Stat. 2049); to the Committee on Oversight and Government Reform.

7568. A letter from the Board Chair and Chief Executive Officer, Farm Credit Administration, transmitting the Administration's FY 2016 Performance and Accountability Report, pursuant to 31 U.S.C. 3515(a)(1); Public Law 101-576, Sec. 303(a)(1) (as amended by Public Law 107-289, Sec. 2(a)); (116 Stat. 2049); to the Committee on Oversight and Government Reform.

7569. A letter from the Chairman, Audit Committee, Farm Credit System Insurance Corporation, transmitting the Corporation's consolidated report to the President addressing the requirements of the Federal Man-

agers' Financial Integrity Act and the Inspector General Act of 1978; to the Committee on Oversight and Government Reform.

7570. A letter from the Members and Chairman, Federal Labor Relations Authority, transmitting the 56th Semiannual Report of the Federal Labor Relations Authority Inspector General for the period April 1, 2016, through September 30, 2016, pursuant to Sec. 5 of the Inspector General Act of 1978, as amended; to the Committee on Oversight and Government Reform.

7571. A letter from the Archivist of the United States, National Archives, transmitting the Archive's Fiscal Year 2016 Agency Financial Report, pursuant to 31 U.S.C. 3515(a)(1); Public Law 101-576, Sec. 303(a)(1) (as amended by Public Law 107-289, Sec. 2(a)); (116 Stat. 2049); to the Committee on Oversight and Government Reform.

7572. A letter from the Chairman, National Mediation Board, transmitting the Board's 2016 Annual Performance and Accountability Report, pursuant to 31 U.S.C. 3515(a)(1); Public Law 101-576, Sec. 303(a)(1) (as amended by Public Law 107-289, Sec. 2(a)); (116 Stat. 2049); to the Committee on Oversight and Government Reform.

7573. A letter from the Associate General Counsel for General Law, Office of the General Counsel, Department of Homeland Security, transmitting a notification of a federal vacancy and designation of acting officer, pursuant to 5 U.S.C. 3349(a); Public Law 105-277, 151(b); (112 Stat. 2681-614); to the Committee on Oversight and Government Reform.

7574. A letter from the Chairman of the Board and Director, Pension Benefit Guaranty Corporation, transmitting the Corporation's Fiscal Year 2016 Agency Financial Report, pursuant to 31 U.S.C. 3515(a)(1); Public Law 101-576, Sec. 303(a)(1) (as amended by Public Law 107-289, Sec. 2(a)); (116 Stat. 2049); to the Committee on Oversight and Government Reform.

7575. A letter from the Chairman, Surface Transportation Board, transmitting the Board's Performance and Accountability Report for FY 2016, pursuant to 31 U.S.C. 3515(a)(1); Public Law 101-576, Sec. 303(a)(1) (as amended by Public Law 107-289, Sec. 2(a)); (116 Stat. 2049); to the Committee on Oversight and Government Reform.

7576. A letter from the Director, U.S. Trade and Development Agency, transmitting the Agency's Performance and Accountability Report, Fiscal Year 2016, pursuant to 31 U.S.C. 3515(a)(1); Public Law 101-576, Sec. 303(a)(1) (as amended by Public Law 107-289, Sec. 2(a)); (116 Stat. 2049); to the Committee on Oversight and Government Reform.

7577. A letter from the Chairman, United States International Trade Commission, transmitting the Commission's Fiscal Year 2016 Agency Financial Report, pursuant to 31 U.S.C. 3515(a)(1); Public Law 101-576, Sec. 303(a)(1) (as amended by Public Law 107-289, Sec. 2(a)); (116 Stat. 2049); to the Committee on Oversight and Government Reform.

7578. A letter from the Section Chief, Regulations Development Section, Bureau of Safety and Environmental Enforcement, Department of the Interior, transmitting the Department's final rule — Oil and Gas and Sulfur Operations in the Outer Continental Shelf — Decommissioning Costs for Pipelines [Docket ID: BSEE-2016-0004; 17XE1700DX EEEE500000 EX1SF0000.DAQ000] (RIN: 1014-AA32) received November 16, 2016, pursuant to 5 U.S.C. 801(a)(1)(A); Public Law 104-121, Sec. 251; (110 Stat. 868); to the Committee on Natural Resources.

7579. A letter from the Acting Director, Office of Sustainable Fisheries, NMFS, National Oceanic and Atmospheric Administration, transmitting the Administration's temporary rule — Fisheries of the Northeastern United States; Northeast Skate Complex; Adjustment to the Skate Bait Inseason Possession Limit [Docket No.: 160301164-6694-02] (RIN: 0648-XE955) received November 16, 2016, pursuant to 5 U.S.C. 801(a)(1)(A); Public Law 104-121, Sec. 251; (110 Stat. 868); to the Committee on Natural Resources.

7580. A letter from the Acting Director, Office of Sustainable Fisheries, NMFS, National Oceanic and Atmospheric Administration, transmitting the Administration's temporary rule — Fisheries of the Exclusive Economic Zone Off Alaska; Pacific Cod by Pot Catcher/Processors in the Bering Sea and Aleutian Islands Management Area [Docket No.: 150916863-6211-02] (RIN: 0648-XE879) received November 16, 2016, pursuant to 5 U.S.C. 801(a)(1)(A); Public Law 104-121, Sec. 251; (110 Stat. 868); to the Committee on Natural Resources.

7581. A letter from the Acting Director, Office of Sustainable Fisheries, NMFS, National Oceanic and Atmospheric Administration, transmitting the Administration's temporary rule — Atlantic Highly Migratory Species; Commercial Aggregated Large Coastal Shark and Hammerhead Shark Management Group Retention Limit Adjustment [Docket No.: 150413357-5999-02] (RIN: 0648-XE914) received November 16, 2016, pursuant to 5 U.S.C. 801(a)(1)(A); Public Law 104-121, Sec. 251; (110 Stat. 868); to the Committee on Natural Resources.

7582. A letter from the Acting Director, Office of Sustainable Fisheries, NMFS, National Oceanic and Atmospheric Administration, transmitting the Administration's temporary rule — Fisheries of the Northeastern United States; Atlantic Bluefish Fishery; Quota Transfer [Docket No.: 151130999-6225-01] (RIN: 0648-XE834) received November 16, 2016, pursuant to 5 U.S.C. 801(a)(1)(A); Public Law 104-121, Sec. 251; (110 Stat. 868); to the Committee on Natural Resources.

7583. A letter from the Acting Director, Office of Sustainable Fisheries, NMFS, National Oceanic and Atmospheric Administration, transmitting the Administration's temporary rule — Fisheries of the Exclusive Economic Zone Off Alaska; Pacific Ocean Perch in the Western Regulatory Area of the Gulf of Alaska [Docket No.: 150818742-6210-02] (RIN: 0648-XE706) received November 16, 2016, pursuant to 5 U.S.C. 801(a)(1)(A); Public Law 104-121, Sec. 251; (110 Stat. 868); to the Committee on Natural Resources.

7584. A letter from the Acting Director, Office of Sustainable Fisheries, NMFS, National Oceanic and Atmospheric Administration, transmitting the Administration's temporary rule — Fisheries of the Exclusive Economic Zone Off Alaska; Dusky Rockfish in the West Yakutat District of the Gulf of Alaska [Docket No.: 150818742-6210-02] (RIN: 0648-XE771) received November 16, 2016, pursuant to 5 U.S.C. 801(a)(1)(A); Public Law 104-121, Sec. 251; (110 Stat. 868); to the Committee on Natural Resources.

7585. A letter from the Acting Director, Office of Sustainable Fisheries, NMFS, National Oceanic and Atmospheric Administration, transmitting the Administration's temporary rule — Fisheries of the Exclusive Economic Zone Off Alaska; Pacific Ocean Perch in the Bering Sea and Aleutian Islands Management Area [Docket No.: 150916863-6211-02] (RIN: 0648-XE795) received November 16, 2016, pursuant to 5 U.S.C. 801(a)(1)(A); Public Law 104-121, Sec. 251; (110 Stat. 868); to the Committee on Natural Resources.

7586. A letter from the Acting Director, Office of Sustainable Fisheries, NMFS, National Oceanic and Atmospheric Administration, transmitting the Administration's temporary rule — Fisheries of the Northeastern United States; Small-Mesh Multispecies Fishery; Adjustment to the Commercial Northern Red Hake Inseason Possession Limit [Docket No.: 120109034-2171-01] (RIN: 0648-XE778) received November 16, 2016, pursuant to 5 U.S.C. 801(a)(1)(A); Public Law 104-121, Sec. 251; (110 Stat. 868); to the Committee on Natural Resources.

7587. A letter from the Acting Director, Office of Sustainable Fisheries, NMFS, National Oceanic and Atmospheric Administration, transmitting the Administration's temporary rule — Snapper-Grouper Fishery of the South Atlantic; 2016 Recreational Accountability Measure and Closure for South Atlantic Golden Tilefish [Docket No.: 120403249-2492-02] (RIN: 0648-XE829) received November 16, 2016, pursuant to 5 U.S.C. 801(a)(1)(A); Public Law 104-121, Sec. 251; (110 Stat. 868); to the Committee on Natural Resources.

7588. A letter from the Section Chief, Regulations Development Section, Bureau of Safety and Environmental Enforcement, Department of the Interior, transmitting the Department's final rule — Civil Penalty Inflation Adjustment [Docket ID: BSEE-2016-0010; 16XE1700DX EX1SF0000.DAQ000 EEEE50000] (RIN: 1014-AA30) received November 16, 2016, pursuant to 5 U.S.C. 801(a)(1)(A); Public Law 104-121, Sec. 251; (110 Stat. 868); to the Committee on the Judiciary.

7589. A letter from the Administrator, FEMA, Department of Homeland Security, transmitting a notification that the cost of response and recovery efforts for FEMA-3376-EM in the State of Louisiana has exceeded the $5 million limit for a single emergency declaration, pursuant to 42 U.S.C. 5193(b)(3); Public Law 93-288, Sec. 503(b)(3) (as amended by Public Law 100-707, Sec. 107(a)); (102 Stat. 4707); to the Committee on Transportation and Infrastructure.

7590. A letter from the Assistant Secretary of the Army, Civil Works, Department of the Army, Department of Defense, transmitting the Corps' Final Houston-Galveston Navigation Channels, Texas Post Authorization Change Report and Section 902 Cost Limit Determination (HGNC 902 PACR) & Appendices March 2016 (Revised May 2016); to the Committee on Transportation and Infrastructure.

7591. A letter from the Management and Program Analyst, FAA, Department of Transportation, transmitting the Department's final rule — Standard Instrument Approach Procedures, and Takeoff Minimums and Obstacle Departure Procedures; Miscellaneous Amendments [Docket No.: 31099; Amdt. No. 3716] received November 17, 2016, pursuant to 5 U.S.C. 801(a)(1)(A); Public Law 104-121, Sec. 251; (110 Stat. 868); to the Committee on Transportation and Infrastructure.

7592. A letter from the Management and Program Analyst, FAA, Department of Transportation, transmitting the Department's final rule — Standard Instrument Approach Procedures, and Takeoff Minimums and Obstacle Departure Procedures; Miscellaneous Amendments [Docket No.: 31098; Amdt. No.: 3715] received November 17, 2016, pursuant to 5 U.S.C. 801(a)(1)(A); Public Law 104-121, Sec. 251; (110 Stat. 868); to the Committee on Transportation and Infrastructure.

7593. A letter from the Management and Program Analyst, FAA, Department of Transportation, transmitting the Department's final rule — Airworthiness Directives; Airbus Helicopters Deutschland GmbH Helicopters [Docket No.: FAA-2016-5306; Directorate Identifier 2015-SW-010-AD; Amendment 39-18697; AD 2016-22-08] received November 17, 2016, pursuant to 5 U.S.C. 801(a)(1)(A); Public Law 104-121, Sec. 251; (110 Stat. 868); to the Committee on Transportation and Infrastructure.

7594. A letter from the Management and Program Analyst, FAA, Department of Transportation, transmitting the Department's final rule — Airworthiness Directives; Diamond Aircraft Industries GmbH Airplanes [Docket No.: FAA-2016-9318; Directorate Identifier 2016-CE-031-AD; Amendment 39-18695; AD 2016-22-06] (RIN: 2120-AA64) received November 17, 2016, pursuant to 5 U.S.C. 801(a)(1)(A); Public Law 104-121, Sec. 251; (110 Stat. 868); to the Committee on Transportation and Infrastructure.

7595. A letter from the Management and Program Analyst, FAA, Department of Transportation, transmitting the Department's final rule — Airworthiness Directives; Embraer S.A. Airplanes [Docket No.: FAA-2016-8160; Directorate Identifier 2016-CE-019-AD; Amendment 39-18691; AD 2016-22-02] (RIN: 2120-AA64) received November 17, 2016, pursuant to 5 U.S.C. 801(a)(1)(A); Public Law 104-121, Sec. 251; (110 Stat. 868); to the Committee on Transportation and Infrastructure.

7596. A letter from the Management and Program Analyst, FAA, Department of Transportation, transmitting the Department's final rule — Airworthiness Directives; Schempp-Hirth Flugzeugbau GmbH Gliders [Docket No.: FAA-2016-6123; Directorate Identifier 2016-CE-007-AD; Amendment 39-18690; AD 2016-22-01] (RIN: 2120-AA64) received November 17, 2016, pursuant to 5 U.S.C. 801(a)(1)(A); Public Law 104-121, Sec. 251; (110 Stat. 868); to the Committee on Transportation and Infrastructure.

7597. A letter from the Management and Program Analyst, FAA, Department of Transportation, transmitting the Department's final rule — Airworthiness Directives; Bell Helicopter Textron [Docket No.: FAA-2015-3821; Directorate Identifier 2014-SW-025-AD; Amendment 39-18696; AD 2016-22-07] (RIN: 2120-AA64) received November 17, 2016, pursuant to 5 U.S.C. 801(a)(1)(A); Public Law 104-121, Sec. 251; (110 Stat. 868); to the Committee on Transportation and Infrastructure.

7598. A letter from the Management and Program Analyst, FAA, Department of Transportation, transmitting the Department's final rule — Airworthiness Directives; Bombardier, Inc. Airplanes [Docket No.: FAA-2015-8464; Directorate Identifier 2015-NM-050-AD; Amendment 39-18692; AD 2016-22-03] (RIN: 2120-AA64) received November 17, 2016, pursuant to 5 U.S.C. 801(a)(1)(A); Public Law 104-121, Sec. 251; (110 Stat. 868); to the Committee on Transportation and Infrastructure.

7599. A letter from the Management and Program Analyst, FAA, Department of Transportation, transmitting the Department's final rule — Airworthiness Directives; Airbus Airplanes [Docket No.: FAA-2016-5589; Directorate Identifier 2014-NM-252-AD; Amendment 39-18678; AD 2016-20-12] (RIN: 2120-AA64) received November 17, 2016, pursuant to 5 U.S.C. 801(a)(1)(A); Public Law 104-121, Sec. 251; (110 Stat. 868); to the Committee on Transportation and Infrastructure.

7600. A letter from the Management and Program Analyst, FAA, Department of Transportation, transmitting the Department's final rule — Airworthiness Directives; Airbus Airplanes [Docket No.: FAA-2016-0465; Directorate Identifier 2015-NM-096-AD; Amendment 39-18679; AD 2016-20-13] (RIN: 2120-AA64) received November 17, 2016, pursuant to 5 U.S.C. 801(a)(1)(A); Public Law 104-121, Sec. 251; (110 Stat. 868); to the Committee on Transportation and Infrastructure.

7601. A letter from the Management and Program Analyst, FAA, Department of Transportation, transmitting the Department's final rule — Airworthiness Directives; Airbus Helicopters Deutschland GmbH (Previously Eurocopter Deutschland GmbH) (Airbus Helicopters) Helicopters [Docket No.: FAA-2014-0578; Directorate Identifier 2013-SW-048-AD; Amendment 39-18684; AD 2016-21-03] (RIN: 2120-AA64) received November 17, 2016, pursuant to 5 U.S.C. 801(a)(1)(A); Public Law 104-121, Sec. 251; (110 Stat. 868); to the Committee on Transportation and Infrastructure.

7602. A letter from the Management and Program Analyst, FAA, Department of Transportation, transmitting the Department's final rule — Airworthiness Directives; The Boeing Company Airplanes [Docket No.: FAA-2015-6538; Directorate Identifier 2015-NM-031-AD; Amendment 39-18668; AD 2016-20-02] (RIN: 2120-AA64) received November 17, 2016, pursuant to 5 U.S.C. 801(a)(1)(A); Public Law 104-121, Sec. 251; (110 Stat. 868); to the Committee on Transportation and Infrastructure.

7603. A letter from the Director, Regulatory Management Division, Environmental Protection Agency, transmitting the Agency's final rule — Ocean Disposal; Designation of a Dredged Material Disposal Site in Eastern Region of Long Island Sound; Connecticut [FRL-9955-13-Region 1] received November 15, 2016, pursuant to 5 U.S.C. 801(a)(1)(A); Public Law 104-121, Sec. 251; (110 Stat. 868); to the Committee on Transportation and Infrastructure.

REPORTS OF COMMITTEES ON PUBLIC BILLS AND RESOLUTIONS

Under clause 2 of rule XIII, reports of committees were delivered to the Clerk for printing and reference to the proper calendar, as follows:

Mr. HENSARLING: Committee on Financial Services. H.R. 5143. A bill to provide greater transparency and congressional oversight of international insurance standards setting processes, and for other purposes; with an amendment (Rept. 114–831). Referred to the Committee of the Whole House on the state of the Union.

Mr. BISHOP of Utah: Committee on Natural Resources. H.R. 2387. A bill to amend the Alaska Native Claims Settlement Act to provide for equitable allotment of land to Alaska Native veterans; with an amendment (Rept. 114–832). Referred to the Committee of the Whole House on the state of the Union.

Mr. BISHOP of Utah: Committee on Natural Resources. H.R. 5259. A bill to direct the Secretary of the Interior to reestablish the Royalty Policy Committee in order to further a more consultative process with key Federal, State, tribal, environmental, and energy stakeholders, and for other purposes; with an amendment (Rept. 114–833). Referred to the Committee of the Whole House on the state of the Union.

PUBLIC BILLS AND RESOLUTIONS

Under clause 2 of rule XII, public bills and resolutions of the following titles were introduced and severally referred, as follows:

By Mr. LUETKEMEYER:

H.R. 6392. A bill to amend the Dodd-Frank Wall Street Reform and Consumer Protection Act to specify when bank holding companies may be subject to certain enhanced supervision, and for other purposes; to the Committee on Financial Services.

By Mr. NUNES (for himself and Mr. SCHIFF):

H.R. 6393. A bill to authorize appropriations for fiscal year 2017 for intelligence and intelligence-related activities of the United States Government, the Community Management Account, and the Central Intelligence Agency Retirement and Disability System, and for other purposes; to the Committee on Intelligence (Permanent Select).

CONSTITUTIONAL AUTHORITY STATEMENT

Pursuant to clause 7 of rule XII of the Rules of the House of Representatives, the following statements are submitted regarding the specific powers granted to Congress in the Constitution to enact the accompanying bill or joint resolution.

By Mr. LUETKEMEYER:

H.R. 6392.

Congress has the power to enact this legislation pursuant to the following:

The constitutional authority on which this bill rests lies in Article 1, Section 7, Clause 2 of the Constitution, which allows for every bill passed by the House of Representatives and the Senate and signed by the President to be codified into law; and therefore implicitly allows Congress to repeal any bill that has been passed by both chambers and signed into law by the President.

Additionally, the Constitution grants to Congress the explicit power to regulate commerce in and among the states, as enumerate in Article 1, Section 8, Clause 3, the Commerce Clause.

By Mr. NUNES:

H.R. 6393.

Congress has the power to enact this legislation pursuant to the following:

The intelligence and intelligence-related activities of the United States Government, including those under Title 50, are carried out to support the national security interests of the United States, to enable the armed forces of the United States, and to support the President in executing the foreign policy of the United States.

Article I, section 8 of the Constitution of the United States provides, in pertinent part, that "Congress shall have power . . . to . . . provide for the common Defense and general Welfare of the United States"; ". . . to raise and support armies . . ."; to "make Rules concerning Captures on Land and Water"; and "To make all laws which shall be necessary and proper for carrying into Execution the foregoing Powers and all other Powers vested in this Constitution in the Government of the United States, or in any Department of Officer thereof."

ADDITIONAL SPONSORS

Under clause 7 of rule XII, sponsors were added to public bills and resolutions, as follows:

H.R. 592: Ms. KUSTER.

H.R. 1631: Ms. KUSTER.

H.R. 1703: Ms. MAXINE WATERS of California.

H.R. 1969: Mr. KENNEDY.

H.R. 3790: Mr. DeSAULNIER.

H.R. 5235: Mr. ROHRABACHER.

H.R. 5689: Ms. McCOLLUM.

H.R. 6058: Ms. PINGREE.

H.R. 6159: Mr. SMITH of Missouri.

H.R. 6179: Mr. GRIJALVA.

H. Con. Res. 165: Ms. FRANKEL of Florida.

H. Res. 808: Mr. COURTNEY.

EXTENSIONS OF REMARKS

HONORING MR. BOBBY SEALE

HON. BARBARA LEE
OF CALIFORNIA
IN THE HOUSE OF REPRESENTATIVES
Tuesday, November 22, 2016

Ms. LEE. Mr. Speaker, I rise today to honor Mr. Bobby Seale on the momentous occasion of his 80th birthday. Mr. Seale has had an incredible career in political activism and community service, dedicating his life to advocating for the rights and betterment of African-Americans across the nation.

Born in Texas in 1936, Mr. Seale grew up entrenched in poverty. After moving around in Texas, living in Dallas, San Antonio, and Port Arthur, Mr. Seale's family finally relocated to Oakland, California, when Mr. Seale was eight years old.

Mr. Seale attended Berkeley High School, where he started to become politically active. In 1955, Mr. Seale dropped out of high school and joined the United States Air Force. After his military service, Mr. Seale worked as a sheet metal mechanic while earning his high school diploma at night.

After earning his high school diploma, Mr. Seale went on to attend Merritt College, where he intended to study engineering. However, during his time at Merritt College, he began to take a deep interest in politics and black history, and joined the Afro-American Association (AAA), a campus group advocating for black separatism. It was through the AAA that Mr. Seale met Mr. Huey P. Newton, a kindred spirit. They quickly became friends and their political activism deepened as they were inspired by the teachings of Malcolm X.

During this time, Mr. Seale was also inspired to give back to his community, spending time teaching youths about black history and personal responsibility at the North Oakland Neighborhood Anti-Poverty Center.

By October 1966, Mr. Seale and Mr. Newton were ready to organize their beliefs and put them into practice, and they formed the Black Panther Party for Self-Defense. Originally formed to protect the African-American community in Oakland from police brutality, the Black Panthers rejected the nonviolent approach of the mainstream Civil Rights Movement. The Black Panthers also focused on serving the community, cooking free breakfast for children before school, distributing clothing, and teaching classes on politics and economics.

A few years later, in 1970, Mr. Seale was arrested in Chicago during a protest at the Democratic National Convention, and he was ultimately sentenced to four years in prison for contempt of court. After his release from prison in 1973, Mr. Seale renounced violence as a means to an end and decided to run for Mayor of Oakland. He finished second out of nine candidates.

In 1974, Mr. Seale resigned as Chairman of the Black Panther Party, having grown tired of politics. He has remained active in the community, writing books and working to improve social services and educational opportunities in black neighborhoods.

On a personal note, I am deeply grateful for "the Chairman's" brilliance and leadership. He was a mentor, a colleague, but most importantly, a true friend. My late beloved mother, Ms. Mildred Massey, was one of Bobby's strongest supporters and believed in him and the Black Panther Party as the "vanguard of the movement." He taught us the importance of grassroots organizing by knocking on doors, walking precincts, and phone banking to communicate our position on issues and most importantly, how to be a true public servant.

Today, California's 13th Congressional District celebrates the extraordinary life and service of Mr. Bobby Seale and wishes him a very happy birthday and a life that continues to be filled with peace and happiness and fulfilled by the great work and leadership he continues to provide.

HONORING JUDGE GORDON BARANCO

HON. BARBARA LEE
OF CALIFORNIA
IN THE HOUSE OF REPRESENTATIVES
Tuesday, November 22, 2016

Ms. LEE. Mr. Speaker, I rise today to recognize the extraordinary career of Judge Gordon Baranco. I would like to congratulate him on his retirement and thank him for his invaluable service to our community.

Born and raised in Oakland, California, Gordon graduated from Oakland High School in 1965. Gordon would become a star basketball player at the University of California, Davis, where he led the Aggies to win three league championships.

Gordon's time spent at UC Davis would coincide with the Vietnam War and the Civil Rights Movement. This time in Gordon's life was critical to his academic and civic development, opening his eyes to injustices here in the United States and abroad.

In 1969, Gordon graduated from UC Davis with a bachelor's degree in political science. Inspired by the idea that the law could be a vehicle to change society, he went on to enroll in law school. He graduated from the King School of Law at UC Davis in 1972.

As an attorney, Gordon practiced as a Graduate Legal Assistant in the office of the California State Attorney General; a Deputy District Attorney in the office of the San Francisco District Attorney; as managing Attorney for the San Francisco Neighborhood Legal Assistance Foundation, and Assistant to the City Attorney in Oakland.

At the young age of 32 he was made the Honorable Gordon Baranco, appointed to the Oakland Piedmont Emeryville Municipal Court by Governor Edmund G. Brown, Jr. After serving as presiding judge of the court, he was appointed by Governor George Deukmejian as a judge of the Alameda County Superior Court.

In 2004, Judge Baranco was instrumental in establishing the Alameda County Homeless and Caring Court, which provides a much needed alternative to the traditional criminal justice court system for the homeless.

On a personal note, Judge Baranco worked with me and helped lead our record remedy and expungement conferences for several years. Because of his boldness and commitment, many returning citizens have been able to move forward with their lives without the troubles of their past once their parole is completed. For this, I, along with so many others, am deeply grateful.

On behalf of the residents of California's 13th Congressional District, Judge Gordon Baranco, salute you. I thank you for a lifetime of service and congratulate you on your achievements. I wish you and your loved ones the very best as you enjoy your well-deserved retirement.

HONORING ZION FIRST CHURCH OF GOD IN CHRIST

HON. BARBARA LEE
OF CALIFORNIA
IN THE HOUSE OF REPRESENTATIVES
Tuesday, November 22, 2016

Ms. LEE. Mr. Speaker, I rise today to honor Zion First Church of God in Christ located in Oakland, California upon its 100th anniversary as a strong religious pillar in the East Bay Community.

After moving to California from Louisiana, Zion First Church of God in Christ was founded in 1916 by Samuel Harrison and was the first Church of God in Christ in Northern California. It was created with the vision to expand the ministry and establish a legacy of spirituality through faith.

Under the leadership of Pastor Harrison, the church thrived and soon needed a building to accommodate its growing membership. In 1921, the church purchased its first building purchase in West Oakland and became a strong faith center for the West Oakland community. During the 1940's, as African Americans migrated to the West for industrial jobs, many families settled in West Oakland. Worship services immediately grew and were so inspirational it was said that people would hang out of their windows to see what was going on in the services.

On January 25, 1977 Pastor Willie E. Pearls was ushered in as the second leader of Zion First Church of God in Christ. Pastor Pearls had moved to California.

In 1978, Zion First upgraded its building to make room for its growing membership. Pastor Pearls moved to California in 1952 and

---

● This "bullet" symbol identifies statements or insertions which are not spoken by a Member of the Senate on the floor.

Matter set in <u>this typeface</u> indicates words inserted or appended, rather than spoken, by a Member of the House on the floor.

joined Zion. First, serving for many years as a youth leader, Deacon, and a special helper to Overseer Harrison before accepting the role as senior pastor.

Pastor Pearls carried on the original vision of the church, helping the community, by giving away food, clothing the homeless, and serving hot breakfast every Sunday to the community.

In 2003, after 33 years of service, Pastor Pearls stepped down and the church elected Pastor Rickie L. Williams. Under his leadership, the church has continued to faithfully serve the West Oakland community through various outreach programs. Although the church was ravaged by fire in September 2013, the congregation bonded together and rebuilt the church on the same property to continue its ministry in the West Oakland community.

On behalf of the residents of California's 13th Congressional District, I extend my sincerest congratulations to Zion First Church of God in Christ on the celebration of its 100th year of worship. I wish Zion First Church of God in Christ many more years of authentic and compassionate service.

IN HONOR OF GEORGE RIVERA AND HIS WINNING SUBMISSION TO THE 2016 VETERANS DAY ESSAY CONTEST FROM NEW YORK'S 14TH CONGRESSIONAL DISTRICT

HON. JOSEPH CROWLEY
OF NEW YORK
IN THE HOUSE OF REPRESENTATIVES
Tuesday, November 22, 2016

Mr. CROWLEY. Mr. Speaker, I rise today to congratulate the winner of the 2016 Veterans Day essay contest from New York's 14th Congressional District. George Rivera, a student from I.S. 61 in Corona, Queens submitted the winning essay on the topic, "What Veterans Day Means To Me." George's essay reads as follows:

Veteran's Day is a public holiday in the United States and it is celebrated on November 11th. On this day, we honor those who fought for our country and thank them for all they have done. The U.S. Armed Forces risk their lives every day for us. The Air Force, Army, Coast Guard, Marine Corps, and the Navy, all make up the United States Armed Forces. Taking time out of our day to honor them is the least that we can do compared to what they have done for us. This holiday is not only for those who served in our military, but also for the ones who are still serving today. Many people take for granted what they do for us; not only this, but some people even forget about them without realizing that without them, we probably would not have the freedom that we have today. These soldiers sacrifice so much for the people they don't even know; they leave their families to fight for our country. Many people enjoy their freedom without knowing that soldiers are dying behind the lines for them to keep their freedom and rights. All of the soldiers show love to our Nation through this big sacrifice.

There are U.S. soldiers located all around the world and I know they miss their families but continue fighting for us. My brother is currently serving in the U.S. Army. Right now he is in Guam which is an island near Japan. I know he misses us but he still strives to keep people from taking our freedom. Throughout U.S. history, many soldiers have lost their lives. In World War I, nearly 11 million military soldiers died, and in World War II even more soldiers died to save our world from tyranny; they wanted to keep the United States safe.

At least two soldiers, on average, die each day trying to fight for our country. Imagine, that is between 600 and 800 soldiers that die every single year, leaving their families with tears. It is really not that hard to honor these men and women; all you can do is take a little time out of your day to visit a Veteran's nursing home and thank all the veterans there. Families worry every single day and hope that their sister, brother, son, daughter, mother, or fathers are okay.

On Veteran's Day, I honor my brother and all U.S. soldiers that are serving. My brother has made me grow as a person, many soldiers have to face struggles and sometimes they have to kill just to keep the rest of us safe. Would you kill someone to keep other people you don't know safe? Not everyone can be a soldier so we should thank and love the soldiers who keep us and our families safe. Without them, our lives would be completely different and probably more dangerous. Even the soldiers who are located in the United States on the borders should earn the same respect as the soldiers who fight in Iraq, Syria, and Afghanistan. Every soldier has the same duty and mindset to keep danger away from the United States. That is what Veteran's Day means to me and I think all the soldiers who have served in the past and who are serving now deserve our respect and gratitude.

HONORING WILLIAM BYRON RUMFORD

HON. BARBARA LEE
OF CALIFORNIA
IN THE HOUSE OF REPRESENTATIVES
Tuesday, November 22, 2016

Ms. LEE. Mr. Speaker, I rise today to honor the extraordinary life of an outstanding member of the East Bay community, the Honorable William Byron Rumford.

He was born in Courtland, Arizona in 1915. As a child, he shined shoes, sold newspapers, and graduated from George Washington Carver High School in Phoenix in 1926. After finishing his studies at Sacramento Junior College in 1931, he earned his pharmacy degree at the University of California, San Francisco. After he graduated, he took a number of exams for employment and was discriminated against at every turn. He fought his way through by appealing his oral examination, ultimately becoming a member of the California Board of Pharmacy.

Mr. Rumford worked in the Bay Area as an assistant pharmacist and as a venereal disease investigator for the state. In 1942, he co-invested in a pharmacy on Sacramento Street in Berkeley, which he later purchased and renamed Rumford's Pharmacy (now known as the Rumford Clinic). Later, he served as the director of the Oakland chapter of the Red Cross, president of the East Bay Health Association, and was on the region's Democratic Central Committee.

Mr. Rumford went on to lead an impactful and significant political career, and ultimately became the first African American legislator from Northern California. Inspired by the disparities he witnessed in his pharmaceutical career, he joined the Berkeley Emergency Housing Committee in 1942 and the Berkeley Rent Board in 1944. In addition, he worked with the unofficial Berkeley Interracial Committee which was intended to ease tensions between the Black community of Berkeley and White Southerners who were moving in. He was also a member of the Appomattox Club, which was one of the first African American political organizations in the country; there was little hope for an African American candidate at that time, so the organization supported White candidates who they believed were right on political issues affecting the African American community.

Mr. Rumford did not seek to become a professional politician; instead, he was a neighborhood pharmacist who was passionate about addressing the biggest issues impacting his community. Eventually, Mr. Rumford ran for election in the California Assembly and won in 1949. At first he represented mostly African American areas of Oakland and a portion of South Berkeley. In 1960, however, the district was enlarged to include all of Berkeley and parts of Albany.

As an Assembly Member, Mr. Rumford produced several effective pieces of legislation. In 1949, he worked tirelessly to pass the Bill to end discrimination in the National Guard. He also introduced legislation early in his Assembly tenure pertaining to fair trade, small businesses, child polio immunizations, atomic energy conversion, and environmental pollution.

Today, Mr. Rumford is best remembered for three pieces of legislation: the California Fair Employment Practices Act of 1959, which lessened the impact of race on hiring decisions; the Good Samaritan Act of 1959, which garnered national attention as the first law in the country to protect professionals in emergency situations; and the law that bore his name: the Rumford Fair Housing Act of 1963, which failed to survive a referendum challenge, but was upheld by the Supreme Court of the United States. This act served as California's main enforcement authority against race-based housing discrimination, by way of housing covenants, until the passage of the Federal Civil Rights Act of 1968.

His tremendous legacy paved the way for civil rights legislation nationally, and has been beautifully honored by the William Byron Rumford Memorial Project. This project is led by a diverse group of community members who see the rapid changing of South Berkeley's demographics as a ripe time to honor his leadership, activism, and community, while preserving the neighborhood's history.

On a personal note, William was a trailblazer. Had it not been for him, I never would have been elected to the CA legislature. I owe him a debt of gratitude and I will be forever grateful.

Today, California's 13th Congressional District salutes the legacy of the Honorable William Byron Rumford. His contributions have truly impacted countless lives through the East Bay area and the country. I join all of Mr. Rumford's loved ones and the community members involved in the William Byron Rumford Memorial Project in celebrating his incredible life and legacy.

HONORING THE 20TH ANNIVERSARY OF INNER CITY ADVISORS FUND GOOD JOBS

HON. BARBARA LEE

OF CALIFORNIA

IN THE HOUSE OF REPRESENTATIVES

Tuesday, November 22, 2016

Ms. LEE. Mr. Speaker, I rise to recognize the 20th anniversary of ICA Fund Good Jobs. Today November 17th, 2016, ICA Fund Good Jobs celebrates its many achievements in supporting small businesses and creating good jobs throughout the Bay Area.

ICA Fund Good Jobs was founded in 1996 as Oakland Advisors (later Inner City Advisors). Its mission is to create jobs for people with high barriers to employment, by helping entrepreneurs with consulting, education, and investment services. ICA focuses on high-growth small businesses in order to create accessible jobs that provide living wages, health benefits, and opportunities for advancement.

In 2013 ICA founded a partner organization called "Fund Good Jobs", which provides small businesses with capital investments and helps reduce the burden of relying on commercial lending for start-up businesses. In 2015 ICA and Fund Good Jobs combined their operations to become a comprehensive support structure for local businesses in the East Bay.

In its 20-year history, ICA Fund Good Jobs has worked with more than 500 companies to create more than 5,000 jobs and generate over $65 million in local employee wealth.

ICA Fund Good Jobs is a certified Community Development Financial Institution, and has used its expertise and capital to support successful startups including Revolution Foods, Blue Bottle Coffee, and newer successes such as Firebrand Artisan Breads and Back to the Roots. These companies and others supported by ICA Fund Good Jobs have spurred economic growth throughout the East Bay, and are examples of the fulfillment of ICA Fund Good Job's mission.

On behalf of the residents of California's 13th Congressional District, I congratulate ICA Fund Good Jobs on 20 years of exemplary service as it continues to solve long-standing problems in new ways, and move the needle on some of the Bay Area's most challenging indicators of socioeconomic inequality. I wish ICA Fund Good Jobs well as it continues to work toward ensuring that every worker has access to a good job.

HONORING MRS. ETHEL MAE MOLO

HON. BARBARA LEE

OF CALIFORNIA

IN THE HOUSE OF REPRESENTATIVES

Tuesday, November 22, 2016

Ms. LEE. Mr. Speaker, I rise today to honor the extraordinary life of Mrs. Ethel Mae Molo, who was affectionately known by family and friends as GG.

Mrs. Molo was born on October 27, 1914 in Homer, Louisiana. After graduating from McDonogh Thirty Five High School she attended and graduated from Xavier University in New Orleans, Louisiana with a Bachelor of Arts degree in Social Work.

After moving to California Ethel married Mr. Raymond Molo, she also had three beautiful children. Once in California she was given the opportunity to hold a position on the Kaiser shipyard as a Rosie the Riveter, helping to support the war efforts for World War II. She later continued her service at the Naval Air station working on aircrafts. After many years as a dispatcher, she retired from the Air Station.

Following her retirement Ethel was very active throughout her community. She worked with political leaders Ronald Dellums, Willie Brown, and Don Peralta on projects in the Bay Area. On a national level she was an active member of the NAACP, for fifteen years she helped fundraise money for Fannie Lou Hamer and the voting rights act in Mississippi.

As a strong woman of faith Mrs. Molo worshiped at the Presbyterian Women of Faith East Oakland Fellowship Circle and was the secretary of her church.

All in all, Ethel was a woman of many colors. Her interests were diverse as were the many people she touched with her hard work and dedication to her community and those that were less fortunate than her.

Traveling, sewing, reading and cooking big meals for her friends and family were among her many hobbies. She spent her golden years reading, comfortably eating her favorite cookies, spending time with her family and watching her game shows.

She leaves to celebrate her life, her three loving children, Dovelyn Burbridge-Winbush, Gene Hennen, and Alfreda Gibson-Hampton. She also leaves six generations of grandchildren, great-grandchildren, and great-great-grandchildren along with her nieces and nephew.

Today, California's 13th Congressional District salutes the legacy of Mrs. Ethel Mae Molo. Her contributions have truly impacted countless lives throughout the Bay Area. I join her loved ones in celebrating her incredible life and offer my most sincere condolences.

RECOGNIZING STEPHEN L. RITCHIE FOR RECEIVING THE AJC'S JUDGE LEARNED HAND HUMAN RELATIONS AWARD

HON. ROBERT J. DOLD

OF ILLINOIS

IN THE HOUSE OF REPRESENTATIVES

Tuesday, November 22, 2016

Mr. DOLD. Mr. Speaker, I rise today to congratulate a highly deserving recipient of the Judge Learned Hand Human Relations Award, Stephen Ritchie. Presented by the American Jewish Committee (AJC), this honor is given to distinguished attorneys who have shown an exceptional commitment to justice, individual rights, and civic leadership.

To those who know Steve, it is no surprise that he is receiving this prestigious recognition. Steve has earned a reputation among his clients and within our community for excellence and leadership. Throughout the past decade, he has consistently been recognized as one of the best lawyers in America, all while showing remarkable dedication to his family and civic and charitable endeavors. Through his service to AJC Chicago, AIPAC's Illinois council, Teach for America, and the United States Holocaust Memorial Museum, Steve has made a true imprint on our community and our nation.

Mr. Speaker, I am honored to consider Steve a friend and congratulate him on receiving the Judge Learned Hand Human Relations Award.

HONORING MS. PATRICIA MARIE JONES

HON. BARBARA LEE

OF CALIFORNIA

IN THE HOUSE OF REPRESENTATIVES

Tuesday, November 22, 2016

Ms. LEE. Mr. Speaker, I rise today to honor the extraordinary life and invaluable service of Ms. Patricia Jones, who passed away August 5, 2016.

Patricia Marie Jones was born on September 3, 1944 in Vallejo, California to Booker T. and Mildred Jones. At a young age the family relocated back to its homeland of Heidelberg, Mississippi where Patricia graduated from Southside High School at the top of her class.

After her high school graduation Patricia moved back to the Bay Area and enrolled at Vallejo Junior college. Patricia earned her Associates Degree. Understanding the power of education, Patricia transferred to San Francisco State University where she would earn her Bachelor's Degree two years later in Journalism. She then enrolled at University of California, Berkeley and in 1973 earned her Master's Degree in City Planning.

Patricia had a distinguished career in public service that included local, state and federal service. She served in the city of Richmond as the city planner, the assistant to the City Manager for External Affairs and Assistant Director of Housing Development. She also served as a Board member of the East Bay Community Foundation. Most recently Patricia served as Assistant Executive Director of the Association of Bay Area Governments, a regional planning agency representing nine cities in the Bay Area.

Patricia was committed to excellence known for her work ethic, integrity, creativity and fierce determination. She excelled at everything she did.

Patricia was also a world traveler and over the years had visited Africa, Asia, Europe, South America and Cuba. She lived a full life and inspired all those around her to do the same.

But no matter her accomplishments, Patricia always put family first; she always made time for them no matter the time of day or size of the problem. She leaves to honor her memory, brothers Terry and Kenneth Jones, along with her many nieces and nephews.

Today, California's 13th Congressional District remembers the extraordinary life of Ms.

Patricia Jones. Her contributions have truly impacted countless lives throughout the Bay Area. I join her loved ones in celebrating her incredible life and offer my most sincere condolences.

HONORING THE 150TH ANNIVERSARY OF THE PACIFIC SCHOOL OF RELIGION

HON. BARBARA LEE
OF CALIFORNIA
IN THE HOUSE OF REPRESENTATIVES

Tuesday, November 22, 2016

Ms. LEE. Mr. Speaker, I rise today to honor the 150th anniversary of the Pacific School of Religion.

Founded in 1866, the Pacific School of Religion (formerly known as the Pacific Theological Seminary) was established to serve as "an institution of the people" and "a child of the churches" by preparing spiritually-rooted leaders through rigorous scholarship, practical training, and immersive footwork. Firmly cemented in the history of social justice in the United States, the school served as a building block for ongoing service including pastoral ministry, non-profit and civic leadership, and public policy.

In 1901, the school moved to its first Berkeley location near the University of California, Berkeley campus. By 1916, because of the school's new nondenominational status and the faculty's growing interest in the importance of the world's religions to the Christian faith, the name was changed to its current name: Pacific School of Religion.

During World War II, former President Arthur C. McGiffert and his colleague John C. Bennett voiced concerns of community members against Japanese internment camps, including the imprisonment of several seminarians. After the war, President McGiffert went on to remedy war-torn communities in both Europe and Asia through the establishment of the Post-War Rehabilitation School at PSR which trained students to minister to these communities.

Similarly, the school provided necessary leadership for other intuitions with similar goals to promote education and dialog in underrepresented communities. The school later formed the Graduate Theological Union, a daring experiment in ecumenical cooperation between Protestant and Catholic institutions. This development aimed to bridge Protestant and Catholic Studies and bring forth new fields of study in religion, such as LGBTQ and Gender Studies.

Over the years, the Pacific School of Religion has gathered some of our nation's leading voices of social change and theological writers, including Georgia Harkness who later became the first tenured woman professor at the school in the 1950s. Today, graduates are well recognized in their respective fields and are a leading force in promoting social justice

and compassion based-practices around the world. Their leadership and commitment to theology and religious studies have been critical starting points to cultivating positive change throughout our nation.

On behalf of California's 13th Congressional District, I extend my sincerest congratulations to the Pacific School of Religion on this important milestone. Thank you to everyone who has contributed to its success over the years. I wish the faculty, students, and administration continued success in the years to come.

HONORING REV. DR. CHARLEY HAMES, JR.

HON. BARBARA LEE
OF CALIFORNIA
IN THE HOUSE OF REPRESENTATIVES

Tuesday, November 22, 2016

Ms. LEE. Mr. Speaker, I rise today to honor the extraordinary career and the service of Rev. Dr. Charley Hames, Jr., as he celebrates with friends, family, and his congregation 25 dedicated years of faithful service and ministry.

Dr. Hames was born to Charley Hames, Sr. and Leona Elizabeth Steadman-Hames on January 10, 1974, on the south side of Chicago, Illinois.

After completing high school, Dr. Hames went on to graduate from Chicago State University where he received his Bachelor of Arts degree in African-American studies. He would then go on to study at Garrett-Evangelical Theological Seminary in Evanston, Illinois and in 2000 he earned his Masters of Divinity. In 2004, Rev. Hames earned and received his Doctor of Ministry degree in Evangelism from the Perkins School of Theology, Southern Methodist University, in Dallas, Texas.

In 2003, Dr. Hames had obediently fulfilled his calling to serve as Senior Pastor of Beebe Memorial Cathedral (BMC) in Oakland. Dr. Hames has received many accolades including being named "Pastor of the Year" by the CME 9th Episcopal District.

A passionate fighter for the men of color in our communities, Dr. Hames was amongst a group of pastors and community leaders selected to meet at the White House in 2012 to discuss the killing of Trayvon Martin with President Barack Obama. He has also been a commentator on CNN to speak about the relationships between police and communities of color. He volunteers as chaplain of 100 Black Men of the Bay Area, Inc., president of the National Action Network's Oakland chapter, Chairman of the Board of the Oakland African-American Chamber of Commerce and is a proud Life member of the Alpha Phi Alpha, Fraternity, making him a true champion of our community.

Dr. Hames is married to Lady Michelle J. Gaskill-Hames who serves as a Senior Vice President with Kaiser Permanente. He is also the proud father of two sons, Charles

Jonathon Hames, Elijah Immanuel Hames and daughter, Jael Deon Hames.

Today, California's 13th Congressional District salutes and honors the outstanding Rev. Dr. Charley Hames, Jr. His dedication and commitment to our local faith community has impacted many lives throughout the district and the nation. I wish Dr. Hames many more years of faithful and compassionate service.

HONORING MR. MICHAEL DAVENPORT

HON. BARBARA LEE
OF CALIFORNIA
IN THE HOUSE OF REPRESENTATIVES

Tuesday, November 22, 2016

Ms. LEE. Mr. Speaker, today I rise with my colleague, Congressman DeSaulnier to honor the extraordinary career and invaluable service to our community from Mr. Michael Davenport.

A native of Richmond, California, Michael attended Richmond public schools and graduated from Harry Ells High School, going on to study at Contra Costa College.

Michael began his career at Ford Motor Company in Richmond, where he worked as a train car unloader and later as an electric forklift mechanic. He also tried his hand in numerous trades, but ultimately found his passion when he began working in the security industry.

In 1996, Michael co-founded DP Security. The company initially operated out of his van, but he was able to grow and establish the company as a reputable business in the community. The company would eventually sign contracts with Richmond Sanitation, Chevron Richmond Refinery, Ford Assembly Building, and many others.

Since its inception, DP Security has employed 180 individuals, the majority of which have been residents of Richmond. Furthermore, Michael has been a civic leader, and has dedicated his life to influencing Richmond's youth by his active involvement in Richmond Little League's baseball organization, Salesian Boys' and Girls' Club, and the Richmond Black Firefighters Youth Academy. He has also been a longtime participant in the Smart Cookie Factory, donating supplies and bicycles to elementary school students.

He has also been a member of the Richmond Police Activities League board, a member of Richmond Main Street, an executive board member of the Richmond Chamber of Commerce, the president of the Kiwanis Club, and the president of the Black Men and Women political organization.

On behalf of the residents of California's 11th and 13th Congressional Districts, I would like to congratulate Michael Davenport on a well-deserved retirement.

SENATE—*Friday, November 25, 2016*

The Senate met at 11 and 3 seconds a.m. and was called to order by the Honorable DANIEL COATS, a Senator from the State of Indiana.

APPOINTMENT OF ACTING PRESIDENT PRO TEMPORE

The PRESIDING OFFICER. The clerk will please read a communication to the Senate from the President pro tempore (Mr. HATCH).

The bill clerk read the following letter:

U.S. SENATE,
PRESIDENT PRO TEMPORE,
Washington, DC, November 25, 2016.
To the Senate:

Under the provisions of rule I, paragraph 3, of the Standing Rules of the Senate, I hereby appoint the Honorable DANIEL COATS, a Senator from the State of Indiana, to perform the duties of the Chair.

ORRIN G. HATCH,
President pro tempore.

Mr. COATS thereupon assumed the Chair as Acting President pro tempore.

ADJOURNMENT UNTIL MONDAY, NOVEMBER 28, 2016, AT 3 P.M.

The ACTING PRESIDENT pro tempore. Under the previous order, the Senate stands adjourned until 3 p.m., Monday, November 28, 2016.

Thereupon, the Senate, at 11 and 34 seconds a.m., adjourned until Monday, November 28, 2016, at 3 p.m.

● This "bullet" symbol identifies statements or insertions which are not spoken by a Member of the Senate on the floor.

HOUSE OF REPRESENTATIVES—*Friday, November 25, 2016*

The House met at 9:30 a.m. and was called to order by the Speaker pro tempore (Mr. UPTON).

DESIGNATION OF THE SPEAKER PRO TEMPORE

The SPEAKER pro tempore laid before the House the following communication from the Speaker:

WASHINGTON, DC,
November 25, 2016.

I hereby appoint the Honorable FRED UPTON to act as Speaker pro tempore on this day.

PAUL D. RYAN,
Speaker of the House of Representatives.

PRAYER

Reverend Vincent De Rosa, St. Joseph's Catholic Church, Washington, D.C., offered the following prayer:

God of all creation, in whom we live and move and have our being, with gratitude for Your countless gifts, we pray for continued peace and prosperity.

Grant our people's Representatives the gifts they need to govern wisely, giving voice to all, especially to the poor and the suffering.

Give them senses open to perceiving Your truth, intellects ready to understand it, and hearts fortified to love it and to administer that truth with mercy and compassion.

Give this House resolve to cling faithfully to the principles of our founding and our future.

Forgive us our failings, humbly admitted before You, and admit all of us one day to virtue's reward.

Amen.

THE JOURNAL

The SPEAKER pro tempore. Pursuant to section 3(a) of House Resolution 921, the Journal of the last day's proceedings is approved.

PLEDGE OF ALLEGIANCE

The SPEAKER pro tempore. The Chair will lead the House in the Pledge of Allegiance.

The SPEAKER pro tempore led the Pledge of Allegiance as follows:

I pledge allegiance to the Flag of the United States of America, and to the Republic for which it stands, one nation under God, indivisible, with liberty and justice for all.

ADJOURNMENT

The SPEAKER pro tempore. Pursuant to section 3(b) of House Resolution 921, the House stands adjourned until noon on Tuesday, November 29, 2016, for morning-hour debate and 2 p.m. for legislative business.

Thereupon (at 9 o'clock and 32 minutes a.m.), under its previous order, the House adjourned until Tuesday, November 29, 2016, at noon.

EXECUTIVE COMMUNICATIONS, ETC.

Under clause 2 of rule XIV, executive communications were taken from the Speaker's table and referred as follows:

7604. A letter from the Secretary, Department of Health and Human Services, transmitting a renewal of the August 12, 2016 declaration of the public health emergency of national significance existing within the Commonwealth of Puerto Rico relating to pregnant women and children born to pregnant women with Zika, pursuant to 42 U.S.C. 247d(a); Public Law 107-188, Sec. 144(a); (116 Stat. 630); to the Committee on Energy and Commerce.

7605. A letter from the Assistant Secretary for Legislative Affairs, Department of Homeland Security, transmitting a legislative proposal titled "U.S. Immigration and Customs Enforcement Pay Reform Act of 2016"; to the Committee on Oversight and Government Reform.

7606. A letter from the Director, Office of Government Ethics, transmitting the Office's final rule — Executive Branch Ethics Program Amendments (RIN: 3209-AA42) received November 17, 2016, pursuant to 5 U.S.C. 801(a)(1)(A); Public Law 104-121, Sec. 251; (110 Stat. 868); to the Committee on Oversight and Government Reform.

7607. A letter from the Administrator, United States Agency for International Development, transmitting the Agency's FY 2016 Agency Financial Report, pursuant to 31 U.S.C. 3515(a)(1); Public Law 101-576, Sec. 303(a)(1) (as amended by Public Law 107-289, Sec. 2(a)); (116 Stat. 2049); to the Committee on Oversight and Government Reform.

7608. A letter from the Secretary, Department of the Interior, transmitting the Department's 2017-2022 Outer Continental Shelf Oil and Gas Leasing Proposed Final Program, pursuant to 43 U.S.C. 1344(e); Aug. 7, 1953, ch. 345, Sec. 18(e) (as amended by Public Law 95-372, Sec. 208); (92 Stat. 649); to the Committee on Natural Resources.

7609. A letter from the Division Chief, Regulatory Affairs, Bureau of Land Management, Department of the Interior, transmitting the Department's final rule — Onshore Oil and Gas Operations; Federal and Indian Oil and Gas Leases; Measurement of Gas [17X.LLWO310000.L13100000.PP0000] (RIN: 1004-AE17) received November 17, 2016, pursuant to 5 U.S.C. 801(a)(1)(A); Public Law 104-121, Sec. 251; (110 Stat. 868); to the Committee on Natural Resources.

7610. A letter from the Division Chief, Regulatory Affairs, Bureau of Land Management, Department of the Interior, transmitting the Department's final rule — Onshore

Oil and Gas Operations; Federal and Indian Oil and Gas Leases; Measurement of Oil [17X.LLWO310000.L13100000.PP0000] (RIN: 1004-AE16) received November 17, 2016, pursuant to 5 U.S.C. 801(a)(1)(A); Public Law 104-121, Sec. 251; (110 Stat. 868); to the Committee on Natural Resources.

7611. A letter from the Division Chief, Regulatory Affairs, Bureau of Land Management, Department of the Interior, transmitting the Department's final rule — Onshore Oil and Gas Operations; Federal and Indian Oil and Gas Leases; Site Security [17X.LLWO310000.L13100000.PP0000] (RIN: 1004-AE15) received November 17, 2016, pursuant to 5 U.S.C. 801(a)(1)(A); Public Law 104-121, Sec. 251; (110 Stat. 868); to the Committee on Natural Resources.

7612. A letter from the Chairman, Surface Transportation Board, transmitting the Board's interim final rule — Civil Monetary Penalty Inflation Adjustment Rule [Docket No.: EP 716 (Sub-No.: 1)] received November 18, 2016, pursuant to 5 U.S.C. 801(a)(1)(A); Public Law 104-121, Sec. 251; (110 Stat. 868); to the Committee on the Judiciary.

7613. A letter from the Chief, Regulatory Coordination Division, U.S. Citizenship and Immigration Services, Department of Homeland Security, transmitting the Department's Major final rule — Retention of EB-1, EB-2, and EB-3 Immigrant Workers and Program Improvements Affecting High-Skilled Nonimmigrant Workers [CIS No.: 2571-15; DHS Docket No: USCIS-2015-0008] (RIN: 1615- AC05) received November 18, 2016, pursuant to 5 U.S.C. 801(a)(1)(A); Public Law 104-121, Sec. 251; (110 Stat. 868); to the Committee on the Judiciary.

7614. A letter from the Trial Attorney, Office of Aviation Enforcement and Proceedings, OST, Department of Transportation, transmitting the Department's final rule — Reporting of Data for Mishandled Baggage and Wheelchairs and Scooters Transported in Aircraft Cargo Compartments [Docket No.: DOT-RITA-2011-0001] (RIN: 2105-AE41 (formerly 2139-AA13)) received November 17, 2016, pursuant to 5 U.S.C. 801(a)(1)(A); Public Law 104-121, Sec. 251; (110 Stat. 868); to the Committee on Transportation and Infrastructure.

7615. A letter from the Trial Attorney, Office of Aviation Enforcement and Proceedings, OST, Department of Transportation, transmitting the Department's final rule — Enhancing Airline Passenger Protections III [Docket No.: DOT-OST-2014-0056] (RIN: 2105-AE11) received November 17, 2016, pursuant to 5 U.S.C. 801(a)(1)(A); Public Law 104-121, Sec. 251; (110 Stat. 868); to the Committee on Transportation and Infrastructure.

7616. A letter from the Management and Program Analyst, FAA, Department of Transportation, transmitting the Department's final rule — Airworthiness Directives; Honeywell International Inc. Turboprop Engines [Docket No.: FAA-2006-23706; Directorate Identifier 2006-NE-03-AD; Amendment 39-18688; AD 2016-21-07] (RIN: 2120-AA64) received November 17, 2016, pursuant to 5 U.S.C. 801(a)(1)(A); Public Law 104-121, Sec. 251; (110 Stat. 868); to the Committee on Transportation and Infrastructure.

☐This symbol represents the time of day during the House proceedings, e.g., ☐1407 is 2:07 p.m.

Matter set in this typeface indicates words inserted or appended, rather than spoken, by a Member of the House on the floor.

7617. A letter from the Management and Program Analyst, FAA, Department of Transportation, transmitting the Department's final rule — Airworthiness Directives; Turbomeca S.A. Turboshaft Engines [Docket No.: FAA-2016-6990; Directorate Identifier 2016-NE-14-AD; Amendment 39-186990; AD 2016-22-10] (RIN: 2120-AA64) received November 17, 2016, pursuant to 5 U.S.C. 801(a)(1)(A); Public Law 104-121, Sec. 251; (110 Stat. 868); to the Committee on Transportation and Infrastructure.

7618. A letter from the Management and Program Analyst, FAA, Department of Transportation, transmitting the Department's final rule — Airworthiness Directives; Pratt & Whitney Division Turbofan Engines [Docket No.: FAA-2016-5423; Directorate Identifier 2016-NE-09-AD; Amendment 39-18694; AD 2016-22-05] (RIN: 2120-AA64) received November 17, 2016, pursuant to 5 U.S.C. 801(a)(1)(A); Public Law 104-121, Sec. 251; (110 Stat. 868); to the Committee on Transportation and Infrastructure.

7619. A letter from the Management and Program Analyst, FAA, Department of Transportation, transmitting the Department's final rule — Airworthiness Directives; Engine Alliance Turbofan Engines [Docket No.: FAA-2012-1293; Directorate Identifier 2012-NE-45-AD; Amendment 39-18700; AD 2016-22-11] (RIN: 2120-AA64) received November 17, 2016, pursuant to 5 U.S.C. 801(a)(1)(A); Public Law 104-121, Sec. 251; (110 Stat. 868); to the Committee on Transportation and Infrastructure.

7620. A letter from the Management and Program Analyst, FAA, Department of Transportation, transmitting the Department's final rule — Amendment of Class D and Class E Airspace; Hagerstown, MD [Docket No.: FAA-2015-4513; Airspace Docket No.: 15-AEA-8] received November 17, 2016, pursuant to 5 U.S.C. 801(a)(1)(A); Public Law 104-121, Sec. 251; (110 Stat. 868); to the Committee on Transportation and Infrastructure.

7621. A letter from the Management and Program Analyst, FAA, Department of Transportation, transmitting the Department's final rule — Amendment of Class E Airspace; Miles City, MT [Docket No.: FAA-2016-7046; Airspace Docket No.: 16-ANM-3] received November 17, 2016, pursuant to 5 U.S.C. 801(a)(1)(A); Public Law 104-121, Sec. 251; (110 Stat. 868); to the Committee on Transportation and Infrastructure.

7622. A letter from the Management and Program Analyst, FAA, Department of Transportation, transmitting the Department's final rule — Amendment of Class D and Class E Airspace; Falmouth, MA [Docket No.: FAA-2016-5444; Airspace Docket No.: 16-ANE-1] received November 17, 2016, pursuant to 5 U.S.C. 801(a)(1)(A); Public Law 104-121, Sec. 251; (110 Stat. 868); to the Committee on Transportation and Infrastructure.

7623. A letter from the Management and Program Analyst, FAA, Department of Transportation, transmitting the Department's final rule — Extension of the Prohibition Against Certain Flights in the Simferopol (UKFV) and Dnipropetrovsk (UKDV) Flight Information Regions (FIRs) [Docket No.: FAA-2014-0225; Amdt. No.: 91-331D] (RIN: 2120-AK92) received November 17, 2016, pursuant to 5 U.S.C. 801(a)(1)(A); Public Law 104-121, Sec. 251; (110 Stat. 868); to the Committee on Transportation and Infrastructure.

ADDITIONAL SPONSORS

Under clause 7 of rule XII, sponsors were added to public bills and resolutions, as follows:

H.R. 346: Ms. MICHELLE LUJAN GRISHAM of New Mexico.

H.R. 6382: Mr. LARSEN of Washington, Mr. CICILLINE, Mr. SMITH of Washington, Mr. HECK of Washington, Mr. BRENDAN F. BOYLE of Pennsylvania, Ms. LEE, Ms. McCOLLUM, Mr. NADLER, Ms. CLARKE of New York, Mr. POLIS, and Mr. BLUMENAUER.

EXTENSIONS OF REMARKS

RECOGNIZING THE LAO HERITAGE FLAG AS THE OFFICIAL SYMBOL OF THE LAO-AMERICAN COMMUNITY OF NEW YORK AND WAT LAO SAMAKHITHAM

HON. CHRISTOPHER P. GIBSON
OF NEW YORK
IN THE HOUSE OF REPRESENTATIVES

Friday, November 25, 2016

Mr. GIBSON. Mr. Speaker, I rise today to recognize the Lao Heritage Flag as the Official Symbol of the Lao-American Community of New York and Wat Lao Samakhitham.

The members of the Lao-American Community in New York are true patriots in every sense of the word. Before arriving in America, many Lao-Americans courageously fought and shed blood in their struggle for freedom during the Southeast Asian conflict in the 1960's and 1970's. As American citizens, they continue to embody an unwavering love of liberty and a desire to serve. There are a significant number of Lao-Americans in New York, and they make great contributions to their local communities.

Lao-American citizens are proud to fly the Lao Heritage Flag alongside the flag of the United States of America. This flag is characterized by the three-headed white elephant, and it is significant to Lao-Americans as a symbol of resilience, freedom, and democracy in Laos, as well as the United States of America. Under this flag, the Lao-American community of New York maintains their Lao cultural heritage while simultaneously celebrating American heritage and customs.

Finally, Mr. Speaker, I would like to acknowledge each member of the vibrant Lao-American community in New York and thank them for their valuable contribution to our State. As a former service member, I believe strongly in the great symbolism of a flag and the pride that accompanies its display. It is my hope that the Lao-American community will always look to the Lao Heritage Flag and be reminded of the prosperity and freedom for Lao-American citizens across the United States.

HONORING THE SERVICE OF MAJOR MATT SCHARDT

HON. CHRISTOPHER P. GIBSON
OF NEW YORK
IN THE HOUSE OF REPRESENTATIVES

Friday, November 25, 2016

Mr. GIBSON. Mr. Speaker, I rise to honor the service of Major Matt Schardt of the United States Army for his extraordinary dedication to duty and service to our Nation. Major Schardt distinguished himself through exceptionally meritorious service from May 5th, 2013 to January 3rd, 2017, while serving as an Army Congressional Fellow and Legislative Liaison in the Army House Liaison Division.

From May 5th, 2013 through January 5th, 2015 Major Schardt served as an Army Congressional Fellow. During this time Matt graduated from The George Washington University with a Master's Degree in legislative politics and served as my military legislative assistant (MLA). As my MLA, Matt served as the national security, foreign affairs, homeland security, intelligence, and veteran's affairs policy advisor for my office. Matt developed, drafted, and managed my legislative initiatives, provided vote recommendations, prepared me for Congressional hearings, and met with senior government officials and constituents. In all of his actions, Matt demonstrated the professionalism Members of Congress and the American public expect of its military officers.

In January, 2015 Major Schardt transitioned from my office to the Army House Liaison Office to serve as an Army legislative liaison. In his role as a legislative liaison in the Army's House Liaison Office, Major Schardt served as the primary liaison between Members of the 114th Congress, their Staffs, Legislative Committees, and the U.S. Army. In this role, Major Schardt planned, coordinated, and accompanied Congressional and Staff Delegations on numerous worldwide fact-finding and investigative missions and worked to increase the trust the U.S. Congress has in the U.S. Army.

Major Schardt is a native of Littleton, Colorado who has served in combat units across the U.S. Army including the 25th Infantry Division and the 4th Infantry Division. A veteran of the conflicts in both Iraq and Afghanistan, Major Schardt is married to the former Amy Meersman of Littleton, Colorado and the proud father of two children—Kyle and Cora. This spring, Major Schardt and his family depart for their next assignment with the 1st Infantry Division at Fort Riley, Kansas.

Mr. Speaker, it is my honor to recognize the selfless service of Major Matt Schardt as he and his family proceed to the next chapter in his remarkable career and continue to serve our great Nation.

SENATE—*Monday, November 28, 2016*

The Senate met at 3 p.m. and was called to order by the President pro tempore (Mr. HATCH).

PRAYER

The Chaplain, Dr. Barry C. Black, offered the following prayer:

Let us pray.

Eternal Savior, how great You are. You are robed with honor and majesty. You are dressed in robes of splendor. Guide our Senators on the right path, helping them to unite in thought and purpose for the common good of our Nation. Lord, remind them that Your desires for them are wiser than their plans so that our lawmakers will cherish the wisdom of Your unfolding providence. May our legislators not become discouraged, but may they anticipate a harvest of blessings at the appropriate time. Help them to find delight in communing with You, knowing that You will plant in their hearts desires that will fulfill Your purposes.

We pray in Your great Name. Amen.

PLEDGE OF ALLEGIANCE

The President pro tempore led the Pledge of Allegiance, as follows:

I pledge allegiance to the Flag of the United States of America, and to the Republic for which it stands, one nation under God, indivisible, with liberty and justice for all.

RESERVATION OF LEADER TIME

The PRESIDING OFFICER (Mrs. ERNST). Under the previous order, the leadership time is reserved.

MORNING BUSINESS

The PRESIDING OFFICER. Under the previous order, the Senate will be in a period of morning business, with Senators permitted to speak therein for up to 10 minutes each.

RECOGNITION OF THE MINORITY LEADER

The PRESIDING OFFICER. The Democratic leader is recognized.

DISPUTE AT STANDING ROCK RESERVATION

Mr. REID. Madam President, this month is Native American Heritage Month. During this month, we honor the contributions of American Indians and also, of course, Alaskan Natives and Hawaiians. We don't have to look very far to see how Native Americans continue fighting for their heritage. They really must fight for their heritage.

If you pick up a newspaper or turn to the news on any channel you want, you will see what is happening at the Standing Rock Reservation in North Dakota. The Standing Rock Sioux Tribe is opposing the construction of a portion of the Dakota Access Pipeline that passes near their reservation where it crosses the Missouri River.

They are concerned that the construction of the pipeline could not only destroy ancestral burial grounds but could also contaminate the water supply for the tribe, as well as for millions of others who depend on water from the Missouri River.

The Standing Rock Sioux are fighting for their land, the right to clean water, clean air, and their history. They are not alone. The Standing Rock Sioux have been joined by thousands of others, including members of hundreds of tribes throughout the United States. Last month, while I was in Nevada, members of the 27 Native American tribes we have in Nevada made it clear to me that they stand in solidarity with the Standing Rock Sioux.

But I do too. Here is why. Here is why I join with the Standing Rock Sioux in calling for an alternative route for the pipeline's construction. It is past time that this situation be resolved peacefully. It has lingered for months, and the debate has descended into violence. Private security guards have unleashed attack dogs on Indians, resulting in men, women, and children being bitten and some very severely. Police have used rubber bullets, tear gas, and compression grenades. Some 300 people have been treated for injuries as a result of this violence against the protesters.

The most severe injury took place a week ago, when one young woman had parts of her arm and hand blown off. The violence at Standing Rock must end. I am confident that President Obama's administration is taking the necessary steps to address the situation. They have done well so far. What is happening at Standing Rock is a movement that has captured the attention of the entire country.

But we should understand the context of what is taking place. We should be mindful that the history of this region is fraught with disputes—very few of which, if any, have been resolved in the favor of the Indians. This region is fraught, I repeat, with disputes between Native Americans and the U.S. Government—disputes that originated more than a century ago but that, in the minds of the Indians, are still very much alive.

Last week, Kevin Gover, the Director of the Smithsonian's National Museum of the American Indian, which is a wonderful place, put the clash at Standing Rock in historic perspective. Here is what he said:

Take Standing Rock, for example . . . if you know what the history of the Sioux Nation is, you know that the treaties were made with the Sioux Nation concerning these lands that no longer belong to the Sioux Nation. And you know that the development of the Missouri River for the past century has always, always involved taking of Indian land. They were building dams up and down the Missouri, and every Indian reservation along the way was flooded. Some of the best land was flooded, which only deepened their poverty and made it that much harder to climb out [of poverty, which they haven't]. So we should know that kind of history.

I agree. This is the history to which he is referring—or at least a part of it. In the 1890s, Congress pushed the Sioux to reservations, took them off their ancestral lands, and jammed them into reservations.

Speaking from the knowledge I have, what they did to the Panamint and Shoshone in Nevada is unbelievable. They put them in the worst places you could find. That is what they did to the Sioux. In the 1890s, they pushed the Sioux into reservations. Then, two decades later, in violation of all of the treaties they had, they built dams on the Missouri River that shrunk the size of the reservations even more.

Then, in the 1940s, the United States built yet another dam, putting the Sioux's most fertile land underwater. I don't intend to have all of the answers. But I do know from experience that progress is possible when cooperation and respect form the foundation of fairness, especially on issues related to tribal rights and environmental concerns.

I take one example that I know a lot about, and that is what happened in Nevada with a really large powerplant—coal-fired—called the Reid Gardner coal-fired plant. It was one of the dirtiest powerplants in the entire country. This coal plant was located less than a football field from the tribal reservation.

Every day it dumped thousands of tons of toxins in the air, such as arsenic, mercury, and lead. Tribal members got sick. Of course, they did. Some 300 people on the reservation were poisoned daily by the pollution. But working with the Moapa Paiutes, I called for closure of the plant. People thought: Why are you doing this? It was the right thing to do. It was the right thing to do for the environment, but, more importantly, it was the fair and just thing to do for the Moapa Band of Paiutes.

Since that time, when we started this initial effort, three of Reid Gardner's four generating units have been shut down—closed. The whole coal facility will be out of business within the next 90 days. That is pretty good. It is gone. Why? Because we had government. Local and State governments, Indian government, and the power company all worked together to address this issue.

It could not have been done without all three of them working together. I have said this publicly. I have had a lot of disputes with the monopoly power company in Nevada, but on this issue I have complimented them because they did the right thing. With the Paiute tribe, instead of having this toxic dump in the form of a coal-fired generating plant right next to them that they breathe every day, they now have a huge solar farm.

It has created lots of construction jobs. That electricity is now being sent to the city of Los Angeles. It has been good for everybody—good for the air of Nevada, good for the Indians with work. It has helped the environment. The power company has made other arrangements for their power. They did it fairly easily.

The simple truth is, based on this whole experience I had, that you need to work together, whether it is the Moapa Paiutes or the Standing Rock Sioux. They are exposed to more pollution than most Americans. That is the way it is.

We don't talk a lot about the people who are severely impacted by a century of practically limitless pollution—Indians. This is not an urban or rural phenomenon. It is everywhere, and it is dangerous. Researchers at the University of Minnesota found that the difference in exposure to nitrogen dioxide alone is equal to roughly 7,000 deaths a year from heart disease.

From South Dakota to Nevada, Native Americans are on the frontlines of these environmental and public health catastrophes. To make matters worse, heavy-polluting industries are fighting to return to the days of limitless pollution under the next administration. Can the people of America expect our newly elected President to intervene on their behalf against the big polluters? Can the Standing Rock Sioux Tribe depend on the man who is financially invested in the Dakota Access Pipeline? Probably not.

This is about more than President-Elect Trump or fossil fuel profits. What is happening at Standing Rock is about respect for people: Where they build their homes, where they raise their families. The violence and aggression against the Standing Rock Sioux in North Dakota is a tragic example of the failure to respect people, of longstanding grievances, for how they and their natural resources have been treated.

No one can see this more than the Indians. The Standing Rock Sioux protest at the Dakota Access Pipeline has everything to do with the history of broken promises and the institutionalized disregard for the rights of their own land as well as the trust relationship between Indian tribes and the Federal Government of the United States. While most stakeholders want a speedy end to this situation, we must understand that overreaction to protesters, violence, and disregard for our history undermines the likelihood of a mutually acceptable solution and rubs salt in already festering wounds.

Profits should not be a determining factor of how this matter is resolved. The Obama administration has recognized that this history means the Dakota Access Pipeline is much more complicated than a water-crossing permit. They are doing the right thing by working with tribes to develop a better consultation process. I appreciate very much what the Obama administration has done. They recognize that history means that the pipeline is more complicated than simply a water crossing.

I appreciate that the President is showing the Standing Rock Sioux the respect to which they are entitled. President Obama has less than 2 months left in his term, and it is becoming clear that the dispute at Standing Rock likely will not be resolved before he leaves office.

I encourage the new administration and the Army Corps of Engineers to continue finding an alternate route. There is one out there. This should not be that hard. There is no reason this situation cannot be remedied in a manner that is fair to all.

Three hundred people have already been injured. Grenades. Dogs being sicced on these Indians. Water being sprayed on them in freezing temperatures—below-freezing temperatures.

Our Native-American tribes are looking to the Federal Government for help. For once, let's get them some help rather than just continue taking from them. They want to believe that after centuries of wrongs, the United States will finally get it right. Indians want to believe that after so long of being treated with no respect, the United States will help and not hurt.

Relocating the pipeline to a more suitable area away from the Standing Rock Indian Reservation would be an easy and historic step in the right direction. For the sake of our country, I hope that happens.

Madam President, I see no one on the floor.

I suggest the absence of a quorum.

The PRESIDING OFFICER. The clerk will call the roll.

The legislative clerk proceeded to call the roll.

Mr. McCONNELL. Madam President, I ask unanimous consent that the order for the quorum call be rescinded.

The PRESIDING OFFICER. Without objection, it is so ordered.

RECOGNITION OF THE MAJORITY LEADER

The PRESIDING OFFICER. The majority leader is recognized.

WORK BEFORE THE SENATE

Mr. McCONNELL. Madam President, over the next few weeks, Senators will work to conclude the business of the 114th Congress as we begin looking forward to the 115th. We have a lot to do, including approving several conference reports and funding the government. It is good to see the respective committees making important progress on conference reports for the National Defense Authorization Act and the Water Resources Development Act.

We will work with our counterparts in the House to consider each of those in the coming days and to send final bills to the President's desk for signature. We will also take up the 21st-century cures bill, which contains resources to promote medical research, including advancing regenerative medicine, among many other important provisions. Sometime soon we will also take up the Iran Sanctions Extension Act, which provides underlying authorities necessary to reimpose sanctions if those sanctions are called for on the country that has continued to exhibit disturbing and very aggressive behavior. And of course we will work to pass the continuing resolution to fund the government.

I would also like to note that my friend from Alaska, Senator MURKOWSKI, is continuing her efforts to advance the Energy Policy Modernization Act, which passed the Senate with large bipartisan support earlier this year. As the chair of the Energy and Natural Resources Committee, she has been a champion of this critical bill and has never stopped working to move it forward. I appreciate her work in that capacity, as well as the many other Members who have been leaders on each of the issues I just named.

I would encourage colleagues on both sides to continue working together so that we can complete our work very soon.

Madam President, I suggest the absence of a quorum.

The PRESIDING OFFICER. The clerk will call the roll.

The legislative clerk proceeded to call the roll.

Mr. DURBIN. Madam President, I ask unanimous consent that the order for the quorum call be rescinded.

The PRESIDING OFFICER. Without objection, it is so ordered.

DACA

Mr. DURBIN. Madam President, during the Presidential campaign, which just concluded, President-Elect Donald Trump made some inflammatory remarks about immigration and immigrants. I condemned those remarks, as did many in both political parties, and I remain concerned about the impact that rhetoric has on America and the people who are living in the United States.

On election night, Mr. Trump said, "Now it is time for America to bind the wounds of division." As one step in bringing our Nation together, Mr. Trump should change his thinking on at least one aspect of immigration, and I hope even more. As the President-elect knows, we are, in fact, a nation of immigrants, and immigration makes America stronger.

Like me, Mr. Trump is the son of an immigrant. His wife will be only the second immigrant in American history to serve as First Lady. During a recent interview, Mr. Trump acknowledged that millions of undocumented immigrants are "terrific people." That is a good start; words matter. The tone the President-elect sets with the language he uses can help to bind the divisions in America, but actions matter as well. I hope that one of President-Elect Trump's first actions will be to pledge to continue the program known as DACA.

It was 6 years ago that I sent a letter to President Barack Obama, and joining me in that letter was Senator Dick Lugar, a Republican Senator from Indiana. It was a bipartisan letter, and we asked President Obama to stop the deportations of young immigrants who grew up in this country. These young people have come to be known as DREAMers. They were brought to the United States as children. They grew up singing the national anthem in their classrooms and pledging allegiance to the only flag they ever knew—the American flag.

These DREAMers are casualties of our broken immigration system. They were brought here as children, toddlers, infants, babies. They didn't have any voice in the decision of their family to come to America. They were brought here to live. We invested in them. We put them in our school systems. It really makes no sense, since many of them have become accomplished and promising young people, to give up on them now and deport them back to countries they have never known.

The President of the United States, Barack Obama, responded. He established the Deferred Action for Childhood Arrivals program, which is known as DACA. DACA provides temporary renewable legal status to immigrant students who arrived in the United States as children. What does it take? A student has to fill out an application form.

When this Executive action went into effect, I joined with Congressman LUIS GUTIÉRREZ of Chicago. We decided on the first day of eligibility we would set up some tables at the Navy Pier in Chicago, and we would welcome young people to come in and sign up. These were undocumented young people who had grown up in the United States, and now they had a chance because of the President's Executive action to ask for temporary protected status and a work permit.

It cost money, almost $500. When they submitted their names, they also submitted their names for a criminal background check to make certain they had no serious criminal offense and they were no threat to this country. Congressman GUTIÉRREZ and I expected several hundred to show up. We had immigration lawyers ready to volunteer to help them fill out the forms.

We were stunned. The night before, at midnight, they started lining up in the dark with their parents, and they waited all night to come into that room and to sign those applications so that they, as undocumented young people in America, would have a fighting chance to become part of America's future. That is all they asked for. They didn't ask for jobs. They didn't ask for government programs. They don't qualify for very many, if any. All they asked for was a chance—a chance to live here and not be deported and a chance to work here.

So far, in the few years that DACA has been in effect, over 740,000 young people have signed up. They came forward, paid their fees, and went through the background checks. They were approved. Now they are working or going to school.

DACA has allowed these DREAMers to make contributions to America that are valuable to all of us. They are soldiers, nurses, teachers, engineers, police officers, and they are aspiring to the highest levels of education in our country. These DACA recipients are making important contributions to our economy.

A new study by the Center for American Progress finds that ending DACA would cost the United States $433.4 billion in gross domestic product over the next 10 years. These are not just bright young students; they are great workers. They will be great professionals. They will help people, and they will make America stronger.

DACA is based on the DREAM Act. The DREAM Act is bipartisan legislation that I first introduced 15 years ago. If you are going to serve in the Senate, you have to be patient. I didn't dream I would be standing here 15 years later, still asking for the Senate to approve the DREAM Act. In the meantime, what President Obama did was to say we will protect these young people while Congress debates the future of immigration reform, but we

will make sure that they can stay in this country without fear of deportation.

If the DREAM Act is enacted into law—and, incidentally, it passed the Senate several years ago—it will give these undocumented students a chance to earn their way to legal status and citizenship. DACA is clearly legal. Like every President before him, President Obama has the authority to set immigration policy for his administration. DACA is also smart and realistic. It is a way to enforce our immigration laws the right way, to make sure that these young people who have done nothing wrong, who have no criminal problems, who have paid their fee and registered with the government are allowed to stay without fear of a knock on the door.

The Department of Homeland Security has only enough funding to deport a small fraction of the undocumented immigrants in our country each year. President Obama has said he wants to focus those resources on those who should not be in the United States, those who could do us harm. That is just common sense. At the same time, the President said we shouldn't waste our resources on deporting young immigrant students who grew up in the United States and are making contributions to our future.

During the campaign, President-Elect Trump pledged to rescind and end DACA. I believe that after his administration studies the issue, there is a chance he will reconsider when he comes to know these "terrific people."

I have come to the floor of the Senate now for over 10 years, telling the stories of these DREAMers. There was a time when they were afraid to come out publicly and tell America who they were. They had been warned by their parents since they were little kids to be careful. If you talk to the wrong person, if you do the wrong thing, if the police knock on the door, you may be deported along with the rest of your family, so be careful.

As kids will, these young people across America have decided they are not going to hide who they are. They want to tell America their story, and I have tried to help them. When they have sent us their biographies, along with photographs, I have come to the floor on about a hundred different occasions to tell the stories of these DREAMers. Each one, in my estimation, is more amazing than the next, and today is no exception.

This is Rey Pineda. In 1990, when Rey was 2 years old, his family came to the United States from Mexico. Rey grew up in Atlanta, GA. He worked hard and was an honor roll student in high school. He became the first member of his family to attend college. In 2010, he graduated with a major in philosophy from Southern Catholic College in Dawsonville, GA.

Rey is a devout Catholic, and he decided to attend Mundelein Seminary in my home State of Illinois. Rey felt that God was calling him to be a priest, but his spiritual path was blocked. Rey is undocumented. Rey is a DREAMer.

Then, in 2012, everything changed. President Obama's Executive action established DACA. In March of 2013, Rey was approved, filed his fee, went through the background check, and did everything he was asked to do. He received his DACA status, and he knew that at least for 2 years he would not be subject to deportation. That allowed him to become a deacon in the Catholic Church 2 months later, in May of 2013.

In 2014, Rey entered the priesthood after he graduated magna cum laude from Mundelein Seminary in Illinois. He has a master of divinity degree. Today, Father Rey Pineda is a priest at the Cathedral of Christ the King in Atlanta, GA. He wrote me a letter, and here is what he said about DACA:

Like many Dreamers, the U.S. is really the only country I know. DACA was an answer to many years of prayers. Without DACA I would not have been able to serve as a priest in my community. I believe my faith in God has brought me to this point in my life; but my faith in America's promise has pushed me to keep fighting for peace, justice, and opportunity in this great country I proudly call home.

If DACA is eliminated—and that threat has been made—Father Rey Pineda will lose his legal status and be subject to deportation, being sent back to a country that he hasn't lived in since he was 2 years old. That would be a tragedy for Father Rey Pineda and his congregation and the hundreds of people who count on him as their priest.

Consider this: There is a chronic shortage of Catholic priests in America. Since 1975, the number of priests has declined by 33 percent while the number of American Catholics has grown by 43 percent. Hundreds of parishes have been forced to close or consolidate. Nearly one out of five Catholic parishes in America have no priest.

This shortage of priests is not limited to the Catholic Church. The problem is so serious that Congress has established a religious worker visa to allow people from overseas to come in on a visa and serve as priests in communities. It is happening all across my State of Illinois, and I bet it is happening in Iowa. If you go to parishes in rural areas, there will be priests from all over the world. I recently met one in Rome who was in Southern Illinois at Pinckneyville, and he was from Nigeria.

At a time when the United States is actively importing ministers and priests from foreign countries, why do we want to deport Father Rey Pineda? This makes no sense. Listen to what Father Rey told me about his role as a priest who is an undocumented immigrant:

I believe my entire journey has prepared me to be compassionate with the sufferings of many people I encounter. I look at my ministry as a calling to build bridges between people from all walks of life. Diversity sometimes brings challenges between people and I want to help heal those differences.

After the most divisive election in recent memory, I believe that Father Rey Pineda and other DREAMers like him have an important role to play in healing the differences that divide America. I am hoping that President-Elect Trump will see this and will continue the DACA program.

Let me be clear. If there is an attempt to shut down DACA, I will do everything in my power as a U.S. Senator to protect the DREAMers who have stepped forward and contributed their talents to our great country.

Many of those DREAMers and their parents spoke to me that day at Navy Pier and ever since. They said: Senator, are you sure? Are you sure that we should sign up with this government? We have spent a lifetime trying to stay out of trouble, stay out of the view of people, not cause any problems, go about our business, raise our families, do our jobs, go to our church. If our children register with this government, will that come back at a future time and be used against us?

At the time, I said—and I believe it now—that America would stand behind these young people. We will not allow them to be deported after what they have been through. We will not tell them that by complying with the requirements of our government, you have penalized yourself in the future. We want to give them a chance. Now is the time for America, this Nation of immigrants, to heal the wounds that divided us during this election. Let's start with the DREAMers, let's start with DACA, let's start with the young people who will make America better and stronger in the years to come. They are the best in this country. Let's make them the best for America's future. I hope and pray the President-elect's words and actions in the coming weeks and months will, in fact, bring us together.

I yield the floor.

I suggest the absence of a quorum.

The PRESIDING OFFICER. The clerk will call the roll.

The bill clerk proceeded to call the roll.

Ms. WARREN. Madam President, I ask unanimous consent that the order for the quorum call be rescinded.

The PRESIDING OFFICER. Without objection, it is so ordered.

21ST CENTURY CURES BILL

Ms. WARREN. Madam President, 3 weeks ago Americans went to the polls. Voters were deeply divided on whether Democrats or Republicans should be in charge. Donald Trump is the President-elect, missing the popular vote by more than 2 million people. But there is one thing Americans are not divided on, one issue on which they sent out a message loud and clear. According to exit polls, 70 percent of voters said that they think the American economy and the lawmakers who oversee it are owned—owned—by big companies and special interests. That is 70 percent of everyone—Republicans, Democrats, and Independents.

In the closing days of this Congress, Big Pharma has its hand out for a bunch of special giveaways and favors that are packed together in something called the 21st Century Cures bill. It is on track to get a vote in the House this week and then get rammed through the Senate. I have been taking a look at the details, and when the American voters say that Congress is owned by big companies, this bill is exactly what they are talking about.

Now we face a choice: Will this Congress say "Yes, we are bought and paid for" or will we stand up and work for the American people?

For more than 2 years, Congress has been working on legislation to help advance medical innovation in the United States. Medical innovation is powerfully important, and I have spent as much time working on this issue as anything I have worked on since I joined the U.S. Senate. From the beginning, I have emphasized one obvious fact: Medical breakthroughs come from increasing investments in basic research. Right now, Congress is choking off investments in the NIH. Adjusted for inflation, Federal spending on medical research over the past dozen years has been cut by 20 percent. Those cuts take the legs out from under future medical innovations in America.

We can name a piece of legislation the "Cures" bill, but if it doesn't include significant, meaningful funding for the National Institutes of Health and the Food and Drug Administration, it won't cure anything. That is why months ago Senate Democrats said any so-called Cures legislation must have significant investment in medical research, and that is why Senate Republicans publicly committed to do exactly that. But now they have reneged on their promise and let Big Pharma hijack the Cures bill.

This final deal has only a tiny fig leaf of funding for NIH and for the opioid crisis, and most of that fig leaf isn't even real. Most of the money won't be there unless future Congresses pass future bills in future years to fund those dollars.

So why bother with a fig leaf in the Cures bill? Why pretend to give money to NIH or opioids? This funding is political cover for huge giveaways to giant drug companies. There are more examples than I can count in this bill. But I am going to talk about three.

First giveaway: Legalize fraud. You know, it is against the law for drug companies to market drugs for uses not approved by the FDA. Now, some drug companies find this rule annoying. After all, they can make a lot more money selling a headache pill as a cure for everything from hair loss to cancer. But pushing treatments without scientific evidence that they work is fraud—fraud that can hurt people. It also undercuts the development of real cures.

That is why some of the largest law enforcement actions against big drug companies over the past 15 years have involved off-label marketing. Drug companies have paid billions of dollars in penalties. Now, one solution would be for those companies to follow the law. But they prefer plan B: Cozy up to enough people in Congress to pass this Cures bill that would shoot holes in the anti-fraud law. In other words, make it easier for drug companies to get away with fraud.

Second giveaway: Cover up bribery. Right now the law requires drug companies to disclose the buckets of money they shower on doctors and hospitals to encourage them to prescribe certain drugs. It is, by the way, all published on a government Web site. You can go look up your doctor and your hospital right now online, if you want to do that.

Now, the drug companies could have responded by ending kickbacks to doctors. But instead, they have chosen plan B again: Cozy up to enough people in Congress to pass this Cures bill, which would let drug companies keep secret any splashy junkets or gifts associated with so-called medical education and make it harder for enforcement agencies to be able to trace those bribes. Senator GRASSLEY, a Republican from Iowa, says he is outraged by this provision. I have to say that I am with Senator GRASSLEY on this one.

Third giveaway: Hand out dangerous special deals to Republican campaign contributors. According to news reports, a major Republican donor stands to benefit financially from selling cellular and regenerative medical therapies. If this guy had it his way, he would be able to sell them to desperate people without a final FDA determination that those therapies were either safe or effective.

Of course, that would be against the law right now. So this megadonor has poured millions of dollars into MITCH MCCONNELL's personal campaign coffers, and into his Republican super PAC, and now he wants his reward. The Cures Act offers to sell government favors. It delivers a special deal so that people can sell these treatments without meeting the FDA gold standards for protecting patient safety and making sure that these drugs actually do some good.

Keep in mind that people could die from using unproven treatments. In fact, people have already died during carefully controlled research experiments on these types of treatments. Congress should not be in the business of selling FDA favors to the highest bidders, risking people's lives to enrich political donors. Let's be clear. What the Republicans are proposing is corrupt, and it is very, very dangerous.

There is more. Republicans decided to hand out gifts for other special interests. The Cures Act, a bill that is supposed to be about medical innovation, has a giveaway to the gun lobby. The bill cuts Medicare funding. It raids money from the Affordable Care Act. It takes health care dollars that should have gone to Puerto Rico. It makes it harder for people with disabilities to get Medicaid services. There is a lot of bad stuff in this bill—a lot of bad stuff.

But not everything in the bill is bad. Republican leaders are playing a crafty game here, trying to buy off Democratic votes, one by one, by tacking on good, bipartisan proposals that Senators in both parties have worked on in good faith for years.

There is a bipartisan mental health bill. There are bipartisan provisions protecting the genetic privacy of patients and bipartisan provisions to give some very limited funding for important priorities, such as the national opioid crisis. There is the Vice President's Cancer Moonshot. There is a proposal in here to improve foster care.

I support most of these proposals. I have worked on many of them for years. I even wrote some of them myself. If this bill becomes law, there is no question it will contain some real legislative accomplishments. But I cannot vote for this bill. I will fight it because I know the differences between compromise and extortion. Compromise is putting together common-sense health proposals supported by Democrats, by Republicans, and by most of the American people, and passing them into law.

Extortion is holding those exact same proposals hostage unless everyone agrees to special favors for campaign donors and giveaways to the richest drug companies in the world. Compromise is when Senators—Democrats and Republicans—find a way forward on issues that matter to their constituents. Extortion is telling those same Senators to forget what their constituents want. We will do nothing with the skyrocketing costs of prescription drugs and nothing to increase medical research.

Instead, every important common-sense bipartisan bill on mental health, genetic privacy, opioid addiction, foster care, and anything else will die today unless Democrats agree to make it easier for drug companies to commit fraud, to give out kickbacks, and to put patients' lives at risk. This demand is enough to make me gag.

Scientists who invent new cures should be celebrated, along with the companies that support them. But let me be perfectly clear. While the drug industry may get a seat at the table, they do not own the table. I do not care how many armies of lawyers and lobbyists they send out. I do not care how many campaign contributions they dump into congressional pockets. I do not care how painful they can make life for politicians who oppose them.

I will not be their lackey. I will work for the hundreds of thousands of scientists and doctors who are committed to saving lives and who are waiting for Congress to fund their work. I will work for the millions of families that have been touched by Alzheimer's, diabetes, cancer, and other deadly diseases who are counting on this research.

I will work for the 70 percent of voters who are sick of a Congress that is owned by big donors and giant corporations. Republicans are taking over Congress. They are taking over the White House. But Republicans do not have majority support in this country. The majority of voters supported Democratic Senate candidates over Republican ones. The majority supported a Democratic Presidential candidate over a Republican one.

The American people did not give Democrats majority support so we can come back to Washington and play dead. They did not send us here to whimper, whine, or grovel. They sent us here to say no to efforts to sell Congress to the highest bidder. They sent us here to stand up for what is right. Now they are watching, waiting, and hoping—hoping that we will show some spine and start fighting back when Congress ignores the message of the American people and returns to the old ways of doing business.

Republicans will control this government, but they cannot hand that control over to big corporations unless Democrats roll over and allow them to do so. It is time for Democrats—Democrats and Republicans, who should be ashamed by this kind of corruption—to make it clear exactly who they work for. Does the Senate work for Big Pharma, which hires lobbyists and people who make giant campaign contributions, or does the Senate work for the American people who actually sent us here?

I yield the floor.

The PRESIDING OFFICER (Mr. COATS). The Senator from Texas.

COMMENTS OF THE SENATOR FROM MASSACHUSETTS

Mr. CORNYN. Mr. President, I confess that I came to the floor to talk about some of the nominations that we are going to see coming from the administration, particularly regarding one of our colleagues, Senator SESSIONS, the Senator from Alabama, to be the next Attorney General.

I am somewhat taken aback by the nature of the comments that I hear coming from the Senator from Massachusetts. I had to refresh my memory of the Senate Standing Rules, which I thought prohibited this sort of ad hominem attack—the claims of corruption, selling legislation for campaign contributions. I thought the rules of decorum of the Senate prohibited that sort of demagoguery.

But I am not sure you can write a rule that would prohibit somebody who is actually determined to defy the very voters they claim to be representing. If our Democratic colleagues like the result of the election that just occurred on November 8, I would say: Keep on keeping on. Keep on with this same sort of ad hominem attacks and attacking the motivation of people, rather than talking about policy.

I thought that is what the Senate was supposed to be all about—not where we come in here and call each other names. It is no wonder that the American people are turned off by what they see as politics as usual. I think what they told us on November 8 is that they actually would like to see us accomplish some things—first of all, starting with listening to them, not telling them what is good for them and saying: Well, if you don't like it, you are going to have to take it because the people in power, the people working in Washington, the elites in America know better than you do what is good for you.

So when I hear the Senator from Massachusetts come in and give essentially a political speech, such as she did, not talking about the merits or the policy but rather making personal attacks against Senators and people who support the policy, I just think this is beneath the dignity of the Senate.

I would hope we would rise to the occasion, in the wake of this historic election and say: You know what, we can do better. The American people deserve better than what they have been getting coming out of Washington. The only way we are going to be able to turn this country around is by, first of all, listening to what the American people are telling us. We know what they said is this: We are not happy with the direction of the country, and we are not happy with what is happening in Washington.

To come in and make the kind of speeches that I just heard a moment ago is disturbing. It is disappointing. We can do better than that. We must do better than that if we are going to regain the confidence of the American people that we are actually worthy of their support as we try to guide this ship of state and try to pass laws that actually will improve the quality of their lives by growing the economy, by making it possible for people to find work who want work so they can provide for their families, to try to make sure that the American people are safe

and secure, and to provide for our common defense.

Those are the sorts of things we ought to be focused on. So it is a little distressing to walk into this Chamber, in what used to be known as the world's greatest deliberative body, and to hear the sort of diatribe and the personal attacks and the name calling that we just heard from the Senator from Massachusetts.

ATTORNEY GENERAL NOMINATION

Mr. CORNYN. Mr. President, the reason I came to the floor is to make note of the fact, as I alluded to a moment ago, that President-Elect Donald Trump announced his intention to nominate one of our own, a Member of the Senate, to be the Nation's top law enforcement officer.

Our friend, the junior Senator from Alabama, Mr. SESSIONS, is undoubtedly qualified and prepared for this role as Attorney General because of the long career he spent protecting and defending our Constitution and the rule of law.

If there is one thing we can do in the U.S. Government to help restore the public's confidence, it will be to re-embrace the concept of equal justice under the law and ensure there is not a double standard by which people are judged—the powerful, the well-connected, and then the rules that apply to everybody else—but, rather, that the same rules apply to all of us. The same laws apply to all of us.

In fact, that is the bulwark of our constitutional democracy. Frankly, I think the American people have seen, in the last two Attorneys General—the current one and her predecessor, Mr. Holder—is essentially an office of the Department of Justice that was not worthy of the name "Justice." It should have been called an extension of the White House political operation because so much of the way they conducted themselves was governed not by the rule of law but by political considerations.

Our friend, the Senator from Alabama, understands firsthand the importance of hard work as well. He is the son of a country store owner from Hybart, AL. He received his law degree from the University of Alabama. He served in the U.S. Army Reserves.

As we know, his service didn't stop there. Guided by a sense of duty for the last five decades, JEFF SESSIONS has dedicated his life to the State of Alabama and to the United States itself, first as a Federal prosecutor—including 12 years as U.S. attorney for the Southern District of Alabama, then as the State's attorney general, and now in the Senate where he has served with distinction for the last decade-plus.

Above all, JEFF SESSIONS has worked for the people of his State and this country with one purpose in mind; that is, to uphold the rule of law.

His career in the Senate reflects this earnest commitment to do what is right, not what is popular, not what is politically convenient but to do what is right, guided by the Constitution, the laws, and inspired by the people he was elected to serve. He has been a defender of our military families and played a leading role in ensuring that rural communities have the health care they need.

I understand the long knives are already starting to come out against President-Elect Trump's nominees and that Senator SESSIONS—our colleague from Alabama—is not going to be spared some of those attacks, but I would ask some of these critics who don't know his entire record to consider the fact that a few years ago he teamed up with the senior Senator from Illinois to reform sentencing charges on crack cocaine, sentencing charges that disproportionately discriminate against African-American communities.

It was a bipartisan solution that in JEFF's words, "achieve fairness without impeding our ability to combat drug violence."

I would also ask these critics to consider the bill he introduced with Senator Ted Kennedy, the now-departed "liberal lion of the Senate," to use grant funding to reduce sexual assaults in prison. The legislation requires the Department of Justice to keep track of these assaults, and it was signed into law by President George W. Bush.

Taken legislatively, these are not the sorts of actions that fit this distorted picture that some of the critics are already starting to draw about Senator SESSIONS and his record in the Senate or his character as a man.

I have had the honor of working closely with JEFF on the Senate Judiciary Committee since I came to the Senate, and I am proud to call him a friend. Those who have watched him day-in and day-out understand his stalwart commitment to the rule of law and his deep and abiding concern for our country.

Of course, we wouldn't be Senators if we didn't sometimes disagree with each other. It is just normal, but Senator SESSIONS has always engaged with seriousness and cordiality and the kind of civility this Chamber and this country could use more of. By the strength of his arguments, he has helped us all to see the weaknesses in our own arguments as he has worked together with his colleagues to try to help us build consensus, which is the only way we get anything done and the way our constitutional system was designed. Only by building consensus can we move our country forward.

We are going to miss Senator SESSIONS in the Senate when he moves on to the executive branch as Attorney General, but it is even more important, at this point in this country's history, to have a champion of the Constitution and the rule of law at the Department of Justice and to help restore the reputation of that Department.

As I said earlier, for years now—during the course of Attorney General Holder's tenure and unfortunately succeeded by Attorney General Lynch—the Department of Justice has twisted the Constitution to further the President's political agenda.

I give just one example. When Congress was performing its legitimate oversight responsibilities into a gun-running operation gone wrong called Fast and Furious, Attorney General Holder was called before the Senate Judiciary Committee, called before our corresponding House committee, and simply defied those committees' lawful and appropriate oversight responsibilities over what the Department of Justice was doing.

To my knowledge, this resulted in his having been the first Attorney General to be held in contempt of Congress—a sitting Attorney General of the United States held in contempt of Congress.

Unfortunately, the Obama administration put politics ahead of our national commitment to the rule of law and too often demonized those who worked to protect us. I have every confidence that Senator SESSIONS, as the Attorney General of the United States, the head of the Department of Justice, and the Trump administration will defend the rule of law and will use his expertise in the Constitution to play an essential role in our President-elect's Cabinet. As a 15-year veteran of the Department, Senator SESSIONS understands better than most what needs to be done to help the Department of Justice refocus its responsibilities and its priorities.

Here is the bottom line. We need people in the highest rungs of our government who will ensure our Constitution is preserved, protected, and defended. Senator SESSIONS, as the next Attorney General of the United States, will do just that.

GETTING OUR WORK DONE

Mr. CORNYN. Mr. President, while the President-elect is considering additional nominees to fill his Cabinet, we in the Senate—working together with our House colleagues—have our own responsibilities to fulfill before the end of this year.

Most pressing is legislation to fund the government, something that unfortunately has been hindered by our Democratic colleagues slow-walking the appropriations process. Actually, calling it slow-walking is a little too generous. What they did is block the normal appropriations process, where the 12 separate appropriations bills would be voted out of committee—which they were, on a bipartisan basis—but then they would come

across the floor of the Senate where amendments would be offered, and we would actually vote on them before sending them to the President to be signed into law.

Instead of this normal process—which is transparent, it is bipartisan, in the best traditions of the Senate—we were denied the opportunity to do that, resulting now in our need to pass a year-end continuing resolution, kicking the funding of the government over to perhaps sometime in the spring. This was strictly as a result of the gamesmanship of our colleagues, many of them blocking the same appropriations bills they voted for, on a bipartisan basis, before the Appropriations Committee itself.

Despite those obstructions, we have actually tried to do some good work. We passed our first bicameral budget since 2009. As I said, the Appropriations Committee voted out all 12 appropriations bills.

Despite the obstructionism we have seen and despite where we find ourselves, I ask all of us to take stock of where we are, given what we saw happen in the historic election of November 8. I think the American people have made very clear they want the government to function and they don't have a lot of tolerance for gamesmanship or partisanship or obstruction, but we cannot move forward with other substantial legislative goals until we address funding for the remainder of this fiscal year. While I am disappointed we find ourselves where we are today—having to pass another short-term continuing resolution until next March or so—this waiting until the last minute is not a good way to do business. I hope next year, with the new administration and with the leadership of Senator MCCONNELL, Speaker RYAN in the House, and with more cooperation from our Democratic colleagues, we can have a regular and open appropriations process, one that will serve the American people much better. It will certainly serve the interests of the Defense Department and other people who need to be able to plan beyond 2 months or 3 months in terms of what they can do with the money Congress is going to appropriate.

Until then, I urge my colleagues on both sides of the aisle to set aside the disputes we have had over the last year and the election itself—which I know some are finding it easier to see the results of the election in the rearview mirror than others, as evidenced by the comments I heard from the Senator from Massachusetts when I came to the floor—but we need to pass a bill that will fund the government and allow us to move forward. I hope we can do that. Then, once we have completed the work for this year, we can come back in the new year with a new administration, a new Congress, and recommit ourselves to doing the people's work

and doing it in a consensus-building, bipartisan way that listens to what our constituents are telling us they want, not the siren call of the people who think they know better than they do what is good for them but to listen to the American people and then get about the work of passing legislation which promotes their interests. This is first to assure for the common defense but, secondly, to make sure our economy starts to grow again so people who want to find work or want better paying jobs can find work available so they can provide for their families and pursue their American dream.

Mr. President, I suggest the absence of a quorum.

The PRESIDING OFFICER. The clerk will call the roll.

The legislative clerk proceeded to call the roll.

Mr. McCONNELL. Mr. President, I ask unanimous consent that the order for the quorum call be rescinded.

The PRESIDING OFFICER. Without objection, it is so ordered.

ARMS SALES NOTIFICATION

Mr. CORKER. Mr. President, section 36(b) of the Arms Export Control Act requires that Congress receive prior notification of certain proposed arms sales as defined by that statute. Upon such notification, the Congress has 30 calendar days during which the sale may be reviewed. The provision stipulates that, in the Senate, the notification of proposed sales shall be sent to the chairman of the Senate Foreign Relations Committee.

In keeping with the committee's intention to see that relevant information is available to the full Senate, I ask unanimous consent to have printed in the RECORD the notifications which have been received. If the cover letter references a classified annex, then such annex is available to all Senators in the office of the Foreign Relations Committee, room SD–423.

There being no objection, the material was ordered to be printed in the RECORD, as follows:

DEFENSE SECURITY
COOPERATION AGENCY,
Arlington, VA, November 28, 2016.
Hon. BOB CORKER,
Chairman, Committee on Foreign Relations,
U.S. Senate, Washington, DC.
DEAR MR. CHAIRMAN: Pursuant to the reporting requirements of Section 36(b)(1) of the Arms Export Control Act, as amended, we are forwarding herewith Transmittal No. 16–72, concerning the Department of the Air Force's proposed Letter(s) of Offer and Acceptance to Poland for defense articles and services estimated to cost $200 million. After this letter is delivered to your office, we plan to issue a news release to notify the public of this proposed sale.

Sincerely,

J. W. RIXEY,
Vice Admiral, USN, Director.
Enclosures.

TRANSMITTAL NO. 16–72

Notice of Proposed Issuance of Letter of Offer Pursuant to Section 36(b)(1) of the Arms Export Control Act, as amended

(i) Prospective Purchaser: Poland

(ii) Total Estimated Value:

Major Defense Equipment* $ 110 million

Other: $ 90 million

Total: $ 200 million

(iii) Description and Quantity or Quantities of Articles or Services under Consideration for Purchase:

Major Defense Equipment (MDE):

Seventy (70) AGM–158B Joint Air-to-Surface Standoff Missiles Extended Range (JASSM–ER)

Two (2) AGM–158B Flight Test Vehicles—Live Fire with TIK & FTS

Two (2) AGM–158B Mass Simulant Vehicles

One (1) AGM–158B Flight Test Vehicle—Captive Carry

Three (3) AGM–158B Separation Test Vehicles

Non-MDE includes:

Two (2) AGM–158B Weapon System Simulators, F–16 operational flight plan upgrade for the Polish F–16C/D, JASSM–ER integration, missile containers, spare and repair parts, support and test equipment, publications and technical documentation, personnel training and training equipment, U.S. Government and contractor engineering, technical and logistics support services, and other related elements of logistical and program support.

(iv) Military Department: Air Force (X7–D–YAD).

(v) Prior Related Cases, if any: PL–D–SAC, PL–D–YAB and amendments.

(vi) Sales Commission, Fee, etc.. Paid, Offered, or Agreed to be Paid: None.

(vii) Sensitivity of Technology Contained in the Defense Article or Defense Services Proposed to be Sold: See Annex Attached.

(viii) Date Report Delivered to Congress: November 28. 2016.

* As defined in Section 47(6) of the Arms Export Control Act.

POLICY JUSTIFICATION

Poland—JASSM–ER with Support

The Government of Poland has requested a possible sale of seventy (70) AGM–158B Joint Air-to-Surface Standoff Missiles Extended Range (JASSM–ER), two (2) AGM–158B Flight Test Vehicles, two (2) AGM–158B Mass Simulant Vehicles, one (1) AGM–158B Flight Test Vehicle—Captive Carry, three (3) AGM–158B Separation Test Vehicles. Also included are two (2) AGM–158B Weapon System Simulators, F–16 operational flight plan upgrade for the Polish F–16C/D, JASSM–ER integration, missile containers, spare and repair parts, support and test equipment, publications and technical documentation, personnel training and training equipment, U.S. Government and contractor engineering, technical and logistics support services, and other related elements of logistical and program support. The total estimated program value is $200 million.

The proposed sale will contribute to the foreign policy and the national security objectives of the United States by helping to improve the security of a NATO ally. Poland continues to be an important force for political stability and economic progress in Central Europe.

The proposed sale will improve Poland's capability to meet current and future threats of enemy air and ground weapons systems. Poland will use the enhanced capability as a deterrent to regional threats and to strengthen its homeland defense. These weapon and capabilities upgrades will allow Poland to strengthen its air-to-ground strike capabilities and increase its contribution to future NATO operations. Poland will have no difficulty absorbing these missiles into its armed forces.

The proposed sale of this equipment and support will not alter the basic military balance in the region.

The prime contractor will be the Lockheed Martin Corporation of Ft. Worth, Texas. There are no known offset agreements proposed in connection with this potential sale.

Implementation of this proposed sale will not require the assignment of any additional U.S. Government or contractor representatives to Poland.

There will be no adverse impact on U.S. defense readiness as a result of this proposed sale.

TRANSMITTAL NO. 16–72

Notice of Proposed Issuance of Letter of Offer Pursuant to Section 36(b)(1) of the Arms Export Control Act

Annex Item No. vii

(vii) Sensitivity of Technology

1. The AGM–158B JASSM ER is an extended range low-observable, highly survivable subsonic cruise missile designed to penetrate next generation air defense systems en-route to target. It is designed to kill hard, medium-hardened, soft and area type targets. The extended range over the baseline was obtained by going from a turbo-jet to a turbo-fan engine and by reconfiguring the fuel tanks for added capacity. Classification of the technical data and information on the AGM–158's performance, capabilities, systems, sub-systems, operations, and maintenance will range from UNCLASSIFIED to SECRET.

2. If a technologically advanced adversary were to obtain knowledge of the specific hardware and software elements, the information could be used to develop countermeasures that might reduce weapon system effectiveness or be used in the development of a system with similar or advanced capabilities.

3. A determination has been made that Poland can provide substantially the same degree of protection for the sensitive technology being released as the U.S. Government. This proposed sale is necessary to further the US foreign policy and national security objectives outlined in the Policy Justification.

4. All defense articles and services listed in this transmittal are authorized for release and export to Poland.

REMOVAL OF NOMINATION OBJECTION

Mr. WYDEN. Mr. President, now more than ever, we need strong leadership at the FCC to protect consumers from consolidated powers in the telecommunications industry. Noncontentious issues should be passed and implemented so Americans have access to wireless broadband and voice services in their communities and access to video programming for the blind and visually impaired can be expanded and consumers can be protected from excessive cable and internet costs.

I was given the assurance that Commissioner Rosenworcel is committed to working toward consensus on all items before the Commission this year, including the Mobility Fund that provides support for wireless and voice service in rural America. For that reason, I lift my hold on her nomination.

TRIBUTE TO ALEJANDRO MAYORKAS

Mr. CARPER. Mr. President, today I wish to express my profound appreciation and best wishes to my friend, Alejandro Mayorkas, who recently stepped down as the Deputy Secretary of the Department of Homeland Security. During his 7 years of public service at DHS, Ali has been a dedicated and thoughtful leader and was instrumental to the advancement and accomplishments at the Department.

Ali arrived at DHS in 2009 with an already impressive record in public service which included over 20 years of distinguished service in law enforcement. As an assistant U.S. attorney for the Central District of California, he aggressively prosecuted drug traffickers, human smugglers, and violent criminals. As U.S. attorney for the Central District of California, he led the largest Federal judicial office in the United States and was appointed by then Attorney General Janet Reno to serve on her advisory committee on ethics and government. Ali continued his public service as the Director of U.S. Citizenship and Immigration Services, USCIS, where he oversaw a $3 billion annual budget and led a workforce of 18,000 individuals. To that end, Ali's accomplishments as the USCIS Director included the development of the special parole program which worked to rescue children who tragically lost their parents to the January 2010 earthquake in Haiti. He continued his humanitarian efforts and dedication to help orphan children by creating a program that allowed international adoption of orphans in Guatemala. These stunning achievements have been widely praised by many who have had the honor to work alongside Ali.

In his most recent role as Deputy Secretary of Homeland Security, Ali served as the second-in-command of the third largest Department in the U.S. Government. In this role, Ali ensured that a $60 billion budget was spent wisely and effectively, while at the same time leading a workforce of nearly 230,000 individuals. Like a true leader, Ali understands the importance of taking care of the Department's employees and recognizes that they are its greatest asset. He worked tirelessly to increase employee morale and, for the last few years, was particularly focused on improving employee engagement with senior leaders. His steadfast dedication to this effort, along with those of Secretary Jeh Johnson, resulted in rising employee satisfaction at DHS this past year. Ali's commitment to making the Department a more unified entity is yet another example of his extraordinary ability to mobilize, manage, and lead people with integrity and selflessness.

Ali's achievements are not limited to domestic operations. As the highest ranking Cuban American in the Obama administration, Ali secured the first homeland security agreement with the Government of Cuba, allowing increased trade, sea and air travel, and tourism between the two nations. His work to facilitate international trade, redesign the Nation's refugee admissions process, and enhance the Visa Waiver Program has resulted in many successful international partnerships.

In order to ensure our Nation's protection in cyber security, Ali has worked closely with international leaders to promote cyber security research and innovation, which has ultimately created a more reliable and effective cyber space at home and abroad. For instance, Ali led delegations in negotiating a cyber security partnership with the State of Israel, as well as the Department's negotiation of a cyber security agreement with China. These efforts and others have been fundamental to the protection of our Nation's cyber community.

Under his leadership, the Department's key counterterrorism efforts have been significantly strengthened. Ali improved national security vetting protocols, enhanced aviation and border security, and distributed counterterrorism intelligence to State, local, and tribal law enforcement. This collaboration has enhanced the Federal Government's national security partnership with first responders and has allowed for a more reliable and fruitful system.

During a time filled with constant threats and endangerments, Ali has continually proven to be a vital leader of DHS operations, ultimately ensuring that our Nation is a safe and secure place. I wish Ali, his wife, Tanya, and their family all the best in this next chapter in their lives. I sincerely thank him for his invaluable service to the Department and to our Nation.

ADDITIONAL STATEMENTS

150TH ANNIVERSARY OF SALINE, MICHIGAN

● Mr. PETERS. Mr. President, today I wish to recognize the 150th anniversary of the city of Saline, MI, which was incorporated as a village in 1866. I appreciate the opportunity to celebrate the history of this wonderful community, which has been consistently ranked as one of the best places to live in the United States.

Before Europeans first settled the area, Native Americans frequently canoed from Lake Erie or traveled over six different trails to hunt in the area and harvest salt, which they used domestically and for trade. In fact, it was the discovery of this important mineral that inspired French voyageurs to name the local river Saline after the French word for "salt". Following the War of 1812, the U.S. Government recognized the need for a military road connecting Detroit and Chicago and hired Mr. Orange Risdon to survey the new route, which would eventually be known as U.S. 12 or Michigan Avenue. Risdon, enchanted by the land around Saline, decided to settle in the area.

Risdon purchased 164 acres from the U.S. Government on April 5, 1825, built a house, and began promoting the area to English and German settlers from New England and New York, as well as a small number of African-American families. The families that joined Risdon agreed to name their new community Saline, which was platted as an unincorporated village in 1832 and became an incorporated village in 1866 after consolidating with the neighboring settlement of Barnegat in 1848.

As an important stop for stagecoaches traveling between Detroit and Chicago, Saline attracted a number of artisan workshops and mills to complement its local agricultural industry. A desire for an affordable and reliable way to transport crops to market inspired farmers and merchants in Saline to raise funds for a railroad line connecting the community with Hillsdale and Ypsilanti, which opened for service on July 4, 1870. The railroad served Saline for nearly 100 years, transporting apples, wool, lumber and livestock, as well as finished goods sold in local stores. By 1875, Saline was the principal agricultural shipping point in southeast Michigan, with 700 residents who enjoyed a 3-story school building, 4 churches, 3 flouring-mills, 2 tanneries, a foundry, 2 hotels, several stores, a newspaper, and daily mail.

Saline continued to grow over the 20th century, even during the Great Depression. The Old Union School was demolished in 1930 and replaced by an Art Deco building that continued to serve as the community's school. In 1932, Saline Valley Farms was established. This farming cooperative consisted of 1,000 acres and attracted struggling families during the Great Depression. Over 100 people lived on the farm with their families, working cooperatively in the farm's dairy, orchards, poultry house, and gardens. The farm's success encouraged members to sell goods to the public with a storefront, as well as delivery vans that brought fresh produce and canned goods to Detroit and its suburbs. Many of the farm's families were attracted from outside Saline but continued to live in the area even after the venture closed in the 1950s.

During World War II, many of Saline's young men and women went to work at the Ford Assembly Plant at Willow Run, which famously produced almost half of all the B–24 Liberator heavy bombers used during the war. In the decades since, Saline has continued to be a thriving community known for its open rural vistas and small town atmosphere. It has also continued to be an important driver of economic growth and innovation as home to a variety of major technical centers and manufacturing sites. Its nearly 10,000 residents enjoy well-maintained historic homes, a district library, a hospital, parks, recreation, art, and a museum. It has held true to the words expressed by Orange Risdon in 1840, when he wished that Saline would continue to "shine in light, knowledge and liberty with the same increasing brilliance that she has shown from infancy to present time." I am proud to represent Saline in the U.S. Senate, and I wish the community many more years of success.●

TRIBUTE TO JAY GRINNEY

● Mr. SESSIONS. Mr. President, today I would like to take the opportunity to recognize Mr. Jay Grinney, the president and chief executive officer of HealthSouth Corporation. Mr. Grinney will be retiring from his position at the end of 2016, and his tenure at HealthSouth has been marked with success and expansion for the company.

Jay Grinney earned his bachelor's degree from St. Olaf College and received a masters of business administration and a masters of health care administration from Washington University. He served as senior vice president at the Methodist hospital system in Houston, the primary teaching affiliate for the Baylor College of Medicine, then went on to become president of the Eastern Group at Hospital Corporation of America, the Nation's largest health care company.

Jay Grinney has been with HealthSouth for over 20 years and served as president and CEO since 2004. Throughout his career, he has maintained a strong work ethic and exercised excellent management of every organization he has led.

Mr. Grinney's leadership at HealthSouth Corporation in particular cannot be underappreciated. HealthSouth is one of the Nation's largest providers of postacute health care services, offering both facility-based and home-based postacute services in 33 States and Puerto Rico through its inpatient rehabilitation clinics. Mr. Grinney became CEO at a critical time in HealthSouth's history and engineered the company's turnaround and repositioning as one of the Nation's leading providers of postacute services. He has overseen the diversification of the company and ensured its financial stability and future. He led the HealthSouth acquisition of Encompass Home Health and Hospice, Reliant Hospital Partners, and CareSouth, successfully expanding the

HealthSouth network to 34 States. Along the way, he established a strong senior management team to ensure growth for HealthSouth in the years to come. For the over 20 years I have known Mr. Grinney, he has proven himself to be a man of great character, and without his guidance, HealthSouth would not be the company it is today.

HealthSouth's head corporation office is located in Birmingham, AL, and HealthSouth operates five rehabilitation hospitals and one outpatient rehabilitation clinic across the State. The company provides jobs to hundreds of Alabamians and quality health care to so many more. Jay Grinney's strong leadership and dedication have enabled this company to continue to provide critical care to our communities.

Mr. Grinney himself is involved with a number of community organizations, serving on the boards of directors of the Birmingham Business Alliance, where he is on the executive committee, the Community Foundation of Greater Birmingham, where he is chairman of the audit committee, and the Public Affairs Research Council of Alabama. He previously served as chairman of the board of directors of the Federation of American Hospitals and as a director on the boards of directors of the Birmingham Civil Rights Institute and the United Way of Central Alabama.

Though Mr. Grinney was not born in Alabama, he embodies all the qualities we most appreciate and respect. I speak for the citizens of Alabama when I thank Jay Grinney for all the work he has done for our State and so many others across the country through his tenure at HealthSouth. Mr. Grinney will be greatly missed, but the effects of his leadership will guarantee the growth and success of this company for years to come.●

MESSAGE FROM THE HOUSE RECEIVED DURING ADJOURNMENT

ENROLLED BILLS SIGNED

Under the authority of the order of the Senate of January 6, 2015, the Secretary of the Senate, on November 21, 2016, during the adjournment of the Senate, received a message from the House of Representatives, announcing that the Acting Speaker pro tempore (Mr. MESSER) had signed the following enrolled bills:

S. 2754. An act to designate the Federal building and United States courthouse located at 300 Fannin Street in Shreveport, Louisiana, as the "Tom Stagg United States Court House."

H.R. 4902. An act to amend title 5, United States Code, to expand law enforcement availability pay to employees of U.S. Customs and Border Protection's Air and Marine Operations.

H.R. 5873. An act to designate the Federal building and United States courthouse located at 511 East San Antonio Avenue in El Paso, Texas, as the "R.E. Thomason Federal Building and United States Courthouse".

Under the authority of the order of the Senate of January 6, 2015, the enrolled bills were signed on November 25, 2016, during the adjournment of the Senate, by the Acting President pro tempore (Mr. COATS).

MESSAGE FROM THE HOUSE

At 3:02 p.m., a message from the House of Representatives, delivered by Mrs. Cole, one of its reading clerks, announced that the House has passed the following bills, in which it requests the concurrence of the Senate:

H.R. 5711. An act to prohibit the Secretary of the Treasury from authorizing certain transactions by a U.S. financial institution in connection with the export or re-export of a commercial passenger aircraft to the Islamic Republic of Iran.

H.R. 5982. An act to amend chapter 8 of title 5, United States Code, to provide for en bloc consideration in resolutions of disapproval for "midnight rules", and for other purposes.

MEASURES REFERRED

The following bills were read the first and the second times by unanimous consent, and referred as indicated:

H.R. 5711. An act to prohibit the Secretary of the Treasury from authorizing certain transactions by a U.S. financial institution in connection with the export or re-export of a commercial passenger aircraft to the Islamic Republic of Iran; to the Committee on Banking, Housing, and Urban Affairs.

H.R. 5982. An act to amend chapter 8 of title 5, United States Code, to provide for en bloc consideration in resolutions of disapproval for "midnight rules", and for other purposes; to the Committee on Homeland Security and Governmental Affairs.

MEASURES READ THE FIRST TIME

The following bill was read the first time:

H.R. 6297. An act to reauthorize the Iran Sanctions Act of 1996.

ENROLLED BILL PRESENTED

The Secretary of the Senate reported that on today, November 28, 2016, she had presented to the President of the United States the following enrolled bill:

S. 2754. An act to designate the Federal building and United States courthouse located at 300 Fannin Street in Shreveport, Louisiana, as the "Tom Stagg United States Court House".

EXECUTIVE AND OTHER COMMUNICATIONS

The following communications were laid before the Senate, together with accompanying papers, reports, and documents, and were referred as indicated:

EC-7618. A communication from the Assistant Secretary for Export Administration, Bureau of Industry and Security, Department of Commerce, transmitting, pursuant to law, the report of a rule entitled "Updated Statements of Legal Authority for the Export Administration Regulations" (RIN0694-AH15) received in the Office of the President of the Senate on November 16, 2016; to the Committee on Banking, Housing, and Urban Affairs.

EC-7619. A communication from the Chief Counsel, Federal Emergency Management Agency, Department of Homeland Security, transmitting, pursuant to law, the report of a rule entitled "Suspension of Community Eligibility; Ulster County, NY, et al." ((44 CFR Part 64) (Docket No. FEMA-2016-0002)) received in the Office of the President of the Senate on November 16, 2016; to the Committee on Banking, Housing, and Urban Affairs.

EC-7620. A communication from the Assistant General Counsel for Legislation, Regulation and Energy Efficiency, Department of Energy, transmitting, pursuant to law, the report of a rule entitled "Energy Conservation Program for Consumer Products and Certain Commercial and Industrial Equipment: Final Determination of Compressors as Covered Equipment" (RIN1904-AC83) received in the Office of the President of Senate on November 15, 2016; to the Committee on Energy and Natural Resources.

EC-7621. A communication from the Section Chief of the Regulations and Standards Branch, Bureau of Safety and Environmental Enforcement, Department of the Interior, transmitting, pursuant to law, the report of a rule entitled "Civil Penalty Inflation Adjustment" (RIN1014-AA30) received in the Office of the President of the Senate on November 16, 2016; to the Committee on Energy and Natural Resources.

EC-7622. A communication from the Section Chief of the Regulations and Standards Branch, Bureau of Safety and Environmental Enforcement, Department of the Interior, transmitting, pursuant to law, the report of a rule entitled "Oil and Gas and Sulfur Operations on the Outer Continental Shelf—Decommissioning Costs for Pipelines" (RIN1014-AA32) received in the Office of the President of the Senate on November 16, 2016; to the Committee on Energy and Natural Resources.

EC-7623. A communication from the Assistant Secretary, Legislative Affairs, Department of State, transmitting, pursuant to law, a report relative to section 36(c) of the Arms Export Control Act (DDTC 16-009); to the Committee on Foreign Relations.

EC-7624. A communication from the Assistant Secretary, Legislative Affairs, Department of State, transmitting, pursuant to law, a report relative to section 36(c) of the Arms Export Control Act (DDTC 16-038); to the Committee on Foreign Relations.

EC-7625. A communication from the Assistant Secretary, Legislative Affairs, Department of State, transmitting, pursuant to law, a report relative to section 36(c) of the Arms Export Control Act (DDTC 16-051); to the Committee on Foreign Relations.

EC-7626. A communication from the Assistant Secretary, Legislative Affairs, Department of State, transmitting, pursuant to law, a report relative to section 36(c) of the Arms Export Control Act (DDTC 16-068); to the Committee on Foreign Relations.

EC-7627. A communication from the Assistant Secretary, Legislative Affairs, Department of State, transmitting, pursuant to law, a report relative to section 36(c) of the Arms Export Control Act (DDTC 16-076); to the Committee on Foreign Relations.

EC-7628. A communication from the Assistant Secretary, Legislative Affairs, Department of State, transmitting, pursuant to law, a report relative to section 36(c) of the Arms Export Control Act (DDTC 16–089); to the Committee on Foreign Relations.

EC–7629. A communication from the Assistant Secretary, Legislative Affairs, Department of State, transmitting, pursuant to law, a report relative to section 36(c) of the Arms Export Control Act (DDTC 16–092); to the Committee on Foreign Relations.

EC–7630. A communication from the Assistant Secretary, Legislative Affairs, Department of State, transmitting, pursuant to law, a report relative to section 36(d) of the Arms Export Control Act (DDTC 16–062); to the Committee on Foreign Relations.

EC–7631. A communication from the Deputy Director of Regulations and Policy Management Staff, Food and Drug Administration, Department of Health and Human Services, transmitting, pursuant to law, the report of a rule entitled "Revision of Organization and Conforming Changes to Regulation" (Docket No. FDA–2012–N–0222) received during adjournment of the Senate in the Office of the President of the Senate on November 14, 2016; to the Committee on Health, Education, Labor, and Pensions.

EC–7632. A communication from the Deputy Director of Regulations and Policy Management Staff, Food and Drug Administration, Department of Health and Human Services, transmitting, pursuant to law, the report of a rule entitled "Amendments to Regulations on Citizen Petitions, Petitions for Stay of Action, and Submission of Documents to Dockets" ((RIN0910–AG26) (Docket No. FDA–2011–N–0697)) received during adjournment of the Senate in the Office of the President of the Senate on November 14, 2016; to the Committee on Health, Education, Labor, and Pensions.

EC–7633. A communication from the Acting Director, Office of Sustainable Fisheries, Department of Commerce, transmitting, pursuant to law, the report of a rule entitled "Atlantic Highly Migratory Species; Atlantic Bluefin Tuna Fisheries" (RIN0648–XE963) received in the Office of the President of the Senate on November 16, 2016; to the Committee on Commerce, Science, and Transportation.

EC–7634. A communication from the Acting Director, Office of Sustainable Fisheries, Department of Commerce, transmitting, pursuant to law, the report of a rule entitled "Atlantic Highly Migratory Species; Atlantic Bluefin Tuna Fisheries" (RIN0648–XE820) received in the Office of the President of the Senate on November 16, 2016; to the Committee on Commerce, Science, and Transportation.

EC–7635. A communication from the Acting Director, Office of Sustainable Fisheries, Department of Commerce, transmitting, pursuant to law, the report of a rule entitled "Snapper-Grouper Fishery of the South Atlantic; 2016 Recreational Accountability Measure and Closure for the South Atlantic Other Porgies Complex" (RIN0648–XE216) received in the Office of the President of the Senate on November 16, 2016; to the Committee on Commerce, Science, and Transportation.

EC–7636. A communication from the Acting Director, Office of Sustainable Fisheries, Department of Commerce, transmitting, pursuant to law, the report of a rule entitled "Snapper-Grouper Fishery of the South Atlantic; 2016 Recreational Accountability Measure and Closure for the South Atlantic Other Jacks Complex" (RIN0648–XE774) received in the Office of the President of the Senate on November 16, 2016; to the Committee on Commerce, Science, and Transportation.

EC–7637. A communication from the Acting Director, Office of Sustainable Fisheries, Department of Commerce, transmitting, pursuant to law, the report of a rule entitled "Coastal Migratory Pelagic Resources of the Gulf of Mexico and South Atlantic; 2016–2017 Commercial Accountability Measures and Closure for King Mackerel in Western Zone of the Gulf of Mexico" (RIN0648–XE959) received in the Office of the President of the Senate on November 16, 2016; to the Committee on Commerce, Science, and Transportation.

EC–7638. A communication from the Acting Director, Office of Sustainable Fisheries, Department of Commerce, transmitting, pursuant to law, the report of a rule entitled "Fisheries of the Northeastern United States; Northeast Skate Complex; Adjustment to the Skate Bait Inseason Possession Limit" (RIN0648–XE955) received in the Office of the President of the Senate on November 16, 2016; to the Committee on Commerce, Science, and Transportation.

EC–7639. A communication from the Acting Director, Office of Sustainable Fisheries, Department of Commerce, transmitting, pursuant to law, the report of a rule entitled "Fisheries of the Northeastern United States; Atlantic Herring Fishery; 2016 Management Area 1A Seasonal Annual Catch Limit Harvested" (RIN0648–XE968) received in the Office of the President of the Senate on November 16, 2016; to the Committee on Commerce, Science, and Transportation.

EC–7640. A communication from the Acting Director, Office of Sustainable Fisheries, Department of Commerce, transmitting, pursuant to law, the report of a rule entitled "Fisheries of the Northeastern United States; Atlantic Bluefish Fishery; Quota Transfer" (RIN0648–XE834) received in the Office of the President of the Senate on November 16, 2016; to the Committee on Commerce, Science, and Transportation.

EC–7641. A communication from the Acting Director, Office of Sustainable Fisheries, Department of Commerce, transmitting, pursuant to law, the report of a rule entitled "Fisheries of the Northeastern United States; Atlantic Bluefish Fishery; Quota Transfer" (RIN0648–XE895) received in the Office of the President of the Senate on November 16, 2016; to the Committee on Commerce, Science, and Transportation.

EC–7642. A communication from the Director, Office of Sustainable Fisheries, Department of Commerce, transmitting, pursuant to law, the report of a rule entitled "Fisheries of the Northeastern United States; Atlantic Bluefish Fishery; Quota Transfer" (RIN0648–XE868) received in the Office of the President of the Senate on November 16, 2016; to the Committee on Commerce, Science, and Transportation.

EC–7643. A communication from the Acting Director, Office of Sustainable Fisheries, Department of Commerce, transmitting, pursuant to law, the report of a rule entitled "Fisheries of the Northeastern United States; Northeast Multispecies Fishery; Gulf of Maine Cod Trimester Total Allowable Catch Area Closure for the Common Pool Fishery" (RIN0648–XE811) received in the Office of the President of the Senate on November 16, 2016; to the Committee on Commerce, Science, and Transportation.

EC–7644. A communication from the Acting Director, Office of Sustainable Fisheries, Department of Commerce, transmitting, pursuant to law, the report of a rule entitled "Fisheries of the Northeastern United States; Small-Mesh Multispecies Fishery; Adjustment to the Commercial Northern Red Hake Inseason Possession Limit" (RIN0648–XE778) received in the Office of the President of the Senate on November 16, 2016; to the Committee on Commerce, Science, and Transportation.

EC–7645. A communication from the Acting Director, Office of Sustainable Fisheries, Department of Commerce, transmitting, pursuant to law, the report of a rule entitled "Fisheries of the Northeastern United States; Atlantic Herring Fishery; 2016 Management Area 1A Seasonal Annual Catch Limit Harvested" (RIN0648–XE968) received in the Office of the President of the Senate on November 16, 2016; to the Committee on Commerce, Science, and Transportation.

EC–7646. A communication from the Acting Director, Office of Sustainable Fisheries, Department of Commerce, transmitting, pursuant to law, the report of a rule entitled "Fisheries of the Exclusive Economic Zone Off Alaska; Inseason Adjustment to the 2016 Gulf of Alaska Pollock Seasonal Apportionments" (RIN0648–XE837) received in the Office of the President of the Senate on November 16, 2016; to the Committee on Commerce, Science, and Transportation.

EC–7647. A communication from the Acting Director, Office of Sustainable Fisheries, Department of Commerce, transmitting, pursuant to law, the report of a rule entitled "Fisheries of the Exclusive Economic Zone Off Alaska; Reallocation of Pacific Cod in the Bering Sea and Aleutian Islands Management Area" (RIN0648–XE851) received in the Office of the President of the Senate on November 16, 2016; to the Committee on Commerce, Science, and Transportation.

EC–7648. A communication from the Acting Director, Office of Sustainable Fisheries, Department of Commerce, transmitting, pursuant to law, the report of a rule entitled "Fisheries of the Exclusive Economic Zone Off Alaska; Sablefish in the Central Regulatory Area of the Gulf of Alaska" (RIN0648–XE967) received in the Office of the President of the Senate on November 16, 2016; to the Committee on Commerce, Science, and Transportation.

EC–7649. A communication from the Acting Director, Office of Sustainable Fisheries, Department of Commerce, transmitting, pursuant to law, the report of a rule entitled "Fisheries of the Exclusive Economic Zone Off Alaska; Reallocation of Pacific Cod in the Bering Sea and Aleutian Islands Management Area" (RIN0648–XE924) received in the Office of the President of the Senate on November 16, 2016; to the Committee on Commerce, Science, and Transportation.

EC–7650. A communication from the Acting Director, Office of Sustainable Fisheries, Department of Commerce, transmitting, pursuant to law, the report of a rule entitled "Fisheries of the Exclusive Economic Zone Off Alaska; Pacific Cod by Pot Catcher/Processors in the Bering Sea and Aleutian Islands Management Area" (RIN0648–XE879) received in the Office of the President of the Senate on November 16, 2016; to the Committee on Commerce, Science, and Transportation.

EC–7651. A communication from the Acting Director, Office of Sustainable Fisheries, Department of Commerce, transmitting, pursuant to law, the report of a rule entitled "Fisheries of the Exclusive Economic Zone Off Alaska; Deep-Water Species Fishery by Vessels Using Trawl Gear in the Gulf of Alaska" (RIN0648–XE835) received in the Office of the President of the Senate on November 16, 2016; to the Committee on Commerce, Science, and Transportation.

EC–7652. A communication from the Director, Office of Sustainable Fisheries, Department of Commerce, transmitting, pursuant to law, the report of a rule entitled "Fisheries of the Exclusive Economic Zone Off Alaska; Pacific Cod in the Bering Sea and Aleutian Islands Management Area" (RIN0648–XE828) received in the Office of the President of the Senate on November 16, 2016; to the Committee on Commerce, Science, and Transportation.

EC–7653. A communication from the Acting Director, Office of Sustainable Fisheries, Department of Commerce, transmitting, pursuant to law, the report of a rule entitled "Fisheries of the Exclusive Economic Zone Off Alaska; Exchange of Flatfish in the Bering Sea and Aleutian Islands Management Area" (RIN0648–XE745) received in the Office of the President of the Senate on November 16, 2016; to the Committee on Commerce, Science, and Transportation.

EC–7654. A communication from the Director, Office of Sustainable Fisheries, Department of Commerce, transmitting, pursuant to law, the report of a rule entitled "Fisheries of the Exclusive Economic Zone Off Alaska; Pacific Cod in the Bering Sea and Aleutian Islands Management Area" (RIN0648–XE828) received in the Office of the President of the Senate on November 16, 2016; to the Committee on Commerce, Science, and Transportation.

EC–7655. A communication from the Director, Office of Sustainable Fisheries, Department of Commerce, transmitting, pursuant to law, the report of a rule entitled "Fisheries of the Exclusive Economic Zone Off Alaska; Deep-Water Species Fishery by Vessels Using Trawl Gear in the Gulf of Alaska" (RIN0648–XE822) received in the Office of the President of the Senate on November 16, 2016; to the Committee on Commerce, Science , and Transportation.

EC–7656. A communication from the Acting Director, Office of Sustainable Fisheries, Department of Commerce, transmitting, pursuant to law, the report of a rule entitled "Fisheries of the Exclusive Economic Zone Off Alaska; Dusky Rockfish in the West Yakutat District of the Gulf of Alaska" (RIN0648–XE837) received in the Office of the President of the Senate on November 16, 2016; to the Committee on Commerce, Science, and Transportation.

EC–7657. A communication from the Acting Director, Office of Sustainable Fisheries, Department of Commerce, transmitting, pursuant to law, the report of a rule entitled "Fisheries of the Exclusive Economic Zone Off Alaska; Pacific Ocean Perch in the Western Regulatory Area of the Gulf of Alaska" (RIN0648–XE706) received in the Office of the President of the Senate on November 16, 2016; to the Committee on Commerce, Science, and Transportation.

EC–7658. A communication from the Acting Director, Office of Sustainable Fisheries, Department of Commerce, transmitting, pursuant to law, the report of a rule entitled "Fisheries of the Exclusive Economic Zone Off Alaska; Pacific Ocean Perch in the Bering Sea and Aleutian Islands" (RIN0648–XE795) received in the Office of the President of the Senate on November 16, 2016; to the Committee on Commerce, Science, and Transportation.

EC–7659. A communication from the Acting Director, Office of Sustainable Fisheries, Department of Commerce, transmitting, pursuant to law, the report of a rule entitled "Magnuson-Stevens Act Provisions; Fisheries Off West Coast States; Pacific Coast Groundfish Fishery; 2015–2016 Biennial Specifications and Management Measures; Inseason Adjustments" (RIN0648–BG27) received in the Office of the President of the

Senate on November 16, 2016; to the Committee on Commerce, Science, and Transportation.

EC–7660. A communication from the Acting Director, Office of Sustainable Fisheries, Department of Commerce, transmitting, pursuant to law, the report of a rule entitled "Fisheries of the Caribbean, Gulf of Mexico, and South Atlantic; Snapper-Grouper Resources of the South Atlantic; Trip Limit Reduction" (RIN0648–XE824) received in the Office of the President of the Senate on November 16, 2016; to the Committee on Commerce, Science, and Transportation.

EC–7661. A communication from the Acting Director, Office of Sustainable Fisheries, Department of Commerce, transmitting, pursuant to law, the report of a rule entitled "Fisheries of the Caribbean, Gulf of Mexico, and South Atlantic; 2016 Commercial Accountability Measures and Closure for Blueline Tilefish in the South Atlantic Region" (RIN0648–XE830) received in the Office of the President of the Senate on November 16, 2016; to the Committee on Commerce, Science, and Transportation.

EC–7662. A communication from the Deputy Under Secretary for Management and Chief Financial Officer, Department of Homeland Security, transmitting, pursuant to law, the fiscal year 2016 Agency Financial Report; to the Committee on Homeland Security and Governmental Affairs.

EC–7663. A communication from the Chairman of the United States International Trade Commission, transmitting, pursuant to law, the Commission's fiscal year 2016 Agency Financial Report; to the Committee on Homeland Security and Governmental Affairs.

EC–7664. A communication from the Chairman of the United States International Trade Commission, transmitting, pursuant to law, the Commission's fiscal year 2016 Agency Financial Report; to the Committee on Homeland Security and Governmental Affairs.

EC–7665. A communication from the Chairman of the Surface Transportation Board, Department of Transportation, transmitting, pursuant to law, the Board's Performance and Accountability Report for fiscal year 2016; to the Committee on Homeland Security and Governmental Affairs.

EC–7666. A communication from the Chairman of the Board, Farm Credit System Insurance Corporation, transmitting, pursuant to law, the Corporation's consolidated report addressing the Federal Managers Financial Integrity Act (FMFIA or Integrity Act) and the Inspector General Act of 1978 (IG Act); to the Committee on Homeland Security and Governmental Affairs.

EC–7667. A communication from the Chairman of the Board, Farm Credit System Insurance Corporation, transmitting, pursuant to law, the Corporation's consolidated report addressing the Federal Managers Financial Integrity Act (FMFIA or Integrity Act) and the Inspector General Act of 1978 (IG Act); to the Committee on Homeland Security and Governmental Affairs.

EC–7668. A communication from the Board Chairman and Chief Executive Officer, Farm Credit Administration, transmitting, pursuant to law, the Administration's Performance and Accountability Report for fiscal year 2016; to the Committee on Homeland Security and Governmental Affairs.

EC–7669. A communication from the Board Chairman and Chief Executive Officer, Farm Credit Administration, transmitting, pursuant to law, the Administration's Performance and Accountability Report for fiscal

year 2016; to the Committee on Homeland Security and Governmental Affairs.

EC–7670. A communication from the Acting Commissioner of Social Security, transmitting, pursuant to law, the Agency Financial Report for fiscal year 2016; to the Committee on Homeland Security and Governmental Affairs.

REPORTS OF COMMITTEES

The following reports of committees were submitted:

By Mr. THUNE, from the Committee on Commerce, Science, and Transportation, with an amendment in the nature of a substitute:

S. 827. A bill to amend the Communications Act of 1934 to ensure the integrity of voice communications and to prevent unjust or unreasonable discrimination among areas of the United States in the delivery of such communications (Rept. No. 114–383).

S. 2206. A bill to reduce the incidence of sexual harassment and assault at the National Oceanic and Atmospheric Administration, to reauthorize the National Oceanic and Atmospheric Administration Commissioned Officer Corps Act of 2002, and to reauthorize the Hydrographic Services Improvement Act of 1998, and for other purposes (Rept. No. 114–384).

S. 2817. A bill to improve understanding and forecasting of space weather events, and for other purposes (Rept. No. 114–385).

S. 3059. A bill to reauthorize and amend the John H. Prescott Marine Mammal Rescue and Response Grant Program and for other purposes (Rept. No. 114–386).

S. 3086. A bill to reauthorize and amend the Marine Debris Act to promote international action to reduce marine debris and for other purposes (Rept. No. 114–387).

By Mr. THUNE, from the Committee on Commerce, Science, and Transportation, without amendment:

S. 3099. A bill to preserve and enhance saltwater fishing opportunities for recreational anglers, and for other purposes (Rept. No. 114–388).

ADDITIONAL COSPONSORS

S. 441

At the request of Mr. NELSON, the name of the Senator from Iowa (Mr. GRASSLEY) was added as a cosponsor of S. 441, a bill to amend the Federal Food, Drug, and Cosmetic Act to clarify the Food and Drug Administration's jurisdiction over certain tobacco products, and to protect jobs and small businesses involved in the sale, manufacturing and distribution of traditional and premium cigars.

S. 974

At the request of Mr. DURBIN, the name of the Senator from New York (Mrs. GILLIBRAND) was added as a cosponsor of S. 974, a bill to amend the Fair Labor Standards Act of 1938 to prohibit employment of children in tobacco-related agriculture by deeming such employment as oppressive child labor.

S. 1566

At the request of Mr. FRANKEN, the name of the Senator from Massachusetts (Ms. WARREN) was added as a cosponsor of S. 1566, a bill to amend the

Public Health Service Act to require group and individual health insurance coverage and group health plans to provide for coverage of oral anticancer drugs on terms no less favorable than the coverage provided for anticancer medications administered by a health care provider.

S. 1831

At the request of Mr. TOOMEY, the name of the Senator from Illinois (Mr. DURBIN) was added as a cosponsor of S. 1831, a bill to revise section 48 of title 18, United States Code, and for other purposes.

S. 2219

At the request of Mrs. ERNST, her name was added as a cosponsor of S. 2219, a bill to require the Secretary of Commerce to conduct an assessment and analysis of the outdoor recreation economy of the United States, and for other purposes.

S. 2659

At the request of Mrs. ERNST, her name was added as a cosponsor of S. 2659, a bill to reaffirm that the Environmental Protection Agency cannot regulate vehicles used solely for competition, and for other purposes.

S. 2748

At the request of Ms. BALDWIN, the name of the Senator from Maryland (Ms. MIKULSKI) was added as a cosponsor of S. 2748, a bill to amend the Public Health Service Act to increase the number of permanent faculty in palliative care at accredited allopathic and osteopathic medical schools, nursing schools, social work schools, and other programs, including physician assistant education programs, to promote education and research in palliative care and hospice, and to support the development of faculty careers in academic palliative medicine.

S. 2800

At the request of Mr. COONS, the name of the Senator from Arizona (Mr. MCCAIN) was added as a cosponsor of S. 2800, a bill to amend the Internal Revenue Code of 1986 and the Higher Education Act of 1965 to provide an exclusion from income for student loan forgiveness for students who have died or become disabled.

S. 2873

At the request of Mr. HATCH, the names of the Senator from Tennessee (Mr. ALEXANDER), the Senator from Montana (Mr. TESTER) and the Senator from Virginia (Mr. WARNER) were added as cosponsors of S. 2873, a bill to require studies and reports examining the use of, and opportunities to use, technology-enabled collaborative learning and capacity building models to improve programs of the Department of Health and Human Services, and for other purposes.

S. 3348

At the request of Mr. WYDEN, the name of the Senator from Michigan (Ms. STABENOW) was added as a cospon-

sor of S. 3348, a bill to amend the Federal Election Campaign Act of 1971 to require candidates of major parties for the office of President to disclose recent tax return information.

S. 3360

At the request of Ms. HIRONO, the name of the Senator from Connecticut (Mr. MURPHY) was added as a cosponsor of S. 3360, a bill to authorize the Secretary of Health and Human Services to award grants to support the access of marginalized youth to sexual health services, and for other purposes.

S. 3476

At the request of Mrs. FEINSTEIN, the name of the Senator from New York (Mrs. GILLIBRAND) was added as a cosponsor of S. 3476, a bill to waive recoupment by the United States of certain bonuses and similar benefits erroneously received by members of the Army National Guard, and for other purposes.

S. 3478

At the request of Mr. RUBIO, the name of the Senator from Illinois (Mr. KIRK) was added as a cosponsor of S. 3478, a bill to require continued and enhanced annual reporting to Congress in the Annual Report on International Religious Freedom on anti-Semitic incidents in Europe, the safety and security of European Jewish communities, and the efforts of the United States to partner with European governments, the European Union, and civil society groups, to combat anti-Semitism, and for other purposes.

S. CON. RES. 30

At the request of Mr. LEE, the name of the Senator from Alaska (Mr. SULLIVAN) was added as a cosponsor of S. Con. Res. 30, a concurrent resolution expressing concern over the disappearance of David Sneddon, and for other purposes.

S. RES. 426

At the request of Mrs. MURRAY, the name of the Senator from New Hampshire (Mrs. SHAHEEN) was added as a cosponsor of S. Res. 426, a resolution expressing the sense of the Senate that the United States should support and protect the right of women working in developing countries to safe workplaces, free from gender-based violence, reprisals, and intimidation.

S. RES. 590

At the request of Mr. WYDEN, the name of the Senator from Connecticut (Mr. MURPHY) was added as a cosponsor of S. Res. 590, a resolution commemorating 100 years of health care services provided by Planned Parenthood.

S. RES. 616

At the request of Mrs. SHAHEEN, the names of the Senator from Delaware (Mr. COONS), the Senator from Ohio (Mr. BROWN), the Senator from Indiana (Mr. DONNELLY) and the Senator from Virginia (Mr. WARNER) were added as cosponsors of S. Res. 616, a resolution supporting the goals and ideals of American Diabetes Month.

AMENDMENTS SUBMITTED AND PROPOSED

SA 5112. Mr. MCCONNELL (for Ms. BALDWIN) proposed an amendment to the bill S. 2325, to require the Secretary of Commerce, acting through the Administrator of the National Oceanic and Atmospheric Administration, to establish a constituent-driven program to provide a digital information platform capable of efficiently integrating coastal data with decision-support tools, training, and best practices and to support collection of priority coastal geospatial data to inform and improve local, State, regional, and Federal capacities to manage the coastal region, and for other purposes.

TEXT OF AMENDMENTS

SA 5112. Mr. MCCONNELL (for Ms. BALDWIN) proposed an amendment to the bill S. 2325, to require the Secretary of Commerce, acting through the Administrator of the National Oceanic and Atmospheric Administration, to establish a constituent-driven program to provide a digital information platform capable of efficiently integrating coastal data with decision-support tools, training, and best practices and to support collection of priority coastal geospatial data to inform and improve local, State, regional, and Federal capacities to manage the coastal region, and for other purposes; as follows:

Strike all after the enacting clause and insert the following:

SECTION 1. SHORT TITLE.

This Act may be cited as the "Digital Coast Act".

SEC. 2. FINDINGS.

Congress makes the following findings:

(1) The Digital Coast is a model approach for effective Federal partnerships with State and local government, nongovernmental organizations, and the private sector.

(2) Access to current, accurate, uniform, and standards-based geospatial information, tools, and training to characterize the United States coastal region is critical for public safety and for the environment, infrastructure, and economy of the United States.

(3) More than half of all people of the United States (153,000,000) currently live on or near a coast and an additional 12,000,000 are expected in the next decade.

(4) Coastal counties in the United States average 300 persons per square mile, compared with the national average of 98.

(5) On a typical day, more than 1,540 permits for construction of single-family homes are issued in coastal counties, combined with other commercial, retail, and institutional construction to support this population.

(6) Over half of the economic productivity of the United States is located within coastal regions.

(7) Highly accurate, high-resolution remote sensing and other geospatial data play an increasingly important role in decision making and management of the coastal zone and economy, including for—

(A) flood and coastal storm surge prediction;

(B) hazard risk and vulnerability assessment;

(C) emergency response and recovery planning;

(D) community resilience to longer range coastal change;

(E) local planning and permitting;

(F) habitat and ecosystem health assessments; and

(G) landscape change detection.

SEC. 3. DEFINITIONS.

In this Act:

(1) COASTAL REGION.—The term "coastal region" means the area of United States waters extending inland from the shoreline to include coastal watersheds and seaward to the territorial sea.

(2) COASTAL STATE.—The term "coastal State" has the meaning given the term "coastal state" in section 304 of the Coastal Zone Management Act of 1972 (16 U.S.C. 1453).

(3) FEDERAL GEOGRAPHIC DATA COMMITTEE.—The term "Federal Geographic Data Committee" means the interagency committee that promotes the coordinated development, use, sharing, and dissemination of geospatial data on a national basis.

(4) REMOTE SENSING AND OTHER GEOSPATIAL.—The term "remote sensing and other geospatial" means collecting, storing, retrieving, or disseminating graphical or digital data depicting natural or manmade physical features, phenomena, or boundaries of the Earth and any information related thereto, including surveys, maps, charts, satellite and airborne remote sensing data, images, LiDAR, and services performed by professionals such as surveyors, photogrammetrists, hydrographers, geodesists, cartographers, and other such services.

(5) SECRETARY.—The term "Secretary" means the Secretary of Commerce, acting through the Administrator of the National Oceanic and Atmospheric Administration.

SEC. 4. ESTABLISHMENT OF THE DIGITAL COAST.

(a) ESTABLISHMENT.—

(1) IN GENERAL.—The Secretary shall establish a program for the provision of an enabling platform that integrates geospatial data, decision-support tools, training, and best practices to address coastal management issues and needs. Under the program, the Secretary shall strive to enhance resilient communities, ecosystem values, and coastal economic growth and development by helping communities address their issues, needs, and challenges through cost-effective and participatory solutions.

(2) DESIGNATION.—The program established under paragraph (1) shall be known as the "Digital Coast" (in this section referred to as the "program").

(b) PROGRAM REQUIREMENTS.—In carrying out the program, the Secretary shall ensure that the program provides data integration, tool development, training, documentation, dissemination, and archive by—

(1) making data and resulting integrated products developed under this section readily accessible via the Digital Coast Internet website of the National Oceanic and Atmospheric Administration, the GeoPlatform.gov and data.gov Internet websites, and such other information distribution technologies as the Secretary considers appropriate;

(2) developing decision-support tools that use and display resulting integrated data and provide training on use of such tools;

(3) documenting such data to Federal Geographic Data Committee standards; and

(4) archiving all raw data acquired under this Act at the appropriate National Oceanic and Atmospheric Administration data center or such other Federal data center as the Secretary considers appropriate.

(c) COORDINATION.—The Secretary shall coordinate the activities carried out under the program to optimize data collection, sharing and integration, and to minimize duplication by—

(1) consulting with coastal managers and decision makers concerning coastal issues, and sharing information and best practices, as the Secretary considers appropriate, with—

(A) coastal States;

(B) local governments; and

(C) representatives of academia, the private sector, and nongovernmental organizations;

(2) consulting with other Federal agencies, including interagency committees, on relevant Federal activities, including activities carried out under the Ocean and Coastal Mapping Integration Act (33 U.S.C. 3501 et seq.), the Coastal Zone Management Act of 1972 (16 U.S.C. 1451 et seq.), the Integrated Coastal and Ocean Observation System Act of 2009 (33 U.S.C. 3601 et seq.), and the Hydrographic Services Improvement Act of 1998 (33 U.S.C. 892 et seq.);

(3) participating, pursuant to section 216 of the E-Government Act of 2002 (Public Law 107–347; 44 U.S.C. 3501 note), in the establishment of such standards and common protocols as the Secretary considers necessary to assure the interoperability of remote sensing and other geospatial data with all users of such information within—

(A) the National Oceanic and Atmospheric Administration;

(B) other Federal agencies;

(C) State and local government; and

(D) the private sector;

(4) coordinating with, seeking assistance and cooperation of, and providing liaison to the Federal Geographic Data Committee pursuant to Office of Management and Budget Circular A–16 and Executive Order 12906 of April 14, 1994 (59 Fed. Reg. 17671), as amended by Executive Order 13286 of March 5, 2003 (68 Fed. Reg. 10619); and

(5) developing and maintaining a best practices document that sets out the best practices used by the Secretary in carrying out the program and providing such document to the United States Geological Survey, the Corps of Engineers, and other relevant Federal agencies.

(d) FILLING NEEDS AND GAPS.—In carrying out the program, the Secretary shall—

(1) maximize the use of remote sensing and other geospatial data collection activities conducted for other purposes and under other authorities;

(2) focus on filling data needs and gaps for coastal management issues, including with respect to areas that, as of the date of the enactment of this Act, were underserved by coastal data and the areas of the Arctic that are under the jurisdiction of the United States;

(3) pursuant to the Ocean and Coastal Mapping Integration Act (33 U.S.C. 3501 et seq.), support continue improvement in existing efforts to coordinate the acquisition and integration of key data sets needed for coastal management and other purposes, including—

(A) coastal elevation data;

(B) land use and land cover data;

(C) socioeconomic and human use data;

(D) critical infrastructure data;

(E) structures data;

(F) living resources and habitat data;

(G) cadastral data; and

(H) aerial imagery; and

(4) integrate the priority supporting data set forth under paragraph (3) with other available data for the benefit of the broadest measure of coastal resource management constituents and applications.

(e) FINANCIAL AGREEMENTS AND CONTRACTS.—

(1) IN GENERAL.—In carrying out the program, the Secretary—

(A) may enter into financial agreements to carry out the program, including—

(i) support to non-Federal entities that participate in implementing the program; and

(ii) grants, cooperative agreements, interagency agreements, contracts, or any other agreement on a reimbursable or non-reimbursable basis, with other Federal, tribal, State, and local governmental and nongovernmental entities; and

(B) may, to the maximum extent practicable, enter into such contracts with private sector entities for such products and services as the Secretary determines may be necessary to collect, process, and provide remote sensing and other geospatial data and products for purposes of the program.

(2) FEES.—

(A) ASSESSMENT AND COLLECTION.—The Secretary may assess and collect fees for the conduct of any training, workshop, or conference that advances the purposes of the program.

(B) AMOUNTS.—The amount of a fee under this paragraph may not exceed the sum of costs incurred, or expected to be incurred, by the Secretary as a direct result of the conduct of the training, workshop, or conference, including for subsistence expenses incidental to the training, workshop, or conference, as applicable.

(C) USE OF FEES.—Amounts collected by the Secretary in the form of fees under this paragraph may be used to pay for—

(i) the costs incurred for conducting an activity described in subparagraph (A); or

(ii) the expenses described in subparagraph (B).

(3) SURVEY AND MAPPING.—Contracts entered into under paragraph (1)(B) shall be considered "surveying and mapping" services as such term is used in and as such contracts are awarded by the Secretary in accordance with the selection procedures in chapter 11 of title 40, United States Code.

(f) OCEAN ECONOMY.—The Secretary may establish publicly available tools that track ocean and Great Lakes economy data for each coastal State.

(g) AUTHORIZATION OF APPROPRIATIONS.—There is authorized to be appropriated to the Secretary $4,000,000 for each fiscal year 2017 through 2021 to carry out the program.

OUTDOOR RECREATION JOBS AND ECONOMIC IMPACT ACT OF 2016

Mr. McCONNELL. Mr. President, I ask unanimous consent that the Senate proceed to the immediate consideration of Calendar No. 667, H.R. 4665.

The PRESIDING OFFICER. The clerk will report the bill by title.

The senior assistant legislative clerk read as follows:

A bill (H.R. 4665) to require the Secretary of Commerce to conduct an assessment and analysis of the outdoor recreation economy of the United States, and for other purposes.

There being no objection, the Senate proceeded to consider the bill.

Mr. McCONNELL. Mr. President, I ask unanimous consent that the bill be considered read a third time and passed and the motion to reconsider be considered made and laid upon the table.

The PRESIDING OFFICER. Without objection, it is so ordered.

The bill (H.R. 4665) was ordered to a third reading, was read the third time, and passed.

TO ENSURE FUNDING FOR THE NATIONAL HUMAN TRAFFICKING HOTLINE

Mr. McCONNELL. Mr. President, I ask unanimous consent that the Committee on Health, Education, Labor, and Pensions be discharged from further consideration of S. 2974, and the Senate proceed to its immediate consideration.

The PRESIDING OFFICER. Without objection, it is so ordered.

The clerk will report the bill by title.

The senior assistant legislative clerk read as follows:

A bill (S. 2974) to ensure funding for the National Human Trafficking Hotline, and for other purposes.

There being no objection, the Senate proceeded to consider the bill.

Mr. McCONNELL. I ask unanimous consent that the bill be read a third time and passed and the motion to reconsider be considered made and laid upon the table.

The PRESIDING OFFICER. Without objection, it is so ordered.

The bill (S. 2974) was ordered to be engrossed for a third reading, was read the third time, and passed, as follows:

S. 2974

Be it enacted by the Senate and House of Representatives of the United States of America in Congress assembled,

SECTION 1. FUNDING FOR THE NATIONAL HUMAN TRAFFICKING HOTLINE; PERFECTING AMENDMENT.

(a) HHS FUNDING FOR TRAFFICKING HOTLINE.—Section 107(b)(1)(B)(ii) of the Trafficking Victims Protection Act of 2000 (22 U.S.C. 7105(b)(1)(B)(ii)) is amended by striking "of amounts made available for grants under paragraph (2),".

(b) PERFECTING AMENDMENT.—Section 603 of the Justice for Victims of Trafficking Act of 2015 (Public Law 114–22; 129 Stat. 259) is amended, in the matter preceding paragraph (1), by striking "Victims of Crime Trafficking" and inserting "Victims of Trafficking".

(c) EFFECTIVE DATE.—The amendments made by this Act shall take effect as if enacted as part of the Justice for Victims of Trafficking Act of 2015 (Public Law 114–22; 129 Stat. 227).

DIGITAL COAST ACT OF 2015

Mr. McCONNELL. Mr. President, I ask unanimous consent that the Senate proceed to the immediate consideration of Calendar No. 660, S. 2325.

The PRESIDING OFFICER. The clerk will report the bill by title.

The senior assistant legislative clerk read as follows:

A bill (S. 2325) to require the Secretary of Commerce, acting through the Administrator of the National Oceanic and Atmospheric Administration, to establish a constituent-driven program to provide a digital information platform capable of efficiently integrating coastal data with decision-support tools, training, and best practices and to support collection of priority coastal geospatial data to inform and improve local, State, regional, and Federal capacities to manage the coastal region, and for other purposes.

There being no objection, the Senate proceeded to consider the bill, which had been reported from the Committee on Commerce, Science, and Transportation, with an amendment to strike all after the enacting clause and insert in lieu thereof the following:

SECTION 1. SHORT TITLE.

This Act may be cited as the "Digital Coast Act of 2015".

SEC. 2. FINDINGS.

Congress makes the following findings:

(1) The Digital Coast is a model approach for effective Federal partnerships with State and local government, nongovernmental organizations, and the private sector.

(2) Access to current, accurate, uniform, and standards-based geospatial information, tools, and training to characterize the United States coastal region is critical for public safety and for the environment, infrastructure, and economy of the United States.

(3) More than half of all people of the United States (153,000,000) currently live on or near a coast and an additional 12,000,000 are expected in the next decade.

(4) Coastal counties in the United States average 300 persons per square mile, compared with the national average of 98.

(5) On a typical day, more than 1,540 permits for construction of single-family homes are issued in coastal counties, combined with other commercial, retail, and institutional construction to support this population.

(6) Over half of the economic productivity of the United States is located within coastal regions.

(7) Highly accurate, high-resolution remote sensing and other geospatial data play an increasingly important role in decisionmaking and management of the coastal zone and economy, including for—

(A) flood and coastal storm surge prediction;

(B) hazard risk and vulnerability assessment;

(C) emergency response and recovery planning;

(D) community resilience to longer range coastal change;

(E) local planning and permitting;

(F) habitat and ecosystem health assessments; and

(G) landscape change detection.

SEC. 3. DEFINITIONS.

In this Act:

(1) COASTAL REGION.—The term "coastal region" means the area of United States waters extending inland from the shoreline to include coastal watersheds and seaward to the territorial sea.

(2) COASTAL STATE.—The term "coastal State" has the meaning given the term "coastal state" in section 304 of the Coastal Zone Management Act of 1972 (16 U.S.C. 1453).

(3) FEDERAL GEOGRAPHIC DATA COMMITTEE.— The term "Federal Geographic Data Committee" means the interagency committee that promotes the coordinated development, use, sharing, and dissemination of geospatial data on a national basis.

(4) REMOTE SENSING AND OTHER GEOSPATIAL.— The term "remote sensing and other geospatial" means collecting, storing, retrieving, or disseminating graphical or digital data depicting natural or manmade physical features, phenomena, or boundaries of the Earth and any information related thereto, including surveys, maps, charts, satellite and airborne remote sensing data, images, LiDAR, and services performed by professionals such as surveyors, photogrammetrists, hydrographers, geodesists, cartographers, and other such services.

(5) SECRETARY.—The term "Secretary" means the Secretary of Commerce, acting through the Administrator of the National Oceanic and Atmospheric Administration.

SEC. 4. ESTABLISHMENT OF THE DIGITAL COAST.

(a) ESTABLISHMENT.—

(1) IN GENERAL.—The Secretary shall establish a program for the provision of an enabling platform that integrates geospatial data, decision-support tools, training, and best practices to address coastal management issues and needs. Under the program, the Secretary shall strive to enhance resilient communities, ecosystem values, and coastal economic growth and development by helping communities address their issues, needs, and challenges through cost-effective and participatory solutions.

(2) DESIGNATION.—The program established under paragraph (1) shall be known as the "Digital Coast" (in this section referred to as the "program").

(b) PROGRAM REQUIREMENTS.—In carrying out the program, the Secretary shall ensure that the program provides data integration, tool development, training, documentation, dissemination, and archive by—

(1) making data and resulting integrated products developed under this section readily accessible via the Digital Coast Internet website of the National Oceanic and Atmospheric Administration, the GeoPlatform.gov and data.gov Internet websites, and such other information distribution technologies as the Secretary considers appropriate;

(2) developing decision-support tools that use and display resulting integrated data and provide training on use of such tools;

(3) documenting such data to Federal Geographic Data Committee standards; and

(4) archiving all raw data acquired under this Act at the appropriate National Oceanic and Atmospheric Administration data center or such other Federal data center as the Secretary considers appropriate.

(c) COORDINATION.—The Secretary shall coordinate the activities carried out under the program to optimize data collection, sharing and integration, and to minimize duplication by—

(1) consulting with coastal managers and decisionmakers concerning coastal issues, and sharing information and best practices, as the Secretary considers appropriate, with—

(A) coastal States;

(B) local governments; and

(C) representatives of academia, the private sector, and nongovernmental organizations;

(2) consulting with other Federal agencies, including interagency committees, on relevant Federal activities, including activities carried out under the Ocean and Coastal Mapping Integration Act (33 U.S.C. 3501 et seq.), the Coastal Zone Management Act of 1972 (16 U.S.C. 1451 et seq.), the Integrated Coastal and Ocean Observation System Act of 2009 (33 U.S.C. 3601 et seq.), and the Hydrographic Services Improvement Act of 1998 (33 U.S.C. 892 et seq.);

(3) participating, pursuant to section 216 of the E-Government Act of 2002 (Public Law 107– 347; 44 U.S.C. 3501 note), in the establishment of such standards and common protocols as the Secretary considers necessary to assure the interoperability of remote sensing and other geospatial data with all users of such information within—

(A) the National Oceanic and Atmospheric Administration;

(B) other Federal agencies;

(C) State and local government; and

(D) the private sector;

(4) coordinating with, seeking assistance and cooperation of, and providing liaison to the Federal Geographic Data Committee pursuant to Office of Management and Budget Circular A– 16 and Executive Order 12906 of April 14, 1994 (59 Fed. Reg. 17671), as amended by Executive Order 13286 of March 5, 2003 (68 Fed. Reg. 10619); and

(5) developing and maintaining a best practices document that sets out the best practices used by the Secretary in carrying out the program and providing such document to the United States Geological Survey, the Corps of Engineers, and other relevant Federal agencies.

(d) FILLING NEEDS AND GAPS.—In carrying out the program, the Secretary shall—

(1) maximize the use of remote sensing and other geospatial data collection activities conducted for other purposes and under other authorities;

(2) focus on filling data needs and gaps for coastal management issues, including with respect to areas that, as of the date of the enactment of this Act, were underserved by coastal data and the areas of the Arctic that are under the jurisdiction of the United States;

(3) pursuant to the Ocean and Coastal Mapping Integration Act (33 U.S.C. 3501 et seq.), support continue improvement in existing efforts to coordinate the acquisition and integration of key data sets needed for coastal management and other purposes, including—

(A) coastal elevation data;

(B) land use and land cover data;

(C) socioeconomic and human use data;

(D) critical infrastructure data;

(E) structures data;

(F) living resources and habitat data;

(G) cadastral data; and

(H) aerial imagery; and

(4) integrate the priority supporting data set forth under paragraph (3) with other available data for the benefit of the broadest measure of coastal resource management constituents and applications.

(e) FINANCIAL AGREEMENTS AND CONTRACTS.—

(1) IN GENERAL.—In carrying out the program, the Secretary—

(A) may enter into financial agreements to carry out the program, including—

(i) support to non-Federal entities that participate in implementing the program;

(ii) grants, cooperative agreements, interagency agreements, contracts, or any other agreement on a reimbursable or non-reimbursable basis, with other Federal, tribal, State, and local governmental and nongovernmental entities; and

(iii) registration fees in support of training, workshops, and conferences that advance the purposes of the program; and

(B) shall enter into such contracts with private sector entities for such products and services as the Secretary determines may be necessary to collect, process, and provide remote sensing and other geospatial data and products for purposes of the program.

(2) SURVEY AND MAPPING.—Contracts entered into under paragraph (1)(B) shall be considered "surveying and mapping" services as such term is used in and as such contracts are awarded by the Secretary in accordance with the selection procedures in chapter 11 of title 40, United States Code.

(f) OCEAN ECONOMY.—The Secretary may establish publically available tools that track ocean and Great Lakes economy data for each coastal state (as that term is defined in section 304 of the of the Coastal Zone Management Act of 1972 (16 U.S.C. 1453)).

(g) AUTHORIZATION OF APPROPRIATIONS.— There is authorized to be appropriated to the Secretary such sums as may be necessary to carry out the program in each of fiscal years 2016 through 2020.

Mr. McCONNELL. Mr. President, I further ask unanimous consent that the committee-reported substitute amendment be withdrawn, that the Baldwin substitute amendment, which is at the desk, be agreed to, that the bill, as amended, be read a third time and passed, and the motion to reconsider be considered made and laid upon the table with no intervening action or debate.

The PRESIDING OFFICER. Without objection, it is so ordered.

The committee-reported substitute amendment was withdrawn.

The amendment (No. 5112) in the nature of a substitute was agreed to.

(The amendment is printed in today's RECORD under "Text of Amendments.")

The bill (S. 2325), as amended, was ordered to be engrossed for a third reading, was read the third time, and passed.

CONSUMER REVIEW FAIRNESS ACT OF 2016

Mr. McCONNELL. Mr. President, I ask unanimous consent that the Senate proceed to the immediate consideration of H.R. 5111, which was received from the House.

The PRESIDING OFFICER. The clerk will report the bill by title.

The senior assistant legislative clerk read as follows:

A bill (H.R. 5111) to prohibit the use of certain clauses in form contracts that restrict the ability of a consumer to communicate regarding the goods or services offered in interstate commerce that were the subject of the contract, and for other purposes.

There being no objection, the Senate proceeded to consider the bill.

Mr. McCONNELL. Mr. President, I ask unanimous consent that the bill be considered read a third time and passed and the motions to reconsider be considered made and laid upon the table.

The PRESIDING OFFICER. Without objection, it is so ordered.

The bill (H.R. 5111) was ordered to a third reading, was read the third time, and passed.

MEASURE READ THE FIRST TIME—H.R. 6297

Mr. McCONNELL. Mr. President, I understand there is a bill at the desk, and I ask for its first reading.

The PRESIDING OFFICER. The clerk will read the bill by title for the first time.

The senior assistant legislative clerk read as follows:

A bill (H.R. 6297) to reauthorize the Iran Sanctions Act of 1996.

Mr. McCONNELL. Mr. President, I now ask for a second reading and, in order to place the bill on the calendar under the provisions of rule XIV, I object to my own request.

The PRESIDING OFFICER. Objection is heard.

The bill will be read for the second time on the next legislative day.

ORDERS FOR TUESDAY, NOVEMBER 29, 2016

Mr. McCONNELL. Mr. President, I ask unanimous consent that when the Senate completes its business today, it adjourn until 10 a.m., Tuesday, November 29; that following the prayer and pledge, the morning hour be deemed expired, the Journal of proceedings be approved to date, and the time for the two leaders be reserved for their use later in the day; further, that following leader remarks, the Senate be in a period of morning business until 11 a.m., with Senators permitted to speak therein for up to 10 minutes each; finally, that the Senate recess from 12:30 p.m. to 2:15 p.m. to allow for the weekly conference meetings.

The PRESIDING OFFICER. Without objection, it is so ordered.

ADJOURNMENT UNTIL 10 A.M. TOMORROW

Mr. McCONNELL. Mr. President, if there is no further business to come before the Senate, I ask unanimous consent that it stand adjourned under the previous order.

There being no objection, the Senate, at 6:30 p.m., adjourned until Tuesday, November 29, 2016, at 10 a.m.

EXTENSIONS OF REMARKS

SENATE COMMITTEE MEETINGS

Title IV of Senate Resolution 4, agreed to by the Senate of February 4, 1977, calls for establishment of a system for a computerized schedule of all meetings and hearings of Senate committees, subcommittees, joint committees, and committees of conference. This title requires all such committees to notify the Office of the Senate Daily Digest—designated by the Rules Committee—of the time, place and purpose of the meetings, when scheduled and any cancellations or changes in the meetings as they occur.

As an additional procedure along with the computerization of this information, the Office of the Senate Daily Digest will prepare this information for printing in the Extensions of Remarks section of the CONGRESSIONAL RECORD on Monday and Wednesday of each week.

Meetings scheduled for Tuesday, November 29, 2016 may be found in the Daily Digest of today's RECORD.

MEETINGS SCHEDULED
NOVEMBER 30

10 a.m.
Committee on Finance
Business meeting to consider the nominations of Charles P. Blahous, III, of Maryland, and Robert D. Reischauer, of Maryland, both to be a Member of the Board of Trustees of the Federal Hospital Insurance Trust Fund, a Member of the Board of Trustees of the Federal Old-Age and Survivors Insurance Trust Fund and the Federal Disability Insurance Trust Fund, and a Member of the Board of Trustees of the Federal Supplementary Medical Insurance Trust Fund.

SD–215

Committee on Homeland Security and Governmental Affairs
To hold hearings to examine initial observations of the new leadership at the Border Patrol.

SD–342

2:30 p.m.
Committee on Commerce, Science, and Transportation
Subcommittee on Space, Science, and Competitiveness
To hold hearings to examine the dawn of artificial intelligence.

SR–253

Special Committee on Aging
To hold hearings to examine financial abuse of older Americans by guardians and others in power.

SD–562

3 p.m.
Select Committee on Intelligence
To receive a closed briefing on certain intelligence matters.

SH–219

DECEMBER 1

9:30 a.m.
Committee on Armed Services
To hold hearings to examine the oversight, acquisition, testing, and employment of the Littoral Combat Ship (LCS) and LCS mission module programs.

SD–G50

10:30 a.m.
Committee on Foreign Relations
To hold hearings to examine the future of counter-terrorism strategy.

SD–419

2 p.m.
Select Committee on Intelligence
To receive a closed briefing on certain intelligence matters.

SH–219

2:30 p.m.
Committee on Homeland Security and Governmental Affairs
Subcommittee on Regulatory Affairs and Federal Management
To hold hearings to examine two Government Accountability Office reports regarding the renewable fuel standard.

SD–342

DECEMBER 6

2:30 p.m.
Committee on Foreign Relations
To hold hearings to examine defeating the Iranian threat network, focusing on options for countering Iranian proxies.

SD–419

Committee on the Judiciary
Subcommittee on Crime and Terrorism
To hold hearings to examine whether additional firewalls are needed to protect Congressional oversight staff from retaliatory criminal referrals.

SD–226

DECEMBER 7

2:15 p.m.
Committee on Indian Affairs
To hold an oversight hearing to examine the Department of the Interior's Land Buy-Back Program for Tribal Nations, four years later.

SD–628

DECEMBER 8

10 a.m.
Committee on Foreign Relations
Subcommittee on State Department and USAID Management, International Operations, and Bilateral International Development
To hold hearings to examine State Department and United States Agency for International Development management challenges and opportunities for the next administration.

SD–419

SENATE—*Tuesday, November 29, 2016*

The Senate met at 10 a.m. and was called to order by the President pro tempore (Mr. HATCH).

PRAYER

The Chaplain, Dr. Barry C. Black, offered the following prayer:

Let us pray.

O God, our help in ages past, our hope for years to come, thank You for the spirit of contentment we can receive from You, bringing quietness and faith to our hearts.

Today, use our Senators for Your purposes, enabling them to live worthy of Your Name. May the words they speak bring edification and unity as our lawmakers build bridges of co-operation. Lord, give them the wisdom to depart from strife, remembering that soft answers turn away anger. Inspire them to avoid contention in their search for common ground. Give them cheerful hearts and optimistic spirits.

We pray in Your great Name. Amen.

PLEDGE OF ALLEGIANCE

The President pro tempore led the Pledge of Allegiance, as follows:

I pledge allegiance to the Flag of the United States of America, and to the Republic for which it stands, one nation under God, indivisible, with liberty and justice for all.

Mr. McCONNELL. Mr. President, I suggest the absence of a quorum.

The PRESIDING OFFICER (Mr. COTTON). The clerk will call the roll.

The senior assistant legislative clerk proceeded to call the roll.

Mr. McCONNELL. Mr. President, I ask unanimous consent that the order for the quorum call be rescinded.

The PRESIDING OFFICER. Without objection, it is so ordered.

RECOGNITION OF THE MAJORITY LEADER

The PRESIDING OFFICER. The majority leader is recognized.

MEASURE PLACED ON THE CALENDAR—H.R. 6297

Mr. McCONNELL. Mr. President, I understand there is a bill at the desk due for a second reading.

The PRESIDING OFFICER. The clerk will read the bill by title for the second time.

The senior assistant legislative clerk read as follows:

A bill (H.R. 6297) to reauthorize the Iran Sanctions Act of 1996.

Mr. McCONNELL. In order to place the bill on the calendar under the provisions of rule XIV, I object to further proceedings.

The PRESIDING OFFICER. Objection is heard.

The bill will be placed on the calendar.

UNANIMOUS CONSENT AGREEMENT—H.R. 6297

Mr. McCONNELL. Mr. President, I now ask unanimous consent that at a time to be determined by the majority leader, after consultation with the Democratic leader, the Senate proceed to the consideration of H.R. 6297, which was received from the House; further that the bill be read a third time and the Senate vote on passage of the bill with no intervening action or debate; finally, if passed, that the motion to reconsider be considered made and laid upon the table.

The PRESIDING OFFICER. The Democratic leader.

Mr. REID. Mr. President, reserving the right to object, the ranking member of the Intelligence Committee, Senator FEINSTEIN, has had some trouble with this. I spoke to her last night. She said to go ahead and let this go. She is totally in agreement now that there would be time for debate on this issue and a vote. We understand that. So I am not objecting to this matter.

The PRESIDING OFFICER. Without objection, it is so ordered.

IRAN SANCTIONS EXTENSION BILL

Mr. McCONNELL. This week, Senators will have a chance to pass the Iran Sanctions Extension Act that recently passed the House on an overwhelming vote. Preserving these sanctions is critical, given Iran's disturbing pattern of aggression and its persistent efforts to expand its sphere of influence across the Middle East.

This is all the more important, given how the administration has ignored Iran's overall efforts to upset the balance of power in the greater Middle East and how it has been held hostage by Iran's threats to withdraw from the nuclear agreement. The authorities extended by this bill give us some of the tools needed to impose sanctions if necessary to hold Iran accountable and help keep Americans safer from this threat.

I expect that next year the new Congress and the new administration will undertake a review of our overall policy toward Iran, and these authorities should remain in place as we address how best to deal with Iranian missile tests, support to Hezbollah, and support of the Syrian regime.

BUSINESS BEFORE THE CONGRESS

Mr. McCONNELL. Mr. President, as we come to the end of this year and of this Congress, we will continue in our efforts to complete the business before us. Members have been working diligently on their respective conference committees to conclude the outstanding conference reports on the Defense authorization bill, the waterways infrastructure and resources bill, and the energy policy modernization bill. I look forward to the full Senate taking up these measures as they are available so that we can pass final legislation to be signed into law.

In the coming days, the Senate will also consider a critical and bipartisan medical innovation bill known as the 21st Century Cures bill, as well as a continuing resolution to keep the government funded and carry us into the spring.

Mr. REID. Mr. President, I suggest the absence of a quorum.

The PRESIDING OFFICER. The clerk will call the roll.

The senior assistant legislative clerk proceeded to call the roll.

Mr. REID. Mr. President, I ask unanimous consent that the order for the quorum call be rescinded.

The PRESIDING OFFICER. Without objection, it is so ordered.

RECOGNITION OF THE MINORITY LEADER

The PRESIDING OFFICER. The Democratic leader is recognized.

UNLV STUDENT NEWSPAPER

Mr. REID. Mr. President, yesterday an amazing thing happened at the University of Nevada at Las Vegas, and it deserves some attention here this morning. I will take just a brief time to talk about that.

The students who operate that newspaper made the bold decision to change the name of the newspaper. It has been going on and has been somewhat controversial now for quite some time. The newspaper will no longer be called the Rebel Yell. There were many who felt that was a disparaging name for the paper. The Civil War ended a long time ago. We should not harken back to the Civil War and the Confederacy for that newspaper.

Now UNLV's newspaper will be called the Scarlet & Gray Free Press. I am happy to have with me today Brian Ahern, who is an able member of my press staff. He was the managing editor of that newspaper. He helped run the newspaper when he was at UNLV.

● This "bullet" symbol identifies statements or insertions which are not spoken by a Member of the Senate on the floor.

I am proud of these students who did this. Seven months ago, when the students announced their intention to change the name of the paper, I publicly supported them. Now that they have followed through, I am all the more amazed by their leadership and courage in doing the right thing. The name change was not easy. There was a lot of debate swirling around this issue on campus and throughout the State. These students were more interested in unifying the student body and rejecting hateful symbols of a racist and divisive past than in hiding behind tradition.

Now it is time for the university's administration to do the right thing and get rid of the "Rebel" mascot. What these young men and women have done is a lesson for all of us. Some politicians, State legislators, and the National Football League can learn a thing or two from these students. I applaud the Scarlet & Gray Free Press for doing the right thing. They have long been an independent voice for the students at UNLV. I congratulate my able staff member, Brian, for urging me to move forward on this matter for many months now.

BUSINESS BEFORE THE CONGRESS

Mr. REID. Mr. President, as the Republican leader mentioned a minute or two ago, the Senate has some important work to do before this Congress can come to a close. One of the pieces of legislation that has to be addressed is the Cures Act, a scaled-back version of the 21st Century Cures legislation the House is scheduled to consider tomorrow.

The staffs of the Senate Health, Education, Labor, and Pensions Committee and the House Energy and Commerce Committee have worked countless hours on this bill. For more than a year, they have missed time with their families and given up vacations in the hope of reaching bipartisan agreement. There are many priorities in this bill to address funding for opioids, which has been an ongoing problem with all of the deaths occurring on a daily basis. We have done nothing to help with that—nothing.

Of course, we are concerned about cancer and the advocacy of Vice President BIDEN and the so-called moonshot, as well as important provisions for the National Institutes of Health. There are other issues outstanding that will need to be resolved in this matter.

It is my understanding that the committee work continues in the House, and we can expect a managers' amendment in the House Rules Committee sometime tonight. We are all eager to see what that is going to be. We know it is different from the Senate bill, which we felt very good about.

By the end of next week, we are going to have to pass new legislation to ensure that the government does not shut down for lack of funding. But we also have to be concerned about what happens with that Cures Act. Is this going to be put over again, as we have put over opioid funding time and again over the past several years, or are we going to move forward with something that is constructive in nature? Right now, there is some angst in my caucus about what we should do.

Now, on funding, I am very disappointed that the Republican leadership appears unwilling to pass a comprehensive bill that reflects the careful and considered judgment of the Appropriations Committee. With only days left in this Congress, we should be working on a bipartisan bill, in a manner that is bipartisan, to set out our priorities. But that is not happening. We should be funding initiatives that serve important needs and eliminate others that are wasteful and have a lower priority. Instead, it appears that we are going to pass another continuing resolution that just sets the government on autopilot, potentially for many months. The exact months we don't know. I guess there is some dispute among the Republican leadership as to how long the CR is going to be.

But this isn't governing. That is punting, for lack of a better description. They are trapped, and the only thing they can do is punt and see what happens later. It is irresponsible, it is wasteful, and it is not the way we should be doing the business of this Congress.

Mr. President, will the Chair announce the business of the day.

RESERVATION OF LEADER TIME

The PRESIDING OFFICER. Under the previous order, the leadership time is reserved.

MORNING BUSINESS

The PRESIDING OFFICER. Under the previous order, the Senate will be in a period of morning business until 11 a.m., with Senators permitted to speak therein for up to 10 minutes each.

The assistant Democratic leader.

DACA

Mr. DURBIN. Mr. President, 15 years ago, a woman contacted my office in Chicago because she had a problem. It turned out that her daughter, who was about 17 years old or 18 years old at the time, had an extraordinary musical talent and had been accepted as a student at the Manhattan School of Music, as well as at the Juilliard School in New York.

The problem was that her daughter was undocumented. She brought her little girl to the United States at the age of 2. This Korean girl, Tereza Lee, was raised in the United States by a family of very modest means, but she showed extraordinary talent at music, so much so that she was accepted at these great schools.

When she went to fill out the application form and they asked for her nationality or citizenship status, she turned to her mother and said: What should I put here?

Her mother said: Well, I never filed any papers after we brought you to this country, so I don't know.

They called our office. The law was very clear. This young girl, who for 15 or 16 years had grown up in Chicago in modest circumstances, gone to school, done well, and excelled in her music, was in fact undocumented. Under the law of the United States of America, the only recourse for her—and it is still the case—was to leave this country for 10 years and apply to come back.

I thought to myself: This little girl had nothing to say when the family decided to move to the United States when she was 2 years of age. She wasn't consulted. She didn't make a conscious decision. She, in fact, did everything she was expected to do in her life. She grew up believing that she would be in America, that she would be part of this country's future, but she has this undocumented status, an uncertain status.

That is why, 15 years ago, I introduced the DREAM Act. It said to young women and men such as Tereza Lee: We will give you a chance. If you were brought to the United States as a child, you have gone through school and done well, and you have no serious criminal issues that worry us, we will give you a chance to earn your way into legal status and ultimately citizenship.

The DREAM Act was introduced 15 years ago. Over the last 15 years, it has passed in the House some years and in the Senate in other years. It has never become the law of the land. It was a few years ago that I wrote a letter to then-President Obama—still President Obama—and asked him, as a cosponsor of my DREAM Act, could he do something to help these young people who were fearful they were going to be deported. Republican Senator Lugar of Indiana joined me in the letter, and later some 20 other Senators joined as well.

President Obama studied it and asked his Attorney General and others to find a path, and he created an Executive action. That Executive action allows those who have been in a status such as Tereza Lee's a chance under the Deferred Action for Childhood Arrivals Program, or the DACA Program, to sign up with the government, to register with the government, to pay a filing fee of almost $500, and to go through a criminal background check. For that, if approved, they receive a 2-year temporary and renewable status.

That status would allow them to stay in the United States without fear of deportation and would allow them to work.

Since the President's Executive action was launched, some 744,000 young people have taken advantage of it.

Many of their parents warned them. They said: Be careful. If you sign up with this government and tell them you are not here legally, they might use it against you.

Some of those students, young people, and their parents came to me with that concern. I said to them: As long as you are following the law, as long as you are paying the fee, submitting yourself to a criminal background check, and understand this is only a temporary situation that can be renewed, do it. Be part of America. Be part of obeying the law, following the law, and, ultimately, I think it will be to your benefit.

When I gave that advice, I could not have imagined that we would be facing a new President in just a few weeks with a totally different view on immigration. That President-elect, Donald Trump, has said some very hurtful and divisive things about immigration during the course of his campaign. Fortunately for us, it appears he is reflecting on those statements now, and some of those he is modifying, if not changing.

I hope he will do the same when it comes to this. These 744,000 DACA-eligible persons who are currently in the program, as well as others, should be given their chance in America. As long as they are no threat to our country, we should capitalize on their talents, on the education that they have received that we paid for, and give them a chance to make America better.

I have stood on the floor many times—and I will today—to tell the story of just one of these students. It is one thing to talk about what they might bring to this country, and it is another thing to get to know them a little bit.

This is a photograph of Yuri Hernandez. Yuri was 3 years old when her family brought her to the United States from Mexico. She grew up in Coos Bay, OR. In high school she was an honor roll student and was active in her community. She was an active member of the Key Club and the Kiwanis service program for students. She was voted homecoming princess of her high school and jubilee princess of Coos Bay.

She attended the University of Portland, where she graduated with a bachelor's degree in social work. She received numerous awards and was involved in many extracurricular and volunteer activities. She was vice president of the Social Work Club, a board member of the National Association of Social Workers, and a member of Oregonians Against Trafficking Humans.

When you hear about her record in college and what she has achieved, remember this: This young lady did not qualify for one penny of Federal assistance. Because she is undocumented, because she is a DREAMer, she was ineligible for the things that many students take for granted in America, such as Pell grants and government loans.

Yuri had to find another way to do this. She had to work her way through school, borrowing money from parents. She faced hardships that many students don't face, but she overcame them. That speaks to her, her character, and her determination.

She volunteered as a tutor for at-risk elementary school students. During her senior year in college, she was a full-time student and a full-time worker to pay for her college education.

Do we need persons in America such as Yuri—so determined, so committed to their future that they are willing to make sacrifices many students don't make? Of course we do.

Yuri is now a graduate student at the University of Michigan School of Social Work. Again, she doesn't qualify for any government assistance to go to school. She is planning on a graduate degree, a master's in social work, in the fall of 2017, and she still finds time to tutor and mentor high school students.

She wants to give back to America. She wrote a letter to me about the DACA Program and said:

DACA opened a lot of doors. I no longer wake up every day fearing that I could be picked up and deported [out of the United States]. . . . DACA changed my life completely and allowed me to use my education.

Would America be better if Yuri were deported, if she were sent away from this country to a country she has never known, one from which she was taken away when she was a child of 3 years of age?

I think the answer is obvious.

For her and for thousands such as her, this is a moment of testing. Will we in the United States of America, this Nation of diverse immigrants, this diverse Nation that believes in fairness and justice, give to those DREAMers, those DACA recipients, their chance to prove themselves? Will we hold these children responsible for decisions made by their parents or will we give them their own chance in life?

Over the last few weeks, I have been home in Illinois, and I have talked to a lot of people who have come to know these DACA recipients and DREAMers. Many of these young people are despondent. With the new President, they are afraid they are going to lose any protection they currently have from deportation. Some of them have been driven to despair. Some have decided to leave the country, and, in some rare cases, there have been cases of suicide from their despondency.

We can do better, America. We can say to these young people that, while

Congress debates immigration and its future, we are going to make certain they are not penalized and hurt in the process.

For Yuri and thousands just like her, we owe it to them to give them their chance.

I yield the floor.

I suggest the absence of a quorum.

The PRESIDING OFFICER. The clerk will call the roll.

The senior assistant legislative clerk proceeded to call the roll.

Mr. WICKER. Mr. President, I ask unanimous consent that the order for the quorum call be rescinded.

The PRESIDING OFFICER. Without objection, it is so ordered.

ECHO BILL

Mr. WICKER. Mr. President, I come to the floor to express my support for the ECHO Act, which the Senate will be voting on in approximately 1 hour.

This represents bipartisan work—another bipartisan achievement during this very productive term of Congress. In this case it is Senators HATCH and SCHATZ who have led us to this morning's vote.

The ECHO Act is named after Project ECHO, an innovative telehealth-inspired model originally conceived at the University of New Mexico. Project ECHO has created promising opportunities for primary care clinicians to receive high-quality specialty training remotely. In this way, the most remote patient in the most underserved area can receive specialized care by his hometown doctor or provider.

I am a longtime supporter of using technology and telehealth to improve patients' access to quality care.

New Mexico is a State with many rural areas, as is my State of Mississippi. For that reason, Mississippi and New Mexico have had to be leaders in innovative health care models for years, such as Project ECHO in New Mexico and the University of Mississippi Medical Center in Jackson, MS.

At UMMC we are national leaders in providing technology-enabled care remotely. While ECHO emphasizes training among professionals, the University of Mississippi Medical Center has used remote technology for clinical care and patient monitoring.

Since 2003, the medical center in Jackson has reached more than one-half million rural Mississippians through the use of telehealth. To date, the program includes more than 30 specialties and can reach patients at more than 200 clinical sites.

Like Senator HATCH, I have reached across the aisle to work with our friend from Hawaii, Senator SCHATZ, to expand an innovative model for the rest of the country. Specifically, I worked this year with Senator SCHATZ on the CONNECT for Health Act, which has been endorsed by nearly 100 organizations. Like CONNECT, the ECHO Act aims at taking a proven approach to technology-enabled care and bringing it to underserved populations across the country.

The CONNECT for Health Act, which is S. 2484, would be a small but significant step toward payment parity for telehealth services under the Medicare Program. In addition to removing specific barriers to telemedicine, the bill would allow for coverage of certain remote patient monitoring services for patients with multiple chronic diseases.

Remote patient monitoring is a model the University of Mississippi Medical Center has used to expand access, improve quality, and reduce hospital admissions for some of our State's most underserved populations.

So I want to thank Senator SCHATZ for his leadership on CONNECT for Health and also ECHO, which again we will be voting on in just a few moments. I extend my utmost appreciation to Senator SCHATZ and to Senator HATCH and the Committee on Finance for including policies inspired by our CONNECT for Health Act in the bipartisan chronic care outline.

I am confident proposals to advance telehealth can improve access and cut costs, and I look forward to seeing CONNECT enacted also, but today I am pleased and thrilled we are taking an important step forward with the passage of the ECHO Act.

I yield the floor.

The PRESIDING OFFICER. The Senator from Maryland.

Mr. CARDIN. Mr. President, I ask unanimous consent to speak for up to 15 minutes.

The PRESIDING OFFICER. Is there objection?

Without objection, it is so ordered.

(The remarks of Mr. CARDIN pertaining to the submission of S. Con. Res. 56 are printed in today's RECORD under "Submitted Resolutions.")

The PRESIDING OFFICER. The Senator from Utah.

────────

ECHO BILL

Mr. HATCH. Mr. President, today, the Senate is voting on S. 2873, the ECHO Act. In April, Senator SCHATZ and I introduced this bill to highlight the impressive work of technology-enabled collaborative learning and capacity-building models.

One such model that has brought promising new ideas to our Nation's healthcare delivery system is Project ECHO, which started in New Mexico and quickly expanded to Utah. Today, Project ECHO is thriving in more than 30 States.

Our bill draws on the success of Project ECHO to improve health services on a national scale. Our proposal is not political; rather, it is the culmina-

tion of a broad bipartisan effort to bring about meaningful healthcare reform that will benefit families across the country in red States and blue States alike.

Our legislation improves medical services for all Americans by providing healthcare professionals in rural and underserved communities with access to a network of peers and specialists who can teach specialty care. By connecting doctors and nurses with teams of experts, patients can receive the care they need when they need it. Most importantly, patients will not have to travel long distances to receive treatments; they can stay close to home and receive treatment from doctors they know and trust.

In today's bustling healthcare environment, policymakers often forget that healthcare delivery works differently in urban and rural settings. To bridge the urban-rural divide, the ECHO Act brings expertise to providers serving rural populations by enabling them to gain the skills they need to care for people living in their communities. Through this exchange, urban providers in return can learn how rural health is operationalized in real time. Ultimately, our proposal prioritizes rural health needs and reconciles differences in care delivery for diverse populations.

Today, I am grateful that a majority of my colleagues have agreed to support this forward-thinking, common-sense legislation. Like the 21st Century Cures bill, our proposal demonstrates our common commitment to improving health care for all patients.

Telehealth is a topic of particular interest in my home State of Utah. Under the existing Project ECHO programs, medical experts based at the University of Utah use videoconferencing to train healthcare professionals who are hundreds, sometimes even thousands, of miles away. As we work to improve telehealth, models like those in the ECHO Act will enable telementorship and provider education to occur via avenues more tailored to health professionals' needs. This customization is an essential step to achieving person-centered health care.

As a body, we must be dedicated to improving health services for all Americans, no matter where they live. Through this bill, we are making significant progress toward achieving that goal. Using groundbreaking new technologies, the ECHO Act will enable us to take better care of our family members, neighbors, and friends. By putting communication front and center, Project ECHO will allow health professionals to share innovations and new discoveries in an efficient, timely manner.

Before turning the floor over to my esteemed colleague from Hawaii, whose collaboration on this proposal has

proven invaluable, I first wish to share how our legislation came to be. Several months ago, doctors at the University of Utah—including Dr. Terry Box and Dr. Vivian Lee, as well as some of the most renowned disease experts in the country—reached out to me to demonstrate how Project ECHO was benefiting families across Utah and the Intermountain Region. Their innovative approach to telehealth piqued my interest. As it turns out, Senator SCHATZ had a very similar experience with his own constituents. After discussing our shared experiences, we joined forces to draft a bill that would allow Americans in rural counties access across the country to reap the benefits of telehealth.

The founder of Project ECHO, Dr. Sanjeev Arora, was an instrumental partner throughout this process. He worked with us to share ideas from ECHO hubs across the country, allowing us to incorporate a broad array of viewpoints. With his help, we were able to hear from countless stakeholders and medical professionals who understood the potential of our legislation. We also worked alongside the leadership of the Health, Education, Labor, and Pensions Committee. With the assistance of Senators ALEXANDER and MURRAY, as well as the majority and minority leaders, we were able to shepherd this legislation through the committee process and bring it to the Senate floor.

This bill was born fresh, from a bottom-up approach, which enabled us to solicit ideas and opinions from numerous healthcare professionals across the country. Thanks to their input and the support of Members on both sides of the aisle, we are poised to pass legislation that will dramatically improve the quality of our Nation's health care.

I wish to thank all those who assisted in this bipartisan effort. Today is a victory for everyone involved. I appreciate the efforts of Senator SCHATZ.

I yield the floor.

The PRESIDING OFFICER. The Senator from Hawaii.

Mr. SCHATZ. Mr. President, I thank the President pro tempore, the Senator from Utah, Mr. HATCH, for his leadership on this and many other issues.

Healthcare policy can be a particularly vexing area for those of us who like to get things done because over the last 8 years we have mostly just been at each other's throats, arguing about the Affordable Care Act. But we are here to talk about a bright spot—something we are not arguing about—which can reduce costs and improve outcomes. Telehealth is the future of health care. It harnesses technology to provide patients with high-quality care, whenever and wherever they need it. That is why we need to update Medicare to take advantage of these new technologies in telemedicine and remote patient monitoring. That is why I and 18 other Senators from both parties have introduced and cosponsored the CONNECT for Health Act.

I thank Senator HATCH for his support in including provisions from our bill in the Senate Finance Committee's chronic care package.

Telehealth will improve the delivery of care to patients, but it will also support providers by giving doctors and nurses the tools to work with and learn from each other. Simply put, a lot of medical education is financially or geographically out of reach for providers on the frontlines, but we can fix that using technology. It is called Project ECHO, and that is what we are about to vote on. Based at the University of New Mexico and with the strong support of Senators HEINRICH and UDALL, Project ECHO has already had a positive impact across the Nation on patients, providers, and communities.

How does it work? Imagine a VTC—video teleconference—with 15 people on the screen. Participants assemble online 2 hours every week for 6 weeks to learn about a selected disease condition—for example, depression. The leader of the VTC is a specialist physician from an academic medical center with a team which would include, for example, a psychologist, a pharmacist, and a social worker. Throughout the 6 weeks, the session time is divided between lessons, case presentations, and discussions. Providers from across the country can learn the latest best practices and develop a network of colleagues to share information and help with the hard questions. This is a game changer. This is the kind of ongoing training for folks in rural areas that has not been available until now.

Project ECHO has already been used for infectious disease outbreaks and public health emergencies, such as H1N1 and Zika; chronic diseases, such as hepatitis C and diabetes; and mental health conditions, such as anxiety and schizophrenia.

The results are impressive. Patients in rural or underserved areas now have more access to better trained doctors in their own communities, which decreases costs and improves outcomes. Providers feel less isolated and more connected to a network of high-quality providers across their State. As a result, they are more likely to stay in underserved areas where they are needed the most. The health system runs more efficiently and effectively. Providers have the training to see and treat more patients.

We still have many questions about this model, which is new, but among them: What are the best successors? What are the barriers to adoption? For which conditions is it best suited? The ECHO Act, as amended, will direct HHS to study this model and give us the answers we need to make decisions at the Federal level about how to best support expanding it nationally.

One final note of thanks. It is not a coincidence that several of the successful health care-related efforts this year have been a result of collaboration with and leadership of Senator HATCH. His bipartisan spirit, his pragmatism, and his understanding of the legislative process make working with him and his staff a true pleasure.

I encourage my colleagues to continue to join us in supporting this revolutionary health care model.

CONCLUSION OF MORNING BUSINESS

The PRESIDING OFFICER (Mr. FLAKE). Morning business is closed.

EXPANDING CAPACITY FOR HEALTH OUTCOMES ACT

The PRESIDING OFFICER. Under the previous order, the Committee on Health, Education, Labor, and Pensions is discharged from and the Senate will proceed to the consideration of S. 2873, which the clerk will report.

The legislative clerk read as follows:

A bill (S. 2873) to require studies and reports examining the use of, and opportunities to use, technology-enabled collaborative learning and capacity building models to improve programs of the Department of Health and Human Services, and for other purposes.

The PRESIDING OFFICER. Under the previous order, there will be 30 minutes of debate, equally divided in the usual form.

The Senator from Hawaii.

Mr. SCHATZ. Mr. President, I ask unanimous consent that the time be equally divided between both sides during the quorum call.

The PRESIDING OFFICER. Without objection, it is so ordered.

Mr. SCHATZ. I suggest the absence of a quorum.

The PRESIDING OFFICER. The clerk will call the roll.

The legislative clerk proceeded to call the roll.

Mr. DAINES. Mr. President, I ask unanimous consent that the order for the quorum call be rescinded.

The PRESIDING OFFICER. Without objection, it is so ordered.

AMENDMENT NO. 5110

Mr. DAINES. Mr. President, I call up amendment No. 5110 and ask unanimous consent that it be reported by number.

The PRESIDING OFFICER. Without objection, it is so ordered.

The clerk will report the amendment by number.

The legislative clerk read as follows:

The Senator from Montana [Mr. DAINES], for Mr. ALEXANDER, proposes an amendment numbered 5110.

The amendment is as follows:

(Purpose: In the nature of a substitute)

Strike all after the enacting clause and insert the following:

SECTION 1. SHORT TITLE.

This Act may be cited as the "Expanding Capacity for Health Outcomes Act" or the "ECHO Act".

SEC. 2. DEFINITIONS.

In this Act:

(1) HEALTH PROFESSIONAL SHORTAGE AREA.—The term "health professional shortage area" means a health professional shortage area designated under section 332 of the Public Health Service Act (42 U.S.C. 254e).

(2) INDIAN TRIBE.—The term "Indian tribe" has the meaning given the term in section 4 of the Indian Self-Determination and Education Assistance Act (25 U.S.C. 5304).

(3) MEDICALLY UNDERSERVED AREA.—The term "medically underserved area" has the meaning given the term "medically underserved community" in section 799B of the Public Health Service Act (42 U.S.C. 295p).

(4) MEDICALLY UNDERSERVED POPULATION.—The term "medically underserved population" has the meaning given the term in section 330(b) of the Public Health Service Act (42 U.S.C. 254b(b)).

(5) NATIVE AMERICANS.—The term "Native Americans" has the meaning given the term in section 736 of the Public Health Service Act (42 U.S.C. 293) and includes Indian tribes and tribal organizations.

(6) SECRETARY.—The term "Secretary" means the Secretary of Health and Human Services.

(7) TECHNOLOGY-ENABLED COLLABORATIVE LEARNING AND CAPACITY BUILDING MODEL.—The term "technology-enabled collaborative learning and capacity building model" means a distance health education model that connects specialists with multiple other health care professionals through simultaneous interactive videoconferencing for the purpose of facilitating case-based learning, disseminating best practices, and evaluating outcomes.

(8) TRIBAL ORGANIZATION.—The term "tribal organization" has the meaning given the term in section 4 of the Indian Self-Determination and Education Assistance Act (25 U.S.C. 5304).

SEC. 3. EXAMINATION AND REPORT ON TECHNOLOGY-ENABLED COLLABORATIVE LEARNING AND CAPACITY BUILDING MODELS.

(a) EXAMINATION.—

(1) IN GENERAL.—The Secretary shall examine technology-enabled collaborative learning and capacity building models and their impact on—

(A) addressing mental and substance use disorders, chronic diseases and conditions, prenatal and maternal health, pediatric care, pain management, and palliative care;

(B) addressing health care workforce issues, such as specialty care shortages and primary care workforce recruitment, retention, and support for lifelong learning;

(C) the implementation of public health programs, including those related to disease prevention, infectious disease outbreaks, and public health surveillance;

(D) the delivery of health care services in rural areas, frontier areas, health professional shortage areas, and medically underserved areas, and to medically underserved populations and Native Americans; and

(E) addressing other issues the Secretary determines appropriate.

(2) CONSULTATION.—In the examination required under paragraph (1), the Secretary shall consult public and private stakeholders with expertise in using technology-enabled collaborative learning and capacity building models in health care settings.

(b) REPORT.—

(1) IN GENERAL.—Not later than 2 years after the date of enactment of this Act, the Secretary shall submit to the Committee on Health, Education, Labor, and Pensions of the Senate and the Committee on Energy and Commerce of the House of Representatives, and post on the appropriate website of the Department of Health and Human Services, a report based on the examination under subsection (a).

(2) CONTENTS.—The report required under paragraph (1) shall include findings from the examination under subsection (a) and each of the following:

(A) An analysis of—

(i) the use and integration of technology-enabled collaborative learning and capacity building models by health care providers;

(ii) the impact of such models on health care provider retention, including in health professional shortage areas in the States and communities in which such models have been adopted;

(iii) the impact of such models on the quality of, and access to, care for patients in the States and communities in which such models have been adopted;

(iv) the barriers faced by health care providers, States, and communities in adopting such models;

(v) the impact of such models on the ability of local health care providers and specialists to practice to the full extent of their education, training, and licensure, including the effects on patient wait times for specialty care; and

(vi) efficient and effective practices used by States and communities that have adopted such models, including potential cost-effectiveness of such models.

(B) A list of such models that have been funded by the Secretary in the 5 years immediately preceding such report, including the Federal programs that have provided funding for such models.

(C) Recommendations to reduce barriers for using and integrating such models, and opportunities to improve adoption of, and support for, such models as appropriate.

(D) Opportunities for increased adoption of such models into programs of the Department of Health and Human Services that are in existence as of the report.

(E) Recommendations regarding the role of such models in continuing medical education and lifelong learning, including the role of academic medical centers, provider organizations, and community providers in such education and lifelong learning.

The PRESIDING OFFICER. Under the previous order, amendment No. 5110 is agreed to.

Mr. DAINES. Mr. President, Montanans have always been on the cutting edge of frontier medicine, using ingenuity to overcome the challenges in frontier and rural America to make sure we have access to high-quality health care. In fact, going back to the time my great-great-grandmother homesteaded near Conrad, MT, our health care providers have worked and continue to work to increase access despite geography, weather, limited resources, and government regulation.

Rural Montanans are often hours away from a hospital and even farther away from any kind of trauma center. Our local providers are the first-line responders. They tackle everything from the common cold to emergency situations. It is their actions that can make the difference between life and death. Rural providers give Montanans access to preventive and behavioral health services. They help ward off chronic illness with early detection and provide care and support through cancer and other debilitating diseases. They deserve our respect and the resources that will help them better serve Montanans. That is why I am honored to join my colleagues in supporting the ECHO Act and making sure it is passed and signed into law. I am thankful for the leadership of the senior Senator from Utah, Senator HATCH, who has been out front leading in this effort.

Geographic location should not dictate the quality of care. This bill will promote opportunities to improve access to high-quality care in rural communities, such as access to specialists and support and training for rural health care providers. In fact, this year the Billings Clinic launched the Montana-based Project ECHO hub in an effort to address a lack of access to mental health and substance abuse resources. The hub connects rural providers with a team of specialists to collaborate, share case studies, and offer support. The hub is built to be flexible, allowing teleclinics on any topic or any disease. It also allows Montana's providers to collaborate with specialists at academic centers, such as the University of Washington and the University of New Mexico. Because of the success of this first hub, the Billings Clinic will launch two more teleclinics next year to help primary care sites across Montana integrate behavioral health services in their practices.

The ECHO Act will promote these programs throughout the country and increase access for all Americans. I am thankful to see strong bipartisan support on the passage of this bill as we work together to improve rural health care.

I thank the Presiding Officer.

I suggest the absence of a quorum.

The PRESIDING OFFICER. The clerk will call the roll.

The legislative clerk proceeded to call the roll.

Mr. VITTER. Mr. President, I ask unanimous consent that the order for the quorum call be rescinded.

The PRESIDING OFFICER. Without objection, it is so ordered.

Mr. VITTER. Mr. President, I ask unanimous consent all time be yielded back.

The PRESIDING OFFICER. Without objection, all time is yielded back.

The bill was ordered to be engrossed for a third reading and was read the third time.

The PRESIDING OFFICER. Under the previous order, the bill having been read the third time, the question is, Shall it pass?

Mr. VITTER. Mr. President, I ask for the yeas and nays.

The PRESIDING OFFICER. Is there a sufficient second?

There appears to be a sufficient second.

The clerk will call the roll.

The bill clerk called the roll.

Mr. CORNYN. The following Senators are necessarily absent: the Senator from Tennessee (Mr. CORKER) and the Senator from Colorado (Mr. GARDNER).

Further, if present and voting, the Senator from Tennessee (Mr. CORKER) would have voted "yea" and the Senator from Colorado (Mr. GARDNER) would have voted "yea."

Mr. DURBIN. I announce that the Senator from Vermont (Mr. SANDERS) is necessarily absent.

The PRESIDING OFFICER (Mr. CRUZ). Are there any other Senators in the Chamber desiring to vote?

The result was announced—yeas 97, nays 0, as follows:

[Rollcall Vote No. 154 Leg.]

YEAS—97

Alexander	Flake	Nelson
Ayotte	Franken	Paul
Baldwin	Gillibrand	Perdue
Barrasso	Graham	Peters
Bennet	Grassley	Portman
Blumenthal	Hatch	Reed
Blunt	Heinrich	Reid
Booker	Heitkamp	Risch
Boozman	Heller	Roberts
Boxer	Hirono	Rounds
Brown	Hoeven	Rubio
Burr	Inhofe	Sasse
Cantwell	Isakson	Schatz
Capito	Johnson	Schumer
Cardin	Kaine	Scott
Carper	King	Sessions
Casey	Kirk	Shaheen
Cassidy	Klobuchar	Shelby
Coats	Lankford	Stabenow
Cochran	Leahy	Sullivan
Collins	Lee	Tester
Coons	Manchin	Thune
Cornyn	Markey	Tillis
Cotton	McCain	Toomey
Crapo	McCaskill	Udall
Cruz	McConnell	Vitter
Daines	Menendez	Warner
Donnelly	Merkley	Warren
Durbin	Mikulski	Whitehouse
Enzi	Moran	Wicker
Ernst	Murkowski	Wyden
Feinstein	Murphy	
Fischer	Murray	

NOT VOTING—3

Corker	Gardner	Sanders

The bill (S. 2873), as amended, was passed.

MORNING BUSINESS

Mr. BLUNT. Mr. President, I ask unanimous consent that the Senate be in a period of morning business, with Senators permitted to speak therein for up to 10 minutes each.

The PRESIDING OFFICER. Without objection, it is so ordered.

NATIONAL ADOPTION MONTH

Mr. BLUNT. Mr. President, I wish to spend a few moments talking about National Adoption Month.

I thank the Senator from Maryland and my colleagues for letting me talk for a few minutes about an issue that I think every single Member of the Senate cares about. The month of November is National Adoption Month. It gives us the opportunity to recognize the recent celebration of National Adoption Day, which was November 19.

As cochair of the Congressional Coalition on Adoption Institute, I have had the opportunity to work with so many of our Members and understand the broad bipartisan support for what we need to do to be looking at and more dedicated to adoption and to child welfare issues.

Last year, Senator KLOBUCHAR and I came to this new role as the Senate's cochairmen of this caucus. I am pleased to be working with her on a resolution that would support National Adoption Month and National Adoption Day again this year.

We also have the good fortune to work with Members of the House. The idea that every child deserves to grow up in a loving, safe family is something I think we can all agree on.

We have a lot of agreement, while we have been working with Members of the Congress, on adoption issues over the last year. Just last week, Senator KLOBUCHAR, Congressman TRENT FRANKS, Congresswoman BRENDA LAWRENCE, and others, along with me, finalized a comment letter to the U.S. Department of State expressing concern over new international adoption regulations.

We have specifically highlighted the negative impact some of the Department's proposed changes could have on the adoption process.

Lately, the adoption process seems to have become more complicated internationally, and we need to make it less complicated.

We worked—many Members, including the Members I just mentioned—very hard on behalf of families who have currently been trying to resolve pending adoption cases from a number of countries, most recently finalizing adoptions out of the Democratic Republic of Congo, Nepal, Uganda, Guatemala, and other countries as well.

In June Senator KLOBUCHAR and I introduced the Vulnerable Children and Families Act, which would help more children living without families or in institutional care to find permanent homes by enhancing our U.S. diplomatic efforts rather than making those efforts more difficult. We need to enhance what we do as a country. We need to enhance what we do through the State Department to where we are more focused on international child welfare, ensuring that intercountry adoption to the United States becomes a more viable and more fully developed option.

I am also continuing to support legislation to ensure that American families have the resources and support they need so that adoption domestically works. Specifically, there is the Adoption Tax Credit Refundability Act and the Supporting Adoptive Families Act.

Before I conclude, I want to make a few comments to highlight three stories of foster children in Missouri who are currently waiting to get the family they would hope to have forever. According to the Missouri Heart Gallery, more than 1,200 Missouri children are in need of permanent homes. One of those children is Jason, age 15, who is an expressive young guy and, in his own words, "likes to play soccer when it is not too hot." He also likes art and music. He feels like he is creative. He is looking for a supportive family to call his own, one who will also help him stay in contact with his brothers and sisters.

Michelle, who is 9 years old, loves to dance and hopes to have her own pets in the future. However, she will tell you she would really rather have a dog than a cat. But what she would really like to find is a family—a family where she could have sisters, a family who would allow her to stay in touch with her biological sister as well.

Lastly, Terrance, age 13, and Terion, age 10, are brothers with a special bond. When you first meet Terrance, he appears shy, but after getting to know him, he really has an incredible sense of humor. He enjoys listening to music, sports, and playing outside. Terion has a smile that just goes on and on. He is very active. He has been on a Little League Baseball team, and he loves to bowl. The brothers are strongly committed to each other. They have a strong bond to each other, beyond just the normal bond of brothers. They want to find a home where they can stay forever and stay together.

Last year, I shared the stories of these two siblings on the Senate Floor. They are still looking for a family to call their own. Like so many children across the United States, Jason, Michelle, Terrance, and Terion are in need of a permanent, safe, loving home as a launching pad for their lives.

I am an adoptive parent. I am always encouraged to see families giving children the most important gift one can give somebody else, and that is a family. I urge my colleagues to join Senator KLOBUCHAR and me in marking November as National Adoption Month by passing this resolution.

I yield the floor.

The PRESIDING OFFICER. The Senator from Maryland.

CONTINUING RESOLUTION

Ms. MIKULSKI. Mr. President, I come to the floor as the vice chair of the Committee on Appropriations. That means I am the Democratic leader on appropriations for this session of Congress, and next to me is the distinguished Senator from Vermont, Mr. LEAHY, who will have that responsibility next year.

I come to the floor to say that, sadly, I am concerned we will not finish our job on appropriations the way we should finish it—to do an omnibus, to get the job done. Alas, the clock is slipping away.

Now, one needs to note that the Committee on Appropriations, during the past year, under the leadership of Senator COCHRAN of Mississippi, worked constructively, worked in a well-paced, well-sequenced way, and we were poised to finish our work, with the Committee on Appropriations reporting all 12 bills for floor consideration 5 months ago. So we were ready 5 months ago to bring them up either as individual bills or in a series of minibuses. But instead of finishing Congress's work to fund the government, we are now contemplating putting the government on autopilot by something called a continuing resolution—a short-term continuing resolution that would only last for maybe 3 months.

I am very frustrated about this. It did not have to be this way. As I said, we have worked very constructively on both sides of the aisle and have been cooperating to do our job. We attempted to write bills that meet the needs of the American people—bills related to national security and economic growth and that meet compelling human needs.

For those Republicans who are obstructionists, they really have been setting us back. For those on both sides of the aisle who want to save money, they are actually going to cost us more money by delaying.

So where are we? There is only one bill—the VA-Military Construction bill, which is signed into law. There are 11 other bills left.

Funding for every mission—let's start with the Department of Defense. Our troops are fighting overseas, and we need to support them. There is Federal law enforcement, foreign policy and embassy security, infrastructure, education—from child care to college affordability. So instead of making choices about what to fund, what to cut, we leave these missions on autopilot, spending the same amount as last year on the same items with the same policies. No business operates this way. No family operates this way. It is irresponsible to spend $1 trillion this way with no thought, delaying important investments, and thus resulting in increasing cost to the taxpayers.

Let me talk about why this really can give you heartburn. Last week, Department of Defense Comptroller Mike McCord warned that a stopgap CR delays ships and weapons our troops need. Hello. Did you hear that? It actually delays the construction of ships and the purchase of weapons our troops need. Without a special provision in the CR, DOD would have to delay planned replacement for their Ohio-class submarines, disrupting contract awards and ultimately delaying production for the length of the CR.

These new subs are necessary. They are the backbone of our nuclear deterrent—our nuclear deterrent. The current ships' nuclear reactors reach the end of their useful lives in the mid-2020s. So this isn't some new whiz-bang thing that might be untried. So without special provisions, other things will be delayed.

What are we trying to do here? We are concerned that people in this country are now facing death from heroin and opioid overdoses. Every Governor in the United States of America has cried out to the Federal Government for help on heroin and opioid overdoses. We have heard on both sides of the aisle advocacy for a comprehensive approach. The problem affects every part of the country—urban and rural—and every socioeconomic category.

Now, our appropriations bill is ready with new spending in law enforcement, prevention, treatment, and education. But in the continuing resolution, we won't get these investments, and more families will suffer. Every leading authority on treatment says when you need it and you are ready to ask for it, you need to get it on the same day. Just as clinicians have to act with urgency, so do we.

What else won't a CR help? It won't help college affordability with full-year Pell grants. It won't bolster security funds for the FBI, for the Border Patrol, for embassy security.

Remember Benghazi? Whoa, when people loved to investigate rather than legislate, Benghazi was in the news. That was at the same time the Congress had cut—particularly, the House had cut—embassy security considerably. But in this bill, working with both sides of the aisle, we were able to come up with the appropriate money for embassy security, border control, and so on.

We also won't have the funds for infrastructure funding, particularly for roads, to improve our ports, and to make our railroads safer.

We won't meet the needs of children—children who are on the march, children who are in desperate need of help in Central America.

I know the other thing we have supported on both sides of the aisle is an innovation agenda, particularly in the area of the medical research of the National Institutes of Health. Hopefully, we are going to be debating the Cures Act, yet right now we have the ability to act with the funding for the National Institutes of Health research and also the great work done at the Department of Defense in research.

All year long I have come to the floor and talked about how appropriations can be used to solve problems, whether it was children exposed to lead in drinking water—the compelling story of Flint, MI. We need to really modernize our water supply. In my own hometown of Baltimore, infrastructure funding could be fantastic. If we replaced the Baltimore water system that was built over 100 years ago, we would improve public health, we would create jobs in Maryland, in Baltimore, and we would leave our communities in a better, safer place by getting the lead out. We need to get the lead out of our water supply, and we need to get the lead out of Congress.

We want to solve problems, create jobs, and protect America. A CR is not the best way to do it. But if we are going to do a CR, it should be for the shortest time possible.

So let me be clear. Senate Democrats are willing to work across the aisle and across the dome. It is our Republican colleagues who need to think about this long and hard. I really urge that you not spend another half year spinning your wheels and not serving the American people, addressing security needs and compelling human needs.

As I get ready to finish my time in being the ranking member on the Committee on Appropriations, I would like to finish it by working constructively, collegially, and in the best interests of the United States of America to get a real bill across the finish line for the longest time possible. That will provide certainty to Federal agencies that are protecting America and protecting our border while we try to protect American jobs.

There is much ahead and that will lie ahead in the new term and with a new administration. We can act with certainty now for at least the funding for next year if we acted, and we acted with a long-term CR.

I could elaborate on more, but, please, let's do our job. Let's work together. There are still a few days where we could get this done the right way.

I yield the floor.

The PRESIDING OFFICER. The Senator from South Dakota.

Mr. THUNE. Mr. President, I ask unanimous consent to conclude my remarks.

The PRESIDING OFFICER. Without objection, it is so ordered.

SENATE ACCOMPLISHMENTS AND PRIORITIES FOR THE 115TH CONGRESS

Mr. THUNE. Mr. President, 2 years ago the American people entrusted Republicans with the Senate majority. At that time, things were in a bad way here in the Senate. Under Democratic control, the legislative process almost ground to a halt. Important bills weren't getting passed, and those that did get passed were frequently drafted behind closed doors, with Republicans and many rank-and-file Democrats shut out of the process, which, of course, means that the American people's voices were frequently shut out of the process.

When Republicans took control, we knew that getting the Senate working again had to be our first priority, and that is what we did. We opened up debate so Senators from both parties could make their voices heard. We started drafting legislation in committee again so that bills were the result of discussion and compromise instead of being dictated by Democratic Party leaders. And we got the Senate passing real, substantial legislation again—a balanced budget, appropriations bills, the first major Energy bill since the Bush administration, and the first significant education reform since 2002.

I am particularly proud of two bills that the committee I chair, the Commerce Committee, worked on—a Federal Aviation Administration bill with major airport security provisions and the first long-term Transportation bill since 2005.

The terrorist attacks in Brussels and Istanbul that occurred this year broadcast airport security challenges—particularly the soft target offered by large crowds in unsecured airport areas. Those were problems we had been working on in the Commerce Committee for months before the attacks, and in July we passed an FAA bill that addresses them and more. The bill we passed requires the TSA to look at ways to improve security checkpoints to make the passenger screening process more efficient and effective, and it significantly increases the security presence in unsecured areas in airports. It also improves vetting of airport employees to address the insider terrorist threat—the risk that an airport employee would give a terrorist access to secure areas. The Senate passed this bill in July, and the President signed it into law a couple days later. I am proud of this law, which is the kind of substantial legislation we should be passing for the American people.

I am also proud of the Transportation bill we passed, part of which came out of our committee. When Congress fails to provide certainty about the way transportation funding will be allocated, States and local governments are left without the certainty they need to authorize projects or to make long-term plans, important investments in infrastructure that support the economy are shelved, and jobs that depend upon transportation are put in jeopardy. The Transportation bill we passed changes all that. It reauthorizes transportation programs for the long term and provides 5 years of guaranteed funding. That means States and local governments will have the certainty they need to invest in big transportation projects and the jobs they create, and that, in turn, means a stronger economy and a more reliable, safe, and effective transportation system.

I am proud of what we were able to accomplish over the past 2 years, but there is a lot left to be done. Some of the most important measures we passed in the 114th Congress went nowhere, thanks to opposition from the Democrats and the White House—an ObamaCare repeal; legislation to overturn some of the Obama administration's most burdensome regulations; legislation to address the dangerous problem of so-called sanctuary cities, which refuse to work with Federal immigration officials to deport illegal immigrants convicted of crimes. I am hopeful that with a Republican President, we will be able to address these issues and many more in the 115th Congress.

Republicans have big plans for the 115th. If there is one thing this election made clear, it is that the Obama economy is not working for American families. Republicans are committed to fixing that.

Growing our economy is going to be our No. 1 priority next Congress. There are a number of things we can do to get our economy healthy again. We can reform our Tax Code to reduce the burden on American families and businesses. Right now, our Nation has the highest corporate tax rate in the developed world. More and more, American companies are focusing their business operations overseas because the tax situation is so much better abroad. That means American jobs are going overseas with them. We have lost our competitive edge in an increasingly global economy. Instead of pushing corporations out of this country, we should bring our Nation's corporate tax rate in line with those of other countries to keep more jobs here in the United States.

Another big thing we can do is repeal some of the burdensome government regulations that are weighing down businesses. While some government regulations are necessary, every administration has to remember that regulations have consequences. The more resources individuals and businesses spend complying with unnecessary government regulations, the less they have to focus on the growth and innovation that drive our economy and create new opportunities for workers. The overregulation of the last 8 years has left businesses with few resources to dedicate to growing and creating jobs.

Another thing we need to do is address our national debt, which has nearly doubled over the past 8 years. All that debt is a drag on the economy. It slows growth and reduces economic opportunity. It is time to get our government back on a budget.

Another way we can help lift the burden on American families is by repealing and replacing ObamaCare. I don't need to tell anyone that the Presi-

dent's health care law is broken. The promise of lower premiums and affordable health care has given way to the reality of giant premium increases and massive deductibles. A Gallup poll released yesterday found that 80 percent of Americans want major changes to ObamaCare or want the law repealed and replaced completely. It is time to give the American people health care reform that actually works.

Another priority for the 115th Congress will be national security. Americans are rightly worried about the threat posed by terrorist groups like ISIS, which has spread violence and devastation not only in the Middle East but across Europe and beyond. Republicans are committed to defeating ISIS abroad and to keeping Americans safe here at home.

We are also committed to keeping Americans safe by securing our borders. We must have secure borders and policies that encourage legal immigration while discouraging illegal immigration.

There are other priorities we need to address: confirming a Supreme Court nominee who will judge based on the law and the Constitution; protecting religious liberty; and the list goes on.

Republicans are aware of the trust the American people have placed in us, and we are committed to earning it. We are going to spend the 115th Congress fighting for the American people's priorities. We have a real chance to get things done in the next Congress, and I look forward to working with my colleagues here in the Senate on both sides of the aisle to address the challenges that are facing our Nation.

Mr. President, I yield the floor.

The PRESIDING OFFICER. The Senator from Vermont.

ORDER OF PROCEDURE

Mr. LEAHY. Mr. President, I ask unanimous consent to continue in morning business for 10 minutes.

The PRESIDING OFFICER. Without objection, it is so ordered.

Mr. LEAHY. I thank the distinguished Presiding Officer.

CONTINUING RESOLUTION

Mr. LEAHY. Mr. President, for the past 2 years, the Republican Party has enjoyed solid majorities in both the House and Senate. They control the schedule and they control the process. They can decide which legislation to call up for debate, and frankly, for all intents and purposes, they can decide whether anything gets done around here.

A good example is the nomination of Merrick Garland to the Supreme Court. If he had been treated like all other Supreme Court nominees throughout the entire history of this country in a Presidential election year, he would

have received a hearing and a vote, and he almost certainly would have been easily confirmed, just as he was when he was nominated to the DC Court of Appeals. Instead, the Republican leadership did not even give Judge Garland a hearing, much less a vote. Republican Senators refused to do their job. And there are countless examples of this.

It would behoove people in this country who complain about the "do nothing" Congress to remind themselves that Congress is controlled by Republicans in both the House and the Senate. They can make it possible for work to get done if they want to, or they can make it impossible. Their track record for the past 2 years speaks for itself. Instead of a Congress that sets the standard for the world's democracies, we have been treated to a lesson of how not to get things done.

The latest example is the fiscal 2017 appropriations bills. I went back and reviewed the record. For months, the Republican leadership extolled the virtues of regular order, and I totally agreed with them on that. They spoke with great optimism and confidence about passing appropriations bills—individual bills, not even an omnibus bill that has become the norm. I agreed with the Republican leadership. They said over and over that they were going to do their job this year and pass these bills, the way we used to. We on the Democratic side fully supported Republicans in that goal. We negotiated 12 individual appropriations bills that were reported, with 1 exception, with bipartisan majorities—in most cases, overwhelming majorities—by the Senate Appropriations Committee. That was 5 months ago.

Senator LINDSEY GRAHAM and I wrote the fiscal year 2017 State and foreign operations bill. As we always do, we wrote a balanced bill, and it was reported unanimously by the Appropriations Committee by a vote of 30 to 0. Our staffs have been meeting for weeks with their House counterparts to hammer out a conference agreement that the House and Senate can vote on and the President can sign. We could easily be finished by December 9, when the current funding resolution expires.

So what is the problem? It is simple. Donald Trump was elected President, and now the Republican leadership has a different idea. Forget all those uplifting speeches about passing appropriations bills. Forget about so-called regular order. Forget about doing our jobs. What is their new plan? Throw 10 months of work into the trash can. Now we will punt the ball down the field for another 4 months. After that, who knows? Maybe we will do it again and have a continuing resolution for the rest of the year. There is no way to predict.

For Members of Congress who may not be familiar with the intricate operations of Federal agencies and would prefer not to think about it, the idea of another 4-month continuing resolution may not be a big deal. For those of us on both sides of the aisle who do know, it is an example of government at its worst. Funding the government by continuing resolution means putting priorities and budgeting decisions on autopilot. It stops us having any kind of a voice in what our government does. It negates the hard work that has gone into reevaluating priorities from one year to the next. It negates the careful process of looking at Federal agencies account by account to make adjustments as warranted. It means largely making a carbon copy of an earlier appropriations bill or bills regardless of changed circumstances or compelling need to modify earlier priorities.

I can give all kinds of examples in the appropriations bills. Here are a few examples of what it means for the State and foreign operations bill, which comprises only 1 percent of the Federal budget.

A continuing resolution will provide $433 million less than Senator GRAHAM's and my bill for economic development, governance, and security programs, such as the Power Africa Initiative. It will mean $59 million less for programs to counter violent extremism. These programs have strong bipartisan support—and did in the Appropriations Committee—because they are the building blocks for stability where we have critical national security interests that affect all Americans.

A continuing resolution will provide $162 million less than our bill for global health, including for maternal and child health programs, such as vaccines for children, and to combat malaria and tuberculosis. These programs literally mean life or death for millions of people, which is why they have bipartisan support—or at least they did before the Republican leadership scrapped the appropriations bills that we passed with overwhelming bipartisan support.

In fact, one of the things a continuing resolution will do is provide $454 million less than Senator GRAHAM's and my bill for security for U.S. diplomatic and consular personnel, for security upgrades to U.S. Embassies and facilities overseas, and for cyber security programs.

I mention that because the Republicans in the other body spent tens of millions of dollars of taxpayers' money decrying the lack of security at our embassies, even after they had already voted to cut money for embassy security, and now they are going to cut another $454 million. Will they stop using their talking points about how we should spend more to protect our diplomats posted overseas? Of course not, because they hope the American people will not pay attention to the fact that they have cut another half billion dollars. When the Republican leadership

blames others for not doing enough on security for our embassies and diplomats, as they have a habit of doing, they need to only look at themselves in the mirror.

At the same time, the continuing resolution provides $538 million more for U.S. contributions to international financial institutions, than the amount Senator GRAHAM and I put in our bill. That is because the 2016 omnibus provided $220 million for the Strategic Climate and Clean Technology Funds, which is not needed in fiscal year 2017 because the United States will not be contributing to either of those funds in fiscal year 2017.

The balance of $318 million is not needed because U.S. contributions to several international financial institutions are lower in fiscal year 2017 than in fiscal year 2016. It boggles the mind. They cut money for the security of our diplomats and embassies, but then they spend half a billion dollars for contributions we don't need to make.

In fact, the continuing resolution provides $161 million more than Senator GRAHAM's and my bill for contributions to international organizations. We don't need to pay that additional amount because of reductions in assessments in exchange rate costs. It would be nice if, instead of wasting this money on things we don't need, we used it to protect our embassies.

The continuing resolution will provide $90 million more than our bill for assessed contributions to international peacekeeping. Again, we don't need to pay that additional amount because of reductions in several peacekeeping missions.

These are just examples for State and foreign operations. Every appropriations bill has its own laundry list of reasons why a continuing resolution makes no sense. It wastes taxpayer dollars and wreaks havoc for the agencies that run the government.

Continuing resolutions beyond a few months are illogical, wasteful, and harmful. We end up spending less for things both Republicans and Democrats strongly support, and we waste money on things we don't need and nobody wants. It is bad government 101. It is what the Republican leadership 10 months ago said they wanted to avoid, and we all agreed with them. But that was then and this is now. Now it's forget what we said before. We have changed our mind. Let's just put the government on autopilot and waste the money.

I heard Senator MCCAIN, the chairman of the Armed Services Committee, denouncing his colleagues for abandoning the regular appropriations process. He knows the problems it will create for the U.S. military.

Senator MIKULSKI, the vice chairwoman of the Appropriations Committee, has called it "absolutely outrageous." She called it "procrasti-

nating" instead of "legislating." I agree with her.

Another 4-month continuing resolution is completely unnecessary, not to mention outrageous, wasteful, and irresponsible. It can still be avoided. Speaking for State and foreign operations, we can complete our conference agreement in less than 1 week. We are perfectly willing to work into the evenings to do that. I suspect the other subcommittees could do the same or close to it. Certainly, we could finish these bills before Christmas.

So why don't we? That is what the Republican leadership said they wanted. That is what regular order is. That is how the Congress is supposed to work. We should do it. We ought to show the American people, for once, that we will actually do the job we were elected to do. That is what this Vermonter wants. I would hope others would also.

I yield the floor.

RECESS

The PRESIDING OFFICER. Under the previous order, the Senate stands in recess until 2:15 p.m.

Thereupon, the Senate, at 12:51 p.m., recessed until 2:15 p.m. and reassembled when called to order by the Presiding Officer (Mr. PORTMAN).

The PRESIDING OFFICER. The Senator from Florida.

Mr. NELSON. Mr. President, are we in a parliamentary procedure to proceed with commentary on the Senate floor?

The PRESIDING OFFICER. We are in morning business, with 10-minute grants.

Mr. NELSON. May I be recognized?

The PRESIDING OFFICER. The Senator from Florida is recognized.

NIH FUNDING

Mr. NELSON. Mr. President, I want to talk about something we all hear about and generally support—that the National Institutes of Health needs help. It was founded in 1887. Its work and investments in the work of others have led to countless discoveries, including in Alzheimer's disease, cancer, and so many other chronic illnesses.

I visited this 300-acre campus in Bethesda, and it is jam-packed with buildings that are teeming with scientists and physicians. Yet that is just the tip of the iceberg because research is being conducted all over the country—indeed, all over the world—by the medical research grants that are given by NIH. This funded research has led to many discoveries and treatments that not only are allowing us to live healthier lives but also contribute to our knowledge and understanding of how diseases and the human body work. Take, for example, the BRAIN Initiative. NIH seeks to unravel the mysteries of the vastly complex human brain, which could allow us to understand an array of conditions affecting the brain.

When I visited yesterday, I met with Dr. Francis Collins, the head of NIH, and a plethora of his brilliant scientists who are working on neurodegenerative diseases—diseases such as concussions, ALS, Parkinson's, and all the many complicated things that come from this complicated organ called the brain. Well, they are on the verge of some real breakthroughs, but that comes at a cost. Dr. Collins stressed the need for consistent, robust funding for NIH.

In 2003, funding for NIH peaked and has since failed to keep up with inflation. In 2009 we came along with a stimulus bill that increased funding for NIH for only 2 years by approximately $4 or $5 billion a year over its base funding of $24 to $25 billion a year.

I will never forget when Dr. Collins told us—after the effect of that second year of the stimulus bill—that he had to cease 700 medical research grants sent out to the medical schools and research institutions all across the country because he simply did not have the money they had planned for, and thus there is the call for consistent and robust funding. Dr. Collins mentioned that the agency's biggest concern was a loss of young researchers. As the next generation of researchers are increasingly facing being denied research grants, they are leaving the research field. I don't think that is what this Nation wants. We need to ensure that NIH maintains a strong pipeline of researchers so that the critical work toward scientific discovery can continue.

This is not a partisan issue. Health and disease research is a bipartisan issue, and so we need to come together to support this consistent and robust funding. Even now, NIH is engaged in developing a prevention tool against the disease that was the dominant conversation last summer—the Zika virus. They are going into their first trials on a vaccine. Zika has affected more than 1,000 people in my State of Florida alone and more than 30,000 people in Puerto Rico. We need a vaccine, but the process of FDA trials takes time.

Now, just to prove that it is not confined to Puerto Rico and Florida, just yesterday the State of Texas reported the first case of locally transmitted Zika virus, which now makes it the second State to officially have local transmission after the State of Florida. The head of the Centers for Disease Control and Prevention, Dr. Frieden, said that Zika could become endemic within our U.S. border, making it more important now than ever to have the Zika vaccine. That is just one other little example of what has been going on at NIH.

We are just about to consider a Cures bill, which has some more robust fund-ing. The whole impetus for the Cures bill was NIH funding. A lot of other things had been attached. There is some controversy, but it would begin to authorize funding that would be stable over a 10-year period. If the United States is going to continue to be looked at as the leader of medical research around the world, we are going to have to provide for the funds for this great institution. We have already seen major breakthroughs in our lifetime, and this funding will help us to see some new incredible breakthroughs accomplished. You have heard of the Moonshot for cancer research. Look at the existing victories that have already been had in cancer research. We are now just on the cusp. What about diseases where we don't have a cure, such as ALS, or amyotrophic lateral sclerosis?

A big reason for my making this speech is for my friend Evan in Jacksonville. He is afflicted with this disease that affects the body's motor nerves. There is something that happens in the brain that does not send the signals all the way through the neurological system to the motor nerves. We first identified that in a famous baseball player, Lou Gehrig. There are 20,000 to 30,000 people in the country afflicted with this disease. We still don't know the reason for it nor have a cure, but yesterday I talked to three different physician scientists who have very promising leads for identifying a gene that has a direct connection to what happens in the brain when someone has ALS. They are trying to determine whether we could go in and clip out that gene so that our progeny would not have this concern.

We have seen what has happened in Alzheimer's. Did you see the 60 Minutes segment last Sunday in which there is this incredible space in Colombia, near Medellin, within a 100-mile diameter, where so many families get the onset of Alzheimer's during their forties, which is quite unusual. They have now identified a protein in the brain where, if you now know the gene that causes that protein, you could go ahead and alert people of the disease, and even though the effects of Alzheimer's has not come on, that person could start a therapy that would work against that protein in the brain. They are right on the cusp of these kinds of exciting discoveries that can help us to live healthier, longer lives.

I implore my colleagues in the Senate not to short-sheet the NIH and the funding that it so desperately needs.

I yield the floor.

The PRESIDING OFFICER. The Senator from California.

ELECTORAL COLLEGE

Mrs. BOXER. Mr. President, I rise today to discuss legislation I introduced to eliminate the Electoral Col-lege and ensure that the candidate who wins the most votes will be elected President. Clearly, this has nothing to do with this past election. There are recounts going on, and we will see where that goes, but the bottom line is that this looks to the future.

The Presidency is the only office in America where the candidate who wins the most votes can still lose the election. There isn't any elected office in the Nation, be it county, city, State, or national level, where this is true. The person who gets more votes—one person, one vote—wins, but that is not true in the Presidential election.

I realized how little sense this made many years ago, but when I tried to explain it to my grandkids after this election, they said: Grandma, who won? Well, I told them, Donald Trump. Well, wait a minute, didn't Mrs. Clinton get more votes? Yes.

What if we did that in sports? I am a major basketball fan. What if the team that got the most points didn't win? What if that happened? What would people think? Well, why not? Well, because not everybody on the team touched the ball, therefore—even though they won by 40 points—they don't win.

This doesn't make sense. This is an outdated system that does not reflect democracy, and it violates the principle of one person, one vote. Every single American, regardless of what State they live in, should be guaranteed that their individual vote matters. Throughout our great history, we have had—this is the 45th President—five elections where the winner of the general election did not win the popular vote, but in our lifetime it has happened twice. We have had two in the last 16 years, and so it really needs to be addressed. This is more than an anomaly. It looks like it could happen one way or the other. We don't know if a Republican or a Democrat gets seated.

Right now, Hillary Clinton's lead in the popular vote is 2.3 million votes. It is expected that she will win by probably more than 2.7 million votes. That would be more than the votes cast in Alaska, Delaware, Washington, DC, Hawaii, Vermont, and the Dakotas combined. We are not talking about a few votes; we are talking about 2.7 million votes—more than the votes cast in Alaska, Delaware, Washington, DC, Hawaii, Vermont, and the Dakotas combined. Clinton would have won the popular vote by a wider margin than not only Al Gore in 2000, but Richard Nixon in 1968 and John Kennedy in 1960.

In 2012 Donald Trump said, "The electoral college is a disaster for democracy." I couldn't agree more. I don't agree with too much of what Donald Trump says, but I sure agree with that. He said, "The electoral college is a disaster for democracy."

After the election, his views did not change:

"You know, I'm not going to change my mind just because I won. But I would rather see it where you went with simple votes."

These are all quotes of his.

"You know, you get 100 million votes and somebody else gets 90 million votes and you win."

After he said that, I think his advisers went a little nuts because by the next morning, he tweeted that the electoral college system was "actually genius." Then he also tweeted this, which was very interesting: "If the election were based on the total popular vote, I would have campaigned in New York, Florida, and California and won even bigger and more easily."

OK. Maybe that is true. Maybe that is true. His point is well-taken.

Presidential candidates should campaign in every single State. Actually, if we got rid of the electoral college, candidates would have to campaign in every State because the vote of every American would matter regardless of where they live. If you get all the popular vote in one State, you will add to your popular vote at the end.

According to nationalpopularvote .com, 94 percent of campaigning by the Presidential candidates in 2016 took place in 12 States—12 States. That was it. Two-thirds of these general election campaign events took place in six States.

In 2015 Gov. Scott Walker of Wisconsin said: "The nation as a whole is not going to elect the next president. Twelve states are." Just think about that. "The nation as a whole is not going to elect the next president."

He was right when he said that in 2015. He was right.

So what message does that send to the people who live in the populous States, like my State, where 39 million Americans live? What message does that send to the 27 million Americans who live in Texas? What message does that send to the smaller States, like North Dakota and Rhode Island, where the candidates don't even bother to campaign for the votes because they are either blue or red? They are not purple, so they don't matter. No wonder voter turnout was just 58 percent in this election. Too many Americans don't believe their vote matters because they are told: Oh, you live in a red State. It is going to Trump. Even if you are for Trump, just stay home.

It is ridiculous. Maybe that person really wanted to vote, but they are convinced that if they live in a bright red State like Alabama, they don't have to vote because it is going for Trump, and if they are for Hillary Clinton and they live in a reliably blue State, they may think: Well, you know what, I am not interested. Why should I bother? My State is blue. What is the difference?

So we have a 58-percent voter turnout. It is altogether ridiculous. Political science experts agree that too

many Americans feel their vote doesn't count. It just doesn't count.

Listen to Doug McAdam, professor of sociology at Stanford University, who asked, "What about all those citizens who live in noncompetitive states?"

He makes my point:

"Consider the loyal Republican who lives in California or the stalwart Mississippi Democrat? Every four years, voting for them is an exercise in political powerlessness, at least when it comes to the presidential race."

What is the difference? Hillary is going to win by so much. Don't worry about it.

But if we were using the popular vote, believe me, every Republican would get out and every Democrat would get out and every Independent would get out because their vote would count.

Every 4 years, a lot of people in different States feel their vote doesn't matter. They feel powerless when it comes to the Presidential race—the only race in the country where the winner doesn't win, maybe. The winner doesn't win. It is crazy. I looked all over to find another example where this is true; it is not true.

William Crotty, professor emeritus of political science at Northeastern University, said that the electoral college "has never worked well. The fact is that it is a terrible system that has no place in an age where democracy is ascendant. It continues to exist from sheer inertia and the protection of entrenched power. It has little to do with democracy."

Well, everybody knows I didn't run again for the Senate. I have a fabulous replacement coming. But I did drop this bill to do away with the electoral college because I am still a Senator, I am still here, and I will be darned if I am going to let this thing pass.

Listen to a professor of law at Fordham University, John Feerick:

"Not only have reasons for the Electoral College long since vanished but the institution has not fulfilled the design of the framers. Today it represents little more than an archaic and undemocratic counting device. There is no good reason for retaining such a formula of electing the president of the United States."

Well, I also saw a poll which shows that 62 percent of the people in this country, regardless of party, think we should do away with it and go to a system where the winner wins. How unique—the winner wins and the loser loses. That is the way it should be in the greatest democracy in the country. Try explaining this to your kids and grandkids. I am telling you, if they are about 11 or 12, explain what happened.

I know changing the system won't be easy. I have been around a long time. I have spent more than half of my life in politics in elected office. So we understand that the legislation would need to be enacted by Congress and would only take effect after being ratified by

three-quarters of the States within 7 years after its passage. This is very difficult. This is a constitutional amendment. So I am not naive, and I understand what we are talking about.

But there is another way to address this; it is called the National Popular Vote plan. It would guarantee that the Presidential candidate who wins the most votes would win the election and be the President, whether it is Donald Trump getting the most votes or Hillary Clinton getting the most votes, et cetera. All it requires is for enough States to act. It is an interstate compact where the States would agree to award their electoral votes to the Presidential candidate who wins the popular vote.

So in California, where we have a number of electoral votes, if Donald Trump wins, they go to Donald Trump regardless of how our State voted. In other words, the votes are counted and then the States give their electoral votes to the winner of the popular vote—pretty simple. So you still have the electoral college, but the result is that the votes are given to the person who wins the national popular vote. The agreement takes effect only once the participating States together hold a majority of electoral votes; that is, 270 out of 538 electoral votes.

So far, the National Popular Vote bill has been enacted into law by 10 States and the District of Columbia, adding up to 165 electoral votes. The legislation has been introduced in every State in the country, and it has support on both sides of the aisle because electing the person who wins is the democratic way.

Trump supporter Newt Gingrich wrote a letter in 2014 endorsing the idea. He wrote:

"No one should become president of the United States without speaking to the needs and hopes of Americans in all 50 States. . . . America would be better served with a presidential election process that treated citizens across the country equally."

Former Republican Congressman Bob Barr said:

"Only when the election process is given back to all of the people of all the states will we be able to choose a President based on what is best for all 50 states and not just a select few."

I will make a point that I don't agree with Newt Gingrich on pretty much anything except this. This is rare. Newt Gingrich said Medicare should wither on the vine. He called Democrats traitors. Believe me, I served with him, I know. And his ethical standards don't meet what I think the standards should be. But setting that aside, here we are on the same side.

"No one should become president of the United States without speaking to the needs and hopes of Americans in all 50 States. . . . America would be better served with a presidential election process that treats citizens across the country equally."

I urge my colleagues to take a close look at the legislation I have introduced, and I urge State legislators and Governors around the country to take a close look at the National Popular Vote bill.

Again, I am going to be honest, it is really hard to pass a constitutional amendment. I am not naive about it. But to pass a law in various States isn't that hard. That should be done. The American people can help. I ask them to call their Senators and Members of Congress about our bill. There is a bill in the House being introduced by CHARLIE RANGEL to do away with the electoral college—very simple—and just let the popular vote stand. Ask them to sign on to this bill, but don't stop there. Write and call your representatives in the State house and push for your State to sign on to the interstate compact.

A lot of people have come up to me after this election and said: You know, I don't feel my voice is heard, period.

This is one of the reasons. Well, make your voice heard on either getting rid of the electoral college or the State compact where the State would give its votes to the winner of the national popular vote.

Voting is the cornerstone of democracy. We have had men and women through the decades die for the right to vote. Many generations of Americans of every gender, race, religion, and ideology have marched and struggled and died to secure this fundamental freedom. Yet we have a system where the winner can lose.

We owe it to the American people who have given so much for the right to vote to make sure that every vote matters and every vote counts. We owe it to them to ensure that the vote of a citizen in my State is worth the same as a vote of someone in a swing State. We owe it to every Republican voter and every Democratic voter and every Independent voter, every Green Party voter—whatever the party—to have that vote count. One person, one vote is the cornerstone of democracy.

By making this critical change where the winner of the popular vote wins and every citizen's vote counts regardless of who they are, where they live, whether they are a Republican, Democrat, or a decline-to-state or Green or whatever party they choose, we would then be engaging voters in every single State. We will lift voter turnouts. We will ensure that every Presidential candidate speaks to the needs of Americans in every State and every region. We will ensure equal representation for all.

You know, sometimes I come down here and I talk about issues that are very controversial. I must tell you, if you ask anyone on the street "Do you think the winner of the popular vote should win the Presidency?" I would say a very strong majority would say

"Of course." If you ask them "Do you know of any office in the land, whether it is Governor, mayor, supervisor, city council, sewer board, sanitation district, you name it, where the winner doesn't win?" they will say "No, I can't think of any." You know what, there are none. So why not do the simple thing and the right thing and the just thing and make sure that the winner of the popular vote is sworn in as our President. I think this will be a huge boon for every single voter in this greatest of all countries.

I yield the floor.

The PRESIDING OFFICER. The Senator from Maryland.

IRAN SANCTIONS EXTENSION BILL

Mr. CARDIN. Mr. President, I noticed the majority leader has given us all notice that, after consultation with the Democratic leader, he intends to bring up the Iran Sanctions Act, H.R. 6297. I point out that this legislation passed the House of Representatives by a vote of 419 to 1.

It is legislation that would extend the Iran Sanctions Act that was passed by this Congress that is set to expire at the end of this year. Let me repeat that. The Iran Sanctions Act, which was enacted originally in 1996—if no action is taken before the end of December, that sanction authorization legislation would expire.

This is our last opportunity to extend the Iran Sanctions Act before it is scheduled to expire at the end of December. It was passed in 1996 by a unanimous vote of this body. Its goal was to deny Iran the ability to be able to have financial support for its nuclear proliferation. Congress had passed several bills that provided sanction opportunities by the administration to impose sanctions in order to get Iran to change its behavior, its illegal activities in pursuing a nuclear weapon, which was against U.S. security interests, destabilizing for the entire region, threatened Israel, threatened the neighboring states. It was, I think, the unanimous view of our body that we had to take whatever steps were possible to prevent Iran from becoming a nuclear weapon power.

The legislation we passed, including the Iran Sanctions Act, allowed the Obama administration to move forward with sanctions against Iran, and they rigorously enforced the sanctions they imposed. I want to acknowledge the work done by the Obama administration in enforcing those sanctions that we gave our authorization to impose.

But the Obama administration went further than that. They then garnered international support to also impose and support the sanctions that we had imposed in the United States, which was strong enough to get Iran to recognize that they had to come to the negotiating table. Clearly, the sanctions

were the motivating factor that allowed for the negotiations of the nuclear agreement that was agreed to 2 years ago.

This legislation is pretty simple. It extends for 10 years the Iran Sanctions Act that was used by the administration and in which we have a temporary—we have relief granted under that law as long as Iran is in compliance with the nuclear agreement. The nuclear agreement, JCPOA, specifically provides for the snapback of sanctions in the event that Iran violates the provisions of the agreement.

In order to have snapbacks, you have to have the sanction regime in place. Therefore, it is incumbent upon us to extend the sanction authorization. This does not impose any new sanctions on Iran. That it does not. It is not in violation of the JCPOA. It just allows us to have effective enforcement to make sure Iran complies with their commitments. I want to underscore that point. During the Senate Foreign Relations Committee hearing, I had a chance to ask the administration's witness, Secretary Lew, that specific question. I asked Secretary Lew—this question was asked July 23, 2015. I said to the witness:

The Iran Sanctions Act expires at the end of 2016. We will still be in the JCPOA a period of time where snapback of sanctions is a viable hedge against Iran's cheating. Congress may well want to extend that law so that power is available immediately if Iran were to violate the agreement. Is that permitted under the JCPOA?

The answer from Secretary Lew:

I think that if it is on expiration, it is one thing. If it is well in advance, it is another. I think the idea of coming out of the box right now is very different from what you would do when it expires.

Well, we are doing exactly what the administration asked us to do. We have held off for over—now it has been over 15 months, 16 months that we have held off before we have taken action to extend the Iran Sanctions Act. If we don't take action now, the authority given by Congress in the 1996 act, which would empower the snapbacks if needed, would not be available. So it is timely for us to act. It is totally consistent with the JCPOA and is not at all inconsistent with our responsibilities under that legislation.

I think, though, that we should have a little bit of a discussion as to what we do moving forward. I should point out that the Iran Sanctions Act, H.R. 6297, is identical to S. 3281, legislation I filed with 19 of my colleagues earlier this year. So I think this enjoys strong bipartisan support, and I urge my colleagues to support it.

Now, looking forward—I did not support the JCPOA. I did not support that agreement for various reasons, but it went into effect. I must tell my colleagues, I think it would be tragic if the United States unilaterally walked away from the Iran nuclear agreement.

What that would do is give the ability to Iran to pursue a nuclear weapons program without inspectors on the ground to let us know what they were doing. They would be able to pursue that, knowing full well that the international community would not be unified in regard to sanctions against Iran. Yes, we would impose sanctions, but our allies around the world would no longer be obligated to follow that, since it was the United States pulling out of the agreement.

Many of those countries already have arrangements, and it would be very difficult to see that they would follow U.S. leadership. In fact, one of the adverse impacts of the United States walking away from the Iran agreement would be that we would lose our standing as an international leader, bringing the international community together to isolate Iran. Instead, we would be isolating the United States. That is not in our national security interest.

So what should we do? Well, as I said earlier, the first step is to pass H.R. 6297 so that we have all of the tools in place. Secondly, let us all join together to rigorously enforce the Iran agreement, the JCPOA. We need to do that. We need to make sure that every part of that agreement is adhered to, including making sure Iran never becomes a nuclear weapons state. We need to continue the use of sanctions on Iran's nonnuclear nefarious activities.

They are still a sponsor of terrorism. We all know that. I was recently in the Middle East. I had a chance to talk to a lot of our strategic partners. They tell me about Iran's activities in their region, how they are supporting efforts to destabilize other sovereign states in the Middle East. They are supporting terrorism.

We also know that they have expanded their ballistic program. That is in contravention to their international obligations. We can impose sanctions and continue to strengthen sanctions against Iran in regard to those activities. They are violating the human rights of the citizens of their own country. We can take actions there.

There are areas where we can continue to work with the international community to deal with Iran's nefarious activities. We should do that. I would just call to my colleagues' attention that several—actually in October of 2015, I introduced S. 2119, along with several of my colleagues, so that the Congress would be in a better position to carry out rigorous enforcement of the JCPOA and to take on Iran, working with our partners, in regard to their other activities.

It provides more information to the Congress on how the sanction relief resources are being used by Iran so that we can track the money. If they use it to support terrorism against the United States or they use it against our interests, we would be able to know about that and take action.

It provides for expedited considerations if Iran commits these types of violations. It makes it very clear that we will continue to work on a regional security strategy so that our partners in the region know that the United States will continue to be on their side against the aggression that we have seen from the Iran regime. To me, that is the responsible action for us to take in order to carry out what should be U.S. leadership in isolating Iran, getting it to change its behavior, recognizing that it has been a major problem for the security of the United States in the region, and we must continue to be actively engaged.

I suggest the absence of a quorum.

The PRESIDING OFFICER (Mr. LANKFORD). The clerk will call the roll.

The senior assistant legislative clerk proceeded to call the roll.

Mr. ALEXANDER. Mr. President, I ask unanimous consent that the order for the quorum call be rescinded.

The PRESIDING OFFICER. Without objection, it is so ordered.

Mr. ALEXANDER. Mr. President, I ask unanimous consent to speak for such time as I may require.

The PRESIDING OFFICER. Without objection, it is so ordered.

21ST CENTURY CURES BILL

Mr. ALEXANDER. Mr. President, tomorrow the U.S. House of Representatives will vote on a piece of legislation that many in this body on both sides of the aisle have worked on and that the majority leader of the Senate has described as the single most important piece of legislation that will pass this year. We call it the 21st Century Cures Act, and it includes three mental health reform acts—the most significant reforms in mental health programs in 10 years.

I ask unanimous consent to have printed in the RECORD at the conclusion of my remarks the more than 200 organizations from all across the country supporting the 21st Century Cures legislation.

Why would the majority leader say it is the most important legislation the Senate might act on—because we do a lot of important stuff around here, whether it is Defense authorization, whether it is cyber security, whether it is the bill to fix No Child Left Behind that we passed in a bipartisan way last December. I think it is because this legislation will affect virtually every American family because we are entering the most exciting period of medical research in our country. That is the first part of it.

The second part, which has to do with mental health, affects so many families. We know that about one out of every five adult Americans suffers from some form of mental illness. This concentrates a large amount of money we actually spend on mental health programs every year from the Federal Government and spends it in a more effective way to actually help people.

In the next few minutes, I would like to acquaint the Senate again with how we have gone about this and remind Senators of how many of us have had a hand in this legislation. It is a remarkable 2 years of work that has involved many, many, many hearings, dozens of meetings, and that has been done in a large committee of 22 Senators of very different points of view in a largely bipartisan way.

I will summarize. The first thing I would mention, the legislation includes $6.3 billion of funding and $1 billion of that is for State opioid grants. Whether it is Senator WHITEHOUSE of Rhode Island or Senator AYOTTE and Senator PORTMAN, probably most Senators of this body have seen on the front pages of their newspapers the tragedies of opioid abuse. I know that is true in Tennessee. This bill helps in two ways. The most immediate way is to provide State grants—Federal dollars to go to States—over the next 2 years to help States fight opioid abuse.

The other way it helps, when we get to the part about 21st Century Cures, is that Dr. Francis Collins, head of the National Institutes of Health—Dr. Collins calls it the "National Institutes of Hope"—says that one of the groundbreaking discoveries we expect to happen in this country is a non-addictive pain medicine. The problem with opioids is, they are addictive. Now, people need it. If you have a back surgery or if you have terrible pain, opioids can help people. We know that, but it is addictive and it is causing problems. What if we had non-addictive pain medicine? So this bill helps that in two ways.

There is other funding in this legislation: $4.8 billion to the National Institutes of Health. The first 1.8 billion of that is for Cancer Moonshot. This is Vice President BIDEN's initiative. He is motivated for many reasons by it. His son died of cancer. Many of us have family members or friends with cancer. There are startling discoveries going on in cancer today. This is $1.8 billion in support of the Vice President's Cancer Moonshot.

Then there is $1.4 billion for the Precision Medicine Initiative. This is one of President Obama's most important initiatives. I know he has said that very realistically he expects it to happen anyway, but he would like to move it along. This helps move it along. What this means is that if the Senator from Oklahoma and I each have a disease, that because of our genetic background, the medicine we might get for that disease should be different. If we know that genetic difference between the two of us, the doctor can prescribe for it. That is called personalized medicine or precision medicine.

Then there is $1.6 billion for the BRAIN Initiative. This includes groundbreaking research in Alzheimer's, for example. I talked to one drug manufacturer that has spent more than $1 billion trying to develop a medicine that will help identify Alzheimer's before it shows symptoms and then another medicine that will slow the progression of Alzheimer's. Imagine what could happen in our country if, for the tens of millions of Americans who are going to suffer with Alzheimer's, we could find that out before they actually have the symptoms and we can then slow down the progression of Alzheimer's. Think of the suffering that would help avoid. Think of the billions of dollars it would save. This is for that kind of research. Dr. Collins says that during this next 10 years, he expects that we will be able to identify individuals at high risk for Alzheimer's before any symptoms appear and provide them with effective medicines to slow or prevent the disease.

It also includes $500 million for the Food and Drug Administration to help pay for the extra work we are giving the FDA.

One Senator was on the floor talking about this bill and suggested this isn't enough money. Let's talk about money just a minute. The United States spends more on biomedical research and development than Europe, Japan, and China—almost as much as those three put together. There has nevertheless been a real need for increased funding for the kinds of things I just mentioned, but the way we do things here is, we have authorization bills, which this is, where we decide what our policies and our programs are going to be. Some of us are on those committees—like the committee I chair, and of which Senator MURRAY of Washington is the ranking Democrat, the Health, Education, Labor, and Pensions Committee in this case. Then we have Appropriations Committees that decide how much we can afford to spend on that. We do that separately.

Last year, this Congress, a Republican majority, I would point out—but Senator BLUNT, chairman of the Appropriations Committee for the Senate, would quickly give Senator MURRAY, the ranking Democrat, full credit—added $2 billion to the National Institutes of Health budget for 1 year. That means $20 billion over 10 years. This year, the same Republican Congress, with the cooperation of the Democratic Members, added another $2 billion to the National Institutes of Health budget. That is another $20 billion over 10 years. The Cures legislation that I have just described is another $5 billion. So that—20, 20, and 5—adds up to 45 billion new dollars approved. The first $20 billion is law, the second $20 billion has just been approved by the Appropriations Committees—hopefully it will become law—and the $5 billion I just described. Now, that is real money.

It is unusual to find an appropriations bill stuck on an authorization bill, but we have done it this time because this is an unusual opportunity, and we have done it in a way that Speaker RYAN and the House of Representatives believe is fiscally responsible. That means it doesn't add any new mandatory spending. That kind of spending has the budget going through the roof so it doesn't do that. It means it is paid for. That means we have reduced other spending to pay for it. When we look at the entire budget, it doesn't add a penny to the entire budget—we call it the discretionary plus the mandatory part—because it is paid for by reducing other spending.

We have set priorities, we have done our job, and the Appropriations Committee has done its job in consecutive years, approving $20 billion more over 10 years for the National Institutes of Health and will add another 5 here just to the National Institutes of Health.

Let's talk about the bipartisan nature of this bill. I am going to go through this fairly quickly, but for those watching, I think it is important to see this because sometimes when bills are popular—and I think this one will be popular. Everyone says: Well, that is easy. Tomorrow, the House of Representatives will vote on the 21st Century Cures bill. It includes the mental health bill—that I will describe in just a minute. I think it will be on suspension, which means they expect a big vote over there. I expect a big vote over here because I don't expect many Senators would want to vote no on a $1 billion grant program that will fight opioid abuse in their home State. I don't think there will be a lot of Senators who want to vote no on more money to fight cancer and to help the Vice President with the Cancer Moonshot. I suspect there will be a lot of Senators who want to vote yes to help the President advance his precision medicine legacy. I know there are families affected by Alzheimer's all over the country who hope Senators vote yes on the BRAIN Initiative. I imagine we will get a big vote when it comes up next Monday and Tuesday, after the House passes it tomorrow, but as we put this bill together, there was plenty of controversy, there was plenty of conflict, but virtually everything we did was bipartisan.

The money I just described is certainly bipartisan—the President's initiative, the Vice President's initiative, the opioid initiative. That is bipartisan, but look at the bills we are talking about.

Here is one called the Advanced Targeted Therapies, which allows researchers to use their own data from previously approved therapies to help find a faster treatment for serious genetic diseases—Senator BENNET, Democrat; Senator WARREN, Democrat; Senator BURR, Republican; Senator HATCH,

Republican—and it passed by voice vote.

I am very quickly going to go through 19 different bills that are the core of the 21st Century Cures legislation. They came out of our committee which has 22 Members, and the largest number of recorded votes against any one of those 19 bills was two because every single one of these bills had a Democratic sponsor and a Republican sponsor, except for one, and that was Senator MURRAY's bill, and she is the ranking Democrat on our committee. So don't let anyone suggest that a bill that has $6.3 billion of appropriations, that include Democratic priorities and bipartisan priorities, and the core of it is 19 bills of FDA and NIH reform that has a Democratic sponsor for every single bill and that was approved by a 22-member committee and only had two recorded votes against it—was the most that was against it—don't let anybody say this is not a bipartisan bill. Anyone who says that simply hasn't spent the time to be involved in the process.

Let's go to the next one.

BURR and FRANKEN, Republican and Democrat, FDA Device Accountability. It will bring innovative devices like artificial knees and insulin pumps to patients more quickly by getting rid of unnecessary regulations.

One of the major things we need to do—and we do it in this bill—is to bring cures and discoveries through the regulatory process more quickly and at less cost. All of us are concerned about the price of drugs. One factor contributing to that cost is that it takes a billion dollars and 13 or 15 years to take a new discovery through the process. We would like to shorten that process as long as we can do it in a way that ensures that it is safe.

The next one is called the Next Generation Researchers Act—Senator BALDWIN, Democrat; Senator COLLINS, Republican. It improves opportunities for our young researchers. It was passed by voice vote. That means there was no objection.

The next one is called the Enhancing Rehabilitation Research at the National Institutes of Health—KIRK, Republican; BENNET, Democrat; HATCH, Republican; MURKOWSKI, Republican; Republicans ISAKSON and COLLINS. Enhancing Rehabilitation Research was passed by voice vote.

Neurological Diseases Research. Here we have ISAKSON and MURPHY, Republican and Democrat, advancing Research for Neurological Diseases.

The next one has do with superbugs and protecting patients. You know about these. You get an infection, and you take a medicine to treat it, but the medicine doesn't work because the infection is a superbug. This bill will clarify that the FDA requires cleaning and validation data for reusable medical devices. In other words, this will make it less likely that will be a problem. That is Senator MURRAY's bill.

Improving Health IT. This is about electronic health records. The government has spent a huge amount of money on that, over $32 billion, including hospitals and doctors to adopt electronic medical records. It is very important to precision medicine, to personalized medicine, because if you can't use all this data, a doctor is not going to prescribe something for the Senator from Oklahoma that is different from something for the Senator from Tennessee.

We found that the electronic medical records system was a mess. We had six hearings on it, and we worked with the Obama administration because they could do some things to fix it and we could do some things to fix it. I thank Secretary Burwell in the Obama administration—I thank her and Andy Slavitt at CMS for the efforts they have made to do what they could do. And these are the things that we could do. Senator MURRAY was involved, Senator CASSIDY, Senator WHITEHOUSE, Senator HATCH, Senator BENNET. It was a bipartisan effort to reduce physician documentation burden—electronic health records to make it more interoperable and to get this system moving again.

Advancing Breakthrough Medical Devices. One of the great successes we have had in legislation was a few years ago when Senator BENNET and Senator BURR, among others, introduced a bill and made it law that brought breakthrough medicines through the Food and Drug Administration more rapidly. More than 49 have been approved and 464 requests for breakthrough designation in about 4 or 5 years. We are applying that same breakthrough strategy to medical devices. Of course, we have bipartisan support for that.

The Advancing Hope Act. If you are a parent of a child with a rare disease, such as brain cancer, this increases the opportunity that the drugs will help.

Medical Electronic Data Technology. We had Senator BENNET, Democrat; Senator HATCH, Republican.

Medical Countermeasure Innovation Act. This is very important. Senators BURR and CASEY have been real leaders in dealing with medical countermeasures. These are in case there is a bioterror attack, anthrax—some kind of man-made or naturally-occurring problem like that. Are we ready to deal with that? This helps to do that.

There are just a few more. Some will say: Why are you going on for so long? Because I would like for people to know when it happens that this Senate is capable of taking a great big, complex subject, and Democrats and Republicans are capable of working together to produce a result that deserves a big vote.

The Combination Products Innovation Act. This helps to bring to the market a products that are made up of medical devices and medicines.

There is a bill by WICKER, BENNET, COLLINS, KLOBUCHAR, ISAKSON, and FRANKEN on Patient Focused Impact Assessment.

There is one to modernize the FDA workforce. Dr. Califf told us that his biggest problem at the FDA is that he can't hire all the people he needs to deal with all of the exciting things going on. This gives him new authority to do that. Everybody thinks that would be an important thing to do. It was approved by voice vote.

Advancing Precision Medicine. This is legislation that I introduced and supported the President's Precision Medicine Initiative, which I have talked about before.

There is other legislation that went through. The point of all of this is that 19 different bills are the core of this 21st Century Cures Act. The most recorded number of votes against this bill was two, and every single one was sponsored by a Democrat as well as a Republican, except for one, which was Senator MURRAY's bill. She is the ranking Democrat on the committee.

In conclusion, we are fortunate to be able to add to the bill the Mental Health Reform Act. Actually, we include three mental health bills, and together they make up the most significant reform of mental health programs that we have had in more than a decade. I want to give particular credit to Senator MURPHY, Democrat, and to Senator CASSIDY, Republican, for working together through some real landmines to get this to a place where it can pass the House almost unanimously and where it will be a part of the bill that we will vote on next week.

I want to thank the majority whip, Senator CORNYN, who also added an important judicial part to this legislation and helped us navigate some difficult issues. In other words, these Senators showed that they know how to legislate. They could have stood up and made a speech. They could have insisted on doing things exactly their way, but they said to look for the area where we might agree on 80 percent of the policy and let's agree that.

This is one of those bills. Look at the number of Republicans and Democrats who have passed that. Here is the second mental health bill we are talking about. You can see the number of Senators. I have taken some time to go through the legislation that will be coming to the Senate early next week and that will be voted on tomorrow in the House of Representatives. I do think it likely represents, as the majority leader has suggested, the most important piece of legislation that we could act on this year. Because it affects virtually every American family, Forbes magazine reported that 78 percent of the American people favored Congress taking action on medical innovation because they have heard people like Dr. Francis Collins, the head of the National Institutes of Health, talk about within the next 10 years having a Zika vaccine and HIV/AIDS vaccine, identifying Alzheimer's before symptoms appear and slow its progression, an artificial pancreas for those with diabetes, and a non-addictive type of pain medicine.

These are magnificent opportunities for us. We have strong leadership at the National Institutes of Health. We have put our money where our mouth is. It is true that we will have to approve it every year, and it is true that we had to reduce other spending in order to have this spending, but that is the way we are supposed to do things.

What we have done is take a bipartisan core of bills; we worked hard for two years in a bipartisan way and produced a result that had very few "no" votes along the way. It includes Democratic priorities as well as Republican priorities. It has the avid interest of the Democratic President of the United States, the Democratic Vice President of the United States. It is a part of the agenda forward in health care for the Republican Speaker of the House, and the Republican majority leader in the Senate says it is the most important bill we are going to act on.

I would think that would get a big vote tomorrow in the House, and I would think it deserves a big vote in the U.S. Senate next week. It has been my privilege to work with Senator MURRAY and the other members of the Committee on Health, Education, and Labor to produce the bill.

I yield the floor.

There being no objection, the material was ordered to be printed in the RECORD, as follows:

ORGANIZATIONS SUPPORTING 21ST CENTURY CURES

IBM, Premier Healthcare Alliance, American Society of Clinical Oncology, National Patient Advocate Foundation, Parent Project Muscular Dystrophy, Alliance of Specialty Medicine, Advanced Medical Technology Association (AdvaMed), Association of American Medical Colleges, Association of Public & Land-Grant Universities/Association of American Universities, United for Medical Research; Epstein Becker Green on behalf of: Coalition for CLIA Waiver Reform, Advanced Medical Technology Association, National Coalition of STD Directors, Abbott, Alere, Becton Dickinson & Company, BioFire Diagnostics, ChemBio Diagnostic Systems, Roche Diagnostics, Sekisui Diagnostics, Spartan Bioscience, TearLab Corporation.

Coalition of 217 rare disease foundations: AKU Society of North America, Alpha–1 Foundation, ALS Association, Alternating Hemiplegia of Childhood Foundation, American Behcet's Disease Association (ABDA), American Brain Tumor Association, American Multiple Endocrine Neoplasia Support (AMEN Support), Association for Frontotemporal Degeneration (AFTD), Association of Gastrointestinal Motility Disorders, Inc. (AGMD), Association for Glycogen Storage Disease, Batten Disease Support and Research Association, BCC Nevus Syndrome

Life Support Network, BRBN Alliance, Children's PKU Network.

Cholangiocarcinoma Foundation, Chromosome Disorder Outreach Inc., Cicatricial Alopecia Research Foundation, Council For Bile Acid Deficiency Diseases, CureCADASIL (CADASIL Association Inc.), CureCMD, Cure HHT, Cutaneous Lymphoma Foundation, The Desmoid Tumor Research Foundation, Inc., Dystonia Advocacy Network, Dystonia Medical Research Foundation, dystrophic epidermolysis bullosa research association of America (debra of America), The Erythromelalgia Association, Everylife Foundation for Rare Diseases, Foundation for Ichthyosis & Related Skin Types, Inc., Foundation for Prader-Willi Research, Foundation to Eradicate Duchenne (FED), Friedreich's Ataxia Research Alliance (FARA), GBS/CIDP Foundation International, The Global Foundation for Peroxisomal Disorders, The Guthy-Jackson Charitable Foundation, Hermansky-Pudlak Syndrome Network Inc., Histiocytosis Association, HLRCC Family Alliance, The Huntington's Disease Society of America, HypoPARAthyroidism Association, Immune Deficiency Foundation, Indian Organization for Rare Disorders, The International Advocate for Glycoprotein Storage Diseases, International FOP Association, International Foundation for CDKL5 Research, International Myeloma Foundation, International Pemphigus and Pemphigoid Foundation (IPPF), International WAGR Syndrome Association, Jack McGovern Coats' Disease Foundation, Kennedy's Disease Association, LAL Solace, The Life Raft Group, Lymphangiomatosis & Gorham's Disease Alliance, The Marfan Foundation, MEBO Research, MitoAction, Moebius Syndrome Foundation, The Morgan Leary Vaughan Fund.

Mucolipidosis Type IV Foundation, Muscular Dystrophy Association (MDA), The Myositis Association, National Adrenal Diseases Foundation, National Alopecia Areata Foundation, National Ataxia Foundation, National Eosinophilia Myalgia Syndrome Network, National Lymphedema Network (NLN), National MPS Society, National Organization for Rare Disorders (NORD), National PKU Alliance, National Spasmodic Dysphonia Association, National Tay-Sachs & Allied Diseases Association, Inc. (NTSAD), NBIA Disorders Association, NephCure Kidney International, Neuroendocrine Tumor Research Foundation, Neurofibromatosis Network, The Oley Foundation, Organic Acidemia Association, Osteogenesis Imperfecta Foundation, Oxalosis and Hyperoxaluria Foundation, Parent Project Muscular Dystrophy (PPMD), Parents and Researchers Interested in Smith-Magenis Syndrome (PRISMS), PKD Foundation, Prader-Willi Syndrome Association (USA), PRP Alliance, Pulmonary Hypertension Association, RASopathies Network USA, Rett Syndrome Research Trust, Scleroderma Foundation, Spastic Paraplegia Foundation, Sturge-Weber Foundation, Tarlov Cyst Disease Foundation, Tuberous Sclerosis Alliance, United Leukodystrophy Foundation, The United Mitochondrial Disease Foundation, US Hereditary Angioedema Association, Vasculitis Foundation, VHL Alliance, Williams Syndrome Association, Wilson Disease Association, Worldwide Syringomyelia & Chiari Task Force, XLH Network.

Mr. ALEXANDER. I suggest the absence of a quorum.

The PRESIDING OFFICER. The clerk will call the roll.

The bill clerk proceeded to call the roll.

Mr. CORNYN. Mr. President, I ask unanimous consent that the order for the quorum call be rescinded.

The PRESIDING OFFICER. Without objection, it is so ordered.

FILLING THE SUPREME COURT VACANCY

Mr. CORNYN. Mr. President, earlier this year the Republican leadership made a somewhat controversial decision, but when you think about it, it shouldn't have been all that controversial. It was to allow the American people, by their selection for the next President of the United States, to express their views about who ought to be nominated to the vacancy left by the untimely death of Justice Antonin Scalia. This is not an easy decision, but the fact remains that the Supreme Court considers rules on some of the most pressing, challenging questions of our time. It does some very important things, such as interpreting the Constitution. They are the final word. It also guarantees liberty by the separation of powers and enforcing the Bill of Rights and the like.

It is no exaggeration to say that the Supreme Court affects the lives of every man, woman, and child in our country, and it is obviously a truism that the people who occupy those seats will have a very clear impact on the future direction of not only the Court but our country.

We have to consider lifetime appointments carefully. As Justice Scalia liked to say during his lifetime, why in the world should people trust nonelected judges to make value judgments and in so doing, substitute their judgment for the views of the duly elected Members of Congress who represent the American people and who are politically accountable? That is why he said judges ought to take a rather limited role, or view of their role, under the Constitution. I agree with him.

The role of the judiciary is not to say what the law should be but, rather, what the law actually is. Unfortunately, we know the Supreme Court of the United States has become such a controversial place in large part because of its tendency to substitute its value judgments for those of the American people or to read into the Constitution words that nobody found in the last 200 years, but miraculously somehow they sprung up with new meaning, resulting in the creation of a new constitutional life that nobody ever dreamed existed before.

It is true that the Supreme Court plays an essential function in our government, and there was simply too much at stake not to let the American people, through their selection of the next President, have a say. Well, suffice it to say, 3 weeks removed from election day, it is clear that we heard

their voice. I think by the selection of Donald Trump as the next President of the United States, the American people clearly realized that even though the Supreme Court wasn't on the ballot, the person who selected the next Supreme Court Justice—perhaps the next two or three—was clearly on the ballot, and there was a clear difference between those choices. I think people realized that Secretary Clinton would likely appoint more judges in the tradition of people like Justice Ginsburg and Justice Sotomayor, people who demonstrated their record of being willing to take some license with the Constitution and the laws and basically rewrite them in their own image.

I think the American people knew they were choosing between activist judges who essentially operated as unaccountable, unelected legislators wearing black robes or judges who believed in the more traditional role for the judiciary—judges who actually interpret the written words on the page passed by the Congress and signed into law or the Constitution itself. I believe that is how our Founding Fathers intended our separation of powers to work.

The judiciary is not supposed to be a substitute for Congress and the political branches; it is supposed to represent a check and balance to make sure that the laws that are passed do not violate the Constitution as written and that the laws that are passed are faithfully enforced according to the words in the statute.

I, for one, look forward to considering President-elect Trump's nominee to the Supreme Court in due time. Since I have been in the Senate, I have had the privilege of participating in the nomination and confirmation of four Justices to the U.S. Supreme Court. As members of the Judiciary Committee, we are at ground zero in that process, and I know Chairman GRASSLEY is already preparing, along with members of the committee, to receive the nomination of President-elect Trump. We don't know whom he will nominate to the Court yet, but he has given the American people a pretty good idea of the type of jurist he would nominate. I think that is one of the reasons millions of Americans voted for him. They wanted an administration committed to the Constitution, and they saw that commitment reflected in the list of men and women President-elect Trump circulated as potential nominees to the Court.

Now that we have heard from the American people, I look forward to going through the confirmation process once again. I am sure it will be a rigorous contest of ideas. I am sure there will be a lot of different views expressed, and that is OK. But in the end, I am confident that we will elect President-elect Trump's nominee to the Supreme Court. I am optimistic that it will be somebody in the tradition of Justice Scalia, somebody who believes in upholding the rule of law in the country.

Having been a member of the State judiciary for 13 years, I have some pretty strong views on this topic. If people want to take on the role of a policymaker, I believe they ought to run for Congress or some legislative office or maybe run for President. They shouldn't seek to be a judge on the Federal court or in the court system because that is not primarily a policymaking role. It is important but perhaps less exciting in some ways or at least is a less visible way of interpreting the Constitution and the laws passed by Congress. That is important and straightforward enough, but it is important that the people who are nominated and confirmed understand what their important but limited role is under our constitutional government.

As I said, we need a Justice like the late Justice Scalia, who believed that the words in the Constitution matter. We need a Justice who brings some sense of humility to the bench. That is a very important quality. I remember Chief Justice Roberts talking about the importance of humility when it comes to the job of judging. When one has a lifetime tenure job and can't be removed from office except by impeachment, that gives them a lot of latitude to do things that perhaps maybe humility would dictate that we not do. So we need people of good character, people with the requisite qualifications and experience and with the right judicial philosophy, I believe. We need a Justice who will fight for the Court to take its proper role as a check against executive or legislative overreach, but it ought to be constrained by the words of the Constitution as written and by the words in the legislation Congress has passed. There is no justification under our Constitution for a judge who simply views their position as license to do what they want or substitute their opinion for that of the elected representatives of the people.

I am optimistic we will be able to move forward with President-elect Trump's nominee to fill the bench and will soon be up to full speed of nine Justices. Through President Obama's tenure, we saw the Senate confirm two of his Justices to the Supreme Court. As I mentioned, those are two of the four confirmations in which I have had the pleasure of participating in the confirmation process. President Obama was able to replace two members of the Court.

In recent months, we heard our friends across the aisle say how important it is to fill the vacancy left by the death of Justice Scalia. We know they disagreed with us on our decision to leave that decision to the voters who selected the next President, but I trust they will feel the same way now—that it is important that we fill this bench without undue delay now that the people have spoken.

It is the American people who I believe have made a choice in the type of Justice they want confirmed to the Court. They have determined that what our country needs is a Justice committed to the rule of law and to the Constitution—not politics, not value judgments, but enforcing the law as written. I look forward to helping the new administration deliver that for the American people.

─────────

JUSTICE FOR ALL REAUTHORIZATION BILL

Mr. CORNYN. Mr. President, today the House will take up a piece of legislation known as the Justice for All Reauthorization Act, a bill that will help victims as they seek to restore their lives and will better equip law enforcement to fight some of the most heinous crimes imaginable. This legislation will help put more of the guilty behind bars and provide key resources to forensic labs across the country while aiming to end the rape kit backlog.

The rape kit backlog in particular has been something that a wonderful woman named Debbie Smith has committed much of her life to, making sure we provide the resources to local forensic labs that test those rape kits because of the power of DNA and forensic testing. One can literally tell with almost certainty whether the evidence contained in a rape kit matches a DNA sample from a suspected sexual offender. Likewise, one can also exclude the suspect from being the one who provided that forensic DNA sample. In other words, you can exonerate as well as convict people as a result of testing from these rape kits.

Being involved in this issue, we initially heard there were as many as 400,000 untested rape kits in America. Some of them had been tested 20 years after the fact only to find that the sexual offender didn't just commit one act of violence or sexual assault but was a serial offender.

There are stories of individual courage on the part of victims of sexual assault who have come forward to tell their story about the impact of this important elimination of the rape kit backlog. There are cities like Houston—Houston, under the leadership of Mayor Parker, basically said they are going to eliminate the rape kit backlog in Houston on their own, with perhaps some Federal assistance. They were able to identify a number of perpetrators in unsolved crimes because they were able to tell that the DNA in these rape kits matched certain hits on the FBI's CODIS list, where they maintain the data bank of DNA samples that are matched against those collected from suspects, collected in forensic examination.

Suffice it to say that this legislation will contribute to ending that rape kit backlog, and I believe that is a good enough reason to support it. It will make sure that brave people like Debbie Smith, who years ago suffered a sexual assault and who has made this one of her causes in life—it will make sure that no woman would have to endure what she had to endure, and that is where law enforcement fails to use all the resources available to it to find her assailant and to bring them to justice.

Most importantly, this legislation will also help strengthen victims' rights and help them pursue their justice in court.

We already passed it once unanimously in the Senate back in June, and I am thankful to the leadership in the House for bringing this bill up in the waning days of the 114th Congress. I look forward to the House bringing up and passing this legislation today and to us taking it up here with any amendments that the House may offer and taking it up here I hope by unanimous consent and passing it before we leave for the holidays.

With that, Mr. President, I yield the floor.

I suggest the absence of a quorum.

The PRESIDING OFFICER. The clerk will call the roll.

The bill clerk proceeded to call the roll.

Mr. WHITEHOUSE. Madam President, I ask unanimous consent that the order for the quorum call be rescinded.

The PRESIDING OFFICER (Ms. AYOTTE). Without objection, it is so ordered.

Mr. WHITEHOUSE. Madam President, I ask unanimous consent to speak for up to 25 minutes in morning business.

The PRESIDING OFFICER. Without objection, it is so ordered.

─────────

CLIMATE CHANGE

Mr. WHITEHOUSE. Madam President, I started my weekly series of speeches about the dangers of climate change in the spring of 2012. My trusty "Time to Wake Up" sign is getting a little battered, showing some wear and tear, but I am still determined to get us to act on climate before it is too late. The Senator from New Hampshire clearly knows what is going on in her State.

It is long past time to wake up to the industry-controlled campaign of calculated misinformation on the dangers of carbon pollution. Opponents of climate action relish operating in the dark. Their slimiest work to undermine science and deny the harmful effects of carbon pollution on human health, natural systems, and the economy is done by hidden hands through front groups. If anything is to change, we first need to acknowledge peer-reviewed science, the expert assessments of our military and national security leaders, and the business case for climate action that iconic American companies are making. But if anything is really going to change, we need to shine a light on the sophisticated scheme of science denial being foisted on the American people.

President Theodore Roosevelt once said: "Far and away the best prize that life offers is the chance to work hard at work worth doing."

We in Congress have the chance to do this worthy work, but big special interests don't want that to happen. So Congress keeps drifting toward climate catastrophe, and I keep delivering my weekly remarks—today for the 150th time.

Thankfully, I am not a lone voice. Many colleagues have been speaking out, particularly our ranking member on the Environment and Public Works Committee, Senator BOXER, and one of our Democratic Party's Presidential contenders, Senator SANDERS. Senator MARKEY has been speaking on climate longer than I have even been in the Senate. Senators SCHUMER, NELSON, BLUMENTHAL, SCHATZ, KING, BALDWIN, BROWN, and COONS have each joined me to speak of the effects of carbon pollution on their home States and economies. Our Democratic leader, Senator REID, has pressed the Senate to face up to this challenge, and 18 fellow Democratic colleagues, including climate champs MERKLEY, WARREN, MARKEY, and SCHUMER joined me in calling out the industry-controlled many-tentacled apparatus deliberately polluting our American discourse with climate science denial.

The climate science that deniers tried to undermine dates back to the 1800s, predating Henry Ford's first production Model T, predating Thomas Edison's first light bulb demonstration, and predating the first commercial oil well in the United States. It was 1824, around the time that President Monroe added the South Portico to the White House, that French scientist Joseph Fourier explained that the Earth's temperature would be much lower if the planet lacked an atmosphere, providing one of the first descriptions of the greenhouse effect. In 1861, the year President Lincoln took office, Irish physicist John Tyndall described the trace components of the atmosphere that were responsible for the greenhouse effect, including carbon dioxide, methane, and water vapor. In 1896, the year Utah joined the Union, Swedish scientist Svante Arrhenius published the first calculation of global warming due to the addition of carbon dioxide from the burning of fossil fuels.

The concentration of carbon dioxide in the Earth's atmosphere at that time was 295 parts per million. Today it is 400 parts per million and rising—indeed, rising at a pace not seen for 66 million years. Scientific research continues to demonstrate planetary warming and the many changes that come with it.

I am from the Ocean State, and we can particularly look at the oceans to see the devastating effects of climate change. Of course, the great, corrupt denial machine the fossil fuel industry supports rarely talks about oceans. But, remember, that machine doesn't care about evidence. It just wants to create phony doubt. But there is not much room for doubt in measurements of warming, rising, and acidifying seas, which are measured with everyday thermometers—with yardsticks, essentially—and pH tests. So faced with all that measurement, they just don't go there.

But the changes happening in the oceans are real. Our unfettered burning of fossil fuels has made our oceans warmer. The oceans have absorbed the vast majority of the heat trapped in our atmosphere by our carbon pollution—the heat equivalent to several Hiroshima-style atomic bombs being set off in the sea every second for the last 20 years. One result of all this heat is the calamity now taking place in the world's coral reefs, the incubators of the sea.

Australia's Great Barrier Reef is the largest coral ecosystem on Earth. Severe bleaching has hit between 60 and 100 percent of corals on the Great Barrier Reef, according to Dr. Terry Hughes of James Cook University in Queensland. Research led by Dr. Andrew King at the University of Melbourne determined that the ocean warming that led to widespread and devastating coral destruction was made 175 times more likely by human-caused climate change.

As one researcher put it, climate change "is the smoking gun." We are not just warming the oceans. The oceans actually absorb carbon dioxide itself, as well as heat. Because carbon dioxide forms carbonic acid when it dissolves in sea water, the seas are acidifying at the fastest rate in 50 million years. On America's northwest coast, oyster hatcheries have already experienced significant losses when their new hatches were unable to grow their shells in the acidified sea water. Off the coasts of Washington, Oregon, and Northern California, 50 percent of tiny sea snails called pteropods—these creatures right here—were measured to have "severe shell damage," mostly from acidified seas. A NOAA study released just last week detailed for the first time the extent to which that damage was caused by human carbon pollution. If this species collapses, the bottom falls out of the oceanic food chain.

In Rhode Island, Narragansett Bay's mean winter water temperature is up nearly 4 degrees Farenheit. Our Rhode Island lobster fishery is crashing, and our winter flounder fishery is practically gone. I know that the New Hampshire fishery is equally stressed. With real alarm, Rhode Island's clammers, lobstermen, fish farmers, and shellfish growers are all watching the damage acidified seas are doing. This is the cost of climate change in the oceans.

We are approaching a point of no return. The U.N. Environment Programme's Emissions Gap Report, released earlier this month, warned that unless reductions in carbon pollution from the energy sector are taken swiftly, it will be nearly impossible to keep warming below 2 degrees Celsius and avoid widespread catastrophes. The report says that the next 3 years are "likely the last chance" to limit global warming to safe limits in this century—likely the last chance to make a difference. But Republicans in this Senate want to do nothing about it.

Once upon a time, Republicans joined Democrats in pushing for action on climate. Senator MCCAIN ran for President on a strong climate change platform and was the lead cosponsor of the Climate Stewardship Act, which would have created a market-based emissions cap-and-trade program to reduce carbon dioxide and other heat-trapping pollutants from the biggest U.S. sources. At the time Senator MCCAIN said:

> While we cannot say with 100 percent confidence what will happen in the future, we do know the emission of greenhouse gases is not healthy for the environment. As many of the top scientists through the world have stated, the sooner we start to reduce these emissions, the better off we will be in the future.

Other Republicans got behind cap-and-trade proposals. Senator CARPER's Clean Air Planning Act at one time or another counted Senators ALEXANDER, GRAHAM, and COLLINS among its supporters. Senator COLLINS later coauthored her own important cap-and-trade bill with Senator CANTWELL.

Senator KIRK voted for the Waxman-Markey cap-and-trade bill in the House. Senator FLAKE, then representing Arizona in the House, was an original cosponsor of the Raise Wages, Cut Carbon Act to reduce payroll taxes for employers and employees in exchange for equal revenue from a carbon tax.

So what happened? Why did this steady heartbeat of Republican climate action suddenly flatline in 2010? Something happened in 2010.

What happened was the Supreme Court's disgraceful 2010 decision in Citizens United v. Federal Election Commission, where, in a nutshell, the Court ruled that corporations are people and money is speech, and so there can be no limit to corporate money influencing American elections.

When Citizens United uncorked all that big, dark money and allowed it to cast its bullying shadow over Congress, Republicans walked back from any major climate legislation. Rather than freeing up open debate, Citizens United effectively ended any honest debate in Congress on the climate crisis.

Unlimited corporate spending in politics can, indeed, corrupt—and not just through floods of anonymous attack advertisements. It can corrupt secretly and, more dangerously, through the mere threat of that spending, through private threats and promises. Sometimes, the fossil fuel industry threat to politicians who don't toe their line is not so subtle. The Koch brothers-backed political juggernaut Americans for Prosperity has openly promised to punish candidates who support curbs on carbon pollution and has openly taken credit for the "political peril"— to use their words—that organization created for Republicans on climate change.

Since 2010, the fossil fuel industry strategy has been to crush Republican opposition to prohibit Republicans from working with Democrats on climate change so that the industry can disguise what is basically old-fashioned special-interest pleading as a partisan issue in America's culture wars.

I don't know if you remember the alien in the movie "Men in Black" who climbed into the skin and clothing of the unfortunate farmer. That is what the fossil fuel industry has done to the Republican Party since Citizens United.

The industry has a lot at stake. The International Monetary Fund has reported the American subsidy for the U.S. fossil fuel industry at nearly $700 billion a year—that is billion with a "b"—and every year. I ask you, how much trouble would an industry go to to protect a $700 billion-per-year subsidy?

A growing body of scholarship is examining the science denial apparatus protecting the fossil fuel industry— how it is funded, how it communicates, and how it propagates the denial message. That research includes work by Harvard's Naomi Oreskes, Michigan State's Aaron McCright, Oklahoma State's Riley Dunlap, Yale's Justin Farrell, Drexel's Robert Brulle, and others.

Industrial powers fighting to obscure the harms their products cause isn't new. They operate from a well-worn playbook that was used for industrial contaminants and health hazards such as DDT, CFCs, and, of course, particularly tobacco. It is the ultimate special interest lobbying.

President-elect Trump campaigned on a pledge of draining the swamp of big special interests controlling Washington. Yet leading the transition at the Environmental Protection Agency for the Trump administration is Myron Ebell, the poster child of industry-backed climate denial. Mr. Ebell is the director of energy and environment at the Competitive Enterprise Institute, a corporate front group that has specialized in undermining tobacco, climate, and other science. CEI received millions of dollars from ExxonMobil, the Koch family, coal companies Murray and Massey, and the identity-laundering groups Donors Trust and Donors Capital. CEI and Myron Ebell are the quintessential DC swamp creatures.

Politico reports that Ebell was a veteran of the tobacco regulation wars. Jeremy Symons of the Environmental Defense Fund credits Ebell with "taking the tobacco playbook and applying it to climate change." And on climate, Jerry Taylor of the libertarian Niskanen Center says Ebell was "involved in marshaling allies, building a skeptic movement and enforcing that political orthodoxy as best he could in the Republican Party."

Ebell criticizes scientists for working outside their degreed fields, but it turns out he isn't even a scientist himself. After college, he studied political theory at the London School of Economics and history at Cambridge.

He has even criticized Pope Francis's encyclical on climate change, calling it "scientifically ill-informed, economically illiterate, intellectually incoherent and morally obtuse." That is rich right there—an outspoken climate contrarian whose organization receives fossil fuel money calling Pope Francis morally obtuse.

Well, the President-elect mocked Republican politicians when they went groveling before the Koch brothers at their "beg-a-thon," as the President-elect called it, but now he is busy filling his staff with Koch operatives. Donald Trump may have won the Presidency, but with operatives like Myron Ebell, the Koch brothers are moving in to run the Presidency.

The new President, however, will hear from our military, he will hear from our National Labs, and he will hear from NASA, which, with a rover driving around on Mars right now, may actually know a little science, that this is deadly serious.

I encourage President-elect Trump to listen to the voices of reason and expertise, not to the swamp things. Don't, Mr. President-elect, be taken in by industry lobbyists and front groups scratching and clawing to protect a $700 billion conflict of interest. Consider, Mr. President-elect, listening to your children, who joined you just 7 years ago in saying climate science was "irrefutable" and portends "catastrophic and irreversible" consequences. That is what you and they said just 7 years ago.

Madam President, let's assume something. Let's assume that all our National Labs, NASA and NOAA, our military leaders, our home State universities across our 50 States, hundreds of major American companies, and the more than 190 different nations that signed the Paris climate agreement are all actually not deluded about climate change, that they are not part of a hoax. If that is so, if these trained expert scientists who don't labor under a $700 billion-per-year conflict of interest are telling the truth, then the fossil fuel industry's science denial operation is a fraud. As a fraud, it is a particularly evil one because in order to achieve its goal, the industry has to drag down the Government of the United States or at least the Congress of the United States to its level. The fossil fuel industry maintains a science denial operation and a political influence operation designed and intended to willfully sabotage the proper operation of a branch of the Government of the United States. We ought to all have a problem when a powerful special interest is willing to damage our American experiment in democracy just to achieve its selfish ends.

As a Senator, John F. Kennedy once said this:

> Let us not despair but act. Let us not seek the Republican answer or the Democratic answer, but the right answer. Let us not seek to fix the blame for the past. Let us accept our own responsibility for the future.

Solutions to climate change need be neither Republican nor Democratic. They do need to be based on sound science and healthy and open debate. And we will be a stronger and more respected country if they are American solutions, if we are leading the world, not tailing along behind other countries.

For a country like ours that claims to stand as an example—as a city on a hill, we call it—a country that benefits from the power of our example around the world, this horrible example of out-of-control special interest influence will have lasting consequences. We have a role to play in this world, we Americans, and it is time we got about it.

I yield the floor.

I suggest the absence of a quorum.

The PRESIDING OFFICER. The clerk will call the roll.

The senior assistant legislative clerk proceeded to call the roll.

Mr. WHITEHOUSE. Madam President, I ask unanimous consent that the order for the quorum call be rescinded.

The PRESIDING OFFICER. Without objection, it is so ordered.

Mr. WHITEHOUSE. Madam President, let me also take a moment to add to my climate remarks my appreciation to Dr. Gifford Wong, who is here with me on the floor today. He has been helpful in my office as a trained expert scientist and has helped with many of these speeches. He is leaving us this week after working as a fellow on my staff for over a year. I am proud to have had him serve in my office, and I wish him well. This is his last climate speech with me.

I yield the floor.

I suggest the absence of a quorum.

The PRESIDING OFFICER. Will the Senator withhold?

Mr. WHITEHOUSE. Yes, the Senator withholds.

The PRESIDING OFFICER. The Senator from Hawaii.

Mr. SCHATZ. Madam President, I want to commend Senator WHITEHOUSE for his 150th climate speech. It takes a lot of passion, a lot of research, and a lot of focus to be willing to stay on one topic in the Senate for that many consecutive speeches. There are a lot of things that are important in the Senate and it is easy to get distracted, but Senator WHITEHOUSE remains steadfast, focused, and passionate, and history will show that SHELDON WHITEHOUSE was right and is right. I am proud to be his colleague.

Mr. WHITEHOUSE. Thank you, sir.

CONTINUING RESOLUTION

Mr. SCHATZ. Madam President, I am here to speak on another topic, actually, and that is what we are about to do with respect to appropriations.

This Congress was told by the majority leader that the Senate would return to the regular order, and I have no doubt he intended to make good on that promise. I know he is an appropriator. I know he is an institutionalist, and he really wanted to get back to the regular order. We were given assurances that keeping the government funded would be an orderly and bipartisan process, and it was true at the committee level, but that was then, and today we are far from that promise.

Today the Republican leadership, led by House leadership, has refused to complete funding bills for the current fiscal year. And what is so confounding for the folks who pay attention and who believe in the appropriations process, who believe in our constitutional prerogative, our constitutional obligation to hold the pursestrings and to use that authority to be a proper check on the executive branch, is that simply kicking the can down the road and passing another short-term CR doesn't result in anything conservative at all.

Many in this Chamber talk passionately about the need to eliminate government waste, fraud, and abuse, and yet a CR does exactly none of that. It does the opposite. It means programs that should be eliminated altogether will keep getting funded and programs that are working well and are critical but are in need of additional funding will remain underfunded. A CR puts the government on autopilot, stopping us from shifting investments to the most critical areas and decreasing funding for programs that are not working or are no longer needed. For example, the CR does not support accelerated counter-ISIL operations in Iraq and Syria; it defers work on the Iron Dome, delaying protection for

Israel from long-range Iranian missiles; it underfunds the DOD's basic operations and maintenance account by $12 billion; and it delays cyber security efforts led by the Department of Homeland Security. The CR also delays critical funding needed to address the opioid crisis—something I know the Presiding Officer cares passionately about. Both House and Senate bills provide large increases to fund drug abuse prevention, but the funding will remain flat under the CR.

We are on autopilot. We are not doing our job. We are abdicating our oversight role in the appropriations process.

There are actually two problems here. One is that things that need to be funded are not funded and things that should be eliminated or funded less are still funded. I don't see what is conservative about that. But the other result in a lot of ways is more insidious from the perspective of the Constitution and from the perspective of this institution, and that is, to the extent and degree that members of the administration, regardless of party, listen to members of the legislative branch, it is because we hold the purse strings. It is because we hold the purse strings. And every time we fail to do an authorization, every time we fail to do an appropriation, we are just shifting authority and clout to the executive. There is nothing conservative about that.

There is a mistaken assumption that running up against our funding deadline will somehow pressure the Congress into doing its job. What is crazy to me is that we have now 5 or 6 or 7 years of proof that doesn't work—this idea that what we should do is take difficult decisions and have them coincide with other difficult decisions and coincide with an even bigger difficult decision and then wrap it all up in a bow and do it at once. There may have been a time in the 1970s, 1980s, or 1990s where we could create these omnibus solutions, where we could get to these grand bargains, but what we need to do now is to hit a few singles. We need to do a few rational things.

The idea that what we should do is take the debt ceiling and the expiration of the CR and put them together just doesn't make any sense. It was proven wrong by the government shutdown of 16 days in the year 2013. The administration estimated that had up to a $6 billion impact on the economy. NIH studies were delayed, national parks were shuttered, transportation and energy projects were postponed, and FDA's routine food safety inspections were pushed back. This is not fiscal conservatism. This is not any kind of conservatism.

The idea of being a conservative, as I understand it—and I will grant you that I am a progressive, so it is not totally clear to me—is the idea that what you do may have unintended con-

sequences and that whatever changes you make ought to be incremental and ought to respect the institutions that have gotten America this far.

This is not a conservative result, to kick the can into the next spring, when we have no idea whether we are going to be able to solve multiple problems at the same time. If we want government to work, piling up all these issues and leaving it to a new administration to deal with in the spring will likely not work. We should finish the work we were elected to do and complete the funding bills for this fiscal year.

I yield the floor.

I suggest the absence of a quorum.

The PRESIDING OFFICER. The clerk will call the roll.

The senior assistant legislative clerk proceeded to call the roll.

Mr. McCONNELL. Mr. President, I ask unanimous consent that the order for the quorum call be rescinded.

The PRESIDING OFFICER (Mr. GARDNER). Without objection, it is so ordered.

TRIBUTE TO BERNARDA "BERNIE" WONG

Mr. DURBIN. Mr. President, I want to take a few moments to acknowledge Bernarda "Bernie" Wong, founder and president of the Chinese American Service League, CASL—and Esther Wong, cofounder and executive director of CASL. Earlier this year, Bernie and Esther announced they would be retiring on December 31, 2016.

Nearly 40 years ago, along with eight Chinese American friends, Bernie and Esther gathered over potluck dinners to discuss the needs of the Chinese community in Chicago. These discussions led to the creation of the Chinese American Service League, commonly referred to as CASL. CASL began with the goal of teaching English as a second language to Chinese immigrants. But today, because of Bernie's leadership, CASL has become one of the largest Asian American social service organizations in the country, providing social support services from early childhood development through elder care.

Born and raised in Hong Kong, Bernie moved to the United States in 1962 at the age of 18. Like many immigrants, Bernie came to the United States to further her education. She was awarded a full scholarship to attend Briar Cliff University in Sioux City, IA, and graduated in 1962 with a degree in social work. Before moving to Chicago, Bernie received her master's degree in social work from Washington University in St. Louis. Social work was in her blood. Her mother used tell her, "Share and give. Even if you don't have much, you share it . . ." And that is exactly what Bernie did, but it didn't come easy. When Bernie first came to Chicago, she faced push back from community leaders. They didn't want an outsider coming in and shining a light on their problems. Some considered it shameful. But that didn't stop Bernie. She went to the United Way and explained what she was trying to do. In 1979, they awarded her a special grant. She used it to start CASL.

Today Bernie's vision for Chinese immigrants in Chicago has grown from an annual budget of $32,000 to $13 million and a handful of employees to 450, serving more than 17,000 of the community's most vulnerable. She once said, "It's my job to know what the people in this community need. Then we can make a program available that will help them." That guiding principle has led Bernie and Esther to launch and oversee each of CASL's programs giving immigrants the tools to succeed in America, such as senior and child care services, family counseling, financial education, and employment training.

Bernie has been the recipient of numerous awards, including the Champion of Change Award given by President Obama for her extraordinary leadership in the community. Her other awards include United Way of Chicago's Executive of the Year Award; Crain's Chicago "100 Most Influential Women of Chicago;" and the Chicago Historical Society's Jane Addams Making History Award. Bernie also chaired the Chicago mayor's advisory council on Asian affairs and was the first Asian appointed to the boards of United Way of Chicago and the Chicago Public Library. And just last month, her years of service were recognized with her very own street: Bernarda "Bernie" Wong Way, right outside the Chinese American Service League. What an honor.

Since CASL's beginning, Esther Wong has been a faithful founding member. For more than two decades, she has served as chair of the program committee. Esther has been integral in CASL's success. So much so that, in 2002, Esther was recruited to assume the newly created executive director position. In this role, Esther has been responsible for expanding CASL's programs to include housing and financial education. She has also overseen several significant infrastructure improvements that have allowed CASL to provide critical safety net programs to the Chicagoland community. As a recipient of the mayor's Commission on Women's Affairs' Woman of the Year Award and the Asian American Coalition of Chicago's Community Services Award, Esther served on countless boards in the Asian American and immigrant community. She continues to serve on the boards of the National Coalition for Asian Pacific American Community Development, the Coalition for Limited English Speaking Elderly, and the Chicago Jobs Council.

I will close with this. A few years ago, the Chicago Tribune interviewed Bernie. They asked how she would like to be remembered if she ever retired.

She recalled a time when a janitor was sitting down eating lunch in the cafeteria. In China, you don't sit with your boss, so he was trying to leave. Bernie said, "No, sit down." He told her, "I've never seen a boss who wanted to include you." That is Bernie Wong's legacy. She simply wants people to know she cares and to make people feel included. After a career spanning nearly four decades at CASL, providing comprehensive and inclusive programs for immigrants and helping generations born in America realize their dreams, one thing is clear: Bernie and Esther care.

I want to congratulate Bernie and Esther on two wonderful careers and thank them for their service to our community. I wish them and their husbands, Albert and David, all the best in the next chapter of their lives.

ISRAELI-PALESTINIAN WOMEN WAGE PEACE MOVEMENT

Mr. LEAHY. Mr. President, for decades people around the world have witnessed seemingly intractable conflict in the Middle East, and those who live there have suffered through generations of violence. While the peace sought for that region has been elusive, organizations such as the Arava Institute for Environmental Studies in Southern Israel have continued the struggle to promote conflict resolution and unity to counter forces of hate and violence. Vermont Rabbi Michael Cohen is one of the founding faculty members of the Arava Institute.

In October, Rabbi Cohen wrote of the Women Wage Peace movement in Israel after thousands of people from different political and religious backgrounds joined together to march in support of peace in that troubled region.

The Women Wage Peace movement, founded by a small group of Israeli women, has grown over the years in both force and numbers. Its mission: to demand a peace agreement between Israel and the Palestinians. The rallies took place throughout the country, with a final march, the March of Hope, taking place in Jerusalem.

Rabbi Cohen, together with many other students, staff, and faculty of the Arava Institute and community members from Kibbutz Ketura where he currently teaches, attended one of the rallies at the official Israeli-Jordanian border crossing along the Eilat promenade, and, the following day, at Qasr al-Yahud, the Jordan River baptismal site.

At the baptismal site one of the members of Kibbutz Ketura recognized a man sitting on the Jordanian side of the river who had visited the Arava Institute earlier in the summer. The man had come to support the March of Hope from the Jordanian side, while members of the Arava Institute showed

their support from the Israeli side. The two men exchanged warm words from across the river epitomizing the goals of the movement.

The Middle East is facing one of its most unstable and dangerous periods in modern history. Entities like the Arava Institute, along with the Women Wage Peace movement, offer hope that peaceful coexistence is possible in the Middle East. Women, men, Israelis, Palestinians, Christians, Muslims, Jews, youth, and elders have joined together to remind us that we are all connected as members of one international community.

I ask unanimous consent that Rabbi Cohen's October 26, 2016, post, "A rabbi in the desert: A reminder of what can be," from the Arava Institute blog be printed in the RECORD.

There being no objection, the material was ordered to be printed in the RECORD, as follows:

[Oct. 26, 2016]

A RABBI IN THE DESERT: A REMINDER OF WHAT CAN BE

When I was five I attended my first political rally. It was the March on Trenton which paralleled the famous March on Washington and Martin Luther King's "I have a Dream Speech." The event in Trenton, New Jersey, as well as others around the country, were held for people who could not make it to the nation's capital to show nationwide support for the message of the event.

Fast forward fifty-three years later, and the grassroots Israeli-Palestinian "Women Wage Peace" movement decided on the same format; rallies throughout the country followed by a rally in Jerusalem. So during the week of the Sukkot holiday, I found myself standing at the official Israeli-Jordanian border crossing between Eilat and Aqaba with members of the southern Arava valley communities including Kibbutz Ketura and students, staff, and faculty of the Arava Institute. The message of the rally was women demanding, with men invited to participate, a model of political leadership that would transform decades of failure when it comes to a settlement of the Palestinian-Israeli conflict. "Right, Center, Left Demand a Peace Agreement" was the slogan of the rally. After a march along the Eilat promenade there were a number of speeches including one by the mayor of Eilat.

The following day many of us got up before the sun so we could travel first to Qasr al-Yahud, the Jordan River Baptist site and then onto Jerusalem. At Qasr al-Yahud we joined together with hundreds of Palestinians. People shared smiles, food, and a sense of doing something important together. It was a powerful sight as we marched, many hand in hand, from the gathering point to the baptismal site.

There, participants mingled with Christian pilgrims who had come to the site for baptism ceremonies. The Jordan River at that point is some fifteen feet wide and on both sides steps allow pilgrims easy access to its holy waters. A member of Kibbutz Ketura pointed out a man with white beard sitting on the Jordanian side of the river who had visited the Arava Institute shortly after our arrival this summer! He owns a farm near that spot and is working with Dr. Clive Lipchin, the Director of our Center for Transboundary Water Management, and Arava alumnus and researcher Suleiman

Halasah, to install the prototype of a new solar desalination system in Jordan. He came to support the March from the Jordanian side of the border. I called across the river and border. He immediately recognized me and we had a conversation much to the delight and surprise of those who listened to us. This extraordinary encounter modelled what the Arava Institute is capable of creating, and by extension what the Women Wage Peace event was all about.

The rally was addressed by Liberian Nobel Peace Prize laureate Leymah Roberta Gbowee, whose story of empowerment, bravery, and strength resonated with the marchers. From Qasr al-Yahud we continued on our way to Jerusalem, where our numbers swelled to 20,000 as we marched past Israeli government ministry buildings, the Knesset, the Prime Minister's office, the President's House, and finally ended up a block from the Prime Minister's residence. The marchers' spirits were uplifted by the sight of so many people snaking their way through the streets and neighborhoods of Jerusalem. At the final rally, Yael Deckelbaum led us in her touching song "Prayer of the Mothers".

The day was called the March of Hope. Hope is one of the great motivating forces in our lives; it allows us to reach forward to what we want. The day was a strong reminder of what can be. The activities of the Arava Institute are daily reminders that hope can also be lived as a reality.

RECOGNIZING ALLENHOLM FARM AND THE ALLEN FAMILY

Mr. LEAHY. Mr. President, Vermonters understand the value of hard work and perseverance, and we take pride in passing those values from generation to generation. Our communities thrive on family-owned businesses built on these values. They form the roots of success in our Green Mountain State, and it is those who own and operate them who are providing the leadership that will carry our State into the future. Today I want to recognize one exceptional Vermont family for the success of their multigenerational Vermont enterprise and their continued commitment to Vermont values.

Founded in 1870, Allenholm Farm is Vermont's largest apple orchard. At its helm is Ray W. Allen, whose great-grandfather Rueben Allen planted the farm's first apple trees more than 150 years ago, and Ray's wife and partner, Pam. After graduating from the University of Vermont with a degree in agriculture, Ray returned to the family farm he had worked as a child, eventually purchasing it from his father in 1960. More than five decades of running the farm haven't slowed Ray down, and he can still be found fixing machinery, giving tours of the orchard, and loading delicious Vermont apples into trucks for shipment.

Like many Vermont businessowners, Ray knows the value of diversification. In addition to the apples it sells to local grocery stores and cider makers, the farm harvests raspberries, blueberries, and cherries, some of which are sold to Vermont's world-renowned Al-

chemist Brewery. Ray and Pam, his wife of 31 years, work together to make hundreds of apple pies that are then baked fresh on demand. The autumn season brings thousands of guests, often multigenerational families themselves, for pick-your-own apples and visits to Willie and Sassafras, the farm's pet donkeys. Visitors may also enjoy maple creemees, a soft serve ice cream that is as unique to the State as the patented Vermont Gold apple variety is to Allenholm Farm.

Ray's dedication to his farm is matched only by his commitment to his family's legacy. As he hands down his knowledge of the apple business to his children, grandchildren, and now great-grandchildren, he passes on something else: a commitment to building on the past to create a successful Vermont for future generations.

I ask unanimous consent that an October 1 story from the Burlington Free Press about the successful Allenholm Farm in South Hero, VT, be printed in the RECORD.

There being no objection, the material was ordered to be printed in the RECORD, as follows:

[From the Burlington Free Press, Oct. 1, 2016]

LOCALVORE SINCE 1870 AT ALLENHOLM FARM IN SOUTH HERO

(By Sally Pollak)

SOUTH HERO.—When the apple pies are sold out, the goats are spitting out grain-filled ice cream cones, and the porta-potties need to be emptied, it's been a busy weekend at Allenholm Farm.

Count last weekend as very busy. Thousands of people visited the South Hero orchard, the owners estimated.

"The groups were really big," co-owner Pam Allen said. "Generational groups."

Allenholm Farm, founded in 1870, is itself multi-generational—seven and counting. The farm in South Hero is thought to be the oldest commercial orchard in the state, according to its owner, Ray W. Allen. Allen, who will turn 80 next month, has owned and operated the farm for 56 years. His great-grandfather, Ruben Allen, planted the first apple trees at the farm almost 150 years ago; the last of the original trees died in 1978.

At one time, Allenholm Farm was a diversified family farm with dairy cows, sheep, hogs and poultry, horses for plowing. These days, the 275-acre farm is primarily an apple orchard, with 2,000 trees growing on roughly 25 acres. The farm also produces cherries, berries, pears and pumpkins.

Farm animals are confined, mostly, to a petting zoo, though a donkey named Willy sometimes strolls down South Street, site of the farm. That's when Ray C. Allen, sheriff of Grand Isle County and son of Ray W. Allen, telephones his stepmother with a message:

"Your husband's ass is in the middle of the road again," the sheriff tells her.

This is family duty, he said. Not law and order.

Ray W. Allen, steadfast and true to the farm, is also a bit of a wanderer. Over the years he has gone off to high school at Lyndon Institute in the Northeast Kingdom; run 25 marathons; appeared on stage in community theater; served as a trustee at the University of Vermont, his alma mater; and volunteered as an EMT—late-night calls before early-morning chores.

Monday morning he was up at 3:15 for a bank run to deposit the weekend's cash. At 4:30, he was back home in his kitchen, hand-mixing pie dough for some of the 2,500 pies Allenholm Farm makes each year. (Ray Allen mixes the dough; Pam Allen makes the filling.)

At 5 a.m., he and his grandson, Brandon Allen, met at the big gray storage shed across from the farmstand to load trucks with boxes of apples for delivery to Hannaford supermarkets.

"It's a good time," Brandon Allen said. "Quality bonding time at 5 in the morning."

STORIED HISTORY OF APPLE PRODUCTION

The Champlain Islands have a long history of quality apple production, said Terry Bradshaw, apple specialist at UVM and director of its Horticulture Research Center. The lake climate—which makes for a cooler summer and protects against frost—provides superior growing and ripening conditions, especially for McIntosh apples, he said. In addition, access to the lake in the early 20th century meant transportation for shipping fruit north to the port of Montreal and south to New York.

"It's historic," Bradshaw said of Allenholm Farm.

The history dates to the founding of Vermont. Pam Allen, Ray Allen's second wife, is a descendant of Thomas Chittenden, Vermont's first governor. Ray Allen descends from Moses Robinson, the state's second governor.

"Illegitimate," Allen said of his ancestry.

More recent farm history includes the end of dairying about half a century ago, and getting in on the craft beer boom. Allen sells his cherries to the Alchemist, the Stowe brewery that makes Heady Topper. The cherries are used in a beer called Petit Mutant. Perks of this job include beer delivery to the farm by Alchemist brewer John Kimmich.

'COOL GUY'

But the main crop is apples, and the primary variety is McIntosh. A crew of six seasonal farm workers from Jamaica are the apple pickers. The men live at the farm in a former dairy barn converted to housing. Winston Waugh, from St. Ann, Jamaica, has worked at Allenholm Farm for about 20 years.

"He's a cool guy," Waugh said of Ray Allen. "He's quite OK."

Picking is hard work, Waugh said, especially in cold weather. It's crucial not to bruise the fruit, he said.

The season's dry weather calls for "selective picking," Allen said, as opposed to stripping a tree of fruit. Selective picking yields 50 to 60 bushels of apples per day per picker, he said. When you strip a tree, an apple-picker brings in about 90 bushels a day.

The size of the apples is important, too. Apples that are three or more inches in diameter are worth $40 a bushel; two-and-a-half to three inches are worth about $30 a bushel; less than two-and-a-half inches sell for $5.50 to $7 a bushel, Allen said.

In the winter and into spring, before the apple trees bloom, Allen is in his orchards pruning trees. He fixes machinery and works in the farm store, which is open until Christmas Eve.

Last spring, Allen had surgery to replace both his knees. He wore them out not from farming or running, but by wearing Western-style boots 365 days a year, he said. Allen didn't want to sit around on the couch, drink beer, and feel sorry for himself, so he challenged himself to be active. Within six days, he was driving around the farm.

"He's a character," his son said.

His roles include welcoming visitors to Allenholm Farm and leading tours. Allen expects future generations will fulfill these and other duties; but he has no plans to retire.

"I would hate to be the one to lose it," he said. "This is the 146th year. I sure don't want to be the first one to lose the farm."

CONSUMER REVIEW FAIRNESS ACT

Mr. THUNE. Mr. President, as chairman of the Commerce, Science, and Transportation Committee, which has jurisdiction over consumer protection matters, I introduced the bipartisan Consumer Review Freedom Act last year, along with Senators SCHATZ and MORAN, and cosponsored by Senators MCCASKILL, DAINES, BLUMENTHAL, NELSON, BOOKER, and WYDEN, to address a growing and alarming trend affecting American consumers in the United States. Some businesses are slipping so-called gag clauses into form contracts to stop consumers from providing critical feedback to the public, even when that feedback is an honest reflection of the consumer experience.

This legislation, and companion legislation agreed to in the House of Representatives would invalidate nondisparagement clauses in form contracts and make it unlawful for a person to offer or enter into a contract containing a nonnegotiable nondisparagement clause. Both bills contain a rule of construction to clarify that the legislation should not be construed to affect the right of a Web site owner to remove a review that "contains the personal information or likeness of another person or is libelous, harassing, abusive, obscene, vulgar, sexually explicit, or inappropriate with respect to race, gender, sexuality, ethnicity, or other intrinsic characteristic."

This language is simply intended to preserve the existing ability of Web site operators to enforce such terms of service. For example, it would—and is intended to—preserve the ability of a business to remove language from its Web site that includes inappropriate or harassing references to someone's religion, physical disability, or similar characteristic. As highlighted at the Commerce Committee hearing on this legislation, the intent is not to regulate speech; the intent is to ensure that consumers are protected against fees and penalties imposed pursuant to form contracts for engaging in honest reviews of goods and services.

I am pleased that the Senate has passed the latest version of this legislation and that it will be headed to the President's desk for signature. I thank my colleagues for their support of this measure.

HONORING CHARLES E. RUDLER

Mr. TOOMEY. Mr. President, today I wish to honor Charles E. Rudler, a World War II infantry soldier and prisoner of war who selflessly served his Nation with distinction.

Born in Linesville, PA, on March 26, 1925, Charles Rudler was an 18-year-old truck driver when he began his service in the U.S. Army in 1943. Serving as a rifleman during WWII, he landed on the beaches of Normandy and fought through northern France, the Ardennes, and Central Europe.

Unfortunately, Rudler was captured while fighting the Nazis and held as a POW through the end of the war at Stalag 3A, a brutal prison and work camp near Brandenburg, Germany. He survived this ordeal and separated from the service at the end of the war with an honorable discharge in 1945.

For his bravery and determination, Rudler has been awarded the WWII Victory Medal, the American Campaign Medal, the Good Conduct Medal, a Purple Heart, and the European-African-Middle Eastern Campaign Medal with four Bronze Stars.

For these reasons, I wish to honor Charles Rudler for his service and sacrifice in defense of our Nation.

ADDITIONAL STATEMENTS

250TH ANNIVERSARY OF LEMPSTER, NEW HAMPSHIRE

● Ms. AYOTTE. Mr. President, today I wish to pay tribute to Lempster, NH— a town in Sullivan County that is celebrating the 250th anniversary of its founding. I am delighted to join citizens across the Granite State in recognizing this historic occasion.

The territory was originally discovered in 1735. In 1753 it was regranted and named Dupplin after a leader of Nova Scotia at the time. Lempster, named for Sir Thomas Fermor of Lempster, England, received its current name after it was regranted a final time in 1767.

Lempster is located in the center of western New Hampshire and consists of three parts: East Lempster, Dodge Hollow, and Keyes Hollow. With a population of 1,154 residents, this close-knit town may be best known for its meetinghouse that is more than 200 years old. The meetinghouse is a source of great pride for Lempster and embodies its deep historical roots.

The town of Lempster is also home to a number of unique landmarks, including New Hampshire's first wind farm. Additionally, Lempster also received the first electric pole under the Rural Electrification Act on December 4, 1939. Nestled among these landmarks are beautiful recreational areas that allow the residents of Lempster and countless visitors the ability to enjoy all that the Granite State has to offer.

On behalf of all Granite Staters, I am pleased to offer my congratulations to the citizens of Lempster on reaching this special milestone, and I thank them for their many contributions to the life and spirit of the State of New Hampshire.●

PLAISTOW FIRE DEPARTMENT'S 101ST ANNIVERSARY

● Ms. AYOTTE. Mr. President, today I wish to recognize the Plaistow Fire Department, as this year marks the 101st anniversary of its founding.

The department was established on August 9, 1915, and was originally known as the Plaistow Volunteer Fire Company. It was formed with the objective of providing better fire protection for the community and served as an active working organization in order to protect the citizens of Plaistow. In 1915, the town noted "we have a village, the best in the State and would seem almost criminal not to protect our property and our beautiful shade trees, which, if destroyed by fire, would be a great loss to the town."

The Plaistow Fire Department is comprised of full-time and on-call staff who are dedicated and professional individuals that are committed to serving the town of Plaistow and our State. Importantly, Plaistow placed an emphasis on inviting all of its residents to contribute to safety and "most earnestly invite the co-operation of every citizen in this matter of fire protection and extend a most cordial welcome to everyone to attend its meetings and try-outs."

Today the Plaistow Fire Department remains committed to responding to every call in a safe and professional manner to protect the lives and property of its citizens. We ask so much of our firefighters and first responders, and we will be forever grateful for the selfless nature of their service.

On behalf of the people of New Hampshire, I join with the residents of Plaistow in celebrating the 101st anniversary of the Plaistow Fire Department and wish them continued success in the years to come.●

TRIBUTE TO ALINE SCHLEIFER ALVES DA COSTA

● Mr. BARRASSO. Mr. President, I would like to take the opportunity to express my appreciation to Aline Schleifer Alves da Costa for her hard work as an intern in my Cheyenne office. I recognize her efforts and contributions to my office as well as to the State of Wyoming.

Aline is a native of Brazil and a graduate of Laramie County Community College. She is a junior at the University of Wyoming, studying international relations. She has demonstrated a strong work ethic, which has made her an invaluable asset to our office. The quality of her work is reflected in her great efforts over the last several months.

I want to thank Aline for the dedication she has shown while working for me and my staff. It is a pleasure to have her as part of our team. I know she will have continued success with all of her future endeavors. I wish her all my best on her journey.

TRIBUTE TO LEANN BENTLEY

● Mr. BARRASSO. Mr. President, I would like to take the opportunity to express my appreciation to Leann Bentley for her hard work as an intern in my Washington, DC, office. I recognize her efforts and contributions to my office as well as to the State of Wyoming.

Leann is a native of Laramie, WY, and a graduate of Laramie High School. She is a junior at the University of Wyoming, studying business marketing with a concentration in sustainability and global markets. She has demonstrated a strong work ethic, which has made her an invaluable asset to our office. The quality of her work is reflected in her great efforts over the last several months.

I want to thank Leann for the dedication she has shown while working for me and my staff. It is a pleasure to have her as part of our team. I know she will have continued success with all of her future endeavors. I wish her all my best on her journey.●

TRIBUTE TO DAULTON GRUBE

● Mr. BARRASSO. Mr. President, I would like to take the opportunity to express my appreciation to Daulton Grube for his hard work as an intern in my Washington, DC, office. I recognize his efforts and contributions to my office as well as to the State of Wyoming.

Daulton is a native of Rock Springs, WY, and a graduate of Rock Springs High School. He attended the University of Wyoming, where he studied microbiology. He has demonstrated a strong work ethic, which has made him an invaluable asset to our office. The quality of his work is reflected in his great efforts over the last several months.

I want to thank Daulton for the dedication he has shown while working for me and my staff. It is a pleasure to have him as part of our team. I know he will have continued success with all of his future endeavors. I wish him all my best on his journey.●

TRIBUTE TO TANNER HANSON

● Mr. BARRASSO. Mr. President, I would like to take the opportunity to express my appreciation to Tanner Hanson for his hard work as an intern in the Senate Committee on Indian Affairs. I recognize his efforts and contributions to my office as well as to the State of Wyoming.

Tanner is a native of Ferndale, WA. He graduated from Reed College, where he studied history. He has demonstrated a strong work ethic, which has made him an invaluable asset to our office. The quality of his work is reflected in his great efforts over the last several months.

I want to thank Tanner for the dedication he has shown while working for me and my staff. It is a pleasure to have him as part of our team. I know he will have continued success with all of his future endeavors. I wish him all my best on his journey.●

TRIBUTE TO THOMAS MYLER

● Mr. BARRASSO. Mr. President, I would like to take the opportunity to express my appreciation to Thomas Myler for his hard work as an intern in my Casper office. I recognize his efforts and contributions to my office as well as to the State of Wyoming.

Thomas is a native of Casper, WY, and a graduate of Natrona County High School. He is currently a second year at Casper College, studying communications and multimedia. He has demonstrated a strong work ethic, which has made him an invaluable asset to our office. The quality of his work is reflected in his great efforts over the last several months.

I want to thank Thomas for the dedication he has shown while working for me and my staff. It is a pleasure to have him as part of our team. I know he will have continued success with all of his future endeavors. I wish him all my best on his journey.●

TRIBUTE TO SAM TANNER

● Mr. BARRASSO. Mr. President, I would like to take the opportunity to express my appreciation to Sam Tanner for his hard work as an intern in the Republican Policy Committee. I recognize his efforts and contributions to my office as well as to the State of Wyoming.

Sam is a native of Utah and a sophomore at Central Wyoming College. He is studying business administration. He has demonstrated a strong work ethic, which has made him an invaluable asset to our office. The quality of his work is reflected in his great efforts over the last several months.

I want to thank Sam for the dedication he has shown while working for me and my staff. It is a pleasure to have him as part of our team. I know he will have continued success with all of his future endeavors. I wish him all my best on his journey.●

TRIBUTE TO ELIZABETH WALSH

● Mr. BARRASSO. Mr. President, I would like to take the opportunity to express my appreciation to Elizabeth Walsh for her hard work as an intern in my Casper office. I recognize her efforts and contributions to my office as well as to the State of Wyoming.

Elizabeth is a native of Glenrock, WY, and a graduate of Natrona County High School. She is currently in her second year of Casper College, where she studies international studies and world languages. She has demonstrated a strong work ethic, which has made her an invaluable asset to our office. The quality of her work is reflected in her great efforts over the last several months.

I want to thank Elizabeth for the dedication she has shown while working for me and my staff. It is a pleasure to have her as part of our team. I know she will have continued success with all of her future endeavors. I wish her all my best on her journey.●

TRIBUTE TO JAMES WILLSON

● Mr. BARRASSO. Mr. President, I would like to take the opportunity to express my appreciation to James Willson for his hard work as an intern in my Washington, DC, office. I recognize his efforts and contributions to my office as well as to the State of Wyoming.

James is a native of Cody, WY, and a graduate of Cody High School. He is a graduate of the University of Wyoming College of Law. He has demonstrated a strong work ethic, which has made him an invaluable asset to our office. The quality of his work is reflected in his great efforts over the last several months.

I want to thank James for the dedication he has shown while working for me and my staff. It is a pleasure to have him as part of our team. I know he will have continued success with all of his future endeavors. I wish him all my best on his journey.●

TRIBUTE TO TOM COURTWAY

● Mr. BOOZMAN. Mr. President, today I wish to honor University of Central Arkansas president Tom Courtway who will retire as president of the university in December after nearly 15 years of dedication to higher education in Arkansas.

President Courtway was appointed the 10th president of UCA in 2011, and he has proven himself to be a driving force in improving and expanding the campus for current and future students.

His career has been marked by leadership and dedicated service, which will endure since he will continue to teach at UCA. During his time leading in higher education, he has always put students first and fought to ensure the community had opportunities to succeed.

President Courtway has been lauded for his steady leadership and has been entrusted to serve time and again. In addition to serving as president of the university, he previously represented UCA as general counsel, vice president, and interim president. President Courtway is a strong leader in central Arkansas' dedication to academic vitality, diversity and integrity.

He has also been actively engaged in the legislative process at the State level on behalf of his community. He served the 45th district in the Arkansas Legislature for 6 years, and he also spent a year as the interim director of the Arkansas Department of Education. President Courtway has served his community and State in a remarkable way, pursuing development and higher education opportunities for the good people of Conway.

I congratulate President Courtway for his outstanding achievements in his career and thank him for his dedication to education, students, and the community. I wish him all the best in retirement and know that his wife, Melissa, and the rest of his family will enjoy the opportunity to spend more time with him.●

TRIBUTE TO JIM SPEARS

● Mr. BOOZMAN. Mr. President, today I wish to honor circuit judge Jim Spears who will be retiring in December after serving the people of Sebastian County, AR, for more than 20 years.

Judge Spears has been an active member of the legal community since graduating from the University of Arkansas School of Law in 1973. Described by those who know him as "kind, fair and approachable," his 24 years presiding over the Sebastian County Circuit's Third Division have been a testament to his commitment to the people of Arkansas.

Those who have stood in court before Judge Spears have expressed their utmost respect and admiration for his conduct and character.

In addition to his passion for the law, his colleagues say that his commitment to civic involvement is equally important to his years on the bench. Judge Spears has worked closely with the Boy Scouts of America and served on the Arkansas Access to Justice Commission and as board chairman of the U.S. Marshals Museum. He has played a critical role in many community projects including leading the effort to create a bronze statue of U.S. Marshal Bass Reeves.

Judge Spears has been honored by many organizations for his efforts, including the Arkansas Bar Association's Citizen Lawyer award in 2004 for his exemplary service to his community.

I am honored to know Judge Spears and want to thank him for his distinguished service as a leader in the justice system and the community. I wish him the best in his well-earned retirement from the bench, and I look forward to watching him use his talents and passion to continue to serve Arkansas in the years to come.

DEDICATION OF THE GRANITE MOUNTAIN HOTSHOTS MEMORIAL STATE PARK

● Mr. McCAIN. Mr. President, today we honor the lives of 19 courageous Granite Mountain Hotshots by celebrating the dedication of the Granite Mountain Hotshots Memorial State Park in Yarnell, AZ. I ask that this letter recognizing the occasion be printed in the RECORD.

The material follows:

> U.S. SENATE,
> *November 29, 2016.*
> ARIZONA STATE PARKS AND TRAILS,
> *Granite Mountain Hotshots Memorial State Park, Yarnell, AZ.*
>
> DEAR FRIENDS: In a proud but solemn moment for all Arizonans, today we celebrate the dedication of the Granite Mountain Hotshots Memorial State Park.
>
> The 2013 Yarnell Hill Fire was a tragedy that resulted in the lives of 19 brave and fearless Granite Mountain Hotshots. That fateful day on June 30, 2013 was the greatest loss of life for firefighters in a wildfire since 1933 and the greatest loss of firefighters in the United States since the September 11th attacks. This Memorial State Park is a most fitting tribute to these remarkable firefighters who selflessly risked their own lives to protect others and their community in the beautiful Arizona town of Yarnell.
>
> I thank Arizona State Parks and the Yarnell Hill Memorial Site Board, who made this designation possible. With this wonderful memorial, I hope the family and friends of those Hotshots who passed may find peace and comfort in this historic designation, which will forever preserve and honor the memory of these brave souls.
>
> My thoughts and prayers are with you all on this occasion, and I send best wishes for a memorable event.
>
> Sincerely,
>
> JOHN McCAIN,
> *U.S. Senator.*●

REMEMBERING RICHARD D. ROGERS

● Mr. MORAN. Mr. President, it is my honor today to honor the life of a revered Kansan, U.S. District Court Judge Richard D. Rogers, who passed away on November 26 of this year at the age of 94.

Richard Rogers was devoted to public service in every sense. He was a decorated veteran, having received the Distinguished Flying Cross for his service flying 33 combat missions as a bombardier in World War II. He served the town of Manhattan, KS, as both its mayor and city commissioner. He served as a State legislator in both chambers of the Kansas Legislature, rising to the title of President of the Senate. And in 1975, President Gerald Ford appointed Richard Rogers to serve as a U.S. District Judge for the District of Kansas, a position he held for more than 40 years.

Judge Rogers represented the very best of the greatest generation, unselfishly giving of himself and his time to improve the lives of those around him. A graduate of Wamego High School, Kansas State University, and later the University of Kansas School of Law, he took an active interest in his State, its people, and their many different walks of life.

His understanding of Kansans carried over to the courtroom where colleagues say Judge Rogers served with great wisdom and fairness. Judge Rogers' contemporaries also remember him as a mentor and friend, someone often consulted for his breadth of knowledge, his geniality, and his humility until he stepped down from his position on the Federal bench on August 7, 2015.

Richard Rogers was a pillar of the Manhattan and Topeka communities, and his integrity, service, and devotion to justice will be forever remembered by the people of Kansas.●

MESSAGES FROM THE PRESIDENT

Messages from the President of the United States were communicated to the Senate by Mr. Pate, one of his secretaries.

EXECUTIVE MESSAGES REFERRED

As in executive session the Presiding Officer laid before the Senate messages from the President of the United States submitting sundry nominations which were referred to the appropriate committees.

(The messages received today are printed at the end of the Senate proceedings.)

PRESIDENTIAL MESSAGE

REPORT RELATIVE TO AN ALTERNATIVE PLAN FOR PAY INCREASES FOR CIVILIAN FEDERAL EMPLOYEES COVERED BY THE GENERAL SCHEDULE AND CERTAIN OTHER PAY SYSTEMS IN JANUARY 2017—PM 57

The PRESIDING OFFICER laid before the Senate the following message from the President of the United States, together with an accompanying report; which was referred to the Committee on Homeland Security and Governmental Affairs:

To the Congress of the United States:

I am transmitting an alternative plan for pay increases for civilian Federal employees covered by the General Schedule and certain other pay systems in January 2017. Title 5, United States Code, authorizes me to implement alternative pay plans for pay increases for civilian Federal employees covered by the General Schedule and certain other pay systems if, because of "national emergency or serious economic conditions affecting the general welfare," I view the adjustments that would otherwise take effect as inappropriate.

Civilian Federal employees made significant sacrifices as a result of the 3-year pay freeze that ended in January 2014. Since the pay freeze ended, annual adjustments for civilian Federal employees have also been lower than private sector pay increases and statutory formulas for adjustments to the General Schedule for 2014 through 2016. However, we must maintain efforts to keep our Nation on a sustainable fiscal course. This is an effort that continues to require tough choices under current economic conditions.

Under current law, locality pay increases averaging 28.49 percent and costing $26 billion would go into effect in January 2017. Federal agency budgets cannot sustain such increases. In my August 31, 2016, alternative pay plan submission, I noted that the alternative plan for locality payments will be limited so that the total combined cost of the 1.0 percent across-the-board base pay increase and the varying locality pay increases will be 1.6 percent of basic payroll, consistent with the assumption in my 2017 Budget. Accordingly, I have determined that under the authority of section 5304a of title 5, United States Code, locality-based comparability payments for the locality pay areas established by the President's Pay Agent, in the amounts set forth in the attached table, shall become effective on the first day of the first applicable pay period beginning on or after January 1, 2017.

The locality-based comparability payments for the locality pay rates in the attached table are based on an allocation of 0.6 percent of payroll as indicated in my August 31, 2016, alternative pay plan for adjustments to the base General Schedule. These decisions will not materially affect our ability to attract and retain a well-qualified Federal workforce.

BARACK OBAMA.
THE WHITE HOUSE, *November 29, 2016.*

MEASURES PLACED ON THE CALENDAR

The following bill was read the second time, and placed on the calendar:

H.R. 6297. An act to reauthorize the Iran Sanctions Act of 1996.

EXECUTIVE AND OTHER COMMUNICATIONS

The following communications were laid before the Senate, together with accompanying papers, reports, and documents, and were referred as indicated:

EC–7671. A communication from the Deputy Secretary, Division of Swap Dealer and Intermediary Oversight, Commodity Futures Trading Commission, transmitting, pursuant to law, the report of a rule entitled "Chief Compliance Officer Annual Report Requirements for Futures Commission Merchants, Swap Dealers, and Major Swap Participants; Amendments to Filing Dates" (RIN3038–AE49) received in the Office of the President of the Senate on November 17, 2016; to the Committee on Agriculture, Nutrition, and Forestry.

EC–7672. A communication from the Assistant Secretary, Legislative Affairs, Department of State, transmitting, pursuant to law, a report entitled "Iran-Related Multilateral Sanctions Regime Efforts" covering the period August 7, 2015 to February 6, 2016; to the Committees on Banking, Housing, and Urban Affairs; Finance; and Foreign Relations.

EC–7673. A communication from the Secretary of the Treasury, transmitting, pursuant to law, a six-month periodic report on the national emergency with respect to the Central African Republic that was declared in Executive Order 13667 of May 12, 2014; to the Committee on Banking, Housing, and Urban Affairs.

EC–7674. A communication from the Secretary of the Treasury, transmitting, pursuant to law, a six-month periodic report on the national emergency with respect to Syria that was declared in Executive Order 13338 of May 11, 2004; to the Committee on Banking, Housing, and Urban Affairs.

EC–7675. A communication from the Administrator and Chief Executive Officer, Bonneville Power Administration, Department of Energy, transmitting, pursuant to law, the Administration's Annual Report for fiscal year 2016; to the Committee on Energy and Natural Resources.

EC–7676. A communication from the Secretary of the Interior, transmitting, pursuant to law, a report entitled "Proposed Final Outer Continental Shelf (OCS) Oil and Gas Leasing Program 2017–2022"; to the Committee on Energy and Natural Resources.

EC–7677. A communication from the Division Chief of Regulatory Affairs, Bureau of Land Management, Department of the Interior, transmitting, pursuant to law, the report of a rule entitled "Onshore Oil and Gas Operations; Federal and Indian Oil and Gas Leases; Measurement of Oil" (RIN1004–AE16) received in the Office of the President of the Senate on November 17, 2016; to the Committee on Energy and Natural Resources.

EC–7678. A communication from the Division Chief of Regulatory Affairs, Bureau of Land Management, Department of the Interior, transmitting, pursuant to law, the report of a rule entitled "Onshore Oil and Gas Operations; Federal and Indian Oil and Gas Leases; Measurement of Gas" (RIN1004–AE17) received in the Office of the President of the Senate on November 17, 2016; to the Committee on Energy and Natural Resources.

EC–7679. A communication from the Division Chief of Regulatory Affairs, Bureau of Land Management, Department of the Interior, transmitting, pursuant to law, the report of a rule entitled "Onshore Oil and Gas Operations; Federal and Indian Oil and Gas Leases; Site Security" (RIN1004–AE15) received in the Office of the President of the Senate on November 17, 2016; to the Committee on Energy and Natural Resources.

EC–7680. A communication from the Division Chief of Regulatory Affairs, Bureau of Land Management, Department of the Interior, transmitting, pursuant to law, the report of a rule entitled "Waste Prevention, Production Subject to Royalties, and Resource Conservation" (RIN1004–AE14) received during adjournment of the Senate in the Office of the President of the Senate on November 18, 2016; to the Committee on Energy and Natural Resources.

EC–7681. A communication from the Secretary of Transportation, transmitting, pursuant to law, the Department's 2016 Report to Congress on the Transportation Infrastructure Finance and Innovation Act; to the Committee on Environment and Public Works.

EC–7682. A communication from the Director of Congressional Affairs, Office of New Reactors, Nuclear Regulatory Commission, transmitting, pursuant to law, the report of a rule entitled "Operating Organization" (NUREG–0800) received during adjournment of the Senate in the Office of the President of the Senate on November 18, 2016; to the Committee on Environment and Public Works.

EC–7683. A communication from the Director of Congressional Affairs, Office of New Reactors, Nuclear Regulatory Commission, transmitting, pursuant to law, the report of a rule entitled "Reactor Operator Qualification Program; Reactor Operator Training" (NUREG–0800) received during adjournment of the Senate in the Office of the President of the Senate on November 18, 2016; to the Committee on Environment and Public Works.

EC–7684. A communication from the Director of Congressional Affairs, Office of New Reactors, Nuclear Regulatory Commission, transmitting, pursuant to law, the report of a rule entitled "Seismic Classification" (NUREG–0800) received during adjournment of the Senate in the Office of the President of the Senate on November 18, 2016; to the Committee on Environment and Public Works.

EC–7685. A communication from the Director of Congressional Affairs, Office of New Reactors, Nuclear Regulatory Commission, transmitting, pursuant to law, the report of a rule entitled "System Quality Group Classification" (NUREG–0800) received during adjournment of the Senate in the Office of the President of the Senate on November 18, 2016; to the Committee on Environment and Public Works.

EC–7686. A communication from the Director of Congressional Affairs, Office of New Reactors, Nuclear Regulatory Commission, transmitting, pursuant to law, the report of a rule entitled "Management and Technical Support Organization" (NUREG–0800) received during adjournment of the Senate in the Office of the President of the Senate on November 18, 2016; to the Committee on Environment and Public Works.

EC–7687. A communication from the Director of Congressional Affairs, Office of New Reactors, Nuclear Regulatory Commission, transmitting, pursuant to law, the report of a rule entitled "Administrative Procedures - General" (NUREG–0800) received during adjournment of the Senate in the Office of the President of the Senate on November 18, 2016; to the Committee on Environment and Public Works.

EC–7688. A communication from the Director of Congressional Affairs, Office of New Reactors, Nuclear Regulatory Commission, transmitting, pursuant to law, the report of a rule entitled "Non-Licensed Plant Staff Training" (NUREG–0800) received during adjournment of the Senate in the Office of the President of the Senate on November 18, 2016; to the Committee on Environment and Public Works.

EC–7689. A communication from the Director of the Regulatory Management Division, Environmental Protection Agency, transmitting, pursuant to law, the report of a rule entitled "Greenhouse Gas Reporting Rule:

Leak Detection Methodology Revisions and Confidentiality Determinations for Petroleum and Natural Gas Systems'' ((RIN2060–AS73) (FRL–9955–12–OAR)) received during adjournment of the Senate in the Office of the President of the Senate on November 18, 2016; to the Committee on Environment and Public Works.

EC–7690. A communication from the Director of the Regulatory Management Division, Environmental Protection Agency, transmitting, pursuant to law, the report of a rule entitled ''Formaldehyde Emission Standards for Composite Wood Products'' (RIN2070–AJ44) (FRL–9949–90)) received during adjournment of the Senate in the Office of the President of the Senate on November 18, 2016; to the Committee on Environment and Public Works.

EC–7691. A communication from the Director of the Regulatory Management Division, Environmental Protection Agency, transmitting, pursuant to law, the report of a rule entitled ''Findings of Failure to Attain the 1997 PM2.5 Standards; California; San Joaquin Valley'' (FRL–9955–53–Region 9) received during adjournment of the Senate in the Office of the President of the Senate on November 18, 2016; to the Committee on Environment and Public Works.; to the Committee on Environment and Public Works.

EC–7692. A communication from the Director of the Regulatory Management Division, Environmental Protection Agency, transmitting, pursuant to law, the report of a rule entitled ''Designation of Areas for Air Quality Planning Purposes; Ohio; Redesignation of the Ohio Portion of the Campbell-Clermont KY–OH Sulfur Dioxide Nonattainment Area'' (FRL–9955–37–Region 5) received during adjournment of the Senate in the Office of the President of the Senate on November 18, 2016; to the Committee on Environment and Public Works.

EC–7693. A communication from the Director of the Regulatory Management Division, Environmental Protection Agency, transmitting, pursuant to law, the report of a rule entitled ''Clarification of Requirements for Method 303 Certification Training'' ((RIN2060–AR97) (FRL–9955–50–OAR)) received during adjournment of the Senate in the Office of the President of the Senate on November 18, 2016; to the Committee on Environment and Public Works.

EC–7694. A communication from the Director of the Regulatory Management Division, Environmental Protection Agency, transmitting, pursuant to law, the report of a rule entitled ''Air Plan Approval; FL Infrastructure Requirements for the 2010 1-hour NO2 NAAQS'' (FRL–9955–49–Region 4) received during adjournment of the Senate in the Office of the President of the Senate on November 18, 2016; to the Committee on Environment and Public Works.

EC–7695. A communication from the Director of the Regulatory Management Division, Environmental Protection Agency, transmitting, pursuant to law, the report of a rule entitled ''Air Plan Approval/Disapproval; AL Infrastructure Requirements'' (FRL–9955–29–Region 4) received during adjournment of the Senate in the Office of the President of the Senate on November 18, 2016; to the Committee on Environment and Public Works.

EC–7696. A communication from the Director of the Regulatory Management Division, Environmental Protection Agency, transmitting, pursuant to law, the report of a rule entitled ''Addition of Hexabromocyclododecane (HBCD) Category; Community Right-to-Know Toxic Chemical Release Reporting'' ((RIN2025–AA42) (FRL–9953–28)) received dur-

ing adjournment of the Senate in the Office of the President of the Senate on November 18, 2016; to the Committee on Environment and Public Works.

EC–7697. A communication from the Director of the Regulatory Management Division, Environmental Protection Agency, transmitting, pursuant to law, the report of a rule entitled ''Spodoptera frugiperda Multiple Nucleopolyhedrovirus strain 3AP2; Exemption from the Requirement of a Tolerance'' (FRL No. 9953–40) received during adjournment of the Senate in the Office of the President of the Senate on November 18, 2016; to the Committee on Agriculture, Nutrition, and Forestry.

EC–7698. A communication from the Director of the Regulatory Management Division, Environmental Protection Agency, transmitting, pursuant to law, the report of a rule entitled ''Endothall; Pesticide Tolerances'' (FRL No. 9953–97) received during adjournment of the Senate in the Office of the President of the Senate on November 18, 2016; to the Committee on Agriculture, Nutrition, and Forestry.

EC–7699. A communication from the Alternate Federal Register Liaison Officer, Office of the Secretary, Department of Defense, transmitting, pursuant to law, the report of a rule entitled ''DoD Environmental Laboratory Accreditation Program (ELAP)'' (RIN0790–AJ16) received in the Office of the President of the Senate on November 28, 2016; to the Committee on Armed Services.

EC–7700. A communication from the Assistant General Counsel for Legislation and Regulations, Office of the Secretary, Department of Housing and Urban Development, transmitting, pursuant to law, the report of a rule entitled ''Establishing a More Effective Fair Market Rent System; Using Small Area Fair Market Rents in the Housing Choice Voucher Program Instead of the Current 50th Percentile FMRs'' (RIN2501–AD74) received in the Office of the President of the Senate on November 28, 2016; to the Committee on Banking, Housing, and Urban Affairs.

EC–7701. A communication from the Assistant General Counsel for Legislation and Regulations, Office of the Secretary, Department of Housing and Urban Development, transmitting, pursuant to law, the report of a rule entitled ''Violence Against Women Reauthorization Act of 2013: Implementation in HUD Housing Programs'' (RIN2501–AD71) received in the Office of the President of the Senate on November 28, 2016; to the Committee on Banking, Housing, and Urban Affairs.

EC–7702. A communication from the Assistant Secretary for Export Administration, Bureau of Industry and Security, Department of Commerce, transmitting, pursuant to law, the report of a rule entitled ''Commerce Control List: Removal of Certain Nuclear Nonproliferation (NP) Column 2 Controls'' (RIN0694–AH04) received in the Office of the President of the Senate on November 28, 2016; to the Committee on Banking, Housing, and Urban Affairs.

EC–7703. A communication from the Assistant Secretary for Export Administration, Bureau of Industry and Security, Department of Commerce, transmitting, pursuant to law, the report of a rule entitled ''Temporary General License: Extension of Validity'' (RIN0694–AG82) received in the Office of the President of the Senate on November 28, 2016; to the Committee on Banking, Housing, and Urban Affairs.

EC–7704. A communication from the Associate General Counsel for Legislation and

Regulations, Office of Community Planning and Development, Department of Housing and Urban Development, transmitting, pursuant to law, the report of a rule entitled ''Equal Access to Housing in HUD's Native American and Native Hawaiian Programs—Regardless of Sexual Orientation of Gender Identity'' (RIN2506–AC40) received in the Office of the President of the Senate on November 28, 2016; to the Committee on Banking, Housing, and Urban Affairs.

EC–7705. A communication from the Regulations Coordinator, Centers for Medicare and Medicaid Services, Department of Health and Human Services, transmitting, pursuant to law, the report of a rule entitled ''Medicaid Program: Final FY 2014 and Preliminary FY 2016 Disproportionate Share Hospital allotments, and Final FY 2014 and Preliminary FY 2016 Institutions for Mental Diseases Disproportionate Share Hospital Limits'' ((RIN0938–ZB30) (CMS–2401-N)) received in the Office of the President of the Senate on November 16, 2016; to the Committee on Finance.

EC–7706. A communication from the Chief of the Publications and Regulations Branch, Internal Revenue Service, Department of the Treasury, transmitting, pursuant to law, the report of a rule entitled ''United States Property Held by Controlled Foreign Corporations in Transactions Involving Partnerships; Rents and Royalties Derived in the Active Conduct of a Trade or Business'' ((RIN1545–BJ48) (TD 9792)) received in the Office of the President of the Senate on November 15, 2016; to the Committee on Finance.

EC–7707. A communication from the Chief of the Publications and Regulations Branch, Internal Revenue Service, Department of the Treasury, transmitting, pursuant to law, the report of a rule entitled ''Transaction of Interest—Section 831(b) Micro-Captive Transactions'' (Notice 2016–66) received in the Office of the President of the Senate on November 15, 2016; to the Committee on Finance.

EC–7708. A communication from the Chief of the Publications and Regulations Branch, Internal Revenue Service, Department of the Treasury, transmitting, pursuant to law, the report of a rule entitled ''Medicaid and Children's Health Insurance Programs: Eligibility Notices, Fair Hearing and Appeal Processes for Medicaid and Other Provisions Related to Eligibility and Enrollment for Medicaid and CHIP'' ((RIN0938–AS27) (CMS–2334-F2)) received in the Office of the President of the Senate on November 28, 2016; to the Committee on Finance.

EC–7709. A communication from the Assistant Secretary, Bureau of Legislative Affairs, Department of State, transmitting, pursuant to law, a report relative to a waiver of section 1003 of Public Law 100–204 regarding the Palestine Liberation Organization Office; to the Committee on Foreign Relations.

EC–7710. A communication from the Assistant Secretary, Legislative Affairs, Department of State, transmitting, pursuant to law, the report of a rule entitled ''Amendment to the International Traffic in Arms Regulations: Revision of U.S. Munitions List Categories VIII and XIX'' (RIN1400–AD89) received in the Office of the President of the Senate on November 15, 2016; to the Committee on Foreign Relations.

EC–7711. A communication from the Assistant Legal Adviser for Treaty Affairs, Department of State, transmitting, pursuant to the Case-Zablocki Act, 1 U.S.C. 112b, as amended, the report of the texts and background statements of international agreements, other than treaties (List 2016–0161—2016–0168); to the Committee on Foreign Relations.

EC–7712. A communication from the Assistant Secretary for Occupational Safety and Health, Department of Labor, transmitting, pursuant to law, the report of a rule entitled "Walking-Working Surfaces and Personal Protective Equipment (Fall Protection Systems)" (RIN1218–AB80) received during adjournment of the Senate in the Office of the President of the Senate on November 18, 2016; to the Committee on Health, Education, Labor, and Pensions.

EC–7713. A communication from the Assistant General Counsel for Regulatory Affairs, Pension Benefit Guaranty Corporation, transmitting, pursuant to law, the report of a rule entitled "Benefits Payable in Terminated Single-Employer Plans; Interest Assumptions for Paying Benefits" (29 CFR Part 4022) received in the Office of the President of the Senate on November 28, 2016; to the Committee on Health, Education, Labor, and Pensions.

EC–7714. A communication from the President and CEO, Inter-American Foundation, transmitting, pursuant to law, the Foundation's fiscal year 2016 Annual Management Report; to the Committee on Homeland Security and Governmental Affairs.

EC–7715. A communication from the Secretary of the Treasury, transmitting, pursuant to law, the Agency Financial Report for fiscal year 2016; to the Committee on Homeland Security and Governmental Affairs.

EC–7716. A communication from the Chair of the Securities and Exchange Commission, transmitting, pursuant to law, the Semiannual Report of the Inspector General and a Management Report for the period from April 1, 2016 through September 30, 2016; to the Committee on Homeland Security and Governmental Affairs.

EC–7717. A communication from the Staff Director, U.S. Commission on Civil Rights, transmitting, pursuant to law, the Commission's Performance and Accountability Report for fiscal year 2016; to the Committee on Homeland Security and Governmental Affairs.

EC–7718. A communication from the Chairman, National Mediation Board, transmitting, pursuant to law, the Board's Annual Performance and Accountability Report for fiscal year 2016; to the Committee on Homeland Security and Governmental Affairs.

EC–7719. A communication from the Chief of the Border Security Regulations Branch, Customs and Border Protection, Department of Homeland Security, transmitting, pursuant to law, the report of a rule entitled "The U.S. Asia-Pacific Economic Cooperation Business Travel Card Program" ((RIN1651–AB01) (CBP Dec. 16–20)) received during adjournment of the Senate in the Office of the President of the Senate on November 21, 2016; to the Committee on Homeland Security and Governmental Affairs.

EC–7720. A communication from the Assistant Secretary for Legislative Affairs, Department of Homeland Security, transmitting proposed legislation entitled "U.S. Immigration and Customs Enforcement Pay Reform Act of 2016"; to the Committee on Homeland Security and Governmental Affairs.

EC–7721. A communication from the President and CEO, Inter-American Foundation, transmitting, pursuant to law, the Foundation's fiscal year 2016 Annual Management Report; to the Committee on Homeland Security and Governmental Affairs.

EC–7722. A communication from the Director, Office of Government Ethics, transmit-

ting, pursuant to law, the report of a rule entitled "Executive Branch Ethics Program Amendments'" (RIN3209–AA42) received in the Office of the President of the Senate on November 17, 2016; to the Committee on Homeland Security and Governmental Affairs.

EC–7723. A communication from the Senior Procurement Executive, Office of Acquisition Policy, General Services Administration, transmitting, pursuant to law, the report of a rule entitled "Federal Acquisition Regulation; Technical Amendments" (FAC 2005–92) received during adjournment of the Senate in the Office of the President of the Senate on November 21, 2016; to the Committee on Homeland Security and Governmental Affairs.

EC–7724. A communication from the Senior Procurement Executive, Office of Acquisition Policy, General Services Administration, transmitting, pursuant to law, the report of a rule entitled "Federal Acquisition Regulation: Removal of Regulations Relating to Telegraphic Communication" ((RIN9000–AN23) (FAC 2005–92)) received during adjournment of the Senate in the Office of the President of the Senate on November 21, 2016; to the Committee on Homeland Security and Governmental Affairs.

EC–7725. A communication from the Senior Procurement Executive, Office of Acquisition Policy, General Services Administration, transmitting, pursuant to law, the report of a rule entitled "Federal Acquisition Regulation; Public Disclosure of Greenhouse Gas Emissions and Reduction Goals-Representation" ((RIN9000–AM90) (FAC 2005–92)) received during adjournment of the Senate in the Office of the President of the Senate on November 21, 2016; to the Committee on Homeland Security and Governmental Affairs.

EC–7726. A communication from the Senior Procurement Executive, Office of Acquisition Policy, General Services Administration, transmitting, pursuant to law, the report of a rule entitled "Federal Acquisition Regulation; Federal Acquisition Circular 2005–92; Introduction" (FAC 2005–92) received during adjournment of the Senate in the Office of the President of the Senate on November 21, 2016; to the Committee on Homeland Security and Governmental Affairs.

EC–7727. A communication from the Chairman, U.S. Nuclear Regulatory Commission, transmitting, pursuant to law, the Commission's Performance and Accountability Report for fiscal year 2016; to the Committee on Homeland Security and Governmental Affairs.

EC–7728. A communication from the Chair, Securities and Exchange Commission, transmitting, pursuant to law, the Commission's Agency Financial Report for fiscal year 2016 and the Uniform Resource Locator (URL) for the report; to the Committee on Homeland Security and Governmental Affairs.

EC–7729. A communication from the Administrator, U.S. Agency for International Development, transmitting, pursuant to law, the Agency's fiscal year 2016 Agency Financial Report and the Uniform Resource Locator (URL) for the report; to the Committee on Homeland Security and Governmental Affairs.

EC–7730. A communication from the Administrator of the U.S. Agency for International Development, transmitting, pursuant to law, the Semiannual Report of the Inspector General for the period from April 1, 2016 through September 30, 2016; to the Committee on Homeland Security and Governmental Affairs.

EC–7731. A communication from the Chairman, Federal Maritime Commission, transmitting, pursuant to law, the Commission's Performance and Accountability Report for fiscal year 2016; to the Committee on Homeland Security and Governmental Affairs.

EC–7732. A communication from the Chairman, Merit Systems Protection Board, transmitting, pursuant to law, the Board's Agency Financial Report for fiscal year 2016; to the Committee on Homeland Security and Governmental Affairs.

EC–7733. A communication from the Chairwoman of the Federal Trade Commission, transmitting, pursuant to law, the Commission's fiscal year 2016 Agency Financial Report and the Uniform Resource Locator (URL) for the report; to the Committee on Homeland Security and Governmental Affairs.

EC–7734. A communication from the Chairman, U.S. Nuclear Regulatory Commission, transmitting, pursuant to law, the Commission's Performance and Accountability Report for fiscal year 2016; to the Committee on Homeland Security and Governmental Affairs.

EC–7735. A communication from the Under Secretary of Defense (Comptroller), transmitting, pursuant to law, a report of a delay in submission of the Department of Defense Agency Financial Report (AFR) for fiscal year 2016; to the Committee on Homeland Security and Governmental Affairs.

EC–7736. A communication from the Staff Director, U.S. Commission on Civil Rights, transmitting, pursuant to law, the Commission's Performance and Accountability Report for fiscal year 2016; to the Committee on Homeland Security and Governmental Affairs.

EC–7737. A communication from the Chairman, National Mediation Board, transmitting, pursuant to law, the Board's Annual Performance and Accountability Report for fiscal year 2016; to the Committee on Homeland Security and Governmental Affairs.

EC–7738. A communication from the Chief of the Publications and Regulations Branch, Internal Revenue Service, Department of the Treasury, transmitting, pursuant to law, the report of a rule entitled "Extension of Import Restrictions Imposed on Certain Archaeological and Ethnological Material from Greece" (RIN1515–AE18) received during adjournment of the Senate in the Office of the President of the Senate on November 21, 2016; to the Committee on Finance.

EC–7739. A communication from the Senior Procurement Executive, Office of Acquisition Policy, General Services Administration, transmitting, pursuant to law, the report of a rule entitled "Federal Acquisition Regulation; Federal Acquisition Circular 2005–92; Small Entity Compliance Guide" (FAC 2005–92) received during adjournment of the Senate in the Office of the President of the Senate on November 21, 2016; to the Committee on Homeland Security and Governmental Affairs.

EC–7740. A communication from the Chief of the Regulatory Coordination Division, Citizenship and Immigration Services, Department of Homeland Security, transmitting, pursuant to law, the report of a rule entitled "Retention of EB–1, EB–2, and EB–3 Immigrant Workers and Program Improvements Affecting High-Skilled Nonimmigrant Workers" (RIN1615–AC05) received during adjournment of the Senate in the Office of the President of the Senate on November 18, 2016; to the Committee on the Judiciary.

EC–7741. A communication from the Deputy General Counsel, Office of Financial Assistance, Small Business Administration, transmitting, pursuant to law, the report of a rule entitled "Debt Refinancing in 504 Loan Program" (RIN3245–AG79) received in the Office of the President of the Senate on November 28, 2016; to the Committee on Small Business and Entrepreneurship.

EC–7742. A communication from the Management and Program Analyst, Federal Aviation Administration, Department of Transportation, transmitting, pursuant to law, the report of a rule entitled "Airworthiness Directives; Airbus Airplanes" ((RIN2120–AA64) (Docket No. FAA–2016–5589)) received in the Office of the President of the Senate on November 17, 2016; to the Committee on Commerce, Science, and Transportation.

EC–7743. A communication from the Management and Program Analyst, Federal Aviation Administration, Department of Transportation, transmitting, pursuant to law, the report of a rule entitled "Airworthiness Directives; Airbus Airplanes" ((RIN2120–AA64) (Docket No. FAA–2016–0465)) received in the Office of the President of the Senate on November 17, 2016; to the Committee on Commerce, Science, and Transportation.

EC–7744. A communication from the Management and Program Analyst, Federal Aviation Administration, Department of Transportation, transmitting, pursuant to law, the report of a rule entitled "Airworthiness Directives; Bombardier, Inc. Airplanes" ((RIN2120–AA64) (Docket No. FAA–2015–8464)) received in the Office of the President of the Senate on November 17, 2016; to the Committee on Commerce, Science, and Transportation.

EC–7745. A communication from the Management and Program Analyst, Federal Aviation Administration, Department of Transportation, transmitting, pursuant to law, the report of a rule entitled "Airworthiness Directives; Airbus Helicopters Deutschland GmbH (Previously Eurocopter Deutschland GmbH) (Airbus Helicopters) Helicopters" ((RIN2120–AA64) (Docket No. FAA–2014–0578)) received in the Office of the President of the Senate on November 17, 2016; to the Committee on Commerce, Science, and Transportation.

EC–7746. A communication from the Management and Program Analyst, Federal Aviation Administration, Department of Transportation, transmitting, pursuant to law, the report of a rule entitled "Airworthiness Directives; Airbus Helicopters Deutschland GmbH (Previously Eurocopter Deutschland GmbH) (Airbus Helicopters) Helicopters" ((RIN2120–AA64) (Docket No. FAA–2016–5306)) received in the Office of the President of the Senate on November 17, 2016; to the Committee on Commerce, Science, and Transportation.

EC–7747. A communication from the Management and Program Analyst, Federal Aviation Administration, Department of Transportation, transmitting, pursuant to law, the report of a rule entitled "Airworthiness Directives; The Boeing Company Airplanes" ((RIN2120–AA64) (Docket No. FAA–2015–6538)) received in the Office of the President of the Senate on November 17, 2016; to the Committee on Commerce, Science, and Transportation.

EC–7748. A communication from the Management and Program Analyst, Federal Aviation Administration, Department of Transportation, transmitting, pursuant to law, the report of a rule entitled "Airworthiness Directives; Bell Helicopter Textron Canada Helicopters" ((RIN2120–AA64) (Docket No. FAA–2016–9144)) received in the Office of the President of the Senate on November 15, 2016; to the Committee on Commerce, Science, and Transportation.

EC–7749. A communication from the Management and Program Analyst, Federal Aviation Administration, Department of Transportation, transmitting, pursuant to law, the report of a rule entitled "Airworthiness Directives; Diamond Aircraft Industries GmbH Airplanes" ((RIN2120–AA64) (Docket No. FAA–2016–9318)) received in the Office of the President of the Senate on November 17, 2016; to the Committee on Commerce, Science, and Transportation.

EC–7750. A communication from the Management and Program Analyst, Federal Aviation Administration, Department of Transportation, transmitting, pursuant to law, the report of a rule entitled "Airworthiness Directives; Embraer S.A. Airplanes" ((RIN2120–AA64) (Docket No. FAA–2016–8160)) received in the Office of the President of the Senate on November 17, 2016; to the Committee on Commerce, Science, and Transportation.

EC–7751. A communication from the Management and Program Analyst, Federal Aviation Administration, Department of Transportation, transmitting, pursuant to law, the report of a rule entitled "Airworthiness Directives; Honeywell International Inc. Turboprop Engines" ((RIN2120–AA64) (Docket No. FAA–2006–23706)) received in the Office of the President of the Senate on November 17, 2016; to the Committee on Commerce, Science, and Transportation.

EC–7752. A communication from the Management and Program Analyst, Federal Aviation Administration, Department of Transportation, transmitting, pursuant to law, the report of a rule entitled "Airworthiness Directives; Pratt and Whitney Division Turbofan Engines" ((RIN2120–AA64) (Docket No. FAA–2016–5423)) received in the Office of the President of the Senate on November 17, 2016; to the Committee on Commerce, Science, and Transportation.

EC–7753. A communication from the Management and Program Analyst, Federal Aviation Administration, Department of Transportation, transmitting, pursuant to law, the report of a rule entitled "Airworthiness Directives; Schempp-Hirth Flugzeugbau GmbH Gliders" ((RIN2120–AA64) (Docket No. FAA–2016–6123)) received in the Office of the President of the Senate on November 17, 2016; to the Committee on Commerce, Science, and Transportation.

EC–7754. A communication from the Management and Program Analyst, Federal Aviation Administration, Department of Transportation, transmitting, pursuant to law, the report of a rule entitled "Airworthiness Directives; Turbomeca S.A. Turboshaft Engines" ((RIN2120–AA64) (Docket No. FAA–2016–6990)) received in the Office of the President of the Senate on November 17, 2016; to the Committee on Commerce, Science, and Transportation.

EC–7755. A communication from the Management and Program Analyst, Federal Aviation Administration, Department of Transportation, transmitting, pursuant to law, the report of a rule entitled "Airworthiness Directives; Engine Alliance Turbofan Engines" ((RIN2120–AA64) (Docket No. FAA–2012–1293)) received in the Office of the President of the Senate on November 17, 2016; to the Committee on Commerce, Science, and Transportation.

EC–7756. A communication from the Management and Program Analyst, Federal Aviation Administration, Department of Transportation, transmitting, pursuant to law, the report of a rule entitled "Prohibition Against Certain Flights in the Simferopol (UKFV) and Dniproptrovsk (UKDV)

Flight Information Regions (FIRs)" ((RIN2120–AK92) (Docket No. FAA–2014–0225)) received in the Office of the President of the Senate on November 17, 2016; to the Committee on Commerce, Science, and Transportation.

EC–7757. A communication from the Management and Program Analyst, Federal Aviation Administration, Department of Transportation, transmitting, pursuant to law, the report of a rule entitled "Airworthiness Directives; Bell Helicopter Textron" ((RIN2120–AA64) (Docket No. FAA–2015–3821)) received in the Office of the President of the Senate on November 17, 2016; to the Committee on Commerce, Science, and Transportation.

EC–7758. A communication from the Trial Attorney, Office of Aviation Enforcement and Proceedings, Department of Transportation, transmitting, pursuant to law, a rule entitled "Organization and Delegation of Powers and Duties in the Transportation Acquisition Regulation" (RIN2105–AE41) received in the Office of the President of the Senate on November 17, 2016; to the Committee on Commerce, Science, and Transportation.

EC–7759. A communication from the Trial Attorney, Office of Aviation Enforcement and Proceedings, Department of Transportation, transmitting, pursuant to law, a rule entitled "Enhancing Airline Passenger Protections III" (RIN2105–AE11) received in the Office of the President of the Senate on November 17, 2016; to the Committee on Commerce, Science, and Transportation.

EC–7760. A communication from the Management and Program Analyst, Federal Aviation Administration, Department of Transportation, transmitting, pursuant to law, the report of a rule entitled "Amendment of Class E Airspace; Miles City, MT" ((RIN2120–AA66) (Docket No. FAA–2016–7046)) received in the Office of the President of the Senate on November 17, 2016; to the Committee on Commerce, Science, and Transportation.

EC–7761. A communication from the Management and Program Analyst, Federal Aviation Administration, Department of Transportation, transmitting, pursuant to law, the report of a rule entitled "Amendment of Class D and Class E Airspace; Falmouth, MA" ((RIN2120–AA66) (Docket No. FAA–2016–5444)) received in the Office of the President of the Senate on November 17, 2016; to the Committee on Commerce, Science, and Transportation.

EC–7762. A communication from the Management and Program Analyst, Federal Aviation Administration, Department of Transportation, transmitting, pursuant to law, the report of a rule entitled "Amendment of Class D and Class E Airspace; Hagerstown, MD" ((RIN2120–AA66) (Docket No. FAA–2015–4513)) received in the Office of the President of the Senate on November 17, 2016; to the Committee on Commerce, Science, and Transportation.

EC–7763. A communication from the Management and Program Analyst, Federal Aviation Administration, Department of Transportation, transmitting, pursuant to law, the report of a rule entitled "Standard Instrument Approach Procedures, and Takeoff Minimums and Obstacle Departure Procedures; Miscellaneous Amendments (43); Amdt. No. 3716" (RIN2120–AA65) received in the Office of the President of the Senate on November 17, 2016; to the Committee on Commerce, Science, and Transportation.

EC–7764. A communication from the Management and Program Analyst, Federal

Aviation Administration, Department of Transportation, transmitting, pursuant to law, the report of a rule entitled "Standard Instrument Approach Procedures, and Take-off Minimums and Obstacle Departure Procedures; Miscellaneous Amendments (1); Amdt. No. 3718" (RIN2120–AA65) received in the Office of the President of the Senate on November 17, 2016; to the Committee on Commerce, Science, and Transportation.

EC–7765. A communication from the Management and Program Analyst, Federal Aviation Administration, Department of Transportation, transmitting, pursuant to law, the report of a rule entitled "Standard Instrument Approach Procedures, and Take-off Minimums and Obstacle Departure Procedures; Miscellaneous Amendments (233); Amdt. No. 371" (RIN2120–AA65) received in the Office of the President of the Senate on November 17, 2016; to the Committee on Commerce, Science, and Transportation.

EC–7766. A communication from the Management and Program Analyst, Federal Aviation Administration, Department of Transportation, transmitting, pursuant to law, the report of a rule entitled "Standard Instrument Approach Procedures, and Take-off Minimums and Obstacle Departure Procedures; Miscellaneous Amendments (85); Amdt. No. 3715" (RIN2120–AA65) received in the Office of the President of the Senate on November 17, 2016; to the Committee on Commerce, Science, and Transportation.

PETITIONS AND MEMORIALS

The following petition or memorial was laid before the Senate and was referred or ordered to lie on the table as indicated:

POM–255. A joint resolution adopted by the Legislature of the State of South Dakota making formal application to the United States Congress to call an Article V convention of the states for the sole purpose of proposing a federal balanced budget amendment to the United States Constitution; to the Committee on the Judiciary.

HOUSE JOINT RESOLUTION NO. 1001

Whereas, the Legislature of the State of South Dakota hereby applies to Congress, under the provisions of Article V of the Constitution of the United States, for the calling of a convention of the states limited to proposing an amendment to the Constitution of the United States requiring that in the absence of a national emergency, the total of all federal appropriations made by Congress for any fiscal year may not exceed the total of all estimated federal revenues for that fiscal year, together with any related and appropriate fiscal restraints; and

Whereas, this application constitutes a continuing application in accordance with Article V of the Constitution of the United States until the legislatures of at least two-thirds of the several states have made applications on the same subject. It supersedes all previous applications by this Legislature on the same subject: Now, therefore, be it

Resolved, by the House of Representatives of the Ninetieth Legislature of the State of South Dakota, the Senate concurring therein, That the State of South Dakota does hereby apply to the Congress of the United States to call an amendment convention pursuant to Article V of the United States Constitution limited to proposing an amendment to the United States Constitution requiring that in the absence of a national emergency, the total of all federal appropriations made by Congress for any fiscal year may not exceed the total of all estimated federal revenues for that fiscal year, together with any related and appropriate fiscal restraints; and be it further

Resolved, This application is to be considered as covering the same subject matter as the presently outstanding balanced budget applications from other states, including previously-adopted applications from Alabama, Alaska, Arkansas, Colorado, Delaware, Florida, Georgia, Indiana, Iowa, Kansas, Louisiana, Maryland, Michigan, Mississippi, Missouri, Nebraska, Nevada, New Hampshire, New Mexico, North Carolina, Ohio, Pennsylvania, Tennessee, and Texas. This application shall be aggregated with same for the purpose of attaining the two-thirds of states necessary to require the calling of a convention for proposing a balanced budget amendment but may not be aggregated with any applications on any other subject; and be it further

Resolved, That the other states be encouraged to make similar applications for an amendment convention pursuant to Article V of the Constitution of the United States; and be it further

Resolved, That this application constitutes a continuing application for such amendment convention pursuant to Article V of the Constitution of the United States until the legislatures of two-thirds of the states have made such applications and such convention has been called by the Congress of the United States; and be it further

Resolved, That the secretary of state transmit copies of this resolution to the President of the United States, the Speaker and the Clerk of the United States House of Representatives, the President and the Clerk of the United States Senate, the members of the South Dakota congressional delegation, and the legislatures of each of the several states, attesting the adoption of this resolution by the Legislature of the State of South Dakota.

INTRODUCTION OF BILLS AND JOINT RESOLUTIONS

The following bills and joint resolutions were introduced, read the first and second times by unanimous consent, and referred as indicated:

By Mr. JOHNSON:

S. 3483. A bill to amend chapter 8 of title 5, United States Code, to provide for en bloc consideration in resolutions of disapproval for "midnight rules", and for other purposes; to the Committee on Homeland Security and Governmental Affairs.

By Mr. TESTER:

S. 3484. A bill to establish an advisory committee to issue nonbinding governmentwide guidelines on making public information available on the Internet, to require publicly available Government information held by the executive branch to be made available on the Internet, to express the sense of Congress that publicly available information held by the legislative and judicial branches should be available on the Internet, and for other purposes; to the Committee on Homeland Security and Governmental Affairs.

SUBMISSION OF CONCURRENT AND SENATE RESOLUTIONS

The following concurrent resolutions and Senate resolutions were read, and referred (or acted upon), as indicated:

By Mr. COONS (for himself and Mr. RUBIO):

S. Res. 620. A resolution reaffirming the United States-Argentina partnership and recognizing Argentina's economic reforms; to the Committee on Foreign Relations.

By Mr. WYDEN (for himself, Ms. BALDWIN, Mr. COONS, Ms. KLOBUCHAR, and Mr. MERKLEY):

S. Res. 621. A resolution designating November 2016 as National Hospice and Palliative Care Month; to the Committee on the Judiciary.

By Mr. BLUNT (for himself, Ms. KLOBUCHAR, Mr. BOOZMAN, Mr. GRASSLEY, Mr. PORTMAN, Mr. GRAHAM, Mr. INHOFE, Mr. DAINES, Mr. MORAN, Mrs. FEINSTEIN, Mr. MARKEY, Mr. HOEVEN, Mr. BENNET, Mrs. FISCHER, Mr. HATCH, Mr. COCHRAN, Mr. LANKFORD, Mr. ROUNDS, Mr. RISCH, Mr. McCAIN, Mr. WICKER, Mr. ENZI, Mr. BOOKER, Mr. PETERS, Mr. CASEY, Mr. TILLIS, Mr. RUBIO, Mr. SCOTT, and Mrs. MURRAY):

S. Res. 622. A resolution expressing support for the goals of National Adoption Day and National Adoption Month by promoting national awareness of adoption and the children awaiting families, celebrating children and families involved in adoption, and encouraging the people of the United States to secure safety, permanency, and well-being, for all children; considered and agreed to.

By Ms. COLLINS (for herself, Ms. MIKULSKI, Mr. BLUMENTHAL, Ms. MURKOWSKI, Mr. TESTER, Mr. WICKER, Mr. WHITEHOUSE, Mr. TOOMEY, Mrs. SHAHEEN, Mr. KIRK, Ms. HIRONO, Mr. ROBERTS, Mr. WYDEN, Mr. INHOFE, Mrs. BOXER, Mr. GARDNER, Mr. COONS, Mr. HATCH, Mr. PETERS, Mr. LANKFORD, Mr. NELSON, Mr. THUNE, Mr. MENENDEZ, Mr. SULLIVAN, Mr. CARPER, Ms. AYOTTE, Ms. BALDWIN, Mr. CRAPO, Mr. HEINRICH, Mr. COTTON, Mr. UDALL, Mr. BLUNT, Mr. CASEY, Mrs. CAPITO, Mr. KING, Mr. ROUNDS, Mr. MARKEY, Mr. BENNET, Mr. FRANKEN, Mr. MANCHIN, and Mr. PERDUE):

S. Res. 623. A resolution recognizing the vital role the Civil Air Patrol has played, and continues to play, in supporting the homeland security and national defense of the United States; considered and agreed to.

By Mr. CARDIN (for himself, Mr. LEAHY, Mr. REID, Mr. DURBIN, Ms. MIKULSKI, Mrs. BOXER, Mr. WYDEN, Mr. REED, Mr. CARPER, Ms. STABENOW, Mr. WHITEHOUSE, Mr. UDALL, Mr. MERKLEY, Mr. BENNET, Mr. FRANKEN, Mr. COONS, Ms. BALDWIN, Mr. MURPHY, Ms. HIRONO, Mr. HEINRICH, Ms. WARREN, Mr. MARKEY, Mr. BOOKER, and Mr. CASEY):

S. Con. Res. 56. A concurrent resolution clarifying any potential misunderstanding as to whether actions taken by President-elect Donald Trump constitute a violation of the Emoluments Clause, and calling on President-elect Trump to divest his interest in, and sever his relationship to, the Trump Organization; to the Committee on Homeland Security and Governmental Affairs.

ADDITIONAL COSPONSORS

S. 298

At the request of Mr. GRASSLEY, the names of the Senator from Vermont (Mr. LEAHY), the Senator from Maine (Ms. COLLINS) and the Senator from Delaware (Mr. CARPER) were added as cosponsors of S. 298, a bill to amend titles XIX and XXI of the Social Security Act to provide States with the option of providing services to children with medically complex conditions under the Medicaid program and Children's Health Insurance Program through a care coordination program focused on improving health outcomes for children with medically complex conditions and lowering costs, and for other purposes.

S. 624

At the request of Mr. BROWN, the name of the Senator from Massachusetts (Ms. WARREN) was added as a cosponsor of S. 624, a bill to amend title XVIII of the Social Security Act to waive coinsurance under Medicare for colorectal cancer screening tests, regardless of whether therapeutic intervention is required during the screening.

S. 849

At the request of Mr. ISAKSON, the name of the Senator from New Hampshire (Mrs. SHAHEEN) was added as a cosponsor of S. 849, a bill to amend the Public Health Service Act to provide for systematic data collection and analysis and epidemiological research regarding Multiple Sclerosis (MS), Parkinson's disease, and other neurological diseases.

S. 979

At the request of Mr. NELSON, the name of the Senator from Wisconsin (Ms. BALDWIN) was added as a cosponsor of S. 979, a bill to amend title 10, United States Code, to repeal the requirement for reduction of survivor annuities under the Survivor Benefit Plan by veterans' dependency and indemnity compensation, and for other purposes.

S. 1476

At the request of Mrs. BOXER, the name of the Senator from Delaware (Mr. COONS) was added as a cosponsor of S. 1476, a bill to require States to report to the Attorney General certain information regarding shooting incidents involving law enforcement officers, and for other purposes.

S. 2126

At the request of Ms. CANTWELL, the name of the Senator from Massachusetts (Mr. MARKEY) was added as a cosponsor of S. 2126, a bill to reauthorize the women's business center program of the Small Business Administration, and for other purposes.

S. 2424

At the request of Mrs. GILLIBRAND, the name of the Senator from Maryland (Mr. CARDIN) was added as a cosponsor of S. 2424, a bill to amend the Public Health Service Act to reauthorize a program for early detection, diagnosis, and treatment regarding deaf and hard-of-hearing newborns, infants, and young children.

S. 2427

At the request of Mr. SCHUMER, the name of the Senator from Minnesota (Mr. FRANKEN) was added as a cosponsor of S. 2427, a bill to prohibit discrimination against individuals with disabilities who need long-term services and supports, and for other purposes.

S. 2551

At the request of Mr. CARDIN, the name of the Senator from Oregon (Mr. WYDEN) was added as a cosponsor of S. 2551, a bill to help prevent acts of genocide and mass atrocities, which threaten national and international security, by enhancing United States civilian capacities to prevent and mitigate such crises.

S. 2680

At the request of Mr. ALEXANDER, the names of the Senator from Ohio (Mr. BROWN) and the Senator from Kansas (Mr. MORAN) were added as cosponsors of S. 2680, a bill to amend the Public Health Service Act to provide comprehensive mental health reform, and for other purposes.

S. 2713

At the request of Mr. ALEXANDER, the name of the Senator from Washington (Mrs. MURRAY) was added as a cosponsor of S. 2713, a bill to provide for the implementation of a Precision Medicine Initiative.

S. 2873

At the request of Mr. HATCH, the name of the Senator from Oklahoma (Mr. INHOFE) was added as a cosponsor of S. 2873, a bill to require studies and reports examining the use of, and opportunities to use, technology-enabled collaborative learning and capacity building models to improve programs of the Department of Health and Human Services, and for other purposes.

S. 2971

At the request of Mr. PORTMAN, the name of the Senator from Ohio (Mr. BROWN) was added as a cosponsor of S. 2971, a bill to authorize the National Urban Search and Rescue Response System.

S. 3065

At the request of Mr. WYDEN, the name of the Senator from Virginia (Mr. KAINE) was added as a cosponsor of S. 3065, a bill to amend parts B and E of title IV of the Social Security Act to invest in funding prevention and family services to help keep children safe and supported at home, to ensure that children in foster care are placed in the least restrictive, most family-like, and appropriate settings, and for other purposes.

S. 3149

At the request of Mr. BROWN, the name of the Senator from New Jersey (Mr. MENENDEZ) was added as a cosponsor of S. 3149, a bill to posthumously award a Congressional Gold Medal to Lawrence Eugene "Larry" Doby in recognition of his achievements and contributions to American major league athletics, civil rights, and the Armed Forces during World War II.

S. 3245

At the request of Mr. MERKLEY, the name of the Senator from Minnesota (Ms. KLOBUCHAR) was added as a cosponsor of S. 3245, a bill to amend title VIII of the Public Health Service Act to extend advanced education nursing grants to support clinical nurse specialist programs, and for other purposes.

S. 3256

At the request of Mr. DURBIN, the name of the Senator from Connecticut (Mr. MURPHY) was added as a cosponsor of S. 3256, a bill to amend the Foreign Assistance Act of 1961 to provide assistance for developing countries to promote quality basic education and to establish the goal of all children in school and learning as an objective of the United States foreign assistance policy, and for other purposes.

S. 3359

At the request of Mr. LEAHY, the names of the Senator from Rhode Island (Mr. WHITEHOUSE), the Senator from Texas (Mr. CORNYN), the Senator from Minnesota (Ms. KLOBUCHAR), the Senator from Utah (Mr. HATCH), the Senator from Delaware (Mr. COONS), the Senator from Connecticut (Mr. BLUMENTHAL), and the Senator from New Hampshire (Ms. AYOTTE) were added as cosponsors of S. 3359, a bill to amend title I of the Omnibus Crime Control and Safe Streets Act of 1968 to authorize grants for heroin and methamphetamine task forces.

S. 3450

At the request of Mr. BROWN, the name of the Senator from New Mexico (Mr. HEINRICH) was added as a cosponsor of S. 3450, a bill to amend the Internal Revenue Code of 1986 to include electric charging of certain vehicles as a qualified transportation fringe benefit excluded from gross income.

S. 3475

At the request of Mr. COONS, the name of the Senator from Vermont (Mr. LEAHY) was added as a cosponsor of S. 3475, a bill to delay the amendments to rule 41 of the Federal Rules of Criminal Procedure.

S. RES. 616

At the request of Mrs. SHAHEEN, the name of the Senator from Michigan (Mr. PETERS) was added as a cosponsor of S. Res. 616, a resolution supporting the goals and ideals of American Diabetes Month.

SUBMITTED RESOLUTIONS

SENATE RESOLUTION 620—REAFFIRMING THE UNITED STATES-ARGENTINA PARTNERSHIP AND RECOGNIZING ARGENTINA'S ECONOMIC REFORMS

Mr. COONS (for himself and Mr. RUBIO) submitted the following resolution; which was referred to the Committee on Foreign Relations:

S. RES. 620

Whereas, on November 22, 2015, the citizens of the Argentine Republic elected Mauricio Macri as their President;

Whereas President Macri has pledged to promote greater national unity, rebuild the economy, combat domestic corruption, strengthen freedom of the press, defend human rights abroad, attract foreign direct investment, return to international credit markets, and reassert Argentina's leadership globally;

Whereas President Macri has emphasized his intention to seek closer ties with the United States and restore the bilateral partnership previously enjoyed by both countries;

Whereas the Argentine Republic is a major non-NATO ally of the United States;

Whereas United States-Argentina relations are historically characterized by comprehensive commercial ties and strong bilateral cooperation on human rights, peacekeeping, science and technology, non-proliferation, and education, as well as on regional and global issues;

Whereas President Barack Obama traveled to Argentina in March 2016 to strengthen engagement on trade and investment, renewable energy, climate change, security, and peacekeeping issues;

Whereas, in an appearance with President Macri at the Casa Rosada in Buenos Aires, President Obama said that "our countries share profound values in common—respect for human rights, for individual freedoms, for democracy, for justice, and for peace";

Whereas the United States Department of the Treasury no longer opposes multilateral development banks lending to Argentina because of the Government of Argentina's "progress on key issues and positive economic policy trajectory";

Whereas President Macri prioritized Argentina resolving its 15-year standoff with private creditors stemming from the 2001–2002 economic crisis;

Whereas the Macri Administration lifted controls on trade, currency, and poultry, enhanced the quality and transparency of government data, and eliminated subsidies on electricity, water, and gas;

Whereas, in April 2016, the Government of Argentina issued $16,500,000,000 in new government bonds and paid $9,300,000,000 to holdout creditors to resolve its default settlements, which facilitated Argentina's return to international financial markets;

Whereas Argentina is Latin America's third largest economy and the International Monetary Fund, in April 2016, claimed the Macri Administration "embarked on an ambitious, much needed transition to remove domestic imbalances and distortions and correct relative prices";

Whereas Secretary of State John Kerry visited Argentina in August 2016 to launch a High-Level Dialogue to develop and sustain cooperation on bilateral, regional, and global challenges, including democratic development and protection of human rights in Latin America; and

Whereas Secretary Kerry, during his visit, stated that "the United States strongly supports President Macri's effort to deepen Argentina's integration with the global economy" and that "our governments will be supporting policies that are aimed at strong, sustainable, and balanced economic growth": Now, therefore, be it

Resolved, That the Senate—

(1) upholds its commitment to the partnership between the United States and Argentina and reaffirms that the Argentine Repub-

lic is a major non-NATO ally of the United States;

(2) encourages the Department of State to coordinate an interagency strategy to increase cooperation with the Government of Argentina on areas of bilateral, regional, and global concern;

(3) commends President Mauricio Macri and his Administration for making far-reaching economic reforms that will benefit the people of Argentina, stimulate economic growth, and deepen Argentina's integration with the global economy;

(4) praises the Government of Argentina for resolving its dispute with international creditors; and

(5) encourages the Government of Argentina to continue to investigate and prosecute those responsible for the 1994 bombing of the Argentine-Israeli Mutual Association (AMIA) in Buenos Aires, as well as the January 2015 death of AMIA special prosecutor Alberto Nisman.

SENATE RESOLUTION 621—DESIGNATING NOVEMBER 2016 AS NATIONAL HOSPICE AND PALLIATIVE CARE MONTH

Mr. WYDEN (for himself, Ms. BALDWIN, Mr. COONS, Ms. KLOBUCHAR, and Mr. MERKLEY) submitted the following resolution; which was referred to the Committee on the Judiciary:

S. RES. 621

Whereas hospice and palliative care services empower individuals to live as fully as possible, surrounded and supported by family and loved ones, despite serious and life-limiting illnesses;

Whereas hospice and palliative care can bring patients and family caregivers high-quality care delivered by an interdisciplinary team of skilled professionals that includes physicians, nurses, social workers, therapists, counselors, health aides, spiritual care providers, and others who make the wishes of each patient and family a priority;

Whereas advance care planning involves an individual making decisions about the health care the individual would want to receive if faced with a serious or life-limiting illness or unable to speak on behalf of the individual;

Whereas hospice and palliative care focus on quality of life through pain management and symptom control, caregiver training and assistance, and emotional and spiritual support, allowing patients to live fully until the end of life, surrounded and supported by loved ones, friends, and committed caregivers;

Whereas every year more than 1,650,000 individuals in the United States living with life-limiting illness, and the families of the individuals, receive care and support from hospice programs in communities throughout the United States;

Whereas more than 430,000 trained volunteers contribute 19,000,000 hours of service to hospice programs annually; and

Whereas hospice and palliative care providers encourage all individuals to learn more about the options of the individuals for care and to share the wishes of the individuals with family, loved ones, and health care professionals: Now, therefore, be it

Resolved, That the Senate—

(1) designates November 2016 as National Hospice and Palliative Care Month; and

(2) encourages the people of the United States—

(A) to increase their understanding and awareness of care at the end of life; and

(B) to observe National Hospice and Palliative Care Month with appropriate activities and programs.

SENATE RESOLUTION 622—EXPRESSING SUPPORT FOR THE GOALS OF NATIONAL ADOPTION DAY AND NATIONAL ADOPTION MONTH BY PROMOTING NATIONAL AWARENESS OF ADOPTION AND THE CHILDREN AWAITING FAMILIES, CELEBRATING CHILDREN AND FAMILIES INVOLVED IN ADOPTION, AND ENCOURAGING THE PEOPLE OF THE UNITED STATES TO SECURE SAFETY, PERMANENCY, AND WELL-BEING, FOR ALL CHILDREN

Mr. BLUNT (for himself, Ms. KLOBUCHAR, Mr. BOOZMAN, Mr. GRASSLEY, Mr. PORTMAN, Mr. GRAHAM, Mr. INHOFE, Mr. DAINES, Mr. MORAN, Mrs. FEINSTEIN, Mr. MARKEY, Mr. HOEVEN, Mr. BENNET, Mrs. FISCHER, Mr. HATCH, Mr. COCHRAN, Mr. LANKFORD, Mr. ROUNDS, Mr. RISCH, Mr. McCAIN, Mr. WICKER, Mr. ENZI, Mr. BOOKER, Mr. PETERS, Mr. CASEY, Mr. TILLIS, Mr. RUBIO, Mr. SCOTT, and Mrs. MURRAY) submitted the following resolution; which was considered and agreed to:

S. RES. 622

Whereas there are millions of unparented children in the world, including 427,910 children in the foster care system in the United States, approximately 111,820 of whom are waiting for families to adopt them;

Whereas 62 percent of the children in foster care in the United States are age 10 or younger;

Whereas the average length of time a child spends in foster care is approximately 2 years;

Whereas for many foster children, the wait for a loving family in which the children are nurtured, comforted, and protected seems endless;

Whereas, in 2015, over 20,000 youth "aged out" of foster care by reaching adulthood without being placed in a permanent home;

Whereas every day, loving and nurturing families are strengthened and expanded when committed and dedicated individuals make an important difference in the life of a child through adoption;

Whereas a 2007 survey conducted by the Dave Thomas Foundation for Adoption demonstrated that although "Americans overwhelmingly support the concept of adoption, and in particular foster care adoption . . . foster care adoptions have not increased significantly over the past 5 years";

Whereas while nearly a quarter of individuals in the United States have considered adoption, a majority of individuals in the United States have misperceptions about the process of adopting children from foster care and the children who are eligible for adoption;

Whereas 50 percent of individuals in the United States believe that children enter the foster care system because of juvenile delinquency, when in reality the vast majority of children who have entered the foster care system were victims of neglect, abandonment, or abuse;

Whereas 39 percent of individuals in the United States believe that foster care adoption is expensive, when in reality there is no substantial cost for adopting from foster care and financial support is available to adoptive parents after the adoption is finalized;

Whereas family reunification, kinship care, and domestic and intercounty adoption promote permanency and stability to a far greater degree than long-term institutionalization or long-term, often disrupted, foster care;

Whereas November is National Adoption Month, and National Adoption Day occurs in November;

Whereas National Adoption Day is a collective national effort to find permanent, loving families for children in the foster care system;

Whereas, since the first National Adoption Day in 2000, nearly 58,500 children have joined permanent families during National Adoption Day; and

Whereas the President traditionally issues an annual proclamation to declare the month of November as National Adoption Month, and National Adoption Day is on November 19, 2016: Now, therefore, be it

Resolved, That the Senate—

(1) supports the goals and ideals of National Adoption Day and National Adoption Month;

(2) recognizes that every child should have a permanent and loving family; and

(3) encourages the people of the United States to consider adoption during the month of November and throughout the year.

SENATE RESOLUTION 623—RECOGNIZING THE VITAL ROLE THE CIVIL AIR PATROL HAS PLAYED, AND CONTINUES TO PLAY, IN SUPPORTING THE HOMELAND SECURITY AND NATIONAL DEFENSE OF THE UNITED STATES

Ms. COLLINS (for herself, Ms. MIKULSKI, Mr. BLUMENTHAL, Ms. MURKOWSKI, Mr. TESTER, Mr. WICKER, Mr. WHITEHOUSE, Mr. TOOMEY, Mrs. SHAHEEN, Mr. KIRK, Ms. HIRONO, Mr. ROBERTS, Mr. WYDEN, Mr. INHOFE, Mrs. BOXER, Mr. GARDNER, Mr. COONS, Mr. HATCH, Mr. PETERS, Mr. LANKFORD, Mr. NELSON, Mr. THUNE, Mr. MENENDEZ, Mr. SULLIVAN, Mr. CARPER, Ms. AYOTTE, Ms. BALDWIN, Mr. CRAPO, Mr. HEINRICH, Mr. COTTON, Mr. UDALL, Mr. BLUNT, Mr. CASEY, Mrs. CAPITO, Mr. KING, Mr. ROUNDS, Mr. MARKEY, Mr. BENNET, Mr. FRANKEN, Mr. MANCHIN, and Mr. PERDUE) submitted the following resolution; which was considered and agreed to:

S. RES. 623

Whereas, on December 1, 1941, a new civilian defense organization known as the Civil Air Patrol was founded, which was to rely on volunteer civilian aviators who would fly in support of the homeland security of the United States;

Whereas with the attack on Pearl Harbor 6 days later and the entry of the United States into World War II, the Civil Air Patrol would find itself serving the United States in ways that were not imagined at the time of the conception of the Civil Air Patrol;

Whereas the Civil Air Patrol initially engaged in coastal patrol operations that were considered critical to the United States war effort, piloting aircraft that in total flew 24,000,000 miles over 18 months, reporting 173 possible enemy submarines, and dropping 82 bombs or depth charges;

Whereas Civil Air Patrol civilian volunteers flew privately owned light aircraft armed with military bombs at the expense of the volunteers, often at low altitude, in bad weather, and up to 60 miles from shore;

Whereas Civil Air Patrol civilian volunteers undertook other vital World War II missions nationwide, which included border patrols, search and rescue operations, courier and cargo services, and air defense and pilot training;

Whereas, unlike many organizations at the time, the Civil Air Patrol welcomed women into its ranks to fly for the Civil Air Patrol, with approximately one-half of the women later joining the Women's Airforce Service Pilots (commonly known as "WASP") after having first flown with the Civil Air Patrol;

Whereas the Civil Air Patrol was open to all pilots interested in flying for the Civil Air Patrol, which allowed African-Americans an opportunity to serve and fly for the United States well before the adoption of the integrated Armed Forces;

Whereas, in 2016, the Civil Air Patrol continues its critical mission in service to the United States, now as a vital partner for the Air Force, serving as the auxiliary force, and, since 2015, as an official component of the total force;

Whereas the Civil Air Patrol remains one of the premier inland search and rescue organizations of the United States, and was credited with saving the lives of 69 individuals through search and rescue operations in 2015;

Whereas the Civil Air Patrol continues to fulfill many other vital missions, including helping train interceptor pilots and unmanned aerial vehicle operators under realistic conditions, aerial observation missions, counterdrug operations, disaster relief support, live organ transport, aerospace education, cadet programs, and Reserve Officer Training Corps orientation flights;

Whereas the continued work of the all-volunteer force of the Civil Air Patrol offers vital support to homeland security and defense missions; and

Whereas the weekly youth and aerospace education programs of the Civil Air Patrol continue to introduce young students to the field of aviation and instill within the students the values of national service and personal responsibility: Now, therefore, be it

Resolved, That the Senate—

(1) applauds the Civil Air Patrol for 75 years of continuous service in times of peace and war;

(2) recognizes the critical emergency services, training support, and mission capabilities that the Civil Air Patrol offers State and national homeland security agencies as well as the United States Armed Forces; and

(3) commends the more than 23,500 youth and 32,500 adult volunteers of the Civil Air Patrol, who hail from a range of professions and across the United States, and dedicate their time to the service of their communities and the United States.

SENATE CONCURRENT RESOLUTION 56—CLARIFYING ANY POTENTIAL MISUNDERSTANDING AS TO WHETHER ACTIONS TAKEN BY PRESIDENT-ELECT DONALD TRUMP CONSTITUTE A VIOLATION OF THE EMOLUMENTS CLAUSE, AND CALLING ON PRESIDENT-ELECT TRUMP TO DIVEST HIS INTEREST IN, AND SEVER HIS RELATIONSHIP TO, THE TRUMP ORGANIZATION

Mr. CARDIN (for himself, Mr. LEAHY, Mr. REID, Mr. DURBIN, Ms. MIKULSKI, Mrs. BOXER, Mr. WYDEN, Mr. REED, Mr. CARPER, Ms. STABENOW, Mr. WHITEHOUSE, Mr. UDALL, Mr. MERKLEY, Mr. BENNET, Mr. FRANKEN, Mr. COONS, Ms. BALDWIN, Mr. MURPHY, Ms. HIRONO, Mr. HEINRICH, Ms. WARREN, Mr. MARKEY, Mr. BOOKER, and Mr. CASEY) submitted the following concurrent resolution; which was referred to the Committee on Homeland Security and Governmental Affairs:

S. CON. RES. 56

Whereas article I, section 9, clause 8 of the United States Constitution (commonly known as the "Emoluments Clause") declares, "No title of Nobility shall be granted by the United States: And no Person holding any Office of Profit or Trust under them, shall, without the Consent of the Congress, accept of any present, Emolument, Office, or Title, of any kind whatever, from any King, Prince, or foreign State.";

Whereas, according to the remarks of Governor Edmund Randolph at the 1787 Constitutional Convention, the Emoluments Clause "was thought proper, in order to exclude corruption and foreign influence, to prohibit any one in office from receiving or holding any emoluments from foreign states";

Whereas the issue of foreign corruption greatly concerned the Founding Fathers of the United States, such that Alexander Hamilton in Federalist No. 22 wrote, "In republics, persons elevated from the mass of the community, by the suffrages of their fellow-citizens, to stations of great pre-eminence and power, may find compensations for betraying their trust, which, to any but minds animated and guided by superior virtue, may appear to exceed the proportion of interest they have in the common stock, and to overbalance the obligations of duty. Hence it is that history furnishes us with so many mortifying examples of the prevalency of foreign corruption in republican governments.";

Whereas the President of the United States is the head of the executive branch of the Federal Government and is expected to have undivided loyalty to the United States, and clearly occupies an "office of profit or trust" within the meaning of article I, section 9, clause 8 of the Constitution, according to the Office of Legal Counsel of the Department of Justice;

Whereas the Office of Legal Counsel of the Department of Justice opined in 2009 that corporations owned or controlled by a foreign government are presumptively foreign states under the Emoluments Clause;

Whereas President-elect Donald J. Trump has a business network, the Trump Organization, that has financial interests around the world and negotiates and concludes transactions with foreign states and entities that are extensions of foreign states;

Whereas Michael Cohen, an attorney for Donald J. Trump and the Trump Organization, has stated that the Trump Organization would be placed into a "blind trust" managed by Donald Trump's children, Donald Trump Jr., Ivanka Trump, and Eric Trump;

Whereas the very nature of a "blind trust" is such that the official will have no control over, will receive no communications about, and will have no knowledge of the identity of the specific assets held in the trust, and that the manager of the trust is independent of the owner, and as such the arrangement proposed by Mr. Cohen is not a blind trust;

Whereas Presidents Ronald Reagan, George H. W. Bush, William J. Clinton, and George W. Bush have set the precedent of using true blind trusts, in which their holdings were liquidated and placed in new investments unknown to them by an independent trustee who managed them free of familial bias;

Whereas the intermingling of the business of the Trump Organization and the work of government has the potential to constitute the foreign corruption so feared by the Founding Fathers and betray the trust of America's citizens;

Whereas the intent of this resolution is to prevent any potential misunderstanding or crisis with regards to whether the actions of Donald J. Trump as President of the United States will violate the Emoluments Clause of the Constitution, Federal law, or fundamental principles of ethics; and

Whereas Congress has an institutional, constitutional obligation to ensure that the President of the United States does not violate the Emoluments Clause and is discharging the obligations of office based on the national interest, not based on personal interest: Now, therefore, be it

Resolved by the Senate (the House of Representatives concurring), That Congress—

(1) calls upon President-elect Donald J. Trump to follow the precedent established by prior presidents and convert his assets to simple, conflict-free holdings, adopt blind trusts managed by an independent trustee with no relationship to Donald J. Trump or his businesses, or take other equivalent measures, in order to ensure compliance with the Emoluments Clause of the United States Constitution;

(2) calls upon President-elect Donald J. Trump not to use the powers or opportunities of his position as President-elect or President of the United States for any purpose related to the Trump Organization; and

(3) regards, in the absence of such actions outlined in paragraph (1) or specific authorization by Congress, dealings that Donald J. Trump, as President of the United States, may have through his companies with foreign governments or entities owned or controlled by foreign governments as potential violations of the Emoluments Clause.

Mr. CARDIN. Mr. President, I come to the floor to speak on behalf of a resolution I will submit today on the enrollment clause, which seems to uphold the values and strictures of one of our Nation's most sacred documents—the Constitution itself.

The Founding Fathers were clear in their belief that any Federal officeholder in the United States must never be put in a position where he or she could be influenced by a foreign governmental actor. Article 1, section 9, clause 8 of the U.S. Constitution, known as the emolument clause, declares that "no title of nobility shall

be granted by the United States: And no person holding any office of profit or trust under them, shall, without the consent of the Congress, accept of any present, emolument, office, or title, of any kind whatever, from any king, prince, or foreign state."

Longstanding precedent has made it plain the President of the United States, as the head of the executive branch of government, clearly occupies an office of profit or trust. As such, the emolument clause clearly applies to and constrains whoever holds the Oval Office of the Presidency.

For those who claim to value a strict interpretation of the Constitution and who place upholding the Constitution above partisan politics, the unambiguous reading and meaning are clear and evident. Put simply, the American public has a right to know the President of the United States is acting in their best interest and not because he or she has received some benefit or gift from a foreign government, such as Russia or China or any foreign entity. They need to know the President of the United States is making decisions about potential trade agreements, sending troops into war, or where we spend America's great resources is based upon what is in the public interest and not because it would advance the President's private pecuniary interests.

The Founding Fathers' concerns on this subject were neither abstract nor baseless. Alexander Hamilton made specific references to these dangers in the Federalist Papers. While the Constitution was being debated in America, the Polish Lithuanian Commonwealth was in the process of being ruthlessly dismembered by her neighbors—Prussia, the Austrian Empire and Russia.

Poland's neighbors bribed Polish Government officials and succeeded in paralyzing the state for decades. The Founding Fathers placed the emoluments clause, an explicit bar on foreign corruption and interference, within the Constitution so we may avoid Poland's fate.

Happily, the emoluments clause has not been a section of the Constitution that has had to be of concern to this body, nor is there voluminous case history detailing its legal interpretation with regard to the highest offices of the executive branch. This is because every President, from George Washington to Barack Obama, has taken great pains to avoid even the appearance of impropriety with regard to their personal wealth and investments, ensuring that such investments never interfere with performing their duties as President of the United States.

That is why, over the past four decades, Presidents Jimmy Carter, Ronald Reagan, George Herbert Walker Bush, Bill Clinton, and George W. Bush all had their assets placed into blind

trusts while they were President. President Obama went even further because he wanted to fulfill his promises of greater transparency. He invested the vast majority of his funds into U.S. Treasury bonds.

I wish the well-established precedent and practice would make it unnecessary to introduce and seek to move this resolution today. I wish President-elect Trump would be inclined to continue the longstanding and bipartisan tradition of Presidential traditions.

In September, Mr. Trump said, if he were elected, he would absolutely sever ties to The Trump Organization. Despite that pledge, it has since become clear that absent intervention by this body, the President-elect may not follow the precedents established by his predecessors. In so doing, he may well—for whatever reason and whatever motive—place himself and our Constitution in jeopardy.

As a separate and coequal branch of government, the Senate has a duty and obligation to safeguard our Constitution. It is to the Constitution, after all, not the person or position, that we swear our oath of office and to nourish the republican virtues that have allowed our Nation and government to flourish.

We must do so because following the election, it appears that President-elect Trump may have changed his mind about the promises he made as he sought office. Mr. Trump's lawyers announced The Trump Organization would be placed into a "blind trust," managed by Don Trump's older children, Donald Trump, Jr., Ivanka Trump, and Eric Trump.

Let me be clear, as the gravity of this issue demands absolute clarity. The financial arrangement described by Mr. Trump and his lawyers is not a blind trust. It just isn't. We can't allow Mr. Trump or his lawyers to trick us or the American people into thinking it is just because they use that term.

A true blind trust, including the ones established by past Presidents, is an arrangement where the official has no control over, will receive no communications about, and will have no knowledge of the identity of the specific assets held in the trust, and the trust's managers operate independently of the owner.

The arrangement described by Mr. Trump and his lawyers is not independent. Mr. Trump is well aware of the specific assets held, and he can receive communications about and take actions to affect the values of such assets. The idea that President-elect Trump's children are or will be truly independent managers is not credible. This is not a blind trust, and this is not an arrangement that will ensure compliance with the emoluments clause of the U.S. Constitution.

Mr. Trump has said there is no one like him who has ever become President of the United States. On that point, he may well be correct. I am very concerned Mr. Trump may violate the U.S. Constitution on the day he takes office and, even if it is not his intent, place himself and our Nation at risk. The purpose of my resolution is to convey to the President-elect there is still time for him to avoid this constitutional conflict.

Some might ask: Why should anyone care? It is not hard to imagine circumstances in which a foreign governmental actor will want to give President Trump gifts so they can curry favor with him and hope to influence his decisions in ways that benefit them when the President's decisions should benefit the American people—precisely the danger our Founding Fathers sought to protect against with the emoluments clause.

This is not an esoteric argument about rules that do not affect real people. The American public has the right to know if President Trump will put our soldiers, sailors, airmen, and marines in harm's way to protect America's national security or to protect the latest Trump Tower in some far-off country. They have the right to know if the trade agreements negotiated by the new administration will benefit American businesses, farmers, workers, and consumers or whether they will benefit some Trump company or hotel.

Donald Trump's business network, The Trump Organization, has financial interests around the world and negotiates and includes transactions with foreign states and entities that are extensions of foreign states.

To give but one example of how bad things can get if Mr. Trump is allowed to stay connected to his businesses: In Azerbaijan, The Trump Organization partnered with billionaire Anar Mammadov to build a 33-story Trump Tower in Baku, the capital of Azerbaijan. Mammadov's father is Azerbaijan's long-time Transportation Minister and a confidant of the President of Azerbaijan. There have been allegations this billionaire's company and the companies he is connected to have profited from more than $1 billion worth of transportation contracts related to his father's position in the Transportation Ministry.

A former U.S. Ambassador to Azerbaijan in the 1990s and an adviser to the Director of National Intelligence under George W. Bush has said of this deal: "These are not business people acting on their own—you're dealing with daddy."

There are a great many nations, none of which we should emulate, where the lines between officials of the foreign government and business entities controlled by that foreign government are blurred or obliterated. For that reason, the Office of Legal Counsel at the Department of Justice has stated that corporations owned or controlled by foreign governments are presumptively

foreign states under the emoluments clause.

We should all be concerned when the President-elect is connected to an organization that has dealings with countries and entities that aren't interested in distinguishing between doing business with President Trump and the profitmaking portion that bears his name. We run the risk of turning the United States of America, our legal system, our immigration system, our financial system, our trade agreements, and our military into subsidiaries of The Trump Organization.

It has already been reported that the Trump International Hotel in Washington, DC, has been patronized by an increasing number of foreign dignitaries and diplomats because of Mr. Trump's election. One diplomat was recorded as saying:

Why wouldn't I stay at his hotel, blocks from the White House, so I can tell the new president, "I love your new hotel"? Isn't it rude to come to his city and say, "I am staying at your competitor"?

Likewise, news reports suggest that one day after a phone call between President-elect Trump and the President of Argentina, permits under review for a Trump building in Buenos Aires were suddenly approved. In China, just days after the Presidential election, Donald Trump scored a legal victory in a decade-long trademark dispute over the right to use the Trump name for real estate agent services in commercial and residential properties in China. The timing of these actions is interesting, to put it mildly.

The appearance of intermingling between the business of The Trump Organization and the work of government has already begun. Despite Mr. Trump's campaign promises to sever ties to The Trump Organization, where he stated that "I'll have my children and my executives run the company and I won't discuss it with them," the Trump Presidential transition team has named Mr. Trump's children, Donald Trump, Jr., Ivanka Trump, and Eric Trump, to the transition team's executive committee—the same children who are supposedly managing The Trump Organization without discussing it with him. In those positions, they have the ability to offer counsel as to which personnel are selected to critical posts in the new Trump administration.

Ivanka Trump reportedly has been present during Mr. Trump's congratulatory calls with Japan's Prime Minister and the President of Argentina. Donald Trump, Jr., reportedly met in secret prior to the election with pro-Russia politicians to discuss Syrian policy. After the election, President-elect Trump met with Indian real estate executives—his partners in developing Trump Towers in India—in which they allegedly discussed with the Trump family about possible additional real estate deals.

The list goes on and on. The totality of these engagements and the potential implications are deeply, deeply disturbing. Yet President-elect Trump has done nothing to assure the American people he will put their interests above the enrichment of himself and his children, and he will assure, as the Founding Fathers intended, that the President is not placed in a position where he might be vulnerable to foreign influence or even the appearance of foreign influence.

While Mr. Trump or his advisers say "Trust us," let us remember what John Adams said: "We are a government of laws and not of men." It was the enduring wisdom of our Founders to recognize that not all men are angels, so we place our trust in the Constitution itself, not in individuals.

Mr. Trump's wealth and business interests must yield to the U.S. Constitution. Those wide-ranging interests make us realize just how critical the Constitution's prohibition of foreign gifts is. The business that the Trump Organization does overseas in places like Scotland, Argentina, India, and Azerbaijan cannot help but not be far from Mr. Trump's mind when he discusses matters of policy with foreign heads of state. This is not because President-elect Trump is any more susceptible to these temptations than anyone else but simply because, as the Founding Fathers recognized, we are humans, not angels.

This insight into human conditions elicited the precise fear articulated by our Founding Fathers: Leaders who receive gifts and payments from foreign governments, being human, may not act in the best interests of the American people. To quote Richard Painter, an expert in ethics and an adviser to George W. Bush: "Imagine where we'd be today if President Franklin Roosevelt had owned apartment buildings in Frankfurt and Berlin. . . . some of us might be speaking German."

I am extremely troubled by Mr. Trump's recent remarks on this subject. On November 22, President-elect Trump stated, "The law's totally on my side, meaning, the president can't have a conflict of interest." In typical Trump sleight of hand, he selectively picks his own facts as he shows a troubling and callous disregard for our Constitution and for the duty he owes to the American people.

While the President, Vice President, Members of Congress, and Federal judges may be granted specific, limited exemptions from conflicts of interest so that they may act and carry out their duties, that law does not supersede the Constitution nor, frankly, have anything to do with the very specific provisions of the emoluments clause preventing foreign governmental financial influence over the President. That the President-elect is not doing enough to avoid such conflicts is what brings me to the floor today and, overall, according to one new poll, is troubling to nearly 60 percent of the people of this country. The limited exception to the conflict of interest statute recognizes that there are certain public officials whose authority to act should not be held in question. That ability to act does not cure the restrictions in the emoluments clause of the Constitution.

The Constitution is the ultimate law of the land, not the President. Mr. Trump apparently does not appreciate the reason that the law on this issue is untested because previous Presidents have had the wisdom and personal forbearance not to seek to put this question to the test. But we have tested the unfortunate proposition that "when the president does it, that means it is not illegal" before, and Congress, in service of the Constitution and the American people, has found that not to be the case. No one is above the law; no one is above the Constitution, including the President of the United States.

President-elect Trump has also tweeted: "Prior to the election it was well known that I have interests in properties around the world." That is undoubtedly true. But the American people, in voting for a candidate, cannot—indeed, would not want to—excuse a potential future violation of the Constitution by that candidate.

President-elect Trump's attempt to imply that because he won the election, the Constitution somehow does not apply to him is irresponsible and disrespectful. It would be disrespectful to the Constitution; it is truly disrespectful to the American people, who are trusting their future, their children, their livelihood, and their safety to decisions Mr. Trump will make once he becomes President.

We must do everything we can to protect our Constitution, our democracy, and the American people from such recklessness.

The aim of my resolution is straightforward. It takes a strict interpretation of the plain words of the Constitution and supports the traditional values and practices adopted by previous Presidents. It simply calls on President-elect Trump to follow the precedent established by prior Presidents and convert his assets to simple, conflict-free holdings, adopt blind trusts managed by truly independent trustees with no relationship to Mr. Trump or his businesses, or to take other, equivalent measures. It calls upon the President-elect to refrain from using the powers or opportunities of his position for any purpose related to The Trump Organization. It makes it clear that if Mr. Trump does not take appropriate actions to sever his ties to his businesses, Congress will have no choice, given the oath to protect and defend the Constitution that each and every Member has taken, but to view any dealings Mr. Trump has through his

companies with foreign governments or entities owned or controlled by foreign governments as a potential violation of the emoluments clause.

As Mr. Painter observed, "It should send a clear message to [Mr. Trump] that he should divest his assets and that [Congress] will regard dealings with his companies that he owns abroad and any entities owned by foreign governments as a potential violation of the Emoluments Clause unless he can prove it was an arm's-length transaction."

It makes it clear to President-elect Trump that we care about the Constitution and our democracy, that the American people really are watching, and that we will not be distracted from caring about these things.

I want to close by observing that because of strong feelings and passions generated by the recent election, some might be tempted to view this resolution and its aims through a distorted prism of politics. Nothing could be further from the truth. I strongly support a smooth transition between the Obama administration and the Trump administration. I want the Trump administration to have support from Congress to succeed on behalf of the American people. But when Mr. Trump deviates from his constitutional responsibilities or recommends policies that are contrary to the core values of our Nation, Members of Congress have an obligation to speak out and to act.

I stand here today because I believe Congress has an institutional, constitutional obligation to ensure that the President of the United States, whosoever that is, does not violate our Constitution, acts lawfully, and is discharging the obligations of the office based on the broad interests of the American people, not his or her own narrow personal interests.

My resolution is not intended to create a misunderstanding or crisis, but to avoid one, so that President-elect Trump can put aside any appearance of impropriety and devote himself to the good work on behalf of the American people. We owe it to President-elect Trump to make very clear what our expectations are ahead of inauguration day. Why? So that we can avoid a Constitutional crisis. Such a crisis would not serve in the best interests of the President, Congress, and the American people.

AMENDMENTS SUBMITTED AND PROPOSED

SA 5113. Mr. MCCONNELL (for Mr. GRASSLEY (for himself, Mrs. GILLIBRAND, Mr. HATCH, Mr. BLUNT, Mr. SCHUMER, and Mr. COONS)) proposed an amendment to the bill S. 2944, to require adequate reporting on the Public Safety Officers' Benefits program, and for other purposes.

SA 5114. Mr. MCCONNELL (for Mr. GRASSLEY) proposed an amendment to the bill S. 2944, supra.

SA 5115. Mr. MCCONNELL (for Mr. CORNYN) proposed an amendment to the bill S. 461, to provide for alternative financing arrangements for the provision of certain services and the construction and maintenance of infrastructure at land border ports of entry, and for other purposes.

SA 5116. Mr. MCCONNELL (for Mr. HELLER (for himself, Mrs. FEINSTEIN, and Mr. REID)) proposed an amendment to the bill S. 3438, to authorize the Secretary of Veterans Affairs to carry out a major medical facility project in Reno, Nevada.

TEXT OF AMENDMENTS

SA 5113. Mr. MCCONNELL (for Mr. GRASSLEY (for himself, Mrs. GILLIBRAND, Mr. HATCH, Mr. BLUNT, Mr. SCHUMER, and Mr. COONS)) proposed an amendment to the bill S. 2944, to require adequate reporting on the Public Safety Officers' Benefits program, and for other purposes; as follows:

Strike all after the enacting clause and insert the following:

SECTION 1. SHORT TITLE.

This Act may be cited as the "Public Safety Officers' Benefits Improvement Act of 2016".

SEC. 2. REPORTS.

Section 1205 of title I of the Omnibus Crime Control and Safe Streets Act of 1968 (42 U.S.C. 3796c) is amended—

(1) in subsection (a), by inserting "Rules, regulations, and procedures issued under this part may include regulations based on standards developed by another Federal agency for programs related to public safety officer death or disability claims." before the last sentence;

(2) in subsection (b)—

(A) by inserting "(1)" before "In making"; and

(B) by adding at the end the following:

"(2) In making a determination under section 1201, the Bureau shall give substantial weight to the evidence and all findings of fact presented by a State, local, or Federal administrative or investigative agency regarding eligibility for death or disability benefits."; and

(3) by adding at the end the following:

"(e)(1)(A) Not later than 30 days after the date of enactment of this subsection, the Bureau shall make available on the public website of the Bureau information on all death, disability, and educational assistance claims submitted under this part that are pending as of the date on which the information is made available.

"(B) Not less frequently than once per week, the Bureau shall make available on the public website of the Bureau updated information with respect to all death, disability, and educational assistance claims submitted under this part that are pending as of the date on which the information is made available.

"(C) The information made available under this paragraph shall include—

"(i) for each pending claim—

"(I) the date on which the claim was submitted to the Bureau;

"(II) the State of residence of the claimant;

"(III) an anonymized, identifying claim number; and

"(IV) the nature of the claim; and

"(ii) the total number of pending claims that were submitted to the Bureau more than 1 year before the date on which the information is made available.

"(2)(A) Not later than 180 days after the date of enactment of this subsection, and every 180 days thereafter, the Bureau shall submit to Congress a report on the death, disability, and educational assistance claims submitted under this part.

"(B) Each report submitted under subparagraph (A) shall include information on—

"(i) the total number of claims for which a final determination has been made during the 180-day period preceding the report;

"(ii) the amount of time required to process each claim for which a final determination has been made during the 180-day period preceding the report;

"(iii) as of the last day of the 180-day period preceding the report, the total number of claims submitted to the Bureau on or before that date for which a final determination has not been made;

"(iv) as of the last day of the 180-day period preceding the report, the total number of claims submitted to the Bureau on or before the date that is 1 year before that date for which a final determination has not been made;

"(v) for each claim described in clause (iv), a detailed description of the basis for delay;

"(vi) as of the last day of the 180-day period preceding the report, the total number of claims submitted to the Bureau on or before that date relating to exposure due to the September 11th, 2001, terrorism attacks for which a final determination has not been made;

"(vii) as of the last day of the 180-day period preceding the report, the total number of claims submitted to the Bureau on or before the date that is 1 year before that date relating to exposure due to the September 11th, 2001, terrorism attacks for which a final determination has not been made;

"(viii) for each claim described in clause (vii), a detailed description of the basis for delay;

"(ix) the total number of claims submitted to the Bureau relating to exposure due to the September 11th, 2001, terrorism attacks for which a final determination was made during the 180-day period preceding the report, and the average award amount for any such claims that were approved;

"(x) the result of each claim for which a final determination was made during the 180-day period preceding the report, including the number of claims rejected and the basis for any denial of benefits;

"(xi) the number of final determinations which were appealed during the 180-day period preceding the report, regardless of when the final determination was first made;

"(xii) the average number of claims processed per reviewer of the Bureau during the 180-day period preceding the report;

"(xiii) for any claim submitted to the Bureau that required the submission of additional information from a public agency, and for which the public agency completed providing all of the required information during the 180-day period preceding the report, the average length of the period beginning on the date the public agency was contacted by the Bureau and ending on the date on which the public agency submitted all required information to the Bureau;

"(xiv) for any claim submitted to the Bureau for which the Bureau issued a subpoena to a public agency during the 180-day period preceding the report in order to obtain information or documentation necessary to determine the claim, the name of the public agency, the date on which the subpoena was issued, and the dates on which the public agency was contacted by the Bureau before the issuance of the subpoena; and

"(xv) information on the compliance of the Bureau with the obligation to offset award amounts under section 1201(f)(3), including—

"(I) the number of claims that are eligible for compensation under both this part and the September 11th Victim Compensation Fund of 2001 (49 U.S.C. 40101 note; Public Law 107–42) (commonly referred to as the 'VCF');

"(II) for each claim described in subclause (I) for which compensation has been paid under the VCF, the amount of compensation paid under the VCF;

"(III) the number of claims described in subclause (I) for which the Bureau has made a final determination; and

"(IV) the number of claims described in subclause (I) for which the Bureau has not made a final determination.

"(3) Not later than 5 years after the date of enactment of the Public Safety Officers' Benefits Improvement Act of 2016, and every 5 years thereafter, the Comptroller General of the United States shall—

"(A) conduct a study on the compliance of the Bureau with the obligation to offset award amounts under section 1201(f)(3); and

"(B) submit to Congress a report on the study conducted under subparagraph (A) that includes an assessment of whether the Bureau has provided the information required under subparagraph (B)(ix) of paragraph (2) of this subsection in each report required under that paragraph.

"(4) In this subsection, the term 'nature of the claim' means whether the claim is a claim for—

"(A) benefits under this subpart with respect to the death of a public safety officer;

"(B) benefits under this subpart with respect to the disability of a public safety officer; or

"(C) education assistance under subpart 2.".

SEC. 3. AGE LIMITATION FOR CHILDREN.

Section 1212(c) of title I of the Omnibus Crime Control and Safe Streets Act of 1968 (42 U.S.C. 3796d–1(c)) is amended—

(1) by striking "No child" and inserting the following:

"(1) IN GENERAL.—Subject to paragraph (2), no child"; and

(2) by adding at the end the following:

"(2) DELAYED APPROVALS.—

"(A) EDUCATIONAL ASSISTANCE APPLICATION.—If a claim for assistance under this subpart is approved more than 1 year after the date on which the application for such assistance is filed with the Attorney General, the age limitation under this subsection shall be extended by the length of the period—

"(i) beginning on the day after the date that is 1 year after the date on which the application is filed; and

"(ii) ending on the date on which the application is approved.

"(B) CLAIM FOR BENEFITS FOR DEATH OR PERMANENT AND TOTAL DISABILITY.—In addition to an extension under subparagraph (A), if any, for an application for assistance under this subpart that relates to a claim for benefits under subpart 1 that was approved more than 1 year after the date on which the claim was filed with the Attorney General, the age limitation under this subsection shall be extended by the length of the period—

"(i) beginning on the day after the date that is 1 year after the date on which the claim for benefits is submitted; and

"(ii) ending on the date on which the claim for benefits is approved.".

SEC. 4. DUE DILIGENCE IN PAYING BENEFIT CLAIMS.

Subpart 1 of part L of title I of the Omnibus Crime Control and Safe Streets Act of 1968 (42 U.S.C. 3796 et seq.) is amended by adding at the end the following:

"SEC. 1206. DUE DILIGENCE IN PAYING BENEFIT CLAIMS.

"(a) IN GENERAL.—The Bureau, with all due diligence, shall expeditiously attempt to obtain the information and documentation necessary to adjudicate a benefit claim filed under this part, including a claim for financial assistance under subpart 2.

"(b) SUFFICIENT INFORMATION UNAVAILABLE.—If a benefit claim filed under this part, including a claim for financial assistance under subpart 2, is unable to be adjudicated by the Bureau because of a lack of information or documentation from a third party, such as a public agency, the Bureau may not abandon the benefit claim unless the Bureau has utilized the investigative tools available to the Bureau to obtain the necessary information or documentation, including subpoenas.".

SEC. 5. PRESUMPTION THAT OFFICER ACTED PROPERLY.

Section 1202 of title I of the Omnibus Crime Control and Safe Streets Act of 1968 (42 U.S.C. 3796a) is amended—

(1) by striking "No benefit" and inserting the following:

"(a) IN GENERAL.—No benefit"; and

(2) by adding at the end the following:

"(b) PRESUMPTION.—In determining whether a benefit is payable under this part, the Bureau shall—

"(1) presume that none of the limitations described in subsection (a) apply; and

"(2) have the burden of establishing by clear and convincing evidence that a limitation described in subsection (a) applies.".

SEC. 6. EFFECTIVE DATE; APPLICABILITY.

The amendments made by this Act shall—

(1) take effect on the date of enactment of this Act; and

(2) apply to any benefit claim or application under part L of title I of the Omnibus Crime Control and Safe Streets Act of 1968 (42 U.S.C. 3796 et seq.) that is—

(A) pending before the Bureau of Justice Assistance on the date of enactment; or

(B) received by the Bureau on or after the date of enactment of this Act.

SA 5114. Mr. McCONNELL (for Mr. GRASSLEY) proposed an amendment to the bill S. 2944, to require adequate reporting on the Public Safety Officers' Benefits program, and for other purposes; as follows:

Amend the title so as to read: "A bill to require adequate reporting on the Public Safety Officers' Benefits program, and for other purposes.".

SA 5115. Mr. McCONNELL (for Mr. CORNYN) proposed an amendment to the bill S. 461, to provide for alternative financing arrangements for the provision of certain services and the construction and maintenance of infrastructure at land border ports of entry, and for other purposes; as follows:

Strike all after the enacting clause and insert the following:

SECTION 1. SHORT TITLE.

This Act may be cited as the "Cross-Border Trade Enhancement Act of 2016".

SEC. 2. PUBLIC-PRIVATE PARTNERSHIPS.

(a) IN GENERAL.—Title IV of the Homeland Security Act of 2002 (6 U.S.C. 202 et seq.) is amended by adding at the end the following:

"Subtitle G—U.S. Customs and Border Protection Public Private Partnerships

"SEC. 481. FEE AGREEMENTS FOR CERTAIN SERVICES AT PORTS OF ENTRY.

"(a) IN GENERAL.—Notwithstanding section 13031(e) of the Consolidated Omnibus Budget Reconciliation Act of 1985 (19 U.S.C. 58c(e)) and section 451 of the Tariff Act of 1930 (19 U.S.C. 1451), the Commissioner of U.S. Customs and Border Protection, upon the request of any entity, may enter into a fee agreement with such entity under which—

"(1) U.S. Customs and Border Protection shall provide services described in subsection (b) at a United States port of entry or any other facility at which U.S. Customs and Border Protection provides or will provide such services;

"(2) such entity shall remit to U.S. Customs and Border Protection a fee imposed under subsection (h) in an amount equal to the full costs that are incurred or will be incurred in providing such services; and

"(3) if space is provided by such entity, each facility at which U.S. Customs and Border Protection services are performed shall be maintained and equipped by such entity, without cost to the Federal Government, in accordance with U.S. Customs and Border Protection specifications.

"(b) SERVICES DESCRIBED.—The services described in this subsection are any activities of any employee or Office of Field Operations contractor of U.S. Customs and Border Protection (except employees of the U.S. Border Patrol, as established under section 411(e)) pertaining to, or in support of, customs, agricultural processing, border security, or immigration inspection-related matters at a port of entry or any other facility at which U.S. Customs and Border Protection provides or will provide services.

"(c) MODIFICATION OF PRIOR AGREEMENTS.—The Commissioner of U.S. Customs and Border Protection, at the request of an entity who has previously entered into an agreement with U.S. Customs and Border Protection for the reimbursement of fees in effect on the date of enactment of this section, may modify such agreement to implement any provisions of this section.

"(d) LIMITATIONS.—

"(1) IMPACTS OF SERVICES.—The Commissioner of U.S. Customs and Border Protection—

"(A) may enter into fee agreements under this section only for services that—

"(i) will increase or enhance the operational capacity of U.S. Customs and Border Protection based on available staffing and workload; and

"(ii) will not shift the cost of services funded in any appropriations Act, or provided from any account in the Treasury of the United States derived by the collection of fees, to entities under this Act; and

"(B) may not enter into a fee agreement under this section if such agreement would unduly and permanently impact services funded in any appropriations Act, or provided from any account in the Treasury of the United States, derived by the collection of fees.

"(2) NUMBER.—There shall be no limit to the number of fee agreements that the Commissioner of U.S. Customs and Border Protection may enter into under this section.

"(e) AIR PORTS OF ENTRY.—

"(1) FEE AGREEMENT.—Except as otherwise provided in this subsection, a fee agreement for U.S. Customs and Border Protection services at an air port of entry may only provide for the payment of overtime costs of U.S. Customs and Border Protection officers and salaries and expenses of U.S. Customs and Border Protection employees to support U.S. Customs and Border Protection officers in performing law enforcement missions.

"(2) SMALL AIRPORTS.—Notwithstanding paragraph (1), U.S. Customs and Border Protection may receive reimbursement in addition to overtime costs if the fee agreement is for services at an air port of entry that has fewer than 100,000 arriving international passengers annually.

"(3) COVERED SERVICES.—In addition to costs described in paragraph (1), a fee agreement for U.S. Customs and Border Protection services at an air port of entry referred to in paragraph (2) may provide for the reimbursement of—

"(A) salaries and expenses of not more that 5 full-time equivalent U.S. Customs and Border Protection Officers beyond the number of such officers assigned to the port of entry on the date on which the fee agreement was signed;

"(B) salaries and expenses of employees of U.S. Customs and Border Protection, other than the officers referred to in subparagraph (A), to support U.S. Customs and Border Protection officers in performing law enforcement functions; and

"(C) other costs incurred by U.S. Customs and Border Protection relating to services described in subparagraph (B), such as temporary placement or permanent relocation of employees, including incentive pay for relocation, as appropriate.

"(f) PORT OF ENTRY SIZE.—The Commissioner of U.S. Customs and Border Protection shall ensure that each fee agreement proposal is given equal consideration regardless of the size of the port of entry.

"(g) DENIED APPLICATION.—

"(1) IN GENERAL.—If the Commissioner of U.S. Customs and Border Protection denies a proposal for a fee agreement under this section, the Commissioner shall provide the entity submitting such proposal with the reason for the denial unless—

"(A) the reason for the denial is law enforcement sensitive; or

"(B) withholding the reason for the denial is in the national security interests of the United States.

"(2) JUDICIAL REVIEW.—Decisions of the Commissioner of U.S. Customs and Border Protection under paragraph (1) are in the discretion of the Commissioner and are not subject to judicial review.

"(h) FEE.—

"(1) IN GENERAL.—The amount of the fee to be charged under an agreement authorized under subsection (a) shall be paid by each entity requesting U.S. Customs and Border Protection services, and shall be for the full cost of providing such services, including the salaries and expenses of employees and contractors of U.S. Customs and Border Protection, to provide such services and other costs incurred by U.S. Customs and Border Protection relating to such services, such as temporary placement or permanent relocation of such employees and contractors.

"(2) TIMING.—The Commissioner of U.S. Customs and Border Protection may require that the fee referred to in paragraph (1) be paid by each entity that has entered into a fee agreement under subsection (a) with U.S. Customs and Border Protection in advance of the performance of U.S. Customs and Border Protection services.

"(3) OVERSIGHT OF FEES.—The Commissioner of U.S. Customs and Border Protection shall develop a process to oversee the services for which fees are charged pursuant to an agreement under subsection (a), including—

"(A) a determination and report on the full costs of providing such services, and a process for increasing such fees, as necessary;

"(B) the establishment of a periodic remittance schedule to replenish appropriations, accounts, or funds, as necessary; and

"(C) the identification of costs paid by such fees.

"(i) DEPOSIT OF FUNDS.—

"(1) ACCOUNT.—Funds collected pursuant to any agreement entered into pursuant to subsection (a)—

"(A) shall be deposited as offsetting collections;

"(B) shall remain available until expended without fiscal year limitation; and

"(C) shall be credited to the applicable appropriation, account, or fund for the amount paid out of such appropriation, account, or fund for any expenses incurred or to be incurred by U.S. Customs and Border Protection in providing U.S. Customs and Border Protection services under any such agreement and any other costs incurred or to be incurred by U.S. Customs and Border Protection relating to such services.

"(2) RETURN OF UNUSED FUNDS.—The Commissioner of U.S. Customs and Border Protection shall return any unused funds collected and deposited into the account described in paragraph (1) if a fee agreement entered into pursuant to subsection (a) is terminated for any reason or the terms of such fee agreement change by mutual agreement to cause a reduction of U.S. Customs and Border Protections services. No interest shall be owed upon the return of any such unused funds.

"(j) TERMINATION.—

"(1) IN GENERAL.—The Commissioner of U.S. Customs and Border Protection shall terminate the services provided pursuant to a fee agreement entered into under subsection (a) with an entity that, after receiving notice from the Commissioner that a fee under subsection (h) is due, fails to pay such fee in a timely manner. If such services are terminated, all costs incurred by U.S. Customs and Border Protection that have not been paid shall become immediately due and payable. Interest on unpaid fees shall accrue based on the rate and amount established under sections 6621 and 6622 of the Internal Revenue Code of 1986.

"(2) PENALTY.—Any entity that, after notice and demand for payment of any fee under subsection (h), fails to pay such fee in a timely manner shall be liable for a penalty or liquidated damage equal to two times the amount of such fee. Any such amount collected under this paragraph shall be deposited into the appropriate account specified under subsection (i) and shall be available as described in such subsection.

"(3) TERMINATION BY THE ENTITY.—Any entity who has previously entered into an agreement with U.S. Customs and Border Protection for the reimbursement of fees in effect on the date of enactment of this section, or under the provisions of this section, may request that such agreement be amended to provide for termination upon advance notice, length, and terms that are negotiated between such entity and U.S. Customs and Border Protection.

"(k) ANNUAL REPORT.—The Commissioner of U.S. Customs and Border Protection shall—

"(1) submit an annual report identifying the activities undertaken and the agreements entered into pursuant to this section to—

"(A) the Committee on Appropriations of the Senate;

"(B) the Committee on Finance of the Senate;

"(C) the Committee on Homeland Security and Governmental Affairs of the Senate;

"(D) the Committee on the Judiciary of the Senate;

"(E) the Committee on Appropriations of the House of Representatives;

"(F) the Committee on Homeland Security of the House of Representatives;

"(G) the Committee on the Judiciary of the House of Representatives; and

"(H) the Committee on Ways and Means of the House of Representatives; and

"(2) not later than 15 days before entering into a fee agreement, notify the members of Congress that represent the State or Congressional District in which the affected port of entry or facility is located of such agreement.

"(l) RULE OF CONSTRUCTION.—Nothing in this section may be construed as imposing on U.S. Customs and Border Protection any responsibilities, duties, or authorities relating to real property.

"SEC. 482. PORT OF ENTRY DONATION AUTHORITY.

"(a) PERSONAL PROPERTY DONATION AUTHORITY.—

"(1) IN GENERAL.—The Commissioner of U.S. Customs and Border Protection, in consultation with the Administrator of General Services, may enter into an agreement with any entity to accept a donation of personal property, money, or nonpersonal services for the uses described in paragraph (3) only with respect to the following locations at which U.S. Customs and Border Protection performs or will be performing inspection services:

"(A) A new or existing sea or air port of entry.

"(B) An existing Federal Government-owned land port of entry.

"(C) A new Federal Government-owned land port of entry if—

"(i) the fair market value of the donation is $50,000,000 or less; and

"(ii) the fair market value, including any personal and real property donations in total, of such port of entry when completed, is $50,000,000 or less.

"(2) LIMITATION ON MONETARY DONATIONS.—Any monetary donation accepted pursuant to this subsection may not be used to pay the salaries of U.S. Customs and Border Protection employees performing inspection services.

"(3) USES.—Donations accepted pursuant to this subsection may be used for activities of the Office of Field Operations set forth in subparagraphs (A) through (F) of section 411(g)(3), which are related to a new or existing sea or air port of entry or a new or existing Federal Government-owned land port of entry described in paragraph (1), including expenses related to—

"(A) furniture, fixtures, equipment, or technology, including the installation or deployment of such items; and

"(B) the operation and maintenance of such furniture, fixtures, equipment, or technology.

"(b) REAL PROPERTY DONATION AUTHORITY.—

"(1) IN GENERAL.—Subject to paragraph (3), the Commissioner of U.S. Customs and Border Protection, and the Administrator of the General Services Administration, as applicable, may enter into an agreement with any entity to accept a donation of real property or money for uses described in paragraph (2) only with respect to the following locations at which U.S. Customs and Border Protec-

tion performs or will be performing inspection services:

"(A) A new or existing sea or air port of entry.

"(B) An existing Federal Government-owned land port of entry.

"(C) A new Federal Government-owned land port of entry if—

"(i) the fair market value of the donation is $50,000,000 or less; and

"(ii) the fair market value, including any personal and real property donations in total, of such port of entry when completed, is $50,000,000 or less.

"(2) USE.—Donations accepted pursuant to this subsection may be used for activities of the Office of Field Operations set forth in section 411(g), which are related to the construction, alteration, operation, or maintenance of a new or existing sea or air port of entry or a new or existing a Federal Government-owned land port of entry described in paragraph (1), including expenses related to—

"(A) land acquisition, design, construction, repair, or alteration; and

"(B) operation and maintenance of such port of entry facility.

"(3) LIMITATION ON REAL PROPERTY DONATIONS.—A donation of real property under this subsection at an existing land port of entry owned by the General Services Administration may only be accepted by the Administrator of General Services.

"(4) SUNSET.—

"(A) IN GENERAL.—The authority to enter into an agreement under this subsection shall terminate on the date that is four years after the date of the enactment of this section.

"(B) RULE OF CONSTRUCTION.—The termination date referred to in subparagraph (A) shall not apply to carrying out the terms of an agreement under this subsection if such agreement is entered into before such termination date.

"(c) GENERAL PROVISIONS.—

"(1) DURATION.—An agreement entered into under subsection (a) or (b) (and, in the case of such subsection (b), in accordance with paragraph (4) of such subsection) may last as long as required to meet the terms of such agreement.

"(2) CRITERIA.—In carrying out an agreement entered into under subsection (a) or (b), the Commissioner of U.S. Customs and Border Protection, in consultation with the Administrator of General Services, shall establish criteria regarding—

"(A) the selection and evaluation of donors;

"(B) the identification of roles and responsibilities between U.S. Customs and Border Protection, the General Services Administration, and donors;

"(C) the identification, allocation, and management of explicit and implicit risks of partnering between the Federal Government and donors;

"(D) decision-making and dispute resolution processes; and

"(E) processes for U.S. Customs and Border Protection, and the General Services Administration, as applicable, to terminate agreements if selected donors are not meeting the terms of any such agreement, including the security standards established by U.S. Customs and Border Protection.

"(3) EVALUATION PROCEDURES.—

"(A) IN GENERAL.—The Commissioner of U.S. Customs and Border Protection, in consultation with the Administrator of General Services, as applicable, shall—

"(i) establish criteria for evaluating a proposal to enter into an agreement under subsection (a) or (b); and

"(ii) make such criteria publicly available.

"(B) CONSIDERATIONS.—Criteria established pursuant to subparagraph (A) shall consider—

"(i) the impact of a proposal referred to in such subparagraph on the land, sea, or air port of entry at issue and other ports of entry or similar facilities or other infrastructure near the location of the proposed donation;

"(ii) such proposal's potential to increase trade and travel efficiency through added capacity;

"(iii) such proposal's potential to enhance the security of the port of entry at issue;

"(iv) the impact of the proposal on reducing wait times at that port of entry or facility and other ports of entry on the same border;

"(v) for a donation under subsection (b)—

"(I) whether such donation satisfies the requirements of such proposal, or whether additional real property would be required; and

"(II) how such donation was acquired, including if eminent domain was used;

"(vi) the funding available to complete the intended use of such donation;

"(vii) the costs of maintaining and operating such donation;

"(viii) the impact of such proposal on U.S. Customs and Border Protection staffing requirements; and

"(ix) other factors that the Commissioner or Administrator determines to be relevant.

"(C) DETERMINATION AND NOTIFICATION.—

"(i) INCOMPLETE PROPOSALS.—

"(I) IN GENERAL.—Not later than 60 days after receiving the proposals for a donation agreement from an entity, the Commissioner of U.S. Customs and Border Protection shall notify such entity as to whether such proposal is complete or incomplete.

"(II) RESUBMISSION.—If the Commissioner of U.S. Customs and Border Protection determines that a proposal is incomplete, the Commissioner shall—

"(aa) notify the appropriate entity and provide such entity with a description of all information or material that is needed to complete review of the proposal; and

"(bb) allow the entity to resubmit the proposal with additional information and material described in item (aa) to complete the proposal.

"(ii) COMPLETE PROPOSALS.—Not later than 180 days after receiving a completed proposal to enter into an agreement under subsection (a) or (b), the Commissioner of U.S. Customs and Border Protection, with the concurrence of the Administrator of General Services, as applicable, shall—

"(I) determine whether to approve or deny such proposal; and

"(II) notify the entity that submitted such proposal of such determination.

"(4) SUPPLEMENTAL FUNDING.—Except as required under section 3307 of title 40, United States Code, real property donations to the Administrator of General Services made pursuant to subsection (a) and (b) at a GSA-owned land port of entry may be used in addition to any other funding for such purpose, including appropriated funds, property, or services.

"(5) RETURN OF DONATIONS.—The Commissioner of U.S. Customs and Border Protection, or the Administrator of General Services, as applicable, may return any donation made pursuant to subsection (a) or (b). No interest shall be owed to the donor with respect to any donation provided under such subsections that is returned pursuant to this subsection.

"(6) PROHIBITION ON CERTAIN FUNDING.—

"(A) IN GENERAL.—Except as provided in subsections (a) and (b) regarding the acceptance of donations, the Commissioner of U.S. Customs and Border Protection and the Administrator of General Services, as applicable, may not, with respect to an agreement entered into under either of such subsections, obligate or expend amounts in excess of amounts that have been appropriated pursuant to any appropriations Act for purposes specified in either of such subsections or otherwise made available for any of such purposes.

"(B) CERTIFICATION REQUIREMENT.—Before accepting any donations pursuant to an agreement under subsection (a) or (b), the Commissioner of U.S. Customs and Border Protection shall certify to the congressional committees set forth in paragraph (7) that the donation will not be used for the construction of a detention facility or a border fence or wall.

"(7) ANNUAL REPORTS.—The Commissioner of U.S. Customs and Border Protection, in collaboration with the Administrator of General Services, as applicable, shall submit an annual report identifying the activities undertaken and agreements entered into pursuant to subsections (a) and (b) to—

"(A) the Committee on Appropriations of the Senate;

"(B) the Committee on Environment and Public Works of the Senate;

"(C) the Committee on Finance of the Senate;

"(D) the Committee on Homeland Security and Governmental Affairs of the Senate;

"(E) the Committee on the Judiciary of the Senate;

"(F) the Committee on Appropriations of the House of Representatives;

"(G) the Committee on Homeland Security of the House of Representatives;

"(H) the Committee on the Judiciary of the House of Representatives;

"(I) the Committee on Transportation and Infrastructure of the House of Representatives; and

"(J) the Committee on Ways and Means of the House of Representatives.

"(d) GAO REPORT.—The Comptroller General of the United States shall submit an annual report to the congressional committees referred to in subsection (c)(7) that evaluates—

"(1) fee agreements entered into pursuant to section 481;

"(2) donation agreements entered into pursuant to subsections (a) and (b); and

"(3) the fees and donations received by U.S. Customs and Border Protection pursuant to such agreements.

"(e) JUDICIAL REVIEW.—Decisions of the Commissioner of U.S. Customs and Border Protection and the Administrator of the General Services Administration under this section regarding the acceptance of real or personal property are in the discretion of the Commissioner and the Administrator and are not subject to judicial review.

"(f) RULE OF CONSTRUCTION.—Except as otherwise provided in this section, nothing in this section may be construed as affecting in any manner the responsibilities, duties, or authorities of U.S. Customs and Border Protection or the General Services Administration.

"SEC. 483. CURRENT AND PROPOSED AGREEMENTS.

"Nothing in this subtitle or in section 4 of the Cross-Border Trade Enhancement Act of 2016 may be construed as affecting—

"(1) any agreement entered into pursuant to section 560 of division D of the Consolidated and Further Continuing Appropriations Act, 2013 (Public Law 113–6) or section 559 of title V of division F of the Consolidated Appropriations Act, 2014 (6 U.S.C. 211 note; Public Law 113–76), as in existence on the day before the date of the enactment of this subtitle, and any such agreement shall continue to have full force and effect on and after such date; or

"(2) a proposal accepted for consideration by U.S. Customs and Border Protection pursuant to such section 559, as in existence on the day before such date of enactment.

"SEC. 484. DEFINITIONS.

"In this subtitle:

"(1) DONOR.—The term 'donor' means any entity that is proposing to make a donation under this Act.

"(2) ENTITY.—The term 'entity' means any—

"(A) person;

"(B) partnership, corporation, trust, estate, cooperative, association, or any other organized group of persons;

"(C) Federal, State or local government (including any subdivision, agency or instrumentality thereof); or

"(D) any other private or governmental entity.".

(b) CLERICAL AMENDMENT.—The table of contents in section 1(b) of the Homeland Security Act of 2002 is amended by adding at the end of the list of items relating to title IV the following:

"Subtitle G—U.S. Customs and Border Protection Public Private Partnerships

"Sec. 481. Fee agreements for certain services at ports of entry.
"Sec. 482. Port of entry donation authority.
"Sec. 483. Current and proposed agreements.
"Sec. 484. Definitions.".

SEC. 3. MODIFICATION OF EXISTING REPORTS TO CONGRESS.

Section 907(b) of the Trade Facilitation and Trade Enforcement Act of 2015 (Public Law 114–125) is amended—

(1) in paragraph (3), by striking "or" at the end;

(2) in paragraph (4), by striking the period at the end and inserting "; or"; and

(3) by adding at the end the following:

"(5) the program for entering into reimbursable fee agreements with U.S. Customs and Border Protection established under section 481 of the Homeland Security Act of 2002.".

SEC. 4. REPEALS.

(a) CONTRACT AUTHORITY.—Section 560 of division D of the Consolidated and Further Continuing Appropriations Act, 2013 (Public Law 113–6) is repealed.

(b) PARTNERSHIP PILOT PROGRAM.—Section 559 of division F of the Consolidated Appropriations Act, 2014 (6 U.S.C. 211 note; Public Law 113–76) is repealed.

SEC. 5. WAIVER OF POLYGRAPH EXAMINATION REQUIREMENT FOR CERTAIN LAW ENFORCEMENT APPLICANTS.

Section 3 of the Anti-Border Corruption Act of 2010 (Public Law 111–376; 6 U.S.C. 221) is amended—

(1) in the matter preceding paragraph (1), by striking "The Secretary" and inserting the following:

"(a) IN GENERAL.—The Secretary";

(2) in subsection (a)(1), as redesignated, by inserting "(except as provided in subsection (b))" after "Border Protection"; and

(3) by adding at the end the following:

"(b) WAIVER.—The Commissioner of U.S. Customs and Border Protection may waive the polygraph examination requirement under subsection (a)(1) for any applicant who—

"(1) is deemed suitable for employment;

"(2) holds a current, active Top Secret/Sensitive Compartmented Information Clearance;

"(3) has a current Single Scope Background Investigation;

"(4) was not granted any waivers to obtain his or her clearance; and

"(5) is a veteran (as defined in section 2108 of title 5, United States Code).".

SA 5116. Mr. MCCONNELL (for Mr. HELLER (for himself, Mrs. FEINSTEIN, and Mr. REID)) proposed an amendment to the bill S. 3438, to authorize the Secretary of Veterans Affairs to carry out a major medical facility project in Reno, Nevada; as follows:

Strike all after the enacting clause and insert the following:

SECTION 1. AUTHORIZATION OF CERTAIN MAJOR MEDICAL FACILITY PROJECTS OF THE DEPARTMENT OF VETERANS AFFAIRS.

(a) IN GENERAL.—The Secretary of Veterans Affairs may carry out the following major medical facility projects, with each project to be carried out in an amount not to exceed the amount specified for that project:

(1) Seismic, life safety, and utilities upgrades and expansion of clinical services in Reno, Nevada, in an amount not to exceed $213,800,000.

(2) Seismic corrections to the mental health and community living center in Long Beach, California, in an amount not to exceed $317,300,000.

(b) AUTHORIZATION OF APPROPRIATIONS.— There is authorized to be appropriated to the Secretary of Veterans Affairs for fiscal year 2017 or the year in which funds are appropriated for the Construction, Major Projects, account $531,100,000 for the projects authorized in subsection (a).

(c) LIMITATION.—The projects authorized in subsection (a) may only be carried out using—

(1) funds appropriated for fiscal year 2017 or the year in which funds are appropriated for the Construction, Major Projects, account pursuant to the authorization of appropriations in subsection (b);

(2) funds available for Construction, Major Projects, for a fiscal year before fiscal year 2017 that remain available for obligation;

(3) funds available for Construction, Major Projects, for a fiscal year after fiscal year 2017 that remain available for obligation;

(4) funds appropriated for Construction, Major Projects, for fiscal year 2017 for a category of activity not specific to a project;

(5) funds appropriated for Construction, Major Projects, for a fiscal year before fiscal year 2017 for a category of activity not specific to a project; and

(6) funds appropriated for Construction, Major Projects, for a fiscal year after fiscal year 2017 for a category of activity not specific to a project.

AUTHORITY FOR COMMITTEES TO MEET

Mr. BLUNT. Mr. President, I have two requests for committees to meet during today's session of the Senate. They have the approval of the Majority and Minority leaders.

Pursuant to Rule XXVI, paragraph 5(a), of the Standing Rules of the Senate, the following committees are authorized to meet during today's session of the Senate:

The Committee on Armed Services is authorized to meet during the session of the Senate on November 29, 2016, at 9:30 a.m.

The Select Committee on Intelligence is authorized to meet during the session of the Senate on November 29, 2016, at 2:30 p.m., in room SH–219 of the Hart Senate Office Building.

FOREIGN TRAVEL FINANCIAL REPORTS

In accordance with the appropriate provisions of law, the Secretary of the Senate herewith submits the following reports for standing committees of the Senate, certain joint committees of the Congress, delegations and groups, and select and special committees of the Senate, relating to expenses incurred in the performance of authorized foreign travel:

CONSOLIDATED REPORT OF EXPENDITURE OF FUNDS FOR FOREIGN TRAVEL BY MEMBERS AND EMPLOYEES OF THE U.S. SENATE, UNDER AUTHORITY OF SEC. 22, P.L. 95–384—22 U.S.C. 1754(b), COMMITTEE ON AGRICULTURE, NUTRITION, AND FORESTRY FOR TRAVEL FROM JULY 1 TO SEPT. 30, 2016

Name and country	Name of currency	Per diem		Transportation		Miscellaneous		Total	
		Foreign currency	U.S. dollar equivalent or U.S. currency	Foreign currency	U.S. dollar equivalent or U.S. currency	Foreign currency	U.S. dollar equivalent or U.S. currency	Foreign currency	U.S. dollar equivalent or U.S. currency
Senator Pat Roberts:									
England	Pound		5,085.86						5,085.86
Total			5,085.86						5,085.86

SENATOR PAT ROBERTS,
Chairman, Committee on Agriculture, Nutrition, and Forestry, Oct. 7, 2016.

CONSOLIDATED REPORT OF EXPENDITURE OF FUNDS FOR FOREIGN TRAVEL BY MEMBERS AND EMPLOYEES OF THE U.S. SENATE, UNDER AUTHORITY OF SEC. 22, P.L. 95–384—22 U.S.C. 1754(b), COMMITTEE ON APPROPRIATIONS FOR TRAVEL FROM JULY 1 TO SEPT. 30, 2016

Name and country	Name of currency	Per diem		Transportation		Miscellaneous		Total	
		Foreign currency	U.S. dollar equivalent or U.S. currency	Foreign currency	U.S. dollar equivalent or U.S. currency	Foreign currency	U.S. dollar equivalent or U.S. currency	Foreign currency	U.S. dollar equivalent or U.S. currency
William Todd:									
Germany	Euro		796.82						796.82
Lithuania	Euro		290.02						290.02
Romania	Leu		500.00						500.00
United States	Dollar				16,331.49				16,331.49
Mary Colleen Gaydos:									
Germany	Euro		796.82						796.82
Lithuania	Euro		290.02						290.02
Romania	Leu		500.00						500.00
United States	Dollar				13,388.51				13,388.51
Laura Friedel:									
Haiti	Gourde		619.00						619.00
United States	Dollar				3,810.79				3,810.79
Sarah Boliek:									
Haiti	Gourde		619.00						619.00
United States	Dollar				3,810.79				3,810.79
Jeff Reczek:									
Haiti	Gourde		619.00						619.00
United States	Dollar				3,810.79				3,810.79
Lisa Bernhardt:									
Haiti	Gourde		375.00						375.00
United States	Dollar				1,651.00				1,651.00
Senator Richard Shelby:									
United Kingdom	Pound		5,085.86						5,085.86
United States	Dollar				7,132.66				7,132.66
Senator Thad Cochran:									
United Kingdom	Pound		5,085.86						5,085.86
United States	Dollar				7,673.76				7,673.76
Kay Webber Cochran:									
United Kingdom	Pound		5,085.86						5,085.86
United States	Dollar				7,673.76				7,673.76
Linda Good:									
United Kingdom	Pound		5,085.86						5,085.86
Brian Potts:									
United Kingdom	Pound		5,085.86						5,085.86
Jacqui Russell:									
United Kingdom	Pound		5,085.86						5,085.86
Jeremy Weirich:									
United Kingdom	Pound		5,085.86						5,085.86
Jean Toal Eisen:									
United Kingdom	Pound		5,085.86						5,085.86
United States	Dollar				561.86				561.86
Virginia Boney:									
United Kingdom	Pound		5,085.86						5,085.86
Senator Lindsey Graham:									
United Kingdom	Pound		3,715.16						3,715.16
Anne Caldwell:									
United Kingdom	Pound		4,985.86						4,985.86
United States	Dollar				596.86				596.86
Rachel Santos:									
Tanzania	Shilling		1,341.50		3,562.00				4,903.50
United States	Dollar				11,367.76				11,367.76
Patrick Carroll:									
Tanzania	Shilling		1,341.50		3,562.00				4,903.50
United States	Dollar				11,367.76				11,367.76
Carlisle Clarke:									
Tanzania	Shilling		1,341.50		3,562.00				4,903.50
United States	Dollar				11,367.76				11,367.76
David Gillies:									
Japan	Yen		1,361.00						1,361.00
United States	Dollar				8,623.66				8,623.66

CONSOLIDATED REPORT OF EXPENDITURE OF FUNDS FOR FOREIGN TRAVEL BY MEMBERS AND EMPLOYEES OF THE U.S. SENATE, UNDER AUTHORITY OF SEC. 22, P.L. 95–384—22 U.S.C. 1754(b), COMMITTEE ON APPROPRIATIONS FOR TRAVEL FROM JULY 1 TO SEPT. 30, 2016—Continued

Name and country	Name of currency	Per diem		Transportation		Miscellaneous		Total	
		Foreign currency	U.S. dollar equivalent or U.S. currency	Foreign currency	U.S. dollar equivalent or U.S. currency	Foreign currency	U.S. dollar equivalent or U.S. currency	Foreign currency	U.S. dollar equivalent or U.S. currency
Kate Kaufer:									
Japan	Yen		1,361.00						1,361.00
Singapore	Dollar		559.00						559.00
United States	Dollar				33,509.26				33,509.26
United States	Dollar		146.81						146.81
Allen Cutler:									
France	Euro		674.00		170.00				844.00
Belgium	Euro		272.00						272.00
United States	Dollar				11,719.00				11,719.00
Alexander Carnes:									
Sudan	Pound		1,856.00		192.42				2,048.42
Djibouti	Franc						20.00		20.00
Ethiopia	Birr		818.05						818.05
United States	Dollar				1,632.88				1,632.88
Robert Henke:									
Germany	Euro		859.32						859.32
Luxembourg	Euro		392.56						392.56
Poland	Zloty		271.92						271.92
Estonia	Euro		226.00						226.00
United States	Dollar				12,403.17				12,403.17
Patrick Magnuson:									
Germany	Euro		859.32						859.32
Luxembourg	Euro		392.56						392.56
Poland	Zloty		271.92						271.92
Estonia	Euro		226.00						226.00
United States	Dollar				12,403.17				12,403.17
Tom Mancinelli:									
Morocco	Dirham		576.00						576.00
Czech Republic	Koruna		389.89						389.89
Ukraine	Hryvnia		737.26						737.26
Estonia	Euro		235.49						235.49
Iceland	Krona		383.00						383.00
William Todd:									
Jordan	Dinar		355.41						355.41
Djibouti	Franc		230.00						230.00
Kuwait	Dinar		788.80						788.80
United States	Dollar				12,385.76				12,385.76
Senator Brian Schatz:									
Korea	Won		790.18						790.18
Philippines	Peso		344.00						344.00
Japan	Yen		1,586.00		1,235.76				2,821.76
Senator Christopher Murphy:									
Korea	Won		790.18						790.18
Philippines	Peso		344.00						344.00
Japan	Yen		1,586.00						1,586.00
Alec Johnson:									
Korea	Won		790.18						790.18
Philippines	Peso		344.00						344.00
Japan	Yen		1,586.00						1,586.00
Chris Hall:									
Korea	Won		790.18						790.18
Philippines	Peso		344.00						344.00
Japan	Yen		1,586.00						1,586.00
Jennifer Santos:									
Korea	Won		790.18						790.18
Philippines	Peso		344.00						344.00
Japan	Yen		1,586.00						1,586.00
Senator Barbara Mikulski:									
Canada	Dollar		922.15						922.15
United States	Dollar				721.14				721.14
Jean Toal Eisen:									
Canada	Dollar		584.43						584.43
United States	Dollar				720.84				720.84
Jason Wheelock:									
Japan	Yen		507.00						507.00
Vietnam	Dong		1,304.00		257.85				1,561.85
Timor-Leste	Dollar		519.75		835.00				1,354.75
Indonesia	Rupiah		833.00						833.00
Hong Kong	Dollar		534.52						534.52
United States	Dollar				4,588.46				4,588.46
Paul Grove:									
Japan	Yen		908.00						908.00
Republic of Korea	Won		345.00						345.00
Philippines	Peso		580.03						580.03
Australia	Dollar		323.00						323.00
Timor-Leste	Dollar		574.89						574.89
Indonesia	Rupiah		724.00						724.00
Hong Kong	Dollar		1,069.04						1,069.04
United States	Dollar				23,751.26				23,751.26
* Delegation expenses:									
Tanzania	Shilling						241.11		241.11
United Kingdom	Pound						17,669.42		17,669.42
Japan	Yen						2,542.31		2,542.31
Romania	Leu						247.00		247.00
Germany	Euro						1,635.00		1,635.00
Canada	Dollar						3,462.18		3,462.18
Germany	Euro						138.98		138.98
Kuwait	Dinar						275.01		275.01
Jordan	Dinar						199.49		199.49
Japan	Yen						6,026.69		6,026.69
Philippines	Peso						1,637.53		1,637.53
Korea	Won						2,756.76		2,756.76
Sudan	Pound						354.55		354.55
Japan	Yen						9.47		9.47
Vietnam	Dong						1,094.99		1,094.99
Timor-Leste	Dollar						692.84		692.84
Indonesia	Rupiah						65.00		65.00
Hong Kong	Dollar						1,676.55		1,676.55
Philippines	Peso						387.40		387.40
Iceland	Krona						32.50		32.50
Ukraine	Hryvnia						93.97		93.97

CONSOLIDATED REPORT OF EXPENDITURE OF FUNDS FOR FOREIGN TRAVEL BY MEMBERS AND EMPLOYEES OF THE U.S. SENATE, UNDER AUTHORITY OF SEC. 22, P.L. 95–384—22 U.S.C. 1754(b), COMMITTEE ON APPROPRIATIONS FOR TRAVEL FROM JULY 1 TO SEPT. 30, 2016—Continued

Name and country	Name of currency	Per diem		Transportation		Miscellaneous		Total	
		Foreign currency	U.S. dollar equivalent or U.S. currency	Foreign currency	U.S. dollar equivalent or U.S. currency	Foreign currency	U.S. dollar equivalent or U.S. currency	Foreign currency	U.S. dollar equivalent or U.S. currency
Estonia	Euro						248.83		248.83
Czech Republic	Koruna						142.32		142.32
Morocco	Dirham						515.83		515.83
Total			101,330.15		236,527.99		42,165.73		380.023.87

* Delegation expenses include payments and reimbursements to the Department of State under authority of Sec. 502(b) of the Mutual Security Act of 1954, as amended by Section 22 of P.L. 95–384, and S. Res. 179 agreed to May 25, 1997.

SENATOR THAD COCHRAN,
Chairman, Committee on Appropriations, Oct. 25, 2016.

CONSOLIDATED REPORT OF EXPENDITURE OF FUNDS FOR FOREIGN TRAVEL BY MEMBERS AND EMPLOYEES OF THE U.S. SENATE, UNDER AUTHORITY OF SEC. 22, P.L. 95–384—22 U.S.C. 1754(b), COMMITTEE ON ARMED SERVICES FOR TRAVEL FROM JULY 1 TO SEPT. 30, 2016

Name and country	Name of currency	Per diem		Transportation		Miscellaneous		Total	
		Foreign currency	U.S. dollar equivalent or U.S. currency	Foreign currency	U.S. dollar equivalent or U.S. currency	Foreign currency	U.S. dollar equivalent or U.S. currency	Foreign currency	U.S. dollar equivalent or U.S. currency
Senator Roger Wicker:									
Georgia	Lari		1,316.67						1,316.67
Italy	Euro		1,118.19						1,118.19
Joseph Lai:									
Georgia	Lari		896.67						896.67
Italy	Euro		707.53						707.53
* Delegation Expenses:									
Georgia	Lari						300.00		300.00
Senator Joni Ernst:									
United States	Dollar				10,949.36				10,949.36
Kosovo	Euro		65.03						65.03
Greece	Euro		238.77						238.77
Kurt Freshley:									
United States	Dollar				14,802.46				14,802.46
Kosovo	Euro		93.85						93.85
Greece	Euro		238.77						238.77
Brenda Safranksi:									
United States	Dollar				10,949.36				10,949.36
Kosovo	Euro		65.03						65.03
Greece	Euro		238.77						238.77
* Delegation Expenses:									
Kosovo	Euro						1,153.35		1,153.35
Greece	Euro						900.00		900.00
Senator John McCain:									
United States	Dollar				20,688.72				20,688.72
Israel	Shekel		436.00						436.00
Pakistan	Rupee		9.00						9.00
Afghanistan	Afghani		48.20						48.20
Kathryn Wheelbarger:									
United States	Dollar				20,688.72				20,688.72
Israel	Shekel		466.00						466.00
Pakistan	Rupee		36.00						36.00
Afghanistan	Afghani		5.50						5.50
Elizabeth O'Bagy:									
United States	Dollar				20,688.72				20,688.72
Israel	Shekel		466.00						466.00
Pakistan	Rupee		36.00						36.00
Afghanistan	Afghani		5.50						5.50
Senator Lindsey Graham:									
United States	Dollar				29,249.02				29,249.02
Israel	Shekel		436.00						436.00
Pakistan	Rupee		15.64						15.64
Afghanistan	Afghani		27.00						27.00
United Kingdom	Pound		559.22						559.22
Craig Abele:									
United States	Dollar				20,688.72				20,688.72
Israel	Shekel		436.00						436.00
Pakistan	Rupee		9.00						9.00
Afghanistan	Afghani		27.00						27.00
Senator Joe Donnelly:									
United States	Dollar				24,402.48				24,402.48
Israel	Shekel		473.66						473.66
Pakistan	Rupee		168.69						168.69
* Delegation Expenses:									
Israel	Shekel						4,929.84		4,929.84
United Kingdom	Pound				5,011.67				5,011.67
Daniel Lerner:									
United States	Dollar				12,901.84				12,901.84
France	Euro		1,712.57						1,712.57
* Delegation Expenses:									
France	Euro				733.00				733.00
Senator Roger Wicker:									
United Kingdom	Pound		4,985.86						4,985.86
Joseph Lai:									
United Kingdom	Pound		4,985.86						4,985.86
Senator James M. Inhofe:									
United Kingdom	Pound		4,464.26						4,464.26
Anthony Lazarski:									
United Kingdom	Pound		4,591.56						4,591.56
Senator Mike Rounds:									
United Kingdom	Pound		4,133.86						4,133.86
Dan Adelstein:									
United Kingdom	Pound		4,133.86						4,133.86
* Delegation Expenses:									
United Kingdom	Pound						5,579.81		5,579.81
Daniel Lerner:									
United States	Dollar				10,079.76				10,079.76
Singapore	Dollar		2,041.09						2,041.09

CONSOLIDATED REPORT OF EXPENDITURE OF FUNDS FOR FOREIGN TRAVEL BY MEMBERS AND EMPLOYEES OF THE U.S. SENATE, UNDER AUTHORITY OF SEC. 22, P.L. 95–384—22 U.S.C. 1754(b), COMMITTEE ON ARMED SERVICES FOR TRAVEL FROM JULY 1 TO SEPT. 30, 2016—Continued

Name and country	Name of currency	Per diem		Transportation		Miscellaneous		Total	
		Foreign currency	U.S. dollar equivalent or U.S. currency	Foreign currency	U.S. dollar equivalent or U.S. currency	Foreign currency	U.S. dollar equivalent or U.S. currency	Foreign currency	U.S. dollar equivalent or U.S. currency
* Delegation Expenses:									
Singapore	Dollar				314.00		534.00		848.00
Christian Brose:									
United States	Dollar				23,447.94				23,447.94
Japan	Yen		589.27						589.27
South Korea	Won		360.54						360.54
Philippines	Peso		427.76						427.76
Australia	Dollar		971.79						971.79
* Delegation Expenses:									
Japan	Yen				281.18				281.18
South Korea	Won				287.42				287.42
Philippines	Peso				326.24				326.24
Australia	Dollar				251.66				251.66
Cord Sterling:									
United States	Dollar				18,656.52				18,656.52
Poland	Zloty		213.53						213.53
Ukraine	Hryvnia		778.92						778.92
Romania	Leu		450.79						450.79
* Delegation Expenses:									
Ukraine	Hryvnia						120.18		120.18
Romania	Leu				322.80				322.80
Adam Barker:									
United States	Dollar				14,001.58				14,001.58
Cameroon	Franc		690.02						690.02
Thomas Goffus:									
United States	Dollar				18,244.86				18,244.86
Germany	Euro		31.00						31.00
Azerbaijan	Manat		317.00						317.00
Georgia	Lari		616.00						616.00
Armenia	Dram		289.00						289.00
Austria	Euro		95.00						95.00
Bosnia & Herzegovina	Marka		493.00						493.00
Montenegro	Euro		525.00						525.00
Albania	Lek		205.00						205.00
Serbia	Dinar		361.00						361.00
Macedonia	Denar		262.00						262.00
Kosovo	Euro		420.00						420.00
Kathryn Wheelbarger:									
United States	Dollar				18,330.86				18,330.86
Germany	Euro		82.00						82.00
Azerbaijan	Manat		317.00						317.00
Georgia	Lari		604.00			.			604.00
Armenia	Dram		289.60						289.60
Austria	Euro		95.00						95.00
Bosnia & Herzegovina	Marka		495.00						495.00
Montenegro	Euro		523.00						523.00
Albania	Lek		204.00						204.00
Serbia	Dinar		350.00						350.00
Macedonia	Denar		266.00						266.00
Kosovo	Euro		433.00						433.00
Dustin Walker:									
United States	Dollar				18,547.66				18,547.66
Germany	Euro		7.50						7.50
Azerbaijan	Manat		233.00						233.00
Georgia	Lari		540.20						540.20
Armenia	Dram		290.00						290.00
Austria	Euro		95.00						95.00
Bosnia & Herzegovina	Marka		482.50						482.50
Montenegro	Euro		425.10						425.10
Albania	Lek		154.00						154.00
Serbia	Dinar		333.20						333.20
Macedonia	Denar		175.50						175.50
Kosovo	Euro		322.05						322.05
Mariah McNamara:									
United States	Dollar				18,244.86				18,244.86
Germany	Euro		58.00						58.00
Azerbaijan	Manat		342.00						342.00
Georgia	Lari		629.00						629.00
Armenia	Dram		290.00						290.00
Austria	Euro		95.00						95.00
Bosnia & Herzegovina	Marka		495.00						495.00
Montenegro	Euro		548.00						548.00
Albania	Lek		198.00						198.00
Serbia	Dinar		372.00						372.00
Macedonia	Denar		256.00						256.00
Kosovo	Euro		433.00						433.00
* Delegation Expenses:									
Azerbaijan	Manat						287.94		287.94
Georgia	Lari						510.82		510.82
Armenia	Dram				480.28				480.28
Bosnia & Herzegovina	Marka						320.33		320.33
Montenegro	Euro						668.00		668.00
Serbia	Dinar				168.00				168.00
Kosovo	Euro						402.58		402.58
Jonathan Epstein:									
United States	Dollar				18,773.96				18,773.96
Kazakhstan	Tenge		572.96						572.96
Armenia	Dram		305.82						305.82
Ukraine	Hryvnia		580.00						580.00
Moldova	Leu		616.04						616.04
Belarus	Ruble		381.00						381.00
* Delegation Expenses:									
Armenia	Dram				258.64				258.64
Ukraine	Hryvnia				257.17				257.17
Cord Sterling:									
United States	Dollar				15,094.82				15,094.82
Philippines	Peso		504.00						504.00
Australia	Dollar		893.33						893.33
Singapore	Dollar		743.00						743.00
Kathryn Wheelbarger:									
United States	Dollar				15,094.82				15,094.82

CONSOLIDATED REPORT OF EXPENDITURE OF FUNDS FOR FOREIGN TRAVEL BY MEMBERS AND EMPLOYEES OF THE U.S. SENATE, UNDER AUTHORITY OF SEC. 22, P.L. 95–384—22 U.S.C. 1754(b), COMMITTEE ON ARMED SERVICES FOR TRAVEL FROM JULY 1 TO SEPT. 30, 2016—Continued

Name and country	Name of currency	Per diem Foreign currency	Per diem U.S. dollar equivalent or U.S. currency	Transportation Foreign currency	Transportation U.S. dollar equivalent or U.S. currency	Miscellaneous Foreign currency	Miscellaneous U.S. dollar equivalent or U.S. currency	Total Foreign currency	Total U.S. dollar equivalent or U.S. currency
Philippines	Peso		504.00						504.00
Australia	Dollar		715.00						715.00
Singapore	Dollar		768.00						768.00
David E. Sayers:									
United States	Dollar				15,094.82				15,094.82
Philippines	Peso		504.00						504.00
Australia	Dollar		715.00						715.00
Singapore	Dollar		768.00						768.00
* Delegation Expenses:									
Australia	Dollar				241.00				241.00
Singapore	Dollar				551.00				551.00
Senator Bill Nelson:									
United States	Dollar				900.20				900.20
Morocco	Dirham		667.83						667.83
Ukraine	Hryvnia		303.27						303.27
Estonia	Euro		285.49						285.49
Iceland	Krona		316.14						316.14
Mathew Williams:									
United States	Dollar				900.20				900.20
Morocco	Dirham		691.29						691.29
Ukraine	Hryvnia		262.86						262.86
Estonia	Euro		207.57						207.57
Iceland	Krona		306.52						306.52
* Delegation Expenses:									
Morocco	Dirham						1,031.65		1,031.65
Ukraine	Hryvnia				241.63				241.63
Estonia	Euro				476.66				476.66
Iceland	Krona						74.28		74.28
Senator Angus King:									
Denmark	Krone				905.38				905.38
Stephen Smith:									
Denmark	Krone		905.25						905.25
Morgan Cashwell:									
Denmark	Krone		895.67						895.67
Delegation Expenses:									
Denmark	Krone				3,928.23				3,928.23
Alex Wong:									
United States	Dollar				6,255.57				6,255.57
Norway	Krone		1,297.07						1,297.07
Sweden	Krona		725.00						725.00
Latvia	Euro		743.11						743.11
* Delegation Expenses:									
Norway	Krone				1,458.74				1,458.74
Sweden	Krona				533.50		493.50		1,027.00
Latvia	Euro				255.64				255.64
Senator Martin Heinrich:									
United States	Dollar				12,178.08				12,178.08
Djibouti	Franc		398.03						398.03
Kuwait	Dinar		949.49						949.49
Iraq	Dinar		61.00						61.00
Austria	Euro		370.24						370.24
Tony Samp:									
United States	Dollar				12,178.08				12,178.08
Djibouti	Franc		398.03						398.03
Kuwait	Dinar		949.49						949.49
Iraq	Dinar		61.00						61.00
Austria	Euro		370.24						370.24
* Delegation Expenses:									
Kuwait	Dinar						309.69		309.69
Iraq	Dinar				3,450.00				3,450.00
Senator Lindsey Graham:									
United States	Dollar				13,357.76				13,357.76
Italy	Euro		1,945.27						1,945.27
* Delegation Expenses:									
Italy	Euro				1,025.64				1,025.64
Anish Goel:									
United States	Dollar				1,861.36				1,861.36
Sweden	Krona		61.49						61.49
Adam Barker:									
United States	Dollar				12,441.46				12,441.46
Germany	Euro		580.88						580.88
Italy	Euro		411.88						411.88
* Delegation Expenses:									
Germany	Euro				600.00				600.00
Italy	Euro				488.51				488.51
Anish Goel:									
United States	Dollar				3,030.62				3,030.62
Peru	Sol		1,167.38						1,167.38
James B. Hickey:									
United States	Dollar				7,407.66				7,407.66
Estonia	Euro		210.94						210.94
Latvia	Euro		727.33						727.33
Germany	Euro		194.55						194.55
Poland	Zloty		687.69						687.69
* Delegation Expenses:									
Latvia	Euro				668.90				668.90
James B. Hickey:									
United States	Dollar				9,950.46				9,950.46
Latvia	Euro		10.00						10.00
Lithuania	Euro		829.65						829.65
* Delegation Expenses:									
Latvia	Euro				269.97				269.97
Lithuania	Euro						37.80		37.80
Total			84,779.28		493,870.17		17,653.77		596,303.22

* Delegation expenses include payments and reimbursements to the Department of State under authority of Sec. 502(b) of the Mutual Security Act of 1954, as amended by Section 22 of P.L. 95–384, and S. Res. 179 agreed to May 25, 1977.

SENATOR JOHN McCAIN,
Chairman, Committee on Armed Services, Nov. 2, 2016.

CONSOLIDATED REPORT OF EXPENDITURE OF FUNDS FOR FOREIGN TRAVEL BY MEMBERS AND EMPLOYEES OF THE U.S. SENATE, UNDER AUTHORITY OF SEC. 22, P.L. 95–384—22 U.S.C. 1754(b), COMMITTEE ON BANKING, HOUSING, AND URBAN AFFAIRS FOR TRAVEL FROM JULY 1 TO SEPT. 30, 2016

Name and country	Name of currency	Per diem		Transportation		Miscellaneous		Total	
		Foreign currency	U.S. dollar equivalent or U.S. currency	Foreign currency	U.S. dollar equivalent or U.S. currency	Foreign currency	U.S. dollar equivalent or U.S. currency	Foreign currency	U.S. dollar equivalent or U.S. currency
Senator Ben Sasse:									
Pakistan	Rupee		28.50						28.50
Afghanistan	Afghani		28.50						28.50
United States	Dollar				13,621.66				13,621.66
Total			57.00		13,621.66		0.00		13,678.66

SENATOR RICHARD C. SHELBY,
Chairman, Committee on Banking, Oct. 25, 2016.

CONSOLIDATED REPORT OF EXPENDITURE OF FUNDS FOR FOREIGN TRAVEL BY MEMBERS AND EMPLOYEES OF THE U.S. SENATE, UNDER AUTHORITY OF SEC. 22, P.L. 95–384—22 U.S.C. 1754(b), COMMITTEE ON COMMERCE, SCIENCE, AND TRANSPORTATION FOR TRAVEL FROM JULY 1 TO SEPT. 30, 2016

Name and country	Name of currency	Per diem		Transportation		Miscellaneous		Total	
		Foreign currency	U.S. dollar equivalent or U.S. currency	Foreign currency	U.S. dollar equivalent or U.S. currency	Foreign currency	U.S. dollar equivalent or U.S. currency	Foreign currency	U.S. dollar equivalent or U.S. currency
B.Bailey Edwards:									
Greenland	Krone		739.59						739.59
Iceland	Krona		244.00						244.00
Nicholas Cummings:									
Greenland	Krone		684.59						684.59
Iceland	Krona		304.00						304.00
Total			1,972.18		0.00		0.00		1,972.18

SENATOR JOHN THUNE,
Chairman, Committee on Commerce, Science, and Transportation,
Nov. 7, 2016.

CONSOLIDATED REPORT OF EXPENDITURE OF FUNDS FOR FOREIGN TRAVEL BY MEMBERS AND EMPLOYEES OF THE U.S. SENATE, UNDER AUTHORITY OF SEC. 22, P.L. 95–384—22 U.S.C. 1754(b), COMMITTEE ON ENERGY AND NATURAL RESOURCES FOR TRAVEL FROM JULY 1 TO SEPT. 30, 2016

Name and country	Name of currency	Per diem		Transportation		Miscellaneous		Total	
		Foreign currency	U.S. dollar equivalent or U.S. currency	Foreign currency	U.S. dollar equivalent or U.S. currency	Foreign currency	U.S. dollar equivalent or U.S. currency	Foreign currency	U.S. dollar equivalent or U.S. currency
David Gillers:									
United States	Dollar				2,539.06				2,539.06
United Kingdom	Pound		1,330.90						1,330.90
Total			1,330.90		2,539.06		0.00		3,869.96

SENATOR LISA MURKOWSKI,
Chairman, Committee on Energy and Natural Resources, Oct. 5, 2016.

CONSOLIDATED REPORT OF EXPENDITURE OF FUNDS FOR FOREIGN TRAVEL BY MEMBERS AND EMPLOYEES OF THE U.S. SENATE, UNDER AUTHORITY OF SEC. 22, P.L. 95–384—22 U.S.C. 1754(b), COMMITTEE ON ENVIRONMENT AND PUBLIC WORKS FOR TRAVEL FROM JULY 1 TO SEPT. 30, 2016

Name and country	Name of currency	Per diem		Transportation		Miscellaneous		Total	
		Foreign currency	U.S. dollar equivalent or U.S. currency	Foreign currency	U.S. dollar equivalent or U.S. currency	Foreign currency	U.S. dollar equivalent or U.S. currency	Foreign currency	U.S. dollar equivalent or U.S. currency
Senator Cory A. Booker:									
United States	Dollar				9,116.29				9,116.29
Iraq	Dinar				4,550.00				4,550.00
Jordan	Dinar		523.31						523.31
Israel	Shekel		1,932.00						1,932.00
Sophia Lalani:									
United States	Dollar				9,467.49				9,467.49
Iraq	Dinar		6.00		4,550.00				4,550.00
Jordan	Dinar		635.22						635.22
Israel	Shekel		1,951.58						1,951.58
Matthew B. Klapper:									
United States	Dollar				9,116.29				9,116.29
Iraq	Dinar				4,550.00				4,550.00
Jordan	Dinar		477.41						477.41
Israel	Shekel		1,846.00						1,846.00
* Delegation Expenses:									
Jordan	Dinar						881.39		881.39
Israel	Shekel						10,440.13		10,440.13
Total			7,371.52		41,350.07		11,321.52		60,043.11

* Delegation expenses include payments and reimbursements to the Department of State under authority of Sec. 502(b) of the Mutual Security Act of 1954, as amended by Section 22 of P.L. 95–384, and S. Res. 179 agreed to May 25, 1977.

SENATOR JAMES INHOFE,
Chairman, Committee on Environment and Public Works, Oct. 27, 2016.

CONSOLIDATED REPORT OF EXPENDITURE OF FUNDS FOR FOREIGN TRAVEL BY MEMBERS AND EMPLOYEES OF THE U.S. SENATE, UNDER AUTHORITY OF SEC. 22, P.L. 95–384—22 U.S.C. 1754(b), COMMITTEE ON FINANCE FOR TRAVEL FROM JULY 1 TO SEPT. 30, 2016

Name and country	Name of currency	Per diem		Transportation		Miscellaneous		Total	
		Foreign currency	U.S. dollar equivalent or U.S. currency	Foreign currency	U.S. dollar equivalent or U.S. currency	Foreign currency	U.S. dollar equivalent or U.S. currency	Foreign currency	U.S. dollar equivalent or U.S. currency
Senator Tim Scott:									
Israel	Shekel		770.00						770.00
United States	Dollar				10,683.39				10,683.39
Jennifer DeCasper:									
Israel	Sheckel		770.00						770.00
United States	Dollar				11,835.39				11,835.39
Brian Goff:									
Israel	Sheckel		770.00						770.00
United States	Dollar				10,683.39				10,683.39
Christopher Campbell:									
Canada	Dollar		3,008.00						3,008.00
United States	Dollar				984.99				984.99
									0.00
Everett Eissenstat:									
Switzerland	Swiss Franc		1,657.01		11,959.06				13,616.07
United States	Dollar				11,959.06				11,959.06
Shane Warren:									
Switzerland	Swiss Franc		1,674.39						1,674.39
United States	Dollar				11,959.06				11,959.06
Christopher Campbell:									
Thailand	Thai Bhat		809.18						809.18
Brunei	Brunei Dollar		347.00						347.00
Singapore	Singapore Dollar		744.47						744.47
United States	Dollar				33,795.22				33,795.22
Everett Eissenstat:									
India	Rupee		464.17						464.17
Thailand	Thai Bhat		526.12						526.12
Brunei	Brunei Dollar		352.14						352.14
Singapore	Singapore Dollar		1,034.36						1,034.36
United States	Dollar				32,656.90				32,656.90
Shane Warren:									
India	Rupee		450.59						450.59
Thailand	Thai Bhat		562.94						562.94
Brunei	Brunei Dollar		347.00						347.00
Singapore	Singapore Dollar		1,120.54						1,120.54
United States	Dollar				32,656.90				32,656.90
Jay Khosla:									
India	Rupee		450.14						450.14
Thailand	Thai Bhat		559.02						559.02
Brunei	Brunei Dollar		347.00						347.00
Singapore	Singapore Dollar		1,068.49						1,068.49
United States	Dollar				32,321.90				32,321.90
* Delegation Expenses									
United States	Dollar						2,180.91		2,180.91
Total			17,832.56		201,495.26		2,180.91		221,508.73

* Delegation expenses include transportation, embassy overtime, as well as official expenses in accordance with the responsibilities of the host country.

SENATOR ORRIN HATCH,
Chairman, Committee on Finance, Oct. 26, 2016.

CONSOLIDATED REPORT OF EXPENDITURE OF FUNDS FOR FOREIGN TRAVEL BY MEMBERS AND EMPLOYEES OF THE U.S. SENATE, UNDER AUTHORITY OF SEC. 22, P.L. 95–384—22 U.S.C. 1754(b), COMMITTEE ON FOREIGN RELATIONS FOR TRAVEL FROM JULY 1 TO SEPT. 30, 2016

Name and country	Name of currency	Per diem		Transportation		Miscellaneous		Total	
		Foreign currency	U.S. dollar equivalent or U.S. currency	Foreign currency	U.S. dollar equivalent or U.S. currency	Foreign currency	U.S. dollar equivalent or U.S. currency	Foreign currency	U.S. dollar equivalent or U.S. currency
Senator John Barrasso:									
United Arab Emirates	Dirham		285.00						285.00
United States	Dollar				15,894.60				15,894.60
Charles Ziegler:									
United Arab Emirates	Dirham		285.00						285.00
United States	Dollar				15,788.16				15,788.16
* Delegation Expenses:									
United Arab Emirates	Dirham						513.92		513.92
Senator Christopher Coons:									
Morocco	Dirham		578.89						578.89
Czech Republic	Koruna		113.29						113.29
Estonia	Kroon		574.93						574.93
Ukraine	Hryvnia		199.62						199.62
Iceland	Kronur		319.88						319.88
Christy Gleason:									
Morocco	Dirham		574.99						574.99
Czech Republic	Koruna		387.75						387.75
Estonia	Kroon		573.05						573.05
Ukraine	Hryvnia		236.46						236.46
Iceland	Kronur		327.37						327.37
* Delegation Expenses:									
Morocco	Dirham						802.38		802.38
Czech Republic	Koruna						284.64		284.64
Estonia	Kroon						497.66		497.66
Ukraine	Hryvnia						130.24		130.24
Iceland	Kronur						452.00		452.00
Senator Edward Markey:									
Cabo Verde	Escudo		182.24						182.24
Senegal	CFA Franc		889.32						889.32
Liberia	Liberian dollar		685.62						685.62
Nigeria	Nairas		1,050.84						1,050.84
Spain	Euro		315.33						315.33
Phillip McGovern:									
Cabo Verde	Escudo		142.71						142.71
Senegal	CFA Franc		678.68						678.68
Liberia	Liberian dollar		645.54						645.54
Nigeria	Nairas		787.52						787.52
Spain	Euro		281.62						281.62

CONSOLIDATED REPORT OF EXPENDITURE OF FUNDS FOR FOREIGN TRAVEL BY MEMBERS AND EMPLOYEES OF THE U.S. SENATE, UNDER AUTHORITY OF SEC. 22, P.L. 95–384—22 U.S.C. 1754(b), COMMITTEE ON FOREIGN RELATIONS FOR TRAVEL FROM JULY 1 TO SEPT. 30, 2016—Continued

Name and country	Name of currency	Per diem		Transportation		Miscellaneous		Total	
		Foreign currency	U.S. dollar equivalent or U.S. currency	Foreign currency	U.S. dollar equivalent or U.S. currency	Foreign currency	U.S. dollar equivalent or U.S. currency	Foreign currency	U.S. dollar equivalent or U.S. currency
* Delegation Expenses:									
Cabo Verde	Escudo						259.01		259.01
Senegal	CFA Franc						1,107.00		1,107.00
Nigeria	Nairas						2,115.75		2,115.75
Spain	Euro						521.52		521.52
Sarah Downs:									
Honduras	Lempira		580.00						580.00
Nicaragua	Cordoba		424.14						424.14
Costa Rica	Costa Rican Colon		561.80						561.80
United States	Dollar				1,719.18				1,719.18
Caleb McCarry:									
Honduras	Lempira		580.00						580.00
Nicaragua	Cordoba		424.14						424.14
Costa Rica	Costa Rican Colon		561.80						561.80
United States	Dollar				1,719.18				1,719.18
* Delegation Expenses:									
Honduras	Lempira						985.00		985.00
Nicaragua	Cordoba						365.51		365.51
Costa Rica	Costa Rican Colon						994.65		994.65
Heather Flynn:									
Burundi	Burundi Francs		597.00						597.00
Ethiopia	Birr		2,105.00						2,105.00
United States	Dollar				5,780.66				5,780.66
* Delegation Expenses:									
Burundi	Burundi Francs						1,108.89		1,108.89
Chris Ford:									
United Kingdom	Pound		1,364.20						1,364.20
France	Euro		677.13						677.13
United States	Dollar				3,427.46				3,427.46
Jim Greene:									
United Kingdom	Pound		1,451.70						1,451.70
Belgium	Euro		948.55						948.55
Germany	Euro		699.94						699.94
Ukraine	Hryvnia		1,388.26						1,388.26
United States	Dollar				3,263.96				3,263.96
Jonathan Tsentas:									
United Kingdom	Pound		1,468.41						1,468.41
Belgium	Euro		988.55						988.55
Germany	Euro		685.82						685.82
Ukraine	Hryvnia		929.00						929.00
United States	Dollar				3,263.96				3,263.96
* Delegation Expenses:									
United Kingdom	Pound						108.14		108.14
Belgium	Euro						235.44		235.44
Ukraine	Hryvnia						345.61		345.61
Josh Klein:									
Greenland	Danish Krone		687.00						687.00
Norway	Norwegian Krone		1,140.83						1,140.83
United States	Dollar				1,798.26				1,798.26
Charlotte Oldham-Moore:									
Kenya	Shilling		1,155.00						1,155.00
Democratic Republic of Congo	Congolese Franc		515.00						515.00
United States	Dollar				6,054.08				6,054.08
* Delegation Expenses:									
Kenya	Shilling						275.00		275.00
Democratic Republic of Congo	Congolese Franc						224.10		224.10
Damian Murphy:									
Afghanistan	Afghanis		134.15						134.15
Pakistan	Rupees		207.00						207.00
United States	Dollar				2,742.76				2,742.76
Margaret Taylor:									
Afghanistan	Afghanis		20.00						20.00
Pakistan	Rupees		407.00						407.00
United States	Dollar				2,742.76				2,742.76
* Delegation Expenses:									
Pakistan	Rupees						249.03		249.03
Morgan Vina:									
Rwanda	Rwandan Francs		642.00						642.00
* Delegation Expenses:									
Rwanda	Rwandan Francs						268.50		268.50
Total			31,459.07		64,195.02		11,843.99		107,498.08

* Delegation expenses include payments and reimbursements to the Department of State under authority of Sec. 502(b) of the Mutual Security Act of 1954, as amended by Section 22 of P.L. 95–384, and S. Res. 179 agreed to May 25, 1977.

SENATOR BOB CORKER,
Chairman, Committee on Foreign Relations, Oct. 27, 2016.

CONSOLIDATED REPORT OF EXPENDITURE OF FUNDS FOR FOREIGN TRAVEL BY MEMBERS AND EMPLOYEES OF THE U.S. SENATE, UNDER AUTHORITY OF SEC. 22, P.L. 95–384—22 U.S.C. 1754(b), COMMITTEE ON HOMELAND SECURITY & GOVERNMENTAL AFFAIRS FOR TRAVEL FROM JAN. 1 TO MAR. 31, 2016

Name and country	Name of currency	Per diem		Transportation		Miscellaneous		Total	
		Foreign currency	U.S. dollar equivalent or U.S. currency	Foreign currency	U.S. dollar equivalent or U.S. currency	Foreign currency	U.S. dollar equivalent or U.S. currency	Foreign currency	U.S. dollar equivalent or U.S. currency
Senator Thomas R. Carper:									
United States	Dollar				1,219.79				1,219.79
Guatemala	Quetzal		92.00						92.00
El Salvador	Dollar		44.17						44.17
Holly Idelson:									
United States	Dollar				1,509.39				1,509.39
Guatemala	Quetzal		24.00						24.00
El Salvador	Dollar		50.17						50.17
Senator Tammy Baldwin:									
Austria	Euro		318.54						318.54
Israel	Shekel		979.80						979.80

CONSOLIDATED REPORT OF EXPENDITURE OF FUNDS FOR FOREIGN TRAVEL BY MEMBERS AND EMPLOYEES OF THE U.S. SENATE, UNDER AUTHORITY OF SEC. 22, P.L. 95–384—22 U.S.C. 1754(b), COMMITTEE ON HOMELAND SECURITY & GOVERNMENTAL AFFAIRS FOR TRAVEL FROM JAN. 1 TO MAR. 31, 2016—Continued

Name and country	Name of currency	Per diem		Transportation		Miscellaneous		Total	
		Foreign currency	U.S. dollar equivalent or U.S. currency	Foreign currency	U.S. dollar equivalent or U.S. currency	Foreign currency	U.S. dollar equivalent or U.S. currency	Foreign currency	U.S. dollar equivalent or U.S. currency
Saudi Arabia	Riyal		447.73						447.73
Turkey	Lira		306.62						306.62
Senator Heidi Heitkamp:									
Austria	Euro		364.94						364.94
Israel	Shekel		847.18						847.18
Saudi Arabia	Riyal		495.30						495.30
Turkey	Lira		356.78						356.78
Senator Cory Booker:									
United States	Dollar				3,160.26				3,160.26
Austria	Euro		330.14						330.14
Israel	Shekel		1,100.00						1,100.00
Saudi Arbaia	Riyal		509.33						509.33
Turkey	Lira		100.51						100.51
Senator Gary Peters:									
Austria	Euro		360.19						360.19
Israel	Shekel		1,081.50						1,081.50
Saudi Arabia	Riyal		490.55						490.55
Turkey	Lira		352.03						352.03
Tessa Gould:									
Austria	Euro		374.30						374.30
Israel	Shekel		1,095.61						1,095.61
Saudi Arabia	Riyal		504.65						504.65
Turkey	Lira		366.13						366.13
Eric Feldman:									
Austria	Euro		297.51						297.51
Israel	Shekel		936.77						936.77
Saudi Arabia	Riyal		482.17						482.17
Turkey	Lira		370.53						370.53
Jeremy Steslicki:									
Austria	Euro		318.54						318.54
Israel	Shekel		976.80						976.80
Saudi Arabia	Riyal		447.73						447.73
Turkey	Lira		306.60						306.60
William "Bill" Murat:									
Austria	Euro		318.84						318.84
Israel	Shekel		977.40						977.40
Saudi Arabia	Riyal		448.03						448.03
Turkey	Lira		306.92						306.92
Matthew Klapper:									
Austria	Euro		330.14						330.14
Israel	Shekel		1,100.00						1,100.00
Saudi Arabia	Riyal		509.33						509.33
Turkey	Lira		128.84						128.84
Sophia Lalani:									
Austria	Euro		330.14						330.14
Israel	Shekel		1,100.00						1,100.00
Saudi Arabia	Riyal		509.33						509.33
Turkey	Lira		246.68						246.68
Jose "Joske" Bautista:									
United States	Dollar				1,855.07				1,855.07
Brazil	Real		580.00						580.00
Argentina	Peso		691.61						691.61
Uruguay	Peso		231.00						231.00
Senator Ben Sasse:									
Burma	Kyat		676.00						676.00
Thailand	Baht		468.21						468.21
Germany	Euro		917.21						917.21
* Delegation Expenses:									
El Salvador							931.69		931.69
Total			24,998.50		7,744.51		931.69		33,674.70

* Delegation expenses include payments and reimbursements to the Department of State under authority of Sec. 502(b) of the Mutual Security Act of 1954, as amended by Section 22 of P.L. 95–384, and S. Res. 179 agreed to May 25, 1977.

SENATOR RON JOHNSON,
Chairman, Committee on Homeland Security & Governmental Affairs,
Sept. 23, 2016.

CONSOLIDATED REPORT OF EXPENDITURE OF FUNDS FOR FOREIGN TRAVEL BY MEMBERS AND EMPLOYEES OF THE U.S. SENATE, UNDER AUTHORITY OF SEC. 22, P.L. 95–384—22 U.S.C. 1754(b), COMMITTEE ON HOMELAND SECURITY & GOVERNMENTAL AFFAIRS FOR TRAVEL FROM JULY 1 TO SEPT. 30, 2016

Name and country	Name of currency	Per diem		Transportation		Miscellaneous		Total	
		Foreign currency	U.S. dollar equivalent or U.S. currency	Foreign currency	U.S. dollar equivalent or U.S. currency	Foreign currency	U.S. dollar equivalent or U.S. currency	Foreign currency	U.S. dollar equivalent or U.S. currency
Jose Bautista:									
United States	Dollar				1,005.56				1,005.56
United Kingdom	Pound		1,527.98						1,527.98
Brooke Ericson:									
United States	Dollar				10,771.76				10,771.76
South Korea	Won		804.59						804.59
Singapore	Dollar		1,170.82						1,170.82
David Luckey:									
United States	Dollar				10,771.76				10,771.76
South Korea	Won		801.59						801.59
Singapore	Dollar		1,166.82						1,166.82
Gabrielle D'Adamo:									
United States	Dollar				10,771.76				10,771.76
South Korea	Won		777.51						777.51
Singapore	Dollar		1,230.85						1,230.85
Gabrielle Batkin:									
United States	Dollar				10,771.76				10,771.76
South Korea	Won		909.59						909.59
Singapore	Dollar		691.00						691.00
Stephen Vina:									
United States	Dollar				10,771.76				10,771.76
South Korea	Won		814.65						814.65

CONSOLIDATED REPORT OF EXPENDITURE OF FUNDS FOR FOREIGN TRAVEL BY MEMBERS AND EMPLOYEES OF THE U.S. SENATE, UNDER AUTHORITY OF SEC. 22, P.L. 95–384—22 U.S.C. 1754(b), COMMITTEE ON HOMELAND SECURITY & GOVERNMENTAL AFFAIRS FOR TRAVEL FROM JULY 1 TO SEPT. 30, 2016—Continued

Name and country	Name of currency	Per diem		Transportation		Miscellaneous		Total	
		Foreign currency	U.S. dollar equivalent or U.S. currency	Foreign currency	U.S. dollar equivalent or U.S. currency	Foreign currency	U.S. dollar equivalent or U.S. currency	Foreign currency	U.S. dollar equivalent or U.S. currency
Singapore	Dollar		1,203.40						1,203.40
Senator Gary Peters:									
Ukraine	Hryvnia		513.63						513.63
Estonia	Euro		172.38						172.38
Iceland	Krona		237.00						237.00
Morocco	Dirham		487.04						487.04
Czech Republic	Koruna		354.93						354.93
David Weinberg:									
Ukraine	Hryvnia		541.71						541.71
Estonia	Euro		193.42						193.42
Iceland	Krona		266.82						266.82
Morocco	Dirham		503.33						503.33
Czech Republic	Koruna		439.89						439.89
* Delegation Expenses:									
South Korea	Won						1,193.88		1,193.88
Total			14,808.95		54,864.36		1,193.88		70,867.19

* Delegation expenses include payments and reimbursements to the Department of State under authority of Sec. 502(b) of the Mutual Security Act of 1954, as amended by Section 22 of P.L. 95–384, and S. Res. 179 agreed to May 25, 1977.

SENATOR RON JOHNSON,
Chairman, Committee on Homeland Security & Governmental Affairs,
Oct. 18, 2016.

CONSOLIDATED REPORT OF EXPENDITURE OF FUNDS FOR FOREIGN TRAVEL BY MEMBERS AND EMPLOYEES OF THE U.S. SENATE, UNDER AUTHORITY OF SEC. 22, P.L. 95–384—22 U.S.C. 1754(b), COMMITTEE ON THE JUDICIARY FOR TRAVEL FROM JULY 1 TO SEPT. 30, 2016

Name and country	Name of currency	Per diem		Transportation		Miscellaneous		Total	
		Foreign currency	U.S. dollar equivalent or U.S. currency	Foreign currency	U.S. dollar equivalent or U.S. currency	Foreign currency	U.S. dollar equivalent or U.S. currency	Foreign currency	U.S. dollar equivalent or U.S. currency
Senator John Cornyn:									
United States	Dollar				13,601.86				13,601.86
Iraq	Dinar		61.00		1,725.00				1,786.00
Afghanistan	Afghani		83.00						83.00
Qatar	Rial		319.65						319.65
Carter Burwell:									
United States	Dollar				12,997.86				12,997.86
Iraq	Dinar		61.00		1,725.00				1,786.00
Afghanistan	Afghani		83.00						83.00
Qatar	Rial		319.65						319.65
* Delegation Expenses:									
Qatar	Rial						244.76		244.76
United Arab Emirates	Dirham						113.61		113.61
Total			927.30		30,049.72		358.37		31,335.39

* Delegation expenses include payments and reimbursements to the Department of State under authority of Sec. 502(b) of the Mutual Security Act of 1954, as amended by Section 22 of P.L. 95–384, and S. Res. 179 agreed to May 25, 1977.

SENATOR CHUCK GRASSLEY,
Chairman, Committee on the Judiciary, Oct. 25, 2016.

CONSOLIDATED REPORT OF EXPENDITURE OF FUNDS FOR FOREIGN TRAVEL BY MEMBERS AND EMPLOYEES OF THE U.S. SENATE, UNDER AUTHORITY OF SEC. 22, P.L. 95–384—22 U.S.C. 1754(b), COMMITTEE ON HEALTH, EDUCATION, LABOR, AND PENSIONS FOR TRAVEL FROM JULY 1 TO SEPT. 30, 2016

Name and country	Name of currency	Per diem		Transportation		Miscellaneous		Total	
		Foreign currency	U.S. dollar equivalent or U.S. currency	Foreign currency	U.S. dollar equivalent or U.S. currency	Foreign currency	U.S. dollar equivalent or U.S. currency	Foreign currency	U.S. dollar equivalent or U.S. currency
Peter Oppenheim:									
South Africa	Rand		2,040.00						2,040.00
Mary Sumpter Lapinski:									
South Africa	Rand		1,978.00						1,978.00
* Delegation Expenses:									
South Africa	Rand						303.13		303.13
Total			4,018.00				303.13		4,321.13

* Delegation expenses include payments and reimbursements to the Department of State under the authority of Sec. 502(b) of the Mutual Security Act of 1954, as amended by Sec. 22 of P.L. 95–384, and S. Res. 179, agreed to May 25, 1977.

SENATOR LAMAR ALEXANDER,
Chairman, Committee on Health, Labor, and Pensions, Oct 25, 2016.

CONSOLIDATED REPORT OF EXPENDITURE OF FUNDS FOR FOREIGN TRAVEL BY MEMBERS AND EMPLOYEES OF THE U.S. SENATE, UNDER AUTHORITY OF SEC. 22, P.L. 95–384—22 U.S.C. 1754(b), COMMITTEE ON SMALL BUSINESS AND ENTREPRENEURSHIP FOR TRAVEL FROM JULY 1 TO SEPT. 30, 2016

Name and country	Name of currency	Per diem		Transportation		Miscellaneous		Total	
		Foreign currency	U.S. dollar equivalent or U.S. currency	Foreign currency	U.S. dollar equivalent or U.S. currency	Foreign currency	U.S. dollar equivalent or U.S. currency	Foreign currency	U.S. dollar equivalent or U.S. currency
Senator David Vitter:									
United Kingdom	Pound		3,207.39						3,207.39
United States	Dollar				15,111.66				15,111.66
Meredith West:									
United Kingdom	Pound		2,969.38						2,969.38
United States	Dollar				21,961.72				21,961.72

Total			6,176.77		37,073.38		0.00		43,250.15

SENATOR DAVID VITTER,
Chairman, Committee on Small Business and Entrepreneurship,
Oct. 27, 2016.

CONSOLIDATED REPORT OF EXPENDITURE OF FUNDS FOR FOREIGN TRAVEL BY MEMBERS AND EMPLOYEES OF THE U.S. SENATE, UNDER AUTHORITY OF SEC. 22, P.L. 95–384—22 U.S.C. 1754(b), U.S. SENATE SELECT COMMITTEE ON INTELLIGENCE FOR TRAVEL FROM JULY 1 TO SEPT. 30, 2016

Name and country	Name of currency	Per diem		Transportation		Miscellaneous		Total	
		Foreign currency	U.S. dollar equivalent or U.S. currency	Foreign currency	U.S. dollar equivalent or U.S. currency	Foreign currency	U.S. dollar equivalent or U.S. currency	Foreign currency	U.S. dollar equivalent or U.S. currency
Chad Tanner:			600.00						600.00
			516.00						516.00
					226.00				226.00
							452.00		452.00
Randy Bookout:			984.13						984.13
							136.66		136.66
Paul Matulic:			984.13						984.13
							136.66		136.66
Ryan White:			984.13						984.13
							136.66		136.66
Chris Joyner:			1,052.00						1,052.00
							251.66		251.66
			680.03						680.03
							362.24		362.24
			395.00						395.00
							287.42		287.42
John Matchison:			1,137.00						1,137.00
					7,900.00				7,900.00
							150.00		150.00
Jongsun Kim:			1,137.00						1,137.00
					7,900.00				7,900.00
							150.00		150.00
Senator Tom Cotton:			250.00						250.00
					6,921.46				6,921.46
Ryan Tully:			250.00						250.00
					6,921.46				6,921.46
Paul Matulic:			1,074.00						1,074.00
			1,236.00						1,236.00
					4,520.00				4,520.00
Hayden Milberg:			1,074.00						1,074.00
			1,236.00						1,236.00
					4,520.00				4,520.00
Senator James Lankford:			480.00						480.00
					1,400.00				1,400.00
							835.00		835.00
Emily Harding:			480.00						480.00
					1,400.00				1,400.00
							835.00		835.00
Adam Farris:			480.00						480.00
					1,400.00				1,400.00
							835.00		835.00
Brian Walsh:			142.00						142.00
			332.00						332.00
			135.00						135.00
					12,847.26				12,847.26
Randy Bookout:			142.00						142.00
			332.00						332.00
			135.00						135.00
					12,847.26				12,847.26
Walter Weiss:			497.00						497.00
			641.00						641.00
			409.50						409.50
					8,722.16				8,722.16
Mike Pevzner:			497.00						497.00
			641.00						641.00
			409.50						409.50
					8,722.16				8,722.16
Senator Tom Cotton:			534.00						534.00
			189.00						189.00
			537.00						537.00
					12,495.86				12,495.86
Ryan Tully:			534.00						534.00
			189.00						189.00
			537.00						537.00
					12,495.86				12,495.86
Total			21,862.42		111,239.48		4,568.30		137,670.20

SENATOR RICHARD BURR,
Chairman, Senate Select Committee on Intelligence, Nov. 7, 2016.

CONSOLIDATED REPORT OF EXPENDITURE OF FUNDS FOR FOREIGN TRAVEL BY MEMBERS AND EMPLOYEES OF THE U.S. SENATE, UNDER AUTHORITY OF SEC. 22, P.L. 95–384—22 U.S.C. 1754(b), COMMISSION ON SECURITY AND COOPERATION IN EUROPE FOR TRAVEL FROM JULY 1 TO SEPT. 30, 2016

Name and country	Name of currency	Per diem		Transportation		Miscellaneous		Total	
		Foreign currency	U.S. dollar equivalent or U.S. currency	Foreign currency	U.S. dollar equivalent or U.S. currency	Foreign currency	U.S. dollar equivalent or U.S. currency	Foreign currency	U.S. dollar equivalent or U.S. currency
Ambassador David Killion:									
Georgia	Lari		885.00						885.00
Italy	Euro		1,110.42						1,110.42
United States	Dollar								
* Delegation Expenses:									
Georgia	Lari		2,490.00						2,490.00
Italy	Euro		305.22						305.22
United Kingdom	Pound		1,487.25						1,487.25
Austria	Euro		1,029.00						1,029.00
United States	Dollar				13,193.56				13,193.56
* Delegation Expenses:									
United Kingdom	Pound		779.72						779.72
Austria	Euro		1,001.70						1,001.70
Poland	Zloty		2,253.44						2,253.44
United States	Dollar				9,522.96				9,522.96
* Delegation Expenses:									
Poland	Zloty		72.92						72.92
Total			11,414.67		22,716.52				34,131.19

* Delegation expenses include payments and reimbursements to the Department of State under authority of Sec. 502(b) of the Mutual Security Act of 1954, as amended by Section 22 of P.L. 95–384, and S. Res. 179 agreed to May 25, 1977.

SENATOR ROGER F. WICKER,
Chairman, Commission on Security and Cooperation in Europe,
Oct. 11, 2016.

CONSOLIDATED REPORT OF EXPENDITURE OF FUNDS FOR FOREIGN TRAVEL BY MEMBERS AND EMPLOYEES OF THE U.S. SENATE, UNDER AUTHORITY OF SEC. 22, P.L. 95–384—22 U.S.C. 1754(b), MAJORITY LEADER FOR TRAVEL FROM JULY 1 TO SEPT. 30, 2016

Name and country	Name of currency	Per diem		Transportation		Miscellaneous		Total	
		Foreign currency	U.S. dollar equivalent or U.S. currency	Foreign currency	U.S. dollar equivalent or U.S. currency	Foreign currency	U.S. dollar equivalent or U.S. currency	Foreign currency	U.S. dollar equivalent or U.S. currency
Thomas Hawkins:									
United States	Dollar				27,610.86				27,610.86
Australia	Dollar		932.31		1,007.00				1,939.31
Philippines	Peso		560.33		1,166.87		199.25		1,926.45
South Korea	Won		395.00		862.27				1,257.27
Japan	Yen		888.30		1,124.71				2,013.01
Thomas Hawkins:									
United States	Dollar				13,100.86				13,100.86
Norway	Krone		749.50						749.50
Sweden	Krona		652.00						652.00
Latvia	Euro		793.11						793.11
Total			4,970.55		44,872.57		199.25		50,042.37

SENATOR MITCH McCONNELL,
Majority Leader, Nov. 18. 2016.

AUTHORIZING RETURN OF PAPERS REQUEST

Mr. McCONNELL. Mr. President, I ask unanimous consent that the Secretary of the Senate be authorized to request the return of the papers with respect to H. Con. Res. 122 so that the enrolling clerk may make a technical correction.

The PRESIDING OFFICER. Without objection, it is so ordered.

PUBLIC SAFETY OFFICERS' BENEFITS IMPROVEMENT ACT OF 2016

Mr. McCONNELL. Mr. President, I ask unanimous consent that the Senate proceed to the immediate consideration of Calendar No. 513, S. 2944.

The PRESIDING OFFICER. The clerk will report the bill by title.

The senior assistant legislative clerk read as follows:

A bill (S. 2944) to require adequate reporting on the Public Safety Officers' Benefit program, and for other purposes.

There being no objection, the Senate proceeded to consider the bill, which had been reported from the Committee on the Judiciary, with amendments, as follows:

(The parts of the bill intended to be stricken are shown in boldface brackets and the parts of the bill intended to be inserted are shown in italics.)

S. 2944

Be it enacted by the Senate and House of Representatives of the United States of America in Congress assembled,

SECTION 1. SHORT TITLE.

This Act may be cited as the "Public Safety Officers' Benefits Improvement Act of 2016".

SEC. 2. REPORTS.

Section 1205 of title I of the Omnibus Crime Control and Safe Streets Act of 1968 (42 U.S.C. 3796c) is amended—

(1) in subsection (a), by inserting "Rules, regulations, and procedures issued under this part may include regulations based on standards developed by another Federal agency for programs related to public safety officer death or disability claims." [after "before the Bureau.";] *before the last sentence;*

(2) in subsection (b)—

(A) by inserting "(1)" before "In making"; and

(B) by adding at the end the following:

"(2) In making a determination under section 1201, the Bureau shall give substantial weight to the evidence and all findings of fact presented by a State, local, or Federal administrative or investigative agency regarding eligibility for death or disability benefits."; and

(3) by adding at the end the following:

"(e)(1)(A) Not later than 30 days after the date of enactment of this subsection, the Bureau shall make available on the public website of the Bureau information on all death, disability, and educational assistance claims submitted under this part that are pending as of the date on which the information is made available.

"(B) Not less frequently than once per week, the Bureau shall make available on the public website of the Bureau updated information with respect to all death, disability, and educational assistance claims submitted under this part that are pending as of the date on which the information is made available.

"(C) The information made available under this paragraph shall include—

"(i) for each pending claim—

"(I) the date on which the claim was submitted to the Bureau;

"(II) the State of residence of the claimant;

"(III) an anonymized, identifying claim number; and

"(IV) the nature of the claim; and

"(ii) the total number of pending claims that were submitted to the Bureau more than 1 year before the date on which the information is made available.

"(2)(A) Not later than 180 days after the date of enactment of this subsection, and every 180 days thereafter, the Bureau shall submit to Congress a report on the death, disability, and educational assistance claims submitted under this part during the 180-day period preceding the report.

"(B) Each report submitted under subparagraph (A) shall include information on—

"(i) the total number of claims, and the nature of each claim, submitted to the Bureau;

"(ii) the number of claims for which a final determination has been made;

"(iii) the number of claims for which a final determination has not been reached and the basis for the delay;

"(iv) the amount of time required to process each claim for which a final determination has been made ⟦and, for any claim which could not be processed within 1 year of being submitted to the Bureau, the basis for any delay⟧;

"(v) the number of claims submitted that are related to exposure due to the September 11th, 2001, terrorism attacks and the average award amount for any such claims for which a final determination has been made;

"(vi) the result of each claim *for which a final determination was made during the 180-day period*, including the number of claims rejected and the basis for any denial of benefits;

"(vii) the number of claims ⟦that were appealed⟧ *for which a final determination was made and appealed during the 180-day period*;

"(viii) the *average* number of claims processed per reviewer of the Bureau; and

⟦"(ix) the average amount of time each agency takes to submit all required information and documents to the Bureau.⟧

"(ix) information on the compliance of the Bureau with the obligation to offset award amounts under section 1201(f)(3), including—

"(I) the number of claims that are eligible for compensation under both this part and the September 11th Victim Compensation Fund of 2001 (49 U.S.C. 40101 note; Public Law 107–42) (commonly referred to as the 'VCF');

"(II) for each claim described in subclause (I) for which compensation has been paid under the VCF, the amount of compensation paid under the VCF;

"(III) the number of claims described in subclause (I) for which the Bureau has made a final determination; and

"(IV) the number of claims described in subclause (I) for which the Bureau has not made a final determination.

"(3) Not later than 5 years after the date of enactment of the Public Safety Officers' Benefits Improvement Act of 2016, and every 5 years thereafter, the Comptroller General of the United States shall—

"(A) conduct a study on the compliance of the Bureau with the obligation to offset award amounts under section 1201(f)(3); and

"(B) submit to Congress a report on the study conducted under subparagraph (A) that includes an assessment of whether the Bureau has provided the information required under subparagraph (B)(ix) of paragraph (2) of this subsection in each report required under that paragraph.

"⟦(3)⟧*(4)* In this subsection, the term 'nature of the claim' means whether the claim is a claim for—

"(A) benefits under this subpart with respect to the death of a public safety officer;

"(B) benefits under this subpart with respect to the disability of a public safety officer; or

"(C) education assistance under subpart 2.".

SEC. 3. AGE LIMITATION FOR CHILDREN.

Section 1212(c) of title I of the Omnibus Crime Control and Safe Streets Act of 1968 (42 U.S.C. 3796d–1(c)) is amended—

(1) by striking "No child" and inserting the following:

"(1) IN GENERAL.—Subject to paragraph (2), no child"; and

(2) by adding at the end the following:

"(2) DELAYED APPROVALS.—

"(A) EDUCATIONAL ASSISTANCE APPLICATION.—If a claim for assistance under this subpart is approved more than 1 year after the date on which the application for such assistance is filed with the Attorney General, the age limitation under this subsection shall be extended by the length of the period—

"(i) beginning on the day after the date that is 1 year after the date on which the application is filed; and

"(ii) ending on the date on which the application is approved.

"(B) CLAIM FOR BENEFITS FOR DEATH OR PERMANENT AND TOTAL DISABILITY.—In addition to an extension under subparagraph (A), if any, for an application for assistance under this subpart that relates to a claim for benefits under subpart 1 that was approved more than 1 year after the date on which the claim was filed with the Attorney General, the age limitation under this subsection shall be extended by the length of the period—

"(i) beginning on the day after the date that is 1 year after the date on which the claim for benefits is submitted; and

"(ii) ending on the date on which the claim for benefits is approved.".

SEC. 4. DUE DILIGENCE IN PAYING BENEFIT CLAIMS.

Subpart 1 of part L of title I of the Omnibus Crime Control and Safe Streets Act of 1968 (42 U.S.C. 3796 et seq.) is amended by adding at the end the following:

"SEC. 1206. DUE DILIGENCE IN PAYING BENEFIT CLAIMS.

"(a) IN GENERAL.—The Bureau, with all due diligence, shall expeditiously attempt to obtain the information and documentation necessary to adjudicate a benefit claim filed under this part, including a claim for financial assistance under subpart 2.

"(b) SUFFICIENT INFORMATION UNAVAILABLE.—If a benefit claim filed under this part, including a claim for financial assistance under subpart 2, is unable to be adjudicated by the Bureau because of a lack of information or documentation from a third party, such as a public agency, the Bureau may not abandon the benefit claim unless the Bureau has utilized the investigative tools available to the Bureau to obtain the necessary information or documentation, including subpoenas.".

SEC. 5. PRESUMPTION THAT OFFICER ACTED PROPERLY.

Section 1202 of title I of the Omnibus Crime Control and Safe Streets Act of 1968 (42 U.S.C. 3796a) is amended—

(1) by striking "No benefit" and inserting the following:

"(a) IN GENERAL.—No benefit"; and

(2) by adding at the end the following:

"(b) PRESUMPTION.—In determining whether a benefit is payable under this part, the Bureau shall—

"(1) presume that none of the limitations described in subsection (a) apply; and

"(2) have the burden of establishing by clear and convincing evidence that a limitation described in subsection (a) applies.".

SEC. 6. EFFECTIVE DATE; APPLICABILITY.

The amendments made by this Act shall—

(1) take effect on the date of enactment of this Act; and

(2) apply to any benefit claim or application under part L of title I of the Omnibus Crime Control and Safe Streets Act of 1968 (42 U.S.C. 3796 et seq.) that is—

(A) pending before the Bureau of Justice Assistance on the date of enactment; or

(B) received by the Bureau on or after the date of enactment of this Act.

Mr. LEAHY. Mr. President, today, the Senate reiterates its commitment to our Nation's law enforcement officers, firefighters, and other first responders. Forty years ago, we created the Public Safety Officers' Benefits Program, PSOB, to support first responders who made the ultimate sacrifice. We have now passed legislation to make much needed improvements to the claims adjudication process, which for too long has been plagued by red tape and delays.

Today's legislation builds upon my past efforts to improve the PSOB program. In 2003, I worked with a bipartisan group of senators to pass the Hometown Heroes Survivors Benefits Act, which recognized that law enforcement officers who suffer fatal heart attacks or strokes in the line of duty also deserve benefits. In 2009, I introduced the Dale Long Emergency Medical Service Providers Protection Act, which became law in 2012 and extended PSOB benefits to nonprofit Emergency Medical Service, EMS, providers. This change covered an estimated 1,200 EMS personnel in Vermont alone. Today's legislation will add transparency to the PSOB's decisionmaking process and should help expedite the review of applications for benefits.

The legislation also includes an amendment I offered in the Judiciary Committee that improved this bill in three important ways. First, it ensured that children are not disqualified from receiving education benefits due to delays within the PSOB program, which can approach 10 years. At a Senate Judiciary hearing in April, a law enforcement official described this as unconscionable. I agree. My amendment ensures it will never happen again. Second, a fallen officer or first responder's family should not have their claim denied simply because their employer fails to provide necessary paperwork to the PSOB office. My amendment requires that the PSOB office use every investigative tool it has to obtain what it needs from third parties to process a claim. This will ensure that officers and their families who are entitled to benefits are not further victimized by delays beyond their control. Finally, as originally drafted, this legislation only applied to claims filed after it becomes law. I want these improvements to help those currently stuck in the backlog, and my amendment fixed this issue.

One hundred twenty-three law enforcement officers have been killed in the line of duty so far in 2016. These families deserve a working and responsive PSOB program. This legislation, while only a modest step, demonstrates our shared commitment to those officers and their families. I urge the House of Representatives to quickly pass this legislation and send it to the President for signature.

Mr. McCONNELL. Mr. President, I ask unanimous consent that the committee-reported amendments be withdrawn; that the Grassley substitute amendment be agreed to; that the bill, as amended, be read a third time and passed; that the Grassley title amendment be agreed to; and that the motions to reconsider be considered made and laid upon the table.

The PRESIDING OFFICER. Without objection, it is so ordered.

The committee-reported amendments were withdrawn.

The amendment (No. 5113) in the nature of a substitute was agreed to.

(The amendment is printed in today's RECORD under "Text of Amendments.")

The bill (S. 2944), as amended, was ordered to be engrossed for a third reading, was read the third time, and passed.

The amendment (No. 5114) was agreed to, as follows:

(Purpose: To amend the title)

Amend the title so as to read: "A bill to require adequate reporting on the Public Safety Officers' Benefits program, and for other purposes.".

CROSS-BORDER TRADE ENHANCEMENT ACT OF 2015

Mr. McCONNELL. Mr. President, I ask unanimous consent that the Senate proceed to the immediate consideration of Calendar No. 559, S. 461.

The PRESIDING OFFICER. The clerk will report the bill by title.

The senior assistant legislative clerk read as follows:

A bill (S. 461) to provide for alternative financing arrangements for the provision of certain services and the construction and maintenance of infrastructure at land border ports of entry, and for other purposes.

There being no objection, the Senate proceeded to consider the bill, which had been reported from the Committee on Homeland Security and Governmental Affairs, with an amendment to strike all after the enacting clause and insert in lieu thereof the following:

SECTION 1. SHORT TITLE.

This Act may be cited as the "Cross-Border Trade Enhancement Act of 2016".

SEC. 2. REPEAL AND TRANSITION PROVISION.

(a) REPEAL.—Subject to subsections (b) and (c), section 560 of the Department of Homeland Security Appropriations Act, 2013 (division D of Public Law 113–6; 127 Stat. 378) and section 559 of the Department of Homeland Security Appropriations Act, 2014 (division F of Public Law 113–76; 6 U.S.C. 211 note) are repealed.

(b) AGREEMENTS IN EFFECT.—Notwithstanding subsection (a), nothing in this Act may be construed as affecting in any manner an agreement entered into pursuant to section 560 of the Department of Homeland Security Appropriations Act, 2013 (division D of Public Law 113–6; 127 Stat. 378) or section 559 of the Department of

Homeland Security Appropriations Act, 2014 (division F of Public Law 113–76; 6 U.S.C. 211 note) that is in effect on the day before the date of the enactment of this Act, and any such agreement shall continue to have full force and effect on and after such date.

(c) PROPOSED AGREEMENTS.—Notwithstanding subsection (a), nothing in this Act may be construed as affecting in any manner a proposal accepted for consideration and further development by U.S. Customs and Border Protection or the General Services Administration pursuant to section 559 of the Department of Homeland Security Appropriations Act, 2014 (division F of Public Law 113–76; 6 U.S.C. 211 note) that was accepted prior to the date of the enactment of this Act.

SEC. 3. DEFINITIONS.

In this Act:

(1) ADMINISTRATION.—The term "Administration" mean the General Services Administration.

(2) ADMINISTRATOR.—The term "Administrator" mean the Administrator of the Administration.

(3) COMMISSIONER.—The term "Commissioner" means the Commissioner of U.S. Customs and Border Protection.

(4) DONATION AGREEMENT.—The term "donation agreement" means an agreement made under section 5(a).

(5) FEE AGREEMENT.—The term "fee agreement" means an agreement made by the Commissioner under section 4(a)(1).

(6) PERSON.—The term "person" means—

(A) an individual;

(B) a corporation, partnership, trust, estate, association, or any other private or public entity;

(C) a Federal, State, or local government;

(D) any subdivision, agency, or instrumentality of a Federal, State, or local government; or

(E) any other governmental entity.

(7) RELEVANT COMMITTEES OF CONGRESS.—The term "relevant committees of Congress" means—

(A) the Committee on Appropriations, the Committee on Environment and Public Works, the Committee on Finance, the Committee on Homeland Security and Governmental Affairs, and the Committee on the Judiciary of the Senate; and

(B) the Committee on Appropriations, the Committee on Homeland Security, the Committee on the Judiciary, and the Committee on Transportation and Infrastructure of the House of Representatives.

SEC. 4. AUTHORITY TO ENTER INTO FEE AGREEMENTS FOR THE PROVISION OF CERTAIN SERVICES OF U.S. CUSTOMS AND BORDER PROTECTION.

(a) FEE AGREEMENTS.—

(1) AUTHORITY FOR FEE AGREEMENTS.—Notwithstanding section 13031(e) of the Consolidated Omnibus Budget Reconciliation Act of 1985 (19 U.S.C. 58c(e)) and section 451 of the Tariff Act of 1930 (19 U.S.C. 1451), the Commissioner may, upon the request of any person, enter into an agreement with that person under which—

(A) U.S. Customs and Border Protection will provide the services described in paragraph (4) at a port of entry or any other facility where U.S. Customs and Border Protection provides or will provide services;

(B) such person will remit a fee imposed under subsection (b) to U.S. Customs and Border Protection in an amount equal to the full costs incurred or that will be incurred in providing such services; and

(C) any additional facilities at which U.S. Customs and Border Protection services are performed or deemed necessary for the provision of services under an agreement entered into under this section shall be provided, maintained, and

equipped by such person, without additional cost to the Federal Government, in accordance with U.S. Customs and Border Protection specifications.

(2) CRITERIA.—The Commissioner shall establish criteria for entering into a partnership under paragraph (1) that include the following:

(A) Selection and evaluation of potential partners.

(B) Identification and documentation of roles and responsibilities between U.S. Customs and Border Protection, the Administration, and private and government partners.

(C) Identification, allocation, and management of explicit and implicit risks of partnering between U.S. Customs and Border Protection, the Administration, and private and government partners.

(D) Decision-making and dispute resolution processes in partnering arrangements.

(E) Criteria and processes for U.S. Customs and Border Protection to terminate agreements if private or government partners are not meeting the terms of such a partnership, including the security standards established by U.S. Customs and Border Protection.

(3) PUBLICATION.—The Commissioner shall make publicly available the criteria established under paragraph (2), and shall notify the relevant committees of Congress not less than 15 days prior to the publication of the criteria and any subsequent changes to such criteria.

(4) SERVICES DESCRIBED.—Services described in this paragraph are any services related to, or in support of, customs, agricultural processing, border security, or inspection-related immigration matters provided by an employee or contractor of U.S. Customs and Border Protection at ports of entry or any other facility where U.S. Customs and Border Protection provides or will provide services.

(5) MODIFICATION OF PRIOR AGREEMENTS.— The Commissioner, at the request of a person who has previously entered into an agreement with U.S. Customs and Border Protection for the reimbursement of fees in effect on the date of enactment of this Act, may modify such agreement to implement any provisions of this Act.

(6) LIMITATION.—The Commissioner may not enter into a reimbursable fee agreement under this subsection if such agreement would unduly and permanently impact services funded in this Act or any appropriations Act, or provided from any account in the Treasury of the United States derived by the collection of fees.

(7) NUMERICAL LIMITATIONS.—Except as provided in paragraphs (8) and (9), there shall be no limit to the number of fee agreements that may be entered into by the Commissioner.

(8) AUTHORITY FOR NUMERICAL LIMITATIONS.—

(A) RESOURCE AVAILABILITY.—If the Commissioner finds that resource or allocation constraints would prevent U.S. Customs and Border Protection from fulfilling, in whole or in part, requests for services under the terms of existing or proposed fee agreements, the Commissioner shall impose annual limits on the number of new fee agreements.

(B) ANNUAL REVIEW.—If the Commissioner limits the number of new fee agreements under this paragraph, the Commissioner shall annually evaluate and reassess such limits and publish the results of such evaluation and affirm any such limits that shall remain in effect in a publicly available format.

(9) AIR PORTS OF ENTRY.—

(A) CERTAIN COSTS.—A fee agreement for U.S. Customs and Border Protection services at an air port of entry may only provide for the reimbursement of—

(i) salaries and expenses of not more than 5 full-time equivalent U.S. Customs and Border Protection officers;

(ii) costs incurred by U.S. Customs and Border Protection for the payment of overtime to employee;

(iii) the salaries and expenses of employees of U.S. Customs and Border Protection (other than officers specified in clause (i)) to support U.S. customs and Border Protection officers in performing law enforcement functions at air ports of entry, including primary and secondary processing of passengers; and

(iv) other costs incurred by U.S. Customs and Border Protection relating to services described in paragraph (4), such as temporary placement or permanent relocation of such employees, including incentive pay for relocation where appropriate.

(B) PRECLEARANCE.—The authority in the section may not be used to enter into new preclearance agreements or initiate the provision of U.S. Customs and Border Protection services outside of the United States.

(C) PERMANENT RELOCATION.—Any fee agreement under this Act to provide for the reimbursement of the permanent relocation of an employee of the U.S. Customs and Border Protection shall certify that the terms of the agreement—

(i) cannot otherwise be sufficiently met by the person and the U.S. Customs and Border Protection;

(ii) would not unduly impact U.S. Customs and Border Protection services at the port of entry from which the relocation of the employee is proposed;

(iii) would be consistent with other applicable laws and regulations regarding the relocation of employees of the U.S. Customs and Border Protection; and

(iv) all costs of the relocation have been approved by the person.

(10) PORT OF ENTRY SIZE CONSIDERATION.—The Commissioner shall—

(A) ensure that each fee agreement proposal is given equal consideration regardless of the size of the port of entry; and

(B) report to the relevant committees of Congress on the number of fee agreement proposals that the Commissioner did not enter into due to numerical limits on the number of fee agreements, if the Commissioner adopts such limits.

(11) DENIED APPLICATION.—If the Commissioner denies a proposal for a fee agreement, the Commission shall provide the person who submitted the proposal the reason for the denial, unless the reason for the denial involves a law enforcement matter or national security interest.

(12) CONSTRUCTION.—Nothing in this section may be construed—

(A) to require a person entering into a fee agreement to cover costs that are otherwise the responsibility of the U.S. Customs and Border Protection or any other agency of the Federal Government and are not incurred, or expected to be incurred, to cover services specifically covered by an agreement entered into under authorities provided by this Act; or

(B) to unduly and permanently reduce the responsibilities or duties of U.S. Customs and Border Protection to provide services at ports of entry that have been authorized or mandated by law and are funded in any appropriation Act or from any accounts in the Treasury of the United States derived by the collection of fees.

(13) JUDICIAL REVIEW.—Decisions of the Commissioner under this subsection are in the discretion of the Commissioner and not subject to judicial review.

(b) FEE.—

(1) IN GENERAL.—A person who enters into a fee agreement shall pay a fee pursuant to such agreement in an amount equal to the full cost of U.S. Customs and Border Protection—

(A) of the salaries and expenses of individuals employed or contracted by U.S. Customs and Border Protection to provide such services; and

(B) of other costs incurred by U.S. Customs and Border Protection related to providing such services, such as temporary placement or permanent relocation of employees, including incentive pay for relocation where appropriate.

(2) ADVANCE PAYMENT.—The Commissioner, with approval from a person requesting services of U.S. Customs and Border Protection services pursuant to a fee agreement, may accept the fee for services prior to providing such services.

(3) OVERSIGHT OF FEES.—The Commissioner shall develop a process to oversee the activities for which fees are charged pursuant to a fee agreement that includes the following:

(A) A determination and report on the full cost of providing services, including direct and indirect costs, as well as a process, through consultation with affected parties and other interested stakeholders, for increasing such fees as necessary.

(B) The establishment of a periodic remittance schedule to replenish appropriations, accounts or funds, as necessary.

(C) The identification of costs paid by such fees.

(4) DEPOSIT OF FUNDS.—Amounts collected pursuant to a fee agreement shall—

(A) be deposited as an offsetting collection;

(B) remain available until expended, without fiscal year limitation; and

(C) be credited to the applicable appropriation, account, or fund for the amount paid out of that appropriation, account, or fund for—

(i) any expenses incurred or to be incurred by U.S. Customs and Border Protection in providing such services; and

(ii) any other costs incurred by U.S. Customs and Border Protection relating to such services.

(5) TERMINATION BY THE COMMISSIONER.—

(A) IN GENERAL.—The Commissioner shall terminate the services provided pursuant to a fee agreement with a person that, after receiving notice from the Commissioner that a fee imposed under the fee agreement is due, fails to pay such fee in a timely manner.

(B) EFFECT OF TERMINATION.—At the time services are terminated pursuant to subparagraph (A), all costs incurred by U.S. Customs and Border Protection which have not been paid, will become immediately due and payable.

(C) INTEREST.—Interest on unpaid fees will accrue based on the quarterly rate(s) established under sections 6621 and 6622 of the Internal Revenue Code of 1986.

(D) PENALTIES.—Any person that fails to pay any fee incurred under a fee agreement in a timely manner, after notice and demand for payment, shall be liable for a penalty or liquidated damage equal to 2 times the amount of such fee.

(E) AMOUNT COLLECTED.—Any amount collected pursuant to a fee agreement shall be deposited into the account specified under paragraph (4) and shall be available as described therein.

(F) RETURN OF UNUSED FUNDS.—The Commissioner shall return any unused funds collected under a fee agreement that is terminated for any reason, or in the event that the terms of such agreement change by mutual agreement to cause a reduction of U.S. Customs and Border Protections services. No interest shall be owed upon the return of any unused funds.

(6) TERMINATION BY THE SPONSOR.—Any person who has previously entered into an agreement with U.S. Customs and Border Protection for the reimbursement of fees in effect on the date of enactment of this Act, or under the provisions of this Act, may request that such agreement make provision for termination at the request of such person upon advance notice, the length and terms of which shall be negotiated between such person and U.S. Customs and Border Protection.

(c) ANNUAL REPORT AND NOTICE TO CONGRESS.—The Commissioner shall—

(1) submit to the relevant committees of Congress an annual report that identifies each fee agreement made during the previous year; and

(2) not less than 15 days before entering into a fee agreement, notify the members of Congress that represent the State or district in which the affected port or facility is located.

(d) MODIFICATION OF EXISTING REPORTS TO CONGRESS.—Section 907(b) of the Trade Facilitation and Trade Enforcement Act of 2015 (Public Law 114–125) is amended—

(1) in paragraph (3), by striking "or" at the end;

(2) in paragraph (4), by striking the period at the end and inserting "; or"; and

(3) by adding at the end the following:

"(5) the program for entering into reimbursable fee agreements for the provision of U.S. Customs and Border Protection services established by the Cross-Border Trade Enhancement Act of 2016.".

SEC. 5. AUTHORITY TO ENTER INTO AGREEMENTS TO ACCEPT DONATIONS FOR PORTS OF ENTRY.

(a) AGREEMENTS AUTHORIZED.—

(1) COMMISSIONER.—The Commissioner, in collaboration with the Administrator as provided under subsection (e), may enter into an agreement with any person to accept a donation of real or personal property, including monetary donations, or nonpersonal services, for activities in subsection (b) at a new or existing land, sea, or air port of entry, or any facility or other infrastructure at a location where U.S. Customs and Border Protection performs or will be performing services within the United States.

(2) ADMINISTRATOR.—Where the Administrator has custody or control of a new or existing land port of entry, facility, or other infrastructure at a location where U.S. Customs and Border Protection performs or will be performing inspection services, the Administrator, in collaboration with the Commissioner, may enter into an agreement with any person to accept a donation of real or personal property, including monetary donations, or nonpersonal services, at that location for activities set forth in subsection (b).

(b) USE.—A donation made under a donation agreement may be used for activities related to construction, alteration, operation or maintenance, including expenses related to—

(1) land acquisition, design, construction, repair, and alteration;

(2) furniture, fixtures, equipment, and technology, including installation and the deployment thereof; and

(3) operation and maintenance of the facility, infrastructure, equipment, and technology.

(c) LIMITATION ON MONETARY DONATIONS.—Any monetary donation accepted pursuant to a donation agreement may not be used to pay the salaries of employees of U.S. Customs and Border Protection who perform inspection services.

(d) TERM OF DONATION AGREEMENT.—The term of a donation agreement may be as long as is required to meet the terms of the agreement.

(e) ROLE OF ADMINISTRATOR.—The Administrator's role, involvement, and authority under this section is limited with respect to donations made at new or existing land ports of entry, facilities, or other infrastructure owned or leased by the Administration.

(f) EVALUATION PROCEDURES.—

(1) REQUIREMENTS FOR PROCEDURES.—Not later than 180 days after the date of enactment, the Commissioner, in consultation with the Administrator as appropriate, shall issue procedures for evaluating proposals for donation agreements on a year-round basis and otherwise consistent with the requirements of this section.

(2) AVAILABILITY.—The procedures issued under paragraph (1) shall be made available to the public.

(3) COST-SHARING ARRANGEMENTS.—In issuing the procedures under paragraph (1), the Commissioner, in consultation with the Administrator, shall evaluate the use of authorities provided under this section to enter into cost-sharing or reimbursement agreements with eligible persons and determine whether such agreements may improve facility conditions or inspection services at new or existing land, sea, or air ports of entry.

(g) DETERMINATION AND NOTIFICATION.—

(1) IN GENERAL.—Not later than 60 days after receiving a proposal for a donation agreement, the Commissioner, and Administrator if applicable, shall notify the person that submitted the proposal as to whether it is complete or incomplete.

(2) INCOMPLETE PROPOSALS.—If the Commissioner, and Administrator if applicable, determines that a proposal is incomplete, the person that submitted the proposal shall be notified and provided with—

(A) a detailed description of all specific information or material that is needed to complete review of the proposal; and

(B) allow the person to resubmit the proposal with additional information and material described under subparagraph (A) to complete the proposal.

(3) COMPLETE APPLICATIONS.—Not later than 180 days after receiving a completed and final proposal for a donation agreement, the Commissioner, and Administrator if applicable, shall—

(A) make a determination whether to deny or approve the proposal; and

(B) notify the person that submitted the proposal of the determination.

(4) CONSIDERATIONS.—In making the determination under paragraph (3)(A), the Commissioner, and Administrator if applicable, shall consider—

(A) the impact of the proposal on reducing wait times at that port of entry or facility and other ports of entry on the same border;

(B) the potential of the proposal to increase trade and travel efficiency through added capacity;

(C) the potential of the proposal to enhance the security of the port of entry or facility;

(D) the funding available to complete the intended use of a donation under this section;

(E) the costs of maintaining and operating such donation;

(F) whether such donation, if real property, satisfies the requirements of such proposal, or whether additional real property would be required;

(G) an explanation of how such donation, if real property, was secured;

(H) the impact of such proposal on staffing requirements; and

(I) other factors that the Commissioner or Administrator determines to be relevant.

(h) SUPPLEMENTAL FUNDING.—Any property, including monetary donations and nonpersonal services, donated pursuant to a donation agreement may be used in addition to any other funds, including appropriated funds, property, or services made available for the same purpose.

(i) RETURN OF DONATION.—If the Commissioner or the Administrator does not use the property or services donated pursuant to a donation agreement, such donated property or services shall be returned to the person that made the donation.

(j) INTEREST PROHIBITED.—No interest may be owed on any donation returned to a person under this subsection.

(k) PROHIBITION ON CERTAIN FUNDING.—The Commissioner, in collaboration with the Administrator if applicable, with respect to an agreement authorized under this section, may not obligate or expend amounts in excess of the value of the donations.

(l) ANNUAL REPORT AND NOTICE TO CONGRESS.—The Commissioner, in collaboration with the Administrator if applicable, shall—

(1) submit to the relevant committees of Congress an annual report that identifies each donation agreement made during the previous year; and

(2) not less than 15 days before entering into a donation agreement, notify the members of Congress that represent the State or district in which the affected port or facility is located.

(m) CONSTRUCTION.—Except as otherwise provided in this section, nothing in this section may be construed—

(1) as affecting in any manner the responsibilities, duties, or authorities of U.S. Customs and Border Protection or the Administration;

(2) to create any right or liability of the parties referred to in this section, except as otherwise set forth in any donation acceptance agreement entered into under this section; or

(3) as affecting any consultation requirement under any other law.

SEC. 6. WAIVER OF POLYGRAPH EXAMINATION REQUIREMENT FOR CERTAIN LAW ENFORCEMENT APPLICANTS.

Section 3 of the Anti-Border Corruption Act of 2010 (Public Law 111–376; 6 U.S.C. 221) is amended—

(1) in the matter preceding paragraph (1), by striking "The Secretary" and inserting the following:

"(a) IN GENERAL.—The Secretary";

(2) in subsection (a)(1), as redesignated, by inserting "(except as provided in subsection (b))" after "Border Protection"; and

(3) by adding at the end the following:

"(b) WAIVER.—The Commissioner of U.S. Customs and Border Protection may waive the polygraph examination requirement under subsection (a)(1) for any applicant who—

"(1) is deemed suitable for employment;

"(2) holds a current, active Top Secret/Sensitive Compartmented Information Clearance;

"(3) has a current Single Scope Background Investigation;

"(4) was not granted any waivers to obtain his or her clearance; and

"(5) is a veteran (as such term is defined in section 2108 of title 5, United States Code).".

SEC. 7. EFFECTIVE PERIOD.

(a) IN GENERAL.—Except as provided in subsection (c), this Act and the amendments made by this Act shall be in effect during the 10-year period beginning on the date of the enactment of this Act.

(b) AGREEMENTS IN EFFECT.—Any agreement made pursuant to this Act that is in effect on the date that is 10 years after the date of the enactment of this Act shall continue to have full force and effect on and after such date and remain in effect under the terms of such agreement.

(c) PERMANENT PROVISIONS.—Section 2, the amendments made by section 2, and the amendments made by section 6 shall take effect on the date of the enactment of this Act.

Mr. McCONNELL. Mr. President, I ask unanimous consent that the committee-reported substitute amendment be withdrawn; that the Cornyn substitute amendment be agreed to; that the bill, as amended, be considered read a third time and passed; and that the motion to reconsider be considered made and laid upon the table.

The PRESIDING OFFICER. Without objection, it is so ordered.

The committee-reported substitute amendment was withdrawn.

The amendment (No. 5115) in the nature of a substitute was agreed to.

(The amendment is printed in today's RECORD under "Text of Amendments.")

The bill (S. 461), as amended, was ordered to be engrossed for a third reading, was read the third time, and passed.

DISTRICT OF COLUMBIA JUDICIAL FINANCIAL TRANSPARENCY ACT

Mr. McCONNELL. Mr. President, I ask unanimous consent that the Senate proceed to the immediate consideration of H.R. 4419, which was received from the House.

The PRESIDING OFFICER. The clerk will report the bill by title.

The senior assistant legislative clerk read as follows:

A bill (H.R. 4419) to update the financial disclosure requirements for judges of the District of Columbia courts and to make other improvements to the District of Columbia courts.

There being no objection, the Senate proceeded to consider the bill.

Mr. McCONNELL. Mr. President, I ask unanimous consent that the bill be considered read a third time and passed and the motion to reconsider be considered made and laid upon the table.

The PRESIDING OFFICER. Without objection, it is so ordered.

The bill (H.R. 4419) was ordered to a third reading, was read the third time, and passed.

PROVIDING FOR AN ANNUITY SUPPLEMENT FOR CERTAIN AIR TRAFFIC CONTROLLERS

Mr. McCONNELL. Mr. President, I ask unanimous consent that the Senate proceed to the immediate consideration of H.R. 5785, which was received from the House.

The PRESIDING OFFICER. The clerk will report the bill by title.

The senior assistant legislative clerk read as follows:

A bill (H.R. 5785) to amend title 5, United States Code, to provide for an annuity supplement for certain air traffic controllers.

There being no objection, the Senate proceeded to consider the bill.

Mr. McCONNELL. I ask unanimous consent that the bill be considered read a third time and passed and the motion to reconsider be considered made and laid upon the table.

The PRESIDING OFFICER. Without objection, it is so ordered.

The bill (H.R. 5785) was ordered to a third reading, was read the third time, and passed.

RECOGNIZING THE NATIONAL GEOSPATIAL-INTELLIGENCE AGENCY ON ITS 20TH ANNIVERSARY

Mr. McCONNELL. Mr. President, I ask unanimous consent that the Armed Services Committee be discharged from further consideration of and the Senate now proceed to the consideration of S. Res. 607.

The PRESIDING OFFICER. Without objection it is so ordered.

The clerk will report the resolution by title.

The senior assistant legislative clerk read as follows:

A resolution (S. Res. 607) recognizing the National Geospatial-Intelligence Agency on its 20th anniversary.

There being no objection, the Senate proceeded to consider the resolution.

Mr. McCONNELL. I ask unanimous consent that the resolution be agreed to, the preamble be agreed to, and the motions to reconsider be considered made and laid upon the table.

The PRESIDING OFFICER. Without objection, it is so ordered.

The resolution (S. Res. 607) was agreed to.

The preamble was agreed to.

(The resolution, with its preamble, is printed in the RECORD of September 29, 2016, under "Submitted Resolutions.")

SUPPORTING THE DESIGNATION OF OCTOBER 8, 2016, AS "40 YEARS OF WOMEN CADETS AT THE UNITED STATES AIR FORCE ACADEMY DAY"

Mr. McCONNELL. Mr. President, I ask unanimous consent that the Armed Services Committee be discharged from further consideration of and the Senate now proceed to the consideration of S. Res. 611.

The PRESIDING OFFICER. Without objection, it is so ordered.

The clerk will report the resolution by title.

The senior assistant legislative clerk read as follows:

A resolution (S. Res. 611) supporting the designation of October 8, 2016, as "40 Years of Women Cadets at the United States Air Force Academy Day."

There being no objection, the Senate proceeded to consider the resolution.

Mr. McCONNELL. I ask unanimous consent that the resolution be agreed to, the preamble be agreed to, and the motions to reconsider be considered made and laid upon the table.

The PRESIDING OFFICER. Without objection, it is so ordered.

The resolution (S. Res. 611) was agreed to.

The preamble was agreed to.

(The resolution, with its preamble, is printed in the RECORD of September 29, 2016, under "Submitted Resolutions.")

EXPRESSING SUPPORT FOR THE GOALS OF NATIONAL ADOPTION DAY AND NATIONAL ADOPTION MONTH

Mr. McCONNELL. Mr. President, I ask unanimous consent that the Senate proceed to the consideration of S. Res. 622, submitted earlier today.

The PRESIDING OFFICER. The clerk will report the resolution by title.

The senior assistant legislative clerk read as follows:

A resolution (S. Res. 622) expressing support for the goals of National Adoption Day and National Adoption Month by promoting national awareness of adoption and the children awaiting families, celebrating children and families involved in adoption, and encouraging the people of the United States to secure safety, permanency, and well-being for all children.

There being no objection, the Senate proceeded to consider the resolution.

Mr. McCONNELL. I ask unanimous consent that the resolution be agreed to, the preamble be agreed to, and the motions to reconsider be considered made and laid upon the table with no intervening action or debate.

The PRESIDING OFFICER. Without objection, it is so ordered.

The resolution (S. Res. 622) was agreed to.

The preamble was agreed to.

(The resolution, with its preamble, is printed in today's RECORD under "Submitted Resolutions.")

RECOGNIZING THE VITAL ROLE THE CIVIL AIR PATROL HAS PLAYED, AND CONTINUES TO PLAY, IN SUPPORTING THE HOMELAND SECURITY AND NATIONAL DEFENSE OF THE UNITED STATES

Mr. McCONNELL. Mr. President, I ask unanimous consent that the Senate proceed to the consideration of S. Res. 623, submitted earlier today.

The PRESIDING OFFICER. The clerk will report the resolution by title.

The senior assistant legislative clerk read as follows:

A resolution (S. Res. 623) recognizing the vital role the Civil Air Patrol has played, and continues to play, in supporting the homeland security and national defense of the United States.

There being no objection, the Senate proceeded to consider the resolution.

Mr. McCONNELL. I ask unanimous consent that the resolution be agreed to, the preamble be agreed to, and the motions to reconsider be considered made and laid upon the table with no intervening action or debate.

The PRESIDING OFFICER. Without objection, it is so ordered.

The resolution (S. Res. 623) was agreed to.

The preamble was agreed to.

(The resolution, with its preamble, is printed in today's RECORD under "Submitted Resolutions.")

AUTHORIZING THE SECRETARY OF VETERANS AFFAIRS TO CARRY OUT A MAJOR MEDICAL FACILITY PROJECT IN RENO, NEVADA

Mr. McCONNELL. Mr. President, I ask unanimous consent that the Committee on Veterans' Affairs be discharged from further consideration of S. 3438 and the Senate proceed to its immediate consideration.

The PRESIDING OFFICER. Without objection, it is so ordered.

The clerk will report the bill by title.

The senior assistant legislative clerk read as follows:

A bill (S. 3438) to authorize the Secretary of Veterans Affairs to carry out a major medical facility project in Reno, Nevada.

There being no objection, the Senate proceeded to consider the bill.

Mr. McCONNELL. Mr. President, I ask unanimous consent that the Heller-Feinstein substitute amendment be agreed to; the bill, as amended, be considered read a third time and passed; and the motion to reconsider be considered made and laid upon the table.

The PRESIDING OFFICER. Without objection, it is so ordered.

The amendment (No. 5116) in the nature of a substitute was agreed to, as follows:

(Purpose: In the nature of a substitute)

Strike all after the enacting clause and insert the following:

SECTION 1. AUTHORIZATION OF CERTAIN MAJOR MEDICAL FACILITY PROJECTS OF THE DEPARTMENT OF VETERANS AFFAIRS.

(a) IN GENERAL.—The Secretary of Veterans Affairs may carry out the following major medical facility projects, with each project to be carried out in an amount not to exceed the amount specified for that project:

(1) Seismic, life safety, and utilities upgrades and expansion of clinical services in Reno, Nevada, in an amount not to exceed $213,800,000.

(2) Seismic corrections to the mental health and community living center in Long Beach, California, in an amount not to exceed $317,300,000.

(b) AUTHORIZATION OF APPROPRIATIONS.— There is authorized to be appropriated to the Secretary of Veterans Affairs for fiscal year 2017 or the year in which funds are appropriated for the Construction, Major Projects, account $531,100,000 for the projects authorized in subsection (a).

(c) LIMITATION.—The projects authorized in subsection (a) may only be carried out using—

(1) funds appropriated for fiscal year 2017 or the year in which funds are appropriated for the Construction, Major Projects, account pursuant to the authorization of appropriations in subsection (b);

(2) funds available for Construction, Major Projects, for a fiscal year before fiscal year 2017 that remain available for obligation;

(3) funds available for Construction, Major Projects, for a fiscal year after fiscal year 2017 that remain available for obligation;

(4) funds appropriated for Construction, Major Projects, for fiscal year 2017 for a category of activity not specific to a project;

(5) funds appropriated for Construction, Major Projects, for a fiscal year before fiscal year 2017 for a category of activity not specific to a project; and

(6) funds appropriated for Construction, Major Projects, for a fiscal year after fiscal year 2017 for a category of activity not specific to a project.

The bill (S. 3438), as amended, was ordered to be engrossed for a third reading, was read the third time, and passed.

ORDERS FOR WEDNESDAY, NOVEMBER 30, 2016

Mr. McCONNELL. Mr. President, I ask unanimous consent that when the Senate completes its business today, it adjourn until 10 a.m., Wednesday, November 30; that following the prayer and pledge, the morning hour be deemed expired, the Journal of proceedings be approved to date, and the time for the two leaders be reserved for their use later in the day; further, that following leader remarks, the Senate be in a period of morning business, with Senators permitted to speak therein for up to 10 minutes each.

The PRESIDING OFFICER. Without objection, it is so ordered.

ADJOURNMENT UNTIL 10 A.M. TOMORROW

Mr. McCONNELL. Mr. President, if there is no further business to come before the Senate, I ask unanimous consent that it stand adjourned under the previous order.

There being no objection, the Senate, at 6:44 p.m., adjourned until Wednesday, November 30, 2016, at 10 a.m.

NOMINATIONS

Executive nominations received by the Senate:

IN THE NAVY

THE FOLLOWING NAMED OFFICER FOR APPOINTMENT IN THE UNITED STATES NAVY TO THE GRADE INDICATED UNDER TITLE 10, U.S.C., SECTION 624:

To be rear admiral

REAR ADM. (LH) BRET C. BATCHELDER

IN THE ARMY

THE FOLLOWING NAMED OFFICER FOR APPOINTMENT TO THE GRADE INDICATED IN THE UNITED STATES ARMY MEDICAL SERVICE CORPS UNDER TITLE 10, U.S.C., SECTIONS 624 AND 3064:

To be lieutenant colonel

CHRISTOPHER S. BESSER

THE FOLLOWING NAMED OFFICER FOR REGULAR APPOINTMENT IN THE GRADE INDICATED IN THE UNITED STATES ARMY MEDICAL SERVICE CORPS UNDER TITLE 10, U.S.C., SECTIONS 531 AND 3064:

To be major

CHAD C. BLACK

THE FOLLOWING NAMED OFFICER FOR APPOINTMENT IN THE GRADE INDICATED IN THE RESERVE OF THE ARMY UNDER TITLE 10, U.S.C., SECTION 12203:

To be colonel

THOMAS D. STARKEY

IN THE MARINE CORPS

THE FOLLOWING NAMED OFFICER FOR REGULAR APPOINTMENT IN THE GRADE INDICATED IN THE UNITED STATES MARINE CORPS UNDER TITLE 10, U.S.C., SECTION 531:

To be major

JOSHUA D. FITZGARRALD

THE FOLLOWING NAMED OFFICER FOR REGULAR APPOINTMENT IN THE GRADE INDICATED IN THE UNITED STATES MARINE CORPS UNDER TITLE 10, U.S.C., SECTION 531:

To be lieutenant colonel

ANTHONY C. LYONS

FOREIGN SERVICE

THE FOLLOWING-NAMED CAREER MEMBERS OF THE SENIOR FOREIGN SERVICE OF THE DEPARTMENT OF STATE FOR THE PERSONAL RANK OF CAREER AMBASSADOR IN RECOGNITION OF ESPECIALLY DISTINGUISHED SERVICE OVER A SUSTAINED PERIOD:

STEPHEN DONALD MULL, OF VIRGINIA

VICTORIA JANE NULAND, OF VIRGINIA

THE FOLLOWING-NAMED CAREER MEMBERS OF THE SENIOR FOREIGN SERVICE OF THE DEPARTMENT OF STATE FOR PROMOTION WITHIN THE SENIOR FOREIGN SERVICE OF THE UNITED STATES OF AMERICA, CLASS OF MINISTER-COUNSELOR:

ROBERT L. ADAMS, OF TEXAS
BRIAN C. AGGELER, OF THE DISTRICT OF COLUMBIA
TANYA CECELIA ANDERSON, OF THE DISTRICT OF COLUMBIA
MICHAEL ADAM BARKIN, OF VIRGINIA
STANLEY H. BENNETT, OF MINNESOTA
RANDY WILLIAM BERRY, OF COLORADO
TIMOTHY A. BETTS, OF THE DISTRICT OF COLUMBIA
VIRGINIA MEADE BLASER, OF VIRGINIA
STEVEN CRAIG BONDY, OF VIRGINIA
MARIA ELENA BREWER, OF VIRGINIA
BRIDGET A. BRINK, OF MICHIGAN
JOHN LESLIE CARWILE, OF VIRGINIA
CARMEN MARGARITA CASTRO, OF VIRGINIA
CRAIG LEWIS CLOUD, OF FLORIDA
THEODORE RAYMOND COLEY, OF VIRGINIA
MARIE CHRISTINE DAMOUR, OF VIRGINIA
NICHOLAS JULIAN DEAN, OF VIRGINIA
ROBIN D. DIALLO, OF MARYLAND
JOHN WALTER DINKELMAN, OF VIRGINIA
MICHAEL J. DODMAN, OF THE DISTRICT OF COLUMBIA
CHRISTINE ANN ELDER, OF WASHINGTON
MICHELLE M. ESPERDY, OF PENNSYLVANIA
NINA MARIA FITE, OF VIRGINIA
BRADLEY ALAN FREDEN, OF ARIZONA
REBECCA ELIZA GONZALES, OF THE DISTRICT OF COLUMBIA
ALYSON LYNN GRUNDER, OF NEW YORK
TODD PHILIP HASKELL, OF FLORIDA
JEFFREY J. HAWKINS, JR., OF MARYLAND
PETER MARK HAYMOND, OF VIRGINIA
BRIAN GEORGE HEATH, OF THE DISTRICT OF COLUMBIA
JONATHAN HENICK, OF CALIFORNIA
ELIZABETH ANN HOPKINS, OF THE DISTRICT OF COLUMBIA
VIRGINIA IDELLE KEENER, OF MARYLAND
KEVIN J. KILPATRICK, OF INDIANA
DOUGLAS A. KONEFF, OF CONNECTICUT
DONALD WILLIAM KORAN, OF VIRGINIA
STEVEN HERBERT KRAFT, OF VIRGINIA
SUZANNE I. LAWRENCE, OF VIRGINIA
THOMAS H. LLOYD, OF VIRGINIA
NAJIB MAHMOOD, OF VIRGINIA
JEAN ELIZABETH MANES, OF FLORIDA
JOSEPH MANSO, OF THE DISTRICT OF COLUMBIA
JENNIFER ALLYN MCINTYRE, OF THE DISTRICT OF COLUMBIA
DAVID MEALE, OF VIRGINIA
JOHN S. MORETTI, OF VIRGINIA
KATHERINE ANNE MUNCHMEYER, OF THE DISTRICT OF COLUMBIA
MICHAEL JOHN MURPHY, OF VIRGINIA
MIREMBE L. NANTONGO, OF VIRGINIA
SUSAN BUTLER NIBLOCK, OF MARYLAND
FRANCISCO LUIS PALMIERI, OF CONNECTICUT
CHARISSE MELANIE PHILLIPS, OF FLORIDA
BETH L. POISSON, OF MARYLAND
LYNETTE JOYCE POULTON, OF VIRGINIA
WAYNE F. QUILLIN, OF NEW YORK
JOSEPH N. RAWLINGS, OF GEORGIA
KURT R. RICE, OF VIRGINIA
JOAN MARIE RICHARDS, OF VIRGINIA
CHRISTOPHER J. SANDROLINI, OF VIRGINIA
STEPHEN M. SCHWARTZ, OF MARYLAND
DOROTHY CAMILLE SHEA, OF THE DISTRICT OF COLUMBIA
GEORGE N. SIBLEY, OF VIRGINIA
ADNAN A. SIDDIQI, OF VIRGINIA
ADAM H. STERLING, OF VIRGINIA
STEPHANIE FAYE SYPTAK-RAMNATH, OF VIRGINIA
MELINDA C. TABLER-STONE, OF VIRGINIA
JOHN STEPHEN TAVENNER, OF TEXAS
DEAN THOMPSON, OF MARYLAND
LISA ANNETTE VICKERS, OF CALIFORNIA
SAMUEL R. WATSON III, OF VIRGINIA
EUGENE STEWART YOUNG, OF VIRGINIA

THE FOLLOWING-NAMED CAREER MEMBERS OF THE FOREIGN SERVICE FOR PROMOTION INTO THE SENIOR FOREIGN SERVICE, AS A CAREER MEMBER OF THE SENIOR FOREIGN SERVICE OF THE UNITED STATES OF AMERICA, CLASS OF COUNSELOR:

DEANNA HANEK ABDEEN, OF VIRGINIA
STEPHEN ANDERSON, OF MONTANA
KEITH MIMS ANDERTON, OF VIRGINIA
DOUGLAS JOSEPH APOSTOL, OF CALIFORNIA
CONSTANCE C. ARVIS, OF VIRGINIA
JENNIFER L. BACHUS, OF KANSAS
DORON D. BARD, OF WASHINGTON
NICHOLAS R. BERLINER, OF VIRGINIA
MARCIA P. BOSSHARDT, OF VIRGINIA
DAVID NOEL BRIZZEE, OF IDAHO
DANA M. BROWN, OF CALIFORNIA
ROBERT G. BURGESS, OF THE DISTRICT OF COLUMBIA
CAROL-ANNE CHANG, OF VIRGINIA
ANGELA COLYVAS-MCGINNIS, OF PENNSYLVANIA
ROBERT E. COPLEY, OF COLORADO
CHAD PARKER CUMMINS, OF CALIFORNIA
JAMES R. DAYRINGER, OF MONTANA
JOHN C. DOCKERY, OF TEXAS
JOEL EHRENDREICH, OF NEW YORK
JEWELL ELIZABETH EVANS, OF THE DISTRICT OF COLUMBIA
ALAN E. EYRE, OF MARYLAND
ERIC A. FICHTE, OF WASHINGTON
TROY DAMIAN FITRELL, OF VIRGINIA

RICHARD HARRIS GLENN, OF VIRGINIA
MATTHEW EUGENE GOSHKO, OF THE DISTRICT OF COLUMBIA
RAMOND F. GREENE III, OF THE DISTRICT OF COLUMBIA
THERESA GRENCIK, OF MARYLAND
ANNE E. GRIMES, OF VIRGINIA
EDWARD G. GRULICH, OF VIRGINIA
MARGARET HAWTHORNE, OF THE DISTRICT OF COLUMBIA
JOHN HENNESSEY-NILAND, OF VIRGINIA
CHRISTINA MARIA HUTH HIGGINS, OF VIRGINIA
MELANIE HARRIS HIGGINS, OF FLORIDA
LISA S. KENNA, OF MARYLAND
JONATHAN STUART KESSLER, OF VIRGINIA
CYNTHIA A. KIERSCHT, OF MINNESOTA
MICHAEL F. KLEINE, OF THE DISTRICT OF COLUMBIA
CHRISTOPHER M. KRAFFT, OF VIRGINIA
HELEN GRACE LAFAVE, OF VIRGINIA
ADAM DUANE LAMOREAUX, OF OREGON
GREGORY F. LAWLESS, OF VIRGINIA
PHILLIP LINDERMAN, OF VIRGINIA
CHARLES LUOMA-OVERSTREET, OF VIRGINIA
MICHAEL MACY, OF FLORIDA
JERROLD L. MALLORY, OF CALIFORNIA
BETTINA A. MALONE, OF VIRGINIA
ANN BARROWS MCCONNELL, OF CALIFORNIA
MEREDITH CLARE MCEVOY, OF VIRGINIA
RICHARD MEI, JR., OF KENTUCKY
ALAN D. MELTZER, OF VIRGINIA
JANE S. W. MESSENGER, OF MARYLAND
JOAQUIN F. MONSERRATE, OF PUERTO RICO
MITCHELL R. MOSS, OF VIRGINIA
PHILLIP R. NELSON, OF MONTANA
ELISHA NYMAN, OF MARYLAND
GARY GLENN OBA, OF ARKANSAS
MARTHA E. PATTERSON, OF TEXAS
ROY ALBERT PERRIN, OF VIRGINIA
DAVID D. POTTER, OF VIRGINIA
VIRGINIA SHER RAMADAN, OF VIRGINIA
WALTER SCOTT REID, OF VIRGINIA
JEFFREY JAMES ROBERTSON, OF CALIFORNIA
HUGO F. RODRIGUEZ, JR., OF THE DISTRICT OF COLUMBIA
RUSSELL A. SCHIEBEL, OF TEXAS
JONATHAN A. SCHOOLS, OF TEXAS
MICAELA A. SCHWEITZER-BLUHM, OF VIRGINIA
MARK WAYNE SEIBEL, OF NORTH CAROLINA
JONATHAN L. SHRIER, OF NEW YORK
SUSAN MARIE SHULTZ, OF THE DISTRICT OF COLUMBIA
EUGENIA M. SIDEREAS, OF THE DISTRICT OF COLUMBIA
DAVID W. SIMONS, OF VIRGINIA
JEFFERSON D. SMITH, OF TEXAS
MATTHEW D. SMITH, OF NEW YORK
WILLARD TENNEY SMITH, OF VIRGINIA
LINDA S. SPECHT, OF VIRGINIA
GAVIN A. SUNDWALL, OF NORTH CAROLINA
REBECCA T. BROWN THOMPSON, OF VIRGINIA
SCOTT BRIAN TICKNOR, OF VIRGINIA
ALAN R. TOUSIGNANT, OF VIRGINIA
PAMELA M. TREMONT, OF VIRGINIA
STEWART D. TUTTLE, JR., OF CALIFORNIA
HEATHER CATHERINE VARIAVA, OF VIRGINIA
AMY HART VRAMPAS, OF THE DISTRICT OF COLUMBIA
JOANNE WAGNER, OF VIRGINIA
SUSAN M. WALSH, OF RHODE ISLAND
EVA ANNE WEIGOLD SCHULTZ, OF VIRGINIA
EDWARD ANTHONY WHITE, OF FLORIDA
ALEISHA WOODWARD, OF UTAH

THE FOLLOWING-NAMED CAREER MEMBERS OF THE FOREIGN SERVICE FOR PROMOTION INTO THE SENIOR FOREIGN SERVICE, AS A CAREER MEMBER OF THE SENIOR FOREIGN SERVICE, CLASS OF COUNSELOR, AND A CONSULAR OFFICER AND A SECRETARY IN THE DIPLOMATIC SERVICE OF THE UNITED STATES OF AMERICA:

WENDY A. BASHNAN, OF SOUTH CAROLINA
JOHN C. BREWER, OF ALABAMA
JULIE S. CABUS, OF VIRGINIA
CORNELL CHASTEN, OF NORTH CAROLINA
NATALIE CROPPER, OF SOUTH CAROLINA
JAIME ESQUIVEL, OF VIRGINIA
YURI P. FEDORENKO, OF MICHIGAN
DONALD E. GONNEVILLE, JR., OF VIRGINIA
MARCIA K. HENKE, OF ALABAMA
PAUL R. HOUSTON, OF VIRGINIA
JOSHUA D. MCDAVID, OF WASHINGTON
GEORGE M. NAVADEL, OF THE DISTRICT OF COLUMBIA
MICHAEL BRITTON PHILLIPS, OF MARYLAND
LARRY D. ROBERTS, JR., OF VIRGINIA
CHRISTOPHER R. ROOKS, OF VIRGINIA
BEHZAD SHAHBAZIAN, OF MARYLAND
HARTAJE K. THIARA, OF THE DISTRICT OF COLUMBIA
JEFFREY A. THOMAS, OF VIRGINIA
TRACY JO THOMAS, OF VIRGINIA
JENNIFER S. TSENG, OF COLORADO
THOMAS R. VANDENBRINK, OF VIRGINIA
JUDITH VARDY, OF FLORIDA

THE FOLLOWING-NAMED CAREER MEMBER OF THE FOREIGN SERVICE FOR PROMOTION INTO THE SENIOR FOREIGN SERVICE, AS A CAREER MEMBER OF THE SENIOR FOREIGN SERVICE OF THE UNITED STATES OF AMERICA, CLASS OF COUNSELOR, EFFECTIVE FEBRUARY 21, 2016:

LAURA ANN GRIESMER, OF WASHINGTON

THE FOLLOWING-NAMED CAREER MEMBERS OF THE SENIOR FOREIGN SERVICE OF THE DEPARTMENT OF STATE FOR PROMOTION WITHIN THE SENIOR FOREIGN SERVICE OF THE UNITED STATES OF AMERICA, CLASS OF CAREER MINISTER:

ROBERT STEPHEN BEECROFT, OF CALIFORNIA
ARNOLD A. CHACON, OF VIRGINIA

TRACEY ANN JACOBSON, OF THE DISTRICT OF COLUMBIA
GEOFFREY R. PYATT, OF CALIFORNIA
MARIE L. YOVANOVITCH, OF CONNECTICUT

THE FOLLOWING–NAMED MEMBERS OF THE FOREIGN SERVICE OF THE DEPARTMENT OF STATE FOR APPOINTMENT AS A FOREIGN SERVICE OFFICER, A CONSULAR OFFICER AND A SECRETARY IN THE DIPLOMATIC SERVICE OF THE UNITED STATES OF AMERICA:

TRISTAN J. ALLEN, OF ARIZONA
CHARLES A. BENTLEY, OF FLORIDA
LADISLAV BERANEK, OF VIRGINIA
MICHAEL C. BONFIELD, OF TEXAS
ANDREW CHIRA, OF THE DISTRICT OF COLUMBIA
JAMES P. CHYNOWETH, OF FLORIDA
RACHAEL M. CULLINS, OF INDIANA
KRISTEN A. FARRELL, OF THE DISTRICT OF COLUMBIA
RYAN A. P. FEEBACK, OF INDIANA
JULIANA K. FINUCANE, OF CALIFORNIA
BENJAMIN M. GULLETT, OF NORTH CAROLINA
CHRISTOPHER J. HALLETT, OF NORTH CAROLINA
MAXWELL S. HARRINGTON, OF CALIFORNIA
JANET ADELE HEG, OF WASHINGTON
MATTHEW R. HERGOTT, OF COLORADO
CHADWICK D. HOUGHTON, OF FLORIDA
RICHARD T. KERR, OF NEW HAMPSHIRE
MICHAEL W. LEACH, OF TEXAS
BOA LEE, OF MINNESOTA
BIC HOANG LEU, OF CONNECTICUT
NATHANIAL S. LINDSEY, OF VIRGINIA
ROBERT S. MACINTOSH, OF MONTANA
CHRISTOPHER T. MCKINNEY, OF TEXAS
DAVID E. MERRELL, OF UTAH
MONIQUE A. NOWICKI, OF VIRGINIA
JESSICA E. PANCHATHA, OF CONNECTICUT
ROBERT M. PASTORE, OF NEW YORK
HILDE LYNN PEARSON, OF VIRGINIA
MICHAEL R. PROSSER, OF FLORIDA
ZAHID M. RAJA, OF TEXAS
ANNE M. REDALEN FRASER, OF MINNESOTA
INGRID K. SPECHT, OF GEORGIA
JOSHUA E. STERN, OF VIRGINIA
JOHN SZYPULA, OF COLORADO
ELIE M. TEICHMAN, OF MARYLAND
JEFFREY S. VANDORN, OF KANSAS
JESSE C. WALTER, OF WISCONSIN
SHANTHINI M. B. WATSON, OF GUAM
CHRISTINA C. WEST, OF TEXAS
DORI ENDERLE WINTER, OF TEXAS
MARION JOHANNA WOHLERS, OF WASHINGTON
WILLIAM F. ZEMAN, OF CONNECTICUT

THE FOLLOWING–NAMED MEMBERS OF THE FOREIGN SERVICE OF THE DEPARTMENT OF STATE TO BE A CONSULAR OFFICER AND A SECRETARY IN THE DIPLOMATIC SERVICE OF THE UNITED STATES OF AMERICA:

ANTHONY ABBA, OF VIRGINIA
TESSIE ANNE ABRAHAM, OF TEXAS
JONATHAN PAUL ACKLEY, OF WASHINGTON
MICHAEL OLUGBENGA AKINWOLEMIWA, OF VIRGINIA
GABRIEL ALLISON, OF VIRGINIA
DIVAH JEANNE ALSHAWA, OF VIRGINIA
GARY PHILLIP ANTHONY, OF NEW YORK
MARYAM K. ARENA, OF VIRGINIA
YARED RIYADH ASNAKE, OF CALIFORNIA
SILVIA CAROLINA ARDON AYALA, OF FLORIDA
KRISTIN D. BAILEY, OF VIRGINIA
MICHELLE MARIE BAILEY, OF VIRGINIA
LAVONDA TANE'E BALDWIN, OF NEW JERSEY
JAMES V. BARR, OF VIRGINIA
MARK BASSOTTI, OF VIRGINIA
JESSE ROSE MACERA BEAUMIER, OF VIRGINIA
JAMES RAYMOND BEHYMER, OF VIRGINIA
ADAM K. BENABDALLAH, OF VIRGINIA
CRAIG D. BENNETT, OF VIRGINIA
EVE SARAH COPELAND BENTOVIM, OF THE DISTRICT OF COLUMBIA
STEPHEN CAREY BIRMINGHAM II, OF CALIFORNIA
JASON BOND, OF OKLAHOMA
ERIC J. BRADSHAW, OF VIRGINIA
HEATHER DAWN BROOKS, OF FLORIDA
PAUL D. BUCKLEW, OF VIRGINIA
PATRICK GENE BURLINGAME, OF PENNSYLVANIA
MICHAEL D. BURRIS, OF VIRGINIA
KRISTIN CATHERINE BYRD BUSHBY, OF MARYLAND
MICHAEL BUSTAMANTE, OF NEW YORK
TERRY B. CARWILE, OF VIRGINIA
KAREN ELIZABETH CASTRO, OF OHIO
GEOFFREY BAYLISS CAUSEY, OF VIRGINIA
SUSAN I. CHESLEY, OF VIRGINIA
JENNIFER DANIELLE CLARK, OF VIRGINIA
CHARLES MEDFORD CLATANOFF, OF VIRGINIA
DAVID ROSS CONCEPCION, OF VIRGINIA
KATHRYN EILEEN CORRIDAN, OF VIRGINIA
EVAN MITCHELL CORZINE, OF VIRGINIA
LISA COSGROVE, OF VIRGINIA
PATRICK DANIEL COUGHLIN, OF NEW YORK
JAYSON CHRISTOPHER CRIDDLE, OF VIRGINIA

JOSEPH EVAN DE BERNARDO, OF VIRGINIA
JOHN JOSEPH DELANEY, OF VIRGINIA
KEYSHA DORCH, OF VIRGINIA
ADAM M. DUNIGAN, OF VIRGINIA
DAWN M. DYETTE, OF VIRGINIA
AARON COOPER EASLICK, OF MICHIGAN
JOEL ELLISON, OF VIRGINIA
SONIA FERNANDES, OF NEW YORK
GREGORY DAVID FERRIS, OF VIRGINIA
ALAN JOSEPH MICHAEL FLESCH, OF OKLAHOMA
MARTA ALYSSA FOLIO, OF VIRGINIA
MILYNDA RAE FOUSHEE, OF VIRGINIA
ELISABETH M. FRENCH, OF VIRGINIA
JAMES E. FRITTER, OF VIRGINIA
CHRISTOPHER S. FULLERTON, OF VIRGINIA
BRYAN J. FURMAN, OF NEW JERSEY
ANDREW R. GALLUCCI, OF VIRGINIA
PAUL ROBERT GIBLIN, OF ARIZONA
SHEIMALIZ ELIZKA GLOVER, OF SOUTH CAROLINA
MATTHEW BERNARD GONZALEZ, OF VIRGINIA
CHARLES H. GRIFFIN, OF VIRGINIA
DAVID CALDERON GUTIERREZ, OF GEORGIA
SAMA EMAD HABIB, OF NEW YORK
ANDREW A. HACKMANN, OF VIRGINIA
LISA M. HAHN, OF CALIFORNIA
SALMAN HAJI, OF NEW MEXICO
GHASSAN HALAWANI, OF VIRGINIA
ALEXANDRA BREANNE HALL, OF GEORGIA
ROBERT JOSEPH HALLIDAY, OF VIRGINIA
BRITTANY CHERELLE HARDY, OF ARIZONA
MICHELLE R HARIG, OF VIRGINIA
KYLE ELIZABETH HARTWELL, OF THE DISTRICT OF COLUMBIA
BENJAMIN ROBERT HARVEY, OF MISSOURI
RYAN ROBERT HEGER, OF VIRGINIA
NELL GARDENIA GULLE HIDALGO, OF VIRGINIA
CARL R. HILL, OF VIRGINIA
KRISTINA LOUISE HILLMAN, OF VIRGINIA
ANDREW WILLIAM HILLSTROM, OF TEXAS
NICOLE STILLWELL HOLLER, OF MARYLAND
JOHN M. HORTON, OF VIRGINIA
JEFFREY PETER HOULE, OF VIRGINIA
JOCELYN DYAN HUGHES, OF VIRGINIA
DEBRA SUE HUNGERFORD, OF VIRGINIA
PORTER ILLI, OF UTAH
ELIZABETH ATKINSON ISAMAN, OF COLORADO
COLE LIHAU JACKSON, OF HAWAII
KEVIN W. JACOBS, OF VIRGINIA
JOSHUA PAUL JOHNSON, OF THE DISTRICT OF COLUMBIA
TIMOTHY ALLEN JOHNSON, OF CALIFORNIA
TIMOTHY C. JOHNSON, OF VIRGINIA
ROBERT OWEN KEANE, OF MASSACHUSETTS
DONALD D. KIM, OF THE DISTRICT OF COLUMBIA
JENNIFER CARTER KIM, OF THE DISTRICT OF COLUMBIA
IAN MIKAEL KITTERMAN, OF THE DISTRICT OF COLUMBIA
SARAH L. KNOBLOCH, OF VIRGINIA
MICHAEL CHARLES KRUEGER, OF VIRGINIA
CHAD R. LAMB, OF VIRGINIA
BRITTANY MARTHA LANING, OF VIRGINIA
LELAND MARCELLUS LAZARUS, OF NEW YORK
JESSICA LEIGH LILLEY, OF VIRGINIA
JAIME DIANE LODA, OF MASSACHUSETTS
CHADWICK W. LUCK, OF VIRGINIA
ORIANA LUQUETTA, OF TEXAS
LEAH NICOLE MAINIERO, OF VIRGINIA
ARMANDO JONATHAN MALDONADO, OF VIRGINIA
TOYA E. MARKS, OF VIRGINIA
TRAVIS B. MARSHALL, OF VIRGINIA
LUIS JAVIER MARTINEZ, OF VIRGINIA
ROBERT EDWARD MCGRAW, JR., OF VIRGINIA
JOHN J. MCHUGH, OF VIRGINIA
MOISES DAVID MENDOZA, OF OREGON
STEPHEN R. MENDOZA, OF VIRGINIA
DENISE MARTON MENENDEZ, OF FLORIDA
KATHLEEN M. MINOR, OF VIRGINIA
KARI ELIZABETH MOORE, OF VIRGINIA
KEVIN SINCLAIR MOSS, OF FLORIDA
CAITLIN ELISE NETTLETON, OF FLORIDA
HUGH PERALTA, OF VIRGINIA
SHANNON BLOTNER PINE, OF VIRGINIA
ANNA MARIA PLACANICA, OF VIRGINIA
DONALD C. PLAISTED, OF VIRGINIA
NICOLE MICHELLE PORTER, OF CALIFORNIA
MATTHEW WILLIAM PRIEST, OF MICHIGAN
DAVID WILLIAM PUCCI, OF VIRGINIA
SUZANNE C. PULKKINEN, OF VIRGINIA
JESS A. PURDY, OF VIRGINIA
MARY–KATHERINE REAM, OF THE DISTRICT OF COLUMBIA
JENNIFER IDA REGAN, OF VIRGINIA
CHRISTOPHER ALEXANDER RIGO, OF VIRGINIA
CLAYTON EARL ROBINSON, OF VIRGINIA
JAMES TRIPOLI ROBINSON, OF VIRGINIA
JOSHUA RASPLICA RODD, OF COLORADO
PEDRO JOSE RODRIGUEZ, OF VIRGINIA
STEPHANIE Z. RODRIGUEZ, OF VIRGINIA

KYLE JAMES ROHRICH, OF NEBRASKA
MELISSA B. ROMO, OF VIRGINIA
NICOLAS ADAM ROSER, OF VIRGINIA
SHAWN DAVID ROSLIN, OF VIRGINIA
MEGHAN ASHLEY WINSOR ROTH, OF VIRGINIA
ROBERT ANTHONY ROWE, OF VIRGINIA
SKARRN RYVNINE, OF FLORIDA
EDDY SANTANA, OF ILLINOIS
JASON W. SCHREYER, OF VIRGINIA
JENNIFER STARR SHELDON, OF KANSAS
TIMOTHY J. SHINGLER, OF VIRGINIA
WILLIAM MASSIE SIEBER, OF DELAWARE
RENNIE ALON SILVA, OF THE DISTRICT OF COLUMBIA
RASHELLE B. SIMONSON, OF VIRGINIA
COREY RAY SKELTON, OF VIRGINIA
AUSTIN T. SLAYMAKER, OF OKLAHOMA
CHRISTINE A. SOLLINGER, OF VIRGINIA
CHARLES LEE SPECHT, OF ILLINOIS
JORDAN MICHAEL STEELMAN, OF VIRGINIA
VICTORIA FISHER STEFFES, OF VIRGINIA
LUCAS M. STELLAR, OF PENNSYLVANIA
MICHELLE NICOLE STOKES, OF TEXAS
KENNETH L. TARPLEY, JR., OF VIRGINIA
BRIDGET TAYLOR, OF VIRGINIA
MICHAEL TEMPLEMAN, OF THE DISTRICT OF COLUMBIA
ANTHONY DOUGLAS TEUSCHER, OF VIRGINIA
BRANDON SCOTT THOMPSON, OF TEXAS
CODY MICHAEL THOMPSON, OF COLORADO
MELISSA ANN TREBIL, OF VIRGINIA
CARDIEL ADRIAN TREVIZO, OF VIRGINIA
ELIZABETH MELODY TROBAUGH, OF WASHINGTON
GREGORY C. TRUNZ, OF VIRGINIA
JAMES LEVERING TYSON III, OF THE DISTRICT OF COLUMBIA
ALAN R. VAN TASSEL, OF VIRGINIA
WILLIAM HARVEY WAGNER, OF VIRGINIA
JERICA J. WARD, OF MARYLAND
SCOTT A WEISEL, OF VIRGINIA
AMANDA B. WHATLEY, OF ALABAMA
JASON L. WILCOX, OF VIRGINIA
KEVIN M. WILLIAMS, OF VIRGINIA
ROBERT FREDERICK WILLIS, OF VIRGINIA
COOPER J. WIMMER, OF VIRGINIA
BRUCE L. WOODYARD, OF VIRGINIA
NICHOLAS ZEIGLER, OF VIRGINIA
MICHAEL DAVID ZGODA, OF THE DISTRICT OF COLUMBIA

DEFENSE NUCLEAR FACILITIES SAFETY BOARD

JOSEPH BRUCE HAMILTON, OF TEXAS, TO BE A MEMBER OF THE DEFENSE NUCLEAR FACILITIES SAFETY BOARD FOR A TERM EXPIRING OCTOBER 18, 2021. (REAPPOINTMENT)

AMTRAK BOARD OF DIRECTORS

SETH HARRIS, OF NEW YORK, TO BE A DIRECTOR OF THE AMTRAK BOARD OF DIRECTORS FOR A TERM OF FIVE YEARS. (NEW POSITION)
JEFFREY R. MORELAND, OF TEXAS, TO BE A DIRECTOR OF THE AMTRAK BOARD OF DIRECTORS FOR A TERM OF FIVE YEARS. (REAPPOINTMENT)

CHEMICAL SAFETY AND HAZARD INVESTIGATION BOARD

RACHEL A. MEIDL, OF WISCONSIN, TO BE A MEMBER OF THE CHEMICAL SAFETY AND HAZARD INVESTIGATION BOARD FOR A TERM OF FIVE YEARS, VICE MARK A. GRIFFON, RESIGNED.

SOCIAL SECURITY ADMINISTRATION

MICHAEL P. LEARY, OF PENNSYLVANIA, TO BE INSPECTOR GENERAL, SOCIAL SECURITY ADMINISTRATION, VICE PATRICK P. O'CARROLL, JR., RESIGNED.

BROADCASTING BOARD OF GOVERNORS

RICHARD STENGEL, OF THE DISTRICT OF COLUMBIA, TO BE A MEMBER OF THE BROADCASTING BOARD OF GOVERNORS FOR A TERM EXPIRING AUGUST 13, 2017, VICE SUSAN MCCUE, RESIGNED.
RICHARD STENGEL, OF THE DISTRICT OF COLUMBIA, TO BE CHAIRMAN OF THE BROADCASTING BOARD OF GOVERNORS, VICE JEFFREY SHELL.

FEDERAL MINE SAFETY AND HEALTH ADMINISTRATION

PATRICK K. NAKAMURA, OF ALABAMA, TO BE A MEMBER OF THE FEDERAL MINE SAFETY AND HEALTH REVIEW COMMISSION FOR A TERM OF SIX YEARS EXPIRING AUGUST 30, 2022. (REAPPOINTMENT)

DEPARTMENT OF DEFENSE

ROBERT P. STORCH, OF THE DISTRICT OF COLUMBIA, TO BE INSPECTOR GENERAL OF THE NATIONAL SECURITY AGENCY. (NEW POSITION)

HOUSE OF REPRESENTATIVES—*Tuesday, November 29, 2016*

The House met at noon and was called to order by the Speaker pro tempore (Mr. WOMACK).

DESIGNATION OF SPEAKER PRO TEMPORE

The SPEAKER pro tempore laid before the House the following communication from the Speaker:

WASHINGTON, DC,
November 29, 2016.

I hereby appoint the Honorable STEVE WOMACK to act as Speaker pro tempore on this day.

PAUL D. RYAN,
Speaker of the House of Representatives.

MORNING-HOUR DEBATE

The SPEAKER pro tempore. Pursuant to the order of the House of January 5, 2016, the Chair will now recognize Members from lists submitted by the majority and minority leaders for morning-hour debate.

The Chair will alternate recognition between the parties, with each party limited to 1 hour and each Member other than the majority and minority leaders and the minority whip limited to 5 minutes, but in no event shall debate continue beyond 1:50 p.m.

RECOGNIZING BILL AND BETTY BURNS

The SPEAKER pro tempore. The Chair recognizes the gentleman from Illinois (Mr. DOLD) for 5 minutes.

Mr. DOLD. Mr. Speaker, I want to take this opportunity to recognize two very special individuals from Lake Villa for their continued dedication to our community. Those individuals are Bill and Betty Burns. They both have consistently been at the forefront of the planning and execution of a number of wonderful community events that really serve as an opportunity to bring everyone together.

Each and every year, Bill and Betty have helped plan the Lake Villa Memorial Day, St. Patrick's Day, and Christmas parades. With their consistent hard work and dedication, these events have been great successes that have been really the glue that has brought our community together, not just on these special days but really a sense of community throughout the entire year.

Last year, Mr. Speaker, the Tenth District recognized them for their service to Lake Villa and to Grayslake with the public servant award for their dedication to our community.

Mr. Speaker, it is really individuals like Bill and Betty Burns that make our community stronger; and there are people like Bill and Betty all over our great Nation that are doing the things necessary to make sure that the little details are not left undone. They do this work tirelessly and thanklessly, in order to make sure our communities are a little bit stronger and a little bit better.

So I want to take this opportunity, Mr. Speaker, to thank Bill and Betty Burns for their tireless service and dedication to our community to make it a much stronger and better place.

RECESS

The SPEAKER pro tempore. Pursuant to clause 12(a) of rule I, the Chair declares the House in recess until 2 p.m. today.

Accordingly (at 12 o'clock and 2 minutes p.m.), the House stood in recess.

□ 1400

AFTER RECESS

The recess having expired, the House was called to order by the Speaker pro tempore (Mr. DENHAM) at 2 p.m.

PRAYER

The Chaplain, the Reverend Patrick J. Conroy, offered the following prayer:

Gracious God, we give You thanks for giving us another day.

You have blessed us with all good gifts, and this past week, with thankful hearts, we gathered with family and loved ones throughout this great land to celebrate our blessings together.

Bless the newly elected Members of the 115th Congress who resume their orientation on Capitol Hill. Give them calm and confidence as they prepare for a new role as servants of our Nation's citizens.

Bless the Members of the people's House who have been entrusted with the privilege to serve our Nation and all Americans in their need. Grant them to work together in respect and affection, faithful in the responsibilities they have been given.

As the end of the 114th Congress approaches, bestow upon them the gifts of wisdom and discernment, that in their actions they will do justice, love with mercy, and walk humbly with You.

May all that is done this day be for Your greater honor and glory.

Amen.

THE JOURNAL

The SPEAKER pro tempore. The Chair has examined the Journal of the last day's proceedings and announces to the House his approval thereof.

Pursuant to clause 1, rule I, the Journal stands approved.

PLEDGE OF ALLEGIANCE

The SPEAKER pro tempore. Will the gentleman from Georgia (Mr. JODY B. HICE) come forward and lead the House in the Pledge of Allegiance.

Mr. JODY B. HICE of Georgia led the Pledge of Allegiance as follows:

I pledge allegiance to the Flag of the United States of America, and to the Republic for which it stands, one nation under God, indivisible, with liberty and justice for all.

RECOGNIZING THE FOOD BANK OF NORTHEAST GEORGIA

(Mr. JODY B. HICE of Georgia asked and was given permission to address the House for 1 minute and to revise and extend his remarks.)

Mr. JODY B. HICE of Georgia. Mr. Speaker, I rise today to recognize the Food Bank of Northeast Georgia for more than 20 years of dedication and service to the people of Georgia. Since 1992, the food bank has worked to combat hunger and alleviate poverty by feeding children, the elderly, the ill, and those in need throughout the northeastern part of Georgia.

Just this past October, my staff and I had the distinct pleasure of lending a hand to the hardworking staff of the food bank and saw their actions, which are indeed remarkable. Just this year alone, the food bank has distributed nearly 12 million pounds of food, which equals about 10½ million meals.

This is truly an outstanding organization that continues to expand its reach and scope through its charitable contributions.

Mr. Speaker, it is my honor to ask my colleagues to join me in recognizing the Food Bank of Northeast Georgia for their outstanding service. I am honored deeply to have them in the 10th District of Georgia. I give my best wishes to the food bank and their staff as they continue to serve those in need.

FLINT, MICHIGAN

(Mr. KILDEE asked and was given permission to address the House for 1 minute.)

□ This symbol represents the time of day during the House proceedings, e.g., □1407 is 2:07 p.m.

Matter set in this typeface indicates words inserted or appended, rather than spoken, by a Member of the House on the floor.

Mr. KILDEE. Mr. Speaker, my hometown of Flint—I am sure you have heard me talk about this before—continues to suffer in this crisis. One hundred thousand people, citizens of that city, still can't drink their water, which has been exposed to high levels of lead.

That crisis is far from over. Flint families don't have access to clean drinking water. They demand—and we should provide—a response from every level of government, including the Federal Government.

That is why I am pleased and appreciate the fact that Democrats and Republicans in the House and the Senate have come together to make a commitment to help the people of Flint. Legislation passed in both bodies provides help for Flint. Now we have to finish that work before we leave this session.

Before we are Democrats or Republicans, we are Americans. We have a tradition in this country of always coming together for those who are facing a crisis, for those who are in great need. It is incumbent now upon Congress to do the same, to come together to help the people of Flint. I look forward to Democrats and Republicans coming together to do that.

RECOGNIZING THE NATIONAL GRANGE ANNIVERSARY

(Mr. THOMPSON of Pennsylvania asked and was given permission to address the House for 1 minute and to revise and extend his remarks.)

Mr. THOMPSON of Pennsylvania. Mr. Speaker, I rise today in recognition of the National Grange's 150th anniversary and to celebrate their century and a half of service to agriculture and rural America.

The National Grange was founded in 1867 by Oliver H. Kelley, an employee at the United States Department of Agriculture. He formed this organization to bring farmers from all over the country together in order to share best agricultural practices, drive educational discussion, and promote the economic and social needs of farmers.

In the 150 years since its founding, the Grange has encouraged families and communities—both rural and urban—to come together at the community, county or district, State, and national level to advocate not only for agriculture, but for an array of causes affecting communities.

For example, the Grange played a critical role in developing rural access, from electricity to rural mail delivery, and was an early supporter of women's suffrage.

I congratulate the National Grange and its members on a century and a half of excellence.

MEDIA IGNORES ILLEGAL IMMIGRATION

(Mr. SMITH of Texas asked and was given permission to address the House for 1 minute and to revise and extend his remarks.)

Mr. SMITH of Texas. Mr. Speaker, a new report by the Wilson Center has found that illegal immigration across the southern border is on pace to break the previous record set in 2014.

This record should not come as a surprise. The administration's policies encourage illegal immigration.

The number of apprehensions at the southern border in August reached its highest point for that month in the last 5 years. This record-setting pace of illegal immigration was largely ignored by the media. Neither the Big Three networks nor the national daily newspapers covered the report.

The administration's failure to enforce immigration laws has caused the new record surge. Americans are understandably concerned about illegal immigration. It is unfortunate that the media does not consider it newsworthy.

COMMUNICATION FROM THE CLERK OF THE HOUSE

The SPEAKER pro tempore laid before the House the following communication from the Clerk of the House of Representatives:

OFFICE OF THE CLERK,
HOUSE OF REPRESENTATIVES,
Washington, DC, November 29, 2016.
Hon. PAUL D. RYAN,
Speaker, House of Representatives,
Washington, DC.

DEAR MR. SPEAKER: Pursuant to the permission granted in Clause 2(h) of Rule II of the Rules of the U.S. House of Representatives, the Clerk received the following message from the Secretary of the Senate on November 29, 2016, at 9:23 a.m.:

That the Senate passed without amendment H.R. 4665.

That the Senate passed without amendment H.R. 5111.

With best wishes, I am

Sincerely,

KAREN L. HAAS.

COMMUNICATION FROM THE CLERK OF THE HOUSE

The SPEAKER pro tempore laid before the House the following communication from the Clerk of the House of Representatives:

OFFICE OF THE CLERK,
HOUSE OF REPRESENTATIVES,
Washington, DC, November 29, 2016.
Hon. PAUL D. RYAN,
Speaker, House of Representatives,
Washington, DC.

DEAR MR. SPEAKER: Pursuant to the permission granted in Clause 2(h) of Rule II of the Rules of the U.S. House of Representatives, the Clerk received the following message from the Secretary of the Senate on November 29, 2016, at 10:45 am.:

That the Senate passed S. 2974.

That the Senate passed S. 2325.

With best wishes, I am

Sincerely,

KAREN L. HAAS.

RECESS

The SPEAKER pro tempore. Pursuant to clause 12(a) of rule I, the Chair declares the House in recess until approximately 3 p.m. today.

Accordingly (at 2 o'clock and 8 minutes p.m.), the House stood in recess.

□ 1501

AFTER RECESS

The recess having expired, the House was called to order by the Speaker pro tempore (Mr. COLLINS of New York) at 3 o'clock and 1 minute p.m.

MESSAGE FROM THE PRESIDENT

A message in writing from the President of the United States was communicated to the House by Mr. Brian Pate, one of his secretaries.

ANNOUNCEMENT BY THE SPEAKER PRO TEMPORE

The SPEAKER pro tempore. Pursuant to clause 8 of rule XX, the Chair will postpone further proceedings today on motions to suspend the rules on which a recorded vote or the yeas and nays are ordered, or on which the vote incurs objection under clause 6 of rule XX.

Record votes on postponed questions will be taken later.

VETERANS TRICARE CHOICE ACT OF 2016

Mr. SMITH of Nebraska. Mr. Speaker, I move to suspend the rules and pass the bill (H.R. 5458) to provide for coordination between the TRICARE program and eligibility for making contributions to a health savings account, and for other purposes, as amended.

The Clerk read the title of the bill.

The text of the bill is as follows:

H.R. 5458

Be it enacted by the Senate and House of Representatives of the United States of America in Congress assembled,

SECTION 1. SHORT TITLE.

This Act may be cited as the "Veterans TRICARE Choice Act of 2016".

SEC. 2. COORDINATION BETWEEN TRICARE PROGRAM AND ELIGIBILITY TO MAKE CONTRIBUTIONS TO HEALTH SAVINGS ACCOUNTS.

(a) IN GENERAL.—Section 223(c)(1)(B) of the Internal Revenue Code of 1986 is amended by striking "and" at the end of clause (ii), by striking the period at the end of clause (iii) and inserting ", and", and by adding at the end the following new clause:

"(iv) coverage under the TRICARE program under chapter 55 of title 10, United States Code, for any period with respect to which an election is in effect under section 1097e of such title providing that the individual is ineligible to be enrolled in (and receive benefits under) such program.".

(b) PROVISIONS RELATING TO ELECTION OF INELIGIBILITY UNDER TRICARE.—

(1) IN GENERAL.—Chapter 55 of title 10, United States Code, is amended by inserting after section 1097d the following new section:

"§ 1097e. TRICARE program: election of eligibility

"(a) ELECTION.—Beginning January 1, 2017, a TRICARE-eligible individual may elect at any time to be ineligible to enroll in (and receive any benefits under) the TRICARE program.

"(b) CHANGE OF ELECTION.—(1) If a TRICARE-eligible individual makes an election under subsection (a), the TRICARE-eligible individual may later elect to be eligible to enroll in the TRICARE program. An election made under this subsection may be made only during a special enrollment period.

"(2) The Secretary shall ensure that a TRICARE-eligible individual who makes an election under subsection (a) may efficiently enroll in the TRICARE program pursuant to an election under paragraph (1), including by maintaining the individual, as appropriate, in the health care enrollment system under section 1099 of this title in an inactive manner.

"(c) PERIOD OF ELECTION.—If a TRICARE-eligible individual makes an election under subsection (a), such election shall be in effect beginning on the date of such election and ending on the date that such individual makes an election under subsection (b)(1) to enroll in the TRICARE program.

"(d) HEALTH SAVINGS ACCOUNT PARTICIPATION.—(1) For provisions allowing participation in a health savings account in connection with coverage under a high deductible health plan during the period that the election under subsection (a) is in effect, see section 223(c)(1)(B)(iv) of the Internal Revenue Code of 1986.

"(2) The Secretary shall submit to the Commissioner of Internal Revenue the name of, and any other information that the Commissioner may require with respect to, each TRICARE-eligible individual who makes an election under subsection (a) or (b), not later than 90 days after such election, for purposes of determining the eligibility of such TRICARE-eligible individual for a health savings account described in paragraph (1).

"(e) RECORDS.—The Secretary shall ensure that a TRICARE-eligible individual who makes an election under subsection (a) is maintained on the Defense Enrollment Eligibility Reporting System, or successor system, regardless of whether the individual is eligible for the TRICARE program during the period of such election.

"(f) PROVISION OF INFORMATION.—The Secretary shall provide to each TRICARE-eligible individual who seeks to make an election under subsection (a) information regarding—

"(1) health savings accounts in connection with coverage under a high deductible health plan described in subsection (d)(1), including a comparison of such health saving accounts and the health care benefits the individual is eligible to receive under the TRICARE program; and

"(2) changing such an election under subsection (b)(1).

"(g) ANNUAL REPORT.—Not later than 60 days after the end of each fiscal year, the Secretary shall submit to the congressional defense committees a report on elections by TRICARE-eligible individuals under this section that includes the following:

"(1) The number of TRICARE-eligible individuals, as of the date of the submittal of the report, who are ineligible to enroll in (and receive any benefits under) the TRICARE program pursuant to an election under subsection (a).

"(2) The number of TRICARE-eligible individuals who made an election described under subsection (a) but, as of the date of the submittal of the report, are enrolled in the TRICARE pro-gram pursuant to a change of election under subsection (b).

"(h) DEFINITIONS.—In this section:

"(1) The term 'TRICARE-eligible individual' means an individual who is—

"(A) eligible to be a covered beneficiary entitled to health care benefits under the TRICARE program (determined without regard to this section); and

"(B) not serving on active duty in the uniformed services.

"(2) The term 'special enrollment period' means the period in which a beneficiary under the Federal Employees Health Benefits program under chapter 89 of title 5 may enroll in or change a plan under such program by reason of a qualifying event or during an open enrollment season. For purposes of this section, such qualifying events shall also include events determined appropriate by the Secretary of Defense, including events relating to a member of the armed forces being ordered to active duty.".

(2) CONFORMING AMENDMENT.—The table of sections at the beginning of chapter 55 of such title is amended by inserting after the item relating to section 1097d the following new item:

"1097e. TRICARE program: election of eligibility.".

(c) EFFECTIVE DATE.—The amendments made by subsection (a) shall apply to months beginning after December 31, 2016.

The SPEAKER pro tempore. Pursuant to the rule, the gentleman from Nebraska (Mr. SMITH) and the gentleman from Washington (Mr. MCDERMOTT) each will control 20 minutes.

The Chair recognizes the gentleman from Nebraska.

GENERAL LEAVE

Mr. SMITH of Nebraska. Mr. Speaker, I ask unanimous consent that all Members may have 5 legislative days within which to revise and extend their remarks and include extraneous material on H.R. 5458, currently under consideration.

The SPEAKER pro tempore. Is there objection to the request of the gentleman from Nebraska?

There was no objection.

Mr. SMITH of Nebraska. Mr. Speaker, I yield myself such time as I may consume.

I rise today in support of H.R. 5458, the Veterans TRICARE Choice Act of 2016. This legislation, introduced by the gentleman from Utah (Mr. STEWART), addresses a gap in current law which prevents veterans and their families with TRICARE coverage who also choose to participate in a high-deductible health plan from utilizing a health savings account, or HSA.

While veterans or their family members who participate in TRICARE may also have private health insurance coverage, including high-deductible plans, they are prohibited from contributing to an HSA affiliated with a high-deductible plan. In order to contribute to an HSA under current law, an individual must permanently renounce their TRICARE eligibility because no mechanism to allow reenrollment currently exists.

H.R. 5458 addresses this issue by allowing certain TRICARE-eligible indi-viduals to voluntarily pause their TRICARE coverage for a period of time in which they choose to contribute to an HSA. The bill also creates special enrollment periods should these individuals choose to reenroll in TRICARE at a later date.

Our veterans devoted their lives to defending our freedoms. We should not allow arbitrary, bureaucratic obstacles to stop them from making the best healthcare choices for themselves and their families. This bill creates a mechanism to improve veterans' health coverage options and provides them greater opportunities to save toward their own healthcare needs. It also ensures patients can be more engaged in their own care while eliminating the inconsistency in our Tax Code.

I applaud the gentleman from Utah (Mr. STEWART) for bringing us this good idea today. I urge support.

Mr. Speaker, I reserve the balance of my time.

COMMITTEE ON ARMED SERVICES,
HOUSE OF REPRESENTATIVES,
Washington, DC, November 17, 2016.

Hon. KEVIN BRADY,
Chairman, Committee on Ways and Means, House of Representatives, Washington, DC.

DEAR MR. CHAIRMAN: I write concerning H.R. 5458, the Veterans TRICARE Choice Act of 2016, which was referred to the Committee on Armed Services. There are certain provisions in the bill that fall within the Rule X jurisdiction of the Committee on Armed Services.

In order to expedite this legislation for floor consideration, the Committee on Armed Services will forgo action on this bill. This decision is conditional on our mutual understanding that forgoing consideration in no way diminishes or alters the jurisdictional interests of the Committee on Armed Services in this bill, any subsequent amendments, or similar legislation. I request you urge the Speaker to appoint members of the Committee on Armed Services to any conference committee convened to consider such provisions.

Please place a copy of this letter and your response acknowledging our jurisdictional interest into the Congressional Record during consideration of the measure on the House floor.

Sincerely,
WILLIAM M. "MAC" THORNBERRY,
Chairman.

———

COMMITTEE ON WAYS AND MEANS,
HOUSE OF REPRESENTATIVES,
Washington, DC, November 28, 2016.

Hon. WILLIAM M. "MAC" THORNBERRY,
Chairman, Committee on Armed Services, House of Representatives, Washington, DC.

DEAR CHAIRMAN THORNBERRY, Thank you for your letter regarding H.R. 5458, the "Veterans TRICARE Choice Act." As you noted, the Committee on Armed Services was granted an additional referral on the bill.

I am most appreciative of your decision to waive formal consideration of H.R. 5458 so that it may proceed expeditiously to the House floor. I acknowledge that although you waived formal consideration of the bill, the Committee on Armed Services is in no way waiving its jurisdiction over the subject matter contained in those provisions of the bill that fall within your Rule X jurisdiction. I would support your effort to seek appointment of an appropriate number of conferees on any House-Senate conference involving this legislation.

I will include a copy of our letters in the Congressional Record during consideration of this legislation on the House floor.

Sincerely,

KEVIN BRADY,
Chairman.

Mr. McDERMOTT. Mr. Speaker, I yield myself such time as I may consume.

While we are here today to debate H.R. 5458, which focuses on one small part of the transition for veterans completing their service and entering the civilian workforce, I wish to take a moment to reflect on a broader issue.

While many veterans enter the workforce, and some may even be offered a health savings account as part of their insurance coverage, many millions depend on Medicare and Medicaid. Now, we in the Congress can't forget the role these programs play in caring for our veterans and their loved ones as they return to the workforce, as they age, or as they live with disabilities.

For more than four decades, Medicare and Medicaid have helped Americans from all walks of life by improving their financial and health security; but if you have been paying attention to the news lately, you know these programs are under grave risk next year with a new Congress and a new President.

As we speak today to honor veterans' service to our country, we must also think about the safety net that has been in place for many years to offer security. For example, today, nearly 1 in 10 veterans lacks health insurance at all. More than 340,000 uninsured veterans and their spouses live in States that have chosen not to expand Medicaid to cover more residents. If those States offered coverage, these veterans would have insurance if we really cared about them—but their Governors apparently don't.

In Florida, more than 55,000 veterans and their spouses would be Medicaid eligible had the State chosen to cover individuals earning less than $21,000 a year. In North Carolina, 32,000 veterans and their spouses, and in Texas 67,000 veterans and their spouses would be eligible. But their Governors saw fit not to care.

Slashing Medicare funding by more than $1 trillion, as Speaker RYAN has proposed, is not a way to help veterans. Yet that is what will be in store next year. That is what people are talking about as what we are going to do in the new year. Turning Medicare into a capped voucher, privatizing the program, shifting more costs on beneficiaries, won't help either.

Now back to the bill at hand. For veterans who are receiving coverage through TRICARE, using employer coverage that offers health savings accounts coupled with high-deductible health plans can cause a problem. Under present law, eligibility for TRICARE coverage disqualifies a retiree from HSA eligibility because the TRICARE program is not a high-deductible plan. This, I believe, is a good thing, and it keeps health care affordable for veterans, especially those who do not have the option for other coverage.

While there is a difference of opinion in the committee on tax-preferred health accounts, the legislation recognizes that some veterans may have that coverage and could run afoul of current law because of enrollment in TRICARE. H.R. 5458 would provide that military retirees may disclaim their eligibility for the TRICARE program. This would allow a retiree who enrolled in a high-deductible health plan to receive or make HSA contributions.

When we considered this bill in the Committee on Ways and Means, the Department of Defense as well as the House Committee on Armed Services had some concerns with the approach in this bill, in particular, that TRICARE eligibility is a statutory entitlement that cannot be waived. If the NDAA conference language is passed later this week, this legislation will no longer be needed as TRICARE enrollment will be voluntary and retirees can move between employer-sponsored insurance and TRICARE, depending on which coverage is best for their current needs. In other words, this bill is going to last about 3 days, until we pass the NDAA on Friday and it is signed into law.

Mr. Speaker, I reserve the balance of my time.

Mr. SMITH of Nebraska. Mr. Speaker, I yield such time as he may consume to the gentleman from Utah (Mr. STEWART), the author of this bill.

Mr. STEWART. Mr. Speaker, I thank the gentleman from Nebraska for the opportunity to speak on behalf of my bill, the Veterans TRICARE Choice Act.

Mr. Speaker, it was my honor to serve for 14 years as a pilot in the Air Force, and for my family—my wife, my children, and me—those were some of the best years of our lives. I continue to be amazed at the quality of those who serve in our military. It shouldn't become cliche to say this: These are some of the finest young men and women that our country has ever produced; they are strong, intelligent, dedicated, courageous individuals who choose to use their talents to serve the rest of us.

It makes me uncomfortable sometimes when I hear those of us who serve in Congress being called public servants when we know that the true public servants are the airmen, the seamen, the soldiers, the marines—and their families; let's not forget their families and their sacrifice as well—those who spend their careers either fighting abroad or preparing for that eventuality. As Americans, we should make it a habit to always thank these servicemembers whenever we see them.

As Members of Congress, it is our job to be wise in our foreign policy, to give our warfighters the resources they need to win and then to ensure that veterans receive the benefits that we have promised them. In fact, that third responsibility is the genesis for this bill, fixing a glitch that was brought to my attention.

As the gentleman has said already, it is just a glitch, just a loophole in the current law that was brought to my attention by a group of airline pilots. These pilots, many of whom are veterans, realized that, as veterans, they were unable to take advantage of all the healthcare benefits offered by their civilian employers. Many of them wanted to use HSAs but, because of the TRICARE eligibility, were legally unable to do that.

Mr. Speaker, HSAs are an innovative healthcare option that House Republicans have advanced as an important part of a market-driven, affordable healthcare system. In fact, HSAs are a critical component to the Speaker's Better Way agenda, which I think many of us are excited to see signed into law in the coming months. With that in mind, it makes no sense to lock veterans out of this benefit based on eligibility for TRICARE.

These pilots came to my office and had a simple request: Give us an on-off switch for TRICARE so the veterans who wish to use an HSA while retaining their right to return to TRICARE in the future can do that if they choose. It made sense, so that is what we did with this bill. The Veterans TRICARE Choice Act allows a veteran to suspend his or her TRICARE benefits for the purpose of enrolling in a health savings plan. If, for whatever reason, the veteran wishes to return to TRICARE, he or she can do so. It is a simple, commonsense fix with broad, bipartisan support.

I would like to thank Representative TULSI GABBARD, a fellow veteran with a distinguished career in the United States Navy and a current member of the Hawaiian National Guard. Representative GABBARD and I have been fortunate to work together on this bill for almost 3 years now, and I am grateful for her work to bring this bill to this point.

I would also like to thank Chairman BRADY, Chairman THORNBERRY, Chairman TIBERI, Chairman HECK, and each of their staffs for their great work and their support in refining the bill and bringing it to the floor today. I am grateful for a similar measure that will be included in the National Defense Authorization Act we will be voting on later this week.

Finally, I would like to thank Nathaniel Johnson, a former member of my staff, a member of the Utah National Guard, a former combat medic who served in Afghanistan, and of course we called him Doc then. I would like to thank Doc, who felt compelled to see this bill through to its conclusion.

Mr. Speaker, our veterans deserve our most profound gratitude. Nothing about their military service should prevent them from accessing the same benefits as their nonveteran coworkers. The very least we can do for them is ensure they receive the benefits we promised them and that the process goes forward as smoothly as possible. I recognize we have lots to do on that front, but I am hopeful the passage of this bill will be one small step forward in that direction.

Mr. Speaker, I urge a "yes" vote.

Mr. McDERMOTT. Mr. Speaker, I yield such time as she may consume to the gentlewoman from Hawaii (Ms. GABBARD).

Ms. GABBARD. Mr. Speaker, the problem that this bill seeks to solve for our veterans is, unfortunately, not uncommon. I have heard from many of my fellow veterans, as has previously been explained, who have similarly not been able to access options widely available to their civilian coworkers because of the current limitations in the law; and that is what this bill seeks to do: correct it.

The Veterans TRICARE Choice Act simply gives veterans and their dependents a choice: They can opt out of TRICARE and contribute to a health savings account with more flexibility and coverage options without fear of permanently losing their TRICARE coverage; and if their situation later changes, they will have the option to reenroll in TRICARE coverage, plain and simple.

Our veterans and their families make tremendous sacrifices in service to our country, and that service should never limit their access to quality health care and their ability to make their own decisions about their own health and the health care for their families in the future.

I would like to thank and congratulate my friend and colleague, CHRIS STEWART, for his leadership on pushing this issue forward, and I encourage my colleagues to join us in supporting H.R. 5458 today.

□ 1515

Mr. SMITH of Nebraska. Mr. Speaker, I reserve the balance of my time.

Mr. McDERMOTT. Mr. Speaker, I yield myself the balance of my time.

Mr. Speaker, this bill is one of those things that you fill time with, and I guess it is not going to hurt anything. So I would recommend that all of my colleagues vote for it. It will be moot on Friday, when we pass the NDAA.

Mr. Speaker, I yield back the balance of my time.

Mr. SMITH of Nebraska. Mr. Speaker, I yield myself such time as I may consume.

Mr. Speaker, I would like to take a moment to again thank Mr. STEWART for his efforts. This is a good bill that, as the gentlewoman from Hawaii mentioned, will help many folks—certainly, those that she has heard from and I know others have as well. I support more veterans having more options. I support the bill's passage and urge my colleagues to support it.

Mr. Speaker, I yield back the balance of my time.

The SPEAKER pro tempore. The question is on the motion offered by the gentleman from Nebraska (Mr. SMITH) that the House suspend the rules and pass the bill, H.R. 5458, as amended.

The question was taken; and (two-thirds being in the affirmative) the rules were suspended and the bill, as amended, was passed.

A motion to reconsider was laid on the table.

RESPONSE ACT OF 2016

Mr. DENHAM. Mr. Speaker, I move to suspend the rules and pass the bill (S. 546) to establish the Railroad Emergency Services Preparedness, Operational Needs, and Safety Evaluation (RESPONSE) Subcommittee under the Federal Emergency Management Agency's National Advisory Council to provide recommendations on emergency responder training and resources relating to hazardous materials incidents involving railroads, and for other purposes, as amended.

The Clerk read the title of the bill.

The text of the bill is as follows:

S. 546

Be it enacted by the Senate and House of Representatives of the United States of America in Congress assembled,

SECTION 1. SHORT TITLE.

This Act may be cited as the "RESPONSE Act of 2016".

SEC. 2. RAILROAD EMERGENCY SERVICES PREPAREDNESS, OPERATIONAL NEEDS, AND SAFETY EVALUATION SUBCOMMITTEE.

Section 508 of the Homeland Security Act of 2002 (6 U.S.C. 318) is amended—

(1) by redesignating subsection (d) as subsection (e); and

(2) by inserting after subsection (c) the following:

"(d) RESPONSE SUBCOMMITTEE.—

"(1) ESTABLISHMENT.—Not later than 30 days after the date of the enactment of the RESPONSE Act of 2016, the Administrator shall establish, as a subcommittee of the National Advisory Council, the Railroad Emergency Services Preparedness, Operational Needs, and Safety Evaluation Subcommittee (referred to in this subsection as the 'RESPONSE Subcommittee').

"(2) MEMBERSHIP.—Notwithstanding subsection (c), the RESPONSE Subcommittee shall be composed of the following:

"(A) The Deputy Administrator, Protection and National Preparedness of the Federal Emergency Management Agency, or designee.

"(B) The Chief Safety Officer of the Pipeline and Hazardous Materials Safety Administration, or designee.

"(C) The Associate Administrator for Hazardous Materials Safety of the Pipeline and Hazardous Materials Safety Administration, or designee.

"(D) The Director of the Office of Emergency Communications of the Department of Homeland Security, or designee.

"(E) The Director for the Office of Railroad, Pipeline and Hazardous Materials Investigations of the National Transportation Safety Board, or designee.

"(F) The Chief Safety Officer and Associate Administrator for Railroad Safety of the Federal Railroad Administration, or designee.

"(G) The Assistant Administrator for Security Policy and Industry Engagement of the Transportation Security Administration, or designee.

"(H) The Assistant Commandant for Response Policy of the Coast Guard, or designee.

"(I) The Assistant Administrator for the Office of Solid Waste and Emergency Response of the Environmental Protection Agency, or designee.

"(J) Such other qualified individuals as the co-chairpersons shall jointly appoint as soon as practicable after the date of the enactment of the RESPONSE Act of 2016 from among the following:

"(i) Members of the National Advisory Council that have the requisite technical knowledge and expertise to address rail emergency response issues, including members from the following disciplines:

"(I) Emergency management and emergency response providers, including fire service, law enforcement, hazardous materials response, and emergency medical services.

"(II) State, local, and tribal government officials.

"(ii) Individuals who have the requisite technical knowledge and expertise to serve on the RESPONSE Subcommittee, including at least 1 representative from each of the following:

"(I) The rail industry.

"(II) Rail labor.

"(III) Persons who offer oil for transportation by rail.

"(IV) The communications industry.

"(V) Emergency response providers, including individuals nominated by national organizations representing State and local governments and emergency responders.

"(VI) Emergency response training providers.

"(VII) Representatives from tribal organizations.

"(VIII) Technical experts.

"(IX) Vendors, developers, and manufacturers of systems, facilities, equipment, and capabilities for emergency responder services.

"(iii) Representatives of such other stakeholders and interested and affected parties as the co-chairpersons consider appropriate.

"(3) CO-CHAIRPERSONS.—The members described in subparagraphs (A) and (B) of paragraph (2) shall serve as the co-chairpersons of the RESPONSE Subcommittee.

"(4) INITIAL MEETING.—The initial meeting of the RESPONSE Subcommittee shall take place not later than 90 days after the date of enactment of the RESPONSE Act of 2016.

"(5) CONSULTATION WITH NONMEMBERS.—The RESPONSE Subcommittee and the program offices for emergency responder training and resources shall consult with other relevant agencies and groups, including entities engaged in federally funded research and academic institutions engaged in relevant work and research, which are not represented on the RESPONSE Subcommittee to consider new and developing technologies and methods that may be beneficial to preparedness and response to rail hazardous materials incidents.

"(6) RECOMMENDATIONS.—The RESPONSE Subcommittee shall develop recommendations, as appropriate, for improving emergency responder training and resource allocation for hazardous materials incidents involving railroads after evaluating the following topics:

"*(A) The quality and application of training for State and local emergency responders related to rail hazardous materials incidents, including training for emergency responders serving small communities near railroads, including the following:*

"*(i) Ease of access to relevant training for State and local emergency responders, including an analysis of—*

"*(I) the number of individuals being trained;*

"*(II) the number of individuals who are applying;*

"*(III) whether current demand is being met;*

"*(IV) current challenges; and*

"*(V) projected needs.*

"*(ii) Modernization of training course content related to rail hazardous materials incidents, with a particular focus on fluctuations in oil shipments by rail, including regular and ongoing evaluation of course opportunities, adaptation to emerging trends, agency and private sector outreach, effectiveness and ease of access for State and local emergency responders.*

"*(iii) Identification of overlap in training content and identification of opportunities to develop complementary courses and materials among governmental and nongovernmental entities.*

"*(iv) Online training platforms, train-the-trainer, and mobile training options.*

"*(B) The availability and effectiveness of Federal, State, local, and nongovernmental funding levels related to training emergency responders for rail hazardous materials incidents, including emergency responders serving small communities near railroads, including—*

"*(i) identifying overlap in resource allocations;*

"*(ii) identifying cost savings measures that can be implemented to increase training opportunities;*

"*(iii) leveraging government funding with nongovernmental funding to enhance training opportunities and fill existing training gaps;*

"*(iv) adaptation of priority settings for agency funding allocations in response to emerging trends;*

"*(v) historic levels of funding across Federal agencies for rail hazardous materials incident response and training, including funding provided by the private sector to public entities or in conjunction with Federal programs; and*

"*(vi) current funding resources across agencies.*

"*(C) The strategy for integrating commodity flow studies, mapping, and rail and hazardous materials databases for State and local emergency responders and increasing the rate of access to the individual responder in existing or emerging communications technology.*

"*(7) REPORT.—*

"*(A) IN GENERAL.—Not later than 1 year after the date of the enactment of the RESPONSE Act of 2016, the RESPONSE Subcommittee shall submit a report to the National Advisory Council that—*

"*(i) includes the recommendations developed under paragraph (6);*

"*(ii) specifies the timeframes for implementing any such recommendations that do not require congressional action; and*

"*(iii) identifies any such recommendations that do require congressional action.*

"*(B) REVIEW.—Not later than 30 days after receiving the report under subparagraph (A), the National Advisory Council shall begin a review of the report. The National Advisory Council may ask for additional clarification, changes, or other information from the RESPONSE Subcommittee to assist in the approval of the recommendations.*

"*(C) RECOMMENDATION.—Once the National Advisory Council approves the recommendations*

of the RESPONSE Subcommittee, the National Advisory Council shall submit the report to—

"*(i) the co-chairpersons of the RESPONSE Subcommittee;*

"*(ii) the head of each other agency represented on the RESPONSE Subcommittee;*

"*(iii) the Committee on Homeland Security and Governmental Affairs of the Senate;*

"*(iv) the Committee on Commerce, Science, and Transportation of the Senate;*

"*(v) the Committee on Homeland Security of the House of Representatives; and*

"*(vi) the Committee on Transportation and Infrastructure of the House of Representatives.*

"*(8) INTERIM ACTIVITY.—*

"*(A) UPDATES AND OVERSIGHT.—After the submission of the report by the National Advisory Council under paragraph (7), the Administrator shall—*

"*(i) provide annual updates to the congressional committees referred to in paragraph (7)(C) regarding the status of the implementation of the recommendations developed under paragraph (6); and*

"*(ii) coordinate the implementation of the recommendations described in paragraph (6)(G)(i), as appropriate.*

"*(B) SUNSET.—The requirements of subparagraph (A) shall terminate on the date that is 2 years after the date of the submission of the report required under paragraph (7)(A).*

"*(9) TERMINATION.—The RESPONSE Subcommittee shall terminate not later than 90 days after the submission of the report required under paragraph (7)(C).*".

The SPEAKER pro tempore. Pursuant to the rule, the gentleman from California (Mr. DENHAM) and the gentleman from Massachusetts (Mr. CAPUANO) each will control 20 minutes.

The Chair recognizes the gentleman from California.

GENERAL LEAVE

Mr. DENHAM. Mr. Speaker, I ask unanimous consent that all Members may have 5 legislative days in which to revise and extend their remarks and include extraneous materials on S. 546, as amended.

The SPEAKER pro tempore. Is there objection to the request of the gentleman from California?

There was no objection.

Mr. DENHAM. Mr. Speaker, I yield myself such time as I may consume.

Mr. Speaker, rail safety is critical to the transport of goods and services throughout our country. As chairman of the Railroads, Pipelines, and Hazardous Materials Subcommittee, I have consistently worked to improve the safety of transporting hazardous materials by rail, especially crude by rail.

In the Passenger Rail Reform and Investment Act of 2015, and later in the FAST Act, Congress required response plans and adopted strong national standards for transporting hazardous materials by rail. Additionally, the Transportation and Infrastructure Committee has held several hearings at both the full committee and subcommittee level to examine how Congress can improve upon what is already a very safe rail network.

I personally have facilitated training for dozens of first responders in my district to ensure they are prepared to respond in the unlikely event of an acci-

dent involving hazardous materials transported by rail. Recently, I traveled with my good friends, Ranking Member CAPUANO and Congressman FARENTHOLD, to Colorado and the Transportation Technology Center to see how the first responder community trains for tank car accidents and the investments our Nation's freight railroad are making to build a safer network.

The bill before us today is an extension of these efforts to build and advance rail safety across our Nation. The RESPONSE Act tasks both government and nongovernmental experts to develop recommendations improving emergency responder training for hazardous materials incidents involving rail.

It requires the evaluation of a number of issues related to rail hazmat incidents, including the quality and application of training for local emergency first responders. Additionally, it looks at overlap in training and ways to modernize training for emergency responders, especially those in small communities near railroads.

This bill will further improve rail safety and enhance responses to rail hazmat incidents. I saw how important this hands-on training can be in August at the Transportation Technology Center in Pueblo. I believe that this bill will build upon the safety of our rail network in communities like mine.

Again, I want to thank the chairman, Mr. KIND, and Senator HEITKAMP for working on this bill.

Mr. Speaker, I reserve the balance of my time.

Mr. CAPUANO. Mr. Speaker, I yield myself such time as I may consume.

Mr. Speaker, I rise in support of this bill as well. I want to thank Ranking Member DENHAM, Chairman SHUSTER, and Ranking Member DEFAZIO for taking the lead on this bill.

Very simply, this is the simplest bill in the world, to be perfectly honest. It gets all the stakeholders together to simply take a look at the current responses we have when there is a disaster relative to rail accidents.

It gets them all in one room to take a look at best practices to figure out what they can do better and to see if resources are allocated well. It is not just Washington insiders. It includes people from the rail industry, people from the labor community, and people from the public safety community at local and State levels. It gets everybody at the table to do things that Congress is not equipped to do appropriately. We are not the safety experts; they are.

There is a time limit. This is not one of those endless committees that is going to sit there forever. For 1 year, they get together, work it out amongst themselves, and come back with recommendations to us so that we can do our job well, which is to support the people actually suppressing these fires and maintaining the safety of our communities.

Again, I rise in support of this bill.

Mr. Speaker, I yield back the balance of my time.

Mr. DENHAM. Mr. Speaker, I yield myself the balance of my time.

Mr. Speaker, in conclusion, this is a great bill. I urge my colleagues to join me in supporting this important piece of legislation.

Mr. Speaker, I yield back the balance of my time.

The SPEAKER pro tempore. The question is on the motion offered by the gentleman from California (Mr. DENHAM) that the House suspend the rules and pass the bill, S. 546, as amended.

The question was taken; and (two-thirds being in the affirmative) the rules were suspended and the bill, as amended, was passed.

A motion to reconsider was laid on the table.

FRED D. THOMPSON FEDERAL BUILDING AND UNITED STATES COURTHOUSE

Mr. DENHAM. Mr. Speaker, I move to suspend the rules and pass the bill (H.R. 6135) to designate the Federal building and United States courthouse located at 719 Church Street in Nashville, Tennessee, as the "Fred D. Thompson Federal Building and United States Courthouse".

The Clerk read the title of the bill.

The text of the bill is as follows:

H.R. 6135

Be it enacted by the Senate and House of Representatives of the United States of America in Congress assembled,

SECTION 1. DESIGNATION.

The Federal building and United States courthouse located at 719 Church Street in Nashville, Tennessee, shall be known and designated as the "Fred D. Thompson Federal Building and United States Courthouse".

SEC. 2. REFERENCES.

Any reference in a law, map, regulation, document, paper, or other record of the United States to the Federal building and United States courthouse referred to in section 1 shall be deemed to be a reference to the "Fred D. Thompson Federal Building and United States Courthouse".

The SPEAKER pro tempore. Pursuant to the rule, the gentleman from California (Mr. DENHAM) and the gentleman from Massachusetts (Mr. CAPUANO) each will control 20 minutes.

The Chair recognizes the gentleman from California.

GENERAL LEAVE

Mr. DENHAM. Mr. Speaker, I ask unanimous consent that all Members may have 5 legislative days in which to revise and extend their remarks and include extraneous materials on H.R. 6135.

The SPEAKER pro tempore. Is there objection to the request of the gentleman from California?

There was no objection.

Mr. DENHAM. Mr. Speaker, I yield myself such time as I may consume.

Mr. Speaker, H.R. 6135 would designate the Federal building and United States courthouse at 719 Church Street in Nashville, Tennessee, as the Fred D. Thompson Federal Building and United States Courthouse.

I would like to thank the gentlewoman from Tennessee (Mrs. BLACKBURN) for her leadership on this legislation.

Senator Thompson was an accomplished lawyer, actor, U.S. Senator, and a great friend. We spent numerous occasions together here in the Washington, D.C., area as he got to know new Members when we came in 2010. I have appreciated his counsel, his friendship, and I look forward to seeing this bill passed.

Mr. Speaker, I reserve the balance of my time.

Mr. CAPUANO. Mr. Speaker, I yield such time as he may consume to the gentleman from Tennessee (Mr. COHEN).

Mr. COHEN. Mr. Speaker, it is my honor to rise on this occasion to have the courthouse in Nashville named for a distinguished American, a friend of mine, Senator Fred Thompson, who is the only University of Memphis graduate to serve in the United States Senate.

Fred was an outstanding attorney and Federal employee. He made Tennessee proud when he was counsel to the Watergate Committee. In a phenomenal fashion, he gave people a good feeling about bipartisanship when a Republican such as Fred Thompson stood up and raised the questions that needed to be raised to end the illegal and crime-ridden episodes of Richard Nixon that were exposed in Watergate.

Despite the fact that Richard Nixon was a Republican, Fred Thompson saw to it that when the President acted in an untowardly fashion, diminishing the Constitution, diminishing our government, all Americans should stand up and oppose such. Fred did it in an admiral way, and Richard Nixon resigned eventually, and Gerald Ford helped save our country. Vice Presidents can do that.

Fred served as an Assistant U.S. Attorney. He was a mentee of Senator Howard Baker, a great Member of the United States Senate and a great American. He was also a private-practicing attorney who had a case concerning pardons. It was a Democrat was doing things that were illegal. Ray Blanton from Tennessee was giving pardons that were improper. Marie Ragghianti stepped forward.

Fred Thompson wrote a book about Marie exposing illegal pardons. Somebody who did the script thought Fred could make a good actor. And Fred made a good actor. He did a lot of TV series and movies and had another ca-

reer besides politician and lawyer: actor.

He came to Memphis one time, I remember specifically, to speak to the Chamber. And he had a droll way about him. He said—and I guess he said it other places, as well—sometimes when I am in Washington, I miss the reality and the sincerity of Hollywood. Well, I laughed when Fred said it. I think about it often here.

When he ran for office, Fred took a little red truck and used it to campaign. He drove that truck around the State. People identified with it. He was ahead of his time. It was kind of like Donald Trump eating McDonald's, I think. He related to the common man with that truck.

I thought about Fred as I was flying up here. I just did get here in time. I was on one of the last of those regional jets, which was kind of like Fred's truck with wings on it. But we made it.

I want to thank Fred Thompson for all he did as an attorney, as an actor, and as a friend to me. He was bipartisan. He was always friendly to me. He was a courteous gentleman.

I came here when Fred won the National Conference of State Legislatures Award for looking out for States' rights. He was the only member of the Senate to vote on a bill that the NCSL was in favor of. And he was right. There was a province that belonged to the States that the Federal Government usurped because it was so wonderful to do and sets good brownie points back home. But Fred didn't do that. He stayed with his position that States' rights should be first and those areas of tort liability should have remained with the States. I came to see Fred get that award.

Fred had a wonderful wife and a wonderful family. One of his sons was a good friend of my mine. He still is. I am honored to be a sponsor of this bill. I am sorry that Fred left us, succumbing to cancer last year, but it is appropriate that we name the U.S. courthouse and Federal building in Nashville after this great American.

Mr. DENHAM. Mr. Speaker, I yield such time as she may consume to the gentlewoman from Tennessee (Mrs. BLACKBURN).

Mrs. BLACKBURN. Mr. Speaker, I want to thank the gentleman from California for his work in moving this legislation forward and also my colleague from Tennessee for joining me on this bill. It is such an honor to bring it forward and to push for the naming of the Federal courthouse in Nashville as the Fred D. Thompson Federal Building and United States Courthouse.

You know, it is so interesting. Fred learned a lot about life and about the law working in the current Federal building. As that building has been outgrown and the need for a new one is in the works, it is so exciting to know that Fred's name will be emblazoned on that building. It is exciting for all of the residents of Lawrence County, Tennessee. That is where Fred grew up. That is in the Seventh Congressional District.

Then, as Fred decided to go to law school and came back to Nashville, he settled in Williamson County, right there in Franklin and Brentwood in suburban Nashville. And that is where I got to know the Thompson family.

☐ 1530

I know this is a very exciting day for them, to know that this is actually taking place, that the House is completing their work and we are sending this on to the Senate for Senators CORKER and ALEXANDER to do their part of the work on this building.

Many people did know Fred Thompson as an actor, and one of the things you would hear people talk about is Fred was a "character actor." But that unassuming manner, the way he valued and embodied integrity, that was just Fred. That was how he lived his life, and he was a great "character actor" because he really played himself.

Whether it was "Marie," whether it was the "Hunt for Red October," whether you were watching him on the small screen or the big screen, he was exactly who he appeared to be, very unassuming, very dedicated, very smart, and a wonderful attorney.

Of course, his public service did start as an Assistant U.S. Attorney in Nashville in the old Federal courthouse, and that did grow. The Watergate Committee, as Congressman COHEN has mentioned, was where Fred really made a mark and where he became extremely close to Senator Howard Baker, who was such a role model for so many generations of Tennesseans and Americans. How exciting it would be for Senator Baker to be here to know Fred's name was going to be on that courthouse in Nashville.

This is the right move for the right person. I encourage all of my colleagues to join in passage of this legislation.

Mr. CAPUANO. Mr. Speaker, I yield back the balance of my time.

Mr. DENHAM. Mr. Speaker, given Senator Thompson's dedication to the law and public service, I believe it is more than fitting to name this courthouse and Federal building in Nashville after him.

I yield back the balance of my time.

The SPEAKER pro tempore. The question is on the motion offered by the gentleman from California (Mr. DENHAM) that the House suspend the rules and pass the bill, H.R. 6135.

The question was taken; and (two-thirds being in the affirmative) the rules were suspended and the bill was passed.

A motion to reconsider was laid on the table.

COMMUNICATION FROM THE CLERK OF THE HOUSE

The SPEAKER pro tempore laid before the House the following communication from the Clerk of the House of Representatives:

OFFICE OF THE CLERK,
HOUSE OF REPRESENTATIVES,
Washington, DC, November 29, 2016.
Hon. PAUL D. RYAN,
Speaker, House of Representatives,
Washington, DC.

DEAR MR. SPEAKER: Pursuant to the permission granted in Clause 2(h) of Rule II of the Rules of the U.S. House of Representatives, the Clerk received the following message from the Secretary of the Senate on November 29, 2016, at 1:48 p.m.:

That the Senate passed S. 2873.
With best wishes, I am,
Sincerely,

KAREN L. HAAS.

JUSTICE FOR ALL REAUTHORIZATION ACT OF 2016

Mr. GOODLATTE. Mr. Speaker, I move to suspend the rules and pass the bill (S. 2577) to protect crime victims' rights, to eliminate the substantial backlog of DNA and other forensic evidence samples to improve and expand the forensic science testing capacity of Federal, State, and local crime laboratories, to increase research and development of new testing technologies, to develop new training programs regarding the collection and use of forensic evidence, to provide post-conviction testing of DNA evidence to exonerate the innocent, to support accreditation efforts of forensic science laboratories and medical examiner offices, to address training and equipment needs, to improve the performance of counsel in State capital cases, and for other purposes, as amended.

The Clerk read the title of the bill.

The text of the bill is as follows:

S. 2577

Be it enacted by the Senate and House of Representatives of the United States of America in Congress assembled,

SECTION 1. SHORT TITLE.

This Act may be cited as the "Justice for All Reauthorization Act of 2016".

SEC. 2. CRIME VICTIMS' RIGHTS.

(a) RESTITUTION DURING SUPERVISED RELEASE.—Section 3583(d) of title 18, United States Code, is amended in the first sentence by inserting ", that the defendant make restitution in accordance with sections 3663 and 3663A, or any other statute authorizing a sentence of restitution," after "supervision".

(b) COLLECTION OF RESTITUTION FROM DEFENDANT'S ESTATE.—Section 3613(b) of title 18, United States Code, is amended by adding at the end the following: "The liability to pay restitution shall terminate on the date that is the later of 20 years from the entry of judgment or 20 years after the release from imprisonment of the person ordered to pay restitution. In the event of the death of the person ordered to pay restitution, the individual's estate will be held responsible for any unpaid balance of the restitution amount, and the lien provided in subsection (c) of this section shall continue until the es-

tate receives a written release of that liability.".

(c) VICTIM INTERPRETERS.—Rule 28 of the Federal Rules of Criminal Procedure is amended in the first sentence by inserting before the period at the end the following: ", including an interpreter for the victim".

(d) GAO STUDY.—

(1) IN GENERAL.—Not later than 180 days after the date of enactment of this Act, the Comptroller General of the United States shall—

(A) conduct a study to determine whether enhancing the restitution provisions under sections 3663 and 3663A of title 18, United States Code, to provide courts broader authority to award restitution for Federal offenses would be beneficial to crime victims and what other factors Congress should consider in weighing such changes; and

(B) submit to Congress a report on the study conducted under subparagraph (A).

(2) CONTENTS.—In conducting the study under paragraph (1), the Comptroller General shall focus on the benefits to crime victims that would result if the restitution provisions under sections 3663 and 3663A of title 18, United States Code, were expanded—

(A) to apply to victims who have suffered harm, injury, or loss that would not have occurred but for the defendant's related conduct;

(B) in the case of an offense resulting in bodily injury resulting in the victim's death, to allow the court to use its discretion to award an appropriate sum to reflect the income lost by the victim's surviving family members or estate as a result of the victim's death;

(C) to require that the defendant pay to the victim an amount determined by the court to restore the victim to the position he or she would have been in had the defendant not committed the offense; and

(D) to require that the defendant compensate the victim for any injury, harm, or loss, including emotional distress, that occurred as a result of the offense.

SEC. 3. REDUCING THE RAPE KIT BACKLOG.

(a) IN GENERAL.—Of the amounts made available to the Attorney General for a DNA Analysis and capacity enhancement program and for other local, State, and Federal forensic activities under the heading "STATE AND LOCAL LAW ENFORCEMENT" under the heading "OFFICE OF JUSTICE PROGRAMS" under the heading "DEPARTMENT OF JUSTICE" in fiscal years 2018, 2019, 2020, and 2021—

(1) not less than 75 percent of such amounts shall be provided for grants for activities described under paragraphs (1), (2), and (3) of section 2(a) of the DNA Analysis Backlog Elimination Act of 2000 (42 U.S.C. 14135(a)); and

(2) not less than 5 percent of such amounts shall be provided for grants for law enforcement agencies to conduct audits of their backlogged rape kits under section 2(a)(7) of the DNA Analysis Backlog Elimination Act of 2000 (42 U.S.C. 14135(a)(7)) to create and operate associated tracking systems and to prioritize testing in those cases in which the statute of limitation will soon expire.

(b) REPORTING.—

(1) REPORT BY GRANT RECIPIENTS.—With respect to amounts made available to the Attorney General for a DNA Analysis and capacity enhancement program and for other local, State, and Federal forensic activities under the heading "STATE AND LOCAL LAW ENFORCEMENT" under the heading "OFFICE OF JUSTICE PROGRAMS" under the heading "DEPARTMENT OF JUSTICE", the Attorney General shall require recipients of the

amounts to report on the effectiveness of the activities carried out using the amounts, including any information the Attorney General needs in order to submit the report required under paragraph (2).

(2) REPORT TO CONGRESS.—Not later than 1 month after the last day of each even-numbered fiscal year, the Attorney General shall submit to the Committee on the Judiciary of the Senate and the Committee on the Judiciary of the House of Representatives a report that includes, for each recipient of amounts described in paragraph (1)—

(A) the amounts distributed to the recipient;

(B) a summary of the purposes for which the amounts were used and an evaluation of the progress of the recipient in achieving those purposes;

(C) a statistical summary of the crime scene samples and arrestee or offender samples submitted to laboratories, the average time between the submission of a sample to a laboratory and the testing of the sample, and the percentage of the amounts that were paid to private laboratories; and

(D) an evaluation of the effectiveness of the grant amounts in increasing capacity and reducing backlogs.

SEC. 4. SEXUAL ASSAULT NURSE EXAMINERS.

Section 304 of the DNA Sexual Assault Justice Act of 2004 (42 U.S.C. 14136a) is amended—

(1) by redesignating subsection (c) as subsection (d); and

(2) by inserting after subsection (b) the following:

"(c) PREFERENCE.—

"(1) IN GENERAL.—In reviewing applications submitted in accordance with a program authorized, in whole or in part, by this section, the Attorney General shall give preference to any eligible entity that certifies that the entity will use the grant funds to—

"(A) improve forensic nurse examiner programs in a rural area or for an underserved population, as those terms are defined in section 4002 of the Violence Against Women Act of 1994 (42 U.S.C. 13925);

"(B) engage in activities that will assist in the employment of full-time forensic nurse examiners to conduct activities under subsection (a); or

"(C) sustain or establish a training program for forensic nurse examiners.

"(2) DIRECTIVE TO THE ATTORNEY GENERAL.—Not later than the beginning of fiscal year 2018, the Attorney General shall coordinate with the Secretary of Health and Human Services to inform Federally Qualified Health Centers, Community Health Centers, hospitals, colleges and universities, and other appropriate health-related entities about the role of forensic nurses and existing resources available within the Department of Justice and the Department of Health and Human Services to train or employ forensic nurses to address the needs of communities dealing with sexual assault, domestic violence, and elder abuse. The Attorney General shall collaborate on this effort with nongovernmental organizations representing forensic nurses.".

SEC. 5. PROTECTING THE VIOLENCE AGAINST WOMEN ACT.

Section 8(e)(1)(A) of the Prison Rape Elimination Act of 2003 (42 U.S.C. 15607(e)(1)(A)) is amended—

(1) in clause (i), by striking "and" at the end;

(2) in clause (ii), by striking the period and inserting "; and"; and

(3) by inserting at the end the following:

"(iii) the program is not administered by the Office on Violence Against Women of the Department of Justice.".

SEC. 6. CLARIFICATION OF VIOLENCE AGAINST WOMEN ACT HOUSING PROTECTIONS.

Section 41411(b)(3)(B)(ii) of the Violence Against Women Act of 1994 (42 U.S.C. 14043e–11(b)(3)(B)(ii)) is amended—

(1) in the first sentence, by inserting "or resident" after "any remaining tenant"; and

(2) in the second sentence, by inserting "or resident" after "tenant" each place it appears.

SEC. 7. STRENGTHENING THE PRISON RAPE ELIMINATION ACT.

The Prison Rape Elimination Act of 2003 (42 U.S.C. 15601 et seq.) is amended—

(1) in section 6(d)(2) (42 U.S.C. 15605(d)(2)), by striking subparagraph (A) and inserting the following:

"(A)(i) include the certification of the chief executive that the State receiving such grant has adopted all national prison rape standards that, as of the date on which the application was submitted, have been promulgated under this Act; or

"(ii) demonstrate to the Attorney General, in such manner as the Attorney General shall require, that the State receiving such grant is actively working to adopt and achieve full compliance with the national prison rape standards described in clause (i);"; and

(2) in section 8(e) (42 U.S.C. 15607(e))—

(A) by striking paragraph (2) and inserting the following:

"(2) ADOPTION OF NATIONAL STANDARDS.—

"(A) IN GENERAL.—For each fiscal year, any amount that a State would otherwise receive for prison purposes for that fiscal year under a grant program covered by this subsection shall be reduced by 5 percent, unless the chief executive officer of the State submits to the Attorney General proof of compliance with this Act through—

"(i) a certification that the State has adopted, and is in full compliance with, the national standards described in subsection (a); or

"(ii) an assurance that the State intends to adopt and achieve full compliance with those national standards so as to ensure that a certification under clause (i) may be submitted in future years, which includes—

"(I) a commitment that not less than 5 percent of such amount shall be used for this purpose; or

"(II) a request that the Attorney General hold 5 percent of such amount in abeyance pursuant to the requirements of subparagraph (E).

"(B) RULES FOR CERTIFICATION.—

"(i) IN GENERAL.—A chief executive officer of a State who submits a certification under this paragraph shall also provide the Attorney General with—

"(I) a list of the prisons under the operational control of the executive branch of the State;

"(II) a list of the prisons listed under subclause (I) that were audited during the most recently concluded audit year;

"(III) all final audit reports for prisons listed under subclause (I) that were completed during the most recently concluded audit year; and

"(IV) a proposed schedule for completing an audit of all the prisons listed under subclause (I) during the following 3 audit years.

"(ii) AUDIT APPEAL EXCEPTION.—Beginning on the date that is 3 years after the date of enactment of the Justice for All Reauthorization Act of 2016, a chief executive officer

of a State may submit a certification that the State is in full compliance pursuant to subparagraph (A)(i) even if a prison under the operational control of the executive branch of the State has an audit appeal pending.

"(C) RULES FOR ASSURANCES.—

"(i) IN GENERAL.—A chief executive officer of a State who submits an assurance under subparagraph (A)(ii) shall also provide the Attorney General with—

"(I) a list of the prisons under the operational control of the executive branch of the State;

"(II) a list of the prisons listed under subclause (I) that were audited during the most recently concluded audit year;

"(III) an explanation of any barriers the State faces to completing required audits;

"(IV) all final audit reports for prisons listed under subclause (I) that were completed during the most recently concluded audit year;

"(V) a proposed schedule for completing an audit of all prisons under the operational control of the executive branch of the State during the following 3 audit years; and

"(VI) an explanation of the State's current degree of implementation of the national standards.

"(ii) ADDITIONAL REQUIREMENT.—A chief executive officer of a State who submits an assurance under subparagraph (A)(ii)(I) shall, before receiving the applicable funds described in subparagraph (A)(ii)(I), also provide the Attorney General with a proposed plan for the expenditure of the funds during the applicable grant period.

"(iii) ACCOUNTING OF FUNDS.—A chief executive officer of a State who submits an assurance under subparagraph (A)(ii)(I) shall, in a manner consistent with the applicable grant reporting requirements, submit to the Attorney General a detailed accounting of how the funds described in subparagraph (A) were used.

"(D) SUNSET OF ASSURANCE OPTION.—

"(i) IN GENERAL.—On the date that is 3 years after the date of enactment of the Justice for All Reauthorization Act of 2016, subclause (II) of subparagraph (A)(ii) shall cease to have effect.

"(ii) ADDITIONAL SUNSET.—On the date that is 6 years after the date of enactment of the Justice for All Reauthorization Act of 2016, clause (ii) of subparagraph (A) shall cease to have effect.

"(iii) EMERGENCY ASSURANCES.—

"(I) REQUEST.—Notwithstanding clause (ii), during the 2-year period beginning 6 years after the date of enactment of the Justice for All Reauthorization Act of 2016, a chief executive officer of a State who certifies that the State has audited not less than 90 percent of prisons under the operational control of the executive branch of the State may request that the Attorney General allow the chief executive officer to submit an emergency assurance in accordance with subparagraph (A)(ii) as in effect on the day before the date on which that subparagraph ceased to have effect under clause (ii) of this subparagraph.

"(II) GRANT OF REQUEST.—The Attorney General shall grant a request submitted under subclause (I) within 60 days upon a showing of good cause.

"(E) DISPOSITION OF FUNDS HELD IN ABEYANCE.—

"(i) IN GENERAL.—If the chief executive officer of a State who has submitted an assurance under subparagraph (A)(ii)(II) subsequently submits a certification under subparagraph (A)(i) during the 3-year period beginning on the date of enactment of the Justice for All Reauthorization Act of 2016, the

Attorney General will release all funds held in abeyance under subparagraph (A)(ii)(II) to be used by the State in accordance with the conditions of the grant program for which the funds were provided.

"(ii) RELEASE OF FUNDS.—If the chief executive officer of a State who has submitted an assurance under subparagraph (A)(ii)(II) is unable to submit a certification during the 3-year period beginning on the date of enactment of the Justice for All Reauthorization Act of 2016, but does assure the Attorney General that ⅔ of prisons under the operational control of the executive branch of the State have been audited at least once, the Attorney General shall release all of the funds of the State held in abeyance to be used in adopting and achieving full compliance with the national standards, if the State agrees to comply with the applicable requirements in clauses (ii) and (iii) of subparagraph (C).

"(iii) REDISTRIBUTION OF FUNDS.—If the chief executive officer of a State who has submitted an assurance under subparagraph (A)(ii)(II) is unable to submit a certification during the 3-year period beginning on the date of enactment of the Justice for All Reauthorization Act of 2016 and does not assure the Attorney General that ⅔ of prisons under the operational control of the executive branch of the State have been audited at least once, the Attorney General shall redistribute the funds of the State held in abeyance to other States to be used in accordance with the conditions of the grant program for which the funds were provided.

"(F) PUBLICATION OF AUDIT RESULTS.—Not later than 1 year after the date of enactment of the Justice for All Reauthorization Act of 2016, the Attorney General shall request from each State, and make available on an appropriate Internet website, all final audit reports completed to date for prisons under the operational control of the executive branch of each State. The Attorney General shall update such website annually with reports received from States under subparagraphs (B)(i) and (C)(i).

"(G) REPORT ON IMPLEMENTATION OF NATIONAL STANDARDS.—Not later than 2 years after the date of enactment of the Justice for All Reauthorization Act of 2016, the Attorney General shall issue a report to the Committee on the Judiciary of the Senate and the Committee on the Judiciary of the House of Representatives on the status of implementation of the national standards and the steps the Department, in conjunction with the States and other key stakeholders, is taking to address any unresolved implementation issues."; and

(B) by adding at the end the following:

"(8) BACKGROUND CHECKS FOR AUDITORS.—An individual seeking certification by the Department of Justice to serve as an auditor of prison compliance with the national standards described in subsection (a) shall, upon request, submit fingerprints in the manner determined by the Attorney General for criminal history record checks of the applicable State and Federal Bureau of Investigation repositories.".

SEC. 8. ADDITIONAL REAUTHORIZATIONS.

(a) DNA RESEARCH AND DEVELOPMENT.—Section 305(c) of the Justice for All Act of 2004 (42 U.S.C. 14136b(c)) is amended by striking "$15,000,000 for each of fiscal years 2005 through 2009" and inserting "$5,000,000 for each of fiscal years 2017 through 2021".

(b) FBI DNA PROGRAMS.—Section 307(a) of the Justice for All Act of 2004 (Public Law 108–405; 118 Stat. 2275) is amended by striking "$42,100,000 for each of fiscal years 2005

through 2009" and inserting "$7,400,000 for fiscal year 2017 and $10,000,000 for each of fiscal years 2018 through 2021".

(c) DNA IDENTIFICATION OF MISSING PERSONS.—Section 308(c) of the Justice for All Act of 2004 (42 U.S.C. 14136d(c)) is amended by striking "fiscal years 2005 through 2009" and inserting "fiscal years 2017 through 2021".

SEC. 9. PAUL COVERDELL FORENSIC SCIENCES IMPROVEMENT GRANTS.

(a) GRANTS.—Part BB of title I of the Omnibus Crime Control and Safe Streets Act of 1968 (42 U.S.C. 3797j) is amended—

(1) in section 2802(2) (42 U.S.C. 3797k(2)), by inserting after "bodies" the following: "and, except with regard to any medical examiner's office, or coroner's office in the State, is accredited by an accrediting body that is a signatory to an internationally recognized arrangement and that offers accreditation to forensic science conformity assessment bodies using an accreditation standard that is recognized by that internationally recognized arrangement, or attests, in a manner that is legally binding and enforceable, to use a portion of the grant amount to prepare and apply for such accreditation not more than 2 years after the date on which a grant is awarded under section 2801";

(2) in section 2803(a) (42 U.S.C. 3797l(a))—

(A) in paragraph (1)—

(i) by striking "Seventy-five percent" and inserting "Eighty-five percent"; and

(ii) by striking "75 percent" and inserting "85 percent";

(B) in paragraph (2), by striking "Twenty-five percent" and inserting "Fifteen percent"; and

(C) in paragraph (3), by striking "0.6 percent" and inserting "1 percent";

(3) in section 2804(a) (42 U.S.C. 3797m(a))—

(A) in paragraph (2)—

(i) by inserting "impression evidence," after "latent prints,"; and

(ii) by inserting "digital evidence, fire evidence," after "toxicology,";

(B) in paragraph (3), by inserting "and medicolegal death investigators" after "laboratory personnel"; and

(C) by inserting at the end the following:

"(4) To address emerging forensic science issues (such as statistics, contextual bias, and uncertainty of measurement) and emerging forensic science technology (such as high throughput automation, statistical software, and new types of instrumentation).

"(5) To educate and train forensic pathologists.

"(6) To fund medicolegal death investigation systems to facilitate accreditation of medical examiner and coroner offices and certification of medicolegal death investigators."; and

(4) in section 2806(a) (42 U.S.C. 3797o(a))—

(A) in paragraph (3), by striking "and" at the end;

(B) by redesignating paragraph (4) as paragraph (5); and

(C) by inserting after paragraph (3) the following:

"(4) the progress of any unaccredited forensic science service provider receiving grant funds toward obtaining accreditation; and".

(b) AUTHORIZATION OF APPROPRIATIONS.—Section 1001(a)(24) of title I of the Omnibus Crime Control and Safe Streets Act of 1968 (42 U.S.C. 3793(a)(24)) is amended—

(1) in subparagraph (H), by striking "and" at the end;

(2) in subparagraph (I), by striking the period at the end and inserting "; and"; and

(3) by adding at the end the following:

"(J) $13,500,000 for fiscal year 2017;

"(K) $18,500,000 for fiscal year 2018;

"(L) $19,000,000 for fiscal year 2019;

"(M) $21,000,000 for fiscal year 2020; and

"(N) $23,000,000 for fiscal year 2021.".

SEC. 10. IMPROVING THE QUALITY OF REPRESENTATION IN STATE CAPITAL CASES.

Section 426 of the Justice for All Act of 2004 (42 U.S.C. 14163e) is amended—

(1) in subsection (a), by striking "$75,000,000 for each of fiscal years 2005 through 2009" and inserting:

"(1) $2,500,000 for fiscal year 2017;

"(2) $7,500,000 for fiscal year 2018;

"(3) $12,500,000 for fiscal year 2019;

"(4) $17,500,000 for fiscal year 2020; and

"(5) $22,500,000 for fiscal year 2021."; and

(2) in subsection (b), by inserting before the period at the end the following: ", or upon a showing of good cause, and at the discretion of the Attorney General, the State may determine a fair allocation of funds across the uses described in sections 421 and 422".

SEC. 11. POST-CONVICTION DNA TESTING.

(a) IN GENERAL.—Section 3600 of title 18, United States Code, is amended—

(1) by striking "under a sentence of" in each place it appears and inserting "sentenced to";

(2) in subsection (a)—

(A) in paragraph (1)(B)(i), by striking "death"; and

(B) in paragraph (3)(A), by striking "and the applicant did not—" and all that follows through "knowingly fail to request" and inserting "and the applicant did not knowingly fail to request";

(3) in subsection (b)(1)—

(A) in subparagraph (A), by striking "and" at the end;

(B) in subparagraph (B), by striking the period at the end and inserting "; and"; and

(C) by adding at the end the following:

"(C) order the Government to—

"(i) prepare an inventory of the evidence related to the case; and

"(ii) issue a copy of the inventory to the court, the applicant, and the Government.";

(4) in subsection (e)—

(A) by amending paragraph (1) to read as follows:

"(1) RESULTS.—

"(A) IN GENERAL.—The results of any DNA testing ordered under this section shall be simultaneously disclosed to the court, the applicant, and the Government.

"(B) RESULTS EXCLUDE APPLICANT.—

"(i) IN GENERAL.—If a DNA profile is obtained through testing that excludes the applicant as the source and the DNA complies with the Federal Bureau of Investigation's requirements for the uploading of crime scene profiles to the National DNA Index System (referred to in this subsection as 'NDIS'), the court shall order that the law enforcement entity with direct or conveyed statutory jurisdiction that has access to the NDIS submit the DNA profile obtained from probative biological material from crime scene evidence to determine whether the DNA profile matches a profile of a known individual or a profile from an unsolved crime.

"(ii) NDIS SEARCH.—The results of a search under clause (i) shall be simultaneously disclosed to the court, the applicant, and the Government."; and

(B) in paragraph (2), by striking "the National DNA Index System (referred to in this subsection as 'NDIS')" and inserting "NDIS"; and

(5) in subsection (g)(2)(B), by striking "death".

(b) PRESERVATION OF BIOLOGICAL EVIDENCE.—Section 3600A of title 18, United States Code, is amended—

(1) in subsection (a), by striking "under a sentence of" and inserting "sentenced to"; and

(2) in subsection (c)—

(A) by striking paragraphs (1) and (2); and

(B) by redesignating paragraphs (3), (4), and (5) as paragraphs (1), (2), and (3), respectively.

SEC. 12. KIRK BLOODSWORTH POST-CONVICTION DNA TESTING PROGRAM.

(a) IN GENERAL.—Section 413 of the Justice for All Act of 2004 (42 U.S.C. 14136 note) is amended—

(1) in the matter preceding paragraph (1), by striking "fiscal years 2005 through 2009" and inserting "fiscal years 2017 through 2021"; and

(2) by striking paragraph (2) and inserting the following:

"(2) for eligible entities that are a State or unit of local government, provide a certification by the chief legal officer of the State in which the eligible entity operates or the chief legal officer of the jurisdiction in which the funds will be used for the purposes of the grants, that the State or jurisdiction—

"(A) provides DNA testing of specified evidence under a State statute or a State or local rule or regulation to persons sentenced to imprisonment or death for a State felony offense, in a manner intended to ensure a reasonable process for resolving claims of actual innocence that ensures post-conviction DNA testing in at least those cases that would be covered by section 3600(a) of title 18, United States Code, had they been Federal cases and, if the results of the testing exclude the applicant as the source of the DNA, permits the applicant to apply for post-conviction relief, notwithstanding any provision of law that would otherwise bar the application as untimely; and

"(B) preserves biological evidence, as defined in section 3600A of title 18, United States Code, under a State statute or a State or local rule, regulation, or practice in a manner intended to ensure that reasonable measures are taken by the State or jurisdiction to preserve biological evidence secured in relation to the investigation or prosecution of, at a minimum, murder, nonnegligent manslaughter and sexual offenses.".

(b) AUTHORIZATION OF APPROPRIATIONS.— Section 412(b) of the Justice for All Act of 2004 (42 U.S.C. 14136e(b)) is amended by striking "$5,000,000 for each of fiscal years 2005 through 2009" and inserting "$10,000,000 for each of fiscal years 2017 through 2021".

SEC. 13. ESTABLISHMENT OF BEST PRACTICES FOR EVIDENCE RETENTION.

(a) IN GENERAL.—Subtitle A of title IV of the Justice for All Act of 2004 (Public Law 108–405; 118 Stat. 2278) is amended by adding at the end the following:

"SEC. 414. ESTABLISHMENT OF BEST PRACTICES FOR EVIDENCE RETENTION.

"(a) IN GENERAL.—The Director of the National Institute of Justice, in consultation with Federal, State, and local law enforcement agencies and government laboratories, shall—

"(1) establish best practices for evidence retention to focus on the preservation of forensic evidence; and

"(2) assist State, local, and tribal governments in adopting and implementing the best practices established under paragraph (1).

"(b) DEADLINE.—Not later than 1 year after the date of enactment of this section, the Director of the National Institute of Justice shall publish the best practices established under subsection (a)(1).

"(c) LIMITATION.—Nothing in this section shall be construed to require or obligate compliance with the best practices established under subsection (a)(1).".

(b) TECHNICAL AND CONFORMING AMENDMENT.—The table of contents in section 1(b) of the Justice for All Act of 2004 (Public Law 108–405; 118 Stat. 2260) is amended by inserting after the item relating to section 413 the following:

"Sec. 414. Establishment of best practices for evidence retention.".

SEC. 14. EFFECTIVE ADMINISTRATION OF CRIMINAL JUSTICE.

(a) SHORT TITLE.—This section may be cited as the "Effective Administration of Criminal Justice Act of 2016".

(b) STRATEGIC PLANNING.—Section 502 of title I of the Omnibus Crime Control and Safe Streets Act of 1968 (42 U.S.C. 3752) is amended—

(1) by inserting "(A) IN GENERAL.—" before "To request a grant"; and

(2) by adding at the end the following:

"(6) A comprehensive Statewide plan detailing how grants received under this section will be used to improve the administration of the criminal justice system, which shall—

"(A) be designed in consultation with local governments, and representatives of all segments of the criminal justice system, including judges, prosecutors, law enforcement personnel, corrections personnel, and providers of indigent defense services, victim services, juvenile justice delinquency prevention programs, community corrections, and reentry services;

"(B) include a description of how the State will allocate funding within and among each of the uses described in subparagraphs (A) through (G) of section 501(a)(1);

"(C) describe the process used by the State for gathering evidence-based data and developing and using evidence-based and evidence-gathering approaches in support of funding decisions;

"(D) describe the barriers at the State and local level for accessing data and implementing evidence-based approaches to preventing and reducing crime and recidivism; and

"(E) be updated every 5 years, with annual progress reports that—

"(i) address changing circumstances in the State, if any;

"(ii) describe how the State plans to adjust funding within and among each of the uses described in subparagraphs (A) through (G) of section 501(a)(1);

"(iii) provide an ongoing assessment of need;

"(iv) discuss the accomplishment of goals identified in any plan previously prepared under this paragraph; and

"(v) reflect how the plan influenced funding decisions in the previous year.

"(b) TECHNICAL ASSISTANCE.—

"(1) STRATEGIC PLANNING.—Not later than 90 days after the date of enactment of this subsection, the Attorney General shall begin to provide technical assistance to States and local governments requesting support to develop and implement the strategic plan required under subsection (a)(6). The Attorney General may enter into agreements with 1 or more non-governmental organizations to provide technical assistance and training under this paragraph.

"(2) PROTECTION OF CONSTITUTIONAL RIGHTS.—Not later than 90 days after the date of enactment of this subsection, the Attorney General shall begin to provide technical assistance to States and local govern-

ments, including any agent thereof with responsibility for administration of justice, requesting support to meet the obligations established by the Sixth Amendment to the Constitution of the United States, which shall include—

"(A) public dissemination of practices, structures, or models for the administration of justice consistent with the requirements of the Sixth Amendment; and

"(B) assistance with adopting and implementing a system for the administration of justice consistent with the requirements of the Sixth Amendment.

"(3) AUTHORIZATION OF APPROPRIATIONS.— For each of fiscal years 2017 through 2021, of the amounts appropriated to carry out this subpart, not less than $5,000,000 and not more than $10,000,000 shall be used to carry out this subsection.".

(c) APPLICABILITY.—The requirement to submit a strategic plan under section 501(a)(6) of title I of the Omnibus Crime Control and Safe Streets Act of 1968, as added by subsection (b), shall apply to any application submitted under such section 501 for a grant for any fiscal year beginning after the date that is 1 year after the date of enactment of this Act.

SEC. 15. OVERSIGHT AND ACCOUNTABILITY.

All grants awarded by the Department of Justice that are authorized under this Act shall be subject to the following:

(1) AUDIT REQUIREMENT.—Beginning in fiscal year 2016, and each fiscal year thereafter, the Inspector General of the Department of Justice shall conduct audits of recipients of grants under this Act to prevent waste, fraud, and abuse of funds by grantees. The Inspector General shall determine the appropriate number of grantees to be audited each year.

(2) MANDATORY EXCLUSION.—A recipient of grant funds under this Act that is found to have an unresolved audit finding shall not be eligible to receive grant funds under this Act during the 2 fiscal years beginning after the 12-month period described in paragraph (5).

(3) PRIORITY.—In awarding grants under this Act, the Attorney General shall give priority to eligible entities that, during the 3 fiscal years before submitting an application for a grant under this Act, did not have an unresolved audit finding showing a violation in the terms or conditions of a Department of Justice grant program.

(4) REIMBURSEMENT.—If an entity is awarded grant funds under this Act during the 2-fiscal-year period in which the entity is barred from receiving grants under paragraph (2), the Attorney General shall—

(A) deposit an amount equal to the grant funds that were improperly awarded to the grantee into the General Fund of the Treasury; and

(B) seek to recoup the costs of the repayment to the fund from the grant recipient that was erroneously awarded grant funds.

(5) DEFINED TERM.—In this section, the term "unresolved audit finding" means an audit report finding in the final audit report of the Inspector General of the Department of Justice that the grantee has utilized grant funds for an unauthorized expenditure or otherwise unallowable cost that is not closed or resolved within a 12-month period beginning on the date when the final audit report is issued.

(6) NONPROFIT ORGANIZATION REQUIREMENTS.—

(A) DEFINITION.—For purposes of this section and the grant programs described in this Act, the term "nonprofit organization" means an organization that is described in section 501(c)(3) of the Internal Revenue Code of 1986 and is exempt from taxation under section 501(a) of such Code.

(B) PROHIBITION.—The Attorney General shall not award a grant under any grant program described in this Act to a nonprofit organization that holds money in offshore accounts for the purpose of avoiding paying the tax described in section 511(a) of the Internal Revenue Code of 1986.

(C) DISCLOSURE.—Each nonprofit organization that is awarded a grant under a grant program described in this Act and uses the procedures prescribed in regulations to create a rebuttable presumption of reasonableness for the compensation of its officers, directors, trustees and key employees, shall disclose to the Attorney General, in the application for the grant, the process for determining such compensation, including the independent persons involved in reviewing and approving such compensation, the comparability data used, and contemporaneous substantiation of the deliberation and decision. Upon request, the Attorney General shall make the information disclosed under this subsection available for public inspection.

(7) ADMINISTRATIVE EXPENSES.—Unless otherwise explicitly provided in authorizing legislation, not more than 7.5 percent of the amounts authorized to be appropriated under this Act may be used by the Attorney General for salaries and administrative expenses of the Department of Justice.

(8) CONFERENCE EXPENDITURES.—

(A) LIMITATION.—No amounts authorized to be appropriated to the Department of Justice under this Act may be used by the Attorney General or by any individual or organization awarded discretionary funds through a cooperative agreement under this Act, to host or support any expenditure for conferences that uses more than $20,000 in Department funds, unless the Deputy Attorney General or the appropriate Assistant Attorney General, Director, or principal deputy as the Deputy Attorney General may designate, provides prior written authorization that the funds may be expended to host a conference.

(B) WRITTEN APPROVAL.—Written approval under subparagraph (A) shall include a written estimate of all costs associated with the conference, including the cost of all food and beverages, audio/visual equipment, honoraria for speakers, and any entertainment.

(C) REPORT.—The Deputy Attorney General shall submit an annual report to the Committee on the Judiciary of the Senate and the Committee on the Judiciary of the House of Representatives on all conference expenditures approved by operation of this paragraph.

(9) PROHIBITION ON LOBBYING ACTIVITY.—

(A) IN GENERAL.—Amounts authorized to be appropriated under this Act may not be utilized by any grant recipient to—

(i) lobby any representative of the Department of Justice regarding the award of grant funding; or

(ii) lobby any representative of a Federal, State, local, or tribal government regarding the award of grant funding.

(B) PENALTY.—If the Attorney General determines that any recipient of a grant under this Act has violated subparagraph (A), the Attorney General shall—

(i) require the grant recipient to repay the grant in full; and

(ii) prohibit the grant recipient from receiving another grant under this Act for not less than 5 years.

(10) PREVENTING DUPLICATIVE GRANTS.—

(A) IN GENERAL.—Before the Attorney General awards a grant to an applicant under

this Act, the Attorney General shall compare potential grant awards with other grants awarded under this Act to determine whether duplicate grants are awarded for the same purpose.

(B) REPORT.—If the Attorney General awards duplicate grants to the same applicant for the same purpose, the Attorney General shall submit to the Committee on the Judiciary of the Senate and the Committee on the Judiciary of the House of Representatives a report that includes—

(i) a list of all duplicate grants awarded, including the total dollar amount of any duplicate grants awarded; and

(ii) the reason the Attorney General awarded the duplicate grants.

SEC. 16. NEEDS ASSESSMENT OF FORENSIC LABORATORIES.

(a) STUDY AND REPORT.—Not later than October 1, 2018, the Attorney General shall conduct a study and submit a report to the Committee on the Judiciary of the Senate and the Committee on the Judiciary of the House of Representatives on the status and needs of the forensic science community.

(b) REQUIREMENTS.—The report required under subsection (a) shall—

(1) examine the status of current workload, backlog, personnel, equipment, and equipment needs of public crime laboratories and medical examiner and coroner offices;

(2) include an overview of academic forensic science resources and needs, from a broad forensic science perspective, including nontraditional crime laboratory disciplines such as forensic anthropology, forensic entomology, and others as determined appropriate by the Attorney General;

(3) consider—

(A) the National Institute of Justice study, Forensic Sciences: Review of Status and Needs, published in 1999;

(B) the Bureau of Justice Statistics census reports on Publicly Funded Forensic Crime Laboratories, published in 2002, 2005, 2009, and 2014;

(C) the National Academy of Sciences report, Strengthening Forensic Science: A Path Forward, published in 2009; and

(D) the Bureau of Justice Statistics survey of forensic providers recommended by the National Commission of Forensic Science and approved by the Attorney General on September 8, 2014;

(4) provide Congress with a comprehensive view of the infrastructure, equipment, and personnel needs of the broad forensic science community; and

(5) be made available to the public.

SEC. 17. CRIME VICTIM ASSISTANCE.

(a) AMENDMENT.—Section 1404(c)(1)(A) of the Victims of Crime Act of 1984 (42 U.S.C. 10603(c)(1)(A)) is amended by inserting "victim services," before "demonstration projects".

(b) SENSE OF CONGRESS.—It is the sense of Congress that the proposed rule entitled "VOCA Victim Assistance Program" published by the Office of Victims of Crime of the Department of Justice in the Federal Register on August 27, 2013 (78 Fed. Reg. 52877), is consistent with section 1404 of the Victims of Crime Act of 1984 (42 U.S.C. 10603).

SEC. 18. IMPROVING THE RESTITUTION PROCESS.

Section 3612 of title 18, United States Code, is amended by adding at the end the following:

"(j) EVALUATION OF OFFICES OF THE UNITED STATES ATTORNEY AND DEPARTMENT COMPONENTS.—

"(1) IN GENERAL.—The Attorney General shall, as part of the regular evaluation process, evaluate each office of the United States

attorney and each component of the Department of Justice on the performance of the office or the component, as the case may be, in seeking and recovering restitution for victims under each provision of this title and the Controlled Substances Act (21 U.S.C. 801 et seq.) that authorizes restitution.

"(2) REQUIREMENT.—Following an evaluation under paragraph (1), each office of the United States attorney and each component of the Department of Justice shall work to improve the practices of the office or component, as the case may be, with respect to seeking and recovering restitution for victims under each provision of this title and the Controlled Substances Act (21 U.S.C. 801 et seq.) that authorizes restitution.

"(k) GAO REPORTS.—

"(1) REPORT.—Not later than 1 year after the date of enactment of this subsection, the Comptroller General of the United States shall prepare and submit to the Committee on the Judiciary of the House of Representatives and the Committee on the Judiciary of the Senate a report on restitution sought by the Attorney General under each provision of this title and the Controlled Substances Act (21 U.S.C. 801 et seq.) that authorizes restitution during the 3-year period preceding the report.

"(2) CONTENTS.—The report required under paragraph (1) shall include statistically valid estimates of—

"(A) the number of cases in which a defendant was convicted and the Attorney General could seek restitution under this title or the Controlled Substances Act (21 U.S.C. 801 et seq.);

"(B) the number of cases in which the Attorney General sought restitution;

"(C) of the cases in which the Attorney General sought restitution, the number of times restitution was ordered by the district courts of the United States;

"(D) the amount of restitution ordered by the district courts of the United States;

"(E) the amount of restitution collected pursuant to the restitution orders described in subparagraph (D);

"(F) the percentage of restitution orders for which the full amount of restitution has not been collected; and

"(G) any other measurement the Comptroller General determines would assist in evaluating how to improve the restitution process in Federal criminal cases.

"(3) RECOMMENDATIONS.—The report required under paragraph (1) shall include recommendations on the best practices for—

"(A) requesting restitution in cases in which restitution may be sought under each provision of this title and the Controlled Substances Act (21 U.S.C. 801 et seq.) that authorizes restitution;

"(B) obtaining restitution orders from the district courts of the United States; and

"(C) collecting restitution ordered by the district courts of the United States.

"(4) REPORT.—Not later than 3 years after the date on which the report required under paragraph (1) is submitted, the Comptroller General of the United States shall prepare and submit to the Committee on the Judiciary of the House of Representatives and the Committee on the Judiciary of the Senate a report on the implementation by the Attorney General of the best practices recommended under paragraph (3).".

The SPEAKER pro tempore. Pursuant to the rule, the gentleman from Virginia (Mr. GOODLATTE) and the gentlewoman from Texas (Ms. JACKSON LEE) each will control 20 minutes.

The Chair recognizes the gentleman from Virginia.

Mr. GOODLATTE. Mr. Speaker, I ask unanimous consent that all Members may have 5 legislative days within which to revise and extend their remarks and include extraneous materials on S. 2577, currently under consideration.

The SPEAKER pro tempore. Is there objection to the request of the gentleman from Virginia?

There was no objection.

Mr. GOODLATTE. Mr. Speaker, I yield myself such time as I may consume.

On October 30, 2004, President George W. Bush signed into law the Justice for All Act of 2004. The law contains four very important sections related to victims of crime and improving the criminal justice process. The law protects the rights of crime victims and eliminates the substantial backlog of DNA samples collected from both crime scenes and convicted offenders. It also improves and expands the DNA testing capacity of Federal, State, and local crime laboratories.

Finally, it establishes the rights of crime victims in Federal criminal proceedings and provides mechanisms for enforcing these rights.

The bill before us today, S. 2577, the Justice for All Reauthorization Act of 2016, is a bipartisan and bicameral bill that builds on the 2004 Justice for All Act. It further improves the criminal justice system and ensures public confidence in it. It strengthens crime victims' rights and programs by increasing access to restitution for Federal crime victims.

The act also further reduces the rape kit backlog and provides resources for forensic labs while protecting the innocent by improving access to post-conviction DNA testing.

The Justice for All Act works to improve the administration of criminal justice programs by increasing accountability for Federal funds and requiring the Justice Department to assist State and local governments to improve their indigent defense systems. Additionally, it ensures the implementation of the Prison Rape Elimination Act.

I commend the gentleman from Texas (Mr. POE) for his hard work on this bill.

Mr. Speaker, I reserve the balance of my time.

Ms. JACKSON LEE. Mr. Speaker, I yield myself such time as I may consume.

Mr. Speaker, I rise in strong support of S. 2577, the Justice for All Reauthorization Act of 2016, and the complementary House bill that was authored by my good friend and colleague from Texas (Mr. POE), and my good friend and colleague from California (Mr. COSTA)—this is an important bill—and, of course, my Senator from the State of Texas, Senator CORNYN.

This bill now comes to the floor of the House as S. 2577. This bipartisan, bicameral legislation advances this Congress' efforts to enhance and improve our Nation's criminal justice system for victims, law enforcement, the courts, and innocent persons, while also fostering public trust and confidence in our criminal justice system.

It also reinforces the important work that the House Judiciary Committee has been doing under Chairman GOODLATTE and Ranking Member CONYERS. My greatest hope, as the ranking member on the Subcommittee on Crime, Terrorism, Homeland Security, and Investigations, is that we can finish our work with the enormity of bills, sentencing reduction, prison reform, juvenile justice reform. I would like to optimistically think we might get these for the holiday season.

S. 2577 would reauthorize and improve upon various programs that began with the initial passage of the appropriately named Justice for All Act. I was proud to support this groundbreaking legislation in 2004, legislation intended to protect all persons who find themselves involved with the criminal justice system, and instill accountability throughout that system.

The programs we enacted in 2004 increased resources to boost the testing capabilities of forensic crime laboratories and eliminate the backlog of DNA samples from sexual assaults, crime scenes, and convicted offenders. I know this firsthand because Harris County—a very large county; fifth in the Nation—experienced this calamity, along with the city of Houston, the fact that these kits and other DNA evidence just couldn't seem to be tested expeditiously.

It also enhanced protections for victims of crimes, and established measures to prevent and overturn wrongful convictions.

The time has come to build upon the foundation we laid in 2004. Fairness and equal treatment under the law are two fundamental values of our Nation's system of justice. When the innocent are jailed for decades for crimes they did not commit, when victims watch their attackers go free because the physical evidence was misplaced or never tested, or when overworked forensic lab technicians provide false reports, the people's trust and belief in the system is diminished.

The bill we are considering today would strengthen crime victims' rights, programs, and services. In addition, it would further reduce the rape kit backlog, provide additional resources to forensic labs, improve access to post-conviction DNA testing, ensure implementation of the Prison Rape Elimination Act, and improve the overall administration of criminal justice systems nationwide, including increas-

ing accountability, transparency, effectiveness and fiscal efficiency.

I hate having to give anecdotal stories, but, unfortunately, again, in Harris County, thousands of pieces of evidence were lost when they were in the possession of one of our local law enforcement structures. We have a lot of law enforcement layers. This happened to be a constable's office.

Mr. Speaker, you know how damaging and dangerous that is to victims' rights, to criminal justice, to the Constitution. That is why this bill is so very important. Being the victim of a crime is a harrowing, disorienting experience. We must do our best to erase or ease the suffering of victims and assist them as they work to rebuild their lives.

Under S. 2577, housing rights for victims of domestic violence would be expanded, and Violence Against Women Act funding would be protected from reductions due to Federal penalties. Other victim-centered programs would be reauthorized by this bill, including programs used to notify victims of their right to be heard in court, to offer victims legal assistance, and to provide interpreters for Federal crime victims who wish to participate in court proceedings.

Additionally, the Government Accountability Office will be required to determine the potential benefits to crime victims, if any, by broadening the authority of Federal courts to award restitution. Our crime victims need relief. We need to give them hope and a sense that we care about them.

The Attorney General will be required to evaluate the effectiveness of the Justice Department components and U.S. Attorney Offices in pursuing and obtaining restitution for crime victims. We all know DNA is a crucial element of many criminal cases, helping to identify suspects, perpetrators of crimes, and to exclude the innocent.

This bill would ensure that victims of sexual assault receive essential services and are able to see their attackers brought to justice by renewing the DNA Backlog grant program and by expanding grants for forensic nurse examiners, giving priority to hiring full-time forensic nurses, establishing programs in rural and underserved areas, and training forensic nurses.

☐ 1545

Agencies across the country would realize further reductions in their rape kit backlogs because the Justice Department would be required, under this legislation, to use at least 75 percent of the funds made available for forensic testing for direct testing of crime scene evidence, including rape kits.

Under this measure, Debbie Smith grant recipients would have to report on the achievement of activities conducted using grant funds. S. 2577 would require the Attorney General to report annually to Congress on how Debbie Smith grant funds are being used to improve DNA testing and reduce the backlogs.

I know that my good friend CAROLYN MALONEY has been involved in these issues as well.

S. 2577 would reauthorize funding for several other DNA grant programs, including the Paul Coverdell Forensic Science Improvement Grant Program, which helps States and local governments that need it greatly speak to the loss of thousands of pieces of evidence in a local law enforcement office.

In that same vein, the Attorney General would be required to conduct a needs assessment for State and local forensic science labs to better utilize Federal funding.

This bill would also enhance protections for the innocent by improving access to postconviction DNA testing, encouraging States to test DNA evidence in criminal cases for which there is untested DNA evidence, expanding State access to postconviction DNA testing funds by narrowing the evidence preservation requirement, and authorizing Federal postconviction DNA testing for individuals who can show exculpatory DNA evidence exists in their case despite having pled guilty.

We have a responsibility to make this criminal justice system fit in the four corners of the Constitution. That includes due process as one of the elements and certainly the response and caring of those individuals who have been victims. We have a responsibility to ensure the safe and humane treatment of individuals, even if they are convicted of crimes and in prison.

Compliance with the Prison Rape Elimination Act would be an all-but-certain result of the incentive structure set in S. 2577, which would require State and local governments to focus more resources on implementation of this legislation's directives, which we really need, while allowing the flexibility necessary to reach full compliance. For example, States that receive Edward Byrne Memorial Justice Assistance Grants would be required to develop a strategic plan setting out how the grant money will be used.

Finally, this bill includes various provisions to ensure Federal funds are used efficiently and effectively.

I believe that this bill answers our concerns on the question of criminal justice reform and constitutional protection for all.

Mr. Speaker, I urge my colleagues to join me in supporting this important legislation.

Mr. Speaker, I rise in strong support of S. 2577, the "Justice for All Reauthorization Act of 2016," as amended.

This bipartisan, bicameral legislation advances this Congress's efforts to enhance and improve our Nation's criminal justice system for victims, law enforcement, the courts, and innocent persons, while also fostering public trust and confidence in our criminal justice system.

S. 2577 would reauthorize and improve upon various programs that began with the initial passage of the appropriately-named Justice for All Act.

I was proud to support this groundbreaking legislation in 2004—legislation intended to protect all persons who find themselves involved with the criminal justice system and instill accountability throughout that system.

The programs we enacted in 2004 increased resources to boost the testing capabilities of forensic crime laboratories and eliminate the backlog of DNA samples from sexual assaults, crime scenes, and convicted offenders.

It also enhanced protections for victims of crimes and established measures to prevent and overturn wrongful convictions.

The time has come to build upon the foundation we laid in 2004.

Fairness and equal treatment under the law are two fundamental values of our Nation's system of justice. When the innocent are jailed for decades for crimes they did not commit, when victims watch their attackers go free because the physical evidence was misplaced or never tested, or when overworked forensic lab technicians provide false reports, the people's trust and belief in the system is diminished.

The bill we are considering today would strengthen crime victims' rights, programs, and services.

In addition, it would—

further reduce the rape kit backlog;

provide additional resources to forensic labs;

improve access to post-conviction DNA testing;

ensure implementation of the Prison Rape Elimination Act; and

improve the overall administration of criminal justice systems nationwide by increasing accountability, transparency, effectiveness, and fiscal efficiency.

Being the victim of a crime is a harrowing, disorienting experience. We must do our best to ease the suffering of victims and assist them as they work to rebuild their lives.

Under S. 2577, housing rights for victims of domestic violence would be expanded and Violence Against Women Act funding would be protected from reductions due to federal penalties.

Other victim-centered programs would be reauthorized by this bill, including programs used to notify victims of their right to be heard in court, to offer victims legal assistance, and to provide interpreters for federal crime victims who wish to participate in court proceedings.

Additionally, the Government Accountability Office would be required to determine the potential benefits to crime victims, if any, by broadening the authority of federal courts to award restitution.

And, the Attorney General would be required to evaluate the effectiveness of Justice Department components and U.S. Attorney Offices in pursuing and obtaining restitution for crime victims.

We all know DNA is a crucial element of many criminal cases, helping to identify suspects and perpetrators of crimes and exclude the innocent.

This bill would ensure that victims of sexual assault receive essential services and are able to see their attackers brought to justice by renewing the DNA Backlog Grant Program and expanding grants for forensic nurse examiners, giving priority to hiring full-time forensic nurses, establishing programs in rural and underserved areas, and training forensic nurses.

Agencies across the country would realize further reductions in their rape kit backlogs because the Justice Department would be required under this legislation to use at least 75 percent of funds made available for forensic testing for direct testing of crime scene evidence, including rape kits.

Under this measure, Debbie Smith Grant recipients would have to report on the achievement of activities conducted using grant funds. S. 2577 would require the Attorney General to report annually to Congress on how Debbie Smith Grant funds are being used to improve DNA testing and reduce the backlogs.

Further, S. 2577 would reauthorize funding for several other DNA grant programs, including the Paul Coverdell Forensic Sciences Improvement Grant Program, which helps states and local governments improve the quality of forensic science services provided.

In that same vein, the Attorney General would be required to conduct a needs assessment for state and local forensic science labs to better utilize federal funding.

This bill would also enhance protections for the innocent by—

improving access to post-conviction DNA testing;

encouraging states to test DNA evidence in criminal cases for which there is untested DNA evidence;

expanding state access to post-conviction DNA testing funds by narrowing the evidence preservation requirement; and

authorizing federal post-conviction DNA testing for individuals who can show exculpatory DNA evidence exists in their case despite having pled guilty.

We have a responsibility to ensure the safe and humane treatment of individuals even if they are convicted of crimes and sentenced to prison.

Compliance with the Prison Rape Elimination Act would be an all but certain result of the incentive structure set forth in S. 2577, which would require state and local governments to focus more resources on implementation of this legislation's directives, while allowing the flexibility necessary to reach full compliance.

For example, states that receive Edward Byrne Memorial Justice Assistance Grant grants would be required to develop a strategic plan setting out how the grant money will be used to improve their criminal systems.

Finally, this bill includes various provisions to ensure federal funds are used efficiently and effectively.

Accordingly, I urge my colleagues to join me in supporting this important legislation and I reserve the balance of my time.

The Justice for All Reauthorization Act is supported by a broad spectrum of organizations involved in, or affected by, our criminal justice system.

These organizations include—

the National Sheriffs Association and the National District Attorneys Association;

the Council of State Governments;
the U.S. Conference of Mayors;
the National Center for Victims of Crime;
the Washington Lawyers Committee for Civil Rights;
the Human Rights Campaign; and
the Innocence Project.

In closing, I want to commend my colleagues in the House, including Judiciary Committee Chairman BOB GOODLATTE, Crime Subcommittee Chairman JIM SENSENBRENNER, and Congressman TED POE, sponsor of the House companion.

And, I also want to acknowledge Senator PATRICK LEAHY for his authorship of the underlying statute and for his leadership in the reauthorization of these critical programs.

For the foregoing reasons, I urge my colleagues to join me in voting for this legislation today.

Mr. Speaker, I reserve the balance of my time.

Mr. GOODLATTE. Mr. Speaker, I have no additional speakers, and I reserve the balance of my time.

Ms. JACKSON LEE. Mr. Speaker, I yield 2 minutes to the gentleman from California (Mr. COSTA), who is an original cosponsor of this legislation.

Mr. COSTA. I thank the gentlewoman from Texas for yielding 2 minutes, and I want to thank her and the chairman, the gentleman from Virginia, for their hard work on this very important piece of legislation.

Mr. Speaker, as the lead Democratic cosponsor of the Justice for All Reauthorization Act and the co-chair of the Congressional Victims' Rights Caucus, along with my good friend and colleague Congressman TED POE, who I know wanted to be here and who has worked so hard on this legislation, we as the chairs of the bipartisan Congressional Victims' Rights Caucus want those groups out there throughout the country to understand how important this legislation is. The broad coalition of groups that are supporting this and the bipartisan group of lawmakers who worked tirelessly to get this legislation on the House floor today is making a difference.

The Justice for All Reauthorization Act will improve our criminal justice system, and it will strengthen programs for victims of crimes. The healing process for the survivors of violent crime, as we all know, can be extremely painful and it can be difficult.

This legislation also helps those survivors by providing resources to reduce, as has been noted already, the rape kit backlog. It also improves housing rights for domestic violence victims. We have these centers in our congressional districts that many of us are familiar with where spouses and children go to escape violence. It also assists with hiring full-time sexual assault nurse examiners in every hospital throughout the country.

Additionally, this bill ensures that the guilty are punished and helps to protect the wrongfully convicted by

improving access to postconviction DNA testing. One thing we have learned for certain over the last decade is that, in law enforcement, DNA testing has become an important tool to apprehend and to prove guilt where, in fact, we did not have that tool before.

These strengthened policies will better provide support for victims of crime throughout the country.

The SPEAKER pro tempore. The time of the gentleman has expired.

Ms. JACKSON LEE. Mr. Speaker, I yield the gentleman an additional 1 minute.

Mr. COSTA. I thank the gentlewoman.

Mr. Speaker, these policies will provide better support for victims of crime throughout the country, especially those who live in rural regions, and we have many rural regions throughout the country. I represent one of those areas in California, the San Joaquin Valley.

I urge my colleagues in the House to support this bill, and I hope the Senate acts swiftly before the end of the year so this Justice for All Reauthorization Act is enacted before Congress adjourns.

Let us remember, Mr. Speaker, that these victims of crimes are members of our families; they are our neighbors; they are people who we know in our communities and in our congressional districts. We know who they are, and we know that these are innocent victims of crime. This legislation goes a long way to address their issues. I urge the support of my colleagues.

Mr. GOODLATTE. Mr. Speaker, I reserve the balance of my time.

Ms. JACKSON LEE. Mr. Speaker, I yield myself such time as I may consume.

Mr. Speaker, I will close my remarks by thanking Mr. COSTA for his leadership. We know that our good friend Congressman TED POE wanted to be here. We thank him for his leadership and the many Members who engaged in this important legislation.

The Justice for All Reauthorization Act is supported by a broad spectrum of organizations involved in or affected by our criminal justice system. Let me share a few: the National Sheriffs' Association, the National District Attorneys Association, the Council of State Governments, the United States Conference of Mayors, the National Center for Victims of Crime, the Washington Lawyers' Committee for Civil Rights, the Human Rights Campaign, and the Innocence Project.

In closing, I would like to commend my colleagues in the House, including Judiciary Committee Chairman BOB GOODLATTE; Crime, Terrorism, Homeland Security, and Investigations Subcommittee Chairman SENSENBRENNER; and Congressman TED POE, the sponsor of the House companion; and the work that we have done on the Judiciary

Committee, as I started out my remarks, in dealing with the enormity of sentencing, passing legislation that will reduce the impact of mandatory minimums, prison reform that we have passed, and certainly looking to reform juvenile justice.

I, too, hope that the legislation that we are speaking of will move and be passed before this session of Congress ends. I would like to think optimistically that we may get some very important bills that we have dealt with in the Judiciary Committee passed as well.

I also want to acknowledge Senator PATRICK LEAHY for his authorship of the underlying statute and for his leadership of the reauthorization of these critical programs, and as I indicated, my senior Senator, JOHN CORNYN, of Texas.

I want to conclude by saying that I left Texas in the backdrop of a Federal court hearing that dealt with the broken bail system, another aspect of criminal justice reform, where 40 percent of individuals on misdemeanors who cannot pay $150 or cannot pay $100 remain incarcerated. What we are doing today is we are joining in a bipartisan manner to begin to approach some of those inequities by this legislation, and I know that we can move forward on many others. So I urge my colleagues to join me in voting for this legislation today, which is an important bill, S. 2577, and the House companion.

Mr. Speaker, I yield back the balance of my time.

Mr. GOODLATTE. Mr. Speaker, I yield myself the balance of my time.

Mr. Speaker, I want to thank the gentleman from Texas (Mr. POE) for his hard work and his leadership on this issue, and I thank the gentleman from California (Mr. COSTA) as well.

This is a very good bill, and I urge my colleagues to vote for the Justice for All Reauthorization Act of 2016.

Mr. Speaker, I yield back the balance of my time.

Mr. POE of Texas. Mr. Speaker, today, I urge the House to pass the Justice for All Reauthorization Act to improve crime victims access to justice, support law enforcement, exonerate the innocent, and strengthen and improve our criminal justice system. In the House, I would like to thank Representative JIM COSTA for joining me in introducing this important legislation. I would also like to thank Senator JOHN CORNYN and Senator PATRICK LEAHY for sponsoring this bill in the Senate.

The Justice for All Act of 2004 enhanced protection for crime victims, provided resources to expand the use of DNA and forensic technology to capture and convict criminals, and established safeguards to reverse wrongful convictions.

This legislation reauthorizes these important programs and also increases crime victims access to restitution and improves housing protections for domestic violence victims. Under this legislation, states will be encouraged to test unexamined DNA evidence in criminal cases to ensure that innocent people are not imprisoned for crimes they did not commit. But one of the most important things this law will do is tackle the national rape kit backlog by providing critically important resources to forensic labs. A victim of rape is sentenced to a lifetime of mental turmoil, but as rape victim Debbie Smith can attest, also knowing that your attacker is still on the streets is far worse.

Debbie was at home doing laundry one afternoon in Williamsburg, Virginia. Suddenly, a masked intruder walked through her backdoor and dragged her outside into a wooded area where he raped her repeatedly. Her attacker told her that if she called the police, he would return to her house and kill her. She was lucky to escape with her life. It was only after her husband begged her to contact the police that she agreed to take a forensic exam. Even though the police had a DNA sample, they didn't test her rape kit. Debbie was left in fear that her rapist would return to her home and kill her for reporting her rape. Finally, after six and a half years, the police tested Debbie's kit and put her attacker behind bars. Debbie has since become a fierce advocate for the elimination of the rape kit testing backlog that occurs all across the nation, and she has been a loud supporter of the Justice for All Reauthorization Act's provisions to address this issue.

As Debbie has said, I know that DNA testing gave me peace, and I want to make sure that other victims have that same opportunity. The Justice for All Reauthorization Act of 2016 is supported by over a thousand victim advocacy groups from around the country. I urge my colleagues to vote to pass this important, bipartisan piece of legislation.

The SPEAKER pro tempore. The question is on the motion offered by the gentleman from Virginia (Mr. GOODLATTE) that the House suspend the rules and pass the bill, S. 2577, as amended.

The question was taken; and (two-thirds being in the affirmative) the rules were suspended and the bill, as amended, was passed.

A motion to reconsider was laid on the table.

FUNDING FOR THE NATIONAL HUMAN TRAFFICKING HOTLINE

Mr. GOODLATTE. Mr. Speaker, I move to suspend the rules and pass the bill (H.R. 5422) to ensure funding for the National Human Trafficking Hotline, and for other purposes.

The Clerk read the title of the bill.

The text of the bill is as follows:

H.R. 5422

Be it enacted by the Senate and House of Representatives of the United States of America in Congress assembled,

SECTION 1. FUNDING FOR THE NATIONAL HUMAN TRAFFICKING HOTLINE; PERFECTING AMENDMENT.

(a) HHS FUNDING FOR TRAFFICKING HOTLINE.—Section 107(b)(1)(B)(ii) of the Trafficking Victims Protection Act of 2000 (22 U.S.C. 7105(b)(1)(B)(ii)) is amended by striking "of amounts made available for grants under paragraph (2),".

(b) PERFECTING AMENDMENT.—Section 603 of the Justice for Victims of Trafficking Act of 2015 (Public Law 114–22; 129 Stat. 259) is amended, in the matter preceding paragraph (1), by striking "Victims of Crime Trafficking" and inserting "Victims of Trafficking".

(c) EFFECTIVE DATE.—The amendments made by this Act shall take effect as if enacted as part of the Justice for Victims of Trafficking Act of 2015 (Public Law 114–22; 129 Stat. 227).

The SPEAKER pro tempore. Pursuant to the rule, the gentleman from Virginia (Mr. GOODLATTE) and the gentlewoman from Texas (Ms. JACKSON LEE) each will control 20 minutes.

The Chair recognizes the gentleman from Virginia.

GENERAL LEAVE

Mr. GOODLATTE. Mr. Speaker, I ask unanimous consent that all Members may have 5 legislative days in which to revise and extend their remarks and include extraneous materials on H.R. 5422, currently under consideration.

The SPEAKER pro tempore. Is there objection to the request of the gentleman from Virginia?

There was no objection.

Mr. GOODLATTE. Mr. Speaker, I yield myself such time as I may consume.

Mr. Speaker, today we consider on suspension H.R. 5422. This bill corrects an inadvertent change made in the Justice for Victims of Trafficking Act of 2015 that caused grant funding for the National Human Trafficking Hotline to be processed through the Department of Justice rather than through the Department of Health and Human Services, as it had been historically.

The National Human Trafficking Hotline is a toll-free hotline, available to answer calls from anywhere in the United States, 24 hours a day, 7 days a week, in more than 200 languages. The hotline's mission is to connect trafficking victims and survivors to critical support services and to equip the antitrafficking community with the tools to effectively combat all forms of human trafficking.

This bill was introduced on June 9, 2015, by Congressman TED POE, a tireless advocate for the prevention of human trafficking and for trafficking victims, and the bill passed out of the Judiciary Committee on November 16 by a voice vote.

While Congressman POE is undergoing treatment for leukemia and is unable to be here, I want to once again let him know that he is in our prayers. We are confident in his recovery and continue to appreciate all his work on these important human trafficking matters. I thank Congressman POE for sponsoring this legislation that corrects an inadvertent drafting oversight, and I urge my colleagues to support the bill.

Mr. Speaker, I reserve the balance of my time.

Ms. JACKSON LEE. Mr. Speaker, I yield myself such time as I may consume.

Mr. Speaker, I rise in strong support of H.R. 5422, a bill that I have cosponsored in order to ensure funding for the National Human Trafficking Hotline, a crucial component in the fight against human trafficking, and also to pay tribute to my neighbor, Congressman TED POE, and join in wishing him a strong recovery. We look forward to continuing to work against the scourge of human trafficking. We have been told, of course, of Houston being the epicenter of such.

As I have said many times before, trafficking in human beings has no place in a civilized society. Congress decided 150 years ago that no individual deserves to be bought, owned, or sold. Our country is now faced with a modern-day version of slavery that denies victims of their humanity and violates the most basic American ideals of liberty and individual autonomy.

Human trafficking is the second fastest growing criminal enterprise: 4,177 sex trafficking cases and 824 trafficking cases were reported in the first 9 months of this year in the United States and its territories. Traffickers use trickery and, most often, coercion and violence to force victims to provide labor or perform sexual acts.

My home city of Houston has been identified as a hub for human trafficking, as I have said. I am proud to say that Houston and the entire State of Texas are working hard to stave off this growing threat.

In an effort to understand the problem and find real solutions, we held several hearings in 2014, including the first-ever field hearing on human trafficking held by the Committee on Homeland Security that I serve on. During that hearing, we heard from victims and survivors of human trafficking. They recounted indignities they suffered as well as the physical and psychological damage done while they were young children but still felt as adults. I am very gratified that Congressman TED POE participated in that hearing, and it was very constructive and instructive as we try to continue working on a solution.

I traveled to a stash house and witnessed the atrocious conditions under which these people are held and forced to engage.

We now know that a comprehensive, collaborative approach that includes lawmakers, law enforcement, victim advocates, community organizations, and social service providers is necessary to identify victims and lead them to safety, restore them, and bring their captors to justice.

□ 1600

The National Human Trafficking Resource Center plays a critical role in the effort to save, protect, and restore victims of human trafficking. The NHTRC is a national anti-trafficking hotline and resource center created and overseen by the Department of Health and Human Services and funded through grant money appropriated to HHS. It is very important.

In 2015, the NHTRC received more than 24,000 signals regarding human trafficking cases or issues related to human trafficking, which includes phone calls, online tips, and emails.

The NHTRC is invaluable to victims, survivors, and stakeholders involving the fight against human trafficking—connecting human trafficking victims and survivors to local, victim-centered support services that provide crisis intervention, urgent or nonurgent care, or lead them to safety; providing tools to fight against human trafficking; and reporting potential trafficking tips to law enforcement. This is a very valuable service and lifeline.

I urge my colleagues to support this legislation.

Mr. Speaker, I reserve the balance of my time.

Mr. GOODLATTE. Mr. Speaker, I reserve the balance of my time.

Ms. JACKSON LEE. Mr. Speaker, I yield 2 minutes to the distinguished gentlewoman from California (Ms. BASS), who has a long history of working with children, of arguing and advocating against the mistreatment of foster care children who find themselves disproportionately involved and subjected to the potential of human trafficking. I thank her for her leadership, for being a cosponsor of this legislation, and a Member of the House Judiciary Committee.

Ms. BASS. Mr. Speaker, I rise in support of the National Human Trafficking Hotline.

I also want to join with my colleagues in wishing well Judge POE, and wishing him a speedy recovery. He has been a leader on this issue for many, many years, and the hotline is a critical feature of how we can address human trafficking in our country.

I also support the resources being managed under Health and Human Services. I believe it reflects the current awareness and knowledge that this really shouldn't be managed by law enforcement. We have all heard the stories of women and children who have been taken from location to location and forced to have sex against their will.

Currently, there are more cases of human trafficking reported in California than in any other State. This hotline has served as a lifeline/vital resource to human trafficking victims and their advocates. In California alone this year, there have been over 3,000 calls received on the hotline, resulting in over 1,000 human trafficking cases being reported, nearly a third of which are minors.

Unfortunately, there is a growing body of evidence that youth who fall through the cracks in the foster care system end up trafficked. As of 2012 in

California, 50 to 80 percent of the commercially exploited children had been involved in the child welfare system. Fifty-eight percent of sexually trafficked girls in the Los Angeles County STAR Court in 2012 were under age and were connected to the foster care system. In Los Angeles, we are fortunate to have a STAR Court, but the purpose of this court is to deal with underage children who have been trafficked.

I recently hosted an event in my district in order to train faith leaders in my community to identify and direct resources to women and girls who had been victims of trafficking. Often, it is members of our communities who are the first line of defense for these girls.

The SPEAKER pro tempore (Mr. NEUGEBAUER). The time of the gentlewoman has expired.

Ms. JACKSON LEE. Mr. Speaker, I yield the gentlewoman from California an additional 1 minute.

Ms. BASS. Mr. Speaker, we must work to break the foster-care-to-child-sex-trafficking-victim pipeline by continuing to fund additional programs, like the National Human Trafficking Hotline, to help identify victims and provide them with the resources that they need.

Mr. GOODLATTE. Mr. Speaker, I continue to reserve the balance of my time.

Ms. JACKSON LEE. Mr. Speaker, I yield myself such time as I may consume.

Let me give my closing remarks and indicate that I am grateful in determining that the Justice for Victims of Trafficking Act, which, unfortunately, was enacted last year, mistakenly directed that funding for the NHTRC be given to the Justice Department instead of HHS, which would still be responsible for administering it. Therefore, we need to change the law to ensure that funding be directed to HHS so that it will continue to fund and oversee NHTRC in the same manner and efficiently as it has in the past. For that reason, this is an important initiative.

I commend again the actions and efforts and commitment of my colleague, Congressman TED POE. I wish him good health and thank him for continuing to work on behalf of human trafficking victims.

This bill is evidence that we have the ability to work together as a unified body to address issues that affect our country and, more importantly, that those victims of this dastardly human trafficking, when they feel so alone and cannot reach out, have a body of Members, House and Senate, who recognize the urgency and importance of this effort to help them restore their lives, but, more importantly, to stand in the way of this terrible and heinous act.

I urge my colleagues to support this legislation.

Mr. Speaker, I yield back the balance of my time.

Mr. Speaker, I rise in support of H.R. 5422, a bill I have cosponsored in order to ensure funding for the National Human Trafficking Hotline, a crucial component in the fight against human trafficking.

As I have said many times before, trafficking in human beings has no place in a civilized society.

Congress decided 150 years ago that no individual deserves to be bought, owned, or sold.

Our country is now faced with a modern-day version of slavery that denies victims of their humanity and violates the most basic American ideals of liberty and individual autonomy.

Human trafficking is the second-fastest growing criminal enterprise.

4,177 sex trafficking cases and 824 labor trafficking cases were reported in the first nine months of this year in the United States and its territories.

Traffickers use trickery and, most often, coercion and violence to force victims to provide labor or perform sexual acts.

My home city of Houston has been identified as a hub for human trafficking. I am proud to say that Houston and the entire state of Texas are working hard to stave off this growing threat.

In an effort to understand the problem and find real solutions, we held several hearings in 2014, including a Field Hearing before the Committee on Homeland Security.

During that hearing, we heard from victims and survivors of human trafficking. They recounted indignities they suffered as well as the physical and psychological damage done while they were young children, but still felt as adults.

I traveled to a stash house and witnessed the atrocious conditions under which these people are held.

We now know that a comprehensive, collaborative approach that includes law makers, law enforcement, victim advocates, community organizations, and social service providers is necessary to identify victims, lead them to safety, restore them, and bring their captors to justice.

The National Human Trafficking Resource Center plays a critical role in the effort to save, protect, and restore victims of human trafficking.

The NHTRC is a national anti-trafficking hotline and resource center, created and overseen by the Department of Health and Human Services, and funded through grant money appropriated to HHS.

In 2015, the NHTRC received more than 24,000 alerts regarding human trafficking cases or issues related to human trafficking, which includes phone calls, online tips, and emails.

The NHTRC is invaluable to victims, survivors, and stakeholders involved in the fight against human trafficking—connecting human trafficking victims and survivors to local, victim-centered support services that provide crisis intervention, urgent or non-urgent care, or lead them to safety; providing tools to fight against human trafficking; and reporting potential trafficking tips to law enforcement.

Unfortunately, the Justice for Victims of Trafficking Act, which was enacted last year, mistakenly directed that funding for the

NHTRC be given to the Justice Department instead of HHS, which would still be responsible for administering it.

Therefore, we need to change the law to ensure that funding be directed to HHS so that it will continue to fund and oversee the NHRTC in the same, efficient manner as it has in the past.

Mr. Speaker, I commend the efforts of my colleague, Congressman TED POE. I wish him good health and thank him for continuing to work on behalf of human trafficking victims.

This bill is evidence that we have the ability to work together as a unified body to address issues that affect our country.

I ask that my colleagues join me in supporting this bill today.

Mr. GOODLATTE. Mr. Speaker, I yield myself the balance of my time.

Let's pass this legislation in honor of Congressman and former Judge TED POE, who has been a champion in the battle against human trafficking. I urge my colleagues to support the bill.

Mr. Speaker, I yield back the balance of my time.

Mr. POE of Texas. Mr. Speaker, Laura was a middle school counselor who noticed that one of her students had begun to act strangely. Laura's instincts were right. Out of the classroom, her student, Alyssa, had started to frequently flee her foster home and was often found in random locations with adult strangers. After some investigation, Laura learned that Alyssa had been lured into the business of having sex with adults. Traffickers did what they do best, identified a vulnerable young woman and lured her into the sex trade. Laura immediately contacted the National Human Trafficking Hotline, reported what had happened to her young student and they were able to advise her on how to proceed and what social services and law enforcement agencies to contact. Because of the hotline, Laura was able to save Alyssa's life.

The National Human Trafficking Hotline serves as an essential lifeline to victims of trafficking, but it also serves as an important source of information to those who suspect they have encountered a victim of trafficking and don't know how to help. This hotline is an essential tool in the fight against human trafficking in the United States.

H.R. 5422 is a bipartisan, non-controversial bill that makes a small technical fix to allow the Department of Health and Human Services (HHS) to continue funding the National Human Trafficking Hotline (NHTH). In the House, I introduced this bill with Representative CAROLYN MALONEY. I would also like to thank Senator JOHN CORNYN and Senator AMY KLOBUCHAR for sponsoring this bill in the Senate.

Without the National Hotline's guidance, Laura may never have known how to help that poor child escape her traffickers. The hotline provides trafficking victims and survivors with access to critical support and emergency services, collects tips about potential trafficking situations and disseminates training and informational materials to help raise awareness in our communities. HHS created and currently oversees and funds the NHTH. As it stands today, the funding for HHS's annual grants has been appropriated to the Department of Justice.

This bill is a simple technical fix to codify the hotline within HHS and to help continue the important work being done by our nation's anti-human trafficking hotline.

Having the hotline under the jurisdiction of DOJ creates an unnecessary and unhelpful additional layer of bureaucracy. It forces HHS to be dependent on funds from DOJ to run the hotline. It is more efficient and effective for HHS to continue using its own finds to operate the NHTH.

I urge the House to pass this simple bipartisan measure to ensure the continued ease of funding to the National Human Trafficking Hotline through the Department of Health and Human Services.

The SPEAKER pro tempore. The question is on the motion offered by the gentleman from Virginia (Mr. GOODLATTE) that the House suspend the rules and pass the bill, H.R. 5422.

The question was taken.

The SPEAKER pro tempore. In the opinion of the Chair, two-thirds being in the affirmative, the ayes have it.

Mr. GOODLATTE. Mr. Speaker, on that I demand the yeas and nays.

The yeas and nays were ordered.

The SPEAKER pro tempore. Pursuant to clause 8 of rule XX, further proceedings on this motion will be postponed.

UNITED STATES-ISRAEL AD-VANCED RESEARCH PARTNER-SHIP ACT OF 2016

Mr. RATCLIFFE. Mr. Speaker, I move to suspend the rules and pass the bill (H.R. 5877) to amend the Homeland Security Act of 2002 and the United States-Israel Strategic Partnership Act of 2014 to promote cooperative homeland security research and antiterrorism programs relating to cybersecurity, and for other purposes, as amended.

The Clerk read the title of the bill.

The text of the bill is as follows:

H.R. 5877

Be it enacted by the Senate and House of Representatives of the United States of America in Congress assembled,

SECTION 1. SHORT TITLE.

This Act may be cited as the "United States-Israel Advanced Research Partnership Act of 2016".

SEC. 2. COOPERATIVE HOMELAND SECURITY RE-SEARCH AND ANTITERRORISM PRO-GRAMS RELATING TO CYBERSECU-RITY.

(a) HOMELAND SECURITY ACT OF 2002.—Section 317 of the Homeland Security Act of 2002 (6 U.S.C. 195c) is amended—

(1) in subsection (e)—

(A) in paragraph (1), by striking "and" after the semicolon;

(B) in paragraph (2), by striking the period at the end and inserting "; and"; and

(C) by inserting after paragraph (2) the following new paragraphs:

"(3) for international cooperative activities identified in the previous reporting period, a status update on the progress of such activities, including whether goals were realized, explaining any lessons learned, and evaluating overall success; and

"(4) a discussion of obstacles encountered in the course of forming, executing, or implementing agreements for international cooperative activities, including administrative, legal, or diplomatic challenges or resource constraints.";

(2) by redesignating subsections (g) and (h) as subsections (h) and (i), respectively; and

(3) by inserting after subsection (f) the following new subsection:

"(g) CYBERSECURITY.—As part of the international cooperative activities authorized in this section, the Under Secretary, in coordination with the Department of State and appropriate Federal officials, may enter into cooperative research activities with Israel to strengthen preparedness against cyber threats and enhance capabilities in cybersecurity.".

(b) UNITED STATES-ISRAEL STRATEGIC PARTNERSHIP ACT OF 2014.—Subsection (c) of section 7 of the United States-Israel Strategic Partnership Act of 2014 (Public Law 113–296; 22 U.S.C. 8606) is amended—

(1) in the heading, by striking "PILOT";

(2) in the matter preceding paragraph (1), by striking "pilot";

(3) in paragraph (2), by striking "and" at the end;

(4) in paragraph (3), by striking the period at the end and inserting "; and"; and

(5) by adding at the end the following new paragraph:

"(4) cybersecurity.".

SEC. 3. PROHIBITION ON ADDITIONAL FUNDING.

No additional funds are authorized to be appropriated to carry out this Act or the amendments made by this Act.

The SPEAKER pro tempore. Pursuant to the rule, the gentleman from Texas (Mr. RATCLIFFE) and the gentleman from Rhode Island (Mr. LANGEVIN) each will control 20 minutes.

The Chair recognizes the gentleman from Texas.

GENERAL LEAVE

Mr. RATCLIFFE. Mr. Speaker, I ask unanimous consent that all Members may have 5 legislative days in which to revise and extend their remarks and include any extraneous materials on the bill under consideration.

The SPEAKER pro tempore. Is there objection to the request of the gentleman from Texas?

There was no objection.

Mr. RATCLIFFE. Mr. Speaker, I yield myself such time as I may consume.

Mr. Speaker, I am very pleased that today the House is considering H.R. 5877, the United States-Israel Advanced Research Partnership Act of 2016.

Israel is our strongest and most trusted ally in the Middle East, and I am grateful to join with the gentleman from Rhode Island (Mr. LANGEVIN), my friend, in working to expand and strengthen this bond through long-term collaboration on cybersecurity efforts between our countries. H.R. 5877 builds on decades of partnership with the State of Israel by amending current law to authorize the Under Secretary of the Science and Technology Directorate at the Department of Homeland Security, in coordination with the Secretary of State, to enter into cooperative research activities with Israel.

H.R. 5877 also amends the U.S.-Israel Strategic Partnership Act of 2014 by further formalizing the program and by adding cybersecurity to the list of research areas authorized under the act. The U.S.-Israel Strategic Partnership Act of 2014 currently authorizes the Secretary of Homeland Security to conduct cooperative research programs to enhance Israel's capabilities in border security, explosives detection, and emergency services. My bill now adds cybersecurity to that important list.

Mr. Speaker, violence and instability in the Middle East present significant challenges for Israel as our major strategic partner in that region of the world, and enhancing collaboration between our countries is, therefore, essential to ensuring Israel's continued ability to defend herself.

Mr. Speaker, I introduced this legislation following an in-depth congressional delegation that I led to Israel earlier this year, along with my colleague, Mr. LANGEVIN. While there, we were able to meet with Israel's top national security figures, including Prime Minister Benjamin Netanyahu, to discuss homeland security and cybersecurity threats to the United States and Israel, and to develop strategies for better cooperation in defending against these threats.

Mr. LANGEVIN and I also met with Israel's cybersecurity firms to learn about their efforts and to discuss the potential application of these innovative technologies to U.S. homeland security. In recent years, Israel's tech sector has been booming with cybersecurity and technology startups, and many United States tech companies now have a presence in Israel. Much of Israel's success in the tech sector results from its development of a very robust cyber workforce, and we discussed ways to apply these lessons here in the United States.

The United States and Israel share a joint recognition that cybersecurity is national security, and that our two nations must closely partner to combat these growing threats. This is exactly why I was so pleased to be able to introduce H.R. 5877, the United States-Israel Advanced Research Partnership Act of 2016, and why I also express my strong support for Mr. LANGEVIN's bill, H.R. 5843, the United States-Israel Cybersecurity Cooperation Enhancement Act of 2016.

I thank my friend and colleague, Mr. LANGEVIN, for his bipartisan partnership on these very important bills. As the co-founder and cochairman of the bipartisan Cybersecurity Caucus, he has long been a leader on cybersecurity issues here in Congress.

Mr. Speaker, I also thank Chairman McCAUL, Ranking Member THOMPSON, and subcommittee Ranking Member RICHMOND for their help in getting this legislation across the finish line today. I also thank Chairman ROYCE and the staff of the Foreign Affairs Committee for their assistance in moving the legislation to the floor today.

I urge all Members to join me in supporting this bill.

Mr. Speaker, I reserve the balance of my time.

HOUSE OF REPRESENTATIVES,
COMMITTEE ON FOREIGN AFFAIRS,
Washington, DC, November 14, 2016.
Hon. MICHAEL MCCAUL,
Chairman, House Committee on Homeland Security.

DEAR CHAIRMAN MCCAUL: Thank you for consulting with the Foreign Affairs Committee regarding H.R. 5877, the United States-Israel Advanced Research Partnership Act of 2016. I agree that the Foreign Affairs Committee may be discharged from further consideration of that measure, so that it may proceed expeditiously to the House floor.

I am writing to confirm our mutual understanding that forgoing further action on this measure does not in any way diminish or alter the jurisdiction of the Committee on Foreign Affairs, or prejudice its jurisdictional prerogatives on this bill or similar legislation in the future. I also request your support for the appointment of Foreign Affairs conferees to any House-Senate conference on this legislation.

I ask that a copy of our exchange of letters on this matter be included in your committee report, and also in the Congressional Record during floor consideration of the bill.

Sincerely,
EDWARD R. ROYCE,
Chairman.

HOUSE OF REPRESENTATIVES,
COMMITTEE ON HOMELAND SECURITY,
Washington, DC, November 15, 2016.
Hon. ED ROYCE,
Chairman, Committee on Foreign Affairs.

DEAR CHAIRMAN ROYCE: Thank you for your letter regarding H.R. 5877, the "United States-Israel Advanced Research Partnership Act of 2016." I appreciate your support in bringing this legislation before the House of Representatives, and accordingly, understand that the Committee on Foreign Affairs will forego further action on the bill.

The Committee on Homeland Security concurs with the mutual understanding that by foregoing further action on this bill at this time, the Committee on Foreign Affairs does not waive any jurisdiction over the subject matter contained in this bill or similar legislation in the future. In addition, should a conference on this bill be necessary, I would support your request to have the Committee on Foreign Affairs represented on the conference committee.

I will insert copies of this exchange in the report on the bill and in the Congressional Record during consideration of this bill on the House floor. I thank you for your cooperation in this matter.

Sincerely,
MICHAEL T. MCCAUL,
Chairman, Committee on Homeland Security.

Mr. LANGEVIN. Mr. Speaker, I yield myself such time as I may consume.

I rise in strong support of H.R. 5877, the United States-Israel Advanced Research Partnership Act of 2016.

Mr. Speaker, both this bill and the subsequent measure that we will consider today are connected, as the chairman mentioned, to a congressional delegation trip that Chairman RATCLIFFE and I took to Israel earlier this year. I thank Chairman RATCLIFFE for his leadership on cybersecurity and other homeland security related issues.

The focus of our trip was cybersecurity, and we learned a great deal about the innovative work the Israelis are doing in this space, both within government and in the private sector.

Israel was one of the first countries to recognize the potential threat posed by interconnected computer systems, and they have been leaders in cybersecurity now for decades. For instance, the first stateful firewall technology was developed by an Israeli firm. Today, these firewalls are ubiquitous across the information security landscape.

☐ 1615

In fact, despite its size, Israel is the second largest exporter of cybersecurity goods and services behind only the United States.

In addition to being a fertile source of public and private sector innovation in the domain, Israel is also the United States' critical strategic partner in the Middle East. In recognizing this confluence of strategic and research interests, the Department of Homeland Security established a memorandum of agreement with the Israeli Ministry of Public Security that was focused on joint homeland security research and development efforts, including cybersecurity. As a founding member of the Homeland Security Committee, I remember when this MOA was first reached, and I think it is a very positive thing that we are working together on these types of issues with Israel.

This MOA provides an excellent foundation for cooperation between our two nations; but one of the common themes we heard during our trip was: Can we be doing even more? After all, it is my firm belief that cybersecurity is the most significant national security challenge of the information age in which we live.

It has certainly been a pleasure working with Mr. RATCLIFFE, who, very quickly during his time here in Congress, has recognized the significance of the challenge that is in front of us.

This national security challenge, of course, is not confined to any nation. On the contrary, our adversaries in cyberspace—most notably Iran—are infiltrating the networks in both of our countries. What is more, the interconnected nature of our information systems leads to a blurring of geography. A cyber threat against Israel could easily migrate to the United States or vice versa, and there is no Internet border patrol, if you will, that will preemptively stop it from spreading.

Some of these challenges can be addressed through collective cyber defense, particularly information sharing, which is why I am grateful that then-Deputy Secretary of Homeland Security Alejandro Mayorkas negotiated an enhanced cybersecurity cooperative agreement with Israel earlier this year that will promote engagement and collaboration by our respective computer emergency readiness teams, or CERTs.

One of the things that I have learned in my near decade as co-chair of the Congressional Cybersecurity Caucus is that the landscape evolves at a dizzying pace. While we must work with our allies to jointly use existing capabilities, it is only through the development of innovative new techniques and technologies that we have any hope of stemming the tide of the cyber attacks that we face.

With that background in mind, Mr. Speaker, I offer my full-throated support for the bill under consideration. H.R. 5877 expands an existing pilot program at the Homeland Security Advanced Research Projects Agency, or HSARPA, to further collaboration on cybersecurity capability development. This program is particularly important because it addresses specific needs from the homeland security community which may not be present in other sectors and which may not be addressed by existing commercial, off-the-shelf products.

Cybersecurity is subject to the same valley of death, if you will, between early applied research and viable commercial product as other cutting-edge fields, and this bill helps ensure that innovative technologies will make it to market that are responsive to the needs of our DHS cybersecurity professionals. This last point, of course, is worth reemphasizing. While we face similar challenges on government networks as other entities, small businesses and government agencies all run Windows on their PCs.

We also face problems that, of course, are unique to nation-states. It is incumbent upon nations that believe in a free and open Internet to work together to preserve its immense benefit and to facilitate collaboration between our countries' innovators. It is natural for us to expand other areas of similar homeland security interests—explosives detection, border security, and emergency services—to include cybersecurity.

I am grateful for Mr. RATCLIFFE's leadership in bringing forth a bill that both cements existing relationships and expands them to the leading threat facing our Nation. I urge my colleagues to support H.R. 5877.

Mr. Speaker, I reserve the balance of my time.

Mr. RATCLIFFE. Mr. Speaker, I again thank Congressman LANGEVIN for his kind words and for his leadership in connection with this bill.

I reserve the balance of my time.

Mr. LANGEVIN. Mr. Speaker, may I inquire as to how much time I have remaining on my side?

The SPEAKER pro tempore. The gentleman from Rhode Island has 14 minutes remaining.

Mr. LANGEVIN. Mr. Speaker, I yield 2 minutes to the gentlewoman from Texas (Ms. JACKSON LEE).

Ms. JACKSON LEE. Mr. Speaker, I rise to commend Mr. RATCLIFFE and Mr. LANGEVIN for their leadership on this issue, and I rise in support of H.R. 5877, which speaks to the crucialness of cybersecurity as does the following bill by Mr. LANGEVIN.

It is interesting that, some years ago, as the chairperson of the Transportation Security Subcommittee, infrastructure was included, and cybersecurity was a part of that. During that tenure, we looked at the vast impact that cyber and security would have on the lives of Americans and on the people around the world. From water systems to sewer systems, an attack on the cyber system could clearly undermine the quality of life of people around the world. Obviously, Israel fully comprehended this in its enhanced level of innovative work when dealing with cybersecurity and particularly, as Mr. LANGEVIN said, in the importance of creating firewalls, which we have been able to see.

I congratulate the sponsors of this legislation and will say that we need to have cybersecurity issues clearly in our eyes' view. I acknowledge the bipartisan work of the Committee on Homeland Security under the leadership of Chairman MCCAUL and Ranking Member THOMPSON, and I acknowledge the Cybersecurity, Infrastructure Protection, and Security Technologies Subcommittee that has Mr. RICHMOND as the ranking member.

I also add my support for H.R. 5843, sponsored by Mr. LANGEVIN, which provides a pilot cybersecurity research program that will require the Department of Homeland Security to establish a grant program to support cybersecurity research and development and the demonstration and commercialization of cybersecurity technology in accordance with the agreement between the Government of the United States and the Government of Israel.

I cannot think of two more important steps that are being made. I hope this legislation will pass before this Congress ends because, if there is any threat that is great to this Nation, it is the unintended impact of cybersecurity.

The SPEAKER pro tempore. The time of the gentlewoman has expired.

Mr. LANGEVIN. I yield the gentlewoman an additional 15 seconds.

Ms. JACKSON LEE. I thank the gentleman.

Mr. Speaker, in the backdrop of seeing technology impact the recent election, I think that we clearly know that we have to be studious, that we have to be thorough, and that we have to make sure that systems work and that systems are protected.

I ask my colleagues to support the underlying bill and also H.R. 5843.

Mr. Speaker, I rise in support of H.R. 5843, United States-Israel Cybersecurity Cooperation Enhancement Act, because it will establish a pilot cybersecurity research program between our nation and our strongest friends in the region for the purpose of strengthening cybersecurity.

I support this bill because the bill requires the Department of Homeland Security (DHS) to establish a grant program to support cybersecurity research and development, and the demonstration and commercialization of cybersecurity technology, in accordance with the Agreement between the Government of the United States of America and the Government of the State of Israel on Cooperation in Science and Technology for Homeland Security Matters.

This bill will codifies and makes available funding for an existing mutual cooperation agreement between the United States and Israel on matters related to cybersecurity.

Grants provided under this bill may be awarded for social science research and technology intended to identify, protect against, respond to, and recover from cybersecurity threats.

To be eligible for a grant, a project must be a joint venture between:

(1) for-profit, nonprofit, or academic entities including U.S. national laboratories in the United States and Israel; or

(2) the governments of the United States and Israel.

Grants shall be awarded only for projects considered unclassified by both the United States and Israel.

Under the terms of this bill DHS must require cost sharing of at least 50% from non-federal sources for grant activities, but it may reduce the nonfederal percentage if necessary on a case-by-case basis.

DHS will also establish an advisory board to monitor the impartial scientific and technical merit method by which grants are awarded and provide periodic reviews of the actions taken to carry out the program.

The grant program terminates seven years after this bill's enactment.

The Science and Technology Homeland Security International Cooperative Programs Office will produce a report every five years by the Science and Technology must contain:

(1) a status update on the progress of such international cooperative activities identified in the previous reporting period; and

(2) a discussion of obstacles encountered in forming, executing, or implementing agreements for such activities.

As a member of the House Committee on Homeland Security since its establishment, and current Ranking Member of the Judiciary Subcommittee on Crime, Terrorism and Homeland Security this bill is of importance to me.

I introduced H.R. 85, the Terrorism Prevention and Critical Infrastructure Protection Act of 2015 out of well-founded concerns regarding the security of critical infrastructure of our nation from terrorists attack.

H.R. 85, directs the Secretary DHS to:

(1) work with critical infrastructure owners and operators and state, local, tribal, and territorial entities to take proactive steps to manage risk and strengthen the security and resilience of the nation's critical infrastructure against terrorist attacks;

(2) establish terrorism prevention policy to engage with international partners to strengthen the security and resilience of domestic critical infrastructure and critical infrastructure located outside of the United States;

(4) establish the Strategic Research Imperatives Program to lead DHS's federal civilian agency approach to strengthen critical infrastructure security and resilience; and

(5) make available research findings and guidance to federal civilian agencies for the identification, prioritization, assessment, remediation, and security of their internal critical infrastructure to assist in the prevention, mediation, and recovery from terrorism events.

H.R. 85, also directs the Secretary of DHS to: (1) appoint a research working group that shall study how best to achieve national unity of effort to protect against terrorism threats and investigate the security and resilience of the nation's information assurance components that provide such protection; and (2) establish a research program to provide strategic guidance, promote a national unity of effort, and coordinate the overall federal effort to promote the security and resilience of the nation's critical infrastructure from terrorist threats.

As we have worked to define and support the mission of the Department of Homeland Security we have worked to keep the efforts of the agency focused not only on the threats we have faced, but also the new ones that may come.

Collaborative agreements that can bolster the ability of DHS to be able to effectively respond to cyber threats is in the best interest of the United States.

It is the responsibility of Congress not only to provide DHS with new guidelines, but also to provide the agency with the funding it needs to do the work of protecting this great nation.

For several Congresses DHS has faced a government shutdown and sequestration that has depleted its resources and stranded its efforts to do all of the work members of this body demands.

As I urge my colleagues to support this bill, I also remind them that the passage of new laws that require more of the agency should also mean that we should require more of ourselves as members of Congress.

We should support the work of the men and women of DHS as they stand to defend this nation from all threats including those that come from cyberspace.

I ask my colleagues to join me in supporting H.R. 5843.

Mr. RATCLIFFE. Mr. Speaker, I reserve the balance of my time.

Mr. LANGEVIN. Mr. Speaker, I yield myself the balance of my time.

This bill will meaningfully improve our homeland security professionals' ability to manage cybersecurity risk. It will do so in a way that also increases the capacity of our Israeli allies to operate securely despite the many and varied threats they face on a daily basis.

Again, I thank Mr. RATCLIFFE for his leadership in bringing this legislation to the floor. It was a pleasure to travel with him to Israel on this factfinding mission, and we both learned a great deal.

I also thank Chairman McCAUL and Ranking Member THOMPSON, as well as Ranking Member RICHMOND of the Subcommittee on Cybersecurity, Infrastructure Protection, and Security Technologies, for their assistance in support of this. I also, of course, thank the staffs on both the Homeland Security Committee, Mr. RATCLIFFE's personal staff, and my personal staff for their hard work in bringing this to the floor. We could not do what we do without their invaluable assistance and due diligence. I urge my colleagues to support this legislation.

Mr. Speaker, I yield back the balance of my time.

Mr. RATCLIFFE. Mr. Speaker, once again, I thank Congressman LANGEVIN, and I urge my colleagues to support H.R. 5877.

I yield back the balance of my time.

The SPEAKER pro tempore. The question is on the motion offered by the gentleman from Texas (Mr. RATCLIFFE) that the House suspend the rules and pass the bill, H.R. 5877, as amended.

The question was taken; and (two-thirds being in the affirmative) the rules were suspended and the bill, as amended, was passed.

A motion to reconsider was laid on the table.

UNITED STATES-ISRAEL CYBERSECURITY COOPERATION ENHANCEMENT ACT OF 2016

Mr. RATCLIFFE. Mr. Speaker, I move to suspend the rules and pass the bill (H.R. 5843) to establish a grant program at the Department of Homeland Security to promote cooperative research and development between the United States and Israel on cybersecurity, as amended.

The Clerk read the title of the bill.

The text of the bill is as follows:

H.R. 5843

Be it enacted by the Senate and House of Representatives of the United States of America in Congress assembled,

SECTION 1. SHORT TITLE.

This Act may be cited as the "United States-Israel Cybersecurity Cooperation Enhancement Act of 2016".

SEC. 2. UNITED STATES-ISRAEL CYBERSECURITY COOPERATION.

(a) GRANT PROGRAM.—

(1) ESTABLISHMENT.—The Secretary, in accordance with the agreement entitled the "Agreement between the Government of the United States of America and the Government of the State of Israel on Cooperation in Science and Technology for Homeland Security Matters", dated May 29, 2008 (or successor agreement), and the requirements specified in paragraph (2), shall establish a grant program at the Department to support—

(A) cybersecurity research and development; and

(B) demonstration and commercialization of cybersecurity technology.

(2) REQUIREMENTS.—

(A) APPLICABILITY.—Notwithstanding any other provision of law, in carrying out a research, development, demonstration, or commercial application program or activity that is authorized under this section, the Secretary shall require cost sharing in accordance with this paragraph.

(B) RESEARCH AND DEVELOPMENT.—

(i) IN GENERAL.—Except as provided in clause (ii), the Secretary shall require not less than 50 percent of the cost of a research, development, demonstration, or commercial application program or activity described in subparagraph (A) to be provided by a non-Federal source.

(ii) REDUCTION.—The Secretary may reduce or eliminate, on a case-by-case basis, the percentage requirement specified in clause (i) if the Secretary determines that such reduction or elimination is necessary and appropriate.

(C) MERIT REVIEW.—In carrying out a research, development, demonstration, or commercial application program or activity that is authorized under this section, awards shall be made only after an impartial review of the scientific and technical merit of the proposals for such awards has been carried out by or for the Department.

(D) REVIEW PROCESSES.—In carrying out a review under subparagraph (C), the Secretary may use merit review processes developed under section 302(14) of the Homeland Security Act of 2002 (6 U.S.C. 182(14)).

(3) ELIGIBLE APPLICANTS.—An applicant shall be eligible to receive a grant under this subsection if the project of such applicant—

(A) addresses a requirement in the area of cybersecurity research or cybersecurity technology, as determined by the Secretary; and

(B) is a joint venture between—

(i)(I) a for-profit business entity, academic institution, National Laboratory (as defined in section 2 of the Energy Policy Act of 2005 (42 U.S.C. 15801)), or nonprofit entity in the United States; and

(II) a for-profit business entity, academic institution, or nonprofit entity in Israel; or

(ii)(I) the Federal Government; and

(II) the Government of Israel.

(4) APPLICATIONS.—To be eligible to receive a grant under this subsection, an applicant shall submit to the Secretary an application for such grant in accordance with procedures established by the Secretary, in consultation with the advisory board established under paragraph (5).

(5) ADVISORY BOARD.—

(A) ESTABLISHMENT.—The Secretary shall establish an advisory board to—

(i) monitor the method by which grants are awarded under this subsection; and

(ii) provide to the Secretary periodic performance reviews of actions taken to carry out this subsection.

(B) COMPOSITION.—The advisory board established under subparagraph (A) shall be composed of three members, to be appointed by the Secretary, of whom—

(i) one shall be a representative of the Federal Government;

(ii) one shall be selected from a list of nominees provided by the United States-Israel Binational Science Foundation; and

(iii) one shall be selected from a list of nominees provided by the United States-Israel Binational Industrial Research and Development Foundation.

(6) CONTRIBUTED FUNDS.—Notwithstanding any other provision of law, the Secretary may accept or retain funds contributed by any person, government entity, or organization for purposes of carrying out this subsection. Such funds shall be available, subject to appropriation, without fiscal year limitation.

(7) REPORT.—Not later than 180 days after the date of completion of a project for which a grant is provided under this subsection, the grant recipient shall submit to the Secretary a report that contains—

(A) a description of how the grant funds were used by the recipient; and

(B) an evaluation of the level of success of each project funded by the grant.

(8) CLASSIFICATION.—Grants shall be awarded under this subsection only for projects that are considered to be unclassified by both the United States and Israel.

(b) TERMINATION.—The grant program and the advisory board established under this section terminate on the date that is seven years after the date of the enactment of this Act.

(c) PROHIBITION ON ADDITIONAL FUNDING.— No additional funds are authorized to be appropriated to carry out this Act.

(d) DEFINITIONS.—In this section—

(1) the term "cybersecurity research" means research, including social science research, into ways to identify, protect against, detect, respond to, and recover from cybersecurity threats;

(2) the term "cybersecurity technology" means technology intended to identify, protect against, detect, respond to, and recover from cybersecurity threats;

(3) the term "cybersecurity threat" has the meaning given such term in section 102 of the Cybersecurity Information Sharing Act of 2015 (enacted as title I of the Cybersecurity Act of 2015 (division N of the Consolidated Appropriations Act, 2016 (Public Law 114–113)));

(4) the term "Department" means the Department of Homeland Security; and

(5) the term "Secretary" means the Secretary of Homeland Security.

The SPEAKER pro tempore. Pursuant to the rule, the gentleman from Texas (Mr. RATCLIFFE) and the gentleman from Rhode Island (Mr. LANGEVIN) each will control 20 minutes.

The Chair recognizes the gentleman from Texas.

GENERAL LEAVE

Mr. RATCLIFFE. Mr. Speaker, I ask unanimous consent that all Members have 5 legislative days in which to revise and extend their remarks and to include any extraneous materials on the bill under consideration.

The SPEAKER pro tempore. Is there objection to the request of the gentleman from Texas?

There was no objection.

Mr. RATCLIFFE. Mr. Speaker, I yield myself such time as I may consume.

I thank my colleague, Mr. LANGEVIN, for offering this very important piece of legislation today.

As I mentioned earlier, both H.R. 5843 and H.R. 5877 were the result of our successful congressional delegation to the State of Israel, where we heard and learned firsthand about the importance of strong collaboration between our two nations—the United States and Israel.

This legislation further builds on the existing agreements between the United States and Israel by authorizing the Secretary to carry out a grant program to bolster the cyber defenses of both countries. It is vitally important that the United States and Israel have robust and innovative cyber defenses in order to stay ahead of our adversaries, and this legislation will help ensure that that is achieved.

Again, I thank Mr. LANGEVIN and his staff for their partnership on this very important issue, and I urge all Members to join me in supporting this bill.

I reserve the balance of my time.

Mr. LANGEVIN. Mr. Speaker, I yield myself such time as I may consume.

I rise in strong support of H.R. 5843, the United States-Israel Cybersecurity Cooperation Enhancement Act of 2016. Much like the previous bill, H.R. 5843 is about enhancing cooperation with our allies in Israel to develop innovative cybersecurity solutions that are directly responsive to the needs of our national security.

Specifically, the bill creates a cybersecurity grant program for joint research and development ventures between Israeli and American entities. Projects would be selected after a merit-review—peer-review—process and would have to address requirements in cybersecurity that are determined by the Secretary of Homeland Security. The grants would also be subject to a cost-sharing requirement, with at least 50 percent of project funds coming from a non-Federal source.

Importantly, H.R. 5843 leverages existing United States-Israel R&D infrastructure, specifically the Binational Industrial Research and Development, or BIRD, Foundation and the Binational Science Foundation, or BSF. Both organizations have a proven track record of encouraging joint research efforts.

BIRD, for instance, has financed R&D and commercialization projects that have led to a cumulative $8 billion in commercial sales since its founding while BSF regularly funds collaborations between the top scientists in our respective countries, as 45 Nobel laureates have received support from the foundation. Using the existing infrastructure, as was done in 2007 when Congress passed the Energy Independence and Security Act, which led to the creation of BIRD Energy, also allows us to capitalize on both foundations' robust networks of American and Israeli entities to help seed these joint efforts.

All of these factors are particularly critical in the fast-moving cybersecurity domain where offensive and defensive tactics and techniques change on a monthly or on even a weekly basis.

□ 1630

As such, advances in the discipline require a near constant reexamining of assumptions, and having people from different backgrounds and security cultures working together engenders an environment where such reexamination is encouraged.

While both the U.S. and Israel have robust cybersecurity communities, further collaboration is needed to spur more advances to combat the threats that we face. Although some of these advances are technological in nature, basic cybersecurity research, such as investigations into the psychology of secure interface design and social engineering, is also supported by the bill.

All told, the programs authorized in H.R. 5843 and H.R. 5877 will both address urgent homeland security needs and build capacity for further transnational collaboration on cybersecurity, all while matching Federal investment with private dollars and funds from the Israeli Government.

As with any bill to make it to the floor, both H.R. 5843 and H.R. 5877 owe much to the dedicated staff who spent hours behind the scenes reviewing the legislation. In particular, I would like to thank Brett DeWitt, Christopher Schepis, and Erik Peterson from the Committee on Homeland Security's Subcommittee on Cybersecurity, Infrastructure Protection, and Security Technologies, who joined Representative RATCLIFFE and me on the congressional delegation trip that we took to Israel, as well as Emily Leviner on Mr. RATCLIFFE's personal staff and Nick Leiserson on my own staff.

I am also very grateful, of course, to Chairman MCCAUL, Ranking Member THOMPSON, and Subcommittee Ranking Member RICHMOND for their continued leadership on the issue of cybersecurity and for their assistance in quickly actualizing the lessons we learned on our trip to Israel.

Finally, once again, I owe a debt of gratitude to the gentleman across the aisle, Mr. RATCLIFFE, who, in just in his first term, has immediately had a substantial impact on our Nation's cybersecurity, as I said previously, and with whom it has been a great pleasure to work.

Mr. Speaker, taken together, H.R. 5843 and H.R. 5877 do three things: they encourage innovative approaches to address top priorities in homeland security R&D; they strengthen ties with Israel, one of our closest allies; and they do so in a public-private partnership that matches Federal investment.

I urge Members to support H.R. 5843.

I reserve the balance of my time.

Mr. RATCLIFFE. Mr. Speaker, I thank Congressman LANGEVIN for his kind words. I would also like to congratulate him on his hard work and his leadership in bringing this bill to the floor today.

I reserve the balance of my time.

Mr. LANGEVIN. Mr. Speaker, I yield myself such time as I may consume.

This bill is about innovation. It is a bill about bringing together the best minds in the U.S. and in Israel to help manage what has become an intractable problem. It is a bill that is sorely needed.

In the past year, just by way of example, we have seen the first cyber attack on a power grid in Ukraine. Many devices that are part of the Internet of Things have been compromised and used to attack Web sites and services.

Most disturbingly, the very foundation of our democracy, our voting system, has been targeted in a Russian information warfare campaign that leverages hacked documents. These are the national and Homeland Security threats that keep me up at night, and they are also the same types of threats that motivate the Israel National Cyber Bureau.

Working together, I believe that we can make meaningful progress to reduce the nation-state specific risk both countries face and better secure the entire Internet ecosystem.

I hope my colleagues in the Senate will move quickly to take up this issue. I would like to particularly thank my dear friend and home State colleague, Senator SHELDON WHITEHOUSE, for his efforts in this regard. He has been the leader in so many ways on the Senate side on cybersecurity, among other things, and has been an invaluable partner to me in this effort.

Again, let me thank Representative RATCLIFFE for his work on this bill and his leadership on the committee.

I urge my colleagues to support this bill.

I yield back the balance of my time.

Mr. RATCLIFFE. Mr. Speaker, I thank Congressman LANGEVIN, and I urge my colleagues to support his bill, H.R. 5843.

I yield back the balance of my time.

The SPEAKER pro tempore. The question is on the motion offered by the gentleman from Texas (Mr. RATCLIFFE) that the House suspend the rules and pass the bill, H.R. 5843, as amended.

The question was taken.

The SPEAKER pro tempore. In the opinion of the Chair, two-thirds being in the affirmative, the ayes have it.

Mr. RATCLIFFE. Mr. Speaker, I object to the vote on the ground that a quorum is not present and make the point of order that a quorum is not present.

The SPEAKER pro tempore. Pursuant to clause 8 of rule XX, further proceedings on this question will be postponed.

The point of no quorum is considered withdrawn.

───────

EXPANSION OF ELIGIBILITY FOR HEADSTONES, MARKERS, AND MEDALLIONS FOR MEDAL OF HONOR RECIPIENTS

Mr. MILLER of Florida. Mr. Speaker, I move to suspend the rules and pass

the bill (H.R. 4757) to amend title 38, United States Code, to expand the eligibility for headstones, markers, and medallions furnished by the Secretary of Veterans Affairs for deceased individuals who were awarded the Medal of Honor and are buried in private cemeteries, as amended.

The Clerk read the title of the bill.

The text of the bill is as follows:

H.R. 4757

Be it enacted by the Senate and House of Representatives of the United States of America in Congress assembled,

SECTION 1. EXPANSION OF ELIGIBILITY FOR HEADSTONES, MARKERS, AND MEDALLIONS FOR MEDAL OF HONOR RECIPIENTS.

Section 2306(d) of title 38, United States Code, is amended by adding at the end the following new paragraph:

"(5)(A) In carrying out this subsection with respect to a deceased individual described in subparagraph (C), the Secretary shall furnish, upon request, a headstone or marker under paragraph (1) or a medallion under paragraph (4) that signifies the deceased's status as a Medal of Honor recipient.

"(B) If the Secretary furnished a headstone, marker, or medallion under paragraph (1) or (4) for a deceased individual described in subparagraph (C) that does not signify the deceased's status as a Medal of Honor recipient, the Secretary shall, upon request, replace such headstone, marker, or medallion with a headstone, marker, or medallion, as the case may be, that so signifies the deceased's status as a Medal of Honor recipient.

"(C) A deceased individual described in this subparagraph is a deceased individual who—

"(i) served in the Armed Forces on or after April 6, 1917;

"(ii) is eligible for a headstone or marker furnished under paragraph (1) or a medallion furnished under paragraph (4) (or would be so eligible for such headstone, marker, or medallion but for the date of the death of the individual); and

"(iii) was awarded the Medal of Honor (including posthumously).".

SEC. 2. EXPANSION OF PRESIDENTIAL MEMORIAL CERTIFICATE PROGRAM.

(a) IN GENERAL.—Section 112(a) of title 38, United States Code, is amended by striking "veterans," and all that follows through "service," and inserting the following: "persons eligible for burial in a national cemetery by reason of any of paragraphs (1), (2), (3), or (7) of section 2402(a) of this title,".

(b) APPLICATION.—The amendment made by subsection (a) shall apply with respect to the death of a person eligible for burial in a national cemetery by reason of paragraph (1), (2), (3), or (7) of section 2402(a) of title 38, United States Code, occurring before, on, or after the date of the enactment of this Act.

The SPEAKER pro tempore. Pursuant to the rule, the gentleman from Florida (Mr. MILLER) and the gentleman from California (Mr. TAKANO) each will control 20 minutes.

The Chair recognizes the gentleman from Florida.

GENERAL LEAVE

Mr. MILLER of Florida. Mr. Speaker, I ask unanimous consent that all Members have 5 legislative days to revise and extend their remarks and to in-

clude any extraneous material on H.R. 4757, as amended.

The SPEAKER pro tempore. Is there objection to the request of the gentleman from Florida?

There was no objection.

Mr. MILLER of Florida. Mr. Speaker, I yield myself such time as I may consume.

Mr. Speaker, I rise to urge all of our colleagues to support H.R. 4757, as amended. This bill would expand two different honors for our Nation's heroes, guaranteeing that their service would never be forgotten.

First, the bill would expand eligibility for a Presidential Memorial Certificate to members of the National Guard or Reserve. Mr. Speaker, Presidential Memorial Certificates are engraved certificates that are signed by the President and sent to a deceased servicemember's family, honoring their loved one's service and sacrifice to our country. My bill would ensure that all service is recognized and cherished because all servicemembers take the exact same oath to support and to defend the Constitution of the United States.

Second, H.R. 4757, as amended, would allow the VA to furnish a headstone, marker, or medallion signifying that the deceased was awarded the Medal of Honor. We all know that veterans who were awarded the Medal of Honor, the highest award for valor, deserve to have their service recognized both in life and after they pass. This bill would make it easier for visitors at any cemetery to pay their respects to Medal of Honor recipients by allowing them to quickly identify our national heroes.

Moreover, these headstones, markers, or medallions will also continue to inspire the next generation of Americans who will be serving our country. I hope that in 100, 200, or even 1,000 years from now future Americans will still take the time to find the graves of these incredibly brave men and women and give thanks that they are living in the greatest Nation in the history of this world. This legislation would help us fulfill our duty as a nation to encourage continued respect and admiration for those that have gone on before us.

I urge all my colleagues to support H.R. 4757, as amended.

I reserve the balance of my time.

Mr. TAKANO. Mr. Speaker, I yield myself such time as I may consume.

I rise to offer my unqualified support for H.R. 4757, Chairman MILLER's bill that updates current law to ensure our Nation's heroes are accorded the recognition they deserve, particularly those afforded the Nation's highest honor for valor, the Medal of Honor.

First, H.R. 4757 directs the VA to provide, upon request, a distinctive headstone, marker, or medallion to Medal of Honor recipients who are buried in private cemeteries. This bill is necessary because current law actually prohibits the Secretary from furnishing these honors to recipients not buried in national cemeteries.

Second, while the VA sends a Presidential Memorial Certificate that expresses the Nation's recognition and gratitude of military service to family members of a deceased veteran, current law limits Presidential Memorial Certificates to the families of those who served in regular armed services or National Guard and Reserve members who were called to Active Duty. H.R. 4757 very rightly expands eligibility for a Presidential Memorial Certificate to members of the Reserve component of the Armed Forces and the Army National Guard or the Air National Guard eligible for interment or inurnment in national cemeteries.

Finally, current law only allows VA to pay for the cost of transporting the remains of a deceased veteran to the nearest open national cemetery. If it is the family's choice instead to be buried in a State or tribal veteran's cemetery, H.R. 4757 authorizes VA to pay the costs associated with transporting the remains of an eligible deceased veteran to that cemetery nearest to the deceased veteran's last residence.

Mr. Speaker, honoring the memory of deceased veterans is our greatest responsibility at the Committee on Veterans' Affairs, and I am pleased to support Chairman MILLER's legislation which refines and improves on the ways we are doing that. I encourage my colleagues to support this important legislation and join me in passing H.R. 4757, as amended.

I yield back the balance of my time.

Mr. MILLER of Florida. Mr. Speaker, I, too, urge all my colleagues to support H.R. 4757, as amended.

I yield back the balance of my time.

The SPEAKER pro tempore. The question is on the motion offered by the gentleman from Florida (Mr. MILLER) that the House suspend the rules and pass the bill, H.R. 4757, as amended.

The question was taken.

The SPEAKER pro tempore. In the opinion of the Chair, two-thirds being in the affirmative, the ayes have it.

Mr. MILLER of Florida. Mr. Speaker, on that I demand the yeas and nays.

The yeas and nays were ordered.

The SPEAKER pro tempore. Pursuant to clause 8 of rule XX, further proceedings on this motion will be postponed.

PROTECTING VETERANS' EDUCATIONAL CHOICE ACT OF 2016

Mr. MILLER of Florida. Mr. Speaker, I move to suspend the rules and pass the bill (H.R. 5047) to direct the Secretary of Veterans Affairs and the Secretary of Labor to provide information to veterans and members of the Armed Forces about articulation agreements between institutions of higher learning, and for other purposes.

The Clerk read the title of the bill.

The text of the bill is as follows:

H.R. 5047

Be it enacted by the Senate and House of Representatives of the United States of America in Congress assembled,

SECTION 1. SHORT TITLE.

This Act may be cited as the "Protecting Veterans' Educational Choice Act of 2016".

SEC. 2. DEPARTMENT OF VETERANS AFFAIRS PROVISION OF INFORMATION ON ARTICULATION AGREEMENTS BETWEEN INSTITUTIONS OF HIGHER LEARNING.

(a) INFORMATION.—Department of Veterans Affairs counselors who provide educational or vocational counseling services pursuant to section 3697A of title 38, United States Code, shall provide to any eligible individual who requests such counseling services information about the articulation agreements of each institution of higher learning in which the veteran is interested.

(b) CERTIFICATION OF ELIGIBILITY.—When the Secretary of Veterans Affairs provides to a veteran a certification of eligibility for educational assistance provided by the Department of Veterans Affairs, the Secretary shall also include detailed information on such educational assistance, including information on requesting education counseling services and on articulation agreements.

(c) DEFINITIONS.—In this section:

(1) The term "institution of higher learning" has the meaning given such term in section 3452(f) of title 38, United States Code.

(2) The term "articulation agreement" has the meaning given such term in section 486A of the Higher Education Act of 1965 (Public Law 89–329; 20 U.S.C. 1093a).

(d) DEADLINE FOR IMPLEMENTATION.—The Secretary of Veterans Affairs shall implement this section not later than 90 days after the date of the enactment of this Act.

The SPEAKER pro tempore. Pursuant to the rule, the gentleman from Florida (Mr. MILLER) and the gentleman from California (Mr. TAKANO) each will control 20 minutes.

The Chair recognizes the gentleman from Florida.

GENERAL LEAVE

Mr. MILLER of Florida. Mr. Speaker, I ask unanimous consent that all Members have 5 legislative days to revise and extend their remarks and to include any extraneous material and other items to H.R. 5047.

The SPEAKER pro tempore. Is there objection to the request of the gentleman from Florida?

There was no objection.

Mr. MILLER of Florida. Mr. Speaker, I yield myself such time as I may consume.

Mr. Speaker, H.R. 5047, the Protecting Veterans' Educational Choice Act of 2016, would further protect student veterans by requiring that, when the Department of Veterans Affairs provides educational counseling or a certificate of eligibility to veterans or servicemembers who are eligible for VA education benefits, the Department also provide information on articulation agreements at institutions of higher learning.

☐ 1645

The Post-9/11 GI Bill has benefitted more than 1.5 million servicemembers,

veterans, and their dependents since its inception in 2009. While many of these beneficiaries complete their entire program of education at one school, we often see individuals who transfer to another school in the middle of their program due to a plethora of circumstances. If they do transfer schools, their previously earned credits can play a large role in determining the length of time it may take for students to complete their program at the new school that they have chosen to go to, and in some cases not all earned credits will transfer. Often, the transferability of certain credits between different institutions of higher learning is not always on an individual's radar when they apply for a certain school or a certain program, and a veteran may or may not have understood how credits transfer when they first initiated their education career.

H.R. 5047 would simply provide our student veterans with additional information as they apply to and attend schools by requiring VA to provide information on articulation agreements at a particular school and that school's agreements with another institution. Our veterans and their dependents deserve full transparency as they set out to use their hard-earned benefits. I thank my colleague, the gentleman from Georgia (Mr. JODY B. HICE) for introducing this bipartisan legislation which has my complete support.

Mr. Speaker, I reserve the balance of my time.

Mr. TAKANO. Mr. Speaker, I yield myself such time as I may consume.

Mr. Speaker, I rise in support of H.R. 5047, the Protecting Veterans' Educational Choice Act of 2016. I thank the gentleman from Georgia (Mr. JODY B. HICE) for introducing this commendable legislation.

This bill would require the VA to include information about the educational services available to all veterans seeking to use their Post-9/11 GI Bill benefits, and it would require VA counselors who provide educational or vocational counseling to inform the veterans about the articulation agreements that exist between schools that govern the transfer of credits. Articulation agreements refer to formal agreements between two or more institutions of higher learning, documenting the credit transfer policies for a specific academic program.

Student veterans have an important decision to make when they choose a college or university to attend with their Post-9/11 GI Bill benefits. It is essential that they understand at the outset whether they could transfer their credits to another college or university down the line.

We have seen too many examples of student veterans depleting their limited GI Bill benefits to attend for-profit colleges, only to find out later that their opportunities to transfer to schools without losing time, money, and credit hours are severely limited.

Ensuring that student veterans know in advance whether a school will give them credit for completed courses if they choose to transfer will help veterans avoid choosing schools where their credits will not transfer, thus saving them both time and their hard-earned Post-9/11 GI Bill benefits.

I thank Representative HICE for introducing this important piece of legislation, which I am proud to cosponsor and support.

Mr. Speaker, I reserve the balance of my time.

Mr. MILLER of Florida. Mr. Speaker, I yield 3 minutes to the gentleman from the 10th District of Georgia (Mr. JODY B. HICE), the sponsor of this particular piece of legislation, the gentleman from the great community of Monroe.

Mr. JODY B. HICE of Georgia. Mr. Speaker, obviously I rise in strong support of this bill, H.R. 5047, the Protecting Veterans' Educational Choice Act of 2016.

Let me just extend a very sincere and heartfelt thank you to Chairman MILLER and Ranking Member TAKANO—who, by the way, is an original cosponsor of this bill—for their support of this bill and overall wide support for this bill. I appreciate the comments that both of my colleagues have made pertaining to this bill.

The Post-9/11 GI Bill, I believe without question, is the most generous educational benefit that our Nation has ever passed. As has already been mentioned, over a million student veterans have benefited tremendously from that particular piece of legislation. Some of the benefits include help to cover cost of tuition, books, supplies, even housing. Yet, in spite of all this, we still find that many of our veterans find themselves still having to take out student loans. Part of the reason for that is, as has been discussed by my colleagues, many of these veterans, as they are going to various schools somewhere in the midst of the process, discover that the credits that they have received from this school won't transfer over here; and somewhere in the middle of that timeframe, much of their GI Bill has already been spent, and so they find themselves in an extremely difficult and awkward position.

I won't reiterate the details of this bill because it has already been done, but the basics of this addresses that problem, Mr. Speaker. It does not have anything to say regarding what school a veteran chooses. They are free to go to whatever school they want to, but what this bill says is up front they need to be aware of whether or not their credits will transfer to another school. They don't need to find that out on the back end. They need to be fully informed on the front end as they

are making these career and educational choices.

I think it is a shame for many of our veterans to feel that they have misused their GI benefits because they weren't informed enough from the beginning of this process. It is incumbent upon Congress, I believe, to ensure that our veterans have as much information as they need at the front end of their educational choices that will best benefit them and their families.

Again, I strongly thank the chairman and the ranking member for their support. I believe this bill is going to go a long way in addressing this problem. I urge my colleagues to support H.R. 5047.

Mr. TAKANO. Mr. Speaker, I strongly support this legislation. I have no other speakers. I urge my colleagues to vote "yes" on H.R. 5047.

I yield back the balance of my time.

Mr. MILLER of Florida. Mr. Speaker, I, too, would encourage all Members to support H.R. 5047.

I yield back the balance of my time.

Mr. VAN HOLLEN. Mr. Speaker, I submit this statement in support of H.R. 5047, the Protecting Veterans' Educational Choice Act of 2016. I will be unable to submit my recorded vote but I fully support this legislation that ensures that veterans will not be unwittingly exploited by deceptive recruiters.

H.R. 5047 is a bipartisan bill that reinforces our commitment to the success of our service members, on and off the battlefield. The bill requires the Department of Veterans Affairs to supply all information regarding articulation agreements to service members who wish to use their VA education benefits. The bill will inform service members, in advance, if and how they can transfer credits and avoid unwittingly misusing their VA education benefits.

In 2010, Congress passed the Post-9/11 Veterans Education Assistance Improvements Act which expanded educational benefits to include more service members and allows them to use their benefits to receive not only traditional degrees but also apprenticeships, vocational training certifications, and on-the-job training. This expansion was vital in providing access to a variety of educational platforms but some for-profit institutions focused on recruiting and scamming service members out of their benefits. H.R. 5047 provides education career counseling to make sure service members are informed of their options.

The SPEAKER pro tempore. The question is on the motion offered by the gentleman from Florida (Mr. MILLER) that the House suspend the rules and pass the bill, H.R. 5047.

The question was taken.

The SPEAKER pro tempore. In the opinion of the Chair, two-thirds being in the affirmative, the ayes have it.

Mr. MILLER of Florida. Mr. Speaker, on that I demand the yeas and nays.

The yeas and nays were ordered.

The SPEAKER pro tempore. Pursuant to clause 8 of rule XX, further proceedings on this motion will be postponed.

WORKING TO INTEGRATE NETWORKS GUARANTEEING MEMBER ACCESS NOW ACT

Mr. MILLER of Florida. Mr. Speaker, I move to suspend the rules and pass the bill (H.R. 5166) to amend title 38, United States Code, to provide certain employees of Members of Congress and certain employees of State or local governmental agencies with access to case-tracking information of the Department of Veterans Affairs, as amended.

The Clerk read the title of the bill.

The text of the bill is as follows:

H.R. 5166

Be it enacted by the Senate and House of Representatives of the United States of America in Congress assembled,

SECTION 1. SHORT TITLE.

This Act may be cited as the "Working to Integrate Networks Guaranteeing Member Access Now Act" or the "WINGMAN Act".

SEC. 2. PROVISION OF ACCESS TO CASE-TRACKING INFORMATION.

(a) IN GENERAL.—Chapter 59 of title 38, United States Code, is amended by adding at the end the following:

"§ 5906. Access of certain congressional employees to veteran records

"(a) IN GENERAL.—(1) The Secretary shall provide to each veteran who submits a claim for benefits under the laws administered by the Secretary an opportunity to permit a covered congressional employee employed in the office of the Member of Congress representing the district where the veteran resides to have access to all of the records of the veteran in the databases of the Veterans Benefits Administration.

"(2) Notwithstanding any other provision of law, upon receipt of permission from the veteran under paragraph (1), the Secretary shall provide read-only access to such records to such a covered congressional employee in a manner that does not allow such employee to modify the data contained in such records or in any part of a database of the Veterans Benefits Administration.

"(3) A Member of Congress may designate not more than two employees of the Member as covered congressional employees.

"(b) COVERED CONGRESSIONAL EMPLOYEES.—(1) In this section, a covered congressional employee is a permanent, full-time employee of a Member of Congress—

"(A) whose responsibilities include assisting the constituents of the Member with issues regarding departments or agencies of the Federal Government;

"(B) who satisfies the criteria required by the Secretary for recognition as an agent or attorney under this chapter; and

"(C) who is designated by a Member of Congress as a covered congressional employee for purposes of this section.

"(2) The Secretary may not impose any requirement other than the requirements under paragraph (1) before treating an employee as a covered congressional employee for purposes of this section.

"(c) NONRECOGNITION.—A covered congressional employee may not be recognized as an agent or attorney under this chapter.

"(d) LIMITATION ON USE OF FUNDS.—None of the amounts made available to carry out this section may be used to design, develop, or administer any training for purposes of providing training to covered congressional employees.

"(e) AUTHORIZATION OF APPROPRIATIONS.—(1) No additional funds are authorized to be appropriated to carry out this section. This section may only be carried out using amounts otherwise authorized to be appropriated.

"(2) For the period of fiscal years 2017 through 2020, not more than $10,000,000 may be made available to carry out this section.

"(f) DEFINITIONS.—In this section:

"(1) The term 'database of the Veterans Benefits Administration' means any database of the Veterans Benefits Administration in which the records of veterans relating to claims for benefits under the laws administered by the Secretary are retained, including information regarding medical records, compensation and pension exams records, rating decisions, statements of the case, supplementary statements of the case, notices of disagreement, Form–9, and any successor form.

"(2) The term 'Member of Congress' means a Representative, a Senator, a Delegate to Congress, or the Resident Commissioner of Puerto Rico.".

(b) CLERICAL AMENDMENT.—The table of sections at the beginning of such chapter is amended by adding at the end the following new item:

"5906. Access of certain congressional employees to veteran records.".

The SPEAKER pro tempore. Pursuant to the rule, the gentleman from Florida (Mr. MILLER) and the gentleman from California (Mr. TAKANO) each will control 20 minutes.

The Chair recognizes the gentleman from Florida.

GENERAL LEAVE

Mr. MILLER of Florida. Mr. Speaker, I ask unanimous consent that all Members may have 5 legislative days within which to revise and extend their remarks and add extraneous material on H.R. 5166, as amended.

The SPEAKER pro tempore. Is there objection to the request of the gentleman from Florida?

There was no objection.

Mr. MILLER of Florida. Mr. Speaker, I yield myself such time as I may consume.

Mr. Speaker, I rise today to urge all of my colleagues to support H.R. 5166, as amended, the WINGMAN Act. I thank our colleagues, the gentleman from Florida (Mr. YOHO) and the gentleman from Illinois (Mr. RODNEY DAVIS), for introducing the WINGMAN Act, which will help Members better serve our constituents.

H.R. 5166 would allow our offices to assist veterans who are seeking information about the status of their claims for disability compensation. Unfortunately, when a congressional staff member contacts the VA for more information about a claim, it can take often weeks or months for the Department of Veterans Affairs to respond. VA's delay in answering congressional inquiries only adds to the veteran's frustration. The veteran simply wants to know the status of his or her claim.

H.R. 5166, as amended, would require VA to give designated permanent, full-time congressional employees access to VA databases so that our staff can tell a veteran the current status of their application for benefits. Moreover, to protect veterans' privacy, the WINGMAN Act mandates that congressional employees first obtain permission before viewing a veteran's information. At the same time, the congressional employee would not be able to alter the electronic file in any way.

Passing this bill will help veterans who simply want to understand where their claim is in the process. I urge my colleagues to support H.R. 5166, as amended.

Mr. Speaker, I reserve the balance of my time.

Mr. TAKANO. Mr. Speaker, I yield myself such time as I may consume.

I rise in support of H.R. 5166, sponsored by Representative YOHO, which would give certified congressional office caseworkers access to veterans' electronic disability claims records at the Veterans Benefits Administration.

The purpose of the bill is to provide faster answers to our veteran constituents who call our offices to help with their VA claims. By the time veterans contact us, many have already faced delays or frustrating experiences trying to get answers themselves. This bill will allow our congressional caseworkers read-only access to disability claims records. This means they will not be able to add or remove anything from a veteran's record.

The bill also includes privacy safeguards, which reinforce the necessity for getting prior consent from a veteran before a caseworker can access a veteran's files. Additionally, the bill requires that congressional employees certified for this access must be full-time employees who provide constituent services.

I am hopeful that as this program is developed, VA will put in place a tracking system to ensure these employees are only assisting constituents from their congressional districts and that congressional staff are held accountable if found to have abused any aspect of this new and unprecedented authority.

In short, Mr. Speaker, there is broad, bipartisan support among our colleagues for helping veterans get timely answers to their claims questions. Allowing full-time congressional staff members access to electronic disability claims records on a read-only basis is a step in the direction of putting the veteran's interest first and foremost.

I support H.R. 5166, as amended, and urge my colleagues to do the same.

Mr. Speaker, I reserve the balance of my time.

Mr. MILLER of Florida. Mr. Speaker, I yield 3 minutes to the gentleman from the Third District of the State of Florida (Mr. YOHO), a primary sponsor of this legislation.

Mr. YOHO. Mr. Speaker, I thank Chairman MILLER, a fellow Floridian, for his support of this measure. Without his help and the help of his team—

Maria and Cecilia in particular—we would not be here today.

This is a monumental bill for our veterans. This comes down to customer service for our veterans. I feel we are in the customer service business. They are not constituents. These are people who have paid the price to defend this country, and it is time that we give them the service that they need.

What this does is it gives us read-only access to a veteran's claim. We have already got a privacy form. We are on a secure system, and this just moves the claim through the process that much quicker so that we can find out why it is hung up. So many times, as the chairman said, the average time it takes for an office to receive the records they request from the VA is 6 months, and at times even over a year. What this will do is, we can look into there, we can read only that particular case, and we can say, You forgot to sign it, you forgot to date it, you forgot to check this box; and we can report immediately back to the veteran. It should free up the VA system.

No single man or woman who has served and protected our freedoms should have to wait to receive the care and benefits that they have more than earned. Unfortunately, they have become statistics, nothing more than numbers on the page, so many times with the VA system. This ends with the passage of the WINGMAN bill. The WINGMAN removes the middleman and allows the staff to access these records directly without waiting on the VA.

Mr. Speaker, I urge all of my colleagues in the House to support this measure and be a good wingman and let our Nation's veterans know that we have their six. Again, I thank the gentleman from Illinois (Mr. RODNEY DAVIS) for his help on this strong bipartisan bill.

□ 1700

Mr. MILLER of Florida. Mr. Speaker, I yield 1 minute to the gentleman from Georgia (Mr. COLLINS).

Mr. COLLINS of Georgia. Mr. Speaker, I come to the floor as a veteran who is currently still serving in the United States Air Force Reserve. I served in Iraq. What Mr. YOHO and Mr. DAVIS have done here is come together to bring common sense to something that really is amazing: we have veterans today who have to call their Congressman to get help, and we are actually hamstrung in trying to help them.

That is not the way it should be. Our veterans deserve the best service that they can have. They deserve it on time, they deserve it in a prompt fashion, and they should not have to call their Congressman. But when they do, we need to give our congressional offices all the tools that they need to help with that.

I just want to compliment these Congressmen for bringing this bill forward and encourage the House to support this. This is a great bill, and it is really the reason why we are here.

Mr. MILLER of Florida. Mr. Speaker, I yield 3 minutes to the gentleman from Illinois (Mr. RODNEY DAVIS), another prime sponsor of this bill, who is from the 13th Congressional District.

Mr. RODNEY DAVIS of Illinois. Mr. Speaker, I want to talk about Carl, an Army veteran from Springfield, Illinois, who couldn't get a response from the VA to receive cancer treatment through the VA Choice program. After multiple communications, my office was finally able to get the authorization from the VA.

Bette, from Staunton, Illinois, the wife of a decorated Vietnam vet who served his country for more than a decade, waited over a year for an answer from the VA about benefits owed to her late husband. Finally, my office was successful in getting Bette, who was experiencing financial difficulty at the time, the accrued benefits owed to her husband.

Kenneth, of Urbana, Illinois, a Bronze Star recipient while serving in Kuwait, Iraq, and Afghanistan, was denied benefits due to a missing doctor's examination because he was deployed at the time and the VA never rescheduled the appointment. He contacted my office, and we worked with the VA to ensure that the benefits were received.

Lawrence, of Palmer, Illinois, another Bronze Star and Purple Heart recipient, simply wanted a copy of his medical records but never heard back from the VA. After several months, he reached out to our office and we were able to get them from the VA.

Another constituent of mine recently asked my office for help after her husband, who was a veteran, passed away. She has been waiting for 6 months for an answer from the VA, and now my office continues to wait for a response from the VA.

These examples not only show the sometimes incompetence and unresponsiveness of certain personnel at the VA, but they also show how important congressional offices are to getting the answers our veterans need and deserve.

Many times when a veteran contacts their Member of Congress for help, it is their last resort. It is not their first call. They don't know where else to turn. Our caseworkers become the middleman between the veteran and the VA.

VA casework in my office remains highest in volume. We currently have over 96 open cases, and we have closed nearly 1,000 in the 4 years that I have been in office. Ask almost any caseworker, and they will tell you the VA is one of the most difficult agencies to get a response from.

It is unacceptable that it takes this long. That is why the WINGMAN Act, H.R. 5166, needs to be passed. It simply allows our certified constituent caseworkers, our advocates, to access certain VA files in order to check the status and progress of claims. This technology will be used to help our veterans get the answers they deserve. It is not going to solve the systemic problems we see at the VA, but it is going to help us hold the VA accountable and get answers for veterans whom we are honored to represent.

I want to thank my colleague, Representative YOHO, for working with me and many others on this important piece of legislation; and, Mr. Speaker, I want to thank Chairman MILLER not only for his help on this, but for his service to this great institution. He is somebody who has put our veterans first as chairman of the Veterans' Affairs Committee and somebody who has spent his career making sure that commonsense proposals like this get enacted so that our veterans, those whom he cares about the most and we care about the most, get the answers and the responses they deserve.

Mr. TAKANO. Mr. Speaker, I ask my colleagues to join me in supporting H.R. 5166, as amended.

Mr. Speaker, I yield back the balance of my time.

Mr. MILLER of Florida. Mr. Speaker, I urge all of my colleagues to support H.R. 5166, as amended.

Mr. Speaker, I yield back the balance of my time.

The SPEAKER pro tempore. The question is on the motion offered by the gentleman from Florida (Mr. MILLER) that the House suspend the rules and pass the bill, H.R. 5166, as amended.

The question was taken; and (two-thirds being in the affirmative) the rules were suspended and the bill, as amended, was passed.

The title of the bill was amended so as to read: "A bill amend title 38, United States Code, to permit veterans to grant access to their records in the databases of the Veterans Benefits Administration to certain designated congressional employees, and for other purposes.".

A motion to reconsider was laid on the table.

───────────

HONORING INVESTMENTS IN RECRUITING AND EMPLOYING AMERICAN MILITARY VETERANS ACT OF 2016

Mr. MILLER of Florida. Mr. Speaker, I move to suspend the rules and pass the bill (H.R. 3286) to encourage effective, voluntary private sector investments to recruit, employ, and retain men and women who have served in the United States military with annual presidential awards to private sector employers recognizing such efforts, and for other purposes, as amended.

The Clerk read the title of the bill.

The text of the bill is as follows:

H.R. 3286

Be it enacted by the Senate and House of Representatives of the United States of America in Congress assembled,

SECTION 1. SHORT TITLE.

This Act may be cited as the "Honoring Investments in Recruiting and Employing American Military Veterans Act of 2016" or the "HIRE Vets Act".

SEC. 2. HIRE VETS MEDALLION PROGRAM.

(a) PROGRAM ESTABLISHED.—Not later than one year after the date of enactment of this Act, the Secretary of Labor shall establish, by rule, a HIRE Vets Medallion Program to solicit voluntary information from employers for purposes of recognizing, by means of an award to be designated a "HIRE Vets Medallion", verified efforts by such employers—

(1) to recruit, employ, and retain veterans; and

(2) to provide community and charitable services supporting the veteran community.

(b) APPLICATION PROCESS.—Beginning in the calendar year following the calendar year in which the Secretary establishes the program—

(1) the Secretary shall annually—

(A) solicit and accept voluntary applications from employers in order to consider whether those employers should receive a HIRE Vets Medallion;

(B) review applications received in each calendar year; and

(C) provide to the President a list of recipients; and

(2) the President shall annually—

(A) notify such recipients of their awards; and

(B) at a time to coincide with the annual commemoration of Veterans Day—

(i) announce the names of such recipients;

(ii) recognize such recipients through publication in the Federal Register; and

(iii) issue to each such recipient—

(I) a HIRE Vets Medallion of the level determined under section 3; and

(II) a certificate stating that such employer is entitled to display such HIRE Vets Medallion during the following calendar year, to be designated a "HIRE Vets Medallion Certificate".

(c) TIMING.—

(1) SOLICITATION PERIOD.—The Secretary shall solicit applications not later than January 31st of each calendar year for the medallions to be awarded in November of that calendar year.

(2) END OF ACCEPTANCE PERIOD.—The Secretary shall stop accepting applications not earlier than April 30th of each calendar year for the medallions to be awarded in November of that calendar year.

(3) REVIEW PERIOD.—The Secretary shall finish reviewing applications not later than August 31st of each calendar year for the medallions to be awarded in November of that calendar year.

(4) RECOMMENDATIONS TO PRESIDENT.—The Secretary shall provide to the President a list of employers to receive HIRE Vets Medallions not later than September 30th of each calendar year for the medallions to be awarded in November of that calendar year.

(5) NOTICE TO RECIPIENTS.—The President shall notify employers who will receive HIRE Vets Medallions not later than October 11th of each calendar year for the medallions to be awarded in November of that calendar year.

SEC. 3. SELECTION OF RECIPIENTS.

(a) APPLICATION REVIEW PROCESS.—

(1) IN GENERAL.—The Secretary shall review all applications received in a calendar

year to determine whether an employer should receive a HIRE Vets Medallion, and, if so, of what level.

(2) APPLICATION CONTENTS.—The Secretary shall require that all applications provide information on the programs and other efforts of applicant employers during the calendar year prior to that in which the medallion is to be awarded, including the categories and activities governing the level of award for which the applicant is eligible under subsection (b).

(3) VERIFICATION.—In reviewing applications, the Secretary shall verify all information provided in the applications, to the extent that such information is relevant in determining whether or not an applicant should receive a HIRE Vets Medallion or in determining the appropriate level of HIRE Vets Medallion for that employer to receive.

(b) AWARDS.—

(1) LARGE EMPLOYERS.—

(A) IN GENERAL.—The Secretary shall establish two levels of HIRE Vets Medallions to be awarded to employers employing 500 or more employees, to be designated the "Gold HIRE Vets Medallion" and the "Platinum HIRE Vets Medallion".

(B) GOLD HIRE VETS MEDALLION.—No employer shall be eligible to receive a Gold HIRE Vets Medallion in a given calendar year unless—

(i) veterans constitute not less than 7 percent of all employees hired by such employer during the prior calendar year;

(ii) such employer has established an employee veteran organization or resource group to assist new veteran employees with integration, including coaching and mentoring; and

(iii) such employer has established programs to enhance the leadership skills of veteran employees during their employment.

(C) PLATINUM HIRE VETS MEDALLION.—No employer shall be eligible to receive a Platinum HIRE Vets Medallion in a given calendar year unless—

(i) veterans constitute not less than 10 percent of all employees hired by such employer during the prior calendar year;

(ii) such employer retains through the end of the prior calendar year not less than 85 percent of veteran employees hired during the calendar year before the prior calendar year;

(iii) such employer employs dedicated human resources professionals to support hiring and retention of veteran employees, including efforts focused on veteran hiring and training;

(iv) such employer provides each of its employees serving on active duty in the United States National Guard or Reserve with compensation sufficient, in combination with the employee's active duty pay, to achieve a combined level of income commensurate with the employee's salary prior to undertaking active duty; and

(v) such employer has established a tuition assistance program to support veteran employees' attendance in postsecondary education during the term of their employment.

(D) EXEMPTION FOR SMALLER EMPLOYERS.—An employer shall be deemed to meet the requirements of subparagraph (C)(iv) if such employer—

(i) employs 5,000 or fewer employees; and

(ii) employs at least one human resources professional whose regular work duties include those described under subparagraph (C)(iii).

(E) ADDITIONAL CRITERIA.—The Secretary may provide, by rule, additional criteria with which to determine qualifications for receipt of each level of HIRE Vets Medallion.

(2) SMALL- AND MEDIUM-SIZED EMPLOYERS.—The Secretary shall establish similar awards in order to recognize achievements in supporting veterans by—

(A) employers with 50 or fewer employees; and

(B) employers with more than 50 but fewer than 500 employees.

(c) DESIGN BY SECRETARY.—The Secretary shall establish the shape, form, and metallic content of each HIRE Vets Medallion.

SEC. 4. DISPLAY OF AWARD.

(a) IN GENERAL.—The recipient of a HIRE Vets Medallion may—

(1) publicly display such medallion through the end of the calendar year following receipt of such medallion; and

(2) publicly display the HIRE Vets Medallion Certificate issued in conjunction with such medallion.

(b) UNLAWFUL DISPLAY PROHIBITED.—It is unlawful for any employer to publicly display a HIRE Vets Medallion, in connection with, or as a part of, any advertisement, solicitation, business activity, or product—

(1) for the purpose of conveying, or in a manner reasonably calculated to convey, a false impression that the employer received the medallion through the HIRE Vets Medallion Program, if such employer did not receive such medallion through the HIRE Vets Medallion Program; or

(2) for the purpose of conveying, or in a manner reasonably calculated to convey, a false impression that the employer received the medallion through the HIRE Vets Medallion Program during the preceding calendar year if it is after the end of the calendar year following the calendar year in which such medallion was issued to such employer through the HIRE Vets Medallion Program.

SEC. 5. APPLICATION FEE AND FUNDING.

(a) FUND ESTABLISHED.—There is established in the Treasury of the United States a fund to be designated the "HIRE Vets Medallion Award Fund".

(b) FEE AUTHORIZED.—The Secretary may assess a reasonable fee on employers that apply for receipt of a HIRE Vets Medallion and the Secretary shall deposit such fees into the HIRE Vets Medallion Award Fund. The Secretary shall establish the amount of the fee such that the amounts collected as fees and deposited into the Fund are sufficient to cover the costs associated with carrying out this Act.

(c) USE OF FUNDS.—Amounts in the HIRE Vets Medallion Award Fund shall be available, subject to appropriation, to the Secretary to carry out the HIRE Vets Medallion Program.

SEC. 6. REPORT TO CONGRESS.

(a) REPORTS.—Beginning not later than two years after the date of enactment of this Act, the Secretary shall submit to Congress annual reports on—

(1) the fees collected from applicants for HIRE Vets Medallions in the prior year and any changes in fees to be proposed in the present year;

(2) the cost of administering the HIRE Vets Medallion Program in the prior year;

(3) the number of applications for HIRE Vets Medallions received in the prior year; and

(4) the HIRE Vets Medallions awarded in the prior year, including the name of each employer to whom a HIRE Vets Medallion was awarded and the level of medallion awarded to each such employer.

(b) COMMITTEES.—The Secretary shall provide the reports required under subsection (a) to the Chairman and Ranking Member of—

(1) the Committees on Education and the Workforce and Veterans' Affairs of the House of Representatives; and

(2) the Committees on Health, Education, Labor, and Pensions and Veterans' Affairs of the Senate.

SEC. 7. DEFINITIONS.

In this Act:

(a) EMPLOYER.—The term "employer" has the meaning given such term under section 4303 of title 38, United States Code, except that such term does not include—

(1) the Federal Government;

(2) any State, as defined in such section; or

(3) any foreign state.

(b) SECRETARY.—The term "Secretary" means the Secretary of Labor.

(c) VETERAN.—The term "veteran" has the meaning given such term under section 101 of title 38, United States Code.

The SPEAKER pro tempore. Pursuant to the rule, the gentleman from Florida (Mr. MILLER) and the gentleman from California (Mr. TAKANO) each will control 20 minutes.

The Chair recognizes the gentleman from Florida.

GENERAL LEAVE

Mr. MILLER of Florida. Mr. Speaker, I ask unanimous consent that all Members may have 5 legislative days in which to revise and extend their remarks and include extraneous material on H.R. 3286, as amended.

The SPEAKER pro tempore. Is there objection to the request of the gentleman from Florida?

There was no objection.

Mr. MILLER of Florida. Mr. Speaker, I yield myself such time as I may consume.

Mr. Speaker, H.R. 3286, as amended, would require the Department of Labor to establish a HIRE Vets Medallion Program to recognize and to award employers with a HIRE Vets Medallion for their efforts to recruit, employ, and retain veterans, as well as their work to provide community and charitable services to veterans in their local communities.

While we still have work to do, it is important to note that the veteran unemployment rate has continued to decrease over recent years and, as of last month, it was at a low of 4.3 percent. While many factors have led to the continued reduction of the unemployment rate for the men and women who have served, our Nation's employers in both the public and the private sectors deserve a lot of the credit, and it is important that we highlight the work that these companies have done and publicly recognize their commitment for hiring veterans.

With this idea in mind, H.R. 3286, as amended, would authorize the Secretary of Labor to create the HIRE Vets Medallion Program, which would recognize employers who hire and retain veterans, as well as companies who provide support services to the veterans in their communities.

Employers would earn either platinum or gold status based on requirements related to the number of veterans hired each year, providing pay equity for guardsmen and Reserve employees who were called up to active military service, and other requirements. Once these employers have earned a HIRE Vets Medallion, they would be able to publicly display their award to illustrate the work they have done on behalf of veterans and the priority that they place on hiring veterans within their workforce.

As we work to continue to decrease the national unemployment rate among our men and women who have served, it is vital that we highlight and step up and thank the employers who have employed these individuals and recognize the benefits of hiring a veteran.

I want to thank Colonel PAUL COOK of California for introducing and advocating for this bill. It has my full and complete support.

Mr. Speaker, I reserve the balance of my time.

Mr. TAKANO. Mr. Speaker, I yield myself such time as I may consume.

Mr. Speaker, I rise in support of H.R. 3286, as amended, the Honoring Investments in Recruiting and Employing American Military Veterans Act of 2016, or the HIRE Vets Act. I thank my colleague and fellow Inland Empire and California Representative Colonel PAUL COOK for introducing this innovative bill.

The HIRE Vets Act directs the Department of Labor's Veterans' Employment and Training Services, otherwise known as DOL VETS, to establish a HIRE Vets Medallion Program. This program will solicit voluntary information from private sector employers who successfully recruit, employ, and retain veterans, and allow these employers to display on their marketing materials a recognized medallion as a symbol of their commendable hiring practices. Employers who provide community and charitable services supporting veterans will also be eligible to display a HIRE Vets Medallion.

Hiring veterans isn't just the right thing to do from a moral perspective; it also makes good business sense. The men and women who served in our military received invaluable training and experience that has been proven to help them thrive in postmilitary employment, whether in the public or private sectors.

Fortunately, we have been seeing encouraging trends in veterans' employment. Thanks to the hard work of DOL VETS, combined with efforts within the private sector and Federal and State governments, the veterans' unemployment rate in October was 4.3 percent. That is lower than the national unemployment rate, which was 4.9 percent. This continues a 24-month trend, with only a single exception.

We can all be very proud of the progress we have made in making sure more veterans are able to find quality, good-paying jobs upon transitioning

into civilian life. That said, we want to remain vigilant to make sure that the men and women who signed up to defend our Nation enjoy opportunities for growth and prosperity when they return home.

Again, I want to thank my colleague, Colonel COOK, for offering this legislation to provide a uniform, recognizable medallion to show our appreciation to companies that hire and retain veteran employees. I am proud to be a cosponsor of this bill and to stand in support of its passage today.

Mr. Speaker, I reserve the balance of my time.

Mr. MILLER of Florida. Mr. Speaker, I yield 3 minutes to the gentleman from California (Mr. COOK), the sponsor of this legislation, from the Eighth District of California.

Mr. COOK. Mr. Speaker, as a combat veteran, I am deeply concerned that the men and women of our Armed Forces continue to struggle to find jobs upon their return to civilian life. These individuals have not only displayed great courage serving their country, but have acquired distinctive skills that make them ideal candidates for employment.

Veterans who serve this country honorably should never struggle to find employment, which is why I have introduced H.R. 3286, the Honoring Investments in Recruiting and Employing American Military Veterans Act, the HIRE Vets Act.

As already mentioned, this bill creates an innovative system to encourage and recognize employers who make veterans a priority in their hiring practices, incentivizing the creation of thousands of jobs for veterans.

This bill goes beyond simply recognizing that a business hires veterans. It is critical that we establish a nationwide gold standard program that creates a strong and consistent brand. This bill is an opportunity for Americans to see which companies truly live up to the employment promises they made to veterans.

It is our duty to ensure veterans receive the benefits and resources they have earned through their services to this country, and that includes encouraging meaningful job opportunities.

I have been around a long while and, of course, have my own experiences from Vietnam, where a lot of veterans returned to their hometown and were shunned; they were ostracized, creating problems in terms of alcohol, drugs, you name it. A lot of it was related to the fact that they couldn't find a job or people didn't want to talk to them. This bill, I think, with the help of businesses, goes a long way to correct a problem we have had for many, many years.

This bill passed out of the House Veterans' Affairs Committee unanimously, and I want to thank Chairman MILLER and Ranking Member TAKANO for their

support. I would also like to thank Representative TULSI GABBARD for being the original cosponsor of this important legislation.

I urge my colleagues to vote in favor of this bill.

□ 1715

Mr. TAKANO. Mr. Speaker, I yield 3 minutes to the gentlewoman from Hawaii (Ms. GABBARD).

Ms. GABBARD. Mr. Speaker, I rise in strong support of H.R. 3286, a bill on which I am proud to have worked with my colleague and fellow veteran, the gentleman from California (Mr. COOK), whose service I honor very much.

Every single day, we have roughly 500 veterans who return to civilian life, joining the more than 2.9 million veterans who have returned home just since 9/11 alone. Now, some choose to take advantage of educational benefits they have earned, and others choose to jump right back into the workforce. Unfortunately, for many of our veterans, making that move is not as simple as submitting a resume and waiting for a call back.

Our veterans, unfortunately, often face sometimes an unfriendly job market or an unfriendly job culture that does not fully understand their needs and the unique challenges of transitioning from military servicemember life to civilian life.

Now, we have taken some important steps to encourage employers to hire more veterans, and we have seen the total percentage of unemployed veterans drop by 1.5 percent over the past year. While this is progress, the fact is, we still have over 400,000 veterans unemployed today. This tells us that more must be done, not only to get them employed but to make sure that they are employed in meaningful, good-paying jobs.

I recently hosted a panel of experts from both the public and private sector where we talked about how we can better empower our veterans in the tech sector specifically. The tech industry has experienced unprecedented growth over the past decade and is the fastest growing sector in our economy. Yet, so far, veterans remain largely underrepresented, making up just 2 percent of this fast-growing industry.

Now, it is not because they are not qualified. It is not because they don't have what it takes to do the job. Through their service and training, our highly trained men and women develop the ability to lead, make decisions under pressure, act as a member of a team and accomplish the mission. The bottom line is they get the job done. These skills make them especially valuable to employers, whether it be in the tech industry or in any other business, nonprofit, or civic leadership position.

That is why I am proud to join my fellow veteran and friend, Congressman

PAUL COOK, today in support of this important legislation because it incentivizes employers to hire and retain veterans by creating a standard of recognition for those who go the extra mile to recruit and retain veterans, and provide services that support our veteran community.

I strongly urge our colleagues to pass this legislation and help serve and empower our veterans and businesses to thrive.

Mr. MILLER of Florida. Mr. Speaker, I have no more requests for time at this point. I reserve the balance of my time.

Mr. TAKANO. Mr. Speaker, I have no further speakers. I yield myself such time as I may consume.

It just strikes me, Colonel COOK, I know we have named this act the HIRE Vets Act, and knowing of your service in Vietnam, and so many of the Vietnam veterans that live in the Inland Empire, we could also call this the Welcome Home Act because nothing is more welcoming than a job.

I share your passion for caring about our veterans in the Inland Empire, and in California, of course, all over our country, and I certainly honor your service to our country.

So I urge all my colleagues to support—to join me in passing H.R. 3286, and I look forward to seeing those medallions in many businesses across your district and mine in California.

Mr. Speaker, I yield back the balance of my time.

Mr. MILLER of Florida. Mr. Speaker, once again, I urge my colleagues to support H.R. 3286, as amended.

I yield back the balance of my time.

The SPEAKER pro tempore. The question is on the motion offered by the gentleman from Florida (Mr. MILLER) that the House suspend the rules and pass the bill, H.R. 3286, as amended.

The question was taken; and (two-thirds being in the affirmative) the rules were suspended and the bill, as amended, was passed.

A motion to reconsider was laid on the table.

NO HERO LEFT UNTREATED ACT

Mr. MILLER of Florida. Mr. Speaker, I move to suspend the rules and pass the bill (H.R. 5600) to direct the Secretary of Veterans Affairs to carry out a pilot program to provide access to magnetic EEG/EKG-guided resonance therapy to veterans, as amended.

The Clerk read the title of the bill.

The text of the bill is as follows:

H.R. 5600

Be it enacted by the Senate and House of Representatives of the United States of America in Congress assembled,

SECTION 1. SHORT TITLE.

This Act may be cited as the "No Hero Left Untreated Act".

SEC. 2. FINDINGS.

Congress finds the following:

(1) Magnetic EEG/EKG-guided resonance therapy has successfully treated more than 400 veterans with post-traumatic stress disorder, traumatic brain injury, military sexual trauma, chronic pain, and opiate addiction.

(2) Recent clinical trials and randomized, placebo-controlled, double-blind studies have produced promising measurable outcomes in the evolution of magnetic EEG/EKG-guided resonance therapy.

(3) These outcomes have resulted in escalating demand from returning warriors and veterans who are seeking access to this treatment.

(4) Congress recognizes the importance of initiating innovative pilot programs that demonstrate the use and effectiveness of new treatment options for post-traumatic stress disorder, traumatic brain injury, military sexual trauma, chronic pain, and opiate addiction.

SEC. 3. MAGNETIC EEG/EKG-GUIDED RESONANCE THERAPY PILOT PROGRAM.

(a) PILOT PROGRAM.—The Secretary of Veterans Affairs shall carry out a pilot program to provide access to magnetic EEG/EKG-guided resonance therapy to treat larger populations of veterans suffering from post-traumatic stress disorder, traumatic brain injury, military sexual trauma, chronic pain, or opiate addiction.

(b) LOCATIONS.—The Secretary shall carry out the pilot program under subsection (a) at not more than two facilities of the Department of Veteran Affairs.

(c) PARTICIPANTS.—In carrying out the pilot program under subsection (a), the Secretary may not provide access to magnetic EEG/EKG-guided resonance therapy to more than 50 veterans.

(d) DURATION.—The Secretary shall carry out the pilot program under subsection (a) for a one-year period.

(e) REPORT.—Not later than 90 days after the date of the termination of the pilot program under subsection (a), the Secretary shall submit to the Committees on Veterans' Affairs of the House of Representatives and the Senate a report on the pilot program.

(f) NO AUTHORIZATION OF APPROPRIATIONS.—No additional funds are authorized to be appropriated to carry out the requirements of this section. Such requirements shall be carried out using amounts otherwise authorized.

The SPEAKER pro tempore. Pursuant to the rule, the gentleman from Florida (Mr. MILLER) and the gentleman from California (Mr. TAKANO) each will control 20 minutes.

The Chair recognizes the gentleman from Florida.

GENERAL LEAVE

Mr. MILLER of Florida. Mr. Speaker, I ask unanimous consent that all Members have 5 legislative days within which to revise their remarks and add extraneous material.

The SPEAKER pro tempore. Is there objection to the request of the gentleman from Florida?

There was no objection.

Mr. MILLER of Florida. Mr. Speaker, I yield myself such time as I may consume.

I do rise today in support of H.R. 5600, as amended, the No Hero Left Untreated Act.

There is no greater priority we have as a grateful nation than to care for those who have been wounded in the service of our country and to ensure that they are provided with the most successful treatments, including those that are new and are promising to assist them on their path to recovery.

H.R. 5600, as amended, would require the Department of Veterans Affairs to carry out a 1-year pilot program to provide access to magnetic EEG/EKG-guided resonance therapy to veterans with post-traumatic stress disorder, traumatic brain injury, chronic pain, opiate addiction, or who have experienced military sexual trauma.

Magnetic EEG/EKG-guided resonance therapy has proven effective in addressing symptoms of post-traumatic stress disorder and traumatic brain injury among veteran patients. For example, in a 2015 study, veteran patients experienced an almost 50 percent reduction in symptom severity after just 2 weeks of using this therapy.

Though the pilot this bill would create is limited, I am hopeful that it will provide the needed data to support the provision of this promising new treatment for many more servicemembers and veterans in the future.

This bill is sponsored by our good friend, Congressman STEVE KNIGHT from California, and I am grateful to him for sponsoring this legislation to increase access to innovative treatment for America's heroes.

I urge all of my colleagues to join me in supporting H.R. 5600, as amended.

Mr. Speaker, I reserve the balance of my time.

Mr. TAKANO. Mr. Speaker, I yield myself such time as I may consume.

I rise today in support of H.R. 5600, as amended, the No Hero Left Untreated Act. This bill is designed to create a pilot program in the VA to determine if magnetic EEG/EKG-guided resonance therapy technology is appropriate for larger populations of veterans suffering from post-traumatic stress disorder, traumatic brain injury, military sexual trauma, chronic pain, or opiate addiction.

Under this treatment, a veteran's EEG and EKG are analyzed to ascertain the brain's patterns of function and detect any possible abnormalities. This information is used to develop a personalized treatment for each patient aimed at restoring the brain to its optimal state.

It is essential that the VA continue to explore new and innovative treatments, like resonance therapy, that can offer breakthroughs for veterans and servicemembers suffering from PTSD and other traumas. For more than 90 years, the Veterans Affairs Research and Development program has been improving the lives of veterans and all Americans through healthcare discovery and innovation.

VA research is unique because of its focus on health issues that affect veterans. It is part of an integrated healthcare system that coordinates care for veterans and affiliates with university medical schools and teaching hospitals to train our healthcare providers and perform groundbreaking medical research.

I look forward to learning more about this treatment and its effects on those veterans who have continued to suffer the wounds of combat trauma here at home. Innovative pilot programs and continued investment in research will help to ensure that our Nation's veterans get the high-quality care they have earned and deserve.

Mr. Speaker, I reserve the balance of my time.

Mr. MILLER of Florida. Mr. Speaker, I yield 3 minutes to the gentleman from the 25th District of California (Mr. KNIGHT), the prime sponsor of this important piece of legislation.

Mr. KNIGHT. Mr. Speaker, I want to thank the chair and ranking member for their support of this piece of legislation.

The No Hero Left Untreated Act is just that. We expect our young warriors to protect our values and our ideals, and we, as Americans, should do nothing less than to take care of them when they return home. The No Hero Left Untreated Act is a new and innovative way of looking at how we can treat our veterans, and I think that that is what people in America are looking for. They are looking for how we can help our veterans in new and innovative ways. Well, this is one of those.

This is a way that we have taken 500 veterans, we have given them this treatment, and about 95 percent of them have said that they have had some difference in their life because of the treatment. Sixty-one percent have said that it is a dramatic change because of this treatment. If we took those numbers and we took them to any kind of treatment or any kind of medical help across this country, I think that all of the physicians and all of the medical industry would say: yes, those are great numbers.

So what we are trying to do here is we are going to put it into two of our medical facilities; put it into two of our VA centers, and we are going to collect some data on the enormous successes that we have seen in the past and hopefully in the future. Then, I hope to come back at a certain time in the future and say: this has been great; the data that we have collected has helped our veterans, has helped our warriors when they have come home. Let's put this across the country.

I expect that everyone in every district across this country, when they see this, these types of successes, would want to put it into their VA facilities. So that is kind of our goal in what we are trying to do here.

Mental and physical injuries are part of battle. Treatment that works should be pushed by our legislative bodies. It shouldn't be stagnated. And that is exactly what this body is doing. We are looking at this, and we are saying: this is working. Why wouldn't we push it?

I thank everyone for looking at this in a bipartisan measure and saying this will help our veterans. Let's move this forward.

This therapy has shown enormous successes, and I think that when the American people look at this and they say, we have got these successes, let's make sure that we push this forward, I think that we should also look at other treatments that might not be having these types of successes and saying, you know what, we can do different changes, and the medical industry, I am sure, would support that.

So that is what we are trying to do with the No Hero Left Untreated Act. That is why we have named it that because that is exactly what we want. We don't want to leave any hero untreated.

I appreciate the support from both sides of the aisle, and I ask for support of this important measure.

Mr. TAKANO. Mr. Speaker, I have no further speakers. I encourage my colleagues to support this legislation and join me in passing H.R. 5600, as amended.

I yield back the balance of my time.

Mr. MILLER of Florida. Mr. Speaker, I too encourage my colleagues to support this piece of legislation.

I yield back the balance of time.

The SPEAKER pro tempore. The question is on the motion offered by the gentleman from Florida (Mr. MILLER) that the House suspend the rules and pass the bill, H.R. 5600, as amended.

The question was taken; and (two-thirds being in the affirmative) the rules were suspended and the bill, as amended, was passed.

A motion to reconsider was laid on the table.

TIBOR RUBIN VA MEDICAL CENTER

Mr. MILLER of Florida. Mr. Speaker, I move to suspend the rules and pass the bill (H.R. 6323) to name the Department of Veterans Affairs health care system in Long Beach, California, the "Tibor Rubin VA Medical Center".

The Clerk read the title of the bill.

The text of the bill is as follows:

H.R. 6323

Be it enacted by the Senate and House of Representatives of the United States of America in Congress assembled,

SECTION 1. NAME OF THE DEPARTMENT OF VETERANS AFFAIRS HEALTH CARE SYSTEM, LONG BEACH, CALIFORNIA.

The Department of Veterans Affairs health care system located at 5901 East 7th Street, Long Beach, California, shall after the date of the enactment of this Act be known and designated as the "Tibor Rubin VA Medical Center". Any reference to such health care system in any law, regulation, map, document, record, or other paper of the United States shall be considered to be a reference to the Tibor Rubin VA Medical Center.

The SPEAKER pro tempore. Pursuant to the rule, the gentleman from Florida (Mr. MILLER) and the gentleman from California (Mr. TAKANO) each will control 20 minutes.

The Chair recognizes the gentleman from Florida.

GENERAL LEAVE

Mr. MILLER of Florida. Mr. Speaker, I ask unanimous consent that all Members may have 5 legislative days within which to revise and extend their remarks and add extraneous material on H.R. 6323.

The SPEAKER pro tempore. Is there objection to the request of the gentleman from Florida?

There was no objection.

Mr. MILLER of Florida. Mr. Speaker, I yield myself such time as I may consume.

I do rise today in support of H.R. 6323, a bill to name the Department of Veterans Affairs healthcare system in Long Beach, California, the Tibor Rubin VA Medical Center.

Mr. Speaker, as a young man, Corporal Tibor Rubin survived 14 months in a German concentration camp in Austria during World War II before it was liberated by the United States Army.

Corporal Rubin was so inspired by the American soldiers who rescued him that he eventually moved to the United States, enlisted in the Army, and became a United States citizen. He was deployed as a member of the 1st Cavalry Division during the Korean war, and was eventually captured by the North Korean military.

During his captivity, he provided crucial moral support and improvised medical support to his fellow prisoners of war. For his service, Corporal Rubin was awarded two Purple Hearts and the Congressional Medal of Honor.

Sadly, he passed away just last year. After such an outstanding life of service and survival, it is only appropriate that we honor Corporal Rubin by naming the Long Beach VA Medical Center after him. H.R. 6323 satisfies the Committee's naming criteria and is supported by the entire California congressional delegation, as well as many local veterans service organizations.

□ 1730

I am grateful to Congressman LOWENTHAL for sponsoring this legislation, and I urge all of my colleagues to join me in supporting it.

Mr. Speaker, I reserve the balance of my time.

Mr. TAKANO. Mr. Speaker, I yield myself such time as I may consume.

Mr. Speaker, I rise today in support of H.R. 6323, to name the Department of Veterans Affairs health care system in Long Beach, California, the Tibor Rubin VA Medical Center.

What a remarkable story about Tibor Rubin. Tibor Rubin survived the Mauthausen concentration camp for 14 months before being liberated by American soldiers in May of 1945. After immigrating to the United States in 1948, he enlisted in the United States Army and volunteered to serve in Korea despite not being required to serve overseas as a non-U.S. citizen.

While in Korea, Corporal Rubin was ordered to defend a road while his division was in retreat. He held that position for 24 hours until the 8th Cavalry could safely withdraw.

Corporal Rubin spent 30 months as a prisoner of war in North Korea, where testimony from his fellow prisoners detailed his willingness to sacrifice for the others. He helped his fellow POWs by sneaking out of the camp at night and foraging for food, stealing from enemy supplies, and bringing back what he could to help the soldiers imprisoned with him. He declined the offer of his Communist captors to return him to Soviet Hungary, his country of origin, to help protect those from his adopted country.

"He shared the food evenly among the GIs," a fellow prisoner wrote. "He also took care of us, nursed us, carried us to the latrine." This GI also added, "Helping his fellow men was the most important thing to him."

For these actions and more, Mr. Rubin was awarded the Medal of Honor in 2005. For all that this brave immigrant did to protect the freedoms of our great country, we are honored to be able to name this VA Medical Center after him.

Mr. Speaker, I urge support for this legislation.

Mr. Speaker, I yield 8 minutes to the gentleman from California (Mr. LOWENTHAL).

Mr. LOWENTHAL. Mr. Speaker, I thank my good friend from California, who has been such a great leader on veterans' issues.

Mr. Speaker, I rise today to honor the life of Holocaust survivor and Medal of Honor recipient and a person that I knew personally before he passed away, Mr. Tibor "Ted" Rubin.

With the support of all 53 members of the California delegation, both California Senators, and many of my State's leading veterans' groups, I recently introduced H.R. 6323, legislation to name the Department of Veterans Affairs Medical Center in Long Beach as the Tibor Rubin VA Medical Center.

As was already noted, Tibor Rubin was born in Hungary on June 18, 1929. During World War II, he survived 14 months in a Nazi concentration camp in Austria, where both his parents and both of his sisters would eventually die.

Liberated by the United States Army, he was inspired by the American soldiers who rescued him, immigrating to the United States and enlisting in the United States Army. He was deployed to Korea as a member of the United States Army's 8th Cavalry Regiment, 1st Cavalry Division during the Korean war.

Despite facing religious discrimination from his sergeant who sent him on the most dangerous patrols and missions and withheld his Medal of Honor commendation, Tibor fought valiantly in several notable engagements. In one such engagement, Tibor enabled the complete withdrawal of his compatriots to the Pusan Perimeter by solely defending a hill under an overwhelming assault by North Korean troops. During this engagement, he inflicted a staggering number of casualties on the attacking force during his personal 24-hour battle, single-handedly slowing the enemy's advance and allowing the 8th Cavalry to withdraw successfully.

Following the successful U.S. Army breakout from the Pusan Perimeter and advance into North Korea, Tibor was personally responsible for the capture of several hundred North Korean soldiers.

In an additional engagement near Usan, Chinese forces attacked his unit during a massive nighttime assault. For nearly 24 hours, he remained at his post with a .30-caliber machine gun at the south end of the unit's line until his ammunition was exhausted. His determined stand slowed the pace of the enemy advance into his sector, permitting the remnants of his unit to retreat southward. However, as the battle raged, Tibor was severely wounded and captured by the Chinese. While in Chinese custody, he refused to be repatriated to Hungary, instead choosing to remain in the prison camp. He would refuse the offer on numerous occasions.

Tibor disregarded his own personal safety and immediately began sneaking out of the camp at night in search of food for his fellow prisoners. Breaking into enemy food storehouses and gardens, he risked certain torture or death if caught.

Tibor provided not only food for the starving soldiers, but also desperately needed medical care and moral support for the sick and wounded of the POW camp. As one of his fellow prisoners recounted about the camp: "Tibor did many good deeds, which he told us were mitzvahs in the Jewish tradition. He was a very religious Jew, and helping his fellow men was the most important thing to him."

Tibor's brave, selfless efforts were directly attributed to saving the lives of as many as 40 of his fellow prisoners. As his Medal of Honor citation reads: "Corporal Rubin's gallant actions in close contact with the enemy and unyielding courage and bravery while a prisoner of war are in the highest traditions of military service and reflect great credit upon himself and the United States Army."

It is worth noting that Tibor was nominated in the field on four occasions for the Medal of Honor. When he was finally presented his Medal of Honor in 2005, it was not presented by President George W. Bush for a single act of heroism. It was instead presented for nearly his entire 3 years of service in the Korean war.

Tibor was fiercely proud of the country he adopted. When he was later asked about his decision to immigrate to the United States, he said: "I always wanted to become a citizen of the United States, and when I became a citizen, it was one of the happiest days in my life.

"I think about the United States, and I am a lucky person to live here.

"When I came to America, it was the first time I was free. It was one of the reasons I joined the U.S. Army, because I wanted to show my appreciation.

"It is the best country in the world, and I am part of it now. I do not have to worry about the Gestapo knocking on my doors."

I am proud to say that after his service, Tibor became a longtime resident of Garden Grove, California, in my district. It was still his home when he passed away on December 5, 2015, and it was the Long Beach VA Hospital where he received his medical services for over 50 years.

It was my great honor to meet Tibor and to represent him in Congress. He was a survivor, a soldier, a nurse, a compatriot, and a wonderful citizen.

Mr. TAKANO. Mr. Speaker, I have no further speakers. What an amazing and inspiring story behind Corporal Rubin.

Mr. Speaker, I urge my colleagues to join me in supporting this legislation, H.R. 6323.

I yield back the balance of my time.

Mr. MILLER of Florida. Mr. Speaker, I, too, encourage all of our colleagues to support this legislation.

Mr. Speaker, I yield back the balance of my time.

The SPEAKER pro tempore. The question is on the motion offered by the gentleman from Florida (Mr. MILLER) that the House suspend the rules and pass the bill, H.R. 6323.

The question was taken; and (two-thirds being in the affirmative) the rules were suspended and the bill was passed.

A motion to reconsider was laid on the table.

REAFFIRMING LONGSTANDING UNITED STATES POLICY IN SUPPORT OF A DIRECT BILATERALLY NEGOTIATED SETTLEMENT OF THE ISRAELI-PALESTINIAN CONFLICT

Mr. ROYCE. Mr. Speaker, I move to suspend the rules and agree to the concurrent resolution (H. Con. Res. 165) expressing the sense of Congress and reaffirming longstanding United States policy in support of a direct bilaterally negotiated settlement of the Israeli-Palestinian conflict and opposition to United Nations Security Council resolutions imposing a solution to the conflict.

The Clerk read the title of the concurrent resolution.

The text of the concurrent resolution is as follows:

H. CON. RES. 165

Whereas the United States has long supported a negotiated settlement leading to a sustainable two-state solution with the democratic, Jewish state of Israel and a democratic Palestinian state living side-by-side in peace and security;

Whereas it is the long-standing policy of the United States Government that a peaceful resolution to the Israeli-Palestinian conflict will only come through direct, bilateral negotiations between the two parties;

Whereas President Barack Obama reiterated this policy at the United Nations General Assembly in 2011, stating, "Peace is hard work. Peace will not come through statements and resolutions at the United Nations—if it were that easy, it would have been accomplished by now. Ultimately, it is the Israelis and the Palestinians who must live side by side. Ultimately, it is the Israelis and the Palestinians—not us—who must reach agreement on the issues that divide them . . .";

Whereas the Palestinian Authority has failed to end incitement to hatred and violence through Palestinian Authority-directed institutions against Israel and Israelis, and end payments to prisoners and the families of those who have engaged in terrorism or acts of violence against Israelis or the State of Israel;

Whereas the Palestinian Authority has continued to provide payments to prisoners and the families of those who have engaged in terrorism or acts of violence against Israelis or the State of Israel, including reports of approximately $300 million in 2016;

Whereas efforts to impose a solution or parameters for a solution can make negotiations more difficult and can set back the cause of peace;

Whereas it is long-standing practice of the United States Government to oppose and, if necessary, veto United Nations Security Council resolutions dictating additional binding parameters on the peace process;

Whereas it is also the historic position of the United States Government to oppose and veto, if necessary, one-sided or anti-Israel resolutions at the United Nations Security Council;

Whereas and for this reason, the United States has vetoed 42 Israel-related resolutions in the United Nations Security Council since 1972;

Whereas the Palestinian Authority must engage in broad, meaningful, and systemic reforms in order to ultimately prepare its institutions and people for statehood and peaceful coexistence with Israel; and

Whereas unilateral recognition of a Palestinian state would bypass negotiations and undermine incentives for the Palestinian Authority to make the changes necessary that are prerequisites for peace: Now, therefore, be it

Resolved by the House of Representatives (the Senate concurring), that it is the sense of Congress that—

(1) a durable and sustainable peace agreement between Israel and the Palestinians will come only through direct bilateral negotiations between the parties;

(2) any widespread international recognition of a unilateral declaration of Palestinian statehood outside of the context of a peace agreement with Israel would cause severe harm to the peace process, and would likely trigger the implementation of penalties under sections 7036 and 7041(j) of the Consolidated Appropriations Act, 2016 (Public Law 114–113);

(3) efforts by outside bodies, including the United Nations Security Council, to impose an agreement or parameters for an agreement are likely to set back the cause of peace;

(4) the United States Government should continue to oppose and veto United Nations Security Council resolutions that seek to impose solutions to final status issues, or are one-sided and anti-Israel; and

(5) the United States Government should continue to support and facilitate the resumption of negotiations without preconditions between Israelis and Palestinians toward a sustainable peace agreement.

The SPEAKER pro tempore. Pursuant to the rule, the gentleman from California (Mr. ROYCE) and the gentleman from California (Mr. SHERMAN) each will control 20 minutes.

The Chair recognizes the gentleman from California (Mr. ROYCE).

GENERAL LEAVE

Mr. ROYCE. Mr. Speaker, I ask unanimous consent that all Members may have 5 legislative days to revise and extend their remarks and to include extraneous materials in the RECORD.

The SPEAKER pro tempore. Is there objection to the request of the gentleman from California?

There was no objection.

Mr. ROYCE. Mr. Speaker, I yield myself such time as I may consume.

Mr. Speaker, I thank the ranking member, the gentleman from New York (Mr. ENGEL), and thank Mr. BRAD SHERMAN of California as well for working with me in a bipartisan manner to bring this important resolution to the floor today.

There is a growing concern in Congress—it is a concern felt on both sides of the aisle—that despite established, bipartisan United States policy, the Obama administration may end the practice of vetoing resolutions in the Security Council that strayed from the principle that the Israeli-Palestinian conflict can only be resolved through direct negotiations between the parties. This administration could also end the related practice of vetoing Security Council resolutions that are one-sided or anti-Israel. This is a real concern. Press reports—including one today—suggest that such a one-sided resolution could be submitted in days.

Worse, the Obama administration could support a resolution at the U.N. Security Council setting parameters for a final settlement between Israel and the Palestinians. U.S. policy has long and wisely been that only Israelis and Palestinians can work out a peace agreement between themselves and that efforts to impose one would be counterproductive. Whatever parameters the U.N. established would be unacceptable to any Israeli Government—a government to the left or a government to the right—making it impossible to see any future peace.

What on Earth today, at this point in time, suggests that Israel has a willing partner in peace?

Not at this moment. Our committee has held hearings to expose the current Palestinian Authority's complicity in inciting violence against the State of Israel as well as against Israelis.

Mr. Speaker, Israel is contending with a deep-seated hatred. It is a deep-seated hatred nurtured, unfortunately, by Palestinian leaders over radio and also in direct communication with the population many, many years, whether it was in the mosques or the schools or the newspapers or on television. As one witness told the committee:

"Incitement" is the term we usually use, but that is not really what we mean. Hatred is what we mean, teaching generations of Palestinians to hate Jews by demonizing and dehumanizing them.

That is the nature of the problem.

Unfortunately, some Palestinians are lured to terrorism with more than just words. Since 2003, it has been Palestinian law to reward Palestinian terrorists in Israeli jails with a monthly paycheck. The Palestinian Authority and the Palestinian Liberation Organization use a so-called martyrs' fund to pay the families of Palestinian prisoners and to pay suicide bombers.

□ 1745

This pay-to-play scheme has got to stop, period. In the face of such hatred, the United States must stand firm. The Israel-Palestinian conflict can only be resolved through direct negotiations between the parties.

I again thank the gentleman from New York (Mr. ENGEL) and the gentleman from California (Mr. SHERMAN), as well, for their work on this resolution.

I reserve the balance of my time.

Mr. SHERMAN. Mr. Speaker, I yield myself such time as I may consume.

I rise today in support of H. Con. Res. 165. This is a bipartisan resolution put forward by the chair and ranking member of our committee, Mr. ROYCE and Mr. ENGEL, cosponsored by myself, with a host of other bipartisan cosponsors.

This resolution comes at a precarious time for the two-state solution, with a new administration preparing to enter office and as turmoil continues in the Middle East. I, myself, have always been a supporter of a negotiated solution between the Israeli and Palestinian sides of this conflict which would result in a secure, democratic Jewish State of Israel alongside a stable and democratic state for the Palestinian people.

This resolution reaffirms this commitment, which has been longstanding

American policy. The United States has provided important leadership as the two parties have negotiated. We would hope to see bilateral negotiations in the future. Peace must be made by the parties themselves. A peace settlement will only come through direct bilateral negotiations. These negotiations are delicate and they are complicated.

As President Barack Obama said in 2011: "Peace is hard work. Peace will not come through statements and resolutions at the United Nations. If it were that easy, it would have been accomplished by now." The President continued: "Ultimately, it is the Israelis and the Palestinians who must live side by side. Ultimately, it is the Israelis and the Palestinians, not us, who must reach agreement on the issues that divide them . . ."

This resolution is consistent with administration policy and consistent with the policy of several prior administrations.

We must heed this advice. Imposing a solution on the parties will not work. In fact, it will be counterproductive to peace. It would undermine incentives for the Palestinian authority to make the necessary changes that are prerequisites for peace. Statehood can be accomplished by ensuring security, eliminating incitement, and demonstrating that the Palestinian side can live peacefully with Israel.

This resolution expresses a sense of Congress as follows:

That the Israeli-Palestinian peace will come only through direct bilateral negotiations;

That recognition of a Palestinian state without a peace deal would cause harm to the peace process;

That efforts by outside bodies to impose an agreement or the parameters for an agreement are likely to set back the peace process;

The United States should veto any one-sided United Nations Security Council resolutions, or those resolutions that would seek to impose solutions on final status issues—again, consistent with the administration policies;

And finally, of course, that America will continue to support negotiations without preconditions between the Israelis and the Palestinians.

The Palestinian people deserve a state of their own. The Israeli people deserve to live in peace as Jews in the State of Israel. In this spirit, I call upon my colleagues to join us in passing this resolution.

I reserve the balance of my time.

Mr. ROYCE. Mr. Speaker, I yield 3 minutes to the gentleman from New Jersey (Mr. SMITH), chairman of the Foreign Affairs Subcommittee on Africa, Global Health, Global Human Rights, and International Organizations.

Mr. SMITH of New Jersey. Mr. Speaker, I thank the gentleman for yielding.

I rise in strong support of H. Con. Res. 165, in support of direct bilateral negotiations to resolve the Israeli-Palestinian conflict, introduced by Chairman ROYCE and Ranking Member ENGEL. This resolution is much more than a restatement of longstanding U.S. policy. It is an urgent defense of our commitments to the State of Israel in the face of innumerable threats.

The United States has long insisted that the only path to peace for the Israelis and Palestinians is through direct, bilateral negotiations. Any so-called resolution imposed from the outside is doomed to failure because it inherently lacks the political support of both parties to the conflict. Peacemaking is hard work, but that reality has not stopped others from looking for a shortcut.

The U.N. Security Council is one such forum that has served as a platform for anti-Israel schemes for many, many years. Thankfully, the United States has always resolutely imposed such unilateralism and, when necessary, through both Democratic and Republican White Houses, has always resolutely used the veto. Since 1972, the United States has used its veto power 42 times to block anti-Israel measures in the Security Council. However, in the closing days of this administration, this longstanding policy is being called into question.

Mr. Speaker, there are many reports that President Obama is considering moving the needle on the peace process before he leaves office by supporting a U.N. Security Council resolution enshrining certain conditions for peace. Just last month, The New York Times editorial board came out forcefully in favor of this scheme. The editorial board wrote: "The best idea under discussion now would be to have the United Nations Security Council, in an official resolution, lay down guidelines for a peace agreement covering such issues as Israel's security, the future of Jerusalem, the fate of Palestinian refugees and borders for both states."

On the contrary, this is just about the worst idea. It would have the effect of dangerously undercutting the peace process. Israel's security, the future of Jerusalem, Palestinian refugees, and borders—anyone familiar with this issue knows—are the four most sensitive matters at stake in this conflict and should not be imposed from without. The United States ought to be very clear when faced with such proposals. Any attempt to determine the fate of these issues outside of direct, bilateral talks undermines the sovereignty of our strong ally Israel, destroys goodwill, and threatens to prolong the conflict further.

The SPEAKER pro tempore. The time of the gentleman has expired.

Mr. ROYCE. I yield the gentleman an additional 1 minute.

Mr. SMITH of New Jersey. Sadly, the drumbeat for unilateral United Nations action on this issue continues. On October 14, the U.N. Security Council held a special debate, titled, "Illegal Israeli Settlements: Obstacles to Peace and the Two-State Solution." The session was held at the request of Security Council members Egypt, Venezuela, Malaysia, Senegal, and Angola, with the backing of the Palestinians. Such one-sided initiatives only damage prospects for peace.

Last April, 390 Members of the House on both sides of the aisle signed a letter to the President. It was signed by so many of us, including some in this room, including NITA LOWEY, KAY GRANGER, KAREN BASS, TED DEUTCH, ILEANA ROS-LEHTINEN, ED ROYCE, ELIOT ENGEL, KEVIN MCCARTHY, STENY HOYER, NANCY PELOSI, and myself—390 in all—that laid out the simple principles that have guided our policy. These principles include:

A refusal to support counterproductive efforts aimed at imposing a solution on the parties;

Opposition to Palestinian efforts to seek recognition of statehood status in international bodies; and

A willingness to oppose, if need be, a one-sided U.N. resolution by way of a veto.

I urge my colleagues to vote for this resolution.

Mr. SHERMAN. Mr. Speaker, I yield 2 minutes to the gentleman from Virginia (Mr. CONNOLLY).

Mr. CONNOLLY. Mr. Speaker, I thank the gentleman from California (Mr. SHERMAN), my friend, for yielding.

I rise today in support of H. Con. Res. 165, reaffirming longstanding U.S. policy in support of a direct, bilaterally negotiated settlement of the Israeli-Palestinian conflict.

For several decades, the United States has maintained a consistent, bipartisan policy toward the conflict that supports a two-state solution and opposes settlement expansion. Explicit congressional support for the two-state solution is critically important, especially in light of President-elect Donald Trump's previous statements on this very subject.

My friends on the other side have indicated an abiding fear that something bad might happen at the U.N. in the waning 52 days of the Obama administration. I don't share that concern. What I am concerned about is the next 4 years and what Donald Trump will do to the longstanding, bipartisan support for a two-state solution that has been the cornerstone of American policy. If he pulls out of that commitment, then you are right, Middle East peace is at risk, but it is not because of what Obama is going to do over the next 52 days.

I urge my colleagues to support this resolution, which reiterates that longstanding, bipartisan support for a two-state solution, and help combat the unpredictability of U.S. foreign policy in these difficult days of transition.

Mr. ROYCE. Mr. Speaker, I yield 4 minutes to the gentlewoman from Florida (Ms. ROS-LEHTINEN), who chairs the Foreign Affairs Subcommittee on the Middle East and North Africa.

Ms. ROS-LEHTINEN. Mr. Speaker, as always, I want to thank our esteemed chairman, the gentleman from California (Mr. ROYCE), as well as our ranking member, the gentleman from New York (Mr. ENGEL), who is so wonderfully represented by the gentleman from California (Mr. SHERMAN). I thank Mr. ROYCE and Mr. ENGEL for authoring this very important resolution, which I am proud to cosponsor. And while I fully support this measure and I urge all of my colleagues to back it as well, I wish that this resolution was not needed; but, sadly, we know better.

The fact that we need to bring this up for debate and pass a resolution urging a United States administration to uphold longstanding U.S. policy as it relates to the peace process is telling and also disappointing, Mr. Speaker.

These next 2 months are going to be crucial for our friend and ally, the democratic Jewish State of Israel, and the U.S.-Israel alliance, which must remain ever strong. Israel is facing a constant barrage by the Palestinians and their supporters at the United Nations, and there are indications that Abu Mazen will once again attempt to further his plan for unilateral statehood through the Security Council.

Ordinarily, any attempt to dictate a two-state solution or impose parameters on negotiations between the Israelis and the Palestinians would be summarily dismissed by the United States. However, sadly, it has become clear over the past year that this administration may be looking to take unprecedented action; and, in fact, we have heard that the administration has been actively seeking ways in which it could force the Israelis into making dangerous concessions.

I have asked Secretary Kerry, I have asked Ambassador Power, our Ambassador to the U.N., I have asked Ambassador Patterson and nearly every administration official who has come before our Foreign Affairs Committee headed by Mr. ROYCE and Mr. ENGEL if President Obama will uphold longstanding U.S. policy and will veto any Security Council resolution related to Israel. Each one has evaded the question, refusing to reaffirm this longstanding, unambiguous, noncontroversial policy.

We hear speak of one-sided resolutions, but that is slick administration talk. Who defines the one-sidedness? It should have been a resounding blanket statement—it is easy—that the President believes that the only way to a real and lasting peace between Israelis and Palestinians must come through direct bilateral negotiations between the two, and lacking that, yes, we will urge the President to veto it. It is not hard.

Peace cannot be forced. Any short-term achievement an imposed solution will bring will be far outweighed by the long-term damage that it will cause.

Mr. Speaker, this is a lameduck administration; and it should go without saying that any action, whether it be at the U.N. or undertaken unilaterally, aimed at forcing solutions to final status issues will be detrimental to the prospects of peace and would harm both Israelis and Palestinians.

I support this measure, strongly, brought forth by Chairman ROYCE and Ranking Member ENGEL. I urge my colleagues to support it to reaffirm longstanding U.S. policy that true peace between the Israelis and the Palestinians can only come between direct bilateral negotiations between them, and to urge the administration to not allow the Palestinian scheme of unilateral statehood to gain any legitimacy at the U.N.

□ 1800

Mr. SHERMAN. Mr. Speaker, I reserve the balance of my time.

Mr. ROYCE. Mr. Speaker, I yield 2 minutes to the gentleman from Illinois (Mr. DOLD), a member of the Committee on Financial Services.

Mr. DOLD. I thank my good friend, the gentleman from California (Mr. ROYCE), for yielding the time.

Mr. Speaker, I, too, stand in strong support of H. Con. Res. 165.

What I find so fascinating is that we need here in the United States to respect Israel's democratically elected leadership. They are a nation, and they are our one true ally; and any efforts by the United Nations or by any other body to try to impose a two-state solution, frankly, I think, is detrimental and reckless. We should never try to force their hand. Frankly, what we find now is it is not the time to try to establish a legacy for an administration that has just a very few short days left by attempting a reckless Hail Mary pass. We here do want a two-state solution, which I think is important to note, but it must be done by direct negotiations by the two parties; and when the United States pressures Israel, all we do is weaken the chances for long-term, durable peace.

My good friend from Virginia talked about his actually being fearful of the next administration. Let me simply say that I hope this body will stand in bipartisan support to ensure that any administration does not pressure Israel. We understand that a long-lasting peace, which is what we are hoping for, comes through direct, bilateral negotiations.

I, for one, am hopeful that this body will stand united to make sure that the world knows that we stand shoulder to shoulder with our one true ally—Israel—and with the hope that the administration and the United Nations Security Council will veto any efforts by the United Nations to try to unilaterally put a statehood in there for the Palestinians. We know that true peace can only happen through direct, bilateral negotiations.

Mr. Speaker, again, I stand in strong support of Mr. ROYCE's and Mr. ENGEL's resolution, and I sincerely hope that my colleagues will stand together, in bipartisan support, to make sure that this administration does not take steps that will weaken Israel's hand in going forward. I hope, in going forward, in administration after administration, that this body will stand as we do today—in bipartisan support.

Mr. SHERMAN. Mr. Speaker, this resolution reaffirms longstanding American policy that can be summarized in five points: talks must be direct and bilateral; a solution cannot be imposed on the parties; both sides must be willing to make important compromises; disagreements should be resolved privately; and the United States should work closely with the State of Israel. This resolution deserves the support of those on both sides of the aisle.

Mr. Speaker, I yield back the balance of my time.

Mr. ROYCE. Mr. Speaker, I yield myself such time as I may consume.

In the past, both Republican and Democratic administrations have recognized that efforts to internationalize the Israeli-Palestinian conflict are not a substitute for direct negotiations between the parties. In fact, such an approach can undermine these negotiations. Direct negotiations between the parties, not a U.N. dictate, are the only way, in our view, to bring about a peaceful coexistence. After all, direct negotiations mean legitimatizing the other party, which, unfortunately, is why Palestinian leaders routinely shun them.

Other past Presidents have pushed peace initiatives in the final hours of their administrations. Indeed, the Obama administration has pointedly not ruled out allowing the U.N. Security Council to dictate the terms of peace negotiations. That, in fact, is what has given rise to our bipartisan concerns about this process. In the absence of a clear answer from the administration as to whether it will continue to use that veto power at the United Nations, this bipartisan approach here, with this resolution, takes a stand.

I strongly urge my colleagues on both sides of the aisle to support the resolution so that the bipartisan policy of encouraging direct negotiations continues and is endorsed loud and clear.

Mr. Speaker, I yield back the balance of my time.

Mr. PRICE of North Carolina. Mr. Speaker, the House's consideration of H. Con. Res. 165 is given special relevance by the presidential transition now underway.

The resolution sends an important message to the incoming Administration:

that the United States Congress reaffirms our nation's commitment to supporting negotiations between Israel and the Palestinians in pursuit of a just and lasting two-state solution, and

that the United States Congress reaffirms a supportive and constructive role, for our country in facilitating resolution of the conflict.

Unfortunately, the resolution also contains overly broad and negative language concerning third-party efforts to facilitate an agreement. Still, it does not preclude the United States from putting forward ideas for bridging differences between the parties, for articulating suggestions that fill in gaps, for offering a nonbinding comprehensive framework to help bring the Israelis and Palestinians to the negotiating table—just as Republican and Democrat Administrations have done in the past.

It is my hope, in fact, that the Obama administration might in the coming weeks "help provide a political horizon for ending the conflict"—I'm quoting now from House Resolution 686, introduced by Representative YARMUTH and myself and cosponsored by 64 members—"by articulating a non-binding vision of what a comprehensive final status agreement might entail that could help foster and guide revived negotiations between the parties."

The resolution also encourages the U.S. government to "firmly articulate 49 years of consistent, bipartisan United States opposition to settlement expansion."

We must be vigilant in protecting 50 years of bipartisan policy to help the Israelis and Palestinians reach as viable two-state solution in order to protect Israel as a secure, democratic, and Jewish state, and to end the cycle of violence that has plagued the region.

As a longstanding supporter of the special relationship between the United States and Israel, I believe the United States must remain steadfast in its commitment to help Israel defend itself, to ensure that Israelis and Palestinians feel that a viable political horizon to ending this conflict continues to exist despite the current absence of ongoing, productive negotiations, and to stand ready to help create better conditions for peace—so that real and achievable progress may prove viable in the months and years ahead.

Ms. MOORE. Mr. Speaker, I thank the ranking member and chairman for their hard work in crafting this resolution. It reiterates a number of points consistent with longstanding U.S. policy on the Israeli-Palestinian conflict, including the current Administration, that I support. It is still to be seen what this policy will look like under the new Administration.

No one disputes the need for the parties to directly work out the issues. I articulated that position in a letter I sent to President Obama when he took office in 2009. I reaffirmed that position again in a letter to the President about a year ago. I continue to support that position.

Additionally, no one disputes the need to oppose unilateral actions by either party that undermines the process. As Vice President BIDEN noted earlier this year, "Actions on either side to undermine trust only take us further away from the path of peace. Actions like

at the U.N. to undermine Israel, or . . . settlement activities." Such actions clearly erode the prospect of a two-state solution, the stated goal for U.S. policy and efforts for a number of years now.

However, I believe that this resolution we are debating is incomplete.

For example, this resolution should not be mischaracterized or misrepresented as opposing constructive steps by the United States, either unilaterally or with the international community, to help preserve and further a negotiated two-state solution between the Israelis and Palestinians.

While no effort can replace the parties themselves reaching agreement, there are a host of ways in which the U.S. and other stakeholders in the international communities, like Arab countries in the region, with a vital interest in peace can support steps to rebuild trust and good will, both of which are sorely lacking and will be needed. It must be made clear that Congress is not discouraging such efforts through this or any other resolution.

The framework for a resolution to the conflict has long been clear for a number of years and formulated a number of times, including President Clinton and President George W. Bush. No U.N. resolution is needed for that.

The issue isn't whether we know where the major issues of disagreement lie, but how to create an environment that encourages the parties to move forward. The U.S. and international support can be helpful and useful to building that environment. It would be foolhardy to hope that somehow the Israelis and Palestinians spontaneously decide to stop pointing fingers and come together and find solutions to some very tough and challenging issues.

The challenges to peace at the moment are tremendous which is why it is important that we should encourage all interested in peace to continue to work for it.

Even Israeli Prime Minister Netanyahu recently expressed appreciation for and a willingness to build on multilateral and regional efforts regarding the conflict between the Israelis and Palestinians, such as the Arab Peace Initiative.

At the end of his Administration, President George W. Bush held a conference at Annapolis where he hosted the leaders of Israel and the Palestinian Authority, but also other "nations that support a two-state solution, reject violence, recognize Israel's right to exist, and commit to all previous agreements between the parties." President Bush also noted that "the world can do more to build the conditions for peace" between the two parties. The U.S. invited 49 countries and international organizations to participate including Members of the Arab League, Permanent Members of the U.N. Security Council, and the International Quartet for Middle East Peace.

In 2007, President George W. Bush argued for the international community to "rise to the moment, and provide decisive support to responsible Palestinian leaders working for peace" and laid out one role for the international community—helping create viable Palestinian institutions necessary for a state.

Former Senator and head of the Senate Foreign Relations Committee, Richard Lugar repeatedly noted that "Both Israel and the Pal-

estinians urgently need international support to fortify their ability and willingness to embrace the difficult choices that will be necessary" to reach a peace deal.

While the world has changed much since that time, the need for the international community to do more to "build conditions for peace" between the two parties has not diminished.

Yet, I am concerned that some may read H. Con. Res. 165 as dismissing all efforts by the U.S. to engage the international community to galvanize broad support for meaningful efforts to move the parties towards peace.

I also want to emphasize that no one should read this resolution as preventing the U.S. from supporting non-binding efforts through the U.N. Security Council to further progress toward a negotiated, conflict-ending agreement. This has long been a part of the U.S. Middle East Peace toolbox.

The U.S. was instrumental in drafting and passing UNSC Resolutions 242 (in 1967) and 338 (in 1973) outlining the international community's desire for a peaceful resolution to the Arab-Israeli conflict through territorial compromise. Democratic and Republican Presidents alike have previously worked through the U.N. Security Council to promote peace.

Under President Reagan, the United States did not veto U.N. Security Council Resolutions criticizing Israel's annexation of the Golan Heights and its activities in the occupied Palestinian territories.

I believe that such efforts remain a viable tool today.

That doesn't mean the U.S. has to support efforts it believes are contrary to peace. It has long been U.S. policy to denounce actions by any party—Israel, the Palestinians, or international actors—that are unwelcomed. This includes opposition to actions by the United Nations—or any other entity—to pass resolutions that are one-sided or anti-Israel. And the Obama Administration has done so when needed.

Additionally, I believe the resolution would have been strengthened by strongly emphasizing that there is no workable alternative to the two-state solution which has been the focus of U.S. peacemaking efforts for years now.

Lastly, I continue to support the current Administration's push for peace between our allies and to urge it to continue to do so even in its waning days. I also urge the incoming Administration to work constructively towards a two-state solution. In a recent poll, 69 percent of American Jewish voters expressed support for President Barack Obama delivering a major speech before leaving office outlining a vision for what Israelis and Palestinians must do to reach a peace agreement.

There is plenty of blame to apportion for why the status quo of violence, instability, and conflict continues unabated.

We owe it to every Israeli and Palestinian who share a vision of two peoples living side by side in peace and security to never quit on working toward a meaningful peace and that should include pursuing every tool and leveraging every ally in that pursuit.

The SPEAKER pro tempore. The question is on the motion offered by the gentleman from California (Mr.

ROYCE) that the House suspend the rules and agree to the concurrent resolution, H. Con. Res. 165.

The question was taken; and (two-thirds being in the affirmative) the rules were suspended and the concurrent resolution was agreed to.

A motion to reconsider was laid on the table.

ENCOURAGING REUNIONS OF DIVIDED KOREAN AMERICAN FAMILIES

Mr. ROYCE. Mr. Speaker, I move to suspend the rules and agree to the concurrent resolution (H. Con. Res. 40) encouraging reunions of divided Korean American families.

The Clerk read the title of the concurrent resolution.

The text of the concurrent resolution is as follows:

H. CON. RES. 40

Whereas the Republic of Korea (hereinafter in this resolution referred to as "South Korea") and the Democratic People's Republic of Korea (hereinafter in this resolution referred to as "North Korea") remain divided since the armistice agreement was signed on July 27, 1953;

Whereas the United States, which as a signatory to the armistice agreement as representing the United Nations Forces Command, and with 28,500 of its troops currently stationed in South Korea, has a stake in peace on the Korean Peninsula and is home to more than 1,700,000 Americans of Korean descent;

Whereas the division on the Korean Peninsula separated more than 10,000,000 Korean family members, including some who are now citizens of the United States;

Whereas there have been 19 rounds of family reunions between South Koreans and North Koreans along the border since 2000;

Whereas Congress signaled its interest in family reunions between United States Citizens and their relatives in North Korea in section 1265 of the National Defense Authorization Act for Fiscal Year 2008 (Public Law 110–181), signed into law by President George W. Bush on January 28, 2008;

Whereas the number of more than 100,000 estimated divided family members in the United States last identified in 2001 has been significantly dwindling as many of them have passed away;

Whereas many Korean Americans are waiting for a chance to meet their relatives in North Korea for the first time in more than 60 years; and

Whereas peace on the Korean Peninsula remains a long-term goal for the Governments of South Korea and the United States, and would mean greater security and stability for the region and the world: Now, therefore, be it

Resolved by the House of Representatives (the Senate concurring), That Congress—

(1) encourages North Korea to allow Korean Americans to meet with their family members from North Korea; and

(2) calls on North Korea to take concrete steps to build goodwill that is conducive to peace on the Korean Peninsula.

The SPEAKER pro tempore. Pursuant to the rule, the gentleman from California (Mr. ROYCE) and the gentleman from California (Mr. SHERMAN) each will control 20 minutes.

The Chair recognizes the gentleman from California (Mr. ROYCE).

GENERAL LEAVE

Mr. ROYCE. Mr. Speaker, I ask unanimous consent that all Members have 5 legislative days to revise and extend their remarks and to include any extraneous material for the RECORD.

The SPEAKER pro tempore. Is there objection to the request of the gentleman from California?

There was no objection.

Mr. ROYCE. Mr. Speaker, I yield myself such time as I may consume.

As the Republican coauthor of this measure, I rise in strong support of H. Con. Res. 40—a resolution I was proud to introduce alongside my good friend, Mr. CHARLIE RANGEL. As always, I appreciate the help from the gentleman from New York, the ranking member, for his assistance in bringing it to the House floor for consideration. It has been a privilege to have worked alongside one of the true champions of peace and stability on the Korean Peninsula, Mr. CHARLIE RANGEL. He is, indeed, a true patriot.

We all know about his bravery and heroism as a young Army officer in the Korean war—spending his days literally freezing behind enemy lines. While wounded, CHARLIE courageously led 40 men from his unit out of a Chinese encirclement, undoubtedly saving many, many lives. For his bravery, CHARLIE earned the Purple Heart and the Bronze Star. Yes, CHARLIE suffered for his country, but his focus has continued to also be on the suffering of the Korean people. A nation was destroyed; millions were killed; families were brutally ripped apart. CHARLIE has never forgotten that. He didn't leave Korea behind, which is why I was happy to work with him on the cause of bringing together the many, many Korean families that have been ripped apart by war.

Sadly, Mr. Speaker, Korea remains a divided peninsula. There is a prosperous and free South Korea and a brutal, totalitarian, impoverished North Korea. This division is a calamity that is acutely felt by South Korean families that have been separated by the DMZ, but it is equally felt here by many Korean American families in the United States. In the decades since the momentous liberation of Korea, millions of Korean families have been separated from their loved ones. Today, an estimated 100,000 Korean Americans have been separated from their relatives in North Korea and have long sought an opportunity to be reunited.

Mr. Speaker, time is running out. Earlier this year, the average Korean separated by the war was 80 years old. A large number is over 90. It is far past time that these war-torn families be given one last opportunity to reunite with the family members they were separated from six decades ago. It is everyone's hope—and, of course, of those in this body—that someday we will see Korea reunited. In the meantime, we can do what we can to encourage the reuniting of these families; so I urge my colleagues to support this resolution.

Mr. Speaker, I reserve the balance of my time.

Mr. SHERMAN. Mr. Speaker, I yield myself such time as I may consume.

I rise to support H. Con. Res. 40. I am pleased to support this measure that was introduced by Congressman CHARLIE RANGEL of New York, and I associate myself with the chairman's remarks in the praise of Charlie's service not only during the Korean war, but after that war, to focus on families that are both here and in Korea who were affected by that conflict.

A decorated veteran of the Korean war, Representative RANGEL has been a tireless advocate for peace and security on the peninsula and for the Korean American community here in the United States. His achievements are many, and as he retires after 40 decades of service here in Congress, he will, of course, be missed.

What Congressman RANGEL and the many cosponsors of H. Con. Res. 40 bring forth today—154 bipartisan cosponsors, including the chair and ranking member of the committee, myself, and so many others—is a reminder not just of the complex security situation on the peninsula, but of the human dimension of a war that has not been formally ended.

As this resolution reminds us, there are 10 million people on the Korean Peninsula and around the world who are victims of this family division, and there are some 100,000 American citizens who are still waiting to see—perhaps for one last time—family members that they have not seen for 60 years, who have remained north of the 38th parallel in the aftermath of the Korean war. There are approximately 1.7 million Korean Americans here in the United States. As I mentioned, over 100,000 of them have relatives who are north of the DMZ, and I am pleased to say that over half of those Korean Americans reside in the State of California.

The Korean Americans who have been divided from their families in North Korea are now in their senior years. Time is running out for these separated families to reunite—perhaps for just one last time—with parents, siblings, children. For many, reunification will be the only contact they will have had in so many decades. As of yet, Korean Americans have not been permitted to participate in family reunions. North Korea should encourage reunions for the sake of their own citizens who are divided family members, for Korean Americans, and for those affected by the war no matter where in the world they live.

H. Con. Res. 40 urges the North Korea regime to resume family reunification visits, which have been suspended for over a year, and to allow families that chance to get together. It also calls on North Korea to take concrete steps to build goodwill that is conducive to peace on the Korean Peninsula. This is particularly important given the nuclear weapons tests and missile tests that we have seen from the north.

The reunification of families is a goodwill gesture that can help put the world and northeast Asia on the road to peace. That is why I support this resolution and urge all of my colleagues to do the same.

Mr. Speaker, I reserve the balance of my time.

Mr. ROYCE. Mr. Speaker, I yield 2 minutes to the gentleman from Illinois (Mr. DOLD).

Mr. DOLD. I thank the gentleman for yielding the time.

Mr. Speaker, this is a critically important humanitarian issue as we talk about families. Each and every one of us just got back from Thanksgiving—an opportunity for us to gather around the table with our families. I think that is something that, often, too many of us take for granted—the opportunity and the ability that we have to jump on a plane or to get on a train and go visit our families. Yet, for so many Korean families, that is something that is beyond the realm of possibility.

It is beyond the realm of possibility because, at the outbreak of the Korean war, many of the Koreans thought that this was just going to be a conflict that was not going to last very long; so families were literally separated at that time and were hoping to be reunited in a very short period of time. What we do know is that, decade after decade, these families have not been able to be reunited. We want to encourage this reuniting of families. There are so many Korean Americans who have family in the north who have not been able to see their families.

□ 1815

Recently, Mr. Speaker, this last year I had an opportunity to travel to Korea and actually had an opportunity to talk to some of the families. A very small few—100 families—were going to have an opportunity to see their loved ones.

Time is of the essence. This is a humanitarian issue because more and more people are passing away and the opportunities to see their loved ones perishes. For the Korean Americans and for the Korean community, their opportunity to pay respects to those who have gone before them is also something that is critical, and they don't have the opportunity to visit them.

So I want to make sure that we stand together in a bipartisan way to encourage the opportunity for families to be able to be reunited.

I thank the gentleman from New York (Mr. RANGEL) for his leadership on this issue. Again, anybody who has served any time in this body knows his love for the Korean people and his record in the Korean war, his heroism in that regard.

I do hope that we, today, will vote to make sure we send a strong signal that the reuniting of families is something we should all stand and be united behind.

Mr. SHERMAN. Mr. Speaker, I yield 5 minutes to the gentleman from New York (Mr. RANGEL), the author of this resolution and a champion for the Korean American community.

Mr. RANGEL. Mr. Speaker, I thank Congressman SHERMAN for giving me this time to speak on this important issue. I will also take this opportunity to thank Chairman ED ROYCE.

So many people ask: After 46 years, what do you consider your major accomplishments? It is hard to explain to those of us who serve in the Congress that you don't list friendships as an accomplishment. There is no question, in knowing ED ROYCE from the people's Republic of California, that he has shattered the wall between Republicans and Democrats, and conservatives and liberals, and he is an American who cares about this Congress and this country. Whether I have talked to him about Africa or about Korea, he has listened and has done the best he could to show what America really feels proud of, and that is seeking peace and justice where we find dictatorships and people destroying the lives of others.

I get so much credit for being a wounded hero in Korea. I volunteered for the Army, but I sure didn't volunteer for Korea. As a matter of fact, it always baffled me how we could go there without a declaration of war. It baffled me how we could make a decision to take a country like Korea with such a beautiful history and have human beings just draw a line and say that this is north, this is south, this is the Soviets, this is the United Nations, and the United States and not realize that these are human beings, mothers and fathers, sons and daughters; that notwithstanding the fact that the south was attacked, notwithstanding that the war still continues technically today, that all people should want to see their families united when all it takes is that, yes, you may see them.

So today I thank Chairman ROYCE so much, Mr. Speaker, and this House for showing America what we are all about. Because it is ironic that we are now talking about Korean Americans, we are talking about divided families USA. We are talking about people who love this country, who fight for this country, but they still have a place they love, and they have family that they want to see before they pass away or before their families are gone.

Isn't this really what makes America different, to find people who love their homeland like Korean Americans love Korea and, at the same time, love this country more and ask us to join with them for what? They ask for peace, equity, and all the things that we care about, but also to meet their family.

There is so much compassion in this. There is so much to show how a line can show you poverty above the line, democracy and progress below the line. But more than anything else, this body is saying today that people who God made of the same blood, the same background, and the same culture, let them meet.

So I would like to include tonight as one of those proudest days that I have served in this august body and, also, to include Representative ED ROYCE as one of the most decent human beings I have also met while serving in this body.

Mr. ROYCE. Mr. Speaker, I reserve the balance of my time.

Mr. SHERMAN. Mr. Speaker, I yield 2 minutes to the gentleman from Virginia (Mr. CONNOLLY).

Mr. CONNOLLY. Mr. Speaker, I too join the chairman and the ranking member in saluting the gentleman from New York (Mr. RANGEL).

I remember him telling the story that he was a teenager at the outbreak of the war in Korea, living in Harlem, and didn't know where Korea was. He sure knows today. He is an iconic figure in the Korean community.

Representative RANGEL, we salute you for your incredible heroism.

Mr. Speaker, I rise in support of H. Con. Res. 40 to encourage the reunion of divided Korean American families. The division of north and south along the 38th parallel offers one of the world's most striking dichotomies. Yet, on both sides of the demilitarized zone resides a shared pain. The pain is that of families ripped apart by the war and an enduring division of one people into two countries. Reunions are a welcome respite from that separation, but, in the end, they provide yet another reminder that family reunification on the Korean Peninsula is all too fleeting.

Many of these Americans—more than 100,000 according to the last estimate—have been waiting to reunite with their family members in North Korea. Too many have already passed away without ever realizing that hope.

This resolution encourages Pyongyang to allow those Korean Americans to meet with their families. It also calls on the North Korean regime to take steps to build goodwill that is conducive to peace in the peninsula.

Earlier this year, we passed the North Korean Sanctions and Policy Enhancement Act, which included my amendment conditioning sanctions relief on the promotion of family reunifications for Koreans and Korean Americans.

It is vital our North Korea policy be informed with an understanding that there are human victims of this ongoing conflict in the North Korean Peninsula.

I ask my colleagues to support the resolution, which demonstrates our commitment to efforts to seek to relieve the pain of separation felt by Korean families.

Mr. ROYCE. Mr. Speaker, I reserve the balance of my time.

Mr. SHERMAN. Mr. Speaker, I salute the author of this resolution, Representative RANGEL, and urge its adoption.

I yield back the balance of my time.

Mr. ROYCE. Mr. Speaker, I yield myself such time as I may consume.

I also want to recognize the staff who have been so instrumental, not only on this resolution but also in maintaining our constructive policy toward Korea, Hannah Kim on Mr. RANGEL's staff and our committee staffers, Hunter Strupp and Jennifer Hendrixson-White.

Earlier, I noted how happy I was to have worked alongside my good friend and colleague, CHARLIE RANGEL, on this measure. As he is retiring at the end of this Congress, I want to once again recognize him as a true champion of U.S.-Korea relations. He truly is. No one, whether it was fighting for his country or advocating on behalf of so many Korean Americans, has done more for this partnership.

As Charlie has often said, since he survived the battle of Kunu-ri and led those freezing soldiers out of that encirclement, he has never, not since that day, never ever had a bad day since. Mr. Speaker, let's hope this streak continues well into the future.

I yield back the balance of my time.

Mr. PASCRELL. Mr. Speaker, as a cosponsor of H. Con. Res. 40, I rise today in strong support of its passage.

Tragically, the division on the Korean Peninsula separated more than 10,000,000 Korean family members, including some who are now citizens of the United States. As a result, many Korean Americans have waited for over 60 years for a chance to meet their relatives in North Korea for the first time.

Although there have been 19 rounds of family reunions between South Koreans and North Koreans, instability has continued to impede the reunion of these divided families. As some family members reach the later years of their lives, time becomes an important factor in giving these families the opportunity to connect.

Congress first signaled its interest in family reunions between United States citizens and their relatives in North Korea in section 1265 of the National Defense Authorization Act for Fiscal Year 2008 (Public Law 110–181), which became law on January 28, 2008. We furthered our commitment to reunification when President Barack Obama signed into law the Continuing Appropriations Act 2011 (Public Law 111–242), which urged the Special Representative on North Korea Policy to prioritize the issues involving Korean divided families.

Enabling Korean Americans to meet their family members from North Korea will help establish the goodwill to lay the foundation for peace on the Korean Peninsula. While peace on the Korean Peninsula remains a long-term goal for the United States and all stakeholders in the region, a first step towards achieving it would be to allow family members to be reunified. This would be a significant step forward for greater security and stability for the region and the world.

I urge my colleagues in the House to swiftly pass H. Con. Res. 40.

The SPEAKER pro tempore. The question is on the motion offered by the gentleman from California (Mr. ROYCE) that the House suspend the rules and agree to the concurrent resolution, H. Con. Res. 40.

The question was taken; and (two-thirds being in the affirmative) the rules were suspended and the concurrent resolution was agreed to.

A motion to reconsider was laid on the table.

TRANSMITTING AN ALTERNATIVE PLAN FOR PAY INCREASES FOR CIVILIAN FEDERAL EMPLOYEES COVERED BY THE GENERAL SCHEDULE AND CERTAIN OTHER PAY SYSTEMS IN JANUARY 2017— MESSAGE FROM THE PRESIDENT OF THE UNITED STATES (H. DOC. NO. 114–185)

The SPEAKER pro tempore laid before the House the following message from the President of the United States; which was read and, together with the accompanying papers, referred to the Committee on Oversight and Government Reform and ordered to be printed:

To the Congress of the United States:

I am transmitting an alternative plan for pay increases for civilian Federal employees covered by the General Schedule and certain other pay systems in January 2017. Title 5, United States Code, authorizes me to implement alternative pay plans for pay increases for civilian Federal employees covered by the General Schedule and certain other pay systems if, because of "national emergency or serious economic conditions affecting the general welfare," I view the adjustments that would otherwise take effect as inappropriate.

Civilian Federal employees made significant sacrifices as a result of the 3-year pay freeze that ended in January 2014. Since the pay freeze ended, annual adjustments for civilian Federal employees have also been lower than private sector pay increases and statutory formulas for adjustments to the General Schedule for 2014 through 2016. However, we must maintain efforts to keep our Nation on a sustainable fiscal course. This is an effort that continues to require tough choices under current economic conditions.

Under current law, locality pay increases averaging 28.49 percent and costing $26 billion would go into effect in January 2017. Federal agency budgets cannot sustain such increases. In my August 31, 2016, alternative pay plan submission, I noted that the alternative plan for locality payments will be limited so that the total combined cost of the 1.0 percent across-the-board base pay increase and the varying locality pay increases will be 1.6 percent of basic payroll, consistent with the assumption in my 2017 Budget. Accordingly, I have determined that under the authority of section 5304a of title 5, United States Code, locality-based comparability payments for the locality pay areas established by the President's Pay Agent, in the amounts set forth in the attached table, shall become effective on the first day of the first applicable pay period beginning on or after January 1, 2017.

The locality-based comparability payments for the locality pay rates in the attached table are based on an allocation of 0.6 percent of payroll as indicated in my August 31, 2016, alternative pay plan for adjustments to the base General Schedule. These decisions will not materially affect our ability to attract and retain a well-qualified Federal workforce.

BARACK OBAMA.
THE WHITE HOUSE, *November 29, 2016.*

RECESS

The SPEAKER pro tempore. Pursuant to clause 12(a) of rule I, the Chair declares the House in recess for a period of less than 15 minutes.

Accordingly (at 6 o'clock and 27 minutes p.m.), the House stood in recess.

□ 1830

AFTER RECESS

The recess having expired, the House was called to order by the Speaker pro tempore (Mr. HOLDING) at 6 o'clock and 30 minutes p.m.

ANNOUNCEMENT BY THE SPEAKER PRO TEMPORE

The SPEAKER pro tempore. Pursuant to clause 8 of rule XX, proceedings will resume on motions to suspend the rules previously postponed.

Votes will be taken in the following order:

H.R. 5422, by the yeas and nays;

H.R. 4757, by the yeas and nays;

H.R. 5843, de novo.

The first electronic vote will be conducted as a 15-minute vote. Remaining electronic votes will be conducted as 5-minute votes.

FUNDING FOR THE NATIONAL HUMAN TRAFFICKING HOTLINE

The SPEAKER pro tempore. The unfinished business is the vote on the motion to suspend the rules and pass the bill (H.R. 5422) to ensure funding for the National Human Trafficking Hotline, and for other purposes, on which the yeas and nays were ordered.

The Clerk read the title of the bill.

The SPEAKER pro tempore. The question is on the motion offered by the gentleman from Virginia (Mr. GOODLATTE) that the House suspend the rules and pass the bill.

The vote was taken by electronic device, and there were—yeas 399, nays 0, not voting 35, as follows:

[Roll No. 588]

YEAS—399

Abraham
Adams
Aderholt
Aguilar
Allen
Amash
Amodei
Ashford
Babin
Barr
Barton
Bass
Beatty
Becerra
Benishek
Bera
Bilirakis
Bishop (GA)
Bishop (MI)
Bishop (UT)
Black
Blackburn
Blum
Blumenauer
Bonamici
Bost
Boustany
Boyle, Brendan F.
Brady (PA)
Brady (TX)
Brat
Bridenstine
Brooks (AL)
Brooks (IN)
Brownley (CA)
Buchanan
Buck
Bucshon
Burgess
Bustos
Butterfield
Byrne
Calvert
Capps
Capuano
Cárdenas
Carney
Carson (IN)
Carter (GA)
Carter (TX)
Cartwright
Castor (FL)
Castro (TX)
Chabot
Chaffetz
Chu, Judy
Cicilline
Clark (MA)
Clarke (NY)
Clay
Cleaver
Clyburn
Coffman
Cohen
Cole
Collins (GA)
Collins (NY)
Comer
Comstock
Conaway
Connolly
Cook
Cooper
Costa
Courtney

Cramer
Crawford
Crenshaw
Crowley
Cuellar
Culberson
Cummings
Curbelo (FL)
Davidson
Davis (CA)
Davis, Danny
DeFazio
DeGette
Delaney
DeLauro
DelBene
Denham
Dent
DeSantis
DeSaulnier
DesJarlais
Deutch
Diaz-Balart
Dingell
Doggett
Dold
Donovan
Doyle, Michael F.
Duckworth
Duffy
Duncan (SC)
Duncan (TN)
Edwards
Ellison
Ellmers (NC)
Emmer (MN)
Eshoo
Esty
Evans
Farenthold
Farr
Fleischmann
Fleming
Flores
Fortenberry
Foster
Foxx
Frankel (FL)
Franks (AZ)
Frelinghuysen
Fudge
Gabbard
Gallego
Garamendi
Garrett
Gibbs
Gibson
Gohmert
Goodlatte
Gowdy
Graham
Granger
Graves (GA)
Graves (LA)
Graves (MO)
Grayson
Green, Al
Green, Gene
Griffith
Grothman
Guthrie
Gutiérrez
Hanabusa
Hanna
Hardy

Harper
Harris
Hartzler
Hastings
Heck (NV)
Heck (WA)
Hensarling
Herrera Beutler
Hice, Jody B.
Higgins
Hill
Himes
Hinojosa
Holding
Honda
Hoyer
Hudson
Huelskamp
Huffman
Huizenga (MI)
Hultgren
Hunter
Hurd (TX)
Israel
Issa
Jackson Lee
Jeffries
Jenkins (KS)
Jenkins (WV)
Johnson (GA)
Johnson (OH)
Johnson, E. B.
Johnson, Sam
Jordan
Joyce
Katko
Keating
Kelly (IL)
Kelly (MS)
Kelly (PA)
Kennedy
Kildee
Kilmer
Kind
King (IA)
King (NY)
Kinzinger (IL)
Kline
Knight
Kuster
Labrador
LaHood
LaMalfa
Lamborn
Lance
Langevin
Larsen (WA)
Larson (CT)
Latta
Lawrence
Lee
Levin
Lewis
Lieu, Ted
Lipinski
LoBiondo
Loebsack
Lofgren
Long
Loudermilk
Love
Lowenthal
Lowey
Lucas
Luetkemeyer

Lujan Grisham (NM)
Luján, Ben Ray (NM)
Lummis
Lynch
MacArthur
Maloney, Carolyn
Maloney, Sean
Marchant
Marino
Massie
Matsui
McCarthy
McClintock
McCollum
McDermott
McGovern
McHenry
McKinley
McMorris Rodgers
McNerney
McSally
Meadows
Meehan
Meeks
Meng
Messer
Mica
Miller (FL)
Moolenaar
Mooney (WV)
Moore
Moulton
Mullin
Mulvaney
Murphy (FL)
Murphy (PA)
Nadler
Napolitano
Neal
Neugebauer
Newhouse
Noem
Nolan
Norcross
Nunes
O'Rourke
Olson
Palazzo
Pallone
Palmer
Pascrell
Paulsen
Payne
Pearce
Pelosi
Perlmutter

Perry
Peters
Peterson
Pingree
Pittenger
Pitts
Pocan
Poliquin
Polis
Pompeo
Posey
Price (NC)
Price, Tom
Quigley
Rangel
Ratcliffe
Reed
Reichert
Ribble
Rice (NY)
Rice (SC)
Richmond
Rigell
Roby
Rogers (AL)
Rogers (KY)
Rohrabacher
Rokita
Rooney (FL)
Ros-Lehtinen
Roskam
Ross
Rothfus
Rouzer
Roybal-Allard
Royce
Ruiz
Ruppersberger
Rush
Russell
Ryan (OH)
Salmon
Sánchez, Linda T.
Sanford
Sarbanes
Scalise
Schakowsky
Schiff
Schrader
Schweikert
Scott (VA)
Scott, Austin
Scott, David
Sensenbrenner
Serrano
Sessions
Sewell (AL)
Sherman
Shimkus

Shuster
Simpson
Sinema
Sires
Slaughter
Smith (MO)
Smith (NE)
Smith (NJ)
Smith (TX)
Smith (WA)
Speier
Stefanik
Stewart
Stivers
Swalwell (CA)
Takano
Thompson (CA)
Thompson (MS)
Thompson (PA)
Thornberry
Tiberi
Tipton
Tonko
Torres
Tsongas
Turner
Upton
Valadao
Van Hollen
Vargas
Velázquez
Visclosky
Wagner
Walberg
Walden
Walker
Walorski
Walters, Mimi
Walz
Wasserman Schultz
Waters, Maxine
Watson Coleman
Webster (FL)
Welch
Wenstrup
Westerman
Wilson (FL)
Wilson (SC)
Wittman
Womack
Woodall
Yarmuth
Yoder
Yoho
Young (AK)
Young (IA)
Young (IN)
Zeldin
Zinke

NOT VOTING—35

Barletta
Beyer
Brown (FL)
Clawson (FL)
Conyers
Costello (PA)
Davis, Rodney
Engel
Fincher
Fitzpatrick
Forbes
Gosar

Grijalva
Guinta
Hahn
Hurt (VA)
Jolly
Jones
Kaptur
Kirkpatrick
McCaul
Miller (MI)
Nugent
Poe (TX)

Renacci
Roe (TN)
Sanchez, Loretta
Stutzman
Titus
Trott
Veasey
Vela
Weber (TX)
Westmoreland
Williams

☐ 1853

Mr. PAYNE changed his vote from "nay" to "yea."

So (two-thirds being in the affirmative) the rules were suspended and the bill was passed.

The result of the vote was announced as above recorded.

A motion to reconsider was laid on the table.

Stated for:

Mr. RODNEY DAVIS of Illinois. Mr. Speaker, on rollcall No. 588, I was unavoidably detained. Had I been present, I would have voted "yes."

EXPANSION OF ELIGIBILITY FOR HEADSTONES, MARKERS, AND MEDALLIONS FOR MEDAL OF HONOR RECIPIENTS

The SPEAKER pro tempore. The unfinished business is the vote on the motion to suspend the rules and pass the bill (H.R. 4757) to amend title 38, United States Code, to expand the eligibility for headstones, markers, and medallions furnished by the Secretary of Veterans Affairs for deceased individuals who were awarded the Medal of Honor and are buried in private cemeteries, as amended, on which the yeas and nays were ordered.

The Clerk read the title of the bill.

The SPEAKER pro tempore. The question is on the motion offered by the gentleman from Florida (Mr. MILLER) that the House suspend the rules and pass the bill, as amended.

This is a 5-minute vote.

The vote was taken by electronic device, and there were—yeas 401, nays 0, not voting 33, as follows:

[Roll No. 589]

YEAS—401

Abraham
Adams
Aderholt
Aguilar
Allen
Amash
Amodei
Ashford
Babin
Barr
Barton
Bass
Beatty
Becerra
Benishek
Bera
Bilirakis
Bishop (GA)
Bishop (MI)
Bishop (UT)
Black
Blackburn
Blum
Blumenauer
Bonamici
Bost
Boustany
Boyle, Brendan F.
Brady (PA)
Brady (TX)
Brat
Bridenstine
Brooks (AL)
Brooks (IN)
Brownley (CA)
Buchanan
Buck
Bucshon
Burgess
Bustos
Butterfield
Byrne
Calvert
Capps
Capuano
Cárdenas
Carney
Carson (IN)
Carter (GA)
Carter (TX)
Cartwright
Castor (FL)
Castro (TX)
Chabot
Chaffetz
Chu, Judy
Cicilline

Clark (MA)
Clarke (NY)
Clay
Cleaver
Clyburn
Coffman
Cohen
Cole
Collins (GA)
Collins (NY)
Comer
Comstock
Conaway
Connolly
Cook
Cooper
Costa
Costello (PA)
Courtney
Cramer
Crawford
Crenshaw
Crowley
Cuellar
Culberson
Cummings
Curbelo (FL)
Davidson
Davis (CA)
Davis, Danny
Davis, Rodney
DeFazio
DeGette
Delaney
DeLauro
DelBene
Denham
Dent
DeSantis
DeSaulnier
DesJarlais
Deutch
Diaz-Balart
Dingell
Doggett
Dold
Donovan
Doyle, Michael F.
Duckworth
Duffy
Duncan (SC)
Duncan (TN)
Edwards
Ellison
Ellmers (NC)
Emmer (MN)
Eshoo

Esty
Evans
Farenthold
Farr
Fleischmann
Fleming
Flores
Fortenberry
Foster
Foxx
Frankel (FL)
Franks (AZ)
Frelinghuysen
Fudge
Gabbard
Gallego
Garamendi
Garrett
Gibbs
Gibson
Gohmert
Goodlatte
Gosar
Gowdy
Graham
Granger
Graves (GA)
Graves (LA)
Grayson
Green, Al
Green, Gene
Griffith
Grothman
Guthrie
Gutiérrez
Hanabusa
Hanna
Hardy
Harper
Harris
Hartzler
Hastings
Heck (NV)
Heck (WA)
Hensarling
Herrera Beutler
Hice, Jody B.
Higgins
Hill
Himes
Hinojosa
Holding
Honda
Hoyer
Hudson
Huelskamp
Huffman
Huizenga (MI)

Hultgren
Hunter
Hurd (TX)
Israel
Issa
Jackson Lee
Jeffries
Jenkins (KS)
Jenkins (WV)
Johnson (GA)
Johnson (OH)
Johnson, E. B.
Johnson, Sam
Jordan
Joyce
Kaptur
Katko
Keating
Kelly (IL)
Kelly (MS)
Kelly (PA)
Kennedy
Kildee
Kilmer
Kind
King (IA)
King (NY)
Kinzinger (IL)
Kline
Knight
Kuster
Labrador
LaHood
LaMalfa
Lamborn
Lance
Langevin
Larsen (WA)
Larson (CT)
Latta
Lawrence
Lee
Levin
Lewis
Lieu, Ted
Lipinski
LoBiondo
Loebsack
Lofgren
Long
Loudermilk
Love
Lowenthal
Lowey
Lucas
Luetkemeyer
Lujan Grisham (NM)
Luján, Ben Ray (NM)
Lummis
Lynch
MacArthur
Maloney, Carolyn
Maloney, Sean
Marchant
Marino
Massie
Matsui
McCarthy
McClintock
McCollum
McDermott
McGovern
McHenry
McKinley
McMorris Rodgers

McNerney
McSally
Meadows
Meehan
Meeks
Meng
Messer
Mica
Miller (FL)
Moolenaar
Mooney (WV)
Moore
Moulton
Mullin
Mulvaney
Murphy (FL)
Murphy (PA)
Nadler
Napolitano
Neal
Neugebauer
Newhouse
Noem
Nolan
Norcross
Nunes
O'Rourke
Olson
Palazzo
Pallone
Palmer
Pascrell
Paulsen
Payne
Pearce
Pelosi
Perlmutter
Perry
Peters
Peterson
Pingree
Pittenger
Pitts
Pocan
Poliquin
Polis
Pompeo
Posey
Price (NC)
Price, Tom
Quigley
Rangel
Ratcliffe
Reed
Reichert
Ribble
Rice (NY)
Rice (SC)
Richmond
Rigell
Roby
Rogers (AL)
Rogers (KY)
Rohrabacher
Rokita
Rooney (FL)
Ros-Lehtinen
Roskam
Ross
Rothfus
Rouzer
Roybal-Allard
Royce
Ruiz
Ruppersberger
Rush
Russell
Salmon

Sánchez, Linda T.
Sanford
Sarbanes
Scalise
Schakowsky
Schiff
Schrader
Schweikert
Scott (VA)
Scott, Austin
Scott, David
Sensenbrenner
Serrano
Sessions
Sewell (AL)
Sherman
Shimkus
Shuster
Simpson
Sinema
Sires
Slaughter
Smith (MO)
Smith (NE)
Smith (NJ)
Smith (TX)
Smith (WA)
Speier
Stefanik
Stewart
Stivers
Swalwell (CA)
Takano
Thompson (CA)
Thompson (MS)
Thompson (PA)
Thornberry
Tiberi
Tipton
Tonko
Torres
Tsongas
Turner
Upton
Valadao
Van Hollen
Vargas
Velázquez
Visclosky
Wagner
Walberg
Walden
Walker
Walorski
Walters, Mimi
Walz
Wasserman Schultz
Waters, Maxine
Watson Coleman
Webster (FL)
Welch
Wenstrup
Westerman
Wilson (FL)
Wilson (SC)
Wittman
Womack
Woodall
Yarmuth
Yoder
Yoho
Young (AK)
Young (IA)
Young (IN)
Zeldin
Zinke

NOT VOTING—33

Barletta
Beyer
Brown (FL)
Clawson (FL)
Conyers
Engel
Fincher
Fitzpatrick
Forbes
Graves (MO)
Grijalva

Guinta
Hahn
Hurt (VA)
Jolly
Jones
Kirkpatrick
McCaul
Miller (MI)
Nugent
Poe (TX)
Renacci

Roe (TN)
Ryan (OH)
Sanchez, Loretta
Stutzman
Titus
Trott
Veasey
Vela
Weber (TX)
Westmoreland
Williams

ANNOUNCEMENT BY THE SPEAKER PRO TEMPORE

The SPEAKER pro tempore (during the vote). There are 2 minutes remaining.

□ 1901

So (two-thirds being in the affirmative) the rules were suspended and the bill, as amended, was passed.

The result of the vote was announced as above recorded.

The title of the bill was amended so as to read: "A bill to expand the eligibility for headstones, markers, and medallions furnished by the Secretary of Veterans Affairs for deceased individuals who were awarded the Medal of Honor and are buried in private cemeteries, and for other purposes.".

A motion to reconsider was laid on the table.

PERSONAL EXPLANATION

Mr. McCAUL. On November 29, 2016, I missed the voting session. If present, I would have voted as follows: "Yes"—H.R. 5422—To ensure funding for the National Human Trafficking Hotline, and for other purposes.

"Yes"—H.R. 4757—To amend title 38, United States Code, to expand the eligibility for headstones, markers, and medallions furnished by the Secretary of Veterans Affairs for deceased individuals who were awarded the Medal of Honor and are buried in private cemeteries, as amended.

UNITED STATES-ISRAEL CYBERSECURITY COOPERATION ENHANCEMENT ACT OF 2016

The SPEAKER pro tempore. The unfinished business is the question on suspending the rules and passing the bill (H.R. 5843) to establish a grant program at the Department of Homeland Security to promote cooperative research and development between the United States and Israel on cybersecurity, as amended.

The Clerk read the title of the bill.

The SPEAKER pro tempore. The question is on the motion offered by the gentleman from Texas (Mr. RATCLIFFE) that the House suspend the rules and pass the bill, as amended.

The question was taken; and (two-thirds being in the affirmative) the rules were suspended and the bill, as amended, was passed.

A motion to reconsider was laid on the table.

REPORT ON H. RES. 933, PROVIDING AMOUNTS FOR FURTHER EXPENSES OF THE COMMITTEE ON ENERGY AND COMMERCE IN THE ONE HUNDRED FOURTEENTH CONGRESS

Mr. HARPER, from the Committee on House Administration, submitted a privileged report (Rept. No. 114–838) providing amounts for further expenses of the Committee on Energy and Commerce in the One Hundred Fourteenth Congress, which was referred to the House Calendar and ordered to be printed.

TREATMENT OF BUILDINGS AND OTHER AREAS WITHIN BOUNDARIES OF REAL ESTATE OR OTHER PROPERTY INTERESTS ACQUIRED BY NATIONAL GALLERY OF ART

Mr. HARPER. Mr. Speaker, I ask unanimous consent to take from the Speaker's table the bill (H.R. 5160) to amend title 40, United States Code, to include as part of the buildings and grounds of the National Gallery of Art any buildings and other areas within the boundaries of any real estate or other property interests acquired by the National Gallery of Art, and ask for its immediate consideration in the House.

The Clerk read the title of the bill.

The SPEAKER pro tempore (Mr. GRAVES of Louisiana). Is there objection to the request of the gentleman from Mississippi?

There was no objection.

The text of the bill is as follows:

H.R. 5160

Be it enacted by the Senate and House of Representatives of the United States of America in Congress assembled,

SECTION 1. TREATMENT OF BUILDINGS AND OTHER AREAS WITHIN BOUNDARIES OF REAL ESTATE OR OTHER PROPERTY INTERESTS ACQUIRED BY NATIONAL GALLERY OF ART.

Section 6301(2) of title 40, United States Code, is amended—

(1) in the matter preceding subparagraph (A), by striking "The National Gallery of Art" and inserting "(A) The National Gallery of Art";

(2) by redesignating subparagraphs (A), (B), and (C) as clauses (i), (ii), and (iii), respectively; and

(3) by adding at the end the following new subparagraph:

"(B) All other buildings, service roads, walks, and other areas within the exterior boundaries of any real estate or land or interest in land (including temporary use) that the National Gallery of Art acquires and that the Director of the National Gallery of Art determines to be necessary for the adequate protection of individuals or property in the National Gallery of Art and suitable for administration as a part of the National Gallery of Art.".

The bill was ordered to be engrossed and read a third time, was read the third time, and passed, and a motion to reconsider was laid on the table.

REPORT ON RESOLUTION PROVIDING FOR CONSIDERATION OF SENATE AMENDMENT TO H.R. 34, TSUNAMI WARNING, EDUCATION, AND RESEARCH ACT OF 2015, AND PROVIDING FOR CONSIDERATION OF H.R. 6392, SYSTEMIC RISK DESIGNATION IMPROVEMENT ACT OF 2016

Mr. BURGESS, from the Committee on Rules, submitted a privileged report (Rept. No. 114–839) on the resolution (H.

Res. 934) providing for consideration of the Senate amendment to the bill (H.R. 34) to authorize and strengthen the tsunami detection, forecast, warning, research, and mitigation program of the National Oceanic and Atmospheric Administration, and for other purposes, and providing for consideration of the bill (H.R. 6392) to amend the Dodd-Frank Wall Street Reform and Consumer Protection Act to specify when bank holding companies may be subject to certain enhanced supervision, and for other purposes, which was referred to the House Calendar and ordered to be printed.

VETERANS MOBILITY SAFETY ACT OF 2016

Mrs. WALORSKI. Mr. Speaker, I ask unanimous consent to take from the Speaker's table the bill (H.R. 3471) to amend title 38, United States Code, to make certain improvements in the provision of automobiles and adaptive equipment by the Department of Veterans Affairs, with the Senate amendment thereto, and concur in the Senate amendment.

The Clerk read the title of the bill.

The SPEAKER pro tempore. The Clerk will report the Senate amendment.

The Clerk read as follows:

Senate amendment:

Strike all after the enacting clause and insert the following:

SECTION 1. SHORT TITLE.

This Act may be cited as the "Veterans Mobility Safety Act of 2016".

SEC. 2. PERSONAL SELECTIONS OF AUTOMOBILES AND ADAPTIVE EQUIPMENT.

Section 3903(b) of title 38, United States Code, is amended—

(1) by striking "Except" and inserting "(1) Except"; and

(2) by adding at the end the following new paragraph:

"(2) The Secretary shall ensure that to the extent practicable an eligible person who is provided an automobile or other conveyance under this chapter is given the opportunity to make personal selections relating to such automobile or other conveyance.".

SEC. 3. COMPREHENSIVE POLICY FOR THE AUTOMOBILES ADAPTIVE EQUIPMENT PROGRAM.

(a) COMPREHENSIVE POLICY.—The Secretary of Veterans Affairs shall develop a comprehensive policy regarding quality standards for providers who provide modification services to veterans under the automobile adaptive equipment program.

(b) SCOPE.—The policy developed under subsection (a) shall cover each of the following:

(1) The Department of Veterans Affairs-wide management of the automobile adaptive equipment program.

(2) The development of standards for safety and quality of equipment and installation of equipment through the automobile adaptive equipment program, including with respect to the defined differentiations in levels of modification complexity.

(3) The consistent application of standards for safety and quality of both equipment and installation throughout the Department.

(4) In accordance with subsection (c)(1), the certification of a provider by a manufacturer if the Secretary designates the quality standards of such manufacturer as meeting or exceeding the standards developed under this section.

(5) In accordance with subsection (c)(2), the certification of a provider by a third party, nonprofit organization if the Secretary designates the quality standards of such organization as meeting or exceeding the standards developed under this section.

(6) The education and training of personnel of the Department who administer the automobile adaptive equipment program.

(7) The compliance of the provider with the Americans with Disabilities Act of 1990 (42 U.S.C. 12101 et seq.) when furnishing automobile adaptive equipment at the facility of the provider.

(8) The allowance, where technically appropriate, for veterans to receive modifications at their residence or location of choice, including standards that ensure such receipt and notification to veterans of the availability of such receipt.

(c) CERTIFICATION OF MANUFACTURERS AND THIRD PARTY, NONPROFIT ORGANIZATIONS.—

(1) CERTIFICATION OF MANUFACTURERS.—The Secretary shall approve a manufacturer as a certifying manufacturer for purposes of subsection (b)(4), if the manufacturer demonstrates that its certification standards meet or exceed the quality standards developed under this section.

(2) CERTIFICATION OF THIRD PARTY, NONPROFIT ORGANIZATIONS.—

(A) IN GENERAL.—The Secretary may approve two or more private, nonprofit organizations as third party, nonprofit certifying organizations for purposes of subsection (b)(5).

(B) LIMITATION.—If at any time there is only one third party, nonprofit certifying organization approved by the Secretary for purposes of subsection (b)(5), such organization shall not be permitted to provide certifications under such subsection until such time as the Secretary approves a second third party, nonprofit certifying organization for purposes of such subsection.

(d) UPDATES.—

(1) INITIAL UPDATES.—Not later than 1 year after the date of the enactment of this Act, the Secretary shall update Veterans Health Administration Handbook 1173.4, or any successor handbook or directive, in accordance with the policy developed under subsection (a).

(2) SUBSEQUENT UPDATES.—Not less frequently than once every 6 years thereafter, the Secretary shall update such handbook, or any successor handbook or directive.

(e) CONSULTATION.—The Secretary shall develop the policy under subsection (a), and revise such policy under subsection (d), in consultation with veterans service organizations, the National Highway Transportation Administration, industry representatives, manufacturers of automobile adaptive equipment, and other entities with expertise in installing, repairing, replacing, or manufacturing mobility equipment or developing mobility accreditation standards for automobile adaptive equipment.

(f) CONFLICTS.—In developing and implementing the policy under subsection (a), the Secretary shall—

(1) minimize the possibility of conflicts of interest, to the extent practicable; and

(2) establish procedures that ensure against the use of a certifying organization referred to in subsection (b)(5) that has a financial conflict of interest regarding the certification of an eligible provider.

(g) BIENNIAL REPORT.—

(1) IN GENERAL.—Not later than 1 year after the date on which the Secretary updates Veterans Health Administration Handbook 1173.4,

or any successor handbook or directive, under subsection (d), and not less frequently than once every other year thereafter through 2022, the Secretary shall submit to the Committee on Veterans' Affairs of the Senate and the Committee on Veterans' Affairs of the House of Representatives a report on the implementation and facility compliance with the policy developed under subsection (a).

(2) CONTENTS.—The report required by paragraph (1) shall include the following:

(A) A description of the implementation plan for the policy developed under subsection (a) and any revisions to such policy under subsection (d).

(B) A description of the performance measures used to determine the effectiveness of such policy in ensuring the safety of veterans enrolled in the automobile adaptive equipment program.

(C) An assessment of safety issues due to improper installations based on a survey of recipients of adaptive equipment from the Department.

(D) An assessment of the adequacy of the adaptive equipment services of the Department based on a survey of recipients of adaptive equipment from the Department.

(E) An assessment of the training provided to the personnel of the Department with respect to administering the program.

(F) An assessment of the certified providers of the Department of adaptive equipment with respect to meeting the minimum standards developed under subsection (b)(2).

(h) DEFINITIONS.—In this section:

(1) AUTOMOBILE ADAPTIVE EQUIPMENT PROGRAM.—The term "automobile adaptive equipment program" means the program administered by the Secretary of Veterans Affairs pursuant to chapter 39 of title 38, United States Code.

(2) VETERANS SERVICE ORGANIZATION.—The term "veterans service organization" means any organization recognized by the Secretary for the representation of veterans under section 5902 of title 38, United States Code.

SEC. 4. APPOINTMENT OF LICENSED HEARING AID SPECIALISTS IN VETERANS HEALTH ADMINISTRATION.

(a) LICENSED HEARING AID SPECIALISTS.—

(1) APPOINTMENT.—Section 7401(3) of title 38, United States Code, is amended by inserting "licensed hearing aid specialists," after "Audiologists,".

(2) QUALIFICATIONS.—Section 7402(b)(14) of such title is amended by inserting ", hearing aid specialist" after "dental technologist".

(b) REQUIREMENTS.—With respect to appointing hearing aid specialists under sections 7401 and 7402 of title 38, United States Code, as amended by subsection (a), and providing services furnished by such specialists, the Secretary shall ensure that—

(1) a hearing aid specialist may only perform hearing services consistent with the hearing aid specialist's State license related to the practice of fitting and dispensing hearing aids without excluding other qualified professionals, including audiologists, from rendering services in overlapping practice areas;

(2) services provided to veterans by hearing aid specialists shall be provided as part of the non-medical treatment plan developed by an audiologist; and

(3) the medical facilities of the Department of Veterans Affairs provide to veterans access to the full range of professional services provided by an audiologist.

(c) CONSULTATION.—In determining the qualifications required for hearing aid specialists and in carrying out subsection (b), the Secretary shall consult with veterans service organizations, audiologists, otolaryngologists, hearing aid specialists, and other stakeholder and industry groups as the Secretary determines appropriate.

(d) ANNUAL REPORT.—

(1) IN GENERAL.—Not later than 1 year after the date of the enactment of this Act, and annually thereafter during the 5-year period beginning on the date of the enactment of this Act, the Secretary of Veterans Affairs shall submit to Congress a report on the following:

(A) Timely access of veterans to hearing health services through the Department of Veterans Affairs.

(B) Contracting policies of the Department with respect to providing hearing health services to veterans in facilities that are not facilities of the Department.

(2) TIMELY ACCESS TO SERVICES.—Each report shall, with respect to the matter specified in paragraph (1)(A) for the 1-year period preceding the submittal of such report, include the following:

(A) The staffing levels of audiologists, hearing aid specialists, and health technicians in audiology in the Veterans Health Administration.

(B) A description of the metrics used by the Secretary in measuring performance with respect to appointments and care relating to hearing health.

(C) The average time that a veteran waits to receive an appointment, beginning on the date on which the veteran makes the request, for the following:

(i) A disability rating evaluation for a hearing-related disability.

(ii) A hearing aid evaluation.

(iii) Dispensing of hearing aids.

(iv) Any follow-up hearing health appointment.

(D) The percentage of veterans whose total wait time for appointments described in subparagraph (C), including an initial and follow-up appointment, if applicable, is more than 30 days.

(3) CONTRACTING POLICIES.—Each report shall, with respect to the matter specified in paragraph (1)(B) for the 1-year period preceding the submittal of such report, include the following:

(A) The number of veterans that the Secretary refers to non-Department audiologists for hearing health care appointments.

(B) The number of veterans that the Secretary refers to non-Department hearing aid specialists for follow-up appointments for a hearing aid evaluation, the dispensing of hearing aids, or any other purpose relating to hearing health.

Mr. KING of New York (during the reading). Mr. Speaker, I ask unanimous consent that the amendment be considered as read.

The SPEAKER pro tempore. Is there objection to the request of the gentleman from New York?

There was no objection.

The SPEAKER pro tempore. Is there objection to the original request of the gentlewoman from Indiana?

There was no objection.

A motion to reconsider was laid on the table.

FIRST RESPONDER ANTHRAX PREPAREDNESS ACT

Mr. KING of New York. Mr. Speaker, I ask unanimous consent to take from the Speaker's table the bill (S. 1915) to direct the Secretary of Homeland Security to make anthrax vaccines available to emergency response providers, and for other purposes, and ask for its immediate consideration in the House.

The Clerk read the title of the bill.

The SPEAKER pro tempore. Is there objection to the request of the gentleman from New York?

There was no objection.

The text of the bill is as follows:

S. 1915

Be it enacted by the Senate and House of Representatives of the United States of America in Congress assembled,

SECTION 1. SHORT TITLE.

This Act may be cited as the "First Responder Anthrax Preparedness Act".

SEC. 2. VOLUNTARY PRE-EVENT ANTHRAX VACCINATION PILOT PROGRAM FOR EMERGENCY RESPONSE PROVIDERS.

(a) PILOT PROGRAM.—

(1) ESTABLISHMENT.—The Secretary of Homeland Security, in coordination with the Secretary of Health and Human Services, shall carry out a pilot program to provide eligible anthrax vaccines from the Strategic National Stockpile under section 319F–2(a) of the Public Health Service Act (42 U.S.C. 247d–6b(a)) that will be nearing the end of their labeled dates of use at the time such vaccines are made available to States for administration to emergency response providers who would be at high risk of exposure to anthrax if such an attack should occur and who voluntarily consent to such administration.

(2) DETERMINATION.—The Secretary of Health and Human Services shall determine whether an anthrax vaccine is eligible to be provided to the Secretary of Homeland Security for the pilot program described in paragraph (1) based on—

(A) a determination that the vaccine is not otherwise allotted for other purposes;

(B) a determination that the provision of the vaccine will not reduce, or otherwise adversely affect, the capability to meet projected requirements for this product during a public health emergency, including a significant reduction of available quantities of vaccine in the Strategic National Stockpile; and

(C) such other considerations as determined appropriate by the Secretary of Health and Human Services.

(3) PRELIMINARY REQUIREMENTS.—Before implementing the pilot program required under this subsection, the Secretary of Homeland Security, in coordination with the Secretary of Health and Human Services, shall—

(A) establish a communication platform for the pilot program;

(B) develop and deliver education and training for the pilot program;

(C) conduct economic analysis of the pilot program, including a preliminary estimate of total costs and expected benefits;

(D) create a logistical platform for the anthrax vaccine request process under the pilot program;

(E) establish goals and desired outcomes for the pilot program; and

(F) establish a mechanism to reimburse the Secretary of Health and Human Services for—

(i) the costs of shipment and transportation of such vaccines provided to the Secretary of Homeland Security from the Strategic National Stockpile under such pilot program, including staff time directly supporting such shipment and transportation; and

(ii) the amount, if any, by which the warehousing costs of the Strategic National Stockpile are increased in order to operate such pilot program.

(4) LOCATION.—

(A) IN GENERAL.—In carrying out the pilot program required under this subsection, the Secretary of Homeland Security shall select not fewer than 2 nor more than 5 States for voluntary participation in the pilot program.

(B) REQUIREMENT.—Each State that participates in the pilot program under this subsection shall ensure that such participation is consistent with the All-Hazards Public Health Emergency Preparedness and Response Plan of the State developed under section 319C–1 of the Public Health Service Act (42 U.S.C. 247d–3a).

(5) GUIDANCE FOR SELECTION.—To ensure that participation in the pilot program under this subsection strategically increases State and local response readiness in the event of an anthrax release, the Secretary of Homeland Security, in coordination with the Secretary of Health and Human Services, shall provide guidance to participating States and units of local government on identifying emergency response providers who are at high risk of exposure to anthrax.

(6) DISTRIBUTION OF INFORMATION.—The Secretary of Homeland Security shall require that each State that participates in the pilot program under this subsection submit a written certification to the Secretary of Homeland Security stating that each emergency response provider within the State that participates in the pilot program is provided with disclosures and educational materials designated by the Secretary of Health and Human Services, which may include—

(A) materials regarding the associated benefits and risks of any vaccine provided under the pilot program, and of exposure to anthrax;

(B) additional material consistent with the Centers for Disease Control and Prevention's clinical guidance; and

(C) notice that the Federal Government is not obligated to continue providing anthrax vaccine after the date on which the pilot program ends.

(7) MEMORANDUM OF UNDERSTANDING.—Before implementing the pilot program under this subsection, the Secretary of Homeland Security shall enter into a memorandum of understanding with the Secretary of Health and Human Services to—

(A) define the roles and responsibilities of each Department for the pilot program; and

(B) establish other performance metrics and policies for the pilot program, as appropriate.

(8) REPORT.—

(A) IN GENERAL.—Notwithstanding subsection (c), not later than 1 year after the date on which the initial vaccines are administered under this section, and annually thereafter until 1 year after the completion of the pilot program under this section, the Secretary of Homeland Security, in coordination with the Secretary of Health and Human Services, shall submit to the Committee on Homeland Security and the Committee on Energy and Commerce of the House of Representatives and the Committee on Homeland Security and Governmental Affairs and the Committee on Health, Education, Labor, and Pensions of the Senate a report on the progress and results of the pilot program, including—

(i) a detailed tabulation of the costs to administer the program, including—

(I) total costs for management and administration;

(II) total costs to ship vaccines;

(III) total number of full-time equivalents allocated to the program; and

(IV) total costs to the Strategic National Stockpile;

(ii) the number and percentage of eligible emergency response providers, as determined by each pilot location, that volunteer to participate;

(iii) the degree to which participants complete the vaccine regimen;

(iv) the total number of doses of vaccine administered; and

(v) recommendations to improve initial and recurrent participation in the pilot program.

(B) FINAL REPORT.—The final report required under subparagraph (A) shall—

(i) consider whether the pilot program required under this subsection should continue after the date described in subsection (c); and

(ii) include—

(I) an analysis of the costs and benefits of continuing the program to provide anthrax vaccines to emergency response providers;

(II) an explanation of the economic, health, and other risks and benefits of administering vaccines through the pilot program rather than post-event treatment; and

(III) in the case of a recommendation under clause (i) to continue the pilot program after the date described in subsection (c), a plan under which the pilot program could be continued.

(b) DEADLINE FOR IMPLEMENTATION.—Not later than 1 year after the date of enactment of this Act, the Secretary of Homeland Security shall begin implementing the pilot program under this section.

(c) SUNSET.—The authority to carry out the pilot program under this section shall expire on the date that is 5 years after the date of enactment of this Act.

The bill was ordered to be read a third time, was read the third time, and passed, and a motion to reconsider was laid on the table.

NORTHERN BORDER SECURITY REVIEW ACT

Mr. KING of New York. Mr. Speaker, I ask unanimous consent to take from the Speaker's table the bill (S. 1808) to require the Secretary of Homeland Security to conduct a Northern Border threat analysis, and for other purposes, and ask for its immediate consideration in the House.

The Clerk read the title of the bill.

The SPEAKER pro tempore. Is there objection to the request of the gentleman from New York?

There was no objection.

The text of the bill is as follows:

S. 1808

Be it enacted by the Senate and House of Representatives of the United States of America in Congress assembled,

SECTION 1. SHORT TITLE.

This Act may be cited as the "Northern Border Security Review Act".

SEC. 2. DEFINITIONS.

In this Act:

(1) APPROPRIATE CONGRESSIONAL COMMITTEES.—The term "appropriate congressional committees" means—

(A) the Committee on Homeland Security and Governmental Affairs of the Senate;

(B) the Committee on Appropriations of the Senate;

(C) the Committee on the Judiciary of the Senate;

(D) the Committee on Homeland Security of the House of Representatives;

(E) the Committee on Appropriations of the House of Representatives; and

(F) the Committee on the Judiciary of the House of Representatives.

(2) NORTHERN BORDER.—The term "Northern Border" means the land and maritime borders between the United States and Canada.

SEC. 3. NORTHERN BORDER THREAT ANALYSIS.

(a) IN GENERAL.—Not later than 180 days after the date of enactment of this Act, the Secretary of Homeland Security shall submit a Northern Border threat analysis to the appropriate congressional committees that includes—

(1) current and potential terrorism and criminal threats posed by individuals and organized groups seeking—

(A) to enter the United States through the Northern Border; or

(B) to exploit border vulnerabilities on the Northern Border;

(2) improvements needed at and between ports of entry along the Northern Border—

(A) to prevent terrorists and instruments of terrorism from entering the United States; and

(B) to reduce criminal activity, as measured by the total flow of illegal goods, illicit drugs, and smuggled and trafficked persons moved in either direction across to the Northern Border;

(3) gaps in law, policy, cooperation between State, tribal, and local law enforcement, international agreements, or tribal agreements that hinder effective and efficient border security, counter-terrorism, anti-human smuggling and trafficking efforts, and the flow of legitimate trade along the Northern Border; and

(4) whether additional U.S. Customs and Border Protection preclearance and pre-inspection operations at ports of entry along the Northern Border could help prevent terrorists and instruments of terror from entering the United States.

(b) ANALYSIS REQUIREMENTS.—For the threat analysis required under subsection (a), the Secretary of Homeland Security shall consider and examine—

(1) technology needs and challenges;

(2) personnel needs and challenges;

(3) the role of State, tribal, and local law enforcement in general border security activities;

(4) the need for cooperation among Federal, State, tribal, local, and Canadian law enforcement entities relating to border security;

(5) the terrain, population density, and climate along the Northern Border; and

(6) the needs and challenges of Department facilities, including the physical approaches to such facilities.

(c) CLASSIFIED THREAT ANALYSIS.—To the extent possible, the Secretary of Homeland Security shall submit the threat analysis required under subsection (a) in unclassified form. The Secretary may submit a portion of the threat analysis in classified form if the Secretary determines that such form is appropriate for that portion.

The bill was ordered to be read a third time, was read the third time, and passed, and a motion to reconsider was laid on the table.

MOMENT OF SILENCE FOR VICTIMS OF WOODMORE ELEMENTARY SCHOOL BUS CRASH

(Mr. FLEISCHMANN asked and was given permission to address the House for 1 minute.)

Mr. FLEISCHMANN. Mr. Speaker, tonight I rise to offer a moment of si-lence. On November 21, while many of us were preparing for the Thanksgiving holiday, tragedy once again struck my hometown of Chattanooga, Tennessee.

Woodmore Elementary School is a beautiful elementary school; young, vibrant children, all so precious. There was a tragic schoolbus crash that happened that day in Chattanooga, Tennessee. The crash took the lives of six young children: Keonte Wilson, Cor'Dayja Jones, Zyaira Mateen, D'Myunn Brown, Zoie Nash, and Zyanna Harris. In addition, several other children were severely injured. Many are still in critical condition.

I know I can speak for all of us, including my dear friends who have joined me from the Tennessee delegation, when I say that we are absolutely heartbroken over this horrific tragedy. Nothing I can say tonight can diminish the gravity of the loss that our community has suffered.

But I must thank the first responders, the Chattanooga Police Department, the local officials, and especially the staff, the doctors at Children's Hospital at Erlanger, for their immediate and compassionate response to this tragedy.

My brothers and sisters in the House, I went with our Governor to see the care and treatment that these children were getting. One young lady about to go up to surgery gave me the thumbs up.

At a time of such tragic loss, these precious lives were lost, and so many are forever hurt. Please join me now in a moment of silence for the victims, for their families, and for our Chattanooga community.

□ 1915

REMEMBERING SAN ANTONIO POLICE OFFICER DETECTIVE BENJAMIN MARCONI

(Mr. CASTRO of Texas asked and was given permission to address the House for 1 minute.)

Mr. CASTRO of Texas. Mr. Speaker, I rise the day after my hometown, San Antonio, laid to rest a hero who was taken from us too soon, Detective Benjamin Marconi.

The son of a San Antonio police officer, Detective Marconi was a 20-year veteran of the force whose life was tragically cut short last week while he was in the field serving our city.

Known for his big smile, his kindness, and his commitment to doing the right thing, Detective Marconi was a beloved member of our community. He leaves behind a son, a grandson, and an extended family who brought him great joy.

Our city mourns the loss of Detective Marconi, an outstanding San Antonian, whom we dearly miss. His passing is a tragic reminder of the risk all of our law enforcement officers take when they go to work each day to keep us safe. We are grateful for his service and theirs.

FIDEL CASTRO'S BRUTAL LEGACY

(Ms. ROS-LEHTINEN asked and was given permission to address the House for 1 minute and to revise and extend her remarks.)

Ms. ROS-LEHTINEN. Mr. Speaker, the Cuban people can finally close one chapter in their 57-year nightmare of oppressive rule: Fidel Castro has died.

When I was just 8 years old, I was forced to flee my native homeland of Cuba with my family. We were not the first, nor were we the last, to leave all that we had behind in search of freedom, democracy, opportunity, and safety.

Many constituents I am so humbled to represent have had family members who did not survive their journey, yet they all risked their lives in fleeing Cuba because they felt the brutality of Fidel Castro. They witnessed firsthand the ruthlessness of the tyrant, and they felt that it was like having their human rights stripped from their very being.

Their stories and their experiences—the firing squads, the gulags, and the torture—Mr. Speaker, will be Fidel Castro's legacy.

EL PASO DREAMERS

(Mr. O'ROURKE asked and was given permission to address the House for 1 minute.)

Mr. O'ROURKE. Mr. Speaker, in this country, there are over 700,000 DREAMers, children and young Americans brought to this country at a young age, through no fault of their own, to improve their lives, their opportunities, and those of their families. They are every bit as much American as you or I or our children.

Pictured next to me is Itzel Campos of El Paso, Texas, a 15-year-old sophomore at Franklin High School, who came to a townhall meeting that we had last night where 300 El Pasoans came out to either tell their stories or show support for DREAMers.

We want to make sure that the President-elect and that the Congress that we have here and the one that will be seated in January do everything within their power to keep these DREAMers in our country, who will earn more than $4 trillion in taxable income during their lives but, more importantly, will contribute to the American Dream, will improve communities like mine, which happens to be the safest city in America in large part because of the immigrants, and especially these DREAMers who call El Paso home, and to give people like Itzel every chance to succeed, to improve their lives and the course of this country.

CONGRATULATIONS TO GOVERNOR NIKKI HALEY

(Mr. WILSON of South Carolina asked and was given permission to address the House for 1 minute and to revise and extend his remarks.)

Mr. WILSON of South Carolina. Mr. Speaker, President-elect Donald Trump nominated South Carolina Governor Nikki Haley to be America's Ambassador to the United Nations.

President-elect Trump has announced:

Governor Haley has a proven record of bringing people together regardless of background or party affiliation to move critical policies forward for the betterment of her State and country. She is also a proven dealmaker, and we look forward to making plenty of deals. She will be a great leader representing us on the world stage.

Governor Haley has led the people of South Carolina through trying times, such as the historic thousand-year flood last year, Hurricane Matthew flooding this year, and the tragic shooting at Mother Emanuel Church in Charleston. She has promoted a pro-business and pro-job environment by recruiting major companies such as Boeing and Volvo, along with Michelin, BMW, and Bridgestone expansions. Governor Haley will be a strong and effective voice for America, advancing freedom and democracy around the world.

Congratulations to Governor Haley and her husband, Michael, and children, Rena and Nalin, on this achievement. Your Lexington County neighbors are very proud of you.

In conclusion, God bless our troops, and may the President, by his actions, never forget September the 11th in the global war on terrorism.

REDUCING RED TAPE

(Mr. LAMALFA asked and was given permission to address the House for 1 minute and to revise and extend his remarks.)

Mr. LAMALFA. Mr. Speaker, I am pleased that the House Subcommittee on Federal Lands is holding a hearing soon on H.R. 5129, the Guide and Outfitter Act—we call it the GO Act—which I have sponsored to make it easier for Americans to access and enjoy their public lands.

I began working on this legislation after an annual endurance run in my district, which had been held for years, was canceled after Federal agencies demanded a costly new study of the event's environmental impacts, a study the small, nonprofit group that held the event couldn't afford. That's right, Federal agencies were concerned that people running on existing trails could have negative impacts on the environment.

The GO Act cuts this red tape by creating a categorical exclusion to ensure activities which have already been permitted do not need duplicative studies in order to continue. It creates a one-stop joint permitting system so races and other events that might stretch across Forest Service lands, BLM, and National Park land, et cetera, don't need to repeat the permit process over and over and over with every single agency.

The bill caps fees to keep them affordable and allows existing permits to be easily extended so that public access and events can continue.

I am proud to say this bill will help get more Americans outside, Mr. Speaker, for less money and with less red tape. That is a goal every Member of this body can support.

AVOIDING TRUMP ADMINISTRATION CONFLICTS OF INTEREST

(Ms. KAPTUR asked and was given permission to address the House for 1 minute.)

Ms. KAPTUR. Mr. Speaker, I am one of those Americans who is very concerned about the conflict of interest that the President-elect faces as he assumes office. I don't think we have ever elected someone to office in this country with his vast wealth, but I must say, as ranking member on the Energy and Water Development, and Related Agencies Subcommittee of the Committee on Appropriations, let me give you one area which causes me concern: where he will separate his private interest from the public interest.

The committee on which I rank handles the Army Corps of Engineers' budget, and we don't have enough money to deal with all the projects around the country, some of which are backed up 20 years. What happens if Mar-a-Lago in Florida faces flooding—or any of the other coastal properties that the President-elect owns—and the Army is trying to make a decision on where to place Federal funds? Will his properties take precedence over thousands of other projects around the country that have been backlogged for years?

I think it is really important that the President-elect create a blind trust and put all of his assets in there. Obviously, he will have a good life in the years ahead, but we simply must not allow the private interests of any American to pollute the public decisions that this country must make.

CLIMATE CHANGE

The SPEAKER pro tempore. Under the Speaker's announced policy of January 6, 2015, the gentleman from Michigan (Mr. BENISHEK) is recognized for 60 minutes as the designee of the majority leader.

Mr. BENISHEK. Mr. Speaker, as a lifelong resident of northern Michigan, I know how important it is to protect and conserve our precious natural resources. Northern Michigan's economy depends on our Great Lakes and our outdoor spaces for tourism, agriculture, and sporting activities.

Generations of people in my district have grown up experiencing the outdoors from the shores of Sleeping Bear Dunes National Lakeshore to Isle Royale National Park. However, we need to make sure that there is a balance and that we do not undertake rash and unproven regulatory policies that are almost guaranteed to negatively impact our economy in the hope of some potential—and often unquantifiable—environmental gain.

I just got back from northern Michigan. As a matter of fact, I was in Ottawa National Forest hunting. What strikes me about the regulatory nature of the Federal Government is it doesn't really take into account what is happening in the wild. The Ottawa National Forest, for example, hasn't been properly managed. The regulations as far as managing the forest make it so difficult that the forest is aging and the trees are actually falling down and rotting rather than being harvested. This is just one of the policies of this administration, and I am really hoping, now that we have a new administration coming forward, there will be a lot of change in the regulatory policies to actually develop policies that make sense for our environment and make sense for our people. That is why I wanted to speak tonight about many of these policies that affect our environment and global warming.

A lot of policies of the last administration, even the administration before that, really don't have the globe at the forefront of solving these problems. What they have been doing is just writing more and more regulations that stop whatever we are doing, and they don't have any particular effect on the global environment.

I am bringing this up for a reason. I just brought this little pollution-by-country chart, and this is the global pollution for the whole world. We know the United States is a pretty big part of that. The EU is a big part of that. India is big, and China is the biggest. The rest of the world provides, probably, the largest. But what strikes me about this is the fact that we in America haven't done things right all the time, but we are constantly striving to make improvements.

My problem with the way that the regulations are written under this administration is the fact that we are killing our economy to improve the global environment, and yet we are a relatively small part of the problem of pollution and global warming—if you believe that it is manmade—and we are not really doing anything about the rest of this.

We are putting so many regulatory burdens on our industry, like, for example, energy production. The cost of energy production is a big part of making steel, for example. Many of the countries around the world are buying steel not so much from us but from China and India because they are polluting the planet in order to produce cheap steel, and we are really helping the environment with all our regulations and everything to the point that we are losing all of our jobs. That doesn't make any sense. If we were allowed to harvest our energy in a very environmentally friendly way, we would have more jobs here in this country. These guys would have less jobs. I want to keep jobs here in America.

This is just one of the examples. Wait until you see some of the pictures I have.

□ 1930

My district was once a huge mining area. We mine iron ore, construction sand and gravel, salt is produced in Michigan, and copper. And these are all good-paying jobs.

I am going to give you a great example of one of the weirdest regulations that have come out of this administration. And that is we do have a mine in my district that recently opened, a new nickel mine, the first nickel mine in this country, I think, in over 50 years. The road to the mine, there is no good road to the mine. There is 68 miles of road through a downtown and around a roundabout to the processing mill to process the nickel ore.

The local county road commission wanted to build a 22-mile road that would bypass the 68 miles of road through a downtown, but they can't get a permit to build the road because EPA blocked it. Now, the Federal Government in Washington, D.C., is telling a local county in my district that they can't build a road because it involves some wetlands. Well, there is about 5 acres of wetlands that have to be filled in order to build this road. Believe me, you can't build a road anywhere in this country without filling in some wetlands in order to have the grade be safe.

We have had environmental laws in this country that said: if you are going to fill in some wetlands to build a road, you have got to create some wetlands somewhere else to mitigate for the fact that you have taken away some habitat from some species maybe and that sort of thing. Well, the road commission put up 100 times the acreage of the wetlands that they were going to use for the roadway to mitigate for that. But that wasn't good enough for the EPA. As a matter of fact, the EPA stopped the road without even listening very well to the mitigation plan.

This was bad for jobs. It makes it difficult for the mine to do business. It makes the longevity of the mine not as good because it is more expensive to process the ore. And it creates more pollution because the trucks are driving 68 miles to the ore processing plant versus the 22 miles on a new road. Besides, the new road would open up a lot of other areas for economic development as well.

Well, this is the type of rule and regulation that doesn't make any sense to the people that want to protect their environment with fewer miles on the road with diesel trucks and also provide economic opportunity in an area that needs jobs. So I am really hopeful that we will continue with a new administration to improve and stop this ridiculous rulemaking that has absolutely no effect on the environment—if anything, it makes it worse—all because people in Washington here under this administration have decided that they know better than the people in Michigan who actually live there, and they can't make a decision for themselves because you can't possibly know it would be good for the environment because you are just living on the UP and you don't really know what is what. That has been my frustration in my time here in Congress. That is a really good example of what is going on.

I want to show you a couple of pictures of some places around the world that aren't managing the environment, such as the United States is. Here we have a factory, a Chinese factory that is putting out all kinds of pollutants without any significant environmental controls on them at all. These are the kind of factories that we are competing with, with our factories, which are much better.

We just had a coal-fired power plant stopped in my district several years ago by the EPA because of this administration's war on coal. This coal plant was a state-of-the-art coal plant. It didn't even produce CO_2 because, in my district, they are able to harness the technology to capture the CO_2 and sell it and actually use it to pump in the ground to help the production of local oil wells. The CO_2 is not an issue. So we are actually competing with people that do this to our environment, and losing jobs overseas because of the tight regulations we have here, but we are not doing anything about this that is going on across the world. None of the policies that we have instituted on our industry are in effect over there. We haven't put any significant demands on the Chinese to make them stop doing this.

I was talking to some biologists from the University of Michigan. We have an environmental research station in my district. The University of Michigan has been studying the environment for the last 100 years or so. And one of the things that I found really interesting was the fact that one of the great concerns about coal mining and coal used for energy production was the mercury in the air. I was talking to these guys from the University of Michigan and they said: we solved the mercury problem in this country decades ago; that is not a problem anymore.

Most of the mercury that is in our environment here in the United States comes from China and India. Because it is over in China and India doesn't mean that it is not a global problem. That stuff goes up in the atmosphere. It takes the jet stream, and it comes all the way over here. The majority of the pollutant mercury in our country is coming from places like this. This administration has done nothing about it except for putting more stringent controls on our energy production, making our energy more expensive, and making people want to buy steel and other products from countries that do this to our environment.

This is not the right way to deal with this issue. If we are going to deal with global pollution, global production of harmful toxins, or global warming, we have to talk to people that are bad actors around the world and make them do their part and not make our industries really the joke of everyone else in the world because they are making money and we are losing our jobs and it doesn't make any sense whatsoever.

Let's see another picture here. This is a pretty good one from India. This is a river in India. This is all trash in the middle of the river in India. I went to India, and I was appalled by how filthy it was and the lack of environmental rules. This is what we are dealing with.

Now, I know the Indians and, perhaps, the Chinese are not as developed as we are, but they are competing in the same environment for industry as we are along the globe. I am hopeful that the coming Trump administration is going to take this kind of stuff seriously, unlike the Obama administration, which his only answer to global warming and global pollution is to put more and more restrictions on our industry, killing jobs in this country and giving more jobs to people around the world that do this.

This picture is a good example of the way things are done across the world. Now, I come from a timber district where we want to harvest responsibly the timber that we have in our national forests. That means cutting trees down as they mature in a logical fashion so that there are a lot of healthy trees in the forest that are not overcome by disease and fire, which is what we have seen out West over the last couple of decades because those forests are not being managed.

Originally, the national forests were developed as a place for multiple use—for harvesting for logs, for entertainment to go hunting and fishing. I hunt and fish in a national forest. But when the trees become over mature and they are not managed in a way that allow new growth, there is a limited amount of species that can exist in that type of a forest.

This is what they do in Indonesia. This is a forest in Indonesia that was clear-cut for miles and miles and miles. This is the way it was left. Now, that is not the way it is done in Michigan, not where I live, not in my Federal forests. The problem is we are not doing enough of the select cuts, the limited clear-cuts that allow spreading of new growth. We are competing on our timber products with people that do this to their environment.

Now, in this country, private forests and State forests are managed with the stewardship program where third-party stewards of the forest, who are registered, licensed, and trained how to manage forests, are given the opportunity to manage forests over decades, over centuries, so that there is always a healthy forest with mid-term growth, long-term growth, new growth. There is a multiple of species that can live amongst that. People can hunt and enjoy that area. I just want to try to, Mr. Speaker, make sure the American people are aware of the fact that our environment is a place where we live, we want it to be good and healthy, and we want it also to be able to provide jobs for the people that live in my district and across the country.

Some of the statistics I could give you about the Chinese, for example, is that in 2012, China was responsible for over a quarter of the pollution worldwide. As you saw in that circle, the total pollution in China currently equals the pollution from the United States and the European Union combined. This is expected to only increase.

Now, China is run by a centralized government that has not traditionally respected the environment or the concerns of the locals when it comes to major decisions or projects. This is the type of policy that we can talk to the Chinese and have a discussion about what they can do to improve their behavior.

India is currently the world's fastest growing economy and already the fourth largest polluter. As the Indian economy grows, these emissions are going to continue to rise.

As you see from Indonesia, there is deforestation and clear-cutting in the rain forest. I want to have responsible and sustainable forestry practices because timber is a renewable resource.

Now, our environmental actions have been incremental in nature, but, until this last administration, they haven't been killing our industry. Now with the Obama administration's war on coal, significant areas of our economy have fallen into disrepair. I am so thankful, frankly, that we have a new administration coming in that is going to, hopefully, put a stop to those policies that have been driving our jobs overseas and making it difficult for us here at home.

I just want to show another graph here for U.S. employment in manufac-

turing industries. Now, starting in 1980 into 2014, as you can see, thousands of jobs in the manufacturing industries have gone down. I am not saying that environmental regulations are the complete cause of this, but I think this should be a pretty major part of our decisionmaking process as to how we do these things.

We have a regulatory and approval process in the United States that most other countries don't even approach or even pretend to go through. Having incremental change consulting with industry and still having strict standards, I think, can all happen at once. But when the current administration has had a policy of killing our industry and not doing anything about these foreign people, we need to put a change to that and turn this manufacturing number around and bring manufacturing back to where it should be.

This slide was made up before the election, so I wasn't sure it was going to happen in the next administration.

□ 1945

Here are the economically significant regulations this government has put out all the way back to 2000. The number of regulations are expected to cost $100 million or more to the American people. You can see that, consistently, from the beginning of the Obama administration that that number has significantly increased. I am so happy to hear that Mr. Trump has promised, for every new regulation, to cut two. Let's start with the cutting.

At the end of the day, we need to protect our environment. However, hamstringing our economy will not save our environment. The other people on the planet provide for most of the pollution and for the other things that people are afraid of in the environment—more than we are by far. All too often, the consequences of overburdening regulations here in America is the flight of manufacturing and industry to nations such as China, Indonesia, and India. I am hopeful that my colleagues here in the House and in the Senate, along with a new administration, will change that and make logical regulations. I think this will benefit our planet. It will certainly benefit the American citizens. We shouldn't be implementing expensive nonsolutions to a problem of which the extent and impact remain uncertain.

I have been criticized in the past for talking about global warming and what the future is going to bring. With anything you talk about with regard to the administration's being over-regulatory, then you are accused of being a polluter of the planet. I ran for election several times, and these are the types of arguments that people will make to try to make you look bad, to make you look as if you want to pollute the planet. I think, really, Americans are tired of that baloney. We want to have a decent living; we want to have a clean planet; we want to make sure that the people around the world have the same values and interests that we do in that, if we are going to work hard to try to make our planet cleaner, they should, too, so that we are competing on an even scale here. With what we are doing now, we are not competing on an even scale.

It is very important that we don't allow people to intimidate us when we say: "I want to have more mining in this country. I want to be able to use coal." They just immediately say that you are an anti-environmentalist, and it is just torture. Most of the people who say this kind of stuff have never been to a community that actually does mining. They just see it from afar. They don't see the end result of a mine that has been rehabilitated and that is covered with green.

They don't have any idea what is really going on. They just use it in fear so that the American people don't really realize the truth of what is going on, and they want their vote. They are causing fear in the American people by their saying: "This guy doesn't want to protect the environment." I mean, I want to protect the environment. I come from one of the most beautiful places in the country, I think. I want it to be clean and healthy for my children as well, and it is going to be really clean and healthy if nobody lives there because there are no jobs. We need to protect our environment, have policies that allow jobs to continue to occur in this country, and have reasonable regulations that make sense and that have sound, scientific studies.

This administration has hid the scientific studies behind closed doors in many cases. I am a physician. I wrote research papers. I had to show my evidence to the world and have other people criticize what I wrote so that they could say: "You didn't do that right," or "your technique was flawed," or "the study you did didn't really show what you said it shows." That is what happens in scientific research—you have to have your research open to criticism. This administration has used science in the way that they say: "The scientists say 'this,'" but they don't want to show you the data because they don't want other people to criticize what they have done. They say that other people who might criticize them are just politicized when they, themselves, are politicized. They also don't want the other side to speak, because they will say: "You are just anti-environment."

We need to have an open discourse of scientists on both sides of issues—and consensus—before we make policies and regulations that kill millions of jobs and that cost families as their raises for the last 8 years have been meager. We need to be sure that science is open and not politicized as it has been in this administration.

I encourage my colleagues to not be afraid to stand up for what is right and for jobs in this country. I encourage the people who may be watching, too, to think about what the politicians they listen to are saying and how it affects jobs and how it really affects the environment because, although we want a clean environment, we are not going to write rules that kill jobs and that do not do anything about the real polluters on this planet, who care nothing about the environment, and who are causing the majority of the problems around the globe.

Mr. Speaker, I yield back the balance of my time.

MAKE IT IN AMERICA: MANUFACTURING

The SPEAKER pro tempore (Mr. GROTHMAN). Under the Speaker's announced policy of January 6, 2015, the gentleman from California (Mr. GARAMENDI) is recognized for 60 minutes as the designee of the minority leader.

Mr. GARAMENDI. Mr. Speaker, our previous speaker spoke about the need to revitalize the American economy, and he talked about the regulatory environment as being one of the impediments. Certainly, there are many, many regulations that could impede economic development, but there are also regulations that might enhance economic development. Today I want to continue with what is now a 6-year effort—oh, yes, let's get this right side up. There we go—to Make It In America. Specifically, today, it is about manufacturing because manufacturing matters.

When I first came to Congress in 2009, we were in the midst of the Great Recession, and millions of Americans had lost their jobs. We saw the Rust Belt literally collapse; we saw factories close; we saw our shipyards opened with nothing happening except in the U.S. naval yards. So here we are some 6 years later: the economy is recovering, and we can talk about regulations; but what I would like to talk about tonight are positive regulations—regulations and laws that grow the American economy, not regulations that would hinder. Specifically, as part of this Make It In America agenda, we have these fundamental policies. If we are going to rebuild the American economy, a big part of it has to be manufacturing. It does matter.

So what are those issues that are involved in rebuilding the American economy?

There are trade issues, and we have heard a lot about that in the recent Presidential campaign. Undoubtedly, the Congress will deal with that;

Taxes. The debate about taxes really was not very clear in the Presidential election, but we are certainly going to be dealing with tax policy here, and we should. There is no doubt that the American tax policy hinders economic growth in many, many ways for small companies and encourages large companies to leave town—to leave America—and leave American workers and communities behind. We have seen too much of that; so tax policy becomes a very, very important part of this;

With regard to energy and labor, I am going to go specifically to those; but just quickly are the educational policies. There is a lot of jabbering around here, on the floor of Congress, and out around the world about educational policies: Are our schools good enough? They don't measure up. We need to have charter schools. We are going to go into that in a big way with our new President; but one of the most important parts of education, when we talk about rebuilding the American economy, is that we have properly trained workers whether they are in the computer field—in computer science—or whether they are in the shipyards welding the parts of a ship. A well-trained, well-prepared workforce is absolutely essential for the growth of the American economy; but education is not the subject today, nor is research;

Infrastructure. It is part of what we are going to talk about today, and I am going to try to do this in, maybe, 10 minutes, but not much longer than that.

What I want to focus on is energy policy and labor. Did you know—does America know—that the United States has become a net exporter of natural gas?

Yes. We do have a boom in the energy industry. It has slowed down a little bit with the drop in the value of crude oil and natural gas; but, nonetheless, as of today, the United States is a net exporter of natural gas. That gas is exported to Canada and Mexico and other parts of the world. When it is exported to other parts of the world, it is exported in ships in liquefied form, called liquefied natural gas, LNG. On ships, liquefied natural gas is part of that export that has turned America from an importing country to an exporting country, which is good for all of us; but let us realize that that natural gas and, for that matter, crude oil, which is also now being exported, is a strategic national asset, a strategic national resource. It is absolutely crucial to the American economy.

I will give you one example—Dow. The big chemical company is bringing back to the United States much of the manufacturing that it once did overseas of plastic and other products because of the strategic national asset called natural gas. The price of natural gas was low enough that that big, international, domestic, American company—Dow—is returning to the United States to manufacture. It is the same thing with oil. These are strategic national assets that we are now exporting.

The question for us in public policy is: Can we, in some way, use this strategic national resource to expand the American economy?

The answer is: absolutely, yes.

It is not just to the benefit of the energy companies. Maybe we could wish them well as they export our strategic national asset to places around the world and gain a healthy profit—okay—but shouldn't that be shared with the rest of America?

I believe it should, and I know it could. Here is how, and it deals with this issue of labor and manufacturing: Make It In America. Manufacturing matters.

Here is the deal. Those export facilities for LNG are big operations—lots of pipe, lots of plumbing, lots of containers, all of which are or could be made in America, creating American jobs. Now, once that natural gas is liquefied—that is, compressed into a liquid—and goes on a ship, the questions are: Where did that ship come from, and who are the sailors on the ship?

It used to be, back when the North Slope of Alaska opened up, that the steel in the Trans-Alaska Pipeline and the ships that would then take that oil to the West Coast ports would be American ships with American sailors. It was the law. It was the regulation. Here you had a situation in which the law and regulations created American jobs for mariners and for the American shipyards.

☐ 2000

If we were to apply that same principle to the export of LNG, that strategic national resource, think of what would happen. This year, 2016, the first export facility in Louisiana, Cheniere, began exporting LNG on ships. They were not American ships. There were no American sailors on those ships. The policy of the North Slope oil was not extended to the export of LNG, to the detriment of American jobs.

So here is what we ought to do. There is an energy bill floating around somewhere in the Senate and the House. Nobody knows exactly where it is. But in that energy bill, there is a section that enhances and speeds up the licensing of six other LNG export facilities around the United States on various coasts—on the East Coast, the Gulf Coast, as well as the West Coast.

Why not take what we did with the North Slope oil, requiring that it be on American-built ships with American sailors, and apply that same principle, same law, to the export of LNG as these new facilities come online?

It is said that the facility on the Gulf Coast, the Cheniere facility in its first part—there are three different pieces of that that will come in over time—the first part of that facility will take 100 ships to export the liquefied natural gas from that one facility. We are probably talking about a few hundred LNG ships to export the liquefied natural gas not only from the existing facility in the Gulf Coast, but to the other facilities that will be built in the future. Perhaps as much as 12 percent of the total natural gas, that strategic national asset, will be exported, requiring hundreds of ships.

What if we passed a law called Energizing America? I like that title. In fact, we are going to introduce it tomorrow, Energizing America. It is a piece of legislation that would require that we provide 15 percent of the total export on American-built ships. Think about it.

Perhaps over the next decade, our shipyards would be building maybe as many as a hundred ships. But let's just say it is 10, 20, 30 ships. Perhaps more than 100,000 people could be employed in the construction of those ships. This would be a good regulation, wouldn't it? It would be a regulation that would put Americans back to work.

It would be a law that would say a strategic national asset of this Nation will also benefit another strategic national asset: the American shipyards.

Our U.S. Navy depends on those shipyards. Every U.S. naval ship is built in America in American shipyards. And if we were to expand those shipyards, we would find more competition for the naval ships, perhaps a lower price. Perhaps we would also be able to employ marine engineers, welders, plumbers, steamfitters, steelworkers, not only at the shipyards, but in the manufacturing of the engines here in the United States.

Make it in America. Build it in America. All it takes is a couple of paragraphs of law. That is all it would take, a couple of paragraphs of law that say between now and 2024, in the next 8 years, 15 percent of that liquefied natural gas must be on American-built ships with American sailors.

Now, it turns out that these American ships and the sailors are a strategic necessity for our U.S. military. Because it turns out that if you are going to project American power around the world, you have to be able to get there with the men, the women, and the materials—and that means ships.

So we would build the U.S. merchant marine. We would build American shipyards so that they would be competitive around the world, and we would employ tens of thousands—and perhaps even hundreds or more thousand—of American workers in our shipyards. It is possible. All it takes is a law.

So when this energy bill starts moving around—and maybe here in the lameduck session—I would propose a simple amendment: between now and 2024, 15 percent of that export of LNG would be on American-built ships with American sailors.

Oh, by the way, there are some older American LNG ships that could be reflagged for the purposes of meeting at least part of that 15 percent in the initial years. And then after 2025, let's ramp it up to 30 percent. Let's keep our shipyards busy. Let's keep our steelworkers, our welders, our plumbers, our marine engineers, our factories busy in the future with a very simple law that would be a really good regulation.

Oh, I can hear the whining of the oil industry and of the natural gas industry, "Oh, it is going to be too expensive." It is not nearly as expensive as not having American jobs and not being able to project American power because we do not have a robust merchant marine and a robust number of American ships.

Consider this fact: after World War II, we had 1,200 American ships, American sailors on them, all American flagged. In the 1980s, we had 500. Today, we have less than 80.

We are seeing the disappearance of the American merchant marine. American sailors, American-flagged ships, American shipyards are all diminishing and very rapidly disappearing. It is up to us, your elected officials—myself, my colleagues, 434 other Members of Congress and the 100 Senators. And, I guess, the new President is interested in making America great again. Hey, here is how you can do it, President-elect Trump. Do it in policies that once again call for making it in America.

So what are my colleagues going to do? Let this opportunity slip? Let this opportunity disappear? Forget about the strategic nature of energy in the United States, the strategic necessity of being able to project American power with American sailors and American ships to go wherever we want?

Oh, yes, I heard somebody say, well, we could contract to have ships sent to move our military: Oh, yeah, hello, Mr. Xi. Oh, yeah, I am phoning. Yeah, I'm phoning from Washington, D.C., and, yeah, can you folks in Beijing send over ships so that we can send men and material to the South China Sea?

It is not likely to happen, right?

We can't depend on other countries. We have to depend on our own abilities, our own shipyards, our own mariners. We can do it.

There are many bad regulations to be sure. There are some that hinder the economy. But I would propose to you that a very good law could be used to build the American economy by simply requiring that the export of liquefied natural gas be done on American ships, 15 percent between now and 2024, and thereafter, 30 percent, echoing what we did back in the 1960s when the North Slope of Alaska opened up and that oil came south.

American steel pipe and American-made ships with American sailors, we can do it once again for the benefit of our country, for our national security, and for American workers and American businesses.

Mr. Speaker, I yield back the balance of my time.

LEAVE OF ABSENCE

By unanimous consent, leave of absence was granted to:

Mr. JONES (at the request of Mr. MCCARTHY) for today and for the balance of the week on account of personal reasons.

Mr. POE of Texas (at the request of Mr. MCCARTHY) for today and for the balance of the week on account of personal reasons.

SENATE BILL REFERRED

A bill of the Senate of the following title was taken from the Speaker's table and, under the rule, referred as follows:

S. 2873. An Act to require studies and reports examining the use of, and opportunities to use, technology-enabled collaborative learning and capacity building models to improve programs of the Department of Health and Human Services, and for other purposes, to the Committee on Energy and Commerce.

BILLS PRESENTED TO THE PRESIDENT

Karen L. Haas, Clerk of the House, reported that on November 28, 2016, she presented to the President of the United States, for his approval, the following bills:

H.R. 4902. To amend title 5, United States Code, to expand law enforcement availability pay to employees of U.S. Customs and Border Protection's Air and Marine Operations.

H.R. 5873. To designate the Federal building and United States courthouse located at 511 East San Antonio Avenue in El Paso, Texas, as the "R.E. Thomason Federal Building and United States Courthouse".

ADJOURNMENT

Mr. GARAMENDI. Mr. Speaker, I move that the House do now adjourn.

The motion was agreed to; accordingly (at 8 o'clock and 10 minutes p.m.), under its previous order, the House adjourned until tomorrow, Wednesday, November 30, 2016, at 10 a.m. for morning-hour debate.

EXPENDITURE REPORTS CONCERNING OFFICIAL FOREIGN TRAVEL

Reports concerning the foreign currencies and U.S. dollars utilized for Official Foreign Travel during the second and third quarters of 2016, pursuant to Public Law 95–384, are as follows:

REPORT OF EXPENDITURES FOR OFFICIAL FOREIGN TRAVEL, COMMITTEE ON ARMED SERVICES, HOUSE OF REPRESENTATIVES, EXPENDED BETWEEN JULY 1 AND SEPT. 30, 2016

Name of Member or employee	Date Arrival	Date Departure	Country	Per diem [1] Foreign currency	Per diem [1] U.S. dollar equivalent or U.S. currency [2]	Transportation Foreign currency	Transportation U.S. dollar equivalent or U.S. currency [2]	Other purposes Foreign currency	Other purposes U.S. dollar equivalent or U.S. currency [2]	Total Foreign currency	Total U.S. dollar equivalent or U.S. currency [2]
Travel to Germany—June 27–July 1, 2016											
Kari Bingen	6/27	7/1	Germany		807.37		66.48				873.85
Commercial transportation							2,121.26				2,121.26
Timothy Morrison	6/27	7/1	Germany		807.37		66.48				873.85
Commercial transportation							2,121.26				2,121.26
William Spencer Johnson	6/27	7/1	Germany		807.37		66.48				873.85
Commercial transportation							2,121.26				2,121.26
Travel to Qatar, Bahrain, Iraq, Kuwait, Afghanistan—July 15–21, 2016											
Hon. William M. "Mac" Thornberry	7/16	7/17	Qatar		162.00						162.00
	7/17	7/17	Bahrain								
	7/17	7/18	Iraq		11.00						11.00
	7/18	7/19	Kuwait		432.00						432.00
	7/19	7/20	Afghanistan		7.00						7.00
	7/20	7/21	Qatar								
Hon. Seth Moulton	7/16	7/17	Qatar		162.00						162.00
	7/17	7/17	Bahrain								
	7/17	7/18	Iraq		11.00						11.00
	7/18	7/19	Kuwait		432.00						432.00
	7/19	7/20	Afghanistan		7.00						7.00
	7/20	7/21	Qatar								
Robert L. Simmons	7/16	7/17	Qatar		162.00						162.00
	7/17	7/17	Bahrain								
	7/17	7/18	Iraq		11.00						11.00
	7/18	7/19	Kuwait		432.00						432.00
	7/19	7/20	Afghanistan		7.00						7.00
	7/20	7/21	Qatar								
Paul Arcangeli	7/16	7/17	Qatar		162.00						162.00
	7/17	7/17	Bahrain								
	7/17	7/18	Iraq		11.00						11.00
	7/18	7/19	Kuwait		432.00						432.00
	7/19	7/20	Afghanistan		7.00						7.00
	7/20	7/21	Qatar								
Kari Bingen	7/16	7/17	Qatar		162.00						162.00
	7/17	7/17	Bahrain								
	7/17	7/18	Iraq		11.00						11.00
	7/18	7/19	Kuwait		432.00						432.00
	7/19	7/20	Afghanistan		7.00						7.00
	7/20	7/21	Qatar								
Delegation expenses			Iraq				7,266.00				7,266.00
Visit to Japan, South Korea, the Philippines—July 15–23, 2016 with CODEL Schatz											
Hon. John Garamendi	7/17	7/19	South Korea		371.78						371.78
	7/19	7/20	the Philippines		295.00						295.00
	7/20	7/23	Japan		599.87						599.87
Visit to United Kingdom—July 16–19, 2016											
Hon. Trent Franks	7/17	7/19	United Kingdom		1,773.39						1,773.39
Commercial transportation							2,121.26				2,121.26
Andrew Walter	7/17	7/19	United Kingdom		1,773.39						1,773.39
Commercial transportation							2,121.26				2,121.26
Visit to Nigeria, Cameroon—July 25–30, 2016 with STAFFDEL Barker											
Katherine Quinn	7/26	7/26	Nigeria								
	7/26	7/29	Cameroon		436.36						436.36
Commercial transportation							13,812.18				13,812.18
Visit to Israel, Latvia, Poland, Germany—August 19–28, 2016											
Hon. Chris Gibson	8/20	8/22	Israel		1,036.00						1,036.00
	8/22	8/24	Poland		535.87						535.87
	8/24	8/24	Latvia								
	8/24	8/25	Germany		269.15						269.15

REPORT OF EXPENDITURES FOR OFFICIAL FOREIGN TRAVEL, COMMITTEE ON ARMED SERVICES, HOUSE OF REPRESENTATIVES, EXPENDED BETWEEN JULY 1 AND SEPT. 30, 2016—
Continued

Name of Member or employee	Date		Country	Per diem [1]		Transportation		Other purposes		Total	
	Arrival	Departure		Foreign currency	U.S. dollar equivalent or U.S. currency [2]	Foreign currency	U.S. dollar equivalent or U.S. currency [2]	Foreign currency	U.S. dollar equivalent or U.S. currency [2]	Foreign currency	U.S. dollar equivalent or U.S. currency [2]
Hon. Paul Cook	8/20	8/22	Israel		1,036.00						1,036.00
	8/22	8/24	Poland		535.87						535.87
	8/24	8/24	Latvia								
	8/24	8/25	Germany		269.15						269.15
Hon. Austin Scott	8/20	8/22	Israel		1,036.00						1,036.00
	8/22	8/24	Poland		535.87						535.87
	8/24	8/24	Latvia								
	8/24	8/25	Germany		269.15						269.15
Hon. Richard B. Nugent	8/20	8/22	Israel		1,036.00						1,036.00
	8/22	8/24	Poland		535.87						535.87
	8/24	8/24	Latvia								
	8/24	8/25	Germany		269.15						269.15
Heath Bope	8/20	8/22	Israel		1,036.00						1,036.00
	8/22	8/24	Poland		535.87						535.87
	8/24	8/24	Latvia								
	8/24	8/25	Germany		269.15						269.15
Visit to Germany, Italy—September 25–29, 2016 with STAFFDEL Barker											
Mark Morehouse	9/26	9/29	Germany		845.18						845.18
	9/27	9/28	Italy		482.77						482.77
Commercial transportation							4,005.76				4,005.76
Katherine Quinn	9/26	9/29	Germany		845.18						845.18
	9/27	9/28	Italy		482.77						482.77
Commercial transportation							4,005.76				4,005.76
Committee total					22,592.90		39,895.44				62,488.34

[1] Per diem constitutes lodging and meals.
[2] If foreign currency is used, enter U.S. dollar equivalent; if U.S. currency is used, enter amount expended.

HON. MAC THORNBERRY, Chairman, Nov. 10, 2016.

(AMENDMENT) REPORT OF EXPENDITURES FOR OFFICIAL FOREIGN TRAVEL, COMMITTEE ON EDUCATION AND THE WORKFORCE, HOUSE OF REPRESENTATIVES, EXPENDED BETWEEN APR. 1 AND JUNE 30, 2016

Name of Member or employee	Date		Country	Per diem [1]		Transportation		Other purposes		Total	
	Arrival	Departure		Foreign currency	U.S. dollar equivalent or U.S. currency [2]	Foreign currency	U.S. dollar equivalent or U.S. currency [2]	Foreign currency	U.S. dollar equivalent or U.S. currency [2]	Foreign currency	U.S. dollar equivalent or U.S. currency [2]
Hon. John Kline	3/31	4/2	Philippines		605.84		(3)				605.84
	4/2	4/7	Australia		1,638.00		(3)				1,638.00
Hon. David "Phil" Roe	3/30	3/31	USA				677.70*				677.70
			Philippines		186.98*						186.98
			Australia		636.00*						636.00
Hon. Robert C. "Bobby" Scott	3/31	4/2	Philippines		605.84		(3)				605.84
	4/2	4/7	Australia		1,638.00		(3)				1,638.00
		4/7	Australia				1,168.86				1,168.86
Hon. Rubén Hinojosa	3/31	4/2	Philippines		605.84		(3)				605.84
	4/2	4/7	Australia		1,638.00		(3)				1,638.00
Juliane Sullivan	3/31	4/2	Philippines		605.84		(3)				605.84
	4/2	4/7	Australia		1,689.00		(3)				1,689.00
Janelle Gardner	3/31	4/2	Philippines		605.84		(3)				605.84
	4/2	4/7	Australia		1,662.00		(3)				1,662.00
Brian Newell	3/31	4/2	Philippines		605.84		(3)				605.84
	4/2	4/7	Australia		1,689.00		(3)				1,689.00
Elizabeth Podgorski	3/31	4/2	Philippines		605.84		(3)				605.84
	4/2	4/7	Australia		1,478.00		(3)				1,478.00
Richard Miller	3/31	4/2	Philippines		605.84		(3)				605.84
	4/2	4/7	Australia		1,662.00		(3)				1,662.00
Krisann Pearce	3/31	4/2	Philippines		605.84		(3)				605.84
	4/2	4/7	Australia		1,662.00		(3)				1,662.00
Hon. Frederica Wilson	6/24	6/27	Panama		837.00		(3)				837.00
Committee total					21,868.54		1,846.56				23,715.10

[1] Per diem constitutes lodging and meals.
[2] If foreign currency is used, enter U.S. dollar equivalent; if U.S. currency is used, enter amount expended.
[3] Military air transportation.
* Traveler departed trip state-side due to a death in the family. Post was unable to cancel rooms in Manila and Sydney.

HON. JOHN KLINE, Chairman, Nov. 7, 2016.

REPORT OF EXPENDITURES FOR OFFICIAL FOREIGN TRAVEL, COMMITTEE ON EDUCATION AND THE WORKFORCE, HOUSE OF REPRESENTATIVES, EXPENDED BETWEEN JULY 1 AND SEPT. 30, 2016

Name of Member or employee	Date		Country	Per diem [1]		Transportation		Other purposes		Total	
	Arrival	Departure		Foreign currency	U.S. dollar equivalent or U.S. currency [2]	Foreign currency	U.S. dollar equivalent or U.S. currency [2]	Foreign currency	U.S. dollar equivalent or U.S. currency [2]	Foreign currency	U.S. dollar equivalent or U.S. currency [2]
HOUSE COMMITTEES											

Please Note: If there were no expenditures during the calendar quarter noted above, please check the box at right to so indicate and return. ☒

[1] Per diem constitutes lodging and meals.
[2] If foreign currency is used, enter U.S. dollar equivalent; if U.S. currency is used, enter amount expended.

HON. JOHN KLINE, Chairman, Nov. 7, 2016.

REPORT OF EXPENDITURES FOR OFFICIAL FOREIGN TRAVEL, SELECT COMMITTEE ON BENGHAZI, HOUSE OF REPRESENTATIVES, EXPENDED BETWEEN JULY 1 AND SEPT. 30, 2016

Name of Member or employee	Date		Country	Per diem [1]		Transportation		Other purposes		Total	
	Arrival	Departure		Foreign currency	U.S. dollar equivalent or U.S. currency [2]	Foreign currency	U.S. dollar equivalent or U.S. currency [2]	Foreign currency	U.S. dollar equivalent or U.S. currency [2]	Foreign currency	U.S. dollar equivalent or U.S. currency [2]

HOUSE COMMITTEES
Please Note: If there were no expenditures during the calendar quarter noted above, please check the box at right to so indicate and return. ☒

[1] Per diem constitutes lodging and meals.
[2] If foreign currency is used, enter U.S. dollar equivalent; if U.S. currency is used, enter amount expended.

HON. TREY GOWDY, Chairman, Nov. 15, 2016.

EXECUTIVE COMMUNICATIONS, ETC.

Under clause 2 of rule XIV, executive communications were taken from the Speaker's table and referred as follows:

7624. A letter from the Deputy Secretary, Division of Swap Dealer and Intermediary Oversight, Commodity Futures Trading Commission, transmitting the Commission's final rule — Chief Compliance Officer Annual Report Requirements for Futures Commission Merchants, Swap Dealers, and Major Swap Participants; Amendments to Filing Dates (RIN: 3038-AE49) received November 17, 2016, pursuant to 5 U.S.C. 801(a)(1)(A); Public Law 104-121, Sec. 251; (110 Stat. 868); to the Committee on Agriculture.

7625. A letter from the Special Inspector General, Office of the Special Inspector General For The Troubled Asset Relief Program, transmitting the Office's quarterly report on the actions undertaken by the Department of the Treasury under the Troubled Asset Relief Program, for the period ending October 26, 2016; to the Committee on Financial Services.

7626. A letter from the Assistant Secretary of Labor, Occupational Safety and Health Administration, Department of Labor, transmitting the Department's Major final rule — Walking-Working Surfaces and Personal Protective Equipment (Fall Protection Systems) [Docket No.: OSHA-2007-0072] (RIN: 1218-AB80) received November 18, 2016, pursuant to 5 U.S.C. 801(a)(1)(A); Public Law 104-121, Sec. 251; (110 Stat. 868); to the Committee on Education and the Workforce.

7627. A letter from the Director, Regulatory Management Division, Environmental Protection Agency, transmitting the Agency's direct final rule — Air Plan Approval; AK; Permitting Fees Revision [EPA-R10-OAR-2016-0591; FRL-9955-48-Region 10] received November 22, 2016, pursuant to 5 U.S.C. 801(a)(1)(A); Public Law 104-121, Sec. 251; (110 Stat. 868); to the Committee on Energy and Commerce.

7628. A letter from the Director, Regulatory Management Division, Environmental Protection Agency, transmitting the Agency's final rule — Air Quality Plans; Tennessee; Infrastructure Requirements for the 2010 Sulfur Dioxide National Ambient Air Quality Standard [EPA-R04-OAR-2015-0154; FRL-9955-58-Region 4] received November 22, 2016, pursuant to 5 U.S.C. 801(a)(1)(A); Public Law 104-121, Sec. 251; (110 Stat. 868); to the Committee on Energy and Commerce.

7629. A letter from the Director, Office of Congressional Affairs, Nuclear Regulatory Commission, transmitting the Commission's final NUREG — Seismic Classification [NUREG-0800, Revision 3] (Section 3.2.1) received November 18, 2016, pursuant to 5 U.S.C. 801(a)(1)(A); Public Law 104-121, Sec. 251; (110 Stat. 868); to the Committee on Energy and Commerce.

7630. A letter from the Director, Office of Congressional Affairs, Nuclear Regulatory Commission, transmitting the Commission's final NUREG — Reactor Operator Requalification Program; Reactor Operator Training [NUREG-0800, Revision 4] (Section 13.2.1) received November 18, 2016, pursuant to 5 U.S.C. 801(a)(1)(A); Public Law 104-121, Sec. 251; (110 Stat. 868); to the Committee on Energy and Commerce.

7631. A letter from the Director, Office of Congressional Affairs, Nuclear Regulatory Commission, transmitting the Commission's final NUREG — Operating Organization [NUREG-0800, Revision 7] (Sections 13.1.2-13.1.3) received November 18, 2016, pursuant to 5 U.S.C. 801(a)(1)(A); Public Law 104-121, Sec. 251; (110 Stat. 868); to the Committee on Energy and Commerce.

7632. A letter from the Director, Office of Congressional Affairs, Nuclear Regulatory Commission, transmitting the Commission's final NUREG — System Quality Group Classification [NUREG-0800, Revision 3] (Section 3.2.2) received November 18, 2016, pursuant to 5 U.S.C. 801(a)(1)(A); Public Law 104-121, Sec. 251; (110 Stat. 868); to the Committee on Energy and Commerce.

7633. A letter from the Director, Office of Congressional Affairs, Nuclear Regulatory Commission, transmitting the Commission's final NUREG — Administrative Procedures — General [NUREG-0800, Revision 2] (Section 13.5.1.1) received November 18, 2016, pursuant to 5 U.S.C. 801(a)(1)(A); Public Law 104-121, Sec. 251; (110 Stat. 868); to the Committee on Energy and Commerce.

7634. A letter from the Director, Office of Congressional Affairs, Nuclear Regulatory Commission, transmitting the Commission's final NUREG — Management and Technical Support Organization [NUREG-0800, Revision 6] (Section 13.1.1) received November 18, 2016, pursuant to 5 U.S.C. 801(a)(1)(A); Public Law 104-121, Sec. 251; (110 Stat. 868); to the Committee on Energy and Commerce.

7635. A letter from the Director, Office of Congressional Affairs, Office of New Reactors, Nuclear Regulatory Commission, transmitting the Commission's final NUREG — Non-Licensed Plant Staff Training; Revision 4, Sec. 13.2.2 (NUREG-0800, Chapter 3) received November 18, 2016, pursuant to 5 U.S.C. 801(a)(1)(A); Public Law 104-121, Sec. 251; (110 Stat. 868); to the Committee on Energy and Commerce.

7636. A letter from the Assistant Secretary, Legislative Affairs, Department of State, transmitting the 2016 Annual Report on the Benjamin A. Gilman International Scholarship Program, pursuant to 22 U.S.C. 2462 note; Public Law 106-309, Sec. 304; (114 Stat. 1095); to the Committee on Foreign Affairs.

7637. A letter from the Assistant Secretary for Export Administration, Bureau of Industry and Security, Department of Commerce, transmitting the Department's final rule — Updated Statements of Legal Authority for the Export Administration Regulations [Docket No.: 161012953-6953-01] (RIN: 0694-AH15) received November 18, 2016, pursuant to 5 U.S.C. 801(a)(1)(A); Public Law 104-121, Sec. 251; (110 Stat. 868); to the Committee on Foreign Affairs.

7638. A letter from the Director, Defense Security Cooperation Agency, Department of Defense, transmitting a proposed Letter of Offer and Acceptance to the Government of Qatar, Transmittal No. 16-58, pursuant to Sec. 36(b)(1) of the Arms Export Control Act, as amended; to the Committee on Foreign Affairs.

7639. A letter from the Director, Defense Security Cooperation Agency, Department of Defense, transmitting a proposed Letter of Offer and Acceptance to the Government of Kuwait, Transmittal No. 16-21, pursuant to Sec. 36(b)(1) of the Arms Export Control Act, as amended; to the Committee on Foreign Affairs.

7640. A letter from the Principal Deputy Assistant Secretary, Bureau of Political-Military Affairs, Department of State, transmitting an addendum to a certification, Transmittal No. DDTC 16-060, pursuant to Public Law 110-429, Sec. 201; to the Committee on Foreign Affairs.

7641. A letter from the Principal Deputy Assistant Secretary, Bureau of Political-Military Affairs, Department of State, transmitting an addendum to a certification, Transmittal No. DDTC 16-091, pursuant to Public Law 110-429, Sec. 201; to the Committee on Foreign Affairs.

7642. A letter from the Principal Deputy Assistant Secretary, Bureau of Political-Military Affairs, Department of State, transmitting an addendum to a certification, Transmittal No. DDTC 16-084, pursuant to Public Law 110-429, Sec. 201; to the Committee on Foreign Affairs.

7643. A letter from the Assistant Secretary, Legislative Affairs, Department of State, transmitting a determination to waive the certification requirement in section 7044(d)(1) regarding FY 2016 Economic Support Funds, pursuant to Public Law 114-113, Div. K, Sec. 7044(d)(2); to the Committee on Foreign Affairs.

7644. A letter from the Assistant Secretary, Legislative Affairs, Department of State, transmitting a determination and certification to waive for a period of six months the restrictions of section 1003 of Public Law 100-204, in accordance with Public Law 114-123, Div. C, Sec. 7041(j)(2)(B)(i); to the Committee on Foreign Affairs.

7645. A letter from the Under Secretary, Comptroller, Department of Defense, transmitting a letter stating that the Department of Defense received an extension from the Office of Management and Budget to submit the Agency Financial Report by December 15, 2016, pursuant to OMB's authority under Sec. 303 of the Chief Financial Officers Act, pursuant to 31 U.S.C. 3515(a)(1); Public Law 101-576, Sec. 303(a)(1) (as amended by Public Law 107-289, Sec. 2(a)); (116 Stat. 2049); to the Committee on Oversight and Government Reform.

7646. A letter from the Secretary, Department of Energy, transmitting the Department's FY 2016 Agency Financial Report, pursuant to 31 U.S.C. 3515(a)(1); Public Law 101-576, Sec. 303(a)(1) (as amended by Public Law 107-289, Sec. 2(a)); (116 Stat. 2049); to the Committee on Oversight and Government Reform.

7647. A letter from the Secretary, Department of the Treasury, transmitting the Department's FY 2016 Agency Financial Report, pursuant to 31 U.S.C. 3515(a)(1); Public Law 101-576, Sec. 303(a)(1) (as amended by Public Law 107-289, Sec. 2(a)); (116 Stat. 2049); to the Committee on Oversight and Government Reform.

7648. A letter from the Chairman, Nuclear Regulatory Commission, transmitting the Commission's FY 2016 Performance and Accountability Report, pursuant to 31 U.S.C. 3515(a)(1); Public Law 101-576, Sec. 303(a)(1) (as amended by Public Law 107-289, Sec. 2(a)); (116 Stat. 2049); to the Committee on Oversight and Government Reform.

7649. A letter from the Chair, Securities and Exchange Commission, transmitting the Commission's Inspector General Semiannual Report to Congress, and Management Report, for the period April 1, 2016 through September 30, 2016, pursuant to 5 U.S.C. app. (Insp. Gen. Act) Sec. 5(b); Public Law 95-452, Sec. 5(b); (92 Stat. 1103); to the Committee on Oversight and Government Reform.

7650. A letter from the Executive Director, National Mining Hall of Fame and Museum, transmitting the annual report and financial audit for the year 2015 of the National Mining Hall of Fame and Museum, pursuant to Sec. 152112 and 10101, respectively, of Title 36 of the U.S. Code; to the Committee on the Judiciary.

7651. A letter from the Management and Program Analyst, FAA, Department of Transportation, transmitting the Department's final rule — Standard Instrument Approach Procedures, and Takeoff Minimums and Obstacle Departure Procedures; Miscellaneous Amendments [Docket No.: 31101; Amdt. No.: 3718] received November 17, 2016, pursuant to 5 U.S.C. 801(a)(1)(A); Public Law 104-121, Sec. 251; (110 Stat. 868); to the Committee on Transportation and Infrastructure.

7652. A letter from the Management and Program Analyst, FAA, Department of Transportation, transmitting the Department's final rule — Standard Instrument Approach Procedures, and Takeoff Minimums, and Obstacle Departure Procedures; Miscellaneous Amendments [Docket No.: 31100; Amdt. No. 3717] received November 17, 2016, pursuant to 5 U.S.C. 801(a)(1)(A); Public Law 104-121, Sec. 251; (110 Stat. 868); to the Committee on Transportation and Infrastructure.

7653. A letter from the Director, Regulatory Management Division, Environmental Protection Agency, transmitting the Agency's final rule — National Pollutant Discharge Elimination System (NPDES) Municipal Separate Storm Sewer System General Permit Remand Rule [EPA-HQ-OW-2015-0671; FRL-9955-11-OW] (RIN: 2040-AF57) received November 22, 2016, pursuant to 5 U.S.C. 801(a)(1)(A); Public Law 104-121, Sec. 251; (110 Stat. 868); to the Committee on Transportation and Infrastructure.

7654. A letter from the Director, Regulatory Management Division, Environmental Protection Agency, transmitting the Agency's final rule — Revision of Certain Federal Water Quality Criteria Applicable to Washington [EPA-HQ-OW-2015-0174; FRL-9955-40-OW] (RIN: 2040-AF56) received November 22,

2016, pursuant to 5 U.S.C. 801(a)(1)(A); Public Law 104-121, Sec. 251; (110 Stat. 868); to the Committee on Transportation and Infrastructure.

7655. A letter from the Chief, Trade and Commercial Regulations Branch, Customs and Border Protection, Department of Homeland Security, transmitting the Department's final rule — Extension of Import Restrictions Imposed on Certain Archaeological and Ethnological Material from Greece [CBP Dec. 16-21] (RIN: 1515-AE18) received November 21, 2016, pursuant to 5 U.S.C. 801(a)(1)(A); Public Law 104-121, Sec. 251; (110 Stat. 868); to the Committee on Ways and Means.

7656. A letter from the Chief, Publications and Regulations Branch, Internal Revenue Service, transmitting the Service's IRB only rule — Treatment of Amounts Paid to Sec. 170(c) Organizations under Employer Leave-Based Donation Programs to Aid Victims of Hurricane Matthew (Notice 2016-69) received November 22, 2016, pursuant to 5 U.S.C. 801(a)(1)(A); Public Law 104-121, Sec. 251; (110 Stat. 868); to the Committee on Ways and Means.

7657. A letter from the Chief, Publications and Regulations Branch, Internal Revenue Service, transmitting the Service's IRB only rule — Applicable Federal Rates — December 2016 (Rev. Rul. 2016-27) received November 22, 2016, pursuant to 5 U.S.C. 801(a)(1)(A); Public Law 104-121, Sec. 251; (110 Stat. 868); to the Committee on Ways and Means.

7658. A letter from the Chief, Publications and Regulations Branch, Internal Revenue Service, transmitting the Service's IRB only rule — SB/SE Fast Track Mediation — Collection (Rev. Proc. 2016-57) received November 22, 2016, pursuant to 5 U.S.C. 801(a)(1)(A); Public Law 104-121, Sec. 251; (110 Stat. 868); to the Committee on Ways and Means.

7659. A letter from the Commission, United States-China Economic and Security Review Commission, transmitting the Commission's 2016 Annual Report to the Congress with Executive Summary and Recommendations, pursuant to 22 U.S.C. 7002(c)(1); Public Law 106-398, Sec. 1238(c)(1) (as amended by Public Law 110-161); (121 Stat. 2285); jointly to the Committees on Ways and Means, Foreign Affairs, and Armed Services.

REPORTS OF COMMITTEES ON PUBLIC BILLS AND RESOLUTIONS

Under clause 2 of rule XIII, reports of committees were delivered to the Clerk for printing and reference to the proper calendar, as follows:

Mr. BISHOP of Utah: Committee on Natural Resources. H.R. 1219. A bill to authorize the Secretary of the Interior to convey certain land and appurtenances of the Arbuckle Project, Oklahoma, to the Arbuckle Master Conservancy District, and for other purposes; with an amendment (Rept. 114–834). Referred to the Committee of the Whole House on the state of the Union.

Mr. CHAFFETZ: Committee on Oversight and Government Reform. H.R. 5790. A bill to provide adequate protections for whistleblowers at the Federal Bureau of Investigation (Rept. 114–835). Referred to the Committee of the Whole House on the state of the Union.

Mr. CHAFFETZ: Committee on Oversight and Government Reform. H.R. 5920. A bill to enhance whistleblower protection for contractor and grantee employees (Rept. 114–836, Pt. 1). Referred to the Committee of the Whole House on the state of the Union.

Mr. CHAFFETZ: Committee on Oversight and Government Reform. H.R. 6302. A bill to provide an increase in premium pay for United States Secret Service agents performing protective services during 2016, and for other purposes (Rept. 114–837). Referred to the Committee of the Whole House on the state of the Union.

Mrs. MILLER of Michigan: Committee on House Administration. H. Res. 933. A resolution providing amounts for further expenses of the Committee on Energy and Commerce in the One Hundred Fourteenth Congress (Rept. 114–838). Referred to the House Calendar.

Mr. BURGESS: Committee on Rules. House Resolution 934. Resolution providing for consideration of the Senate amendment to the bill (H.R. 34) to authorize and strengthen the tsunami detection, forecast, warning, research, and mitigation program of the National Oceanic and Atmospheric Administration, and for other purposes, and providing for consideration of the bill (H.R. 6392) to amend the Dodd-Frank Wall Street Reform and Consumer Protection Act to specify when bank holding companies may be subject to certain enhanced supervision, and for other purposes (Rept. 114–839). Referred to the House Calendar.

DISCHARGE OF COMMITTEE

Pursuant to clause 2 of rule XIII, the Committee on Armed Services discharged from further consideration. H.R. 5920 referred to the Committee of the Whole House on the state of the Union, and ordered to be printed.

PUBLIC BILLS AND RESOLUTIONS

Under clause 2 of rule XII, public bills and resolutions of the following titles were introduced and severally referred, as follows:

By Mr. McNERNEY (for himself and Mr. KINZINGER of Illinois):
H.R. 6394. A bill to require the Federal Communications Commission to submit to Congress a report on promoting broadband Internet access service for veterans; to the Committee on Energy and Commerce.

By Mr. HUDSON:
H.R. 6395. A bill to amend the Internal Revenue Code of 1986 to exempt the spouses of active duty members of the Armed Forces from the determination of whether an employer is subject to the employer health insurance mandate; to the Committee on Ways and Means.

By Mr. BUCHANAN (for himself, Mr. RENACCI, Mr. KIND, and Mr. NEAL):
H.R. 6396. A bill to amend the Internal Revenue Code of 1986 to modify the qualification requirements with respect to certain multiple employer plans with pooled plan providers, and for other purposes; to the Committee on Education and the Workforce, and in addition to the Committee on Ways and Means, for a period to be subsequently determined by the Speaker, in each case for consideration of such provisions as fall within the jurisdiction of the committee concerned.

By Mr. COLLINS of New York:
H.R. 6397. A bill to amend the Internal Revenue Code of 1986 to ensure that new wind turbines located near certain military installations are ineligible for the renewable electricity production credit and the energy credit; to the Committee on Ways and Means.

By Mr. ISRAEL:
H.R. 6398. A bill to amend the Small Business Act to provide for the inclusion of unmarried women in the criteria for awarding

a grant to a women's business center; to the Committee on Small Business.

By Mr. KELLY of Pennsylvania (for himself and Mr. MICHAEL F. DOYLE of Pennsylvania):

H.R. 6399. A bill to amend title XVIII of the Social Security Act to create a Medicare hospital wage index metropolitan floor, and for other purposes; to the Committee on Ways and Means.

By Mr. PALLONE:

H.R. 6400. A bill to revise the boundaries of certain John H. Chafee Coastal Barrier Resources System units in New Jersey; to the Committee on Natural Resources.

By Mr. SABLAN (for himself and Mrs. RADEWAGEN):

H.R. 6401. A bill to amend Public Law 94-241 with respect to the Northern Mariana Islands; to the Committee on Natural Resources, and in addition to the Committee on the Judiciary, for a period to be subsequently determined by the Speaker, in each case for consideration of such provisions as fall within the jurisdiction of the committee concerned.

By Ms. LINDA T. SÁNCHEZ of California (for herself and Mr. ROE of Tennessee):

H.R. 6402. A bill to amend the Internal Revenue Code of 1986 and the Employee Retirement Income Security Act of 1974 to avoid duplicative annual reporting, and for other purposes; to the Committee on Ways and Means, and in addition to the Committee on Education and the Workforce, for a period to be subsequently determined by the Speaker, in each case for consideration of such provisions as fall within the jurisdiction of the committee concerned.

By Ms. SCHAKOWSKY (for herself, Mr. GENE GREEN of Texas, Mr. GRIJALVA, Mr. HONDA, and Mrs. BUSTOS):

H. Res. 932. A resolution expressing the sense of the House of Representatives with respect to third-party charges on consumer telephone bills; to the Committee on Energy and Commerce.

By Ms. GABBARD (for herself and Mr. YOUNG of Alaska):

H. Res. 935. A resolution expressing the sense of the House that Congress should recognize the benefits of charitable giving and express support for the designation of #GivingTuesday; to the Committee on Ways and Means.

By Mr. WELCH:

H. Res. 936. A resolution expressing the sense of the House of Representatives that all students should have access to the digital tools necessary to further their education and compete in the 21st century economy; to the Committee on Education and the Workforce.

CONSTITUTIONAL AUTHORITY STATEMENT

Pursuant to clause 7 of rule XII of the Rules of the House of Representatives, the following statements are submitted regarding the specific powers granted to Congress in the Constitution to enact the accompanying bill or joint resolution.

By Mr. McNERNEY:

H.R. 6394.

Congress has the power to enact this legislation pursuant to the following:

Article I, Section 8 of the Constitution of the United States grants Congress the authority to enact this bill.

By Mr. HUDSON:

H.R. 6395.

Congress has the power to enact this legislation pursuant to the following:

Article 1, Section 8 of the Constitution.

By Mr. BUCHANAN:

H.R. 6396.

Congress has the power to enact this legislation pursuant to the following:

Article I, sec. 8

By Mr. COLLINS of New York:

H.R. 6397.

Congress has the power to enact this legislation pursuant to the following:

Article 1, Section 8 of the Constitution of the United States

By Mr. ISRAEL:

H.R. 6398.

Congress has the power to enact this legislation pursuant to the following:

This bill is enacted pursuant to the powers granted to the Congress by Article I, Section 8, Clauses 3 and 8 of the United States Constitution.

By Mr. KELLY of Pennsylvania:

H.R. 6399.

Congress has the power to enact this legislation pursuant to the following:

United States Constitution, Article I, Section 8

By Mr. PALLONE:

H.R. 6400.

Congress has the power to enact this legislation pursuant to the following:

Article I, section 8 of the Constitution of the United States grants Congress the authority to enact this bill.

By Mr. SABLAN:

H.R. 6401.

Congress has the power to enact this legislation pursuant to the following:

Under Article I, Section 8, Clauses 1, 3, 4, and Article IV, Section 3, Clause 2 of the Constitution of the United States.

By Ms. LINDA T. SÁNCHEZ of California:

H.R. 6402.

Congress has the power to enact this legislation pursuant to the following:

Article I, Section 7

ADDITIONAL SPONSORS

Under clause 7 of rule XII, sponsors were added to public bills and resolutions, as follows:

H.R. 241: Ms. MCSALLY.
H.R. 449: Mrs. BEATTY.
H.R. 592: Mr. ROYCE.
H.R. 604: Mr. FARENTHOLD.
H.R. 729: Ms. ROS-LEHTINEN.
H.R. 846: Ms. EDDIE BERNICE JOHNSON of Texas.
H.R. 855: Mr. HECK of Washington.
H.R. 994: Mr. HECK of Washington.
H.R. 1116: Mr. DAVID SCOTT of Georgia.
H.R. 1171: Mr. COURTNEY.
H.R. 1202: Mr. LEWIS.
H.R. 1211: Mr. HECK of Washington.
H.R. 1356: Mr. HECK of Washington.
H.R. 1422: Mr. LANGEVIN.
H.R. 1427: Mrs. DINGELL.
H.R. 1457: Mr. LIPINSKI.
H.R. 1526: Mr. AUSTIN SCOTT of Georgia.
H.R. 1552: Ms. ESTY.
H.R. 1559: Mr. ROTHFUS.
H.R. 1608: Ms. STEFANIK, Mr. GRAVES of Missouri, Mr. BRIDENSTINE, and Mr. MCNERNEY.
H.R. 2050: Mr. LEVIN.
H.R. 2293: Mr. CLAY and Mr. DIAZ-BALART.
H.R. 2368: Ms. LINDA T. SÁNCHEZ of California.
H.R. 2411: Mr. HECK of Washington.
H.R. 2434: Mr. LIPINSKI.

H.R. 2450: Mr. COURTNEY, Ms. WASSERMAN SCHULTZ, Mr. LYNCH, Ms. SLAUGHTER, Mr. GARAMENDI, and Mr. YARMUTH.
H.R. 2903: Mr. COLE.
H.R. 3226: Mr. CARSON of Indiana and Mr. LEWIS.
H.R. 3229: Mr. RENACCI.
H.R. 3268: Mr. REICHERT.
H.R. 3355: Mr. ASHFORD, Mr. BROOKS of Alabama, and Mr. MOULTON.
H.R. 3365: Mr. HECK of Washington.
H.R. 3381: Mr. REICHERT.
H.R. 3474: Mr. PALLONE.
H.R. 3666: Ms. SCHAKOWSKY.
H.R. 3706: Ms. BROWNLEY of California and Mr. DEUTCH.
H.R. 3846: Mr. JOHNSON of Ohio, Ms. STEFANIK, Mr. SESSIONS, and Mr. PALAZZO.
H.R. 4013: Mr. COHEN.
H.R. 4212: Mr. CÁRDENAS, Mrs. BLACKBURN, Miss RICE of New York, Ms. PINGREE, and Mr. SWALWELL of California.
H.R. 4220: Mr. LAMBORN.
H.R. 4275: Mrs. BLACKBURN.
H.R. 4380: Mr. PETERS.
H.R. 4625: Mr. HECK of Washington.
H.R. 4818: Mr. YOHO and Mr. CHAFFETZ.
H.R. 4919: Ms. BASS.
H.R. 5082: Mr. WALKER.
H.R. 5167: Ms. PINGREE and Mr. ROKITA.
H.R. 5180: Mr. DUNCAN of South Carolina.
H.R. 5235: Mr. LAMALFA.
H.R. 5262: Ms. MCSALLY, Mr. SCHWEIKERT, and Mr. GOSAR.
H.R. 5369: Ms. MCCOLLUM and Ms. DELAURO.
H.R. 5410: Mr. ROSKAM.
H.R. 5474: Mr. FOSTER.
H.R. 5489: Mr. THORNBERRY.
H.R. 5584: Mr. COHEN.
H.R. 5667: Mr. RICHMOND, Mr. SIMPSON, and Mr. KILMER.
H.R. 5681: Mr. HARPER and Mrs. BEATTY.
H.R. 5721: Mr. BILIRAKIS, Mr. STIVERS, Mr. RENACCI, Mrs. BLACKBURN, and Mr. CROWLEY.
H.R. 5916: Ms. LOFGREN.
H.R. 5932: Mr. COHEN.
H.R. 5974: Mr. BISHOP of Michigan.
H.R. 5999: Mr. LEVIN, Mr. CALVERT, Mr. YODER, Mr. McKINLEY, Ms. SLAUGHTER, and Mr. GRAVES of Missouri.
H.R. 6020: Mr. RYAN of Ohio and Mr. TAKANO.
H.R. 6021: Mr. RYAN of Ohio and Mr. TAKANO.
H.R. 6030: Mrs. BEATTY.
H.R. 6045: Ms. STEFANIK.
H.R. 6099: Ms. TSONGAS, Mr. KILMER, and Ms. DELBENE.
H.R. 6100: Mr. SMITH of Nebraska, Mr. PERRY, Mr. PALAZZO, Mr. POLIQUIN, Mr. LABRADOR, and Mr. OLSON.
H.R. 6108: Mr. OLSON, Mr. LIPINSKI, and Mr. GIBBS.
H.R. 6116: Ms. DELAURO.
H.R. 6117: Mr. GARAMENDI and Mr. MCNERNEY.
H.R. 6139: Mr. STIVERS.
H.R. 6159: Mr. RENACCI.
H.R. 6185: Mrs. ELLMERS of North Carolina.
H.R. 6208: Mrs. TORRES, Mr. LEVIN, Mrs. COMSTOCK, and Mr. GENE GREEN of Texas.
H.R. 6283: Mr. EMMER of Minnesota.
H.R. 6299: Mr. LAMALFA.
H.R. 6316: Ms. SPEIER.
H.R. 6336: Mr. HUFFMAN and Mr. POLIS.
H.R. 6340: Ms. SCHAKOWSKY, Mr. BEYER, Mr. MCGOVERN, Ms. VELÁZQUEZ, Mr. MCDERMOTT, Mr. BRENDAN F. BOYLE of Pennsylvania, Mr. NADLER, Mr. COHEN, Mr. CICILLINE, Ms. MENG, Ms. MCCOLLUM, Ms. BONAMICI, Ms. MOORE, Mr. MEEKS, Mr. TED LIEU of California, Mr. CAPUANO, Ms. KAPTUR, Mr. BLUMENAUER, Mr. SCHIFF, Mr. GUTIÉRREZ, Ms.

LEE, Mr. DEUTCH, Mrs. NAPOLITANO, Mr. HASTINGS, Ms. SPEIER, Mr. GRAYSON, Mr. GALLEGO, Mr. POLIS, Mr. JOHNSON of Georgia, Ms. CLARKE of New York, Mr. CASTRO of Texas, Ms. JACKSON LEE, Mr. LANGEVIN, Mr. MICHAEL F. DOYLE of Pennsylvania, and Ms. EDWARDS.

H.R. 6346: Mr. HONDA.

H.R. 6374: Mr. LOUDERMILK.

H.R. 6382: Ms. VELÁZQUEZ, Mr. RYAN of Ohio, Mr. YARMUTH, Mr. TAKANO, Ms. MOORE, Mr. BEYER, and Mr. KILDEE.

H.R. 6392: Mr. MURPHY of Florida, Ms. SINEMA, Ms. SEWELL of Alabama, Mr. DAVID SCOTT of Georgia, Mr. WILLIAMS, Mr. STIVERS, Mr. HILL, Mr. SESSIONS, and Mrs. LOVE.

H.J. Res. 102: Mr. SMITH of Washington.

H. Con. Res. 40: Mr. LARSON of Connecticut, Mrs. MIMI WALTERS of California, and Mr. BRADY of Texas.

H. Con. Res. 145: Ms. JACKSON LEE and Mr. RYAN of Ohio.

H. Con. Res. 159: Mr. SHERMAN, Mr. LUETKEMEYER, and Mr. GROTHMAN.

H. Con. Res. 161: Mr. YOHO and Mr. BILIRAKIS.

H. Con. Res. 162: Mr. McGOVERN and Ms. TITUS.

H. Con. Res. 165: Ms. SINEMA, Mr. DEUTCH, Mr. ROKITA, Mr. SHERMAN, Mr. CICILLINE, Ms. ROS-LEHTINEN, Mr. BROOKS of Alabama, Mr. DIAZ-BALART, Mrs. LOWEY, and Mr. MOULTON.

H. Res. 752: Mr. HUDSON, Mr. TED LIEU of California, Mrs. LAWRENCE, Ms. PINGREE, Ms. ROS-LEHTINEN, Mr. ELLISON, Mrs. BLACK, Miss RICE of New York, Ms. LINDA T. SÁNCHEZ of California, Ms. STEFANIK, Mr. TONKO, Mr. FOSTER, Mr. BILIRAKIS, Mr. KENNEDY, Mr. VARGAS, and Ms. PLASKETT.

H. Res. 838: Mr. BISHOP of Michigan.

H. Res. 854: Mr. TED LIEU of California.

H. Res. 871: Mr. BARR.

H. Res. 925: Mr. LUETKEMEYER and Mr. SCOTT of Virginia.

H. Res. 926: Ms. ADAMS, Ms. CLARKE of New York, Mr. CLAY, Mr. CONYERS, Mr. CUMMINGS, Mr. ELLISON, Mr. AL GREEN of Texas, Mr. HASTINGS, Mr. MEEKS, Ms. MOORE, Mrs. WATSON COLEMAN, Ms. WILSON of Florida, Mr. RYAN of Ohio, Mr. RICHMOND, Mr. CARSON of Indiana, Mrs. LAWRENCE, and Ms. PLASKETT.

CONGRESSIONAL EARMARKS, LIMITED TAX BENEFITS, OR LIMITED TARIFF BENEFITS

Under clause 9 of rule XXI, lists or statements on congressional earmarks, limited tax benefits, or limited tariff benefits were submitted as follows:

OFFERED BY MR. LUETKEMEYER

H.R. 6392 does not contain any congressional earmarks, limited tax benefits, or limited tariff benefits as defined in clause 9 of rule XXI.

EXTENSIONS OF REMARKS

HONORING JIMMIE MARTINEZ

HON. BLAKE FARENTHOLD
OF TEXAS

IN THE HOUSE OF REPRESENTATIVES

Tuesday, November 29, 2016

Mr. FARENTHOLD. Mr. Speaker, I rise today to remember the life and memory of Mr. Jimmie Martinez of Lumberton, Texas, who passed away earlier this month at the age of fifty-four.

A former classmate of mine at Incarnate Word Academy, Jimmie committed himself to public service after graduation, joining the Nueces County Emergency Service District in Flour Bluff as a firefighter and EMT. He also served the Annaville Emergency Service District and Lumberton Fire and EMS as Assistant Fire Marshal and as a firefighter and EMT.

Jimmie served as the president of the twenty-one-county East Texas Firefighters' and Fire Marshals' Association, received the firefighter of the year award, the medal of valor and more.

Most importantly, Jimmie was a friend to all—always willing to go out of his way to help those in need. He often volunteered on the weekends at his old firehouse in Flour Bluff to give them an extra hand. Jimmie was a great man and a dedicated public servant, and I say on behalf of the entire Coastal Bend community, thank you Jimmie. You will be missed.

IN HONOR OF MR. LUIS VALDEZ

HON. SAM FARR
OF CALIFORNIA

IN THE HOUSE OF REPRESENTATIVES

Tuesday, November 29, 2016

Mr. FARR. Mr. Speaker, I rise today to join President Obama in honoring a truly great American, Mr. Luis Valdez of San Juan Bautista, California. This past September, Luis participated in a White House ceremony where the President presented him with a National Medal of the Arts in recognition of his lifetime of contributions to the arts of the Unites States. The recognition highlights the incredible contribution Luis has made as a playwright, actor, writer, and director.

Luis Valdez was born in Delano, California, in 1940. He was the second of ten children and grew up in a family of migrant farm workers. Luis began work in the fields at a young age and followed the harvest with his family up and down California's Central Valley. He attended numerous schools before his family finally settled in San Jose. He entered San Jose State University on a scholarship for math and physics but switched his major to English and began to pursue his passion for theater. The imagination of theater had held a grip on Luis from an early age. In grammar school, he had organized plays and put on puppet shows in his garage. While still at SJSU, Luis won a playwriting contest with The Theft, and produced a full length play called The Shrunken Head of Pancho Villa.

In 1965, Luis returned to Delano and joined with Cesar Chavez in the UFW's effort to organize farmworkers. It was then that he had the inspiration to combine his passions for theater and social justice and created a farm workers theater troupe simply called El Teatro Campesino. The group specialized in short one act plays based on the farm worker experience that aimed to educate both farmworkers and the broader public. By 1967, El Teatro began to explore broader Chicano themes and Luis left the group to share that vision with a broader audience. He founded the Centro Campesino Cultural in Del Rey and later Fresno to produce plays in a theater setting.

Luis quickly developed a reputation as the Godfather of Chicano theater and helped organize other Chicano theater groups throughout the Southwest. During this period he wrote and produced numerous plays, including La Virgen de Tepeyac, La carpa de los resquachis, and Corridos: Tales of Passion and Revolucion. However, Luis is best known for his seminal play Zoot Suit which he first produced in Los Angeles in 1978. The next year, Zoot Suit became the first play written by a Chicano produced on Broadway. A film version followed in 1981. This film experience led Luis to other television and movie projects, including the hit movie La Bamba in 1987 that told the story of Richie Valens.

All along Luis remained committed to the campesino movement that he helped form and that helped to form him. In 1971, he moved his theater group to San Juan Bautisa in my California district. He became a founding member of the California Arts Council and is a member of the College of Fellows of the American Theater.

Mr. Speaker, I know I speak for the whole House when I extend our congratulations to Luis Valdez for his most recent of honors. It comes on top of a lifetime of achievement giving voice to those voices that have been so often missed or dismissed by our broader society. Mindful of recent events, his voice is more important than ever.

HONORING ELAINE KOHRMAN

HON. MICHELLE LUJAN GRISHAM
OF NEW MEXICO

IN THE HOUSE OF REPRESENTATIVES

Tuesday, November 29, 2016

Ms. MICHELLE LUJAN GRISHAM of New Mexico. Mr. Speaker, I rise today to acknowledge Forest Supervisor Elaine Kohrman for her leadership during the on-going effort to update the Cibola Forest Plan so that it reflects the perspectives and recommendations of all communities with historical ties to the land.

As the Supervisor for the Cibola National Forest and National Grasslands, Kohrman has successfully brought together representatives of communities that have a long history of animosity and distrust of the federal government.

Kohrman's inclusive approach fostered an environment that encouraged leaders of several New Mexico land grants to come together as leaders to provide their perspectives as part of the Forest Plan revision process. Six of the land grants, including San Antonio de las Huertas, Cañon de Carnué, Chilili, Torreón, Tajique, and Manzano have signed Memorandums of Understanding to co-host and co-convene the land grant communities as part of the public engagement process. The New Mexico Land Grant Council is also a participant by MOU and represents statewide issues in this process. Their active participation has been instrumental in developing and elevating a better understanding for employees, other co-operating agencies and public interests of their status and historic ties to the land and the continued uses of the Cibola to support their cultural identity.

As a result of this involvement, the Cibola National Forest was recently recognized by the New Mexico Land Grant Consejo for "turning the page" and promoting good faith consultation with the land grant communities.

Kohrman has also welcomed participation from affected tribes and pueblos that are actively engaging with other participants, other than just the Forest Service. Five pueblos, including Acoma, Isleta, Cochiti, San Felipe and Santa Ana, have also signed MOU's to participate, leading to consideration of issues related to the protection of sacred sites and strengthening tribal partnerships.

I greatly appreciate Elaine Kohrman's efforts to promote a model of the Forest Service working as a partner, rather than being in the middle of issues. As a result of the more collaborative process, contentious issues are addressed in a more productive manner. I hope this collaboration can serve as a template for similar efforts throughout the Forest Service and the federal government.

CELEBRATING THE LIFE AND WORK OF DAVID FLORES

HON. JOHN R. CARTER
OF TEXAS

IN THE HOUSE OF REPRESENTATIVES

Tuesday, November 29, 2016

Mr. CARTER of Texas. Mr. Speaker, I rise today to celebrate the life and work of David Flores of Georgetown, Texas. After nearly four decades of impeccable work as County Auditor, David is beginning his richly-deserved retirement.

County Auditors play a vital role in maintaining the fiscal integrity in county government and few have taken on this important responsibility with greater professionalism than

---

David. He knows that second-rate work isn't acceptable. The people of Texas deserve that level of excellence when it comes to managing their precious tax dollars. David doesn't let them down.

David's positive impacts on the counties he's served cannot be overstated. Under his leadership, Williamson County's bond rating went from "low investment grade" to AAA, the highest rating available. He's established thoughtful standards for county purchases and has provided superb oversight for $1 billion in capital projects. Central Texas is better because of his leadership and hard work.

David's commitment to excellence doesn't stop when the work day ends. He has been a trustee for the Texas County and District Retirement System and is a past president for the Texas Association of County Auditors. David shouldered the demanding responsibilities as the Chairman of the Investment Committee for the Texas Association of Counties from 2008 to 2012. Over the years, he's deservedly received numerous awards and commendations as well as the admiration of his peers and colleagues.

Retirement is to be celebrated and enjoyed. It is not the end of a career, but rather the beginning of a new adventure. I heartily salute David Flores' work and contributions to his community. I'm sure I echo the thoughts of all when I wish him the best in both his retirement and all his future endeavors.

HONORING DENNIS R. LEBER OF PENNSYLVANIA

HON. SCOTT PERRY

OF PENNSYLVANIA

IN THE HOUSE OF REPRESENTATIVES

Tuesday, November 29, 2016

Mr. PERRY. Mr. Speaker, today I honor my constituent, Dennis R. Leber, on his pending retirement upon more than 17 years of combined service with the United States House of Representatives and the United States Air Force.

Mr. Leber began his career as an Air Force telecommunications specialist, then spent several decades in the private sector communications and networking industry. Upon completion of his private sector career, Mr. Leber served two years as a contractor with the U.S. House of Representatives and House Information Resources (HIR) Group, where he completes his professional career this December, upon 11 years of service as a Senior Network Systems Engineer in this august institution.

Mr. Leber's dedication and professionalism touched the lives of many people and challenged all with whom he served to be the best. His presence and dedication will be missed, but we wish him well and Godspeed in his future adventures.

On behalf of Pennsylvania's Fourth Congressional District, I commend and congratulate Dennis R. Leber upon his retirement and thank him for his tireless service to the citizens of the United States of America.

IN HONOR OF MAJOR TOOLE

HON. SAM FARR

OF CALIFORNIA

IN THE HOUSE OF REPRESENTATIVES

Tuesday, November 29, 2016

Mr. FARR. Mr. Speaker, I rise to recognize Major Travis N. Toole for his dedication to duty and service as an Army Officer. In 2014, Travis was selected to be an Army Congressional Fellow in my office. His portfolio included working with Team Monterey, all the Department of Defense entities located in Monterey, CA. Team Monterey includes the Defense Language Institute and the Naval Postgraduate School, Guard and Reserve facilities, SATCOM, and nine other critical DoD and Navy missions all located in Monterey, after the closure of the former Fort Ord.

Major Toole staffed me for the House Appropriations Subcommittee on Military Construction and Veterans Affairs and brought his expertise as an Engineer to the portfolio that led to significant accomplishments. He was instrumental in working the halls of the Pentagon on behalf of the California National Guard to secure funding for a bridge replacement, a number one priority of the Guard for several years. His diligence to constituent services enabled him to help a local transit provider navigate the Army bureaucracy for ultimate payment of transit services. He was well respected by the Military Construction Appropriations staff for his contributions to the Subcommittee hearings and markup.

When Travis returned to the Pentagon as an Army Congressional Budget Liaison, he worked closely with the House and Senate Military Constructions Appropriations Subcommittees, ensuring Army's budget positions were extremely well represented and articulated to the Committees. He assisted the Subcommittee staff with their oversight responsibilities in Korea, Japan and many CONUS facilities, and accompanied Members visiting Afghanistan during the Christmas holiday.

The next step for Major Toole will be further military education at the Command and General Staff College at Fort Belvoir, Virginia.

A native of Cincinnati, Ohio, Major Toole was commissioned as an Engineer officer after his graduation from Ohio University with a Bachelor of Arts degree. He has subsequently earned a Master's degree in Legislative Affairs from the George Washington University. He has served in a broad range of assignments during his Army career. Major Toole's previous assignments include serving as a Mobility Support Platoon Leader for the 562nd Engineer Company, 172nd Stryker Brigade Combat Team, and a Sapper Platoon Leader and Executive Officer for the 73rd Engineer Company, 1st Brigade 25th Infantry Division at Fort Wainwright, Alaska.

He then served as a Current Operations Officer for the 130th Engineer Brigade and commanded the 34th Sapper Company, 65th Engineer Battalion at Schofield Barracks, Hawaii. Travis has led Soldiers in combat as a Platoon Leader, Battalion Operations Officer, and Company Commander while deployed in direct support of combat operations in Iraq on three separate occasions.

Throughout his distinguished Army career, Travis has positively affected his Soldiers, peers, and superiors. His extraordinary leadership, thoughtful judgment, and exemplary work have made our country safer. On behalf of a grateful nation, I commend Major Travis Toole for his service to our nation and wish him all the best as he continues his journey in the United States Army.

HONORING ADDISON RUSSELL FOR ADDISON RUSSELL DAY AT PACE HIGH SCHOOL IN PACE, FLORIDA

HON. JEFF MILLER

OF FLORIDA

IN THE HOUSE OF REPRESENTATIVES

Tuesday, November 29, 2016

Mr. MILLER of Florida. Mr. Speaker, it is with great pleasure that I rise to recognize Addison Russell for his incredible athletic talent and honor him for Addison Russell Day at Pace High School. His natural ability to lead by example both on and off the field has distinguished him among his peers and built the foundation for his successful career.

Born and raised in Pace, Florida, Russell began his freshman year at Pace High School in 2009 where he became the 5th freshman in the school's history to play on the varsity baseball team. In 2010, he led Pace High School to a class 5A Florida High School Athletic Association baseball state championship and again as runner-up in 2012. In 2011, Russell was selected to be a member of the USA Baseball 18U National Team at the COPABE 18U/AAA Pan American Games. Russell hit a grand slam in the Championship game against Team Canada, allowing his team to take home the gold medal and Russell to be named at the First-Team All-Tournament as Shortstop.

Upon graduating from high school, Russell was drafted by the Oakland Athletics with the 11th overall pick of the first round in the 2012 Major League Baseball Draft. He was then traded to the Chicago Cubs on July 4, 2014 and on April 21, 2015 Russell made his major league debut against the Pittsburgh Pirates.

Russell represented the Cubs in the 2016 Major League Baseball All-Star Game as the starting shortstop for the National League. Then, during game six of the 2016 World Series, Addison hit the 19th grand slam in the history of the Series and also tied the Major League Baseball record for six RBIs by one player in a game on a team facing elimination from the fall classic.

Mr. Speaker, Northwest Florida is proud to honor Addison Russell on November 29, 2016 with Addison Russell Day at Pace High School. My wife Vicki and I extend Russell, wife, Melisa; and children, Aiden and Mila; our best wishes for their continued success.

CELEBRATING THE 9TH ANNUAL LAKESHORE CLASSIC BASKETBALL INVITATIONAL

HON. PETER J. VISCLOSKY

OF INDIANA

IN THE HOUSE OF REPRESENTATIVES

Tuesday, November 29, 2016

Mr. VISCLOSKY. Mr. Speaker, it is with great honor and respect that I recognize the

Gary Chamber of Commerce as the organization celebrates the 9th annual Lakeshore Classic Basketball Invitational. In observance of this special event, the Gary Chamber of Commerce hosted a celebratory corporate luncheon at the Diamond Center in Gary, Indiana, on Monday, November 21, 2016, followed by the basketball invitational at West Side Leadership Academy on Friday, November 25 and Saturday, November 26, 2016.

The theme for this year's Lakeshore Classic is "Step Up for Education," which emphasizes the importance of combining athletics, academics, and the significant role of teachers, parents, coaches, and community leaders in the educational processes. To enhance this vision, the Gary Chamber of Commerce chose David J. Johns, Executive Director for the White House Initiative on Educational Excellence for African Americans, as a guest speaker for the corporate luncheon. This initiative works with federal agencies and partners nationwide to improve the range of educational programs for African Americans. David is not only passionate about empowering youth and conducting research to improve the perception of African American males, he is also heavily committed to educational improvement in the African American community. Through his passion and tireless contributions to education, Mr. Johns has proven to be an extraordinary advocate and example to all youth and is an inspiration to us all.

At this time, I would like to recognize the schools who participated in the Lakeshore Classic basketball tournament. These teams are dedicated to achieving academic excellence and to demonstrating exceptional sportsmanship. The participating teams include the Gary West Side Lady Cougars, Gary West Side Cougars, John Marshall Lady Commandos, John Marshall Commandos, East Chicago Central Cardinals, Thea Bowman Eagles, Charles A. Tindley Tigers, and the Griffith Panthers.

Mr. Speaker, at this time, I ask you to join me in recognizing the Gary Chamber of Commerce, as well as the organizers and sponsors of the 9th annual Lakeshore Classic. Their leadership, enthusiasm, and dedication to our youth and Northwest Indiana is worthy of the highest praise.

RECOGNIZING PEACH TREE HEALTH ON ITS 25TH ANNIVERSARY

HON. JOHN GARAMENDI

OF CALIFORNIA

IN THE HOUSE OF REPRESENTATIVES

Tuesday, November 29, 2016

Mr. GARAMENDI. Mr. Speaker, I rise today to recognize Peach Tree Health for its 25 years of providing quality and affordable healthcare to medically underserved communities in the 3rd District of California.

Peach Tree Health is a federally qualified health center and an independent non-profit corporation based in Marysville, California. It has successfully extended its services throughout three counties within the 3rd District without sacrificing its core values of compassion, integrity, excellence, and cooperation in providing care for almost 30,000 patients.

In August, Peach Tree Health opened its first clinic in Sacramento County, launching a unique vision care service designed to maximize access to any child regardless of their family's ability to pay. In 2017, Peach Tree Health will be opening a comprehensive Pediatric Center in Yuba City, California, that will offer health and dental services.

The Department of Health and Human Services recently awarded Peach Tree Health a federal grant that will allow it to enhance its health information technology, further enhancing the quality of care it provides.

Congratulations to Peach Tree Health on this important milestone and its continued work offering personalized health services at affordable rates. Its services are of great importance to communities throughout the 3rd District and I look forward to working with them in the future.

IN RECOGNITION OF PICATINNY ARSENAL'S STEM PROGRAM

HON. DONALD M. PAYNE, JR.

OF NEW JERSEY

IN THE HOUSE OF REPRESENTATIVES

Tuesday, November 29, 2016

Mr. PAYNE. Mr. Speaker, I rise today to recognize the Science, Technology, Engineering, and Mathematics (STEM) education program developed by the United States Army Armament Research, Development and Engineering Center (ARDEC) at Picatinny Arsenal in New Jersey.

This STEM Educational Outreach Program supports public and private schools, colleges and universities, and professional development training throughout the state of New Jersey. Participants of the program have the opportunity to visit with exceptional engineers and scientists in their laboratories, gain funding for their student robotics teams and sponsorship for student competitions, and benefit from the creation of new instructional materials. Approximately 200 Picatinny scientists and engineers have volunteered to support STEM education by making over 1,000 classroom visits, staffing over 100 educational field trips to Picatinny Arsenal's laboratories, participating in the annual "Introduce a Girl to Engineering" Open House, assisting nearly 800 teachers, and inspiring 50,000 students in over 400 schools, including many throughout the 10th Congressional District of New Jersey.

This program has been developed to inspire students and educators through fresh and stimulating classroom activities in all avenues of STEM education. It has been custom tailored to meet the specific needs of individual schools using cutting edge technologies that are critical in order to compete in this current employment market. On behalf of the New Jersey youth, I am humbled to see such dedication from ARDEC's staff and professionals who are dedicated to transferring their knowledge of emerging technologies in STEM and look forward to the next generation of scientists and engineers from NJ–10.

CELEBRATING THE LIFE OF MICHAEL SIMONOFF

HON. TED LIEU

OF CALIFORNIA

IN THE HOUSE OF REPRESENTATIVES

Tuesday, November 29, 2016

Mr. TED LIEU of California. Mr. Speaker, I rise today to celebrate the life of Michael Scott Simonoff—a beloved husband, father, and son—who passed away following a motorcycle accident on Wednesday, November 9, 2016.

Michael was born in 1967 to Jerome and Carol Simonoff in New York and spent his formative years in Plainview, Long Island. He graduated from John F. Kennedy High School in 1985 and attended the University of Denver where he received a Bachelor's of Science in Accounting and a CPA license. He went on to earn a law degree from Whittier Law School in Southern California in 1998.

While Michael is recognized for his business acumen, he was also extraordinarily generous with his time and resources. He started his own firm, the Simonoff Group that provided office services, consulting, and bookkeeping to businesses. As a member of the California State Bar, Michael also used his legal expertise to negotiate complex real estate deals.

His ceaseless generosity is manifested in his final act of goodness. Michael donated his organs to ensure others in need could have the gift of life. His family hopes this beautiful gift will allow others to live their lives to the fullest and extend Michael's free and beautiful spirit.

Michael is survived by his wife, Elayne Howitt, and two sons, Joel Simonoff and Sam Simonoff and two stepsons Adam Howitt and Josh Howitt of Encino, California. He also leaves behind his parents Jerome and Carol Simonoff of Marina Del Rey, California, his brother Zachary Simonoff, sister-in-law Lisa Swenski of Lorain, Ohio, his sister Rachael Wexler, brother-in-law Eric Wexler as well as his niece Amanda Wexler and nephew Harrison (Harry) Wexler of Pacific Palisades, California. He is survived by many good friends and extended family.

A funeral was held for Michael on Sunday November 13, 2016 at the Mount Sinai Cemetery. In the spirit of Michael's generosity, the Simonoff family requested that in lieu of flowers, donations be made to charities of their choice. I wish Michael's family nothing but peace and solace as they mourn the loss of a cherished husband, father, and son. I ask that my colleagues join me in recognizing Michael Simonoff's beautiful life.

HONORING THE LATE DR. LUNA ISAAC MISHOE

HON. ALCEE L. HASTINGS

OF FLORIDA

IN THE HOUSE OF REPRESENTATIVES

Tuesday, November 29, 2016

Mr. HASTINGS. Mr. Speaker, I rise today to honor Dr. Luna Isaac Mishoe, former President of Delaware State College and a veteran of World War II. Revered as a mentor, guide, and instructor, Dr. Mishoe was a symbol of hope for many young African American individuals.

One of America's most distinguished mathematicians and physicists, Dr. Mishoe was only the 17th African American in this country to earn a Ph.D. in Mathematics. Indeed, Dr. Mishoe was a very well educated man: he held a Bachelor of Science Degree in mathematics and chemistry from Allen University, a Master of Science Degree in mathematics and physics from the University of Michigan, and a Doctor of Philosophy in mathematics from New York University, as well as a year of post-doctoral research in mathematics at Oxford University. And, at the age of 63, while serving as President of Delaware State, Dr. Mishoe graduated once again, this time with a Bachelor of Science Degree in Accounting and Business Administration, and a Master of Business Administration Degree from the Wharton School of the University of Pennsylvania. His tenacious desire to pursue his education is truly inspiring.

At the age of 53, Dr. Mishoe accepted the role as president of Delaware State College, where he oversaw the overall growth and development of the University. The school continued to expand under Dr. Mishoe's 27-year tenure, and he saw to it that greater emphasis be placed on the development and improvement of academic programs dedicated to the education of all people. Enrollment progressively increased from 386 students in 1960 to 2,327 in 1987.

Dr. Mishoe's phenomenal leadership generated an exemplary environment at DSU. Serving the second longest tenure, Dr. Mishoe was able to improve the physical infrastructure by completing the construction of Conwell Hall for men, Laws Hall for women, building of Business and Economics, and Evers Hall. Through his ability to create the first master's degree program in Education Curriculum and Instruction in 1981, and later, establishing six other graduate degree programs, Dr. Mishoe upheld the University's mission of integrating the highest standard of excellence.

Prior to entering academia, Dr. Mishoe served in the Air Force during World War II. During this time of racial conflict, Dr. Mishoe fought battles abroad and for civil rights at home. It was recently determined by the National Office of the Tuskegee Airmen that Dr. Mishoe is a documented Original Tuskegee Airman. He also served as a Special Consultant for the Ballistics Research Laboratory at the U.S. Army Ordnance Proving Ground in Maryland, prior to taking the helm at DSC.

Dr. Mishoe sadly passed away at the age of 72 on January 18, 1989, and is remembered as a dynamic community leader by his family, friends, students, and the many people whose lives he touched. I am very pleased to honor his life and legacy.

TRIBUTE TO JAGUAR TRACK CLUB

HON. DONALD M. PAYNE, JR.
OF NEW JERSEY
IN THE HOUSE OF REPRESENTATIVES
Tuesday, November 29, 2016

Mr. PAYNE. Mr. Speaker, I rise today to mark the 20th anniversary of the Jaguar Track Club, a competitive track program for youth ages 7–18 in South Orange, Maplewood, and surrounding communities in the 10th district of New Jersey. Founders Maurice and Daneen Cooper, Andrea Johnson, and Carl Lea held their first practice at Underhill Field in April 1996 and have been serving the public ever since.

The program's motto is "train your body to lead, train your body to follow." Not only are these young athletes exercising their bodies physically, but they are working their minds concurrently to become productive members of society. Each youth is trained to run sprint, middle, and long distances, as well as field events such as hurdles, shot put, discus, and long jump. However, the program also builds self-esteem, promotes physical fitness, teaches positive social skills, develops responsibility, and requires maintenance of academic excellence.

Over 2,000 athletes have gone through the Jaguar Track Club; many have continued their love for track in college and beyond. A number of the youth have achieved the distinction of All American, participated in Olympic trials, and even represented the United States in the Olympics.

On December 28, 2016, the Jaguar Track Club will celebrate its 20th anniversary and the common bond shared of being a Jaguar. I am honored to recognize the athletes, parents, and coaches that have all participated throughout these past two decades. Congratulations once again to the Jaguar Track Club.

HONORING CARLO A. SCISSURA

HON. DANIEL M. DONOVAN, JR.
OF NEW YORK
IN THE HOUSE OF REPRESENTATIVES
Tuesday, November 29, 2016

Mr. DONOVAN. Mr. Speaker, I rise today to recognize the tireless dedication of Brooklyn's Carlo A. Scissura for his service to the community.

For the last two decades, Carlo has devoted his life to public service. In 1999, Carlo was elected to Community School Board 20 where he served for five years. During his time on the board, Carlo worked closely with parents and teachers to fight for drug and alcohol abuse prevention programs. He was then appointed to the Community Education Council for district 20 where he served as President and Chairman of the Legislative Committee. Carlo was fundamental in having the School Construction Authority approve the largest capital construction plan for District 20. He has also served on the staffs of a local State Senator, Assemblyman, and Borough President.

Since 2012, Carlo has served as President and CEO of the Brooklyn Chamber of Commerce. Under Carlo's leadership, the Chamber has advocated fiercely for businesses and economic development in Brooklyn. In the last four years, the Chamber has launched multiple initiatives such as Explore Brooklyn, Brooklyn-Made, and Chamber on the Go. These programs have proven successful and beneficial to all businesses that call Kings County their home. The Chamber will be sad to see Carlo leave as his life takes a new turn down the path of success.

Mr. Speaker, Carlo Scissura's dedication to charity and improving his community is the essence of the model New Yorker. I thank him, and the Chamber thanks him for his service, dedication, and all of his great work. I am proud to honor this great American from New York's 11th District.

WITH THANKS FOR THE LIFE OF JUDGE DAVID A. KATZ

HON. MARCY KAPTUR
OF OHIO
IN THE HOUSE OF REPRESENTATIVES
Tuesday, November 29, 2016

Ms. KAPTUR. Mr. Speaker, I rise today in this season of thanksgiving when we are especially grateful for family and friends to pay tribute to one such friend, The Honorable David A. Katz. Judge Katz passed from this life during the summer on July 26, 2016.

A justice with the United States District Court, Northern District of Ohio, Judge Katz was appointed by President Bill Clinton in 1994 and had served on senior status since 2005. His tenure was marked by strong jurisprudence and included his tireless perseverance of a new federal courthouse in Toledo. A highly regarded and well respected jurist, the flags flew at half staff the day after his death to honor his public service. In issuing the order, chief judge for the Northern District of Ohio Solomon Oliver, Jr. summed up Judge Katz' service most succinctly when he stated, "Judge Katz' contribution to our court has been immeasurable. He came to the court with a keen sense of fairness and a very large dose of common sense. He could always be counted on. He was highly respected by the lawyers in the community. Though he had many strengths, one of his greatest was his ability to resolve complex cases involving multiple parties. As Chief Judge, I often sought and received his wise counsel. Every judge on our court highly valued David's friendship. We will all miss him greatly."

David Katz was born in Toledo to parents Ruth and Samuel Katz and raised in Findlay, Ohio. He married Joan Siegel in 1955. He graduated from Ohio State University's College of Law in 1957. He began private practice with the Toledo firm of Spengler Nathanson where he ably practiced until his judicial appointment. Strong in his faith and proud of his Jewish heritage, Judge Katz gave of his time and talents to the Toledo Jewish Community Foundation, where the David A. Katz Philanthropic Fund was established.

Even with all of the public accolades, Judge Katz' proudest and most important achievement was his family. A family man to his core, he cherished his wife, their children, grandchildren and great-granddaughter above all else. Though a public man and elder statesman whose imprimatur is writ large through the decisions he rendered and his contributions to our community, his true legacy is given to his family. As his family and friends remember Judge David A. Katz in thanksgiving for his life, we recall the words in the poem by Sylvan Kamens & Rabbi Jack Riemer, entitled We Remember Them.

At the rising sun and at its going down; We remember them.

At the blowing of the wind and in the chill of winter; We remember them.
At the opening of the buds and in the rebirth of spring; We remember them.
At the blueness of the skies and in the warmth of summer; We remember them.
At the rustling of the leaves and in the beauty of the autumn; We remember them.
At the beginning of the year and when it ends; We remember them.
As long as we live, they too will live, for they are now a part of us as We remember them.
When we are weary and in need of strength; We remember them.
When we are lost and sick at heart; We remember them.
When we have decisions that are difficult to make; We remember them.
When we have joy we crave to share; We remember them.
When we have achievements that are based on theirs; We remember them.
For as long as we live, they too will live, for they are now a part of us as We remember them.

CONGRATULATING PETER GILEA ON RECEIVING THE BRONZE MEDALLION AND KNIGHTED INTO THE U.S. ARMY CAVALRY AND ARMOR ASSOCIATION'S ORDER OF ST. GEORGE

HON. PETER J. ROSKAM
OF ILLINOIS
IN THE HOUSE OF REPRESENTATIVES
Tuesday, November 29, 2016

Mr. ROSKAM. Mr. Speaker, I rise today to honor a World War II veteran from the Sixth Congressional District of Illinois, Peter Gilea. Peter was recently named a knight of the U.S. Army Cavalry and Armor Association's Order of St. George and presented with the Bronze Medallion. The honor is awarded to Armor and Cavalrymen who perform outstanding service to the U.S. Army Armored Force.

Peter Gilea was drafted and went into the army January 25, 1943. He went through his training with the 735th Independent Tank Battalion, which he also helped establish and on February 12, 1944 his unit left the United States and arrived in Scotland on February 24, 1944. While serving as a commander on a Sherman tank with the 735th Tank Battalion in Europe, he received five campaign battle stars, which include fighting in Normandy, the pursuit through France and action in Luxembourg during the important allied victory of the Battle of the Bulge. Peter also received the Bronze Star Medal for bravery, two Purple Hearts, European-African-Middle Eastern Campaign Medal, Good Conduct Medal, American Defense Medal, World War II Victory Medal and the French Legion of Honor Medal.

His courage and commitment to defending the freedoms we cherish will forever be a credit to his patriotism and sacrifice. His bravery during campaigns through Normandy, Northern France, Rhineland, Ardennes-Alsace, and Central Europe was pivotal in the destruction of the oppressive and evil Nazi regime. It is because of men like Peter Gilea that we enjoy the rights and liberties we value so deeply.

Mr. Speaker, please join me in congratulating Peter Gilea for receiving the Bronze Medallion and receiving a knighthood into the Order of St. George. Once again, congratulations, and I wish Peter all the best in the years to come.

RECOGNIZING DAVID WILDY, WINNER OF THE 2016 SWISHER SWEETS/SUNBELT EXPO SOUTHEASTERN FARMER OF THE YEAR AWARD

HON. AUSTIN SCOTT
OF GEORGIA
IN THE HOUSE OF REPRESENTATIVES
Tuesday, November 29, 2016

Mr. AUSTIN SCOTT of Georgia. Mr. Speaker, Representative CRAWFORD and I would like to recognize Mr. David Wildy of Manila, Arkansas for being selected as the 2016 Swisher Sweets/Sunbelt Expo Southeastern Farmer of the Year. Receiving the award over nine other state finalists, Mr. Wildy was honored at the Willie B. Withers Luncheon on October 18, 2016, the opening day of the Sunbelt Ag Expo in Moultrie, Georgia.

Upon graduating from the University of Arkansas in 1975, Mr. Wildy became the fifth-generation Wildy to take over the family's century old farm, where he oversees the farm's cotton, corn, soybean, wheat, peanut and potato production. Throughout his career, Mr. Wildy has found success not only in developing his family farm but also in strengthening agriculture in his home state of Arkansas. In farming communities across the Southeast, Mr. Wildy is known as a generous man who shares his farm's resources with agricultural scientists and researchers from private industries, public universities, and the U.S. Department of Agriculture.

Mr. Wildy has also achieved distinction as a hard-working public servant and philanthropist in his community. He has served as President of the Mississippi County Farm Bureau, member of the USDA-Farm Service Agency in Mississippi County, member of the University of Arkansas Agriculture Development Council, member of the Arkansas Northeastern College Foundation Board of Governors, board member of the St. Francis Levee District of Arkansas, and board member of the Arkansas Certified Crop Advisor. Mr. Wildy has also championed education in his community, providing scholarships to local high school graduates and giving books to elementary school students.

Through his actions, service, and devotion to his farm and his community, Mr. Wildy has demonstrated profound leadership and dedication to the agriculture industry. On behalf of the House Agriculture Committee, we would like to thank David Wildy for his service and congratulate him on the honor of being the 2016 Swisher Sweets/Sunbelt Expo Southeastern Farmer of the Year.

IN RECOGNITION OF CAMDEN, ARKANSAS'S AEROJET ROCKETDYNE EMPLOYEES

HON. BRUCE WESTERMAN
OF ARKANSAS
IN THE HOUSE OF REPRESENTATIVES
Tuesday, November 29, 2016

Mr. WESTERMAN. Mr. Speaker, I rise today to recognize the 675 employees at Aerojet Rocketdyne's Camden, Arkansas, production facility and their upcoming achievement of the milestone shipment of the 2,700th PAC–3 Cost Reduction Initiative Rocket Motor, 500,000th PAC–3 Attitude Control Motor, and completion of the first full rate production contract of the PAC–3 Missile Segment Enhancement Rocket Motor, to Lockheed Martin and the United States Army.

Aerojet Rocketdyne is a world-recognized aerospace and defense leader principally serving the missile, space propulsion, and armaments markets. This most significant milestone will be commemorated with a celebration ceremony held in Camden, Arkansas, on Thursday, December 8, 2016.

The PAC–3 missile, powered by Aerojet Rocketdyne propulsion, is a high velocity interceptor that defeats incoming targets by direct, body-to-body impact. The "hit-to-kill" PAC–3 missile is the world's most advanced, capable, and powerful terminal air defense missile, and when deployed in a Patriot battery, significantly increases the Patriot system's firepower. It is capable of defeating the entire threat of tactical ballistic missiles, cruise missiles, and aircraft. One hundred percent effective in Operation Iraqi Freedom, the PAC–3 missile is a quantum leap ahead of any other air defense missile when it comes to the ability to protect the Warfighter.

Aerojet Rocketdyne has manufactured the PAC–3 Solid Rocket Motors and Attitude Control Motors since 1998 at its Camden facility. Production of the Missile Segment Enhancement Rocket Motor began in 2014. The PAC–3 rocket motors are a noteworthy element of Aerojet Rocketdyne's industry-leading tactical propulsion portfolio produced in Camden, generating significant employment opportunities for the area.

On the occasion of this milestone, I am proud to recognize the dedicated, hardworking employees of Aerojet Rocketdyne in Camden and their achievements so far. These Arkansans are working hard to ensure our men and women in uniform have the resources they need to carry out their missions effectively and quickly, and they deserve our sincere appreciation.

MAMMOTH LAKES TRAIL AND PUBLIC ACCESS TENTH ANNIVERSARY

HON. PAUL COOK
OF CALIFORNIA
IN THE HOUSE OF REPRESENTATIVES
Tuesday, November 29, 2016

Mr. COOK. Mr. Speaker, I rise today to recognize the tenth anniversary of the Mammoth Lakes Trail and Public Access (MLTPA), a non-profit organization which has devoted their efforts to the planning and creation of a four-season trail system in Mammoth Lakes and the immediate Eastern Sierra. MLTPA is an effective, independent leader in recreational wilderness regions of California, preserving America's natural beauty and encouraging a prosperous local economy. In 2005, the MLTPA began planning and raising over twenty million dollars which it invested to connect people with nature. Public access was improved so more people could come and enjoy the area's great outdoors and through collaborative partnerships and recreation opportunities, community participation increased. MLTPA has made a significant difference in connecting the community to the local government and businesses in order to bring people to the region by providing a safe and sustainable trail network. Mammoth Lakes Trail and Public Access has increased awareness about the future of the community and its relationship to the surrounding public lands. MLTPA has led a collaborative effort with the local government, federal agencies, and other non-profits. Its upcoming projects include the acceleration of various transportation projects which aim to link the Town's bicycle, pedestrian, transit, and parking alternatives. I congratulate them on their ten years of success and look forward to all their success in the years to come.

TRIBUTE TO CHARLES JOE HELMS

HON. LUKE MESSER
OF INDIANA
IN THE HOUSE OF REPRESENTATIVES
Tuesday, November 29, 2016

Mr. MESSER. Mr. Speaker, I rise today to pay tribute to the life of my good friend Charles Joe Helms of Butlerville, Indiana.

Charlie was born on May 8, 1948 in Richmond, Indiana, to Myron and Esther Dennis Helms. Charlie lived a long, full life dedicated to his family and his community. Charlie is survived by his loving wife, Vickie; three sons, Jon, Lennie, and Arnie; daughter, Nichelle Burkhardt; stepdaughters, Traci Baldwin, Amy McCanlis, and Bekah Hunsucker; one sister, Lynda Schmidt; and seven grandchildren.

Raised in Indiana, Charlie graduated from Brookville High School before serving his country in the U.S. Navy. Following his service, he worked for Ford Motor Company in Connersville and then General Motors Delphi in Dayton, Ohio for several years. Charlie officially retired in 2010, after working for the Muscatatuck Urban Training Center.

As the Good Book says in Acts 20:35, "It is more blessed to give than to receive." Charlie truly lived this scripture throughout his life. Everyone who knew him, knew of his steadfast faith and compassion for serving the Hoosier community. Charlie was a member of the Nebraska Church of God, Masonic Lodge Number 219 in Butlerville and American Legion Post Number 77 in Brookville. In his free time, he enjoyed exploring the outdoors, boating and spending time with his family

I am lucky to have called Charlie Helms a close friend. I know first-hand his faith, his ex-

traordinary friendship and his consistent encouragement. I will never forget his support and belief in me.

Charlie will be missed dearly by his family and his community, but his memory will live on in those who were blessed to know him.

Today, it is my privilege to honor the life of Charlie Helms. My thoughts and prayers go out to Charlie's family, and may God comfort those he left behind with His peace and strength.

IN RECOGNITION OF THE SACRAMENTO JAPANESE AMERICAN CITIZENS LEAGUE 2016 HONOREES

HON. DORIS O. MATSUI
OF CALIFORNIA
IN THE HOUSE OF REPRESENTATIVES
Tuesday, November 29, 2016

Ms. MATSUI. Mr. Speaker, I rise today to recognize the Sacramento Chapter of the Japanese American Citizens League's 2016 honorees. As the members of the Sacramento Japanese American Citizens League (JACL) join together for their annual community recognition and installation banquet, I ask all of my colleagues to join me in recognizing these outstanding leaders in our community.

As one of the oldest and largest Japanese American Citizens League chapters in our nation, the Sacramento chapter remains a leader in the fight for civil rights of all Americans, while supporting programs that enhance our culture and community. Each year, the Sacramento JACL honors inspiring individuals and companies that are committed to public service and upholding the values of the JACL. This year, I join the members of the Sacramento JACL in honoring the following individuals: Dr. Donna Yee and Priscilla Ouachita, as well as members from the Dharma School Courtyard Kitchen of the Sacramento Buddhist Church—Sam and Gladys Adachi, Billy and Grace Hatano, Reiko Kurahara, Mike and Rachel Nagai, Sachiko Sawada and Akaiye Shimada.

Dr. Donna Yee, Chief Executive Officer of Asian Community Center Senior Services, has worked tirelessly for over forty years to ensure that seniors and their families have much needed access to resources and programs vital to their well-being. The ACC provides assisted and independent living as well as supporting programs including transportation, home respite services, and caregiver support.

Priscilla Ouchida, a longtime community advocate, has much experience and numerous accomplishments in the quest for civil rights and promoting the cultural heritage of Japanese-Americans. Serving as the Executive Director of the JACL, the Chief of Staff and Legislative Director for Senator Joe Simitian, and the Chief of Staff and Legislative Director for Senator Patrick Johnston, Ms. Ouchida is a valued leader in our community.

Sam and Gladys Adachi, Billy and Grace Hatano, Reiko Kurahara, Mike and Rachel Nagai, Sachiko Sawada and Akaiye Shimada from the Dharma School Courtyard Kitchen of the Sacramento Buddhist Church have been

preparing meals for over 35 years. They manage to do all this from donations from local businesses and church membership.

Mr. Speaker, as these individuals are being recognized by the Japanese American Citizens League, I ask my colleagues to join me in thanking them for their outstanding service to our Sacramento community.

HONORING MS. DEBORAH WILLIAMS

HON. BARBARA LEE
OF CALIFORNIA
IN THE HOUSE OF REPRESENTATIVES
Tuesday, November 29, 2016

Ms. LEE. Mr. Speaker, I rise today to honor the extraordinary life and invaluable career of Ms. Deborah Hudson-Williams, who passed away on November 18, 2016.

Deborah was born on September 15, 1952 in Oakland California, to Girver and Gertrude Hudson, and grew up in a large working-class family which her father supported through his career as an electrician at General Electric. Her father was also active with the United Auto Workers (UAW), and his work would inspire her own career, when she followed him into working for the UAW.

Ms. Williams was incredibly passionate about the rights of workers, and she was very active in the UAW, including many years when she worked at the New United Motor Manufacturing, Inc., (NUMMI) plant in Fremont, California. She also served as the chairperson for the UAW's Political Action Committee in the Bay Area, which enabled her to support candidates and policies that worked to improve the quality of life for middle-class families like her own.

In addition to working to support the men and women of her union, Ms. Williams was politically active in many areas, including working with the National Association of Negro Business and Professional Women's Clubs (NANBPWC), the A. Philip Randolph Organization, the NAACP, and the Oakland East Bay Democratic Club.

She is survived by many siblings, including four brothers: Anthony Hudson (Linda) Las Vegas, NV, Girver Hudson Jr. (Linda) California, Michael Hudson (Delores) Oakland, Mark Hudson, Oakland; and seven sisters, Brenda Brooks, Oakland, Francine Wesley (Noel) San Pablo, Cheryl Moore, Oakland, Patricia Henry (Clarence) Oakland, Mada Hudson, Oakland, Beverly Hudson, Pittsburg, Karen Cox (Mobil), Oakland.

On a personal note, Debbie was a loyal supporter whose wise counsel I always appreciated and who always came through for me right on time, every time. Most importantly, she was a dear friend who I will deeply miss.

On behalf on California's 13th Congressional District, I would like to offer my sincerest condolences to her family, friends, and the community she cared so much about. Ms. Williams' legacy as a strong advocate for working men and women will be remembered and honored throughout the Bay Area.

CELEBRATING THE REPUBLIC OF KAZAKHSTAN'S 25 YEARS OF INDEPENDENCE

HON. ALCEE L. HASTINGS
OF FLORIDA
IN THE HOUSE OF REPRESENTATIVES
Tuesday, November 29, 2016

Mr. HASTINGS. Mr. Speaker, I rise today to recognize the Republic of Kazakhstan, which on December 16, 2016 will celebrate its independence day. For twenty five years, Kazakhstan and its people have stood out as a steadfast and true friend to the United States on an array of security and economic issues and have made tremendous strides in democratization and economic development.

Since its independence, Kazakhstan has stood out as a reliable strategic partner in Central Asia to the United States and the North Atlantic Treaty Organization (NATO). Kazakhstan contributes to the reconstruction of Afghanistan, finances the education of thousands of Afghan immigrants and refugees, and has provided supply line access and support to the International Security Assistance Force (ISAF) Coalition. For the past thirteen years, Kazakh, American, and NATO security forces have conducted joint military training programs in the Central Asian steppes. According to the National Bank of Kazakhstan, American companies invested $24 billion in the Kazakh economy from 2005 to 2016.

However, the cornerstone of strong U.S.-Kazakhstan relations is nuclear nonproliferation. After the dissolution of the Soviet Union, Kazakhstan inherited a nuclear weapons stockpile of 1,400 nuclear warheads, the fourth largest stockpile of nuclear weapons in the world. President Nursultan Nazarbayev expressed his early commitment to nuclear disarmament by decommissioning all 1,400 nuclear weapons.

The government in Astana has remained committed to the global cause of nonproliferation ever since. Recently the country established the first-ever Low Enriched Uranium Fuel Bank backed by the International Atomic Energy Agency (IAEA) in order to ensure the stability of civil nuclear energy use worldwide. As a nonpermanent member of the UN Security Council, President Nazarbayev has relentlessly pursued the cause of nuclear disarmament.

Kazakhstan is also on the road to becoming a regional hub for sustainable economic activity in Central Asia. Its New Silk Road Initiative, the "Bright Path" stimulus plan, and the 2050 Strategy each mark President Nazarbayev's commitment to developing transportation and telecommunications infrastructure and his commitment to diversifying Kazakhstan's overall economy. Relatedly, Kazakhstan will host an International Exposition in 2017 that aims to create a global discourse among states, NGOs, and corporations about ensuring sustainable access to energy while reducing carbon emissions. These promising strides in economic development will not only help the Kazakh people, but will benefit American companies doing business in Kazakhstan.

Mr. Speaker, I once again want to congratulate President Nazarbayev and the Kazakh people on the joyous occasion of their twenty fifth anniversary of independence, and I look forward to a continued, strong and resilient friendship between our two countries.

2016 NATIONAL NATIVE AMERICAN HERITAGE MONTH

HON. BETTY McCOLLUM
OF MINNESOTA
IN THE HOUSE OF REPRESENTATIVES
Tuesday, November 29, 2016

Ms. McCOLLUM. Mr. Speaker, each November we celebrate the contributions of First Americans with National Native American Heritage Month. The people of the 567 diverse, federally recognized tribal nations—including the 11 Ojibwe and Dakota nations in Minnesota—play a complex and vital role in our nation's history, and make our communities and our country stronger today.

Despite centuries of violent discrimination and abusive policies, our country's Native American cultures and nations have endured. Tribal governments and Native communities have made monumental progress. Our federal trust relationship with tribal nations has grown stronger in the current era of self-governance among Native American tribes—a proud accomplishment that will continue to require the federal government's full and respectful engagement.

As a co-chair of the Congressional Native American Caucus and the Ranking Member of the Interior-Environment Appropriations Subcommittee, I have had the honor to meet with hundreds of tribal leaders to discuss the needs of Indian Country. Working together, we have succeeded in making substantial progress on education, health, and criminal justice issues through measures like the Indian Health Care Improvement Act, increased funding for the Bureau of Indian Education, and special tribal jurisdiction in domestic violence cases.

Despite these concrete steps, we have much more work to do to address disparities, invest in Indian Country, and create more opportunities for all Native Americans—especially Native youth. As we honor the achievements and resilience of our First Americans, I pledge to continue working to ensure that our Native American brothers and sisters have every opportunity to succeed.

IN RECOGNITION OF JOHN SHIREY

HON. DORIS O. MATSUI
OF CALIFORNIA
IN THE HOUSE OF REPRESENTATIVES
Tuesday, November 29, 2016

Ms. MATSUI. Mr. Speaker, I rise today to recognize John Shirey as he retires after over 44 years of public service. As his loved ones, friends, and colleagues celebrate his decorated career, I ask my colleagues to join me in celebrating his work as Sacramento's City Manager.

John earned his Bachelor of Science degree in industrial engineering at Purdue University and then completed his Master's degree in public administration at the University of Southern California. He served diligently as the Assistant City Manager of City of Long Beach, starting a long career of public service in California. For a few years he served as City Manager of Cincinnati, Ohio. After returning to California, John began his time as Executive Director of the California Redevelopment Association, an organization responsible for over 350 redevelopment agencies. Consistent with his dedication to the public good, John dedicated nine years to urban redevelopment, and thereafter became the City Manager of Sacramento in September of 2011. During his tenure as City Manager, Mr. Shirey has balanced not only an annual budget that nears $900 million, but also a work force of around 4,100 employees. His expertise and knowledge have served the city well, and he will be missed.

Mr. Shirey played a pivotal role in keeping our Sacramento Kings where they belong, which is in California's capital city. His motivation and drive were integral to the construction of the Golden 1 Center, which is a jewel in Sacramento's downtown that will drive economic development and commerce for decades to come. John has also made a continual effort to support the homeless in Sacramento. His hard work and integrity have helped make Sacramento a better place.

Mr. Speaker, as John and his family, friends, and colleagues gather to celebrate his retirement, I ask my colleagues to join me in wishing him the best in retirement and thanking him for his contributions to the Sacramento region.

IN HONOR OF FRANK JOHNSON

HON. SANFORD D. BISHOP, JR.
OF GEORGIA
IN THE HOUSE OF REPRESENTATIVES
Tuesday, November 29, 2016

Mr. BISHOP of Georgia. Mr. Speaker, it is with a heavy heart and solemn remembrance that I rise today to pay tribute to a respected community leader and outstanding citizen, Frank Johnson. Sadly, Mr. Johnson passed away on Sunday, November 20, 2016. Funeral services were held on Saturday, November 26, 2016.

Frank Johnson served our nation honorably among the ranks of the first black Marines, known as the Montford Point Marines because they received basic training at the segregated Montford Point Base adjacent to Camp Lejeune, North Carolina. Mr. Johnson later worked at Robins Air Force Base until he retired.

Although Mr. Johnson fought to protect our cherished freedoms and liberties, he did not benefit from all those freedoms and liberties for he did not have the right to vote due to the color of his skin. This inspired Mr. Johnson to join the march over the Edmund Pettus Bridge in Selma, Alabama on March 7, 1965. When the group of protesters reached the other side of the bridge, they were brutally attacked by police, giving the historic day the name "Bloody Sunday."

Frank Johnson's life was about helping people. He was known as the "mayor" of Macon's Unionville neighborhood for his efforts to revitalize the area and improve the quality of life for its residents. He was involved in the Unionville Improvement Association and helped with community clean-ups. Mr. Johnson wanted a recreation center for Unionville's young people to enjoy. He got that and more—a recreation center was opened on Mercer University Drive on the site where he grew up playing and it was named after him. The Frank Johnson Community Center is currently undergoing renovations and will reopen soon.

Mr. Johnson devoted decades of service to the people of Macon through his meaningful contribution of energy, love, and genuine passion. He was an honorable human being who loved deeply and, in return, was deeply loved. Frank Johnson is survived by his wife of 62 years, Dorothy, and his daughter, Cheryl.

Maya Angelou once said, "A great soul serves everyone all the time. A great soul never dies." Frank Johnson is one such great soul, who served humanity in a special way. Each day he graced the people around him with an enthusiastic sincerity of presence. His impression on this earth extends beyond himself to the very wellbeing of the Macon community, and for it he will be remembered by the community for time to come.

Mr. Speaker, my wife Vivian and I, along with the more than 730,000 people of the Second Congressional District salute Frank Johnson for his dedicated service and exceptional impact on Macon, Georgia. I ask my colleagues in the House of Representatives to join us in extending our deepest sympathies to Mr. Johnson's family, friends and loved ones during this difficult time. We pray that they will be consoled and comforted by an abiding faith and the Holy Spirit in the days, weeks and months ahead.

IN RECOGNITION OF THE SACRAMENTO BRANCH OF THE NAACP'S CENTENNIAL CELEBRATION

HON. DORIS O. MATSUI
OF CALIFORNIA
IN THE HOUSE OF REPRESENTATIVES
Tuesday, November 29, 2016

Ms. MATSUI. Mr. Speaker, I rise today to recognize the Sacramento branch of the NAACP as they celebrate their 100th anniversary. The NAACP's time-honored chapter in Sacramento has been a leader in the difficult yet rewarding work of the civil rights movement. I ask all my colleagues to join me in honoring the significant contributions to civil rights in our community and nation of the Sacramento NAACP.

The Sacramento branch was founded in 1916, seven years after the establishment of the first NAACP office in New York. The Sacramento branch was one of the first formed in the West and has continued to lead the peaceful, but powerful, fight against violence and civil rights abuses. This year's Gala embodies the valued work of the branch over the years, which has helped the community express its voice and assert its rights. Through the faith, perseverance, and never-ending courage of the Sacramento NAACP, our community has seen the rights of many expanded and protected.

Over the years the Sacramento branch of the NAACP has seen many great leaders. This legacy began with Rev. T. Allen, the first president of the branch who fought tirelessly to see that liberties would be defended. This fight has continued with every subsequent leader. This year's Gala is a testament to their hard work, which has included providing free legal services to fight discrimination, sponsoring bills that ensure the rights of children and families, and fighting for education in the community.

For 100 years the Sacramento branch of the NAACP has been striving to ensure political, educational, social, and economic equality for all. The NAACP has always been and will continue to be an instrumental organization in facilitating the advancement of minorities. I ask all my colleagues to join me in celebrating the 100th anniversary of the Sacramento chapter of the NAACP.

HONORING STEVE LATOURETTE

HON. BOB GOODLATTE
OF VIRGINIA
IN THE HOUSE OF REPRESENTATIVES
Tuesday, November 29, 2016

Mr. GOODLATTE. Mr. Speaker, I rise to pay tribute to a good friend and former colleague, Steve LaTourette, who sadly passed away earlier this year after battling pancreatic cancer.

I first met Steve after he was elected to serve the 19th Congressional District of Ohio in 1994. One of the longtime leaders of the House Transportation and Infrastructure Committee, Steve worked diligently on improving the infrastructure needs of not just his district and Ohio, but the nation. He played an important role in crafting highway authorization legislation, and in his last few years in the House, served as a member of the Appropriations Committee's Transportation Subcommittee as well.

Steve was also someone who sought out consensus and results in the legislative process. As one of the heads of Republican Main Street Partnership, a moderate Republican organization, Steve looked for ways to advance policy ideas that would benefit the American people and bring as many folks together as possible on common ground.

While Steve is no longer with us today, his sense of humor, leadership, and intelligence are not forgotten. I know that folks in Ohio and across the nation will remember his good works in Congress on behalf of his constituents and the American people. True public servants like Steve LaTourette are missed when they leave the House, and mourned when they pass away too soon.

Our thoughts and prayers go out to Steve's wife, children, and his entire family. He will be missed.

HONORING THE LIFE OF DR. FRANK J. INDIHAR

HON. BETTY McCOLLUM
OF MINNESOTA
IN THE HOUSE OF REPRESENTATIVES
Tuesday, November 29, 2016

Ms. McCOLLUM. Mr. Speaker, my dear friend, Frank J. Indihar, MD passed away on October 23, 2016. He leaves a legacy of both medical excellence and committed service to my community, the state of Minnesota, and our nation.

From 2002 through 2008, Dr. Indihar led Bethesda Hospital as Chief Executive Officer, after serving as its Medical Director for several years and decades as a practicing physician. Bethesda Hospital, located steps from the State Capitol in Saint Paul, is a long-term acute care hospital with a reputation for first-class specialty care. Under his management, Bethesda improved its programs and services and undertook major facility renovations.

The entire Midwest greatly benefited from Dr. Indihar's long list of accomplishments at Bethesda, including establishing the Capistrant Center for Parkinson's Disease and Movement Disorders, starting an innovative clinic to treat young people injured from concussions, and creating a therapeutic garden for patients, families, and employees.

With Bethesda's specialty in treating brain injuries, Dr. Indihar was a key resource to me as we worked to ensure that our servicemembers and veterans receive the health care they need, including assessment and treatment for those who sustained traumatic brain injuries during their service in Iraq and Afghanistan. Dr. Indihar greatly assisted me with my work on this issue in Congress.

As a Major in the United States Army Medical Corps, Dr. Indihar began his medical career serving in Vietnam and Washington, DC, and was awarded a Bronze Star with Oak Leaf Cluster in 1970 for his brave and meritorious service. In 1973, he served as Chief Resident in Internal Medicine Service at the Minneapolis VA Medical Center.

Throughout his distinguished career, Dr. Indihar demonstrated a steadfast commitment to excellence in medicine. Among his numerous professional positions, he was President of the Ramsey County Medical Society and served as Delegate and Chair of the Minnesota delegation to the American Medical Association House of Delegates for many years. His dedication to medicine was especially apparent through his lifelong mentorship of medical students.

Frank was known as a Renaissance man and demonstrated strong support for the arts community in Minnesota. He also made extensive civic contributions to the boards of Catholic Services to the Elderly, the Minnesota Orchestra, New Connections, and the Saint Paul Seminary.

I wish to extend my sincere condolences to Frank's wife, Anita Pampusch, as well as his sisters, nephew and nieces, and grandnieces. My heartfelt condolences also go out to his colleagues at Bethesda Hospital and HealthEast for their loss.

It was an honor to work with Frank, and I valued our continued friendship in his retirement. He was a kind and extraordinary person who will be deeply missed.

IN RECOGNITION OF THE 2016 URBAN LAND INSTITUTE VISION HONORS AWARD RECIPIENTS

HON. DORIS O. MATSUI
OF CALIFORNIA
IN THE HOUSE OF REPRESENTATIVES
Tuesday, November 29, 2016

Ms. MATSUI. Mr. Speaker, I rise today to recognize the Urban Land Institute (ULI) of Sacramento and the 2016 ULI Vision Honors Award recipients. As the members of the Urban Land Institute of Sacramento gather at the annual Vision Honors dinner to recognize the projects and individuals that have shown exemplary leadership in smart planning, urban growth, and sustainable communities, I ask all my colleagues to join me in honoring their contributions to the Sacramento region.

The ULI's mission has long been to promote the responsible use of land for the benefit of local communities, and every year ULI recognizes leaders in the community who have upheld this mission. The ULI Principles Vision Honors Awardee is Mr. Mike McKeever, the outgoing Chief Executive Officer of the Sacramento Area Council of Governments. For over a decade, Mr. McKeever led SACOG with a steady hand and contributed to the advancement of the region's infrastructure. His nationally acclaimed Blueprint regional planning scenario has become a model for sustainability planning and smart growth. Navigating an organization that represents six counties and 22 local cities is no easy task, but Mike proved time and again that he could bring people together and build a consensus among divergent viewpoints. I applaud Mike for his time at SACOG and his work that is not only improving the efficiency of Sacramento's transit network, but is also increasing the region's environmental friendliness through its plan to reduce emissions.

The 2016 ULI Project of the Year award is presented to the Sacramento Kings and the City of Sacramento for the Golden 1 Center/ Downtown Commons Project. The Golden 1 Center is a groundbreaking project in the heart of Sacramento's downtown that ties the most advanced technology in the world with environmental sustainability. As the first LEED Platinum-designated arena in the world, the Golden 1 Center counteracts climate change through its use of solar energy and its water efficiency. Even more importantly, it promotes environmental awareness and sustainability to its estimated 1.2 million annual visitors. The Golden 1 Center/Downtown Commons Project also contributes to a thriving local community through its commitment to sourcing 90 percent of all food services from local farms and businesses.

The ULI Member/Achiever of the Year Vision Honors Awardee is Mr. Jeffrey M. Goldman, AICP, Principal of AECOM. Mr. Goldman has over 30 years of experience in community planning, development codes, community outreach, and CEQA compliance. Over the last decade, Mr. Goldman has led the Sacramento AECOM office with an increased focus on sustainability, climate mitigation, adaptation, and community resilience. Mr. Goldman has become a leader in coordinating climate action planning documents for local jurisdictions and has furthered sustainability through his numerous environmentally conscious development plans for the Sacramento region, as well as his community-based housing and restoration projects.

Mr. Speaker, as these leaders are being recognized for their forward-thinking contributions to the Sacramento community, I ask all my colleagues to join me in honoring the impact they have made in the Sacramento region.

TUESDAYS IN TEXAS: SUSANA DICKINSON

HON. TED POE
OF TEXAS
IN THE HOUSE OF REPRESENTATIVES
Tuesday, November 29, 2016

Mr. POE of Texas. Mr. Speaker, the year was 1836. To many, this year does not signify much. For Texans everywhere, 1836 shaped the course of our history and spirit.

In February of 1836, the troops of General Santa Anna invaded the Alamo where many Texians gave their lives in the struggle for independence. General Santa Anna and his troops numbered between 1,800 and 6,000 men. The 200 Texians occupying the Alamo stood ready to defend their country. All of the men in the Alamo would give their lives for Texan independence that night. General Santa Anna had ordered his men to take no prisoners.

Among the few that survived were Susana Dickinson and her daughter, Angelina. Susana Dickinson and her daughter had moved to San Antonio because her husband, Almeron Dickinson, had wanted them close to him. When the Mexican troops arrived in San Antonio, Almeron Dickinson moved his family into the Alamo. Although Susana and Angelina survived the siege of the Alamo, Almerson and the rest of the men did not.

Susana was found hiding in the powder magazine by General Juan Almonte and sent to General Santa Anna, where she found her daughter sitting on his lap. General Santa Anna released her with the condition that she go to Camp Gonzalez and warn the Texas troops that he would kill them as he had killed the men in the Alamo. However, in accordance with true Texas spirit, it is believed that instead of delivering a threat, she delivered a war cry for the Texans.

As a result of the siege and her husband's death, Susana was forced to live in poverty for years. She faced multiple unsuccessful marriages and a difficult life but her spirit remained strong. As a survivor of the Alamo, she lived to tell about the heroic fight for freedom against an oppressive and cruel dictator. The Alamo stands as a pillar of hope and is the single most significant structure in Texas history. Susana Dickinson's story of the brave, heroic men who drew a line in the sand and fought for Texas's freedom will live in the history books, reminding future generations of Texans just what this great state stands for. Her spirit and bravery will live on in Texas history.

And that's just the way it is.

IN RECOGNITION OF DR. SHETAL SHAH AND HIS EXPERTISE IN CHILD HEALTH POLICY

HON. STEVE ISRAEL
OF NEW YORK
IN THE HOUSE OF REPRESENTATIVES
Tuesday, November 29, 2016

Mr. ISRAEL. Mr. Speaker, I rise today to recognize a constituent, physician and researcher, Dr. Shetal I. Shah, MD, FAAP for his vigorous advocacy efforts in support of child and newborn health. For over 10 years, Dr. Shah has been an engaged physician-advocate in his roles as Legislative Chairman and Executive Committee member of the Long Island Chapter of the American Academy of Pediatrics. A lifelong member of New York's Third Congressional District, Dr. Shah's medical expertise—coupled with his policy insights and practical, first-hand knowledge of how pediatric and neonatal medicine are practiced in the region—have been a vital resource for my office in interpreting child health legislation. His work has provided practice insights into how national policy will directly affect newborns, children, pediatricians and healthcare systems across my congressional district and across Long Island.

Throughout my tenure in the United States Congress, Dr. Shah has volunteered his time to work with my office to increase pediatric medication safety, support pediatric stem cell research, improve rates of life-saving immunizations, expand access for children to pediatricians, and reduce the effects of gun violence and tobacco on children. His work to promote increased funding for pediatric research, international vaccination funding and healthcare for children has also been helpful to my work in Congress.

I was particularly grateful to receive Dr. Shah's assistance during the debate regarding passage of the 2010 Patient Protection and Affordable Care Act. He was a vocal proponent of how Medicaid Expansion, partnered with Health Insurance Exchanges and the State Child Health Insurance Program—would significantly increase health care access and preventive care for children on Long Island and across the nation. These meetings helped me to critically evaluate this signature legislative achievement.

Dr. Shah has been well recognized for his advocacy efforts over the past decade and I am thankful to be able to extend my appreciation to him for his work. Dr. Shah is co-chairman of the Advocacy Committee of the Society for Pediatric Research, a selective organization consisting of the leading pediatric scientists, policy analysts and researchers in the nation. He is also an appointed member of the Pediatric Policy Council, a consortium of pediatric advocates from the leading medical organizations dedicated to child health. His work in health policy on behalf of children has been honored by the American Medical Association, the March of Dimes, the American Academy of Pediatrics and the Institute for Medicine as a Professor at Columbia University. A former Fulbright Scholar, Dr. Shah is well prepared for his work. A 1996 graduate of Princeton University, Dr. Shah subsequently earned his medical degree—with honors in research—

from Cornell University Medical College. He completed a three-year residency in pediatrics at Duke University School of Medicine followed by a three-year fellowship in neonatal-perinatal medicine at New York University School of Medicine before returning to Long Island. Currently he is a Clinical Professor of Pediatrics and Neonatal Medicine at New York Medical College and a neonatologist at Maria Fareri Children's Hospital.

Mr. Speaker, as I prepare to leave the United States Congress, I wish to thank impactful and engaged citizens such as Dr. Shah for his work with my office on behalf of children. His expert child health care policy analysis has helped elevate and focus debate on our most important constituents—our children.

On behalf of New York's third congressional district, I ask my colleagues to join with me in congratulating Dr. Shetal Shah, MD FAAP and extend to him thanks on behalf of a grateful United States Congress.

REMEMBERING DAVE HUTTON

HON. MARK SANFORD
OF SOUTH CAROLINA
IN THE HOUSE OF REPRESENTATIVES
Tuesday, November 29, 2016

Mr. SANFORD. Mr. Speaker, I rise today in remembrance of Dave Hutton of Daufuskie Island, located in the First District of South Carolina. He died earlier this month doing what he loved—living life fully and at full speed. In this case, he was on a hunting trip with friends. He was only twenty-seven years old.

In that vein, Mark Twain once observed that the fear of death results from of a fear of life, but someone whose life is well lived is prepared to die at any time. Dave was indeed an example of life robustly lived, and much of his time spent on this earth was in the service of others.

A man of large stature and spirit, his presence was one that welcomed you and that could not be ignored. As a native of Daufuskie Island, it comes as no surprise that Dave was among those who remained behind to watch over it when Hurricane Matthew hit back in October. A member of the so-called "Daufuskie 100"—the name for the number of residents who rode out the storm, he was someone that those on the island looked to as a leader. Indeed, when I last saw Dave, he was leading the cleanup effort from the driver's seat of his bulldozer.

That was par for the course for him. He couldn't help but lead. Even as a toddler, Dave encouraged his mother to give the change to charity whenever they went out to eat, an early indication that a life filled with service was to come. Dave's story is one of leading by example, one of both talking the talk and walking the walk, and I think there is a lesson that all of us can learn from within those pages.

In his memory, I would ask that we take a moment today for reflection, and pause in asking how we can live up to his example of leadership. For those of us who knew him, even in the briefest of life's moments, he will be missed. Accordingly, I want to offer my condolences to his mother, Martha, as well as to the other family and friends he leaves behind. Daufuskie has lost one of its strongest spirits. But inasmuch as Daufuskie is a heavenly place for all who are called to its shores, I look forward to landing at the ultimate heavenly place that calls all of us one day home—and seeing him there. Dave will be more than just waiting for us. Perhaps on a shinier dozer, he will have cleared a path for islanders and non-islanders alike. He will be giving perhaps a touch too much direction and leadership—but this indeed is the Dave of Dave.

Until that reunion, Godspeed.

HONORING HARRIET SOL

HON. THEODORE E. DEUTCH
OF FLORIDA
IN THE HOUSE OF REPRESENTATIVES
Tuesday, November 29, 2016

Mr. DEUTCH. Mr. Speaker, I, along with Congresswoman LOIS FRANKEL, rise today in memory of Harriet Sol, who passed away on November 20th. Her strength of character and her ever-outgoing and optimistic attitude is greatly missed by her loved ones and all who knew her.

From the man she met on a Northeast train who eventually became her husband to the many recipients of her charity work, Harriet made an impact on everyone she met.

Harriet never shied away from a new challenge to help others. Upon retirement, she and her husband Ed settled into life in Delray Beach, where her selfless efforts fundraising for the Andy Roddick Foundation for Children in Distress and for the local National Football League chapter charity earned her the "Volunteer of the Year" award at the Lakes of Delray.

As vice president of the United South County Democratic Club and an active volunteer for the Palm Beach County Democratic Club, Harriet was known as a passionate activist and outreach expert.

Harriet worked hard to better our community, and we have lost a great friend and mentor. It was an honor to have known her and to have represented her in the United States Congress.

HONORING CONTRA COSTA COMMUNITY COLLEGE CHANCELLOR HELEN BENJAMIN

HON. MARK DeSAULNIER
OF CALIFORNIA
IN THE HOUSE OF REPRESENTATIVES
Tuesday, November 29, 2016

Mr. DeSAULNIER. Mr. Speaker, I, along with Congressmen MIKE THOMPSON, JERRY McNERNEY, and ERIC SWALWELL, rise today to honor Helen Benjamin for her long commitment to the future of our youth and her belief in the power of education to improve our lives and our communities. Over the last 27 years, Helen's leadership has been instrumental to the vibrant academic culture of the Contra Costa Community College District, spending the past twelve years as Chancellor.

Helen was born in the City of Alexandria, Louisiana, and attended Bishop College in Texas and earned her Master's and doctoral degrees from Texas Woman's University. Helen began her professional career as a public school teacher before taking a position at a four-year institution and moving to a community college. Helen joined the Contra Costa Community College District in the early 1990s as the Los Medanos College Dean of Language Arts and Humanistic Studies and Related Occupations. She also participated in the inaugural class of the League for Innovation in the Community College's Expanding Leadership Diversity program.

Helen has held several positions within the district over the years, including President of Contra Costa Community College, before becoming Chancellor in 2005. She leaves behind a legacy of passionate advocacy for higher education, cultural diversity, professional development, and expanding opportunities for the students and faculty at the district's three main campuses of Diablo Valley College, Los Medanos College, and Contra Costa College. Helen has also been a guiding force in the expansion of the college district with a new campus in San Ramon and the consideration of a new campus in Brentwood.

Helen is highly respected throughout the Bay Area and beyond as an inspiring public servant. I, along with Congressmen MIKE THOMPSON, JERRY McNERNEY, and ERIC SWALWELL, wish Helen and her family well in her retirement and thank her for her years of dedicated service to those seeking to improve their lives through education.

RECOGNIZING THE SERVICE OF ESPERANZA WORLEY

HON. EDDIE BERNICE JOHNSON
OF TEXAS
IN THE HOUSE OF REPRESENTATIVES
Tuesday, November 29, 2016

Ms. EDDIE BERNICE JOHNSON of Texas. Mr. Speaker, today I want to recognize the deep and selfless commitment of a public servant who holds a special place in my heart. 2016 will mark the final year that Esperanza Worley works in my District office. We share that, a deep love for Dallas. I have known her since before I was elected into office, and she has worked on our team every single day of my Congressional career. Though my team and the constituents of Texas' 30th District will lose an exceptional and caring advocate, they will gain a friend who will be rightfully enjoying some much-deserved retirement.

Her attention to detail and warm demeanor have made her an excellent congressional staffer, but an even better friend to all of us. Mr. Speaker, I want to recognize the selfless dedication Esperanza Worley has given to the people she has worked with and for in Dallas and beyond. For this she deserves our utmost respect, admiration, and praise—though her humility will likely not allow her to accept it. But more than anything, I want to show how much we like her, and wish her the best.

ANNE OTTERSON

HON. SUSAN A. DAVIS

OF CALIFORNIA

IN THE HOUSE OF REPRESENTATIVES

Tuesday, November 29, 2016

Mrs. DAVIS of California. Mr. Speaker, San Diego recently lost a giant presence in our community with the passing of Anne Otterson.

Anne was a beloved part of San Diego, and she concentrated so much of her life to giving back. Through her work as an activist and philanthropist with Project Concern International (PCI) and the University of California San Diego, she left behind an enormous impact on the community.

A former Fulbright scholar, she was very quick and intelligent, but in a way that was inclusive and encouraging of those around her.

Anne had an ability to bring people in. She was always listening and wanted to learn about other people's experiences.

She had a dedication to helping her community and used her resources and talents to do just that. Anne was a celebrated chef and teacher at the local culinary school Perfect Pan School of Cooking. She took that passion to the next level and used it for the good of others by establishing the annual Celebrity Chefs Cook Gala in 1981—this event has gone on for decades and has raised over $9 million for cancer research and care at UCSD's Moores Cancer Centers.

Anne had a wonderful sense of humor, she was engaging, and had a presence that made people feel good. People just liked being around her.

I was lucky enough to have spent time with Anne, and what always struck me about her was her strong sense of service. Her genuine interest was advancing PCI's mission: spreading women's empowerment, democracy and creating opportunity.

Of all her many accomplishments, Anne considered her children and grandchildren to be her greatest achievements. She leaves behind a proud legacy.

I also love what she described as her philosophy of life—I think it spells out the way she saw the world and how we can all learn from her. Anne said, "Laugh at yourself, be curious and care about others, and listen to the world about you—whether it is the babbling brook, the melodious sounds of a flute, or the plaintive cry of oppressed people."

These are the words that Anne Otterson lived by and they are an inspiration that lives on.

SENATE—*Wednesday, November 30, 2016*

The Senate met at 10 a.m. and was called to order by the Honorable TOM COTTON, a Senator from the State of Arkansas.

PRAYER

The Chaplain, Dr. Barry C. Black, offered the following prayer:

Let us pray.

O Lord our God, giver of everlasting life, nothing can separate us from Your limitless love.

Use our lawmakers today for Your glory, inspiring them to cultivate tough minds and tender hearts. Lord, help them to remember that nothing is impossible to those who place their trust in You. May the power of faith create in them both the desire and the ability to do Your will. As our Senators humble themselves in prayer, prepare their hearts and minds to serve Your purposes on Earth.

Lord, give Your consolation to those experiencing sorrow and Your love to us all.

We pray in Your merciful Name. Amen.

PLEDGE OF ALLEGIANCE

The Presiding Officer led the Pledge of Allegiance, as follows:

I pledge allegiance to the Flag of the United States of America, and to the Republic for which it stands, one nation under God, indivisible, with liberty and justice for all.

APPOINTMENT OF ACTING PRESIDENT PRO TEMPORE

The PRESIDING OFFICER. The clerk will please read a communication to the Senate from the President pro tempore (Mr. HATCH).

The senior assistant legislative clerk read the following letter:

U.S. SENATE,
PRESIDENT PRO TEMPORE,
Washington, DC, November 30, 2016.
To the Senate:
Under the provisions of rule I, paragraph 3, of the Standing Rules of the Senate, I hereby appoint the Honorable TOM COTTON, a Senator from the State of Arkansas, to perform the duties of the Chair.

ORRIN G. HATCH,
President pro tempore.

Mr. COTTON thereupon assumed the Chair as Acting President pro tempore.

RECOGNITION OF THE MAJORITY LEADER

The ACTING PRESIDENT pro tempore. The majority leader is recognized.

WORK BEFORE THE SENATE

Mr. McCONNELL. Mr. President, the Senate has a number of issues to wrap up, including the conference reports on the Water Resources Development Act, the Energy Policy Modernization Act, and, of course, the National Defense Authorization Act as well.

The action taken by the Senate yesterday will allow us to have a final vote on the critical Iran Sanctions Extension Act sometime this week. Later today, the House is set to vote on the 21st Century Cures bill, an important medical research and innovation bill which contains a number of bipartisan priorities.

Once their work is complete, the Senate will consider this measure and send it to the President's desk. Talks on the continuing resolution are ongoing. I will have more to say about that in the coming days.

RECOGNITION OF THE MINORITY LEADER

The ACTING PRESIDENT pro tempore. The Democratic leader is recognized.

TRIBUTE TO BARBARA BOXER

Mr. REID. Mr. President, I have served in Congress now for 34 years. Throughout that time, I have tried to be pleasant and helpful to my colleagues. I feel very fortunate to have become personally close and friends with Members of Congress from all over this great country. BARBARA BOXER and I were Members of the House class of 1982. Such fond memories do I have of that class—TOM CARPER, DICK DURBIN, and scores of others. We had a huge class.

At first glance, BARBARA BOXER and HARRY REID had very little in common. She was from California. It is a heavily populated and liberal State. I was from Nevada, a much smaller State in area and in population. I was the only Democrat in my State's Congressional delegation. But I was stunned when I was asked to join this huge California Congressional delegation. Being from Nevada and being part of the largest Congressional delegation in America was extremely helpful to me.

The Californians were good to me in so many different ways, just allowing me to be part of their meetings every Wednesday morning. I was flattered when I was asked to be secretary-treasurer of that large delegation. I have so many memories of the work we did together, California and Nevada.

Howard Berman, who was the leader of that freshman class from California, was the head of the steering committee. Don Edwards was the chairman of the delegation at those meetings we had every morning. The Burton brothers and just so many others went out of their way to help me.

I came to know quickly that BARBARA BOXER was no ordinary public servant. She was relentless—I mean relentless—and dedicated and very principled. She was raised by hard-working, first-generation immigrants in Brooklyn, NY. She attended Brooklyn College, graduated with a degree in economics. Over the decades, we have gotten to know each other's families very well. We talk about each other's children. We have exchanged family experiences many, many times.

My favorite story of BARBARA BOXER's family is the time when she was a girl coming home from elementary school, with her mom, from a window that was up high, yelling down to her little daughter coming home from school—excitedly yelling out the window of the upstairs apartment: Daddy passed the bar. Daddy passed the bar.

BARBARA knew that her dad did not go to bars. But she quickly learned from her excited mother that she was talking about her dad having passed the very, very difficult New York bar examination. I always remember that story.

In 1965, BARBARA moved to Northern California from faraway New York. But in California, they sat down their roots and raised their two children, Doug and Nicole. Stew became a very prominent lawyer and BARBARA, a stockbroker.

It was in California where BARBARA began to make her mark very quickly as a trailblazer. In 1976, after having been in California not very long, in that very big county, part of the metropolitan area of San Francisco, she became a member of the Marin County Board of Supervisors. She was elected to that post. She quickly became the board's first woman president.

Shortly thereafter in 1982, BARBARA ran successfully for Congress. Her campaign slogan tells us all you need to know about her because that year her slogan was: "BARBARA BOXER Gives a Damn." That was on all of her campaign literature, posters, everything. So I guess with a slogan like that, it should not be any surprise that she won handily.

In 1992, she was elected to the Senate. She stood no chance to win. Everybody told her that—all of the editorials, not only of the California papers but all over the country. BARBARA

● This "bullet" symbol identifies statements or insertions which are not spoken by a Member of the Senate on the floor.

BOXER was in with the big time, and things were going to change for this upstart Member of the House of Representatives. She had tried to move too quickly. She should have stayed in the House, but she won by a really nice margin. This surprised everybody except her.

In 1992, she was elected to the Senate—the year that was popularly referred to as the "Year of the Woman," and rightfully so. She was part of the memorable class that came here in 1982: DIANNE FEINSTEIN, PATTY MURRAY, Carol Moseley Braun, and, of course, the underdog, BARBARA BOXER.

In the Senate, BARBARA and I have worked together on matters of importance to Nevada, California, and our Nation. I have watched BARBARA BOXER lead on so many important issues. I am going to name only a handful of them. She worked to designate more than 1 million acres in California as a wilderness, keeping that land in a pristine condition for our children, our grandchildren, and generations to come. I say "our" because the wilderness in California or in Nevada does not belong to California or Nevada, it belongs to the people of this country. She fought for the Pinnacles National Monument to become America's 59th national park. It became such.

She helped lead the fight to stop drilling in the Arctic National Wildlife Refuge, and, of course, along the California shoreline. She has spoken about that so many times. It succeeded. We have had no oil spills on the coast of California because of a number of reasons, but there is no one more responsible for that nondegradation than BARBARA BOXER.

She advocated to eliminate government military waste as a Member of the House of Representatives and the Senate. It was her first breakthrough where she exposed the outrageous, exorbitant cost of purchases made by the military. She did that while she was in the House. Why was she taking on the establishment? Well, that is who she is; that is who she was.

She discovered that our military paid defense contractors unbelievable amounts of money: for a hammer—a claw hammer—$430; for a toilet seat, $640; for a coffee maker, $7,622. That is quite a coffee maker. For an aluminum ladder, which must have been one that would get you over the fence that Trump is going to build between Mexico and the United States, it cost $74,165.

It is legendary what she has done with the military. Ever since she did that, the military was no longer untouchable. BARBARA BOXER proved that. She put an end to all of the wasteful spending. Yes, she did—BARBARA BOXER—not all of it; some things slipped through the cracks, but she sure headed everyone in the right direction.

Maybe of lesser importance, but something we all watched very carefully in the House—it did not happen overnight, but she caused the all-male House gym to admit female Members of Congress. She went up against some big people to do that—the very well-known Dan Rostenkowski, the chairman of the Ways and Means Committee, and others—but she won.

BARBARA and I have worked together to protect Lake Tahoe. We share that. The States of California and Nevada share that alpine glacial lake. There is only one other lake like it in the world, and that is in Siberia, Lake Baikal. We feel good about what we have been able to do to promote the richness of this beautiful national treasure, Lake Tahoe.

She has also promoted clean energy. I can remember her going after a substance that was in gasoline to put in a car that ruined the environment. She came out strongly against that. Again, she prevailed. We no longer do that. She has also done a lot to protect our public lands.

I mentioned just a little bit of what she has done. I can say without any hesitation that BARBARA BOXER has been one of the best and most effective environmental leaders in the history of this country. That says a lot. She has made California and the entire country a cleaner, healthier, and a better place, especially as chair and ranking member of the Committee on Environment and Public Works. I loved that committee. It was a committee I was placed on when I first came to the Senate. I had the good fortune to be chairman of that committee twice.

She has done so much in her advocacy. For a lot of the things she was not able to declare a legislative victory, but she certainly declared a victory in the minds of the American people because she took on the big guys without any fear.

BARBARA is also a champion of women. She has been a groundbreaker on issues like sexual harassment and women's rights in the workplace, access to women's health, and clinic violence. She took that on. BARBARA BOXER has worked to protect women's access to health care and make sure that Planned Parenthood continues to help millions of women who depend on their services every year.

I lament the fact that BARBARA will not be here because, as you know, the new Republican majority has threatened to do away with Planned Parenthood. I don't know what they expect to do with the 2 million women who go there every year for help, but that is what they have said they are going to do.

I can remember, oh so clearly, because it was such a difficult time, working on the Affordable Care Act in my office just a short distance from here. BARBARA was there the better

part of 2 days. We were facing incredibly contentious issues regarding women's health, and this required close attention. But it worked out. We were able to accomplish this in spite of some people who said we couldn't do that.

BARBARA has always been ideological, pure but with a sound mix of pragmatism on ObamaCare and other issues relating to women. I told her personally—and I said it publicly, but I wish to say it again—that I have enjoyed working with her. She has helped and mentored me and led me to understand issues important to the women of America like no one else, and I appreciate it very much.

I can remember writing her a letter in my longhand, my cursive. In that letter I told her a number of things, but this is something I said—a direct quote:

BARBARA, I have three brothers. I've never had a sister. You are the sister I've never had.

That was what I said. To this day, we still refer to each other as brother and sister.

Stew and BARBARA are an exemplary team. They are partners in every sense of the word "partner." Landra and I have been guests in their Southern California home. We have been together many times in Nevada.

For decades, BARBARA and I have worked together politically, campaigning in different parts of the country, different parts of California, and different parts of Nevada. We have raised money together for the cause of Democrats. We have raised money for each other. It has always been a pleasure to work with her on this and other issues.

BARBARA and I came to Washington together in 1982, 34 years ago. BARBARA and I will be leaving Washington together after 34 memorable years together.

Senator BARBARA BOXER, congratulations on your historic career as a Senator for 40 million Californians and 300 million citizens of the United States.

BARBARA, remember, you are and always will be my sister.

Godspeed, BARBARA.

The ACTING PRESIDENT pro tempore. The Senator from California.

Mrs. BOXER. Senator REID, my leader, I can't tell you how humble I feel to hear you talk about my career and to put it, in many ways, in a historic place.

I am going to have a lot to say about your career, what you have meant to me. Today I won't get into it, but you are a man—you just don't throw words around. I know how humble you are because every time I try to praise you, even in a situation with just a few people around you, you look down like you are doing now. It makes you uncomfortable. I don't want to make you uncomfortable. So here is what I am going to say today. I am going to make you uncomfortable in the near future when I talk about your career and what it has meant to me. But today, hearing you talk about what you just said, weaving our friendship, our work together, and our family friendship has meant a lot to me.

Obviously, I am going to miss you, but I will say this. As we enter into uncharted territories in terms of politics, I know you and I are not going to lose our voices. We will have a platform. We are not leaving because we are tired of the fight. We are not leaving because we have nothing more to say, we are leaving because we think it is time for the next generation. I look forward to working with you in the future—and I mean that sincerely—just fighting for the things we care about, whether it is Lake Tahoe or whether it is clean air, whether it is fighting against the ravages of climate change, whether it is fighting for the right of the American people, from children to seniors, to have affordable health care. We are not going into the wilderness. That I was able to protect more than a million acres—I am so proud you mentioned that.

Today you have humbled me with your words. I will always be your sister. Thank you very much.

I yield the floor.

RESERVATION OF LEADER TIME

The ACTING PRESIDENT pro tempore. Under the previous order, the leadership time is reserved.

MORNING BUSINESS

The ACTING PRESIDENT pro tempore. Under the previous order, the Senate will be in a period of morning business, with Senators permitted to speak therein for up to 10 minutes each.

Mrs. BOXER. Mr. President, I suggest the absence of a quorum.

The ACTING PRESIDENT pro tempore. The clerk will call the roll.

The senior assistant legislative clerk proceeded to call the roll.

Mr. DURBIN. Mr. President, I ask unanimous consent that the order for the quorum call be rescinded.

The ACTING PRESIDENT pro tempore. Without objection, it is so ordered.

DACA

Mr. DURBIN. Mr. President, there are many disagreements in this Chamber and between the House and the Senate, but I think there is one thing we fundamentally agree on. Our system of immigration in this country is broken. There are many different ways to approach it in changing it, improving it, and fixing it, but most of us concede something is wrong. If we have 11 to 12 million people living in the United States who are not documented or not legal, by our definition—and that has been going on for years, sometimes decades—it raises a serious question about whether our immigration system works, whether it is responsive, and whether it serves the best interests of the United States.

Many of the people who are here once came to the United States on visitors' visas that they were supposed to ultimately see come to an end and leave, but they stayed. They got married. They had children in the United States who became citizens. Those who think that families represent the large share of undocumented people don't take a look at the families individually. They should. You may find in one household of a mother, father, and two or three children that only one person is undocumented, and it might be the mother.

The one thing we also came to discover was that there were many people here who were undocumented, technically illegal under our system, and they were in that condition through no fault of their own. Well, who could that be? Children—children who were brought here as toddlers, infants, small kids, and brought in with their families. They had no voice in the decision to come to America, but the family did, and they grew up here. Some of them came at a very early age. They didn't speak the language of their original country. They never visited that country.

From the start, they thought they were Americans. They went to school, went to class, put their hands over their hearts and pledged allegiance to the only flag they ever knew. They sang the only national anthem they really knew, and they believed they were Americans. At some point in their lives, maybe someone in the household said: Let me tell you a stark truth here: You are not legal by this Nation's standards.

It was because of that group that I introduced a bill 15 years ago called the DREAM Act. The DREAM Act really defined this category of people who are undocumented, were brought here as children, grew up in America, graduated from our schools, and didn't create any criminal record in their lifetime, and they were hoping and praying that they would get a chance to stay in a legal status as citizens. That is what the DREAM Act was all about. It is just for these—they have come to be known as DREAMers—who came here as children and infants, to be given that choice.

It was a few years ago that I wrote a letter to President Obama—signed by Senator Lugar of Indiana, a Republican, who shared my feelings—and asked the President if he could do something to protect these young people from being deported. We had a number of Senators join me in a subsequent letter, and the President acted, creating something called DACA, the Deferred Action for Childhood Arrivals Program.

What it boiled down to was that, if these undocumented young people who came here as young children would step forward, identify themselves to our government, pay about $500 in a filing fee, and go through a criminal background check, we would give them a 2-year temporary protection from being deported and give them a temporary right to work in this country.

The DACA Program turned out to be a big success as 740,000 young people were eligible, signed up, and were cleared to be approved for this DACA status.

Then came a change in administrations, which will happen in just a few weeks. Questions started being raised. What is going to happen to these young people—the ones who complied with the law as they were told it existed, who did a risky thing in identifying themselves to a government, paid their fee, went through the background check, and now are in the United States? I have met so many of them—thousands of them across this country, the DREAMers, those who are DACA eligible, those who are DACA approved. They are amazing stories.

At the Loyola University Stritch School of Medicine in Chicago, they decided to open a competition in their medical school to allow these DACA-eligibles to apply—not to give them a special number of billets or positions in the school but to say: You can apply with everyone else.

For many of these young people from across the United States who dreamed of being a doctor one day, this was the answer to a prayer, and they were ready for it. They competed and they won. I believe there are about 25, maybe more, who are currently medical students at Loyola in Chicago aspiring to be doctors. Now their life is complicated. They can't borrow money from the government to go to school. They are not eligible for any Federal assistance because they are technically undocumented.

So we created a program through our State where they would be able to borrow the money to go to school on one condition; for every year of schooling that is provided by these loans, they have to pledge 1 year as doctors to serve in underserved areas of our State, whether it is in the inner city or the rural areas.

So here are, at the moment, 25 aspiring DREAMers in the Loyola School of Medicine who will be giving us years of service in underserved communities in our State. Is that good for Illinois? Is it good for America? You bet it is. I am from downstate Illinois. There are many rural towns in our State that would beg for these doctors to come in so they can keep a local hospital open so they can have good medical talent when they need it.

These DREAMers, who are now protected DACA today, are questioning what their future will be with a new President. There were some powerful words spoken during the course of this campaign about immigration, but I am heartened by the fact that President-elect Trump, after the election, said he wanted to try to bind the wounds of this country. When asked specifically about immigrants, after some of the harsh things he said during the campaign, he said many of these immigrants are terrific people.

Well, let me say to the President-elect, if you are looking for terrific people when it comes to immigrants, take a look at these DACA young people, take a look at these DREAMers. They are amazing.

I believe I have come to the floor 100 times, maybe more, to tell these DREAMer stories because it is one thing, as I have just done, to describe them in general, but it is another thing to get to meet them. Some of these young people have had the courage to step up and say: You can tell my story. I will send you a photo.

The story of one today is of Valentina Garcia Gonzalez. Valentina was 6 years old when her family brought her to the United States from Uruguay in South America. She grew up in the suburbs of Atlanta, GA. A very bright child, she learned English quickly. She said:

After that, I became my parents' right hand. Everything and anything that involved speaking to the outside world meant I was in the front, translating and representing my parents. It was a lot of responsibility for a young undocumented kid.

In addition to this responsibility, Valentina turned out to be quite a good student. In middle school she received the President's Education Award not once but twice—once from President Bush and then again from President Obama.

In high school, Valentina was an honor graduate and an Advanced Placement Scholar. She was a leader in student government, a member of the Beta Club—a national academic honors program—and Peer Leaders, where she mentored younger students. She somehow also found time to be president of the school's environmental group and managed the varsity basketball team.

Valentina was quite a student, but Georgia State law bans undocumented students from attending that State's top public universities. As a result, she applied and was accepted to Dartmouth College, an Ivy League school in Hanover, NH. She is now a sophomore at Dartmouth, where she is a premed student majoring in neuroepidemiology. You see, Valentina's dream is to become a doctor, to help people, and to give back to her community.

To help pay for her few tuition, she works as a projectionist at a local theater. Keep in mind, as an undocumented student, she is ineligible for any Federal Government assistance. She still finds time to volunteer as a mentor for kids in the local community schools, and in a letter to me she said the following about DACA, President Obama's program:

I am beyond grateful because, by receiving DACA, the U.S. has given me an opportunity to give back to this country that has given me so much. This is my country. I have worked hard to prove myself worthy in the eyes of my American counterparts and knowing that I am in a weird limbo in regards to my legal status doesn't make me sleep any easier. My name is registered with the government, so I might be deported if they decide to end DACA.

Let me say clearly to Valentina and the other DREAMers like her. I am going to do everything in my power as a U.S. Senator to ensure that DACA continues and to protect them from deportation. Many came forward, against the best advice of their parents, who say: You are registering with a government that can deport you. But they had confidence that if they followed the law, as it was described to them, if they were open and honest, America would treat them fairly.

That is all I am asking. For the 740,000 currently protected by DACA, and for the others who are eligible for it, who will go through a background check and pay their fee, we are asking for fairness. These young people came here as kids. They had no voice in the decision to come to America. Now they want us to be their voice in terms of their future in America.

Would America be better if Valentina was deported back to Uruguay, a country where she hasn't lived since she was 6 years old? Will it be stronger if we lose Valentina as a doctor, serving a critical part of America? The answer is clear.

Now is the time for America, this Nation of immigrants, to come together and heal the wounds that divided us during the election. I hope President-elect Trump will understand and will continue the DACA Program that provides some fairness, some opportunity for these amazing young people.

Mr. President, I yield the floor.

The ACTING PRESIDENT pro tempore. The Senator from Wyoming.

THE BUDGET

Mr. ENZI. Mr. President, I want to start off by reminding everybody of an old but very short Hans Christian Andersen story about an emperor who was convinced by two very clever weavers that they could make clothes that would be invisible to anybody who was unfit for a position or stupid or incompetent. As a result, everybody thought they could see the clothes, until one little boy said: The emperor doesn't have any clothes. And then everybody gasped and realized that was the case.

Well, we have kind of been weaving a budget through the years that is kind of like the emperor's clothes. We want everybody to be able to see them and think we are fit and competent and not stupid, but as this year quickly draws to a close, we are once again approaching a Federal spending deadline that will likely be postponed with yet another temporary spending bill. In the last 40 years, Congress has enacted 175 of these continuing resolutions to avoid doing its job. This will be the 176th continuing resolution since the modern budget process was established.

The November election results show the American people are eager for change. With a new President taking the oath of office on January 20, Congress has an opportunity and a responsibility to get back to work. One of our top priorities must be fixing America's broken budget process to provide our Nation with a responsible fiscal blueprint and help guide our spending decisions now and into the future.

Let me tell you about America's coming fiscal crisis. America is on a course for a fiscal disaster. Sadly, that is not going to surprise many people. We all know the statistics: $20 trillion in debt, on track to grow to $29 trillion in 10 years, unchecked entitlement spending that assumes 70 percent of the budget, and the imminent return of trillion-dollar deficits.

Everyone knows we are in deep trouble, but what is surprising is that Congress is not considering ways to fix it. The country's finances are in a perilous position and the Federal Government has refused to act. We pretend to see the clothes.

That is because, when it comes to spending money, Congress is kind of like a binge eater. We don't want to start our diet until right after the next dessert, and we never seem to run out of ideas for new desserts. That attitude has led to a mammoth, oversized debt burden that will crush future generations' prosperity.

The first step to spending within our means is to establish healthy habits. We should stock the fridge with fruits and vegetables, not cake and cookies. Unfortunately, America's broken budget process does the opposite. It makes it easy for Congress to spend and spend without ever checking its fiscal waistline. Congress never has to consider the fiscally healthy options that would put our budget on a better path.

America's looming fiscal crisis actually has its roots in the way America's budget and spending process is laid out. This money funds activities that most people would associate with good government, such as national defense, education, and infrastructure spending. This is the portion of the budget that attracts the most congressional scrutiny. We have limits in place that make it difficult to spend more than what is allotted, and those limits are subject to fierce debate and negotiations every 2 years or so. We also must pass spending bills to fund these government activities every year, forcing a public debate about where taxpayers' dollars should be spent. This portion of the budget is not growing rapidly and is not the cause of our unsustainable fiscal course.

The real culprit is the other 70 percent of the Federal budget. This portion is spent automatically without regular congressional action or review. Let me say that again. The real culprit is the other 70 percent of the Federal budget. This portion is spent automatically without regular Congressional action or review. In just 15 years, it will consume all government revenues as debt, interest payments and entitlements continue to grow rapidly. There are no effective limits to the amount that can be spent on that side of the budget, at least until this spending drives America into bankruptcy.

This is how the budget process makes it easy to spend money. There is regular review and strict limits on the small and shrinking portion of the budget—the 30 percent—but the much larger automatic spending programs are not regularly reviewed and can grow almost without limit. Some automatic spending programs have a dedicated but insufficient source of revenue. For example, Social Security, Medicare, and unemployment benefits are funded in part—in part—by payroll taxes and insurance premiums.

This makes sense. If Congress is not going to regularly review a program, there should at least be a source of funding to ensure the program is sustainable. However, the automatic programs that receive dedicated revenues are grossly underfunded, and many others do not receive any dedicated revenues. That means our government is making promises to pay for these programs even though they do not have any idea where the money will come from.

Let me repeat that. The automatic programs that receive dedicated revenues are grossly underfunded, and many others don't even receive any dedicated revenues. That means our government is making promises to pay for these programs even though they do not have any idea where the money will come from.

This chart gives us a little bit of an idea. The chart shows the dedicated revenues for some of the largest automatic spending programs. For example, Social Security and Medicare are each funded in part with a dedicated payroll tax. However, payroll taxes are less than benefit payments. We can see the Social Security spending gap over the next 10 years is two and three-tenths trillion, or $2,321 billion. Medicare's receipts cover only 54 percent of spend-

ing, leaving a funding gap of four and four-tenths, or $4,365 billion.

These annual cashflow deficits grow worse every year of the budget window, and they will continue to deteriorate at a faster rate outside the budget window as millions of baby boomers continue to retire.

Now, I like to phrase this a little differently. On Social Security, the amount of spending versus the amount of revenue—$12,000 billion in spending but only $10,000 billion in revenue, which leaves a program deficit of $2,321 billion. It is not being funded by Social Security now. Instead of revenue as a percentage of spending, I like to say we overspend by 18 percent.

On Medicare, $9,590 billion—that is a lot of money—in spending, but the revenue is only $5,225 billion. That is a deficit of $4,365 billion. So revenue as a percentage of spending is 54 percent, but it is 46 percent overspent.

Some people will say we shouldn't worry about these programs because we collected money from previous generations that will cover the cost of these programs. They say we have "trust funds" to pay for these programs. But you can't trust these government trust funds. There is no way the Federal Government puts away cash to be used later; instead, they took these excesses as they came in, in past years, when we had fewer baby boomers, and that cash was spent in exchange for bonds being put in a drawer. The bonds are with the full faith and trust of the Federal Government, but that is not real money. In order to spend that, money has to be put in the drawer. Yes, there was a surplus in Social Security, but it was spent. Now we will continue to manufacture money to make those payments, but the government has no way to invest money.

As an accountant, I can tell you that the Federal budget operates on a cash basis, and previous Congresses spent that cash as soon as it came in—all the cash. There is no real money socked away to cover these costs. So when it comes time to pay for these programs, the only money the Treasury Department can rely on is these dedicated revenues. As the chart shows, they are not sufficient to cover spending, so the Treasury Department has to take extra money from taxpayers or borrow it in public debt markets.

Overall, the nonpartisan Congressional Budget Office estimates that the government will spend over $35 trillion on automatic spending programs over the next 10 years, but this chart shows these programs will only collect $15.5 trillion, or $15,538 billion—$15,538 billion but the spending will be $35,333 billion. As a percentage of spending, that is 44 percent. Actually, that is overspending of 56 percent. We aren't even taking in half of what we promised. So guess what happens next. The Treasury Department will ask taxpayers and

public debt markets for an additional $20 trillion to pay for these programs.

That is why America is facing trillion-dollar deficits—overspending. "Deficit" is another word for "overspending." It doesn't sound quite as bad as "overspending." But that is why we are facing trillion-dollar overspending amounts in each year. That is why America's debt is $20 trillion, on the way to $29 trillion; it is overspending.

Let me talk about rising interest rates. To make matters worse, the historically low interest rates America pays on its debts are poised to rise, according to the latest signals from the Federal Reserve. That is why we have to do something, and we have to do something now. The interest is a mandatory expense—there is no way to avoid it—and it doesn't have any source of revenue other than the general fund. Now, we pay almost 2 percent interest on our $14 trillion in publicly held debt—$14,000 billion and we pay 2 percent on it. That is roughly $220 billion a year, excluding the share paid to Federal revenues which goes back to the Federal budget. But a 2-percent interest rate is not the norm for our government. When interest rates rise, as they are expected to do in the next few years, the $220 billion could more than triple. That will be $700 billion, maybe $800 billion a year spent on only the interest on our Nation's debt. That is more than we spend on national defense. That interest is a mandatory expense with no source of revenue.

So what is the bad news and the good news? That is the bad news, but there is good news too. Both the House Budget Committee, under the leadership of Chairman Tom Price, and the Senate Budget Committee have been working on solutions that would improve the way Congress considers budget legislation. Over the last year, the Senate Budget Committee has held a series of public hearings with expert witnesses, consulted with budget practitioners from both sides of the aisle, and sought advice from former chairmen. Members considered all the ideas presented and even entertained proposals to abolish the Budget Committee if it could be replaced with a better government structure. This yearlong effort demonstrated what successful budget reform should look like. I intend to pursue these reforms at every opportunity and enact as many as possible in the coming months.

At a minimum, we need to fix budget procedures in the Senate so that the congressional budget is easier to pass and harder to ignore and easier to understand. The budget resolution is the only regular tool we have that forces Congress to examine all spending and revenues, including automatic spending, over a 10-year period. Unfortunately, the budget resolution has devolved into a purely political exercise, and that is often ignored. The last passed budget was good for about 3 months before waivers overrode the budget.

Congress cannot continue to lurch from crisis to crisis without meaningful, long-term budget plans. My reforms would fix congressional budgeting by reducing the political impediments to passing budget resolution. Budget proceedings would be more orderly and transparent, with less political "gotcha" amendments that define consideration of a budget resolution here in the Senate. My reforms would also make the budget meaningful by requiring a higher vote threshold for legislation that spends billions of taxpayer dollars without offsetting it—and offsetting it in a real way.

We also need to revise the concepts and rules that determine how we budget and estimate the cost of legislation. These outdated rules haven't been comprehensively reviewed and updated since 1967 and often lead to confusing or inaccurate estimates. A new commission of experts should update our Federal budget concepts for the 21st century.

We should also create new rules that encourage Congress to consider the annual appropriations measures on time under regular order. The current process has been completed on time only four times in the last 40 years. The last time was 1998, and that is when there was a lot of Social Security extra money spent. This is a disgrace. Congress should do its job on time and in an orderly fashion. It should not be negotiating a year's worth of spending in the weeks before the holidays like a college student cramming for midterms or maybe stuffing on spending like everybody is a budget Thanksgiving.

One of my proposals borrows an idea from the Wyoming State Legislature. They set aside a certain number of days every other year to consider only budget legislation. If a member wants to consider a nonbudget bill, which perhaps would be an emergency, they have to convince two-thirds of their colleagues to agree to take it up without any debate; otherwise, they stick to the spending.

I will also encourage enactment of Senator PORTMAN's bill to end government shutdowns and legislation to move the annual spending process to a biennial cycle so that it does not have to complete all 12 spending bills each year. Each agency would have 2 years of planning that they would be able to count on.

We need a fiscal course correction. Addressing America's long-term debt crisis is a daunting challenge that cannot be left to future generations as it has been in the past. But the annual budget process is not designed to force through the serious reforms needed to put America's budget back on a sus-

tainable trajectory, nor should an annual majority-driven process be empowered to do so. That is why former Senators Kent Conrad and Judd Gregg, the former Democratic and Republican Budget Committee chairs, have advocated for a bipartisan task force, operating outside the annual budget process, to solve the country's long-term fiscal crisis. A BRAC-style commission similar to what has been introduced by Senator COATS should be created to set a sustainable, long-term fiscal target and recommend policy options to achieve that target, and Congress must take up and consider those recommendations.

This institution cannot continue to willfully ignore these serious threats to our country's future prosperity. This is the major issue of our time, and substantive solutions should be considered on the floor of the House and Senate. I know it is fun to invent and spend on new programs, but Congress has to be the adult in the room. They have to recognize whether their emperor has clothes or not. They can't pretend to see.

These bipartisan reforms wouldn't solve all of our budget problems, but they are a promising first step toward unsticking the budget gridlock that has gripped Washington in recent years. More importantly, they would create healthy fiscal habits that would force Congress to recognize and be able to address the daunting fiscal challenges this country faces. This crisis isn't going to go away, and only Members of Congress can fix it. The American people have spoken, and we owe it to them to put this country on a better path. These reforms are a necessary first step, and Congress must enact them as soon as possible.

Mr. President, I yield the floor.

The ACTING PRESIDENT pro tempore. The majority whip.

Mr. CORNYN. Mr. President, while he is still in the Chamber, let me express my gratitude to the chairman of the Budget Committee, Senator ENZI, for his leadership on these very difficult but very important issues.

One of the things I am most concerned about is that there no longer seems to be bipartisan consensus toward how to deal with our spending problems. We look at annual budget deficits and we look at the increase in the debt, and we know we have no current means to pay that back. While the Federal Reserve has basically made money free—in other words, interest rates are so low now, we don't have to pay our debt holders as much money now as we will in the future—we all know this is a ticking time bomb, with only about 30 percent of our Federal spending being discretionary or appropriated funds and roughly 70 percent being on autopilot. As our interest rates go up more and more, that is going to crowd out more of that 30 per-

cent that we need to spend on our Nation's priorities, like national security.

This is a very serious issue, and I am grateful to the Senator from Wyoming, the chairman of the Budget Committee, for his leadership. I look forward to working with him as we work together to try to come up with meaningful solutions.

21ST CENTURY CURES BILL

Mr. CORNYN. Mr. President, we are winding down the final days of the 114th Congress, and some of the work we have been engaged in is coming to fruition.

I spoke to the chairman of the Environment and Public Works Committee, who told me he thought the WRDA bill—the water resources development bill—was coming together and would likely be voted on in the House tomorrow.

I believe that Senator MCCAIN and Chairman THORNBERRY in the House—the Armed Services Committee—have a national defense authorization bill that on Friday will be voted on in the House and then will be coming over here to the Senate.

We know that we have to, by the December 9 deadline, pass an appropriations bill that will keep the lights on for the Federal Government for an undetermined, at this point, period of time, probably sometime into next spring, when we will have a new President and a new administration.

This afternoon in the House, they are going to be voting on another important piece of legislation that I wanted to talk about briefly. It is called the 21st Century Cures Act. This has been a product of a lot of methodical and very deliberate hard work on both sides of the aisle in both Chambers, and it will make a big difference in the lives of Americans because it will help make our country healthier and stronger.

As its name suggests, it will help develop medical treatments and cures for some of the most tragic health problems facing families today. Recently, I was at the 75th anniversary celebration at the MD Anderson hospital in Houston, TX, and it is the premier cancer facility in the country. Some time ago, the hospital started their own MD Anderson Moon Shots Program and is doing all that it can do to study and research various forms of cancer with the goal to eliminate cancer as a public health threat. Of course, we know that Vice President BIDEN, who was part of that 75th anniversary celebration at MD Anderson in Houston, and this administration have their own Cancer Moonshot Program to help eliminate cancer, and that will also be part of this 21st Century Cures bill. The whole idea of the Moonshot, even to the current generation, reminds us that at one time we thought putting a man on the Moon was impossible, outside the realm of possibility, but because of a vision and because of a commitment and a desire to push the bounds of our capabilities, they persevered and we found a way. MD Anderson's Moon Shots Program serves as another example of American ingenuity, ambition, and dogged determination to make the lives of our families and the future generations better than our own.

Fortunately, as I said, this Cures bill the House will be voting on today, which we will vote on next week, will provide funding for cancer and Alzheimer's research, among other terrible diseases, so that the best medical community in the world can help make great strides in fighting them.

This legislation will also fund the battle against opioid abuse, prescription drug abuse—something we have discussed a lot here on the floor during the last year because of the devastation that it has brought about in many parts of the country. Of course, we know that when the opioids aren't available, cheap heroin imported into the United States from south of our border is part of that scourge as well.

Overdoses and the abuse of opioid drugs are tearing families apart. This bill will provide additional grant funding to States to combat it and to help people who are already in the grips of this terrible addiction to find a way to freedom.

I am particularly glad that this legislation includes bipartisan mental health reforms that I introduced in this Chamber last year, known as the Mental Health and Safe Communities Act. I want to express my gratitude to Senator ALEXANDER, Senator MURRAY, and others on a bipartisan basis and bicameral basis for working with us to make sure we include mental health reform as a component of the 21st Century Cures legislation.

We all know that mental health problems are something that American families have to deal with. I dare say there is probably not a family in America that doesn't have to deal with this in some way or another—either at work, with people you go to church with, or with people you live next door to. In some way or another, mental health problems are rampant.

A lot of that has to do with well-intended but unintended consequences of deinstitutionalization of our mentally ill back in the 1990s. The idea was that it was not appropriate to institutionalize people with mental illness, and so we ought to deinstitutionalize them. But we contemplated that there would be some sort of safety net after they went back to their communities where they could get treatment and where they would get the care they needed. Unfortunately, what has happened and what my legislation is designed to address is that our jails have become the de facto default mental health treatment facilities in this country.

I recently was at a meeting of a large county sheriffs association in Washington, DC, and a friend of mine, the current sheriff of Bexar County, TX, Sheriff Pamerleau, said: How would you like to meet the largest mental health provider in America? I said: Well, sure.

She walked across the floor and introduced me to the sheriff of Los Angeles County, who runs the Los Angeles County jails. You get my point. We are warehousing people in jails and other places and not giving them the treatment they need in order to get their basic underlying problem taken care of. Of course, people with untreated mental illness frequently engage in petty crimes—trespassing and other things—which end them up in jail. But if they don't get treated, they are going to stay in that turnstile and keep coming back.

We all know the problem of homelessness in our streets. You walk down the street in Washington, DC, or any city in the country—such as Austin, TX—and you see people who have obvious symptoms of mental illness who are not being treated. What this legislation does is to provide a pathway to treatment, primarily by using preexisting appropriations to make grants to our States and local communities so they can deal with these using the very best practices in the country. For example, the Federal Government already spends about $2 billion a year on grants to State and local law enforcement. Doesn't it make sense to prioritize dealing with these mental health problems and particularly with the best practices in places such as San Antonio, TX, where the mental health community and law enforcement and other leaders have come together to try to come up with a program to divert people with mental illness to treatment and to provide additional training to law enforcement, to deescalate some of the conflicts that occur—for example, when the police show up and confront somebody with obvious mental illness. If the police don't get the kind of training they need, then that could end up in a tragedy, either for the person being arrested or for the police officers.

It is really important that we deal with this in a sensible way, and this legislation helps to do that—again, using some of that $2 billion in grant funding we give to State and local law enforcement but prioritizing and authorizing some of the very best practices occurring in communities around the country so that more people can benefit from these programs.

This also provides families additional tools. For example, if you have a family member who is suffering from severe mental illness—let's say they are an adult—there is not a whole lot you can do about it if they refuse to seek treatment or comply with their doc-

tor's orders. There is a means—a very difficult means—for temporary institutionalization. For example, you have to get a doctor's order and then go to court and get somebody put in a State hospital or an institution, but they are not there forever. They may be there for 30 days or so, until their symptoms abate because they are complying with their doctor's orders and taking their medication.

The great news in mental health treatment is there are a lot of miraculous treatments, and if the person afflicted with mental illness will comply with their doctor's orders and take their medication, they can lead relatively normal and productive lives. But the great problem is that so often people refuse to take their medication. They start feeling better. They quit, and they become sicker and sicker, until they become a danger both to themselves and the community.

One of the things this legislation does is to provide an additional procedure, called assisted outpatient treatment, which gives local courts and civil courts the authority to consider a petition whereby a family member can come in and say: My son, my daughter, my husband, my relative is having serious problems with their mental illness and they are noncompliant with their treatments. Judge, will you please enter an order, which essentially is like probation, saying that periodically you have to come back and report to the court on your compliance with the order, but part of that is to follow your doctor's orders and to take your medication. I am not saying it is a panacea, but it provides family members another tool when their loved ones become mentally ill and when there are no good options for the family members to assure that they will get the treatment or remain compliant with their doctor's orders by taking their medication.

I applaud the House for taking up these critical reforms. I know Congressman TIM MURPHY has worked on this long and hard in the House. There are a lot of other people who have worked on this mental health reform. In this Chamber, Senator BILL CASSIDY has been a champion and CHRIS MURPHY, among others. Really, the persons who have gotten us this far—there are two of them—are Senator ALEXANDER and Senator MURRAY, the chairman and the ranking member of the HELP Committee. But it has taken a bipartisan, bicameral effort to try to get us to this point, and I am glad that we will be voting on this next week, after the House passes it today.

With that, I yield the floor.

The PRESIDING OFFICER (Mr. SULLIVAN). The Senator from Oregon.

UNANIMOUS CONSENT REQUEST—
S. 2952

Mr. WYDEN. Mr. President, absent Senate action, at midnight tonight, this Senate will make one of the biggest mistakes in surveillance policy in years and years. Without a single congressional hearing, without a shred of meaningful public input, without any opportunity for Senators to ask their questions in a public forum, one judge with one warrant would be able to authorize the hacking of thousands—possibly millions—of devices, cell phones, and tablets. This would come about through the adoption of an obscure rule of criminal procedure called rule 41. Rule 41 isn't something folks are talking about in coffee shops in Alaska, in Oregon, and in other parts of the country, but I am convinced Americans are sure going to come to Members of Congress if one of their hospitals—one of their crucial medical programs—is hacked by the government. It is a fact that one of the highest profile victims of cyber attacks are medical facilities, our hospitals.

The Justice Department has said this is no big deal. You basically ought to trust us. We are just going to take care of this. I will tell you, generally, changes to the Federal rules of procedure are designed for modest, almost housekeeping kinds of procedural changes, not major shifts in policies. When you are talking about these kinds of rules, they talk about who might receive a copy of a document in a bankruptcy proceeding. That is what the Rules Enabling Act was for. It wasn't for something that was sweeping, that was unprecedented, that could have calamitous ramifications for Americans the way government hacking would. As I have indicated, this would go forward without a chance for any Member of the Senate to formally weigh in.

The government says it can go forward with this rule 41 and conduct these massive hacks—large-scale hacks—without causing any collateral damage whatsoever and ensuring that Americans' rights are protected. Oddly enough—again, breaking with the way these matters are usually handled—the government will not tell the Congress or the American people how it would protect those rights or how it would prevent collateral damage or even how it would carry out these hacks. In effect, the policy is "trust us."

I think that right at the heart of our obligations is to do vigorous oversight. I always thought Ronald Reagan had a valid point when he said: You can trust but you ought to verify. That is especially important under this policy, where innocent Americans could be victimized twice—once by their hackers and a second time by their government.

We are going to have the opportunity to do something about it before this goes into effect in just over 12 hours. I want to emphasize that those of us who would like the chance for Members of Congress to weigh in and be heard—our concern has been bipartisan. Senator COONS. Senator DAINES. We have worked in a bipartisan fashion on this for months.

This morning we are going to offer three unanimous consent requests to block or delay this particular change in order to make sure our colleagues have an opportunity to do what I think is Senate 101: to have a hearing and have a review that is bipartisan, where Senators get to ask questions, to be able to get public input in a meaningful kind of fashion.

I urge every Senator to think, and think carefully, before they prevent this body from performing the vigorous oversight Americans demand of Congress. That is right at the heart of what Senator COONS, Senator DAINES, and I will be talking about. This rule change will give the government unprecedented authority to hack into Americans' personal phones, computers, and other devices. Frankly, I was concerned about this before the election, but we now know that the administration—it is a new administration—will be led by the individual who said he wanted the power to hack his political opponents the same way Russia does. These mass hacks could affect cell phones, desktop computers, traffic lights, not to mention a whole host of different areas. During these hacks and searches, there is a considerable chance that the hacked devices will be damaged or broken, and that would obviously be a significant matter. Don't take my word for it.

Mr. President, I ask unanimous consent to have an article that I wrote with renowned security experts Matt Blaze and Susan Landau printed in the RECORD.

There being no objection, the material was ordered to be printed in the RECORD, as follows:

[From Wired.com, Sept. 14, 2016]

THE FEDS WILL SOON BE ABLE TO LEGALLY HACK ALMOST ANYONE

(By Senator Ron Wyden, Matt Blaze and Susan Landau)

Digital devices and software programs are complicated. Behind the pointing and clicking on screen are thousands of processes and routines that make everything work. So when malicious software—malware—invades a system, even seemingly small changes to the system can have unpredictable impacts.

That's why it's so concerning that the Justice Department is planning a vast expansion of government hacking. Under a new set of rules, the FBI would have the authority to secretly use malware to hack into thousands or hundreds of thousands of computers that belong to innocent third parties and even crime victims. The unintended consequences could be staggering.

The new plan to drastically expand the government's hacking and surveillance authorities is known formally as amendments to Rule 41 of the Federal Rules of Criminal Procedure, and the proposal would allow the government to hack a million computers or more with a single warrant. If Congress doesn't pass legislation blocking this proposal, the new rules go into effect on December 1. With just six work weeks remaining on the Senate schedule and a long Congressional to-do list, time is running out.

The government says it needs this power to investigate a network of devices infected with malware and controlled by a criminal—what's known as a "botnet." But the Justice Department has given the public far too little information about its hacking tools and how it plans to use them. And the amendments to Rule 41 are woefully short on protections for the security of hospitals, lifesaving computer systems, or the phones and electronic devices of innocent Americans.

Without rigorous and periodic evaluation of hacking software by independent experts, it would be nothing short of reckless to allow this massive expansion of government hacking.

If malware crashes your personal computer or phone, it can mean a loss of photos, documents and records—a major inconvenience. But if a hospital's computer system or other critical infrastructure crashes, it puts lives at risk. Surgical directives are lost. Medical histories are inaccessible. Patients can wait hours for care. If critical information isn't available to doctors, people could die. Without new safeguards on the government's hacking authority, the FBI could very well be responsible for this kind of tragedy in the future.

No one believes the government is setting out to damage victims' computers. But history shows just how hard it is to get hacking tools right. Indeed, recent experience shows that tools developed by law enforcement have actually been co-opted and used by criminals and miscreants. For example, the FBI digital wiretapping tool Carnivore, later renamed DCS 3000, had weaknesses (which were eventually publicly identified) that made it vulnerable to spoofing by unauthorized parties, allowing criminals to hijack legitimate government searches. Cisco's Law Enforcement access standards, the guidelines for allowing government wiretaps through Cisco's routers, had similar weaknesses that security researchers discovered.

The government will likely argue that its tools for going after large botnets have yet to cause the kind of unintended damage we describe. But it is impossible to verify that claim without more transparency from the agencies about their operations. Even if the claim is true, today's botnets are simple, and their commands can easily be found online. So even if the FBI's investigative techniques are effective today, in the future that might not be the case. Damage to devices or files can happen when a software program searches and finds pieces of the botnet hidden on a victim's computer. Indeed, damage happens even when changes are straightforward: recently an anti-virus scan shut down a device in the middle of heart surgery.

Compounding the problem is that the FBI keeps its hacking techniques shrouded in secrecy. The FBI's statements to date do not inspire confidence that it will take the necessary precautions to test malware before deploying them in the field. One FBI special agent recently testified that a tool was safe because he tested it on his home computer, and it "did not make any changes to the security settings on my computer." This obviously falls far short of the testing needed to vet a complicated hacking tool that could be unleashed on millions of devices.

Why would Congress approve such a short-sighted proposal? It didn't. Congress had no role in writing or approving these changes, which were developed by the US court system through an obscure procedural process. This process was intended for updating minor procedural rules, not for making major policy decisions.

This kind of vast expansion of government mass hacking and surveillance is clearly a policy decision. This is a job for Congress, not a little-known court process.

If Congress had to pass a bill to enact these changes, it almost surely would not pass as written. The Justice Department may need new authorities to identify and search anonymous computers linked to digital crimes. But this package of changes is far too broad, with far too little oversight or protections against collateral damage.

Congress should block these rule changes from going into effect by passing the bipartisan, bicameral Stopping Mass Hacking Act. Americans deserve a real debate about the best way to update our laws to address online threats.

Mr. WYDEN. In the op-ed, we point out that legislators and the public know next to nothing about how the government conducts the searches and that the government itself is planning to use software that has not been properly vetted by outside security experts. A bungled government hack could damage systems at hospitals, the power grid, transportation, or other critical infrastructure, and Congress has not had a single hearing on this issue—not one.

In addition, the Rules Enabling Act gives Congress the opportunity to weigh in, which is exactly what my colleagues hope to be doing now on this important issue.

Because of these serious damages, I introduced a bill called the Stop Mass Hacking Act with a number of my colleagues, including Senators DAINES and PAUL. This bill would stop these changes from taking effect, and I am here this morning to ask unanimous consent that the bill be taken up and passed.

Mr. President, I ask unanimous consent that the Judiciary Committee be discharged from further consideration of S. 2952 and the Senate proceed to its immediate consideration, that the bill be read a third time and passed, and the motion to reconsider be considered made and laid upon the table with no intervening action or debate.

The PRESIDING OFFICER. Is there objection?

The majority whip.

Mr. CORNYN. Mr. President, reserving the right to object, I respect our colleague's right to come to the floor and ask unanimous consent. I understand that there are three unanimous consent requests, and I will be objecting to all three of them. I will reserve my statement as to why I am objecting after the third request.

At this point, I object to the unanimous consent request.

The PRESIDING OFFICER. Objection is heard.

Mr. WYDEN. Mr. President, I wish to recognize my colleague from Montana, and after my colleague from Montana speaks, my friend from Delaware will address the Senate.

The PRESIDING OFFICER. The Senator from Montana.

Mr. DAINES. Mr. President, I thank my colleague from Oregon, Senator WYDEN, for talking about this important issue on the floor today.

We shop online with our credit cards, order medicine with our electronic health care records, talk to friends, share personal information, Skype, post beliefs and photos on social media, or Snapchat fun moments, all the while believing everything is safe and secure. It is more important now than ever to ensure that the information we store on our devices is kept safe and that our right to privacy is protected, and that is what we are really talking about here today. How can we ensure that our information is both safe and secure from hacking and government surveillance?

Certainly technology has made our lives easier, but it has also made it easier for criminals to commit crimes and evade law enforcement. In short, our laws aren't keeping up with 21st-century technology advances. But the government's solution to this problem we are talking about today, the change to rule 41 of the Federal Rules of Criminal Procedure, represents a major policy shift in the way the government investigates cyber crime. This proposed solution essentially gives the government a blank check to infringe upon our civil liberties. The change greatly expands the hacking power of the Federal Government, allowing the search of potentially millions of Americans' devices with a single warrant. What this means is that the victims of hacks could be hacked again by their very own government.

You would think such a drastic policy change that directly impacts our Fourth Amendment right would need to come before Congress. It would need to have a hearing and be heard before the American people with full transparency. But, in fact, we have had no hearings. There has been no real debate on this issue.

My colleagues and I have introduced bipartisan, bicameral legislation to stop the rule change and ensure that the American people have a voice. The American people deserve transparency, and Congress needs time to review this policy to ensure that the privacy rights of Americans are protected.

The fact that the Department of Justice is insisting this rule change take effect on December 1—that is tonight at midnight—frankly, should send a shiver down the spines of all Americans.

My colleagues and I are here today to not only wake up Americans to this great expansion of powers by our government but also to urge our colleagues to join this bipartisan effort to stop rule 41 changes without duly considering the impact to our civil liberties. Our civil liberties and our Fourth Amendment can be chipped away little by little until we barely recognize them anymore. We simply can't give unlimited power for unlimited hacking which puts Americans' civil liberties at risk.

Again, I thank my colleagues from Delaware and Oregon for joining me here today, and I yield to my friend and colleague from Delaware, Senator COONS.

The PRESIDING OFFICER. The Senator from Delaware.

UNANIMOUS CONSENT REQUEST— S. 3475

Mr. COONS. Mr. President, I thank my colleagues, Senator WYDEN and Senator DAINES. They have worked tirelessly to address this pressing issue of the pending change to privacy protections contained in a proposed change to the Federal Rules of Criminal Procedure.

As you have heard, if Congress fails to act today and thoroughly consider and debate these rule changes, they will go into effect at midnight tonight. They will take effect tomorrow, December 1. I believe it is essential that these rules strike a careful balance, giving law enforcement the tools they need to investigate cyber attacks and cyber crimes to keep us safe while also protecting Americans' constitutional rights to freedom from unreasonable searchs, our right to privacy.

Neither the Senate nor House has held a single hearing or markup to evaluate these changes to the Federal Rules of Criminal Procedure. The body of government closest to the people has utterly failed to weigh in on an issue that can immediately and directly impact our constituents—our citizens. While the proposed changes are not necessarily bad or good, they are serious and present significant privacy concerns that warrant careful consideration and debate.

All Americans should want criminal investigations to proceed quickly and thoroughly, but, as I have said, I am concerned that these changes would remove important judicial safeguards by having one judge decide on a search that would give our government the ability to search and possibly alter thousands of computers owned by innocent and unknowing American citizens all over our country.

Members of Congress should have an opportunity to consider this information seriously. We should carefully evaluate the merits of these proposed changes and their ramifications. I think it is our duty to have a frank and open discussion so we can think about the unintended consequences and protect our constituents' rights. Two weeks ago, I introduced legislation that would give Congress the time to have that conversation. The Review the Rule Act, or S. 3475, would delay the changes to rule 41 until July 1, 2017. That bill is cosponsored by Senators WYDEN, LEAHY, BALDWIN, and FRANKEN, as well as Republican Senators DAINES, LEE, and PAUL. That list of Senators from every part of our ideological spectrum is just a reminder that this is not a partisan issue. This is a bipartisan group of Senators raising questions and challenges to a proposal by the Obama administration's Justice Department.

I think it is important to remind anyone watching or listening that we want to ensure that the American people are kept safe from hackers and online criminal activity. We want law enforcement to have the tools to investigate and address potential threats, but we shouldn't have to sacrifice our rights to privacy and protection from unreasonable searches and seizures just to achieve that protection.

I encourage my colleagues to join me in supporting this legislation and working together to evaluate these changes to the Federal Rules of Criminal Procedure.

Mr. President, I ask unanimous consent that the Judiciary Committee be discharged from further consideration of S. 3475 and that the Senate proceed to its immediate consideration. I further ask that the bill be read a third time and passed and the motion to reconsider be considered made and laid upon the table.

The PRESIDING OFFICER. Is there objection?

The majority whip.

Mr. CORNYN. Mr. President, I object.

The PRESIDING OFFICER. Objection is heard.

Mr. CORNYN. Mr. President, I understand that the Senator from Montana will not be offering a unanimous consent request, so if it is all right with my colleagues, I wish to explain why I have objected.

Excuse me. I will yield back to the Senator from Oregon.

The PRESIDING OFFICER. The Senator from Oregon.

Mr. WYDEN. Mr. President, I will still be offering a third proposal, so I ask my colleague if he wishes to speak now or after the third request.

Mr. CORNYN. Mr. President, I appreciate the courtesy of my friend and colleague from Washington—excuse me, Oregon, but I will reserve my remarks until after he makes the next UC request.

The PRESIDING OFFICER. The Senator from Oregon.

Mr. WYDEN. Mr. President, when the Oregon Ducks go to the NCAA title game in basketball, I will invite my friend to sit with me and he will see Oregon in action.

UNANIMOUS CONSENT REQUEST— S. 3485

Mr. WYDEN. Senator CORNYN has now objected to passage of the two bills relating to rule 41, and he is certainly within his right to do so. I wish to offer the theory—not exactly a radical one, in my view—that if we can't pass bills with respect to mass surveillance or have hearings, we at least ought to have a vote so that the American people can actually determine if their Senators support authorizing unprecedented, sweeping government hacking without a single hearing. There is a lot more debate in this body over the tax treatment of race horses than massive expansion of surveillance authority.

In a moment, I will ask unanimous consent that the body move to an immediate rollcall vote on the Stalling Mass Damaging Hacking Act which would delay rule 41 changes until March 31. I don't condone Congress kicking cans down the road. This is one example of where, with a short delay, it would be possible to have at least one hearing in both bodies so that Congress would have a chance to debate a very significant change in our hacking policy.

Congress has not weighed, considered, amended, or acted like anything resembling an elected legislature on this issue. There have been some who have looked into the issue, but—I call it Senate 101—we should at least have a hearing on a topic with enormous potential consequences for millions of Americans. That had not been done, despite a bipartisan bill being introduced in the House and the Senate, days after the changes were approved. Lawmakers and the public ought to know more about a novel, complicated, and controversial topic, and they would be in a position to have that information if there was a hearing and Members of both sides of the aisle could ask important questions.

Since the Senate has not had a hearing on this issue, lawmakers have still been trying to get answers to important questions. Twenty-three elected representatives from the House and Senate, Democrats and Republicans spanning the philosophical spectrum, have asked substantive questions that the Department of Justice has failed to answer, and they barely went through the motions. They spectacularly failed to respond to both concerns of Democrats and Republicans in both the Senate and in the House.

I ask unanimous consent that the letter that was sent to the DOJ, signed by myself and 22 bipartisan colleagues from the House and Senate, be printed in the RECORD.

There being no objection, the material was ordered to be printed in the RECORD, as follows:

CONGRESS OF THE UNITED STATES,
Washington, DC, October 27, 2016.
Hon. LORETTA LYNCH,
U.S. Attorney General,
Department of Justice, Washington, DC.

DEAR ATTORNEY GENERAL LYNCH: We write to request information regarding the Department of Justice's proposed amendments to Rule 41 of the Federal Rules of Criminal Procedure. These amendments were approved by the Supreme Court and transmitted to Congress pursuant to the Rules Enabling Act on April 30, 2016. Absent congressional action the amendments will take effect on December 1, 2016.

The proposed amendments to Rule 41 have the potential to significantly expand the Department's ability to obtain a warrant to engage in "remote access," or hacking of computers and other electronic devices. We are concerned about the full scope of the new authority that would be provided to the Department of Justice. We believe that Congress—and the American public—must better understand the Department's need for the proposed amendments, how the Department intends to use its proposed new powers, and the potential consequences to our digital security before these rules go into effect. In light of the limited time for congressional consideration of the proposed amendments, we request that you provide us with the following information two weeks after your receipt of this letter.

1. How would the government prevent "forum shopping" under the proposed amendments? The proposed amendments would allow prosecutors to seek a warrant in any district "where activities related to a crime may have occurred." Will the Department issue guidance to prosecutors on how this should be interpreted?

2. We are concerned that the deployment of software to search for and possibly disable a botnet may have unintended consequences on internet-connected devices, from smartphones to medical devices. Please describe the testing that is conducted on the viability of 'network investigative techniques' ("NITs") to safely search devices such as phones, tablets, hospital information systems, and internet-connected video monitoring systems.

3. Will law enforcement use authority under the proposed amendments to disable or otherwise render inoperable software that is damaging or has damaged a protected device? In other words, will network investigative techniques be used to "clean" infected devices, including devices that belong to innocent Americans? Has the Department ever attempted to "clean" infected computers in the past? If so, under what legal authority?

4. What methods will the Department use to notify users and owners of devices that have been searched, particularly in potential cases where tens of thousands of devices are searched?

5. How will the Department maintain proper chain of custody when analyzing or removing evidence from a suspect's device? Please describe how the Department intends to address technical issues such as fluctuations of internet speed and limitations on the ability to securely transfer data.

6. Please describe any differences in legal requirements between obtaining a warrant for a physical search versus obtaining a warrant for a remote electronic search. In particular, and if applicable, please describe how the principle of probable cause may be used to justify the remote search of tens of thousands of devices. Is it sufficient probable cause for a search that a device merely be "damaged" and connected to a crime?

7. If the Department were to search devices belonging to innocent Americans to combat a complicated computer crime, please describe what procedures the Department would use to protect the private information of victims and prevent further damage to accessed devices.

Sincerely,

Ron Wyden; Patrick Leahy; Tammy Baldwin; Christopher A. Coons; Ted Poe; John Conyers, Jr.; Justin Amash; Jason Chaffetz; Steve Daines; Al Franken; Mazie K. Hirono; Mike Lee; Jon Tester; Elizabeth Warren; Martin Heinrich; Judy Chu; Steve Cohen; Suzan DelBene; Louie Gohmert; Henry C. "Hank" Johnson; Ted W. Lieu; Zoe Lofgren; Jerrold Nadler.

Mr. WYDEN. I also ask unanimous consent that the response from the Department of Justice, which I have characterized as extraordinarily unresponsive to what legislators have said, be printed in the RECORD as well.

There being no objection, the material was ordered to be printed in the RECORD, as follows:

U.S. DEPARTMENT OF JUSTICE,
OFFICE OF LEGISLATIVE AFFAIRS,
Washington, DC, November 18, 2016.

Hon. RON WYDEN,
U.S. Senate,
Washington, DC.

DEAR SENATOR WYDEN: This responds to your letter to the Attorney General, dated October 27, 2016, regarding proposed amendments to Rule 41 of the Federal Rules of Criminal Procedure, recently approved by the Supreme Court. We are sending identical responses to the Senators and Members who joined in your letter.

The amendments to Rule 41, which are scheduled to take effect on December 1, 2016, mark the end of a three-year deliberation process, which included extensive written comments and public testimony. After hearing the public's views, the federal judiciary's Advisory Committee on the Federal Rules of Criminal Procedure, which includes federal and state judges, law professors, attorneys in private practice, and others in the legal community, approved the amendments and rejected criticisms of the proposal. The amendments were then considered and unanimously approved by the Standing Committee on Rules and the Judicial Conference, and adopted by the United States Supreme Court.

It is important to note that the amendments do not change any of the traditional protections and procedures under the Fourth Amendment, such as the requirement that the government establish probable cause. Rather, the amendments would merely ensure that venue exists so that at least one court is available to consider whether a particular warrant application comports with the Fourth Amendment.

Further, the amendments would not authorize the government to undertake any search or seizure or use any remote search technique, whether inside or outside the United States, that is not already permitted under current law. The use of remote searches is not new, and warrants for remote searches are currently issued under Rule 41. In addition, courts already permit the search of multiple computers pursuant to a single warrant, so long as the necessary legal requirements are met with respect to each computer. Nothing in the amendments changes the existing legal requirements.

The amendments apply in two narrow circumstances. First, where a criminal suspect has hidden the location of his computer using technological means, the changes to Rule 41 would ensure that federal agents know which magistrate judge to go to in order to apply for a warrant. For example, if agents are investigating criminals who are sexually exploiting children and uploading videos of that exploitation for others to see—but concealing their locations through anonymizing technology—agents will be able to apply for a search warrant to discover where they are located.

An investigation of the Playpen website—a Tor site used by more than 100,000 pedophiles to encourage sexual abuse and exploitation of children and to trade sexually explicit images of the abuse—illustrates the importance of this change. During the investigation, authorities were able to wrest control of the site from its administrators, and then obtained approval from a federal court to use a remote search tool to undo the anonymity promised by Tor. The search would occur only if a Playpen user accessed child pornography on the site (a federal crime), in which case the tool would cause the user's computer to transmit to investigators a limited amount of information, including the user's true IP address, to help locate and identify the user and his computer. Based on that information, investigators could then conduct a traditional, real-world investigation, such as by running a criminal records check, interviewing neighbors, or applying for an additional warrant to search a suspect's house for incriminating evidence. Those court-authorized remote searches in the Playpen case have led to more than 200 active prosecutions—including the prosecution of at least 48 alleged abusers—and the identification or rescue of at least 49 American children who were subject to sexual abuse. Nonetheless, despite the success of the Playpen investigation, Federal courts have ordered the suppression of evidence in some of the resulting prosecutions because of the lack of clear venue in the current version of Rule 41. In other cases, courts have declined to suppress evidence because the law was not clear, but have suggested that they would do so in future cases.

Second, where the crime involves criminals hacking computers located in five or more different judicial districts, the changes to Rule 41 would ensure that federal agents may identify one judge to review an application for a search warrant rather than be required to submit separate warrant applications in each district—up to 94—where a computer is affected. For example, agents may seek a search warrant to assist in the investigation of a ransomware scheme facilitated by a botnet that enables criminals abroad to extort thousands of Americans. Such botnets, which range in size from hundreds to millions of infected computers and may be used for a variety of criminal purposes, represent one of the fastest-growing species of computer crime and are among the key cybersecurity threats facing American citizens and businesses. Absent the amendments to Rule 41, however, the requirement to obtain up to 94 simultaneous search warrants may prevent cyber investigators from taking needed action to liberate computers infected with such malware. This change would not permit indiscriminate surveillance of thousands of victim computers—that is not permissible now and will continue to be prohibited when the amendment goes into effect. This is because other than identifying a court to consider the warrant application, the amendment makes no change to the substantive law governing when a warrant application should be granted or denied.

The amended rule limits forum shopping by restricting the venue in which a magistrate judge may issue a warrant for a remote search to "any district where activities related to a crime may have occurred." Often, this language will leave only a single district in which investigators can seek a warrant. For example, where a victim has received death threats, extortion demands, or ransomware demands from a criminal hiding behind Internet anonymizing technologies, the victim's district would likely be the only district in which a warrant could be issued for a remote search to identify the perpetrator.

In cases involving widespread criminal conduct, activities related to the crime may have occurred in multiple districts, and thus there may be multiple districts in which investigators may seek a warrant under the new amendment. For many years, however, existing laws have recognized the need for warrants to be issued in a district connected to criminal activity even when the information sought may not be present in the district. The language of the new Rule 41(6)(6) amendment limiting warrant venue to "any district where activities related to a crime may have occurred" was copied verbatim from the existing warrant venue provisions in Rule 41(6)(3) and (b)(5), which authorize judges to issue out-of-district warrants in cases involving terrorism and searches of U.S. territories and overseas diplomatic premises. Thus, the new venue provision of Rule 41(b)(6) for remote searches is consistent with existing practices in these other contexts. Similarly, warrants for email and other stored electronic communications are sought tens of thousands of times a year in a wide range of investigations. Such warrants may be issued in any district by a court that "has jurisdiction over the offense being investigated." 18 U.S.C. §§ 2703 & 2711(3).

As with law enforcement activities in the physical world, law enforcement actions to prevent or redress online crime can never be completely free of risk. Before we conduct online investigations, the Department of Justice (the Department) carefully considers both the need to prevent harm to the public caused by criminals and the potential risks of taking action. In particular, when conducting complex online operations, we typically work closely with sophisticated computer security researchers both inside and outside the government. As part of operational planning, investigators conduct pre-deployment verification and validation of computer tools. Such testing is designed to ensure that tools work as intended and do not create unintended consequences. That kind of careful consideration of any future technical measures will continue, and we welcome continued collaboration with the private sector and cybersecurity experts in the development and use of botnet mitigation techniques. The Department's anti-botnet successes have demonstrated that the Department can disrupt and dismantle botnets while avoiding collateral damage to victims. And of course, choosing to do nothing has its own cost: leaving victims' computers under the control of criminals who will continue to invade their privacy, extort money from them through ransomware, or steal their financial information.

Law enforcement could obtain identifying information (such as an IP address) from infected computers comprising a botnet in order to make sure owners are warned of the infection (typically, by their Internet service provider). Or law enforcement might engage in an online operation that is designed to disrupt the botnet and restore full control over computers to their legal owners. Both of these techniques, however, could involve conduct that some courts might hold constitutes a search or seizure under the Fourth Amendment. In general, we anticipate that the items to be searched or seized from victim computers pursuant to a botnet warrant will be quite limited. For example, we believe that it may be reasonable in a botnet investigation to take steps to measure the size of the botnet by having each victim computer report a unique identifier; but it would not be lawful in such circumstances to search the victims' unrelated private files. Whether or not a warrant authorizing a remote search is proper is a question of Fourth Amendment law, which is not changed by the amendments to Rule 41. Simply put, the amendments do not authorize the government to undertake any search or seizure or use any remote search technique that is not already permitted under the Fourth Amendment. They merely ensure that searches that are appropriate under the Fourth Amendment and necessary to help free victim computers from criminal control are not, as a practical matter, blocked by outmoded venue rules.

The amendment's notice requirement mandates that when executing a warrant for a remote search, "the officer must make reasonable efforts to serve a copy of the warrant on the person whose property was searched or whose information was seized or copied," and that "[s]ervice may be accomplished by any means, including electronic means, reasonably calculated to reach that person." What means are reasonably available to notify an individual who has concealed his location and identity will of course vary from case to case. If the remote search is successful in identifying the suspect, then notice can be provided in the traditional manner (following existing rules for delaying notice where appropriate in ongoing investigations). If the search is unsuccessful, then investigators would have to consider other means that may be available, for example through a known email address. In an investigation involving botnet victims, the Department would make reasonable efforts to notify victims of any search conducted pursuant to warrant. For example, if investigators obtained victims' IP addresses at a particular date and time in order to measure the size of the botnet, investigators could ask the victims' Internet service providers to notify the individuals whose computers were identified as being under the control of criminal bot herders. Under such an approach, it would not even be necessary for investigators to learn the identities of specific victims. The Department will, of course, also consider other appropriate mechanisms to provide notice consistent with the amended Rule 41.

Under the Federal Rules of Evidence, the government must establish the authenticity of any item of electronic evidence it moves to admit in evidence. To do so, it must offer evidence "sufficient to support a finding that the item is" what the government claims it to be, and a criminal defendant may object to the admission of evidence on the basis that the government has not established its authenticity. The amendments to Rule 41 do not make any change to the law governing the admissibility of lawfully obtained evidence at trial, whether on the basis of authenticity or any other basis, and to our knowledge authenticity objections have not played a substantial role in prior federal criminal trials at which evidence obtained as a result of remote searches was introduced.

Protecting victims' privacy is one of the Department's top priorities. To the extent that investigators collect any information concerning botnet victims, the Department will take all appropriate steps to safeguard any such information from improper use or disclosure. The Department presently and vigorously protects the private information collected pursuant to search warrants for computers and documents seized from a home or business and the Department will follow the same exacting standards for any warrant executed under the amendments to Rule 41.

We hope that this information is helpful. Please do not hesitate to contact this office if we may provide additional assistance regarding this or any other matter.

Sincerely,

PETER J. KADZIK,
Assistant Attorney General.

Mr. WYDEN. Colleagues are going to see that substantive, clear questions, posed by Democrats and Republicans in writing, were not responded to.

Because of the lack of genuine answers from the Justice Department to this letter, signed by 23 Members of Congress, and the substantial nature of these unprecedented changes in surveillance policy, I ask now for unanimous consent for a vote on the SMDH Act to give Congress time to debate these sweeping changes to government's hacking authority.

I ask unanimous consent that the Senate proceed to the immediate consideration of S. 3485, introduced earlier today; that at a time to be determined by the majority leader, in consultation with the Democratic leader, but no later than 4 p.m. today, the Senate proceed to vote in relation to this bill.

The PRESIDING OFFICER. Is there objection?

The majority whip.

Mr. CORNYN. Mr. President, I object.

The PRESIDING OFFICER. Objection is heard.

Mr. CORNYN. Mr. President, I know sometimes that when people hear us engage in these debates, they think we don't like each other and we can't work together; that we are so polarized, we are dysfunctional. Actually, these Senators are my friends in addition to being colleagues. Let me just explain how I think their concerns are misplaced.

First of all, we all care about, on the spectrum of privacy to security, how that is dialed in. As the Presiding Officer knows, as the former attorney general of Alaska, we always try to strike the right balance between individual privacy and safety and security and law enforcement, and sometimes we have differences of opinion as to where exactly on that spectrum that ought to be struck, but the fundamental problem with the requests that have been made today is, Federal Rule Of Criminal Procedure 41 has already been the subject of a lengthy 3-year process with a lot of thoughtful input, public hearings, and deliberation.

As the Presiding Officer knows, the courts have the inherent power to write their own rules of procedure, and that is what this is, part of the Federal Rules of Criminal Procedure. What happens is a pretty challenging process when we want to change a Federal rule of criminal procedure. We have to get it approved by the Rules Advisory Committee. It is made up of judges, law professors, and practicing lawyers. Then it has to be approved by the Judicial Conference. Then, as in this case, they have to be endorsed by the U.S. Supreme Court, which is Federal Rule of Criminal Procedure 41, which happened on May 1, 2016.

If there was any basis for the claim that this is somehow a hacking of personal information without due process of law or without adequate consideration, I just—I think the process by which the Supreme Court has set up, through the Rules Advisory Committee and through the Judicial Conference, dispels any concerns that the objections that were raised were not adequately considered.

I am also told, Senator GRAHAM from South Carolina chaired a subcommittee hearing of the Senate Judiciary Committee—I believe it was last spring—on this very issue. So there has been some effort in the Congress to do oversight and to look into this, although perhaps it didn't get the sort of attention that it has gotten now.

The biggest, most important point to me is that for everybody who cares about civil liberties and for everybody who cares about the personal right of privacy we all have in our homes and the expectation of privacy we have against intrusion by the government without due process, this still requires the government to come forward and do what it always has to do when it seeks a search warrant under the Fourth Amendment. You still have to go before a judge—an impartial magistrate—you still have to show probable cause that a crime has been committed, and the defendant can still challenge the lawfulness of the search. The defendant always reserves that right to challenge the lawfulness of the search. I believe all of these constitutional protections, all of these procedural protections, all the concerns about lack of adequate deliberation can be dispelled by the simple facts.

There is a challenge when cyber criminals use the Internet and social media to prey on innocent children, to traffic in human beings, to buy and sell drugs, and there has to be a way for law enforcement—for the Federal Government—to get a search warrant approved by a judge based on the showing of probable cause to be able to get that evidence so the law can be enforced and these cyber criminals can be prosecuted. That is what we are talking about. All this rule 41 does is creates a circumstance where if the criminal is using an anonymizer, or some way to scramble the IP address—the Internet Protocol address of the computer they are operating from—then this rule of procedure allows the U.S. attorney, the Justice Department, to go to any court that will then require probable cause, that will then allow the defendant to challenge that search warrant—but to provide a means by which you can go to court and get a search warrant and investigate the facts and, if a crime has been committed, to make sure that person is prosecuted under the letter of the law.

I appreciate the concerns my colleagues have expressed, that somehow we have gotten the balance between security and privacy wrong, but I believe that as a result of the process by which the Rules Advisory Committee, the Judicial Conference, and the Supreme Court have approved this rule after 3 years of deliberation, including public hearings, scholarly input by academicians, practicing lawyers, law professors and the like, I think that ought to allay their concerns that somehow this is an unthought-through or hasty rule that is going to have unintended consequences. I think the fundamental protection we all have under the Fourth Amendment of the Constitution against unreasonable searches and seizures and the requirement that the government come to court in front of a judge and show probable cause that a crime has been committed, and that even once the search warrant is issued, that the defendant can challenge the lawfulness of the search—all of that ought to allay the concerns of my colleagues that somehow we have gotten that balance between privacy and security right because I think this does strike an appropriate balance.

Those are the reasons I felt compelled to object to the unanimous consent requests, and I appreciate the courtesy of each of my colleagues.

The PRESIDING OFFICER. The Senator from Oregon.

Mr. WYDEN. Mr. President, before he leaves the floor, I wish to engage my friend for a moment with respect to his remarks. He is absolutely right that we have been friends since we arrived here, and we are working together on a whole host of projects right now. So this is debate about differences of opinion with respect to some of the key issues. I wish to make a couple of quick points in response to my colleague.

My colleague said there had been an inclusive process for discussing this. As far as I can tell, the vast amount of discussion basically took place between the judges and the government. My guess is, if you and I walked into a coffee shop in Houston or Dallas, or in my home State, in Coos Bay or Eugene, people wouldn't have any idea what was going to happen tonight at midnight. Tonight at midnight is going to be a significant moment in this discussion.

My colleague made the point with respect to security and privacy. I definitely feel those two are not mutually exclusive; we can have both, but it is going to take smart policies. My colleague has done a lot of important work on the Freedom of Information Act issues. These are complicated, important issues, and nobody up here has had a chance to weigh in. There has been a process with some judges, and I guess some folks got a chance to submit a brief. Maybe there was a notice in the Federal Register; that is the way it usually works, but nobody at home knows anything about that. My guess is, none of our hospitals know anything about something like this, and it has real implications for them because our medical facilities—something we all agree on that have been major sources of cyber hackings—they have been major kinds of targets.

Again, this is not the kind of thing where somebody is saying something derogatory about somebody personally; we just have a difference of opinion with respect to the process. To me, at home, when people hear about a government process, they say: Hey, I guess that means I get a chance to weigh in. That is why I have townhall meetings in every county every year because that is what the people think the process is, not judges talking among themselves.

The second point my friend touched on was essentially the warrant policies and that he supports the Fourth Amendment and this is about the Fourth Amendment. I think that is worth debating. To me, at a minimum, this is an awful novel approach to the Fourth Amendment. One judge, one warrant for thousands and potentially millions of computers which could result in more damage to the citizen after the citizen has already been hit once with the hack. So my colleague said this is what the fourth Amendment is about. I think that is a fair point for debate. I would argue this is an awful novel approach to the Fourth Amendment. This is not what I think most people think the Fourth Amendment is. Hey, this is about me and somebody is going to have to get a warrant about me. It is about individuals. To me, the Senate has now—and we still have officially 12 hours to do something about it—but as of now, the Senate has given consent to an expansion of government hacking and surveillance. In effect, the Senate, by not acting, has put a stamp of approval on a major policy change that has not had a single hearing, no oversight, no discussion. In effect, the Senate—this is not even Senate 101. That is what everybody thinks Senators are supposed to be about. When we are talking about search and seizure, that is an issue for Congress to debate, and the Justice Department shouldn't have the ability to, at a minimum, as I indicated in my

conversation with my colleague from Texas, come up with a very novel approach to the Fourth Amendment without elected officials being able to weigh in.

Now I will close by way of saying that when Americans find out that the Congress is allowing the Justice Department to just wave its arms in the air and grant itself new powers under the Fourth Amendment without the Senate even being a part of a single hearing, I think law abiding Americans are going to ask: So what were you people in the Senate thinking about? What are you thinking about when the FBI starts hacking the victims of a botnet attack or when a mass attack breaks their device or an entire hospital system, in effect, has great damage done, faces great damage, and possibly puts lives at risk?

My hope is that Congress would add protections for Americans surrounding the whole issue of government hacking. I have said again and again and again that the smart technology policy, the smart surveillance policy from the get-go is built around the idea that security and liberty are not mutually exclusive, that a smart policy will do both, but increasingly, policies coming out of here aren't doing a whole lot of either. In this case, I think the Senate is abdicating its obligations. Certainly, in the digital era, Americans do not throw their Fourth Amendment rights out the window because they use a device that connects to the Internet.

So I am going to close by way of saying that I think this debate about government hacking is far from over. My guess is that Senators are going to hear from their constituents about this policy sooner rather than later, and we will be back on the floor then, looking to do what should have been done prior to midnight tonight, which is to have hearings, to involve the public—not just Justices and maybe a few people who can figure out how to find that section of the Federal Register so they can weigh in.

Americans are going to continue to demand from all of us in the Senate policies that protect their security and their liberty. They are right to do so. That cause will be harmed if the Senate doesn't take steps between now and midnight.

With that, Mr. President, I yield the floor.

I suggest the absence of a quorum.

The PRESIDING OFFICER. The clerk will call the roll.

The legislative clerk proceeded to call the roll.

Ms. WARREN. Mr. President, I ask unanimous consent that the order for the quorum call be rescinded.

The PRESIDING OFFICER. Without objection, it is so ordered.

21ST CENTURY CURES BILL

Ms. WARREN. Mr. President, I am glad to be here with my colleagues today to have a chance to talk about the 21st Century Cures bill. On Monday I came to the Senate floor to speak against a deal that was emerging in the House of Representatives around this bill.

When Congress first started working on this proposal 2 years ago, the idea was for Democrats and Republicans to work together to improve medical innovation and access to lifesaving cures. For over 2 years a lot of people worked really hard on that effort. We had a chance to bring down the cost of skyrocketing drugs. We had a chance to support medical research so we could start to cure diseases such as Alzheimer's and diabetes. We had a chance to help coal miners whose health care is on the ropes and who are running out of time. Unfortunately, the Cures bill introduced in the House last week didn't do any of those things. Instead, it was a typical Washington deal—a deal that ignored what voters want, and held a bunch of commonsense, bipartisan health proposals hostage unless Congress also agreed to pass a giant giveaway to drug companies.

So how did this happen? Lobbyists. Kaiser Health News estimated that the new Cures bill has generated more lobbying than almost all of the 11,000 bills that have been proposed during this Congress. At one point, there were about three lobbyists for every single Member of Congress. Every one of those lobbyists wanted favors. Wow. Did they get some doozies here: a provision to make it easier for drug companies to commit off-label marketing fraud—taking pills that are approved for one use and using them for a whole lot of other purposes—without any evidence that it is either safe or effective, a provision making it easier for drug companies to hide gifts they give to doctors who prescribe certain drugs, a giveaway to a major super PAC donor who stands to benefit financially through pushing regenerative therapies through FDA, even if they don't meet the FDA's gold standard for safety and effectiveness.

This bill is not about doing what the American people want. This bill is about doing what drug companies and donors want. On Monday, I made it clear that I oppose this. Since then, two things have happened. First, since Monday, the public has gotten wind of this deal and they don't like it. In the last 24 hours, more than 100,000 people have signed petitions calling on Congress to just reject the deal. Second, since Monday, we have seen the bill changed a little.

Last night, after they got some heat, the House took out the provision letting drug companies hide kickbacks to donors. Good. I guess they were having a hard time explaining to anybody why it made any sense to help drug companies cover up bribery. The lobbyists are disappointed about that, but they are still pushing for the bill because even though the kickbacks are out, letting drug companies get away with fraud is still in.

Giveaways are bad in this bill, but that is not the only thing that is a problem with this bill. What is not in the bill also hurts. Seventy years ago, Congress promised to provide for the health and welfare of American coal miners and their families. Now 120,000 coal miners, their widows, and their families will see massive cuts to their health benefits and retirement pensions. Why? Because the bipartisan mine workers protection act was left out of this bill. Without it, 12,500 coal miners will lose their health insurance on December 31 of this year. Another 10,000 will lose their coverage next year and on and on into the future.

According to exit polls, 70 percent of voters say they think the American economy and the lawmakers who oversee it are owned—owned by big companies and special interests. Bills like the 21st Century Cures Act are the reason why. There is so much we could do with this bill.

This Congress could step up for thousands of American coal miners. For their entire lives, these coal miners have sacrificed everything for their families, for their communities, and for this country. They have literally sacrificed their health. They are running out of time. We could help.

This Congress could step up to help millions of people who are struggling with exploding drug prices. We could help bring down the cost of drugs. This Congress could step up to help the millions of families who have been touched by Alzheimer's, diabetes, cancer, and other deadly disease.

We could help by providing more funding for the research that would generate real cures. This Congress could step up to deal with drug companies that think they are above the law, giant corporations that think they can break the rules and then get Congress to do special favors for them. We can just say: No, that is not what we are in business to do. The American people are not clamoring for the Cures bill, at least not this version.

Tens of thousands of people have asked us not to pass it. Even the conservative group Heritage Action for America has come out strongly against this deal. I don't agree with all of their objections, but they explain, "In Washington terms, backroom negotiators have turned the Cures bill into a Christmas tree loaded with handouts for special interests, all at the expense of the taxpayer."

Boy, got that one right. This kind of backroom dealing that helps those with money and connections and leaves scraps for everyone else is why people hate Washington. It is the reason I will oppose this bill.

The PRESIDING OFFICER (Mr. SASSE). The Senator from Illinois.

Mr. DURBIN. Mr. President, I thank the Senator from Massachusetts for calling us together on the floor to discuss this important bill, the 21st Century Cures Act. It is a bill I followed closely because I started off introducing the American Cures Act.

My goal in medical research was inspired by Dr. Francis Collins at the NIH. He just told me point blank: If you want to increase the output of medical research, find cures for diseases and help innocent people, increase the spending at the NIH by 5 percent real growth a year for 10 years, and I will light up the scoreboard.

That is what I set out to do. That is what the American Cures Act set out to do, including the Centers for Disease Control and the Department of Defense medical research. As is usually the case in Congress, it is no surprise when someone sees an idea and thinks they can do it a little differently and a little better so, in the House of Representatives, Congressman FRED UPTON and Congresswoman DIANA DEGETTE introduced the 21st Century Cures Act.

Theirs was a different approach. I guess it reflected a difference in philosophy. What we see today is what has happened to an originally good idea as it worked its way through the House of Representatives over a long period of time. The simple concept of increasing medical research spending at NIH by 5 percent a year has now become a very complicated formula.

Frankly, it is one I have very mixed feelings over. I look at it and think: It would have been so simple for us to make a national commitment on a bipartisan basis to increase NIH funding by 5 percent a year and to do it over 10 years. I know we would see the difference.

Just to put things in perspective so we understand them, there are certain diseases now which are costing us dearly: Alzheimer's. We know about that, don't we. There is hardly a family in America who does not have someone in their family or a friend who has been stricken by Alzheimer's. Think of this for a moment. An American is diagnosed with the Alzheimer's disease once every 67 seconds—once every 67 seconds.

Twenty percent—twenty percent of all the money we spend on Medicare in America is spent for Alzheimer's and dementia—one out of five dollars—but you add to that, one out of three dollars in Medicare is spent on diabetes, so between diabetes and Alzheimer's, over half of our Medicare budget is going to those patients.

When we talk about the need to develop new drugs to intervene and, with God's blessing, to cure some of these diseases, we are talking about not only alleviating human suffering, we are talking about the very real cost of government and health care—the very real cost that we bear as individuals, as families, as businesses, as a government, and as taxpayers.

In this bill are some positive things, this 21st Century Cures bill. I do want to highlight them because they are worthy; the fact that we are now going to commit ourselves to deal with issues such as opioids. The opioid-heroin epidemic in America is real, and we are not investing in what we need to treat it and deal with it. We need to have substance abuse treatment—much, much more than we have today.

One out of six or eight people who are currently addicted are receiving treatment. We need to do dramatically better. This bill puts money into that. It also includes language, including some parts I offered as an amendment, that will deal with mental illness. Mental illness and substance abuse treatment are basically on the same track in terms of helping people. This bill addresses that. I am glad it does. I think that is very positive.

What is disappointing about this bill—there are several things. First, the money we are spending in this bill largely comes from one source, prevention—health care prevention funding in the Affordable Care Act. How important is that? Do you know how that money is being spent? We have something called the 317 vaccination program. What it says is, if you come from one of the poorest families in America, we will pay for our children to be vaccinated so they don't have to worry about the diseases that can change the life or even take the life of an infant.

The 317 vaccine program, half of the money comes from the prevention funds we are raiding for medical research. Does that make sense; that we are going to take money away from prevention and vaccination to invest in new drugs to treat diseases? We can prevent these diseases in the first place with adequate vaccinations.

It is a warped sense of justice in America that we would eliminate the health care prevention funds to pay for health care research funds. It is a zero sum as far as I am concerned. It is not just a matter of vaccinations. When you look at other things: 43 percent of the money that is spent on diabetes in America—prevention of diabetes in America—is through the prevention fund in the Affordable Care Act.

That figure tells us that if we can invest on getting people to change their lifestyles, sometimes very slightly, or to take certain drugs, they can avoid the onset of diabetes. So we are cutting the prevention funds for diabetes in order to pay for more research for cures for diabetes. Does that make sense?

Let me ask you about this: tobacco. A lot of my career in Congress has been focused on tobacco, the No. 1 avoidable cause of death in America today. Tobacco cessation programs pay off many times over. They are paid for by the prevention funds we are now raiding for medical research. We are taking away the funds to prevent tobacco addiction, and we are going to put more investment in trying to find cures for lung disease. There is something wrong with this thinking—completely wrong with this thinking.

At the outset, I would say going to the prevention programs to pay for research programs is not clear thinking on the part of the people that are putting this together. We are told: Well, you better do it because the Republicans will take control of the White House and Congress next year and they are going to wipe out all of the prevention funds. They want to do away with the Affordable Care Act. We will pay a heavy price for that. We are starting to make that payment today.

The second thing I want to say is, I am totally underwhelmed by the amount of money in this bill. When you take a look at the amount of money that is being spent here, it has dramatically changed as we have debated this bill. Originally, this was a $9.3 billion program for medical research, pretty hefty. Over a 5-year-period of time, this would have had a dramatic impact in a short period of time.

Well, that changed. It is about half of that now. It is spread over 10 years. So the amount of money actually going to the National Institutes of Health any given year is interesting—$400 million, $500 million—but it does not match what was originally promised in the 21st Century Cures Act. Of course, the question is, if this money is put in out of prevention funding, will it be additive? Will it be more?

Let me close by saying this. I know there are many who have strong feelings about this bill. I think it is a step in the right direction, but as Senator WARREN has told us, it is at a hefty cost when it comes to some of the favors included in this bill for people who have friends in high places when it comes to the Congress.

Here is what I can tell you with certainty. We have been able, for 2 successive years in the appropriations process, to do something important and historic. Let me tip a hat to my colleague from Missouri, Senator ROY BLUNT, a Republican, who took up this cause in the Appropriations Committee and provided 5-percent real growth in spending for the National Institutes of Health last year and would do it again this year if the Republican leadership would allow us to bring his appropriations bill to the floor.

We know we can make substantial new investments in NIH medical research. We have a bipartisan will to achieve it. We have the Appropriations Committee ready to act. Instead, what I am afraid of is this bill, which is a modest investment in medical research, will be the end of the conversation for many Members of Congress.

When the time comes months from now, whether this passes or not—it probably will pass—but when the time comes months from now for us to debate medical research, many will say: Oh, we already checked that box. We have already done that with the 21st Century Cures bill.

This bill is a pale imitation of the original bill. It is only a fraction of the funding which the Appropriations Committee has already put in to enhance medical research at the NIH. It overpromises and underdelivers. Some of the aspects of it—the troubling aspects—are off-label drugs and special favors for the contributors when it comes to medical treatment are out of place here.

If we did not learn any lesson in this last election about draining the swamp, well, shame on us because the American people told us do it differently—do it openly. Bring in transparency and honesty in this effort. When it comes to medical research, we should expect nothing less.

I yield the floor.

The PRESIDING OFFICER. The Senator from Oregon.

Mr. MERKLEY. Mr. President, I am delighted to join my colleagues from Massachusetts and Illinois to express strong objections to the 21st Century Cures Act, a bill that is being considered in the House today and will be considered in the Senate.

This bill proceeds to make effective $6.3 billion in cuts to programs while laying out a vision of what might possibly be spent in the future to assist in medical research. This is very much an imbalance. Real cuts—and as I will point out, those cuts hit things that matter with a promise of some of future possible action. We have seen these promises made and broken time and time and time again in this Chamber. If you are going to make a real commitment, then why isn't the real commitment in this bill?

I ask my colleagues from across the aisle: Why isn't the real commitment to these programs in this bill? Why isn't the spending in this bill? Why isn't the spending on precision medicine that is promised to be considered in the future in this bill? Why isn't the funding for the Cancer Moonshot promised to be considered at some point in the future actually in this bill? Why isn't the program to help address an understanding of and pursue cures for Alzheimer's, which is actually just a promise to be considered in the future—why isn't that actually in this bill? Why isn't the work promised to be considered in the future for adult stem cell research, which could have application to multiple cures and multiple diseases, actually in this bill?

Well, I will tell you what is in this bill. What is in this bill is a provision that loosens the rules governing how companies market their drugs and the anti-fraud laws that go along with them—headache pills being advertised on television as a cure for the common cold and hair loss, perhaps. This is just what Big Pharma wants: freedom, freedom to mislead consumers about what drugs actually have been proven to do.

I will tell you what else is in this bill. It allows people to sell untested treatments and drugs without final FDA approval that has demonstrated the treatments are safe. Two big factors deregulating responsible provisions for Big Pharma are in this bill. But all of those rainbows, all those stars promised—those are for future consideration, to dress up special interest provisions for Big Pharma.

I will tell you what else is in this bill. There are special interest provisions for Big Tobacco, taking away $3.5 billion in prevention funds from the public health fund, $3.5 billion real dollars in prevention. The tobacco companies hate prevention programs because they make their money from addicts. Their goal in life is to get people addicted. This prevention fund is to prevent people from getting addicted. As you ponder all the diseases that stem from the use of tobacco—cancer of the lungs, cancer of the esophagus, heart disease in one form or another, all kinds of forms of decimation due to the daily inhaling of these toxins—that is what the tobacco industry thrives on, and they thrive on it from addiction.

Here we have a fund designed to help people avoid the addiction that takes away from their quality of life, often for decades of their time on our beautiful, blue-green planet, and, instead, encourages a process through which people will not only suffer personally but have massive medical bills, driving up the cost of health care in America for everyone, driving up the cost of insurance for everyone in America.

Since its launch in 2012, the Tips campaign has helped more than 400,000 smokers quit for good. According to the Centers for Disease Control and Prevention, it saved 50,000 lives. At a cost of less than $400 for each year of life saved, in public health circles it is considered a best buy, dollars well spent that improve the quality of thousands of people's lives and reduce costs in the health care system. That is a win-win.

But what is in this bill? An assault on that win-win to help the tobacco companies get more addicts.

The chronic diseases and unhealthy behaviors the prevention fund is intended to address impose tremendous costs. Tobacco use alone costs about $170 billion a year. Last year in health care expenses, more than 60 percent of it was paid by taxpayers through Medicare and Medicaid, so we all feel the impact of this.

What else gets cut? Oh, Medicare funding gets cut. If you are for taking apart the preeminent health care sys-

tem so that our seniors can retire without the stress of worrying about access to health care, then vote for this bill. This is an assault on Medicare—big favors for Big Pharma, big favors for Big Tobacco, and an assault on Medicare. It doesn't trim some Medicare programs that maybe are not as effective as others and help the others be stronger, more effective. No, it just takes away from Medicare.

Those are the things that are in this act, but what is not in this act? The mine workers protection act championed by my colleague from West Virginia, Senator MANCHIN. The mine workers protection act isn't in here, but the provisions expire for thousands of mine workers in the near future. There are 12,500 coal miners who will lose their health insurance on December 31. Another 10,000 will lose their health coverage next year and on into the future if we don't restore this program. If this bill is about health care, why isn't the coal miners' provision in here? I think it should be, but it is not.

What else isn't in here? Senator WYDEN's provision to help children who are foster children gain access to programs to help them address mental health and addiction. That was in here yesterday. That would have been a positive talking point for this bill yesterday, but it was stripped out last night. This bill isn't ready, not just for prime time; it is not ready for consideration at all.

If we are going to cut real programs to fund other real programs such as the Moonshot and Alzheimer's research, strengthening NIH, then get it into this bill. Don't just put in the real cuts and then say there is some promise and an invitation to chase a rainbow down the road. Put it in the bill.

The things that are in here are powerful, deregulatory giveaways to Big Pharma and Big Tobacco, making the lives of our citizens worse, not better. That is why we should kill this bill.

Thank you.

Mr. President, I suggest the absence of a quorum.

The PRESIDING OFFICER. The clerk will call the roll.

The legislative clerk proceeded to call the roll.

Mr. KAINE. Mr. President, I ask unanimous consent that the order for the quorum call be rescinded.

The PRESIDING OFFICER. Without objection, it is so ordered.

HONORING OUR ARMED FORCES

CHIEF PETTY OFFICER SCOTT C. DAYTON

Mr. KAINE. Mr. President, I rise today to honor Naval CPO Scott Dayton, a Virginian who became America's first combat casualty in Syria. Scott was a resident of Woodbridge, VA, here in Northern Virginia. He enlisted in the military in 1993, in the Navy, and had a distinguished 23-year career, fin-

ishing his time in one of the most dangerous billets in the military—as a bomb disposal expert.

Scott was working in Syria pursuant to Operation Inherent Resolve, and on Thanksgiving day he was killed. He was a 42-year-old Virginian based out of Virginia Beach, but he was killed working to dispose of bombs about 30 miles from Raqqa, Syria, which is one of the two main headquarters of ISIS.

Scott Dayton was a decorated sailor in his 23-year military career. He won virtually every award there was, including a Bronze Star—19 different awards and commendations. Because his death occurred over a holiday weekend, there wasn't a lot of attention paid to it, but it was something I really wanted to come to the floor today to talk about because he is the first combat death in Syria of an American servicemember in Operation Inherent Resolve.

I wish we were paying more attention to this, and that is what I want to devote the rest of my comments to.

USE OF MILITARY FORCE AUTHORIZATION

Mr. KAINE. We began Operation Inherent Resolve, which is a war against ISIS, on August 7, 2014. President Obama announced at the time that we were engaging in targeted airstrikes against ISIS because of their advance toward Erbil. There is a U.S. consulate in Erbil, and so that was part of the President's inherent powers to defend the Nation—to protect our consulate.

Within a very few weeks, we had completely protected American interests, and President Obama said now is the time to go on offense against ISIS. The President appeared before the American public in a televised speech the evening of September 10, 2014, and said that we had taken care of the imminent threat to the United States but now we needed to go into an offensive war to "degrade and ultimately destroy the Islamic state." And that description of what the mission is has now been broadened, in the words of current Secretary of Defense Ash Carter, to focus on ISIS's lasting defeat.

Since the war against ISIS began in August 2014, more than 5,000 members of the U.S. military have served in Operation Inherent Resolve either in Iraq or Syria. Right now, just as an example, from my home State, there is a carrier, the USS *Eisenhower*—homeported in Norfolk—that is in the gulf now as part of Operation Inherent Resolve. The U.S. military has launched over 12,600 airstrikes. We are carrying out special forces operations. We are assisting the Iraqi military, Syrians fighting the Islamic State in Syria, as well as the Kurdish Peshmerga in the northern part of Iraq.

Because of the work of American troops and those they are working with, we have made major gains against ISIS in northern Iraq. The territory they control in northern Iraq has dramatically shrunk. We have made major gains in shrinking their territory in northern Syria, and that is to be credited to brave folks like CPO Scott Dayton. But the threat posed by the Islamic State continues, and increasingly, as their battle space shrinks in real estate, they undertake efforts off that battleground to try to destabilize us around the world.

This fight against ISIL, which is a key—maybe the key—national security priority involving U.S. combat operations in Iraq and Syria, will likely continue for the long foreseeable future, even after the complete liberation of Mosul and Raqqa, which I am confident will occur. The war has cost $10 billion—800 days of operations at an average of $12.6 million a day.

I began by honoring Scott Dayton, but Scott Dayton is not the only military member who has lost his life in this war. Five have been killed in combat in total, and 28 American servicemembers have lost their lives supporting Operation Inherent Resolve. As we speak, there are more than 300 special forces now in Syria fighting a very complex battlefield where Turkish, Syrian, Russian, Iranian, Lebanese Hezbollah, and Kurdish forces are operating in close proximity, as evidenced by recent developments and the growing humanitarian catastrophe in Aleppo.

I continue to believe—and I will say this in a very personal way as a military dad—that the troops we have deployed overseas deserve to know Congress is behind this mission. As this war has expanded into 2-plus years—I don't know whether that would have been the original expectation—with more and more of our troops risking and losing their lives far from home, I am concerned—and again raise something I have raised often on this floor—that there is a tacit agreement to avoid debating this war in the one place where it ought to be debated—in the Halls of Congress.

The President maintains that he can conduct this war without a new authorization from Congress, relying upon an authorization that was passed on September 14, 2001. When the new Congress is sworn in, in early January—I think 80 percent of those Members of Congress were not here when the September 14, 2001, authorization was passed, so the 80 percent of us who were not here in 2001 have never had a meaningful debate or vote regarding this war against ISIL.

I have been very critical of this President. I am a supporter of the President. I am a friend of the President. I respect the Office of the President. But I have been very critical of this President for not vigorously attempting to get an authorization done.

When the President spoke about the need to go on offense against ISIL in September of 2014, it took him 6 months from the start of hostilities to even deliver to Congress a proposed authorization. I actually think that is the way the system is supposed to work, that the President delivers the proposed authorization. But I have also been harshly critical of the article I branch because regardless of whether the President promptly delivers an authorization, under article I of the Constitution, it is Congress that has the obligation to initiate war.

As the current Presiding Officer knows because he is not only a Senator but a historian, the founding documents of this country are so unusual still today in making the initiation of war a legislative rather than Executive function. Madison and the other drafters of the Constitution knew that the history of war was a history of making it about the Executive—the King, the Monarch, the Sultan, the Emperor—but we decided that we would be different and that war would only be initiated by a vote of the people's elected legislative body and at that point would be conducted by only 1 commander-in-chief, not by 435. We have not had the debate. We have not had the vote.

This has been ironic because for 4 years I have been in a Congress that has been very quick to criticize the President for using Executive action. This is an Executive action that most clearly is in the legislative wheelhouse; yet it has been an Executive action that the body—and I am making this as a bipartisan and bicameral comment—has been very willing to allow the President to make.

I introduced a resolution for the first time to get Congress to debate and do this job in September of 2014, 2 days after the President spoke to the Nation about the need to take military action against ISIL. That authorization led to a Senate Foreign Relations Committee hearing and a vote in December of 2014 to authorize military action against ISIL, but that committee resolution never received any debate or vote on the Senate floor.

In 2015, working together with a Senate colleague from Arizona, Senator FLAKE, we decided we really needed to show our opposition to ISIL. Our belief that appropriate military force from the United States should be used against them was bipartisan, and so we introduced a bipartisan authorization of military force on June 8, 2015, in an attempt to move forward with some congressional debate on this most important issue. Aside from a few informal discussions in the Senate Foreign Relations Committee, there has never been a markup, never been a discussion, never been a committee vote or a floor vote.

So 2½ years of war against the Islamic State and 15 years now after the passage of the authorization in September of 2014, we see that authorization has been stretched way beyond what it was intended to do. The authorization of September 14, 2001, was a 60-word authorization giving the President the tools to go after the perpetrators of the attacks of 9/11. ISIL didn't exist on September 11, 2001; it was formed in 2003. President Obama recently announced that the authorization is now going to be expanded to allow use of military action against Al-Shabaab, the African terrorist group—a dangerous terrorist group, to be sure—but Al-Shabaab did not begin until 2007.

So an original authorization that was very specific by this body to allow action against the perpetrators of the 9/11 attacks is now being used all over the globe against organizations that didn't even exist when the 9/11 attacks occurred. Just to give an example, the 2001 authorization has been cited by Presidents Bush and Obama in at least 37 instances to justify sending Armed Forces to 14 nations. Pursuant to the authorization to go after the perpetrators of the 9/11 attacks, we have authorized military action in the Bush and Obama administrations in Libya, Turkey, Georgia, Syria, Iraq, Afghanistan, Yemen, Eritrea, Ethiopia, Djibouti, Somalia, Kenya, and the Philippines, as well as authorizing military activity in Cuba at Guantanamo to maintain detainees.

Just in the last week, the New York Times reported that President Obama is expanding the legal scope of the war against Al Qaeda by easing targeting and restrictions against Al-Shabaab, but again this was a group that didn't exist until 2007, 6 years after the 9/11 attacks.

Mr. President, I will conclude and say that having been very vocal about this issue for a number of years, it has been disappointing. Although we are all used to not getting our way in all kinds of ways, it has been disappointing to me that we have not been willing to take up this matter.

I do think a transition to a new administration and a transition to a new Congress that will be sworn in, in early January always gives you the opportunity to review the status of affairs and make a decision about what to do. I believe it is time for us to review the progress of the war against nonstate terrorist groups—Al Qaeda, ISIS, Al-Shabaab, Boko Haram, Al-Nusra. It is time for us to review U.S. military action against nonstate terrorist organizations. It is time for us to redraft the 2001 authorization that has been stretched far beyond its original intent. It is time for us to recognize that this is a continuing threat that is not going away anytime soon. But I guess what I will say is most important is that it is time for Congress to reassert its rightful place in this most important set of decisions. Of all the powers we would have as Congress, I can't think of any that are more important than the power to declare war. I view that as the most important, the most difficult, the most challenging, the power we should approach with the most sense of gravity. That is the most important thing we should do. It should never be an easy vote. It should always be a hard vote, but it should be a necessary vote. I think the inability or unwillingness of Congress to grapple with this sends a message that is unfortunate. It sends a message of lack of resolve to allies. It might even send a message of lack of resolve to our adversary.

But what I am most concerned about are people like CPO Scott Dayton, people who are serving in a theater of war, who are risking their lives in a theater of war, who have been giving their lives in a theater of war and doing it without the knowledge that Congress supports the mission they are on.

As I conclude, Article I and Article II allocation of responsibilities are not just about what is constitutional. I think it reflects a value, and the value is this: We shouldn't order people into harm's way to risk their lives unless there is a political consensus that the mission is worth it. Anyone who volunteers for military service knows it is going to be difficult, and we will not be able to change that. But if we are going to order people into combat and order them to risk their lives—and even if they are not harmed, they may see things happen to colleagues of theirs that could affect them the rest of their lives. If we are going to order them to do that, then there should at least be a national political consensus that the mission is worth it. The way the Constitution sets that up is the President makes a proposal, but then Congress— the people's elected body—votes and says: Yes, the mission is worth it.

Now that we have had that vote, now that we have had that debate and we have educated the public about what is at stake, and now that we have said the mission is worth it, it is fair then to ask our 2 million Active-Duty Guard and Reserves—folks like Chief Petty Officer Scott Dayton, folks like my oldest son—to go and risk their lives on a mission like this. But if we are unwilling to have the debate and have the vote, it seems to me to be almost the height of public immorality to force people to risk and give their lives in support of a mission that we are unwilling to discuss.

Again, I offer these words in honor of a brave Virginian who lost his life on Thanksgiving Day, November 24. I hope that the growing number of people who are losing their lives in Operation Inherent Resolve may spur this body to take this responsibility with more gravity.

Mr. President, I yield the floor.

The PRESIDING OFFICER. The Senator from Ohio.

Mr. BROWN. Mr. President I thank my colleague from Virginia, who is always speaking up for our men and women in uniform and for our Nation's veterans.

MINE WORKERS' HEALTH CARE AND PENSIONS AND THE 21ST CENTURY CURES BILL

Mr. BROWN. Mr. President, right now our Nation's retired coal miners— and I know Senator KAINE and Senator WARREN care about this, too—are on the brink of losing the health care and retirement benefits that they have earned over a lifetime of hard work.

It is within the power of this Congress to stop this, to help the mine workers, and to do right by these hard-working Americans. Many of them are veterans. Most of them wore their bodies out to give their families a better life. There is no more fitting action that we can take during this holiday season than to honor this promise that the American Government has made to our Nation's mine workers since Harry Truman made that promise. The workers held up their end of the bargain. It is despicable that we are not holding up ours and that we are preparing to leave town without lifting a finger to help these workers.

United Mine Workers of America's health care and pension plan covers some 100,000 mine workers; 6,800 live in Ohio. If Congress fails to act, thousands of retired miners could lose their health care this year. I emphasize that it is retirement security they worked for, security they fought for, and security they sacrificed raises and their own health for.

Understand this: Too many people that dress in suits, work here, draw good salaries, and draw good benefits don't understand what happens at the bargaining table for workers in our country. They often give up raises today to defer that money so that they have retirements and pensions in the future.

Say that again: People at the bargaining table give up dollars today. Rather than take a little higher pay today, they are willing to defer that so they will have better pensions and health care. This Congress, this Senate leadership is blocking us from doing that.

These are workers who worked for decades in the mines—hard, back-breaking work but work that had dignity. I live in a place that some national media people, including President-elect Trump, have referred to as the "rust belt." When they say "rust belt," that is a direct attack on the dignity of work. It demeans their work. It diminishes who they are. It is saying that those people, such as miners, steelworkers, and others who make things, are in the past.

For these mine workers, every year in their work in the mines, they have earned and contributed to a health plan and pension plan. I have met with some of these workers—Ohioans like Norm Skinner, Dave Dilly, and Babe Erdos. I have heard their stories. They knew they were signing up for tough, dangerous work. They worked in the mines, after all. They knew that. But they also know their work had dignity. That work was part of a covenant we used to have in this country—a covenant that said: If you work hard, if you put in the hours, if you contribute to retirement, if you provide for your own health care in the future, you will be able to support yourself and your family. It is what built our country. It is what created the middle class.

Today, the value of that work is eroding. Too often, too many major corporations in this country are choosing profits over people. We haven't lifted a finger, frankly. The political agenda here—some people who run this Senate simply don't have respect for the mine workers, for the union. They seem to have some anti-union sensibilities about this. Whatever it is, they are not lifting a finger to help these workers who put in the effort and who are in trouble through no fault of their own.

There is no reason to leave town. We shouldn't be going home for the holidays without taking care of the 6,800 mine workers in Ohio, a number of mine workers in West Virginia, thousands of mine workers in Virginia, Eastern Kentucky, and Southwest Pennsylvania.

This is a bipartisan solution. It will not cost taxpayers a dime. If this bipartisan mine workers legislation were brought to the floor today, it would pass with majorities in each party. We shouldn't be taking up other legislation. Until we do this, it should be part of the Cures Act that we will be voting on later.

The Cures Act has important components to it, good steps on mental health, on hospital reimbursement. It has my National Pediatric Research Network Act in it. But it is a 900-page bill negotiated entirely in the House. It has major flaws.

It does include funding for NIH, funds to fight the opioid epidemic. We know how important that is. But the funding isn't mandatory. It will be subject to the whims of future Congresses. This is pretty good happy talk, and we are saying the right things. We are putting language in this bill, but it doesn't guarantee the money will be there. It is so important to my State.

A new report released this week showed Ohio had the most drug overdoses that resulted in death in the country in 2014, not the most per capita. We had more drug overdose deaths than California, three times our population; Texas, twice our population; more than Illinois, Pennsylvania, New York, Florida—all States with more people than we have. More Ohioans died from drug overdoses from OxyContin or oxycodone or heroin or the new synthetic drugs we are seeing more and more. We have to do more.

The billion dollars in grants in this bill are critically important, but it needs to be mandatory funding. It can't be that down the road some powerful Member of the House or Senate stands in the way of actually getting these communities the money. We can't fight year after year to get these dollars appropriated.

The Cures Act gives significant concessions to Big Pharma, which is the big drug industry, the drug giants in this country, but it does absolutely nothing to combat drug prices. We give concessions to the big drug companies, but we do nothing to fight the high cost of drugs in this bill.

We shouldn't be spending time on this flawed bill until we keep our promises to the 12,000 mine workers I mentioned. These miners worked in some of the most dangerous conditions of any jobs in this country. They deserve the full pension and health benefits they were promised. They have worked a lifetime to earn these benefits. They kept faith with us. We must keep faith with them. It is simply irresponsible and immoral for us to leave town and not take care of the mine workers.

Mr. President, I suggest the absence of a quorum.

The PRESIDING OFFICER. The clerk will call the roll.

The senior assistant legislative clerk proceeded to call the roll.

Mr. SASSE. Mr. President, I ask unanimous consent that the order for the quorum call be rescinded.

The PRESIDING OFFICER (Mr. BARRASSO). Without objection, it is so ordered.

USE OF MILITARY FORCE AUTHORIZATION

Mr. SASSE. Mr. President, I had not intended to speak today. I was presiding in the chair, but I simply want to take one minute to associate myself with the comments of the Senator from Virginia, Mr. KAINE, who just spoke about our war against ISIS.

I think two points he said are worth underscoring for us in this body:

No. 1, we are obviously at war with ISIS. We should acknowledge that we are at war with ISIS.

No. 2, why is it important that we do this? It is important for the troops who are at war for us to acknowledge the reality of the fact that we are at war. It is important for their families. It is important for debate and deliberation in this body and in the country more broadly. And, frankly, it is important for the future of this body to honor a constitutional intent that distinguishes between Article I, the legislature, and Article II, the Executive.

In the American system, in Madison and the other Founders' genius, they recognized that many foreign wars have not made sense in human history because Executives get wrapped up in war without broader deliberation about the consequences of their actions.

To be clear, we should absolutely be at war with ISIS, and we are at war with ISIS. But in the American constitutional system, it is the obligation of the 535 of us who serve in the Congress—and particularly the 100 who serve in the Senate—to represent our people and to have this debate before the people about the fact that we are at war with ISIS.

Then, the Commander in Chief, as Chief Executive, should prosecute that war in a way that the American people know has the sanction and the validation of both branches and of all the people across 50 States.

This is not the action of one President acting unilaterally. It is a bad precedent to set for us to continue to drift and to remain at war now 15 years post the authorization that was against the perpetrators of the 9/11 attack, now using that old authorization to conduct a war, now on a second continent—now in Africa as well—but without any current discussion or authorization.

The use of military force is something that should be deliberated about in this body. I again want to associate myself with the comments of the Senator from Virginia that, given that we are at war with ISIS, we should formally be declaring war against ISIS.

The PRESIDING OFFICER (Mr. PERDUE). The Senator from Wyoming.

OBAMACARE

Mr. BARRASSO. Mr. President, Democrats in Washington continue to try to understand the results of the election. I have heard them blame Republicans, I have heard them blame Russian hackers, I have heard them blame the FBI, and I have even heard them blame the press. What I have not heard is a single Washington Democrat admit that one reason Democrats lost on November 8 could be their disastrous health care law. Well, the health care law has definitely been on the minds of the voters.

On October 31, just 1 week before election day, the Milwaukee Journal Sentinel had an article with the headline, "Rates for Obamacare Plans Jump in Wisconsin." This article said that tens of thousands of middle-class people in Wisconsin who don't qualify for Washington subsidies "will pay the full cost of double-digit premium increases."

The article quoted one insurance broker, saying:

I've talked with people who are exasperated. They are just at wit's end.

That is what the insurance broker said.

It is not just the price increases. In at least five States, there is only one company selling plans on the ObamaCare exchange. My State of Wyoming is one of those. People are being told their plan will no longer include their doctor or maybe even a hospital near where they live. The average deductible for a silver plan next year is going to be almost $3,600. There is damage that ObamaCare is doing to American families right now. People are seeing it.

That article was in a Wisconsin newspaper, a State in which, apparently—according to the polls—Donald Trump was running behind, RON JOHNSON was running behind, but both of them carried the State handedly. Here we have an election where people expressed their opinion, and the Democrats seem to want to deny the main reason for it.

The American people have placed their faith now in Republicans, and we, in turn, earned that trust. We will do it through both Executive action and legislative action with regard to the health care law. First, President Trump will have a great opportunity to start making things better for the American people by changing some of the regulations that are a huge part of the health care law.

Remember, this health care law is 2,700 pages long, and within those 2,700 pages there are more than 1,800 places where the law gives the Secretary of Health and Human Services the power to write different rules and different regulations and different requirements to try to spell out what the 2,700-page law says. The Obama administration absolutely abused that power. The administration added more than 40,000 pages—40,000 pages of regulations and of redtape that were never actually in the law itself.

In the Trump administration, there is going to be a new Secretary of Health and Human Services. He is a physician—an orthopedic surgeon. Once confirmed, I believe he will be able to interpret, reinterpret, and then reapply the law in ways that actually help American families instead of so many ways that hurt American families because the interpretation in the past favored Big Government over people.

This includes applying the law to make it easier for businesses to provide insurance to people who work for them. It means giving power back to the States to come up with ideas that work for all of the citizens. The nominated Secretary of Health and Human Services is not just a doctor, but he also served in the State legislature, and he knows that at the State level you can make much better decisions for the people of that State than when Washington comes up with a one-size-fits-all decision.

Republicans want to make sure the power goes back to where it belongs—with the people, the families, and the States. That is where it belongs. The

Executive action can start pretty quickly, and it can be abridged to the important work that the Congress is going to have to do. We are going to work hard in the Senate and in the House to undo some of the damage—significant amounts of the damage—that ObamaCare has caused. It is undoing the damage because people all around this country have suffered under this health care law. It means repealing the health care law and wiping the slate clean.

ObamaCare can't be fixed by tinkering with it here and there—not with another attempted bailout of the insurance companies, which the President has continued to promote. This solution isn't to add more government on top of what we already have.

The health care law began collapsing a long time ago, and Republicans are now ready to clear away the rubble. Then, we will write a new law with a multiple step-by-step process—a law that reforms America's broken health care insurance system so patients can get the care they need from a doctor they choose at lower costs—one that puts American families in control of their health care and a law that is simpler, fairer, more effective, and more accountable.

We have seen the mistakes that the Democrats have made with the health care law. We have seen that every State is different. So we are going to be looking to push as much authority out of Washington and back to the States. We have seen that too many mandates and regulations drive up costs, and they drive up the costs without improving the quality of care. We have seen that when Washington writes bad laws, the unintended consequences are severe.

These are all things that Republicans have said since the very beginning. The failure of ObamaCare has proven that the Republicans were right. The election has proven that the American people want a new approach. American families don't want us to tinker with ObamaCare. They just want affordable health care.

I want to make a couple of things clear. First of all, nobody is talking about taking people off of insurance without a replacement plan in place. We all understand that there needs to be a transition over time. People have already been hurt too much when they lost their insurance, when their rates went up because of ObamaCare, and with the mandates and the government saying they know better than families across the country.

We will be working to make the transition as smooth as possible for everyone. That is why we are including a transition period in a repeal bill that Congress passed last year and sent to the President's desk. The President, of course, vetoed it. Our goal is to do no harm.

As we write a new health care law, we will be looking to make it real reform that is actually centered on patients. We can increase the use of health savings accounts. That will give more people the chance to control how they spend their own money on their health care. We can support innovative insurance plans that pay for prescription drugs that work best for patients and not just the ones preferred by insurance companies. We will be talking about ways to protect people with preexisting conditions and letting young people stay on their parents' insurance. These are important parts of the health care law.

Republicans are going to consider any ideas—any ideas that can help us to give people what they wanted all along—access to the care they need from a doctor they choose at lower cost.

Democrats promised that they would listen to other people's ideas, and then they went behind a closed door in an office back there and they wrote the law, ignoring all of the suggestions by Republicans and without any Republican support at all.

We are not going to make that mistake. We will be looking for Democrats' help. We will be looking for Democrats to work with. We will be listening to Democrats' ideas, and we will be working very hard to win Democratic votes for any new law.

Reforming health care in this country is not going to be easy. It is not something we are going to do for the purpose of scoring political points or to discredit President Obama. I will tell you, as a doctor, that it is something we must do to protect American families and their health, as well as their health care.

I suggest the absence of a quorum.

The PRESIDING OFFICER. The clerk will call the roll.

The senior assistant legislative clerk proceeded to call the roll.

Mr. HOEVEN. Mr. President, I ask unanimous consent that the order for the quorum call be rescinded.

The PRESIDING OFFICER. Without objection, it is so ordered.

DAKOTA ACCESS PIPELINE

Mr. HOEVEN. Mr. President, I rise to speak and also to respond to the comments of some of my colleagues on the Dakota Access Pipeline and the ongoing protests in my State of North Dakota.

Here we have a chart showing the Dakota Access Pipeline. It is a 1,172-mile pipeline from the Bakken oil fields near Stanley, ND, to refineries and terminals that actually connect to Patoka, IL, and then that light crude can go into eastern refineries. It will move 470,000 barrels of oil daily from the Bakken in North Dakota and Montana to eastern markets and to refineries

that depend on that light sweet crude. This is high quality. This is the lightest, sweetest crude we produce. It is very high quality oil.

It is also important to understand this oil is already moving. It is already moving to these markets right now by rail and by truck. This oil is already being moved.

This pipeline actually increases the efficiency and the safety with which we move this oil that is already being transported to eastern markets.

Furthermore, the project has undergone years of State regulatory reviews and an extensive Federal environmental assessment which found no significant environmental impact. Again, the environmental assessment found no significant environmental impact. It has been twice challenged and twice upheld, including by the Obama administration's own appointees in Federal court. The Federal courts found that the Army Corps had followed the appropriate process that the Standing Rock Tribe was properly consulted and that the project can lawfully proceed.

Everyone has a right to be heard, but it must be done lawfully and peacefully, whether this is during the permitting process with its opportunities for comment or disputing the outcome through the court system. Of course, that is why we have the court system. It hears grievances and provides dispute resolution.

The ongoing protest activities which are occurring in North Dakota—which at times have been violent—are being prolonged and intensified by the Obama administration's refusal to approve the final remaining easement at Lake Oahe. This inaction has inflamed tensions, strained State and local resources and, most importantly, is needlessly putting people at risk, including Tribal members, protesters, law enforcement officers, construction workers, and area residents—our farmers and ranchers who live and work in the area of the pipeline.

It is past time that the final easement is approved and construction is completed. We need to get this issue resolved. It is past time to get this issue resolved. As the record demonstrates, it should be done on its merits through the previously established regulatory and legal process. In other words, follow the law. We are a country of laws. Follow the law.

Further, the Federal law enforcement agencies should help our State and local law enforcement officers to ensure the law is followed to prevent violent and unlawful protests and see that the peace is maintained. Our law enforcement officers have worked professionally, diligently, and tirelessly to protect the public.

To further describe the situation, let me provide some background. The company developed the route for the Dakota Access Pipeline beginning in 2014.

The current path will run parallel to an existing Northern Border Gas pipeline which was placed into service in 1982, as well as an existing high-voltage electric transmission line. In North Dakota, this is an already established right-of-way for energy infrastructure. You have an existing gas line that goes through this same route and you have a high-voltage transmission line as well.

Approximately 99 percent of the route for the Dakota Access Pipeline crosses private land. Only 3 percent of the work needed to build the pipeline requires Federal approval of any kind, and only 1 percent of the pipeline affects U.S. waterways. To date, the pipeline is already 98 percent complete in North Dakota, and it is 86 percent complete overall, from North Dakota to Illinois. That includes the route around and up to the final two-tenths-of-a-mile portion of the Missouri River, which is where most of this protest is occurring. This area of the river, known as Lake Oahe, is controlled by the Army Corps for flood control purposes and requires one remaining Federal easement.

The segment at the center of this debate is a small section planned to traverse under Lake Oahe which would occur at a depth of 92 to 117 feet below the riverbed. In other words, the pipeline doesn't enter the river at all. It is about 100 feet below the river. That is very important to understand. In fact, where it crosses underneath the river, it is 100 percent adjacent to an existing natural gas pipeline. In other words, it follows a pipeline that is already built and is there now, an existing natural gas pipeline. This was done so any ground disturbances would not harm any cultural or Tribal features. That is why they followed this right-of-way.

Let's put this into perspective a little bit. We have another chart that helps do that. Remember, we are talking about crossing the river in one place, right? We are talking about a pipeline that is going to cross this river in one spot.

Let's put that into a broader context, into a broader perspective. The Congressional Research Service estimates there are 38,410 crude oil pipeline river and water body crossings in the United States. So in our network of oil pipelines around the country, we cross water more than 38,000 times. We are talking about doing it one more time here. But we already do it more than 38,000 times all over the country. This chart shows you that.

In North Dakota alone, we cross bodies of water more than 1,000 times—more than 1,000 times. So this is hardly something new and different. The Congressional Research Service estimates that there are 3,410 crude oil pipeline river and water body crossings in the United States already existing, including 1,079 in North Dakota alone. So I guess we go from 1,079 to 1,080 just in our State. These crossings range from rivers, streams, and lakes to ponds, canals and ditches.

So let's talk about tribal consultation. In total, the Army Corps held 389 meetings, conferred with more than 55 tribes, and conducted a 1,261-page environmental assessment before finding that this infrastructure project has no significant environmental impact. So they did all of that study, all of that consultation. Conclusion: This project has no significant environmental impact.

So the Federal court then reviewed this decision once the protests started. The Federal court reviewed the Corps' work. In the September 9 Federal court opinion, U.S. District Judge James Boasberg noted that the company surveyed nearly twice as many miles in North Dakota as the 357-mile route that would eventually be used for the pipeline. So they surveyed a lot more than they actually used.

Why did they do that? The Federal judge noted that where the surveys revealed evidence of historically important or cultural resources, such as stone features, the company modified the route on its own—140 times in North Dakota alone. So 140 times the company modified its route to make sure they avoided any cultural or sensitive features. Remember, they are using an existing corridor that already has a gas pipeline and already has a high-voltage transmission line. They still modified it 140 times to make sure they avoid any culturally sensitive resources.

Additionally, in another instance, the Corps ordered the company to actually change the route where it crossed the James River, which is another river further east that has not been protested—it crosses that river too—to avoid burial sites there. They actually changed the route to make sure they avoided any sensitive sites.

The pipeline company and the Army Corps have documented dozens of attempts to engage with the Standing Rock Sioux Tribe to help identify historical resources and provide feedback in the planning process. Judge Boasberg, I might mention again, was appointed by the Obama administration. Judge Boasberg, a U.S. Federal court judge here in the District of Colombia, wrote: "The tribe largely refused to engage in consultations, and chose to hold out for more, namely the chance to conduct its own cultural surveys over the entire length of the pipeline."

Remember, the entire length of the pipeline goes all the way from North Dakota to Illinois. All right, let's go to the third chart. Further, I am going to put this up because the tribe appealed to the court to stop construction on the pipeline. The court said no. They have followed the law. They have done this appropriately.

I think here is a good quote from the judge's decision. Judge Boasberg wrote:

As it was previously mentioned, this Court does not lightly countenance any depredation of lands that hold significance to the Standing Rock Sioux. Aware of the indignities visited upon the Tribe over the last centuries, the Court scrutinizes the permitting process here with particular care. Having done so, the Court must nonetheless conclude that the Tribe has not demonstrated that an injunction is warranted here.

So the Judge says that he came into reviewing the Corps process trying to find if they had not covered all the bases properly. He came with a mindset to make sure they had exercised due diligence. He said they had.

In the spring of 2016, I helped arrange meetings between Colonel Henderson—COL John Henderson is the district director from Omaha, NE, for our district—and the Standing Rock Sioux Tribe, at the request of the Standing Rock Sioux Tribe. It was during these meetings that Army Corps Colonel Henderson imposed additional conditions on the pipeline, including a double-walled piping in response to tribal concerns about environmental safety. So he is now adding additional features after that consultation.

A tribal monitoring plan has also been required, which requires Dakota Access to allow tribal monitors at certain sites when construction is occurring. So he added even more conditions after further consultation. In July 2016, the Army Corps issued its final environmental assessment, which concluded with a "Finding of No Significant Impact" and "No Historic Properties Affected" determinations.

The environmental assessment establishes that the Corps made a good-faith effort to consult with the tribes and that it considered all tribal comments. In addition, Dakota Access has developed response and action plans. They will include state-of-the-art monitoring systems, shutoff valves and other safety features to minimize the risk of spills and reduce or remediate any potential damage.

So, let's take a look at just some of these—just some of these. There are many of them. Again, it is at least 92 feet under the river. So if you had a break in the pipeline, it would have to come up somehow through almost 100 feet of bedrock—come up through 100 feet of bedrock somehow to get into the river.

But if you did have a rupture, you have automatic shutoff valves that are monitored 24 hours a day, 7 days a week. Remember that additional condition that the Corps added after consultation? It is a double-walled pipe. So it is a double-walled pipe.

These are just some of the safety features. In addition, the Army Corps required the company to implement numerous mitigation plans, including: One, an environmental construction plan; two, a stormwater pollution prevention plan; three, a spill prevention, control, and countermeasure plan; four, a horizontal directional drilling construction plan; five, a horizontal directional drilling contingency plan; six, an unanticipated cultural resources discovery plan; seven, a geographical response plan; eight, a facility response plan; and, nine, a tribal monitoring plan, among other measures. Those are just some of them.

So let's talk about the protests. The Obama administration's inaction on the final Federal easement crossing the Missouri River has created undue hardship and uncertainty for area residents, for private landowners, for our farmers and ranchers that live and work in the area, for tribal members, for construction workers who have been chased off the construction site by protesters, and certainly for our law enforcement personnel who have had to be out there day and night for months.

Now we have winter weather conditions. Recently, with a very severe snowstorm, you have really life-threatening conditions out there for somebody who is trying to camp out in the middle of winter. Since the protests started earlier this year, State and local agencies have been put to the test in maintaining public safety, which have been threatened by ongoing and often violent protest activity.

There have been instances of trespassing, vandalism, and theft. Construction equipment has been set on fire. Workers have been chased off the work site. Workers who were just trying to lawfully do their job were chased off the work site. Fires were started on privately owned ranchland. This is not on the reservation. It is on private land. Residents have endured the challenges caused by roads being blocked or closed, either by protest activity. They have shut down highways. Protest activities have shut down highways. Roads are being blocked or closed by protest activity that has shut down roads or by law enforcement's response to ensure safety, at a time when farmers and ranchers are busy harvesting, hauling hay, shipping calves, and moving their herds from summer pastures.

In addition, law enforcement is investigating cases of butchered, mutilated, injured, and missing cattle, horses, and bison in areas adjacent to the site occupied by the protesters. Law enforcement has worked to protect everyone. Again, I will emphasize that. Law enforcement has worked to protect everyone. They have been patient, professional, and diligent. They have not used concussion grenades.

More than 500 protesters have been arrested for breaking the law, and over 90 percent of them are from out of State. Over 90 percent of the more than 500 protesters that have been arrested are from out of State, and many, if not most, are not Native American. They are environmental activists from other parts of the country. If you want more information on law enforcement, go to YouTube, "Know the Truth Morton County," which is a Web site that the Morton County Sheriff's Department uses to provide updates on their efforts to maintain law and order at the protest site.

The motto of law enforcement is to "serve and protect." That is exactly what they are doing. So in conclusion, in accordance with the findings of the Army Corps of Engineer's environmental assessment and the court decisions, the Army Corps needs to follow established legal and regulatory criteria and approve the final easement so that construction can be completed.

In addition, Federal resources should be deployed expeditiously to protect people and property in the area of violent protests to help support State and local law enforcement efforts.

As I said, this issue needs to be resolved. It is past time to get this issue resolved.

I yield the floor.

The PRESIDING OFFICER (Mrs. FISCHER). The Senator from New Hampshire.

CONTINUING RESOLUTION

Mrs. SHAHEEN. Madam President, I came to the floor this afternoon to talk about our failure, once again, to go through a regular appropriations process. I share what I know is a disappointment on the part of many of our colleagues that this Congress is choosing, once again, to disregard the regular appropriations process and resort to a short-term continuing resolution.

This will have serious negative impacts on our country's national security and on the economy. As ranking member on the Appropriations Subcommittee on Homeland Security, I applaud the chair of that subcommittee, Senator HOEVEN, who was just on the floor, for the bipartisan work that has gone on. But as I look at the potential impact on homeland security, our failure to get an appropriations bill will have serious negative consequences for our Nation's emergency preparedness, for our transportation security, and for cyber security, just to name a few.

Closer to home in our local communities, it will hurt law enforcement as well as efforts to combat the opioid epidemic. At the beginning of this 114th Congress, the majority leader pledged to return the Senate to regular order. Now, translated into simple English for people who may be watching, regular order means doing our job and doing it the right way when it comes to the budget process.

It means meeting our Constitutional responsibility to produce an annual appropriations bill for the American people—legislation that will allow government at all levels and people from all walks of life to plan, to invest, to build, and to move our Nation forward. But instead, we are again being presented with an inadequate short-term stopgap bill, a continuing resolution that does not get the job done for the American people.

I applaud the Appropriations Committee chair, Senator COCHRAN, and our vice chair, Senator MIKULSKI, and the great work that has been done by all of the members of the Appropriations Committee. Senators COCHRAN and MIKULSKI have led the committee in a diligent good-faith effort to craft appropriations bills that meet our Nation's current needs and challenges, but unfortunately all those efforts will now be cast aside.

As Vice Chair MIKULSKI said yesterday, Republican leaders have decided to "procrastinate rather than legislate." This has brought us to the final days of the 114th Congress with no regular order and no annual appropriations bills. This has very serious consequences nationally as well as in our States and local communities. For example, just on homeland security, over the last year the Appropriations Subcommittee on Homeland Security has crafted a bipartisan bill to ramp up emergency preparedness at the local level to meet the rising threat of cyber attacks and to address challenges in transportation security, including at our airports. All of these improvements and gains will be lost for the time of the continuing resolution.

Over the last year, we have seen terrorist attacks in San Bernardino, Orlando, and sadly, just this last week, in Columbus, OH. Yet, because of the continuing resolution, the Federal Emergency Management Agency will be unable to award more than $2 billion in homeland security preparedness grants to State and local governments. These are grants that allow States and local communities to plan and to practice their emergency response before disasters happen. That is how we cut response time, and that is how we save lives, but because of Congress's failure to do our jobs and pass annual appropriations bills, these preparedness grants will not be able to go forward.

Another area that is a critical national priority is cyber security. Last year Federal agencies reported more than 77,000 cyber security incidents. Local businesses that own and operate much of the infrastructure, from banks to sewage systems, are under greater threat of cyber attack. Late last month hackers attacked the New Hampshire-based company of Dyn, which is part of the backbone of the Internet. This attack on Dyn took down large swathes of Internet all across the globe. Dyn responded admirably to the attack, but there will be more and more sophisticated attacks in the future. To address these challenges, our appropriations bill in Homeland Security tripled the number of Federal cyber security advisers, and it increased cyber security funds to harden systems in Federal agencies. But, again, because of the continuing resolution, all of these advances will be put on hold for the duration of the CR.

Of course, our Nation faces ongoing challenges in transportation security. To address increasing airline passenger volume and long security wait times, we have added nearly 1,400 transportation security officers, converted about 3,000 part-time officers to full-time status, funded 50 new bomb-sniffing K–9 teams, and added new screening equipment. To sustain these efforts through fiscal year 2017, the Transportation Security Administration needs a funding increase, but under the continuing resolution, these funds will not be available. This increases the prospect of staffing shortfalls, and it means that more and more Americans will be standing in long lines, angry and frustrated at airports across this country.

The damage done by the continuing resolution will be felt in each of our States and in communities all across America. This week I heard from the executive director of New Hampshire's Coalition Against Domestic and Sexual Violence, Lyn Schollett. She and her colleagues across New Hampshire are very troubled by the prospect of the continuing resolution. She told me that crisis centers, which are critical to help victims of domestic violence, will be stretched. They will have unpredictability that will make it even harder for programs to train and retain competent staff. It will affect their ability to serve victims of domestic violence across New Hampshire.

As a member of the Armed Services Committee, I am also very aware—as so many of us on that committee are—of the harmful effect of continuing resolutions on our military. Just yesterday I joined with other members of the Senate Navy Caucus to hear from the Chief of Naval Operations, ADM John Richardson. He pointed out that the Navy and all the other services have lived with 9 years of continuing resolutions. I want to say that again. Nine years of continuing resolutions. Nine years of not being able to count on a budget process that would allow them to plan. He talked about how this chronic budget chaos has been very costly. He said that military planners now operate from the assumption that there will be a CR and that any planning for the first quarter of the fiscal year is rendered unreliable. Year after year, this has resulted in project delays, multiple contracting actions for the same work, and it winds up costing more. It winds up costing the taxpayers more, it winds up costing our military more, and it winds up having an impact on all of the missions we have asked our men and women in uniform to take on.

During the current continuing resolution period running through Decem-

ber 9, the Navy had planned to award $24 billion in research and development contracts, but now, because of the CR, it will award only $16 billion in contracts. In my home State of New Hampshire, the CR limits the ability of the Portsmouth Naval Shipyard—one of the four premier public shipyards in the country—to award contracts for critical infrastructure projects. This can interfere with submarine maintenance schedules, which then impacts the readiness of the submarine fleet. Again, I think it is important to point out that this costs us more. It doesn't save money to have a continuing resolution. That is a whole misunderstanding on the part of some people. It costs more.

Every Senator understands that our failure to pass a full-year appropriations bill for fiscal year 2017 will do serious harm to people in communities all across America. As I just said, as we have seen in past years, it is going to cost us more money.

The Constitution vests in Congress the profound responsibility to appropriate funds to meet the Nation's needs. We have a duty to do so in a timely and responsible manner.

I appreciate—I understand, based on news reports, that the reason we are going to a short-term continuing resolution is because the incoming administration says they want to put a stamp on government spending. Well, that is not the way the process is supposed to work. In future fiscal years, there will be the opportunity for the new administration to put their imprint on government spending. They will have a lot to do in the coming months of the new administration with the nominees and the process of vetting and approval of nominees and with new legislation. Why set up a budget battle 3 months into the new administration when we don't need to, when we have appropriations bills that have been through committee, in most cases have been agreed to by House and Senate negotiators, and we could move forward with that process, just as leadership of this body has committed to do?

At the beginning of this Congress, the Senate's Republican leaders pledged to restore regular order to the appropriations process. Instead, once again we are presented with a short-term stop-gap funding bill that short-changes critical national needs and priorities. I believe the American people deserve better.

Madam President, I yield the floor.

The PRESIDING OFFICER. The Senator from Vermont.

Mr. LEAHY. Madam President, I see the distinguished Senator from Arkansas on the floor. I suggest we go to him next, but I ask unanimous consent that I be recognized when he finishes his comments.

The PRESIDING OFFICER. Is there objection?

Without objection, it is so ordered.

The Senator from Arkansas.

TRIBUTE TO JAMES A. ROSS

Mr. COTTON. Madam President, today I wish to recognize James A. Ross of Cotter as the Arkansan of the Week for exemplifying what it means to be a great Arkansan.

After serving in the U.S. Navy, Jim and his wife Mary Lou moved to Cotter in 1959 to raise their three boys because they saw Arkansas as a State that puts people first.

Jim worked as a carpenter and played a role in the construction of many buildings in Cotter, Mountain Home, and other areas in North Central Arkansas. Until his retirement, he worked tirelessly to ensure the success and stability of his family, his church, and his community.

Jim is a popular guy in Cotter. He has always been an active member of the community. He served as the Cotter school board secretary and worked to help build the current Cotter City Hall. Additionally, Jim has served as a deacon for First Baptist Church in Cotter for over 40 years.

Jim and Mary Lou have been married for over 64 years. Jim now spends his time enjoying his three children and a number of grandchildren and great-grandchildren. In fact, it was one of those grandkids, Cameron, who nominated Jim for Arkansan of the Week. In his nomination, Cameron wrote:

Jim's faith drives his every move, and at 86-years-old, he still gives as much back to the community as he possibly can. On any given day you can find him driving around town waving at passersby, or working in his garden in front of his green-and-brown house with sunflowers painted on it.

Cameron continued:

Jim Ross is a great Arkansan, not because he has done one major thing, but because he has done countless little things to further his city, his state, and his nation.

I couldn't agree more. Jim truly embodies what it means to be the Arkansan of the Week. We could all take a few lessons from him about commitment to faith, family, and community. Jim and Mary Lou came to Arkansas because they saw it as a State that puts people first, and it is people like Jim who make that recognition a reality.

Madam President, I yield the floor.

The PRESIDING OFFICER. The Senator from Vermont.

APPROPRIATIONS

Mr. LEAHY. Madam President, first, I should note how much I agree with the senior Senator from New Hampshire and her comments about the appropriations process. I mentioned on the floor yesterday that in the Appropriations Committee, we reported 12 bills, including the State and foreign operations bill. It passed, 30 to 0. It and the other bills have now been put on a shelf to collect dust by the House Republican leadership. We will probably never get a chance to vote on them. By doing so, by deciding to put the government on autopilot and drafting another continuing resolution instead, they will reduce by almost $500 million the amount that the Senate provided for fiscal year 2017 for the security of our diplomats and embassies abroad. It is very similar to what the House did when they refused to support the Senate's higher amount for embassy security prior to the Benghazi attack. They didn't want to admit it, as they spent tens of millions of dollars of taxpayers' money investigating the lack of security in Benghazi, blaming everyone but themselves. It will be interesting to see if they acknowledge that they are again cutting funds for embassy security.

PRESIDENT-ELECT'S BUSINESS DEALINGS

Mr. LEAHY. Madam President, on another matter, I have noted for months, actually for years, in the lead-up to the November 8 election, that congressional Republicans spent millions of taxpayers' dollars to air their unsubstantiated concerns about corruption at the highest levels of our government. If they were trying to get on television doing it, we might want to take a look at what they said. They said the Clinton Foundation should be dissolved, notwithstanding the amount of good work it is doing around the world. Every action, every meeting, every activity of the Clinton Foundation should be revealed, they said. We cannot allow such a foundation to run so close to the Oval Office, they said.

So it is ironic, sadly ironic, actually it is madly ironic, that since November 8, I have heard neither a shout nor a whisper from congressional Republicans echoing the same concerns about our President-elect's personal and profitable business dealings. No outrage that the President-elect's family may charge the American taxpayers millions of dollars to rent space for the Secret Service at Trump Tower. No demand that the President-elect—the chairman and president of The Trump Corporation—dissolve the interests he owns. Today we hear how the President-elect plans to address these conflicts of interest which he calls a "visual" problem rather than an ethical one. But unless he does what I and others have called for—divest his interest in and sever his relationship to the Trump Organization and put the proceeds in a true blind trust—it is nothing more than lipservice. Until we know more about what role his family will have, both in his business interests and the government's operation under a Trump administration, no one should

consider this serious concern as addressed.

And here is the duplicity of congressional Republicans' double standard. After years of partisan witch hunts and millions of wasted taxpayer dollars investigating bogus allegations against Hillary Clinton, and by extension the Clinton Foundation, if they fail to demand the same of Donald Trump that they demanded of her, they will, as E.J. Dionne said so eloquently in his column in the Washington Post, "be fully implicated in any Trump scandal that results from a shameful and partisan double standard."

Madam President, I am hearing from Vermonters. They are worried. They are uncertain. Some of them are scared. Congress could do a great service to all our constituents if it led by example, not just by convenient spoken platitudes that might give you a few seconds on the evening news. If my colleagues want to actually be the leaders that they claim they are, do not start by validating an offensive and dangerous double standard. Have the same standard for Republicans as you do for Democrats. You can't condemn Democrats on something but say it is perfectly okay if Republicans do it. It doesn't work that way.

Madam President, I ask unanimous consent that the column from the Washington Post of November 27, 2016, by E.J. Dionne entitled "An ethical double standard for Trump—and the GOP?" be printed in the RECORD.

There being no objection, the material was ordered to be printed in the RECORD, as follows:

[From the Washington Post, Nov. 27, 2016]

AN ETHICAL DOUBLE STANDARD FOR TRUMP—AND THE GOP?

(By E.J. Dionne Jr.)

Republicans are deeply concerned about ethics in government and the vast potential for corruption stemming from conflicts of interest. We know this because of the acute worries they expressed over how these issues could have cast a shadow over a Hillary Clinton presidency.

"If Hillary Clinton wins this election and they don't shut down the Clinton Foundation and come clean with all of its past activities, then there's no telling the kind of corruption that you might see out of the Clinton White House," Sen. Tom Cotton (R-Ark.) told conservative talk show host Hugh Hewitt.

Presumably Cotton will take the lead in advising Donald Trump to "shut down" his business activities and "come clean" on what came before. Surely Cotton wants to be consistent.

The same must be true of Reince Priebus, the Republican National Committee chair whom Trump tapped as his chief of staff. "When that 3 a.m. phone call comes, Americans deserve to have a president on the line who is not compromised by foreign donations," Priebus said earnestly in a statement on Aug. 18.

Priebus, you would think, believes this even more strongly about a president whose enterprises might reap direct profits for himself or members of his family from foreign businesses or governments. Priebus must

thus be hard at work right now on a plan for Trump to sell off his assets.

"The deals that she and her husband were pocketing—hundreds of thousands of foreign money," Rep. Darrell Issa (R-Calif.) told the Breitbart website, the right-wing outlet once led by the soon-to-be White House chief strategist, Stephen K. Bannon. Issa added that Clinton wanted her activities "to be behind closed doors" and "did that because she doesn't know where the line is."

We can assume that Issa will press the president-elect about the dangers of doing business deals "behind closed doors" and instruct him about where the ethical "line" should be.

And it would be truly heartening to know that Rep. Jason Chaffetz (R-Utah), a vociferous critic of the Clinton Foundation ("There's a connection between what the foundation is doing and what the secretary of state's office is doing"), plans to apply the same benchmarks to Trump.

After all, when the chairman of the House Oversight and Government Reform Committee was asked last August on CNN if Trump should release his tax returns, his answer was both colorful and unequivocal. "If you're going to run and try to become the president of the United States," Chaffetz replied, "you're going to have to open up your kimono and show everything, your tax returns, your medical records. You are . . . just going to have to do that."

I eagerly await Chaffetz's news conference reiterating his kimono policy, since he made very clear that he sees his role as nonpartisan. "My job is not to be a cheerleader for the president," he said. "My job is to hold them accountable and to provide that oversight. That's what we do." Early, comprehensive hearings on the problems Trump's business dealings would pose to his independence and trustworthiness as our commander in chief would be a fine way to prove Chaffetz meant this.

Republicans did an extraordinary job raising doubts about Clinton—helped, we learned courtesy of The Post, by a Russian disinformation campaign. Does the GOP want to cast itself as a band of hypocrites who cared not at all about ethics and were simply trying to win an election?

APPROPRIATIONS

Mr. LEAHY. I do not see anybody else seeking recognition, but let me just say just a little bit more on these issues. Yesterday I commended my Republican colleague, Senator McCain. He complained about the decision of his own party to do away with regular order in our appropriations process. He's absolutely right. We should have debated and passed those bills the way we used to do. Ten months ago that's what the Republican leadership said they wanted to do, and they are in control here. And we worked hard in the Appropriations Committee, Republicans and Democrats together, and reported out all our appropriations bills. Hundreds and hundreds of hours of work by members, even more by their staffs.

Almost every one of these bills was bipartisan, and they passed usually by a unanimous vote or close to it. All that goes for naught. I commented about just one of these, and of course that is the State and foreign operations bill. Both before Benghazi and since Benghazi, the Republican chairman of the subcommittee and I have put in money, a considerable amount of money, for the security of our embassies and our personnel abroad. Rather than acknowledge their own responsibility for having cut funding for security prior to Benghazi, the House Republicans wasted tens of millions of dollars on hearings to blame the administration. Madam President, maybe double standards make for a sound bite on the evening news, especially if it sounds good and the people putting it on haven't done the research to find out what's really going on.

But it's no consolation to the men and women serving at our embassies and throughout the world to represent the American people. Oftentimes in danger, as we just saw within the last couple of days in the Philippines. It does them no good to see Congress spend tens of millions of dollars to decry the lack of security, tens of millions of taxpayers' dollars on hearings that proved nothing, to get on television for political purposes, and then scrapping the appropriations bills and supporting instead a continuing resolution that will cut funds for embassy security by half a billion dollars.

Madam President, I suggest the absence of a quorum.

The PRESIDING OFFICER. The clerk will call the roll.

The senior assistant legislative clerk proceeded to call the roll.

Mr. GRASSLEY. Madam President, I ask unanimous consent that the order for the quorum call be rescinded.

The PRESIDING OFFICER. Without objection, it is so ordered.

UNANIMOUS CONSENT REQUEST— H.R. 5963

Mr. GRASSLEY. Madam President, soon I will offer a unanimous consent request with regard to a bill that would reform and reauthorize Federal juvenile justice programs. This bill is known as the Supporting Youth Opportunity and Preventing Delinquency Act of 2016. It passed the other Chamber last month by a vote of 382–29.

The bipartisan House bill is modeled closely to one that I introduced over a year ago with the Senator from Rhode Island, Mr. WHITEHOUSE. That legislation was titled the "Juvenile Justice and Delinquency Prevention Reauthorization Act." It has 19 Senate cosponsors and cleared the Senate Judiciary Committee, which I chair, without a single dissenting vote last year. The House companion before us today also won the unanimous approval of a committee in the other Chamber before passing the House with overwhelming support a few weeks ago.

The two bills are remarkably similar in most respects, indicating their ob-

jectives. One such objective is to extend the Juvenile Justice and Delinquency Prevention Act for 5 more years. That Federal statute was last reauthorized in 2002, and it is long overdue for an update. Congress is still funding juvenile justice programs that expired in 2007, nearly a decade ago.

I think my colleagues know of the hard work of Senator ENZI, chairman of the Budget Committee, and a program that he has of the hundreds of billions of dollars of taxpayer money we are spending that has not been authorized by the authorizing committees. So getting a lot of bills that have expired reauthorized is in the spirit of what Senator ENZI is trying to promote among the 15, 16, or however many committees we have in the Senate that don't do their work on a regular basis.

The centerpiece of the 1974 act is its core protections for youth. Over 40 years ago, Congress committed to making Federal grants available to States that observed these core protections, of which there are now four.

The first core protection discourages the detention of children and youth for extremely minor infractions, such as truancy, underage tobacco use, disobeying parents, and running away. No State would ever jail an adult; that is an important emphasis. No State would ever jail an adult for this same conduct. And research shows that nothing much positive comes out of locking up children for conduct that isn't even criminal.

The second core protection calls for juveniles to be kept out of adult facilities except in certain very rare instances. The third calls for juveniles to be separated from adults when they are held in adult facilities. And the fourth calls for States to try to reduce disproportionate minority contact in their juvenile justice system.

That is from 1974, and those goals are still legitimate goals. Under our proposed legislation, as under this current law, if a State commits to meeting these core protections for youth, it can expect to continue receiving Federal grant money to support its juvenile justice activities.

Our second objective for this legislation is to make reforms to current law so that taxpayer-supported juvenile justice programs will yield best possible outcomes. To that end, our bill reflects the latest research that works best with at-risk children and youth.

We added provisions to promote the rehabilitation of runaways who are at high risk of being trafficked. We included language to discourage shackling of pregnant juveniles during childbirth. After learning that a handful of States receiving Federal grant funds are locking up children as young as 8 or 9 for minor infractions, such as truancy, we called for a phaseout of valid court orders permitting that practice. Last but not least, we responded to

concerns voiced by whistleblowers by adding accountability measures to protect the taxpayers and promote more oversight of justice reforms.

These accountability measures are something I have been working on both as ranking member of the Judiciary Committee and chairman of that committee for a long period of time, not just on the juvenile justice program but on a lot of other programs where taxpayer money is being wasted by having different standards in some programs versus the others, particularly when the bureaucracy at the Justice Department is not policing what States do and they let the States get out. We have all kinds of GAO reports or reports from inspectors general that come back to us saying that this money to the States is not following the intent that was intended by Congress. I think all Senators assume a responsibility to make sure that taxpayer money will go as far as it can. So we worked some of those accountability issues into every bill I can get out of the Justice Department that affects these programs.

Groups such as the Campaign for Youth Justice, the Coalition for Juvenile Justice, Boys Town, Fight Crime: Invest in Kids, among many others, endorsed the legislation and contributed input. We also consulted the National Criminal Justice Association, the National District Attorneys Association, and a coalition of roughly two dozen anti-human trafficking groups that endorsed the legislation as well.

The House bill before us today includes many or most of the same provisions that Senator WHITEHOUSE and I championed, and it enjoys the support of virtually all of the same 100-plus organizations that endorsed the versions we sponsored in this Chamber. The House made a few key changes to preserve more flexibility for States.

Speaking of those 100-plus organizations, I feel a responsibility to them to work as hard as I can to get this legislation passed because they have worked so hard at the grass roots level.

Let me go back to the flexibility we give to the States that the House put in. States that object to phasing out the detention of status offenders over a period of 3 years can invoke a 1-year hardship exception. That hardship exception is renewable every year for an indefinite period, and that is at the State's option.

The House-passed measure also includes a modified version of legislation by Senators Inhofe, Casey, and Vitter in this Chamber. That language would encourage the rehabilitation of youth who are at risk because of involvement in gangs or the criminal justice system.

The House bill shouldn't be controversial, which is why we are requesting unanimous consent to have the Senate pass it today. Again, I remind my colleagues that the other

Chamber passed it by an overwhelming vote in September, after the Education Committee, under Chairman JOHN KLINE's leadership, reported the measure without a single dissenting vote.

I also thank our cosponsors, which include the ranking member of the Judiciary Committee, Senator LEAHY, as well as ranking member Senator FEINSTEIN, for their support of this legislation.

Unfortunately, when we sought to bring up the Senate version by unanimous consent back in February, a single Senator objected, preventing its passage. He has objected to the language that would require States to embrace one of the 42-year core principles.

Before this Congress comes to a close, we have a great opportunity to pass an important piece of legislation to help some of the most vulnerable children and youth in the United States. But it is not only these at-risk children who would benefit due to the reforms we have included in this bill; the legislation would benefit taxpayers as well.

I see Senator WHITEHOUSE on the floor. Before I ask unanimous consent, I wish to yield to him for the purpose of his speaking on the bill.

The PRESIDING OFFICER. Is there objection?

Without objection, it is so ordered.

The Senator from Rhode Island.

Mr. WHITEHOUSE. Madam President, I thank Chairman GRASSLEY.

The chairman and I have been working on this bill since 2014. What we heard from juvenile justice practitioners around the country is that a lot of the policies which had been in place for dealing with juvenile offenders were stale and ineffective and that there were better ways to do business than were currently being supported by this grant. So we have worked for years to get this program, the Juvenile Justice and Delinquency Prevention Act, reauthorized.

I see Senator COTTON on the floor, and he can speak for himself, but I think the crux of today's concerns are that the JJDPA would phase out over time—over 3 years, in fact—the ability for States to take its money. You don't have to take the money, but if you take the money, you have to phase out locking up young people—kids—for status offenses, for offenses for which an adult could not be locked up. It is simply not good practice. That is one of the reasons the National Council of Juvenile and Family Court Judges has supported this bill—they know it is bad practice. Indeed, the members of the National Council of Juvenile and Family Court Judges from the State of Arkansas support this measure.

The bill the chairman referred to that passed the House by such an astonishingly strong vote was voted for by every Member of the Arkansas delegation in the House of Representatives,

and the senior Senator from the State of Arkansas supports this bill. We hope the junior Senator from Arkansas would be willing to take the legendary advice of Ben Franklin that perhaps we should doubt, each of us, a little bit of our own infallibility and give us a chance to let this bill go forward.

If Arkansas doesn't like this, there is a provision that the House put in that allows any State to declare itself outside of the provision under a self-declared hardship provision. That is an indefinite. That is not a 3-year phase-in; that is indefinite. So if the Arkansas courts really want to lock up juveniles for status offenses that no adult could be locked up for, all they have to do is declare under that provision. They may or may not want to do that. The fact that every other member of Arkansas' delegation in Congress appears to support this and that the family court members from the council appear to support it suggests that may not be the case.

In any event, we would like the ability to go forward. We are prepared to move this bill right now. I would be delighted to join the chairman of the Judiciary Committee in his motion for unanimous consent that the bill be adopted.

I would add for the record that these law enforcement leaders in Arkansas have expressed their support for the bill: Chief Alcon of the Mayflower Police Department; Chief Benton of the Ward Police Department; Chief Coffman of the Judsonia Police Department; Chief Harvey of the Lowell Police Department; Chief Kizer of the Bryant Police Department; Chief Lane of the Benton Police Department; Chief Reid of the Glenwood Police Department; Chief Sims of the Dardanelle Police Department; and Sheriff Sims of the Lafayette County Sheriff's Office.

Madam President, I yield the floor.

The PRESIDING OFFICER. The Senator from Iowa.

Mr. GRASSLEY. Madam President, I see my colleague from Arkansas on the floor. He is right so many times; I am sorry that we disagree on this issue. I don't believe the Senator will make me wrong on that point, but I do want to respect his right. He is such a good legislator.

Madam President, I ask unanimous consent that the Senate proceed to the immediate consideration of Calendar No. 649, H.R. 5963. I further ask that the bill be considered read a third time and passed and the motion to reconsider be considered made and laid upon the table.

The PRESIDING OFFICER. Is there objection?

The Senator from Arkansas.

Mr. COTTON. Madam President, reserving the right to object, I share mutual esteem with the Senator from Iowa. I hate to find myself on the opposite side of an issue with him. We had

this conversation in February as well, almost 9 months ago.

There are many fine provisions in this legislation, as the chairman of the Judiciary Committee outlined, including his legendary work on holding agencies and recipients of Federal funds accountable and working with the GAO to ferret out fraud and abuses.

My objection to this legislation is very specific. It is not, as the Senator from Rhode Island said, about the jailing of juveniles for so-called status offenses; that is, for something a juvenile would do—such as smoking cigarettes, running away from home, skipping school—that wouldn't be a crime if you were 18 years old. So for all these young pages down here who are not supposed to be smoking cigarettes, the law currently says you cannot put them in jail for smoking cigarettes—and you shouldn't smoke cigarettes regardless. However, if a juvenile goes before a juvenile judge and the juvenile judge issues a valid court order and tells him "Don't smoke any more cigarettes, don't skip school, and don't run away from home" and that juvenile flaunts the authority of the judge, that judge needs some mechanism to enforce his orders. That is no longer a status offense; that is contempt of court. In my many conversations with Arkansans—be it judges, prosecutors, parents, or public defenders—they have said repeatedly that the judge needs that authority to get the attention of that juvenile delinquent.

I want this legislation to pass, as I said 9 months ago in a colloquy with the Senator from Rhode Island. I thought we had an agreement worked out about a provision on the inherent authority of judges. It didn't work out, but we worked together in good faith on it. On multiple occasions, I worked with the chairman of the Judiciary Committee to resolve some of these issues.

Some activists say that we shouldn't do this to kids who are so young, so I proposed an age floor in the teenage years. Some say they might be corrupted or hardened by even more hardcore juvenile delinquents in a detention facility. I said let's impose a separation requirement. Some activists have said that they could be detained indefinitely. I said that is fine too; let's put a time limit on how long they can be detained. But repeatedly we have been told this legislation cannot be changed.

I would submit to the Senate that these are all small, reasonable changes that would allow this legislation to move forward quickly in the Senate here in these final couple weeks and again on the suspension calendar in the House of Representatives. But when Arkansans have specifically passed justice reform legislation in recent years in our legislature and they retained this authority of juvenile judges not to detain delinquents for their status offenses but because they disobeyed a valid court order, I don't think we in Washington should dictate a single one-size-fits-all solution for every State in the Union.

This legislation or legislation like it has come before the Senate multiple times in recent years, and every time it is hung up on this specific issue. I want to protect Arkansas' interests. I want to ensure that judges can enforce their own orders. I want to do what is best for the people of my State and our criminal justice system. I also want to pass this legislation. So I would offer to both proponents of this legislation that we continue to try to address some of these proposals I have made, but until then, I am going to have to, regrettably, object.

The PRESIDING OFFICER. Objection is heard.

Mr. GRASSLEY. Madam President, I am disappointed that the Senator from Arkansas continues to impose the only remaining roadblock to passage of this critical piece of legislation.

Back in February, Senator COTTON indicated a willingness to work with Senator WHITEHOUSE and me to resolve our sole point of disagreement. Senator CORNYN tried to resolve our differences as well. As you can see, we are still at an impasse.

Our disagreement stems from a 42-year-old provision of the federal juvenile justice law that encourages States to phase out the detention of children who commit infractions, such as running away from home, skipping school, disobeying parents, or underage tobacco use. This statutory provision—which has been on the books since 1974—extends a "carrot" in the form of Federal grant funds, to any State that commits to deinstitutionalizing juveniles who commit extremely minor infractions, also known as "status offenses."

The reason for this core protection is simple: Locking up children for conduct, like running away or underage tobacco use, which could never, ever result in an adult's being jailed, defies logic and common sense.

For example, when you lock up a child for truancy, you ensure that the child will miss even more school and fall even further behind in schoolwork. At the same time you have done little, if anything, to resolve the underlying issue that led to the truancy. Similarly, very little is accomplished by locking up a repeat runaway who is being abused at home.

I urge my colleague to consider what happens when a judge sends an especially young child, who has committed the most minor infraction, known as a "status offense," in juvenile detention with hardened or violent offenders. That young child, who has committed no crime whatsoever, is particularly vulnerable to abuse by older juveniles in detention.

Consider, too, that some of these children come from broken homes or have mental health issues. They are among the most vulnerable members of our communities and need our help. They don't need to be dumped in a detention facility where they will be exposed to violent criminals who have committed much more serious crimes than skipping school.

In the decades since 1974, Congress made good on its pledge to appropriate resources for every State that committed to fulfill the core requirements under the federal juvenile justice statute. About half of the States, recognizing that the detention of status offenders is mostly ineffective and tremendously costly, have made good on their commitment under this grant program. These States have phased out the practice of locking up status offenders entirely.

In another couple dozen States, judges invoke the "valid court order" exception sparingly. The exception is just that, an exception to be invoked only rarely. Status offenders end up in detention only occasionally in these states.

But in a tiny handful of States, some judges send status offenders to detention much more regularly. It has been reported that some of the children in detention for status offenses in one state are as young as 8 or 9. Juvenile advocates have charged that some judges are sending status offenders to detention as a general practice, which has led to calls for reform.

The Arkansas legislature has chosen to retain the option of jailing children for status offenses as a last resort option. This bill does not change that. This bill is not a mandate that would override the State's law. It merely lays out conditions for receiving Federal grant money. Arkansas is still free to not comply with the conditions set forth in this legislation.

I want to remind my colleague that over 100 nonprofit groups, numerous judges, and about 1000 law enforcement officers support this legislation. They agree that detaining child status offenders is not good public policy, based on significant research that points to the same conclusion.

I would also remind my colleagues that judges have multiple other options to hold these juveniles accountable. The other options include, for example, suspending the juvenile's driver's license, imposing fines, or ordering the juvenile into counseling, with or without parents. Counseling and other community-based alternatives not only cost much less, but are more effective than locking up children alongside violent criminals, research suggests.

This one issue is holding up a bill that is vital to help the children in our country.

Once again, I would like to point out that this legislation does not affect

State law in Arkansas. We are merely imposing conditions to receiving Federal grant money. If this bill passes, which I hope will happen today, Arkansas is free to continue to invoke "the valid court exception." So I ask that the Senator lift his hold on this critical piece of legislation.

Madam President, I yield the floor.

The PRESIDING OFFICER. The Senator from Pennsylvania.

STOP DANGEROUS SANCTUARY CITIES ACT

Mr. TOOMEY. Madam President, I have spoken before on the floor about the tremendous dangers that arise from cities across America that choose to be sanctuary cities. Recent events compel me to come back to the floor today.

Just this week, Federal law enforcement officers finally found Winston Enrique Perez Pilarte. Pilarte was an illegal immigrant from the Dominican Republic. In July of 2015, a little over a year ago, Philadelphia police arrested Pilarte, a 40-year-old man, for the rape of a child. He had previously been convicted of drug trafficking, resisting arrest, and theft—convicted, sentenced, and went to jail—but he was released and rearrested. In 2015, when he was rearrested, he managed to raise the money necessary for bail. When the background check was done, Federal law enforcement asked the city of Philadelphia to hold him temporarily, after he had raised the money for bail, rather than simply releasing him—to hold him temporarily so they could pick him up and begin deportation proceedings. The city refused to cooperate, and they instead released this dangerous, previously convicted man who was here illegally, released him back onto the streets of Philadelphia. Pilarte roamed the streets of Philadelphia for a full year, doing who knows what, until just this week when Federal officials managed to find him and took him into custody.

Consider the case of Jose Palermo Ramirez. In 2013 this 43-year-old illegal immigrant was convicted of indecent assault on a 7-year-old girl. Federal immigration officials asked the city in this case to notify them when Palermo Ramirez completed his sentence and prior to his release so they could pick him up and begin the deportation proceedings of this person who was here illegally and obviously a dangerous and convicted criminal, but the city refused. Instead, they released this convicted child molester back out onto the city streets. Luckily for Pennsylvania families, Federal law enforcement officers were able to find and deport him, despite the lack of help from the city.

Maybe the most heartbreaking story is that of Ramon Ochoa. Ramon Ochoa is a Honduran immigrant who came here illegally in 2009. He was caught and he was deported. He found his way back into the United States and managed to get to Philadelphia. Last year Philadelphia police arrested him, and they had him in custody on charges of aggravated assault, making terrorist threats, resisting arrest, and harassment.

Again, when the background check was done, Federal law enforcement officials realized they knew who this was. He was here illegally, he had been deported previously, and he was violent and dangerous. They asked the city to cooperate with them so they could pick him up and begin deportation proceedings. Once again, Philadelphia refused. Instead, they released him back onto the city streets, where he continued to prey on others, and just 4 months ago, Ochoa was arrested, this time for raping a child under the age of 13.

How can this possibly happen? How can this possibly happen, that a city would knowingly, willfully, and repeatedly choose to release dangerous criminals, including child molesters who don't even have a right to be in the United States in the first place because they came here illegally? It is just unbelievable, but this is what is happening, and it happens because Philadelphia is a sanctuary city. Let's be clear about what that means. That means it is the legal policy of the city of Philadelphia to forbid local law enforcement from even cooperating, even sharing information with Federal immigration officials when the person in question came here illegally. In many cases, we confer this special legal privilege on dangerous, violent criminals because they came here illegally. It is unbelievable.

This isn't the police's fault. Police would much rather be cooperating with Federal immigration officials. They are not allowed to because local politicians in cities across America have decided they will not allow it to take place. This is absurd. This is very dangerous, and small children in my State are paying the price for this.

This is why earlier this year I introduced legislation, which is called the Stop Dangerous Sanctuary Cities Act, and it would solve this problem. It does it with two components. The first is to eliminate the perceived, and understandably perceived, legal liability that communities have, municipalities have, and here is the nature of their concern. There is a court order that says if the Department of Homeland Security issues a detainer request—the request that you detain a person who is here illegally that they believe is violent—and you comply with that request, you detain the person, and it turns out the Department of Homeland Security had the wrong guy, the concern on the part of our municipalities is they can be sued for that.

My legislation solves that problem. It says: In a case like that, where a municipality complies with a bona fide detainer request, if the person is wrongly held and they have a cause of action they can take, they can do so, but that has to be against the Federal Government. It has to be against the entity that asked for the detainer.

That makes perfect sense, and it completely eliminates any legal liability on the part of the municipality that would then cooperate with these detainer requests and information requests. That is the first part, eliminate any danger of a legal liability.

The second part is, if a city, nevertheless, chooses that it wants to be a sanctuary city, then we should withhold some of the Federal funding we currently send to these cities. Specifically, my legislation would withhold community development block grants—very cherished by the city governments all across America—if they choose to endanger all of us by continuing to be sanctuary cities.

We had a vote on this. Last summer we had a vote. A majority of this body voted in favor of my legislation to bring an end to sanctuary cities this way, but unfortunately we didn't have the 60 votes we needed to overcome Senator REID's filibuster on this.

I am suggesting we revisit this because these appalling crimes are continuing to be committed, as of course they will, if cities keep releasing violent criminals back out onto our streets. In the meantime, I will suggest there is something that President-elect Trump can do when he becomes President, and that would be he could issue an Executive order which would, I think, significantly limit dangerous sanctuary cities.

Let me be clear. The Executive action he could legally pursue would not be permanent. I don't think it would be as effective as the legislation I have introduced. It wouldn't have the legal force of a new law, but it would be a good start, and it would be fully consistent with his constitutional powers. That would be progress. I think it is very clear that we have to act.

How important is the rule of law to all of us? How important is the safety and security of the American people? How important are the childhoods of the victims we are hearing about repeatedly as recently as just this week? To me, the answer is clear. These are very important priorities, and we need to act. While we await the opportunity to enact this legislation, I hope our new President will take the Executive order steps he can to at least diminish this problem.

I yield the floor.

I suggest the absence of a quorum.

The PRESIDING OFFICER. The clerk will call the roll.

The senior assistant legislative clerk proceeded to call the roll.

Mr. ALEXANDER. Mr. President, I ask unanimous consent that the order for the quorum call be rescinded.

The PRESIDING OFFICER (Mr. TOOMEY). Without objection, it is so ordered.

Mr. ALEXANDER. Mr. President, I ask unanimous consent to use the time that I may require and that following my remarks, Senator CASSIDY and Senator MURPHY be recognized.

The PRESIDING OFFICER. Without objection, it is so ordered.

SEVIER COUNTY, TENNESSEE, WILDFIRES

Mr. ALEXANDER. Mr. President, I come to the floor to speak on two matters. The first is the matter of wildfires in Tennessee.

Anybody who has been watching television the last few days has seen the devastation caused by the runaway wildfires just outside the Great Smoky Mountains National Park in Gatlinburg, TN. We are not used to that in Tennessee. I know we have debates on the floor, and we have colleagues who see the fires in the West where it doesn't rain much, a few inches of rain a year, but in the Great Smoky Mountains where I live—I live just outside of the park—we have 80, 83 inches of rain a year. We have dense forests, and this time of year the leaves are all over the ground, and usually there is a lot of rain to tamp that down.

For the last few months, we have not had rain, and so the forest floor is like a tinderbox. On Monday, in the chimney tops area of the Great Smoky Mountains National Park, a fire started—maybe it was a campfire—and then winds as high as 80 to 90 miles an hour came and swept the fire through the park and into the resort town of Gatlinburg.

There were stories of firefighters getting back in their trucks to avoid the bears who were fleeing the fire. There were stories of cars catching fire as motorists drove to escape the fire. A couple from Alabama said they watched their windshield wipers melt on the car as they drove down the mountain. At least four people have been killed and others are missing. Fortunately, by now the fires have been pretty much been put out. There were no fire outbreaks that were new in Pigeon Forge, which is nearby. Gatlinburg had some more fire outbreaks, but the rain that fell last night helped to put most of those out. The small town of Gatlinburg, a picturesque community on the edge of the Smokies where people have vacationed and have gone for their honeymoons, had to evacuate 14,000 citizens.

The Red Cross in addition to other independent groups operated six shelters. The mayor of Gatlinburg told people that his home burned up in 15 minutes. The city manager's home burned down. We have had a tremendous response from the Governor of our State, Governor Haslam, who was on the spot the next day with many of his State officials. There were 400 firefighters and more than 100 firetrucks that came from all parts of Tennessee. There were National Guardsmen and highway patrolmen. The Governor said they haven't seen a fire like that in Tennessee in 100 years. As I said, 14,000 citizens have been evacuated.

This is a heartbreaking story for all of us who know and love the Great Smoky Mountains and the people who live near there. I want the residents in Sevier County, Gatlinburg, and that area to know that Senator CORKER and I—and all of us in the Federal delegation—will do whatever we can appropriately do to help. That starts with helping pay for 75 percent of the cost of fighting fires, and, after that, cooperating with Governor Haslam as the State looks for ways to help individuals who might be hurt by this.

I know the mayor of Gatlinburg, the city manager, and Larry Waters, the county mayor, would want me to say that this is a resilient town and resilient people, and they are going to be fine, but it is going to be tough and hard. Fire always is. But Dollywood will be open at 2 p.m. on Friday, and people will be coming back. They have about 10 million people visit the Great Smoky Mountains National Park every year. We don't want people to stay away, but I do want the people of Gatlinburg and Sevier County to know how much we care for them and how determined we are to help them help themselves so they can get back on their feet.

21ST CENTURY CURES BILL

Mr. ALEXANDER. Mr. President, the second subject I came here to talk about is the 21st Century Cures Act and the mental health legislation, both of which are being debated in the U.S. House of Representatives. There will be a vote on that legislation this afternoon at about 5:30.

This is legislation that has the strong support of the President of the United States, the active support of the Vice President of the United States. House Speaker RYAN has said that it is an important part of his agenda for health care for the future, and the majority leader, Senator MCCONNELL, has said he believes it is the most important piece of legislation Congress could enact this year. One reason it has been successful is that it has been so bipartisan in its making, both in the House and in the Senate.

Let me begin by thanking President Obama and Vice President BIDEN for their strong support and their interest. The President supports precision medicine—the idea of personalized medicine. For example, if the Senator from Pennsylvania and I each have the same disease, we might not take exactly the same medicine because our genetics

might be different. We now know enough about it that if we can help doctors have that information, they can prescribe medicines that will help us live longer.

The President and the executive office of the President have issued a Statement of Administration Policy that is one of the strongest I have seen. I hope it persuades both Republicans and Democrats to be supportive of this legislation.

Mr. President, I ask unanimous consent that at the conclusion of my remarks, the Statement of Administration Policy be printed in the RECORD.

Mr. President, I mentioned the bipartisan nature of the legislation, and I will give two examples of that. My two colleagues, who are on the floor, will give the second example, which is the mental health bill.

This has been complex, no doubt about it. Yesterday I spoke at length on the floor about that. I ask that my colleagues recognize the core of this legislation, which is the following: There were 19 different bills that went through the Senate's Health, Education, Labor, and Pensions Committee—22 Members of the Senate. After many hearings, the largest number of recorded votes against any of those 19 bills was 2. We have a very diverse committee. We have some of the most liberal Members and some of the most conservative Members, and we were able to work out 19 bills that are the core of this legislation on a complex issue like this, and the largest number of votes recorded against any of the 19 bills was 2.

Secondly, every single one of those 19 bills but one had a Democratic sponsor and a Republican sponsor—usually more than one.

In addition to that, there is money attached to the bill. That is very unusual because this is an authorization bill, but the House did it, and we did it as well. We recognized the importance of this to the American people, and we did it in a fiscally responsible way. It is $6.3 billion. It doesn't add a penny to the overall budget because for every increase in the discretionary budget, we reduced the same amount in the mandatory budget.

What is the funding for? The National Institutes of Health will get $4.8 billion for research on urgent matters; $1.8 billion for the Cancer Moonshot that the Vice President is leading; $1.4 billion for precision medicine; $1.6 billion for the BRAIN Initiative, including Alzheimer's; and then $1 billion for State grants to help States fight the opioid abuse epidemic. That money has been accelerated so that all of this money is spent in the first 2 years and all of the Cancer Moonshot money is spent in the first 5 years. Speaker RYAN arranged for this money in the following way: While it has to be approved each year by the Appropriations

Committee, it cannot be spent on anything other than what it has been designated for. So that $1 billion can be spent only on opioid abuse.

I cannot imagine that the House of Representatives, if it overwhelmingly passes the 21st Century Cures bill in a vote, will not complete its promise to spend $1 billion on opioid abuse this year and next year. I cannot imagine the U.S. Senate, which I also expect will approve this by a large vote, doing the same. I also can't imagine Democrats and Republicans going home and having to explain why they would vote no on $1 billion worth of State grants for opioid money when all year we have been talking about what an urgent epidemic it is or having to explain why they voted no for $1.4 billion for Cancer Moonshot when so many advances are being made or voting against $1.4 billion for precision medicine when the President so eloquently made the case of why it is important or $1.6 billion for the BRAIN Initiative at a time when Dr. Francis Collins, the head of the National Institutes of Health, tells us that we are close to identifying Alzheimer's before there are symptoms and we could have the medicine that will permit us to retard its progression. Think of the grief that will save millions of families. Think of the billions of dollars that will save for our country.

This bill has had the participation of dozens of Members of the U.S. Senate but none more effective and important than the Senator from Louisiana, Mr. CASSIDY, and the Senator from Connecticut, CHRIS MURPHY. Even though they are both relatively new to the Senate, they have taken the mental health bill and navigated landmines as if they have been here 25 years. They have worked across the aisle with each other, and they have worked with Democrats and Republicans in the House of Representatives to produce a bill that passed overwhelmingly in the House and will be added to the bill today by amendment. It has also been approved by our Health, Education, Labor, and Pensions Committee here, and I thought it would be helpful today—and an example of the bipartisan support for the bill—to ask Senator CASSIDY and Senator MURPHY to describe the mental health bill.

Senator MCCONNELL says the 21st Century Cures bill is the most important piece of legislation that Congress will enact and pass this year. I believe that the mental health bill, which has three parts that we will enact this year—a part from our committee and part from judiciary—is the most significant piece of mental health legislation in terms of reforms of programs that the Congress will have passed in more than a decade.

There being no objection, the material was ordered to be printed in the RECORD, as follows:

EXECUTIVE OFFICE OF THE PRESI-
DENT, OFFICE OF MANAGEMENT
AND BUDGET,
Washington, DC, November 29, 2016.

STATEMENT OF ADMINISTRATION POLICY

HOUSE AMENDMENT TO THE SENATE AMEND-
MENT TO H.R. 34—21ST CENTURY CURES ACT

The Administration strongly supports passage of the bipartisan House Amendment to
the Senate Amendment to H.R. 34, the 21st
Century Cures Act, which dedicates more
than $6 billion to implement key priorities
such as the President's proposal to combat
the heroin and prescription opioid epidemic;
the Vice President's Cancer Moonshot; and
the President's signature biomedical research initiatives, the Precision Medicine
and Brain Research through Advancing Innovative Neurotechnologies (BRAIN) Initiatives. It also takes important steps to improve mental health, including provisions
that build on the work of the President's
Mental Health and Substance Use Disorder
Parity Task Force, and includes policies to
further modernize the drug approval process.

The legislation includes $1 billion over two
years, including $500 million in Fiscal Year
2017, to combat the prescription opioid and
heroin epidemic, consistent with the President's budget request. More Americans now
die every year from drug overdoses than they
do in motor vehicle crashes, and the majority involve opioids. The opioid epidemic is
devastating families and communities and
straining the capacity of law enforcement
and the healthcare system. The resources included in the bill will allow states to expand
access to treatment to help individuals seeking help to find it and to start the road to recovery, with preference given to states with
an incidence or prevalence of opioid use disorders that is substantially higher relative
to other states.

The Administration is committed to taking immediate action to lay the groundwork
to ensure that the funds in the bill would be
disbursed quickly and effectively so we can
begin to address these important public
health challenges.

The bill also includes $1.8 billion, including
$1 billion over the next three years, to sup-
port the Vice President's Cancer Moonshot.
The Moonshot aims to accelerate research
efforts and make new therapies available to
more patients, while also improving our ability to prevent cancer and detect it at an
early stage. The resources in this legislation
will support investment in promising new
therapies like cancer immunotherapy, new
prevention tools, cancer vaccine development, novel early detection tools, and pediatric cancer interventions. As the Vice
President and scientific experts have said,
we are at an inflection point in cancer research and this investment could help seize
this opportunity.

The legislation also dedicates support for
other key research initiatives. In 2013, the
President launched the BRAIN Initiative
with the goal of helping researchers find new
ways to treat, cure, and prevent brain disorders, such as Alzheimer's disease, epilepsy,
and traumatic brain injury. In 2015, he
launched the Precision Medicine Initiative
to pioneer a new model of patient-powered
research that promises to accelerate biomedical discoveries and provide clinicians
with new tools, knowledge, and therapies to
select which treatments will work best for
which patients. The bill creates dedicated
funding of $1.5 billion for the BRAIN Initia-
tive and $1.4 billion for the Precision Medi-
cine Initiative to continue these signature
Presidential Initiatives, which have broad
bipartisan support, over the next decade.

The legislation also includes bipartisan
mental health reforms. These include a renewed emphasis on evidence-based strategies
for treating serious mental illness, improved
coordination between primary care and behavioral health services, reauthorization of
important programs focused on suicide prevention and other prevention services, and
mental health and substance use disorder
parity provisions that build on the work of
the President's Mental Health and Substance
Use Disorder Parity Task Force.

In addition, the bill takes multiple steps to
further the progress made in this Administration in improving the drug development
process. It enhances the ongoing efforts to
better incorporate patients' voices into the
Food and Drug Administration's (FDA) decision-making processes; supports FDA's efforts to modernize clinical trial design; and
improves FDA's ability to hire and retain
scientific experts. The legislation includes
strong protections for individuals' health
data, as well as provisions preventing unnecessary restrictions on the sharing of health
information technology data with patients
and providers.

There are also provisions in the bill that
raise concerns, but that have been modified
from previous versions to help address concerns, such as provisions that allow for the
marketing of drugs to payors for off-label
uses. In addition, a number of effective dates
will be challenging to meet, especially without additional administrative funding. The
requirement to sell additional inventory
from the Strategic Petroleum Reserve, when
added to the sale requirements of the Bipartisan Budget Act and the FAST Act, continues a bad precedent of selling off longer
term energy security assets to satisfy near
term budget scoring needs.

That said, this legislation offers advances
in health that far outweigh these concerns.
As such, the Administration strongly supports passage of the House Amendment to
the Senate Amendment to H.R. 34, the 21st
Century Cures Act.

The PRESIDING OFFICER. The Senator from Louisiana.

Mr. CASSIDY. Mr. President, I thank
Senator ALEXANDER for yielding and
for his leadership, and I thank Senator
MURRAY for her leadership. I thank
Senator MURPHY for his cooperation
and collaboration in passing this legislation.

I will speak to mental health as Senator, a doctor, a family member, and as
a friend of those with mental illness.
Because of these different hats, passing
comprehensive mental health reform
has been a priority since day one. Senator CHRIS MURPHY and I introduced
the Mental Health Reform Act in 2015,
shortly after arriving in the Senate.
Since then, Senators ALEXANDER and
ranking member MURRAY have made
mental health reform a priority, and I
thank them once more for their vital
work to include the provisions the four
of us introduced in the Mental Health
Reform Act of 2016 in the 21st Century
Cures Act.

In some way, everyone is affected by
serious mental illness. This is not a
partisan issue. It crosses any division
of age, gender, demographics, and certainly political party. If I go to a townhall meeting in Louisiana in an area

that is not so wealthy and speak of the
need to address mental health, heads
nod yes. If I go to another townhall
meeting in another area that is very
wealthy and mention the need to address mental health, all heads nod yes.
Everyone nods their head yes because
mental health is an issue in the back of
everyone's mind.

Earlier I mentioned that everyone
has a family member or friend who has
a serious mental illness—maybe not,
but it might be that person whom you
went to high school with and her life
turned out far differently. Perhaps her
marriage broke up, perhaps her children are in foster care, or perhaps she
is homeless. If you think—not even
hard—that person will come to your
mind. The largest problem affecting
Americans with serious mental illness
is lack of access to care.

Just a few weeks ago, I spoke to a
neuropsychologist in Baton Rouge, Dr.
Paul Dammers. He said he sees 15 to 20
patients a day and is booked up to 6
months in advance. If your loved one is
having a mental health crisis, they
should not have to wait 6 months to receive treatment. He stressed the significance of the barrier to treatment
posed by the shortage of mental health
professionals. Thank God for Dr.
Dammers and for all the work he and
the other mental health specialists do
to help those with mental illness return to wholeness, but they need help.
Access delayed is access denied, and access is hampered by a shortage of mental health providers and too few beds
for those with serious mental illness
who need to be hospitalized. Too often
patients cannot get the care they need,
and too often they have a long delay
between diagnosis and treatment.
Without appropriate treatment options, prisons, jails, and emergency
rooms become the de facto mental facility.

Sheriff Greg Champagne from St.
Charles Parish, LA, and past President
of the National Sheriffs' Association
quotes a statistic that sheriffs are the
No. 1 providers of mental health services in any parish or county in the
country. Incarceration has become our
top mental health treatment strategy.
More than three times as many mentally ill are housed at any one time in
prisons and jails than being treated in
hospitals.

Now, it is clear it is time to fix our
broken mental health care system. The
21st Century Cures Act provides incentives to build an adequate and skilled
mental health workforce to expand access to mental health care, providing
quick and effective diagnosis and treatment. Our goal is that the person who
has her first psychotic episode when
she is 18 will be restored to wholeness
so that when she is 50, she looks back
upon that as a distant memory but not
as a life-defining event.

This bill also addresses privacy issues
that keep some patients from receiving

the best treatment possible. As an effect of the government regulation HIPAA—an important law protecting patient privacy—nonetheless, when it comes to a patient with mental illness as an adult, the doctor feels as if she or he is not allowed to share vital information for their care with a third party, even if that third party is their caregiver. A woman I went to high school with has an adult son with serious mental illness, and she relates that she is the one who brings him to the hospital and she is the one who gives him his medicines. Yet, when he is discharged, she is not told what medicines he takes. She is not told when he takes them, and she is not told when to bring him for follow up.

Privacy is important, but when government regulation gets in the way of a doctor and a patient and a family trying to make sure their loved one is cared for, something needs to change.

This legislation also provides incentives to build an adequate and skilled mental health workforce but also to train that workforce to better understand these rules of disclosing patient information. This allows doctors to better serve their patients and ensure they are getting the proper care they need. It also—again, as a physician, this next provision just matters so much to me—promotes access to services through the integration of primary and behavioral health. Right now, if someone with a serious mental illness goes to see their psychiatrist and the psychiatrist notes that their hypertension is out of control and she wants to send the patient down the hallway to see her colleague, the family practitioner, the Federal program won't pay for that. She refers the patient to the emergency room instead. Conversely, the family practitioner treating the hypertension knows that the patient is psychotic. They are not allowed to send the patient down to the psychiatrist on the same day.

Now, in private insurance programs, this is not an issue. It has only been an issue in Medicaid. This law begins to change that. I will note that patients with psychiatric illness die 20 years younger than do patients who have a physical illness but do not have a psychiatric illness. We must do better by those with serious mental illness.

Another thing this bill does is to establish a grant program focused on intensive early intervention for children who demonstrate the first signs that may evolve into serious mental illness later in life. Drs. Howard Osofsky and Joy Osofsky of the Health Science Center in New Orleans did research after Hurricane Katrina and found that you can detect from ages 0 to 3 evidence of a child who may have a problem with mental illness later in life. This bill provides grants for early intervention for the infants and children, which will address the effects of trauma and the

adverse experiences that up to 10 to 15 percent of children under the age of 5 have. A second grant program supports pediatricians consulting with mental health teams. This is modeled after successful programs in Massachusetts and Connecticut.

This legislation does many important things to change how we treat mental illness. By expanding access to mental health resources, clarifying the rules on disclosure of patient information with family caretakers, and integrating primary and behavioral health, the 21st Century Cures Act will begin to fix our broken mental health system and prevent more people affected by mental illness from being denied the care they need.

Thank you, and I yield the floor.

The PRESIDING OFFICER. The Senator from Connecticut.

Mr. MURPHY. Mr. President, I wish to thank Senator CASSIDY and Senator ALEXANDER for being such amazing partners in bringing this legislation from its introduction last summer to the floor of the House and soon to the floor of the Senate. I will say a little bit more about them and their teams, but it really has been a pleasure. I have learned a lot, especially from Senator ALEXANDER, about how to overcome some tough obstacles and pitfalls while bringing something this big and this meaningful through the process.

I accept the premise that there is something fundamentally broken about the way things work here in Washington, DC. Cable news fame and getting ready for the next election all matter way too much here, and it means that there are a lot of big issues, like immigration reform and entitlement reform and infrastructure, that don't get done because politics get in the way. But there are, frankly, a lot more breakthroughs that happen here than most Americans know about, and a lot of them happen on the HELP Committee. There are, more often than one would think, moments where politics get put to the side or temporarily squeezed out of the way and something really important happens here. This is one of those moments.

Senator CASSIDY really explained the contours of this bill very well. So I want to provide just a little bit of the context for it. I have been working on this issue of mental health since I was 25 years old, in the Connecticut State legislature, and I ran for Congress in part because I knew that I couldn't fix what was broken in Connecticut's mental health system without addressing the myriad of Federal funding sources, laws, and regulations that create today what is kind of currently a dystopian web of uncoordinated, misaligned behavioral health care in this country.

The consequences of this failed health care system are all around us, and they are just increasingly impossible to ignore. Senator CASSIDY spoke

about some of them. But it is personal because every single one of us knows someone in our family or our next door neighbor who suffered from a serious mental illness and failed to get the care they need. All of us recognize that this suicide crisis is spiraling out of control. We have seen a 25-percent increase in suicides in just the last 15 years. When we visit our hospitals, no matter what State we are in, we all notice that one of the major building campaigns that is happening is additions to the emergency departments to take care of this tsunami of mentally ill patients who are walking into these ERs because they have absolutely nowhere else to go.

Lastly, for as much back-patting as we have done for ourselves in the last 50 years because of our decision to close mental institutions all across the country, we have essentially just recreated these institutions all over again. They are now called prisons. A recent article in the Boston Globe by the now famous Spotlight investigative team found that prisoners in that State essentially had to self-mutilate themselves in prison in order to get any mental health care. The Spotlight team concluded that "there may be no worse place for mentally ill people to receive care than prisons." Yet we have essentially decided in this country to exchange the old insane asylums for new ones.

Mainly, though, I stay awake thinking about a meeting that I had earlier this year with moms—with a bunch of mothers in West Hartford, CT. These were moms that were at their wit's end. They were fairly affluent. They were well educated. They had learned the ins and outs of this broken system. Yet they still had no answers about what to do with their deeply mentally ill children. Many of them were adults. So, technically, they were not under the supervision of their parents any longer. They were petrified—petrified that their kids would end up in those prisons or, worse, that they would end up dead because there was no way for them to find proper care for their children's mental illness. These moms told the story dozens of times, courageously so. They wept and they trembled with me as they were telling these horror stories.

Yet, of course, for all of the disaster that exists in our under-resourced, uncoordinated behavioral health system, there is lots of hope. Why? Because recovery is possible. Check that, actually. It is not possible, it is actually probable, if you can find the right therapy, the right set of supports, and perhaps the right set of medications needed.

Over the last 20 years of public service, I have met plenty of people who have beaten this disease, who have trained their minds to work differently, and who are leading full and happy lives. The simple problem is that the resources here are just too far out of reach and sometimes nonexistent for millions of constituents living with mental illness.

So that brings us to this moment and how this place actually does work for good sometimes. Two years ago, I approached Senator CASSIDY right here on this very floor, just days after his swearing in, and I told him that I had heard that when he was a House Member, he would come to hearings on mental illness in the House with a dog-eared, wornout copy of a book called "Crazy" by Pete Early. I don't agree with everything in that book, but it is a story of a father who had the same story to tell as all of those moms in West Hartford. I asked Bill if his enthusiasm for this book meant that he was interested in working on mental health policy, and he said: Absolutely. For the next 6 months, he and I worked together to meet with everybody we could find, both nationally and in our States, who could tell us what was wrong with our mental health system, and we decided to do something big.

A lot of us work with Members of the other party on small bills. They are meaningful pieces of legislation, but they are kind of one-offs. They fix one problem here or there. We decided to write a big, sweeping bill—one that would tackle as many problems in the behavioral health system as we could all at once. We had a head start because of our friend in the House of Representatives, Representative TIM MURPHY, had already introduced a comprehensive reform bill. So in August of that year, after hundreds of these meetings and forums, we introduced our own version of TIM MURPHY's bill—the Mental Health Reform Act. Today, about 16 months after introduction, the House is going to pass this bill as a major component of the Cures package, as Senator ALEXANDER said. My hope is that we will have a bipartisan vote here some time very soon.

Senator CASSIDY and I will be the first to admit that it doesn't come close to solving all the problems that people with mental illness confront. Most importantly, it doesn't include new Medicaid or Medicare money to address some of these huge shortages that patients and families face. But it does require insurance companies to stop discriminating against people with mental illness by rejecting claims for mental health at a rate that is much higher than they do for physical health. This strengthening of our Nation's mental health parity law is probably the bill's most important provision in my mind. I am convinced it is going to result in hundreds of millions of dollars in new care for people with mental illness. I wish to thank Senator ALEXANDER and Senator MURRAY for supporting this provision, even though it was at times controversial.

The bill also elevates the place of mental illness within the Department of Health and Human Services by creating a new assistant secretary who is going to oversee all of this funding that often is done in a really uncoordinated way. It creates new programming to assist young children who show the first signs of mental illness. We get at it early. It reauthorizes important suicide prevention programs that have been shown to work, and it clarifies that parents don't need to be totally cut out of their adult child's care—that doctors can share information with parents if it is in the best interests of the patient to do so.

Frankly, that is just the tip of the iceberg. Senator CASSIDY went much deeper. There are a lot of other provisions in this bill that will make it less likely that people with mental illness face continued barriers to care.

Over the past 2 years, this bill has faced a lot of uncertain moments, and that is where Senators ALEXANDER and MURRAY come in. They have really helped us navigate through some tough waters. I give a lot of credit as well to Senator CORNYN. Senator FRANKEN contributed a big section of this bill that reforms the way the mentally ill are treated in the criminal justice system. Senator CORNYN, in particular, helped us overcome a major hurdle in this bill this fall.

Finally, I just want to thank all of the staff people who have worked on this. I want to thank Brenda Destro in Senator CASSIDY's office. I want to thank Mary Sumpter Lapinski and Laura Pence in Senator ALEXANDER's office; Evan Schatz, Nick Bath, and Colin Goldfinch in Senator MURRAY's office. First and foremost, I want to thank Joe Dunn in my office, who in many ways is the parent of this bill from beginning to end, and all the people in our office who worked underneath him.

When and if the Senate approves this bill and the President signs it into law, maybe the most important thing that will happen here is that we will show that this place can work together to address a big problem that really has no partisanship to it. Mental illness doesn't care if you are a Republican or if you are a Democrat. Mental illness doesn't care if you voted for Hillary Clinton or Donald Trump, and it doesn't care if you think you are not the kind of person who could suffer from mental illness. It doesn't discriminate. Yet we do. We continue to push those with mental illness into the shadows. Our unwillingness to fund the better coordinated care system that we know we need is a clear message to these patients that they are something less inside our health care system.

That begins to change with the passage of this legislation. I think, accurately described by Senator ALEXANDER, it is probably the most significant piece of mental health legislation we have passed in over a decade. I can say that maybe there is nothing I have worked on in my 20 years of elected office of which I am more proud. I commend this bill to all of my colleagues.

I yield the floor.

The PRESIDING OFFICER. The Senator from Tennessee.

Mr. ALEXANDER. Mr. President, once again, I want to thank Senator MURPHY and Senator CASSIDY for their exceptional passion, leadership, and professionalism on a big issue. We all will have a chance to support their work when the bill comes over from the House on Monday as a part of the 21st Century Cures legislation.

I want to reiterate what Senator MURPHY said about Mr. CORNYN, the Senator from Texas. He played a key role in developing parts of the legislation that came through the Judiciary Committee and he, like Senator MURPHY and Senator CASSIDY, had to negotiate a few landmines in order for the bill to be considered and included as it has been. I want to pay my respects to Senator CORNYN and thank him for his leadership on the bill.

I yield the floor.

The PRESIDING OFFICER. The Senator from South Dakota.

────────────

EMERGENCY CARE FAIRNESS BILL

Mr. ROUNDS. Mr. President, let me begin by thanking my colleagues who are here today, the Senator from Tennessee, the Senator from Louisiana, and the Senator from Connecticut, for the hard work they are doing to create new legislation that will improve the health care of Americans in the future, but I come today as well to speak about legislation which has already passed that was designed to improve the health care of veterans across the entire United States.

I come to speak in favor and in support of the Emergency Care Fairness Act of 2009, which recently has come under attack by the VA and legislation introduced on this floor. In 2009, the 111th Congress passed the Emergency Care Fairness Act to fix a very big loophole in the law which hurt our Nation's veterans. Prior to 2009, the VA was not authorized to cover any costs of emergency room care at non-VA facilities for veterans who were covered by any type of third-party insurance. That meant that if a veteran had a limited insurance policy that covered even $1 of an emergency room bill, the VA would not pay a dime to cover costs that were not paid for by their insurance. Meanwhile, if a veteran had no insurance and was rushed to the emergency room, the VA was authorized to cover all of his or her costs. Clearly, this made no sense. Under the system, the VA penalized veterans for owning third-party insurance, particularly Medicare.

Leaders in both the House and the Senate got to work to fix this issue and introduced bills in both Chambers of Congress to allow the VA to pay the remaining balance of emergency care after a veteran's third-party insurance was applied. This made good common sense. At the time, the chairman of the Senate Veterans' Affairs Committee, Senator Daniel Akaka of Hawaii, stated the following on this very floor: "The bill I am introducing would amend current law so that a veteran who had outside insurance would be eligible for reimbursement in the event that any outside insurance does not cover the full amount of the emergency care."

Mr. President, congressional intent does not get any clearer than that.

While the Emergency Care Fairness Act was being considered in committee, the VA is on the record as having supported the intent of the bill. Everything was going according to plan and the President signed the bill into law in February of 2010. The problem arose when after the law was passed, the VA implemented a new regulation which continued to deny veterans' legitimate emergency room claims. Despite having previously supported the Emergency Care Fairness Act, the VA reversed course and elected not to comply. This went on for 6 years, and hundreds of thousands of veterans had their emergency room claims denied by the VA.

It was not until a veteran from Minnesota named Richard Staab had a heart attack in 2015 that the VA's illegal regulation was challenged in court. Mr. Staab was rushed to the emergency room following his heart attack and accrued $48,000 in medical expenses. Because he carried limited Medicare insurance, the VA denied his claim for reimbursement, as it had done for so many veterans, even though his Medicare didn't come close to covering the cost of his treatment.

Mr. Staab sued the VA, and in April of this year, his case was heard by the U.S. Court of Appeals for Veterans Claims. After hearing the case, the court unanimously ruled in Mr. Staab's favor and ruled that the VA was in violation of the law by denying his claim and specifically ruled that the VA's regulation was in violation of congressional intent of the Emergency Care Fairness Act.

Part of the Court's ruling stated: "Therefore, it is clear from the plain language of the statute that Congress intended the VA to reimburse a veteran for that portion of expenses not covered by a health plan contract."

This was a huge win for veterans.

Unfortunately, today the VA has appealed the decision of the U.S. Circuit Court of Appeals. This is an egregious dereliction of duty and a clear effort to avoid complying with the original intent of Congress back in 2009. Just since the VA's appeal of the ruling, over 100,000 veterans' claims have been put in a pending status. That equates to thousands upon thousands of veterans who are waiting for the VA to help them pay their bills.

It is a fact that those most affected by the VA's noncompliance with the Emergency Care Fairness Act are elderly veterans, many of whom are living on fixed incomes and have limited resources to pay medical bills. Often these veterans find themselves dealing with collection agencies as a result of emergency care received in their communities. In an era where we know that more than 20 veterans commit suicide every day, with 65 percent of those veterans aged 50 years or older, this is unacceptable.

I want to tell a short story about a constituent of mine who was a veteran that was supposed to be covered by the Emergency Care Fairness Act. His name is Mr. Alfred Dymock. Mr. Dymock is 90 years old, and he served in the Army Air Corps during the Korean war. He flew over 100 combat missions during the war and earned a Bronze Star and Distinguished Flying Cross for his heroic service. Mr. Dymock receives all his medical care at the VA as a disabled veteran but also carries his Medicare Part A, as does nearly every American over the age of 65.

During a 1-month span earlier this year, Mr. Dymock collapsed twice in the middle of the night while he was in the bathroom. One time he hit his head and was bleeding. Because his 85-year-old wife was unable to pick him up, she appropriately called 9-1-1 each time. In both instances, the ambulance took him to Rapid City Regional Hospital, even though he requested to go to the Fort Meade VA hospital, the VA facility where he normally receives all of his care. The paramedics did not want to take him on the 25-mile drive to Fort Meade because they feared he was having a heart attack and may not survive even in that short of a drive. As a result of these two incidents, Mr. Dymock's emergency room bills totaled over $44,000.

After Medicare Part A paid its share, Mr. Dymock still owes Rapid City Regional nearly $10,000. The VA has denied Mr. Dymock's claims to cover this amount because he, like nearly every other American, is eligible for Medicare Part A.

The Dymocks do not own a home. They live in an apartment. They live solely on their Social Security and on Mr. Dymock's VA disability payments. If the VA continues to deny his claims, the Dymocks have no ability to pay these medical bills.

Today, Mr. Dymock is in hospice care with Stage 4 kidney disease and liver disease. His daughter writes to me that even as frail and ill as Mr. Dymock is, he wants to know before he dies that his bills are covered so he can have peace.

It was veterans like Mr. Dymock in Rapid City, SD, that Congress intended to help when it passed the Emergency Care Fairness Act in 2009. Today I call on the VA to drop their appeal of the court's ruling and begin writing new regulations that comply with the law as Congress intended to properly reimburse our veterans for their emergency room care.

I fully understand there is a cost associated with this course of action. Taking care of our veterans and complying with the law in this case is not a cost issue. I believe it is a moral issue, and in this case, it is also a legal issue. Complying with the intent of the Emergency Care Fairness Act is also simply the right thing to do.

Should the VA agree, I stand ready to support them in their efforts to take care of our veterans and to give them medical care which they need, both from the VA and in the private sector.

While we certainly have a long way to go to fix VA health care, I fully believe that implementing the Emergency Care Fairness Act as it was intended is a step in the right direction. I look forward to working with the Secretary of the VA and my colleagues on the Senate Veterans' Affairs Committee on a broad range of initiatives that continue to improve health care for our veterans.

It is my goal to keep our veterans at the center of all we do. I urge my colleagues to join me in standing up for our veterans in supporting the Emergency Care Fairness Act of 2009.

Thank you, Mr. President.

I yield the floor.

The PRESIDING OFFICER. The Senator from Georgia.

21ST CENTURY CURES BILL

Mr. ISAKSON. Mr. President, first of all, I commend the Senator from North Dakota who is a Member of the Veterans' Affairs Committee for his diligent efforts, his thoughtful words, and all he does for veterans on the Health, Education, Labor, and Pensions Committee, and I appreciate what he said and support his efforts.

As a 71-year-old citizen of this country, one who has been in business, has been fortunate to be married 49 years to a wonderful woman and raised a family, one who has been in public life for 40 years, you learn that there are three kinds of people in the world: those who make things happen, those who watch things happen, and those who wonder what the hell is happening.

We have the chairman of the Health, Education, Labor, and Pensions Committee, Senator LAMAR ALEXANDER, who is one of those people who makes things happen. What we are going to do on the Cures bill in this body next week is nothing short of remarkable, but it is an example of somebody who cares and is ready to do the hard work that legislating can bring about.

It is a bill that incorporates many of the provisions of this administration and Members of this Senate, things that have been worked on for years and things that will save and improve lives in America.

For me, it is personal for two or three reasons. One reason is the pediatric rare disease provision. In 2005 I met a young lady named Alexa Rohrbach. Alexa was 5 years old when I met her. She came to lobby me about finding cures for incurable diseases and incurable cancers. She had a cancer called neuroblastoma. She won my heart over. I have her picture in my office. I had dinner with her parents 2 weeks ago in Atlanta at the Rally Foundation annual dinner.

Alexa got her angel wings 2 years ago and is in Heaven looking down today, but I am testifying on Alexa's behalf that the more we can do to accelerate research and development for cures of rare diseases, the more we can make the lives of people happy and long, rather than short and sad. Alexa Rohrbach was an inspiration to me, and I speak today for the 21st Century Cures bill, in part, because of Alexa Rohrbach because if this bill had been in place before I met her in person, she would have been saved from the rare disease she had. We would not have to talk about her in the past tense but only in the present.

The second reason is, there are things I worked on for a long time that are coming to full fruition. One of the measures is home infusion. I have a wonderful son named Kevin, who was almost killed in an automobile accident when he was 18 years old in 1989.

Kevin got a bad leg infection. He had the bottom part of his leg blown off and lost a lot of the bone, and they had to put a lot of replacements in, a lot of metal rods. He had to lie in a hospital bed with antibiotics running through his system to keep his bone marrow from getting infected.

When he came home, for the next 6 months he had to be administered antibiotics daily. My wife and I administered those through home infusion. He was able to recover from this disease at home, in his own bed, with his own parents attending to him. Under the law today, for home infusion to be reimbursable, it is only reimbursable if you are in the doctor's office or if you are in the hospital. If you are doing it at home with visiting nurses or any other way, you can't do it.

What costs more, a hospital or home visit? Obviously, a hospital. This bill provides a way for us to find a way forward to reimburse home infusions at home. It is the safest, best, most efficient, and least expensive way to deliver home infusions, incentivized by the 21st Century Cures bill.

We also know that neurological diseases such as Parkinson's, MS, and Alzheimer's are more prevalent than ever before. They are the No. 1 disease for people my age and the generations to follow. This bill creates a neurological disease registry of all these diseases which have common characteristics to help the CDC in early diagnosis and early treatment. I, as one who suffers from one of those diseases, can tell you the more you learn from one you can tell about another.

I commend Senator ALEXANDER in his efforts to bring that forward so we have a neurological disease registry that works, that we have an expedited review process for drugs of rare cancers in children, and so we do the things we need to do to cure the bad diseases of the 20th century so the lives of the people in the 21st century are better.

Chairman ALEXANDER is a unique individual. He is a former college president, a U.S. Senator, candidate for president of a university, and a great chairman of the Health, Education, Labor, and Pensions Committee. If we pass this bill as a trademark to him next week, it will be, in large measure, because of his belief that if you give everybody a chance to be a part of the same thing, whether Republican or Democrat, rich or poor, northerner or southerner, they will work together to do the right thing for the American people. Senator LAMAR ALEXANDER deserves our credit, deserves our appreciation, and I thank him for allowing me as a member of the committee to have the chance to work on the 21st Century Cures legislation.

REMEMBERING CARL W. KNOBLOCH, JR.

Mr. ISAKSON. Mr. President, I wish to pay tribute to a great American and a great Georgian who passed away last week in Atlanta, GA. The cities of Wilson, WY, and Atlanta, GA, lost a great citizen last week, America lost a great patriot, and philanthropy lost one of its greatest contributors.

Carl Knobloch passed away last Friday. Carl was a personal friend of mine and a unique individual and a unique inspiration to me and many others. He was a gentleman who went to the Hill School, then went to Harvard, and then went to Yale. He was a leading intercollegiate fencer and won an international medal for his intercollegiate fencing ability.

He went into business using everything he learned as a Baker Scholar at Yale University. He went into business. His first business was a drive-in theater in Zimbabwe. His second business was an oil and gas business in Africa. He then went on to build businesses all over the United States of America dealing with natural resources, dealing with gas and oil. He was a specialist in taking companies that were failing and turning them around and making them profitable. Do you know how he did it? He believed that everybody who had helped him succeed ought to have equity in the projects he succeeded in, so he made people who owned failing companies that he took over equity partners so that when he turned the company around, they profited from the work they put in to save the company. That is a great leader of business.

He also was a great subscriber to Theodore Roosevelt's great statement, which he made as President of the United States, which I want to read verbatim:

> The nation behaves well if it treats the natural resources as assets, which it must turn over to the next generation.

Therefore, a great American businessman, Carl Knobloch, formed the Knobloch Family Foundation to take much of his wealth and much of the wealth he gained and direct it toward saving the natural resources of the United States of America. Whether it was our wildlife, whether it was our land, whether it was our oceans, whether it was our plains, or whether it was our beach fronts, whatever it was, where he could save and conserve our assets, he did. He put most of his lifelong earnings into that.

He and his beautiful wife Emily were great friends of my family. Emily will miss him dearly, as I will miss him.

I know America is a better country today because of Carl Knobloch. The environment is safer in America because of Carl Knobloch. The United States of America has lost a great patriot and a great friend.

I pay tribute to my friend Carl Knobloch of Wilson, WY, and Atlanta, GA.

I yield the floor.

I suggest the absence of a quorum.

The PRESIDING OFFICER (Mr. GARDNER). The clerk will call the roll.

The bill clerk proceeded to call the roll.

Mr. GRAHAM. Mr. President, I ask unanimous consent that the order for the quorum call be rescinded.

The PRESIDING OFFICER. Without objection, it is so ordered.

AMENDING THE JUSTICE AGAINST SPONSORS OF TERRORISM BILL

Mr. GRAHAM. Mr. President, I would like to address the body for just a moment. Senator MCCAIN is on his way. We are talking about a problem we are trying to solve that is an important problem for our Nation as a whole and I think eventually for all of those who serve our Nation abroad.

Recently, we passed a bill 99 to 1—I cannot remember the number—that would allow victims of the 9/11 attack to bring a lawsuit under a claims act basically against a foreign entity, a government, for any complicity they may have had in the 9/11 attack.

I just want people to understand that basically here is the deal: Sovereign immunity exists for us. It exists for sovereign governments, but it is waived. If you get hurt by a Federal Government employee, even though sovereign immunity is available to the U.S. Government, we have a Federal Tort Claims Act, and you can bring a claim if somebody—if a postal truck hits you, you can bring a claim under the Federal Tort Claims Act. We waive sovereign immunity in limited circumstances. The same is true if you are in New York or Washington and someone driving a car, working for a foreign government, hits you. You can actually bring a lawsuit. If there is a tort committed against you or your family by a foreign entity, just as long as the people are within the scope of their employment, you can sue.

What about terrorism? We are not talking about car wrecks. We are not talking about slip-and-falls. We are talking about something that nobody really thought of when they created the exception to foreign immunity; that is, an act of terror.

So here is where Senator MCCAIN and I come out. We want 9/11 families and other people who may be victims of state-sponsored terrorism to have the ability to take the perpetrator to court. What we don't want is our government or any other government sued for a discretionary planning function, an exercise of sovereignty in the normal course of business.

Let me tell you why this is important. We are using drones all over the world to go after terrorists. We went inside Pakistan to kill bin Laden. Sometimes these drone attacks are designed to kill terrorists and unfortunately civilians are injured and sometimes killed. The United States is not intentionally trying to kill these civilians. We are not joining with a terrorist organization to kill innocent people. We are actually exercising national security discretion. You don't want countries that are involved in making political decisions to defend themselves to be exposed in court.

So what we have done to amend the law that was passed overwhelmingly is to create a caveat to the law. You can sue a foreign state for tortious acts, but when it comes to terrorism, when a terrorist entity takes innocent lives, the only time you can sue that country is if the foreign state knowingly engaged in the financing or sponsorship of terrorism, whether directly or indirectly. Why is that important? That protects us as we go throughout the world trying to kill terrorists who are trying to kill us all, and sometimes we hit innocent people. It protects the United States in its efforts to defend itself in a very dangerous world. We don't want to be sued under those circumstances. We try to do right by innocent people, but we don't want to expose the Federal Government or its employees to being hauled into foreign courts or international tribunals to be accused of war crimes.

So we are trying to work with Senator SCHUMER and Senator CORNYN, who deserve a lot of credit for trying to help the 9/11 families. Here is what we are asking: We are asking that we put a caveat to the law that just passed, saying that you can bring a lawsuit, but if you are suing based on a discretionary function of a government to form an alliance with somebody or to make a military decision or a political decision, the only time that government is liable is if they knowingly engage with a terrorist organization directly or indirectly, including financing. I am OK with that because our country is not going to fall in league with terrorists and finance them to hurt other people.

If we don't make this change, here is what I fear: that other countries will pass laws like this. They will say that the United States is liable for engaging in drone attacks or other activity in the War on Terror and haul us into court as a nation and haul the people to whom we give the responsibility to defend the Nation into foreign court.

The fix is not the following: The statutes say that military members and CIA officers and other people cannot ever be sued or held liable. That won't work. I don't want any nation state, including ours, to be sued for a discretionary act unless that discretionary act encompasses knowingly engaging in the financing or sponsorship of terrorism, whether directly or indirectly.

You can not fix this problem without making this change. Here is the problem: Every time a drone is launched, every time Americans go in harm's way, every time a diplomatic engages in activity abroad, we are subjecting them and our Nation to lawsuits, potential imprisonment. We need to fix this because if we don't fix this, it will come back to haunt us.

So the right to sue exists, but when it comes to a discretionary act, such as launching a drone, the only way a country can be sued when terrorism is involved is if you can prove the country knowingly engaged in supporting that terrorist network directly or indirectly. That fixes the problem we face as a nation. That would send a signal to the world that we are not opening a Pandora's box. It would allow the 9/11 families to move forward, but their burden would have to be that any government they sued knowingly engaged in activity with a terrorist who launched 9/11. I think this is the right compromise. If we don't change the law along the lines I have just indicated, we are going to create a new class of victims—those who serve on foreign shores under the banner of the United States—and that is not helping the 9/11 families.

I hope that these negotiations will bear fruit and that we can get this fixed this year. If not, next year Senator MCCAIN and I will introduce legislation along the lines I have described. We are not going to stop until we have this problem fixed because it is a real problem for people serving the United States in real time.

The PRESIDING OFFICER. The Senator from Arizona.

Mr. MCCAIN. Mr. President, I ask unanimous consent to engage in a colloquy with the Senator from South Carolina.

The PRESIDING OFFICER. Without objection, it is so ordered.

Mr. MCCAIN. My friend is correct. He and I were both Members of this body the day the 9/11 attacks took place as we fled the Capitol and watched the Pentagon. Of course, none of us will ever forget the horror and terror of that day, nor will we ever stint in our commitment to making sure the families of those who sacrificed their lives and were wantonly murdered on that terrible day are adequately compensated in every possible way for the tragedy—and we can never fully repay them. But it is a reality. None of us will ever forget it. But that does not mean, that cannot mean that we would endorse legislation that would hold the government of a nation responsible for an act that was committed from that country.

We know that today as we speak, in Iraq, in Mosul, there are weapons factories. There are chemical weapons factories designed to attack different places in the world.

I would ask my friend, if there is an attack from Mosul and lives are lost, and of course the government of Iraq doesn't know anything about it, is the government of Iraq now liable, held responsible for the actions of terrorists within their country without them knowing that those activities are taking place?

Unfortunately, there are terrorist organizations in many nations throughout the world, as Al Qaeda has metastasized and terrorism has spread throughout the regions. Acts of terror are committed and innocent people are killed every single day. Does that mean the governments of those countries are to be held responsible? Obviously, I think the answer is no.

What we are doing with this well intentioned legislation, which all of us are supportive of—but what we do not intend and should not intend is to hold a foreign government responsible for actions that were taken by a terrorist or terrorist organizations. We know that some of those who committed the attacks of 9/11 were Saudi citizens, but that does not then necessarily mean the Saudi Government is responsible for the actions of terrorists. Unfortunately, this legislation does not define that. That is why it is so important.

There are several aspects of this legislation that need to be fixed, but the most important aspect is the phrase that says that this nation has to "knowingly" assist a terrorist group. If you can prove that any government was behind a terrorist attack of the United States of America, that government, that nation, should be held responsible. Those who are injured or harmed should be compensated in every possible way, but to hold a nation's government responsible for acts of terror that were taken by individuals or organizations within that country, without them even knowing about it, then that opens a Pandora's box of incredible proportions.

For example, is the Government of Saudi Arabia responsible for the acts that took place on 9/11? Is the government of other Middle Eastern citizens from other Middle Eastern nations? For example, are organizations that exist within—again, I use Iraq and other countries where terrorist organizations exist, and there are many. Libya is another example.

The Government of Libya is not responsible for acts of terror committed by terrorist organizations that exist and are functioning today within Libya.

All the Senator from South Carolina and I are saying is, we do not in any way want to prevent the families, loved ones, and those who have suffered so much agony and pain over this horrendous and horrific attack that took place on 9/11—in fact, I am proud of our record of support of everything we could possibly do for those families, but we are going to invoke the law of unintended consequences.

For example, if we are going to sue—if a nation that has significant investments in the United States of America, whether it be in the stock market or other investments, and that country knows it is going to be sued and possibly have its assets frozen, any thinking government is going to withdraw those assets so they cannot be frozen as the court proceedings go on. That is just a small example.

The other example is our Middle Eastern friends doubt us. They doubt us because when the redline was crossed and we said we would act, we didn't. They doubt us when we see the rise of terrorist organizations, Al Qaeda, ISIS, and their spread. They doubt our commitment. If they believe that because of the actions of an organization or citizens from within their country they are going to be brought to court, prosecuted, sued for damages and held liable, obviously, I think their course of action would be to withdraw.

We don't want our friends to withdraw from the United States of America nor do we want to see long, drawn-out legal cases which, frankly, don't benefit them nearly as much as the trial lawyers.

The changes that Senator GRAHAM and I are proposing are modest. Logically, I think you should not pursue or prosecute a government that did not knowingly—the word isn't "abetted" or "orchestrated"—but knowingly stand by and assist a terrorist group. They shouldn't be dragged into our courts. If we don't fix it, our ability to defend ourselves would be undermined.

I just wish to emphasize one point the Senator from South Carolina made. We have had drone strikes in many countries in the world. Pakistan is another example. All of us have supported the efforts, many of them successful, in destroying those leaders who were responsible for the deaths of American servicemen and servicewomen. It is a weapon in the war against terror, but sometimes, as in war, mistakes were made and innocent civilians were killed along with those terrorists. Does that mean the United States of America, the government, is now liable? I am afraid that some in the tort profession would view this as an opening to bring suits against the United States of America. In fact, we are already hearing that is being contemplated in some places.

I hope Senator SCHUMER and Senator CORNYN will look at these concerns that we and our friends have, especially in the Middle East, and make these very modest modifications, which are modest in nature but of the most significant impact.

Mr. GRAHAM. If I could add to what Senator MCCAIN said, the language we are talking about putting back into the statute was originally there. Somebody took the discretionary function language out of the original bill. I guess a lot of them missed it. The more you think about what we are trying to do, we are trying to make sure foreign governments that intentionally engage in acts of terrorism are held liable at every level in the courts, the courts of public opinion, and could suffer reprisals from the United States.

Let's go back to Libya, the Lockerbie bombing. It is clear to me, the Libyan Government orchestrated the downing of that aircraft. Over time, evidence was developed and lawsuits were brought. I think Qadhafi's people did that.

Right now Libya is just a mess. Whatever government they have cannot be held responsible for what ISIL is doing in Libya, unless they knowingly engage in the financing and sponsorship of terrorism.

Here is the point. We are supporting the YPG Kurds in Syria to help destroy ISIL. They are a Kurdish group who are sort of the ideological cousins to the PKK inside Turkey who are defined by Turkey and most everybody else as a terrorist organization. With some reservations, I support trying to get the YPG Kurds to help us destroy ISIL, but I don't want that help to expose us if,

for some reason, unbeknownst to us, they fall in league with the PKK and attack somebody in Turkey.

We didn't knowingly do that. We are trying to sign them up, a discretionary function, to get allies to go after ISIL. I don't want to be responsible for anything they may do in the future unless we were knowingly part of it.

This is what I will tell Senators SCHUMER and CORNYN. I appreciate what you have done on behalf of 9/11 families. This was the original language that I think needs to be put in because here is where we stand right now. As a nation, we are opening ourselves to lawsuits all over the world. It will not be enough in this statute to exempt soldiers and CIA operatives because down the road another country may not do that. Once you expose yourself to liability, who can be sued is in the hands of another country.

What I want to do is let the United States be clear in two areas. To any country that engages in acts of terror against us, we are coming after you—not just through the courts but hopefully militarily. To our allies and people around the world who are having to make hard decisions, such as Saudi Arabia and Yemen, trying to form alliances to deal with Houthis sponsored by Iran, we don't want to open Pandora's box, that when a country has to make alliances with people—such as we are doing with the Kurds—that we own everything they do. It has to be for a liability, to attach "knowing."

In the case of 9/11, if the Saudi Arabian Government knowingly engaged in the financing or sponsorship of terrorism, whether directly or indirectly, they could be held liable under the law we just passed—if you adopt our language. Without our language, there is no "knowing" requirement. That is not fair to them, it is not smart for us, and we need to get this fixed while we still have time because as I speak, people are engaged in combat, diplomacy, and the dark art of espionage all over the world.

If we don't fix this, we are going to create a new class of victims. We are going to put people at risk of being captured, killed, tortured, and imprisoned abroad. That doesn't help the 9/11 families.

The war started there. It is still very much going on. As we try to make sure that we look backward to address the wrongs of the past and help the 9/11 families, which we should, we also owe it to those who are in the fight today not to unnecessarily expose them.

If you want allies—which we desperately need—we need to think long and hard about the exposure they have here at home because we could be in the same boat over there.

All we are saying to any ally of the United States is, you can't be sued in the United States for an act of terrorism unless you knowingly were involved, and the same applies to us in your country.

Because it could be interpreted that someone from that country or someone in that country committed an act of terror, therefore, the government of that country is held responsible. That is not right. That is not what this should be all about. Certainly, there are a number of government sponsors of terrorism, but the people who are affected by—the governments that are affected by this legislation are also not worthy, or not necessarily, and certainly they will react in a rather negative fashion. We will be opening a Pandora's box, which we will have to close with great difficulty and certainly with great regret.

I yield the floor.

I suggest the absence of a quorum.

The PRESIDING OFFICER. The clerk will call the roll.

The bill clerk proceeded to call the roll.

Mrs. FISCHER. Mr. President, I ask unanimous consent that the order for the quorum call be rescinded.

The PRESIDING OFFICER. Without objection, it is so ordered.

TRIBUTE TO ADMIRAL CECIL D. HANEY

Mrs. FISCHER. Mr. President, I rise today to recognize ADM Cecil D. Haney at the conclusion of his tenure as commander of U.S. Strategic Command and on his upcoming retirement from the U.S. Navy.

Admiral Haney has been an exemplary officer, and he has been an outstanding leader. Over the course of his 38-year career in the Navy, he has made countless sacrifices for our country. I commend his service and the sacrifices of his family, including his wife Bonny, his daughter Elizabeth, and his two sons, Thomas and Joey. I express our great appreciation for his leadership and devotion to our Nation's security.

I first met Admiral Haney in 2013, when he was nominated to succeed General Kehler as the commander of STRATCOM. Over the past 3 years, it has been my great pleasure to work with him, and I am grateful for his wise counsel and his firm resolve to always do what is best for our Nation and for the men and women he leads.

Secretary Carter has pointed out on many occasions that our nuclear forces remain the bedrock of our Nation's security, and as the commander of U.S. Strategic Command, Admiral Haney spent the last 3 years ensuring that this bedrock remained strong. Every day our Nation relies on its nuclear forces to deter strategic attack on the United States and our allies. Admiral Haney has ably led the forces that comprise our nuclear deterrent as they perform this highest priority mission.

He has also been a strong advocate for the modernization of our aging nuclear infrastructure—no small task in a time of capped budgets. His ability to work closely with Members of Congress and his clear-eyed assessments—such as the statement he delivered to the Committee on Armed Services last year that "there is no margin to absorb risk" in our plans to modernize our nuclear enterprise—have helped maintain congressional consensus on the importance of following through with those modernization commitments.

Admiral Haney has also shown strong leadership and provided valuable advocacy with respect to the other capabilities for which the command is responsible. For example, he led the effort to establish the Joint Interagency Combined Space Operations Center, which will become a crucial command and control node, ensuring our Nation has the ability to protect and defend critical national space infrastructure.

Admiral Haney's selection as commander of the U.S. Strategic Command was a fitting capstone to a career of service that never strayed far from the nuclear mission. He began his career in 1978 as a distinguished graduate from the U.S. Naval Academy. Rising quickly through the Navy, he went on to command the USS *Honolulu*, Submarine Squadron 1, Submarine Group 2, and to become the director of the Submarine Warfare Division and the Naval Warfare Integration Group. In 2010, he became the deputy commander of U.S. Strategic Command, after which he served as commander of the U.S. Pacific Fleet.

In each role, Admiral Haney has set a strong example for those under his command by faithfully discharging his duties with professionalism and dedication.

With nearly four decades of dedicated service to our Nation, Admiral Haney deserves our most heartfelt gratitude and praise. So I thank the admiral and wish him the best and also the best to his family.

I yield the floor.

I suggest the absence of a quorum.

The PRESIDING OFFICER. The clerk will call the roll.

The senior assistant legislative clerk proceeded to call the roll.

Mr. CRUZ. Mr. President, I ask unanimous consent that the order for the quorum call be rescinded.

The PRESIDING OFFICER. Without objection, it is so ordered.

CASTRO REGIME

Mr. CRUZ. Mr. President, it was Armando Valladares, a Cuban dissident and poet who was imprisoned for 22 years under the Castro regime, who so powerfully observed in his memoir:

My response to those who still try to justify Castro's tyranny with the excuse that he has built schools and hospitals is this: Stalin, Hitler and Pinochet also built schools and hospitals, and like Castro, they also tortured and assassinated opponents. They built concentration and extermination camps and eradicated all liberties, committing the worst crimes against humanity.

This week we witnessed a powerful moment for people all across the country and especially for Cuban-Americans like myself. Cuba's longtime oppressive dictator Fidel Castro is dead. Let me be absolutely clear. We are not mourning the death of some revolutionary romantic or a distinguished statesman. We are not grieving for the protector of peace or a judicious steward of his people. Today we are thankful. We are thankful that a man who has imprisoned and tortured and degraded the lives of so many is no longer with us. He has departed for warmer climes.

This brutal dictator is dead, and I would like to pay tribute to the millions who have suffered at the hands of the Castro regime. We remember them, and we honor the brave souls who fought the lonely fight against the totalitarian Communist dictatorship imposed on Cuba. Yet, at the same time, it seems the race is on to see which world leader can most fulsomely praise Fidel Castro's legacy while delicately averting his eyes from his less than savory characteristics. Two duly-elected leaders of democracies who should know better, Canadian Prime Minister Justin Trudeau and American President Barack Obama, have been leading the way.

Mr. Trudeau praised Castro as a "larger than life leader who served his people for almost half a century" and "a legendary revolutionary and orator, [who] made significant improvements to the education and healthcare of his island nation." Tell that to the people in the prisons. Tell that to the people who have been tortured and murdered by Fidel Castro.

Mr. Obama likewise offered his "condolences" to the Cuban people and blandly suggested that "history will record and judge the enormous impact of this singular figure." Now, he added, we can "look to the future."

What is it about young leftists, what is it about young Socialists that they idolize Communist dictators who torture and murder people? Fidel Castro and Che Guevara and all of their goons were not these sexy, unshaven revolutionaries on posters in college dorm rooms that make leftists go all tingly inside; they were brutal monsters, and we should always remember their victims.

Earlier this week, I publicly called that no U.S. Government official should attend Castro's funeral unless and until his brother Raul releases the political prisoners—first and foremost, those who have been detained just since Fidel's death. Unfortunately, in this administration, my call went unheeded. Two high-level U.S. Government officials attended Fidel's memorial service yesterday. This unofficial delegation included Ben Rhodes, assistant to the President, National Security Advisor for Strategic Communications, and Jeffrey DeLaurentis, the top U.S. diplomat in Cuba.

Yesterday, when asked about a U.S. presence for the memorial service, White House Press Secretary Josh Earnest said, "We believe that this was an appropriate way for the United States to show our commitment to an ongoing future-oriented relationship with the Cuban people" and that "this is an appropriate way to show respect, to participate in the events that are planned for this evening, while also acknowledging some of the differences that remain between our two countries." I am afraid I must ask Mr. Earnest whether any of these "differences" were publicly acknowledged while Rhodes and DeLaurentis were commemorating the legacy of Fidel Castro. How exactly do you commemorate it—cheers to the tyrant? I suspect that those "differences" were not mentioned in the funeral pamphlet. Mr. Earnest also claimed last night: "Certainly no one from the White House and no other delegations will be sent to Cuba to participate in any of the other events."

Well, that is comforting. Let's hold him to those words. My hope and prayers are that these officials do not attend the funeral. Although I must say, it is quite convenient that Rhodes had a preplanned trip to Cuba this week. Earnest remarked that "Mr. Rhodes has played a leading role in crafting the normalization policy that President Obama announced about two years ago" and "he has been the principal interlocutor with the Cuban government from the White House in crafting this policy and implementing it successfully."

I suppose it is appropriate that the Federal Government official who played an integral role in allowing billions of dollars to flow to Cuba—to flow directly to Raul and Fidel Castro—be there to commemorate Fidel's death. It is billions of dollars that have gone to strengthen the repressive machinery, to strengthen the regime. If a U.S. company or a European company wants to hire a Cuban worker, they can't do it. It is against the law.

It is unlike many other countries. It is unlike China or other places where you can hire a local worker. Instead, you must hire the government. There is one and only one person you can hire. The foreign companies pay the Cuban Government, and the Cuban Government, in its benevolence, keeps 93 cents of every dollar and pays the Cuban workers 7 cents out of every dollar.

Ninety-three cents of every dollar of the billions that Barack Obama has funneled to Castro has gone to the government of Raul Castro and Fidel Castro to fund the secret police, to fund the prisons, and to fund the torture,

while our diplomatic brigade pat themselves on the back as to what enlightened diplomats they are.

The life and legacy of Fidel Castro is no cause for celebration or commemoration. His contributions consist of a ruined country and a broken people. Cuba is almost like the land that time forgot. You can go and see cars from the 1950s—meticulously maintained, held together almost with rubber bands and chewing gum. It is not that the citizens there have a fondness for antiquities. It is that the repressive communist economy has trapped them, has mired them in poverty where 1950s cars are all they have, and where the last 60 years didn't happen, other than the jackboot of the oppressive police state.

I will point out that on this issue I am not a disinterested observer. My own family's experience has been acute. My father, born and raised in Cuba, fought in the Revolution. He initially believed in the principles of freedom that he thought the Revolution was about. He fought against Batista, a cruel dictator, and was tortured and imprisoned by Batista's police state.

Then my aunt, Tia Sonia, who is younger than my father, stayed and was there after the Revolution occurred and suddenly discovered the Revolution was based on a lie. The kids who thought they were fighting for freedom discovered instead an even worse tyrant than that who preceded him—a communist dictator who would line up dissidents and shoot them.

My Tia Sonia participated in the counterrevolution. She fought against the Castro tyranny. I will tell you, when she was a high school girl, she and her two best friends were arrested, were thrown into prison by the Castro regime, and, like her brother, she faced terrible treatment in a Cuban prison. What they did in Cuban jails to teenage girls should not happen to anyone.

This is the legendary figure that Trudeau and Obama celebrate. The night that the news broke that Castro had died, I received a text from my cousin Bibi—my Tia Sonia's daughter and someone whom I grow up with like a sister. Bibi texted me. She said: Fidel Castro is dead. I am glad that I was able to make that call to let my mother know.

I image when Bibi called my Tia Sonia it was an extraordinary moment. My aunt was asleep at the time. Bibi sent me a second text. I couldn't help to think about all the conversations at the dinner table with my grandparents about the day that Castro dies. Texts just like that millions of people sent all over the world, especially in the Cuban-American community. People had dreamed for years, for decades about the day this tyrant would die and face eternal judgment.

The betrayal, brutality, and the violence experienced by my father and by my aunt were all too typical of the

millions of Cubans who have suffered under the Castro regime over the last six decades. This is not the stuff of Cold War history that would be swept under the rug simply because Fidel is dead.

Consider, for example, the dissidents Guillermo Farinas and Elizardo Sanchez, who came to the United States. I had the opportunity to sit down and visit with them and interview them both. They warned me in the summer of 2013 that the Castros, then on the ropes of the reduction of Venezuelan patronage, were plotting to cement their hold on power by pretending to liberalize in order to get the American economic embargo lifted. Their motto was Vladimir Putin's motto—his consolidation of power in Russia, which Sanchez called "Putinismo."

Their plan was to get the United States to pay for it. Sadly, it worked. The year, after I met with Farinas and Sanchez, Mr. Obama announced his famous "thaw" with the Castros, and the American dollars started flowing. As we know now, there was no corresponding political liberalization—simply, American dollars funding a brutal dictatorship. Last September, Mr. Farinas concluded his 25th hunger strike against the Castros' oppression.

Then there is the case of prominent dissident Oswaldo Paya, who died in 2012 in a car crash that is widely believed to have been orchestrated by the Castro regime. His daughter, Rosa Maria, has pressed relentlessly for answers on her father's apparent murder, and, thus, she has become a target herself. Just 3 years after her father's death, the Obama administration honored the Castros with a new embassy in Washington, DC, and at the launch of that embassy, Rosa Maria tried to attend the State Department press conference as an accredited journalist. She was spotted by the Cuban delegation, who demanded that she be removed if she dared to ask any questions. The Americans complied, in an act of thuggery more typical with Havana than Washington.

What does it say of John Kerry and the State Department? What does it say of the Obama administration when a communist tyrant or their police force says: There is a dissident, a journalist who might ask inconvenient questions; will you silence her and muzzle her? And the response from the Obama administration is only too happy to comply—no inconvenient questions about the apparent murder of your father. We have different priorities.

Last summer I had the honor to meet with Dr. Oscar Biscet, an early truth teller about the disgusting practice of postbirth abortions. I want you to think about that concept for a second—postbirth abortions, otherwise known as the murder of infants, which are far too widespread in Cuba. Dr. Biscet has been repeatedly jailed and tortured for his fearless opposition to the Castros.

I asked him, as I had Mr. Farinas and Mr. Sanchez, whether his ability to travel signaled a growing freedom on the island? He answered—just as they had 3 years earlier: No. In fact, he said, the repression had grown worse since the so-called thaw.

Didn't we realize, he asked me, that all those American dollars were flowing to the Castros' pockets and funding the next generation of their police state? That is the true legacy of Fidel Castro—that he was able to institutionalize his dictatorship so that it would survive him.

Fidel Castro's death cannot bring back the thousands of victims, nor can it bring lasting comfort to their families. For 60 years, Fidel Castro systematically exploited and oppressed the people of Cuba, and now that tyrannical reign has fallen to his brother Raul, every bit as vicious as Fidel was.

I was with my father shortly after he found out the news that Fidel Castro was dead. I asked my dad: What do you think happens now? My father shrugged and said sadly: Not much of anything. Raul has been in charge for years now. The system has gotten stronger.

What Obama has done in funneling billions of dollars to the Castros has strengthened tyranny just 90 miles from our shores. Those billions—those American dollars—are being used to oppress dissidents. In 2016 roughly 10,000 political arrests occurred in Cuba. That is five times as many as occurred in 2010. What does it say about President Obama's foreign policy that under him political arrests have increased to 500 percent where they were just 5 years ago? This tyrannical regime has gotten stronger because of a weak President and a weak foreign policy.

There is a real danger that we will now fall into a trap of thinking that Fidel's death represents material change in Cuba. It does not. The moment to exert maximum pressure would have been 8 years ago, when Fidel's failing health forced him to pass control to his brother Raul. Rather than leverage the transition in our favor, the Obama administration decided to start negotiations with Raul in the mistaken belief that he would prove more reasonable than his brother. It is an unfortunate pattern that this administration has repeated with Kim Jong Un, Hasan Ruhani, and Nicolas Maduro. They don't seem to learn the lesson about the brutality of tyrants. The administration lifted the embargo that had been exerting economic pressure and having real meaningful effect.

Efforts to be diplomatically polite about Fidel's death suggest the administration still hopes that Raul can be brought around. All historical evidence points to the opposite conclusion. Raul is not a different Castro. He is his brother's chosen successor, who has spent the last 8 years implementing his dynastic plan. Unlike Cuba, however, the United States has an actual democracy, and our recent election suggests there is significant resistance among the American people to the Obama administration's pattern of appeasement and weakness toward hostile dictators. We can, we should, and we are sending clear signals that the policy of weakness and appeasement is at an end.

Among other things, we should halt the dangerous "security cooperation" we have begun with the Castro regime, which extends to military exercises, counternarcotics efforts, communications, and navigation—all of which places our sensitive information in the hands of a hostile government that would not hesitate to share it with other enemies, from Iran to North Korea.

I hope all my colleagues will join me in calling for these alterations. The Communist dictator Raul Castro is not our friend, and we should not be sharing military secrets in military cooperation with his military only to have those used against us. A dictator is dead, but his dark, repressive legacy will not automatically follow him to the grave. Change can come to Cuba, but only if America learns from history and prevents Fidel's successor from playing the same old tricks.

It is very much my hope and belief that with a new President coming into office in January, President Trump and a new administration, that U.S. foreign policy—not just with Cuba but with our enemies, whether they be Iran, ISIS, or North Korea—will no longer be a policy of weakness and appeasement but instead will use U.S. strength to defend this Nation and press for change. This ought to be a moment where Cubans are dancing in the street because they are being liberated but, instead, if anyone dances in the street right now, they will be thrown in jail.

Obama is sending his condolences to the Cuban people on the passing of a dictator who has imprisoned, tortured, and oppressed them for 60 years. Those are condolences they can do without. Cuba is not a free society. You aren't allowed to speak or worship freely. They tear down churches. They repress the most basic liberty to worship God.

We need leadership to prompt real and meaningful change in Cuba. Valladares wrote in his memoir:

The mass execution was ordered by Raul Castro and attended by him personally. Nor was it an isolated instance; other officers in Castro's guerrilla forces shot ex-soldiers en masse without a trial, without any charges of any kind lodged against them, simply as an act of reprisal against the defeated army.

I have never been to my father's homeland. I have never been to Cuba. My father has not returned to Cuba in over 60 years. I look forward to one day visiting Cuba, hopefully with my dad, my Tia Sonia, my cousin Bibi, and seeing a free Cuba where people can live according to their beliefs without fear of imprisonment, violence, or oppression, but under the dictator Raul Castro, today is not that day.

The people of Cuba need to know that there are still those in America who understand that and stand with them, not the corrupt and vicious crime family that has oppressed them for so long, that has enriched themselves, accumulating millions and millions of dollars in personal wealth, living like emperors and kings while they have oppressed the people of Cuba.

Those in Hollywood, those in the academy, and those in the Obama administration think that communism is about equality. There is nothing equal about Cuban communism other than a quality of suffering, other than a quality of misery, other than a quality of hopelessness. In the Cuban Communist regime, the army acts as the enforcers for the dictators who live opulent lifestyles while oppressing the masses. There is a word for that. It is called evil. It is not simply an interesting way to govern a society. It is the face of oppression, the face of dictatorship, the face of evil. Let there be no mistake, Fidel Castro was evil. Anyone who systematically murders, tortures, and oppresses people for over six decades embodies it, and I have no doubt that right now, today, Fidel Castro is facing the ultimate judgment. That is cause for celebration, and I look forward to celebrating the end of his dictatorship and repressive regime and the return of freedom to Cuba.

I thank the Presiding Officer.

I yield the floor and suggest the absence of a quorum.

The PRESIDING OFFICER (Mr. Lee). The clerk will call the roll.

The legislative clerk proceeded to call the roll.

Mr. BLUMENTHAL. Mr. President, I ask unanimous consent that the order for the quorum call be rescinded.

The PRESIDING OFFICER (Mr. Perdue). Without objection, it is so ordered.

DACA

Mr. BLUMENTHAL. Mr. President, our Nation's immigration system is broken. There would be scant, if any, disagreement with that proposition in this Chamber. There would be no disagreement among anyone who is familiar with this broken immigration system. Far too often, that system is not only broken but violates the essential fundamental values and core convictions of the American people, values that are embodied in our Constitution, in the daily ethics we preach and live about fairness and welcoming people who are different from ourselves, people who have come here to escape persecution in their native lands, much as my father did in 1935 at the age of 17.

He came alone, he spoke virtually no English, had not much more than the shirt on his back, and knew virtually no one. That is the way people still come to this great country, the greatest country in the history of the world.

The immigration system that enabled him to come here is now fraught with strictures and failings and irrational barriers that work against not only the interests of people seeking freedom and opportunity but our national interests. That interest is best served when we make possible the talent, gifts, and energy of immigrants. We are a nation of immigrants, and we should be working to reform the immigration system for our national interest.

No one exemplifies more poignantly and eloquently the flaws in our present system than young people known as the DREAMers. For a while, not that long ago, I resolved that I would come to the floor every week with a photograph of a different DREAMer from Connecticut who would demonstrate with a face, if not a voice, why some relief for our DREAMers is essential to our national interests.

DREAMers are members of our society, brought to this country as children, some before they even learned to speak, but now, for almost all of them, English is their native language. This Nation is the only home they have ever known. They pledge allegiance to the flag in school and at events with their hand over their hearts, just as we all do and just as we begin every day the proceedings of this Chamber. Many of them know and never take for granted the gifts of living in the greatest, freest, strongest nation ever to exist on the planet. They know it. They never take it for granted because they hear stories from their aunts and uncles, maybe even their parents about what life was like in the place they left when they were brought here as infants and small children.

So they go to our schools. They learn skills. They go to colleges, and many go on to higher education. They have skills and training and gifts and talents that would be extraordinarily useful and important. There is one problem: They are not citizens. They are not citizens. They are in constant danger of deportation. They are stuck in a potentially illegal and devastating situation because they have no path to citizenship in a country that should welcome them and make it possible for them to come out of the shadows.

In recognition of those overwhelming merits, President Obama used his well-established Executive authority to institute the DACA Program. Understand that the DACA Program does not grant citizenship, it just defers and delays deportation proceedings. Countless young men and women came out of the shadows and made known their presence to the U.S. Government to become part of the DACA Program, disclosing their illegal status. They are now fearful. In fact, fearful is a clear understatement. They are terrified. I have met with many of them. I have known many of them over the years. I have come to admire and respect their patriotism, their aspirations, and their dreams.

As DREAMers, their dream is American citizenship, which all too often many of us take for granted. Their dream is American citizenship in the best sense of it—giving back to the country that they regard as their home, giving back by using those talents as nurses and doctors to help the sick, as engineers and scientists to build inventions and advance our knowledge, as entrepreneurs to build businesses and employ people and create jobs and drive the economy forward. In fact, immigration reform and these programs are thought to be job creators and sources of economic profit.

The DACA Program was a temporary effort, a respite for them in their striving to gain some permanency and some reliable status so they could be secure and feel safe in this country. Their terror now is well-founded, in fact, because the threat to them from the incoming administration is that they will be, in fact, deported en masse or perhaps their parents will be with them, and the American dream will become a fantasy—in fact, a nightmare.

We are talking about young men, one of them well known to me in Bridgeport, who was brought to Connecticut from Brazil at the age of 5. He studied in the Bridgeport public schools from kindergarten to high school, and then he went on to attend Fairfield University. He majored in chemistry, minored in mathematics. He excelled, so that during his senior year at Fairfield, he was accepted at the University of California, Berkeley's Physical Chemistry Program. But he had to live under the threat of deportation because he had no way to apply for lawful permanent status while he was continuing his studies here in America, potentially contributing greatly to the American quality of life.

There is the New Britain woman who was born in Mexico and brought to America when she was 6 years old. The journey for her was terrifying. She could not understand what was happening. She certainly had no idea that she was entering America in a way that would affect her the rest of her life at 6 years old. The idea that she was here in an illegal status was incomprehensible. Her family settled in Connecticut. She began school immediately in New Britain, and she went through the public schools there and graduated from New Britain High School in 2008. She decided to attend college out of State at Bay Path College, earning a great many leadership positions there. She became the first in her family to graduate from college and then received a master's degree in occupational therapy. She has dreamed about helping people—maybe at nonprofit—to make sure that families with low incomes have access to occupational therapy.

I think, too, of the young woman I know who was born in Venezuela. She was brought here when she was 11 years old. She remembers her mother telling her that she was going to America to learn English. Her mother also told her that she could be successful if she was bilingual and if she worked hard and studied. That is exactly what she did with her family when they settled in Norwalk, CT. She began to go to school right away. Life at the beginning was difficult. There was a lot to learn. By the time she was a junior in high school, she stopped trying to get perfect grades because she feared colleges would not accept her simply because she was undocumented, and even after she was accepted, she could not afford it, but she persevered. She attended community college, which was a huge financial burden. After Norwalk Community College, she went on to Western Connecticut State University. She persevered and she climbed those obstacles that many young American young people don't face, but she pursued a double major in accounting and finance. She hopes to become an accountant and pursue a career in business. But she has no pathway to citizenship or even lawful status. She fears that her dream will be unreachable.

That is why DACA is so important, why it should be extended, why we need to reform a broken immigration system that keeps the DREAMers and all of those 11 million people in the shadows without a path to earned citizenship, why we need to go back to the bipartisan reform proposal that passed overwhelmingly in this body with strong support on both sides of the aisle and then was denied a vote in the House of Representatives. That bipartisan effort needs to be resolved.

In the meantime, the DREAMers should be given lawful status so they can pursue their studies and their careers and give back to the greatest country in the history of the world.

I yield the floor.

I suggest the absence of a quorum.

The PRESIDING OFFICER. The clerk will call the roll.

The senior assistant legislative clerk proceeded to call the roll.

Mr. DAINES. Mr. President, I ask unanimous consent that the order for the quorum call be rescinded.

The PRESIDING OFFICER. Without objection, it is so ordered.

DONALD TRUMP'S FINANCIAL PLANS

Ms. WARREN. Mr. President, I ask unanimous consent that the following statement by former Representative Barney Frank entitled "Trump's financial plans promise another Great Recession" be printed in the RECORD.

There being no objection, the material was ordered to be printed in the RECORD, as follows:

[From the Boston Globe, Nov. 28, 2016]

TRUMP'S FINANCIAL PLANS PROMISE ANOTHER GREAT RECESSION

(By Barney Frank)

Apparently, one aspect of American greatness that Donald Trump seeks to recreate is the Great Recession of 2008. He calls for a complete repeal of all the rules that were adopted to govern the financial industry in response to that crisis, restoring to it the freedom to create unlimited debt throughout the economy, with no requirement that serious attention be given to the ability of the indebted to meet their obligations.

By the '90s, the business of lending had been transformed by securitization. Lenders sold the right to repayment of loans, eliminating their incentive to worry about the borrowers' solvency. The financial institutions that bought the loans then packaged them into securities and sold pieces of these throughout the economy. Other large institutions then sold insurance against the failure of these securities to pay. The use of derivative forms greatly magnified the amounts of money at stake.

When imprudently granted mortgage loans began to default, so did securities, leading to investor losses, and demands that the insurers make good on their pledges. Faced with a shutdown of the economy caused by the spreading inability of the indebted to repay, and the consequent refusal of anyone to advance funds to anyone else, the Bush administration bailed out multinational insurance company AIG, asked Congress for general bailout authority, and intensified the work that it had begun along with Congress to create rules to prevent a recurrence.

Modified by the Obama administration and Congress, these rules evolved into the Dodd-Frank Wall Street Reform and Consumer Protection Act, which was designed to prohibit abusive practices, and diminish the negative impact from the misjudgments that are inevitable in a system in which risk-taking is necessary.

Here are some of the most significant changes that will result if Trump succeeds in wiping the law off the books, with real-world reminders of the "great" financial system he would restore.

The abolition of the law's restrictions on granting mortgages to borrowers who are highly unlikely to repay means we will see successors to Countrywide, the mortgage-granting machine that gave us countrywide defaults.

The removal of the regulations governing trading in derivatives means Goldman Sachs, J.P. Morgan Chase, and others can return to the unrestricted dissemination throughout the economy of securities composed of bad mortgages, even when, in Goldman's case, the packager knew enough about the weakness of what it was selling to bet its own money that it would fail to pay off.

An end to the rule that participants in derivative trades either do so through exchanges or otherwise demonstrate that they have the funds to meet their obligations to

their trading partners brings back the situation that prevailed when three of the five leading investment companies—Bear Stearns, Merrill Lynch, and Lehman Brothers—were unable either to pay their own debts or collect what they were owed by others, and AIG told Federal officials it was 170 billion dollars short of meeting its obligations to pay off what it owed those who had bought their credit default swaps (insurance against the failure of mortgage-backed securities).

This leads to the next result of a return to the good old days: It will put Federal officials back to having to choose between letting a company go bankrupt—Lehman—with its disruptive effect, or bailing it out—AIG. We repealed the provision that allowed the Fed to advance 170 billion dollars to pay AIG's debts while letting it stay in business. It replacement—which Trump would repeal, reinstating the unrestricted bailout authority—empowers officials to pay only as much off the debt of the bankrupt entity as is needed to maintain economic stability, but only after putting it out of business, and with a requirement that no money paid out from taxpayers be recouped by assessment on the surviving large financial companies.

Trump's plan to wipe out the provision that purchasers of loans who then package them for resale to bear responsibility for the first 5 percent of the losses that occur means the investing public will once again be wholly dependent on the rating agencies—whose blend of incompetence and dishonesty was chronicled in The Big Short." (My one objection to the way in which the law has been administrated is the failure to apply this provision to home mortgages, but the power to do so remains in the law if experience calls for it.)

The disappearance of the Consumer Financial Protection Bureau will return to the status quo in which consumers harmed by the abusive behavior of a massive financial institutions could only turn to the federal agencies whose primary mission was to worry about the health of these entities. Had there not been a consumer bureau, Wells Fargo might still be creating false credit card accounts.

I do favor some adjustments to lessen the scrutiny given to small and medium-size banks, although not in the area of consumer protection.

But the major beneficiaries of total repeal are the largest financial entities. I understand why those who believe absolutely in an unregulated market advocate a return to the process that risks repeating 2008. I do not understand how this stance complies with Trump's promise to vindicate the interests of average working people against those who stand at the top of the economic structure.

NAVAL SUPPORT ACTIVITY CRANE'S 75TH ANNIVERSARY

Mr. DONNELLY. Mr. President, today, I wish to recognize the incredible Hoosier workforce at Naval Support Activity Crane as it celebrates its 75th anniversary on Thursday, December 1.

Crane was established on December 1, 1941, as a naval ammunition depot to produce, test, and store ordnance away from American coastlines. Today this Indiana facility is the third largest naval installation in the world and one of our Nation's most important military laboratories.

With more than 5,000 employees, Crane supports not only our national security, but our local, regional, and State economies as well. The Hoosier men and women at Crane Army Ammunition Activity and Naval Surface Warfare Center Crane work on some of our most critical and sensitive military missions. Its dedication and hard work helps keep our Nation safe and ensures that our servicemembers are able to successfully complete their missions and return home safely.

The 750 Hoosiers of the Crane Army Ammunition Activity produce, store, and supply conventional munitions for ground, sea, and air forces. Its expertise is essential to the ability of our warfighters to succeed on the battlefield.

At Naval Surface Warfare Center Crane, Hoosiers support America's national defense through work on our nuclear deterrent, electronic warfare capabilities, missile defense technology, and special operations. Its efforts give our Nation a strategic edge. The technological developments generated at NSWC Crane directly support the most critical components of U.S. national security in an efficient, cost-effective way.

As our Nation faces new challenges from advanced adversaries, the need for cutting-edge technology is more important than ever. The Department of Defense has lauded Crane for its work to ensure we have the most technologically advanced military in the world in new areas like hypersonic systems. NSA Crane has also demonstrated leadership in creating effective partnerships between the military, academic institutions, and the industrial base. These partnerships allow Crane to leverage independent expertise and expand the knowledge and capacity of those serving at the facility.

In June, it was an honor to host Secretary of Defense Ash Carter at Crane, marking the first time a Secretary of Defense has visited the base in its 75 year history. Secretary Carter got to see Crane's innovative work firsthand and called the base a "national treasure" that will continue to be an integral part of our national security efforts for years to come. I am proud to echo that statement and truly believe that Crane represents the best of Indiana's tradition of service to our country.

Because of the hard-working employees and military personnel at NSA Crane, our Armed Forces are well equipped to defend our Nation and support our allies across the globe. Its continued devotion to our servicemembers and our country should serve as an example for all.

I am very proud of NSA Crane's 75-year record of accomplishments and continued dedication to creating state-of-the-art solutions for our Armed Forces. I believe that NSA Crane and its elite personnel serve a unique and essential function for the Department of Defense. On behalf of Hoosiers, I congratulate Crane on this special anniversary and for making Indiana, our country, and our world safer. I look forward to Crane's next 75 years of excellence.

ADDITIONAL STATEMENTS

REMEMBERING DAVID "BOO" FERRISS

● Mr. COCHRAN. Mr. President, I wish to recognize the life and service of Major League All-Star pitcher and longtime head baseball coach at Delta State University, David "Boo" Ferriss, who passed away on November 24, 2016.

Boo Ferriss was born in Shaw, MS, and was raised in the Mississippi Delta region. He joined the baseball team as a student at Mississippi State University in 1941 before signing a Major League contract with the Boston Red Sox organization in 1942. Ferriss's early career with the Red Sox included a 2-year hiatus to serve in World War II. Discharged in 1945, he was called up to play for the Red Sox, helping lead the team to the 1946 World Series. Despite suffering a shoulder injury in 1947, Ferriss played for the Red Sox until 1950, finishing with a 65–30 record as a pitcher.

Following his retirement from professional baseball, Ferriss went on to become the head coach of the Delta State University baseball team, a position he held with great success for nearly 26 years. He led the Statesmen to three Division II World Series and four Gulf South Conference Championships. Induction into the Mississippi Sports Hall of Fame and the Red Sox Hall of Fame are among the numerous awards made to honor Ferriss's achievements. In 2003, the Mississippi Sports Hall of Fame established the Ferriss Trophy, which has become the Heisman Trophy for Mississippi college baseball players.

Boo Ferriss's accomplishments extended beyond the ballfield. He was an active member of the Covenant Presbyterian Church in Cleveland, MS, and a founder of the Fellowship of Christian Athletes in Mississippi. He was a dedicated family man, married for 67 years to his wife, Miriam. They raised two children, Dr. David Ferriss and Margaret Ferriss White, and have two grandchildren and three great-grandchildren. Coach Ferriss will be remembered as a great Mississippian who dedicated his life to the game that he loved and to a generation of players that he educated on the field and in life.

For myself and all those who knew Boo Ferriss, I commemorate his years of service and a life well lived.●

REMEMBERING DOUG ALEXANDER

● Mr. DAINES. Mr. President, in the Capitol in Washington, DC, there is a corridor that highlights the discovery and expansion of America. Just above one of the doors, there is a quote that reminds me of the people who have helped shape Montana, and that makes me proud to be a Westerner. The quote from Horace Greenley reads, "Go West, young men, go West and grow up with the country."

Today I honor a man who was a fourth-generation Montanan and arguably one of Montana State University's biggest fans, Doug Alexander. Doug will be deeply missed as a member of the Bozeman and Bobcat community. Doug was born in Miles City, MT, in 1942 and attended many Montana schools before graduating from Montana State University in 1964. Even after he graduated, he remained very involved with is fraternity Sigma Nu serving as an adviser to the chapter, a friend and mentor to many members, eventually pinning his son Dan with his own Sigma Nu badge in the early 1990s. At the beginning of his career, Doug served his country proudly in the National Guard and was discharged as a first lieutenant in 1970.

Doug maintained adventure in his life, owning many small businesses across the State. However, it was when he acquired Bozeman's Story Motor Supply that he made his way back to the place he loved. It was Doug's compassion for his business and the community that made him such a strong leader and employer for Bozeman. He even joined the Montana Petroleum Marketers Association where he enlisted others to join and eventually lead the association as its national director in 1988 and 1989, where his service and dedication landed him in the Western Petroleum Marketers Association Hall of Fame.

Doug maintained his support of MSU through a position on the foundation board, the Football Quarterback Club, and the Rodeo team, among others. Suffice it to say, MSU wouldn't be where it is today without Doug Alexander and his incredible loyalty to his alma mater. I had the pleasure of being a Sunrise Rotary member with Doug for many years after he cofounded it in 1992. I am thankful for Doug's passion and am thankful that his legacy will be continued by many others in the years to come.●

TRIBUTE TO JAMES "JIM" FRENCH

● Mr. SCOTT. Mr. President, I would like to wish Mr. James "Jim" French of Charleston, SC, a happy 90th birthday.

Mr. French, a committed, passionate, and award-winning journalist, served as a U.S. Navy chief journalist for 26 years. After retiring, he founded the Charleston Chronicle in 1971. His work at the Charleston Chronicle focused on offering solutions for the problems within the Black community and successfully led to receive hundreds of awards from organizations throughout the Lowcountry and Nation.

Mr. French's legacy will forever be defined not just by his work and service, but by some many people he has touched in the Charleston community.

I would like to recognize Mr. Jim French for his service to our country and our amazing State; he truly represents the very best of South Carolina.

Happy 90th birthday, Mr. French. May God bless you.●

RECOGNIZING THE PHILLIS WHEATLEY LITERARY AND SOCIAL CLUB

● Mr. SCOTT. Mr. President, I would like to congratulate the Phillis Wheatley Literary and Social Club, one of Charleston's earliest Black women's clubs, on their 100th anniversary.

Named after a prominent African-American poet, Phillis Wheatley, the club was established by Jeanette Keeble Cox in 1916 as the Wheatley Community Club. Mrs. Cox was the wife of Benjamin F. Cox, the first African-American principal of the Avery Normal Institute.

The Phillis Wheatley Club has remained committed to bringing hope and opportunities to each of its members. This year, we recognize the club's ongoing legacy, and I believe this centennial celebration is a testament to its positive influence.

It is with honor and admiration that we recognize the Phillis Wheatley Club, and its great impact on so many women's lives, accomplishing its mission "to promote interest in literary and community work and to lift others as they climb high heights."●

RECOGNIZING ALVAREZ CONSTRUCTION

● Mr. VITTER. Mr. President, known for their resiliency and perseverance, Louisianans possess great strength and determination when facing adversity. This includes the folks who move to Louisiana and build a life there, such as Jairo Alvarez-Botero, a Colombian immigrant, who settled in Baton Rouge to build Alvarez Construction and has spent decades giving back to his community. For its many years of success and community service, I would like to recognize Alvarez Construction of Baton Rouge, LA, as Small Business of the Week.

In 1963 Jairo Alvarez-Botero came to the United States to learn English and put himself through college. With the mindset that there is "no such thing as impossible," Jairo graduated from Albany Business College with honors and returned to his home country of Colombia to start a family. However, as the country's political and economic stability continued to waver, in the early 1980s, Jairo and his wife, Anita, decided to immigrate to the United States to provide a brighter future for their three children, Carlos, Ana, and Sebastian.

Landing in Baton Rouge, the Alvarez family tried several business ventures before finding success in construction. In 1991, Jairo and his eldest son, Carlos, launched Alvarez Construction. They built three homes that first year, then six more the following year. Starting with individual single-family residential homes, Alvarez Construction eventually expanded its operations to include real estate and residential development.

After Hurricane Katrina, Jairo recognized the immediate need for increased construction in Baton Rouge and began developing an affordable subdivision for displaced first-time home buyers. In 2007, Alvarez Construction had several hundred houses under construction and 200 full-time workers. In the years since, the family-owned and operated small business has continued to achieve success, developing the St. Jude Dream Home and entire multiuse communities across the greater Baton Rouge area.

Jairo developed cancer in 2005 and spent years battling the disease. He passed away in 2013 as the patriarch of a successful construction and development business that was very involved in the Baton Rouge community. Appreciative of the opportunities the United States had afforded him, Jairo had made it a priority for his firm to participate in various volunteer programs that give back to the community, such as the St. Jude Dream Home Campaign and Wheels to Succeed, a foundation that provides adapted three-wheeled cycles for children with physical disabilities.

Today each member of the Alvarez family continues to play a major role in the business's success. Anita and Ana are in charge of administration, including accounting, bookkeeping, and staffing. With a business administration degree from Louisiana State University, Carlos is a licensed broker and responsible for the production, building, and selling aspects of the firm. As an expert in landscape architecture, Sebastian manages the firm's land development and subdivision infrastructure.

Congratulations to the Alvarez family and the Alvarez Construction Company for being recognized as Small Business of the Week. I look forward to your continued growth and success.●

MESSAGES FROM THE HOUSE
ENROLLED BILL SIGNED

At 1:27 p.m., a message from the House of Representatives, delivered by Mrs. Cole, one of its reading clerks, announced that the Speaker has signed the following enrolled bill:

H.R. 4665. An act to require the Secretary of Commerce to conduct an assessment and analysis of the outdoor recreation economy of the United States, and for other purposes.

The enrolled bill was subsequently signed by the President pro tempore (Mr. HATCH).

At 4:45 p.m., a message from the House of Representatives, delivered by Mrs. Cole, one of its reading clerks, announced that the House has passed the following bills, without amendment:

S. 1808. An act to require the Secretary of Homeland Security to conduct a Northern Border threat analysis, and for other purposes.

S. 1915. An act to direct the Secretary of Homeland Security to make anthrax vaccines available to emergency response providers, and for other purposes.

The message also announced that the House has passed the following bills, in which it requests the concurrence of the Senate:

H.R. 3286. An act to encourage effective, voluntary private sector investments to recruit, employ, and retain men and women who have served in the United States military with annual presidential awards to private sector employers recognizing such efforts, and for other purposes.

H.R. 4757. An act to expand the eligibility for headstones, markers, and medallions furnished by the Secretary of Veterans Affairs for deceased individuals who were awarded the Medal of Honor and are buried in private cemeteries, and for other purposes.

H.R. 5160. An act to amend title 40, United States Code, to include as part of the buildings and grounds of the National Gallery of Art any buildings and other areas within the boundaries of any real estate or other property interests acquired by the National Gallery of Art.

H.R. 5166. An act amend title 38, United States Code, to permit veterans to grant access to their records in the databases of the Veterans Benefits Administration to certain designated congressional employees, and for other purposes.

H.R. 5422. An act to ensure funding for the National Human Trafficking Hotline, and for other purposes.

H.R. 5458. An act to provide for coordination between the TRICARE program and eligibility for making contributions to a health savings account, and for other purposes.

H.R. 5600. An act to direct the Secretary of Veterans Affairs to carry out a pilot program to provide access to magnetic EEG/EKG-guided resonance therapy to veterans.

H.R. 5843. An act to establish a grant program at the Department of Homeland Security to promote cooperative research and development between the United States and Israel on cybersecurity.

H.R. 5877. An act to amend the Homeland Security Act of 2002 and the United States-Israel Strategic Partnership Act of 2014 to promote cooperative homeland security research and antiterrorism programs relating to cybersecurity, and for other purposes.

H.R. 6135. An act to designate the Federal building and United States courthouse located at 719 Church Street in Nashville, Tennessee, as the "Fred D. Thompson Federal Building and United States Courthouse".

H.R. 6323. An act to name the Department of Veterans Affairs health care system in Long Beach, California, the "Tibor Rubin VA Medical Center".

The message further announced that the House agrees to the amendment of the Senate to the bill (H.R. 3471) to amend title 38, United States Code, to make certain improvements in the provision of automobiles and adaptive equipment by the Department of Veterans Affairs.

The message also announced that the House agrees to the following concurrent resolutions, in which it requests the concurrence of the Senate:

H. Con. Res. 40. Concurrent resolution encouraging reunions of divided Korean American families.

H. Con. Res. 165. Concurrent resolution expressing the sense of Congress and reaffirming longstanding United States policy in support of a direct bilaterally negotiated settlement of the Israeli-Palestinian conflict and opposition to United Nations Security Council resolutions imposing a solution to the conflict.

The message further announced that the House passed the following bills, with amendment, in which it requests the concurrence of the Senate:

S. 546. An act to establish the Railroad Emergency Services Preparedness, Operational Needs, and Safety Evaluation (RESPONSE) Subcommittee under the Federal Emergency Management Agency's National Advisory Council to provide recommendations on emergency responder training and resources relating to hazardous materials incidents involving railroads, and for other purposes.

S. 2577. An act to protect crime victims' rights, to eliminate the substantial backlog of DNA and other forensic evidence samples to improve and expand the forensic science testing capacity of Federal, State, and local crime laboratories, to increase research and development of new testing technologies, to develop new training programs regarding the collection and use of forensic evidence, to provide post-conviction testing of DNA evidence to exonerate the innocent, to support accreditation efforts of forensic science laboratories and medical examiner offices, to address training and equipment needs, to improve the performance of counsel in State capital cases, and for other purposes.

The message also announced that the Clerk of the House be directed to return to the Senate the resolution (H. Con. Res. 122) supporting efforts to stop the theft, illegal possession or sale, transfer, and export of tribal cultural items of American Indians, Alaska Natives, and Native Hawaiians in the United States and internationally, together with all accompanying papers, in compliance with a request of the Senate for the return thereof, to make a technical correction in the engrossment of the aforesaid resolution.

INTRODUCTION OF BILLS AND JOINT RESOLUTIONS

The following bills and joint resolutions were introduced, read the first and second times by unanimous consent, and referred as indicated:

By Mr. WYDEN (for himself, Mr. PAUL, Mr. COONS, and Ms. BALDWIN):

S. 3485. A bill to delay the amendments to rule 41 of the Federal Rules of Criminal Procedure; to the Committee on the Judiciary.

By Mr. WARNER (for himself, Mr. LANKFORD, and Mr. BOOKER):

S. 3486. A bill to amend chapter 31 of title 5, United States Code, to establish in statute the Presidential Innovation Fellows Program; to the Committee on Homeland Security and Governmental Affairs.

By Mr. VITTER:

S. 3487. A bill to amend title XVIII of the Social Security Act to provide Medicare entitlement to immunosuppressive drugs for kidney transplant recipients; to the Committee on Finance.

By Mr. CRUZ:

S. 3488. A bill to protect freedom of speech in America's electoral process and ensure transparency in campaign finance; to the Committee on Rules and Administration.

SUBMISSION OF CONCURRENT AND SENATE RESOLUTIONS

The following concurrent resolutions and Senate resolutions were read, and referred (or acted upon), as indicated:

By Mr. BROWN (for himself and Mr. ISAKSON):

S. Res. 624. A resolution supporting the goals, activities, and ideals of World Prematurity Month; to the Committee on the Judiciary.

By Mr. BROWN (for himself and Mr. ISAKSON):

S. Res. 625. A resolution supporting the goals, activities, and ideals of World Prematurity Day; to the Committee on the Judiciary.

By Mr. CORNYN (for himself and Mr. CRUZ):

S. Res. 626. A resolution recognizing the 75th anniversary of the establishment of the University of Texas MD Anderson Cancer Center in Houston, Texas; considered and agreed to.

By Mr. HATCH (for himself, Mr. WHITEHOUSE, Mr. ROBERTS, Mr. MARKEY, Mr. FLAKE, Mr. COTTON, and Mr. GARDNER):

S. Con. Res. 57. A concurrent resolution honoring in praise and remembrance the extraordinary life, steady leadership, and remarkable, 70-year reign of King Bhumibol Adulyadej of Thailand; to the Committee on Foreign Relations.

ADDITIONAL COSPONSORS

S. 386

At the request of Mr. THUNE, the name of the Senator from Texas (Mr. CRUZ) was added as a cosponsor of S. 386, a bill to limit the authority of States to tax certain income of employees for employment duties performed in other States.

S. 1524

At the request of Mr. BLUNT, the name of the Senator from New York (Mrs. GILLIBRAND) was added as a cosponsor of S. 1524, a bill to enable concrete masonry products manufacturers to establish, finance, and carry out a coordinated program of research, education, and promotion to improve, maintain, and develop markets for concrete masonry products.

S. 1714

At the request of Mr. MANCHIN, the name of the Senator from New Mexico (Mr. HEINRICH) was added as a cosponsor of S. 1714, a bill to amend the Surface Mining Control and Reclamation Act of 1977 to transfer certain funds to the Multiemployer Health Benefit Plan and the 1974 United Mine Workers of America Pension Plan, and for other purposes.

S. 1915

At the request of Ms. AYOTTE, the name of the Senator from Wisconsin (Mr. JOHNSON) was added as a cosponsor of S. 1915, a bill to direct the Secretary of Homeland Security to make anthrax vaccines available to emergency response providers, and for other purposes.

S. 2469

At the request of Mr. BLUMENTHAL, the name of the Senator from Nevada (Mr. REID) was added as a cosponsor of S. 2469, a bill to repeal the Protection of Lawful Commerce in Arms Act.

S. 2612

At the request of Mr. LEAHY, the name of the Senator from Minnesota (Ms. KLOBUCHAR) was added as a cosponsor of S. 2612, a bill to ensure United States jurisdiction over offenses committed by United States personnel stationed in Canada in furtherance of border security initiatives.

S. 2782

At the request of Mr. BLUNT, the name of the Senator from New Hampshire (Mrs. SHAHEEN) was added as a cosponsor of S. 2782, a bill to amend the Public Health Service Act to provide for the participation of pediatric subspecialists in the National Health Service Corps program, and for other purposes.

S. 2989

At the request of Ms. MURKOWSKI, the names of the Senator from Wisconsin (Ms. BALDWIN), the Senator from New Hampshire (Ms. AYOTTE) and the Senator from Illinois (Mr. KIRK) were added as cosponsors of S. 2989, a bill to award a Congressional Gold Medal, collectively, to the United States merchant mariners of World War II, in recognition of their dedicated and vital service during World War II.

S. 3021

At the request of Mr. INHOFE, the name of the Senator from Montana (Mr. DAINES) was added as a cosponsor of S. 3021, a bill to amend title 38, United States Code, to authorize the use of Post-9/11 Educational Assistance to pursue independent study programs at certain educational institutions that are not institutions of higher learning.

S. 3043

At the request of Ms. KLOBUCHAR, the name of the Senator from Arkansas (Mr. BOOZMAN) was added as a cosponsor of S. 3043, a bill to direct the Secretary of Veterans Affairs to carry out a pilot program establishing a patient self-scheduling appointment system, and for other purposes.

S. 3373

At the request of Mr. WARNER, the names of the Senator from North Dakota (Ms. HEITKAMP) and the Senator from Arkansas (Mr. BOOZMAN) were added as cosponsors of S. 3373, a bill to amend the Federal Deposit Insurance Act to ensure that the reciprocal deposits of an insured depository institution are not considered to be funds obtained by or through a deposit broker, and for other purposes.

S. 3386

At the request of Mrs. MCCASKILL, the name of the Senator from Minnesota (Ms. KLOBUCHAR) was added as a cosponsor of S. 3386, a bill to amend title 36, United States Code, to designate May 1 as "Silver Star Service Banner Day".

S. 3391

At the request of Mr. REED, the name of the Senator from Montana (Mr. TESTER) was added as a cosponsor of S. 3391, a bill to reauthorize the Museum and Library Services Act.

S. 3447

At the request of Mr. SULLIVAN, the names of the Senator from Wisconsin (Mr. JOHNSON) and the Senator from West Virginia (Mr. MANCHIN) were added as cosponsors of S. 3447, a bill to direct the Secretary of the Army to place in Arlington National Cemetery a memorial honoring the helicopter pilots and crew members of the Vietnam era, and for other purposes.

S. 3475

At the request of Mr. COONS, the name of the Senator from Oregon (Mr. MERKLEY) was added as a cosponsor of S. 3475, a bill to delay the amendments to rule 41 of the Federal Rules of Criminal Procedure.

S. CON. RES. 56

At the request of Mr. CARDIN, the names of the Senator from Connecticut (Mr. BLUMENTHAL), the Senator from Ohio (Mr. BROWN) and the Senator from Washington (Mrs. MURRAY) were added as cosponsors of S. Con. Res. 56, a concurrent resolution clarifying any potential misunderstanding as to whether actions taken by President-elect Donald Trump constitute a violation of the Emoluments Clause, and calling on President-elect Trump to divest his interest in, and sever his relationship to, the Trump Organization.

S. RES. 616

At the request of Mrs. SHAHEEN, the names of the Senator from Michigan (Ms. STABENOW) and the Senator from Hawaii (Ms. HIRONO) were added as cosponsors of S. Res. 616, a resolution supporting the goals and ideals of American Diabetes Month.

S. RES. 621

At the request of Mr. WYDEN, the name of the Senator from West Virginia (Mrs. CAPITO) was added as a cosponsor of S. Res. 621, a resolution designating November 2016 as National Hospice and Palliative Care Month.

STATEMENTS ON INTRODUCED BILLS AND JOINT RESOLUTIONS

By Mr. CRUZ:

S. 3488. A bill to protect freedom of speech in America's electoral process and ensure transparency in campaign finance; to the Committee on Rules and Administration.

Mr. CRUZ. Mr. President, today I am introducing the SuperPAC Elimination Act. Another election cycle has come and gone without addressing a glaring issue that remains significant: free speech and transparency in campaign finance. Our current campaign finance system is absurd. Right now, a large percentage—sometimes a majority—of campaign expenditures are made by independent third-party SuperPACs that are prohibited from communicating with candidates. That makes no sense. Candidates should define their own messages, and citizens should be free to support whatever candidates they choose to support. Restrictions to political contributions are always presented under the guise of preventing corruption and holding politicians accountable, when in fact they accomplish exactly the opposite: protecting incumbent politicians. My legislation would put Americans on a level playing field with the media and politicians when it comes to influencing elections and exercising our First Amendment rights. Specifically, it would remove the caps on direct contributions to candidates from individuals and requires donations of more than $200 to be disclosed within 24 hours. Establishing unlimited contributions paired with immediate disclosure is the best way to promote transparency, eliminate the viability of SuperPACs going forward, and ensure that free speech is protected in the electoral process. I look forward to working with my colleagues in the Senate to shed light on the political arena and empower individual Americans by passing this important legislation.

SUBMITTED RESOLUTIONS

SENATE RESOLUTION 624—SUPPORTING THE GOALS, ACTIVITIES, AND IDEALS OF WORLD PREMATURITY MONTH

Mr. BROWN (for himself and Mr. ISAKSON) submitted the following resolution; which was referred to the Committee on the Judiciary:

S. RES. 624

Whereas, according to the World Health Organization, complications from preterm birth are the world's leading killer of children younger than 5 years of age;

Whereas preterm birth is a global problem, exacting a harsh toll on families from all parts of society in every country;

Whereas, in 2015, complications from preterm birth accounted for 1,000,000 deaths of children younger than 5 years of age worldwide;

Whereas there are stark inequalities with respect to the survival rates of preterm babies born around the world;

Whereas up to 75 percent of deaths resulting from preterm birth worldwide could be prevented through proven low-cost interventions;

Whereas countries can improve maternal health and the survival rate of babies born prematurely by making strategic investments in health care systems to ensure access to—

(1) high quality prenatal and postnatal care;

(2) quality childbirth services;

(3) emergency obstetric care; and

(4) comprehensive care for affected newborns;

Whereas, according to the Centers for Disease Control and Prevention, premature birth is the leading contributor to infant death in the United States and poses the risk of lifelong health problems for babies who survive;

Whereas, while the preterm birth rate in the United States decreased from a peak of 12.8 percent in 2006 to 9.6 percent in 2015, the rate remains too high;

Whereas many communities in the United States experience significant racial and ethnic disparities in preterm birth rates;

Whereas, in 2005, the Institute of Medicine estimated that the annual societal economic cost associated with preterm birth in the United States was $26,200,000,000; and

Whereas preterm births can be prevented through evidence-based public health programs, including through the reduction of risk factors, such as tobacco use and early elective deliveries, and the promotion of healthy timing and spacing of pregnancy: Now, therefore, be it

Resolved, That the Senate—

(1) recognizes November 2016 as "World Prematurity Month";

(2) supports efforts in the United States, and recognizes efforts abroad, to—

(A) reduce the impact of preterm births by improving maternal health; and

(B) advance the care and treatment of infants who are born preterm; and

(3) honors individuals working in the United States and internationally to reduce the number of preterm births.

SENATE RESOLUTION 625—SUPPORTING THE GOALS, ACTIVITIES, AND IDEALS OF WORLD PREMATURITY DAY

Mr. BROWN (for himself and Mr. ISAKSON) submitted the following resolution; which was referred to the Committee on the Judiciary:

S. RES. 625

Whereas, according to the World Health Organization, complications from preterm birth are the world's leading killer of children younger than 5 years of age;

Whereas preterm birth is a global problem, exacting a harsh toll on families from all parts of society in every country;

Whereas, in 2015, complications from preterm birth accounted for 1,000,000 deaths of children younger than 5 years of age worldwide;

Whereas there are stark inequalities with respect to the survival rates of preterm babies born around the world;

Whereas up to 75 percent of deaths resulting from preterm birth worldwide could be prevented through proven low-cost interventions;

Whereas countries can improve maternal health and the survival rate of babies born prematurely by making strategic investments in health care systems to ensure access to—

(1) high quality prenatal and postnatal care;

(2) quality childbirth services;

(3) emergency obstetric care; and

(4) comprehensive care for affected newborns;

Whereas, according to the Centers for Disease Control and Prevention, premature birth is the leading contributor to infant death in the United States and poses the risk of lifelong health problems for babies who survive;

Whereas, while the preterm birth rate in the United States decreased from a peak of 12.8 percent in 2006 to 9.6 percent in 2015, the rate remains too high;

Whereas many communities in the United States experience significant racial and ethnic disparities in preterm birth rates;

Whereas, in 2005, the Institute of Medicine estimated that the annual societal economic cost associated with preterm birth in the United States was $26,200,000,000; and

Whereas preterm births can be prevented through evidence-based public health programs, including through the reduction of risk factors, such as tobacco use and early elective deliveries: Now, therefore, be it

Resolved, That the Senate—

(1) recognizes November 17, 2016, as "World Prematurity Day";

(2) supports efforts in the United States, and recognizes efforts abroad, to—

(A) reduce the impact of preterm births by improving maternal health; and

(B) advance the care and treatment of infants who are born preterm; and

(3) honors individuals working in the United States and internationally to reduce the number of preterm births.

SENATE RESOLUTION 626—RECOGNIZING THE 75TH ANNIVERSARY OF THE ESTABLISHMENT OF THE UNIVERSITY OF TEXAS MD ANDERSON CANCER CENTER IN HOUSTON, TEXAS

Mr. CORNYN (for himself and Mr. CRUZ) submitted the following resolution; which was considered and agreed to:

S. RES. 626

Whereas the University of Texas MD Anderson Cancer Center (referred to in this preamble as "MD Anderson Cancer Center") has provided continuous health services for 75 years;

Whereas the Texas legislature established MD Anderson Cancer Center in 1941 as part of the University of Texas system with an appropriation of $500,000 and a matching funding grant from the MD Anderson Foundation to build a cancer hospital and research center;

Whereas MD Anderson Cancer Center is 1 of the original 3 comprehensive cancer centers in the United States that was established by the National Cancer Act of 1971 (Public Law 92–216);

Whereas as of November 2016, MD Anderson Cancer Center is 1 of the largest and most respected centers devoted exclusively to cancer patient care, research, education, and prevention in the world;

Whereas the mission of MD Anderson Cancer Center—

(1) is to eliminate cancer in Texas, the United States, and the world through exceptional programs that integrate patient care, research, and prevention; and

(2) includes education for undergraduate and graduate student trainees, professionals, employees, and the public;

Whereas MD Anderson Cancer Center is dedicated to embracing the 3 core values of caring, integrity, and discovery;

Whereas hundreds of thousands of Texans have received quality medical care from MD Anderson Cancer Center during its 75 years of service;

Whereas MD Anderson Cancer Center has invested hundreds of millions of dollars towards scientific breakthroughs in the fight against cancer, including nearly $800,000,000 in fiscal year 2015;

Whereas MD Anderson Cancer Center is home to the largest cancer clinical trial program in the world, with more than 9,400 patients participating in almost 1,200 clinical trials;

Whereas MD Anderson has educated tens of thousands of health professionals, including physicians, scientists, nurses, and allied health professionals during its 75 years of service;

Whereas MD Anderson has employed tens of thousands of hardworking individuals who have devoted their lives to the care, concern, and healing of patients;

Whereas the commitment of MD Anderson Cancer Center to individuals who have served in the United States military earned MD Anderson Cancer Center a place on the 2015 Best for Vets employer list;

Whereas MD Anderson Cancer Center—

(1) was ranked number 1 for cancer care in the survey of best hospitals published in U.S. News and World Report in 2016; and

(2) has been named 1 of the top 2 cancer centers in the United States every year since that survey began in 1990; and

Whereas the nursing program at MD Anderson Cancer Center holds the American Nurses Credentialing Center's Magnet Nursing Services Recognition status, which recognizes health care organizations for quality patient care, nursing excellence, and innovations in professional nursing practice: Now, therefore, be it

Resolved, That the Senate—

(1) recognizes the 75th anniversary of the establishment of MD Anderson Cancer Center in Houston, Texas; and

(2) commends MD Anderson Cancer Center and its employees for providing quality care to hundreds of thousands of patients over the last 75 years.

SENATE CONCURRENT RESOLUTION 57—HONORING IN PRAISE AND REMEMBRANCE THE EXTRAORDINARY LIFE, STEADY LEADERSHIP, AND REMARKABLE, 70-YEAR REIGN OF KING BHUMIBOL ADULYADEJ OF THAILAND

Mr. HATCH (for himself, Mr. WHITEHOUSE, Mr. ROBERTS, Mr. MARKEY, Mr. FLAKE, Mr. COTTON, and Mr. GARDNER) submitted the following concurrent resolution; which was referred to the Committee on Foreign Relations:

S. CON. RES. 57

Whereas His Majesty King Bhumibol Adulyadej enjoyed a special relationship with the United States, having been born in Cambridge, Massachusetts, in 1927 while his father was completing his medical studies at Harvard University;

Whereas King Bhumibol Adulyadej ascended to the throne on June 9, 1946, and celebrated his 70th year as King of Thailand in 2016;

Whereas, at the time of his death, King Bhumibol Adulyadej was the longest-serving head of state in the world and the longest-reigning monarch in the history of Thailand;

Whereas His Majesty dedicated his life to the well-being of the Thai people and the sustainable development of Thailand;

Whereas His Majesty led by example and virtue with the interest of the people at heart, earning His Majesty the deep reverence of the Thai people and the respect of people around the world;

Whereas His Majesty reached out to the poorest and most vulnerable people of Thailand, regardless of their status, ethnicity, or religion, listened to their problems, and empowered them to take their lives into their own hands;

Whereas, in 2006, His Majesty received the first United Nations Human Development Award, recognizing him as the "Development King" for the extraordinary contribution of His Majesty to human development;

Whereas His Majesty was recognized internationally in the areas of intellectual property, innovation, and creativity, and in 2006, the World Intellectual Property Organization presented His Majesty with the Global Leadership Award;

Whereas His Majesty was an anchor of peace and stability for Thailand during the turbulent decades of the Cold War;

Whereas His Majesty was always a trusted friend of the United States in advancing a strong and enduring alliance and partnership between the United States and Thailand;

Whereas His Majesty addressed a joint session of Congress on June 29, 1960, during which His Majesty reaffirmed the strong friendship and good will between the United States and Thailand;

Whereas the United States and Thailand remain strong security allies, as memorialized in the Southeast Asia Collective Defense Treaty (commonly known as the "Manila Pact of 1954") and later expanded under the Thanat-Rusk Communique of 1962;

Whereas, for decades, Thailand has hosted the annual Cobra Gold military exercises, the largest multilateral exercises in Asia, to improve regional defense cooperation;

Whereas Thailand has allowed the Armed Forces of the United States to use the Utapao Air Base to coordinate international humanitarian relief efforts;

Whereas President George W. Bush designated Thailand as a major non-NATO ally on December 30, 2003;

Whereas close cooperation and mutual sacrifices in the face of common threats have bound the United States and Thailand together and established a firm foundation for the advancement of a mutually beneficial relationship; and

Whereas, on October 13, 2016, at the age of 88, His Majesty King Bhumibol Adulyadej passed away, leaving behind a lasting legacy for Thailand: Now, therefore, be it

Resolved by the Senate (the House of Representatives concurring), That Congress—

(1) honors the extraordinary life, steady leadership, and remarkable, 70-year reign of His Majesty King Bhumibol Adulyadej of Thailand;

(2) extends our deepest sympathies to the members of the Royal Family and to the people of Thailand in their bereavement; and

(3) celebrates the alliance and friendship between Thailand and the United States that reflects common interests, a 183-year diplomatic history, and a multifaceted partnership that has contributed to peace, stability, and prosperity in the Asia-Pacific region.

AUTHORITY FOR COMMITTEES TO MEET

Mr. ALEXANDER. Mr. President, I have five requests for committees to meet during today's session of the Senate. They have the approval of the Majority and Minority leaders.

Pursuant to Rule XXVI, paragraph 5(a), of the Standing Rules of the Senate, the following committees are authorized to meet during today's session of the Senate:

COMMITTEE ON COMMERCE, SCIENCE, AND TRANSPORTATION

The Committee on Commerce, Science, and Transportation is authorized to meet during the session of the Senate on November 30, 2016, at 2:30 p.m., in room SR–253 of the Russell Senate Office Building to conduct a Subcommittee hearing entitled "The Dawn of Artificial Intelligence."

COMMITTEE ON FINANCE

The Committee on Finance is authorized to meet during the session of the Senate on November 30, 2016, at 10 a.m., in room SD–215 of the Dirksen Senate Office Building.

COMMITTEE ON HOMELAND SECURITY AND GOVERNMENTAL AFFAIRS

The Committee on Homeland Security and Governmental Affairs is authorized to meet during the session of the Senate on November 30, 2016, at 10 a.m., to conduct a hearing entitled "Initial Observations of the New Leadership at the U.S. Border Patrol."

SELECT COMMITTEE ON INTELLIGENCE

The Select Committee on Intelligence is authorized to meet during the session of the Senate on November 30, 2016, at 3 p.m., in room SH–219 of the Hart Senate Office Building.

SPECIAL COMMITTEE ON AGING

The Special Committee on Aging is authorized to meet during the session of the Senate on November 30, 2016, in room SD–562 of the Dirksen Senate Office Building, at 2:30 p.m., to conduct a hearing entitled "Trust Betrayed: Financial Abuse of Older Americans by Guardians and Others in Power."

PRIVILEGES OF THE FLOOR

Mr. MURPHY. Mr. President, I ask unanimous consent that Dr. Laura Willing, a health fellow in my office, be granted floor privileges for the remainder of the calendar year.

The PRESIDING OFFICER. Without objection, it is so ordered.

NATIONAL URBAN SEARCH AND RESCUE RESPONSE SYSTEM ACT OF 2016

Mr. DAINES. Mr. President, I ask unanimous consent that the Senate proceed to the immediate consideration of Calendar No. 578, S. 2971.

The PRESIDING OFFICER. The clerk will report the bill by title.

The senior assistant legislative clerk read as follows:

A bill (S. 2971) to authorize the National Urban Search and Rescue Response System.

There being no objection, the Senate proceeded to consider the bill, which had been reported from the Committee on Homeland Security and Governmental Affairs, with an amendment, as follows:

(The part of the bill intended to be stricken is shown in boldface brackets and the part of the bill intended to be inserted is shown in italics.)

S. 2971

Be it enacted by the Senate and House of Representatives of the United States of America in Congress assembled,

SECTION 1. SHORT TITLE.

This Act may be cited as the "National Urban Search and Rescue Response System Act of 2016".

SEC. 2. NATIONAL URBAN SEARCH AND RESCUE RESPONSE SYSTEM.

(a) IN GENERAL.—Title III of the Robert T. Stafford Disaster Relief and Emergency Assistance Act (42 U.S.C. 5141 et seq.) is amended by adding at the end the following:

"SEC. 327. NATIONAL URBAN SEARCH AND RESCUE RESPONSE SYSTEM.

"(a) DEFINITIONS.—In this section, the following definitions shall apply:

"(1) ADMINISTRATOR.—The term 'Administrator' means the Administrator of the Federal Emergency Management Agency.

"(2) AGENCY.—The term 'Agency' means the Federal Emergency Management Agency.

"(3) HAZARD.—The term 'hazard' has the meaning given the term in section 602.

"(4) NONEMPLOYEE SYSTEM MEMBER.—The term 'nonemployee System member' means a System member not employed by a sponsoring agency or participating agency.

"(5) PARTICIPATING AGENCY.—The term 'participating agency' means a State or local government, nonprofit organization, or private organization that has executed an agreement with a sponsoring agency to participate in the System.

"(6) SPONSORING AGENCY.—The term 'sponsoring agency' means a State or local government that is the sponsor of a task force designated by the Administrator to participate in the System.

"(7) SYSTEM.—The term 'System' means the National Urban Search and Rescue Response System to be administered under this section.

"(8) SYSTEM MEMBER.—The term 'System member' means an individual who is not a full-time employee of the Federal Government and who serves on a task force or on a System management or other technical team.

"(9) TASK FORCE.—The term 'task force' means an urban search and rescue team designated by the Administrator to participate in the System.

"(b) GENERAL AUTHORITY.—Subject to the requirements of this section, the Administrator shall continue to administer the emergency response system known as the National Urban Search and Rescue Response System.

"(c) FUNCTIONS.—In administering the System, the Administrator shall provide for a national network of standardized search and rescue resources to assist States and local governments in responding to hazards.

"(d) TASK FORCES.—

"(1) DESIGNATION.—The Administrator shall designate task forces to participate in the System. The Administration shall determine the criteria for such participation.

"(2) SPONSORING AGENCIES.—Each task force shall have a sponsoring agency. The Administrator shall enter into an agreement with the sponsoring agency with respect to the participation of each task force in the System.

"(3) COMPOSITION.—

"(A) PARTICIPATING AGENCIES.—A task force may include, at the discretion of the sponsoring agency, 1 or more participating agencies. The sponsoring agency shall enter into an agreement with each participating agency with respect to the participation of the participating agency on the task force.

"(B) OTHER INDIVIDUALS.—A task force may also include, at the discretion of the sponsoring agency, other individuals not otherwise associated with the sponsoring agency or a participating agency. The sponsoring agency of a task force may enter into a separate agreement with each such individual with respect to the participation of the individual on the task force.

"(e) MANAGEMENT AND TECHNICAL TEAMS.—The Administrator shall maintain such management teams and other technical teams as the Administrator determines are necessary to administer the System.

"(f) APPOINTMENT OF SYSTEM MEMBERS INTO FEDERAL SERVICE.—

"(1) IN GENERAL.—The Administrator may appoint a System member into Federal service for a period of service to provide for the participation of the System member in exercises, preincident staging, major disaster and emergency response activities, and training events sponsored or sanctioned by the Administrator.

"(2) NONAPPLICABILITY OF CERTAIN CIVIL SERVICE LAWS.—The Administrator may make appointments under paragraph (1) without regard to the provisions of title 5, United States Code, governing appointments in the competitive service.

"(3) RELATIONSHIP TO OTHER AUTHORITIES.—The authority of the Administrator to make appointments under this subsection shall not affect any other authority of the Administrator under this Act.

"(4) LIMITATION.—A System member who is appointed into Federal service under paragraph (1) shall not be considered an employee of the United States for purposes other than those specifically set forth in this section.

"(g) COMPENSATION.—

"(1) PAY OF SYSTEM MEMBERS.—Subject to such terms and conditions as the Administrator may impose by regulation, the Administrator shall make payments to the sponsoring agency of a task force—

"(A) to reimburse each employer of a System member on the task force for compensation paid by the employer to the System member for any period during which the System member is appointed into Federal service under subsection (f)(1); and

"(B) to make payments directly to a nonemployee System member on the task force for any period during which the nonemployee System member is appointed into Federal service under subsection (f)(1).

"(2) REIMBURSEMENT FOR EMPLOYEES FILLING POSITIONS OF SYSTEM MEMBERS.—

"(A) IN GENERAL.—Subject to such terms and conditions as the Administrator may impose by regulation, the Administrator shall make payments to the sponsoring agency of a task force to be used to reimburse each employer of a System member on the task force for compensation paid by the employer to an employee filling a position normally filled by the System member for any period during which the System member is appointed into Federal service under subsection (f)(1).

"(B) LIMITATION.—Costs incurred by an employer shall be eligible for reimbursement under subparagraph (A) only to the extent that the costs are in excess of the costs that would have been incurred by the employer had the System member not been appointed into Federal service under subsection (f)(1).

"(3) METHOD OF PAYMENT.—A System member shall not be entitled to pay directly from the Agency for a period during which the System member is appointed into Federal Service under subsection (f)(1).

"(h) PERSONAL INJURY, ILLNESS, DISABILITY, OR DEATH.—

"(1) IN GENERAL.—A System member who is appointed into Federal service under subsection (f)(1) and who suffers personal injury, illness, disability, or death as a result of a personal injury sustained while acting in the scope of such appointment, shall, for the purposes of subchapter I of chapter 81 of title 5, United States Code, be treated as though the member were an employee (as defined by section 8101 of that title) who had sustained the injury in the performance of duty.

"(2) ELECTION OF BENEFITS.—

"(A) IN GENERAL.—A System member (or, in the case of the death of the System member, the System member's dependent) who is entitled under paragraph (1) to receive benefits under subchapter I of chapter 81 of title 5, United States Code, by reason of personal injury, illness, disability, or death, and to receive benefits from a State or local government by reason of the same personal injury, illness, disability or death shall elect to—

"(i) receive benefits under such subchapter; or

"(ii) receive benefits from the State or local government.

"(B) DEADLINE.—A System member or dependent shall make an election of benefits under subparagraph (A) not later than 1 year after the date of the personal injury, illness, disability, or death that is the reason for the benefits, or until such later date as the Secretary of Labor may allow for reasonable cause shown.

"(C) EFFECT OF ELECTION.—An election of benefits made under this paragraph is irrevocable unless otherwise provided by law.

"(3) REIMBURSEMENT FOR STATE OR LOCAL BENEFITS.—Subject to such terms and conditions as the Administrator may impose by regulation, if a System member or dependent elects to receive benefits from a State or local government under paragraph (2)(A), the Administrator shall reimburse the State or local government for the value of the benefits.

"(4) PUBLIC SAFETY OFFICER CLAIMS.—Nothing in this subsection shall be construed to bar any claim by, or with respect to, any System member who is a public safety officer, as defined in section 1204 of title I of the Omnibus Crime Control and Safe Streets Act of 1968 (42 U.S.C. [3769b] *3796b*), for any benefits authorized under part L of title I of that Act (42 U.S.C. 3796 et seq.).

"(i) LIABILITY.—A System member appointed into Federal service under subsection (f)(1), while acting within the scope of the appointment, shall be considered to be an employee of the Federal Government under section 1346(b) of title 28, United States Code, and chapter 171 of that title, relating to tort claims procedure.

"(j) EMPLOYMENT AND REEMPLOYMENT RIGHTS.—With respect to a System member who is not a regular full-time employee of a sponsoring agency or participating agency, the following terms and conditions apply:

"(1) SERVICE.—Service as a System member shall be considered to be 'service in the uniformed services' for purposes of chapter 43 of title 38, United States Code, relating to employment and reemployment rights of individuals who have performed service in the uniformed services (regardless of whether the individual receives compensation for such participation). All rights and obligations of such persons and procedures for assistance, enforcement, and investigation shall be as provided for in such chapter.

"(2) PRECLUSION.—Preclusion of giving notice of service by necessity of appointment under this section shall be considered to be preclusion by 'military necessity' for purposes of section 4312(b) of title 38, United States Code, pertaining to giving notice of absence from a position of employment. A determination of such necessity shall be made by the Administrator and shall not be subject to judicial review.

"(k) LICENSES AND PERMITS.—If a System member holds a valid license, certificate, or other permit issued by any State or other governmental jurisdiction evidencing the member's qualifications in any professional, mechanical, or other skill or type of assistance required by the System, the System member is deemed to be performing a Federal activity when rendering aid involving such skill or assistance during a period of appointment into Federal service under subsection (f)(1).

"(l) PREPAREDNESS COOPERATIVE AGREEMENTS.—Subject to the availability of appropriations for such purpose, the Administrator shall enter into an annual preparedness cooperative agreement with each sponsoring agency. Amounts made available to a sponsoring agency under such a preparedness cooperative agreement shall be for the following purposes:

"(1) Training and exercises, including training and exercises with other Federal, State, and local government response entities.

"(2) Acquisition and maintenance of equipment, including interoperable communications and personal protective equipment.

"(3) Medical monitoring required for responder safety and health in anticipation of and following a major disaster, emergency, or other hazard, as determined by the Administrator.

"(m) RESPONSE COOPERATIVE AGREEMENTS.—The Administrator shall enter into a response cooperative agreement with each sponsoring agency, as appropriate, under which the Administrator agrees to reimburse the sponsoring agency for costs incurred by the sponsoring agency in responding to a major disaster or emergency.

"(n) OBLIGATIONS.—The Administrator may incur all necessary obligations consistent with this section in order to ensure the effectiveness of the System.

"(o) EQUIPMENT MAINTENANCE AND REPLACEMENT.—Not later than 180 days after the date of enactment of this section, the Administrator shall submit to the appropriate congressional committees (as defined in section 2 of the Homeland Security Act of 2002 (6 U.S.C. 101)) a report on the development of a plan, including implementation steps and timeframes, to finance, maintain, and replace System equipment.

"(p) AUTHORIZATION OF APPROPRIATIONS.—There is authorized to be appropriated to carry out the System and the provisions of this section such sums as are necessary for each of fiscal years 2017, 2018, and 2019.".

(b) CONFORMING AMENDMENTS.—

(1) APPLICABILITY OF TITLE 5, UNITED STATES CODE.—Section 8101(1) of title 5, United States Code, is amended—

(A) in subparagraph (D), by striking "and" at the end;

(B) by transferring subparagraph (F) to between subparagraph (E) and the matter following subparagraph (E);

(C) in subparagraph (F)—

(i) by striking "United States Code,"; and

(ii) by adding "and" at the end; and

(D) by inserting after subparagraph (F) the following:

"(G) an individual who is a System member of the National Urban Search and Rescue Response System during a period of appointment into Federal service pursuant to section 327 of the Robert T. Stafford Disaster Relief and Emergency Assistance Act;".

(2) INCLUSION AS PART OF UNIFORMED SERVICES FOR PURPOSES OF USERRA.—Section 4303 of title 38, United States Code, is amended—

(A) in paragraph (13), by inserting ", a period for which a System member of the National Urban Search and Rescue Response System is absent from a position of employment due to an appointment into Federal service under section 327 of the Robert T. Stafford Disaster Relief and Emergency Assistance Act" before ", and a period"; and

(B) in paragraph (16), by inserting "System members of the National Urban Search and Rescue Response System during a period of appointment into Federal service under section 327 of the Robert T. Stafford Disaster Relief and Emergency Assistance Act," after "Public Health Service,".

Mr. DAINES. Mr. President, I ask unanimous consent that the committee-reported amendment be agreed to, the bill, as amended, be considered read a third time and passed, and the motion to reconsider be considered made and laid upon the table.

The PRESIDING OFFICER. Without objection, it is so ordered.

The committee-reported amendment was agreed to.

The bill (S. 2971), as amended, was ordered to be engrossed for a third reading, was read the third time, and passed, as follows:

S. 2971

Be it enacted by the Senate and House of Representatives of the United States of America in Congress assembled,

SECTION 1. SHORT TITLE.

This Act may be cited as the "National Urban Search and Rescue Response System Act of 2016".

SEC. 2. NATIONAL URBAN SEARCH AND RESCUE RESPONSE SYSTEM.

(a) IN GENERAL.—Title III of the Robert T. Stafford Disaster Relief and Emergency Assistance Act (42 U.S.C. 5141 et seq.) is amended by adding at the end the following:

"SEC. 327. NATIONAL URBAN SEARCH AND RESCUE RESPONSE SYSTEM.

"(a) DEFINITIONS.—In this section, the following definitions shall apply:

"(1) ADMINISTRATOR.—The term 'Administrator' means the Administrator of the Federal Emergency Management Agency.

"(2) AGENCY.—The term 'Agency' means the Federal Emergency Management Agency.

"(3) HAZARD.—The term 'hazard' has the meaning given the term in section 602.

"(4) NONEMPLOYEE SYSTEM MEMBER.—The term 'nonemployee System member' means a System member not employed by a sponsoring agency or participating agency.

"(5) PARTICIPATING AGENCY.—The term 'participating agency' means a State or local government, nonprofit organization, or private organization that has executed an agreement with a sponsoring agency to participate in the System.

"(6) SPONSORING AGENCY.—The term 'sponsoring agency' means a State or local government that is the sponsor of a task force designated by the Administrator to participate in the System.

"(7) SYSTEM.—The term 'System' means the National Urban Search and Rescue Response System to be administered under this section.

"(8) SYSTEM MEMBER.—The term 'System member' means an individual who is not a full-time employee of the Federal Government and who serves on a task force or on a System management or other technical team.

"(9) TASK FORCE.—The term 'task force' means an urban search and rescue team designated by the Administrator to participate in the System.

"(b) GENERAL AUTHORITY.—Subject to the requirements of this section, the Administrator shall continue to administer the emergency response system known as the National Urban Search and Rescue Response System.

"(c) FUNCTIONS.—In administering the System, the Administrator shall provide for a national network of standardized search and rescue resources to assist States and local governments in responding to hazards.

"(d) TASK FORCES.—

"(1) DESIGNATION.—The Administrator shall designate task forces to participate in the System. The Administration shall determine the criteria for such participation.

"(2) SPONSORING AGENCIES.—Each task force shall have a sponsoring agency. The Administrator shall enter into an agreement with the sponsoring agency with respect to the participation of each task force in the System.

"(3) COMPOSITION.—

"(A) PARTICIPATING AGENCIES.—A task force may include, at the discretion of the sponsoring agency, 1 or more participating agencies. The sponsoring agency shall enter into an agreement with each participating agency with respect to the participation of the participating agency on the task force.

"(B) OTHER INDIVIDUALS.—A task force may also include, at the discretion of the sponsoring agency, other individuals not otherwise associated with the sponsoring agency or a participating agency. The sponsoring agency of a task force may enter into a separate agreement with each such individual with respect to the participation of the individual on the task force.

"(e) MANAGEMENT AND TECHNICAL TEAMS.— The Administrator shall maintain such management teams and other technical teams as the Administrator determines are necessary to administer the System.

"(f) APPOINTMENT OF SYSTEM MEMBERS INTO FEDERAL SERVICE.—

"(1) IN GENERAL.—The Administrator may appoint a System member into Federal service for a period of service to provide for the participation of the System member in exercises, preincident staging, major disaster and emergency response activities, and training events sponsored or sanctioned by the Administrator.

"(2) NONAPPLICABILITY OF CERTAIN CIVIL SERVICE LAWS.—The Administrator may make appointments under paragraph (1) without regard to the provisions of title 5, United States Code, governing appointments in the competitive service.

"(3) RELATIONSHIP TO OTHER AUTHORITIES.— The authority of the Administrator to make appointments under this subsection shall not affect any other authority of the Administrator under this Act.

"(4) LIMITATION.—A System member who is appointed into Federal service under paragraph (1) shall not be considered an employee of the United States for purposes other than those specifically set forth in this section.

"(g) COMPENSATION.—

"(1) PAY OF SYSTEM MEMBERS.—Subject to such terms and conditions as the Administrator may impose by regulation, the Administrator shall make payments to the sponsoring agency of a task force—

"(A) to reimburse each employer of a System member on the task force for compensation paid by the employer to the System member for any period during which the System member is appointed into Federal service under subsection (f)(1); and

"(B) to make payments directly to a nonemployee System member on the task force for any period during which the nonemployee System member is appointed into Federal service under subsection (f)(1).

"(2) REIMBURSEMENT FOR EMPLOYEES FILLING POSITIONS OF SYSTEM MEMBERS.—

"(A) IN GENERAL.—Subject to such terms and conditions as the Administrator may impose by regulation, the Administrator shall make payments to the sponsoring agency of a task force to be used to reimburse each employer of a System member on the task force for compensation paid by the employer to an employee filling a position normally filled by the System member for any period during which the System member is appointed into Federal service under subsection (f)(1).

"(B) LIMITATION.—Costs incurred by an employer shall be eligible for reimbursement under subparagraph (A) only to the extent that the costs are in excess of the costs that would have been incurred by the employer had the System member not been appointed into Federal service under subsection (f)(1).

"(3) METHOD OF PAYMENT.—A System member shall not be entitled to pay directly from the Agency for a period during which the System member is appointed into Federal Service under subsection (f)(1).

"(h) PERSONAL INJURY, ILLNESS, DISABILITY, OR DEATH.—

"(1) IN GENERAL.—A System member who is appointed into Federal service under subsection (f)(1) and who suffers personal injury, illness, disability, or death as a result of a personal injury sustained while acting in the scope of such appointment, shall, for the purposes of subchapter I of chapter 81 of title 5, United States Code, be treated as though the member were an employee (as defined by section 8101 of that title) who had sustained the injury in the performance of duty.

"(2) ELECTION OF BENEFITS.—

"(A) IN GENERAL.—A System member (or, in the case of the death of the System member, the System member's dependent) who is entitled under paragraph (1) to receive benefits under subchapter I of chapter 81 of title 5, United States Code, by reason of personal injury, illness, disability, or death, and to receive benefits from a State or local government by reason of the same personal injury, illness, disability or death shall elect to—

"(i) receive benefits under such subchapter; or

"(ii) receive benefits from the State or local government.

"(B) DEADLINE.—A System member or dependent shall make an election of benefits under subparagraph (A) not later than 1 year after the date of the personal injury, illness, disability, or death that is the reason for the benefits, or until such later date as the Secretary of Labor may allow for reasonable cause shown.

"(C) EFFECT OF ELECTION.—An election of benefits made under this paragraph is irrevocable unless otherwise provided by law.

"(3) REIMBURSEMENT FOR STATE OR LOCAL BENEFITS.—Subject to such terms and conditions as the Administrator may impose by regulation, if a System member or dependent elects to receive benefits from a State or local government under paragraph (2)(A), the Administrator shall reimburse the State or local government for the value of the benefits.

"(4) PUBLIC SAFETY OFFICER CLAIMS.—Nothing in this subsection shall be construed to bar any claim by, or with respect to, any System member who is a public safety officer, as defined in section 1204 of title I of the Omnibus Crime Control and Safe Streets Act of 1968 (42 U.S.C. 3796b), for any benefits authorized under part L of title I of that Act (42 U.S.C. 3796 et seq.).

"(i) LIABILITY.—A System member appointed into Federal service under subsection (f)(1), while acting within the scope of the appointment, shall be considered to be an employee of the Federal Government under section 1346(b) of title 28, United States Code, and chapter 171 of that title, relating to tort claims procedure.

"(j) EMPLOYMENT AND REEMPLOYMENT RIGHTS.—With respect to a System member who is not a regular full-time employee of a sponsoring agency or participating agency, the following terms and conditions apply:

"(1) SERVICE.—Service as a System member shall be considered to be 'service in the uniformed services' for purposes of chapter 43 of title 38, United States Code, relating to employment and reemployment rights of individuals who have performed service in the uniformed services (regardless of whether the individual receives compensation for such participation). All rights and obligations of such persons and procedures for assistance, enforcement, and investigation shall be as provided for in such chapter.

"(2) PRECLUSION.—Preclusion of giving notice of service by necessity of appointment under this section shall be considered to be preclusion by 'military necessity' for purposes of section 4312(b) of title 38, United States Code, pertaining to giving notice of absence from a position of employment. A determination of such necessity shall be made by the Administrator and shall not be subject to judicial review.

"(k) LICENSES AND PERMITS.—If a System member holds a valid license, certificate, or other permit issued by any State or other governmental jurisdiction evidencing the member's qualifications in any professional, mechanical, or other skill or type of assistance required by the System, the System member is deemed to be performing a Federal activity when rendering aid involving such skill or assistance during a period of appointment into Federal service under subsection (f)(1).

"(l) PREPAREDNESS COOPERATIVE AGREEMENTS.—Subject to the availability of appropriations for such purpose, the Administrator shall enter into an annual preparedness cooperative agreement with each sponsoring agency. Amounts made available to a sponsoring agency under such a preparedness cooperative agreement shall be for the following purposes:

"(1) Training and exercises, including training and exercises with other Federal, State, and local government response entities.

"(2) Acquisition and maintenance of equipment, including interoperable communications and personal protective equipment.

"(3) Medical monitoring required for responder safety and health in anticipation of and following a major disaster, emergency, or other hazard, as determined by the Administrator.

"(m) RESPONSE COOPERATIVE AGREEMENTS.—The Administrator shall enter into a response cooperative agreement with each sponsoring agency, as appropriate, under which the Administrator agrees to reimburse the sponsoring agency for costs incurred by the sponsoring agency in responding to a major disaster or emergency.

"(n) OBLIGATIONS.—The Administrator may incur all necessary obligations consistent with this section in order to ensure the effectiveness of the System.

"(o) EQUIPMENT MAINTENANCE AND REPLACEMENT.—Not later than 180 days after the date of enactment of this section, the Administrator shall submit to the appropriate congressional committees (as defined in section 2 of the Homeland Security Act of 2002 (6 U.S.C. 101)) a report on the development of a plan, including implementation steps and timeframes, to finance, maintain, and replace System equipment.

"(p) AUTHORIZATION OF APPROPRIATIONS.— There is authorized to be appropriated to carry out the System and the provisions of this section such sums as are necessary for each of fiscal years 2017, 2018, and 2019.''.

(b) CONFORMING AMENDMENTS.—

(1) APPLICABILITY OF TITLE 5, UNITED STATES CODE.—Section 8101(1) of title 5, United States Code, is amended—

(A) in subparagraph (D), by striking "and" at the end;

(B) by transferring subparagraph (F) to between subparagraph (E) and the matter following subparagraph (E);

(C) in subparagraph (F)—

(i) by striking "United States Code,"; and

(ii) by adding "and" at the end; and

(D) by inserting after subparagraph (F) the following:

"(G) an individual who is a System member of the National Urban Search and Rescue Response System during a period of appointment into Federal service pursuant to section 327 of the Robert T. Stafford Disaster Relief and Emergency Assistance Act;''.

(2) INCLUSION AS PART OF UNIFORMED SERVICES FOR PURPOSES OF USERRA.—Section 4303 of title 38, United States Code, is amended—

(A) in paragraph (13), by inserting ", a period for which a System member of the National Urban Search and Rescue Response System is absent from a position of employment due to an appointment into Federal service under section 327 of the Robert T. Stafford Disaster Relief and Emergency Assistance Act" before ", and a period"; and

(B) in paragraph (16), by inserting "System members of the National Urban Search and Rescue Response System during a period of appointment into Federal service under section 327 of the Robert T. Stafford Disaster Relief and Emergency Assistance Act," after "Public Health Service,".

BETTER ONLINE TICKET SALES ACT OF 2016

Mr. DAINES. Mr. President, I ask unanimous consent that the Senate proceed to the immediate consideration of Calendar No. 648, S. 3183.

The PRESIDING OFFICER. The clerk will report the bill by title.

The senior assistant legislative clerk read as follows:

A bill (S. 3183) to prohibit the circumvention of control measures used by Internet ticket sellers to ensure equitable consumer access to tickets for any given event, and for other purposes.

There being no objection, the Senate proceeded to consider the bill, which had been reported from the Committee on Commerce, Science, and Transportation, with an amendment to strike all after the enacting clause and insert in lieu thereof the following:

SECTION 1. SHORT TITLE.

This Act may be cited as the "Better Online Ticket Sales Act of 2016" or the "BOTS Act of 2016".

SEC. 2. UNFAIR AND DECEPTIVE ACTS AND PRACTICES RELATING TO CIRCUMVENTION OF TICKET ACCESS CONTROL MEASURES.

(a) CONDUCT PROHIBITED.—

(1) IN GENERAL.—Except as provided in paragraph (2), it shall be unlawful for any person—

(A) to circumvent a security measure, access control system, or other technological control or measure on an Internet website or online service that is used by the ticket issuer to enforce posted event ticket purchasing limits or to maintain the integrity of posted online ticket purchasing order rules; or

(B) to sell or offer to sell any event ticket in interstate commerce obtained in violation of subparagraph (A) if the person selling or offering to sell the ticket either—

(i) participated directly in or had the ability to control the conduct in violation of subparagraph (A); or

(ii) knew or should have known that the event ticket was acquired in violation of subparagraph (A).

(2) EXCEPTION.—It shall not be unlawful under this section for a person to create or use any computer software or system—

(A) to investigate, or further the enforcement or defense, of any alleged violation of this section or other statute or regulation; or

(B) to engage in research necessary to identify and analyze flaws and vulnerabilities of measures, systems, or controls described in paragraph (1)(A), if these research activities are conducted to advance the state of knowledge in the field of computer system security or to assist in the development of computer security product.

(b) ENFORCEMENT BY THE FEDERAL TRADE COMMISSION.—

(1) UNFAIR OR DECEPTIVE ACTS OR PRACTICES.—A violation of subsection (a) shall be treated as a violation of a rule defining an unfair or a deceptive act or practice under section 18(a)(1)(B) of the Federal Trade Commission Act (15 U.S.C. 57a(a)(1)(B)).

(2) POWERS OF COMMISSION.—

(A) IN GENERAL.—The Commission shall enforce this section in the same manner, by the same means, and with the same jurisdiction, powers, and duties as though all applicable terms and provisions of the Federal Trade Commission Act (15 U.S.C. 41 et seq.) were incorporated into and made a part of this section.

(B) PRIVILEGES AND IMMUNITIES.—Any person who violates subsection (a) shall be subject to the penalties and entitled to the privileges and immunities provided in the Federal Trade Commission Act (15 U.S.C. 41 et seq.).

(C) AUTHORITY PRESERVED.—Nothing in this section shall be construed to limit the authority of the Federal Trade Commission under any other provision of law.

(c) ENFORCEMENT BY STATES.—

(1) IN GENERAL.—In any case in which the attorney general of a State has reason to believe that an interest of the residents of the State has been or is threatened or adversely affected by the engagement of any person subject to subsection (a) in a practice that violates such subsection, the attorney general of the State may, as parens patriae, bring a civil action on behalf of the residents of the State in an appropriate district court of the United States—

(A) to enjoin further violation of such subsection by such person;

(B) to compel compliance with such subsection; and

(C) to obtain damages, restitution, or other compensation on behalf of such residents.

(2) RIGHTS OF FEDERAL TRADE COMMISSION.—

(A) NOTICE TO FEDERAL TRADE COMMISSION.—

(i) IN GENERAL.—Except as provided in clause (iii), the attorney general of a State shall notify the Commission in writing that the attorney general intends to bring a civil action under paragraph (1) not later than 10 days before initiating the civil action.

(ii) CONTENTS.—The notification required by clause (i) with respect to a civil action shall include a copy of the complaint to be filed to initiate the civil action.

(iii) EXCEPTION.—If it is not feasible for the attorney general of a State to provide the notification required by clause (i) before initiating a civil action under paragraph (1), the attorney general shall notify the Commission immediately upon instituting the civil action.

(B) INTERVENTION BY FEDERAL TRADE COMMISSION.—The Commission may—

(i) intervene in any civil action brought by the attorney general of a State under paragraph (1); and

(ii) upon intervening—

(I) be heard on all matters arising in the civil action; and

(II) file petitions for appeal of a decision in the civil action.

(3) INVESTIGATORY POWERS.—Nothing in this subsection may be construed to prevent the attorney general of a State from exercising the powers conferred on the attorney general by the laws of the State to conduct investigations, to administer oaths or affirmations, or to compel the attendance of witnesses or the production of documentary or other evidence.

(4) PREEMPTIVE ACTION BY FEDERAL TRADE COMMISSION.—If the Commission institutes a civil action or an administrative action with respect to a violation of subsection (a), the attorney general of a State may not, during the pendency of such action, bring a civil action under paragraph (1) against any defendant named in the complaint of the Commission for the violation with respect to which the Commission instituted such action.

(5) VENUE; SERVICE OF PROCESS.—

(A) VENUE.—Any action brought under paragraph (1) may be brought in—

(i) the district court of the United States that meets applicable requirements relating to venue under section 1391 of title 28, United States Code; or

(ii) another court of competent jurisdiction.

(B) SERVICE OF PROCESS.—In an action brought under paragraph (1), process may be served in any district in which the defendant—

(i) is an inhabitant; or

(ii) may be found.

(6) ACTIONS BY OTHER STATE OFFICIALS.—

(A) IN GENERAL.—In addition to civil actions brought by attorneys general under paragraph (1), any other consumer protection officer of a State who is authorized by the State to do so may bring a civil action under paragraph (1), subject to the same requirements and limitations that apply under this subsection to civil actions brought by attorneys general.

(B) SAVINGS PROVISION.—Nothing in this subsection may be construed to prohibit an authorized official of a State from initiating or continuing any proceeding in a court of the State for a violation of any civil or criminal law of the State.

SEC. 3. DEFINITIONS.

In this Act:

(1) COMMISSION.—The term "Commission" means the Federal Trade Commission.

(2) EVENT.—The term "event" means any concert, theatrical performance, sporting event, show, or similarly scheduled activity, taking place in a venue with a seating or attendance capacity exceeding 200 persons that—

(A) is open to the general public; and

(B) is promoted, advertised, or marketed in interstate commerce or for which event tickets are generally sold or distributed in interstate commerce.

(3) EVENT TICKET.—The term "event ticket" means any physical, electronic, or other form of a certificate, document, voucher, token, or other evidence indicating that the bearer, possessor, or person entitled to possession through purchase or otherwise has—

(A) a right, privilege, or license to enter an event venue or occupy a particular seat or area in an event venue with respect to one or more events; or

(B) an entitlement to purchase such a right, privilege, or license with respect to one or more future events.

(4) TICKET ISSUER.—The term "ticket issuer" means any person who makes event tickets available, directly or indirectly, to the general public, and may include—

(A) the operator of the venue;

(B) the sponsor or promoter of an event;

(C) a sports team participating in an event or a league whose teams are participating in an event;

(D) a theater company, musical group, or similar participant in an event; and

(E) an agent for any such person.

Mr. DAINES. I ask unanimous consent that the committee-reported substitute amendment be agreed to, the bill, as amended, be considered read a third time and passed, and the motion to reconsider be considered made and laid upon the table.

The PRESIDING OFFICER. Without objection, it is so ordered.

The committee-reported amendment in the nature of a substitute was agreed to.

The bill (S. 3183), as amended, was ordered to be engrossed for a third reading, was read the third time, and passed.

PROGRAM MANAGEMENT IMPROVEMENT ACCOUNTABILITY ACT

Mr. DAINES. Mr. President, I ask the Chair to lay before the Senate the message to accompany S. 1550.

The Presiding Officer laid before the Senate the following message from the House of Representatives:

Resolved, That the bill from the Senate (S. 1550). entitled "An Act to amend title 31, United States Code, to establish entities tasked with improving program and project management in certain Federal agencies, and for other, purposes.", do pass with an amendment.

Mr. DAINES. Mr. President, I move to concur in the House amendment; and I ask unanimous consent that the motion be agreed to and the motion to reconsider be considered made and laid upon the table.

The PRESIDING OFFICER. Without objection, it is so ordered.

GAO CIVILIAN TASK AND DELIVERY ORDER PROTEST AUTHORITY ACT OF 2016

Mr. DAINES. Mr. President, I ask unanimous consent that the Senate proceed to the immediate consideration of H.R. 5995, which was received from the House.

The PRESIDING OFFICER. The clerk will report the bill by title.

The senior assistant legislative clerk read as follows:

A bill (H.R. 5995) to strike the sunset on certain provisions relating to the authorized protest of a task or delivery order under section 4106 of title 41, United States Code.

There being no objection, the Senate proceeded to consider the bill.

Mr. DAINES. Mr. President, I ask unanimous consent that the bill be considered read a third time and passed and the motion to reconsider be considered made and laid upon the table.

The PRESIDING OFFICER. Without objection, it is so ordered.

The bill (H.R. 5995) was ordered to a third reading, was read the third time, and passed.

DR. OTIS BOWEN VETERAN HOUSE

Mr. DAINES. Mr. President, I ask unanimous consent that the Committee on Veterans' Affairs be discharged from further consideration of H.R. 5509 and the Senate proceed to its immediate consideration.

The PRESIDING OFFICER. Without objection, it is so ordered.

The clerk will report the bill by title.

The senior assistant legislative clerk read as follows:

A bill (H.R. 5509) to name the Department of Veterans Affairs temporary lodging facility in Indianapolis, Indiana, as the "Dr. Otis Bowen Veteran House."

There being no objection, the Senate proceeded to consider the bill.

Mr. DAINES. Mr. President, I ask unanimous consent that the bill be considered read a third time and passed and the motion to reconsider be considered made and laid upon the table.

The PRESIDING OFFICER. Without objection, it is so ordered.

The bill (H.R. 5509) was ordered to a third reading, was read the third time, and passed.

HONORING ARNOLD PALMER

Mr. DAINES. Mr. President, I ask unanimous consent that the Judiciary Committee be discharged from further consideration of and the Senate now proceed to the consideration of S. Res. 605.

The PRESIDING OFFICER. Without objection, it is so ordered.

The clerk will report the resolution by title.

The senior assistant legislative clerk read as follows:

A resolution (S. Res. 605) honoring Arnold Palmer.

There being no objection, the Senate proceeded to consider the resolution.

Mr. DAINES. Mr. President, I ask unanimous consent that the resolution be agreed to, the preamble be agreed to, and the motions to reconsider be considered made and laid upon the table.

The PRESIDING OFFICER. Without objection, it is so ordered.

The resolution (S. Res. 605) was agreed to.

The preamble was agreed to.

(The resolution, with its preamble, is printed in the RECORD of September 29, 2016, under "Submitted Resolutions.")

EXPRESSING SUPPORT FOR THE DESIGNATION OF THE FIRST FRIDAY IN OCTOBER 2016 AS "MANUFACTURING DAY"

Mr. DAINES. Mr. President, I ask unanimous consent that the Commerce, Science, and Transportation Committee be discharged from further consideration of and the Senate now proceed to the consideration of S. Res. 610.

The PRESIDING OFFICER. Without objection, it is so ordered.

The clerk will report the resolution by title.

The senior assistant legislative clerk read as follows:

A resolution (S. Res. 610) expressing support for the designation of the first Friday in October 2016 as "Manufacturing Day."

There being no objection, the Senate proceeded to consider the resolution.

Mr. DAINES. Mr. President, I ask unanimous consent that the resolution be agreed to, the preamble be agreed to, and the motions to reconsider be considered made and laid upon the table.

The PRESIDING OFFICER. Without objection, it is so ordered.

The resolution (S. Res. 610) was agreed to.

The preamble was agreed to.

(The resolution, with its preamble, is printed in the RECORD of September 29, 2016, under "Submitted Resolutions.")

RECOGNIZING THE 75TH ANNIVERSARY OF THE ESTABLISHMENT OF THE UNIVERSITY OF TEXAS MD ANDERSON CANCER CENTER IN HOUSTON, TEXAS

Mr. DAINES. Mr. President, I ask unanimous consent that the Senate proceed to the consideration of S. Res. 626, submitted earlier today.

The PRESIDING OFFICER. The clerk will report the resolution by title.

The senior assistant legislative clerk read as follows:

A resolution (S. Res. 626) recognizing the 75th anniversary of the establishment of the University of Texas MD Anderson Cancer Center in Houston, Texas.

There being no objection, the Senate proceeded to consider the resolution.

Mr. DAINES. Mr. President, I ask unanimous consent that the resolution be agreed to, the preamble be agreed to, and the motions to consider be considered made and laid upon the table with no intervening action or debate.

The PRESIDING OFFICER. Without objection, it is so ordered.

The resolution (S. Res. 626) was agreed to.

The preamble was agreed to.

(The resolution, with its preamble, is printed in today's RECORD under "Submitted Resolutions.")

SILVER STAR SERVICE BANNER DAY

Mr. DAINES. Mr. President, I ask unanimous consent that the Committee on the Judiciary be discharged from further consideration of S. 3386 and the Senate proceed to its immediate consideration.

The PRESIDING OFFICER. Without objection, it is so ordered.

The clerk will report the bill by title.

The senior assistant legislative clerk read as follows:

A bill (S. 3386) to amend title 36, United States Code, to designate May 1 as "Silver Star Service Banner Day."

There being no objection, the Senate proceeded to consider the bill.

Mr. DAINES. Mr. President, I ask unanimous consent that the bill be read a third time and passed and the motion to reconsider be considered made and laid upon the table.

The PRESIDING OFFICER. Without objection, it is so ordered.

The bill (S. 3386) was ordered to be engrossed for a third reading, was read the third time, and passed, as follows:

S. 3386

Be it enacted by the Senate and House of Representatives of the United States of America in Congress assembled,

SECTION 1. SHORT TITLE.

This Act may be cited as the "Silver Star Service Banner Day Act".

SEC. 2. FINDINGS.

Congress finds the following:

(1) Congress has always honored the sacrifices made by the wounded and ill members of the Armed Forces.

(2) The Silver Star Service Banner has come to represent the members of the Armed Forces and veterans who were wounded or became ill in combat in the wars fought by the United States.

(3) The Silver Star Families of America was formed to help the people of the United States remember the sacrifices made by the wounded and ill members of the Armed Forces by designing and manufacturing Silver Star Service Banners and Silver Star Flags for that purpose.

(4) The sole mission of the Silver Star Families of America is to evoke memories of the sacrifices of members of the Armed Forces and veterans on behalf of the United States through the presence of a Silver Star Service Banner in a window or a Silver Star Flag flying.

(5) The sacrifices of members of the Armed Forces and veterans on behalf of the United States should never be forgotten.

(6) May 1 is an appropriate date to designate as "Silver Star Service Banner Day".

SEC. 3. DESIGNATION.

(a) IN GENERAL.—Chapter 1 of title 36, United States Code, is amended by adding at the end the following:

"§ 145. Silver Star Service Banner Day

"(a) DESIGNATION.—May 1 is Silver Star Service Banner Day.

"(b) PROCLAMATION.—The President is requested to issue each year a proclamation calling on the people of the United States to observe Silver Star Service Banner Day with appropriate programs, ceremonies, and activities.".

(b) TECHNICAL AND CONFORMING AMENDMENT.—The table of sections for chapter 1 of title 36, United States Code, is amended by inserting after the item relating to section 144 the following:

"145. Silver Star Service Banner Day.".

ORDERS FOR THURSDAY, DECEMBER 1, 2016

Mr. DAINES. Mr. President, I ask unanimous consent that when the Senate completes its business today, it adjourn until 9:30 a.m., Thursday, December 1; that following the prayer and pledge, the morning hour be deemed expired, the Journal of proceedings be approved to date, and the time for the two leaders be reserved for their use later in the day; further, that following leader remarks, the Senate be in a period of morning business, with Senators permitted to speak therein for up to 10 minutes each; finally, that the Senate proceed to the consideration of H.R. 6297 at 1:45 p.m. tomorrow, as provided for under the previous order.

The PRESIDING OFFICER. Without objection, it is so ordered.

ADJOURNMENT UNTIL 9:30 A.M. TOMORROW

Mr. DAINES. Mr. President, if there is no further business to come before the Senate, I ask unanimous consent that it stand adjourned under the previous order.

There being no objection, the Senate, at 6:42 p.m., adjourned until Thursday, December 1, 2016, at 9:30 a.m.

HOUSE OF REPRESENTATIVES—*Wednesday, November 30, 2016*

The House met at 10 a.m. and was called to order by the Speaker pro tempore (Mr. BOST).

DESIGNATION OF SPEAKER PRO TEMPORE

The SPEAKER pro tempore laid before the House the following communication from the Speaker:

WASHINGTON, DC,
November 30, 2016.

I hereby appoint the Honorable MIKE BOST to act as Speaker pro tempore on this day.

PAUL D. RYAN,
Speaker of the House of Representatives.

MORNING-HOUR DEBATE

The SPEAKER pro tempore. Pursuant to the order of the House of January 5, 2016, the Chair will now recognize Members from lists submitted by the majority and minority leaders for morning-hour debate.

The Chair will alternate recognition between the parties, with each party limited to 1 hour and each Member other than the majority and minority leaders and the minority whip limited to 5 minutes, but in no event shall debate continue beyond 11:50 a.m.

THERE IS MORE THAT UNITES US THAN DIVIDES US

The SPEAKER pro tempore. The Chair recognizes the gentleman from Illinois (Mr. QUIGLEY) for 5 minutes.

Mr. QUIGLEY. Mr. Speaker, equality, justice, and opportunity for all cannot coexist in a society where bigotry, misogyny, anti-Semitism, and other kinds of hatred are accepted or even encouraged. Only one of these two sets of values has made our country great, while the other has the ability to further divide and ultimately destroy us.

Following the President-elect's appointment of Steve Bannon as White House Chief Strategist, my office received hundreds of calls and letters from concerned constituents deeply worried about an administration that pits people against one another, creates scapegoats, and goes against the better angels of our nature.

If the President-elect wants to be the President for all Americans, he simply cannot surround himself with individuals that tolerate, inspire, or participate in hate speech.

With reports of bias-based attacks continuing to rise following the election, we must remain focused on ensuring that no American, regardless of race, religion, gender, or sexual orientation, feels marginalized or afraid in his or her own community.

We must remember that there will always be more that unites us than divides us. It is up to us to stop hatred wherever we see it, especially in the halls of government.

DEMOCRACY FOR CUBA

The SPEAKER pro tempore. The Chair recognizes the gentlewoman from Florida (Ms. ROS-LEHTINEN) for 5 minutes.

Ms. ROS-LEHTINEN. Mr. Speaker, over the years, I have come down here regularly to the Chamber, one of the most iconic symbols of our wonderful democracy, and urged the United States to do more to support the cause of freedom for my native homeland, the island nation of Cuba.

In tow would be posters just like the one I have here today, depicting images of the real Cuba, the Cuba in which opposition to the Castro regime is met with violence and harassment, extrajudicial punishment and confinement in one of the many Cuban gulags built by Fidel Castro. These images would show what the regime under Fidel Castro would do to the Ladies in White depicted here. These women, clad in white, carrying flowers, march peacefully to mass at a Catholic church every Sunday, praying for their loved ones wrongfully imprisoned by the regime, only to be harassed and beaten by Castro's thugs.

I came to this floor to offer my support for these brave women; like Laura Pollan, who was mysteriously killed, no doubt by the regime, and Berta Soler, pictured here.

Mr. Speaker, I have come to this very floor denouncing the Castro regime's treatment of opposition leaders like Jorge Luis Garcia "Antunez" Perez, who was imprisoned for 17 years by Castro for speaking out against communism and refusing the regime's communist reeducation program.

I spoke out in support of Dr. Oscar Elias Biscet, who was sentenced to 25 years in Castro's prisons for crimes committed against Cuban sovereignty, which, in Cuba, is code for calling for reforms; and he was awarded the Presidential Medal of Freedom by George W. Bush.

I stood here for Coco Farinas, right over here. Coco Farinas went on a 50-day hunger strike just recently to bring attention to the plight of the Cuban people.

I also spoke in favor of Cuban rapper El Sexto, pictured here, who was jailed just last week, again, when the regime announced the tyrant's death.

I stood here in solidarity with Cubans, freedom fighters like Antonio Rodiles, pictured here, who was arrested hours before President Obama landed in Cuba earlier this year. Round up the usual suspects.

I have come to this well time and time again to call attention to the abuses being committed by Fidel Castro against the Cuban people, the people of the homeland that I was forced to flee along with my family when I was a little girl, and to the people who have had everything taken away from them and could not speak for themselves.

And I have come repeatedly to this very podium to call my colleagues' attention to the threat that Fidel Castro and his regime pose to the U.S. and our national security. This thug, Fidel Castro, who attempted to infiltrate every level of our government through his intelligence service, like convicted spy Ana Belen Montes, who is currently still serving her prison sentence in a Texas jail.

This despot, who aligned himself with the greatest threats to the U.S., like Iran and Russia, and allowed Russia to put up a facility in Cuba in order to spy on our Nation; this autocrat, who told the Ayatollah in Iran that both Iran and Cuba would bring the U.S. to its knees, and who tried to bring the world to nuclear war during the Cuban Missile Crisis.

Yet, this is a man who some world leaders and media want to romanticize. They whitewash his horrific crimes and claim that he was a legendary folk hero.

The truth is, Mr. Speaker, Fidel Castro was a sadistic murderer, a tyrant, and a hypocrite. He was a thug who took control over all industries and Cuba and decried capitalism. Yet, somehow, he was likely worth about $1 billion when he died.

When 11 million Cubans are barely struggling to get by under his Communist regime, this is a tyrant who died with more wealth than the entire island nation.

Mr. Speaker, Fidel Castro is dead, and Cuba and the world are better for it. Now we have an opportunity to move forward by reversing some of this administration's concessions to the Castro regime and press for reforms.

It is time for the Cuban people to have the opportunity to achieve freedom and democracy for which they

---

have been yearning. We must pressure the regime in the island of Cuba.

We must not relent until there are free and fair elections, until all political prisoners are freed, and until the people's basic and fundamental human rights are restored. Is that too much to ask for the enslaved and oppressed people of Cuba?

Let that be how we honor the countless Cubans who have lost their lives or who have suffered under the terrible dictatorship of Fidel Castro. That is some legacy.

DRAINING THE SWAMP

The SPEAKER pro tempore. The Chair recognizes the gentleman from Oregon (Mr. DEFAZIO) for 5 minutes.

Mr. DEFAZIO. Mr. Speaker, I remember the closing ad in the Trump campaign. He was going to drain the swamp. Good. And then he had the CEO of Goldman Sachs up there, who represented the global elite who robbed the working class of their savings and homes. Pretty powerful stuff, and I will tell you what, I pretty much agreed with it.

Now, he is already working on draining the swamp, so things are showing up in D.C. that you haven't seen for a while. I was walking down the street by Trump Tower International last night and I found this laying in the street.

Now, I haven't seen this since a guy named Henry "Hank" Paulson, former CEO of Goldman Sachs, was Secretary of the Treasury under George Bush and he came to Congress after Wall Street destroyed our economy with reckless gambling and asked for an unlimited bailout of Wall Street, the key to the Treasury.

Now, I opposed that and, for one proud day, the House of Representatives didn't bail out Wall Street. Unfortunately, the Senate came back to town. They got scared by Wall Street tanking the market. They bailed out Wall Street and a number of my colleagues in the House changed their votes, so they all got bailed out. Well enough, good.

Now, that is Goldman Sachs that says please return to Goldman Sachs. Well, Donald Trump is returning the key to the Treasury to Goldman Sachs. Ain't that great? That's draining the swamp folks; draining the swamp.

A guy named Mnuchin—now he is a film producer, but he made a fortune at Goldman Sachs; his dad worked at Goldman Sachs for 33 years; his brother still works at Goldman Sachs—is going to get the key to the Treasury.

Now, he also made a fortune during the TARP bailout by buying an asset, IndyMac, and dispossessing tens of thousands of people of their homes.

So I would say that Mr. Trump, the candidate, and the ad was right. These people at Goldman Sachs and elsewhere are the global elite who have stolen people's savings, who have taken away their homes.

But now he is putting them back in charge. Mr. Mnuchin is getting the key to the Treasury, Goldman Sachs executive, dad, lifetime Goldman Sachs executive, brother still working at Goldman Sachs.

How the heck is that draining the swamp?

PRESIDENT-ELECT TRUMP MAY HAVE WON THE POPULAR VOTE

The SPEAKER pro tempore. The Chair recognizes the gentleman from Alabama (Mr. BROOKS) for 5 minutes.

Mr. BROOKS of Alabama. Mr. Speaker, President-elect Donald Trump opined in a tweet on November 27 that: "In addition to winning the electoral college in a landslide, I won the popular vote if you deduct the millions of people who voted illegally."

As would be expected, a circus of left-wing, media pundits immediately pounced on President-elect Trump's opinion in an effort to silence serious discussion of the noncitizen voter fraud problem.

For example, PolitiFact, a self-proclaimed purveyor of truth, gave Trump's statement a "Pants on Fire" evaluation and stated: "Neither Trump nor his allies have presented any evidence of widespread illegal voting. In reality, studies have consistently shown that voter fraud is nowhere near common enough to call into question millions and millions of votes."

The truth is, PolitiFact and its allies ignore contrary studies and information. But isn't that what you would expect of PolitiFact and its leftwing media allies that have, in effect, become the communications wing of the Democratic Party?

A 2014 study by professors at Old Dominion University and George Mason University estimated that noncitizens vote 80 percent of the time for Democrats.

Does anyone really expect Democrats and their media and pundit allies to object to or scrutinize illegal votes that may be the deciding factor in the election of Democrat candidates?

Let me give but one example of how tens of millions of noncitizens are a threat to register to vote, and vote, in America's elections.

Alabama is my home State. Our laws limit voting to American citizens. That sounds pretty reasonable to me, that only Americans should vote in American elections. In order to limit American elections to American citizens, Alabama code section 31–13–28 requires proof of citizenship to register to vote. The code lists 13 different documents that are conclusive proof of citizenship, things like driver's licenses, birth certificates, passports, naturalization documents, adoption papers, military service documents. Further, an American can offer any other document that is proof of citizenship.

In January of 2016, the United States Election Assistance Commission approved Alabama's proof of citizenship voter registration requirement. The League of Women Voters then challenged proof of citizenship laws in the Washington, D.C., Federal courts.

In an astonishing ruling in September of 2016, a mere 6 weeks before the election, the United States Court of Appeals for the District of Columbia entered a preliminary injunction that barred Alabama, Kansas, Georgia and, indirectly, any other State from requiring proof of citizenship to register to vote.

The Court of Appeals' ruling opens the floodgates for voting by tens of millions of illegal aliens and other citizens on American soil, thus blatantly undermining the American Republic for which so many Americans fought and died.

The dissenting opinion of the Court of Appeals' Senior Circuit Judge Randolph well-described the Court's ruling, and I quote:

"Of utmost importance is that on the eve of a Presidential election, and elections for Federal office, a court has issued an injunction forbidding Kansas, Georgia, and Alabama from enforcing their election laws, laws requiring those who seek to register to prove that they are citizens of this country.

"That order is unconstitutional.

"In my view, the appeal should have been disposed on the ground that the League of Women Voters and their allies have not even come close to demonstrating the type of harm entitling them to an order suspending these State laws."

□ 1015

Notwithstanding Judge Randolph's dissent, the bad guys prevailed.

Now, what does all that mean? It means that, right before the Presidential election, Federal courts created a massive legal hole that empowers noncitizens to register to vote and, once registered, to vote in America's elections with impunity, thereby undermining and diluting the vote of lawful Americans and striking at the very heart of our democracy.

It means that President-elect Trump may very well be right that he "won the popular vote if you deduct the millions of people who voted illegally."

Quite frankly, Mr. Speaker, we will never know for sure if hundreds of thousands or millions of noncitizens voted in the 2016 elections. Worse yet, if the leftwing media pundits continue to summarily dismiss and turn a blind eye to the problem, it will be harder to stop future elections from being stolen.

FAREWELL ADDRESS

The SPEAKER pro tempore. The Chair recognizes the gentleman from

Washington (Mr. McDermott) for 5 minutes.

Mr. McDERMOTT. Mr. Speaker, it is hard to condense 28 years into 5 minutes, but that is what I am going to try to do here.

This is a wonderful opportunity that I have had to represent the Seventh District of the State of Washington, and I want to thank the people who sent me here. To represent people for 28 years, having their trust, is a great responsibility and a great honor.

My constituents have witnessed the good times and the bad. They have offered encouragement when I did what they thought was right and were gracious to point out to me when they thought that I had veered from where they thought I should be. I have enduring thanks for what they did for me.

I also want to thank my colleagues here in the House, my colleagues in the Washington State delegation, all the staff who have served me over these 28 years, and, of course, my family, who allowed me to serve here in the Congress.

When I envisioned what might be my final speech on the floor of the House, I had hoped for a brighter political future than the one currently unfolding. For me and for millions of Americans, it is difficult to see the coming 4 years as anything short of calamitous. Never has the role of congressional oversight been as critical to the integrity of our Republic as it is now, and I beg my colleagues to remain vigilant as we confront this menacing wave of nativism, misogyny, and racism that is raging in our country.

The systems of checks and balances underpin the very survival of the democracy, and this body must not fail in its constitutional responsibility to scrutinize every executive action and to pass sanction when the rights of the people are threatened. This is the people's House, designed not just to reflect the will of the people, but also to ensure the rights of the people endure.

The right to worship as you choose, the right to marry whom you love, the right to equal pay, the right to a livable wage, the right to affordable health care, the right to reproductive choice, and, of course, the basic founding rights affirmed by our earliest tenets and enshrined as "inalienable" are always at risk without the people's advocate to protect them.

As President Obama said in his second inaugural:

History may deem equality for all as self-evident, but we know these rights have never been self-executing; that while freedom is a gift from God, it must be secured by the people here on Earth.

Mr. Speaker, you have a dark and difficult road ahead. Please do not lose sight of the fundamental decency and respect for our fellow citizens that has always made this country great.

It is fashionable these days to ridicule the Congress, but I depart this institution steadfast in the belief that the government—and the Federal Government, in particular—can, should, and does make a positive impact on the lives of all Americans.

Moreover, I am a proud member of the Democratic Party. We may spend the next couple of years massaging our message and regrouping our strength, but the values that define us as a party are as true and as important today as they ever were. This is still the party of social and economic justice; it is still the party of environmental protection; it is still the party of international diplomacy; it is still the party of guaranteed health care and quality education; and this will always—always—be the party of ethnic, racial, and gender inclusion. We are a party of service, of dignity, and of hope.

I came to this House 28 years ago to work on health care, and with President Obama, we were able to get it started. It is incumbent on this body not to leave the American people out in the cold when they are sick or ailing or worried about whether they can go to the hospital and pay for what they have got.

Mr. Speaker, it has been an honor to serve here. I leave here. It has been a good run, and I thank everyone who has been helpful to me during that period of time.

Mr. Speaker, it's hard to condense 28 remarkable years into five minutes, and it's even harder to thank each of those people with whom I have worked and who have helped me over the course of this fortunate career.

First, I want to thank the people of the 7th District of Washington State. It has been my privilege to serve them in the United States Congress. I leave forever grateful for their unwavering trust and support.

My constituents have witnessed the good times and the bad; they offered encouragement when I did something right, and were gracious to point me in the right direction when I had wandered off the path. They have my enduring thanks.

I also want to thank my colleagues here in the House; my colleagues in the Washington State delegation; all the staff who have served with me over the last 28 years; and of course my family who has supported me in my public service.

When I envisioned giving what is perhaps my final speech on the floor of the U.S. House of Representatives, I had hoped for a brighter political future than the one currently unfolding.

For me, and for millions of Americans, it is difficult to see the coming four years as nothing short of calamitous.

Never has the role of Congressional oversight been as critical to the integrity of our republic as it is now and I beg my colleagues to remain vigilant as we confront this menacing wave of nativism, misogyny, and racism that is raging our country.

The system of checks and balances underpin the very survival of our democracy and this body must not fail in its Constitutional responsibility to scrutinize executive action and to pass sanction when the rights of the people are threatened.

This is the "People's House," designed not just to reflect the will of the people, but also to ensure that the rights of those people endure.

The right to worship as you choose; the right to marry who you love; the right to equal pay; the right to a livable wage; the right to affordable healthcare; the right to reproductive choice; and of course, those basic founding rights, affirmed by our earliest tenets and enshrined as "inalienable," are always at risk without the people's advocates to uphold them.

As President Obama said in his Second Inaugural, history may deem equality for all as self-evident, but we know these rights have "never been self-executing; that while freedom is a gift from God, it must be secured by His people here on Earth."

My colleagues, you have a dark and difficult road ahead. Please do not lose sight of the fundamental decency and respect for our fellow citizens that has always made this country great.

It is fashionable these days to ridicule the Congress, but I depart this institution steadfast in the belief that government, and the federal government in particular, can, should, and does make a positive impact on the lives of Americans.

Moreover, I am a proud member of the Democratic Party. We may spend the next couple of years honing our message and regrouping our electoral strength, but the values that define us as a party are as true and important today as they ever were.

This is still the party of social and economic justice; this is still the party of environmental protection; this is still the party of international diplomacy; this is still the party of guaranteed healthcare and quality education.

And this will always be the party of ethnic, racial, and gender inclusion.

We are the party of service, of dignity, and of I hope.

I came to the House 28 years ago as a proud liberal. And that is how I am going to leave.

Mr. Speaker, it has been an honor, and my privilege.

WAR ON COAL

The SPEAKER pro tempore. The Chair recognizes the gentleman from West Virginia (Mr. JENKINS) for 5 minutes.

Mr. JENKINS of West Virginia. Mr. Speaker, coal communities throughout West Virginia and Appalachia are struggling. This administration's war on coal and market forces have combined to close coal mines and send thousands of coal miners to the unemployment lines.

While we work to repeal onerous and overreaching regulations and reopen mines, we also need to diversify our economy. That means attracting new industries to our coal communities and creating new opportunities for investment.

I have introduced, today, H.R. 6403, legislation that will help us do just that. The Creating Opportunities for Rural Economies Act would allocate a portion of available new markets tax credits to be used for development in communities impacted by the downturn in coal.

Over the next 3 years, it would mean $525 million in credits for heavily impacted communities in West Virginia and Appalachia. These tax credits can be used to help spur investment for new businesses. They can go toward developing new mixed-use facilities, food and grocery stores in underserved communities, manufacturing, healthcare services, and so much more.

I want to thank Senator SHELLEY MOORE CAPITO for her leadership in the Senate on this important issue and legislation. Our coal communities deserve our support and help as they work to diversify their economies.

MINERS' PENSIONS

Mr. JENKINS of West Virginia. Mr. Speaker, with only weeks left in this Congress—2, to be exact—our retired coal miners and widows are wondering if we will act to protect them. At the end of the year, the healthcare benefits for many miners and their widows will dry up, and their pensions could be cut in the months and years ahead.

When they went down into the mines, they were made a promise: when you retire, you will have a good pension and healthcare benefits. Now that promise is in jeopardy. The pensions and benefits they worked their whole lives for are in jeopardy.

Mr. Speaker, time is running out to do the right thing by our miners and their families. But we have a solution: the Coal Healthcare and Pensions Protection Act, legislation I am a proud cosponsor of. It is a bipartisan bill, and a similar bill is pending in the Senate.

Congress needs to act to fulfill this promise, to keep our word to the miners of West Virginia and other coal States. These miners and their families deserve no less than what they worked their entire lives to earn: the peace of mind that comes with a pension.

Mr. Speaker, I urge my colleagues to keep the promise and support this important legislation. Time is running out to stand up for our miners and their families.

STRENGTHENING THE PARTNERSHIP BETWEEN ISRAEL AND THE UNITED STATES

The SPEAKER pro tempore. The Chair recognizes the gentleman from Pennsylvania (Mr. COSTELLO) for 5 minutes.

Mr. COSTELLO of Pennsylvania. Mr. Speaker, I rise today in support of recent efforts to strengthen the partnership between Israel and the United States by this Congress.

Our countries have a long and important friendship. That is why my and

this Congress' support of H.R. 5877, the United States-Israel Advanced Research Partnership Act, and H.R. 5843, the United States-Israel Cybersecurity Cooperation Enhancement Act, two bills that advance the vital goal of bolstering the U.S.-Israeli partnership on security, are so important. These bills focus specifically on strengthening cybersecurity collaboration through grants, research, and antiterrorism programs.

Knowing of the security challenges Israel faces in its region, these measures would reinforce our commitment to our most critical ally in the Middle East at a time when the evolving threat of a cybersecurity attack has never been more serious. It is imperative we continue to work together on the security issues faced by our respective countries.

STUDENT VETERANS

Mr. COSTELLO of Pennsylvania. Mr. Speaker, I rise today in support of bipartisan legislation to improve and simplify the decisionmaking process for our student veterans.

H.R. 5047, the Protecting Veterans' Educational Choice Act, would help veterans clearly understand if and how their coursework credits might transfer between schools. The legislation would require the Department of Veterans Affairs to provide student veterans with detailed information about education assistance benefits, including how to request free education counseling services at the VA.

For our veterans who wish to obtain or complete a degree, access to this information can not only save them countless administrative headaches, but also precious time and money. I am proud to support measures such as this bill that would streamline the transition for veterans into civilian life and provide them with the tools and resources to succeed.

I urge my colleagues to support this bill.

FINDING CURES

Mr. COSTELLO of Pennsylvania. Mr. Speaker, I rise today in support of H.R. 34, the 21st Century Cures Act, a bipartisan bill that focuses solely on solutions for patients.

All of us have been affected, whether directly or indirectly, by tragic diseases. That is why advancing and improving medical innovation and providing much-needed resources that are required for finding cures, which this bill would do, are such important goals.

The 21st Century Cures Act would target diseases that do not yet have a cure. Bringing safe, effective drugs and devices to Pennsylvanians and Americans in a more efficient manner will benefit our families and communities. This bill would also bring much-needed certainty to job creators and help keep Pennsylvania at the forefront of medical innovation.

In Congress, we have a responsibility to ensure that resources are available to help defeat these yet incurable diseases. This bill is a significant step forward toward this goal.

The 21st Century Cures Act also includes important mental health reform measures. I have focused much of my attention since coming into office on ways to make Pennsylvania communities healthier and safer, and families across my district have shared their stories about how mental health issues impact individuals, families, and communities. Much-needed reforms are included in this bill: empowering patients and caregivers, ensuring availability of treatment, encouraging students to choose careers in mental health, providing for those on the front lines, and maintaining transparency in government programs.

I urge my colleagues to support this legislation.

HOMENET AUTOMOTIVE WINS TECH AWARD

Mr. COSTELLO of Pennsylvania. Mr. Speaker, I want to congratulate HomeNet Automotive, a company in my district, on receiving the Tech360 Technology Team of the Year Award from the Chester County Economic Development Council.

I had the opportunity to visit HomeNet Automotive over the summer and enjoyed learning about their innovative company, which is bringing jobs and forward-looking technology to our community.

HomeNet Automotive makes the SnapLot Photo Capture App, which provides car dealers with the ability to update the inventory it displays on their Web sites. A tech team from the company based in East Whiteland, Chester County, updated the technology to improve its ease of use for dealers. The app is currently used by dealers nationwide as well as at Manheim Auto Auctions, with the possibility of expanding with Manheim into Europe.

I am very proud of that company in Pennsylvania's Sixth Congressional District.

RECOGNIZING RYAN VARGO

Mr. COSTELLO of Pennsylvania. Mr. Speaker, I wish to bring attention to the leadership of Ryan Vargo, a senior up at Pottsgrove School District, and his role in helping expand recreational opportunity at the Upper Pottsgrove Township Park. He spearheaded a project to install donated playground equipment at Hollenbach Park off North Hanover Street, adding recreational opportunity for children in the Pottsgrove community.

It is a testament to how our country and its future is great when we look at student leaders and what they are doing in their teenage years to help improve communities across this Commonwealth and across this country.

☐ 1030

MINNESOTA'S BEST AND BRIGHTEST

The SPEAKER pro tempore. The Chair recognizes the gentleman from Minnesota (Mr. EMMER) for 5 minutes.

Mr. EMMER of Minnesota. Mr. Speaker, I rise today to celebrate five outstanding students in my district who have earned a Fulbright scholarship this year.

Austin Barkley of Sartell, Paul Creager of Stillwater, Amy Grant of Big Lake, Natalie Hoidal of Forest Lake, and Jenna Maus of Kimball will each have the once-in-a-lifetime opportunity to lecture, study, teach English, or do research in foreign countries that range from Mexico to Malaysia. Each of these Fulbright scholars will not only have the ability to promote healthy relations and diplomacy with foreign nations, but they will also bring home the knowledge and leadership experience they will gain while abroad.

Many past participants of this program have gone on to achieve success in a variety of fields, with some even serving here in Congress. I have no doubt we will see great things from each of these exceptional individuals, and I congratulate and wish them luck on their exciting adventure.

MINNESOTA'S TOP FARM FAMILY

Mr. EMMER of Minnesota. Mr. Speaker, I rise today to congratulate Bruce and Sharon Johnson of East Bethel and the Minnesota Fresh Farm for being named the Anoka County Farm Family of the Year by the University of Minnesota. For the past 2 decades, the University of Minnesota has chosen top farming families for their work promoting our State's great agricultural industry.

The Minnesota Fresh Farm has been passed down from one generation of the Johnson family to the next and is currently being farmed by Bruce and Sharon Johnson, along with their son, Luke; and his wife, Liz.

This year, the Johnson family was chosen for the efforts they have made to educate Minnesota's youth about farming. This includes working with the Opportunity Services in Anoka, an organization that helps individuals with special needs so they can enjoy farming and the great outdoors. The Johnson family were also chosen because of their focus on sustainable production methods and growing food without using pesticides.

I want to congratulate the Johnson family and thank them for their efforts to promote the farming life and Minnesota's agricultural industry.

INVESTING IN MINNESOTA'S FUTURE

Mr. EMMER of Minnesota. Mr. Speaker, I rise today to celebrate a great Minnesota company that is actively helping our Nation's students develop skills that will help them shine in their future success. I am proud that Minnesota's own Best Buy Foundation is giving grants to form programs that will give students the chance to master important technology skills, like coding and graphic design.

The world that we are living in is rapidly transforming and technology is quickly becoming more than just a luxury—it is becoming a way of life and a key ingredient to our Nation's future success.

What is perhaps most commendable about Best Buy's grant program is that it targets teens who live in underserved communities. If we as a Nation hope to remain not only relevant, but competitive, then everybody must have the chance to strive. I would like to thank the Best Buy Foundation for recognizing the importance of serving the underserved.

STEARNS COUNTY HEROES

Mr. EMMER of Minnesota. Mr. Speaker, I rise today to honor 12 Stearns County dispatchers who received medals of merit for their work during the horrific attack at the Crossroads Center Mall.

What seemed like a normal night at a mall in central Minnesota quickly turned into a nightmare when a man began to attack shoppers with a knife. As the attacks unfolded, chaos ensued.

What kept this dangerous situation from getting even worse was the dedicated work of these 12 professionals. In 2 hours, they took 250 calls and they made numerous calls to emergency responders to keep them abreast on the most current details of the attack. As a result of their work, there was no loss of life and all shoppers and first responders were able to return home safely to their loved ones that night.

While words can never express the full extent of our gratitude, I am proud to stand here today to thank these men and women for their heroic efforts.

RECOGNIZING REPRESENTATIVE RON STEPHENS

The SPEAKER pro tempore. The Chair recognizes the gentleman from Georgia (Mr. CARTER) for 5 minutes.

Mr. CARTER of Georgia. Mr. Speaker, I rise today to recognize my lifelong friend, Representative Ron Stephens from Savannah, Georgia, for being awarded the Distinguished Alumnus Award from Armstrong State University.

Chairman Stephens represents the 164th District in the Georgia General Assembly. During his time in the legislature, he has done a remarkable job representing his constituents.

Currently, he is the chairman of the House Economic Development and Tourism Committee and a member of the Appropriations, Rules, and Ways and Means Committees, allowing him to advocate important issues for his constituency. In addition, Governor Nathan Deal appointed Mr. Stephens to the Georgia Tourism Foundation.

Before his time in the Georgia General Assembly, Chairman Stephens was already working for the betterment of his community. He began his career in pharmacy and served the medical needs of others for 37 years. Thereafter, he served as a councilman in Garden City, Georgia.

I am proud of my lifelong friend for his work, and I am overjoyed that he is receiving the Distinguished Alumnus Award from Armstrong State University.

RECOGNIZING COACH DOYLE KELLEY

Mr. CARTER of Georgia. Mr. Speaker, I rise today to honor Mr. Doyle Kelley from Savannah, Georgia, who passed away on September 30.

Mr. Kelley, known throughout the Savannah community as Coach Kelley, dedicated his life to teaching and mentoring students.

After graduating from Armstrong State University in 1969, Coach Kelley started coaching Jenkins High School's basketball team, sparking his commitment to students. Coach Kelley's passion shows not only in his incredible success on the court, but also the notorious testimonials from students about how he changed their lives for the better.

After he moved to coach basketball at Savannah Christian Preparatory School, he had 427 victories in basketball, along with 18 State championships in three sports, but the number of students he positively impacted is far greater.

After his successful years in the sport, Coach Kelley served as the high school principal for 14 years at Savannah Christian until his retirement.

His caring and compassionate nature was seen by everyone in the community, from friends, colleagues, students, and certainly family members. Coach Kelley's presence in the community will be deeply missed and felt by all who had the pleasure of knowing him.

HONORING WINSTON HENCELY

Mr. CARTER of Georgia. Mr. Speaker, I rise today to ask for your thoughts and prayers for Mr. Winston Hencely.

Mr. Hencely was injured in the suicide attack on Bagram Air Base in Afghanistan on November 12. Four brave Americans were killed in the attack and Mr. Hencely was one of 16 soldiers who were injured. He was immediately transported to Germany for treatment and surgery, but is currently in critical condition.

This attack is a sobering reminder of the harsh reality that our soldiers must endure during their deployment.

I encourage everyone to keep our Nation's soldiers in their thoughts and, especially, Mr. Winston Hencely during his time of need.

Mr. Hencely, thank you for your service to our country, and we will be with you every step of the way.

RECOGNIZING JOHN RUTLEDGE

Mr. CARTER of Georgia. Mr. Speaker, I rise today to recognize the life of Mr. John Rutledge, who passed away on September 11, 2016, at the age of 96.

Mr. Rutledge's life has been quite extraordinary as he has been on hand for some incredible events in our Nation's history.

On December 7, 1941, Mr. Rutledge was aboard the USS *California* during the attack on Pearl Harbor, narrowly escaping with his life. The next year, he was at the Battle of Midway in the Pacific Ocean, covering the battle as a photographer and filming the burning of Japanese ships.

Mr. Rutledge continued his service to our Nation long after his time with the military and fighting in World War II. For the next 20 years, he taught science classes at Pensacola High School.

I am proud to honor someone who dedicated so much of his life to the betterment of our Nation.

Mr. Rutledge, you will be greatly missed.

FINDING CURES

The SPEAKER pro tempore. The Chair recognizes the gentlewoman from Missouri (Mrs. WAGNER) for 5 minutes.

Mrs. WAGNER. Mr. Speaker, today I rise in support of legislation that begins making strides toward enhancing our ability to combat some of the toughest diseases of our time—the 21st Century Cures Act.

From improving the development and approval process of drugs and devices, to bettering our ability to diagnose and treat diseases like Alzheimer's and diabetes, this legislation will have a positive impact on countless lives.

I further applaud provisions in the bill that address mental health issues and opioid abuse, both crises that tear families apart in my home district of St. Louis and across our Nation.

However, I also rise today to say that passing this bill must not be the end of our efforts, but, rather, the beginning—the beginning as we look towards a better day for thousands of children fighting against pediatric cancers.

Mr. Speaker, the 21st Century Cures Act legislation outlines that rare and pediatric diseases and conditions should remain a biomedical research priority. While the bill provides an additional $4.8 billion to the National Institutes of Health, I see little that suggests a sufficient amount of this money will be dedicated to pediatric research and care.

This past October, I had the opportunity to tour the Cardinals Kids Cancer Center at Mercy Hospital in St. Louis and meet with families affected by pediatric cancer, including the Les- lie family. The Leslies' son, Caleb, was diagnosed with Ewing's sarcoma, a rare type of bone cancer, when he was just 10 years old. Despite the incredible strength that Caleb showed in his more than 2-year fight with cancer, he ultimately lost the battle on July 22, 2015.

I was shocked when the Leslies told me that childhood cancer receives only 4 percent of the National Cancer Institute's annual research budget—only 4 percent—an absurdly small amount of money for a population with countless life years ahead of them.

In fiscal year 2016, the NCI was appropriated $5.21 billion, and only $208 million of this went toward childhood cancer research. Childhood cancer does not discriminate based on gender, race, or social class. These are diseases that could affect any of our children at any time.

It is my hope that going forward, as both a lawmaker and a mother of three children, that we can prioritize NCI research funding to give every child a fighting chance at a healthy and happy future.

I am committed to giving families like the Leslies solace, solace in knowing that maybe one less family will have to suffer the tragic loss that they endured.

GATLINBURG FIRE

The SPEAKER pro tempore. The Chair recognizes the gentlewoman from Tennessee (Mrs. BLACK) for 5 minutes.

Mrs. BLACK. Mr. Speaker, Tennesseans have experienced the worst of Mother Nature this week—from the tornadoes in my own district to the historic wildfires that ravaged the Gatlinburg community. These fires forced a mass evacuation, destroyed hundreds of homes and businesses, and tragically caused three known fatalities so far.

Today I rise to call for prayer for our neighbors in the beautiful Smoky Mountains region of our State, to remember those precious lives lost, and to recognize our heroic first responders who have worked diligently to contain the damage.

As the work continues, we pray that healing rain would fall, literally, across eastern Tennessee this week, that businesses would be able to quickly reopen, and that visitors would once again flock to this treasured region of our State to experience all that Gatlinburg has to offer.

FIDEL CASTRO

The SPEAKER pro tempore. The Chair recognizes the gentleman from Florida (Mr. DeSANTIS) for 5 minutes.

Mr. DeSANTIS. Mr. Speaker, last week marked the death of the tyrant in Cuba, Fidel Castro. This is a man whose regime was marked by the suppression of God-given rights—the right to religion, to speech, to assemble.

The people who disagreed with the regime in Castro's Cuba were jailed or tortured. People who had spent their lives building businesses, restaurants, and hotels had their property confiscated after the Cuban revolution. People were executed by the thousands who ran afoul of the regime.

☐ 1045

Now, in pre-Castro Cuba, you had economic opportunity and prosperity, but you did have a yearning for democratic reforms. It was effectively an authoritarian system, and Castro capitalized on this by pointing out that we needed to have free elections. There were people who supported Castro initially because they thought he was going to usher in democratic reforms. He duped people. Once he had the opportunity to seize power, he sided with the Soviet Union and imposed a Stalinist tyranny on the small island nation.

I think it is interesting, when people look back, to see how poorly Cuba has done under his rule. Compare that with a lot of the Cuban exiles who left Castro's tyranny. These are people—many of them—who came to Florida. A lot of them didn't speak the language. They were in a new country and didn't necessarily have a whole lot of advantages; yet Cuban Americans, in our country, have excelled at all levels—in business, in government, in athletics, in entertainment. You name it.

Meanwhile, you look at the people, over the last decades, in Cuba, and unless you are attached to the ruling class—the regime—to the intelligence services, or to the military, you basically have no shot to do anything to advance your life and to make the most of your God-given abilities. Of the Cuban exiles who came to Florida, a lot of them were responsible for really putting Miami on the map. I think that shows that, when you have folks fleeing from a tyranny and going to freedom, they can succeed beyond people's wildest dreams, but the people who are suffering under the tyranny just have nowhere to go.

It is funny because, if you look at some of the media reports, Castro is lauded by some as an egalitarian—that this was a big deal that he was an egalitarian. Look, I have to admit that part of that was true. I mean, he was an egalitarian in the sense that he inflicted the equal suffering—equal misery—upon broad cross-sections of the Cuban people. That much is true, but it is obviously false in the sense that his thing was not egalitarianism. It was to amass power for himself. He died a billionaire. This was the avant-garde of the working class, supposedly. He was a billionaire while many Cubans struggled to even eat, and, certainly, they could not prosper.

We also shouldn't forget that this was a very reckless leader. He brought the world to the brink of a nuclear confrontation in 1962 during the Cuban Missile Crisis. Once the Soviet Union expired and we had access to these files, Castro was urging Khrushchev to nuke the United States. So you had Khrushchev—this crusty, Communist, Soviet leader—having to be the voice of reason in telling Castro: no, we are not going to do that, or we will end up in a thermonuclear war. If it had been up to Fidel Castro, those nuclear bombs would have been launched.

This is not a complicated legacy. This is not the George Washington of Cuba, as some have said. Washington refused power. He won a war, refused power, and could have aggrandized power for himself. He did the exact opposite. Castro wrecked Cuba and turned it into an island prison in order to amass power and wealth for himself, and that is his legacy.

The most damning evidence of his failure, of his tyranny, and of his evil nature are the tens of thousands of people who perished while fleeing Cuba and going through the Straits of Florida. Those watery graves really stand as a monument to Castro's barbarity because these were people who knew that, very likely, they were not going to be able to make it as these were shark-infested waters. Yet even the small chance of their escaping freedom and Castro's tyranny was so oppressive that they were willing to do that while knowing that they would, most likely, meet their own demise.

As we look forward, let's be honest about the nature of this regime. Let's commit to having policies that will actually put pressure on the regime and that will help those people who are still in Cuba and who are trying to fight the good fight for freedom, for free elections, and for democratic reforms.

RECESS

The SPEAKER pro tempore. Pursuant to clause 12(a) of rule I, the Chair declares the House in recess until noon today.

Accordingly (at 10 o'clock and 48 minutes a.m.), the House stood in recess.

□ 1200

AFTER RECESS

The recess having expired, the House was called to order by the Speaker at noon.

PRAYER

Rabbi Shea Hecht, Hadar Hatorah Yeshiva, Brooklyn, New York, offered the following prayer:

Heavenly Father, help us be honest enough to admit our shortcomings, brilliant enough to accept flattery without arrogance, tall enough to tower above deceit, strong enough to treasure love, brave enough to welcome criticism, compassionate enough to understand human frailties, wise enough to recognize our mistakes, humble enough to appreciate greatness, and righteous enough to be devoted to the love of God.

Almighty God, inspire the leaders in Congress to inspire all the people. Bestow Your infinite blessings upon all the citizens of this great country.

We pray for the safety of our Armed Forces and that every soldier return home safely after fulfilling Your mission.

We pray that the world be a better place for all mankind; that we rid ourselves of prejudice and hatred, poverty and addiction, greed, jealousy, and selfishness, and that all these ills are replaced with love and harmony, peace and tranquility, respect and dignity, sanctity of marriage, family and community.

May this country, the greatest country of the world, go from strength to strength.

Amen.

THE JOURNAL

The SPEAKER. The Chair has examined the Journal of the last day's proceedings and announces to the House his approval thereof.

Pursuant to clause 1, rule I, the Journal stands approved.

PLEDGE OF ALLEGIANCE

The SPEAKER. Will the gentleman from New York (Mr. HIGGINS) come forward and lead the House in the Pledge of Allegiance.

Mr. HIGGINS led the Pledge of Allegiance as follows:

I pledge allegiance to the Flag of the United States of America, and to the Republic for which it stands, one nation under God, indivisible, with liberty and justice for all.

WELCOMING RABBI SHEA HECHT

The SPEAKER. Without objection, the gentleman from New York (Mr. GIBSON) is recognized for 1 minute.

There was no objection.

Mr. GIBSON. Mr. Speaker, I rise today to thank Rabbi Shea Hecht for his opening prayer. Rabbi Hecht, a Chabad Rabbi, is the chairman of the board of the National Committee for the Furtherance of Jewish Education.

Rabbi Hecht has brought together people of different faiths, races, and backgrounds in New York to promote peace through understanding. These principles hold true in New York, as they do throughout the country and right here in this body.

One thing that my time in Congress has reinforced in me is that prayer matters. The daily opening prayers here in the Chamber set the tone for my day and often help me reflect on how to be a better husband, father, and Congressman.

I join Rabbi Hecht in his pursuit for peace at home and abroad and thank him for his meaningful prayer. I certainly thank his family as well, including Rabbis Hanoch and Yitzchok, rabbis in the Hudson Valley.

Mr. Speaker, I am very grateful.

ANNOUNCEMENT BY THE SPEAKER

The SPEAKER. The Chair will entertain up to 15 requests for 1-minute speeches on each side of the aisle.

CONGRATULATING CHAIRMAN TOM PRICE

(Mr. WILSON of South Carolina asked and was given permission to address the House for 1 minute and to revise and extend his remarks.)

Mr. WILSON of South Carolina. Mr. Speaker, Tuesday morning, President-elect Donald Trump made an extraordinary cabinet selection by appointing Chairman Dr. TOM PRICE to serve as America's Secretary of Health and Human Services.

President-elect Trump announced: "Chairman PRICE, a renowned physician, has earned a reputation for being a tireless problem solver and the go-to expert on healthcare policy, making him the ideal choice to serve in this capacity. He is exceptionally qualified to shepherd our commitment to repeal and replace ObamaCare and bring affordable and accessible healthcare to every American."

I am grateful to have served alongside Chairman PRICE in the House of Representatives and I was honored to be an original cosponsor of his legislation, the Empowering Patients First Act. This is a comprehensive healthcare plan that puts Americans in control of their healthcare plans and choices, not the government.

Congratulations to Dr. TOM PRICE, his wife, State representative Betty, and their son, Robert, my former intern, on this deserved honor. I look forward to watching his success in this new role for the American people.

In conclusion, God bless our troops, and may the President, by his actions, never forget September the 11th in the global war on terrorism.

PIONEERING MEDICAL RESEARCH LEGISLATION

(Mr. HIGGINS asked and was given permission to address the House for 1 minute.)

Mr. HIGGINS. Mr. Speaker, I rise today in support of the 21st Century Cures Act and the hope and help it brings to those whose lives have been touched by disease or addiction.

In my western New York community, opioid overdoses doubled from 2014 to 2015, and, tragically, that number is expected to double again this year. This bill delivers funds to help States and families fight the epidemic.

This legislation also makes substantial investments in pioneering research for those fighting cancer, Alzheimer's, and other debilitating diseases, bringing us closer to the promise of better treatments and cures for the afflicted and hope to those who love and care for them.

The 21st Century Cures Act also provides tens of billions of dollars more in research funds to accelerate promising cancer research in our Nation's leading cancer centers, including Buffalo's Roswell Park Cancer Institute.

RECOGNIZING NATIONAL ADOPTION MONTH

(Mr. THOMPSON of Pennsylvania asked and was given permission to address the House for 1 minute and to revise and extend his remarks.)

Mr. THOMPSON of Pennsylvania. Mr. Speaker, I rise today in recognition of National Adoption Month, which is observed each November.

The goal of National Adoption Month is to increase national awareness of adoption and to bring attention to the need for permanent families for children and youth in the foster care system. As of September 30 of last year, there were more than 110,000 children across our Nation waiting to be adopted.

This year, the initiative focuses on older youth adoptions, which has a special significance to me. When I was 11 years old, my family welcomed a foster care child, Bob, into our home. Bob, throughout the years, has been a part of my life since I was 11 and will be my brother for life. In fact, it is because of Bob that I developed a lifelong passion for scouting and was eventually motivated to a call to public service.

I commend the men and women across our Nation who have selflessly decided to open their homes to these boys and girls, providing good homes at a very challenging time for these young people.

To all the parents who have either adopted a child or participated in foster care: Thank you.

HATE CRIMES

(Ms. GRAHAM asked and was given permission to address the House for 1 minute.)

Ms. GRAHAM. Mr. Speaker, today I rise to speak out against hate. Across our country, incidents of hate crimes and harassment are on the rise.

Just this last week, the trend reared its ugly head in my hometown of Tallahassee. A community office was vandalized with the letters KKK painted across the door.

With the rise in hate, we have also seen an increase in indifference. Too many are turning a blind eye. But there can be no tolerance for racism, bigotry or anti-Semitism in the United States of America.

The opposite of love is not hate. It is indifference. I won't be indifferent. I won't be silent. I am asking each of you to speak out against acts of hate wherever you see them. We cannot be bullied or intimidated. We must fight back. Together, we are stronger than any hatred.

HELPING DISABLED VETERANS

(Mrs. WALORSKI asked and was given permission to address the House for 1 minute and to revise and extend her remarks.)

Mrs. WALORSKI. Mr. Speaker, I rise today to applaud the unanimous passage last night of the Veterans Mobility Safety Act.

With this commonsense bill on its way to the President's desk, we are making sure the mobility equipment veterans depend on is safe. The VA helps disabled veterans update their vehicles with things like wheelchair lifts and easier steering and braking to improve their quality of life. But outdated policies and lack of standards in the program have led to safety issues for veterans and the driving public.

With my bill, the VA will develop new policies and standards to ensure veterans have access to safe, high-quality mobility equipment.

I thank Chairman MILLER for his tireless work on veterans' issues, as well as my colleagues, Representatives BROWNLEY and RUIZ, Paralyzed Veterans of America, and the National Mobility Equipment Dealers Association for their work on this bill.

Mr. Speaker, we owe a debt of gratitude to our disabled veterans, and that includes making sure the mobility equipment they need is safe and reliable. With this bill, we are doing just that.

FIDEL CASTRO'S DEATH

(Ms. ROS-LEHTINEN asked and was given permission to address the House for 1 minute and to revise and extend her remarks.)

Ms. ROS-LEHTINEN. Mr. Speaker, in the wake of the announcement of Fidel Castro's death, some world leaders and some in the media were quick to express their sorrow and sympathy for Castro.

They fawned over a dictator, as Canadian Prime Minister Justin Trudeau claimed he was "a legendary revolutionary and orator."

It is precisely this ignorance of Castro's true nature that is so alarming. Fidel Castro was a ruthless tyrant who ruled with an iron fist. Castro was responsible for the deaths of countless Cubans, and he beat, jailed, and even tortured his opposition.

Castro was a despot who confiscated private property and businesses. He subjugated Cuban citizens, and he took away all their freedoms and their rights.

Fidel Castro was an avowed enemy of the United States. This is a thug who should be condemned and not eulogized.

REMEMBERING REGIS BOBONIS OF SEWICKLEY, PENNSYLVANIA

(Mr. ROTHFUS asked and was given permission to address the House for 1 minute and to revise and extend his remarks.)

Mr. ROTHFUS. Mr. Speaker, today I rise to remember an outstanding member of the Sewickley, Pennsylvania, community: the late Regis Bobonis, who passed away this past November 25.

This great American was a man of many firsts. He was the first African American news reporter for the Pittsburgh Post-Gazette and the first African American television news reporter in Pittsburgh. Following his career in communications, he served as the public relations director for Mercy Hospital for 25 years.

Prior to these achievements, Regis Bobonis served as a Petty Officer 3rd Class during World War II, and he was a committed husband, father, and grandfather. He and his late wife, Hurley Williams, remained married for 53 years before her passing.

Through his work for the Daniel B. Matthews Historical Society in Sewickley, Mr. Bobonis discovered there were more Tuskegee Airmen from western Pennsylvania than any other State in the Nation. His discovery led him to spearhead the campaign that resulted in the largest outdoor memorial to the Tuskegee Airmen, which is in Sewickley Cemetery, pictured to my left.

Mr. Bobonis' sterling example and lasting contributions to our community will not be forgotten. May his family be consoled, and may he rest in peace.

BRIDGES TO HOPE

(Mr. WESTERMAN asked and was given permission to address the House for 1 minute.)

Mr. WESTERMAN. Mr. Speaker, I believe the number one way to move people from poverty to self-reliance is not a government program. If we want to make a difference in the lives of the impoverished, we must help them find a pathway to employment.

In my hometown of Hot Springs, Arkansas, a nonprofit has taken this mission to heart. Cooperative Christian Ministries and Clinic works with disadvantaged residents to give them skills that will give them a step up in the workforce. The ministry's program, Bridges to Hope, has worked with local employers in Hot Springs to put its graduates to work, and it is seeing great success. According to a report by the local Sentinel-Record newspaper, Oaklawn Race Track has employed four graduates, all of whom have had a 100 percent success rate, according to Oaklawn General Manager Eric Jackson.

The first Bridges to Hope class graduated only 90 days ago, but its success is already resounding as residents in the Fourth Congressional District of Arkansas are finding satisfaction and self-reliance through employment.

I thank Bridges of Hope for its work in my hometown, and I hope to see its efforts not only grow, but also be replicated, because there is a better way to fight poverty and it is still the best anti-poverty program of all time—a job.

DEPARTMENT OF LABOR OVERTIME RULE UPDATE

(Mr. ALLEN asked and was given permission to address the House for 1 minute and to revise and extend his remarks.)

Mr. ALLEN. Mr. Speaker, last week, a Texas judge granted an emergency injunction against the Department of Labor's overtime rule.

This disastrous overtime rule is yet another attempt by this administration to legislate outside of reason and job description to impose their "we know what is best for you" agenda.

This rule, set to go into effect December 1, would double the overtime salary threshold almost overnight. For Americans, this overtime rule would mean fewer job prospects, less flexibility, and less opportunity.

I have stood before this body many times telling the stories of small businesses that have come to me and warned me of the struggles their employees and families would face because of this overtime rule.

Schools and universities back home in my district were negatively impacted by this rule and the possibility of having to inform employees of a partial paycheck right before the holidays. Despite outcry and outrage from folks back home, the administration pushed forward with its unpopular overtime rule.

Thankfully, the courts got it right. I thank the courts for standing up for the rule of law and the American people.

□ 1215

THE OHIO STATE UNIVERSITY KEEPS STUDENTS SAFE

(Mr. TIBERI asked and was given permission to address the House for 1 minute and to revise and extend his remarks.)

Mr. TIBERI. Mr. Speaker, I rise today to recognize The Ohio State University, their emergency management team, and all our police officers and first responders who took swift action on Monday to keep our students safe and stop an attacker wielding a knife. My thoughts and prayers are with the victims who were injured, and I wish them a quick and full recovery.

As a fellow Buckeye, it is difficult to even fathom that senseless violence like this can happen even on one of our own campuses. I walked those sidewalks as a student, and just a few days ago I was with my wife on campus.

With the unpredictable threats and the potential emergencies we face today, we must be prepared, and we must always be vigilant.

I am sincerely grateful to The Ohio State University that they were ready. An OSU police officer, who is also a graduate of the university, is a hero for stopping a potential terror attack that ISIS has claimed responsibility for. The university effectively utilized emergency response protocol to keep thousands of students on campus out of harm's way.

Mr. Speaker, America's universities and colleges are places where students should safely engage with their classmates, where they are challenged, and where they find opportunities to succeed in our great Nation. That is certainly the case at The Ohio State University.

As we continue to pray for our students' safety and security, we must stand with the Buckeye community. We are Buckeye strong.

HONORING WAYNE STATE UNIVERSITY POLICE K9 OFFICER COLLIN ROSE

(Mr. BISHOP of Michigan asked and was given permission to address the House for 1 minute and to revise and extend his remarks.)

Mr. BISHOP of Michigan. Mr. Speaker, I rise today with a heavy heart to pay tribute to a fallen Wayne State University Police K9 Officer Collin Rose, who died in the line of duty on Tuesday, November 22, 2016.

Officer Rose was a man of the community, who visited schools and trained police dogs. He was a Ferris State University Criminal Justice and Law Enforcement Academy graduate. And tragically, Officer Rose became the fifth officer to be shot in the United States in a matter of days.

It is completely unacceptable. This trend of violence and murder against the very people who serve and protect us, there are no words. It must stop.

These brave men and women in uniform are more than their occupation. They are husbands, they are wives, they are brothers, and sisters. They are

our children. In Officer Rose's case, he was somebody's fiance, preparing to get married in less than a year from now.

As much as we think that their job is to protect us, it is our job to ensure their safety as well. Our communities must work with the police to open dialogue and voice concerns peacefully. Every single American must respect our police and men and women in uniform.

Please join me today in praying for Officer Rose's family, friends, and the entire Wayne State Police Force during this time of tragedy. His life and legacy will never be forgotten.

SUPPORT INNOVATION, RESEARCH, AND LIFESAVING CURES TO DISEASES

(Mr. YODER asked and was given permission to address the House for 1 minute and to revise and extend his remarks.)

Mr. YODER. Mr. Speaker, I rise today in support of innovation, research, and lifesaving cures to diseases that affect every family in every neighborhood of America.

We are set to begin a new era in Washington in January, but we still have the opportunity to accomplish meaningful change before the end of this year. We have the opportunity to save lives by passing the 21st Century Cures Act and getting it signed into law.

For example, right now, each year, 700,000 people die with Alzheimer's disease annually. By 2050, estimates are that our country will spend over $1 trillion alone just to treat patients with Alzheimer's. Yet, we spend just a few hundred million dollars a year on Alzheimer's research.

This weekend, 60 Minutes highlighted an NIH-backed Alzheimer's study and the amazing work our researchers are doing to find a cure for this dreadful disease.

21st Century Cures increases our commitment to studies like these by adding almost $5 billion in new investment for research over the next 10 years.

Mr. Speaker, if we support 21st Century Cures, we not only save lives, but our investment will pay for itself a thousand times over.

COMMUNICATION FROM THE CLERK OF THE HOUSE

The SPEAKER pro tempore (Mr. DUNCAN of Tennessee) laid before the House the following communication from the Clerk of the House of Representatives:

OFFICE OF THE CLERK,
HOUSE OF REPRESENTATIVES,
Washington, DC, November 30, 2016.
Hon. PAUL D. RYAN,
The Speaker, House of Representatives,
Washington, DC.

DEAR MR. SPEAKER: Pursuant to the permission granted in Clause 2(h) of Rule II of the Rules of the U.S. House of Representatives, the Clerk received the following message from the Secretary of the Senate on November 30, 2016, at 9:18 a.m.:

That the Senate request return of official papers to make a technical correction to the engrossment H. Con. Res 122.

That the Senate passed S. 2944.

That the Senate passed S. 3438.

That the Senate passed S. 461.

That the Senate passed without amendment H.R. 4419.

That the Senate passed without amendment H.R. 5785.

With best wishes, I am,

Sincerely,

KAREN L. HAAS.

REQUESTING RETURN OF H. CON. RES. 122, PROTECTION OF THE RIGHT OF TRIBES TO STOP THE EXPORT OF CULTURAL AND TRADITIONAL PATRIMONY RESOLUTION

The SPEAKER pro tempore laid before the House the following privileged message from the Senate:

In the Senate of the United States, November 29, 2016.

Ordered, That the Secretary be directed to request the House of Representatives to return to the Senate the Concurrent resolution (H. Con. Res. 122) entitled "Concurrent resolution supporting efforts to stop the theft, illegal possession or sale, transfer, and export of tribal cultural items of American Indians, Alaska Natives, and Native Hawaiians in the United States and internationally.", together with all accompanying papers, and that upon the compliance of the request, the Enrolling Clerk of the Senate may make a technical correction in the engrossment of the aforesaid bill.

Attest:

JULIE E. ADAMS,
Secretary.

The SPEAKER pro tempore. Without objection, the request of the Senate is agreed to, and H. Con. Res. 122 and the Senate amendment thereto will be returned to the Senate.

There was no objection.

CONFERENCE REPORT ON S. 2943, NATIONAL DEFENSE AUTHORIZATION ACT FOR FISCAL YEAR 2017

Mr. THORNBERRY submitted the following conference report and statement on the bill (S. 2943) to authorize appropriations for fiscal year 2017 for military activities of the Department of Defense, for military construction, and for defense activities of the Department of Energy, to prescribe military personnel strengths for such fiscal year, and for other purposes:

CONFERENCE REPORT (H. REPT. 114-840)

The committee of conference on the disagreeing votes of the two Houses on the amendment of the House to the bill (S. 2943), to authorize appropriations for fiscal year 2017 for military activities of the Department of Defense, for military construction, and for defense activities of the Department of Energy, to prescribe military personnel strengths for such fiscal year, and for other purposes, having met, after full and free conference, have agreed to recommend and do recommend to their respective Houses as follows:

That the Senate recede from its disagreement to the amendment of the House and agree to the same with an amendment as follows:

In lieu of the matter proposed to be inserted by the House amendment, insert the following:

SECTION 1. SHORT TITLE.

This Act may be cited as the "National Defense Authorization Act for Fiscal Year 2017".

SEC. 2. ORGANIZATION OF ACT INTO DIVISIONS; TABLE OF CONTENTS.

(a) *DIVISIONS.*—This Act is organized into five divisions as follows:

(1) Division A—Department of Defense Authorizations.

(2) Division B—Military Construction Authorizations.

(3) Division C—Department of Energy National Security Authorizations and Other Authorizations.

(4) Division D—Funding Tables.

(5) Division E—Uniform Code of Military Justice Reform.

(b) *TABLE OF CONTENTS.*—The table of contents for this Act is as follows:

Sec. 1. Short title.

Sec. 2. Organization of Act into divisions; table of contents.

Sec. 3. Congressional defense committees.

Sec. 4. Budgetary effects of this Act.

DIVISION A—DEPARTMENT OF DEFENSE AUTHORIZATIONS

TITLE I—PROCUREMENT

Subtitle A—Authorization of Appropriations

Sec. 101. Authorization of appropriations.

Subtitle B—Army Programs

Sec. 111. Multiyear procurement authority for AH–64E Apache helicopters.

Sec. 112. Multiyear procurement authority for UH–60M and HH–60M Black Hawk helicopters.

Sec. 113. Distributed Common Ground System–Army increment 1.

Sec. 114. Assessment of certain capabilities of the Department of the Army.

Subtitle C—Navy Programs

Sec. 121. Determination of vessel delivery dates.

Sec. 122. Incremental funding for detail design and construction of LHA replacement ship designated LHA 8.

Sec. 123. Littoral Combat Ship.

Sec. 124. Limitation on use of sole-source shipbuilding contracts for certain vessels.

Sec. 125. Limitation on availability of funds for the Advanced Arresting Gear Program.

Sec. 126. Limitation on availability of funds for procurement of U.S.S. Enterprise (CVN–80).

Sec. 127. Sense of Congress on aircraft carrier procurement schedules.

Sec. 128. Report on P–8 Poseidon aircraft.

Sec. 129. Design and construction of replacement dock landing ship designated LX(R) or amphibious transport dock designated LPD–29.

Subtitle D—Air Force Programs

Sec. 131. EC–130H Compass Call recapitalization program.

Sec. 132. Repeal of requirement to preserve certain retired C–5 aircraft.

Sec. 133. Repeal of requirement to preserve F–117 aircraft in recallable condition.

Sec. 134. Prohibition on availability of funds for retirement of A–10 aircraft.

Sec. 135. Limitation on availability of funds for destruction of A–10 aircraft in storage status.

Sec. 136. Prohibition on availability of funds for retirement of Joint Surveillance Target Attack Radar System aircraft.

Sec. 137. Elimination of annual report on aircraft inventory.

Subtitle E—Defense-wide, Joint, and Multiservice Matters

Sec. 141. Standardization of 5.56mm rifle ammunition.

Sec. 142. Fire suppressant and fuel containment standards for certain vehicles.

Sec. 143. Limitation on availability of funds for destruction of certain cluster munitions.

Sec. 144. Report on Department of Defense munitions strategy for the combatant commands.

Sec. 145. Modifications to reporting on use of combat mission requirements funds.

Sec. 146. Report on alternative management structures for the F–35 joint strike fighter program.

Sec. 147. Comptroller General review of F–35 Lightning II aircraft sustainment support.

Sec. 148. Briefing on acquisition strategy for Ground Mobility Vehicle.

Sec. 149. Study and report on optimal mix of aircraft capabilities for the Armed Forces.

TITLE II—RESEARCH, DEVELOPMENT, TEST, AND EVALUATION

Subtitle A—Authorization of Appropriations

Sec. 201. Authorization of appropriations.

Subtitle B—Program Requirements, Restrictions, and Limitations

Sec. 211. Laboratory quality enhancement program.

Sec. 212. Modification of mechanisms to provide funds for defense laboratories for research and development of technologies for military missions.

Sec. 213. Making permanent authority for defense research and development rapid innovation program.

Sec. 214. Authorization for National Defense University and Defense Acquisition University to enter into cooperative research and development agreements.

Sec. 215. Manufacturing Engineering Education Grant Program.

Sec. 216. Notification requirement for certain rapid prototyping, experimentation, and demonstration activities.

Sec. 217. Increased micro-purchase threshold for research programs and entities.

Sec. 218. Improved biosafety for handling of select agents and toxins.

Sec. 219. Designation of Department of Defense senior official with principal responsibility for directed energy weapons.

Sec. 220. Restructuring of the distributed common ground system of the Army.

Sec. 221. Limitation on availability of funds for the countering weapons of mass destruction system Constellation.

Sec. 222. Limitation on availability of funds for Defense Innovation Unit Experimental.

Sec. 223. Limitation on availability of funds for Joint Surveillance Target Attack Radar System (JSTARS) recapitalization program.

Sec. 224. Acquisition program baseline and annual reports on follow-on modernization program for F–35 Joint Strike Fighter.

Subtitle C—Reports and Other Matters

Sec. 231. Strategy for assured access to trusted microelectronics.

Sec. 232. Pilot program on evaluation of commercial information technology.

Sec. 233. Pilot program for the enhancement of the research, development, test, and evaluation centers of the Department of Defense.

Sec. 234. Pilot program on modernization and fielding of electromagnetic spectrum warfare systems and electronic warfare capabilities.

Sec. 235. Pilot program on disclosure of certain sensitive information to federally funded research and development centers.

Sec. 236. Pilot program on enhanced interaction between the Defense Advanced Research Projects Agency and the service academies.

Sec. 237. Independent review of F/A–18 physiological episodes and corrective actions.

Sec. 238. B–21 bomber development program accountability matrices.

Sec. 239. Study on helicopter crash prevention and mitigation technology.

Sec. 240. Strategy for Improving Electronic and Electromagnetic Spectrum Warfare Capabilities.

Sec. 241. Sense of Congress on development and fielding of fifth generation airborne systems.

TITLE III—OPERATION AND MAINTENANCE

Subtitle A—Authorization of Appropriations

Sec. 301. Authorization of appropriations.

Subtitle B—Energy and Environment

Sec. 311. Modified reporting requirement related to installations energy management.

Sec. 312. Waiver authority for alternative fuel procurement requirement.

Sec. 313. Utility data management for military facilities.

Sec. 314. Alternative technologies for munitions disposal.

Sec. 315. Report on efforts to reduce high energy costs at military installations.

Sec. 316. Sense of Congress on funding decisions relating to climate change.

Subtitle C—Logistics and Sustainment

Sec. 321. Revision of deployability rating system and planning reform.

Sec. 322. Revision of guidance relating to corrosion control and prevention executives.

Sec. 323. Pilot program for inclusion of certain industrial plants in the Armament Retooling and Manufacturing Support Initiative.

Sec. 324. Repair, recapitalization, and certification of dry docks at naval shipyards.

Sec. 325. Private sector port loading assessment.

Sec. 326. Strategy on revitalizing Army organic industrial base.

Subtitle D—Reports

Sec. 331. Modifications to Quarterly Readiness Report to Congress.

Sec. 332. Report on average travel costs of members of the reserve components.

Sec. 333. Report on HH–60G sustainment and Combat Rescue Helicopter program.

Subtitle E—Other Matters

Sec. 341. Air navigation matters.

Sec. 342. Contract working dogs.

Sec. 343. Plan, funding documents, and management review relating to explosive ordnance disposal.

Sec. 344. Process for communicating availability of surplus ammunition.

Sec. 345. Mitigation of risks posed by window coverings with accessible cords in certain military housing units.

Sec. 346. Access to military installations by transportation companies.

Sec. 347. Access to wireless high-speed Internet and network connections for certain members of the Armed Forces.

Sec. 348. Limitation on availability of funds for Office of the Under Secretary of Defense for Intelligence.

Sec. 349. Limitation on development and fielding of new camouflage and utility uniforms.

Sec. 350. Plan for improved dedicated adversary air training enterprise of the Air Force.

Sec. 351. Independent review and assessment of the Ready Aircrew Program of the Air Force.

Sec. 352. Study on space-available travel system of the Department of Defense.

Sec. 353. Evaluation of motor carrier safety performance and safety technology.

TITLE IV—MILITARY PERSONNEL AUTHORIZATIONS

Subtitle A—Active Forces

Sec. 401. End strengths for active forces.

Sec. 402. Revisions in permanent active duty end strength minimum levels.

Subtitle B—Reserve Forces

Sec. 411. End strengths for Selected Reserve.

Sec. 412. End strengths for reserves on active duty in support of the reserves.

Sec. 413. End strengths for military technicians (dual status).

Sec. 414. Fiscal year 2017 limitation on number of non-dual status technicians.

Sec. 415. Maximum number of reserve personnel authorized to be on active duty for operational support.

Sec. 416. Technical corrections to annual authorization for personnel strengths.

Subtitle C—Authorization of Appropriations

Sec. 421. Military personnel.

TITLE V—MILITARY PERSONNEL POLICY

Subtitle A—Officer Personnel Policy

Sec. 501. Reduction in number of general and flag officers on active duty and authorized strength after December 31, 2022, of such general and flag officers.

Sec. 502. Repeal of statutory specification of general or flag officer grade for various positions in the Armed Forces.

Sec. 503. Number of Marine Corps general officers.

Sec. 504. Promotion eligibility period for officers whose confirmation of appointment is delayed due to nonavailability to the Senate of probative information under control of non-Department of Defense agencies.

Sec. 505. Continuation of certain officers on active duty without regard to requirement for retirement for years of service.

Sec. 506. Equal consideration of officers for early retirement or discharge.

Sec. 507. Modification of authority to drop from rolls a commissioned officer.

Sec. 508. Extension of force management authorities allowing enhanced flexibility for officer personnel management.

Sec. 509. Pilot programs on direct commissions to cyber positions.

Sec. 510. Length of joint duty assignments.

Sec. 510A. Revision of definitions used for joint officer management.

Subtitle B—Reserve Component Management

Sec. 511. Authority for temporary waiver of limitation on term of service of Vice Chief of the National Guard Bureau.

Sec. 512. Rights and protections available to military technicians.

Sec. 513. Inapplicability of certain laws to National Guard technicians performing active Guard and Reserve duty.

Sec. 514. Extension of removal of restrictions on the transfer of officers between the active and inactive National Guard.

Sec. 515. Extension of temporary authority to use Air Force reserve component personnel to provide training and instruction regarding pilot training.

Sec. 516. Expansion of eligibility for deputy commander of combatant command having United States among geographic area of responsibility to include officers of the Reserves.

Subtitle C—General Service Authorities

Sec. 521. Matters relating to provision of leave for members of the Armed Forces, including prohibition on leave not expressly authorized by law.

Sec. 522. Transfer of provision relating to expenses incurred in connection with leave canceled due to contingency operations.

Sec. 523. Expansion of authority to execute certain military instruments.

Sec. 524. Medical examination before administrative separation for members with post-traumatic stress disorder or traumatic brain injury in connection with sexual assault.

Sec. 525. Reduction of tenure on the temporary disability retired list.

Sec. 526. Technical correction to voluntary separation pay and benefits.

Sec. 527. Consolidation of Army marketing and pilot program on consolidated Army recruiting.

Subtitle D—Member Whistleblower Protections and Correction of Military Records

Sec. 531. Improvements to whistleblower protection procedures.

Sec. 532. Modification of whistleblower protection authorities to restrict contrary findings of prohibited personnel action by the Secretary concerned.

Sec. 533. Availability of certain Correction of Military Records and Discharge Review Board information through the Internet.

Sec. 534. Improvements to authorities and procedures for the correction of military records.

Sec. 535. Treatment by discharge review boards of claims asserting post-traumatic stress disorder or traumatic brain injury in connection with combat or sexual trauma as a basis for review of discharge.

Sec. 536. Comptroller General of the United States review of integrity of Department of Defense whistleblower program.

Subtitle E—Military Justice and Legal Assistance Matters

Sec. 541. United States Court of Appeals for the Armed Forces.
Sec. 542. Effective prosecution and defense in courts-martial and pilot programs on professional military justice development for judge advocates.
Sec. 543. Inclusion in annual reports on sexual assault prevention and response efforts of the Armed Forces of information on complaints of retaliation in connection with reports of sexual assault in the Armed Forces.
Sec. 544. Extension of the requirement for annual report regarding sexual assaults and coordination with release of Family Advocacy Program report.
Sec. 545. Metrics for evaluating the efforts of the Armed Forces to prevent and respond to retaliation in connection with reports of sexual assault in the Armed Forces.
Sec. 546. Training for Department of Defense personnel who investigate claims of retaliation.
Sec. 547. Notification to complainants of resolution of investigations into retaliation.
Sec. 548. Modification of definition of sexual harassment for purposes of investigations by commanding officers of complaints of harassment.
Sec. 549. Improved Department of Defense prevention of and response to hazing in the Armed Forces.

Subtitle F—National Commission on Military, National, and Public Service

Sec. 551. Purpose, scope, and definitions.
Sec. 552. Preliminary report on purpose and utility of registration system under Military Selective Service Act.
Sec. 553. National Commission on Military, National, and Public Service.
Sec. 554. Commission hearings and meetings.
Sec. 555. Principles and procedure for Commission recommendations.
Sec. 556. Executive Director and staff.
Sec. 557. Termination of Commission.

Subtitle G—Member Education, Training, Resilience, and Transition

Sec. 561. Modification of program to assist members of the Armed Forces in obtaining professional credentials.
Sec. 562. Inclusion of alcohol, prescription drug, opioid, and other substance abuse counseling as part of required preseparation counseling.
Sec. 563. Inclusion of information in Transition Assistance Program regarding effect of receipt of both veteran disability compensation and voluntary separation pay.
Sec. 564. Training under Transition Assistance Program on career and employment opportunities associated with transportation security cards.
Sec. 565. Extension of suicide prevention and resilience program.
Sec. 566. Congressional notification in advance of appointments to service academies.
Sec. 567. Report and guidance on Job Training, Employment Skills Training, Apprenticeships, and Internships and SkillBridge initiatives for members of the Armed Forces who are being separated.
Sec. 568. Military-to-mariner transition.

Subtitle H—Defense Dependents' Education and Military Family Readiness Matters

Sec. 571. Continuation of authority to assist local educational agencies that benefit dependents of members of the Armed Forces and Department of Defense civilian employees.
Sec. 572. One-year extension of authorities relating to the transition and support of military dependent students to local educational agencies.
Sec. 573. Annual notice to members of the Armed Forces regarding child custody protections guaranteed by the Servicemembers Civil Relief Act.
Sec. 574. Requirement for annual Family Advocacy Program report regarding child abuse and domestic violence.
Sec. 575. Reporting on allegations of child abuse in military families and homes.
Sec. 576. Repeal of Advisory Council on Dependents' Education.
Sec. 577. Support for programs providing camp experience for children of military families.
Sec. 578. Comptroller General of the United States assessment and report on Exceptional Family Member Programs.
Sec. 579. Impact aid amendments.

Subtitle I—Decorations and Awards

Sec. 581. Posthumous advancement of Colonel George E. "Bud" Day, United States Air Force, on the retired list.
Sec. 582. Authorization for award of medals for acts of valor during certain contingency operations.
Sec. 583. Authorization for award of the Medal of Honor to Gary M. Rose and James C. McCloughan for acts of valor during the Vietnam War.
Sec. 584. Authorization for award of Distinguished-Service Cross to First Lieutenant Melvin M. Spruiell for acts of valor during World War II.
Sec. 585. Authorization for award of the Distinguished Service Cross to Chaplain (First Lieutenant) Joseph Verbis LaFleur for acts of valor during World War II.
Sec. 586. Review regarding award of Medal of Honor to certain Asian American and Native American Pacific Islander war veterans.

Subtitle J—Miscellaneous Reports and Other Matters

Sec. 591. Repeal of requirement for a chaplain at the United States Air Force Academy appointed by the President.
Sec. 592. Extension of limitation on reduction in number of military and civilian personnel assigned to duty with service review agencies.
Sec. 593. Annual reports on progress of the Army and the Marine Corps in integrating women into military occupational specialities and units recently opened to women.
Sec. 594. Report on feasibility of electronic tracking of operational active-duty service performed by members of the Ready Reserve of the Armed Forces.
Sec. 595. Report on discharge by warrant officers of pilot and other flight officer positions in the Navy, Marine Corps, and Air Force currently discharged by commissioned officers.

Sec. 596. Body mass index test.
Sec. 597. Report on career progression tracks of the Armed Forces for women in combat arms units.

TITLE VI—COMPENSATION AND OTHER PERSONNEL BENEFITS

Subtitle A—Pay and Allowances

Sec. 601. Fiscal year 2017 increase in military basic pay.
Sec. 602. Publication by Department of Defense of actual rates of basic pay payable to members of the Armed Forces by pay grade for annual or other pay periods.
Sec. 603. Extension of authority to provide temporary increase in rates of basic allowance for housing under certain circumstances.
Sec. 604. Reports on a new single-salary pay system for members of the Armed Forces.

Subtitle B—Bonuses and Special and Incentive Pays

Sec. 611. One-year extension of certain bonus and special pay authorities for reserve forces.
Sec. 612. One-year extension of certain bonus and special pay authorities for health care professionals.
Sec. 613. One-year extension of special pay and bonus authorities for nuclear officers.
Sec. 614. One-year extension of authorities relating to title 37 consolidated special pay, incentive pay, and bonus authorities.
Sec. 615. One-year extension of authorities relating to payment of other title 37 bonuses and special pays.
Sec. 616. Aviation incentive pay and bonus matters.
Sec. 617. Conforming amendment to consolidation of special pay, incentive pay, and bonus authorities.
Sec. 618. Technical amendments relating to 2008 consolidation of certain special pay authorities.

Subtitle C—Travel and Transportation Allowances

Sec. 621. Maximum reimbursement amount for travel expenses of members of the Reserves attending inactive duty training outside of normal commuting distances.

Subtitle D—Disability Pay, Retired Pay, and Survivor Benefits

PART I—AMENDMENTS IN CONNECTION WITH RETIRED PAY REFORM

Sec. 631. Election period for members in the service academies and inactive Reserves to participate in the modernized retirement system.
Sec. 632. Effect of separation of members from the uniformed services on participation in the Thrift Savings Plan.
Sec. 633. Continuation pay for full Thrift Savings Plan members who have completed 8 to 12 years of service.
Sec. 634. Combat-related special compensation coordinating amendment.

PART II—OTHER MATTERS

Sec. 641. Use of member's current pay grade and years of service and retired pay cost-of-living adjustments, rather than final retirement pay grade and years of service, in a division of property involving disposable retired pay.
Sec. 642. Equal benefits under Survivor Benefit Plan for survivors of reserve component members who die in the line of duty during inactive-duty training.

Sec. 643. Authority to deduct Survivor Benefit Plan premiums from combat-related special compensation when retired pay not sufficient.

Sec. 644. Extension of allowance covering monthly premium for Service-members' Group Life Insurance while in certain overseas areas to cover members in any combat zone or overseas direct support area.

Sec. 645. Authority for payment of pay and allowances and retired and retainer pay pursuant to power of attorney.

Sec. 646. Extension of authority to pay special survivor indemnity allowance under the Survivor Benefit Plan.

Sec. 647. Repeal of obsolete authority for combat-related injury rehabilitation pay.

Sec. 648. Independent assessment of the Survivor Benefit Plan.

Subtitle E—Commissary and Nonappropriated Fund Instrumentality Benefits and Operations

Sec. 661. Protection and enhancement of access to and savings at commissaries and exchanges.

Sec. 662. Acceptance of Military Star Card at commissaries.

Subtitle F—Other Matters

Sec. 671. Recovery of amounts owed to the United States by members of the uniformed services.

Sec. 672. Modification of flat rate per diem requirement for personnel on long-term temporary duty assignments.

TITLE VII—HEALTH CARE PROVISIONS

Subtitle A—Reform of TRICARE and Military Health System

Sec. 701. TRICARE Select and other TRICARE reform.

Sec. 702. Reform of administration of the Defense Health Agency and military medical treatment facilities.

Sec. 703. Military medical treatment facilities.

Sec. 704. Access to urgent and primary care under TRICARE program.

Sec. 705. Value-based purchasing and acquisition of managed care support contracts for TRICARE program.

Sec. 706. Establishment of high performance military-civilian integrated health delivery systems.

Sec. 707. Joint Trauma System.

Sec. 708. Joint Trauma Education and Training Directorate.

Sec. 709. Standardized system for scheduling medical appointments at military treatment facilities.

Subtitle B—Other Health Care Benefits

Sec. 711. Extended TRICARE program coverage for certain members of the National Guard and dependents during certain disaster response duty.

Sec. 712. Continuity of health care coverage for Reserve Components.

Sec. 713. Provision of hearing aids to dependents of retired members.

Sec. 714. Coverage of medically necessary food and vitamins for certain conditions under the TRICARE program.

Sec. 715. Eligibility of certain beneficiaries under the TRICARE program for participation in the Federal Employees Dental and Vision Insurance Program.

Sec. 716. Applied behavior analysis.

Sec. 717. Evaluation and treatment of veterans and civilians at military treatment facilities.

Sec. 718. Enhancement of use of telehealth services in military health system.

Sec. 719. Authorization of reimbursement by Department of Defense to entities carrying out State vaccination programs for costs of vaccines provided to covered beneficiaries.

Subtitle C—Health Care Administration

Sec. 721. Authority to convert military medical and dental positions to civilian medical and dental positions.

Sec. 722. Prospective payment of funds necessary to provide medical care for the Coast Guard.

Sec. 723. Reduction of administrative requirements relating to automatic renewal of enrollments in TRICARE Prime.

Sec. 724. Modification of authority of Uniformed Services University of the Health Sciences to include undergraduate and other medical education and training programs.

Sec. 725. Adjustment of medical services, personnel authorized strengths, and infrastructure in military health system to maintain readiness and core competencies of health care providers.

Sec. 726. Program to eliminate variability in health outcomes and improve quality of health care services delivered in military medical treatment facilities.

Sec. 727. Acquisition strategy for health care professional staffing services.

Sec. 728. Adoption of core quality performance metrics.

Sec. 729. Improvement of health outcomes and control of costs of health care under TRICARE program through programs to involve covered beneficiaries.

Sec. 730. Accountability for the performance of the military health system of certain leaders within the system.

Sec. 731. Establishment of advisory committees for military treatment facilities.

Subtitle D—Reports and Other Matters

Sec. 741. Extension of authority for joint Department of Defense-Department of Veterans Affairs Medical Facility Demonstration Fund and report on implementation of information technology capabilities.

Sec. 742. Pilot program on expansion of use of physician assistants to provide mental health care to members of the Armed Forces.

Sec. 743. Pilot program for prescription drug acquisition cost parity in the TRICARE pharmacy benefits program.

Sec. 744. Pilot program on display of wait times at urgent care clinics and pharmacies of military medical treatment facilities.

Sec. 745. Requirement to review and monitor prescribing practices at military treatment facilities of pharmaceutical agents for treatment of post-traumatic stress.

Sec. 746. Department of Defense study on preventing the diversion of opioid medications.

Sec. 747. Incorporation into survey by Department of Defense of questions on experiences of members of the Armed Forces with family planning services and counseling.

Sec. 748. Assessment of transition to TRICARE program by families of members of reserve components called to active duty and elimination of certain charges for such families.

Sec. 749. Oversight of graduate medical education programs of military departments.

Sec. 750. Study on health of helicopter and tiltrotor pilots.

Sec. 751. Comptroller General reports on health care delivery and waste in military health system.

TITLE VIII—ACQUISITION POLICY, ACQUISITION MANAGEMENT, AND RELATED MATTERS

Subtitle A—Acquisition Policy and Management

Sec. 801. Rapid acquisition authority amendments.

Sec. 802. Authority for temporary service of Principal Military Deputies to the Assistant Secretaries of the military departments for acquisition as Acting Assistant Secretaries.

Sec. 803. Modernization of services acquisition.

Sec. 804. Defense Modernization Account amendments.

Subtitle B—Department of Defense Acquisition Agility

Sec. 805. Modular open system approach in development of major weapon systems.

Sec. 806. Development, prototyping, and deployment of weapon system components or technology.

Sec. 807. Cost, schedule, and performance of major defense acquisition programs.

Sec. 808. Transparency in major defense acquisition programs.

Sec. 809. Amendments relating to technical data rights.

Subtitle C—Amendments to General Contracting Authorities, Procedures, and Limitations

Sec. 811. Modified restrictions on undefinitized contractual actions.

Sec. 812. Amendments relating to inventory and tracking of purchases of services.

Sec. 813. Use of lowest price technically acceptable source selection process.

Sec. 814. Procurement of personal protective equipment.

Sec. 815. Amendments related to detection and avoidance of counterfeit electronic parts.

Sec. 816. Amendments to special emergency procurement authority.

Sec. 817. Compliance with domestic source requirements for footwear furnished to enlisted members of the Armed Forces upon their initial entry into the Armed Forces.

Sec. 818. Extension of authority for enhanced transfer of technology developed at Department of Defense laboratories.

Sec. 819. Modified notification requirement for exercise of waiver authority to acquire vital national security capabilities.

Sec. 820. Defense cost accounting standards.

Sec. 821. Increased micro-purchase threshold applicable to Department of Defense procurements.

Sec. 822. Enhanced competition requirements.

Sec. 823. Revision to effective date of senior executive benchmark compensation for allowable cost limitations.

Sec. 824. Treatment of independent research and development costs on certain contracts.

Sec. 825. Exception to requirement to include cost or price to the Government as a factor in the evaluation of proposals for certain multiple-award task or delivery order contracts.

Sec. 826. Extension of program for comprehensive small business contracting plans.

Sec. 827. *Treatment of side-by-side testing of certain equipment, munitions, and technologies manufactured and developed under cooperative research and development agreements as use of competitive procedures.*

Sec. 828. *Defense Acquisition Challenge Program amendments.*

Sec. 829. *Preference for fixed-price contracts.*

Sec. 830. *Requirement to use firm fixed-price contracts for foreign military sales.*

Sec. 831. *Preference for performance-based contract payments.*

Sec. 832. *Contractor incentives to achieve savings and improve mission performance.*

Sec. 833. *Sunset and repeal of certain contracting provisions.*

Sec. 834. *Flexibility in contracting award program.*

Sec. 835. *Protection of task order competition.*

Sec. 836. *Contract closeout authority.*

Sec. 837. *Closeout of old Department of the Navy contracts.*

Subtitle D—Provisions Relating to Major Defense Acquisition Programs

Sec. 841. *Change in date of submission to Congress of Selected Acquisition Reports.*

Sec. 842. *Amendments relating to independent cost estimation and cost analysis.*

Sec. 843. *Revisions to Milestone B determinations.*

Sec. 844. *Review and report on sustainment planning in the acquisition process.*

Sec. 845. *Revision to distribution of annual report on operational test and evaluation.*

Sec. 846. *Repeal of major automated information systems provisions.*

Sec. 847. *Revisions to definition of major defense acquisition program.*

Sec. 848. *Acquisition strategy.*

Sec. 849. *Improved life-cycle cost control.*

Sec. 850. *Authority to designate increments or blocks of items delivered under major defense acquisition programs as major subprograms for purposes of acquisition reporting.*

Sec. 851. *Reporting of small business participation on Department of Defense programs.*

Sec. 852. *Waiver of congressional notification for acquisition of tactical missiles and munitions greater than quantity specified in law.*

Sec. 853. *Multiple program multiyear contract pilot demonstration program.*

Sec. 854. *Key performance parameter reduction pilot program.*

Sec. 855. *Mission integration management.*

Subtitle E—Provisions Relating to Acquisition Workforce

Sec. 861. *Project management.*

Sec. 862. *Authority to waive tenure requirement for program managers for program definition and program execution periods.*

Sec. 863. *Purposes for which the Department of Defense Acquisition Workforce Development Fund may be used; advisory panel amendments.*

Sec. 864. *Department of Defense Acquisition Workforce Development Fund determination adjustment.*

Sec. 865. *Limitations on funds used for staff augmentation contracts at management headquarters of the Department of Defense and the military departments.*

Sec. 866. *Senior Military Acquisition Advisors in the Defense Acquisition Corps.*

Sec. 867. *Authority of the Secretary of Defense under the acquisition demonstration project.*

Subtitle F—Provisions Relating to Commercial Items

Sec. 871. *Market research for determination of price reasonableness in acquisition of commercial items.*

Sec. 872. *Value analysis for the determination of price reasonableness.*

Sec. 873. *Clarification of requirements relating to commercial item determinations.*

Sec. 874. *Inapplicability of certain laws and regulations to the acquisition of commercial items and commercially available off-the-shelf items.*

Sec. 875. *Use of commercial or non-Government standards in lieu of military specifications and standards.*

Sec. 876. *Preference for commercial services.*

Sec. 877. *Treatment of commingled items purchased by contractors as commercial items.*

Sec. 878. *Treatment of services provided by nontraditional contractors as commercial items.*

Sec. 879. *Defense pilot program for authority to acquire innovative commercial items, technologies, and services using general solicitation competitive procedures.*

Sec. 880. *Pilot programs for authority to acquire innovative commercial items using general solicitation competitive procedures.*

Subtitle G—Industrial Base Matters

Sec. 881. *Greater integration of the national technology and industrial base.*

Sec. 882. *Integration of civil and military roles in attaining national technology and industrial base objectives.*

Sec. 883. *Pilot program for distribution support and services for weapon systems contractors.*

Sec. 884. *Nontraditional and small contractor innovation prototyping program.*

Subtitle H—Other Matters

Sec. 885. *Report on bid protests.*

Sec. 886. *Review and report on indefinite delivery contracts.*

Sec. 887. *Review and report on contractual flow-down provisions.*

Sec. 888. *Requirement and review relating to use of brand names or brand-name or equivalent descriptions in solicitations.*

Sec. 889. *Inclusion of information on common grounds for sustaining bid protests in annual Government Accountability Office reports to Congress.*

Sec. 890. *Study and report on contracts awarded to minority-owned and women-owned businesses.*

Sec. 891. *Authority to provide reimbursable auditing services to certain non-Defense Agencies.*

Sec. 892. *Selection of service providers for auditing services and audit readiness services.*

Sec. 893. *Amendments to contractor business system requirements.*

Sec. 894. *Improved management practices to reduce cost and improve performance of certain Department of Defense organizations.*

Sec. 895. *Exemption from requirement for capital planning and investment control for information technology equipment included as integral part of a weapon or weapon system.*

Sec. 896. *Modifications to pilot program for streamlining awards for innovative technology projects.*

Sec. 897. *Rapid prototyping funds for the military departments.*

Sec. 898. *Establishment of Panel on Department of Defense and AbilityOne Contracting Oversight, Accountability, and Integrity; Defense Acquisition University training.*

Sec. 899. *Coast Guard major acquisition programs.*

Sec. 899A. *Enhanced authority to acquire products and services produced in Africa in support of certain activities.*

TITLE IX—DEPARTMENT OF DEFENSE ORGANIZATION AND MANAGEMENT

Subtitle A—Office of the Secretary of Defense and Related Matters

Sec. 901. *Organization of the Office of the Secretary of Defense.*

Sec. 902. *Responsibilities and reporting of the Chief Information Officer of the Department of Defense.*

Sec. 903. *Maximum number of personnel in the Office of the Secretary of Defense and other Department of Defense headquarters offices.*

Sec. 904. *Repeal of Financial Management Modernization Executive Committee.*

Subtitle B—Organization and Management of the Department of Defense Generally

Sec. 911. *Organizational strategy for the Department of Defense.*

Sec. 912. *Policy, organization, and management goals and priorities of the Secretary of Defense for the Department of Defense.*

Sec. 913. *Secretary of Defense delivery unit.*

Sec. 914. *Performance of civilian functions by military personnel.*

Sec. 915. *Repeal of requirements relating to efficiencies plan for the civilian personnel workforce and service contractor workforce of the Department of Defense.*

Subtitle C—Joint Chiefs of Staff and Combatant Command Matters

Sec. 921. *Joint Chiefs of Staff and related combatant command matters.*

Sec. 922. *Organization of the Department of Defense for management of special operations forces and special operations.*

Sec. 923. *Establishment of unified combatant command for cyber operations.*

Sec. 924. *Assigned forces of the combatant commands.*

Sec. 925. *Modifications to the requirements process.*

Sec. 926. *Review of combatant command organization.*

Subtitle D—Organization and Management of Other Department of Defense Offices and Elements

Sec. 931. *Qualifications for appointment of the Secretaries of the military departments.*

Sec. 932. *Enhanced personnel management authorities for the Chief of the National Guard Bureau.*

Sec. 933. *Reorganization and redesignation of Office of Family Policy and Office of Community Support for Military Families with Special Needs.*

Sec. 934. Redesignation of Assistant Secretary of the Air Force for Acquisition as Assistant Secretary of the Air Force for Acquisition, Technology, and Logistics.

Subtitle E—Strategies, Reports, and Related Matters

Sec. 941. National defense strategy.
Sec. 942. Commission on the National Defense Strategy for the United States.
Sec. 943. Reform of the national military strategy.
Sec. 944. Form of annual national security strategy report.
Sec. 945. Modification to independent study of national security strategy formulation process.

Subtitle F—Other Matters

Sec. 951. Enhanced security programs for Department of Defense personnel and innovation initiatives.
Sec. 952. Modification of authority of the Secretary of Defense relating to protection of the Pentagon Reservation and other Department of Defense facilities in the National Capital Region.
Sec. 953. Modifications to requirements for accounting for members of the Armed Forces and Department of Defense civilian employees listed as missing.
Sec. 954. Modifications to corrosion report.

TITLE X—GENERAL PROVISIONS

Subtitle A—Financial Matters

Sec. 1001. General transfer authority.
Sec. 1002. Report on auditable financial statements.
Sec. 1003. Increased use of commercial data integration and analysis products for the purpose of preparing financial statement audits.
Sec. 1004. Sense of Congress on sequestration.
Sec. 1005. Requirement to transfer funds from Department of Defense Acquisition Workforce Development Fund to the Treasury.

Subtitle B—Counterdrug Activities

Sec. 1011. Codification and modification of authority to provide support for counterdrug activities and activities to counter transnational organized crime of civilian law enforcement agencies.
Sec. 1012. Secretary of Defense review of curricula and program structures of National Guard counterdrug schools.
Sec. 1013. Extension of authority to support unified counterdrug and counterterrorism campaign in Colombia.
Sec. 1014. Enhancement of information sharing and coordination of military training between Department of Homeland Security and Department of Defense.

Subtitle C—Naval Vessels and Shipyards

Sec. 1021. Definition of short-term work with respect to overhaul, repair, or maintenance of naval vessels.
Sec. 1022. Warranty requirements for shipbuilding contracts.
Sec. 1023. National Sea-Based Deterrence Fund.
Sec. 1024. Availability of funds for retirement or inactivation of Ticonderoga-class cruisers or dock landing ships.

Subtitle D—Counterterrorism

Sec. 1031. Frequency of counterterrorism operations briefings.

Sec. 1032. Prohibition on use of funds for transfer or release of individuals detained at United States Naval Station, Guantanamo Bay, Cub, to the United States.
Sec. 1033. Prohibition on use of funds to construct or modify facilities in the United States to house detainees transferred from United States Naval Station, Guantanamo Bay, Cuba.
Sec. 1034. Prohibition on use of funds for transfer or release to certain countries of individuals detained at United States Naval Station, Guantanamo Bay, Cuba.
Sec. 1035. Prohibition on use of funds for realignment of forces at or closure of United States Naval Station, Guantanamo Bay, Cuba.
Sec. 1036. Congressional notification requirements for sensitive military operations.

Subtitle E—Miscellaneous Authorities and Limitations

Sec. 1041. Expanded authority for transportation by the Department of Defense of non-Department of Defense personnel and cargo.
Sec. 1042. Reduction in minimum number of Navy carrier air wings and carrier air wing headquarters required to be maintained.
Sec. 1043. Modification to support for non-Federal development and testing of material for chemical agent defense.
Sec. 1044. Protection of certain Federal spectrum operations.
Sec. 1045. Prohibition on use of funds for retirement of legacy maritime mine countermeasures platforms.
Sec. 1046. Extension of authority of Secretary of Transportation to issue non-premium aviation insurance.
Sec. 1047. Evaluation of Navy alternate combination cover and unisex combination cover.
Sec. 1048. Independent evaluation of Department of Defense excess property program.
Sec. 1049. Waiver of certain polygraph examination requirements.
Sec. 1050. Use of Transportation Worker Identification Credential to gain access at Department of Defense installations.
Sec. 1051. Limitation on availability of funds for destruction of certain landmines and briefing on development of replacement anti-personnel landmine munitions.
Sec. 1052. Transition of Air Force to operation of remotely piloted aircraft by enlisted personnel.
Sec. 1053. Prohibition on divestment of Marine Corps Search and Rescue Units.
Sec. 1054. Support for the Associate Director of the Central Intelligence Agency for Military Affairs.
Sec. 1055. Notification on the provision of defense sensitive support.
Sec. 1056. Prohibition on enforcement of military commission rulings preventing members of the Armed Forces from carrying out otherwise lawful duties based on member sex.

Subtitle F—Studies and Reports

Sec. 1061. Temporary continuation of certain Department of Defense reporting requirements.

Sec. 1062. Reports on programs managed under alternative compensatory control measures in the Department of Defense.
Sec. 1063. Matters for inclusion in report on designation of countries for which rewards may be paid under Department of Defense rewards program.
Sec. 1064. Annual reports on unfunded priorities of the Armed Forces and the combatant commands and annual report on combatant command requirements.
Sec. 1065. Management and reviews of electromagnetic spectrum.
Sec. 1066. Requirement for notice and reporting to Committees on Armed Services on certain expenditures of funds by Defense Intelligence Agency.
Sec. 1067. Congressional notification of biological select agent and toxin theft, loss, or release involving the Department of Defense.
Sec. 1068. Report on service-provided support and enabling capabilities to United States special operations forces.
Sec. 1069. Report on citizen security responsibilities in the Northern Triangle of Central America.
Sec. 1070. Report on counterproliferation activities and programs.
Sec. 1071. Report on testing and integration of minehunting sonar systems to improve Littoral Combat Ship minehunting capabilities.
Sec. 1072. Quarterly reports on parachute jumps conducted at Fort Bragg and Pope Army Airfield and Air Force support for such jumps.
Sec. 1073. Study on military helicopter noise.
Sec. 1074. Independent review of United States military strategy and force posture in the United States Pacific Command area of responsibility.
Sec. 1075. Assessment of the joint ground forces of the Armed Forces.

Subtitle G—Other Matters

Sec. 1081. Technical and clerical amendments.
Sec. 1082. Increase in maximum amount available for equipment, services, and supplies provided for humanitarian demining assistance.
Sec. 1083. Liquidation of unpaid credits accrued as a result of transactions under a cross-servicing agreement.
Sec. 1084. Modification of requirements relating to management of military technicians.
Sec. 1085. Streamlining of the National Security Council.
Sec. 1086. National biodefense strategy.
Sec. 1087. Global Cultural Knowledge Network.
Sec. 1088. Sense of Congress regarding Connecticut's Submarine Century.
Sec. 1089. Sense of Congress regarding the reporting of the MV–22 mishap in Marana, Arizona, on April 8, 2000.
Sec. 1090. Cost of Wars.
Sec. 1091. Reconnaissance Strike Group matters.
Sec. 1092. Border security metrics.
Sec. 1093. Program to commemorate the 100th anniversary of the Tomb of the Unknown Soldier.
Sec. 1094. Sense of Congress regarding the OCONUS basing of the KC–46A aircraft.
Sec. 1095. Designation of a Department of Defense Strategic Arctic Port.
Sec. 1096. Recovery of excess rifles, ammunition, and parts granted to foreign countries and transfer to certain persons.

TITLE XI—CIVILIAN PERSONNEL MATTERS
Subtitle A—Department of Defense Matters Generally
Sec. 1101. Civilian personnel management.
Sec. 1102. Repeal of requirement for annual strategic workforce plan for the Department of Defense.
Sec. 1103. Training for employment personnel of Department of Defense on matters relating to authorities for recruitment and retention at United States Cyber Command.
Sec. 1104. Public-private talent exchange.
Sec. 1105. Temporary and term appointments in the competitive service in the Department of Defense.
Sec. 1106. Direct-hire authority for the Department of Defense for post-secondary students and recent graduates.
Sec. 1107. Temporary increase in maximum amount of voluntary separation incentive pay authorized for civilian employees of the Department of Defense.
Sec. 1108. Extension of rate of overtime pay for Department of the Navy employees performing work aboard or dockside in support of the nuclear-powered aircraft carrier forward deployed in Japan.
Sec. 1109. Limitation on number of DOD SES positions.
Sec. 1110. Direct hire authority for financial management experts in the Department of Defense workforce.
Sec. 1111. Repeal of certain basis for appointment of a retired member of the Armed Forces to Department of Defense position within 180 days of retirement.

Subtitle B—Department of Defense Science and Technology Laboratories and Related Matters
Sec. 1121. Permanent personnel management authority for the Department of Defense for experts in science and engineering.
Sec. 1122. Codification and modification of certain authorities for certain positions at Department of Defense research and engineering laboratories.
Sec. 1123. Modification to information technology personnel exchange program.
Sec. 1124. Pilot program on enhanced pay authority for certain research and technology positions in the science and technology reinvention laboratories of the Department of Defense.
Sec. 1125. Temporary direct hire authority for domestic defense industrial base facilities, the Major Range and Test Facilities Base, and the Office of the Director of Operational Test and Evaluation.

Subtitle C—Governmentwide Matters
Sec. 1131. Elimination of two-year eligibility limitation for noncompetitive appointment of spouses of members of the Armed Forces.
Sec. 1132. Temporary personnel flexibilities for domestic defense industrial base facilities and Major Range and Test Facilities Base civilian personnel.
Sec. 1133. One-year extension of temporary authority to grant allowances, benefits, and gratuities to civilian personnel on official duty in a combat zone.

Sec. 1134. Advance payments for employees relocating within the United States and its territories.
Sec. 1135. Eligibility of employees in a time-limited appointment to compete for a permanent appointment at any Federal agency.
Sec. 1136. Review of official personnel file of former Federal employees before rehiring.
Sec. 1137. One-year extension of authority to waive annual limitation on premium pay and aggregate limitation on pay for Federal civilian employees working overseas.
Sec. 1138. Administrative leave.
Sec. 1139. Direct hiring for Federal wage schedule employees.
Sec. 1140. Record of investigation of personnel action in separated employee's official personnel file.

TITLE XII—MATTERS RELATING TO FOREIGN NATIONS
Subtitle A—Assistance and Training
Sec. 1201. One-year extension of logistical support for coalition forces supporting certain United States military operations.
Sec. 1202. Special Defense Acquisition Fund matters.
Sec. 1203. Codification of authority for support of special operations to combat terrorism.
Sec. 1204. Independent evaluation of strategic framework for Department of Defense security cooperation.
Sec. 1205. Sense of Congress regarding an assessment, monitoring, and evaluation framework for security cooperation.

Subtitle B—Matters Relating to Afghanistan and Pakistan
Sec. 1211. Extension and modification of Commanders' Emergency Response Program.
Sec. 1212. Extension of authority to acquire products and services produced in countries along a major route of supply to Afghanistan.
Sec. 1213. Extension and modification of authority to transfer defense articles and provide defense services to the military and security forces of Afghanistan.
Sec. 1214. Special immigrant status for certain Afghans.
Sec. 1215. Modification to semiannual report on enhancing security and stability in Afghanistan.
Sec. 1216. Prohibition on use of funds for certain programs and projects of the Department of Defense in Afghanistan that cannot be safely accessed by United States Government personnel.
Sec. 1217. Improvement of oversight of United States Government efforts in Afghanistan.
Sec. 1218. Extension and modification of authority for reimbursement of certain coalition nations for support provided to United States military operations.

Subtitle C—Matters Relating to Syria, Iraq, and Iran
Sec. 1221. Modification and extension of authority to provide assistance to the vetted Syrian opposition.
Sec. 1222. Modification and extension of authority to provide assistance to counter the Islamic State of Iraq and the Levant.

Sec. 1223. Extension and modification of authority to support operations and activities of the Office of Security Cooperation in Iraq.
Sec. 1224. Limitation on provision of man-portable air defense systems to the vetted Syrian opposition during fiscal year 2017.
Sec. 1225. Modification of annual report on military power of Iran.
Sec. 1226. Quarterly report on confirmed ballistic missile launches from Iran.

Subtitle D—Matters Relating to the Russian Federation
Sec. 1231. Military response options to Russian Federation violation of INF Treaty.
Sec. 1232. Limitation on military cooperation between the United States and the Russian Federation.
Sec. 1233. Extension and modification of authority on training for Eastern European national military forces in the course of multilateral exercises.
Sec. 1234. Prohibition on availability of funds relating to sovereignty of the Russian Federation over Crimea.
Sec. 1235. Annual report on military and security developments involving the Russian Federation.
Sec. 1236. Limitation on use of funds to vote to approve or otherwise adopt any implementing decision of the Open Skies Consultative Commission and related requirements.
Sec. 1237. Extension and enhancement of Ukraine Security Assistance Initiative.
Sec. 1238. Reports on INF Treaty and Open Skies Treaty.

Subtitle E—Reform of Department of Defense Security Cooperation
Sec. 1241. Enactment of new chapter for defense security cooperation.
Sec. 1242. Military-to-military exchanges.
Sec. 1243. Consolidation and revision of authorities for payment of personnel expenses necessary for theater security cooperation.
Sec. 1244. Transfer and revision of certain authorities on payment of expenses of training and exercises with friendly foreign forces.
Sec. 1245. Transfer and revision of authority to provide operational support to forces of friendly foreign countries.
Sec. 1246. Department of Defense State Partnership Program.
Sec. 1247. Transfer of authority on Regional Defense Combating Terrorism Fellowship Program.
Sec. 1248. Consolidation of authorities for service academy international engagement.
Sec. 1249. Consolidated annual budget for security cooperation programs and activities of the Department of Defense.
Sec. 1250. Department of Defense security cooperation workforce development.
Sec. 1251. Reporting requirements.
Sec. 1252. Quadrennial review of security sector assistance programs and authorities of the United States Government.
Sec. 1253. Other conforming amendments and authority for administration.

Subtitle F—Human Rights Sanctions
Sec. 1261. Short title.
Sec. 1262. Definitions.
Sec. 1263. Authorization of imposition of sanctions.

Sec. 1264. Reports to Congress.
Sec. 1265. Sunset.

Subtitle G—Miscellaneous Reports

Sec. 1271. Modification of annual report on military and security developments involving the People's Republic of China.
Sec. 1272. Monitoring and evaluation of overseas humanitarian, disaster, and civic aid programs of the Department of Defense.
Sec. 1273. Strategy for United States defense interests in Africa.
Sec. 1274. Report on the potential for cooperation between the United States and Israel on directed energy capabilities.
Sec. 1275. Annual update of Department of Defense Freedom of Navigation Report.
Sec. 1276. Assessment of proliferation of certain remotely piloted aircraft systems.

Subtitle H—Other Matters

Sec. 1281. Enhancement of interagency support during contingency operations and transition periods.
Sec. 1282. Two-year extension and modification of authorization of non-conventional assisted recovery capabilities.
Sec. 1283. Authority to destroy certain specified World War II-era United States-origin chemical munitions located on San Jose Island, Republic of Panama.
Sec. 1284. Sense of Congress on military exchanges between the United States and Taiwan.
Sec. 1285. Limitation on availability of funds to implement the Arms Trade Treaty.
Sec. 1286. Prohibition on use of funds to invite, assist, or otherwise assure the participation of Cuba in certain joint or multilateral exercises.
Sec. 1287. Global Engagement Center.
Sec. 1288. Modification of United States International Broadcasting Act of 1994.
Sec. 1289. Redesignation of South China Sea Initiative.
Sec. 1290. Measures against persons involved in activities that violate arms control treaties or agreements with the United States.
Sec. 1291. Agreements with foreign governments to develop land-based water resources in support of and in preparation for contingency operations.
Sec. 1292. Enhancing defense and security cooperation with India.
Sec. 1293. Coordination of efforts to develop free trade agreements with sub-Saharan African countries.
Sec. 1294. Extension and expansion of authority to support border security operations of certain foreign countries.
Sec. 1295. Modification and clarification of United States-Israel anti-tunnel cooperation authority.
Sec. 1296. Maintenance of prohibition on procurement by Department of Defense of People's Republic of China-origin items that meet the definition of goods and services controlled as munitions items when moved to the ''600 series'' of the Commerce Control List.
Sec. 1297. International sales process improvements.
Sec. 1298. Efforts to end modern slavery.

TITLE XIII—COOPERATIVE THREAT REDUCTION

Sec. 1301. Specification of Cooperative Threat Reduction funds.
Sec. 1302. Funding allocations.
Sec. 1303. Limitation on availability of funds for Cooperative Threat Reduction in People's Republic of China.

TITLE XIV—OTHER AUTHORIZATIONS

Subtitle A—Military Programs

Sec. 1401. Working capital funds.
Sec. 1402. Chemical Agents and Munitions Destruction, Defense.
Sec. 1403. Drug Interdiction and Counter-Drug Activities, Defense-wide.
Sec. 1404. Defense Inspector General.
Sec. 1405. Defense Health Program.

Subtitle B—National Defense Stockpile

Sec. 1411. Authority to dispose of certain materials from and to acquire additional materials for the National Defense Stockpile.
Sec. 1412. National Defense Stockpile matters.

Subtitle C—Chemical Demilitarization Matters

Sec. 1421. National Academies of Sciences study on conventional munitions demilitarization alternative technologies.

Subtitle D—Other Matters

Sec. 1431. Authority for transfer of funds to joint Department of Defense-Department of Veterans Affairs Medical Facility Demonstration Fund for Captain James A. Lovell Health Care Center, Illinois.
Sec. 1432. Authorization of appropriations for Armed Forces Retirement Home.

TITLE XV—AUTHORIZATION OF ADDITIONAL APPROPRIATIONS FOR OVERSEAS CONTINGENCY OPERATIONS

Subtitle A—Authorization of Appropriations

Sec. 1501. Purpose and treatment of certain authorizations of appropriations.
Sec. 1502. Procurement.
Sec. 1503. Research, development, test, and evaluation.
Sec. 1504. Operation and maintenance.
Sec. 1505. Military personnel.
Sec. 1506. Working capital funds.
Sec. 1507. Drug Interdiction and Counter-Drug Activities, Defense-wide.
Sec. 1508. Defense Inspector General.
Sec. 1509. Defense Health program.

Subtitle B—Financial Matters

Sec. 1511. Treatment as additional authorizations.
Sec. 1512. Special transfer authority.

Subtitle C—Limitations, Reports, and Other Matters

Sec. 1521. Afghanistan Security Forces Fund.
Sec. 1522. Joint Improvised Explosive Device Defeat Fund.
Sec. 1523. Extension of authority to use Joint Improvised Explosive Device Defeat Fund for training of foreign security forces to defeat improvised explosive devices.
Sec. 1524. Overseas contingency operations.
Sec. 1525. Extension and modification of authorities on Counterterrorism Partnerships Fund.

TITLE XVI—STRATEGIC PROGRAMS, CYBER, AND INTELLIGENCE MATTERS

Subtitle A—Space Activities

Sec. 1601. Repeal of provision permitting the use of rocket engines from the Russian Federation for the evolved expendable launch vehicle program.
Sec. 1602. Exception to the prohibition on contracting with Russian suppliers of rocket engines for the evolved expendable launch vehicle program.
Sec. 1603. Rocket propulsion system to replace RD-180.
Sec. 1604. Plan for use of allied launch vehicles.
Sec. 1605. Analysis of alternatives for wideband communications.
Sec. 1606. Modification of pilot program for acquisition of commercial satellite communication services.
Sec. 1607. Space-based environmental monitoring.
Sec. 1608. Prohibition on use of certain non-allied positioning, navigation, and timing systems.
Sec. 1609. Limitation of availability of funds for the Joint Space Operations Center Mission System.
Sec. 1610. Limitations on availability of funds for the Global Positioning System Next Generation Operational Control System.
Sec. 1611. Availability of funds for certain secure voice conferencing capabilities.
Sec. 1612. Space-based infrared system and advanced extremely high frequency program.
Sec. 1613. Pilot program on commercial weather data.
Sec. 1614. Plans on transfer of acquisition and funding authority of certain weather missions to National Reconnaissance Office.
Sec. 1615. Five-year plan for Joint Interagency Combined Space Operations Center.
Sec. 1616. Organization and management of national security space activities of the Department of Defense.
Sec. 1617. Review of charter of Operationally Responsive Space Program Office.
Sec. 1618. Backup and complementary positioning, navigation, and timing capabilities of Global Positioning System.
Sec. 1619. Report on use of spacecraft assets of the space-based infrared system wide-field-of-view program.
Sec. 1620. Provision of certain information to Government Accountability Office by National Reconnaissance Office.
Sec. 1621. Cost-benefit analysis of commercial use of excess ballistic missile solid rocket motors.
Sec. 1622. Independent assessment of Global Positioning System Next Generation Operational Control System.

Subtitle B—Defense Intelligence and Intelligence-Related Activities

Sec. 1631. Report on United States Central Command Intelligence Fusion Center.
Sec. 1632. Prohibition on availability of funds for certain relocation activities for NATO Intelligence Fusion Cell.
Sec. 1633. Survey and review of Defense Intelligence Enterprise.

Subtitle C—Cyberspace-Related Matters

Sec. 1641. Special emergency procurement authority to facilitate the defense against or recovery from a cyber attack.
Sec. 1642. Limitation on termination of dual-hat arrangement for Commander of the United States Cyber Command.
Sec. 1643. Cyber mission forces matters.
Sec. 1644. Requirement to enter into agreements relating to use of cyber opposition forces.

Sec. 1645. *Cyber protection support for Department of Defense personnel in positions highly vulnerable to cyber attack.*
Sec. 1646. *Limitation on full deployment of joint regional security stacks.*
Sec. 1647. *Advisory committee on industrial security and industrial base policy.*
Sec. 1648. *Change in name of National Defense University's Information Resources Management College to College of Information and Cyberspace.*
Sec. 1649. *Evaluation of cyber vulnerabilities of F-35 aircraft and support systems.*
Sec. 1650. *Evaluation of cyber vulnerabilities of Department of Defense critical infrastructure.*
Sec. 1651. *Strategy to incorporate Army reserve component cyber protection teams into Department of Defense cyber mission force.*
Sec. 1652. *Strategic Plan for the Defense Information Systems Agency.*
Sec. 1653. *Plan for information security continuous monitoring capability and comply-to-connect policy; limitation on software licensing.*
Sec. 1654. *Reports on deterrence of adversaries in cyberspace.*
Sec. 1655. *Sense of Congress on cyber resiliency of the networks and communications systems of the National Guard.*

Subtitle D—Nuclear Forces

Sec. 1661. *Improvements to Council on Oversight of National Leadership Command, Control, and Communications System.*
Sec. 1662. *Treatment of certain sensitive information by State and local governments.*
Sec. 1663. *Procurement authority for certain parts of intercontinental ballistic missile fuzes.*
Sec. 1664. *Prohibition on availability of funds for mobile variant of ground-based strategic deterrent missile.*
Sec. 1665. *Limitation on availability of funds for extension of New START Treaty.*
Sec. 1666. *Certifications regarding integrated tactical warning and attack assessment mission of the Air Force.*
Sec. 1667. *Matters relating to intercontinental ballistic missiles.*
Sec. 1668. *Requests for forces to meet security requirements for land-based nuclear forces.*
Sec. 1669. *Report on Russian and Chinese political and military leadership survivability, command and control, and continuity of government programs and activities.*
Sec. 1670. *Review by Comptroller General of the United States of recommendations relating to nuclear enterprise of Department of Defense.*
Sec. 1671. *Sense of Congress on nuclear deterrence.*
Sec. 1672. *Sense of Congress on importance of independent nuclear deterrent of United Kingdom.*

Subtitle E—Missile Defense Programs

Sec. 1681. *National missile defense policy.*
Sec. 1682. *Extensions of prohibitions relating to missile defense information and systems.*
Sec. 1683. *Non-terrestrial missile defense intercept and defeat capability for the ballistic missile defense system.*
Sec. 1684. *Review of the missile defeat policy and strategy of the United States.*

Sec. 1685. *Maximizing Aegis Ashore capability and developing medium range discrimination radar.*
Sec. 1686. *Technical authority for integrated air and missile defense activities and programs.*
Sec. 1687. *Hypersonic defense capability development.*
Sec. 1688. *Conventional Prompt Global Strike weapons system.*
Sec. 1689. *Required testing by Missile Defense Agency of ground-based midcourse defense element of ballistic missile defense system.*
Sec. 1690. *Iron Dome short-range rocket defense system and Israeli cooperative missile defense program codevelopment and coproduction.*
Sec. 1691. *Limitations on availability of funds for lower tier air and missile defense capability of the Army.*
Sec. 1692. *Pilot program on loss of unclassified, controlled technical information.*
Sec. 1693. *Plan for procurement of medium-range discrimination radar to improve homeland missile defense.*
Sec. 1694. *Review of Missile Defense Agency budget submissions for ground-based midcourse defense and evaluation of alternative ground-based interceptor deployments.*
Sec. 1695. *Semiannual notifications on missile defense tests and costs.*
Sec. 1696. *Reports on unfunded priorities of the Missile Defense Agency.*

Subtitle F—Other Matters

Sec. 1697. *Protection of certain facilities and assets from unmanned aircraft.*
Sec. 1698. *Harmful interference to Department of Defense Global Positioning System.*

TITLE XVII—GUAM WORLD WAR II LOYALTY RECOGNITION ACT

Sec. 1701. *Short title.*
Sec. 1702. *Recognition of the suffering and loyalty of the residents of Guam.*
Sec. 1703. *Guam World War II Claims Fund.*
Sec. 1704. *Payments for Guam World War II claims.*
Sec. 1705. *Adjudication.*
Sec. 1706. *Grants program to memorialize the occupation of Guam during World War II.*
Sec. 1707. *Authorization of appropriations.*

TITLE XVIII—MATTERS RELATING TO SMALL BUSINESS PROCUREMENT

Subtitle A—Improving Transparency and Clarity for Small Businesses

Sec. 1801. *Plain language rewrite of requirements for small business procurements.*
Sec. 1802. *Transparency in small business goals.*

Subtitle B—Clarifying the Roles of Small Business Advocates

Sec. 1811. *Scope of review by procurement center representatives.*
Sec. 1812. *Duties of the Office of Small and Disadvantaged Business Utilization.*
Sec. 1813. *Improving contractor compliance.*
Sec. 1814. *Improving education on small business regulations.*

Subtitle C—Strengthening Opportunities for Competition in Subcontracting

Sec. 1821. *Good faith in subcontracting.*
Sec. 1822. *Pilot program to provide opportunities for qualified subcontractors to obtain past performance ratings.*
Sec. 1823. *Amendments to the Mentor-Protege Program of the Department of Defense.*

Subtitle D—Miscellaneous Provisions

Sec. 1831. *Improvements to size standards for small agricultural producers.*

Sec. 1832. *Uniformity in service-disabled veteran definitions.*
Sec. 1833. *Office of Hearings and Appeals.*
Sec. 1834. *Extension of SBIR and STTR programs.*
Sec. 1835. *Issuance of guidance on small business matters.*

Subtitle E—Improving Cyber Preparedness for Small Businesses

Sec. 1841. *Small Business Development Center Cyber Strategy and outreach.*
Sec. 1842. *Role of small business development centers in cybersecurity and preparedness.*
Sec. 1843. *Additional cybersecurity assistance for small business development centers.*
Sec. 1844. *Prohibition on additional funds.*

TITLE XIX—DEPARTMENT OF HOMELAND SECURITY COORDINATION

Sec. 1901. *Department of Homeland Security coordination.*
Sec. 1902. *Office of Strategy, Policy, and Plans of the Department of Homeland Security.*
Sec. 1903. *Management and execution.*
Sec. 1904. *Chief Human Capital Officer of the Department of Homeland Security.*
Sec. 1905. *Department of Homeland Security transparency.*
Sec. 1906. *Transparency in research and development.*
Sec. 1907. *United States Government review of certain foreign fighters.*
Sec. 1908. *National strategy to combat terrorist travel.*
Sec. 1909. *National Operations Center.*
Sec. 1910. *Department of Homeland Security strategy for international programs.*
Sec. 1911. *State and high-risk urban area working groups.*
Sec. 1912. *Cybersecurity strategy for the Department of Homeland Security.*
Sec. 1913. *EMP and GMD planning, research and development, and protection and preparedness.*

DIVISION B—MILITARY CONSTRUCTION AUTHORIZATIONS

Sec. 2001. *Short title.*
Sec. 2002. *Expiration of authorizations and amounts required to be specified by law.*
Sec. 2003. *Effective date.*

TITLE XXI—ARMY MILITARY CONSTRUCTION

Sec. 2101. *Authorized Army construction and land acquisition projects.*
Sec. 2102. *Family housing.*
Sec. 2103. *Authorization of appropriations, Army.*
Sec. 2104. *Modification of authority to carry out certain fiscal year 2014 project.*
Sec. 2105. *Extension of authorizations of certain fiscal year 2013 projects.*
Sec. 2106. *Extension of authorizations of certain fiscal year 2014 projects.*

TITLE XXII—NAVY MILITARY CONSTRUCTION

Sec. 2201. *Authorized Navy construction and land acquisition projects.*
Sec. 2202. *Family housing.*
Sec. 2203. *Improvements to military family housing units.*
Sec. 2204. *Authorization of appropriations, Navy.*
Sec. 2205. *Modification of authority to carry out certain fiscal year 2014 project.*
Sec. 2206. *Extension of authorizations of certain fiscal year 2013 projects.*

Sec. 2207. Extension of authorizations of certain fiscal year 2014 projects.
Sec. 2208. Status of "net negative" policy regarding Navy acreage on Guam.

TITLE XXIII—AIR FORCE MILITARY CONSTRUCTION

Sec. 2301. Authorized Air Force construction and land acquisition projects.
Sec. 2302. Family housing.
Sec. 2303. Improvements to military family housing units.
Sec. 2304. Authorization of appropriations, Air Force.
Sec. 2305. Modification of authority to carry out certain fiscal year 2016 project.
Sec. 2306. Extension of authorization of certain fiscal year 2013 project.
Sec. 2307. Extension of authorization of certain fiscal year 2014 project.
Sec. 2308. Restriction on acquisition of property in Northern Mariana Islands.

TITLE XXIV—DEFENSE AGENCIES MILITARY CONSTRUCTION

Sec. 2401. Authorized Defense Agencies construction and land acquisition projects.
Sec. 2402. Authorized energy conservation projects.
Sec. 2403. Authorization of appropriations, Defense Agencies.
Sec. 2404. Modification of authority to carry out certain fiscal year 2014 project.
Sec. 2405. Extension of authorizations of certain fiscal year 2013 projects.
Sec. 2406. Extension of authorizations of certain fiscal year 2014 projects.

TITLE XXV—INTERNATIONAL PROGRAMS

Subtitle A—North Atlantic Treaty Organization Security Investment Program

Sec. 2501. Authorized NATO construction and land acquisition projects.
Sec. 2502. Authorization of appropriations, NATO.

Subtitle B—Host Country In-Kind Contributions

Sec. 2511. Republic of Korea funded construction projects.

TITLE XXVI—GUARD AND RESERVE FORCES FACILITIES

Subtitle A—Project Authorizations and Authorization of Appropriations

Sec. 2601. Authorized Army National Guard construction and land acquisition projects.
Sec. 2602. Authorized Army Reserve construction and land acquisition projects.
Sec. 2603. Authorized Navy Reserve and Marine Corps Reserve construction and land acquisition projects.
Sec. 2604. Authorized Air National Guard construction and land acquisition projects.
Sec. 2605. Authorized Air Force Reserve construction and land acquisition projects.
Sec. 2606. Authorization of appropriations, National Guard and Reserve.

Subtitle B—Other Matters

Sec. 2611. Modification of authority to carry out certain fiscal year 2014 project.
Sec. 2612. Modification of authority to carry out certain fiscal year 2015 project.
Sec. 2613. Modification of authority to carry out certain fiscal year 2016 project.
Sec. 2614. Extension of authorization of certain fiscal year 2013 project.
Sec. 2615. Extension of authorizations of certain fiscal year 2014 projects.

TITLE XXVII—BASE REALIGNMENT AND CLOSURE ACTIVITIES

Sec. 2701. Extension of authorizations of certain fiscal year 2014 projects.
Sec. 2702. Prohibition on conducting additional Base Realignment and Closure (BRAC) round.

TITLE XXVIII—MILITARY CONSTRUCTION GENERAL PROVISIONS

Subtitle A—Military Construction Program and Military Family Housing

Sec. 2801. Modification of criteria for treatment of laboratory revitalization projects as minor military construction projects.
Sec. 2802. Classification of facility conversion projects as repair projects.
Sec. 2803. Limited authority for scope of work increase.
Sec. 2804. Extension of temporary, limited authority to use operation and maintenance funds for construction projects outside the United States.
Sec. 2805. Authority to expand energy conservation construction program to include energy resiliency projects.
Sec. 2806. Additional entities eligible for participation in defense laboratory modernization pilot program.
Sec. 2807. Extension of temporary authority for acceptance and use of contributions for certain construction, maintenance, and repair projects mutually beneficial to the Department of Defense and Kuwait military forces.

Subtitle B—Real Property and Facilities Administration

Sec. 2811. Acceptance of military construction projects as payments in-kind and in-kind contributions.
Sec. 2812. Allotment of space and provision of services to WIC offices operating on military installations.
Sec. 2813. Sense of Congress regarding inclusion of stormwater systems and components within the meaning of "wastewater system" under the Department of Defense authority for conveyance of utility systems.
Sec. 2814. Assessment of public schools on Department of Defense installations.
Sec. 2815. Prior certification required for use of Department of Defense facilities by other Federal agencies for temporary housing support.

Subtitle C—Land Conveyances

Sec. 2821. Land conveyance, High Frequency Active Auroral Research Program facility and adjacent property, Gakona, Alaska.
Sec. 2822. Land conveyance, Campion Air Force Radar Station, Galena, Alaska.
Sec. 2823. Lease, Joint Base Elmendorf-Richardson, Alaska.
Sec. 2824. Transfer of administrative jurisdictions, Navajo Army Depot, Arizona.
Sec. 2825. Exchange of property interests, San Diego Unified Port District, California.
Sec. 2826. Release of property interests retained in connection with land conveyance, Eglin Air Force Base, Florida.
Sec. 2827. Land exchange, Fort Hood, Texas.
Sec. 2828. Land Conveyance, P-36 Warehouse, Colbern United States Army Reserve Center, Laredo, Texas.
Sec. 2829. Land conveyance, St. George National Guard Armory, St. George, Utah.

Sec. 2829A. Land acquisitions, Arlington County, Virginia.
Sec. 2829B. Release of restrictions, Richland Innovation Center, Richland, Washington.
Sec. 2829C. Modification of land conveyance, Rocky Mountain Arsenal National Wildlife Refuge.
Sec. 2829D. Closure of St. Marys Airport.
Sec. 2829E. Transfer of Fort Belvoir Mark Center Campus from the Secretary of the Army to the Secretary of Defense and applicability of certain provisions of law relating to the Pentagon Reservation.
Sec. 2829F. Return of certain lands at Fort Wingate, New Mexico, to the original inhabitants.

Subtitle D—Military Memorials, Monuments, and Museums

Sec. 2831. Cyber Center for Education and Innovation-Home of the National Cryptologic Museum.
Sec. 2832. Renaming site of the Dayton Aviation Heritage National Historical Park, Ohio.
Sec. 2833. Women's military service memorials and museums.
Sec. 2834. Petersburg National Battlefield boundary modification.

Subtitle E—Designations and Other Matters

Sec. 2841. Designation of portion of Moffett Federal Airfield, California, as Moffett Air National Guard Base.
Sec. 2842. Redesignation of Mike O'Callaghan Federal Medical Center.
Sec. 2843. Replenishment of Sierra Vista subwatershed regional aquifer, Arizona.
Sec. 2844. Limited exceptions to restriction on development of public infrastructure in connection with realignment of Marine Corps forces in Asia-Pacific region.
Sec. 2845. Duration of withdrawal and reservation of public land, Naval Air Weapons Station China Lake, California.

TITLE XXIX—OVERSEAS CONTINGENCY OPERATIONS MILITARY CONSTRUCTION

Sec. 2901. Authorized Navy construction and land acquisition projects.
Sec. 2902. Authorized Air Force construction and land acquisition projects.
Sec. 2903. Authorization of appropriations.

TITLE XXX—UTAH TEST AND TRAINING RANGE AND RELATED MATTERS

Subtitle A—Authorization for Temporary Closure of Certain Public Land Adjacent to the Utah Test and Training Range

Sec. 3001. Definitions.
Sec. 3002. Memorandum of agreement.
Sec. 3003. Temporary closures.
Sec. 3004. Liability.
Sec. 3005. Community resource advisory group.
Sec. 3006. Savings clauses.

Subtitle B—Bureau of Land Management Land Exchange With State of Utah

Sec. 3011. Definitions.
Sec. 3012. Exchange of Federal land and non-Federal land.
Sec. 3013. Status and management of non-Federal land acquired by the United States.
Sec. 3014. Hazardous substances.

DIVISION C—DEPARTMENT OF ENERGY NATIONAL SECURITY AUTHORIZATIONS AND OTHER AUTHORIZATIONS

TITLE XXXI—DEPARTMENT OF ENERGY NATIONAL SECURITY PROGRAMS

Subtitle A—National Security Programs and Authorizations

Sec. 3101. National Nuclear Security Administration.

Sec. 3102. *Defense environmental cleanup.*
Sec. 3103. *Other defense activities.*
Sec. 3104. *Nuclear energy.*

Subtitle B—Program Authorizations, Restrictions, and Limitations

Sec. 3111. *Independent acquisition project reviews of capital assets acquisition projects.*
Sec. 3112. *Protection of certain nuclear facilities and assets from unmanned aircraft.*
Sec. 3113. *Common financial reporting system for the nuclear security enterprise.*
Sec. 3114. *Rough estimate of total life cycle cost of tank waste cleanup at Hanford Nuclear Reservation.*
Sec. 3115. *Annual certification of shipments to Waste Isolation Pilot Plant.*
Sec. 3116. *Disposition of weapons-usable plutonium.*
Sec. 3117. *Design basis threat.*
Sec. 3118. *Industry best practices in operations at National Nuclear Security Administration facilities and sites.*
Sec. 3119. *Pilot program on unavailability for overhead costs of amounts specified for laboratory-directed research and development.*
Sec. 3120. *Research and development of advanced naval nuclear fuel system based on low-enriched uranium.*
Sec. 3121. *Increase in certain limitations applicable to funds for conceptual and construction design of the Department of Energy.*
Sec. 3122. *Prohibition on availability of funds for programs in Russian Federation.*
Sec. 3123. *Limitation on availability of funds for Federal salaries and expenses.*
Sec. 3124. *Limitation on availability of funds for defense environmental cleanup program direction.*
Sec. 3125. *Limitation on availability of funds for acceleration of nuclear weapons dismantlement.*

Subtitle C—Plans and Reports

Sec. 3131. *Independent assessment of technology development under defense environmental cleanup program.*
Sec. 3132. *Updated plan for verification and monitoring of proliferation of nuclear weapons and fissile material.*
Sec. 3133. *Report on the use of highly-enriched uranium for naval reactors.*
Sec. 3134. *Analysis of approaches for supplemental treatment of low-activity waste at Hanford Nuclear Reservation.*
Sec. 3135. *Clarification of annual report and certification on status of security of atomic energy defense facilities.*
Sec. 3136. *Report on service support contracts and authority for appointment of certain personnel.*
Sec. 3137. *Elimination of certain reporting requirements.*
Sec. 3138. *Report on United States nuclear deterrence.*

TITLE XXXII—DEFENSE NUCLEAR FACILITIES SAFETY BOARD

Sec. 3201. *Authorization.*

TITLE XXXIV—NAVAL PETROLEUM RESERVES

Sec. 3401. *Authorization of appropriations.*

TITLE XXXV—MARITIME MATTERS

Subtitle A—Maritime Administration, Coast Guard, and Shipping Matters

Sec. 3501. *Authorization of the Maritime Administration.*

Sec. 3502. *Authority to extend certain age restrictions relating to vessels in the Maritime Security Fleet.*
Sec. 3503. *Corrections to provisions enacted by Coast Guard Authorization Acts.*
Sec. 3504. *Status of National Defense Reserve Fleet vessels.*
Sec. 3505. *NDRF national security multi-mission vessel.*
Sec. 3506. *Superintendent of United States Merchant Marine Academy.*
Sec. 3507. *Use of National Defense Reserve Fleet scrapping proceeds.*
Sec. 3508. *Floating dry docks.*
Sec. 3509. *Transportation worker identification credentials for individuals undergoing separation, discharge, or release from the Armed Forces.*
Sec. 3510. *Actions to address sexual harassment and sexual assault at the United States Merchant Marine Academy.*
Sec. 3511. *Sexual assault response coordinators and sexual assault victim advocates.*
Sec. 3512. *Report from the Department of Transportation Inspector General.*
Sec. 3513. *Sexual assault prevention and response working group.*
Sec. 3514. *Sea Year compliance.*
Sec. 3515. *State maritime academy physical standards and reporting.*
Sec. 3516. *Appointments.*
Sec. 3517. *Maritime workforce working group.*
Sec. 3518. *Maritime extreme weather task force.*
Sec. 3519. *Workforce plans and onboarding policies.*
Sec. 3520. *Drug and alcohol policy.*
Sec. 3521. *Vessel transfers.*
Sec. 3522. *Clarifying amendment; continuation boards.*
Sec. 3523. *Polar icebreaker recapitalization plan.*
Sec. 3524. *GAO report on icebreaking capability in United States.*

Subtitle B—Pribilof Islands Transition Completion

Sec. 3531. *Short title.*
Sec. 3532. *Conveyance of property.*
Sec. 3533. *Transfer, use, and disposal of tract 43.*

Subtitle C—Sexual Harassment and Assault Prevention at the National Oceanic and Atmospheric Administration

Sec. 3541. *Actions to address sexual harassment at National Oceanic and Atmospheric Administration.*
Sec. 3542. *Actions to address sexual assault at National Oceanic and Atmospheric Administration.*
Sec. 3543. *Rights of the victim of a sexual assault.*
Sec. 3544. *Change of station.*
Sec. 3545. *Applicability of policies to crews of vessels secured by National Oceanic and Atmospheric Administration under contract.*
Sec. 3546. *Annual report on sexual assaults in the National Oceanic and Atmospheric Administration.*
Sec. 3547. *Sexual assault defined.*

DIVISION D—FUNDING TABLES

Sec. 4001. *Authorization of amounts in funding tables.*

TITLE XLI—PROCUREMENT

Sec. 4101. *Procurement.*
Sec. 4102. *Procurement for overseas contingency operations.*
Sec. 4103. *Procurement for overseas contingency operations for base requirements.*

TITLE XLII—RESEARCH, DEVELOPMENT, TEST, AND EVALUATION

Sec. 4201. *Research, development, test, and evaluation.*

Sec. 4202. *Research, development, test, and evaluation for overseas contingency operations.*
Sec. 4203. *Research, development, test, and evaluation for overseas contingency operations for base requirements.*

TITLE XLIII—OPERATION AND MAINTENANCE

Sec. 4301. *Operation and maintenance.*
Sec. 4302. *Operation and maintenance for overseas contingency operations.*
Sec. 4303. *Operation and maintenance for overseas contingency operations for base requirements.*

TITLE XLIV—MILITARY PERSONNEL

Sec. 4401. *Military personnel.*
Sec. 4402. *Military personnel for overseas contingency operations.*
Sec. 4403. *Military personnel for overseas contingency operations for base requirements.*

TITLE XLV—OTHER AUTHORIZATIONS

Sec. 4501. *Other authorizations.*
Sec. 4502. *Other authorizations for overseas contingency operations.*
Sec. 4503. *Other authorizations for overseas contingency operations for base requirements.*

TITLE XLVI—MILITARY CONSTRUCTION

Sec. 4601. *Military construction.*
Sec. 4602. *Military construction for overseas contingency operations.*
Sec. 4603. *Military construction for overseas contingency operations for base requirements.*

TITLE XLVII—DEPARTMENT OF ENERGY NATIONAL SECURITY PROGRAMS

Sec. 4701. *Department of Energy national security programs.*

DIVISION E—UNIFORM CODE OF MILITARY JUSTICE REFORM

Sec. 5001. *Short title.*

TITLE LI—GENERAL PROVISIONS

Sec. 5101. *Definitions.*
Sec. 5102. *Clarification of persons subject to UCMJ while on inactive-duty training.*
Sec. 5103. *Staff judge advocate disqualification due to prior involvement in case.*
Sec. 5104. *Conforming amendment relating to military magistrates.*
Sec. 5105. *Rights of victim.*

TITLE LII—APPREHENSION AND RESTRAINT

Sec. 5121. *Restraint of persons charged.*
Sec. 5122. *Modification of prohibition of confinement of members of the Armed Forces with enemy prisoners and certain others.*

TITLE LIII—NON-JUDICIAL PUNISHMENT

Sec. 5141. *Modification of confinement as non-judicial punishment.*

TITLE LIV—COURT-MARTIAL JURISDICTION

Sec. 5161. *Courts-martial classified.*
Sec. 5162. *Jurisdiction of general courts-martial.*
Sec. 5163. *Jurisdiction of special courts-martial.*
Sec. 5164. *Summary court-martial as non-criminal forum.*

TITLE LV—COMPOSITION OF COURTS-MARTIAL

Sec. 5181. *Technical amendment relating to persons authorized to convene general courts-martial.*
Sec. 5182. *Who may serve on courts-martial and related matters.*
Sec. 5183. *Number of court-martial members in capital cases.*

Sec. 5184. Detailing, qualifications, and other matters relating to military judges.
Sec. 5185. Military magistrates.
Sec. 5186. Qualifications of trial counsel and defense counsel.
Sec. 5187. Assembly and impaneling of members and related matters.

TITLE LVI—PRE-TRIAL PROCEDURE

Sec. 5201. Charges and specifications.
Sec. 5202. Certain proceedings conducted before referral.
Sec. 5203. Preliminary hearing required before referral to general court-martial.
Sec. 5204. Disposition guidance.
Sec. 5205. Advice to convening authority before referral for trial.
Sec. 5206. Service of charges and commencement of trial.

TITLE LVII—TRIAL PROCEDURE

Sec. 5221. Duties of assistant defense counsel.
Sec. 5222. Sessions.
Sec. 5223. Technical amendment relating to continuances.
Sec. 5224. Conforming amendments relating to challenges.
Sec. 5225. Statute of limitations.
Sec. 5226. Former jeopardy.
Sec. 5227. Pleas of the accused.
Sec. 5228. Subpoena and other process.
Sec. 5229. Refusal of person not subject to UCMJ to appear, testify, or produce evidence.
Sec. 5230. Contempt.
Sec. 5231. Depositions.
Sec. 5232. Admissibility of sworn testimony by audiotape or videotape from records of courts of inquiry.
Sec. 5233. Conforming amendment relating to defense of lack of mental responsibility.
Sec. 5234. Voting and rulings.
Sec. 5235. Votes required for conviction, sentencing, and other matters.
Sec. 5236. Findings and sentencing.
Sec. 5237. Plea agreements.
Sec. 5238. Record of trial.

TITLE LVIII—SENTENCES

Sec. 5301. Sentencing.
Sec. 5302. Effective date of sentences.
Sec. 5303. Sentence of reduction in enlisted grade.

TITLE LIX—POST-TRIAL PROCEDURE AND REVIEW OF COURTS-MARTIAL

Sec. 5321. Post-trial processing in general and special courts-martial.
Sec. 5322. Limited authority to act on sentence in specified post-trial circumstances.
Sec. 5323. Post-trial actions in summary courts-martial and certain general and special courts-martial.
Sec. 5324. Entry of judgment.
Sec. 5325. Waiver of right to appeal and withdrawal of appeal.
Sec. 5326. Appeal by the United States.
Sec. 5327. Rehearings.
Sec. 5328. Judge advocate review of finding of guilty in summary court-martial.
Sec. 5329. Transmittal and review of records.
Sec. 5330. Courts of Criminal Appeals.
Sec. 5331. Review by Court of Appeals for the Armed Forces.
Sec. 5332. Supreme Court review.
Sec. 5333. Review by Judge Advocate General.
Sec. 5334. Appellate defense counsel in death penalty cases.
Sec. 5335. Authority for hearing on vacation of suspension of sentence to be conducted by qualified judge advocate.
Sec. 5336. Extension of time for petition for new trial.

Sec. 5337. Restoration.
Sec. 5338. Leave requirements pending review of certain court-martial convictions.

TITLE LX—PUNITIVE ARTICLES

Sec. 5401. Reorganization of punitive articles.
Sec. 5402. Conviction of offense charged, lesser included offenses, and attempts.
Sec. 5403. Soliciting commission of offenses.
Sec. 5404. Malingering.
Sec. 5405. Breach of medical quarantine.
Sec. 5406. Missing movement; jumping from vessel.
Sec. 5407. Offenses against correctional custody and restriction.
Sec. 5408. Disrespect toward superior commissioned officer; assault of superior commissioned officer.
Sec. 5409. Willfully disobeying superior commissioned officer.
Sec. 5410. Prohibited activities with military recruit or trainee by person in position of special trust.
Sec. 5411. Offenses by sentinel or lookout.
Sec. 5412. Disrespect toward sentinel or lookout.
Sec. 5413. Release of prisoner without authority; drinking with prisoner.
Sec. 5414. Penalty for acting as a spy.
Sec. 5415. Public records offenses.
Sec. 5416. False or unauthorized pass offenses.
Sec. 5417. Impersonation offenses.
Sec. 5418. Insignia offenses.
Sec. 5419. False official statements; false swearing.
Sec. 5420. Parole violation.
Sec. 5421. Wrongful taking, opening, etc. of mail matter.
Sec. 5422. Improper hazarding of vessel or aircraft.
Sec. 5423. Leaving scene of vehicle accident.
Sec. 5424. Drunkenness and other incapacitation offenses.
Sec. 5425. Lower blood alcohol content limits for conviction of drunken or reckless operation of vehicle, aircraft, or vessel.
Sec. 5426. Endangerment offenses.
Sec. 5427. Communicating threats.
Sec. 5428. Technical amendment relating to murder.
Sec. 5429. Child endangerment.
Sec. 5430. Rape and sexual assault offenses.
Sec. 5431. Deposit of obscene matter in the mail.
Sec. 5432. Fraudulent use of credit cards, debit cards, and other access devices.
Sec. 5433. False pretenses to obtain services.
Sec. 5434. Robbery.
Sec. 5435. Receiving stolen property.
Sec. 5436. Offenses concerning Government computers.
Sec. 5437. Bribery.
Sec. 5438. Graft.
Sec. 5439. Kidnapping.
Sec. 5440. Arson; burning property with intent to defraud.
Sec. 5441. Assault.
Sec. 5442. Burglary and unlawful entry.
Sec. 5443. Stalking.
Sec. 5444. Subornation of perjury.
Sec. 5445. Obstructing justice.
Sec. 5446. Misprision of serious offense.
Sec. 5447. Wrongful refusal to testify.
Sec. 5448. Prevention of authorized seizure of property.
Sec. 5449. Wrongful interference with adverse administrative proceeding.
Sec. 5450. Retaliation.
Sec. 5451. Extraterritorial application of certain offenses.
Sec. 5452. Table of sections.

TITLE LXI—MISCELLANEOUS PROVISIONS

Sec. 5501. Technical amendments relating to courts of inquiry.
Sec. 5502. Technical amendment to Article 136.

Sec. 5503. Articles of Uniform Code of Military Justice to be explained to officers upon commissioning.
Sec. 5504. Military justice case management; data collection and accessibility.

TITLE LXII—MILITARY JUSTICE REVIEW PANEL AND ANNUAL REPORTS

Sec. 5521. Military Justice Review Panel.
Sec. 5522. Annual reports.

TITLE LXIII—CONFORMING AMENDMENTS AND EFFECTIVE DATES

Sec. 5541. Amendments to UCMJ subchapter tables of sections.
Sec. 5542. Effective dates.

SEC. 3. CONGRESSIONAL DEFENSE COMMITTEES.

In this Act, the term "congressional defense committees" has the meaning given that term in section 101(a)(16) of title 10, United States Code.

SEC. 4. BUDGETARY EFFECTS OF THIS ACT.

The budgetary effects of this Act, for the purposes of complying with the Statutory Pay-As-You-Go Act of 2010, shall be determined by reference to the latest statement titled "Budgetary Effects of PAYGO Legislation" for this Act, jointly submitted for printing in the Congressional Record by the Chairmen of the House and Senate Budget Committees, provided that such statement has been submitted prior to the vote on passage in the House acting first on the conference report or amendment between the Houses.

DIVISION A—DEPARTMENT OF DEFENSE AUTHORIZATIONS

TITLE I—PROCUREMENT

Subtitle A—Authorization of Appropriations

Sec. 101. Authorization of appropriations.

Subtitle B—Army Programs

Sec. 111. Multiyear procurement authority for AH–64E Apache helicopters.
Sec. 112. Multiyear procurement authority for UH–60M and HH–60M Black Hawk helicopters.
Sec. 113. Distributed Common Ground System—Army increment 1.
Sec. 114. Assessment of certain capabilities of the Department of the Army.

Subtitle C—Navy Programs

Sec. 121. Determination of vessel delivery dates.
Sec. 122. Incremental funding for detail design and construction of LHA replacement ship designated LHA 8.
Sec. 123. Littoral Combat Ship.
Sec. 124. Limitation on use of sole-source shipbuilding contracts for certain vessels.
Sec. 125. Limitation on availability of funds for the Advanced Arresting Gear Program.
Sec. 126. Limitation on availability of funds for procurement of U.S.S. Enterprise (CVN–80).
Sec. 127. Sense of Congress on aircraft carrier procurement schedules.
Sec. 128. Report on P–8 Poseidon aircraft.
Sec. 129. Design and construction of replacement dock landing ship designated LX(R) or amphibious transport dock designated LPD–29.

Subtitle D—Air Force Programs

Sec. 131. EC–130H Compass Call recapitalization program.
Sec. 132. Repeal of requirement to preserve certain retired C–5 aircraft.
Sec. 133. Repeal of requirement to preserve F–117 aircraft in recallable condition.
Sec. 134. Prohibition on availability of funds for retirement of A–10 aircraft.
Sec. 135. Limitation on availability of funds for destruction of A–10 aircraft in storage status.

Sec. 136. Prohibition on availability of funds for retirement of Joint Surveillance Target Attack Radar System aircraft.

Sec. 137. Elimination of annual report on aircraft inventory.

Subtitle E—Defense-wide, Joint, and Multiservice Matters

Sec. 141. Standardization of 5.56mm rifle ammunition.

Sec. 142. Fire suppressant and fuel containment standards for certain vehicles.

Sec. 143. Limitation on availability of funds for destruction of certain cluster munitions.

Sec. 144. Report on Department of Defense munitions strategy for the combatant commands.

Sec. 145. Modifications to reporting on use of combat mission requirements funds.

Sec. 146. Report on alternative management structures for the F-35 joint strike fighter program.

Sec. 147. Comptroller General review of F-35 Lightning II aircraft sustainment support.

Sec. 148. Briefing on acquisition strategy for Ground Mobility Vehicle.

Sec. 149. Study and report on optimal mix of aircraft capabilities for the Armed Forces.

Subtitle A—Authorization of Appropriations

SEC. 101. AUTHORIZATION OF APPROPRIATIONS.

Funds are hereby authorized to be appropriated for fiscal year 2017 for procurement for the Army, the Navy and the Marine Corps, the Air Force, and Defense-wide activities, as specified in the funding table in section 4101.

Subtitle B—Army Programs

SEC. 111. MULTIYEAR PROCUREMENT AUTHORITY FOR AH-64E APACHE HELICOPTERS.

(a) AUTHORITY FOR MULTIYEAR PROCUREMENT.—Subject to section 2306b of title 10, United States Code, the Secretary of the Army may enter into one or more multiyear contracts, beginning with the fiscal year 2017 program year, for the procurement of AH-64E Apache helicopters.

(b) CONDITION FOR OUT-YEAR CONTRACT PAYMENTS.—A contract entered into under subsection (a) shall provide that any obligation of the United States to make a payment under the contract for a fiscal year after fiscal year 2017 is subject to the availability of appropriations for that purpose for such later fiscal year.

SEC. 112. MULTIYEAR PROCUREMENT AUTHORITY FOR UH-60M AND HH-60M BLACK HAWK HELICOPTERS.

(a) AUTHORITY FOR MULTIYEAR PROCUREMENT.—Subject to section 2306b of title 10, United States Code, the Secretary of the Army may enter into one or more multiyear contracts, beginning with the fiscal year 2017 program year, for the procurement of UH-60M and HH-60M Black Hawk helicopters.

(b) CONDITION FOR OUT-YEAR CONTRACT PAYMENTS.—A contract entered into under subsection (a) shall provide that any obligation of the United States to make a payment under the contract for a fiscal year after fiscal year 2017 is subject to the availability of appropriations for that purpose for such later fiscal year.

SEC. 113. DISTRIBUTED COMMON GROUND SYSTEM-ARMY INCREMENT 1.

(a) TRAINING FOR OPERATORS.—The Secretary of the Army shall take such actions as may be necessary to improve and tailor training for covered units in the versions of increment 1 that are in use on the date of the enactment of this Act.

(b) FIELDING OF CAPABILITY.—

(1) IN GENERAL.—The Secretary shall rapidly identify and field a capability for fixed and deployable multi-source ground processing systems for covered units.

(2) COMMERCIALLY AVAILABLE CAPABILITIES.—In carrying out paragraph (1), the Secretary shall procure commercially available off-the-shelf technologies that—

(A) meet essential tactical requirements for processing, analyzing, and displaying intelligence information;

(B) can integrate and communicate with covered units at the tactical unit level and at higher unit levels;

(C) are substantially easier for personnel to use than the Distributed Common Ground System–Army; and

(D) require less training than the Distributed Common Ground System–Army.

(c) LIMITATION ON THE AWARD OF CONTRACT.—The Secretary may not enter into a contract for the design, development, or procurement of any data architecture, data integration, or "cloud" capability, or any data analysis or data visualization and workflow capability (including warfighting function tools relating to increment 1 of the Distributed Common Ground System–Army) for covered units unless the contract—

(1) is awarded not later than 180 days after the date of the enactment of this Act;

(2) is awarded in accordance with applicable law and regulations providing for the use of competitive procedures or procedures applicable to the procurement of commercial items including parts 12 and 15 of the Federal Acquisition Regulation;

(3) is a fixed-price contract; and

(4) provides that the technology to be procured under the contract will—

(A) begin initial fielding rapidly after the contract award;

(B) achieve initial operating capability not later than nine months after the date on which the contract is awarded; and

(C) achieve full operating capability not later than 18 months after the date on which the contract is awarded.

(d) WAIVER.—

(1) IN GENERAL.—The Secretary of Defense may waive the limitation in subsection (c) if the Secretary submits to the appropriate congressional committees a written statement declaring that such limitation would adversely affect ongoing operational activities.

(2) NONDELEGATION.—The Secretary of Defense may not delegate the waiver authority under paragraph (1).

(e) DEFINITIONS.—In this section:

(1) APPROPRIATE CONGRESSIONAL COMMITTEES.—The term "appropriate congressional committees" means—

(A) the congressional defense committees;

(B) the Select Committee on Intelligence of the Senate; and

(C) the Permanent Select Committee on Intelligence of the House of Representatives.

(2) COVERED UNITS.—The term "covered units" means military units that use increment 1 of the Distributed Common Ground System–Army, including tactical units and operators at the division, brigade, and battalion levels, and tactical units below the battalion level.

SEC. 114. ASSESSMENT OF CERTAIN CAPABILITIES OF THE DEPARTMENT OF THE ARMY.

(a) ASSESSMENT.—The Secretary of Defense, in consultation with the Secretary of the Army and the Chief of Staff of the Army, shall conduct an assessment of the following capabilities with respect to the Department of the Army:

(1) The capacity of AH-64 Apache-equipped attack reconnaissance battalions to meet future needs.

(2) Air defense artillery capacity and responsiveness, including—

(A) the capacity of short-range air defense artillery to address existing and emerging threats, including threats posed by unmanned aerial systems, cruise missiles, and manned aircraft; and

(B) the potential for commercial off-the-shelf solutions.

(3) Chemical, biological, radiological, and nuclear capabilities and modernization needs.

(4) Field artillery capabilities, including—

(A) modernization needs;

(B) munitions inventory shortfalls; and

(C) changes in doctrine and war plans consistent with the Memorandum of the Secretary of Defense dated June 19, 2008, regarding the Department of Defense policy on cluster munitions and unintended harm to civilians.

(5) Fuel distribution and water purification capacity and responsiveness.

(6) Watercraft and port-opening capabilities and responsiveness.

(7) Transportation capacity and responsiveness, particularly with respect to the transportation of fuel, water, and cargo.

(8) Military police capacity.

(9) Tactical mobility and tactical wheeled vehicle capacity, including heavy equipment prime movers.

(b) REPORT.—Not later than April 1, 2017, the Secretary of Defense shall submit to the congressional defense committees a report that includes—

(1) the assessment conducted under subsection (a);

(2) recommendations for reducing or eliminating shortfalls in responsiveness and capacity with respect to each of the capabilities described in such subsection; and

(3) an estimate of the costs of implementing such recommendations.

(c) FORM.—The report under subsection (b) shall be submitted in unclassified form, but may include a classified annex.

Subtitle C—Navy Programs

SEC. 121. DETERMINATION OF VESSEL DELIVERY DATES.

(a) DETERMINATION OF VESSEL DELIVERY DATES.—

(1) IN GENERAL.—Chapter 633 of title 10, United States Code, is amended by inserting after section 7300 the following new section:

"**§ 7301. Determination of vessel delivery dates**

"(a) IN GENERAL.—The delivery of a covered vessel shall be deemed to occur on the date on which—

"(1) the Secretary of the Navy determines that the vessel is assembled and complete; and

"(2) custody of the vessel and all systems contained in the vessel transfers to the Navy.

"(b) INCLUSION IN BUDGET AND ACQUISITION REPORTS.—The delivery dates of covered vessels shall be included—

"(1) in the materials submitted to Congress by the Secretary of Defense in support of the budget of the President for each fiscal year (as submitted to Congress under section 1105(a) of title 31, United States Code); and

"(2) in any relevant Selected Acquisition Report submitted to Congress under section 2432 of this title.

"(c) COVERED VESSEL DEFINED.—In this section, the term 'covered vessel' means any vessel of the Navy that is under construction on or after the date of the enactment of this section using amounts authorized to be appropriated for the Department of Defense for shipbuilding and conversion, Navy.".

(2) CLERICAL AMENDMENT.—The table of sections at the beginning of such chapter is amended by inserting after the item relating to section 7300 the following new item:

"7301. Determination of vessel delivery dates.".

(b) CERTIFICATION.—

(1) IN GENERAL.—Not later than January 1, 2017, the Secretary of the Navy shall certify to the congressional defense committees that the delivery dates of the following vessels have been adjusted in accordance with section 7301 of title 10, United States Code, as added by subsection (a):

(A) The U.S.S. John F. Kennedy (CVN–79).

(B) The U.S.S. Zumwalt (DDG–1000).

(C) The U.S.S. Michael Monsoor (DDG–1001).

(D) The U.S.S. Lyndon B. Johnson (DDG–1002).

(E) Any other vessel of the Navy that is under construction on the date of the enactment of this Act.

(2) CONTENTS.—The certification under paragraph (1) shall include—

(A) an identification of each vessel for which the delivery date was adjusted; and

(B) the delivery date of each such vessel, as so adjusted.

SEC. 122. INCREMENTAL FUNDING FOR DETAIL DESIGN AND CONSTRUCTION OF LHA REPLACEMENT SHIP DESIGNATED LHA 8.

(a) AUTHORITY TO USE INCREMENTAL FUNDING.—The Secretary of the Navy may enter into and incrementally fund a contract for detail design and construction of the LHA Replacement ship designated LHA 8 and, subject to subsection (b), funds for payments under the contract may be provided from amounts authorized to be appropriated for the Department of Defense for Shipbuilding and Conversion, Navy, for fiscal years 2017 and 2018.

(b) CONDITION FOR OUT-YEAR CONTRACT PAYMENTS.—A contract entered into under subsection (a) shall provide that any obligation of the United States to make a payment under the contract for any subsequent fiscal year is subject to the availability of appropriations for that purpose for such subsequent fiscal year.

SEC. 123. LITTORAL COMBAT SHIP.

(a) REPORT ON LITTORAL COMBAT SHIP MISSION PACKAGES.—

(1) IN GENERAL.—The Secretary of Defense shall include in the materials submitted in support of the budget of the President (as submitted to Congress under section 1105(a) of title 31, United States Code) for each fiscal year through fiscal year 2022 a report on Littoral Combat Ship mission packages.

(2) ELEMENTS.—Each report under paragraph (1) shall include, with respect to each Littoral Combat Ship mission package and increment, the following:

(A) A description of the status of and plans for development, production, and sustainment, including—

(i) projected unit costs compared to originally estimated unit costs for each system that comprises the mission package;

(ii) projected development costs, procurement costs, and 20-year sustainment costs compared to original estimates of such costs for each system that comprises the mission package;

(iii) demonstrated performance compared to required performance for each system that comprises the mission package and for the mission package as a whole;

(iv) problems relating to realized and potential costs, schedule, or performance; and

(v) any development plans, production plans, or sustainment and mitigation plans that may be implemented to address such problems.

(B) A description, including dates, of each developmental test, operational test, integrated test, and follow-on test event that is—

(i) completed in the fiscal year preceding the fiscal year covered by the report; and

(ii) expected to be completed in the fiscal year covered by the report and any of the following five fiscal years.

(C) The date on which initial operational capability is expected to be attained and a description of the performance level criteria that must be demonstrated to declare that such capability has been attained.

(D) A description of—

(i) the systems that attained initial operational capability in the fiscal year preceding the fiscal year covered by the report; and

(ii) the performance level demonstrated by such systems compared to the performance level required of such systems.

(E) The acquisition inventory objective for each system.

(F) An identification of—

(i) each location (including the city, State, and country) to which systems were delivered in the fiscal year preceding the fiscal year covered by the report; and

(ii) the quantity of systems delivered to each such location.

(G) An identification of—

(i) each location (including the city, State, and country) to which systems are projected to be delivered in the fiscal year covered by the report and any of the following five fiscal years; and

(ii) the quantity of systems projected to be delivered to each such location.

(b) CERTIFICATION OF LITTORAL COMBAT SHIP MISSION PACKAGE PROGRAM OF RECORD.—

(1) IN GENERAL.—The Under Secretary of Defense for Acquisition, Technology, and Logistics shall include in the materials submitted in support of the budget of the President (as submitted to Congress under section 1105(a) of title 31, United States Code) for fiscal year 2018 the certification described in paragraph (2).

(2) CERTIFICATION.—The certification described in this paragraph is a certification with respect to Littoral Combat Ship mission packages that includes, as of the fiscal year covered by the certification, the program of record quantity for—

(A) surface warfare mission packages;

(B) anti-submarine warfare mission packages; and

(C) mine countermeasures mission packages.

(c) LIMITATIONS.—

(1) LIMITATION ON DEVIATION FROM ACQUISITION STRATEGY.—

(A) IN GENERAL.—The Secretary of Defense may not revise or deviate from revision three of the Littoral Combat Ship acquisition strategy, until the date on which the Secretary submits to the congressional defense committees the certification described in subparagraph (B).

(B) CERTIFICATION.—The certification described in this subparagraph is a certification that includes—

(i) the rationale of the Secretary for revising or deviating from revision three of the Littoral Combat Ship acquisition strategy;

(ii) a description of each such revision or deviation; and

(iii) the Littoral Combat Ship acquisition strategy that is in effect following the implementation of such revisions or deviations.

(2) LIMITATION ON SELECTION OF SINGLE CONTRACTOR.—The Secretary of Defense may not select only a single prime contractor to construct the Littoral Combat Ship or any successor frigate class ship unless such selection—

(A) is conducted using competitive procedures and for the limited purpose of awarding a contract or contracts for—

(i) an engineering change proposal for a frigate class ship; or

(ii) the construction of a frigate class ship; and

(B) occurs only after a frigate design has—

(i) reached sufficient maturity and completed a preliminary design review; or

(ii) demonstrated an equivalent level of design completeness.

(d) DEFINITIONS.—In this section:

(1) LITTORAL COMBAT SHIP MISSION PACKAGE.—The term "Littoral Combat Ship mission package" means a mission module for a Littoral Combat Ship combined with the crew detachment and support aircraft for such ship.

(2) MISSION MODULE.—The term "mission module" means the mission systems (including vehicles, communications, sensors, and weapons systems) combined with support equipment (including support containers and standard interfaces) and software (including software relating to the computing environment and multiple vehicle communications system of the mission package).

(3) REVISION THREE.—The term "revision three of the Littoral Combat Ship acquisition strategy" means the third revision of the Littoral Combat Ship acquisition strategy approved by the Under Secretary of Defense for Acquisition, Technology, and Logistics on March 29, 2016.

(e) REPEAL OF QUARTERLY REPORTING REQUIREMENT.—Section 126 of the National Defense Authorization Act for Fiscal Year 2013 (Public Law 112–239; 126 Stat. 1657) is amended—

(1) by striking subsection (b); and

(2) by striking "(a) DESIGNATION REQUIRED.—".

SEC. 124. LIMITATION ON USE OF SOLE-SOURCE SHIPBUILDING CONTRACTS FOR CERTAIN VESSELS.

(a) LIMITATION.—None of the funds authorized to be appropriated by this Act or otherwise made available for the Department of Defense for fiscal year 2017 for joint high speed vessels or expeditionary fast transports may be used to enter into or prepare to enter into a contract on a sole-source basis for the construction of such vessels or transports unless the Secretary of the Navy submits to the congressional defense committees the certification described in subsection (b) and the report described in subsection (c).

(b) CERTIFICATION.—The certification described in this subsection is a certification by the Secretary of the Navy that—

(1) awarding a contract for the construction of one or more joint high speed vessels or expeditionary fast transports on a sole-source basis is in the national security interests of the United States;

(2) the construction of the vessels or transports will not result in exceeding the requirement for the ship class, as described in the most recent Navy force structure assessment;

(3) the contract will be a fixed-price contract;

(4) the price of the contract will be fair and reasonable, as determined by the service acquisition executive of the Navy; and

(5) the contract will provide for the United States to have Government purpose rights in the data for the ship design.

(c) REPORT.—The report described in this subsection is a report that includes—

(1) an explanation of the rationale for awarding a contract for the construction of joint high speed vessels or expeditionary fast transports on a sole-source basis; and

(2) a description of—

(A) actions that may be carried out to ensure that, if additional ships in the class are procured after the award of the contract referred to in paragraph (1), the contracts for the ships shall be awarded using competitive procedures; and

(B) with respect to each such action, an implementation schedule and any associated cost savings, as compared to a contract awarded on a sole-source basis.

SEC. 125. LIMITATION ON AVAILABILITY OF FUNDS FOR THE ADVANCED ARRESTING GEAR PROGRAM.

(a) ADVANCED ARRESTING GEAR FOR U.S.S. ENTERPRISE.—None of the funds authorized to be appropriated by this Act or otherwise made available for fiscal year 2017 for the research

and development, design, procurement, or advanced procurement of materials for advanced arresting gear for the U.S.S. Enterprise (CVN–80) may be obligated or expended until the Secretary of Defense submits to the congressional defense committees the report described in section 2432 of title 10, United States Code, for the most recently concluded fiscal quarter for the Advanced Arresting Gear Program in accordance with subsection (c)(1).

(b) ADVANCED ARRESTING GEAR FOR U.S.S. JOHN F. KENNEDY.—None of the funds authorized to be appropriated by this Act or otherwise made available for fiscal year 2017 for the research and development, design, procurement, or advanced procurement of materials for advanced arresting gear for the U.S.S. John F. Kennedy (CVN–79) may be obligated or expended unless—

(1) the decision to install advanced arresting gear on the vessel is determined by the milestone decision authority for the Program; and

(2) the milestone decision authority for the Program submits notification of such determination to the congressional defense committees.

(c) ADDITIONAL REQUIREMENTS.—

(1) TREATMENT OF BASELINE ESTIMATE.—The Secretary of Defense shall deem the Baseline Estimate for the Advanced Arresting Gear Program for fiscal year 2009 as the original Baseline Estimate for the Program.

(2) UNIT COST REPORTS AND CRITICAL COST GROWTH.—

(A) Subject to subparagraph (B), the Secretary shall carry out sections 2433 and 2433a of title 10, United States Code, with respect to the Advanced Arresting Gear Program, as if the Department had submitted a Selected Acquisition Report for the Program that included the Baseline Estimate for the Program for fiscal year 2009 as the original Baseline Estimate, except that the Secretary shall not carry out subparagraph (B) or subparagraph (C) of section 2433a(c)(1) of such title with respect to the Program.

(B) In carrying out the review required by section 2433a of such title, the Secretary shall not approve a contract, enter into a new contract, exercise an option under a contract, or otherwise extend the scope of a contract for advanced arresting gear for the U.S.S. Enterprise (CVN–80), except to the extent determined necessary by the milestone decision authority, on a non-delegable basis, to ensure that the Program can be restructured as intended by the Secretary without unnecessarily wasting resources.

(d) DEFINITIONS.—In this section:

(1) BASELINE ESTIMATE.—The term "Baseline Estimate" has the meaning given the term in section 2433(a)(2) of title 10, United States Code.

(2) MILESTON DECISION AUTHORITY.—The term "milestone decision authority" has the meaning given the term in section 2366b(g)(3) of title 10, United States Code.

(3) ORIGINAL BASELINE ESTIMATE.—The term "original Baseline Estimate" has the meaning given the term in section 2435(d)(1) of title 10, United States Code.

(4) SELECTED ACQUISITION REPORT.—The term "Selected Acquisition Report" means a Selected Acquisition Report submitted to Congress under section 2432 of title 10, United States Code.

SEC. 126. LIMITATION ON AVAILABILITY OF FUNDS FOR PROCUREMENT OF U.S.S. ENTERPRISE (CVN–80).

(a) LIMITATION.—Of the funds authorized to be appropriated by this Act or otherwise made available for fiscal year 2017 for advance procurement or procurement for the U.S.S. Enterprise (CVN–80), not more than 25 percent may be obligated or expended until the date on which the Secretary of the Navy and the Chief of Naval Operations jointly submit to the congressional defense committees the report under subsection (b).

(b) INITIAL REPORT ON CVN–79 AND CVN–80.—Not later than December 1, 2016, the Secretary of the Navy and the Chief of Naval Operations shall jointly submit to the congressional defense committees a report that includes a description of actions that may be carried out (including descoping requirements, if necessary) to achieve a ship end cost of—

(1) not more than $12,000,000,000 for the CVN–80; and

(2) not more than $11,000,000,000 for the U.S.S. John F. Kennedy (CVN–79).

(c) ANNUAL REPORT ON CVN–79 AND CVN–80.—

(1) IN GENERAL.—Together with the budget of the President for each fiscal year through fiscal year 2021 (as submitted to Congress under section 1105(a) of title 31, United States Code) the Secretary of the Navy and the Chief of Naval Operations shall submit a report on the efforts of the Navy to achieve the ship end costs described in subsection (b) for the CVN–79 and CVN–80.

(2) ELEMENTS.—The report under paragraph (1) shall include, with respect to the procurement of the CVN–79 and the CVN–80, the following:

(A) A description of the progress made toward achieving the ship end costs described in subsection (b), including realized cost savings.

(B) A description of low value-added or unnecessary elements of program cost that have been reduced or eliminated.

(C) Cost savings estimates for current and planned initiatives.

(D) A schedule that includes—

(i) a plan for spending with phasing of key obligations and outlays;

(ii) decision points describing when savings may be realized; and

(iii) key events that must occur to execute initiatives and achieve savings.

(E) Instances of lower Government estimates used in contract negotiations.

(F) A description of risks that may result from achieving the procurement end costs specified in subsection (b).

(G) A description of incentives or rewards provided or planned to be provided to prime contractors for meeting the procurement end costs specified in subsection (b).

SEC. 127. SENSE OF CONGRESS ON AIRCRAFT CARRIER PROCUREMENT SCHEDULES.

(a) FINDINGS.—Congress finds the following:

(1) In the Congressional Budget Office report titled "An Analysis of the Navy's Fiscal Year 2016 Shipbuilding Plan", the Office stated as follows: "To prevent the carrier force from declining to 10 ships in the 2040s, 1 short of its inventory goal of 11, the Navy could accelerate purchases after 2018 to 1 every four years, rather than 1 every five years".

(2) In a report submitted to Congress on March 17, 2015, the Secretary of the Navy indicated the Department of the Navy has a requirement of 11 aircraft carriers.

(b) SENSE OF CONGRESS.—It is the sense of Congress that—

(1) the plan of the Department of the Navy to schedule the procurement of one aircraft carrier every five years will reduce the overall aircraft carrier inventory to 10 aircraft carriers, a level insufficient to meet peacetime and war plan requirements; and

(2) to accommodate the required aircraft carrier force structure, the Department of the Navy should—

(A) begin to program construction for the next aircraft carrier to be built after the U.S.S. Enterprise (CVN–80) in fiscal year 2022; and

(B) program the required advance procurement activities to accommodate the construction of such carrier.

SEC. 128. REPORT ON P–8 POSEIDON AIRCRAFT.

(a) REPORT REQUIRED.—Not later than October 1, 2017, the Secretary of the Navy shall submit to the congressional defense committees a report on potential upgrades to the capabilities of the P–8 Poseidon aircraft.

(b) ELEMENTS.—The report under subsection (a) shall include, with respect to the P–8 Poseidon aircraft, the following:

(1) A review of potential upgrades to the sensors onboard the aircraft, including upgrades to intelligence sensors, surveillance sensors, and reconnaissance sensors such as those being fielded on MQ–4 Global Hawk aircraft platforms.

(2) An assessment of the ability of the Navy to use long-range multispectral imaging systems onboard the aircraft that are similar to such systems being used onboard the MQ–4 Global Hawk aircraft.

SEC. 129. DESIGN AND CONSTRUCTION OF REPLACEMENT DOCK LANDING SHIP DESIGNATED LX(R) OR AMPHIBIOUS TRANSPORT DOCK DESIGNATED LPD–29.

(a) IN GENERAL.—The Secretary of the Navy may enter into a contract, beginning with the fiscal year 2017 program year, for the design and construction of the replacement dock landing ship designated LX(R) or the amphibious transport dock designated LPD–29 using amounts authorized to be appropriated for the Department of Defense for Shipbuilding and Conversion, Navy.

(b) USE OF INCREMENTAL FUNDING.—With respect to the contract entered into under subsection (a), the Secretary may use incremental funding to make payments under the contract.

(c) CONDITION FOR OUT-YEAR CONTRACT PAYMENTS.—The contract entered into under subsection (a) shall provide that any obligation of the United States to make a payment under such contract for any fiscal year after fiscal year 2017 is subject to the availability of appropriations for that purpose for such fiscal year.

Subtitle D—Air Force Programs

SEC. 131. EC–130H COMPASS CALL RECAPITALIZATION PROGRAM.

(a) AUTHORIZATION.—Subject to subsection (b), the Secretary of the Air Force may carry out a program to transfer the primary mission equipment of the EC–130H Compass Call fleet to an aircraft platform that the Secretary determines—

(1) is more operationally effective and survivable than the existing EC–130H Compass Call aircraft platform; and

(2) meets the requirements of the combatant commands.

(b) LIMITATION.—

(1) Except as provided in paragraph (2), none of the funds authorized to be appropriated by this Act or otherwise made available for fiscal year 2017 or any other fiscal year for procurement may be obligated or expended on the program under subsection (a) until the date on which the Secretary of the Air Force determines that there is a high likelihood that the program will meet the requirements of the combatant commands.

(2) The limitation in paragraph (1)—

(A) shall not apply to the development and procurement of the first two aircraft under the program; and

(B) shall not limit the authority of the Secretary to enter into a contract that may include an option for the future production of aircraft under the program if—

(i) the exercise of such option is at the discretion of the Secretary; and

(ii) such option is not exercised until the Secretary determines that there is a high likelihood that the program will meet the requirements of the combatant commands.

SEC. 132. REPEAL OF REQUIREMENT TO PRESERVE CERTAIN RETIRED C-5 AIRCRAFT.

Section 141 of the National Defense Authorization Act for Fiscal Year 2013 (Public Law 112–239; 126 Stat. 1659) is amended by striking subsection (d).

SEC. 133. REPEAL OF REQUIREMENT TO PRESERVE F-117 AIRCRAFT IN RECALLABLE CONDITION.

Section 136 of the John Warner National Defense Authorization Act for Fiscal Year 2007 (Public Law 109–364; 120 Stat. 2114) is amended by striking subsection (b).

SEC. 134. PROHIBITION ON AVAILABILITY OF FUNDS FOR RETIREMENT OF A-10 AIRCRAFT.

(a) PROHIBITION ON AVAILABILITY OF FUNDS FOR RETIREMENT.—None of the funds authorized to be appropriated by this Act or otherwise made available for fiscal year 2017 for the Air Force may be obligated or expended to retire, prepare to retire, or place in storage or on backup aircraft inventory status any A-10 aircraft.

(b) ADDITIONAL LIMITATION ON RETIREMENT.—In addition to the prohibition in subsection (a), the Secretary of the Air Force may not retire, prepare to retire, or place in storage or on backup aircraft inventory status any A-10 aircraft until a period of 90 days has elapsed following the date on which the Secretary submits to the congressional defense committees the report under subsection (e)(2).

(c) PROHIBITION ON SIGNIFICANT REDUCTIONS IN MANNING LEVELS.—None of the funds authorized to be appropriated by this Act or otherwise made available for fiscal year 2017 for the Air Force may be obligated or expended to make significant reductions to manning levels with respect to any A-10 aircraft squadrons or divisions.

(d) MINIMUM INVENTORY REQUIREMENT.—The Secretary of the Air Force shall ensure the Air Force maintains a minimum of 171 A-10 aircraft designated as primary mission aircraft inventory until a period of 90 days has elapsed following the date on which the Secretary submits to the congressional defense committees the report under subsection (e)(2).

(e) REPORTS REQUIRED.—

(1) The Director of Operational Test and Evaluation shall submit to the congressional defense committees a report that includes—

(A) the results and findings of the initial operational test and evaluation of the F-35 aircraft program; and

(B) a comparison test and evaluation that examines the capabilities of the F-35A and A-10C aircraft in conducting close air support, combat search and rescue, and forward air controller airborne missions.

(2) Not later than 180 days after the date of the submission of the report under paragraph (1), the Secretary of the Air Force shall submit to the congressional defense committees a report that includes—

(A) the views of the Secretary with respect to the results of the initial operational test and evaluation of the F-35 aircraft program as summarized in the report under paragraph (1), including any issues or concerns of the Secretary with respect to such results;

(B) a plan for addressing any deficiencies and carrying out any corrective actions identified in such report; and

(C) short-term and long-term strategies for preserving the capability of the Air Force to conduct close air support, combat search and rescue, and forward air controller airborne missions.

(f) SPECIAL RULE.—

(1) Subject to paragraph (2), the Secretary of the Air Force may carry out the transition of the A-10 unit at Fort Wayne Air National Guard Base, Indiana, to an F-16 unit as described by the Secretary in the Force Structure Actions map submitted in support of the budget of the President for fiscal year 2017 (as submitted to Congress under section 1105(a) of title 31, United States Code).

(2) Subsections (a) through (e) shall apply with respect to any A-10 aircraft affected by the transition described in paragraph (1).

SEC. 135. LIMITATION ON AVAILABILITY OF FUNDS FOR DESTRUCTION OF A-10 AIRCRAFT IN STORAGE STATUS.

(a) LIMITATION.—None of the funds authorized to be appropriated by this Act or otherwise made available for the Air Force for fiscal year 2017 or any fiscal year thereafter may be obligated or expended to scrap, destroy, or otherwise dispose of any potential donor A-10 aircraft until the date on which the Secretary of the Air Force submits to the congressional defense committees the report required under section 134(e)(2).

(b) NOTIFICATION AND CERTIFICATION.—Not later than 45 days before taking any action to scrap, destroy, or otherwise dispose of any A-10 aircraft in any storage status in the 309th Aerospace Maintenance and Regeneration Group, the Secretary of the Air Force shall—

(1) notify the congressional defense committees of the intent of the Secretary to take such action; and

(2) certify that the A-10 aircraft subject to such action does not have serviceable wings or other components that could be used to prevent the permanent removal of any active inventory A-10 aircraft from flyable status.

(c) PLAN TO PREVENT REMOVAL A-10 AIRCRAFT FROM FLYABLE STATUS.—The Secretary of the Air Force shall—

(1) include with the materials submitted to Congress in support of the budget of the Department of Defense for fiscal year 2018 (as submitted with the budget of the President under section 1105(a) of title 31, United States Code) a plan to prevent the permanent removal of any active inventory A-10 aircraft from flyable status due to unserviceable wings or any other required component during the period covered by the future years defense plan submitted to Congress under section 221 of title 10, United States Code; and

(2) carry out such plan to prevent the permanent removal of any active inventory A-10 aircraft from flyable status.

(d) POTENTIAL DONOR A-10 AIRCRAFT DEFINED.—In this section, the term "potential donor A-10 aircraft" means any A-10 aircraft in any storage status in the 309th Aerospace Maintenance and Regeneration Group that has serviceable wings or other components that could be used to prevent any active inventory A-10 aircraft from being permanently removed from flyable status due to unserviceable wings or other components.

SEC. 136. PROHIBITION ON AVAILABILITY OF FUNDS FOR RETIREMENT OF JOINT SURVEILLANCE TARGET ATTACK RADAR SYSTEM AIRCRAFT.

(a) PROHIBITION.—Except as provided by subsection (b) and in addition to the prohibition under section 144 of the National Defense Authorization Act for Fiscal Year 2016 (Public Law 114–92; 129 Stat. 758), none of the funds authorized to be appropriated or otherwise made available for fiscal year 2018 for the Air Force may be obligated or expended to retire, or prepare to retire, any Joint Surveillance Target Attack Radar System aircraft.

(b) EXCEPTION.—The prohibition in subsection (a) shall not apply to individual Joint Surveillance Target Attack Radar System aircraft that the Secretary of the Air Force determines, on a case-by-case basis, to be non-operational because of mishaps, other damage, or being uneconomical to repair.

SEC. 137. ELIMINATION OF ANNUAL REPORT ON AIRCRAFT INVENTORY.

Section 231a of title 10, United States Code, is amended—

(1) by striking subsection (e); and

(2) by redesignating subsection (f) as subsection (e).

Subtitle E—Defense-wide, Joint, and Multiservice Matters

SEC. 141. STANDARDIZATION OF 5.56MM RIFLE AMMUNITION.

(a) REPORT.—If, on the date that is 180 days after the date of the enactment of this Act, the Army and the Marine Corps are using in combat two different types of enhanced 5.56mm rifle ammunition, the Secretary of Defense shall, on such date, submit to the congressional defense committees a report explaining the reasons that the Army and the Marine Corps are using different types of such ammunition.

(b) STANDARDIZATION REQUIREMENT.—Except as provided in subsection (c), not later than one year after the date of the enactment of this Act, the Secretary of Defense shall ensure that the Army and the Marine Corps are using in combat one standard type of enhanced 5.56mm rifle ammunition.

(c) EXCEPTION.—Subsection (b) shall not apply in a case in which the Secretary of Defense—

(1) determines that a state of emergency requires the Army and the Marine Corps to use in combat different types of enhanced 5.56mm rifle ammunition; and

(2) certifies to the congressional defense committees that such a determination has been made.

SEC. 142. FIRE SUPPRESSANT AND FUEL CONTAINMENT STANDARDS FOR CERTAIN VEHICLES.

(a) GUIDANCE REQUIRED.—

(1) The Secretary of the Army shall issue guidance regarding fire suppressant and fuel containment standards for covered vehicles of the Army.

(2) The Secretary of the Navy shall issue guidance regarding fire suppressant and fuel containment standards for covered vehicles of the Marine Corps.

(b) ELEMENTS.—The guidance regarding fire suppressant and fuel containment standards issued pursuant to subsection (a) shall—

(1) meet the survivability requirements applicable to each class of covered vehicles;

(2) include standards for vehicle armor, vehicle fire suppression systems, and fuel containment technologies in covered vehicles; and

(3) balance cost, survivability, and mobility.

(c) REPORT TO CONGRESS.—Not later than 180 days after the date of the enactment of this Act, the Secretary of the Army and the Secretary of the Navy shall each submit to the congressional defense committees a report that includes—

(1) the policy guidance established pursuant to subsection (a), set forth separately for each class of covered vehicle; and

(2) any other information the Secretaries determine to be appropriate.

(d) COVERED VEHICLES.—In this section, the term "covered vehicles" means ground vehicles acquired on or after October 1, 2018, under a major defense acquisition program (as such term is defined in section 2430 of title 10, United States Code), including light tactical vehicles, medium tactical vehicles, heavy tactical vehicles, and ground combat vehicles.

SEC. 143. LIMITATION ON AVAILABILITY OF FUNDS FOR DESTRUCTION OF CERTAIN CLUSTER MUNITIONS.

(a) LIMITATION.—Except as provided in subsection (b), none of the funds authorized to be appropriated by this Act or otherwise made available for fiscal year 2017 for the Department of Defense may be obligated or expended for the destruction of cluster munitions until the date on which the Secretary of Defense submits the report required by subsection (c).

(b) *EXCEPTION FOR SAFETY.*—The limitation under subsection (a) shall not apply to the destruction of cluster munitions that the Secretary determines—

(1) are unserviceable as a result of an inspection, test, field incident, or other significant failure to meet performance or logistics requirements; or

(2) are unsafe or could pose a safety risk if not demilitarized or destroyed.

(c) *REPORT REQUIRED.*—

(1) IN GENERAL.—Not later than March 1, 2017, the Secretary of Defense shall submit to the congressional defense committees a report that includes each of the following elements:

(A) A description of the policy of the Department of Defense regarding the use of cluster munitions, including an explanation of the process through which commanders may seek waivers to use such munitions.

(B) A 10-year projection of the requirements and inventory levels for all cluster munitions that takes into account future production of cluster munitions, any plans for demilitarization of such munitions, any plans for the recapitalization of such munitions, the age of the munitions, storage and safety considerations, and other factors that will affect the size of the inventory.

(C) A 10-year projection for the cost to achieve the inventory levels projected in subparagraph (B), including the cost for potential demilitarization or disposal of such munitions.

(D) A 10-year projection for the cost to develop and produce new cluster munitions that comply with the Memorandum of the Secretary of Defense dated June 19, 2008, regarding the Department of Defense policy on cluster munitions and unintended harm to civilians that the Secretary determines are necessary to meet the demands of current operational plans.

(E) An assessment, by the Chairman of the Joint Chiefs of Staff, of the effects of the projected cluster inventory on operational plans.

(F) Any other matters that the Secretary determines should be included in the report.

(2) FORM OF REPORT.—The report required by paragraph (1) shall be submitted in unclassified form, but may include a classified annex.

(d) *CLUSTER MUNITIONS DEFINED.*—In this section, the term "cluster munitions" includes systems delivered by aircraft, cruise missiles, artillery, mortars, missiles, tanks, rocket launchers, or naval guns that deploy payloads of explosive submunitions that detonate via target acquisition, impact, or altitude, or that self-destruct.

SEC. 144. REPORT ON DEPARTMENT OF DEFENSE MUNITIONS STRATEGY FOR THE COMBATANT COMMANDS.

(a) *REPORT REQUIRED.*—Not later than April 1, 2017, the Secretary of Defense shall submit to the congressional defense committees a report on the munitions strategy for the combatant commands for the six-year period beginning on January 1, 2017.

(b) *ELEMENTS.*—The report required by subsection (a) shall include the following:

(1) For each year covered by the report, an identification of the munitions requirements of the combatant commands, including—

(A) plans, programming, and budgeting for each type of munition; and

(B) the inventory of each type of munition.

(2) An assessment of any gaps and shortfalls with respect to munitions determined to be essential to the ability of the combatant commands to fulfill mission requirements.

(3) An assessment of how current and planned munitions programs may affect operational concepts and capabilities of the combatant commands.

(4) An identification of limitations in relevant industrial bases and a description of necessary munitions investments.

(5) An assessment of how munitions capability and capacity may be affected by changes consistent with the memorandum of the Secretary of Defense dated June 19, 2008, regarding the policy of the Department of Defense on cluster munitions and unintended harm to civilians.

(6) Any other matters the Secretary determines appropriate.

SEC. 145. MODIFICATIONS TO REPORTING ON USE OF COMBAT MISSION REQUIREMENTS FUNDS.

Section 123 of the Ike Skelton National Defense Authorization Act for Fiscal Year 2011 (Public Law 111–383; 124 Stat. 4158; 10 U.S.C. 167 note) is amended—

(1) in the section heading, by striking "**QUARTERLY**" and inserting "**ANNUAL**";

(2) in the subsection heading of subsection (a), by striking "QUARTERLY" and inserting "ANNUAL"; and

(3) by striking "quarter" each place it appears and inserting "year".

SEC. 146. REPORT ON ALTERNATIVE MANAGEMENT STRUCTURES FOR THE F–35 JOINT STRIKE FIGHTER PROGRAM.

(a) IN GENERAL.—Not later than March 31, 2017, the Secretary of Defense shall submit to the congressional defense committees a report on potential alternative management structures for the F–35 joint strike fighter program.

(b) *ELEMENTS.*—The report under subsection (a) shall include the following:

(1) An analysis of potential alternative management structures for the F–35 joint strike fighter program, including—

(A) continuation of the joint program office for the program;

(B) the establishment of separate program offices for the program in the Department of the Air Force and the Department of the Navy;

(C) the establishment of separate program offices for each variant of the F–35A, F–35B, and F–35C;

(D) division of responsibilities for the program between a joint program office and the military departments; and

(E) such other alternative management structures as the Secretary determines to be appropriate.

(2) An evaluation of the benefits and drawbacks of each alternative management structure analyzed in the report with respect to—

(A) cost;

(B) alignment of responsibility and accountability; and

(C) the adequacy of representation from military departments and program partners.

(c) *FORM.*—The report under subsection (a) shall be submitted in unclassified form, but may include a classified annex.

SEC. 147. COMPTROLLER GENERAL REVIEW OF F–35 LIGHTNING II AIRCRAFT SUSTAINMENT SUPPORT.

(a) *REVIEW.*—Not later than September 30, 2017, the Comptroller General of the United States shall submit to the congressional defense committees a report on the sustainment support structure for the F–35 Lightning II aircraft program.

(b) *ELEMENTS.*—The review under subsection (a) shall include, with respect to the F–35 Lightning II aircraft program, the following:

(1) The status of the sustainment support strategy for the program, including goals for personnel training, required infrastructure, and fleet readiness.

(2) Approaches, including performance-based logistics, considered in developing the sustainment support strategy for the program.

(3) Other information regarding sustainment and logistics support for the program that the

Comptroller General determines to be of critical importance to the long-term viability of the program.

SEC. 148. BRIEFING ON ACQUISITION STRATEGY FOR GROUND MOBILITY VEHICLE.

(a) *BRIEFING REQUIRED.*—Not later than 180 days after the date of the enactment of this Act, the Under Secretary of Defense for Acquisition, Technology, and Logistics, in consultation with the Secretary of the Army, shall provide a briefing to the congressional defense committees on the acquisition strategy for the Ground Mobility Vehicle for use with the Global Response Force of the 82nd Airborne Division.

(b) *ELEMENTS.*—The briefing under subsection (a) shall include an assessment of the following:

(1) The feasability of acquiring the Ground Mobility Vehicle—

(A) as a commercially available off-the-shelf item (as such term is defined in section 104 of title 41, United States Code); or

(B) as a modified version of such an item.

(2) Whether acquiring the Ground Mobility Vehicle in a manner described in paragraph (1) would satisfy the requirements of the program and reduce the life-cycle cost of the program.

(3) Whether the acquisition strategy for the Ground Mobility Vehicle meets the focus areas specified in the most recent version of the Better Buying Power initiative of the Secretary of Defense.

(4) Whether including an active safety system in the Ground Mobility Vehicle, such as the electronic stability control system used on the joint light tactical vehicle, would reduce the risk of vehicle rollover.

SEC. 149. STUDY AND REPORT ON OPTIMAL MIX OF AIRCRAFT CAPABILITIES FOR THE ARMED FORCES.

(a) *STUDY.*—

(1) IN GENERAL.—The Secretary of Defense shall conduct a study to determine—

(A) an optimal mix of short-range fighter-class strike aircraft and long-range strike aircraft for the use of the Armed Forces during the covered period;

(B) an optimal mix of manned aerial platforms and unmanned aerial platforms for the use of the Armed Forces during such period; and

(C) an optimal mix of other aircraft and capabilities for the use of the Armed Forces during such period, including—

(i) long-range, medium-range, and short-range intelligence, surveillance, reconnaissance, or strike aircraft, or combination of such aircraft;

(ii) aircraft with varying observability characteristics;

(iii) land-based and sea-based aircraft;

(iv) advanced legacy fourth-generation aircraft platforms of proven design;

(v) next generation air superiority capabilities; and

(vi) advanced technology innovations.

(2) CONSIDERATIONS.—In making the determinations under paragraph (1), the Secretary shall consider defense strategy, critical assumptions, priorities, force size, and cost.

(b) *REPORT.*—

(1) IN GENERAL.—Not later than April 14, 2017, the Secretary shall submit to the appropriate congressional committees a report that includes the following:

(A) The results of the study conducted under subsection (a).

(B) A discussion of the specific assumptions, observations, conclusions, and recommendations of the study.

(C) A description of the modeling and analysis techniques used for the study.

(D) A plan for fielding complementary aircraft and capabilities identified as an optimal mix in the study under subsection (a).

(E) A plan to meet objectives and fulfill the warfighting capability and capacity requirements of the combatant commands using the aircraft and capabilities described in subsection (a).

(2) FORM.—*The report under paragraph (1) may be submitted in classified form, but shall include an unclassified executive summary.*

(3) NONDUPLICATION OF EFFORT.—*If any information required under paragraph (1) has been included in another report or notification previously submitted to any of the appropriate congressional committees by law, the Secretary may provide a list of such reports and notifications at the time of submitting the report required under such paragraph instead of including such information in such report.*

(4) DEFINITIONS.—*In this subsection:*

(A) The term "appropriate congressional committees" means the congressional defense committees, the Select Committee on Intelligence of the Senate, and the Permanent Select Committee on Intelligence of the House of Representatives.

(B) The term "covered period" means the period beginning on the date of the enactment of this Act and ending on January 1, 2030.

TITLE II—RESEARCH, DEVELOPMENT, TEST, AND EVALUATION

Subtitle A—Authorization of Appropriations

Sec. 201. Authorization of appropriations.

Subtitle B—Program Requirements, Restrictions, and Limitations

Sec. 211. Laboratory quality enhancement program.

Sec. 212. Modification of mechanisms to provide funds for defense laboratories for research and development of technologies for military missions.

Sec. 213. Making permanent authority for defense research and development rapid innovation program.

Sec. 214. Authorization for National Defense University and Defense Acquisition University to enter into cooperative research and development agreements.

Sec. 215. Manufacturing Engineering Education Grant Program.

Sec. 216. Notification requirement for certain rapid prototyping, experimentation, and demonstration activities.

Sec. 217. Increased micro-purchase threshold for research programs and entities.

Sec. 218. Improved biosafety for handling of select agents and toxins.

Sec. 219. Designation of Department of Defense senior official with principal responsibility for directed energy weapons.

Sec. 220. Restructuring of the distributed common ground system of the Army.

Sec. 221. Limitation on availability of funds for the countering weapons of mass destruction system Constellation.

Sec. 222. Limitation on availability of funds for Defense Innovation Unit Experimental.

Sec. 223. Limitation on availability of funds for Joint Surveillance Target Attack Radar System (JSTARS) recapitalization program.

Sec. 224. Acquisition program baseline and annual reports on follow-on modernization program for F–35 Joint Strike Fighter.

Subtitle C—Reports and Other Matters

Sec. 231. Strategy for assured access to trusted microelectronics.

Sec. 232. Pilot program on evaluation of commercial information technology.

Sec. 233. Pilot program for the enhancement of the research, development, test, and evaluation centers of the Department of Defense.

Sec. 234. Pilot program on modernization and fielding of electromagnetic spectrum warfare systems and electronic warfare capabilities.

Sec. 235. Pilot program on disclosure of certain sensitive information to federally funded research and development centers.

Sec. 236. Pilot program on enhanced interaction between the Defense Advanced Research Projects Agency and the service academies.

Sec. 237. Independent review of F/A–18 physiological episodes and corrective actions.

Sec. 238. B–21 bomber development program accountability matrices.

Sec. 239. Study on helicopter crash prevention and mitigation technology.

Sec. 240. Strategy for Improving Electronic and Electromagnetic Spectrum Warfare Capabilities.

Sec. 241. Sense of Congress on development and fielding of fifth generation airborne systems.

Subtitle A—Authorization of Appropriations

SEC. 201. AUTHORIZATION OF APPROPRIATIONS.

Funds are hereby authorized to be appropriated for fiscal year 2017 for the use of the Department of Defense for research, development, test, and evaluation, as specified in the funding table in section 4201.

Subtitle B—Program Requirements, Restrictions, and Limitations

SEC. 211. LABORATORY QUALITY ENHANCEMENT PROGRAM.

(a) IN GENERAL.—*The Secretary of Defense, acting through the Assistant Secretary of Defense for Research and Engineering, shall carry out a program to be known as the "Laboratory Quality Enhancement Program" under which the Secretary shall establish the panels described in subsection (b) and direct such panels—*

(1) to review and make recommendations to the Secretary with respect to—

(A) existing policies and practices affecting the science and technology reinvention laboratories to improve the mission effectiveness of such laboratories; and

(B) new initiatives proposed by the science and technology reinvention laboratories;

(2) to support implementation of current and future initiatives affecting the science and technology reinvention laboratories; and

(3) to conduct assessments or data analysis on such other issues as the Secretary determines to be appropriate.

(b) PANELS.—*The panels described in this subsection are:*

(1) A panel on personnel, workforce development, and talent management.

(2) A panel on facilities, equipment, and infrastructure.

(3) A panel on research strategy, technology transfer, and industry and university partnerships.

(4) A panel on governance and oversight processes.

(c) COMPOSITION OF PANELS.—*(1) Each panel described in paragraphs (1) through (3) of subsection (b) may be composed of subject matter and technical management experts from—*

(A) laboratories and research centers of the Army, Navy, and Air Force;

(B) appropriate Defense Agencies;

(C) the Office of the Assistant Secretary of Defense for Research and Engineering; and

(D) such other entities as the Secretary determines to be appropriate.

(2) The panel described in subsection (b)(4) shall be composed of—

(A) the Director of the Army Research Laboratory;

(B) the Director of the Air Force Research Laboratory;

(C) the Director of the Naval Research Laboratory;

(D) the Director of the Engineer Research and Development Center of the Army Corps of Engineers; and

(E) such other members as the Secretary determines to be appropriate.

(d) GOVERNANCE OF PANELS.—*(1) The chairperson of each panel shall be selected by its members.*

(2) Each panel, in coordination with the Assistant Secretary of Defense for Research and Engineering, shall transmit to the Science and Technology Executive Committee of the Department of Defense such information or findings on topics requiring decision or approval as the panel considers appropriate.

(e) DISCHARGE OF CERTAIN AUTHORITIES TO CONDUCT PERSONNEL DEMONSTRATION PROJECTS.—*Subparagraph (C) of section 342(b)(3) of the National Defense Authorization Act for Fiscal Year 1995 (Public Law 103–337; 108 Stat. 2721), as added by section 1114(a) of the Floyd D. Spence National Defense Authorization Act for Fiscal Year 2001 (as enacted into law by Public Law 106–398; 114 Stat. 1654A–315), is amended by inserting before the period at the end the following: "through the Assistant Secretary of Defense for Research and Engineering (who shall place an emphasis in the exercise of such authorities on enhancing efficient operations of the laboratory and who may, in exercising such authorities, request administrative support from science and technology reinvention laboratories to review, research, and adjudicate personnel demonstration project proposals)".*

(f) SCIENCE AND TECHNOLOGY REINVENTION LABORATORY DEFINED.—*In this section, the term "science and technology reinvention laboratory" means a science and technology reinvention laboratory designated under section 1105 of the National Defense Authorization Act for Fiscal Year 2010 (Public Law 111–84; 10 U.S.C. 2358 note), as amended.*

SEC. 212. MODIFICATION OF MECHANISMS TO PROVIDE FUNDS FOR DEFENSE LABORATORIES FOR RESEARCH AND DEVELOPMENT OF TECHNOLOGIES FOR MILITARY MISSIONS.

(a) AMOUNT AUTHORIZED UNDER CURRENT MECHANISM.—*Paragraph (1) of subsection (a) of section 219 of the Duncan Hunter National Defense Authorization Act for Fiscal Year 2009 (10 U.S.C. 2358 note) is amended in the matter before subparagraph (A) by striking "not more than three percent" and inserting "not less two percent and not more than four percent".*

(b) ADDITIONAL MECHANISM TO PROVIDE FUNDS.—*Such subsection is further amended by adding at the end the following new paragraph:*

"(3) FEE.—After consultation with the science and technology executive of the military department concerned, the director of a defense laboratory may charge customer activities a fixed percentage fee, in addition to normal costs of performance, in order to obtain funds to carry out activities authorized by this subsection. The fixed fee may not exceed four percent of costs.".

(c) MODIFICATION OF COST LIMIT COMPLIANCE FOR INFRASTRUCTURE PROJECTS.—*Subsection (b)(4) of such section is amended by adding at the end the following new subparagraph:*

"(C) Section 2802 of such title, with respect to construction projects that exceed the cost specified in subsection (a)(2) of section 2805 of such title for certain unspecified minor military construction projects for laboratories.".

(d) REPEAL OF SUNSET.—*Such section is amended by striking subsection (d).*

SEC. 213. MAKING PERMANENT AUTHORITY FOR DEFENSE RESEARCH AND DEVELOPMENT RAPID INNOVATION PROGRAM.

Section 1073 of the Ike Skelton National Defense Authorization Act for Fiscal Year 2011 (Public Law 111–383; 10 U.S.C. 2359 note) is amended—

(1) in subsection (d), by striking "for each of fiscal years 2011 through 2023 may be used for any such fiscal year" and inserting "for a fiscal year may be used for such fiscal year"; and

(2) by striking subsection (f).

SEC. 214. AUTHORIZATION FOR NATIONAL DEFENSE UNIVERSITY AND DEFENSE ACQUISITION UNIVERSITY TO ENTER INTO COOPERATIVE RESEARCH AND DEVELOPMENT AGREEMENTS.

(a) NATIONAL DEFENSE UNIVERSITY.—Section 2165 of title 10, United States Code, is amended by adding at the end the following new subsection:

"(f) COOPERATIVE RESEARCH AND DEVELOPMENT AGREEMENTS.—(1) In engaging in research and development projects pursuant to subsection (a) of section 2358 of this title by a contract, cooperative agreement, or grant pursuant to subsection (b)(1) of such section, the Secretary may enter into such contract or cooperative agreement or award such grant through the National Defense University.

"(2) The National Defense University shall be considered a Government-operated Federal laboratory for purposes of section 12 of the Stevenson-Wydler Technology Innovation Act of 1980 (15 U.S.C. 3710a).".

(b) DEFENSE ACQUISITION UNIVERSITY.—Section 1746 of title 10, United States Code, is amended by adding at the end the following new subsection:

"(d) COOPERATIVE RESEARCH AND DEVELOPMENT AGREEMENTS.—(1) In engaging in research and development projects pursuant to subsection (a) of section 2358 of this title by a contract, cooperative agreement, or grant pursuant to subsection (b)(1) of such section, the Secretary may enter into such contract or cooperative agreement or award such grant through the Defense Acquisition University.

"(2) The Defense Acquisition University shall be considered a Government-operated Federal laboratory for purposes of section 12 of the Stevenson-Wydler Technology Innovation Act of 1980 (15 U.S.C. 3710a).".

SEC. 215. MANUFACTURING ENGINEERING EDUCATION GRANT PROGRAM.

Section 2196 of title 10, United States Code, is amended to read as follows:

"§2196. Manufacturing engineering education program

"(a) ESTABLISHMENT OF MANUFACTURING ENGINEERING EDUCATION PROGRAM.—(1) The Secretary of Defense shall establish a program under which the Secretary makes grants or other awards to support—

"(A) the enhancement of existing programs in manufacturing engineering education to further a mission of the department; or

"(B) the establishment of new programs in manufacturing engineering education that meet such requirements.

"(2) Grants and awards under this section may be made to industry, not-for-profit institutions, institutions of higher education, or to consortia of such institutions or industry.

"(3) The Secretary shall establish the program in consultation with the Secretary of Education, the Director of the National Science Foundation, the Director of the Office of Science and Technology Policy, and the secretaries of such other relevant Federal agencies as the Secretary considers appropriate.

"(4) The Secretary shall ensure that the program is coordinated with Department programs associated with advanced manufacturing.

"(5) The program shall be known as the 'Manufacturing Engineering Education Program'.

"(b) GEOGRAPHICAL DISTRIBUTION OF GRANTS AND AWARDS.—In awarding grants and other awards under this subsection, the Secretary shall, to the maximum extent practicable, avoid geographical concentration of awards.

"(c) COVERED PROGRAMS.—A program of engineering education supported pursuant to this section shall meet the requirements of this section.

"(d) COMPONENTS OF PROGRAM.—The program of education for which such a grant is made shall be a consolidated and integrated multidisciplinary program of education with an emphasis on the following components:

"(1) Multidisciplinary instruction that encompasses the total manufacturing engineering enterprise and that may include—

"(A) manufacturing engineering education and training through classroom activities, laboratory activities, thesis projects, individual or team projects, internships, cooperative work-study programs, and interactions with industrial facilities, consortia, or such other activities and organizations in the United States and foreign countries as the Secretary considers appropriate;

"(B) faculty development programs;

"(C) recruitment of educators highly qualified in manufacturing engineering to teach or develop manufacturing engineering courses;

"(D) presentation of seminars, workshops, and training for the development of specific manufacturing engineering skills;

"(E) activities involving interaction between students and industry, including programs for visiting scholars, personnel exchange, or industry executives;

"(F) development of new, or updating and modification of existing, manufacturing curriculum, course offerings, and education programs;

"(G) establishment of programs in manufacturing workforce training;

"(H) establishment of joint manufacturing engineering programs with defense laboratories and depots; and

"(I) expansion of manufacturing training and education programs and outreach for members of the armed forces, dependents and children of such members, veterans, and employees of the Department of Defense.

"(2) Opportunities for students to obtain work experience in manufacturing through such activities as internships, summer job placements, or cooperative work-study programs.

"(3) Faculty and student engagement with industry that is directly related to, and supportive of, the education of students in manufacturing engineering because of—

"(A) the increased understanding of manufacturing engineering challenges and potential solutions; and

"(B) the enhanced quality and effectiveness of the instruction that result from that increased understanding.

"(e) PROPOSALS.—The Secretary of Defense shall solicit proposals for grants and other awards to be made pursuant to this section for the support of programs of manufacturing engineering education that are consistent with the purposes of this section.

"(f) MERIT COMPETITION.—Applications for awards shall be evaluated on the basis of merit pursuant to competitive procedures prescribed by the Secretary.

"(g) SELECTION CRITERIA.—The Secretary may select a proposal for an award pursuant to this section if the proposal, at a minimum, does each of the following:

"(1) Contains innovative approaches for improving engineering education in manufacturing technology.

"(2) Demonstrates a strong commitment by the proponents to apply the resources necessary to achieve the objectives for which the award is to be made.

"(3) Provides for effective engagement with industry or government organizations that supports the instruction to be provided in the proposed program and is likely to improve manufacturing engineering and technology.

"(4) Demonstrates a significant level of involvement of United States industry in the proposed instructional and research activities.

"(5) Is likely to attract superior students and promote careers in manufacturing engineering.

"(6) Proposes to involve fully qualified personnel who are experienced in manufacturing engineering education and technology.

"(7) Proposes a program that, within three years after the award is made, is likely to attract from sources other than the Federal Government the financial and other support necessary to sustain such program.

"(8) Proposes to achieve a significant level of participation by women, members of minority groups, and individuals with disabilities through active recruitment of students from among such persons.

"(9) Trains students in advanced manufacturing and in relevant emerging technologies and production processes.

"(h) INSTITUTION OF HIGHER EDUCATION DEFINED.—In this section, the term 'institution of higher education' has the meaning given such term in section 101(a) of the Higher Education Act of 1965 (20 U.S.C. 1001(a)).".

SEC. 216. NOTIFICATION REQUIREMENT FOR CERTAIN RAPID PROTOTYPING, EXPERIMENTATION, AND DEMONSTRATION ACTIVITIES.

(a) NOTICE REQUIRED.—The Secretary of the Navy shall not initiate a covered activity until a period of 10 business days has elapsed following the date on which the Secretary submits to the congressional defense committees the notice described in subsection (b) with respect to such activity.

(b) ELEMENTS OF NOTICE.—The notice described in this subsection is a written notice of the intention of the Secretary to initiate a covered activity. Each such notice shall include the following:

(1) A description of the activity.

(2) Estimated costs and funding sources for the activity, including a description of any cost-sharing or in-kind support arrangements with other participants.

(3) A description of any transition agreement, including the identity of any partner organization that may receive the results of the covered activity under such an agreement.

(4) Identification of major milestones and the anticipated date of completion of the activity.

(c) COVERED ACTIVITY.—In this section, the term "covered activity" means a rapid prototyping, experimentation, or demonstration activity carried out under program element 0603382N.

(d) SUNSET.—The requirements of this section shall terminate five years after the date of the enactment of this Act.

SEC. 217. INCREASED MICRO-PURCHASE THRESHOLD FOR RESEARCH PROGRAMS AND ENTITIES.

(a) INCREASED MICRO-PURCHASE THRESHOLD FOR BASIC RESEARCH PROGRAMS AND ACTIVITIES OF THE DEPARTMENT OF DEFENSE SCIENCE AND TECHNOLOGY REINVENTION LABORATORIES.—

(1) IN GENERAL.—Chapter 137 of title 10, United States Code, is amended by adding at the end the following new section:

"§2338. Micro-purchase threshold for basic research programs and activities of the Department of Defense science and technology reinvention laboratories

"Notwithstanding subsection (a) of section 1902 of title 41, the micro-purchase threshold for the Department of Defense for purposes of such section is $10,000 for purposes of basic research programs and for the activities of the Department of Defense science and technology reinvention laboratories.".

(2) CLERICAL AMENDMENT.—The table of sections at the beginning of such chapter is amended by adding at the end the following new item:

"2338. Micro-purchase threshold for basic research programs and activities of the Department of Defense science and technology reinvention laboratories.".

(b) INCREASED MICRO-PURCHASE THRESHOLD FOR UNIVERSITIES, INDEPENDENT RESEARCH INSTITUTES, AND NONPROFIT RESEARCH ORGANIZATIONS.—Section 1902 of title 41, United States Code, is amended—

(1) in subsection (a)—

(A) by striking "For purposes" and inserting "(1) Except as provided in section 2338 of title 10 and paragraph (2) of this subsection, for purposes"; and

(B) by adding at the end the following new paragraph:

"(2) For purposes of this section, the micro-purchase threshold for procurement activities administered under sections 6303 through 6305 of title 31 by institutions of higher education (as defined in section 101(a) of the Higher Education Act of 1965 (20 U.S.C. 1001(a)), or related or affiliated nonprofit entities, or by nonprofit research organizations or independent research institutes is—

"(A) $10,000; or

"(B) such higher threshold as determined appropriate by the head of the relevant executive agency and consistent with clean audit findings under chapter 75 of title 31, internal institutional risk assessment, or State law."; and

(2) in subsections (d) and (e), by striking "not greater than $3,000" and inserting "with a price not greater than the micro-purchase threshold".

SEC. 218. IMPROVED BIOSAFETY FOR HANDLING OF SELECT AGENTS AND TOXINS.

(a) QUALITY CONTROL AND QUALITY ASSURANCE PROGRAM.—The Secretary of Defense, acting through the executive agent for the biological select agent and toxin biosafety program of the Department of Defense, shall carry out a program to implement certain quality control and quality assurance measures at each covered facility.

(b) QUALITY CONTROL AND QUALITY ASSURANCE MEASURES.—Subject to subsection (c), the quality control and quality assurance measures implemented at each covered facility under subsection (a) shall include the following:

(1) Designation of an external manager to oversee quality assurance and quality control.

(2) Environmental sampling and inspection.

(3) Production procedures that prohibit operations where live biological select agents and toxins are used in the same laboratory where viability testing is conducted.

(4) Production procedures that prohibit work on multiple organisms or multiple strains of one organism within the same biosafety cabinet.

(5) A video surveillance program that uses video monitoring as a tool to improve laboratory practices in accordance with regulatory requirements.

(6) Formal, recurring data reviews of production in an effort to identify data trends and nonconformance issues before such issues affect end products.

(7) Validated protocols for production processes to ensure that process deviations are adequately vetted prior to implementation.

(8) Maintenance and calibration procedures and schedules for all tools, equipment, and irradiators.

(c) WAIVER.—In carrying out the program under subsection (a), the Secretary may waive any of the quality control and quality assurance measures required under subsection (b) in the interest of national defense.

(d) STUDY AND REPORT REQUIRED.—

(1) STUDY.—The Secretary of Defense shall carry out a study to evaluate—

(A) the feasibility of consolidating covered facilities within a unified command to minimize risk;

(B) opportunities to partner with industry for the production of biological select agents and toxins and related services in lieu of maintaining such capabilities within the Department of the Army; and

(C) whether operations under the biological select agent and toxin production program should be transferred to another government or commercial laboratory that may be better suited to execute production for non-Department of Defense customers.

(2) REPORT.—Not later than February 1, 2017, the Secretary shall submit to the congressional defense committees a report on the results of the study under paragraph (1).

(e) COMPTROLLER GENERAL REVIEW.—Not later than September 1, 2017, the Comptroller General of the United States shall submit to the congressional defense committees a report that includes the following:

(1) A review of—

(A) the actions taken by the Department of Defense to address the findings and recommendations of the report of the Department of the Army titled "Individual and Institutional Accountability for the Shipment of Viable Bacillus Anthracis from Dugway Proving Grounds", dated December 15, 2015, including any actions taken to address the culture of complacency in the biological select agent and toxin production program identified in such report; and

(B) the progress of the Secretary in carrying out the program under subsection (a).

(2) An analysis of the study and report under subsection (d).

(f) DEFINITIONS.—In this section:

(1) The term "biological select agent and toxin" means any agent or toxin identified under—

(A) section 331.3 of title 7, Code of Federal Regulations;

(B) section 121.3 or section 121.4 of title 9, Code of Federal Regulations; or

(C) section 73.3 or section 73.4 of title 42, Code of Federal Regulations.

(2) The term "covered facility" means any facility of the Department of Defense that produces biological select agents and toxins.

SEC. 219. DESIGNATION OF DEPARTMENT OF DEFENSE SENIOR OFFICIAL WITH PRINCIPAL RESPONSIBILITY FOR DIRECTED ENERGY WEAPONS.—

(a) DESIGNATION OF SENIOR OFFICIAL.—

(1) IN GENERAL.—Not later than 180 days after the date of the enactment of this Act, the Secretary of Defense shall designate a senior official already serving within the Department of Defense as the official with principal responsibility for the development and demonstration of directed energy weapons for the Department.

(2) DEVELOPMENT OF STRATEGIC PLAN.—

(A) IN GENERAL.—The senior official designated under paragraph (1) shall develop a detailed strategic plan to develop, mature, and transition directed energy technologies to acquisition programs of record.

(B) ROADMAP.—Such strategic plan shall include a strategic roadmap for the development and fielding of directed energy weapons and key enabling capabilities for the Department, identifying and coordinating efforts across military departments to achieve overall joint mission effectiveness.

(3) ACCELERATION OF DEVELOPMENT AND FIELDING OF DIRECTED ENERGY WEAPONS CAPABILITIES.—

(A) IN GENERAL.—To the degree practicable, the senior official designated under paragraph (1) shall use the flexibility of the policies of the Department in effect on the day before the date of the enactment of this Act, or any successor policies, to accelerate the development and fielding of directed energy capabilities.

(B) ENGAGEMENT.—The Secretary shall use the flexibility of the policies of the Department

in effect on the day before the date of the enactment of this Act, or any successor policies, to ensure engagement with defense and private industries, research universities, and unaffiliated, nonprofit research institutions.

(4) ADVICE FOR EXERCISES AND DEMONSTRATIONS.—The senior official designated under paragraph (1) shall, to the degree practicable, provide technical advice and support to entities in the Department of Defense and the military departments conducting exercises or demonstrations with the purpose of improving the capabilities of or operational viability of technical capabilities supporting directed energy weapons, including supporting military utility assessments of the relevant cost and benefits of directed energy weapon systems.

(5) SUPPORT FOR DEVELOPMENT OF REQUIREMENTS.—The senior official designated under paragraph (1) shall coordinate with the military departments, Defense Agencies, and the Joint Directed Energy Transition Office to define requirements for directed energy capabilities that address the highest priority warfighting capability gaps of the Department.

(6) AVAILABILITY OF INFORMATION.—The Secretary of Defense shall ensure that the senior official designated under paragraph (1) has access to such information on programs and activities of the military departments and other defense agencies as the Secretary considers appropriate to coordinate departmental directed energy efforts.

(b) JOINT DIRECTED ENERGY TRANSITION OFFICE.—

(1) REDESIGNATION.—The High Energy Laser Joint Technology Office of the Department of Defense is hereby redesignated as the "Joint Directed Energy Transition Office" (in this subsection referred to as the "Office"), and shall report to the official designated under subsection (a)(1).

(2) ADDITIONAL FUNCTIONS.—In addition to the functions and duties of the Office in effect on the day before the date of the enactment of this Act, the Office shall assist the senior official designated under paragraph (1) of subsection (a) in carrying out paragraphs (2) through (5) of such subsection.

(3) FUNDING.—The Secretary may make available such funds to the Office for basic research, applied research, advanced technology development, prototyping, studies and analyses, and organizational support as the Secretary considers appropriate to support the efficient and effective development of directed energy systems and technologies and transition of those systems and technologies into acquisition programs or operational use.

SEC. 220. RESTRUCTURING OF THE DISTRIBUTED COMMON GROUND SYSTEM OF THE ARMY.

(a) IN GENERAL.—Not later that April 1, 2017, the Secretary of the Army shall restructure versions of the distributed common ground system of the Army after Increment 1—

(1) by discontinuing development of new software code, excluding the configuration and testing of system interfaces to commercial, open source, and existing Government off the shelf (GOTS) software, of any component of the system for which there is commercial, open source, or Government off the shelf software that is capable of fulfilling at least 80 percent of the system requirements applicable to such component; and

(2) by conducting a review of the acquisition strategy of the program to ensure that procurement of commercial software is the preferred method of meeting program requirements for major system components.

(b) LIMITATION.—The Secretary of the Army shall not award any contract for the development of new component software capability for the distributed common ground system of the Army if such a capability is already a commercial item or open source, except for configuration of capabilities that are incidental to and necessary for the proper functioning of the system.

(c) *REPORT REQUIRED.—*

(1) *REQUIREMENT.—Not later than March 1, 2018,* the Under Secretary of Defense for Acquisition, Technology and Logistics, in consultation with the Director, Operational Test and Evaluation, shall submit to the congressional defense committees a report on the Increment 2 of the distributed common ground system of the Army.

(2) *ELEMENTS OF REPORT.—The report required by paragraph (1) shall include, at a minimum, the following:*

(A) The overall assessment of the system and each individual major component of the system.

(B) The status of alignment with the Intelligence Community Information Technology Enterprise (IC-ITE).

(C) The ease of use of Increment 2 as compared with Increment 1 for operators in deployed environments.

(D) The extent to which a common, synchronized view of all system data is globally available to all system users, at all times.

(E) The level of maturity of the technologies underlying core system components and application programming interfaces.

(F) The extent to which program operators can move data seamlessly between different components of the system.

SEC. 221. LIMITATION ON AVAILABILITY OF FUNDS FOR THE COUNTERING WEAPONS OF MASS DESTRUCTION SYSTEM CONSTELLATION.

(a) *LIMITATION.—Not more than 50 percent of the funds authorized to be appropriated by this Act or otherwise made available for fiscal year 2017 for the countering weapons of mass destruction situational awareness information system commonly known as "Constellation" may be obligated or expended for research, development, or prototyping for such system until the report required by subsection (b)(4) has been delivered to the congressional defense committees.*

(b) *INDEPENDENT REVIEW AND ASSESSMENT.—*

(1) *IN GENERAL.—The Secretary of Defense shall provide for an independent review and assessment of the requirements and implementation for research, development, and prototyping for the Constellation system prior to a Milestone A decision or other operational use.*

(2) *ELEMENTS OF INDEPENDENT REVIEW.—The independent review provided for under paragraph (1) shall include the following:*

(A) A review of the major software components of the system and an explanation of the requirements of the Department of Defense with respect to each such component.

(B) A review of the requirements validated in the Information System Initial Capabilities Document (ISICD) and capability gaps identified for duplication and redundancy with other validated information technology requirements and capability gaps.

(C) Identification of elements and applications of the system that cannot be implemented using the existing technical infrastructure and tools of the Department of Defense or the infrastructure and tools in development.

(D) An overview of a security plan to achieve an accredited cross-domain solution system, including security milestones and proposed security architecture to mitigate both insider and outsider threats.

(E) Identification of the planned categories of end-users of the system, linked to organizations, mission requirements, and concept of operations, the expected total number of end-users, and the associated permissions granted to such users.

(3) *ENTITY CONDUCTING INDEPENDENT REVIEW AND ASSESSMENT.—The Secretary shall ensure that—*

(A) the independent review and assessment provided for under paragraph (1) is conducted by a federally funded research and development center selected (or entered into an arrangement with) by the Secretary or such other entity as the Secretary considers appropriate; and

(B) such center or entity provides periodic updates to the congressional defense committees on such independent review and assessment prior to the completion of the independent review and assessment.

(4) *REPORT ON INDEPENDENT REVIEW AND ASSESSMENT.—The Secretary shall submit to the congressional defense committees a report containing—*

(A) the findings of the center or entity selected (or entered into an arrangement with) under paragraph (3)(A) with respect to the independent review and assessment conducted by such center or entity pursuant to such paragraph; and

(B) an assessment of the need to continue Constellation research, development, and prototyping.

SEC. 222. LIMITATION ON AVAILABILITY OF FUNDS FOR DEFENSE INNOVATION UNIT EXPERIMENTAL.

(a) *LIMITATION.—*

(1) *OPERATION AND MAINTENANCE.—Of the funds specified in subsection (c)(1), not more than 75 percent may be obligated or expended until the date on which the Secretary of Defense submits to the congressional defense committees the report under subsection (b).*

(2) *RESEARCH, DEVELOPMENT, TEST, AND EVALUATION.—Of the funds specified in subsection (c)(2), not more than 25 percent may be obligated or expended until the date on which the Secretary submits to the congressional defense committees the report under subsection (b).*

(b) *REPORT REQUIRED.—The Secretary of Defense shall submit to the congressional defense committees a report on the Defense Innovation Unit Experimental. Such report shall include the following:*

(1) The charter and mission statement of the Unit.

(2) A description of—

(A) the management and operations of the Unit, including—

(i) the governance structure of the Unit;

(ii) the process for coordinating and deconflicting the activities of the Unit with similar activities of the Small Business Innovation Research Program, military departments, Defense Agencies, and other departments and agencies of the Federal Government, including activities carried out by In-Q-Tel, the Defense Advanced Research Projects Agency, and Department of Defense laboratories;

(iii) the direct staffing requirements of the Unit, including a description of the desired skills and expertise of such staff at each location;

(iv) the number of civilian and military personnel provided by the military departments and Defense Agencies to support the Unit; and

(v) any planned expansion to new sites, the metrics used to identify such sites, and an explanation of how such expansion will provide access to innovations of nontraditional defense contractors (as such term is defined in section 2302 of title 10, United States Code) that are not otherwise accessible; and

(B) policies and practices that will enable the Unit to best support Department of Defense missions, including—

(i) the metrics used to measure the effectiveness of the Unit;

(ii) how compliance with Department of Defense or Federal Government requirements could

affect the ability of nontraditional defense contractors (as such term is defined in section 2302 of title 10, United States Code) to market products and obtain funding;

(iii) how to treat intellectual property that has been developed with little or no government funding;

(iv) detailed justification for the expansion of the mission of the Unit, including authority to use research and development agreements, contracts, and merit-based prize competitions to explore emerging technologies and additional physical locations;

(v) a description of how existing Department of Defense agencies, services, entities, and other elements are authorized to better use streamlined acquisition procedures, research and development agreements, contracts, and merit-based prize competitions to explore emerging technologies, including modification of guidance and procedures to permit effective and streamlined implementation of authorities provided by Congress for rapid execution;

(vi) an account of the successes and failures of contracts already awarded by the unit;

(vii) recommendations on practices, policies, and authorities that will permit increased public-private partnership in financing and funding of research and technology development efforts; and

(viii) a description of technology transition strategies to ensure that research and technology programs funded by the Unit will be effectively and efficiently transitioned into operational use or acquisition programs, including a description of the role of Defense laboratories in such technology transition efforts.

(3) Any other information the Secretary determines to be appropriate.

(c) *FUNDS SPECIFIED.—The funds specified in this subsection are as follows:*

(1) Funds authorized to be appropriated by this Act or otherwise made available for fiscal year 2017 for operation and maintenance, Defense-wide, for the Defense Innovation Unit Experimental.

(2) Funds authorized to be appropriated by this Act or otherwise made available for fiscal year 2017 for research, development, test, and evaluation, Defense-wide, for the Defense Innovation Unit Experimental.

SEC. 223. LIMITATION ON AVAILABILITY OF FUNDS FOR JOINT SURVEILLANCE TARGET ATTACK RADAR SYSTEM (JSTARS) RECAPITALIZATION PROGRAM.

(a) *IN GENERAL.—Except as provided in subsection (b), none of the funds authorized to be appropriated by this Act or otherwise made available for fiscal year 2017 or any other fiscal year for the Air Force may be made available for the Air Force's Joint Surveillance Target Attack Radar System (JSTARS) recapitalization program unless the contract for engineering and manufacturing development uses a firm fixed-price contract structure.*

(b) *NATIONAL SECURITY WAIVER AUTHORITY.—The Secretary of Defense may waive the limitation in subsection (a) if the Secretary determines that such a waiver is in the national security interests of the United States.*

SEC. 224. ACQUISITION PROGRAM BASELINE AND ANNUAL REPORTS ON FOLLOW-ON MODERNIZATION PROGRAM FOR F–35 JOINT STRIKE FIGHTER.

(a) *LIMITATION.—The Secretary of Defense may not award any follow-on modernization development contracts for the F–35 Joint Strike Fighter until the Secretary has submitted the report required by subsection (b)(1) in accordance with such subsection.*

(b) *ACQUISITION PROGRAM BASELINE.—*

(1) *IN GENERAL.—Not later than March 31, 2017, the Secretary of Defense shall submit to the congressional defense committees a report*

that contains the basic elements of an acquisition program baseline for Block 4 Modernization.

(2) ELEMENTS.—The report required by paragraph (1) shall include the following:

(A) Cost estimates for development, production, and modification.

(B) Projected key schedule dates, including dates for the completion of—

(i) a capabilities development document;

(ii) an independent cost estimate;

(iii) an initial preliminary design review;

(iv) a development contract award; and

(v) a critical design review.

(C) Technical performance parameters.

(D) Technology readiness levels.

(E) Annual funding profiles for development and procurement.

(c) REVIEW BY COMPTROLLER GENERAL OF THE UNITED STATES.—Not later than 60 days after the date on which the report required by subsection (b)(1) is submitted to the congressional defense committees in accordance with such subsection, the Comptroller General of the United States shall—

(1) review such report; and

(2) brief the congressional defense committees on the findings of the Comptroller General with respect to such review.

(d) ANNUAL REPORTS BY SECRETARY OF DEFENSE.—Not later than one year after the date on which the Secretary awards a development contract for follow-on modernization of the F–35 Joint Strike Fighter and not less frequently than once each year thereafter until March 31, 2023, the Secretary shall submit to the congressional defense committees a report on the cost, schedule, and performance progress against the baseline set forth in the report submitted pursuant to subsection (b)(1).

Subtitle C—Reports and Other Matters

SEC. 231. STRATEGY FOR ASSURED ACCESS TO TRUSTED MICROELECTRONICS.

(a) STRATEGY.—The Secretary of Defense shall develop a strategy to ensure that the Department of Defense has assured access to trusted microelectronics by not later than September 30, 2019.

(b) ELEMENTS.—The strategy under subsection (a) shall include the following:

(1) Definitions of the various levels of trust required by classes of Department of Defense systems.

(2) Means of classifying systems of the Department of Defense based on the level of trust such systems are required to maintain with respect to microelectronics.

(3) Means by which trust in microelectronics can be assured.

(4) Means to increase the supplier base for assured microelectronics to ensure multiple supply pathways.

(5) An assessment of the microelectronics needs of the Department of Defense in future years, including the need for trusted, radiation-hardened microelectronics.

(6) An assessment of the microelectronic needs of the Department of Defense that may not be fulfilled by entities outside the Department of Defense.

(7) The resources required to assure access to trusted microelectronics, including infrastructure, workforce, and investments in science and technology.

(8) A research and development strategy to ensure that the Department of Defense can, to the maximum extent practicable, use state of the art commercial microelectronics capabilities or their equivalent, while satisfying the needs for trust.

(9) Recommendations for changes in authorities, regulations, and practices, including acquisition policies, financial management, public-private partnership policies, or in any other relevant areas, that would support the achievement of the goals of the strategy.

(c) SUBMISSION AND UPDATES.—(1) Not later than one year after the date of the enactment of this Act, the Secretary shall submit to the congressional defense committees the strategy developed under subsection (a). The strategy shall be submitted in unclassified form, but may include a classified annex.

(2) Not later than two years after submitting the strategy under paragraph (1) and not less frequently than once every two years thereafter until September 30, 2024, the Secretary shall update the strategy as the Secretary considers appropriate to support Department of Defense missions.

(d) DIRECTIVE REQUIRED.—Not later than September 30, 2019, the Secretary of Defense shall issue a directive for the Department of Defense describing how Department of Defense entities may access assured and trusted microelectronics supply chains for Department of Defense systems.

(e) REPORT AND CERTIFICATION.—Not later than September 30, 2020, the Secretary of the Defense shall submit to the congressional defense committees—

(1) a report on—

(A) the status of the implementation of the strategy developed under subsection (a);

(B) the actions being taken to achieve full implementation of such strategy, and a timeline for such implementation; and

(C) the status of the implementation of the directive required by subsection (d); and

(2) a certification of whether the Department of Defense has an assured means for accessing a sufficient supply of trusted microelectronics, as required by the strategy developed under subsection (a).

(f) DEFINITIONS.—In this section:

(1) The term "assured" refers, with respect to microelectronics, to the ability of the Department of Defense to guarantee availability of microelectronics parts at the necessary volumes and with the performance characteristics required to meet the needs of the Department of Defense.

(2) The terms "trust" and "trusted" refer, with respect to microelectronics, to the ability of the Department of Defense to have confidence that the microelectronics function as intended and are free of exploitable vulnerabilities, either intentionally or unintentionally designed or inserted as part of the system at any time during its life cycle.

SEC. 232. PILOT PROGRAM ON EVALUATION OF COMMERCIAL INFORMATION TECHNOLOGY.

(a) PILOT PROGRAM.—The Director of the Defense Information Systems Agency may carry out a pilot program to evaluate commercially available information technology tools to better understand the potential impact of such tools on networks and computing environments of the Department of Defense.

(b) ACTIVITIES.—Activities under the pilot program may include the following:

(1) Prototyping, experimentation, operational demonstration, military user assessments, and other means of obtaining quantitative and qualitative feedback on the commercial information technology products.

(2) Engagement with the commercial information technology industry to—

(A) forecast military requirements and technology needs; and

(B) support the development of market strategies and program requirements before finalizing acquisition decisions and strategies.

(3) Assessment of novel or innovative commercial technology for use by the Department of Defense.

(4) Assessment of novel or innovative contracting mechanisms to speed delivery of capabilities to the Armed Forces.

(5) Solicitation of operational user input to shape future information technology requirements of the Department of Defense.

(c) LIMITATION ON AVAILABILITY OF FUNDS.—Of the amounts authorized to be appropriated for research, development, test, and evaluation, Defense-wide, for each of fiscal years 2017 through 2022, not more than $15,000,000 may be expended on the pilot program in any such fiscal year.

SEC. 233. PILOT PROGRAM FOR THE ENHANCEMENT OF THE RESEARCH, DEVELOPMENT, TEST, AND EVALUATION CENTERS OF THE DEPARTMENT OF DEFENSE.

(a) PILOT PROGRAM REQUIRED.—

(1) IN GENERAL.—The Secretary of Defense and the secretaries of the military departments shall jointly carry out a pilot program to demonstrate methods for the more effective development of technology and management of functions at eligible centers.

(2) ELIGIBLE CENTERS.—For purposes of the pilot program, the eligible centers are—

(A) the science and technology reinvention laboratories, as specified in section 1105(a) of the National Defense Authorization Act for Fiscal Year 2010 (10 U.S.C. 2358 note);

(B) the test and evaluation centers which are activities specified as part of the Major Range and Test Facility Base in Department of Defense Directive 3200.11; and

(C) the Defense Advanced Research Projects Agency.

(b) SELECTION.—

(1) IN GENERAL.—The secretaries described in subsection (a) shall ensure that participation in the pilot program includes—

(A) the Defense Advanced Research Projects Agency; and

(B) in accordance with paragraph (2)—

(i) five additional eligible centers described in subparagraph (A) of subsection (a)(2) from each of the military departments; and

(ii) five additional eligible centers described in subparagraph (B) of such subsection from each of the military departments.

(2) SELECTION PROCEDURES.—(A) The head of an eligible center described in subparagraph (A) or (B) of subsection (a)(2) seeking to participate in the pilot program shall submit to the appropriate reviewer an application therefor at such time, in such manner, and containing such information as the appropriate reviewer shall specify.

(B) Not later than 120 days after the date of the enactment of this Act, each appropriate reviewer shall—

(i) evaluate each application received under subparagraph (A); and

(ii) approve or disapprove of the application.

(C) If the head of an eligible center submits an application under subparagraph (A) in accordance with the requirements specified by the appropriate reviewer for purposes of such subparagraph and the appropriate reviewer neither approves nor disapproves such application pursuant to subparagraph (B)(ii) on or before the date that is 120 days after the date of the enactment of this Act, such eligible center shall be considered a participant in the pilot program.

(D) For purposes of this paragraph, the appropriate reviewer is—

(i) in the case of an eligible center described in subparagraph (A) of subsection (a)(2), the Laboratory Quality Enhancement Program; and

(ii) in the case of an eligible center described in subparagraph (B) of such subsection, the Director of the Test Resource Management Center.

(c) PARTICIPATION IN PROGRAM.—

(1) IN GENERAL.—Subject to paragraph (2), the head of each eligible center selected under subsection (b)(1) shall propose and implement alternative and innovative methods of effective management and operations of eligible centers, rapid

project delivery, support, experimentation, prototyping, and partnership with universities and private sector entities to—

(A) generate greater value and efficiencies in research and development activities;

(B) enable more efficient and effective operations of supporting activities, such as—

(i) facility management, construction, and repair;

(ii) business operations;

(iii) personnel management policies and practices; and

(iv) intramural and public outreach; and

(C) enable more rapid deployment of warfighter capabilities.

(2) IMPLEMENTATION.—(A) The head of an eligible center described in subparagraph (A) or (B) of subsection (a)(2) shall implement each method proposed under paragraph (1) unless such method is disapproved in writing by the Assistant Secretary concerned within 60 days of receiving a proposal from an eligible center selected under subsection (b)(1) by such Assistant Secretary.

(B) The Director of the Defense Advanced Research Projects Agency shall implement each method proposed under paragraph (1) unless such method is disapproved in writing by the Chief Management Officer within 60 days of receiving a proposal from the Director.

(C) In this paragraph, the term "Assistant Secretary concerned" means—

(i) the Assistant Secretary of the Air Force for Acquisition, with respect to matters concerning the Air Force;

(ii) the Assistant Secretary of the Army for Acquisition, Technology, and Logistics, with respect to matters concerning the Army; and

(iii) the Assistant Secretary of the Navy for Research, Development, and Acquisition, with respect to matters concerning the Navy.

(d) WAIVER AUTHORITY FOR DEMONSTRATION AND IMPLEMENTATION.—Until the termination of the pilot program under subsection (e), the head of an eligible center selected under subsection (b)(1) may waive any regulation, restriction, requirement, guidance, policy, procedure, or departmental instruction that would affect the implementation of a method proposed under subsection (c)(1), unless such implementation would be prohibited by a provision of a Federal statute or common law.

(e) TERMINATION.—The pilot program shall terminate on September 30, 2022.

(f) REPORT.—

(1) IN GENERAL.—Not later than one year after the date of the enactment of this Act, the Secretary of Defense shall submit to the congressional defense committees a report on the pilot program.

(2) CONTENTS.—The report required by paragraph (1) shall include the following:

(A) Identification of the eligible centers participating in the pilot program.

(B) Identification of the eligible centers whose applications to participate in the pilot program were disapproved under subsection (b), including justifications for such disapprovals.

(C) A description of the methods implemented pursuant to subsection (c).

(D) A description of the methods that were proposed pursuant to paragraph (1) of subsection (c) but disapproved under paragraph (2) of such subsection.

(E) An assessment of how methods implemented pursuant to subsection (c) have contributed to the objectives identified in subparagraphs (A), (B), and (C) of paragraph (1) of such subsection.

SEC. 234. PILOT PROGRAM ON MODERNIZATION AND FIELDING OF ELECTROMAGNETIC SPECTRUM WARFARE SYSTEMS AND ELECTRONIC WARFARE CAPABILITIES.

(a) PILOT PROGRAM.—

(1) IN GENERAL.—The Secretary of Defense may carry out a pilot program on the modernization and fielding of electromagnetic spectrum warfare systems and electronic warfare systems.

(2) SELECTION.—If the Secretary carries out the pilot program under paragraph (1), the Electronic Warfare Executive Committee shall select from the list described in section 240(b)(4) a total of 10 electromagnetic spectrum warfare systems and electronic warfare systems across at least two military departments for modernization and fielding under the pilot program.

(b) TERMINATION.—The pilot program authorized by subsection (a) shall terminate on September 30, 2023.

(c) FUNDING.—For the purposes of this pilot program, funds authorized to be appropriated for electromagnetic spectrum warfare and electronic warfare may be used for the development and fielding of electromagnetic spectrum warfare systems and electronic warfare capabilities.

(d) DEFINITIONS.—In this section:

(1) The term "electromagnetic spectrum warfare" means electronic warfare that encompasses military communications and sensing operations that occur in the electromagnetic operational domain.

(2) The term "electronic warfare" means military action involving the use of electromagnetic and directed energy to control the electromagnetic spectrum or to attack the enemy.

SEC. 235. PILOT PROGRAM ON DISCLOSURE OF CERTAIN SENSITIVE INFORMATION TO FEDERALLY FUNDED RESEARCH AND DEVELOPMENT CENTERS.

(a) IN GENERAL.—The Secretary of Defense shall carry out a pilot program on—

(1) permitting officers and employees of the Department of Defense to disclose sensitive information to federally funded research and development centers of the Department for the sole purpose of the performance of administrative, technical, or professional services under and within the scope of the contracts with the parent organizations of such federally funded research and development centers; and

(2) appropriately protecting proprietary information from unauthorized disclosure or use by such centers.

(b) FFRDCs.—The pilot program shall be carried out with one or more federally funded research and development centers of the Department selected by the Secretary for participation in the pilot program.

(c) FFRDC PERSONNEL.—Sensitive information may be disclosed to personnel of a federally funded research and development center under the pilot program only if such personnel and contractors agree to be subject to, and comply with, appropriate ethics standards and requirements applicable to Government personnel, including the Ethics in Government Act of 1978, section 1905 of title 18, United States Code, and chapter 21 of title 41, United States Code.

(d) CONDITIONS ON DISCLOSURE.—Sensitive information may be disclosed under the pilot program only if the federally funded research and development center concerned and its parent organization agree to and acknowledge in the parent organization's contract with the Department of Defense that—

(1) sensitive information furnished to the federally funded research and development center will be accessed and used only for the purposes stated in the contract between the parent organization of the federally funded research and development center and the Department of Defense;

(2) the federally funded research and development center will take all precautions necessary to prevent disclosure of the sensitive information furnished to anyone not authorized access to the information in order to perform the applicable contract;

(3) sensitive information furnished under the pilot program shall not be used by the federally funded research and development center or parent organization to compete against a third party for a Government or non-Government contract or funding, or to support other current or future research or technology development activities performed by the federally funded research and development center; and

(4) any personnel of a federally funded research and development center participating in the pilot program may not disclose or use any trade secrets or any nonpublic information accessed under the pilot program, unless specifically authorized by this section.

(e) DURATION.—(1) The pilot program may commence at any time after the review and issuance of policy guidance, updated appropriately, pertaining to the identification, mitigation, and prevention of potentially unfair competitive advantage conferred to federally funded research and development center personnel with access to sensitive information who serve as technical advisors to acquisition programs.

(2) The pilot program shall terminate on the date that is three years after the date of the commencement of the pilot program.

(f) ASSESSMENT.—Not later than two years after the commencement of the pilot program, the Comptroller General of the United States shall submit to the Committees on Armed Services of the Senate and the House of Representatives a report on the pilot program, including an assessment of the effectiveness of activities under the pilot program in improving acquisition processes and the effectiveness of protections of private-sector intellectual property in the course of such activities.

(g) SENSITIVE INFORMATION DEFINED.—In this section, the term "sensitive information" means confidential commercial, financial, or proprietary information, technical data, contract performance, contract performance evaluation, management, and administration data, or other privileged information owned by other contractors of the Department of Defense that is exempt from public disclosure under section 552(b)(4) of title 5, United States Code, or which would otherwise be prohibited from disclosure under section 1832 or 1905 of title 18, United States Code.

SEC. 236. PILOT PROGRAM ON ENHANCED INTERACTION BETWEEN THE DEFENSE ADVANCED RESEARCH PROJECTS AGENCY AND THE SERVICE ACADEMIES.

(a) IN GENERAL.—The Secretary of Defense, acting through the Director of the Defense Advanced Research Projects Agency, shall carry out a pilot program to enhance interaction between the Defense Advanced Research Projects Agency and the service academies to promote technology transition, education, and training in science, technology, engineering, and mathematics fields that are relevant to the Department of Defense.

(b) AWARDS OF FUNDS.—(1) In carrying out the pilot program, the Secretary, acting through the Director, shall provide funds to contractors and grantees of the Defense Advanced Research Projects Agency in order to encourage such contractors and grantees to develop research partnerships with the service academies to support more efficient and effective technology transition of research programs and products.

(2) It shall be the responsibility of the Director to ensure that such funds are used effectively and that sufficient efforts are made to build appropriate partnerships.

(c) SERVICE ACADEMY TECHNOLOGY TRANSITION NETWORKS.—In carrying out the pilot program, the Director shall prioritize the leveraging of—

(1) the technology transition networks that service academies maintain among their academic departments and resident research centers; and

(2) *partnerships with Department of Defense laboratories, other Federal degree granting institutions, academia, and industry.*

(d) TERMINATION.—*The authority to carry out the pilot program shall terminate on September 30, 2020.*

(e) SERVICE ACADEMIES DEFINED.—*In this section, the term "service academies" means the following:*

(1) *The United States Military Academy.*

(2) *The United States Naval Academy.*

(3) *Th United States Air Force Academy.*

(4) *The United States Coast Guard Academy.*

(5) *The United States Merchant Marine Academy.*

SEC. 237. INDEPENDENT REVIEW OF F/A–18 PHYSIOLOGICAL EPISODES AND CORRECTIVE ACTIONS.

(a) INDEPENDENT REVIEW REQUIRED.—*The Secretary of the Navy shall conduct an independent review of the plans, programs, and research of the Department of the Navy with respect to—*

(1) *physiological events affecting aircrew of the F/A–18 Hornet and the F/A–18 Super Hornet aircraft during the covered period; and*

(2) *the efforts of the Navy and Marine Corps to prevent and mitigate the affects of such physiological events.*

(b) CONDUCT OF REVIEW.—*In conducting the review under subsection (a), the Secretary of the Navy shall—*

(1) *designate an appropriate senior official in the Office of the Secretary of the Navy to oversee the review; and*

(2) *consult experts from outside the Department of Defense in appropriate technical and medical fields.*

(c) REVIEW ELEMENTS.—*The review under subsection (a) shall include an evaluation of—*

(1) *any data of the Department of the Navy relating to the increased frequency of physiological events affecting aircrew of the F/A–18 Hornet and the F/A–18 Super Hornet aircraft during the covered period;*

(2) *aircraft mishaps potentially related to such physiological events;*

(3) *the cost and effectiveness of all material, operational, maintenance, and other measures carried out by the Department of the Navy to mitigate such physiological events during the covered period;*

(4) *material, operational, maintenance, or other measures that may reduce the rate of such physiological events in the future; and*

(5) *the performance of—*

(A) *the onboard oxygen generation system in the F/A–18 Super Hornet;*

(B) *the overall environmental control system in the F/A–18 Hornet and F/A–18 Super Hornet; and*

(C) *other relevant subsystems of the F/A–18 Hornet and F/A–18 Super Hornet, as determined by the Secretary.*

(d) REPORT REQUIRED.—*Not later than December 1, 2017, the Secretary of Navy shall submit to the congressional defense committees a report that includes the results of the review under subsection (a).*

(e) COVERED PERIOD.—*In this section, the term "covered period" means the period beginning on January 1, 2009, and ending on the date of the submission of the report under subsection (d).*

SEC. 238. B–21 BOMBER DEVELOPMENT PROGRAM ACCOUNTABILITY MATRICES.

(a) SUBMITTAL OF MATRICES.—*Concurrent with the President's annual budget request submitted to Congress under section 1105 of title 31, United States Code, for fiscal year 2018, the Secretary of the Air Forces shall submit to the congressional defense committees and the Comptroller General of the United States the matrices described in subsection (b) relating to the B–21 bomber aircraft program.*

(b) MATRICES DESCRIBED.—*The matrices described in this subsection are the following:*

(1) EMD GOALS.—*A matrix that identifies, in six month increments, key milestones, development events, and specific performance goals for the EMD phase of the B–21 bomber aircraft program, which shall be subdivided, at a minimum, according to the following:*

(A) *Technology readiness levels of major components and key demonstration events.*

(B) *Design maturity.*

(C) *Software maturity.*

(D) *Manufacturing readiness levels for critical manufacturing operations and key demonstration events.*

(E) *Manufacturing operations.*

(F) *System verification and key flight test events.*

(G) *Reliability.*

(2) COST.—*A matrix expressing, in six month increments, the total cost for the Air Force service cost position for the EMD phase and low initial rate of production lots of the B–21 bomber aircraft and a matrix expressing the total cost for the prime contractor's estimate for such EMD phase and production lots, both of which shall be phased over the entire EMD period and subdivided according to the costs of the following:*

(A) *Air vehicle.*

(B) *Propulsion.*

(C) *Mission systems.*

(D) *Vehicle subsystems.*

(E) *Air vehicle software.*

(F) *Systems engineering.*

(G) *Program management.*

(H) *System test and evaluation.*

(I) *Support and training systems.*

(J) *Contract fee.*

(K) *Engineering changes.*

(L) *Direct mission support, including Congressional General Reductions.*

(M) *Government testing.*

(c) SEMIANNUAL UPDATE OF MATRICES.—

(1) IN GENERAL.—*Not later than 180 days after the date on which the Secretary of the Air Force submits the matrices required by subsection (a), concurrent with the submittal of each annual budget request to Congress under section 1105 of title 31, United States Code, thereafter, and not later than 180 days after each such submittal, the Secretary of the Air Force shall submit to the congressional defense committees and the Comptroller General of the United States updates to the matrices described in subsection (b).*

(2) ELEMENTS.—*Each update submitted under paragraph (1) shall detail progress made toward the goals identified in the matrix described in subsection (b)(1) and provide updated cost estimates.*

(3) TREATMENT OF INITIAL MATRICES AS BASELINE.—*The matrices submitted pursuant to subsection (a) shall be treated as the baseline for the full EMD phase and low rate initial production of the B–21 bomber aircraft program for purposes of the updates submitted pursuant to paragraph (1) of this subsection.*

(d) ASSESSMENT BY COMPTROLLER GENERAL OF THE UNITED STATES.—*Not later than the date that is 45 days after the date on which the Comptroller General of the United States receives an update to a matrix under subsection (d)(1), the Comptroller General shall review the sufficiency of such matrix and submit to the congressional defense committees an assessment of such matrix, including by identifying cost, schedule, or performance trends.*

SEC. 239. STUDY ON HELICOPTER CRASH PREVENTION AND MITIGATION TECHNOLOGY.

(a) STUDY REQUIRED.—*The Secretary of Defense shall seek to enter into a contract with a federally funded research and development center to conduct a study on technologies with the*

potential to prevent and mitigate helicopter crashes.

(b) ELEMENTS.—*The study required under subsection (a) shall include the following:*

(1) *Identification of technologies with the potential—*

(A) *to prevent helicopter crashes (such as collision avoidance technologies and battle space and terrain situational awareness technologies); and*

(B) *to improve survivability among individuals involved in such crashes (such as adaptive flight control technologies and improved energy absorbing technologies).*

(2) *A cost-benefit analysis of each technology identified under paragraph (1) that takes into account the cost of developing and deploying the technology compared to the potential of the technology to prevent casualties or injuries.*

(3) *A list that ranks the technologies identified under paragraph (1) based on—*

(A) *the results of the cost-benefit analysis under paragraph (2); and*

(B) *the readiness level of each technology.*

(4) *An analysis of helicopter crashes that—*

(A) *compares the casualty rates of cockpit occupants to the casualty rates of occupants of cargo compartments and troop seats; and*

(B) *identifies the root causes of the casualties described in subparagraph (A).*

(c) BRIEFING.—*Not later than one year after the date of the enactment of this Act, the Secretary shall provide to the Committees on Armed Services of the Senate and the House of Representatives (and the other congressional defense committees on request) a briefing that includes—*

(1) *the results of the study required under subsection (a); and*

(2) *the list described in subsection (b)(3).*

SEC. 240. STRATEGY FOR IMPROVING ELECTRONIC AND ELECTROMAGNETIC SPECTRUM WARFARE CAPABILITIES.

(a) STRATEGY REQUIRED.—*Not later than April 1, 2017, the Under Secretary of Defense for Acquisition, Technology and Logistics, acting through the Electronic Warfare Executive Committee, shall submit to the congressional defense committees a strategy on the electronic and electromagnetic spectrum warfare capabilities of the Department of Defense.*

(b) ELEMENTS.—*The strategy required by subsection (a) shall include the following:*

(1) *A strategy for advancing and accelerating research, development, test, and evaluation, and fielding, of electronic warfare capabilities to meet current and projected requirements, including intra-service ground and air interoperabilities, as well as recommendations for streamlining acquisition processes with respect to such capabilities.*

(2) *A methodology for synchronizing and overseeing electronic warfare strategies, operational concepts, and programs across the Department of Defense, including electronic warfare programs that support or enable cyber operations.*

(3) *A description of the training and operational support required for fielding and sustaining current and planned investments in electronic warfare capabilities, including the requirements for conducting large-scale simulated exercises and training in contested electronic warfare environments.*

(4) *A comprehensive list of investments of the Department of Defense in electronic warfare capabilities, including the capabilities to be developed, procured, or sustained in—*

(A) *the budget of the President for fiscal year 2018 submitted to Congress under section 1105(a) of title 31, United States Code; and*

(B) *the future-years defense program submitted to Congress under section 221 of title 10, United States Code, for that fiscal year.*

(5) *A description of the threat environment for electromagnetic spectrum for current and future warfare needs.*

(6) An assessment of progress on increasing interoperability between Services and Agencies, as well as increasing application of innovative electromagnetic spectrum warfighting methods and operational concepts that provide advantages within the electromagnetic spectrum operational domain.

(7) Specific attributes needed in future electronic and electromagnetic spectrum warfare capabilities, such as networking, adaptability, agility, multifunctionality, and miniaturization, and progress toward incorporating such attributes in new electronic warfare systems.

(8) Capability gaps with respect to asymmetric and near-peer adversaries identified pursuant to a capability gap assessment.

(9) A joint strategy on achieving near realtime system adaption to rapidly advancing modern digital electronics.

(10) Any other information the Secretary determines to be appropriate.

(c) FORM.—The strategy required by subsection (a) shall be submitted in unclassified form, but may include a classified annex.

(d) ELECTRONIC WARFARE EXECUTIVE COMMITTEE DEFINED.—In this section the term "Electronic Warfare Executive Committee" means the committee established on March 17, 2015, and chartered on August 11, 2015, by the Deputy Secretary of Defense to serve as the principal forum within the Department of Defense to inform, coordinate, and evaluate electronic warfare matters to maintain a strong technological advantage in United States capabilities.

SEC. 241. SENSE OF CONGRESS ON DEVELOPMENT AND FIELDING OF FIFTH GENERATION AIRBORNE SYSTEMS.

(a) FINDINGS.—Congress makes the following findings:

(1) The term "fifth generation", with respect to airborne systems, means those airborne systems capable of operating effectively in highly contested battle spaces defined by the most capable currently fielded threats, and those reasonably expected to be operational in the foreseeable future.

(2) Continued modernization of Department of Defense airborne systems such as fighters, bombers, and intelligence, surveillance, and reconnaissance (ISR) aircraft with fifth generation capabilities is required because—

(A) adversary integrated air defense systems (IADS) have created regions where fourth generation airborne systems may be limited in their ability to effectively operate;

(B) adversary aircraft, air-to-air missiles, and airborne electronic attack or electronic protection systems are advancing beyond the capabilities of fourth generation airborne systems; and

(C) fifth generation airborne systems provide a wider variety of options for a given warfighting challenge, preserve the technological advantage of the United States over near-peer threats, and serve as a force multiplier by increasing situational awareness and combat effectiveness of fourth generation airborne systems.

(b) SENSE OF CONGRESS.—It is the sense of Congress that development and fielding of fifth generation airborne system systems should include the following:

(1) Multispectral (radar, infrared, visual, emissions) low observable (LO) design features, self-protection jamming, and other capabilities that significantly delay or deny threat system detection, tracking, and engagement.

(2) Integrated avionics that autonomously fuse and prioritize onboard multispectral sensors and offboard information data to provide an accurate realtime operating picture and data download for postmission exploitation and analysis.

(3) Resilient communications, navigation, and identification techniques designed to effectively counter adversary attempts to deny or confuse friendly systems.

(4) Robust and secure networks linking individual platforms to create a common, accurate, and highly integrated picture of the battle space for friendly forces.

(5) Advanced onboard diagnostics capable of monitoring system health, accurately reporting system faults, and increasing overall system performance and reliability.

(6) Integrated platform and subsystem designs to maximize lethality and survivability while enabling decision superiority.

(7) Maximum consideration for the fielding of unmanned platforms either employed in concert with fifth generation manned platforms or as standalone unmanned platforms, to increase warfighting effectiveness and reduce risk to personnel during high risk missions.

(8) Advanced air-to-air, air-to-ground, and other weapons able to leverage fifth generation capabilities.

(9) Comprehensive and high-fidelity live, virtual, and constructive training systems, updated range infrastructure, and sufficient threat-representative adversary training assets to maximize fifth generation force proficiency, effectiveness, and readiness while protecting sensitive capabilities.

TITLE III—OPERATION AND MAINTENANCE

Subtitle A—Authorization of Appropriations

Sec. 301. *Authorization of appropriations.*

Subtitle B—Energy and Environment

Sec. 311. *Modified reporting requirement related to installations energy management.*

Sec. 312. *Waiver authority for alternative fuel procurement requirement.*

Sec. 313. *Utility data management for military facilities.*

Sec. 314. *Alternative technologies for munitions disposal.*

Sec. 315. *Report on efforts to reduce high energy costs at military installations.*

Sec. 316. *Sense of Congress on funding decisions relating to climate change.*

Subtitle C—Logistics and Sustainment

Sec. 321. *Revision of deployability rating system and planning reform.*

Sec. 322. *Revision of guidance relating to corrosion control and prevention executives.*

Sec. 323. *Pilot program for inclusion of certain industrial plants in the Armament Retooling and Manufacturing Support Initiative.*

Sec. 324. *Repair, recapitalization, and certification of dry docks at naval shipyards.*

Sec. 325. *Private sector port loading assessment.*

Sec. 326. *Strategy on revitalizing Army organic industrial base.*

Subtitle D—Reports

Sec. 331. *Modifications to Quarterly Readiness Report to Congress.*

Sec. 332. *Report on average travel costs of members of the reserve components.*

Sec. 333. *Report on HH–60G sustainment and Combat Rescue Helicopter program.*

Subtitle E—Other Matters

Sec. 341. *Air navigation matters.*

Sec. 342. *Contract working dogs.*

Sec. 343. *Plan, funding documents, and management review relating to explosive ordnance disposal.*

Sec. 344. *Process for communicating availability of surplus ammunition.*

Sec. 345. *Mitigation of risks posed by window coverings with accessible cords in certain military housing units.*

Sec. 346. *Access to military installations by transportation companies.*

Sec. 347. *Access to wireless high-speed Internet and network connections for certain members of the Armed Forces.*

Sec. 348. *Limitation on availability of funds for Office of the Under Secretary of Defense for Intelligence.*

Sec. 349. *Limitation on development and fielding of new camouflage and utility uniforms.*

Sec. 350. *Plan for improved dedicated adversary air training enterprise of the Air Force.*

Sec. 351. *Independent review and assessment of the Ready Aircrew Program of the Air Force.*

Sec. 352. *Study on space-available travel system of the Department of Defense.*

Sec. 353. *Evaluation of motor carrier safety performance and safety technology.*

Subtitle A—Authorization of Appropriations

SEC. 301. AUTHORIZATION OF APPROPRIATIONS.

Funds are hereby authorized to be appropriated for fiscal year 2017 for the use of the Armed Forces and other activities and agencies of the Department of Defense for expenses, not otherwise provided for, for operation and maintenance, as specified in the funding table in section 4301.

Subtitle B—Energy and Environment

SEC. 311. MODIFIED REPORTING REQUIREMENT RELATED TO INSTALLATIONS ENERGY MANAGEMENT.

Subsection (a) of section 2925 of title 10, United States Code, is amended—

(1) in the subsection heading, by inserting ", RESILIENCY, AND MISSION ASSURANCE" after "ANNUAL REPORT RELATED TO INSTALLATIONS ENERGY MANAGEMENT";

(2) by striking paragraphs (2), (3), (4), (5), (6), (7), (8), and (10);

(3) by redesignating paragraphs (9) and (11) as paragraphs (3), and (4), respectively; and

(4) by inserting after paragraph (1), the following:

"(2) A description of the energy savings, return on investment, and enhancements to installation mission assurance realized by the fulfillment of the goals described in paragraph (1).".

SEC. 312. WAIVER AUTHORITY FOR ALTERNATIVE FUEL PROCUREMENT REQUIREMENT.

(a) IN GENERAL.—The Secretary of Defense may waive the requirement under section 526 of the Energy Independence and Security Act of 2007 (Public Law 110–140; 42 U.S.C. 17142) if the Secretary determines it is in the national security interest of the United States.

(b) NOTIFICATION REQUIREMENT.—The Secretary of Defense shall notify the congressional defense committees not later than 15 days after exercising the waiver authority under subsection (a).

SEC. 313. UTILITY DATA MANAGEMENT FOR MILITARY FACILITIES.

(a) PILOT PROGRAM.—The Secretary of Defense, in consultation with the Secretary of Energy, may carry out a pilot program to investigate the use of utility data management services to perform utility bill aggregation, analysis, third-party payment, storage, and distribution for the Department of Defense.

(b) USE OF FUNDS.—Of the funds authorized to be appropriated by this Act or otherwise made available for fiscal year 2017 for operation and maintenance, Navy, for enterprise information, not more than $250,000 may be obligated or expended to carry out the pilot program under subsection (a).

SEC. 314. ALTERNATIVE TECHNOLOGIES FOR MUNITIONS DISPOSAL.

In carrying out the disposal of munitions in the stockpile of conventional munitions awaiting demilitarization and disposal, the Secretary of the Army may use cost-competitive technologies that minimize waste generation and air emissions as alternatives to disposal by open burning, open detonation, direct contact combustion, and incineration.

SEC. 315. REPORT ON EFFORTS TO REDUCE HIGH ENERGY COSTS AT MILITARY INSTALLATIONS.

(a) *REPORT.—*

(1) *REPORT REQUIRED.*—Not later than 270 days after the date of the enactment of this Act, the Under Secretary of Defense for Acquisition, Technology, and Logistics, in conjunction with the assistant secretaries responsible for installations and environment for the military services and the Defense Logistics Agency, shall submit to the congressional defense committees a report detailing the efforts to achieve cost savings at military installations with high levels of energy intensity.

(2) *ELEMENTS.*—The report required under paragraph (1) shall include the following elements:

(A) A comprehensive, installation-specific assessment of feasible and mission-appropriate energy initiatives supporting energy production and consumption at military installations with high levels of energy intensity.

(B) An assessment of current sources of energy in areas with high energy costs and potential future sources that are technologically feasible, cost-effective, and mission-appropriate for military installations.

(C) A comprehensive implementation strategy to include required investment for feasible energy efficiency options determined to be the most beneficial and cost-effective, where appropriate, and consistent with Department of Defense priorities.

(D) An explanation of how military services are working collaboratively in order to leverage lessons learned on potential energy efficiency solutions.

(E) An assessment of the extent to which activities administered under the Federal Energy Management Program could be used to assist with the implementation strategy.

(F) An assessment of State and local partnership opportunities that could achieve efficiency and cost savings, and any legislative authorities required to carry out such partnerships or agreements.

(3) *COORDINATION WITH STATE AND LOCAL AND OTHER ENTITIES.*—In preparing the report required under paragraph (1), the Under Secretary may work in conjunction and coordinate with the States containing areas of high levels of energy intensity, local communities, and other Federal departments and agencies.

(b) *DEFINITIONS.*—In this section, the term "high levels of energy intensity" means costs for the provision of energy by kilowatt of electricity or British thermal unit of heat or steam for a military installation in the United States that is in the highest 20 percent of all military installations for a military department.

SEC. 316. SENSE OF CONGRESS ON FUNDING DECISIONS RELATING TO CLIMATE CHANGE.

It is the sense of Congress that—

(1) decisions relating to the funding of the Department of Defense for fiscal year 2017 should prioritize the support and enhancement of the combat capabilities of the Department, in addition to seeking efficiency and efficacy;

(2) funds should be allocated among the programs of the Department in the manner that best serves the national security interests of the United States; and

(3) decisions relating to energy efficiency, energy use, and climate change should adhere to the principles described in paragraphs (1) and (2).

Subtitle C—Logistics and Sustainment

SEC. 321. REVISION OF DEPLOYABILITY RATING SYSTEM AND PLANNING REFORM.

(a) *DEPLOYMENT PRIORITIZATION AND READINESS.—*

(1) *IN GENERAL.*—Chapter 1003 of title 10, United States Code, is amended by inserting after section 10102 the following new section:

"§ 10102a. Deployment prioritization and readiness of Army components

"(a) *DEPLOYMENT PRIORITIZATION.*—The Secretary of the Army shall maintain a system for identifying the priority of deployment for units of all components of the Army.

"(b) *DEPLOYABILITY READINESS RATING.*—The Secretary of the Army shall maintain a readiness rating system for units of all components of the Army that provides an accurate assessment of the deployability of a unit and those shortfalls of a unit that require the provision of additional resources. The system shall ensure—

"(1) that the personnel readiness rating of a unit reflects—

"(A) both the percentage of the overall personnel requirement of the unit that is manned and deployable and the fill and deployability rate for critical occupational specialties necessary for the unit to carry out its basic mission requirements; and

"(B) the number of personnel in the unit who are qualified in their primary military occupational specialty; and

"(2) that the equipment readiness assessment of a unit—

"(A) documents all equipment required for deployment;

"(B) reflects only that equipment that is directly possessed by the unit;

"(C) specifies the effect of substitute items; and

"(D) assesses the effect of missing components and sets on the readiness of major equipment items.".

(2) *CLERICAL AMENDMENT.*—The table of sections at the beginning of chapter 1003 of such title is amended by inserting after the item relating to section 10102 the following new item:

"10102a. Deployment prioritization and readiness of Army components.".

(b) *REPEAL OF SUPERSEDED PROVISIONS OF LAW.*—Sections 1121 and 1135 of the Army National Guard Combat Readiness Reform Act of 1992 (title XI of Public Law 102–484; 10 U.S.C. 10105 note) are repealed.

SEC. 322. REVISION OF GUIDANCE RELATING TO CORROSION CONTROL AND PREVENTION EXECUTIVES.

(a) *IN GENERAL.*—Not later than 90 days after the date of the enactment of this Act, the Under Secretary of Defense for Acquisition, Technology, and Logistics, in coordination with the Director of Corrosion Policy and Oversight for the Department of Defense, shall revise guidance relating to corrosion control and prevention executives to—

(1) clarify the role of each such executive with respect to assisting the Office of Corrosion Policy and Oversight in holding the appropriate project management office in each military department accountable for submitting the annual report required under section 903(b)(5) of the Duncan Hunter National Defense Authorization Act for Fiscal Year 2009 (Public Law 110–417; 10 U.S.C. 2228 note); and

(2) ensure that corrosion control and prevention executives emphasize the reduction of corrosion and the effects of corrosion on the military equipment and infrastructure of the Department of Defense, as required in the long-term strategy of the Department of Defense under section 2228(d) of title 10, United States Code.

(b) *CORROSION CONTROL AND PREVENTION EXECUTIVE DEFINED.*—In this section, the term "corrosion control and prevention executive" means the employee of a military department designated as the corrosion control and prevention executive of the department under section 903(a) of the Duncan Hunter National Defense Authorization Act for Fiscal Year 2009 (Public Law 110–417; 10 U.S.C. 2228 note).

SEC. 323. PILOT PROGRAM FOR INCLUSION OF CERTAIN INDUSTRIAL PLANTS IN THE ARMAMENT RETOOLING AND MANUFACTURING SUPPORT INITIATIVE.

During the five-year period beginning on the date of the enactment of this Act, the Secretary of Defense may treat a Government-owned, contractor-operated industrial plant of the Department of Defense as an eligible facility under section 4551(2) of title 10, United States Code.

SEC. 324. REPAIR, RECAPITALIZATION, AND CERTIFICATION OF DRY DOCKS AT NAVAL SHIPYARDS.

(a) *SPECIAL AUTHORITY TO TRANSFER AUTHORIZATIONS.*—In addition to the authority to transfer funds provided under section 1001, the Secretary of Defense may transfer not more than $250,000,000 of authorizations made available to the Department of Defense in this Act for fiscal year 2017 to the Department of the Navy for the repair, recapitalization, and certification of dry docks at Government-owned, Government-operated shipyards of the Navy.

(b) *NOTICE TO CONGRESS.*—The Secretary shall promptly notify Congress of each transfer made under subsection (a).

(c) *TERMS AND CONDITIONS.—*

(1) *IN GENERAL.*—Except as provided in paragraph (2), transfers under this section shall be subject to the same terms and conditions as transfers under section 1001.

(2) *EFFECT ON DOLLAR LIMIT.*—A transfer of funds under this section shall not be counted toward the dollar limitation described in section 1001(a)(2).

SEC. 325. PRIVATE SECTOR PORT LOADING ASSESSMENT.

(a) *ASSESSMENTS REQUIRED.*—During the period beginning on the date of the enactment of this Act and ending on the date of the final briefing under subsection (c), the Secretary of the Navy shall conduct quarterly assessments of naval ship maintenance and loading activities carried out by private sector entities at each covered port.

(b) *ELEMENTS OF ASSESSMENTS.*—Each assessment under subsection (a) shall include, with respect to each covered port, the following:

(1) Resources per day, including daily ship availabilities and the workforce available to carry out maintenance and loading activities, for the fiscal year preceding the quarter covered by the assessment through the end of such quarter.

(2) Projected resources per day, including daily ship availabilities and the workforce available to carry out maintenance and loading activities, through the end of the second fiscal year beginning after the quarter covered by the assessment.

(3) A description of the methods by which the Secretary communicates projected workloads to private sector entities engaged in ship maintenance activities and ship loading activities.

(4) A description of any processes that have been implemented to allow for timely feedback from private sector entities engaged in ship maintenance activities and ship loading activities.

(c) *BRIEFINGS REQUIRED.*—Not later than 30 days after the date of the enactment of this Act, and on a quarterly basis thereafter until September 30, 2021, the Secretary shall provide to the Committees on Armed Services of the Senate and House of Representatives (and other congressional defense committees on request)—

(1) a briefing on the results of the assessments conducted under subsection (a); and

(2) a chart depicting the information described in paragraphs (1) and (2) of subsection (b) with respect to each covered port.

(d) COVERED PORTS.—In this section, the term "covered ports" means port facilities used by the Department of Defense in each of the following locations:

(1) Mayport, Florida.

(2) Norfolk, Virginia.

(3) Pearl Harbor, Hawaii.

(4) Puget Sound, Washington.

(5) San Diego, California.

SEC. 326. STRATEGY ON REVITALIZING ARMY ORGANIC INDUSTRIAL BASE.

(a) STRATEGY.—Not later than October 1, 2017, the Secretary of Army shall submit to the congressional defense committees a strategy to revitalize the organic industrial base of the Army.

(b) ELEMENTS.—The strategy under subsection (a) shall include, with respect to the organic industrial base of the Army, the following:

(1) A plan to ensure the long-term viability of the organic industrial base.

(2) An assessment of legacy items of the Army that are sustained by the Defense Logistics Agency.

(3) A description of how the organic industrial base may be used to address diminishing manufacturing sources and material shortages.

(4) A description of critical capabilities that are required across the organic industrial base.

(5) An assessment of infrastructure across the organic industrial base.

(6) An assessment of manufacturing sources in the organic industrial base and the private sector.

(7) An explanation of how contracting may be used to meet organic industrial base requirements.

(8) An assessment of current and future workloads across the organic industrial base.

(9) An assessment of the processes used to identify critical capabilities for the organic industrial base and the methods used to determine workloads.

(10) An assessment of existing labor rates.

(11) A description of manufacturing skills that are needed to sustain readiness.

(12) A description of how public-private partnerships may be used to improve the organic industrial base.

(13) A description of how working capital funds may be used to improve the organic industrial base.

(14) An assessment of operating expenses and the potential for reducing or recovering such expenses.

(15) Identification of the tooling, equipment, and facilities upgrades necessary for a facility in the organic industrial base to manufacture the legacy items of the Defense Logistics Agency, including items described in section 333(a) of the National Defense Authorization Act for Fiscal Year 2016 (Public Law 114–92; 129 Stat. 792).

(16) An assessment of the suitability of manufacturing the legacy items of the Defense Logistics Agency in a facility in the organic industrial base.

(c) DEFINITIONS.—In this section:

(1) LEGACY ITEMS.—The term "legacy items" means manufactured items that are no longer produced by the private sector but continue to be used for weapons systems of the Department of Defense, but does not include information systems and information technology (as those terms are defined in section 11101 of title 40, United States Code).

(2) ORGANIC INDUSTRIAL BASE.—The term "organic industrial base" means United States military facilities, including arsenals, depots, munition plants and centers, and storage sites, that advance a vital national security interest by

producing, maintaining, repairing, and storing materiel, munitions, and hardware.

Subtitle D—Reports

SEC. 331. MODIFICATIONS TO QUARTERLY READINESS REPORT TO CONGRESS.

(a) DEADLINE FOR REPORT.—Subsection (a) of section 482 of title 10, United States Code, is amended by striking "Not later than 45 days after the end of each calendar-year quarter" and inserting "Not later than 30 days after the end of each calendar-year quarter".

(b) ELIMINATION OF REPORTING REQUIREMENTS RELATED TO PREPOSITIONED STOCKS AND NATIONAL GUARD CIVIL SUPPORT MISSION READINESS.—Such section is further amended—

(1) in subsection (a), by striking "subsections (b), (d), (e), (f), (g), (h), and (i)" and inserting "subsections (b), (d), (e), (f), and (g)";

(2) by striking subsections (d) and (e); and

(3) by redesignating subsections (f), (g), (h), (i), and (j) as subsections (d), (e), (f), (g), and (i) respectively.

(c) INCLUSION OF INFORMATION ON CANNIBALIZATION RATES.—Such section, as amended by subsection (b), is further amended by inserting after subsection (g), as redesignated by paragraph (3) of such subsection (b), the following new subsection:

"(h) CANNIBALIZATION RATES.—Each report under this section shall include a separate unclassified report containing the information collected pursuant to section 117(c)(7) of this title.".

SEC. 332. REPORT ON AVERAGE TRAVEL COSTS OF MEMBERS OF THE RESERVE COMPONENTS.

Not later than 180 days after the date of the enactment of this Act, the Comptroller General of the United States shall submit to the congressional defense committees a report on the travel expenses of members of reserve components associated with performing active duty service, active service, full-time National Guard duty, active Guard and Reserve duty, and inactive-duty training, as such terms are defined in section 101(d) of title 10, United States Code. Such report shall include the average annual cost for all travel expenses for a member of a reserve component.

SEC. 333. REPORT ON HH–60G SUSTAINMENT AND COMBAT RESCUE HELICOPTER PROGRAM.

(a) REPORT ON SUSTAINMENT PLAN.—Not later than one year after the date of the enactment of this Act, the Secretary of Defense shall submit to the congressional defense committees a report that sets forth a plan to modernize, sustain training, and conduct depot-level maintenance and repair for all components of the HH–60 helicopter fleet until total force combat rescue units have been fully equipped with HH–60W Combat Rescue Helicopters.

(b) ELEMENTS.—The report required by subsection (a) shall include a description of the plans of the Air Force—

(1) to modernize legacy HH–60G combat rescue helicopters;

(2) to maintain the training pipeline for the HH–60G aircrew and the maintenance force required to maintain full readiness through the end of fiscal year 2029; and

(3) to carry out depot-level maintenance and repair (as that term is defined in section 2460 of title 10, United States Code) to ensure the legacy HH–60G fleet of helicopters is maintained to meet readiness rates through the end of fiscal year 2029.

(c) FORM.—The report required by subsection (a) shall be submitted in unclassified form, but may include a classified annex.

Subtitle E—Other Matters

SEC. 341. AIR NAVIGATION MATTERS.

(a) EXPANSION OF DEFINITION OF STRUCTURES INTERFERING WITH AIR COMMERCE AND NATIONAL DEFENSE.—

(1) NOTICE.—Section 44718(a) of title 49, United States Code, is amended—

(A) in paragraph (1), by striking "and" at the end;

(B) in paragraph (2), by striking the period at the end and inserting "; or"; and

(C) by adding at the end the following:

"(3) the interests of national security, as determined by the Secretary of Defense.".

(2) STUDIES.—Section 44718(b) of title 49, United States Code, is amended to read as follows:

"(b) STUDIES.—

"(1) IN GENERAL.—Under regulations prescribed by the Secretary, if the Secretary decides that constructing or altering a structure may result in an obstruction of the navigable airspace, an interference with air navigation facilities and equipment or the navigable airspace, or, after consultation with the Secretary of Defense, an adverse impact on military operations and readiness, the Secretary of Transportation shall conduct an aeronautical study to decide the extent of any adverse impact on the safe and efficient use of the airspace, facilities, or equipment. In conducting the study, the Secretary shall—

"(A) consider factors relevant to the efficient and effective use of the navigable airspace, including—

"(i) the impact on arrival, departure, and en route procedures for aircraft operating under visual flight rules;

"(ii) the impact on arrival, departure, and en route procedures for aircraft operating under instrument flight rules;

"(iii) the impact on existing public-use airports and aeronautical facilities;

"(iv) the impact on planned public-use airports and aeronautical facilities;

"(v) the cumulative impact resulting from the proposed construction or alteration of a structure when combined with the impact of other existing or proposed structures; and

"(vi) other factors relevant to the efficient and effective use of navigable airspace; and

"(B) include the finding made by the Secretary of Defense under subsection (f).

"(2) REPORT.—On completing the study, the Secretary of Transportation shall issue a report disclosing the extent of the—

"(A) adverse impact on the safe and efficient use of the navigable airspace that the Secretary finds will result from constructing or altering the structure; and

"(B) unacceptable risk to the national security of the United States, as determined by the Secretary of Defense under subsection (f).

"(3) SEVERABILITY.—A determination by the Secretary of Transportation on hazard to air navigation under this section shall remain independent of a determination of unacceptable risk to the national security of the United States by the Secretary of Defense under subsection (f).".

(3) NATIONAL SECURITY FINDING; DEFINITIONS.—Section 44718 of title 49, United States Code, is amended by adding at the end the following:

"(f) NATIONAL SECURITY FINDING.—As part of an aeronautical study conducted under subsection (b), the Secretary of Defense shall—

"(1) make a finding on whether the construction, alteration, establishment, or expansion of a structure or sanitary landfill included in the study would result in an unacceptable risk to the national security of the United States; and

"(2) transmit the finding to the Secretary of Transportation for inclusion in the report required under subsection (b)(2).

"(g) DEFINITIONS.—In this section, the following definitions apply:

"(1) ADVERSE IMPACT ON MILITARY OPERATIONS AND READINESS.—The term 'adverse impact on military operations and readiness' has

the meaning given the term in section 211.3 of title 32, Code of Federal Regulations, as in effect on January 6, 2014.

''(2) UNACCEPTABLE RISK TO THE NATIONAL SECURITY OF THE UNITED STATES.—The term 'unacceptable risk to the national security of the United States' has the meaning given the term in section 211.3 of title 32, Code of Federal Regulations, as in effect on January 6, 2014.''.

(4) CONFORMING AMENDMENTS.—

(A) SECTION HEADING.—Section 44718 of title 49, United States Code, is amended in the section heading by inserting "**or national security**" after "**air commerce**".

(B) CLERICAL AMENDMENT.—The table of sections at the beginning of chapter 447 of title 49, United States Code, is amended by striking the item relating to section 44718 and inserting the following:

''44718. Structures interfering with air commerce or national security.''.

(b) PERFORMANCE-BASED NAVIGATION.—Section 213(c) of the FAA Modernization and Reform Act of 2012 (Public Law 112–95; 49 U.S.C. 40101 note) is amended by adding at the end the following:

''(3) NOTIFICATIONS AND CONSULTATIONS.—Not later than 90 days before applying a categorical exclusion under this subsection to a new procedure at an OEP airport, the Administrator shall—

''(A) notify and consult with the operator of the airport at which the procedure would be implemented; and

''(B) consider consultations or other engagement with the community in the which the airport is located to inform the public of the procedure.

''(4) REVIEW OF CERTAIN CATEGORICAL EXCLUSIONS.—

''(A) IN GENERAL.—The Administrator shall review any decision of the Administrator made on or after February 14, 2012, and before the date of the enactment of this paragraph to grant a categorical exclusion under this subsection with respect to a procedure to be implemented at an OEP airport that was a material change from procedures previously in effect at the airport to determine if the implementation of the procedure had a significant effect on the human environment in the community in which the airport is located.

''(B) CONTENT OF REVIEW.—If, in conducting a review under subparagraph (A) with respect to a procedure implemented at an OEP airport, the Administrator, in consultation with the operator of the airport, determines that implementing the procedure had a significant effect on the human environment in the community in which the airport is located, the Administrator shall—

''(i) consult with the operator of the airport to identify measures to mitigate the effect of the procedure on the human environment; and

''(ii) in conducting such consultations, consider the use of alternative flight paths that do not substantially degrade the efficiencies achieved by the implementation of the procedure being reviewed.

''(C) HUMAN ENVIRONMENT DEFINED.—In this paragraph, the term 'human environment' has the meaning given such term in section 1508.14 of title 40, Code of Federal Regulations (as in effect on the day before the date of the enactment of this paragraph).''.

SEC. 342. CONTRACT WORKING DOGS.

(a) REQUIRED CONTRACT CLAUSE.—

(1) IN GENERAL.—Chapter 141 of title 10, United States Code, is amended by adding at the end the following new section:

''§2410r. Contract working dogs: requirement to transfer animals to 341st Training Squadron after service life

''(a) IN GENERAL.—Each contract entered into by the Secretary of Defense for the provision of a contract working dog shall require that the dog be transferred to the 341st Training Squadron after the service life of the dog has terminated as described in subsection (b) for reclassification as a military animal and placement for adoption in accordance with section 2583 of this title.

''(b) SERVICE LIFE.—The service life of a contract working dog has terminated and the dog is available for transfer to the 341st Training Squadron pursuant to a contract under subsection (a) only if the contracting officer concerned has determined that—

''(1) the final contractual obligation of the dog preceding such transfer is with the Department of Defense; and

''(2) the dog cannot be used by another department or agency of the Federal Government due to age, injury, or performance.

''(c) CONTRACT WORKING DOG.—In this section, the term 'contract working dog' means a dog—

''(1) that performs a service for the Department of Defense pursuant to a contract; and

''(2) that is trained and kenneled by an entity that provides such a dog pursuant to such a contract.''.

(2) CLERICAL AMENDMENT.—The table of sections at the beginning of such chapter is amended by adding at the end the following new item:

''2410r. Contract working dogs: requirement to transfer animals to 341st Training Squadron after service life.''.

(b) INCLUSION IN DEFINITION OF MILITARY ANIMAL.—Paragraph (1) of section 2583(h) of title 10, United States Code, is amended to read as follows:

''(1) A military working dog, which may include a contract working dog (as such term is defined in section 2410r) that has been transferred to the 341st Training Squadron.''.

SEC. 343. PLAN, FUNDING DOCUMENTS, AND MANAGEMENT REVIEW RELATING TO EXPLOSIVE ORDNANCE DISPOSAL.

(a) PLAN REQUIRED.—

(1) IN GENERAL.—The Secretary of Defense shall develop a plan to establish an explosive ordnance disposal program in the Department of Defense to ensure close and continuous coordination among the military departments on matters relating to explosive ordnance disposal.

(2) ROLES, RESPONSIBILITIES, AND AUTHORITIES.—The plan under paragraph (1) shall include provisions under which—

(A) the Secretary of Defense shall—

(i) assign responsibility for the coordination and integration of explosive ordnance disposal to a joint office or entity in the Office of the Secretary of Defense; and

(ii) designate the Secretary of the Navy (or a designee of the Secretary of the Navy) as the executive agent for the Department of Defense to coordinate and integrate research, development, test, and evaluation activities and procurement activities of the military departments relating to explosive ordnance disposal; and

(B) the Secretary of each military department shall assess the needs of the military department concerned with respect to explosive ordnance disposal and may carry out research, development, test, and evaluation activities and procurement activities to address such needs.

(b) ANNUAL EXPLOSIVE ORDNANCE DISPOSAL FUNDING DOCUMENTS.—

(1) IN GENERAL.—The Secretary of Defense shall submit to Congress, as a part of the defense budget materials for each fiscal year after fiscal year 2017, a consolidated funding display, in classified and unclassified form, that identifies the funding source for all explosive ordnance disposal activities within the Department of Defense.

(2) ELEMENTS.—The funding display under paragraph (1) for a fiscal year shall include a single program element from each military department for each of the following:

(A) Research, development, test, and evaluation.

(B) Procurement.

(C) Operation and maintenance.

(D) Any other program element used to fund explosive ordnance disposal activities (but not including any program element relating to military construction).

(c) MANAGEMENT REVIEW AND ASSESSMENT.—

(1) IN GENERAL.—The Secretary of Defense shall review and assess the effectiveness of current management structures in supporting the explosive ordnance disposal needs of the combatant commands and the military departments.

(2) ELEMENTS.—The review and assessment under paragraph (1) shall include the following:

(A) A review of the organizational structures and responsibilities within the Office of the Secretary of Defense that provide policy and oversight of the policies, programs, acquisition activities, and personnel of the military departments relating to explosive ordnance disposal.

(B) A review of the organizational structures and responsibilities within the military departments that—

(i) man, equip, and train explosive ordnance disposal forces; and

(ii) support such forces with manpower, technology, equipment, and readiness.

(C) A review of the organizational structures and responsibilities of the Secretary of the Navy as the executive agent for explosive ordnance disposal technology and training.

(D) Budget displays for each military department that support research, development, test, and evaluation; procurement; and operation and maintenance, relating to explosive ordnance disposal.

(E) An assessment of the adequacy of the organizational structures and responsibilities and the alignment of funding within the military departments in supporting the needs of the combatant commands and the military departments with respect to explosive ordnance disposal.

(d) BRIEFING.—Not later than March 1, 2017, the Secretary shall provide to the Committees on Armed Services of the Senate and the House of Representatives a briefing that includes—

(1) details of the plan required under subsection (a);

(2) the results of the review and assessment under subsection (c);

(3) a description of any measures undertaken to improve joint coordination, oversight, and management of programs relating to explosive ordnance disposal;

(4) recommendations to the Secretary to improve the capabilities and readiness of explosive ordnance disposal forces; and

(5) an explanation of the advantages and disadvantages of assigning responsibility for the coordination and integration of explosive ordnance disposal to a single joint office or entity in the Office of the Secretary of Defense.

(e) DEFINITIONS.—In this section:

(1) EXPLOSIVE ORDNANCE.—The term "explosive ordnance" means any munition containing explosives, nuclear fission or fusion materials, or biological or chemical agents, including—

(A) bombs and warheads;

(B) guided and ballistic missiles;

(C) artillery, mortar, rocket, and small arms munitions;

(D) mines, torpedoes, and depth charges;

(E) demolition charges;

(F) pyrotechnics;

(G) clusters and dispensers;

(H) cartridge and propellant actuated devices;

(I) electro-explosive devices; and

(J) clandestine and improvised explosive devices.

(2) DISPOSAL.—The term "disposal" means, with respect to explosive ordnance, the detection, identification, field evaluation, defeat, disablement, or rendering safe, recovery and exploitation, and final disposition of the ordnance.

SEC. 344. PROCESS FOR COMMUNICATING AVAILABILITY OF SURPLUS AMMUNITION.

(a) IN GENERAL.—The Secretary of Defense shall implement a formal process to provide Federal Government agencies outside the Department of Defense with information on the availability of surplus, serviceable ammunition from the Department of Defense for the purpose of reducing costs relating to the storage and disposal of such ammunition.

(b) IMPLEMENTATION DEADLINE.—The Secretary shall implement the process described in subsection (a) beginning not later than 180 days after the date of the enactment of this Act.

SEC. 345. MITIGATION OF RISKS POSED BY WINDOW COVERINGS WITH ACCESSIBLE CORDS IN CERTAIN MILITARY HOUSING UNITS.

(a) REMOVAL OF CERTAIN WINDOW COVERINGS.—Not later than three years after the date of enactment of this Act, the Secretary of Defense shall remove and replace disqualified window coverings from—

(1) military housing units owned by the Department of Defense in which children under the age of 9 may reside; and

(2) military housing units leased by the Department of Defense in which children under the age of 9 may reside if the lease for such units requires the Department to provide window coverings.

(b) PROHIBITION ON DISQUALIFIED WINDOW COVERINGS IN MILITARY HOUSING UNITS ACQUIRED OR CONSTRUCTED BY CONTRACT.—All contracts entered into by the Secretary of Defense after September 30, 2017, for the acquisition or construction of military family housing, including military family housing acquired or constructed pursuant to subchapter IV of chapter 169 of title 10, United States Code, shall prohibit the use of disqualified window coverings in such housing.

(c) DISQUALIFIED WINDOW COVERING DEFINED.—In this section, the term "disqualified window covering" means—

(1) a window covering with an accessible cord that exceeds 8 inches in length; or

(2) a window covering with an accessible continuous loop cord that does not have a cord tension device that prevents operation when the cord is not anchored to the wall.

SEC. 346. ACCESS TO MILITARY INSTALLATIONS BY TRANSPORTATION COMPANIES.

(a) IN GENERAL.—Not later than one year after the date of the enactment of this Act, the Secretary of Defense shall establish policies under which covered drivers may be authorized to access military installations.

(b) ELEMENTS.—The policies established under subsection (a)—

(1) shall include the terms and conditions under which a covered driver may be authorized to access a military installation;

(2) may require a transportation company and a covered driver to enter into a written agreement with the Department of Defense as a precondition for obtaining authorization to access a military installation;

(3) shall be consistent across military installations, to the extent practicable;

(4) shall be designed to promote the expeditious entry of covered drivers onto military installations for purposes of providing commercial transportation services;

(5) shall place appropriate restrictions on entry into sensitive areas of military installations;

(6) shall be designed, to the extent practicable, to give covered drivers access to barracks areas, housing areas, temporary lodging facilities, hospitals, and community support facilities;

(7) shall require transportation companies—

(A) to track, in real-time, the location of the entry and exit of covered drivers onto and off of military installations; and

(B) to provide, on demand, the information described in subparagraph (A) to appropriate personnel and agencies of the Department; and

(8) shall take into account force protection requirements and ensure the protection and safety of members of the Armed Forces, civilian employees of the Department of Defense, and the families of such members and employees.

(c) CONFIDENTIALITY OF INFORMATION.—The Secretary shall ensure that any information provided to the Department by a transportation company under subsection (b)(7)—

(1) is treated as confidential and proprietary information of the company that is exempt from public disclosure pursuant to section 552 of title 5, United States Code (commonly known as the "Freedom of Information Act"); and

(2) except as provided in subsection (b)(7), is not disclosed to any person or entity without the express written consent of the company unless disclosure of such information is required by a court order.

(d) DEFINITIONS.—In this section:

(1) TRANSPORTATION COMPANY.—The term "transportation company" means a corporation, partnership, sole proprietorship, or other entity outside of the Department of Defense that provides a commercial transportation service to a rider, including a company that uses a digital network to connect riders to covered drivers for the purpose of providing such transportation service.

(2) COVERED DRIVER.—The term "covered driver"—

(A) means an individual—

(i) who is an employee of a transportation company or who is affiliated with a transportation company; and

(ii) who provides a commercial transportation service to a rider; and

(B) includes a vehicle operated by such individual for the purpose of providing such service.

SEC. 347. ACCESS TO WIRELESS HIGH-SPEED INTERNET AND NETWORK CONNECTIONS FOR CERTAIN MEMBERS OF THE ARMED FORCES.

(a) IN GENERAL.—In providing members of the Armed Forces with access to high-speed wireless Internet and network connections at military installations outside the United States, the Secretary of Defense may provide such access without charge to the members and their dependents.

(b) CONTRACT AUTHORITY.—The Secretary may enter into contracts for the purpose of carrying out subsection (a).

SEC. 348. LIMITATION ON AVAILABILITY OF FUNDS FOR OFFICE OF THE UNDER SECRETARY OF DEFENSE FOR INTELLIGENCE.

Of the funds authorized to be appropriated by this Act or otherwise made available for fiscal year 2017 for Operation and Maintenance, Defense-wide, for the Office of the Under Secretary of Defense for Intelligence, not more than 90 percent may be obligated or expended until the Secretary of Defense issues guidance on the process by which members of the Armed Forces may carry an appropriate firearm on a military installation, as required by section 526 of the National Defense Authorization Act for Fiscal Year 2016 (Public Law 114–92; 129 Stat. 813; 10 U.S.C. 2672 note).

SEC. 349. LIMITATION ON DEVELOPMENT AND FIELDING OF NEW CAMOUFLAGE AND UTILITY UNIFORMS.

None of the funds authorized to be appropriated by this Act or otherwise made available for the Department of Defense may be obligated or expended to develop or field new camouflage uniforms, new utility uniforms, or new families of uniforms until the date that is one year after the date on which the Secretary of Defense submits to the congressional defense committees notice of the intent of the Secretary to develop or field such uniforms.

SEC. 350. PLAN FOR IMPROVED DEDICATED ADVERSARY AIR TRAINING ENTERPRISE OF THE AIR FORCE.

(a) IN GENERAL.—The Chief of Staff of the Air Force shall develop a plan for an improved dedicated adversary air training enterprise for the Air Force—

(1) to maximize warfighting effectiveness and synergies of the current and planned fourth and fifth generation combat air forces through optimized training and readiness;

(2) to harness intelligence analysis, emerging live-virtual-constructive training technologies, range infrastructure improvements, and results of experimentation and prototyping efforts in operational concept development;

(3) to challenge the combat air forces of the Air Force with threat representative adversary-to-friendly aircraft ratios, known and emerging adversary tactics, and high fidelity replication of threat airborne and ground capabilities; and

(4) to achieve training and readiness goals and objectives of the Air Force with demonstrated institutional commitment to the adversary air training enterprise through the application of Air Force policy and resources, partnering with the other Armed Forces, allies, and friends, and employing the use of industry contracted services.

(b) ELEMENTS.—The plan under subsection (a) shall include, with respect to an improved dedicated adversary air training enterprise, the following:

(1) Goals and objectives.

(2) Concepts of operations.

(3) Timelines for the phased implementation of the enterprise.

(4) Analysis of readiness improvements that may result from the enterprise.

(5) Prioritized resource requirements.

(6) Such other matters as the Chief of Staff considers appropriate.

(c) WRITTEN PLAN AND BRIEFING.—Not later than March 3, 2017, the Chief of Staff shall provide to the Committees on Armed Services of the Senate and the House of Representatives—

(1) a written version of the plan developed under subsection (a); and

(2) a briefing on such plan.

SEC. 351. INDEPENDENT REVIEW AND ASSESSMENT OF THE READY AIRCREW PROGRAM OF THE AIR FORCE.

(a) INDEPENDENT REVIEW AND ASSESSMENT.—The Secretary of the Air Force shall enter into a contract with an independent entity with appropriate expertise—

(1) to conduct a review and assessment of—

(A) the assumptions underlying the annual continuation training requirements of the Air Force; and

(B) the overall effectiveness of the Ready Aircrew Program of the Air Force in managing aircrew training requirements; and

(2) to make recommendations for the improved management of such training requirements.

(b) REPORT.—

(1) IN GENERAL.—Not later than 120 days after the date of the enactment of this Act, the Secretary of the Air Force shall submit to the congressional defense committees a report on the review and assessment conducted under subsection (a).

(2) ELEMENTS.—The report under paragraph (1) shall include an examination of the following:

(A) For the aircrews of each type of combat aircraft and by mission type—

(i) the number of sorties required to reach minimum and optimal levels of proficiency, respectively;

(ii) the optimal mix of live and virtual training sorties; and

(iii) the optimal mix of experienced aircrews versus inexperienced aircrews.

(B) The availability of assets and infrastructure to support the achievement of aircrew proficiency levels and an explanation of any requirements relating to such assets and infrastructure.

(C) The accumulated flying hours or other measurements used to determine if an aircrew qualifies for designation as an experienced aircrew, and whether different measurements should be used.

(D) Any actions taken or planned to be taken to implement recommendations resulting from the independent review and assessment under subsection (a), including an estimate of the resources required to implement such recommendations.

(E) Any other matters the Secretary determines are appropriate to ensure a comprehensive review and assessment.

(c) COMPTROLLER GENERAL REVIEW.—

(1) IN GENERAL.—The Comptroller General of the United States shall submit to the congressional defense committees a review of the report described in subsection (b). Such review shall include an assessment of—

(A) the extent to which the report addressed the elements described in paragraph (2) of such subsection;

(B) the adequacy and completeness of the assumptions reviewed to establish the annual training requirements of the Air Force;

(C) any actions the Air Force plans to carry out to incorporate the results of the report into annual training documents; and

(D) any other matters the Comptroller General determines are relevant.

(2) BRIEFING.—Not later than 60 days after the date on which the Secretary of the Air Force submits the report under subsection (b) and prior to submitting the review required under paragraph (1), the Comptroller General shall provide a briefing to the congressional defense committees on the preliminary results of the review conducted under such paragraph.

SEC. 352. STUDY ON SPACE-AVAILABLE TRAVEL SYSTEM OF THE DEPARTMENT OF DEFENSE.

(a) STUDY REQUIRED.—Not later than 90 days after the date of the enactment of this Act, the Secretary of Defense shall seek to enter into a contract with a federally funded research and development center to conduct an independent study on the space-available travel system of the Department of Defense.

(b) REPORT REQUIRED.—Not later than 180 days after entering into a contract with a federally funded research and development center under subsection (a), the Secretary shall submit to the congressional defense committees a report summarizing the results of the study conducted under such subsection.

(c) ELEMENTS.—The report under subsection (b) shall include, with respect to the space-available travel system, the following:

(1) A determination of—

(A) the capacity of the system as of the date of the enactment of this Act;

(B) the projected capacity of the system for the 10-year period following such date of enactment; and

(C) the projected number of reserve retirees, active duty retirees, and dependents of such retirees that will exist by the end of such 10-year period.

(2) Estimates of system capacity based the projections described in paragraph (1).

(3) A discussion of the efficiency of the system and data regarding the use of available space with respect to each category of passengers eligible for space-available travel under existing regulations.

(4) A description of the effect on system capacity if eligibility for space-available travel is extended to—

(A) drilling reserve component personnel and dependents of such personnel on international flights;

(B) dependents of reserve component retirees who are less than 60 years of age;

(C) retirees who are less than 60 years of age on international flights;

(D) drilling reserve component personnel traveling to drilling locations; and

(E) members or former members of the Armed Forces who have a disability rated as total, if space-available travel is provided to such members on the same basis as such travel is provided to members of the Armed Forces entitled to retired or retainer pay.

(5) A discussion of logistical and management problems, including congestion at terminals, waiting times, lodging availability, and personal hardships experienced by travelers.

(6) An evaluation of the cost of the system and whether space-available travel is and can remain cost-neutral.

(7) An evaluation of the feasibility of expanding the categories of passengers eligible for space-available travel to include—

(A) in the case of overseas travel, retired members of an active or reserve component, including retired members of reserve components, who, but for being under the eligibility age applicable to the member under section 12731 of title 10, United States Code, would be eligible for retired pay under chapter 1223 of such title;

(B) unremarried widows and widowers of active or reserve component members of the Armed Forces; and

(C) members or former members of the Armed Forces who have a disability rated as total, if space-available travel is provided to such members on the same basis as such travel is provided to members of the Armed Forces entitled to retired or retainer pay.

(8) Such other factors relating to the efficiency and cost of the system as the Secretary determines to be appropriate.

(d) ADDITIONAL RESPONSIBILITIES.—In addition to carrying out subsections (a) through (c), the Secretary of Defense shall—

(1) analyze the methods used to prioritize among the categories of individuals eligible for space-available travel and make recommendations for—

(A) re-ordering the priority of such categories; and

(B) adding additional categories of eligible individuals; and

(2) collect data on travelers who request but do not obtain available travel spaces under the space-available travel system.

(e) DISABILITY RATED AS TOTAL DEFINED.—In this section, the term "disability rated as total" has the meaning given the term in section 1414(e)(3) of title 10, United States Code.

SEC. 353. EVALUATION OF MOTOR CARRIER SAFETY PERFORMANCE AND SAFETY TECHNOLOGY.

(a) IN GENERAL.—The Secretary of Defense shall evaluate the need for proven safety technology in vehicles transporting shipments under the Transportation Protective Services program of the United States Transportation Command, including—

(1) electronic logging devices;

(2) roll stability control;

(3) forward collision avoidance systems;

(4) lane departure warning systems; and

(5) speed limiters.

(b) CONSIDERATIONS.—In carrying out subsection (a), the Secretary shall—

(1) consider the need to avoid catastrophic accidents and exposure of security-sensitive materials; and

(2) take into the account the findings of the Government Accountability Office report numbered GAO–16–82 and titled "Defense Transportation; DoD Needs to Improve the Evaluation of Safety and Performance Information for Carriers Transporting Security-Sensitive Materials".

TITLE IV—MILITARY PERSONNEL AUTHORIZATIONS

Subtitle A—Active Forces

Sec. 401. End strengths for active forces.
Sec. 402. Revisions in permanent active duty end strength minimum levels.

Subtitle B—Reserve Forces

Sec. 411. End strengths for Selected Reserve.
Sec. 412. End strengths for reserves on active duty in support of the reserves.
Sec. 413. End strengths for military technicians (dual status).
Sec. 414. Fiscal year 2017 limitation on number of non-dual status technicians.
Sec. 415. Maximum number of reserve personnel authorized to be on active duty for operational support.
Sec. 416. Technical corrections to annual authorization for personnel strengths.

Subtitle C—Authorization of Appropriations

Sec. 421. Military personnel.

Subtitle A—Active Forces

SEC. 401. END STRENGTHS FOR ACTIVE FORCES.

The Armed Forces are authorized strengths for active duty personnel as of September 30, 2017, as follows:

(1) The Army, 476,000.

(2) The Navy, 323,900.

(3) The Marine Corps, 185,000.

(4) The Air Force, 321,000.

SEC. 402. REVISIONS IN PERMANENT ACTIVE DUTY END STRENGTH MINIMUM LEVELS.

Section 691(b) of title 10, United States Code, is amended by striking paragraphs (1) through (4) and inserting the following new paragraphs:

"(1) For the Army, 476,000.

"(2) For the Navy, 323,900.

"(3) For the Marine Corps, 185,000.

"(4) For the Air Force, 321,000.".

Subtitle B—Reserve Forces

SEC. 411. END STRENGTHS FOR SELECTED RESERVE.

(a) IN GENERAL.—The Armed Forces are authorized strengths for Selected Reserve personnel of the reserve components as of September 30, 2017, as follows:

(1) The Army National Guard of the United States, 343,000.

(2) The Army Reserve, 199,000.

(3) The Navy Reserve, 58,000.

(4) The Marine Corps Reserve, 38,500.

(5) The Air National Guard of the United States, 105,700.

(6) The Air Force Reserve, 69,000.

(7) The Coast Guard Reserve, 7,000.

(b) END STRENGTH REDUCTIONS.—The end strengths prescribed by subsection (a) for the Selected Reserve of any reserve component shall be proportionately reduced by—

(1) the total authorized strength of units organized to serve as units of the Selected Reserve of such component which are on active duty (other than for training) at the end of the fiscal year; and

(2) the total number of individual members not in units organized to serve as units of the Selected Reserve of such component who are on active duty (other than for training or for unsatisfactory participation in training) without their consent at the end of the fiscal year.

(c) END STRENGTH INCREASES.—Whenever units or individual members of the Selected Reserve for any reserve component are released

from active duty during any fiscal year, the end strength prescribed for such fiscal year for the Selected Reserve of such reserve component shall be increased proportionately by the total authorized strengths of such units and by the total number of such individual members.

SEC. 412. END STRENGTHS FOR RESERVES ON ACTIVE DUTY IN SUPPORT OF THE RESERVES.

Within the end strengths prescribed in section 411(a), the reserve components of the Armed Forces are authorized, as of September 30, 2017, the following number of Reserves to be serving on full-time active duty or full-time duty, in the case of members of the National Guard, for the purpose of organizing, administering, recruiting, instructing, or training the reserve components:

(1) The Army National Guard of the United States, 30,155.

(2) The Army Reserve, 16,261.

(3) The Navy Reserve, 9,955.

(4) The Marine Corps Reserve, 2,261.

(5) The Air National Guard of the United States, 14,764.

(6) The Air Force Reserve, 2,955.

SEC. 413. END STRENGTHS FOR MILITARY TECHNICIANS (DUAL STATUS).

(a) IN GENERAL.—The authorized number of military technicians (dual status) as of September 30, 2017, for the reserve components of the Army and the Air Force (notwithstanding section 129 of title 10, United States Code) shall be the following:

(1) For the Army National Guard of the United States, 25,507.

(2) For the Army Reserve, 7,570.

(3) For the Air National Guard of the United States, 22,103.

(4) For the Air Force Reserve, 10,061.

(b) VARIANCE.—Notwithstanding section 115 of title 10, United States Code, the end strength prescribed by subsection (a) for a reserve component specified in that subsection may be increased—

(1) by 3 percent, upon determination by the Secretary of Defense that such action is in the national interest; and

(2) by 2 percent, upon determination by the Secretary of the military department concerned that such action would enhance manning and readiness in essential units or in critical specialties or ratings.

SEC. 414. FISCAL YEAR 2017 LIMITATION ON NUMBER OF NON-DUAL STATUS TECHNICIANS.

(a) LIMITATIONS.—

(1) NATIONAL GUARD.—Within the limitation provided in section 10217(c)(2) of title 10, United States Code, the number of non-dual status technicians employed by the National Guard as of September 30, 2017, may not exceed the following:

(A) For the Army National Guard of the United States, 1,600.

(B) For the Air National Guard of the United States, 350.

(2) ARMY RESERVE.—The number of non-dual status technicians employed by the Army Reserve as of September 30, 2017, may not exceed 420.

(3) AIR FORCE RESERVE.—The number of non-dual status technicians employed by the Air Force Reserve as of September 30, 2017, may not exceed 90.

(b) NON-DUAL STATUS TECHNICIANS DEFINED.—In this section, the term "non-dual status technician" has the meaning given that term in section 10217(a) of title 10, United States Code.

SEC. 415. MAXIMUM NUMBER OF RESERVE PERSONNEL AUTHORIZED TO BE ON ACTIVE DUTY FOR OPERATIONAL SUPPORT.

During fiscal year 2017, the maximum number of members of the reserve components of the Armed Forces who may be serving at any time on full-time operational support duty under section 115(b) of title 10, United States Code, is the following:

(1) The Army National Guard of the United States, 17,000.

(2) The Army Reserve, 13,000.

(3) The Navy Reserve, 6,200.

(4) The Marine Corps Reserve, 3,000.

(5) The Air National Guard of the United States, 16,000.

(6) The Air Force Reserve, 14,000.

SEC. 416. TECHNICAL CORRECTIONS TO ANNUAL AUTHORIZATION FOR PERSONNEL STRENGTHS.

Section 115 of title 10, United States Code, is amended—

(1) in subsection (b)(1)—

(A) in subparagraph (B), by striking "502(f)(2)" and inserting "502(f)(1)(B)"; and

(B) in subparagraph (C), by striking "502(f)(2)" and inserting "502(f)(1)(B)"; and

(2) in subsection (i)(7), by striking "502(f)(1)" and inserting "502(f)(1)(A)".

Subtitle C—Authorization of Appropriations

SEC. 421. MILITARY PERSONNEL.

(a) AUTHORIZATION OF APPROPRIATIONS.—Funds are hereby authorized to be appropriated for fiscal year 2017 for the use of the Armed Forces and other activities and agencies of the Department of Defense for expenses, not otherwise provided for, for military personnel, as specified in the funding table in section 4401.

(b) CONSTRUCTION OF AUTHORIZATION.—The authorization of appropriations in subsection (a) supersedes any other authorization of appropriations (definite or indefinite) for such purpose for fiscal year 2017.

TITLE V—MILITARY PERSONNEL POLICY

Subtitle A—Officer Personnel Policy

Sec. 501. Reduction in number of general and flag officers on active duty and authorized strength after December 31, 2022, of such general and flag officers.

Sec. 502. Repeal of statutory specification of general or flag officer grade for various positions in the Armed Forces.

Sec. 503. Number of Marine Corps general officers.

Sec. 504. Promotion eligibility period for officers whose confirmation of appointment is delayed due to nonavailability to the Senate of probative information under control of non-Department of Defense agencies.

Sec. 505. Continuation of certain officers on active duty without regard to requirement for retirement for years of service.

Sec. 506. Equal consideration of officers for early retirement or discharge.

Sec. 507. Modification of authority to drop from rolls a commissioned officer.

Sec. 508. Extension of force management authorities allowing enhanced flexibility for officer personnel management.

Sec. 509. Pilot programs on direct commissions to cyber positions.

Sec. 510. Length of joint duty assignments.

Sec. 510A. Revision of definitions used for joint officer management.

Subtitle B—Reserve Component Management

Sec. 511. Authority for temporary waiver of limitation on term of service of Vice Chief of the National Guard Bureau.

Sec. 512. Rights and protections available to military technicians.

Sec. 513. Inapplicability of certain laws to National Guard technicians performing active Guard and Reserve duty.

Sec. 514. Extension of removal of restrictions on the transfer of officers between the active and inactive National Guard.

Sec. 515. Extension of temporary authority to use Air Force reserve component personnel to provide training and instruction regarding pilot training.

Sec. 516. Expansion of eligibility for deputy commander of combatant command having United States among geographic area of responsibility to include officers of the Reserves.

Subtitle C—General Service Authorities

Sec. 521. Matters relating to provision of leave for members of the Armed Forces, including prohibition on leave not expressly authorized by law.

Sec. 522. Transfer of provision relating to expenses incurred in connection with leave canceled due to contingency operations.

Sec. 523. Expansion of authority to execute certain military instruments.

Sec. 524. Medical examination before administrative separation for members with post-traumatic stress disorder or traumatic brain injury in connection with sexual assault.

Sec. 525. Reduction of tenure on the temporary disability retired list.

Sec. 526. Technical correction to voluntary separation pay and benefits.

Sec. 527. Consolidation of Army marketing and pilot program on consolidated Army recruiting.

Subtitle D—Member Whistleblower Protections and Correction of Military Records

Sec. 531. Improvements to whistleblower protection procedures.

Sec. 532. Modification of whistleblower protection authorities to restrict contrary findings of prohibited personnel action by the Secretary concerned.

Sec. 533. Availability of certain Correction of Military Records and Discharge Review Board information through the Internet.

Sec. 534. Improvements to authorities and procedures for the correction of military records.

Sec. 535. Treatment by discharge review boards of claims asserting post-traumatic stress disorder or traumatic brain injury in connection with combat or sexual trauma as a basis for review of discharge.

Sec. 536. Comptroller General of the United States review of integrity of Department of Defense whistleblower program.

Subtitle E—Military Justice and Legal Assistance Matters

Sec. 541. United States Court of Appeals for the Armed Forces.

Sec. 542. Effective prosecution and defense in courts-martial and pilot programs on professional military justice development for judge advocates.

Sec. 543. Inclusion in annual reports on sexual assault prevention and response efforts of the Armed Forces of information on complaints of retaliation in connection with reports of sexual assault in the Armed Forces.

Sec. 544. Extension of the requirement for annual report regarding sexual assaults and coordination with release of Family Advocacy Program report.

Sec. 545. Metrics for evaluating the efforts of the Armed Forces to prevent and respond to retaliation in connection with reports of sexual assault in the Armed Forces.

Sec. 546. Training for Department of Defense personnel who investigate claims of retaliation.

Sec. 547. Notification to complainants of resolution of investigations into retaliation.

Sec. 548. Modification of definition of sexual harassment for purposes of investigations by commanding officers of complaints of harassment.

Sec. 549. Improved Department of Defense prevention of and response to hazing in the Armed Forces.

Subtitle F—National Commission on Military, National, and Public Service

Sec. 551. Purpose, scope, and definitions.

Sec. 552. Preliminary report on purpose and utility of registration system under Military Selective Service Act.

Sec. 553. National Commission on Military, National, and Public Service.

Sec. 554. Commission hearings and meetings.

Sec. 555. Principles and procedure for Commission recommendations.

Sec. 556. Executive Director and staff.

Sec. 557. Termination of Commission.

Subtitle G—Member Education, Training, Resilience, and Transition

Sec. 561. Modification of program to assist members of the Armed Forces in obtaining professional credentials.

Sec. 562. Inclusion of alcohol, prescription drug, opioid, and other substance abuse counseling as part of required preseparation counseling.

Sec. 563. Inclusion of information in Transition Assistance Program regarding effect of receipt of both veteran disability compensation and voluntary separation pay.

Sec. 564. Training under Transition Assistance Program on career and employment opportunities associated with transportation security cards.

Sec. 565. Extension of suicide prevention and resilience program.

Sec. 566. Congressional notification in advance of appointments to service academies.

Sec. 567. Report and guidance on Job Training, Employment Skills Training, Apprenticeships, and Internships and SkillBridge initiatives for members of the Armed Forces who are being separated.

Sec. 568. Military-to-mariner transition.

Subtitle H—Defense Dependents' Education and Military Family Readiness Matters

Sec. 571. Continuation of authority to assist local educational agencies that benefit dependents of members of the Armed Forces and Department of Defense civilian employees.

Sec. 572. One-year extension of authorities relating to the transition and support of military dependent students to local educational agencies.

Sec. 573. Annual notice to members of the Armed Forces regarding child custody protections guaranteed by the Servicemembers Civil Relief Act.

Sec. 574. Requirement for annual Family Advocacy Program report regarding child abuse and domestic violence.

Sec. 575. Reporting on allegations of child abuse in military families and homes.

Sec. 576. Repeal of Advisory Council on Dependents' Education.

Sec. 577. Support for programs providing camp experience for children of military families.

Sec. 578. Comptroller General of the United States assessment and report on Exceptional Family Member Programs.

Sec. 579. Impact aid amendments.

Subtitle I—Decorations and Awards

Sec. 581. Posthumous advancement of Colonel George E. "Bud" Day, United States Air Force, on the retired list.

Sec. 582. Authorization for award of medals for acts of valor during certain contingency operations.

Sec. 583. Authorization for award of the Medal of Honor to Gary M. Rose and James C. McCloughan for acts of valor during the Vietnam War.

Sec. 584. Authorization for award of Distinguished-Service Cross to First Lieutenant Melvin M. Spruiell for acts of valor during World War II.

Sec. 585. Authorization for award of the Distinguished Service Cross to Chaplain (First Lieutenant) Joseph Verbis LaFleur for acts of valor during World War II.

Sec. 586. Review regarding award of Medal of Honor to certain Asian American and Native American Pacific Islander war veterans.

Subtitle J—Miscellaneous Reports and Other Matters

Sec. 591. Repeal of requirement for a chaplain at the United States Air Force Academy appointed by the President.

Sec. 592. Extension of limitation on reduction in number of military and civilian personnel assigned to duty with service review agencies.

Sec. 593. Annual reports on progress of the Army and the Marine Corps in integrating women into military occupational specialities and units recently opened to women.

Sec. 594. Report on feasability of electronic tracking of operational active-duty service performed by members of the Ready Reserve of the Armed Forces.

Sec. 595. Report on discharge by warrant officers of pilot and other flight officer positions in the Navy, Marine Corps, and Air Force currently discharged by commissioned officers.

Sec. 596. Body mass index test.

Sec. 597. Report on career progression tracks of the Armed Forces for women in combat arms units.

Subtitle A—Officer Personnel Policy

SEC. 501. REDUCTION IN NUMBER OF GENERAL AND FLAG OFFICERS ON ACTIVE DUTY AND AUTHORIZED STRENGTH AFTER DECEMBER 31, 2022, OF SUCH GENERAL AND FLAG OFFICERS.

(a) REDUCTION IN NUMBER OF GENERAL AND FLAG OFFICERS BY DECEMBER 31, 2022.—

(1) REQUIRED REDUCTION.—Except as otherwise provided by an Act enacted after the date of the enactment of this Act that expressly modifies the requirements of this paragraph, by not later than December 31, 2022, the Secretary of Defense shall reduce the number of general and flag officers on active duty by 110 from the aggregate authorized number of general and flag officers authorized by sections 525 and 526 of title 10, United States Code, as of December 31, 2015.

(2) DISTRIBUTION OF AUTHORIZED POSITIONS.—Effective as of December 31, 2022, and reflecting the reduction required by paragraph (1), authorized general and flag officer positions shall be distributed among the Army, Navy, Air Force, Marine Corps, and joint pool as follows:

(A) The Army is authorized 220 positions in the general officer grades.

(B) The Navy is authorized 151 positions in the flag officer grades.

(C) The Air Force is authorized 187 positions in the general officer grades.

(D) The Marine Corps is authorized 62 positions in the general officer grades.

(E) The joint pool is authorized 232 positions in the general or flag officer grades, to be distributed as follows:

(i) 82 positions in the general officer grades from the Army.

(ii) 60 positions in the flag officer grades from the Navy.

(iii) 69 positions in the general officer grades from the Air Force.

(iv) 21 positions in the general officer grades from the Marine Corps.

(3) TEMPORARY ADDITIONAL JOINT POOL ALLOCATION.—In addition to the positions authorized by paragraph (2), the 30 general and flag officer positions designated for overseas contingency operations are authorized as an additional maximum temporary allocation to the joint pool.

(b) PLAN TO ACHIEVE REQUIRED REDUCTION AND DISTRIBUTION.—

(1) PLAN REQUIRED.—Utilizing the study conducted under subsection (c), the Secretary of Defense shall develop a plan to achieve, by the date specified in subsection (a)(1)—

(A) the reduction required by such subsection in the number of general and flag officers; and

(B) the distribution of authorized positions required by subsection (a)(2).

(2) SUBMISSION OF PLAN.—When the budget for the Department of Defense for fiscal year 2019 is submitted to Congress pursuant to section 1105 of title 31, United States Code, the Secretary of Defense shall submit to the Committees on Armed Services of the Senate and the House of Representatives a report setting forth the plan developed under this subsection.

(3) PROGRESS REPORTS.—The Secretary of Defense shall include with the budget for the Department of Defense for each of fiscal years 2020, 2021, and 2022 a report describing and assessing the progress of the Secretary in implementing the plan developed under this subsection.

(c) STUDY FOR PURPOSES OF PLAN.—

(1) STUDY REQUIRED.—For purposes of complying with subsection (a) and preparing the plan required by subsection (b), the Secretary of Defense shall conduct a comprehensive and deliberate global manpower study of requirements for general and flag officers with the goal of identifying—

(A) the requirement justification for each general or flag officer position in terms of overall force structure, scope of responsibility, command and control requirements, and force readiness and execution;

(B) an additional 10 percent reduction in the aggregate number of authorized general officer and flag officer positions after the reductions required by subsection (a); and

(C) an appropriate redistribution of all general officer and flag officer positions within the reductions so identified.

(2) SUBMISSION OF STUDY RESULTS.—Not later than April 1, 2017, the Secretary of Defense shall submit to the Committees on Armed Services of the Senate and the House of Representatives a report setting forth the results of the

study conducted under this subsection, including the justification for general and flag officer position to be retained and the reductions identified by general and flag officer position.

(3) INTERIM REPORT.—If practicable before the date specified in paragraph (2), the Secretary of Defense shall submit to the Committees on Armed Services of the Senate and the House of Representatives an interim report describing the progress made toward the completion of the study under this subsection, including—

(A) the specific general and flag officer positions that have been evaluated;

(B) the results of that evaluation; and

(C) recommendations for achieving the additional 10 percent reduction in the aggregate number of authorized general officer and flag officer positions to be identified under paragraph (1)(C) and recommendations for redistribution of general and flag officer positions that have been developed to that point.

(d) EXCLUSIONS.—

(1) RELATED TO JOINT DUTY ASSIGNMENTS.— For purposes of complying with subsection (a), the Secretary of Defense may exclude—

(A) a general or flag officer released from a joint duty assignment, but only during the 60-day period beginning on the date the officer departs the joint duty assignment, except that the Secretary may authorize the Secretary of a military department to extend the 60-day period by an additional 120 days, but not more than three officers on active duty from each Armed Force may be covered by the additional extension at the same time; and

(B) the number of officers required to serve in joint duty assignments for each Armed Force as authorized by the Secretary under section 526a(b) of title 10, United States Code, as added by subsection (h) of this section.

(2) RELATED TO RELIEF FROM CHIEF OF STAFF DUTY.—For purposes of complying with subsection (a), the Secretary of Defense may exclude an officer who continues to hold the grade of general or admiral under section 601(b)(5) of title 10, United States Code, after relief from the position of Chairman of the Joint Chiefs of Staff, Chief of Staff of the Army, Chief of Naval Operations, Chief of Staff of the Air Force, or Commandant of the Marine Corps.

(3) RELATED TO RETIREMENT, SEPARATION, RELEASE, OR RELIEF.—For purposes of complying with subsection (a), the Secretary of Defense may exclude the following officers:

(A) An officer of an Armed Force in the grade of brigadier general or above or, in the case of the Navy, in the grade of rear admiral (lower half) or above, who is on leave pending the retirement, separation, or release of that officer from active duty, but only during the 60-day period beginning on the date of the commencement of such leave of such officer.

(B) An officer of an Armed Force who has been relieved from a position designated under section 601(a) of title 10, United States Code, or by law to carry one of the grades specified in such section, but only during the 60-day period beginning on the date on which the assignment of the officer to the first position is terminated or until the officer is assigned to a second such position, whichever occurs first.

(e) SECRETARIAL AUTHORITY TO GRANT EXCEPTIONS TO LIMITATIONS.—

(1) IN GENERAL.—Subject to paragraph (2), the Secretary of Defense may alter the reduction otherwise required by subsection (a)(1) in the number of general and flag officer or the distribution of authorized positions otherwise required by subsection (a)(2) in the interest of the national security of the United States.

(2) NOTICE TO CONGRESS OF EXCEPTIONS.—Not later than 30 days after authorizing a number of general or flag officers in excess of the number required as a result of the reduction required by

subsection (a)(1) or altering the distribution of authorized positions under subsection (a)(2), the Secretary of Defense shall submit to the Committees on Armed Services of the Senate and the House of Representatives written notice of such exception, including a statement of the reason for such exception and the anticipated duration of the exception.

(f) ORDERLY TRANSITION FOR OFFICERS RECENTLY ASSIGNED TO POSITIONS TO BE ELIMINATED.—

(1) COVERED OFFICERS.—In order to provide an orderly transition for personnel in general or flag officer positions to be eliminated pursuant to the plan prepared under subsection (b), any general or flag officer who has not completed, as of December 31, 2022, at least 24 months in a position to be eliminated pursuant to the plan may remain in the position until the last day of the month that is 24 months after the month in which the officer assumed the duties of the position.

(2) REPORT TO CONGRESS ON COVERED OFFICERS.—The Secretary of Defense shall include in the annual report required by section 526(j) of title 10, United States Code, in 2020 a description of the positions in which an officer will remain pursuant to paragraph (1), including the latest date on which the officer may remain in such position pursuant to that paragraph.

(3) NOTICE TO CONGRESS ON DETACHMENT OF COVERED OFFICERS.—The Secretary of Defense shall submit to the Committees on Armed Services of the Senate and the House of Representatives a notice on the date on which each officer covered by paragraph (1) is detached from the officer's position pursuant to such paragraph.

(g) RELATION TO SUBSEQUENT GENERAL OR FLAG NOMINATIONS.—

(1) NOTICE TO SENATE WITH NOMINATION.—In order to help achieve the requirements of the plan required by subsection (b), effective 30 days after the commencement of the implementation of the plan, the Secretary of Defense shall include with each nomination of an officer to a grade above colonel or captain (in the case of the Navy) that is forwarded by the President to the Senate for appointment, by and with the advice and consent of the Senate, a certification to the Committee on Armed Services of the Senate that the appointment of the officer to the grade concerned will not interfere with achieving the reduction required by subsection (a)(1) in the number of general and flag officer positions or the distribution of authorized positions required by subsection (a)(2).

(2) IMPLEMENTATION.—Not later than 120 days after the date of the submission of the plan required by subsection (b), the Secretary of Defense shall revise applicable guidance of the Department of Defense on general and flag officer authorizations in order to ensure that—

(A) the achievement of the reductions required pursuant to subsection (a) is incorporated into the planning for the execution of promotions by the military departments and for the joint pool;

(B) to the extent practicable, the resulting grades for general and flag officer positions are uniformly applied to positions of similar duties and responsibilities across the military departments and the joint pool; and

(C) planning achieves a reduction in the headquarters functions and administrative and support activities and staffs of the Department of Defense and the military departments commensurate with the achievement of the reductions required pursuant to subsection (a).

(h) AUTHORIZED STRENGTH AFTER DECEMBER 31, 2022, OF GENERAL AND FLAG OFFICERS ON ACTIVE DUTY.—

(1) IN GENERAL.—Chapter 32 of title 10, United States Code, is amended by inserting after section 526 the following new section:

"§ 526a. Authorized strength after December 31, 2022: general officers and flag officers on active duty

"(a) LIMITATIONS.—The number of general officers on active duty in the Army, Air Force, and Marine Corps, and the number of flag officers on active duty in the Navy, after December 31, 2022, may not exceed the number specified for the armed force concerned as follows:

"(1) For the Army, 220.

"(2) For the Navy, 151.

"(3) For the Air Force, 187.

"(4) For the Marine Corps, 62.

"(b) LIMITED EXCLUSION FOR JOINT DUTY REQUIREMENTS.—

"(1) IN GENERAL.—The Secretary of Defense may designate up to 232 general officer and flag officer positions that are joint duty assignments for purposes of chapter 38 of this title for exclusion from the limitations in subsection (a).

"(2) MINIMUM NUMBER.—Unless the Secretary of Defense determines that a lower number is in the best interest of the Department of Defense, the minimum number of officers serving in positions designated under paragraph (1) for each armed force shall be as follows:

"(A) For the Army, 75.

"(B) For the Navy, 53.

"(C) For the Air Force, 68.

"(D) For the Marine Corps, 17.

"(c) EXCLUSION OF CERTAIN OFFICERS PENDING SEPARATION OR RETIREMENT OR BETWEEN SENIOR POSITIONS.—The limitations of this section do not apply to—

"(1) an officer of an armed force in the grade of brigadier general or above or, in the case of the Navy, in the grade of rear admiral (lower half) or above, who is on leave pending the retirement, separation, or release of that officer from active duty, but only during the 60-day period beginning on the date of the commencement of such leave of such officer; or

"(2) an officer of an armed force who has been relieved from a position designated under section 601(a) of this title or by law to carry one of the grades specified in such section, but only during the 60-day period beginning on the date on which the assignment of the officer to the first position is terminated or until the officer is assigned to a second such position, whichever occurs first.

"(d) TEMPORARY EXCLUSION FOR ASSIGNMENT TO CERTAIN TEMPORARY BILLETS.—

"(1) IN GENERAL.—The limitations in subsection (a) do not apply to a general officer or flag officer assigned to a temporary joint duty assignment designated by the Secretary of Defense.

"(2) DURATION OF EXCLUSION.—A general officer or flag officer assigned to a temporary joint duty assignment as described in paragraph (1) may not be excluded under this subsection from the limitations in subsection (a) for a period of longer than one year.

"(e) EXCLUSION OF OFFICERS DEPARTING FROM JOINT DUTY ASSIGNMENTS.—The limitations in subsection (a) do not apply to an officer released from a joint duty assignment, but only during the 60-day period beginning on the date the officer departs the joint duty assignment. The Secretary of Defense may authorize the Secretary of a military department to extend the 60-day period by an additional 120 days, except that not more than three officers on active duty from each armed force may be covered by the additional extension at the same time.

"(f) ACTIVE-DUTY BASELINE.—

"(1) NOTICE AND WAIT REQUIREMENTS.—If the Secretary of a military department proposes an action that would increase above the baseline the number of general officers or flag officers of an armed force under the jurisdiction of that Secretary who would be on active duty and would count against the statutory limit applicable to that armed force under subsection (a), the

action shall not take effect until after the end of the 60-calendar day period beginning on the date on which the Secretary provides notice of the proposed action, including the rationale for the action, to the Committees on Armed Services of the Senate and the House of Representatives.

"(2) BASELINE DEFINED.—In paragraph (1), the term 'baseline' for an armed force means the lower of—

"(A) the statutory limit of general officers or flag officers of that armed force under subsection (a); or

"(B) the actual number of general officers or flag officers of that armed force who, as of January 1, 2023, counted toward the statutory limit of general officers or flag officers of that armed force under subsection (a).

"(g) JOINT DUTY ASSIGNMENT BASELINE.—

"(1) NOTICE AND WAIT REQUIREMENT.—If the Secretary of Defense, the Secretary of a military department, or the Chairman of the Joint Chiefs of Staff proposes an action that would increase above the baseline the number of general officers and flag officers of the armed forces in joint duty assignments who count against the statutory limit under subsection (b)(1), the action shall not take effect until after the end of the 60-calendar day period beginning on the date on which such Secretary or the Chairman, as the case may be, provides notice of the proposed action, including the rationale for the action, to the Committees on Armed Services of the Senate and the House of Representatives.

"(2) BASELINE DEFINED.—In paragraph (1), the term 'baseline' means the lower of—

"(A) the statutory limit on general officer and flag officer positions that are joint duty assignments under subsection (b)(1); or

"(B) the actual number of general officers and flag officers who, as of January 1, 2023, were in joint duty assignments counted toward the statutory limit under subsection (b)(1).

"(h) ANNUAL REPORT.—Not later than March 1 each year, the Secretary of Defense shall submit to the Committees on Armed Services of the Senate and the House of Representatives a report specifying the following:

"(1) The numbers of general officers and flag officers who, as of January 1 of the calendar year in which the report is submitted, counted toward the service-specific limits of subsection (a).

"(2) The number of general officers and flag officers in joint duty assignments who, as of such January 1, counted toward the statutory limit under subsection (b)(1).".

"(2) CONFORMING AMENDMENT.—Section 526 of title 10, United States Code, is amended by adding at the end the following new subsection:

"(k) CESSATION OF APPLICABILITY.—The provisions of this section shall not apply to number of general officers and flag officers in the armed forces after December 31, 2022. For provisions applicable to the number of such officers after that date, see section 526a of this title.".

"(3) CLERICAL AMENDMENT.—The table of sections at the beginning of chapter 32 of title 10, United States Code, is amended by inserting after the item relating to section 526 the following new item:

"526a. Authorized strength after December 31, 2022: general officers and flag officers on active duty.".

SEC. 502. REPEAL OF STATUTORY SPECIFICATION OF GENERAL OR FLAG OFFICER GRADE FOR VARIOUS POSITIONS IN THE ARMED FORCES.

(a) ASSISTANTS TO CJCS FOR NG MATTERS AND RESERVE MATTERS.—

(1) IN GENERAL.—Section 155a of title 10, United States Code, is repealed.

(2) CLERICAL AMENDMENT.—The table of sections at the beginning of chapter 5 of such title is amended by striking the item relating to section 155a.

(b) LEGAL COUNSEL TO CJCS.—Section 156 of title 10, United States Code, is amended—

(1) by striking subsection (c); and

(2) by redesignating subsection (d) as subsection (c).

(c) DIRECTOR OF TEST RESOURCE MANAGEMENT CENTER.—Section 196(b)(1) of title 10, United States Code, is amended by striking the second and third sentences.

(d) DIRECTOR OF MISSILE DEFENSE AGENCY.—

(1) IN GENERAL.—Section 203 of title 10, United States Code, is repealed.

(2) CLERICAL AMENDMENT.—The table of sections at the beginning of chapter 8 of such title is amended by striking the item relating to section 203.

(e) JOINT 4-STAR POSITIONS.—Section 604(b) of title 10, United States Code, is amended by striking paragraph (3).

(f) SENIOR MEMBERS OF MILITARY STAFF COMMITTEE OF UN.—Section 711 of title 10, United States Code, is amended by striking the second sentence.

(g) CHIEF OF STAFF TO PRESIDENT.—

(1) IN GENERAL.—Section 720 of title 10, United States Code, is repealed.

(2) CLERICAL AMENDMENT.—The table of sections at the beginning of chapter 41 of such title is amended by striking the item relating to section 720.

(h) ATTENDING PHYSICIAN TO CONGRESS.—

(1) IN GENERAL.—Section 722 of title 10, United States Code, is repealed.

(2) CLERICAL AMENDMENT.—The table of sections at the beginning of chapter 41 of such title is amended by striking the item relating to section 722.

(i) PHYSICIAN TO WHITE HOUSE.—

(1) IN GENERAL.—Section 744 of title 10, United States Code, is repealed.

(2) CLERICAL AMENDMENT.—The table of sections at the beginning of chapter 43 of such title is amended by striking the item relating to section 744.

(j) CHIEF OF LEGISLATIVE LIAISON OF THE ARMY.—Section 3023(a) of title 10, United States Code, is amended by striking the second sentence.

(k) CHIEFS OF BRANCHES OF THE ARMY.—Section 3036(b) of title 10, United States Code, is amended in the flush matter following paragraph (2)—

(1) by striking the first sentence; and

(2) in the second sentence, by striking ", and while so serving, has the grade of lieutenant general".

(l) JUDGE ADVOCATE GENERAL OF THE ARMY.—Section 3037(a) of title 10, United States Code, is amended by striking the last two sentences.

(m) CHIEF OF ARMY RESERVE.—Section 3038(c) of title 10, United States Code, is amended—

(1) in the subsection heading, by striking "; GRADE";

(2) by striking "(1)"; and

(3) by striking paragraph (2).

(n) DEPUTY AND ASSISTANT CHIEFS OF BRANCHES OF THE ARMY.—

(1) IN GENERAL.—Section 3039 of title 10, United States Code, is repealed.

(2) CLERICAL AMENDMENT.—The table of sections at the beginning of chapter 305 of such title is amended by striking the item relating to section 3039.

(o) CHIEF OF ARMY NURSE CORPS.—Section 3069(b) of title 10, United States Code, is amended by striking the second sentence.

(p) ASSISTANT CHIEFS OF ARMY MEDICAL SPECIALIST CORPS.—

(1) IN GENERAL.—Section 3070 of title 10, United States Code, is amended—

(A) in subsection (a), by striking "and assistant chiefs";

(B) by striking subsection (c); and

(C) by redesignating subsection (d) as subsection (c).

(2) CONFORMING AMENDMENT.—The heading of such section is amended to read as follows:

"**§ 3070. Army Medical Specialist Corps: organization; Chief**".

(3) CLERICAL AMENDMENT.—The table of sections at the beginning of chapter 307 of such title is amended by striking the item relating to section 3070 and inserting the following new item:

"3070. Army Medical Specialist Corps: organization; Chief.".

(q) JUDGE ADVOCATE GENERAL'S CORPS OF THE ARMY.—Section 3072 of title 10, United States Code, is amended—

(1) by striking paragraph (3); and

(2) by redesignating paragraphs (4) and (5) as paragraphs (3) and (4), respectively.

(r) CHIEF OF VETERINARY CORPS OF THE ARMY.—

(1) IN GENERAL.—Section 3084 of title 10, United States Code, is amended by striking the second sentence.

(2) CONFORMING AMENDMENT.—The heading of such section is amended to read as follows:

"**§ 3084. Chief of Veterinary Corps**".

(3) CLERICAL AMENDMENT.—The table of sections at the beginning of chapter 307 of such title is amended by striking the item relating to section 3084 and inserting the following new item:

"3084. Chief of Veterinary Corps.".

(s) ARMY AIDES.—

(1) IN GENERAL.—Section 3543 of title 10, United States Code, is repealed.

(2) CLERICAL AMENDMENT.—The table of sections at the beginning of chapter 343 of such title is amended by striking the item relating to section 3543.

(t) PRINCIPAL MILITARY DEPUTY TO ASSISTANT SECRETARY OF THE NAVY FOR RD&A.—Section 5016(b)(4)(B) of title 10, United States Code, is amended by striking "a vice admiral of the Navy or a lieutenant general of the Marine Corps" and inserting "an officer of the Navy or the Marine Corps".

(u) CHIEF OF NAVAL RESEARCH.—Section 5022 of title 10, United States Code, is amended—

(1) by striking "(1)"; and

(2) by striking paragraph (2).

(v) CHIEF OF LEGISLATIVE AFFAIRS OF THE NAVY.—Section 5027(a) of title 10, United States Code, is amended by striking the second sentence.

(w) DIRECTOR FOR EXPEDITIONARY WARFARE.—Section 5038 of title 10, United States Code, is amended—

(1) by striking subsection (b); and

(2) by redesignating subsections (c) and (d) as subsections (b) and (c), respectively.

(x) SJA TO COMMANDANT OF THE MARINE CORPS.—Section 5046(a) of title 10, United States Code, is amended by striking the last sentence.

(y) LEGISLATIVE ASSISTANT TO COMMANDANT OF THE MARINE CORPS.—Section 5047 of title 10, United States Code, is amended by striking the second sentence.

(z) BUREAU CHIEFS OF THE NAVY.—

(1) IN GENERAL.—Section 5133 of title 10, United States Code, is repealed.

(2) CLERICAL AMENDMENT.—The table of sections at the beginning of chapter 513 of such title is amended by striking the item relating to section 5133.

(aa) CHIEF OF DENTAL CORPS OF THE NAVY.—Section 5138 of title 10, United States Code, is amended—

(1) in subsection (a), by striking "not below the grade of rear admiral (lower half)"; and

(2) in subsection (c), by striking the first sentence.

(bb) BUREAU OF NAVAL PERSONNEL.—

(1) IN GENERAL.—Section 5141 of title 10, United States Code, is amended—

(A) in subsection (a), by striking the first sentence; and

(B) in subsection (b), by striking the first sentence.

(2) CONFORMING AMENDMENT.—The heading of such section is amended to read as follows:

"§5141. Chief of Naval Personnel; Deputy Chief of Naval Personnel".

(3) CLERICAL AMENDMENT.—The table of sections at the beginning of chapter 513 of such title is amended by striking the item relating to section 5141 and inserting the following new item:

"5141. Chief of Naval Personnel; Deputy Chief of Naval Personnel.".

(cc) CHIEF OF CHAPLAINS OF THE NAVY.—Section 5142 of title 10, United States Code, is amended by striking subsection (e).

(dd) CHIEF OF NAVY RESERVE.—Section 5143(c) of title 10, United States Code, is amended—

(1) in the subsection heading, by striking "; GRADE";

(2) by striking "(1)"; and

(3) by striking paragraph (2).

(ee) COMMANDER, MARINE FORCES RESERVE.—Section 5144(c) of title 10, United States Code, is amended—

(1) in the subsection heading, by striking "; GRADE";

(2) by striking "(1)"; and

(3) by striking paragraph (2).

(ff) JUDGE ADVOCATE GENERAL OF THE NAVY.—Section 5148(b) of title 10, United States Code, is amended by striking the last sentence.

(gg) DEPUTY AND ASSISTANT JUDGE ADVOCATES GENERAL OF THE NAVY.—Section 5149 of title 10, United States Code, is amended—

(1) in subsection (a)(1)—

(A) in the first sentence, by striking ", by and with the advice and consent of the Senate,"; and

(B) by striking the second sentence; and

(2) in each of subsections (b) and (c), by striking the second and last sentences.

(hh) CHIEFS OF STAFF CORPS OF THE NAVY.—Section 5150 of title 10, United States Code, is amended—

(1) in subsection (b)(2), by striking "Subject to subsection (c), the Secretary" and inserting "The Secretary"; and

(2) by striking subsection (c).

(ii) PRINCIPAL MILITARY DEPUTY TO ASSISTANT SECRETARY OF THE AIR FORCE FOR ACQUISITION.—Section 8016(b)(4)(B) of title 10, United States Code, is amended by striking "a lieutenant general" and inserting "an officer".

(jj) CHIEF OF LEGISLATIVE LIAISON OF THE AIR FORCE.—Section 8023(a) of title 10, United States Code, is amended by striking the second sentence.

(kk) JUDGE ADVOCATE GENERAL AND DEPUTY JUDGE ADVOCATE GENERAL OF THE AIR FORCE.—Section 8037 of title 10, United States Code, is amended—

(1) in subsection (a), by striking the last sentence; and

(2) in subsection (d)(1), by striking the last sentence.

(ll) CHIEF OF THE AIR FORCE RESERVE.—Section 8038(c) of title 10, United States Code, is amended—

(1) in the subsection heading, by striking "; GRADE";

(2) by striking "(1)"; and

(3) by striking paragraph (2).

(mm) CHIEF OF CHAPLAINS OF THE AIR FORCE.—Section 8039 of title 10, United States Code, is amended—

(1) in subsection (a)(1)—

(A) by striking subparagraph (A); and

(B) by redesignating subparagraphs (B) and (C) as subparagraphs (A) and (B), respectively; and

(2) by striking subsection (c).

(nn) CHIEF OF AIR FORCE NURSES.—

(1) IN GENERAL.—Section 8069 of title 10, United States Code, is amended—

(A) in subsection (a)—

(i) in the subsection heading, by striking "POSITIONS OF CHIEF AND ASSISTANT CHIEF" and inserting "POSITION OF CHIEF"; and

(ii) by striking "and assistant chief";

(B) in subsection (b), by striking the second sentence; and

(C) by striking subsection (c).

(2) CONFORMING AMENDMENT.—The heading of such section is amended to read as follows:

"§8069. Air Force nurses: Chief; appointment".

(3) CLERICAL AMENDMENT.—The table of sections at the beginning of chapter 807 of such title is amended by striking the item relating to section 8069 and inserting the following new item:

"8069. Air Force nurses: Chief; appointment.".

(oo) ASSISTANT SURGEON GENERAL FOR DENTAL SERVICES OF THE AIR FORCE.—Section 8081 of title 10, United States Code, is amended by striking the second sentence.

(pp) AIR FORCE AIDES.—

(1) IN GENERAL.—Section 8543 of title 10, United States Code, is repealed.

(2) CLERICAL AMENDMENT.—The table of sections at the beginning of chapter 843 of such title is amended by striking the item relating to section 8543.

(qq) DEAN OF FACULTY OF THE AIR FORCE ACADEMY.—Section 9335(b) of title 10, United States Code, is amended by striking the first and third sentences.

(rr) VICE CHIEF OF THE NATIONAL GUARD BUREAU.—Section 10505(a) of title 10, United States Code, is amended—

(1) in subsection (a)(1)—

(A) in subparagraph (C), by adding "and" at the end;

(B) in subparagraph (D), by striking "; and" at the end and inserting a period; and

(C) by striking subparagraph (E); and

(2) by striking subsection (c).

(ss) OTHER SENIOR NATIONAL GUARD BUREAU OFFICERS.—Section 10506(a)(1) of title 10, United States Code, is amended in each of subparagraphs (A) and (B)—

(1) by striking "general"; and

(2) by striking ", and shall hold the grade of lieutenant general while so serving,".

SEC. 503. NUMBER OF MARINE CORPS GENERAL OFFICERS.

(a) DISTRIBUTION OF COMMISSIONED OFFICERS ON ACTIVE DUTY IN GENERAL OFFICER AND FLAG OFFICER GRADES.—Section 525(a)(4) of title 10, United States Code, is amended—

(1) in subparagraph (B), by striking "15" and inserting "17"; and

(2) in subparagraph (C), by striking "23" and inserting "22".

(b) GENERAL AND FLAG OFFICERS ON ACTIVE DUTY.—Section 526(a)(4) of such title is amended by striking "61" and inserting "62".

(c) DEPUTY COMMANDANTS.—Section 5045 of such title is amended by striking "six" and inserting "seven".

SEC. 504. PROMOTION ELIGIBILITY PERIOD FOR OFFICERS WHOSE CONFIRMATION OF APPOINTMENT IS DELAYED DUE TO NONAVAILABILITY TO THE SENATE OF PROBATIVE INFORMATION UNDER CONTROL OF NON-DEPARTMENT OF DEFENSE AGENCIES.

Section 629(c) of title 10, United States Code, is amended—

(1) by redesignating paragraph (3) as paragraph (4); and

(2) by inserting after paragraph (2) the following new paragraph (3):

"(3) Paragraph (1) does not apply when the Senate is not able to obtain information necessary to give its advice and consent to the appointment concerned because that information is under the control of a department or agency of the Federal Government other than the Department of Defense.".

SEC. 505. CONTINUATION OF CERTAIN OFFICERS ON ACTIVE DUTY WITHOUT REGARD TO REQUIREMENT FOR RETIREMENT FOR YEARS OF SERVICE.

(a) AUTHORITY FOR CONTINUATION ON ACTIVE DUTY.—

(1) IN GENERAL.—Subchapter IV of chapter 36 of title 10, United States Code, is amended by inserting after section 637 the following new section:

"§637a. Continuation on active duty: officers in certain military specialties and career tracks

"(a) IN GENERAL.—The Secretary of the military department concerned may authorize an officer in a grade above grade O–4 to remain on active duty after the date otherwise provided for the retirement of the officer in section 633, 634, 635, or 636 of this title, as applicable, if the officer has a military occupational specialty, rating, or specialty code in a military specialty designated pursuant to subsection (b).

"(b) MILITARY SPECIALTIES.—Each Secretary of a military department shall designate the military specialties in which a military occupational specialty, rating, or specialty code, as applicable, assigned to members of the armed forces under the jurisdiction of such Secretary authorizes the members to be eligible for continuation on active duty as provided in subsection (a).

"(c) DURATION OF CONTINUATION.—An officer continued on active duty pursuant to this section shall, if not earlier retired, be retired on the first day of the month after the month in which the officer completes 40 years of active service.

"(d) REGULATIONS.—The Secretaries of the military departments shall carry out this section in accordance with regulations prescribed by the Secretary of Defense. The regulations shall specify the criteria to be used by the Secretaries of the military departments in designating military specialities for purposes of subsection (b).".

(2) CLERICAL AMENDMENT.—The table of sections at the beginning of subchapter IV of chapter 36 of title 10, United States Code, is amended by inserting after the item relating to section 637 the following new item:

"637a. Continuation on active duty: officers in certain military specialties and career tracks.".

(b) CONFORMING AMENDMENTS.—The following provisions of title 10, United States Code, are amended by inserting "or 637a" after "637(b)":

(1) Section 633(a).

(2) Section 634(a).

(3) Section 635.

(4) Section 636(a).

SEC. 506. EQUAL CONSIDERATION OF OFFICERS FOR EARLY RETIREMENT OR DISCHARGE.

Section 638a of title 10, United States Code, is amended—

(1) in subsection (b), by adding at the end the following new paragraph:

"(4) Convening selection boards under section 611(b) of this title to consider for early retirement or discharge regular officers on the active-duty list in a grade below lieutenant colonel or commander—

"(A) who have served at least one year of active duty in the grade currently held; and

"(B) whose names are not on a list of officers recommended for promotion.";

(2) by redesignating subsection (e) as subsection (f); and

(3) by inserting after subsection (d) the following new subsection (e):

"(e)(1) In the case of action under subsection (b)(4), the Secretary of the military department

concerned shall specify the total number of officers described in that subsection that a selection board convened under section 611(b) of this title pursuant to the authority of that subsection may recommend for early retirement or discharge. Officers who are eligible, or are within two years of becoming eligible, to be retired under any provision of law (other than by reason of eligibility pursuant to section 4403 of the National Defense Authorization Act for Fiscal Year 1993 (Public Law 102–484)), if selected by the board, shall be retired or retained until becoming eligible to retire under section 3911, 6323, or 8911 of this title, and those officers who are otherwise ineligible to retire under any provision of law shall, if selected by the board, be discharged.

"(2) In the case of action under subsection (b)(4), the Secretary of the military department concerned may submit to a selection board convened pursuant to that subsection—

"(A) the names of all eligible officers described in that subsection, whether or not they are eligible to be retired under any provision of law, in a particular grade and competitive category; or

"(B) the names of all eligible officers described in that subsection in a particular grade and competitive category, whether or not they are eligible to be retired under any provision of law, who are also in particular year groups, specialties, or retirement categories, or any combination thereof, with that competitive category.

"(3) The number of officers specified under paragraph (1) may not be more than 30 percent of the number of officers considered.

"(4) An officer who is recommended for discharge by a selection board convened pursuant to the authority of subsection (b)(4) and whose discharge is approved by the Secretary concerned shall be discharged on a date specified by the Secretary concerned.

"(5) Selection of officers for discharge under this subsection shall be based on the needs of the service.".

SEC. 507. MODIFICATION OF AUTHORITY TO DROP FROM ROLLS A COMMISSIONED OFFICER.

Section 1161(b) of title 10, United States Code, is amended by inserting "or the Secretary of Defense, or in the case of a commissioned officer of the Coast Guard, the Secretary of the department in which the Coast Guard is operating when it is not operating in the Navy," after "President".

SEC. 508. EXTENSION OF FORCE MANAGEMENT AUTHORITIES ALLOWING ENHANCED FLEXIBILITY FOR OFFICER PERSONNEL MANAGEMENT.

(a) TEMPORARY EARLY RETIREMENT AUTHORITY.—Section 4403(i) of the National Defense Authorization Act for Fiscal Year 1993 (10 U.S.C. 1293 note) is amended by striking "December 31, 2018" and inserting "December 31, 2025".

(b) CONTINUATION ON ACTIVE DUTY.—Section 638a(a)(2) of title 10, United States Code, is amended by striking "December 31, 2018" and inserting "December 31, 2025".

(c) VOLUNTARY SEPARATION PAY.—Section 1175a(k)(1) of such title is amended by striking "December 31, 2018" and inserting "December 31, 2025".

(d) SERVICE-IN-GRADE WAIVERS.—Section 1370(a)(2)(F) of such title is amended by striking "2018" and inserting "2025".

SEC. 509. PILOT PROGRAMS ON DIRECT COMMISSIONS TO CYBER POSITIONS.

(a) PILOT PROGRAMS AUTHORIZED.—Each Secretary of a military department may carry out a pilot program to improve the ability of an Armed Force under the jurisdiction of the Secretary to recruit cyber professionals.

(b) ELEMENTS.—Under a pilot program established under this section, an individual who

meets educational, physical, and other requirements determined appropriate by the Secretary of the military department concerned may receive an original appointment as a commissioned officer in a cyber specialty.

(c) CONSULTATION.—In developing a pilot program for the Army or the Air Force under this section, the Secretary of the Army and the Secretary of the Air Force may consult with the Secretary of the Navy with respect to an existing, similar program carried out by the Secretary of the Navy.

(d) DURATION.—

(1) COMMENCEMENT.—The Secretary of a military department may commence a pilot program under this section on or after January 1, 2017.

(2) TERMINATION.—All pilot programs under this section shall terminate no later than December 31, 2022.

(e) STATUS REPORT.—Not later than January 1, 2020, each Secretary of a military department who conducts a pilot program under this section shall submit to the Committees on Armed Services of the Senate and the House of Representatives a report containing an evaluation of the success of the program in obtaining skilled cyber personnel for the Armed Forces.

SEC. 510. LENGTH OF JOINT DUTY ASSIGNMENTS.

(a) IN GENERAL.—Subsection (a) of section 664 of title 10, United States Code, is amended by striking "assignment—" and all that follows and inserting "assignment shall be not less than two years.".

(b) REPEAL OF AUTHORITY FOR SHORTER LENGTH FOR OFFICERS INITIALLY ASSIGNED TO CRITICAL OCCUPATIONAL SPECIALTIES.—Such section is further amended by striking subsection (c).

(c) EXCLUSIONS FROM TOUR LENGTH.—Subsection (d) of such section is amended—

(1) in the matter preceding paragraph (1), by striking "the standards prescribed in subsection (a)" and inserting "the requirement in subsection (a)";

(2) in paragraph (1)(D), by striking "assignment—" and all that follows and inserting "assignment as prescribed by the Secretary of Defense in regulations.";

(3) by striking paragraph (2);

(4) by redesignating paragraph (3) as paragraph (2); and

(5) in paragraph (2), as redesignated by paragraph (4) of this subsection, by striking "the applicable standard prescribed in subsection (a)" and inserting "the requirement in subsection (a)".

(d) REPEAL OF AVERAGE TOUR LENGTH REQUIREMENTS.—Such section is further amended by striking subsection (e).

(e) FULL TOUR OF DUTY.—Subsection (f) of such section is amended—

(1) in paragraph (1), by striking "standards prescribed in subsection (a)" and inserting "the requirement in subsection (a)";

(2) by striking paragraphs (2) and (4);

(3) by redesignating paragraphs (3), (5), and (6) as paragraphs (2), (3), and (4), respectively; and

(4) in paragraph (4), as redesignated by paragraph (3) of this subsection, by striking ", but not less than two years".

(f) CONSTRUCTIVE CREDIT.—Subsection (h) of such section is amended—

(1) by striking "(1)";

(2) by striking "accord" and inserting "award"; and

(3) by striking paragraph (2).

(g) CONFORMING AMENDMENTS.—Such section is further amended—

(1) by redesignating subsections (d), (f), (g), and (h), as amended by this section, as subsections (c), (d), (e), and (f), respectively;

(2) in paragraph (2) of subsection (c), as so redesignated and amended, by striking "subsection (f)(3)" and inserting "subsection (d)(2)".

(3) paragraph (2) of subsection (d), as so redesignated and amended, by striking "subsection (g)" and inserting "subsection (e)";

(4) in subsection (e), as so redesignated and amended, by striking "subsection (f)(3)" and inserting "subsection (d)(2)"; and

(5) in subsection (f), as so redesignated and amended, by striking "paragraphs (1), (2), and (4) of subsection (f)" and inserting "subsection (d)(1)".

SEC. 510A. REVISION OF DEFINITIONS USED FOR JOINT OFFICER MANAGEMENT.

(a) DEFINITION OF JOINT MATTERS.—Paragraph (1) of section 668(a) of title 10, United States Code, is amended to read as follows:

"(1) In this chapter, the term 'joint matters' means matters related to any of the following:

"(A) The development or achievement of strategic objectives through the synchronization, coordination, and organization of integrated forces in operations conducted across domains, such as land, sea, or air, in space, or in the information environment, including matters relating to any of the following:

"(i) National military strategy.

"(ii) Strategic planning and contingency planning.

"(iii) Command and control, intelligence, fires, movement and maneuver, protection or sustainment of operations under unified command.

"(iv) National security planning with other departments and agencies of the United States.

"(v) Combined operations with military forces of allied nations.

"(B) Acquisition matters conducted by members of the armed forces and covered under chapter 87 of this title involved in developing, testing, contracting, producing, or fielding of multi-service programs or systems.

"(C) Other matters designated in regulation by the Secretary of Defense in consultation with the Chairman of the Joint Chiefs of Staff.".

(b) DEFINITION OF INTEGRATED FORCES.—Section 668(a)(2) of title 10, United States Code, is amended in the matter preceding subparagraph (A)—

(1) by striking "integrated military forces" and inserting "integrated forces"; and

(2) by striking "the planning or execution (or both) of operations involving" and inserting "achieving unified action with".

(c) DEFINITION OF JOINT DUTY ASSIGNMENT.—Section 668(b)(1) of title 10, United States Code, is amended by striking subparagraph (A) and inserting the following new subparagraph:

"(A) shall be limited to assignments in which—

"(i) the preponderance of the duties of the officer involve joint matters and

"(ii) the officer gains significant experience in joint matters; and".

(d) REPEAL OF DEFINITION OF CRITICAL OCCUPATIONAL SPECIALITY.—Section 668 of title 10, United States Code, is amended by striking subsection (d).

Subtitle B—Reserve Component Management

SEC. 511. AUTHORITY FOR TEMPORARY WAIVER OF LIMITATION ON TERM OF SERVICE OF VICE CHIEF OF THE NATIONAL GUARD BUREAU.

Section 10505(a)(4) of title 10, United States Code, is amended by striking "paragraph (3)(B) for a limited period of time" and inserting "paragraph (3) for not more than 90 days".

SEC. 512. RIGHTS AND PROTECTIONS AVAILABLE TO MILITARY TECHNICIANS.

(a) IN GENERAL.—Section 709 of title 32, United States Code, is amended—

(1) in subsection (f)—

(A) in paragraph (4), by striking "; and" and inserting "when the appeal concerns activity occurring while the member is in a military pay status, or concerns fitness for duty in the reserve components;";

(B) by redesignating paragraph (5) as paragraph (6); and

(C) by inserting after paragraph (4) the following new paragraph (5):

"(5) with respect to an appeal concerning any activity not covered by paragraph (4), the provisions of sections 7511, 7512, and 7513 of title 5, and section 717 of the Civil Rights Act of 1991 (42 U.S.C. 2000e–16) shall apply; and"; and

(2) in subsection (g), by striking "Sections" and inserting "Except as provided in subsection (f), sections".

(b) DEFINITIONS.—Section 709 of title 32, United States Code, is further amended by adding at the end the following new subsection:

"(j) In this section:

"(1) The term 'military pay status' means a period of service where the amount of pay payable to a technician for that service is based on rates of military pay provided for under title 37.

"(2) The term 'fitness for duty in the reserve components' refers only to military-unique service requirements that attend to military service generally, including service in the reserve components or service on active duty.".

(c) CONFORMING AMENDMENT.—Section 7511 of title 5, United States Code, is amended by striking paragraph (5).

SEC. 513. INAPPLICABILITY OF CERTAIN LAWS TO NATIONAL GUARD TECHNICIANS PERFORMING ACTIVE GUARD AND RESERVE DUTY.

Section 709(g) of title 32, United States Code, as amended by section 512(a)(2), is further amended—

(1) by inserting "(1)" after "(g)"; and

(2) by adding at the end the following new paragraph:

"(2) In addition to the sections referred to in paragraph (1), section 6323(a)(1) of title 5 also does not apply to a person employed under this section who is performing active Guard and Reserve duty (as that term is defined in section 101(d)(6) of title 10).".

SEC. 514. EXTENSION OF REMOVAL OF RESTRICTIONS ON THE TRANSFER OF OFFICERS BETWEEN THE ACTIVE AND INACTIVE NATIONAL GUARD.

Section 512 of the National Defense Authorization Act for Fiscal Year 2014 (Public Law 113–66; 127 Stat. 752; 32 U.S.C. prec. 301 note) is amended—

(1) in subsection (a) in the matter preceding paragraph (1), by striking "December 31, 2016" and inserting "December 31, 2019"; and

(2) in subsection (b) in the matter preceding paragraph (1), by striking "December 31, 2016" and inserting "December 31, 2019".

SEC. 515. EXTENSION OF TEMPORARY AUTHORITY TO USE AIR FORCE RESERVE COMPONENT PERSONNEL TO PROVIDE TRAINING AND INSTRUCTION REGARDING PILOT TRAINING.

Section 514(a)(1) of the National Defense Authorization Act for Fiscal Year 2016 (Public Law 114–92; 129 Stat. 810) is amended by inserting "and fiscal year 2017" after "During fiscal year 2016".

SEC. 516. EXPANSION OF ELIGIBILITY FOR DEPUTY COMMANDER OF COMBATANT COMMAND HAVING UNITED STATES AMONG GEOGRAPHIC AREA OF RESPONSIBILITY TO INCLUDE OFFICERS OF THE RESERVES.

Section 164(e)(4) of title 10, United States Code, is amended—

(1) by striking "the National Guard" and inserting "a reserve component of the armed forces"; and

(2) by striking "a National Guard officer" and inserting "a reserve component officer".

Subtitle C—General Service Authorities

SEC. 521. MATTERS RELATING TO PROVISION OF LEAVE FOR MEMBERS OF THE ARMED FORCES, INCLUDING PROHIBITION ON LEAVE NOT EXPRESSLY AUTHORIZED BY LAW.

(a) PRIMARY AND SECONDARY CAREGIVER LEAVE.—Section 701 of title 10, United States Code, is amended—

(1) by striking subsections (i) and (j); and

(2) by inserting after subsection (h) the following new subsections (i) and (j):

"(i)(1)(A) Under regulations prescribed by the Secretary of Defense, a member of the armed forces described in paragraph (2) who is the primary caregiver in the case of the birth of a child is allowed up to twelve weeks of total leave, including up to six weeks of medical convalescent leave, to be used in connection with such birth.

"(B) Under the regulations prescribed for purposes of this subsection, a member of the armed forces described in paragraph (2) who is the primary caregiver in the case of the adoption of a child is allowed up to six weeks of total leave to be used in connection with such adoption.

"(2) Paragraph (1) applies to the following members:

"(A) A member on active duty.

"(B) A member of a reserve component performing active Guard and Reserve duty.

"(C) A member of a reserve component subject to an active duty recall or mobilization order in excess of 12 months.

"(3) The Secretary shall prescribe in the regulations referred to in paragraph (1) a definition of the term 'primary caregiver' for purposes of this subsection.

"(4) Notwithstanding paragraph (1)(A), a member may receive more than six weeks of medical convalescent leave in connection with the birth of a child, but only if the additional medical convalescent leave—

"(A) is specifically recommended, in writing, by the medical provider of the member to address a diagnosed medical condition; and

"(B) is approved by the commander of the member.

"(5) Any leave taken by a member under this subsection, including leave under paragraphs (1) and (4), may be taken only in one increment in connection with such birth or adoption.

"(6)(A) Any leave authorized by this subsection that is not taken within one year of such birth or adoption shall be forfeited.

"(B) Any leave authorized by this subsection for a member of a reserve component on active duty that is not taken by the time the member is separated from active duty shall be forfeited at that time.

"(7) The period of active duty of a member of a reserve component may not be extended in order to permit the member to take leave authorized by this subsection.

"(8) Under the regulations prescribed for purposes of this subsection, a member taking leave under paragraph (1) may, as a condition for taking such leave, be required—

"(A) to accept an extension of the member's current service obligation, if any, by one week for every week of leave taken under paragraph (1); or

"(B) to incur a reduction in the member's leave account by one week for every week of leave taken under paragraph (1).

"(9)(A) Leave authorized by this subsection is in addition to any other leave provided under other provisions of this section.

"(B) Medical convalescent leave under paragraph (4) is in addition to any other leave provided under other provisions of this subsection.

"(10)(A) Subject to subparagraph (B), a member taking leave under paragraph (1) during a period of obligated service shall not be eligible for terminal leave, or to sell back leave, at the end such period of obligated service.

"(B) Under the regulations for purposes of this subsection, the Secretary concerned may waive, whether in whole or in part, the applicability of subparagraph (A) to a member who reenlists at the end of the member's period of obligated service described in that subparagraph if the Secretary determines that the waiver is in the interests of the armed force concerned.

"(j)(1) Under regulations prescribed by the Secretary of Defense, a member of the armed forces described in subsection (i)(2) who is the secondary caregiver in the case of the birth of a child or the adoption of a child is allowed up to 21 days of leave to be used in connection with such birth or adoption.

"(2) The Secretary shall prescribe in the regulations referred to in paragraph (1) a definition of the term 'secondary caregiver' for purposes of this subsection.

"(3) Any leave taken by a member under this subsection may be taken only in one increment in connection with such birth or adoption.

"(4) Under the regulations prescribed for purposes of this subsection, paragraphs (6) through (10) of subsection (i) (other than paragraph (9)(B) of such subsection) shall apply to leave, and the taking of leave, authorized by this subsection.".

(b) PROHIBITION ON LEAVE NOT EXPRESSLY AUTHORIZED BY LAW.—

(1) PROHIBITION.—Chapter 40 of title 10, United States Code, is amended by inserting after section 704 the following new section:

"§ 704a. Administration of leave: prohibition on authorizing, granting, or assigning leave not expressly authorized by law

"No member or category of members of the armed forces may be authorized, granted, or assigned leave, including uncharged leave, not expressly authorized by a provision of this chapter or another statute unless expressly authorized by an Act of Congress enacted after the date of the enactment of the National Defense Authorization Act for Fiscal Year 2017.".

(2) CLERICAL AMENDMENT.—The table of sections at the beginning of chapter 40 of title 10, United States Code, is amended by inserting after the item relating to section 704 the following new item:

"704a. Administration of leave: prohibition on authorizing, granting, or assigning leave not expressly authorized by law.".

SEC. 522. TRANSFER OF PROVISION RELATING TO EXPENSES INCURRED IN CONNECTION WITH LEAVE CANCELED DUE TO CONTINGENCY OPERATIONS.

(a) ENACTMENT IN TITLE 10, UNITED STATES CODE, OF AUTHORITY FOR REIMBURSEMENT OF EXPENSES.—Chapter 40 of title 10, United States Code, is amended by inserting after section 709 the following new section:

"§ 709a. Expenses incurred in connection with leave canceled due to contingency operations: reimbursement

"(a) AUTHORIZATION TO REIMBURSE.—The Secretary concerned may reimburse a member of the armed forces under the jurisdiction of the Secretary for travel and related expenses (to the extent not otherwise reimbursable under law) incurred by the member as a result of the cancellation of previously approved leave when—

"(1) the leave is canceled in connection with the member's participation in a contingency operation; and

"(2) the cancellation occurs within 48 hours of the time the leave would have commenced.

"(b) REGULATIONS.—The Secretary of Defense and, in the case of the Coast Guard when it is not operating as a service in the Navy, the Secretary of Homeland Security shall prescribe regulations to establish the criteria for the applicability of subsection (a).

"(c) CONCLUSIVENESS OF SETTLEMENT.—The settlement of an application for reimbursement under subsection (a) is final and conclusive.".

(b) CLERICAL AMENDMENT.—The table of sections at the beginning of chapter 40 of such title is amended by inserting after the item relating to section 709 the following new item:

"709a. Expenses incurred in connection with leave canceled due to contingency operations: reimbursement.".

(c) REPEAL OF SUPERSEDED AUTHORITY.—Section 453 of title 37, United States Code, is amended by striking subsection (g).

SEC. 523. EXPANSION OF AUTHORITY TO EXECUTE CERTAIN MILITARY INSTRUMENTS.

(a) EXPANSION OF AUTHORITY TO EXECUTE MILITARY TESTAMENTARY INSTRUMENTS.—Section 1044d(c) of title 10, United States Code, is amended—

(1) by striking paragraph (2) and inserting the following:

"(2) the execution of the instrument is notarized by—

"(A) a military legal assistance counsel;

"(B) a person who is authorized to act as a notary under section 1044a of this title who—

"(i) is not an attorney; and

"(ii) is supervised by a military legal assistance counsel; or

"(C) a State-licensed notary employed by a military department or the Coast Guard who is supervised by a military legal assistance counsel;"; and

(2) in paragraph (3), by striking *"presiding attorney"* and inserting *"person notarizing the instrument in accordance with paragraph (2)".*

(b) EXPANSION OF AUTHORITY TO NOTARIZE DOCUMENTS TO CIVILIANS SERVING IN MILITARY LEGAL ASSISTANCE OFFICES.—Section 1044a(b) of title 10, United States Code, is amended by adding at the end the following new paragraph:

"(6) All civilian paralegals serving at military legal assistance offices, supervised by a military legal assistance counsel (as defined in section 1044d(g) of this title).".

SEC. 524. MEDICAL EXAMINATION BEFORE ADMINISTRATIVE SEPARATION FOR MEMBERS WITH POST-TRAUMATIC STRESS DISORDER OR TRAUMATIC BRAIN INJURY IN CONNECTION WITH SEXUAL ASSAULT.

Section 1177(a)(1) of title 10, United States Code, is amended—

(1) by inserting *", or sexually assaulted,"* after *"deployed overseas in support of a contingency operation"*; and

(2) by inserting *"or based on such sexual assault,"* after *"while deployed,".*

SEC. 525. REDUCTION OF TENURE ON THE TEMPORARY DISABILITY RETIRED LIST.

(a) REDUCTION OF TENURE.—Section 1210 of title 10, United States Code, is amended—

(1) in subsection (b), by striking *"five years"* and inserting *"three years"*; and

(2) in subsection (h), by striking *"five years"* and inserting *"three years".*

(b) APPLICABILITY.—The amendments made by subsection (a) shall take effect on January 1, 2017, and shall apply to members of the Armed Forces whose names are placed on the temporary disability retired list on or after that date.

SEC. 526. TECHNICAL CORRECTION TO VOLUNTARY SEPARATION PAY AND BENEFITS.

Section 1175a(j) of title 10, United States Code, is amended—

(1) in paragraph (2)—

(A) by striking *"or 12304"* and inserting *"12304, 12304a, or 12304b"*; and

(B) by striking *"502(f)(1)"* and inserting *"502(f)(1)(A)"*; and

(2) in paragraph (3), by striking *"502(f)(2)"* and inserting *"502(f)(1)(B)".*

SEC. 527. CONSOLIDATION OF ARMY MARKETING AND PILOT PROGRAM ON CONSOLIDATED ARMY RECRUITING.

(a) CONSOLIDATION OF ARMY MARKETING.—Not later than October 1, 2017, the Secretary of the Army shall consolidate into a single organization within the Department of the Army all functions relating to the marketing of the Army and each of the components of the Army in order to assure unity of effort and cost effectiveness in the marketing of the Army and each of the components of the Army.

(b) PILOT PROGRAM ON CONSOLIDATED ARMY RECRUITING.—

(1) PILOT PROGRAM REQUIRED.—Not later than 180 days after the date of the enactment of this Act, the Secretary of the Army shall carry out a pilot program to consolidate the recruiting efforts of the Regular Army, Army Reserve, and Army National Guard under which a recruiter in one of the components participating in the pilot program may recruit individuals to enlist in any of the components regardless of the funding source of the recruiting activity.

(2) CREDIT TOWARD ENLISTMENT GOALS.—Under the pilot program, a recruiter shall receive credit toward periodic enlistment goals for each enlistment regardless of the component in which the individual enlists.

(3) DURATION.—The Secretary shall carry out the pilot program for a period of not less than three years.

(c) BRIEFING AND REPORTS.—

(1) BRIEFING ON CONSOLIDATION PLAN.—Not later than March 1, 2017, the Secretary of the Army shall provide to the Committees on Armed Services of the Senate and the House of Representatives a briefing on the Secretary's plan to carry out the Army marketing consolidation required by subsection (a).

(2) INTERIM REPORT ON PILOT PROGRAM.—

(A) IN GENERAL.—Not later than one year after the date on which the pilot program under subsection (b) commences, the Secretary shall submit to the congressional committees specified in paragraph (1) a report on the pilot program.

(B) ELEMENTS.—The report under subparagraph (A) shall include each of the following:

(i) An analysis of the effects that consolidated recruiting efforts has on the overall ability of recruiters to attract and place qualified candidates.

(ii) A determination of the extent to which consolidating recruiting efforts affects efficiency and recruiting costs.

(iii) An analysis of any challenges associated with a recruiter working to recruit individuals to enlist in a component in which the recruiter has not served.

(iv) An analysis of the satisfaction of recruiters and the component recruiting commands with the pilot program.

(3) FINAL REPORT ON PILOT PROGRAM.—Not later than 180 days after the date on which the pilot program is completed, the Secretary shall submit to the congressional committees specified in paragraph (1) a final report on the pilot program. The final report shall include any recommendations of the Secretary with respect to extending or making permanent the pilot program and a description of any related legislative actions that the Secretary considers appropriate.

Subtitle D—Member Whistleblower Protections and Correction of Military Records

SEC. 531. IMPROVEMENTS TO WHISTLEBLOWER PROTECTION PROCEDURES.

(a) ACTIONS TREATABLE AS PROHIBITED PERSONNEL ACTIONS.—Paragraph (2) of section 1034(b) of title 10, United States Code, is amended to read as follows:

*"(2)(A) The actions considered for purposes of this section to be a personnel action prohibited by this subsection shall include any action pro-*hibited by paragraph (1), including any of the following:

"(i) The threat to take any unfavorable action.

"(ii) The withholding, or threat to withhold, any favorable action.

"(iii) The making of, or threat to make, a significant change in the duties or responsibilities of a member of the armed forces not commensurate with the member's grade.

"(iv) The failure of a superior to respond to any retaliatory action or harassment (of which the superior had actual knowledge) taken by one or more subordinates against a member.

"(v) The conducting of a retaliatory investigation of a member.

"(B) In this paragraph, the term 'retaliatory investigation' means an investigation requested, directed, initiated, or conducted for the primary purpose of punishing, harassing, or ostracizing a member of the armed forces for making a protected communication.

"(C) Nothing in this paragraph shall be construed to limit the ability of a commander to consult with a superior in the chain of command, an inspector general, or a judge advocate general on the disposition of a complaint against a member of the armed forces for an allegation of collateral misconduct or for a matter unrelated to a protected communication. Such consultation shall provide an affirmative defense against an allegation that a member requested, directed, initiated, or conducted a retaliatory investigation under this section.".

(b) ACTION IN RESPONSE TO HARDSHIP IN CONNECTION WITH PERSONNEL ACTIONS.—Section 1034 of title 10, United States Code, is amended—

(1) in subsection (c)(4)—

(A) by redesignating subparagraph (E) as subparagraph (F); and

(B) by inserting after subparagraph (D) the following new subparagraph (E):

"(E) If the Inspector General makes a preliminary determination in an investigation under subparagraph (D) that, more likely than not, a personnel action prohibited by subsection (b) has occurred and the personnel action will result in an immediate hardship to the member alleging the personnel action, the Inspector General shall promptly notify the Secretary of the military department concerned or the Secretary of Homeland Security, as applicable, of the hardship, and such Secretary shall take such action as such Secretary considers appropriate."; and

(2) in subsection (e)(1), by striking *"subsection (c)(4)(E)"* and inserting *"subsection (c)(4)(F)".*

(c) PERIODIC NOTICE TO MEMBERS ON PROGRESS OF INSPECTOR GENERAL INVESTIGATIONS.—Paragraph (3) of section 1034(e) of title 10, United States Code, is amended to read as follows:

"(3)(A) Not later than 180 days after the commencement of an investigation of an allegation under subsection (c)(4), and every 180 days thereafter until the transmission of the report on the investigation under paragraph (1) to the member concerned, the Inspector General conducting the investigation shall submit a notice on the investigation described in subparagraph (B) to the following:

"(i) The member.

"(ii) The Secretary of Defense.

"(iii) The Secretary of the military department concerned, or the Secretary of Homeland Security in the case of a member of the Coast Guard when the Coast Guard is not operating as a service in the Navy.

"(B) Each notice on an investigation under subparagraph (A) shall include the following:

"(i) A description of the current progress of the investigation.

"(ii) An estimate of the time remaining until the completion of the investigation and the

transmittal of the report required by paragraph (1) to the member concerned.''.

(d) CORRECTION OF RECORDS.—Paragraph (2) of section 1034(g) of title 10, United States Code, is amended to read as follows:

''(2) In resolving an application described in paragraph (1) for which there is a report of the Inspector General under subsection (e)(1), a correction board—

''(A) shall review the report of the Inspector General;

''(B) may request the Inspector General to gather further evidence;

''(C) may receive oral argument, examine and cross-examine witnesses, and take depositions; and

''(D) shall consider a request by a member or former member in determining whether to hold an evidentiary hearing.''.

(e) UNIFORM STANDARDS FOR INSPECTOR GENERAL INVESTIGATIONS OF PROHIBITED PERSONNEL ACTIONS AND OTHER MATTERS.—

(1) IN GENERAL.—Not later than one year after the date of the enactment of this Act, the Inspector General of the Department of Defense shall prescribe uniform standards for the following:

(A) The investigation of allegations of prohibited personnel actions under section 1034 of title 10, United States Code (as amended by this section), by the Inspector General and the Inspectors General of the military departments.

(B) The training of the staffs of the Inspectors General referred to in subparagraph (A) on the conduct of investigations described in that subparagraph.

(2) USE.—Commencing 180 days after prescription of the standards required by paragraph (1), the Inspectors General referred to in that paragraph shall comply with such standards in the conduct of investigations described in that paragraph and in the training of the staffs of such Inspectors General in the conduct of such investigations.

SEC. 532. MODIFICATION OF WHISTLEBLOWER PROTECTION AUTHORITIES TO RESTRICT CONTRARY FINDINGS OF PROHIBITED PERSONNEL ACTION BY THE SECRETARY CONCERNED.

(a) IN GENERAL.—Section 1034(f) of title 10, United States Code, is amended—

(1) in the subsection heading, by striking ''VIOLATIONS'' and inserting ''SUBSTANTIATED VIOLATIONS''; and

(2) in paragraph (1), by striking ''there is sufficient basis'' and all that follows and inserting ''corrective or disciplinary action should be taken. If the Secretary concerned determines that corrective or disciplinary action should be taken, the Secretary shall take appropriate corrective or disciplinary action.''.

(b) ACTIONS FOLLOWING DETERMINATIONS.—Paragraph (2) of such section is amended—

(1) in the matter preceding subparagraph (A)—

(A) by striking ''the Secretary concerned determines under paragraph (1)'' and inserting ''the Inspector General determines''; and

(B) by striking ''the Secretary shall'' and inserting ''the Secretary concerned shall'';

(2) in subparagraph (A), by inserting '', including referring the report to the appropriate board for the correction of military records'' before the semicolon; and

(3) by striking subparagraph (B) and inserting the following new subparagraph (B):

''(B) submit to the Inspector General a report on the actions taken by the Secretary pursuant to this paragraph, and provide for the inclusion of a summary of the report under this subparagraph (with any personally identifiable information redacted) in the semiannual report to Congress of the Inspector General of the Department of Defense or the Inspector General of the Department of Homeland Security, as applica-

ble, under section 5 of the Inspector General Act of 1978 (5 U.S.C. App.).''.

(c) EFFECTIVE DATE.—The amendments made by this section shall take effect on the date of the enactment of this Act, and shall apply with respect to reports received by the Secretaries of the military departments and the Secretary of Homeland Security under section 1034(e) of title 10, United States Code, on or after that date.

SEC. 533. AVAILABILITY OF CERTAIN CORRECTION OF MILITARY RECORDS AND DISCHARGE REVIEW BOARD INFORMATION THROUGH THE INTERNET.

(a) BOARD FOR THE CORRECTION OF MILITARY RECORDS.—Section 1552 of title 10, United States Code, is amended—

(1) by redesignating subsection (h) as subsection (i); and

(2) by inserting after subsection (g) the following new subsection (h):

''(h) Each board established under this section shall make available to the public each calender quarter, on an Internet website of the military department concerned or the Department of Homeland Security, as applicable, that is available to the public the following:

''(1) The number of claims considered by such board during the calendar quarter preceding the calender quarter in which such information is made available, including cases in which a mental health condition of the claimant, including post-traumatic stress disorder or traumatic brain injury, is alleged to have contributed, whether in whole or part, to the original characterization of the discharge or release of the claimant.

''(2) The number of claims submitted during the calendar quarter preceding the calender quarter in which such information is made available that relate to service by a claimant during a war or contingency operation, catalogued by each war or contingency operation.

''(3) The number of military records corrected pursuant to the consideration described in paragraph (1) to upgrade the characterization of discharge or release of claimants.''.

(b) DISCHARGE REVIEW BOARD.—Section 1553 of title 10, United States Code, is amended by adding at the end the following new subsection:

''(f) Each board established under this section shall make available to the public each calender quarter, on an Internet website of the military department concerned or the Department of Homeland Security, as applicable, that is available to the public the following:

''(1) The number of motions or requests for review considered by such board during the calendar quarter preceding the calender quarter in which such information is made available, including cases in which a mental health condition of the former member, including post-traumatic stress disorder or traumatic brain injury, is alleged to have contributed, whether in whole or part, to the original characterization of the discharge or dismissal of the former member.

''(2) The number of claims submitted during the calendar quarter preceding the calender quarter in which such information is made available that relate to service by a claimant during a war or contingency operation, catalogued by each war or contingency operation.

''(3) The number of discharges or dismissals corrected pursuant to the consideration described in paragraph (1) to upgrade the characterization of discharge or dismissal of former members.''.

SEC. 534. IMPROVEMENTS TO AUTHORITIES AND PROCEDURES FOR THE CORRECTION OF MILITARY RECORDS.

(a) PROCEDURES OF BOARDS.—Paragraph (3) of section 1552(a) of title 10, United States Code, is amended—

(1) by inserting ''(A)'' after ''(3)''; and

(2) by adding at the end the following new subparagraphs:

''(B) If a board makes a preliminary determination that a claim under this section lacks sufficient information or documents to support the claim, the board shall notify the claimant, in writing, indicating the specific information or documents necessary to make the claim complete and reviewable by the board.

''(C) If a claimant is unable to provide military personnel or medical records applicable to a claim under this section, the board shall make reasonable efforts to obtain the records. A claimant shall provide the board with documentary evidence of the efforts of the claimant to obtain such records. The board shall inform the claimant of the results of the board's efforts, and shall provide the claimant copies of any records so obtained upon request of the claimant.

''(D) Any request for reconsideration of a determination of a board under this section, no matter when filed, shall be reconsidered by a board under this section if supported by materials not previously presented to or considered by the board in making such determination.''.

(b) PUBLICATION OF FINAL DECISIONS OF BOARDS.—Such section is further amended by adding at the end the following new paragraph:

''(5) Each final decision of a board under this subsection shall be made available to the public in electronic form on a centralized Internet website. In any decision so made available to the public there shall be redacted all personally identifiable information.''.

(c) TRAINING OF MEMBERS OF BOARDS.—

(1) IN GENERAL.—Not later than one year after the date of the enactment of this Act, each Secretary concerned shall develop and implement a comprehensive training curriculum for members of boards for the correction of military records under the jurisdiction of such Secretary in the duties of such boards under section 1552 of title 10, United States Code. The curriculum shall address all areas of administrative law applicable to the duties of such boards.

(2) UNIFORM CURRICULA.—The Secretary of Defense and the Secretary of Homeland Security shall jointly ensure that the curricula developed and implemented pursuant to this subsection are, to the extent practicable, uniform.

(3) TRAINING.—

(A) IN GENERAL.—Each member of a board for the correction of military records shall undergo retraining (consistent with the curriculum developed and implemented pursuant to this subsection) regarding the duties of boards for the correction of military records under section 1552 of title 10, United States Code, at least once every five years during the member's tenure on the board.

(B) CURRENT MEMBERS.—Each member of a board for the correction of military records as of the date of the implementation of the curriculum required by paragraph (1) (in this paragraph referred to as the ''curriculum implementation date'') shall undergo training described in subparagraph (A) not later than 90 days after the curriculum implementation date.

(C) NEW MEMBERS.—Each individual who becomes a member of a board for the correction of military records after the curriculum implementation date shall undergo training described in subparagraph (A) by not later than 90 days after the date on which such individual becomes a member of the board.

(4) REPORTS.—Not later than 18 months after the date of the enactment of this Act, each Secretary concerned shall submit to Congress a report setting forth the following:

(A) A description and assessment of the progress made by such Secretary in implementing training requirements for members of boards for the correction of military records under the jurisdiction of such Secretary.

(B) A detailed description of the training curriculum required of such Secretary by paragraph (1).

(C) A description and assessment of any impediments to the implementation of training requirements for members of boards for the correction of military records under the jurisdiction of such Secretary.

(5) SECRETARY CONCERNED DEFINED.—In this subsection, the term "Secretary concerned" means a "Secretary concerned" as that term is used in section 1552 of title 10, United States Code.

SEC. 535. TREATMENT BY DISCHARGE REVIEW BOARDS OF CLAIMS ASSERTING POST-TRAUMATIC STRESS DISORDER OR TRAUMATIC BRAIN INJURY IN CONNECTION WITH COMBAT OR SEXUAL TRAUMA AS A BASIS FOR REVIEW OF DISCHARGE.

Section 1553(d) of title 10, United States Code, is amended by adding at the end the following new paragraph:

"(3)(A) In addition to the requirements of paragraphs (1) and (2), in the case of a former member described in subparagraph (B), the Board shall—

"(i) review medical evidence of the Secretary of Veterans Affairs or a civilian health care provider that is presented by the former member; and

"(ii) review the case with liberal consideration to the former member that post-traumatic stress disorder or traumatic brain injury potentially contributed to the circumstances resulting in the discharge of a lesser characterization.

"(B) A former member described in this subparagraph is a former member described in paragraph (1) or a former member whose application for relief is based in whole or in part on matters relating to post-traumatic stress disorder or traumatic brain injury as supporting rationale, or as justification for priority consideration, whose post-traumatic stress disorder or traumatic brain injury is related to combat or military sexual trauma, as determined by the Secretary concerned.".

SEC. 536. COMPTROLLER GENERAL OF THE UNITED STATES REVIEW OF INTEGRITY OF DEPARTMENT OF DEFENSE WHISTLEBLOWER PROGRAM.

(a) REPORT REQUIRED.—Not later than 18 months after the date of the enactment of this Act, the Comptroller General of the United States shall submit to the Committees on Armed Services of the Senate and the House of Representatives a report setting forth a review of the integrity of the Department of Defense whistleblower program.

(b) ELEMENTS.—The review for purposes of the report required by subsection (a) shall include the following elements:

(1) An assessment of the extent to which the Department of Defense whistleblower program meets executive branch policies and goals for whistleblower protections.

(2) An assessment of the adequacy of procedures to handle and address complaints submitted by employees in the Office of the Inspector General of the Department of Defense to ensure that such employees themselves are able to disclose a suspected violation of law, rule, or regulation without fear of reprisal.

(3) An assessment of the extent to which there have been violations of standards used in regard to the protection of confidentiality provided to whistleblowers by the Inspector General of the Department of Defense.

(4) An assessment of the extent to which there have been incidents of retaliatory investigations against whistleblowers within the Office of the Inspector General.

(5) An assessment of the extent to which the Inspector General of the Department of Defense has thoroughly investigated and substantiated allegations within the past 10 years against civilian officials of the Department of Defense appointed to their positions by and with the advice

and consent of the Senate, and whether Congress has been notified of the results of such investigations.

(6) An assessment of the ability of the Inspector General of the Department of Defense and the Inspectors General of the military departments to access agency information necessary to the execution of their duties, including classified and other sensitive information, and an assessment of the adequacy of security procedures to safeguard such classified or sensitive information when so accessed.

Subtitle E—Military Justice and Legal Assistance Matters

SEC. 541. UNITED STATES COURT OF APPEALS FOR THE ARMED FORCES.

(a) CLARIFICATION OF AUTHORITY OF JUDGES OF THE COURT TO ADMINISTER OATHS AND ACKNOWLEDGMENTS.—Subsection (c) of section 936 of title 10, United States Code (article 136 of the Uniform Code of Military Justice), is amended to read as follows:

"(c) Each judge and senior judge of the United States Court of Appeals for the Armed Forces shall have the powers relating to oaths, affirmations, and acknowledgments provided to justices and judges of the United States by section 459 of title 28.".

(b) MODIFICATION OF TERM OF JUDGES OF THE COURT TO RESTORE ROTATION OF JUDGES.—

(1) EARLY RETIREMENT AUTHORIZED FOR ONE CURRENT JUDGE.—If the judge of the United States Court of Appeals for the Armed Forces who is the junior in seniority of the two judges of the court whose terms of office under section 942(b)(2) of title 10, United States Code (article 142(b)(2) of the Uniform Code of Military Justice), expire on July 31, 2021, chooses to retire one year early, that judge—

(A) may retire from service on the court effective August 1, 2020; and

(B) shall be treated, upon such retirement, for all purposes as having completed a term of service for which the judge was appointed as a judge of the court.

(2) STAGGERING OF FUTURE APPOINTMENTS.—Section 942(b)(2) of title 10, United States Code (article 142(b)(2) of the Uniform Code of Military Justice), is amended—

(A) by inserting "(A)" after "(2)";

(B) by redesignating subparagraphs (A) and (B) as clauses (i) and (ii), respectively; and

(C) by adding at the end the following new subparagraph:

"(B) If at the time of the appointment of a judge the date that is otherwise applicable under subparagraph (A) for the expiration of the term of service of the judge is the same as the date for the expiration of the term of service of a judge already on the court, then the term of the judge being appointed shall expire on the first July 31 after such date on which no term of service of a judge already on the court will expire.".

(3) APPLICATION OF AMENDMENTS.—The amendments made by paragraph (2) shall apply with respect to appointments to the United States Court of Appeals for the Armed Forces that are made on or after the date of the enactment of this Act.

(c) REPEAL OF REQUIREMENT RELATING TO POLITICAL PARTY STATUS OF JUDGES OF THE COURT.—Section 942(b)(3) of title 10, United States Code (article 142(b)(3) of the Uniform Code of Military Justice), is amended by striking "Not more than three of the judges of the court may be appointed from the same political party, and no" and by inserting "No".

(d) MODIFICATION OF DAILY RATE OF COMPENSATION FOR SENIOR JUDGES PERFORMING JUDICIAL DUTIES WITH THE COURT.—Section 942(e)(2) of title 10, United States Code (article 142(e)(2) of the Uniform Code of Military Justice), is amended by striking "equal to" and all

that follows and inserting "equal to the difference between—

"(A) the daily equivalent of the annual rate of pay provided for a judge of the court; and

"(B) the daily equivalent of the annuity of the judge under section 945 of this title (article 145), the applicable provisions of title 5, or any other retirement system for employees of the Federal Government under which the senior judge receives an annuity.".

(e) REPEAL OF DUAL COMPENSATION PROVISION RELATING TO JUDGES OF THE COURT.—Section 945 of title 10, United States Code (article 145 of the Uniform Code of Military Justice), is amended—

(1) in subsection (d), by striking "subsection (g)(1)(B)" and inserting "subsection (f)(1)(B)";

(2) by striking subsection (f); and

(3) by redesignating subsections (g), (h), and (i) as subsections (f), (g), and (h), respectively.

SEC. 542. EFFECTIVE PROSECUTION AND DEFENSE IN COURTS-MARTIAL AND PILOT PROGRAMS ON PROFESSIONAL MILITARY JUSTICE DEVELOPMENT FOR JUDGE ADVOCATES.

(a) PROGRAM FOR EFFECTIVE PROSECUTION AND DEFENSE.—The Secretary concerned shall carry out a program to ensure that—

(1) trial counsel and defense counsel detailed to prosecute or defend a court-martial have sufficient experience and knowledge to effectively prosecute or defend the case; and

(2) a deliberate professional developmental process is in place to ensure effective prosecution and defense in all courts-martial.

(b) MILITARY JUSTICE EXPERIENCE DESIGNATORS OR SKILL IDENTIFIERS.—The Secretary concerned shall establish and use a system of military justice experience designators or skill identifiers for purposes of identifying judge advocates with skill and experience in military justice proceedings in order to ensure that judge advocates with experience and skills identified through such experience designators or skill identifiers are assigned to develop less experienced judge advocates in the prosecution and defense in courts-martial under a program carried out pursuant to subsection (a).

(c) PILOT PROGRAMS ON PROFESSIONAL DEVELOPMENTAL PROCESS FOR JUDGE ADVOCATES.—

(1) PURPOSE.—The Secretary concerned shall carry out a pilot program to assess the feasibility and advisability of establishing a deliberate professional developmental process for judge advocates under the jurisdiction of the Secretary that leads to judge advocates with military justice expertise serving as military justice practitioners capable of prosecuting and defending complex cases in military courts-martial.

(2) ADDITIONAL MATTERS.—A pilot program may also assess such other matters related to professional military justice development for judge advocates as the Secretary concerned considers appropriate.

(3) DURATION.—Each pilot program shall be for a period of five years.

(4) REPORT.—Not later than four years after the date of the enactment of this Act, the Secretary concerned shall submit to the Committees on Armed Services of the Senate and the House of Representatives a report on the pilot programs conducted under this section. The report shall include the following:

(A) A description and assessment of each pilot program.

(B) Such recommendations as the Secretary considers appropriate in light of the pilot programs, including whether any pilot program should be extended or made permanent.

(d) SECRETARY CONCERNED DEFINED.—In this section, the term "Secretary concerned" has the meaning given that term in section 101(a)(9) of title 10, United States Code.

SEC. 543. INCLUSION IN ANNUAL REPORTS ON SEXUAL ASSAULT PREVENTION AND RESPONSE EFFORTS OF THE ARMED FORCES OF INFORMATION ON COMPLAINTS OF RETALIATION IN CONNECTION WITH REPORTS OF SEXUAL ASSAULT IN THE ARMED FORCES.

Section 1631(b) of the Ike Skelton National Defense Authorization Act for Fiscal Year 2011 (Public Law 111–383; 10 U.S.C. 1561 note) is amended by adding at the end the following new paragraph:

"(12) Information on each claim of retaliation in connection with a report of sexual assault in the Armed Force made by or against a member of such Armed Force as follows:

"(A) A narrative description of each complaint.

"(B) The nature of such complaint, including whether the complainant claims professional or social retaliation.

"(C) The gender of the complainant.

"(D) The gender of the individual claimed to have committed the retaliation.

"(E) The nature of the relationship between the complainant and the individual claimed to have committed the retaliation.

"(F) The nature of the relationship, if any, between the individual alleged to have committed the sexual assault concerned and the individual claimed to have committed the retaliation.

"(G) The official or office that received the complaint.

"(H) The organization that investigated or is investigating the complaint.

"(I) The current status of the investigation.

"(J) If the investigation is complete, a description of the results of the investigation, including whether the results of the investigation were provided to the complainant.

"(K) If the investigation determined that retaliation occurred, whether the retaliation was an offense under chapter 47 of title 10, United States Code (the Uniform Code of Military Justice).".

SEC. 544. EXTENSION OF THE REQUIREMENT FOR ANNUAL REPORT REGARDING SEXUAL ASSAULTS AND COORDINATION WITH RELEASE OF FAMILY ADVOCACY PROGRAM REPORT.

Section 1631 of the Ike Skelton National Defense Authorization Act for Fiscal Year 2011 (Public Law 111–383; 124 Stat. 4433; 10 U.S.C. 1561 note) is amended—

(1) in subsection (a), by striking "March 1, 2017" and inserting "March 1, 2021"; and

(2) by adding at the end the following new subsection:

"(g) COORDINATION OF RELEASE DATE BETWEEN ANNUAL REPORTS REGARDING SEXUAL ASSAULTS AND FAMILY ADVOCACY REPORT.—The Secretary of Defense shall ensure that the reports required under subsection (a) for a given year are delivered to the Committees on Armed Services of the Senate and House of Representatives simultaneously with the Family Advocacy Program report for that year regarding child abuse and domestic violence, as required by section 574 of the National Defense Authorization Act for Fiscal Year 2017.".

SEC. 545. METRICS FOR EVALUATING THE EFFORTS OF THE ARMED FORCES TO PREVENT AND RESPOND TO RETALIATION IN CONNECTION WITH REPORTS OF SEXUAL ASSAULT IN THE ARMED FORCES.

(a) METRICS REQUIRED.—The Sexual Assault Prevention and Response Office of the Department of Defense shall establish and issue to the military departments metrics to be used to evaluate the efforts of the Armed Forces to prevent and respond to retaliation in connection with reports of sexual assault in the Armed Forces.

(b) BEST PRACTICES.—For purposes of enhancing and achieving uniformity in the efforts of the Armed Forces to prevent and respond to retaliation in connection with reports of sexual assault in the Armed Forces, the Sexual Assault Prevention and Response Office shall identify and issue to the military departments best practices to be used in the prevention of and response to retaliation in connection with such reports.

SEC. 546. TRAINING FOR DEPARTMENT OF DEFENSE PERSONNEL WHO INVESTIGATE CLAIMS OF RETALIATION.

(a) TRAINING REGARDING NATURE AND CONSEQUENCES OF RETALIATION.—The Secretary of Defense shall ensure that the personnel of the Department of Defense specified in subsection (b) who investigate claims of retaliation receive training on the nature and consequences of retaliation, and, in cases involving reports of sexual assault, the nature and consequences of sexual assault trauma. The training shall include such elements as the Secretary shall specify for purposes of this section.

(b) COVERED PERSONNEL.—The personnel of the Department of Defense covered by subsection (a) are the following:

(1) Personnel of military criminal investigation services.

(2) Personnel of Inspectors General offices.

(3) Personnel of any command of the Armed Forces who are assignable by the commander of such command to investigate claims of retaliation made by or against members of such command.

(c) RETALIATION DEFINED.—In this section, the term "retaliation" has the meaning given the term by the Secretary of Defense in the strategy required by section 539 of the National Defense Authorization Act of Fiscal Year 2016 (Public Law 114–92; 129 Stat. 818) or a subsequent meaning specified by the Secretary.

SEC. 547. NOTIFICATION TO COMPLAINANTS OF RESOLUTION OF INVESTIGATIONS INTO RETALIATION.

(a) NOTIFICATION REQUIRED.—

(1) MEMBERS OF THE ARMY, NAVY, AIR FORCE, AND MARINE CORPS.—Under regulations prescribed by the Secretary of Defense, upon the conclusion of an investigation by an office, element, or personnel of the Department of Defense or of the Armed Forces of a complaint by a member of the Armed Forces of retaliation, the member shall be informed in writing of the results of the investigation, including whether the complaint was substantiated, unsubstantiated, or dismissed.

(2) MEMBERS OF COAST GUARD.—The Secretary of Homeland Security shall provide in a similar manner for notification in writing of the results of investigations by offices, elements, or personnel of the Department of Homeland Security or of the Coast Guard of complaints of retaliation made by members of the Coast Guard when it is not operating as a service in the Navy.

(b) RETALIATION DEFINED.—In this section, the term "retaliation" has the meaning given the term by the Secretary of Defense in the strategy required by section 539 of the National Defense Authorization Act of Fiscal Year 2016 (Public Law 114–92; 129 Stat. 818) or a subsequent meaning specified by the Secretary.

SEC. 548. MODIFICATION OF DEFINITION OF SEXUAL HARASSMENT FOR PURPOSES OF INVESTIGATIONS BY COMMANDING OFFICERS OF COMPLAINTS OF HARASSMENT.

(a) IN GENERAL.—Section 1561(e) of title 10, United States Code, is amended—

(1) in paragraph (1)—

(A) in the matter preceding subparagraph (A), by striking "constituting a form of sex discrimination"; and

(B) in subparagraph (B), by striking "the work environment" and inserting "the environment"; and

(2) in paragraph (3), by striking "in the workplace".

(b) EFFECTIVE DATE.—The amendments made by subsection (a) shall take effect on the date of the enactment of this Act, and shall apply with respect to complaints described in section 1561 of title 10, United States Code, that are first received by a commanding officer or officer in charge on or after that date.

SEC. 549. IMPROVED DEPARTMENT OF DEFENSE PREVENTION OF AND RESPONSE TO HAZING IN THE ARMED FORCES.

(a) ANTI-HAZING DATABASE.—The Secretary of Defense shall provide for the establishment and use of a comprehensive and consistent data-collection system for the collection of reports, including anonymous reports, of incidents of hazing involving a member of the Armed Forces. The Secretary shall issue department-wide guidance regarding the availability and use of the database, including information on protected classes, such as race and religion, who are often the victims of hazing.

(b) IMPROVED TRAINING.—Each Secretary of a military department, in consultation with the Chief of Staff of each Armed Force under the jurisdiction of such Secretary, shall seek to improve training to assist members of the Armed Forces better recognize, prevent, and respond to hazing at all command levels.

(c) ANNUAL REPORTS ON HAZING.—

(1) REPORT REQUIRED.—Not later than January 31 of each year through January 31, 2021, each Secretary of a military department, in consultation with the Chief of Staff of each Armed Force under the jurisdiction of such Secretary, shall submit to the Committees on Armed Services of the Senate and the House of Representatives a report containing a description of efforts during the previous year—

(A) to prevent and respond to incidents of hazing involving members of the Armed Forces;

(B) to track and encourage reporting, including reporting anonymously, incidents of hazing in the Armed Force; and

(C) to ensure the consistent implementation of anti-hazing policies.

(2) ADDITIONAL ELEMENTS.—Each report required by this subsection also shall address the same elements originally addressed in the anti-hazing reports required by section 534 of the National Defense Authorization Act for Fiscal Year 2013 (Public Law 112–239; 126 Stat. 1726).

Subtitle F—National Commission on Military, National, and Public Service

SEC. 551. PURPOSE, SCOPE, AND DEFINITIONS.

(a) PURPOSE.—The purpose of this subtitle is to establish the National Commission on Military, National, and Public Service to—

(1) conduct a review of the military selective service process (commonly referred to as "the draft"); and

(2) consider methods to increase participation in military, national, and public service in order to address national security and other public service needs of the Nation.

(b) SCOPE OF REVIEW.—In order to provide the fullest understanding of the matters required under the review under subsection (a), the Commission shall consider—

(1) the need for a military selective service process, including the continuing need for a mechanism to draft large numbers of replacement combat troops;

(2) means by which to foster a greater attitude and ethos of service among United States youth, including an increased propensity for military service;

(3) the feasibility and advisability of modifying the military selective service process in order to obtain for military, national, and public service individuals with skills (such as medical, dental, and nursing skills, language skills, cyber skills, and science, technology, engineering, and mathematics (STEM) skills) for which the Nation has a critical need, without regard to age or sex; and

(4) the feasibility and advisability of including in the military selective service process, as so modified, an eligibility or entitlement for the receipt of one or more Federal benefits (such as educational benefits, subsidized or secured student loans, grants or hiring preferences) specified by the Commission for purposes of the review.

(c) DEFINITIONS.—In this subtitle:

(1) The term "military service" means active service (as that term is defined in subsection (d)(3) of section 101 of title 10, United States Code) in one of the uniformed services (as that term is defined in subsection (a)(5) of such section).

(2) The term "national service" means civilian employment in Federal or State Government in a field in which the Nation and the public have critical needs.

(3) The term "public service" means civilian employment in any non-governmental capacity, including with private for-profit organizations and non-profit organizations (including with appropriate faith-based organizations), that pursues and enhances the common good and meets the needs of communities, the States, or the Nation in sectors related to security, health, care for the elderly, and other areas considered appropriate by the Commission for purposes of this subtitle.

SEC. 552. PRELIMINARY REPORT ON PURPOSE AND UTILITY OF REGISTRATION SYSTEM UNDER MILITARY SELECTIVE SERVICE ACT.

(a) REPORT REQUIRED.—To assist the Commission in carrying out its duties under this subtitle, the Secretary of Defense shall—

(1) submit, not later than July 1, 2017, to the Committees on Armed Services of the Senate and the House of Representatives and to the Commission a report on the current and future need for a centralized registration system under the Military Selective Service Act (50 U.S.C. 3801 et seq.); and

(2) provide a briefing on the results of the report.

(b) ELEMENTS OF REPORT.—The report required by subsection (a) shall include the following:

(1) A detailed analysis of the current benefits derived, both directly and indirectly, from the Military Selective Service System, including—

(A) the extent to which mandatory registration benefits military recruiting;

(B) the extent to which a national registration capability serves as a deterrent to potential enemies of the United States; and

(C) the extent to which expanding registration to include women would impact these benefits.

(2) An analysis of the functions currently performed by the Selective Service System that would be assumed by the Department of Defense in the absence of a national registration capability.

(3) An analysis of the systems, manpower, and facilities that would be needed by the Department to physically mobilize inductees in the absence of the Selective Service System.

(4) An analysis of the feasibility and utility of eliminating the current focus on mass mobilization of primarily combat troops in favor of a system that focuses on mobilization of all military occupational specialties, and the extent to which such a change would impact the need for both male and female inductees.

(5) A detailed analysis of the Department's personnel needs in the event of an emergency requiring mass mobilization, including—

(A) a detailed timeline, along with the factors considered in arriving at this timeline, of when the Department would require—

(i) the first inductees to report for service;

(ii) the first 100,000 inductees to report for service; and

(iii) the first medical personnel to report for service; and

(B) an analysis of any additional critical skills that would be needed in the event of a national emergency, and a timeline for when the Department would require the first inductees to report for service.

(6) A list of the assumptions used by the Department when conducting its analysis in preparing the report.

(c) COMPTROLLER GENERAL REVIEW.—Not later than December 1, 2017, the Comptroller General of the United States shall submit to the Committees on Armed Services of the Senate and the House of Representatives and to the Commission a review of the procedures used by the Department of Defense in evaluating selective service requirements.

SEC. 553. NATIONAL COMMISSION ON MILITARY, NATIONAL, AND PUBLIC SERVICE.

(a) ESTABLISHMENT.—There is established in the executive branch an independent commission to be known as the National Commission on Military, National, and Public Service (in this subtitle referred to as the "Commission"). The Commission shall be considered an independent establishment of the Federal Government as defined by section 104 of title 5, United States Code, and a temporary organization under section 3161 of such title.

(b) MEMBERSHIP.—

(1) NUMBER AND APPOINTMENT.—The Commission shall be composed of 11 members appointed as follows:

(A) The President shall appoint three members.

(B) The Majority Leader of the Senate shall appoint one member.

(C) The Minority Leader of the Senate shall appoint one member.

(D) The Speaker of the House of Representatives shall appoint one member.

(E) The Minority Leader of the House of Representatives shall appoint one member.

(F) The Chairman of the Committee on Armed Services of the Senate shall appoint one member.

(G) The ranking minority member of the Committee on Armed Services of the Senate shall appoint one member.

(H) The Chairman of the Committee on Armed Services of the House of Representatives shall appoint one member.

(I) The ranking minority member of the Committee on Armed Services of the House of Representatives shall appoint one member.

(2) DEADLINE FOR APPOINTMENT.—Members shall be appointed to the Commission under paragraph (1) not later than 90 days after the Commission establishment date.

(3) EFFECT OF LACK OF APPOINTMENT BY APPOINTMENT DATE.—If one or more appointments under subparagraph (A) of paragraph (1) is not made by the appointment date specified in paragraph (2), the authority to make such appointment or appointments shall expire, and the number of members of the Commission shall be reduced by the number equal to the number of appointments so not made. If an appointment under subparagraph (B), (C), (D), (E), (F), (G), (H), or (I) of paragraph (1) is not made by the appointment date specified in paragraph (2), the authority to make an appointment under such subparagraph shall expire, and the number of members of the Commission shall be reduced by the number equal to the number otherwise appointable under such subparagraph.

(c) CHAIR AND VICE CHAIR.—The Commission shall elect a Chair and Vice Chair from among its members.

(d) TERMS.—Members shall be appointed for the life of the Commission. A vacancy in the Commission shall not affect its powers, and shall be filled in the same manner as the original appointment was made.

(e) STATUS AS FEDERAL EMPLOYEES.—Notwithstanding the requirements of section 2105 of title 5, United States Code, including the required supervision under subsection (a)(3) of such section, the members of the Commission shall be deemed to be Federal employees.

(f) PAY FOR MEMBERS OF THE COMMISSION.—

(1) IN GENERAL.—Each member, other than the Chair, of the Commission shall be paid at a rate equal to the daily equivalent of the annual rate of basic pay payable for level IV of the Executive Schedule under section 5315 of title 5, United States Code, for each day (including travel time) during which the member is engaged in the actual performance of duties vested in the Commission.

(2) CHAIR.—The Chair of the Commission shall be paid at a rate equal to the daily equivalent of the annual rate of basic pay payable for level III of the Executive Schedule under section 5314, of title 5, United States Code, for each day (including travel time) during which the member is engaged in the actual performance of duties vested in the Commission.

(g) USE OF GOVERNMENT INFORMATION.—The Commission may secure directly from any department or agency of the Federal Government such information as the Commission considers necessary to carry out its duties. Upon such request of the chair of the Commission, the head of such department or agency shall furnish such information to the Commission.

(h) POSTAL SERVICES.—The Commission may use the United States mails in the same manner and under the same conditions as departments and agencies of the United States.

(i) AUTHORITY TO ACCEPT GIFTS.—The Commission may accept, use, and dispose of gifts or donations of services, goods, and property from non-Federal entities for the purposes of aiding and facilitating the work of the Commission. The authority in this subsection does not extend to gifts of money.

(j) PERSONAL SERVICES.—

(1) AUTHORITY TO PROCURE.—The Commission may—

(A) procure the services of experts or consultants (or of organizations of experts or consultants) in accordance with the provisions of section 3109 of title 5, United States Code; and

(B) pay in connection with such services travel expenses of individuals, including transportation and per diem in lieu of subsistence, while such individuals are traveling from their homes or places of business to duty stations.

(2) LIMITATION.—The total number of experts or consultants procured pursuant to paragraph (1) may not exceed five experts or consultants.

(3) MAXIMUM DAILY PAY RATES.—The daily rate paid an expert or consultant procured pursuant to paragraph (1) may not exceed the daily rate paid a person occupying a position at level IV of the Executive Schedule under section 5315 of title 5, United States Code.

(k) FUNDING.—Of the amounts authorized to be appropriated by this Act for fiscal year 2017 for the Department of Defense, up to $15,000,000 shall be made available to the Commission to carry out its duties under this subtitle. Funds made available to the Commission under the preceding sentence shall remain available until expended.

SEC. 554. COMMISSION HEARINGS AND MEETINGS.

(a) IN GENERAL.—The Commission shall conduct hearings on the recommendations it is taking under consideration. Any such hearing, except a hearing in which classified information is to be considered, shall be open to the public. Any hearing open to the public shall be announced on a Federal website at least 14 days in advance. For all hearings open to the public, the Commission shall release an agenda and a listing of materials relevant to the topics to be discussed. The Commission is authorized and encouraged to hold hearings and meetings in

various locations throughout the country to provide maximum opportunity for public comment and participation in the Commission's execution of its duties.

(b) MEETINGS.—

(1) INITIAL MEETING.—The Commission shall hold its initial meeting not later than 30 days after the date as of which all members have been appointed.

(2) SUBSEQUENT MEETINGS.—After its initial meeting, the Commission shall meet upon the call of the chair or a majority of its members.

(3) PUBLIC MEETINGS.—Each meeting of the Commission shall be held in public unless any member objects or classified information is to be considered.

(c) QUORUM.—Six members of the Commission shall constitute a quorum, but a lesser number may hold hearings or meetings.

(d) PUBLIC COMMENTS.—

(1) SOLICITATION.—The Commission shall seek written comments from the general public and interested parties on matters of the Commission's review under this subtitle. Comments shall be requested through a solicitation in the Federal Register and announcement on the Internet website of the Commission.

(2) PERIOD FOR SUBMITTAL.—The period for the submittal of comments pursuant to the solicitation under paragraph (1) shall end not earlier than 30 days after the date of the solicitation and shall end on or before the date on which recommendations are transmitted to the Commission under section 555(d).

(3) USE BY COMMISSION.—The Commission shall consider the comments submitted under this subsection when developing its recommendations.

(e) SPACE FOR USE OF COMMISSION.—Not later than 90 days after the date of the enactment of this Act, the Administrator of General Services, in consultation with the Secretary, shall identify and make available suitable excess space within the Federal space inventory to house the operations of the Commission. If the Administrator is not able to make such suitable excess space available within such 90-day period, the Commission may lease space to the extent the funds are available.

(f) CONTRACTING AUTHORITY.—The Commission may acquire administrative supplies and equipment for Commission use to the extent funds are available.

SEC. 555. PRINCIPLES AND PROCEDURE FOR COMMISSION RECOMMENDATIONS.

(a) CONTEXT OF COMMISSION REVIEW.—The Commission shall—

(1) conduct a review of the military selective service process; and

(2) consider methods to increase participation in military, national, and public service opportunities to address national security and other public service needs of the Nation.

(b) DEVELOPMENT OF COMMISSION RECOMMENDATIONS.—The Commission shall develop recommendations on the matters subject to its review under subsection (a) that are consistent with the principles established by the President under subsection (c).

(c) PRESIDENTIAL PRINCIPLES.—

(1) IN GENERAL.—Not later than three months after the Commission establishment date, the President shall establish and transmit to the Commission and Congress principles for reform of the military selective service process, including means by which to best acquire for the Nation skills necessary to meet the military, national, and public service requirements of the Nation in connection with that process.

(2) ELEMENTS.—The principles required under this subsection shall address the following:

(A) Whether, in light of the current and predicted global security environment and the changing nature of warfare, there continues to

be a continuous or potential need for a military selective service process designed to produce large numbers of combat members of the Armed Forces, and if so, whether such a system should include mandatory registration by all citizens and residents, regardless of sex.

(B) The need, and how best to meet the need, of the Nation, the military, the Federal civilian sector, and the private sector (including the non-profit sector) for individuals possessing critical skills and abilities, and how best to employ individuals possessing those skills and abilities for military, national, or public service.

(C) How to foster within the Nation, particularly among United States youth, an increased sense of service and civic responsibility in order to enhance the acquisition by the Nation of critically needed skills through education and training, and how best to acquire those skills for military, national, or public service.

(D) How to increase a propensity among United States youth for service in the military, or alternatively in national or public service, including how to increase the pool of qualified applicants for military service.

(E) The need in Government, including the military, and in the civilian sector to increase interest, education, and employment in certain critical fields, including science, technology, engineering, and mathematics (STEM), national security, cyber, linguistics and foreign language, education, health care, and the medical professions.

(F) How military, national, and public service may be incentivized, including through educational benefits, grants, federally-insured loans, Federal or State hiring preferences, or other mechanisms that the President considers appropriate.

(G) Any other matters the President considers appropriate for purposes of this subtitle.

(d) CABINET RECOMMENDATIONS.—Not later than seven months after the Commission establishment date, the Secretary of Defense, the Attorney General, the Secretary of Homeland Security, the Secretary of Labor, and such other Government officials, and such experts, as the President shall designate for purposes of this subsection shall jointly transmit to the Commission and Congress recommendations for the reform of the military selective service process and military, national, and public service in connection with that process.

(e) COMMISSION REPORT AND RECOMMENDATIONS.—

(1) REPORT.—Not later than 30 months after the Commission establishment date, the Commission shall transmit to the President and Congress a report containing the findings and conclusions of the Commission, together with the recommendations of the Commission regarding the matters reviewed by the Commission pursuant to this subtitle. The Commission shall include in the report legislative language and recommendations for administrative action to implement the recommendations of the Commission. The findings and conclusions in the report shall be based on the review and analysis by the Commission of the recommendations made under subsection (d).

(2) REQUIREMENT FOR APPROVAL.—The recommendations of the Commission must be approved by at least five members of the Commission before the recommendations may be transmitted to the President and Congress under paragraph (1).

(3) PUBLIC AVAILABILITY.—The Commission shall publish a copy of the report required by paragraph (1) on an Internet website available to the public on the same date on which it transmits that report to the President and Congress under that paragraph.

(f) JUDICIAL REVIEW PRECLUDED.—Actions under this section of the President, the officials

specified or designated under subsection (d), and the Commission shall not be subject to judicial review.

SEC. 556. EXECUTIVE DIRECTOR AND STAFF.

(a) EXECUTIVE DIRECTOR.—The Commission shall appoint and fix the rate of basic pay for an Executive Director in accordance with section 3161 of title 5, United States Code.

(b) STAFF.—Subject to subsections (c) and (d), the Executive Director, with the approval of the Commission, may appoint and fix the rate of basic pay for additional personnel as staff of the Commission in accordance with section 3161 of title 5, United States Code.

(c) LIMITATIONS ON STAFF.—

(1) NUMBER OF DETAILEES FROM EXECUTIVE DEPARTMENTS.—Not more than one-third of the personnel employed by or detailed to the Commission may be on detail from the Department of Defense and other executive branch departments.

(2) PRIOR DUTIES WITHIN EXECUTIVE BRANCH.—A person may not be detailed from the Department of Defense or other executive branch department to the Commission if, in the year before the detail is to begin, that person participated personally and substantially in any matter concerning the preparation of recommendations for the military selective service process and military and public service in connection with that process.

(d) LIMITATIONS ON PERFORMANCE REVIEWS.—No member of the uniformed services, and no officer or employee of the Department of Defense or other executive branch department (other than a member of the uniformed services or officer or employee who is detailed to the Commission), may—

(1) prepare any report concerning the effectiveness, fitness, or efficiency of the performance of the staff of the Commission or any person detailed to that staff;

(2) review the preparation of such a report (other than for administrative accuracy); or

(3) approve or disapprove such a report.

SEC. 557. TERMINATION OF COMMISSION.

Except as otherwise provided in this subtitle, the Commission shall terminate not later than 36 months after the Commission establishment date.

Subtitle G—Member Education, Training, Resilience, and Transition

SEC. 561. MODIFICATION OF PROGRAM TO ASSIST MEMBERS OF THE ARMED FORCES IN OBTAINING PROFESSIONAL CREDENTIALS.

(a) SCOPE OF PROGRAM.—Section 2015(a)(1) of title 10, United States Code, is amended by striking "incident to the performance of their military duties".

(b) QUALITY ASSURANCE OF CERTIFICATION PROGRAMS AND STANDARDS.—Section 2015(c) of title 10, United States Code, is amended—

(1) in paragraph (1), by striking "is accredited by an accreditation body that" and all that follows and inserting "meets one of the requirements specified in paragraph (2)."; and

(2) by striking paragraph (2) and inserting the following new paragraph (2):

"(2) The requirements for a credentialing program specified in this paragraph are that the credentialing program—

"(A) is accredited by a nationally-recognized, third-party personnel certification program accreditor;

"(B)(i) is sought or accepted by employers within the industry or sector involved as a recognized, preferred, or required credential for recruitment, screening, hiring, retention, or advancement purposes; and

"(ii) where appropriate, is endorsed by a nationally-recognized trade association or organization representing a significant part of the industry or sector;

"*(C) grants licenses that are recognized by the Federal Government or a State government; or*

"*(D) meets credential standards of a Federal agency.*".

SEC. 562. INCLUSION OF ALCOHOL, PRESCRIPTION DRUG, OPIOID, AND OTHER SUBSTANCE ABUSE COUNSELING AS PART OF REQUIRED PRESEPARATION COUNSELING.

Section 1142(b)(11) of title 10, United States Code, is amended by inserting before the period the following: "*and information concerning the availability of treatment options and resources to address substance abuse, including alcohol, prescription drug, and opioid abuse*".

SEC. 563. INCLUSION OF INFORMATION IN TRANSITION ASSISTANCE PROGRAM REGARDING EFFECT OF RECEIPT OF BOTH VETERAN DISABILITY COMPENSATION AND VOLUNTARY SEPARATION PAY.

Section 1144(b) of title 10, United States Code, is amended by adding at the end the following new paragraph:

"*(10) Provide information regarding the required deduction, pursuant to subsection (h) of section 1175a of this title, from disability compensation paid by the Secretary of Veterans Affairs of amounts equal to any voluntary separation pay received by the member under such section.*".

SEC. 564. TRAINING UNDER TRANSITION ASSISTANCE PROGRAM ON CAREER AND EMPLOYMENT OPPORTUNITIES ASSOCIATED WITH TRANSPORTATION SECURITY CARDS.

(a) IN GENERAL.—Section 1144(b) of title 10, United States Code, as amended by section 563, is further amended by adding at the end the following new paragraph:

"*(11) Acting through the Secretary of the department in which the Coast Guard is operating, provide information on career and employment opportunities available to members with transportation security cards issued under section 70105 of title 46.*".

(b) DEADLINE FOR IMPLEMENTATION.—The program carried out under section 1144 of title 10, United States Code, shall satisfy the requirements of subsection (b)(11) of such section (as added by subsection (a) of this section) by not later than 180 days after the date of the enactment of this Act.

SEC. 565. EXTENSION OF SUICIDE PREVENTION AND RESILIENCE PROGRAM.

Section 10219(g) of title 10, United States Code, is amended by striking "October 1, 2017" and inserting "October 1, 2018".

SEC. 566. CONGRESSIONAL NOTIFICATION IN ADVANCE OF APPOINTMENTS TO SERVICE ACADEMIES.

(a) UNITED STATES MILITARY ACADEMY.—Section 4342(a) of title 10, United States Code, is amended in the matter after paragraph (10) by adding at the end the following new sentence: "When a nominee of a Senator, Representative, or Delegate is selected for appointment as a cadet, the Senator, Representative, or Delegate shall be notified at least 48 hours before the official notification or announcement of the appointment is made.".

(b) UNITED STATES NAVAL ACADEMY.—Section 6954(a) of title 10, United States Code, is amended in the matter after paragraph (10) by adding at the end the following new sentence: "When a nominee of a Senator, Representative, or Delegate is selected for appointment as a midshipman, the Senator, Representative, or Delegate shall be notified at least 48 hours before the official notification or announcement of the appointment is made.".

(c) UNITED STATES AIR FORCE ACADEMY.—Section 9342(a) of title 10, United States Code, is amended in the matter after paragraph (10) by adding at the end the following new sentence:

"When a nominee of a Senator, Representative, or Delegate is selected for appointment as a cadet, the Senator, Representative, or Delegate shall be notified at least 48 hours before the official notification or announcement of the appointment is made.".

(d) UNITED STATES MERCHANT MARINE ACADEMY.—Section 51302 of title 46, United States Code, is amended by adding at the end the following:

"*(e) CONGRESSIONAL NOTIFICATION IN ADVANCE OF APPOINTMENTS.—When a nominee of a Senator, Representative, or Delegate is selected for appointment as a cadet, the Senator, Representative, or Delegate shall be notified at least 48 hours before the official notification or announcement of the appointment is made.*".

(e) APPLICATION OF AMENDMENTS.—The amendments made by this section shall apply with respect to the appointment of cadets and midshipmen to the United States Military Academy, the United States Naval Academy, the United States Air Force Academy, and the United States Merchant Marine Academy for classes entering these service academies after January 1, 2018.

SEC. 567. REPORT AND GUIDANCE ON JOB TRAINING, EMPLOYMENT SKILLS TRAINING, APPRENTICESHIPS, AND INTERNSHIPS AND SKILLBRIDGE INITIATIVES FOR MEMBERS OF THE ARMED FORCES WHO ARE BEING SEPARATED.

(a) REPORT REQUIRED.—Not later than 180 days after the date of the enactment of this Act, the Under Secretary of Defense for Personnel and Readiness shall submit to the Committees on Armed Services of the Senate and the House of Representatives, and make available to the public, a report evaluating the success of the Job Training, Employment Skills Training, Apprenticeships, and Internships (known as JTEST–AI) and SkillBridge initiatives, under which civilian businesses and companies make available to members of the Armed Forces who are being separated from the Armed Forces training or internship opportunities that offer a high probability of employment for the members after their separation.

(b) ELEMENTS.—In preparing the report required by subsection (a), the Under Secretary of Defense for Personnel and Readiness shall use the effectiveness metrics described in Enclosure 5 of Department of Defense Instruction No. 1322.29. The report shall include the following:

(1) An assessment of the successes of the Job Training, Employment Skills Training, Apprenticeships, and Internships and SkillBridge initiatives.

(2) Recommendations by the Under Secretary on ways in which the administration of the initiatives could be improved.

(3) Recommendations by civilian companies participating in the initiatives on ways in which the administration of the initiatives could be improved.

SEC. 568. MILITARY-TO-MARINER TRANSITION.

(a) REPORT.—Not later than 180 days after the date of the enactment of this Act, the Secretary of Defense and the Secretary of the department in which the Coast Guard is operating shall jointly report to the Committee on Armed Services and the Committee on Transportation and Infrastructure of the House of Representatives and the Committee on Armed Services and the Committee on Commerce, Science, and Transportation of the Senate on steps the Departments of Defense and Homeland Security have taken or intend to take—

(1) to maximize the extent to which United States Armed Forces service, training, and qualifications are creditable toward meeting the laws and regulations governing United States merchant mariner license, certification, and document laws and the International Convention on Standards of Training, Certification and Watchkeeping for Seafarers, 1978, including steps to enhance interdepartmental coordination; and

(2) to promote better awareness among Armed Forces personnel who serve in vessel operating positions of the requirements for postservice use of Armed Forces training, education, and practical experience in satisfaction of requirements for merchant mariner credentials under section 11.213 of title 46, Code of Federal Regulations, and the need to document such service in a manner suitable for post-service use.

(b) LIST OF TRAINING PROGRAMS.—The report under subsection (a) shall include a list of Army, Navy, and Coast Guard training programs open to Army, Navy, and Coast Guard vessel operators, respectively, that shows—

(1) which programs have been approved for credit toward merchant mariner credentials;

(2) which programs are under review for such approval;

(3) which programs are not relevant to the training needed for merchant mariner credentials; and

(4) which programs could become eligible for credit toward merchant mariner credentials with minor changes.

Subtitle H—Defense Dependents' Education and Military Family Readiness Matters

SEC. 571. CONTINUATION OF AUTHORITY TO ASSIST LOCAL EDUCATIONAL AGENCIES THAT BENEFIT DEPENDENTS OF MEMBERS OF THE ARMED FORCES AND DEPARTMENT OF DEFENSE CIVILIAN EMPLOYEES.

(a) ASSISTANCE TO SCHOOLS WITH SIGNIFICANT NUMBERS OF MILITARY DEPENDENT STUDENTS.—Of the amount authorized to be appropriated for fiscal year 2017 by section 301 and available for operation and maintenance for Defense-wide activities as specified in the funding table in division D, $30,000,000 shall be available only for the purpose of providing assistance to local educational agencies under subsection (a) of section 572 of the National Defense Authorization Act for Fiscal Year 2006 (Public Law 109–163; 20 U.S.C. 7703b).

(b) IMPACT AID FOR CHILDREN WITH SEVERE DISABILITIES.—Of the amount authorized to be appropriated for fiscal year 2017 by section 301 and available for operation and maintenance for Defense-wide activities as specified in the funding table in section 4301, $5,000,000 shall be available for payments under section 363 of the Floyd D. Spence National Defense Authorization Act for Fiscal Year 2001 (as enacted into law by Public Law 106–398; 114 Stat. 1654A–77; 20 U.S.C. 7703a).

(c) LOCAL EDUCATIONAL AGENCY DEFINED.—In this section, the term "local educational agency" has the meaning given that term in section 8013(9) of the Elementary and Secondary Education Act of 1965 (20 U.S.C. 7713(9)).

SEC. 572. ONE-YEAR EXTENSION OF AUTHORITIES RELATING TO THE TRANSITION AND SUPPORT OF MILITARY DEPENDENT STUDENTS TO LOCAL EDUCATIONAL AGENCIES.

(a) EXTENSION.—Section 574(c)(3) of the John Warner National Defense Authorization Act for Fiscal Year 2007 (20 U.S.C. 7703b note) is amended by striking "September 30, 2016" and inserting "September 30, 2017".

(b) INFORMATION TO BE INCLUDED WITH FUTURE REQUESTS FOR EXTENSION.—The budget justification materials that accompany any budget of the President for a fiscal year after fiscal year 2017 (as submitted to Congress pursuant to section 1105 of title 31, United States Code) that includes a request for the extension of section 574(c) of the John Warner National Defense Authorization Act for Fiscal Year 2007 shall include the following:

(1) A full accounting of the expenditure of funds pursuant to such section 574(c) during the

last fiscal year ending before the date of the submittal of the budget.

(2) An assessment of the impact of the expenditure of such funds on the quality of opportunities for elementary and secondary education made available for military dependent students.

SEC. 573. ANNUAL NOTICE TO MEMBERS OF THE ARMED FORCES REGARDING CHILD CUSTODY PROTECTIONS GUARANTEED BY THE SERVICEMEMBERS CIVIL RELIEF ACT.

The Secretaries of each of the military departments shall ensure that each member of the Armed Forces with dependents receives annually, and prior to each deployment, notice of the child custody protections afforded to members of the Armed Forces under the Servicemembers Civil Relief Act (50 U.S.C. 3901 et seq.).

SEC. 574. REQUIREMENT FOR ANNUAL FAMILY ADVOCACY PROGRAM REPORT REGARDING CHILD ABUSE AND DOMESTIC VIOLENCE.

(a) ANNUAL REPORT ON CHILD ABUSE AND DOMESTIC VIOLENCE.—Not later than April 30, 2017, and annually thereafter through April 30, 2021, the Secretary of Defense shall submit to the Committees on Armed Services of the House of Representatives and the Senate a report on the child abuse and domestic abuse incident data from the Department of Defense Family Advocacy Program central registry of child abuse and domestic abuse incidents for the preceding calendar year.

(b) CONTENTS.—The report shall contain each of the following:

(1) The number of incidents reported during the year covered by the report involving—

(A) spouse physical or sexual abuse;

(B) intimate partner physical or sexual abuse;

(C) child physical or sexual abuse; and

(D) child or domestic abuse resulting in a fatality.

(2) An analysis of the number of such incidents that met the criteria for substantiation.

(3) An analysis of—

(A) the types of abuse reported;

(B) for cases involving children as the reported victims of the abuse, the ages of the abused children; and

(C) other relevant characteristics of the reported victims.

(4) An analysis of the military status, sex, and pay grade of the alleged perpetrator of the child or domestic abuse.

(5) An analysis of the effectiveness of the Family Advocacy Program.

(c) COORDINATION OF RELEASE DATE BETWEEN ANNUAL REPORTS REGARDING SEXUAL ASSAULTS AND FAMILY ADVOCACY PROGRAM REPORT.—The Secretary of Defense shall ensure that the sexual assault reports required to be submitted under section 1631(d) of the Ike Skelton National Defense Authorization Act for Fiscal Year 2011 (Public Law 111–383; 10 U.S.C. 1561 note) for a year are delivered to the Committees on Armed Services of the House of Representatives and the Senate simultaneously with the report for that year required under this section.

SEC. 575. REPORTING ON ALLEGATIONS OF CHILD ABUSE IN MILITARY FAMILIES AND HOMES.

(a) REPORTS TO FAMILY ADVOCACY PROGRAM OFFICES.—

(1) IN GENERAL.—The following information shall be reported immediately to the Family Advocacy Program office at the military installation to which the member of the Armed Forces concerned is assigned:

(A) Credible information (which may include a reasonable belief), obtained by any individual within the chain of command of the member, that a child in the family or home of the member has suffered an incident of child abuse.

(B) Information, learned by a member of the Armed Forces engaged in a profession or activity described in section 226(b) of the Victims of Child Abuse Act of 1990 (42 U.S.C. 13031(b)) for members of the Armed Forces and their dependents, that gives reason to suspect that a child in the family or home of the member has suffered an incident of child abuse.

(2) REGULATIONS.—The Secretary of Defense and the Secretary of Homeland Security (with respect to the Coast Guard when it is not operating as a service in the Navy) shall jointly prescribe regulations to carry out this subsection.

(3) CHILD ABUSE DEFINED.—In this subsection, the term "child abuse" has the meaning given that term in section 226(c) of the Victims of Child Abuse Act of 1990 (42 U.S.C. 13031(c)).

(b) REPORTS TO STATE CHILD WELFARE SERVICES.—Section 226 of the Victims of Child Abuse Act of 1990 (42 U.S.C. 13031) is amended—

(1) in subsection (a), by inserting " and to the agency or agencies provided for in subsection (e), if applicable" before the period;

(2) by redesignating subsections (e) and (f) as subsections (f) and (g), respectively; and

(3) by inserting after subsection (d) the following new subsection (e):

"(e) REPORTERS AND RECIPIENT OF REPORT INVOLVING CHILDREN AND HOMES OF MEMBERS OF THE ARMED FORCES.—

"(1) RECIPIENTS OF REPORTS.—In the case of an incident described in subsection (a) involving a child in the family or home of member of the Armed Forces (regardless of whether the incident occurred on or off a military installation), the report required by subsection (a) shall be made to the appropriate child welfare services agency or agencies of the State in which the child resides. The Attorney General, the Secretary of Defense, and the Secretary of Homeland Security (with respect to the Coast Guard when it is not operating as a service in the Navy) shall jointly, in consultation with the chief executive officers of the States, designate the child welfare service agencies of the States that are appropriate recipients of reports pursuant to this subsection. Any report on an incident pursuant to this subsection is in addition to any other report on the incident pursuant to this section.

"(2) MAKERS OF REPORTS.—For purposes of the making of reports under this section pursuant to this subsection, the persons engaged in professions and activities described in subsection (b) shall include members of the Armed Forces who are engaged in such professions and activities for members of the Armed Forces and their dependents.".

SEC. 576. REPEAL OF ADVISORY COUNCIL ON DEPENDENTS' EDUCATION.

Section 1411 of the Defense Dependents' Education Act of 1978 (20 U.S.C. 929) is repealed.

SEC. 577. SUPPORT FOR PROGRAMS PROVIDING CAMP EXPERIENCE FOR CHILDREN OF MILITARY FAMILIES.

(a) AUTHORITY TO PROVIDE SUPPORT.—The Secretary of Defense may provide financial or non-monetary support to qualified nonprofit organizations in order to assist such organizations in carrying out programs to support the attendance at a camp, or camp-like setting, of children of military families who have experienced the death of a family member or other loved one or who have another family member living with a substance use disorder or post-traumatic stress disorder.

(b) APPLICATION FOR SUPPORT.—

(1) IN GENERAL.—Each organization seeking support pursuant to subsection (a) shall submit to the Secretary of Defense an application therefor containing such information as the Secretary shall specify for purposes of this section.

(2) CONTENTS.—Each application submitted under paragraph (1) shall include the following:

(A) A description of the program for which support is being sought, including the location of the setting or settings under the program, the duration of such setting or settings, any local partners participating in or contributing to the program, and the ratio of counselors, trained volunteers, or both to children at such setting or settings.

(B) An estimate of the number of children of military families to be supported using the support sought.

(C) A description of the type of activities that will be conducted using the support sought, including the manner in which activities are particularly supportive to children of military families described in subsection (a).

(D) A description of the outreach conducted or to be conducted by the organization to military families regarding the program.

(c) USE OF SUPPORT.—Support provided by the Secretary of Defense to an organization pursuant to subsection (a) shall be used by the organization to support attendance at a camp, or camp-like setting, of children of military families described in subsection (a).

SEC. 578. COMPTROLLER GENERAL OF THE UNITED STATES ASSESSMENT AND REPORT ON EXCEPTIONAL FAMILY MEMBER PROGRAMS.

(a) ASSESSMENT AND REPORT REQUIRED.—

(1) ASSESSMENT.—The Comptroller General of the United States shall conduct an assessment on the effectiveness of each Exceptional Family Member Program of the Armed Forces.

(2) REPORT.—Not later than December 31, 2017, the Comptroller General shall submit to the Committees on Armed Services of the Senate and the House of Representatives a report containing the results of the assessment conducted under this subsection.

(b) ELEMENTS.—The assessment and report under subsection (a) shall address the following:

(1) The differences between each Exceptional Family Member Program of the Armed Forces.

(2) The manner in which Exceptional Family Member Programs are implemented on joint bases and installations.

(3) The extent to which military family members are screened for potential coverage under an Exceptional Family Member Program and the manner of such screening.

(4) The degree to which conditions of military family members who qualify for coverage under an Exceptional Family Member Program are taken into account in making assignments of military personnel.

(5) The types of services provided to address the needs of military family members who qualify for coverage under an Exceptional Family Member Program.

(6) The extent to which the Department of Defense has implemented specific directives for providing family support and enhanced case management services, such as special needs navigators, to military families with special needs children.

(7) The extent to which the Department has conducted periodic reviews of best practices in the United States for the provision of medical and educational services to military family members with special needs.

(8) The necessity in the Department for an advisory panel on community support for military families members with special needs.

(9) The development and implementation of the uniform policy for the Department regarding families with special needs required by section 1781c(e) of title 10, United States Code.

(10) The implementation by each Armed Force of the recommendations in the Government Accountability Report entitled "Military Dependent Students, Better Oversight Needed to Improve Services for Children with Special Needs" (GAO–12–680).

SEC. 579. IMPACT AID AMENDMENTS.

(a) MILITARY "BUILD TO LEASE" PROGRAM HOUSING.—Notwithstanding section 5(d) of the

Every Student Succeeds Act (Public Law 114–95; 129 Stat. 1806), the amendment made by section 7004(1) of such Act (Public Law 114–95; 129 Stat. 2077)—

(1) for fiscal year 2016—

(A) shall be applied as if amending section 8003(a)(5)(A) of the Elementary and Secondary Education Act of 1965, as in effect on the day before the date of enactment of the Every Student Succeeds Act (Public Law 114–95; 129 Stat. 1802); and

(B) shall be applicable with respect to appropriations for use under title VIII of the Elementary and Secondary Education Act of 1965 (Public Law 114–95; 129 Stat. 1802); and

(2) for fiscal year 2017 and each succeeding fiscal year, shall be in effect with respect to appropriations for use under title VII of the Elementary and Secondary Education Act of 1965, as amended by the Every Student Succeeds Act (Public Law 114–95; 129 Stat. 1802).

(b) ELIGIBILITY FOR HEAVILY IMPACTED LOCAL EDUCATIONAL AGENCIES.—

(1) AMENDMENT.—Subclause (I) of section 7003(b)(2)(B)(i) of the Elementary and Secondary Education Act of 1965 (20 U.S.C. 7703(b)(2)(B)(i)(I)) is amended to read as follows:

"(I) is a local educational agency—

"(aa) whose boundaries are the same as a Federal military installation; or

"(bb)(AA) whose boundaries are the same as an island property designated by the Secretary of the Interior to be property that is held in trust by the Federal Government; and

"(BB) that has no taxing authority;".

(2) EFFECTIVE DATE.—The amendment made by paragraph (1) shall take effect with respect to appropriations for use under title VII of the Elementary and Secondary Education Act of 1965, as amended by the Every Student Succeeds Act (Public Law 114–95; 129 Stat. 1802), beginning with fiscal year 2017 and as if enacted as part of title VII of the Every Student Succeeds Act.

(c) SPECIAL RULE REGARDING THE PER-PUPIL EXPENDITURE REQUIREMENT.—

(1) REFERENCES.—Except as otherwise expressly provided, any reference in this subsection to a section or other provision of title VII of the Elementary and Secondary Education Act of 1965 shall be considered to be a reference to the section or other provision of such title VII as amended by the Every Student Succeeds Act (Public Law 114–95; 129 Stat. 1802).

(2) IN GENERAL.—Notwithstanding section 5(d) of the Every Student Succeeds Act (Public Law 114–95; 129 Stat. 1806) or section 7003(b)(2) of the Elementary and Secondary Education Act of 1965 (20 U.S.C. 7703(b)(2)), with respect to any application submitted under section 7005 of such Act (20 U.S.C. 7705) for eligibility consideration under subclause (II) or (V) of section 7003(b)(2)(B)(i) of such Act for fiscal year 2017, 2018, or 2019, the Secretary of Education shall determine that a local educational agency meets the per-pupil expenditure requirement for purposes of such subclause (II) or (V), as applicable, only if—

(A) in the case of a local educational agency that received a basic support payment for fiscal year 2001 under section 8003(b)(2)(B) of the Elementary and Secondary Education Act of 1965 (20 U.S.C. 7703(b)(2)(B)) (as such section was in effect for such fiscal year), the agency, for the year for which the application is submitted, has a per-pupil expenditure that is less than the average per-pupil expenditure of the State in which the agency is located or the average per-pupil expenditure of all States (whichever average per-pupil expenditure is greater), except that a local educational agency with a total student enrollment of less than 350 students shall be deemed to have satisfied such per-pupil expenditure requirement; or

(B) in the case of a local educational agency that did not receive a basic support payment for fiscal year 2015 under such section 8003(b)(2)(B), as so in effect, the agency, for the year for which the application is submitted—

(i) has a total student enrollment of 350 or more students and a per-pupil expenditure that is less than the average per-pupil expenditure of the State in which the agency is located; or

(ii) has a total student enrollment of less than 350 students and a per-pupil expenditure that is less than the average per-pupil expenditure of a comparable local educational agency or 3 comparable local educational agencies (whichever average per-pupil expenditure is greater), in the State in which the agency is located.

(d) PAYMENTS FOR ELIGIBLE FEDERALLY CONNECTED CHILDREN.—

(1) AMENDMENTS.—Section 7003(b)(2) of the Elementary and Secondary Education Act of 1965 (20 U.S.C. 7703(b)(2)), as amended by subsection (b) and sections 7001 and 7004 of the Every Student Succeeds Act (Public Law 114–95; 129 Stat. 2074, 2077), is further amended—

(A) in subclause (IV) of subparagraph (B)(i)—

(i) in the matter preceding item (aa), by inserting "received a payment for fiscal year 2015 under section 8003(b)(2)(E) (as such section was in effect for such fiscal year) and" before "has";

(ii) in item (aa), by striking "50" and inserting "35"; and

(iii) by striking item (bb) and inserting the following:

"(bb)(AA) not less than 3,500 of such children are children described in subparagraphs (A) and (B) of subsection (a)(1); or

"(BB) not less than 7,000 of such children are children described in subparagraph (D) of subsection (a)(1);"; and

(B) in subparagraph (D)—

(i) in clause (i)—

(I) in subclause (I), by striking "clause (ii)" and inserting "clauses (ii), (iii), and (iv)"; and

(II) in subclause (II)—

(aa) by inserting "received a payment for fiscal year 2015 under section 8003(b)(2)(E) (as such section was in effect for such fiscal year) and" after "agency that";

(bb) by striking "50 percent" and inserting "35 percent";

(cc) by striking "subsection (a)(1) and not less than 5,000" and inserting the following: "subsection (a)(1) and—

"(aa) not less than 3,500"; and

(dd) by striking "subsection (a)(1)." and inserting the following: "subsection (a)(1); or

"(bb) not less than 7,000 of such children are children described in subparagraph (D) of subsection (a)(1).";

(ii) in clause (ii), by striking "shall be 1.35." and inserting the following: "shall be—

"(I) for fiscal year 2016, 1.35;

"(II) for each of fiscal years 2017 and 2018, 1.38;

"(III) for fiscal year 2019, 1.40;

"(IV) for fiscal year 2020, 1.42; and

"(V) for fiscal year 2021 and each fiscal year thereafter, 1.45."; and

(iii) by adding at the end the following:

"(iii) FACTOR FOR CHILDREN WHO LIVE OFF BASE.—For purposes of calculating the maximum amount described in clause (i), the factor used in determining the weighted student units under subsection (a)(2) with respect to children described in subsection (a)(1)(D) shall be—

"(I) for fiscal year 2016, .20;

"(II) for each of fiscal years 2017 and 2018, .22;

"(III) for each of fiscal years 2019 and 2020, .25; and

"(IV) for fiscal year 2021 and each fiscal year thereafter—

"(aa) .30 with respect to each of the first 7,000 children; and

"(bb) .25 with respect to the number of children that exceeds 7,000.

"(iv) SPECIAL RULE.—Notwithstanding clauses (ii) and (iii), for fiscal year 2020 or any succeeding fiscal year, if the number of students who are children described in subparagraphs (A) and (B) of subsection (a)(1) for a local educational agency subject to this subparagraph exceeds 7,000 for such year or the number of students who are children described in subsection (a)(1)(D) for such local educational agency exceeds 12,750 for such year, then—

"(I) the factor used, for the fiscal year for which the determination is being made, to determine the weighted student units under subsection (a)(2) with respect to children described in subparagraphs (A) and (B) of subsection (a)(1) shall be 1.40; and

"(II) the factor used, for such fiscal year, to determine the weighted student units under subsection (a)(2) with respect to children described in subsection (a)(1)(D) shall be .20.".

(2) EFFECTIVE DATE.—The amendments made by paragraph (1) shall take effect with respect to appropriations for use under title VII of the Elementary and Secondary Education Act of 1965 beginning with fiscal year 2017 and as if enacted as part of title VII of the Every Student Succeeds Act (Public Law 114–95; 129 Stat. 2074).

(3) SPECIAL RULES.—

(A) APPLICABILITY FOR FISCAL YEAR 2016.—Notwithstanding any other provision of law, in making basic support payments under section 8003(b)(2) of the Elementary and Secondary Education Act of 1965 (20 U.S.C. 7703(b)(2)) for fiscal year 2016, the Secretary of Education shall carry out subparagraphs (B)(i) and (E) of such section as if the amendments made to subparagraphs (B)(i)(IV) and (D) of section 7003(b)(2) of such Act (as amended and redesignated by this subsection and the Every Student Succeeds Act (Public Law 114–95; 129 Stat. 1802)) had also been made to the corresponding provisions of section 8003(b)(2) of the Elementary and Secondary Education Act of 1965, as in effect on the day before the date of enactment of the Every Student Succeeds Act.

(B) LOSS OF ELIGIBILITY.—For fiscal year 2016 or any succeeding fiscal year, if a local educational agency is eligible for a basic support payment under subclause (IV) of section 7003(b)(2)(B)(i) of the Elementary and Secondary Education Act of 1965 (as amended by this section and the Every Student Succeeds Act (Public Law 114–95; 129 Stat. 1802)) or through a corresponding provision under subparagraph (A), such local educational agency shall be ineligible to apply for a payment for such fiscal year under any other subclause of such section (or, for fiscal year 2016, any other item of section 8003(b)(2)(B)(i)(II) of the Elementary and Secondary Education Act of 1965).

(C) PAYMENT AMOUNTS.—If, before the date of enactment of this Act, a local educational agency receives 1 or more payments under section 8003(b)(2)(E) of the Elementary and Secondary Education Act of 1965 (20 U.S.C. 7703(b)(2)(E)) for fiscal year 2016, the sum of which is greater than the amount the Secretary of Education determines the local educational agency is entitled to receive under such section in accordance with subparagraph (A)—

(i) the Secretary shall allow the local educational agency to retain the larger amount; and

(ii) such local educational agency shall not be eligible to receive any additional payment under such section for fiscal year 2016.

Subtitle I—Decorations and Awards

SEC. 581. POSTHUMOUS ADVANCEMENT OF COLONEL GEORGE E. "BUD" DAY, UNITED STATES AIR FORCE, ON THE RETIRED LIST.

(a) ADVANCEMENT.—Colonel George E. "Bud" Day, United States Air Force (retired), is entitled to hold the rank of brigadier general while on the retired list of the Air Force.

(b) ADDITIONAL BENEFITS NOT TO ACCRUE.—The advancement of George E. "Bud" Day on the retired list of the Air Force under subsection (a) shall not affect the retired pay or other benefits from the United States to which George E. "Bud" Day would have been entitled based upon his military service or affect any benefits to which any other person may become entitled based on his military service.

SEC. 582. AUTHORIZATION FOR AWARD OF MEDALS FOR ACTS OF VALOR DURING CERTAIN CONTINGENCY OPERATIONS.

(a) AUTHORIZATION.—Notwithstanding the time limitations specified in sections 3744, 6248, and 8744 of title 10, United States Code, or any other time limitation with respect to the awarding of certain medals to persons who served in the Armed Forces, the President may award a medal specified in subsection (c) to a member or former member of the Armed Forces identified as warranting award of that medal pursuant to the review of valor award nominations for Operation Enduring Freedom, Operation Iraqi Freedom, Operation New Dawn, Operation Freedom's Sentinel, and Operation Inherent Resolve that was directed by the Secretary of Defense on January 7, 2016.

(b) AWARD OF MEDAL OF HONOR.—If, pursuant to the review referred to in subsection (a), the President decides to award to a member or former member of the Armed Forces the Medal of Honor, the medal may only be awarded after the Secretary of Defense submits to the Committees on Armed Services of the Senate and the House of Representatives a letter identifying the intended recipient of the Medal of Honor and the rationale for awarding the Medal of Honor to such intended recipient.

(c) MEDALS.—The medals covered by subsection (a) are any of the following:

(1) The Medal of Honor under section 3741, 6241, or 8741 of title 10, United States Code.

(2) The Distinguished-Service Cross under section 3742 of such title.

(3) The Navy Cross under section 6242 of such title.

(4) The Air Force Cross under section 8742 of such title.

(5) The Silver Star under section 3746, 6244, or 8746 of such title.

(d) TERMINATION.—No medal may be awarded under the authority of this section after December 31, 2019.

SEC. 583. AUTHORIZATION FOR AWARD OF THE MEDAL OF HONOR TO GARY M. ROSE AND JAMES C. MCCLOUGHAN FOR ACTS OF VALOR DURING THE VIETNAM WAR.

(a) GARY M. ROSE.—

(1) AUTHORIZATION.—Notwithstanding the time limitations specified in section 3744 of title 10, United States Code, or any other time limitation with respect to the awarding of certain medals to persons who served in the Armed Forces, the President is authorized to award the Medal of Honor under section 3741 of such title to Gary M. Rose for the acts of valor described in paragraph (2).

(2) ACTS OF VALOR DESCRIBED.—The acts of valor referred to in paragraph (1) are the actions of Gary M. Rose in Laos from September 11 through 14, 1970, during the Vietnam War while a member of the United States Army, Military Assistance Command Vietnam-Studies and Observation Group (MACVSOG).

(b) JAMES C. MCCLOUGHAN.—

(1) AUTHORIZATION.—Notwithstanding the time limitations specified in section 3744 of title 10, United States Code, or any other time limitation with respect to the awarding of certain medals to persons who served in the Armed Forces, the President is authorized to award the Medal of Honor under section 3741 of such title to James C. McCloughan for the acts of valor described in paragraph (2).

(2) ACTS OF VALOR DESCRIBED.—The acts of valor referred to in paragraph (1) are the actions of James C. McCloughan during combat operations between May 13, 1969, and May 15, 1969, while serving as a Combat Medic with Company C, 3d Battalion, 21st Infantry, 196th Light Infantry Brigade, American Division, Republic of Vietnam, for which he was previously awarded the Bronze Star Medal with "V" Device.

SEC. 584. AUTHORIZATION FOR AWARD OF DISTINGUISHED-SERVICE CROSS TO FIRST LIEUTENANT MELVIN M. SPRUIELL FOR ACTS OF VALOR DURING WORLD WAR II.

(a) WAIVER OF TIME LIMITATIONS.—Notwithstanding the time limitations specified in section 3744 of title 10, United States Code, or any other time limitation with respect to the awarding of certain medals to persons who served in the Armed Forces, the Secretary of the Army may award the Distinguished-Service Cross under section 3742 of such title to First Lieutenant Melvin M. Spruiell of the Army for the acts of valor during World War II described in subsection (b).

(b) ACTS OF VALOR DESCRIBED.—The acts of valor referred to in subsection (a) are the actions of First Lieutenant Melvin M. Spruiell on June 10 and 11, 1944, as a member of the Army serving in France with the 377th Parachute Field Artillery, 101st Airborne Division.

SEC. 585. AUTHORIZATION FOR AWARD OF THE DISTINGUISHED SERVICE CROSS TO CHAPLAIN (FIRST LIEUTENANT) JOSEPH VERBIS LAFLEUR FOR ACTS OF VALOR DURING WORLD WAR II.

(a) AUTHORIZATION.—Notwithstanding the time limitations specified in section 3744 of title 10, United States Code, or any other time limitation with respect to the awarding of certain medals to persons who served in the Armed Forces, the Secretary of the Army may award the Distinguished Service Cross under section 3742 of that title to Chaplain (First Lieutenant) Joseph Verbis LaFleur for the acts of valor referred to in subsection (b).

(b) ACTS OF VALOR DESCRIBED.—The acts of valor referred to in subsection (a) are the actions of Chaplain (First Lieutenant) Joseph Verbis LaFleur while interned as a prisoner-of-war by Japan from December 30, 1941, to September 7, 1944.

SEC. 586. REVIEW REGARDING AWARD OF MEDAL OF HONOR TO CERTAIN ASIAN AMERICAN AND NATIVE AMERICAN PACIFIC ISLANDER WAR VETERANS.

(a) REVIEW REQUIRED.—The Secretary of each military department shall review the service records of each Asian American and Native American Pacific Islander war veteran described in subsection (b) to determine whether that veteran should be awarded the Medal of Honor.

(b) COVERED VETERANS.—The Asian American and Native American Pacific Islander war veterans whose service records are to be reviewed under subsection (a) are any former members of the Armed Forces whose service records identify them as an Asian American or Native American Pacific Islander war veteran who was awarded the Distinguished-Service Cross, the Navy Cross, or the Air Force Cross during the Korean War or the Vietnam War.

(c) CONSULTATIONS.—In carrying out the review under subsection (a), the Secretary of each military department shall consult with such veterans service organizations as the Secretary considers appropriate.

(d) RECOMMENDATIONS BASED ON REVIEW.—If the Secretary concerned determines, based upon the review under subsection (a) of the service records of any Asian American or Native American Pacific Islander war veteran, that the award of the Medal of Honor to that veteran is warranted, the Secretary shall submit to the President a recommendation that the President award the Medal of Honor to that veteran.

(e) AUTHORITY TO AWARD MEDAL OF HONOR.—A Medal of Honor may be awarded to an Asian American or Native American Pacific Islander war veteran in accordance with a recommendation of the Secretary concerned under subsection (d).

(f) CONGRESSIONAL NOTIFICATION.—No Medal of Honor may be awarded pursuant to subsection (e) until the Secretary of Defense submits to the Committees on Armed Services of the Senate and the House of Representatives notice of the recommendations under subsection (d), including the name of each Asian American or Native American Pacific Islander war veteran recommended to be awarded a Medal of Honor and the rationale for such recommendation.

(g) WAIVER OF TIME LIMITATIONS.—An award of the Medal of Honor may be made under subsection (e) without regard to—

(1) section 3744, 6248, or 8744 of title 10, United States Code, as applicable; and

(2) any regulation or other administrative restriction on—

(A) the time for awarding the Medal of Honor; or

(B) the awarding of the Medal of Honor for service for which a Distinguished-Service Cross, Navy Cross, or Air Force Cross has been awarded.

(h) DEFINITION.—In this section, the term "Native American Pacific Islander" means a Native Hawaiian or Native American Pacific Islander, as those terms are defined in section 815 of the Native American Programs Act of 1974 (42 U.S.C. 2992c).

Subtitle J—Miscellaneous Reports and Other Matters

SEC. 591. REPEAL OF REQUIREMENT FOR A CHAPLAIN AT THE UNITED STATES AIR FORCE ACADEMY APPOINTED BY THE PRESIDENT.

(a) REPEAL.—Section 9337 of title 10, United States Code, is repealed.

(b) CLERICAL AMENDMENT.—The table of sections at the beginning of chapter 903 of such title is amended by striking the item related to section 9337.

SEC. 592. EXTENSION OF LIMITATION ON REDUCTION IN NUMBER OF MILITARY AND CIVILIAN PERSONNEL ASSIGNED TO DUTY WITH SERVICE REVIEW AGENCIES.

Section 1559(a) of title 10, United States Code, is amended by striking "December 31, 2016" and inserting "December 31, 2019".

SEC. 593. ANNUAL REPORTS ON PROGRESS OF THE ARMY AND THE MARINE CORPS IN INTEGRATING WOMEN INTO MILITARY OCCUPATIONAL SPECIALTIES AND UNITS RECENTLY OPENED TO WOMEN.

(a) REPORTS REQUIRED.—Not later than April 1, 2017, and each year thereafter through 2020, the Chief of Staff of the Army and the Commandant of the Marine Corps shall each submit to the Committees on Armed Services of the Senate and the House of Representatives a report on the current status of the implementation by the Army and the Marine Corps, respectively, of the policy of Secretary of Defense dated March 9, 2016, to open to women military occupational specialties and units previously closed to women.

(b) ELEMENTS.—Each report shall include, current as of the date of such report and for the Armed Force covered by such report, the following:

(1) The status of gender-neutral standards throughout the Entry Level Training continuum.

(2) The propensity of applicants to apply for and access into newly-opened ground combat programs, by gender and program.

(3) Success rates in Initial Screening Tests and Military Occupational Speciality (MOS) Classification Standards for newly-opened ground combat military occupational specialties, by gender.

(4) Attrition rates and the top three causes of attrition throughout the Entry Level Training continuum, by gender and military occupational specialty.

(5) Reclassification rates and the top three causes of reclassification throughout the Entry Level Training continuum, by gender and military occupational specialty.

(6) Injury rates and the top five causes of injury throughout the Entry Level Training continuum, by gender and military occupational specialty.

(7) Injury rates and nondeployability rates in newly-opened ground combat military occupational specialties, by gender and military occupational specialty.

(8) Lateral move approval rates into newly-opened military occupational specialties, by gender and military occupational specialty.

(9) Reenlistment and retention rates in newly-opened ground combat military occupational specialties, by gender and military occupational specialty.

(10) Promotion rates in newly-opened ground combat military occupational specialties, by grade and gender.

(11) Actions taken to address matters relating to equipment sizing and supply, and facilities, in connection with the implementation by such Armed Force of the policy referred to in paragraph (1).

(c) APPLICABILITY TO SOCOM.—In addition to the reports required by subsection (a), the Commander of the United States Special Operations Command shall submit to the Committees on Armed Services of the Senate and the House of Representatives, on the dates provided for in subsection (a), a report on the current status of the implementation by the United States Special Operations Command of the policy of Secretary of Defense referred to in subsection (a). Each report shall include the matters specified in subsection (b) with respect to the United States Special Operations Command.

SEC. 594. REPORT ON FEASABILITY OF ELECTRONIC TRACKING OF OPERATIONAL ACTIVE-DUTY SERVICE PERFORMED BY MEMBERS OF THE READY RESERVE OF THE ARMED FORCES.

Not later than March 1, 2017, the Secretary of Defense shall submit to the Committees on Armed Services of the Senate and the House of Representatives a report on the feasability of establishing an electronic means by which members of the Ready Reserve of the Armed Forces can track their operational active-duty service performed after January 28, 2008, under section 12301(a), 12301(d), 12301(g), 12302, or 12304 of title 10, United States Code. The means assessed for purposes of the report shall include a tour calculator that specifies early retirement credit authorized for each qualifying tour of active duty, as well as cumulative early reserve retirement credit authorized to date under section 12731(f) of such title.

SEC. 595. REPORT ON DISCHARGE BY WARRANT OFFICERS OF PILOT AND OTHER FLIGHT OFFICER POSITIONS IN THE NAVY, MARINE CORPS, AND AIR FORCE CURRENTLY DISCHARGED BY COMMISSIONED OFFICERS.

(a) REPORT REQUIRED.—Not later than 180 days after the date of the enactment of this Act, the Secretary of the Navy and the Secretary of the Air Force shall each submit to the Committees on Armed Services of the Senate and the House of Representatives a report on the feasibility and advisability of the discharge by warrant officers of pilot and other flight officer positions in the Armed Forces under the jurisdiction of such Secretary that are currently discharged by commissioned officers.

(b) ELEMENTS.—Each report under subsection (a) shall set forth, for each Armed Force covered by such report, the following:

(1) An assessment of the feasibility and advisability of the discharge by warrant officers of pilot and other flight officer positions that are currently discharged by commissioned officers.

(2) An identification of each such position, if any, for which the discharge by warrant officers is assessed to be feasible and advisable.

SEC. 596. BODY MASS INDEX TEST.

(a) REVIEW REQUIRED.—Each Secretary of a military department shall review—

(1) the current body mass index test procedure used by each Armed Force under the jurisdiction of that Secretary; and

(2) other methods to measure body fat with a more holistic health and wellness approach.

(b) ELEMENTS.—The review required under subsection (a) shall—

(1) address nutrition counseling;

(2) determine the best methods to be used by the Armed Forces to assess body fat percentages; and

(3) improve the accuracy of body fat measurements.

SEC. 597. REPORT ON CAREER PROGRESSION TRACKS OF THE ARMED FORCES FOR WOMEN IN COMBAT ARMS UNITS.

Not later than 30 days after the date of the enactment of this Act, the Secretary of Defense shall submit to Congress a report setting forth a description, for each Armed Force, of the following:

(1) The career progression track for entry level women as officers in combat arms units of such Armed Force.

(2) The career progression track for laterally transferred women as officers in combat arms units of such Armed Force.

(3) The career progression track for entry level women as enlisted members in combat arms units of such Armed Force.

(4) The career progression track for laterally transferred women as enlisted members in combat arms units of such Armed Force.

TITLE VI—COMPENSATION AND OTHER PERSONNEL BENEFITS

Subtitle A—Pay and Allowances

Sec. 601. Fiscal year 2017 increase in military basic pay.
Sec. 602. Publication by Department of Defense of actual rates of basic pay payable to members of the Armed Forces by pay grade for annual or other pay periods.
Sec. 603. Extension of authority to provide temporary increase in rates of basic allowance for housing under certain circumstances.
Sec. 604. Reports on a new single-salary pay system for members of the Armed Forces.

Subtitle B—Bonuses and Special and Incentive Pays

Sec. 611. One-year extension of certain bonus and special pay authorities for reserve forces.
Sec. 612. One-year extension of certain bonus and special pay authorities for health care professionals.
Sec. 613. One-year extension of special pay and bonus authorities for nuclear officers.
Sec. 614. One-year extension of authorities relating to title 37 consolidated special pay, incentive pay, and bonus authorities.
Sec. 615. One-year extension of authorities relating to payment of other title 37 bonuses and special pays.
Sec. 616. Aviation incentive pay and bonus matters.
Sec. 617. Conforming amendment to consolidation of special pay, incentive pay, and bonus authorities.
Sec. 618. Technical amendments relating to 2008 consolidation of certain special pay authorities.

Subtitle C—Travel and Transportation Allowances

Sec. 621. Maximum reimbursement amount for travel expenses of members of the Reserves attending inactive duty training outside of normal commuting distances.

Subtitle D—Disability Pay, Retired Pay, and Survivor Benefits

PART I—AMENDMENTS IN CONNECTION WITH RETIRED PAY REFORM

Sec. 631. Election period for members in the service academies and inactive Reserves to participate in the modernized retirement system.
Sec. 632. Effect of separation of members from the uniformed services on participation in the Thrift Savings Plan.
Sec. 633. Continuation pay for full Thrift Savings Plan members who have completed 8 to 12 years of service.
Sec. 634. Combat-related special compensation coordinating amendment.

PART II—OTHER MATTERS

Sec. 641. Use of member's current pay grade and years of service and retired pay cost-of-living adjustments, rather than final retirement pay grade and years of service, in a division of property involving disposable retired pay.
Sec. 642. Equal benefits under Survivor Benefit Plan for survivors of reserve component members who die in the line of duty during inactive-duty training.
Sec. 643. Authority to deduct Survivor Benefit Plan premiums from combat-related special compensation when retired pay not sufficient.
Sec. 644. Extension of allowance covering monthly premium for Service-members' Group Life Insurance while in certain overseas areas to cover members in any combat zone or overseas direct support area.
Sec. 645. Authority for payment of pay and allowances and retired and retainer pay pursuant to power of attorney.
Sec. 646. Extension of authority to pay special survivor indemnity allowance under the Survivor Benefit Plan.
Sec. 647. Repeal of obsolete authority for combat-related injury rehabilitation pay.
Sec. 648. Independent assessment of the Survivor Benefit Plan.

Subtitle E—Commissary and Nonappropriated Fund Instrumentality Benefits and Operations

Sec. 661. Protection and enhancement of access to and savings at commissaries and exchanges.

Sec. 662. Acceptance of Military Star Card at commissaries.

Subtitle F—Other Matters

Sec. 671. Recovery of amounts owed to the United States by members of the uniformed services.

Sec. 672. Modification of flat rate per diem requirement for personnel on long-term temporary duty assignments.

Subtitle A—Pay and Allowances

SEC. 601. FISCAL YEAR 2017 INCREASE IN MILITARY BASIC PAY.

(a) WAIVER OF SECTION 1009 ADJUSTMENT.—The adjustment to become effective during fiscal year 2017 required by section 1009 of title 37, United States Code, in the rates of monthly basic pay authorized members of the uniformed services shall not be made.

(b) INCREASE IN BASIC PAY.—Effective on January 1, 2017, the rates of monthly basic pay for members of the uniformed services are increased by 2.1 percent.

SEC. 602. PUBLICATION BY DEPARTMENT OF DEFENSE OF ACTUAL RATES OF BASIC PAY PAYABLE TO MEMBERS OF THE ARMED FORCES BY PAY GRADE FOR ANNUAL OR OTHER PAY PERIODS.

Any pay table published or otherwise issued by the Department of Defense to indicate the rates of basic pay of the Armed Forces in effect for members of the Armed Forces for a calendar year or other period shall state the rate of basic pay to be received by members in each pay grade for such year or period as specified or otherwise provided by applicable law, including any rate to be so received pursuant during such year or period by the operation of a ceiling under section 203(a)(2) of title 37, United States Code, or a similar provision in an annual defense authorization Act.

SEC. 603. EXTENSION OF AUTHORITY TO PROVIDE TEMPORARY INCREASE IN RATES OF BASIC ALLOWANCE FOR HOUSING UNDER CERTAIN CIRCUMSTANCES.

Section 403(b)(7)(E) of title 37, United States Code, is amended by striking "December 31, 2016" and inserting "December 31, 2017".

SEC. 604. REPORTS ON A NEW SINGLE-SALARY PAY SYSTEM FOR MEMBERS OF THE ARMED FORCES.

(a) REPORT ON PLAN TO IMPLEMENT NEW PAY STRUCTURE.—Not later than March 1, 2017, the Secretary of Defense shall submit to the Committees on Armed Services of the Senate and the House of Representative a report that sets forth the following:

(1) The military pay tables as of January 1, 2017, reflecting the Regular Military Compensation of members of the Armed Forces as of that date in the range of grades, dependency statuses, and assignment locations.

(2) A comprehensive description of the manner in which the Department of Defense would begin, by not later than January 1, 2018, to implement a transition between the current pay structure for members of the Armed Forces and a new pay structure for members of the Armed Forces as provided for by this section.

(b) REPORT ON ELEMENTS OF NEW PAY STRUCTURE.—Not later than January 1, 2018, the Secretary shall submit to the Committees on Armed Services of the Senate and the House of Representative a report that sets forth the following:

(1) A description and comparison of the current pay structure for members of the Armed Forces and a new pay structure for members of the Armed Forces, including new pay tables, that uses a single-salary pay system (as adjusted by the same cost-of-living adjustment that the Department of Defense uses worldwide for civilian employees) based on the assumptions in subsection (c).

(2) A proposal for such legislative and administrative action as the Secretary considers appropriate to implement the new pay structure, and to provide for a transition between the current pay structure and the new pay structure.

(3) A comprehensive schedule for the implementation of the new pay structure and for the transition between the current pay structure and the new pay structure, including all significant deadlines.

(c) NEW PAY STRUCTURE.—The new pay structure described pursuant to subsection (b)(1) shall assume the repeal of the basic allowance for housing and basic allowance subsistence for members of the Armed Forces in favor of a single-salary pay system, and shall include the following:

(1) A statement of pay comparability with the civilian sector adequate to effectively recruit and retain a high-quality All-Volunteer Force.

(2) The level of pay necessary by grade and years of service to meet pay comparability as described in paragraph (1) in order to recruit and retain a high-quality All-Volunteer Force.

(3) Necessary modifications to the military retirement system, including the retired pay multiplier, to ensure that members of the Armed Forces under the pay structure are situated similarly to where they would otherwise be under the military retirement system that will take effect on January 1, 2018, by reason part I of subtitle D of the National Defense Authorization Act for Fiscal Year 2016 (Public Law 114–92; 129 Stat. 842), and the amendments made by that part.

(d) COST CONTAINMENT.—The single-salary pay system under the new pay structure provided for by this section shall be a single-salary pay system that will result in no or minimal additional costs to the Government, both in terms of annual discretionary outlays and entitlements, when compared with the continuation of the current pay system for members of the Armed Forces.

Subtitle B—Bonuses and Special and Incentive Pays

SEC. 611. ONE-YEAR EXTENSION OF CERTAIN BONUS AND SPECIAL PAY AUTHORITIES FOR RESERVE FORCES.

The following sections of title 37, United States Code, are amended by striking "December 31, 2016" and inserting "December 31, 2017":

(1) Section 308b(g), relating to Selected Reserve reenlistment bonus.

(2) Section 308c(i), relating to Selected Reserve affiliation or enlistment bonus.

(3) Section 308d(c), relating to special pay for enlisted members assigned to certain high-priority units.

(4) Section 308g(f)(2), relating to Ready Reserve enlistment bonus for persons without prior service.

(5) Section 308h(e), relating to Ready Reserve enlistment and reenlistment bonus for persons with prior service.

(6) Section 308i(f), relating to Selected Reserve enlistment and reenlistment bonus for persons with prior service.

(7) Section 478a(e), relating to reimbursement of travel expenses for inactive-duty training outside of normal commuting distance.

(8) Section 910(g), relating to income replacement payments for reserve component members experiencing extended and frequent mobilization for active duty service.

SEC. 612. ONE-YEAR EXTENSION OF CERTAIN BONUS AND SPECIAL PAY AUTHORITIES FOR HEALTH CARE PROFESSIONALS.

(a) TITLE 10 AUTHORITIES.—The following sections of title 10, United States Code, are amended by striking "December 31, 2016" and inserting "December 31, 2017":

(1) Section 2130a(a)(1), relating to nurse officer candidate accession program.

(2) Section 16302(d), relating to repayment of education loans for certain health professionals who serve in the Selected Reserve.

(b) TITLE 37 AUTHORITIES.—The following sections of title 37, United States Code, are amended by striking "December 31, 2016" and inserting "December 31, 2017":

(1) Section 302c-1(f), relating to accession and retention bonuses for psychologists.

(2) Section 302d(a)(1), relating to accession bonus for registered nurses.

(3) Section 302e(a)(1), relating to incentive special pay for nurse anesthetists.

(4) Section 302g(e), relating to special pay for Selected Reserve health professionals in critically short wartime specialties.

(5) Section 302h(a)(1), relating to accession bonus for dental officers.

(6) Section 302j(a), relating to accession bonus for pharmacy officers.

(7) Section 302k(f), relating to accession bonus for medical officers in critically short wartime specialties.

(8) Section 302l(g), relating to accession bonus for dental specialist officers in critically short wartime specialties.

SEC. 613. ONE-YEAR EXTENSION OF SPECIAL PAY AND BONUS AUTHORITIES FOR NUCLEAR OFFICERS.

The following sections of title 37, United States Code, are amended by striking "December 31, 2016" and inserting "December 31, 2017":

(1) Section 312(f), relating to special pay for nuclear-qualified officers extending period of active service.

(2) Section 312b(c), relating to nuclear career accession bonus.

(3) Section 312c(d), relating to nuclear career annual incentive bonus.

SEC. 614. ONE-YEAR EXTENSION OF AUTHORITIES RELATING TO TITLE 37 CONSOLIDATED SPECIAL PAY, INCENTIVE PAY, AND BONUS AUTHORITIES.

The following sections of title 37, United States Code, are amended by striking "December 31, 2016" and inserting "December 31, 2017":

(1) Section 331(h), relating to general bonus authority for enlisted members.

(2) Section 332(g), relating to general bonus authority for officers.

(3) Section 333(i), relating to special bonus and incentive pay authorities for nuclear officers.

(4) Section 334(i), relating to special aviation incentive pay and bonus authorities for officers.

(5) Section 335(k), relating to special bonus and incentive pay authorities for officers in health professions.

(6) Section 336(g), relating to contracting bonus for cadets and midshipmen enrolled in the Senior Reserve Officers' Training Corps.

(7) Section 351(h), relating to hazardous duty pay.

(8) Section 352(g), relating to assignment pay or special duty pay.

(9) Section 353(i), relating to skill incentive pay or proficiency bonus.

(10) Section 355(h), relating to retention incentives for members qualified in critical military skills or assigned to high priority units.

SEC. 615. ONE-YEAR EXTENSION OF AUTHORITIES RELATING TO PAYMENT OF OTHER TITLE 37 BONUSES AND SPECIAL PAYS.

The following sections of title 37, United States Code, are amended by striking "December 31, 2016" and inserting "December 31, 2017":

(1) Section 301b(a), relating to aviation officer retention bonus.

(2) Section 307a(g), relating to assignment incentive pay.

(3) Section 308(g), relating to reenlistment bonus for active members.

(4) Section 309(e), relating to enlistment bonus.

(5) Section 316a(g), relating to incentive pay for members of precommissioning programs pursuing foreign language proficiency.

(6) Section 324(g), relating to accession bonus for new officers in critical skills.

(7) Section 326(g), relating to incentive bonus for conversion to military occupational specialty to ease personnel shortage.

(8) Section 327(h), relating to incentive bonus for transfer between Armed Forces.

(9) Section 330(f), relating to accession bonus for officer candidates.

SEC. 616. AVIATION INCENTIVE PAY AND BONUS MATTERS.

(a) MAXIMUM INCENTIVE PAY AND BONUS AMOUNTS.—Paragraph (1) of section 334(c) of title 37, United States Code, is amended by striking subparagraphs (A) and (B) and inserting the following new subparagraphs:

"(A) aviation incentive pay under subsection (a) shall be paid at a monthly rate not to exceed $1,000 per month; and

"(B) an aviation bonus under subsection (b) may not exceed $35,000 for each 12-month period of obligated service agreed to under subsection (d).".

(b) ANNUAL BUSINESS CASE FOR PAYMENT OF AVIATION BONUS.—Such section is further amended—

(1) by redesignating paragraphs (2) and (3) as paragraphs (3) and (4), respectively; and

(2) by inserting after paragraph (1) the following new paragraph (2):

"(2) ANNUAL BUSINESS CASE FOR PAYMENT OF AVIATION BONUS AMOUNTS.—

"(A) IN GENERAL.—The Secretary concerned shall determine the amount of the aviation bonus payable under paragraph (1)(B) under agreements entered into under subsection (d) during a fiscal year solely through a business case analysis of the amount required to be paid under such agreements in order to address anticipated manning shortfalls for such fiscal year by aircraft type category.

"(B) BUDGET JUSTIFICATION DOCUMENTS.—The budget justification documents in support of the budget of the President for a fiscal year (as submitted to Congress pursuant to section 1105 of title 31) shall set forth for each uniformed service the following:

"(i) The amount requested for the payment of aviation bonuses under subsection (b) using amounts authorized to be appropriated for the fiscal year concerned by aircraft type category.

"(ii) The business case analysis supporting the amount so requested by aircraft type category.

"(iii) For each aircraft type category, whether or not the amount requested will permit the payment during the fiscal year concerned of the maximum amount of the aviation bonus authorized by paragraph (1)(B).

"(iv) If any amount requested is to address manning shortfalls, a description of any plans of the Secretary concerned to address such shortfalls by nonmonetary means.".

SEC. 617. CONFORMING AMENDMENT TO CONSOLIDATION OF SPECIAL PAY, INCENTIVE PAY, AND BONUS AUTHORITIES.

Section 332(c)(1)(B) of title 37, United States Code, is amended by striking "$12,000" and inserting "$20,000".

SEC. 618. TECHNICAL AMENDMENTS RELATING TO 2008 CONSOLIDATION OF CERTAIN SPECIAL PAY AUTHORITIES.

(a) FAMILY CARE PLANS.—Section 586 of the National Defense Authorization Act for Fiscal Year 2008 (Public Law 110–181; 10 U.S.C. 991 note) is amended by inserting "or 351" after "section 310".

(b) DEPENDENTS' MEDICAL CARE.—Section 1079(g)(1) of title 10, United States Code, is amended by inserting "or 351" after "section 310".

(c) RETENTION ON ACTIVE DUTY DURING DISABILITY EVALUATION PROCESS.—Section

1218(d)(1) of title 10, United States Code, is amended by inserting "or 351" after "section 310".

(d) STORAGE SPACE.—Section 362(1) of the John Warner National Defense Authorization Act for Fiscal Year 2007 (Public Law 109–364; 10 U.S.C. 2825 note) is amended by inserting ", or paragraph (1) or (3) of section 351(a)," after "section 310".

(e) STUDENT ASSISTANCE PROGRAMS.—Sections 455(o)(3)(B) and 465(a)(2)(D) of the Higher Education Act of 1965 (20 U.S.C. 1087e(o)(3)(B), 1087ee(a)(2)(D)) are amended by inserting ", or paragraph (1) or (3) of section 351(a)," after "section 310".

(f) ARMED FORCES RETIREMENT HOME.—Section 1512(a)(3)(A) of the Armed Forces Retirement Home Act of 1991 (24 U.S.C. 412(a)(3)(A)) is amended by inserting "or 351" after "section 310".

(g) VETERANS OF FOREIGN WARS MEMBERSHIP.—Section 230103(3) of title 36, United States Code, is amended by inserting "or 351" after "section 310".

(h) MILITARY PAY AND ALLOWANCES.—Title 37, United States Code, is amended—

(1) in section 212(a), by inserting ", or paragraph (1) or (3) of section 351(a)," after "section 310";

(2) in section 402a(b)(3)(B), by inserting "or 351" after "section 310";

(3) in section 481a(a), by inserting "or 351" after "section 310";

(4) in section 907(d)(1)(H), by inserting "or 351" after "section 310"; and

(5) in section 910(b)(2)(B), by inserting ", or paragraph (1) or (3) of section 351(a)," after "section 310".

(i) EXCLUSIONS FROM INCOME FOR PURPOSE OF SUPPLEMENTAL SECURITY INCOME.—Section 1612(b)(20) of the Social Security Act (42 U.S.C. 1382a(b)(20)) is amended by inserting ", or paragraph (1) or (3) of section 351(a)," after "section 310".

(j) EXCLUSIONS FROM INCOME FOR PURPOSE OF HEAD START PROGRAM.—Section 645(a)(3)(B)(i) of the Head Start Act (42 U.S.C. 9840(a)(3)(B)(i)) is amended by inserting "or 351" after "section 310".

(k) EXCLUSIONS FROM GROSS INCOME FOR FEDERAL INCOME TAX PURPOSES.—Section 112(c)(5)(B) of the Internal Revenue Code of 1986 is amended by inserting ", or paragraph (1) or (3) of section 351(a)," after "section 310".

Subtitle C—Travel and Transportation Allowances

SEC. 621. MAXIMUM REIMBURSEMENT AMOUNT FOR TRAVEL EXPENSES OF MEMBERS OF THE RESERVES ATTENDING INACTIVE DUTY TRAINING OUTSIDE OF NORMAL COMMUTING DISTANCES.

Section 478a(c) of title 37, United States Code, is amended—

(1) by striking "The amount" and inserting the following: "(1) Except as provided by paragraph (2), the amount"; and

(2) by adding at the end the following new paragraph:

"(2) The Secretary concerned may authorize, on a case-by-case basis, a higher reimbursement amount for a member under subsection (a) when the member—

"(A) resides—

"(i) in the same State as the training location; and

"(ii) outside of an urbanized area with a population of 50,000 or more, as determined by the Bureau of the Census; and

"(B) is required to commute to a training location—

"(i) using an aircraft or boat on account of limited or nonexistent vehicular routes to the training location or other geographical challenges; or

"(ii) from a permanent residence located more than 75 miles from the training location.".

Subtitle D—Disability Pay, Retired Pay, and Survivor Benefits

PART I—AMENDMENTS IN CONNECTION WITH RETIRED PAY REFORM

SEC. 631. ELECTION PERIOD FOR MEMBERS IN THE SERVICE ACADEMIES AND INACTIVE RESERVES TO PARTICIPATE IN THE MODERNIZED RETIREMENT SYSTEM.

(a) IN GENERAL.—Paragraph (4)(C) of section 1409(b) of title 10, United States Code, is amended—

(1) in clause (i), by striking "and (iii)" and inserting ", (iii), (iv), and (v)"; and

(2) by adding at the end the following new clauses:

"(iv) CADETS AND MIDSHIPMEN, ETC.—A member of a uniformed service who serves as a cadet, midshipman, or member of the Senior Reserve Officers' Training Corps during the election period specified in clause (i) shall make the election described in subparagraph (B)—

"(I) on or after the date on which such cadet, midshipman, or member of the Senior Reserve Officers' Training Corps is appointed as a commissioned officer or otherwise begins to receive basic pay; and

"(II) not later than 30 days after such date or the end of such election period, whichever is later.

"(v) INACTIVE RESERVES.—A member of a reserve component who is not in an active status during the election period specified in clause (i) shall make the election described in subparagraph (B)—

"(I) on or after the date on which such member is transferred from an inactive status to an active status or active duty; and

"(II) not later than 30 days after such date or the end of such election period, whichever is later.".

(b) EFFECTIVE DATE.—The amendments made by subsection (a) shall take effect on January 1, 2018, immediately after the coming into effect of the amendments made by section 631(a) of the National Defense Authorization Act for Fiscal Year 2016 (Public Law 114–92; 129 Stat. 842), to which the amendments made by subsection (a) relate.

SEC. 632. EFFECT OF SEPARATION OF MEMBERS FROM THE UNIFORMED SERVICES ON PARTICIPATION IN THE THRIFT SAVINGS PLAN.

Effective as of the date of the enactment of this Act, paragraph (2) of section 632(c) of the National Defense Authorization Act for Fiscal Year 2016 (Public Law 114–92; 129 Stat. 847) is repealed, and the amendment proposed to be made by that paragraph shall not be made or go into effect.

SEC. 633. CONTINUATION PAY FOR FULL THRIFT SAVINGS PLAN MEMBERS WHO HAVE COMPLETED 8 TO 12 YEARS OF SERVICE.

(a) CONTINUATION PAY.—Subsection (a) of section 356 of title 37, United States Code, is amended—

(1) by striking paragraph (1) and inserting the following new paragraph (1):

"(1) has completed not less than 8 and not more than 12 years of service in a uniformed service; and"; and

(2) in paragraph (2), by striking "an additional 4 years" and inserting "not less than 3 additional years".

(b) PAYMENT AMOUNT.—Subsection (b) of such section is amended by striking all the matter preceding paragraph (1) and inserting the following:

"(b) PAYMENT AMOUNT.—The Secretary concerned shall determine the payment amount under this section as a multiple of a full TSP

member's monthly basic pay. The multiple for a full TSP member who is a member of a regular component or a reserve component, if the member is performing active Guard and Reserve duty (as defined in section 101(d)(6) of title 10), shall not be less than 2.5 times the member's monthly basic pay. The multiple for a full TSP member who is a member of a reserve component not performing active Guard or Reserve duty (as so defined) shall not be less than 0.5 times the monthly basic pay to which the member would be entitled if the member were a member of a regular component. The maximum amount the Secretary concerned may pay a member under this section is—".

(c) TIMING OF PAYMENT.—Subsection (d) of such section is amended to read as follows:

"(d) TIMING OF PAYMENT.—The Secretary concerned shall pay continuation pay under subsection (a) to a full TSP member when the member has completed not less than 8 and not more than 12 years of service in a uniformed service.".

(d) CONFORMING AND CLERICAL AMENDMENTS.—

(1) HEADING.—The heading of such section is amended to read as follows:

"§356. Continuation pay: full TSP members with 8 to 12 years of service".

(2) TABLE OF SECTIONS.—The table of sections at the beginning of chapter 5 of such title is amended by striking the item relating to section 356 and inserting the following new item:

"356. Continuation pay: full TSP members with 8 to 12 years of service.".

(e) EFFECTIVE DATE.—The amendments made by this section shall take effect on January 1, 2018, immediately after the coming into effect of the amendments providing for section 356 of title 37, United States Code, to which the amendments made by this section relate.

SEC. 634. COMBAT-RELATED SPECIAL COMPENSATION COORDINATING AMENDMENT.

(a) IN GENERAL.—Section 1413a(b)(3)(B) of title 10, United States Code, is amended by striking "2½ percent" and inserting "the retired pay percentage (determined for the member under section 1409(b) of this title)".

(b) EFFECTIVE DATE.—The amendment made by subsection (a) shall take effect on January 1, 2018, immediately after the coming into effect of the amendments made by part I of subtitle D of title VI of the National Defense Authorization Act for Fiscal Year 2016 (Public Law 114–92; 129 Stat. 842), to which the amendment made by subsection (a) relates.

PART II—OTHER MATTERS

SEC. 641. USE OF MEMBER'S CURRENT PAY GRADE AND YEARS OF SERVICE AND RETIRED PAY COST-OF-LIVING ADJUSTMENTS, RATHER THAN FINAL RETIREMENT PAY GRADE AND YEARS OF SERVICE, IN A DIVISION OF PROPERTY INVOLVING DISPOSABLE RETIRED PAY.

(a) IN GENERAL.—Section 1408(a)(4) of title 10, United States Code, is amended—

(1) by redesignating subparagraphs (A), (B), (C), (D) as clauses (i), (ii), (iii), (iv), respectively;

(2) by inserting "(A)" after "(4)";

(3) in subparagraph (A), as designated by paragraph (2), by inserting "(as determined pursuant to subparagraph (B))" after "member is entitled"; and

(4) by adding at the end the following new subparagraph:

"(B) For purposes of subparagraph (A), the total monthly retired pay to which a member is entitled shall be—

"(i) the amount of basic pay payable to the member for the member's pay grade and years of service at the time of the court order, as increased by

"(ii) each cost-of-living adjustment that occurs under section 1401a(b) of this title between the time of the court order and the time of the member's retirement using the adjustment provisions under that section applicable to the member upon retirement.".

(b) APPLICATION OF AMENDMENTS.—The amendments made by subsection (a) shall apply with respect to any division of property as part of a final decree of divorce, dissolution, annulment, or legal separation involving a member of the Armed Forces to which section 1408 of title 10, United States Code, applies that becomes final after the date of the enactment of this Act.

SEC. 642. EQUAL BENEFITS UNDER SURVIVOR BENEFIT PLAN FOR SURVIVORS OF RESERVE COMPONENT MEMBERS WHO DIE IN THE LINE OF DUTY DURING INACTIVE-DUTY TRAINING.

(a) TREATMENT OF INACTIVE-DUTY TRAINING IN SAME MANNER AS ACTIVE DUTY.—Section 1451(c)(1)(A) of title 10, United States Code, is amended—

(1) in clause (i)—

(A) by inserting "or 1448(f)" after "section 1448(d)"; and

(B) by inserting "or (iii)" after "clause (ii)"; and

(2) in clause (iii)—

(A) by striking "section 1448(f) of this title" and inserting "section 1448(f)(1)(A) of this title by reason of the death of a member or former member not in line of duty"; and

(B) by striking "active service" and inserting "service".

(b) CONSISTENT TREATMENT OF DEPENDENT CHILDREN.—Paragraph (2) of section 1448(f) of title 10, United States Code, is amended to read as follows:

"(2) DEPENDENT CHILDREN ANNUITY.—

"(A) ANNUITY WHEN NO ELIGIBLE SURVIVING SPOUSE.—In the case of a person described in paragraph (1), the Secretary concerned shall pay an annuity under this subchapter to the dependent children of that person under section 1450(a)(2) of this title as applicable.

"(B) OPTIONAL ANNUITY WHEN THERE IS AN ELIGIBLE SURVIVING SPOUSE.—The Secretary may pay an annuity under this subchapter to the dependent children of a person described in paragraph (1) under section 1450(a)(3) of this title, if applicable, instead of paying an annuity to the surviving spouse under paragraph (1), if the Secretary concerned, in consultation with the surviving spouse, determines it appropriate to provide an annuity for the dependent children under this paragraph instead of an annuity for the surviving spouse under paragraph (1).".

(c) DEEMED ELECTIONS.—Section 1448(f) of title 10, United States Code, is further amended by adding at the end the following new paragraph:

"(5) DEEMED ELECTION TO PROVIDE AN ANNUITY FOR DEPENDENT.—Paragraph (6) of subsection (d) shall apply in the case of a member described in paragraph (1) who dies after November 23, 2003, when no other annuity is payable on behalf of the member under this subchapter.".

(d) AVAILABILITY OF SPECIAL SURVIVOR INDEMNITY ALLOWANCE.—Section 1450(m)(1)(B) of title 10, United States Code, is amended by inserting "or (f)" after "subsection (d)".

(e) APPLICATION OF AMENDMENTS.—

(1) PAYMENT.—No annuity benefit under subchapter II of chapter 73 of title 10, United States Code, shall accrue to any person by reason of the amendments made by this section for any period before the date of the enactment of this Act.

(2) ELECTIONS.—For any death that occurred before the date of the enactment of this Act with respect to which an annuity under such subchapter is being paid (or could be paid) to a surviving spouse, the Secretary concerned may,

within six months of that date and in consultation with the surviving spouse, determine it appropriate to provide an annuity for the dependent children of the decedent under paragraph 1448(f)(2)(B) of title 10, United States Code, as added by subsection (b), instead of an annuity for the surviving spouse. Any such determination and resulting change in beneficiary shall be effective as of the first day of the first month following the date of the determination.

SEC. 643. AUTHORITY TO DEDUCT SURVIVOR BENEFIT PLAN PREMIUMS FROM COMBAT-RELATED SPECIAL COMPENSATION WHEN RETIRED PAY NOT SUFFICIENT.

(a) AUTHORITY.—Subsection (d) of section 1452 of title 10, United States Code, is amended—

(1) by redesignating paragraph (2) as paragraph (3); and

(2) by inserting after paragraph (1) the following new paragraph (2):

"(2) DEDUCTION FROM COMBAT-RELATED SPECIAL COMPENSATION WHEN RETIRED PAY NOT ADEQUATE.—In the case of a person who has elected to participate in the Plan and who has been awarded both retired pay and combat-related special compensation under section 1413a of this title, if a deduction from the person's retired pay for any period cannot be made in the full amount required, there shall be deducted from the person's combat-related special compensation in lieu of deduction from the person's retired pay the amount that would otherwise have been deducted from the person's retired pay for that period.".

(b) CONFORMING AMENDMENTS TO SECTION 1452.—

(1) Subsection (d) of such section is further amended—

(A) in the subsection heading, by inserting "OR NOT SUFFICIENT" after "NOT PAID";

(B) in paragraph (1), by inserting before the period at the end the following: ", except to the extent that the required deduction is made pursuant to paragraph (2)"; and

(C) in paragraph (3), as redesignated by subsection (a)(1), by striking "Paragraph (1) does not" and inserting "Paragraphs (1) and (2) do not".

(2) Subsection (f)(1) of such section is amended by inserting "or combat-related special compensation" after "from retired pay".

(3) Subsection (g)(4) of such section is amended—

(A) in the paragraph heading, by inserting "OR CRSC" after "RETIRED PAY"; and

(B) by inserting "or combat-related special compensation" after "from the retired pay".

(c) CONFORMING AMENDMENTS TO OTHER PROVISIONS OF SBP STATUTE.—

(1) Section 1449(b)(2) of such title is amended—

(A) in the paragraph heading, by inserting "OR CRSC" after "RETIRED PAY"; and

(B) by inserting "or combat-related special compensation" after "from retired pay".

(2) Section 1450(e) of such title is amended—

(A) in the subsection heading, by inserting "OR CRSC" after "RETIRED PAY"; and

(B) in paragraph (1), by inserting "or combat-related special compensation" after "from the retired pay".

SEC. 644. EXTENSION OF ALLOWANCE COVERING MONTHLY PREMIUM FOR SERVICEMEMBERS' GROUP LIFE INSURANCE WHILE IN CERTAIN OVERSEAS AREAS TO COVER MEMBERS IN ANY COMBAT ZONE OR OVERSEAS DIRECT SUPPORT AREA.

(a) EXPANSION OF COVERAGE.—Subsection (a) of section 437 of title 37, United States Code, is amended—

(1) by inserting "(1)" before "In the case of";

(2) by striking "who serves in the theater of operations for Operation Enduring Freedom or

Operation Iraqi Freedom" and inserting "who serves in a designated duty assignment"; and

(3) by adding at the end the following new paragraph:

"(2) In this subsection, the term 'designated duty assignment' means a permanent or temporary duty assignment outside the United States or its possessions in support of a contingency operation in an area that—

"(A) has been designated a combat zone; or

"(B) is in direct support of an area that has been designated a combat zone.".

(b) CONFORMING AMENDMENTS.—

(1) CROSS-REFERENCE.—Subsection (b) of such section is amended by striking "theater of operations" and inserting "designated duty assignment".

(2) SECTION HEADING.—The heading of such section is amended to read as follows:

"§ 437. Allowance to cover monthly premiums for Servicemembers' Group Life Insurance: members serving in a designated duty assignment".

(3) TABLE OF SECTIONS.—The item relating to section 437 in the table of sections at the beginning of chapter 7 of such title is amended to read as follows:

"437. Allowance to cover monthly premium for Servicemembers' Group Life Insurance: members serving in a designated duty assignment.".

(c) EFFECTIVE DATE.—The amendments made by this section shall apply to service by members of the Armed Forces in a designated duty assignment (as defined in subsection (a)(2) of section 437 of title 37, United States Code) for any month beginning on or after the date of the enactment of this Act.

SEC. 645. AUTHORITY FOR PAYMENT OF PAY AND ALLOWANCES AND RETIRED AND RETAINER PAY PURSUANT TO POWER OF ATTORNEY.

Section 602 of title 37, United States Code, is amended—

(1) in subsection (a)—

(A) by striking ", in the opinion of a board of medical officers or physicians,"; and

(B) by striking "use or benefit" and all that follows through "any person designated" and inserting the following: "use or benefit to—

"(1) a legal committee, guardian, or other representative that has been appointed by a court of competent jurisdiction;

"(2) an individual to whom the member has granted authority to manage such funds pursuant to a valid and legally executed durable power of attorney; or

"(3) any person designated";

(2) in subsection (b)—

(A) by striking "The board shall consist" and inserting "An individual may not be designated under subsection (a)(3) to receive payments unless a board consisting"; and

(B) by inserting "determines that the member is mentally incapable of managing the member's affairs. Any such board shall be" after "treatment of mental disorders,";

(3) in subsection (c), by striking "designated" and inserting "authorized to receive payments";

(4) in subsection (d), by inserting ", unless a court of competent jurisdiction orders payment of such fee, commission, or other charge" before the period;

(5) by striking subsection (e);

(6) by redesignating subsection (f) as subsection (e); and

(7) in subsection (e), as redesignated by paragraph (6)—

(A) by inserting "under subsection (a)(3)" after "who is designated"; and

(B) by striking "$1,000" and inserting "$25,000".

SEC. 646. EXTENSION OF AUTHORITY TO PAY SPECIAL SURVIVOR INDEMNITY ALLOWANCE UNDER THE SURVIVOR BENEFIT PLAN.

Section 1450(m) of title 10, United States Code, is amended—

(1) in paragraph (2)(I), by striking "fiscal year 2017" and inserting "each of fiscal years 2017 and 2018"; and

(2) in paragraph (6)—

(A) by striking "September 30, 2017" and inserting "May 31, 2018"; and

(B) by striking "October 1, 2017" both places it appears and inserting "June 1, 2018".

SEC. 647. REPEAL OF OBSOLETE AUTHORITY FOR COMBAT-RELATED INJURY REHABILITATION PAY.

(a) REPEAL.—Section 328 of title 37, United States Code, is repealed.

(b) CLERICAL AMENDMENT.—The table of sections at the beginning of chapter 5 of such title is amended by striking the item relating to section 328.

SEC. 648. INDEPENDENT ASSESSMENT OF THE SURVIVOR BENEFIT PLAN.

(a) ASSESSMENT REQUIRED.—The Secretary of Defense shall provide for an independent assessment of the Survivor Benefit Plan (SBP) under subchapter II of chapter 73 of title 10, United States Code, by a Federally-funded research and development center (FFRDC).

(b) ASSESSMENT ELEMENTS.—The assessment conducted pursuant to subsection (a) shall include, but not be limited to, the following:

(1) The purposes of the Survivor Benefit Plan, the manner in which the Plan interacts with other Federal programs to provide financial stability and resources for survivors of members of the Armed Forces and military retirees, and a comparison between the benefits available under the Plan, on the one hand, and benefits available to Government and private sector employees, on the other hand, intended to provide financial stability and resources for spouses and other dependents when a primary family earner dies.

(2) The effectiveness of the Survivor Benefit Plan in providing survivors with intended benefits, including the provision of survivor benefits for survivors of members of the Armed Forces dying on active duty and members dying while in reserve active-status.

(3) The feasibility and advisability of providing survivor benefits through alternative insurance products available commercially for similar purposes, the extent to which the Government could subsidize such products at no cost in excess of the costs of the Survivor Benefit Plan, and the extent to which such products might meet the needs of survivors, especially those on fixed incomes, to maintain financial stability.

(c) REPORT.—Not later than one year after the date of the enactment of this Act, the Secretary shall submit to the Committees on Armed Services of the Senate and the House of Representatives a report setting forth the results of the assessment conducted pursuant to subsection (a), together with such recommendations as the Secretary considers appropriate for legislative or administration action in light of the results of the assessment.

Subtitle E—Commissary and Nonappropriated Fund Instrumentality Benefits and Operations

SEC. 661. PROTECTION AND ENHANCEMENT OF ACCESS TO AND SAVINGS AT COMMISSARIES AND EXCHANGES.

(a) OPTIMIZATION STRATEGY.—Section 2481(c) of title 10, United States Code, is amended by adding at the end the following paragraph:

"(3)(A) The Secretary of Defense shall develop and implement a comprehensive strategy to optimize management practices across the defense commissary system and the exchange system that reduce reliance of those systems on appropriated funding without reducing benefits to the patrons of those systems or the revenue generated by nonappropriated fund entities or instrumentalities of the Department of Defense for the morale, welfare, and recreation of members of the armed forces.

"(B) The Secretary shall ensure that savings generated due to such optimization practices are shared by the defense commissary system and the exchange system through contracts or agreements that appropriately reflect the participation of the systems in the development and implementation of such practices.

"(C) If the Secretary determines that the reduced reliance on appropriated funding pursuant to subparagraph (A) is insufficient to maintain the benefits to the patrons of the defense commissary system, and if the Secretary converts the defense commissary system to a nonappropriated fund entity or instrumentality pursuant to paragraph (1) of section 2484(j) of this title, the Secretary shall transfer appropriated funds pursuant to paragraph (2) of such section to ensure the maintenance of such benefits.

"(4) On not less than a quarterly basis, the Secretary shall provide to the congressional defense committees a briefing on the defense commissary system, including—

"(A) an assessment of the savings the system provides patrons;

"(B) the status of implementing section 2484(i) of this title;

"(C) the status of implementing section 2484(j) of this title, including whether the system requires any appropriated funds pursuant to paragraph (2) of such section;

"(D) the status of carrying out a program for such system to sell private label merchandise; and

"(E) any other matters the Secretary considers appropriate.".

(b) AUTHORIZATION TO SUPPLEMENT APPROPRIATIONS THROUGH BUSINESS OPTIMIZATION.—Section 2483(c) of such title is amended by adding at the end the following new sentence: "Such appropriated amounts may also be supplemented with additional funds derived from improved management practices implemented pursuant to sections 2481(c)(3) and 2487(c) of this title and the variable pricing program implemented pursuant to section 2484(i) of this title.".

(c) VARIABLE PRICING PILOT PROGRAM.—Section 2484 of such title is amended by adding at the end the following new subsections:

"(i) VARIABLE PRICING PROGRAM.—(1) Notwithstanding subsection (e), and subject to subsection (k), the Secretary of Defense may establish a variable pricing program pursuant to which prices may be established in response to market conditions and customer demand, in accordance with the requirements of this subsection. Notwithstanding the amount of the uniform surcharge assessed in subsection (d), the Secretary may provide for an alternative surcharge of not more than five percent of sales proceeds under the variable pricing program to be made available for the purposes specified in subsection (h).

"(2) Subject to subsection (k), before establishing a variable pricing program under this subsection, the Secretary shall establish the following:

"(A) Specific, measurable benchmarks for success in the provision of high quality grocery merchandise, discount savings to patrons, and levels of customer satisfaction while achieving savings for the Department of Defense.

"(B) A baseline of overall savings to patrons achieved by commissary stores prior to the initiation of the variable pricing program, based on a comparison of prices charged by those stores on a regional basis with prices charged by relevant local competitors for a representative market basket of goods.

"(3) The Secretary shall ensure that the defense commissary system implements the variable pricing program by conducting price comparisons using the methodology established for paragraph (2)(B) and adjusting pricing as necessary to ensure that pricing in the variable pricing program achieves overall savings to patrons that are consistent with the baseline savings established for the relevant region pursuant to such paragraph.

"(j) CONVERSION TO NONAPPROPRIATED FUND ENTITY OR INSTRUMENTALITY.—(1) Subject to subsection (k), if the Secretary of Defense determines that the variable pricing program has met the benchmarks for success established pursuant to paragraph (2)(A) of subsection (i) and the savings requirements established pursuant to paragraph (3) of such subsection over a period of at least six months, the Secretary may convert the defense commissary system to a nonappropriated fund entity or instrumentality, with operating expenses financed in whole or in part by receipts from the sale of products and the sale of services. Upon such conversion, appropriated funds shall be transferred to the defense commissary system only in accordance with paragraph (2) or section 2491 of this title. The requirements of section 2483 of this title shall not apply to the defense commissary system operating as a nonappropriated fund entity or instrumentality.

"(2) If the Secretary determines that the defense commissary system operating as a nonappropriated fund entity or instrumentality is likely to incur a loss in any fiscal year as a result of compliance with the savings requirement established in subsection (i), the Secretary shall authorize a transfer of appropriated funds available for such purpose to the commissary system in an amount sufficient to offset the anticipated loss. Any funds so transferred shall be considered to be nonappropriated funds for such purpose.

"(3)(A) The Secretary may identify positions of employees in the defense commissary system who are paid with appropriated funds whose status may be converted to the status of an employee of a nonappropriated fund entity or instrumentality.

"(B) The status and conversion of employees in a position identified by the Secretary under subparagraph (A) shall be addressed as provided in section 2491(c) of this title for employees in morale, welfare, and recreation programs, including with respect to requiring the consent of such employee to be so converted.

"(C) No individual who is an employee of the defense commissary system as of the date of the enactment of this subsection shall suffer any loss of or decrease in pay as a result of a conversion made under this paragraph.

"(k) OVERSIGHT REQUIRED TO ENSURE CONTINUED BENEFIT TO PATRONS.—(1) With respect to each action described in paragraph (2), the Secretary of Defense may not carry out such action until—

"(A) the Secretary provides to the congressional defense committees a briefing on such action, including a justification for such action; and

"(B) a period of 30 days has elapsed following such briefing.

"(2) The actions described in this paragraph are the following:

"(A) Establishing the representative market basket of goods pursuant to subsection (i)(2)(B).

"(B) Establishing the variable pricing program under subsection (i)(1).

"(C) Converting the defense commissary system to a nonappropriated fund entity or instrumentality under subsection (j)(1).".

(d) ESTABLISHMENT OF COMMON BUSINESS PRACTICES.—Section 2487 of such title is amended—

(1) by redesignating subsection (c) as subsection (d); and

(2) by inserting after subsection (b) the following new subsection (c):

"(c) COMMON BUSINESS PRACTICES.—(1) Notwithstanding subsections (a) and (b), the Secretary of Defense may establish common business processes, practices, and systems—

"(A) to exploit synergies between the defense commissary system and the exchange system; and

"(B) to optimize the operations of the defense retail systems as a whole and the benefits provided by the commissaries and exchanges.

"(2) The Secretary may authorize the defense commissary system and the exchange system to enter into contracts or other agreements—

"(A) for products and services that are shared by the defense commissary system and the exchange system; and

"(B) for the acquisition of supplies, resale goods, and services on behalf of both the defense commissary system and the exchange system.

"(3) For the purpose of a contract or agreement authorized under paragraph (2), the Secretary may—

"(A) use funds appropriated pursuant to section 2483 of this title to reimburse a nonappropriated fund entity or instrumentality for the portion of the cost of a contract or agreement entered by the nonappropriated fund entity or instrumentality that is attributable to the defense commissary system; and

"(B) authorize the defense commissary system to accept reimbursement from a nonappropriated fund entity or instrumentality for the portion of the cost of a contract or agreement entered by the defense commissary system that is attributable to the nonappropriated fund entity or instrumentality.".

(e) AUTHORITY FOR EXPERT COMMERCIAL ADVICE.—Section 2485 of such title is amended by adding at the end the following new subsection:

"(i) EXPERT COMMERCIAL ADVICE.—The Secretary of Defense may enter into a contract with an entity to obtain expert commercial advice, commercial assistance, or other similar services not otherwise carried out by the Defense Commissary Agency, to implement section 2481(c), subsections (i) and (j) of section 2484, and section 2487(c) of this title.".

(f) CLARIFICATION OF REFERENCES TO "THE EXCHANGE SYSTEM".—Section 2481(a) of such title is amended by adding at the end the following new sentence: "Any reference in this chapter to 'the exchange system' shall be treated as referring to each separate administrative entity within the Department of Defense through which the Secretary has implemented the requirement under this subsection for a worldwide system of exchange stores.".

(g) OPERATION OF DEFENSE COMMISSARY SYSTEM AS A NONAPPROPRIATED FUND ENTITY.—In the event that the defense commissary system is converted to a nonappropriated fund entity or instrumentality as authorized by section 2484(j)(1) of title 10, United States Code, as added by subsection (c) of this section, the Secretary of Defense may—

(1) provide for the transfer of commissary assets, including inventory and available funds, to the nonappropriated fund entity or instrumentality; and

(2) ensure that revenues accruing to the defense commissary system are appropriately credited to the nonappropriated fund entity or instrumentality.

(h) CONFORMING CHANGE.—Section 2643(b) of such title is amended by adding at the end the following new sentence: "Such appropriated funds may be supplemented with additional funds derived from improved management practices implemented pursuant to sections 2481(c)(3) and 2487(c) of this title.".

SEC. 662. ACCEPTANCE OF MILITARY STAR CARD AT COMMISSARIES.

(a) IN GENERAL.—The Secretary of Defense shall ensure that—

(1) commissary stores accept as payment the Military Star Card; and

(2) any financial liability of the United States relating to such acceptance as payment be assumed by the Army and Air Force Exchange Service.

(b) MILITARY STAR CARD DEFINED.—In this section, the term "Military Star Card" means a credit card administered under the Exchange Credit Program by the Army and Air Force Exchange Service.

Subtitle F—Other Matters

SEC. 671. RECOVERY OF AMOUNTS OWED TO THE UNITED STATES BY MEMBERS OF THE UNIFORMED SERVICES.

(a) STATUTE OF LIMITATIONS.—Section 1007(c)(3) of title 37, United States Code, is amended by adding at the end the following new subparagraphs:

"(C)(i) In accordance with clause (ii), if the indebtedness of a member of the uniformed services to the United States occurs, through no fault of the member, as a result of the overpayment of pay or allowances to the member or upon the settlement of the member's accounts, the Secretary concerned may not recover the indebtedness from the member, including a retired or former member, using deductions from the pay of the member, deductions from retired or separation pay, or any other collection method unless recovery of the indebtedness commences before the end of the 10-year period beginning on the date on which the indebtedness was incurred.

"(ii) Clause (i) applies with respect to indebtedness incurred on or after the date of the enactment of the National Defense Authorization Act for Fiscal Year 2017.

"(D)(i) Not later than January 1 of each of 2017 through 2027, the Director of the Defense Finance and Accounting Service shall review all cases occurring during the 10-year period prior to the date of the review of indebtedness of a member of the uniformed services, including a retired or former member, to the United States in which—

"(I) the recovery of the indebtedness commenced after the end of the 10-year period beginning on the date on which the indebtedness was incurred; or

"(II) the Director did not otherwise notify the member of such indebtedness during such 10-year period.

"(ii) The Director shall submit to the congressional defense committees and the Committees on Veterans' Affairs of the House of Representatives and the Senate each review conducted under clause (i), including the amounts owed to the United States by the members included in such review.".

(b) REMISSION OR CANCELLATION OF INDEBTEDNESS OF RESERVES NOT ON ACTIVE DUTY.—

(1) ARMY.—Section 4837(a) of title 10, United States Code, is amended by striking "on active duty as a member of the Army" and inserting "as a member of the Army, whether as a regular or a reserve in active status".

(2) NAVY.—Section 6161(a) of such title is amended by striking "on active duty as a member of the naval service" and inserting "as a member of the naval service, whether as a regular or a reserve in active status".

(3) AIR FORCE.—Section 9837(a) of such title is amended by striking "on active duty as a member of the Air Force" and inserting "as a member of the Air Force, whether as a regular or a reserve in active status".

(4) COAST GUARD.—Section 461(1) of title 14, United States Code, is amended by striking "on active duty as a member of the Coast Guard" and inserting "as a member of the Coast Guard, whether as a regular or a reserve in active status".

(5) EFFECTIVE DATE.—The amendments made by this subsection shall take effect on the date of the enactment of this Act, and shall apply with respect to debt incurred on or after October 7, 2001.

(c) BENEFITS PAID TO MEMBERS OF CALIFORNIA NATIONAL GUARD.—

(1) REVIEW OF CERTAIN BENEFITS PAID.—

(A) IN GENERAL.—The Secretary of Defense shall conduct a review of all bonus pays, special pays, student loan repayments, and similar special payments that were paid to members of the National Guard of the State of California during the period beginning on January 1, 2004, and ending on December 31, 2015.

(B) EXCEPTION.—A review is not required under this paragraph for benefits paid as described in subparagraph (A) that were reviewed before the date of the enactment of this Act and in which fraud or other ineligibility was identified in connection with payment.

(C) CONDUCT OF REVIEW.—The Secretary shall establish a process to expedite the review required by this paragraph. The Secretary shall allocate appropriate personnel and other resources of the Department of Defense for the process, and for such other purposes as the Secretary considers appropriate, in order to achieve the completion of the review by the date specified in subparagraph (D).

(D) COMPLETION.—The review required by this paragraph shall be completed by not later than July 30, 2017.

(2) REVIEW.—

(A) IN GENERAL.—In conducting the review of benefits paid to members of the National Guard of the State of California pursuant to paragraph (1), the board of review concerned shall—

(i) carry out a complete review of all bonus pay and special pay contracts awarded to such members during the period described in paragraph (1)(A) for which the Department has reason to believe a recoupment of pay may be warranted in order to determine whether such members were eligible for the contracts so awarded and whether the contracts so awarded accurately specified the amounts of pay for which members were eligible;

(ii) carry out a complete review of all student loan repayment contracts awarded to such members during the period for which the Department has reason to believe a recoupment of payment may be warranted in order to determine whether such members were eligible for the contracts so awarded and whether the contracts so awarded accurately specified the amounts of payment for which members were eligible;

(iii) carry out a complete review of any other similar special payments paid to such members during the period for which the Department has reason to believe a recoupment of payments may be warranted in order to determine whether such members were eligible for payment and in such amount;

(iv) if any member is determined not to have been eligible for a bonus pay, special pay, student loan repayment, or other special payment paid, determine whether waiver of recoupment is warranted; and

(v) if any bonus pay, special pay, student loan repayment, or other special payment paid to any such member during the period has been recouped, determine whether the recoupment was unwarranted.

(B) WAIVER OF RECOUPMENT.—For purposes of clause (iv) of subparagraph (A), the board of review shall determine that waiver of recoupment is warranted with respect to a particular member unless the board makes an affirmative determination, by a preponderance of the evidence, that the member knew or reasonably should have known that the member was ineligible for the bonus pay, special pay, student loan repayment, or other special payment otherwise subject to recoupment.

(C) PROPRIETY OF RECOUPMENT.—For purposes of clause (v) of subparagraph (A), the board of review shall determine that recoupment was unwarranted with respect to a particular member unless the board makes an affirmative determination, by a preponderance of the evidence, that the member knew or reasonably should have known that the member was ineligible for the bonus pay, special pay, student loan repayment, or other special payment recouped.

(D) STANDARD OF REVIEW.—In applying subparagraph (B) or (C) in making a determination under clause (iv) or (v) of subparagraph (A), as applicable, with respect to a member, the board of review shall evaluate the evidence in a light most favorable to the member.

(3) PARTICIPATION OF MEMBERS.—

(A) IN GENERAL.—A member subject to a determination under clause (iv) or (v) of paragraph (2)(A) may submit to the board of review concerned such documentary and other evidence as the member considers appropriate to assist the board of review in the determination.

(B) NOTICE.—The Secretary shall notify, in writing, each member subject to a determination under clause (iv) or (v) of paragraph (2)(A) of the review under paragraph (1) and the applicability of the determination process under such clause to such member. The notice shall be provided at a time designed to give each member a reasonable opportunity to submit documentary and other evidence as authorized by subparagraph (A). The notice shall provide each member the following:

(i) Notice of the opportunity for such member to submit evidence to assist the board of review.

(ii) A description of resources available to such member to submit such evidence.

(C) CONSIDERATION.—In making a determination under clause (iv) or (v) of paragraph (2)(A) with respect to a member, the board of review shall undertake a comprehensive review of any submissions made by the member pursuant to this paragraph.

(4) ACTIONS FOLLOWING REVIEW.—

(A) WAIVER OF RECOUPMENT.—Upon completion of a review pursuant to paragraph (2)(A)(iv) with respect to a member—

(i) the board of review shall submit to the Secretary concerned a notice setting forth—

(I) the determination of the board pursuant to that paragraph with respect to the member; and

(II) the recommendation of the board whether or not the recoupment of the bonus pay, special pay, student loan repayment, or other special payment covered by the determination should be waived; and

(ii) the Secretary may waive recoupment of the pay, repayment, or other payment from the member.

(B) REPAYMENT OF AMOUNT RECOUPED.—Upon completion of a review pursuant to paragraph (2)(A)(v) with respect to a member—

(i) the board of review shall submit to the Secretary concerned a notice setting forth—

(I) the determination of the board pursuant to that paragraph with respect to the member; and

(II) the recommendation of the board whether or not the recouped bonus pay, special pay, student loan repayment, or other special payment covered by the determination should be repaid the member; and

(ii) the Secretary may repay the member the amount so recouped.

(C) CONSUMER CREDIT AND RELATED MATTERS.—If the Secretary concerned waives recoupment of a bonus pay, special pay, student loan repayment, or other special payment paid a member pursuant to paragraph (4)(A)(ii), or repays a member an amount of a bonus pay, special pay, student loan repayment, or other special payment recouped pursuant to paragraph (4)(B)(ii), the Secretary shall—

(i) in the event the Secretary had previously notified a consumer reporting agency of the existence of the debt subject to the relief granted the member pursuant to this paragraph, notify such consumer reporting agency that such debt was never valid; and

(ii) if the member is experiencing or has experienced financial hardship as a result of the actions of the United States to obtain recoupment of such debt, assist the member, to the extent practicable, in addressing such financial hardship in accordance with such mechanisms as the Secretary shall develop for purposes of this clause.

(D) EFFECT OF CONSUMER CREDIT NOTIFICATION.—A consumer reporting agency notified of the invalidity of a debt pursuant to subparagraph (C)(i) may not, after the date of the notice, make any consumer report containing any information relating to the debt.

(E) DEFINITIONS.—In this paragraph, the terms "consumer reporting agency" and "consumer report" have the meaning given such terms in section 603 of the Fair Credit Reporting Act (15 U.S.C. 1681a).

(5) FUNDING.—Amounts for activities under this subsection, including for the conduct of the review required by paragraph (1), for activities in connection with the review, for repayments pursuant to paragraph (4)(B), and for activities under paragraph (4)(C), shall be derived from amounts available for the National Guard of the United States for the State of California.

(6) SECRETARY OF DEFENSE REPORT.—

(A) IN GENERAL.—Not later than August 1, 2017, the Secretary of Defense shall submit to the Committees on Armed Services of the Senate and the House of Representatives a report on the review conducted pursuant to paragraph (1).

(B) ELEMENTS.—The report under this paragraph shall include the following:

(i) The total amount of bonus pays, special pays, student loan repayments, and other special pays paid to members of the National Guard of the State of California during the period beginning on September 1, 2001, and ending on December 31, 2015.

(ii) The number of bonus pay and special pay contracts reviewed pursuant to paragraph (2)(A)(i), and the amounts of such pays paid under each such contract.

(iii) The number of student loan repayment contracts reviewed pursuant to paragraph (2)(A)(ii), and the amounts of such payments made pursuant to each such contract.

(iv) The number of other special pay payments reviewed pursuant to paragraph (2)(A)(iii), and the amounts of such payments made to each particular member so paid.

(v) The number of bonus pay and special pay contracts, student loan repayments, and other special pay payments that were determined pursuant to the review to be paid in error, and the total amount, if any, recouped from each member concerned.

(vi) Any additional fraud or other ineligibility identified in the course of the review in the payment of bonus pays, special pays, student loan repayments, and other special pays paid to the members of the National Guard of the State of California during the period beginning on September 1, 2001, and ending on December 31, 2015.

(7) COMPTROLLER GENERAL REPORT.—

(A) IN GENERAL.—Not later than one year after the date of the enactment of this Act, the Comptroller General of the United States shall submit to the Committees on Armed Services of the Senate and the House of Representatives a report on the actions of the National Guard of the State of California relating to the payment of bonus pays, special pays, student loan repayments, and other special pays from 2004 through 2015.

(B) ELEMENTS.—The report under this paragraph shall include the following:

(i) An assessment whether the National Guard of the State of California and the National Guard Bureau have established policies and procedures that will minimize the chance of improper payment of such pays and repayments and of managerial abuse in the payment of such pays and repayments.

(ii) An assessment whether the procedures, processes, and resources of the Defense Finance and Accounting Service and the Defense Office of Hearings and Appeals were appropriate to identify and respond to fraud or other ineligibility in connection with the payment of such pays and repayments, and to do so in a timely manner.

(iii) Any recommendations the Comptroller General considers appropriate to streamline the procedures and processes for the waiver of recoupment of the payment of such pays and repayments by the United States when recoupment is unwarranted.

SEC. 672. MODIFICATION OF FLAT RATE PER DIEM REQUIREMENT FOR PERSONNEL ON LONG-TERM TEMPORARY DUTY ASSIGNMENTS.

(a) MODIFICATION OF FLAT RATE.—

(1) IN GENERAL.—The Secretary of Defense shall take such action as may be necessary to provide that, to the extent that regulations implementing travel and transportation authorities for military and civilian personnel of the Department of Defense impose a flat rate per diem for meals and incidental expenses for authorized travelers on long-term temporary duty assignments that is at a reduced rate compared to the per diem rate otherwise applicable, the Secretary concerned may waive the applicability of such reduced rate and pay such travelers actual expenses up to the full per diem rate for such travel in any case when the Secretary concerned determines that the reduced flat rate per diem for meals and incidental expenses is not sufficient under the circumstances of the temporary duty assignment.

(2) APPLICABILITY.—The Secretary concerned may exercise the authority provided pursuant to paragraph (1) with respect to per diem payable for any day on or after the date of the enactment of this Act.

(b) DELEGATION OF AUTHORITY.—The authority pursuant to subsection (a) may be delegated by the Secretary concerned to an officer at the level of lieutenant general or vice admiral, or above. Such authority may not be delegated to an officer below that level.

(c) WAIVER OF COLLECTION OF RECEIPTS.—The Secretary concerned or an officer to whom the authority pursuant to subsection (a) is delegated pursuant to subsection (b) may waive any requirement for the submittal of receipts by travelers on long-term temporary duty assignments for the purpose of receiving the full per diem rate pursuant to subsection (a) if the Secretary concerned or officer, as described in subsection (b), personally certifies that requiring travelers to submit receipts for that purpose will negatively affect mission performance or create an undue administrative burden.

(d) SECRETARY CONCERNED DEFINED.—In this section, the term "Secretary concerned" has the meaning given that term in section 101 of title 37, United States Code.

TITLE VII—HEALTH CARE PROVISIONS

Subtitle A—Reform of TRICARE and Military Health System

Sec. 701. TRICARE Select and other TRICARE reform.
Sec. 702. Reform of administration of the Defense Health Agency and military medical treatment facilities.
Sec. 703. Military medical treatment facilities.
Sec. 704. Access to urgent and primary care under TRICARE program.
Sec. 705. Value-based purchasing and acquisition of managed care support contracts for TRICARE program.
Sec. 706. Establishment of high performance military-civilian integrated health delivery systems.
Sec. 707. Joint Trauma System.
Sec. 708. Joint Trauma Education and Training Directorate.
Sec. 709. Standardized system for scheduling medical appointments at military treatment facilities.

Subtitle B—Other Health Care Benefits

Sec. 711. Extended TRICARE program coverage for certain members of the National Guard and dependents during certain disaster response duty.
Sec. 712. Continuity of health care coverage for Reserve Components.
Sec. 713. Provision of hearing aids to dependents of retired members.
Sec. 714. Coverage of medically necessary food and vitamins for certain conditions under the TRICARE program.
Sec. 715. Eligibility of certain beneficiaries under the TRICARE program for participation in the Federal Employees Dental and Vision Insurance Program.
Sec. 716. Applied behavior analysis.
Sec. 717. Evaluation and treatment of veterans and civilians at military treatment facilities.
Sec. 718. Enhancement of use of telehealth services in military health system.
Sec. 719. Authorization of reimbursement by Department of Defense to entities carrying out State vaccination programs for costs of vaccines provided to covered beneficiaries.

Subtitle C—Health Care Administration

Sec. 721. Authority to convert military medical and dental positions to civilian medical and dental positions.
Sec. 722. Prospective payment of funds necessary to provide medical care for the Coast Guard.
Sec. 723. Reduction of administrative requirements relating to automatic renewal of enrollments in TRICARE Prime.
Sec. 724. Modification of authority of Uniformed Services University of the Health Sciences to include undergraduate and other medical education and training programs.
Sec. 725. Adjustment of medical services, personnel authorized strengths, and infrastructure in military health system to maintain readiness and core competencies of health care providers.
Sec. 726. Program to eliminate variability in health outcomes and improve quality of health care services delivered in military medical treatment facilities.
Sec. 727. Acquisition strategy for health care professional staffing services.
Sec. 728. Adoption of core quality performance metrics.
Sec. 729. Improvement of health outcomes and control of costs of health care under TRICARE program through programs to involve covered beneficiaries.
Sec. 730. Accountability for the performance of the military health system of certain leaders within the system.
Sec. 731. Establishment of advisory committees for military treatment facilities.

Subtitle D—Reports and Other Matters

Sec. 741. Extension of authority for joint Department of Defense-Department of Veterans Affairs Medical Facility Demonstration Fund and report on implementation of information technology capabilities.
Sec. 742. Pilot program on expansion of use of physician assistants to provide mental health care to members of the Armed Forces.
Sec. 743. Pilot program for prescription drug acquisition cost parity in the TRICARE pharmacy benefits program.
Sec. 744. Pilot program on display of wait times at urgent care clinics and pharmacies of military medical treatment facilities.
Sec. 745. Requirement to review and monitor prescribing practices at military treatment facilities of pharmaceutical agents for treatment of post-traumatic stress.
Sec. 746. Department of Defense study on preventing the diversion of opioid medications.
Sec. 747. Incorporation into survey by Department of Defense of questions on experiences of members of the Armed Forces with family planning services and counseling.
Sec. 748. Assessment of transition to TRICARE program by families of members of reserve components called to active duty and elimination of certain charges for such families.
Sec. 749. Oversight of graduate medical education programs of military departments.
Sec. 750. Study on health of helicopter and tiltrotor pilots.
Sec. 751. Comptroller General reports on health care delivery and waste in military health system.

Subtitle A—Reform of TRICARE and Military Health System

SEC. 701. TRICARE SELECT AND OTHER TRICARE REFORM.

(a) ESTABLISHMENT OF TRICARE SELECT.—

(1) IN GENERAL.—Chapter 55 of title 10, United States Code, is amended by inserting after section 1074n the following new section:

"**§ 1075. TRICARE Select**

"(a) ESTABLISHMENT.—(1) Not later than January 1, 2018, the Secretary of Defense shall establish a self-managed, preferred-provider network option under the TRICARE program. Such option shall be known as 'TRICARE Select'.

"(2) The Secretary shall establish TRICARE Select in all areas. Under TRICARE Select, eligible beneficiaries will not have restrictions on the freedom of choice of the beneficiary with respect to health care providers.

"(b) ENROLLMENT ELIGIBILITY.—(1) The beneficiary categories for purposes of eligibility to enroll in TRICARE Select and cost-sharing requirements applicable to such category are as follows:

"(A) An 'active-duty family member' category that consists of beneficiaries who are covered by section 1079 of this title (as dependents of active duty members).

"(B) A 'retired' category that consists of beneficiaries covered by subsection (c) of section 1086 of this title, other than Medicare-eligible beneficiaries described in subsection (d)(2) of such section.

"(C) A 'reserve and young adult' category that consists of beneficiaries who are covered by—

"(i) section 1076d of this title;

"(ii) section 1076e; or

"(iii) section 1110b.

"(2) A covered beneficiary who elects to participate in TRICARE Select shall enroll in such option under section 1099 of this title.

"(c) COST-SHARING REQUIREMENTS.—The cost-sharing requirements under TRICARE Select are as follows:

"(1) With respect to beneficiaries in the active-duty family member category or the retired category by reason of being a member or former member of the uniformed services who originally enlists or is appointed in the uniformed services on or after January 1, 2018, or by reason of being a dependent of such a member, the cost-sharing requirements shall be calculated pursuant to subsection (d)(1).

"(2)(A) Except as provided by subsection (e), with respect to beneficiaries described in subparagraph (B) in the active-duty family member category or the retired category, the cost-sharing requirements shall be calculated as if the beneficiary were enrolled in TRICARE Extra or TRICARE Standard as if TRICARE Extra or TRICARE Standard, as the case may be, were still being carried out by the Secretary.

"(B) Beneficiaries described in this subparagraph are beneficiaries who are eligible to enroll in the TRICARE program by reason of being a member or former member of the uniformed services who originally enlists or is appointed in the uniformed services before January 1, 2018, or by reason of being a dependent of such a member.

"(3) With respect to beneficiaries in the reserve and young adult category, the cost-sharing requirements shall be calculated pursuant to subsection (d)(1) as if the beneficiary were in the active-duty family member category or the retired category, as applicable, except that the premiums calculated pursuant to section 1076d, 1076e, or 1110b of this title, as the case may be, shall apply instead of any enrollment fee required under this section.

"(d) COST-SHARING AMOUNTS FOR CERTAIN BENEFICIARIES.—(1) Beneficiaries described in subsection (c)(1) enrolled in TRICARE Select shall be subject to cost-sharing requirements in accordance with the amounts and percentages under the following table during calendar year 2018 and as such amounts are adjusted under paragraph (2) for subsequent years:

"TRICARE Select	Active-Duty Family Member (Individual/Family)	Retired (Individual/Family)
Annual Enrollment	$0	$450 / $900
Annual deductible	E4 & below: $50 / $100 E5 & above: $150 / $300	$150 / $300 Network $300 / $600 out of network
Annual catastrophic cap	$1,000	$3,500
Outpatient visit civilian network	$15 primary care $25 specialty care Out of network: 20%	$25 primary care $40 specialty care 25% of out of network
ER visit civilian network	$40 network 20% out of network	$80 network 25% out of network
Urgent care civilian network	$20 network 20% out of network	$40 network 25% out of network
Ambulatory surgery civilian network	$25 network 20% out of network	$95 network 25% out of network
Ambulance civilian network	$15	$60
Durable medical equipment civilian network	10% of negotiated fee	20% network
Inpatient visit civilian network	$60 per network admission 20% out of network	$175 per admission network 25% out of network
Inpatient skilled nursing/rehab civilian	$25 per day network $50 per day out of network	$50 per day network Lesser of $300 per day or 20% of billed charges out of network

"(2) Each dollar amount expressed as a fixed dollar amount in the table set forth in paragraph (1), and the amounts specified under paragraphs (1) and (2) of subsection (e), shall be annually indexed to the amount by which retired pay is increased under section 1401a of this title, rounded to the next lower multiple of $1. The remaining amount above such multiple of $1 shall be carried over to, and accumulated with, the amount of the increase for the subsequent year or years and made when the aggregate amount of increases carried over under this clause for a year is $1 or more.

"(3) Enrollment fees, deductible amounts, and catastrophic caps under this section are on a calendar-year basis.

"(e) EXCEPTIONS TO CERTAIN COST-SHARING AMOUNTS FOR CERTAIN BENEFICIARIES ELIGIBLE PRIOR TO 2018.—(1) Subject to paragraph (4), and in accordance with subsection (d)(2), the Secretary shall establish an annual enrollment fee for beneficiaries described in subsection (c)(2)(B) in the retired category who enroll in TRICARE Select (other than such beneficiaries covered by paragraph (3)). Such enrollment fee shall be $150 for an individual and $300 for a family.

"(2) For the calendar year for which the Secretary first establishes the annual enrollment fee under paragraph (1), the Secretary shall adjust the catastrophic cap amount to be $3,500 for beneficiaries described in subsection (c)(2)(B) in the retired category who are enrolled in TRICARE Select (other than such beneficiaries covered by paragraph (3)).

"(3) The enrollment fee established pursuant to paragraph (1) and the catastrophic cap adjusted under paragraph (2) for beneficiaries described in subsection (c)(2)(B) in the retired category shall not apply with respect to the following beneficiaries:

"(A) Retired members and the family members of such members covered by paragraph (1) of section 1086(c) of this title by reason of being retired under chapter 61 of this title or being a dependent of such a member.

"(B) Survivors covered by paragraph (2) of such section 1086(c).

"(4) The Secretary may not establish an annual enrollment fee under paragraph (1) until 90 days has elapsed following the date on which the Comptroller General of the United States is required to submit the review under paragraph (5).

"(5) Not later than February 1, 2020, the Comptroller General of the United States shall submit to the Committees on Armed Services of the House of Representatives and the Senate a review of the following:

"(A) Whether health care coverage for covered beneficiaries has changed since the enactment of this section.

"(B) Whether covered beneficiaries are able to obtain appointments for health care according to the access standards established by the Secretary of Defense.

"(C) The percent of network providers that accept new patients under the TRICARE program.

"(D) The satisfaction of beneficiaries under TRICARE Select.

"(f) EXCEPTION TO COST-SHARING REQUIREMENTS FOR TRICARE FOR LIFE BENEFICIARIES.—A beneficiary enrolled in TRICARE for Life is subject to cost-sharing requirements pursuant to section 1086(d)(3) of this title and calculated as if the beneficiary were enrolled in TRICARE Standard as if TRICARE Standard were still being carried out by the Secretary.

"(g) CONSTRUCTION.—Nothing in this section may be construed as affecting the availability of TRICARE Prime and TRICARE for Life or the cost-sharing requirements for TRICARE for Life under section 1086(d)(3) of this title.

"(h) DEFINITIONS.—In this section:

"(1) The terms 'active-duty family member category', 'retired category', and 'reserve and young adult category' mean the respective categories of TRICARE Select enrollment described in subsection (b).

"(2) The term 'network' means—

"(A) with respect to health care services, such services provided to beneficiaries by TRICARE-authorized civilian health care providers who have entered into a contract under this chapter with a contractor under the TRICARE program; and

"(B) with respect to providers, civilian health care providers who have agreed to accept a pre-negotiated rate as the total charge for services provided by the provider and to file claims for beneficiaries.

"(3) The term 'out-of-network' means, with respect to health care services, such services provided by TRICARE-authorized civilian providers who have not entered into a contract under this chapter with a contractor under the TRICARE program.".

(2) CLERICAL AMENDMENT.—The table of sections at the beginning of chapter 55 of title 10, United States Code, is amended by inserting after the item relating to section 1074n, the following new item:

"1075. TRICARE Select.".

(b) TRICARE PRIME COST SHARING.—

(1) IN GENERAL.—Chapter 55 of title 10, United States Code, is amended by inserting after section 1075, as added by subsection (a), the following new section:

"§ 1075a. TRICARE Prime: cost sharing

"(a) COST-SHARING REQUIREMENTS.—The cost-sharing requirements under TRICARE Prime are as follows:

"(1) There are no cost-sharing requirements for beneficiaries who are covered by section 1074(a) of this title.

"(2) With respect to beneficiaries in the active-duty family member category or the retired category (as described in section 1075(b)(1) of this title) by reason of being a member or former member of the uniformed services who originally enlists or is appointed in the uniformed services on or after January 1, 2018, or by reason of being a dependent of such a member, the cost-sharing requirements shall be calculated pursuant to subsection (b)(1).

"(3)(A) With respect to beneficiaries described in subparagraph (B) in the active-duty family member category or the retired category (as described in section 1075(b)(1) of this title), the cost-sharing requirements shall be calculated in accordance with the other provisions of this chapter without regard to subsection (b).

"(B) Beneficiaries described in this subparagraph are beneficiaries who are eligible to enroll in the TRICARE program by reason of being a member or former member of the uniformed services who originally enlists or is appointed in the uniformed services before January 1, 2018, or by reason of being a dependent of such a member.

"(b) COST-SHARING AMOUNTS.—(1) Beneficiaries described in subsection (a)(2) enrolled in TRICARE Prime shall be subject to cost-sharing requirements in accordance with the amounts and percentages under the following table during calendar year 2018 and as such amounts are adjusted under paragraph (2) for subsequent years:

"TRICARE Prime	Active-Duty Family Member (Individual/Family)	Retired (Individual/Family)
Annual Enrollment	$0	$350 / $700
Annual deductible	No	No
Annual catastrophic cap	$1,000	$3,500
Outpatient visit civilian network	$0	$20 primary care
		$30 specialty care
ER visit civilian network	$0	$60 network
Urgent care civilian network	$0	$30 network
Ambulatory surgery civilian network	$0	$60 network
Ambulance civilian network	$0	$40
Durable medical equipment civilian network	$0	20% of negotiated fee, network
Inpatient visit civilian network	$0	$150 per admission
Inpatient skilled nursing/rehab civilian	$0	$30 per day network

"(2) Each dollar amount expressed as a fixed dollar amount in the table set forth in paragraph (1) shall be annually indexed to the amount by which retired pay is increased under section 1401a of this title, rounded to the next lower multiple of $1. The remaining amount above such multiple of $1 shall be carried over to, and accumulated with, the amount of the increase for the subsequent year or years and made when the aggregate amount of increases carried over under this clause for a year is $1 or more.

"(3) Enrollment fees, deductible amounts, and catastrophic caps under this section are on a calendar-year basis.

"(c) SPECIAL RULE FOR AMOUNTS WITHOUT REFERRALS.—Notwithstanding subsection (b)(1), the cost-sharing amount for a beneficiary enrolled in TRICARE Prime who does not obtain a referral for care under paragraph (1) of section 1075f(a) of this title (or a waiver pursuant to paragraph (2) of such section for such care) shall be an amount equal to 50 percent of the allowed point-of-service charge for such care.".

(2) CLERICAL AMENDMENT.—The table of sections at the beginning of chapter 55 of title 10, United States Code, is amended by inserting after the item relating to section 1075, as added by subsection (a), the following new item:

"1075a. TRICARE Prime: cost sharing.".

(c) REFERRALS AND PREAUTHORIZATION FOR TRICARE PRIME.—Section 1095f of title 10, United States Code, is amended to read as follows:

"§ 1095f. TRICARE program: referrals and preauthorizations under TRICARE Prime

"(a) REFERRALS.—(1) Except as provided by paragraph (2), a beneficiary enrolled in TRICARE Prime shall be required to obtain a referral for care through a designated primary care manager (or other care coordinator) prior to obtaining care under the TRICARE program.

"(2) The Secretary may waive the referral requirement in paragraph (1) in such circumstances as the Secretary may establish for purposes of this subsection.

"(3) The cost-sharing amounts for a beneficiary enrolled in TRICARE Prime who does not obtain a referral for care under paragraph (1) (or a waiver pursuant to paragraph (2) for such care) shall be determined under section 1075a(c) of this title.

"(b) PREAUTHORIZATION.—A beneficiary enrolled in TRICARE Prime shall be required to obtain preauthorization only with respect to a referral for the following:

"(1) Inpatient hospitalization.

''(2) Inpatient care at a skilled nursing facility.

''(3) Inpatient care at a rehabilitation facility.

''(c) PROHIBITION REGARDING PRIOR AUTHORIZATION FOR CERTAIN REFERRALS.—The Secretary of Defense shall ensure that no contract for managed care support under the TRICARE program includes any requirement that a managed care support contractor require a primary care or specialty care provider to obtain prior authorization before referring a patient to a specialty care provider that is part of the network of health care providers or institutions of the contractor.''.

(d) ENROLLMENT PERIODS.—

(1) ANNUAL PERIODS AND QUALIFYING EVENTS.—Section 1099(b) of title 10, United States Code, is amended by amending paragraph (1) to read as follows:

''(1) allow covered beneficiaries to elect to enroll in a health care plan, or modify a previous election, from eligible health care plans designated by the Secretary of Defense during—

''(A) an annual open enrollment period; and

''(B) any period based on a qualifying event experienced by the beneficiary, as determined appropriate by the Secretary; or''.

(2) APPLICATION.—The Secretary of Defense shall implement the initial annual open enrollment period pursuant to section 1099(b)(1) of title 10, United States Code, as amended by paragraph (1), during 2018.

(3) GRACE PERIOD DURING FIRST YEAR.—

(A) At any time during the one-year period beginning on the date on which the initial annual open enrollment period begins pursuant to section 1099(b)(1) of title 10, United States Code, as amended by paragraph (1), a covered beneficiary may make an election, or modify such an election, described in such section.

(B) If during such one-year period an individual who is eligible to enroll in the TRICARE program, but does not elect to enroll in such program, receives health care services for an episode of care that would be covered under the TRICARE program if such individual were enrolled in the TRICARE program, the Secretary—

(i) shall pay the out-of-network fees only for the first episode of care and inform the individual of the opportunity to enroll in the TRICARE program; and

(ii) may not pay any costs relating to any subsequent episode of care if such individual is not enrolled in the TRICARE program.

(4) TRANSITION PLAN.—Not later than March 1, 2017, the Secretary shall provide to the Committees on Armed Services of the Senate and the House of Representatives a briefing on the transition plan of the Department of Defense for implementing an annual enrollment period for TRICARE Prime and TRICARE Select pursuant to section 1099(b)(1) of title 10, United States Code, as amended by paragraph (1). Such plan shall include strategies to notify each beneficiary of the changes to the TRICARE options and the changes to the enrollment process.

(e) TERMINATION OF TRICARE STANDARD AND TRICARE EXTRA.—Beginning on January 1, 2018, the Secretary of Defense may not carry out TRICARE Standard and TRICARE Extra under the TRICARE program. The Secretary shall ensure that any individual who is covered under TRICARE Standard or TRICARE Extra as of December 31, 2017, enrolls in TRICARE Prime or TRICARE Select, as the case may be, as of January 1, 2018, for the individual to continue coverage under the TRICARE program.

(f) IMPLEMENTATION PLAN.—

(1) IN GENERAL.—Not later than June 1, 2017, the Secretary of Defense shall submit to the Committees on Armed Services of the House of Representatives and the Senate an implementation plan to improve access to health care for TRICARE beneficiaries pursuant to the amendments made by this section.

(2) ELEMENTS.—The plan under paragraph (1) shall—

(A) ensure that at least 85 percent of the beneficiary population under TRICARE Select is covered by the network by January 1, 2018;

(B) ensure access standards for appointments for health care that meet or exceed those of high-performing health care systems in the United States, as determined by the Secretary;

(C) establish mechanisms for monitoring compliance with access standards;

(D) establish health care provider-to-beneficiary ratios;

(E) monitor on a monthly basis complaints by beneficiaries with respect to network adequacy and the availability of health care providers;

(F) establish requirements for mechanisms to monitor the responses to complaints by beneficiaries;

(G) establish mechanisms to evaluate the quality metrics of the network providers established under section 728;

(H) include any recommendations for legislative action the Secretary determines necessary to carry out the plan; and

(I) include any other elements the Secretary determines appropriate.

(g) GAO REVIEWS.—

(1) IMPLEMENTATION PLAN.—Not later than December 1, 2017, the Comptroller General of the United States shall submit to the Committees on Armed Services of the House of Representatives and the Senate a review of the implementation plan of the Secretary under paragraph (1) of subsection (f), including an assessment of the adequacy of the plan in meeting the elements specified in paragraph (2) of such subsection.

(2) NETWORK.—Not later than September 1, 2017, the Comptroller General shall submit to the Committees on Armed Services of the House of Representatives and the Senate a review of the network established under TRICARE Extra, including the following:

(A) An identification of the percent of beneficiaries who are covered by the network.

(B) An assessment of the extent to which beneficiaries are able to obtain appointments under TRICARE Extra.

(C) The percent of network providers under TRICARE Extra that accept new patients under the TRICARE program.

(D) An assessment of the satisfaction of beneficiaries under TRICARE Extra.

(h) PILOT PROGRAM ON INCORPORATION OF VALUE-BASED HEALTH CARE IN PURCHASED CARE COMPONENT OF TRICARE PROGRAM.—

(1) IN GENERAL.—Not later than January 1, 2018, the Secretary of Defense shall carry out a pilot program to demonstrate and assess the feasibility of incorporating value-based health care methodology in the purchased care component of the TRICARE program by reducing copayments or cost shares for targeted populations of covered beneficiaries in the receipt of high-value medications and services and the use of high-value providers under such purchased care component, including by exempting certain services from deductible requirements.

(2) REQUIREMENTS.—In carrying out the pilot program under paragraph (1), the Secretary shall—

(A) identify each high-value medication and service that is covered under the purchased care component of the TRICARE program for which a reduction or elimination of the copayment or cost share for such medication or service would encourage covered beneficiaries to use the medication or service;

(B) reduce or eliminate copayments or cost shares for covered beneficiaries to receive high-value medications and services;

(C) reduce or eliminate copayments or cost shares for covered beneficiaries to receive health care services from high-value providers;

(D) credit the amount of any reduction or elimination of a copayment or cost share under subparagraph (B) or (C) for a covered beneficiary towards meeting a deductible applicable to the covered beneficiary in the purchased care component of the TRICARE program to the same extent as if such reduction or elimination had not applied; and

(E) develop a process to reimburse high-value providers at rates higher than those rates for health care providers that are not high-value providers.

(3) REPORT ON VALUE-BASED HEALTH CARE METHODOLOGY.—Not later than 180 days after the date of the enactment of this Act, the Secretary shall submit to the Committees on Armed Services of the Senate and the House of Representatives a report that includes the following:

(A) A list of each high-value medication and service identified under paragraph (2)(A) for which the copayment or cost share amount will be reduced or eliminated under the pilot program to encourage covered beneficiaries to use such medications and services through the purchased care component of the TRICARE program.

(B) For each high-value medication and service identified under paragraph (2)(A), the amount of the copayment or cost share required under the purchased care component of the TRICARE program and the amount of any reduction or elimination of such copayment or cost share pursuant to the pilot program.

(C) A description of a plan to identify and communicate to covered beneficiaries, through multiple communication media—

(i) the list of high-value medications and services described in subparagraph (A); and

(ii) a list of high-value providers.

(D) A description of modifications, if any, to existing health care contracts that may be required to implement value-based health care methodology in the purchased care component of the TRICARE program under the pilot program and the estimated costs of those contract modifications.

(4) COMPTROLLER GENERAL PRELIMINARY REVIEW AND ASSESSMENT.—

(A) Not later than March 1, 2021, the Comptroller General of the United States shall submit to the Committees on Armed Services of the Senate and the House of Representatives a review and assessment of the preliminary results of the pilot program.

(B) The review and assessment required under subparagraph (A) shall include the following:

(i) An assessment of the extent of the use of value-based health care methodology in the purchased care component of the TRICARE program under the pilot program.

(ii) An analysis demonstrating how reducing or eliminating the copayment or cost share for each high-value medication and service identified under paragraph (2)(A) resulted in—

(I) increased adherence to medication regimens;

(II) improvement of quality measures;

(III) improvement of health outcomes;

(IV) reduction of number of emergency room visits or hospitalizations; and

(V) enhancement of experience of care for covered beneficiaries.

(iii) Such recommendations for incentivizing the use of high-value medications and services to improve health outcomes and the experience of care for beneficiaries as the Comptroller General considers appropriate.

(5) REVIEW AND ASSESSMENT OF PILOT PROGRAM.—

(A) Not later than January 1, 2023, the Secretary shall submit to the Committees on Armed Services of the Senate and the House of Representatives a review and assessment of the pilot program.

(B) The review and assessment required under subparagraph (A) shall include the following:

(i) An assessment of the extent of the use of value-based health care methodology in the purchased care component of the TRICARE program under the pilot program.

(ii) An analysis demonstrating how reducing or eliminating the copayment or cost share for each high-value medication and service identified under paragraph (2)(A) resulted in—

(I) increased adherence to medication regimens;

(II) improvement of quality measures;

(III) improvement of health outcomes; and

(IV) enhancement of experience of care for covered beneficiaries.

(iii) A cost-benefit analysis of the implementation of value-based health care methodology in the purchased care component of the TRICARE program under the pilot program.

(iv) Such recommendations for incentivizing the use of high-value medications and services to improve health outcomes and the experience of care for covered beneficiaries as the Secretary considers appropriate.

(6) TERMINATION.—The Secretary may not carry out the pilot program after December 31, 2022.

(i) DEFINITIONS.—In this section:

(1) The terms "uniformed services", "covered beneficiary", "TRICARE Extra", "TRICARE for Life", "TRICARE Prime", and "TRICARE Standard", have the meaning given those terms in section 1072 of title 10, United States Code, as amended by subsection (j).

(2) The term "TRICARE Select" means the self-managed, preferred-provider network option under the TRICARE program established by section 1075 of such title, as added by subsection (a).

(3) The term "chronic conditions" includes diabetes, chronic obstructive pulmonary disease, asthma, congestive heart failure, hypertension, history of stroke, coronary artery disease, mood disorders, and such other diseases or conditions as the Secretary considers appropriate.

(4) The term "high-value medications and services" means prescription medications and clinical services for the management of chronic conditions that the Secretary determines would improve health outcomes and create health value for covered beneficiaries (such as preventive care, primary and specialty care, diagnostic tests, procedures, and durable medical equipment).

(5) The term "high-value provider" means an individual or institutional health care provider that provides health care under the purchased care component of the TRICARE program and that consistently improves the experience of care, meets established quality of care and effectiveness metrics, and reduces the per capita costs of health care.

(6) The term "value-based health care methodology" means a methodology for identifying specific prescription medications and clinical services provided under the TRICARE program for which reduction of copayments, cost shares, or both, would improve the management of specific chronic conditions because of the high value and clinical effectiveness of such medications and services for such chronic conditions.

(j) CONFORMING AMENDMENTS.—

(1) IN GENERAL.—Title 10, United States Code, is amended as follows:

(A) Section 1072 is amended—

(i) by striking paragraph (7) and inserting the following:

"(7) The term 'TRICARE program' means the various programs carried out by the Secretary of Defense under this chapter and any other provision of law providing for the furnishing of medical and dental care and health benefits to members and former members of the uniformed serv-

ices and their dependents, including the following health plan options:

"(A) TRICARE Prime.

"(B) TRICARE Select.

"(C) TRICARE for Life."; and

(ii) by adding at the end the following new paragraphs:

"(11) The term 'TRICARE Extra' means the preferred-provider option of the TRICARE program made available prior to January 1, 2018, under which TRICARE Standard beneficiaries may obtain discounts on cost sharing as a result of using TRICARE network providers.

"(12) The term 'TRICARE Select' means the self-managed, preferred-provider network option under the TRICARE program established by section 1075 of this title.

"(13) The term 'TRICARE for Life' means the Medicare wraparound coverage option of the TRICARE program made available to the beneficiary by reason of section 1086(d) of this title.

"(14) The term 'TRICARE Prime' means the managed care option of the TRICARE program.

"(15) The term 'TRICARE Standard' means the TRICARE program made available prior to January 1, 2018, covering—

"(A) medical care to which a dependent described in section 1076(a)(2) of this title is entitled; and

"(B) health benefits contracted for under the authority of section 1079(a) of this title and subject to the same rates and conditions as apply to persons covered under that section.".

(B) Section 1076d is amended—

(i) in subsection (d)(1), by inserting after "coverage." the following: "Such premium shall apply instead of any enrollment fees required under section 1075 of this section."; and

(ii) in subsection (f), by striking paragraph (2) and inserting the following new paragraph:

"(2) The term 'TRICARE Reserve Select' means the TRICARE Select self-managed, preferred-provider network option under section 1075 made available to beneficiaries by reason of this section and in accordance with subsection (d)(1)."; and

(iii) by striking "TRICARE Standard" each place it appears (including in the heading of such section) and inserting "TRICARE Reserve Select".

(C) Section 1076e is amended—

(i) in subsection (d)(1), by inserting after "coverage." the following: "Such premium shall apply instead of any enrollment fees required under section 1075 of this section."; and

(ii) in subsection (f), by striking paragraph (2) and inserting the following new paragraph:

"(2) The term 'TRICARE Retired Reserve' means the TRICARE Select self-managed, preferred-provider network option under section 1075 made available to beneficiaries by reason of this section and in accordance with subsection (d)(1).";

(iii) in subsection (b), by striking "TRICARE Standard coverage at" and inserting "TRICARE coverage at"; and

(iv) by striking "TRICARE Standard" each place it appears (including in the heading of such section) and inserting "TRICARE Retired Reserve".

(D) Section 1079a is amended—

(i) in the section heading, by striking "CHAMPUS" and inserting "TRICARE program"; and

(ii) by striking "the Civilian Health and Medical Program of the Uniformed Services" and inserting "the TRICARE program".

(E) Section 1099(c) is amended by striking paragraph (2) and inserting the following new paragraph:

"(2) A plan under the TRICARE program.".

(F) Section 1110b(c)(1) is amended by inserting after "(b)." the following: "Such premium shall apply instead of any enrollment fees required under section 1075 of this section.".

(2) CLERICAL AMENDMENTS.—The table of sections at the beginning of chapter 55 of title 10, United States Code, is further amended—

(A) in the item relating to section 1076d, by striking "TRICARE Standard" and inserting "TRICARE Reserve Select";

(B) in the item relating to section 1076e, by striking "TRICARE Standard" and inserting "TRICARE Retired Reserve";

(C) in the item relating to section 1079a, by striking "CHAMPUS" and inserting "TRICARE program"; and

(D) in the item relating to section 1095f, by striking "for specialty health care" and inserting "and preauthorizations under TRICARE Prime".

(3) CONFORMING STYLE.—Any new language inserted or added to title 10, United States Code, by an amendment made by this subsection shall conform to the typeface and typestyle of the matter in which the language is so inserted or added.

(k) APPLICATION.—The amendments made by this section shall apply with respect to the provision of health care under the TRICARE program beginning on January 1, 2018.

SEC. 702. REFORM OF ADMINISTRATION OF THE DEFENSE HEALTH AGENCY AND MILITARY MEDICAL TREATMENT FACILITIES.

(a) ADMINISTRATION.—

(1) IN GENERAL.—Chapter 55 of title 10, United States Code, is amended by inserting after section 1073b the following new section:

"§ 1073c. Administration of Defense Health Agency and military medical treatment facilities

"(a) ADMINISTRATION OF MILITARY MEDICAL TREATMENT FACILITIES.—(1) Beginning October 1, 2018, the Director of the Defense Health Agency shall be responsible for the administration of each military medical treatment facility, including with respect to—

"(A) budgetary matters;

"(B) information technology;

"(C) health care administration and management;

"(D) administrative policy and procedure;

"(E) miliary medical construction; and

"(F) any other matters the Secretary of Defense determines appropriate.

"(2) The commander of each military medical treatment facility shall be responsible for—

"(A) ensuring the readiness of the members of the armed forces and civilian employees at such facility; and

"(B) furnishing the health care and medical treatment provided at such facility.

"(3) The Secretary of Defense shall establish within the Defense Health Agency a professional staff to provide policy, oversight, and direction to carry out subsection (a). The Secretary shall carry out this paragraph by appointing the positions specified in subsections (b) and (c).

"(b) DHA ASSISTANT DIRECTOR.—(1) There is in the Defense Health Agency an Assistant Director for Health Care Administration. The Assistant Director shall—

"(A) be a career appointee within the Department; and

"(B) report directly to the Director of the Defense Health Agency.

"(2) The Assistant Director shall be appointed from among individuals who have equivalent education and experience as a chief executive officer leading a large, civilian health care system.

"(3) The Assistant Director shall be responsible for the following:

"(A) Establishing priorities for health care administration and management.

"(B) Establishing policies, procedures, and direction for the provision of direct care at military medical treatment facilities.

"(C) Establishing priorities for budgeting matters with respect to the provision of direct care at military medical treatment facilities.

"(D) Establishing policies, procedures, and direction for clinic management and operations at military medical treatment facilities.

"(E) Establishing priorities for information technology at and between the military medical treatment facilities.

"(c) DHA DEPUTY ASSISTANT DIRECTORS.—(1)(A) There is in the Defense Health Agency a Deputy Assistant Director for Information Operations.

"(B) The Deputy Assistant Director for Information Operations shall be responsible for policies, management, and execution of information technology operations at and between the military medical treatment facilities.

"(2)(A) There is in the Defense Health Agency a Deputy Assistant Director for Financial Operations.

"(B) The Deputy Assistant Director for Financial Operations shall be responsible for the policy, procedures, and direction of budgeting matters and financial management with respect to the provision of direct care across the military health system.

"(3)(A) There is in the Defense Health Agency a Deputy Assistant Director for Health Care Operations.

"(B) The Deputy Assistant Director for Health Care Operations shall be responsible for the policy, procedures, and direction of health care administration in the military medical treatment facilities.

"(4)(A) There is in the Defense Health Agency a Deputy Assistant Director for Medical Affairs.

"(B) The Deputy Assistant Director for Medical Affairs shall be responsible for policy, procedures, and direction of clinical quality and process improvement, patient safety, infection control, graduate medical education, clinical integration, utilization review, risk management, patient experience, and civilian physician recruiting.

"(5) Each Deputy Assistant Director appointed under paragraphs (1) through (4) shall report directly to the Assistant Director for Health Care Administration.

"(d) CERTAIN RESPONSIBILITIES OF DHA DIRECTOR.—(1) In addition to the other duties of the Director of the Defense Health Agency, the Director shall coordinate with the Joint Staff Surgeon to ensure that the Director most effectively carries out the responsibilities of the Defense Health Agency as a combat support agency under section 193 of this title.

"(2) The responsibilities of the Director shall include the following:

"(A) Ensuring that the Defense Health Agency meets the operational needs of the commanders of the combatant commands.

"(B) Coordinating with the military departments to ensure that the staffing at the military medical treatment facilities supports readiness requirements for members of the armed forces and health care personnel.

"(e) DEFINITIONS.—In this section:

"(1) The term 'career appointee' has the meaning given that term in section 3132(a)(4) of title 5.

"(2) The term 'Defense Health Agency' means the Defense Agency established pursuant to Department of Defense Directive 5136.13, or such successor Defense Agency.".

(2) CLERICAL AMENDMENT.—The table of sections at the beginning of such chapter is amended by inserting after the item relating to section 1073b the following new item:

"1073c. Administration of Defense Health Agency and military medical treatment facilities.".

(b) POSITIONS OF SURGEON GENERAL IN THE ARMED FORCES.—

(1) SURGEON GENERAL OF THE ARMY.—Section 3036 of title 10, United States Code, is amended—

(A) in subsection (d), by striking "(1)";

(B) by redesignating subsection (e) as subsection (g);

(C) by inserting after subsection (d) a new subsection (e);

(D) by transferring paragraphs (2) and (3) of subsection (d) to subsection (e), as added by subparagraph (C), and redesignating such paragraphs as paragraphs (1) and (2), respectively; and

(E) by adding after subsection (e), as added by subparagraph (C), the following new subsection (f):

"(f)(1) The Surgeon General serves as the principal advisor to the Secretary of the Army and the Chief of Staff of the Army on all health and medical matters of the Army, including strategic planning and policy development relating to such matters.

"(2) The Surgeon General serves as the chief medical advisor of the Army to the Director of the Defense Health Agency on matters pertaining to military health readiness requirements and safety of members of the Army.

"(3) The Surgeon General, acting under the authority, direction, and control of the Secretary of the Army, shall recruit, organize, train, and equip, medical personnel of the Army.".

(2) SURGEON GENERAL OF THE NAVY.—

(A) IN GENERAL.—Section 5137 of title 10, United States Code, is amended to read as follows:

"§ 5137. Surgeon General: appointment; duties

"(a) APPOINTMENT.—The Surgeon General of the Navy shall be appointed by the President, by and with the advice and consent of the Senate, for a term of four years, from officers on the active-duty list of the Navy in any corps of the Navy Medical Department.

"(b) DUTIES.—(1) The Surgeon General serves as the Chief of the Bureau of Medicine and Surgery and serves as the principal advisor to the Secretary of the Navy and the Chief of Naval Operations on all health and medical matters of the Navy and the Marine Corps, including strategic planning and policy development relating to such matters.

"(2) The Surgeon General serves as the chief medical advisor of the Navy and the Marine Corps to the Director of the Defense Health Agency on matters pertaining to military health readiness requirements and safety of members of the Navy and the Marine Corps.

"(3) The Surgeon General, acting under the authority, direction, and control of the Secretary of the Navy, shall recruit, organize, train, and equip, medical personnel of the Navy and the Marine Corps.".

(B) CLERICAL AMENDMENT.—The table of sections at the beginning of chapter 513 of such title is amended by striking the item relating to section 5137 and inserting the following new item:

"5137. Surgeon General: appointment; duties.".

(3) SURGEON GENERAL OF THE AIR FORCE.—

(A) IN GENERAL.—Section 8036 of title 10, United States Code, is amended to read as follows:

"§ 8036. Surgeon General: appointment; duties

"(a) APPOINTMENT.—The Surgeon General of the Air Force shall be appointed by the President, by and with the advice and consent of the Senate from officers of the Air Force who are in the Air Force medical department.

"(b) DUTIES.—(1) The Surgeon General serves as the principal advisor to the Secretary of the Air Force and the Chief of Staff of the Air Force on all health and medical matters of the Air Force, including strategic planning and policy development relating to such matters.

"(2) The Surgeon General serves as the chief medical advisor of the Air Force to the Director of the Defense Health Agency on matters pertaining to military health readiness requirements and safety of members of the Air Force.

"(3) The Surgeon General, acting under the authority, direction, and control of the Secretary of the Air Force, shall recruit, organize, train, and equip, medical personnel of the Air Force.".

(B) CLERICAL AMENDMENT.—The table of sections at the beginning of chapter 805 of such title is amended by striking the item relating to section 8036 and inserting the following new item:

"8036. Surgeon General: appointment; duties.".

(c) APPOINTMENTS.—The Secretary of Defense shall make appointments of the positions under section 1073c of title 10, United States Code, as added by subsection (a)—

(1) by not later than October 1, 2018; and

(2) by not increasing the number of full-time equivalent employees of the Defense Health Agency.

(d) IMPLEMENTATION PLAN.—

(1) IN GENERAL.—The Secretary of Defense shall develop a plan to implement section 1073c of title 10, United States Code, as added by subsection (a).

(2) ELEMENTS.—The plan developed under paragraph (1) shall include the following:

(A) How the Secretary will carry out subsection (a) of such section 1073c.

(B) Efforts to eliminate duplicative activities carried out by the elements of the Defense Health Agency and the military departments.

(C) Efforts to maximize efficiencies in the activities carried out by the Defense Health Agency.

(D) How the Secretary will implement such section 1073c in a manner that reduces the number of members of the Armed Forces, civilian employees who are full-time equivalent employees, and contractors relating to the headquarters activities of the military health system, as of the date of the enactment of this Act.

(e) REPORTS.—

(1) INTERIM REPORT.—Not later than March 1, 2017, the Secretary shall submit to the Committees on Armed Services of the House of Representatives and the Senate a report containing—

(A) a preliminary draft of the plan developed under subsection (d)(1); and

(B) any recommendations for legislative actions the Secretary determines necessary to carry out the plan.

(2) FINAL REPORT.—Not later than March 1, 2018, the Secretary shall submit to the Committees on Armed Services of the House of Representatives and the Senate a report containing the final version of the plan developed under subsection (d)(1).

(3) COMPTROLLER GENERAL REVIEWS.—

(A) The Comptroller General of the United States shall submit to the Committees on Armed Services of the House of Representatives and the Senate—

(i) a review of the preliminary draft of the plan submitted under paragraph (1) by not later than September 1, 2017; and

(ii) a review of the final version of the plan submitted under paragraph (2) by not later than September 1, 2018.

(B) Each review of the plan conducted under subparagraph (A) shall determine whether the Secretary has addressed the required elements for the plan under subsection (d)(2).

SEC. 703. MILITARY MEDICAL TREATMENT FACILITIES.

(a) ADMINISTRATION.—

(1) IN GENERAL.—Chapter 55 of title 10, United States Code, as amended by section 702, is further amended by inserting after section 1073c the following new section:

"§ 1073d. Military medical treatment facilities

"(a) IN GENERAL.—To support the medical readiness of the armed forces and the readiness of medical personnel, the Secretary of Defense, in consultation with the Secretaries of the military departments, shall maintain the military medical treatment facilities described in subsections (b), (c), and (d).

"(b) MEDICAL CENTERS.—(1) The Secretary of Defense shall maintain medical centers in areas with a large population of members of the armed forces and covered beneficiaries.

"(2) Medical centers shall serve as referral facilities for members and covered beneficiaries who require comprehensive health care services that support medical readiness.

"(3) Medical centers shall consist of the following:

"(A) Inpatient and outpatient tertiary care facilities that incorporate specialty and subspecialty care.

"(B) Graduate medical education programs.

"(C) Residency training programs.

"(D) Level one or level two trauma care capabilities.

"(4) The Secretary may designate a medical center as a regional center of excellence for unique and highly specialized health care services, including with respect to polytrauma, organ transplantation, and burn care.

"(c) HOSPITALS.—(1) The Secretary of Defense shall maintain hospitals in areas where civilian health care facilities are unable to support the health care needs of members of the armed forces and covered beneficiaries.

"(2) Hospitals shall provide—

"(A) inpatient and outpatient health services to maintain medical readiness; and

"(B) such other programs and functions as the Secretary determines appropriate.

"(3) Hospitals shall consist of inpatient and outpatient care facilities with limited specialty care that the Secretary determines—

"(A) is cost effective; or

"(B) is not available at civilian health care facilities in the area of the hospital.

"(d) AMBULATORY CARE CENTERS.—(1) The Secretary of Defense shall maintain ambulatory care centers in areas where civilian health care facilities are able to support the health care needs of members of the armed forces and covered beneficiaries.

"(2) Ambulatory care centers shall provide the outpatient health services required to maintain medical readiness, including with respect to partnerships established pursuant to section 706 of the National Defense Authorization Act for Fiscal Year 2017.

"(3) Ambulatory care centers shall consist of outpatient care facilities with limited specialty care that the Secretary determines—

"(A) is cost effective; or

"(B) is not available at civilian health care facilities in the area of the ambulatory care center.".

(2) CLERICAL AMENDMENT.—The table of sections at the beginning of such chapter, as amended by section 702, is further amended by inserting after the item relating to section 1073c the following new item:

"1073d. Military medical treatment facilities.".

(3) SATELLITE CENTERS.—In addition to the centers of excellence designated under section 1073d(b)(4) of title 10, United States Code, as added by paragraph (1), the Secretary of Defense may establish satellite centers of excellence to provide specialty care for certain conditions, including with respect to—

(A) post-traumatic stress;

(B) traumatic brain injury; and

(C) such other conditions as the Secretary considers appropriate.

(b) EXCEPTION.—In carrying out section 1073d of title 10, United States Code, as added by sub-section (a)(1), the Secretary of Defense may not restructure or realign the infrastructure of, or modify the health care services provided by, a military medical treatment facility unless the Secretary determines that, if such a restructure, realignment, or modification will eliminate the ability of a covered beneficiary to access health care services at a military medical treatment facility, the covered beneficiary will be able to access such health care services through the purchased care component of the TRICARE program.

(c) UPDATE OF STUDY.—

(1) IN GENERAL.—The Secretary of Defense, in collaboration with the Secretaries of the military departments, shall update the report described in paragraph (2) to address the restructuring or realignment of military medical treatment facilities pursuant to section 1073d of title 10, United States Code, as added by subsection (a), including with respect to any expansions or consolidations of such facilities.

(2) REPORT DESCRIBED.—The report described in this paragraph is the Military Health System Modernization Study dated May 29th, 2015, required by section 713(a)(2) of the Carl Levin and Howard P. "Buck" McKeon National Defense Authorization Act for Fiscal Year 2015 (Public Law 113–291; 128 Stat. 3414).

(3) SUBMISSION.—Not later than 270 days after the date of the enactment of this Act, the Secretary of Defense shall submit to the congressional defense committees the updated report under paragraph (1).

(d) IMPLEMENTATION PLAN.—

(1) IN GENERAL.—Not later than two years after the date of the enactment of this Act, the Secretary of Defense shall submit to the congressional defense committees an implementation plan to restructure or realign the military medical treatment facilities pursuant to section 1073d of title 10, United States Code, as added by subsection (a).

(2) ELEMENTS.—The implementation plan under paragraph (1) shall include the following:

(A) With respect to each military medical treatment facility—

(i) whether the facility will be realigned or restructured under the plan;

(ii) whether the functions of such facility will be expanded or consolidated;

(iii) the costs of such realignment or restructuring;

(iv) a description of any changes to the military and civilian personnel assigned to such facility as of the date of the plan;

(v) a timeline for such realignment or restructuring;

(vi) the justifications for such realignment or restructuring, including an assessment of the capacity of the civilian health care facilities located near such facility;

(vii) a comprehensive assessment of the health care services provided at the facility;

(viii) a description of the current accessibility of covered beneficiaries to health care services provided at the facility and proposed modifications to that accessibility, including with respect to types of services provided;

(ix) a description of the current availability of urgent care, emergent care, and specialty care at the facility and in the TRICARE provider network in the area in which the facility is located, and proposed modifications to the availability of such care;

(x) a description of the current level of coordination between the facility and local health care providers in the area in which the facility is located and proposed modifications to such level of coordination; and

(xi) a description of any unique challenges to providing health care at the facility, with a focus on challenges relating to rural, remote, and insular areas, as appropriate.

(B) A description of the relocation of the graduate medical education programs and the residency programs.

(C) A description of the plans to assist members of the Armed Forces and covered beneficiaries with travel and lodging, if necessary, in connection with the receipt of specialty care services at regional centers of excellence designated under subsection (b)(4) of such section 1073d.

(D) A description of how the Secretary will carry out subsection (b).

(3) GAO REPORT.—Not later than 60 days after the date on which the Secretary of Defense submits the report under paragraph (1), the Comptroller General of the United States shall submit to the Committees on Armed Services of the Senate and the House of Representatives a review of such report.

(e) DEFINITIONS.—In this section, the terms "covered beneficiary" and "TRICARE program" have the meaning given those terms in section 1072 of title 10, United States Code.

SEC. 704. ACCESS TO URGENT AND PRIMARY CARE UNDER TRICARE PROGRAM.

(a) IN GENERAL.—Chapter 55 of title 10, United States Code, is amended by inserting after section 1077 the following new section:

"§ 1077a. Access to military medical treatment facilities and other facilities

"(a) URGENT CARE.—(1) The Secretary of Defense shall ensure that military medical treatment facilities, at locations the Secretary determines appropriate, provide urgent care services for members of the armed forces and covered beneficiaries until 11:00 p.m. each day.

"(2) With respect to areas in which a military medical treatment facility covered by paragraph (1) is not located, the Secretary shall ensure that members of the armed forces and covered beneficiaries may access urgent care clinics through the health care provider network under the TRICARE program.

"(3) A covered beneficiary may access urgent care services without the need for pre-authorization for such services.

"(4) The Secretary shall—

"(A) publish information about changes in access to urgent care under the TRICARE program—

"(i) on the primary publicly available Internet website of the Department; and

"(ii) on the primary publicly available Internet website of each military medical treatment facility; and

"(B) ensure that such information is made available on the publicly available Internet website of each current managed care support contractor that has established a health care provider network under the TRICARE program.

"(b) NURSE ADVICE LINE.—The Secretary shall ensure that the nurse advice line of the Department directs covered beneficiaries seeking access to care to the source of the most appropriate level of health care required to treat the medical conditions of the beneficiaries, including urgent care services described in subsection (a).

"(c) PRIMARY CARE CLINICS.—(1) The Secretary shall ensure that primary care clinics at military medical treatment facilities are available for members of the armed forces and covered beneficiaries between the hours determined appropriate under paragraph (2), including with respect to expanded hours described in subparagraph (B) of such paragraph.

"(2)(A) The Secretary shall determine the hours that each primary care clinic at a military medical treatment facility is available for members of the armed forces and covered beneficiaries based on—

"(i) the needs of the military medical treatment facility to meet the access standards under the TRICARE Prime program; and

"(ii) the primary care utilization patterns of members and covered beneficiaries at such military medical treatment facility.

"(B) The primary care clinic hours at a military medical treatment facility determined under subparagraph (A) shall include expanded hours beyond regular business hours during weekdays and the weekend if the Secretary determines under such subparagraph that sufficient demand exists at the military medical treatment facility for such expanded primary care clinic hours.''.

(b) CLERICAL AMENDMENT.—The table of sections at the beginning of such chapter is amended by inserting after the item relating to section 1077 the following new item:

"1077a. Access to military medical treatment facilities and other facilities''.

(c) IMPLEMENTATION.—The Secretary of Defense shall implement—

(1) subsection (a) of section 1077a of title 10, United States Code, as added by subsection (a) of this section, by not later than one year after the date of the enactment of this Act; and

(2) subsection (c) of such section by not later than 180 days after the date of the enactment of this Act.

SEC. 705. VALUE-BASED PURCHASING AND ACQUISITION OF MANAGED CARE SUPPORT CONTRACTS FOR TRICARE PROGRAM.

(a) VALUE-BASED HEALTH CARE.—

(1) IN GENERAL.—The Secretary of Defense shall develop and implement value-based incentive programs as part of any contract awarded under chapter 55 of title 10, United States Code, for the provision of health care services to covered beneficiaries to encourage health care providers under the TRICARE program (including physicians, hospitals, and other persons and facilities involved in providing such health care services) to improve the following:

(A) The quality of health care provided to covered beneficiaries under the TRICARE program.

(B) The experience of covered beneficiaries in receiving health care under the TRICARE program.

(C) The health of covered beneficiaries.

(2) VALUE-BASED INCENTIVE PROGRAMS.—

(A) DEVELOPMENT.—In developing value-based incentive programs under paragraph (1), the Secretary shall—

(i) link payments to health care providers under the TRICARE program to improved performance with respect to quality, cost, and reducing the provision of inappropriate care;

(ii) consider the characteristics of the population of covered beneficiaries affected by the value-based incentive program;

(iii) consider how the value-based incentive program would affect the receipt of health care under the TRICARE program by such covered beneficiaries;

(iv) establish or maintain an assurance that such covered beneficiaries will have timely access to health care during the operation of the value-based incentive program;

(v) ensure that such covered beneficiaries do not incur any additional costs by reason of the value-based incentive program; and

(vi) consider such other factors as the Secretary considers appropriate.

(B) SCOPE AND METRICS.—With respect to a value-based incentive program developed and implemented under paragraph (1), the Secretary shall ensure that—

(i) the size, scope, and duration of the value-based incentive program is reasonable in relation to the purpose of the value-based incentive program; and

(ii) the value-based incentive program relies on the core quality performance metrics adopted pursuant to section 728.

(3) USE OF EXISTING MODELS.—In developing a value-based incentive program under paragraph (1), the Secretary may adapt a value-based incentive program conducted by a TRICARE managed care support contractor, the Centers for Medicare & Medicaid Services, or any other Federal Government, State government, or commercial health care program.

(b) TRANSFER OF CONTRACTING RESPONSIBILITY.—With respect to the acquisition of any managed care support contracts under the TRICARE program initiated after the date of the enactment of this Act, the Secretary of Defense shall transfer contracting responsibility for the solicitation and award of such contracts from the Defense Health Agency to the Office of the Under Secretary of Defense for Acquisition, Technology, and Logistics.

(c) ACQUISITION OF CONTRACTS.—

(1) STRATEGY.—Not later than January 1, 2018, the Secretary of Defense shall develop and implement a strategy to ensure that managed care support contracts under the TRICARE program entered into with private sector entities, other than overseas medical support contracts—

(A) improve access to health care for covered beneficiaries;

(B) improve health outcomes for covered beneficiaries;

(C) improve the quality of health care received by covered beneficiaries;

(D) enhance the experience of covered beneficiaries in receiving health care; and

(E) lower per capita costs to the Department of Defense of health care provided to covered beneficiaries.

(2) APPLICABILITY OF STRATEGY.—

(A) IN GENERAL.—The strategy required by paragraph (1) shall apply to all managed care support contracts under the TRICARE program entered into with private sector entities.

(B) MODIFICATION OF CONTRACTS.—Contracts entered into prior to the implementation of the strategy required by paragraph (1) shall be modified to ensure consistency with such strategy.

(3) LOCAL, REGIONAL, AND NATIONAL HEALTH PLANS.—In developing and implementing the strategy required by paragraph (1), the Secretary shall ensure that local, regional, and national health plans have an opportunity to participate in the competition for managed care support contracts under the TRICARE program.

(4) CONTINUOUS INNOVATION.—The strategy required by paragraph (1) shall include incentives for the incorporation of innovative ideas and solutions into managed care support contracts under the TRICARE program through the use of teaming agreements, subcontracts, and other contracting mechanisms that can be used to develop and continuously refresh high-performing networks of health care providers at the national, regional, and local level.

(5) ELEMENTS OF STRATEGY.—The strategy required by paragraph (1) shall provide for the following with respect to managed care support contracts under the TRICARE program:

(A) The maximization of flexibility in the design and configuration of networks of individual and institutional health care providers, including a focus on the development of high-performing networks of health care providers.

(B) The establishment of an integrated medical management system between military medical treatment facilities and health care providers in the private sector that, when appropriate, effectively coordinates and integrates health care across the continuum of care.

(C) With respect to telehealth services—

(i) the maximization of the use of such services to provide real-time interactive communications between patients and health care providers and remote patient monitoring; and

(ii) the use of standardized payment methods to reimburse health care providers for the provision of such services.

(D) The use of value-based reimbursement methodologies, including through the use of value-based incentive programs under subsection (a), that transfer financial risk to health care providers and managed care support contractors.

(E) The use of financial incentives for contractors and health care providers to receive an equitable share in the cost savings to the Department resulting from improvement in health outcomes for covered beneficiaries and the experience of covered beneficiaries in receiving health care.

(F) The use of incentives that emphasize prevention and wellness for covered beneficiaries receiving health care services from private sector entities to seek such services from high-value health care providers.

(G) The adoption of a streamlined process for enrollment of covered beneficiaries to receive health care and timely assignment of primary care managers to covered beneficiaries.

(H) The elimination of the requirement for a referral to be authorized prior receiving specialty care services at a facility of the Department of Defense or through the TRICARE program.

(I) The use of incentives to encourage covered beneficiaries to participate in medical and lifestyle intervention programs.

(6) RURAL, REMOTE, AND ISOLATED AREAS.—In developing and implementing the strategy required by paragraph (1), the Secretary shall—

(A) assess the unique characteristics of providing health care services in Alaska, Hawaii, and the territories and possessions of the United States, and in rural, remote, or isolated locations in the contiguous 48 States;

(B) consider the various challenges inherent in developing robust networks of health care providers in those locations;

(C) develop a provider reimbursement rate structure in those locations that ensures—

(i) timely access of covered beneficiaries to health care services;

(ii) the delivery of high-quality primary and specialty care;

(iii) improvement in health outcomes for covered beneficiaries; and

(iv) an enhanced experience of care for covered beneficiaries; and

(D) ensure that managed care support contracts under the TRICARE program in those locations will—

(i) establish individual and institutional provider networks that will provide timely access to care for covered beneficiaries, including pursuant to such networks relating to an Indian tribe or tribal organization that is party to the Alaska Native Health Compact with the Indian Health Service or has entered into a contract with the Indian Health Service to provide health care in rural Alaska or other locations in the United States; and

(ii) deliver high-quality care, better health outcomes, and a better experience of care for covered beneficiaries.

(d) REPORT PRIOR TO CERTAIN CONTRACT MODIFICATIONS.—Not later than 60 days before the date on which the Secretary of Defense first modifies a contract awarded under chapter 55 of title 10, United States Code, to implement a value-based incentive program under subsection (a), or the managed care support contract acquisition strategy under subsection (c), the Secretary shall submit to the Committees on Armed Services of the Senate and the House of Representatives a report on any implementation plan of the Secretary with respect to such value-based incentive program or managed care support contract acquisition strategy.

(e) COMPTROLLER GENERAL REPORT.—

(1) IN GENERAL.—Not later than 180 days after the date on which the Secretary submits the report under subsection (d), the Comptroller General of the United States shall submit to the

Committees on Armed Services of the Senate and the House of Representatives a report that assesses the compliance of the Secretary of Defense with the requirements of subsection (a) and subsection (c).

(2) ELEMENTS.—The report required by paragraph (1) shall include an assessment of the following:

(A) Whether the approach of the Department of Defense for acquiring managed care support contracts under the TRICARE program—

(i) improves access to care;

(ii) improves health outcomes;

(iii) improves the experience of care for covered beneficiaries; and

(iv) lowers per capita health care costs.

(B) Whether the Department has, in its requirements for managed care support contracts under the TRICARE program, allowed for—

(i) maximum flexibility in network design and development;

(ii) integrated medical management between military medical treatment facilities and network providers;

(iii) the maximum use of the full range of telehealth services;

(iv) the use of value-based reimbursement methods that transfer financial risk to health care providers and managed care support contractors;

(v) the use of prevention and wellness incentives to encourage covered beneficiaries to seek health care services from high-value providers;

(vi) a streamlined enrollment process and timely assignment of primary care managers;

(vii) the elimination of the requirement to seek authorization for referrals for specialty care services;

(viii) the use of incentives to encourage covered beneficiaries to engage in medical and lifestyle intervention programs; and

(ix) the use of financial incentives for contractors and health care providers to receive an equitable share in cost savings resulting from improvements in health outcomes and the experience of care for covered beneficiaries.

(C) Whether the Department has considered, in developing requirements for managed care support contracts under the TRICARE program, the following:

(i) The unique characteristics of providing health care services in Alaska, Hawaii, and the territories and possessions of the United States, and in rural, remote, or isolated locations in the contiguous 48 States;

(ii) The various challenges inherent in developing robust networks of health care providers in those locations.

(iii) A provider reimbursement rate structure in those locations that ensures—

(I) timely access of covered beneficiaries to health care services;

(II) the delivery of high-quality primary and specialty care;

(III) improvement in health outcomes for covered beneficiaries; and

(IV) an enhanced experience of care for covered beneficiaries.

(f) DEFINITIONS.—In this section:

(1) The terms "covered beneficiary" and "TRICARE program" have the meaning given those terms in section 1072 of title 10, United States Code.

(2) The term "high-performing networks of health care providers" means networks of health care providers that, in addition to such other requirements as the Secretary of Defense may specify for purposes of this section, do the following:

(A) Deliver high quality health care as measured by leading health quality measurement organizations such as the National Committee for Quality Assurance and the Agency for Healthcare Research and Quality.

(B) Achieve greater efficiency in the delivery of health care by identifying and implementing within such network improvement opportunities that guide patients through the entire continuum of care, thereby reducing variations in the delivery of health care and preventing medical errors and duplication of medical services.

(C) Improve population-based health outcomes by using a team approach to deliver case management, prevention, and wellness services to high-need and high-cost patients.

(D) Focus on preventive care that emphasizes—

(i) early detection and timely treatment of disease;

(ii) periodic health screenings; and

(iii) education regarding healthy lifestyle behaviors.

(E) Coordinate and integrate health care across the continuum of care, connecting all aspects of the health care received by the patient, including the patient's health care team.

(F) Facilitate access to health care providers, including—

(i) after-hours care;

(ii) urgent care; and

(iii) through telehealth appointments, when appropriate.

(G) Encourage patients to participate in making health care decisions.

(H) Use evidence-based treatment protocols that improve the consistency of health care and eliminate ineffective, wasteful health care practices.

SEC. 706. ESTABLISHMENT OF HIGH PERFORMANCE MILITARY-CIVILIAN INTEGRATED HEALTH DELIVERY SYSTEMS.

(a) IN GENERAL.—Not later than January 1, 2018, the Secretary of Defense shall establish military-civilian integrated health delivery systems through partnerships with other health systems, including local or regional health systems in the private sector—

(1) to improve access to health care for covered beneficiaries;

(2) to enhance the experience of covered beneficiaries in receiving health care;

(3) to improve health outcomes for covered beneficiaries;

(4) to share resources between the Department of Defense and the private sector, including such staff, equipment, and training assets as may be required to carry out such integrated health delivery systems;

(5) to maintain services within military treatment facilities that are essential for the maintenance of operational medical force readiness skills of health care providers of the Department; and

(6) to provide members of the Armed Forces with additional training opportunities to maintain such readiness skills.

(b) ELEMENTS OF SYSTEMS.—Each military-civilian integrated health delivery system established under subsection (a) shall—

(1) deliver high quality health care as measured by leading national health quality measurement organizations;

(2) achieve greater efficiency in the delivery of health care by identifying and implementing within each such system improvement opportunities that guide patients through the entire continuum of care, thereby reducing variations in the delivery of health care and preventing medical errors and duplication of medical services;

(3) improve population-based health outcomes by using a team approach to deliver case management, prevention, and wellness services to high-need and high-cost patients;

(4) focus on preventive care that emphasizes—

(A) early detection and timely treatment of disease;

(B) periodic health screenings; and

(C) education regarding healthy lifestyle behaviors;

(5) coordinate and integrate health care across the continuum of care, connecting all aspects of the health care received by the patient, including the patient's health care team;

(6) facilitate access to health care providers, including—

(A) after-hours care;

(B) urgent care; and

(C) through telehealth appointments, when appropriate;

(7) encourage patients to participate in making health care decisions;

(8) use evidence-based treatment protocols that improve the consistency of health care and eliminate ineffective, wasteful health care practices; and

(9) improve coordination of behavioral health services with primary mental health care.

(c) AGREEMENTS.—

(1) IN GENERAL.—In establishing military-civilian integrated health delivery systems through partnerships under subsection (a), the Secretary shall seek to enter into memoranda of understanding or contracts between military treatment facilities and health maintenance organizations, health care centers of excellence, public or private academic medical institutions, regional health organizations, integrated health systems, accountable care organizations, and such other health systems as the Secretary considers appropriate.

(2) PRIVATE SECTOR CARE.—Memoranda of understanding and contracts entered into under paragraph (1) shall ensure that covered beneficiaries are eligible to enroll in and receive medical services under the private sector components of military-civilian integrated health delivery systems established under subsection (a).

(3) VALUE-BASED REIMBURSEMENT METHODOLOGIES.—The Secretary shall incorporate value-based reimbursement methodologies, such as capitated payments, bundled payments, or pay for performance, into memoranda of understanding and contracts entered into under paragraph (1) to reimburse entities for medical services provided to covered beneficiaries under such memoranda of understanding and contracts.

(4) QUALITY OF CARE.—Each memorandum of understanding or contract entered into under paragraph (1) shall ensure that the quality of services received by covered beneficiaries through a military-civilian integrated health delivery system under such memorandum of understanding or contract is at least comparable to the quality of services received by covered beneficiaries from a military treatment facility.

(d) COVERED BENEFICIARY DEFINED.—In this section, the term "covered beneficiary" has the meaning given that term in section 1072 of title 10, United States Code.

SEC. 707. JOINT TRAUMA SYSTEM.

(a) PLAN.—

(1) IN GENERAL.—Not later than 180 days after the date of the enactment of this Act, the Secretary of Defense shall submit to the Committees on Armed Services of the House of Representatives and the Senate an implementation plan to establish a Joint Trauma System within the Defense Health Agency that promotes improved trauma care to members of the Armed Forces and other individuals who are eligible to be treated for trauma at a military medical treatment facility.

(2) IMPLEMENTATION.—The Secretary shall implement the plan under paragraph (1) after a 90-day period has elapsed following the date on which the Comptroller General of the United States is required to submit to the Committees on Armed Services of the House of Representatives and the Senate the review under subsection (c). In implementing such plan, the Secretary shall take into account any recommendation made by the Comptroller General under such review.

(b) ELEMENTS.—The Joint Trauma System described in subsection (a)(1) shall include the following elements:

(1) Serve as the reference body for all trauma care provided across the military health system.

(2) Establish standards of care for trauma services provided at military medical treatment facilities.

(3) Coordinate the translation of research from the centers of excellence of the Department of Defense into standards of clinical trauma care.

(4) Coordinate the incorporation of lessons learned from the trauma education and training partnerships pursuant to section 709 into clinical practice.

(c) REVIEW.—Not later than 180 days after the date on which the Secretary submits to the Committees on Armed Services of the House of Representatives and the Senate the implementation plan under subsection (a)(1), the Comptroller General of the United States shall submit to such committees a review of such plan to determine if each element under subsection (b) is included in such plan.

(d) REVIEW OF MILITARY TRAUMA SYSTEM.— In establishing a Joint Trauma System, the Secretary of Defense may seek to enter into an agreement with a non-governmental entity with subject matter experts to—

(1) conduct a system-wide review of the military trauma system, including a comprehensive review of combat casualty care and wartime trauma systems during the period beginning on January 1, 2001, and ending on the date of the review, including an assessment of lessons learned to improve combat casualty care in future conflicts; and

(2) make publicly available a report containing such review and recommendations to establish a comprehensive trauma system for the Armed Forces.

SEC. 708. JOINT TRAUMA EDUCATION AND TRAINING DIRECTORATE.

(a) ESTABLISHMENT.—The Secretary of Defense shall establish a Joint Trauma Education and Training Directorate (in this section referred to as the "Directorate") to ensure that the traumatologists of the Armed Forces maintain readiness and are able to be rapidly deployed for future armed conflicts. The Secretary shall carry out this section in collaboration with the Secretaries of the military departments.

(b) DUTIES.—The duties of the Directorate are as follows:

(1) To enter into and coordinate the partnerships under subsection (c).

(2) To establish the goals of such partnerships necessary for trauma teams led by traumatologists to maintain professional competency in trauma care.

(3) To establish metrics for measuring the performance of such partnerships in achieving such goals.

(4) To develop methods of data collection and analysis for carrying out paragraph (3).

(5) To communicate and coordinate lessons learned from such partnerships with the Joint Trauma System established under section 707.

(6) To develop standardized combat casualty care instruction for all members of the Armed Forces, including the use of standardized trauma training platforms.

(7) To develop a comprehensive trauma care registry to compile relevant data from point of injury through rehabilitation of members of the Armed Forces.

(8) To develop quality of care outcome measures for combat casualty care.

(9) To direct the conduct of research on the leading causes of morbidity and mortality of members of the Armed Forces in combat.

(c) PARTNERSHIPS.—

(1) IN GENERAL.—The Secretary may enter into partnerships with civilian academic medical centers and large metropolitan teaching hospitals that have level I civilian trauma centers to provide integrated combat trauma teams, including forward surgical teams, with maximum exposure to a high volume of patients with critical injuries.

(2) TRAUMA TEAMS.—Under the partnerships entered into with civilian academic medical centers and large metropolitan teaching hospitals under paragraph (1), trauma teams of the Armed Forces led by traumatologists of the Armed Forces shall embed within the trauma centers of the medical centers and hospitals on an enduring basis.

(3) SELECTION.—The Secretary shall select civilian academic medical centers and large metropolitan teaching hospitals to enter into partnerships under paragraph (1) based on patient volume, acuity, and other factors the Secretary determines necessary to ensure that the traumatologists of the Armed Forces and the associated clinical support teams have adequate and continuous exposure to critically injured patients.

(4) CONSIDERATION.—In entering into partnerships under paragraph (1), the Secretary may consider the experiences and lessons learned by the military departments that have entered into memoranda of understanding with civilian medical centers for trauma care.

(d) PERSONNEL MANAGEMENT PLAN.—

(1) PLAN.—The Secretary shall establish a personnel management plan for the following wartime medical specialties:

(A) Emergency medical services and prehospital care.

(B) Trauma surgery.

(C) Critical care.

(D) Anesthesiology.

(E) Emergency medicine.

(F) Other wartime medical specialties the Secretary determines appropriate for purposes of the plan.

(2) ELEMENTS.—The elements of the plan established under paragraph (1) shall include, at a minimum, the following:

(A) An accession plan for the number of qualified medical personnel to maintain wartime medical specialties on an annual basis in order to maintain the required number of trauma teams as determined by the Secretary.

(B) The number of positions required in each such medical specialty.

(C) Crucial organizational and operational assignments for personnel in each such medical specialty.

(D) Career pathways for personnel in each such medical specialty.

(3) IMPLEMENTATION.—The Secretaries of the military departments shall carry out the plan established under paragraph (1).

(e) IMPLEMENTATION PLAN.—Not later than July 1, 2017, the Secretary of Defense shall submit to the Committees on Armed Services of the House of Representatives and the Senate an implementation plan for establishing the Joint Trauma Education and Training Directorate under subsection (a), entering into partnerships under subsection (c), and establishing the plan under subsection (d).

(f) LEVEL I CIVILIAN TRAUMA CENTER DEFINED.—In this section, the term "level I civilian trauma center" means a comprehensive regional resource that is a tertiary care facility central to the trauma system and is capable of providing total care for every aspect of injury from prevention through rehabilitation.

SEC. 709. STANDARDIZED SYSTEM FOR SCHEDULING MEDICAL APPOINTMENTS AT MILITARY TREATMENT FACILITIES.

(a) STANDARDIZED SYSTEM.—

(1) IN GENERAL.—Not later than January 1, 2018, the Secretary of Defense shall implement a system for scheduling medical appointments at military treatment facilities that is standardized throughout the military health system to enable timely access to care for covered beneficiaries.

(2) LACK OF VARIANCE.—The system implemented under paragraph (1) shall ensure that the appointment scheduling processes and procedures used within the military health system do not vary among military treatment facilities.

(b) SOLE SYSTEM.—Upon implementation of the system under subsection (a), no military treatment facility may use an appointment scheduling process other than such system.

(c) SCHEDULING OF APPOINTMENTS.—

(1) IN GENERAL.—Under the system implemented under subsection (a), each military treatment facility shall use a centralized appointment scheduling capability for covered beneficiaries that includes the ability to schedule appointments manually via telephone as described in paragraph (2) or automatically via a device that is connected to the Internet through an online scheduling system described in paragraph (3).

(2) TELEPHONE APPOINTMENT PROCESS.—

(A) IN GENERAL.—In the case of a covered beneficiary who contacts a military treatment facility via telephone to schedule an appointment under the system implemented under subsection (a), the Secretary shall implement standard processes to ensure that the needs of the covered beneficiary are met during the first such telephone call.

(B) MATTERS INCLUDED.—The standard processes implemented under subparagraph (A) shall include the following:

(i) The ability of a covered beneficiary, during the telephone call to schedule an appointment, to also schedule wellness visits or follow-up appointments during the 180-day period beginning on the date of the request for the visit or appointment.

(ii) The ability of a covered beneficiary to indicate the process through which the covered beneficiary prefers to be reminded of future appointments, which may include reminder telephone calls, emails, or cellular text messages to the covered beneficiary at specified intervals prior to appointments.

(3) ONLINE SYSTEM.—

(A) IN GENERAL.—The Secretary shall implement an online scheduling system that is available 24 hours per day, seven days per week, for purposes of scheduling appointments under the system implemented under subsection (a).

(B) CAPABILITIES OF ONLINE SYSTEM.—The online scheduling system implemented under subparagraph (A) shall have the following capabilities:

(i) An ability to send automated email and text message reminders, including repeat reminders, to patients regarding upcoming appointments.

(ii) An ability to store appointment records to ensure rapid access by medical personnel to appointment data.

(d) STANDARDS FOR PRODUCTIVITY OF HEALTH CARE PROVIDERS.—

(1) IN GENERAL.—The Secretary shall implement standards for the productivity of health care providers at military treatment facilities.

(2) MATTERS CONSIDERED.—In developing standards under paragraph (1), the Secretary shall consider—

(A) civilian benchmarks for measuring the productivity of health care providers;

(B) the optimal number of medical appointments for each health care provider that would be required, as determined by the Secretary, to maintain access of covered beneficiaries to health care from the Department; and

(C) the readiness requirements of the Armed Forces.

(e) PLAN.—

(1) IN GENERAL.—Not later than January 1, 2017, the Secretary shall submit to the Committees on Armed Services of the Senate and the

House of Representatives a comprehensive plan to implement the system required under subsection (a).

(2) ELEMENTS.—The plan required under paragraph (1) shall include the following:

(A) A description of the manual appointment process to be used at military treatment facilities under the system required under subsection (a).

(B) A description of the automated appointment process to be used at military treatment facilities under such system.

(C) A timeline for the full implementation of such system throughout the military health system.

(f) BRIEFING.—Not later than February 1, 2018, the Secretary shall brief the Committees on Armed Services of the Senate and the House of Representatives on the implementation of the system required under subsection (a) and the standards for the productivity of health care providers required under subsection (d).

(g) REPORT ON MISSED APPOINTMENTS.—

(1) IN GENERAL.—Not later than March 1 each year, the Secretary of Defense shall submit to the Committees on Armed Services of the Senate and the House of Representatives a report on the total number of medical appointments at military treatment facilities for which a covered beneficiary failed to appear without prior notification during the one-year period preceding the submittal of the report.

(2) ELEMENTS.—Each report under paragraph (1) shall include for each military treatment facility the following:

(A) An identification of the top five reasons for a covered beneficiary missing an appointment.

(B) A comparison of the number of missed appointments for specialty care versus primary care.

(C) An estimate of the cost to the Department of Defense of missed appointments.

(D) An assessment of strategies to reduce the number of missed appointments.

(h) COVERED BENEFICIARY DEFINED.—In this section, the term "covered beneficiary" has the meaning given that term in section 1072 of title 10, United States Code.

Subtitle B—Other Health Care Benefits

SEC. 711. EXTENDED TRICARE PROGRAM COVERAGE FOR CERTAIN MEMBERS OF THE NATIONAL GUARD AND DEPENDENTS DURING CERTAIN DISASTER RESPONSE DUTY.

(a) IN GENERAL.—Chapter 55 of title 10, United States Code, is amended by inserting after section 1076e the following new section:

"§ 1076f. TRICARE program: extension of coverage for certain members of the National Guard and dependents during certain disaster response duty

"(a) EXTENDED COVERAGE.—During a period in which a member of the National Guard is performing disaster response duty, the member may be treated as being on active duty for a period of more than 30 days for purposes of the eligibility of the member and dependents of the member for health care benefits under the TRICARE program if such period immediately follows a period in which the member served on full-time National Guard duty under section 502(f) of title 32, including pursuant to chapter 9 of such title, unless the Governor of the State (or, with respect to the District of Columbia, the mayor of the District of Columbia) determines that such extended eligibility is not in the best interest of the member or the State.

"(b) CONTRIBUTION BY STATE.—(1) The Secretary shall charge a State for the costs of providing coverage under the TRICARE program to members of the National Guard of the State and the dependents of the members pursuant to subsection (a). Such charges shall be paid from the funds of the State or from any other non-Federal funds.

"(2) Any amounts received by the Secretary under paragraph (1) shall be credited to the appropriation available for the Defense Health Program Account under section 1100 of this title, shall be merged with sums in such Account that are available for the fiscal year in which collected, and shall be available under subsection (b) of such section, including to carry out subsection (a) of this section.

"(c) DEFINITIONS.—In this section:

"(1) The term 'disaster response duty' means duty performed by a member of the National Guard in State status pursuant to an emergency declaration by the Governor of the State (or, with respect to the District of Columbia, the mayor of the District of Columbia) in response to a disaster or in preparation for an imminent disaster.

"(2) The term 'State' means each of the several States, the District of Columbia, the Commonwealth of Puerto Rico, and any territory or possession of the United States.".

(b) CLERICAL AMENDMENT.—The table of sections at the beginning of such chapter is amended by inserting after the item relating to section 1076e the following new item:

"1076f. TRICARE program: extension of coverage for certain members of the National Guard and dependents during certain disaster response duty.".

SEC. 712. CONTINUITY OF HEALTH CARE COVERAGE FOR RESERVE COMPONENTS.

(a) STUDY.—

(1) IN GENERAL.—The Secretary of Defense shall conduct a study of options for providing health care coverage that improves the continuity of health care provided to current and former members of the Selected Reserve of the Ready Reserve who are not—

(A) serving on active duty;

(B) eligible for the Transitional Assistance Management Program under section 1145 of title 10, United States Code; or

(C) eligible for the Federal Employees Health Benefit Program.

(2) ELEMENTS.—The study under paragraph (1) shall address the following:

(A) Whether to allow current and former members of the Selected Reserve to participate in the Federal Employees Health Benefit Program.

(B) Whether to pay a stipend to current and former members to continue coverage in a health plan obtained by the member.

(C) Whether to allow current and former members to participate in the TRICARE program under section 1076d of title 10, United States Code.

(D) Whether to amend section 1076f of title 10, United States Code, as added by section 711, to require the extension of TRICARE program coverage for members of the National Guard assigned to Homeland Response Force Units mobilized for a State emergency pursuant to chapter 9 of title 32, United States Code.

(E) The findings and recommendations under section 748.

(F) Any other options for providing health care coverage to current and former members of the Selected Reserve the Secretary considers appropriate.

(3) CONSULTATION.—In carrying out the study under paragraph (1), the Secretary shall consult with, and obtain the opinions of, current and former members of the Selected Reserve, including the leadership of the Selected Reserve.

(4) SUBMISSION.—

(A) REPORT.—Not later than 180 days after the date of the enactment of this Act, the Secretary shall submit to the congressional defense committees a report on the study under paragraph (1).

(B) MATTERS INCLUDED.—The report under subparagraph (A) shall include the following:

(i) A description of the health care coverage options addressed by the Secretary under paragraph (2).

(ii) Identification of such health care coverage option that the Secretary recommends as the best option.

(iii) The justifications for such recommended best option.

(iv) The number and proportion of the current and former members of the Selected Reserve projected to participate in such recommended best option.

(v) A determination of the appropriate cost sharing for such recommended best option with respect to the percentage contribution as a monthly premium for current members of the Selected Reserve.

(vi) An estimate of the cost of implementing such recommended best option.

(vii) Any legislative language required to implement such recommended best option.

(b) PILOT PROGRAM.—

(1) AUTHORIZATION.—The Secretary of Defense and the Director may jointly carry out a pilot program, at the election of the Secretary, under which the Director provides commercial health insurance coverage to eligible reserve component members who enroll in a health benefits plan under paragraph (4) as an individual, for self plus one coverage, or for self and family coverage.

(2) ELEMENTS.—The pilot program shall—

(A) provide for enrollment by eligible reserve component members, at the election of the member, in a health benefits plan under paragraph (4) during an open enrollment period established by the Director for purposes of this subsection;

(B) include a variety of national and regional health benefits plans that—

(i) meet the requirements of this subsection;

(ii) are broadly representative of the health benefits plans available in the commercial market; and

(iii) do not contain unnecessary restrictions, as determined by the Director; and

(C) offer a sufficient number of health benefits plans in order to provide eligible reserve component beneficiaries with an ample choice of health benefits plans, as determined by the Director.

(3) DURATION.—If the Secretary elects to carry out the pilot program, the Secretary and the Director shall carry out the pilot program for not less than five years.

(4) HEALTH BENEFITS PLANS.—

(A) IN GENERAL.—In providing health insurance coverage under the pilot program, the Director shall contract with qualified carriers for a variety of health benefits plans.

(B) DESCRIPTION OF PLANS.—Health benefits plans contracted for under this subsection—

(i) may vary by type of plan design, covered benefits, geography, and price;

(ii) shall include maximum limitations on out-of-pocket expenses paid by an eligible reserve component beneficiary for the health care provided; and

(iii) may not exclude an eligible reserve component member who chooses to enroll.

(C) QUALITY OF PLANS.—The Director shall ensure that each health benefits plan offered under this subsection offers a high degree of quality, as determined by criteria that include—

(i) access to an ample number of medical providers, as determined by the Director;

(ii) adherence to industry-accepted quality measurements, as determined by the Director;

(iii) access to benefits described in paragraph (5), including ease of referral for health care services; and

(iv) inclusion in the services covered by the plan of advancements in medical treatments and technology as soon as practicable in accordance with generally accepted standards of medicine.

(5) BENEFITS.—A health benefits plan offered by the Director under this subsection shall include, at a minimum, the following benefits:

(A) The health care benefits provided under chapter 55 of title 10, United States Code, excluding pharmaceutical, dental, and extended health care option benefits.

(B) Such other benefits as the Director determines appropriate.

(6) CARE AT FACILITIES OF UNIFORMED SERVICES.—

(A) IN GENERAL.—If an eligible reserve component beneficiary receives benefits described in paragraph (5) at a facility of the uniformed services, the health benefits plan under which the beneficiary is covered shall be treated as a third-party payer under section 1095 of title 10, United States Code, and shall pay charges for such benefits as determined by the Secretary.

(B) MILITARY MEDICAL TREATMENT FACILITIES.—The Secretary, in consultation with the Director—

(i) may contract with qualified carriers with which the Director has contracted under paragraph (4) to provide health insurance coverage for health care services provided at military treatment facilities under this subsection; and

(ii) may receive payments under section 1095 of title 10, United States Code, from qualified carriers for health care services provided at military medical treatment facilities under this subsection.

(7) SPECIAL RULE RELATING TO ACTIVE DUTY PERIOD.—

(A) IN GENERAL.—An eligible reserve component member may not receive benefits under a health benefits plan under this subsection during any period in which the member is serving on active duty for more than 30 days.

(B) TREATMENT OF DEPENDENTS.—Subparagraph (A) does not affect the coverage under a health benefits plan of any dependent of an eligible reserve component member.

(8) ELIGIBILITY FOR FEDERAL EMPLOYEES HEALTH BENEFITS PROGRAM.—An individual is not eligible to enroll in or be covered under a health benefits plan under this subsection if the individual is eligible to enroll in a health benefits plan under the Federal Employees Health Benefits Program.

(9) COST SHARING.—

(A) RESPONSIBILITY FOR PAYMENT.—

(i) IN GENERAL.—Except as provided in clause (ii), an eligible reserve component member shall pay an annual premium amount calculated under subparagraph (B) for coverage under a health benefits plan under this subsection and additional amounts described in subparagraph (C) for health care services in connection with such coverage.

(ii) ACTIVE DUTY PERIOD.—

(I) IN GENERAL.—During any period in which an eligible reserve component member is serving on active duty for more than 30 days, the eligible reserve component member is not responsible for paying any premium amount under subparagraph (B) or additional amounts under subparagraph (C).

(II) COVERAGE OF DEPENDENTS.—With respect to a dependent of an eligible reserve component member that is covered under a health benefits plan under this subsection, during any period described in subclause (I) with respect to the member, the Secretary shall, on behalf of the dependent, pay 100 percent of the total annual amount of a premium for coverage of the dependent under the plan and such cost-sharing amounts as may be applicable under the plan.

(B) PREMIUM AMOUNT.—

(i) IN GENERAL.—The annual premium calculated under this subparagraph is an amount equal to 28 percent of the total annual amount of a premium under the health benefits plan selected.

(ii) TYPES OF COVERAGE.—The premium amounts calculated under this subparagraph shall include separate calculations for—

(I) coverage as an individual;

(II) self plus one coverage; and

(III) self and family coverage.

(C) ADDITIONAL AMOUNTS.—The additional amounts described in this subparagraph with respect to an eligible reserve component member are such cost-sharing amounts as may be applicable under the health benefits plan under which the member is covered.

(10) CONTRACTING.—

(A) IN GENERAL.—In contracting for health benefits plans under paragraph (4), the Director may contract with qualified carriers in a manner similar to the manner in which the Director contracts with carriers under section 8902 of title 5, United States Code, including that—

(i) a contract under this subsection shall be for a uniform term of not less than one year, but may be made automatically renewable from term to term in the absence of notice of termination by either party;

(ii) a contract under this subsection shall contain a detailed statement of benefits offered and shall include such maximums, limitations, exclusions, and other definitions of benefits determined by the Director in accordance with paragraph (5);

(iii) a contract under this subsection shall ensure that an eligible reserve component member who is eligible to enroll in a health benefits plan pursuant to such contract is able to enroll in such plan; and

(iv) the terms of a contract under this subsection relating to the nature, provision, or extent of coverage or benefits (including payments with respect to benefits) shall supersede and preempt any conflicting State or local law.

(B) EVALUATION OF FINANCIAL SOLVENCY.—The Director shall perform a thorough evaluation of the financial solvency of an insurance carrier before entering into a contract with the insurance carrier under subparagraph (A).

(11) RECOMMENDATIONS AND DATA.—

(A) IN GENERAL.—The Secretary of Defense, in consultation with the Secretary of Homeland Security, shall provide recommendations and data to the Director with respect to—

(i) matters involving military medical treatment facilities;

(ii) matters unique to eligible reserve component members and dependents of such members; and

(iii) such other strategic guidance necessary for the Director to administer this subsection as the Secretary of Defense, in consultation with the Secretary of Homeland Security, considers appropriate.

(B) LIMITATION ON IMPLEMENTATION.—The Director shall not implement any recommendation provided by the Secretary of Defense under subparagraph (A) if the Director determines that the implementation of the recommendation would result in eligible reserve components beneficiaries receiving less generous health benefits under this subsection than the health benefits commonly available to individuals under the Federal Employees Health Benefits Program during the same period.

(12) TRANSMISSION OF INFORMATION.—On an annual basis during each year in which the pilot program is carried out, the Director shall provide the Secretary with information on the use of health care benefits under the pilot program, including—

(A) the number of eligible reserve component beneficiaries participating in the pilot program, listed by the health benefits plan under which the beneficiary is covered;

(B) the number of health benefits plans offered under the pilot program and a description of each such plan; and

(C) the costs of the health care provided under the plans.

(13) FUNDING.—

(A) IN GENERAL.—The Secretary of Defense and the Director shall jointly establish an appropriate mechanism to fund the pilot program.

(B) AVAILABILITY OF AMOUNTS.—Amounts shall be made available to the Director pursuant to the mechanism established under subparagraph (A), without fiscal year limitation—

(i) for payments to health benefits plans under this subsection; and

(ii) to pay the costs of administering this subsection.

(14) REPORTS.—

(A) INITIAL REPORTS.—Not later than one year after the date on which the Secretary establishes the pilot program, and annually thereafter for the following three years, the Secretary shall submit to the Committees on Armed Services of the Senate and the House of Representatives a report on the pilot program.

(B) MATTERS INCLUDED.—The report under subparagraph (A) shall include, with respect to the year covered by the report, the following:

(i) The number of eligible reserve component beneficiaries participating in the pilot program, listed by the health benefits plan under which the beneficiary is covered.

(ii) The number of health benefits plans offered under the pilot program.

(iii) The cost of the pilot program to the Department of Defense.

(iv) The estimated cost savings, if any, to the Department of Defense.

(v) The average cost to the eligible reserve component beneficiary.

(vi) The effect of the pilot program on the medical readiness of the members of the reserve components.

(vii) The effect of the pilot program on access to health care for members of the reserve components.

(C) FINAL REPORT.—Not later than 180 days before the date on which the pilot program will terminate pursuant to paragraph (3), the Secretary shall submit to the Committees on Armed Services of the Senate and the House of Representatives a report on the pilot program that includes—

(i) the matters specified under subparagraph (B); and

(ii) the recommendation of the Secretary regarding whether to make the pilot program permanent or to terminate the pilot program.

(c) DEFINITIONS.—In this section:

(1) The term "Director" means the Director of the Office of Personnel Management.

(2) The term "eligible reserve component beneficiary" means an eligible reserve component member enrolled in, or a dependent of such a member described in subparagraph (A), (D), or (I) of section 1072(2) of title 10, United States Code, covered under, a health benefits plan under subsection (b).

(3) The term "eligible reserve component member" means a member of the Selected Reserve of the Ready Reserve of an Armed Force.

(4) The term "extended health care option" means the program of extended benefits under subsections (d) and (e) of section 1079 of title 10, United States Code.

(5) The term "Federal Employees Health Benefits Program" means the health insurance program under chapter 89 of title 5, United States Code.

(6) The term "qualified carrier" means an insurance carrier that is licensed to issue group health insurance in any State, the District of Columbia, the Commonwealth of Puerto Rico, the Commonwealth of the Northern Mariana Islands, Guam, and any territory or possession of the United States.

SEC. 713. PROVISION OF HEARING AIDS TO DEPENDENTS OF RETIRED MEMBERS.

Section 1077 of title 10, United States Code, is amended—

(1) in subsection (a)(16), by striking "A hearing aid" and inserting "Except as provided by subsection (g), a hearing aid"; and

(2) by adding at the end the following new subsection:

"(g) In addition to the authority to provide a hearing aid under subsection (a)(16), hearing aids may be sold under this section to dependents of former members of the uniformed services at cost to the United States.".

SEC. 714. COVERAGE OF MEDICALLY NECESSARY FOOD AND VITAMINS FOR CERTAIN CONDITIONS UNDER THE TRICARE PROGRAM.

(a) IN GENERAL.—Section 1077 of title 10, United States Code, as amended by section 713, is further amended—

(1) in subsection (a)—

(A) in paragraph (3), by inserting before the period at the end the following: ", including, in accordance with subsection (g), medically necessary vitamins"; and

(B) by adding at the end the following new paragraph:

"(18) In accordance with subsection (g), medically necessary food and the medical equipment and supplies necessary to administer such food (other than durable medical equipment and supplies).".; and

(2) by adding at the end the following new subsection:

"(h)(1) Vitamins that may be provided under subsection (a)(3) are vitamins used for the management of a covered disease or condition pursuant to the prescription, order, or recommendation (as applicable) of a physician or other health care professional qualified to make such prescription, order, or recommendation.

"(2) Medically necessary food that may be provided under subsection (a)(18)—

"(A) is food, including a low protein modified food product or an amino acid preparation product, that is—

"(i) furnished pursuant to the prescription, order, or recommendation (as applicable) of a physician or other health care professional qualified to make such prescription, order, or recommendation, for the dietary management of a covered disease or condition;

"(ii) a specially formulated and processed product (as opposed to a naturally occurring foodstuff used in its natural state) for the partial or exclusive feeding of an individual by means of oral intake or enteral feeding by tube;

"(iii) intended for the dietary management of an individual who, because of therapeutic or chronic medical needs, has limited or impaired capacity to ingest, digest, absorb, or metabolize ordinary foodstuffs or certain nutrients, or who has other special medically determined nutrient requirements, the dietary management of which cannot be achieved by the modification of the normal diet alone;

"(iv) intended to be used under medical supervision, which may include in a home setting; and

"(v) intended only for an individual receiving active and ongoing medical supervision under which the individual requires medical care on a recurring basis for, among other things, instructions on the use of the food; and

"(B) may not include—

"(i) food taken as part of an overall diet designed to reduce the risk of a disease or medical condition or as weight-loss products, even if the food is recommended by a physician or other health care professional;

"(ii) food marketed as gluten-free for the management of celiac disease or non-celiac gluten sensitivity;

"(iii) food marketed for the management of diabetes; or

"(iv) such other products as the Secretary determines appropriate.

"(3) In this subsection, the term 'covered disease or condition' means—

"(A) inborn errors of metabolism;

"(B) medical conditions of malabsorption;

"(C) pathologies of the alimentary tract or the gastrointestinal tract;

"(D) a neurological or physiological condition; and

"(E) such other diseases or conditions the Secretary determines appropriate.".

(b) EFFECTIVE DATE.—The amendments made by subsection (a) shall apply to health care provided under chapter 55 of such title on or after the date that is one year after the date of the enactment of this Act.

SEC. 715. ELIGIBILITY OF CERTAIN BENEFICIARIES UNDER THE TRICARE PROGRAM FOR PARTICIPATION IN THE FEDERAL EMPLOYEES DENTAL AND VISION INSURANCE PROGRAM.

(a) IN GENERAL.—

(1) DENTAL BENEFITS.—Section 8951 of title 5, United States Code, is amended—

(A) in paragraph (3), by striking "paragraph (1) or (2)" and inserting "paragraph (1), (2), or (8)"; and

(B) by adding at the end the following new paragraph:

"(8) The term 'covered TRICARE-eligible individual' means an individual entitled to dental care under chapter 55 of title 10, pursuant to section 1076c of such title, who the Secretary of Defense determines should be an eligible individual for purposes of this chapter.".

(2) VISION BENEFITS.—Section 8981 of title 5, United States Code, is amended—

(A) in paragraph (3), by striking "paragraph (1) or (2)" and inserting "paragraph (1), (2), or (8)"; and

(B) by adding at the end the following new paragraph:

"(8)(A) The term 'covered TRICARE-eligible individual'—

"(i) means an individual entitled to medical care under chapter 55 of title 10, pursuant to section 1076d, 1076e, 1079(a), 1086(c), or 1086(d) of such title, who the Secretary of Defense determines in accordance with an agreement entered into under subparagraph (B) should be an eligible individual for purposes of this chapter; and

"(ii) does not include an individual covered under section 1110b of title 10.

"(B) The Secretary of Defense shall enter into an agreement with the Director of the Office relating to classes of individuals described in subparagraph (A)(i) who should be eligible individuals for purposes of this chapter.".

(b) CONFORMING AMENDMENTS.—

(1) DENTAL BENEFITS.—Section 8958(c) of title 5, United States Code, is amended—

(A) in paragraph (1), by striking "or" at the end;

(B) in paragraph (2), by striking the period at the end and inserting a semicolon; and

(C) by adding at the end the following new paragraphs:

"(3) in the case of a covered TRICARE-eligible individual who receives pay from the Federal Government or an annuity from the Federal Government due to the death of a member of the uniformed services (as defined in section 101 of title 10), and is not a former spouse of a member of the uniformed services, be withheld from—

"(A) the pay (including retired pay) of such individual; or

"(B) the annuity paid to such individual; or

"(4) in the case of a covered TRICARE-eligible individual who is not described in paragraph (3), be billed to such individual directly.".

(2) VISION BENEFITS.—Section 8988(c) of title 5, United States Code, is amended—

(A) in paragraph (1), by striking "or" at the end;

(B) in paragraph (2), by striking the period at the end and inserting a semicolon; and

(C) by adding at the end the following new paragraphs:

"(3) in the case of a covered TRICARE-eligible individual who receives pay from the Federal Government or an annuity from the Federal Government due to the death of a member of the uniformed services (as defined in section 101 of title 10), and is not a former spouse of a member of the uniformed services, be withheld from—

"(A) the pay (including retired pay) of such individual; or

"(B) the annuity paid to such individual; or

"(4) in the case of a covered TRICARE-eligible individual who is not described in paragraph (3), be billed to such individual directly.".

(3) PLAN FOR DENTAL INSURANCE FOR CERTAIN RETIREES, SURVIVING SPOUSES, AND OTHER DEPENDENTS.—Subsection (a) of section 1076c of title 10, United States Code, is amended to read as follows:

"(a) REQUIREMENT FOR PLAN.—(1) The Secretary of Defense shall establish a dental insurance plan for retirees of the uniformed services, certain unremarried surviving spouses, and dependents in accordance with this section.

"(2) The Secretary may satisfy the requirement under paragraph (1) by entering into an agreement with the Director of the Office of Personnel Management to allow persons described in subsection (b) to enroll in an insurance plan under chapter 89A of title 5 that provides benefits similar to those benefits required to be provided under subsection (d).".

(c) APPLICABILITY.—The amendments made by this section shall apply with respect to the first contract year for chapter 89A or 89B of title 5, United States Code, as applicable, that begins on or after January 1, 2018.

SEC. 716. APPLIED BEHAVIOR ANALYSIS.

(a) RATES OF REIMBURSEMENT.—

(1) IN GENERAL.—In furnishing applied behavior analysis under the TRICARE program to individuals described in paragraph (2) during the period beginning on the date of the enactment of this Act and ending on December 31, 2018, the Secretary of Defense shall ensure that the reimbursement rates for providers of applied behavior analysis are not less than the rates that were in effect on March 31, 2016.

(2) INDIVIDUALS DESCRIBED.—Individuals described in this paragraph are individuals who are covered beneficiaries by reason of being a member or former member of the Army, Navy, Air Force, or Marine Corps, including the reserve components thereof, or a dependent of such a member or former member.

(b) ANALYSIS.—

(1) IN GENERAL.—Upon the completion of the Department of Defense Comprehensive Autism Care Demonstration, the Assistant Secretary of Defense for Health Affairs shall conduct an analysis to—

(A) use data gathered during the demonstration to set future reimbursement rates for providers of applied behavior analysis under the TRICARE program;

(B) review comparative commercial insurance claims for purposes of setting such future rates, including by—

(i) conducting an analysis of the comparative total of commercial insurance claims billed for applied behavior analysis; and

(ii) reviewing any covered beneficiary limitations on access to applied behavior analysis services at various military installations throughout the United States; and

(C) determine whether the use of applied behavioral analysis under the demonstration has improved outcomes for covered beneficiaries with autism spectrum disorder.

(2) SUBMISSION.—The Assistant Secretary shall submit to the Committees on Armed Services of the Senate and the House of Representatives the analysis conducted under paragraph (1).

(c) DEFINITIONS.—In this section, the terms "covered beneficiary" and "TRICARE program" have the meaning given those terms in section 1072 of title 10, United States Code.

SEC. 717. EVALUATION AND TREATMENT OF VETERANS AND CIVILIANS AT MILITARY TREATMENT FACILITIES.

(a) IN GENERAL.—The Secretary of Defense shall authorize a veteran (in consultation with the Secretary of Veterans Affairs) or civilian to be evaluated and treated at a military treatment facility if the Secretary of Defense determines that—

(1) the evaluation and treatment of the individual is necessary to attain the relevant mix and volume of medical casework required to maintain medical readiness skills and competencies of health care providers at the facility;

(2) the health care providers at the facility have the competencies, skills, and abilities required to treat the individual; and

(3) the facility has available space, equipment, and materials to treat the individual.

(b) PRIORITY OF COVERED BENEFICIARIES.— The evaluation and treatment of covered beneficiaries at military treatment facilities shall be prioritized ahead of the evaluation and treatment of veterans and civilians at such facilities under subsection (a).

(c) REIMBURSEMENT FOR TREATMENT.—

(1) CIVILIANS.—A military treatment facility that evaluates or treats an individual (other than an individual described in paragraph (2)) under subsection (a) shall bill the individual and accept reimbursement from the individual or a third-party payer (as that term is defined in section 1095(h) of title 10, United States Code) on behalf of such individual for the costs of any health care services provided to the individual under such subsection.

(2) VETERANS.—The Secretary of Defense shall enter into a memorandum of agreement with the Secretary of Veterans Affairs under which the Secretary of Veterans Affairs will pay a military treatment facility using a prospective payment methodology (including interagency transfers of funds or obligational authority and similar transactions) for the costs of any health care services provided at the facility under subsection (a) to individuals eligible for such health care services from the Department of Veterans Affairs.

(3) USE OF AMOUNTS.—The Secretary of Defense shall make available to a military treatment facility any amounts collected by such facility under paragraph (1) or (2) for health care services provided to an individual under subsection (a).

(d) COVERED BENEFICIARY DEFINED.—In this section, the term "covered beneficiary" has the meaning given that term in section 1072 of title 10, United States Code.

SEC. 718. ENHANCEMENT OF USE OF TELEHEALTH SERVICES IN MILITARY HEALTH SYSTEM.

(a) INCORPORATION OF TELEHEALTH.—

(1) IN GENERAL.—Not later than 18 months after the date of the enactment of this Act, the Secretary of Defense shall incorporate, throughout the direct care and purchased care components of the military health system, the use of telehealth services, including mobile health applications—

(A) to improve access to primary care, urgent care, behavioral health care, and specialty care;

(B) to perform health assessments;

(C) to provide diagnoses, interventions, and supervision;

(D) to monitor individual health outcomes of covered beneficiaries with chronic diseases or conditions;

(E) to improve communication between health care providers and patients; and

(F) to reduce health care costs for covered beneficiaries and the Department of Defense.

(2) TYPES OF TELEHEALTH SERVICES.—The telehealth services required to be incorporated under paragraph (1) shall include those telehealth services that—

(A) maximize the use of secure messaging between health care providers and covered beneficiaries to improve the access of covered beneficiaries to health care and reduce the number of visits to medical facilities for health care needs;

(B) allow covered beneficiaries to schedule appointments; and

(C) allow health care providers, through video conference, telephone or tablet applications, or home health monitoring devices—

(i) to assess and evaluate disease signs and symptoms;

(ii) to diagnose diseases;

(iii) to supervise treatments; and

(iv) to monitor health outcomes.

(b) COVERAGE OF ITEMS OR SERVICES.—An item or service furnished to a covered beneficiary via a telecommunications system shall be covered under the TRICARE program to the same extent as the item or service would be covered if furnished in the location of the covered beneficiary.

(c) REIMBURSEMENT RATES FOR TELEHEALTH SERVICES.—The Secretary shall develop standardized payment methods to reimburse health care providers for telehealth services provided to covered beneficiaries in the purchased care component of the TRICARE program, including by using reimbursement rates that incentivize the provision of telehealth services.

(d) REDUCTION OR ELIMINATION OF COPAYMENTS.—The Secretary shall reduce or eliminate, as the Secretary considers appropriate, copayments or cost shares for covered beneficiaries in connection with the receipt of telehealth services under the purchased care component of the TRICARE program.

(e) REPORTS.—

(1) INITIAL REPORT.—

(A) IN GENERAL.—Not later than 180 days after the date of the enactment of this Act, the Secretary shall submit to the Committees on Armed Services of the Senate and the House of Representatives a report describing the full range of telehealth services to be available in the direct care and purchased care components of the military health system and the copayments and cost shares, if any, associated with those services.

(B) REIMBURSEMENT PLAN.—The report required under subparagraph (A) shall include a plan to develop standardized payment methods to reimburse health care providers for telehealth services provided to covered beneficiaries in the purchased care component of the TRICARE program, as required under subsection (c).

(2) FINAL REPORT.—

(A) IN GENERAL.—Not later than three years after the date on which the Secretary begins incorporating, throughout the direct care and purchased care components of the military health system, the use of telehealth services as required under subsection (a), the Secretary shall submit to the Committees on Armed Services of the Senate and the House of Representatives a report describing the impact made by the use of telehealth services, including mobile health applications, to carry out the actions specified in subparagraphs (A) through (F) of subsection (a)(1).

(B) ELEMENTS.—The report required under subparagraph (A) shall include an assessment of the following:

(i) The satisfaction of covered beneficiaries with telehealth services furnished by the Department of Defense.

(ii) The satisfaction of health care providers in providing telehealth services furnished by the Department.

(iii) The effect of telehealth services furnished by the Department on the following:

(I) The ability of covered beneficiaries to access health care services in the direct care and purchased care components of the military health system.

(II) The frequency of use of telehealth services by covered beneficiaries.

(III) The productivity of health care providers providing care furnished by the Department.

(IV) The reduction, if any, in the use by covered beneficiaries of health care services in military treatment facilities or medical facilities in the private sector.

(V) The number and types of appointments for the receipt of telehealth services furnished by the Department.

(VI) The savings, if any, realized by the Department by furnishing telehealth services to covered beneficiaries.

(f) REGULATIONS.—

(1) INTERIM FINAL RULE.—Not later than 180 days after the date of the enactment of this Act, the Secretary shall prescribe an interim final rule to implement this section.

(2) FINAL RULE.—Not later than 180 days after prescribing the interim final rule under paragraph (1) and considering public comments with respect to such interim final rule, the Secretary shall prescribe a final rule to implement this section.

(3) OBJECTIVES.—The regulations prescribed under paragraphs (1) and (2) shall accomplish the objectives set forth in subsection (a) and ensure quality of care, patient safety, and the integrity of the TRICARE program.

(g) DEFINITIONS.—In this section, the terms "covered beneficiary" and "TRICARE program" have the meaning given those terms in section 1072 of title 10, United States Code.

SEC. 719. AUTHORIZATION OF REIMBURSEMENT BY DEPARTMENT OF DEFENSE TO ENTITIES CARRYING OUT STATE VACCINATION PROGRAMS FOR COSTS OF VACCINES PROVIDED TO COVERED BENEFICIARIES.

(a) REIMBURSEMENT.—

(1) IN GENERAL.—The Secretary of Defense may reimburse an amount determined under paragraph (2) to an entity carrying out a State vaccination program for the cost of vaccines provided to covered beneficiaries through such program.

(2) AMOUNT OF REIMBURSEMENT.—

(A) IN GENERAL.—Except as provided in subparagraph (B), the amount determined under this paragraph with respect to a State vaccination program shall be the amount assessed by the entity carrying out such program to purchase vaccines provided to covered beneficiaries through such program.

(B) LIMITATION.—The amount determined under this paragraph to provide vaccines to covered beneficiaries through a State vaccination program may not exceed the amount that the Department would reimburse an entity under the TRICARE program for providing vaccines to the number of covered beneficiaries who were involved in the applicable State vaccination program.

(b) DEFINITIONS.—In this section:

(1) COVERED BENEFICIARY; TRICARE PROGRAM.—The terms "covered beneficiary" and "TRICARE program" have the meanings given those terms in section 1072 of title 10, United States Code.

(2) STATE VACCINATION PROGRAM.—The term "State vaccination program" means a vaccination program that provides vaccinations to individuals in a State and is carried out by an entity (including an agency of the State) within the State.

Subtitle C—Health Care Administration

SEC. 721. AUTHORITY TO CONVERT MILITARY MEDICAL AND DENTAL POSITIONS TO CIVILIAN MEDICAL AND DENTAL POSITIONS.

(a) LIMITED AUTHORITY FOR CONVERSION.—

(1) AUTHORITY.—Chapter 49 of title 10, United States Code, is amended by inserting after section 976 the following new section:

"§ 977. Conversion of military medical and dental positions to civilian medical and dental positions: limitation

"(a) PROCESS.—The Secretary of Defense, in collaboration with the Secretaries of the military departments, shall establish a process to define the military medical and dental personnel requirements necessary to meet operational medical force readiness requirements.

"(b) REQUIREMENTS RELATING TO CONVERSION.—A military medical or dental position within the Department of Defense may be converted to a civilian medical or dental position if the Secretary determines that the position is not necessary to meet operational medical force readiness requirements, as determined pursuant to subsection (a).

"(c) GRADE OR LEVEL CONVERTED.—In carrying out a conversion under subsection (b), the Secretary of Defense—

"(1) shall convert the applicable military position to a civilian position with a level of compensation commensurate with the skills and experience necessary to carry out the duties of such civilian position; and

"(2) may not place any limitation on the grade or level to which the military position is so converted.

"(d) DEFINITIONS.—In this section:

"(1) The term 'military medical or dental position' means a position for the performance of health care functions within the armed forces held by a member of the armed forces.

"(2) The term 'civilian medical or dental position' means a position for the performance of health care functions within the Department of Defense held by an employee of the Department or of a contractor of the Department.

"(3) The term 'conversion', with respect to a military medical or dental position, means a change of the position to a civilian medical or dental position, effective as of the date of the manning authorization document of the military department making the change (through a change in designation from military to civilian in the document, the elimination of the listing of the position as a military position in the document, or through any other means indicating the change in the document or otherwise).".

(2) CLERICAL AMENDMENT.—The table of sections at the beginning of chapter 49 of such title is amended by inserting after the item relating to section 976 the following new item:

"977. Conversion of military medical and dental positions to civilian medical and dental positions: limitation.".

(3) EFFECTIVE DATE OF CONVERSION AUTHORITY.—The Secretary of Defense may not carry out section 977(b) of title 10, United States Code, as added by paragraph (1), until the date that is 180 days after the date on which the Secretary submits the report under subsection (b).

(b) REPORT.—Not later than 90 days after the date of the enactment of this Act, the Secretary of Defense shall submit to the Committees on Armed Services of the Senate and the House of Representatives a report that includes the following:

(1) A description of the process established under section 977(a) of title 10, United States Code, as added by subsection (a), to define the military medical and dental personnel requirements necessary to meet operational medical force readiness requirements.

(2) A complete list, by position, of the military medical and dental personnel requirements nec-

essary to meet operational medical force readiness requirements.

(c) CONFORMING REPEAL.—Section 721 of the National Defense Authorization Act for Fiscal Year 2008 (Public Law 110–181; 122 Stat. 198; 10 U.S.C. 129c note) is repealed.

SEC. 722. PROSPECTIVE PAYMENT OF FUNDS NECESSARY TO PROVIDE MEDICAL CARE FOR THE COAST GUARD.

(a) IN GENERAL.—Chapter 13 of title 14, United States Code, is amended by adding at the end the following:

"§ 520. Prospective payment of funds necessary to provide medical care

"(a) PROSPECTIVE PAYMENT REQUIRED.—In lieu of the reimbursement required under section 1085 of title 10, the Secretary of Homeland Security shall make a prospective payment to the Secretary of Defense of an amount that represents the actuarial valuation of treatment or care—

"(1) that the Department of Defense shall provide to members of the Coast Guard, former members of the Coast Guard, and dependents of such members and former members (other than former members and dependents of former members who are a Medicare-eligible beneficiary or for whom the payment for treatment or care is made from the Medicare-Eligible Retiree Health Care Fund) at facilities under the jurisdiction of the Department of Defense or a military department; and

"(2) for which a reimbursement would otherwise be made under section 1085.

"(b) AMOUNT.—The amount of the prospective payment under subsection (a) shall be—

"(1) in the case of treatment or care to be provided to members of the Coast Guard and their dependents, derived from amounts appropriated for the operating expenses of the Coast Guard;

"(2) in the case of treatment or care to be provided former members of the Coast Guard and their dependents, derived from amounts appropriated for retired pay;

"(3) determined under procedures established by the Secretary of Defense;

"(4) paid during the fiscal year in which treatment or care is provided; and

"(5) subject to adjustment or reconciliation as the Secretaries determine appropriate during or promptly after such fiscal year in cases in which the prospective payment is determined excessive or insufficient based on the services actually provided.

"(c) NO PROSPECTIVE PAYMENT WHEN SERVICE IN NAVY.—No prospective payment shall be made under this section for any period during which the Coast Guard operates as a service in the Navy.

"(d) RELATIONSHIP TO TRICARE.—This section shall not be construed to require a payment for, or the prospective payment of an amount that represents the value of, treatment or care provided under any TRICARE program.".

(b) CLERICAL AMENDMENT.—The analysis for chapter 13 of title 14, United States Code, is amended by adding at the end the following:

"520. Prospective payment of funds necessary to provide medical care.".

(c) REPEAL.—Section 217 of the Coast Guard Authorization Act of 2016 (Public Law 114–120), as amended by section 3503, and the item relating to that section in the table of contents in section 2 of such Act, are repealed.

SEC. 723. REDUCTION OF ADMINISTRATIVE REQUIREMENTS RELATING TO AUTOMATIC RENEWAL OF ENROLLMENTS IN TRICARE PRIME.

Section 1097a(b) of title 10, United States Code, is amended—

(1) in paragraph (1), by striking "(1) An" and inserting "An"; and

(2) by striking paragraph (2).

SEC. 724. MODIFICATION OF AUTHORITY OF UNIFORMED SERVICES UNIVERSITY OF THE HEALTH SCIENCES TO INCLUDE UNDERGRADUATE AND OTHER MEDICAL EDUCATION AND TRAINING PROGRAMS.

(a) IN GENERAL.—Section 2112(a) of title 10, United States Code, is amended to read as follows:

"(a)(1) There is established a Uniformed Services University of the Health Sciences (in this chapter referred to as the 'University') with authority to grant appropriate certificates, certifications, undergraduate degrees, and advanced degrees.

"(2) The University shall be so organized as to graduate not fewer than 100 medical students annually.

"(3) The headquarters of the University shall be at a site or sites selected by the Secretary of Defense within 25 miles of the District of Columbia.".

(b) ADMINISTRATION.—Section 2113 of such title is amended—

(1) in subsection (d)—

(A) in the first sentence, by striking "located in or near the District of Columbia";

(B) in the third sentence, by striking "in or near the District of Columbia"; and

(C) by striking the fifth sentence; and

(2) in subsection (e)(3), by inserting after "programs" the following: ", including certificate, certification, and undergraduate degree programs,".

(c) REPEAL OF EXPIRED PROVISION.—Section 2112a of such title is amended—

(1) by striking subsection (b); and

(2) in subsection (a), by striking "(a) CLOSURE PROHIBITED.—".

SEC. 725. ADJUSTMENT OF MEDICAL SERVICES, PERSONNEL AUTHORIZED STRENGTHS, AND INFRASTRUCTURE IN MILITARY HEALTH SYSTEM TO MAINTAIN READINESS AND CORE COMPETENCIES OF HEALTH CARE PROVIDERS.

(a) IN GENERAL.—Except as provided by subsection (c), not later than one year after the date of the enactment of this Act, the Secretary of Defense shall implement measures to maintain the critical wartime medical readiness skills and core competencies of health care providers within the Armed Forces.

(b) MEASURES.—The measures under subsection (a) shall include measures under which the Secretary ensures the following:

(1) Medical services provided through the military health system at military medical treatment facilities—

(A) maintain the critical wartime medical readiness skills and core competencies of health care providers within the Armed Forces; and

(B) ensure the medical readiness of the Armed Forces.

(2) The authorized strengths for military and civilian personnel throughout the military health system—

(A) maintain the critical wartime medical readiness skills and core competencies of health care providers within the Armed Forces; and

(B) ensure the medical readiness of the Armed Forces.

(3) The infrastructure in the military health system, including infrastructure of military medical treatment facilities—

(A) maintains the critical wartime medical readiness skills and core competencies of health care providers within the Armed Forces; and

(B) ensures the medical readiness of the Armed Forces.

(4) Any covered beneficiary who may be affected by the measures implemented under subsection (a) will be able to receive through the purchased care component of the TRICARE program any medical services that will not be available to such covered beneficiary at a military

medical treatment facility by reason of such measures.

(c) EXCEPTION.—The Secretary is not required to implement measures under subsection (a)(1) with respect to military medical treatment facilities located in a foreign country if the Secretary determines that providing medical services in addition to the medical services described in such subsection is necessary to ensure that covered beneficiaries located in that foreign country have access to a similar level of care available to covered beneficiaries located in the United States.

(d) DEFINITIONS.—In this section:

(1) The term "clinical and logistical capabilities" means those capabilities relating to the provision of health care that are necessary to accomplish operational requirements, including—

(A) combat casualty care;

(B) medical response to and treatment of injuries sustained from chemical, biological, radiological, nuclear, or explosive incidents;

(C) diagnosis and treatment of infectious diseases;

(D) aerospace medicine;

(E) undersea medicine;

(F) diagnosis, treatment, and rehabilitation of specialized medical conditions;

(G) diagnosis and treatment of diseases and injuries that are not related to battle; and

(H) humanitarian assistance.

(2) The terms "covered beneficiary" and "TRICARE program" have the meanings given those terms in section 1072 of title 10, United States Code.

(3) The term "critical wartime medical readiness skills and core competencies" means those essential medical capabilities, including clinical and logistical capabilities, that are—

(A) necessary to be maintained by health care providers within the Armed Forces for national security purposes; and

(B) vital to the provision of effective and timely health care during contingency operations.

SEC. 726. PROGRAM TO ELIMINATE VARIABILITY IN HEALTH OUTCOMES AND IMPROVE QUALITY OF HEALTH CARE SERVICES DELIVERED IN MILITARY MEDICAL TREATMENT FACILITIES.

(a) PROGRAM.—Beginning not later than January 1, 2018, the Secretary of Defense shall implement a program—

(1) to establish best practices for the delivery of health care services for certain diseases or conditions at military medical treatment facilities, as selected by the Secretary;

(2) to incorporate such best practices into the daily operations of military medical treatment facilities selected by the Secretary for purposes of the program, with priority in selection given to facilities that provide specialty care; and

(3) to eliminate variability in health outcomes and to improve the quality of health care services delivered at military medical treatment facilities selected by the Secretary for purposes of the program.

(b) USE OF CLINICAL PRACTICE GUIDELINES.—In carrying out the program under subsection (a), the Secretary shall develop, implement, monitor, and update clinical practice guidelines reflecting the best practices established under paragraph (1) of such subsection.

(c) DEVELOPMENT.—In developing the clinical practice guidelines under subsection (b), the Secretary shall ensure that such development includes a baseline assessment of health care delivery and outcomes at military medical treatment facilities to evaluate and determine evidence-based best practices, within the direct care component of the military health system and the private sector, for treating the diseases or conditions selected by the Secretary under subsection (a)(1).

(d) IMPLEMENTATION.—The Secretary shall implement the clinical practice guidelines under

subsection (b) in military medical treatment facilities selected by the Secretary under subsection (a)(2) using means determined appropriate by the Secretary, including by communicating with the relevant health care providers of the evidence upon which the guidelines are based and by providing education and training on the most appropriate implementation of the guidelines.

(e) MONITORING.—The Secretary shall monitor the implementation of the clinical practice guidelines under subsection (b) using appropriate means, including by monitoring the results in clinical outcomes based on specific metrics included as part of the guidelines.

(f) UPDATING.—The Secretary shall periodically update the clinical practice guidelines under subsection (b) based on the results of monitoring conducted under subsection (e) and by continuously assessing evidence-based best practices within the direct care component of the military health system and the private sector.

(g) CONTINUOUS CYCLE.—The Secretary shall establish a continuous cycle of carrying out subsections (c) through (f) with respect to the clinical practice guidelines established under subsection (a).

SEC. 727. ACQUISITION STRATEGY FOR HEALTH CARE PROFESSIONAL STAFFING SERVICES.

(a) ACQUISITION STRATEGY.—

(1) IN GENERAL.—The Secretary of Defense shall develop and carry out a performance-based, strategic sourcing acquisition strategy with respect to entering into contracts for the services of health care professional staff at military medical treatment facilities located in a State.

(2) ELEMENTS.—The acquisition strategy under paragraph (1) shall include the following:

(A) Except as provided by subparagraph (B), a requirement that all the military medical treatment facilities that provide direct care use contracts described under paragraph (1).

(B) A process for a military medical treatment facility to obtain a waiver of the requirement under subparagraph (A) in order to use an acquisition strategy not described in paragraph (1).

(C) Identification of the responsibilities of the military departments and the elements of the Department of Defense in carrying out such strategy.

(D) Projection of the demand by covered beneficiaries for health care services, including with respect to primary care and expanded-hours urgent care services.

(E) Estimation of the workload gaps at military medical treatment facilities for health care services, including with respect to primary care and expanded-hours urgent care services.

(F) Methods to analyze, using reliable and detailed data covering the entire direct care component of the military health system, the amount of funds expended on contracts for the services of health care professional staff.

(G) Methods to identify opportunities to consolidate requirements for such services and reduce cost.

(H) Methods to measure cost savings that are realized by using such contracts instead of purchased care.

(I) Metrics to determine the effectiveness of such strategy.

(J) Metrics to evaluate the success of the strategy in achieving its objectives, including metrics to assess the effects of the strategy on the timeliness of beneficiary access to professional health care services in military medical treatment facilities.

(K) Such other matters as the Secretary considers appropriate.

(b) REPORT.—Not later than July 1, 2017, the Secretary shall submit to the Committees on

Armed Services of the Senate and the House of Representatives a report on the status of implementing the acquisition strategy under paragraph (1) of subsection (a), including how each element under subparagraphs (A) through (K) of paragraph (2) of such subsection is being carried out.

(c) DEFINITIONS.—In this section:

(1) The term "covered beneficiary" has the meaning given that term in section 1072 of title 10, United States Code.

(2) The term "State" means the several States and the District of Columbia.

(d) CONFORMING REPEAL.—Section 725 of the Carl Levin and Howard P. "Buck" McKeon National Defense Authorization Act for Fiscal Year 2015 (Public Law 113–291; 10 U.S.C. 1091 note) is repealed.

SEC. 728. ADOPTION OF CORE QUALITY PERFORMANCE METRICS.

(a) ADOPTION.—

(1) IN GENERAL.—Not later than 180 days after the date of the enactment of this Act, the Secretary of Defense shall adopt, to the extent appropriate, the core quality performance metrics agreed upon by the Core Quality Measures Collaborative for use by the military health system and in contracts awarded to carry out the TRICARE program.

(2) CORE MEASURES.—The core quality performance metrics described in paragraph (1) shall include the following sets:

(A) Accountable care organizations, patient centered medical homes, and primary care.

(B) Cardiology.

(C) Gastroenterology.

(D) HIV and hepatitis C.

(E) Medical oncology.

(F) Obstetrics and gynecology.

(G) Orthopedics.

(H) Such other sets of core quality performance metrics released by the Core Quality Measures Collaborative as the Secretary considers appropriate.

(b) PUBLICATION.—

(1) ONLINE AVAILABILITY.—Section 1073b of title 10, United States Code, is amended—

(A) in paragraph (1)—

(i) by striking "Not later than" and all that follows through "2016, the Secretary" and inserting "The Secretary"; and

(ii) by adding at the end the following new sentence: "Such data shall include the core quality performance metrics adopted by the Secretary under section 728 of the National Defense Authorization Act for Fiscal Year 2017."; and

*(B) in the section heading, by inserting "**and publication of certain data**" after "**reports**".*

(2) CLERICAL AMENDMENT.—The table of sections at the beginning of chapter 55 of title 10, United States Code, is amended by striking the item relating to section 1073b and inserting the following:

"1073b. Recurring reports and publication of certain data.".

(c) DEFINITIONS.—In this section:

(1) The term "Core Quality Measures Collaborative" means the collaboration between the Centers for Medicare & Medicaid Services, major health insurance companies, national physician organizations, and other entities to reach consensus on core performance measures reported by health care providers.

(2) The term "TRICARE program" has the meaning given that term in section 1072 of title 10, United States Code.

SEC. 729. IMPROVEMENT OF HEALTH OUTCOMES AND CONTROL OF COSTS OF HEALTH CARE UNDER TRICARE PROGRAM THROUGH PROGRAMS TO INVOLVE COVERED BENEFICIARIES.

(a) MEDICAL INTERVENTION INCENTIVE PROGRAM.—

(1) IN GENERAL.—The Secretary of Defense shall establish a program to incentivize covered

beneficiaries to participate in medical intervention programs established by the Secretary, such as comprehensive disease management programs, that may include lowering fees for enrollment in the TRICARE program by a certain percentage or lowering copayment and cost-share amounts for health care services during a particular year for covered beneficiaries with chronic diseases or conditions described in paragraph (2) who met participation milestones, as determined by the Secretary, in the previous year in such medical intervention programs.

(2) CHRONIC DISEASES OR CONDITIONS DESCRIBED.—Chronic diseases or conditions described in this paragraph may include diabetes, chronic obstructive pulmonary disease, asthma, congestive heart failure, hypertension, history of stroke, coronary artery disease, mood disorders, obesity, and such other diseases or conditions as the Secretary determines appropriate.

(b) LIFESTYLE INTERVENTION INCENTIVE PROGRAM.—The Secretary shall establish a program to incentivize lifestyle interventions for covered beneficiaries, such as smoking cessation and weight reduction, that may include lowering fees for enrollment in the TRICARE program by a certain percentage or lowering copayment and cost share amounts for health care services during a particular year for covered beneficiaries who met participation milestones, as determined by the Secretary, in the previous year with respect to such lifestyle interventions, such as quitting smoking or achieving a lower body mass index by a certain percentage.

(c) HEALTHY LIFESTYLE MAINTENANCE INCENTIVE PROGRAM.—The Secretary shall establish a program to incentivize the maintenance of a healthy lifestyle among covered beneficiaries, such as exercise and weight maintenance, that may include lowering fees for enrollment in the TRICARE program by a certain percentage or lowering copayment and cost-share amounts for health care services during a particular year for covered beneficiaries who met participation milestones, as determined by the Secretary, in the previous year with respect to the maintenance of a healthy lifestyle, such as maintaining smoking cessation or maintaining a normal body mass index.

(d) REPORT.—

(1) IN GENERAL.—Not later than January 1, 2020, the Secretary shall submit to the Committees on Armed Services of the Senate and the House of Representatives a report on the implementation of the programs established under subsections (a), (b), and (c).

(2) ELEMENTS.—The report required by paragraph (1) shall include the following:

(A) A detailed description of the programs implemented under subsections (a), (b), and (c).

(B) An assessment of the impact of such programs on—

(i) improving health outcomes for covered beneficiaries; and

(ii) lowering per capita health care costs for the Department of Defense.

(e) REGULATIONS.—Not later than January 1, 2018, the Secretary shall prescribe an interim final rule to carry out this section.

(f) DEFINITIONS.—In this section, the terms "covered beneficiary" and "TRICARE program" have the meaning given those terms in section 1072 of title 10, United States Code.

SEC. 730. ACCOUNTABILITY FOR THE PERFORMANCE OF THE MILITARY HEALTH SYSTEM OF CERTAIN LEADERS WITHIN THE SYSTEM.

(a) IN GENERAL.—Commencing not later than 180 days after the date of the enactment of this Act, the Secretary of Defense, in consultation with the Secretaries of the military departments, shall incorporate into the annual performance review of each military and civilian leader in the military health system, as determined by the Secretary of Defense, measures of accountability

for the performance of the military health system described in subsection (b).

(b) MEASURES OF ACCOUNTABILITY FOR PERFORMANCE.—The measures of accountability for the performance of the military health system incorporated into the annual performance review of an individual pursuant to this section shall include measures to assess performance and assure accountability for the following:

(1) Quality of care.

(2) Access of beneficiaries to care.

(3) Improvement in health outcomes for beneficiaries.

(4) Patient safety.

(5) Such other matters as the Secretary of Defense, in consultation with the Secretaries of the military departments, considers appropriate.

(c) REPORT ON IMPLEMENTATION.—

(1) IN GENERAL.—Not later than 180 days after the date of the enactment of this Act, the Secretary of Defense shall submit to the Committees on Armed Services of the Senate and the House of Representatives a report on the incorporation of measures of accountability for the performance of the military health system into the annual performance reviews of individuals as required by this section.

(2) ELEMENTS.—The report required by paragraph (1) shall include the following:

(A) A comprehensive plan for the use of measures of accountability for performance in annual performance reviews pursuant to this section as a means of assessing and assuring accountability for the performance of the military health system.

(B) The identification of each leadership position in the military health system determined under subsection (a) and a description of the specific measures of accountability for performance to be incorporated into the annual performance reviews of each such position pursuant to this section.

SEC. 731. ESTABLISHMENT OF ADVISORY COMMITTEES FOR MILITARY TREATMENT FACILITIES.

(a) IN GENERAL.—The Secretary of Defense shall establish, under such regulations as the Secretary may prescribe, an advisory committee for each military treatment facility.

(b) STATUS OF CERTAIN MEMBERS OF ADVISORY COMMITTEES.—A member of an advisory committee established under subsection (a) who is not a member of the Armed Forces on active duty or an employee of the Federal Government shall, with the approval of the commanding officer or director of the military treatment facility concerned, be treated as a volunteer under section 1588 of title 10, United States Code, in carrying out the duties of the member under this section.

(c) DUTIES.—Each advisory committee established under subsection (a) for a military treatment facility shall provide to the commanding officer or director of such facility advice on the administration and activities of such facility as it relates to the experience of care for beneficiaries at such facility.

Subtitle D—Reports and Other Matters

SEC. 741. EXTENSION OF AUTHORITY FOR JOINT DEPARTMENT OF DEFENSE-DEPARTMENT OF VETERANS AFFAIRS MEDICAL FACILITY DEMONSTRATION FUND AND REPORT ON IMPLEMENTATION OF INFORMATION TECHNOLOGY CAPABILITIES.

(a) IN GENERAL.—Section 1704(e) of the National Defense Authorization Act for Fiscal Year 2010 (Public Law 111–84; 123 Stat. 2573), as amended by section 722 of the Carl Levin and Howard P. "Buck" McKeon National Defense Authorization Act for Fiscal Year 2015 (Public Law 113–291) and section 723 of the National Defense Authorization Act for Fiscal Year 2016 (Public Law 114–92), is further amended by striking "September 30, 2017" and inserting "September 30, 2018".

(b) REPORT ON IMPLEMENTATION OF INFORMATION TECHNOLOGY CAPABILITIES.—Not later than March 30, 2017, the Secretary of Defense shall submit to the Committees on Armed Services of the Senate and the House of Representatives a report on plans to implement all information technology capabilities required by the executive agreement entered into under section 1701(a) of the National Defense Authorization Act for Fiscal Year 2010 (Public Law 111–84; 123 Stat. 2567) that remain unimplemented as of the date of the report.

SEC. 742. PILOT PROGRAM ON EXPANSION OF USE OF PHYSICIAN ASSISTANTS TO PROVIDE MENTAL HEALTH CARE TO MEMBERS OF THE ARMED FORCES.

(a) IN GENERAL.—The Secretary of Defense may conduct a pilot program to assess the feasibility and advisability of expanding the use by the Department of Defense of physician assistants specializing in psychiatric medicine at medical facilities of the Department of Defense in order to meet the increasing demand for mental health care providers at such facilities through the use of a psychiatry fellowship program for physician assistants.

(b) REPORT ON PILOT PROGRAM.—

(1) IN GENERAL.—If the Secretary conducts the pilot program under this section, not later than 90 days after the date on which the Secretary completes the conduct of the pilot program, the Secretary shall submit to the Committees on Armed Services of the Senate and the House of Representatives a report on the pilot program.

(2) ELEMENTS.—The report submitted under paragraph (1) shall include the following:

(A) A description of the implementation of the pilot program, including a detailed description of the education and training provided under the pilot program.

(B) An assessment of potential cost savings, if any, to the Department of Defense resulting from the pilot program.

(C) A description of improvements, if any, to the access of members of the Armed Forces to mental health care resulting from the pilot program.

(D) A recommendation as to the feasibility and advisability of extending or expanding the pilot program.

SEC. 743. PILOT PROGRAM FOR PRESCRIPTION DRUG ACQUISITION COST PARITY IN THE TRICARE PHARMACY BENEFITS PROGRAM.

(a) AUTHORITY TO ESTABLISH PILOT PROGRAM.—The Secretary of Defense may conduct a pilot program to evaluate whether, in carrying out the TRICARE pharmacy benefits program under section 1074g of title 10, United States Code, extending additional discounts for prescription drugs filled at retail pharmacies will maintain or reduce prescription drug costs for the Department of Defense.

(b) ELEMENTS OF PILOT PROGRAM.—In carrying out the pilot program under subsection (a), the Secretary shall require that for prescription medications, including non-generic maintenance medications, that are dispensed to TRICARE beneficiaries that are not Medicare eligible, through any TRICARE participating retail pharmacy, including small business pharmacies, manufacturers shall pay rebates such that those medications are available to the Department at the lowest rate available. In addition to utilizing the authority under section 1074g(f) of title 10, United States Code, the Secretary shall have the authority to enter into a blanket purchase agreement with prescription drug manufacturers for supplemental discounts for prescription drugs dispensed in the pilot to be paid in the form of manufacturer's rebates.

(c) CONSULTATION.—The Secretary shall develop the pilot program in consultation with—

(1) the Secretaries of the military departments;

(2) the Chief of the Pharmacy Operations Division of the Defense Health Agency; and

(3) *stakeholders, including TRICARE beneficiaries and retail pharmacies.*

(d) DURATION OF PILOT PROGRAM.—*If the Secretary carries out the pilot program under subsection (a), the Secretary shall commence such pilot program no later than October 1, 2017, and shall terminate such program no later than September 30, 2018.*

(e) REPORTS.—*If the Secretary carries out the pilot program under subsection (a), the Secretary of Defense shall submit to the Committees on Armed Services of the Senate and the House of Representatives reports on the pilot program as follows:*

(1) *Not later than 90 days after the date of the enactment of this Act, a report containing an implementation plan for the pilot program.*

(2) *Not later than 180 days after the date on which the pilot program commences, an interim report on the pilot program.*

(3) *Not later than 90 days after the date on which the pilot program terminates, a final report describing the results of the pilot program, including—*

(A) *any recommendations of the Secretary to expand such program;*

(B) *an analysis of the changes in prescription drug costs for the Department of Defense relating to the pilot program;*

(C) *an analysis of the impact on beneficiary access to prescription drugs;*

(D) *a survey of beneficiary satisfaction with the pilot program; and*

(E) *a summary of any fraud and abuse activities related to the pilot and actions taken in response by the Department.*

SEC. 744. PILOT PROGRAM ON DISPLAY OF WAIT TIMES AT URGENT CARE CLINICS AND PHARMACIES OF MILITARY MEDICAL TREATMENT FACILITIES.

(a) PILOT PROGRAM AUTHORIZED.—*Beginning not later than one year after the date of the enactment of this Act, the Secretary of Defense shall carry out a pilot program for the display of wait times in urgent care clinics and pharmacies of military medical treatment facilities selected under subsection (b).*

(b) SELECTION OF FACILITIES.—

(1) CATEGORIES.—*The Secretary shall select not fewer than four military medical treatment facilities from each of the following categories to participate in the pilot program:*

(A) *Medical centers.*

(B) *Hospitals.*

(C) *Ambulatory care centers.*

(2) OCONUS LOCATIONS.—*Of the military medical treatment facilities selected under each category described in subparagraphs (A) through (C) of paragraph (1), not fewer than one shall be located outside of the continental United States.*

(3) CONTRACTOR-OPERATED FACILITIES.—*The Secretary may select Government-owned, contractor-operated facilities among those military medical treatment facilities selected under paragraph (1).*

(c) URGENT CARE CLINICS.—

(1) PLACEMENT.—*With respect to each military medical treatment facility participating in the pilot program with an urgent care clinic, the Secretary shall place in a conspicuous location at the urgent care clinic an electronic sign that displays the current average wait time determined under paragraph (2) for a patient to be seen by a qualified medical professional.*

(2) DETERMINATION.—*In carrying out paragraph (1), every 30 minutes, the Secretary shall determine the average wait time to display under such paragraph by calculating, for the four-hour period preceding the calculation, the average length of time beginning at the time of the arrival of a patient at the urgent care clinic and ending at the time at which the patient is first seen by a qualified medical professional.*

(d) PHARMACIES.—

(1) PLACEMENT.—*With respect to each military medical treatment facility participating in the pilot program with a pharmacy, the Secretary shall place in a conspicuous location at the pharmacy an electronic sign that displays the current average wait time to receive a filled prescription for a pharmaceutical agent.*

(2) DETERMINATION.—*In carrying out paragraph (1), every 30 minutes, the Secretary shall determine the average wait time to display under such paragraph by calculating, for the four-hour period preceding the calculation, the average length of time beginning at the time of submission by a patient of a prescription for a pharmaceutical agent and ending at the time at which the pharmacy dispenses the pharmaceutical agent to the patient.*

(e) DURATION.—*The Secretary shall carry out the pilot program for a period that is not more than two years.*

(f) REPORT.—

(1) SUBMISSION.—*Not later than 90 days after the completion of the pilot program, the Secretary shall submit to the Committees on Armed Services of the House of Representatives and the Senate a report on the pilot program.*

(2) ELEMENTS.—*The report under paragraph (1) shall include—*

(A) *the costs for displaying the wait times under subsections (c) and (d);*

(B) *any changes in patient satisfaction;*

(C) *any changes in patient behavior with respect to using urgent care and pharmacy services;*

(D) *any changes in pharmacy operations and productivity;*

(E) *a cost-benefit analysis of posting such wait times; and*

(F) *the feasibility of expanding the posting of wait times in emergency departments in military medical treatment facilities.*

(g) QUALIFIED MEDICAL PROFESSIONAL DEFINED.—*In this section, the term "qualified medical professional" means a doctor of medicine, a doctor of osteopathy, a physician assistant, or an advanced registered nurse practitioner.*

SEC. 745. REQUIREMENT TO REVIEW AND MONITOR PRESCRIBING PRACTICES AT MILITARY TREATMENT FACILITIES OF PHARMACEUTICAL AGENTS FOR TREATMENT OF POST-TRAUMATIC STRESS.

(a) IN GENERAL.—*Not later than 180 days after the date of the enactment of this Act, the Secretary of Defense shall—*

(1) *conduct a comprehensive review of the prescribing practices at military treatment facilities of pharmaceutical agents for the treatment of post-traumatic stress;*

(2) *implement a process or processes to monitor the prescribing practices at military treatment facilities of pharmaceutical agents that are discouraged from use under the VA/DOD Clinical Practice Guideline for Management of Post-Traumatic Stress; and*

(3) *implement a plan to address any deviations from such guideline in prescribing practices of pharmaceutical agents for management of post-traumatic stress at such facilities.*

(b) PHARMACEUTICAL AGENT DEFINED.—*In this section, the term "pharmaceutical agent" has the meaning given that term in section 1074g(g) of title 10, United States Code.*

SEC. 746. DEPARTMENT OF DEFENSE STUDY ON PREVENTING THE DIVERSION OF OPIOID MEDICATIONS.

(a) STUDY.—*The Secretary of Defense shall conduct a study on the feasibility and effectiveness in preventing the diversion of opioid medications of the following measures:*

(1) *Requiring that, in appropriate cases, opioid medications be dispensed in vials using affordable technologies designed to prevent access to the medications by anyone other than the intended patient, such as a vial with a locking-cap closure mechanism.*

(2) *Providing education on the risks of opioid medications to individuals for whom such medications are prescribed, and to their families, with special consideration given to raising awareness among adolescents on such risks.*

(b) BRIEFING.—

(1) IN GENERAL.—*Not later than one year after the date of the enactment of this Act, the Secretary shall provide to the Committees on Armed Services of the Senate and the House of Representatives a briefing on the results of the study conducted under subsection (a).*

(2) ELEMENTS.—*The briefing under paragraph (1) shall include an assessment of the cost effectiveness of the measures studied under subsection (a).*

SEC. 747. INCORPORATION INTO SURVEY BY DEPARTMENT OF DEFENSE OF QUESTIONS ON EXPERIENCES OF MEMBERS OF THE ARMED FORCES WITH FAMILY PLANNING SERVICES AND COUNSELING.

Not later than 90 days after the date of the enactment of this Act, the Secretary of Defense shall initiate action to integrate into the Health Related Behavior Survey of Active Duty Military Personnel questions designed to obtain information on the experiences of members of the Armed Forces—

(1) *in accessing family planning services and counseling; and*

(2) *in using family planning methods, including information on which method was preferred and whether deployment conditions affected the decision on which family planning method or methods to be used.*

SEC. 748. ASSESSMENT OF TRANSITION TO TRICARE PROGRAM BY FAMILIES OF MEMBERS OF RESERVE COMPONENTS CALLED TO ACTIVE DUTY AND ELIMINATION OF CERTAIN CHARGES FOR SUCH FAMILIES.

(a) ASSESSMENT OF TRANSITION TO TRICARE PROGRAM.—

(1) IN GENERAL.—*Not later than 180 days after the date of the enactment of this Act, the Secretary of Defense shall complete an assessment of the extent to which families of members of the reserve components of the Armed Forces serving on active duty pursuant to a call or order to active duty for a period of more than 30 days experience difficulties in transitioning from health care arrangements relied upon when the member is not in such an active duty status to health care benefits under the TRICARE program.*

(2) ELEMENTS.—*The assessment under paragraph (1) shall address the following:*

(A) *The extent to which family members of members of the reserve components of the Armed Forces are required to change health care providers when they become eligible for health care benefits under the TRICARE program.*

(B) *The extent to which health care providers in the private sector with whom such family members have established relationships when not covered under the TRICARE program are providers who—*

(i) *are in a preferred provider network under the TRICARE program;*

(ii) *are participating providers under the TRICARE program; or*

(iii) *will agree to treat covered beneficiaries at a rate not to exceed 115 percent of the maximum allowable charge under the TRICARE program.*

(C) *The extent to which such family members encounter difficulties associated with a change in health care claims administration, health care authorizations, or other administrative matters when transitioning to health care benefits under the TRICARE program.*

(D) *Any particular reasons for, or circumstances that explain, the conditions described in subparagraphs (A), (B), and (C).*

(E) *The effects of the conditions described in subparagraphs (A), (B), and (C) on the health care experience of such family members.*

(F) Recommendations for changes in policies and procedures under the TRICARE program, or other administrative action by the Secretary, to remedy or mitigate difficulties faced by such family members in transitioning to health care benefits under the TRICARE program.

(G) Recommendations for legislative action to remedy or mitigate such difficulties.

(H) Such other matters as the Secretary determines relevant to the assessment.

(3) REPORT.—

(A) IN GENERAL.—Not later than 180 days after completing the assessment under paragraph (1), the Secretary shall submit to the Committees on Armed Services of the Senate and the House of Representatives a report detailing the results of the assessment.

(B) ANALYSIS OF RECOMMENDATIONS.—The report required by subparagraph (A) shall include an analysis of each recommendation for legislative action addressed under paragraph (2)(G), together with a cost estimate for implementing each such action.

(b) EXPANSION OF AUTHORITY TO ELIMINATE BALANCE BILLING.—Section 1079(h)(4)(C)(ii) of title 10, United States Code, is amended by striking "in support of a contingency operation under a provision of law referred to in section 101(a)(13)(B) of this title".

(c) DEFINITIONS.—In this section, the terms "covered beneficiary" and "TRICARE program" have the meanings given those terms in section 1072 of title 10, United States Code.

SEC. 749. OVERSIGHT OF GRADUATE MEDICAL EDUCATION PROGRAMS OF MILITARY DEPARTMENTS.

(a) PROCESS.—Not later than one year after the date of the enactment of this Act, the Secretary of Defense shall establish and implement a process to provide oversight of the graduate medical education programs of the military departments to ensure that such programs fully support the operational medical force readiness requirements for health care providers of the Armed Forces and the medical readiness of the Armed Forces. The process shall include the following:

(1) A process to review such programs to ensure, to the extent practicable, that such programs are—

(A) conducted jointly among the military departments; and

(B) focused on, and related to, operational medical force readiness requirements.

(2) A process to minimize duplicative programs relating to such programs among the military departments.

(3) A process to ensure that—

(A) assignments of faculty, support staff, and students within such programs are coordinated among the military departments; and

(B) the Secretary optimizes resources by using military medical treatment facilities as training platforms when and where most appropriate.

(4) A process to review and, if necessary, restructure or realign, such programs to sustain and improve operational medical force readiness.

(b) REPORT.—Not later than 30 days after the date on which the Secretary establishes the process under subsection (a), the Secretary shall submit to the Committees on Armed Services of the Senate and the House of Representatives a report that describes such process. The report shall include a description of each graduate medical education program of the military departments, categorized by the following:

(1) Programs that provide direct support to operational medical force readiness.

(2) Programs that provide indirect support to operational medical force readiness.

(3) Academic programs that provide other medical support.

(c) COMPTROLLER GENERAL REVIEW AND REPORT.—

(1) REVIEW.—The Comptroller General of the United States shall conduct a review of the process established under subsection (a), including with respect to each process described in paragraphs (1) through (4) of such subsection.

(2) REPORT.—Not later than 180 days after the date on which the Secretary submits the report under subsection (b), the Comptroller General shall submit to the Committees on Armed Services of the Senate and the House of Representatives the review conducted under paragraph (1), including an assessment of the elements of the process established under subsection (a).

SEC. 750. STUDY ON HEALTH OF HELICOPTER AND TILTROTOR PILOTS.

(a) STUDY REQUIRED.—The Secretary of Defense shall carry out a study of career helicopter and tiltrotor pilots to assess potential links between the operation of helicopter and tiltrotor aircraft and acute and chronic medical conditions experienced by such pilots.

(b) ELEMENTS.—The study under subsection (a) shall include the following:

(1) A study of career helicopter and tiltrotor pilots compared to a control population that—

(A) takes into account the amount of time such pilots operated aircraft;

(B) examines the severity and rates of acute and chronic injuries experienced by such pilots; and

(C) determines whether such pilots experience a higher degree of acute and chronic medical conditions than the control population.

(2) If a higher degree of acute and chronic medical conditions is observed among such pilots, an explanation of—

(A) the specific causes of the conditions (such as whole body vibration, seat and cockpit ergonomics, landing loads, hard impacts, and pilot-worn gear); and

(B) any costs associated with treating the conditions if the causes are not mitigated.

(3) A review of relevant scientific literature and prior research.

(4) Such other information as the Secretary determines to be appropriate.

(c) DURATION.—The duration of the study under subsection (a) shall be not more than two years.

(d) REPORT.—Not later than 30 days after the completion of the study under subsection (a), the Secretary shall submit to the Committees on Armed Services of the Senate and the House of Representatives a report on the study.

SEC. 751. COMPTROLLER GENERAL REPORTS ON HEALTH CARE DELIVERY AND WASTE IN MILITARY HEALTH SYSTEM.

(a) IN GENERAL.—Not later than one year after the date of the enactment of this Act, and not less frequently than once each year thereafter for four years, the Comptroller General of the United States shall submit to the Committees on Armed Services of the Senate and the House of Representatives a report assessing the delivery of health care in the military health system, with an emphasis on identifying potential waste and inefficiency.

(b) ELEMENTS.—

(1) IN GENERAL.—The reports submitted under subsection (a) shall, within the direct and purchased care components of the military health system, evaluate the following:

(A) Processes for ensuring that health care providers adhere to clinical practice guidelines.

(B) Processes for reporting and resolving adverse medical events.

(C) Processes for ensuring program integrity by identifying and resolving medical fraud and waste.

(D) Processes for coordinating care within and between the direct and purchased care components of the military health system.

(E) Procedures for administering the TRICARE program.

(F) Processes for assessing and overseeing the efficiency of clinical operations of military hospitals and clinics, including access to care for covered beneficiaries at such facilities.

(2) ADDITIONAL INFORMATION.—The reports submitted under subsection (a) may include, if the Comptroller General considers feasible—

(A) an estimate of the costs to the Department of Defense relating to any waste or inefficiency identified in the report; and

(B) such recommendations for action by the Secretary of Defense as the Comptroller General considers appropriate, including eliminating waste and inefficiency in the direct and purchased care components of the military health system.

(c) DEFINITIONS.—In this section, the terms "covered beneficiary" and "TRICARE program" have the meaning given those terms in section 1072 of title 10, United States Code.

TITLE VIII—ACQUISITION POLICY, ACQUISITION MANAGEMENT, AND RELATED MATTERS

Subtitle A—Acquisition Policy and Management

Sec. 801. *Rapid acquisition authority amendments.*

Sec. 802. *Authority for temporary service of Principal Military Deputies to the Assistant Secretaries of the military departments for acquisition as Acting Assistant Secretaries.*

Sec. 803. *Modernization of services acquisition.*

Sec. 804. *Defense Modernization Account amendments.*

Subtitle B—Department of Defense Acquisition Agility

Sec. 805. *Modular open system approach in development of major weapon systems.*

Sec. 806. *Development, prototyping, and deployment of weapon system components or technology.*

Sec. 807. *Cost, schedule, and performance of major defense acquisition programs.*

Sec. 808. *Transparency in major defense acquisition programs.*

Sec. 809. *Amendments relating to technical data rights.*

Subtitle C—Amendments to General Contracting Authorities, Procedures, and Limitations

Sec. 811. *Modified restrictions on undefinitized contractual actions.*

Sec. 812. *Amendments relating to inventory and tracking of purchases of services.*

Sec. 813. *Use of lowest price technically acceptable source selection process.*

Sec. 814. *Procurement of personal protective equipment.*

Sec. 815. *Amendments related to detection and avoidance of counterfeit electronic parts.*

Sec. 816. *Amendments to special emergency procurement authority.*

Sec. 817. *Compliance with domestic source requirements for footwear furnished to enlisted members of the Armed Forces upon their initial entry into the Armed Forces.*

Sec. 818. *Extension of authority for enhanced transfer of technology developed at Department of Defense laboratories.*

Sec. 819. *Modified notification requirement for exercise of waiver authority to acquire vital national security capabilities.*

Sec. 820. *Defense cost accounting standards.*

Sec. 821. *Increased micro-purchase threshold applicable to Department of Defense procurements.*

Sec. 822. *Enhanced competition requirements.*

Sec. 823. *Revision to effective date of senior executive benchmark compensation for allowable cost limitations.*

Sec. 824. Treatment of independent research and development costs on certain contracts.
Sec. 825. Exception to requirement to include cost or price to the Government as a factor in the evaluation of proposals for certain multiple-award task or delivery order contracts.
Sec. 826. Extension of program for comprehensive small business contracting plans.
Sec. 827. Treatment of side-by-side testing of certain equipment, munitions, and technologies manufactured and developed under cooperative research and development agreements as use of competitive procedures.
Sec. 828. Defense Acquisition Challenge Program amendments.
Sec. 829. Preference for fixed-price contracts.
Sec. 830. Requirement to use firm fixed-price contracts for foreign military sales.
Sec. 831. Preference for performance-based contract payments.
Sec. 832. Contractor incentives to achieve savings and improve mission performance.
Sec. 833. Sunset and repeal of certain contracting provisions.
Sec. 834. Flexibility in contracting award program.
Sec. 835. Protection of task order competition.
Sec. 836. Contract closeout authority.
Sec. 837. Closeout of old Department of the Navy contracts.

Subtitle D—Provisions Relating to Major Defense Acquisition Programs

Sec. 841. Change in date of submission to Congress of Selected Acquisition Reports.
Sec. 842. Amendments relating to independent cost estimation and cost analysis.
Sec. 843. Revisions to Milestone B determinations.
Sec. 844. Review and report on sustainment planning in the acquisition process.
Sec. 845. Revision to distribution of annual report on operational test and evaluation.
Sec. 846. Repeal of major automated information systems provisions.
Sec. 847. Revisions to definition of major defense acquisition program.
Sec. 848. Acquisition strategy.
Sec. 849. Improved life-cycle cost control.
Sec. 850. Authority to designate increments or blocks of items delivered under major defense acquisition programs as major subprograms for purposes of acquisition reporting.
Sec. 851. Reporting of small business participation on Department of Defense programs.
Sec. 852. Waiver of congressional notification for acquisition of tactical missiles and munitions greater than quantity specified in law.
Sec. 853. Multiple program multiyear contract pilot demonstration program.
Sec. 854. Key performance parameter reduction pilot program.
Sec. 855. Mission integration management.

Subtitle E—Provisions Relating to Acquisition Workforce

Sec. 861. Project management.
Sec. 862. Authority to waive tenure requirement for program managers for program definition and program execution periods.
Sec. 863. Purposes for which the Department of Defense Acquisition Workforce Development Fund may be used; advisory panel amendments.

Sec. 864. Department of Defense Acquisition Workforce Development Fund determination adjustment.
Sec. 865. Limitations on funds used for staff augmentation contracts at management headquarters of the Department of Defense and the military departments.
Sec. 866. Senior Military Acquisition Advisors in the Defense Acquisition Corps.
Sec. 867. Authority of the Secretary of Defense under the acquisition demonstration project.

Subtitle F—Provisions Relating to Commercial Items

Sec. 871. Market research for determination of price reasonableness in acquisition of commercial items.
Sec. 872. Value analysis for the determination of price reasonableness.
Sec. 873. Clarification of requirements relating to commercial item determinations.
Sec. 874. Inapplicability of certain laws and regulations to the acquisition of commercial items and commercially available off-the-shelf items.
Sec. 875. Use of commercial or non-Government standards in lieu of military specifications and standards.
Sec. 876. Preference for commercial services.
Sec. 877. Treatment of commingled items purchased by contractors as commercial items.
Sec. 878. Treatment of services provided by nontraditional contractors as commercial items.
Sec. 879. Defense pilot program for authority to acquire innovative commercial items, technologies, and services using general solicitation competitive procedures.
Sec. 880. Pilot programs for authority to acquire innovative commercial items using general solicitation competitive procedures.

Subtitle G—Industrial Base Matters

Sec. 881. Greater integration of the national technology and industrial base.
Sec. 882. Integration of civil and military roles in attaining national technology and industrial base objectives.
Sec. 883. Pilot program for distribution support and services for weapon systems contractors.
Sec. 884. Nontraditional and small contractor innovation prototyping program.

Subtitle H—Other Matters

Sec. 885. Report on bid protests.
Sec. 886. Review and report on indefinite delivery contracts.
Sec. 887. Review and report on contractual flow-down provisions.
Sec. 888. Requirement and review relating to use of brand names or brand-name or equivalent descriptions in solicitations.
Sec. 889. Inclusion of information on common grounds for sustaining bid protests in annual Government Accountability Office reports to Congress.
Sec. 890. Study and report on contracts awarded to minority-owned and women-owned businesses.
Sec. 891. Authority to provide reimbursable auditing services to certain non-Defense Agencies.
Sec. 892. Selection of service providers for auditing services and audit readiness services.
Sec. 893. Amendments to contractor business system requirements.

Sec. 894. Improved management practices to reduce cost and improve performance of certain Department of Defense organizations.
Sec. 895. Exemption from requirement for capital planning and investment control for information technology equipment included as integral part of a weapon or weapon system.
Sec. 896. Modifications to pilot program for streamlining awards for innovative technology projects.
Sec. 897. Rapid prototyping funds for the military departments.
Sec. 898. Establishment of Panel on Department of Defense and AbilityOne Contracting Oversight, Accountability, and Integrity; Defense Acquisition University training.
Sec. 899. Coast Guard major acquisition programs.
Sec. 899A. Enhanced authority to acquire products and services produced in Africa in support of certain activities.

Subtitle A—Acquisition Policy and Management

SEC. 801. RAPID ACQUISITION AUTHORITY AMENDMENTS.

Section 806 of the Bob Stump National Defense Authorization Act for Fiscal Year 2003 (Public Law 107–314; 10 U.S.C. 2302 note) is amended—

(1) in subsection (a)(1)—

(A) in subparagraph (A), by striking "; or" and inserting a semicolon;

(B) in subparagraph (B), by striking "; and" and inserting "; or"; and

(C) by adding at the end the following new subparagraph:

"(C) developed or procured under the rapid fielding or rapid prototyping acquisition pathways under section 804 of the National Defense Authorization Act for Fiscal Year 2016 (Public Law 114–92; 10 U.S.C. 2302 note); and";

(2) in subsection (b), by adding at the end the following new paragraph:

"(3) Specific procedures in accordance with the guidance developed under section 804(a) of the National Defense Authorization Act for Fiscal Year 2016 (Public Law 114–92; 10 U.S.C. 2302 note).''; and

(3) in subsection (c)—

(A) in paragraph (2)(A)—

(i) by striking "Whenever the Secretary" and inserting "(i) Except as provided under clause (ii), whenever the Secretary"; and

(ii) by adding at the end the following new clause:

"(ii) Clause (i) does not apply to acquisitions initiated in the case of a determination by the Secretary that funds are necessary to immediately initiate a project under the rapid fielding or rapid prototyping acquisition pathways under section 804 of the National Defense Authorization Act for Fiscal Year 2016 (Public Law 114–92; 10 U.S.C. 2302 note) if the designated official for acquisitions using such pathways is the service acquisition executive.";

(B) in paragraph (3)—

(i) in subparagraph (A), by inserting "or upon the Secretary making a determination that funds are necessary to immediately initiate a project under the rapid fielding or rapid prototyping acquisition pathways under section 804 of the National Defense Authorization Act for Fiscal Year 2016 (Public Law 114–92; 10 U.S.C. 2302 note) based on a compelling national security need," after "of paragraph (1),";

(ii) in subparagraph (B)—

(I) by striking "The authority" and inserting "Except as provided under subparagraph (C), the authority";

(II) in clause (ii), by striking "; and" and inserting a semicolon;

(III) in clause (iii), by striking the period at the end and inserting "; and"; and

(IV) by adding at the end the following new clause:

"(iv) in the case of a determination by the Secretary that funds are necessary to immediately initiate a project under the rapid fielding or rapid prototyping acquisition pathways under section 804 of the National Defense Authorization Act for Fiscal Year 2016 (Public Law 114–92; 10 U.S.C. 2302 note), in an amount not more than $200,000,000 during any fiscal year."; and

(iii) by adding at the end the following new subparagraph:

"(C) For each of fiscal years 2017 and 2018, the limits set forth in clauses (i) and (ii) of subparagraph (B) do not apply to the exercise of authority under such clauses provided that the total amount of supplies and associated support services acquired as provided under such subparagraph does not exceed $800,000,000 during such fiscal year.";

(C) in paragraph (4)—

(i) by redesignating subparagraphs (C), (D), and (E) as subparagraphs (D), (E), and (F), respectively; and

(ii) by inserting after subparagraph (B) the following new subparagraph:

"(C) In the case of a determination by the Secretary under paragraph (3)(A) that funds are necessary to immediately initiate a project under the rapid fielding or rapid prototyping acquisition pathways under section 804 of the National Defense Authorization Act for Fiscal Year 2016 (Public Law 114–92; 10 U.S.C. 2302 note), the Secretary shall notify the congressional defense committees of the determination within 10 days after the date of the use of such funds."; and

(D) in paragraph (5)—

(i) by striking "Any acquisition" and inserting "(A) Any acquisition"; and

(ii) by adding at the end the following new subparagraph:

"(B) Subparagraph (A) does not apply to acquisitions initiated in the case of a determination by the Secretary that funds are necessary to immediately initiate a project under the rapid fielding or rapid prototyping acquisition pathways under section 804 of the National Defense Authorization Act for Fiscal Year 2016 (Public Law 114–92; 10 U.S.C. 2302 note).".

SEC. 802. AUTHORITY FOR TEMPORARY SERVICE OF PRINCIPAL MILITARY DEPUTIES TO THE ASSISTANT SECRETARIES OF THE MILITARY DEPARTMENTS FOR ACQUISITION AS ACTING ASSISTANT SECRETARIES.

(a) ASSISTANT SECRETARY OF THE ARMY FOR ACQUISITION, LOGISTICS, AND TECHNOLOGY.—Section 3016(b)(5)(B) of title 10, United States Code, is amended by adding at the end the following new sentence: "In the event of a vacancy in the position of Assistant Secretary of the Army for Acquisition, Logistics, and Technology, the Principal Military Deputy may serve as Acting Assistant Secretary for a period of not more than one year.".

(b) ASSISTANT SECRETARY OF THE NAVY FOR RESEARCH, DEVELOPMENT, AND ACQUISITION.—Section 5016(b)(4)(B) of such title is amended by adding at the end the following new sentence: "In the event of a vacancy in the position of Assistant Secretary of the Navy for Research, Development, and Acquisition, the Principal Military Deputy may serve as Acting Assistant Secretary for a period of not more than one year.".

(c) ASSISTANT SECRETARY OF THE AIR FORCE FOR ACQUISITION.—Section 8016(b)(4)(B) of such title is amended by adding at the end the following new sentence: "In the event of a vacancy in the position of Assistant Secretary of

the Air Force for Acquisition, the Principal Military Deputy may serve as Acting Assistant Secretary for a period of not more than one year.".

SEC. 803. MODERNIZATION OF SERVICES ACQUISITION.

(a) REVIEW OF SERVICES ACQUISITION CATEGORIES.—Not later than 180 days after the date of the enactment of this Act, the Secretary of Defense shall review and, if necessary, revise Department of Defense Instruction 5000.74, dated January 5, 2016 (in this section referred to as the "Acquisition of Services Instruction"), and other guidance pertaining to the acquisition of services. In conducting the review, the Secretary shall examine—

(1) how the acquisition community should consider the changing nature of the technology and professional services markets, particularly the convergence of hardware and services; and

(2) the services acquisition portfolio groups referenced in the Acquisition of Services Instruction and other guidance in order to ensure the portfolio groups are fully reflective of changes to the technology and professional services market.

(b) GUIDANCE REGARDING TRAINING AND DEVELOPMENT OF THE ACQUISITION WORKFORCE.—

(1) IN GENERAL.—Not later than 180 days after the date of the enactment of this Act, the Secretary of Defense shall issue guidance addressing the training and development of the Department of Defense workforce engaged in the procurement of services, including those personnel not designated as members of the acquisition workforce.

(2) IDENTIFICATION OF TRAINING AND PROFESSIONAL DEVELOPMENT OPPORTUNITIES AND ALTERNATIVES.—The guidance required under paragraph (1) shall identify training and professional development opportunities and alternatives, not limited to existing Department of Defense institutions, that focus on and provide relevant training and professional development in commercial business models and contracting.

(3) TREATMENT OF TRAINING AND PROFESSIONAL DEVELOPMENT.—Any training and professional development provided pursuant to this subsection outside Department of Defense institutions shall be deemed to be equivalent to similar training certified or provided by the Defense Acquisition University.

SEC. 804. DEFENSE MODERNIZATION ACCOUNT AMENDMENTS.

(a) FUNDS AVAILABLE FOR ACCOUNT.—Section 2216(b)(1) of title 10, United States Code, is amended by striking "commencing".

(b) TRANSFERS TO ACCOUNT.—Section 2216(c) of such title is amended—

(1) in paragraph (1)(A)—

(A) by striking "or the Secretary of Defense with respect to Defense-wide appropriations accounts" and inserting ", or the Secretary of Defense with respect to Defense-wide appropriations accounts,"; and

(B) by striking "that Secretary" and inserting "the Secretary concerned";

(2) in paragraph (1)(B)—

(A) by inserting after "following funds" the following: "that have been appropriated for fiscal years after fiscal year 2016 and are";

(B) in clause (i)—

(i) by striking "for procurement" and inserting "for new obligations";

(ii) by striking "a particular procurement" and inserting "an acquisition program"; and

(iii) by striking "that procurement" and inserting "that program";

(C) by striking clause (ii); and

(D) by redesignating clause (iii) as clause (ii);

(3) in paragraph (2)—

(A) by striking ", other than funds referred to in subparagraph (B)(iii) of such paragraph,"; and

(B) by striking "if—" and all that follows through "(B) the balance of funds" and inserting "if the balance of funds";

(4) in paragraph (3)—

(A) by striking "credited to" both places it appears and inserting "deposited in"; and

(B) by inserting "and obligation" after "available for transfer"; and

(5) by striking paragraph (4).

(c) AUTHORIZED USE OF FUNDS.—Section 2216(d) of such title is amended—

(1) in paragraph (1)—

(A) by striking "commencing"; and

(B) by striking "Secretary of Defense" and inserting "Secretary concerned";

(2) in paragraph (2), by striking "a procurement program" and inserting "an acquisition program";

(3) by amending paragraph (3) to read as follows:

"(3) For research, development, test, and evaluation, for procurement, and for sustainment activities necessary for paying costs of unforeseen contingencies that are approved by the milestone decision authority concerned, that could prevent an ongoing acquisition program from meeting critical schedule or performance requirements."; and

(4) by inserting at the end the following new paragraph:

"(4) For paying costs of changes to program requirements or system configuration that are approved by the configuration steering board for a major defense acquisition program.".

(d) LIMITATIONS.—Section 2216(e) of such title is amended—

(1) in paragraph (1), by striking "procurement program" both places it appears and inserting "acquisition program"; and

(2) in paragraph (2), by striking "authorized appropriations" and inserting "authorized appropriations, unless the procedures for initiating a new start program are complied with".

(e) TRANSFER OF FUNDS.—Section 2216(f)(1) of such title is amended by striking "Secretary of Defense" and inserting "Secretary of a military department, or the Secretary of Defense with respect to Defense-wide appropriations accounts,".

(f) AVAILABILITY OF FUNDS BY APPROPRIATION.—Section 2216(g) of such title is amended—

(1) by striking "in accordance with the provisions of appropriations Acts"; and

(2) by adding at the end the following: "Funds deposited in the Defense Modernization Account shall remain available for obligation until the end of the third fiscal year that follows the fiscal year in which the amounts are deposited in the account.".

(g) SECRETARY TO ACT THROUGH COMPTROLLER.—Section 2216(h)(2) of such title is amended—

(1) by redesignating subparagraphs (A), (B), and (C) as subparagraphs (B), (C), and (D), respectively;

(2) by inserting before subparagraph (B), as so redesignated, the following new subparagraph (A):

"(A) the establishment and management of subaccounts for each of the military departments and Defense Agencies concerned for the use of funds in the Defense Modernization Account, consistent with each military department's or Defense Agency's deposits in the Account;";

(3) in subparagraph (C), as so redesignated, by inserting "and subaccounts" after "Account"; and

(4) in subparagraph (D), as so redesignated, by striking "subsection (c)(1)(B)(iii)" and inserting "subsection (c)(1)(B)(ii)".

(h) DEFINITIONS.—Paragraph (1) of section 2216(i) of such title is amended to read as follows:

"(1) The term 'major defense acquisition program' has the meaning given the term in section 2430(a) of this title.".

(j) EXPIRATION OF AUTHORITY.—Section 2216(j)(1) of such title is amended by striking "terminates at the close of September 30, 2006" and inserting "terminates at the close of September 30, 2022".

Subtitle B—Department of Defense Acquisition Agility

SEC. 805. MODULAR OPEN SYSTEM APPROACH IN DEVELOPMENT OF MAJOR WEAPON SYSTEMS.

(a) MODULAR OPEN SYSTEM APPROACH.—

(1) IN GENERAL.—Part IV of subtitle A of title 10, United States Code, is amended by inserting after chapter 144A the following new chapter:

"CHAPTER 144B—WEAPON SYSTEMS DEVELOPMENT AND RELATED MATTERS

"Subchapter   Sec.

"I. Modular Open System Approach in Development of Weapon Systems ... 2446a

"II. Development, Prototyping, and Deployment of Weapon System Components and Technology 2447a

"III. Cost, Schedule, and Performance of Major Defense Acquisition Programs 2448a

"SUBCHAPTER I—MODULAR OPEN SYSTEM APPROACH IN DEVELOPMENT OF WEAPON SYSTEMS

"Sec.

"2446a. Requirement for modular open system approach in major defense acquisition programs; definitions.

"2446b. Requirement to address modular open system approach in program capabilities development and acquisition weapon system design.

"2446c. Requirements relating to availability of major system interfaces and support for modular open system approach.

"§ 2446a. Requirement for modular open system approach in major defense acquisition programs; definitions

"(a) MODULAR OPEN SYSTEM APPROACH REQUIREMENT.—A major defense acquisition program that receives Milestone A or Milestone B approval after January 1, 2019, shall be designed and developed, to the maximum extent practicable, with a modular open system approach to enable incremental development and enhance competition, innovation, and interoperability.

"(b) DEFINITIONS.—In this chapter:

"(1) The term 'modular open system approach' means, with respect to a major defense acquisition program, an integrated business and technical strategy that—

"(A) employs a modular design that uses major system interfaces between a major system platform and a major system component, between major system components, or between major system platforms;

"(B) is subjected to verification to ensure major system interfaces comply with, if available and suitable, widely supported and consensus-based standards;

"(C) uses a system architecture that allows severable major system components at the appropriate level to be incrementally added, removed, or replaced throughout the life cycle of a major system platform to afford opportunities for enhanced competition and innovation while yielding—

"(i) significant cost savings or avoidance;

"(ii) schedule reduction;

"(iii) opportunities for technical upgrades;

"(iv) increased interoperability, including system of systems interoperability and mission integration; or

"(v) other benefits during the sustainment phase of a major weapon system; and

"(D) complies with the technical data rights set forth in section 2320 of this title.

"(2) The term 'major system platform' means the highest level structure of a major weapon system that is not physically mounted or installed onto a higher level structure and on which a major system component can be physically mounted or installed.

"(3) The term 'major system component'—

"(A) means a high level subsystem or assembly, including hardware, software, or an integrated assembly of both, that can be mounted or installed on a major system platform through well-defined major system interfaces; and

"(B) includes a subsystem or assembly that is likely to have additional capability requirements, is likely to change because of evolving technology or threat, is needed for interoperability, facilitates incremental deployment of capabilities, or is expected to be replaced by another major system component.

"(4) The term 'major system interface'—

"(A) means a shared boundary between a major system platform and a major system component, between major system components, or between major system platforms, defined by various physical, logical, and functional characteristics, such as electrical, mechanical, fluidic, optical, radio frequency, data, networking, or software elements; and

"(B) is characterized clearly in terms of form, function, and the content that flows across the interface in order to enable technological innovation, incremental improvements, integration, and interoperability.

"(5) The term 'program capability document' means, with respect to a major defense acquisition program, a document that specifies capability requirements for the program, such as a capability development document or a capability production document.

"(6) The terms 'program cost targets' and 'fielding target' have the meanings provided in section 2448a(a) of this title.

"(7) The term 'major defense acquisition program' has the meaning provided in section 2430 of this title.

"(8) The term 'major weapon system' has the meaning provided in section 2379(f) of this title.

"§ 2446b. Requirement to address modular open system approach in program capabilities development and acquisition weapon system design

"(a) PROGRAM CAPABILITY DOCUMENT.—A program capability document for a major defense acquisition program shall identify and characterize—

"(1) the extent to which requirements for system performance are likely to evolve during the life cycle of the system because of evolving technology, threat, or interoperability needs; and

"(2) for requirements that are expected to evolve, the minimum acceptable capability that is necessary for initial operating capability of the major defense acquisition program.

"(b) ANALYSIS OF ALTERNATIVES.—The Director of Cost Assessment and Performance Evaluation, in formulating study guidance for analyses of alternatives for major defense acquisition programs and performing such analyses under section 139a(d)(4) of this title, shall ensure that any such analysis for a major defense acquisition program includes consideration of evolutionary acquisition, prototyping, and a modular open system approach.

"(c) ACQUISITION STRATEGY.—In the case of a major defense acquisition program that uses a modular open system approach, the acquisition strategy required under section 2431a of this title shall—

"(1) clearly describe the modular open system approach to be used for the program;

"(2) differentiate between the major system platform and major system components being de-

veloped under the program, as well as major system components developed outside the program that will be integrated into the major defense acquisition program;

"(3) clearly describe the evolution of major system components that are anticipated to be added, removed, or replaced in subsequent increments;

"(4) identify additional major system components that may be added later in the life cycle of the major system platform;

"(5) clearly describe how intellectual property and related issues, such as technical data deliverables, that are necessary to support a modular open system approach, will be addressed; and

"(6) clearly describe the approach to systems integration and systems-level configuration management to ensure mission and information assurance.

"(d) REQUEST FOR PROPOSALS.—The milestone decision authority for a major defense acquisition program that uses a modular open system approach shall ensure that a request for proposals for the development or production phases of the program shall describe the modular open system approach and the minimum set of major system components that must be included in the design of the major defense acquisition program.

"(e) MILESTONE B.—A major defense acquisition program may not receive Milestone B approval under section 2366b of this title until the milestone decision authority determines in writing that—

"(1) in the case of a program that uses a modular open system approach—

"(A) the program incorporates clearly defined major system interfaces between the major system platform and major system components, between major system components, and between major system platforms;

"(B) such major system interfaces are consistent with the widely supported and consensus-based standards that exist at the time of the milestone decision, unless such standards are unavailable or unsuitable for particular major system interfaces; and

"(C) the Government has arranged to obtain appropriate and necessary intellectual property rights with respect to such major system interfaces upon completion of the development of the major system platform; or

"(2) in the case of a program that does not use a modular open system approach, that the use of a modular open system approach is not practicable.

"§ 2446c. Requirements relating to availability of major system interfaces and support for modular open system approach

"The Secretary of each military department shall—

"(1) coordinate with the other military departments, the defense agencies, defense and other private sector entities, national standards-setting organizations, and, when appropriate, with elements of the intelligence community with respect to the specification, identification, development, and maintenance of major system interfaces and standards for use in major system platforms, where practicable;

"(2) ensure that major system interfaces incorporate commercial standards and other widely supported consensus-based standards that are validated, published, and maintained by recognized standards organizations to the maximum extent practicable;

"(3) ensure that sufficient systems engineering and development expertise and resources are available to support the use of a modular open system approach in requirements development and acquisition program planning;

"(4) ensure that necessary planning, programming, and budgeting resources are provided to specify, identify, develop, and sustain the modular open system approach, associated major

system interfaces, systems integration, and any additional program activities necessary to sustain innovation and interoperability; and

"(5) ensure that adequate training in the use of a modular open system approach is provided to members of the requirements and acquisition workforce.".

(2) CLERICAL AMENDMENT.—The table of chapters for title 10, United States Code, is amended by adding after the item relating to chapter 144A the following new item:

"**144B. Weapon Systems Development and Related Matters** ....2446a".

(3) CONFORMING AMENDMENT.—Section 2366b(a)(3) of such title is amended—

(A) by striking "and" at the end of subparagraph (K); and

(B) by inserting after subparagraph (L) the following new subparagraph:

"(M) the requirements of section 2446b(e) of this title are met; and".

(4) EFFECTIVE DATE.—Subchapter I of chapter 144B of title 10, United States Code, as added by paragraph (1), shall take effect on January 1, 2017.

(b) REQUIREMENT TO INCLUDE MODULAR OPEN SYSTEM APPROACH IN SELECTED ACQUISITION REPORTS.—Section 2432(c)(1) of such title is amended—

(1) by striking "and" at the end of subparagraph (F);

(2) by redesignating subparagraph (G) as subparagraph (H); and

(3) by inserting after subparagraph (F) the following new subparagraph (G):

"(G) for each major defense acquisition program that receives Milestone B approval after January 1, 2019, a brief summary description of the key elements of the modular open system approach as defined in section 2446a of this title or, if a modular open system approach was not used, the rationale for not using such an approach; and".

SEC. 806. DEVELOPMENT, PROTOTYPING, AND DEPLOYMENT OF WEAPON SYSTEM COMPONENTS OR TECHNOLOGY.

(a) DEVELOPMENT, PROTOTYPING, AND DEPLOYMENT OF WEAPON SYSTEM COMPONENTS OR TECHNOLOGY.—

(1) IN GENERAL.—Chapter 144B of title 10, United States Code, as added by section 805, is further amended by adding at the end the following new subchapter:

"SUBCHAPTER II—DEVELOPMENT, PROTOTYPING, AND DEPLOYMENT OF WEAPON SYSTEM COMPONENTS OR TECHNOLOGY

"Sec.
"2447a. Weapon system component or technology prototype projects: display of budget information.
"2447b. Weapon system component or technology prototype projects: oversight.
"2447c. Requirements and limitations for weapon system component or technology prototype projects.
"2447d. Mechanisms to speed deployment of successful weapon system component or technology prototypes.
"2447e. Definition of weapon system component.

"**§2447a. Weapon system component or technology prototype projects: display of budget information**

"(a) REQUIREMENTS FOR BUDGET DISPLAY.—In the defense budget materials for any fiscal year after fiscal year 2017, the Secretary of Defense shall, with respect to advanced component development and prototype activities (within the research, development, test, and evaluation budget), set forth the amounts requested for each of the following:

"(1) Acquisition programs of record.

"(2) Development, prototyping, and experimentation of weapon system components or

other technologies, including those based on commercial items and technologies, separate from acquisition programs of record.

"(3) Other budget line items as determined by the Secretary of Defense.

"(b) ADDITIONAL REQUIREMENTS.—For purposes of subsection (a)(2), the amounts requested for development, prototyping, and experimentation of weapon system components or other technologies shall be—

"(1) structured into either capability, weapon system component, or technology portfolios that reflect the priority areas for prototype projects; and

"(2) justified with general descriptions of the types of capability areas and technologies being funded or expected to be funded during the fiscal year concerned.

"(c) DEFINITIONS.—In this section, the terms 'budget' and 'defense budget materials' have the meaning given those terms in section 234 of this title.

"**§2447b. Weapon system component or technology prototype projects: oversight**

"(a) ESTABLISHMENT.—The Secretary of each military department shall establish an oversight board or identify a similar existing group of senior advisors for managing prototype projects for weapon system components and other technologies and subsystems, including the use of funds for such projects, within the military department concerned.

"(b) MEMBERSHIP.—Each oversight board shall be comprised of senior officials with—

"(1) expertise in requirements; research, development, test, and evaluation; acquisition; sustainment; or other relevant areas within the military department concerned;

"(2) awareness of technology development activities and opportunities in the Department of Defense, industry, and other sources; and

"(3) awareness of the component capability requirements of major weapon systems, including scheduling and fielding goals for such component capabilities.

"(c) FUNCTIONS.—The functions of each oversight board are as follows:

"(1) To issue a strategic plan every three years that prioritizes the capability and weapon system component portfolio areas for conducting prototype projects, based on assessments of—

"(A) high priority warfighter needs;

"(B) capability gaps or readiness issues with major weapon systems;

"(C) opportunities to incrementally integrate new components into major weapon systems based on commercial technology or science and technology efforts that are expected to be sufficiently mature to prototype within three years; and

"(D) opportunities to reduce operation and support costs of major weapon systems.

"(2) To annually recommend funding levels for weapon system component or technology development and prototype projects across capability or weapon system component portfolios.

"(3) To annually recommend to the service acquisition executive of the military department concerned specific weapon system component or technology development and prototype projects, subject to the requirements and limitations in section 2447c of this title.

"(4) To ensure projects are managed by experts within the Department of Defense who are knowledgeable in research, development, test, and evaluation and who are aware of opportunities for incremental deployment of component capabilities and other technologies to major weapon systems or directly to support warfighting capabilities.

"(5) To ensure projects are conducted in a manner that allows for appropriate experimentation and technology risk.

"(6) To ensure projects have a plan for technology transition of the prototype into a fielded

system, program of record, or operational use, as appropriate, upon successful achievement of technical and project goals.

"(7) To ensure necessary technical, contracting, and financial management resources are available to support each project.

"(8) To submit to the congressional defense committees a semiannual notification that includes the following:

"(A) each weapon system component or technology prototype project initiated during the preceding six months, including an explanation of each project and its required funding.

"(B) the results achieved from weapon system component prototype and technology projects completed and tested during the preceding six months.

"**§2447c. Requirements and limitations for weapon system component or technology prototype projects**

"(a) LIMITATION ON PROTOTYPE PROJECT DURATION.—A prototype project shall be completed within two years of its initiation.

"(b) MERIT-BASED SELECTION PROCESS.—A prototype project shall be selected by the service acquisition executive of the military department concerned through a merit-based selection process that identifies the most promising, innovative, and cost-effective prototypes that address one or more of the elements set forth in subsection (c)(1) of section 2447b of this title and are expected to be successfully demonstrated in a relevant environment.

"(c) TYPE OF TRANSACTION.—Prototype projects shall be funded through contracts, cooperative agreements, or other transactions.

"(d) FUNDING LIMIT.—(1) Each prototype project may not exceed a total amount of $10,000,000 (based on fiscal year 2017 constant dollars), unless—

"(A) the Secretary of the military department, or the Secretary's designee, approves a larger amount of funding for the project, not to exceed $50,000,000; and

"(B) the Secretary, or the Secretary's designee, submits to the congressional defense committees, within 30 days after approval of such funding for the project, a notification that includes—

"(i) the project;

"(ii) expected funding for the project; and

"(iii) a statement of the anticipated outcome of the project.

"(2) The Secretary of Defense may adjust the amounts (and the base fiscal year) provided in paragraph (1) on the basis of Department of Defense escalation rates.

"(e) RELATED PROTOTYPE AUTHORITIES.—Prototype projects that exceed the duration and funding limits established in this section shall be pursued under the rapid prototyping process established by section 804 of the National Defense Authorization Act for Fiscal Year 2016 (Public Law 114–92; 10 U.S.C. 2302 note). In addition, nothing in this subchapter shall affect the authority to carry out prototype projects under section 2371b or any other section of this title related to prototyping.

"**§2447d. Mechanisms to speed deployment of successful weapon system component or technology prototypes**

"(a) SELECTION OF PROTOTYPE PROJECT FOR PRODUCTION AND RAPID FIELDING.—A weapon system component or technology prototype project may be selected by the service acquisition executive of the military department concerned for a follow-on production contract or other transaction without the use of competitive procedures, notwithstanding the requirements of section 2304 of this title, if—

"(1) the follow-on production project addresses a high priority warfighter need or reduces the costs of a weapon system;

"(2) competitive procedures were used for the selection of parties for participation in the original prototype project;

"(3) the participants in the original prototype project successfully completed the requirements of the project; and

"(4) a prototype of the system to be procured was demonstrated in a relevant environment.

"(b) SPECIAL TRANSFER AUTHORITY.—(1) The Secretary of a military department may, as specified in advance by appropriations Acts, transfer funds that remain available for obligation in procurement appropriation accounts of the military department to fund the low-rate initial production of the rapid fielding project until required funding for full-rate production can be submitted and approved through the regular budget process of the Department of Defense.

"(2) The funds transferred under this subsection to fund the low-rate initial production of a rapid fielding project shall be for a period not to exceed two years, the amount for such period may not exceed $50,000,000, and the special transfer authority provided in this subsection may not be used more than once to fund procurement of a particular new or upgraded system.

"(3) The special transfer authority provided in this subsection is in addition to any other transfer authority available to the Department of Defense.

"(c) NOTIFICATION TO CONGRESS.—Within 30 days after the service acquisition executive of a military department selects a weapon system component or technology project for a follow-on production contract or other transaction, the service acquisition executive shall notify the congressional defense committees of the selection and provide a brief description of the rapid fielding project.

"**§2447e. Definition of weapon system component**

"In this subchapter, the term 'weapon system component' has the meaning given the term 'major system component' in section 2446a of this title.".

(2) EFFECTIVE DATE.—Subchapter II of chapter 144B of title 10, United States Code, as added by paragraph (1), shall take effect on January 1, 2017.

(b) ADDITION TO REQUIREMENTS NEEDED BEFORE MILESTONE A APPROVAL.—Section 2366a(b) of such title is amended—

(1) by striking "and" at the end of paragraph (7);

(2) by redesignating paragraph (8) as paragraph (9); and

(3) by inserting after paragraph (7) the following new paragraph (8):

"(8) that, with respect to a program initiated after January 1, 2019, technology shall be developed in the program (after Milestone A approval) only if the milestone decision authority determines with a high degree of confidence that such development will not delay the fielding target of the program, or, if the milestone decision authority does not make such determination for a major system component being developed under the program, the milestone decision authority ensures that the technology related to the major system component shall be sufficiently matured and demonstrated in a relevant environment (after Milestone A approval) separate from the program using the prototyping authorities in subchapter II of chapter 144B of this title or other authorities, as appropriate, and have an effective plan for adoption or insertion by the relevant program; and".

SEC. 807. COST, SCHEDULE, AND PERFORMANCE OF MAJOR DEFENSE ACQUISITION PROGRAMS.

(a) COST, SCHEDULE, AND PERFORMANCE OF MAJOR DEFENSE ACQUISITION PROGRAMS.—

(1) IN GENERAL.—Chapter 144B of title 10, United States Code, as added by section 805, is amended by adding at the end the following new subchapter:

"SUBCHAPTER III—COST, SCHEDULE, AND PERFORMANCE OF MAJOR DEFENSE ACQUISITION PROGRAMS

"Sec.

"2448a. Program cost, fielding, and performance goals in planning major defense acquisition programs.

"2448b. Independent technical risk assessments.

"**§2448a. Program cost, fielding, and performance goals in planning major defense acquisition programs**

"(a) PROGRAM COST AND FIELDING TARGETS.—(1) Before funds are obligated for technology development, systems development, or production of a major defense acquisition program, the Secretary of Defense shall ensure, by establishing the goals described in paragraph (2), that the milestone decision authority for the major defense acquisition program approves a program that will—

"(A) be affordable;

"(B) incorporate program planning that anticipates the evolution of capabilities to meet changing threats, technology insertion, and interoperability; and

"(C) be fielded when needed.

"(2) The goals described in this paragraph are goals for—

"(A) the procurement unit cost and sustainment cost (referred to in this section as the 'program cost targets');

"(B) the date for initial operational capability (referred to in this section as the 'fielding target'); and

"(C) technology maturation, prototyping, and a modular open system approach to evolve system capabilities and improve interoperability.

"(b) DELEGATION.—The responsibilities of the Secretary of Defense in subsection (a) may be delegated only to the Deputy Secretary of Defense.

"(c) DEFINITIONS.—In this section:

"(1) The term 'procurement unit cost' has the meaning provided in section 2432(a)(2) of this title.

"(2) The term 'initial capabilities document' has the meaning provided in section 2366a(d)(2) of this title.

"**§2448b. Independent technical risk assessments**

"(a) IN GENERAL.—With respect to a major defense acquisition program, the Secretary of Defense shall ensure that an independent technical risk assessment is conducted—

"(1) before any decision to grant Milestone A approval for the program pursuant to section 2366a of this title, that identifies critical technologies and manufacturing processes that need to be matured; and

"(2) before any decision to grant Milestone B approval for the program pursuant to section 2366b of this title, any decision to enter into low-rate initial production or full-rate production, or at any other time considered appropriate by the Secretary, that includes the identification of any critical technologies or manufacturing processes that have not been successfully demonstrated in a relevant environment.

"(b) CATEGORIZATION OF TECHNICAL RISK LEVELS.—The Secretary shall issue guidance and a framework for categorizing the degree of technical and manufacturing risk in a major defense acquisition program.".

(2) EFFECTIVE DATE.—Subchapter III of chapter 144B of title 10, United States Code, as added by paragraph (1), shall apply with respect to major defense acquisition programs that reach Milestone A after October 1, 2017.

(b) MODIFICATION OF MILESTONE DECISION AUTHORITY.—Effective January 1, 2017, subsection (d) of section 2430 of title 10, United States Code, as added by section 825(a) of the National Defense Authorization Act for Fiscal Year 2016 (Public Law 114–92; 129 Stat. 907), is amended—

(1) in paragraph (2)(A), by inserting "subject to paragraph (5)," before "the Secretary determines"; and

(2) by adding at the end the following new paragraph:

"(5) The authority of the Secretary of Defense to designate an alternative milestone decision authority for a program with respect to which the Secretary determines that the program is addressing a joint requirement, as set forth in paragraph (2)(A), shall apply only for a major defense acquisition program that reaches Milestone A after October 1, 2016, and before October 1, 2019.".

(c) ADHERENCE TO REQUIREMENTS IN MAJOR DEFENSE ACQUISITION PROGRAMS.—Section 2547 of title 10, United States Code, is amended—

(1) by redesignating subsections (b) and (c) as subsections (c) and (d), respectively;

(2) by inserting after subsection (a) the following new subsection (b):

"(b) ADHERENCE TO REQUIREMENTS IN MAJOR DEFENSE ACQUISITION PROGRAMS.—The Secretary of the military department concerned shall ensure that the program document supporting a Milestone B or subsequent decision for a major defense acquisition program may not be approved until the chief of the armed force concerned determines in writing that the requirements in the document are necessary and realistic in relation to the program cost and fielding targets established under section 2448a(a) of this title."; and

(3) by adding at the end of subsection (d), as so redesignated, the following new paragraph:

"(3) The term 'program capability document' has the meaning provided in section 2446a(b)(5) of this title.".

(d) AMENDMENT RELATING TO DETERMINATION REQUIRED BEFORE MILESTONE A APPROVAL.—Section 2366a(b)(4) of title 10, United States Code, is amended by inserting after "areas of risk" the following: ", including risks determined by the identification of critical technologies required under section 2448b(a)(1) of this title or any other risk assessment".

(e) AMENDMENT RELATING TO CERTIFICATION REQUIRED BEFORE MILESTONE B APPROVAL.—Section 2366b(a) of title 10, United States Code, is amended—

(1) in paragraph (2), by striking "assessment by the Assistant Secretary" and all that follows through "Test and Evaluation" and inserting "technical risk assessment conducted under section 2448b of this title"; and

(2) in paragraph (3), as amended by section 805(a)(3)(B)—

(A) by striking "and" at the end of subparagraph (C);

(B) by redesignating subparagraphs (D) through (M) as subparagraphs (E) through (N), respectively; and

(C) by inserting after subparagraph (C) the following new subparagraph (D):

"(D) the estimated procurement unit cost for the program and the estimated date for initial operational capability for the baseline description for the program (established under section 2435) do not exceed the program cost and fielding targets established under section 2448a(a) of this title, or, if such estimated cost is higher than the program cost targets or if such estimated date is later than the fielding target, the program cost targets have been increased or the fielding target has been delayed by the Secretary of Defense after a request for such increase or delay by the milestone decision authority;".

SEC. 808. TRANSPARENCY IN MAJOR DEFENSE ACQUISITION PROGRAMS.

(a) MILESTONE A REPORT.—

(1) IN GENERAL.—Section 2366a(c) of title 10, United States Code, is amended to read as follows:

"(c) SUBMISSIONS TO CONGRESS ON MILESTONE A.—

"(1) BRIEF SUMMARY REPORT.—Not later than 15 days after granting Milestone A approval for a major defense acquisition program, the milestone decision authority for the program shall provide to the congressional defense committees and, in the case of intelligence or intelligence-related activities, the congressional intelligence committees a brief summary report that contains the following elements:

"(A) The program cost and fielding targets established by the Secretary of Defense under section 2448a(a) of this title.

"(B) The estimated cost and schedule for the program established by the military department concerned, including—

"(i) the dollar values estimated for the program acquisition unit cost and total life-cycle cost; and

"(ii) the planned dates for each program milestone and initial operational capability.

"(C) The independent estimated cost for the program established pursuant to section 2334(a)(6) of this title, and any independent estimated schedule for the program, including—

"(i) as assessment of the major contributors to the program acquisition unit cost and total life-cycle cost; and

"(ii) the planned dates for each program milestone and initial operational capability.

"(D) A summary of the technical or manufacturing risks associated with the program, as determined by the military department concerned, including identification of any critical technologies or manufacturing processes that need to be matured.

"(E) A summary of the independent technical risk assessment conducted or approved under section 2448b of this title, including identification of any critical technologies or manufacturing processes that need to be matured.

"(F) A summary of any sufficiency review conducted by the Director of Cost Assessment and Program Evaluation of the analysis of alternatives performed for the program (as referred to in section 2366a(b)(6) of this title).

"(G) Any other information the milestone decision authority considers relevant.

"(2) ADDITIONAL INFORMATION.—(A) At the request of any of the congressional defense committees or, in the case of intelligence or intelligence-related activities, the congressional intelligence committees, the milestone decision authority shall submit to the committee an explanation of the basis for a determination made under subsection (b) with respect to a major defense acquisition program, together with a copy of the written determination, or further information or underlying documentation for the information in a brief summary report submitted under paragraph (1), including the independent cost and schedule estimates and the independent technical risk assessments referred to in that paragraph.

"(B) The explanation or information shall be submitted in unclassified form, but may include a classified annex.".

(2) DEFINITIONS.—Section 2366a(d) of such title is amended by adding at the end the following new paragraphs:

"(8) The term 'fielding target' has the meaning given that term in section 2448a(a) of this title.

"(9) The term 'major system component' has the meaning given that term in section 2446a(b)(3) of this title.

"(10) The term 'congressional intelligence committees' has the meaning given that term in section 437(c) of this title.".

(b) MILESTONE B REPORT.—

(1) IN GENERAL.—Section 2366b(c) of title 10, United States Code, is amended to read as follows:

"(c) SUBMISSIONS TO CONGRESS ON MILESTONE B.—

"(1) BRIEF SUMMARY REPORT.—Not later than 15 days after granting Milestone B approval for a major defense acquisition program, the milestone decision authority for the program shall provide to the congressional defense committees and, in the case of intelligence or intelligence-related activities, the congressional intelligence committees a brief summary report that contains the following elements:

"(A) The program cost and fielding targets established by the Secretary of Defense under section 2448a(a) of this title.

"(B) The estimated cost and schedule for the program established by the military department concerned, including—

"(i) the dollar values estimated for the program acquisition unit cost, average procurement unit cost, and total life-cycle cost; and

"(ii) the planned dates for each program milestone, initial operational test and evaluation, and initial operational capability.

"(C) The independent estimated cost for the program established pursuant to section 2334(a)(6) of this title, and any independent estimated schedule for the program, including—

"(i) the dollar values and ranges estimated for the program acquisition unit cost, average procurement unit cost, and total life-cycle cost; and

"(ii) the planned dates for each program milestone, initial operational test and evaluation, and initial operational capability.

"(D) A summary of the technical and manufacturing risks associated with the program, as determined by the military department concerned, including identification of any critical technologies or manufacturing processes that have not been successfully demonstrated in a relevant environment.

"(E) A summary of the independent technical risk assessment conducted or approved under section 2448b of this title, including identification of any critical technologies or manufacturing processes that have not been successfully demonstrated in a relevant environment.

"(F) A statement of whether a modular open system approach is being used for the program.

"(G) Any other information the milestone decision authority considers relevant.

"(2) CERTIFICATIONS AND DETERMINATIONS.—(A) The certifications and determination under subsection (a) with respect to a major defense acquisition program shall be submitted to the congressional defense committees with the first Selected Acquisition Report submitted under section 2432 of this title after completion of the certification.

"(B) The milestone decision authority shall retain records of the basis for the certifications and determination under paragraphs (1), (2), and (3) of subsection (a).

"(3) ADDITIONAL INFORMATION.—(A) At the request of any of the congressional defense committees or, in the case of intelligence or intelligence-related activities, the congressional intelligence committees, the milestone decision authority shall submit to the committee an explanation of the basis for the certifications and determination under paragraphs (1), (2), and (3) of subsection (a) with respect to a major defense acquisition program or further information or underlying documentation for the information in a brief summary report submitted under paragraph (1), including the independent cost and schedule estimates and the independent technical risk assessments referred to in that paragraph.

"(B) The explanation or information shall be submitted in unclassified form, but may include a classified annex.".

(2) DEFINITIONS.—Section 2366b(g) of such title is amended by adding at the end the following new paragraphs:

"(6) The term 'fielding target' has the meaning given that term in section 2448a(a) of this title.

"(7) The term 'major system component' has the meaning given that term in section 2446a(b)(3) of this title.

"(8) The term 'congressional intelligence committees' has the meaning given that term in section 437(c) of this title.".

(c) MILESTONE C REPORT.—

(1) IN GENERAL.—Chapter 139 of such title is amended by inserting after section 2366b the following new section:

"§ 2366c. Major defense acquisition programs: submissions to Congress on Milestone C

"(a) BRIEF SUMMARY REPORT.—Not later than 15 days after granting Milestone C approval for a major defense acquisition program, the milestone decision authority for the program shall provide to the congressional defense committees and, in the case of intelligence or intelligence-related activities, the congressional intelligence committees a brief summary report that contains the following:

"(1) The estimated cost and schedule for the program established by the military department concerned, including—

"(A) the dollar values estimated for the program acquisition unit cost, average procurement unit cost, and total life-cycle cost; and

"(B) the planned dates for initial operational test and evaluation and initial operational capability.

"(2) The independent estimated cost for the program established pursuant to section 2334(a)(6) of this title, and any independent estimated schedule for the program, including—

"(A) the dollar values estimated for the program acquisition unit cost, average procurement unit cost, and total life-cycle cost; and

"(B) the planned dates for initial operational test and evaluation and initial operational capability.

"(3) A summary of any production, manufacturing, and fielding risks associated with the program.

"(b) ADDITIONAL INFORMATION.—At the request of any of the congressional defense committees or, in the case of intelligence or intelligence-related activities, the congressional intelligence committees, the milestone decision authority shall submit to the committee further information or underlying documentation for the information in a brief summary report submitted under subsection (a), including the independent cost and schedule estimates and the independent technical risk assessments referred to in that subsection.

"(c) CONGRESSIONAL INTELLIGENCE COMMITTEES DEFINED.—In this section, the term 'congressional intelligence committees' has the meaning given that term in section 437(c) of this title.".

(2) CLERICAL AMENDMENT.—The table of sections at the beginning of such chapter is amended by inserting after the item relating to section 2366b the following new item:

"2366c. Major defense acquisition programs: submissions to Congress on Milestone C.".

SEC. 809. AMENDMENTS RELATING TO TECHNICAL DATA RIGHTS.

(a) RIGHTS RELATING TO ITEM OR PROCESS DEVELOPED EXCLUSIVELY AT PRIVATE EXPENSE.—Subsection (a)(2)(C)(iii) of section 2320 of title 10, United States Code, is amended by inserting after "or process data" the following: ", including such data pertaining to a major system component".

(b) RIGHTS RELATING TO INTERFACE OR MAJOR SYSTEM INTERFACE.—Subsection (a)(2) of section 2320 of such title is further amended—

(1) by redesignating subparagraphs (F) and (G) as subparagraphs (H) and (I), respectively;

(2) in subparagraph (B), by striking "Except as provided in subparagraphs (C) and (D),," and inserting "Except as provided in subparagraphs (C), (D), and (G),";

(3) in subparagraph (D)(i)(II), by striking "is necessary" and inserting "is a release, disclosure, or use of technical data pertaining to an interface between an item or process and other items or processes necessary";

(4) in subparagraph (E)—

(A) by striking "In the case" and inserting "Except as provided in subparagraphs (F) and (G), in the case"; and

(B) by striking "negotiations). The United States shall have" and all that follows through "such negotiated rights shall" and inserting the following: "negotiations) and shall be based on negotiations between the United States and the contractor, except in any case in which the Secretary of Defense determines, on the basis of criteria established in the regulations, that negotiations would not be practicable. The establishment of such rights shall"; and

(5) by inserting after subparagraph (E) the following new subparagraphs (F) and (G):

"(F) INTERFACES DEVELOPED WITH MIXED FUNDING.—Notwithstanding subparagraph (E), the United States shall have government purpose rights in technical data pertaining to an interface between an item or process and other items or processes that was developed in part with Federal funds and in part at private expense, except in any case in which the Secretary of Defense determines, on the basis of criteria established in the regulations, that negotiation of different rights in such technical data would be in the best interest of the United States.

"(G) MAJOR SYSTEM INTERFACES DEVELOPED EXCLUSIVELY AT PRIVATE EXPENSE OR WITH MIXED FUNDING.—Notwithstanding subparagraphs (B) and (E), the United States shall have government purpose rights in technical data pertaining to a major system interface developed exclusively at private expense or in part with Federal funds and in part at private expense and used in a modular open system approach pursuant to section 2446a of this title, except in any case in which the Secretary of Defense determines that negotiation of different rights in such technical data would be in the best interest of the United States. Such major system interface shall be identified in the contract solicitation and the contract. For technical data pertaining to a major system interface developed exclusively at private expense for which the United States asserts government purpose rights, the Secretary of Defense shall negotiate with the contractor the appropriate and reasonable compensation for such technical data.".

(c) AMENDMENT RELATING TO DEFERRED ORDERING.—Subsection (b)(9) of section 2320 of such title is amended—

(1) by striking "at any time" and inserting ", until the date occurring six years after acceptance of the last item (other than technical data) under a contract or the date of contract termination, whichever is later,";

(2) by striking "or utilized in the performance of a contract" and inserting "in the performance of the contract"; and

(3) by striking clause (ii) of subparagraph (B) and inserting the following:

"(ii) is described in subparagraphs (D)(i)(II), (F), and (G) of subsection (a)(2); and".

(d) DEFINITIONS.—Section 2320 of such title is further amended—

(1) in subsection (f), by inserting "COVERED GOVERNMENT SUPPORT CONTRACTOR DEFINED.—" before "In this section"; and

(2) by adding at the end the following new subsection:

"(g) ADDITIONAL DEFINITIONS.—In this section, the terms 'major system component', 'major

system interface', and 'modular open system approach' have the meanings provided in section 2446a of this title.".*

(e) AMENDMENTS TO ADD CERTAIN HEADINGS FOR READABILITY.—Section 2320(a) of such title is further amended—

(1) in subparagraph (A) of paragraph (2), by inserting after "(A)" the following: "DEVELOPMENT EXCLUSIVELY WITH FEDERAL FUNDS.—";

(2) in subparagraph (B) of such paragraph, by inserting after "(B)" the following: "DEVELOPMENT EXCLUSIVELY AT PRIVATE EXPENSE.—";

(3) in subparagraph (C) of such paragraph, by inserting after "(C)" the following: "EXCEPTION TO SUBPARAGRAPH (B).—";

(4) in subparagraph (D) of such paragraph, by inserting after "(D)" the following: "EXCEPTION TO SUBPARAGRAPH (B).—"; and

(5) in subparagraph (E) of such paragraph, by inserting after "(E)" the following: "DEVELOPMENT WITH MIXED FUNDING.—".

(f) GOVERNMENT-INDUSTRY ADVISORY PANEL AMENDMENTS.—Section 813(b) of the National Defense Authorization Act for Fiscal Year 2016 (Public Law 114–92; 129 Stat. 892) is amended—

(1) by adding at the end of paragraph (1) the following: "The panel shall develop recommendations for changes to sections 2320 and 2321 of title 10, United States Code, and the regulations implementing such sections.";

(2) in paragraph (3)—

(A) by redesignating subparagraphs (D) and (E) as subparagraphs (E) and (F), respectively; and

(B) by inserting after subparagraph (C) the following new subparagraph (D):

"(D) Ensuring that the Department of Defense and Department of Defense contractors have the technical data rights necessary to support the modular open system approach requirement set forth in section 2446a of title 10, United States Code, taking into consideration the distinct characteristics of major system platforms, major system interfaces, and major system components developed exclusively with Federal funds, exclusively at private expense, and with a combination of Federal funds and private expense."; and

(3) by amending paragraph (4) to read as follows:

"(4) FINAL REPORT.—Not later than February 1, 2017, the advisory panel shall submit its final report and recommendations to the Secretary of Defense and the congressional defense committees. Not later than 60 days after receiving the report, the Secretary shall submit any comments or recommendations to the congressional defense committees.".

Subtitle C—Amendments to General Contracting Authorities, Procedures, and Limitations

SEC. 811. MODIFIED RESTRICTIONS ON UNDEFINITIZED CONTRACTUAL ACTIONS.

Section 2326 of title 10, United States Code, is amended—

(1) in subsection (e)—

(A) by redesignating paragraphs (1) and (2) as subparagraphs (A) and (B);

(B) by inserting "(1)" before "The head"; and

(C) by adding at the end the following new paragraph:

"(2) If a contractor submits a qualifying proposal to definitize an undefinitized contractual action and the contracting officer for such action definitizes the contract after the end of the 180-day period beginning on the date on which the contractor submitted the qualifying proposal, the head of the agency concerned shall ensure that the profit allowed on the contract accurately reflects the cost risk of the contractor as such risk existed on the date the contractor submitted the qualifying proposal.";

(2) by redesignating subsections (f) and (g) as subsections (h) and (i), respectively;

(3) by inserting after subsection (e) the following new subsections:

"(f) TIME LIMIT.—No undefinitized contractual action may extend beyond 90 days without a written determination by the Secretary of the military department concerned, the head of the Defense Agency concerned, the commander of the combatant command concerned, or the Under Secretary of Defense for Acquisition, Technology, and Logistics (as applicable) that it is in the best interests of the military department, the Defense Agency, the combatant command, or the Department of Defense, respectively, to continue the action.

"(g) FOREIGN MILITARY CONTRACTS.—(1) Except as provided in paragraph (2), a contracting officer of the Department of Defense may not enter into an undefinitized contractual action for a foreign military sale unless the contractual action provides for agreement upon contractual terms, specifications, and price by the end of the 180-day period described in subsection (b)(1)(A).

"(2) The requirement under paragraph (1) may be waived in accordance with subsection (b)(4)."; and

(4) in subsection (i), as redesignated by paragraph (2)—

(A) in paragraph (1)—

(i) by striking subparagraph (A); and

(ii) by redesignating subparagraphs (B), (C), and (D) as subparagraphs (A), (B), and (C), respectively; and

(B) in paragraph (2), by striking "complete and meaningful audits" and all that follows through the period and inserting "a meaningful audit of the information contained in the proposal.".

SEC. 812. AMENDMENTS RELATING TO INVENTORY AND TRACKING OF PURCHASES OF SERVICES.

(a) INCREASED THRESHOLD.—Subsection (a) of section 2330a of title 10, United States Code, is amended by striking "in excess of the simplified acquisition threshold" and inserting "in excess of $3,000,000".

(b) SPECIFICATION OF SERVICES.—Subsection (a) of such section is further amended by striking the period at the end and inserting the following: ", for services in the following service acquisition portfolio groups:

"(1) Logistics management services.

"(2) Equipment related services.

"(3) Knowledge-based services.

"(4) Electronics and communications services.".

(c) INVENTORY SUMMARY.—Subsection (c) of such section is amended—

(1) by striking "(c) INVENTORY.—" and inserting "(c) INVENTORY SUMMARY.—"; and

(2) in paragraph (1), by striking "submit to Congress an annual inventory" and all that follows through "for or on behalf" and inserting "prepare an annual inventory, and submit to Congress a summary of the inventory, of activities performed during the preceding fiscal year pursuant to staff augmentation contracts on behalf".

(d) ELIMINATION OF CERTAIN REQUIREMENTS.—Such section is further amended—

(1) by striking subsections (d), (g), and (h); and

(2) by redesignating subsections (e), (f), (i), and (j) as subsections (d), (e), (g), and (h), respectively.

(e) SPECIFICATION OF SERVICES TO BE REVIEWED.—Subsection (d), as so redesignated, of such section, is amended in paragraph (1) by inserting after "responsible" the following: ", with particular focus and attention on the following categories of high-risk product service codes (also referred to as Federal supply codes):

"(A) Special studies or analysis that is not research and development.

"(B) Information technology and telecommunications.

"(C) Support, including professional, administrative, and management.".

(f) COMPTROLLER GENERAL REPORT.—Such section is further amended by inserting after subsection (e), as so redesignated, the following new subsection (f):

"(f) COMPTROLLER GENERAL REPORT.—Not later than March 31, 2018, the Comptroller General of the United States shall submit to the congressional defense committees a report on the status of the data collection required in subsection (a) and an assessment of the efforts by the Department of Defense to implement subsection (e).".

(g) DEFINITIONS.—Subsection (h), as so redesignated, of such section is amended by adding at the end the following new paragraphs:

"(6) The term 'service acquisition portfolio groups' means the groups identified in Department of Defense Instruction 5000.74, Defense Acquisition of Services (January 5, 2016) or successor guidance.

"(7) The term 'staff augmentation contracts' means services contracts for personnel who are physically present in a Government work space on a full-time or permanent part-time basis, for the purpose of advising on, providing support to, or assisting a Government agency in the performance of the agency's missions, including authorized personal services contracts (as that term is defined in section 2330a(g)(5) of this title).".

SEC. 813. USE OF LOWEST PRICE TECHNICALLY ACCEPTABLE SOURCE SELECTION PROCESS.

(a) STATEMENT OF POLICY.—It shall be the policy of the Department of Defense to avoid using lowest price technically acceptable source selection criteria in circumstances that would deny the Department the benefits of cost and technical tradeoffs in the source selection process.

(b) REVISION OF DEFENSE FEDERAL ACQUISITION REGULATION SUPPLEMENT.—Not later than 120 days after the date of the enactment of this Act, the Secretary of Defense shall revise the Defense Federal Acquisition Regulation Supplement to require that, for solicitations issued on or after the date that is 120 days after the date of the enactment of this Act, lowest price technically acceptable source selection criteria are used only in situations in which—

(1) the Department of Defense is able to comprehensively and clearly describe the minimum requirements expressed in terms of performance objectives, measures, and standards that will be used to determine acceptability of offers;

(2) the Department of Defense would realize no, or minimal, value from a contract proposal exceeding the minimum technical or performance requirements set forth in the request for proposal;

(3) the proposed technical approaches will require no, or minimal, subjective judgment by the source selection authority as to the desirability of one offeror's proposal versus a competing proposal;

(4) the source selection authority has a high degree of confidence that a review of technical proposals of offerors other than the lowest bidder would not result in the identification of factors that could provide value or benefit to the Department;

(5) the contracting officer has included a justification for the use of a lowest price technically acceptable evaluation methodology in the contract file; and

(6) the Department of Defense has determined that the lowest price reflects full life-cycle costs, including for operations and support.

(c) AVOIDANCE OF USE OF LOWEST PRICE TECHNICALLY ACCEPTABLE SOURCE SELECTION CRITERIA IN CERTAIN PROCUREMENTS.—To the maximum extent practicable, the use of lowest price technically acceptable source selection criteria shall be avoided in the case of a procurement that is predominately for the acquisition of—

(1) information technology services, cybersecurity services, systems engineering and technical assistance services, advanced electronic testing, audit or audit readiness services, or other knowledge-based professional services;

(2) personal protective equipment; or

(3) knowledge-based training or logistics services in contingency operations or other operations outside the United States, including in Afghanistan or Iraq.

(d) REPORTING.—Not later than December 1, 2017, and annually thereafter for three years, the Comptroller General of the United States shall submit to the congressional defense committees a report on the number of instances in which lowest price technically acceptable source selection criteria is used for a contract exceeding $10,000,000, including an explanation of how the situations listed in subsection (b) were considered in making a determination to use lowest price technically acceptable source selection criteria.

SEC. 814. PROCUREMENT OF PERSONAL PROTECTIVE EQUIPMENT.

(a) LIMITATION.—Not later than 90 days after the date of the enactment of this Act, the Defense Federal Acquisition Regulation Supplement shall be revised—

(1) to prohibit the use by the Department of Defense of reverse auctions or lowest price technically acceptable contracting methods for the procurement of personal protective equipment if the level of quality or failure of the item could result in combat casualties; and

(2) to establish a preference for the use of best value contracting methods for the procurement of such equipment.

(b) CONFORMING AMENDMENT.—Section 884 of the National Defense Authorization Act for Fiscal Year 2016 (Public Law 114–92; 129 Stat. 948; 10 U.S.C. 2302 note) is hereby repealed.

SEC. 815. AMENDMENTS RELATED TO DETECTION AND AVOIDANCE OF COUNTERFEIT ELECTRONIC PARTS.

Section 818 of the National Defense Authorization Act for Fiscal Year 2012 (Public Law 112–81; 10 U.S.C. 2302 note) is amended—

(1) in paragraph (3) of subsection (c)—

(A) by striking the heading and inserting "SUPPLIERS MEETING ANTICOUNTERFEITING REQUIREMENTS.—";

(B) in subparagraph (A)(i), by striking "trusted suppliers in accordance with regulations issued pursuant to subparagraph (C) or (D) who" and inserting "suppliers that meet anticounterfeiting requirements in accordance with regulations issued pursuant to subparagraph (C) or (D) and that";

(C) in subparagraphs (A)(ii) and (A)(iii), by striking "trusted suppliers" each place it appears and inserting "suppliers that meet anticounterfeiting requirements";

(D) in subparagraph (C), by striking "as trusted suppliers those" and inserting "suppliers";

(E) in subparagraph (D) in the matter preceding clause (i), by striking "trusted suppliers" and inserting "suppliers that meet anticounterfeiting requirements"; and

(F) in subparagraphs (D)(i) and (D)(iii), by striking "trusted" each place it appears; and

(2) in subsection (e)(2)(A)(v), by striking "use of trusted suppliers" and inserting "the use of suppliers that meet applicable anticounterfeiting requirements".

SEC. 816. AMENDMENTS TO SPECIAL EMERGENCY PROCUREMENT AUTHORITY.

Section 1903(a) of title 41, United States Code, is amended—

(1) by striking "or" at the end of paragraph (1);

(2) by striking the period at the end of paragraph (2) and inserting a semicolon; and

(3) by adding after paragraph (2) the following new paragraphs:

"(3) in support of a request from the Secretary of State or the Administrator of the United States Agency for International Development to facilitate the provision of international disaster assistance pursuant to chapter 9 of part I of the Foreign Assistance Act of 1961 (22 U.S.C. 2292 et seq.); or

"(4) in support of an emergency or major disaster (as those terms are defined in section 102 of the Robert T. Stafford Disaster Relief and Emergency Assistance Act (42 U.S.C. 5122)).".

SEC. 817. COMPLIANCE WITH DOMESTIC SOURCE REQUIREMENTS FOR FOOTWEAR FURNISHED TO ENLISTED MEMBERS OF THE ARMED FORCES UPON THEIR INITIAL ENTRY INTO THE ARMED FORCES.

Section 418 of title 37, United States Code, is amended by adding at the end the following new subsection:

"(d)(1) In the case of athletic footwear needed by members of the Army, Navy, Air Force, or Marine Corps upon their initial entry into the armed forces, the Secretary of Defense shall furnish such footwear directly to the members instead of providing a cash allowance to the members for the purchase of such footwear.

"(2) In procuring athletic footwear to comply with paragraph (1), the Secretary of Defense shall—

"(A) procure athletic footwear that complies with the requirements of section 2533a of title 10, without regard to the applicability of any simplified acquisition threshold under chapter 137 of title 10 (or any other provision of law); and

"(B) procure additional athletic footwear, for two years following the date of the enactment of the National Defense Authorization Act for Fiscal Year 2017, that is necessary to provide a member described in paragraph (1) with sufficient choices in athletic shoes so as to minimize the incidence of athletic injuries and potential unnecessary harm and risk to the safety and well-being of members in initial entry training.

"(3) This subsection does not prohibit the provision of a cash allowance to a member described in paragraph (1) for the purchase of athletic footwear if such footwear—

"(A) is medically required to meet unique physiological needs of the member; and

"(B) cannot be met with athletic footwear that complies with the requirements of this subsection.".

SEC. 818. EXTENSION OF AUTHORITY FOR ENHANCED TRANSFER OF TECHNOLOGY DEVELOPED AT DEPARTMENT OF DEFENSE LABORATORIES.

Section 801(e) of the National Defense Authorization Act for Fiscal Year 2014 (Public Law 113–66; 127 Stat. 804; 10 U.S.C. 2514 note) is amended by striking "2017" and inserting "2021".

SEC. 819. MODIFIED NOTIFICATION REQUIREMENT FOR EXERCISE OF WAIVER AUTHORITY TO ACQUIRE VITAL NATIONAL SECURITY CAPABILITIES.

Subsection (d) of section 806 of the National Defense Authorization Act for Fiscal Year 2016 (Public Law 114–92; 10 U.S.C. 2302 note) is amended to read as follows:

"(d) NOTIFICATION REQUIREMENT.—Not later than 10 days after exercising the waiver authority under subsection (a), the Secretary of Defense shall provide a written notification to Congress providing the details of the waiver and the expected benefits it provides to the Department of Defense.".

SEC. 820. DEFENSE COST ACCOUNTING STANDARDS.

(a) AMENDMENTS TO THE COST ACCOUNTING STANDARDS BOARD.—

(1) IN GENERAL.—Section 1501 of title 41, United States Code, is amended—

(A) in subsection (b)(1)(B)(ii), by inserting "and, if possible, is a representative of a public accounting firm" after "systems";

(B) by redesignating subsections (c) through (f) as subsections (f) through (i), respectively;

(C) by inserting after subsection (b) the following new subsections:

"(c) DUTIES.—The Board shall—

"(1) ensure that the cost accounting standards used by Federal contractors rely, to the maximum extent practicable, on commercial standards and accounting practices and systems;

"(2) within one year after the date of enactment of this subsection, and on an ongoing basis thereafter, review any cost accounting standards established under section 1502 of this title and conform such standards, where practicable, to Generally Accepted Accounting Principles; and

"(3) annually review disputes involving such standards brought to the boards established in section 7105 of this title or Federal courts, and consider whether greater clarity in such standards could avoid such disputes.

"(d) MEETINGS.—The Board shall meet not less than once each quarter and shall publish in the Federal Register notice of each meeting and its agenda before such meeting is held.

"(e) REPORT.—The Board shall annually submit a report to the congressional defense committees, the Committee on Oversight and Government Reform of the House of Representatives, and the Committee on Homeland Security and Governmental Affairs of the Senate describing the actions taken during the prior year—

"(1) to conform the cost accounting standards established under section 1502 of this title with Generally Accepted Accounting Principles; and

"(2) to minimize the burden on contractors while protecting the interests of the Federal Government."; and

(D) by amending subsection (f) (as so redesignated) to read as follows:

"(f) SENIOR STAFF.—The Administrator, after consultation with the Board—

"(1) without regard to the provisions of title 5 governing appointments in the competitive service—

"(A) shall appoint an executive secretary; and

"(B) may appoint, or detail pursuant to section 3341 of title 5, two additional staff members; and

"(2) may pay those employees without regard to the provisions of chapter 51 and subchapter III of chapter 53 of title 5 relating to classification and General Schedule pay rates, except that those employees may not receive pay in excess of the maximum rate of basic pay payable for level IV of the Executive Schedule.".

(2) VALUE OF CONTRACTS ELIGIBLE FOR WAIVER.—Section 1502(b)(3)(A) of title 41, United States Code, is amended by striking "$15,000,000" and inserting "$100,000,000".

(3) CONFORMING AMENDMENTS.—Section 1501(i) of title 41, United States Code (as redesignated by paragraph (1)), is amended—

(A) in paragraph (1), by striking "subsection (e)(1)" and inserting "subsection (h)(1)"; and

(B) in paragraph (3), by striking "subsection (e)(2)" and inserting "subsection (h)(2)".

(b) DEFENSE COST ACCOUNTING STANDARDS BOARD.—

(1) IN GENERAL.—Chapter 7 of title 10, United States Code, is amended by adding at the end the following new section:

"§ 190. Defense Cost Accounting Standards Board

"(a) ORGANIZATION.—The Defense Cost Accounting Standards Board is an independent board in the Office of the Secretary of Defense.

"(b) MEMBERSHIP.—(1) The Board consists of seven members. One member is the Chief Finan-

cial Officer of the Department of Defense or a designee of the Chief Financial Officer, who serves as Chairman. The other six members, all of whom shall have experience in contract pricing, finance, or cost accounting, are as follows:

"(A) Three representatives of the Department of Defense appointed by the Secretary of Defense; and

"(B) Three individuals from the private sector, each of whom is appointed by the Secretary of Defense, and—

"(i) one of whom is a representative of a non-traditional defense contractor (as defined in section 2302(9) of this title); and

"(ii) one of whom is a representative from a public accounting firm.

"(2) A member appointed under paragraph (1)(A) may not continue to serve after ceasing to be an officer or employee of the Department of Defense.

"(c) DUTIES OF THE CHAIRMAN.—The Chief Financial Officer of the Department of Defense, after consultation with the Defense Cost Accounting Standards Board, shall prescribe rules and procedures governing actions of the Board under this section.

"(d) DUTIES.—The Defense Cost Accounting Standards Board—

"(1) shall review cost accounting standards established under section 1502 of title 41 and recommend changes to such cost accounting standards to the Cost Accounting Standards Board established under section 1501 of such title;

"(2) has exclusive authority, with respect to the Department of Defense, to implement such cost accounting standards to achieve uniformity and consistency in the standards governing measurement, assignment, and allocation of costs to contracts with the Department of Defense; and

"(3) shall develop standards to ensure that commercial operations performed by Government employees at the Department of Defense adhere to cost accounting standards (based on cost accounting standards established under section 1502 of title 41 or Generally Accepted Accounting Principles) that inform managerial decision-making.

"(e) COMPENSATION.—(1) Members of the Defense Cost Accounting Standards Board who are officers or employees of the Department of Defense shall not receive additional compensation for services but shall continue to be compensated by the Department of Defense.

"(2) Each member of the Board appointed from the private sector shall receive compensation at a rate not to exceed the daily equivalent of the rate for level IV of the Executive Schedule for each day (including travel time) in which the member is engaged in the actual performance of duties vested in the Board.

"(3) While serving away from home or regular place of business, Board members and other individuals serving on an intermittent basis shall be allowed travel expenses in accordance with section 5703 of title 5.

"(f) AUDITING REQUIREMENTS.—(1) Notwithstanding any other provision of law, contractors with the Department of Defense may present, and the Defense Contract Audit Agency shall accept without performing additional audits, a summary of audit findings prepared by a commercial auditor if—

"(A) the auditor previously performed an audit of the allowability, measurement, assignment to accounting periods, and allocation of indirect costs of the contractor; and

"(B) such audit was performed using relevant commercial accounting standards (such as Generally Accepted Accounting Principles) and relevant commercial auditing standards established by the commercial auditing industry for the relevant accounting period.

"(2) The Defense Contract Audit Agency may audit direct costs of Department of Defense cost

contracts and shall rely on commercial audits of indirect costs without performing additional audits, except that in the case of companies or business units that have a predominance of cost-type contracts as a percentage of sales, the Defense Contract Audit Agency may audit both direct and indirect costs.".

(2) CLERICAL AMENDMENT.—The table of sections at the beginning of chapter 7 of such title is amended by adding after the item relating to section 189 the following new item:

"190. Defense Cost Accounting Standards Board.".

(c) REPORT.—Not later than December 31, 2019, the Comptroller General of the United States shall submit to the congressional defense committees a report on the adequacy of the method used by the Cost Accounting Standards Board established under section 1501 of title 41, United States Code, to apply cost accounting standards to indirect and fixed price incentive contracts.

(d) EFFECTIVE DATE.—The amendments made by this section shall take effect on October 1, 2018.

SEC. 821. INCREASED MICRO-PURCHASE THRESHOLD APPLICABLE TO DEPARTMENT OF DEFENSE PROCUREMENTS.

(a) INCREASED MICRO-PURCHASE THRESHOLD.—Chapter 137 of title 10, United States Code, is amended by adding at the end the following new section:

"§ 2338. Micro-purchase threshold

"Notwithstanding subsection (a) of section 1902 of title 41, the micro-purchase threshold for the Department of Defense for purposes of such section is $5,000.".

(b) CLERICAL AMENDMENT.—The table of sections at the beginning of such chapter is amended by adding at the end the following new item:

"2338. Micro-purchase threshold.".

SEC. 822. ENHANCED COMPETITION REQUIREMENTS.

Section 2306a of title 10, United States Code, is amended—

(1) in subsection (a)(1)(A), by inserting "that is only expected to receive one bid" after "entered into using procedures other than sealed-bid procedures"; and

(2) in subsection (b)—

(A) in paragraph (1)(A)(i), by striking "price competition" and inserting "competition that results in at least two or more responsive and viable competing bids"; and

(B) by adding at the end the following new paragraph:

"(6) DETERMINATION BY PRIME CONTRACTOR.— A prime contractor required to submit certified cost or pricing data under subsection (a) with respect to a prime contract shall be responsible for determining whether a subcontract under such contract qualifies for an exception under paragraph (1)(A) from such requirement.".

SEC. 823. REVISION TO EFFECTIVE DATE OF SENIOR EXECUTIVE BENCHMARK COMPENSATION FOR ALLOWABLE COST LIMITATIONS.

(a) REPEAL OF RETROACTIVE APPLICABILITY.— Section 803(c) of the National Defense Authorization Act for Fiscal Year 2012 (Public Law 112–81; 125 Stat. 1485; 10 U.S.C. 2324 note) is amended by striking "amendments made by" and all that follows and inserting "amendments made by this section shall apply with respect to costs of compensation incurred after January 1, 2012, under contracts entered into on or after December 31, 2011.".

(b) APPLICABILITY.—The amendment made by subsection (a) shall take effect as of December 31, 2011, and shall apply as if included in the National Defense Authorization Act for Fiscal Year 2012 as enacted.

SEC. 824. TREATMENT OF INDEPENDENT RE-SEARCH AND DEVELOPMENT COSTS ON CERTAIN CONTRACTS.

(a) INDEPENDENT RESEARCH AND DEVELOPMENT COSTS: ALLOWABLE COSTS.—

(1) IN GENERAL.—Section 2372 of title 10, United States Code, is amended to read as follows:

"§ 2372. Independent research and development costs: allowable costs

"(a) REGULATIONS.—The Secretary of Defense shall prescribe regulations governing the payment by the Department of Defense of expenses incurred by contractors for independent research and development costs. Such regulations shall provide that expenses incurred for independent research and development shall be reported independently from other allowable indirect costs.

"(b) COSTS TREATED AS FAIR AND REASONABLE, AND ALLOWABLE, EXPENSES.—The regulations prescribed under subsection (a) shall provide that independent research and development costs shall be considered a fair and reasonable, and allowable, indirect expense on Department of Defense contracts.

"(c) ADDITIONAL CONTROLS.—Subject to subsection (d), the regulations prescribed under subsection (a) may include the following provisions:

"(1) Controls on the reimbursement of costs to the contractor for expenses incurred for independent research and development to ensure that such costs were incurred for independent research and development.

"(2) Implementation of regular methods for transmission—

"(A) from the Department of Defense to contractors, in a reasonable manner, of timely and comprehensive information regarding planned or expected needs of the Department of Defense for future technology and advanced capability; and

"(B) from contractors to the Department of Defense, in a reasonable manner, of information regarding progress by the contractor on the independent research and development programs of the contractor.

"(d) LIMITATIONS ON REGULATIONS.—Regulations prescribed under subsection (a) may not include provisions that would infringe on the independence of a contractor to choose which technologies to pursue in its independent research and development program if the chief executive officer of the contractor determines that expenditures will advance the needs of the Department of Defense for future technology and advanced capability as transmitted pursuant to subsection (c)(3)(A).

"(e) EFFECTIVE DATE.—The regulations prescribed under subsection (a) shall apply to indirect costs incurred on or after October 1, 2017.".

(2) CLERICAL AMENDMENT.—The table of sections at the beginning of chapter 139 is amended by striking the item relating to section 2372 and inserting the following new item:

"2372. Independent research and development costs: allowable costs".

(b) BID AND PROPOSAL COSTS: ALLOWABLE COSTS.—

(1) IN GENERAL.—Chapter 139 of title 10, United States Code, is amended by inserting after section 2372 the following new section:

"§ 2372a. Bid and proposal costs: allowable costs

"(a) REGULATIONS.—The Secretary of Defense shall prescribe regulations governing the payment by the Department of Defense of expenses incurred by contractors for bid and proposal costs. Such regulations shall provide that expenses incurred for bid and proposal costs shall be reported independently from other allowable indirect costs.

"(b) COSTS ALLOWABLE AS INDIRECT EXPENSES.—The regulations prescribed under subsection (a) shall provide that bid and proposal costs shall be allowable as indirect expenses on covered contracts, as defined in section 2324(l) of this title, to the extent that those costs are allocable, reasonable, and not otherwise unallowable by law or under the Federal Acquisition Regulation.

"(c) GOAL FOR REIMBURSABLE BID AND PROPOSAL COSTS.—The Secretary shall establish a goal each fiscal year limiting the amount of reimbursable bid and proposal costs paid by the Department of Defense to an amount equal to not more than one percent of the total aggregate industry sales to the Department of Defense. To achieve such goal, the Secretary may not limit the payment of allowable bid and proposal costs for the covered year.

"(d) PANEL.—(1) If the Department of Defense exceeds the goal established under subsection (c) for a fiscal year, within 180 days after exceeding the goal, the Secretary shall establish an advisory panel. The panel shall be supported by the Defense Acquisition University and the National Defense University, including administrative support.

"(2) The panel shall be composed of nine individuals who are recognized experts in acquisition and procurement policy appointed by the Secretary. In making such appointments, the Secretary shall ensure that the members of the panel reflect diverse experiences in the public and private sector.

"(3) The panel shall review laws, regulations, and practices that contribute to the expenses incurred by contractors for bids and proposals in the fiscal year concerned and recommend changes to such laws, regulations, and practices that may reduce expenses incurred by contractors for bids and proposals.

"(4)(A) Not later than six months after the establishment of the panel, the panel shall submit to the Secretary and the congressional defense committees an interim report on the findings of the panel.

"(B) Not later than one year after the establishment of the panel, the panel shall submit to the Secretary and the congressional defense committees a final report on the findings of the panel.

"(5) The panel shall terminate on the day the panel submits the final report under paragraph (4)(B).

"(6) The Secretary of Defense may use amounts available in the Department of Defense Acquisition Workforce Development Fund established under section 1705 of this title to support the activities of the panel established under this subsection.

"(e) EFFECTIVE DATE.—The regulations prescribed under subsection (a) shall apply to indirect costs incurred on or after October 1, 2017.".

(2) CLERICAL AMENDMENT.—The table of sections at the beginning of chapter 139 of such title is amended by inserting the following new item:

"2372a. Bid and proposal costs: allowable costs".

(c) REPORT ON ELEMENTS CONTRIBUTING TO EXPENSES INCURRED BY CONTRACTORS FOR BIDS AND PROPOSALS.—

(1) IN GENERAL.—Not later than 90 days after the date of the enactment of this Act, the Secretary of Defense shall enter into a contract with an independent entity to study the laws, regulations, and practices relating to expenses incurred by contractors for bids and proposals.

(2) REPORT.—Not later than 180 days after receipt of the contract required by paragraph (1), the independent entity shall submit to the Department of Defense and the congressional defense committees a report on the laws, regulations, or practices relating to expenses incurred

by contractors for bids and recommendations for changes to such laws, regulations, or practices that may reduce expenses incurred by contractors for bids and proposals.

(d) DEFENSE CONTRACT AUDIT AGENCY: ANNUAL REPORT.—

(1) IN GENERAL.—Subsection (a) of section 2313a of title 10, United States Code, is amended—

(A) by redesignating paragraphs (4) and (5) as paragraphs (6) and (7), respectively; and

(B) by inserting after paragraph (3) the following new paragraphs:

"(3) a summary, set forth separately by dollar amount and percentage, of indirect costs for independent research and development incurred by contractors in the previous fiscal year;

"(4) a summary, set forth separately by dollar amount and percentage, of indirect costs for bid and proposal costs incurred by contractors in the previous fiscal year;".

(2) EFFECTIVE DATE.—The amendments made by this subsection shall take effect on October 1, 2018.

SEC. 825. EXCEPTION TO REQUIREMENT TO INCLUDE COST OR PRICE TO THE GOVERNMENT AS A FACTOR IN THE EVALUATION OF PROPOSALS FOR CERTAIN MULTIPLE-AWARD TASK OR DELIVERY ORDER CONTRACTS.

(a) EXCEPTION TO REQUIREMENT TO INCLUDE COST OR PRICE AS FACTOR.—Section 2305(a)(3) of title 10, United States Code, is amended—

(1) in subparagraph (A)—

(A) in clause (i), by inserting "(except as provided in subparagraph (C))" after "shall"; and

(B) in clause (ii), by inserting "(except as provided in subparagraph (C))" after "shall"; and

(2) by adding at the end the following new subparagraphs:

"(C) If the head of an agency issues a solicitation for multiple task or delivery order contracts under section 2304a(d)(1)(B) of this title for the same or similar services and intends to make a contract award to each qualifying offeror—

"(i) cost or price to the Federal Government need not, at the Government's discretion, be considered under clause (ii) of subparagraph (A) as an evaluation factor for the contract award; and

"(ii) if, pursuant to clause (i), cost or price to the Federal Government is not considered as an evaluation factor for the contract award—

"(I) the disclosure requirement of clause (iii) of subparagraph (A) shall not apply; and

"(II) cost or price to the Federal Government shall be considered in conjunction with the issuance pursuant to section 2304c(b) of this title of a task or delivery order under any contract resulting from the solicitation.

"(D) In subparagraph (C), the term 'qualifying offeror' means an offeror that—

"(i) is determined to be a responsible source;

"(ii) submits a proposal that conforms to the requirements of the solicitation; and

"(iii) the contracting officer has no reason to believe would likely offer other than fair and reasonable pricing.

"(E) Subparagraph (C) shall not apply to multiple task or delivery order contracts if the solicitation provides for sole source task or delivery order contracts pursuant to section 8(a) of the Small Business Act (15 U.S.C. 637(a)).".

(b) AMENDMENT TO PROCEDURES RELATING TO ORDERS UNDER MULTIPLE-AWARD CONTRACTS.—Section 2304c(b) of title 10, United States Code, is amended—

(1) in paragraph (3), by striking "or" at the end;

(2) in paragraph (4), by striking the period at the end and inserting "; or"; and

(3) by adding at the end the following new paragraph:

"(5) the task or delivery order satisfies one of the exceptions in section 2304(c) of this title to the requirement to use competitive procedures.".

SEC. 826. EXTENSION OF PROGRAM FOR COMPREHENSIVE SMALL BUSINESS CONTRACTING PLANS.

Section 834(e) of the National Defense Authorization Act for Fiscal Years 1990 and 1991 (15 U.S.C. 637 note) is amended by striking "December 31, 2017" and inserting "December 31, 2027".

SEC. 827. TREATMENT OF SIDE-BY-SIDE TESTING OF CERTAIN EQUIPMENT, MUNITIONS, AND TECHNOLOGIES MANUFACTURED AND DEVELOPED UNDER COOPERATIVE RESEARCH AND DEVELOPMENT AGREEMENTS AS USE OF COMPETITIVE PROCEDURES.

Section 2350a(g) of title 10, United States Code, is amended by inserting after paragraph (2) the following new paragraph:

"(3) The use of side-by-side testing under this subsection may be considered to be the use of competitive procedures for purposes of chapter 137 of this title, when procuring items within 5 years after an initial determination that the items have been successfully tested and found to satisfy United States military requirements or to correct operational deficiencies.".

SEC. 828. DEFENSE ACQUISITION CHALLENGE PROGRAM AMENDMENTS.

(a) EXPANSION OF SCOPE TO INCLUDE SYSTEMS-OF-SYSTEMS AND FUNCTIONS.—Paragraph (2) of subsection (a) of section 2359b of title 10, United States Code, is amended by striking "or system" and all that follows through the end of the paragraph and inserting the following: "system, or system-of-systems level of an existing Department of Defense acquisition program, or to address any broader functional challenge to Department of Defense missions that may not fall within an acquisition program, that would result in improvements in performance, affordability, manufacturability, or operational capability of that acquisition program or function.".

(b) TREATMENT OF CHALLENGE PROPOSAL PROCEDURES AS USE OF COMPETITIVE PROCEDURES.—Such section is further amended—

(1) by redesignating subsections (j) and (k) as subsections (k) and (l), respectively; and

(2) by inserting after subsection (i) the following new subsection:

"(j) TREATMENT OF USE OF CERTAIN PROCEDURES AS USE OF COMPETITIVE PROCEDURES.—The use of general solicitation competitive procedures established under subsection (c) shall be considered to be the use of competitive procedures for purposes of chapter 137 of this title.".

(c) EXTENSION OF SUNSET FOR PILOT PROGRAM FOR PROGRAMS OTHER THAN MAJOR DEFENSE ACQUISITION PROGRAMS.—Such section is further amended in paragraph (5) of subsection (l), as redesignated by subsection (b)(1) of this subsection, by striking "2016" and inserting "2021".

(d) CONFORMING AMENDMENTS.—Such section is further amended—

(1) in subsection (c)(3), by inserting "or functions" after "acquisition programs";

(2) in subsection (c)(4)(A)—

(A) by striking "and" at the end of clause (i);

(B) by striking the period at the end of clause (ii) and inserting "; and"; and

(C) by adding at the end the following new clause:

"(iii) any functional challenges of importance to Department of Defense missions.";

(3) in subsection (c)(5), by adding at the end the following new subparagraph:

"(D) Whether the challenge proposal is likely to result in improvements to any functional challenges of importance to Department of Defense missions, and whether the proposal could be implemented rapidly, at an acceptable cost, and without unacceptable disruption to such missions."; and

(4) in subsection (c)(5)(B) and in subsection (e)(1), by striking "or system" and inserting "system, or system-of-systems".

SEC. 829. PREFERENCE FOR FIXED-PRICE CONTRACTS.

(a) ESTABLISHMENT OF PREFERENCE.—Not later than 180 days after the date of the enactment of this Act, the Defense Federal Acquisition Regulation Supplement shall be revised to establish a preference for fixed-price contracts, including fixed-price incentive fee contracts, in the determination of contract type.

(b) APPROVAL REQUIREMENT FOR CERTAIN COST-TYPE CONTRACTS.—

(1) IN GENERAL.—A contracting officer of the Department of Defense may not enter into a cost-type contract described in paragraph (2) unless the contract is approved by the service acquisition executive of the military department concerned, the head of the Defense Agency concerned, the commander of the combatant command concerned, or the Under Secretary of Defense for Acquisition, Technology, and Logistics (as applicable).

(2) COVERED CONTRACTS.—A contract described in this paragraph is—

(A) a cost-type contract in excess of $50,000,000, in the case of a contract entered into on or after October 1, 2018, and before October 1, 2019; and

(B) a cost-type contract in excess of $25,000,000, in the case of a contract entered into on or after October 1, 2019.

SEC. 830. REQUIREMENT TO USE FIRM FIXED-PRICE CONTRACTS FOR FOREIGN MILITARY SALES.

(a) REQUIREMENT.—Not later than 180 days after the date of the enactment of this Act, the Secretary of Defense shall prescribe regulations to require the use of firm fixed-price contracts for foreign military sales.

(b) EXCEPTIONS.—The regulations prescribed pursuant to subsection (a) shall include exceptions that may be exercised if the foreign country that is the counterparty to a foreign military sale—

(1) has established in writing a preference for a different contract type; or

(2) requests in writing that a different contract type be used for a specific foreign military sale.

(c) WAIVER AUTHORITY.—The regulations prescribed pursuant to subsection (a) shall include a waiver that may be exercised by the Secretary of Defense or his designee if the Secretary or his designee determines on a case-by-case basis that a different contract type is in the best interest of the United States and American taxpayers.

(d) PILOT PROGRAM FOR ACCELERATION OF FOREIGN MILITARY SALES.—

(1) IN GENERAL.—The Secretary of Defense shall establish a pilot program to reform and accelerate the contracting and pricing processes associated with full rate production of major weapon systems for no more than 10 foreign military sales contracts by—

(A) basing price reasonableness determinations on actual cost and pricing data for purchases of the same product for the Department of Defense; and

(B) reducing the cost and pricing data to be submitted in accordance with section 2306a of title 10, United States Code.

(2) EXPIRATION OF AUTHORITY.—Authority for the pilot program under this subsection expires on January 1, 2020.

SEC. 831. PREFERENCE FOR PERFORMANCE-BASED CONTRACT PAYMENTS.

(a) IN GENERAL.—Section 2307(b) of title 10, United States Code, is amended—

(1) in the subsection heading, by inserting "PREFERENCE FOR" before "PERFORMANCE-BASED";

(2) by redesignating paragraphs (1), (2), and (3) as subparagraphs (A), (B), and (C), respectively;

(3) by striking "Wherever practicable, payment under subsection (a) shall be made" and

inserting "(1) Whenever practicable, payments under subsection (a) shall be made using performance-based payments"; and

(4) by adding at the end the following new paragraphs:

"(2) Performance-based payments shall not be conditioned upon costs incurred in contract performance but on the achievement of performance outcomes listed in paragraph (1).

"(3) The Secretary of Defense shall ensure that nontraditional defense contractors and other private sector companies are eligible for performance-based payments, consistent with best commercial practices.

"(4)(A) In order to receive performance-based payments, a contractor's accounting system shall be in compliance with Generally Accepted Accounting Principles, and there shall be no requirement for a contractor to develop Government-unique accounting systems or practices as a prerequisite for agreeing to receive performance-based payments.

"(B) Nothing in this section shall be construed to grant the Defense Contract Audit Agency the authority to audit compliance with Generally Accepted Accounting Principles.".

(b) REGULATIONS.—Not later than 120 days after the date of the enactment of this Act, the Secretary of Defense shall revise the Department of Defense Federal Acquisition Regulation Supplement to conform with section 2307(b) of title 10, United States Code, as amended by subsection (a).

SEC. 832. CONTRACTOR INCENTIVES TO ACHIEVE SAVINGS AND IMPROVE MISSION PERFORMANCE.

Not later than 180 days after the date of the enactment of this Act, the Defense Acquisition University shall develop and implement a training program for Department of Defense acquisition personnel on fixed-priced incentive fee contracts, public-private partnerships, performance-based contracting, and other authorities in law and regulation designed to give incentives to contractors to achieve long-term savings and improve administrative practices and mission performance.

SEC. 833. SUNSET AND REPEAL OF CERTAIN CONTRACTING PROVISIONS.

(a) SUNSETS.—

(1) PLANTATIONS AND FARMS: OPERATION, MAINTENANCE, AND IMPROVEMENT.—Section 2421 of title 10, United States Code, is amended by adding at the end the following new subsection:

"(e) SUNSET.—The authority under this section shall terminate on September 30, 2018.".

(2) REQUIREMENT TO ESTABLISH COST, PERFORMANCE, AND SCHEDULE GOALS FOR MAJOR DEFENSE ACQUISITION PROGRAMS AND EACH PHASE OF RELATED ACQUISITION CYCLES.—Section 2220 of title 10, United States Code, is amended by adding at the end the following new subsection:

"(c) SUNSET.—The authority under this section shall terminate on September 30, 2018.".

(b) REPEALS.—

(1) LIMITATION ON USE OF OPERATION AND MAINTENANCE FUNDS FOR PURCHASE OF INVESTMENT ITEMS.—

(A) IN GENERAL.—Section 2245a of title 10, United States Code, is repealed.

(B) CLERICAL AMENDMENT.—The table of sections at the beginning of subchapter I of chapter 134 of such title is amended by striking the item relating to section 2245a.

(C) CONFORMING AMENDMENT.—Section 166a(e)(1)(A) of such title is amended by striking "the investment unit cost threshold in effect under section 2245a of this title" and inserting "$250,000".

(2) INFORMATION TECHNOLOGY PURCHASES: TRACKING AND MANAGEMENT.—

(A) IN GENERAL.—Section 2225 of title 10, United States Code, is repealed.

(B) CLERICAL AMENDMENT.—The table of sections at the beginning of chapter 131 of such title is amended by striking the item relating to section 2225.

(C) CONFORMING AMENDMENTS.—

(i) Section 812 of the Floyd D. Spence National Defense Authorization Act for Fiscal Year 2001 (Public Law 106–393; 114 Stat. 1654A–213; 10 U.S.C. 2225 note) is amended by striking subsections (b) and (c).

(ii) Section 2330a(j) of title 10, United States Code, is amended—

(I) by striking paragraph (2);

(II) by redesignating paragraphs (3), (4), and (5) as paragraphs (2), (3), and (4), respectively; and

(III) by adding at the end the following new paragraphs:

"(5) SIMPLIFIED ACQUISITION THRESHOLD.— The term 'simplified acquisition threshold' has the meaning given the term in section 134 of title 41.

"(6) SMALL BUSINESS ACT DEFINITIONS.—

"(A) The term 'small business concern' has the meaning given such term under section 3 of the Small Business Act (15 U.S.C. 632).

"(B) The terms 'small business concern owned and controlled by socially and economically disadvantaged individuals' and 'small business concern owned and controlled by women' have the meanings given such terms, respectively, in section 8(d)(3) of the Small Business Act (15 U.S.C. 637(d)(3)).".

(iii) Section 222(d) of the National Defense Authorization Act for Fiscal Year 2012 (Public Law 112–81; 10 U.S.C. 2358 note) is amended by striking "as defined in section 2225(f)(3)" and inserting "as defined in section 2330a(j)".

(3) PROCUREMENT OF COPIER PAPER CONTAINING SPECIFIED PERCENTAGES OF POST-CONSUMER RECYCLED CONTENT.—

(A) IN GENERAL.—Section 2378 of title 10, United States Code, is repealed.

(B) CLERICAL AMENDMENT.—The table of sections at the beginning of chapter 140 of such title is amended by striking the item relating to section 2378.

(4) LIMITATION ON PROCUREMENT OF TABLE AND KITCHEN EQUIPMENT FOR OFFICERS' QUARTERS.—

(A) IN GENERAL.—Section 2387 of title 10, United States Code, is repealed.

(B) CLERICAL AMENDMENT.—The table of sections at the beginning of chapter 141 of such title is amended by striking the item relating to section 2387.

(5) IMPLEMENTATION OF ELECTRONIC COMMERCE CAPABILITY.—

(A) REPEAL.—

(i) Section 2302c of title 10, United States Code, is repealed.

(ii) Section 2301 of title 41, United States Code, is amended by adding at the end the following new subsection:

"(f) INAPPLICABILITY TO DEPARTMENT OF DEFENSE.—In this section, the term 'executive agency' does not include the Department of Defense.".

(B) CLERICAL AMENDMENT.—The table of sections at the beginning of chapter 137 of such title is amended by striking the item relating to section 2302c.

SEC. 834. FLEXIBILITY IN CONTRACTING AWARD PROGRAM.

(a) ESTABLISHMENT OF AWARD PROGRAM.— The Secretary of Defense shall create an award to recognize those acquisition programs and professionals that make the best use of the flexibilities and authorities granted by the Federal Acquisition Regulation and Department of Defense Instruction 5000.02 (Operation of the Defense Acquisition System).

(b) PURPOSE OF AWARD.—The award established under subsection (a) shall recognize outstanding performers whose approach to program management emphasizes innovation and local adaptation, including the use of—

(1) simplified acquisition procedures;

(2) inherent flexibilities within the Federal Acquisition Regulation;

(3) commercial contracting approaches;

(4) public-private partnership agreements and practices;

(5) cost-sharing arrangements;

(6) innovative contractor incentive practices; and

(7) other innovative implementations of acquisition flexibilities.

SEC. 835. PROTECTION OF TASK ORDER COMPETITION.

(a) AMENDMENT TO VALUE OF AUTHORIZED TASK ORDER PROTESTS.—Section 2304c(e)(1)(B) of title 10, United States Code, is amended by striking "$10,000,000" and inserting "$25,000,000".

(b) REPEAL OF EFFECTIVE DATE.—Section 4106(f) of title 41, United States Code, is amended by striking paragraph (3).

SEC. 836. CONTRACT CLOSEOUT AUTHORITY.

(a) AUTHORITY.—The Secretary of Defense may close out a contract or group of contracts as described in subsection (b) through the issuance of one or more modifications to such contracts without completing a reconciliation audit or other corrective action. To accomplish closeout of such contracts—

(1) remaining contract balances may be offset with balances in other contract line items within a contract regardless of the year or type of appropriation obligated to fund each contract line item and regardless of whether the appropriation for such contract line item has closed; and

(2) remaining contract balances may be offset with balances on other contracts regardless of the year or type of appropriation obligated to fund each contract and regardless of whether the appropriation has closed.

(b) COVERED CONTRACTS.—This section covers any contract or group of contracts between the Department of Defense and a defense contractor, each one of which—

(1) was entered into prior to fiscal year 2000;

(2) has no further supplies or services deliverables due under the terms and conditions of the contract; and

(3) is determined by the Secretary of Defense to be not otherwise reconcilable because—

(A) the records have been destroyed or lost; or

(B) the records are available but the Secretary of Defense has determined that the time or effort required to determine the exact amount owed to the United States Government or amount owed to the contractor is disproportionate to the amount at issue.

(c) NEGOTIATED SETTLEMENT AUTHORITY.— Any contract or group of contracts covered by this section may be closed out through a negotiated settlement with the contractor.

(d) WAIVER AUTHORITY.—

(1) IN GENERAL.—The Secretary of Defense is authorized to waive any provision of acquisition law or regulation to carry out the authority under subsection (a).

(2) NOTIFICATION REQUIREMENT.—The Secretary of Defense shall notify the congressional defense committees not later than 10 days after exercising the authority under subsection (d). The notice shall include an identification of each provision of law or regulation waived.

(e) ADJUSTMENT AND CLOSURE OF RECORDS.— After closeout of any contract described in subsection (b) using the authority under this section, the payment or accounting offices concerned may adjust and close any open finance and accounting records relating to the contract.

(f) NO LIABILITY.—No liability shall attach to any accounting, certifying, or payment official, or any contracting officer, for any adjustments or closeout made pursuant to the authority under this section.

(g) REGULATIONS.—The Secretary of Defense shall prescribe regulations for the administration of the authority under this section.

SEC. 837. CLOSEOUT OF OLD DEPARTMENT OF THE NAVY CONTRACTS.

(a) AUTHORITY.—The Secretary of the Navy may close out contracts described in subsection (b) through the issuance of one or more modifications to such contracts without completing further reconciliation audits or corrective actions other than those described in this section. To accomplish closeout of such contracts—

(1) remaining contract balances may be offset with balances in other contract line items within a contract regardless of the year or type of appropriation obligated to fund each contract line item and regardless of whether the appropriation for such contract line item has closed; and

(2) remaining contract balances may be offset with balances on other contracts regardless of the year or type of appropriation obligated to fund each contract and regardless of whether the appropriation has closed.

(b) CONTRACTS COVERED.—The contracts covered by this section are a group of contracts that are with one contractor and identified by the Secretary, each one of which is a contract—

(1) to design, construct, repair, or support the construction or repair of Navy submarines that—

(A) was entered into between fiscal years 1974 and 1998; and

(B) has no further supply or services deliverables due under the terms and conditions of the contract;

(2) with respect to which the Secretary of the Navy has established the total final contract value; and

(3) with respect to which the Secretary of the Navy has determined that the final allowable cost may have a negative or positive unliquidated obligation balance for which it would be difficult to determine the year or type of appropriation because—

(A) the records for the contract have been destroyed or lost; or

(B) the records for the contract are available but the contracting officer, in collaboration with the certifying official, has determined that a discrepancy is of such a minimal value that the time and effort required to determine the cause of an out-of-balance condition is disproportionate to the amount of the discrepancy.

(c) CLOSEOUT TERMS.—The contracts described in subsection (b) may be closed out—

(1) upon receipt of $581,803 from the contractor to be deposited into the Treasury as miscellaneous receipts;

(2) without seeking further amounts from the contractor; and

(3) without payment to the contractor of any amounts that may be due under any such contracts.

(d) WAIVER AUTHORITY.—

(1) IN GENERAL.—The Secretary of the Navy is authorized to waive any provision of acquisition law or regulation to carry out the authority under subsection (a).

(2) NOTIFICATION REQUIREMENT.—The Secretary of the Navy shall notify the congressional defense committees not later than 10 days after exercising the authority under paragraph (1). The notice shall include an identification of each provision of law or regulation waived.

(e) ADJUSTMENT AND CLOSURE OF RECORDS.— After closeout of any contract described in subsection (b) using the authority under this section, the payment or accounting offices concerned may adjust and close any open finance and accounting records relating to the contract.

(f) NO LIABILITY.—No liability shall attach to any accounting, certifying, or payment official or contracting officer for any adjustments or closeout made pursuant to the authority under this section.

(g) EXPIRATION OF AUTHORITY.—The authority under this section shall expire upon receipt of the funds identified in subsection (c)(1).

Subtitle D—Provisions Relating to Major Defense Acquisition Programs

SEC. 841. CHANGE IN DATE OF SUBMISSION TO CONGRESS OF SELECTED ACQUISITION REPORTS.

Section 2432(f) of title 10, United States Code, is amended by striking "45" the first place it occurs and inserting "30".

SEC. 842. AMENDMENTS RELATING TO INDEPENDENT COST ESTIMATION AND COST ANALYSIS.

(a) AMENDMENTS.—Section 2334 of title 10, United States Code, is amended—

(1) in subsection (a)(3), by striking "selection of confidence levels" both places it appears and inserting "discussion of risk";

(2) in subsection (a)(6)—

(A) by inserting "or approve" after "conduct";

(B) by striking "major defense acquisition programs" and all that follows through "Authority—" and inserting "all major defense acquisition programs and major subprograms—"; and

(C) in subparagraph (B), by striking "or upon the request" and all that follows through the semicolon at the end and inserting ", upon the request of the Under Secretary of Defense for Acquisition, Technology, and Logistics, or upon the request of the milestone decision authority";

(3) by redesignating subsections (b), (c), (d), (e), and (f) as subsections (c), (d), (e), (f), and (h), respectively;

(4) by inserting after subsection (a) the following new subsection (b):

"(b) INDEPENDENT COST ESTIMATE REQUIRED BEFORE APPROVAL.—(1) A milestone decision authority may not approve entering a milestone phase of a major defense acquisition program or major subprogram unless an independent cost estimate has been conducted or approved by the Director of Cost Assessment and Program Evaluation and considered by the milestone decision authority that—

"(A) for the technology maturation and risk reduction phase, includes the identification and sensitivity analysis of key cost drivers that may affect life-cycle costs of the program or subprogram; and

"(B) for the engineering and manufacturing development phase, or production and deployment phase, includes a cost estimate of the full life-cycle cost of the program or subprogram.

"(2) The regulations governing the content and submission of independent cost estimates required by subsection (a) shall require that the independent cost estimate of the full life-cycle cost of a program or subprogram include—

"(A) all costs of development, procurement, military construction, operations and support, and trained manpower to operate, maintain, and support the program or subprogram upon full operational deployment, without regard to funding source or management control; and

"(B) an analysis to support decisionmaking that identifies and evaluates alternative courses of action that may reduce cost and risk, and result in more affordable programs and less costly systems.";

(5) in subsection (d), as so redesignated, in paragraph (3), by striking "confidence level" and inserting "discussion of risk";

(6) in subsection (e), as so redesignated—

(A) by amending the subsection heading to read as follows: "DISCUSSION OF RISK IN COST ESTIMATES.—";

(B) by amending paragraph (1) to read as follows:

"(1) issue guidance requiring a discussion of risk, the potential impacts of risk on program costs, and approaches to mitigate risk in cost estimates for major defense acquisition programs and major subprograms;";

(C) in paragraph (2)—

(i) by striking "such confidence level provides" and inserting "cost estimates are developed, to the extent practicable, based on historical actual cost information that is based on demonstrated contractor and Government performance and that such estimates provide"; and

(ii) by inserting "or subprogram" after "the program"; and

(D) in paragraph (3), by striking "disclosure required by paragraph (1)" and inserting "information required in the guidance under paragraph (1)"; and

(7) by inserting after subsection (f), as so redesignated, the following new subsection:

"(g) GUIDELINES AND COLLECTION OF COST DATA.—(1) The Director of Cost Assessment and Program Evaluation shall, in consultation with the Under Secretary of Defense for Acquisition, Technology, and Logistics, develop policies, procedures, guidance, and a collection method to ensure that quality acquisition cost data are collected to facilitate cost estimation and comparison across acquisition programs.

"(2) The program manager and contracting officer for each acquisition program in an amount greater than $100,000,000, in consultation with the cost estimating component of the relevant military department or Defense Agency, shall ensure that cost data are collected in accordance with the requirements of paragraph (1).

"(3) The requirement under paragraph (1) may be waived only by the Director of Cost Assessment and Program Evaluation.".

(b) CONFORMING AMENDMENTS TO ADD SUBPROGRAMS.—Section 2334 of such title is further amended—

(1) in subsection (a)(2), by inserting "or major subprogram" before "under chapter 144";

(2) in paragraphs (3), (4), and (5) of subsection (a) and in subsection (c)(1) (as redesignated by subsection (a) of this section), by striking "major defense acquisition programs and major automated information system programs" and inserting "major defense acquisition programs and major subprograms" each place it appears;

(3) in paragraphs (1) and (2) of subsection (d) (as so redesignated), and in subsection (f)(4) (as so redesignated), by striking "major defense acquisition program or major automated information system program" and inserting "major defense acquisition program or major subprogram" each place it appears;

(4) in subsection (d)(4) (as so redesignated), by inserting before the period "or major subprogram";

(5) in subsection (e)(3)(B) (as so redesignated), by inserting "or major subprogram" after "major defense acquisition program"; and

(6) in subsection (f)(3) (as so redesignated), by striking "major defense acquisition program and major automated information system program" and inserting "major defense acquisition program and major subprogram".

(c) REPEAL.—Chapter 144 of such title is amended—

(1) by striking section 2434; and

(2) in the table of sections at the beginning of such chapter, by striking the item relating to such section.

SEC. 843. REVISIONS TO MILESTONE B DETERMINATIONS.

Section 2366b(a)(3) of title 10, United States Code, is amended—

(1) in subparagraph (B), by striking "acquisition cost in" and all that follows through the semicolon, and inserting "life-cycle cost;"; and

(2) in subparagraph (D), by striking "funding is" and all that follows through "made," and inserting "funding is expected to be available to execute the product development and production plan for the program,".

SEC. 844. REVIEW AND REPORT ON SUSTAINMENT PLANNING IN THE ACQUISITION PROCESS.

(a) REQUIREMENT FOR REVIEW.—The Secretary of Defense shall conduct a review of the extent to which sustainment matters are considered in decisions related to the requirements, research and development, acquisition, cost estimating, and programming and budgeting processes for major defense acquisition programs. The review shall include the following:

(1) A determination of whether information related to the operation and sustainment of major defense acquisition programs, including cost data and intellectual property requirements, is available to inform decisions made during those processes.

(2) If such information exists, an evaluation of the completeness, timeliness, quality, and suitability of the information for aiding in decisions made during those processes.

(3) A determination of whether information related to the operation and sustainment of existing major weapon systems is used to forecast the operation and sustainment needs of major weapon systems proposed for or under development.

(4) A description of the potential benefits from improved completeness, timeliness, quality, and suitability of data on operation and support costs and increased consideration of such data.

(5) Recommendations for improving access to, analyses of, and consideration of operation and support cost data.

(6) An assessment of product support strategies for major weapon systems required by section 2337 of title 10, United States Code, or other similar life-cycle sustainment strategies, including an evaluation of—

(A) the stage at which such strategies are developed during the life of a major weapon system;

(B) the content and completeness of such strategies, including whether such strategies address—

(i) all aspects of total life-cycle management of a major weapon system, including product support, logistics, product support engineering, supply chain integration, maintenance, and software sustainment; and

(ii) the capabilities, capacity, and resource constraints of the organic industrial base and the materiel commands of the military department concerned;

(C) the extent to which such strategies or their elements are or should be incorporated into the acquisition strategy required by section 2431a of title 10, United States Code;

(D) the extent to which such strategies influence the planning for major defense acquisition programs; and

(E) the extent to which such strategies influence decisions related to the life-cycle management and product support of major weapon systems.

(7) An assessment of how effectively the military departments consider sustainment matters at key decision points for acquisition and life-cycle management in accordance with the requirements of sections 2431a, 2366a, 2366b, and 2337 of title 10, United States Code, and section 832 of the National Defense Authorization Act for Fiscal Year 2012 (Public Law 112–81; 10 U.S.C. 2430 note).

(8) Recommendations for improving the consideration of sustainment during the requirements, acquisition, cost estimating, programming and budgeting processes.

(9) An assessment of whether research and development efforts and adoption of commercial technologies is prioritized to reduce sustainment costs.

(10) An assessment of whether alternate financing methods, including share-in-savings approaches, public-private partnerships, and

energy savings performance contracts, could be used to encourage the development and adoption of technologies and practices that will reduce sustainment costs.

"(11) An assessment of private sector best practices in assessing and reducing sustainment costs for complex systems.

"(b) AGREEMENT WITH INDEPENDENT ENTITY.— Not later than 60 days after the date of the enactment of this Act, the Secretary shall enter into an agreement with an independent entity with appropriate expertise to conduct the review required by subsection (a). The Secretary shall ensure that the independent entity has access to all data, information, and personnel required, and is funded, to satisfactorily complete the review required by subsection (a). The agreement also shall require the entity to provide to the Secretary a report on the findings of the entity.

"(c) BRIEFING.—Not later than April 1, 2017, the Secretary shall provide a briefing to the Committees on Armed Services of the Senate and House of Representatives on the preliminary findings of the independent entity.

"(d) SUBMISSION TO CONGRESS.—Not later than August 1, 2017, the Secretary shall submit to the congressional defense committees a copy of the report of the independent entity, along with comments on the report, proposed revisions or clarifications to laws related to lifecycle management or sustainment planning for major weapon systems, and a description of any actions the Secretary may take to revise or clarify regulations and practices related to life-cycle management or sustainment planning for major weapon systems".

SEC. 845. REVISION TO DISTRIBUTION OF ANNUAL REPORT ON OPERATIONAL TEST AND EVALUATION.

Section 139(h) of title 10, United States Code, is amended—

(1) in paragraph (2)—

(A) by inserting "the Secretaries of the military departments," after "Logistics,"; and

(B) by striking "10 days" and all that follows through "title 31" and inserting "January 31 of each year, through January 31, 2021"; and

(2) in paragraph (5), by inserting after "Secretary" the following: "of Defense and the Secretaries of the military departments".

SEC. 846. REPEAL OF MAJOR AUTOMATED INFORMATION SYSTEMS PROVISIONS.

Effective September 30, 2017—

(1) chapter 144A of title 10, United States Code, is repealed;

(2) the tables of chapters at the beginning of subtitle A of such title, and at the beginning of part IV of subtitle A, are amended by striking the item relating to chapter 144A; and

(3) section 2334(a)(2) of title 10, United States Code, is amended by striking "or a major automated information system under chapter 144A of this title".

SEC. 847. REVISIONS TO DEFINITION OF MAJOR DEFENSE ACQUISITION PROGRAM.

(a) IN GENERAL.—Section 2430 of title 10, United States Code, is amended in subsection (a)—

(1) by redesignating paragraphs (1) and (2) as subparagraphs (A) and (B), respectively;

(2) by striking "In this chapter" and inserting "(1) Except as provided under paragraph (2), in this chapter"; and

(3) by adding at the end the following new paragraph:

"(2) In this chapter, the term 'major defense acquisition program' does not include an acquisition program or project that is carried out using the rapid fielding or rapid prototyping acquisition pathway under section 804 of the National Defense Authorization Act for Fiscal Year 2016 (Public Law 114–92; 10 U.S.C. 2302 note).".

(b) ANNUAL REPORTING.—The Secretary of Defense shall include in each comprehensive annual Selected Acquisition Report submitted under section 2432 of title 10, United States Code, a listing of all programs or projects being developed or procured under the exceptions to the definition of major defense acquisition program set forth in paragraph (2) of section 2430(a) of United States Code, as added by subsection (a)(1)(C) of this section.

SEC. 848. ACQUISITION STRATEGY.

Section 2431a of title 10, United States Code, is amended—

(1) in subsection (b), by inserting ", or the milestone decision authority, when the milestone decision authority is the service acquisition executive of the military department that is managing the program," after "the Under Secretary of Defense for Acquisition, Technology, and Logistics";

(2) in subsection (c)—

(A) in paragraph (1), by inserting ", or the milestone decision authority, when the milestone decision authority is the service acquisition executive of the military department that is managing the program," after "the Under Secretary"; and

(B) in paragraph (2)(C), by striking ", in accordance with section 2431b of this title"; and

(3) in subsection (d)—

(A) in paragraph (1), by striking "(1) Subject to the authority, direction, and control of the Under Secretary of Defense for Acquisition, Technology, and Logistics, the" and inserting "The"; and

(B) in paragraph (2), by inserting "because of a change described in paragraph (1)(F)" after "for a program or system".

SEC. 849. IMPROVED LIFE-CYCLE COST CONTROL.

(a) MODIFIED GUIDANCE FOR RAPID FIELDING PATHWAY.—Section 804(c)(3) of the National Defense Authorization Act for Fiscal Year 2016 (Public Law 114–92; 10 U.S.C. 2302 note) is amended—

(1) in subparagraph (C), by striking "; and" and inserting a semicolon;

(2) in subparagraph (D), by striking the period at the end and inserting "; and"; and

(3) by adding at the end the following new subparagraph:

"(E) a process for identifying and exploiting opportunities to use the rapid fielding pathway to reduce total ownership costs.".

(b) LIFE-CYCLE COST MANAGEMENT.—Section 805(2) of such Act (Public Law 114–92; 10 U.S.C. 2302 note) is amended by inserting "life-cycle cost management," after "budgeting,".

(c) SUSTAINMENT REVIEWS.—

(1) IN GENERAL.—Chapter 144 of title 10, United States Code, is amended by adding at the end the following new section:

"**§ 2441. Sustainment reviews**

"(a) IN GENERAL.—The Secretary of each military department shall conduct a sustainment review of each major weapon system not later than five years after declaration of initial operational capability of a major defense acquisition program and throughout the life cycle of the weapon system to assess the product support strategy, performance, and operation and support costs of the weapon system. For any review after the first one, the Secretary concerned shall use availability and reliability thresholds and cost estimates as the basis for the circumstances that prompt such a review. The results of the sustainment review shall be documented in a memorandum by the relevant decision authority.

"(b) ELEMENTS.—At a minimum, the review required under subsection (a) shall include the following elements:

"(1) An independent cost estimate for the remainder of the life cycle of the program.

"(2) A comparison of actual costs to the amount of funds budgeted and appropriated in the previous five years, and if funding shortfalls exist, an explanation of the implications on equipment availability.

"(3) A comparison between the assumed and achieved system reliabilities.

"(4) An analysis of the most cost-effective source of repairs and maintenance.

"(5) An evaluation of the cost of consumables and depot-level repairables.

"(6) An evaluation of the costs of information technology, networks, computer hardware, and software maintenance and upgrades.

"(7) As applicable, an assessment of the actual fuel efficiencies compared to the projected fuel efficiencies as demonstrated in tests or operations.

"(8) As applicable, a comparison of actual manpower requirements to previous estimates.

"(9) An analysis of whether accurate and complete data are being reported in the cost systems of the military department concerned, and if deficiencies exist, a plan to update the data and ensure accurate and complete data are submitted in the future.

"(c) COORDINATION.—The review required under subsection (a) shall be conducted in coordination with the requirements of section 2337 of this title and section 832 of the National Defense Authorization Act for Fiscal Year 2012 (Public Law 112–81; 10 U.S.C. 2430 note).

"(2) CLERICAL AMENDMENT.—The table of sections at the beginning of such chapter is amended by adding at the end the following new item:

"2441. Sustainment reviews.".

(d) COMMERCIAL OPERATIONAL AND SUPPORT SAVINGS INITIATIVE.—

(1) IN GENERAL.—The Secretary of Defense may establish a commercial operational and support savings initiative to improve readiness and reduce operations and support costs by inserting existing commercial items or technology into military legacy systems through the rapid development of prototypes and fielding of production items based on current commercial technology.

(2) PROGRAM PRIORITY.—The commercial operational and support savings initiative shall fund programs that—

(A) reduce the costs of owning and operating a military system, including the costs of personnel, consumables, goods and services, and sustaining the support and investment associated with the peacetime operation of a weapon system;

(B) take advantage of the commercial sector's technological innovations by inserting commercial technology into fielded weapon systems; and

(C) emphasize prototyping and experimentation with new technologies and concepts of operations.

(3) FUNDING PHASES.—

(A) IN GENERAL.—Projects funded under the commercial operational and support savings initiative shall consist of two phases, Phase I and Phase II.

(B) PHASE I.—(i) Funds made available during Phase I shall be used to perform the non-recurring engineering, testing, and qualification that are typically needed to adapt a commercial item or technology for use in a military system.

(ii) Phase I shall include—

(I) establishment of cost and performance metrics to evaluate project success;

(II) establishment of a transition plan and agreement with a military department or Defense Agency for adoption and sustainment of the technology or system; and

(III) the development, fabrication, and delivery of a demonstrated prototype to a military department for installation into a fielded Department of Defense system.

(iii) Programs shall be terminated if no agreement is established within two years of project initiation.

(iv) The Office of the Secretary of Defense may provide up to 50 percent of Phase I funding for a project. The military department or Defense Agency concerned may provide the remainder of Phase I funding, which may be provided out of operation and maintenance funding.

(v) Phase I funding shall not exceed three years.

(vi) Phase I projects shall be selected based on a merit-based process using criteria to be established by the Secretary of Defense.

(C) PHASE II.—(i) Phase II shall include the purchase of limited production quantities of the prototype kits and transition to a program of record for continued sustainment.

(ii) Phase II awards may be made without competition if general solicitation competitive procedures were used for the selection of parties for participation in a Phase I project.

(iii) Phase II awards may be made as firm fixed-price awards.

(4) TREATMENT AS COMPETITIVE PROCEDURES.—The use of a merit-based process for selection of projects under the commercial operational and support savings initiative shall be considered to be the use of competitive procedures for purposes of chapter 137 of title 10, United States Code.

SEC. 850. AUTHORITY TO DESIGNATE INCREMENTS OR BLOCKS OF ITEMS DELIVERED UNDER MAJOR DEFENSE ACQUISITION PROGRAMS AS MAJOR SUBPROGRAMS FOR PURPOSES OF ACQUISITION REPORTING.

Section 2430a(1)(B) of title 10, United States Code, is amended by striking "major defense acquisition program to purchase satellites requires the delivery of satellites in two or more increments or blocks" and inserting "major defense acquisition program requires the delivery of two or more increments or blocks".

SEC. 851. REPORTING OF SMALL BUSINESS PARTICIPATION ON DEPARTMENT OF DEFENSE PROGRAMS.

(a) REPORT REQUIREMENT.—Not later than March 31 of each year, the Secretary of Defense shall submit to the congressional defense committees a report covering the following matters for the preceding fiscal year:

(1) For each prime contract goal established by section 15(g)(1)(A) of the Small Business Act (15 U.S.C. 644(g)(1)(A)), the total value and percentage of prime contracts awarded by the Department of Defense and attributed to each prime contract goal for prime contracts awarded for major defense acquisition programs.

(2) For each subcontract goal established by section 15(g)(1)(A) of the Small Business Act (15 U.S.C. 644(g)(1)(A)), the total value and percentage of first tier subcontract awards attributed to each subcontract goal for subcontracts awarded in support of prime contracts awarded by the Department of Defense for major defense acquisition programs.

(3) For the prime contract and subcontract goals negotiated with the Department of Defense pursuant to section 15(g)(2) of the Small Business Act (15 U.S.C. 644(g)(2))—

(A) the information reported by the Department of Defense to the Small Business Administration pursuant to section 15(h)(1) of the Small Business Act (15 U.S.C. 644(h)(1)); and

(B) the information required by subparagraph (A) calculated after excluding—

(i) contracts awarded pursuant to chapter 85 of title 41, United States Code (popularly referred to as the Javits-Wagner-O'Day Act);

(ii) contracts awarded to the American Institute in Taiwan;

(iii) contracts awarded and performed outside of the United States;

(iv) acquisition on behalf of foreign governments, entities, or international organizations; and

(v) contracts for major defense acquisition programs.

(b) SUNSET.—The requirement to submit a report under subsection (a) shall not apply after the Secretary submits the report covering fiscal year 2020.

SEC. 852. WAIVER OF CONGRESSIONAL NOTIFICATION FOR ACQUISITION OF TACTICAL MISSILES AND MUNITIONS GREATER THAN QUANTITY SPECIFIED IN LAW.

Section 2308(c) of title 10, United States Code, is amended—

(1) by inserting "(1)" before "The head";

(2) by inserting ", except as provided in paragraph (2)," after "but"; and

(3) by adding at the end the following new paragraph:

"(2) A notification is not required under paragraph (1) if the end item being acquired in a higher quantity is an end item under a tactical missile program or a munitions program.".

SEC. 853. MULTIPLE PROGRAM MULTIYEAR CONTRACT PILOT DEMONSTRATION PROGRAM.

(a) AUTHORITY.—The Secretary of Defense may conduct a multiyear contract, over a period of up to four years, for the purchase of units for multiple defense programs that are produced at common facilities at a high rate, and which maximize commonality, efficiencies, and quality, in order to provide maximum benefit to the Department of Defense. Contracts awarded under this section should allow for significant savings, as determined consistent with the authority under section 2306b of title 10, United States Code, to be achieved as compared to using separate annual contracts under individual programs to purchase such units, and may include flexible delivery across the overall period of performance.

(b) SCOPE.—The contracts authorized in subsection (a) shall at a minimum provide for the acquisition of units from three discrete programs from two of the military departments.

(c) DOCUMENTATION.—Each contract awarded under subsection (a) shall include the documentation required to be provided for a multiyear contract proposal under section 2306b(i) of title 10.

(d) DEFINITIONS.—In this section:

(1) The term "high rate" means total annual production across the multiple defense programs of more than 200 end-items per year.

(2) The term "common facilities" means production facilities operating within the same general and allowable rate structure.

(e) SUNSET.—No new contracts may be awarded under the authority of this section after September 30, 2021.

SEC. 854. KEY PERFORMANCE PARAMETER REDUCTION PILOT PROGRAM.

(a) IN GENERAL.—The Secretary of Defense may carry out a pilot program under which the Secretary may identify at least one acquisition program in each military department for reduction of the total number of key performance parameters established for the program, for purposes of determining whether operational and programmatic outcomes of the program are improved by such reduction.

(b) LIMITATION ON KEY PERFORMANCE PARAMETERS.—Any acquisition program identified for the pilot program carried out under subsection (a) shall establish no more than three key performance parameters, each of which shall describe a program-specific performance attribute. Any key performance parameters for such a program that are required by statute shall be treated as key system attributes.

SEC. 855. MISSION INTEGRATION MANAGEMENT.

(a) IN GENERAL.—The Secretary of Defense shall establish mission integration management activities for each mission area specified in subsection (b).

(b) COVERED MISSION AREAS.—The mission areas specified in this subsection are mission areas that involve multiple Armed Forces and multiple programs and, at a minimum, include the following:

(1) Close air support.

(2) Air defense and offensive and defensive counter-air.

(3) Interdiction.

(4) Intelligence, surveillance, and reconnaissance.

(5) Any other overlapping mission area of significance, as jointly designated by the Deputy Secretary of Defense and the Vice Chairman of the Joint Chiefs of Staff for purposes of this subsection.

(c) QUALIFICATIONS.—Mission integration management activities shall be performed by qualified personnel from the acquisition and operational communities.

(d) RESPONSIBILITIES.—The mission integration management activities for a mission area under this section shall include—

(1) development of technical infrastructure for engineering, analysis, and test, including data, modeling, analytic tools, and simulations;

(2) the conduct of tests, demonstrations, exercises, and focused experiments for compelling challenges and opportunities;

(3) overseeing the implementation of section 2446c of title 10, United States Code;

(4) sponsoring and overseeing research on and development of (including tests and demonstrations) automated tools for composing systems of systems on demand;

(5) developing mission-based inputs for the requirements process, assessment of concepts, prototypes, design options, budgeting and resource allocation, and program and portfolio management; and

(6) coordinating with commanders of the combatant commands on the development of concepts of operation and operational plans.

(e) SCOPE.—The mission integration management activities for a mission area under this subsection shall extend to the supporting elements for the mission area, such as communications, command and control, electronic warfare, and intelligence.

(f) FUNDING.—There is authorized to be made available annually such amounts as the Secretary of Defense determines appropriate from the Rapid Prototyping Fund established under section 804(d) of the National Defense Authorization Act for Fiscal Year 2016 (Public Law 114–92; 10 U.S.C. 2302 note) for mission integration management activities listed in subsection (d).

(g) STRATEGY.—The Secretary of Defense shall submit to the congressional defense committees, at the same time as the budget for the Department of Defense for fiscal year 2018 is submitted to Congress pursuant to section 1105 of title 31, United States Code, a strategy for mission integration management, including a resourcing strategy for mission integration managers to carry out the responsibilities specified in this section.

Subtitle E—Provisions Relating to Acquisition Workforce

SEC. 861. PROJECT MANAGEMENT.

(a) DEPUTY DIRECTOR FOR MANAGEMENT.—

(1) ADDITIONAL FUNCTIONS.—Section 503 of title 31, United States Code, is amended by adding at the end the following:

"(c) PROGRAM AND PROJECT MANAGEMENT.—

"(1) REQUIREMENT.—Subject to the direction and approval of the Director, the Deputy Director for Management or a designee shall—

"(A) adopt governmentwide standards, policies, and guidelines for program and project management for executive agencies;

"(B) oversee implementation of program and project management for the standards, policies,

and guidelines established under subparagraph (A);

"(C) chair the Program Management Policy Council established under section 1126(b);

"(D) establish standards and policies for executive agencies, consistent with widely accepted standards for program and project management planning and delivery;

"(E) engage with the private sector to identify best practices in program and project management that would improve Federal program and project management;

"(F) conduct portfolio reviews to address programs identified as high risk by the Government Accountability Office;

"(G) not less than annually, conduct portfolio reviews of agency programs in coordination with Project Management Improvement Officers designated under section 1126(a)(1) to assess the quality and effectiveness of program management; and

"(H) establish a 5-year strategic plan for program and project management.

"(2) APPLICATION TO DEPARTMENT OF DEFENSE.—Paragraph (1) shall not apply to the Department of Defense to the extent that the provisions of that paragraph are substantially similar to or duplicative of—

"(A) the provisions of chapter 87 of title 10; or

"(B) policy, guidance, or instruction of the Department related to program management.".

(2) DEADLINE FOR STANDARDS, POLICIES, AND GUIDELINES.—Not later than 1 year after the date of enactment of this Act, the Deputy Director for Management of the Office of Management and Budget shall issue the standards, policies, and guidelines required under section 503(c) of title 31, United States Code, as added by paragraph (1).

(3) REGULATIONS.—Not later than 90 days after the date on which the standards, policies, and guidelines are issued under paragraph (2), the Deputy Director for Management of the Office of Management and Budget, in consultation with the Program Management Policy Council established under section 1126(b) of title 31, United States Code, as added by subsection (b)(1), and the Director of the Office of Management and Budget, shall issue any regulations as are necessary to implement the requirements of section 503(c) of title 31, United States Code, as added by paragraph (1).

(b) PROGRAM MANAGEMENT IMPROVEMENT OFFICERS AND PROGRAM MANAGEMENT POLICY COUNCIL.—

(1) AMENDMENT.—Chapter 11 of title 31, United States Code, is amended by adding at the end the following:

"§ 1126. Program Management Improvement Officers and Program Management Policy Council

"(a) PROGRAM MANAGEMENT IMPROVEMENT OFFICERS.—

"(1) DESIGNATION.—The head of each agency described in section 901(b) shall designate a senior executive of the agency as the Program Management Improvement Officer of the agency.

"(2) FUNCTIONS.—The Program Management Improvement Officer of an agency designated under paragraph (1) shall—

"(A) implement program management policies established by the agency under section 503(c); and

"(B) develop a strategy for enhancing the role of program managers within the agency that includes the following:

"(i) Enhanced training and educational opportunities for program managers that shall include—

"(I) training in the relevant competencies encompassed with program and project manager within the private sector for program managers; and

"(II) training that emphasizes cost containment for large projects and programs.

"(ii) Mentoring of current and future program managers by experienced senior executives and program managers within the agency.

"(iii) Improved career paths and career opportunities for program managers.

"(iv) A plan to encourage the recruitment and retention of highly qualified individuals to serve as program managers.

"(v) Improved means of collecting and disseminating best practices and lessons learned to enhance program management across the agency.

"(vi) Common templates and tools to support improved data gathering and analysis for program management and oversight purposes.

"(3) APPLICATION TO DEPARTMENT OF DEFENSE.—This subsection shall not apply to the Department of Defense to the extent that the provisions of this subsection are substantially similar to or duplicative of the provisions of chapter 87 of title 10. For purposes of paragraph (1), the Under Secretary of Defense for Acquisition, Technology, and Logistics (or a designee of the Under Secretary) shall be considered the Program Management Improvement Officer.

"(b) PROGRAM MANAGEMENT POLICY COUNCIL.—

"(1) ESTABLISHMENT.—There is established in the Office of Management and Budget a council to be known as the 'Program Management Policy Council' (in this subsection referred to as the 'Council').

"(2) PURPOSE AND FUNCTIONS.—The Council shall act as the principal interagency forum for improving agency practices related to program and project management. The Council shall—

"(A) advise and assist the Deputy Director for Management of the Office of Management and Budget;

"(B) review programs identified as high risk by the Government Accountability Office and make recommendations for actions to be taken by the Deputy Director for Management of the Office of Management and Budget or a designee;

"(C) discuss topics of importance to the workforce, including—

"(i) career development and workforce development needs;

"(ii) policy to support continuous improvement in program and project management; and

"(iii) major challenges across agencies in managing programs;

"(D) advise on the development and applicability of standards governmentwide for program management transparency; and

"(E) review the information published on the website of the Office of Management and Budget pursuant to section 1122.

"(3) MEMBERSHIP.—

"(A) COMPOSITION.—The Council shall be composed of the following members:

"(i) Five members from the Office of Management and Budget as follows:

"(I) The Deputy Director for Management.

"(II) The Administrator of the Office of Electronic Government.

"(III) The Administrator of Federal Procurement Policy.

"(IV) The Controller of the Office of Federal Financial Management.

"(V) The Director of the Office of Performance and Personnel Management.

"(ii) The Program Management Improvement Officer from each agency described in section 901(b).

"(iii) Any other full-time or permanent part-time officer or employee of the Federal Government or member of the Armed Forces designated by the Chairperson.

"(B) CHAIRPERSON AND VICE CHAIRPERSON.—

"(i) IN GENERAL.—The Deputy Director for Management of the Office of Management and Budget shall be the Chairperson of the Council.

A Vice Chairperson shall be elected by the members and shall serve a term of not more than 1 year.

"(ii) DUTIES.—The Chairperson shall preside at the meetings of the Council, determine the agenda of the Council, direct the work of the Council, and establish and direct subgroups of the Council as appropriate.

"(4) MEETINGS.—The Council shall meet not less than twice per fiscal year and may meet at the call of the Chairperson or a majority of the members of the Council.

"(5) SUPPORT.—The head of each agency with a Project Management Improvement Officer serving on the Council shall provide administrative support to the Council, as appropriate, at the request of the Chairperson.".

(2) REPORT REQUIRED.—Not later than 1 year after the date of the enactment of this Act, the Director of the Office of Management and Budget, in consultation with each Program Management Improvement Officer designated under section 1126(a)(1) of title 31, United States Code, shall submit to Congress a report containing the strategy developed under section 1126(a)(2)(B) of such title, as added by paragraph (1).

(c) PROGRAM AND PROJECT MANAGEMENT PERSONNEL STANDARDS.—

(1) DEFINITION.—In this subsection, the term "agency" means each agency described in section 901(b) of title 31, United States Code, other than the Department of Defense.

(2) REGULATIONS REQUIRED.—Not later than 180 days after the date on which the standards, policies, and guidelines are issued under section 503(c) of title 31, United States Code, as added by subsection (a)(1), the Director of the Office of Personnel Management, in consultation with the Director of the Office of Management and Budget, shall issue regulations that—

(A) identify key skills and competencies needed for a program and project manager in an agency;

(B) establish a new job series, or update and improve an existing job series, for program and project management within an agency; and

(C) establish a new career path for program and project managers within an agency.

(d) GAO REPORT ON EFFECTIVENESS OF POLICIES ON PROGRAM AND PROJECT MANAGEMENT.—Not later than 3 years after the date of enactment of this Act, the Comptroller General of the United States shall issue, in conjunction with the high risk list of the Government Accountability Office, a report examining the effectiveness of the following on improving Federal program and project management:

(1) The standards, policies, and guidelines for program and project management issued under section 503(c) of title 31, United States Code, as added by subsection (a)(1).

(2) The 5-year strategic plan established under section 503(c)(1)(H) of title 31, United States Code, as added by subsection (a)(1).

(3) Program Management Improvement Officers designated under section 1126(a)(1) of title 31, United States Code, as added by subsection (b)(1).

(4) The Program Management Policy Council established under section 1126(b)(1) of title 31, United States Code, as added by subsection (b)(1).

SEC. 862. AUTHORITY TO WAIVE TENURE REQUIREMENT FOR PROGRAM MANAGERS FOR PROGRAM DEFINITION AND PROGRAM EXECUTION PERIODS.

(a) PROGRAM DEFINITION PERIOD.—Section 826(e) of the National Defense Authorization Act for Fiscal Year 2016 (Public Law 114–92) is amended by striking "The Secretary may waive" and inserting "The service acquisition executive, in the case of a major defense acquisition program of a military department, or the

Under Secretary of Defense for Acquisition, Technology, and Logistics, in the case of a Defense-wide or Defense Agency major defense acquisition program, may waive''.

(b) PROGRAM EXECUTION PERIOD.—Section 827(e) of the National Defense Authorization Act for Fiscal Year 2016 (Public Law 114–92) is amended by striking ''The immediate supervisor of a program manager for a major defense acquisition program may waive'' and inserting ''The service acquisition executive, in the case of a major defense acquisition program of a military department, or the Under Secretary of Defense for Acquisition, Technology, and Logistics, in the case of a Defense-wide or Defense Agency major defense acquisition program, may waive''.

SEC. 863. PURPOSES FOR WHICH THE DEPARTMENT OF DEFENSE ACQUISITION WORKFORCE DEVELOPMENT FUND MAY BE USED; ADVISORY PANEL AMENDMENTS.

(a) IN GENERAL.—Section 1705 of title 10, United States Code, is amended—

(1) in subsection (e)—

(A) in paragraph (1), by inserting ''and to develop acquisition tools and methodologies, and undertake research and development activities, leading to acquisition policies and practices that will improve the efficiency and effectiveness of defense acquisition efforts'' after ''workforce of the Department''; and

(B) in paragraph (4), by striking ''other than for the purpose of'' and all that follows through the period at the end and inserting ''other than for the purposes of—

''(A) providing advanced training to Department of Defense employees;

''(B) developing acquisition tools and methodologies and performing research on acquisition policies and best practices that will improve the efficiency and effectiveness of defense acquisition efforts; and

''(C) supporting human capital and talent management of the acquisition workforce, including benchmarking studies, assessments, and requirements planning.''; and

(2) in subsection (f), by striking ''Each report shall include'' and all that follows through the period at the end of paragraph (5).

(b) TECHNICAL AMENDMENTS.—Such section is further amended—

(1) in subsection (d)(2)(C), by striking ''in each'' and inserting ''in such'';

(2) in subsection (f)—

(A) by striking ''Not later than 120 days after the end of each fiscal year'' and inserting ''Not later than February 1 each year''; and

(B) by striking ''such fiscal year'' the first place it appears and inserting ''the preceding fiscal year''; and

(3) in subsection (g)(1)—

(A) by striking ''of of'' and inserting ''of''; and

(B) by striking '', as defined in subsection (h),''.

(c) LIMITATION ON AVAILABILITY OF FUNDS FOR CERTAIN PURPOSES.—Of the amounts authorized to be appropriated by this Act or otherwise made available for fiscal year 2017, not more than $35,000,000 may be obligated or expended for the purposes set forth in subparagraphs (B) and (C) of section 1705(e)(4) of title 10, United States Code, as added by subsection (a).

(d) AMENDMENTS TO ADVISORY PANEL ON STREAMLINING AND CODIFYING ACQUISITION REGULATIONS.—Section 809 of the National Defense Authorization Act for Fiscal Year 2016 (Public Law 114–92; 129 Stat. 889) is amended—

(1) by amending subsection (a) to read as follows:

''(a) ESTABLISHMENT.—The Secretary of Defense shall establish an independent advisory panel on streamlining acquisition regulations.

The panel shall be supported by the Defense Acquisition University and the National Defense University, including administrative support.''; and

(2) in subsection (d)—

(A) in paragraph (1), by striking ''and analysis'' and inserting '', analysis, and logistics support''; and

(B) by adding at the end the following new paragraph:

''(3) AUTHORITIES.—The panel shall have the authorities provided in section 3161 of title 5, United States Code.''.

SEC. 864. DEPARTMENT OF DEFENSE ACQUISITION WORKFORCE DEVELOPMENT FUND DETERMINATION ADJUSTMENT.

(a) CREDIT TO RAPID PROTOTYPING FUND.—Notwithstanding section 1705(d)(2)(B) of title 10, United States Code, of the funds credited to the Department of Defense Acquisition Workforce Development Fund in fiscal year 2017 pursuant to such section, $225,000,000 shall be transferred to the Rapid Prototyping Fund established under section 804(d) of the National Defense Authorization Act for Fiscal Year 2016 (Public Law 114–92; 10 U.S.C. 2302 note). Of the $225,000,000 so transferred, $75,000,000 shall be credited to each of the military department-specific funds established under section 804(d)(2) of such Act (as added by section 897 of this Act).

(b) TECHNICAL AND CONFORMING AMENDMENTS.—Section 804(d)(1) of the National Defense Authorization Act for Fiscal Year 2016 (Public Law 114–92; 10 U.S.C. 2302 note) is amended—

(1) in the first sentence, by inserting a comma after ''may be available'';

(2) at the end of the first sentence, by inserting before the period the following: ''and other purposes specified in law''; and

(3) in the last sentence, by striking ''shall consist of'' and all that follows through ''this Act.'' and inserting the following: ''shall consist of—

''(i) amounts appropriated to the Fund;

''(ii) amounts credited to the Fund pursuant to section 828 of this Act; and

''(iii) any other amounts appropriated to, credited to, or transferred to the Fund.''.

SEC. 865. LIMITATIONS ON FUNDS USED FOR STAFF AUGMENTATION CONTRACTS AT MANAGEMENT HEADQUARTERS OF THE DEPARTMENT OF DEFENSE AND THE MILITARY DEPARTMENTS.

(a) LIMITATIONS.—

(1) FOR FISCAL YEARS 2017 AND 2018.—The total amount obligated by the Department of Defense for fiscal year 2017 or 2018 for contract services for staff augmentation contracts at management headquarters of the Department and the military departments may not exceed an amount equal to the aggregate amount expended by the Department for contract services for staff augmentation contracts at management headquarters of the Department and the military departments in fiscal year 2016 adjusted for net transfers from funding for overseas contingency operations (in this subsection referred to as the ''fiscal year 2016 staff augmentation contracts funding amount'').

(2) FOR FISCAL YEARS 2018 THROUGH 2022.—The total amount obligated by the Department for any fiscal year after fiscal year 2018 and before fiscal year 2023 for contract services for staff augmentation contracts at management headquarters of the Department and the military departments may not exceed an amount equal to 75 percent of the fiscal year 2016 staff augmentation contracts funding amount.

(b) DEFINITIONS.—In this section:

(1) The term ''contract services'' has the meaning given that term in section 235 of title 10, United States Code.

(2) The term ''staff augmentation contracts'' means services contracts for personnel who are

physically present in a Government work space on a full-time or permanent part-time basis, for the purpose of advising on, providing support to, or assisting a Government agency in the performance of the agency's missions, including authorized personal services contracts (as that term is defined in section 2330a(g)(5) of title 10, United States Code).

SEC. 866. SENIOR MILITARY ACQUISITION ADVISORS IN THE DEFENSE ACQUISITION CORPS.

(a) POSITIONS.—

(1) IN GENERAL.—Subchapter II of chapter 87 of title 10, United States Code, is amended by adding at the end the following new section:

''§ 1725. Senior Military Acquisition Advisors

''(a) POSITION.—

''(1) IN GENERAL.—The Secretary of Defense may establish in the Defense Acquisition Corps a position to be known as 'Senior Military Acquisition Advisor'.

''(2) APPOINTMENT.—A Senior Military Acquisition Advisor shall be appointed by the President, by and with the advice and consent of the Senate.

''(3) SCOPE OF POSITION.—An officer who is appointed as a Senior Military Acquisition Advisor—

''(A) shall serve as an advisor to, and provide senior level acquisition expertise to, the service acquisition executive of that officer's military department in accordance with this section; and

''(B) shall be assigned as an adjunct professor at the Defense Acquisition University.

''(b) CONTINUATION ON ACTIVE DUTY.—An officer who is appointed as a Senior Military Acquisition Advisor may continue on active duty while serving in such position without regard to any mandatory retirement date that would otherwise be applicable to that officer by reason of years of service or age. An officer who is continued on active duty pursuant to this section is not eligible for consideration for selection for promotion.

''(c) RETIRED GRADE.—Upon retirement, an officer who is a Senior Military Acquisition Advisor may, in the discretion of the President, be retired in the grade of brigadier general or rear admiral (lower half) if—

''(1) the officer has served as a Senior Military Acquisition Advisor for a period of not less than three years; and

''(2) the officer's service as a Senior Military Acquisition Advisor has been distinguished.

''(d) SELECTION AND TENURE.—

''(1) IN GENERAL.—Selection of an officer for recommendation for appointment as a Senior Military Acquisition Advisor shall be made competitively, and shall be based upon demonstrated experience and expertise in acquisition.

''(2) OFFICERS ELIGIBLE.—Officers shall be selected for recommendation for appointment as Senior Military Acquisition Advisors from among officers of the Defense Acquisition Corps who are serving in the grade of colonel or, in the case of the Navy, captain, and who have at least 12 years of acquisition experience. An officer selected for recommendation for appointment as a Senior Military Acquisition Advisor shall have at least 30 years of active commissioned service at the time of appointment.

''(3) TERM.—The appointment of an officer as a Senior Military Acquisition Advisor shall be for a term of not longer than five years.

''(e) LIMITATION.—

''(1) LIMITATION ON NUMBER AND DISTRIBUTION.—There may not be more than 15 Senior Military Acquisition Advisors at any time, of whom—

''(A) not more than five may be officers of the Army;

''(B) not more than five may be officers of the Navy and Marine Corps; and

"(C) not more than five may be officers of the Air Force.

"(2) NUMBER IN EACH MILITARY DEPARTMENT.—Subject to paragraph (1), the number of Senior Military Acquisition Advisors for each military department shall be as required and identified by the service acquisition executive of such military department and approved by the Under Secretary of Defense for Acquisition, Technology, and Logistics.

"(f) ADVICE TO SERVICE ACQUISITION EXECUTIVE.—An officer who is a Senior Military Acquisition Advisor shall have as the officer's primary duty providing strategic, technical, and programmatic advice to the service acquisition executive of the officer's military department on matters pertaining to the Defense Acquisition System, including matters pertaining to procurement, research and development, advanced technology, test and evaluation, production, program management, systems engineering, and lifecycle logistics.".

"(2) CLERICAL AMENDMENT.—The table of sections at the beginning of subchapter II of chapter 87 of such title is amended by adding at the end the following new item:

"1725. Senior Military Acquisition Advisors.".

(b) EXCLUSION FROM OFFICER GRADE-STRENGTH LIMITATIONS.—Section 523(b) of such title is amended by adding at the end the following new paragraph:

"(9) Officers who are Senior Military Acquisition Advisors under section 1725 of this title, but not to exceed 15.".

SEC. 867. AUTHORITY OF THE SECRETARY OF DEFENSE UNDER THE ACQUISITION DEMONSTRATION PROJECT.

(a) AMENDMENT.—Section 1762(b) of title 10, United States Code, is amended by adding at the end the following new paragraph:

"(4) The Secretary of Defense shall exercise the authorities granted to the Office of Personnel Management under section 4703 of title 5 for purposes of the demonstration project authorized under this section.".

(b) EFFECTIVE DATE.—Paragraph (4) of section 1762(b) of title 10, United States Code, as added by subsection (a), shall take effect on the first day of the first month beginning 60 days after the date of the enactment of this Act.

Subtitle F—Provisions Relating to Commercial Items

SEC. 871. MARKET RESEARCH FOR DETERMINATION OF PRICE REASONABLENESS IN ACQUISITION OF COMMERCIAL ITEMS.

Section 2377 of title 10, United States Code, is amended—

(1) by redesignating subsection (d) as subsection (e), and in that subsection by striking "subsection (c)" and inserting "subsections (c) and (d)"; and

(2) by inserting after subsection (c) the following new subsection (d):

"(d) MARKET RESEARCH FOR PRICE ANALYSIS.—The Secretary of Defense shall ensure that procurement officials in the Department of Defense conduct or obtain market research to support the determination of the reasonableness of price for commercial items contained in any bid or offer submitted in response to an agency solicitation. To the extent necessary to support such market research, the procurement official for the solicitation—

"(1) in the case of items acquired under section 2379 of this title, shall use information submitted under subsection (d) of that section; and

"(2) in the case of other items, may require the offeror to submit relevant information.".

SEC. 872. VALUE ANALYSIS FOR THE DETERMINATION OF PRICE REASONABLENESS.

Subsection 2379(d) of title 10, United States Code, is amended—

(1) by redesignating paragraph (2) as paragraph (3); and

(2) by inserting after paragraph (1) the following new paragraph (2):

"(2) An offeror may submit information or analysis relating to the value of a commercial item to aid in the determination of the reasonableness of the price of such item. A contracting officer may consider such information or analysis in addition to the information submitted pursuant to paragraphs (1)(A) and (1)(B).".

SEC. 873. CLARIFICATION OF REQUIREMENTS RELATING TO COMMERCIAL ITEM DETERMINATIONS.

Paragraphs (1) and (2) of section 2380 of title 10, United States Code, are amended to read as follows:

"(1) establish and maintain a centralized capability with necessary expertise and resources to provide assistance to the military departments and Defense Agencies in making commercial item determinations, conducting market research, and performing analysis of price reasonableness for the purposes of procurements by the Department of Defense; and

"(2) provide to officials of the Department of Defense access to previous Department of Defense commercial item determinations, market research, and analysis used to determine the reasonableness of price for the purposes of procurements by the Department of Defense.".

SEC. 874. INAPPLICABILITY OF CERTAIN LAWS AND REGULATIONS TO THE ACQUISITION OF COMMERCIAL ITEMS AND COMMERCIALLY AVAILABLE OFF-THE-SHELF ITEMS.

(a) AMENDMENT TO TITLE 10, UNITED STATES CODE.—Section 2375 of title 10, United States Code, is amended to read as follows:

"§2375. Relationship of commercial item provisions to other provisions of law

"(a) APPLICABILITY OF GOVERNMENT-WIDE STATUTES.—(1) No contract for the procurement of a commercial item entered into by the head of an agency shall be subject to any law properly listed in the Federal Acquisition Regulation pursuant to section 1906(b) of title 41.

"(2) No subcontract under a contract for the procurement of a commercial item entered into by the head of an agency shall be subject to any law properly listed in the Federal Acquisition Regulation pursuant to section 1906(c) of title 41.

"(3) No contract for the procurement of a commercially available off-the-shelf item entered into by the head of an agency shall be subject to any law properly listed in the Federal Acquisition Regulation pursuant to section 1907 of title 41.

"(b) APPLICABILITY OF DEFENSE-UNIQUE STATUTES TO CONTRACTS FOR COMMERCIAL ITEMS.—(1) The Defense Federal Acquisition Regulation Supplement shall include a list of defense-unique provisions of law and of contract clause requirements based on government-wide acquisition regulations, policies, or executive orders not expressly authorized in law that are inapplicable to contracts for the procurement of commercial items. A provision of law or contract clause requirement properly included on the list pursuant to paragraph (2) does not apply to purchases of commercial items by the Department of Defense. This section does not render a provision of law or contract clause requirement not included on the list inapplicable to contracts for the procurement of commercial items.

"(2) A provision of law or contract clause requirement described in subsection (e) that is enacted after January 1, 2015, shall be included on the list of inapplicable provisions of law and contract clause requirements required by paragraph (1) unless the Under Secretary of Defense for Acquisition, Technology, and Logistics makes a written determination that it would not be in the best interest of the Department of Defense to exempt contracts for the procurement of commercial items from the applicability of the provision or contract clause requirement.

"(c) APPLICABILITY OF DEFENSE-UNIQUE STATUTES TO SUBCONTRACTS FOR COMMERCIAL ITEMS.—(1) The Defense Federal Acquisition Regulation Supplement shall include a list of provisions of law and of contract clause requirements based on government-wide acquisition regulations, policies, or executive orders not expressly authorized in law that are inapplicable to subcontracts under a Department of Defense contract or subcontract for the procurement of commercial items. A provision of law or contract clause requirement properly included on the list pursuant to paragraph (2) does not apply to those subcontracts under a contract for the procurement of commercial items.

"(2) A provision of law or contract clause requirement described in subsection (e) shall be included on the list of inapplicable provisions of law and contract clause requirements required by paragraph (1) unless the Under Secretary of Defense for Acquisition, Technology, and Logistics makes a written determination that it would not be in the best interest of the Department of Defense to exempt subcontracts under a contract for the procurement of commercial items from the applicability of the provision or contract clause requirement.

"(3) In this subsection, the term 'subcontract' includes a transfer of commercial items between divisions, subsidiaries, or affiliates of a contractor or subcontractor. The term does not include agreements entered into by a contractor for the supply of commodities that are intended for use in the performance of multiple contracts with the Department of Defense and other parties and are not identifiable to any particular contract.

"(4) This subsection does not authorize the waiver of the applicability of any provision of law or contract clause requirement with respect to any first-tier subcontract under a contract with a prime contractor reselling or distributing commercial items of another contractor without adding value.

"(d) APPLICABILITY OF DEFENSE-UNIQUE STATUTES TO CONTRACTS FOR COMMERCIALLY AVAILABLE, OFF-THE-SHELF ITEMS.—(1) The Defense Federal Acquisition Regulation Supplement shall include a list of provisions of law and of contract clause requirements based on government-wide acquisition regulations, policies, or executive orders not expressly authorized in law that are inapplicable to contracts for the procurement of commercially available off-the-shelf items. A provision of law or contract clause requirement properly included on the list pursuant to paragraph (2) does not apply to Department of Defense contracts for the procurement of commercially available off-the-shelf items. This section does not render a provision of law or contract clause requirement not included on the list inapplicable to contracts for the procurement of commercially available off-the-shelf items.

"(2) A provision of law or contract clause requirement described in subsection (e) shall be included on the list of inapplicable provisions of law and contract clause requirements required by paragraph (1) unless the Under Secretary of Defense for Acquisition, Technology, and Logistics makes a written determination that it would not be in the best interest of the Department of Defense to exempt contracts for the procurement of commercially available off-the-shelf items from the applicability of the provision or contract clause requirement.

"(e) COVERED PROVISION OF LAW OR CONTRACT CLAUSE REQUIREMENT.—A provision of law or contract clause requirement referred to in subsections (b)(2), (c)(2), and (d)(2) is a provision of law or contract clause requirement that the Under Secretary of Defense for Acquisition, Technology, and Logistics determines sets forth policies, procedures, requirements, or restrictions for the procurement of property or services by the Federal Government, except for a provision of law or contract clause requirement that—

"(1) provides for criminal or civil penalties;

"(2) requires that certain articles be bought from American sources pursuant to section 2533a of this title, or requires that strategic materials critical to national security be bought from American sources pursuant to section 2533b of this title; or

"(3) specifically refers to this section and provides that, notwithstanding this section, it shall be applicable to contracts for the procurement of commercial items.".

(b) CHANGES TO DEFENSE FEDERAL ACQUISITION REGULATION SUPPLEMENT.—

(1) IN GENERAL.—To the maximum extent practicable, the Under Secretary of Defense for Acquisition, Technology, and Logistics shall ensure that—

(A) the Defense Federal Acquisition Regulation Supplement does not require the inclusion of contract clauses in contracts for the procurement of commercial items or contracts for the procurement of commercially available off-the-shelf items, unless such clauses are—

(i) required to implement provisions of law or executive orders applicable to such contracts; or

(ii) determined to be consistent with standard commercial practice; and

(B) the flow-down of contract clauses to subcontracts under contracts for the procurement of commercial items or commercially available off-the-shelf items is prohibited unless such flow-down is required to implement provisions of law or executive orders applicable to such subcontracts.

(2) SUBCONTRACTS.—In this subsection, the term "subcontract" includes a transfer of commercial items between divisions, subsidiaries, or affiliates of a contractor or subcontractor. The term does not include agreements entered into by a contractor for the supply of commodities that are intended for use in the performance of multiple contracts with the Department of Defense and other parties and are not identifiable to any particular contract.

SEC. 875. USE OF COMMERCIAL OR NON-GOVERNMENT STANDARDS IN LIEU OF MILITARY SPECIFICATIONS AND STANDARDS.

(a) IN GENERAL.—The Secretary of Defense shall ensure that the Department of Defense uses commercial or non-Government specifications and standards in lieu of military specifications and standards, including for procuring new systems, major modifications, upgrades to current systems, non-developmental and commercial items, and programs in all acquisition categories, unless no practical alternative exists to meet user needs. If it is not practicable to use a commercial or non-Government standard, a Government-unique specification may be used.

(b) LIMITED USE OF MILITARY SPECIFICATIONS.—

(1) IN GENERAL.—Military specifications shall be used in procurements only to define an exact design solution when there is no acceptable commercial or non-Government standard or when the use of a commercial or non-Government standard is not cost effective.

(2) WAIVER.—A waiver for the use of military specifications in accordance with paragraph (1) shall be approved by either the appropriate milestone decision authority, the appropriate service acquisition executive, or the Under Secretary of Defense for Acquisition, Technology, and Logistics.

(c) REVISION TO DFARS.—Not later than 180 days after the date of the enactment of this Act,

the Under Secretary of Defense for Acquisition, Technology, and Logistics shall revise the Defense Federal Acquisition Regulation Supplement to encourage contractors to propose commercial or non-Government standards and industry-wide practices that meet the intent of the military specifications and standards.

(d) DEVELOPMENT OF NON-GOVERNMENT STANDARDS.—The Under Secretary for Acquisition, Technology, and Logistics shall form partnerships with appropriate industry associations to develop commercial or non-Government standards for replacement of military specifications and standards where practicable.

(e) EDUCATION, TRAINING, AND GUIDANCE.—The Under Secretary of Defense for Acquisition, Technology, and Logistics shall ensure that training, education, and guidance programs throughout the Department are revised to incorporate specifications and standards reform.

(f) LICENSES.—The Under Secretary of Defense for Acquisition, Technology, and Logistics shall negotiate licenses for standards to be used across the Department of Defense and shall maintain an inventory of such licenses that is accessible to other Department of Defense organizations.

SEC. 876. PREFERENCE FOR COMMERCIAL SERVICES.

Not later than 90 days after the date of the enactment of this Act, the Secretary of Defense shall revise the guidance issued pursuant to section 855 of the National Defense Authorization Act for Fiscal Year 2016 (Public Law 114–92; 10 U.S.C. 2377 note) to provide that—

(1) the head of an agency may not enter into a contract in excess of $10,000,000 for facilities-related services, knowledge-based services (except engineering services), construction services, medical services, or transportation services that are not commercial services unless the service acquisition executive of the military department concerned, the head of the Defense Agency concerned, the commander of the combatant command concerned, or the Under Secretary of Defense for Acquisition, Technology, and Logistics (as applicable) determines in writing that no commercial services are suitable to meet the agency's needs as provided in section 2377(c)(2) of title 10, United States Code; and

(2) the head of an agency may not enter into a contract in an amount above the simplified acquisition threshold and below $10,000,000 for facilities-related services, knowledge-based services (except engineering services), construction services, medical services, or transportation services that are not commercial services unless the contracting officer determines in writing that no commercial services are suitable to meet the agency's needs as provided in section 2377(c)(2) of such title.

SEC. 877. TREATMENT OF COMMINGLED ITEMS PURCHASED BY CONTRACTORS AS COMMERCIAL ITEMS.

(a) IN GENERAL.—Chapter 140 of title 10, United States Code, is amended by adding at the end the following new section:

"§ 2380B. Treatment of commingled items purchased by contractors as commercial items

"Notwithstanding 2376(1) of this title, items valued at less than $10,000 that are purchased by a contractor for use in the performance of multiple contracts with the Department of Defense and other parties and are not identifiable to any particular contract shall be treated as a commercial item for purposed of this chapter.".

(b) CLERICAL AMENDMENT.—The table of sections for such chapter is amended by inserting after the item relating to section 2380A the following new item:

"2380B. Treatment of items purchased prior to release of prime contract requests for proposals as commercial items.".

SEC. 878. TREATMENT OF SERVICES PROVIDED BY NONTRADITIONAL CONTRACTORS AS COMMERCIAL ITEMS.

(a) IN GENERAL.—Section 2380A of title 10, United States Code, is amended—

(1) by striking "Notwithstanding" and inserting the following:

"(a) GOODS AND SERVICES PROVIDED BY NONTRADITIONAL DEFENSE CONTRACTORS.—Notwithstanding"; and

(2) by adding at the end the following new subsection:

"(b) SERVICES PROVIDED BY CERTAIN NONTRADITIONAL CONTRACTORS.—Notwithstanding section 2376(1) of this title, services provided by a business unit that is a nontraditional defense contractor (as that term is defined in section 2302(9) of this title) shall be treated as commercial items for purposes of this chapter, to the extent that such services use the same pool of employees as used for commercial customers and are priced using methodology similar to methodology used for commercial pricing.".

(b) CONFORMING AMENDMENTS.—

(1) SECTION HEADING.—Section 2380A of title 10, United States Code, as amended by subsection (a), is further amended by striking the section heading and inserting the following:

"§ 2380a. Treatment of certain items as commercial items".

(2) TABLE OF SECTIONS.—The table of sections at the beginning of chapter 140 of title 10, United States Code, is amended by striking the item relating to section 2380A and inserting the following new item:

"2380a. Treatment of certain items as commercial items.".

SEC. 879. DEFENSE PILOT PROGRAM FOR AUTHORITY TO ACQUIRE INNOVATIVE COMMERCIAL ITEMS, TECHNOLOGIES, AND SERVICES USING GENERAL SOLICITATION COMPETITIVE PROCEDURES.

(a) AUTHORITY.—The Secretary of Defense and the Secretaries of the military departments may carry out a pilot program, to be known as the "defense commercial solutions opening pilot program", under which the Secretary may acquire innovative commercial items, technologies, and services through a competitive selection of proposals resulting from a general solicitation and the peer review of such proposals.

(b) TREATMENT AS COMPETITIVE PROCEDURES.—Use of general solicitation competitive procedures for the pilot program under subsection (a) shall be considered to be use of competitive procedures for purposes of chapter 137 of title 10, United States Code.

(c) LIMITATIONS.—

(1) IN GENERAL.—The Secretary may not enter into a contract or agreement under the pilot program for an amount in excess of $100,000,000 without a written determination from the Under Secretary for Acquisition, Logistics, and Technology or the relevant service acquisition executive of the efficacy of the effort to meet mission needs of the Department of Defense or the relevant military department.

(2) FIXED-PRICE REQUIREMENT.—Contracts or agreements entered into under the program shall be fixed-price, including fixed-price incentive fee contracts.

(3) TREATMENT AS COMMERCIAL ITEMS.—Notwithstanding section 2376(1) of title 10, United States Code, items, technologies, and services acquired under the pilot program shall be treated as commercial items.

(d) GUIDANCE.—Not later than six months after the date of the enactment of this Act, the Secretary shall issue guidance for the implementation of the pilot program under this section within the Department of Defense. Such guidance shall be issued in consultation with the Director of the Office of Management and Budget and shall be posted for access by the public.

(e) CONGRESSIONAL NOTIFICATION REQUIRED.—

(1) IN GENERAL.—Not later than 45 days after the award of a contract for an amount exceeding $100,000,000 using the authority in subsection (a), the Secretary of Defense shall notify the congressional defense committees of such award.

(2) ELEMENTS.—Notice of an award under paragraph (1) shall include the following:

(A) Description of the innovative commercial item, technology, or service acquired.

(B) Description of the requirement, capability gap, or potential technological advancement with respect to which the innovative commercial item, technology, or service acquired provides a solution or a potential new capability.

(C) Amount of the contract awarded.

(D) Identification of contractor awarded the contract.

(f) DEFINITION.—In this section, the term "innovative" means—

(1) any technology, process, or method, including research and development, that is new as of the date of submission of a proposal; or

(2) any application that is new as of the date of submission of a proposal of a technology, process, or method existing as of such date.

(g) SUNSET.—The authority to enter into contracts under the pilot program shall expire on September 30, 2022.

SEC. 880. PILOT PROGRAMS FOR AUTHORITY TO ACQUIRE INNOVATIVE COMMERCIAL ITEMS USING GENERAL SOLICITATION COMPETITIVE PROCEDURES.

(a) AUTHORITY.—

(1) IN GENERAL.—The head of an agency may carry out a pilot program, to be known as a "commercial solutions opening pilot program", under which innovative commercial items may be acquired through a competitive selection of proposals resulting from a general solicitation and the peer review of such proposals.

(2) HEAD OF AN AGENCY.—In this section, the term "head of an agency" means the following:

(A) The Secretary of Homeland Security.

(B) The Administrator of General Services.

(3) APPLICABILITY OF SECTION.—This section applies to the following agencies:

(A) The Department of Homeland Security.

(B) The General Services Administration.

(b) TREATMENT AS COMPETITIVE PROCEDURES.—Use of general solicitation competitive procedures for the pilot program under subsection (a) shall be considered, in the case of the Department of Homeland Security and the General Services Administration, to be use of competitive procedures for purposes of division C of title 41, United States Code (as defined in section 152 of such title).

(c) LIMITATION.—The head of an agency may not enter into a contract under the pilot program for an amount in excess of $10,000,000.

(d) GUIDANCE.—The head of an agency shall issue guidance for the implementation of the pilot program under this section within that agency. Such guidance shall be issued in consultation with the Office of Management and Budget and shall be posted for access by the public.

(e) REPORT REQUIRED.—

(1) IN GENERAL.—Not later than three years after the date of the enactment of this Act, the head of an agency shall submit to the congressional committees specified in paragraph (3) a report on the activities the agency carried out under the pilot program.

(2) ELEMENTS OF REPORT.—Each report under this subsection shall include the following:

(A) An assessment of the impact of the pilot program on competition.

(B) A comparison of acquisition timelines for—

(i) procurements made using the pilot program; and

(ii) procurements made using other competitive procedures that do not use general solicitations.

(C) A recommendation on whether the authority for the pilot program should be made permanent.

(3) SPECIFIED CONGRESSIONAL COMMITTEES.—The congressional committees specified in this paragraph are the Committee on Homeland Security and Governmental Affairs of the Senate and the Committee on Oversight and Government Reform of the House of Representatives.

(f) INNOVATIVE DEFINED.—In this section, the term "innovative" means—

(1) any new technology, process, or method, including research and development; or

(2) any new application of an existing technology, process, or method.

(g) TERMINATION.—The authority to enter into a contract under a pilot program under this section terminates on September 30, 2022.

Subtitle G—Industrial Base Matters

SEC. 881. GREATER INTEGRATION OF THE NATIONAL TECHNOLOGY AND INDUSTRIAL BASE.

(a) PLAN REQUIRED.—Not later than January 1, 2018, the Secretary of Defense shall develop a plan to reduce the barriers to the seamless integration between the persons and organizations that comprise the national technology and industrial base (as defined in section 2500 of title 10, United States Code). The plan shall include at a minimum the following elements:

(1) A description of the various components of the national technology and industrial base, including government entities, universities, nonprofit research entities, nontraditional and commercial item contractors, and private contractors that conduct commercial and military research, produce commercial items that could be used by the Department of Defense, and produce items designated and controlled under section 38 of the Arms Export Control Act (also known as the "United States Munitions List").

(2) Identification of the barriers to the seamless integration of the transfer of knowledge, goods, and services among the persons and organizations of the national technology and industrial base.

(3) Identification of current authorities that could contribute to further integration of the persons and organizations of the national technology and industrial base, and a plan to maximize the use of those authorities.

(4) Identification of changes in export control rules, procedures, and laws that would enhance the civil-military integration policy objectives set forth in section 2501(b) of title 10, United States Code, for the national technology and industrial base to increase the access of the Armed Forces to commercial products, services, and research and create incentives necessary for nontraditional and commercial item contractors, universities, and nonprofit research entities to modify commercial products or services to meet Department of Defense requirements.

(5) Recommendations for increasing integration of the national technology and industrial base that supplies defense articles to the Armed Forces and enhancing allied interoperability of forces through changes to the text or the implementation of—

(A) section 126.5 of title 22, Code of Federal Regulations (relating to exemptions that are applicable to Canada under the International Traffic in Arms Regulations);

(B) the Treaty Between the Government of the United States of America and the Government of Australia Concerning Defense Trade Cooperation, done at Sydney on September 5, 2007;

(C) the Treaty Between the Government of the United States of America and the Government of the United Kingdom of Great Britain and Northern Ireland Concerning Defense Trade Cooperation, done at Washington and London on June 21 and 26, 2007; and

(D) any other agreements among the countries comprising the national technology and industrial base.

(b) AMENDMENT TO DEFINITION OF NATIONAL TECHNOLOGY AND INDUSTRIAL BASE.—Section 2500(1) of title 10, United States Code, is amended by inserting ", the United Kingdom of Great Britain and Northern Ireland, Australia," after "United States".

(c) REPORTING REQUIREMENT.—The Secretary of Defense shall report on the progress of implementing the plan in subsection (a) in the report required under section 2504 of title 10, United States Code.

SEC. 882. INTEGRATION OF CIVIL AND MILITARY ROLES IN ATTAINING NATIONAL TECHNOLOGY AND INDUSTRIAL BASE OBJECTIVES.

Section 2501(b) of title 10, United States Code, is amended by striking "It is the policy of Congress that the United States attain" and inserting "The Secretary of Defense shall ensure that the United States attains".

SEC. 883. PILOT PROGRAM FOR DISTRIBUTION SUPPORT AND SERVICES FOR WEAPON SYSTEMS CONTRACTORS.

(a) AUTHORITY.—The Secretary of Defense may carry out a six-year pilot program under which the Secretary may make available storage and distribution services support to a contractor in support of the performance by the contractor of a contract for the production, modification, maintenance, or repair of a weapon system that is entered into by the Department of Defense.

(b) SUPPORT CONTRACTS.—

(1) IN GENERAL.—Any storage and distribution services to be provided under the pilot program under this section to a contractor in support of the performance of a contract described in subsection (a) shall be provided under a separate contract that is entered into by the Director of the Defense Logistics Agency with that contractor. The requirements of section 2208(h) of title 10, United States Code, and the regulations prescribed pursuant to such section shall apply to any such separate support contract between the Director of the Defense Logistics Agency and the contractor.

(2) LIMITATION.—Not more than five support contracts between the Director and the contractor may be awarded under the pilot program.

(c) SCOPE OF SUPPORT AND SERVICES.—The storage and distribution support services that may be provided under this section in support of the performance of a contract described in subsection (a) are storage and distribution of materiel and repair parts necessary for the performance of that contract.

(d) REGULATIONS.—Before exercising the authority under the pilot program under this section, the Secretary of Defense shall prescribe in regulations such requirements, conditions, and restrictions as the Secretary determines appropriate to ensure that storage and distribution services are provided under the pilot program only when it is in the best interests of the United States to do so. The regulations shall include, at a minimum, the following:

(1) A requirement for the solicitation of offers for a contract described in subsection (a), for which storage and distribution services are to be made available under the pilot program, including—

(A) a statement that the storage and distribution services are to be made available under the authority of the pilot program under this section to any contractor awarded the contract, but only on a basis that does not require acceptance of the support and services; and

(B) a description of the range of the storage and distribution services that are to be made available to the contractor.

(2) A requirement for the rates charged a contractor for storage and distribution services provided to a contractor under the pilot program to reflect the full cost to the United States of the resources used in providing the support and

services, including the costs of resources used, but not paid for, by the Department of Defense.

(3) With respect to a contract described in subsection (a) that is being performed for a department or agency outside the Department of Defense, a prohibition, in accordance with applicable contracting procedures, on the imposition of any charge on that department or agency for any effort of Department of Defense personnel or the contractor to correct deficiencies in the performance of such contract.

(4) A prohibition on the imposition of any charge on a contractor for any effort of the contractor to correct a deficiency in the performance of storage and distribution services provided to the contractor under this section.

(5) A requirement that storage and distribution services provided under the pilot program may not interfere with the mission of the Defense Logistics Agency or of any military department involved with the pilot program.

(6) A requirement that any support contract for storage and distribution services entered into under the pilot program shall include a clause to indemnify the Government against any failure by the contractor to perform the support contract, and to remain responsible for performance of the primary contract.

(e) RELATIONSHIP TO TREATY OBLIGATIONS.— The Secretary shall ensure that the exercise of authority under the pilot program under this section does not conflict with any obligation of the United States under any treaty or other international agreement.

(f) REPORTS.—

(1) SECRETARY OF DEFENSE.—Not later than the end of the fourth year of operation of the pilot program, the Secretary of Defense shall submit to the Committees on Armed Services of the Senate and House of Representatives a report describing—

(A) the cost effectiveness for both the Government and industry of the pilot program; and

(B) how support contracts under the pilot program affected meeting the requirements of primary contracts.

(2) COMPTROLLER GENERAL.—Not later than the end of the fifth year of operation of the pilot program, the Comptroller General of the United States shall review the report of the Secretary under paragraph (1) for sufficiency and provide such recommendations in a report to the Committees on Armed Services of the Senate and House of Representatives as the Comptroller General considers appropriate.

(g) SUNSET.—The authority to enter into contracts under the pilot program shall expire six years after the date of the enactment of this Act. Any contracts entered into before such date shall continue in effect according to their terms.

SEC. 884. NONTRADITIONAL AND SMALL CONTRACTOR INNOVATION PROTOTYPING PROGRAM.

(a) IN GENERAL.—The Secretary of Defense shall conduct a pilot program for nontraditional defense contractors and small business concerns to design, develop, and demonstrate innovative prototype military platforms of significant scope for the purpose of demonstrating new capabilities that could provide alternatives to existing acquisition programs and assets. The Secretary shall establish the pilot program within the Departments of the Army, Navy, and Air Force, the Missile Defense Agency, and the United States Special Operations Command.

(b) FUNDING.—There is authorized to be made available $250,000,000 from the Rapid Prototyping Fund established under section 804(d) of the National Defense Authorization Act for Fiscal Year 2016 (Public Law 114–92; 10 U.S.C. 2302 note) to carry out the pilot program.

(c) PLAN.—

(1) IN GENERAL.—The Secretary of Defense shall submit to the congressional defense com-

mittees, concurrent with the budget for the Department of Defense for fiscal year 2018, as submitted to Congress pursuant to section 1105 of title 31, United States Code, a plan to fund and carry out the pilot program in future years.

(2) ELEMENTS.—The plan submitted under paragraph (1) shall consider maximizing use of—

(A) broad agency announcements or other merit-based selection procedures;

(B) the Department of Defense Acquisition Challenge Program authorized under section 2359b of title 10, United States Code;

(C) the foreign comparative test program;

(D) projects carried out under the Rapid Innovation Program of the Department of Defense or pursuant to a Phase III agreement (as defined in section 9(r)(2) of the Small Business Act (15 U.S.C. 638(r)(2))); and

(E) streamlined procedures for acquisition provided under section 804 of the National Defense Authorization Act for Fiscal Year 2016 (Public Law 114–92; 10 U.S.C. 2302 note) and procedures for alternative acquisition pathways established under section 805 of such Act (10 U.S.C. 2302 note).

(d) PROGRAMS TO BE INCLUDED.—As part of the pilot program, the Secretary of Defense shall allocate up to $50,000,000 on a fixed price contractual basis for fiscal year 2017 or pursuant to the plan submitted under subsection (c) for demonstrations of the following capabilities:

(1) Swarming of multiple unmanned air vehicles.

(2) Unmanned, modular fixed-wing aircraft that can be rapidly adapted to multiple missions and serve as a fifth generation weapons augmentation platform.

(3) Vertical takeoff and landing tiltrotor aircraft.

(4) Integration of a directed energy weapon on an air, sea, or ground platform.

(5) Swarming of multiple unmanned underwater vehicles.

(6) Commercial small synthetic aperture radar (SAR) satellites with on-board machine learning for automated, real-time feature extraction and predictive analytics.

(7) Active protection system to defend against rocket-propelled grenades and anti-tank missiles.

(8) Defense against hypersonic weapons, including sensors.

(9) Other systems as designated by the Secretary.

(e) DEFINITIONS.—In this section:

(1) NONTRADITIONAL DEFENSE CONTRACTOR.— The term "nontraditional defense contractor" has the meaning given the term in section 2302(9) of title 10, United States Code.

(2) SMALL BUSINESS CONCERN.—The term "small business concern" has the meaning given the term in section 3 of the Small Business Act (15 U.S.C. 632).

(f) SUNSET.—The authority under this section expires at the close of September 30, 2026.

Subtitle H—Other Matters

SEC. 885. REPORT ON BID PROTESTS.

(a) REPORT REQUIRED.—Not later than 270 days after the date of the enactment of this Act, the Secretary of Defense shall enter into a contract with an independent research entity that is a not-for-profit entity or a federally funded research and development center with appropriate expertise and analytical capability to carry out a comprehensive study on the prevalence and impact of bid protests on Department of Defense acquisitions, including protests filed with contracting agencies, the Government Accountability Office, and the Court of Federal Claims.

(b) ELEMENTS.—The report required by subsection (a) shall cover Department of Defense contracts and include, at a minimum, the following elements:

(1) For employees of the Department, including the contracting officers, program executive officers, and program managers, the extent and manner in which the bid protest system affects or is perceived to affect—

(A) the development of a procurement to avoid protests rather than improve acquisition;

(B) the quality or quantity of pre-proposal discussions, discussions of proposals, or post-award debriefings;

(C) the decision to use lowest price technically acceptable procurement methods;

(D) the decision to make multiple awards or encourage teaming;

(E) the ability to meet an operational or mission need or address important requirements;

(F) the decision to use sole source award methods; and

(G) the decision to exercise options on existing contracts.

(2) With respect to a company bidding on contracts or task or delivery orders, the extent and manner in which the bid protest system affects or is perceived to affect—

(A) the decision to offer a bid or proposal on single award or multiple award contracts when the company is the incumbent contractor;

(B) the decision to offer a bid or proposal on single award or multiple award contracts when the company is not the incumbent contractor;

(C) the ability to engage in pre-proposal discussions, discussions of proposals, or post-award debriefings;

(D) the decision to participate in a team or joint venture; and

(E) the decision to file a protest with the agency concerned, the Government Accountability Office, or the Court of Federal Claims.

(3) A description of trends in the number of bid protests filed with agencies, the Government Accountability Office, and Federal courts, the effectiveness of each forum for contracts and task or delivery orders, and the rate of such bid protests compared to contract obligations and the number of contracts.

(4) An analysis of bid protests filed by incumbent contractors, including—

(A) the rate at which such protesters are awarded bridge contracts or contract extensions over the period that the protest remains unresolved; and

(B) an assessment of the cost and schedule impact of successful and unsuccessful bid protests filed by incumbent contractors on contracts for services with a value in excess of $100,000,000.

(5) A comparison of the number of protests, the values of contested orders or contracts, and the outcome of protests for—

(A) awards of contracts compared to awards of task or delivery orders;

(B) contracts or orders primarily for products, compared to contracts or orders primarily for services;

(C) protests filed pre-award to challenge the solicitation compared to those filed post-award;

(D) contracts or awards with single protestors compared to multiple protestors; and

(E) contracts with single awards compared to multiple award contracts.

(6) An analysis of the number and disposition of protests filed with the contracting agency.

(7) A description of trends in the number of bid protests filed as a percentage of contracts and as a percentage of task or delivery orders awarded during the same period of time, overall and set forth separately by the value of the contract or order, as follows:

(A) Contracts valued in excess of $3,000,000,000.

(B) Contracts valued between $500,000,000 and $3,000,000,000.

(C) Contracts valued between $50,000,000 and $500,000,000.

(D) Contracts valued between $10,000,000 and $50,000,000.

(E) Contracts valued under $10,000,000.

(8) An assessment of the cost and schedule impact of successful and unsuccessful bid protests filed on contracts valued in excess of $3,000,000,000.

(9) An analysis of how often protestors are awarded the contract that was the subject of the bid protest.

(10) A summary of the results of protests in which the contracting agencies took unilateral corrective action, including—

(A) at what point in the bid protest process the agency agreed to take corrective action;

(B) the average time for remedial action to be completed; and

(C) a determination regarding—

(i) whether or to what extent the decision to take the corrective action was a result of a determination by the agency that there had been a probable violation of law or regulation; or

(ii) whether or to what extent such corrective action was a result of some other factor.

(11) A description of the time it takes agencies to implement corrective actions after a ruling or decision, and the percentage of those corrective actions that are subsequently protested, including the outcome of any subsequent protest.

(12) An analysis of those contracts with respect to which a company files a protest (referred to as the "initial protest") and later files another protest (referred to as the "subsequent protest"), analyzed by the forum of the initial protest and the subsequent protest, including any difference in the outcome, between the forums.

(13) An analysis of the effect of the quantity and quality of debriefings on the frequency of bid protests.

(14) An analysis of the time spent at each phase of the procurement process attempting to prevent a protest, addressing a protest, or taking corrective action in response to a protest, including the efficacy of any actions attempted to prevent the occurrence of a protest.

(c) BRIEFING.—Not later than March 1, 2017, the Secretary, or his designee, shall brief the Committees on Armed Services of the Senate and House of Representatives on interim findings of the independent entity.

(d) REPORT.—Not later than one year after the date of the enactment of this Act, the independent entity that conducts the study under subsection (a) shall provide to the Secretary of Defense and the congressional defense committees a report on the results of the study, along with any related recommendations.

SEC. 886. REVIEW AND REPORT ON INDEFINITE DELIVERY CONTRACTS.

(a) REPORT.—The Comptroller General of the United States shall deliver, not later than March 31, 2018, a report to Congress on the use by the Department of Defense of indefinite delivery contracts entered into during fiscal years 2015, 2016, and 2017.

(b) ELEMENTS.—The report under subsection (a) shall address, at a minimum, the following:

(1) A review of Department of Defense policies for entering into and using indefinite delivery contracts, including requirements for competition, as well as the guidance, if any, on the appropriate number of vendors that should receive multiple award indefinite delivery contracts.

(2) The number and value of all indefinite delivery contracts entered into by the Department of Defense, including the number and value of such contracts entered into with a single vendor.

(3) An assessment of the number and value of indefinite delivery contracts entered into by the Department of Defense that included competition between multiple vendors.

(4) Selected case studies of indefinite delivery contracts, including an assessment of whether any such contracts may have limited future op-

portunities for competition for the services or items required.

(5) Recommendations for potential changes to current law or Department of Defense acquisition regulations or guidance to promote competition with respect to indefinite delivery contracts.

SEC. 887. REVIEW AND REPORT ON CONTRACTUAL FLOW-DOWN PROVISIONS.

(a) REVIEW REQUIRED.—The Secretary of Defense shall conduct a review of contractual flow-down provisions related to major defense acquisition programs on contractors and suppliers, including small businesses, contractors for commercial items, nontraditional defense contractors, universities, and not-for-profit research institutions. The review shall—

(1) identify the flow-down provisions that exist in the Federal Acquisition Regulation and the Defense Federal Acquisition Regulation Supplement;

(2) identify the flow-down provisions that are critical for national security;

(3) examine the extent to which clauses in contracts with the Department of Defense are being applied inappropriately in subcontracts under the contracts;

(4) assess the applicability of flow-down provisions for the purchase of commodity items that are acquired in bulk for multiple acquisition programs;

(5) determine the unnecessary costs or burdens, if any, of flow-down provisions on the supply chain;

(6) determine the effect, if any, of flow-down provisions on the participation rate of small businesses, contractors for commercial items, nontraditional defense contractors, universities, and not-for-profit research organizations in defense acquisition efforts; and

(7) determine the effect, if any, of flow-down provisions on Department of Defense access to advanced research and technology capabilities available in the private sector.

(b) CONTRACT.—Not later than 60 days after the date of the enactment of this Act, the Secretary of Defense shall enter into a contract with an independent entity with appropriate expertise to conduct the review required by subsection (a).

(c) REPORT.—Not later than August 1, 2017, the Secretary shall submit to the congressional defense committees a report on the findings of the independent entity, along with a description of any actions that the Secretary proposes to address the findings of the independent entity.

SEC. 888. REQUIREMENT AND REVIEW RELATING TO USE OF BRAND NAMES OR BRAND-NAME OR EQUIVALENT DESCRIPTIONS IN SOLICITATIONS.

(a) REQUIREMENT.—The Secretary of Defense shall ensure that competition in Department of Defense contracts is not limited through the use of specifying brand names or brand-name or equivalent descriptions, or proprietary specifications or standards, in solicitations unless a justification for such specification is provided and approved in accordance with section 2304(f) of title 10, United States Code.

(b) REVIEW OF ANTI-COMPETITIVE SPECIFICATIONS IN INFORMATION TECHNOLOGY ACQUISITIONS.—

(1) REVIEW REQUIRED.—Not later than 180 days after the date of the enactment of this Act, the Under Secretary of Defense for Acquisition, Technology, and Logistics shall conduct a review of the policy, guidance, regulations, and training related to specifications included in information technology acquisitions to ensure current policies eliminate the unjustified use of potentially anti-competitive specifications. In conducting the review, the Under Secretary shall examine the use of brand names or proprietary specifications or standards in solicitations for

procurements of goods and services, as well as the current acquisition training curriculum related to those areas.

(2) BRIEFING REQUIRED.—Not later than 270 days after the date of the enactment of this Act, the Under Secretary shall provide a briefing to the Committees on Armed Services of the Senate and House of Representatives on the results of the review required by paragraph (1).

(3) ADDITIONAL GUIDANCE.—Not later than one year after the date of the enactment of this Act, the Under Secretary shall revise policies, guidance, and training to incorporate such recommendations as the Under Secretary considers appropriate from the review required by paragraph (1).

SEC. 889. INCLUSION OF INFORMATION ON COMMON GROUNDS FOR SUSTAINING BID PROTESTS IN ANNUAL GOVERNMENT ACCOUNTABILITY OFFICE REPORTS TO CONGRESS.

The Comptroller General of the United States shall include in the annual report to Congress on the Government Accountability Office each year a list of the most common grounds for sustaining protests relating to bids for contracts during such year.

SEC. 890. STUDY AND REPORT ON CONTRACTS AWARDED TO MINORITY-OWNED AND WOMEN-OWNED BUSINESSES.

(a) STUDY.—The Comptroller General of the United States shall carry out a study on the number and types of contracts for the procurement of goods or services for the Department of Defense awarded to minority-owned and women-owned businesses during fiscal years 2010 through 2015. In conducting the study, the Comptroller General shall identify minority-owned businesses according to the categories identified in the Federal Procurement Data System (described in section 1122(a)(4)(A) of title 41, United States Code).

(b) REPORT.—Not later than 1 year after the date of the enactment of this Act, the Comptroller General shall submit to the congressional defense committees a report on the results of the study under subsection (a).

SEC. 891. AUTHORITY TO PROVIDE REIMBURSABLE AUDITING SERVICES TO CERTAIN NON-DEFENSE AGENCIES.

Section 893(a) of the National Defense Authorization Act for Fiscal Year 2016 (Public Law 114–92; 10 U.S.C. 2313 note) is amended—

(1) in paragraph (1), by inserting "except as provided in paragraph (2)," after "this Act,"; and

(2) by amending paragraph (2) to read as follows:

"(2) EXCEPTION FOR NATIONAL NUCLEAR SECURITY ADMINISTRATION.—Notwithstanding paragraph (1), the Defense Contract Audit Agency may provide audit support on a reimbursable basis for the National Nuclear Security Administration.".

SEC. 892. SELECTION OF SERVICE PROVIDERS FOR AUDITING SERVICES AND AUDIT READINESS SERVICES.

The Department of Defense shall select service providers for auditing services and audit readiness services based on the best value to the Department, as determined by the resource sponsor for an auditing contract, rather than based on the lowest price technically acceptable service provider.

SEC. 893. AMENDMENTS TO CONTRACTOR BUSINESS SYSTEM REQUIREMENTS.

(a) BUSINESS SYSTEM REQUIREMENTS.—Section 893 of the Ike Skelton National Defense Authorization Act for Fiscal Year 2011 (Public Law 111–383; 10 U.S.C. 2302 note) is amended in subsection (b)(1), by striking "system requirements" and inserting "clear and specific business system requirements that are identified and made publicly available".

(b) THIRD-PARTY INDEPENDENT AUDITOR REVIEWS.—Section 893 of such Act is further amended—

(1) by redesignating subsections (c), (d), (e), (f), and (g) as subsections (d), (e), (f), (g), and (h), respectively; and

(2) by inserting after subsection (b) the following new subsection (c):

"(c) REVIEW BY THIRD-PARTY INDEPENDENT AUDITORS.—The review process for contractor business systems pursuant to subsection (b)(2) shall—

"(1) if a registered public accounting firm attests to the internal control assessment of a contractor, pursuant to section 404(b) of the Sarbanes-Oxley Act of 2002 (15 U.S.C. 7262(b)), allow the contractor, subject to paragraph (3), to submit certified documentation from such registered public accounting firm that the contractor business systems of the contractor meet the business system requirements referred to in subsection (b)(1) and to thereby eliminate the need for further review of the contractor business systems by the Secretary of Defense;

"(2) limit the review, subject to paragraph (3), of the contractor business systems of a contractor that is not a covered contractor to confirming that the contractor uses the same contractor business system for its Government and commercial work and that the outputs of the contractor business system based on statistical sampling are reasonable; and

"(3) allow a milestone decision authority to require a review of a contractor business system of a contractor that submits documentation pursuant to paragraph (1) or that is not a covered contractor after determining in writing that such a review is necessary to appropriately manage contractual risk.".

(c) AMENDMENT TO DEFINITION OF COVERED CONTRACTOR.—Section 893 of such Act is further amended in subsection (g), as so redesignated, by striking "means a contractor" and all that follows and inserting "means a contractor that has covered contracts with the United States Government accounting for greater than 1 percent of its total gross revenue, except that the term does not include any contractor that is exempt, under section 1502 of title 41, United States Code, or regulations implementing that section, from using full cost accounting standards established in that section.".

(d) REPEAL OF OBSOLETE DEADLINE.—Section 893 of such Act is further amended in subsection (a) by striking "Not later than 270 days after the date of the enactment of this Act, the" and inserting "The".

SEC. 894. IMPROVED MANAGEMENT PRACTICES TO REDUCE COST AND IMPROVE PERFORMANCE OF CERTAIN DEPARTMENT OF DEFENSE ORGANIZATIONS.

(a) IN GENERAL.—Beginning not later than 180 days after the date of the enactment of this Act, the Secretary of Defense shall designate units, subunits, or entities of the Department of Defense, other than Centers of Industrial and Technical Excellence designated pursuant to section 2474 of title 10, United States Code, that conduct work that is commercial in nature or is not inherently governmental to prioritize efforts to conduct business operations in a manner that uses modern, commercial management practices and principles to reduce the costs and improve the performance of such organizations.

(b) ADOPTION OF MODERN BUSINESS PRACTICES.—The Secretary shall ensure that each such unit, subunit, or entity of the Department described in subsection (a) is authorized to adopt and implement best commercial and business management practices to achieve the goals described in such subsection.

(c) WAIVERS.—The Secretary shall authorize waivers of Department of Defense, military service, and Defense Agency regulations, as appropriate, to achieve the goals in subsection (a), including in the following areas:

(1) Financial management.

(2) Human resources.

(3) Facility and plant management.

(4) Acquisition and contracting.

(5) Partnerships with the private sector.

(6) Other business and management areas as identified by the Secretary.

(d) GOALS.—The Secretary of Defense shall identify savings goals to be achieved through the implementation of the commercial and business management practices adopted under subsection (b), and establish a schedule for achieving the savings.

(e) BUDGET ADJUSTMENT.—The Secretary shall establish policies to adjust organizational budget allocations, at the Secretary's discretion, for purposes of—

(1) using savings derived from implementation of best commercial and business management practices for high priority military missions of the Department of Defense;

(2) creating incentives for the most efficient and effective development and adoption of new commercial and business management practices by organizations; and

(3) investing in the development of new commercial and business management practices that will result in further savings to the Department of Defense.

(f) BUDGET BASELINES.—Beginning not later than one year after the date of the enactment of this Act, each such unit, subunit, or entity of the Department described in subsection (a) shall, in accordance with such guidance as the Secretary of Defense shall establish for purposes of this section—

(1) establish an annual baseline cost estimate of its operations; and

(2) certify that costs estimated pursuant to paragraph (1) are wholly accounted for and presented in a format that is comparable to the format for the presentation of such costs for other elements of the Department or consistent with best commercial practices.

SEC. 895. EXEMPTION FROM REQUIREMENT FOR CAPITAL PLANNING AND INVESTMENT CONTROL FOR INFORMATION TECHNOLOGY EQUIPMENT INCLUDED AS INTEGRAL PART OF A WEAPON OR WEAPON SYSTEM.

(a) WAIVER AUTHORITY.—Notwithstanding subsection (c)(2) of section 11103 of title 40, United States Code, a national security system described in subsection (a)(1)(D) of such section shall not be subject to the requirements of paragraphs (2) through (5) of section 11312(b) of such title unless the milestone decision authority determines in writing that application of such requirements is appropriate and in the best interests of the Department of Defense.

(b) MILESTONE DECISION AUTHORITY DEFINED.—In this section, the term "milestone decision authority" has the meaning given the term in section 2366a(d)(7) of title 10, United States Code.

SEC. 896. MODIFICATIONS TO PILOT PROGRAM FOR STREAMLINING AWARDS FOR INNOVATIVE TECHNOLOGY PROJECTS.

Section 873 of the National Defense Authorization Act for Fiscal Year 2016 (Public Law 114–92; 10 U.S.C. 2306a note) is amended—

(1) in subsection (a)(2), by inserting "or Small Business Technology Transfer Program" after "Small Business Innovation Research Program";

(2) in subsection (b)—

(A) by inserting "subparagraphs (A), (B), and (C) of section 2313(a)(2) of title 10, United States Code, and" before "subsection (b) of section 2313"; and

(B) in paragraph (2), by inserting ", and if such performance audit is initiated within 18 months of the contract completion" before the period at the end;

(3) by redesignating subsections (c), (d), and (e) as subsections (f), (g), and (h), respectively; and

(4) by inserting after subsection (b) the following new subsections:

"(c) TREATMENT AS COMPETITIVE PROCEDURES.—Use of a technical, merit-based selection procedure or the Small Business Innovation Research Program or Small Business Technology Transfer Program for the pilot program under this section shall be considered to be use of competitive procedures for purposes of chapter 137 of title 10, United States Code.

"(d) DISCRETION TO USE NON-CERTIFIED ACCOUNTING SYSTEMS.—In executing programs under this pilot program, the Secretary of Defense shall establish procedures under which a small business or nontraditional contractor may engage an independent certified public accountant for the review and certification of its accounting system for the purposes of any audits required by regulation, unless the head of the agency determines that this is not appropriate based on past performance of the specific small business or nontraditional defense contractor, or based on analysis of other information specific to the award.

"(e) GUIDANCE AND TRAINING.—The Secretary of Defense shall ensure that acquisition and auditing officials are provided guidance and training on the flexible use and tailoring of authorities under the pilot program to maximize efficiency and effectiveness.".

SEC. 897. RAPID PROTOTYPING FUNDS FOR THE MILITARY DEPARTMENTS.

Section 804(d) of the National Defense Authorization Act for Fiscal Year 2016 (Public Law 114–92; 10 U.S.C. 2302 note), as amended by section 864 of this Act, is further amended—

(1) in the subsection heading, by striking "FUND" and inserting "FUNDS";

(2) in paragraph (1), by striking "IN GENERAL.—The Secretary" and inserting the following: "DEPARTMENT OF DEFENSE RAPID PROTOTYPING FUND.—

"(A) IN GENERAL.—The Secretary";

(3) by redesignating paragraphs (2) and (3) as subparagraphs (B) and (C), respectively, and moving such subparagraphs, as so redesignated, two ems to the right;

(4) in subparagraph (B), as redesignated by paragraph (3), by striking "this subsection" and inserting "this paragraph"; and

(5) by inserting after paragraph (1) the following new paragraph:

"(2) RAPID PROTOTYPING FUNDS FOR THE MILITARY DEPARTMENTS.—The Secretary of each military department may establish a military department-specific fund (and, in the case of the Secretary of the Navy, including the Marine Corps) to provide funds, in addition to other funds that may be available to the military department concerned, for acquisition programs under the rapid fielding and prototyping pathways established pursuant to this section. Each military department-specific fund shall consist of amounts appropriated or credited to the fund.".

SEC. 898. ESTABLISHMENT OF PANEL ON DEPARTMENT OF DEFENSE AND ABILITYONE CONTRACTING OVERSIGHT, ACCOUNTABILITY, AND INTEGRITY; DEFENSE ACQUISITION UNIVERSITY TRAINING.

(a) ESTABLISHMENT OF PANEL ON DEPARTMENT OF DEFENSE AND ABILITYONE CONTRACTING OVERSIGHT, ACCOUNTABILITY, AND INTEGRITY.—

(1) IN GENERAL.—The Secretary of Defense shall establish a panel to be known as the "Panel on Department of Defense and AbilityOne Contracting Oversight, Accountability, and Integrity" (hereafter in this section referred to as the "Panel"). The Panel shall be

supported by the Defense Acquisition University, established under section 1746 of title 10, United States Code, and the National Defense University, including administrative support.

(2) COMPOSITION.—The Panel shall be composed of the following:

(A) A representative of the Under Secretary of Defense for Acquisition, Technology, and Logistics, who shall be the chairman of the Panel.

(B) A representative from the AbilityOne Commission.

(C) A representative of the service acquisition executive of each military department and Defense Agency (as such terms are defined, respectively, in section 101 of title 10, United States Code).

(D) A representative of the Under Secretary of Defense (Comptroller).

(E) A representative of the Inspector General of the Department of Defense and the AbilityOne Commission.

(F) A representative from each of the Army Audit Agency, the Navy Audit Service, the Air Force Audit Agency, and the Defense Contract Audit Agency.

(G) The President of the Defense Acquisition University, or a designated representative.

(H) One or more subject matter experts on veterans employment from a veterans service organization.

(I) A representative of the Commission Directorate of Veteran Employment of the AbilityOne Commission whose duties include maximizing opportunities to employ significantly disabled veterans in accordance with the regulations of the AbilityOne Commission.

(J) One or more representatives from the Department of Justice who are subject matter experts on compliance with disability rights laws applicable to contracts of the Department of Defense and the AbilityOne Commission.

(K) One or more representatives from the Department of Justice who are subject matter experts on Department of Defense contracts, Federal Prison Industries, and the requirements of the Javits-Wagner-O'Day Act.

(L) Such other representatives as may be determined appropriate by the Under Secretary of Defense for Acquisition, Technology, and Logistics.

(b) MEETINGS.—The Panel shall meet as determined necessary by the chairman of the Panel, but not less often than once every three months.

(c) DUTIES.—The Panel shall—

(1) review the status of and progress relating to the implementation of the recommendations of report number DODIG–2016–097 of the Inspector General of the Department of Defense titled "DoD Generally Provided Effective Oversight of AbilityOne Contracts", published on June 17, 2016;

(2) recommend actions the Department of Defense and the AbilityOne Commission may take to eliminate waste, fraud, and abuse with respect to contracts of the Department of Defense and the AbilityOne Commission;

(3) recommend actions the Department of Defense and the AbilityOne Commission may take to ensure opportunities for the employment of significantly disabled veterans and the blind and other severely disabled individuals;

(4) recommend changes to law, regulations, and policy that the Panel determines necessary to eliminate vulnerability to waste, fraud, and abuse with respect to the performance of contracts of the Department of Defense;

(5) recommend criteria for veterans with disabilities to be eligible for employment opportunities through the programs of the AbilityOne Commission that considers the definitions of disability used by the Secretary of Veterans Affairs and the AbilityOne Commission;

(6) recommend ways the Department of Defense and the AbilityOne Commission may ex-plore opportunities for competition among qualified nonprofit agencies or central nonprofit agencies and ensure an equitable selection and allocation of work to qualified nonprofit agencies;

(7) recommend changes to business practices, information systems, and training necessary to ensure that—

(A) the AbilityOne Commission complies with regulatory requirements related to the establishment and maintenance of the procurement list established pursuant to section 8503 of title 41, United States Code; and

(B) the Department of Defense complies with the statutory and regulatory requirements for use of such procurement list; and

(8) any other duties determined necessary by the Secretary of Defense.

(d) CONSULTATION.—To carry out the duties described in subsection (c), the Panel may consult or contract with other executive agencies and with experts from qualified nonprofit agencies or central nonprofit agencies on—

(1) compliance with disability rights laws applicable to contracts of the Department of Defense and the AbilityOne Commission;

(2) employment of significantly disabled veterans; and

(3) vocational rehabilitation.

(e) AUTHORITY.—To carry out the duties described in subsection (c), the Panel may request documentation or other information needed from the AbilityOne Commission, central nonprofit agencies, and qualified nonprofit agencies.

(f) PANEL RECOMMENDATIONS AND MILESTONE DATES.—

(1) MILESTONE DATES FOR IMPLEMENTING RECOMMENDATIONS.—After consulting with central nonprofit agencies and qualified nonprofit agencies, the Panel shall suggest milestone dates for the implementation of the recommendations made under subsection (c) and shall notify the congressional defense committees, the Committee on Oversight and Government Reform of the House of Representatives, the Committee on Homeland Security and Governmental Affairs of the Senate, qualified nonprofit agencies, and central nonprofit agencies of such dates.

(2) NOTIFICATION OF IMPLEMENTATION OF RECOMMENDATIONS.—After the establishment of milestone dates under paragraph (1), the Panel may review the activities, including contracts, of the AbilityOne Commission, the central nonprofit agencies, and the relevant qualified nonprofit agencies to determine if the recommendations made under subsection (c) are being substantially implemented in good faith by the AbilityOne Commission or such agencies. If the Panel determines that the AbilityOne Commission or any such agency is not implementing the recommendations, the Panel shall notify the Secretary of Defense, the congressional defense committees, the Committee on Oversight and Government Reform of the House of Representatives, and the Committee on Homeland Security and Governmental Affairs of the Senate.

(g) REMEDIES.—

(1) IN GENERAL.—Upon receiving notification under subsection (f)(2) and subject to the limitation in paragraph (2), the Secretary of Defense may take one of the following actions:

(A) With respect to a notification relating to the AbilityOne Commission, the Secretary may suspend compliance with the requirement to procure a product or service in section 8504 of title 41, United States Code, until the date on which the Secretary notifies Congress, in writing, that the AbilityOne Commission is substantially implementing the recommendations made under subsection (c).

(B) With respect to a notification relating to a qualified nonprofit agency, the Secretary may terminate a contract with such agency that is in existence on the date of receipt of such notification, or elect to not enter into a contract with such agency after such date, until the date on which the AbilityOne Commission certifies to the Secretary that such agency is substantially implementing the recommendations made under subsection (c).

(C) With respect to a notification relating to a central nonprofit agency, the Secretary may include a term in a contract entered into after the date of receipt of such notification with a qualified nonprofit agency that is under such central nonprofit agency that states that such qualified nonprofit agency shall not pay a fee to such central nonprofit agency until the date on which the AbilityOne Commission certifies to the Secretary that such central nonprofit agency is substantially implementing the recommendations made under subsection (c).

(2) LIMITATION.—If the Secretary of Defense takes any of the actions described in paragraph (1), the Secretary shall coordinate with the AbilityOne Commission or the relevant central nonprofit agency, as appropriate, to fully implement the recommendations made under subsection (c). On the date on which such recommendations are fully implemented, the Secretary shall notify Congress, in writing, and the Secretary's authority under paragraph (1) shall terminate.

(h) PROGRESS REPORTS.—

(1) CONSULTATION ON RECOMMENDATIONS.—Before submitting the progress report required under paragraph (2), the Panel shall consult with the AbilityOne Commission on draft recommendations made pursuant to subsection (c). The Panel shall include any recommendations of the AbilityOne Commission in the progress report submitted under paragraph (2).

(2) PROGRESS REPORT.—Not later than 180 days after the date of the enactment of this Act, the Panel shall submit to the Secretary of Defense, the Chairman of the AbilityOne Commission, the congressional defense committees, the Committee on Oversight and Government Reform of the House of Representatives, and the Committee on Homeland Security and Governmental Affairs of the Senate a progress report on the activities of the Panel.

(i) ANNUAL REPORT.—

(1) CONSULTATION ON REPORT.—Before submitting the annual report required under paragraph (2), the Panel shall consult with the AbilityOne Commission on the contents of the report. The Panel shall include any recommendations of the AbilityOne Commission in the report submitted under paragraph (2).

(2) REPORT.—Not later than September 30, 2017, and annually thereafter for the next three years, the Panel shall submit to the Secretary of Defense, the Chairman of the AbilityOne Commission, the congressional defense committees, the Committee on Oversight and Government Reform of the House of Representatives, and the Committee on Homeland Security and Governmental Affairs of the Senate a report that includes—

(A) a summary of findings and recommendations for the year covered by the report;

(B) a summary of the progress of the relevant qualified nonprofit agencies or central nonprofit agencies in implementing recommendations of the previous year's report, if applicable;

(C) an examination of the current structure of the AbilityOne Commission to eliminate waste, fraud, and abuse and to ensure contracting integrity and accountability for any violations of law or regulations;

(D) recommendations for any changes to the acquisition and contracting practices of the Department of Defense and the AbilityOne Commission to improve the delivery of goods and services to the Department of Defense; and

(E) recommendations for administrative safeguards to ensure the Department of Defense and the AbilityOne Commission are in compliance with the requirements of the Javits-Wagner-O'Day Act, Federal civil rights law, and regulations and policy related to the performance of contracts of the Department of Defense with qualified nonprofit agencies and the contracts of the AbilityOne Commission with central nonprofit agencies.

(j) SUNSET.—The Panel shall terminate on the date of submission of the last annual report required under subsection (i).

(k) INAPPLICABILITY OF FACA.—The requirements of the Federal Advisory Committee Act (5 U.S.C. App.) shall not apply to the Panel established pursuant to subsection (a).

(l) DEFENSE ACQUISITION UNIVERSITY TRAINING.—

(1) IN GENERAL.—The Secretary of Defense shall establish a training program at the Defense Acquisition University established under section 1746 of title 10, United States Code. Such training shall include—

(A) information about—

(i) the mission of the AbilityOne Commission;

(ii) the employment of significantly disabled veterans through contracts from the procurement list maintained by the AbilityOne Commission;

(iii) reasonable accommodations and accessibility requirements for the blind and other severely disabled individuals; and

(iv) Executive orders and other subjects related to the blind and other severely disabled individuals, as determined by the Secretary of Defense; and

(B) procurement, acquisition, program management, and other training specific to procuring goods and services for the Department of Defense pursuant to the Javits-Wagner-O'Day Act.

(2) ACQUISITION WORKFORCE ASSIGNMENT.—Members of the acquisition workforce (as defined in section 101 of title 10, United States Code) who have participated in the training described in paragraph (1) are eligible for a detail to the AbilityOne Commission.

(3) ABILITYONE COMMISSION ASSIGNMENT.—Career employees of the AbilityOne Commission may participate in the training program described in paragraph (1) on a non-reimbursable basis for up to three years and on a non-reimbursable or reimbursable basis thereafter.

(4) FUNDING.—Amounts from the Department of Defense Acquisition Workforce Development Fund established under section 1705 of title 10, United States Code, are authorized for use for the detail of members of the acquisition workforce to the AbilityOne Commission.

(m) DEFINITIONS.—In this section:

(1) The term "AbilityOne Commission" means the Committee for Purchase From People Who Are Blind or Severely Disabled established under section 8502 of title 41, United States Code.

(2) The terms "blind", "qualified nonprofit agency for the blind", "qualified nonprofit agency for other severely disabled", and "severely disabled individual" have the meanings given such terms under section 8501 of such title.

(3) The term "central nonprofit agency" means a central nonprofit agency designated under section 8503(c) of such title.

(4) The term "executive agency" has the meaning given such term in section 133 of such title.

(5) The term "Javits-Wagner-O'Day Act" means chapter 85 of such title.

(6) The term "qualified nonprofit agency" means—

(A) a qualified nonprofit agency for the blind; or

(B) a qualified nonprofit agency for other severely disabled.

(7) The term "significantly disabled veteran" means a veteran (as defined in section 101 of title 38, United States Code) who is a severely disabled individual.

SEC. 899. COAST GUARD MAJOR ACQUISITION PROGRAMS.

(a) FUNCTIONS OF CHIEF ACQUISITION OFFICER.—Section 56(c) of title 14, United States Code, is amended by striking "and" after the semicolon at the end of paragraph (8), striking the period at the end of paragraph (9) and inserting "; and", and adding at the end the following:

"(10)(A) keeping the Commandant informed of the progress of major acquisition programs (as that term is defined in section 581);

"(B) informing the Commandant on a continuing basis of any developments on such programs that may require new or revisited trade-offs among cost, schedule, technical feasibility, and performance, including—

"(i) significant cost growth or schedule slippage; and

"(ii) requirements creep (as that term is defined in section 2547(c)(1) of title 10); and

"(C) ensuring that the views of the Commandant regarding such programs on cost, schedule, technical feasibility, and performance trade-offs are strongly considered by program managers and program executive officers in all phases of the acquisition process.".

(b) CUSTOMER SERVICE MISSION OF DIRECTORATE.—

(1) IN GENERAL.—Chapter 15 of title 14, United States Code, is amended—

(A) in section 561(b)—

(i) in paragraph (1), by striking "; and" and inserting a semicolon;

(ii) in paragraph (2), by striking the period and inserting "; and"; and

(iii) by adding at the end the following:

"(3) to meet the needs of customers of major acquisition programs in the most cost-effective manner practicable.";

(B) in section 562, by repealing subsection (b) and redesignating subsections (c), (d), (f), and (g) as subsections (b), (c), (d), and (e), respectively;

(C) in section 563, by striking "Not later than 180 days after the date of enactment of the Coast Guard Authorization Act of 2010, the Commandant shall commence implementation of" and inserting "The Commandant shall maintain";

(D) by adding at the end of section 564 the following:

"(c) ACQUISITION OF UNMANNED AERIAL SYSTEMS.—

"(1) IN GENERAL.—During any fiscal year for which funds are appropriated for the design or construction of the Offshore Patrol Cutter, the Commandant—

"(A) may not award a contract for design of an unmanned aerial system for use by the Coast Guard; and

"(B) may acquire an unmanned aerial system only—

"(i) if such a system has been acquired by, or has been used by, the Department of Defense or the Department of Homeland Security, or a component thereof, before the date on which the Commandant acquires the system; and

"(ii) through an agreement with such a department or component, unless the unmanned aerial system can be obtained at less cost through independent contract action.

"(2) LIMITATIONS ON APPLICATION.—

"(A) SMALL UNMANNED AERIAL SYSTEMS.—The limitations in paragraph (1)(B) do not apply to any small unmanned aerial system that consists of—

"(i) an unmanned aircraft weighing less than 55 pounds on takeoff, including all components and equipment on board or otherwise attached to the aircraft; and

"(ii) associated elements (including communication links and the components that control such aircraft) that are required for the safe and efficient operation of such aircraft.

"(B) PREVIOUSLY FUNDED SYSTEMS.—The limitations in paragraph (1) do not apply to the design or acquisition of an unmanned aerial system for which funds for research, development, test, and evaluation have been received from the Department of Defense or the Department of Homeland Security";

(E) in subchapter II, by adding at the end the following:

"§578. Role of Vice Commandant in major acquisition programs

"The Vice Commandant—

"(1) shall represent the customer of a major acquisition program with regard to trade-offs made among cost, schedule, technical feasibility, and performance with respect to such program; and

"(2) shall advise the Commandant in decisions regarding the balancing of resources against priorities, and associated trade-offs referred to in paragraph (1), on behalf of the customer of a major acquisition program.

"§579. Extension of major acquisition program contracts

"(a) IN GENERAL.—Notwithstanding section 564(a)(2) of this title and section 2304 of title 10, and subject to subsections (b) and (c) of this section, the Secretary may acquire additional units procured under a Coast Guard major acquisition program contract, by extension of such contract without competition, if the Director of the Cost Analysis Division of the Department of Homeland Security determines that the costs that would be saved through award of a new contract in accordance with such sections would not exceed the costs of such an award.

"(b) LIMITATION ON NUMBER OF ADDITIONAL UNITS.—The number of additional units acquired under a contract extension under this section may not exceed the number of additional units for which such determination is made.

"(c) DETERMINATION OF COSTS UPON REQUEST.—The Director of the Cost Analysis Division of the Department of Homeland Security shall, at the request of the Secretary, determine for purposes of this section—

"(1) the costs that would be saved through award of a new major acquisition program contract in accordance with section 564(a)(2) for the acquisition of a number of additional units specified by the Secretary; and

"(2) the costs of such award, including the costs that would be incurred due to acquisition schedule delays and asset design changes associated with such award.

"(d) NUMBER OF EXTENSIONS.—A contract may be extended under this section more than once."; and

(F) in section 581—

(i) by redesignating paragraphs (7) through (10) as paragraphs (9) through (12), respectively, and by redesignating paragraphs (3) through (6) as paragraphs (4) through (7), respectively;

(ii) by inserting after paragraph (2) the following:

"(3) CUSTOMER OF A MAJOR ACQUISITION PROGRAM.—The term 'customer of a major acquisition program' means the operating field unit of the Coast Guard that will field the system or systems acquired under a major acquisition program."; and

(iii) by inserting after paragraph (7), as so redesignated, the following:

"(8) MAJOR ACQUISITION PROGRAM.—The term 'major acquisition program' means an ongoing acquisition undertaken by the Coast Guard with a life-cycle cost estimate greater than or equal to $300,000,000.".

(2) CLERICAL AMENDMENT.—The analysis at the beginning of such chapter is amended by adding at the end of the items relating to subchapter II the following:

"578. Role of Vice Commandant in major acquisition programs.

"579. Extension of major acquisition program contracts.".

(c) REVIEW REQUIRED.—

(1) REQUIREMENT.—The Commandant of the Coast Guard shall conduct a review of—

(A) the authorities provided to the Commandant in chapter 15 of title 14, United States Code, and other relevant statutes and regulations related to Coast Guard acquisitions, including developing recommendations to ensure that the Commandant plays an appropriate role in the development of requirements, acquisition processes, and the associated budget practices;

(B) implementation of the strategy prepared in accordance with section 562(b)(2) of title 14, United States Code, as in effect before the enactment of the National Defense Authorization Act for Fiscal Year 2017; and

(C) acquisition policies, directives, and regulations of the Coast Guard to ensure such policies, directives, and regulations establish a customer-oriented acquisition system.

(2) REPORT.—Not later than March 1, 2017, the Commandant shall submit to the Committee on Transportation and Infrastructure of the House of Representatives and the Committee on Commerce, Science, and Transportation of the Senate a report containing, at a minimum, the following:

(A) The recommendations developed by the Commandant under paragraph (1) and other results of the review conducted under such paragraph.

(B) The actions the Commandant is taking, if any, within the Commandant's existing authority to implement such recommendations.

(3) MODIFICATION OF POLICIES, DIRECTIVES, AND REGULATIONS.—Not later than one year after the date of the enactment of this Act, the Commandant of the Coast Guard shall modify the acquisition policies, directives, and regulations of the Coast Guard as necessary to ensure the development and implementation of a customer-oriented acquisition system, pursuant to the review under paragraph (1)(C).

(d) ANALYSIS OF USING MULTIYEAR CONTRACTING.—

(1) IN GENERAL.—No later than one year after the date of the enactment of this Act, the Secretary of the department in which the Coast Guard is operating shall submit to the Committee on Transportation and Infrastructure of the House of Representatives and the Committee on Commerce, Science, and Transportation of the Senate an analysis of the use of multiyear contracting, including procurement authority provided under section 2306b of title 10, United States Code, and authority similar to that granted to the Navy under section 121(b) of the National Defense Authorization Act for Fiscal Year 1998 (Public Law 105–85; 111 Stat. 1648) and section 150 of the Continuing Appropriations Act, 2011 (Public Law 111–242; 124 Stat. 3519), to acquire any combination of at least five—

(A) Fast Response Cutters, beginning with hull 43; and

(B) Offshore Patrol Cutters, beginning with hull 5.

(2) CONTENTS.—The analysis under paragraph (1) shall include the costs and benefits of using multiyear contracting, the impact of multiyear contracting on delivery timelines, and whether the acquisitions examined would meet the tests for the use of multiyear procurement authorities.

SEC. 899A. ENHANCED AUTHORITY TO ACQUIRE PRODUCTS AND SERVICES PRODUCED IN AFRICA IN SUPPORT OF CERTAIN ACTIVITIES.

(a) IN GENERAL.—Except as provided in subsection (c), in the case of a product or service to be acquired in support of covered activities in a covered African country for which the Secretary of Defense makes a determination described in subsection (b), the Secretary may conduct a procurement in which—

(1) competition is limited to products or services from the host nation;

(2) a preference is provided for products or services from the host nation; or

(3) a preference is provided for products or services from a covered African country, other than the host nation.

(b) DETERMINATION.—

(1) IN GENERAL.—A determination described in this subsection is a determination by the Secretary of any of the following:

(A) That the product or service concerned is to be used only in support of covered activities.

(B) That it is in the national security interests of the United States to limit competition or provide a preference as described in subsection (a) because such limitation or preference is necessary—

(i) to reduce overall United States transportation costs and risks in shipping products in support of operations, exercises, theater security cooperation activities, and other missions in the African region;

(ii) to reduce delivery times in support of covered activities; or

(iii) to promote regional security and stability in Africa.

(C) That the product or service is of equivalent quality to a product or service that would have otherwise been acquired without such limitation or preference.

(2) REQUIREMENT FOR EFFECTIVENESS OF ANY PARTICULAR DETERMINATION.—A determination under paragraph (1) shall not be effective for purposes of a limitation or preference under subsection (a) unless the Secretary also determines that—

(A) the limitation or preference will not adversely affect—

(i) United States military operations or stability operations in the African region; or

(ii) the United States industrial base; and

(B) in the case of air transportation, an air carrier holding a certificate under section 41102 of title 49, United States Code, is not reasonably available to provide the air transportation.

(c) INAPPLICABILITY OF AUTHORITY TO PROCUREMENT OF ITEMS ON ABILITYONE PROCUREMENT CATALOG.—The authority under subsection (a) may not be used for the procurement of any good that is contained in the procurement list described in section 8503(a) of title 41, United States Code, if such good can be produced and delivered by a qualified non profit agency for the blind or a nonprofit agency for other severely disabled in a timely fashion to support mission requirements.

(d) REPORT ON USE OF AUTHORITY.—Not later than December 31, 2017, the Secretary shall submit to the congressional defense committees a report on the use of the authority in subsection (a). The report shall include, but not be limited to, the following:

(1) The number of determinations made by the Secretary pursuant to subsection (b).

(2) A list of the countries providing products or services as a result of determinations made pursuant to subsection (b).

(3) A description of the products and services acquired using the authority.

(4) The extent to which the use of the authority has met the one or more of the objectives specified in clause (i), (ii), or (iii) of subsection (b)(1)(B).

(5) Such recommendations for improvements to the authority as the Secretary considers appropriate.

(6) Such other matters as the Secretary considers appropriate.

(e) DEFINITIONS.—In this section:

(1) COVERED ACTIVITIES.—The term "covered activities" means Department of Defense activities in the African region or a regional neighbor.

(2) COVERED AFRICAN COUNTRY.—The term "covered African country" means a country in Africa that has signed a long-term agreement with the United States related to the basing or operational needs of the United States Armed Forces.

(3) HOST NATION.—The term "host nation" means a nation that allows the Armed Forces and supplies of the United States to be located on, to operate in, or to be transported through its territory.

(4) PRODUCT OR SERVICE OF A COVERED AFRICAN COUNTRY.—The term "product or service of a covered African country" means the following:

(A) A product from a covered African country that is wholly grown, mined, manufactured, or produced in the covered African country.

(B) A service from a covered African country that is performed by a person or entity that—

(i) is properly licensed or registered by appropriate authorities of the covered African country; and

(ii) as determined by the Chief of Mission concerned—

(I) is operating primarily in the covered African country; or

(II) is making a significant contribution to the economy of the covered African country through payment of taxes or use of products, materials, or labor that are primarily grown, mined, manufactured, produced, or sourced from the covered African country.

(f) CONFORMING AMENDMENT.—Section 1263 of the National Defense Authorization Act for Fiscal Year 2015 (Public Law 113–291; 128 Stat. 3581) is repealed.

TITLE IX—DEPARTMENT OF DEFENSE ORGANIZATION AND MANAGEMENT

Subtitle A—Office of the Secretary of Defense and Related Matters

Sec. 901. Organization of the Office of the Secretary of Defense.
Sec. 902. Responsibilities and reporting of the Chief Information Officer of the Department of Defense.
Sec. 903. Maximum number of personnel in the Office of the Secretary of Defense and other Department of Defense headquarters offices.
Sec. 904. Repeal of Financial Management Modernization Executive Committee.

Subtitle B—Organization and Management of the Department of Defense Generally

Sec. 911. Organizational strategy for the Department of Defense.
Sec. 912. Policy, organization, and management goals and priorities of the Secretary of Defense for the Department of Defense.
Sec. 913. Secretary of Defense delivery unit.
Sec. 914. Performance of civilian functions by military personnel.
Sec. 915. Repeal of requirements relating to efficiencies plan for the civilian personnel workforce and service contractor workforce of the Department of Defense.

Subtitle C—Joint Chiefs of Staff and Combatant Command Matters

Sec. 921. Joint Chiefs of Staff and related combatant command matters.
Sec. 922. Organization of the Department of Defense for management of special operations forces and special operations.
Sec. 923. Establishment of unified combatant command for cyber operations.
Sec. 924. Assigned forces of the combatant commands.

Sec. 925. Modifications to the requirements process.

Sec. 926. Review of combatant command organization.

Subtitle D—Organization and Management of Other Department of Defense Offices and Elements

Sec. 931. Qualifications for appointment of the Secretaries of the military departments.

Sec. 932. Enhanced personnel management authorities for the Chief of the National Guard Bureau.

Sec. 933. Reorganization and redesignation of Office of Family Policy and Office of Community Support for Military Families with Special Needs.

Sec. 934. Redesignation of Assistant Secretary of the Air Force for Acquisition as Assistant Secretary of the Air Force for Acquisition, Technology, and Logistics.

Subtitle E—Strategies, Reports, and Related Matters

Sec. 941. National defense strategy.

Sec. 942. Commission on the National Defense Strategy for the United States.

Sec. 943. Reform of the national military strategy.

Sec. 944. Form of annual national security strategy report.

Sec. 945. Modification to independent study of national security strategy formulation process.

Subtitle F—Other Matters

Sec. 951. Enhanced security programs for Department of Defense personnel and innovation initiatives.

Sec. 952. Modification of authority of the Secretary of Defense relating to protection of the Pentagon Reservation and other Department of Defense facilities in the National Capital Region.

Sec. 953. Modifications to requirements for accounting for members of the Armed Forces and Department of Defense civilian employees listed as missing.

Sec. 954. Modifications to corrosion report.

Subtitle A—Office of the Secretary of Defense and Related Matters

SEC. 901. ORGANIZATION OF THE OFFICE OF THE SECRETARY OF DEFENSE.

(a) UNDER SECRETARY OF DEFENSE FOR RESEARCH AND ENGINEERING.—

(1) IN GENERAL.—Effective on February 1, 2018, chapter 4 of title 10, United States Code, is amended by striking section 133 and inserting the following new section:

"§ 133a. Under Secretary of Defense for Research and Engineering

"(a) UNDER SECRETARY OF DEFENSE.—There is an Under Secretary of Defense for Research and Engineering, appointed from civilian life by the President, by and with the advice and consent of the Senate. The Under Secretary shall be appointed from among persons who have an extensive technology, science, or engineering background and experience with managing complex or advanced technological programs. A person may not be appointed as Under Secretary within seven years after relief from active duty as a commissioned officer of a regular component of an armed force.

"(b) DUTIES AND POWERS.—Subject to the authority, direction, and control of the Secretary of Defense, the Under Secretary shall perform such duties and exercise such powers as the Secretary may prescribe, including—

"(1) serving as the chief technology officer of the Department of Defense with the mission of advancing technology and innovation for the armed forces (and the Department);

"(2) establishing policies on, and supervising, all defense research and engineering, technology development, technology transition, prototyping, experimentation, and developmental testing activities and programs, including the allocation of resources for defense research and engineering, and unifying defense research and engineering efforts across the Department; and

"(3) serving as the principal advisor to the Secretary on all research, engineering, and technology development activities and programs in the Department.

"(c) PRECEDENCE IN DEPARTMENT OF DEFENSE.—

"(1) PRECEDENCE IN MATTERS OF RESPONSIBILITY.—With regard to all matters for which the Under Secretary has responsibility by the direction of the Secretary of Defense or by law, the Under Secretary takes precedence in the Department of Defense after the Secretary and the Deputy Secretary of Defense.

"(2) PRECEDENCE IN OTHER MATTERS.—With regard to all matters other than the matters for which the Under Secretary has responsibility by the direction of the Secretary or by law, the Under Secretary takes precedence in the Department of Defense after the Secretary, the Deputy Secretary, and the Secretaries of the military departments.".

(2) SERVICE OF INCUMBENT USD FOR ATL IN POSITION.—The individual serving as Under Secretary of Defense for Acquisition, Technology, and Logistics under section 133 of title 10, United States Code, as of February 1, 2018, may continue to serve as Under Secretary of Defense for Research and Engineering commencing as of that date, without further appointment under section 133a of such title, as added by paragraph (1).

(b) UNDER SECRETARY OF DEFENSE FOR ACQUISITION AND SUSTAINMENT.—Effective on February 1, 2018, chapter 4 of title 10, United States Code, is further amended by inserting after section 133a, as added by subsection (a), the following new section:

"§ 133b. Under Secretary of Defense for Acquisition and Sustainment

"(a) UNDER SECRETARY OF DEFENSE.—There is an Under Secretary of Defense for Acquisition and Sustainment, appointed from civilian life by the President, by and with the advice and consent of the Senate. The Under Secretary shall be appointed from among persons who have an extensive system development, engineering, production, or management background and experience with managing complex programs. A person may not be appointed as Under Secretary within seven years after relief from active duty as a commissioned officer of a regular component of an armed force.

"(b) DUTIES AND POWERS.—Subject to the authority, direction, and control of the Secretary of Defense, the Under Secretary shall perform such duties and exercise such powers as the Secretary may prescribe, including—

"(1) serving as the chief acquisition and sustainment officer of the Department of Defense with the mission of delivering and sustaining timely, cost-effective capabilities for the armed forces (and the Department);

"(2) establishing policies on, and supervising, all elements of the Department relating to acquisition (including system design, development, and production, and procurement of goods and services) and sustainment (including logistics, maintenance, and materiel readiness);

"(3) establishing policies for access to, and maintenance of, the defense industrial base and materials critical to national security, and policies on contract administration;

"(4) serving as—

"(A) the principal advisor to the Secretary on acquisition and sustainment in the Department;

"(B) the senior procurement executive for the Department for the purposes of section 1702(c) of title 41; and

"(C) the Defense Acquisition Executive for purposes of regulations and procedures of the Department providing for a Defense Acquisition Executive;

"(5) overseeing the modernization of nuclear forces and the development of capabilities to counter weapons of mass destruction, and serving as the chairman of the Nuclear Weapons Council and the co-chairman of the Council on Oversight of the National Leadership Command, Control, and Communications System;

"(6) the authority to direct the Secretaries of the military departments and the heads of all other elements of the Department with regard to matters for which the Under Secretary has responsibility, except that the Under Secretary shall exercise supervisory authority over service acquisition programs for which the service acquisition executive is the milestone decision authority; and

"(7) to the extent directed by the Secretary, exercising overall supervision of all personnel (civilian and military) in the Office of the Secretary of Defense with regard to matters for which the Under Secretary has responsibility, unless otherwise provided by law.

"(c) PRECEDENCE IN DEPARTMENT OF DEFENSE.—

"(1) PRECEDENCE IN MATTERS OF RESPONSIBILITY.—With regard to all matters for which the Under Secretary has responsibility by the direction of the Secretary of Defense or by law, the Under Secretary takes precedence in the Department of Defense after the Secretary, the Deputy Secretary of Defense, and the Under Secretary of Defense for Research and Engineering.

"(2) PRECEDENCE IN OTHER MATTERS.—With regard to all matters other than the matters for which the Under Secretary has responsibility by the direction of the Secretary or by law, the Under Secretary takes precedence in the Department of Defense after the Secretary, the Deputy Secretary, the Under Secretary of Defense for Research and Engineering, and the Secretaries of the military departments.".

"(c) CHIEF MANAGEMENT OFFICER.—

"(1) IN GENERAL.—Effective on February 1, 2018, there is a Chief Management Officer of the Department of Defense.

"(2) APPOINTMENT.—The Chief Management Officer shall be appointed from civilian life by the President, by and with the advice and consent of the Senate. The Chief Management Officer shall be appointed from among persons who have an extensive management or business background and experience with managing large or complex organizations. A person may not be appointed as Chief Management Officer within seven years after relief from active duty as a commissioned officer of a regular component of an Armed Force

"(3) DUTIES AND POWERS.—Subject to the authority, direction, and control of the Secretary of Defense, the Chief Management Officer shall perform such duties and exercise such powers as the Secretary may prescribe, including—

"(A) serving as the chief management officer of the Department of Defense with the mission of managing the business operations of the Department;

"(B) establishing policies on, and supervising, all business operations of the Department, including business transformation, business planning and processes, performance management, and business information technology management and improvement activities and programs, including the allocation of resources for business operations, and unifying business management efforts across the Department;

(C) serving as the principal advisor to the Secretary on all business operations activities and programs in the Department; and

(D) the authority to direct the Secretaries of the military departments and the heads of all other elements of the Department with regard to matters for which the Chief Management Officer has responsibility.

(4) CONFORMING AMENDMENTS.—Effective on February 1, 2018, section 132 of title 10, United States Code, is amended—

(A) by striking subsection (c); and

(B) by redesignating subsections (d) and (e) as subsections (c) and (d), respectively.

(d) REPEAL OF PENDING AUTHORITY TO ESTABLISH UNDER SECRETARY OF DEFENSE FOR BUSINESS MANAGEMENT AND INFORMATION.—Subsection (a) of section 901 of the Carl Levin and Howard P. "Buck" McKeon National Defense Authorization Act for Fiscal Year 2015 (Public Law 113–291; 128 Stat. 3462) is repealed.

(e) REPEAL OF CERTAIN ASD AND DIRECTOR POSITIONS.—Chapter 4 of title 10, United States Code, is further amended—

(1) in section 138(b)—

(A) by striking paragraphs (6), (7), (8), and (9); and

(B) by redesignating paragraph (10) as paragraph (6); and

(2) by striking sections 139b and 139c.

(f) OFFICE OF THE SECRETARY OF DEFENSE.— Effective on February 1, 2018, section 131(b)(2) of title 10, United States Code, is amended—

(1) by redesignating subparagraphs (B) through (E) as subparagraphs (C) through (F), respectively; and

(2) by striking subparagraph (A) and inserting the following new subparagraphs:

"(A) The Under Secretary of Defense for Research and Engineering.

"(B) The Under Secretary of Defense for Acquisition and Sustainment.".

(g) TABLE OF SECTION AMENDMENTS.—

(1) TABLE OF SECTIONS EFFECTIVE ON ENACTMENT.—The table of sections at the beginning of chapter 4 of title 10, United States Code, is amended by striking the items relating to sections 139b and 139c.

(2) TABLE OF SECTIONS EFFECTIVE ON DELAYED EFFECTIVE DATE.—Effective on February 1, 2018, the table of sections at the beginning of chapter 4 of such title is further amended by striking the item relating to section 133 and inserting the following new items:

"133a. Under Secretary of Defense for Research and Engineering.

"133b. Under Secretary of Defense for Acquisition and Sustainment.".

(h) EXECUTIVE SCHEDULE LEVEL II.—Effective on February 1, 2018, section 5313 of title 5, United States Code, is amended by striking the item relating to the Under Secretary of Defense for Acquisition, Technology, and Logistics and inserting the following new items:

"Under Secretary of Defense for Research and Engineering.

"Under Secretary of Defense for Acquisition and Sustainment.".

(i) REVIEW REQUIRED.—

(1) IN GENERAL.—The Secretary of Defense shall conduct a review and identify a recommended organizational and management structure for the Department of Defense that implements the organizational policy guidance expressed in this section and the amendments made by this section.

(2) ELEMENTS .—The review and recommendations shall address, but not be limited to, the following:

(A) The organizational and management structure of the Department including the disposition of leadership positions, subordinate organizations, and defined relationships across such leadership positions and organizations.

(B) The recommended disposition within the Office of the Secretary of Defense of the various Assistant Secretaries of Defense, Deputy Assistant Secretaries of Defense, and Directors affected by the organizational policy guidance.

(C) The specific delineation of roles, responsibilities, and authorities, as directed by the Secretary, for the organizational and management structure covered by subparagraph (A).

(j) REPORTS.—

(1) INTERIM REPORT.—Not later than March 1, 2017, the Secretary of Defense shall submit to the congressional defense committees an interim report on the review and recommended organizational and management structure for the Department of Defense as required by subsection (i).

(2) FINAL REPORT.—Not later than August 1, 2017, the Secretary shall submit to the congressional defense committees a final report on the review and recommended organizational and management structure, including—

(A) a proposed implementation plan for how the Department would implement its recommendations;

(B) recommendations for revisions to appointments and qualifications, duties and powers, and precedent in the Department;

(C) recommendations for such legislative and administrative action, including conforming and other amendments to law, as the Secretary considers appropriate to implement the plan; and

(D) any other matters that the Secretary considers appropriate.

SEC. 902. RESPONSIBILITIES AND REPORTING OF THE CHIEF INFORMATION OFFICER OF THE DEPARTMENT OF DEFENSE.

(a) IN GENERAL.—Section 142(b)(1) of title 10, United States Code, is amended—

(1) in subparagraph (C), by striking "and" at the end;

(2) in subparagraph (D), by striking the period at the end and inserting a semicolon; and

(3) by adding at the end the following new subparagraphs:

"(E) exercises authority, direction, and control over the Defense Information Systems Agency, or any successor organization;

"(F) has the responsibilities for policy, oversight, guidance, and coordination for all Department of Defense matters related to electromagnetic spectrum, including coordination with other Federal and industry agencies, coordination for classified programs, and in coordination with the Under Secretary for Personnel and Readiness, policies related to spectrum management workforce;

"(G) has the responsibilities for policy, oversight, guidance, and coordination for nuclear command and control systems;

"(H) has the responsibilities for policy, oversight, and guidance for matters related to precision navigation and timing; and

"(I) has the responsibilities for policy, oversight, and guidance for the architecture and programs related to the networking and cyber defense architecture of the Department.".

(b) DIRECT REPORTING.—Section 151(b)(5) of such title is amended by inserting before the period at the end the following: ", who reports directly to the Secretary and Deputy Secretary without intervening authority".

SEC. 903. MAXIMUM NUMBER OF PERSONNEL IN THE OFFICE OF THE SECRETARY OF DEFENSE AND OTHER DEPARTMENT OF DEFENSE HEADQUARTERS OFFICES.

(a) OFFICE OF THE SECRETARY OF DEFENSE.— Section 143(b) of title 10, United States Code, is amended by striking "and civilian personnel" and inserting ", civilian, and detailed personnel".

(b) JOINT STAFF.—

(1) IN GENERAL.—Section 155 of such title is amended by adding at the end the following new subsection:

"(h) PERSONNEL LIMITATIONS.—(1) The total number of members of the armed forces and civilian employees assigned or detailed to permanent duty for the Joint Staff may not exceed 2,069.

"(2) Not more than 1,500 members of the armed forces on the active-duty list may be assigned or detailed to permanent duty for the Joint Staff.

"(3) The limitations in paragraphs (1) and (2) do not apply in time of war.

"(4) Each limitation in paragraphs (1) and (2) may be exceeded by a number equal to 15 percent of such limitation in time of national emergency.".

(2) EFFECTIVE DATE.—The amendment made by paragraph (1) shall take effect on December 31, 2019.

(c) OFFICE OF THE SECRETARY OF THE ARMY.— Section 3014(f) of such title is amended—

(1) in paragraph (4), by striking "time of war" and all that follows and inserting "time of war."; and

(2) by adding at the end the following new paragraph:

"(5) Each limitation in paragraphs (1) and (2) may be exceeded by a number equal to 15 percent of such limitation in time of national emergency.".

(d) OFFICE OF THE SECRETARY OF THE NAVY.— Section 5014(f) of such title is amended—

(1) in paragraph (4), by striking "time of war" and all that follows and inserting "time of war."; and

(2) by adding at the end the following new paragraph:

"(5) Each limitation in paragraphs (1) and (2) may be exceeded by a number equal to 15 percent of such limitation in time of national emergency.".

(e) OFFICE OF THE SECRETARY OF THE AIR FORCE.—Section 8014(f) of such title is amended—

(1) in paragraph (4), by striking "time of war" and all that follows and inserting "time of war."; and

(2) by adding at the end the following new paragraph:

"(5) Each limitation in paragraphs (1) and (2) may be exceeded by a number equal to 15 percent of such limitation in time of national emergency.".

SEC. 904. REPEAL OF FINANCIAL MANAGEMENT MODERNIZATION EXECUTIVE COMMITTEE.

(a) REPEAL.—Section 185 of title 10, United States Code, is repealed.

(b) CLERICAL AMENDMENT.—The table of sections at the beginning of chapter 7 of such title is amended by striking the item relating to section 185.

Subtitle B—Organization and Management of the Department of Defense Generally

SEC. 911. ORGANIZATIONAL STRATEGY FOR THE DEPARTMENT OF DEFENSE.

(a) ORGANIZATIONAL STRATEGY REQUIRED.—

(1) IN GENERAL.—Not later than September 1, 2017, the Secretary of Defense shall formulate and issue to the Department of Defense an organizational strategy for the Department that—

(A) identifies the critical objectives and other organizational outputs for the Department that span multiple functional boundaries and would benefit from the use of cross-functional teams under this section to ensure collaboration and integration across organizations within the Department;

(B) improves the manner in which the Department integrates the expertise and capacities of the functional components of the Department for effective and efficient achievement of such objectives and outputs;

(C) improves the management of relationships and processes involving the Office of the Secretary of Defense, the Joint Staff, the combatant

commands, the military departments, and the Defense Agencies with regard to such objectives and outputs;

(D) improves the ability of the Department to work effectively in interagency processes with regard to such objectives and outputs in order to better serve the President; and

(E) achieves an organizational structure that enhances performance with regard to such objectives and outputs.

(2) ELEMENTS.—The strategy shall provide for the following:

(A) The appropriate use of cross-functional teams to manage critical objectives and outputs of the Department described in paragraph (1)(A).

(B) The furtherance and advancement of a collaborative, team-oriented, results-driven, and innovative culture within the Department that fosters an open debate of ideas and alternative courses of action, and supports cross-functional teaming and integration.

(b) ACTIONS IN SUPPORT OF STRATEGY.—

(1) STUDY.—The Department of Defense shall conduct a study of the following in order to determine how best to implement effective cross-functional teams in the Department to achieve the strategic objectives of the Secretary of Defense:

(A) Lessons learned, as reflected in academic literature, business and management school case studies, and the work of leading management consultant firms, on the successful and failed application of cross-functional teams in the private sector and government, and on the cultural factors necessary to support effective cross-functional teams.

(B) The historical and current use by the Department of cross-functional working groups, integrated process teams, councils, and committees, and the reasons why such entities have or have not achieved high levels of teamwork or effectiveness.

(2) CONDUCT OF STUDY.—The study required by paragraph (1) shall be conducted by an independent organization with widely acknowledged expertise in modern organizational management and teaming selected by the Secretary for purposes of the study.

(3) SCHEDULE.—The Secretary shall award any necessary contract for the study required by paragraph (1) pursuant to paragraph (2) by not later than March 15, 2017, and shall provide the results of the study to the congressional defense committees by not later than July 15, 2017.

(c) CROSS-FUNCTIONAL TEAMS.—In support of the strategy required by subsection (a):

(1) IN GENERAL.—The Secretary of Defense shall establish cross-functional teams to address critical objectives and outputs for such teams as are determined to be appropriate in accordance with the organizational strategy issued under subsection (a), with initial teams established by not later than September 30, 2017.

(2) PURPOSES.—The purposes of cross-functional teams established pursuant to this subsection shall be, as determined appropriate by the Secretary—

(A) to provide for effective collaboration and integration across organizational and functional boundaries in the Department of Defense;

(B) to develop, at the direction of the Secretary, recommendations for comprehensive and fully integrated policies, strategies, plans, and resourcing decisions;

(C) to make decisions on cross-functional issues, to the extent authorized by the Secretary and within parameters established by the Secretary; and

(D) to provide oversight for and, as directed by the Secretary, supervise the implementation of approved policies, strategies, plans, and resourcing decisions approved by the Secretary.

(3) GUIDANCE ON TEAMS.—Not later than September 30, 2017, the Secretary shall issue guidance—

(A) addressing the role, authorities, reporting relationships, resourcing, manning, training, and operations of cross-functional teams established pursuant to this subsection;

(B) delineating decision-making authority of such teams;

(C) providing that the leaders of functional components of the Department that provide personnel to such teams respect and respond to team needs and activities; and

(D) emphasizing that personnel selected for assignment to such teams shall faithfully represent the views and expertise of their functional components while contributing to the best of their ability to the success of the team concerned.

(4) PARTICIPANTS.—In establishing a cross-functional team pursuant to this subsection, the Secretary shall consider personnel from the Office of the Secretary of Defense, the Joint Staff, the military departments, and the Defense Agencies in all functional areas that the Secretary considers appropriate.

(5) TEAM PERSONNEL.—For each cross-functional team established by the Secretary pursuant to this subsection, the Secretary shall—

(A) assign as leader of such team a senior qualified and experienced individual, who shall report directly to the Secretary regarding the activities of such team;

(B) delegate to the team leader designated pursuant to subparagraph (A) authority to select members of such team from among civilian employees of the Department and members of the Armed Forces in any grade who are recommended for membership on such team by the head of a functional component of the Department within the Office of the Secretary of Defense, the Joint Staff, and the military departments, by the commander of a combatant command, or by the director of a Defense Agency;

(C) provide the team leader with necessary full time support from team members, and the means to co-locate team members;

(D) ensure that team members and all leaders in functional organizations that are in the supervisory chain for personnel serving on such team receive training in elements of successful cross-functional teams, including teamwork, collaboration, conflict resolution, and appropriately representing the views and expertise of their functional components; and

(E) ensure that the congressional defense committees are provided information on the progress and results of such team upon request.

(6) TEAM STRATEGIES AND DECISION-MAKING AUTHORITY.—

(A) IN GENERAL.—The Secretary shall ensure that the objectives of each cross-functional team established pursuant to this subsection are clearly established in writing, through a memorandum, statement, charter, or similar document.

(B) METRICS.—To improve team performance and accountability, the Secretary shall task each team, as appropriate, to establish a strategy to achieve the objectives specified by the Secretary, metrics for evaluation of the achievement of such objectives by such team, and the alignment of individual and team goals for the achievement of such objectives by such team.

(C) DELEGATION OF AUTHORITY.—The Secretary may delegate to a team any decision-making authority that, and shall delegate such authority as, the Secretary considers appropriate to permit such team to achieve the objectives established by the Secretary.

(7) REVIEW OF TEAMS.—Not later than 18 months after the date on which the first cross-functional team is established pursuant to this subsection, the Secretary shall complete an analysis, with support from external experts in organizational and management sciences, of the successes and failures of teams established pur-

suant to this subsection, and determine how to apply the lessons learned from that analysis.

(8) REPORT ON ESTABLISHMENT.—Not later than 18 months after the date of the enactment of this Act, the Secretary shall submit to Congress a report on the establishment of cross-functional teams under this subsection, including descriptions from the leaders of teams established prior to the date on which this report is submitted of the manner in which the teams were designed and how they functioned.

(d) DIRECTIVE ON COLLABORATIVE CULTURE AND BEHAVIOR.—The guidance issued by the Secretary of Defense pursuant to subsection (c)(3) shall also—

(1) articulate the shared purposes, values, and principles for the operation of the Office of the Secretary of Defense that are required to promote a team-oriented, collaborative, results-driven culture within the Office to support the primary objectives of the Department of Defense;

(2) ensure that collaboration across functional and organizational boundaries is an important factor in the performance review of leaders of cross-functional teams established pursuant to subsection (c), members of teams, and other appropriate leaders of the Department; and

(3) identify key practices that senior leaders of the Department should follow with regard to leadership, organizational practice, collaboration, and the functioning of cross-functional teams, and the types of personnel behavior that senior leaders should encourage and discourage.

(e) STREAMLINING OF ORGANIZATIONAL STRUCTURE AND PROCESSES OF OSD.—Not later than 18 months after the date of the enactment of this Act, the Secretary of Defense shall take such actions as the Secretary considers appropriate to streamline the organizational structure and processes of the Office of the Secretary of Defense in order to increase spans of control, achieve a reduction in layers of management, eliminate unnecessary duplication between the Office and the Joint Staff, and reduce the time required to complete standard processes and activities.

(f) TRAINING FOR INDIVIDUALS NOMINATED FOR APPOINTMENT FOR OSD POSITIONS CONFIRMED BY THE SENATE.—

(1) IN GENERAL.—Within three months of the appointment of an individual to a position in the Office of the Secretary of Defense appointable by and with the advice and consent of the Senate, the individual shall complete a course of instruction in leadership, modern organizational practice, collaboration, and the operation of teams described in subsection (c).

(2) WAIVER.—The President may waive the requirement in paragraph (1) with respect to an individual if the Secretary determines in writing that the individual possesses, through training and experience, the skill and knowledge otherwise to be provided through a course of instruction as described in that paragraph.

(g) COMPTROLLER GENERAL OF THE UNITED STATES ASSESSMENTS.—

(1) BIANNUAL REPORT ON ASSESSMENTS.—Not later than six months after the date of the enactment of this Act, and every six months thereafter through December 31, 2019, the Comptroller General of the United States shall submit to the Committees on Armed Services of the Senate and the House of Representatives a report setting forth a comprehensive assessment of the actions taken under this section during the six-month period ending on the date of such report and cumulatively since the date of the enactment of this Act.

(2) ASSESSMENT TEAM.—The Comptroller General may establish within the Government Accountability Office a team of analysts to assist the Comptroller General in the performance assessments required by this subsection.

SEC. 912. POLICY, ORGANIZATION, AND MANAGEMENT GOALS AND PRIORITIES OF THE SECRETARY OF DEFENSE FOR THE DEPARTMENT OF DEFENSE.

(a) IN GENERAL.—A Secretary of Defense serving in that position pursuant to an appointment to that position after January 20, 2017, shall submit to the Committees on Armed Services of the Senate and the House of Representatives, not later than each of the deadlines specified in subsection (b), a report on the policy, organization, and management goals and priorities of the Secretary for the Department of Defense. Each report shall include, current as of the date of such report, an identification of the following:

(1) Policy goals and priorities, including specific and measurable performance and implementation targets.

(2) Organization and management goals and priorities, including specific and measurable performance and implementation targets that address, but are not limited to, the following:

(A) The elimination or consolidation of any unnecessary or redundant functions within the Department.

(B) Force management and shaping, including recommendations for such legislative action as is required to meet force management and shaping goals and priorities.

(C) The delayering or reorganization of headquarters organizations across the Department.

(3) Any other goals or priorities for the Department the Secretary considers appropriate.

(b) DEADLINES.—The deadlines for the submittal of reports under subsection (a) are April 1, 2017, and February 1 of each year thereafter though 2022.

(c) BRIEFINGS SATISFY LATER REPORTING REQUIREMENTS.—Any report required under subsection (a) after the initial report may be provided in the form of a briefing.

SEC. 913. SECRETARY OF DEFENSE DELIVERY UNIT.

(a) IN GENERAL.—The Secretary of Defense serving in that position as of March 1, 2017, may establish within the Office of the Secretary of Defense a unit of personnel that shall be responsible for providing expertise and support throughout the Department of Defense in an effort to improve the implementation of policies and priorities across the Department. The unit may be known as the "delivery unit".

(b) COMPOSITION.—The unit established pursuant to subsection (a) shall consist of not more than 30 individuals selected by the Secretary primarily from among individuals outside the Government who have significant experience and expertise in management consulting, organizational architecture, relationship management, or data analytics.

(c) DUTIES.—The unit established pursuant to subsection (a) shall have the duties as follows:

(1) To advise the Secretary on improving the implementation and delivery of policies and priorities of the Department, including making recommendations on establishing performance or implementation targets, assisting in the development of delivery plans to achieve targets, and monitoring and measuring progress.

(2) To work across organizations, missions, and functions of the Department in order to identify obstacles to improving the implementation of policies and priorities of the Department, including organization, culture, and incentives, and to recommend options to the Secretary for addressing such obstacles.

(d) SUNSET.—The unit established pursuant to subsection (a) shall sunset on January 31, 2021.

SEC. 914. PERFORMANCE OF CIVILIAN FUNCTIONS BY MILITARY PERSONNEL.

Section 129a of title 10, United States Code, is amended by adding at the end the following new subsection:

"(g) PERFORMANCE OF CIVILIAN FUNCTIONS BY MILITARY PERSONNEL.—(1) Functions performed by civilian personnel should not be performed by military personnel except—

"(A) if the Secretary of the military department concerned determines in writing based on mission requirements that the performance of such functions by military personnel, including a permanent conversion of such functions to performance by military personnel, is cost-effective or required by a mission; or

"(B) if the performance of such functions by military personnel is required to address critical staffing needs resulting from a reduction in personnel or budgetary resources by reason of an Act of Congress, in which case such functions may not be performed by military personnel for a period in excess of one year.

"(2) In determining the workforce mix between civilian and military personnel, the Secretary of a military department shall reserve military personnel for the performance of the functions that, in the estimation of the Secretary, are required to be performed by military personnel in order to achieve national defense goals or in order to enable the proper functioning of the military department. In making workforce decisions, the Secretary shall account for the relative budgetary impact of military versus civilian personnel in determining the functions required to be performed by military personnel.".

SEC. 915. REPEAL OF REQUIREMENTS RELATING TO EFFICIENCIES PLAN FOR THE CIVILIAN PERSONNEL WORKFORCE AND SERVICE CONTRACTOR WORKFORCE OF THE DEPARTMENT OF DEFENSE.

Section 955 of the National Defense Authorization Act for Fiscal Year 2013 (Public Law 112–239; 126 Stat. 1896; 10 U.S.C. 129a note) is repealed.

Subtitle C—Joint Chiefs of Staff and Combatant Command Matters

SEC. 921. JOINT CHIEFS OF STAFF AND RELATED COMBATANT COMMAND MATTERS.

(a) FUNCTIONS OF JOINT CHIEFS OF STAFF.—

(1) CONSULTATION BY CHAIRMAN.—Subsection (c)(1) of section 151 of title 10, United States Code, is amended by striking "as he considers appropriate" and inserting "as necessary".

(2) MODIFICATION OF ADVICE AND OPINIONS OF MEMBERS OTHER THAN CHAIRMAN.—Such section is further amended—

(A) in subsection (b)(2), by striking "subsections (d) and (e)" and inserting "subsection (d)";

(B) in subsection (d)—

(i) by redesignating paragraphs (1) and (2) as paragraphs (2) and (3), respectively; and

(ii) by inserting before paragraph (1), as redesignated by clause (i), the following new paragraph (1):

"(1) After first informing the Secretary of Defense and the Chairman, the members of the Joint Chiefs of Staff, individually or collectively, in their capacity as military advisors, may provide advice to the President, the National Security Council, the Homeland Security Council, or the Secretary of Defense on a particular matter on the judgment of the military member."; and

(C) by striking subsection (e).

(b) TERM AND REAPPOINTMENT OF CHAIRMAN OF THE JOINT CHIEFS OF STAFF.—

(1) IN GENERAL.—Section 152(a) of title 10, United States Code, is amended—

(A) in paragraph (1), by striking "two years, beginning on October 1 of odd-numbered years" and all that follows and inserting "four years, beginning on October 1 of an odd-numbered year. The limitation does not apply in time of war."; and

(B) by striking paragraph (3) and inserting the following new paragraph (3):

"(3) The President may extend to eight years the combined period of service of an officer as Chairman and Vice Chairman if the President determines that such action is in the national interest. The limitation in this paragraph does not apply in time of war.".

(2) EFFECTIVE DATE.—The amendments made by paragraph (1) shall take effect on January 1, 2019, and shall apply to individuals appointed as Chairman of the Joint Chiefs of Staff on or after that date.

(c) FUNCTIONS OF CHAIRMAN OF JOINT CHIEFS OF STAFF.—The text of section 153 of title 10, United States Code, is amended to read as follows:

"Subject to the authority, direction, and control of the President and the Secretary of Defense, the Chairman of the Joint Chiefs of Staff shall be responsible for the following

"(1) STRATEGIC DIRECTION.—Assisting the President and the Secretary in providing for the strategic direction of the armed forces.

"(2) STRATEGIC AND CONTINGENCY PLANNING.—In matters relating to strategic and contingency planning—

"(A) developing strategic frameworks and preparing strategic plans, as required, to guide the use and employment of military force and related activities across all geographic regions and military functions and domains, and to sustain military efforts over different durations of time, as necessary;

"(B) advising the Secretary on the production of the national defense strategy required by section 113(g) of this title and the national security strategy required by section 108 of the National Security Act of 1947 (50 U.S.C. 3043);

"(C) preparing military analysis, options, and plans, as the Chairman considers appropriate, to recommend to the President and the Secretary;

"(D) providing for the preparation and review of contingency plans which conform to policy guidance from the President and the Secretary; and

"(E) preparing joint logistic and mobility plans to support national defense strategies and recommending the assignment of responsibilities to the armed forces in accordance with such plans.

"(3) GLOBAL MILITARY INTEGRATION.—In matters relating to global military strategic and operational integration—

"(A) providing advice to the President and the Secretary on ongoing military operations; and

"(B) advising the Secretary on the allocation and transfer of forces among geographic and functional combatant commands, as necessary, to address transregional, multi-domain, and multifunctional threats.

"(4) COMPREHENSIVE JOINT READINESS.—In matters relating to comprehensive joint readiness—

"(A) evaluating the overall preparedness of the joint force to perform the responsibilities of that force under national defense strategies and to respond to significant contingencies worldwide;

"(B) assessing the risks to United States missions, strategies, and military personnel that stem from shortfalls in military readiness across the armed forces, and developing risk mitigation options;

"(C) advising the Secretary on critical deficiencies and strengths in joint force capabilities (including manpower, logistics, and mobility support) identified during the preparation and review of national defense strategies and contingency plans and assessing the effect of such deficiencies and strengths on meeting national security objectives and policy and on strategic plans;

"(D) advising the Secretary on the missions and functions that are likely to require contractor or other external support to meet national security objectives and policy and strategy, and the risks associated with such support; and

"(E) establishing and maintaining, after consultation with the commanders of the unified and specified combatant commands, a uniform system of evaluating the preparedness of each such command, and groups of commands collectively, to carry out missions assigned to the command or commands.

"(5) JOINT CAPABILITY DEVELOPMENT.—In matters relating to joint capability development—

"(A) identifying new joint military capabilities based on advances in technology and concepts of operation needed to maintain the technological and operational superiority of the armed forces, and recommending investments and experiments in such capabilities to the Secretary;

"(B) performing military net assessments of the joint capabilities of the armed forces of the United States and its allies in comparison with the capabilities of potential adversaries;

"(C) advising the Secretary under section 163(b)(2) of this title on the priorities of the requirements identified by the commanders of the unified and specified combatant commands;

"(D) advising the Secretary on the extent to which the program recommendations and budget proposals of the military departments and other components of the Department of Defense for a fiscal year conform with the priorities established in national defense strategies and with the priorities established for the requirements of the unified and specified combatant commands;

"(E) advising the Secretary on new and alternative joint military capabilities, and alternative program recommendations and budget proposals, within projected resource levels and guidance provided by the Secretary, in order to achieve greater conformance with the priorities referred to in subparagraph (D);

"(F) assessing joint military capabilities and identifying, approving, and prioritizing gaps in such capabilities to meet national defense strategies, pursuant to section 181 of this title; and

"(G) recommending to the Secretary appropriate trade-offs among life-cycle cost, schedule, performance, and procurement quantity objectives in the acquisition of materiel and equipment to support the strategic and contingency plans required by this paragraph in the most effective and efficient manner.

"(6) JOINT FORCE DEVELOPMENT ACTIVITIES.—In matters relating to joint force development activities—

"(A) developing doctrine for the joint employment of the armed forces;

"(B) formulating policies and technical standards, and executing actions, for the joint training of the armed forces;

"(C) formulating policies for coordinating the military education of members of the armed forces;

"(D) formulating policies for concept development and experimentation for the joint employment of the armed forces;

"(E) formulating policies for gathering, developing, and disseminating joint lessons learned for the armed forces; and

"(F) advising the Secretary on development of joint command, control, communications, and cybercapability, including integration and interoperability of such capability, through requirements, integrated architectures, data standards, and assessments.

"(7) OTHER MATTERS.—In other matters—

"(A) recommending to the Secretary, in accordance with section 166 of this title, a budget proposal for activities of each unified and specified combatant command;

"(B) providing for representation of the United States on the Military Staff Committee of the United Nations in accordance with the Charter of the United Nations; and

"(C) performing such other duties as may be prescribed by law or by the President or the Secretary.".

(d) VICE CHAIRMAN OF THE JOINT CHIEFS OF STAFF MATTERS.—

(1) TERM OF SERVICE.—Paragraph (3) of section 154(a) of title 10, United States Code, is amended by striking "for a term of two years" and all that follows and inserting "for a single term of four years, beginning on October 1 of an odd-numbered year, except that the term may not begin in the same year as the term of a Chairman. In time of war, there is no limit on the number of reappointments.".

(2) INELIGIBILITY FOR SERVICE AS CHAIRMAN OR ANY OTHER POSITION IN THE ARMED FORCES.—Such section is further amended by adding at the end the following new paragraph:

"(4)(A) The Vice Chairman shall not be eligible for promotion to the position of Chairman or any other position in the armed forces.

"(B) The President may waive subparagraph (A) if the President determines such action is necessary in the national interest.".

(3) EFFECTIVE DATE.—The amendments made by this subsection shall take effect on January 1, 2021, and shall apply to individuals appointed as Vice Chairman of the Joint Chiefs of Staff on or after that date.

(e) COMMANDERS OF THE COMBATANT COMMANDS.—Section 164 of title 10, United States Code, is amended—

(1) in subsection (b), by adding at the end the following new paragraph:

"(3) Among the full range of command responsibilities specified in subsection (c) and as provided for in section 161 of this title, the primary duties of the commander of a combatant command shall be as follows:

"(A) To produce plans for the employment of the armed forces to execute national defense strategies and respond to significant military contingencies.

"(B) To take actions, as necessary, to deter conflict.

"(C) To command United States armed forces as directed by the Secretary and approved by the President."; and

(2) by adding at the end the following new subsection:

"(h) SUPPORT TO CHAIRMAN OF THE JOINT CHIEFS OF STAFF.—The commander of a combatant command shall provide such information to the Chairman of the Joint Chiefs of Staff as may be necessary for the Chairman to perform the duties of the Chairman under section 153 of this title.".

SEC. 922. ORGANIZATION OF THE DEPARTMENT OF DEFENSE FOR MANAGEMENT OF SPECIAL OPERATIONS FORCES AND SPECIAL OPERATIONS.

(a) RESPONSIBILITY OF ASSISTANT SECRETARY OF DEFENSE FOR SPECIAL OPERATIONS AND LOW INTENSITY CONFLICT.—Section 138(b)(4) of title 10, United States Code, is amended by adding at the end the following new sentence: "Subject to the authority, direction, and control of the Secretary of Defense, the Assistant Secretary shall do the following:

"(A) Exercise authority, direction, and control of all special-operations peculiar administrative matters relating to the organization, training, and equipping of special operations forces.

"(B) Assist the Secretary and the Under Secretary of Defense for Policy in the development and supervision of policy, program planning and execution, and allocation and use of resources for the activities of the Department of Defense for the following:

"(i) Irregular warfare, combating terrorism, and the special operations activities specified by section 167(k) of this title.

"(ii) Integrating the functional activities of the headquarters of the Department to most efficiently and effectively provide for required special operations forces and capabilities.

"(iii) Such other matters as may be specified by the Secretary and the Under Secretary.".

(b) SPECIAL OPERATIONS POLICY AND OVERSIGHT COUNCIL.—

(1) IN GENERAL.—Chapter 4 of title 10, United States Code, as amended by section 901(e)(2) of this Act, is further amended by inserting after section 139a the following new section:

"§ 139b. Special Operations Policy and Oversight Council

"(a) IN GENERAL.—In order to fulfill the responsibilities specified in section 138(b)(4) of this title, the Assistant Secretary of Defense for Special Operations and Low Intensity Conflict, or the designee of the Assistant Secretary, shall establish and lead a team to be known as the 'Special Operations Policy and Oversight Council' (in this section referred to as the 'Council').

"(b) PURPOSE.—The purpose of the Council is to integrate the functional activities of the headquarters of the Department of Defense in order to most efficiently and effectively provide for special operations forces and capabilities. In fulfilling this purpose, the Council shall develop and continuously improve policy, joint processes, and procedures that facilitate the development, acquisition, integration, employment, and sustainment of special operations forces and capabilities.

"(c) MEMBERSHIP.—The Council shall include the following:

"(1) The Assistant Secretary, who shall act as leader of the Council.

"(2) Appropriate senior representatives of each of the following:

"(A) The Under Secretary of Defense for Research and Engineering.

"(B) The Under Secretary of Defense for Management and Support.

"(C) The Under Secretary of Defense (Comptroller).

"(D) The Under Secretary of Defense for Personnel and Readiness.

"(E) The Under Secretary of Defense for Intelligence.

"(F) The General Counsel of the Department of Defense.

"(G) The other Assistant Secretaries of Defense under the Under Secretary of Defense for Policy.

"(H) The military departments.

"(I) The Joint Staff.

"(J) The United States Special Operations Command.

"(K) Such other officials or Agencies, elements, or components of the Department of Defense as the Secretary of Defense considers appropriate.

"(d) OPERATION.—The Council shall operate continuously.".

(2) CLERICAL AMENDMENT.—The table of sections at the beginning of chapter 4 of such title, as amended by section 901(g)(1) of this Act, is further amended by inserting after the item relating to section 139a the following new item:

"139b. Special Operations Policy and Oversight Council.".

(c) US SPECIAL OPERATIONS COMMAND MATTERS.—

(1) AUTHORITY OF COMMANDER.—Subsection (e)(2) of section 167 of title 10, United States Code, is amended—

(A) in the matter preceding subparagraph (A), by striking "The commander" and inserting "Subject to the authority, direction, and control of the Assistant Secretary of Defense for Special Operations and Low Intensity Conflict, the commander"; and

(B) by striking subparagraph (J) and inserting the following new subparagraph (J):

"(J) Monitoring the promotions of special operations forces and coordinating with the military departments regarding the assignment, retention, training, professional military education, and special and incentive pays of special operations forces.".

(2) ADMINISTRATIVE CHAIN OF COMMAND.— Such section is further amended—

(A) by redesignating subsections (f) through (k) as subsections (g), through (l), respectively; and

(B) by inserting after subsection (e) the following new subsection (f):

"(f) ADMINISTRATIVE CHAIN OF COMMAND.— (1) Unless otherwise directed by the President, the administrative chain of command to the special operations command runs—

"(A) from the President to the Secretary of Defense;

"(B) from the Secretary of Defense to the Assistant Secretary of Defense for Special Operations and Low Intensity Conflict; and

"(C) from the Assistant Secretary of Defense for Special Operations and Low Intensity Conflict to the commander of the special operations command.

"(2) For purposes of this subsection, administrative chain of command refers to the exercise of authority, direction and control with respect to the special operations-peculiar administration and support of the special operations command, including the readiness and organization of special operations forces, resources and equipment, and civilian personnel. It does not refer to the exercise of authority, direction, and control of operational matters that are subject to the operational chain of command of the commanders of combatant commands or the exercise of authority, direction, and control of personnel, resources, equipment, and other matters that are not special operations-peculiar that are the purview of the armed forces.".

SEC. 923. ESTABLISHMENT OF UNIFIED COMBATANT COMMAND FOR CYBER OPERATIONS.

(a) ESTABLISHMENT OF CYBER COMMAND.— Chapter 6 of title 10, United States Code, is amended by inserting after section 167a the following new section:

"§ 167b. Unified combatant command for cyber operations

"(a) ESTABLISHMENT.—With the advice and assistance of the Chairman of the Joint Chiefs of Staff, the President, through the Secretary of Defense, shall establish under section 161 of this title a unified combatant command for cyber operations forces (hereinafter in this section referred to as the 'cyber command'). The principal function of the command is to prepare cyber operations forces to carry out assigned missions.

"(b) ASSIGNMENT OF FORCES.—Unless otherwise directed by the Secretary of Defense, all active and reserve cyber operations forces of the armed forces stationed in the United States shall be assigned to the cyber command.

"(c) GRADE OF COMMANDER.—The commander of the cyber command shall hold the grade of general or, in the case of an officer of the Navy, admiral while serving in that position, without vacating that officer's permanent grade. The commander of such command shall be appointed to that grade by the President, by and with the advice and consent of the Senate, for service in that position.

"(d) COMMAND OF ACTIVITY OR MISSION.—(1) Unless otherwise directed by the President or the Secretary of Defense, a cyber operations activity or mission shall be conducted under the command of the commander of the unified combatant command in whose geographic area the activity or mission is to be conducted.

"(2) The commander of the cyber command shall exercise command of a selected cyber operations mission if directed to do so by the President or the Secretary of Defense.

"(e) AUTHORITY OF COMBATANT COMMANDER.—(1) In addition to the authority prescribed in section 164(c) of this title, the commander of the cyber command shall be responsible for, and shall have the authority to con-

duct, all affairs of such command relating to cyber operations activities.

"(2)(A) Subject to the authority, direction, and control of the Principal Cyber Advisor, the commander of such command shall be responsible for, and shall have the authority to conduct, the following functions relating to cyber operations activities (whether or not relating to the cyber command):

"(i) Developing strategy, doctrine, and tactics.

"(ii) Preparing and submitting to the Secretary of Defense program recommendations and budget proposals for cyber operations forces and for other forces assigned to the cyber command.

"(iii) Exercising authority, direction, and control over the expenditure of funds—

"(I) for forces assigned directly to the cyber command; and

"(II) for cyber operations forces assigned to unified combatant commands other than the cyber command, with respect to all matters covered by section 807 of the National Defense Authorization Act for Fiscal Year 2014 (Public Law 114–92; 129 Stat. 886; 10 U.S.C. 2224 note) and, with respect to a matter not covered by such section, to the extent directed by the Secretary of Defense.

"(iv) Training and certification of assigned joint forces.

"(v) Conducting specialized courses of instruction for commissioned and noncommissioned officers.

"(vi) Validating requirements.

"(vii) Establishing priorities for requirements.

"(viii) Ensuring the interoperability of equipment and forces.

"(ix) Formulating and submitting requirements for intelligence support.

"(x) Monitoring the promotion of cyber operations forces and coordinating with the military departments regarding the assignment, retention, training, professional military education, and special and incentive pays of cyber operation forces.

"(B) The authority, direction, and control exercised by the Principal Cyber Advisor for purposes of this section is authority, direction, and control with respect to the administration and support of the cyber command, including readiness and organization of cyber operations forces, cyber operations-peculiar equipment and resources, and civilian personnel.

"(C) Nothing in this section shall be construed as providing the Principal Cyber Advisor authority, direction, and control of operational matters that are subject to the operational chain of command of the combatant commands or the exercise of authority, direction, and control of personnel, resources, equipment, and other matters that are not cyber-operations peculiar and that are in the purview of the armed forces.

"(3) The commander of the cyber command shall be responsible for—

"(A) ensuring the combat readiness of forces assigned to the cyber command; and

"(B) monitoring the preparedness to carry out assigned missions of cyber forces assigned to unified combatant commands other than the cyber command.

"(C) The staff of the commander shall include an inspector general who shall conduct internal audits and inspections of purchasing and contracting actions through the cyber operations command and such other inspector general functions as may be assigned.

"(f) INTELLIGENCE AND SPECIAL ACTIVITIES.— This section does not constitute authority to conduct any activity which, if carried out as an intelligence activity by the Department of Defense, would require a notice to the Select Committee on Intelligence of the Senate and the Permanent Select Committee on Intelligence of the House of Representatives under title V of the National Security Act of 1947 (50 U.S.C. 3091 et seq.).".

(b) CLERICAL AMENDMENT.—The table of sections at the beginning of chapter 6 of such title is amended by inserting after the item relating to section 167a the following new item:

"167b. Unified combatant command for cyber operations.".

SEC. 924. ASSIGNED FORCES OF THE COMBATANT COMMANDS.

Section 162(a) of title 10, United States Code, is amended—

(1) in paragraph (1)—

(A) by striking "Except as provided in paragraph (2)" and inserting "As directed by the Secretary of Defense";

(B) by striking "all forces" and inserting "specified forces"; and

(C) by striking the second sentence;

(2) by striking paragraph (2) and inserting the following new paragraph (2):

"(2) A force not assigned to a combatant command or to the United States element of the North American Aerospace Defense Command under paragraph (1) shall remain assigned to the military department concerned for carrying out the responsibilities of the Secretary of the military department concerned as specified in section 3013, 5013, or 8013 of this title, as applicable."; and

(3) in paragraph (4)—

(A) by striking "operating with the geographic area" and

(B) by striking "assigned to, and".

SEC. 925. MODIFICATIONS TO THE REQUIREMENTS PROCESS.

(a) IN GENERAL.—The text of section 181 of title 10, United States Code, is amended to read as follows:

"(a) IN GENERAL.—There is a Joint Requirements Oversight Council in the Department of Defense.

"(b) MISSION.—In addition to other matters assigned to it by the President or Secretary of Defense, the Joint Requirements Oversight Council shall assist the Chairman of the Joint Chiefs of Staff in—

"(1) assessing joint military capabilities, and identifying, approving, and prioritizing gaps in such capabilities, to meet applicable requirements in the national defense strategy under section 118 of this title;

"(2) reviewing and validating whether a capability proposed by an armed force, Defense Agency, or other entity of the Department of Defense fulfills a gap in joint military capabilities;

"(3) developing recommendations, in consultation with the advisors to the Council under subsection (d), for program cost and fielding targets pursuant to section 2448a of this title that—

"(A) require a level of resources that is consistent with the level of priority assigned to the associated capability gap; and

"(B) have an estimated period of time for the delivery of an initial operational capability that is consistent with the urgency of the associated capability gap;

"(4) establishing and approving joint performance requirements that—

"(A) ensure interoperability, where appropriate, between and among joint military capabilities; and

"(B) are necessary, as designated by the Chairman of the Joint Chiefs of Staff, to fulfill capability gaps of more than one armed force, Defense Agency, or other entity of the Department;

"(5) reviewing performance requirements for any existing or proposed capability that the Chairman of the Joint Chiefs of Staff determines should be reviewed by the Council;

"(6) identifying new joint military capabilities based on advances in technology and concepts of operation; and

"(7) identifying alternatives to any acquisition program that meets approved joint military

capability requirements for the purposes of sections 2366a(b), 2366b(a)(4), and 2433(e)(2) of this title.

''(c) COMPOSITION.—

''(1) IN GENERAL.—The Joint Requirements Oversight Council is composed of the following:

''(A) The Vice Chairman of the Joint Chiefs of Staff, who is the Chair of the Council and is the principal adviser to the Chairman of the Joint Chiefs of Staff for making recommendations about joint military capabilities or joint performance requirements.

''(B) An Army officer in the grade of general.

''(C) A Navy officer in the grade of admiral.

''(D) An Air Force officer in the grade of general.

''(E) A Marine Corps officer in the grade of general.

''(2) SELECTION OF MEMBERS.—Members of the Council under subparagraphs (B), (C), (D), and (E) of paragraph (1) shall be selected by the Chairman of the Joint Chiefs of Staff, after consultation with the Secretary of Defense, from officers in the grade of general or admiral, as the case may be, who are recommended for selection by the Secretary of the military department concerned.

''(3) RECOMMENDATIONS.—In making any recommendation to the Chairman of the Joint Chiefs of Staff as described in paragraph (1)(A), the Vice Chairman of the Joint Chiefs of Staff shall provide the Chairman any dissenting view of members of the Council under paragraph (1) with respect to such recommendation.

''(d) ADVISORS.—

''(1) IN GENERAL.—The following officials of the Department of Defense shall serve as advisors to the Joint Requirements Oversight Council on matters within their authority and expertise:

''(A) The Under Secretary of Defense for Policy.

''(B) The Under Secretary of Defense for Intelligence.

''(C) The Under Secretary of Defense for Acquisition, Technology, and Logistics.

''(D) The Under Secretary of Defense (Comptroller).

''(E) The Director of Cost Assessment and Program Evaluation.

''(F) The Director of Operational Test and Evaluation.

''(G) The commander of a combatant command when matters related to the area of responsibility or functions of that command are under consideration by the Council.

''(2) INPUT FROM COMBATANT COMMANDS.—The Council shall seek and consider input from the commanders of the combatant commands in carrying out its mission under paragraphs (1) and (2) of subsection (b).

''(3) INPUT FROM CHIEFS OF STAFF.—The Council shall seek, and strongly consider, the views of the Chiefs of Staff of the armed forces, in their roles as customers of the acquisition system, on matters pertaining to a capability proposed by an armed force, Defense Agency, or other entity of the Department of Defense under subsection (b)(2) and joint performance requirements pursuant to subsection (b)(3).

''(e) PERFORMANCE REQUIREMENTS AS RESPONSIBILITY OF ARMED FORCES.—The Chief of Staff of an armed force is responsible for all performance requirements for that armed force and, except for performance requirements specified in subsections (b)(4) and (b)(5), such performance requirements do not need to be validated by the Joint Requirements Oversight Council.

''(f) ANALYTIC SUPPORT.—The Secretary of Defense shall ensure that analytical organizations within the Department of Defense, such as the Office of Cost Assessment and Program Evaluation, provide resources and expertise in operations research, systems analysis, and cost

estimation to the Joint Requirements Oversight Council to assist the Council in performing the mission in subsection (b).

''(g) AVAILABILITY OF OVERSIGHT INFORMATION TO CONGRESSIONAL DEFENSE COMMITTEES.—The Secretary of Defense shall ensure that, in the case of a recommendation by the Chairman of the Joint Chiefs of Staff to the Secretary that is approved by the Secretary, oversight information with respect to such recommendation that is produced as a result of the activities of the Joint Requirements Oversight Council is made available in a timely fashion to the congressional defense committees.

''(h) DEFINITIONS.—In this section:

''(1) The term 'joint military capabilities' means the collective capabilities across the joint force, including both joint and force-specific capabilities, that are available to conduct military operations.

''(2) The term 'performance requirement' means a performance attribute of a particular system considered critical or essential to the development of an effective military capability.

''(3) The term 'joint performance requirement' means a performance requirement that is critical or essential to ensure interoperability or fulfill a capability gap of more than one armed force, Defense Agency, or other entity of the Department of Defense, or impacts the joint force in other ways such as logistics.

''(4) The term 'oversight information' means information and materials comprising analysis and justification that are prepared to support a recommendation that is made to, and approved by, the Secretary of Defense.''.

(b) PROGRAM COST AND FIELD TARGETS.—The Secretary of Defense shall establish a process to develop program cost and fielding targets pursuant to section 2448a of title 10, United States Code, that—

(1) is co-chaired by the Deputy Secretary of Defense and the Vice Chairman of the Joint Chiefs of Staff;

(2) is supported by—

(A) the Joint Staff, to provide expertise on joint military capabilities, capability gaps, and performance requirements;

(B) the Office of Cost Assessment and Program Evaluation, to provide expertise in resource allocation, operations research, systems analysis, and cost estimation; and

(C) other Department of Defense organizations determined appropriate by the Secretary; and

(3) ensures that appropriate trade-offs are made among life-cycle cost, schedule, and performance objectives and procurement quantity objectives.

SEC. 926. REVIEW OF COMBATANT COMMAND ORGANIZATION.

(a) REVIEWS REQUIRED.—

(1) IN GENERAL.—The entities specified in paragraph (2) shall each conduct a review of the organizational structures of the combatant commands, and shall develop recommendations for improving the overall effectiveness of the combatant commands, and addressing threats that span multiple regions, functions, and domains.

(2) ENTITIES.—The entities specified in this paragraph are the following:

(A) The Secretary of Defense, in consultation with the Chairman of the Joint Chiefs of Staff.

(B) An independent entity with appropriate expertise, selected by the Secretary and with which the Secretary shall enter into a contract by not later than 30 days after the date of the enactment of this Act.

(b) ELEMENTS.—Each review under subsection (a) shall include an examination of the following:

(1) The evolution of combatant command mission requirements and the ability of combatant commands to satisfy those mission requirements.

(2) The evolution of the organizational structures, compositions, and sizes of the combatant commands, and how such factors may have contributed to combatant command performance in satisfying mission requirements, planning, and maintaining force readiness.

(3) The resources of combatant commands, including the degree to which combatant command force requirements are resourced.

(4) The benefits, drawbacks, and resource implications of eliminating or consolidating combatant commands, or of altering the relationships among combatant commands and their component command organizations or the command and control structures of the combatant commands.

(5) Organizational structures of the combatant commands, including Joint Task Forces or task-organized forces operating below the combatant command level, and the benefits, drawbacks, and resource implications of alternative organizational structures.

(c) REPORT.—Not later than September 30, 2017, the Secretary shall submit to the congressional defense committees a report on the findings and recommendations of each review required by subsection (a).

Subtitle D—Organization and Management of Other Department of Defense Offices and Elements

SEC. 931. QUALIFICATIONS FOR APPOINTMENT OF THE SECRETARIES OF THE MILITARY DEPARTMENTS.

(a) SECRETARY OF THE ARMY.—Section 3013(a)(1) of title 10, United States Code, is amended by inserting after the first sentence the following new sentence: ''The Secretary shall, to the greatest extent practicable, be appointed from among persons most highly qualified for the position by reason of background and experience, including persons with appropriate management or leadership experience.''.

(b) SECRETARY OF THE NAVY.—Section 5013(a)(1) of such title is amended by inserting after the first sentence the following new sentence: ''The Secretary shall, to the greatest extent practicable, be appointed from among persons most highly qualified for the position by reason of background and experience, including persons with appropriate management or leadership experience.''.

(c) SECRETARY OF THE AIR FORCE.—Section 8013(a)(1) of such title is amended by inserting after the first sentence the following new sentence: ''The Secretary shall, to the greatest extent practicable, be appointed from among persons most highly qualified for the position by reason of background and experience, including persons with appropriate management or leadership experience.''.

SEC. 932. ENHANCED PERSONNEL MANAGEMENT AUTHORITIES FOR THE CHIEF OF THE NATIONAL GUARD BUREAU.

Section 10508 of title 10, United States Code, is amended—

(1) by inserting ''(a) MANPOWER REQUIREMENTS OF NATIONAL GUARD BUREAU.—'' before ''The manpower requirements''; and

(2) by adding at the end the following new subsection:

''(b) PERSONNEL FOR FUNCTIONS OF NATIONAL GUARD BUREAU.—

''(1) IN GENERAL.—The Chief of the National Guard Bureau may program for, appoint, employ, administer, detail, and assign persons under sections 2103, 2105, and 3101 of title 5, or section 328 of title 32, within the National Guard Bureau and the National Guard of each State, the Commonwealth of Puerto Rico, the District of Columbia, Guam, and the Virgin Islands to execute the functions of the National Guard Bureau and the missions of the National Guard, and missions as assigned by the Chief of the National Guard Bureau.

"(2) ADMINISTRATION THROUGH ADJUTANTS GENERAL.—The Chief of the National Guard Bureau may designate the adjutants general referred to in section 314 of title 32 to appoint, employ, and administer the National Guard employees authorized by this subsection.

"(3) ADMINISTRATIVE ACTIONS.—Notwithstanding the Intergovernmental Personnel Act of 1970 (42 U.S.C. 4701 et seq.) and under regulations prescribed by the Chief of the National Guard Bureau, all personnel actions or conditions of employment, including adverse actions under title 5, pertaining to a person appointed, employed, or administered by an adjutant general under this subsection shall be accomplished by the adjutant general of the jurisdiction concerned. For purposes of any administrative complaint, grievance, claim, or action arising from, or relating to, such a personnel action or condition of employment:

"(A) The adjutant general of the jurisdiction concerned shall be considered the head of the agency and the National Guard of the jurisdiction concerned shall be considered the employing agency of the individual and the sole defendant or respondent in any administrative action.

"(B) The National Guard of the jurisdiction concerned shall defend any administrative complaint, grievance, claim, or action, and shall promptly implement all aspects of any final administrative order, judgment, or decision.

"(C) In any civil action or proceeding brought in any court arising from an action under this section, the United States shall be the sole defendant or respondent.

"(D) The Attorney General of the United States shall defend the United States in actions arising under this section described in subparagraph (C).

"(E) Any settlement, judgment, or costs arising from an action described in subparagraph (A) or (C) shall be paid from appropriated funds allocated to the National Guard of the jurisdiction concerned.".

SEC. 933. REORGANIZATION AND REDESIGNATION OF OFFICE OF FAMILY POLICY AND OFFICE OF COMMUNITY SUPPORT FOR MILITARY FAMILIES WITH SPECIAL NEEDS.

(a) OFFICE OF FAMILY POLICY.—

(1) REDESIGNATION AS OFFICE OF MILITARY FAMILY READINESS POLICY.—Section 1781(a) of title 10, United States Code, is amended—

(A) by striking "Office of Family Policy" and inserting "Office of Military Family Readiness Policy"; and

(B) by striking "Director of Family Policy" and inserting "Director of Military Family Readiness Policy".

(2) INCLUSION OF DIRECTOR ON MILITARY FAMILY READINESS COUNCIL.—Subsection (b)(1)(E) of section 1781a of such title is amended by striking "Office of Community Support for Military Families with Special Needs" and inserting "Office of Military Family Readiness Policy".

(3) CONFORMING AMENDMENT.—Section 131(b)(8)(G) of such title is amended by striking "Director of Family Policy" and inserting "Director of Military Family Readiness Policy".

(4) HEADING AND CLERICAL AMENDMENTS.—

(A) SECTION HEADING.—The heading of section 1781 of such title is amended to read as follows:

"§ 1781. Office of Military Family Readiness Policy".

(B) CLERICAL AMENDMENT.—The table of sections at the beginning of chapter 88 of such title is amended by striking the item relating to section 1781 and inserting the following new item:

"1781. Office of Military Family Readiness Policy.".

(b) OFFICE OF COMMUNITY SUPPORT FOR MILITARY FAMILIES WITH SPECIAL NEEDS.—

(1) REDESIGNATION AS OFFICE OF SPECIAL NEEDS.—Subsection (a) of section 1781c of title 10, United States Code, is amended by striking "Office of Community Support for Military Families with Special Needs" and inserting "Office of Special Needs".

(2) REORGANIZATION UNDER OFFICE OF MILITARY FAMILY READINESS POLICY.—Such subsection is further amended by striking "Office of the Under Secretary of Defense for Personnel and Readiness" and inserting "Office of Military Family Readiness Policy".

(3) REPEAL OF REQUIREMENT FOR HEAD OF OFFICE TO BE MEMBER OF SENIOR EXECUTIVE SERVICE OR GENERAL OR FLAG OFFICER.—Such section is further amended by striking subsection (c).

(4) CONFORMING AMENDMENTS.—Such section is further amended—

(A) by redesignating subsections (d) through (i) as subsections (c) through (h), respectively;

(B) by striking "subsection (e)" each place it appears and inserting "subsection (d)";

(C) in subsection (c), as so redesignated, by striking "subsection (f)" in paragraph (2) and inserting "subsection (e)"; and

(D) in subsection (g), as so redesignated—

(i) in paragraph (2)(A), by striking "subsection (d)(3)" and inserting "subsection (c)(3)"; and

(ii) in paragraph (2)(B), by striking "subsection (d)(4)" and inserting "subsection (c)(4)".

(5) HEADING AND CLERICAL AMENDMENTS.—

(A) SECTION HEADING.—The heading of such section is amended to read as follows:

"§ 1781c. Office of Special Needs".

(B) CLERICAL AMENDMENT.—The table of sections at the beginning of chapter 88 of such title is amended by striking the item relating to section 1781c and inserting the following new item:

"1781c. Office of Special Needs.".

SEC. 934. REDESIGNATION OF ASSISTANT SECRETARY OF THE AIR FORCE FOR ACQUISITION AS ASSISTANT SECRETARY OF THE AIR FORCE FOR ACQUISITION, TECHNOLOGY, AND LOGISTICS.

(a) REDESIGNATION.—Section 8016(b)(4)(A) of title 10, United States Code, is amended—

(1) by striking "Assistant Secretary of the Air Force for Acquisition" and inserting "Assistant Secretary of the Air Force for Acquisition, Technology, and Logistics"; and

(2) by inserting ", technology, and logistics" after "acquisition".

(b) REFERENCES.—Any reference to the Assistant Secretary of the Air Force for Acquisition in any law, regulation, map, document, record, or other paper of the United States shall be deemed to be a reference to the Assistant Secretary of the Air Force for Acquisition, Technology, and Logistics.

Subtitle E—Strategies, Reports, and Related Matters

SEC. 941. NATIONAL DEFENSE STRATEGY.

(a) NATIONAL DEFENSE STRATEGY.—Subsection (g) of section 113 of title 10, United States Code, is amended to read as follows:

"(g)(1)(A) Except as provided in subparagraph (E), in January every four years, and intermittently otherwise as may be appropriate, the Secretary of Defense shall provide to the Secretaries of the military departments, the Chiefs of Staff of the armed forces, the commanders of the unified and specified combatant commands, and the heads of all Defense Agencies and Field Activities of the Department of Defense and other elements of the Department specified in paragraphs (1) through (10) of section 111(b) of this title, and to the congressional defense committees, a defense strategy. Each strategy shall be known as the 'national defense strategy', and shall support the most recent national security strategy report of the President under section 108 of the National Security Act of 1947 (50 U.S.C. 3043).

"(B) Each national defense strategy shall including the following:

"(i) The priority missions of the Department of Defense, and the assumed force planning scenarios and constructs.

"(ii) The assumed strategic environment, including the most critical and enduring threats to the national security of the United States and its allies posed by state or non-state actors, and the strategies that the Department will employ to counter such threats and provide for the national defense.

"(iii) A strategic framework prescribed by the Secretary that guides how the Department will prioritize among the threats described in clause (ii) and the missions specified pursuant to clause (i), how the Department will allocate and mitigate the resulting risks, and how the Department will make resource investments.

"(iv) The roles and missions of the armed forces to carry out the missions described in clause (i), and the assumed roles and capabilities provided by other United States Government agencies and by allies and international partners.

"(v) The force size and shape, force posture, defense capabilities, force readiness, infrastructure, organization, personnel, technological innovation, and other elements of the defense program necessary to support such strategy.

"(vi) The major investments in defense capabilities, force structure, force readiness, force posture, and technological innovation that the Department will make over the following five-year period in accordance with the strategic framework described in clause (iii).

"(C) The Secretary shall seek the military advice and assistance of the Chairman of the Joint Chiefs of Staff in preparing each national defense strategy required by this subsection.

"(D) Each national defense strategy under this subsection shall be presented to the congressional defense committees in classified form with an unclassified summary.

"(E) In a year following an election for President, which election results in the appointment by the President of a new Secretary of Defense, the Secretary shall present the national defense strategy required by this subsection as soon as possible after appointment by and with the advice and consent of the Senate.

"(F) In February of each year in which the Secretary does not submit a new defense strategy as required by paragraph (A), the Secretary shall submit to the congressional defense committees an assessment of the current national defense strategy, including an assessment of the implementation of the strategy by the Department and an assessment whether the strategy requires revision as a result of changes in assumptions, policy, or other factors.

"(2) In implementing a national defense strategy under paragraph (1), the Secretary, with the advice and assistance of the Chairman of the Joint Chiefs of Staff, shall provide annually to the Secretaries of the military departments, the Chiefs of Staff of the armed forces, the commanders of the unified and specified combatant commands, and the heads of all Defense Agencies and Field Activities of the Department and other elements of the Department specified in paragraphs (1) through (10) of section 111(b) of this title, written policy guidance for the preparation and review of the program recommendations and budget proposals of their respective components to guide the development of forces. Such guidance shall include—

"(A) the national security interests and objectives;

"(B) the priority military missions of the Department, including the assumed force planning scenarios and constructs;

"(C) the force size and shape, force posture, defense capabilities, force readiness, infrastructure, organization, personnel, technological innovation, and other elements of the defense program necessary to support the strategy;

"(D) the resource levels projected to be available for the period of time for which such recommendations and proposals are to be effective; and

"(E) a discussion of any changes in the defense strategy and assumptions underpinning the strategy, as required by paragraph (1).

"(3) In implementing the guidance under paragraph (2), the Secretary, with the approval of the President and after consultation with the Chairman of the Joint Chiefs of Staff, shall provide, every two years or more frequently as needed, to the Chairman written policy guidance for the preparation and review of contingency plans, including plans for providing support to civil authorities in an incident of national significance or a catastrophic incident, for homeland defense, and for military support to civil authorities. Such guidance shall include guidance on the employment of forces, including specific force levels and specific supporting resource levels projected to be available for the period of time for which such plans are to be effective.

"(4) Not later than February 15 in any calendar year in which any written guidance is required pursuant to paragraph (2) or (3), the Secretary shall provide to the congressional defense committees a detailed classified briefing summarizing such guidance developed pursuant to such paragraphs.".

(b) CONFORMING REPEAL.—

(1) IN GENERAL.—Section 118 of title 10, United States Code, is repealed.

(2) CLERICAL AMENDMENT.—The table of sections at the beginning of chapter 2 of such title is amended by striking the item relating to section 118.

SEC. 942. COMMISSION ON THE NATIONAL DEFENSE STRATEGY FOR THE UNITED STATES.

(a) ESTABLISHMENT.—There is hereby established a commission to be known as the "Commission on the National Defense Strategy for the United States" (in this section referred to as the "Commission"). The purpose of the Commission is to examine and make recommendations with respect to the national defense strategy for the United States.

(b) COMPOSITION.—

(1) MEMBERSHIP.—The Commission shall be composed of 12 members appointed as follows:

(A) Three members appointed by the chair of the Committee on Armed Services of the House of Representatives.

(B) Three members appointed by the ranking minority member of the Committee on Armed Services of the House of Representatives.

(C) Three members appointed by the chair of the Committee on Armed Services of the Senate.

(D) Three members appointed by the ranking minority member of the Committee on Armed Services of the Senate.

(2) CHAIR; VICE CHAIR.—

(A) CHAIR.—The chair of the Committee on Armed Services of the House of Representative and the chair of the Committee on Armed Services of the Senate shall jointly designate one member of the Commission to serve as chair of the Commission.

(B) VICE CHAIR.—The ranking minority member of the Committee on Armed Services of the House of Representative and the ranking minority member of the Committee on Armed Services of the Senate shall jointly designate one member of the Commission to serve as vice chair of the Commission.

(3) PERIOD OF APPOINTMENT; VACANCIES.—Members shall be appointed for the life of the Commission. Any vacancy in the Commission shall be filled in the same manner as the original appointment.

(c) DUTIES.—

(1) REVIEW.—The Commission shall review the current national defense strategy of the United States, including the assumptions, missions, force posture and structure, and strategic and military risks associated with the strategy.

(2) ASSESSMENT AND RECOMMENDATIONS.—The Commission shall conduct a comprehensive assessment of the strategic environment, the threats to the United States, the size and shape of the force, the readiness of the force, the posture and capabilities of the force, the allocation of resources, and strategic and military risks in order to provide recommendations on the national defense strategy for the United States.

(d) COOPERATION FROM GOVERNMENT.—

(1) COOPERATION.—In carrying out its duties, the Commission shall receive the full and timely cooperation of the Secretary of Defense in providing the Commission with analysis, briefings, and other information necessary for the fulfillment of its responsibilities.

(2) LIAISON.—The Secretary shall designate at least one officer or employee of the Department of Defense to serve as a liaison officer between the Department and the Commission.

(e) REPORT.—

(1) FINAL REPORT.—Not later than December 1, 2017, the Commission shall submit to the President, the Secretary of Defense, the Committee on Armed Services of the House of Representatives, and the Committee on Armed Services of the Senate a report on the Commission's findings, conclusions, and recommendations. The report shall address, but not be limited to, each of the following:

(A) The strategic environment, including threats to the United States and the potential for conflicts arising from such threats, security challenges, and the national security interests of the United States.

(B) The military missions for which the Department of Defense should prepare and the force planning construct.

(C) The roles and missions of the Armed Forces to carry out those missions and the roles and capabilities provided by other United States Government agencies and by allies and international partners.

(D) The force planning construct, size and shape, posture and capabilities, readiness, infrastructure, organization, personnel, and other elements of the defense program necessary to support the strategy.

(E) The resources necessary to support the strategy, including budget recommendations.

(F) The risks associated with the strategy, including the relationships and tradeoffs between missions, risks, and resources.

(2) INTERIM BRIEFING.—Not later than June 1, 2017, the Commission shall provide to the Committee on Armed Services of the House of Representatives, and the Committee on Armed Services of the Senate a briefing on the status of its review and assessment, and include a discussion of any interim recommendations.

(3) FORM.—The report submitted to Congress under paragraph (1) shall be submitted in unclassified form, but may include a classified annex.

(f) FUNDING.—Of the amounts authorized to be appropriated by to this Act for the Department of Defense, $5,000,000 is available to fund the activities of the Commission.

(g) TERMINATION.—The Commission shall terminate 6 months after the date on which it submits the report required by subsection (e).

SEC. 943. REFORM OF THE NATIONAL MILITARY STRATEGY.

(a) IN GENERAL.—Paragraph (1) of section 153(b) of title 10, United States Code, is amended to read as follows:

"(1) NATIONAL MILITARY STRATEGY.—(A) The Chairman shall determine each even-numbered year whether to prepare a new National Military Strategy in accordance with this paragraph or to update a strategy previously prepared in accordance with this paragraph. The Chairman shall provide such National Military Strategy or update to the Secretary of Defense in time for transmittal to Congress pursuant to paragraph (3), including in time for inclusion in the report of the Secretary of Defense, if any, under paragraph (4).

"(B) Each National Military Strategy (or update) under this paragraph shall be based on a comprehensive review conducted by the Chairman in conjunction with the other members of the Joint Chiefs of Staff and the commanders of the unified and specified combatant commands. Each update shall address only those parts of the most recent National Military Strategy for which the Chairman determines, on the basis of the review, that a modification is needed.

"(C) Each National Military Strategy (or update) submitted under this paragraph shall describe how the military will support the objectives of the United States as articulated in—

"(i) the most recent National Security Strategy prescribed by the President pursuant to section 108 of the National Security Act of 1947 (50 U.S.C. 3043);

"(ii) the most recent annual report of the Secretary of Defense submitted to the President and Congress pursuant to section 113 of this title;

"(iii) the most recent national defense strategy presented by the Secretary of Defense pursuant to section 113 of this title;

"(iv) the most recent policy guidance provided by the Secretary of Defense pursuant to section 113(g) of this title; and

"(v) any other national security or defense strategic guidance issued by the President or the Secretary of Defense.

"(D) At a minimum, each National Military Strategy (or update) submitted under this paragraph shall—

"(i) assess the strategic environment, threats, opportunities, and challenges that affect the national security of the United States;

"(ii) assess military ends, ways, and means to support the objectives referred to in subparagraph (C);

"(iii) provide the framework for the assessment by the Chairman of military strategic and operational risks, and for the development of risk mitigation options;

"(iv) develop military options to address threats and opportunities;

"(v) assess joint force capabilities, capacities, and resources; and

"(vi) establish military guidance for the development of the joint force and the total force building on guidance by the President and the Secretary of Defense as referred to in subparagraph (C).".

(b) MODIFICATION TO RISK ASSESSMENT.—Paragraph (2) of such section is amended—

(1) in the third sentence of subparagraph (A), by striking "of the report" and inserting "in the report"; and

(2) in subparagraph (B)—

(A) by inserting "(or update)" after "National Military Strategy" each place it appears;

(B) in clause (ii), by striking "strategic risks to United States interests" and all that follows and inserting "military strategic and operational risks to United States interests and the military strategic and operational risks in executing the National Military Strategy (or update).";

(C) in clause (iii), by striking "distinguishing between the concepts of probability and consequences";

(D) in clause (iv)(II), by striking "most"; and

(E) in clause (v), by striking "or support of—" and all the follows and inserting "of external support, as appropriate.".

(c) FORM.—Paragraph (3) of such section is amended by adding at the end the following new subparagraph:

"(C) The National Military Strategy (or update) and Risk Assessment submitted under this subsection shall be classified in form, but shall include an unclassified summary.".

SEC. 944. FORM OF ANNUAL NATIONAL SECURITY STRATEGY REPORT.

Section 108(c) of the National Security Act of 1947 (50 U.S.C. 3043(c)) is amended by striking "in both a classified form and an unclassified form" and inserting "to Congress in classified form, but may include an unclassified summary".

SEC. 945. MODIFICATION TO INDEPENDENT STUDY OF NATIONAL SECURITY STRATEGY FORMULATION PROCESS.

Section 1064(b)(2) of the National Defense Authorization Act for Fiscal Year 2016 (Public Law 114–92; 129 Stat. 989) is amended—

(1) in subparagraph (D), by inserting ", including Congress," after "Federal Government"; and

(2) by adding at the end the following new subparagraph:

"(E) The capabilities and limitations of the Department of Defense workforce responsible for conducting strategic planning, including recommendations for improving the workforce through training, education, and career management.".

Subtitle F—Other Matters

SEC. 951. ENHANCED SECURITY PROGRAMS FOR DEPARTMENT OF DEFENSE PERSONNEL AND INNOVATION INITIATIVES.

(a) ENHANCEMENT OF SECURITY PROGRAMS GENERALLY.—

(1) PERSONNEL BACKGROUND AND SECURITY PLAN REQUIRED.—The Secretary of Defense shall develop an implementation plan for the Defense Security Service to conduct, after October 1, 2017, background investigations for personnel of the Department of Defense whose investigations are adjudicated by the Consolidated Adjudication Facility of the Department. The Secretary shall submit the implementation plan to the congressional defense committees by not later than August 1, 2017.

(2) PLAN FOR POTENTIAL TRANSFER OF INVESTIGATIVE PERSONNEL TO DEPARTMENT OF DEFENSE.—Not later than October 1, 2017, the Secretary and the Director of the Office of Personnel Management shall develop a plan to transfer Government investigative personnel and contracted resources to the Department in proportion to the background and security investigative workload that would be assumed by the Department if the plan required by paragraph (1) were implemented.

(3) REPORT.—Not later than August 1, 2017, the Secretary shall submit to the congressional defense committees a report on the number of full-time equivalent employees of the management headquarters of the Department that would be required by the Defense Security Service to carry out the plan developed under paragraph (1).

(4) COLLECTION, STORAGE, AND RETENTION OF INFORMATION BY INSIDER THREAT PROGRAMS.—In order to enable detection and mitigation of potential insider threats, the Secretary shall ensure that insider threat programs of the Department collect, store, and retain information from the following:

(A) Personnel security.

(B) Physical security.

(C) Information security.

(D) Law enforcement.

(E) Counterintelligence.

(F) User activity monitoring.

(G) Information assurance.

(H) Such other data sources as the Secretary considers necessary and appropriate.

(b) ELEMENTS OF SYSTEM.—

(1) IN GENERAL.—In developing a system for the performance of background investigations for personnel in carrying out subsection (a), the Secretary shall—

(A) conduct a review of security clearance business processes and, to the extent practicable, modify such processes to maximize compatibility with the security clearance information technology architecture to minimize the need for customization of the system;

(B) conduct business process mapping of the business processes described in subparagraph (A);

(C) use spiral development and incremental acquisition practices to rapidly deploy the system, including through the use of prototyping and open architecture principles;

(D) establish a process to identify and limit interfaces with legacy systems and to limit customization of any commercial information technology tools used;

(E) establish automated processes for measuring the performance goals of the system;

(F) incorporate capabilities for the continuous monitoring of network security and the mitigation of insider threats to the system;

(G) institute a program to collect and maintain data and metrics on the background investigation process; and

(H) establish a council (to be known as the "Department of Defense Background Investigations Rate Council") to advise and advocate for rate efficiencies for background clearance investigation rates, and to negotiate rates for background investigation services provided to outsides entities and agencies when requested.

(2) COMPLETION DATE.—The Secretary shall complete the development and implementation of the system described in paragraph (1) by not later than September 30, 2019.

(c) ESTABLISHMENT OF ENHANCED SECURITY PROGRAM TO SUPPORT DEPARTMENT OF DEFENSE INNOVATION INITIATIVE.—

(1) IN GENERAL.—Not later than 180 days after the date of the enactment of this Act, the Secretary shall establish a personnel security program, and take such other actions as the Secretary considers appropriate, to support the Innovation Initiative of the Department to better leverage commercial technology.

(2) POLICIES AND PROCEDURES.—In establishing the program required by paragraph (1), the Secretary shall develop policies and procedures to rapidly and inexpensively investigate and adjudicate security clearances for personnel from commercial companies with innovative technologies and solutions to enable such companies to receive relevant threat reporting and to propose solutions for a broader set of Department requirements.

(3) ACCESS TO CLASSIFIED INFORMATION.—The Secretary shall ensure that access to classified information under the program required by paragraph (1) is not contingent on a company already being under contract with the Department.

(4) AWARD OF SECURITY CLEARANCES.—The Secretary may award secret clearances under the program required by paragraph (1) for limited purposes and periods relating to the acquisition or modification of capabilities and services.

(d) UPDATED GUIDANCE AND REVIEW OF POLICIES.—

(1) REVIEW OF APPLICABLE LAWS.—The Secretary shall review laws, regulations, and executive orders relating to the maintenance of personnel security clearance information by the Federal Government, including the investigation timeline metrics established in the Intelligence Reform and Prevention of Terrorism Act of 2004 (Public Law 108–458). The review should also identify recommendations to eliminate duplica-

tive or outdated authorities in current executive orders, regulations and guidance. Not later than 90 days after the date of the enactment of this Act, the Secretary shall provide to the Committees on Armed Services of the Senate and the House of Representatives a briefing that includes—

(A) the results of the review; and

(B) recommendations, if any, for consolidating and clarifying laws, regulations, and executive orders relating to the maintenance of personnel security clearance information by the Federal Government.

(2) RECIPROCITY DIRECTIVE.—Not later than 180 days after the date of the enactment of this Act, the Secretary shall coordinate with the Security Executive Agent, in consultation with the Suitability Executive Agent, to issue an updated reciprocity directive that accounts for security policy changes associated with new position designation regulations under section 1400 of title 5, Code of Federal Regulations, new continuous evaluation policies, and new Federal investigative standards.

(3) IMPLEMENTATION DIRECTIVES.—The Secretary, working with the Security Executive Agent and the Suitability Executive Agent, shall jointly develop and issue directives on—

(A) completing the implementation of the National Security Sensitive Position designations required by section 1400 of title 5, Code of Federal Regulations; and

(B) aligning to the maximum practical extent the investigative and adjudicative standards and criteria for positions requiring access to classified information and national security sensitive positions not requiring access to classified information to ensure effective and efficient reciprocity and consistent designation of like-positions across the Federal Government.

(e) WAIVER OF CERTAIN DEADLINES.—For each of fiscal years 2017 through 2019, the Secretary may waive any background investigation timeline specified in the Intelligence Reform and Prevention of Terrorism Act of 2004 if the Secretary submits to the appropriate committees of Congress a written notification on the waiver not later than 30 days before the beginning of the fiscal year concerned.

(f) DEFINITIONS.—In this section:

(1) The term "appropriate committees of Congress" has the meaning given that term in section 3001(a)(8) of the Intelligence Reform and Prevention of Terrorism Act of 2004 (50 U.S.C. 3341(a)(8)).

(2) The term "business process mapping" has the meaning given that term in section 2222(i) of title 10, United States Code.

(3) The term "insider threat" means, with respect to the Department, a threat presented by a person who—

(A) has, or once had, authorized access to information, a facility, a network, a person, or a resource of the Department; and

(B) wittingly, or unwittingly, commits—

(i) an act in contravention of law or policy that resulted in, or might result in, harm through the loss or degradation of government or company information, resources, or capabilities; or

(ii) a destructive act, which may include physical harm to another in the workplace.

SEC. 952. MODIFICATION OF AUTHORITY OF THE SECRETARY OF DEFENSE RELATING TO PROTECTION OF THE PENTAGON RESERVATION AND OTHER DEPARTMENT OF DEFENSE FACILITIES IN THE NATIONAL CAPITAL REGION.

(a) LAW ENFORCEMENT AUTHORITY.—Subsection (b) of section 2674 of title 10, United States Code, is amended—

(1) by redesignating paragraph (2) as paragraph (5); and

(2) by striking the matter in such subsection preceding such paragraph and inserting the following:

"(b)(1) The Secretary shall protect the buildings, grounds, and property located in the National Capital Region that are occupied by, or under the jurisdiction, custody, or control of, the Department of Defense, and the persons on that property.

"(2) The Secretary may designate military or civilian personnel to perform law enforcement functions and military, civilian, or contract personnel to perform security functions for such buildings, grounds, property, and persons, including, with regard to civilian personnel designated under this section, duty in areas outside the property referred to in paragraph (1) to the extent necessary to protect that property and persons on that property. Subject to the authorization of the Secretary, any such military or civilian personnel so designated may exercise the authorities listed in paragraphs (1) through (5) of section 2672(c) of this title.

"(3) The powers granted under paragraph (2) to military and civilian personnel designated under that paragraph shall be exercised in accordance with guidelines prescribed by the Secretary and approved by the Attorney General.

"(4) Nothing in this subsection shall be construed to—

"(A) preclude or limit the authority of any Defense Criminal Investigative Organization or any other Federal law enforcement agency;

"(B) restrict the authority of the Secretary of Homeland Security under the Homeland Security Act of 2002 (6 U.S.C. 101 et seq.) or the authority of the Administrator of General Services, including the authority to promulgate regulations affecting property under the custody and control of that Secretary or the Administrator, respectively;

"(C) expand or limit section 21 of the Internal Security Act of 1950 (50 U.S.C. 797);

"(D) affect chapter 47 of this title (the Uniform Code of Military Justice);

"(E) restrict any other authority of the Secretary of Defense or the Secretary of a military department; or

"(F) restrict the authority of the Director of the National Security Agency under section 11 of the National Security Agency Act of 1959 (50 U.S.C. 3609).".

(b) RATES OF BASIC PAY FOR CIVILIAN LAW ENFORCEMENT PERSONNEL.—Paragraph (5) of such subsection, as redesignated by subsection (a)(1) of this section, is amended by inserting ", whichever is greater" before the period at the end.

(c) CODIFICATION OF AUTHORITY TO PROVIDE PHYSICAL PROTECTION AND PERSONAL SECURITY WITHIN UNITED STATES TO CERTAIN SENIOR LEADERS IN DOD AND OTHER SPECIFIED PERSONS.—

(1) IN GENERAL.—Chapter 41 of title 10, United States Code, is amended by inserting after section 713 a new section 714 consisting of—

(A) a heading as follows:

"§ 714. Senior leaders of the Department of Defense and other specified persons: authority to provide protection within the United States"; and

(B) a text consisting of the text of subsections (a) through (d) of section 1074 of the National Defense Authorization Act for Fiscal Year 2008 (10 U.S.C. 113 note).

(2) CLERICAL AMENDMENT.—The table of sections at the beginning of chapter 41 of such title is amended by adding at the end the following new item:

"714. Senior leaders of the Department of Defense and other specified persons: authority to provide protection within the United States.".

(3) REPEAL OF CODIFIED PROVISION.—Section 1074 of the National Defense Authorization Act for Fiscal Year 2008 is repealed.

(4) CONFORMING AND STYLISTIC AMENDMENTS DUE TO CODIFICATION.—Section 714 of title 10,

United States Code, as added by paragraph (1), is amended—

(A) in subsections (a), (b)(1), and (d)(1), by striking "Armed Forces" and inserting "armed forces";

(B) in subsection (c)—

(i) by striking "section:" and all that follows through "Forces' and" and inserting "section, the terms 'qualified members of the armed forces' and"; and

(ii) by redesignating subparagraphs (A) through (E) as paragraphs (1) through (5), respectively, and realigning the left margin of such paragraphs, as so redesignated, two ems to the left; and

(C) in subsection (d)(2), by striking ", United States Code".

(5) AMENDMENTS FOR CONSISTENCY WITH TITLE 10 USAGE AS TO SERVICE CHIEFS.—Such section is further amended—

(A) in subsection (a)—

(i) in paragraph (6), by striking "Chiefs of the Services" and inserting "Members of the Joint Chiefs of Staff in addition to the Chairman and Vice Chairman";

(ii) by striking paragraph (7); and

(iii) by redesignating paragraph (8) as paragraph (7); and

(B) in subsection (b)(1), by striking "through (8)" and inserting "through (7)".

(6) AMENDMENTS FOR CONSISTENCY WITH TITLE 10 USAGE AS TO "MILITARY MEMBER".—Subsection (b)(2)(A) of such section is amended—

(A) by striking ", military member,"; and

(B) by inserting after "of the Department of Defense" the following: "or member of the armed forces".

SEC. 953. MODIFICATIONS TO REQUIREMENTS FOR ACCOUNTING FOR MEMBERS OF THE ARMED FORCES AND DEPARTMENT OF DEFENSE CIVILIAN EMPLOYEES LISTED AS MISSING.

(a) LIMITATION OF DEFENSE POW/MIA ACCOUNTING AGENCY TO MISSING PERSONS FROM PAST CONFLICTS.—Section 1501(a) of title 10, United States Code, is amended—

(1) in paragraph (1)(A), by inserting "from past conflicts" after "matters relating to missing persons";

(2) in paragraph (2)—

(A) by striking subparagraph (A);

(B) by redesignating subparagraphs (B), (C), (D), (E), and (F) as subparagraphs (A), (B), (C), (D), and (E), respectively; and

(C) by inserting "from past conflicts" after "missing persons" each place it appears;

(3) in paragraph (4)—

(A) by striking "for personal recovery (including search, rescue, escape, and evasion) and"; and

(B) by inserting "from past conflicts" after "missing persons"; and

(4) by striking paragraph (5).

(b) ACTION UPON DISCOVERY OR RECEIPT OF INFORMATION.—Section 1505(c) of such title is amended by striking "designated Agency Director" in paragraphs (1), (2), and (3) and inserting "Secretary of Defense".

(c) DEFINITION OF "ACCOUNTED FOR".—Section 1513(3)(B) of such title is amended by inserting "to the extent practicable" after "are recovered".

SEC. 954. MODIFICATIONS TO CORROSION REPORT.

(a) MODIFICATIONS TO REPORT TO CONGRESS.—Section 2228(e)(1) of title 10, United States Code, is amended—

(1) in the matter preceding subparagraph (A), by inserting after "2009" the following: "and ending with the budget for fiscal year 2022";

(2) by amending subparagraph (B) to read as follows:

"(B) The estimated composite return on investment achieved by implementing the strategy, and documented in the assessments by the De-

partment of Defense of completed corrosion projects and activities.";

(3) by amending subparagraph (D) to read as follows:

"(D) If the full amount of funding requirements is not requested in the budget, the reasons for not including the full amount and a description of the impact on readiness, logistics, and safety of not fully funding required corrosion prevention and mitigation activities."; and

(4) in subparagraph (F), by striking "pilot".

(b) REPORT TO DIRECTOR OF CORROSION POLICY AND OVERSIGHT.—Section 2228(e)(2) of such title is amended—

(1) by inserting "(A)" before "Each report";

(2) by striking "a copy of" and all that follows through the period and inserting "a summary of the most recent report required by subparagraph (B)."; and

(3) by adding at the end the following new subparagraph:

"(B) Not later than December 31 of each year, through December 31, 2020, the corrosion control and prevention executive of a military department shall submit to the Director of Corrosion Policy and Oversight a report containing recommendations pertaining to the corrosion control and prevention program of the military department. Such report shall include recommendations for the funding levels necessary for the executive to carry out the duties of the executive under this section. The report required under this subparagraph shall—

"(i) provide a summary of key accomplishments, goals, and objectives of the corrosion control and prevention program of the military department; and

"(ii) include the performance measures used to ensure that the corrosion control and prevention program achieved the goals and objectives described in clause (i).".

(c) CONFORMING REPEAL.—Section 903(b) of the Duncan Hunter National Defense Authorization Act for Fiscal Year 2009 (10 U.S.C. 2228 note) is amended by striking paragraph (5).

TITLE X—GENERAL PROVISIONS

Subtitle A—Financial Matters

Sec. 1001. General transfer authority.
Sec. 1002. Report on auditable financial statements.
Sec. 1003. Increased use of commercial data integration and analysis products for the purpose of preparing financial statement audits.
Sec. 1004. Sense of Congress on sequestration.
Sec. 1005. Requirement to transfer funds from Department of Defense Acquisition Workforce Development Fund to the Treasury.

Subtitle B—Counterdrug Activities

Sec. 1011. Codification and modification of authority to provide support for counterdrug activities and activities to counter transnational organized crime of civilian law enforcement agencies.
Sec. 1012. Secretary of Defense review of curricula and program structures of National Guard counterdrug schools.
Sec. 1013. Extension of authority to support unified counterdrug and counterterrorism campaign in Colombia.
Sec. 1014. Enhancement of information sharing and coordination of military training between Department of Homeland Security and Department of Defense.

Subtitle C—Naval Vessels and Shipyards

Sec. 1021. Definition of short-term work with respect to overhaul, repair, or maintenance of naval vessels.
Sec. 1022. Warranty requirements for shipbuilding contracts.

Sec. 1023. National Sea-Based Deterrence Fund.
Sec. 1024. Availability of funds for retirement or inactivation of Ticonderoga-class cruisers or dock landing ships.

Subtitle D—Counterterrorism

Sec. 1031. Frequency of counterterrorism operations briefings.
Sec. 1032. Prohibition on use of funds for transfer or release of individuals detained at United States Naval Station, Guantanamo Bay, Cub, to the United States.
Sec. 1033. Prohibition on use of funds to construct or modify facilities in the United States to house detainees transferred from United States Naval Station, Guantanamo Bay, Cuba.
Sec. 1034. Prohibition on use of funds for transfer or release to certain countries of individuals detained at United States Naval Station, Guantanamo Bay, Cuba.
Sec. 1035. Prohibition on use of funds for realignment of forces at or closure of United States Naval Station, Guantanamo Bay, Cuba.
Sec. 1036. Congressional notification requirements for sensitive military operations.

Subtitle E—Miscellaneous Authorities and Limitations

Sec. 1041. Expanded authority for transportation by the Department of Defense of non-Department of Defense personnel and cargo.
Sec. 1042. Reduction in minimum number of Navy carrier air wings and carrier air wing headquarters required to be maintained.
Sec. 1043. Modification to support for non-Federal development and testing of material for chemical agent defense.
Sec. 1044. Protection of certain Federal spectrum operations.
Sec. 1045. Prohibition on use of funds for retirement of legacy maritime mine countermeasures platforms.
Sec. 1046. Extension of authority of Secretary of Transportation to issue non-premium aviation insurance.
Sec. 1047. Evaluation of Navy alternate combination cover and unisex combination cover.
Sec. 1048. Independent evaluation of Department of Defense excess property program.
Sec. 1049. Waiver of certain polygraph examination requirements.
Sec. 1050. Use of Transportation Worker Identification Credential to gain access at Department of Defense installations.
Sec. 1051. Limitation on availability of funds for destruction of certain landmines and briefing on development of replacement anti-personnel landmine munitions.
Sec. 1052. Transition of Air Force to operation of remotely piloted aircraft by enlisted personnel.
Sec. 1053. Prohibition on divestment of Marine Corps Search and Rescue Units.
Sec. 1054. Support for the Associate Director of the Central Intelligence Agency for Military Affairs.
Sec. 1055. Notification on the provision of defense sensitive support.
Sec. 1056. Prohibition on enforcement of military commission rulings preventing members of the Armed Forces from carrying out otherwise lawful duties based on member sex.

Subtitle F—Studies and Reports

Sec. 1061. Temporary continuation of certain Department of Defense reporting requirements.
Sec. 1062. Reports on programs managed under alternative compensatory control measures in the Department of Defense.
Sec. 1063. Matters for inclusion in report on designation of countries for which rewards may be paid under Department of Defense rewards program.
Sec. 1064. Annual reports on unfunded priorities of the Armed Forces and the combatant commands and annual report on combatant command requirements.
Sec. 1065. Management and reviews of electromagnetic spectrum.
Sec. 1066. Requirement for notice and reporting to Committees on Armed Services on certain expenditures of funds by Defense Intelligence Agency.
Sec. 1067. Congressional notification of biological select agent and toxin theft, loss, or release involving the Department of Defense.
Sec. 1068. Report on service-provided support and enabling capabilities to United States special operations forces.
Sec. 1069. Report on citizen security responsibilities in the Northern Triangle of Central America.
Sec. 1070. Report on counterproliferation activities and programs.
Sec. 1071. Report on testing and integration of minehunting sonar systems to improve Littoral Combat Ship minehunting capabilities.
Sec. 1072. Quarterly reports on parachute jumps conducted at Fort Bragg and Pope Army Airfield and Air Force support for such jumps.
Sec. 1073. Study on military helicopter noise.
Sec. 1074. Independent review of United States military strategy and force posture in the United States Pacific Command area of responsibility.
Sec. 1075. Assessment of the joint ground forces of the Armed Forces.

Subtitle G—Other Matters

Sec. 1081. Technical and clerical amendments.
Sec. 1082. Increase in maximum amount available for equipment, services, and supplies provided for humanitarian demining assistance.
Sec. 1083. Liquidation of unpaid credits accrued as a result of transactions under a cross-servicing agreement.
Sec. 1084. Modification of requirements relating to management of military technicians.
Sec. 1085. Streamlining of the National Security Council.
Sec. 1086. National biodefense strategy.
Sec. 1087. Global Cultural Knowledge Network.
Sec. 1088. Sense of Congress regarding Connecticut's Submarine Century.
Sec. 1089. Sense of Congress regarding the reporting of the MV–22 mishap in Marana, Arizona, on April 8, 2000.
Sec. 1090. Cost of Wars.
Sec. 1091. Reconnaissance Strike Group matters.
Sec. 1092. Border security metrics.
Sec. 1093. Program to commemorate the 100th anniversary of the Tomb of the Unknown Soldier.
Sec. 1094. Sense of Congress regarding the OCONUS basing of the KC–46A aircraft.
Sec. 1095. Designation of a Department of Defense Strategic Arctic Port.
Sec. 1096. Recovery of excess rifles, ammunition, and parts granted to foreign countries and transfer to certain persons.

Subtitle A—Financial Matters

SEC. 1001. GENERAL TRANSFER AUTHORITY.

(a) AUTHORITY TO TRANSFER AUTHORIZATIONS.—

(1) AUTHORITY.—Upon determination by the Secretary of Defense that such action is necessary in the national interest, the Secretary may transfer amounts of authorizations made available to the Department of Defense in this division for fiscal year 2017 between any such authorizations for that fiscal year (or any subdivisions thereof). Amounts of authorizations so transferred shall be merged with and be available for the same purposes as the authorization to which transferred.

(2) LIMITATION.—Except as provided in paragraph (3), the total amount of authorizations that the Secretary may transfer under the authority of this section may not exceed $4,500,000,000.

(3) EXCEPTION FOR TRANSFERS BETWEEN MILITARY PERSONNEL AUTHORIZATIONS.—A transfer of funds between military personnel authorizations under title IV shall not be counted toward the dollar limitation in paragraph (2).

(b) LIMITATIONS.—The authority provided by subsection (a) to transfer authorizations—

(1) may only be used to provide authority for items that have a higher priority than the items from which authority is transferred; and

(2) may not be used to provide authority for an item that has been denied authorization by Congress.

(c) EFFECT ON AUTHORIZATION AMOUNTS.—A transfer made from one account to another under the authority of this section shall be deemed to increase the amount authorized for the account to which the amount is transferred by an amount equal to the amount transferred.

(d) NOTICE TO CONGRESS.—The Secretary shall promptly notify Congress of each transfer made under subsection (a).

SEC. 1002. REPORT ON AUDITABLE FINANCIAL STATEMENTS.

Not later than 90 days after the date of the enactment of this Act, the Secretary of Defense shall submit to the congressional defense committees a report ranking all military departments and Defense Agencies in order of how advanced they are in achieving auditable financial statements as required by law. The report should not include information otherwise available in other reports to Congress.

SEC. 1003. INCREASED USE OF COMMERCIAL DATA INTEGRATION AND ANALYSIS PRODUCTS FOR THE PURPOSE OF PREPARING FINANCIAL STATEMENT AUDITS.

(a) DEPLOYMENT OF DATA ANALYTICS CAPABILITIES.—The Secretary of Defense shall use competitive procedures under chapter 137 of title 10, United States Code, to procure or develop, as soon as practicable, technologies or services, including those based on commercially available information technologies and services to improve data collection and analyses to support preparation of auditable financial statements for the Department of Defense.

(b) USE OF FUNDING AND RESOURCES.—The Secretary of Defense may use science and technology funding, prototypes, and test and evaluation resources as appropriate in support of this deployment.

(c) REPORT ON PERFORMANCE.—Not later than 180 days after the date of the enactment of this Act, the Secretary of Defense, in consultation with the Chief Financial Officer and the Chief Management Officer of the Department of Defense, shall submit to the congressional defense committees a report on the capabilities procured pursuant to subsection (a), including the results of using such capabilities in connection with auditing a financial statement of the Department of Defense.

SEC. 1004. SENSE OF CONGRESS ON SEQUESTRATION.

It is the sense of the Congress that—

(1) the fiscal challenges of the Federal Government are a top priority for Congress, and sequestration—non-strategic, across-the-board budget cuts—remains an unreasonable and inadequate budgeting tool to address the deficits and debt of the Federal Government;

(2) budget caps imposed by the Budget Control Act of 2011 (Public Law 112–25) impose unacceptable limitations on the budget and increase risk to the national security of the United States; and

(3) the budget caps imposed by the Budget Control Act of 2011 must be modified or eliminated through a bipartisan legislative agreement.

SEC. 1005. REQUIREMENT TO TRANSFER FUNDS FROM DEPARTMENT OF DEFENSE ACQUISITION WORKFORCE DEVELOPMENT FUND TO THE TREASURY.

(a) TRANSFER REQUIRED.—During fiscal year 2017, the Secretary of Defense shall transfer, from amounts available in the Department of Defense Acquisition Workforce Development Fund from amounts credited to the Fund pursuant to section 1705(d)(2) of title 10, United States Code, $475,000,000 to the Secretary of the Treasury for deposit in the general fund of the Treasury.

(b) ADDITIONAL AUTHORITY.—The transfer authority provided by this section is in addition to any other transfer authority contained in this Act.

Subtitle B—Counterdrug Activities

SEC. 1011. CODIFICATION AND MODIFICATION OF AUTHORITY TO PROVIDE SUPPORT FOR COUNTERDRUG ACTIVITIES AND ACTIVITIES TO COUNTER TRANSNATIONAL ORGANIZED CRIME OF CIVILIAN LAW ENFORCEMENT AGENCIES.

(a) CODIFICATION AND MODIFICATION.—

(1) IN GENERAL.—Chapter 18 of title 10, United States Code, is amended by adding at the end the following new section:

"§ 384. Support for counterdrug activities and activities to counter transnational organized crime

"(a) SUPPORT TO OTHER AGENCIES.—The Secretary of Defense may provide support for the counterdrug activities or activities to counter transnational organized crime of any other department or agency of the Federal Government or of any State, local, tribal, or foreign law enforcement agency for any of the purposes set forth in subsection (b) or (c), as applicable, if—

"(1) in the case of support described in subsection (b), such support is requested—

"(A) by the official who has responsibility for the counterdrug activities or activities to counter transnational organized crime of the department or agency of the Federal Government, in the case of support for other departments or agencies of the Federal Government; or

"(B) by the appropriate official of a State, local, or tribal government, in the case of support for State, local, or tribal law enforcement agencies; or

"(2) in the case of support described in subsection (c), such support is requested by an appropriate official of a department or agency of the Federal Government, in coordination with the Secretary of State, that has counterdrug responsibilities or responsibilities for countering transnational organized crime.

"(b) TYPES OF SUPPORT FOR AGENCIES OF UNITED STATES.—The purposes for which the Secretary may provide support under subsection (a) for other departments or agencies of the Federal Government or a State, local, or tribal law enforcement agencies, are the following:

"(1) The maintenance and repair of equipment that has been made available to any department or agency of the Federal Government or to any State, local, or tribal government by the Department of Defense for the purposes of—

"(A) preserving the potential future utility of such equipment for the Department of Defense; and

"(B) upgrading such equipment to ensure compatibility of that equipment with other equipment used by the Department.

"(2) The maintenance, repair, or upgrading of equipment (including computer software), other than equipment referred to in paragraph (1) for the purpose of—

"(A) ensuring that the equipment being maintained or repaired is compatible with equipment used by the Department of Defense; and

"(B) upgrading such equipment to ensure the compatibility of that equipment with equipment used by the Department.

"(3) The transportation of personnel of the United States and foreign countries (including per diem expenses associated with such transportation), and the transportation of supplies and equipment, for the purpose of facilitating counterdrug activities or activities to counter transnational organized crime within or outside the United States.

"(4) The establishment (including an unspecified minor military construction project) and operation of bases of operations or training facilities for the purpose of facilitating counterdrug activities or activities to counter transnational organized crime of the Department of Defense or any Federal, State, local, or tribal law enforcement agency within or outside the United States.

"(5) Counterdrug or counter-transnational organized crime related training of law enforcement personnel of the Federal Government, of State, local, and tribal governments, including associated support expenses for trainees and the provision of materials necessary to carry out such training.

"(6) The detection, monitoring, and communication of the movement of—

"(A) air and sea traffic within 25 miles of and outside the geographic boundaries of the United States; and

"(B) surface traffic outside the geographic boundary of the United States and within the United States not to exceed 25 miles of the boundary if the initial detection occurred outside of the boundary.

"(7) Construction of roads and fences and installation of lighting to block drug smuggling corridors across international boundaries of the United States.

"(8) Establishment of command, control, communications, and computer networks for improved integration of law enforcement, active military, and National Guard activities.

"(9) The provision of linguist and intelligence analysis services.

"(10) Aerial and ground reconnaissance.

"(c) TYPES OF SUPPORT FOR FOREIGN LAW ENFORCEMENT AGENCIES.—

"(1) PURPOSES.—The purposes for which the Secretary may provide support under subsection (a) for foreign law enforcement agencies are the following:

"(A) The transportation of personnel of the United States and foreign countries (including per diem expenses associated with such transportation), and the transportation of supplies and equipment, for the purpose of facilitating counterdrug activities or activities to counter transnational organized crime within or outside the United States.

"(B) The establishment (including small scale construction) and operation of bases of operations or training facilities for the purpose of facilitating counterdrug activities or activities to counter transnational organized crime of a foreign law enforcement agency outside the United States.

"(C) The detection, monitoring, and communication of the movement of—

"(i) air and sea traffic within 25 miles of and outside the geographic boundaries of the United States; and

"(ii) surface traffic outside the geographic boundaries of the United States.

"(D) Establishment of command, control, communications, and computer networks for improved integration of United States Federal and foreign law enforcement entities and United States Armed Forces.

"(E) The provision of linguist and intelligence analysis services.

"(F) Aerial and ground reconnaissance.

"(2) COORDINATION WITH SECRETARY OF STATE.—In providing support for a purpose described in this subsection, the Secretary shall coordinate with the Secretary of State.

"(d) CONTRACT AUTHORITY.—In carrying out subsection (a), the Secretary may acquire services or equipment by contract for support provided under that subsection if the Department of Defense would normally acquire such services or equipment by contract for the purpose of conducting a similar activity for the Department.

"(e) LIMITED WAIVER OF PROHIBITION.—Notwithstanding section 376 of this title, the Secretary may provide support pursuant to subsection (a) in any case in which the Secretary determines that the provision of such support would adversely affect the military preparedness of the United States in the short term if the Secretary determines that the importance of providing such support outweighs such short-term adverse effect.

"(f) CONDUCT OF TRAINING OR OPERATION TO AID CIVILIAN AGENCIES.—In providing support pursuant to subsection (a), the Secretary may plan and execute otherwise valid military training or operations (including training exercises undertaken pursuant to section 1206(a) of the National Defense Authorization Act for Fiscal Years 1990 and 1991 (Public Law 101–189; 103 Stat. 1564) for the purpose of aiding civilian law enforcement agencies.

"(g) RELATIONSHIP TO OTHER SUPPORT AUTHORITIES.—

"(1) ADDITIONAL AUTHORITY.—The authority provided in this section for the support of counterdrug activities or activities to counter transnational organized crime by the Department of Defense is in addition to, and except as provided in paragraph (2), not subject to the other requirements of this chapter.

"(2) EXCEPTION.—Support under this section shall be subject to the provisions of section 375 and, except as provided in subsection (e), section 376 of this title.

"(h) CONGRESSIONAL NOTIFICATION.—

"(1) IN GENERAL.—Not less than 15 days before providing support for an activity under subsection (a), the Secretary of Defense shall submit to the appropriate committees of Congress a written and electronic notice of the following:

"(A) In the case of support for a purpose described in subsection (c)—

"(i) the country the capacity of which will be built or enabled through the provision of such support;

"(ii) the budget, implementation timeline with milestones, anticipated delivery schedule for support, and completion date for the purpose or project for which support is provided;

"(iii) the source and planned expenditure of funds provided for the project or purpose;

"(iv) a description of the arrangements, if any, for the sustainment of the project or purpose and the source of funds to support sustainment of the capabilities and performance outcomes achieved using such support, if applicable;

"(v) a description of the objectives for the project or purpose and evaluation framework to be used to develop capability and performance metrics associated with operational outcomes for the recipient;

"(vi) information, including the amount, type, and purpose, about the support provided the country during the three fiscal years preceding the fiscal year for which the support covered by the notice is provided under this section under—

"(I) this section;

"(II) section 23 of the Arms Export Control Act (22 U.S.C. 2763);

"(III) peacekeeping operations;

"(IV) the International Narcotics Control and Law Enforcement program under section 481 of the Foreign Assistance Act of 1961 (22 U.S.C. 2291);

"(V) Nonproliferation, Anti-Terrorism, Demining, and Related Programs;

"(VI) counterdrug activities authorized by section 1004 of the National Defense Authorization Act for Fiscal Year 1991 (10 U.S.C. 374 note) and section 1033 of the National Defense Authorization Act for Fiscal Year 1998 (Public Law 105–85); or

"(VII) any other significant program, account, or activity for the provision of security assistance that the Secretary of Defense and the Secretary of State consider appropriate;

"(vii) an evaluation of the capacity of the recipient country to absorb the support provided; and

"(viii) an evaluation of the manner in which the project or purpose for which the support is provided fits into the theater security cooperation strategy of the applicable geographic combatant command.

"(B) In the case of support for a purpose described in subsection (b) or (c), a description of any small scale construction project for which support is provided.

"(2) COORDINATION WITH SECRETARY OF STATE.—In providing notice under this subsection for a purpose described in subsection (c), the Secretary of Defense shall coordinate with the Secretary of State.

"(i) DEFINITIONS.—In this section:

"(1) The term 'appropriate committees of Congress' means—

"(A) the Committee on Armed Services, the Committee on Appropriations, and the Committee on Foreign Affairs of the House of Representatives; and

"(B) the Committee on Armed Services, the Committee on Appropriations, and the Committee on Foreign Relations of the Senate.

"(2) The term 'Indian tribe' means a Federally recognized Indian tribe.

"(3) The term 'small scale construction' means construction at a cost not to exceed $750,000 for any project.

"(4) The term 'tribal government' means the governing body of an Indian tribe, the status of whose land is 'Indian country' as defined in section 1151 of title 18 or held in trust by the United States for the benefit of the Indian tribe.

"(5) The term 'tribal law enforcement agency' means the law enforcement agency of a tribal government.

"(6) The term 'transnational organized crime' means self-perpetuating associations of individuals who operate transnationally for the purpose of obtaining power, influence, monetary, or commercial gains, wholly or in part by illegal means, while protecting their activities through a pattern of corruption or violence or through a transnational organization structure and the exploitation of transnational commerce or communication mechanisms.''.

(2) CLERICAL AMENDMENT.—The table of sections at the beginning of chapter 18 of such title is amended by adding at the end the following new item:

"384. Support for counterdrug activities and activities to counter transnational organized crime.''.

(b) REPEAL OF SUPERSEDED AUTHORITY.—Section 1004 of the National Defense Authorization Act for Fiscal Year 1991 (10 U.S.C. 374 note) is repealed.

SEC. 1012. SECRETARY OF DEFENSE REVIEW OF CURRICULA AND PROGRAM STRUCTURES OF NATIONAL GUARD COUNTERDRUG SCHOOLS.

(a) IN GENERAL.—Section 901 of the Office of National Drug Control Policy Reauthorization Act of 2006 (Public Law 109–469; 32 U.S.C. 112 note) is amended—

(1) by redesignating subsections (e) through (g) as subsections (f) through (h), respectively; and

(2) by inserting after subsection (d) the following new subsection (e):

"(e) CURRICULUM REVIEW.—The Secretary of Defense shall review the curriculum and program structure of each school established under this section.''.

(b) TECHNICAL AMENDMENT.—Subsection (d)(1) of such section is amended by striking "section 112(b) of that title 32'' and inserting "section 112(b) of title 32''.

SEC. 1013. EXTENSION OF AUTHORITY TO SUPPORT UNIFIED COUNTERDRUG AND COUNTERTERRORISM CAMPAIGN IN COLOMBIA.

Section 1021 of the Ronald W. Reagan National Defense Authorization Act for Fiscal Year 2005 (Public Law 108–375; 118 Stat. 2042), as most recently amended by section 1011 of the National Defense Authorization Act for Fiscal Year 2016 (Public Law 114–92; 129 Stat. 962), is further amended—

(1) in subsection (a)(1), by striking "2017'' and inserting "2019''; and

(2) in subsection (c), by striking "2017'' and inserting "2019''.

SEC. 1014. ENHANCEMENT OF INFORMATION SHARING AND COORDINATION OF MILITARY TRAINING BETWEEN DEPARTMENT OF HOMELAND SECURITY AND DEPARTMENT OF DEFENSE.

(a) IN GENERAL.—The Secretary of Homeland Security shall ensure that the information needs of the Department of Homeland Security relating to civilian law enforcement activities in proximity to the international borders of the United States are identified and communicated to the Secretary of Defense for the purposes of the planning and executing of military training by the Department of Defense.

(b) FORMAL MECHANISM OF NOTIFICATION.—

(1) IN GENERAL.—Not later than 180 days after the date of the enactment of this Act, the Secretary of Homeland Security, in coordination with the Secretary of Defense, shall establish a formal mechanism through which the information needs of the Department of Homeland Security relating to civilian law enforcement activities in proximity to the international borders of the United States are identified and communicated to the Secretary of Defense for the purposes of the planning and executing military training by the Department of Defense.

(2) DISSEMINATION TO THE ARMED FORCES.—To the extent practicable, the Secretary of Defense shall ensure that such information needs are disseminated to the Armed Forces in a timely manner so the Armed Forces may take into account the information needs of civilian law enforcement when planning and executing training in accordance with section 371 of title 10, United States Code.

(3) COORDINATION OF TRAINING.—To the maximum extent practicable, the Secretary of Defense shall ensure that the planning and execution of training described in paragraph (2) is co-ordinated with the Department of Homeland Security.

(c) SHARING OF CERTAIN INFORMATION.—Not later than 180 days after the date of the enactment of this Act, the Secretary of Homeland Security and the Secretary of Defense shall jointly formulate guidance to ensure that the information relevant to civilian law enforcement matters that is collected by the Armed Forces during the normal course of military training or operations in proximity to the international borders of the United States is provided promptly to relevant officials in accordance with section 371 of title 10, United States Code.

(d) ANNUAL REPORTS.—

(1) DEPARTMENT OF DEFENSE REPORT.—

(A) IN GENERAL.—Not later than March 31 of each year, the Secretary of Defense shall submit to the congressional defense committees, the Committee on Homeland Security of the House of Representatives, and the Committee on Homeland Security and Governmental Affairs of the Senate a report on any assistance provided by the Department of Defense to the border security mission of the Department of Homeland Security at the international borders of the United States during the fiscal year preceding the fiscal year during which the report is submitted.

(B) ELEMENTS.—Each report submitted under subparagraph (A) shall include each of the following:

(i) A description of the military training and operational activities of each military component leveraged, pursuant to section 371 of title 10, United States Code, to support the border security mission of the Department of Homeland Security at the southern border of the United States.

(ii) For each activity described in clause (i), each of the following, identified by component:

(I) The Department of Homeland Security information need that was supported.

(II) The military training or operational activity leveraged to provide support.

(III) The duration of the support.

(IV) The cost of the support.

(iii) A description of any Department of Defense activities provided in response to a request for assistance from the Department of Homeland Security.

(iv) For each activity described in clause (iii)—

(I) The stated rationale of the Department of Homeland Security for requesting assistance from the Department of Defense.

(II) The capability provided by the Department of Defense.

(III) The duration of the assistance provided by the capability.

(IV) The statutory authority under which the assistance was provided.

(V) The cost of the assistance provided.

(VI) Whether the Department of Defense was reimbursed by the Department of Homeland Security for the assistance provided.

(VII) In the case of assistance for which the Department of Defense was not reimbursed, the justification for non-reimbursement.

(v) A description of any Department of Defense excess property provided to U. S. Customs and Border Protection.

(vi) The status of the implementation of this section.

(vii) A description of any other activity the Secretary of Defense determines relevant.

(2) DEPARTMENT OF HOMELAND SECURITY REPORT.—Not later than March 31 of each year, the Secretary of Homeland Security shall submit to the congressional defense committees, the Committee on Homeland Security of the House of Representatives, and the Committee on Homeland Security and Governmental Affairs of the Senate a report on—

(A) any activities of the Department of Homeland Security to reduce, mitigate, or eliminate the demand for Department of Defense support at the international borders of the United States; and

(B) the status of implementation of this section.

(3) TERMINATION.—The requirement to submit a report under paragraph (1) or (2) shall terminate on January 31, 2020.

Subtitle C—Naval Vessels and Shipyards

SEC. 1021. DEFINITION OF SHORT-TERM WORK WITH RESPECT TO OVERHAUL, REPAIR, OR MAINTENANCE OF NAVAL VESSELS.

Section 7299a(c)(4) of title 10, United States Code, is amended by striking "six months" and inserting "10 months".

SEC. 1022. WARRANTY REQUIREMENTS FOR SHIPBUILDING CONTRACTS.

(a) WARRANTY REQUIREMENTS.—

(1) IN GENERAL.—Chapter 633 of title 10, United States Code, is amended by adding at the end the following new section:

"§ 7318. Warranty requirements for shipbuilding contracts

"(a) REQUIREMENT.—A contracting officer for a contract for new construction for which funds are expended from the Shipbuilding and Conversion, Navy account shall require, as a condition of the contract, that the work performed under the contract is covered by a warranty for a period of at least one year.

"(b) WAIVER.—If the contracting officer for a contract covered by the requirement under subsection (a) determines that a limited liability of warranted work is in the best interest of the Government, the contracting officer may agree to limit the liability of the work performed under the contract to a level that the contracting officer determines is sufficient to protect the interests of the Government and in keeping with historical levels of warranted work on similar vessels.".

(2) CLERICAL AMENDMENT.—The table of sections at the beginning of such chapter is amended by adding at the end the following new item:

"7318. Warranty requirements for shipbuilding contracts.".

(b) EFFECTIVE DATE.—Section 7318 of title 10, United States Code, as added by subsection (a), shall take effect on the later of the following dates:

(1) The date of the enactment of the National Defense Authorization for Fiscal Year 2018.

(2) September 30, 2017.

SEC. 1023. NATIONAL SEA-BASED DETERRENCE FUND.

(a) AUTHORITY FOR MULTIYEAR PROCUREMENT OF CRITICAL COMPONENTS TO SUPPORT CONTINUOUS PRODUCTION OF THE COMMON MISSILE COMPARTMENT.—Section 2218a of title 10, United States Code, is amended—

(1) by redesignating subsections (i) and (j) as subsections (j) and (k), respectively; and

(2) by inserting after subsection (h) the following new subsection (i):

"(i) AUTHORITY FOR MULTIYEAR PROCUREMENT OF CRITICAL COMPONENTS TO SUPPORT CONTINUOUS PRODUCTION OF THE COMMON MISSILE COMPARTMENT.—(1) To implement the continuous production of the common missile compartment, the Secretary of the Navy may use funds deposited in the Fund, in conjunction with funds appropriated for the procurement of other nuclear-powered vessels, to enter into one or more multiyear contracts (including economic ordering quantity contracts), for the procurement of critical contractor-furnished and Government-furnished components for the common missile compartments of national sea-based deterrence vessels. The authority under this subsection extends to the procurement of equivalent critical parts, components, systems, and subsystems common with and required for other nuclear-powered vessels.

"(2) In each annual budget request submitted to Congress, the Secretary shall clearly identify funds requested for the common missile compartment and the individual ships and programs for which such funds are requested.

"(3) Any contract entered into pursuant to paragraph (1) shall provide that any obligation of the United States to make a payment under the contract is subject to the availability of appropriations for that purpose and that the total liability to the Government for the termination of the contract shall be limited to the total amount of funding obligated for the contract as of the date of the termination.".

(b) DEFINITION OF NATIONAL SEA-BASED DETERRENCE VESSEL.—Subsection (k)(2) of such section, as redesignated by subsection (b), is amended—

(1) by striking "any vessel" and inserting "any submersible vessel constructed or purchased after fiscal year 2016 that is"; and

(2) by inserting "and" before "that carries".

SEC. 1024. AVAILABILITY OF FUNDS FOR RETIREMENT OR INACTIVATION OF TICONDEROGA-CLASS CRUISERS OR DOCK LANDING SHIPS.

None of the funds authorized to be appropriated by this Act or otherwise made available for the Department of Defense for fiscal year 2017 may be obligated or expended—

(1) to retire, prepare to retire, or inactivate a cruiser or dock landing ship; or

(2) to place more than six cruisers and one dock landing ship in the modernization program under section 1026(a)(2) of the Carl Levin and Howard P. "Buck" McKeon National Defense Authorization Act for Fiscal Year 2015 (Public Law 113–291; 128 Stat. 3490).

Subtitle D—Counterterrorism

SEC. 1031. FREQUENCY OF COUNTERTERRORISM OPERATIONS BRIEFINGS.

(a) IN GENERAL.—Subsection (a) of section 485 of title 10, United States Code is amended by striking "quarterly" and inserting "monthly".

(b) SECTION HEADING.—The section heading for such section is amended by striking "**Quarterly**" and inserting "**Monthly**".

(c) CLERICAL AMENDMENT.—The table of sections at the beginning of chapter 23 of such title is amended by striking the item relating to section 485 and inserting the following new item:

"485. Monthly counterterrorism operations briefings.".

SEC. 1032. PROHIBITION ON USE OF FUNDS FOR TRANSFER OR RELEASE OF INDIVIDUALS DETAINED AT UNITED STATES NAVAL STATION, GUANTANAMO BAY, CUB, TO THE UNITED STATES.

No amounts authorized to be appropriated or otherwise made available for the Department of Defense may be used during the period beginning on the date of the enactment of this Act and ending on December 31, 2017, to transfer, release, or assist in the transfer or release to or within the United States, its territories, or possessions of Khalid Sheikh Mohammed or any other detainee who—

(1) is not a United States citizen or a member of the Armed Forces of the United States; and

(2) is or was held on or after January 20, 2009, at United States Naval Station, Guantanamo Bay, Cuba, by the Department of Defense.

SEC. 1033. PROHIBITION ON USE OF FUNDS TO CONSTRUCT OR MODIFY FACILITIES IN THE UNITED STATES TO HOUSE DETAINEES TRANSFERRED FROM UNITED STATES NAVAL STATION, GUANTANAMO BAY, CUBA.

(a) IN GENERAL.—No amounts authorized to be appropriated or otherwise made available to the Department of Defense may be used during the period beginning on the date of the enactment of this Act and ending on December 31, 2017, to construct or modify any facility in the

United States, its territories, or possessions to house any individual detained at Guantanamo for the purposes of detention or imprisonment in the custody or under the control of the Department of Defense unless authorized by Congress.

(b) EXCEPTION.—The prohibition in subsection (a) shall not apply to any modification of facilities at United States Naval Station, Guantanamo Bay, Cuba.

(c) INDIVIDUAL DETAINED AT GUANTANAMO DEFINED.—In this section, the term "individual detained at Guantanamo" has the meaning given that term in section 1034(f)(2) of the National Defense Authorization Act for Fiscal Year 2016 (Public Law 114–92; 129 Stat. 971; 10 U.S.C. 801 note).

SEC. 1034. PROHIBITION ON USE OF FUNDS FOR TRANSFER OR RELEASE TO CERTAIN COUNTRIES OF INDIVIDUALS DETAINED AT UNITED STATES NAVAL STATION, GUANTANAMO BAY, CUBA.

No amounts authorized to be appropriated or otherwise made available for the Department of Defense may be used during the period beginning on the date of the enactment of this Act and ending on December 31, 2017, to transfer, release, or assist in the transfer or release of any individual detained in the custody or under the control of the Department of Defense at United States Naval Station, Guantanamo Bay, Cuba, to the custody or control of any country, or any entity within such country, as follows:

(1) Libya.

(2) Somalia.

(3) Syria.

(4) Yemen.

SEC. 1035. PROHIBITION ON USE OF FUNDS FOR REALIGNMENT OF FORCES AT OR CLOSURE OF UNITED STATES NAVAL STATION, GUANTANAMO BAY, CUBA.

No amounts authorized to be appropriated or otherwise made available for the Department of Defense for fiscal year 2017 may be used—

(1) to close or abandon United States Naval Station, Guantanamo Bay, Cuba;

(2) to relinquish control of Guantanamo Bay to the Republic of Cuba; or

(3) to implement a material modification to the Treaty Between the United States of America and Cuba signed at Washington, D.C. on May 29, 1934, that constructively closes United States Naval Station, Guantanamo Bay.

SEC. 1036. CONGRESSIONAL NOTIFICATION REQUIREMENTS FOR SENSITIVE MILITARY OPERATIONS.

(a) TIMING OF NOTIFICATIONS.—Subsection (a) of section 130f of title 10, United States Code, is amended in the first sentence, by inserting "no later than 48 hours" before "following such operation".

(b) PROCEDURES.—Subsection (b) of such section is amended—

(1) In paragraph (1), by adding at the end the following new sentence: "The Secretary shall promptly notify the congressional defense committees in writing of any changes to such procedures at least 14 days prior to the adoption of any such changes"; and

(2) by adding at the end the following new paragraph:

"(3) In the event of an unauthorized disclosure of a sensitive military operation covered by this section, the Secretary shall ensure, to the maximum extent practicable, that the congressional defense committees are notified immediately of the sensitive military operation concerned. The notification under this paragraph may be verbal or written, but in the event of a verbal notification a written notification shall be provided by not later than 48 hours after the provision of the verbal notification.".

(c) BRIEFING REQUIREMENTS.—Such section is further amended—

(1) in subsection (a), by striking the second sentence; and

(2) in subsection (c), by inserting before the period at the end the following: ", including Department of Defense support to such operations conducted under the National Security Act of 1947 (50 U.S.C. 3001 et seq.)".

(d) DEFINITION OF SENSITIVE MILITARY OPERATION.—Subsection (d) of such section is amended by striking "means" and all that follows and inserting "means the following:"

"(1) A lethal operation or capture operation—

"(A) conducted by the armed forces outside a declared theater of active armed conflict; or

"(B) conducted by a foreign partner in coordination with the armed forces that targets a specific individual or individuals.

"(2) An operation conducted by the armed forces outside a declared theater of active armed conflict in self-defense or in defense of foreign partners, including during a cooperative operation.".

(e) REPEAL OF EXCEPTION TO NOTIFICATION REQUIREMENT.—Such section is further amended—

(1) by striking subsection (e); and

(2) by redesignating subsection (f) as subsection (e).

(f) CONFORMING AMENDMENTS.—

(1) SECTION HEADING AMENDMENT.—The heading of such section is amended to read as follows:

"§ 130f. Notification requirements for sensitive military operations".

(2) TABLE OF SECTIONS AMENDMENT.—The table of sections at the beginning of chapter 3 of such title is amended by striking the item relating to section 130f and inserting the following new item:

"130f. Notification requirements for sensitive military operations.".

Subtitle E—Miscellaneous Authorities and Limitations

SEC. 1041. EXPANDED AUTHORITY FOR TRANSPORTATION BY THE DEPARTMENT OF DEFENSE OF NON-DEPARTMENT OF DEFENSE PERSONNEL AND CARGO.

(a) TRANSPORTATION OF ALLIED AND CIVILIAN PERSONNEL AND CARGO.—Subsection (c) of section 2649 of title 10, United States Code, is amended—

(1) in the subsection heading, by striking "PERSONNEL" and inserting "AND CIVILIAN PERSONNEL AND CARGO";

(2) by striking "Until January 6, 2016, when" and inserting "When"; and

(3) by striking "allied forces or civilians", and inserting "allied and civilian personnel and cargo".

(b) COMMERCIAL INSURANCE.—Such section is further amended by adding at the end the following new subsection:

"(d) COMMERCIAL INSURANCE.—The Secretary may enter into a contract or other arrangement with one or more commercial providers to make insurance products available to non-Department of Defense shippers using the Defense Transportation System to insure against the loss or damage of the shipper's cargo. Any such contract or arrangement shall provide that—

"(1) any insurance premium is collected by the commercial provider;

"(2) any claim for loss or damage is processed and paid by the commercial provider;

"(3) the commercial provider agrees to hold the United States harmless and waive any recourse against the United States for amounts paid to an insured as a result of a claim; and

"(4) the contract between the commercial provider and the insured shall contain a provision whereby the insured waives any claim against the United States for loss or damage that is within the scope of enumerated risks covered by the insurance product.".

(c) CONFORMING CROSS-REFERENCE AMENDMENTS.—Subsection (b) of such section is

amended by striking "this section" both places it appears and inserting "subsection (a)".

SEC. 1042. REDUCTION IN MINIMUM NUMBER OF NAVY CARRIER AIR WINGS AND CARRIER AIR WING HEADQUARTERS REQUIRED TO BE MAINTAINED.

(a) CODIFICATION AND REDUCTION.—Section 5062 of title 10, United States Code, is amended by adding at the end the following new subsection:

"(e) The Secretary of the Navy shall ensure that—

"(1) the Navy maintains a minimum of 9 carrier air wings until the earlier of—

"(A) the date on which additional operationally deployable aircraft carriers can fully support a 10th carrier air wing; or

"(B) October 1, 2025;

"(2) after the earlier of the two dates referred to in subparagraphs (A) and (B) of paragraph (1), the Navy maintains a minimum of 10 carrier air wings; and

"(3) for each such carrier air wing, the Navy maintains a dedicated and fully staffed headquarters.".

(b) REPEAL OF SUPERSEDED REQUIREMENT.—Section 1093 of the National Defense Authorization Act for Fiscal Year 2012 (Public Law 112–81; 125 Stat. 1606; 10 U.S.C. 5062 note) is repealed.

SEC. 1043. MODIFICATION TO SUPPORT FOR NON-FEDERAL DEVELOPMENT AND TESTING OF MATERIAL FOR CHEMICAL AGENT DEFENSE.

Section 1034 of the National Defense Authorization Act for Fiscal Year 2008 (Public Law 110–181) is amended—

(1) in subsection (d)—

(A) by striking "report on the use of the authority under subsection (a)" and all that follows and inserting "report that includes—"

"(A) a description of—

"(i) each use of the authority under subsection (a); and

"(ii) for each such use, the specific material made available and to whom it was made available; and

"(B) a description of—

"(i) any instance in which the Department of Defense made available to a State, a unit of local government, or a private entity any biological select agent or toxin for the development or testing of any biodefense technology; and

"(ii) for each such instance, the specific material made available and to whom it was made available."; and

(B) by adding at the end the following new paragraph:

"(3) The requirement to submit a report under paragraph (1) shall terminate on January 31, 2021."; and

(2) in subsection (e), by striking "this section" and all that follows and inserting "this section:"

"(1) The terms 'precursor', 'protective purposes', and 'toxic chemical' have the meanings given those terms in the convention referred to in subsection (c), in paragraph 2, paragraph 9(b), and paragraph 1, respectively, of article II of that convention.

"(2) The term 'biological select agent or toxin' means any agent or toxin identified under any of the following:

"(A) Section 331.3 of title 7, Code of Federal Regulations.

"(B) Section 121.3 or section 121.4 of title 9, Code of Federal Regulations.

"(C) Section 73.3 or section 73.4 of title 42, Code of Federal Regulations.".

SEC. 1044. PROTECTION OF CERTAIN FEDERAL SPECTRUM OPERATIONS.

Section 1004 of the Bipartisan Budget Act of 2015 (Public Law 114–74; 47 U.S.C. 921 note) is amended by adding at the end the following:

"(d) PROTECTION OF CERTAIN FEDERAL SPECTRUM OPERATIONS.—If the report required by

subsection (a) determines that reallocation and auction of the spectrum described in the report would harm national security by impacting existing terrestrial Federal spectrum operations at the Nevada Test and Training Range, the Commission, in coordination with the Secretary shall, prior to the auction described in subsection (c)(1)(B), establish rules for licensees in such spectrum sufficient to mitigate harmful interference to such operations.

"(e) RULE OF CONSTRUCTION.—Nothing in this section shall be construed to affect any requirement under section 1062(b) of the National Defense Authorization Act for Fiscal Year 2000 (47 U.S.C. 921 note; Public Law 106–65).".

SEC. 1045. PROHIBITION ON USE OF FUNDS FOR RETIREMENT OF LEGACY MARITIME MINE COUNTERMEASURES PLATFORMS.

(a) PROHIBITIONS.—Except as provided under subsection (b), none of the funds authorized to be appropriated by this Act or otherwise made available for fiscal year 2017 for the Navy may be obligated or expended to—

(1) retire, prepare to retire, transfer, or place in storage any AVENGER-class mine countermeasures ship or associated equipment;

(2) retire, prepare to retire, transfer, or place in storage any SEA DRAGON (MH–53) helicopter or associated equipment;

(3) make any reductions to manning levels with respect to any AVENGER-class mine countermeasures ship; or

(4) make any reductions to manning levels with respect to any SEA DRAGON (MH–53) helicopter squadron or detachment.

(b) WAIVER.—The Secretary of the Navy may waive the limitations under subsection (a) if the Secretary certifies to the congressional defense committees that the Secretary has—

(1) identified a replacement capability and the necessary quantity of such systems to meet all combatant commander mine countermeasures operational requirements that are currently being met by the AVENGER-class ships and SEA DRAGON helicopters to be retired, transferred, or placed in storage;

(2) achieved initial operational capability of all systems described in paragraph (1); and

(3) deployed a sufficient quantity of systems described in paragraph (1) that have achieved initial operational capability to continue to meet or exceed all combatant commander mine countermeasures operational requirements currently being met by the AVENGER-class ships and SEA DRAGON helicopters.

SEC. 1046. EXTENSION OF AUTHORITY OF SECRETARY OF TRANSPORTATION TO ISSUE NON-PREMIUM AVIATION INSURANCE.

Section 44310(b) of title 49, United States Code, is amended by striking "December 31, 2018" and inserting "December 31, 2019".

SEC. 1047. EVALUATION OF NAVY ALTERNATE COMBINATION COVER AND UNISEX COMBINATION COVER.

(a) MANDATORY POSSESSION OR WEAR DATE.—The Secretary of the Navy shall change the mandatory possession or wear date of the alternate combination cover or the unisex combination cover from October 31, 2016, to October 31, 2018.

(b) EVALUATION AND REPORT.—Not later than February 1, 2017, the Secretary of the Navy shall submit to the Committees on Armed Services of the Senate and House of Representatives a report on the evaluation of the Navy female service dress uniforms based on surveying a representative group of female officer and enlisted service members. Such evaluation shall include each of the following:

(1) An identification of the operational need addressed by the alternate combination cover or the unisex combination cover.

(2) An assessment of the individual cost of service dress uniform items to members of the

Armed Forces as a percentage of their monthly pay.

(3) The composition of each uniform item's wear test group.

(4) An identification of the costs to the Navy and to individual members of the Armed Forces for uniform changes identified in the Navy administrative message 236/15 dated October 9, 2015.

(5) The opinions of a representative group of female officer and enlisted service members of the Navy active and reserve components.

(6) Any other rationale the Secretary determines appropriate.

SEC. 1048. INDEPENDENT EVALUATION OF DEPARTMENT OF DEFENSE EXCESS PROPERTY PROGRAM.

(a) IN GENERAL.—The Secretary of Defense shall enter into an agreement with a federally funded research and development center, or another appropriate independent entity, with relevant expertise to conduct an evaluation of the Department of Defense excess property program under section 2576a of title 10, United States Code. Not later than 180 days after the date of the enactment of this Act, the Secretary shall submit such evaluation to the congressional defense committees

(b) ELEMENTS OF EVALUATION.—The evaluation required under paragraph (1) shall include each of the following:

(1) A review of the current listing of "authorized", "controlled", and "prohibited" items as defined by Executive Order 13688 and by Department of Defense policy, guidance, and instruction, as well as why each item is currently assigned to each category.

(2) A review of the preferences and any associated prioritization provided to Federal, State, and local law enforcement agency requests for excess equipment to be used in border security, counterdrug, and counterterrorism activities, pursuant to section 2576a(a)(1)(A) of title 10 United States Code, including the overall numbers and percentages of equipment provided and used under these preferential categories.

(3) Whether the Department of Defense has bought a type of equipment and declared as excess the same type of equipment during the same year, and if so, how much such equipment.

(4) The type of information being collected by State coordinators and the Defense Logistics Agency when a request for equipment is made, and whether or not that information is sufficient to demonstrate a need for the equipment requested by the law enforcement agency making the request.

(5) The extent to which State coordinators and the Defense Logistics Agency deny requests for equipment and the reasons for such denials.

(6) The extent to which law enforcement agencies have been suspended from participating in the program and the reasons for such suspensions.

(7) Any other matters the Secretary determines appropriate.

SEC. 1049. WAIVER OF CERTAIN POLYGRAPH EXAMINATION REQUIREMENTS.

The Secretary of Homeland Security, acting through the Commissioner of U.S. Customs and Border Protection, may waive the polygraph examination requirement under section 3 of the Anti-Border Corruption Act of 2010 (Public Law 111–376) for any applicant who—

(1) the Commissioner determines is suitable for employment;

(2) holds a current, active Top Secret clearance and is able to access sensitive compartmented information;

(3) has a current single scope background investigation;

(4) was not granted any waivers to obtain the clearance; and

(5) is a veteran (as such term is defined in section 2108 or 2109a of title 5, United States Code).

SEC. 1050. USE OF TRANSPORTATION WORKER IDENTIFICATION CREDENTIAL TO GAIN ACCESS AT DEPARTMENT OF DEFENSE INSTALLATIONS.

(a) ACCESS TO INSTALLATIONS FOR CREDENTIALED TRANSPORTATION WORKERS.—During the period that the Secretary is developing and fielding physical access standards, capabilities, processes, and electronic access control systems, the Secretary shall, to the maximum extent practicable, ensure that the Transportation Worker Identification Credential (TWIC) shall be accepted as a valid credential for unescorted access to Department of Defense installations by transportation workers.

(b) CREDENTIALED TRANSPORTATION WORKERS WITH SECRET CLEARANCE.—TWIC-carrying transportation workers who also have a current Secret Level Clearance issued by the Department of Defense shall be considered exempt from further vetting when seeking unescorted access at Department of Defense facilities. Access security personnel shall verify such person's security clearance in a timely manner and provide them with unescorted access to complete their freight service.

SEC. 1051. LIMITATION ON AVAILABILITY OF FUNDS FOR DESTRUCTION OF CERTAIN LANDMINES AND BRIEFING ON DEVELOPMENT OF REPLACEMENT ANTI-PERSONNEL LANDMINE MUNITIONS.

(a) LIMITATION.—Except as provided in subsection (b), none of the funds authorized to be appropriated by this Act or otherwise made available for fiscal year 2017 for the Department of Defense may be obligated or expended for the destruction of anti-personnel landmine munitions before the date on which the Secretary of Defense submits the report required by section 1058(c) of the National Defense Authorization Act for Fiscal Year 2016 (Public Law 114–92; 129 Stat. 986).

(b) EXCEPTION FOR SAFETY.—Subsection (a) shall not apply to any anti-personnel landmine munitions that the Secretary determines are unsafe or could pose a safety risk if not demilitarized or destroyed.

(c) BRIEFING REQUIRED.—

(1) IN GENERAL.—Not later than 180 days after the date of the enactment of this Act, the Secretary of Defense shall provide to the congressional defense committees a briefing on the current state of research and development into operational alternatives to anti-personnel landmine munitions.

(2) FORM OF BRIEFING.—The briefing required by paragraph (1) may contain classified information.

(d) ANTI-PERSONNEL LANDMINE MUNITIONS DEFINED.—In this section, the term "anti-personnel landmine munitions" includes anti-personnel landmines and sub-munitions as defined by the Convention on the Prohibition of the Use, Stockpiling, Production and Transfer of Anti-Personnel Mines and on their Destruction, as determined by the Secretary.

SEC. 1052. TRANSITION OF AIR FORCE TO OPERATION OF REMOTELY PILOTED AIRCRAFT BY ENLISTED PERSONNEL.

(a) TRANSITION REQUIRED.—The Secretary of the Air Force shall transition the Air Force to an organizational model for all Air Force remotely piloted aircraft that uses a significant number of enlisted personnel as operators of such aircraft rather than officers only.

(b) DEADLINES.—

(1) REGULAR COMPONENT.—For the regular component of the Air Force, the transition required by subsection (a) shall be completed not later than September 30, 2020.

(2) RESERVE COMPONENTS.—For the Air Force Reserve and Air National Guard, the transition required by subsection (a) shall be completed not later than September 30, 2023.

(c) TRANSITION MATTERS.—The transition required by subsection (a) shall account for the following:

(1) Training infrastructure for enlisted personnel operating Air Force remotely piloted aircraft.

(2) Supervisory roles for officers and senior enlisted personnel for enlisted personnel operating Air Force remotely piloted aircraft.

(d) REPORTS.—

(1) INITIAL REPORT.—Not later than March 1, 2017, the Secretary of the Air Force shall submit to the Committees on Armed Services of the Senate and the House of Representatives a report that sets forth a detailed description of the plan for the transition required by subsection (a), including the following:

(A) The objectives of the transition.

(B) The timeline of the transition.

(C) The resources required to implement the transition.

(D) Recommendations for any legislation action required to implement the transition.

(E) The assumptions used to complete the transition.

(F) Risks associated with implementing the transition.

(2) REPORTS ON PROGRESS OF IMPLEMENTATION.—Not later than March 1, 2018, and each March 1 thereafter until the transition required by subsection (a) is completed, the Secretary shall submit to the committees referred to in paragraph (1) a report on the progress of the Air Force in implementing the plan required under that paragraph and in achieving the transition required by subsection (a).

SEC. 1053. PROHIBITION ON DIVESTMENT OF MARINE CORPS SEARCH AND RESCUE UNITS.

None of the amounts authorized to be appropriated by this Act or otherwise made available for fiscal year 2017 for the Navy or the Marine Corps may be obligated or expended—

(1) to retire, prepare to retire, transfer, or place in storage any Marine Corps Search and Rescue Unit (SRU) aircraft; or

(2) to make any change or revision to manning levels with respect to any Marine Corps Search and Rescue Unit squadron.

SEC. 1054. SUPPORT FOR THE ASSOCIATE DIRECTOR OF THE CENTRAL INTELLIGENCE AGENCY FOR MILITARY AFFAIRS.

(a) SELECTION OF ASSOCIATE DIRECTOR.—The Associate Director of the Central Intelligence Agency for Military Affairs shall be selected by the Secretary of Defense, with the concurrence of the Director of the Central Intelligence Agency, from among commissioned officers of the Armed Forces who are general or flag officers.

(b) SUPPORT FOR ACTIVITIES.—

(1) IN GENERAL.—In order to improve the provision of support to, and the receipt of support from, the Central Intelligence Agency, and to improve deconfliction of the activities of the Central Intelligence Agency and the Department of Defense, the Secretary of Defense and the Under Secretary of Defense for Intelligence shall ensure that the Associate Director of the Central Intelligence Agency for Military Affairs has access to, and support from, offices, agencies, and programs of the Department necessary for the purposes of the Associate Director as follows:

(A) To facilitate and coordinate Department of Defense support for the Central Intelligence Agency requested by the Director of the Central Intelligence Agency and approved by the Secretary, including oversight of Department of Defense military and civilian personnel detailed or assigned to the Central Intelligence Agency.

(B) To prioritize, communicate, and coordinate Department of Defense requests for, and the provision of support to, the Department of Defense from the Central Intelligence Agency, including support requested by and provided to the commanders of the combatant commands and subordinate task forces and commands.

(2) POLICIES.—The Under Secretary shall develop and supervise the implementation of policies to integrate and communicate Department of Defense requirements and requests for support from the Central Intelligence Agency that are coordinated by the Associate Director pursuant to paragraph (1)(B).

SEC. 1055. NOTIFICATION ON THE PROVISION OF DEFENSE SENSITIVE SUPPORT.

(a) LIMITATION.—The Secretary of Defense may provide defense sensitive support to a non-Department of Defense Federal department or agency only after the Secretary has determined that such support—

(1) is consistent with the mission and functions of the Department of Defense; and

(2) does—

(A) not significantly interfere with the mission or functions of the Department; or

(B) interfere with the mission and functions of the Department of Defense but such support is in the national security interest of the United States.

(b) NOTICE REQUIRED.—

(1) IN GENERAL.—Except as provided in paragraph (3), before providing defense sensitive support to a non-Department of Defense Federal department or agency, the Secretary of Defense shall notify the congressional defense committees, and, when the part of the Department of Defense providing the sensitive support is a member of the intelligence community, the congressional intelligence committees of the Secretary's intent to provide such support.

(2) CONTENTS.—Notice provided under paragraph (1) shall include the following:

(A) A description of the support to be provided.

(B) A description of how the support is consistent with the mission and functions of the Department.

(C) A description of how the support—

(i) does not significantly interfere with the mission or functions of the Department; or

(ii) significantly interferes with the mission or functions of the Department but is in the national security interest of the United States.

(3) TIME SENSITIVE SUPPORT.—In the event that the provision of defense sensitive support is time-sensitive, the Secretary—

(A) may provide notification under paragraph (1) after providing the support; and

(B) shall provide such notice as soon as practicable after providing such support, but not later than 48 hours after providing the support.

(c) DEFENSE SENSITIVE SUPPORT DEFINED.—In this section, the term "defense sensitive support" means support provided by the Department of Defense to a non-Department of Defense Federal department or agency that requires special protection from disclosure.

SEC. 1056. PROHIBITION ON ENFORCEMENT OF MILITARY COMMISSION RULINGS PREVENTING MEMBERS OF THE ARMED FORCES FROM CARRYING OUT OTHERWISE LAWFUL DUTIES BASED ON MEMBER SEX.

(a) PROHIBITION.—No order, ruling, finding, or other determination of a military commission may be construed or implemented to prohibit or restrict a member of the Armed Forces from carrying out duties otherwise lawfully assigned to such member to the extent that the basis for such prohibition or restriction is the sex of such member.

(b) APPLICABILITY TO PRIOR ORDERS, ETC..—The prohibition or restriction described in subsection (a) shall, upon motion, apply to any order, ruling, finding, or other determination described in that subsection that was issued before the date of the enactment of this Act in a military commission and is still effective as of the date of such motion.

(c) MILITARY COMMISSION DEFINED.—In this section, the term "military commission" means a military commission established under chapter 47A of title 10, United States Code, and any military commission otherwise established or convened by law.

Subtitle F—Studies and Reports

SEC. 1061. TEMPORARY CONTINUATION OF CERTAIN DEPARTMENT OF DEFENSE REPORTING REQUIREMENTS.

(a) EXCEPTIONS TO REPORTS TERMINATION PROVISION.—Section 1080 of the National Defense Authorization Act for Fiscal Year 2016 (Public Law 114–92; 129 Stat. 1000; 10 U.S.C. 111 note) does not apply to any report required to be submitted to Congress by the Department of Defense, or by any officer, official, component, or element of the Department, pursuant to a provision of law specified in this section, notwithstanding the enactment of the reporting requirement by an annual national defense authorization Act or the inclusion of the report in the list of reports prepared by the Secretary of Defense pursuant to subsection (c) of such section 1080.

(b) FINAL TERMINATION DATE FOR SUBMITTAL OF EXEMPTED REPORTS.—

(1) IN GENERAL.—Except as provided in paragraph (2), each report required pursuant to a provision of law specified in this section that is still required to be submitted to Congress as of December 31, 2021, shall no longer be required to be submitted to Congress after that date.

(2) REPORTS EXEMPTED FROM TERMINATION.—The termination dates specified in paragraph (1) and section 1080 of the National Defense Authorization Act for Fiscal Year 2016 do not apply to the following:

(A) The submission of the reports on the National Military Strategy and Risk Assessment under section 153(b)(3) of title 10, United States Code.

(B) The submission of the future-years defense program (including associated annexes) under section 221 of title 10, United States Code.

(C) The submission of the future-years mission budget for the military programs of the Department of Defense under section 221 of such title.

(D) The submission of audits of contracting compliance by the Inspector General of the Department of Defense under section 1601(b) of the National Defense Authorization Act for Fiscal Year 2014 (Public Law 113–66; 10 U.S.C. 2533a note).

(c) REPORTS REQUIRED BY TITLE 10, UNITED STATES CODE.—Subject to subsection (b), subsection (a) applies to reporting requirements contained in the following sections of title 10, United States Code:

(1) Section 113(i).

(2) Section 117(e).

(3) 118a(d).

(4) Section 119(a) and (b).

(5) Section 127b(f).

(6) Section 139(h).

(7) Section 139b(d).

(8) Sections 153(c).

(9) Section 171a(e) and (g)(2).

(10) Section 179(f).

(11) Section 196(d)(1), (d)(4), and (e)(3).

(12) Section 223a(a).

(13) Section 225(c)

(14) Section 229.

(15) Section 231.

(16) Section 231a.

(17) Section 238.

(18) Section 341(f) of title 10, United States Code, as amended by section 1246 of this Act.

(19) Section 401(d).

(20) Section 407(d).

(21) Section 481a(c).

(22) Section 482(a).

(23) Section 488(c).

(24) Section 494(b).

(25) Section 526(j).

(26) Section 946(c) (Article 146 of the Uniform Code of Military Justice).

(27) Section 981(c).

(28) Section 1116(d).

(29) Section 1566(c)(3).

(30) Section 1557(e).

(31) Section 1781a(e).

(32) Section 1781c(h).

(33) Section 2011(e).

(34) Section 2166(i).

(35) Section 2218(h).

(36) Section 2228(e).

(37) Section 2229(d).

(38) Section 2229a.

(39) Section 2249c(c).

(40) Section 2275.

(41) Section 2276(e).

(42) Section 2367(d).

(43) Section 2399(g).

(44) Section 2445b.

(45) Section 2464(d).

(46) Section 2466(d).

(47) Section 2504.

(48) Section 2561(c).

(49) Section 2684a(g).

(50) Section 2687a.

(51) Section 2711.

(52) Sections 2884(b) and (c).

(53) Section 2911(a) and (b)(3).

(54) Section 2925.

(55) Section 2926(c)(4).

(56) Section 4361(d)(4)(B).

(57) Section 4721(e).

(58) Section 6980(d)(4)(B).

(59) Section 7310(c).

(60) Section 9361(d)(4)(B).

(61) Section 10216(c).

(62) Section 10541.

(63) Section 10543.

(d) REPORTS REQUIRED BY NATIONAL DEFENSE AUTHORIZATION ACT FOR FISCAL YEAR 2015.—Subject to subsection (b), subsection (a) applies to reporting requirements contained in the following sections of the Carl Levin and Howard P. "Buck" McKeon National Defense Authorization Act for Fiscal Year 2015 (Public Law 113–291):

(1) Section 546(d) (10 U.S.C. 1561 note).

(2) Section 1003 (10 U.S.C. 221 note).

(3) Section 1026(d) (128 Stat. 3490).

(4) Section 1055 (128 Stat. 3498).

(5) Section 1204(b) (10 U.S.C. 2249e note).

(6) Section 1205(e) (128 Stat. 3537).

(7) Section 1206(e) (10 U.S.C. 2282 note).

(8) Section 1211 (128 Stat. 3544).

(9) Section 1225 (128 Stat. 3550).

(10) Section 1235 (128 Stat. 3558).

(11) Section 1245 (128 Stat. 3566).

(12) Section 1253(b) (22 U.S.C. 2151 note).

(13) Section 1275(b) (128 Stat. 3591).

(14) Section 1343 (128 Stat. 3605; 50 U.S.C. 3743).

(15) Section 1650 (128 Stat. 3653).

(16) Section 1662(c)(2) and (d)(2) (128 Stat. 3657; 10 U.S.C. 2431 note).

(17) Section 2821(a)(3) (10 U.S.C. 2687 note).

(e) REPORTS REQUIRED BY NATIONAL DEFENSE AUTHORIZATION ACT FOR FISCAL YEAR 2014.—Subject to subsection (b), subsection (a) applies to reporting requirements contained in the following sections of the National Defense Authorization Act for Fiscal Year 2014 (Public Law 113–66):

(1) Section 704(e) (10 U.S.C. 1074 note).

(2) Sections 713(f), (g), and (h) (10 U.S.C. 1071 note).

(3) Section 904(d)(2) (10 U.S.C. 111 note).

(4) Section 1205(f)(3) (32 U.S.C. 107 note).

(f) REPORTS REQUIRED BY NATIONAL DEFENSE AUTHORIZATION ACT FOR FISCAL YEAR 2013.—Subject to subsection (b), subsection (a) applies to reporting requirements contained in the following sections of the National Defense Authorization Act for Fiscal Year 2013 (Public Law 112–239):

(1) Section 524(c)(2) (10 U.S.C. 1222 note).

(2) Section 904(h)(1) and (2) (10 U.S.C. 133 note).

(3) Section 1009 (126 Stat. 1906).

(4) Section 1023 (126 Stat. 1911).

(5) Section 1052(b)(4) (126 Stat. 1936; 49 U.S.C. 40101 note).

(g) REPORTS REQUIRED BY NATIONAL DEFENSE AUTHORIZATION ACT FOR FISCAL YEAR 2011.— Subject to subsection (b), subsection (a) applies to reporting requirements contained in the following sections of the Ike Skelton National Defense Authorization Act for Fiscal Year 2011 (Public Law 111–383):

(1) Section 123 (10 U.S.C. 167 note).

(2) Section 1216(c) (124 Stat. 4392).

(3) Section 1217(i) (22 U.S.C. 7513 note).

(4) Section 1631(d) (10 U.S.C. 1561 note).

(h) REPORTS REQUIRED BY NATIONAL DEFENSE AUTHORIZATION ACT FOR FISCAL YEAR 2010.— Subject to subsection (b), subsection (a) applies to reporting requirements contained in the following sections of the National Defense Authorization Act for Fiscal Year 2010 (Public Law 111–84):

(1) Section 711(d) (10 U.S.C. 1071 note).

(2) Section 1003(b) (10 U.S.C. 2222 note).

(3) Section 1244(d) (22 U.S.C. 1928 note).

(4) Section 1245 (123 Stat. 2542).

(5) Section 1806 (10 U.S.C. 948a note).

(i) REPORTS REQUIRED BY OTHER LAWS.— Subject to subsection (b), subsection (a) applies to reporting requirements contained in the following provisions of law:

(1) Sections 1412(i) and (j) of the National Defense Authorization Act, 1986 (50 U.S.C. 1521), as amended by section 1421 of the Ike Skelton National Defense Authorization Act for Fiscal Year 2011 (Public Law 111–383).

(2) Section 1703 of the National Defense Authorization Act for Fiscal Year 1994 (50 U.S.C. 1523).

(3) Section 717(c) of the National Defense Authorization Act for Fiscal Year 1996 (Public Law 104–106; 10 U.S.C. 1073 note).

(4) Section 234 of the National Defense Authorization Act for Fiscal Year 1998 (50 U.S.C. 2367).

(5) Section 1309(c) of the National Defense Authorization Act for Fiscal Year 1998 (Public Law 105–85; 10 U.S.C. 113 note).

(6) Section 1237(b)(2) of the National Defense Authorization Act for Fiscal Year 1999 (Public Law 105–261; 50 U.S.C. 1701 note).

(7) Section 1202 of the National Defense Authorization Act for Fiscal Year 2000 (Public Law 106–65; 10 U.S.C. 113 note).

(8) Section 232(h)(2) of the National Defense Authorization Act for Fiscal Year 2002 (Public Law 107–107; 10 U.S.C. 2431 note).

(9) Section 366(a)(5) and (c)(2) of the Bob Stump National Defense Authorization Act for Fiscal Year 2003 (Public Law 107–314; 10 U.S.C. 113 note).

(10) Section 1208(f) of the Ronald W. Reagan National Defense Authorization Act for Fiscal Year 2005 (Public Law 108–375; 118 Stat. 2086).

(11) Section 1208(d) of the National Defense Authorization Act for 2006 (Public Law 109–163; 119 Stat. 3459).

(12) Section 1405(d) of the National Defense Authorization Act for Fiscal Year 2006 (Public Law 109–163; 10 U.S.C. 801 note).

(13) Section 122(f)(1) of the John Warner National Defense Authorization Act for Fiscal Year 2007 (Public Law 109–364; 120 Stat. 2104).

(14) Section 721 of the John Warner National Defense Authorization Act for Fiscal Year 2007 (Public Law 109–364; 120 Stat. 2294).

(15) Section 1017(e) of the John Warner National Defense Authorization Act for Fiscal Year 2007 (Public Law 109–364; 10 U.S.C. 2631 note).

(16) Section 1517(f) of the John Warner National Defense Authorization Act for Fiscal Year 2007 (Public Law 109–364; 120 Stat. 2443).

(17) Section 911(f)(2) of the National Defense Authorization Act for Fiscal Year 2008 (Public Law 110–181; 10 U.S.C. 2271 note).

(18) Section 1034(d) of the National Defense Authorization Act for Fiscal Year 2008 (Public Law 110–181; 122 Stat. 309).

(19) Section 1107(d) of the National Defense Authorization Act for Fiscal Year 2008 (Public Law 110–181; 122 Stat. 358).

(20) Section 1233(f) of the National Defense Authorization Act for Fiscal Year 2008 (Public Law 110–181; 122 Stat. 393).

(21) Section 1234(e) of the National Defense Authorization Act for Fiscal Year 2008 (Public Law 110–181; 122 Stat. 394).

(22) Section 219(c) of the Duncan Hunter National Defense Authorization Act for Fiscal Year 2009 (Public Law 110–417; 10 U.S.C. 2358 note).

(23) Section 533(i) of the Duncan Hunter National Defense Authorization Act for Fiscal Year 2010 (Public Law 110–417).

(24) Section 1047(d)(2) of the Duncan Hunter National Defense Authorization Act for Fiscal Year 2010 (Public Law 110–417; 10 U.S.C. 2366b note)

(25) Section 1201(b)(1) of the National Defense Authorization Act for Fiscal Year 2012 (Public Law 112–81; 125 Stat. 1619).

(26) Section 1236 of the National Defense Authorization Act for Fiscal Year 2012 (Public Law 112–81; 125 Stat. 1641).

(27) Section 103A(b)(3) of the Sikes Act (16 U.S.C. 670c–1(b)(3)).

(28) Section 1511(h) of the Armed Forces Retirement Home Act of 1991 (24 U.S.C. 411(h)).

(29) Section 901(f) of the Office of National Drug Control Policy Reauthorization Act of 2006 (Public Law 109–469; 32 U.S.C. 112 note), as added by section 1008 of the National Defense Authorization Act for Fiscal Year 2013 (Public Law 112–239).

(30) Section 14 of the Strategic and Critical Materials Stock Piling Act (50 U.S.C. 98h–5).

(31) Section 105A(b) of the Uniformed and Overseas Citizens Absentee Voting Act (52 U.S.C. 20308(b)), as added by section 586 of the National Defense Authorization Act for Fiscal Year 2010 (Public Law 111–84).

(32) Section 112(f) of title 32, United States Code.

(33) Section 310b(i)(2) of title 37, United States Code.

(j) CONFORMING AMENDMENT.—Section 1080(a) of the National Defense Authorization Act for Fiscal Year 2016 (Public Law 114–92; 129 Stat. 1000; 10 U.S.C. 111 note) is amended—

(1) by striking "on the date that is two years after the date of the enactment of this Act" and inserting "November 25, 2017"; and

(2) by striking "effective".

(k) REPORT TO CONGRESS.—Not later than February 1, 2017, the Secretary of Defense shall submit to the congressional defense committees a report that includes each of the following:

(1) A list of all reports that are required to be submitted to Congress as of the date of the enactment of this Act that will no longer be required to be submitted to Congress as of November 25, 2017.

(2) For each such report, a citation to the provision of law under which the report is or was required to be submitted.

SEC. 1062. REPORTS ON PROGRAMS MANAGED UNDER ALTERNATIVE COMPENSATORY CONTROL MEASURES IN THE DEPARTMENT OF DEFENSE.

(a) IN GENERAL.—Chapter 2 of title 10, United States Code, is amended by adding at the end the following new section:

"§ 119a. Programs managed under alternative compensatory control measures: congressional oversight

"(a) ANNUAL REPORT ON CURRENT PROGRAMS UNDER AACMS.—

"(1) IN GENERAL.—Not later than March 1 each year, the Secretary of Defense shall submit to the congressional defense committees a report on the programs being managed under alternative compensatory control measures in the Department of Defense.

"(2) ELEMENTS.—Each report under paragraph (1) shall set forth the following:

"(A) The total amount requested for programs being managed under alternative compensatory control measures in the Department in the budget of the President under section 1105 of title 31 for the fiscal year beginning in the fiscal year in which such report is submitted.

"(B) For each program in that budget that is a program being managed under alternative compensatory control measures in the Department—

"(i) a brief description of the program;

"(ii) a brief discussion of the major milestones established for the program;

"(iii) the actual cost of the program for each fiscal year during which the program has been conducted before the fiscal year during which that budget is submitted; and

"(iv) the estimated total cost of the program and the estimated cost of the program for—

"(I) the current fiscal year;

"(II) the fiscal year for which that budget is submitted; and

"(III) each of the four succeeding fiscal years during which the program is expected to be conducted.

"(3) ELEMENTS ON PROGRAMS COVERED BY MULTIYEAR BUDGETING.—In the case of a report under paragraph (1) submitted in a year during which the budget of the President for the fiscal year concerned does not, because of multiyear budgeting for the Department, include a full budget request for the Department, the report required by paragraph (1) shall set forth—

"(A) the total amount already appropriated for the next fiscal year for programs being managed under alternative compensatory control measures in the Department, and any additional amount requested in that budget for such programs for such fiscal year; and

"(B) for each program that is a program being managed under alternative compensatory control measures in the Department, the information specified in paragraph (2)(B).

"(b) ANNUAL REPORT ON NEW PROGRAMS UNDER AACMS.—

"(1) IN GENERAL.—Not later than February 1 each year, the Secretary shall submit to the congressional defense committees a report that, with respect to each new program being managed under alternative compensatory control measures in the Department, provides—

"(A) notice of the designation of the program as a program being managed under alternative compensatory control measures in the Department; and

"(B) a justification for such designation.

"(2) ADDITIONAL ELEMENTS.—A report under paragraph (1) with respect to a program shall include—

"(A) the current estimate of the total program cost for the program; and

"(B) an identification of existing programs or technologies that are similar to the technology, or that have a mission similar to the mission, of the program that is the subject of the report.

"(3) NEW PROGRAM BEING MANAGED UNDER ALTERNATIVE COMPENSATORY CONTROL MEASURES DEFINED.—In this subsection, the term 'new program being managed under alternative compensatory control measures' means a program in the Department that has not previously been covered by a report under this subsection.

"(c) REPORT ON CHANGE IN CLASSIFICATION OR DECLASSIFICATION OF PROGRAMS.—

"(1) IN GENERAL.—Whenever a change in the classification of a program being managed

under alternative compensatory control measures in the Department is planned to be made, or whenever classified information concerning a program being managed under alternative compensatory control measures in the Department is to be declassified and made public, the Secretary shall submit to the congressional defense committees a report containing a description of the proposed change, the reasons for the proposed change, and notice of any public announcement planned to be made with respect to the proposed change.

"(2) DEADLINE FOR REPORT.—Except as provided in paragraph (3), a report required by paragraph (1) shall be submitted not less than 14 days before the date on which the proposed change or public announcement concerned is to occur.

"(3) EXCEPTION.—If the Secretary determines that because of exceptional circumstances the requirement in paragraph (2) cannot be met with respect to a proposed change or public announcement concerning a program covered by paragraph (1), the Secretary may submit the report required by that paragraph regarding the proposed change or public announcement at any time before the proposed change or public announcement is made, and shall include in the report an explanation of the exceptional circumstances.

"(d) MODIFICATION OF CRITERIA OR POLICY FOR DESIGNATING PROGRAMS UNDER ACCMS.—Whenever there is a modification or termination of the policy or criteria used for designating a program as a program being managed under alternative compensatory control measures in the Department, the Secretary shall promptly notify the congressional defense committees of such modification or termination. Any such notification shall contain the reasons for the modification or termination and, in the case of a modification, the provisions of the policy or criteria as modified.

"(e) WAIVER.—

"(1) IN GENERAL.—The Secretary may waive any requirement in subsection (a), (b), or (c) that certain information be included in a report under such subsection if the Secretary determines that inclusion of that information in the report would adversely affect the national security. Any such waiver shall be made on a case-by-case basis.

"(2) NOTICE TO CONGRESS.—If the Secretary exercises the authority in paragraph (1), the Secretary shall provide the information described in the applicable subsection with respect to the program concerned, and the justification for the waiver, jointly to the chairman and ranking minority member of each of the congressional defense committees.

"(f) LIMITATION ON INITIATION OF PROGRAMS UNDER ACCMS.—

"(1) NOTICE AND WAIT.—Except as provided in paragraph (2), a program to be managed under alternative compensatory control measures in the Department may not be initiated until—

"(A) the congressional defense committees are notified of the program; and

"(B) a period of 30 days elapses after such notification is received.

"(2) EXCEPTION.—If the Secretary determines that waiting for the regular notification process before initiating a program as described in paragraph (1) would cause exceptionally grave damage to the national security, the Secretary may begin a program to be managed under alternative compensatory control measures in the Department before such waiting period elapses. The Secretary shall notify the congressional defense committees within 10 days of initiating a program under this paragraph, including a justification for the determination of the Secretary that waiting for the regular notification process would cause exceptionally grave damage to the national security.".

(b) CLERICAL AMENDMENT.—The table of sections at the beginning of chapter 2 of such title is amended by adding at the end the following new item:

"119a. Programs managed under alternative compensatory control measures: congressional oversight.".

SEC. 1063. MATTERS FOR INCLUSION IN REPORT ON DESIGNATION OF COUNTRIES FOR WHICH REWARDS MAY BE PAID UNDER DEPARTMENT OF DEFENSE REWARDS PROGRAM.

Section 127b(h) of title 10, United States Code, is amended—

(1) in paragraph (2), by inserting "and justification" after "reason"; and

(2) by amending paragraph (3) to read as follows:

"(3) An estimate of the amount or value of the rewards to be paid as monetary payment or payment-in-kind under this section.".

SEC. 1064. ANNUAL REPORTS ON UNFUNDED PRIORITIES OF THE ARMED FORCES AND THE COMBATANT COMMANDS AND ANNUAL REPORT ON COMBATANT COMMAND REQUIREMENTS.

(a) ANNUAL REPORTS REQUIRED.—

(1) IN GENERAL.—Chapter 9 of title 10, United States Code, is amended by inserting after section 222 the following new section:

"§222a. Unfunded priorities of the armed forces and combatant commands: annual report

"(a) ANNUAL REPORT.—Not later than 10 days after the date on which the budget of the President for a fiscal year is submitted to Congress pursuant to section 1105 of title 31, each officer specified in subsection (b) shall submit to the Secretary of Defense and the Chairman of the Joint Chiefs of Staff, and to the congressional defense committees, a report on the unfunded priorities of the armed force or forces or combatant command under the jurisdiction or command of such officer.

"(b) OFFICERS.—The officers specified in this subsection are the following:

"(1) The Chief of Staff of the Army.

"(2) The Chief of Naval Operations.

"(3) The Chief of Staff of the Air Force.

"(4) The Commandant of the Marine Corps.

"(5) The commanders of the combatant commands established under section 161 of this title.

"(c) ELEMENTS.—

"(1) IN GENERAL.—Each report under this subsection shall specify, for each unfunded priority covered by such report, the following:

"(A) A summary description of such priority, including the objectives to be achieved if such priority is funded (whether in whole or in part).

"(B) The additional amount of funds recommended in connection with the objectives under subparagraph (A).

"(C) Account information with respect to such priority, including the following (as applicable):

"(i) Line Item Number (LIN) for applicable procurement accounts.

"(ii) Program Element (PE) number for applicable research, development, test, and evaluation accounts.

"(iii) Sub-activity group (SAG) for applicable operation and maintenance accounts.

"(2) PRIORITIZATION OF PRIORITIES.—Each report shall present the unfunded priorities covered by such report in order of urgency of priority.

"(d) UNFUNDED PRIORITY DEFINED.—In this section, the term 'unfunded priority', in the case of a fiscal year, means a program, activity, or mission requirement that—

"(1) is not funded in the budget of the President for the fiscal year as submitted to Congress pursuant to section 1105 of title 31;

"(2) is necessary to fulfill a requirement associated with an operational or contingency plan

of a combatant command or other validated requirement; and

"(3) would have been recommended for funding through the budget referred to in paragraph (1) by the officer submitting the report required by subsection (a) in connection with the budget if—

"(A) additional resources been available for the budget to fund the program, activity, or mission requirement; or

"(B) the program, activity, or mission requirement has emerged since the budget was formulated.".

(2) CLERICAL AMENDMENT.—The table of sections at the beginning of chapter 9 of such title is amended by inserting after the item relating to section 222 the following new item:

"222a. Unfunded priorities of the armed forces and combatant commands: annual report.".

(b) REPEAL OF SUPERSEDED PROVISION.—Section 1003 of the National Defense Authorization Act for Fiscal Year 2013 (Public Law 113–239; 126 Stat. 1903) is repealed.

(c) SUBMITTAL OF ANNUAL REPORT ON COMBATANT COMMAND REQUIREMENTS.—Section 153(c)(1) of title 10, United States Code, is amended by striking "At or about the time that the budget is submitted to Congress for a fiscal year under section 1105(a) of title 31" and inserting "Not later than 25 days after the date on which the budget of the President for a fiscal year is submitted to Congress pursuant to section 1105(a) of title 31".

SEC. 1065. MANAGEMENT AND REVIEWS OF ELECTROMAGNETIC SPECTRUM.

(a) MANAGEMENT AND REVIEWS.—

(1) IN GENERAL.—Section 488 of title 10, United States Code, is amended to read as follows:

"§488. Management and review of electromagnetic spectrum

"(a) ORGANIZATION.—The Secretary of Defense shall—

"(1) ensure the effective organization and management of the electromagnetic spectrum used by the Department of Defense; and

"(2) establish an enduring review and evaluation process that—

"(A) considers all requirements relating to such spectrum; and

"(B) ensures that all users of such spectrum, regardless of the classification of such uses, are involved in the decision-making process of the Department concerning the potential sharing, reassigning, or reallocating of such spectrum, or the relocation of the uses by the Department of such spectrum.

"(b) REPORTS.—(1) From time to time as the Secretary and the Chairman of the Joint Chiefs of Staff determine useful for the effective oversight of the access by the Department to electromagnetic spectrum, but not less frequently than every two years, the Secretary and the Chairman shall jointly submit to the congressional defense committees a report on national policy plans regarding implications for such access in bands identified for study for potential reallocation, or under consideration for potential reallocation, by the Policy and Plans Steering Group established by the National Telecommunications and Information Administration.

"(2) Each report under paragraph (1) shall address, with respect to the electromagnetic spectrum used by the Department that is covered by the report, the implications to the missions of the Department resulting from sharing, reassigning, or reallocating the spectrum, or relocating the uses by the Department of such spectrum, if the Secretary and the Chairman jointly determine that such sharing, reassigning, reallocating, or relocation—

"(A) would potentially create a loss of essential military capability to the missions of the Department, as determined under feasibility assessments to ensure comparable capability; or

"(B) would not likely be possible within the 10-year period beginning on the date of the report.".

(2) CLERICAL AMENDMENT.—The table of sections at the beginning of chapter 23 of such title is amended by striking the item relating to section 488 and inserting the following new item:

"488. Management and review of electromagnetic spectrum.".

(b) ISSUANCE OF INSTRUCTION OR DIRECTIVE.—The Secretary of Defense shall—

(1) not later than 180 days after the date of the enactment of this Act, issue a Department of Defense Instruction or a Department of Defense Directive to carry out section 488(a) of title 10, United States Code, as amended by subsection (a); and

(2) upon the date of the issuance of the instruction or directive issued under paragraph (1), submit to the congressional defense committees such instruction or directive.

(c) INITIAL REVIEW.—Not later than 180 days after the date of the enactment of this Act, the Secretary of Defense and the Chairman of the Joint Chiefs of Staff shall jointly submit to the congressional defense committees a report described in section 488(b) of title 10, United States Code, as amended by subsection (a), with respect to—

(1) the plan by the National Telecommunications and Information Administration titled "Sixth Interim Progress Report on the Ten-Year Plan and Timetable" issued in June 2016; and

(2) the seventh such interim progress report issued (or to be issued) by the National Telecommunications and Information Administration.

SEC. 1066. REQUIREMENT FOR NOTICE AND REPORTING TO COMMITTEES ON ARMED SERVICES ON CERTAIN EXPENDITURES OF FUNDS BY DEFENSE INTELLIGENCE AGENCY.

Section 105(c) of the National Security Act of 1947 (50 U.S.C. 3038(c)) is amended by inserting ", the Committee on Armed Services of the Senate, and the Committee on Armed Services of the House of Representatives" after "committees" each place it appears.

SEC. 1067. CONGRESSIONAL NOTIFICATION OF BIOLOGICAL SELECT AGENT AND TOXIN THEFT, LOSS, OR RELEASE INVOLVING THE DEPARTMENT OF DEFENSE.

(a) NOTIFICATION REQUIREMENT.—Not later than 15 days after notice of any theft, loss, or release of a biological select agent or toxin involving the Department of Defense is provided to the Centers for Disease Control and Prevention or the Animal and Plant Health Inspection Service, as specified by section 331.19 of part 7 of the Code of Federal Regulations, the Secretary of Defense shall provide to the congressional defense committees notice of such theft, loss, or release.

(b) ELEMENTS.—Notice of a theft, loss, or release of a biological select agent or toxin under subsection (a) shall include each of the following:

(1) The name of the agent or toxin and any identifying information, including the strain or other relevant characterization information.

(2) An estimate of the quantity of the agent or toxin stolen, lost, or released.

(3) The location or facility from which the theft, loss, or release occurred.

(4) In the case of a release, any hazards posed by the release and the number of individuals potentially exposed to the agent or toxin.

(5) Actions taken to respond to the theft, loss, or release.

SEC. 1068. REPORT ON SERVICE-PROVIDED SUPPORT AND ENABLING CAPABILITIES TO UNITED STATES SPECIAL OPERATIONS FORCES.

(a) REPORT REQUIRED.—Not later than 180 days after the date of the enactment of this Act, the Secretary of Defense shall submit to the congressional defense committees a written report on service-common support and enabling capabilities contributed from each of the military services to special operations forces. Such report shall include each of the following:

(1) A definition of the terms "service-common" and "special operations-peculiar".

(2) A description of the factors and process used by the Department of Defense to determine whether combat support, combat service support, base operating support, and enabling capabilities are service-common or special operations-peculiar.

(3) A detailed accounting of the resources allocated by each military service to provide combat support, combat service support, base operating support, and enabling capabilities for special operations forces.

(4) An identification of any change in the level or type of service-common support and enabling capabilities provided by each of the military services to special operations forces in the current fiscal year when compared to the preceding fiscal year, including the rationale for any such change and any mitigating actions.

(5) An assessment of the specific effects that the budget request for the current fiscal year and any anticipated future manpower and force structure changes are likely to have on the ability of each of the military services to provide service-common support and enabling capabilities to special operations forces.

(6) Any other matters the Secretary determines relevant.

(b) ANNUAL UPDATES.—For each of fiscal years 2018 through 2020, at the same time the Secretary of Defense submits to Congress the budget request for such fiscal year, the Secretary shall submit to the congressional defense committees an update to the report required under subsection (a).

(c) FORM OF REPORT.—The report required under subsection (a) and each update provided under subsection (b) shall be submitted in unclassified form, but may contain a classified annex.

SEC. 1069. REPORT ON CITIZEN SECURITY RESPONSIBILITIES IN THE NORTHERN TRIANGLE OF CENTRAL AMERICA.

(a) IN GENERAL.—Not later than 180 days after the date of the enactment of this Act, the Secretary of Defense and the Secretary of State shall jointly prepare and submit to the appropriate congressional committees a report on military units that have been assigned to policing or citizen security responsibilities in Guatemala, Honduras, and El Salvador.

(b) MATTERS TO BE INCLUDED.—The report required by subsection (a) shall include each of the following:

(1) The following information, as of the date of the enactment of this Act, with respect to military units assigned to policing or citizen security responsibilities in each of Guatemala, Honduras, and El Salvador:

(A) The proportion of individuals in each such country's military who participate in policing or citizen security activities relative to the total number of individuals in that country's military.

(B) Of the military units assigned to policing or citizen security responsibilities, the types of units conducting police activities.

(C) The role of the Department of Defense and the Department of State in training individuals for purposes of participation in such military units.

(D) The number of individuals who participated in such military units who received train-

ing by the Department of Defense, and the types of training they received.

(2) Any other information that the Secretary of Defense or the Secretary of State determines to be necessary to help better understand the relationships of the militaries of Guatemala, Honduras, and El Salvador to public security in such countries.

(3) A description of the plan of the United States to assist the militaries of Guatemala, Honduras, and El Salvador to carry out their responsibilities in a manner that adheres to democratic principles.

(c) FORM.—The report required by subsection (a) shall be submitted in unclassified form, but may contain a classified annex.

(d) PUBLIC AVAILABILITY.—The unclassified matter of the report required by subsection (a) shall be posted on a publicly available Internet website of the Department of Defense and a publicly available Internet website of the Department of State.

(e) APPROPRIATE CONGRESSIONAL COMMITTEES.—In this section, the term "appropriate congressional committees" means the Committee on Armed Services and the Committee on Foreign Affairs of the House of Representatives and the Committee on Armed Services and the Committee on Foreign Relations of the Senate.

SEC. 1070. REPORT ON COUNTERPROLIFERATION ACTIVITIES AND PROGRAMS.

(a) IN GENERAL.—Not later than July 1, 2017, the Secretary of Defense shall submit to the congressional defense committees a report on the counterproliferation activities and programs of the Department of Defense.

(b) MATTERS INCLUDED.—The report required under subsection (a) shall include each of the following:

(1) A complete list and assessment of existing and proposed capabilities and technologies for support of United States nonproliferation policy and counterproliferation policy, with regard to—

(A) interdiction;

(B) elimination;

(C) threat reduction cooperation;

(D) passive defenses;

(E) security cooperation and partner activities;

(F) offensive operations;

(G) active defenses; and

(H) weapons of mass destruction consequence management.

(2) For the existing and proposed capabilities and technologies identified under paragraph (1), an identification of goals, a description of ongoing efforts, and recommendations for further enhancements.

(3) A complete description of requirements and priorities for the development and deployment of highly effective capabilities and technologies, including identifying areas for capability enhancement and deficiencies in existing capabilities and technologies.

(4) A comprehensive discussion of the near-term, mid-term, and long-term programmatic options for meeting requirements and eliminating deficiencies, including the annual funding requirements and completion dates established for each such option.

(5) An outline of interagency activities and initiatives.

(6) Any other matters the Secretary considers appropriate.

(c) FORMS OF REPORT.—The report under subsection (a) shall be submitted in unclassified form, but may contain a classified annex.

SEC. 1071. REPORT ON TESTING AND INTEGRATION OF MINEHUNTING SONAR SYSTEMS TO IMPROVE LITTORAL COMBAT SHIP MINEHUNTING CAPABILITIES.

(a) REPORT TO CONGRESS.—Not later than April 1, 2018, the Secretary of the Navy shall submit to the congressional defense committees a report that contains the findings of an assessment of all operational minehunting Synthetic Aperture Sonar (hereinafter referred to as "SAS") technologies suitable to meet the requirements for use on the Littoral Combat Ship Mine Countermeasures Mission Package.

(b) ELEMENTS.—The report required by subsection (a) shall include—

(1) an explanation of the future acquisition strategy for the minehunting mission package;

(2) specific details regarding the capabilities of all in-production SAS systems available for integration into the Littoral Combat Ship Mine Countermeasure Mission Package;

(3) an assessment of key performance parameters for the Littoral Combat Ship Mine Countermeasures Mission Package with each of the assessed SAS technologies; and

(4) a review of the Department of the Navy's efforts to evaluate SAS technologies in operation with allied Navies for future use on the Littoral Combat Ship Mine Countermeasures Mission Package.

(c) SYSTEM TESTING.—The Secretary of the Navy is encouraged to perform at-sea testing and experimentation of sonar systems in order to provide data in support of the assessment required by subsection (a).

SEC. 1072. QUARTERLY REPORTS ON PARACHUTE JUMPS CONDUCTED AT FORT BRAGG AND POPE ARMY AIRFIELD AND AIR FORCE SUPPORT FOR SUCH JUMPS.

For the period beginning on January 31, 2017, and ending on January 31, 2018, the Secretary of the Air Force and the Secretary of the Army shall jointly submit to the Committees on Armed Services of the House of Representatives and the Senate quarterly reports on the parachute drop requirements for the XVIII Airborne Corps, the 82nd Airborne Division, and the United States Army Special Operations Command. Each such report shall include, for the calendar quarter covered by the report—

(1) the total parachute drop requirement, by month;

(2) the total parachute drops requested, by month;

(3) the total parachute drops for which the Secretary of the Air Force entered into a contract, by month;

(4) the total parachute drops executed by non-Air Force entities pursuant to contracts, by month;

(5) the total parachute drops executed by the Air Force, by month;

(6) if the total parachute drop requirement was not fulfilled for the quarter, the reasons why such requirement was not fulfilled and the assessment of the Secretary of the Army of any effects on Army readiness caused by the unfulfilled portion of the requirement; and

(7) any other clarifying information, as appropriate, the Secretaries determine the Committees would need to understand important aspects of the Air Force implementing off-site airlift support for XVIII Airborne Corps, the 82nd Airborne Division, and the United States Army Special Operations Command, and the ability of the Air Force to meet the training requirements of the Army and the United States Special Operations Command.

SEC. 1073. STUDY ON MILITARY HELICOPTER NOISE.

(a) IN GENERAL.—The Secretary of Defense, in coordination with the Administrator of the Federal Aviation Administration, shall—

(1) conduct a study on the effects of military helicopter noise on National Capital Region communities and individuals; and

(2) develop recommendations for the reduction of the effects of military helicopter noise on individuals, structures, and property values in the National Capital Region.

(b) FOCUS.—In conducting the study under subsection (a), the Secretary and the Administrator shall focus on air traffic control, airspace design, airspace management, and types of aircraft to address helicopter noise problems and shall take into account the needs of law enforcement, emergency, and military operations.

(c) CONSIDERATION OF VIEWS.—In conducting the study under subsection (a), the Secretary shall consider the views of representatives of—

(1) members of the Armed Forces;

(2) law enforcement agencies;

(3) community stakeholders, including residents and local government officials; and

(4) organizations with an interest in reducing military helicopter noise.

(d) REPORT.—

(1) IN GENERAL.—Not later than 90 days after the date of the enactment of this Act, the Secretary shall submit to Congress a report on the results of the study conducted under subsection (a).

(2) AVAILABILITY TO THE PUBLIC.—The Secretary shall make the report required under paragraph (1) publicly available.

SEC. 1074. INDEPENDENT REVIEW OF UNITED STATES MILITARY STRATEGY AND FORCE POSTURE IN THE UNITED STATES PACIFIC COMMAND AREA OF RESPONSIBILITY.

(a) INDEPENDENT REVIEW.—

(1) IN GENERAL.—In fiscal year 2018, the Secretary of Defense shall commission an independent review of United States policy in the Indo-Asia-Pacific region, with a focus on issues expected to be critical during the ten-year period beginning on the date of such review, including the national security interests and military strategy of the United States in the Indo-Asia-Pacific region.

(2) CONDUCT OF REVIEW.—The review conducted pursuant to paragraph (1) shall be conducted by an independent organization that has—

(A) recognized credentials and expertise in national security and military affairs; and

(B) access to policy experts throughout the United States and from the Indo-Asia-Pacific region.

(3) ELEMENTS.—Each review conducted pursuant to paragraph (1) shall include the following elements:

(A) An assessment of the risks to United States national security interests in the United States Pacific Command area of responsibility during the ten-year period beginning on the date of such review as a result of changes in the security environment.

(B) An assessment of the current and planned United States force posture adjustments with respect to the Indo-Asia-Pacific region.

(C) An evaluation of any key capability gaps and shortfalls of the United States in the Indo-Asia-Pacific region, including undersea warfare (including submarines), naval and maritime, ballistic missile defense, cyber, munitions, anti-access area denial, land-force power projection, and intelligence, surveillance, and reconnaissance capabilities.

(D) An analysis of the willingness and capacity of allies, partners, and regional organizations to contribute to the security and stability of the Indo-Asia-Pacific region, including potential required adjustments to United States military strategy based on that analysis.

(E) An evaluation of theater security cooperation efforts of the United States Pacific Command in the context of current and projected threats, and desired capabilities and priorities of the United States and its allies and partners.

(F) An evaluation of the seams between United States Pacific Command and adjacent geographic combatant commands, including an appraisal of the Arctic ambitions of actors in the Indo-Asia-Pacific region in the context of current and projected capabilities, and recommendations to mitigate the effects of those seams.

(G) The views of noted policy leaders and regional experts, including military commanders, in the Indo-Asia-Pacific region.

(b) REPORT.—

(1) SUBMITTAL TO SECRETARY OF DEFENSE.—Not later than 180 days after commencing the review under subsection (a), the independent organization conducting the review shall submit to the Secretary of Defense a report containing the findings of the review. The report shall be submitted in unclassified form, but may contain an classified annex.

(2) SUBMITTAL TO CONGRESS.—Not later than 90 days after the date of receipt of a report required by paragraph (1), the Secretary shall submit to the congressional defense committees the report, together with any comments on the report that the Secretary considers appropriate.

SEC. 1075. ASSESSMENT OF THE JOINT GROUND FORCES OF THE ARMED FORCES.

(a) IN GENERAL.—The Secretary of Defense, in consultation with the Chairman of the Joint Chiefs of Staff, the Chief of Staff of the Army, and the Commandant of the Marine Corps, shall provide for and oversee an assessment of the joint ground forces of the Armed Forces.

(b) REPORT.—Not later than one year after the date of the enactment of this Act, the Secretary shall submit to the Committees on Armed Services of the Senate and the House of Representatives a report on the assessment described in subsection (a). The report shall include the following:

(1) A description of any gaps in the capabilities and capacities of the joint ground forces that threaten the successful execution of decisive operational maneuver by the joint ground forces.

(2) Recommendations for actions to be taken to eliminate or otherwise address such gaps in capabilities or capacities.

(3) An assessment by each of the Chief of Staff of the Army and the Commandant of the Marine Corps of any specific gaps in the capability and capacity of the Army and Marine Corps, respectively, that threaten the successful execution of decisive operational maneuver.

Subtitle G—Other Matters

SEC. 1081. TECHNICAL AND CLERICAL AMENDMENTS.

(a) TITLE 10, UNITED STATES CODE.—Title 10, United States Code, is amended as follows:

(1) Section 130h is amended by striking "subsection (a) and (b)" both places it appears and inserting "subsections (a) and (b)".

(2) Section 187(a)(2)(C) is amended by striking "Acquisition, Logistics, and Technology" and inserting "Acquisition, Technology, and Logistics".

(3) Section 196(c)(1)(A)(ii) is amended by striking "section 139(i)" and inserting "section 139(j)".

(4) Subsection (b)(1)(B) of section 1415 is amended by adding a period at the end of clause (ii).

(5) Section 1705(g)(1) is amended by striking "of of" and inserting "of".

(6) Section 2222 is amended—

(A) in subsection (d)(1)(B), by inserting "to" before "eliminate";

(B) in subsection (g)(1)(E), by inserting "the system" before "is in compliance"; and

(C) in subsection (i)(5), by striking "PROGRAM" in the heading.

(7) Subsection (d) of section 2431b is amended to read as follows:

"(d) DEFINITIONS.—

"(1) CONCURRENCY.—The term 'concurrency' means, with respect to an acquisition strategy, the combination with or overlap of program phases or activities.

''*(2) MAJOR DEFENSE ACQUISITION PROGRAM AND MAJOR SYSTEM.—The terms 'major defense acquisition program' and 'major system' have the meanings provided in section 2431a of this title.''.*

(b) AMENDMENTS RELATED TO ELIMINATION OF TITLE 50 APPENDIX.—

(1) MILITARY SELECTIVE SERVICE ACT CITATION CHANGES.—

(A) TITLE 10, UNITED STATES CODE.—Title 10, United States Code, is amended as follows:

(i) Section 101(d)(6)(B)(v) is amended by striking ''(50 U.S.C. App. 460(b)(2))'' and inserting ''(50 U.S.C. 3809(b)(2))''.

(ii) Section 513(c) is amended—

(I) by striking ''(50 U.S.C. App. 451 et seq.)'' and inserting ''(50 U.S.C. 3801 et seq.)''; and

(II) by inserting ''(50 U.S.C. 3806(c)(2)(A))'' after ''of that Act''.

(iii) Section 523(b)(7) is amended by striking ''(50 U.S.C. App. 460(b)(2))'' and inserting ''(50 U.S.C. 3809(b)(2))''.

(iv) Section 651(a) is amended by striking ''(50'' and all that follows through ''shall serve'' and inserting ''(50 U.S.C. 3806(d)(1))''.

(v) Section 671(c)(1) is amended by striking ''(50 U.S.C. App. 454(a))'' and inserting ''(50 U.S.C. 3803(a))''.

(vi) Section 1475(a)(5)(B) is amended by striking ''(50 U.S.C. App. 451 et seq.)'' and inserting ''(50 U.S.C. 3801 et seq.)''.

(vii) Section 12103 is amended—

(I) in subsections (b) and (d), by striking ''(50 U.S.C. App. 451 et seq.)'' both places it appears and inserting ''(50 U.S.C. 3801 et seq.)''; and

(II) in subsection (d), by striking ''section 6(c)(2)(A)(ii) and (iii) of such Act'' and inserting ''clauses (ii) and (iii) of section 6(c)(2)(A) of such Act (50 U.S.C. 3806(c)(2)(A))''.

(viii) Section 12104(a) is amended by striking ''(50 U.S.C. App. 451 et seq.)'' both places it appears and inserting ''(50 U.S.C. 3801 et seq.)''.

(ix) Section 12208(a) is amended by striking ''(50 U.S.C. App. 451 et seq.)'' both places it appears and inserting ''(50 U.S.C. 3801 et seq.)''.

(B) TITLE 37, UNITED STATES CODE.—Section 209(a)(1) of title 37, United States Code, is amended by striking ''(50 U.S.C. App. 456(d)(1))'' and inserting ''(50 U.S.C. 3806(d)(1))''.

(2) SERVICEMEMBERS CIVIL RELIEF ACT CITATION CHANGES.—Title 10, United States Code, is amended as follows:

(A) Section 987 is amended—

(i) in subsection (e)(2), by inserting ''(50 U.S.C. 3901 et seq.)'' before the semicolon; and

(ii) in subsection (g), by striking ''(50 U.S.C. App. 527)'' and inserting ''(50 U.S.C. 3937)''.

(B) Section 1408(b)(1)(D) is amended by striking ''(50 U.S.C. App. 501 et seq.)'' and inserting ''(50 U.S.C. 3901 et seq.)''.

(3) EXPORT ADMINISTRATION ACT OF 1979 CITATION CHANGES.—Title 10, United States Code, is amended as follows:

(A) Section 130(a) is amended by striking ''(50 U.S.C. App. 2401–2420)'' and inserting ''(50 U.S.C. 4601 et seq.)''.

(B) Section 2249a(a)(1) is amended by striking ''(50 U.S.C. App. 2405(j)(1)(A))'' and inserting ''(50 U.S.C. 4605(j)(1)(A))''.

(C) Section 2327 is amended—

(i) in subsection (a), by striking ''(50 U.S.C. App. 2405(j)(1)(A))'' and inserting ''(50 U.S.C. 4605(j)(1)(A))''; and

(ii) in subsection (b)(2), by striking ''(50 U.S.C. App. 2405(j)(1)(A))'' and inserting ''(50 U.S.C. 4605(j)(1)(A))''.

(D) Section 2410i(a) is amended by striking ''(50 U.S.C. App. 2402(5)(A))'' and inserting ''(50 U.S.C. 4602(5)(A))''.

(E) Section 7430(e) is amended by striking ''(50 U.S.C. App. 2401 et seq.)'' and inserting ''(50 U.S.C. 4601 et seq.)''.

(4) DEFENSE PRODUCTION ACT OF 1950 CITATION CHANGES.—Title 10, United States Code, is amended as follows:

(A) Section 139c is amended—

(i) in subsection (b)—

(I) in paragraph (11), by striking ''(50 U.S.C. App. 2171)'' and inserting ''(50 U.S.C. 4567)''; and

(II) in paragraph (12)—

(aa) by striking ''(50 U.S.C. App. 2062(b))'' and inserting ''(50 U.S.C. 4502(b))''; and

(bb) by striking ''(50 U.S.C. App. 2061 et seq.)'' and inserting ''(50 U.S.C. 4501 et seq.)''; and

(ii) in subsection (c), by striking ''(50 U.S.C. App. 2170(k))'' and inserting ''(50 U.S.C. 4565(k))''.

(B) Section 2537(c) is amended by striking ''(50 U.S.C. App. 2170(a))'' and inserting ''(50 U.S.C. 4565(a))''.

(C) Section 9511(6) is amended by striking ''(50 U.S.C. App. 2071)'' and inserting ''(50 U.S.C. 4511)''.

(D) Section 9512(e) is amended by striking ''(50 U.S.C. App. 2071)'' and inserting ''(50 U.S.C. 4511)''.

(5) MERCHANT SHIP SALES ACT OF 1946 CITATION CHANGES.—Section 2218 of title 10, United States Code, is amended—

(A) in subsection (c)(1)(E), by striking ''(50 U.S.C. App. 1744)'' and inserting ''(50 U.S.C. 4405)''; and

(B) in subsection (k)(3)(B), by striking ''(50 U.S.C. App. 1744)'' and inserting ''(50 U.S.C. 4405)''.

(c) NATIONAL DEFENSE AUTHORIZATION ACT FOR FISCAL YEAR 2016.—Effective as of November 25, 2015, and as if included therein as enacted, the National Defense Authorization Act for Fiscal Year 2016 (Public Law 114–92) is amended as follows:

(1) Section 563(a) is amended by striking ''Section 5(c)(5)'' and inserting ''Section 5(c)(2)''.

(2) Section 804(d)(3) is amended by inserting ''within 5 business days after such transfer'' before the period at the end of the first sentence.

(3) Section 809(e)(2)(A) is amended by striking ''repealed'' and inserting ''rescinded''.

(4) Section 883(a)(2) is amended by striking ''such chapter'' and inserting ''chapter 131 of such title''.

(5) Section 883 is amended by adding at the end the following new subsection:

''(f) CONFORMING AMENDMENTS.—

''(1) Effective on the effective date specified in subsection (a)(1) of section 901 of the Carl Levin and Howard P. 'Buck' McKeon National Defense Authorization Act for Fiscal Year 2015 (Public Law 113–291; 128 Stat. 3462; 10 U.S.C. 132a note), section 2222 of title 10, United States Code, is amended—

''(A) by striking 'Deputy Chief Management Officer of the Department of Defense' each place it appears in subsections (c)(2), (e)(1), (g)(2)(A), (g)(2)(B)(ii), and (i)(5)(B) and inserting 'Under Secretary of Defense for Business Management and Information'; and

''(B) by striking 'Deputy Chief Management Officer' in subsection (f)(1) and inserting 'Under Secretary of Defense for Business Management and Information'.

''(2) The second paragraph (3) of section 901(k) of such Act (Public Law 113–291; 128 Stat. 3468; 10 U.S.C. 2222 note) is repealed.''.

(6) Section 1079(a) is amended to read as follows:

''(a) ANNUAL REPORT ON PRIZES FOR ADVANCED TECHNOLOGY ACHIEVEMENTS.—Section 2374a of title 10, United States Code, is amended—

''(1) by striking subsection (f); and

''(2) by redesignating subsection (g) as subsection (f).''.

(7) Section 1086(f)(11)(A) is amended by striking ''Not later than\ one year'' and inserting ''Not later than one year''.

(d) COORDINATION WITH OTHER AMENDMENTS MADE BY THIS ACT.—For purposes of applying

amendments made by provisions of this Act other than this section, the amendments made by this section shall be treated as having been enacted immediately before any such amendments by other provisions of this Act.

SEC. 1082. INCREASE IN MAXIMUM AMOUNT AVAILABLE FOR EQUIPMENT, SERVICES, AND SUPPLIES PROVIDED FOR HUMANITARIAN DEMINING ASSISTANCE.

Section 407(c)(3) of title 10, United States Code, is amended by striking ''$10,000,000'' and inserting ''$15,000,000''.

SEC. 1083. LIQUIDATION OF UNPAID CREDITS ACCRUED AS A RESULT OF TRANSACTIONS UNDER A CROSS-SERVICING AGREEMENT.

(a) LIQUIDATION OF UNPAID CREDITS.—Section 2345 of title 10, United States Code, is amended by adding at the end the following new subsection:

''(c)(1) Any credits of the United States accrued as a result of the provision of logistic support, supplies, and services under the authority of this subchapter that remain unliquidated more than 18 months after the date of delivery of the logistic support, supplies, or services may, at the option of the Secretary of Defense, with the concurrence of the Secretary of State, be liquidated by offsetting the credits against any amount owed by the Department of Defense, pursuant to a transaction or transactions concluded under the authority of this subchapter, to the government or international organization to which the logistic support, supplies, or services were provided by the United States.

''(2) The amount of any credits offset pursuant to paragraph (1) shall be credited as specified in section 2346 of this title as if it were a receipt of the United States.''.

(b) EFFECTIVE DATE.—Subsection (c) of section 2345 of title 10, United States Code, as added by subsection (a), shall apply with respect to credits accrued by the United States that—

(1) were accrued prior to, and remain unpaid as of, the date of the enactment of this Act; or

(2) are accrued after the date of the enactment of this Act.

SEC. 1084. MODIFICATION OF REQUIREMENTS RELATING TO MANAGEMENT OF MILITARY TECHNICIANS.

(a) CONVERSION OF CERTAIN MILITARY TECHNICIAN (DUAL STATUS) POSITIONS.—Subsection (a) of section 1053 of the National Defense Authorization Act for Fiscal Year 2016 (Public Law 114–92; 129 Stat. 981; 10 U.S.C. 10216 note) is amended—

(1) by striking paragraph (1) and inserting the following new paragraph (1):

''(1) IN GENERAL.—By not later than October 1, 2017, the Secretary of Defense shall convert not fewer than 20 percent of all military technician positions to positions filled by individuals who are employed under section 3101 of title 5, United States Code, or section 1601 of title 10, United States Code, and are not military technicians. The positions to be converted are described in paragraph (2).'';

(2) in paragraph (2), by striking ''in the report'' and all that follows and inserting ''by the Army Reserve, the Air Force Reserve, the National Guard Bureau, State adjutants general, and the Secretary of Defense in the course of reviewing all military technician positions for purposes of implementing this section.''; and

(3) in paragraph (3), by striking ''may fill'' and inserting ''shall fill''.

(b) CONVERSION OF ARMY RESERVE, AIR FORCE RESERVE, AND NATIONAL GUARD NON-DUAL STATUS POSITIONS.—Subsection (e) of section 10217 of title 10, United States Code, is amended is amended to read as follows:

"(e) CONVERSION OF POSITIONS.—(1) No individual may be newly hired or employed, or rehired or reemployed, as a non-dual status technician for purposes of this section after September 30, 2017.

"(2) By not later than October 1, 2017, the Secretary of Defense shall convert all non-dual status technicians to positions filled by individuals who are employed under section 3101 of title 5 or section 1601 of this title and are not military technicians.

"(3) In the case of a position converted under paragraph (2) for which there is an incumbent employee on October 1, 2017, the Secretary shall fill that position, as converted, with the incumbent employee without regard to any requirement concerning competition or competitive hiring procedures.

"(4) Any individual newly hired or employed, or rehired or employed, to a position required to be filled by reason of paragraph (1) shall an individual employed in such position under section 3101 of title 5 or section 1601 of this title.".

(c) REPORT ON CONVERSION OF MILITARY TECHNICIAN POSITIONS TO PERSONNEL PERFORMING ACTIVE GUARD AND RESERVE DUTY.—

*(1) IN GENERAL.—*Not later than March 1, 2017, the Secretary of Defense, shall in consultation with the Chief of the National Guard Bureau, submit to the Committees on Armed Services of the Senate and the House of Representatives a report on the feasibility and advisability of converting any remaining military technicians (dual status) to personnel performing active Guard and Reserve duty under section 328 of title 32, United States Code, or other applicable provisions of law. The report shall include the following:

(A) An analysis of the fully-burdened costs of the conversion taking into account the new modernized military retirement system.

(B) An assessment of the ratio of members of the Armed Forces performing active Guard and Reserve duty and civilian employees of the Department of Defense under title 5, United States Code, required to best contribute to the readiness of the National Guard and the Reserves.

*(2) ACTIVE GUARD AND RESERVE DUTY DEFINED.—*In this subsection, the term "active Guard and Reserve duty" has the meaning given that term in section 101(d)(6) of title 10, United States Code.

SEC. 1085. STREAMLINING OF THE NATIONAL SECURITY COUNCIL.

*(a) IN GENERAL.—*Section 101 of the National Security Act of 1947 (50 U.S.C. 3021) is amended to read as follows:

"SEC. 101. NATIONAL SECURITY COUNCIL.

*"(a) NATIONAL SECURITY COUNCIL.—*There is a council known as the National Security Council (in this section referred to as the 'Council').

*"(b) FUNCTIONS.—*Consistent with the direction of the President, the functions of the Council shall be to—

"(1) advise the President with respect to the integration of domestic, foreign, and military policies relating to the national security so as to enable the Armed Forces and the other departments and agencies of the United States Government to cooperate more effectively in matters involving the national security;

"(2) assess and appraise the objectives, commitments, and risks of the United States in relation to the actual and potential military power of the United States, and make recommendations thereon to the President; and

"(3) make recommendations to the President concerning policies on matters of common interest to the departments and agencies of the United States Government concerned with the national security.

"(c) MEMBERSHIP.—

*"(1) IN GENERAL.—*The Council consists of the President, the Vice President, the Secretary of State, the Secretary of Defense, the Secretary of Energy, and such other officers of the United States Government as the President may designate.

*"(2) ATTENDANCE AND PARTICIPATION IN MEETINGS.—*The President may designate such other officers of the United States Government as the President considers appropriate, including the Director of National Intelligence, the Director of National Drug Control Policy, and the Chairman of the Joint Chiefs of Staff, to attend and participate in meetings of the Council.

*"(d) PRESIDING OFFICERS.—*At meetings of the Council, the President shall preside or, in the absence of the President, a member of the Council designated by the President shall preside.

"(e) STAFF.—

*"(1) IN GENERAL.—*The Council shall have a staff headed by a civilian executive secretary appointed by the President.

*"(2) STAFF.—*Consistent with the direction of the President and subject to paragraph (3), the executive secretary may, subject to the civil service laws and chapter 51 and subchapter III of chapter 53 of title 5, United States Code, appoint and fix the compensation of such personnel as may be necessary to perform such duties as may be prescribed by the President in connection with performance of the functions of the Council.

*"(3) NUMBER OF PROFESSIONAL STAFF.—*The professional staff for which this subsection provides shall not exceed 200 persons, including persons employed by, assigned to, detailed to, under contract to serve on, or otherwise serving or affiliated with the staff. The limitation in this paragraph does not apply to personnel serving substantially in support or administrative positions.

*"(f) SPECIAL ADVISOR TO THE PRESIDENT ON INTERNATIONAL RELIGIOUS FREEDOM.—*It is the sense of Congress that there should be within the staff of the Council a Special Adviser to the President on International Religious Freedom, whose position should be comparable to that of a director within the Executive Office of the President. The Special Adviser should serve as a resource for executive branch officials, compiling and maintaining information on the facts and circumstances of violations of religious freedom (as defined in section 3 of the International Religious Freedom Act of 1998 (22 U.S.C. 6402)), and making policy recommendations. The Special Adviser should serve as liaison with the Ambassador at Large for International Religious Freedom, the United States Commission on International Religious Freedom, Congress and, as advisable, religious nongovernmental organizations.".

*(b) EFFECTIVE DATE OF LIMITATION ON NUMBER OF PROFESSIONAL STAFF.—*The limitation on the number of professional staff of the National Security Council specified in subsection (e)(3) of section 101 of the National Security Act of 1947, as amended by subsection (a) of this section, shall take effect on the date that is 18 months after the date of the enactment of this Act.

SEC. 1086. NATIONAL BIODEFENSE STRATEGY.

*(a) STRATEGY AND IMPLEMENTATION PLAN REQUIRED.—*The Secretary of Defense, the Secretary of Health and Human Services, the Secretary of Homeland Security, and the Secretary of Agriculture shall jointly develop a national biodefense strategy and associated implementation plan, which shall include a review and assessment of biodefense policies, practices, programs and initiatives. Such Secretaries shall review and, as appropriate, revise the strategy biennially.

*(b) ELEMENTS.—*The strategy and associated implementation plan required under subsection (a) shall include each of the following:

(1) An inventory and assessment of all existing strategies, plans, policies, laws, and interagency agreements related to biodefense, including prevention, deterrence, preparedness, detection, response, attribution, recovery, and mitigation.

(2) A description of the biological threats, including biological warfare, bioterrorism, naturally occurring infectious diseases, and accidental exposures.

(3) A description of the current programs, efforts, or activities of the United States Government with respect to preventing the acquisition, proliferation, and use of a biological weapon, preventing an accidental or naturally occurring biological outbreak, and mitigating the effects of a biological epidemic.

(4) A description of the roles and responsibilities of the Executive Agencies, including internal and external coordination procedures, in identifying and sharing information related to, warning of, and protection against, acts of terrorism using biological agents and weapons and accidental or naturally occurring biological outbreaks.

(5) An articulation of related or required interagency capabilities and whole-of-Government activities required to support the national biodefense strategy.

(6) Recommendations for strengthening and improving the current biodefense capabilities, authorities, and command structures of the United States Government.

(7) Recommendations for improving and formalizing interagency coordination and support mechanisms with respect to providing a robust national biodefense.

(8) Any other matters the Secretary of Defense, the Secretary of Health and Human Services, the Secretary of Homeland Security, and the Secretary of Agriculture determine necessary.

*(c) SUBMITTAL TO CONGRESS.—*Not later than 275 days after the date of the enactment of this Act, the Secretary of Defense, the Secretary of Health and Human Services, the Secretary of Homeland Security, and the Secretary of Agriculture shall submit to the appropriate congressional committees the strategy and associated implementation plan required by subsection (a). The strategy and implementation plan shall be submitted in unclassified form, but may include a classified annex.

*(d) BRIEFINGS.—*Not later than March 1, 2017, and annually thereafter until March 1, 2019, the Secretary of Defense, the Secretary of Health and Human Services, the Secretary of Homeland Security, and the Secretary of Agriculture shall provide to the Committee on Armed Services of the House of Representatives, the Committee on Energy and Commerce of the House of Representatives, the Committee on Homeland Security of the House of Representatives, and the Committee on Agriculture of the House of Representatives a joint briefing on the strategy developed under subsection (a) and the status of the implementation of such strategy.

*(e) GAO REVIEW.—*Not later than 180 days after the date of the submittal of the strategy and implementation plan under subsection (c), the Comptroller General of the United States shall conduct a review of the strategy and implementation plan to analyze gaps and resources mapped against the requirements of the National Biodefense Strategy and existing United States biodefense policy documents.

*(f) APPROPRIATE CONGRESSIONAL COMMITTEES DEFINED.—*In this section, the term "appropriate congressional committees" means the following:

(1) The congressional defense committees.

(2) The Committee on Energy and Commerce of the House of Representatives and the Committee on Health, Education, Labor, and Pensions of the Senate.

(3) The Committee on Homeland Security of the House of Representatives and the Committee

on Homeland Security and Governmental Affairs of the Senate.

(4) The Committee on Agriculture of the House of Representatives and the Committee on Agriculture, Nutrition, and Forestry of the Senate.

SEC. 1087. GLOBAL CULTURAL KNOWLEDGE NETWORK.

(a) PROGRAM AUTHORIZED.—The Secretary of the Army shall carry out a program to support the socio-cultural understanding needs of the Department of the Army, to be known as the Global Cultural Knowledge Network.

(b) GOALS.—The Global Cultural Knowledge Network shall support the following goals:

(1) Provide socio-cultural analysis support to any unit deployed, or preparing to deploy, to an exercise or operation in the assigned region of responsibility of the unit being supported.

(2) Make recommendations or support policy or doctrine development to increase the social science expertise of military and civilian personnel of the Department of the Army.

(3) Provide reimbursable support to other military departments or Federal agencies if requested through an operational needs request process.

(c) ELEMENTS OF THE PROGRAM.—The Global Cultural Knowledge Network shall include the following elements:

(1) A center in the continental United States (referred to in this section as a "reach-back center") to support requests for information, research, and analysis.

(2) Outreach to academic institutions and other Federal agencies involved in social science research to increase the network of resources for the reach-back center.

(3) Training with operational units during annual training exercises or during pre-deployment training.

(4) The training, contracting, and human resources capacity to rapidly respond to contingencies in which social science expertise is requested by operational commanders through an operational needs request process.

(d) DIRECTIVE REQUIRED.—The Secretary of the Army shall issue a directive within one year after the date of the enactment of this Act for the governance of the Global Cultural Knowledge Network, including oversight and process controls for auditing the activities of personnel of the Network, the employment of the Global Cultural Knowledge Network by operational forces, and processes for requesting support by operational Army units and other Department of Defense and Federal entities.

(e) PROHIBITION ON DEPLOYMENTS UNDER GLOBAL CULTURAL KNOWLEDGE NETWORK.—

(1) PROHIBITION.—The Secretary of the Army may not deploy social scientists of the Global Cultural Knowledge Network in a conflict zone.

(2) WAIVER.—The Secretary of the Army may waive the prohibition in paragraph (1) if the Secretary submits, at least 10 days before the deployment, to the Committees on Armed Services of the House of Representatives and the Senate—

(A) notice of the waiver; and

(B) a certification that there is a compelling national security interest for the deployment or there will be a benefit to the safety and welfare of members of the Armed Forces from the deployment.

(3) ELEMENTS OF WAIVER NOTICE.—A waiver notice under this subsection also shall include the following:

(A) The operational unit, or units, requesting support, including the location or locations where the social scientists are to be deployed.

(B) The number of Global Cultural Knowledge Network personnel to be deployed and the anticipated duration of such deployments.

(C) The anticipated resource needs for such deployment.

SEC. 1088. SENSE OF CONGRESS REGARDING CONNECTICUT'S SUBMARINE CENTURY.

(a) FINDINGS.—Congress makes the following findings:

(1) On March 2, 1867, Congress enacted a naval appropriations Act that authorized the Secretary of the Navy to "receive and accept a deed of gift, when offered by the State of Connecticut, of a tract of land with not less than one mile of shore front on the Thames River near New London, Connecticut, to be held by the United States for naval purposes".

(2) The people of Connecticut and the towns and cities in the southeastern region of Connecticut subsequently gifted land to establish a military installation to fulfil the Nation's need for a naval facility on the Atlantic coast.

(3) On April 11, 1868, the Navy accepted the deed of gift of land from Connecticut to establish a naval yard and storage depot along the eastern shore of the Thames River in Groton, Connecticut.

(4) Between 1868 and 1912, the New London Navy Yard supported a diverse range of missions, including berthing inactive Civil War era ironclad warships and serving as a coaling station for refueling naval ships traveling in New England waters.

(5) Congress rejected the Navy's proposal to close New London Navy Yard in 1912, following an impassioned effort by Congressman Edwin W. Higgins, who stated that "this action proposed is not only unjust but unreasonable and unsound as a military proposition".

(6) The outbreak of World War I and the enemy use of submarines to sink allied military and civilian ships in the Atlantic sparked a new focus on developing submarine capabilities in the United States.

(7) October 18, 1915, marked the arrival at the New London Navy Yard of the submarines G–1, G–2, and G–4 under the care of the tender USS Ozark and the arrival of submarines E–1, D–1, and D–3 under the care of the tender USS Tonopah. November 1, 1915, marked the arrival of the first ship built as a submarine tender, the USS Fulton (AS–1).

(8) On June 21, 1916, Commander Yeates Stirling assumed the command of the newly designated Naval Submarine Base New London, the New London Submarine Flotilla, and the Submarine School.

(9) In the 100 years since the arrival of the first submarines to the base, Naval Submarine Base New London has grown to occupy more than 680 acres along the east side of the Thames River, with more than 160 major facilities, 15 nuclear submarines, and more than 70 tenant commands and activities, including the Submarine Learning Center, Naval Submarine School, the Naval Submarine Medical Research Laboratory, the Naval Undersea Medical Institute, and the newly established Undersea Warfighting Development Center.

(10) In addition to being the site of the first submarine base in the United States, Connecticut was home to the foremost submarine manufacturers of the time, the Lake Torpedo Boat Company in Bridgeport and the Electric Boat Company in Groton, which later became General Dynamics Electric Boat.

(11) General Dynamics Electric Boat, its talented workforce, and its Connecticut-based and nationwide network of suppliers have delivered more than 200 submarines from its current location in Groton, Connecticut, including the first nuclear-powered submarine, the USS Nautilus (SSN 571), and nearly half of the nuclear submarines ever built by the United States.

(12) The Submarine Force Museum, located adjacent to Naval Submarine Base New London in Groton, Connecticut, is the only submarine museum operated by the United States Navy and today serves as the primary repository for artifacts, documents, and photographs relating to the bold and courageous history of the Submarine Force and highlights as its core exhibit the Historic Ship Nautilus (SSN 571) following her retirement from service.

(13) Reflecting the close ties between Connecticut and the Navy that began with the gift of land that established the base, the State of Connecticut has set aside $40,000,000 in funding for critical infrastructure investments to support the mission of the base, including construction of a new dive locker building, expansion of the Submarine Learning Center, and modernization of energy infrastructure.

(14) On September 29, 2015, Connecticut Governor Dannel Malloy designated October 2015 through October 2016 as Connecticut's Submarine Century, a year-long observance that celebrates 100 years of submarine activity in Connecticut, including the Town of Groton's distinction as the Submarine Capital of the World, to coincide with the centennial anniversary of the establishment of Naval Submarine Base New London and the Naval Submarine School.

(15) Whereas Naval Submarine Base New London still proudly proclaims its motto of "The First and Finest".

(16) Congressman Higgins' statement before Congress in 1912 that "Connecticut stands ready, as she always has, to bear her part of the burdens of the national defense" remains true today.

(b) SENSE OF CONGRESS.—Congress—

(1) commends the longstanding dedication and contribution to the Navy and submarine force by the people of Connecticut, both through the initial deed of gift that established what would become Naval Submarine Base New London and through their ongoing commitment to support the mission of the base and the Navy personnel assigned to it;

(2) honors the submariners who have trained and served at Naval Submarine Base New London throughout its history in support of the Nation's security and undersea superiority;

(3) recognizes the contribution of the industry and workforce of Connecticut in designing, building, and sustaining the Navy's submarine fleet; and

(4) encourages the recognition of Connecticut's Submarine Century by Congress, the Navy, and the American people by honoring the contribution of the people of Connecticut to the defense of the United States and the important role of the submarine force in safeguarding the security of the United States for more than a century.

SEC. 1089. SENSE OF CONGRESS REGARDING THE REPORTING OF THE MV–22 MISHAP IN MARANA, ARIZONA, ON APRIL 8, 2000.

It is the sense of Congress that—

(1) in the report accompanying H.R. 1735 of the 114th Congress (House Report 114–102), the Committee on Armed Services of the House of Representatives encouraged the Secretary of Defense to "publicly clarify the causes of the MV-22 mishap at Marana Northwest Regional Airport, Arizona, in a way consistent with the results of all investigations as soon as possible";

(2) the Deputy Secretary of Defense Robert O. Work did an excellent job reviewing the investigations of such mishap and concluded that there was a misrepresentation of facts by the media which incorrectly identified pilot error as the cause of the mishap which the Deputy Secretary publicly made known in March 2016; and

(3) Congress is grateful for the successful conclusion to this tragic situation.

SEC. 1090. COST OF WARS.

The Secretary of Defense, in consultation with the Commissioner of the Internal Revenue Service and the Director of the Bureau of Economic Analysis, shall post on the public Internet website of the Department of Defense the costs to each United States taxpayer of each of the wars in Afghanistan, Iraq, and Syria.

SEC. 1091. RECONNAISSANCE STRIKE GROUP MATTERS.

(a) MODELING OF ALTERNATIVE ARMY DESIGN AND OPERATIONAL CONCEPT.—

(1) ANALYSES REQUIRED.—The Chairman of the Joint Chiefs of Staff and the Chief of Staff of the Army, in consultation with the commanding general of the United States European Command, shall each conduct a separate analysis of alternative Army operational concepts and organizational designs, known as the Reconnaissance Strike Group, as recommended by the National Commission on the Future of the United States Army.

(2) ASSESSMENT OF ANALYSES.— The Chairman of the Joint Chiefs of Staff and Chief of Staff of the Army shall then each separately assess the operational merits, feasible force mix under programmed end-strength, estimated costs for assessed potential force structure changes, and strategic force sufficiency and risk of each analysis conducted under paragraph (1).

(b) REPORTS REQUIRED.—Not later than one year after the date of the enactment of this Act, the Chairman of the Joint Chiefs of Staff and the Chief of Staff of the Army shall each submit to the Committees on Armed Services of the Senate and House of Representatives a separate report on the alternative designs and operational concepts analyzed under subsection (a)(1). Each such report shall include an assessment of the merits and sufficiency of such designs and concepts, the potential for future experimentation (such as a follow-on pilot program), and the recommendation of the Chairman and Chief of Staff, as the case may be, regarding the Reconnaissance Strike Group.

(c) INDEPENDENT ASSESSMENTS REQUIRED.— Before submittal of the reports required under subsection (b), the Chairman of the Joint Chiefs of Staff and the Chief of Staff of the Army shall each select a Federally Funded Research and Development Center to review and evaluate each report. The review and evaluation of each report shall be submitted to the Committees on Armed Services of the Senate and House of Representatives together with the reports under subsection (b).

SEC. 1092. BORDER SECURITY METRICS.

(a) DEFINITIONS.—In this section:

(1) APPROPRIATE CONGRESSIONAL COMMITTEES.—The term "appropriate congressional committees" means—

(A) the Committee on Homeland Security and Governmental Affairs of the Senate; and

(B) the Committee on Homeland Security of the House of Representatives.

(2) CONSEQUENCE DELIVERY SYSTEM.—The term "Consequence Delivery System" means the series of consequences applied by U.S. Border Patrol in collaboration with other Federal agencies to persons unlawfully entering the United States, in order to prevent unlawful border crossing recidivism.

(3) GOT AWAY.—The term "got away" means an unlawful border crosser who—

(A) is directly or indirectly observed making an unlawful entry into the United States;

(B) is not apprehended; and

(C) is not a turn back.

(4) KNOWN MARITIME MIGRANT FLOW.—The term "known maritime migrant flow" means the sum of the number of undocumented migrants—

(A) interdicted in the waters over which the United States has jurisdiction;

(B) identified at sea either directly or indirectly, but not interdicted;

(C) if not described in subparagraph (A) or (B), who were otherwise reported, with a significant degree of certainty, as having entered, or attempted to enter, the United States through the maritime border.

(5) MAJOR VIOLATOR.—The term "major violator" means a person or entity that has engaged in serious criminal activities at any land, air, or sea port of entry, including the following:

(A) Possession of illicit drugs.

(B) Smuggling of prohibited products.

(C) Human smuggling.

(D) Possession of illegal weapons.

(E) Use of fraudulent documents.

(F) Any other offense that is serious enough to result in an arrest.

(6) SECRETARY.—The term "the Secretary" means the Secretary of Homeland Security.

(7) SITUATIONAL AWARENESS.—The term "situational awareness" means knowledge and understanding of current unlawful cross-border activity, including the following:

(A) Threats and trends concerning illicit trafficking and unlawful crossings.

(B) The ability to forecast future shifts in such threats and trends.

(C) The ability to evaluate such threats and trends at a level sufficient to create actionable plans.

(D) The operational capability to conduct persistent and integrated surveillance of the international borders of the United States.

(8) TRANSIT ZONE.—The term "transit zone" means the sea corridors of the western Atlantic Ocean, the Gulf of Mexico, the Caribbean Sea, and the eastern Pacific Ocean through which undocumented migrants and illicit drugs transit, either directly or indirectly, to the United States.

(9) TURN BACK.—The term "turn back" means an unlawful border crosser who, after making an unlawful entry into the United States, responds to United States enforcement efforts by returning promptly to the country from which such crosser entered.

(10) UNLAWFUL BORDER CROSSING EFFECTIVENESS RATE.—The term "unlawful border crossing effectiveness rate" means the percentage that results from dividing the number of apprehensions and turn backs by the sum of the number of apprehensions, estimated undetected unlawful entries, turn backs, and got aways.

(11) UNLAWFUL ENTRY.—The term "unlawful entry" means an unlawful border crosser who enters the United States and is not apprehended by a border security component of the Department of Homeland Security.

(b) METRICS FOR SECURING THE BORDER BETWEEN PORTS OF ENTRY.—

(1) IN GENERAL.—Not later than 180 days after the date of the enactment of this section, the Secretary shall develop metrics, informed by situational awareness, to measure the effectiveness of security between ports of entry. The Secretary shall annually implement the metrics developed under this subsection, which shall include the following:

(A) Estimates, using alternative methodologies where appropriate, including recidivism data, survey data, known-flow data, and technologically-measured data, of the following:

(i) The rate of apprehension of attempted unlawful border crossers.

(ii) The number of detected unlawful entries.

(iii) The number of estimated undetected unlawful entries.

(iv) Turn backs.

(v) Got aways.

(B) A measurement of situational awareness achieved in each U.S. Border Patrol sector.

(C) An unlawful border crossing effectiveness rate in each U.S. Border Patrol sector.

(D) A probability of detection rate, which compares the estimated total unlawful border crossing attempts not detected by U.S. Border Patrol to the unlawful border crossing effectiveness rate under subparagraph (C), as informed by subparagraph (A).

(E) The number of apprehensions in each U.S. Border Patrol sector.

(F) The number of apprehensions of unaccompanied alien children, and the nationality of such children, in each U.S. Border Patrol sector.

(G) The number of apprehensions of family units, and the nationality of such family units, in each U.S. Border Patrol sector.

(H) An illicit drugs seizure rate for drugs seized by U.S. Border Patrol between ports of entry, which compares the ratio of the amount and type of illicit drugs seized between ports of entry in any fiscal year to the average of the amount and type of illicit drugs seized between ports of entry in the immediately preceding five fiscal years.

(I) Estimates of the impact of the Consequence Delivery System on the rate of recidivism of unlawful border crossers over multiple fiscal years.

(J) An examination of each consequence under the Consequence Delivery System referred to in subparagraph (I), including the following:

(i) Voluntary return.

(ii) Warrant of arrest or notice to appear.

(iii) Expedited removal.

(iv) Reinstatement of removal.

(v) Alien transfer exit program.

(vi) Criminal consequence program.

(vii) Standard prosecution.

(viii) Operation Against Smugglers Initiative on Safety and Security.

(2) METRICS CONSULTATION.—To ensure that authoritative data sources are utilized in the development of the metrics described in paragraph (1), the Secretary shall—

(A) consult with the heads of the appropriate components of the Department of Homeland Security; and

(B) where appropriate, with the heads of other agencies, including the Office of Refugee Resettlement of the Department of Health and Human Services and the Executive Office for Immigration Review of the Department of Justice.

(3) MANNER OF COLLECTION.—The data collected to inform the metrics developed in accordance with paragraph (1) shall be collected and reported in a consistent and standardized manner across all U.S. Border Patrol sectors, informed by situational awareness.

(c) METRICS FOR SECURING THE BORDER AT PORTS OF ENTRY.—

(1) IN GENERAL.—Not later than 180 days after the date of the enactment of this section, the Secretary shall develop metrics, informed by situational awareness, to measure the effectiveness of security at ports of entry. The Secretary shall annually implement the metrics developed under this subsection, which shall include the following:

(A) Estimates, using alternative methodologies where appropriate, including recidivism data, survey data, and randomized secondary screening data, of the following:

(i) Total inadmissible travelers who attempt to, or successfully, enter the United States at a port of entry.

(ii) The rate of refusals and interdictions for travelers who attempt to, or successfully, enter the United States at a port of entry.

(iii) The number of unlawful entries at a port of entry.

(B) The amount and type of illicit drugs seized by the Office of Field Operations of U.S. Customs and Border Protection at ports of entry during the previous fiscal year.

(C) An illicit drugs seizure rate for drugs seized by the Office of Field Operations, which compares the ratio of the amount and type of illicit drugs seized by the Office of Field Operations in any fiscal year to the average of the amount and type of illicit drugs seized by the Office of Field Operations in the immediately preceding five fiscal years.

(D) The number of infractions related to travelers and cargo committed by major violators who are interdicted by the Office of Field Operations at ports of entry, and the estimated number of such infractions committed by major violators who are not so interdicted.

(E) In consultation with the heads of the Office of National Drug Control Policy and the United States Southern Command, a cocaine seizure effectiveness rate, which is the percentage resulting from dividing the amount of cocaine seized by the Office of Field Operations by the total estimated cocaine flow rate at ports of entry along the United States land border with Mexico and Canada.

(F) A measurement of how border security operations affect crossing times, including the following:

(i) A wait time ratio that compares the average wait times to total commercial and private vehicular traffic volumes at each land port of entry.

(ii) An infrastructure capacity utilization rate that measures traffic volume against the physical and staffing capacity at each land port of entry.

(iii) A secondary examination rate that measures the frequency of secondary examinations at each land port of entry.

(iv) An enforcement rate that measures the effectiveness of such secondary examinations at detecting major violators.

(G) A seaport scanning rate that includes the following:

(i) The number of all cargo containers that are considered potentially "high-risk", as determined by the Executive Assistant Commissioner of the Office of Field Operations.

(ii) A comparison of the number of potentially high-risk cargo containers scanned by the Office of Field Operations at each sea port of entry during a fiscal year to the total number of high-risk cargo containers entering the United States at each such sea port of entry during the previous fiscal year.

(iii) The number of potentially high-risk cargo containers scanned upon arrival at a United States sea port of entry.

(iv) The number of potentially high-risk cargo containers scanned before arrival at a United States sea port of entry.

(2) METRICS CONSULTATION.—To ensure that authoritative data sources are utilized in the development of the metrics described in paragraph (1), the Secretary shall—

(A) consult with the heads of the appropriate components of the Department of Homeland Security; and

(B) where appropriate, work with heads of other appropriate agencies, including the Office of Refugee Resettlement of the Department of Health and Human Services and the Executive Office for Immigration Review of the Department of Justice.

(3) MANNER OF COLLECTION.—The data collected to inform the metrics developed in accordance with paragraph (1) shall be collected and reported in a consistent and standardized manner across all United States ports of entry, informed by situational awareness.

(d) METRICS FOR SECURING THE MARITIME BORDER.—

(1) IN GENERAL.—Not later than 180 days after the date of the enactment of this section, the Secretary shall develop metrics, informed by situational awareness, to measure the effectiveness of security in the maritime environment. The Secretary shall annually implement the metrics developed under this subsection, which shall include the following:

(A) Situational awareness achieved in the maritime environment.

(B) A known maritime migrant flow rate.

(C) An illicit drugs removal rate for drugs removed inside and outside of a transit zone, which compares the amount and type of illicit drugs removed, including drugs abandoned at sea, by the maritime security components of the Department of Homeland Security in any fiscal year to the average of the amount and type of illicit drugs removed by such maritime components for the immediately preceding five fiscal years.

(D) In consultation with the heads of the Office of National Drug Control Policy and the United States Southern Command, a cocaine removal effectiveness rate for cocaine removed inside a transit zone and outside a transit zone, which compares the amount of cocaine removed by the maritime security components of the Department of Homeland Security by the total documented cocaine flow rate, as contained in Federal drug databases.

(E) A response rate, which compares the ability of the maritime security components of the Department of Homeland Security to respond to and resolve known maritime threats, whether inside or outside a transit zone, by placing assets on-scene, to the total number of events with respect to which the Department has known threat information.

(F) An intergovernmental response rate, which compares the ability of the maritime security components of the Department of Homeland Security or other United States Government entities to respond to and resolve actionable maritime threats, whether inside or outside a transit zone, with the number of such threats detected.

(2) METRICS CONSULTATION.—To ensure that authoritative data sources are utilized in the development of the metrics described in paragraph (1), the Secretary shall—

(A) consult with the heads of the appropriate components of the Department of Homeland Security; and

(B) where appropriate, work with the heads of other agencies, including the Drug Enforcement Agency, the Department of Defense, and the Department of Justice.

(3) MANNER OF COLLECTION.—The data used by the Secretary shall be collected and reported in a consistent and standardized manner by the maritime security components of the Department of Homeland Security, informed by situational awareness.

(e) AIR AND MARINE SECURITY METRICS IN THE LAND DOMAIN.—

(1) IN GENERAL.—Not later than 180 days after the date of the enactment of this section, the Secretary shall develop metrics, informed by situational awareness, to measure the effectiveness of the aviation assets and operations of Air and Marine Operations of U.S. Customs and Border Protection. The Secretary shall annually implement the metrics developed under this subsection, which shall include the following:

(A) A flight hour effectiveness rate, which compares Air and Marine Operations flight hours requirements to the number of flight hours flown by Air and Marine Operations.

(B) A funded flight hour effectiveness rate, which compares the number of funded flight hours appropriated to Air and Marine Operations to the number of actual flight hours flown by Air and Marine Operations.

(C) A readiness rate, which compares the number of aviation missions flown by Air and Marine Operations to the number of aviation missions cancelled by Air and Marine Operations due to maintenance, operations, or other causes.

(D) The number of missions cancelled by Air and Marine Operations due to weather compared to the total planned missions.

(E) The number of individuals detected by Air and Marine Operations through the use of unmanned aerial systems and manned aircraft.

(F) The number of apprehensions assisted by Air and Marine Operations through the use of unmanned aerial systems and manned aircraft.

(G) The number and quantity of illicit drug seizures assisted by Air and Marine Operations through the use of unmanned aerial systems and manned aircraft.

(H) The number of times that actionable intelligence related to border security was obtained through the use of unmanned aerial systems and manned aircraft.

(2) METRICS CONSULTATION.—To ensure that authoritative data sources are utilized in the development of the metrics described in paragraph (1), the Secretary shall—

(A) consult with the heads of the appropriate components of the Department of Homeland Security; and

(B) as appropriate, work with the heads of other departments and agencies, including the Department of Justice.

(3) MANNER OF COLLECTION.—The data collected to inform the metrics developed in accordance with paragraph (1) shall be collected and reported in a consistent and standardized manner by Air and Marine Operations, informed by situational awareness.

(f) DATA TRANSPARENCY.—The Secretary shall—

(1) in accordance with applicable privacy laws, make data related to apprehensions, inadmissible aliens, drug seizures, and other enforcement actions available to the public, law enforcement communities, and academic research communities; and

(2) provide the Office of Immigration Statistics of the Department of Homeland Security with unfettered access to the data referred to in paragraph (1).

(g) EVALUATION BY THE GOVERNMENT ACCOUNTABILITY OFFICE AND THE SECRETARY.—

(1) METRICS REPORT.—

(A) MANDATORY DISCLOSURES.—The Secretary shall submit to the appropriate congressional committees and the Comptroller General of the United States an annual report containing the metrics required under this section and the data and methodology used to develop such metrics.

(B) PERMISSIBLE DISCLOSURES.—The Secretary, for the purpose of validation and verification, may submit the annual report described in subparagraph (A) to—

(i) the Center for Borders, Trade, and Immigration Research of the Centers of Excellence network of the Department of Homeland Security;

(ii) the head of a national laboratory within the Department of Homeland Security laboratory network with prior expertise in border security; and

(iii) a Federally Funded Research and Development Center.

(2) GAO REPORT.—Not later than 270 days after receiving the first report under paragraph (1)(A) and biennially thereafter for the following ten years with respect to every other such report, the Comptroller General of the United States shall submit to the appropriate congressional committees a report that—

(A) analyzes the suitability and statistical validity of the data and methodology contained in each such report; and

(B) includes recommendations on—

(i) the feasibility of other suitable metrics that may be used to measure the effectiveness of border security; and

(ii) improvements that need to be made to the metrics being used to measure the effectiveness of border security.

(3) STATE OF THE BORDER REPORT.—Not later than 60 days after the end of each fiscal year through fiscal year 2026, the Secretary shall submit to the appropriate congressional committees a "State of the Border" report that—

(A) provides trends for each metric under this section for the last ten fiscal years, to the greatest extent possible;

(B) provides selected analysis into related aspects of illegal flow rates, including undocumented migrant flows and stock estimation techniques;

(C) provides selected analysis into related aspects of legal flow rates; and

(D) includes any other information that the Secretary determines appropriate.

(4) METRICS UPDATE.—

(A) IN GENERAL.—After submitting the tenth report to the Comptroller General under paragraph (1), the Secretary may reevaluate and update any of the metrics developed in accordance with this section to ensure that such metrics are suitable to measure the effectiveness of border security.

(B) CONGRESSIONAL NOTIFICATION.—Not later than 30 days before updating the metrics pursuant to subparagraph (A), the Secretary shall notify the appropriate congressional committees of such updates.

SEC. 1093. PROGRAM TO COMMEMORATE THE 100TH ANNIVERSARY OF THE TOMB OF THE UNKNOWN SOLDIER.

(a) COMMEMORATIVE PROGRAM.—

(1) IN GENERAL.—The Secretary of Defense shall conduct a program to commemorate the 100th anniversary of the Tomb of the Unknown Soldier. In conducting the commemorative program, the Secretary shall coordinate, support, and facilitate other programs and activities of the Federal Government and State and local governments.

(2) WORK WITH NONGOVERNMENTAL ORGANIZATIONS.—In conducting the commemorative program, the Secretary may work with nongovernmental organizations working to support the commemoration of the Tomb of the Unknown Soldier. No public funds may be used to undertake activities sponsored by such organizations.

(b) SCHEDULE.—The Secretary shall determine the schedule of major events and priority of efforts for the commemorative program in order to ensure achievement of the objectives specified in subsection (c).

(c) COMMEMORATIVE ACTIVITIES AND OBJECTIVES.—The commemorative program may include activities and ceremonies to achieve the following objectives:

(1) To honor America's commitment to never forget or forsake those who served and sacrificed for our Country, including personnel who were held as prisoners of war or listed as missing in action, and to thank and honor the families of these veterans.

(2) To highlight the service of the Armed Forces in times of war or armed conflict and contributions of Federal agencies and governmental and nongovernmental organizations that served with, or in support of, the Armed Forces.

(3) To pay tribute to the contributions made on the home front by the people of the United States in times of war or armed conflict.

(4) To educate the American Public about service and sacrifice on behalf of the United States of America and the principles that define and unite us.

(5) To recognize the contributions and sacrifices made by the allies of the United States during times of war or armed conflict.

(d) NAMES AND SYMBOLS.—The Secretary shall have the sole and exclusive right to use the name "The United States of America Tomb of the Unknown Soldier Commemoration", and such seal, emblems, and badges incorporating such name as the Secretary may lawfully adopt. Nothing in this section may be construed to supersede rights that are established or vested before the date of the enactment of this Act.

(e) COMMEMORATION FUND.—

(1) IN GENERAL.—Upon the establishment of the commemorative program under subsection (a), the Secretary of the Treasury shall establish in the Treasury of the United States an account

to be known as the "Tomb of the Unknown Soldier Commemoration Fund" (in this subsection referred to as the "Fund"). The Fund shall be administered by the Secretary of Defense.

(2) DEPOSITS.—There shall be deposited into the Fund the following:

(A) Amounts appropriated to the Fund.

(B) Proceeds derived from the use by the Secretary of Defense of the exclusive rights described in subsection (d).

(C) Donations made in support of the commemorative program by private and corporate donors.

(D) Funds transferred to the Fund by the Secretary of Defense from funds appropriated for fiscal year 2017 and subsequent years for the Department of Defense.

(3) USE OF FUND.—The Secretary of Defense shall use the assets of the Fund only for the purpose of conducting the commemorative program. The Secretary shall prescribe such regulations regarding the use of the Fund as the Secretary considers appropriate.

(4) AVAILABILITY.—Amounts deposited under paragraph (2) shall constitute the assets of the Fund and remain available until expended.

(5) BUDGET REQUEST.—The Secretary of Defense may establish a separate budget line for the commemorative program. In the budget justification materials submitted by the Secretary in support of the budget of the President for any fiscal year for which the Secretary establishes the separate budget line (as submitted to Congress pursuant to section 1105 of title 31, United States Code), the Secretary shall—

(A) identify and explain any amounts expended for the commemorative program in the fiscal year preceding the budget request;

(B) identify and explain the amounts being requested to support the commemorative program for the fiscal year of the budget request; and

(C) present a summary of the fiscal status of the Fund.

(f) ACCEPTANCE OF VOLUNTARY SERVICES.—

(1) AUTHORITY TO ACCEPT SERVICES.—Notwithstanding section 1342 of title 31, United States Code, the Secretary of Defense may accept from any person voluntary services to be provided in furtherance of the commemorative program. The Secretary shall prohibit the solicitation of any voluntary services if the nature or circumstances of such solicitation would compromise the integrity or the appearance of integrity of any program of the Department of Defense or of any individual involved in the program.

(2) REIMBURSEMENT OF INCIDENTAL EXPENSES.—The Secretary may provide for reimbursement of incidental expenses incurred by a person providing voluntary services under this subsection. The Secretary shall determine which expenses are eligible for reimbursement under this paragraph.

(g) FINAL REPORT.—Not later than 60 days after the end of the commemorative program, if established by the Secretary of Defense under subsection (a), the Secretary shall submit to Congress a report containing an accounting of the following:

(1) All of the funds deposited into and expended from the Tomb of the Unknown Soldier Commemoration Fund.

(2) Any other funds expended under this section.

(3) Any unobligated funds remaining in the Fund.

SEC. 1094. SENSE OF CONGRESS REGARDING THE OCONUS BASING OF THE KC–46A AIRCRAFT.

(a) FINDING.—Congress finds that the Department of Defense is continuing its process of permanently stationing the KC–46A aircraft at installations in the Continental United States (in this section referred to as "CONUS") and for-

ward-basing outside the Continental United States (in this section referred to as "OCONUS").

(b) SENSE OF CONGRESS.—It is the sense of Congress that the Secretary of the Air Force, as part of the strategic basing process for the KC–46A aircraft, should continue to place emphasis on and consider the benefits derived from outside the continental United States (OCONUS) locations that—

(1) support day-to-day air refueling operations, combatant commander operations plans, and flexibility for contingency ops, and have—

(A) a strategic location that is essential to the defense of the United States and its interests;

(B) receivers for boom or probe-and-drogue training opportunities with joint and international partners; and

(C) sufficient airfield and airspace availability and capacity to meet requirements; and

(2) possess facilities that—

(A) take full advantage of existing infrastructure to provide—

(i) runway, hangars, and aircrew and maintenance operations; and

(ii) sufficient fuels receipt, storage, and distribution for 5-day peacetime operating stock; and

(B) minimize overall construction and operational costs.

SEC. 1095. DESIGNATION OF A DEPARTMENT OF DEFENSE STRATEGIC ARCTIC PORT.

(a) SENSE OF CONGRESS.—It is the sense of Congress that the Arctic is a region of growing strategic importance to the national security interest of the United States and that the Department of Defense must better align its posture and capabilities to meet the growing array of challenges in the region.

(b) ARCTIC DEFINED.—In this section, the term "Arctic" has the meaning given that term in section 112 of the Arctic Research and Policy Act of 1984 (15 U.S.C. 4111).

(c) REPORT REQUIRED.—Not later than 180 days after the date of the enactment of this Act, the Secretary of Defense, in consultation with the Chairman of the Joint Chiefs of Staff, the Commanding General of the United States Army Corps of Engineers, the Commandant of the Coast Guard, and the Administrator of the Maritime Administration, shall submit to the congressional defense committees a report containing an assessment of the future security requirements for one or more strategic ports in the Arctic.

(d) CONTENTS OF REPORT.—Consistent with the updated military strategy for the protection of United States national security interests in the Arctic region set forth in the reports required under section 1068 of the National Defense Authorization Act for Fiscal Year 2016 (Public Law 114–92; 129 Stat. 992), the report required under subsection (c) shall include—

(1) the amount of sufficient and suitable space needed to create capacity for port and other necessary infrastructure for at least one of each of type of Navy or Coast Guard vessel, including an Arleigh Burke class destroyer of the Navy, or a national security cutter or a heavy polar ice breaker of the Coast Guard;

(2) the amount of sufficient and suitable space needed to create capacity for equipment and fuel storage, technological infrastructure, and civil infrastructure to support military and civilian operations, including—

(A) aerospace warning;

(B) maritime surface and subsurface warning;

(C) maritime control and defense;

(D) maritime domain awareness;

(E) homeland defense;

(F) defense support to civil authorities;

(G) humanitarian relief;

(H) search and rescue;

(I) disaster relief;

(J) oil spill response;

(K) medical stabilization and evacuation; and

(L) meteorological measurements and fore-casting;

(3) an identification of proximity and road access to an airport designated as a commercial service airport by the Federal Aviation Administration that is capable of supporting military and civilian aircraft for operations designated in paragraph (2); and

(4) a description of the requirements, to include infrastructure and installations, communications, and logistics necessary to improve response effectiveness to support military and civilian operations designated in paragraph (2).

(e) DESIGNATION OF STRATEGIC ARCTIC PORTS.—

(1) DESIGNATION CRITERIA AND RECOMMENDATIONS.—Upon completion of the report required under subsection (c), the Secretary of Defense, in consultation with the Chairman of the Joint Chiefs of Staff, the Commanding General of the United States Army Corps of Engineers, the Commandant of the Coast Guard, the Administrator of the Maritime Administration, shall—

(A) establish criteria for the designation of a port as a "Department of Defense Strategic Arctic Port"; and

(B) if the report required under subsection (c) includes a determination that one or more strategic Arctic ports are necessary to fulfill future security requirements in the Arctic, not later than 18 months after the date of the completion of the report, submit to the congressional defense committees recommendations for the designation of one or more ports as Department of Defense Strategic Arctic Ports.

(2) COST ESTIMATES.—The recommendations submitted under paragraph (1)(B) shall include the estimated cost of sufficient construction necessary to initiate and sustain expected operations at the ports designated as Department of Defense Strategic Arctic Ports.

(f) RULE OF CONSTRUCTION.—Nothing in this section may be construed to authorize any additional appropriations for the Department of Defense for the establishment of any port recommended pursuant to this section.

SEC. 1096. RECOVERY OF EXCESS RIFLES, AMMUNITION, AND PARTS GRANTED TO FOREIGN COUNTRIES AND TRANSFER TO CERTAIN PERSONS.

(a) RECOVERY.—Subchapter II of chapter 407 of title 36, United States Code, is amended by inserting after section 40728A the following new section:

"§ 40728B. Recovery of excess rifles, ammunition, and parts granted to foreign countries and transfer to certain persons

"(a) AUTHORITY TO RECOVER.—(1) Subject to paragraph (2) and subsection (b), the Secretary of the Army may acquire from any person any rifle, ammunition, repair parts, or other supplies described in section 40731(a) of this title which were—

"(A) provided to any country on a grant basis under the conditions imposed by section 505 of the Foreign Assistance Act of 1961 (22 U.S.C. 2314) that became excess to the needs of such country; and

"(B) lawfully acquired by such person.

"(2) The Secretary of the Army may not acquire anything under paragraph (1) except for transfer to a person in the United States under subsection (c).

"(3) The Secretary of the Army may accept rifles, ammunition, repair parts, or other supplies under paragraph (1) notwithstanding section 1342 of title 31.

"(b) COST OF RECOVERY.—The Secretary of the Army may not acquire anything under subsection (a) if the United States would incur any cost for such acquisition.

"(c) AVAILABILITY FOR TRANSFER.—Any rifles, ammunition, repair parts, or supplies acquired

under subsection (a) shall be available for transfer in the United States to the person from whom acquired if such person—

"(1) is licensed as a manufacturer, importer, or dealer pursuant to section 923(a) of title 18; and

"(2) uses an ammunition depot of the Army that is an eligible facility for receipt of any rifles, ammunition, repair parts, or supplies under this paragraph.

"(d) MARKET VALUE.—The Secretary of the Army may only transfer an item under subsection (c) if the Secretary receives fair market value for the item.

"(e) CONTRACTS.—Notwithstanding subsection (k) of section 2304 of title 10, the Secretary may enter into such contracts or cooperative agreements on a sole source basis pursuant to paragraphs (4) and (5) of subsection (c) of such section to carry out this section.

"(f) AECA.—Transfers authorized under this section may only be made in accordance with applicable provisions of the Arms Export Control Act (22 U.S.C. 2778).

"(g) RIFLE DEFINED.—In this section, the term 'rifle' has the meaning given such term in section 921 of title 18.".

(b) SALE.—Section 40732 of such title is amended—

(1) by adding at the end the following new subsection:

"(d) SALES BY OTHER PERSONS.—A person who receives a rifle or any ammunition, repair parts, or supplies under section 40728B(c) of this title may sell, at fair market value, such rifle, ammunition, repair parts, or supplies. With respect to rifles other than caliber .22 rimfire and caliber .30 rifles, the seller shall obtain a license as a dealer in rifles and abide by all requirements imposed on persons licensed under chapter 44 of title 18, including maintaining acquisition and disposition records, and conducting background checks."; and

(2) in subsection (c)(1), by striking "The corporation may not" and inserting "No person acquiring a firearm under this chapter may".

(c) CLERICAL AMENDMENT.—The table of sections at the beginning of chapter 407 of such title is amended by inserting after the item relating to section 40728A the following new item:

"40728B. Recovery of excess rifles, ammunition, and parts granted to foreign countries and transfer to certain persons.".

(d) REPORT.—

(1) REPORT REQUIRED.—Not later than 180 days after the date of the enactment of this Act, the Secretary of the Army shall submit to the Committee on Armed Services and the Committee on Foreign Relations of the Senate and the Committee on Armed Services and the Committee on Foreign Affairs of the House of Representatives a report on the acquisition and transfer of excess rifles, ammunition, repair parts, and other supplies described in section 40731(a) of title 36, United States Code, that were provided to a country on a grant basis under the conditions imposed by section 505 of the Foreign Assistance Act of 1961. The report shall include each of the following:

(A) A list of excess rifles, ammunition, repair parts, and other supplies known to the United States Army as eligible for transfer under section 40731(a) of title 36, United States Code.

(B) An assessment of whether and how the Secretary of the Army intends to use the authorities under section 40728B of title 36, United States Code, as added by this section.

(C) Any other issue that the Secretary of the Army considers appropriate.

(2) PROHIBITION ON TRANSFERS PENDING SUBMITTAL OF REPORT.—No rifle, ammunition, repair part, or supplies acquired under section 40728B(a) of title 36, United States Code, may be

transferred until the date that is 90 days after the date of the submittal of the report required under paragraph (1).

TITLE XI—CIVILIAN PERSONNEL MATTERS

Subtitle A—Department of Defense Matters Generally

Sec. 1101. Civilian personnel management.

Sec. 1102. Repeal of requirement for annual strategic workforce plan for the Department of Defense.

Sec. 1103. Training for employment personnel of Department of Defense on matters relating to authorities for recruitment and retention at United States Cyber Command.

Sec. 1104. Public-private talent exchange.

Sec. 1105. Temporary and term appointments in the competitive service in the Department of Defense.

Sec. 1106. Direct-hire authority for the Department of Defense for post-secondary students and recent graduates.

Sec. 1107. Temporary increase in maximum amount of voluntary separation incentive pay authorized for civilian employees of the Department of Defense.

Sec. 1108. Extension of rate of overtime pay for Department of the Navy employees performing work aboard or dockside in support of the nuclear-powered aircraft carrier forward deployed in Japan.

Sec. 1109. Limitation on number of DOD SES positions.

Sec. 1110. Direct hire authority for financial management experts in the Department of Defense workforce.

Sec. 1111. Repeal of certain basis for appointment of a retired member of the Armed Forces to Department of Defense position within 180 days of retirement.

Subtitle B—Department of Defense Science and Technology Laboratories and Related Matters

Sec. 1121. Permanent personnel management authority for the Department of Defense for experts in science and engineering.

Sec. 1122. Codification and modification of certain authorities for certain positions at Department of Defense research and engineering laboratories.

Sec. 1123. Modification to information technology personnel exchange program.

Sec. 1124. Pilot program on enhanced pay authority for certain research and technology positions in the science and technology reinvention laboratories of the Department of Defense.

Sec. 1125. Temporary direct hire authority for domestic defense industrial base facilities, the Major Range and Test Facilities Base, and the Office of the Director of Operational Test and Evaluation.

Subtitle C—Governmentwide Matters

Sec. 1131. Elimination of two-year eligibility limitation for noncompetitive appointment of spouses of members of the Armed Forces.

Sec. 1132. Temporary personnel flexibilities for domestic defense industrial base facilities and Major Range and Test Facilities Base civilian personnel.

Sec. 1133. *One-year extension of temporary authority to grant allowances, benefits, and gratuities to civilian personnel on official duty in a combat zone.*

Sec. 1134. *Advance payments for employees relocating within the United States and its territories.*

Sec. 1135. *Eligibility of employees in a time-limited appointment to compete for a permanent appointment at any Federal agency.*

Sec. 1136. *Review of official personnel file of former Federal employees before rehiring.*

Sec. 1137. *One-year extension of authority to waive annual limitation on premium pay and aggregate limitation on pay for Federal civilian employees working overseas.*

Sec. 1138. *Administrative leave.*

Sec. 1139. *Direct hiring for Federal wage schedule employees.*

Sec. 1140. *Record of investigation of personnel action in separated employee's official personnel file.*

Subtitle A—Department of Defense Matters Generally

SEC. 1101. CIVILIAN PERSONNEL MANAGEMENT.

(a) MODIFICATION OF MANAGEMENT LIMITATIONS.—Section 129 of title 10, United States Code, is amended—

(1) in subsection (a)—

(A) in the first sentence, by striking "solely";

(B) in the second sentence—

(i) by striking "The management of such personnel in any fiscal year shall not be subject to any" and inserting "Any"; and

(ii) by inserting before the period the following: "shall be developed on the basis of those factors and shall be subject to adjustment solely for reasons of changed circumstances"; and

(C) in the third sentence, by striking "unless such reduction" and all that follows and inserting "except in accordance with the requirements of this section and section 129a of this title.";

(2) by striking subsections (b), (c), (e), and (f);

(3) by redesignating subsection (d) as subsection (b); and

(4) by adding at the end the following new subsection (c):

"(c)(1) Not later than February 1 of each year—

"(A) the Secretary of Defense shall submit to the congressional defense committees a report on the management of the civilian workforce of the Office of the Secretary of Defense and the Defense Agencies and Field Activities; and

"(B) the Secretary of each military department shall submit to the congressional defense committees a report on the management of the civilian workforces under the jurisdiction of such Secretary.

"(2) Each report under paragraph (1) shall contain, with respect to the civilian workforce under the jurisdiction of the official submitting the report, the following:

"(A) An assessment of the projected size of such civilian workforce in the current year and for each year in the future-years defense program.

"(B) If the projected size of such civilian workforce has changed from the previous year's projected size, an explanation of the reasons for the increase or decrease from the previous projection, including an explanation of any efforts that have been taken to identify offsetting reductions and avoid unnecessary overall growth in the size of the civilian workforce.

"(C) In the case of a transfer of functions between military, civilian, and contractor workforces, an explanation of the reasons for the transfer and the steps that have been taken to control the overall cost of the function to the Department.".

(b) CONFORMING AMENDMENTS.—

(1) SECTION HEADING.—The heading of such section is amended to read as follows:

"§ 129. Civilian personnel management".

(2) CLERICAL AMENDMENT.—The item relating to such section in the table of sections at the beginning of chapter 3 of such title is amended to read as follows:

"129. Civilian personnel management.".

SEC. 1102. REPEAL OF REQUIREMENT FOR ANNUAL STRATEGIC WORKFORCE PLAN FOR THE DEPARTMENT OF DEFENSE.

(a) REPEAL.—Section 115b of title 10, United States Code, is repealed.

(b) CLERICAL AMENDMENT.—The table of sections at the beginning of chapter 2 of such title is amended by striking the item relating to section 115b.

SEC. 1103. TRAINING FOR EMPLOYMENT PERSONNEL OF DEPARTMENT OF DEFENSE ON MATTERS RELATING TO AUTHORITIES FOR RECRUITMENT AND RETENTION AT UNITED STATES CYBER COMMAND.

(a) TRAINING REQUIRED.—Section 1599f of title 10, United States Code, is amended—

(1) by redesignating subsections (f), (g), (h), (i), and (j) as subsections (g), (h), (i), (j), and (k), respectively; and

(2) by inserting after subsection (e) the following new subsection (f):

"(f) TRAINING.—(1) The Secretary shall provide training to covered personnel on hiring and pay matters relating to authorities under this section.

"(2) For purposes of this subsection, covered personnel are employees of the Department who—

"(A) carry out functions relating to—

"(i) the management of human resources and the civilian workforce of the Department; or

"(ii) the writing of guidance for the implementation of authorities regarding hiring and pay under this section; or

"(B) are employed in supervisory positions or have responsibilities relating to the hiring of individuals for positions in the Department and to whom the Secretary intends to delegate authority under this section.".

(b) REPORTS.—

(1) INITIAL REPORT.—Not later than 180 days after the date of the enactment of this Act, the Secretary of Defense shall submit to the appropriate committees of Congress (as defined in section 1599f of title 10, United States Code) a report on the training the Secretary intends to provide to each of the employees described in subsection (f)(2) of such section (as added by subsection (a) of this section) and the frequency with which the Secretary intends to provide such training.

(2) ONGOING REPORTS.—Subsection (h)(2)(E) of such section, as redesignated by subsection (a)(1) of this section, is amended by striking "supervisors of employees in qualified positions at the Department on the use of the new authorities" and inserting "employees described in subsection (f)(2) on the use of authorities under this section".

SEC. 1104. PUBLIC-PRIVATE TALENT EXCHANGE.

(a) AUTHORITY.—Chapter 81 of title 10, United States Code, is amended by adding at the end the following new section:

"§ 1599g. Public-private talent exchange

"(a) ASSIGNMENT AUTHORITY.—Under regulations prescribed by the Secretary of Defense, the Secretary may, with the agreement of a private-sector organization and the consent of the employee, arrange for the temporary assignment of an employee to such private-sector organization, or from such private-sector organization to a Department of Defense organization under this section.

"(b) AGREEMENTS.—(1) The Secretary of Defense shall provide for a written agreement among the Department of Defense, the private-sector organization, and the employee concerned regarding the terms and conditions of the employee's assignment under this section. The agreement—

"(A) shall require that the employee of the Department of Defense, upon completion of the assignment, will serve in the Department of Defense, or elsewhere in the civil service if approved by the Secretary, for a period equal to twice the length of the assignment;

"(B) shall provide that if the employee of the Department of Defense or of the private-sector organization (as the case may be) fails to carry out the agreement, such employee shall be liable to the United States for payment of all expenses of the assignment, unless that failure was for good and sufficient reason, as determined by the Secretary of Defense; and

"(C) shall contain language ensuring that such employee of the Department does not improperly use pre-decisional or draft deliberative information that such employee may be privy to or aware of related to Department programing, budgeting, resourcing, acquisition, or procurement for the benefit or advantage of the private-sector organization.

"(2) An amount for which an employee is liable under paragraph (1) shall be treated as a debt due the United States.

"(3) The Secretary may waive, in whole or in part, collection of a debt described in paragraph (2) based on a determination that the collection would be against equity and good conscience and not in the best interests of the United States, after taking into account any indication of fraud, misrepresentation, fault, or lack of good faith on the part of the employee.

"(c) TERMINATION.—An assignment under this section may, at any time and for any reason, be terminated by the Department of Defense or the private-sector organization concerned.

"(d) DURATION.—(1) An assignment under this section shall be for a period of not less than three months and not more than two years, renewable up to a total of four years. No employee of the Department of Defense may be assigned under this section for more than a total of 4 years inclusive of all such assignments.

"(2) An assignment under this section may be for a period in excess of two years, but not more than four years, if the Secretary determines that such assignment is necessary to meet critical mission or program requirements.

"(e) STATUS OF FEDERAL EMPLOYEES ASSIGNED TO PRIVATE-SECTOR ORGANIZATIONS.—(1) An employee of the Department of Defense who is assigned to a private-sector organization under this section shall be considered, during the period of assignment, to be on detail to a regular work assignment in the Department for all purposes. The written agreement established under subsection (b)(1) shall address the specific terms and conditions related to the employee's continued status as a Federal employee.

"(2) In establishing a temporary assignment of an employee of the Department of Defense to a private-sector organization, the Secretary of Defense shall—

"(A) ensure that the normal duties and functions of such employee can be reasonably performed by other employees of the Department of Defense without the transfer or reassignment of other personnel of the Department of Defense, including members of the armed forces;

"(B) ensure that the normal duties and functions of such employees are not, as a result of and during the course of such temporary assignment, performed or augmented by contractor personnel in violation of the provisions of section 2461 of this title; and

"(C) certify that the temporary assignment of such employee shall not have an adverse or negative impact on mission attainment, warfighter support, or organizational capabilities associated with the assignment.

"(f) TERMS AND CONDITIONS FOR PRIVATE-SECTOR EMPLOYEES.—An employee of a private-sector organization who is assigned to a Department of Defense organization under this section—

"(1) shall continue to receive pay and benefits from the private-sector organization from which such employee is assigned and shall not receive pay or benefits from the Department of Defense, except as provided in paragraph (2);

"(2) is deemed to be an employee of the Department of Defense for the purposes of—

"(A) chapters 73 and 81 of title 5;

"(B) sections 201, 203, 205, 207, 208, 209, 603, 606, 607, 643, 654, 1905, and 1913 of title 18;

"(C) sections 1343, 1344, and 1349(b) of title 31;

"(D) the Federal Tort Claims Act and any other Federal tort liability statute;

"(E) the Ethics in Government Act of 1978; and

"(F) chapter 21 of title 41;

"(3) shall not have access to any trade secrets or to any other nonpublic information which is of commercial value to the private-sector organization from which such employee is assigned;

"(4) may perform work that is considered inherently governmental in nature only when requested in writing by the Secretary of Defense; and

"(5) may not be used to circumvent the provision of section 2461 of this title nor to circumvent any limitation or restriction on the size of the Department's workforce.

"(g) PROHIBITION AGAINST CHARGING CERTAIN COSTS TO THE FEDERAL GOVERNMENT.—A private-sector organization may not charge the Department or any other agency of the Federal Government, as direct or indirect costs under a Federal contract, the costs of pay or benefits paid by the organization to an employee assigned to a Department organization under this section for the period of the assignment.

"(h) CONSIDERATIONS.—In carrying out this section, the Secretary of Defense—

"(1) shall ensure that, of the assignments made under this section each year, at least 20 percent are from small business concerns (as defined by section 3703(e)(2)(A) of title 5);

"(2) shall take into consideration the question of how assignments under this section might best be used to help meet the needs of the Department of Defense with respect to the training of employees; and

"(3) shall take into consideration, where applicable, areas of particular private sector expertise, such as cybersecurity.".

(b) TABLE OF SECTIONS AMENDMENT.—The table of sections at the beginning of such chapter is amended by adding at the end the following new item:

"1599g. Public-private talent exchange.".

SEC. 1105. TEMPORARY AND TERM APPOINTMENTS IN THE COMPETITIVE SERVICE IN THE DEPARTMENT OF DEFENSE.

(a) APPOINTMENT.—

(1) IN GENERAL.—The Secretary of Defense may make a temporary appointment or a term appointment in the Department when the need for the services of an employee in the Department is not permanent.

(2) EXTENSION.—The Secretary may extend a temporary appointment or a term appointment made under paragraph (1).

(b) APPOINTMENTS FOR CRITICAL HIRING NEEDS.—

(1) IN GENERAL.—If there is a critical hiring need, the Secretary of Defense may make a noncompetitive temporary appointment or a noncompetitive term appointment in the Department of Defense, without regard to the requirements of sections 3327 and 3330 of title 5, United States

Code, for a period that is not more than 18 months.

(2) NO EXTENSION AVAILABLE.—An appointment made under paragraph (1) may not be extended.

(c) REGULATIONS.—The Secretary may prescribe regulations to carry out this section.

(d) DEFINITIONS.—In this section:

(1) The term "temporary appointment" means the appointment of an employee in the competitive service for a period that is not more than one year.

(2) The term "term appointment" means the appointment of an employee in the competitive service for a period that is more than one year and not more than five years, unless the Secretary of Defense, before the appointment of the employee, authorizes a longer period.

SEC. 1106. DIRECT-HIRE AUTHORITY FOR THE DEPARTMENT OF DEFENSE FOR POST-SECONDARY STUDENTS AND RECENT GRADUATES.

(a) HIRING AUTHORITY.—Without regard to sections 3309 through 3318, 3327, and 3330 of title 5, United States Code, the Secretary of Defense may recruit and appoint qualified recent graduates and current post-secondary students to competitive service positions in professional and administrative occupations within the Department of Defense.

(b) LIMITATION ON APPOINTMENTS.—Subject to subsection (c)(2), the total number of employees appointed by the Secretary under subsection (a) during a fiscal year may not exceed the number equal to 15 percent of the number of hires made into professional and administrative occupations of the Department at the GS–11 level and below (or equivalent) under competitive examining procedures during the previous fiscal year.

(c) REGULATIONS.—

(1) IN GENERAL.—The Secretary shall administer this section in accordance with regulations prescribed by the Secretary for purposes of this section.

(2) LOWER LIMIT ON APPOINTMENTS.—The regulations may establish a lower limit on the number of individuals appointable under subsection (a) during a fiscal year than is otherwise provided for under subsection (b), based on such factors as the Secretary considers appropriate.

(3) PUBLIC NOTICE AND ADVERTISING.—To the extent practical, as determined by the Secretary, the Secretary shall publicly advertise positions available under this section. In carrying out the preceding sentence, the Secretary shall—

(A) take into account merit system principles, mission requirements, costs, and organizational benefits of any advertising of positions; and

(B) advertise such positions in the manner the Secretary determines is most likely to provide diverse and qualified candidates and ensure potential applicants have appropriate information relevant to the positions available.

(d) SUNSET.—The authority provided under this section shall terminate on September 30, 2021.

(e) DEFINITIONS.—In this section:

(1) The term "current post-secondary student" means a person who—

(A) is currently enrolled in, and in good academic standing at, a full-time program at an institution of higher education;

(B) is making satisfactory progress toward receipt of a baccalaureate or graduate degree; and

(C) has completed at least one year of the program.

(2) The term "institution of higher education" has the meaning given the term in section 101 of the Higher Education Act of 1965 (20 U.S.C. 1001).

(3) The term "recent graduate", with respect to appointment of a person under this section, means a person who was awarded a degree by an institution of higher education not more than two years before the date of the appoint-

ment of such person, except that in the case of a person who has completed a period of obligated service in a uniformed service of more than four years, such term means a person who was awarded a degree by an institution of higher education not more than four years before the date of the appointment of such person.

SEC. 1107. TEMPORARY INCREASE IN MAXIMUM AMOUNT OF VOLUNTARY SEPARATION INCENTIVE PAY AUTHORIZED FOR CIVILIAN EMPLOYEES OF THE DEPARTMENT OF DEFENSE.

During the period beginning on the date of enactment of this Act and ending on September 30, 2018, section 9902(f)(5)(A)(ii) of title 5, United States Code, shall be applied by substituting "an amount determined by the Secretary, not to exceed $40,000" for "$25,000".

SEC. 1108. EXTENSION OF RATE OF OVERTIME PAY FOR DEPARTMENT OF THE NAVY EMPLOYEES PERFORMING WORK ABOARD OR DOCKSIDE IN SUPPORT OF THE NUCLEAR-POWERED AIRCRAFT CARRIER FORWARD DEPLOYED IN JAPAN.

Section 5542(a)(6)(B) of title 5, United States Code, is amended by striking "September 30, 2017" and inserting "September 30, 2018".

SEC. 1109. LIMITATION ON NUMBER OF DOD SES POSITIONS.

(a) LIMITATION ON NUMBER OF DOD SES POSITIONS.—

(1) IN GENERAL.—Not later than December 31, 2022, the total number of Senior Executive Service positions authorized under section 3133 of title 5, United States Code, for the Department of Defense may not exceed 1,260.

(2) HIGHLY QUALIFIED EXPERTS.—Of the total number of positions authorized under paragraph (1), not more than 200 of such positions may be occupied by an individual appointed under the authority provided in section 9903 of such title.

(b) PLAN TO ACHIEVE REQUIRED LIMITATION.—

(1) IN GENERAL.—The Secretary of Defense shall develop a plan to achieve the limitation required by subsection (a) that includes—

(A) the distribution of Senior Executive Service positions across the Office of the Secretary of Defense, the Joint Staff, the Military Departments, the Defense Agencies and Field Activities, the unified and specified combatant commands, and other key elements of the Department of Defense;

(B) the by-year reductions to Senior Executive Service positions consistent with the distribution required under subparagraph (A); and

(C) recommendations for any legislative action that may be necessary for personnel management and shaping authorities to achieve the required limitation.

(2) SUBMISSION OF PLAN.—Not less than one year after the date of the enactment of this Act, the Secretary of Defense shall submit to the Committees on Armed Services of the Senate and the House of Representatives a report setting forth the plan developed under paragraph (1).

(3) PROGRESS REPORTS.—The Secretary of Defense shall provide to the Committees on Armed Services of the Senate and the House of Representatives semi-annual progress report briefings describing and assessing the progress of the Secretary in implementing the plan developed under paragraph (1).

(c) CONFORMING AMENDMENT.—Section 3133(c) of title 5, United States Code, is amended by adding at the end the following new sentence: "Beginning in 2023, the number of such positions authorized under the preceding sentence for the Department of Defense may not exceed the limitation provided in section 1109 of the National Defense Authorization Act for Fiscal Year 2017.".

(d) DEFINITION OF SENIOR EXECUTIVE SERVICE POSITION.—In this section, the term "Senior Executive Service position" has the meaning given such term in section 3132(a)(2) of title 5, United States Code.

SEC. 1110. DIRECT HIRE AUTHORITY FOR FINANCIAL MANAGEMENT EXPERTS IN THE DEPARTMENT OF DEFENSE WORKFORCE.

(a) AUTHORITY.—Each Secretary concerned may appoint qualified candidates possessing a finance, accounting, management, or actuarial science degree, or a related degree or equivalent experience, to positions specified in subsection (c) for the Defense Agencies or the applicable military department without regard to the provisions of subchapter I of chapter 33 of title 5, United States Code.

(b) SECRETARY CONCERNED.—For purposes of this section, the Secretary concerned is as follows:

(1) The Secretary of Defense with respect to the Defense Agencies.

(2) The Secretary of a military department with respect to such military department.

(c) POSITIONS.—The positions specified in this subsection are the positions within the Department of Defense workforce as follows:

(1) Financial management positions.

(2) Accounting positions.

(3) Auditing positions.

(4) Actuarial positions.

(5) Cost estimation positions.

(6) Operational research positions.

(7) Business and business administration positions.

(d) LIMITATION.—Authority under this section may not, in any calendar year and with respect to any Defense Agency or military department, be exercised with respect to a number of candidates greater than the number equal to 10 percent of the total number of the financial management, accounting, auditing, and actuarial positions within the financial management workforce of such Defense Agency or military department that are filled as of the close of the fiscal year last ending before the start of such calendar year.

(e) NATURE OF APPOINTMENT.—Any appointment under this section shall be treated as an appointment on a full-time equivalent basis, unless such appointment is made on a term or temporary basis.

(f) EMPLOYEE DEFINED.—In this section, the term "employee" has the meaning given that term in section 2105 of title 5, United States Code.

(g) TERMINATION.—The authority to make appointments under this section shall not be available after December 31, 2022.

SEC. 1111. REPEAL OF CERTAIN BASIS FOR APPOINTMENT OF A RETIRED MEMBER OF THE ARMED FORCES TO DEPARTMENT OF DEFENSE POSITION WITHIN 180 DAYS OF RETIREMENT.

Section 3326(b) of title 5, United States Code, is amended—

(1) in paragraph (1), by adding "or" at the end;

(2) in paragraph (2), by striking "; or" and inserting a period; and

(3) by striking paragraph (3).

Subtitle B—Department of Defense Science and Technology Laboratories and Related Matters

SEC. 1121. PERMANENT PERSONNEL MANAGEMENT AUTHORITY FOR THE DEPARTMENT OF DEFENSE FOR EXPERTS IN SCIENCE AND ENGINEERING.

(a) PERMANENT PERSONNEL MANAGEMENT AUTHORITY.—

(1) IN GENERAL.—Chapter 81 of title 10, United States Code, as amended by section 1104 of this Act, is further amended by adding at the end the following new section:

"**§ 1599h. Personnel management authority to attract experts in science and engineering**

"(a) PROGRAMS AUTHORIZED.—

"(1) LABORATORIES OF THE MILITARY DEPARTMENTS.—The Secretary of Defense may carry out a program of personnel management authority provided in subsection (b) in order to facilitate recruitment of eminent experts in science or engineering for such laboratories of the military departments as the Secretary shall designate for purposes of the program for research and development projects of such laboratories.

"(2) DARPA.—The Director of the Defense Advanced Research Projects Agency may carry out a program of personnel management authority provided in subsection (b) in order to facilitate recruitment of eminent experts in science or engineering for research and development projects and to enhance the administration and management of the Agency.

"(3) DOTE.—The Director of the Office of Operational Test and Evaluation may carry out a program of personnel management authority provided in subsection (b) in order to facilitate recruitment of eminent experts in science or engineering to support operational test and evaluation missions of the Office.

"(b) PERSONNEL MANAGEMENT AUTHORITY.—Under a program under subsection (a), the official responsible for administration of the program may—

"(1) without regard to any provision of title 5 governing the appointment of employees in the civil service—

"(A) in the case of the laboratories of the military departments designated pursuant to subsection (a)(1), appoint scientists and engineers to a total of not more than 40 scientific and engineering positions in such laboratories;

"(B) in the case of the Defense Advanced Research Projects Agency, appoint individuals to a total of not more than 100 positions in the Agency, of which not more than 5 such positions may be positions of administration or management of the Agency; and

"(C) in the case of the Office of Operational Test and Evaluation, appoint scientists and engineers to a total of not more than 10 scientific and engineering positions in the Office;

"(2) notwithstanding any provision of title 5 governing the rates of pay or classification of employees in the executive branch, prescribe the rates of basic pay for positions to which employees are appointed under paragraph (1)—

"(A) in the case of employees appointed pursuant to paragraph (1)(B) to any of 5 positions designated by the Director of the Defense Advanced Research Projects Agency for purposes of this subparagraph, at rates not in excess of a rate equal to 150 percent of the maximum rate of basic pay authorized for positions at Level I of the Executive Schedule under section 5312 of title 5; and

"(B) in the case of any other employee appointed pursuant to paragraph (1), at rates not in excess of the maximum rate of basic pay authorized for senior-level positions under section 5376 of title 5; and

"(3) pay any employee appointed under paragraph (1), other than an employee appointed to a position designated as described in paragraph (2)(A), payments in addition to basic pay within the limit applicable to the employee under subsection (d).

"(c) LIMITATION ON TERM OF APPOINTMENT.—

"(1) IN GENERAL.—Except as provided in paragraph (2), the service of an employee under an appointment under subsection (b)(1) may not exceed four years.

"(2) EXTENSION.—The official responsible for the administration of a program under subsection (a) may, in the case of a particular employee under the program, extend the period to which service is limited under paragraph (1) by up to two years if the official determines that such action is necessary to promote the efficiency of a laboratory of a military department,

the Defense Advanced Research Projects Agency, or the Office of Operational Test and Evaluation, as applicable.

"(d) MAXIMUM AMOUNT OF ADDITIONAL PAYMENTS PAYABLE.—Notwithstanding any other provision of this section or section 5307 of title 5, no additional payments may be paid to an employee under subsection (b)(3) in any calendar year if, or to the extent that, the employee's total annual compensation in such calendar year will exceed the maximum amount of total annual compensation payable at the salary set in accordance with section 104 of title 3.".

(2) CLERICAL AMENDMENT.—The table of sections at the beginning of chapter 81 of such title, as so amended, is further amended by adding at the end the following new item:

"1599h. Personnel management authority to attract experts in science and engineering.".

(b) REPEAL OF SUPERSEDED AUTHORITY.—Section 1101 of the Strom Thurmond National Defense Authorization Act for Fiscal Year 1999 (Public Law 105–261; 5 U.S.C. 3104 note) is repealed.

(c) APPLICABILITY OF PERSONNEL MANAGEMENT AUTHORITY TO PERSONNEL CURRENTLY EMPLOYED UNDER SUPERSEDED AUTHORITY.—

(1) IN GENERAL.—Any individual employed as of the date of the enactment of this Act under section 1101(b)(1) of the Strom Thurmond National Defense Authorization Act for Fiscal Year 1999 (5 U.S.C. 3104 note) (as in effect on the day before such date) shall remain employed under section 1599h of title 10, United States Code (as added by subsection (a)), after such date in accordance with such section 1599h and the applicable program carried out under such section 1599h.

(2) DATE OF APPOINTMENT.—For purposes of subsection (c) of section 1599h of title 10, United States Code (as so added), the date of the appointment of any employee who remains employed as described in paragraph (1) shall be the date of the appointment of such employee under section 1101(b)(1) of the Strom Thurmond National Defense Authorization Act for Fiscal Year 1999 (5 U.S.C. 3104 note) (as so in effect).

SEC. 1122. CODIFICATION AND MODIFICATION OF CERTAIN AUTHORITIES FOR CERTAIN POSITIONS AT DEPARTMENT OF DEFENSE RESEARCH AND ENGINEERING LABORATORIES.

(a) CODIFICATION.—

(1) IN GENERAL.—Chapter 139 of title 10, United States Code, is amended by inserting after section 2358 the following new section:

"**§ 2358a. Authorities for certain positions at science and technology reinvention laboratories**

"(a) AUTHORITY TO MAKE DIRECT APPOINTMENTS.—

"(1) CANDIDATES FOR SCIENTIFIC AND ENGINEERING POSITIONS AT SCIENCE AND TECHNOLOGY REINVENTION LABORATORIES.—The director of any Science and Technology Reinvention Laboratory (hereinafter in this section referred to as an 'STRL') may appoint qualified candidates possessing a bachelor's degree to positions described in paragraph (1) of subsection (b) as an employee in a laboratory described in that paragraph without regard to the provisions of subchapter I of chapter 33 of title 5 (other than sections 3303 and 3328 of such title).

"(2) VETERAN CANDIDATES FOR SIMILAR POSITIONS AT RESEARCH AND ENGINEERING FACILITIES.—The director of any STRL may appoint qualified veteran candidates to positions described in paragraph (2) of subsection (b) as an employee at a laboratory, agency, or organization specified in that paragraph without regard to the provisions of subchapter I of chapter 33 of title 5.

"(3) STUDENTS ENROLLED IN SCIENTIFIC AND ENGINEERING PROGRAMS.—The director of any

STRL may appoint qualified candidates enrolled in a program of undergraduate or graduate instruction leading to a bachelor's or an advanced degree in a scientific, technical, engineering or mathematical course of study at an institution of higher education (as that term is defined in sections 101 and 102 of the Higher Education Act of 1965 (20 U.S.C. 1001, 1002)) to positions described in paragraph (3) of subsection (b) as an employee in a laboratory described in that paragraph without regard to the provisions of subchapter I of chapter 33 of title 5 (other than sections 3303 and 3328 of such title).

"(4) NONCOMPETITIVE CONVERSION TO PERMANENT APPOINTMENT.—With respect to any student appointed by the director of an STRL under paragraph (3) to a temporary or term appointment, upon graduation from the applicable institution of higher education (as defined in such paragraph), the director may noncompetitively convert such student to a permanent appointment within the STRL without regard to the provisions of subchapter I of chapter 33 of title 5 (other than sections 3303 and 3328 of such title), provided the student meets all eligibility and Office of Personnel Management qualification requirements for the position.

"(b) COVERED POSITIONS.—

"(1) CANDIDATES FOR SCIENTIFIC AND ENGINEERING POSITIONS.—The positions described in this paragraph are scientific and engineering positions that may be temporary, term, or permanent in any laboratory designated by section 1105(a) of the National Defense Authorization Act for Fiscal Year 2010 (Public Law 111–84; 10 U.S.C. 2358 note) as a Department of Defense science and technology reinvention laboratory.

"(2) QUALIFIED VETERAN CANDIDATES.—The positions described in this paragraph are scientific, technical, engineering, and mathematics positions, including technicians, in the following:

"(A) Any laboratory referred to in paragraph (1).

"(B) Any other Department of Defense research and engineering agency or organization designated by the Secretary for purposes of subsection (a)(2).

"(3) CANDIDATES ENROLLED IN SCIENTIFIC AND ENGINEERING PROGRAMS.—The positions described in this paragraph are scientific and engineering positions that may be temporary or term in any laboratory designated by section 1105(a) of the National Defense Authorization Act for Fiscal Year 2010 (Public Law 111–84; 10 U.S.C. 2358 note) as a Department of Defense science and technology reinvention laboratory.

"(c) LIMITATION ON NUMBER OF APPOINTMENTS ALLOWABLE IN A CALENDAR YEAR.—The authority under subsection (a) may not, in any calendar year and with respect to any laboratory, agency, or organization described in subsection (b), be exercised with respect to a number of candidates greater than the following:

"(1) In the case of a laboratory described in subsection (b)(1), with respect to appointment authority under subsection (a)(1), the number equal to 6 percent of the total number of scientific and engineering positions in such laboratory that are filled as of the close of the fiscal year last ending before the start of such calendar year.

"(2) In the case of a laboratory, agency, or organization described in subsection (b)(2), with respect to appointment authority under subsection (a)(2), the number equal to 3 percent of the total number of scientific, technical, engineering, mathematics, and technician positions in such laboratory, agency, or organization that are filled as of the close of the fiscal year last ending before the start of such calendar year.

"(3) In the case of a laboratory described in subsection (b)(3), with respect to appointment authority under subsection (a)(3), the number

equal to 10 percent of the total number of scientific and engineering positions in such laboratory that are filled as of the close of the fiscal year last ending before the start of such calendar year.

"(d) SENIOR SCIENTIFIC TECHNICAL MANAGERS.—

"(1) ESTABLISHMENT.—There is hereby established in each STRL a category of senior professional scientific and technical positions, the incumbents of which shall be designated as 'senior scientific technical managers' and which shall be positions classified above GS–15 of the General Schedule, notwithstanding section 5108(a) of title 5. The primary functions of such positions shall be—

"(A) to engage in research and development in the physical, biological, medical, or engineering sciences, or another field closely related to the mission of such STRL; and

"(B) to carry out technical supervisory responsibilities.

"(2) APPOINTMENTS.—The positions described in paragraph (1) may be filled, and shall be managed, by the director of the STRL involved, under criteria established pursuant to section 342(b) of the National Defense Authorization Act for Fiscal Year 1995 (Public Law 103–337; 10 U.S.C. 2358 note), relating to personnel demonstration projects at laboratories of the Department of Defense, except that the director of the laboratory involved shall determine the number of such positions at such laboratory, not to exceed 2 percent of the number of scientists and engineers employed at such laboratory as of the close of the last fiscal year before the fiscal year in which any appointments subject to that numerical limitation are made.

"(e) EXCLUSION FROM PERSONNEL LIMITATIONS.—

"(1) IN GENERAL.—The director of an STRL shall manage the workforce strength, structure, positions, and compensation of such STRL—

"(A) without regard to any limitation on appointments, positions, or funding with respect to such STRL, subject to subparagraph (B); and

"(B) in a manner consistent with the budget available with respect to such STRL.

"(2) EXCEPTIONS.—Paragraph (1) shall not apply to Senior Executive Service positions (as defined in section 3132(a) of title 5) or scientific and professional positions authorized under section 3104 of such title.

"(f) DEFINITIONS.—In this section:

"(1) The term 'employee' has the meaning given that term in section 2105 of title 5.

"(2) The term 'veteran' has the meaning given that term in section 101 of title 38.".

(2) CLERICAL AMENDMENT.—The table of sections at the beginning of chapter 139 of such title is amended by inserting after the item relating to section 2358 the following new item:

"2358a. Authorities for certain positions at science and technology reinvention laboratories.".

(b) REPEAL OF SUPERSEDED SECTION.—Section 1107 of the National Defense Authorization Act for Fiscal Year 2014 (10 U.S.C. 2358 note) is hereby repealed.

SEC. 1123. MODIFICATION TO INFORMATION TECHNOLOGY PERSONNEL EXCHANGE PROGRAM.

Section 1110 of the National Defense Authorization Act for Fiscal Year 2010 (Public Law 111–84; 5 U.S.C. 3702 note) is amended—

(1) in the section heading, by inserting "**CYBER AND**" before "**INFORMATION**".

(2) in subsections (a)(1)(A), (a)(1)(C), and (g)(2), by inserting "cyber operations or" before "information";

(3) in subsection (d), by striking "2018" and inserting "2022";

(4) in subsection (g)(1), by inserting "to or" before "from"; and

(5) in subsection (h), by striking "10" and inserting "50".

SEC. 1124. PILOT PROGRAM ON ENHANCED PAY AUTHORITY FOR CERTAIN RESEARCH AND TECHNOLOGY POSITIONS IN THE SCIENCE AND TECHNOLOGY REINVENTION LABORATORIES OF THE DEPARTMENT OF DEFENSE.

(a) PILOT PROGRAM AUTHORIZED.—The Secretary of Defense may carry out a pilot program to assess the feasibility and advisability of using the pay authority specified in subsection (d) to fix the rate of basic pay for positions described in subsection (c) in order to assist the military departments in attracting and retaining high quality acquisition and technology experts in positions responsible for managing and performing complex, high-cost research and technology development efforts in the science and technology reinvention laboratories of the Department of Defense.

(b) APPROVAL REQUIRED.—The pilot program may be carried out in a military department only with the approval of the Service Acquisition Executive of the military department concerned.

(c) POSITIONS.—The positions described in this subsection are positions in the science and technology reinvention laboratories of the Department of Defense that—

(1) require expertise of an extremely high level in a scientific, technical, professional, or acquisition management field; and

(2) are critical to the successful accomplishment of an important research or technology development mission.

(d) RATE OF BASIC PAY.—The pay authority specified in this subsection is authority as follows:

(1) Authority to fix the rate of basic pay for a position at a rate not to exceed 150 percent of the rate of basic pay payable for level I of the Executive Schedule, upon the approval of the Service Acquisition Executive concerned.

(2) Authority to fix the rate of basic pay for a position at a rate in excess of 150 percent of the rate of basic pay payable for level I of the Executive Schedule, upon the approval of the Secretary of the military department concerned.

(e) LIMITATIONS.—

(1) IN GENERAL.—The authority in subsection (a) may be used only to the extent necessary to competitively recruit or retain individuals exceptionally well qualified for positions described in subsection (c).

(2) NUMBER OF POSITIONS.—The authority in subsection (a) may not be used with respect to more than five positions in each military department at any one time.

(3) TERM OF POSITIONS.—The authority in subsection (a) may be used only for positions having a term of less than five years.

(f) TERMINATION.—

(1) IN GENERAL.—The authority to fix rates of basic pay for a position under this section shall terminate on October 1, 2021.

(2) CONTINUATION OF PAY.—Nothing in paragraph (1) shall be construed to prohibit the payment after October 1, 2021, of basic pay at rates fixed under this section before that date for positions having terms that continue after that date.

(g) SCIENCE AND TECHNOLOGY REINVENTION LABORATORIES OF THE DEPARTMENT OF DEFENSE DEFINED.—In this section, the term "science and technology reinvention laboratories of the Department of Defense" means the laboratories designated as science and technology reinvention laboratories by section 1105(a) of the National Defense Authorization Act for Fiscal Year 2010 (10 U.S.C. 2358 note).

SEC. 1125. TEMPORARY DIRECT HIRE AUTHORITY FOR DOMESTIC DEFENSE INDUSTRIAL BASE FACILITIES, THE MAJOR RANGE AND TEST FACILITIES BASE, AND THE OFFICE OF THE DIRECTOR OF OPERATIONAL TEST AND EVALUATION.

(a) DEFENSE INDUSTRIAL BASE FACILITY AND MRTFB.—During fiscal years 2017 and 2018, the Secretary of Defense may appoint, without regard to the provisions of subchapter I of chapter 33 of title 5, United States Code, other than sections 3303 and 3328 of such title, qualified candidates to positions in the competitive service at any defense industrial base facility or the Major Range and Test Facilities Base.

(b) OFFICE OF THE DIRECTOR OF OPERATIONAL TEST AND EVALUATION.—During fiscal years 2017 through 2021, the Secretary of Defense may, acting through the Director of Operational Test and Evaluation, appoint qualified candidates possessing an advanced degree to scientific and engineering positions within the Office of the Director of Operational Test and Evaluation without regard to the provisions of subchapter I of chapter 33 of title 5, United States Code, other than sections 3303 and 3328 of such title.

(c) DEFINITION OF DEFENSE INDUSTRIAL BASE FACILITY.—In this section, the term "defense industrial base facility" means any Department of Defense depot, arsenal, or shipyard located within the United States.

Subtitle C—Governmentwide Matters

SEC. 1131. ELIMINATION OF TWO-YEAR ELIGIBILITY LIMITATION FOR NONCOMPETITIVE APPOINTMENT OF SPOUSES OF MEMBERS OF THE ARMED FORCES.

Section 3330d(c) of title 5, United States Code, is amended by adding at the end the following new paragraph:

"(3) NO TIME LIMITATION ON APPOINTMENT.—A relocating spouse of a member of the Armed Forces remains eligible for noncompetitive appointment under this section for the duration of the spouse's relocation to the permanent duty station of the member.".

SEC. 1132. TEMPORARY PERSONNEL FLEXIBILITIES FOR DOMESTIC DEFENSE INDUSTRIAL BASE FACILITIES AND MAJOR RANGE AND TEST FACILITIES BASE CIVILIAN PERSONNEL.

(a) IN GENERAL.—Notwithstanding chapter 33 of title 5, United States Code, or any other provision of law relating to the examination, certification, and appointment of individuals in the competitive service, during fiscal years 2017 and 2018, an employee of a defense industrial base facility or the Major Range and Test Facilities Base serving under a time-limited appointment in the competitive service is eligible to compete for a permanent appointment in the competitive service at (A) any such facility, Base, or any other component of the Department of Defense when such facility, Base, or component (as the case may be) is accepting applications from individuals within the facility, Base, or component's workforce under merit promotion procedures, or (B) any agency when the agency is accepting applications from individuals outside its own workforce under merit promotion procedures of the applicable agency, if—

(1) the employee was appointed initially under open, competitive examination under subchapter I of chapter 33 of such title to the time-limited appointment;

(2) the employee has served under 1 or more time-limited appointments by a defense industrial base facility or the Major Range and Test Facilities Base for a period or periods totaling more than 24 months without a break of 2 or more years; and

(3) the employee's performance has been at an acceptable level of performance throughout the period or periods (as the case may be) referred to in paragraph (2).

(b) WAIVER OF AGE REQUIREMENT.—In determining the eligibility of a time-limited employee under this section to be examined for or appointed in the competitive service, the Office of Personnel Management or other examining agency shall waive requirements as to age, unless the requirement is essential to the performance of the duties of the position.

(c) STATUS.—An individual appointed under this section—

(1) becomes a career-conditional employee, unless the employee has otherwise completed the service requirements for career tenure; and

(2) acquires competitive status upon appointment.

(d) FORMER EMPLOYEES.—A former employee of a defense industrial base facility or the Major Range and Test Facilities Base who served under a time-limited appointment and who otherwise meets the requirements of this section shall be deemed a time-limited employee for purposes of this section if—

(1) such employee applies for a position covered by this section within the period of 2 years after the most recent date of separation; and

(2) such employee's most recent separation was for reasons other than misconduct or performance.

(e) BENEFITS.—Any employee of a defense industrial base facility or the Major Range and Test Facilities Base serving under a time-limited appointment in the competitive service shall be provided with benefits that are comparable to the benefits provided to similar employees not serving under time-limited appointments at the defense industrial base facility or the Major Range and Test Facilities Base concerned, including professional development opportunities, eligibility for awards programs, and designation as status applicants for purposes of eligibility for positions in the civil service.

(f) DEFINITION OF DEFENSE INDUSTRIAL BASE FACILITY.—In this section, the term "defense industrial base facility" means any Department of Defense depot, arsenal, or shipyard located within the United States.

SEC. 1133. ONE-YEAR EXTENSION OF TEMPORARY AUTHORITY TO GRANT ALLOWANCES, BENEFITS, AND GRATUITIES TO CIVILIAN PERSONNEL ON OFFICIAL DUTY IN A COMBAT ZONE.

Paragraph (2) of section 1603(a) of the Emergency Supplemental Appropriations Act for Defense, the Global War on Terror, and Hurricane Recovery, 2006 (Public Law 109–234; 120 Stat. 443), as added by section 1102 of the Duncan Hunter National Defense Authorization Act for Fiscal Year 2009 (Public Law 110–417; 122 Stat. 4616) and as most recently amended by section 1102 of the National Defense Authorization Act for Fiscal Year 2016 (Public Law 114–92; 129 Stat. 1022), is further amended by striking "2017" and inserting "2018".

SEC. 1134. ADVANCE PAYMENTS FOR EMPLOYEES RELOCATING WITHIN THE UNITED STATES AND ITS TERRITORIES.

(a) IN GENERAL.—Subsection (a) of section 5524a of title 5, United States Code, is amended—

(1) by striking "(a) The head" and inserting "(a)(1) The head"; and

(2) by adding at the end the following:

"(2) The head of each agency may provide for the advance payment of basic pay, covering not more than 4 pay periods, to an employee who is assigned to a position in the agency that is located—

"(A) outside of the employee's commuting area; and

"(B) in the United States, the Commonwealth of Puerto Rico, the Commonwealth of the Northern Mariana Islands, or any territory or possession of the United States.".

(b) CONFORMING AMENDMENTS.—Subsection (b) of such section is amended—

(1) in paragraph (1), by inserting "or assigned" after "appointed"; and

(2) in paragraph (2)(B)—

(A) by inserting "or assignment" after "appointment"; and

(B) by inserting "or assigned" after "appointed".

(c) CLERICAL AMENDMENTS.—

*(1) SECTION HEADING.—The heading of such section is amended by inserting "**and employees relocating within the United States and its territories**" after "**appointees**".*

(2) TABLE OF SECTIONS.—The item relating to such section in the table of sections of chapter 55 of such title is amended to read as follows:

"5524a. Advance payments for new appointees and employees relocating within the United States and its territories.".

SEC. 1135. ELIGIBILITY OF EMPLOYEES IN A TIME-LIMITED APPOINTMENT TO COMPETE FOR A PERMANENT APPOINTMENT AT ANY FEDERAL AGENCY.

Section 9602 of title 5, United States Code, is amended—

(1) in subsection (a) by striking "any land management agency or any other agency (as defined in section 101 of title 31) under the internal merit promotion procedures of the applicable agency" and inserting "such land management agency when such agency is accepting applications from individuals within the agency's workforce under merit promotion procedures, or any agency, including a land management agency, when the agency is accepting applications from individuals outside its own workforce under the merit promotion procedures of the applicable agency"; and

(2) in subsection (d) by inserting "of the agency from which the former employee was most recently separated" after "deemed a time-limited employee".

SEC. 1136. REVIEW OF OFFICIAL PERSONNEL FILE OF FORMER FEDERAL EMPLOYEES BEFORE REHIRING.

(a) IN GENERAL.—Subchapter I of chapter 33 of title 5, United States Code, is amended by adding at the end the following:

"§ 3330e. Review of official personnel file of former Federal employees before rehiring

"(a) If a former Government employee is a candidate for a position within the competitive service or the excepted service, prior to making any determination with respect to the appointment or reinstatement of such employee to such position, the appointing authority shall review and consider merit-based information relating to such employee's former period or periods of service such as official personnel actions, employee performance ratings, and disciplinary actions, if any, in such employee's official personnel record file.

"(b) In subsection (a), the term 'former Government employee' means an individual whose most recent position with the Government prior to becoming a candidate as described under subsection (a) was within the competitive service or the excepted service.

"(c) The Office of Personnel Management shall prescribe regulations to carry out the purpose of this section. Such regulations may not contain provisions that would increase the time required for agency hiring actions.".

(b) APPLICATION.—The amendment made by subsection (a) shall apply to any former Government employee (as described in section 3330e of title 5, United States Code, as added by such subsection) appointed or reinstated on or after the date that is 180 days after the date of enactment of this Act.

(c) CLERICAL AMENDMENT.—The table of sections of subchapter I of chapter 33 of title 5, United States Code, is amended by adding at the end the following:

"*3330e. Review of official personnel file of former Federal employees before rehiring.*".

SEC. 1137. ONE-YEAR EXTENSION OF AUTHORITY TO WAIVE ANNUAL LIMITATION ON PREMIUM PAY AND AGGREGATE LIMITATION ON PAY FOR FEDERAL CIVILIAN EMPLOYEES WORKING OVERSEAS.

Section 1101(a) of the Duncan Hunter National Defense Authorization Act for Fiscal Year 2009 (Public Law 110–417; 122 Stat. 4615), as most recently amended by section 1108 of the National Defense Authorization Act for Fiscal Year 2016 (Public Law 114–92; 129 Stat. 1027), is further amended by striking "through 2016" and inserting "through 2017".

SEC. 1138. ADMINISTRATIVE LEAVE.

(a) SHORT TITLE.—This section may be cited as the "Administrative Leave Act of 2016".

(b) SENSE OF CONGRESS.—It is the sense of Congress that—

(1) agency use of administrative leave, and leave that is referred to incorrectly as administrative leave in agency recording practices, has exceeded reasonable amounts—

(A) in contravention of—

(i) established precedent of the Comptroller General of the United States; and

(ii) guidance provided by the Office of Personnel Management; and

(B) resulting in significant cost to the Federal Government;

(2) administrative leave should be used sparingly;

(3) prior to the use of paid leave to address personnel issues, an agency should consider other actions, including—

(A) temporary reassignment; and

(B) transfer;

(4) an agency should prioritize and expeditiously conclude an investigation in which an employee is placed in administrative leave so that, not later than the conclusion of the leave period—

(A) the employee is returned to duty status; or

(B) an appropriate personnel action is taken with respect to the employee;

(5) data show that there are too many examples of employees placed in administrative leave for 6 months or longer, leaving the employees without any available recourse to—

(A) return to duty status; or

(B) challenge the decision of the agency;

(6) an agency should ensure accurate and consistent recording of the use of administrative leave so that administrative leave can be managed and overseen effectively; and

(7) other forms of excused absence authorized by law should be recorded separately from administrative leave, as defined by the amendments made by this section.

(c) ADMINISTRATIVE LEAVE.—

(1) IN GENERAL.—Subchapter II of chapter 63 of title 5, United States Code, is amended by adding at the end the following:

"§ 6329a. Administrative leave

"(a) DEFINITIONS.—In this section—

"(1) the term 'administrative leave' means leave—

"(A) without loss of or reduction in—

"(i) pay;

"(ii) leave to which an employee is otherwise entitled under law; or

"(iii) credit for time or service; and

"(B) that is not authorized under any other provision of law;

"(2) the term 'agency'—

"(A) means an Executive agency (as defined in section 105 of this title);

"(B) includes the Department of Veterans Affairs; and

"(C) does not include the Government Accountability Office; and

"(3) the term 'employee'—

"(A) has the meaning given the term in section 2105; and

"(B) does not include an intermittent employee who does not have an established regular tour of duty during the administrative workweek.

"(b) ADMINISTRATIVE LEAVE.—

"(1) IN GENERAL.—During any calendar year, an agency may place an employee in administrative leave for a period of not more than a total of 10 work days.

"(2) RECORDS.—An agency shall record administrative leave separately from leave authorized under any other provision of law.

"(c) REGULATIONS.—

"(1) OPM REGULATIONS.—Not later than 270 calendar days after the date of enactment of this section, the Director of the Office of Personnel Management shall—

"(A) prescribe regulations to carry out this section; and

"(B) prescribe regulations that provide guidance to agencies regarding—

"(i) acceptable agency uses of administrative leave; and

"(ii) the proper recording of—

"(I) administrative leave; and

"(II) other leave authorized by law.

"(2) AGENCY ACTION.—Not later than 270 calendar days after the date on which the Director of the Office of Personnel Management prescribes regulations under paragraph (1), each agency shall revise and implement the internal policies of the agency to meet the requirements of this section.

"(d) RELATION TO OTHER LAWS.—Notwithstanding subsection (a) of section 7421 of title 38, this section shall apply to an employee described in subsection (b) of that section.".

(2) TECHNICAL AND CONFORMING AMENDMENT.—The table of sections for subchapter II of chapter 63 of title 5, United States Code, is amended by inserting after the item relating to section 6329 the following:

"6329a. Administrative leave.".

(d) INVESTIGATIVE LEAVE AND NOTICE LEAVE.—

(1) IN GENERAL.—Subchapter II of chapter 63 of title 5, United States Code, as amended by this section, is further amended by adding at the end the following:

"§ 6329b. Investigative leave and notice leave

"(a) DEFINITIONS.—In this section—

"(1) the term 'agency'—

"(A) means an Executive agency (as defined in section 105 of this title);

"(B) includes the Department of Veterans Affairs; and

"(C) does not include the Government Accountability Office;

"(2) the term 'Chief Human Capital Officer' means—

"(A) the Chief Human Capital Officer of an agency designated or appointed under section 1401; or

"(B) the equivalent;

"(3) the term 'committees of jurisdiction', with respect to an agency, means each committee of the Senate or House of Representatives with jurisdiction over the agency;

"(4) the term 'Director' means the Director of the Office of Personnel Management;

"(5) the term 'employee'—

"(A) has the meaning given the term in section 2105; and

"(B) does not include—

"(i) an intermittent employee who does not have an established regular tour of duty during the administrative workweek; or

"(ii) the Inspector General of an agency;

"(6) the term 'investigative entity' means—

"(A) an internal investigative unit of an agency granting investigative leave under this section;

"(B) the Office of Inspector General of an agency granting investigative leave under this section;

"(C) the Attorney General; and

"(D) the Office of Special Counsel;

"(7) the term 'investigative leave' means leave—

"(A) without loss of or reduction in—

"(i) pay;

"(ii) leave to which an employee is otherwise entitled under law; or

"(iii) credit for time or service;

"(B) that is not authorized under any other provision of law; and

"(C) in which an employee who is the subject of an investigation is placed;

"(8) the term 'notice leave' means leave—

"(A) without loss of or reduction in—

"(i) pay;

"(ii) leave to which an employee is otherwise entitled under law; or

"(iii) credit for time or service;

"(B) that is not authorized under any other provision of law; and

"(C) in which an employee who is in a notice period is placed; and

"(9) the term 'notice period' means a period beginning on the date on which an employee is provided notice required under law of a proposed adverse action against the employee and ending on the date on which an agency may take the adverse action.

"(b) LEAVE FOR EMPLOYEES UNDER INVESTIGATION OR IN A NOTICE PERIOD.—

"(1) AUTHORITY.—An agency may, in accordance with paragraph (2), place an employee in—

"(A) investigative leave if the employee is the subject of an investigation;

"(B) notice leave if the employee is in a notice period; or

"(C) notice leave following a placement in investigative leave if, not later than the day after the last day of the period of investigative leave—

"(i) the agency proposes or initiates an adverse action against the employee; and

"(ii) the agency determines that the employee continues to meet 1 or more of the criteria described in paragraph (2)(A).

"(2) REQUIREMENTS.—An agency may place an employee in leave under paragraph (1) only if the agency has—

"(A) made a determination with respect to the employee that the continued presence of the employee in the workplace during an investigation of the employee or while the employee is in a notice period, as applicable, may—

"(i) pose a threat to the employee or others;

"(ii) result in the destruction of evidence relevant to an investigation;

"(iii) result in loss of or damage to Government property; or

"(iv) otherwise jeopardize legitimate Government interests;

"(B) considered—

"(i) assigning the employee to duties in which the employee no longer poses a threat described in clauses (i) through (iv) of subparagraph (A);

"(ii) allowing the employee to take leave for which the employee is eligible;

"(iii) if the employee is absent from duty without approved leave, carrying the employee in absence without leave status; and

"(iv) for an employee subject to a notice period, curtailing the notice period if there is reasonable cause to believe the employee has committed a crime for which a sentence of imprisonment may be imposed; and

"(C) determined that none of the available options under clauses (i) through (iv) of subparagraph (B) is appropriate.

"(3) DURATION OF LEAVE.—

"(A) INVESTIGATIVE LEAVE.—Upon the expiration of the 10 work day period described in section 6329a(b)(1) with respect to an employee, and if an agency determines that an extended investigation of the employee is necessary, the agency may place the employee in investigative leave for a period of not more than 30 work days.

"(B) NOTICE LEAVE.—Placement of an employee in notice leave shall be for a period not longer than the duration of the notice period.

"(4) EXPLANATION OF LEAVE.—

"(A) IN GENERAL.—If an agency places an employee in leave under this subsection, the agency shall provide the employee a written explanation of whether the employee was placed in investigative leave or notice leave.

"(B) EXPLANATION.—The written notice under subparagraph (A) shall describe the limitations of the leave placement, including—

"(i) the applicable limitations under paragraph (3); and

"(ii) in the case of a placement in investigative leave, an explanation that, at the conclusion of the period of leave, the agency shall take an action under paragraph (5).

"(5) AGENCY ACTION.—Not later than the day after the last day of a period of investigative leave for an employee under paragraph (1), an agency shall—

"(A) return the employee to regular duty status;

"(B) take 1 or more of the actions under clauses (i) through (iv) of paragraph (2)(B);

"(C) propose or initiate an adverse action against the employee as provided under law; or

"(D) extend the period of investigative leave under subsections (c) and (d).

"(6) RULE OF CONSTRUCTION.—Nothing in paragraph (5) shall be construed to prevent the continued investigation of an employee, except that the placement of an employee in investigative leave may not be extended for that purpose except as provided in subsections (c) and (d).

"(c) INITIAL EXTENSION OF INVESTIGATIVE LEAVE.—

"(1) IN GENERAL.—Subject to paragraph (4), if the Chief Human Capital Officer of an agency, or the designee of the Chief Human Capital Officer, approves such an extension after consulting with the investigator responsible for conducting the investigation to which an employee is subject, the agency may extend the period of investigative leave for the employee under subsection (b) for not more than 30 work days.

"(2) MAXIMUM NUMBER OF EXTENSIONS.—The total period of additional investigative leave for an employee under paragraph (1) may not exceed 90 work days.

"(3) DESIGNATION GUIDANCE.—Not later than 270 days after the date of enactment of this section, the Chief Human Capital Officers Council shall issue guidance to ensure that if the Chief Human Capital Officer of an agency delegates the authority to approve an extension under paragraph (1) to a designee, the designee is at a sufficiently high level within the agency to make an impartial and independent determination regarding the extension.

"(4) EXTENSIONS FOR OIG EMPLOYEES.—

"(A) APPROVAL.—In the case of an employee of an Office of Inspector General—

"(i) the Inspector General or the designee of the Inspector General, rather than the Chief Human Capital Officer or the designee of the Chief Human Capital Officer, shall approve an extension of a period of investigative leave for the employee under paragraph (1); or

"(ii) at the request of the Inspector General, the head of the agency within which the Office of Inspector General is located shall designate an official of the agency to approve an extension of a period of investigative leave for the employee under paragraph (1).

"(B) GUIDANCE.—Not later than 270 calendar days after the date of enactment of this section, the Council of the Inspectors General on Integrity and Efficiency shall issue guidance to ensure that if the Inspector General or the head of an agency, at the request of the Inspector General, delegates the authority to approve an extension under subparagraph (A) to a designee, the designee is at a sufficiently high level within the Office of Inspector General or the agency, as applicable, to make an impartial and independent determination regarding the extension.

"(d) FURTHER EXTENSION OF INVESTIGATIVE LEAVE.—

"(1) REPORT.—After reaching the limit under subsection (c)(2) and if an investigative entity submits a certification under paragraph (2) of this subsection, an agency may further extend a period of investigative leave for an employee for periods of not more than 30 work days each if, not later than 5 business days after granting each further extension, the agency submits to the Committee on Homeland Security and Governmental Affairs of the Senate and the Committee on Oversight and Government Reform of the House of Representatives, along with any other committees of jurisdiction, a report containing—

"(A) the title, position, office or agency subcomponent, job series, pay grade, and salary of the employee;

"(B) a description of the duties of the employee;

"(C) the reason the employee was placed in investigative leave;

"(D) an explanation as to why—

"(i) the employee poses a threat described in clauses (i) through (iv) of subsection (b)(2)(A); and

"(ii) the agency is not able to reassign the employee to another position within the agency;

"(E) in the case of an employee required to telework under section 6502(c) during the investigation of the employee—

"(i) the reasons that the agency required the employee to telework under that section; and

"(ii) the duration of the teleworking requirement;

"(F) the status of the investigation of the employee;

"(G) the certification described in paragraph (2); and

"(H) in the case of a completed investigation of the employee—

"(i) the results of the investigation; and

"(ii) the reason that the employee remains in investigative leave.

"(2) CERTIFICATION.—If, after an employee has reached the limit under subsection (c)(2), an investigative entity determines that additional time is needed to complete the investigation of the employee, the investigative entity shall—

"(A) certify to the appropriate agency that additional time is needed to complete the investigation of the employee; and

"(B) include in the certification an estimate of the amount of time that is necessary to complete the investigation of the employee.

"(3) NO EXTENSIONS AFTER COMPLETION OF INVESTIGATION.—An agency may not further extend a period of investigative leave of an employee under paragraph (1) on or after the date that is 30 calendar days after the completion of the investigation of the employee by an investigative entity.

"(e) CONSULTATION GUIDANCE.—Not later than 270 calendar days after the date of enactment of this section, the Council of the Inspectors General on Integrity and Efficiency, in consultation with the Attorney General and the Special Counsel, shall issue guidance on best practices for consultation between an investigator and an agency on the need to place an employee in investigative leave during an investigation of the employee, including during a criminal investigation, because the continued presence of the employee in the workplace during the investigation may—

"(1) pose a threat to the employee or others;

"(2) result in the destruction of evidence relevant to an investigation;

"(3) result in loss of or damage to Government property; or

"(4) otherwise jeopardize legitimate Government interests.

"(f) REPORTING AND RECORDS.—

"(1) IN GENERAL.—An agency shall keep a record of the placement of an employee in investigative leave or notice leave by the agency, including—

"(A) the basis for the determination made under subsection (b)(2)(A);

"(B) an explanation of why an action under clauses (i) through (iv) of subsection (b)(2)(B) was not appropriate;

"(C) the length of the period of leave;

"(D) the amount of salary paid to the employee during the period of leave;

"(E) the reasons for authorizing the leave, including, if applicable, the recommendation made by an investigator under subsection (c)(1);

"(F) whether the employee is required to telework under section 6502(c) during the investigation, including the reasons for requiring the employee to telework; and

"(G) the action taken by the agency at the end of the period of leave, including, if applicable, the granting of any extension of a period of investigative leave under subsection (c) or (d).

"(2) AVAILABILITY OF RECORDS.—An agency shall make a record kept under paragraph (1) available—

"(A) to any committee of jurisdiction, upon request;

"(B) to the Office of Personnel Management; and

"(C) as otherwise required by law, including for the purposes of the Administrative Leave Act of 2016 and the amendments made by that Act.

"(g) RECOURSE TO THE OFFICE OF SPECIAL COUNSEL.—For purposes of subchapter II of chapter 12 and section 1221, placement on investigative leave under subsection (b) of this section for a period of not less than 70 work days shall be considered a personnel action under paragraph (8) or (9) of section 2302(b).

"(h) REGULATIONS.—

"(1) OPM ACTION.—Not later than 270 calendar days after the date of enactment of this section, the Director shall prescribe regulations to carry out this section, including guidance to agencies regarding—

"(A) acceptable purposes for the use of—

"(i) investigative leave; and

"(ii) notice leave;

"(B) the proper recording of—

"(i) the leave categories described in subparagraph (A); and

"(ii) other leave authorized by law;

"(C) baseline factors that an agency shall consider when making a determination that the continued presence of an employee in the workplace may—

"(i) pose a threat to the employee or others;

"(ii) result in the destruction of evidence relevant to an investigation;

"(iii) result in loss or damage to Government property; or

"(iv) otherwise jeopardize legitimate Government interests; and

"(D) procedures and criteria for the approval of an extension of a period of investigative leave under subsection (c) or (d).

"(2) AGENCY ACTION.—Not later than 270 calendar days after the date on which the Director prescribes regulations under paragraph (1), each agency shall revise and implement the internal policies of the agency to meet the requirements of this section.

"(i) RELATION TO OTHER LAWS.—Notwithstanding subsection (a) of section 7421 of title 38, this section shall apply to an employee described in subsection (b) of that section.".

(2) GAO REPORT.—Not later than 5 years after the date of enactment of this Act, and every 5 years thereafter, the Comptroller General of the United States shall submit to the Committee on Homeland Security and Governmental Affairs of the Senate and the Committee on Oversight and Government Reform of the House of Representatives a report on the results of an evaluation of the implementation of the authority provided under sections 6329a and 6329b of title 5, United States Code, as added by subsection (c)(1) of this section and paragraph (1) of this subsection, respectively, including—

(A) the number of times that an agency, under subsection (c)(1) of such section 6329b—

(i) consulted with the investigator responsible for conducting the investigation to which an employee was subject with respect to the decision of the agency to grant an extension under that subsection; and

(ii) did not have a consultation described in clause (i), including the reasons that the agency failed to have such a consultation;

(B) an assessment of the use of the authority provided under subsection (d) of such section 6329b by agencies, including data regarding the number and length of extensions granted under that subsection;

(C) an assessment of the compliance with the requirements of subsection (f) of such section 6329b by agencies;

(D) a review of the practice of agency placement of an employee in investigative or notice leave under subsection (b) of such section 6329b because of a determination under subsection (b)(2)(A)(iv) of that section that the employee jeopardized legitimate Government interests, including the extent to which such determinations were supported by evidence; and

(E) an assessment of the effectiveness of subsection (g) of such section 6329b in preventing and correcting the use of extended investigative leave as a tool of reprisal for making a protected disclosure or engaging in protected activity as described in paragraph (8) or (9) of section 2302(b) of title 5, United States Code.

(3) TELEWORK.—Section 6502 of title 5, United States Code, is amended by adding at the end the following:

"(c) REQUIRED TELEWORK.—If an agency places an employee in investigative leave under section 6329b, the agency may require the employee to, through telework, perform duties similar to the duties that the employee performs onsite if—

"(1) the agency determines that such a requirement would not—

"(A) pose a threat to the employee or others;

"(B) result in the destruction of evidence relevant to an investigation;

"(C) result in the loss of or damage to Government property; or

"(D) otherwise jeopardize legitimate Government interests;

"(2) the employee is eligible to telework under subsections (a) and (b) of this section; and

"(3) the agency determines that it would be appropriate for the employee to perform the duties of the employee through telework.".

(4) TECHNICAL AND CONFORMING AMENDMENT.—The table of sections for subchapter II of chapter 63 of title 5, United States Code, is amended by inserting after the item relating to section 6329a, as added by this section, the following:

"6329b. Investigative leave and notice leave.".

(e) WEATHER AND SAFETY LEAVE.—

(1) IN GENERAL.—Subchapter II of chapter 63 of title 5, United States Code, as amended by this section, is further amended by adding at the end the following:

"**§ 6329c. Weather and safety leave**

"(a) DEFINITIONS.—In this section—

"(1) the term 'agency'—

"(A) means an Executive agency (as defined in section 105 of this title);

"(B) includes the Department of Veterans Affairs; and

"(C) does not include the Government Accountability Office; and

"(2) the term 'employee'—

"(A) has the meaning given the term in section 2105; and

"(B) does not include an intermittent employee who does not have an established regular tour of duty during the administrative workweek.

"(b) LEAVE FOR WEATHER AND SAFETY ISSUES.—An agency may approve the provision of leave under this section to an employee or a group of employees without loss of or reduction in the pay of the employee or employees, leave to which the employee or employees are otherwise entitled, or credit to the employee or employees for time or service only if the employee or group of employees is prevented from safely traveling to or performing work at an approved location due to—

"(1) an act of God;

"(2) a terrorist attack; or

"(3) another condition that prevents the employee or group of employees from safely traveling to or performing work at an approved location.

"(c) RECORDS.—An agency shall record leave provided under this section separately from leave authorized under any other provision of law.

"(d) REGULATIONS.—Not later than 270 days after the date of enactment of this section, the Director of the Office of Personnel Management shall prescribe regulations to carry out this section, including—

"(1) guidance to agencies regarding the appropriate purposes for providing leave under this section; and

"(2) the proper recording of leave provided under this section.

"(e) RELATION TO OTHER LAWS.—Notwithstanding subsection (a) of section 7421 of title 38, this section shall apply to an employee described in subsection (b) of that section.".

(2) TECHNICAL AND CONFORMING AMENDMENT.—The table of sections for subchapter II of chapter 63 of title 5, United States Code, is amended by inserting after the item relating to section 6329b, as added by this section, the following:

"6329c. Weather and safety leave.".

SEC. 1139. DIRECT HIRING FOR FEDERAL WAGE SCHEDULE EMPLOYEES.

The Director of the Office of Personnel Management shall permit an agency with delegated examining authority under 1104(a)(2) of title 5, United States Code, to use direct-hire authority under section 3304(a)(3) of such title for a permanent or non-permanent position or group of positions in the competitive services at GS–15 (or equivalent) and below, or for prevailing rate employees, if the Director determines that there is either a severe shortage of candidates or a critical hiring need for such positions.

SEC. 1140. RECORD OF INVESTIGATION OF PERSONNEL ACTION IN SEPARATED EMPLOYEE'S OFFICIAL PERSONNEL FILE.

(a) IN GENERAL.—Subchapter I of chapter 33 of title 5, United States Code, is amended by inserting after section 3321 the following:

"**§ 3322. Voluntary separation before resolution of personnel investigation**

"(a) With respect to any employee occupying a position in the competitive service or the excepted service who is the subject of a personnel investigation and resigns from Government employment prior to the resolution of such investigation, the head of the agency from which such employee so resigns shall, if an adverse

finding was made with respect to such employee pursuant to such investigation, make a permanent notation in the employee's official personnel record file. The head shall make such notation not later than 40 days after the date of the resolution of such investigation.

"(b) Prior to making a permanent notation in an employee's official personnel record file under subsection (a), the head of the agency shall—

"(1) notify the employee in writing within 5 days of the resolution of the investigation and provide such employee a copy of the adverse finding and any supporting documentation;

"(2) provide the employee with a reasonable time, but not less than 30 days, to respond in writing and to furnish affidavits and other documentary evidence to show why the adverse finding was unfounded (a summary of which shall be included in any notation made to the employee's personnel file under subsection (d)); and

"(3) provide a written decision and the specific reasons therefore to the employee at the earliest practicable date.

"(c) An employee is entitled to appeal the decision of the head of the agency to make a permanent notation under subsection (a) to the Merit Systems Protection Board under section 7701.

"(d)(1) If an employee files an appeal with the Merit Systems Protection Board pursuant to subsection (c), the agency head shall make a notation in the employee's official personnel record file indicating that an appeal disputing the notation is pending not later than 2 weeks after the date on which such appeal was filed.

"(2) If the head of the agency is the prevailing party on appeal, not later than 2 weeks after the date that the Board issues the appeal decision, the head of the agency shall remove the notation made under paragraph (1) from the employee's official personnel record file.

"(3) If the employee is the prevailing party on appeal, not later than 2 weeks after the date that the Board issues the appeal decision, the head of the agency shall remove the notation made under paragraph (1) and the notation of an adverse finding made under subsection (a) from the employee's official personnel record file.

"(e) In this section, the term 'personnel investigation' includes—

"(1) an investigation by an Inspector General; and

"(2) an adverse personnel action as a result of performance, misconduct, or for such cause as will promote the efficiency of the service under chapter 43 or chapter 75.".

(b) APPLICATION.—The amendment made by subsection (a) shall apply to any employee described in section 3322 of title 5, United States Code, (as added by such subsection) who leaves the service after the date of enactment of this Act.

(c) CLERICAL AMENDMENT.—The table of sections of subchapter I of chapter 33 of title 5, United States Code, is amended by inserting after the item relating to section 3321 the following:

"3322. Voluntary separation before resolution of personnel investigation.".

TITLE XII—MATTERS RELATING TO FOREIGN NATIONS

Subtitle A—Assistance and Training

Sec. 1201. One-year extension of logistical support for coalition forces supporting certain United States military operations.

Sec. 1202. Special Defense Acquisition Fund matters.

Sec. 1203. Codification of authority for support of special operations to combat terrorism.

Sec. 1204. *Independent evaluation of strategic framework for Department of Defense security cooperation.*

Sec. 1205. *Sense of Congress regarding an assessment, monitoring, and evaluation framework for security cooperation.*

Subtitle B—Matters Relating to Afghanistan and Pakistan

Sec. 1211. *Extension and modification of Commanders' Emergency Response Program.*

Sec. 1212. *Extension of authority to acquire products and services produced in countries along a major route of supply to Afghanistan.*

Sec. 1213. *Extension and modification of authority to transfer defense articles and provide defense services to the military and security forces of Afghanistan.*

Sec. 1214. *Special immigrant status for certain Afghans.*

Sec. 1215. *Modification to semiannual report on enhancing security and stability in Afghanistan.*

Sec. 1216. *Prohibition on use of funds for certain programs and projects of the Department of Defense in Afghanistan that cannot be safely accessed by United States Government personnel.*

Sec. 1217. *Improvement of oversight of United States Government efforts in Afghanistan.*

Sec. 1218. *Extension and modification of authority for reimbursement of certain coalition nations for support provided to United States military operations.*

Subtitle C—Matters Relating to Syria, Iraq, and Iran

Sec. 1221. *Modification and extension of authority to provide assistance to the vetted Syrian opposition.*

Sec. 1222. *Modification and extension of authority to provide assistance to counter the Islamic State of Iraq and the Levant.*

Sec. 1223. *Extension and modification of authority to support operations and activities of the Office of Security Cooperation in Iraq.*

Sec. 1224. *Limitation on provision of man-portable air defense systems to the vetted Syrian opposition during fiscal year 2017.*

Sec. 1225. *Modification of annual report on military power of Iran.*

Sec. 1226. *Quarterly report on confirmed ballistic missile launches from Iran.*

Subtitle D—Matters Relating to the Russian Federation

Sec. 1231. *Military response options to Russian Federation violation of INF Treaty.*

Sec. 1232. *Limitation on military cooperation between the United States and the Russian Federation.*

Sec. 1233. *Extension and modification of authority on training for Eastern European national military forces in the course of multilateral exercises.*

Sec. 1234. *Prohibition on availability of funds relating to sovereignty of the Russian Federation over Crimea.*

Sec. 1235. *Annual report on military and security developments involving the Russian Federation.*

Sec. 1236. *Limitation on use of funds to vote to approve or otherwise adopt any implementing decision of the Open Skies Consultative Commission and related requirements.*

Sec. 1237. *Extension and enhancement of Ukraine Security Assistance Initiative.*

Sec. 1238. *Reports on INF Treaty and Open Skies Treaty.*

Subtitle E—Reform of Department of Defense Security Cooperation

Sec. 1241. *Enactment of new chapter for defense security cooperation.*

Sec. 1242. *Military-to-military exchanges.*

Sec. 1243. *Consolidation and revision of authorities for payment of personnel expenses necessary for theater security cooperation.*

Sec. 1244. *Transfer and revision of certain authorities on payment of expenses of training and exercises with friendly foreign forces.*

Sec. 1245. *Transfer and revision of authority to provide operational support to forces of friendly foreign countries.*

Sec. 1246. *Department of Defense State Partnership Program.*

Sec. 1247. *Transfer of authority on Regional Defense Combating Terrorism Fellowship Program.*

Sec. 1248. *Consolidation of authorities for service academy international engagement.*

Sec. 1249. *Consolidated annual budget for security cooperation programs and activities of the Department of Defense.*

Sec. 1250. *Department of Defense security cooperation workforce development.*

Sec. 1251. *Reporting requirements.*

Sec. 1252. *Quadrennial review of security sector assistance programs and authorities of the United States Government.*

Sec. 1253. *Other conforming amendments and authority for administration.*

Subtitle F—Human Rights Sanctions

Sec. 1261. *Short title.*

Sec. 1262. *Definitions.*

Sec. 1263. *Authorization of imposition of sanctions.*

Sec. 1264. *Reports to Congress.*

Sec. 1265. *Sunset.*

Subtitle G—Miscellaneous Reports

Sec. 1271. *Modification of annual report on military and security developments involving the People's Republic of China.*

Sec. 1272. *Monitoring and evaluation of overseas humanitarian, disaster, and civic aid programs of the Department of Defense.*

Sec. 1273. *Strategy for United States defense interests in Africa.*

Sec. 1274. *Report on the potential for cooperation between the United States and Israel on directed energy capabilities.*

Sec. 1275. *Annual update of Department of Defense Freedom of Navigation Report.*

Sec. 1276. *Assessment of proliferation of certain remotely piloted aircraft systems.*

Subtitle H—Other Matters

Sec. 1281. *Enhancement of interagency support during contingency operations and transition periods.*

Sec. 1282. *Two-year extension and modification of authorization of non-conventional assisted recovery capabilities.*

Sec. 1283. *Authority to destroy certain specified World War II-era United States-origin chemical munitions located on San Jose Island, Republic of Panama.*

Sec. 1284. *Sense of Congress on military exchanges between the United States and Taiwan.*

Sec. 1285. *Limitation on availability of funds to implement the Arms Trade Treaty.*

Sec. 1286. *Prohibition on use of funds to invite, assist, or otherwise assure the participation of Cuba in certain joint or multilateral exercises.*

Sec. 1287. *Global Engagement Center.*

Sec. 1288. *Modification of United States International Broadcasting Act of 1994.*

Sec. 1289. *Redesignation of South China Sea Initiative.*

Sec. 1290. *Measures against persons involved in activities that violate arms control treaties or agreements with the United States.*

Sec. 1291. *Agreements with foreign governments to develop land-based water resources in support of and in preparation for contingency operations.*

Sec. 1292. *Enhancing defense and security cooperation with India.*

Sec. 1293. *Coordination of efforts to develop free trade agreements with sub-Saharan African countries.*

Sec. 1294. *Extension and expansion of authority to support border security operations of certain foreign countries.*

Sec. 1295. *Modification and clarification of United States-Israel anti-tunnel cooperation authority.*

Sec. 1296. *Maintenance of prohibition on procurement by Department of Defense of People's Republic of China-origin items that meet the definition of goods and services controlled as munitions items when moved to the "600 series" of the Commerce Control List.*

Sec. 1297. *International sales process improvements.*

Sec. 1298. *Efforts to end modern slavery.*

Subtitle A—Assistance and Training

SEC. 1201. ONE-YEAR EXTENSION OF LOGISTICAL SUPPORT FOR COALITION FORCES SUPPORTING CERTAIN UNITED STATES MILITARY OPERATIONS.

Section 1234 of the National Defense Authorization Act for Fiscal Year 2008 (Public Law 110–181; 122 Stat. 394), as most recently amended by section 1201 of the National Defense Authorization Act for Fiscal Year 2016 (Public Law 114–92; 129 Stat. 1035), is further amended—

(1) in subsection (a), by striking "fiscal year 2016" and inserting "fiscal year 2017";

(2) in subsection (d), by striking "during the period beginning on October 1, 2015, and ending on December 31, 2016" and inserting "during the period beginning on October 1, 2016, and ending on December 31, 2017"; and

(3) in subsection (e)(1), by striking "December 31, 2016" and inserting "December 31, 2017".

SEC. 1202. SPECIAL DEFENSE ACQUISITION FUND MATTERS.

(a) INCREASE IN SIZE.—Effective as of October 1, 2016, paragraph (1) of section 114(c) of title 10, United States Code, is amended by striking "$1,070,000,000" and inserting "$2,500,000,000".

(b) LIMITED AVAILABILITY OF CERTAIN AMOUNTS.—Such section is further amended—

(1) in paragraph (2)(A), by striking "limitation in paragraph (1)" and inserting "limitations in paragraphs (1) and (3)"; and

(2) by adding at the end the following new paragraph:

''(3) Of the amount available in the Special Defense Acquisition Fund in any fiscal year after fiscal year 2016, $500,000,000 may be used in such fiscal year only to procure and stock precision guided munitions that may be required by partner and allied forces to enhance the effectiveness of current or future contributions of such forces to overseas contingency operations conducted or supported by the United States.''.

''(c) REPORTS.—

''(1) INITIAL PLAN ON USE OF AUTHORITY.—Before exercising authority for use of amounts in the Special Defense Acquisition Fund in excess of the size of that Fund as of September 30, 2016, by reason of the amendments made by this section, the Secretary of Defense shall, with the concurrence of the Secretary of State, submit to the appropriate committees of Congress a report on the plan for the use of such amounts.

''(2) QUARTERLY SPENDING PLAN.—Not later than 30 days before the beginning of each fiscal year quarter, the Secretary of Defense shall, with the concurrence of the Secretary of State, submit to the appropriate committees of Congress a detailed plan for the use of amounts in the Special Defense Acquisition Fund for such fiscal year quarter.

''(3) ANNUAL UPDATES.—Not later than 90 days after the end of each fiscal year, the Secretary of Defense shall, with the concurrence of the Secretary of State, submit to the appropriate committees of Congress a report setting forth the inventory of defense articles and services acquired, possessed, and transferred through the Special Defense Acquisition Fund in such fiscal year.

''(4) APPROPRIATE COMMITTEES OF CONGRESS DEFINED.—In this subsection, the term ''appropriate committees of Congress'' has the meaning given that term in section 301(1) of title 10, United States Code (as added by section 1241(a)(3) of this Act).

SEC. 1203. CODIFICATION OF AUTHORITY FOR SUPPORT OF SPECIAL OPERATIONS TO COMBAT TERRORISM.

(a) CODIFICATION OF AUTHORITY.—

(1) IN GENERAL.—Chapter 3 of title 10, United States Code, is amended by inserting before section 128 the following new section:

''§ 127e. Support of special operations to combat terrorism

''(a) AUTHORITY.—The Secretary of Defense may, with the concurrence of the relevant Chief of Mission, expend up to $100,000,000 during any fiscal year to provide support to foreign forces, irregular forces, groups, or individuals engaged in supporting or facilitating ongoing military operations by United States special operations forces to combat terrorism.

''(b) FUNDS.—Funds for support under this section in a fiscal year shall be derived from amounts authorized to be appropriated for that fiscal year for the Department of Defense for operation and maintenance.

''(c) PROCEDURES.—The authority in this section shall be exercised in accordance with such procedures as the Secretary shall establish for purposes of this section. The Secretary shall notify the congressional defense committees of any material modification of such procedures.

''(d) NOTIFICATION.—

''(1) IN GENERAL.—Not later than 15 days before exercising the authority in this section to make funds available to initiate support of an approved military operation or changing the scope or funding level of any support for such an operation by $1,000,000 or an amount equal to 20 percent of such funding level (whichever is less), or not later than 48 hours after exercising such authority if the Secretary determines that extraordinary circumstances that impact the national security of the United States exist, the Secretary shall notify the congressional defense committees of the use of such authority with re-

spect to that operation. Any such notification shall be in writing.

''(2) ELEMENTS.—A notification required by this subsection shall include the following:

''(A) The type of support provided or to be provided to United States special operations forces.

''(B) The type of support provided or to be provided to the recipient of the funds.

''(C) The amount obligated under the authority to provide support.

''(e) LIMITATION ON DELEGATION.—The authority of the Secretary to make funds available under this section for support of a military operation may not be delegated.

''(f) INTELLIGENCE ACTIVITIES.—This section does not constitute authority to conduct a covert action, as such term is defined in section 503(e) of the National Security Act of 1947 (50 U.S.C. 3093(e)).

''(g) BIANNUAL REPORTS.—

''(1) REPORT ON PRECEDING CALENDAR YEAR.—Not later than March 1 each year, the Secretary shall submit to the congressional defense committees a report on the support provided under this section during the preceding calendar year.

''(2) REPORT ON CURRENT CALENDAR YEAR.—Not later than September 1 each year, the Secretary shall submit to the congressional defense committees a report on the support provided under this section during the first half of the calendar year in which the report is submitted.

''(3) ELEMENTS.—Each report required by this subsection shall include, for the period covered by such report, the following:

''(A) A summary of the ongoing military operations by United States special operations forces to combat terrorism that were supported or facilitated by foreign forces, irregular forces, groups, or individuals for which support was provided under this section.

''(B) A description of the support or facilitation provided by such foreign forces, irregular forces, groups, or individuals to United States special operations forces.

''(C) The type of recipients that were provided support under this section, identified by authorized category (foreign forces, irregular forces, groups, or individuals).

''(D) The total amount obligated for support under this section, including budget details.

''(E) The total amount obligated in prior fiscal years under this section and applicable preceding authority.

''(F) The intended duration of support provided under this section.

''(G) A description of the support or training provided to the recipients of support under this section.

''(H) A value assessment of the support provided under this section, including a summary of significant activities undertaken by foreign forces, irregular forces, groups, or individuals to support operations by United States special operations forces to combat terrorism.''.

(2) CLERICAL AMENDMENT.—The table of sections at the beginning of chapter 3 of such title is amended by inserting before the item relating to section 128 the following new item:

''127e. Support of special operations to combat terrorism.''.

(b) REPEAL OF SUPERSEDED AUTHORITY.—Section 1208 of the Ronald W. Reagan National Defense Authorization Act for Fiscal Year 2005 (Public Law 108–375) is repealed.

SEC. 1204. INDEPENDENT EVALUATION OF STRATEGIC FRAMEWORK FOR DEPARTMENT OF DEFENSE SECURITY COOPERATION.

(a) EVALUATION REQUIRED.—

(1) IN GENERAL.—The Secretary of Defense shall enter into an agreement with a federally funded research and development center, or another appropriate independent entity, with ex-

pertise in security cooperation to conduct an evaluation of the implementation of the strategic framework for Department of Defense security cooperation, as directed by section 1202 of the National Defense Authorization Act for Fiscal Year 2016 (Public Law 114–92; 129 Stat. 1036; 10 U.S.C. 113 note).

(2) ELEMENTS.—The evaluation under paragraph (1) shall include the following:

(A) An evaluation of the Department of Defense's implementation of each of the required elements of the strategic framework.

(B) An evaluation of the impact of the strategic framework on Department of Defense security cooperation activities, including the extent to which such activities are being planned, prioritized, and executed in accordance with the strategic framework.

(C) Recommendations of areas in which additional guidance, or additional specificity within existing guidance, is necessary to achieve greater alignment between Department of Defense security cooperation activities and the strategic goals and priorities identified within the strategic framework.

(D) Any other matters the entity that conducts the evaluation considers appropriate.

(b) REPORT REQUIRED.—

(1) IN GENERAL.—Not later than November 1, 2018, the Secretary of Defense shall submit to the congressional defense committees, the Committee on Foreign Relations of the Senate, and the Committee on Foreign Affairs of the House of Representatives a report that includes the evaluation under subsection (a) and any other matters the Secretary considers appropriate.

(2) FORM.—The report required under paragraph (1) shall be submitted in unclassified form, but may include a classified annex.

SEC. 1205. SENSE OF CONGRESS REGARDING AN ASSESSMENT, MONITORING, AND EVALUATION FRAMEWORK FOR SECURITY COOPERATION.

It is the sense of Congress that—

(1) the Secretary of Defense should develop and maintain an assessment, monitoring, and evaluation framework for security cooperation with foreign countries to ensure accountability and foster implementation of best practices; and

(2) such framework—

(A) should be consistent with interagency approaches and existing best practices;

(B) should be sufficiently resourced and appropriately placed within the Department of Defense to enable the rigorous examination and measurement of security cooperation efforts towards meeting stated objectives and outcomes; and

(C) should be used to inform security cooperation planning, policies, and resource decisions as well as ensure the effectiveness and efficiency of security cooperation efforts.

Subtitle B—Matters Relating to Afghanistan and Pakistan

SEC. 1211. EXTENSION AND MODIFICATION OF COMMANDERS' EMERGENCY RESPONSE PROGRAM.

(a) EXTENSION.—Section 1201 of the National Defense Authorization Act for Fiscal Year 2012 (Public Law 112–81; 125 Stat. 1619), as most recently amended by section 1211 of the National Defense Authorization Act for Fiscal Year 2016 (Public Law 114–92; 129 Stat. 1042), is further amended—

(1) in subsection (a)—

(A) by striking ''During fiscal year 2016'' and inserting ''During the period beginning on October 1, 2016, and ending on December 31, 2018''; and

(B) by striking ''in such fiscal year'' and inserting ''in such period'';

(2) in subsection (b), by striking ''fiscal year 2016'' and inserting ''fiscal year 2017 and fiscal year 2018''; and

(3) in subsection (f), by striking "in fiscal year 2016" and inserting "during the period beginning on October 1, 2016, and ending on December 31, 2018".

(b) AUTHORITY FOR CERTAIN PAYMENTS TO REDRESS INJURY AND LOSS IN AFGHANISTAN, IRAQ, AND SYRIA.—

(1) IN GENERAL.—During the period beginning on October 1, 2016, and ending on December 31, 2018, amounts available pursuant to section 1201 of the National Defense Authorization Act for Fiscal Year 2012, as amended by this section, shall also be available for ex gratia payments for damage, personal injury, or death that is incident to combat operations of the Armed Forces in Afghanistan, Iraq, or Syria.

(2) NOTICE.—The Secretary of Defense shall, upon each exercise of the authority in this subsection, submit to the congressional defense committees a report setting forth the following:

(A) The amount that will be used for payments pursuant to this subsection.

(B) The manner in which claims for payments shall be verified.

(C) The officers or officials who shall be authorized to approve claims for payments.

(D) The manner in which payments shall be made.

(3) AUTHORITIES APPLICABLE TO PAYMENT.—Any payment made pursuant to this subsection shall be made in accordance with the authorities and limitations in section 8121 of the Department of Defense Appropriations Act, 2015 (division C of Public Law 113–235), other than subsection (h) of such section.

(4) CONSTRUCTION WITH RESTRICTION ON AMOUNT OF PAYMENTS.—For purposes of the application of subsection (e) of such section 1201, as so amended, to any payment pursuant to this subsection, such payment shall be deemed to be a project described by such subsection (e).

SEC. 1212. EXTENSION OF AUTHORITY TO ACQUIRE PRODUCTS AND SERVICES PRODUCED IN COUNTRIES ALONG A MAJOR ROUTE OF SUPPLY TO AFGHANISTAN.

Section 801(f) of the National Defense Authorization Act for Fiscal Year 2010 (Public Law 111–84; 123 Stat. 2399), as most recently amended by section 1214 of the National Defense Authorization Act for Fiscal Year 2016 (Public Law 114–92; 129 Stat. 1045), is further amended by striking "December 31, 2016" and inserting "December 31, 2018".

SEC. 1213. EXTENSION AND MODIFICATION OF AUTHORITY TO TRANSFER DEFENSE ARTICLES AND PROVIDE DEFENSE SERVICES TO THE MILITARY AND SECURITY FORCES OF AFGHANISTAN.

(a) EXPIRATION.—Subsection (h) of section 1222 of the National Defense Authorization Act for Fiscal Year 2013 (Public Law 112–239; 126 Stat. 1992), as most recently amended by section 1215 of the National Defense Authorization Act for Fiscal Year 2016 (Public Law 114–92; 129 Stat. 1045), is further amended by striking "December 31, 2016" and inserting "December 31, 2017".

(b) CONVERSION OF QUARTERLY REPORTS INTO ANNUAL REPORTS.—Effective on January 1, 2017, subsection (f) of such section 1222, as so amended, is further amended—

(1) in the subsection heading, by striking "QUARTERLY" and inserting "ANNUAL"; and

(2) in paragraph (1)—

(A) by striking "Not later than 90 days" and all that follows through "in which the authority in subsection (a) is exercised" and inserting "Not later than March 31 of any year following a year in which the authority in subsection (a) is exercised"; and

(B) by striking "during the 90-day period ending on the date of such report" and inserting "during the preceding year".

(c) EXCESS DEFENSE ARTICLES.—Subsection (i)(2) of such section 1222, as so amended, is fur-

ther amended by striking "During fiscal years 2013, 2014, 2015, and 2016" each place it appears and inserting "Through December 31, 2017,".

SEC. 1214. SPECIAL IMMIGRANT STATUS FOR CERTAIN AFGHANS.

(a) ALIENS DESCRIBED.—Section 602(b)(2)(A)(ii)(I) of the Afghan Allies Protection Act of 2009 (8 U.S.C. 1101 note) is amended to read as follows:

"(I)(aa) by, or on behalf of, the United States Government, in the case of an alien submitting an application for Chief of Mission approval pursuant to subparagraph (D) before the date of the enactment of the National Defense Authorization Act for Fiscal Year 2017; or

"(bb) by, or on behalf of, the United States Government, in the case of an alien submitting an application for Chief of Mission approval pursuant to subparagraph (D) on or after the date of the enactment of the National Defense Authorization Act for Fiscal Year 2017, which employment required the alien—

"(AA) to serve as an interpreter or translator for personnel of the Department of State or the United States Agency for International Development in Afghanistan, particularly while traveling away from United States embassies or consulates with such personnel;

"(BB) to serve as an interpreter or translator for United States military personnel in Afghanistan, particularly while traveling off-base with such personnel; or

"(CC) to perform sensitive and trusted activities for the United States Government in Afghanistan; or".

(b) NUMERICAL LIMITATIONS.—Section 602(b)(3)(F) of such Act is amended—

(1) in the matter preceding clause (i), by striking "7,000" and inserting "8,500"; and

(2) in each of clauses (i) and (ii), by striking "December 31, 2016;" and inserting "December 31, 2020".

(c) REPORT.—Section 602(b)(14) of such Act is amended—

(1) by striking "Not later than 60 days after the date of the enactment of this paragraph," and inserting "Not later than December 31, 2016, and annually thereafter through January 31, 2021,"; and

(2) in subparagraph (A)(i), by striking "under this section;" and inserting "under subclause (I) or (II)(bb) of paragraph (2)(A)(ii);".

SEC. 1215. MODIFICATION TO SEMIANNUAL REPORT ON ENHANCING SECURITY AND STABILITY IN AFGHANISTAN.

(a) REPORTS REQUIRED.—Subsection (a)(2) of section 1225 of the Carl Levin and Howard P. "Buck" McKeon National Defense Authorization Act for Fiscal Year 2015 (Public Law 113–291; 128 Stat. 3550) is amended by striking "December 15, 2017" and inserting "December 15, 2019".

(b) MATTERS TO BE INCLUDED.—Subsection (b) of such section is amended by adding at the end the following:

"(8) AFGHAN PERSONNEL AND PAY SYSTEM.—A description of the status of the implementation of the Afghan Personnel and Pay System (APPS) at the Afghan Ministry of Interior and the Afghan Ministry of Defense for personnel funds provided through the Afghanistan Security Forces Fund, including, with respect to each such Ministry—

"(A) the expected completion date for full implementation of the APPS;

"(B) the extent to which the APPS is being utilized;

"(C) an explanation of any challenges or delays affecting full implementation of the APPS;

"(D) a description of the steps taken to mitigate fraud, waste, and abuse in the disbursement of personnel funds prior to full implementation of the APPS; and

"(E) an estimate of cost savings by reason of full implementation of the APPS.".

SEC. 1216. PROHIBITION ON USE OF FUNDS FOR CERTAIN PROGRAMS AND PROJECTS OF THE DEPARTMENT OF DEFENSE IN AFGHANISTAN THAT CANNOT BE SAFELY ACCESSED BY UNITED STATES GOVERNMENT PERSONNEL.

(a) PROHIBITION.—

(1) IN GENERAL.—Amounts available to the Department of Defense may not be obligated or expended for a construction or other infrastructure program or project of the Department in Afghanistan if military or civilian personnel of the United States Government or their representatives with authority to conduct oversight of such program or project cannot safely access such program or project.

(2) APPLICABILITY.—Paragraph (1) shall apply only with respect to a program or project that is initiated on or after the date of the enactment of this Act.

(b) WAIVER.—

(1) IN GENERAL.—The prohibition in subsection (a) may be waived with respect to a program or project otherwise covered by that subsection if a determination described in paragraph (2) is made as follows:

(A) In the case of a program or project with an estimated lifecycle cost of less than $1,000,000, by the contracting officer assigned to oversee the program or project.

(B) In the case of a program or project with an estimated lifecycle cost of $1,000,000 or more, but less than $20,000,000, by the Commander of the Combined Security Transition Command-Afghanistan.

(C) In the case of a program or project with an estimated lifecycle cost of $20,000,000 or more, but less than $40,000,000, by the Commander of United States Forces-Afghanistan.

(D) In the case of a program or project with an estimated lifecycle cost of $40,000,000 or more, by the Secretary of Defense.

(2) DETERMINATION.—A determination described in this paragraph with respect to a program or project is a determination of each of the following:

(A) That the program or project clearly contributes to United States national interests or strategic objectives.

(B) That the Government of Afghanistan has requested or expressed a need for the program or project.

(C) That the program or project has been coordinated with the Government of Afghanistan, and with any other implementing agencies or international donors.

(D) That security conditions permit effective implementation and oversight of the program or project.

(E) That the program or project includes safeguards to detect, deter, and mitigate corruption and waste, fraud, and abuse of funds.

(F) That adequate arrangements have been made for the sustainment of the program or project following its completion, including arrangements with respect to funding and technical capacity for sustainment.

(G) That meaningful metrics have been established to measure the progress and effectiveness of the program or project in meeting its objectives.

(3) NOTICE ON CERTAIN WAIVERS.—In the event a waiver is issued under paragraph (1) for a program or project described in subparagraph (D) of that paragraph, the Secretary of Defense shall notify Congress of the waiver not later than 15 days after the issuance of the waiver.

SEC. 1217. IMPROVEMENT OF OVERSIGHT OF UNITED STATES GOVERNMENT EFFORTS IN AFGHANISTAN.

(a) REPORT ON IG OVERSIGHT ACTIVITIES IN AFGHANISTAN DURING FISCAL YEAR 2017.—Not later than 60 days after the date of the enactment of this Act, the Lead Inspector General for

Operation Freedom's Sentinel, as designated pursuant to section 8L of the Inspector General Act of 1978 (5 U.S.C. App.), shall, in coordination with the Inspector General of the Department of State, the Inspector General of the United States Agency for International Development, and the Special Inspector General for Afghanistan Reconstruction, submit to the appropriate committees of Congress a report on the oversight activities of United States Inspectors General in Afghanistan planned for fiscal year 2017.

(b) ELEMENTS.—The report required by subsection (a) shall include the following:

(1) A description of the requirements, responsibilities, and focus areas of each Inspector General of the United States planning to conduct oversight activities in Afghanistan during fiscal year 2017.

(2) A comprehensive list of the funding to be used for the oversight activities described in paragraph (1).

(3) A list of the oversight activities and products anticipated to be produced by each Inspector General of the United States in connection with oversight activities in Afghanistan during fiscal year 2017.

(4) An identification of any anticipated overlap among the planned oversight activities of Inspectors General of the United States in Afghanistan during fiscal year 2017, and a justification for such overlap.

(5) A description of the processes by which the Inspectors General of the United States coordinate and reduce redundancies in requests for information to United States Government officials executing funds in Afghanistan.

(6) A description of the specific professional standards expected to be used to ensure the quality of different types of products issued by the Inspectors General regarding Afghanistan, including periodic reports to Congress and audits of Federal establishments, organizations, programs, activities, and functions.

(7) Any other matters the Lead Inspector General for Operation Freedom's Sentinel considers appropriate.

(c) APPROPRIATE COMMITTEES OF CONGRESS DEFINED.—In this section, the term "appropriate committees of Congress" means—

(1) the Committee on Armed Services, the Committee on Foreign Relations, the Committee on Homeland Security and Governmental Affairs, and the Committee Appropriations of the Senate; and

(2) the Committee on Armed Services, the Committee on Foreign Affairs, the Committee on Homeland Security, and the Committee Appropriations of the House of Representatives.

SEC. 1218. EXTENSION AND MODIFICATION OF AUTHORITY FOR REIMBURSEMENT OF CERTAIN COALITION NATIONS FOR SUPPORT PROVIDED TO UNITED STATES MILITARY OPERATIONS.

(a) EXTENSION.—Subsection (a) of section 1233 of the National Defense Authorization Act for Fiscal Year 2008 (Public Law 110–181; 122 Stat. 393), as most recently amended by section 1212 of the National Defense Authorization Act for Fiscal Year 2016 (Public Law 114–92; 129 Stat. 1043), is further amended by striking "fiscal year 2016" and inserting "the period beginning on October 1, 2016, and ending on December 31, 2017,".

(b) MODIFICATION OF AUTHORITIES.—Such section, as so amended, is further amended—

(1) in subsection (a), by striking "the Secretary of Defense may reimburse any key cooperating nation" and all that follows and inserting "the Secretary of Defense may reimburse—

"(1) any key cooperating nation (other than Pakistan) for—

"(A) logistical and military support provided by that nation to or in connection with United States military operations in Afghanistan, Iraq, or Syria; and

"(B) logistical, military, and other support, including access, provided by that nation to or in connection with United States military operations described in subparagraph (A); and

"(2) Pakistan for certain activities meant to enhance the security situation in the Afghanistan-Pakistan border region and for counterterrorism."; and

(2) in subsection (b), by striking "in Iraq or in Operation Enduring Freedom in Afghanistan" and inserting "in Afghanistan, Iraq, or Syria".

(c) LIMITATION ON AMOUNTS AVAILABLE.—Subsection (d)(1) of such section, as so amended, is further amended—

(1) in the second sentence, by striking "during fiscal year 2016 may not exceed $1,160,000,000" and inserting "during the period beginning on October 1, 2016, and ending on December 31, 2017, may not exceed $1,100,000,000";

(2) in the third sentence, by striking "fiscal year 2016" and inserting "the period beginning on October 1, 2016, and ending on December 31, 2017,"; and

(3) by striking the first sentence.

(d) REIMBURSEMENT OF PAKISTAN FOR SECURITY ENHANCEMENT ACTIVITIES.—Such section, as so amended, is further amended—

(1) by redesignating subsections (e), (f), and (g) as subsections (f), (g), and (h), respectively; and

(2) by inserting after subsection (d) the following:

"(e) REIMBURSEMENT OF PAKISTAN FOR SECURITY ENHANCEMENT ACTIVITIES.—

"(1) ACTIVITIES.—Reimbursement authorized by subsection (a)(2) may be provided for activities as follows:

"(A) Counterterrorism activities, including the following:

"(i) Eliminating infrastructure, training areas, and sanctuaries used by terrorist groups, and preventing the establishment of new or additional infrastructure, training areas, and sanctuaries.

"(ii) Direct action against individuals that are involved in or supporting terrorist activities.

"(iii) Any other activity recognized by the Secretary of Defense as a counterterrorism activity for purposes of subsection (a)(2).

"(B) Border security activities along the Afghanistan-Pakistan border, including the following:

"(i) Building and maintaining border outposts.

"(ii) Strengthening cooperative efforts between the Pakistan military and the Afghan National Defense and Security Forces, including border security cooperation.

"(iii) Maintaining access to and securing key ground lines of communication.

"(iv) Providing training and equipment for the Pakistan Frontier Corps Khyber Pakhtunkhwa.

"(v) Improving interoperability between the Pakistan military and the Pakistan Frontier Corps Khyber Pakhtunkhwa.

"(C) Any activities carried out by the Pakistan military that the Secretary of Defense determines and reports to the appropriate congressional committees have enhanced the security of United States personnel stationed in Afghanistan or enhanced the effectiveness of United States military personnel in conducting counterterrorism operations and training, advising, and assisting the Afghan National Defense and Security Forces.

"(2) REPORT.—Not later than December 31, 2017, the Secretary of Defense shall submit to the appropriate congressional committees a report on the expenditure of funds under the authority in subsection (a)(2), including a description of the following:

"(A) The purpose for which such funds were expended.

"(B) Each organization on whose behalf such funds were expended, including the amount expended on such organization and the number of members of such organization supported by such amount.

"(C) Any limitation imposed on the expenditure of funds under subsection (a)(2), including on any recipient of funds or any use of funds expended.

"(3) INFORMATION ON CLAIMS DISALLOWED OR DEFERRED BY THE UNITED STATES.—

"(A) IN GENERAL.—The Secretary of Defense shall submit to the appropriate congressional committees, in the manner specified in subparagraph (B), an itemized description of the costs claimed by the Government of Pakistan for activities specified in paragraph (1) provided by Government of Pakistan to the United States for which the United States will disallow or defer reimbursement to the Government of Pakistan under the authority in subsection (a)(2).

"(B) MANNER OF SUBMITTAL.—

"(i) IN GENERAL.—To the maximum extent practicable, the Secretary shall submit each itemized description of costs required by subparagraph (A) not later than 180 days after the date on which a decision to disallow or defer reimbursement for the costs claimed is made.

"(ii) FORM.—Each itemized description of costs under clause (i) shall be submitted in an unclassified form, but may include a classified annex.".

(e) EXTENSION OF NOTICE REQUIREMENT RELATING TO REIMBURSEMENT OF PAKISTAN FOR SUPPORT PROVIDED BY PAKISTAN.—Section 1232(b)(6) of the National Defense Authorization Act for Fiscal Year 2008 (122 Stat. 393), as most recently amended by section 1212(c) of the National Defense Authorization Act for Fiscal Year 2016 (129 Stat. 1043), is further amended by striking "September 30, 2016" and inserting "December 31, 2017".

(f) EXTENSION OF LIMITATION ON REIMBURSEMENT OF PAKISTAN PENDING CERTIFICATION ON PAKISTAN.—Section 1227(d)(1) of the National Defense Authorization Act for Fiscal Year 2013 (Public Law 112–239; 126 Stat. 2001), as most recently amended by section 1212(d) of the National Defense Authorization Act for Fiscal Year 2016 (129 Stat. 1043), is further amended by striking "for fiscal year 2016 or any prior fiscal year" and inserting "for any period prior to December 31, 2017".

(g) ADDITIONAL LIMITATION ON REIMBURSEMENT OF PAKISTAN PENDING CERTIFICATION ON PAKISTAN.—Of the total amount of reimbursements and support authorized for Pakistan during the period beginning on October 1, 2016, and ending on December 31, 2017, pursuant to the third sentence of section 1233(d)(1) of the National Defense Authorization Act for Fiscal Year 2008 (as amended by subsection (b)(2)), $400,000,000 shall not be eligible for the waiver under section 1227(d)(2) of the National Defense Authorization Act for Fiscal Year 2013 (126 Stat. 2001) unless the Secretary of Defense certifies to the congressional defense committees that—

(1) Pakistan continues to conduct military operations that are contributing to significantly disrupting the safe haven and freedom of movement of the Haqqani Network in Pakistan;

(2) Pakistan has taken steps to demonstrate its commitment to prevent the Haqqani Network from using any Pakistani territory as a safe haven;

(3) the Government of Pakistan actively coordinates with the Government of Afghanistan to restrict the movement of militants, such as the Haqqani Network, along the Afghanistan-Pakistan border; and

(4) Pakistan has shown progress in arresting and prosecuting Haqqani Network senior leaders and mid-level operatives.

Subtitle C—Matters Relating to Syria, Iraq, and Iran

SEC. 1221. MODIFICATION AND EXTENSION OF AUTHORITY TO PROVIDE ASSISTANCE TO THE VETTED SYRIAN OPPOSITION.

(a) IN GENERAL.—Subsection (a) of section 1209 of the Carl Levin and Howard P. "Buck" McKeon National Defense Authorization Act for Fiscal Year 2015 (Public Law 113–291; 128 Stat. 3541) is amended by striking "December 31, 2016" and inserting "December 31, 2018".

(b) REPROGRAMMING REQUIREMENT.—Subsection (f) of such section, as amended by section 1225(e) of the National Defense Authorization Act for Fiscal Year 2016 (Public Law 114–92; 129 Stat. 1055), is further amended in paragraph (1) by striking "December 31, 2016" and inserting "December 31, 2018".

SEC. 1222. MODIFICATION AND EXTENSION OF AUTHORITY TO PROVIDE ASSISTANCE TO COUNTER THE ISLAMIC STATE OF IRAQ AND THE LEVANT.

(a) AUTHORITY.—Subsection (a) of section 1236 of the Carl Levin and Howard P. "Buck" McKeon National Defense Authorization Act for Fiscal Year 2015 (Public Law 113–291; 128 Stat. 3559) is amended by striking "December 31, 2016" and inserting "December 31, 2018".

(b) FUNDING.—Subsection (g) of such section, as amended by section 1223 of the National Defense Authorization Act for Fiscal Year 2016 (Public Law 114–92; 129 Stat. 1049), is further amended—

(1) by striking the first sentence and inserting the following: "Of the amounts authorized to be appropriated in the National Defense Authorization Act for Fiscal Year 2017 for Overseas Contingency Operations in title XV for fiscal year 2017, there are authorized to be appropriated $630,000,000 to carry out this section."; and

(2) by striking the second sentence.

(c) ADDITIONAL ASSESSMENT ON CERTAIN ACTIONS BY GOVERNMENT OF IRAQ.—Subsection (i) of such section, as added by section 1223(e) of the National Defense Authorization Act for Fiscal Year 2016 (Public Law 114–92; 129 Stat. 1050), is amended in paragraph (1)(A) by striking "National Defense Authorization Act for Fiscal Year 2016" and inserting "National Defense Authorization Act for Fiscal Year 2017, and annually thereafter".

(d) PROHIBITION ON ASSISTANCE AND REPORT ON EQUIPMENT OR SUPPLIES TRANSFERRED TO OR ACQUIRED BY VIOLENT EXTREMIST ORGANIZATIONS.—Subsection (f) of section 1223 of the National Defense Authorization Act for Fiscal Year 2016 (Public Law 114–92; 129 Stat. 1050) is amended—

(1) in paragraph (1)—

(A) by striking ", as so amended,"; and

(B) by inserting "(and annually thereafter until December 31, 2018)" after "certifies to the appropriate congressional committees, after the date of the enactment of this Act"; and

(2) in paragraph (2), by striking ", as so amended,".

SEC. 1223. EXTENSION AND MODIFICATION OF AUTHORITY TO SUPPORT OPERATIONS AND ACTIVITIES OF THE OFFICE OF SECURITY COOPERATION IN IRAQ.

(a) EXTENSION OF AUTHORITY.—Subsection (f)(1) of section 1215 of the National Defense Authorization Act for Fiscal Year 2012 (Public Law 112–81; 125 Stat. 1631; 10 U.S.C. 113 note), as most recently amended by section 1221 of the National Defense Authorization Act for Fiscal Year 2016 (Public Law 114–92; 129 Stat. 1047), is further amended by striking "fiscal year 2016" and inserting "fiscal year 2017".

(b) LIMITATION ON AMOUNT.—Subsection (c) of such section is amended—

(1) by striking "fiscal year 2016" and inserting "fiscal year 2017"; and

(2) by striking "$80,000,000" and inserting "$70,000,000".

(c) SOURCE OF FUNDS.—Subsection (d) of such section is amended by striking "fiscal year 2016" and inserting "fiscal year 2017".

SEC. 1224. LIMITATION ON PROVISION OF MANPORTABLE AIR DEFENSE SYSTEMS TO THE VETTED SYRIAN OPPOSITION DURING FISCAL YEAR 2017.

(a) NOTICE AND WAIT.—If a determination is made during fiscal year 2017 to use funds available to the Department of Defense for that fiscal year to provide man-portable air defense systems (MANPADs) to the vetted Syrian opposition pursuant to the authority in section 1209 of the Carl Levin and Howard P. "Buck" McKeon National Defense Authorization Act for Fiscal Year 2015 (Public Law 113–291; 128 Stat. 3541), such funds may not be used for that purpose until—

(1) the Secretary of Defense and the Secretary of State jointly submit to the appropriate congressional committees a report on the determination; and

(2) 30 days elapses after the date of the submittal of such report to the appropriate congressional committees.

(b) ELEMENTS.—The report under subsection (a) shall set forth the following:

(1) A description of each element of the vetted Syrian opposition that will provided man-portable air defense systems as described in subsection (a), including—

(A) the geographic location of such element;

(B) a detailed intelligence assessment of such element;

(C) a description of the alignment of such element within the broader conflict in Syria; and

(D) a description and assessment of the assurance, if any, received by the commander of such element in connection with the provision of man-portable air defense systems.

(2) The number and type of man-portable air defense systems to be so provided.

(3) The logistics plan for providing and resupplying each element to be so provided man-portable air defense systems with additional man-portable air defense systems.

(4) The duration of support to be provided in connection with the provision of man-portable air defense systems.

(5) The justification for the provision of man-portable air defense systems to each element of the vetted Syrian opposition, including an explanation of the purpose and expected employment of such systems.

(6) Any other matters that the Secretary of Defense and the Secretary of State jointly consider appropriate.

(c) APPROPRIATE CONGRESSIONAL COMMITTEES DEFINED.—In this section, the term "appropriate congressional committees" has the meaning given that term in section 1209(e)(2) of the Carl Levin and Howard P. "Buck" McKeon National Defense Authorization Act for Fiscal Year 2015.

SEC. 1225. MODIFICATION OF ANNUAL REPORT ON MILITARY POWER OF IRAN.

(a) IN GENERAL.—Section 1245(b)(3) of the National Defense Authorization Act for Fiscal Year 2010 (10 U.S.C. 113 note) is amended by striking subparagraph (F) and inserting the following new subparagraph (F):

"(F) Iran's cyber capabilities, including—

"(i) Iran's ability to use proxies and other actors to mask its cyber operations;

"(ii) Iran's ability to target United States governmental and nongovernmental entities and activities; and

"(iii) cooperation with or assistance from state and non-state actors in support or enhancement of Iran's cyber capabilities;".

(b) EFFECTIVE DATE.—The amendment made by subsection (a) shall take effect on January 1, 2018, and shall apply with respect to reports required to be submitted under section 1245 of the National Defense Authorization Act for Fiscal Year 2010 on or after that date.

SEC. 1226. QUARTERLY REPORT ON CONFIRMED BALLISTIC MISSILE LAUNCHES FROM IRAN.

(a) QUARTERLY REPORT ON CONFIRMED LAUNCHES.—Not later than the last day of the first fiscal year quarter beginning after the date of the enactment of this Act, and every 90 days thereafter, the Director of National Intelligence shall submit to the appropriate committees of Congress a report describing any confirmed ballistic missile launch by Iran during the previous calendar quarter.

(b) QUARTERLY REPORT ON IMPOSITION OF SANCTIONS IN CONNECTION WITH LAUNCHES.—Not later than the last day of the second fiscal year quarter beginning after the date of the enactment of this Act, and every 90 days thereafter, the Secretary of State and the Secretary of Treasury shall jointly submit to the appropriate committees of Congress a report setting forth a description of the following:

(1) The efforts, if any, to impose unilateral sanctions against appropriate entities or individuals in connection with a confirmed ballistic missile launch from Iran.

(2) The diplomatic efforts, if any, to impose multilateral sanctions against appropriate entities or individuals in connection with such a confirmed ballistic missile launch.

(3) Any other matters the Secretaries consider appropriate.

(c) CONCURRENT SUBMITTAL OF QUARTERLY REPORTS.—The report on a calendar quarter under subsection (a) shall be submitted concurrently with the report on the calendar quarter under subsection (b).

(d) FORM.—Each report under this section shall, to the extent practicable, be submitted in unclassified form, but may include a classified annex.

(e) SUNSET.—No report is required under this section after December 31, 2019.

(f) APPROPRIATE COMMITTEES OF CONGRESS DEFINED.—In this section, the term "appropriate committees of Congress" means—

(1) the Committee on Armed Services, the Committee on Foreign Relations, the Committee on Banking, Housing, and Urban Affairs, and the Select Committee on Intelligence of the Senate; and

(2) the Committee on Armed Services, the Committee on Foreign Affairs, the Committee on Financial Services, and the Permanent Select Committee on Intelligence of the House of Representatives.

Subtitle D—Matters Relating to the Russian Federation

SEC. 1231. MILITARY RESPONSE OPTIONS TO RUSSIAN FEDERATION VIOLATION OF INF TREATY.

An amount equal to $10,000,000 of the amount authorized to be appropriated or otherwise made available to the Department of Defense for fiscal year 2017 to provide support services to the Executive Office of the President shall be withheld from obligation or expenditure until the Secretary of Defense completes the meaningful development of the military capabilities described in paragraph (1) of section 1243(d) of the National Defense Authorization Act for Fiscal Year 2016 (Public Law 114–92; 129 Stat. 1062), as required to be addressed in the plan under that paragraph, in accordance with the requirements described in paragraph (3) of such section.

SEC. 1232. LIMITATION ON MILITARY COOPERATION BETWEEN THE UNITED STATES AND THE RUSSIAN FEDERATION.

(a) LIMITATION.—None of the funds authorized to be appropriated for fiscal year 2017 for the Department of Defense may be used for any bilateral military-to-military cooperation between the Governments of the United States and the Russian Federation until the Secretary of Defense, in coordination with the Secretary of State, certifies to the appropriate congressional committees that—

(1) the Russian Federation has ceased its occupation of Ukrainian territory and its aggressive activities that threaten the sovereignty and territorial integrity of Ukraine and members of the North Atlantic Treaty Organization; and

(2) the Russian Federation is abiding by the terms of and taking steps in support of the Minsk Protocols regarding a ceasefire in eastern Ukraine.

(b) NONAPPLICABILITY.—The limitation in subsection (a) shall not apply to—

(1) any activities necessary to ensure the compliance of the United States with its obligations or the exercise of rights of the United States under any bilateral or multilateral arms control or nonproliferation agreement or any other treaty obligation of the United States; and

(2) any activities required to provide logistical or other support to the conduct of United States or North Atlantic Treaty Organization military operations in Afghanistan or the withdrawal from Afghanistan.

(c) WAIVER.—The Secretary of Defense may waive the limitation in subsection (a) if the Secretary of Defense, in coordination with the Secretary of State—

(1) determines that the waiver is in the national security interest of the United States; and

(2) submits to the appropriate congressional committees—

(A) a notification that the waiver is in the national security interest of the United States and a description of the national security interest covered by the waiver; and

(B) a report explaining why the Secretary of Defense cannot make the certification under subsection (a).

(d) EXCEPTION FOR CERTAIN MILITARY BASES.—The certification requirement specified in paragraph (1) of subsection (a) shall not apply to military bases of the Russian Federation in Ukraine's Crimean peninsula operating in accordance with its 1997 agreement on the Status and Conditions of the Black Sea Fleet Stationing on the Territory of Ukraine.

(e) APPROPRIATE CONGRESSIONAL COMMITTEES DEFINED.—In this section, the term "appropriate congressional committees" means—

(1) the Committee on Armed Services and the Committee on Foreign Relations of the Senate; and

(2) the Committee on Armed Services and the Committee on Foreign Affairs of the House of Representatives.

SEC. 1233. EXTENSION AND MODIFICATION OF AUTHORITY ON TRAINING FOR EASTERN EUROPEAN NATIONAL MILITARY FORCES IN THE COURSE OF MULTILATERAL EXERCISES.

(a) FORCES ELIGIBLE FOR TRAINING.—Subsection (a) of section 1251 of the National Defense Authorization Act for Fiscal Year 2016 (Public Law 114–92; 129 Stat. 1070; 10 U.S.C. 2282 note) is amended by striking "national military forces" and inserting "national security forces".

(b) ADDITIONAL SOURCE OF FUNDING.—Subsection (d)(2) of such section is amended by adding at the end the following new subparagraph:

"(C) Amounts authorized to be appropriated for a fiscal year for overseas contingency operations for operation and maintenance, Army, and available for additional activities for the European Deterrence Initiative for that fiscal year.".

(c) ONE-YEAR EXTENSION.—Subsection (h) of such section is amended—

(1) by striking "September 30, 2017" and inserting "September 30, 2018"; and

(2) by striking "through 2017" and inserting "through 2018".

(d) CONFORMING AMENDMENT.—The heading of such section is amended to read as follows:

"SEC. 1251. TRAINING FOR EASTERN EUROPEAN NATIONAL SECURITY FORCES IN THE COURSE OF MULTILATERAL EXERCISES.".

SEC. 1234. PROHIBITION ON AVAILABILITY OF FUNDS RELATING TO SOVEREIGNTY OF THE RUSSIAN FEDERATION OVER CRIMEA.

(a) PROHIBITION.—None of the funds authorized to be appropriated by this Act or otherwise made available for fiscal year 2017 for the Department of Defense may be obligated or expended to implement any activity that recognizes the sovereignty of the Russian Federation over Crimea.

(b) WAIVER.—The Secretary of Defense, with the concurrence of the Secretary of State, may waive the restriction on the obligation or expenditure of funds required by subsection (a) if the Secretary—

(1) determines that to do so is in the national security interest of the United States; and

(2) submits to the Committee on Armed Services and the Committee on Foreign Relations of the Senate and the Committee on Armed Services and the Committee on Foreign Affairs of the House of Representatives a notification of the waiver at the time the waiver is invoked.

SEC. 1235. ANNUAL REPORT ON MILITARY AND SECURITY DEVELOPMENTS INVOLVING THE RUSSIAN FEDERATION.

(a) ADDITIONAL MATTERS TO BE INCLUDED IN REPORT.—Subsection (b) of section 1245 of the Carl Levin and Howard P. "Buck" McKeon National Defense Authorization Act for Fiscal Year 2015 (Public Law 113–291; 128 Stat. 3566), as amended by section 1248 of the National Defense Authorization Act for Fiscal Year 2016 (Public Law 114–92; 129 Stat. 1066), is further amended—

(1) by redesignating paragraphs (10) through (18) as paragraphs (12) through (20), respectively;

(2) by inserting after paragraph (9) the following new paragraphs:

"(10) In consultation with the Secretary of State, the Secretary of the Treasury, and the Director of National Intelligence, an assessment of Russia's diplomatic, economic, and intelligence operations in Ukraine.

"(11) A summary of all Russian foreign military deployments, as of the date that is one month before the date of submission of the report, including for each deployment the estimated number of forces deployed, the types of capabilities deployed (including any advanced weapons), the length of deployment as of such date, and, if known, any basing agreement with the host nation.";

(3) by striking paragraph (14), as redesignated by paragraph (1) of this subsection, and inserting the following new paragraph:

"(14) An analysis of the nuclear strategy and associated doctrine of Russia and of the capabilities, range, and readiness of all Russian nuclear systems and delivery methods."; and

(4) in paragraph (18)(B), as redesignated by paragraph (1) of this subsection, by striking "day before the date of submission of the report" and inserting "date that is one month before the date of submission of the report".

(b) PUBLISHING REQUIREMENT.—Such section is further amended—

(1) by redesignating subsections (d), (e), and (f) as subsections (e), (f), and (g), respectively; and

(2) by inserting after subsection (c) the following new subsection:

"(d) PUBLISHING REQUIREMENT.—Upon submission of the report required under subsection (a) in both classified and unclassified form, the Secretary of Defense shall publish the unclassified form on the website of the Department of Defense.".

(c) SUNSET.—Subsection (g) of such section, as redesignated by subsection (b)(1) of this section, is amended by striking "June 1, 2018" and inserting "January 31, 2021".

SEC. 1236. LIMITATION ON USE OF FUNDS TO VOTE TO APPROVE OR OTHERWISE ADOPT ANY IMPLEMENTING DECISION OF THE OPEN SKIES CONSULTATIVE COMMISSION AND RELATED REQUIREMENTS.

(a) LIMITATION.—None of the funds authorized to be appropriated or otherwise made available by this Act or any other Act for fiscal year 2017 or any subsequent fiscal year may be used to vote to approve or otherwise adopt any implementing decision of the Open Skies Consultative Commission pursuant to Article X of the Open Skies Treaty to authorize approval of requests by state parties to the Treaty to certify infra-red or synthetic aperture radar sensors pursuant to Article IV of the Treaty unless and until the Secretary of Defense, jointly with the relevant United States Government officials, submits to the appropriate congressional committees the following:

(1) A certification that the implementing decision would not be detrimental or otherwise harmful to the national security of the United States.

(2) A report on the Open Skies Treaty that includes the following:

(A) The annual costs to the United States associated with countermeasures to combat potential abuses of observation flights by the Russian Federation carried out under the Treaty over European and United States territories involving infra-red or synthetic aperture radar sensors.

(B) A plan, and its estimated comparative cost, to replace the Treaty architecture with a more robust sharing of overhead commercial imagery, consistent with United States national security, with covered state parties, excluding the Russian Federation.

(C) An evaluation by the Director of National Intelligence of matters concerning how an observation flight described in subparagraph (A) could implicate intelligence activities of the Russian Federation in the United States and United States counterintelligence activities and vulnerabilities.

(D) An assessment of how such information is used by the Russian Federation, for what purpose, and how the information fits into the Russian Federation's overall collection posture.

(b) CERTIFICATION.—Not later than 90 days before the date on which the United States votes to approve or otherwise adopt any implementing decision of the Open Skies Consultative Commission as described in subsection (a), the Secretary of State shall—

(1) submit to the appropriate congressional committees a certification that—

(A) the Russian Federation—

(i) is not taking any actions that are inconsistent with the terms of the Open Skies Treaty;

(ii) is not exceeding the imagery limits set forth in the Treaty; and

(iii) is allowing observation flights by covered state parties over all of Moscow, Chechnya, Kaliningrad and within 10 kilometers of its border with Georgia's occupied territories of Abkhazia and South Ossetia without restriction and without inconsistency to requirements under the Treaty; and

(B) covered state parties have been notified and briefed on concerns of the intelligence community (as defined in section 3 of the National Security Act of 1947 (50 U.S.C. 3003)) regarding infra-red or synthetic aperture radar sensors used under the Open Skies Treaty; or

(2) if the Secretary of State is unable to make a certification under paragraph (1), submit to

the appropriate congressional committees a report that contains the reasons why the Secretary cannot make such certification and a justification why it is in the national interest of the United States to vote to approve or otherwise adopt such implementing decision.

(c) QUARTERLY REPORT.—

(1) IN GENERAL.—The Secretary of Defense, jointly with the Secretary of Energy, the Secretary of Homeland Security, the Director of the Federal Bureau of Investigation, and the Director of National Intelligence, shall submit to the appropriate congressional committees on a quarterly basis a report on all observation flights by the Russian Federation over the United States during the preceding calendar quarter.

(2) CONTENTS.—The report required under paragraph (1) shall include the following with respect to each such observation flight:

(A) A description of the flight path.

(B) An analysis of whether and the extent to which any United States critical infrastructure was the subject of image capture activities of such observation flight.

(C) An estimate for the mitigation costs imposed on the Department of Defense or other United States Government agencies by such observation flight.

(D) An assessment of how such information is used by the Russian Federation, for what purpose, and how the information fits into the Russian Federation's overall collection posture.

(3) SUNSET.—The requirements of this subsection shall terminate 5 years after the date of the enactment of this Act.

(d) ADDITIONAL LIMITATION.—

(1) IN GENERAL.—Not more than 65 percent of the funds authorized to be appropriated or otherwise made available by this Act or any other Act for fiscal year 2017 may be used to carry out any activities to implement the Open Skies Treaty until the requirements described in paragraph (2) are met.

(2) REQUIREMENTS DESCRIBED.—The requirements described in this paragraph are the following:

(A) The Director of National Intelligence and the Director of the National Geospatial-Intelligence Agency jointly submit to the appropriate congressional committees a report on the following:

(i) Whether it is possible, consistent with United States national security interests, to provide enhanced access to United States commercial imagery or other United States capabilities, consistent with the protection of sources and methods and United States national security, to covered state parties that is qualitatively similar to that derived by observation flights over the territory of the United States or over the territory of a covered state party under the Open Skies Treaty, on a more timely basis.

(ii) What the cost would be to provide enhanced access to such commercial imagery or other capabilities as compared to the current imagery sharing through the Treaty.

(iii) Whether any new agreements would be needed to provide enhanced access to such commercial imagery or other capabilities and what would be required to obtain such agreements.

(iv) Whether transitioning to such commercial imagery or other capabilities from the current imagery sharing through the Treaty would reduce opportunities by the Russian Federation to exceed imagery limits and reduce utility for Russian intelligence collection against the United States or covered state parties.

(v) How such commercial imagery or other capabilities would compare to the current imagery sharing through the Treaty.

(B) The Secretary of State, in consultation with the Director of the National Geospatial Intelligence Agency and the Secretary of Defense, submits to the appropriate congressional committees a report that—

(i) details the costs for implementation of the Open Skies Treaty, including—

(I) mitigation costs relating to national security; and

(II) aircraft, sensors, and related overhead and implementation costs for covered state parties; and

(ii) describes the impact on contributions and participation by covered state parties and relationships among covered state parties in the context of the Open Skies Treaty, the North Atlantic Treaty Organization, and any other venues for United States partnership dialogue and activity.

(e) FORM.—Each certification, report, and notice required under this section shall be submitted in unclassified form, but may contain a classified annex if necessary.

(f) DEFINITIONS.—In this section:

(1) APPROPRIATE CONGRESSIONAL COMMITTEES.—The term "appropriate congressional committees" means—

(A) the Committee on Armed Services, the Committee on Foreign Relations, and the Select Committee on Intelligence of the Senate; and

(B) the Committee on Armed Services, the Committee on Foreign Affairs, and the Permanent Select Committee on Intelligence of the House of Representatives.

(2) COVERED STATE PARTY.—The term "covered state party" means a foreign country that—

(A) is a state party to the Open Skies Treaty; and

(B) is a United States ally.

(3) INFRA-RED OR SYNTHETIC APERTURE RADAR SENSOR.—The term "infra-red or synthetic aperture radar sensor" means a sensor that is classified as—

(A) an infra-red line-scanning device under category C of paragraph 1 of Article IV of the Open Skies Treaty; or

(B) a sideways-looking synthetic aperture radar under category D of paragraph 1 of Article IV of the Open Skies Treaty.

(4) OBSERVATION FLIGHT.—The term "observation flight" has the meaning given such term in Article II of the Open Skies Treaty.

(5) OPEN SKIES TREATY; TREATY.—The term "Open Skies Treaty" or "Treaty" means the Treaty on Open Skies, done at Helsinki March 24, 1992, and entered into force January 1, 2002.

(6) RELEVANT UNITED STATES GOVERNMENT OFFICIALS.—The term "relevant United States Government officials" means the following:

(A) The Secretary of Energy.

(B) The Secretary of Homeland Security.

(C) The Director of the Federal Bureau of Investigation.

(D) The Director of National Intelligence.

(E) The Commander of U.S. Strategic Command and the Commander of U.S. Northern Command in the case of an observation flight over the territory of the United States.

(F) The Commander of U.S. European Command in the case of an observation flight other than an observation flight described in subparagraph (E).

(7) SENSOR.—The term "sensor" has the meaning given such term in Article II of the Open Skies Treaty.

SEC. 1237. EXTENSION AND ENHANCEMENT OF UKRAINE SECURITY ASSISTANCE INITIATIVE.

(a) FUNDING.—Section 1250 of the National Defense Authorization Act for Fiscal Year 2016 (Public Law 114–92; 129 Stat. 1068) is amended—

(1) in subsection (a), by striking "Of the amounts" and all that follows through "shall be available to" and inserting "Amounts available for a fiscal year under subsection (f) shall be available to";

(2) by redesignating subsection (f) as subsection (h); and

(3) by inserting after subsection (e) the following new subsection (f):

"(f) FUNDING.—From amounts authorized to be appropriated for the fiscal year concerned for the Department of Defense for overseas contingency operations, up to the following shall be available for purposes of subsection (a):

"(1) For fiscal year 2016, $300,000,000.

"(2) For fiscal year 2017, $350,000,000.".

(b) ADDITIONAL AUTHORIZED ASSISTANCE.—Subsection (b) of such section is amended by adding at the end the following new paragraphs:

"(10) Equipment and technical assistance to the State Border Guard Service of Ukraine for the purpose of developing a comprehensive border surveillance network for Ukraine.

"(11) Training for staff officers and senior leadership of the military.".

(c) AVAILABILITY OF FUNDS.—Subsection (c) of such section is amended—

(1) by striking paragraphs (1) and (2) and inserting the following new paragraphs:

"(1) ASSISTANCE FOR UKRAINE.—Not more than $175,000,000 of the funds available for fiscal year 2017 pursuant to subsection (f)(2) may be used for purposes of subsection (a) until the certification described in paragraph (2) is made.

"(2) CERTIFICATION.—The certification described in this paragraph is a certification by the Secretary of Defense, in coordination with the Secretary of State, that the Government of Ukraine has taken substantial actions to make defense institutional reforms, in such areas as civilian control of the military, cooperation and coordination with Verkhovna Rada efforts to exercise oversight of the Ministry of Defense and military forces, increased transparency and accountability in defense procurement, and improvement in transparency, accountability, and potential opportunities for privatization in the defense industrial sector, for purposes of decreasing corruption, increasing accountability, and sustaining improvements of combat capability enabled by assistance under subsection (a). The certification shall include an assessment of the substantial actions taken to make such defense institutional reforms and the areas in which additional action is needed.";

(2) in paragraph (3), by striking the matter preceding subparagraph (A) and inserting the following:

"(3) OTHER PURPOSES.—If in fiscal year 2017 funds are not available for purposes of subsection (a) by reason of the lack of a certification described in paragraph (2), such funds may be used in that fiscal year for the purposes as follows, with not more than $100,000,000 available for the purposes as follows for any particular country:"; and

(3) by adding at the end the following new paragraph:

"(4) NOTICE TO CONGRESS.—Not later than 15 days before providing assistance or support under paragraph (3), the Secretary of Defense shall submit to the congressional defense committees, the Committee on Foreign Relations of the Senate, and the Committee on Foreign Affairs of the House of Representatives a notification containing the following:

"(A) The recipient foreign country.

"(B) A detailed description of the assistance or support to be provided, including—

"(i) the objectives of such assistance or support;

"(ii) the budget for such assistance or support; and

"(iii) the expected or estimated timeline for delivery of such assistance or support.

"(C) Such other matters as the Secretary considers appropriate.".

(d) CONSTRUCTION WITH OTHER AUTHORITY.—Such section is further amended by inserting after subsection (f), as amended by subsection (a)(3) of this section, the following new subsection (g):

"(g) CONSTRUCTION WITH OTHER AUTHORITY.—The authority to provide assistance and support pursuant to subsection (a), and the authority to provide assistance and support under subsection (c), is in addition to authority to provide assistance and support under title 10, United States Code, the Foreign Assistance Act of 1961, the Arms Export Control Act, or any other provision of law.''.

(e) EXTENSION.—Subsection (h) of such section, as redesignated by subsection (a)(2) of this section, is amended by striking "December 31, 2017" and inserting "December 31, 2018".

(f) EXTENSION OF REPORTS ON MILITARY ASSISTANCE TO UKRAINE.—Section 1275(e) of the Carl Levin and Howard P. "Buck" McKeon National Defense Authorization Act for Fiscal Year 2015 (Public Law 113–291; 128 Stat. 3592), as amended by section 1250(g) of the National Defense Authorization Act for Fiscal Year 2016, is further amended by striking "December 31, 2017" and inserting "January 31, 2021".

SEC. 1238. REPORTS ON INF TREATY AND OPEN SKIES TREATY.

(a) REPORTS.—Not later than 90 days after the date of the enactment of this Act, the Chairman of the Joint Chiefs of Staff shall submit to the appropriate congressional committees the following reports:

(1) A report on the Open Skies Treaty containing—

(A) an assessment, conducted by the Chairman jointly with the Secretary of Defense and the Secretary of State, of whether and why the Treaty remains in the national security interest of the United States, including if there are compliance concerns related to implementation of the Treaty by the Russian Federation;

(B) a specific plan by the Chairman jointly with the Secretary of Defense and the Secretary of State on remedying any such compliance concerns; and

(C) a military assessment conducted by the Chairman of such compliance concerns.

(2) A report on the INF Treaty containing—

(A) an assessment, conducted by the Chairman jointly with the Secretary of Defense and the Secretary of State, of whether and why the Treaty remains in the national security interest of the United States, including how any ongoing violations bear on the assessment if such a violation is not resolved in the near-term;

(B) a specific plan by the Chairman jointly with the Secretary of Defense and the Secretary of State to remedy violation of the Treaty by the Russian Federation, and a judgment of whether the Russian Federation intends to take the steps required to establish verifiable evidence that the Russian Federation has resumed its compliance with the Treaty if such non-compliance and inconsistencies are not resolved by the date of the enactment of this Act; and

(C) a military assessment conducted by the Chairman of the risks posed by violation of the Treaty by the Russian Federation.

(b) UPDATE.—Not later than February 15, 2018, the Chairman, the Secretary of Defense, and the Secretary of State shall jointly submit to the appropriate congressional committees an update to each report under subsection (a).

(c) DEFINITIONS.—In this section:

(1) The term "appropriate congressional committees" means—

(A) the Committee on Armed Services, the Committee on Foreign Affairs, and the Permanent Select Committee on Intelligence of the House of Representatives; and

(B) the Committee on Armed Services, the Committee on Foreign Relations, and the Select Committee on Intelligence of the Senate.

(2) The term "INF Treaty" means the Treaty Between the United States of America and the Union of Soviet Socialist Republics on the Elimination of Their Intermediate-Range and Shorter-Range Missiles, commonly referred to as the "Intermediate-Range Nuclear Forces (INF) Treaty", signed at Washington December 8, 1987, and entered into force June 1, 1988.

(3) The term "Open Skies Treaty" means the Treaty on Open Skies, done at Helsinki March 24, 1992, and entered into force January 1, 2002.

Subtitle E—Reform of Department of Defense Security Cooperation

SEC. 1241. ENACTMENT OF NEW CHAPTER FOR DEFENSE SECURITY COOPERATION.

(a) STATUTORY REORGANIZATION.—Part I of subtitle A of title 10, United States Code, is amended—

(1) by redesignating chapters 13, 15, 17, and 18 as chapters 12, 13, 14, and 15, respectively;

(2) by redesignating sections 261, 311, 312, 331, 332, 333, 334, 335, 351, 371, 372, 373, 374, 375, 376, 377, 378, 379, 380, 381, 382, 383, and 384 (as added by section 1011 of this Act) as sections 241, 246, 247, 251, 252, 253, 254, 255, 261, 271, 272, 273, 274, 275, 276, 277, 278, 279, 280, 281, 282, 283, and 284, respectively; and

(3) by inserting after chapter 15, as redesignated by paragraph (1), the following new chapter:

"CHAPTER 16—SECURITY COOPERATION

"Subchapter	Sec.
"I. General Matters	301
"II. Military-to-Military Engagements	311
"III. Training With Foreign Forces	321
"IV. Support for Operations and Capacity Building	331
"V. Educational and Training Activities	341
"VI. Limitations on Use of Department of Defense Funds	361
"VII. Administrative and Miscellaneous Matters	381

"SUBCHAPTER I—GENERAL MATTERS

"Sec.
"301. Definitions.

"§ 301. Definitions

"In this chapter:

"(1) The terms 'appropriate congressional committees' and 'appropriate committees of Congress' mean—

"(A) the Committee on Armed Services, the Committee on Foreign Relations, and the Committee on Appropriations of the Senate; and

"(B) the Committee on Armed Services, the Committee on Foreign Affairs, and the Committee on Appropriations of the House of Representatives.

"(2) The term 'defense article' has the meaning given that term in section 644 of the Foreign Assistance Act of 1961 (22 U.S.C. 2403).

"(3) The term 'defense service' has the meaning given that term in section 644 of the Foreign Assistance Act of 1961 (22 U.S.C. 2403).

"(4) The term 'developing country' has the meaning prescribed by the Secretary of Defense for purposes of this chapter in accordance with section 1241(n) of the National Defense Authorization Act for Fiscal Year 2017.

"(5) The term 'incremental expenses', with respect to a foreign country—

"(A) means the reasonable and proper costs of rations, fuel, training ammunition, transportation, and other goods and services consumed by the country as a direct result of the country's participation in activities authorized by this chapter; and

"(B) does not include—

"(i) any form of lethal assistance (excluding training ammunition); or

"(ii) pay, allowances, and other normal costs of the personnel of the country.

"(6) The term 'national security forces', in the case of a foreign country, means the following:

"(A) National military and national-level security forces of the foreign country that have the functional responsibilities for which training is authorized in section 333(a) of this title.

"(B) With respect to operations referred to in section 333(a)(2) of this title, military and civilian first responders of the foreign country at the national or local level that have such operations among their functional responsibilities.

"(7) The term 'security cooperation programs and activities of the Department of Defense' means any program, activity (including an exercise), or interaction of the Department of Defense with the security establishment of a foreign country to achieve a purpose as follows:

"(A) To build and develop allied and friendly security capabilities for self-defense and multinational operations.

"(B) To provide the armed forces with access to the foreign country during peacetime or a contingency operation.

"(C) To build relationships that promote specific United States security interests.

"(8) The term 'small-scale construction' means construction at a cost not to exceed $750,000 for any project.

"(9) The term 'training' has the meaning given the term 'military education and training' in section 644 of the Foreign Assistance Act of 1961 (22 U.S.C. 2403).

"SUBCHAPTER II—MILITARY-TO-MILITARY ENGAGEMENTS

"Sec.
"311. Exchange of defense personnel between United States and friendly foreign countries: authority.
"312. Payment of personnel expenses necessary for theater security cooperation.
"313. Bilateral or regional cooperation programs: awards and mementos to recognize superior noncombat achievements or performance.

"SUBCHAPTER III—TRAINING WITH FOREIGN FORCES

"Sec.
"321. Training with friendly foreign countries: payment of training and exercise expenses.
"322. Special operations forces: training with friendly foreign forces.

"SUBCHAPTER IV—SUPPORT FOR OPERATIONS AND CAPACITY BUILDING

"Sec.
"331. Friendly foreign countries: authority to provide support for conduct of operations.
"332. Friendly foreign countries; international and regional organizations: defense institution capacity building.
"333. Foreign security forces: authority to build capacity.

"SUBCHAPTER V—EDUCATIONAL AND TRAINING ACTIVITIES

"Sec.
"341. Department of Defense State Partnership Program.
"342. Regional centers for security studies.
"343. Western Hemisphere Institute for Security Cooperation.
"344. Participation in multinational military centers of excellence.
"345. Regional Defense Combating Terrorism Fellowship Program.
"346. Distribution to certain foreign personnel of education and training materials and information technology to enhance military interoperability with the armed forces.
"347. International engagement authorities for service academies.
"348. Aviation Leadership Program.

"349. Inter-American Air Forces Academy.

"350. Inter-European Air Forces Academy.

"SUBCHAPTER VI—LIMITATIONS ON USE OF DEPARTMENT OF DEFENSE FUNDS

"Sec.

"361. Prohibition on providing financial assistance to terrorist countries.

"362. Prohibition on use of funds for assistance to units of foreign security forces that have committed a gross violation of human rights.

"SUBCHAPTER VII—ADMINISTRATIVE AND MISCELLANEOUS MATTERS

"Sec.

"381. Consolidated budget.

"382. Execution and administration of programs and activities.

"383. Assessment, monitoring, and evaluation of programs and activities.

"384. Department of Defense security cooperation workforce development.

"385. Department of Defense support for other departments and agencies of the United States Government that advance Department of Defense security cooperation objectives.

"386. Annual report.".

(b) TRANSFER OF SECTION 1051B.—Section 1051b of title 10, United States Code, is transferred to chapter 16 of such title, as added by subsection (a)(3), inserted after the table of sections at the beginning of subchapter II of such chapter, and redesignated as section 313.

(c) CODIFICATION OF SECTION 1081 OF FY 2012 NDAA.—

(1) CODIFICATION.—Chapter 16 of title 10, United States Code, as added by subsection (a)(3), is amended by inserting after the table of sections at the beginning of subchapter IV a new section 332 consisting of—

(A) a heading as follows:

"**§ 332. Friendly foreign countries; international and regional organizations: defense institution capacity building**"; and

(B) a text consisting of the text of subsections (a), (b), and (d) of section 1081 of the National Defense Authorization Act for Fiscal Year 2012 (10 U.S.C. 168 note).

(2) CONFORMING AMENDMENT.—Section 332 of title 10, United States Code, as so amended, is further amended by redesignating subsection (d) as subsection (c).

(3) CONFORMING REPEAL.—Section 1081 of the National Defense Authorization Act for Fiscal Year 2012 is repealed.

(d) SUPERSEDING AUTHORITY TO TRAIN AND EQUIP FOREIGN SECURITY FORCES.—

(1) SUPERSEDING AUTHORITY.—Chapter 16 of title 10, United States Code, as added by subsection (a)(3), is amended by inserting after section 332, as added by subsection (c), the following new section:

"**§ 333. Foreign security forces: authority to build capacity**

"(a) AUTHORITY.—The Secretary of Defense is authorized to conduct or support a program or programs to provide training and equipment to the national security forces of one or more foreign countries for the purpose of building the capacity of such forces to conduct one or more of the following:

"(1) Counterterrorism operations.

"(2) Counter-weapons of mass destruction operations.

"(3) Counter-illicit drug trafficking operations.

"(4) Counter-transnational organized crime operations.

"(5) Maritime and border security operations.

"(6) Military intelligence operations.

"(7) Operations or activities that contribute to an international coalition operation that is determined by the Secretary to be in the national interest of the United States.

"(b) CONCURRENCE AND COORDINATION WITH SECRETARY OF STATE.—

"(1) CONCURRENCE IN CONDUCT OF PROGRAMS.—The concurrence of the Secretary of State is required to conduct or support any program authorized by subsection (a).

"(2) JOINT DEVELOPMENT AND PLANNING OF PROGRAMS.—The Secretary of Defense and the Secretary of State shall jointly develop and plan any program carried out pursuant to subsection (a).

"(3) IMPLEMENTATION OF PROGRAMS.—The Secretary of Defense and the Secretary of State shall coordinate the implementation of any program under subsection (a). The Secretary of Defense and the Secretary of State shall each designate an individual responsible for program coordination under this paragraph at the lowest appropriate level in the Department concerned.

"(4) COORDINATION IN PREPARATION OF CERTAIN NOTICES.—Any notice required by this section to be submitted to the appropriate committees of Congress shall be prepared in coordination with the Secretary of State.

"(c) TYPES OF CAPACITY BUILDING.—

"(1) AUTHORIZED ELEMENTS.—A program under subsection (a) may include the provision and sustainment of defense articles, training, defense services, supplies (including consumables), and small-scale construction.

"(2) REQUIRED ELEMENTS.—A program under subsection (a) shall include elements that promote the following:

"(A) Observance of and respect for the law of armed conflict, human rights and fundamental freedoms, and the rule of law.

"(B) Respect for civilian control of the military.

"(3) HUMAN RIGHTS TRAINING.—In order to meet the requirement in paragraph (2)(A) with respect to particular national security forces under a program under subsection (a), the Secretary of Defense shall certify, prior to the initiation of the program, that the Department of Defense is already undertaking, or will undertake as part of the security sector assistance provided to the foreign country concerned, human rights training that includes a comprehensive curriculum on human rights and the law of armed conflict, as applicable, to such national security forces.

"(4) INSTITUTIONAL CAPACITY BUILDING.—In order to meet the requirement in paragraph (2)(B) with respect to a particular foreign country under a program under subsection (a), the Secretary shall certify, prior to the initiation of the program, that the Department is already undertaking, or will undertake as part of the program, a program of institutional capacity building with appropriate institutions of such foreign country that is complementary to the program with respect to such foreign country under subsection (a). The purpose of the program of institutional capacity building shall be to enhance the capacity of such foreign country to exercise responsible civilian control of the national security forces of such foreign country.

"(d) LIMITATIONS.—

"(1) ASSISTANCE OTHERWISE PROHIBITED BY LAW.—The Secretary of Defense may not use the authority in subsection (a) to provide any type of assistance described in subsection (c) that is otherwise prohibited by any provision of law.

"(2) PROHIBITION ON ASSISTANCE TO UNITS THAT HAVE COMMITTED GROSS VIOLATIONS OF HUMAN RIGHTS.—The provision of assistance pursuant to a program under subsection (a) shall be subject to the provisions of section 362 of this title.

"(3) DURATION OF SUSTAINMENT SUPPORT.—Sustainment support may not be provided pursuant to a program under subsection (a), or for equipment previously provided by the Department of Defense under any authority available to the Secretary during fiscal year 2015 or 2016, for a period in excess of five years unless the notice on the program pursuant to subsection (e) includes the information specified in paragraph (7) of subsection (e).

"(e) NOTICE AND WAIT ON ACTIVITIES UNDER PROGRAMS.—Not later than 15 days before initiating activities under a program under subsection (a), the Secretary of Defense shall submit to the appropriate committees of Congress a written and electronic notice of the following:

"(1) The foreign country, and specific unit, whose capacity to engage in activities specified in subsection (a) will be built under the program, and the amount, type, and purpose of the support to be provided.

"(2) A detailed evaluation of the capacity of the foreign country and unit to absorb the training or equipment to be provided under the program.

"(3) The cost, implementation timeline, and delivery schedule for assistance under the program.

"(4) A description of the arrangements, if any, for the sustainment of the program and the estimated cost and source of funds to support sustainment of the capabilities and performance outcomes achieved under the program beyond its completion date, if applicable.

"(5) Information, including the amount, type, and purpose, on the security assistance provided the foreign country during the three preceding fiscal years pursuant to authorities under this title, the Foreign Assistance Act of 1961, and any other train and equip authorities of the Department of Defense.

"(6) A description of the elements of the theater security cooperation plan of the geographic combatant command concerned, and of the interagency integrated country strategy, that will be advanced by the program.

"(7) In the case of a program described in subsection (d)(3), each of the following:

"(A) A written justification that the provision of sustainment support described in that subsection for a period in excess of five years will enhance the security interest of the United States.

"(B) To the extent practicable, a plan to transition such sustainment support from funding through the Department to funding through another security sector assistance program of the United States Government or funding through partner nations.

"(f) QUARTERLY MONITORING REPORTS.—The Director of the Defense Security Cooperation Agency shall, on a quarterly basis, submit to the appropriate committees of Congress a report setting forth, for the preceding calendar quarter, the following:

"(1) Information, by recipient country, of the delivery and execution status of all defense articles, training, defense services, supplies (including consumables), and small-scale construction under programs under subsection (a).

"(2) Information on the timeliness of delivery of defense articles, defense services, supplies (including consumables), and small-scale construction when compared with delivery schedules for such articles, services, supplies, and construction previously provided to Congress.

"(3) Information, by recipient country, on the status of funds allocated for programs under subsection (a), including amounts of unobligated funds, unliquidated obligations, and disbursements.

"(g) FUNDING.—

"(1) SOLE SOURCE OF FUNDS.—Amounts for programs carried out pursuant to subsection (a) in a fiscal year, and for other purposes in connection with such programs as authorized by this section, may be derived only from amounts authorized to be appropriated for such fiscal year for the Department of Defense for operation and maintenance, Defense-wide, and available for the Defense Security Cooperation Agency for such programs and purposes.

"(2) AVAILABILITY OF FUNDS FOR PROGRAMS ACROSS FISCAL YEARS.—

"(A) IN GENERAL.—Amounts available in a fiscal year to carry out the authority in subsection (a) may be used for programs under that authority that begin in such fiscal year and end not later than the end of the second fiscal year thereafter.

"(B) ACHIEVEMENT OF FULL OPERATIONAL CAPACITY.—If, in accordance with subparagraph (A), equipment or training is delivered under a program under the authority in subsection (a) in the fiscal year after the fiscal year in which the program begins, amounts for defense articles, training, defense services, supplies (including consumables), and small-scale construction associated with such equipment or training and necessary to ensure that the recipient unit achieves full operational capability for such equipment or training may be used in the fiscal year in which the foreign country takes receipt of such equipment and in the next two fiscal years.".

(2) FUNDING FOR FISCAL YEAR 2017.—Amounts may be available for fiscal year 2017 for programs and other purposes described in subsection (g) of section 333 of title 10, United States Code, as added by paragraph (1), as follows:

(A) Amounts authorized to be appropriated by section 301 for operation and maintenance, Defense-wide, and available for the Defense Security Cooperation Agency for such programs and purposes as specified in the funding table in section 4301.

(B) Amounts authorized to be appropriated by section 1407 for Drug Interdiction and Counter-Drug Activities, Defense-Wide, as specified in the funding table in section 4501.

(C) Amounts authorized to be appropriated by section 1504 for operation and maintenance, Defense-wide, for overseas contingency operations and available for the Defense Security Cooperation Agency for such programs and purposes as specified in the funding table in section 4302.

(D) Amounts authorized to be appropriated by section 1504 for operation and maintenance, Defense-wide, for overseas contingency operations and available for the Counter Islamic State of Iraq and the Levant Fund as specified in the funding table in section 4302, which amounts may be available for such programs and other purposes with respect to a country other than Iraq or Syria if—

(i) such programs and other purposes are for the purpose of countering the Islamic State of Iraq and the Levant; and

(ii) notice on the use of such amounts for such programs and other purposes is provided to Congress in accordance with subsection (e) of section 333 of title 10, United States Code, as so added.

(E) Amounts authorized to be appropriated by section 1507 for Drug Interdiction and Counter-Drug Activities, Defense-Wide, for overseas contingency operations as specified in the funding table in section 4502 or 4503.

(F) Amounts available for fiscal years before fiscal year 2017 for the Counterterrorism Partnerships Fund that remain available for obligation in fiscal year 2017.

(3) LIMITATION ON AVAILABILITY OF FUNDS FOR FISCAL YEAR 2017.—Of the amounts available for fiscal year 2017 pursuant to paragraph (2) for programs and other purposes described in subsection (g) of section 333 of title 10, United States Code, as so added, not more than 65 percent of such amounts may be used for such purposes until the guidance required by paragraph

(4) is submitted to the congressional defense committees as required by paragraph (4).

(4) GUIDANCE.—Not later than 180 days after the date of the enactment of this Act, the Secretary of Defense shall prescribe, and submit to the congressional defense committees, initial policy guidance on roles, responsibilities, and processes in connection with programs and activities authorized by section 333 of title 10, United States Code, as so added. Not later than 270 days after the date of the enactment of this Act, the Secretary shall prescribe, and submit to the congressional defense committees, final policy guidance on roles, responsibilities, and processes in connection with such programs and activities.

(5) CONFORMING REPEALS.—Effective as of the date that is 270 days after the date of the enactment of this Act, the following provisions of law are repealed:

(A) Section 2282 of title 10, United States Code.

(B) The following provisions of the National Defense Authorization Act for Fiscal Year 2014 (Public Law 113–66):

(i) Section 1204 (127 Stat. 896; 10 U.S.C. 401 note).

(ii) Section 1207 (127 Stat. 902; 22 U.S.C. 2151 note).

(C) Section 1033 of the National Defense Authorization Act for Fiscal Year 1998 (Public Law 105–85; 111 Stat. 1881).

(6) CLERICAL AMENDMENT.—Effective as of the date that is 270 days after the date of the enactment of this Act, the table of sections at the beginning of chapter 136 of title 10, United States Code, is amended by striking the item relating to section 2282.

(e) TRANSFER AND MODIFICATION OF SECTION 184 AND CODIFICATION OF RELATED PROVISIONS.—

(1) TRANSFER AND REDESIGNATION.—Section 184 of title 10, United States Code, is transferred to chapter 16 of such title as added by subsection (a)(3), inserted after the table of sections at the beginning of subchapter V of such chapter, and redesignated as section 342.

(2) MODIFICATION OF AUTHORITIES AND CODIFICATION OF REIMBURSEMENT-RELATED PROVISIONS.—Section 342 of title 10, United States Code, as so transferred and redesignated, is amended—

(A) in subsection (a), by striking "and exchange of ideas" and inserting "exchange of ideas, and training";

(B) in subsection (b)—

(i) in paragraph (1)(B), by striking "and exchange of ideas" and inserting "exchange of ideas, and training"; and

(ii) in paragraph (3), by striking ", except as specifically provided by law after October 17, 2006";

(C) in subsection (c), by adding at the end the following new sentence: "The regulations shall prioritize within the respective areas of focus of each Regional Center the functional areas for engagement of territorial and maritime security, transnational and asymmetric threats, and defense sector governance."; and

(D) in subsection (f)—

(i) in paragraph (3)—

(I) by inserting "(A)" after "(3)";

(II) in subparagraph (A), as so designated, by striking "civilian government officials" and inserting "personnel"; and

(III) by adding at the end the following new subparagraph:

"(B)(i) The Secretary of Defense may, with the concurrence of the Secretary of State, waive reimbursement otherwise required under this subsection of the costs of activities of the Regional Centers for personnel of nongovernmental and international organizations who participate in activities of the Regional Centers

that enhance cooperation of nongovernmental organizations and international organizations with United States forces if the Secretary of Defense determines that attendance of such personnel without reimbursement is in the national security interest of the United States.

"(ii) The amount of reimbursement that may be waived under clause (i) in any fiscal year may not exceed $1,000,000."; and

(ii) in paragraph (5), by striking "under the Latin American cooperation authority" and all that follows and inserting "under section 312 of this title are also available for the costs of the operation of the Regional Centers.".

(3) CODIFICATION OF PROVISIONS RELATING TO SPECIFIC CENTERS.—Such section 342, as so transferred and redesignated, is further amended by adding at the end the following new subsections:

"(h) AUTHORITIES SPECIFIC TO MARSHALL CENTER.—(1) The Secretary of Defense may authorize participation by a European or Eurasian country in programs of the George C. Marshall Center for Security Studies (in this subsection referred to as the 'Marshall Center') if the Secretary determines, after consultation with the Secretary of State, that such participation is in the national interest of the United States.

"(2)(A) In the case of any person invited to serve without compensation on the Marshall Center Board of Visitors, the Secretary of Defense may waive any requirement for financial disclosure that would otherwise apply to that person solely by reason of service on such Board.

"(B) A member of the Marshall Center Board of Visitors may not be required to register as an agent of a foreign government solely by reason of service as a member of the Board.

"(C) Notwithstanding section 219 of title 18, a non-United States citizen may serve on the Marshall Center Board of Visitors even though registered as a foreign agent.

"(3)(A) The Secretary of Defense may waive reimbursement of the costs of conferences, seminars, courses of instruction, or similar educational activities of the Marshall Center for military officers and civilian officials from states located in Europe or the territory of the former Soviet Union if the Secretary determines that attendance by such personnel without reimbursement is in the national security interest of the United States.

"(B) Costs for which reimbursement is waived pursuant to subparagraph (A) shall be paid from appropriations available for the Center.

"(i) AUTHORITIES SPECIFIC TO INOUYE CENTER.—(1) The Secretary of Defense may waive reimbursement of the cost of conferences, seminars, courses of instruction, or similar educational activities of the Daniel K. Inouye Center for Security Studies for military officers and civilian officials of foreign countries if the Secretary determines that attendance by such personnel, without reimbursement, is in the national security interest of the United States.

"(2) Costs for which reimbursement is waived pursuant to paragraph (1) shall be paid from appropriations available for the Center.".

(4) ANNUAL REVIEW OF PROGRAM STRUCTURE AND PROGRAMS OF CENTERS.—Such section 342, as amended by this subsection, is further amended by adding at the end the following new subsection:

"(j) ANNUAL REVIEW OF PROGRAM STRUCTURE AND PROGRAMS OF CENTERS.—(1) The Secretary shall on an annual basis review the program and structure of each Regional Center in order to determine whether such Regional Center is appropriately aligned with the strategic priorities of the Department of Defense and the applicable geographic combatant commands.

"(2) The Secretary may revise the program, structure, or both of a Regional Center following an annual review under paragraph (1) in order to more appropriately align the Regional Center with strategic priorities and the geographic combatant commands as described in that paragraph..''.

(5) REPEAL OF CODIFIED PROVISIONS.—The following provisions of law are repealed:

(A) Section 941(b) of the Duncan Hunter National Defense Authorization Act for Fiscal Year 2009 (Public Law 110–417; 10 U.S.C. 184 note).

(B) Section 1065 of the National Defense Authorization Act for Fiscal Year 1997 (Public Law 104–201; 10 U.S.C. 113 note).

(C) Section 1306 of the National Defense Authorization Act for Fiscal Year 1995 (Public Law 103–337; 108 Stat. 2892).

(D) Section 8073 of the Department of Defense Appropriations Act, 2003 (Public Law 107–248; 10 U.S.C. prec. 2161 note).

(f) TRANSFER OF SECTION 2166.—

(1) TRANSFER AND REDESIGNATION.—Section 2166 of title 10, United States Code, is transferred to chapter 16 of such title, as added by subsection (a)(3), inserted after section 342, as transferred and redesignated by subsection (e), and redesignated as section 343.

(2) CONFORMING STYLISTIC AMENDMENTS.—Such section 343, as so transferred and redesignated, is amended by striking ''nations'' each place it appears in subsections (b) and (c) and inserting ''countries''.

(g) TRANSFER OF SECTION 2350M.—

(1) TRANSFER AND REDESIGNATION.—Section 2350m of title 10, United States Code, is transferred to chapter 16 of such title, as added by subsection (a)(3), inserted after section 343, as transferred and redesignated by subsection (f), and redesignated as section 344.

(2) CONFORMING AMENDMENTS.—Such section 344, as so transferred and redesignated, is amended—

(A) by striking subsection (e); and

(B) by redesignating subsection (f) as subsection (e).

(h) TRANSFER OF SECTION 2249D.—

(1) TRANSFER AND REDESIGNATION.—Section 2249d of title 10, United States Code, is transferred to chapter 16 of such title, as added by subsection (a)(3), inserted after section 344, as transferred and redesignated by subsection (g), and redesignated as section 346.

(2) CONFORMING AND STYLISTIC AMENDMENTS.—Such section 346, as so transferred and redesignated, is amended—

(A) by striking ''nations'' in subsections (a) and (d) and inserting ''countries''; and

(B) by striking subsections (f) and (g).

(i) REENACTMENT OF CHAPTER 905.—

(1) CONSOLIDATION OF SECTIONS 9381, 9382, AND 9383.—Chapter 16 of title 10, United States Code, as added by subsection (a)(3), is amended by inserting after section 346, as transferred and redesignated by subsection (h), the following new section:

"§348. Aviation Leadership Program

"(a) IN GENERAL.—Under regulations prescribed by the Secretary of Defense, the Secretary of the Air Force may carry out an Aviation Leadership Program to provide undergraduate pilot training and necessary related training to personnel of the air forces of friendly, developing foreign countries. Training under this section shall include language training and programs to promote better awareness and understanding of the democratic institutions and social framework of the United States.

"(b) SUPPLIES AND CLOTHING.—(1) The Secretary of the Air Force may, under such conditions as the Secretary may prescribe, provide to a person receiving training under this section—

"(A) transportation incident to the training;

"(B) supplies and equipment to be used during the training;

"(C) flight clothing and other special clothing required for the training; and

"(D) billeting, food, and health services.

"(2) The Secretary may authorize such expenditures from the appropriations of the Air Force as the Secretary considers necessary for the efficient and effective maintenance of the Program in accordance with this section.

"(c) ALLOWANCES.—The Secretary of the Air Force may pay to a person receiving training under this section a living allowance at a rate to be prescribed by the Secretary, taking into account the amount of living allowances authorized for a member of the armed forces under similar circumstances.''.

(2) CONFORMING REPEAL.—Chapter 905 of such title is repealed.

(j) TRANSFER OF SECTION 9415.—

(1) IN GENERAL.—Section 9415 of title 10, United States Code, is transferred to chapter 16 of such title, as added by subsection (a)(3), inserted after section 348, as added by subsection (i), and redesignated as section 349.

(2) CONFORMING AMENDMENT FOR STANDARDIZATION WITH CERTAIN OTHER AIR FORCES ACADEMY AUTHORITY.—Such section 349, as so transferred and amended, is amended—

(A) by redesignating subsection (b) as subsection (c); and

(B) by inserting after subsection (a) the following new subsection (b):

"(b) LIMITATIONS.—

"(1) CONCURRENCE OF SECRETARY OF STATE.—Military personnel of a foreign country may be provided education and training under this section only with the concurrence of the Secretary of State.

"(2) ASSISTANCE OTHERWISE PROHIBITED BY LAW.—Education and training may not be provided under this section to the military personnel of any country that is otherwise prohibited from receiving such type of assistance under any other provision of law.''.

(k) CODIFICATION OF SECTION 1268 OF FY 2015 NDAA.—

(1) CODIFICATION.—Chapter 16 of title 10, United States Code, as added by subsection (a)(3), is amended by inserting after section 349, as transferred and redesignated by subsection (j), a new section 350 consisting of—

(A) a heading as follows:

"§350. Inter-European Air Forces Academy''; and

(B) a text consisting of the text of subsections (a) through (f) of section 1268 of the Carl Levin and Howard P. ''Buck'' McKeon National Defense Authorization Act for Fiscal Year 2015 (Public Law 113–291; 128 Stat. 3585; 10 U.S.C. 9411 note).

(2) CONFORMING REPEAL.—Section 1268 of the Carl Levin and Howard P. ''Buck'' McKeon National Defense Authorization Act for Fiscal Year 2015 is repealed.

(l) TRANSFER OF SECTIONS 2249A AND 2249E.—

(1) TRANSFER AND REDESIGNATION.—Sections 2249a and 2249e of title 10, United States Code, are transferred to chapter 16 of such title, as added by subsection (a)(3), inserted after the table of sections at the beginning of subchapter VI of such chapter, and redesignated as sections 361 and 362, respectively.

(2) CONFORMING REPEAL RELATING TO SUPERSEDED DEFINITION OF CONGRESSIONAL COMMITTEES.—Section 362 of such title, as transferred and redesignated by paragraph (1), is amended by striking subsection (f).

(m) ADMINISTRATIVE MATTERS.—Chapter 16 of title 10, United States Code, as added by subsection (a)(3), is amended by inserting after the table of sections at the beginning of subchapter VII the following new sections:

"§382. Execution and administration of programs and activities

"(a) POLICY OVERSIGHT AND RESOURCE ALLOCATION.—The Secretary of Defense shall assign responsibility for the oversight of strategic policy and guidance and responsibility for overall resource allocation for security cooperation programs and activities of the Department of Defense to a single official and office in the Office of the Secretary of Defense at the level of Under Secretary of Defense or below.

"(b) EXECUTION AND ADMINISTRATION OF CERTAIN PROGRAMS AND ACTIVITIES.—

"(1) IN GENERAL.—The Director of the Defense Security Cooperation Agency shall be responsible for the execution and administration of all security cooperation programs and activities of the Department of Defense involving the provision of defense articles, military training, and other defense-related services by grant, loan, cash sale, or lease.

"(2) DESIGNATION OF RESPONSIBILITY.—The Director may designate an element of an armed force, combatant command, Defense Agency, Department of Defense Field Activity, or other element or organization of the Department of Defense to execute and administer security cooperation programs and activities described in paragraph (1) if the Director determines that the designation will achieve maximum effectiveness, efficiency, and economy in the activities for which designated.

"(c) AVAILABILITY OF FUNDS.—

"(1) IN GENERAL.—Funds available to the Defense Security Cooperation Agency, and other funds available to the Department of Defense for security cooperation programs and activities of the Department of Defense, may be used to implement security cooperation programs and activities of the Department of Defense authorized by this chapter.

"(2) BUDGET JUSTIFICATION.—Funds necessary for implementing security cooperation programs and activities of the Department of Defense under this chapter for a fiscal year shall be identified, with appropriate justification, in the consolidated budget for such fiscal year required by section 381 of this title.

"§383. Assessment, monitoring, and evaluation of programs and activities

"(a) PROGRAM REQUIRED.—The Secretary of Defense shall maintain a program of assessment, monitoring, and evaluation in support of the security cooperation programs and activities of the Department of Defense.

"(b) PROGRAM ELEMENTS AND REQUIREMENTS.—

"(1) ELEMENTS.—The program under subsection (a) shall provide for the following:

"(A) Initial assessments of partner capability requirements, potential programmatic risks, baseline information, and indicators of efficacy for purposes of planning, monitoring, and evaluation of security cooperation programs and activities of the Department of Defense.

"(B) Monitoring of implementation of such programs and activities in order to measure progress in execution and, to the extent possible, achievement of desired outcomes.

"(C) Evaluation of the efficiency and effectiveness of such programs and activities in achieving desired outcomes.

"(D) Identification of lessons learned in carrying out such programs and activities, and development of recommendation for improving future security cooperation programs and activities of the Department of Defense.

"(2) BEST PRACTICES.—The program shall be conducted in accordance with international best practices, interagency standards, and, if applicable, the Government Performance and Results Act of 1993 (Public Law 103–62), and the amendments made by that Act, and the GPRA Modernization Act of 2010 (Public Law 111–352), and the amendments made by that Act.

"(c) AVAILABILITY OF FUNDS.—

"(1) IN GENERAL.—Funds available to the Defense Security Cooperation Agency, and other funds available to the Department of Defense for security cooperation programs and activities of the Department of Defense, may be used to carry out the program required by subsection (a).

"(2) BUDGET JUSTIFICATION.—Funds described in paragraph (1) for a fiscal year shall be identified, with appropriate justification, in the consolidated budget for such fiscal year required by section 381 of this title.

"(d) REPORTS.—

"(1) REPORTS TO CONGRESS.—The Secretary shall submit to the congressional defense committees each year a report on the program under subsection (a) during the previous year. Each report shall include, for the year covered by such report, the following:

"(A) A description of the activities under the program.

"(B) An evaluation of the lessons learned and best practices identified through activities under the program.

"(2) INFORMATION FOR THE PUBLIC ON EVALUATIONS.—The Secretary shall make available to the public, on an Internet website of the Department of Defense available to the public, a summary of each evaluation conducted pursuant to subsection (b)(1)(C). In making a summary so available, the Secretary may redact or omit any information that the Secretary determines should not be disclosed to the public in order to protect the interest of the United States or the foreign country or countries covered by such evaluation.

"§ 385. Department of Defense support for other departments and agencies of the United States Government that advance Department of Defense security cooperation objectives

"(a) SUPPORT AUTHORIZED.—Subject to subsection (c), the Secretary of Defense is authorized to support other departments and agencies of the United States Government for the purpose of implementing or supporting foreign assistance programs and activities described in subsection (b) that advance security cooperation objectives of the Department of Defense.

"(b) FOREIGN ASSISTANCE PROGRAMS AND ACTIVITIES.—The foreign assistance programs and activities described in this subsection are foreign assistance programs and activities that—

"(1) are necessary for the effectiveness of one or more programs of the Department of Defense relating to security cooperation conducted pursuant to an authority in this chapter; and

"(2) cannot be carried out by the Department.

"(c) ANNUAL LIMITATION ON AMOUNT OF SUPPORT.—The amount of support provided pursuant to subsection (a) in any fiscal year may not exceed $75,000,000.

"(d) NOTICE AND WAIT.—If a determination is made to transfer funds in connection with the provision of support pursuant to subsection (a) for a program or activity, the transfer may not occur until—

"(1) the Secretary and the head of the department or agency to receive the funds jointly submit to the congressional defense committees a notice on the transfer, which notice shall include—

"(A) a detailed description of the purpose and estimated cost of such program or activity;

"(B) a detailed description of the security cooperation objectives of the Department, include the theater campaign plan of the combatant command concerned, that will be advanced;

"(C) a justification why such program or activity will advance such objectives;

"(D) a justification why such program or activity cannot be carried out by the Department;

"(E) an identification of any funds programmed or obligated by the department or agency other than the Department on such program or activity; and

"(F) a timeline for the provision of such support; and

"(2) a period of 30 days elapses after the date of the submittal of the notice pursuant to paragraph (1).".

"(n) PRESCRIPTION OF TERM "DEVELOPING COUNTRY".—

"(1) IN GENERAL.—The Secretary of Defense shall prescribe the meaning of the term "developing country" for purposes of chapter 16 of title 10, United States Code, as added by subsection (a)(3), and may from time to time prescribe a revision to the meaning of that term for those purposes.

"(2) INITIAL PRESCRIPTION.—The Secretary shall first prescribe the meaning of the term by not later than 270 days after the date of the enactment of this Act.

"(3) NOTICE TO CONGRESS.—Whenever the Secretary prescribes the meaning of the term pursuant to paragraph (1), the Secretary shall notify the appropriate committees of Congress of the meaning of the term as so prescribed.

"(4) APPROPRIATE COMMITTEES OF CONGRESS DEFINED.—In this subsection, the term "appropriate committees of Congress" has the meaning given that term in section 301(1) of title 10, United States Code, as so added.

"(o) CLERICAL AMENDMENTS.—Title 10, United States Code, is amended as follows:

"(1) The tables of chapters at the beginning of subtitle A, and at the beginning of part I of subtitle A, are amended—

"(A) by revising the chapter references relating to chapters 13, 15, 17, and 18 (and the section references therein) to conform to the redesignations made by paragraphs (1) and (2) of subsection (a); and

"(B) by inserting after the item relating to chapter 15, as revised pursuant to subparagraph (A), the following new item:

"16. Security Cooperation .... 301".

"(2) The section references in the tables of sections at the beginning of chapters 12, 13, 14, and 15, as redesignated by paragraph (1) of subsection (a), are revised to conform to the redesignations made by paragraph (2) of such subsection.

"(3) The table of sections at the beginning of chapter 7 is amended by striking the item relating to section 184.

"(4) The table of sections at the beginning of chapter 53 is amended by striking the item relating to section 1051b.

"(5) The table of sections at the beginning of chapter 108 is amended by striking the item relating to section 2166.

"(6) The table of sections at the beginning of subchapter I of chapter 134 is amended by striking the items relating to sections 2249a, 2249d, and 2249e.

"(7) The table of sections at the beginning of subchapter II of chapter 138 is amended by striking the item relating to section 2350m.

"(8) The tables of chapters at the beginning of subtitle D, and at the beginning of part III of subtitle D, are amended by striking the item relating to chapter 905.

"(9) The table of sections at the beginning of chapter 907 is amended by striking the item relating to section 9415.

SEC. 1242. MILITARY-TO-MILITARY EXCHANGES.

(a) CODIFICATION IN NEW CHAPTER ON SECURITY COOPERATION ACTIVITIES.—Chapter 16 of title 10, United States Code, as added by section 1241(a)(3) of this Act, is amended by inserting after the table of sections at the beginning of subchapter II a new section 311 consisting of—

(1) a heading as follows:

"§ 311. Exchange of defense personnel between United States and friendly foreign countries: authority"; and

(2) a text consisting of the text of section 1082 of the National Defense Authorization Act for

Fiscal Year 1997 (Public Law 104–201; 110 Stat. 2672; 10 U.S.C. 168 note).

(b) REVISIONS TO INCORPORATE PERMANENT NONRECIPROCAL EXCHANGE AUTHORITY.—Section 311 of title 10, United States Code, as added by subsection (a), is amended—

(1) in subsection (a)—

(A) in paragraph (1), by adding at the end the following new sentence: "Any exchange of personnel under such an agreement is subject to paragraph (3).";

(B) in paragraph (2)—

(i) in the matter preceding subparagraph (A), by striking "an ally of the United States or another friendly foreign country for the exchange" and inserting "a friendly foreign country or international or regional security organization for the reciprocal or non-reciprocal exchange";

(ii) in subparagraph (A), by striking "military" and inserting "members of the armed forces"; and

(iii) in subparagraph (B)—

(I) by inserting "or security" after "defense"; and

(II) by inserting before the period at the end the following: "or international or regional security organization"; and

(C) by adding at the end the following new paragraph:

"(3) An exchange of personnel under an international defense personnel exchange agreement under this section may only be made with the concurrence of the Secretary to State to the extent the exchange is with either of the following:

"(A) A non-defense security ministry of a foreign government.

"(B) An international or regional security organization.";

(2) in subsection (b)(2), by inserting before the period at the end the following: ", subject to the concurrence of the Secretary of State";

(3) in subsection (c)—

(A) by striking "Each government shall be required under" and inserting "In the case of"; and

(B) by inserting after "exchange agreement" the following: "that provides for reciprocal exchanges, each government shall be required"; and

(4) in subsection (f), by inserting "defense or security ministry of that" after "military personnel of the".

(c) CONFORMING REPEALS.—The following provisions of law are repealed:

(1) Section 1082 of the National Defense Authorization Act for Fiscal Year 1997 (Public Law 104–201; 110 Stat. 2672; 10 U.S.C. 168 note).

(2) Section 1207 of the National Defense Authorization Act for Fiscal Year 2010 (10 U.S.C. 168 note).

SEC. 1243. CONSOLIDATION AND REVISION OF AUTHORITIES FOR PAYMENT OF PERSONNEL EXPENSES NECESSARY FOR THEATER SECURITY COOPERATION.

(a) CONSOLIDATION AND REVISION OF AUTHORITIES IN NEW CHAPTER ON SECURITY COOPERATION ACTIVITIES.—Chapter 16 of title 10, United States Code, as added by section 1241(a)(3) of this Act, is amended by inserting after section 311, as added by section 1242(a) of this Act, the following new section:

"§ 312. Payment of personnel expenses necessary for theater security cooperation

"(a) AUTHORITY.—The Secretary of Defense may pay expenses specified in subsection (b) that the Secretary considers necessary for theater security cooperation.

"(b) TYPES OF EXPENSES.—The expenses that may be paid under the authority provided in subsection (a) are the following:

"(1) PERSONNEL EXPENSES.—The Secretary of Defense may pay travel, subsistence, and similar personnel expenses of, and special compensation for, the following that the Secretary considers necessary for theater security cooperation:

"(A) Defense personnel of friendly foreign governments.

"(B) With the concurrence of the Secretary of State, other personnel of friendly foreign governments and non-governmental personnel.

"(2) ADMINISTRATIVE SERVICES AND SUPPORT FOR LIAISON OFFICERS.—The Secretary of Defense may provide administrative services and support for the performance of duties by a liaison officer of a foreign country while the liaison officer is assigned temporarily to any headquarters in the Department of Defense.

"(3) TRAVEL, SUBSISTENCE, AND MEDICAL CARE FOR LIAISON OFFICERS.—The Secretary of Defense may pay the expenses of a liaison officer in connection with the assignment of that officer as described in paragraph (2) if the assignment is requested by the commander of a combatant command, the Chief of Staff of the Army, the Chief of Naval Operations, the Chief of Staff of the Air Force, the Commandant of the Marine Corps, or the head of a Defense Agency as follows:

"(A) Travel and subsistence expenses.

"(B) Personal expenses directly necessary to carry out the duties of that officer in connection with that assignment.

"(C) Expenses for medical care at a civilian medical facility if—

"(i) adequate medical care is not available to the liaison officer at a local military medical treatment facility;

"(ii) the Secretary determines that payment of such medical expenses is necessary and in the best interests of the United States; and

"(iii) medical care is not otherwise available to the liaison officer pursuant to any treaty or other international agreement.

"(D) Mission-related travel expenses if such travel meets each of the following conditions:

"(i) The travel is in support of the national security interests of the United States.

"(ii) The officer or official making the request directs round-trip travel from the assigned location to one or more travel locations.

"(4) CONFERENCES, SEMINARS, AND SIMILAR MEETINGS.—The authority provided by paragraph (1) includes authority to pay travel and subsistence expenses for personnel described in that paragraph in connection with the attendance of such personnel at any conference, seminar, or similar meeting that is in direct support of enhancing interoperability between the United States armed forces and the national security forces of a friendly foreign country for the purposes of conducting operations, the provision of equipment or training, or the planning for, or the execution of, bilateral or multilateral training, exercises, or military operations.

"(5) OTHER EXPENSES.—In addition to the personnel expenses payable under paragraph (1), the Secretary of Defense may pay such other limited expenses in connection with conferences, seminars, and similar meetings covered by paragraph (4) as the Secretary considers appropriate in the national security interests of the United States.

"(c) LIMITATIONS ON EXPENSES PAYABLE.—

"(1) PERSONNEL FROM DEVELOPING COUNTRIES.—The authority provided in subsection (a) may be used only for the payment of expenses of, and special compensation for, personnel from developing countries, except that the Secretary of Defense may authorize the payment of such expenses and special compensation for personnel from a country other than a developing country if the Secretary determines that such payment is necessary to respond to extraordinary circumstances and is in the national security interest of the United States.

"(2) NON-DEFENSE LIAISON OFFICERS.—In the case of a non-defense liaison officer of a foreign country, the authority of the Secretary of Defense under subsection (a) to pay expenses specified in paragraph (2) or (3) of subsection (b) may be exercised only if the assignment of that liaison officer as a liaison officer with the Department of Defense was accepted by the Secretary of Defense with the coordination of the Secretary of State.

"(d) REIMBURSEMENT.—The Secretary of Defense may provide the services and support specified in subsection (b)(2) with or without reimbursement from (or on behalf of) the recipients. The terms of reimbursement (if any) shall be specified in the appropriate agreements used to assign the liaison officer.

"(e) MONETARY LIMITATIONS ON EXPENSES PAYABLE.—

"(1) TRAVEL AND SUBSISTENCE EXPENSES GENERALLY.—Travel and subsistence expenses authorized to be paid under subsection (a) may not, in the case of any individual, exceed the amount that would be paid under chapter 7 or 8 of title 37 to a member of the armed forces (of a comparable grade) for authorized travel of a similar nature.

"(2) TRAVEL AND RELATED EXPENSES OF LIAISON OFFICERS.—The amount paid for expenses specified in subsection (b)(3) for any liaison officer in any fiscal year may not exceed $150,000.

"(f) REGULATIONS.—The Secretary of Defense shall prescribe regulations for the administration of this section. Such regulations shall be submitted to the Committees on Armed Services of the Senate and the House of Representatives.

"(g) ADMINISTRATIVE SERVICES AND SUPPORT DEFINED.—In this section, the term 'administrative services and support' includes base or installation support services, office space, utilities, copying services, fire and police protection, training programs conducted to familiarize, orient, or certify liaison personnel regarding unique aspects of the assignments of the liaison personnel, and computer support.".

(b) CONFORMING AMENDMENTS.—

(1) REPEALS.—Sections 1050, 1050a, 1051, and 1051a of title 10, United States Code, are repealed.

(2) CLERICAL AMENDMENTS.—The table of sections at the beginning of chapter 53 of such title is amended by striking the items relating to sections 1050, 1050a, 1051, and 1051a.

(c) SAVINGS PROVISION FOR FISCAL YEAR 2017.—The authority under section 1050 of title 10, United States Code, as in effect on the day before the date of the enactment of this Act, shall continue to apply with respect to the Inter-American Defense College during fiscal year 2017 under regulations prescribed by the Secretary of Defense.

SEC. 1244. TRANSFER AND REVISION OF CERTAIN AUTHORITIES ON PAYMENT OF EXPENSES OF TRAINING AND EXERCISES WITH FRIENDLY FOREIGN FORCES.

(a) TRANSFER AND REVISION OF AUTHORITY ON PAYMENT OF EXPENSES OF DEVELOPING COUNTRIES.—Section 2010 of title 10, United States Code, is transferred to chapter 16 of such title, as added by section 1241(a)(3) of this Act, inserted after the table of sections at the beginning of subchapter III, redesignated as section 321, and amended to read as follows:

"§321. Training with friendly foreign countries: payment of training and exercise expenses

"(a) TRAINING AUTHORIZED.—

"(1) TRAINING WITH FOREIGN FORCES GENERALLY.—The armed forces under the jurisdiction of the Secretary of Defense may train with the military forces or other security forces of a friendly foreign country if the Secretary determines that it is in the national security interest of the United States to do so.

"(2) LIMITATION ON TRAINING OF GENERAL PURPOSE FORCES.—The general purpose forces of the United States armed forces may train only with the military forces of a friendly foreign country.

"(3) TRAINING TO SUPPORT MISSION ESSENTIAL TASKS.—Any training conducted pursuant to paragraph (1) shall, to the maximum extent practicable, support the mission essential tasks for which the unit of the United States armed forces participating in such training is responsible.

"(4) ELEMENTS OF TRAINING.—Any training conducted pursuant to paragraph (1) shall, to the maximum extent practicable, include elements that promote—

"(A) observance of and respect for human rights and fundamental freedoms; and

"(B) respect for legitimate civilian authority within the foreign country concerned.

"(b) AUTHORITY TO PAY TRAINING AND EXERCISE EXPENSES.—Under regulations prescribed pursuant to subsection (e), the Secretary of a military department or the commander of a combatant command may pay, or authorize payment for, any of the following expenses:

"(1) Expenses of training forces assigned or allocated to that command in conjunction with training, and training with, the military forces or other security forces of a friendly foreign country under subsection (a).

"(2) Expenses of deploying such forces for that training.

"(3) The incremental expenses of a friendly foreign country as the direct result of participating in such training, as specified in the regulations.

"(4) The incremental expenses of a friendly foreign country as the direct result of participating in an exercise with the armed forces under the jurisdiction of the Secretary of Defense.

"(5) Small-scale construction that is directly related to the effective accomplishment of the training described in paragraph (1) or an exercise described in paragraph (4).

"(c) PURPOSE OF TRAINING AND EXERCISES.—

"(1) IN GENERAL.—The primary purpose of the training and exercises for which payment may be made under subsection (b) shall be to train United States forces.

"(2) SELECTION OF FOREIGN PARTNERS.—Training and exercises with friendly foreign countries under subsection (a) should be planned and prioritized consistent with applicable guidance relating to the security cooperation programs and activities of the Department of Defense.

"(d) AVAILABILITY OF FUNDS FOR ACTIVITIES THAT CROSS FISCAL YEARS.—Amounts available for the authority to pay expenses in subsection (b) for a fiscal year may be used to pay expenses under that subsection for training and exercises that begin in such fiscal year but end in the next fiscal year.

"(e) QUARTERLY NOTICE ON PLANNED TRAINING.—Not later than the end of the first calendar quarter beginning after the date of the enactment of the National Defense Authorization Act for Fiscal Year 2017, and every calendar quarter thereafter, the Secretary of Defense shall submit to the appropriate committees of Congress a notice setting forth the schedule of planned training engagement pursuant to subsection (a) during the calendar quarter first following the calendar quarter in which such notice is submitted.

"(f) REGULATIONS.—

"(1) IN GENERAL.—The Secretary of Defense shall prescribe regulations for the administration of this section. The Secretary shall submit the regulations to the Committees on Armed Services of the Senate and the House of Representatives.

"(2) ELEMENTS.—The regulations required under this section shall provide the following:

"(A) A requirement that training and exercise activities may be carried out under this section only with the prior approval of the Secretary.

"(B) Accounting procedures to ensure that the expenditures pursuant to this section are appropriate.

"(C) Procedures to limit the payment of incremental expenses to friendly foreign countries only to developing countries, except in the case of exceptional circumstances as specified in the regulations.''.

(b) TRANSFER OF AUTHORITY FOR PAYMENT OF EXPENSES IN CONNECTION WITH SPECIAL OPERATIONS FORCES TRAINING.—Section 2011 of title 10, United States Code, is transferred to chapter 16 of such title, inserted after section 321, as transferred and amended by subsection (a) of this section, and redesignated as section 322.

(c) CONFORMING REPEAL.—Section 1203 of the National Defense Authorization Act for Fiscal Year 2014 (Public Law 113–66; 127 Stat. 894; 10 U.S.C. 2011 note) is repealed.

(d) CLERICAL AMENDMENT.—The table of sections at the beginning of chapter 101 of title 10, United States Code, is amended by striking the items relating to sections 2010 and 2011.

SEC. 1245. TRANSFER AND REVISION OF AUTHORITY TO PROVIDE OPERATIONAL SUPPORT TO FORCES OF FRIENDLY FOREIGN COUNTRIES.

(a) TRANSFER AND REVISION.—Section 127d of title 10, United States Code, is transferred to chapter 16 of such title, as added by section 1241(a)(3) of this Act, inserted after the table of sections at the beginning of subchapter IV, redesignated as section 331, and amended to read as follows:

"§ 331. Friendly foreign countries: authority to provide support for conduct of operations

"(a) AUTHORITY.—The Secretary of Defense may provide support to friendly foreign countries in connection with the conduct of operations designated pursuant to subsection (b).

"(b) DESIGNATED OPERATIONS.—

"(1) IN GENERAL.—The Secretary of Defense shall designate the operations for which support may be provided under the authority in subsection (a).

"(2) NOTICE TO CONGRESS.—The Secretary shall notify the appropriate committees of Congress of the designation of any operation pursuant to this subsection.

"(3) ANNUAL REVIEW FOR CONTINUING DESIGNATION.—The Secretary shall undertake on an annual basis a review of the operations currently designated pursuant to this subsection in order to determine whether each such operation merits continuing designation for purposes of this section for another year. If the Secretary determines that any operation so reviewed merits continuing designation for purposes of this section for another year, the Secretary—

"(A) may continue the designation of such operation under this subsection for such purposes for another year; and

"(B) if the Secretary so continues the designation of such operation, shall notify the appropriate committees of Congress of the continuation of designation of such operation.

"(c) TYPES OF SUPPORT AUTHORIZED.—The types of support that may be provided under the authority in subsection (a) are the following:

"(1) Logistic support, supplies, and services to security forces of a friendly foreign country participating in—

"(A) an operation with the armed forces under the jurisdiction of the Secretary of Defense; or

"(B) a military or stability operation that benefits the national security interests of the United States.

"(2) Logistic support, supplies, and services—

"(A) to military forces of a friendly foreign country solely for the purpose of enhancing the interoperability of the logistical support systems of military forces participating in a combined operation with the United States in order to facilitate such operation; or

"(B) to a nonmilitary logistics, security, or similar agency of a friendly foreign government if such provision would directly benefit the armed forces under the jurisdiction of the Secretary of Defense.

"(3) Procurement of equipment for the purpose of the loan of such equipment to the military forces of a friendly foreign country participating in a United States-supported coalition or combined operation and the loan of such equipment to those forces to enhance capabilities or to increase interoperability with the armed forces under the jurisdiction of the Secretary of Defense and other coalition partners.

"(4) Provision of specialized training to personnel of friendly foreign countries in connection with such an operation, including training of such personnel before deployment in connection with such operation.

"(5) Small-scale construction to support military forces of a friendly foreign country participating in a United States-supported coalition or combined operation when the construction is directly linked to the ability of such forces to participate in such operation effectively and is limited to the geographic area where such operation is taking place.

"(d) CERTIFICATION REQUIRED.—

"(1) OPERATIONS IN WHICH THE UNITED STATES IS NOT PARTICIPATING.—The Secretary of Defense may provide support under subsection (a) to a friendly foreign country with respect to an operation in which the United States is not participating only—

"(A) if the Secretary of Defense and the Secretary of State jointly certify to the appropriate committees of Congress that the operation is in the national security interests of the United States; and

"(B) after the expiration of the 15-day period beginning on the date of such certification.

"(2) ACCOMPANYING REPORT.—Any certification under paragraph (1) shall be accompanied by a report that includes the following:

"(A) A description of the operation, including the geographic area of the operation.

"(B) A list of participating countries.

"(C) A description of the type of support and the duration of support to be provided.

"(D) A description of the national security interests of the United States supported by the operation.

"(E) Such other matters as the Secretary of Defense and the Secretary of State consider significant to a consideration of such certification.

"(e) SECRETARY OF STATE CONCURRENCE.—The provision of support under subsection (a) may be made only with the concurrence of the Secretary of State.

"(f) SUPPORT OTHERWISE PROHIBITED BY LAW.—The Secretary of Defense may not use the authority in subsection (a) to provide any type of support described in subsection (c) that is otherwise prohibited by any provision of law.

"(g) LIMITATIONS ON VALUE.—

"(1) The aggregate value of all logistic support, supplies, and services provided under paragraphs (1), (4), and (5) of subsection (c) in any fiscal year may not exceed $450,000,000.

"(2) The aggregate value of all logistic support, supplies, and services provided under subsection (c)(2) in any fiscal year may not exceed $5,000,000.

"(h) LOGISTIC SUPPORT, SUPPLIES, AND SERVICES DEFINED.—In this section, the term 'logistic support, supplies, and services' has the meaning given that term in section 2350(1) of this title.''.

(b) CLERICAL AMENDMENT.—The table of sections at the beginning of chapter 3 of such title is amended by striking the item relating to section 127d.

(c) CONFORMING REPEAL.—Section 1207 of the National Defense Authorization Act for Fiscal Year 2016 (Public Law 114–92; 129 Stat. 1040; 10 U.S.C. 2282 note) is repealed.

SEC. 1246. DEPARTMENT OF DEFENSE STATE PARTNERSHIP PROGRAM.

(a) CODIFICATION IN NEW CHAPTER ON SECURITY COOPERATION ACTIVITIES.—Chapter 16 of title 10, United States Code, as added by section 1241(a)(3) of this Act, is amended by inserting after the table of sections at the beginning of subchapter V a new section 341 consisting of—

(1) a heading as follows:

"§ 341. Department of Defense State Partnership Program"; and

(2) a text consisting of subsections (a) through (g) of section 1205 of the National Defense Authorization Act for Fiscal Year 2014 (32 U.S.C. 107 note).

(b) PROHIBITION ON ACTIVITIES WITH UNITS HAVING COMMITTED GROSS VIOLATIONS OF HUMAN RIGHTS.—Subsection (b) of section 341 of title 10, United States Code, as added by subsection (a) of this section, is amended—

(1) by striking "(b) LIMITATION.—An activity" and inserting the following:

"(b) LIMITATIONS.—

"(1) IN GENERAL.—An activity"; and

(2) by adding at the end the following new paragraph:

"(2) PROHIBITION ON ACTIVITIES WITH UNITS THAT HAVE COMMITTED GROSS VIOLATIONS OF HUMAN RIGHTS.—The conduct of any activities under a program established under subsection (a) shall be subject to the provisions of section 362 of this title.''.

(c) REVISIONS TO STRIKE OBSOLETE PROVISIONS AND CONFORM TO PROVISIONS IN NEW CHAPTER.—Such section 341, as so added, is further amended—

(1) by striking subsection (d) and inserting the following new subsection (d):

"(d) REGULATIONS.—This section shall be carried out in accordance with such regulations as the Secretary of Defense shall prescribe for purposes of this section. Such regulations shall include accounting procedures to ensure that expenditures of funds to carry out this section are accounted for and appropriate.''; and

(2) in subsection (g), by striking "under title 10" and all that follows and inserting "under title 10 as in effect on December 26, 2013.''.

(d) ANNUAL REPORTS.—

(1) REPORTS UNDER CODIFIED AUTHORITY.—Subsection (f) of such section 341, as so added, is amended—

(A) by striking "(f) REPORTS AND NOTIFICATIONS.—" and all that follows through "(B) MATTERS TO BE INCLUDED.—" and inserting the following:

"(f) ANNUAL REPORTS.—

"(1) IN GENERAL.—Not later than February 1 following each of fiscal years 2016, 2017, and 2018, the Secretary of Defense shall submit to the appropriate congressional committees a report on activities under each program established under subsection (a) during such fiscal year.

"(2) MATTERS TO BE INCLUDED.—''; and

(B) in paragraph (2), as redesignated by subparagraph (A) of this paragraph—

(i) by redesignating clauses (i) through (vi) as subparagraphs (A) through (F), respectively, and realigning the margin of each such subparagraph two ems to the left; and

(ii) in subparagraph (F), as redesignated by clause (i) of this subparagraph, by striking "clause (v)" and inserting "subparagraph (E)".

(2) REPORTS UNDER CODIFIED REPORTING AUTHORITY IN NEW CHAPTER ON SECURITY COOPERATION ACTIVITIES.—Effective as of January 1, 2020—

(A) section 386(c)(1) of title 10, United States Code, as added by section 1251(d)(1) of this Act, is amended by inserting "341," after "333,"; and

(B) section 341 of title 10, United States Code, as added and amended by this section, is further amended—

(i) by striking subsection (f); and

(ii) by redesignating subsection (g) as subsection (f).

(e) CONFORMING REPEAL.—Section 1205 of the National Defense Authorization Act for Fiscal Year 2014 is repealed.

SEC. 1247. TRANSFER OF AUTHORITY ON REGIONAL DEFENSE COMBATING TERRORISM FELLOWSHIP PROGRAM.

(a) TRANSFER AND REDESIGNATION.—Section 2249c of title 10, United States Code, is transferred to chapter 16 of such title, as added by section 1241(a)(3) of this Act, inserted after section 344, as transferred and redesignated by section 1241(g) of this Act, and redesignated as section 345.

(b) CONFORMING AMENDMENT IN CONNECTION WITH TRANSFER TO NEW CHAPTER.—Subsection (c) of such section 345, as so transferred and redesignated, is amended by striking "to Congress" and inserting "to the appropriate committees of Congress".

(c) HEADING AMENDMENT.—The heading of such section 345, as so transferred and redesignated, is amended to read as follows:

"§345. Regional Defense Combating Terrorism Fellowship Program".

(d) CLERICAL AMENDMENT.—The table of sections at the beginning of subchapter I of chapter 134 of such title is amended by striking the item relating to section 2249c.

SEC. 1248. CONSOLIDATION OF AUTHORITIES FOR SERVICE ACADEMY INTERNATIONAL ENGAGEMENT.

(a) CONSOLIDATION OF AUTHORITIES.—Chapter 16 of title 10, United States Code, as added by section 1241(a)(3) of this Act, is amended by inserting after section 346, as transferred and redesignated by section 1241(h) of this Act, the following new section:

"§347. International engagement authorities for service academies

"(a) SELECTION OF PERSONS FROM FOREIGN COUNTRIES TO RECEIVE INSTRUCTION AT SERVICE ACADEMIES.—

"(1) ATTENDANCE AUTHORIZED.—

"(A) IN GENERAL.—The Secretary of each military department may permit persons from foreign countries to receive instruction at the Service Academy under the jurisdiction of the Secretary. Such persons shall be in addition to—

"(i) in the case of the United States Military Academy, the authorized strength of the Corps of the Cadets of the Academy under 4342 of this title;

"(ii) in the case of the United States Naval Academy, the authorized strength of the Brigade of Midshipmen of the Academy under section 6954 of this title; and

"(iii) in the case of the United States Air Force Academy, the authorized strength of the Cadet Wing of the Academy under 9342 of this title.

"(B) LIMITATION ON NUMBER.—The number of persons permitted to receive instruction at each Service Academy under this subsection may not be more than 60 at any one time.

"(2) DETERMINATION OF FOREIGN COUNTRIES FROM WHICH PERSONS MAY BE SELECTED.—The Secretary of a military department, upon approval by the Secretary of Defense, shall determine—

"(A) the countries from which persons may be selected for appointment under this subsection to the Service Academy under the jurisdiction of that Secretary; and

"(B) the number of persons that may be selected from each country.

"(3) QUALIFICATIONS AND SELECTION.—The Secretary of each military department—

"(A) may establish entrance qualifications and methods of competition for selection among individual applicants under this subsection; and

"(B) shall select those persons who will be permitted to receive instruction at the Service Academy under the jurisdiction of the Secretary under this subsection.

"(4) SELECTION PRIORITY TO PERSONS WITH NATIONAL SERVICE OBLIGATION UPON GRADUATION.—In selecting persons to receive instruction under this subsection from among applicants from the countries approved under paragraph (2), the Secretary of the military department concerned shall give a priority to persons who have a national service obligation to their countries upon graduation from the Service Academy concerned.

"(5) PAY, ALLOWANCES, AND EMOLUMENTS OF PERSONS ADMITTED.—A person receiving instruction under this subsection is entitled to the pay, allowances, and emoluments of a cadet or midshipman appointed from the United States, and from the same appropriations.

"(6) REIMBURSEMENT OF COSTS BY FOREIGN COUNTRIES FROM WHICH PERSONS ARE ADMITTED.—

"(A) REIMBURSEMENT REQUIRED.—Each foreign country from which a cadet or midshipman is permitted to receive instruction at one of the Service Academies under this subsection shall reimburse the United States for the cost of providing such instruction, including the cost of pay, allowances, and emoluments provided under paragraph (5). The Secretaries of the military departments shall prescribe the rates for reimbursement under this paragraph, except that the reimbursement rates may not be less than the cost to the United States of providing such instruction, including pay, allowances, and emoluments, to a cadet or midshipman appointed from the United States.

"(B) WAIVER AUTHORITY.—The Secretary of Defense may waive, in whole or in part, the requirement for reimbursement of the cost of instruction for a cadet or midshipman under subparagraph (A). In the case of a partial waiver, the Secretary of Defense shall establish the amount waived.

"(7) APPLICABILITY OF ACADEMY REGULATIONS, ETC.—

"(A) IN GENERAL.—Except as the Secretary of the military department concerned determines, a person receiving instruction under this subsection at the Service Academy under the jurisdiction of that Secretary is subject to the same regulations governing admission, attendance, discipline, resignation, discharge, dismissal, and graduation as a cadet or midshipman at that Academy appointed from the United States.

"(B) CLASSIFIED INFORMATION.—The Secretary of the military department concerned may prescribe regulations with respect to access to classified information by a person receiving instruction under this subsection at the Service Academy under the jurisdiction of that Secretary that differ from the regulations that apply to a cadet or midshipman at that Academy appointed from the United States.

"(8) INELIGIBILITY FOR APPOINTMENT IN THE UNITED STATES ARMED FORCES.—A person receiving instruction at a Service Academy under this subsection is not entitled to an appointment in an armed force of the United States by reason of graduation from the Academy.

"(9) INAPPLICABILITY OF REQUIREMENT FOR TAKING OATH OF ADMISSION.—A person receiving instruction under this subsection is not subject to section 4346(d), 6958(d), or 9346(d) of this title, as the case may be.

"(b) EXCHANGE PROGRAMS WITH FOREIGN MILITARY ACADEMIES.—

"(1) EXCHANGE PROGRAMS AUTHORIZED.—The Secretary of a military department may permit a student enrolled at a military academy of a foreign country to receive instruction at the Service Academy under the jurisdiction of that Secretary in exchange for a cadet or midshipman receiving instruction at that foreign military academy pursuant to an exchange agreement entered into between the Secretary and appropriate officials of the foreign country. A student receiving instruction at a Service Academy under the exchange program under this subsection shall be in addition to persons receiving instruction at the Academy under subsection (a).

"(2) LIMITATIONS ON NUMBER AND DURATION OF EXCHANGES.—An exchange agreement under this subsection between the Secretary and a foreign country shall provide for the exchange of students on a one-for-one basis each fiscal year. Not more than 100 cadets or midshipmen from each Service Academy and a comparable number of students from foreign military academies participating in the exchange program may be exchanged during any fiscal year. The duration of an exchange may not exceed the equivalent of one academic semester at a Service Academy.

"(3) COSTS AND EXPENSES.—

"(A) NO PAY AND ALLOWANCES.—A student from a military academy of a foreign country is not entitled to the pay, allowances, and emoluments of a cadet or midshipman by reason of attendance at a Service Academy under the exchange program, and the Department of Defense may not incur any cost of international travel required for transportation of such a student to and from the sponsoring foreign country.

"(B) SUBSISTENCE, TRANSPORTATION, ETC..— The Secretary of the military department concerned may provide a student from a foreign country under the exchange program, during the period of the exchange, with subsistence, transportation within the continental United States, clothing, health care, and other services to the same extent that the foreign country provides comparable support and services to the exchanged cadet or midshipman in that foreign country.

"(C) SOURCE OF FUNDS.—A Service Academy shall bear all costs of the exchange program from funds appropriated for that Academy and from such additional funds as may be available to that Academy from a source, other than appropriated funds, to support cultural immersion, regional awareness, or foreign language training activities in connection with the exchange program.

"(D) LIMITATION ON EXPENDITURES.—Expenditures in support of the exchange program from funds appropriated for each Academy may not exceed $1,000,000 during any fiscal year.

"(4) APPLICATION OF OTHER LAWS.—Paragraphs (7), (8), and (9) of subsection (a) shall apply with respect to a student enrolled at a military academy of a foreign country while attending a Service Academy under the exchange program.

"(5) REGULATIONS.—The Secretary of the military department concerned shall prescribe regulations to implement this subsection. Such regulations may include qualification criteria and methods of selection for students of foreign military academies to participate in the exchange program.

"(c) FOREIGN AND CULTURAL EXCHANGE ACTIVITIES.—

"(1) ATTENDANCE AUTHORIZED.—The Secretary of a military department may authorize the Service Academy under the jurisdiction of that Secretary to permit students, officers, and other representatives of a foreign country to attend that Academy for periods of not more than four weeks if the Secretary determines that the attendance of such persons contributes significantly to the development of foreign language, cross-cultural interactions and understanding, and cultural immersion of cadets or midshipmen, as the case may be.

"(2) EFFECT OF ATTENDANCE.—Persons attending a Service Academy under paragraph (1) are not considered to be students enrolled at that Academy and are in addition to persons receiving instruction at that Academy under subsection (a) or (b).

"(3) FINANCIAL MATTERS.—

"(A) COSTS AND EXPENSES.—The Secretary of a military department may pay the travel, subsistence, and similar personal expenses of persons incurred to attend the Service Academy under the jurisdiction of that Secretary under paragraph (1).

"(B) SOURCE OF FUNDS.—Each Service Academy shall bear the costs of the attendance of persons at that Academy under paragraph (1) from funds appropriated for that Academy and from such additional funds as may be available to that Academy from a source, other than appropriated funds, to support cultural immersion, regional awareness, or foreign language training activities in connection with their attendance.

"(C) LIMITATION ON EXPENDITURES.—Expenditures from appropriated funds in support of activities under this subsection for any Service Academy may not exceed $40,000 during any fiscal year.

"(d) SERVICE ACADEMY DEFINED.—In this section, the term 'Service Academy' means the following:

"(1) The United States Military Academy.

"(2) The United States Naval Academy.

"(3) The United States Air Force Academy.".

(b) CONFORMING REPEALS.—

(1) REPEALS.—Sections 4344, 4345, 4345a, 6957, 6957a, 6957b, 9344, 9345, and 9345a of title 10, United States Code, are repealed.

(2) CLERICAL AMENDMENTS.—

(A) The table of sections at the beginning of chapter 403 of such title is amended by striking the items relating to sections 4344, 4345, and 4345a.

(B) The table of sections at the beginning of chapter 603 of such title is amended by striking the items relating to sections 6957, 6957a, and 6957b.

(C) The table of sections at the beginning of chapter 903 of such title is amended by striking the items relating to sections 9344, 9345, and 9345a.

SEC. 1249. CONSOLIDATED ANNUAL BUDGET FOR SECURITY COOPERATION PROGRAMS AND ACTIVITIES OF THE DEPARTMENT OF DEFENSE.

(a) IN GENERAL.—Chapter 16 of title 10, United States Code, as added by section 1241(a)(3) of this Act, is amended by inserting after the table at the beginning of subchapter VII the following new section:

"§ 381. Consolidated budget

"(a) CONSOLIDATED BUDGET.—The budget of the President for each fiscal year, as submitted to Congress by the President pursuant to section 1105 of title 31, shall set forth by budget function and as a separate item the amounts requested for the Department of Defense for such fiscal year for all security cooperation programs and activities of the Department of Defense, including the military departments, to be conducted in such fiscal year, including the specific country or region and the applicable authority, to the extent practicable.

"(b) QUARTERLY REPORT ON USE OF FUNDS.—Not later than 30 days after the end of each calendar quarter, the Secretary shall submit to the appropriate committees of Congress a report on the obligation and expenditure of funds for security cooperation programs and activities of the Department of Defense during such calendar quarter.".

(b) APPLICABILITY.—The amendment made by subsection (a) shall take effect on the date of the enactment of this Act, and shall apply as follows:

(1) Subsection (a) of section 381 of title 10, United States Code, as added by subsection (a), shall apply to budgets submitted to Congress by the President pursuant to section 1105 of title 31, United States Code, for each fiscal year after fiscal year 2018.

(2) Subsection (b) of such section 381, as so added, shall apply to calendar quarters beginning on or after the date of the enactment of this Act.

SEC. 1250. DEPARTMENT OF DEFENSE SECURITY COOPERATION WORKFORCE DEVELOPMENT.

(a) IN GENERAL.—Chapter 16 of title 10, United States Code, as added by section 1241(a)(3) of this Act, is amended by inserting after section 383, as added by section 1241(m) of this Act, the following new section:

"§ 384. Department of Defense security cooperation workforce development

"(a) PROGRAM REQUIRED.—The Secretary of Defense shall carry out a program to be known as the 'Department of Defense Security Cooperation Workforce Development Program' (in this section referred to as the 'Program') to oversee the development and management of a professional workforce supporting security cooperation programs and activities of the Department of Defense, including—

"(1) assessment, planning, monitoring, execution, evaluation, and administration of such programs and activities under this chapter; and

"(2) execution of security assistance programs and activities under the Foreign Assistance Act of 1961 and the Arms Export Control Act by the Department of Defense.

"(b) PURPOSE.—The purpose of the Program is to improve the quality and professionalism of the security cooperation workforce in order to ensure that the workforce—

"(1) has the capacity, in both personnel and skills, needed to properly perform its mission, provide appropriate support to the assessment, planning, monitoring, execution, evaluation, and administration of security cooperation programs and activities described in subsection (a), and ensure that the Department receives the best value for the expenditure of public resources on such programs and activities; and

"(2) is assigned in a manner that ensures personnel with the appropriate level of expertise and experience are assigned in sufficient numbers to fulfill requirements for the security cooperation programs and activities of the Department of Defense and the execution of security assistance programs and activities described in subsection (a)(2).

"(c) ELEMENTS.—The Program shall consist of such elements relating to the development and management of the security cooperation workforce as the Secretary considers appropriate for the purposes specified in subsection (b), including elements on training, certification, assignment, and career development of personnel of the security cooperation workforce.

"(d) MANAGEMENT.—The Program shall be managed by the Director of the Defense Security Cooperation Agency.

"(e) GUIDANCE.—

"(1) INTERIM GUIDANCE.—Not later than 180 days after the date of the enactment of the National Defense Authorization Act for Fiscal Year 2017, the Secretary shall issue interim guidance for the execution and administration of the Program.

"(2) FINAL GUIDANCE.—Not later than one year after the date of the enactment of the National Defense Authorization Act for Fiscal Year 2017, the Secretary shall issue final guidance for the execution and administration of the Program.

"(3) SCOPE OF GUIDANCE.—The guidance shall do the following:

"(A) Provide direction to the Department of Defense on the establishment of professional career paths for the personnel of the security cooperation workforce, addressing training and education standards, promotion opportunities and requirements, retention policies, and scope of workforce demands.

"(B) Provide for a mechanism to identify and define training and certification requirements for security cooperation positions in the Department and a means to track workforce skills and certifications.

"(C) Provide for a mechanism to establish a program of professional certification in Department of Defense security cooperation for personnel of the security cooperation workforce in different career tracks and levels of competency based on requisite training and experience.

"(D) Establish requirements for training and professional development associated with each level of certification provided for under subparagraph (C).

"(E) Establish and maintain a school to train, educate, and certify the security cooperation workforce according to standards developed for purposes of subparagraph (C).

"(F) Provide for a mechanism for assigning appropriately certified personnel of the security cooperation workforce to assignments associated with key positions in connection with security cooperation programs and activities.

"(G) Identify the appropriate composition of career and temporary personnel necessary to constitute the security cooperation workforce.

"(H) Identify specific positions throughout the security cooperation workforce to be managed and assigned through the Program.

"(f) SOURCE OF FUNDS.—

"(1) IN GENERAL.—Funds available to the Defense Security Cooperation Agency, and other funds available to the Department of Defense for security cooperation programs and activities of the Department of Defense, may be used to carry out the Program.

"(2) BUDGET JUSTIFICATION.—Funds necessary to carry out the Program as described in paragraph (1) for a fiscal year shall be identified, with appropriate justification, in the consolidated budget for such fiscal year required by section 381 of this title.

"(g) USE OF FUNDS.—Amounts available for use for the Program may be transferred to any account of the military departments or the Defense Agencies for purposes of the Program.

"(h) SECURITY COOPERATION WORKFORCE DEFINED.—In this section, the term 'security cooperation workforce' means the following:

"(1) Members of the armed forces and civilian employees of the Department of Defense working in the security cooperation organizations of United States missions overseas.

"(2) Members of the armed forces and civilian employees of the Department of Defense in the geographic combatant commands and functional combatant commands responsible for planning, monitoring, or conducting security cooperation activities.

"(3) Members of the armed forces and civilian employees of the Department of Defense in the military departments performing security cooperation activities, including activities in connection with the acquisition and development of technology release policies.

"(4) Other military and civilian personnel of Defense Agencies and Field Activities who perform security cooperation activities.

"(5) Personnel of the Department of Defense who perform assessments, monitoring, or evaluations of security cooperation programs and activities of the Department of Defense, including assessments under section 383 of this title.

"(6) Other members of the armed forces or civilian employees of the Department of Defense who contribute significantly to the security cooperation programs and activities of the Department of Defense by virtue of their assigned duties, as determined pursuant to the guidance issued under subsection (e).".

(b) REPORTS ON WORKFORCE DEVELOPMENT.—

(1) IN GENERAL.—Not later than March 1, 2018, and each year thereafter through 2021, the Secretary of Defense shall submit to the appropriate committees of Congress a report on the Department of Defense Security Cooperation Workforce Development Program required by section 384 of title 10, United States Code, as added by subsection (a), for the fiscal year beginning in the year in which such report is submitted.

(2) ELEMENTS.—Each report under this subsection shall include, for the fiscal year covered by such report, the following:

(A) The funds requested or allocated for the Department of Defense Security Cooperation Workforce Development Program and for the security cooperation workforce.

(B) A description of how the funds identified pursuant to subparagraph (A) will be implemented for the following:

(i) To address any gaps in the skills and competencies of the current or anticipated security cooperation workforce

(ii) To provide incentives to retain qualified, experienced personnel in the security cooperation workforce.

(iii) To provide incentives to attract and recruit new, high-quality personnel to the security cooperation workforce.

(C) Any other matters the Secretary considers appropriate.

(3) DEFINITIONS.—In this subsection:

(A) The term "appropriate committees of Congress" has the meaning given that term in section 301(1) of title 10, United States Code, as added by section 1241(a)(3) of this Act.

(B) The term "security cooperation workforce" has the meaning given that term in section 384(h) of title 10, United States Code, as added by subsection (a).

SEC. 1251. REPORTING REQUIREMENTS.

(a) CODIFICATION IN NEW CHAPTER ON SECURITY COOPERATION ACTIVITIES.—Chapter 16 of title 10, United States Code, as added by section 1241(a)(3) of this Act, is amended by inserting after section 385, as added by section 1241(m) of this Act, a new section 386 consisting of—

(1) a heading as follows:

"§386. Annual report"; and

(2) a text consisting of subsections (a) through (e) of section 1211 of the Carl Levin and Howard P. "Buck" McKeon National Defense Authorization Act for Fiscal Year 2015 (Public Law 113–291; 128 Stat. 3544).

(b) REVISIONS TO PROVIDE FOR PERMANENT, ANNUAL REPORT.—Subsection (a) of section 386 of title 10, United States Code, as added by subsection (a) of this section, is amended—

(1) by striking "BIENNIAL" and all that follows through "the Secretary of Defense" and inserting "ANNUAL REPORT REQUIRED.—Not later than January 31 of each year beginning in 2018, the Secretary of Defense";

(2) by striking "congressional defense committees" and inserting "appropriate congressional committees";

(3) by inserting "under the authorities in subsection (c)" after "Department of Defense";

(4) by striking "security assistance" and inserting "assistance";

(5) by striking "the two fiscal years" and inserting "the fiscal year"; and

(6) by striking "under the authorities in subsection (c)" after "submitted".

(c) ELEMENTS OF REPORT.—Subsection (b) of such section 386, as so added, is amended—

(1) in paragraph (1), by inserting ", duration," after "purpose";

(2) in paragraph (2), by striking "The cost" and inserting "The cost and expenditures";

(3) by adding at the end the following:

"(4) For each foreign country in which defense articles, defense services, supplies (including consumables), small-scale construction, or reimbursement were provided, a description of the extent of participation, if any, by the military forces and security forces or other government organizations of such foreign country.

"(5) The number of members of the United States armed forces involved in providing such defense articles, defense services, supplies (including consumables), and small-scale construction, and, if applicable, a description of the military benefits for such members involved in providing such training, equipment, or assistance.

"(6) A summary, by authority, of the activities carried out under each authority specified in subsection (c).".

(d) MODIFICATION TO SPECIFIED AUTHORITIES.—Subsection (c) of such section 386, as so added, is amended—

(1) by striking paragraph (1) and inserting the following new paragraph (1):

"(1) Sections 311, 321, 331, 332, 333, 344, 348, 349, and 350 of this title.";

(2) by striking paragraphs (4), (5), (7), (10), (11), and (12);

(3) by redesignating paragraphs (6), (8), (9), and (13) through (16) as paragraphs (4) through (10), respectively;

(4) by inserting after paragraph (10), as redesignated by paragraph (3) of this subsection, the following new paragraphs:

"(11) Section 401 of this title, relating to humanitarian and civic assistance provided in conjunction with military operations.

"(12) Section 1206 of the Carl Levin and Howard P. 'Buck' McKeon National Defense Authorization Act for Fiscal Year 2015 (128 Stat. 3538; 10 U.S.C. 2282 note), relating to authority to conduct human rights training of security forces and associated security ministries of foreign countries.";

(5) by redesignating paragraph (17) as paragraph (13); and

(6) by striking "of title 10, United States Code" each place it appears and inserting "of this title".

(e) MODIFICATION OF NONDUPLICATION OF EFFORT REQUIREMENT.—Subsection (d) of such section 386, as so added, is amended—

(1) by striking "If any information" and inserting the following:

"(1) IN GENERAL.—Except as provided in paragraph (2), if any information"; and

(2) by adding at the end the following new paragraph:

"(2) EXCEPTION.—Paragraph (1) does not apply with respect to information required under subsection (a) that is required to be submitted as described in paragraphs (1) and (2) of subsection (b).".

(f) FORM.—Subsection (e) of such section 386, as so added, is amended by inserting "that may also include other sensitive information" after "annex".

(g) CONFORMING REPEAL.—Section 1211 of the Carl Levin and Howard P. "Buck" McKeon National Defense Authorization Act for Fiscal Year 2015 is repealed.

SEC. 1252. QUADRENNIAL REVIEW OF SECURITY SECTOR ASSISTANCE PROGRAMS AND AUTHORITIES OF THE UNITED STATES GOVERNMENT.

(a) STATEMENT OF POLICY.—It is the policy of the United States that the principal goals of the security sector assistance programs and authorities of the United States Government are as follows:

(1) To assist partner nations in building sustainable capability to address common security challenges with the United States.

(2) To promote partner nation support for United States interests.

(3) To promote universal values, such as good governance, transparent and accountable oversight of security forces, rule of law, transparency, accountability, delivery of fair and effective justice, and respect for human rights.

(4) To strengthen collective security and multinational defense arrangements and organizations of which the United States is a participant.

(b) QUADRENNIAL REVIEW.—

(1) REVIEW REQUIRED.—Not later than January 31, 2018, and every four years thereafter though 2034, the President shall complete a review of the security sector assistance programs, policies, authorities, and resources of the United States Government across the United States Government.

(2) ELEMENTS.—Each review under this subsection shall include the following:

(A) An examination whether the current security sector assistance programs, policies, authorities, and resources of the United States Government are sufficient to achieve the goals specified in subsection (a), and an identification of any gaps or shortfalls needing mitigation.

(B) An examination of the success of such programs and resources in achieving such goals, based on a review of relevant departmental and interagency programmatic and strategic evaluations.

(C) An examination of the extent to which the security sector assistance of the United States Government is aligned with national security and foreign policy objectives, conducted in support of clear and coherent policy guidance, and planned and executed in accordance with identified best practices.

(D) The development of recommendations, as appropriate, for improving the security sector assistance programs, policies, authorities, and resources of the United States Government to more effectively achieve the goals specified in subsection (a) and support other national security objectives.

(3) SUBMITTAL TO CONGRESS.—Not later than 60 days after the completion of a review under this subsection, the President shall submit to the appropriate committees of Congress a report setting forth a summary of the review, including any recommendations developed pursuant to paragraph (2)(D).

(4) APPROPRIATE COMMITTEES OF CONGRESS DEFINED.—In this subsection, the term "appropriate committees of Congress" has the meaning given that term in section section 301(1) of title 10, United States Code, as added by section 1241(a)(3) of this Act.

SEC. 1253. OTHER CONFORMING AMENDMENTS AND AUTHORITY FOR ADMINISTRATION.

(a) REPEAL OF OTHER SUPERSEDED, OBSOLETE, OR DUPLICATIVE STATUTES.—

(1) IN GENERAL.—The following provisions of title 10, United States Code, are repealed:

(A) Section 168, relating to military-to-military contacts and comparable activities.

(B) Section 1051c, relating to assignment of members of foreign military forces to improve education and training in information security through multilateral, bilateral, or regional cooperation programs.

(C) Section 2562, relating to a limitation on use of excess construction or fire equipment from Department of Defense stocks in foreign assistance or military sales programs.

(D) Sections 4681 and 9681, relating to sale of surplus war material to States and foreign governments.

(2) CLERICAL AMENDMENTS.—Title 10, United States Code, is amended as follows:

(A) The table of sections at the beginning of chapter 6 is amended by striking the item relating to section 168.

(B) The table of sections at the beginning of chapter 53 is amended by striking the item relating to section 1051c.

(C) The table of sections at the beginning of chapter 152 is amended by striking the item relating to section 2562.

(D) The table of sections at the beginning of chapter 443 is amended by striking the item relating to section 4681.

(E) The table of sections at the beginning of chapter 943 is amended by striking the item relating to section 9681.

(b) SAVINGS CLAUSE.—Any determination or other action made or taken before the date of the enactment of this Act under a provision of law transferred or repealed by this subchapter that is in effect as of the date of the enactment of this Act and is necessary for the administration of a successor authority to such provision of law under chapter 16 of title 10, United States Code, by reason of the enactment of such chapter by this subchapter shall remain in effect, in accordance with the terms of such determination or action when made or taken, for purposes of the administration of such successor authority.

(c) REPORT ON DISCHARGE OF CERTAIN ACTIVITIES UNDER NEW SECURITY COOPERATION AUTHORITY.—

(1) IN GENERAL.—Not later than October 1, 2017, the Secretary of Defense shall submit to the congressional defense committees a report setting forth a description of any gaps that exist between applicable authorities in chapter 16 of title 10, United States Code, as added by section 1241(a)(3) of this Act, and the current law or other authorities under which activities under the initiatives specified in paragraph (2) are carried out.

(2) INITIATIVES.—The initiatives specified in this paragraph are the following:

(A) The Southeast Asia Maritime Security Initiative.

(B) The Ukraine Security Assistance Initiative.

(3) ELEMENTS.—The report under paragraph (1) shall include the following:

(A) A description of each discrete set of activities under an initiative specified in paragraph (2) for which gaps exist between the applicable authorities in chapter 16 of title 10, United States Code, as so added, and current law or other authorities under which such activities are carried out.

(B) For each discrete set of activities covered by subparagraph (A), the following:

(i) A description of the gaps described in subparagraph (A).

(ii) Recommendations for legislative or administrative action to address such gaps.

Subtitle F—Human Rights Sanctions

SEC. 1261. SHORT TITLE.

This subtitle may be cited as the "Global Magnitsky Human Rights Accountability Act".

SEC. 1262. DEFINITIONS.

In this subtitle:

(1) FOREIGN PERSON.—The term "foreign person" has the meaning given that term in section 595.304 of title 31, Code of Federal Regulations (as in effect on the day before the date of the enactment of this Act).

(2) GROSS VIOLATIONS OF INTERNATIONALLY RECOGNIZED HUMAN RIGHTS.—The term "gross violations of internationally recognized human rights" has the meaning given that term in section 502B(d)(1) of the Foreign Assistance Act of 1961 (22 U.S.C. 2304(d)(1)).

(3) PERSON.—The term "person" has the meaning given that term in section 591.308 of title 31, Code of Federal Regulations (as in effect on the day before the date of the enactment of this Act).

(4) UNITED STATES PERSON.—The term "United States person" has the meaning given that term in section 595.315 of title 31, Code of Federal Regulations (as in effect on the day before the date of the enactment of this Act).

SEC. 1263. AUTHORIZATION OF IMPOSITION OF SANCTIONS.

(a) IN GENERAL.—The President may impose the sanctions described in subsection (b) with respect to any foreign person the President determines, based on credible evidence—

(1) is responsible for extrajudicial killings, torture, or other gross violations of internationally recognized human rights committed against individuals in any foreign country who seek—

(A) to expose illegal activity carried out by government officials; or

(B) to obtain, exercise, defend, or promote internationally recognized human rights and freedoms, such as the freedoms of religion, expression, association, and assembly, and the rights to a fair trial and democratic elections;

(2) acted as an agent of or on behalf of a foreign person in a matter relating to an activity described in paragraph (1);

(3) is a government official, or a senior associate of such an official, that is responsible for, or complicit in, ordering, controlling, or otherwise directing, acts of significant corruption, including the expropriation of private or public assets for personal gain, corruption related to government contracts or the extraction of natural resources, bribery, or the facilitation or transfer of the proceeds of corruption to foreign jurisdictions; or

(4) has materially assisted, sponsored, or provided financial, material, or technological support for, or goods or services in support of, an activity described in paragraph (3).

(b) SANCTIONS DESCRIBED.—The sanctions described in this subsection are the following:

(1) INADMISSIBILITY TO UNITED STATES.—In the case of a foreign person who is an individual—

(A) ineligibility to receive a visa to enter the United States or to be admitted to the United States; or

(B) if the individual has been issued a visa or other documentation, revocation, in accordance with section 221(i) of the Immigration and Nationality Act (8 U.S.C. 1201(i)), of the visa or other documentation.

(2) BLOCKING OF PROPERTY.—

(A) IN GENERAL.—The blocking, in accordance with the International Emergency Economic Powers Act (50 U.S.C. 1701 et seq.), of all transactions in all property and interests in property of a foreign person if such property and interests in property are in the United States, come within the United States, or are or come within the possession or control of a United States person.

(B) INAPPLICABILITY OF NATIONAL EMERGENCY REQUIREMENT.—The requirements of section 202 of the International Emergency Economic Powers Act (50 U.S.C. 1701) shall not apply for purposes of this section.

(C) EXCEPTION RELATING TO IMPORTATION OF GOODS.—

(i) IN GENERAL.—The authority to block and prohibit all transactions in all property and interests in property under subparagraph (A) shall not include the authority to impose sanctions on the importation of goods.

(ii) GOOD.—In this subparagraph, the term "good" has the meaning given that term in section 16 of the Export Administration Act of 1979 (50 U.S.C. 4618) (as continued in effect pursuant to the International Emergency Economic Powers Act (50 U.S.C. 1701 et seq.)).

(c) CONSIDERATION OF CERTAIN INFORMATION IN IMPOSING SANCTIONS.—In determining whether to impose sanctions under subsection (a), the President shall consider—

(1) information provided jointly by the chairperson and ranking member of each of the appropriate congressional committees; and

(2) credible information obtained by other countries and nongovernmental organizations that monitor violations of human rights.

(d) REQUESTS BY APPROPRIATE CONGRESSIONAL COMMITTEES.—

(1) IN GENERAL.—Not later than 120 days after receiving a request that meets the requirements of paragraph (2) with respect to whether a foreign person has engaged in an activity described in subsection (a), the President shall—

(A) determine if that person has engaged in such an activity; and

(B) submit a classified or unclassified report to the chairperson and ranking member of the committee or committees that submitted the request with respect to that determination that includes—

(i) a statement of whether or not the President imposed or intends to impose sanctions with respect to the person; and

(ii) if the President imposed or intends to impose sanctions, a description of those sanctions.

(2) REQUIREMENTS.—

(A) REQUESTS RELATING TO HUMAN RIGHTS VIOLATIONS.—A request under paragraph (1) with respect to whether a foreign person has engaged in an activity described in paragraph (1) or (2) of subsection (a) shall be submitted to the President in writing jointly by the chairperson and ranking member of one of the appropriate congressional committees.

(B) REQUESTS RELATING TO CORRUPTION.—A request under paragraph (1) with respect to whether a foreign person has engaged in an activity described in paragraph (3) or (4) of subsection (a) shall be submitted to the President in writing jointly by the chairperson and ranking member of—

(i) one of the appropriate congressional committees of the Senate; and

(ii) one of the appropriate congressional committees of the House of Representatives.

(e) EXCEPTION TO COMPLY WITH UNITED NATIONS HEADQUARTERS AGREEMENT AND LAW ENFORCEMENT OBJECTIVES.—Sanctions under subsection (b)(1) shall not apply to an individual if admitting the individual into the United States would further important law enforcement objectives or is necessary to permit the United States to comply with the Agreement regarding the Headquarters of the United Nations, signed at Lake Success June 26, 1947, and entered into force November 21, 1947, between the United Nations and the United States, or other applicable international obligations of the United States.

(f) ENFORCEMENT OF BLOCKING OF PROPERTY.—A person that violates, attempts to violate, conspires to violate, or causes a violation of a sanction described in subsection (b)(2) that is imposed by the President or any regulation, license, or order issued to carry out such a sanction shall be subject to the penalties set forth in subsections (b) and (c) of section 206 of the International Emergency Economic Powers Act (50 U.S.C. 1705) to the same extent as a person that commits an unlawful act described in subsection (a) of that section.

(g) TERMINATION OF SANCTIONS.—The President may terminate the application of sanctions under this section with respect to a person if the President determines and reports to the appropriate congressional committees not later than 15 days before the termination of the sanctions that—

(1) credible information exists that the person did not engage in the activity for which sanctions were imposed;

(2) the person has been prosecuted appropriately for the activity for which sanctions were imposed;

(3) the person has credibly demonstrated a significant change in behavior, has paid an appropriate consequence for the activity for which sanctions were imposed, and has credibly committed to not engage in an activity described in subsection (a) in the future; or

(4) the termination of the sanctions is in the national security interests of the United States.

(h) REGULATORY AUTHORITY.—The President shall issue such regulations, licenses, and orders as are necessary to carry out this section.

(i) IDENTIFICATION OF SANCTIONABLE FOREIGN PERSONS.—The Assistant Secretary of State for Democracy, Human Rights, and Labor, in consultation with the Assistant Secretary of State for Consular Affairs and other bureaus of the Department of State, as appropriate, is authorized to submit to the Secretary of State, for review and consideration, the names of foreign persons who may meet the criteria described in subsection (a).

(j) APPROPRIATE CONGRESSIONAL COMMITTEES DEFINED.—In this section, the term "appropriate congressional committees" means—

(1) the Committee on Banking, Housing, and Urban Affairs and the Committee on Foreign Relations of the Senate; and

(2) the Committee on Financial Services and the Committee on Foreign Affairs of the House of Representatives.

SEC. 1264. REPORTS TO CONGRESS.

(a) IN GENERAL.—The President shall submit to the appropriate congressional committees, in accordance with subsection (b), a report that includes—

(1) a list of each foreign person with respect to which the President imposed sanctions pursuant to section 1263 during the year preceding the submission of the report;

(2) a description of the type of sanctions imposed with respect to each such person;

(3) the number of foreign persons with respect to which the President—

(A) imposed sanctions under section 1263(a) during that year; and

(B) terminated sanctions under section 1263(g) during that year;

(4) the dates on which such sanctions were imposed or terminated, as the case may be;

(5) the reasons for imposing or terminating such sanctions; and

(6) a description of the efforts of the President to encourage the governments of other countries to impose sanctions that are similar to the sanctions authorized by section 1263.

(b) DATES FOR SUBMISSION.—

(1) INITIAL REPORT.—The President shall submit the initial report under subsection (a) not later than 120 days after the date of the enactment of this Act.

(2) SUBSEQUENT REPORTS.—

(A) IN GENERAL.—The President shall submit a subsequent report under subsection (a) on December 10, or the first day thereafter on which both Houses of Congress are in session, of—

(i) the calendar year in which the initial report is submitted if the initial report is submitted before December 10 of that calendar year; and

(ii) each calendar year thereafter.

(B) CONGRESSIONAL STATEMENT.—Congress notes that December 10 of each calendar year has been recognized in the United States and internationally since 1950 as "Human Rights Day".

(c) FORM OF REPORT.—

(1) IN GENERAL.—Each report required by subsection (a) shall be submitted in unclassified form, but may include a classified annex.

(2) EXCEPTION.—The name of a foreign person to be included in the list required by subsection (a)(1) may be submitted in the classified annex authorized by paragraph (1) only if the President—

(A) determines that it is vital for the national security interests of the United States to do so;

(B) uses the annex in a manner consistent with congressional intent and the purposes of this subtitle; and

(C) not later than 15 days before submitting the name in a classified annex, provides to the appropriate congressional committees notice of, and a justification for, including the name in the classified annex despite any publicly available credible information indicating that the person engaged in an activity described in section 1263(a).

(d) PUBLIC AVAILABILITY.—

(1) IN GENERAL.—The unclassified portion of the report required by subsection (a) shall be made available to the public, including through publication in the Federal Register.

(2) NONAPPLICABILITY OF CONFIDENTIALITY REQUIREMENT WITH RESPECT TO VISA RECORDS.—The President shall publish the list required by subsection (a)(1) without regard to the requirements of section 222(f) of the Immigration and Nationality Act (8 U.S.C. 1202(f)) with respect to confidentiality of records pertaining to the issuance or refusal of visas or permits to enter the United States.

(e) APPROPRIATE CONGRESSIONAL COMMITTEES DEFINED.—In this section, the term "appropriate congressional committees" means—

(1) the Committee on Appropriations, the Committee on Banking, Housing, and Urban Affairs, the Committee on Foreign Relations, and the Committee on the Judiciary of the Senate; and

(2) the Committee on Appropriations, the Committee on Financial Services, the Committee on Foreign Affairs, and the Committee on the Judiciary of the House of Representatives.

SEC. 1265. SUNSET.

(a) IN GENERAL.—The authority to impose sanctions under this subtitle shall terminate on the date that is 6 years after the date of the enactment of this Act.

(b) CONTINUATION IN EFFECT OF SANCTIONS.—Sanctions imposed under this subtitle on or before the date specified in subsection (a), and in effect as of such date, shall remain in effect until terminated in accordance with the requirements of section 1263(g).

Subtitle G—Miscellaneous Reports

SEC. 1271. MODIFICATION OF ANNUAL REPORT ON MILITARY AND SECURITY DEVELOPMENTS INVOLVING THE PEOPLE'S REPUBLIC OF CHINA.

(a) ANNUAL REPORT.—Subsection (a) of section 1202 of the National Defense Authorization Act for Fiscal Year 2000 (Public Law 106–65; 113 Stat. 781; 10 U.S.C. 113 note) is amended by striking "March 1 each year" and inserting "January 31 of each year through January 31, 2021".

(b) MATTERS TO BE INCLUDED.—Subsection (b) of such section, as most recently amended by section 1252(a) of the Carl Levin and Howard P. "Buck" McKeon National Defense Authorization Act for Fiscal Year 2015 (Public Law 113–291; 128 Stat. 3571), is further amended by adding at the end the following:

"(21) A summary of the order of battle of the People's Liberation Army, including anti-ship ballistic missiles, theater ballistic missiles, and land attack cruise missile inventory.

"(22) A description of the People's Republic of China's military and nonmilitary activities in the South China Sea.".

(c) EFFECTIVE DATE.—The amendments made by this section take effect on the date of the enactment of this Act and apply with respect to reports required to be submitted under subsection (a) of section 1202 of the National Defense Authorization Act for Fiscal Year 2000 on or after that date.

SEC. 1272. MONITORING AND EVALUATION OF OVERSEAS HUMANITARIAN, DISASTER, AND CIVIC AID PROGRAMS OF THE DEPARTMENT OF DEFENSE.

(a) IN GENERAL.—Of the amounts authorized to be appropriated by this Act for Overseas Humanitarian, Disaster, and Civic Aid, the Secretary of Defense is authorized to use up to 5 percent of such amounts to conduct monitoring and evaluation of programs that are funded using such amounts during fiscal years 2017 and 2018.

(b) BRIEFING.—Not later than 90 days after the date of the enactment of this Act, the Secretary of Defense shall provide to the appropriate congressional committees a briefing on mechanisms to evaluate the programs conducted pursuant to the authorities listed in subsection (a).

(c) DEFINITION.—In subsection (b), the term "appropriate congressional committees" means—

(1) the Committee on Armed Services and the Committee on Foreign Relations of the Senate; and

(2) the Committee on Armed Services and the Committee on Foreign Affairs of the House of Representatives.

SEC. 1273. STRATEGY FOR UNITED STATES DEFENSE INTERESTS IN AFRICA.

(a) REQUIRED REPORT.—Not later than one year after the date of the enactment of this Act, the Secretary of Defense, in coordination with the Secretary of State, shall submit to the congressional defense committees a report that contains the strategy for United States defense interests in Africa.

(b) MATTERS TO BE INCLUDED.—The report required by subsection (a) shall address the following:

(1) United States national security interests in Africa, including an assessment of threats to global and regional United States national security interests emanating from the continent.

(2) United States defense objectives in Africa.

(3) Courses of action to accomplish United States defense objectives in Africa, including those conducted in cooperation with other Federal agencies.

(4) Measures to improve coordination between United States Africa Command and other combatant commands to achieve unity of effort to counter threats that cross combatant command boundaries.

(5) Department of Defense capabilities and resources required to achieve defense objectives in Africa, and the mitigation plan to address any gaps in such capabilities or resources that affect the implementation of the strategy required by subsection (a).

(6) Security cooperation initiatives to advance defense objectives in Africa.

(7) Any other matters the Secretary of Defense determines to be appropriate.

(c) FORM.—The report required by subsection (a) shall be submitted in unclassified form, but may contain a classified annex if necessary.

SEC. 1274. REPORT ON THE POTENTIAL FOR COOPERATION BETWEEN THE UNITED STATES AND ISRAEL ON DIRECTED ENERGY CAPABILITIES.

(a) REPORT.—Not later than 180 days after the date of the enactment of this Act, the Secretary of Defense shall submit to the appropriate committees of Congress a report on the potential for cooperative development by the United States and Israel of a directed energy capability to defeat ballistic missiles, cruise missiles, unmanned aerial vehicles, mortars, and improvised explosive devices that threaten the United States, deployed forces of the United States, or Israel. The report shall include the following:

(1) An assessment of the technological maturity of United States and Israeli directed energy capabilities to defeat adversary threat systems.

(2) An assessment of the respective military capability gaps of each country that such directed energy developments could address.

(3) An assessment of the opportunities for the United States and Israel to cooperate to develop directed energy capabilities to defeat adversary threat systems, including estimated costs of pursuing such opportunities.

(4) An assessment of whether such opportunities should be pursued, including any potential risks from the pursuit of such opportunities.

(5) Any other matters the Secretary considers appropriate.

(b) FORM.—The report shall be submitted in unclassified form, but may include a classified annex.

(c) APPROPRIATE COMMITTEES OF CONGRESS DEFINED.—In this section, the term "appropriate committees of Congress" means—

(1) the Committee on Armed Services, the Committee on Foreign Relations, and the Committee on Appropriations of the Senate; and

(2) the Committee on Armed Services, the Committee on Foreign Affairs, and the Committee on Appropriations of the House of Representatives.

SEC. 1275. ANNUAL UPDATE OF DEPARTMENT OF DEFENSE FREEDOM OF NAVIGATION REPORT.

(a) IN GENERAL.—The Secretary of Defense shall submit to the Committees on Armed Services of the Senate and the House of Representatives on an annual basis a report setting forth an update of the most current Department of Defense Freedom of Navigation Report under the Freedom of Navigation Operations (FONOPS) program. The purpose of each report shall be to document the types and locations of excessive claims that the Armed Forces of the United States have challenged in the previous year in order to preserve the rights, freedoms, and uses of the sea and airspace guaranteed to all countries by international law.

(b) ELEMENTS.—Each report under this section shall include, for the year covered by such report, the following:

(1) Each excessive maritime claim challenged by the United States under the program referred to in subsection (a), including the country making each such claim.

(2) The nature of each claim, including the geographic location or area covered by such claim (including the body of water and island grouping, when applicable).

(3) The specific legal challenge asserted through the program.

(c) FORM.—Each report under this section shall be submitted in unclassified form.

(d) SUNSET.—No report is required under this section after December 31, 2021.

SEC. 1276. ASSESSMENT OF PROLIFERATION OF CERTAIN REMOTELY PILOTED AIRCRAFT SYSTEMS.

(a) REPORT ON ASSESSMENT OF PROLIFERATION OF REMOTELY PILOTED AIRCRAFT SYSTEMS.—Not later than 6 months after the date of the enactment of this Act, the Chairman of the Joint Chiefs of Staff shall submit to the congressional defense committees a report setting forth an assessment, obtained by the Chairman for purposes of the report, of the impact to United States national security interests of the proliferation of remotely piloted aircraft that are assessed to be "Category I" items under the Missile Technology Control Regime (MTCR).

(b) INDEPENDENT ASSESSMENT.—

(1) IN GENERAL.—The assessment obtained for purposes of subsection (a) shall be conducted by a federally funded research and development center (FFRDC), or another appropriate independent entity with expertise in the procurement and operation of remotely piloted aircraft, selected by the Chairman for purposes of the assessment.

(2) USE OF PREVIOUS STUDIES.—The entity conducting the assessment may use and incorporate information from previous studies on matters appropriate to the assessment.

(c) ELEMENTS.—The assessment obtained for purposes of subsection (a) shall include the following:

(1) A qualitative and quantitative assessment of the scope and scale of the proliferation of remotely piloted aircraft that are "Category I" items under the Missile Technology Control Regime.

(2) An assessment of the threat posed to United States interests as a result of the proliferation of such aircraft to adversaries.

(3) An assessment of the impact of the proliferation of such aircraft on the combat capa-

bilities of and interoperability with partners and allies of the United States.

(4) An analysis of the degree to which the United States has limited the proliferation of such aircraft as a result of the application of a "strong presumption of denial" for exports of such aircraft.

(5) An assessment of the benefits and risks of continuing to limit exports of such aircraft.

(6) Such other matters as the Chairman considers appropriate.

(d) FORM.—The report under subsection (a) shall be submitted in unclassified form, but may include a classified annex.

Subtitle H—Other Matters

SEC. 1281. ENHANCEMENT OF INTERAGENCY SUPPORT DURING CONTINGENCY OPERATIONS AND TRANSITION PERIODS.

(a) AUTHORITY.—The Secretary of Defense and the Secretary of State may enter into an agreement under which each Secretary may provide covered support, supplies, and services on a reimbursement basis, or by exchange of covered support, supplies, and services, to the other Secretary during a contingency operation and related transition period for up to 2 years following the end of such contingency operation.

(b) AGREEMENT.—An agreement entered into under this section shall be in writing and shall include the following terms:

(1) The price charged by a supplying agency shall be the direct costs that such agency incurred by providing the covered support, supplies, or services to the requesting agency under this section.

(2) Credits and liabilities of the agencies accrued as a result of acquisitions and transfers of covered support, supplies, and services under this section shall be liquidated not less often than once every 3 months by direct payment to the agency supplying such support, supplies, or services by the agency receiving such support, supplies, or services.

(3) Exchange entitlements accrued as a result of acquisitions and transfers of covered support, supplies, and services under this section shall be satisfied within 12 months after the date of the delivery of the covered support, supplies, or services. Exchange entitlements not so satisfied shall be immediately liquidated by direct payment to the agency supplying such covered support, supplies, or services.

(c) EFFECT OF OBLIGATION AND AVAILABILITY OF FUNDS.—An order placed by an agency pursuant to an agreement under this section is deemed to be an obligation in the same manner that a similar order placed under a contract with, or a contract for similar goods or services awarded to, a private contractor is an obligation. Appropriations remain available to pay an obligation to the servicing agency in the same manner as appropriations remain available to pay an obligation to a private contractor.

(d) DEFINITIONS.—In this section:

(1) COVERED SUPPORT, SUPPLIES, AND SERVICES.—The term "covered support, supplies, and services" means food, billeting, transportation (including airlift), petroleum, oils, lubricants, communications services, medical services, ammunition, base operations support, use of facilities, spare parts and components, repair and maintenance services, and calibration services.

(2) CONTINGENCY OPERATION.—The term "contingency operation" has the meaning given that term in section 101(a)(13) of title 10, United States Code.

(e) CREDITING OF RECEIPTS.—Any receipt as a result of an agreement entered into under this section shall be credited, at the option of the Secretary of Defense with respect to the Department of Defense and the Secretary of State with respect to the Department of State, to—

(1) the appropriation, fund, or account used in incurring the obligation; or

(2) an appropriate appropriation, fund, or account currently available for the purposes for which the expenditures were made.

(f) NOTIFICATION.—Not later than 30 days after the end of a fiscal year in which covered support, supplies, and services are provided or exchanged pursuant to an agreement under this section, the Secretary of Defense and the Secretary of State shall jointly submit to the congressional defense committees, the Committee on Foreign Relations of the Senate, and the Committee on Foreign Affairs of the House of Representatives a notification that contains a copy of such agreement and a description of such covered support, supplies, and services.

SEC. 1282. TWO-YEAR EXTENSION AND MODIFICATION OF AUTHORIZATION OF NON-CONVENTIONAL ASSISTED RECOVERY CAPABILITIES.

(a) EXTENSION OF AUTHORITY.—Subsection (h) of section 943 of the Duncan Hunter National Defense Authorization Act for Fiscal Year 2009 (Public Law 110–417; 122 Stat. 4579), as most recently amended by section 1271 of the National Defense Authorization Act for Fiscal Year 2016 (Public Law 114–92; 129 Stat. 1075), is further amended by striking "2018" and inserting "2021".

(b) MODIFICATION TO AUTHORIZED ACTIVITIES.—Subsection (c) of such section is amended by inserting ", or other individuals, as determined by the Secretary of Defense, with respect to already established non-conventional assisted recovery capabilities" before the period at the end of the first sentence.

SEC. 1283. AUTHORITY TO DESTROY CERTAIN SPECIFIED WORLD WAR II-ERA UNITED STATES-ORIGIN CHEMICAL MUNITIONS LOCATED ON SAN JOSE ISLAND, REPUBLIC OF PANAMA.

(a) AUTHORITY.—

(1) IN GENERAL.—Subject to subsection (b), the Secretary of Defense may destroy the chemical munitions described in subsection (c).

(2) EX GRATIA ACTION.—The action authorized by this section is "ex gratia" on the part of the United States, as the term "ex gratia" is used in section 321 of the Strom Thurmond National Defense Authorization Act for Fiscal Year 1999 (Public Law 105–261; 10 U.S.C. 2701 note).

(3) CONSULTATION BETWEEN SECRETARY OF DEFENSE AND SECRETARY OF STATE.—The Secretary of Defense and the Secretary of State shall consult and develop any arrangements with the Republic of Panama with respect to this section.

(b) CONDITIONS.—The Secretary of Defense may exercise the authority under subsection (a) only if the Republic of Panama has—

(1) revised the declaration of the Republic of Panama under the Convention on the Prohibition of the Development, Production, Stockpiling and Use of Chemical Weapons and on Their Destruction to indicate that the chemical munitions described in subsection (c) are "old chemical weapons" rather than "abandoned chemical weapons"; and

(2) affirmed, in writing, that it understands (A) that the United States intends only to destroy the munitions described in subsections (c) and (d), and (B) that the United States is not legally obligated and does not intend to destroy any other munitions, munitions constituents, and associated debris that may be located on San Jose Island as a result of research, development, and testing activities conducted on San Jose Island during the period of 1943 through 1947.

(c) CHEMICAL MUNITIONS.—The chemical munitions described in this subsection are the eight United States-origin chemical munitions located on San Jose Island, Republic of Panama, that were identified in the 2002 Final Inspection Report of the Technical Secretariat of the Organization for the Prohibition of Chemical Weapons.

(d) LIMITED INCIDENTAL AUTHORITY TO DESTROY OTHER MUNITIONS.—In exercising the authority under subsection (a), the Secretary of Defense may destroy other munitions located on San Jose Island, Republic of Panama, but only to the extent essential and required to reach and destroy the chemical munitions described in subsection (c).

(e) SOURCE OF FUNDS.—Of the amounts authorized to be appropriated by this Act, the Secretary of Defense may use up to $30,000,000 from amounts made available for Chemical Agents and Munitions Destruction, Defense to carry out the authority in subsection (a).

(f) SUNSET.—The authority under subsection (a) shall terminate on the date that is 3 years after the date of the enactment of this Act.

SEC. 1284. SENSE OF CONGRESS ON MILITARY EXCHANGES BETWEEN THE UNITED STATES AND TAIWAN.

(a) MILITARY EXCHANGES BETWEEN SENIOR OFFICERS AND OFFICIALS OF THE UNITED STATES AND TAIWAN.—The Secretary of Defense should carry out a program of exchanges of senior military officers and senior officials between the United States and Taiwan designed to improve military to military relations between the United States and Taiwan.

(b) EXCHANGES DESCRIBED.—For the purposes of this section, an exchange is an activity, exercise, event, or observation opportunity between members of the Armed Forces and officials of the Department of Defense, on the one hand, and armed forces personnel and officials of Taiwan, on the other hand.

(c) FOCUS OF EXCHANGES.—The exchanges under the program described in subsection (a) should include exchanges focused on the following:

(1) Threat analysis.

(2) Military doctrine.

(3) Force planning.

(4) Logistical support.

(5) Intelligence collection and analysis.

(6) Operational tactics, techniques, and procedures.

(7) Humanitarian assistance and disaster relief.

(d) CIVIL-MILITARY AFFAIRS.—The exchanges under the program described in subsection (a) should include activities and exercises focused on civil-military relations, including parliamentary relations.

(e) LOCATION OF EXCHANGES.—The exchanges under the program described in subsection (a) should be conducted in both the United States and Taiwan.

(f) DEFINITIONS.—In this section:

(1) The term "senior military officer", with respect to the Armed Forces, means a general or flag officer of the Armed Forces on active duty.

(2) The term "senior official", with respect to the Department of Defense, means a civilian official of the Department of Defense at the level of Assistant Secretary of Defense or above.

SEC. 1285. LIMITATION ON AVAILABILITY OF FUNDS TO IMPLEMENT THE ARMS TRADE TREATY.

(a) IN GENERAL.—None of the funds authorized to be appropriated by this Act or otherwise made available for fiscal year 2017 for the Department of Defense may be obligated or expended to implement the Arms Trade Treaty, or to make any change to existing programs, projects, or activities as approved by Congress in furtherance of, pursuant to, or otherwise to implement the Arms Trade Treaty, unless the Arms Trade Treaty has received the advice and consent of the Senate and has been the subject of implementing legislation, as required, by Congress.

(b) RULE OF CONSTRUCTION.—Nothing in this section shall be construed to preclude the Department of Defense from assisting foreign countries in bringing their laws and regulations up to United States standards.

SEC. 1286. PROHIBITION ON USE OF FUNDS TO INVITE, ASSIST, OR OTHERWISE ASSURE THE PARTICIPATION OF CUBA IN CERTAIN JOINT OR MULTILATERAL EXERCISES.

(a) PROHIBITION.—The Secretary of Defense may not use any funds authorized to be appropriated or otherwise made available for fiscal year 2017 for the Department of Defense to invite, assist, or otherwise assure the participation of the Government of Cuba in any joint or multilateral exercise or related security conference between the Governments of the United States and Cuba until the Secretary of Defense and the Secretary of State, in consultation with the Director of National Intelligence, certify to the appropriate congressional committees that—

(1) the Cuban military has ceased committing human rights abuses against civil rights activists and other citizens of Cuba;

(2) the Cuban military has ceased providing military intelligence, weapons training, strategic planning, and security logistics to the military and security forces of Venezuela;

(3) the Cuban military and other security forces in Cuba have ceased all persecution, intimidation, arrest, imprisonment, and assassination of dissidents and members of faith-based organizations;

(4) the Government of Cuba no longer demands that the United States relinquish control of Guantanamo Bay, in violation of an international treaty; and

(5) the officials of the Cuban military that were indicted in the murder of United States citizens during the shootdown of planes operated by the Brothers to the Rescue humanitarian organization in 1996 are brought to justice.

(b) EXCEPTIONS.—The prohibition in subsection (a) shall not apply with respect to—

(1) payments in furtherance of the lease agreement, or other financial transactions necessary for maintenance and improvements of the military base at Guantanamo Bay, Cuba, including any adjacent areas under the control or possession of the United States;

(2) assistance or support in furtherance of democracy-building efforts for Cuba described in section 109 of the Cuban Liberty and Democratic Solidarity (LIBERTAD) Act of 1996 (22 U.S.C. 6039);

(3) customary and routine financial transactions necessary for the maintenance, improvements, or regular duties of the United States mission in Havana, including outreach to the pro-democracy opposition; or

(4) any joint or multilateral exercise or operation related to humanitarian assistance or disaster response.

(c) APPROPRIATE CONGRESSIONAL COMMITTEES DEFINED.—In this section, the term "appropriate congressional committees" means—

(1) the Committee on Armed Services and the Committee on Foreign Relations of the Senate; and

(2) the Committee on Armed Services and the Committee on Foreign Affairs of the House of Representatives.

SEC. 1287. GLOBAL ENGAGEMENT CENTER.

(a) ESTABLISHMENT.—

(1) IN GENERAL.—Not later than 180 days after the date of the enactment of this Act, the Secretary of State, in coordination with the Secretary of Defense and the heads of other relevant Federal departments and agencies, shall establish within the Department of State a Global Engagement Center (in this section referred to as the "Center").

(2) PURPOSE.—The purpose of the Center shall be to lead, synchronize, and coordinate efforts of the Federal Government to recognize, understand, expose, and counter foreign state and non-state propaganda and disinformation efforts aimed at undermining United States national security interests.

(b) FUNCTIONS.—The Center shall carry out the following functions:

(1) Integrate interagency and international efforts to track and evaluate counterfactual narratives abroad that threaten the national security interests of the United States and United States allies and partner nations.

(2) Analyze relevant information, data, analysis, and analytics from United States Government agencies, United States allies and partner nations, think tanks, academic institutions, civil society groups, and other nongovernmental organizations.

(3) As needed, support the development and dissemination of fact-based narratives and analysis to counter propaganda and disinformation directed at the United States and United States allies and partner nations.

(4) Identify current and emerging trends in foreign propaganda and disinformation in order to coordinate and shape the development of tactics, techniques, and procedures to expose and refute foreign misinformation and disinformation and proactively promote fact-based narratives and policies to audiences outside the United States.

(5) Facilitate the use of a wide range of technologies and techniques by sharing expertise among Federal departments and agencies, seeking expertise from external sources, and implementing best practices.

(6) Identify gaps in United States capabilities in areas relevant to the purpose of the Center and recommend necessary enhancements or changes.

(7) Identify the countries and populations most susceptible to propaganda and disinformation based on information provided by appropriate interagency entities.

(8) Administer the information access fund established pursuant to subsection (f).

(9) Coordinate with United States allies and partner nations in order to amplify the Center's efforts and avoid duplication.

(10) Maintain, collect, use, and disseminate records (as such term is defined in section 552a(a)(4) of title 5, United States Code) for research and data analysis of foreign state and non-state propaganda and disinformation efforts and communications related to public diplomacy efforts intended for foreign audiences. Such research and data analysis shall be reasonably tailored to meet the purposes of this paragraph and shall be carried out with due regard for privacy and civil liberties guidance and oversight.

(c) HEAD OF CENTER.—

(1) APPOINTMENT.—The head of the Center shall be an individual who is an official of the Federal Government, who shall be appointed by the President.

(2) COMPLIANCE WITH PRIVACY AND CIVIL LIBERTIES LAWS.—The President shall designate a senior official to develop guidance for the Center relating to relevant privacy and civil liberties laws and to ensure compliance with such guidance.

(d) EMPLOYEES OF THE CENTER.—

(1) DETAILEES.—Any Federal Government employee may be detailed to the Center without reimbursement, and such detail shall be without interruption or loss of civil service status or privilege for a period of not more than 3 years.

(2) PERSONAL SERVICE CONTRACTORS.—The Secretary of State may hire United States citizens or aliens as personal services contractors for purposes of personnel resources of the Center, if—

(A) the Secretary determines that existing personnel resources are insufficient;

(B) the period in which services are provided by a personal services contractor, including options, does not exceed 3 years, unless the Secretary determines that exceptional circumstances justify an extension of up to one additional year;

(C) not more than 50 United States citizens or aliens are employed as personal services contractors under the authority of this paragraph at any time; and

(D) the authority of this paragraph is only used to obtain specialized skills or experience or to respond to urgent needs.

(e) TRANSFER OF AMOUNTS AUTHORIZED.—

(1) IN GENERAL.—If amounts authorized to be appropriated or otherwise made available to carry out the functions of the Center—

(A) for fiscal year 2017 are less than $80,000,000, the Secretary of Defense is authorized to transfer, from amounts authorized to be appropriated by this Act for the Department of Defense for fiscal year 2017, to the Secretary of State an amount, not to exceed $60,000,000, to be available to carry out the functions of the Center for fiscal year 2017; and

(B) for fiscal year 2018 are less than $80,000,000, the Secretary of Defense is authorized to transfer, from amounts authorized to be appropriated by an Act authorizing funds for the Department of Defense for fiscal year 2018, to the Secretary of State an amount, not to exceed $60,000,000, to be available to carry out the functions of the Center for fiscal year 2018.

(2) NOTICE REQUIREMENT.—The Secretary of Defense shall notify the congressional defense committees of a proposed transfer under paragraph (1) not less than 15 days prior to making such transfer.

(3) INAPPLICABILITY OF REPROGRAMMING REQUIREMENTS.—The authority to transfer amounts under paragraph (1) shall not be subject to any reprogramming requirement under any other provision of law.

(f) INFORMATION ACCESS FUND.—

(1) AUTHORITY FOR GRANTS.—The Center is authorized to provide grants or contracts of financial support to civil society groups, media content providers, nongovernmental organizations, federally funded research and development centers, private companies, or academic institutions for the following purposes:

(A) To support local independent media who are best placed to refute foreign disinformation and manipulation in their own communities.

(B) To collect and store examples in print, online, and social media, disinformation, misinformation, and propaganda directed at the United States and its allies and partners.

(C) To analyze and report on tactics, techniques, and procedures of foreign information warfare with respect to disinformation, misinformation, and propaganda.

(D) To support efforts by the Center to counter efforts by foreign entities to use disinformation, misinformation, and propaganda to influence the policies and social and political stability of the United States and United States allies and partner nations.

(2) FUNDING AVAILABILITY AND LIMITATIONS.—The Secretary of State shall provide that each organization that applies to receive funds under this subsection is selected in accordance with the relevant existing regulations to ensure its bona fides, capability, and experience, and its compatibility with United States interests and objectives.

(g) REPORTS.—

(1) IN GENERAL.—Not later than one year after the date on which the Center is established, the Secretary of State shall submit to the appropriate congressional committees a report evaluating the success of the Center in carrying out its functions under subsection (b) and outlining steps to improve any areas of deficiency.

(2) DEFINITION.—In this subsection, the term "appropriate congressional committees" means—

(A) the Committee on Foreign Relations, the Committee on Armed Services, the Committee on Homeland Security and Governmental Affairs, and the Committee on Appropriations of the Senate; and

(B) the Committee on Foreign Affairs, the Committee on Armed Services, the Committee on Homeland Security, and the Committee on Appropriations of the House of Representatives.

(h) LIMITATION.—None of the funds authorized to be appropriated or otherwise made available to carry out this section shall be used for purposes other than countering foreign propaganda and misinformation that threatens United States national security.

(i) TERMINATION.—The Center shall terminate on the date that is 8 years after the date of the enactment of this Act.

SEC. 1288. MODIFICATION OF UNITED STATES INTERNATIONAL BROADCASTING ACT OF 1994.

The United States International Broadcasting Act of 1994 (22 U.S.C. 6201 et seq.; Public Law 103–236) is amended—

(1) by amending section 304 (22 U.S.C. 6203) to read as follows:

"SEC. 304. ESTABLISHMENT OF THE CHIEF EXECUTIVE OFFICER OF THE BROADCASTING BOARD OF GOVERNORS.

"(a) CONTINUED EXISTENCE WITHIN EXECUTIVE BRANCH.—The Broadcasting Board of Governors shall continue to exist within the Executive branch of Government as an entity described in section 104 of title 5, United States Code.

"(b) CHIEF EXECUTIVE OFFICER.—

"(1) IN GENERAL.—The head of the Broadcasting Board of Governors shall be a Chief Executive Officer, who shall be appointed by the President, by and with the advice and consent of the Senate. Notwithstanding any other provision of law, until such time as a Chief Executive Officer is appointed and has qualified, the current or acting Chief Executive Officer appointed by the Board may continue to serve and exercise the authorities and powers under this Act.

"(2) TERM.—The first Chief Executive Officer appointed pursuant to paragraph (1) shall serve for an initial term of three years.

"(3) COMPENSATION.—A Chief Executive Officer appointed pursuant to paragraph (1) shall be compensated at the annual rate of basic pay for level III of the Executive Schedule under section 5314 of title 5, United States Code.

"(c) TERMINATION OF DIRECTOR OF INTERNATIONAL BROADCASTING BUREAU.—Effective on the date of the enactment of this section, the position of the Director of the International Broadcasting Bureau shall be terminated, and all of the responsibilities, offices, authorities, and immunities of the Director or the Board under this or any other Act or authority before such date of enactment shall be transferred or available to, assumed by, or overseen by the Chief Executive Officer, as head of the Board.

"(d) IMMUNITY FROM CIVIL LIABILITY.—Notwithstanding any other provision of law, all limitations on liability that apply to the Chief Executive Officer shall also apply to members of the boards of directors of RFE/RL, Inc., Radio Free Asia, the Middle East Broadcasting Networks, or any organization that consolidates such entities when such members are acting in their official capacities.";

(2) in section 305 (22 U.S.C. 6204)—

(A) in subsection (a)—

(i) by striking "Board" each place it appears and inserting "Chief Executive Officer";

(ii) in paragraph (1), by inserting "direct and" before "supervise";

(iii) in paragraph (5)—

(I) by inserting "and cooperative agreements" after "grants"; and

(II) by striking "in accordance with sections 308 and 309" and inserting "in furtherance of the purposes of this Act and on behalf of other agencies, accordingly";

(iv) in paragraph (6)—

(I) by striking "International Broadcasting Bureau" and inserting "Board"; and

(II) by striking "subject to the limitations in sections 308 and 309 and";

(v) in paragraph (10)—

(I) by inserting ", rent, or lease" after "procure"; and

(II) by striking "personal property" and inserting "property for journalism, media, production, and broadcasting, and related support services, notwithstanding any other provision of law relating to such acquisition, rental, or lease, and under the same terms and conditions as authorized under section 501(b) of the United States Information and Educational Exchange Act of 1948 (22 U.S.C. 1461(b)), and for multiyear contracts and leases for periods of up to 20 years subject to the requirements of subsections (b) through (f) of section 3903 of title 41, United States Code";

(vi) in paragraph (11)—

(I) by striking "staff";

(II) by striking "as the Board" and inserting "as the Chief Executive Officer"; and

(III) by striking "subject" and inserting "which shall not be subject";

(vii) in paragraph (13)—

(I) by striking "Bureau" and inserting "Board"; and

(II) by striking "Board has taken" and inserting "Chief Executive Officer has taken";

(viii) in paragraph (14)—

(I) by inserting "transmission or" before "relay"; and

(II) by inserting "or any other grantee authorized under this Act" after "Radio Free Asia";

(ix) in paragraph (15)(A), by striking—

(I) "temporary and intermittent"; and

(II) "to the same extent as is authorized by section 3109 of title 5, United States Code,";

(x) in paragraph (16), by striking "Board determines" and inserting "Chief Executive Officer determines";

(xi) in paragraph (18), by striking "the Bureau" and inserting "the Chief Executive Officer"; and

(xii) by adding at the end the following new paragraphs:

"(20) Notwithstanding any other provision of law, including section 308(a), to condition, if appropriate, any grant or cooperative agreement to RFE/RL, Inc., Radio Free Asia, or the Middle East Broadcasting Networks, or any organization that is established through the consolidation of such entities, on authority to determine membership of their respective boards, and the consolidation of such grantee entities into a single grantee organization under terms and conditions established by the Board.

"(21) To redirect or reprogram funds within the scope of any grant or cooperative agreement, or between grantees, as necessary (and not later than 15 days before any such redirection of funds between language services, to notify the Committee on Appropriations and the Committee on Foreign Affairs of the House of Representatives and the Committee on Appropriations and the Committee on Foreign Relations of the Senate regarding such redirection), and to condition grants or cooperative agreements, if appropriate, on such grants or cooperative agreements or any similar amendments as authorized under section 308(a), including authority to name and replace the board of any grantee authorized under this Act, including with Federal officials, to meet the purposes of this Act.

"*(22) To change the name of the Board pursuant to congressional notification 60 days prior to any such change.*";

(B) by striking subsections (b) and (c); and

(C) by redesignating subsection (d) as subsection (b); and

(D) in subsection (b) (as so redesignated)—

(i) by striking "and the Board" and inserting "and the Chief Executive Officer"; and

(ii) by striking "International Broadcasting Bureau" and inserting "Board";

(3) by amending section 306 (22 U.S.C. 6205) to read as follows:

"SEC. 306. ESTABLISHMENT OF THE INTERNATIONAL BROADCASTING ADVISORY BOARD.

"*(a) IN GENERAL.—Except as provided in subsection (b)(2), the International Broadcasting Advisory Board (referred to in this section as the 'Advisory Board') shall consist of five members, including the Secretary of State, appointed by the President and in accordance with subsection (d), to advise the Chief Executive Officer of the Broadcasting Board of Governors, as appropriate.*

"*(b) RETENTION OF EXISTING BBG BOARD MEMBERS.—*

"*(1) IN GENERAL.—The presidentially appointed and Senate-confirmed members of the Board of the Broadcasting Board of Governors who are serving on unexpired terms as of the date of the enactment of this section shall—*

"*(A) constitute the first Advisory Board; and*

"*(B) hold office for the remainder of their original terms of office without reappointment to the Advisory Board.*

"*(2) EFFECT OF ADDITIONAL MEMBERS.—If, on the date of the enactment of this section, more than five members described in subsection (a) are serving their original terms of office on the Broadcasting Board of Governors, each such member may serve on the Advisory Board for a period equal to the time remaining on each such member's respective term without reappointment.*

"*(c) TERMS OF OFFICE.—*

"*(1) IN GENERAL.—Except as provided in paragraph (2), the term of office of each member of the Advisory Board appointed pursuant to subsection (a) shall be three years.*

"*(2) VACANCIES.—If a vacancy on the Advisory Board occurs before the expiration of the term of the member who created such vacancy—*

"*(A) the President shall appoint a new member to fill such vacancy in accordance with subsection (d); and*

"*(B) the member appointed pursuant to such subsection shall serve for the remainder of such term.*

"*(3) SERVICE BEYOND TERM PROHIBITED.—Members may not serve beyond the term for which they were appointed.*

"*(d) SELECTION OF THE BOARD.—In identifying individuals for appointment to the Advisory Board under subsection (a), the President shall appoint United States citizens—*

"*(1) who, with the exception of the Secretary of State, are not regular, full-time employees of the United States Government; and*

"*(2) distinguished in the fields of public diplomacy, mass communications, print, broadcast or digital media, or foreign affairs, of whom—*

"*(A) one individual should be appointed from among a list of at least three individuals submitted by the Chair of the Committee on Foreign Affairs of the House of Representatives;*

"*(B) one individual should be appointed from among a list of at least three individuals submitted by the Ranking Member of the Committee on Foreign Affairs of the House of Representatives;*

"*(C) one individual should be appointed from among a list of at least three individuals submitted by the Chair of the Committee on Foreign Relations of the Senate; and*

"*(D) one individual should be appointed from among a list of at least three individuals submitted by the Ranking Member of the Committee on Foreign Relations of the Senate.*

"*(e) FUNCTIONS OF THE BOARD.—The members of the Advisory Board shall perform the following advisory functions:*

"*(1) To provide the Chief Executive Officer of the Broadcasting Board of Governors with counsel and recommendations for improving the effectiveness and efficiency of the agency and its programming.*

"*(2) To meet with the Chief Executive Officer at least twice annually and at additional meetings at the request of the Chief Executive Officer.*

"*(3) To report periodically or upon request to the congressional committees specified in subsection (d)(2) regarding its counsel and recommendations for improving the effectiveness and efficiency of the Broadcasting Board of Governors and its programming.*

"*(4) To obtain information from the Chief Executive Officer, as needed, for the purposes of fulfilling the functions described in this subsection.*

"*(f) COMPENSATION.—Members of the Advisory Board, including the Secretary of State, may not receive any fee, salary, or remuneration of any kind for their service as members.*";

(4) by striking section 307 (22 U.S.C. 6206);

(5) in section 308 (22 U.S.C. 6207)—

(A) in subsection (a)(1), by striking "of the Broadcasting Board of Governors established under section 304 and no other members" and inserting "authorized under section 305(a)(20)";

(B) by amending subsection (d) to read as follows:

"*(d) ALTERNATIVE GRANTEE.—If the Chief Executive Officer determines at any time that RFE/RL, Incorporated is not carrying out the functions described in this section in an effective and economical manner, the Board may award the grant to carry out such functions to another entity.*"; and

(C) in subsection (g)(4)—

(i) by striking "International Broadcasting Bureau" and inserting "any other grantee of the Board"; and

(ii) by striking "by the Board" and inserting "by the Chief Executive Officer"; and

(D) in subsection (i), by striking "(1) Effective" and inserting "Effective";

(6) in section 309 (22 U.S.C. 6208)—

(A) in subsection (f)(2), by striking "Chairman of the Board" and inserting "Chief Executive Officer of the Board";

(B) by redesignating subsection (g) as subsection (h); and

(C) by inserting after subsection (f) the following new subsection:

"*(g) ALTERNATIVE GRANTEE.—If the Chief Executive Officer determines at any time that Radio Free Asia is not carrying out the functions described in this section in an effective and economical manner, the Board may award the grant to carry out such functions to another entity.*";

(7) by inserting after section 309 (22 U.S.C. 6208) the following new sections:

"SEC. 310. BROADCAST ENTITIES REPORTING TO CHIEF EXECUTIVE OFFICER.

"*(a) CONSOLIDATION OF GRANTEE ORGANIZATIONS.—*

"*(1) IN GENERAL.—The Chief Executive Officer, subject to the regular notification procedures of the Committee on Appropriations and the Committee on Foreign Affairs of the House of Representatives and the Committee on Appropriations and the Committee on Foreign Relations of the Senate, who is authorized to incorporate a grantee, may condition annual grants to RFE/RL, Inc., Radio Free Asia, and the Middle East Broadcasting Networks on the consoli-*

dation of such grantees into a single, consolidated private, non-profit corporation (in accordance with section 501(c)(3) of the Internal Revenue Code and exempt from tax under section 501(a) of such Code), in such a manner and under such terms and conditions as determined by the Chief Executive Officer, which may broadcast and provide news and information to audiences wherever the agency may broadcast, for activities that the Chief Executive Officer determines are consistent with the purposes of this Act, including the terms and conditions of subsections (g)(5), (h), (i), and (j) of section 308, except that the Agency may select any name for such a consolidated grantee.*

"*(2) SPECIAL RULE.—No State or political subdivision of a State may establish, enforce, or continue in effect any provision of law or legal requirement that is different from, or is in conflict with, any requirement or authority applicable under this Act relating to the consolidation, incorporation, structure, or dissolution of any grantee under this Act.*

"*(b) MISSION.—The consolidated grantee established under subsection (a) shall—*

"*(1) counter state-sponsored propaganda which undermines the national security or foreign policy interests of the United States and its allies;*

"*(2) provide uncensored local and regional news and analysis to people in societies where a robust, indigenous, independent, and free media does not exist;*

"*(3) help countries improve their indigenous capacity to enhance media professionalism and independence, and develop partnerships with local media outlets, as appropriate; and*

"*(4) promote unrestricted access to uncensored sources of information, especially via the internet, and use all effective and efficient mediums of communication to reach target audiences.*

"*(c) FEDERAL STATUS.—Nothing in this or any other Act, or any action taken pursuant to this or any other Act, may be construed to make such a consolidated grantee described in subsection (a) or RFE/RL, Inc., Radio Free Asia, or the Middle East Broadcasting Networks or any other grantee or entity provided funding by the agency a Federal agency or instrumentality. Employees or staff of such grantees or entities may not be Federal employees. For purposes of this section and this Act, the term 'grant' includes agreements under section 6305 of title 31, United States Code, and the term 'grantee' includes recipients of such agreements.*

"*(d) LEADERSHIP OF GRANTEE ORGANIZATIONS.—Officers and directors of RFE/RL Inc., Radio Free Asia, and the Middle East Broadcasting Networks or any organization that is established through the consolidation of such entities, or authorized under this Act, shall serve at the pleasure of and may be named by the Chief Executive Officer of the Board.*

"*(e) MAINTENANCE OF THE EXISTING INDIVIDUAL GRANTEE BRANDS.—RFE/RL, Incorporated, Radio Free Asia, and the Middle East Broadcasting Networks, Incorporated should remain brand names under which news and related programming and content may be disseminated by the consolidated grantee. Additional brands may be created as necessary.*

"SEC. 310A. INSPECTOR GENERAL AUTHORITIES.

"*(a) IN GENERAL.—The Inspector General of the Department of State and the Foreign Service shall exercise the same authorities with respect to the Broadcasting Board of Governors as the Inspector General exercises under the Inspector General Act of 1978 and section 209 of the Foreign Service Act of 1980 (22 U.S.C. 3929) with respect to the Department of State.*

"*(b) RESPECT FOR JOURNALISTIC INTEGRITY OF BROADCASTERS.—The Inspector General of the Department of State and the Foreign Service shall respect the journalistic integrity of all the* broadcasters covered by this Act and may not evaluate the philosophical or political perspectives reflected in the content of broadcasts.

"SEC. 310B. ROLE OF THE SECRETARY OF STATE IN FOREIGN POLICY GUIDANCE.

"To assist the Board in carrying out its functions, the Chief Executive Officer shall regularly consult with and seek from the Secretary of State guidance on foreign policy issues."; and

(8) in section 314 (22 U.S.C. 6213)—

(A) by redesignating paragraphs (2) and (3) as paragraphs (3) and (4), respectively; and

(B) by inserting after paragraph (1) the following new paragraph:

"(4) the terms 'Board' and 'Chief Executive Officer of the Board' mean the Broadcasting Board of Governors and the position, respectively, authorized in accordance with this Act;".

SEC. 1289. REDESIGNATION OF SOUTH CHINA SEA INITIATIVE.

(a) REDESIGNATION AS SOUTHEAST ASIA MARITIME SECURITY INITIATIVE.—Subsection (a)(2) of section 1263 of the National Defense Authorization Act for Fiscal Year 2016 (Public Law 114–92; 129 Stat. 1073; 10 U.S.C. 2282 note) is amended by striking "the 'South China Sea Initiative'" and inserting "the 'Southeast Asia Maritime Security Initiative'".

(b) CONFORMING AMENDMENT.—The heading of such section is amended to read as follows:

"SEC. 1263. SOUTHEAST ASIA MARITIME SECURITY INITIATIVE.".

SEC. 1290. MEASURES AGAINST PERSONS INVOLVED IN ACTIVITIES THAT VIOLATE ARMS CONTROL TREATIES OR AGREEMENTS WITH THE UNITED STATES.

(a) REPORTS ON PERSONS THAT VIOLATE TREATIES OR AGREEMENTS.—

(1) IN GENERAL.—Not later than 30 days after the submittal to Congress of an annual report on the status of United States policy and actions with respect to arms control, nonproliferation, and disarmament pursuant to section 403 of the Arms Control and Disarmament Act (22 U.S.C. 2593a), the Secretary of the Treasury shall submit to the appropriate congressional committees a report, consistent with the protection of intelligence sources and methods, identifying every person with respect to whom there is credible information indicating that—

(A) the person—

(i)(I) is an individual who is a citizen, national, or permanent resident of a country described in paragraph (2); or

(II) is an entity organized under the laws of a country described in paragraph (2); and

(ii) has engaged in any activity that contributed to or is a significant factor in the President's or the Secretary of State's determination that such country is not in full compliance with its obligations as further described in paragraph (2); or

(B) the person has provided material support for such non-compliance to a person described in subparagraph (A).

(2) COUNTRY DESCRIBED.—A country described in this paragraph is a country (other than a country described in paragraph (3)) that the President or the Secretary of State has determined, in the most recent annual report described in paragraph (1), to be not in full compliance with its obligations undertaken in all arms control, nonproliferation, and disarmament agreements or commitments to which the United States is a participating state.

(3) EXCLUDED COUNTRIES.—The following countries are not described for purposes of paragraph (2):

(A) The United States.

(B) Any country determined by the Director of National Intelligence to be closely cooperating in intelligence matters with the United States in the period covered by the most recent annual re-

port described in paragraph (1), regardless of the extent of the compliance of such country with the obligations described in paragraph (2) during such period.

(b) IMPOSITION OF MEASURES.—Except as provided in subsections (d), (e), and (f), the President shall impose the measures described in subsection (c) with respect to each person identified in a report under subsection (a).

(c) MEASURES DESCRIBED.—

(1) IN GENERAL.—The measures to be imposed with respect to a person under subsection (b) are the head of any executive agency (as defined in section 133 of title 41, United States Code) may not enter into, renew, or extend a contract for the procurement of goods or services with the person.

(2) EXCEPTION FOR MAJOR ROUTES OF SUPPLY.—The requirement to impose measures under paragraph (1) shall not apply with respect to any contract for the procurement of goods or services along a major route of supply to a zone of active combat or major contingency operation.

(3) REQUIREMENT TO REVISE REGULATIONS.—

(A) IN GENERAL.—Not later than 90 days after the date of the enactment of this Act, the Federal Acquisition Regulation, the Defense Federal Acquisition Regulation Supplement, and the Uniform Administrative Requirements, Cost Principles, and Audit Requirements for Federal Awards shall be revised to implement paragraph (1).

(B) CERTIFICATIONS.—The revisions to the Federal Acquisition Regulation under subparagraph (A) shall include a requirement for a certification from each person that is a prospective contractor that the person, and any person owned or controlled by the person, does not engage in any activity described in subsection (a)(1)(A)(ii).

(C) REMEDIES.—If the head of an executive agency determines that a person has submitted a false certification under subparagraph (B) on or after the date on which the applicable revision of the Federal Acquisition Regulation required by this paragraph becomes effective—

(i) the head of that executive agency shall terminate a contract with such person or debar or suspend such person from eligibility for Federal contracts for a period of not less than 2 years;

(ii) any such debarment or suspension shall be subject to the procedures that apply to debarment and suspension under the Federal Acquisition Regulation under subpart 9.4 of part 9 of title 48, Code of Federal Regulations; and

(iii) the Administrator of General Services shall include on the List of Parties Excluded from Federal Procurement and Nonprocurement Programs maintained by the Administrator under part 9 of the Federal Acquisition Regulation each person that is debarred, suspended, or proposed for debarment or suspension by the head of an executive agency on the basis of a determination of a false certification under subparagraph (B).

(d) WAIVER FOR LACK OF KNOWING VIOLATION.—

(1) IN GENERAL.—The President may waive the application of measures on a case-by-case basis under subsection (b) with respect to a person if the President—

(A) determines that—

(i)(I) in the case of a person described in subsection (a)(1)(A), the person did not knowingly engage in any activity described in such subsection;

(II) in the case of a person described in subsection (a)(1)(B), the person conducted or facilitated a transaction or transactions with, or provided financial services to, a person described in subsection (a)(1)(A) that did not knowingly engage in any activity described in such subsection; and

(III) in the case of a person described in subsection (a)(1)(A) or (a)(1)(B), the person has terminated the activity for which otherwise covered by such subsection or has provided verifiable assurances that the person will terminate such activity; and

(ii) the waiver is in the national security interest of the United States; and

(B) submits to the appropriate congressional committees a report on the determination and the reasons for the determination.

(2) FORM OF REPORT.—The report required by paragraph (1)(B) shall be submitted in unclassified form, but may include a classified annex.

(e) WAIVER TO PREVENT DISCLOSURE OF INTELLIGENCE SOURCES AND METHODS.—The President may waive the application of measures on a case-by-case basis under subsection (b) with respect to a person if the President—

(1) determines that the waiver is necessary to prevent the disclosure of intelligence sources or methods; and

(2) submits to the appropriate congressional committees a report, consistent with the protection of intelligence sources and methods, on the determination and the reasons for the determination.

(f) TIMING OF IMPOSITION.—

(1) IN GENERAL.—Except as provided in paragraph (2), the President shall immediately impose measures under subsection (b) against a person described in subsection (a)(1) upon the submittal to Congress of the report identifying the person pursuant to subsection (a)(1) unless the President determines and certifies to the appropriate congressional committees that the government of the country concerned has taken specific and effective actions, including, as appropriate, the imposition of appropriate penalties, to terminate the involvement of the person in the activities that resulted in the identification of the person in the report.

(2) DELAY.—

(A) IN GENERAL.—The President may delay the imposition of measures against a person for up to 120 days after the date of the submittal to Congress of the report identifying the person pursuant to subsection (a)(1) if the President initiates consultations with the government concerned with respect to the taking of actions described in paragraph (1).

(B) ADDITIONAL DELAY.—The President may delay the imposition of measures for up to an additional 120 days after the delay authorized by subparagraph (A) if the President determines and certifies to the appropriate congressional committees that the government concerned is in the process of taking the actions described in paragraph (1).

(3) REPORT.—Not later than 60 days after the submittal to Congress of the report identifying a person pursuant to subsection (a)(1), the President shall submit to the appropriate congressional committees a report on the status of consultations, if any, with the government concerned under this subsection, and the basis for any determination under paragraph (1).

(g) TERMINATION.—

(1) TERMINATION THROUGH COMPLIANCE OF COUNTRY WITH ARMS CONTROL AND OTHER AGREEMENTS.—The measures imposed with respect to a person under subsection (b) shall terminate on the date on which the President submits to Congress a subsequent annual report pursuant to section 403 of the Arms Control and Disarmament Act that does not contain a determination of the President that the country described in subsection (a)(2) with respect to which the measures were imposed with respect to the person is a country that is not in full compliance with its obligations undertaken in all arms control, nonproliferation, and disarmament agreements or commitments to which the United States is a participating state.

(2) TERMINATION THROUGH CESSATION BY PERSON OF VIOLATING ACTIVITIES.—In addition to termination provided for by paragraph (1), the measures imposed with respect to a person under subsection (b) in connection with a particular activity shall terminate upon a determination of the President that the person has ceased such activity. The termination of measures imposed with respect to a person in connection with a particular activity pursuant to this paragraph shall not result in the termination of any measures imposed with respect to the person in connection with any other activity for which measures were imposed under subsection (b).

(h) APPROPRIATE CONGRESSIONAL COMMITTEES DEFINED.—In this section, the term "appropriate congressional committees" means—

(1) the Committee on Armed Services, the Committee on Foreign Affairs, and the Permanent Select Committee on Intelligence of the House of Representatives; and

(2) the Committee on Armed Services, the Committee on Foreign Relations, and the Select Committee on Intelligence of the Senate.

SEC. 1291. AGREEMENTS WITH FOREIGN GOVERNMENTS TO DEVELOP LAND-BASED WATER RESOURCES IN SUPPORT OF AND IN PREPARATION FOR CONTINGENCY OPERATIONS.

(a) AGREEMENTS AUTHORIZED.—The Secretary of Defense, with the concurrence of the Secretary of State, is authorized to enter into agreements with the governments of foreign countries to develop land-based water resources in support of and in preparation for contingency operations, including water selection, pumping, purification, storage, distribution, cooling, consumption, water reuse, water source intelligence, research and development, training, acquisition of water support equipment, and water support operations.

(b) NOTIFICATION REQUIRED.—Not later than 30 days after entering into an agreement under subsection (a), the Secretary of Defense shall notify the appropriate congressional committees of the existence of the agreement and provide a summary of the terms of the agreement.

(c) DEFINITION.—In this section, the term "appropriate congressional committees" means—

(1) the Committee on Armed Services and the Committee on Foreign Relations of the Senate; and

(2) the Committee on Armed Services and the Committee on Foreign Affairs of the House of Representatives.

SEC. 1292. ENHANCING DEFENSE AND SECURITY COOPERATION WITH INDIA.

(a) ACTIONS.—

(1) IN GENERAL.—The Secretary of Defense and Secretary of State should jointly take such actions as may be necessary to—

(A) recognize India's status as a major defense partner of the United States;

(B) designate an individual within the executive branch who has experience in defense acquisition and technology—

(i) to reinforce and ensure, through interagency policy coordination, the success of the Framework for the United States-India Defense Relationship; and

(ii) to help resolve remaining issues impeding United States-India defense trade, security cooperation, and co-production and co-development opportunities;

(C) approve and facilitate the transfer of advanced technology, consistent with United States conventional arms transfer policy, to support combined military planning with India's military for missions such as humanitarian assistance and disaster relief, counter piracy, freedom of navigation, and maritime domain awareness missions, and to promote weapons systems interoperability;

(D) strengthen the effectiveness of the U.S.-India Defense Trade and Technology Initiative and the durability of the Department of Defense's "India Rapid Reaction Cell";

(E) collaborate with the Government of India to develop mutually agreeable mechanisms to verify the security of defense articles, defense services, and related technology, such as appropriate cyber security and end use monitoring arrangements, consistent with United States export control laws and policy;

(F) promote policies that will encourage the efficient review and authorization of defense sales and exports to India;

(G) encourage greater government-to-government and commercial military transactions between the United States and India;

(H) support the development and alignment of India's export control and procurement regimes with those of the United States and multilateral control regimes; and

(I) continue to enhance defense and security cooperation with India in order to advance United States interests in the South Asia and greater Indo-Asia-Pacific regions.

(2) REPORT.—Not later than 180 days after the date of the enactment of this Act, and annually thereafter, the Secretary of Defense and Secretary of State shall jointly submit to the congressional defense committees and the Committee on Foreign Relations of the Senate and the Committee on Foreign Affairs of the House of Representatives a report on how the United States is supporting its defense relationship with India in relation to the actions described in paragraph (1).

(b) BILATERAL COORDINATION.—To enhance cooperation and encourage military-to-military engagement between the United States and India, the Secretary of Defense should take appropriate actions to ensure that exchanges between senior military officers and senior civilian defense officials of the United States Government and the Government of India—

(1) are at a level appropriate to enhance engagement between the militaries of the two countries for threat analysis, military doctrine, force planning, mutual security interests, logistical support, intelligence, tactics, techniques and procedures, humanitarian assistance, and disaster relief;

(2) include exchanges of general and flag officers between the two countries;

(3) enhance cooperative military operations, including maritime security, counter-piracy, counter-terror cooperation, and domain awareness, in the Indo-Asia-Pacific region;

(4) accelerate the development of combined military planning for missions such as those identified in subsection (a)(1)(C) or in paragraph (1) of this subsection, or other missions in the national security interests of both countries; and

(5) solicit and recognize actions and efforts by India that would allow the United States to treat India as a major defense partner.

(c) ASSESSMENT REQUIRED.—

(1) IN GENERAL.—The Secretary of Defense and Secretary of State shall jointly, on an ongoing basis, conduct an assessment of the extent to which India possesses capabilities to support and carry out military operations of mutual interest to the United States and India, including an assessment of the defense export control regulations and policies that need appropriate modification, in recognition of India's capabilities and its status as a major defense partner.

(2) USE OF ASSESSMENT.—The President shall ensure that the assessment described in paragraph (1) is used, consistent with United States conventional arms transfer policy, to inform the review by the United States of requests to export defense articles, defense services, or related technology to India under the Arms Export Control Act (22 U.S.C. 2751 et seq.), and to inform any regulatory and policy adjustments that may be appropriate.

SEC. 1293. COORDINATION OF EFFORTS TO DEVELOP FREE TRADE AGREEMENTS WITH SUB-SAHARAN AFRICAN COUNTRIES.

(a) COORDINATION BETWEEN THE UNITED STATES TRADE REPRESENTATIVE AND OTHER AGENCIES.—The United States Trade Representative shall consult and coordinate with other relevant Federal agencies to assist countries identified under paragraph (1) of section 110(b) of the Trade Preferences Extension Act of 2015 (Public Law 114–27; 129 Stat. 370; 19 U.S.C. 3705 note) in the most recent report required by that section, including through the deployment of resources from those agencies to such countries and through trade capacity building, in addressing the plan developed under paragraph (3) of that section.

(b) COORDINATION OF USAID WITH FREE TRADE AGREEMENT POLICY.—

(1) AUTHORIZATION OF FUNDS.—Funds made available to the United States Agency for International Development under section 496 of the Foreign Assistance Act of 1961 (22 U.S.C. 2293) after the date of the enactment of this Act may be used, in consultation with the United States Trade Representative—

(A) to assist eligible countries, including by deploying resources to such countries, in addressing the plan developed under section 116(b) of the African Growth and Opportunity Act (19 U.S.C. 3723(b)); and

(B) to assist eligible countries in the implementation of the commitments of those countries under agreements with the United States and under the WTO Agreement (as defined in section 2(9) of the Uruguay Round Agreements Act (19 U.S.C. 3501(9))) and agreements annexed to the WTO Agreement.

(2) DEFINITIONS.—In this subsection:

(A) ELIGIBLE COUNTRY.—The term "eligible country" means a sub-Saharan African country that receives—

(i) benefits under the African Growth and Opportunity Act (19 U.S.C. 3701 et seq.); and

(ii) funding from the United States Agency for International Development.

(B) SUB-SAHARAN AFRICAN COUNTRY.—The term "sub-Saharan African country" has the meaning given that term in section 107 of the African Growth and Opportunity Act (19 U.S.C. 3706).

SEC. 1294. EXTENSION AND EXPANSION OF AUTHORITY TO SUPPORT BORDER SECURITY OPERATIONS OF CERTAIN FOREIGN COUNTRIES.

(a) EXPANSION OF AUTHORITY.—Section 1226 of the National Defense Authorization Act for Fiscal Year 2016 (Public Law 114–92; 129 Stat. 1056; 22 U.S.C. 2551 note) is amended—

(1) in subsection (a)(1)—

(A) by striking "the Government of Jordan and the Government of Lebanon" and inserting "the Government of Egypt, the Government of Jordan, the Government of Lebanon, and the Government of Tunisia";

(B) by striking "efforts of the armed forces" and inserting "efforts as follows:

"(A) Efforts of the armed forces"; and

(C) by adding at the end the following new subparagraph:

"(B) Efforts of the armed forces of Egypt and the armed forces of Tunisia to increase security and sustain increased security along the border of Egypt and the border of Tunisia with Libya, as applicable."; and

(2) in subsection (c)(4), by striking "along the border" and all that follows and inserting "along the border of the country as specified in subsection (a)(1).".

(b) FUNDS AVAILABLE FOR SUPPORT.—Subsection (b) of such section is amended—

(1) in paragraphs (1) and (2), by striking "Amounts" and inserting "In fiscal year 2016, amounts"; and

(2) by adding at the end the following new paragraph:

"(3) In any fiscal year after fiscal year 2016, amounts authorized to be appropriated for such fiscal year and available for Operation and Maintenance, Defense-Wide, and the Counter Islamic State of Iraq and the Levant Fund for such fiscal year.".

(c) EXTENSION.—Subsection (f) of such section is amended by striking "December 31, 2018" and inserting "December 31, 2019".

(d) CONFORMING AMENDMENT.—The heading of such section is amended to read as follows:

"SEC. 1226. SUPPORT TO CERTAIN GOVERNMENTS FOR BORDER SECURITY OPER-ATIONS.".

SEC. 1295. MODIFICATION AND CLARIFICATION OF UNITED STATES-ISRAEL ANTI-TUNNEL COOPERATION AUTHORITY.

(a) AMOUNT OF SUPPORT PROVIDABLE BY THE UNITED STATES.—Paragraph (4) of section 1279(b) of the National Defense Authorization Act for Fiscal Year 2016 (Public Law 114–92; 129 Stat. 1079; 22 U.S.C. 8606 note) is amended by striking "$25,000,000" and inserting "$50,000,000".

(b) SCOPE OF REQUIREMENT FOR MATCHING CONTRIBUTION BY ISRAEL.—Paragraph (3) of such section is amended by inserting before the period at the end the following: "in the calendar year in which the support is provided".

(c) USE OF CERTAIN AMOUNT FOR RDT&E ACTIVITIES IN THE UNITED STATES.—Of the amount contributed by the United States for activities under section 1279 of the National Defense Authorization Act for Fiscal Year 2016, not less than 50 percent of such amount shall be used in fiscal year 2017 for research, development, test, and evaluation activities for purposes of such section in the United States.

SEC. 1296. MAINTENANCE OF PROHIBITION ON PROCUREMENT BY DEPARTMENT OF DEFENSE OF PEOPLE'S REPUBLIC OF CHINA-ORIGIN ITEMS THAT MEET THE DEFINITION OF GOODS AND SERVICES CONTROLLED AS MUNITIONS ITEMS WHEN MOVED TO THE "600 SERIES" OF THE COMMERCE CONTROL LIST.

(a) IN GENERAL.—Section 1211 of the National Defense Authorization Act for Fiscal Year 2006 (Public Law 109–163; 10 U.S.C. 2302 note) is amended—

(1) in subsection (b), by inserting "or in the 600 series of the control list of the Export Administration Regulations" after "in Arms Regulations"; and

(2) in subsection (e), by adding at the end the following new paragraph:

"(3) The term '600 series of the control list of the Export Administration Regulations' means the 600 series of the Commerce Control List contained in Supplement No. 1 to part 774 of subtitle B of title 15 of the Code of Federal Regulations.".

(b) TECHNICAL CORRECTIONS TO ITAR REFERENCES.—Such section is further amended by striking "Trafficking" both places it appears and inserting "Traffic".

SEC. 1297. INTERNATIONAL SALES PROCESS IMPROVEMENTS.

(a) PLAN REQUIRED.—Not later than 180 days after the date of the enactment of this Act, the Secretary of Defense shall develop a plan to improve the management and use of fees collected on transfer of defense articles and services via sale, lease, or grant to international customers under programs over which the Defense Security Cooperation Agency has administration responsibilities. The plan shall include options to use fees more effectively—

(1) to improve the staffing and processes of the licensing review cycle at the Defense Technology Security Administration and other reviewing authorities; and

(2) to maintain a cadre of contracting officers and acquisition officials who specialize in foreign military sales contracting.

(b) PROCESS FOR GATHERING INPUT.—The Secretary of Defense shall establish a process for contractors to provide input, feedback, and adjudication of any differences regarding the appropriateness of governmental pricing and availability estimates prior to the delivery to potential foreign customers of formal responses to Letters of Request for Pricing and Availability.

SEC. 1298. EFFORTS TO END MODERN SLAVERY.

(a) ACTIONS BY THE SECRETARY OF DEFENSE.—

(1) IN GENERAL.—Not later than 90 days after the date of the enactment of this Act, the Secretary of Defense shall provide to the appropriate congressional committees a briefing on the policies and guidance of the Department of Defense with respect to the education and training on human slavery and the appropriate role of the United States Armed Forces in combatting trafficking in persons that is received by personnel of the Armed Forces, including uniformed personnel and civilians engaged in partnership with foreign nations.

(2) ELEMENTS.—The briefing required under paragraph (1) shall address—

(A) resources available for Armed Forces personnel who become aware of instances of human slavery or trafficking in persons while deployed overseas; and

(B) guidance on the requirement to make official reports through the chain of command, the roles and responsibilities of military and civilian officials of the United States Armed Forces and host nations, circumstances in which members of the Armed Forces are authorized to take immediate action to prevent loss of life or serious injury, and the authority to use appropriate force to stop or prevent sexual abuse or exploitation of children.

(b) GRANT AUTHORIZATION.—The Secretary of State is authorized to make a grant or grants of funding to provide support for transformational programs and projects that seek to achieve a measurable and substantial reduction of the prevalence of modern slavery in targeted populations within partner countries (or jurisdictions thereof).

(c) MONITORING AND EVALUATION.—Any grantee shall—

(1) develop specific and detailed criteria for the monitoring and evaluation of supported projects;

(2) implement a system for measuring progress against baseline data that is rigorously designed based on international corporate and nongovernmental best practices;

(3) ensure that each supported project is regularly and rigorously monitored and evaluated, on a not less than biennial basis, by an independent monitoring and evaluation entity, against the specific and detailed criteria established pursuant to paragraph (1), and that the progress of the project towards its stated goals is measured by such entity against baseline data;

(4) support the development of a scientifically sound, representative survey methodology for measuring prevalence with reference to existing research and experience, and apply the methodology consistently to determine the baseline prevalence in target populations and outcomes in order to periodically assess progress in reducing prevalence; and

(5) establish, and revise on a not less than annual basis, specific and detailed criteria for the suspension and termination, as appropriate, of projects supported by the grantee that regularly or consistently fail to meet the criteria required by this section.

(d) AUDITING.—

(1) IN GENERAL.—Any grantee shall be subject to the same auditing, recordkeeping, and reporting obligations required under subsections (e),

(f), (g), and (i) of section 504 of the National Endowment for Democracy Act (22 U.S.C. 4413).

(2) COMPTROLLER GENERAL AUDIT AUTHORITY.—

(A) IN GENERAL.—The Comptroller General of the United States may evaluate the financial transactions of the grantee as well as the programs or activities the grantee carries out pursuant to this section.

(B) ACCESS TO RECORDS.—Any grantee shall provide the Comptroller General, or the Comptroller General's duly authorized representatives, access to such records as the Comptroller General determines necessary to conduct evaluations authorized by this section.

(e) ANNUAL REPORT.—Any grant recipient shall submit a report to the Secretary of State annually and the Secretary shall transmit it to the appropriate congressional committees within 30 days. Such report shall include the names of each of the projects or sub-grantees receiving such funding pursuant to this section and the amount of funding provided for, along with a detailed description of, each such project.

(f) RULE OF CONSTRUCTION REGARDING AVAILABILITY OF FISCAL YEAR 2016 APPROPRIATIONS.—The enactment of this section is deemed to meet the condition of the first proviso of paragraph (2) of section 7060(f) of the Department of State, Foreign Operations, and Related Appropriations Act, 2016 (division K of Public Law 114–113), and the funds referred to in such paragraph shall be made available in accordance with, and for the purposes set forth in, such paragraph.

(g) AUTHORIZATION OF APPROPRIATIONS; SUNSET.—

(1) AUTHORIZATION OF APPROPRIATIONS FOR FISCAL YEARS 2017 THROUGH 2020.—There is authorized to be appropriated to the Department of State for the purpose of making a grant or grants authorized under this section, for each fiscal year from 2017 through 2020, $37,500,000.

(2) SUNSET.—The authorities of subsections (b) through (f) shall expire on September 30, 2020.

(h) COMPTROLLER GENERAL REVIEW OF EXISTING PROGRAMS.—

(1) IN GENERAL.—Not later than September 30, 2018, and September 30, 2020, the Comptroller General of the United States shall submit to Congress a report on all of the programs conducted by the Department of State, the United States Agency for International Development, the Department of Labor, the Department of Defense, and the Department of the Treasury that address human trafficking and modern slavery, including a detailed analysis of the effectiveness of such programs in limiting human trafficking and modern slavery and specific recommendations on which programs are not effective at reducing the prevalence of human trafficking and modern slavery and how the funding for such programs may be redirected to more effective efforts.

(2) CONSIDERATION OF REPORT.—The Comptroller General of the United States shall brief the appropriate congressional committees on the report submitted under paragraph (1). The appropriate congressional committees shall review and consider the reports and shall, as appropriate, consider modifications to authorization levels and programs within the jurisdiction of such committees to address the recommendations made in the report.

(i) APPROPRIATE CONGRESSIONAL COMMITTEES DEFINED.—In this section, the term "appropriate congressional committees" means—

(1) the Committee on Foreign Relations, the Committee on Armed Services, and the Committee on Appropriations of the Senate; and

(2) the Committee on Foreign Affairs, the Committee on Armed Services, and the Committee on Appropriations of the House of Representatives.

TITLE XIII—COOPERATIVE THREAT REDUCTION

Sec. 1301. Specification of Cooperative Threat Reduction funds.
Sec. 1302. Funding allocations.
Sec. 1303. Limitation on availability of funds for Cooperative Threat Reduction in People's Republic of China.

SEC. 1301. SPECIFICATION OF COOPERATIVE THREAT REDUCTION FUNDS.

(a) FISCAL YEAR 2017 COOPERATIVE THREAT REDUCTION FUNDS DEFINED.—In this title, the term "fiscal year 2017 cooperative threat reduction funds" means the funds appropriated pursuant to the authorization of appropriations in section 301 and made available by the funding table in division D for the Department of Defense Cooperative Threat Reduction Program established under section 1321 of the Department of Defense Cooperative Threat Reduction Act (50 U.S.C. 3711).

(b) AVAILABILITY OF FUNDS.—Funds appropriated pursuant to the authorization of appropriations in section 301 and made available by the funding table in division D for the Department of Defense Cooperative Threat Reduction Program shall be available for obligation for fiscal years 2017, 2018, and 2019.

SEC. 1302. FUNDING ALLOCATIONS.

(a) IN GENERAL.—Of the $325,604,000 authorized to be appropriated to the Department of Defense for fiscal year 2017 in section 301 and made available by the funding table in division D for the Department of Defense Cooperative Threat Reduction Program established under section 1321 of the Department of Defense Cooperative Threat Reduction Act (50 U.S.C. 3711), the following amounts may be obligated for the purposes specified:

(1) For strategic offensive arms elimination, $11,791,000.

(2) For chemical weapons destruction, $2,942,000.

(3) For global nuclear security, $16,899,000.

(4) For cooperative biological engagement, $213,984,000.

(5) For proliferation prevention, $50,709,000, of which—

(A) $4,000,000 may be obligated for purposes relating to nuclear nonproliferation assisted or caused by additive manufacture technology (commonly referred to as "3D printing");

(B) $4,000,000 may be obligated for monitoring the "proliferation pathways" under the Joint Comprehensive Plan of Action;

(C) $4,000,000 may be obligated for enhancing law enforcement cooperation and intelligence sharing; and

(D) $4,000,000 may be obligated for the Proliferation Security Initiative under subtitle B of title XVIII of the Implementing Recommendations of the 9/11 Commission Act of 2007 (50 U.S.C. 2911 et seq.).

(6) For threat reduction engagement, $2,000,000.

(7) For activities designated as Other Assessments/Administrative Costs, $27,279,000.

(b) MODIFICATIONS TO CERTAIN REQUIREMENTS.—The Department of Defense Cooperative Threat Reduction Act (50 U.S.C. 3701 et seq.) is amended as follows:

(1) Section 1321(g)(1) (50 U.S.C. 3711(g)(1)) is amended by striking "15 days" and inserting "45 days".

(2) Section 1322(b) (50 U.S.C. 3712(b)) is amended—

(A) by striking "At the time at which" and inserting "Not later than 15 days before the date on which";

(B) in paragraph (1), by striking "; and" and inserting a semicolon;

(C) in paragraph (2), by striking the period and inserting "; and"; and

(D) by adding at the end the following new paragraph:

"(3) a discussion of—

"(A) whether authorities other than the authority under this section are available to the Secretaries to perform such project or activity to meet the threats or goals identified under subsection (a)(1); and

"(B) if such other authorities exist, why the Secretaries were not able to use such authorities for such project or activity.".

(3) Section 1323(b)(3) (50 U.S.C. 3713(b)(3)) is amended by striking "at the time at which" and inserting "not later than seven days before the date on which".

(4) Section 1324 (50 U.S.C. 3714) is amended—

(A) in subsection (a)(1)(C), by striking "15 days" and inserting "45 days"; and

(B) in subsection (b)(3), by striking "15 days" and inserting "45 days".

(c) JOINT COMPREHENSIVE PLAN OF ACTION DEFINED.—In this section, the term "Joint Comprehensive Plan of Action" means the Joint Comprehensive Plan of Action, signed at Vienna July 14, 2015, by Iran and by the People's Republic of China, France, Germany, the Russian Federation, the United Kingdom, and the United States, with the High Representative of the European Union for Foreign Affairs and Security Policy, and all implementing materials and agreements related to the Joint Comprehensive Plan of Action, and transmitted by the President to Congress on July 19, 2015, pursuant to section 135(a) of the Atomic Energy Act of 1954, as amended by the Iran Nuclear Agreement Review Act of 2015 (Public Law 114–17; 129 Stat. 201).

SEC. 1303. LIMITATION ON AVAILABILITY OF FUNDS FOR COOPERATIVE THREAT REDUCTION IN PEOPLE'S REPUBLIC OF CHINA.

(a) IN GENERAL.—The Department of Defense Cooperative Threat Reduction Act (50 U.S.C. 3701 et seq.) is amended by inserting after section 1334 the following new section:

"SEC. 1335. LIMITATION ON AVAILABILITY OF FUNDS FOR COOPERATIVE THREAT REDUCTION ACTIVITIES IN PEOPLE'S REPUBLIC OF CHINA.

"(a) SEMIANNUAL INSTALLMENTS.—In carrying out activities under the Program in the People's Republic of China, the Secretary of Defense shall ensure that Cooperative Threat Reduction funds for such activities are obligated or expended in semiannual installments.

"(b) REQUIRED REPORTS.—

"(1) ADDITIONAL INFORMATION.—With respect to carrying out activities under the Program in the People's Republic of China, the Secretary of Defense shall submit to the congressional defense committees the reports required by section 1321(g) on a semiannual basis by not later than 15 days before any obligation of Cooperative Threat Reduction funds for such activities during the covered semiannual period. In addition to the matters required by such section, each such report shall include, in coordination with the Secretary of State—

"(A) whether China has taken material steps to—

"(i) disrupt the proliferation activities of Li Fangwei (also known as Karl Lee, or any other alias known by the United States); and

"(ii) arrest Li Fangwei pursuant the indictment charged in the United States District Court for the Southern District of New York on April 29, 2014;

"(B) whether China has proliferated to any non-nuclear weapons state, or any nuclear weapons state in violation of the Treaty on the Non-Proliferation of Nuclear Weapons, any item that contributes to a ballistic missile or nuclear weapons delivery system; and

"(C) the number, type, and summary of any demarches between the United States and China with respect to the matters described in subparagraphs (A) and (B).

"(2) ADDITIONAL SUBMISSIONS.—At the same time as the Secretary of Defense submits to the congressional defense committees the information described in subparagraphs (A), (B), and (C) of paragraph (1) as part of the reports required by section 1321(g), the Secretary shall submit to the Committee on Foreign Affairs of the House of Representatives and the Committee on Foreign Relations of the Senate such information.

"(3) COVERAGE.—With respect to the information described in subparagraphs (A), (B), and (C) of paragraph (1)—

"(A) the first report described in such paragraph that is submitted after the date of the enactment of this section shall cover the preceding 12-month period before the date of such submission; and

"(B) each subsequent report shall cover the semiannual period preceding the date of such submission.

"(4) FORM.—The information described in subparagraphs (A), (B), and (C) of paragraph (1) shall be submitted in unclassified form, but may include a classified annex.".

(b) CONFORMING AMENDMENTS.—Section 1321(g) of such Act (50 U.S.C. 3711(g)) is amended—

(1) in paragraph (1)—

(A) in the heading, by striking "ANNUAL REQUIREMENT" and inserting "REPORTS REQUIREMENT"; and

(B) by striking "that fiscal year" and inserting "that fiscal year (or, in accordance with section 1335(b), the semiannual period covered by the report)"; and

(2) in paragraph (3), by striking "Paragraph (1)" and inserting "Except for Cooperative Threat Reduction funds subject to section 1335, paragraph (1)".

TITLE XIV—OTHER AUTHORIZATIONS

Subtitle A—Military Programs

Sec. 1401. Working capital funds.
Sec. 1402. Chemical Agents and Munitions Destruction, Defense.
Sec. 1403. Drug Interdiction and Counter-Drug Activities, Defense-wide.
Sec. 1404. Defense Inspector General.
Sec. 1405. Defense Health Program.

Subtitle B—National Defense Stockpile

Sec. 1411. Authority to dispose of certain materials from and to acquire additional materials for the National Defense Stockpile.
Sec. 1412. National Defense Stockpile matters.

Subtitle C—Chemical Demilitarization Matters

Sec. 1421. National Academies of Sciences study on conventional munitions demilitarization alternative technologies.

Subtitle D—Other Matters

Sec. 1431. Authority for transfer of funds to joint Department of Defense-Department of Veterans Affairs Medical Facility Demonstration Fund for Captain James A. Lovell Health Care Center, Illinois.
Sec. 1432. Authorization of appropriations for Armed Forces Retirement Home.

Subtitle A—Military Programs

SEC. 1401. WORKING CAPITAL FUNDS.

Funds are hereby authorized to be appropriated for fiscal year 2017 for the use of the Armed Forces and other activities and agencies of the Department of Defense for providing capital for working capital and revolving funds, as specified in the funding table in section 4501.

SEC. 1402. CHEMICAL AGENTS AND MUNITIONS DESTRUCTION, DEFENSE.

(a) AUTHORIZATION OF APPROPRIATIONS.—Funds are hereby authorized to be appropriated for the Department of Defense for fiscal year 2017 for expenses, not otherwise provided for, for Chemical Agents and Munitions Destruction, Defense, as specified in the funding table in section 4501.

(b) USE.—Amounts authorized to be appropriated under subsection (a) are authorized for—

(1) the destruction of lethal chemical agents and munitions in accordance with section 1412 of the Department of Defense Authorization Act, 1986 (50 U.S.C. 1521); and

(2) the destruction of chemical warfare materiel of the United States that is not covered by section 1412 of such Act.

SEC. 1403. DRUG INTERDICTION AND COUNTER-DRUG ACTIVITIES, DEFENSE-WIDE.

Funds are hereby authorized to be appropriated for the Department of Defense for fiscal year 2017 for expenses, not otherwise provided for, for Drug Interdiction and Counter-Drug Activities, Defense-wide, as specified in the funding table in section 4501.

SEC. 1404. DEFENSE INSPECTOR GENERAL.

Funds are hereby authorized to be appropriated for the Department of Defense for fiscal year 2017 for expenses, not otherwise provided for, for the Office of the Inspector General of the Department of Defense, as specified in the funding table in section 4501.

SEC. 1405. DEFENSE HEALTH PROGRAM.

Funds are hereby authorized to be appropriated for fiscal year 2017 for the Defense Health Program, as specified in the funding table in section 4501, for use of the Armed Forces and other activities and agencies of the Department of Defense in providing for the health of eligible beneficiaries.

Subtitle B—National Defense Stockpile

SEC. 1411. AUTHORITY TO DISPOSE OF CERTAIN MATERIALS FROM AND TO ACQUIRE ADDITIONAL MATERIALS FOR THE NATIONAL DEFENSE STOCKPILE.

(a) DISPOSAL AUTHORITY.—Pursuant to section 5(b) of the Strategic and Critical Materials Stock Piling Act (50 U.S.C. 98d(b)), the National Defense Stockpile Manager may dispose of the following materials contained in the National Defense Stockpile in the following quantities:

(1) 27 short tons of beryllium.

(2) 111,149 short tons of chromium, ferroalloy.

(3) 2,973 short tons of chromium metal.

(4) 8,380 troy ounces of platinum.

(5) 275,741 pounds of contained tungsten metal powder.

(6) 12,433,796 pounds of contained tungsten ores and concentrates.

(b) ACQUISITION AUTHORITY.—

(1) AUTHORITY.—Using funds available in the National Defense Stockpile Transaction Fund, the National Defense Stockpile Manager may acquire the following materials determined to be strategic and critical materials required to meet the defense, industrial, and essential civilian needs of the United States:

(A) High modulus and high strength carbon fibers.

(B) Tantalum.

(C) Germanium.

(D) Tungsten rhenium metal.

(E) Boron carbide powder.

(F) Europium.

(G) Silicon carbide fiber.

(2) AMOUNT OF AUTHORITY.—The National Defense Stockpile Manager may use up to $55,000,0000 in the National Defense Stockpile Transaction Fund for acquisition of the materials specified paragraph (1).

(3) FISCAL YEAR LIMITATION.—The authority under paragraph (1) is available for purchases during fiscal year 2017 through fiscal year 2021.

SEC. 1412. NATIONAL DEFENSE STOCKPILE MATTERS.

(a) MATERIALS CONSTITUTING THE NATIONAL DEFENSE STOCKPILE.—Section 4 of the Strategic and Critical Materials Stock Piling Act (50 U.S.C. 98c) is amended—

(1) in subsection (b), by striking "required for" and inserting "suitable for transfer or disposal through"; and

(2) in subsection (c)—

(A) by striking "(1)" and all that follows through "(2)"; and

(B) by striking "this subsection" and inserting "subsection (b)".

(b) QUALIFICATION OF DOMESTIC SOURCES.—Section 15(a) of such Act (50 U.S.C. 98h–6(a)) is amended—

(1) in paragraph (1), by striking "and" at the end ;

(2) in paragraph (2), by striking the period at the end and inserting a semicolon; and

(3) by adding at the end the following new paragraphs:

"(3) by qualifying existing domestic facilities and domestically produced strategic and critical materials to meet the requirements of defense and essential civilian industries in times of national emergency when existing domestic sources of supply are either insufficient or vulnerable to single points of failure; and

"(4) by contracting with domestic facilities to recycle strategic and critical materials, thereby increasing domestic supplies when such materials would otherwise be insufficient to support defense and essential civilian industries in times of national emergency.".

Subtitle C—Chemical Demilitarization Matters

SEC. 1421. NATIONAL ACADEMIES OF SCIENCES STUDY ON CONVENTIONAL MUNITIONS DEMILITARIZATION ALTERNATIVE TECHNOLOGIES.

(a) IN GENERAL.—The Secretary of the Army shall enter into an arrangement with the Board on Army Science and Technology of the National Academies of Sciences, Engineering, and Medicine to conduct a study of the conventional munitions demilitarization program of the Department of Defense.

(b) ELEMENTS.—The study required pursuant to subsection (a) shall include the following:

(1) A review of the current conventional munitions demilitarization stockpile, including types of munitions and types of materials contaminated with propellants or energetics, and the disposal technologies used.

(2) An analysis of disposal, treatment, and reuse technologies, including technologies currently used by the Department and emerging technologies used or being developed by private or other governmental agencies, including a comparison of cost, throughput capacity, personnel safety, and environmental impacts.

(3) An identification of munitions types for which alternatives to open burning, open detonation, or non-closed loop incineration/combustion are not used.

(4) An identification and evaluation of any barriers to full-scale deployment of alternatives to open burning, open detonation, or non-closed loop incineration/combustion, and recommendations to overcome such barriers.

(5) An evaluation whether the maturation and deployment of governmental or private technologies currently in research and development would enhance the conventional munitions demilitarization capabilities of the Department.

(c) SUBMITTAL TO CONGRESS.—Not later than 18 months after the date of the enactment of this Act, the Secretary shall submit to the congressional defense committees the study conducted pursuant to subsection (a).

Subtitle D—Other Matters

SEC. 1431. AUTHORITY FOR TRANSFER OF FUNDS TO JOINT DEPARTMENT OF DEFENSE-DEPARTMENT OF VETERANS AFFAIRS MEDICAL FACILITY DEMONSTRATION FUND FOR CAPTAIN JAMES A. LOVELL HEALTH CARE CENTER, ILLINOIS.

(a) AUTHORITY FOR TRANSFER OF FUNDS.—Of the funds authorized to be appropriated by section 1405 and available for the Defense Health Program for operation and maintenance, $122,400,000 may be transferred by the Secretary of Defense to the Joint Department of Defense-Department of Veterans Affairs Medical Facility Demonstration Fund established by subsection (a)(1) of section 1704 of the National Defense Authorization Act for Fiscal Year 2010 (Public Law 111–84; 123 Stat. 2571). For purposes of subsection (a)(2) of such section 1704, any funds so transferred shall be treated as amounts authorized and appropriated specifically for the purpose of such a transfer.

(b) USE OF TRANSFERRED FUNDS.—For the purposes of subsection (b) of such section 1704, facility operations for which funds transferred under subsection (a) may be used are operations of the Captain James A. Lovell Federal Health Care Center, consisting of the North Chicago Veterans Affairs Medical Center, the Navy Ambulatory Care Center, and supporting facilities designated as a combined Federal medical facility under an operational agreement covered by section 706 of the Duncan Hunter National Defense Authorization Act for Fiscal Year 2009 (Public Law 110–417; 122 Stat. 4500).

SEC. 1432. AUTHORIZATION OF APPROPRIATIONS FOR ARMED FORCES RETIREMENT HOME.

There is hereby authorized to be appropriated for fiscal year 2017 from the Armed Forces Retirement Home Trust Fund the sum of $64,300,000 for the operation of the Armed Forces Retirement Home.

TITLE XV—AUTHORIZATION OF ADDITIONAL APPROPRIATIONS FOR OVERSEAS CONTINGENCY OPERATIONS

Subtitle A—Authorization of Appropriations

Sec. 1501. Purpose and treatment of certain authorizations of appropriations.
Sec. 1502. Procurement.
Sec. 1503. Research, development, test, and evaluation.
Sec. 1504. Operation and maintenance.
Sec. 1505. Military personnel.
Sec. 1506. Working capital funds.
Sec. 1507. Drug Interdiction and Counter-Drug Activities, Defense-wide.
Sec. 1508. Defense Inspector General.
Sec. 1509. Defense Health program.

Subtitle B—Financial Matters

Sec. 1511. Treatment as additional authorizations.
Sec. 1512. Special transfer authority.

Subtitle C—Limitations, Reports, and Other Matters

Sec. 1521. Afghanistan Security Forces Fund.
Sec. 1522. Joint Improvised Explosive Device Defeat Fund.
Sec. 1523. Extension of authority to use Joint Improvised Explosive Device Defeat Fund for training of foreign security forces to defeat improvised explosive devices.
Sec. 1524. Overseas contingency operations.
Sec. 1525. Extension and modification of authorities on Counterterrorism Partnerships Fund.

Subtitle A—Authorization of Appropriations

SEC. 1501. PURPOSE AND TREATMENT OF CERTAIN AUTHORIZATIONS OF APPROPRIATIONS.

(a) PURPOSE.—The purpose of this subtitle is to authorize appropriations for the Department of Defense for fiscal year 2017 to provide additional funds—

(1) for overseas contingency operations being carried out by the Armed Forces; and

(2) pursuant to sections 1502, 1503, 1504, 1505, and 1507 for expenses, not otherwise provided for, for procurement, research, development, test, and evaluation, operation and maintenance, military personnel, and defense-wide drug interdiction and counter-drug activities, as specified in the funding tables in sections 4103, 4203, 4303, 4403, and 4503.

(b) SUPPORT OF BASE BUDGET REQUIREMENTS; TREATMENT.—Funds identified in subsection (a)(2) are being authorized to be appropriated in support of base budget requirements as requested by the President for fiscal year 2017 pursuant to section 1105(a) of title 31, United States Code. The Director of the Office of Management and Budget shall apportion the funds identified in such subsection to the Department of Defense without restriction, limitation, or constraint on the execution of such funds in support of base requirements, including any restriction, limitation, or constraint imposed by, or described in, the document entitled "Criteria for War/Overseas Contingency Operations Funding Requests" transmitted by the Director to the Department of Defense on September 9, 2010, or any successor or related guidance.

SEC. 1502. PROCUREMENT.

Funds are hereby authorized to be appropriated for fiscal year 2017 for procurement accounts for the Army, the Navy and the Marine Corps, the Air Force, and Defense-wide activities, as specified in—

(1) the funding table in section 4102; or

(2) the funding table in section 4103.

SEC. 1503. RESEARCH, DEVELOPMENT, TEST, AND EVALUATION.

Funds are hereby authorized to be appropriated for fiscal year 2017 for the use of the Department of Defense for research, development, test, and evaluation, as specified in—

(1) the funding table in section 4202; or

(2) the funding table in section 4203.

SEC. 1504. OPERATION AND MAINTENANCE.

Funds are hereby authorized to be appropriated for fiscal year 2017 for the use of the Armed Forces and other activities and agencies of the Department of Defense for expenses, not otherwise provided for, for operation and maintenance, as specified in—

(1) the funding table in section 4302, or

(2) the funding table in section 4303.

SEC. 1505. MILITARY PERSONNEL.

Funds are hereby authorized to be appropriated for fiscal year 2017 for the use of the Armed Forces and other activities and agencies of the Department of Defense for expenses, not otherwise provided for, for military personnel, as specified in—

(1) the funding table in section 4402; or

(2) the funding table in section 4403.

SEC. 1506. WORKING CAPITAL FUNDS.

Funds are hereby authorized to be appropriated for fiscal year 2017 for the use of the Armed Forces and other activities and agencies of the Department of Defense for providing capital for working capital and revolving funds, as specified in the funding table in section 4502.

SEC. 1507. DRUG INTERDICTION AND COUNTER-DRUG ACTIVITIES, DEFENSE-WIDE.

Funds are hereby authorized to be appropriated for the Department of Defense for fiscal year 2017 for expenses, not otherwise provided for, for Drug Interdiction and Counter-Drug Activities, Defense-wide, as specified in—

(1) the funding table in section 4502; or

(2) the funding table in section 4503.

SEC. 1508. DEFENSE INSPECTOR GENERAL.

Funds are hereby authorized to be appropriated for the Department of Defense for fiscal year 2017 for expenses, not otherwise provided for, for the Office of the Inspector General of the Department of Defense, as specified in the funding table in section 4502.

SEC. 1509. DEFENSE HEALTH PROGRAM.

Funds are hereby authorized to be appropriated for the Department of Defense for fiscal year 2017 for expenses, not otherwise provided for, for the Defense Health Program, as specified in the funding table in section 4502.

Subtitle B—Financial Matters

SEC. 1511. TREATMENT AS ADDITIONAL AUTHORIZATIONS.

The amounts authorized to be appropriated by this title are in addition to amounts otherwise authorized to be appropriated by this Act.

SEC. 1512. SPECIAL TRANSFER AUTHORITY.

(a) AUTHORITY TO TRANSFER AUTHORIZATIONS.—

(1) AUTHORITY.—Upon determination by the Secretary of Defense that such action is necessary in the national interest, the Secretary may transfer amounts of authorizations made available to the Department of Defense in this title for fiscal year 2017 between any such authorizations for that fiscal year (or any subdivisions thereof).

(2) EFFECT OF TRANSFER.—Amounts of authorizations transferred under this subsection shall be merged with and be available for the same purposes as the authorization to which transferred.

(3) LIMITATIONS.—The total amount of authorizations that the Secretary may transfer under the authority of this subsection may not exceed $3,500,000,000.

(4) EXCEPTION.—In the case of the authorizations of appropriations contained in sections 1502, 1503, 1504, 1505, and 1507 that are provided for the purpose specified in section 1501(a)(2), the transfer authority provided under section 1001, rather than the transfer authority provided by this subsection, shall apply to any transfer of amounts of such authorizations.

(b) TERMS AND CONDITIONS.—Transfers under this section shall be subject to the same terms and conditions as transfers under section 1001.

(c) ADDITIONAL AUTHORITY.—The transfer authority provided by this section is in addition to the transfer authority provided under section 1001.

Subtitle C—Limitations, Reports, and Other Matters

SEC. 1521. AFGHANISTAN SECURITY FORCES FUND.

(a) CONTINUATION OF PRIOR AUTHORITIES AND NOTICE AND REPORTING REQUIREMENTS.—Funds available to the Department of Defense for the Afghanistan Security Forces Fund for fiscal year 2017 shall be subject to the conditions contained in subsections (b) through (g) of section 1513 of the National Defense Authorization Act for Fiscal Year 2008 (Public Law 110–181; 122 Stat. 428), as amended by section 1531(b) of the Ike Skelton National Defense Authorization Act for Fiscal Year 2011 (Public Law 111–383; 124 Stat. 4424).

(b) EQUIPMENT DISPOSITION.—

(1) ACCEPTANCE OF CERTAIN EQUIPMENT.—Subject to paragraph (2), the Secretary of Defense may accept equipment that is procured using amounts in the Afghanistan Security Forces Fund authorized under this Act and is intended for transfer to the security forces of Afghanistan, but is not accepted by such security forces.

(2) CONDITIONS ON ACCEPTANCE OF EQUIPMENT.—Before accepting any equipment under the authority provided by paragraph (1), the Commander of United States forces in Afghanistan shall make a determination that the equipment was procured for the purpose of meeting requirements of the security forces of Afghanistan, as agreed to by both the Government of Afghanistan and the United States, but is no longer required by such security forces or was damaged before transfer to such security forces.

(3) ELEMENTS OF DETERMINATION.—In making a determination under paragraph (2) regarding equipment, the Commander of United States forces in Afghanistan shall consider alternatives to Secretary of Defense acceptance of the equipment. An explanation of each determination, including the basis for the determination and the alternatives considered, shall be included in the relevant quarterly report required under paragraph (5).

(4) TREATMENT AS DEPARTMENT OF DEFENSE STOCKS.—Equipment accepted under the authority provided by paragraph (1) may be treated as stocks of the Department of Defense upon notification to the congressional defense committees of such treatment.

(5) QUARTERLY REPORTS ON EQUIPMENT DISPOSITION.—Not later than 90 days after the date of the enactment of this Act and every 90-day period thereafter during which the authority provided by paragraph (1) is exercised, the Secretary of Defense shall submit to the congressional defense committees a report describing the equipment accepted under this subsection, section 1531(d) of the National Defense Authorization Act for Fiscal Year 2014 (Public Law 113–66; 127 Stat. 938; 10 U.S.C. 2302 note), and section 1532(b) of the Carl Levin and Howard P. "Buck" McKeon National Defense Authorization Act for Fiscal Year 2015 (Public Law 113–291; 128 Stat. 3612) during the period covered by the report. Each report shall include a list of all equipment that was accepted during the period covered by the report and treated as stocks of the Department and copies of the determinations made under paragraph (2), as required by paragraph (3).

(c) PLAN TO PROMOTE SECURITY OF AFGHAN WOMEN.—

(1) REPORTING REQUIREMENT.—The Secretary of Defense, with the concurrence of the Secretary of State, shall include in each report required under section 1225 of the Carl Levin and Howard P. "Buck" McKeon National Defense Authorization Act for Fiscal Year 2015 (Public Law 113–291; 128 Stat. 3550)—

(A) a current assessment of the security of Afghan women and girls, including information regarding efforts to increase the recruitment and retention of women in the Afghan National Security Forces; and

(B) a current assessment of the implementation of the plans for the recruitment, integration, retention, training, treatment, and provision of appropriate facilities and transportation for women in the Afghan National Security Forces, including the challenges associated with such implementation and the steps being taken to address those challenges.

(2) PLAN REQUIRED.—

(A) IN GENERAL.—The Secretary of Defense, with the concurrence of the Secretary of State, shall support, to the extent practicable, the efforts of the Government of Afghanistan to promote the security of Afghan women and girls during and after the security transition process through the development and implementation by the Government of Afghanistan of an Afghan-led plan that should include the elements described in this paragraph.

(B) TRAINING.—The Secretary of Defense, with the concurrence of the Secretary of State and working with the NATO-led Resolute Support mission, should encourage the Government of Afghanistan to develop—

(i) measures for the evaluation of the effectiveness of existing training for Afghan National Security Forces on this issue;

(ii) a plan to increase the number of female security officers specifically trained to address cases of gender-based violence, including ensuring the Afghan National Police's Family Response Units have the necessary resources and are available to women across Afghanistan;

(iii) mechanisms to enhance the capacity for units of National Police's Family Response Units to fulfill their mandate as well as indicators measuring the operational effectiveness of these units;

(iv) a plan to address the development of accountability mechanisms for Afghanistan National Army and Afghanistan National Police personnel who violate codes of conduct relating to the human rights of women and girls, including female members of the Afghan National Security Forces;

(v) a plan to address the development of accountability mechanisms for Afghanistan National Army and Afghanistan National Police personnel who violate codes of conduct relating to protecting children from sexual abuse; and

(vi) a plan to develop training for the Afghanistan National Army and the Afghanistan National Police to increase awareness and responsiveness among Afghanistan National Army and Afghanistan National Police personnel regarding the unique security challenges women confront when serving in those forces.

(C) ENROLLMENT AND TREATMENT.—The Secretary of Defense, with the concurrence of the Secretary of State and in cooperation with the Afghan Ministries of Defense and Interior, shall seek to assist the Government of Afghanistan in including as part of the plan developed under subparagraph (A) the development and implementation of a plan to increase the number of female members of the Afghanistan National Army and the Afghanistan National Police and to promote their equal treatment, including through such steps as providing appropriate equipment, modifying facilities, and ensuring literacy and gender awareness training for recruits.

(D) ALLOCATION OF FUNDS.—

(i) IN GENERAL.—Of the funds available to the Department of Defense for the Afghan Security Forces Fund for fiscal year 2017, it is the goal that $25,000,000, but in no event less than $10,000,000, shall be used for—

(I) the recruitment, integration, retention, training, and treatment of women in the Afghan National Security Forces; and

(II) the recruitment, training, and contracting of female security personnel for future elections.

(ii) TYPES OF PROGRAMS AND ACTIVITIES.—Such programs and activities may include—

(I) efforts to recruit women into the Afghan National Security Forces, including the special operations forces;

(II) programs and activities of the Afghan Ministry of Defense Directorate of Human Rights and Gender Integration and the Afghan Ministry of Interior Office of Human Rights, Gender and Child Rights;

(III) development and dissemination of gender and human rights educational and training materials and programs within the Afghan Ministry of Defense and the Afghan Ministry of Interior;

(IV) efforts to address harassment and violence against women within the Afghan National Security Forces;

(V) improvements to infrastructure that address the requirements of women serving in the Afghan National Security Forces, including appropriate equipment for female security and police forces, and transportation for policewomen to their station;

(VI) support for Afghanistan National Police Family Response Units; and

(VII) security provisions for high-profile female police and army officers.

(d) REPORTING REQUIREMENT.—

(1) SEMI-ANNUAL REPORTS.—Not later than January 31 and July 31 of each year through January 31, 2021, the Secretary of Defense shall submit to the congressional defense committees a report summarizing the details of any obligation or transfer of funds from the Afghanistan Security Forces Fund during the preceding six-calendar month period.

(2) CONFORMING REPEALS.—(A) Section 1513 of the National Defense Authorization Act for Fiscal Year 2008 (Public Law 110–181; 122 Stat. 428), as amended by section 1531(b) of the Ike Skelton National Defense Authorization Act for Fiscal Year 2011 (Public Law 111–383; 124 Stat. 4424), is further amended by striking subsection (g).

(B) Section 1517 of the John Warner National Defense Authorization Act for Fiscal Year 2007 (Public Law 109–364; 120 Stat. 2442) is amended by striking subsection (f).

SEC. 1522. JOINT IMPROVISED EXPLOSIVE DEVICE DEFEAT FUND.

(a) USE AND TRANSFER OF FUNDS.—Subsection 1532(a) of the National Defense Authorization Act for Fiscal Year 2016 (Public Law 114–92; 129 Stat. 1091) is amended by striking "fiscal year 2016" and inserting "fiscal years 2016 and 2017".

(b) EXTENSION OF INTERDICTION OF IMPROVISED EXPLOSIVE DEVICE PRECURSOR CHEMICALS AUTHORITY.—Subsection (c) of section 1532 of the National Defense Authorization Act for Fiscal Year 2013 (Public Law 112–239; 126 Stat. 2057) is amended—

(1) in paragraph (1)—

(A) by striking "for fiscal year 2013 and for fiscal year 2016," and inserting "for fiscal years 2013, 2016, and 2017";

(B) by inserting "with the concurrence of the Secretary of State" after "may be available to the Secretary of Defense";

(C) by striking "of the Government of Pakistan" and inserting "of foreign governments"; and

(D) by striking "from Pakistan to locations in Afghanistan";

(2) in paragraph (2), by striking "of the Government of Pakistan" and inserting "of foreign governments"; and

(3) in paragraph (4), as most recently amended by section 1532(b)(2) of the National Defense Authorization Act for Fiscal Year 2016 (Public Law 114–92; 129 Stat. 1091), by striking "December 31, 2016" and inserting "December 31, 2017".

(c) NOTICE TO CONGRESS.—Paragraph (3) of such subsection is amended to read as follows:

"*(3) NOTICE TO CONGRESS.*— None of the funds made available pursuant to paragraph (1) may be obligated or expended to supply training, equipment, supplies, or services to a foreign country before the date that is 15 days after the date on which the Secretary of Defense, in coordination with the Secretary of State, submits to the Committee on Armed Services and the Committee on Foreign Relations of the Senate and the Committee on Armed Services and the Committee on Foreign Affairs of the House of Representatives a notice that contains—

"*(A)* the foreign country for which training, equipment, supplies, or services are proposed to be supplied;

"*(B)* a description of the training, equipment, supplies, and services to be provided using such funds;

"*(C)* a detailed description of the amount of funds proposed to be obligated or expended to supply such training, equipment, supplies or services, including any funds proposed to be obligated or expended to support the participation of another department or agency of the United States and a description of the training, equipment, supplies, or services proposed to be supplied;

"*(D)* an evaluation of the effectiveness of the efforts of the foreign country identified under subparagraph (A) to counter the flow of improvised explosive device precursor chemicals; and

"*(E)* an overall plan for countering the flow of precursor chemicals in the foreign country identified under subparagraph (A).".

SEC. 1523. EXTENSION OF AUTHORITY TO USE JOINT IMPROVISED EXPLOSIVE DEVICE DEFEAT FUND FOR TRAINING OF FOREIGN SECURITY FORCES TO DEFEAT IMPROVISED EXPLOSIVE DEVICES.

Section 1533(e) of the National Defense Authorization Act for Fiscal Year 2016 (Public Law 114–92; 129 Stat. 1093) is amended by striking "September 30, 2018" and inserting "September 30, 2020".

SEC. 1524. OVERSEAS CONTINGENCY OPERATIONS.

Funds are hereby authorized to be appropriated for fiscal year 2017 for the Department of Defense for overseas contingency operations in such amounts as may be designated as provided in section 251(b)(2)(A)(ii) of the Balanced Budget and Emergency Deficit Control Act of 1985.

SEC. 1525. EXTENSION AND MODIFICATION OF AUTHORITIES ON COUNTERTERRORISM PARTNERSHIPS FUND.

(a) EXTENSION.—Section 1534 of the Carl Levin and Howard P. "Buck" McKeon National Defense Authorization Act for Fiscal Year 2015 (Public Law 113–291; 128 Stat. 3616) is amended—

(1) in subsection (a), by striking "Amounts authorized to be appropriated for fiscal year 2015 by this title" and inserting "Subject to subsection (b), amounts authorized to be appropriated through fiscal year 2017"; and

(2) in subsection (h), by striking "December 31, 2016" and inserting "December 31, 2017".

(b) LIMITATION ON USE OF FUNDS AUTHORIZED FOR FISCAL YEAR 2016.—Such section is further amended—

(1) by redesignating subsections (b) through (h) as subsections (c) through (i), respectively; and

(2) by inserting after subsection (a) the following new subsection (b):

"*(b) LIMITATION ON USE OF FUNDS AUTHORIZED FOR FISCAL YEAR 2016.*—Amounts authorized to be appropriated for fiscal year 2016 for the Counterterrorism Partnerships Fund may only be used for the purposes specified in subsection (a)(2). In the use of such amounts, any reference in this section to 'subsection (a)' shall be deemed to be a reference to 'subsection (a)(2)'.".

(c) ADMINISTRATION OF FUND.—Subsection (e) of such section, as redesignated by subsection (b)(1) of this section, is amended—

(1) by striking paragraph (3); and

(2) by redesignating paragraphs (4), (5), and (6) as paragraphs (3), (4), and (5), respectively.

(d) REPORTS.—Subsection (h) of such section, as redesignated by subsection (b)(1) of this section, is amended—

(1) in the matter preceding paragraph (1)—

(A) by striking "and 2017" and inserting "2017, and 2018"; and

(B) by striking "and 2016" and inserting "2016, and 2017";

(2) in paragraph (4), by striking "subsection (d)(5)" and inserting "subsection (e)(4)"; and

(3) in paragraph (5), by striking "subsection (f)" and inserting "subsection (g)".

TITLE XVI—STRATEGIC PROGRAMS, CYBER, AND INTELLIGENCE MATTERS

Subtitle A—Space Activities

Sec. 1601. Repeal of provision permitting the use of rocket engines from the Russian Federation for the evolved expendable launch vehicle program.

Sec. 1602. Exception to the prohibition on contracting with Russian suppliers of rocket engines for the evolved expendable launch vehicle program.

Sec. 1603. Rocket propulsion system to replace RD–180.
Sec. 1604. Plan for use of allied launch vehicles.
Sec. 1605. Analysis of alternatives for wideband communications.
Sec. 1606. Modification of pilot program for acquisition of commercial satellite communication services.
Sec. 1607. Space-based environmental monitoring.
Sec. 1608. Prohibition on use of certain non-allied positioning, navigation, and timing systems.
Sec. 1609. Limitation of availability of funds for the Joint Space Operations Center Mission System.
Sec. 1610. Limitations on availability of funds for the Global Positioning System Next Generation Operational Control System.
Sec. 1611. Availability of funds for certain secure voice conferencing capabilities.
Sec. 1612. Space-based infrared system and advanced extremely high frequency program.
Sec. 1613. Pilot program on commercial weather data.
Sec. 1614. Plans on transfer of acquisition and funding authority of certain weather missions to National Reconnaissance Office.
Sec. 1615. Five-year plan for Joint Interagency Combined Space Operations Center.
Sec. 1616. Organization and management of national security space activities of the Department of Defense.
Sec. 1617. Review of charter of Operationally Responsive Space Program Office.
Sec. 1618. Backup and complementary positioning, navigation, and timing capabilities of Global Positioning System.
Sec. 1619. Report on use of spacecraft assets of the space-based infrared system wide-field-of-view program.
Sec. 1620. Provision of certain information to Government Accountability Office by National Reconnaissance Office.
Sec. 1621. Cost-benefit analysis of commercial use of excess ballistic missile solid rocket motors.
Sec. 1622. Independent assessment of Global Positioning System Next Generation Operational Control System.

Subtitle B—Defense Intelligence and Intelligence-Related Activities

Sec. 1631. Report on United States Central Command Intelligence Fusion Center.
Sec. 1632. Prohibition on availability of funds for certain relocation activities for NATO Intelligence Fusion Cell.
Sec. 1633. Survey and review of Defense Intelligence Enterprise.

Subtitle C—Cyberspace-Related Matters

Sec. 1641. Special emergency procurement authority to facilitate the defense against or recovery from a cyber attack.
Sec. 1642. Limitation on termination of dual-hat arrangement for Commander of the United States Cyber Command.
Sec. 1643. Cyber mission forces matters.
Sec. 1644. Requirement to enter into agreements relating to use of cyber opposition forces.
Sec. 1645. Cyber protection support for Department of Defense personnel in positions highly vulnerable to cyber attack.

Sec. 1646. Limitation on full deployment of joint regional security stacks.
Sec. 1647. Advisory committee on industrial security and industrial base policy.
Sec. 1648. Change in name of National Defense University's Information Resources Management College to College of Information and Cyberspace.
Sec. 1649. Evaluation of cyber vulnerabilities of F-35 aircraft and support systems.
Sec. 1650. Evaluation of cyber vulnerabilities of Department of Defense critical infrastructure.
Sec. 1651. Strategy to incorporate Army reserve component cyber protection teams into Department of Defense cyber mission force.
Sec. 1652. Strategic Plan for the Defense Information Systems Agency.
Sec. 1653. Plan for information security continuous monitoring capability and comply-to-connect policy; limitation on software licensing.
Sec. 1654. Reports on deterrence of adversaries in cyberspace.
Sec. 1655. Sense of Congress on cyber resiliency of the networks and communications systems of the National Guard.

Subtitle D—Nuclear Forces

Sec. 1661. Improvements to Council on Oversight of National Leadership Command, Control, and Communications System.
Sec. 1662. Treatment of certain sensitive information by State and local governments.
Sec. 1663. Procurement authority for certain parts of intercontinental ballistic missile fuzes.
Sec. 1664. Prohibition on availability of funds for mobile variant of ground-based strategic deterrent missile.
Sec. 1665. Limitation on availability of funds for extension of New START Treaty.
Sec. 1666. Certifications regarding integrated tactical warning and attack assessment mission of the Air Force.
Sec. 1667. Matters relating to intercontinental ballistic missiles.
Sec. 1668. Requests for forces to meet security requirements for land-based nuclear forces.
Sec. 1669. Report on Russian and Chinese political and military leadership survivability, command and control, and continuity of government programs and activities.
Sec. 1670. Review by Comptroller General of the United States of recommendations relating to nuclear enterprise of Department of Defense.
Sec. 1671. Sense of Congress on nuclear deterrence.
Sec. 1672. Sense of Congress on importance of independent nuclear deterrent of United Kingdom.

Subtitle E—Missile Defense Programs

Sec. 1681. National missile defense policy.
Sec. 1682. Extensions of prohibitions relating to missile defense information and systems.
Sec. 1683. Non-terrestrial missile defense intercept and defeat capability for the ballistic missile defense system.
Sec. 1684. Review of the missile defeat policy and strategy of the United States.
Sec. 1685. Maximizing Aegis Ashore capability and developing medium range discrimination radar.
Sec. 1686. Technical authority for integrated air and missile defense activities and programs.

Sec. 1687. Hypersonic defense capability development.
Sec. 1688. Conventional Prompt Global Strike weapons system.
Sec. 1689. Required testing by Missile Defense Agency of ground-based midcourse defense element of ballistic missile defense system.
Sec. 1690. Iron Dome short-range rocket defense system and Israeli cooperative missile defense program codevelopment and coproduction.
Sec. 1691. Limitations on availability of funds for lower tier air and missile defense capability of the Army.
Sec. 1692. Pilot program on loss of unclassified, controlled technical information.
Sec. 1693. Plan for procurement of medium-range discrimination radar to improve homeland missile defense.
Sec. 1694. Review of Missile Defense Agency budget submissions for ground-based midcourse defense and evaluation of alternative ground-based interceptor deployments.
Sec. 1695. Semiannual notifications on missile defense tests and costs.
Sec. 1696. Reports on unfunded priorities of the Missile Defense Agency.

Subtitle F—Other Matters

Sec. 1697. Protection of certain facilities and assets from unmanned aircraft.
Sec. 1698. Harmful interference to Department of Defense Global Positioning System.

Subtitle A—Space Activities

SEC. 1601. REPEAL OF PROVISION PERMITTING THE USE OF ROCKET ENGINES FROM THE RUSSIAN FEDERATION FOR THE EVOLVED EXPENDABLE LAUNCH VEHICLE PROGRAM.

Section 8048 of the Department of Defense Appropriations Act, 2016 (division C of Public Law 114–113; 129 Stat. 2363) is repealed.

SEC. 1602. EXCEPTION TO THE PROHIBITION ON CONTRACTING WITH RUSSIAN SUPPLIERS OF ROCKET ENGINES FOR THE EVOLVED EXPENDABLE LAUNCH VEHICLE PROGRAM.

Section 1608 of the Carl Levin and Howard P. "Buck" McKeon National Defense Authorization Act for Fiscal Year 2015 (Public Law 113–291; 128 Stat. 3626; 10 U.S.C. 2271 note), as amended by section 1607 of the National Defense Authorization Act for Fiscal Year 2016 (Public Law 114–92; 129 Stat. 1100), is further amended by striking subsection (c) and inserting the following new subsection:

"(c) EXCEPTION.—The prohibition in subsection (a) shall not apply to any of the following:

"(1) The placement of orders or the exercise of options under the contract numbered FA8811–13–C–0003 and awarded on December 18, 2013.

"(2) Contracts that are awarded during the period beginning on the date of the enactment of the National Defense Authorization Act for Fiscal Year 2017 and ending December 31, 2022, for the procurement of property or services for space launch activities that include the use of a total of 18 rocket engines designed or manufactured in the Russian Federation, in addition to the Russian-designed or Russian-manufactured engines to which paragraph (1) applies.".

SEC. 1603. ROCKET PROPULSION SYSTEM TO REPLACE RD–180.

Section 1604 of the Carl Levin and Howard P. "Buck" McKeon National Defense Authorization Act for Fiscal Year 2015 (Public Law 113–291; 128 Stat. 3623; 10 U.S.C. 2273 note), as amended by section 1606 of the National Defense Authorization Act for Fiscal Year 2016 (Public Law 114–92; 129 Stat. 1099), is further amended by striking subsection (d) and inserting the following new subsections:

"(d) USE OF FUNDS UNDER DEVELOPMENT PROGRAM.—

"(1) DEVELOPMENT OF ROCKET PROPULSION SYSTEM.—The funds described in paragraph (2)—

"(A) may be obligated or expended for—

"(i) the development of the rocket propulsion system to replace non-allied space launch engines pursuant to subsection (a); and

"(ii) the necessary interfaces to, or integration of, the rocket propulsion system with an existing or new launch vehicle; and

"(B) except as provided by paragraph (3), may not be obligated or expended to develop or procure a launch vehicle, an upper stage, a strap-on motor, or related infrastructure.

"(2) FUNDS DESCRIBED.—The funds described in this paragraph are the following:

"(A) Funds authorized to be appropriated by the National Defense Authorization Act for Fiscal Year 2017 or otherwise made available for fiscal year 2017 for the Department of Defense for the development of the rocket propulsion system under subsection (a).

"(B) Funds authorized to be appropriated by this Act or the National Defense Authorization Act for Fiscal Year 2016 or otherwise made available for fiscal years 2015 or 2016 for the Department of Defense for the development of the rocket propulsion system under subsection (a) that are unobligated as of the date of the enactment of the National Defense Authorization Act for Fiscal Year 2017.

"(3) OTHER PURPOSES.—The Secretary may obligate or expend not more than a total of the amount calculated under paragraph (4) of the funds that are authorized to be appropriated by the National Defense Authorization Act for Fiscal Year 2017 or otherwise made available for fiscal year 2017 for the rocket propulsion system and launch system investment for activities not authorized by paragraph (1)(A), including for developing a launch vehicle, an upper stage, a strap-on motor, or related infrastructure. The Secretary may exceed such limit calculated under paragraph (4) in fiscal year 2017 for such purposes if—

"(A) the Secretary certifies to the appropriate congressional committees that, as of the date of the certification—

"(i) the development of the rocket propulsion system is being carried out pursuant to paragraph (1)(A) in a manner that ensures that the rocket propulsion system will meet each requirement under subsection (a)(2); and

"(ii) such obligation or expenditure will not negatively affect the development of the rocket propulsion system, including with respect to meeting such requirements; and

"(B) the reprogramming or transfer is carried out in accordance with established procedures for reprogramming or transfers, including with respect to presenting a request for a reprogramming of funds.

"(4) CALCULATION OF AMOUNTS FOR OTHER PURPOSES.—In carrying out paragraph (3), the Secretary shall calculate the amount of the funds specified in such paragraph as follows:

"(A) If the total amount of funds that are authorized to be appropriated by the National Defense Authorization Act for Fiscal Year 2017 or otherwise made available for fiscal year 2017 for the rocket propulsion system and launch system investment is equal to or less than $320,000,000, such amount shall equal 31 percent.

"(B) If the total amount of funds that are authorized to be appropriated by the National Defense Authorization Act for Fiscal Year 2017 or otherwise made available for fiscal year 2017 for the rocket propulsion system and launch system investment is greater than $320,000,000, such amount shall equal the difference of—

"(i) the amount of funds so authorized to be appropriated, minus

"(ii) $220,000,000.

"(e) DEFINITIONS.—In this section:

"(1) The term 'appropriate congressional committees' means—

"(A) the congressional defense committees; and

"(B) the Permanent Select Committee on Intelligence of the House of Representatives and the Select Committee on Intelligence of the Senate.

"(2) The term 'rocket propulsion system' means, with respect to the development authorized by subsection (a), a main booster, first-stage rocket engine or motor. The term does not include a launch vehicle, an upper stage, a strap-on motor, or related infrastructure.".

SEC. 1604. PLAN FOR USE OF ALLIED LAUNCH VEHICLES.

(a) PLAN.—The Secretary of Defense, in coordination with the Director of National Intelligence, shall develop a plan to use allied launch vehicles to meet the requirements for achieving the policy relating to assured access to space set forth in section 2273 of title 10, United States Code, in the event that such requirements cannot be met, for a limited period, using only launch vehicles of the United States.

(b) ASSESSMENTS.—In developing the plan required by subsection (a), the Secretary shall conduct assessments of the following:

(1) What satellites of the United States would be appropriate to be launched on an allied launch vehicle.

(2) The relevant laws, regulations, and policies governing the launch of national security satellites and whether any legislative, regulatory, or policy actions (including with respect to waivers) would be necessary to allow for the launch of a national security satellite on an allied launch vehicle.

(3) The certification requirements for using allied launch vehicles pursuant to the plan and the estimated cost, schedule, and actions that would be necessary to certify allied launch vehicles.

(4) Any other matters the Secretary determines appropriate.

(c) SUBMISSION TO CONGRESS.—Not later than 180 days after the date of the enactment of this Act, the Secretary shall submit to the appropriate congressional committees a report on the plan required by subsection (a) and the assessments required by subsection (b).

(d) DEFINITIONS.—In this section:

(1) The term "allied launch vehicle" means a launch vehicle of the government of a country that is an ally of the United States. The term does not include a launch vehicle of the Government of the Russian Federation, the Government of the People's Republic of China, the Government of the Islamic Republic of Iran, or the Government of the Democratic People's Republic of Korea.

(2) The term "appropriate congressional committees" means—

(A) the congressional defense committees; and

(B) the Permanent Select Committee on Intelligence of the House of Representatives and the Select Committee on Intelligence of the Senate.

(3) The term "national security satellite" means a satellite launched for national security purposes, including such a satellite launched by the Air Force, the Navy, or the National Reconnaissance Office, or any other element of the Department of Defense.

SEC. 1605. ANALYSIS OF ALTERNATIVES FOR WIDE-BAND COMMUNICATIONS.

Section 1611 of the National Defense Authorization Act for Fiscal Year 2016 (Public Law 114–92; 129 Stat. 1103) is amended by striking subsection (b) and inserting the following new subsections:

"(b) SCOPE.—

"(1) STUDY GUIDANCE.—In conducting the analysis of alternatives under subsection (a),

the Secretary shall develop study guidance that requires such analysis to include the full range of military and commercial satellite communications capabilities, acquisition processes, and service delivery models.

"(2) OTHER CONSIDERATIONS.—The Secretary shall ensure that—

"(A) any cost assessments of military or commercial satellite communications systems included in the analysis of alternatives conducted under subsection (a) include detailed full life-cycle costs, as applicable, including with respect to—

"(i) military personnel, military construction, military infrastructure operation, maintenance costs, and ground and user terminal impacts; and

"(ii) any other costs regarding military or commercial satellite communications systems the Secretary determines appropriate; and

"(B) such analysis identifies any considerations relating to the use of military versus commercial systems.

"(c) COMPTROLLER GENERAL REPORT.—

"(1) SUBMISSION.—Upon completion of the analysis of alternatives conducted under subsection (a), the Secretary shall submit such analysis to the Comptroller General of the United States.

"(2) REPORT.—Not later than 120 days after the date on which the Comptroller General receives the analysis of alternatives under paragraph (1), the Comptroller General shall submit to the congressional defense committees a report containing—

"(A) a review of the analysis; and

"(B) an assessment of the types of analyses the Secretary has conducted to understand the costs and benefits of the use of KA-band commercial satellite communications by the Department of Defense.

"(3) MATTERS INCLUDED.—The report under paragraph (2) shall include the following:

"(A) With respect to the review of the analysis of alternatives conducted under subsection (a)—

"(i) whether, and to what extent, the Secretary—

"(I) conducted such analysis using best practices;

"(II) fully addressed the concerns of the acquisition, operational, and user communities; and

"(III) complied with subsection (b); and

"(ii) a description of how the Secretary identified the requirements and assessed and addressed the cost, schedule, and risks posed for each alternative included in such analysis.

"(B) With respect to the assessment under paragraph (2)(B)—

"(i) whether the Secretary has evaluated the use of KA-band commercial satellite communications, based on total cost, capabilities, and interoperability with existing or planned terminals; and

"(ii) such other matters as the Comptroller General considers appropriate.

"(d) BRIEFINGS.—Not later than 90 days after the date of the enactment of the National Defense Authorization Act for Fiscal Year 2017, and semiannually thereafter until the date on which the analysis of alternatives conducted under subsection (a) is completed, the Secretary shall provide the Committees on Armed Services of the House of Representatives and the Senate (and any other congressional defense committee upon request) a briefing on such analysis.".

SEC. 1606. MODIFICATION OF PILOT PROGRAM FOR ACQUISITION OF COMMERCIAL SATELLITE COMMUNICATION SERVICES.

(a) IMPLEMENTATION OF GOALS.—Section 1605 of the Carl Levin and Howard P. "Buck" McKeon National Defense Authorization Act for Fiscal Year 2015 (Public Law 113–291; 10 U.S.C. 2208 note), as amended by section 1612 of the

National Defense Authorization Act for Fiscal Year 2016 (Public Law 114–92; 129 Stat. 1103), is further amended by adding at the end the following new subsection:

"(e) IMPLEMENTATION OF GOALS.—In developing and carrying out the pilot program under subsection (a)(1), by not later than September 30, 2017, the Secretary shall take actions to begin the implementation of each goal specified in subsection (b).".

(b) LIMITATION.—Of the funds authorized to be appropriated by this Act or otherwise made available for fiscal year 2017 for the headquarters operations of the Air Force Space Command, not more than 95 percent may be obligated or expended until the date on which the Secretary of Defense submits to the congressional defense committees a plan to demonstrate that the pilot program under section 1605 of the Carl Levin and Howard P. "Buck" McKeon National Defense Authorization Act for Fiscal Year 2015 (Public Law 113–291; 10 U.S.C. 2208 note) will achieve order-of-magnitude improvements in satellite communications capability, as required by subsection (b)(5) of such section.

SEC. 1607. SPACE-BASED ENVIRONMENTAL MONITORING.

(a) ROLES OF DOD AND NOAA.—

(1) MECHANISMS.—The Secretary of Defense and the Administrator of the National Oceanic and Atmospheric Administration shall jointly establish mechanisms to collaborate and coordinate in defining the roles and responsibilities of the Department of Defense and the National Oceanic and Atmospheric Administration to—

(A) carry out space-based environmental monitoring; and

(B) plan for future non-governmental space-based environmental monitoring capabilities, as appropriate.

(2) RULE OF CONSTRUCTION.—Nothing in paragraph (1) may be construed to authorize a joint satellite program of the Department of Defense and the National Oceanic and Atmospheric Administration.

(b) REPORT.—Not later than 120 days after the date of the enactment of this Act, the Secretary and the Administrator shall jointly submit to the appropriate congressional committees a report on the mechanisms established under subsection (a)(1).

(c) APPROPRIATE CONGRESSIONAL COMMITTEES DEFINED.—In this section, the term "appropriate congressional committees" means—

(1) the congressional defense committees;

(2) the Committee on Science, Space, and Technology of the House of Representatives; and

(3) the Committee on Commerce, Science, and Transportation of the Senate.

SEC. 1608. PROHIBITION ON USE OF CERTAIN NON-ALLIED POSITIONING, NAVIGATION, AND TIMING SYSTEMS.

(a) PROHIBITION.—During the period beginning not later than 60 days after the date of the enactment of this Act and ending on September 30, 2018, the Secretary of Defense shall ensure that the Armed Forces and each element of the Department of Defense do not use a non-allied positioning, navigation, and timing system or service provided by such a system.

(b) WAIVER.—The Secretary may waive the prohibition in subsection (a) if—

(1) the Secretary determines that the waiver is—

(A) in the national security interest of the United States; and

(B) necessary to mitigate exigent operational concerns;

(2) the Secretary notifies, in writing, the appropriate congressional committees of such waiver; and

(3) a period of 30 days has elapsed following the date of such notification.

(c) ASSESSMENT.—Not later than 120 days after the date of the enactment of this Act, the Secretary of Defense, the Chairman of the Joint Chiefs of Staff, and the Director of National Intelligence shall jointly submit to the appropriate congressional committees an assessment of the risks to national security and to the operations and plans of the Department of Defense from using a non-allied positioning, navigation, and timing system or service provided by such a system. Such assessment shall—

(1) address risks regarding—

(A) espionage, counterintelligence, and targeting;

(B) the use of the Global Positioning System by allies and partners of the United States and others; and

(C) harmful interference to the Global Positioning System; and

(2) include any other matters the Secretary, the Chairman, and the Director determine appropriate.

(d) DEFINITIONS.—In this section:

(1) The term "appropriate congressional committees" means—

(A) the congressional defense committees; and

(B) the Permanent Select Committee on Intelligence of the House of Representatives and the Select Committee on Intelligence of the Senate.

(2) The term "non-allied positioning, navigation, and timing system" means any of the following systems:

(A) The Beidou system.

(B) The Glonass global navigation satellite system.

SEC. 1609. LIMITATION OF AVAILABILITY OF FUNDS FOR THE JOINT SPACE OPERATIONS CENTER MISSION SYSTEM.

None of the funds authorized to be appropriated by this Act or otherwise made available for fiscal year 2017 for increment 3 of the Joint Space Operations Center Mission System may be obligated or expended until the date on which the Secretary of the Air Force, in coordination with the Commander of the United States Strategic Command, submits to the congressional defense committees a report on such increment, including—

(1) an acquisition strategy and strategic plan for such increment that includes—

(A) the space battlement management, communication, and control capabilities, as of the date of the enactment of this Act;

(B) the plan to develop and perform space battlement management, communication, and control capabilities in the future; and

(C) the critical elements described in subparagraphs (A) and (B) that will require common software and hardware in other similar space battle management software and systems to promote a common operating environment and reduce acquisition costs and long-term maintenance requirements;

(2) the warfighter requirements of such increment;

(3) the funding and schedule for such increment;

(4) the strategy for use of commercially available capabilities, as appropriate, relating to such increment to rapidly address warfighter requirements, including the market research and evaluation of such commercial capabilities; and

(5) the relationship of such increment with the other related activities and investments of the Department of Defense.

SEC. 1610. LIMITATIONS ON AVAILABILITY OF FUNDS FOR THE GLOBAL POSITIONING SYSTEM NEXT GENERATION OPERATIONAL CONTROL SYSTEM.

(a) LIMITATION UNTIL CERTIFICATION.—Of the funds authorized to be appropriated by this Act or otherwise made available for fiscal year 2017 for the Global Positioning System Next Generation Operational Control System (in this section

referred to as "OCX"), not more than five percent may be obligated or expended for the current product development contract for the OCX, or for any other purpose in connection with the OCX, until the date on which the Secretary of Defense submits to Congress the certification on the OCX required pursuant to section 2433a(b) of title 10, United States Code, as a result of the determination not to terminate the procurement of the OCX.

(b) ADDITIONAL LIMITATION UNTIL INITIAL BRIEFING.—In addition to the limitation in subsection (a), of the funds authorized to be appropriated by this Act or otherwise made available for fiscal year 2017 for the OCX, not more than 50 percent may be obligated or expended for the current product development contract for the OCX, or for any other purpose in connection with the OCX, unless—

(1) the Secretary has submitted to Congress the certification described in subsection (a); and

(2) not earlier than January 15, 2017, the Secretary provides to the congressional defense committees a briefing on the OCX with respect to—

(A) the status of the OCX program, including information on the risks, costs, and schedule, and technical information;

(B) contingency plans and investments, and the status of such plans and investments;

(C) an assessment of the OCX by the Director of Operational Test and Evaluation; and

(D) the total program cost that is validated by the Director of Cost Assessment and Program and a five-year budget that is based on an updated and rebaselined program cost.

(c) ADDITIONAL LIMITATION UNTIL SECOND BRIEFING.—In addition to the limitations in subsection (a) and (b), of the funds authorized to be appropriated by this Act or otherwise made available for fiscal year 2017 for the OCX, not more than 75 percent may be obligated or expended for the current product development contract for the OCX, or for any other purpose in connection with the OCX, unless—

(1) the Secretary has submitted to Congress the certification described in subsection (a);

(2) the Secretary has provided to the congressional defense committees the briefing under subsection (b)(2); and

(3) not earlier than March 15, 2017, the Secretary provides to the congressional defense committees an update to such briefing.

(d) ADJUSTMENT OF BRIEFING DATES.—The Secretary may provide the briefing under subsection (b)(2) or subsection (c)(3), respectively, before the date specified by such subsection if the Secretary determines that providing such briefing before such date is necessary for the national security interests of the United States.

SEC. 1611. AVAILABILITY OF FUNDS FOR CERTAIN SECURE VOICE CONFERENCING CAPABILITIES.

Of the funds authorized to be appropriated or otherwise made available by the Carl Levin and Howard P. "Buck" McKeon National Defense Authorization Act for Fiscal Year 2015 (Public Law 113–291) or the National Defense Authorization Act for Fiscal Year 2016 (Public Law 114–92) or otherwise made available for fiscal years 2015 or 2016 for research, development, test, and evaluation, Air Force, and available for obligation as of the date of the enactment of this Act, not more than $10,200,000 may be used to support the accomplishment by the Air Force of integration and associated critical testing and systems engineering activities for the Presidential and National Voice Conferencing program and the Advanced Extremely High Frequency Extended Data Rate, worldwide, secure, survivable voice conferencing capability for the President and national leaders, as described in the reprogramming action prior approval request submitted by the Under Secretary of Defense (Comptroller) to Congress on March 3, 2016.

SEC. 1612. SPACE-BASED INFRARED SYSTEM AND ADVANCED EXTREMELY HIGH FREQUENCY PROGRAM.

(a) LIMITATION ON DEVELOPMENT AND ACQUISITION OF ALTERNATIVES.—

(1) LIMITATION.—Except as provided by paragraph (4), the Secretary of Defense may not develop or acquire an alternative to the space-based infrared system program of record or develop or acquire an alternative to the advanced extremely high frequency program of record until the date on which the Commander of the United States Strategic Command and the Director of the Space Security and Defense Program, in consultation with the Defense Intelligence Officer for Science and Technology of the Defense Intelligence Agency, jointly submit to the appropriate congressional committees the assessments described in paragraph (2) for the respective program.

(2) ASSESSMENT.—The assessments described in this paragraph are—

(A) an assessment of the resilience and mission assurance of each alternative to the space-based infrared system being considered by the Secretary of the Air Force; and

(B) an assessment of the resilience and mission assurance of each alternative to the advanced extremely high frequency program being considered by the Secretary of the Air Force.

(3) ELEMENTS.—An assessment described in paragraph (2) shall include, with respect to each alternative to the space-based infrared system program of record and each alternative to the advanced extremely high frequency program of record being considered by the Secretary of the Air Force, the following:

(A) The requirements for resilience and mission assurance.

(B) The criteria to measure such resilience and mission assurance.

(C) How the alternative affects—

(i) deterrence and full spectrum warfighting;

(ii) warfighter requirements and relative costs to include ground station and user terminals;

(iii) the potential order of battle of adversaries; and

(iv) the required capabilities of the broader space security and defense enterprise.

(4) EXCEPTION.—The limitation in paragraph (1) shall not apply to efforts to examine and develop technology insertion opportunities for the space-based infrared system program of record or the satellite communications programs of record.

(b) APPROPRIATE CONGRESSIONAL COMMITTEES DEFINED.—In this section, the term "appropriate congressional committees" means the following:

(1) With respect to the submission of the assessment described in subparagraph (A) of subsection (a)(2), the—

(A) the congressional defense committees; and

(B) the Permanent Select Committee on Intelligence of the House of Representatives.

(2) With respect to the submission of the assessment described in subparagraph (B) of subsection (a)(2), the congressional defense committees.

SEC. 1613. PILOT PROGRAM ON COMMERCIAL WEATHER DATA.

(a) IN GENERAL.—Not later than 180 days after the date of the enactment of this Act, the Secretary of Defense shall establish a pilot program to assess the viability of commercial satellite weather data to support requirements of the Department of Defense.

(b) DURATION.—The Secretary may carry out the pilot program under subsection (a) for a period not exceeding one year.

(c) BRIEFINGS.—

(1) INTERIM BRIEFING.—Not later than 60 days after the date of the enactment of this Act, the Secretary of Defense shall provide a briefing to the Committees on Armed Services of the House

of Representatives and the Senate (and to any other congressional defense committee upon request) demonstrating how the Secretary plans to implement the pilot program under subsection (a).

(2) FINAL BRIEFING.—Not later than 90 days after the pilot program under subsection (a) is completed, the Secretary shall provide a briefing to the Committees on Armed Services of the House of Representatives and the Senate (and to any other congressional defense committee upon request) on the utility, cost, and other considerations regarding the purchase of commercial satellite weather data to support the requirements of the Department of Defense.

SEC. 1614. PLANS ON TRANSFER OF ACQUISITION AND FUNDING AUTHORITY OF CERTAIN WEATHER MISSIONS TO NATIONAL RECONNAISSANCE OFFICE.

(a) LIMITATION.—Except as provided by subsection (c), of the funds authorized to be appropriated by this Act or otherwise made available for fiscal year 2017 for research, development, test, and evaluation, Air Force, for the weather satellite follow-on system, not more than 50 percent may be obligated or expended until the date on which the Secretary of the Air Force submits to the appropriate congressional committees the plan under subsection (b)(1).

(b) PLANS FOR TRANSFER OF AUTHORITY.—

(1) AIR FORCE PLAN.—Except as provided by subsection (c), the Secretary of the Air Force shall develop a plan for the Air Force to transfer, beginning with fiscal year 2018, the acquisition authority and the funding authority for covered space-based environmental monitoring missions from the Air Force to the National Reconnaissance Office, including a description of the amount of funds that would be necessary to be transferred from the Air Force to the National Reconnaissance Office during fiscal years 2018 through 2022 to carry out such plan.

(2) NRO PLAN.—

(A) Except as provided by subsection (c), the Director of the National Reconnaissance Office shall develop a plan for the National Reconnaissance Office to address how to carry out covered space-based environmental monitoring missions. Such plan shall include—

(I) a description of the related national security requirements for such missions;

(ii) a description of the appropriate manner to meet such requirements; and

(iii) the amount of funds that would be necessary to be transferred from the Air Force to the National Reconnaissance Office during fiscal years 2018 through 2022 to carry out such plan.

(B) In developing the plan under subparagraph (A), the Director may conduct pre-acquisition activities, including with respect to requests for information, analyses of alternatives, study contracts, modeling and simulation, and other activities the Director determines necessary to develop such plan.

(C) Except as provided by subsection (c), the Director shall submit to the appropriate congressional committees such plan by not later than July 1, 2017.

(3) INDEPENDENT COST ESTIMATE.—The Director of the Cost Assessment Improvement Group of the Office of the Director of National Intelligence, in coordination with the Director of Cost Assessment and Program Evaluation, shall certify to the appropriate congressional committees that the amounts of funds identified under paragraphs (1) and (2)(A)(iii) as being necessary to transfer are appropriate and include funding for positions and personnel to support program office costs.

(c) WAIVER BASED ON REPORT AND CERTIFICATION OF AIR FORCE ACQUISITION PROGRAM.—The Secretary of the Air Force may waive the limitation in subsection (a) and the requirement to develop a plan under subsection (b)(1), and

the Director of the National Reconnaissance Office may waive the requirement to develop a plan under subsection (b)(2), if the Under Secretary of Defense for Acquisition, Technology, and Logistics and the Chairman of the Joint Chiefs of Staff jointly submit to the appropriate congressional committees a report by not later than July 1, 2017, that contains—

(1) a certification that the Secretary of the Air Force is carrying out a formal acquisition program that has received Milestone A approval to address the cloud characterization and theater weather imagery requirements of the Department of Defense; and

(2) an identification of the cost, schedule, requirements, and acquisition strategy of such acquisition program.

(d) DEFINITIONS.—In this section:

(1) The term "appropriate congressional committees" means—

(A) the congressional defense committees; and

(B) the Permanent Select Committee on Intelligence of the House of Representatives the Select Committee on Intelligence of the Senate.

(2) The term "covered space-based environmental monitoring missions" means the acquisition programs necessary to meet the national security requirements for cloud characterization and theater weather imagery.

(3) The term "Milestone A approval" has the meaning given that term in section 2366a(d) of title 10, United States Code.

SEC. 1615. FIVE-YEAR PLAN FOR JOINT INTER-AGENCY COMBINED SPACE OPERATIONS CENTER.

(a) PLAN.—Not later than 90 days after the date of the enactment of this Act, the Secretary of Defense, in coordination with the Director of National Intelligence, shall submit to the appropriate congressional committees a plan for the Joint Interagency Combined Space Operations Center for the five-year period beginning on such date of enactment that includes—

(1) a description of the roles, responsibilities, and objective of the Center;

(2) an estimate of funding during the period covered by the current future-years defense program under section 221 of title 10, United States Code, needed for the Center that includes a description of contributions from other Federal agencies;

(3) an estimate of the personnel needed for the Center, listed by military personnel, civilian personnel, and contractor personnel, and the organization or commercial entity such personnel are representing;

(4) a description of planned activities of the Center;

(5) a description of planned use of commercial capabilities by the Center, as appropriate;

(6) a description of how the Center will complement and support the mission of the Joint Space Operations Center; and

(7) a description of the command and control of the related operations of the Joint Interagency Combined Space Operations Center.

(b) APPROPRIATE CONGRESSIONAL COMMITTEES DEFINED.—In this section, the term "appropriate congressional committees" means—

(1) the congressional defense committees; and

(2) the Permanent Select Committee on Intelligence of the House of Representatives and the Select Committee on Intelligence of the Senate.

SEC. 1616. ORGANIZATION AND MANAGEMENT OF NATIONAL SECURITY SPACE ACTIVITIES OF THE DEPARTMENT OF DEFENSE.

(a) FINDINGS.—Congress finds the following:

(1) National security space capabilities are a vital element of the national defense of the United States.

(2) The advantages of the United States in national security space are now threatened to an unprecedented degree by growing and serious counterspace capabilities of potential foreign

adversaries, and the space advantages of the United States must be protected.

(3) The Department of Defense has recognized the threat and has taken initial steps necessary to defend space, however the organization and management may not be strategically postured to fully address this changed domain of operations over the long term.

(4) The defense of space is currently a priority for the leaders of the Department, however the space mission is managed within competing priorities of each of the Armed Forces.

(5) Space elements provide critical capabilities to all of the Armed Forces in the joint fight, however the disparate activities throughout the Department have no single leader that is empowered to make decisions affecting the space forces of the Department.

(b) SENSE OF CONGRESS.—It is the sense of Congress that, to modernize and fully address the growing threat to the national security space advantage of the United States, the Secretary of Defense must evaluate the range of options and take further action to strengthen the leadership, management, and organization of the national security space activities of the Department of Defense, including with respect to—

(1) unifying, integrating, and de-conflicting activities to provide for stronger prioritization, accountability, coherency, focus, strategy, and integration of the joint space program of the Department;

(2) streamlining decision-making, limiting unnecessary bureaucracy, and empowering the appropriate level of authority, while enabling effective oversight;

(3) maintaining the involvement of each of the Armed Forces and adapting the culture and improving the capabilities of the workforce to ensure the workforce has the appropriate training, experience, and tools to accomplish the mission; and

(4) reviewing authorities and preparing for a conflict that could extend to space.

(c) RECOMMENDATIONS.—Not later than 180 days after the date of the enactment of this Act, the Secretary of Defense and the Director of the Office of Management and Budget shall each separately submit to the appropriate congressional committees recommendations to—

(1) in accordance with subsection (b), strengthen the leadership, management, and organization of the Department of Defense with respect to the national security space activities of the Department; and

(2) address the findings covered in the report of the Comptroller General of the United States numbered GAO–16–592R regarding space acquisition and oversight of the Department of Defense.

(d) APPROPRIATE CONGRESSIONAL COMMITTEES.—In this section, the term "appropriate congressional committees" means the following:

(1) The congressional defense committees.

(2) The Permanent Select Committee on Intelligence of the House of Representatives and the Select Committee on Intelligence of the Senate.

SEC. 1617. REVIEW OF CHARTER OF OPERATIONALLY RESPONSIVE SPACE PROGRAM OFFICE.

(a) REVIEW.—The Secretary of Defense shall conduct a review of charter of the Operationally Responsive Space Program Office established by section 2273a of title 10, United States Code (in this section referred to as the "Office").

(b) ELEMENTS.—The review under subsection (a) shall include the following:

(1) A review of the key operationally responsive space needs with respect to the warfighter and with respect to national security.

(2) How the Office could fit into the broader resilience and space security strategy of the Department of Defense.

(3) An assessment of the potential of the Office to focus on the reconstitution capabilities

with small satellites using low-cost launch vehicles and existing infrastructure.

(4) An assessment of the potential of the Office to leverage existing or planned commercial capabilities.

(5) A review of the necessary workforce specialties and acquisition authorities of the Office.

(6) A review of the funding profile of the Office.

(7) A review of the organizational placement and reporting structure of the Office.

(c) REPORT.—Not later than 180 days after the date of the enactment of this Act, the Secretary shall submit to the congressional defense committees a report containing the review under subsection (a), including any recommendations for legislative actions based on such review.

SEC. 1618. BACKUP AND COMPLEMENTARY POSITIONING, NAVIGATION, AND TIMING CAPABILITIES OF GLOBAL POSITIONING SYSTEM.

(a) STUDY.—

(1) IN GENERAL.—The covered Secretaries shall jointly conduct a study to assess and identify the technology-neutral requirements to backup and complement the positioning, navigation, and timing capabilities of the Global Positioning System for national security and critical infrastructure.

(2) REPORT.—Not later than one year after the date of the enactment of this Act, the covered Secretaries shall submit to the appropriate congressional committees a report on the study under paragraph (1). Such report shall include—

(A) with respect to the Department of each covered Secretary, the identification of the respective requirements to backup and complement the positioning, navigation, and timing capabilities of the Global Positioning System for national security and critical infrastructure;

(B) an analysis of alternatives to meet such requirements, including, at a minimum—

(i) an analysis of appropriate technology options;

(ii) an analysis of the viability of a public-private partnership to establish a complementary positioning, navigation, and timing system; and

(iii) an analysis of the viability of service level agreements to operate a complementary positioning, navigation, and timing system; and

(C) a plan to meet such requirements that includes—

(i) for each such Department, the estimated costs, schedule, and system level technical considerations, including end user equipment and integration considerations; and

(ii) identification of the appropriate resourcing for each such Department in accordance with the respective requirements of the Department, including domestic or international requirements.

(b) SINGLE DESIGNATED OFFICIAL.—Each covered Secretary shall designate a single senior official of the Department of the Secretary to act as the primary representative of such Department for purposes of conducting the study under subsection (a)(1).

(c) DEFINITIONS.—In this section:

(1) The term "appropriate congressional committees" means—

(A) the congressional defense committees;

(B) the Committee on Science, Space, and Technology, the Committee on Transportation and Infrastructure, and the Committee on Homeland Security of the House of Representatives; and

(C) the Committee on Commerce, Science, and Transportation and the Committee on Homeland Security and Governmental Affairs of the Senate.

(2) The term "covered Secretaries" means the Secretary of Defense, the Secretary of Transportation, and the Secretary of Homeland Security.

SEC. 1619. REPORT ON USE OF SPACECRAFT ASSETS OF THE SPACE-BASED INFRARED SYSTEM WIDE-FIELD-OF-VIEW PROGRAM.

(a) REPORT.—Not later than 180 days after the date of the enactment of this Act, the Secretary of Defense, in coordination with the Director of National Intelligence, shall submit to the appropriate congressional committees a report on the advisability and feasibility of using available spacecraft assets of the space-based infrared system wide-field-of-view program to satisfy other mission requirements of the Department of Defense or the intelligence community.

(b) MATTERS COVERED.—The report required by subsection (a) shall include, at a minimum, the following:

(1) An evaluation of using the space-based infrared system wide-field-of-view spacecraft bus for other urgent national security space priorities.

(2) An evaluation of the cost and schedule impact, if any, to the space-based infrared system wide-field-of-view program if the spacecraft bus is used for another purpose.

(c) FORM.—The report required by subsection (a) shall be submitted in unclassified form, but may contain a classified annex if necessary to protect the national security interests of the United States.

(d) APPROPRIATE CONGRESSIONAL COMMITTEES DEFINED.—In this section, the term "appropriate congressional committees" means—

(1) the congressional defense committees; and

(2) the Permanent Select Committee on Intelligence of the House of Representatives and the Select Committee on Intelligence of the Senate.

SEC. 1620. PROVISION OF CERTAIN INFORMATION TO GOVERNMENT ACCOUNTABILITY OFFICE BY NATIONAL RECONNAISSANCE OFFICE.

(a) IN GENERAL.—The Director of the National Reconnaissance Office shall provide to the Comptroller General of the United States, in a timely manner, access to the cost, schedule, and performance information the Comptroller General requires to conduct assessments, as required by any of the appropriate congressional committees, of programs of the National Reconnaissance Office.

(b) APPROPRIATE CONGRESSIONAL COMMITTEES DEFINED.—In this section, the term "appropriate congressional committees" means—

(1) the congressional defense committees; and

(2) the Select Committee on Intelligence of the Senate and the Permanent Select Committee on Intelligence of the House of Representatives.

SEC. 1621. COST-BENEFIT ANALYSIS OF COMMERCIAL USE OF EXCESS BALLISTIC MISSILE SOLID ROCKET MOTORS.

(a) IN GENERAL.—The Comptroller General of the United States shall conduct an analysis of the costs and benefits of allowing the use of solid rocket motors from missiles described in section 50134(c) of title 51, United States Code, for commercial space launch purposes. Such analysis shall include an evaluation of the effect, if any, of allowing such use on national security, the Department of Defense, the solid rocket motor industrial base, the commercial space launch market, and any other areas the Comptroller General considers appropriate.

(b) BRIEFINGS.—

(1) INTERIM BRIEFING.—Not later than March 15, 2017, the Comptroller General shall provide to the appropriate congressional committees an interim briefing on the analysis under subsection (a).

(2) FINAL BRIEFING.—Not later than 180 days after the date of the enactment of this Act, the Comptroller General shall provide to the appropriate congressional committees a final briefing on the analysis under subsection (a).

(3) APPROPRIATE CONGRESSIONAL COMMITTEES DEFINED.—In this subsection, the term "appropriate congressional committees" means the following:

(A) The congressional defense committees.

(B) The Committee on Commerce, Science, and Transportation of the Senate and the Committee on Science, Space, and Technology of the House of Representatives.

SEC. 1622. INDEPENDENT ASSESSMENT OF GLOBAL POSITIONING SYSTEM NEXT GENERATION OPERATIONAL CONTROL SYSTEM.

(a) IN GENERAL.—Not later than 60 days after the date of the enactment of this Act, the Secretary of Defense shall seek to enter into an arrangement with a federally funded research and development center, or other appropriate independent entity, to assess the acquisition strategy of the Air Force for the Global Positioning System Next Generation Operational Control System (in this section referred to as "OCX").

(b) ELEMENTS.—The assessment required by subsection (a) shall include the following:

(1) An assessment of the ability of the Air Force to complete blocks zero through two of the OCX operating system on a schedule necessary to transition the OCX to full operation.

(2) An estimate of the cost of completing blocks zero through two on the schedule described in paragraph (1), taking into account—

(A) the rate of software defects;

(B) earned value management; and

(C) information assurance requirements.

(3) An assessment of the ability of the Air Force to implement contingency plans for sustaining the Global Positioning System constellation to mitigate the effects of delays to the implementation of the OCX and to alleviate challenges with respect to the operations and checkout of the Global Positioning System III satellites.

(4) An assessment of any risks to the viability and required availability of the Global Positioning System constellation associated with efforts to complete blocks zero through two as described in paragraph (1) or the contingency plans described in paragraph (3).

(5) An assessment of whether there are well-defined methods for terminating the OCX program (including an analysis of the ability of alternative systems to satisfy the requirements of the Department of Defense), in the event of the inability of the Air Force to successfully complete blocks zero through two or other requirements for the OCX while ensuring that the Global Positioning System constellation meets requirements for the availability of that System.

(6) Any other matters the entity conducting the assessment determines appropriate.

(c) SUBMISSION.—Not later than one year after the date of the enactment of this Act, the Secretary shall submit to the congressional defense committees a report on the results of the assessment required by subsection (a).

Subtitle B—Defense Intelligence and Intelligence-Related Activities

SEC. 1631. REPORT ON UNITED STATES CENTRAL COMMAND INTELLIGENCE FUSION CENTER.

(a) REPORT ON PROCEDURES.—Not later than March 1, 2017, the Commander of the United States Central Command shall submit to the appropriate congressional committees a report on the steps taken by the Commander to formalize and disseminate procedures for establishing, staffing, and operating the Intelligence Fusion Center of the United States Central Command.

(b) APPROPRIATE CONGRESSIONAL COMMITTEES DEFINED.—In this section, the term "appropriate congressional committees" means—

(1) the congressional defense committees; and

(2) the Permanent Select Committee on Intelligence of the House of Representatives.

SEC. 1632. PROHIBITION ON AVAILABILITY OF FUNDS FOR CERTAIN RELOCATION ACTIVITIES FOR NATO INTELLIGENCE FUSION CELL.

(a) PROHIBITION.—None of the funds authorized to be appropriated by this Act or otherwise made available for fiscal year 2017 for operation and maintenance may be obligated or expended for the procurement of fit-out supplies and equipment to support the relocation of the NATO Intelligence Fusion Cell from Royal Air Force Molesworth, United Kingdom, to Royal Air Force Croughton, United Kingdom.

(b) REPORT.—Not later than 120 days after the date of the enactment of this Act, the Secretary of Defense, in coordination with the Director of National Intelligence, shall submit to the appropriate congressional committees a report on the NATO Intelligence Fusion Cell that outlines—

(1) the current facility and support requirements and associated costs, including any adjustments of such requirements and costs, for the NATO Intelligence Fusion Cell to be located and operationally viable at Royal Air Force Croughton; and

(2) the operational requirements of, and costs associated with, any operations of the United States collocated with the NATO Intelligence Fusion Cell.

(c) APPROPRIATE CONGRESSIONAL COMMITTEES DEFINED.—In this section, the term "appropriate congressional committees" means—

(1) the congressional defense committees; and

(2) the Permanent Select Committee on Intelligence of the House of Representatives and the Select Committee on Intelligence of the Senate.

SEC. 1633. SURVEY AND REVIEW OF DEFENSE INTELLIGENCE ENTERPRISE.

(a) SURVEY AND REVIEW.—

(1) IN GENERAL.—Not later than 120 days after the date of the enactment of this Act, the Chairman of the Joint Chiefs of Staff shall—

(A) review the organization, resources, and processes of the Defense Intelligence Enterprise, including the defense intelligence agencies and intelligence elements of the combatant commands and military departments, to assess the capabilities and capacity of such Enterprise, along with the intelligence community, to meet present and future defense intelligence requirements; and

(B) conduct a survey of each geographic combatant command to assess—

(i) the current state of intelligence support to military operations;

(ii) the prioritization and allocation of intelligence resources within each combatant command; and

(iii) whether intelligence resources are balanced between support to theater commanders and support to operational commanders.

(2) ELEMENTS.—The review and survey required by paragraph (1) shall include the following:

(A) A comprehensive assessment of the Defense Intelligence Enterprise and whether such Enterprise—

(i) is organized and has resources to meet current and future defense intelligence requirements;

(ii) is balancing resources appropriately between operational and strategic defense intelligence requirements;

(iii) is responding with sufficient agility to emerging or unexpected requirements; and

(iv) is sufficiently integrated with combatant commands, subordinate commands, and joint task forces.

(B) With respect to each geographic combatant command surveyed—

(i) information on the total intelligence workforce assigned to the combatant command, including civilians, military, and contract personnel;

(ii) detailed information on the allocation of intelligence resources to meet combatant commander priorities;

(iii) detailed information on the intelligence priorities of the commander of the combatant command and intelligence resources allocated to each priority; and

(iv) detailed information on the intelligence resources, including personnel and assets, dedicated to each of the following:

(I) Direct support to the combatant commander.

(II) Contingency planning.

(III) Ongoing operations.

(IV) Crisis response.

(b) REPORT.—

(1) SUBMISSION.—Not later than 270 days after the date of the enactment of this Act, the Chairman of the Joint Chiefs of Staff shall submit to the appropriate congressional committees and the Under Secretary of Defense for Intelligence a report on the findings of the Chairman with respect to the review and survey required by subsection (a)(1).

(2) CONTENT.—The report required by paragraph (1) shall include—

(A) a detailed analysis of how each combatant command uses the intelligence resources available to such command; and

(B) the recommendations of the Chairman, if any, to improve the Defense Intelligence Enterprise to fulfill operational military requirements.

(c) DEFINITIONS.—In this section:

(1) The term "appropriate congressional committees" means—

(A) the congressional defense committees; and

(B) the Permanent Select Committee on Intelligence of the House of Representatives.

(2) The term "Defense Intelligence Enterprise" means the organizations, infrastructure, and measures, including policies, processes, procedures, and products, of the intelligence, counterintelligence, and security components of each of the following:

(A) The Department of Defense.

(B) The Joint Staff.

(C) The combatant commands.

(D) The military departments.

(E) Other elements of the Department of Defense that perform national intelligence, defense intelligence, intelligence-related, counterintelligence, or security functions.

Subtitle C—Cyberspace-Related Matters

SEC. 1641. SPECIAL EMERGENCY PROCUREMENT AUTHORITY TO FACILITATE THE DEFENSE AGAINST OR RECOVERY FROM A CYBER ATTACK.

Section 1903(a)(2) of title 41, United States Code, is amended by inserting "cyber," before "nuclear,".

SEC. 1642. LIMITATION ON TERMINATION OF DUAL-HAT ARRANGEMENT FOR COMMANDER OF THE UNITED STATES CYBER COMMAND.

(a) LIMITATION ON TERMINATION OF DUAL-HAT ARRANGEMENT.—The Secretary of Defense may not terminate the dual-hat arrangement until the date on which the Secretary and the Chairman of the Joint Chiefs of Staff jointly certify to the appropriate committees of Congress that—

(1) the Secretary and the Chairman carried out the assessment under subsection (b);

(2) each of the conditions described in paragraph (2)(C) of such subsection has been met; and

(3) termination of the dual-hat arrangement will not pose risks to the military effectiveness of the United States Cyber Command that are unacceptable to the national security interests of the United States.

(b) ASSESSMENT.—

(1) IN GENERAL.—The Secretary and the Chairman shall jointly assess the military and intelligence necessity and benefit of the dual-hat arrangement.

(2) ELEMENTS.—The assessment under paragraph (1) shall include the following elements:

(A) An evaluation of the operational dependence of the United States Cyber Command on the National Security Agency.

(B) An evaluation of the ability of the United States Cyber Command and the National Security Agency to carry out their respective roles and responsibilities independently.

(C) A determination of whether the following conditions have been met:

(i) Robust operational infrastructure has been deployed that is sufficient to meet the unique cyber mission needs of the United States Cyber Command and the National Security Agency, respectively.

(ii) Robust command and control systems and processes have been established for planning, deconflicting, and executing military cyber operations.

(iii) The tools and weapons used in cyber operations are sufficient for achieving required effects.

(iv) Capabilities have been established to enable intelligence collection and operational preparation of the environment for cyber operations.

(v) Capabilities have been established to train cyber operations personnel, test cyber capabilities, and rehearse cyber missions.

(vi) The cyber mission force has achieved full operational capability.

(c) DEFINITIONS.—In this section:

(1) APPROPRIATE COMMITTEES OF CONGRESS.— The term "appropriate committees of Congress" means—

(A) the Committee on Armed Services, the Committee on Appropriations, and the Select Committee on Intelligence of the Senate; and

(B) the Committee on Armed Services, the Committee on Appropriations, and the Permanent Select Committee on Intelligence of the House of Representatives.

(2) DUAL-HAT ARRANGEMENT.—The term "dual-hat arrangement" means the arrangement under which the Commander of the United States Cyber Command also serves as the Director of the National Security Agency.

SEC. 1643. CYBER MISSION FORCES MATTERS.

(a) ACTIONS PENDING FULL IMPLEMENTATION OF PLAN FOR CYBER MISSION FORCE POSITIONS.—Until the Secretary of Defense completes implementation of the authority in subsection (a) of section 1599f of title 10, United States Code, for United States Cyber Command workforce positions in accordance with the implementation plan required by subsection (d) of such section, the Secretary shall do each of the following:

(1) Notwithstanding sections 3309 through 3318 of title 5, United States Code, provide for and implement an interagency transfer agreement between excepted service position systems and competitive service position systems in military departments and Defense Agencies concerned to satisfy the requirements for cyber workforce positions from among a mix of employees in the excepted service and the competitive service in such military departments and Defense Agencies.

(2) Implement in the defense civilian cyber personnel system a classification system commonly known as a "Rank-in-person" classification system similar to such classification system used by the National Security Agency as of the date of the enactment of this Act.

(3) Approve direct hiring authority for cyber workforce positions up to the GG or GS-15 level in accordance with the criteria in section 3304 of title 5, United States Code.

(4) Notwithstanding section 5333 of title 5, United States Code, authorize officials conducting hiring in the competitive service for cyber workforce positions to set starting salaries at up to a step-five level with no justification and at up to a step-ten level with justification that meets published guidelines applicable to the excepted service.

(b) OTHER MATTERS.—The Principal Cyber Advisor, acting through the cross-functional team established by section 932(c)(3) of the National Defense Authorization Act for Fiscal Year 2014 (Public Law 113–66; 10 U.S.C. 2224

note) and in consultation with the Commander of the United States Cyber Command, shall supervise—

(1) the development of training standards for computer network operations tool developers for military, civilian, and contractor personnel supporting the cyber mission forces;

(2) the rapid enhancement of capacity to train personnel to those standards to meet the needs of the cyber mission forces for tool development; and

(3) actions necessary to ensure timely completion of personnel security investigations and adjudications of security clearances for tool development personnel.

SEC. 1644. REQUIREMENT TO ENTER INTO AGREEMENTS RELATING TO USE OF CYBER OPPOSITION FORCES.

(a) REQUIREMENT FOR AGREEMENTS.—Not later than September 30, 2017, the Secretary of Defense shall ensure that each commander of a combatant command establishes appropriate agreements with the Secretary relating to the use of cyber opposition forces. Each agreement shall require the command—

(1) to support a high state of mission readiness in the command through the use of one or more cyber opposition forces in continuous exercises and other training activities as considered appropriate by the commander of the command; and

(2) in conducting such exercises and training activities, meet the standard required under subsection (b).

(b) JOINT STANDARD FOR CYBER OPPOSITION FORCES.—Not later than March 31, 2017, the Secretary of Defense shall issue a joint training and certification standard for use by all cyber opposition forces within the Department of Defense.

(c) JOINT STANDARD FOR PROTECTION OF CONTROL SYSTEMS.—Not later than June 30, 2017, the Secretary of Defense shall issue a joint training and certification standard for the protection of control systems for use by all cyber operations forces within the Department of Defense. Such standard shall—

(1) provide for applied training and exercise capabilities; and

(2) use expertise and capabilities from other departments and agencies of the Federal Government, as appropriate.

(d) BRIEFING REQUIRED.—Not later than September 30, 2017, the Secretary of Defense shall provide to the Committees on Armed Services of the Senate and the House of Representatives a briefing that includes—

(1) a list of each combatant command that has established an agreement under subsection (a);

(2) with respect to each such agreement—

(A) special conditions in the agreement placed on any cyber opposition force used by the command;

(B) the process for making decisions about deconfliction and risk mitigation of cyber opposition force activities in continuous exercises and training;

(C) identification of cyber opposition forces trained and certified to operate at the joint standard, as issued under subsection (b);

(D) identification of the annual exercises that will include participation of the cyber opposition forces; and

(E) identification of any shortfalls in resources that may prevent annual exercises using cyber opposition forces; and

(3) any other matters the Secretary of Defense considers appropriate.

SEC. 1645. CYBER PROTECTION SUPPORT FOR DEPARTMENT OF DEFENSE PERSONNEL IN POSITIONS HIGHLY VULNERABLE TO CYBER ATTACK.

(a) AUTHORITY TO PROVIDE CYBER PROTECTION SUPPORT.—

(1) IN GENERAL.—Subject to a determination by the Secretary of Defense, the Secretary may

provide cyber protection support for the personal technology devices of the personnel described in paragraph (2).

(2) AT-RISK PERSONNEL.—The personnel described in this paragraph are personnel of the Department of Defense—

(A) who the Secretary determines to be highly vulnerable to cyber attacks and hostile information collection activities because of the positions occupied by such personnel in the Department; and

(B) whose personal technology devices are highly vulnerable to cyber attacks and hostile information collection activities.

(b) NATURE OF CYBER PROTECTION SUPPORT.— Subject to the availability of resources, the cyber protection support provided to personnel under subsection (a) may include training, advice, assistance, and other services relating to cyber attacks and hostile information collection activities.

(c) LIMITATION ON SUPPORT.—Nothing in this section shall be construed—

(1) to encourage personnel of the Department of Defense to use personal technology devices for official business; or

(2) to authorize cyber protection support for senior Department personnel using personal devices and networks in an official capacity.

(d) REPORT.—Not later than 180 days after the date of the enactment of this Act, the Secretary shall submit to the Committees on Armed Services of the Senate and the House of Representatives a report on the provision of cyber protection support under subsection (a). The report shall include—

(1) a description of the methodology used to make the determination under subsection (a)(2); and

(2) guidance for the use of cyber protection support and tracking of support requests for personnel receiving cyber protection support under subsection (a).

(e) PERSONAL TECHNOLOGY DEVICES DEFINED.—In this section, the term "personal technology devices" means technology devices used by Department of Defense personnel outside of the scope of their employment with the Department and includes networks to which such devices connect.

SEC. 1646. LIMITATION ON FULL DEPLOYMENT OF JOINT REGIONAL SECURITY STACKS.

(a) LIMITATION.—The Secretary of a military department or the head of a Defense Agency may not declare that such department or Defense Agency has achieved full operational capability for the deployment of joint regional security stacks until the date on which—

(1) the department or Defense Agency concerned completes operational test and evaluation activities to determine the effectiveness, suitability, and survivability of the joint regional security stacks system of such department or Defense Agency; and

(2) written certification that such testing and evaluation activities have been completed is provided to the Secretary of such department or the head of such Defense Agency by the appropriate operational test and evaluation organization of such department or Defense Agency.

(b) WAIVER.—

(1) IN GENERAL.—The Secretary of a military department or the head of a Defense Agency may waive the requirements of subsection (a) if a certification described in paragraph (2) is provided to the Secretary of Defense, and signed by—

(A) the Secretary of the military department or the head of the Defense Agency concerned;

(B) the Director of Operational Test and Evaluation for the Department of Defense; and

(C) the Chief Information Officer of the Department of Defense.

(2) CERTIFICATION.—A certification described in this subsection is a written certification that—

(A) the testing and evaluation activities required under subsection (a) are unnecessary, accompanied by an explanation of the reasons such activities are unnecessary;

(B) the effectiveness, suitability, and survivability of the joint regional security stacks system of the military department or Defense Agency concerned has been demonstrated by methods other than the testing and evaluation activities required under subsection (a), accompanied by supporting data; or

(C) national security needs justify full deployment of the joint regional security stacks system of the military department or Defense Agency concerned before the test and evaluation activities required under subsection (a) can be completed, accompanied by an explanation of such justification and a risk management plan.

SEC. 1647. ADVISORY COMMITTEE ON INDUSTRIAL SECURITY AND INDUSTRIAL BASE POLICY.

(a) ADVISORY COMMITTEE.—Not later than April 30, 2017, the Secretary of Defense shall establish an advisory committee (referred to in this section as the "Committee") to review, assess, and make recommendations with respect to industrial security and industrial base policy.

(b) DUTIES.—The Committee shall—

(1) review and assess—

(A) the national industrial security program for cleared facilities and the protection of the information and networking systems of cleared defense contractors;

(B) policies and practices relating to physical security and installation access at installations of the Department of Defense;

(C) information security and cyber defense policies, practices, and reporting relating to the unclassified information and networking systems of defense contractors;

(D) policies, practices, regulations, and reporting relating to industrial base issues; and

(E) any other matters the Secretary determines to be appropriate; and

(2) make recommendations to the Secretary based on such review and assessment.

(c) MEMBERS.—The Committee shall be composed of 10 members appointed by the Secretary of Defense of which five members shall be representatives of non-governmental entities and five members shall be representatives of departments or agencies of the Federal Government.

(d) MEETINGS.—The Committee shall meet not less often than once annually until the date on which the Committee terminates under subsection (e).

(e) TERMINATION.—The Committee shall terminate on September 30, 2022.

SEC. 1648. CHANGE IN NAME OF NATIONAL DEFENSE UNIVERSITY'S INFORMATION RESOURCES MANAGEMENT COLLEGE TO COLLEGE OF INFORMATION AND CYBERSPACE.

(a) IN GENERAL.—Section 2165(b)(5) of title 10, United States Code, is amended by striking "Information Resources Management College" and inserting "College of Information and Cyberspace".

(b) REFERENCES.—Any reference in any law, regulation, document, record, or other paper of the United States to the Information Resources Management College shall be considered to be a reference to the College of Information and Cyberspace.

SEC. 1649. EVALUATION OF CYBER VULNERABILITIES OF F–35 AIRCRAFT AND SUPPORT SYSTEMS.

(a) EVALUATION AND REPORT.—

(1) EVALUATION.—Not later than 120 days after the date of the enactment of this Act, the Secretary of Defense shall complete an evaluation of the cyber vulnerabilities of the F–35 aircraft and the support systems of the aircraft under section 1647(a)(1) of the National Defense Authorization Act for Fiscal Year 2016 (Public Law 114–92; 129 Stat. 1118).

(2) REPORT.—Not later than 180 days after the date of the enactment of this Act, the Secretary shall submit to the congressional defense committees a report on the evaluation completed under paragraph (1) that includes—

(A) the findings of the Secretary with respect to the evaluation;

(B) identification of any major information assurance deficiencies relating to the F–35 aircraft or the support systems of the aircraft (including the autonomic logistics information system); and

(C) a cyber vulnerability mitigation strategy for F–35 aircraft and the support systems of the aircraft.

(3) WAIVER PROHIBITED.—Notwithstanding section 1647(a)(2) of the National Defense Authorization Act for Fiscal Year 2016 (Public Law 114–92; 129 Stat. 1118), the Secretary may not waive the requirements of paragraphs (1) and (2).

(b) TOOLS AND SOLUTIONS FOR ASSESSING AND MITIGATING CYBER VULNERABILITIES.—Section 1647 of the National Defense Authorization Act for Fiscal Year 2016 (Public Law 114–92; 129 Stat. 1118) is amended—

(1) by redesignating subsections (d) and (e) as subsections (e) and (f), respectively; and

(2) by inserting after subsection (c) the following new subsection:

"(d) TOOLS AND SOLUTIONS FOR ASSESSING AND MITIGATING CYBER VULNERABILITIES.—In addition to carrying out the evaluation of cyber vulnerabilities of major weapon systems of the Department under this section, the Secretary may—

"(1) develop tools to improve the detection and evaluation of cyber vulnerabilities;

"(2) conduct non-recurring engineering for the design of solutions to mitigate cyber vulnerabilities; and

"(3) establish Department-wide information repositories to share findings relating to the evaluation and mitigation of cyber vulnerabilities.".

SEC. 1650. EVALUATION OF CYBER VULNERABILITIES OF DEPARTMENT OF DEFENSE CRITICAL INFRASTRUCTURE.

(a) PLAN FOR EVALUATION.—

(1) IN GENERAL.—Not later than 180 days after the date of the enactment of this Act, the Secretary shall submit to the congressional defense committees a plan for the evaluation of the cyber vulnerabilities of the critical infrastructure of the Department of Defense.

(2) ELEMENTS.—The plan under paragraph (1) shall include—

(A) an identification of each of the military installations to be evaluated; and

(B) an estimate of the cost of the evaluation.

(3) PRIORITY IN EVALUATION.—The plan under paragraph (1) shall prioritize the evaluation of military installations based on the criticality of the infrastructure supporting such installations, as determined by the Chairman of the Joint Chiefs of Staff based on an assessment of—

(A) the Armed Forces stationed at such military installations; and

(B) threats to such military installations.

(4) INTEGRATION WITH OTHER EFFORTS.—The plan under paragraph (1) shall build upon other efforts of Department of Defense relating to the identification and mitigation of cyber vulnerabilities of major weapon systems and critical infrastructure of the Department and shall not duplicate such efforts.

(b) PILOT PROGRAM.—

(1) IN GENERAL.—Not later than 30 days after the date on which the Secretary submits the plan under subsection (a), the Secretary, acting through a covered research laboratory, shall initiate a pilot program under which the Secretary shall assess the feasibility and advisability of applying new, innovative methodologies or engineering approaches—

(A) to improve the defense of control systems against cyber attacks;

(B) to increase the resilience of military installations against cybersecurity threats;

(C) to prevent or mitigate the potential for high-consequence cyber attacks; and

(D) to inform future requirements for the development of such control systems.

(2) LOCATIONS.—The Secretary shall carry out the pilot program under paragraph (1) at not fewer than two military installations selected by the Secretary from among military installations that support the most critical mission-essential functions of the Department of Defense as identified in the plan under subsection (a).

(3) TOOLS.—In carrying out the pilot program under paragraph (1), the Secretary may use tools and solutions developed under subsection (e).

(4) REPORT.—Not later than December 31, 2019, the Secretary shall submit to the congressional defense committees a final report on the pilot program that includes—

(A) a description of the activities carried out under the pilot program at each military installation concerned;

(B) an assessment of the value of the methodologies or tools applied during the pilot program in increasing the resilience of military installations against cybersecurity threats;

(C) recommendations for administrative or legislative actions to improve the ability of the Department to employ methodologies and tools for reducing cyber vulnerabilities in other activities of the Department of Defense; and

(D) recommendations for including such methodologies or tools as requirements for relevant activities, including technical requirements for systems or military construction projects.

(5) TERMINATION.—The authority of the Secretary to carry out the pilot program under this subsection shall terminate on September 30, 2019.

(c) EVALUATION.—

(1) IN GENERAL.—Not later than December 31, 2020, the Secretary shall complete an evaluation of the cyber vulnerabilities of the critical infrastructure of the Department of Defense in accordance with the plan under subsection (a).

(2) RISK MITIGATION STRATEGIES.—The Secretary shall develop strategies for mitigating the risks of cyber vulnerabilities identified in the course of the evaluation under paragraph (1).

(d) STATUS ON PROGRESS.—The Secretary shall include in each quarterly cyber operations briefing submitted to Congress under section 484 of title 10, United States Code, a summary of any activities carried out as part of—

(1) the pilot program under subsection (b); or

(2) the evaluation under subsection (c).

(e) TOOLS AND SOLUTIONS.—The Secretary may—

(1) develop tools that improve assessments of cyber vulnerabilities of Department of Defense critical infrastructure;

(2) conduct non-recurring engineering for the design of mitigation solutions for such vulnerabilities; and

(3) establish Department-wide information repositories to share findings relating to such assessments and to share such mitigation solutions.

(f) DEFINITIONS.—In this section:

(1) CRITICAL INFRASTRUCTURE OF THE DEPARTMENT OF DEFENSE.—The term "critical infrastructure of the Department of Defense" means any asset of the Department of Defense of such extraordinary importance to the functioning of the Department and the operation of the Armed Forces that the incapacitation or destruction of such asset by a cyber attack would have a debilitating effect on the ability of the Department to fulfill its missions.

(2) COVERED RESEARCH LABORATORY.—The term "covered research laboratory" means—

(A) a research laboratory of the Department of Defense; or

(B) a research laboratory of the Department of Energy approved by the Secretary of Energy to carry out the pilot program under subsection (b).

SEC. 1651. STRATEGY TO INCORPORATE ARMY RESERVE COMPONENT CYBER PROTECTION TEAMS INTO DEPARTMENT OF DEFENSE CYBER MISSION FORCE.

(a) STRATEGY REQUIRED.—Not later than 180 days after the date of the enactment of this Act, the Secretary of the Army shall provide to the Committees on Armed Services of the Senate and the House of Representatives a briefing on a strategy for incorporating reserve component cyber protection teams into the cyber mission force of the Department of Defense.

(b) ELEMENTS OF STRATEGY.—The strategy required by subsection (a) shall include, at minimum, the following:

(1) A timeline for incorporating reserve component cyber protection teams into the cyber mission force of the Department of Defense, including a timeline for the appropriate training of such teams.

(2) Identification of the specific reserve component cyber protection teams to be incorporated into the cyber mission force of the Department of Defense.

(3) An assessment of how the incorporation of reserve component cyber protection teams into the cyber mission force of the Department of Defense might be used to enhance readiness through improved individual and collective training capabilities.

(4) A status report on the progress of the Army in issuing additional guidance that clarifies how reserve component cyber protection teams of the Army National Guard can support State and civil operations in National Guard status under title 32, United States Code.

(5) Other matters as considered appropriate by the Secretary of the Army.

(c) RESERVE COMPONENT CYBER PROTECTION TEAMS DEFINED.—In this section, the term "reserve component cyber protection teams" means cyber protection teams of—

(1) the Army National Guard; and

(2) the other reserve components of the Army.

SEC. 1652. STRATEGIC PLAN FOR THE DEFENSE INFORMATION SYSTEMS AGENCY.

(a) STRATEGIC PLAN REQUIRED.—Not later than 180 days after the date of the enactment of this Act and not less often than once every 2 fiscal years thereafter until September 30, 2022, the Director of the Defense Information Systems Agency, in consultation with the Under Secretary of Defense for Acquisition, Technology, and Logistics and the Chief Information Officer of the Department of Defense, shall develop or update, as appropriate, a strategic plan for the Agency that includes—

(1) a comprehensive review of the requirements and mission of the Agency with respect to research, development, test, and evaluation; and

(2) an assessment of the adequacy of the activities, facilities, workforce, and resources of the Agency in meeting such requirements and fulfilling such mission.

(b) COVERED PERIOD.—Each strategic plan under subsection (a) shall cover the period of five fiscal years beginning with the fiscal year in which the plan is developed or updated.

(c) ELEMENTS.—Each strategic plan under subsection (a) shall include the following elements:

(1) A statement of the mission of the Defense Information Systems Agency that—

(A) addresses the critical operations and functions carried out by the Agency; and

(B) includes an assessment of projected changes to such operations and functions for the period covered by the plan.

(2) An assessment of the personnel, facilities, and research, development, test, and evaluation requirements of the Department of Defense that are needed to support the operations of the Agency for the period covered by the plan.

(3) An identification of performance metrics for measuring the successful achievement of objectives for the period covered by the plan.

(4) An assessment of the programs and plans of the Agency with respect to research, development, test, and evaluation, including the projected resources, personnel, and supporting infrastructure needed to carry out such programs and plans.

(5) An assessment of the facilities and resources of the Agency that are used for research, development, test, and evaluation activities.

(6) A description of the plans and business case analyses supporting any significant modifications to the facilities, workforce, and resources of the Agency (including any modifications involving the expansion, divestment, consolidation, or curtailment of activities) that are proposed, projected, or recommended by the Director.

(7) Any other matters determined to be appropriate by the Director.

SEC. 1653. PLAN FOR INFORMATION SECURITY CONTINUOUS MONITORING CAPABILITY AND COMPLY-TO-CONNECT POLICY; LIMITATION ON SOFTWARE LICENSING.

(a) INFORMATION SECURITY MONITORING PLAN AND POLICY.—

(1) PLAN AND POLICY.—The Chief Information Officer of the Department of Defense and the Commander of the United States Cyber Command shall jointly develop—

(A) a plan for a modernized, Department-wide automated information security continuous monitoring capability that includes—

(i) a proposed information security architecture for the capability;

(ii) a concept of operations for the capability; and

(iii) requirements with respect to the functionality and interoperability of the tools, sensors, systems, processes, and other components of the continuous monitoring capability; and

(B) a comply-to-connect policy that requires systems to automatically comply with the configurations of the networks of the Department as a condition of connecting to such networks.

(2) CONSULTATION.—In developing the plan and policy under paragraph (1), the Chief Information Officer and the Commander shall consult with the Principal Cyber Advisor to the Secretary of Defense.

(3) IMPLEMENTATION.—The Chief Information Officer and the Commander shall each issue such directives as they each consider appropriate to ensure compliance with the plan and policy developed under paragraph (1).

(4) INCLUSION IN BUDGET MATERIALS.—The Secretary of Defense shall include funding and program plans relating to the plan and policy under paragraph (1) in the budget materials submitted by the Secretary in support of the budget of the President for fiscal year 2019 (as submitted to Congress under section 1105(a) of title 31, United States Code).

(5) INTEGRATION WITH OTHER CAPABILITIES.—The Chief Information Officer and the Commander shall ensure that information generated through automated and automation-assisted processes for continuous monitoring, asset management, and comply-to-connect policies and processes shall be accessible and usable in machine-readable form to appropriate cyber protection teams and computer network defense service providers.

(6) SOFTWARE LICENSE COMPLIANCE MATTERS.—The plan and policy required by paragraph (1) shall comply with the software license inventory requirements of the plan issued pursuant to section 937 of the National Defense Authorization Act for Fiscal Year 2013 (Public Law 112–239; 10 U.S.C. 2223 note) and updated pursuant to section 935 of the National Defense Authorization Act for Fiscal Year 2014 (Public Law 113–66; 10 U.S.C. 2223 note).

(b) LIMITATION ON FUTURE SOFTWARE LICENSING.—

(1) IN GENERAL.—Subject to paragraph (2), none of the funds authorized to be appropriated by this Act or otherwise made available for fiscal year 2017 or any fiscal year thereafter for the Department of Defense may be obligated or expended on a contract for a software license with a cost of more than $5,000,000 in a fiscal year unless the Department is able, through automated means—

(A) to count the number of such licenses in use; and

(B) to determine the security status of each instance of use of the software licensed.

(2) EFFECTIVE DATE.—Paragraph (1) shall apply—

(A) beginning on January 1, 2018, with respect to any contract entered into by the Secretary of Defense on or after such date for the licensing of software; and

(B) beginning on January 1, 2020, with respect to any contract entered into by the Secretary for the licensing of software that was in effect on December 31, 2017.

SEC. 1654. REPORTS ON DETERRENCE OF ADVERSARIES IN CYBERSPACE.

(a) REPORT OF THE SECRETARY OF DEFENSE.—

(1) IN GENERAL.—Not later than 180 days after the date of the enactment of this Act, the Secretary of Defense, in consultation with the Chairman of the Joint Chiefs of Staff, shall submit to the President and the congressional defense committees a report on the military and nonmilitary options available to the United States for deterring and responding to imminent threats in cyberspace and malicious cyber activities carried out against the United States by foreign governments and terrorist organizations.

(2) ELEMENTS.—The report under paragraph (1) shall include the following:

(A) A description of the military and nonmilitary options described in paragraph (1), including citations to relevant provisions of law, regulation, or directives or other policy documents of the Federal Government.

(B) Descriptions of relevant authorities, rules of engagement, command and control structures, and response plans relating to such options, including—

(i) authorities that have been delegated by the President to the Secretary of Defense for the conduct of cyber operations;

(ii) operational authorities delegated by the Secretary to the Commander of the United States Cyber Command for military cyber operations;

(iii) identification of how the law of war applies to cyber operations of the Department of Defense;

(iv) an assessment of the effectiveness of each such option; and

(v) an integrated priorities list for cyber deterrence capabilities of the Department of Defense that identifies, at a minimum, high priority capability needs prioritized by armed force, function, risk areas, and long-term strategic planning issues.

(b) REPORT OF THE PRESIDENT.—

(1) IN GENERAL.—Not later than 180 days after the date on which the Secretary of Defense submits the report under subsection (a), the President shall submit to the congressional defense committees a report describing the types of actions carried out in cyberspace against the United States that may warrant a military response.

(2) ELEMENTS.—The report under paragraph (1) shall include the following:

(A) Discussion of the types of actions carried out in cyberspace that may warrant a military response or operation.

(B) A description of the role of the military in responding to acts of aggression in cyberspace against the United States.

(C) A description of the circumstances required for a military response to a cyber attack against the United States.

(D) A plan for articulating a declaratory policy on the use of cyber weapons by the United States.

SEC. 1655. SENSE OF CONGRESS ON CYBER RESILIENCY OF THE NETWORKS AND COMMUNICATIONS SYSTEMS OF THE NATIONAL GUARD.

It is the sense of Congress that, to the greatest extent practicable, the National Guard should continuously seek ways to improve, expand, and provide resources for its communications and networking systems to enhance the performance and resilience of such systems in the face of cyber attacks, disruptions, and other threats.

Subtitle D—Nuclear Forces

SEC. 1661. IMPROVEMENTS TO COUNCIL ON OVERSIGHT OF NATIONAL LEADERSHIP COMMAND, CONTROL, AND COMMUNICATIONS SYSTEM.

(a) RESPONSIBILITIES.—Subsection (d) of section 171a of title 10, United States Code, is amended—

(1) in paragraph (1), by inserting before the period the following: ", and including with respect to the integrated tactical warning and attack assessment systems, processes, and enablers, and continuity of the governmental functions of the Department of Defense"; and

(2) in paragraph (2)(C), by inserting before the period the following: "(including space system architectures and associated user terminals and ground segments)".

(b) ENSURING CAPABILITIES.—Such section is further amended—

(1) by redesignating subsection (i) as subsection (k); and

(2) by inserting after subsection (h) the following new subsections:

"(i) REPORTS ON SPACE ARCHITECTURE DEVELOPMENT.—(1) Not less than 90 days before each of the dates on which a system described in paragraph (2) achieves Milestone A or Milestone B approval, the Under Secretary of Defense for Acquisitions, Technology, and Logistics shall submit to the congressional defense committees a report prepared by the Council detailing the implications of any changes to the architecture of such a system with respect to the systems, capabilities, and programs covered under subsection (d).

"(2) A system described in this paragraph is any of the following:

"(A) Advanced extremely high frequency satellites.

"(B) The space-based infrared system.

"(C) The integrated tactical warning and attack assessment system and its command and control system.

"(D) The enhanced polar system.

"(3) In this subsection, the terms 'Milestone A approval' and 'Milestone B approval' have the meanings given such terms in section 2366(e) of this title.

"(j) NOTIFICATION OF REDUCTION OF CERTAIN WARNING TIME.—(1) None of the funds authorized to be appropriated or otherwise made available to the Department of Defense for any fiscal year may be used to change any command, control, and communications system described in subsection (d)(1) in a manner that reduces the warning time provided to the national leadership of the United States with respect to a warning of a strategic missile attack on the United States unless—

"(A) the Secretary of Defense notifies the congressional defense committees of such proposed change and reduction; and

"(B) a period of one year elapses following the date of such notification.

"(2) Not later than March 1, 2017, and each year thereafter, the Council shall determine whether the integrated tactical warning and attack assessment system and its command and control system have met all warfighter requirements for operational availability, survivability, and endurability. If the Council determines that such systems have not met such requirements, the Secretary of Defense and the Chairman of the Joint Chiefs of Staff shall jointly submit to the congressional defense committees—

"(A) an explanation for such negative determination;

"(B) a description of the mitigations that are in place or being put in place as a result of such negative determination; and

"(C) the plan of the Secretary and the Chairman to ensure that the Council is able to make a positive determination in the following year.".

(c) REPORTING REQUIREMENTS.—Subsection (e) of such section is amended—

(1) in the matter preceding paragraph (1), by striking "At the same time" and all that follows through "title 31," and inserting the following: "During the period preceding January 31, 2021, at the same time each year that the budget of the President is submitted to Congress pursuant to section 1105(a) of title 31, and from time to time after such period at the discretion of the Council,"; and

(2) by adding at the end the following new paragraph:

"(6) An assessment of the readiness of the command, control, and communications system for the national leadership of the United States and of each layer of the system, as that layer relates to nuclear command, control, and communications.".

SEC. 1662. TREATMENT OF CERTAIN SENSITIVE INFORMATION BY STATE AND LOCAL GOVERNMENTS.

(a) SPECIAL NUCLEAR MATERIAL.—

(1) IN GENERAL.—Section 128 of title 10, United States Code, is amended by adding at the end the following new subsection:

"(d) Information that the Secretary prohibits to be disseminated pursuant to subsection (a) that is provided to a State or local government shall remain under the control of the Department of Defense, and a State or local law authorizing or requiring a State or local government to disclose such information shall not apply to such information.".

*(2) CONFORMING AMENDMENT.—The heading of such section is amended by striking "**Physical protection**" and inserting "**Control and physical protection**".".*

(3) CLERICAL AMENDMENT.—The table of sections at the beginning of chapter 3 of such title is amended by striking the item relating to section 128 and inserting the following new item:

"128. Control and physical protection of special nuclear material: limitation on dissemination of unclassified information.".

(b) CRITICAL INFRASTRUCTURE SECURITY INFORMATION.—Section 130e of such title is amended—

(1) by transferring subsection (c) to the end of such section and redesignating such subsection, as so transferred, as subsection (f); and

(2) by striking subsection (b) and inserting the following new subsections:

"(b) DESIGNATION OF DEPARTMENT OF DEFENSE CRITICAL INFRASTRUCTURE SECURITY INFORMATION.—In addition to any other authority or requirement regarding protection from dissemination of information, the Secretary may designate information as being Department of Defense

Defense critical infrastructure security information, including during the course of creating such information, to ensure that such information is not disseminated without authorization. Information so designated is subject to the determination process under subsection (a) to determine whether to exempt such information from disclosure described in such subsection.

"(c) INFORMATION PROVIDED TO STATE AND LOCAL GOVERNMENTS.—(1) Department of Defense critical infrastructure security information covered by a written determination under subsection (a) or designated under subsection (b) that is provided to a State or local government shall remain under the control of the Department of Defense.

"(2)(A) A State or local law authorizing or requiring a State or local government to disclose Department of Defense critical infrastructure security information that is covered by a written determination under subsection (a) shall not apply to such information.

"(B) If a person requests pursuant to a State or local law that a State or local government disclose information that is designated as Department of Defense critical infrastructure security information under subsection (b), the State or local government shall provide the Secretary an opportunity to carry out the determination process under subsection (a) to determine whether to exempt such information from disclosure pursuant to subparagraph (A).".

SEC. 1663. PROCUREMENT AUTHORITY FOR CERTAIN PARTS OF INTERCONTINENTAL BALLISTIC MISSILE FUZES.

(a) AVAILABILITY OF FUNDS.—Notwithstanding section 1502(a) of title 31, United States Code, of the amount authorized to be appropriated for fiscal year 2017 by section 101 and available for Missile Procurement, Air Force, as specified in the funding table in section 4101, $17,095,000 shall be available for the procurement of covered parts pursuant to contracts entered into under section 1645(a) of the Carl Levin and Howard P. "Buck" McKeon National Defense Authorization Act for Fiscal Year 2015 (Public Law 113–291; 128 Stat. 3651).

(b) COVERED PARTS DEFINED.—In this section, the term "covered parts" means commercially available off-the-shelf items as defined in section 104 of title 41, United States Code.

SEC. 1664. PROHIBITION ON AVAILABILITY OF FUNDS FOR MOBILE VARIANT OF GROUND-BASED STRATEGIC DETERRENT MISSILE.

None of the funds authorized to be appropriated by this Act or otherwise made available for any of fiscal years 2017 or 2018 may be obligated or expended to retain the option for, or develop, a mobile variant of the ground-based strategic deterrent missile.

SEC. 1665. LIMITATION ON AVAILABILITY OF FUNDS FOR EXTENSION OF NEW START TREATY.

(a) LIMITATION.—None of the funds authorized to be appropriated by this Act or otherwise made available for fiscal year 2017 or any other fiscal year for the Department of Defense may be obligated or expended to extend the New START Treaty unless—

(1) the Chairman of the Joint Chiefs of Staff submits the report under subsection (b);

(2) the Director of National Intelligence submits the National Intelligence Estimate under subsection (c)(2); and

(3) a period of 120 days elapses following the submission of both the report and the National Intelligence Estimate.

(b) REPORT.—The Chairman of the Joint Chiefs of Staff shall submit to the appropriate congressional committees a report detailing the following:

(1) The impacts on the nuclear forces and force planning of the United States with respect

to a State Party to the New START Treaty developing a capability to conduct a rapid reload of its ballistic missiles.

(2) Whether any State Party to the New START Treaty has significantly increased its upload capability with non-deployed nuclear warheads and the degree to which such developments impact crisis stability and the nuclear forces, force planning, use concepts, and deterrent strategy of the United States.

(3) The extent to which non-treaty-limited nuclear or strategic conventional systems pose a threat to the United States or the allies of the United States.

(4) The extent to which violations of arms control treaty and agreement obligations pose a risk to the national security of the United States and the allies of the United States, including the perpetuation of violations ongoing as of the date of the enactment of this Act, as well as potential further violations.

(5) The extent to which—

(A) the "escalate-to-deescalate" nuclear use doctrine of the Russian Federation is deterred under the current nuclear force structure, weapons capabilities, and declaratory policy of the United States; and

(B) deterring the implementation of such a doctrine has been integrated into the war plans of the United States.

(6) The status of the nuclear weapons, nuclear weapons infrastructure, and nuclear command and control modernization activities of the United States, and the impact such status has on plans to—

(A) implement the reduction of the nuclear weapons of the United States; or

(B) further reduce the numbers and types of such weapons.

(7) Whether, and if so, the reasons that, the New START Treaty, and the extension of the treaty as of the date of the report, is in the national security interests of the United States.

(c) NATIONAL INTELLIGENCE ESTIMATE.—

(1) PRODUCTION.—The Director of National Intelligence shall produce a National Intelligence Estimate on the following:

(A) The nuclear forces and doctrine of the Russian Federation.

(B) The nuclear weapons research and production capability of Russia.

(C) The compliance of Russia with respect to arms control obligations (including treaties, agreements, and other obligations).

(D) The doctrine of Russia with respect to targeting adversary critical infrastructure and the relationship between such doctrine and other Russian war planning, including, at a minimum, "escalate-to-deescalate" concepts.

(2) SUBMISSION.—The Director of National Intelligence shall submit, consistent with the protection of sources and methods, to the appropriate congressional committees the National Intelligence Estimate produced under paragraph (1).

(d) DEFINITIONS.—In this section:

(1) The term "appropriate congressional committees" means—

(A) the Committees on Armed Services of the House of Representatives and the Senate;

(B) the Committee on Foreign Affairs of the House of Representatives and the Committee on Foreign Relations of the Senate; and

(C) the Permanent Select Committee on Intelligence of the House of Representatives and the Select Committee on Intelligence of the Senate.

(2) The term "New START Treaty" means the Treaty between the United States of America and the Russian Federation on Measures for the Further Reduction and Limitation of Strategic Offensive Arms, signed on April 8, 2010, and entered into force on February 5, 2011.

SEC. 1666. CERTIFICATIONS REGARDING INTEGRATED TACTICAL WARNING AND ATTACK ASSESSMENT MISSION OF THE AIR FORCE.

(a) ANNUAL CERTIFICATION.—Not later than March 31, 2017, and each year thereafter through 2020, the Commander of the United States Strategic Command shall certify to the Secretary of Defense and the congressional defense committees that—

(1) the Air Force is appropriately organized, staffed, trained, and equipped to carry out the portions of the integrated tactical warning and attack assessment mission assigned to the Air Force that are survivable and endurable; and

(2) the programs and plans of the Air Force for sustaining, modernizing, training, and exercising capabilities relating to such mission are sufficient to ensure the success of the mission.

(b) INABILITY TO CERTIFY.—If the Commander does not make a certification under subsection (a) by March 31 of any year in which a certification is required under such subsection, the Secretary of the Air Force shall take immediate actions to consolidate all terrestrial and aerial components of the integrated tactical warning and attack assessment system of the Air Force that are survivable and endurable under the major command of the Air Force commanded by the single general officer that is responsible for all aspects of the Air Force nuclear mission, as described by Air Force Program Action Directive D16–01 dated August 2, 2016.

(c) RULE OF CONSTRUCTION.—Nothing in this section may be construed to affect any responsibilities and authorities relating to the integrated tactical warning and attack assessment system in effect on the date of the enactment of this Act pursuant to the Agreement Between the Government of the United States of America and the Government of Canada on the North American Aerospace Defense Command and the terms of reference for the North American Aerospace Defense Command.

SEC. 1667. MATTERS RELATING TO INTERCONTINENTAL BALLISTIC MISSILES.

(a) PROHIBITION.—

(1) IN GENERAL.—Except as provided by paragraph (2), none of the funds authorized to be appropriated by this Act or otherwise made available for fiscal year 2017 for the Department of Defense shall be obligated or expended for—

(A) reducing, or preparing to reduce, the responsiveness or alert level of the intercontinental ballistic missiles of the United States; or

(B) reducing, or preparing to reduce, the quantity of deployed intercontinental ballistic missiles of the United States to a number less than 400.

(2) EXCEPTION.—The prohibition in paragraph (1) shall not apply to any of the following activities:

(A) The maintenance or sustainment of intercontinental ballistic missiles.

(B) Ensuring the safety, security, or reliability of intercontinental ballistic missiles.

(C) Reduction in the number of deployed intercontinental ballistic missiles that are carried out in compliance with—

(i) the limitations of the New START Treaty (as defined in section 494(a)(2)(D) of title 10, United States Code); and

(ii) section 1644 of the Carl Levin an Howard P. "Buck" McKeon National Defense Authorization Act for Fiscal Year 2015 (Public Law 113–291; 128 Stat. 3651; 10 U.S.C. 494 note).

(b) REPORT.—

(1) IN GENERAL.—Not later than 60 days after the date of the enactment of this Act, the Secretary of the Air Force and the Chairman of the Nuclear Weapons Council shall submit to the congressional defense committees a report regarding efforts to carry out section 1057 of the National Defense Authorization Act for Fiscal Year 2014 (Public Law 113–66; 10 U.S.C. 495 note).

(2) ELEMENTS.—The report under paragraph (1) shall include the following with respect to the period of the expected lifespan of the Minuteman III system:

(A) The number of nuclear warheads required to support the capability to redeploy multiple independently retargetable reentry vehicles across the full intercontinental ballistic missile fleet.

(B) The current and planned (through 2030) readiness state of nuclear warheads intended to support the capability to redeploy multiple independently retargetable reentry vehicles across the full intercontinental ballistic missile fleet, including which portion of the active or inactive stockpile such warheads are classified within.

(C) The current and planned (through 2030) reserve of components or subsystems required to redeploy multiple independently retargetable reentry vehicles across the full intercontinental ballistic missile fleet, including the plans or industrial capability and capacity to produce more such components or subsystems, if needed.

(D) The current and planned (through 2030) time required to commence redeployment of multiple independently retargetable reentry vehicles across the intercontinental ballistic missile fleet, including the time required to finish deployment across the full fleet.

(E) The estimated cost of maintaining the capability and warheads required to redeploy multiple independently retargetable reentry vehicles across the full intercontinental ballistic missile fleet.

SEC. 1668. REQUESTS FOR FORCES TO MEET SECURITY REQUIREMENTS FOR LAND-BASED NUCLEAR FORCES.

(a) EXPEDITED DECISION FOR SECURING LAND-BASED MISSILE FIELDS.—To mitigate any risk posed to the nuclear forces of the United States by the failure to replace the UH–1N helicopter, the Secretary of Defense shall, in consultation with the Chairman of the Joint Chiefs of Staff—

(1) decide if the land-based missile fields using UH–1N helicopters meet security requirements and if there are any shortfalls or gaps in meeting such requirements;

(2) not later than 30 days after the date of the enactment of this Act, submit to Congress a report on the decision relating to a request for forces required by paragraph (1); and

(3) if the Chairman determines the implementation of the decision to be warranted to mitigate any risk posed to the nuclear forces of the United States—

(A) not later than 60 days after such date of enactment, implement that decision; or

(B) if the Secretary cannot implement that decision during the period specified in subparagraph (A), not later than 45 days after such date of enactment, submit to Congress a report that includes a proposal for the date by which the Secretary can implement that decision and a plan to carry out that proposal.

(b) LIMITATION.—Of the funds authorized to be appropriated by this Act or otherwise made available for fiscal year 2017 for the travel and representational expenses of the Under Secretary of Defense for Acquisition, Technology, and Logistics, not more than 75 percent may be obligated or expended until the date on which the Under Secretary certifies to the congressional defense committees that there is a acquisition process in place to ensure that a UH–1N replacement aircraft is under contract in fiscal year 2018.

SEC. 1669. REPORT ON RUSSIAN AND CHINESE POLITICAL AND MILITARY LEADERSHIP SURVIVABILITY, COMMAND AND CONTROL, AND CONTINUITY OF GOVERNMENT PROGRAMS AND ACTIVITIES.

(a) REPORT.—Not later than January 15, 2017, the Director of National Intelligence shall submit to the appropriate congressional committees,

consistent with the protection of sources and methods, a report on the leadership survivability, command and control, and continuity of government programs and activities with respect to the People's Republic of China and the Russian Federation, respectively. The report shall include the following:

(1) The goals and objectives of such programs and activities of each respective country.

(2) An assessment of how such programs and activities fit into the political and military doctrine and strategy of each respective country.

(3) An assessment of the size and scope of such activities, including the location and description of above-ground and underground facilities important to the political and military leadership survivability, command and control, and continuity of government programs and activities of each respective country.

(4) An identification of which facilities various senior political and military leaders of each respective country are expected to operate out of during crisis and wartime.

(5) A technical assessment of the political and military means and methods for command and control in wartime of each respective country.

(6) An identification of key officials and organizations of each respective country involved in managing and operating such facilities, programs, and activities, including the command structure for each organization involved in such programs and activities.

(7) An assessment of how senior leaders of each respective country measure the effectiveness of such programs and activities.

(8) An estimate of the annual cost of such programs and activities.

(9) An assessment of the degree of enhanced survivability such programs and activities can be expected to provide in various military scenarios ranging from limited conventional conflict to strategic nuclear employment.

(10) An assessment of the type and extent of foreign assistance, if any, in such programs and activities.

(11) An assessment of the status and the effectiveness of the intelligence collection of the United States on such programs and capabilities, and any gaps in such collection.

(12) Any other matters the Director determines appropriate.

(b) COUNCIL ASSESSMENT.—Not later than 90 days after the date on which the Director submits the report under subsection (a), the Council on Oversight of the National Leadership Command, Control, and Communications System established by section 171a of title 10, United States Code, shall submit to the appropriate congressional committees an assessment of how the command, control, and communications systems for the national leadership of the People's Republic of China and the Russian Federation, respectively, compare to such system of the United States.

(c) STRATCOM.—Together with the assessment submitted under subsection (b), the Commander of the United States Strategic Command shall submit to the appropriate congressional committees the views of the Commander on the report under subsection (a), including a detailed description for how the leadership survivability, command and control, and continuity of government programs and activities of the People's Republic of China and the Russian Federation, respectively, are considered in the plans and options under the responsibility of the Commander under the unified command plan.

(d) FORMS.—Each report or assessment submitted under this section may be submitted in unclassified form, but may include a classified annex.

(e) APPROPRIATE CONGRESSIONAL COMMITTEES DEFINED.—In this section, the term "appropriate congressional committees" means—

(1) the congressional defense committees; and

(2) the Permanent Select Committee on Intelligence of the House of Representatives and the Select Committee on Intelligence of the Senate.

SEC. 1670. REVIEW BY COMPTROLLER GENERAL OF THE UNITED STATES OF RECOMMENDATIONS RELATING TO NUCLEAR ENTERPRISE OF DEPARTMENT OF DEFENSE.

(a) IN GENERAL.—During each of fiscal years 2017 through 2021, the Comptroller General of the United States shall conduct a review of the following:

(1) The processes of the Department of Defense for addressing the recommendations of the Department of Defense Internal Nuclear Enterprise Review, the Independent Review of the Department of Defense Nuclear Enterprise, and other recommendations affecting the health of the nuclear enterprise of the Department of Defense identified or tracked by the Nuclear Deterrence Enterprise Review Group, including the process used by the Director of Cost Assessment and Program Evaluation to evaluate the implementation of such recommendations.

(2) The processes used to implement recommendations from other assessments of the nuclear enterprise of the Department of Defense, including the National Leadership Command Capability and Nuclear Command, Control, and Communications Enterprise Review.

(b) BRIEFING.—After conducting each review under subsection (a), the Comptroller General shall provide to the congressional defense committees a briefing on the review.

(c) CONFORMING REPEAL.—Section 1658 of the National Defense Authorization Act for Fiscal Year 2016 (Public Law 114–92; 129 Stat. 1125) is repealed.

SEC. 1671. SENSE OF CONGRESS ON NUCLEAR DETERRENCE.

It is the sense of Congress that—

(1) the nuclear forces of the United States continue to play a fundamental role in deterring aggression against the interests of the United States and the allies of the United States in an increasingly dangerous world in which foreign adversaries, including the Russian Federation, are making explicit nuclear threats against the United States and such allies;

(2) strong United States nuclear forces assure the allies of the United States that the extended deterrence guarantees of the United States are credible and that the resolve of the United States remains strong even in the face of nuclear provocations, including nuclear coercion and blackmail;

(3) the prevention of war through effective deterrence requires survivable and flexible nuclear forces that are well exercised and ready to respond to nuclear escalation if necessary;

(4) possessing a range of capabilities and options to counter nuclear threats assures the allies of the United States and enhances the credibility of United States nuclear deterrence by reinforcing the resolve of the United States in the minds of such allies and potential adversaries;

(5) the declared policy of the United States with respect to the use of nuclear weapons must be coordinated and communicate clearly that the use of nuclear weapons against the United States or its vital interests would ultimately fail and subject the aggressor to incalculable consequences;

(6) in support of a strong and credible nuclear deterrent, the United States must—

(A) maintain a nuclear force with a diverse, flexible range of nuclear yield and delivery modes that are ready, capable, and credible;

(B) afford the highest priority to the modernization of the nuclear triad, dual-capable aircraft, and related command and control elements; and

(C) ensure the broadest participation of allies of the United States in nuclear defense planning, training, and exercises to demonstrate the commitment of the United States and such allies and their solidarity against nuclear threats and coercion; and

(7) with respect to the North Atlantic Treaty Organization (NATO)—

(A) NATO has made it clear at the NATO summit in Warsaw, Poland, in July 2018, that—

(i) "the fundamental purpose of NATO's nuclear capability is to preserve peace, prevent coercion, and deter aggression"; and

(ii) "Nuclear weapons are unique. Any employment of nuclear weapons against NATO would fundamentally alter the nature of a conflict. The circumstances in which NATO might have to use nuclear weapons are extremely remote. If the fundamental security of any of its members were to be threatened however, NATO has the capabilities and resolve to impose costs on an adversary that would be unacceptable and far outweigh the benefits that an adversary could hope to achieve."; and

(B) accordingly, effective deterrence requires that NATO conduct realistic nuclear planning and exercises, and modernize the full suite of dual-capable aircraft and associated command and control networks and facilities.

SEC. 1672. SENSE OF CONGRESS ON IMPORTANCE OF INDEPENDENT NUCLEAR DETERRENT OF UNITED KINGDOM.

It is the sense of Congress that—

(1) the United States believes that the independent nuclear deterrent and decision-making of the United Kingdom provides a crucial contribution to international stability, the North Atlantic Treaty Organization alliance, and the national security of the United States;

(2) nuclear deterrence is and will continue to be the highest priority mission of the Department of Defense and the United States benefits when the closest ally of the United States clearly and unequivocally sets similar priorities;

(3) the United States sees the nuclear deterrent of the United Kingdom as central to trans-Atlantic security and to the commitment of the United Kingdom to NATO to spend two percent of gross domestic product on defense;

(4) the commitment of the United Kingdom to maintain a continuous at-sea deterrence posture today and in the future complements the deterrent capabilities of the United States and provides a credible "second center of decision making" which ensures potential attackers cannot discount the solidarity of the mutual relationship of the United States and the United Kingdom;

(5) the United States Navy must execute the Ohio-class replacement submarine program on time and within budget, seeking efficiencies and cost savings wherever possible, to ensure that the program delivers a Common Missile Compartment, the Trident II (D5) Strategic Weapon System, and associated equipment and production capabilities, that support the successful development and deployment of the Dreadnought submarines of the United Kingdom; and

(6) the close technical collaboration, especially expert mutual scientific peer review, provides valuable resilience and cost effectiveness to the respective deterrence programs of the United States and the United Kingdom.

Subtitle E—Missile Defense Programs

SEC. 1681. NATIONAL MISSILE DEFENSE POLICY.

(a) POLICY.—It is the policy of the United States to maintain and improve an effective, robust layered missile defense system capable of defending the territory of the United States, allies, deployed forces, and capabilities against the developing and increasingly complex ballistic missile threat with funding subject to the annual authorization of appropriations and the annual appropriation of funds for National Missile Defense.

(b) CONFORMING REPEAL.—Section 2 of the National Missile Defense Act of 1999 (Public Law 106–38; 10 U.S.C. 2431 note) is repealed.

SEC. 1682. EXTENSIONS OF PROHIBITIONS RELATING TO MISSILE DEFENSE INFORMATION AND SYSTEMS.

(a) PROHIBITION ON INTEGRATION OF CERTAIN MISSILE DEFENSE SYSTEMS.—

(1) IN GENERAL.—Section 130h of title 10, United States Code, is amended—

(A) by redesignating subsection (d) as subsection (e);

(B) by inserting after subsection (c) the following new subsection (d):

"(d) INTEGRATION.—None of the funds authorized to be appropriated or otherwise made available for any fiscal year for the Department of Defense may be obligated or expended to integrate a missile defense system of the Russian Federation or a missile defense system of the People's Republic of China into any missile defense system of the United States."; and

*(C) by striking the section heading and inserting the following: "**Prohibitions relating to missile defense information and systems**".*

(2) CLERICAL AMENDMENT.—The table of sections at the beginning of chapter 3 of title 10, United States Code, is amended by striking the item relating to section 130h and inserting the following new item:

"130h. Prohibitions relating to missile defense information and systems.".

(3) CONFORMING REPEALS.—Sections 1672 and 1673 of the National Defense Authorization Act for Fiscal Year 2016 (Public Law 114–92; 129 Stat. 1130) are repealed.

(b) EXTENSION OF SUNSET.—Section 130h(e) of title 10, United States Code, as redesignated by subsection (a)(1), is amended to read as follows:

"(e) SUNSET.—The prohibitions in subsections (a), (b), and (d) shall expire on January 1, 2019.".

SEC. 1683. NON-TERRESTRIAL MISSILE DEFENSE INTERCEPT AND DEFEAT CAPABILITY FOR THE BALLISTIC MISSILE DEFENSE SYSTEM.

Section 1685 of the National Defense Authorization Act for Fiscal Year 2016 (Public Law 114–92; 129 Stat. 1142) is amended—

(1) in subsection (c)(2), by inserting before the semicolon at the end the following: "for each fiscal year over the five-fiscal-year period beginning with the fiscal year following the fiscal year in which the report is submitted, assuming such potential program of record is technically feasible and could be deployed by December 31, 2027"; and

(2) by adding at the end the following new subsection:

"(d) COMMENCEMENT OF RDT&E.—Not later than 60 days after the submittal of the report required by subsection (c), the Director may commence coordination and activities associated with research, development, test, and evaluation on the programs described in subsection (c)(2).".

SEC. 1684. REVIEW OF THE MISSILE DEFEAT POLICY AND STRATEGY OF THE UNITED STATES.

(a) NEW REVIEW.—The Secretary of Defense and the Chairman of the Joint Chiefs of Staff shall jointly conduct a new review of the missile defeat capability, policy, and strategy of the United States, with respect to—

(1) left- and right-of-launch ballistic missile defense for—

(A) both regional and homeland purposes; and

(B) the full range of active, passive, kinetic, and nonkinetic defense measures across the full spectrum of land-, air-, sea-, and space-based platforms;

(2) the integration of offensive and defensive forces for the defeat of ballistic missiles, including against weapons initially deployed on ballistic missiles, such as hypersonic glide vehicles; and

(3) cruise missile defense of the homeland.

(b) ELEMENTS.—The review under subsection (a) shall address the following:

(1) The missile defeat policy, strategy, and objectives of the United States in relation to the national security strategy of the United States and the military strategy of the United States.

(2) The role of deterrence in the missile defeat policy and strategy of the United States.

(3) The missile defeat posture, capability, and force structure of the United States.

(4) With respect to both the five- and ten-year periods beginning on the date of the review, the planned and desired end-state of the missile defeat programs of the United States, including regarding the integration and interoperability of such programs with the joint forces and the integration and interoperability of such programs with allies, and specific benchmarks, milestones, and key steps required to reach such end-states.

(5) The process for determining requirements, force structure, and inventory objectives for missile defeat capabilities under such programs, including input from the joint military requirements process.

(6) The organization, execution, and oversight of acquisition for the missile defeat programs of the United States.

(7) The roles and responsibilities of the Office of the Secretary of Defense, Defense Agencies, combatant commands, the Joint Chiefs of Staff, the military departments, and the intelligence community in such programs and the process for ensuring accountability of each stakeholder.

(8) Standards for the military utility, operational effectiveness, suitability, and survivability of the missile defeat systems of the United States.

(9) The method in which resources for the missile defeat mission are planned, programmed, and budgeted within the Department of Defense.

(10) The near-term and long-term costs and cost effectiveness of such programs.

(11) The options for affecting the offense-defense cost curve.

(12) The role of international cooperation in the missile defeat policy and strategy of the United States and the plans, policies, and requirements for integration and interoperability of missile defeat capability with allies.

(13) Options for increasing the frequency of the codevelopment of missile defeat capabilities with allies of the United States in the near-term and far-term.

(14) Declaratory policy governing the employment of missile defeat capabilities and the military options and plans and employment options of such capabilities.

(15) The role of multi-mission defense and other assets of the United States, including space and terrestrial sensors and plans to achieve multi-mission capability in current, planned, and other future assets and acquisition programs.

(16) The indications and warning required to meet the missile defeat strategy and objectives of the United States described in paragraph (1) and the key enablers and programs to achieve such indications and warning.

(17) The impact of the mobility, countermeasures, and denial and deception capabilities of adversaries on the indications and warning described in paragraph (16) and the consequences on the missile defeat capability, objectives, and military options of the United States and the plans of the combatant commanders.

(18) Any other matters the Secretary determines relevant.

(c) REPORTS.—

(1) RESULTS.—Not later than January 31, 2018, the Secretary shall submit to the congressional defense committees a report setting forth the results of the review under subsection (a).

(2) FORM.—The report required by paragraph (1) shall be submitted in unclassified form, but may include a classified annex.

(3) ANNUAL IMPLEMENTATION UPDATES.—During the five-year period beginning on the date of the submission of the report under paragraph (1), the Director of Cost Assessment and Program Evaluation shall submit to the Secretary of Defense, the Chairman of the Joint Chiefs of Staff, and the congressional defense committees annual status updates detailing the progress of the Secretary in implementing the missile defeat strategy of the United States.

(4) THREAT REPORT.—Not later than 180 days after the date of the enactment of this Act, the Director of National Intelligence shall submit to the congressional defense committees, the Permanent Select Committee on Intelligence of the House of Representatives, and the Select Committee on Intelligence of the Senate a report containing an unclassified summary, consistent with the protection of intelligence sources and methods, of—

(A) as of the date of the report required by this paragraph, the ballistic and cruise missile threat to the United States, deployed forces of the United States, and friends and allies of the United States from short-, medium-, intermediate-, and long-range nuclear and non-nuclear ballistic and cruise missile threats; and

(B) an assessment of such threat in 2026.

(5) DECLARATORY POLICY, CONCEPT OF OPERATIONS, AND EMPLOYMENT GUIDELINES FOR LEFT-OF-LAUNCH CAPABILITY.—Not later than 120 days after the date of the enactment of this Act, the Secretary of Defense and the Chairman of the Joint Chiefs of Staff shall jointly submit to the congressional defense committees the following:

(A) The unclassified declaratory policy of the United States regarding the use of the left-of-launch capability of the United States against potential targets.

(B) Both the classified and unclassified concept of operations for the use of such capability across and between the combatant commands.

(C) Both the classified and unclassified employment strategy, plans, and options for such capability.

(d) NOTIFICATION.—

(1) LIMITATION.—None of the funds authorized to be appropriated by this Act or otherwise made available for fiscal year 2017 or fiscal year 2018 for the Secretary of Defense may be obligated or expended to change the non-standard acquisition processes and responsibilities described in paragraph (2) until—

(A) the Secretary notifies the congressional defense committees of such proposed change; and

(B) a period of 180 days has elapsed following the date of such notification.

(2) NON-STANDARD ACQUISITION PROCESSES AND RESPONSIBILITIES DESCRIBED.—The non-standard acquisition processes and responsibilities described in this paragraph are such processes and responsibilities described in—

(A) the memorandum of the Secretary of Defense titled "Missile Defense Program Direction" signed on January 2, 2002; and

(B) Department of Defense Directive 5134.09, as in effect on the date of the enactment of this Act.

(e) DESIGNATION REQUIRED.—

(1) AUTHORITY.—Not later than March 31, 2018, the Secretary of Defense shall designate a military department or Defense Agency with acquisition authority with respect to—

(A) the capability to defend the homeland from cruise missiles; and

(B) left-of-launch ballistic missile defeat capability.

(2) DISCRETION.—The Secretary may designate a single military department or Defense Agency

with the acquisition authority described in paragraph (1) or designate a separate military department or Defense Agency for each function specified in such paragraph.

(3) *VALIDATION.*—In making a designation under paragraph (1), the Secretary shall include a description of the manner in which the military requirements for such capabilities will be validated.

(f) *DEFINITIONS.*—In this section:

(1) The term "Defense Agency" has the meaning given that term in section 101(a)(11) of title 10, United States Code.

(2) The term "intelligence community" has the meaning given that term in section 3 of the National Security Act of 1947 (50 U.S.C. 3003).

SEC. 1685. MAXIMIZING AEGIS ASHORE CAPABILITY AND DEVELOPING MEDIUM RANGE DISCRIMINATION RADAR.

(a) *ANTI-AIR WARFARE CAPABILITY OF AEGIS ASHORE SITES.*—

(1) *AUTHORIZATION.*—Using funds authorized to be appropriated by sections 101 and 201 of this Act or otherwise made available for fiscal year 2017 for procurement and research, development, test, and evaluation, the Secretary of Defense shall continue the development, procurement, and deployment of anti-air warfare capabilities at each Aegis Ashore site in Romania and Poland.

(2) *LONG-LEAD COMPONENTS.*—Of the funds specified in paragraph (1), not more than $25,000,000 may be obligated or expended for the procurement of long-lead components to provide the anti-air warfare capabilities described in such paragraph.

(3) *REPROGRAMMING AND TRANSFERS.*—Any reprogramming or transfer made to carry out paragraph (1) shall be carried out in accordance with established procedures for reprogramming or transfers.

(b) *AEGIS ASHORE CAPABILITY EVALUATION.*— Not later than 120 days after the date of the enactment of this Act, the Secretary of Defense and the Chairman of the Joint Chiefs of Staff shall jointly submit to the congressional defense committees an evaluation of the ballistic missile and air threat against the continental United States and the efficacy (including with respect to cost, ideal and optimal deployment locations, and potential deployment schedule) of deploying one or more Aegis Ashore sites and Aegis Ashore components for the ballistic and cruise missile defense of the continental United States.

(c) *AEGIS ASHORE SITE AND MEDIUM RANGE DISCRIMINATION RADAR ON THE PACIFIC MISSILE RANGE FACILITY.*—

(1) *LIMITATION.*—During fiscal year 2017, the Secretary of Defense may not reduce the manning levels or test capability, as such levels and capability existed on January 1, 2015, of the Aegis Ashore site at the Pacific Missile Range Facility in Hawaii, including by putting such site into a "cold" or "stand by" status.

(2) *ENVIRONMENTAL IMPACT STATEMENT.*—

(A) Not later than 60 days after the date of the enactment of this Act, the Director of the Missile Defense Agency shall notify the congressional defense committees on whether the preferred alternative for fielding a medium range ballistic missile defense sensor for the defense of Hawaii identified by the report under section 1689(b)(2) of the National Defense Authorization Act for Fiscal Year 2016 (Public Law 114–92; 129 Stat. 1144) would require an update to the environmental impact statement required for constructing the Aegis Ashore site at the Pacific Missile Range Facility.

(B) In carrying out the preferred alternative for fielding a medium range ballistic missile defense sensor for the defense of Hawaii, if the Director determines that an updated environmental impact statement, a new environmental impact statement, or another action is required

or recommended pursuant to the National Environmental Policy Act of 1969 (42 U.S.C. et seq.), the Director shall commence such action by not later than 60 days after the date on which the Director makes the notification under subparagraph (A).

(3) *EVALUATION.*—Not later than 60 days after the date of the enactment of this Act, the Secretary of Defense and the Chairman of the Joint Chiefs of Staff shall jointly submit to the congressional defense committees an evaluation of the ballistic missile and air threat against Hawaii (including with respect to threats to the Armed Forces and installations located in Hawaii) and the efficacy (including with respect to cost and potential alternatives) of—

(A) making the Aegis Ashore site at the Pacific Missile Range Facility operational;

(B) deploying the preferred alternative for fielding a medium range ballistic missile defense sensor for the defense of Hawaii described in paragraph (2)(A); and

(C) any other alternative the Secretary and the Chairman determine appropriate.

(d) *FORMS.*—The evaluations submitted under subsections (b) and (c)(3) shall each be submitted in unclassified form, but may each include a classified annex.

SEC. 1686. TECHNICAL AUTHORITY FOR INTEGRATED AIR AND MISSILE DEFENSE ACTIVITIES AND PROGRAMS.

(a) *AUTHORITY.*—

(1) *IN GENERAL.*—The Director of the Missile Defense Agency is the technical authority of the Department of Defense for integrated air and missile defense activities and programs, including joint engineering and integration efforts for such activities and programs, including with respect to defining and controlling the interfaces of such activities and programs and the allocation of technical requirements for such activities and programs.

(2) *DETAILEES.*—

(A) In carrying out the technical authority under paragraph (1), the Director may seek to have staff detailed to the Missile Defense Agency from the Joint Functional Component Command for Integrated Missile Defense and the Joint Integrated Air and Missile Defense Organization in a number the Director determines necessary in accordance with subparagraph (B).

(B) In detailing staff under subparagraph (A) to carry out the technical authority under paragraph (1), the total number of staff, including detailees, of the Missile Defense Agency who carry out such authority may not exceed the number that is twice the number of such staff carrying out such authority as of January 1, 2016.

(b) *ASSESSMENTS AND PLANS.*—

(1) *BIENNIAL SUBMISSION.*—Not later than January 31, 2017, and biennially thereafter through 2021, the Director shall submit to the congressional defense committees an assessment of the state of integration and interoperability of the integrated air and missile defense capabilities of the Department of Defense.

(2) *ELEMENTS.*—Each assessment under paragraph (1) shall include the following:

(A) Identification of any gaps in the integration and interoperability of the integrated air and missile defense capabilities of the Department.

(B) A description of the options to improve such capabilities and remediate such gaps.

(C) A plan to carry out such improvements and remediations, including milestones and costs for such plan.

(3) *FORM.*—Each assessment under paragraph (1) shall be submitted in classified form unless the Director determines that submitting such assessment in unclassified form is useful and expedient.

SEC. 1687. HYPERSONIC DEFENSE CAPABILITY DEVELOPMENT.

(a) *EXECUTIVE AGENT.*—The Director of the Missile Defense Agency shall serve as the executive agent for the Department of Defense for the development of a capability by the United States to counter hypersonic boost-glide vehicle capabilities and conventional prompt strike capabilities that may be employed against the United States, the allies of the United States, and the deployed forces of the United States.

(b) *DUTIES.*—In carrying out subsection (a), the Director shall—

(1) develop architectures for a hypersonic defense capability, from detecting threats to intercepting such threats, that—

(A) involves systems of the military departments and the Defense Agencies; and

(B) includes both kinetic and nonkinetic options for such interception; and

(2) not later than September 30, 2017, establish a program of record to develop a hypersonic defense capability.

(c) *REPORTS REQUIRED.*—Not later than March 31, 2017—

(1) the Director shall submit to the congressional defense committees a report on the architectures and sensors evaluated pursuant to subsection (b); and

(2) the Chairman of the Joint Chiefs of Staff shall submit to the congressional defense committees a report on the military capability or capabilities and capability gaps relating to the threat posed by hypersonic boost-glide vehicles and maneuvering ballistic missiles to the United States, the allies of the United States, and the deployed forces of the United States.

(d) *NOTIFICATION OF FUNDING PROCEDURES.*— Not later than 90 days after the date on which the Director submits the report under subsection (c)(1), the Director shall notify the congressional defense committees with respect to whether the Director intends to use established procedures for reprogramming or transfers to carry out subsection (a) to conduct activities regarding experimentation, modeling and simulation, or research and development, to develop a hypersonic defense capability.

(e) *DEFINITIONS.*—In this section:

(1) The term "Defense Agencies" has the meaning given that term in section 101(a)(11) of title 10, United States Code.

(2) The term "executive agent" has the meaning given the term "DoD Executive Agent" in Department of Defense Directive 5101.1, or any successor directive relating to the responsibilities of an executive agent of the Department of Defense.

(3) The term "hypersonic defense capability" means the capability to counter hypersonic boost-glide vehicles and conventional prompt strike ballistic missiles.

SEC. 1688. CONVENTIONAL PROMPT GLOBAL STRIKE WEAPONS SYSTEM.

(a) *MILESTONE A APPROVAL DECISION.*—The Secretary of Defense shall make a decision regarding Milestone A approval (as defined in section 2366(e) of title 10, United States Code) for the conventional prompt global strike weapons system not later than the earlier of—

(1) September 30, 2020; or

(2) the date that is 240 days after the date of the successful completion of intermediate range flight 2 of such system.

(b) *LIMITATION ON AVAILABILITY OF FUNDS.*— Of the funds authorized to be appropriated by this Act or otherwise made available for fiscal year 2017 for research, development, test, and evaluation, Defense-wide, for the conventional prompt global strike weapons system, not more than 75 percent may be obligated or expended until the date on which the Chairman of the Joint Chiefs of Staff, in consultation with the Commander of the United States European Command, the Commander of the United States Pacific Command, and the Commander of the

United States Strategic Command, submits to the congressional defense committees a report on—

(1) whether there are warfighter requirements or integrated priorities list submitted needs for a limited operational conventional prompt strike capability; and

(2) whether the program plan and schedule proposed by the program office in the Office of the Under Secretary of Defense for Acquisition, Technology, and Logistics supports such requirements and integrated priorities lists submissions.

SEC. 1689. REQUIRED TESTING BY MISSILE DEFENSE AGENCY OF GROUND-BASED MIDCOURSE DEFENSE ELEMENT OF BALLISTIC MISSILE DEFENSE SYSTEM.

(a) TESTING REQUIRED.—Except as provided in subsection (c), not less frequently than once each fiscal year, the Director of the Missile Defense Agency shall administer a flight test of the ground-based midcourse defense element of the ballistic missile defense system.

(b) REQUIREMENTS.—The Director shall ensure that each test carried out under subsection (a) provides, when possible, for one or more of the following:

(1) The validation of technical improvements made to increase system performance and reliability.

(2) The evaluation of the operational effectiveness of the ground-based midcourse defense element of the ballistic missile defense system.

(3) The use of threat-representative targets and critical engagement conditions.

(4) The evaluation of new configurations of interceptors before they are fielded.

(5) The satisfaction of the "fly before buy" acquisition approach for new interceptor components or software.

(6) The evaluation of the interoperability of the ground-based midcourse defense element with other elements of the ballistic missile defense systems.

(c) EXCEPTIONS.—The Director may forgo a test under subsection (a) in a fiscal year under one or more of the following conditions:

(1) Such a test would jeopardize national security.

(2) Insufficient time considerations between post-test analysis and subsequent pre-test design.

(3) Insufficient funding.

(4) An interceptor is unavailable.

(5) A target is unavailable or is insufficiently representative of threats.

(6) The test range or necessary test assets are unavailable.

(7) Inclement weather.

(8) Any other condition the Director considers appropriate.

(d) CERTIFICATION.—Not later than 45 days after forgoing a test for a condition or conditions under subsection (c)(8), the Under Secretary of Defense for Acquisition, Technology, and Logistics shall submit to the congressional defense committees a certification setting forth the condition or conditions that caused the test to be forgone under such subsection.

(e) REPORT.—Not later than 45 days after forgoing a test for any condition specified in subsection (c), the Director shall submit to the congressional defense committees a report setting forth the rationale for forgoing the test and a plan to restore an intercept flight test in the Integrated Master Test Plan of the Missile Defense Agency. In the case of a test forgone for a condition or conditions under subsection (c)(8), the report required by this subsection is in addition to the certification required by subsection (d).

SEC. 1690. IRON DOME SHORT-RANGE ROCKET DEFENSE SYSTEM AND ISRAELI COOPERATIVE MISSILE DEFENSE PROGRAM CODEVELOPMENT AND COPRODUCTION.

(a) IRON DOME SHORT-RANGE ROCKET DEFENSE SYSTEM.—

(1) AVAILABILITY OF FUNDS.—Of the funds authorized to be appropriated by this Act or otherwise made available for fiscal year 2017 for procurement, Defense-wide, and available for the Missile Defense Agency, not more than $62,000,000 may be provided to the Government of Israel to procure Tamir interceptors for the Iron Dome short-range rocket defense system through coproduction of such interceptors in the United States by industry of the United States.

(2) CONDITIONS.—

(A) AGREEMENT.—Funds described in paragraph (1) for the Iron Dome short-range rocket defense program shall be available subject to the terms and conditions in the Agreement Between the Department of Defense of the United States of America and the Ministry of Defense of the State of Israel Concerning Iron Dome Defense System Procurement, signed on March 5, 2014, subject to an amended bilateral international agreement for coproduction for Tamir interceptors. In negotiations by the Missile Defense Agency and the Missile Defense Organization of the Government of Israel regarding such production, the goal of the United States is to maximize opportunities for coproduction of the Tamir interceptors described in paragraph (1) in the United States by industry of the United States.

(B) CERTIFICATION.—Not later than 30 days prior to the initial obligation of funds described in paragraph (1), the Director of the Missile Defense Agency and the Under Secretary of Defense for Acquisition, Technology, and Logistics shall jointly submit to the appropriate congressional committees—

(i) a certification that the amended bilateral international agreement specified in subparagraph (A) is being implemented as provided in such agreement; and

(ii) an assessment detailing any risks relating to the implementation of such agreement.

(b) ISRAELI COOPERATIVE MISSILE DEFENSE PROGRAM CODEVELOPMENT AND COPRODUCTION.—

(1) IN GENERAL.—Subject to paragraph (2), of the funds authorized to be appropriated for fiscal year 2017 for procurement, Defense-wide, and available for the Missile Defense Agency—

(A) not more than $150,000,000 may be provided to the Government of Israel to procure the David's Sling Weapon System, including for coproduction of parts and components in the United States by United States industry; and

(B) not more than $120,000,000 may be provided to the Government of Israel for the Arrow 3 Upper Tier Interceptor Program, including for coproduction of parts and components in the United States by United States industry.

(2) CERTIFICATION.—

(A) CRITERIA.—Except as provided by paragraph (3), the Under Secretary of Defense for Acquisition, Technology, and Logistics shall submit to the appropriate congressional committees a certification that—

(i) the Government of Israel has demonstrated the successful completion of the knowledge points, technical milestones, and production readiness reviews required by the research, development, and technology agreements for the David's Sling Weapon System and the Arrow 3 Upper Tier Development Program, respectively;

(ii) funds specified in subparagraphs (A) and (B) of paragraph (1) will be provided on the basis of a one-for-one cash match made by Israel for such respective systems or in another matching amount that otherwise meets best efforts (as mutually agreed to by the United States and Israel);

(iii) the United States has entered into a bilateral international agreement with Israel that establishes, with respect to the use of such funds—

(I) in accordance with clause (iv), the terms of coproduction of parts and components of such respective systems on the basis of the greatest practicable coproduction of parts, components, and all-up rounds (if appropriate) by United States industry and minimizes nonrecurring engineering and facilitization expenses to the costs needed for coproduction;

(II) complete transparency on the requirement of Israel for the number of interceptors and batteries of such respective systems that will be procured, including with respect to the procurement plans, acquisition strategy, and funding profiles of Israel;

(III) technical milestones for coproduction of parts and components and procurement of such respective systems; and

(IV) joint approval processes for third-party sales of such respective systems and the components of such respective systems;

(iv) the level of coproduction described in clause (iii)(I) for the Arrow 3 Upper Tier Interceptor Program and the David's Sling Weapon System is not less than 50 percent; and

(v) of the funds specified in subparagraph (B) of paragraph (1), not more than $5,000,000 may be obligated or expended to cover costs related to any delays, including delays with respect to exchanging technical data or specifications, of the Arrow 3 Upper Tier Interceptor Program.

(B) NUMBER.—In carrying out subparagraph (A), the Under Secretary may submit—

(i) one certification covering both the David's Sling Weapon System and the Arrow 3 Upper Tier Interceptor Program; or

(ii) separate certifications for each respective system.

(C) TIMING.—The Under Secretary shall submit to the congressional defense committees the certification under subparagraph (A) by not later than 60 days before the funds specified in paragraph (1) for the respective system covered by the certification are provided to the Government of Israel.

(3) WAIVER.—The Under Secretary may waive the certification required by paragraph (2) if the Under Secretary certifies to the appropriate congressional committees that the Under Secretary has received sufficient data from the Government of Israel to demonstrate—

(A) the funds specified in subparagraphs (A) and (B) of paragraph (1) are provided to Israel solely for funding the procurement of long-lead components and critical hardware in accordance with a production plan, including a funding profile detailing Israeli contributions for production, including long-lead production, of either David's Sling Weapon System or the Arrow 3 Upper Tier Interceptor Program;

(B) such long-lead components have successfully completed knowledge points, technical milestones, and production readiness reviews; and

(C) the long-lead procurement will be conducted in a manner that maximizes coproduction in the United States without incurring nonrecurring engineering activity or cost other than such activity or cost required for suppliers of the United States to start or restart production in the United States.

(c) LIMITATION ON FUNDING FOR DAVID'S SLING WEAPON SYSTEM.—None of the amounts appropriated or otherwise made available pursuant to subsection (a)(1) of section 1679 of the National Defense Authorization Act for Fiscal Year 2016 (Public Law 114–92; 129 Stat. 1135) that remain available and are unobligated as of the date of the enactment of this Act may be obligated or expended until the appropriate congressional committees receive the plan required by subsection (d) of such section.

(d) APPROPRIATE CONGRESSIONAL COMMITTEES DEFINED.—In this section, the term "appropriate congressional committees" means the following:

(1) The congressional defense committees.

(2) The Committee on Foreign Affairs of the House of Representatives and the Committee on Foreign Relations of the Senate.

SEC. 1691. LIMITATIONS ON AVAILABILITY OF FUNDS FOR LOWER TIER AIR AND MISSILE DEFENSE CAPABILITY OF THE ARMY.

(a) LIMITATION.—Of the funds authorized to be appropriated by this Act or otherwise made available for fiscal year 2017 for lower tier missile defense capability (PE 0604114A) radar replacement, not more than 75 percent may be obligated or expended until each of the following occurs:

(1) The Director of the Missile Defense Agency, in coordination with the Chief of Staff of the Army, submits to the congressional defense committees a report on the manner in which the Director, acting as the technical integrating authority for air and missile defense, will ensure that the lower tier air and missile defense radar will meet the requirements of the commanders of the combatant commands for interoperability with the ballistic missile defense system and other air and missile defense capabilities deployed and planned to be deployed by the United States, including the establishment of key military requirements for such integrated capability and program development milestones.

(2) The Chairman of the Joint Chiefs of Staff—

(A) certifies to the congressional defense committees that the planned lower tier air and missile defense radar of the Army is being designed to fully support the required attributes for modularity sought by the commanders of the geographic combatant commands, including a description of such required attributes and the key milestones that will be used to ensure such modularity is achieved; and

(B) notifies the congressional defense committees of any objective requirements not met in the threshold requirement for the air and missile defense capability of the Army, including an assessment of any resulting capability gaps to military air and missile defense capability.

(b) ADDITIONAL LIMITATION.—In addition to the limitation in subsection (a), of the funds authorized to be appropriated by this Act or otherwise made available for fiscal year 2017 for lower tier missile defense capability (PE 0604114A) radar replacement, not more than 90 percent may be obligated or expended until the date on which the Chief of Staff of the Army, in coordination with the Secretary of the Army, submits to the congressional defense committees a determination regarding—

(1) whether the technology demonstration and knowledge points progression of the technology maturation and risk reduction phase of the lower tier air and missile defense radar acquisition program support a fair, full, and open acquisition program that can begin low-rate initial production earlier than 2021; and

(2) if such production can begin earlier than 2021, what steps the Chief of Staff is taking to achieve such an earlier production date.

(c) NOTIFICATION ON DELEGATION.—Not later than 30 days after the date of the enactment of this Act, the Under Secretary of Defense for Acquisition, Technology, and Logistics shall notify the congressional defense committees as to whether the Under Secretary will delegate to the Secretary of the Army the acquisition authority for the lower tier air and missile defense radar program of the Army.

(d) NOTIFICATION ON FUNDING.—Not later than 30 days after the completion of the technology demonstration phase of the lower tier air and missile defense radar acquisition program,

the Secretary of the Army shall notify the congressional defense committees whether the Secretary could carry out a reprogramming or transfer of funds previously authorized to be appropriated for another purpose (in accordance with established procedures for reprogramming or transfers) to meaningfully accelerate the acquisition program and, if so, how.

SEC. 1692. PILOT PROGRAM ON LOSS OF UNCLASSIFIED, CONTROLLED TECHNICAL INFORMATION.

(a) PILOT PROGRAM.—Beginning not later than 90 days after the date of the enactment of this Act, the Director of the Missile Defense Agency shall carry out a pilot program to implement improvements to the data protection options in the programs of the Missile Defense Agency (including the contractors of the Agency), particularly with respect to unclassified, controlled technical information and controlled unclassified information.

(b) PRIORITY.—In carrying out the pilot program under subsection (a), the Director shall give priority to implementing data protection options that are used by the private sector and have been proven successful.

(c) DURATION.—The Director shall carry out the pilot program under subsection (a) for not more than a 5-year period.

(d) NOTIFICATION.—Not later than 30 days before the date on which the Director commences the pilot program under subsection (a), the Director shall notify the congressional defense committees, the Committee on Oversight and Government Reform of the House of Representatives, and the Committee on Homeland Security and Governmental Affairs of the Senate of—

(1) the data protection options that the Director is considering to implement under the pilot program and the potential costs of such options; and

(2) such option that is the preferred option of the Director.

(e) DATA PROTECTION OPTIONS.—In this section, the term "data protection options" means actions to improve processes, practices, and systems that relate to the safeguarding, hygiene, and data protection of information.

SEC. 1693. PLAN FOR PROCUREMENT OF MEDIUM-RANGE DISCRIMINATION RADAR TO IMPROVE HOMELAND MISSILE DEFENSE.

(a) PLAN.—

(1) DEVELOPMENT.—The Director of the Missile Defense Agency shall develop a plan to—

(A) procure a medium-range discrimination radar or equivalent sensor for a location the Director determines will improve homeland missile defense for the defense of Hawaii from the limited ballistic missile threat (including accidental or unauthorized launch); and

(B) field such radar or equivalent sensor by not later than December 31, 2021.

(2) SUBMISSION.—Not later than 60 days after the date of the enactment of this Act, the Director shall submit to the congressional defense committees the plan developed under paragraph (1).

(b) REQUEST FOR PROPOSALS.—Not later than October 1, 2017, the Director shall issue a request for proposals for the medium-range discrimination radar or equivalent sensor specified in subsection (a)(1)(A).

SEC. 1694. REVIEW OF MISSILE DEFENSE AGENCY BUDGET SUBMISSIONS FOR GROUND-BASED MIDCOURSE DEFENSE AND EVALUATION OF ALTERNATIVE GROUND-BASED INTERCEPTOR DEPLOYMENTS.

(a) BUDGET SUFFICIENCY.—

(1) REPORT.—Not later than 180 days after the date of the enactment of this Act, the Director of Cost Assessment and Program Evaluation shall submit to the congressional defense committees a report on the ground-based midcourse defense system.

(2) ELEMENTS.—The report under paragraph (1) shall include an evaluation of each of the following:

(A) The modernization requirements for the ground-based midcourse system, including all command and control, ground systems, sensors and sensor interfaces, boosters and kill vehicles, and integration of known future systems and components.

(B) The obsolescence of such systems and components.

(C) The industrial base requirements relating to the ground-based midcourse system, as determined by the Director of the Missile Defense Agency.

(D) The extent to which the estimated levels of annual funding included in the most recent budget and the future-years defense program submitted under section 221 of title 10, United States Code, fully fund the requirements under subparagraph (A).

(3) UPDATES.—Not later than 30 days after the date on which each budget is submitted through January 31, 2021, the Director shall submit to the congressional defense committees an update to the report under paragraph (1).

(b) EVALUATION OF TRANSPORTABLE GROUND-BASED INTERCEPTOR.—Not later than 180 days after the date of the enactment of this Act, the Director of the Missile Defense Agency shall submit to the congressional defense committees a report on transportable ground-based interceptors. Such report shall detail the views of the Director regarding—

(1) the cost that is unconstrained by current projected budget levels for the Missile Defense Agency (including a detailed program development production and deployment cost and schedule for the earliest technically possible deployment), the associated manning, and the comparative cost (including as compared to developing a fixed ground-based interceptor site), technical readiness, and feasibility of a transportable ground-based interceptor as a means to deploy additional ground-based interceptors for the defense of the United States and the operational value of a transportable ground-based interceptor for the defense of the homeland against a limited ballistic missile attack, including from accidental or unauthorized ballistic missile launch;

(2) the type and number of flight and or intercept tests that would be required to validate the capability and compatibility of a transportable ground-based interceptor in the ballistic missile defense system;

(3) the enabling capabilities, and the cost of such capabilities, to support such a system;

(4) any safety consideration of a transportable ground-based interceptor; and

(5) other matters that the Director determines pertinent to such a system.

(c) FORM.—The report submitted under subsection (b) shall be submitted in unclassified form, but may include a classified annex.

(d) DEFINITIONS.—In this section, the terms "budget" and "defense budget materials" have the meanings given those terms in section 231 of title 10, United States Code.

SEC. 1695. SEMIANNUAL NOTIFICATIONS ON MISSILE DEFENSE TESTS AND COSTS.

(a) NOTIFICATIONS.—Not less than once every 180-day period beginning 90 days after the date of the enactment of this Act and ending on January 31, 2021, the Director of the Missile Defense Agency shall submit to the congressional defense committees a notification on—

(1) the outcome of each planned flight test, including intercept tests, occurring during the period covered by the notification; and

(2) flight tests, including intercept tests, planned to occur after the date of the notification.

(b) ELEMENTS.—Each notification shall include the following:

(1) With respect to each test described in subsection (a)(1)—

(A) the cost;

(B) any changes made to the scope or objectives of the test, or future tests, and an explanation for such changes;

(C) in the event of a failure of the test or a decision to delay or cancel the test—

(i) the reasons such test did not succeed or occur;

(ii) the funds expended on such attempted test; and

(iii) in the case of a test failure or cancelled test that is the result of contractor performance, the contractor liability, if appropriate, as compared to the cost of such test and potential retest; and

(D) the plan to conduct a retest, if necessary, and an estimate of the cost of such retest.

(2) With respect to each test described in subsection (a)(2)—

(A) any changes made to the scope of the test;

(B) whether the test was to occur earlier but was delayed; and

(C) an explanation for any such changes or delays.

(3) The status of any open failure review boards or any failure review boards completed during the period covered by the notification.

(c) FORM.—Each notification submitted under subsection (a) shall be submitted in unclassified form, but may include a classified annex.

SEC. 1696. REPORTS ON UNFUNDED PRIORITIES OF THE MISSILE DEFENSE AGENCY.

(a) REPORTS.—Not later than 10 days after the date on which the budget of the President for each of fiscal years 2018 and 2019 is submitted to Congress pursuant to section 1105 of title 31, United States Code, the Director of the Missile Defense Agency shall submit to the Secretary of Defense and the Chairman of the Joint Chiefs of Staff, and to the congressional defense committees, a report on the unfunded priorities of the Missile Defense Agency.

(b) ELEMENTS.—

(1) IN GENERAL.—Each report under subsection (a) shall specify, for each unfunded priority covered by such report, the following:

(A) A summary description of such priority, including the objectives to be achieved if such priority is funded (whether in whole or in part).

(B) The additional amount of funds recommended in connection with the objectives under subparagraph (A).

(C) Account information with respect to such priority, including the following (as applicable):

(i) Line Item Number (LIN) for applicable procurement accounts.

(ii) Program Element (PE) number for applicable research, development, test, and evaluation accounts.

(iii) Sub-activity group (SAG) for applicable operation and maintenance accounts.

(2) PRIORITIZATION OF PRIORITIES.—Each report under subsection (a) shall present the unfunded priorities covered by such report in order of urgency of priority.

(c) UNFUNDED PRIORITY DEFINED.—In this section, the term ''unfunded priority'', in the case of a fiscal year, means a program, activity, or mission requirement of the Missile Defense Agency that—

(1) is not funded in the budget of the President for the fiscal year as submitted to Congress pursuant to section 1105 of title 31, United States Code;

(2) is necessary to fulfill a requirement associated with an operational or contingency plan of a combatant command or other validated requirement; and

(3) would have been recommended for funding through the budget referred to in paragraph (1) by the Director of the Missile Defense Agency in connection with the budget if—

(A) additional resources had been available for the budget to fund the program, activity, or mission requirement; or

(B) the program, activity, or mission requirement has emerged since the budget was formulated.

Subtitle F—Other Matters

SEC. 1697. PROTECTION OF CERTAIN FACILITIES AND ASSETS FROM UNMANNED AIRCRAFT.

(a) IN GENERAL.—Chapter 3 of title 10, United States Code, is amended by adding at the end the following new section:

"§ 130i. Protection of certain facilities and assets from unmanned aircraft

''(a) AUTHORITY.—Notwithstanding any provision of title 18, the Secretary of Defense may take, and may authorize the armed forces to take, such actions described in subsection (b)(1) that are necessary to mitigate the threat (as defined by the Secretary of Defense, in consultation with the Secretary of Transportation) that an unmanned aircraft system or unmanned aircraft poses to the safety or security of a covered facility or asset.

''(b) ACTIONS DESCRIBED.—(1) The actions described in this paragraph are the following:

''(A) Detect, identify, monitor, and track the unmanned aircraft system or unmanned aircraft, without prior consent, including by means of intercept or other access of a wire, oral, or electronic communication used to control the unmanned aircraft system or unmanned aircraft.

''(B) Warn the operator of the unmanned aircraft system or unmanned aircraft, including by passive or active, and direct or indirect physical, electronic, radio, and electromagnetic means.

''(C) Disrupt control of the unmanned aircraft system or unmanned aircraft, without prior consent, including by disabling the unmanned aircraft system or unmanned aircraft by intercepting, interfering, or causing interference with wire, oral, electronic, or radio communications used to control the unmanned aircraft system or unmanned aircraft.

''(D) Seize or exercise control of the unmanned aircraft system or unmanned aircraft.

''(E) Seize or otherwise confiscate the unmanned aircraft system or unmanned aircraft.

''(F) Use reasonable force to disable, damage, or destroy the unmanned aircraft system or unmanned aircraft.

''(2) The Secretary of Defense shall develop the actions described in paragraph (1) in coordination with the Secretary of Transportation.

''(c) FORFEITURE.—Any unmanned aircraft system or unmanned aircraft described in subsection (a) that is seized by the Secretary of Defense is subject to forfeiture to the United States.

''(d) REGULATIONS.—The Secretary of Defense and the Secretary of Transportation may prescribe regulations and shall issue guidance in the respective areas of each Secretary to carry out this section.

''(e) DEFINITIONS.—In this section:

''(1) The term 'covered facility or asset' means any facility or asset that—

''(A) is identified by the Secretary of Defense for purposes of this section;

''(B) is located in the United States (including the territories and possessions of the United States); and

''(C) relates to—

''(i) the nuclear deterrence mission of the Department of Defense, including with respect to nuclear command and control, integrated tactical warning and attack assessment, and continuity of government;

''(ii) the missile defense mission of the Department; or

''(iii) the national security space mission of the Department.

''(2) The terms 'unmanned aircraft' and 'unmanned aircraft system' have the meanings given those terms in section 331 of the FAA Modernization and Reform Act of 2012 (Public Law 112–95; 49 U.S.C. 40101 note).''.

(b) CLERICAL AMENDMENT.—The table of sections at the beginning of such chapter is amended by inserting after the item relating to section 130h the following new item:

''130i. Protection of certain facilities and assets from unmanned aircraft.''.

SEC. 1698. HARMFUL INTERFERENCE TO DEPARTMENT OF DEFENSE GLOBAL POSITIONING SYSTEM.

(a) FEDERAL COMMUNICATIONS COMMISSION CONDITIONS ON COMMERCIAL TERRESTRIAL OPERATIONS.—Part I of title III of the Communications Act of 1934 (47 U.S.C. 301 et seq.) is amended by adding at the end the following:

"SEC. 343. CONDITIONS ON COMMERCIAL TERRESTRIAL OPERATIONS.

''(a) IN GENERAL.—The Commission shall not permit commercial terrestrial operations in the 1525–1559 megahertz band or the 1626.5–1660.5 megahertz band until the date that is 90 days after the Commission resolves concerns of widespread harmful interference by such operations in such band to covered GPS devices.

''(b) NOTICE TO CONGRESS.—

''(1) IN GENERAL.—At the conclusion of the decision regarding whether to permit such operations in such band, the Commission shall submit to the congressional committees described in paragraph (2) official copies of the documents containing the final decision of the Commission. If the decision is to permit such operations in such band, such documents shall contain or be accompanied by an explanation of how the concerns described in subsection (a) have been resolved.

''(2) CONGRESSIONAL COMMITTEES DESCRIBED.—The congressional committees described in this paragraph are the following:

''(A) The Committee on Energy and Commerce and the Committee on Armed Services of the House of Representatives.

''(B) The Committee on Commerce, Science, and Transportation and the Committee on Armed Services of the Senate.

''(c) COVERED GPS DEVICE DEFINED.—In this section, the term 'covered GPS device' means a Global Positioning System device of the Department of Defense.''.

(b) SECRETARY OF DEFENSE REVIEW OF HARMFUL INTERFERENCE.—

(1) REVIEW.—Not later than 90 days after the date of the enactment of this Act, and every 90 days thereafter until the date referred to in paragraph (3), the Secretary of Defense shall conduct a review to—

(A) assess the ability of covered GPS devices to receive signals from Global Positioning System satellites without widespread harmful interference; and

(B) determine if commercial communications services are causing or will cause widespread harmful interference with covered GPS devices.

(2) NOTICE TO CONGRESS.—

(A) NOTICE.—If the Secretary of Defense determines during a review under paragraph (1) that commercial communications services are causing or will cause widespread harmful interference with covered GPS devices, the Secretary shall promptly submit to the congressional defense committees notice of such interference.

(B) CONTENTS.—The notice required under subparagraph (A) shall include—

(i) a list and description of the covered GPS devices that are being or expected to be interfered with by commercial communications services;

(ii) a description of the source of, and the entity causing or expected to cause, the interference with such devices;

(iii) a description of the manner in which such source or such entity is causing or expected to cause such interference;

(iv) a description of the magnitude of harm caused or expected to be caused by such interference;

(v) a description of the duration of and the conditions and circumstances under which such interference is occurring or expected to occur;

(vi) a description of the impact of such interference on the national security interests of the United States; and

(vii) a description of the plans of the Secretary to address, alleviate, or mitigate such interference, including the cost of such plans.

(C) FORM.—The notice required under subparagraph (A) shall be submitted in unclassified form, but may include a classified annex.

(3) TERMINATION DATE.—The date referred to in this paragraph is the earlier of—

(A) the date that is two years after the date of the enactment of this Act; or

(B) the date on which the Secretary—

(i) determines that commercial communications services are not causing any widespread harmful interference with covered GPS devices; and

(ii) submits to the congressional defense committees notice of the determination made under clause (i).

(c) COVERED GPS DEVICE DEFINED.—In this section, the term "covered GPS device" means a Global Positioning System device of the Department of Defense.

(d) CONFORMING REPEAL.—Section 911 of the National Defense Authorization Act for Fiscal Year 2012 (Public Law 112–81; 125 Stat. 1534) is repealed.

TITLE XVII—GUAM WORLD WAR II LOYALTY RECOGNITION ACT

Sec. 1701. Short title.
Sec. 1702. Recognition of the suffering and loyalty of the residents of Guam.
Sec. 1703. Guam World War II Claims Fund.
Sec. 1704. Payments for Guam World War II claims.
Sec. 1705. Adjudication.
Sec. 1706. Grants program to memorialize the occupation of Guam during World War II.
Sec. 1707. Authorization of appropriations.

SEC. 1701. SHORT TITLE.

This title may be cited as the "Guam World War II Loyalty Recognition Act".

SEC. 1702. RECOGNITION OF THE SUFFERING AND LOYALTY OF THE RESIDENTS OF GUAM.

(a) RECOGNITION OF THE SUFFERING OF THE RESIDENTS OF GUAM.—The United States recognizes that, as described by the Guam War Claims Review Commission, the residents of Guam, on account of their United States nationality, suffered unspeakable harm as a result of the occupation of Guam by Imperial Japanese military forces during World War II, by being subjected to death, rape, severe personal injury, personal injury, forced labor, forced march, or internment.

(b) RECOGNITION OF THE LOYALTY OF THE RESIDENTS OF GUAM.—The United States forever will be grateful to the residents of Guam for their steadfast loyalty to the United States, as demonstrated by the countless acts of courage they performed despite the threat of death or great bodily harm they faced at the hands of the Imperial Japanese military forces that occupied Guam during World War II.

SEC. 1703. GUAM WORLD WAR II CLAIMS FUND.

(a) ESTABLISHMENT OF FUND.—The Secretary of the Treasury shall establish in the Treasury of the United States a special fund (in this title referred to as the "Claims Fund") for the payment of claims submitted by compensable Guam victims and survivors of compensable Guam decedents in accordance with sections 1704 and 1705.

(b) COMPOSITION OF FUND.—The Claims Fund established under subsection (a) shall be composed of amounts deposited into the Claims Fund under subsection (c) and any other payments made available for the payment of claims under this title.

(c) PAYMENT OF CERTAIN DUTIES, TAXES, AND FEES COLLECTED FROM GUAM DEPOSITED INTO FUND.—

(1) IN GENERAL.—Notwithstanding section 30 of the Organic Act of Guam (48 U.S.C. 1421h), the excess of—

(A) any amount of duties, taxes, and fees collected under such section after fiscal year 2014, over

(B) the amount of duties, taxes, and fees collected under such section during fiscal year 2014,

shall be deposited into the Claims Fund.

(2) APPLICATION.—Paragraph (1) shall not apply after the date for which the Secretary of the Treasury determines that all payments required to be made under section 1704 have been made.

(d) LIMITATION ON PAYMENTS MADE FROM FUND.—

(1) IN GENERAL.—No payment may be made in a fiscal year under section 1704 until funds are deposited into the Claims Fund in such fiscal year under subsection (c).

(2) AMOUNTS.—For each fiscal year in which funds are deposited into the Claims Fund under subsection (c), the total amount of payments made in a fiscal year under section 1704 may not exceed the amount of funds available in the Claims Fund for such fiscal year.

(e) DEDUCTIONS FROM FUND FOR ADMINISTRATIVE EXPENSES.—The Secretary of the Treasury shall deduct from any amounts deposited into the Claims Fund an amount equal to 5 percent of such amounts as reimbursement to the Federal Government for expenses incurred by the Foreign Claims Settlement Commission and by the Department of the Treasury in the administration of this title. The amounts so deducted shall be covered into the Treasury as miscellaneous receipts.

SEC. 1704. PAYMENTS FOR GUAM WORLD WAR II CLAIMS.

(a) PAYMENTS FOR DEATH, PERSONAL INJURY, FORCED LABOR, FORCED MARCH, AND INTERNMENT.—After the Secretary of the Treasury receives the certification from the Chairman of the Foreign Claims Settlement Commission as required under section 1705(b)(8), the Secretary of the Treasury shall make payments, subject to the availably of appropriations, to compensable Guam victims and survivors of a compensable Guam decedents as follows:

(1) COMPENSABLE GUAM VICTIM.—Before making any payments under paragraph (2), the Secretary shall make payments to compensable Guam victims as follows:

(A) In the case of a victim who has suffered an injury described in subsection (c)(2)(A), $15,000.

(B) In the case of a victim who is not described in subparagraph (A), but who has suffered an injury described in subsection (c)(2)(B), $12,000.

(C) In the case of a victim who is not described in subparagraph (A) or (B), but who has suffered an injury described in subsection (c)(2)(C), $10,000.

(2) SURVIVORS OF COMPENSABLE GUAM DECEDENTS.—In the case of a compensable Guam decedent, the Secretary shall pay $25,000 for distribution to survivors of the decedent in accordance with subsection (b). The Secretary shall make payments under this paragraph only after all payments are made under paragraph (1).

(b) DISTRIBUTION OF SURVIVOR PAYMENTS.—A payment made under subsection (a)(2) to the survivors of a compensable Guam decedent shall be distributed as follows:

(1) In the case of a decedent whose spouse is living as of the date of the enactment of this Act, but who had no living children as of such date, the payment shall be made to such spouse.

(2) In the case of a decedent whose spouse is living as of the date of the enactment of this Act and who had one or more living children as of such date, 50 percent of the payment shall be made to the spouse and 50 percent shall be made to such children, to be divided among such children to the greatest extent possible into equal shares.

(3) In the case of a decedent whose spouse is not living as of the date of the enactment of this Act and who had one or more living children as of such date, the payment shall be made to such children, to be divided among such children to the greatest extent possible into equal shares.

(4) In the case of a decedent whose spouse is not living as of the date of the enactment of this Act and who had no living children as of such date, but who—

(A) had a parent who is living as of such date, the payment shall be made to the parent; or

(B) had two parents who are living as of such date, the payment shall be divided equally between the parents.

(5) In the case of a decedent whose spouse is not living as of the date of the enactment of this Act, who had no living children as of such date, and who had no parents who are living as of such date, no payment shall be made.

(c) DEFINITIONS.—For purposes of this title:

(1) COMPENSABLE GUAM DECEDENT.—The term "compensable Guam decedent" means an individual determined under section 1705 to have been a resident of Guam who died as a result of the attack and occupation of Guam by Imperial Japanese military forces during World War II, or incident to the liberation of Guam by United States military forces, and whose death would have been compensable under the Guam Meritorious Claims Act of 1945 (Public Law 79–224) if a timely claim had been filed under the terms of such Act.

(2) COMPENSABLE GUAM VICTIM.—The term "compensable Guam victim" means an individual who is not deceased as of the date of the enactment of this Act and who is determined under section 1705 to have suffered, as a result of the attack and occupation of Guam by Imperial Japanese military forces during World War II, or incident to the liberation of Guam by United States military forces, any of the following:

(A) Rape or severe personal injury (such as loss of a limb, dismemberment, or paralysis).

(B) Forced labor or a personal injury not under subparagraph (A) (such as disfigurement, scarring, or burns).

(C) Forced march, internment, or hiding to evade internment.

(3) DEFINITIONS OF SEVERE PERSONAL INJURIES AND PERSONAL INJURIES.—Not later than 180 days after the date of the enactment of this Act, the Foreign Claims Settlement Commission shall promulgate regulations to specify the injuries that constitute a severe personal injury or a personal injury for purposes of subparagraphs (A) and (B), respectively, of paragraph (2).

SEC. 1705. ADJUDICATION.

(a) AUTHORITY OF FOREIGN CLAIMS SETTLEMENT COMMISSION.—

(1) IN GENERAL.—The Foreign Claims Settlement Commission shall adjudicate claims and determine the eligibility of individuals for payments under section 1704.

(2) RULES AND REGULATIONS.—Not later than 180 days after the date of the enactment of this Act, the Chairman of the Foreign Claims Settlement Commission shall publish in the Federal

Register such rules and regulations as may be necessary to enable the Commission to carry out the functions of the Commission under this title.

(b) CLAIMS SUBMITTED FOR PAYMENTS.—

(1) SUBMITTAL OF CLAIM.—For purposes of subsection (a)(1) and subject to paragraph (2), the Foreign Claims Settlement Commission may not determine an individual is eligible for a payment under section 1704 unless the individual submits to the Commission a claim in such manner and form and containing such information as the Commission specifies.

(2) FILING PERIOD FOR CLAIMS AND NOTICE.—

(A) FILING PERIOD.—An individual filing a claim for a payment under section 1704 shall file such claim not later than one year after the date on which the Foreign Claims Settlement Commission publishes the notice described in subparagraph (B).

(B) NOTICE OF FILING PERIOD.—Not later than 180 days after the date of the enactment of this Act, the Foreign Claims Settlement Commission shall publish a notice of the deadline for filing a claim described in subparagraph (A)—

(i) in the Federal Register; and

(ii) in newspaper, radio, and television media in Guam.

(3) ADJUDICATORY DECISIONS.—The decision of the Foreign Claims Settlement Commission on each claim filed under this title shall—

(A) be by majority vote;

(B) be in writing;

(C) state the reasons for the approval or denial of the claim; and

(D) if approved, state the amount of the payment awarded and the distribution, if any, to be made of the payment.

(4) DEDUCTIONS IN PAYMENT.—The Foreign Claims Settlement Commission shall deduct, from a payment made to a compensable Guam victim or survivors of a compensable Guam decedent under this section, amounts paid to such victim or survivors under the Guam Meritorious Claims Act of 1945 (Public Law 79–224) before the date of the enactment of this Act.

(5) INTEREST.—No interest shall be paid on payments made by the Foreign Claims Settlement Commission under section 1704.

(6) LIMITED COMPENSATION FOR PROVISION OF REPRESENTATIONAL SERVICES.—

(A) LIMIT ON COMPENSATION.—Any agreement under which an individual who provided representational services to an individual who filed a claim for a payment under this title that provides for compensation to the individual who provided such services in an amount that is more than one percent of the total amount of such payment shall be unlawful and void.

(B) PENALTIES.—Whoever demands or receives any compensation in excess of the amount allowed under subparagraph (A) shall be fined not more than $5,000 or imprisoned not more than one year, or both.

(7) APPEALS AND FINALITY.—Objections and appeals of decisions of the Foreign Claims Settlement Commission shall be to the Commission, and upon rehearing, the decision in each claim shall be final, and not subject to further review by any court or agency.

(8) CERTIFICATIONS FOR PAYMENT.—After a decision approving a claim becomes final, the Chairman of the Foreign Claims Settlement Commission shall certify such decision to the Secretary of the Treasury for authorization of a payment under section 1704.

(9) TREATMENT OF AFFIDAVITS.—For purposes of section 1704 and subject to paragraph (2), the Foreign Claims Settlement Commission shall treat a claim that is accompanied by an affidavit of an individual that attests to all of the material facts required for establishing the eligibility of such individual for payment under such section as establishing a prima facie case of the eligibility of the individual for such payment

without the need for further documentation, except as the Commission may otherwise require. Such material facts shall include, with respect to a claim for a payment made under section 1704(a), a detailed description of the injury or other circumstance supporting the claim involved, including the level of payment sought.

(10) RELEASE OF RELATED CLAIMS.—Acceptance of a payment under section 1704 by an individual for a claim related to a compensable Guam decedent or a compensable Guam victim shall be in full satisfaction of all claims related to such decedent or victim, respectively, arising under the Guam Meritorious Claims Act of 1945 (Public Law 79–224), the implementing regulations issued by the United States Navy pursuant to such Act (Public Law 79–224), or this title.

SEC. 1706. GRANTS PROGRAM TO MEMORIALIZE THE OCCUPATION OF GUAM DURING WORLD WAR II.

(a) ESTABLISHMENT.—Subject to subsection (b), the Secretary of the Interior shall establish a grant program under which the Secretary shall award grants for research, educational, and media activities for purposes of appropriately illuminating and interpreting the causes and circumstances of the occupation of Guam during World War II and other similar occupations during the war that—

(1) memorialize the events surrounding such occupation; or

(2) honor the loyalty of the people of Guam during such occupation.

(b) ELIGIBILITY.—The Secretary of the Interior may not award a grant under subsection (a) unless the person seeking the grant submits an application to the Secretary for such grant, in such time, manner, and form and containing such information as the Secretary specifies.

SEC. 1707. AUTHORIZATION OF APPROPRIATIONS.

(a) GUAM WORLD WAR II CLAIMS PAYMENTS AND ADJUDICATION.—For the purposes of carrying out sections 1704 and 1705, there is authorized to be appropriated for any fiscal year beginning after the date of enactment of this Act, an amount equal to the amount deposited into the Claims Fund in a fiscal year under section 1703. Not more than 5 percent of funds make available under this subsection shall be used for administrative costs. Amounts appropriated under this section may remain available until expended.

(b) GUAM WORLD WAR II GRANTS PROGRAM.—For purposes of carrying out section 1706, there are authorized to be appropriated $5,000,000 for each fiscal year beginning after the date of the enactment of this Act.

TITLE XVIII—MATTERS RELATING TO SMALL BUSINESS PROCUREMENT

Subtitle A—Improving Transparency and Clarity for Small Businesses

Sec. 1801. Plain language rewrite of requirements for small business procurements.

Sec. 1802. Transparency in small business goals.

Subtitle B—Clarifying the Roles of Small Business Advocates

Sec. 1811. Scope of review by procurement center representatives.

Sec. 1812. Duties of the Office of Small and Disadvantaged Business Utilization.

Sec. 1813. Improving contractor compliance.

Sec. 1814. Improving education on small business regulations.

Subtitle C—Strengthening Opportunities for Competition in Subcontracting

Sec. 1821. Good faith in subcontracting.

Sec. 1822. Pilot program to provide opportunities for qualified subcontractors to obtain past performance ratings.

Sec. 1823. Amendments to the Mentor-Protege Program of the Department of Defense.

Subtitle D—Miscellaneous Provisions

Sec. 1831. Improvements to size standards for small agricultural producers.

Sec. 1832. Uniformity in service-disabled veteran definitions.

Sec. 1833. Office of Hearings and Appeals.

Sec. 1834. Extension of SBIR and STTR programs.

Sec. 1835. Issuance of guidance on small business matters.

Subtitle E—Improving Cyber Preparedness for Small Businesses

Sec. 1841. Small Business Development Center Cyber Strategy and outreach.

Sec. 1842. Role of small business development centers in cybersecurity and preparedness.

Sec. 1843. Additional cybersecurity assistance for small business development centers.

Sec. 1844. Prohibition on additional funds.

Subtitle A—Improving Transparency and Clarity for Small Businesses

SEC. 1801. PLAIN LANGUAGE REWRITE OF REQUIREMENTS FOR SMALL BUSINESS PROCUREMENTS.

Section 15(a) of the Small Business Act (15 U.S.C. 644(a)) is amended to read as follows:

"(a) SMALL BUSINESS PROCUREMENTS.—

"(1) IN GENERAL.—For purposes of this Act, small business concerns shall receive any award or contract if such award or contract is, in the determination of the Administrator and the contracting agency, in the interest of—

"(A) maintaining or mobilizing the full productive capacity of the United States;

"(B) war or national defense programs; or

"(C) assuring that a fair proportion of the total purchase and contracts for goods and services of the Government in each industry category (as defined under paragraph (2)) are awarded to small business concerns.

"(2) INDUSTRY CATEGORY DEFINED.—

"(A) IN GENERAL.—In this subsection, the term 'industry category' means a discrete group of similar goods and services, as determined by the Administrator in accordance with the North American Industry Classification System codes used to establish small business size standards, except that the Administrator shall limit an industry category to a greater extent than provided under the North American Industry Classification System codes if the Administrator receives evidence indicating that further segmentation of the industry category is warranted—

"(i) due to special capital equipment needs;

"(ii) due to special labor requirements;

"(iii) due to special geographic requirements, except as provided in subparagraph (B);

"(iv) due to unique Federal buying patterns or requirements; or

"(v) to recognize a new industry.

"(B) EXCEPTION FOR GEOGRAPHIC REQUIREMENTS.—The Administrator may not further segment an industry category based on geographic requirements unless—

"(i) the Government typically designates the geographic area where work for contracts for goods or services is to be performed;

"(ii) Government purchases comprise the major portion of the entire domestic market for such goods or services; and

"(iii) it is unreasonable to expect competition from business concerns located outside of the general geographic area due to the fixed location of facilities, high mobilization costs, or similar economic factors.

"(3) DETERMINATIONS WITH RESPECT TO AWARDS OR CONTRACTS.—Determinations made pursuant to paragraph (1) may be made for individual awards or contracts, any part of an award or contract or task order, or for classes of awards or contracts or task orders.

"(4) INCREASING PRIME CONTRACTING OPPORTUNITIES FOR SMALL BUSINESS CONCERNS.—

"(A) DESCRIPTION OF COVERED PROPOSED PROCUREMENTS.—The requirements of this paragraph shall apply to a proposed procurement that includes in its statement of work goods or services currently being supplied or performed by a small business concern and, as determined by the Administrator—

"(i) is in a quantity or of an estimated dollar value which makes the participation of a small business concern as a prime contractor unlikely;

"(ii) in the case of a proposed procurement for construction, seeks to bundle or consolidate discrete construction projects; or

"(iii) is a solicitation that involves an unnecessary or unjustified bundling of contract requirements.

"(B) NOTICE TO PROCUREMENT CENTER REPRESENTATIVES.—With respect to proposed procurements described in subparagraph (A), at least 30 days before issuing a solicitation and concurrent with other processing steps required before issuing the solicitation, the contracting agency shall provide a copy of the proposed procurement to the procurement center representative of the contracting agency (as described in subsection (l)) along with a statement explaining—

"(i) why the proposed procurement cannot be divided into reasonably small lots (not less than economic production runs) to permit offers on quantities less than the total requirement;

"(ii) why delivery schedules cannot be established on a realistic basis that will encourage the participation of small business concerns in a manner consistent with the actual requirements of the Government;

"(iii) why the proposed procurement cannot be offered to increase the likelihood of the participation of small business concerns;

"(iv) in the case of a proposed procurement for construction, why the proposed procurement cannot be offered as separate discrete projects; or

"(v) why the contracting agency has determined that the bundling of contract requirements is necessary and justified.

"(C) ALTERNATIVES TO INCREASE PRIME CONTRACTING OPPORTUNITIES FOR SMALL BUSINESS CONCERNS.—If the procurement center representative believes that the proposed procurement will make the participation of small business concerns as prime contractors unlikely, the procurement center representative, within 15 days after receiving the statement described in subparagraph (B), shall recommend to the contracting agency alternative procurement methods for increasing prime contracting opportunities for small business concerns.

"(D) FAILURE TO AGREE ON AN ALTERNATIVE PROCUREMENT METHOD.—If the procurement center representative and the contracting agency fail to agree on an alternative procurement method, the Administrator shall submit the matter to the head of the appropriate department or agency for a determination.

"(5) CONTRACTS FOR SALE OF GOVERNMENT PROPERTY.—With respect to a contract for the sale of Government property, small business concerns shall receive any such contract if, in the determination of the Administrator and the disposal agency, the award of such contract is in the interest of assuring that a fair proportion of the total sales of Government property be made to small business concerns.

"(6) SALE OF ELECTRICAL POWER OR OTHER PROPERTY.—Nothing in this subsection shall be construed to change any preferences or priorities established by law with respect to the sale of electrical power or other property by the Federal Government.

"(7) COSTS EXCEEDING FAIR MARKET PRICE.—A contract may not be awarded under this sub- section if the cost of the contract to the awarding agency exceeds a fair market price.".*

SEC. 1802. TRANSPARENCY IN SMALL BUSINESS GOALS.

Section 15(h)(3) of the Small Business Act (15 U.S.C. 644(h)(3)) is amended to read as follows:

"(3) PROCUREMENT DATA.—

"(A) FEDERAL PROCUREMENT DATA SYSTEM.—

"(i) IN GENERAL.—To assist in the implementation of this section, the Administrator shall have access to information collected through the Federal Procurement Data System, Federal Subcontracting Reporting System, or any new or successor system.

"(ii) GSA REPORT.—On the date that the Administrator makes available the report required under paragraph (2), the Administrator of the General Services Administration shall submit to the President and Congress, and shall make available on a public website, a report in the same form and manner, and including the same information, as the report required under paragraph (2). The report shall include all procurements made for the period covered by the report and may not exclude any contract awarded.

"(B) AGENCY PROCUREMENT DATA SOURCES.—To assist in the implementation of this section, the head of each contracting agency shall provide, upon request of the Administrator, procurement information collected through agency data collection sources in existence at the time of the request. Contracting agencies shall not be required to establish new data collection systems to provide such data.".

Subtitle B—Clarifying the Roles of Small Business Advocates

SEC. 1811. SCOPE OF REVIEW BY PROCUREMENT CENTER REPRESENTATIVES.

(a) Section 15(l) of the Small Business Act (15 U.S.C. 644(l)) is amended by adding at the end the following new paragraph:

"(9) SCOPE OF REVIEW.—The Administrator—

"(A) may not limit the scope of review by the procurement center representative for any solicitation of a contract or task order without regard to whether the contract or task order or part of the contract or task order is set aside for small business concerns, whether 1 or more contracts or task order awards are reserved for small business concerns under a multiple award contract, or whether or not the solicitation would result in a bundled or consolidated contract (as defined in subsection (s)) or a bundled or consolidated task order; and

"(B) shall, unless the contracting agency requests a review, limit the scope of review by the procurement center representative for any solicitation of a contract or task order if such solicitation is awarded by or for the Department of Defense and—

"(i) is conducted pursuant to section 22 of the Arms Export Control Act (22 U.S.C. 2762);

"(ii) is a humanitarian operation as defined in section 401(e) of title 10, United States Code;

"(iii) is for a contingency operation, as defined in section 101(a)(13) of title 10, United States Code;

"(iv) is to be awarded pursuant to an agreement with the government of a foreign country in which Armed Forces of the United States are deployed; or

"(v) both the place of award and the place of performance are outside of the United States and its territories.".

(b) Section 15(g)(2)(B) of the Small Business Act (15 U.S.C. 644(g)(2)(B)) is amended by inserting after the period at the end the following new sentence: "Contracts excluded from review by procurement center representatives pursuant to subsection (l)(9)(B) shall not be considered when establishing these goals.".

SEC. 1812. DUTIES OF THE OFFICE OF SMALL AND DISADVANTAGED BUSINESS UTILIZATION.

Section 15(k) of the Small Business Act (15 U.S.C. 644(k)) is amended—

(1) by striking "section 8, 15 or 44" and inserting "section 8, 15, 31, 36, or 44";

(2) by striking "sections 8 and 15" each place such term appears and inserting "sections 8, 15, 31, 36, and 44";

(3) in paragraph (10), by striking "section 8(a)" and inserting "section 8, 15, 31, or 36";

(4) in paragraph (17)(C), by striking the period at the end and inserting a semicolon;

(5) by inserting after paragraph (17) the following new paragraph:

"(18) shall review summary data provided by purchase card issuers of purchases made by the agency greater than the micro-purchase threshold (as defined under section 1902 of title 41, United Stated Code) and less than the simplified acquisition threshold to ensure that the purchases have been made in compliance with the provisions of this Act and have been properly recorded in the Federal Procurement Data System, if the method of payment is a purchase card issued by the Department of Defense pursuant to section 2784 of title 10, United States Code, or by the head of an executive agency pursuant to section 1909 of title 41, United States Code;"; and

(6) in paragraph (16)—

(A) in subparagraph (B), by striking "and" at the end; and

(B) by adding at the end the following new subparagraph:

"(D) any failure of the agency to comply with section 8, 15, 31, or 36;".

SEC. 1813. IMPROVING CONTRACTOR COMPLIANCE.

(a) REQUIREMENTS FOR THE OFFICE OF SMALL AND DISADVANTAGED BUSINESS UTILIZATION.—Section 15(k) of the Small Business Act (15 U.S.C. 644(k)(8)), as amended by this Act, is further amended by inserting after paragraph (18) (as inserted by section 1812 of this Act) the following new paragraph:

"(19) shall provide assistance to a small business concern awarded a contract or subcontract under this Act or under title 10 or title 41, United States Code, in finding resources for education and training on compliance with contracting regulations (including the Federal Acquisition Regulation) after award of such a contract or subcontract; and".

(b) REQUIREMENTS UNDER THE MENTOR-PROTEGE PROGRAM OF THE DEPARTMENT OF DEFENSE.—Section 831(e)(1) of the National Defense Authorization Act for Fiscal Year 1991 (Public Law 101–510; 104 Stat. 1607; 10 U.S.C. 2302 note) is amended—

(1) in subparagraph (B), by striking "and" at the end;

(2) in subparagraph (C), by striking the period at the end and inserting "; and"; and

(3) by adding at the end the following new subparagraph:

"(D) the assistance the mentor firm will provide to the protege firm in understanding contract regulations of the Federal Government and the Department of Defense (including the Federal Acquisition Regulation and the Defense Federal Acquisition Regulation Supplement) after award of a subcontract under this section, if applicable.".

(c) RESOURCES FOR SMALL BUSINESS CONCERNS.—Section 15 of the Small Business Act (15 U.S.C. 644) is amended by adding at the end the following new subsection:

"(u) POST-AWARD COMPLIANCE RESOURCES.—The Administrator shall provide to small business development centers and entities participating in the Procurement Technical Assistance Cooperative Agreement Program under chapter 142 of title 10, United States Code, and shall make available on the website of the Administration, a list of resources for small business concerns seeking education and assistance on compliance with contracting regulations (including the Federal Acquisition Regulation) after award of a contract or subcontract.".

(d) REQUIREMENTS FOR PROCUREMENT CENTER REPRESENTATIVES.—Section 15(l)(2) of the Small Business Act (15 U.S.C. 644(l)(2)) is amended—

(1) by redesignating subparagraph (I) as subparagraph (J);

(2) in subparagraph (H), by striking "and" at the end; and

(3) by inserting after subparagraph (H) the following new subparagraph:

"(I) assist small business concerns with finding resources for education and training on compliance with contracting regulations (including the Federal Acquisition Regulation) after award of a contract or subcontract; and".

(e) REQUIREMENTS UNDER THE MENTOR-PROTEGE PROGRAM OF THE SMALL BUSINESS ADMINISTRATION.—Section 45(b)(3) of the Small Business Act (15 U.S.C. 657r(b)(3)) is amended by adding at the end the following new subparagraph:

"(K) The types of assistance provided by a mentor to assist with compliance with the requirements of contracting with the Federal Government after award of a contract or subcontract under this section.".

SEC. 1814. IMPROVING EDUCATION ON SMALL BUSINESS REGULATIONS.

(a) REGULATORY CHANGES AND TRAINING MATERIALS.—Section 15 of the Small Business Act (15 U.S.C. 644), as amended by section 1813, is further amended by adding at the end the following new subsection:

"*(v) REGULATORY CHANGES AND TRAINING MATERIALS.*—Not less than annually, the Administrator shall provide to the Defense Acquisition University (established under section 1746 of title 10, United States Code), the Federal Acquisition Institute (established under section 1201 of title 41, United States Code), the individual responsible for mandatory training and education of the acquisition workforce of each agency (described under section 1703(f)(1)(C) of title 41, United States Code), small business development centers, and entities participating in the Procurement Technical Assistance Cooperative Agreement Program under chapter 142 of title 10, United States Code—

"(1) a list of all changes made in the prior year to regulations promulgated—

"(A) by the Administrator that affect Federal acquisition; and

"(B) by the Federal Acquisition Council that implement amendments to this Act; and

"(2) any materials the Administrator has developed that explain, train, or assist Federal agencies or departments or small business concerns with compliance with the regulations described in paragraph (1).".

(b) TRAINING TO BE UPDATED.—After receipt of information from the Administrator of the Small Business Administration pursuant to section 15(v) of the Small Business Act, the Defense Acquisition University (established under section 1746 of title 10, United States Code) and the Federal Acquisition Institute (established under section 1201 of title 41, United States Code) shall periodically update the training provided to the acquisition workforce to incorporate such information.

Subtitle C—Strengthening Opportunities for Competition in Subcontracting

SEC. 1821. GOOD FAITH IN SUBCONTRACTING.

(a) TRANSPARENCY IN SUBCONTRACTING GOALS.—Section 8(d)(9) of the Small Business Act (15 U.S.C. 637(d)(9)) is amended—

(1) by striking "(9) The failure" and inserting the following:

"(9) MATERIAL BREACH.—The failure";

(2) in subparagraph (A), by striking "or" at the end;

(3) in subparagraph (B), by inserting "or" at the end;

(4) by inserting after subparagraph (B) the following new subparagraph:

"(C) assurances provided under paragraph (6)(E),"; and

(5) by moving the margins of subparagraphs (A) and (B), and the matter after subparagraph (C) (as inserted by paragraph (4)), 2 ems to the right.

(b) REVIEW OF SUBCONTRACTING PLANS.—Section 15(k) of the Small Business Act (15 U.S.C. 644(k)) as amended by this Act, is further amended by inserting after paragraph (19) (as inserted by section 1813 of this Act) the following new paragraph:

"(20) shall review all subcontracting plans required by paragraph (4) or (5) of section 8(d) to ensure that the plan provides maximum practicable opportunity for small business concerns to participate in the performance of the contract to which the plan applies.".

(c) GOOD FAITH COMPLIANCE.—Not later than 270 days after the date of enactment of this title, the Administrator of the Small Business Administration shall provide examples of activities that would be considered a failure to make a good faith effort to comply with the requirements imposed on an entity (other than a small business concern as defined under section 3 of the Small Business Act (15 U.S.C. 632)) that is awarded a prime contract containing the clauses required under paragraph (4) or (5) of section 8(d) of the Small Business Act (15 U.S.C. 637(d)).

SEC. 1822. PILOT PROGRAM TO PROVIDE OPPORTUNITIES FOR QUALIFIED SUBCONTRACTORS TO OBTAIN PAST PERFORMANCE RATINGS.

Section 8(d) of the Small Business Act (15 U.S.C. 637(d)) is amended by adding at the end the following new paragraph:

"(17) PILOT PROGRAM PROVIDING PAST PERFORMANCE RATINGS FOR OTHER SMALL BUSINESS SUBCONTRACTORS.—

"(A) ESTABLISHMENT.—The Administrator shall establish a pilot program for a small business concern without a past performance rating as a prime contractor performing as a first tier subcontractor for a covered contract (as defined in paragraph 13(A)) to request a past performance rating in the system used by the Federal Government to monitor or record contractor past performance.

"(B) APPLICATION.—A small business concern described in subparagraph (A) shall submit an application to the appropriate official for a past performance rating no later than 270 days after the small business concern completed the work for which it seeks a past performance rating or 180 days after the prime contractor completes work on the covered contract, whichever is earlier. Such application shall include written evidence of the past performance factors for which the small business concern seeks a rating and a suggested rating.

"(C) DETERMINATION.—The appropriate official shall submit the application from the small business concern to the Office of Small and Disadvantaged Business Utilization for the covered contract and to the prime contractor for review. The Office of Small and Disadvantaged Business Utilization and the prime contractor shall, not later than 30 days after receipt of the application, submit to the appropriate official a response regarding the application.

"(i) AGREEMENT ON RATING.—If the Office of Small and Disadvantaged Business Utilization and the prime contractor agree on a past performance rating, or if either the Office of Small and Disadvantaged Business Utilization or the prime contractor fail to respond and the responding person agrees with the rating of the applicant small business concern, the appropriate official shall enter the agreed-upon past performance rating in the system described in subparagraph (A).

"(ii) DISAGREEMENT ON RATING.—If the Office of Small and Disadvantaged Business Utiliza-

tion and the prime contractor fail to respond within 30 days or if they disagree about the rating, or if either the Office of Small and Disadvantaged Business Utilization or the prime contractor fail to respond and the responding person disagrees with the rating of the applicant small business concern, the Office of Small and Disadvantaged Business Utilization or the prime contractor shall submit a notice contesting the application to the appropriate official. The appropriate official shall follow the requirements of subparagraph (D).

"(D) PROCEDURE FOR RATING.—Not later than 14 calendar days after receipt of a notice under subparagraph (C)(ii), the appropriate official shall submit such notice to the applicant small business concern. Such concern may submit comments, rebuttals, or additional information relating to the past performance of such concern not later 14 calendar days after receipt of such notice. The appropriate official shall enter into the system described in subparagraph (A) a rating that is neither favorable nor unfavorable along with the initial application from such concern, any responses of the Office of Small and Disadvantaged Business Utilization and the prime contractor, and any additional information provided by such concern. A copy of the information submitted shall be provided to the contracting officer (or designee of such officer) for the covered contract.

"(E) USE OF INFORMATION.—A small business subcontractor may use a past performance rating given under this paragraph to establish its past performance for a prime contract.

"(F) DURATION.—The pilot program established under this paragraph shall terminate 3 years after the date on which the first applicant small business concern receives a past performance rating for performance as a first tier subcontractor.

"(G) REPORT.—The Comptroller General of the United States shall begin an assessment of the pilot program 1 year after the establishment of such program. Not later than 6 months after beginning such assessment, the Comptroller General shall submit a report to the Committee on Small Business and Entrepreneurship of the Senate and the Committee on Small Business of the House of Representatives, which shall include—

"(i) the number of small business concerns that have received past performance ratings under the pilot program;

"(ii) the number of applications in which the contracting officer (or designee) or the prime contractor contested the application of the small business concern;

"(iii) any suggestions or recommendations the Comptroller General or the small business concerns participating in the program have to address disputes between the small business concern, the contracting officer (or designee), and the prime contractor on past performance ratings;

"(iv) the number of small business concerns awarded prime contracts after receiving a past performance rating under this pilot program; and

"(v) any suggestions or recommendation the Comptroller General has to improve the operation of the pilot program.

"(H) APPROPRIATE OFFICIAL DEFINED.—In this paragraph, the term 'appropriate official' means—

"(i) a commercial market representative;

"(ii) another individual designated by the senior official appointed by the Administrator with responsibilities under sections 8, 15, 31, and 36; or

"(iii) the Office of Small and Disadvantaged Business Utilization of a Federal agency, if the head of the Federal agency and the Administrator agree.".

SEC. 1823. AMENDMENTS TO THE MENTOR-PRO-TEGE PROGRAM OF THE DEPART-MENT OF DEFENSE.

Section 831 of the National Defense Authorization Act for Fiscal Year 1991 (Public Law 101–510; 104 Stat. 1607; 10 U.S.C. 2302 note) is amended—

(1) by amending subsection (d) to read as follows:

"(d) MENTOR FIRM ELIGIBILITY.—

"(1) Subject to subsection (c)(1), a mentor firm may enter into an agreement with one or more protege firms under subsection (e) and provide assistance under the program pursuant to that agreement if the mentor firm—

"(A) is eligible for award of Federal contracts; and

"(B) demonstrates that it—

"(i) is qualified to provide assistance that will contribute to the purpose of the program;

"(ii) is of good financial health and character and does not appear on a Federal list of debarred or suspended contractors; and

"(iii) can impart value to a protege firm because of experience gained as a Department of Defense contractor or through knowledge of general business operations and government contracting, as demonstrated by evidence that—

"(I) during the fiscal year preceding the fiscal year in which the mentor firm enters into the agreement, the total amount of the Department of Defense contracts awarded such mentor firm and the subcontracts awarded such mentor firm under Department of Defense contracts was equal to or greater than $100,000,000; or

"(II) the mentor firm demonstrates the capability to assist in the development of protege firms, and is approved by the Secretary of Defense pursuant to criteria specified in the regulations prescribed pursuant to subsection (k).

"(2) A mentor firm may not enter into an agreement with a protege firm if the Administrator of the Small Business Administration has made a determination finding affiliation between the mentor firm and the protege firm.

"(3) If the Administrator of the Small Business Administration has not made such a determination and if the Secretary has reason to believe (based on the regulations promulgated by the Administrator regarding affiliation) that the mentor firm is affiliated with the protege firm, the Secretary shall request a determination regarding affiliation from the Administrator of the Small Business Administration.";

(2) in subsection (n), by amending paragraph (9) to read as follows:

"(9) The term 'affiliation', with respect to a relationship between a mentor firm and a protege firm, means a relationship described under section 121.103 of title 13, Code of Federal Regulations (or any successor regulation).''; and

(3) in subsection (f)(6)—

(A) in subparagraph (B), by striking "or" at the end;

(B) in subparagraph (C), by striking the period at the end and inserting "; or"; and

(C) by adding at the end the following new subparagraph:

"(D) women's business centers described in section 29 of the Small Business Act (15 U.S.C. 656).''.

Subtitle D—Miscellaneous Provisions

SEC. 1831. IMPROVEMENTS TO SIZE STANDARDS FOR SMALL AGRICULTURAL PRODUCERS.

(a) AMENDMENT TO DEFINITION OF AGRICULTURAL ENTERPRISES.—Paragraph (1) of section 18(b) of the Small Business Act (15 U.S.C. 647(b)(1)) is amended by striking "businesses" and inserting "small business concerns".

(b) EQUAL TREATMENT OF SMALL FARMS.—Paragraph (1) of section 3(a) of the Small Business Act (15 U.S.C. 632(a)(1)) is amended by striking "operation: Provided," and all that follows through the period at the end and inserting "operation.''.

(c) UPDATED SIZE STANDARDS.—Size standards established for agricultural enterprises under section 3(a) of the Small Business Act (15 U.S.C. 632(a)) shall be subject to the rolling review procedures established under section 1344(a) of the Small Business Jobs Act of 2010 (15 U.S.C. 632 note).

SEC. 1832. UNIFORMITY IN SERVICE-DISABLED VETERAN DEFINITIONS.

(a) SMALL BUSINESS DEFINITION OF SMALL BUSINESS CONCERN CONSOLIDATED.—Section 3(q) of the Small Business Act (15 U.S.C. 632(q)) is amended—

(1) by amending paragraph (2) to read as follows:

"(2) SMALL BUSINESS CONCERN OWNED AND CONTROLLED BY SERVICE-DISABLED VETERANS.—The term 'small business concern owned and controlled by service-disabled veterans' means any of the following:

"(A) A small business concern—

"(i) not less than 51 percent of which is owned by one or more service-disabled veterans or, in the case of any publicly owned business, not less than 51 percent of the stock (not including any stock owned by an ESOP) of which is owned by one or more service-disabled veterans; and

"(ii) the management and daily business operations of which are controlled by one or more service-disabled veterans or, in the case of a veteran with permanent and severe disability, the spouse or permanent caregiver of such veteran.

"(B) A small business concern—

"(i) not less than 51 percent of which is owned by one or more service-disabled veterans with a disability that is rated by the Secretary of Veterans Affairs as a permanent and total disability who are unable to manage the daily business operations of such concern; or

"(ii) in the case of a publicly owned business, not less than 51 percent of the stock (not including any stock owned by an ESOP) of which is owned by one or more such veterans.

"(C)(i) During the time period described in clause (ii), a small business concern that was a small business concern described in subparagraph (A) or (B) immediately prior to the death of a service-disabled veteran who was the owner of the concern, the death of whom causes the concern to be less than 51 percent owned by one or more service-disabled veterans, if—

"(I) the surviving spouse of the deceased veteran acquires such veteran's ownership interest in such concern;

"(II) such veteran had a service-connected disability (as defined in section 101(16) of title 38, United States Code) rated as 100 percent disabling under the laws administered by the Secretary of Veterans Affairs or such veteran died as a result of a service-connected disability; and

"(III) immediately prior to the death of such veteran, and during the period described in clause (ii), the small business concern is included in the database described in section 8127(f) of title 38, United States Code.

"(ii) The time period described in this clause is the time period beginning on the date of the veteran's death and ending on the earlier of—

"(I) the date on which the surviving spouse remarries;

"(II) the date on which the surviving spouse relinquishes an ownership interest in the small business concern; or

"(III) the date that is 10 years after the date of the death of the veteran."; and

(2) by adding at the end the following new paragraphs:

"(6) ESOP.—The term 'ESOP' has the meaning given the term 'employee stock ownership plan' in section 4975(e)(7) of the Internal Revenue Code of 1986 (26 U.S.C. 4975(e)(7)).

"(7) SURVIVING SPOUSE.—The term 'surviving spouse' has the meaning given such term in section 101(3) of title 38, United States Code.''.

(b) VETERANS AFFAIRS DEFINITION OF SMALL BUSINESS CONCERN CONSOLIDATED.—

(1) IN GENERAL.—Section 8127 of title 38, United States Code, is amended—

(A) by striking subsection (h) and redesignating subsections (i) through (l) as subsections (h) through (k), respectively; and

(B) in subsection (k), as so redesignated—

(i) by amending paragraph (2) to read as follows:

"(2) The term 'small business concern owned and controlled by veterans' has the meaning given that term under section 3(q)(3) of the Small Business Act (15 U.S.C. 632(q)(3)).''; and

(ii) by adding at the end the following new paragraph:

"(3) The term 'small business concern owned and controlled by veterans with service-connected disabilities' has the meaning given the term 'small business concern owned and controlled by service-disabled veterans' under section 3(q)(2) of the Small Business Act (15 U.S.C. 632(q)(2)).''.

(2) CONFORMING AMENDMENTS.—Such section is further amended—

(A) in subsection (b), by inserting "or a small business concern owned and controlled by veterans with service-connected disabilities" after "a small business concern owned and controlled by veterans";

(B) in subsection (c), by inserting "or a small business concern owned and controlled by veterans with service-connected disabilities" after "a small business concern owned and controlled by veterans";

(C) in subsection (d) by inserting "or small business concerns owned and controlled by veterans with service-connected disabilities" after "small business concerns owned and controlled by veterans" both places it appears; and

(D) in subsection (f)(1), by inserting ", small business concerns owned and controlled by veterans with service-connected disabilities," after "small business concerns owned and controlled by veterans".

(c) TECHNICAL CORRECTION.—Section 8(d)(3) of the Small Business Act (15 U.S.C. 637(d)(3)), is amended by adding at the end the following new subparagraph:

"(H) In this contract, the term 'small business concern owned and controlled by service-disabled veterans' has the meaning given that term in section 3(q).''.

(d) REGULATIONS RELATING TO DATABASE OF THE SECRETARY OF VETERANS AFFAIRS.—

(1) REQUIREMENT TO USE CERTAIN SMALL BUSINESS ADMINISTRATION REGULATIONS.—Section 8127(f)(4) of title 38, United States Code, is amended by striking "verified" and inserting "verified, using regulations issued by the Administrator of the Small Business Administration with respect to the status of the concern as a small business concern and the ownership and control of such concern,''.

(2) PROHIBITION ON SECRETARY OF VETERANS AFFAIRS ISSUING CERTAIN REGULATIONS.—Section 8127(f) of title 38, United States Code, is amended by adding at the end the following new paragraph:

"(7) The Secretary may not issue regulations related to the status of a concern as a small business concern and the ownership and control of such small business concern.''.

(e) DELAYED EFFECTIVE DATE.—The amendments made by subsections (a), (b), (c), and (d) shall take effect on the date on which the Administrator of the Small Business Administration and the Secretary of Veterans Affairs jointly issue regulations implementing such sections.

(f) APPEALS OF INCLUSION IN DATABASE.—

(1) IN GENERAL.—Section 8127(f) of title 38, United States Code, as amended by this section, is further amended by adding at the end the following new paragraph:

"(8)(A) If a small business concern is not included in the database because the Secretary does not verify the status of the concern as a small business concern or the ownership or control of the concern, the concern may appeal the denial of verification to the Office of Hearings and Appeals of the Small Business Administration (as established under section 5(i) of the Small Business Act). The decision of the Office of Hearings and Appeals shall be considered a final agency action.

"(B)(i) If an interested party challenges the inclusion in the database of a small business concern owned and controlled by veterans or a small business concern owned and controlled by veterans with service-connected disabilities based on the status of the concern as a small business concern or the ownership or control of the concern, the challenge shall be heard by the Office of Hearings and Appeals of the Small Business Administration as described in subparagraph (A). The decision of the Office of Hearings and Appeals shall be considered final agency action.

"(ii) In this subparagraph, the term 'interested party' means—

"(I) the Secretary; or

"(II) in the case of a small business concern that is awarded a contract, the contracting officer of the Department or another small business concern that submitted an offer for the contract that was awarded to the small business concern that is the subject of a challenge made under clause (i).

"(C) For each fiscal year, the Secretary shall reimburse the Administrator of the Small Business Administration in an amount necessary to cover any cost incurred by the Office of Hearings and Appeals of the Small Business Administration for actions taken by the Office under this paragraph. The Administrator is authorized to accept such reimbursement. The amount of any such reimbursement shall be determined jointly by the Secretary and the Administrator and shall be provided from fees collected by the Secretary under multiple-award schedule contracts. Any disagreement about the amount shall be resolved by the Director of the Office of Management and Budget.".

(2) EFFECTIVE DATE.—Paragraph (8) of subsection (f) of title 38, United States Code, as added by paragraph (1), shall apply with respect to a verification decision made by the Secretary of Veterans Affairs on or after the date of the enactment of this Act.

SEC. 1833. OFFICE OF HEARINGS AND APPEALS.

(a) CLARIFICATION AS TO JURISDICTION.—Section 5(i)(1)(B) of the Small Business Act (15 U.S.C. 634(i)(1)(B)) is amended to read as follows:

"(B) JURISDICTION.—

"(i) IN GENERAL.—Except as provided in clause (ii), the Office of Hearings and Appeals shall hear appeals of agency actions under or pursuant to this Act, the Small Business Investment Act of 1958 (15 U.S.C. 661 et seq.), and title 13 of the Code of Federal Regulations, and shall hear such other matters as the Administrator may determine appropriate.

"(ii) EXCEPTION.—The Office of Hearings and Appeals shall not adjudicate disputes that require a hearing on the record, except disputes pertaining to the small business programs described in this Act.".

(b) NEW RULES OR GUIDANCE FOR PETITIONS FOR RECONSIDERATION.—Section 3(a)(9) of the Small Business Act (15 U.S.C. 632(a)(9)) is amended by adding at the end the following new subparagraph:

"(E) RULES OR GUIDANCE.—The Office of Hearings and Appeals shall begin accepting petitions for reconsideration described in subparagraph (A) after the date on which the Administration issues a rule or other guidance implementing this paragraph. Notwithstanding the provisions of subparagraph (B), petitions for reconsideration of size standards revised, modified, or established in a Federal Register final rule published between November 25, 2015, and the effective date of such rule or other guidance shall be considered timely if filed within 30 days of such effective date.".

SEC. 1834. EXTENSION OF SBIR AND STTR PROGRAMS.

(a) SBIR.—Section 9(m) of the Small Business Act (15 U.S.C. 638(m)) is amended by striking "September 30, 2017" and inserting "September 30, 2022".

(b) STTR.—Section 9(n)(1) of the Small Business Act (15 U.S.C. 638(n)(1)) is amended by striking "fiscal year 2017" and inserting "fiscal year 2022".

SEC. 1835. ISSUANCE OF GUIDANCE ON SMALL BUSINESS MATTERS.

Not later than 180 days after the date of enactment of this Act, the Administrator of the Small Business Administration and the Secretary of Veterans Affairs shall issue guidance pertaining to the amendments made by this title to the Small Business Act and section 8127 of title 38, United States Code. The Administrator and the Secretary shall provide notice and opportunity for comment on such guidance for a period of not less than 60 days.

Subtitle E—Improving Cyber Preparedness for Small Businesses

SEC. 1841. SMALL BUSINESS DEVELOPMENT CENTER CYBER STRATEGY AND OUTREACH.

(a) SMALL BUSINESS DEVELOPMENT CENTER CYBER STRATEGY.—

(1) IN GENERAL.—Not later than 180 days after the date of the enactment of this Act, the Administrator of the Small Business Administration and the Secretary of Homeland Security shall work collaboratively to develop a cyber strategy for small business development centers to be known as the "Small Business Development Center Cyber Strategy".

(2) CONSULTATION.—In developing the strategy under this subsection, the Administrator of the Small Business Administration and the Secretary of Homeland Security shall consult with entities representing the concerns of small business development centers, including any association recognized under section 21(a)(3)(A) of the Small Business Act (15 U.S.C. 648(a)(3)(A)).

(3) CONTENT.—The strategy required under paragraph (1) shall include, at minimum, the following:

(A) Plans for allowing small business development centers (hereinafter in this paragraph referred to as "SBDCs") to access existing cyber programs of the Department of Homeland Security and other appropriate Federal agencies to enhance services and streamline cyber assistance to small business concerns.

(B) To the extent practicable, methods for providing counsel and assistance to improve a small business concern's cybersecurity infrastructure, awareness of cyber threat indicators, and cyber training programs for employees, including—

(i) working to ensure individuals are aware of best practices in the areas of cybersecurity, awareness of cyber threat indicators, and cyber training;

(ii) working with individuals to develop cost-effective plans for implementing best practices in these areas;

(iii) entering into agreements, where practical, with Information Sharing and Analysis Centers or similar entities that share cyber information to gain an awareness of actionable cyber threat indicators that may be beneficial to small business concerns; and

(iv) providing referrals to area specialists when necessary.

(C) An analysis of—

(i) how Federal Government programs, projects, and activities can be leveraged by SBDCs to improve access to high-quality cyber support for small business concerns;

(ii) additional resources SBDCs may need to effectively carry out their role; and

(iii) how SBDCs can leverage existing partnerships and develop new partnerships with Federal, State, and local government entities as well as private entities to improve the quality of cyber support services to small business concerns.

(4) DELIVERY OF STRATEGY.—Not later than 1 year after the date of the enactment of this Act, the Small Business Administrator and the Secretary of Homeland Security shall submit to the Committees on Homeland Security and Small Business of the House of Representatives and the Committees on Homeland Security and Governmental Affairs and Small Business and Entrepreneurship of the Senate the Small Business Development Center Cyber Strategy developed under paragraph (1).

(5) DEFINITIONS.—In this subsection, the following definitions shall apply:

(A) CYBER THREAT INDICATOR.—The term "cyber threat indicator" has the meaning given such term in section 227(a) of the Homeland Security Act of 2002 (6 U.S.C. 148(a)).

(B) SMALL BUSINESS DEVELOPMENT CENTER.—The term "small business development center" has the meaning given such term in section 3 of the Small Business Act (15 U.S.C. 632).

(b) CYBERSECURITY OUTREACH FOR SMALL BUSINESS DEVELOPMENT CENTERS.—Section 227 of the Homeland Security Act of 2002 (6 U.S.C. 148) is amended—

(1) by redesignating subsection (l) as subsection (m); and

(2) by inserting after subsection (k) the following new subsection:

"(l) CYBERSECURITY OUTREACH.—

"(1) IN GENERAL.—The Secretary may leverage small business development centers to provide assistance to small business concerns by disseminating information on cyber threat indicators, defense measures, cybersecurity risks, incidents, analyses, and warnings to help small business concerns in developing or enhancing cybersecurity infrastructure, awareness of cyber threat indicators, and cyber training programs for employees.

"(2) DEFINITIONS.—For purposes of this subsection, the terms 'small business concern' and 'small business development center' have the meaning given such terms, respectively, under section 3 of the Small Business Act.".

SEC. 1842. ROLE OF SMALL BUSINESS DEVELOPMENT CENTERS IN CYBERSECURITY AND PREPAREDNESS.

Section 21 of the Small Business Act (15 U.S.C. 648) is amended—

(1) in subsection (a)(1), by striking "and providing access to business analysts who can refer small business concerns to available experts:" and inserting "providing access to business analysts who can refer small business concerns to available experts; and, to the extent practicable, providing assistance in furtherance of the Small Business Development Center Cyber Strategy developed under section 1841(a) of the National Defense Authorization Act for Fiscal Year 2017:"; and

(2) in subsection (c)(2)—

(A) in subparagraph (E), by striking "and" at the end;

(B) in subparagraph (F), by striking the period at the end and inserting "; and"; and

(C) by adding at the end of the following new subparagraph:

"(G) access to cybersecurity specialists to counsel, assist, and inform small business concern clients, in furtherance of the Small Business Development Center Cyber Strategy developed under section 1841(a) of the National Defense Authorization Act for Fiscal Year 2017.".

SEC. 1843. ADDITIONAL CYBERSECURITY ASSISTANCE FOR SMALL BUSINESS DEVELOPMENT CENTERS.

Section 21(a) of the Small Business Act (15 U.S.C. 648(a)) is amended by adding at the end the following new paragraph:

"(8) CYBERSECURITY ASSISTANCE.—

"(A) IN GENERAL.—The Department of Homeland Security, and any other Federal department or agency in coordination with the Department of Homeland Security, may leverage small business development centers to provide assistance to small business concerns by disseminating information relating to cybersecurity risks and other homeland security matters to help small business concerns in developing or enhancing cybersecurity infrastructure, awareness of cyber threat indicators, and cyber training programs for employees.

"(B) DEFINITIONS.—In this paragraph, the terms 'cybersecurity risk' and 'cyber threat indicator' have the meanings given such terms, respectively, under section 227(a) of the Homeland Security Act of 2002 (6 U.S.C. 148(a)).".

SEC. 1844. PROHIBITION ON ADDITIONAL FUNDS.

No additional funds are authorized to be appropriated to carry out sections 1841 through 1843 or the amendments made by such sections.

TITLE XIX—DEPARTMENT OF HOMELAND SECURITY COORDINATION

Sec. 1901. Department of Homeland Security coordination.
Sec. 1902. Office of Strategy, Policy, and Plans of the Department of Homeland Security.
Sec. 1903. Management and execution.
Sec. 1904. Chief Human Capital Officer of the Department of Homeland Security.
Sec. 1905. Department of Homeland Security transparency.
Sec. 1906. Transparency in research and development.
Sec. 1907. United States Government review of certain foreign fighters.
Sec. 1908. National strategy to combat terrorist travel.
Sec. 1909. National Operations Center.
Sec. 1910. Department of Homeland Security strategy for international programs.
Sec. 1911. State and high-risk urban area working groups.
Sec. 1912. Cybersecurity strategy for the Department of Homeland Security.
Sec. 1913. EMP and GMD planning, research and development, and protection and preparedness.

SEC. 1901. DEPARTMENT OF HOMELAND SECURITY COORDINATION.

(a) IN GENERAL.—Subsection (d) of section 103 of the Homeland Security Act of 2002 (6 U.S.C. 113) is amended by adding at the end the following new paragraph:

"(5) Any Director of a Joint Task Force under section 708.".

(b) JOINT TASK FORCES.—Title VII of the Homeland Security Act of 2002 (6 U.S.C. 341 et seq.) is amended by adding at the end the following new section:

"SEC. 708. JOINT TASK FORCES.

"(a) DEFINITION.—In this section, the term 'situational awareness' means knowledge and unified understanding of unlawful cross-border activity, including—

"(1) threats and trends concerning illicit trafficking and unlawful crossings;

"(2) the ability to forecast future shifts in such threats and trends;

"(3) the ability to evaluate such threats and trends at a level sufficient to create actionable plans; and

"(4) the operational capability to conduct continuous and integrated surveillance of the air, land, and maritime borders of the United States.

"(b) JOINT TASK FORCES.—

"(1) ESTABLISHMENT.—The Secretary may establish and operate departmental Joint Task Forces to conduct joint operations using personnel and capabilities of the Department for the purposes specified in paragraph (2).

"(2) PURPOSES.—

"(A) IN GENERAL.—Subject to subparagraph (B), the purposes referred to in paragraph (1) are or relate to the following:

"(i) Securing the land and maritime borders of the United States.

"(ii) Homeland security crises.

"(iii) Establishing regionally-based operations.

"(B) LIMITATION.—

"(i) IN GENERAL.—The Secretary may not establish a Joint Task Force for any major disaster or emergency declared under the Robert T. Stafford Disaster Relief and Emergency Assistance Act (42 U.S.C. 5121 et seq.) or an incident for which the Federal Emergency Management Agency has primary responsibility for management of the response under title V of this Act, including section 504(a)(3)(A), unless the responsibilities of such a Joint Task Force—

"(I) do not include operational functions related to incident management, including coordination of operations; and

"(II) are consistent with the requirements of paragraphs (3) and (4)(A) of section 503(c) and section 509(c) of this Act, and section 302 of the Robert T. Stafford Disaster Relief and Emergency Assistance Act (42 U.S.C. 5143).

"(ii) RESPONSIBILITIES AND FUNCTIONS NOT REDUCED.—Nothing in this section may be construed to reduce the responsibilities or functions of the Federal Emergency Management Agency or the Administrator of the Agency under title V of this Act or any other provision of law, including the diversion of any asset, function, or mission from the Agency or the Administrator of the Agency pursuant to section 506.

"(3) JOINT TASK FORCE DIRECTORS.—

"(A) DIRECTOR.—Each Joint Task Force established and operated pursuant to paragraph (1) shall be headed by a Director, appointed by the President, for a term of not more than two years. The Secretary shall submit to the President recommendations for such appointments after consulting with the heads of the components of the Department with membership on any such Joint Task Force. Any Director appointed by the President shall be—

"(i) a current senior official of the Department with not less than one year of significant leadership experience at the Department; or

"(ii) if no suitable candidate is available at the Department, an individual with—

"(I) not less than one year of significant leadership experience in a Federal agency since the establishment of the Department; and

"(II) a demonstrated ability in, knowledge of, and significant experience working on the issues to be addressed by any such Joint Task Force.

"(B) EXTENSION.—The Secretary may extend the appointment of a Director of a Joint Task Force under subparagraph (A) for not more than two years if the Secretary determines that such an extension is in the best interest of the Department.

"(4) JOINT TASK FORCE DEPUTY DIRECTORS.—For each Joint Task Force, the Secretary shall appoint a Deputy Director who shall be an official of a different component or office of the Department than the Director of such Joint Task Force.

"(5) RESPONSIBILITIES.—The Director of a Joint Task Force, subject to the oversight, direction, and guidance of the Secretary, shall—

"(A) when established for the purpose referred to in paragraph (2)(A)(i), maintain situational awareness within the areas of responsibility of the Joint Task Force, as determined by the Secretary;

"(B) provide operational plans and requirements for standard operating procedures and contingency operations within the areas of responsibility of the Joint Task Force, as determined by the Secretary;

"(C) plan and execute joint task force activities within the areas of responsibility of the Joint Task Force, as determined by the Secretary;

"(D) set and accomplish strategic objectives through integrated operational planning and execution;

"(E) exercise operational direction over personnel and equipment from components and offices of the Department allocated to the Joint Task Force to accomplish the objectives of the Joint Task Force;

"(F) when established for the purpose referred to in paragraph (2)(A)(i), establish operational and investigative priorities within the areas of responsibility of the Joint Task Force, as determined by the Secretary;

"(G) coordinate with foreign governments and other Federal, State, and local agencies, as appropriate, to carry out the mission of the Joint Task Force; and

"(H) carry out other duties and powers the Secretary determines appropriate.

"(6) PERSONNEL AND RESOURCES.—

"(A) IN GENERAL.—The Secretary may, upon request of the Director of a Joint Task Force, and giving appropriate consideration of risk to the other primary missions of the Department, allocate to such Joint Task Force on a temporary basis personnel and equipment of components and offices of the Department.

"(B) COST NEUTRALITY.—A Joint Task Force may not require more resources than would have otherwise been required by the Department to carry out the duties assigned to such Joint Task Force if such Joint Task Force had not been established.

"(C) LOCATION OF OPERATIONS.—In establishing a location of operations for a Joint Task Force, the Secretary shall, to the extent practicable, use existing facilities that integrate efforts of components of the Department and State, local, tribal, or territorial law enforcement or military entities.

"(D) CONSIDERATION OF IMPACT.—When reviewing requests for allocation of component personnel and equipment under subparagraph (A), the Secretary shall consider the impact of such allocation on the ability of the donating component or office to carry out the primary missions of the Department, and in the case of the Coast Guard, the missions specified in section 888.

"(E) LIMITATION.—Personnel and equipment of the Coast Guard allocated under this paragraph may be used only to carry out operations and investigations related to the missions specified in section 888.

"(F) REPORT.—The Secretary shall, at the time the budget of the President is submitted to Congress for a fiscal year under section 1105(a) of title 31, United States Code, submit to the Committee on Homeland Security and the Committee on Transportation and Infrastructure of the House of Representatives and the Committee on Homeland Security and Governmental Affairs and the Committee on Commerce, Science, and Transportation of the Senate a report on the total funding, personnel, and other resources that each component or office of the Department allocated under this paragraph to each Joint Task Force to carry out the mission of such Joint Task Force during the fiscal year immediately preceding each such report, and a description of the degree to which the resources drawn from each component or office impact the primary mission of such component or office.

"(7) COMPONENT RESOURCE AUTHORITY.—As directed by the Secretary—

"(A) each Director of a Joint Task Force shall be provided sufficient resources from relevant components and offices of the Department and the authority necessary to carry out the missions and responsibilities of such Joint Task Force required under this section;

"(B) the resources referred to in subparagraph (A) shall be under the operational authority, direction, and control of the Director of the Joint Task Force to which such resources are assigned; and

"(C) the personnel and equipment of each Joint Task Force shall remain under the administrative direction of the head of the component or office of the Department that provided such personnel or equipment.

"(8) JOINT TASK FORCE STAFF.—Each Joint Task Force shall have a staff, composed of officials from relevant components and offices of the Department, to assist the Director of such Joint Task Force in carrying out the mission and responsibilities of such Joint Task Force.

"(9) ESTABLISHMENT OF PERFORMANCE METRICS.—The Secretary shall—

"(A) establish outcome-based and other appropriate performance metrics to evaluate the effectiveness of each Joint Task Force;

"(B) not later than 120 days after the date of the enactment of this section and 120 days after the establishment of a new Joint Task Force, as appropriate, submit to the Committee on Homeland Security and the Committee on Transportation and Infrastructure of the House of Representatives and the Committee on Homeland Security and Governmental Affairs and the Committee on Commerce, Science, and Transportation of the Senate the metrics established under subparagraph (A).

"(C) not later than January 31 of each year beginning in 2017, submit to each committee specified in subparagraph (B) a report that contains the evaluation described in subparagraph (A).

"(10) JOINT DUTY TRAINING PROGRAM.—

"(A) IN GENERAL.—The Secretary shall—

"(i) establish a joint duty training program in the Department for the purposes of—

"(I) enhancing coordination within the Department; and

"(II) promoting workforce professional development; and

"(ii) tailor such joint duty training program to improve joint operations as part of the Joint Task Forces.

"(B) ELEMENTS.—The joint duty training program established under subparagraph (A) shall address, at a minimum, the following topics:

"(i) National security strategy.

"(ii) Strategic and contingency planning.

"(iii) Command and control of operations under joint command.

"(iv) International engagement.

"(v) The homeland security enterprise.

"(vi) Interagency collaboration.

"(vii) Leadership.

"(viii) Specific subject matters relevant to the Joint Task Force, including matters relating to the missions specified in section 888, to which the joint duty training program is assigned.

"(C) TRAINING REQUIRED.—

"(i) DIRECTORS AND DEPUTY DIRECTORS.—Except as provided in clauses (iii) and (iv), an individual shall complete the joint duty training program before being appointed Director or Deputy Director of a Joint Task Force.

"(ii) JOINT TASK FORCE STAFF.—Each official serving on the staff of a Joint Task Force shall complete the joint duty training program within the first year of assignment to such Joint Task Force.

"(iii) EXCEPTION.—Clause (i) shall not apply to the first Director or Deputy Director appointed to a Joint Task Force on or after the date of the enactment of this section.

"(iv) WAIVER.—The Secretary may waive the application of clause (i) if the Secretary determines that such a waiver is in the interest of homeland security or necessary to carry out the mission for which a Joint Task Force was established.

"(11) NOTIFICATION OF JOINT TASK FORCE FORMATION.—

"(A) IN GENERAL.—Not later than 90 days before establishing a Joint Task Force under this subsection, the Secretary shall submit to the majority leader of the Senate, the minority leader of the Senate, the Speaker of the House of Representatives, the majority leader of the House of Representatives, the minority leader of the House of Representatives, and the Committee on Homeland Security and the Committee on Transportation and Infrastructure of the House of Representatives and the Committee on Homeland Security and Governmental Affairs and the Committee on Commerce, Science, and Transportation of the Senate a notification regarding such establishment.

"(B) WAIVER AUTHORITY.—The Secretary may waive the requirement under subparagraph (A) in the event of an emergency circumstance that imminently threatens the protection of human life or property.

"(12) REVIEW.—

"(A) IN GENERAL.—Not later than January 31, 2018, and January 31, 2021, the Inspector General of the Department shall submit to the Committee on Homeland Security and the Committee on Transportation and Infrastructure of the House of Representatives and the Committee on Homeland Security and Governmental Affairs and the Committee on Commerce, Science, and Transportation of the Senate a review of the Joint Task Forces established under this subsection.

"(B) CONTENTS.—The reviews required under subparagraph (A) shall include—

"(i) an assessment of the effectiveness of the structure of each Joint Task Force; and

"(ii) recommendations for enhancements to such structure to strengthen the effectiveness of each Joint Task Force.

"(13) SUNSET.—This section expires on September 30, 2022.

"(c) JOINT DUTY ASSIGNMENT PROGRAM.—After establishing the joint duty training program under subsection (b)(10), the Secretary shall establish a joint duty assignment program within the Department for the purposes of enhancing coordination in the Department and promoting workforce professional development.".

(c) TRANSITION.—An individual serving as a Director of a Joint Task Force of the Department of Homeland Security in existence on the day before the date of the enactment of this section may serve as the Director of such Joint Task Force on and after such date of enactment until a Director of such Joint Task Force is appointed pursuant to subparagraph (A) of section 708(b)(3), as added by subsection (a) of this section.

(d) CONFORMING AMENDMENTS.—The Homeland Security Act of 2002 is amended—

(1) in subsection (c) of section 506 (6 U.S.C. 316)—

(A) in paragraph (1), by inserting ", including through a Joint Task Force established under section 708," after "reduce"; and

(B) in paragraph (2), by inserting "including a Joint Task Force established under section 708," after "Department,"; and

(2) in paragraph (2) of section 509(c) (6 U.S.C. 319)—

(A) in the paragraph heading, by inserting "; JOINT TASK FORCE" after "OFFICIAL"; and

(B) in the matter preceding subparagraph (A), by inserting "or Director of a Joint Task Force established under section 708" before "shall".

(e) CLERICAL AMENDMENT.—The table of contents in section 1(b) of the Homeland Security Act of 2002 is amended by inserting after the item relating to section 707 the following new item:

"Sec. 708. Joint Task Forces.".

SEC. 1902. OFFICE OF STRATEGY, POLICY, AND PLANS OF THE DEPARTMENT OF HOMELAND SECURITY.

(a) OFFICE OF STRATEGY, POLICY, AND PLANS.—Title VII of the Homeland Security Act of 2002 (6 U.S.C. 341 et seq.), as amended by section 1901 of this title, is further amended by adding at the end the following new section:

"SEC. 709. OFFICE OF STRATEGY, POLICY, AND PLANS.

"(a) IN GENERAL.—There is established in the Department an Office of Strategy, Policy, and Plans.

"(b) HEAD OF OFFICE.—The Office of Strategy, Policy, and Plans shall be headed by an Under Secretary for Strategy, Policy, and Plans, who shall serve as the principal policy advisor to the Secretary. The Under Secretary for Strategy, Policy, and Plans shall be appointed by the President, by and with the advice and consent of the Senate.

"(c) FUNCTIONS.—The Under Secretary for Strategy, Policy, and Plans shall—

"(1) lead, conduct, and coordinate Department-wide policy development and implementation and strategic planning;

"(2) develop and coordinate policies to promote and ensure quality, consistency, and integration for the programs, components, offices, and activities across the Department;

"(3) develop and coordinate strategic plans and long-term goals of the Department with risk-based analysis and planning to improve operational mission effectiveness, including consultation with the Secretary regarding the quadrennial homeland security review under section 707;

"(4) manage Department leadership councils and provide analytics and support to such councils;

"(5) manage international coordination and engagement for the Department;

"(6) review and incorporate, as appropriate, external stakeholder feedback into Department policy; and

"(7) carry out such other responsibilities as the Secretary determines appropriate.

"(d) DEPUTY UNDER SECRETARY.—

"(1) IN GENERAL.—The Secretary may—

"(A) establish within the Office of Strategy, Policy, and Plans a position of Deputy Under Secretary to support the Under Secretary for Strategy, Policy, and Plans in carrying out the Under Secretary's responsibilities; and

"(B) appoint a career employee to such position.

"(2) LIMITATION ON ESTABLISHMENT OF DEPUTY UNDER SECRETARY POSITIONS.—A Deputy Under Secretary position (or any substantially similar position) within the Office of Strategy, Policy, and Plans may not be established except for the position provided for by paragraph (1), unless the Secretary receives prior authorization from Congress.

"(3) DEFINITIONS.—For purposes of paragraph (1)—

"(A) the term 'career employee' means any employee (as such term is defined in section 2105 of title 5, United States Code), but does not include a political appointee; and

"(B) the term 'political appointee' means any employee who occupies a position which has been excepted from the competitive service by reason of its confidential, policy-determining, policy-making, or policy-advocating character.

"(e) COORDINATION BY DEPARTMENT COMPONENTS.—To ensure consistency with the policy priorities of the Department, the head of each component of the Department shall coordinate with the Office of Strategy, Policy, and Plans in establishing or modifying policies or strategic planning guidance with respect to each such component.

"(f) HOMELAND SECURITY STATISTICS AND JOINT ANALYSIS.—

"(1) HOMELAND SECURITY STATISTICS.—The Under Secretary for Strategy, Policy, and Plans shall—

"(A) establish standards of reliability and validity for statistical data collected and analyzed by the Department;

"(B) be provided by the heads of all components of the Department with statistical data maintained by the Department regarding the operations of the Department;

"(C) conduct or oversee analysis and reporting of such data by the Department as required by law or as directed by the Secretary; and

"(D) ensure the accuracy of metrics and statistical data provided to Congress.

"(2) TRANSFER OF RESPONSIBILITIES.—There shall be transferred to the Under Secretary for Strategy, Policy, and Plans the maintenance of all immigration statistical information of U.S. Customs and Border Protection, U.S. Immigration and Customs Enforcement, and United States Citizenship and Immigration Services, which shall include information and statistics of the type contained in the publication entitled 'Yearbook of Immigration Statistics' prepared by the Office of Immigration Statistics, including region-by-region statistics on the aggregate number of applications and petitions filed by an alien (or filed on behalf of an alien) and denied, and the reasons for such denials, disaggregated by category of denial and application or petition type.

"(g) LIMITATION.—Nothing in this section overrides or otherwise affects the requirements specified in section 888.".

(b) CONFORMING AMENDMENT.—Subparagraph (B) of section 707(a)(3) of the Homeland Security Act of 2002 (6 U.S.C. 347(a)(3)) is amended by inserting before the semicolon the following: ", including the Under Secretary for Strategy, Policy, and Plans".

(c) CLERICAL AMENDMENT.—The table of contents in section 1(b) of the Homeland Security Act of 2002 , as amended by section 1901 of this title, is further amended by inserting after the item relating to section 708 the following new item:

"Sec. 709. Office of Strategy, Policy, and Plans.".

SEC. 1903. MANAGEMENT AND EXECUTION.

(a) IN GENERAL.—Section 103 of the Homeland Security Act of 2002 (6 U.S.C. 113) is amended—

(1) in subsection (a)(1)—

(A) in subparagraph (F), by inserting before the period at the end the following: ", who shall be first assistant to the Deputy Secretary of Homeland Security for purposes of subchapter III of chapter 33 of title 5, United States Code"; and

(B) by adding at the end the following:

"(K) An Under Secretary for Strategy, Policy, and Plans."; and

(2) by adding at the end the following:

"(g) VACANCIES.—

"(1) ABSENCE, DISABILITY, OR VACANCY OF SECRETARY OR DEPUTY SECRETARY.—Notwithstanding chapter 33 of title 5, United States Code, the Under Secretary for Management shall serve as the Acting Secretary if by reason of absence, disability, or vacancy in office, neither the Secretary nor Deputy Secretary is available to exercise the duties of the Office of the Secretary.

"(2) FURTHER ORDER OF SUCCESSION.—Notwithstanding chapter 33 of title 5, United States Code, the Secretary may designate such other officers of the Department in further order of succession to serve as Acting Secretary.

"(3) NOTIFICATION OF VACANCIES.—The Secretary shall notify the Committee on Homeland Security and Governmental Affairs of the Senate and the Committee on Homeland Security of the House of Representatives of any vacancies that require notification under sections 3345 through 3349d of title 5, United States Code (commonly known as the 'Federal Vacancies Reform Act of 1998').".

(b) UNDER SECRETARY FOR MANAGEMENT.—Section 701 of the Homeland Security Act of 2002 (6 U.S.C. 341) is amended—

(1) in subsection (a)—

(A) by striking paragraph (9) and inserting the following:

"(9) The management integration and transformation within each functional management discipline of the Department, including information technology, financial management, acquisition management, and human capital management, to ensure an efficient and orderly consolidation of functions and personnel in the Department, including—

"(A) the development of centralized data sources and connectivity of information systems to the greatest extent practicable to enhance program visibility, transparency, and operational effectiveness and coordination;

"(B) the development of standardized and automated management information to manage and oversee programs and make informed decisions to improve the efficiency of the Department;

"(C) the development of effective program management and regular oversight mechanisms, including clear roles and processes for program governance, sharing of best practices, and access to timely, reliable, and evaluated data on all acquisitions and investments; and

"(D) the overall supervision, including the conduct of internal audits and management analyses, of the programs and activities of the Department, including establishment of oversight procedures to ensure a full and effective review of the efforts by components of the Department to implement policies and procedures of the Department for management integration and transformation.";

(B) by redesignating paragraphs (10) and (11) as paragraphs (12) and (13), respectively; and

(C) by inserting after paragraph (9) the following:

"(10) The development of a transition and succession plan, before December 1 of each year in which a Presidential election is held, to guide the transition of Department functions to a new Presidential administration, and making such plan available to the next Secretary and Under Secretary for Management and to the congressional homeland security committees.

"(11) Reporting to the Government Accountability Office every six months to demonstrate measurable, sustainable progress made in implementing the corrective action plans of the Department to address the designation of the management functions of the Department on the biannual high risk list of the Government Accountability Office, until the Comptroller General of the United States submits to the appropriate congressional committees written notification of removal of the high-risk designation.";

(2) by striking subsection (b) and inserting the following:

"(b) WAIVERS FOR CONDUCTING BUSINESS WITH SUSPENDED OR DEBARRED CONTRACTORS.—Not later than five days after the date on which the Chief Procurement Officer or Chief Financial Officer of the Department issues a waiver of the requirement that an agency not engage in business with a contractor or other recipient of funds listed as a party suspended or debarred from receiving contracts, grants, or other types of Federal assistance in the System for Award Management maintained by the General Serv-

ices Administration, or any successor thereto, the Under Secretary for Management shall submit to the congressional homeland security committees and the Inspector General of the Department notice of the waiver and an explanation of the finding by the Under Secretary that a compelling reason exists for the waiver.";

(3) by redesignating subsection (d) as subsection (e); and

(4) by inserting after subsection (c) the following:

"(d) SYSTEM FOR AWARD MANAGEMENT CONSULTATION.—The Under Secretary for Management shall require that all Department contracting and grant officials consult the System for Award Management (or successor system) as maintained by the General Services Administration prior to awarding a contract or grant or entering into other transactions to ascertain whether the selected contractor is excluded from receiving Federal contracts, certain subcontracts, and certain types of Federal financial and non-financial assistance and benefits.".

SEC. 1904. CHIEF HUMAN CAPITAL OFFICER OF THE DEPARTMENT OF HOMELAND SECURITY.

Section 704 of the Homeland Security Act of 2002 (6 U.S.C. 344) is amended to read as follows:

"SEC. 704. CHIEF HUMAN CAPITAL OFFICER.

"(a) IN GENERAL.—The Chief Human Capital Officer shall report directly to the Under Secretary for Management.

"(b) RESPONSIBILITIES.—In addition to the responsibilities set forth in chapter 14 of title 5, United States Code, and other applicable law, the Chief Human Capital Officer of the Department shall—

"(1) develop and implement strategic workforce planning policies that are consistent with Government-wide leading principles and in line with Department strategic human capital goals and priorities, taking into account the special requirements of members of the Armed Forces serving in the Coast Guard;

"(2) develop performance measures to provide a basis for monitoring and evaluating Department-wide strategic workforce planning efforts;

"(3) develop, improve, and implement policies, including compensation flexibilities available to Federal agencies where appropriate, to recruit, hire, train, and retain the workforce of the Department, in coordination with all components of the Department;

"(4) identify methods for managing and overseeing human capital programs and initiatives, in coordination with the head of each component of the Department;

"(5) develop a career path framework and create opportunities for leader development in coordination with all components of the Department;

"(6) lead the efforts of the Department for managing employee resources, including training and development opportunities, in coordination with each component of the Department;

"(7) work to ensure the Department is implementing human capital programs and initiatives and effectively educating each component of the Department about these programs and initiatives;

"(8) identify and eliminate unnecessary and duplicative human capital policies and guidance;

"(9) provide input concerning the hiring and performance of the Chief Human Capital Officer or comparable official in each component of the Department; and

"(10) ensure that all employees of the Department are informed of their rights and remedies under chapters 12 and 23 of title 5, United States Code.

"(c) COMPONENT STRATEGIES.—

"(1) IN GENERAL.—Each component of the Department shall, in coordination with the Chief

Human Capital Officer of the Department, develop a 5-year workforce strategy for the component that will support the goals, objectives, and performance measures of the Department for determining the proper balance of Federal employees and private labor resources.

"(2) STRATEGY REQUIREMENTS.—In developing the strategy required under paragraph (1), each component shall consider the effect on human resources associated with creating additional Federal full-time equivalent positions, converting private contractors to Federal employees, or relying on the private sector for goods and services.

"(d) ANNUAL SUBMISSION.—Not later than 90 days after the date on which the Secretary submits the annual budget justification for the Department, the Secretary shall submit to the congressional homeland security committees a report that includes a table, delineated by component with actual and enacted amounts, including—

"(1) information on the progress within the Department of fulfilling the workforce strategies developed under subsection (c);

"(2) the number of on-board staffing for Federal employees from the prior fiscal year;

"(3) the total contract hours submitted by each prime contractor as part of the service contract inventory required under section 743 of the Financial Services and General Government Appropriations Act, 2010 (division C of Public Law 111–117; 31 U.S.C. 501 note); and

"(4) the number of full-time equivalent personnel identified under the Intergovernmental Personnel Act of 1970 (42 U.S.C. 4701 et seq.).

"(e) LIMITATION.—Nothing in this section overrides or otherwise affects the requirements specified in section 888.".

SEC. 1905. DEPARTMENT OF HOMELAND SECURITY TRANSPARENCY.

(a) FEASIBILITY STUDY.—The Administrator of the Federal Emergency Management Agency shall initiate a study to determine the feasibility of gathering data and providing information to Congress on the use of Federal grant awards, for expenditures of more than $5,000, by entities that receive a Federal grant award under the Urban Area Security Initiative and the State Homeland Security Grant Program under sections 2003 and 2004 of the Homeland Security Act of 2002 (6 U.S.C. 604 and 605), respectively.

(b) REPORT.—Not later than one year after the date of the enactment of this Act, the Administrator of the Federal Emergency Management Agency shall submit to the Committee on Homeland Security of the House of Representatives and the Committee on Homeland Security and Governmental Affairs a report on the results of the study required under subsection (a).

SEC. 1906. TRANSPARENCY IN RESEARCH AND DEVELOPMENT.

(a) IN GENERAL.—Title III of the Homeland Security Act of 2002 (6 U.S.C. 181 et seq.) is amended by adding at the end the following new section:

"SEC. 319. TRANSPARENCY IN RESEARCH AND DEVELOPMENT.

"(a) REQUIREMENT TO LIST RESEARCH AND DEVELOPMENT PROGRAMS.—

"(1) IN GENERAL.—The Secretary shall maintain a detailed list of the following:

"(A) Each classified and unclassified research and development project, and all appropriate details for each such project, including the component of the Department responsible for each such project.

"(B) Each task order for a Federally Funded Research and Development Center not associated with a research and development project.

"(C) Each task order for a University-based center of excellence not associated with a research and development project.

"(D) The indicators developed and tracked by the Under Secretary for Science and Technology with respect to transitioned projects pursuant to subsection (c).

"(2) EXCEPTION FOR CERTAIN COMPLETED PROJECTS.—Paragraph (1) shall not apply to a project completed or otherwise terminated before the date of the enactment of this section.

"(3) UPDATES.—The list required under paragraph (1) shall be updated as frequently as possible, but not less frequently than once per quarter.

"(4) RESEARCH AND DEVELOPMENT DEFINED.—For purposes of the list required under paragraph (1), the Secretary shall provide a definition for the term 'research and development'.

"(b) REQUIREMENT TO REPORT TO CONGRESS ON ALL PROJECTS.—Not later than January 1, 2017, and annually thereafter, the Secretary shall submit to the Committee on Homeland Security of the House of Representatives and the Committee on Homeland Security and Governmental Affairs of the Senate a classified and unclassified report, as applicable, that lists each ongoing classified and unclassified project at the Department, including all appropriate details of each such project.

"(c) INDICATORS OF SUCCESS OF TRANSITIONED PROJECTS.—

"(1) IN GENERAL.—For each project that has been transitioned to practice from research and development, the Under Secretary for Science and Technology shall develop and track indicators to demonstrate the uptake of the technology or project among customers or end-users.

"(2) REQUIREMENT.—To the fullest extent possible, the tracking of a project required under paragraph (1) shall continue for the three-year period beginning on the date on which such project was transitioned to practice from research and development.

"(d) DEFINITIONS.—In this section:

"(1) ALL APPROPRIATE DETAILS.—The term 'all appropriate details' means, with respect to a research and development project—

"(A) the name of such project, including both classified and unclassified names if applicable;

"(B) the name of the component of the Department carrying out such project;

"(C) an abstract or summary of such project;

"(D) funding levels for such project;

"(E) project duration or timeline;

"(F) the name of each contractor, grantee, or cooperative agreement partner involved in such project;

"(G) expected objectives and milestones for such project; and

"(H) to the maximum extent practicable, relevant literature and patents that are associated with such project.

"(2) CLASSIFIED.—The term 'classified' means anything containing—

"(A) classified national security information as defined in section 6.1 of Executive Order 13526 (50 U.S.C. 3161 note) or any successor order;

"(B) Restricted Data or data that was formerly Restricted Data, as defined in section 11y. of the Atomic Energy Act of 1954 (42 U.S.C. 2014(y));

"(C) material classified at the Sensitive Compartmented Information (SCI) level, as defined in section 309 of the Intelligence Authorization Act for Fiscal Year 2001 (50 U.S.C. 3345); or

"(D) information relating to a special access program, as defined in section 6.1 of Executive Order 13526 (50 U.S.C. 3161 note) or any successor order.

"(3) CONTROLLED UNCLASSIFIED INFORMATION.—The term 'controlled unclassified information' means information described as 'Controlled Unclassified Information' under Executive Order 13556 (50 U.S.C. 3501 note) or any successor order.

"(4) PROJECT.—The term 'project' means a research or development project, program, or activity administered by the Department, whether ongoing, completed, or otherwise terminated.

"(e) LIMITATION.—Nothing in this section overrides or otherwise affects the requirements specified in section 888.".

(b) CLERICAL AMENDMENT.—The table of contents in section 1(b) of the Homeland Security Act of 2002 is amended by inserting after the item relating to section 318 the following new item:

"Sec. 319. Transparency in research and development.".

SEC. 1907. UNITED STATES GOVERNMENT REVIEW OF CERTAIN FOREIGN FIGHTERS.

(a) REVIEW.—Not later than 30 days after the date of the enactment of this Act, the President shall initiate a review of known instances since 2011 in which a person has traveled or attempted to travel to a conflict zone in Iraq or Syria from the United States to join or provide material support or resources to a terrorist organization.

(b) SCOPE OF REVIEW.—The review under subsection (a) shall—

(1) include relevant unclassified and classified information held by the United States Government related to each instance described in subsection (a);

(2) ascertain which factors, including operational issues, security vulnerabilities, systemic challenges, or other issues, which may have undermined efforts to prevent the travel of persons described in subsection (a) to a conflict zone in Iraq or Syria from the United States, including issues related to the timely identification of suspects, information sharing, intervention, and interdiction; and

(3) identify lessons learned and areas that can be improved to prevent additional travel by persons described in subsection (a) to a conflict zone in Iraq or Syria, or other terrorist safe haven abroad, to join or provide material support or resources to a terrorist organization.

(c) INFORMATION SHARING.—The President shall direct the heads of relevant Federal agencies to provide the appropriate information that may be necessary to complete the review required under this section.

(d) SUBMISSION TO CONGRESS.—Not later than 120 days after the date of the enactment of this Act, the President, consistent with the protection of classified information, shall submit a report to the majority leader of the Senate, the minority leader of the Senate, the Speaker of the House of Representatives, the majority leader of the House of Representatives, the minority leader of the House of Representatives, and the appropriate congressional committees that includes the results of the review required under this section, including information on travel routes of greatest concern, as appropriate.

(e) DEFINITIONS.—In this section:

(1) APPROPRIATE CONGRESSIONAL COMMITTEES.—The term "appropriate congressional committees" means—

(A) the Committee on Homeland Security and Governmental Affairs of the Senate;

(B) the Select Committee on Intelligence of the Senate;

(C) the Committee on the Judiciary of the Senate;

(D) the Committee on Armed Services of the Senate;

(E) the Committee on Foreign Relations of the Senate;

(F) the Committee on Banking, Housing, and Urban Affairs of the Senate;

(G) the Committee on Appropriations of the Senate;

(H) the Committee on Homeland Security of the House of Representatives;

(I) the Permanent Select Committee on Intelligence of the House of Representatives;

(J) the Committee on the Judiciary of the House of Representatives;

(K) the Committee on Armed Services of the House of Representatives;

(L) the Committee on Foreign Affairs of the House of Representatives;

(M) the Committee on Appropriations of the House of Representatives; and

(N) the Committee on Financial Services of the House of Representatives.

(2) MATERIAL SUPPORT OR RESOURCES.—The term "material support or resources" has the meaning given such term in section 2339A of title 18, United States Code.

SEC. 1908. NATIONAL STRATEGY TO COMBAT TERRORIST TRAVEL.

(a) SENSE OF CONGRESS.—It is the sense of Congress that it should be the policy of the United States to—

(1) continue to regularly assess the evolving terrorist threat to the United States;

(2) catalog existing Federal Government efforts to obstruct terrorist and foreign fighter travel into, out of, and within the United States, and overseas;

(3) identify such efforts that may benefit from reform or consolidation, or require elimination;

(4) identify potential security vulnerabilities in United States defenses against terrorist travel; and

(5) prioritize resources to address any such security vulnerabilities in a risk-based manner.

(b) NATIONAL STRATEGY AND UPDATES.—

(1) IN GENERAL.—Not later than 180 days after the date of the enactment of this Act, the President shall submit to the majority leader of the Senate, the minority leader of the Senate, the Speaker of the House of Representatives, the majority leader of the House of Representatives, the minority leader of the House of Representatives, and the appropriate congressional committees a national strategy to combat terrorist travel. The strategy shall address efforts to intercept terrorists and foreign fighters and constrain the domestic and international travel of such persons. Consistent with the protection of classified information, the strategy shall be submitted in unclassified form, including, as appropriate, a classified annex.

(2) UPDATED STRATEGIES.—Not later than 180 days after the date on which a new President is inaugurated, the President shall submit to the majority leader of the Senate, the minority leader of the Senate, the Speaker of the House of Representatives, the majority leader of the House of Representatives, the minority leader of the House of Representatives, and the appropriate congressional committees an updated version of the strategy described in paragraph (1).

(3) CONTENTS.—The strategy and updates required under this subsection shall—

(A) include an accounting and description of all Federal Government programs, projects, and activities designed to constrain domestic and international travel by terrorists and foreign fighters;

(B) identify specific security vulnerabilities within the United States and outside of the United States that may be exploited by terrorists and foreign fighters;

(C) delineate goals for—

(i) closing the security vulnerabilities identified under subparagraph (B); and

(ii) enhancing the ability of the Federal Government to constrain domestic and international travel by terrorists and foreign fighters; and

(D) describe the actions that will be taken to achieve the goals delineated under subparagraph (C) and the means needed to carry out such actions, including—

(i) steps to reform, improve, and streamline existing Federal Government efforts to align with the current threat environment;

(ii) new programs, projects, or activities that are requested, under development, or undergoing implementation;

(iii) new authorities or changes in existing authorities needed from Congress;

(iv) specific budget adjustments being requested to enhance United States security in a risk-based manner; and

(v) the Federal departments and agencies responsible for the specific actions described in this subparagraph.

(4) SUNSET.—The requirement to submit updated national strategies under this subsection shall terminate on the date that is seven years after the date of the enactment of this Act.

(c) DEVELOPMENT OF IMPLEMENTATION PLANS.—For each national strategy required under subsection (b), the President shall direct the heads of relevant Federal agencies to develop implementation plans for each such agency.

(d) IMPLEMENTATION PLANS.—

(1) IN GENERAL.—The President shall submit to the majority leader of the Senate, the minority leader of the Senate, the Speaker of the House of Representatives, the majority leader of the House of Representatives, the minority leader of the House of Representatives, and the appropriate congressional committees an implementation plan developed under subsection (c) with each national strategy required under subsection (b). Consistent with the protection of classified information, each such implementation plan shall be submitted in unclassified form, but may include a classified annex.

(2) ANNUAL UPDATES.—The President shall submit to the majority leader of the Senate, the minority leader of the Senate, the Speaker of the House of Representatives, the majority leader of the House of Representatives, the minority leader of the House of Representatives, and the appropriate congressional committees an annual updated implementation plan during the ten-year period beginning on the date of the enactment of this Act.

(e) DEFINITION.—In this section, the term "appropriate congressional committees" means—

(1) in the House of Representatives—

(A) the Committee on Homeland Security;

(B) the Committee on Armed Services;

(C) the Permanent Select Committee on Intelligence;

(D) the Committee on the Judiciary;

(E) the Committee on Foreign Affairs;

(F) the Committee on Appropriations; and

(2) in the Senate—

(A) the Committee on Homeland Security and Governmental Affairs;

(B) the Committee on Armed Services;

(C) the Select Committee on Intelligence;

(D) the Committee on the Judiciary;

(E) the Committee on Foreign Relations; and

(F) the Committee on Appropriations.

(f) SPECIAL RULE FOR CERTAIN RECEIPT.—The definition under subsection (e) shall be treated as including the Committee on Transportation and Infrastructure of the House of Representatives and the Committee on Commerce, Science, and Transportation of the Senate for purposes of receipt of those portions of—

(1) the national strategy (including updates thereto), and

(2) the implementation plan (including updates thereto),

required under this section that relate to maritime travel into and out of the United States.

SEC. 1909. NATIONAL OPERATIONS CENTER.

Section 515 of the Homeland Security Act of 2002 (6 U.S.C. 321d) is amended—

(1) in subsection (a)—

(A) by striking "emergency managers and decision makers" and inserting "emergency managers, decision makers, and other appropriate officials"; and

(B) by inserting "and steady-state activity" before the period at the end;

(2) in subsection (b)—

(A) in paragraph (1)—

(i) by striking "and tribal governments" and inserting "tribal, and territorial governments, the private sector, and international partners";

(ii) by striking "in the event of" and inserting "for events, threats, and incidents involving"; and

(iii) by striking "and" at the end;

(B) in paragraph (2), by striking the period at the end and inserting "; and"; and

(C) by adding at the end the following:

"(3) enter into agreements with other Federal operations centers and other homeland security partners, as appropriate, to facilitate the sharing of information.";

(4) in subsection (c)—

(A) in the subsection heading, by striking "Fire Service" and inserting "Emergency Responder";

(B) by striking paragraph (1) and inserting the following:

"(1) ESTABLISHMENT OF POSITIONS.—The Secretary shall establish a position, on a rotating basis, for a representative of State and local emergency responders at the National Operations Center established under subsection (b) to ensure the effective sharing of information between the Federal Government and State and local emergency response services.";

(C) by striking paragraph (2); and

(D) by redesignating paragraph (3) as paragraph (2).

SEC. 1910. DEPARTMENT OF HOMELAND SECURITY STRATEGY FOR INTERNATIONAL PROGRAMS.

(a) IN GENERAL.—Not later than 180 days after the date of the enactment of this Act, the Secretary of Homeland Security shall submit to the Committee on Homeland Security of the House of Representatives and the Committee on Homeland Security and Governmental Affairs of the Senate a comprehensive three-year strategy for international programs of the Department of Homeland Security in which personnel and resources of the Department are deployed abroad for vetting and screening of persons seeking to enter the United States.

(b) CONTENTS.—The strategy required under subsection (a) shall include, at a minimum, the following:

(1) Specific Department of Homeland Security risk-based goals for international programs of the Department in which personnel and resources of the Department are deployed abroad for vetting and screening of persons seeking to enter the United States.

(2) A risk-based method for determining whether to establish new international programs in new locations, given resource constraints, or expand existing international programs of the Department, in which personnel and resources of the Department are deployed abroad for vetting and screening of persons seeking to enter the United States.

(3) Alignment with the highest Department-wide and Government-wide strategic priorities of resource allocations on international programs of the Department in which personnel and resources of the Department are deployed abroad for vetting and screening of persons seeking to enter the United States.

(4) A common reporting framework for the submission of reliable, comparable cost data by components of the Department on overseas expenditures attributable to international programs of the Department in which personnel and resources of the Department are deployed abroad for vetting and screening of persons seeking to enter the United States.

(c) CONSIDERATIONS.—In developing the strategy required under subsection (a), the Secretary of Homeland Security shall consider, at a minimum, the following:

(1) Information on existing operations of international programs of the Department of

Homeland Security in which personnel and resources of the Department are deployed abroad for vetting and screening of persons seeking to enter the United States that includes corresponding information for each location in which each such program operates.

(2) The number of Department personnel deployed to each location at which an international program referred to in subparagraph (A) is in operation during the current and preceding fiscal year.

(3) Analysis of the impact of each international program referred to in paragraph (1) on domestic activities of components of the Department of Homeland Security.

(4) Analysis of barriers to the expansion of an international program referred to in paragraph (1).

(d) FORM.—The strategy required under subsection (a) shall be submitted in unclassified form but may contain a classified annex if the Secretary of Homeland Security determines that such is appropriate.

SEC. 1911. STATE AND HIGH-RISK URBAN AREA WORKING GROUPS.

Subsection (b) of section 2021 of the Homeland Security Act of 2002 (6 U.S.C. 611) is amended to read as follows:

"(b) PLANNING COMMITTEES.—

"(1) IN GENERAL.—Any State or high-risk urban area receiving a grant under section 2003 or 2004 shall establish a State planning committee or urban area working group to assist in preparation and revision of the State, regional, or local homeland security plan or the threat and hazard identification and risk assessment, as the case may be, and to assist in determining effective funding priorities for grants under such sections.

"(2) COMPOSITION.—

"(A) IN GENERAL.—The State planning committees and urban area working groups referred to in paragraph (1) shall include at least one representative from each of the following significant stakeholders:

"(i) Local or tribal government officials.

"(ii) Emergency response providers, which shall include representatives of the fire service, law enforcement, emergency medical services, and emergency managers.

"(iii) Public health officials and other appropriate medical practitioners.

"(iv) Individuals representing educational institutions, including elementary schools, community colleges, and other institutions of higher education.

"(v) State and regional interoperable communications coordinators, as appropriate.

"(vi) State and major urban area fusion centers, as appropriate.

"(B) GEOGRAPHIC REPRESENTATION.—The members of the State planning committee or urban area working group, as the case may be, shall be a representative group of individuals from the counties, cities, towns, and Indian tribes within the State or high-risk urban area, including, as appropriate, representatives of rural, high-population, and high-threat jurisdictions.

"(3) EXISTING PLANNING COMMITTEES.—Nothing in this subsection may be construed to require that any State or high-risk urban area create a State planning committee or urban area working group, as the case may be, if that State or high-risk urban area has established and uses a multijurisdictional planning committee or commission that meets the requirements of this subsection.".

SEC. 1912. CYBERSECURITY STRATEGY FOR THE DEPARTMENT OF HOMELAND SECURITY.

(a) IN GENERAL.—Subtitle C of title II of the Homeland Security Act of 2002 (6 U.S.C. 141 et seq.) is amended by inserting after section 228 the following new section:

"SEC. 228A. CYBERSECURITY STRATEGY.

"(a) IN GENERAL.—Not later than 90 days after the date of the enactment of this section, the Secretary shall develop a departmental strategy to carry out cybersecurity responsibilities as set forth in law.

"(b) CONTENTS.—The strategy required under subsection (a) shall include the following:

"(1) Strategic and operational goals and priorities to successfully execute the full range of the Secretary's cybersecurity responsibilities.

"(2) Information on the programs, policies, and activities that are required to successfully execute the full range of the Secretary's cybersecurity responsibilities, including programs, policies, and activities in furtherance of the following:

"(A) Cybersecurity functions set forth in the section 227 (relating to the national cybersecurity and communications integration center).

"(B) Cybersecurity investigations capabilities.

"(C) Cybersecurity research and development.

"(D) Engagement with international cybersecurity partners.

"(c) CONSIDERATIONS.—In developing the strategy required under subsection (a), the Secretary shall—

"(1) consider—

"(A) the cybersecurity strategy for the Homeland Security Enterprise published by the Secretary in November 2011;

"(B) the Department of Homeland Security Fiscal Years 2014–2018 Strategic Plan; and

"(C) the most recent Quadrennial Homeland Security Review issued pursuant to section 707; and

"(2) include information on the roles and responsibilities of components and offices of the Department, to the extent practicable, to carry out such strategy.

"(d) IMPLEMENTATION PLAN.—Not later than 90 days after the development of the strategy required under subsection (a), the Secretary shall issue an implementation plan for the strategy that includes the following:

"(1) Strategic objectives and corresponding tasks.

"(2) Projected timelines and costs for such tasks.

"(3) Metrics to evaluate performance of such tasks.

"(e) CONGRESSIONAL OVERSIGHT.—The Secretary shall submit to Congress for assessment the following:

"(1) A copy of the strategy required under subsection (a) upon issuance.

"(2) A copy of the implementation plan required under subsection (d) upon issuance, together with detailed information on any associated legislative or budgetary proposals.

"(f) CLASSIFIED INFORMATION.—The strategy required under subsection (a) shall be in an unclassified form but may contain a classified annex.

"(g) RULE OF CONSTRUCTION.—Nothing in this section may be construed as permitting the Department to engage in monitoring, surveillance, exfiltration, or other collection activities for the purpose of tracking an individual's personally identifiable information.

"(h) DEFINITION.—In this section, the term 'Homeland Security Enterprise' means relevant governmental and nongovernmental entities involved in homeland security, including Federal, State, local, and tribal government officials, private sector representatives, academics, and other policy experts.".

(b) CLERICAL AMENDMENT.—The table of contents in section 1(b) of the Homeland Security Act of 2002 is amended by inserting after the item relating to section 228 the following new item:

"Sec. 228A. Cybersecurity strategy.".

SEC. 1913. EMP AND GMD PLANNING, RESEARCH AND DEVELOPMENT, AND PROTECTION AND PREPAREDNESS.

(a) IN GENERAL.—The Homeland Security Act of 2002 (6 U.S.C. 101 et seq.) is amended—

(1) in section 2 (6 U.S.C. 101)—

(A) by redesignating paragraphs (9) through (18) as paragraphs (11) through (20), respectively;

(B) by redesignating paragraphs (7) and (8) as paragraphs (8) and (9), respectively;

(C) by inserting after paragraph (6) the following new paragraph:

"(7) The term 'EMP' means an electromagnetic pulse caused by a nuclear device or nonnuclear device, including such a pulse caused by an act of terrorism."; and

(D) by inserting after paragraph (9), as so redesignated, the following new paragraph:

"(10) The term 'GMD' means a geomagnetic disturbance caused by a solar storm or another naturally occurring phenomenon.";

(2) in subsection (d) of section 201 (6 U.S.C. 121), by adding at the end the following new paragraph:

"(26)(A) Not later than six months after the date of the enactment of this paragraph, to conduct an intelligence-based review and comparison of the risks and consequences of EMP and GMD facing critical infrastructure, and submit to the Committee on Homeland Security and the Permanent Select Committee on Intelligence of the House of Representatives and the Committee on Homeland Security and Governmental Affairs and the Select Committee on Intelligence of the Senate—

"(i) a recommended strategy to protect and prepare the critical infrastructure of the homeland against threats of EMP and GMD; and

"(ii) not less frequently than every two years thereafter for the next six years, updates of the recommended strategy.

"(B) The recommended strategy under subparagraph (A) shall—

"(i) be based on findings of the research and development conducted under section 319;

"(ii) be developed in consultation with the relevant Federal sector-specific agencies (as defined under Presidential Policy Directive-21) for critical infrastructure;

"(iii) be developed in consultation with the relevant sector coordinating councils for critical infrastructure;

"(iv) be informed, to the extent practicable, by the findings of the intelligence-based review and comparison of the risks and consequences of EMP and GMD facing critical infrastructure conducted under subparagraph (A); and

"(v) be submitted in unclassified form, but may include a classified annex.

"(C) The Secretary may, if appropriate, incorporate the recommended strategy into a broader recommendation developed by the Department to help protect and prepare critical infrastructure from terrorism, cyber attacks, and other threats if, as incorporated, the recommended strategy complies with subparagraph (B).";

(3) in title III (6 U.S.C. 181 et seq.), by adding at the end the following new section:

"SEC. 319. EMP AND GMD MITIGATION RESEARCH AND DEVELOPMENT.

"(a) IN GENERAL.—In furtherance of domestic preparedness and response, the Secretary, acting through the Under Secretary for Science and Technology, and in consultation with other relevant executive agencies, relevant State, local, and tribal governments, and relevant owners and operators of critical infrastructure, shall, to the extent practicable, conduct research and development to mitigate the consequences of threats of EMP and GMD.

"(b) SCOPE.—The scope of the research and development under subsection (a) shall include the following:

"(1) An objective scientific analysis—

"(A) evaluating the risks to critical infrastructure from a range of threats of EMP and GMD; and

"(B) which shall—

"(i) be conducted in conjunction with the Office of Intelligence and Analysis; and

"(ii) include a review and comparison of the range of threats and hazards facing critical infrastructure of the electrical grid.

"(2) Determination of the critical utilities and national security assets and infrastructure that are at risk from threats of EMP and GMD.

"(3) An evaluation of emergency planning and response technologies that would address the findings and recommendations of experts, including those of the Commission to Assess the Threat to the United States from Electromagnetic Pulse Attack, which shall include a review of the feasibility of rapidly isolating one or more portions of the electrical grid from the main electrical grid.

"(4) An analysis of technology options that are available to improve the resiliency of critical infrastructure to threats of EMP and GMD, including an analysis of neutral current blocking devices that may protect high-voltage transmission lines.

"(5) The restoration and recovery capabilities of critical infrastructure under differing levels of damage and disruption from various threats of EMP and GMD, as informed by the objective scientific analysis conducted under paragraph (1).

"(6) An analysis of the feasibility of a real-time alert system to inform electrical grid operators and other stakeholders within milliseconds of a high-altitude nuclear explosion.

"(c) EXEMPTION FROM DISCLOSURE.—

"(1) INFORMATION SHARED WITH THE FEDERAL GOVERNMENT.—Section 214, and any regulations issued pursuant to such section, shall apply to any information shared with the Federal Government under this section.

"(2) INFORMATION SHARED BY THE FEDERAL GOVERNMENT.—Information shared by the Federal Government with a State, local, or tribal government under this section shall be exempt from disclosure under any provision of State, local, or tribal freedom of information law, open government law, open meetings law, open records law, sunshine law, or similar law requiring the disclosure of information or records.''; and

"(4) in title V (6 U.S.C. 311 et seq.), by adding at the end the following new section:

"SEC. 527. NATIONAL PLANNING AND EDUCATION.

"The Secretary shall, to the extent practicable—

"(1) include in national planning frameworks the threat of an EMP or GMD event; and

"(2) conduct outreach to educate owners and operators of critical infrastructure, emergency planners, and emergency response providers at all levels of government regarding threats of EMP and GMD.''.

(b) TECHNICAL AND CONFORMING AMENDMENTS.—

(1) The table of contents in section 1(b) of the Homeland Security Act of 2002 is amended—

(A) by inserting after the item relating to section 317 the following new item:

"Sec. 319. EMP and GMD mitigation research and development.''; and

(B) by inserting after the item relating to section 525 the following:

"Sec. 526. Integrated Public Alert and Warning System modernization.

"Sec. 527. National planning and education.''.

(2) Section 501(13) of the Homeland Security Act of 2002 (6 U.S.C. 311(13)) is amended by striking "section 2(11)(B)'' and inserting "section 2(13)(B)''.

(3) Section 712(a) of title 14, United States Code, is amended by striking "section 2(16) of the Homeland Security Act of 2002 (6 U.S.C. 101(16))'' and inserting "section 2 of the Homeland Security Act of 2002 (6 U.S.C. 101)''.

(c) DEADLINE FOR INITIAL RECOMMENDED STRATEGY.—Not later than one year after the date of the enactment of this section, the Secretary of Homeland Security shall submit the recommended strategy required under paragraph (26) of section 201(d) of the Homeland Security Act of 2002 (6 U.S.C. 121(d)), as added by this section.

(d) REPORT.—Not later than 180 days after the date of the enactment of this section, the Secretary of Homeland Security shall submit to Congress a report describing the progress made in, and an estimated date by which the Department of Homeland Security will have completed—

(1) including threats of EMP and GMD (as those terms are defined in section 2 of the Homeland Security Act of 2002, as amended by this section) in national planning, as described in section 527 of the Homeland Security Act of 2002, as added by this section;

(2) research and development described in section 319 of the Homeland Security Act of 2002, as added by this section;

(3) development of the recommended strategy required under paragraph (26) of section 201(d) of the Homeland Security Act of 2002 (6 U.S.C. 121(d)), as added by this section; and

(4) beginning to conduct outreach to educate emergency planners and emergency response providers at all levels of government regarding threats of EMP and GMD events.

(e) NO REGULATORY AUTHORITY.—Nothing in this section, including the amendments made by this section, shall be construed to grant any regulatory authority.

(f) NO NEW AUTHORIZATION OF APPROPRIATIONS.—This section, including the amendments made by this section, may be carried out only by using funds appropriated under the authority of other laws.

DIVISION B—MILITARY CONSTRUCTION AUTHORIZATIONS

SEC. 2001. SHORT TITLE.

This division may be cited as the "Military Construction Authorization Act for Fiscal Year 2017''.

SEC. 2002. EXPIRATION OF AUTHORIZATIONS AND AMOUNTS REQUIRED TO BE SPECIFIED BY LAW.

(a) EXPIRATION OF AUTHORIZATIONS AFTER THREE YEARS.—Except as provided in subsection (b), all authorizations contained in titles XXI through XXVII and title XXIX for military construction projects, land acquisition, family housing projects and facilities, and contributions to the North Atlantic Treaty Organization Security Investment Program (and authorizations of appropriations therefor) shall expire on the later of—

(1) October 1, 2019; or

(2) the date of the enactment of an Act authorizing funds for military construction for fiscal year 2020.

(b) EXCEPTION.—Subsection (a) shall not apply to authorizations for military construction projects, land acquisition, family housing projects and facilities, and contributions to the North Atlantic Treaty Organization Security Investment Program (and authorizations of appropriations therefor), for which appropriated funds have been obligated before the later of—

(1) October 1, 2019; or

(2) the date of the enactment of an Act authorizing funds for fiscal year 2020 for military construction projects, land acquisition, family housing projects and facilities, or contributions to the North Atlantic Treaty Organization Security Investment Program.

SEC. 2003. EFFECTIVE DATE.

Titles XXI through XXVII and title XXIX shall take effect on the later of—

(1) October 1, 2016; or

(2) the date of the enactment of this Act.

TITLE XXI—ARMY MILITARY CONSTRUCTION

Sec. 2101. Authorized Army construction and land acquisition projects.

Sec. 2102. Family housing.

Sec. 2103. Authorization of appropriations, Army.

Sec. 2104. Modification of authority to carry out certain fiscal year 2014 project.

Sec. 2105. Extension of authorizations of certain fiscal year 2013 projects.

Sec. 2106. Extension of authorizations of certain fiscal year 2014 projects.

SEC. 2101. AUTHORIZED ARMY CONSTRUCTION AND LAND ACQUISITION PROJECTS.

(a) INSIDE THE UNITED STATES.—Using amounts appropriated pursuant to the authorization of appropriations in section 2103(a) and available for military construction projects inside the United States as specified in the funding table in section 4601, the Secretary of the Army may acquire real property and carry out military construction projects for the installations or locations inside the United States, and in the amounts, set forth in the following table:

Army: Inside the United States

State	Installation	Amount
Alaska	Fort Wainwright	$47,000,000
California	Concord	$12,600,000
Colorado	Fort Carson	$13,100,000
Georgia	Fort Gordon	$100,600,000
	Fort Stewart	$14,800,000
Missouri	Fort Leonard Wood	$6,900,000
Texas	Fort Hood	$7,600,000
Utah	Camp Williams	$7,400,000
Virginia	Fort Belvoir	$23,000,000

(b) OUTSIDE THE UNITED STATES.—Using amounts appropriated pursuant to the authorization of appropriations in section 2103(a) and available for military construction projects out-side the United States as specified in the funding table in section 4601, the Secretary of the Army may acquire real property and carry out the military construction project for the instal-lations or locations outside the United States, and in the amount, set forth in the following table:

Army: Outside the United States

Country	Installation	Amount
Cuba	Guantanamo Bay	$33,000,000
Germany	East Camp Grafenwoehr	$22,000,000
	Garmisch	$9,600,000
	Wiesbaden Army Airfield	$19,200,000

SEC. 2102. FAMILY HOUSING.

(a) CONSTRUCTION AND ACQUISITION.—Using amounts appropriated pursuant to the authorization of appropriations in section 2103(a) and available for military family housing functions as specified in the funding table in section 4601, the Secretary of the Army may construct or acquire family housing units (including land acquisition and supporting facilities) at the installations or locations, in the number of units, and in the amounts set forth in the following table:

Army: Family Housing

State/Country	Installation	Units	Amount
Korea	Camp Humphreys	Family Housing New Construction	$297,000,000
	Camp Walker	Family Housing New Construction	$54,554,000

(b) PLANNING AND DESIGN.—Using amounts appropriated pursuant to the authorization of appropriations in section 2103(a) and available for military family housing functions as specified in the funding table in section 4601, the Secretary of the Army may carry out architectural and engineering services and construction design activities with respect to the construction or improvement of family housing units in an amount not to exceed $2,618,000.

SEC. 2103. AUTHORIZATION OF APPROPRIATIONS, ARMY.

(a) AUTHORIZATION OF APPROPRIATIONS.—Funds are hereby authorized to be appropriated for fiscal years beginning after September 30, 2016, for military construction, land acquisition, and military family housing functions of the Department of the Army as specified in the funding table in section 4601.

(b) LIMITATION ON TOTAL COST OF CONSTRUCTION PROJECTS.—Notwithstanding the cost variations authorized by section 2853 of title 10, United States Code, and any other cost variation authorized by law, the total cost of all projects carried out under section 2101 of this Act may not exceed the total amount authorized to be appropriated under subsection (a), as specified in the funding table in section 4601.

SEC. 2104. MODIFICATION OF AUTHORITY TO CARRY OUT CERTAIN FISCAL YEAR 2014 PROJECT.

In the case of the authorization contained in the table in section 2101(a) of the Military Construction Authorization Act for Fiscal Year 2014 (division B of Public Law 113–66; 127 Stat. 986) for Joint Base Lewis-McChord, Washington, for construction of an aircraft maintenance hangar at the installation, the Secretary of the Army may construct an aircraft washing apron.

SEC. 2105. EXTENSION OF AUTHORIZATIONS OF CERTAIN FISCAL YEAR 2013 PROJECTS.

(a) EXTENSION.—Notwithstanding section 2002 of the Military Construction Authorization Act for Fiscal Year 2013 (division B of Public Law 112–239; 126 Stat. 2118), the authorizations set forth in the table in subsection (b), as provided in section 2101 of that Act (126 Stat. 2119) and extended by section 2107 of the Military Construction Authorization Act for Fiscal Year 2016 (division B of Public Law 114–92; 129 Stat. 1148), shall remain in effect until October 1, 2017, or the date of the enactment of an Act authorizing funds for military construction for fiscal year 2018, whichever is later.

(b) TABLE.—The table referred to in subsection (a) is as follows:

Army: Extension of 2013 Project Authorizations

State/Country	Installation or Location	Project	Amount
Kansas	Fort Riley	Unmanned Aerial Vehicle Complex	$12,200,000
Virginia	Fort Belvoir	Secure Admin/Operations Facility	$172,200,000
Italy	Camp Ederle	Barracks	$36,000,000
Japan	Sagami	Vehicle Maintenance Shop	$18,000,000

SEC. 2106. EXTENSION OF AUTHORIZATIONS OF CERTAIN FISCAL YEAR 2014 PROJECTS.

(a) EXTENSION.—Notwithstanding section 2002 of the Military Construction Authorization Act for Fiscal Year 2014 (division B of Public Law 113–66; 127 Stat. 985), the authorizations set forth in the table in subsection (b), as provided in section 2101 of that Act (127 Stat. 986) shall remain in effect until October 1, 2017, or the date of the enactment of an Act authorizing funds for military construction for fiscal year 2018, whichever is later.

(b) TABLE.—The table referred to in subsection (a) is as follows:

Army: Extension of 2014 Project Authorizations

State or Country	Installation or Location	Project	Amount
Maryland	Fort Detrick	Entry Control Point	$2,500,000
Marshall Islands	Kwajalein Atoll	Pier	$63,000,000
Japan	Kyotango City	Company Operations Complex	$33,000,000

TITLE XXII—NAVY MILITARY CONSTRUCTION

Sec. 2201. Authorized Navy construction and land acquisition projects.

Sec. 2202. Family housing.

Sec. 2203. Improvements to military family housing units.

Sec. 2204. Authorization of appropriations, Navy.

Sec. 2205. Modification of authority to carry out certain fiscal year 2014 project.

Sec. 2206. Extension of authorizations of certain fiscal year 2013 projects.

Sec. 2207. Extension of authorizations of certain fiscal year 2014 projects.

Sec. 2208. Status of "net negative" policy regarding Navy acreage on Guam.

SEC. 2201. AUTHORIZED NAVY CONSTRUCTION AND LAND ACQUISITION PROJECTS.

(a) INSIDE THE UNITED STATES.—Using amounts appropriated pursuant to the authorization of appropriations in section 2204(a) and available for military construction projects inside the United States as specified in the funding table in section 4601, the Secretary of the Navy may acquire real property and carry out *military construction projects for the installa-* | *tions or locations inside the United States, and in the amounts, set forth in the following table:*

Navy: Inside the United States

State	Installation or Location	Amount
Arizona	Yuma	$48,355,000
California	Coronado	$104,501,000
	Lemoore	$26,723,000
	Miramar	$193,600,000
	Seal Beach	$21,007,000
Florida	Eglin Air Force Base	$20,489,000
Guam	Joint Region Marianas	$89,185,000
Hawaii	Barking Sands	$43,384,000
	Kaneohe Bay	$72,565,000
Maine	Kittery	$47,892,000
Maryland	Patuxent River	$40,576,000
Nevada	Fallon	$13,523,000
North Carolina	Camp Lejeune	$18,482,000
	Cherry Point Marine Corps Air Station	$12,515,000
South Carolina	Beaufort	$83,490,000
	Parris Island	$29,882,000
Virginia	Norfolk	$27,000,000
Washington	Bangor	$113,415,000
	Bremerton	$6,704,000
	Whidbey Island	$75,976,000

(b) OUTSIDE THE UNITED STATES.—Using amounts appropriated pursuant to the authorization of appropriations in section 2204(a) and available for military construction projects out- *side the United States as specified in the funding table in section 4601, the Secretary of the Navy may acquire real property and carry out military construction projects for the installa-* *tion or location outside the United States, and in the amounts, set forth in the following table:*

Navy: Outside the United States

Country	Installation or Location	Amount
Japan	Kadena Air Base	$26,489,000
	Sasebo	$16,420,000
Spain	Rota	$23,607,000
Worldwide Unspecified	Unspecified Worldwide Locations	$41,380,000

SEC. 2202. FAMILY HOUSING.

(a) CONSTRUCTION AND ACQUISITION.—Using amounts appropriated pursuant to the authorization of appropriations in section 2204(a) and *available for military family housing functions as specified in the funding table in section 4601, the Secretary of the Navy may construct or acquire family housing units (including land ac-* *quisition and supporting facilities) at the installation or location, in the number of units, and in the amount set forth in the following table:*

Navy: Family Housing

State	Installation or Location	Units	Amount
Mariana Islands	Guam	Replace Andersen Housing PH 1	$78,815,000

(b) PLANNING AND DESIGN.—Using amounts appropriated pursuant to the authorization of appropriations in section 2204(a) and available for military family housing functions as specified in the funding table in section 4601, the Secretary of the Navy may carry out architectural and engineering services and construction design activities with respect to the construction or improvement of family housing units in an amount not to exceed $4,149,000.

SEC. 2203. IMPROVEMENTS TO MILITARY FAMILY HOUSING UNITS.

Subject to section 2825 of title 10, United States Code, and using amounts appropriated pursuant to the authorization of appropriations in section 2204(a) and available for military family housing functions as specified in the funding table in section 4601, the Secretary of the Navy may improve existing military family housing units in an amount not to exceed $11,047,000.

SEC. 2204. AUTHORIZATION OF APPROPRIATIONS, NAVY.

(a) AUTHORIZATION OF APPROPRIATIONS.— Funds are hereby authorized to be appropriated for fiscal years beginning after September 30, 2016, for military construction, land acquisition, and military family housing functions of the Department of the Navy, as specified in the funding table in section 4601.

(b) LIMITATION ON TOTAL COST OF CONSTRUCTION PROJECTS.—Notwithstanding the cost variations authorized by section 2853 of title 10, United States Code, and any other cost variation authorized by law, the total cost of all projects carried out under section 2201 of this Act may not exceed the total amount authorized to be appropriated under subsection (a), as specified in the funding table in section 4601.

SEC. 2205. MODIFICATION OF AUTHORITY TO CARRY OUT CERTAIN FISCAL YEAR 2014 PROJECT.

In the case of the authorization contained in the table in section 2201 of the Military Construction Authorization Act for Fiscal Year 2014 (division B of Public Law 113–66; 127 Stat. 989) for Pearl City, Hawaii, for construction of a water transmission line at that location, the Secretary of the Navy may construct a 591-meter (1,940-foot) long 16-inch diameter water trans- mission line as part of the network required to provide the main water supply to Joint Base Pearl Harbor-Hickam, Hawaii.

SEC. 2206. EXTENSION OF AUTHORIZATIONS OF CERTAIN FISCAL YEAR 2013 PROJECTS.

(a) EXTENSION.—Notwithstanding section 2002 of the Military Construction Authorization Act for Fiscal Year 2013 (division B of Public Law 112–239; 126 Stat. 2118), the authorizations set forth in the table in subsection (b), as provided in section 2201 of that Act (126 Stat. 2122) and extended by section 2206 of the Military Construction Authorization Act for Fiscal Year 2016 (division B of Public Law 114–92; 129 Stat. 1151), shall remain in effect until October 1, 2017, or the date of the enactment of an Act authorizing funds for military construction for fiscal year 2018, whichever is later.

(b) TABLE.—The table referred to in subsection (a) is as follows:

Navy: Extension of 2013 Project Authorizations

State/Country	Installation or Location	Project	Amount
California	Camp Pendleton	Comm. Information Systems Ops Complex	$78,897,000
Greece	Souda Bay	Intermodal Access Road	$4,630,000
South Carolina	Beaufort	Recycling/Hazardous Waste Facility	$3,743,000
Worldwide Unspecified	Various Worldwide Locations	BAMS Operational Facilities	$34,048,000

SEC. 2207. EXTENSION OF AUTHORIZATIONS OF CERTAIN FISCAL YEAR 2014 PROJECTS.

(a) EXTENSION.—Notwithstanding section 2002 of the Military Construction Authorization Act for Fiscal Year 2014 (division B of Public Law 113–66; 127 Stat. 985), the authorizations set forth in the table in subsection (b), as provided in section 2201 of that Act (127 Stat. 989), shall remain in effect until October 1, 2017, or the date of the enactment of an Act authorizing funds for military construction for fiscal year 2018, whichever is later.

(b) TABLE.—The table referred to in subsection (a) is as follows:

Navy: Extension of 2014 Project Authorizations

State/Country	Installation or Location	Project	Amount
Hawaii	Kaneohe	Aircraft Maintenance Hangar Upgrades	$31,820,000
	Pearl City	Water Transmission Line	$30,100,000
Illinois	Great Lakes	Unaccompanied Housing	$35,851,000
Maine	Bangor	NCTAMS VLF Commercial Power Connection	$13,800,000
Nevada	Fallon	Wastewater Treatment Plant	$11,334,000
Virginia	Quantico	Academic Instruction Facility TECOM Schools	$25,731,000
	Quantico	Fuller Road Improvements	$9,013,000

SEC. 2208. STATUS OF "NET NEGATIVE" POLICY REGARDING NAVY ACREAGE ON GUAM.

(a) REPORT ON STATUS.—

(1) REPORT.—Not later than 6 months after the date of the enactment of this Act, the Secretary of the Navy shall submit a report to the congressional defense committees regarding the status of the implementation of the "net negative" policy regarding the total number of acres of the real property controlled by the Department of the Navy on Guam, as described in subsection (b).

(2) CONTENTS.—The report required under paragraph (1) shall include the following information:

(A) A description of the real property controlled by the Navy on Guam which the Navy has transferred to the control of Guam after January 20, 2011, or which the Navy plans to transfer to the control of Guam, as well as a description of the specific legal authority under which the Navy has transferred or will transfer each such property.

(B) The methodology and process the Navy will use to determine the total number of acres of real property that the Navy will transfer or has transferred to the control of Guam as part of the "net negative" policy, and the date on which the Navy will transfer or has transferred control of any such property.

(C) A description of the real property controlled by the Navy on Guam which the Navy plans to retain under its control and the reasons for retaining such property, including a detailed explanation of the reasons for retaining any such property which has not been developed or for which no development has been proposed under the current installation master plans for major military installations (as described in section 2864 of title 10, United States Code).

(3) EXCLUSION OF CERTAIN PROPERTY.—In preparing and submitting the report under this subsection, the Secretary may not take into account any real property which has been transferred to the Government of Guam prior to January 20, 2011, to include property under the Guam Excess Lands Act (Public Law 103–339) or the Guam Land Use Plan (GLUP) 1977, or pursuant to base realignment and closure authorized under the Defense Base Closure and Realignment Act of 1990 (part A of title XXIX of Public Law 101–510; 10 U.S.C. 2687 note).

(b) POLICY DESCRIBED.—The "net negative" policy described in this section is the policy of the Secretary of the Navy, as expressed in the statement released by Under Secretary of the Navy on January 20, 2011, that the relocation of Marines to Guam occurring during 2011 will not cause the total number of acres of real property controlled by the Navy on Guam upon the completion of such relocation to exceed the total number of acres of real property controlled by the Navy on Guam prior to such relocation.

TITLE XXIII—AIR FORCE MILITARY CONSTRUCTION

Sec. 2301. Authorized Air Force construction and land acquisition projects.
Sec. 2302. Family housing.
Sec. 2303. Improvements to military family housing units.
Sec. 2304. Authorization of appropriations, Air Force.
Sec. 2305. Modification of authority to carry out certain fiscal year 2016 project.
Sec. 2306. Extension of authorization of certain fiscal year 2013 project.
Sec. 2307. Extension of authorization of certain fiscal year 2014 project.
Sec. 2308. Restriction on acquisition of property in Northern Mariana Islands.

SEC. 2301. AUTHORIZED AIR FORCE CONSTRUCTION AND LAND ACQUISITION PROJECTS.

(a) INSIDE THE UNITED STATES.—Using amounts appropriated pursuant to the authorization of appropriations in section 2304(a) and available for military construction projects inside the United States as specified in the funding table in section 4601, the Secretary of the Air Force may acquire real property and carry out military construction projects for the installations or locations inside the United States, and in the amounts, set forth in the following table:

Air Force: Inside the United States

State	Installation or Location	Amount
Alabama	Maxwell Air Force Base	$15,000,000
Alaska	Clear Air Force Station	$20,000,000
	Eielson Air Force Base	$295,600,000
	Joint Base Elmendorf-Richardson	$29,000,000
Arizona	Luke Air Force Base	$20,000,000
California	Edwards Air Force Base	$24,000,000
Colorado	Buckley Air Force Base	$13,500,000
Delaware	Dover Air Force Base	$39,000,000
Florida	Eglin Air Force Base	$123,600,000
	Patrick Air Force Base	$13,500,000
Georgia	Moody Air Force Base	$30,900,000
Guam	Joint Region Marianas	$80,658,000
Illinois	Scott Air Force Base	$41,000,000
Kansas	McConnell Air Force Base	$19,800,000
Louisiana	Barksdale Air Force Base	$21,000,000
Maryland	Joint Base Andrews	$66,500,000

Air Force: Inside the United States—*Continued*

State	Installation or Location	Amount
Massachusetts	Hanscom Air Force Base	$30,965,000
Montana	Malmstrom Air Force Base	$14,600,000
Nevada	Nellis Air Force Base	$10,600,000
New Mexico	Cannon Air Force Base	$21,000,000
	Holloman Air Force Base	$10,600,000
	Kirtland Air Force Base	$7,300,000
Ohio	Wright-Patterson Air Force Base	$12,600,000
Oklahoma	Altus Air Force Base	$11,600,000
	Tinker Air Force Base	$43,000,000
South Carolina	Joint Base Charleston	$17,000,000
Texas	Joint Base San Antonio	$67,300,000
Utah	Hill Air Force Base	$44,500,000
Virginia	Joint Base Langley-Eustis	$59,200,000
Washington	Fairchild Air Force Base	$27,000,000
Wyoming	F.E. Warren Air Force Base	$5,550,000

(b) OUTSIDE THE UNITED STATES.—*Using amounts appropriated pursuant to the authorization of appropriations in section 2304(a) and available for military construction projects outside the United States as specified in the funding table in section 4601, the Secretary of the Air Force may acquire real property and carry out military construction projects for the installation or location outside the United States, and in the amount, set forth in the following table:*

Air Force: Outside the United States

Country	Installation or Location	Amount
Australia	Darwin	$30,400,000
Germany	Ramstein Air Base	$13,437,000
	Spangdahlem Air Base	$43,465,000
Japan	Kadena Air Base	$19,815,000
	Yokota Air Base	$32,020,000
Mariana Islands	Unspecified Location	$9,000,000
Turkey	Incirlik Air Base	$13,449,000
United Arab Emirates	Al Dhafra	$35,400,000
United Kingdom	Royal Air Force Croughton	$69,582,00

SEC. 2302. FAMILY HOUSING.

Using amounts appropriated pursuant to the authorization of appropriations in section 2304(a) and available for military family housing functions as specified in the funding table in section 4601, the Secretary of the Air Force may carry out architectural and engineering services and construction design activities with respect to the construction or improvement of family housing units in an amount not to exceed $4,368,000.

SEC. 2303. IMPROVEMENTS TO MILITARY FAMILY HOUSING UNITS.

Subject to section 2825 of title 10, United States Code, and using amounts appropriated pursuant to the authorization of appropriations in section 2304(a) and available for military family housing functions as specified in the funding table in section 4601, the Secretary of the Air Force may improve existing military family housing units in an amount not to exceed $56,984,000.

SEC. 2304. AUTHORIZATION OF APPROPRIATIONS, AIR FORCE.

(a) AUTHORIZATION OF APPROPRIATIONS.—Funds are hereby authorized to be appropriated for fiscal years beginning after September 30, 2016, for military construction, land acquisition, and military family housing functions of the Department of the Air Force, as specified in the funding table in section 4601.

(b) LIMITATION ON TOTAL COST OF CONSTRUCTION PROJECTS.—Notwithstanding the cost variations authorized by section 2853 of title 10, United States Code, and any other cost variation authorized by law, the total cost of all projects carried out under section 2301 of this Act may not exceed the total amount authorized to be appropriated under subsection (a), as specified in the funding table in section 4601.

SEC. 2305. MODIFICATION OF AUTHORITY TO CARRY OUT CERTAIN FISCAL YEAR 2016 PROJECT.

In the case of the authorization contained in the table in section 2301(a) of the Military Construction Authorization Act for Fiscal Year 2016 (division B of Public Law 114–92; 129 Stat. 1153) for Malmstrom Air Force Base, Montana, for construction of a Tactical Response Force Alert Facility at the installation, the Secretary of the Air Force may construct an emergency power generator system consistent with the Air Force's construction guidelines.

SEC. 2306. EXTENSION OF AUTHORIZATION OF CERTAIN FISCAL YEAR 2013 PROJECT.

(a) EXTENSION.—Notwithstanding section 2002 of the Military Construction Authorization Act for Fiscal Year 2013 (division B of Public Law 112–239; 126 Stat. 2118), the authorization set forth in the table in subsection (b), as provided in section 2301 of that Act (126 Stat. 2126) and extended by section 2309 of the Military Construction Authorization Act for Fiscal Year 2016 (division B of Public Law 114–92; 129 Stat. 1155), shall remain in effect until October 1, 2017, or the date of the enactment of an Act authorizing funds for military construction for fiscal year 2018, whichever is later.

(b) TABLE.—The table referred to in subsection (a) is as follows:

Air Force: Extension of 2013 Project Authorization

State/Country	Installation or Location	Project	Amount
Portugal	Lajes Field	Sanitary Sewer Lift/Pump Station	$2,000,000

SEC. 2307. EXTENSION OF AUTHORIZATION OF CERTAIN FISCAL YEAR 2014 PROJECT.

(a) EXTENSION.—Notwithstanding section 2002 of the Military Construction Authorization Act for Fiscal Year 2014 (division B of Public Law 113–66; 127 Stat. 985), the authorization set forth in the table in subsection (b), as provided in section 2301 of that Act (127 Stat. 992), shall remain in effect until October 1, 2017, or the date of the enactment of an Act authorizing funds for military construction for fiscal year 2018, whichever is later.

(b) TABLE.—The table referred to in subsection (a) is as follows:

Air Force: Extension of 2014 Project Authorizations

Country	Installation or Location	Project	Amount
Worldwide Unspecified (Italy)	Aviano Air Base	Guardian Angel Operations Facility	$22,047,000

SEC. 2308. RESTRICTION ON ACQUISITION OF PROPERTY IN NORTHERN MARIANA ISLANDS.

The Secretary of the Air Force may not use any of the amounts authorized to be appropriated under section 2304 to acquire property or interests in property at an unspecified location in the Commonwealth of the Northern Mariana Islands, as specified in the funding table set forth in section 2301(b) and the funding table in section 4601, until the congressional defense committees have received from the Secretary a report providing the following information:

(1) The specific location of the property or interest in property to be acquired.

(2) The total cost, scope, and location of the military construction projects and the acquisition of property or interests in property required to support the Secretary's proposed divert activities and exercises in the Commonwealth of the Northern Mariana Islands.

(3) An analysis of any alternative locations that the Secretary considered acquiring, including other locations or interests within the Commonwealth of the Northern Mariana Islands or the Freely Associated States. For purposes of this paragraph, the term "Freely Associated States" means the Republic of the Marshall Islands, the Federated States of Micronesia, and the Republic of Palau.

TITLE XXIV—DEFENSE AGENCIES MILITARY CONSTRUCTION

Sec. 2401. Authorized Defense Agencies construction and land acquisition projects.
Sec. 2402. Authorized energy conservation projects.
Sec. 2403. Authorization of appropriations, Defense Agencies.

Sec. 2404. Modification of authority to carry out certain fiscal year 2014 project.
Sec. 2405. Extension of authorizations of certain fiscal year 2013 projects.
Sec. 2406. Extension of authorizations of certain fiscal year 2014 projects.

SEC. 2401. AUTHORIZED DEFENSE AGENCIES CONSTRUCTION AND LAND ACQUISITION PROJECTS.

(a) INSIDE THE UNITED STATES.—Using amounts appropriated pursuant to the authorization of appropriations in section 2403(a) and available for military construction projects inside the United States as specified in the funding table in section 4601, the Secretary of Defense may acquire real property and carry out military construction projects for the installations or locations inside the United States, and in the amounts, set forth in the following table:

Defense Agencies: Inside the United States

State	Installation or Location	Amount
Alaska	Clear Air Force Station	$155,000,000
	Fort Greely	$9,560,000
	Joint Base Elmendorf-Richardson	$4,900,000
Arizona	Fort Huachuca	$4,493,000
California	Coronado	$175,412,000
	Travis Air Force Base	$26,500,000
Delaware	Dover Air Force Base	$44,115,000
Florida	Patrick Air Force Base	$10,100,000
Georgia	Fort Benning	$4,820,000
	Fort Gordon	$25,000,000
Maine	Portsmouth	$27,100,000
Maryland	Bethesda Naval Hospital	$510,000,000
	Fort Meade	$38,000,000
Missouri	St. Louis	$801,000
North Carolina	Camp Lejeune	$31,000,000
	Fort Bragg	$86,593,000
South Carolina	Joint Base Charleston	$17,000,000
Texas	Red River Army Depot	$44,700,000
	Sheppard Air Force Base	$91,910,000
Virginia	Pentagon	$20,216,000

(b) OUTSIDE THE UNITED STATES.—Using amounts appropriated pursuant to the authorization of appropriations in section 2403(a) and available for military construction projects outside the United States as specified in the funding table in section 4601, the Secretary of Defense may acquire real property and carry out military construction projects for the installations or locations outside the United States, and in the amounts, set forth in the following table:

Defense Agencies: Outside the United States

Country	Installation or Location	Amount
Diego Garcia	Diego Garcia	$30,000,000
Germany	Kaiserslautern	$45,221,000
Japan	Ikakuni	$6,664,000
	Kadena Air Base	$161,224,000
	Yokota Air Base	$113,731,000
Kwajalein	Kwajalein Atoll	$85,500,000
United Kingdom	Royal Air Force Croughton	$71,424,000
	Royal Air Force Lakenheath	$13,500,000
Wake Island	Wake Island	$11,670,000

SEC. 2402. AUTHORIZED ENERGY CONSERVATION PROJECTS.

(a) INSIDE THE UNITED STATES.—Using amounts appropriated pursuant to the authorization of appropriations in section 2403(a) and available for energy conservation projects as specified in the funding table in section 4601, the Secretary of Defense may carry out energy conservation projects under chapter 173 of title 10, United States Code, in the amount set forth in the following table:

Energy Conservation Projects: Inside the United States

State	Installation or Location	Amount
California	Edwards Air Force Base	$8,400,000
	Naval Base San Diego	$4,230,000
	Fort Hunter Liggett	$5,400,000
Colorado	Fort Carson	$5,000,000
	Schriever Air Force Base	$3,295,000
Florida	SUBASE Kings Bay NAS Jacksonville	$3,230,000
Guam	NAVBASE Guam	$8,540,000
Hawaii	NSAH Wahiawa Kunia Oahu	$14,890,000
Ohio	Wright Patterson Air Force Base	$14,400,000
Utah	Dugway Proving Ground	$7,500,000
	Tooele Army Depot	$8,200,000
Various Locations	Various Locations	$28,088,000

(b) OUTSIDE THE UNITED STATES.—Using amounts appropriated pursuant to the authorization of appropriations in section 2403(a) and available for energy conservation projects outside the United States as specified in the funding table in section 4601, the Secretary of Defense may carry out energy conservation projects under chapter 173 of title 10, United States Code, for the installations or locations outside the United States, and in the amounts, set forth in the following table:

Energy Conservation Projects: Outside the United States

Country	Installation or Location	Amount
Cuba	Guantanamo Bay	$6,080,000
Diego Garcia	NSF Diego Garcia	$17,010,000
Japan	Kadena Air Base	$4,007,000
	Misawa Air Base	$5,315,000
Spain	Rota	$3,710,000
Various Locations	Various Locations	$2,705,000

SEC. 2403. AUTHORIZATION OF APPROPRIATIONS, DEFENSE AGENCIES.

(a) AUTHORIZATION OF APPROPRIATIONS.—Funds are hereby authorized to be appropriated for fiscal years beginning after September 30, 2016, for military construction, land acquisition, and military family housing functions of the Department of Defense (other than the military departments), as specified in the funding table in section 4601.

(b) LIMITATION ON TOTAL COST OF CONSTRUCTION PROJECTS.—Notwithstanding the cost variations authorized by section 2853 of title 10, United States Code, and any other cost variation authorized by law, the total cost of all projects carried out under section 2401 of this Act may not exceed the total amount authorized to be appropriated under subsection (a), as specified in the funding table in section 4601.

SEC. 2404. MODIFICATION OF AUTHORITY TO CARRY OUT CERTAIN FISCAL YEAR 2014 PROJECT.

In the case of the authorization in the table in section 2401(b) of the Military Construction Authorization Act for Fiscal Year 2014 (division B of Public Law 113–66; 127 Stat. 996), for Royal Air Force Lakenheath, United Kingdom, for construction of a high school, the Secretary of Defense may construct a combined middle/high school.

SEC. 2405. EXTENSION OF AUTHORIZATIONS OF CERTAIN FISCAL YEAR 2013 PROJECTS.

(a) EXTENSION.—Notwithstanding section 2002 of the Military Construction Authorization Act for Fiscal Year 2013 (division B of Public Law 112–239; 126 Stat. 2118), the authorizations set forth in the table in subsection (b), as provided in section 2401 of that Act (126 Stat. 2127) and amended by section 2406(a) of the Military Construction Authorization Act for Fiscal Year 2016 (division B of Public Law 114–92; 129 Stat. 1160), shall remain in effect until October 1, 2017, or the date of the enactment of an Act authorizing funds for military construction for fiscal year 2018, whichever is later.

(b) TABLE.—The table referred to in subsection (a) is as follows:

Defense Agencies: Extension of 2013 Project Authorizations

State/Country	Installation or Location	Project	Amount
Japan	Camp Zama	Renovate Zama High School	$13,273,000
Pennsylvania	New Cumberland	Replace reservoir	$4,300,000

SEC. 2406. EXTENSION OF AUTHORIZATIONS OF CERTAIN FISCAL YEAR 2014 PROJECTS.

(a) EXTENSION.—Notwithstanding section 2002 of the Military Construction Authorization Act for Fiscal Year 2014 (division B of Public Law 113–66; 127 Stat. 985), the authorizations set forth in the table in subsection (b), as provided in section 2401 of that Act (127 Stat. 995), shall remain in effect until October 1, 2017, or the date of the enactment of an Act authorizing funds for military construction for fiscal year 2018, whichever is later.

(b) TABLE.—The table referred to in subsection (a) is as follows:

Defense Agencies: Extension of 2014 Project Authorizations

State/Country	Installation or Location	Project	Amount
California	Brawley	SOF Desert Warfare Training Center	$23,095,000
Germany	Kaiserslautern	Replace Kaiserslautern Elementary School	$49,907,000
	Ramstein Air Base	Replace Ramstein High School	$98,762,000
Hawaii	Joint Base Pearl Harbor-Hickam	DISA Pacific Facility Upgrade	$2,615,000
Massachusetts	Hanscom Air Force Base	Replace Hanscom Primary School	$36,213,000
United Kingdom	RAF Lakenheath	Replace Lakenheath High School	$69,638,000
Virginia	Marine Corps Base Quantico	Replace Quantico Middle/High School	$40,586,000
	Pentagon	PFPA Support Operations Center	$14,800,000
	Pentagon	Raven Rock Administrative Facility Upgrade	$32,000,000
	Pentagon	Boundary Channel Access Control Point	$6,700,000

TITLE XXV—INTERNATIONAL PROGRAMS

Subtitle A—North Atlantic Treaty Organization Security Investment Program

Sec. 2501. Authorized NATO construction and land acquisition projects.
Sec. 2502. Authorization of appropriations, NATO.

Subtitle B—Host Country In-Kind Contributions

Sec. 2511. Republic of Korea funded construction projects.

Subtitle A—North Atlantic Treaty Organization Security Investment Program

SEC. 2501. AUTHORIZED NATO CONSTRUCTION AND LAND ACQUISITION PROJECTS.

The Secretary of Defense may make contributions for the North Atlantic Treaty Organization Security Investment Program as provided in section 2806 of title 10, United States Code, in an amount not to exceed the sum of the amount authorized to be appropriated for this purpose in section 2502 and the amount collected from the North Atlantic Treaty Organization as a result of construction previously financed by the United States.

SEC. 2502. AUTHORIZATION OF APPROPRIATIONS, NATO.

Funds are hereby authorized to be appropriated for fiscal years beginning after September 30, 2016, for contributions by the Secretary of Defense under section 2806 of title 10, United States Code, for the share of the United States of the cost of projects for the North Atlantic Treaty Organization Security Investment Program authorized by section 2501 as specified in the funding table in section 4601.

Subtitle B—Host Country In-Kind Contributions

SEC. 2511. REPUBLIC OF KOREA FUNDED CONSTRUCTION PROJECTS.

Pursuant to agreement with the Republic of Korea for required in-kind contributions, the Secretary of Defense may accept military construction projects for the installations or locations, and in the amounts, set forth in the following table:

Republic of Korea Funded Construction Projects

Country	Component	Installation or Location	Project	Amount
Korea	Army	CP Tango	Repair Collective Protection System (CPS)	$11,600,000
	Army	Camp Humphreys	Duplex Company Operations, Zoeckler Station	$10,200,00
	Army	Camp Humphreys	Vehicle Maintenance Facility & Company Ops Complex (3rd CAB)	$49,500,000
	Army	Camp Humphreys	8th Army Correctional Facility	$14,600,000
	Navy	Camp Mujuk	Marine Air Ground Task Force Operations Center	$68,000,000
	Navy	Camp Mujuk	Camp Mujuk Life Support Area (LSA) Barracks #2	$14,100,000
	Navy	Camp Mujuk	Camp Mujuk Life Support Area (LSA) Barracks #3	$14,100,000
	Air Force	Kunsan Air Base	3rd Generation Hardened Aircraft Shelters (HAS); Phases 4, 5, 6	$132,500,000
	Air Force	Kunsan Air Base	Upgrade Electrical Distribution System	$13,000,000
	Air Force	Osan Air Base	Construct Korea Air Operations Center	$160,000,000
	Air Force	Osan Air Base	Air Freight Terminal Facility	$40,000,000
	Air Force	Osan Air Base	Construct F-16 Quick Turn Pad	$7,500,000
	Defense-Wide	Camp Carroll	Sustainment Facilities Upgrade Phase I – DLA Warehouse	$74,600,000
	Defense-Wide	USAG Humphreys	Elementary School	$42,000,000
	Defense-Wide	Icheon Special Warfare Command	Special Operations Command, Korea (SOCKOR) Contingency Operations Center and Barracks	$9,900,000
	Defense-Wide	K–16 Air Base	Special Operations Forces (SOF) Operations Facility, B-606	$11,000,000

TITLE XXVI—GUARD AND RESERVE FORCES FACILITIES

Subtitle A—Project Authorizations and Authorization of Appropriations

Sec. 2601. Authorized Army National Guard construction and land acquisition projects.
Sec. 2602. Authorized Army Reserve construction and land acquisition projects.
Sec. 2603. Authorized Navy Reserve and Marine Corps Reserve construction and land acquisition projects.
Sec. 2604. Authorized Air National Guard construction and land acquisition projects.
Sec. 2605. Authorized Air Force Reserve construction and land acquisition projects.
Sec. 2606. Authorization of appropriations, National Guard and Reserve.

Subtitle B—Other Matters

Sec. 2611. Modification of authority to carry out certain fiscal year 2014 project.
Sec. 2612. Modification of authority to carry out certain fiscal year 2015 project.
Sec. 2613. Modification of authority to carry out certain fiscal year 2016 project.
Sec. 2614. Extension of authorization of certain fiscal year 2013 project.
Sec. 2615. Extension of authorizations of certain fiscal year 2014 projects.

Subtitle A—Project Authorizations and Authorization of Appropriations

SEC. 2601. AUTHORIZED ARMY NATIONAL GUARD CONSTRUCTION AND LAND ACQUISITION PROJECTS.

Using amounts appropriated pursuant to the authorization of appropriations in section 2606 and available for the National Guard and Reserve as specified in the funding table in section 4601, the Secretary of the Army may acquire real property and carry out military construction projects for the Army National Guard locations inside the United States, and in the amounts, set forth in the following table:

Army National Guard

State	Location	Amount
Colorado	Fort Carson	$16,500,000
Hawaii	Hilo	$31,000,000
Iowa	Davenport	$23,000,000
Kansas	Fort Leavenworth	$29,000,000
New Hampshire	Hooksett	$11,000,000
	Rochester	$8,900,000
Oklahoma	Ardmore	$22,000,000
Pennsylvania	Fort Indiantown Gap	$20,000,000
	York	$9,300,000
Rhode Island	East Greenwich	$20,000,000
Utah	Camp Williams	$37,000,000
Wyoming	Camp Guernsey	$31,000,000
	Laramie	$21,000,000

SEC. 2602. AUTHORIZED ARMY RESERVE CONSTRUCTION AND LAND ACQUISITION PROJECTS.

Using amounts appropriated pursuant to the authorization of appropriations in section 2606 and available for the National Guard and Reserve as specified in the funding table in section 4601, the Secretary of the Army may acquire real property and carry out military construction projects for the Army Reserve locations inside the United States, and in the amounts, set forth in the following table:

Army Reserve

State	Location	Amount
Arizona	Phoenix	$30,000,000
California	Camp Parks	$19,000,000
	Fort Hunter Liggett	$21,500,000
Virginia	Dublin	$6,000,000
Wisconsin	Fort McCoy	$11,400,000

SEC. 2603. AUTHORIZED NAVY RESERVE AND MARINE CORPS RESERVE CONSTRUCTION AND LAND ACQUISITION PROJECTS.

Using amounts appropriated pursuant to the authorization of appropriations in section 2606 and available for the National Guard and Reserve as specified in the funding table in section 4601, the Secretary of the Navy may acquire real property and carry out military construction projects for the Navy Reserve and Marine Corps Reserve locations inside the United States, and in the amounts, set forth in the following table:

Navy Reserve and Marine Corps Reserve

State	Location	Amount
Louisiana	New Orleans	$11,207,000
New York	Brooklyn	$1,964,000
	Syracuse	$13,229,000
Texas	Galveston	$8,414,000

SEC. 2604. AUTHORIZED AIR NATIONAL GUARD CONSTRUCTION AND LAND ACQUISITION PROJECTS.

Using amounts appropriated pursuant to the authorization of appropriations in section 2606 and available for the National Guard and Reserve as specified in the funding table in section 4601, the Secretary of the Air Force may acquire real property and carry out military construction projects for the Air National Guard locations inside the United States, and in the amounts, set forth in the following table:

Air National Guard

State	Location	Amount
Connecticut	Bradley IAP	$6,300,000
Florida	Jacksonville IAP	$9,000,000
Hawaii	Joint Base Pearl Harbor-Hickam	$11,000,000
Iowa	Sioux Gateway Airport	$12,600,000
Maryland	Joint Base Andrews	$5,000,000
Minnesota	Duluth IAP	$7,600,000
New Hampshire	Pease International Trade Port	$1,500,000
North Carolina	Charlotte/Douglas IAP	$50,600,000
Ohio	Toledo Express Airport	$6,000,000
South Carolina	McEntire ANGS	$8,400,000
Texas	Ellington Field	$4,500,000
Vermont	Burlington IAP	$4,500,000

SEC. 2605. AUTHORIZED AIR FORCE RESERVE CONSTRUCTION AND LAND ACQUISITION PROJECTS.

Using amounts appropriated pursuant to the authorization of appropriations in section 2606 and available for the National Guard and Reserve as specified in the funding table in section 4601, the Secretary of the Air Force may acquire real property and carry out military construction projects for the Air Force Reserve locations inside the United States, and in the amounts, set forth in the following table:

Air Force Reserve

State	Location	Amount
North Carolina	Seymour Johnson Air Force Base	$97,950,000
Pennsylvania	Pittsburgh International Airport	$85,000,000

SEC. 2606. AUTHORIZATION OF APPROPRIATIONS, NATIONAL GUARD AND RESERVE.

Funds are hereby authorized to be appropriated for fiscal years beginning after September 30, 2016, for the costs of acquisition, architectural and engineering services, and construction of facilities for the Guard and Reserve Forces, and for contributions therefor, under chapter 1803 of title 10, United States Code (including the cost of acquisition of land for those facilities), as specified in the funding table in section 4601.

Subtitle B—Other Matters

SEC. 2611. MODIFICATION OF AUTHORITY TO CARRY OUT CERTAIN FISCAL YEAR 2014 PROJECT.

In the case of the authorization contained in the table in section 2602 of the Military Construction Authorization Act for Fiscal Year 2014 (division B of Public Law 113–66; 127 Stat. 1001) for Bullville, New York, for construction of a new Army Reserve Center at that location, the Secretary of the Army may add to or alter the existing Army Reserve Center at Bullville, New York.

SEC. 2612. MODIFICATION OF AUTHORITY TO CARRY OUT CERTAIN FISCAL YEAR 2015 PROJECT.

In the case of the authorization contained in the table in section 2603 of the Military Construction Authorization Act for Fiscal Year 2015 (division B of Public Law 113–291; 128 Stat. 3689) for Pittsburgh, Pennsylvania, for construction of a Reserve Training Center at that location, the Secretary of the Navy may acquire approximately 8.5 acres (370,260 square feet) of adjacent land, obtain necessary interest in land, and construct road improvements and associated supporting facilities to provide required access to the Reserve Training Center.

SEC. 2613. MODIFICATION OF AUTHORITY TO CARRY OUT CERTAIN FISCAL YEAR 2016 PROJECT.

In the case of the authorization contained in the table in section 2602 of the Military Construction Authorization Act for Fiscal Year 2016 (division B of Public Law 114–92; 129 Stat. 1163) for MacDill Air Force Base, Florida, for construction of an Army Reserve Center/Aviation Support Facility at that location, the Secretary

of the Army may relocate and construct replacement skeet and grenade launcher ranges necessary to clear the site for the new Army Reserve facilities.

SEC. 2614. EXTENSION OF AUTHORIZATION OF CERTAIN FISCAL YEAR 2013 PROJECT.

(a) EXTENSION.—Notwithstanding section 2002 of the Military Construction Authorization Act for Fiscal Year 2013 (division B of Public Law 112–239; 126 Stat. 2118), the authorizations set forth in the table in subsection (b), as provided

in section 2603 of that Act (126 Stat. 2135) and extended by section 2614 of the Military Construction Authorization Act for Fiscal Year 2016 (division B of Public Law 114–92; 129 Stat. 1166), shall remain in effect until October 1, 2017, or the date of the enactment of an Act authorizing funds for military construction for fiscal year 2018, whichever is later.

(b) TABLE.—The table referred to in subsection (a) is as follows:

National Guard and Reserve: Extension of 2013 Project Authorization

State	Installation or Location	Project	Amount
Iowa	Fort Des Moines	Joint Reserve Center	$19,162,000

SEC. 2615. EXTENSION OF AUTHORIZATIONS OF CERTAIN FISCAL YEAR 2014 PROJECTS.

(a) EXTENSION.—Notwithstanding section 2002 of the Military Construction Authorization Act

for Fiscal Year 2014 (division B of Public Law 113–66; 127 Stat. 985), the authorizations set forth in the table in subsection (b), as provided in sections 2602, 2603, 2604, and 2605 of that Act (127 Stat. 1001, 1002), shall remain in effect until

October 1, 2017, or the date of the enactment of an Act authorizing funds for military construction for fiscal year 2018, whichever is later.

(b) TABLE.—The table referred to in subsection (a) is as follows:

National Guard and Reserve: Extension of 2014 Project Authorizations

State	Installation or Location	Project	Amount
California	Camp Parks	Army Reserve Center	$17,500,000
	March Air Force Base	NOSC Moreno Valley Reserve Training Center	$11,086,000
Florida	Homestead ARB	Entry Control Complex	$9,800,000
Maryland	Fort Meade	175th Network Warfare Squadron Facility	$4,000,000
	Martin State Airport	Cyber/ISR Facility	$8,000,000
New York	Bullville	Army Reserve Center	$14,500,000

TITLE XXVII—BASE REALIGNMENT AND CLOSURE ACTIVITIES

Sec. 2701. Extension of authorizations of certain fiscal year 2014 projects.

Sec. 2702. Prohibition on conducting additional Base Realignment and Closure (BRAC) round.

SEC. 2701. EXTENSION OF AUTHORIZATIONS OF CERTAIN FISCAL YEAR 2014 PROJECTS.

Funds are hereby authorized to be appropriated for fiscal years beginning after September 30, 2016, for base realignment and closure activities, including real property acquisition and military construction projects, as authorized by the Defense Base Closure and Realignment Act of 1990 (part A of title XXIX of Public Law 101–510; 10 U.S.C. 2687 note) and funded through the Department of Defense Base Closure Account established by section 2906 of such Act (as amended by section 2711 of the Military Construction Authorization Act for Fiscal Year 2013 (division B of Public Law 112–239; 126 Stat. 2140)), as specified in the funding table in section 4601.

SEC. 2702. PROHIBITION ON CONDUCTING ADDITIONAL BASE REALIGNMENT AND CLOSURE (BRAC) ROUND.

Nothing in this Act shall be construed to authorize an additional Base Realignment and Closure (BRAC) round.

TITLE XXVIII—MILITARY CONSTRUCTION GENERAL PROVISIONS

Subtitle A—Military Construction Program and Military Family Housing

Sec. 2801. Modification of criteria for treatment of laboratory revitalization projects as minor military construction projects.

Sec. 2802. Classification of facility conversion projects as repair projects.

Sec. 2803. Limited authority for scope of work increase.

Sec. 2804. Extension of temporary, limited authority to use operation and maintenance funds for construction projects outside the United States.

Sec. 2805. Authority to expand energy conservation construction program to include energy resiliency projects.

Sec. 2806. Additional entities eligible for participation in defense laboratory modernization pilot program.

Sec. 2807. Extension of temporary authority for acceptance and use of contributions for certain construction, maintenance, and repair projects mutually beneficial to the Department of Defense and Kuwait military forces.

Subtitle B—Real Property and Facilities Administration

Sec. 2811. Acceptance of military construction projects as payments in-kind and in-kind contributions.

Sec. 2812. Allotment of space and provision of services to WIC offices operating on military installations.

Sec. 2813. Sense of Congress regarding inclusion of stormwater systems and components within the meaning of "wastewater system" under the Department of Defense authority for conveyance of utility systems.

Sec. 2814. Assessment of public schools on Department of Defense installations.

Sec. 2815. Prior certification required for use of Department of Defense facilities by other Federal agencies for temporary housing support.

Subtitle C—Land Conveyances

Sec. 2821. Land conveyance, High Frequency Active Auroral Research Program facility and adjacent property, Gakona, Alaska.

Sec. 2822. Land conveyance, Campion Air Force Radar Station, Galena, Alaska.

Sec. 2823. Lease, Joint Base Elmendorf-Richardson, Alaska.

Sec. 2824. Transfer of administrative jurisdictions, Navajo Army Depot, Arizona.

Sec. 2825. Exchange of property interests, San Diego Unified Port District, California.

Sec. 2826. Release of property interests retained in connection with land conveyance, Eglin Air Force Base, Florida.

Sec. 2827. Land exchange, Fort Hood, Texas.

Sec. 2828. Land Conveyance, P–36 Warehouse, Colbern United States Army Reserve Center, Laredo, Texas.

Sec. 2829. Land conveyance, St. George National Guard Armory, St. George, Utah.

Sec. 2829A. Land acquisitions, Arlington County, Virginia.

Sec. 2829B. Release of restrictions, Richland Innovation Center, Richland, Washington.

Sec. 2829C. Modification of land conveyance, Rocky Mountain Arsenal National Wildlife Refuge.

Sec. 2829D. Closure of St. Marys Airport.

Sec. 2829E. Transfer of Fort Belvoir Mark Center Campus from the Secretary of the Army to the Secretary of Defense and applicability of certain provisions of law relating to the Pentagon Reservation.

Sec. 2829F. Return of certain lands at Fort Wingate, New Mexico, to the original inhabitants.

Subtitle D—Military Memorials, Monuments, and Museums

Sec. 2831. Cyber Center for Education and Innovation-Home of the National Cryptologic Museum.

Sec. 2832. Renaming site of the Dayton Aviation Heritage National Historical Park, Ohio.

Sec. 2833. Women's military service memorials and museums.
Sec. 2834. Petersburg National Battlefield boundary modification.

Subtitle E—Designations and Other Matters
Sec. 2841. Designation of portion of Moffett Federal Airfield, California, as Moffett Air National Guard Base.
Sec. 2842. Redesignation of Mike O'Callaghan Federal Medical Center.
Sec. 2843. Replenishment of Sierra Vista subwatershed regional aquifer, Arizona.
Sec. 2844. Limited exceptions to restriction on development of public infrastructure in connection with realignment of Marine Corps forces in Asia-Pacific region.
Sec. 2845. Duration of withdrawal and reservation of public land, Naval Air Weapons Station China Lake, California.

Subtitle A—Military Construction Program and Military Family Housing

SEC. 2801. MODIFICATION OF CRITERIA FOR TREATMENT OF LABORATORY REVITALIZATION PROJECTS AS MINOR MILITARY CONSTRUCTION PROJECTS.

(a) INCREASE IN THRESHOLD.—Section 2805(d) of title 10, United States Code, is amended by striking "$4,000,000" each place it appears in paragraph (1)(A), (1)(B), and (2) and inserting "$6,000,000".

(b) NOTICE REQUIREMENTS.—Section 2805(d) of such title is amended—
(1) by striking the second sentence of paragraph (2); and
(2) by amending paragraph (3) to read as follows:
"(3) If the Secretary concerned makes a decision to carry out an unspecified minor military construction project to which this subsection applies, the Secretary concerned shall notify in writing the appropriate committees of Congress of that decision, of the justification for the project, and of the estimated cost of the project. The project may then be carried out only after the end of the 21-day period beginning on the date the notification is received by the committees or, if earlier, the end of the 14-day period beginning on the date on which a copy of the notification is provided in an electronic medium pursuant to section 480 of this title.".

(c) EXTENSION OF SUNSET.—Paragraph (5) of section 2805(d) of such title is amended by striking "2018" and inserting "2025".

SEC. 2802. CLASSIFICATION OF FACILITY CONVERSION PROJECTS AS REPAIR PROJECTS.

Subsection (e) of section 2811 of title 10, United States Code, is amended to read as follows:
"(e) REPAIR PROJECT DEFINED.—In this section, the term 'repair project' means a project—
"(1) to restore a real property facility, system, or component to such a condition that it may effectively be used for its designated functional purpose; or
"(2) to convert a real property facility, system, or component to a new functional purpose without increasing its external dimensions.".

SEC. 2803. LIMITED AUTHORITY FOR SCOPE OF WORK INCREASE.

(a) IN GENERAL.—Section 2853 of title 10, United States Code, is amended—
(1) in subsection (b)(2), by striking "The scope of work" and inserting "Except as provided in subsection (d), the scope of work";
(2) by redesignating subsections (d) and (e) as subsections (e) and (f), respectively; and
(3) by inserting after subsection (c) the following new subsection (d):
"(d) The limitation in subsection (b)(2) on an increase in the scope of work does not apply if—

"(1) the increase in the scope of work is not more than 10 percent of the amount specified for that project, construction, improvement, or acquisition in the justification data provided to Congress as part of the request for authorization of the project, construction, improvement, or acquisition;
"(2) the increase is approved by the Secretary concerned;
"(3) the Secretary concerned notifies the congressional defense committees in writing of the increase in scope and the reasons therefor; and
"(4) a period of 21 days has elapsed after the date on which the notification is received by the committees or, if over sooner, a period of 14 days has elapsed after the date on which a copy of the notification is provided in an electronic medium pursuant to section 480 of this title.".

(b) CROSS-REFERENCE AMENDMENTS.—(1) Subsection (a) of such section is amended by striking "subsection (c) or (d)" and inserting "subsection (c), (d), or (e)".
(2) Subsection (f) of such section, as redesignated by subsection (a)(2), is amended by striking "through (d)" and inserting "through (e)".
(c) ADDITIONAL TECHNICAL AMENDMENT.—Subsection (a) of such section is further amended by inserting "of this title" after "section 2805(a)".

SEC. 2804. EXTENSION OF TEMPORARY, LIMITED AUTHORITY TO USE OPERATION AND MAINTENANCE FUNDS FOR CONSTRUCTION PROJECTS OUTSIDE THE UNITED STATES.

(a) EXTENSION OF AUTHORITY.—Subsection (h) of section 2808 of the Military Construction Authorization Act for Fiscal Year 2004 (division B of Public Law 108–136; 117 Stat. 1723), as most recently amended by section 2802 of the Military Construction Authorization Act for Fiscal Year 2016 (division B of Public Law 114–92; 129 Stat. 1169), is amended—
(1) in paragraph (1), by striking "December 31, 2016" and inserting "December 31, 2017"; and
(2) in paragraph (2), by striking "fiscal year 2017" and inserting "fiscal year 2018".
(b) LIMITATION ON USE OF AUTHORITY.—Subsection (c)(1) of such section is amended—
(1) by striking "October 1, 2015" and inserting "October 1, 2016";
(2) by striking "December 31, 2016" and inserting "December 31, 2017"; and
(3) by striking "fiscal year 2017" and inserting "fiscal year 2018".

SEC. 2805. AUTHORITY TO EXPAND ENERGY CONSERVATION CONSTRUCTION PROGRAM TO INCLUDE ENERGY RESILIENCY PROJECTS.

(a) EXPANSION OF AUTHORITY TO ENERGY RESILIENCY AND ENERGY SECURITY PROJECTS.—
(1) IN GENERAL.—Section 2914 of title 10, United States Code, is amended—
(A) in the section heading, by inserting "**RESILIENCY AND**" before "**CONSERVATION CONSTRUCTION PROJECTS**"; and
(B) in subsection (a), by striking "military construction project for energy conservation" and inserting "military construction project for energy resiliency, energy security, or energy conservation".
(2) CLERICAL AMENDMENT.—The table of sections at the beginning of chapter 173 of such title is amended by striking the item relating to section 2914 and inserting the following new item:
"2914. Energy resiliency and conservation construction projects.".

(b) NOTICE AND REPORTING REQUIREMENTS FOR PROJECTS.—
(1) CONTENTS OF NOTIFICATIONS.—
(A) CONTENTS.—Section 2914(b) of title 10, United States Code, is amended—
(i) by striking "When a decision" and inserting "(1) When a decision"; and

(ii) by adding at the end the following new paragraph:
"(2) The Secretary of Defense shall include in each notification submitted under paragraph (1) the following information:
"(A) In the case of a military construction project for energy conservation, the justification and current cost estimate for the project, the expected savings-to-investment ratio, simple payback estimates, and the project's measurement and verification cost estimate.
"(B) In the case of a military construction project for energy resiliency or energy security, the rationale for how the project would enhance mission assurance, support mission critical functions, and address known vulnerabilities.".
(B) EFFECTIVE DATE.—The amendment made by subparagraph (A) shall apply with respect to notifications provided during fiscal year 2017 or any succeeding fiscal year.
(2) ANNUAL REPORT.—Section 2914 of such title is amended by adding at the end the following new subsection:
"(c) ANNUAL REPORT.—Not later than 90 days after the end of each fiscal year (beginning with fiscal year 2017), the Secretary of Defense shall submit to the appropriate committees of Congress a report on the status of the planned and active projects carried out under this section (including completed projects), and shall include in the report with respect to each such project the following information:
"(1) The title, location, a brief description of the scope of work, the original project cost estimate, and the current working cost estimate.
"(2) In the case of a military construction project for energy conservation—
"(A) the original expected savings-to-investment ratio and simple payback estimates and measurement and verification cost estimate;
"(B) the most current expected savings-to-investment ratio and simple payback estimates and measurement and verification plan and costs; and
"(C) a brief description of the measurement and verification plan and planned funding source.
"(3) In the case of a military construction project for energy resiliency or energy security, the rationale for how the project would enhance mission assurance, support mission critical functions, and address known vulnerabilities.
"(4) Such other information as the Secretary considers appropriate.".

SEC. 2806. ADDITIONAL ENTITIES ELIGIBLE FOR PARTICIPATION IN DEFENSE LABORATORY MODERNIZATION PILOT PROGRAM.

Section 2803(a) of the National Defense Authorization Act for Fiscal Year 2016 (Public Law 114–92; 129 Stat. 1169; 10 U.S.C. 2358 note) is amended by adding at the end the following:
"(4) A Department of Defense research, development, test, and evaluation facility that is not designated as a Science and Technology Reinvention Laboratory, but nonetheless is involved with developmental test and evaluation.".

SEC. 2807. EXTENSION OF TEMPORARY AUTHORITY FOR ACCEPTANCE AND USE OF CONTRIBUTIONS FOR CERTAIN CONSTRUCTION, MAINTENANCE, AND REPAIR PROJECTS MUTUALLY BENEFICIAL TO THE DEPARTMENT OF DEFENSE AND KUWAIT MILITARY FORCES.

Section 2804(f) of the National Defense Authorization Act for Fiscal Year 2016 (Public Law 114–92; 129 Stat. 1171; 10 U.S.C. 2350j note) is amended by striking "September 30, 2020" and inserting "September 30, 2030".

Subtitle B—Real Property and Facilities Administration

SEC. 2811. ACCEPTANCE OF MILITARY CONSTRUCTION PROJECTS AS PAYMENTS IN-KIND AND IN-KIND CONTRIBUTIONS.

(a) PAYMENTS-IN-KIND AND IN-KIND CONTRIBUTIONS.—Subsection (f) of section 2687a of title 10, United States Code, is amended to read as follows:

"(f) ACCEPTANCE OF MILITARY CONSTRUCTION PROJECTS AS PAYMENTS-IN-KIND AND IN-KIND CONTRIBUTIONS.—(1)(A) Except as provided in subparagraph (B), a military construction project costing more than $6,000,000 may be accepted as payment-in-kind or as an in-kind contribution required by a bilateral agreement with a host country only if that military construction project is authorized by law.

"(B) Subparagraph (A) does not apply to a military construction project that—

"(i) was specified in a bilateral agreement with a host country that was entered into before December 26, 2013;

"(ii) was the subject of negotiation between the United States and a host country as of the date of the enactment of the Military Construction Authorization Act for Fiscal Year 2015; or

"(iii) was accepted as payment-in-kind for the residual value of improvements made by the United States at military installations released to the host country under section 2921 of the Military Construction Authorization Act for Fiscal Year 1991 (division B of Public Law 101–510; 10 U.S.C. 2687 note) before December 26, 2013.

"(2)(A) If the Secretary of Defense accepts a military construction project to be built for Department of Defense personnel outside the United States as a payment-in-kind or an in-kind contribution required by a bilateral agreement with a host country, the Secretary shall submit to the congressional defense committees a written notification at least 30 days before the initiation date for any such military construction project.

"(B) A notification under subparagraph (A) with respect to a proposed military construction project shall include the following:

"(i) The requirements for, and purpose and description of, the proposed project.

"(ii) The cost of the proposed project.

"(iii) The scope of the proposed project.

"(iv) The schedule for the proposed project.

"(v) Such other details as the Secretary considers relevant.

"(C) Subparagraph (A) shall not apply to a military construction project authorized in a Military Construction Authorization Act.

"(3) To the extent that a payment-in-kind or an in-kind contribution is provided under a bilateral agreement with a host country with respect to a military construction project for which funds have already been obligated or expended by the Secretary of Defense, the Secretary shall return to the Treasury funds in an amount equal to the value of the funds already obligated or expended for the project.

"(4) In this subsection, the term 'military construction project' has the meaning given such term in section 2801 of this title.".

(b) CONFORMING AMENDMENT.—Section 2802 of such title is amended by striking subsection (d).

(c) REPEAL.—Section 2803 of the Carl Levin and Howard "Buck" McKeon National Defense Authorization Act for Fiscal Year 2015 (Public Law 113–291; 128 Stat. 3696) is repealed, and the provisions of law amended by subsections (a) and (b) of that section shall be restored as if such section had not been enacted into law.

SEC. 2812. ALLOTMENT OF SPACE AND PROVISION OF SERVICES TO WIC OFFICES OPERATING ON MILITARY INSTALLATIONS.

(a) ALLOTMENT OF SPACE AND PROVISION OF SERVICES AUTHORIZED.—Chapter 152 of title 10, United States Code, is amended by inserting after section 2566 the following new section:

"§ 2567. Space and services: provision to WIC offices

"(a) ALLOTMENT OF SPACE AND PROVISION OF SERVICES AUTHORIZED.—Upon application by a WIC office, the Secretary of a military department may allot space on a military installation under the jurisdiction of the Secretary to the WIC office without charge for rent or services if the Secretary determines that—

"(1) the WIC office provides or will provide services solely to members of the armed forces assigned to the installation, civilian employees of the Department of Defense employed at the installation, or dependents of such members or employees;

"(2) space is available on the installation;

"(3) operation of the WIC office will not hinder military mission requirements; and

"(4) the security situation at the installation permits the presence of a non-Federal entity on the installation.

"(b) DEFINITIONS.—In this section:

"(1) The term 'services' includes the provision of lighting, heating, cooling, and electricity.

"(2) The term 'WIC office' means a local agency (as defined in subsection (b)(6) of section 17 of the Child Nutrition Act of 1966 (42 U.S.C. 1786)) that participates in the special supplemental nutrition program for women, infants, and children under such section.".

(b) CLERICAL AMENDMENT.—The table of sections at the beginning of chapter 152 of title 10, United States Code, is amended by inserting after the item relating to section 2566 the following new item:

"2567. Space and services: provision to WIC offices".

SEC. 2813. SENSE OF CONGRESS REGARDING INCLUSION OF STORMWATER SYSTEMS AND COMPONENTS WITHIN THE MEANING OF "WASTEWATER SYSTEM" UNDER THE DEPARTMENT OF DEFENSE AUTHORITY FOR CONVEYANCE OF UTILITY SYSTEMS.

It is the sense of Congress that the reference to a system for the collection or treatment of wastewater in the definition of "utility system" in section 2688 of title 10, United States Code, which authorizes the Department of Defense to convey utility systems, includes stormwater systems and components.

SEC. 2814. ASSESSMENT OF PUBLIC SCHOOLS ON DEPARTMENT OF DEFENSE INSTALLATIONS.

(a) REPORT REQUIRED.—

(1) UPDATE OF 2011 ASSESSMENT ON SCHOOL CAPACITY AND CONDITION.—Not later than one year after the date of the enactment of this Act, the Secretary of Defense shall submit to the congressional defense committees an update of the assessment on the capacity and facility condition deficiencies of elementary and secondary public schools on military installations conducted by the Secretary in July 2011 under section 8109 of the Department of Defense and Full-Year Continuing Appropriations Act, 2011 (Public Law 112–10; 125 Stat. 82). In updating the assessment, the Secretary shall take into consideration factors including—

(A) schools that have had changes in their condition or capacity since the original assessment; and

(B) the capacity and facility condition deficiencies of schools that may have been inadvertently omitted from the original assessment.

(2) ADDITIONAL INFORMATION.—The Secretary shall include in the update submitted under paragraph (1) a report on the status of the funds already appropriated, and the schedule for the completion of projects already approved, under the programs funded under section 8109 of the Department of Defense and Full-Year Continuing Appropriations Act, 2011 (Public Law 112–10; 125 Stat. 82), section 8118 of the Consolidated Appropriations Act, 2012 (Public Law 112–74; 125 Stat. 833), section 8108 of the Consolidated and Further Continuing Appropriations Act, 2013 (Public Law 113–6; 127 Stat. 322), and section 8107 of the Consolidated and Further Continuing Appropriations Act, 2015 (Public Law 113–235; 128 Stat. 2255).

(b) COMPTROLLER GENERAL EVALUATION.—Not later than 180 days after the date of the submission of the report under subsection (a), the Comptroller General of the United States shall submit to the congressional defense committees an evaluation of the updated assessment prepared by the Secretary of Defense under paragraph (1) of subsection (a), including an evaluation of the accuracy and analytical sufficiency of the updated assessment.

SEC. 2815. PRIOR CERTIFICATION REQUIRED FOR USE OF DEPARTMENT OF DEFENSE FACILITIES BY OTHER FEDERAL AGENCIES FOR TEMPORARY HOUSING SUPPORT.

The Secretary of Defense shall not sign a memorandum of agreement with another Federal agency to provide the agency with a vacant facility for purposes of temporary housing support unless the Secretary first submits to the Committees on Armed Services of the House of Representatives and Senate a certification that the provision of the facility to the agency for such purpose will not negatively affect military training, operations, readiness, or other military requirements, including National Guard and Reserve readiness.

Subtitle C—Land Conveyances

SEC. 2821. LAND CONVEYANCE, HIGH FREQUENCY ACTIVE AURORAL RESEARCH PROGRAM FACILITY AND ADJACENT PROPERTY, GAKONA, ALASKA.

(a) CONVEYANCES AUTHORIZED.—

(1) CONVEYANCE TO UNIVERSITY OF ALASKA.—The Secretary of the Air Force may convey to the University of Alaska (in this section referred to as the "University") all right, title, and interest of the United States in and to a parcel of real property, including improvements thereon, consisting of approximately 1,158 acres near the Gulkana Village, Alaska, which was purchased by the Secretary of the Air Force from Ahtna, Incorporated, in January 1989, contain a High Frequency Active Auroral Research Program facility, and comprise a portion of the property more particularly described in subsection (b), for the purpose of permitting the University to use the conveyed property for public purposes.

(2) CONVEYANCE TO ALASKA NATIVE CORPORATION.—The Secretary of the Air Force may convey to Ahtna, Incorporated (in this section referred to as "Ahtna"), all right, title, and interest of the United States in and to a parcel of real property, including improvements thereon, consisting of approximately 4,259 acres near Gulkana Village, Alaska, which was purchased by the Secretary of the Air Force from Ahtna, Incorporated, in January 1989 and comprise the portion of the property more particularly described in subsection (b) that does not contain the High Frequency Active Auroral Research Program facility. The property to be conveyed under this paragraph does not include any of the property authorized for conveyance to the University under paragraph (1).

(b) PROPERTY DESCRIBED.—Subject to the property exclusions specified in subsection (c), the real property authorized for conveyance under subsection (a) consists of portions of sections within township 7 north, range 1 east; township 7 north, range 2 east; township 8 north, range 1 east; and township 8 north, range 2 east; Copper River Meridian, Chitina Recording District, Third Judicial District, State of Alaska, as follows:

(1) Township 7 north, range 1 east:
(A) Section 1.
(B) E½, S½NW¼, SW¼ of section 2.
(C) S½SE¼, NE¼SE¼ of section 3.
(D) E½ of section 10.
(E) Sections 11 and 12.
(F) That portion of N½, N½S½ of section 13, excluding all lands lying southerly and easterly of the Glenn Highway right-of-way.
(G) N½, N½S½ of section 14.
(H) NE¼, NE¼SE¼ of section 15.
(2) Township 7 north, range 2 east:
(A) W½ of section 6.
(B) NW¼ of section 7, and the portion of N½SW¼ and NW¼SE¼ of such section lying northerly of the Glenn Highway right-of-way.
(3) Township 8 north, range 1 east:
(A) SE¼SE¼ of section 35.
(B) E½, SW¼, SE¼NW¼ of section 36.
(4) Township 8 north, range 2 east:
(A) W½ of section 31.
(c) EXCLUSION OF CERTAIN PROPERTY.—The real property authorized for conveyance under subsection (a) may not include the following:
(1) Public easements reserved pursuant to section 17(b) of the Alaska Native Claims Settlement Act (43 U.S.C. 1616(b)), as described in the Warranty Deed from Ahtna, Incorporated, to the United States, dated March 1, 1990, recorded in Book 31, pages 665 through 668 in the Chitina Recording District, Third Judicial District, Alaska.
(2) Easement for an existing trail as described in such Warranty Deed from Ahtna, Incorporated, to the United States.
(3) The subsurface estate.
(d) CONSIDERATION.—
(1) CONVEYANCE TO UNIVERSITY.—As consideration for the conveyance of property under subsection (a)(1), the University shall provide the United States with consideration in an amount that is acceptable to the Secretary of the Air Force, whether in the form of cash payment, in-kind consideration, or a combination thereof.
(2) CONVEYANCE TO AHTNA.—As consideration for the conveyance of property under subsection (a)(2), Ahtna shall provide the United States with consideration in an amount that is acceptable to the Secretary, whether in the form of cash payment, in-kind consideration, a land exchange under the Alaska Native Claims Settlement Act (43 U.S.C. 1601 et seq.), or a combination thereof.
(3) TREATMENT OF CASH CONSIDERATION RECEIVED.—Any cash payment received by the Secretary as consideration for a conveyance under subsection (a) shall be deposited in the special account in the Treasury established under subsection (b) of section 572 of title 40, United States Code, and shall be available in accordance with paragraph (5)(B) of such subsection.
(e) REVERSIONARY INTEREST.—If the Secretary of the Air Force determines at any time that the real property conveyed under subsection (a)(1) is not being used by the University in accordance with the purposes of the conveyance specified in such subsection, all right, title, and interest in and to the property, including any improvements thereto, shall, at the option of the Secretary, revert to and become the property of the United States, and the United States shall have the right of immediate entry onto such property. A determination by the Secretary under this subsection shall be made on the record after an opportunity for a hearing.
(f) PAYMENT OF COSTS OF CONVEYANCE.—
(1) PAYMENT REQUIRED.—The Secretary of the Air Force shall require the recipient of real property under this section to cover all costs to be incurred by the Secretary, or to reimburse the Secretary for such costs incurred by the Secretary, to carry out the conveyance of that property, including survey costs, costs for environmental documentation, and any other ad-

ministrative costs related to the conveyance. If amounts are collected in advance of the Secretary incurring the actual costs, and the amount collected exceeds the costs actually incurred by the Secretary to carry out the conveyance, the Secretary shall refund the excess amount to the recipient.
(2) TREATMENT OF AMOUNTS RECEIVED.— Amounts received under paragraph (1) as reimbursement for costs incurred by the Secretary to carry out a conveyance under this section shall be credited and made available to the Secretary as provided in section 2695(c) of title 10, United States Code.
(g) CONVEYANCE AGREEMENT.—The conveyance of property under this section shall be accomplished using a quitclaim deed or other legal instrument and upon terms and conditions mutually satisfactory to the Secretary of the Air Force and the recipient of the property, including such additional terms and conditions as the Secretary considers appropriate to protect the interests of the United States.

SEC. 2822. LAND CONVEYANCE, CAMPION AIR FORCE RADAR STATION, GALENA, ALASKA.

(a) CONVEYANCE AUTHORIZED.—The Secretary of the Air Force may convey, without consideration, to the Town of Galena, Alaska (in this section referred to as the "Town"), all right, title, and interest of the United States in and to a parcel of real property, including improvements thereon, at the former Campion Air Force Station, Alaska, as further described in subsection (b), for the purpose of permitting the Town to use the conveyed property for public purposes. The conveyance under this subsection is subject to valid existing rights.
(b) DESCRIPTION OF PROPERTY.—The property to be conveyed under subsection (a) consists of up to approximately 1,300 acres of the remaining land withdrawn under Public Land Order No. 843 of June 24, 1952, and Public Land Order No. 1405 of April 4, 1957, for use by the Secretary of the Air Force as the former Campion Air Force Station. The portions of the former Air Force Station that are not authorized to be conveyed under subsection (a) are those portions that are subject to environmental land use restrictions or are undergoing environmental remediation by the Secretary of the Air Force as of the date of such conveyance.
(c) REVERSIONARY INTEREST.—If the Secretary of the Air Force determines at any time that the real property conveyed under subsection (a) is not being used in accordance with the purpose of the conveyance specified in such subsection, all right, title, and interest in and to the land, including any improvements thereto, shall, at the option of the Secretary, revert to and become the property of the United States, and the United States shall have the right of immediate entry onto such real property. A determination by the Secretary under this subsection shall be made on the record after an opportunity for a hearing.
(d) CONVEYANCE AGREEMENT.—The conveyance of land under this section shall be accomplished using a quitclaim deed or other legal instrument and upon terms and conditions mutually satisfactory to the Secretary of the Air Force, after consulting with the Secretary of the Interior, and the Town, including such additional terms and conditions as the Secretary of the Air Force, after consulting with the Secretary of the Interior, considers appropriate to protect the interests of the United States.
(e) PAYMENT OF COSTS OF CONVEYANCE.—
(1) PAYMENT REQUIRED.—The Secretary of the Air Force shall require the Town to cover all costs (except costs for environmental remediation of the property) to be incurred by the Secretary of the Air Force and by the Secretary of the Interior, or to reimburse the appropriate

Secretary for such costs incurred by the Secretary, to carry out the conveyance under this section, including survey costs, costs for environmental documentation, and any other administrative costs related to the conveyance. If amounts are collected from the Town in advance of the Secretary incurring the actual costs, and the amount collected exceeds the costs actually incurred by the Secretary to carry out the conveyance, the appropriate Secretary shall refund the excess amount to the Town.
(2) TREATMENT OF AMOUNTS RECEIVED.— Amounts received under paragraph (1) as reimbursement for costs incurred by the Secretary of the Air Force or by the Secretary of the Interior to carry out the conveyance under subsection (a) shall be credited to the fund or account that was used to cover the costs incurred by the appropriate Secretary in carrying out the conveyance, or to an appropriate fund or account currently available to the appropriate Secretary for the purposes for which the costs were paid. Amounts so credited shall be merged with amounts in such fund or account and shall be available for the same purposes, and subject to the same conditions and limitations, as amounts in such fund or account.
(f) MAP AND LEGAL DESCRIPTION.—As soon as practicable after the date of the enactment of this Act, the Secretary of the Air Force, in consultation with the Secretary of the Interior, shall finalize a map and the legal description of the real property to be conveyed under subsection (a). The Secretary of the Air Force may correct any minor errors in the map or the legal description. The map and legal description shall be on file and available for public inspection in the appropriate offices of the Bureau of Land Management.
(g) SUPERSEDENCE OF PUBLIC LAND ORDERS.— Public Land Order Nos. 843 and 1405 are hereby superseded, but only insofar as the orders affect the lands conveyed to the Town under subsection (a).

SEC. 2823. LEASE, JOINT BASE ELMENDORF-RICHARDSON, ALASKA.

(a) LEASES AUTHORIZED.—
(1) LEASE TO MUNICIPALITY OF ANCHORAGE.— The Secretary of the Air Force may lease to the Municipality of Anchorage, Alaska, certain real property, to include improvements thereon, at Joint Base Elmendorf-Richardson ("JBER"), Alaska, as more particularly described in subsection (b) for the purpose of permitting the Municipality to use the leased property for recreational purposes.
(2) LEASE TO MOUNTAIN VIEW LIONS CLUB.— The Secretary of the Air Force may lease to the Mountain View Lions Club certain real property, to include improvements thereon, at JBER, as more particularly described in subsection (b) for the purpose of the installation, operation, maintenance, protection, repair, and removal of recreational equipment.
(b) DESCRIPTION OF PROPERTY.—
(1) The real property to be leased under subsection (a)(1) consists of the real property described in Department of the Air Force Lease No. DACA85-1-99-14.
(2) The real property to be leased under subsection (a)(2) consists of real property described in Department of the Air Force Lease No. DACA85-1-97-36.
(c) TERM AND CONDITIONS OF LEASES.—
(1) TERM OF LEASES.—The term of the leases authorized under subsection (a) shall not exceed 25 years.
(2) OTHER TERMS AND CONDITIONS.—Except as otherwise provided in this section—
(A) the remaining terms and conditions of the lease under subsection (a)(1) shall consist of the same terms and conditions described in Department of the Air Force Lease No. DACA85-1-99-14; and

(B) the remaining terms and conditions of the lease under subsection (a)(2) shall consist of the same terms and conditions described in Department of the Air Force Lease No. DACA85–1–97–36.

(d) ADDITIONAL TERMS AND CONDITIONS.—The Secretary may require such additional terms and conditions in connection with the leases under this section as the Secretary considers appropriate to protect the interests of the United States.

SEC. 2824. TRANSFER OF ADMINISTRATIVE JURISDICTIONS, NAVAJO ARMY DEPOT, ARIZONA.

(a) IN GENERAL.—All administrative jurisdiction of the Secretary of Agriculture over 28,423 acres of National Forest System land located within the Kaibab National Forest and the Coconino National Forest shown on the map entitled "Navajo Army Depot Jurisdiction" and dated July 19, 2016, is hereby transferred to the Secretary of the Army.

(b) VOLUNTEER MOUNTAIN LOOKOUT.—

(1) AGREEMENT.—The Secretary of the Army and the Secretary of Agriculture shall enter into an agreement to authorize the Secretary of Agriculture to occupy, access by vehicle, and use Volunteer Mountain Lookout for the purposes of wildfire detection and reporting for as long as needed by the Secretary of Agriculture.

(2) MAINTENANCE.—The Secretary of Agriculture shall be responsible for maintaining the Volunteer Mountain Lookout structure. The Secretary of the Army, in coordination with the Secretary of Agriculture, shall be responsible for maintaining road access to Volunteer Mountain Lookout.

(c) RESTORATION OR REMEDIATION.—The Secretary of the Army shall be responsible for, and fund any environmental restoration or remediation that is required for, the abatement of any release of hazardous substances, pollutants, contaminants, or petroleum products on the land referenced in subsection (a), and shall hold harmless the Secretary of Agriculture from any financial obligation to contribute to any such restoration or remediation.

(d) REVOCATION.—Public Land Order 59 (dated November 12, 1942) and Public Land Order 176 (dated September 29, 1943) are hereby revoked.

(e) REVERSIONARY INTEREST.—On the request of the owners of the Camp Navajo railroad 1 parcel and the Camp Navajo railroad 2 parcel, any reversionary interest of the United States pursuant to the Act of July 27, 1866 (14 Stat. 292, chapter 278), in and to the Camp Navajo railroad 1 parcel shall be transferred to the Camp Navajo railroad 2 parcel.

(f) RELEASE.—On transfer of the reversionary interest under subsection (e), the Camp Navajo railroad 1 parcel shall no longer be subject to the reversionary interest described in that subsection.

(g) DEFINITIONS.—In this section:

(1) CAMP NAVAJO RAILROAD 1 PARCEL.—The term "Camp Navajo railroad 1 parcel" means the land described in the deed recorded in Coconino County, Arizona, on October 6, 2014, as document number 3703647.

(2) CAMP NAVAJO RAILROAD 2 PARCEL.—The term "Camp Navajo railroad 2 parcel" means the parcel of land as described in the deed recorded in Coconino County, Arizona, on June 2, 2006, as document number 3386576.

SEC. 2825. EXCHANGE OF PROPERTY INTERESTS, SAN DIEGO UNIFIED PORT DISTRICT, CALIFORNIA.

(a) EXCHANGE OF PROPERTY INTERESTS AUTHORIZED.—

(1) INTERESTS TO BE CONVEYED.—The Secretary of the Navy (hereafter referred to as the "Secretary") may convey to the San Diego Unified Port District (hereafter referred to as the "District") all right, title, and interest of the United States in and to a parcel of real property, including any improvements thereon and, without limitation, any leasehold interests of the United States therein, consisting of approximately 0.33 acres and identified as Parcel No. 4 on District Drawing No. 018–107 (April 2013). This parcel contains 48 parking spaces central to the mission conducted on the site of the Navy's leasehold interest at 1220 Pacific Highway, San Diego, California.

(2) INTERESTS TO BE ACQUIRED.—In exchange for the property interests described in paragraph (1), the Secretary may accept from the District property interests of equal value and similar utility, as determined by the Secretary, located within immediate proximity to the property described in paragraph (1), that provide the rights to an equivalent number of parking spaces of equal value (subject to subsection (c)(1)).

(b) ENCUMBRANCES.—

(1) NO ACCEPTANCE OF PROPERTY WITH ENCUMBRANCES PRECLUDING USE AS PARKING SPACES.—In an exchange of property interests under subsection (a), the Secretary may not accept any property under subsection (a)(2) unless the property is free of encumbrances that would preclude the Department of the Navy from using the property for parking spaces, as determined under paragraph (2).

(2) DETERMINATION OF FREEDOM FROM ENCUMBRANCES.—For purposes of paragraph (1), a property shall be considered to be free of encumbrances that would preclude the Department of the Navy from using the property for parking spaces if—

(A) the District guarantees and certifies that the property is free of such encumbrances under its own authority to preclude the use of the property for parking spaces; and

(B) the District obtains guarantees and certifications from appropriate entities of the State and units of local government that the property is free of any such encumbrances that may be in place pursuant to the Tidelands Trust, the North Embarcadero Visionary Plan, the Downtown Community Plan, or any other law, regulation, plan, or document.

(c) EQUALIZATION.—

(1) TRANSFER OF RIGHTS TO ADDITIONAL PARKING SPACES.—If the value of the property interests described in subsection (a)(1) is greater than the value of the property interests and rights to parking spaces described in subsection (a)(2), the values shall be equalized by the transfer to the Secretary of rights to additional parking spaces.

(2) NO AUTHORIZATION OF CASH EQUALIZATION PAYMENTS FROM SECRETARY.—If the value of the property interests and parking rights described in subsection (a)(2) are greater than the value of the property interests described in subsection (a)(1), the Secretary may not make a cash equalization payment to equalize the values.

(d) PAYMENT OF COSTS OF CONVEYANCE.—

(1) PAYMENT REQUIRED.—The Secretary shall require the District to cover all costs to be incurred by the Secretary, or to reimburse the Secretary for such costs incurred by the Secretary, to carry out the exchange of property interests under this section, including survey costs, costs related to environmental documentation, real estate due diligence such as appraisals, and any other administrative costs related to the exchange of property interests. If amounts are collected from the District in advance of the Secretary incurring the actual costs and the amount collected exceeds the costs actually incurred by the Secretary to carry out the exchange of property interests, the Secretary shall refund the excess amount to the District.

(2) TREATMENT OF AMOUNTS RECEIVED.—Amounts received as reimbursement under paragraph (1) shall be credited to the fund or account that was used to cover those costs incurred by the Secretary in carrying out the exchange of property interests. Amounts so credited shall be merged with amounts in such fund or account and shall be available for the same purposes, and subject to the same conditions and limitations, as amounts in such fund or account.

(e) DESCRIPTION OF PROPERTY.—The exact acreage and legal description of the property interests to be exchanged under this section shall be determined by surveys satisfactory to the Secretary.

(f) CONVEYANCE AGREEMENT.—The exchange of property interests under this section shall be accomplished using a lease, lease amendment, or other legal instrument and upon terms and conditions mutually satisfactory to the Secretary and the District, including such additional terms and conditions as the Secretary considers appropriate to protect the interests of the United States.

SEC. 2826. RELEASE OF PROPERTY INTERESTS RETAINED IN CONNECTION WITH LAND CONVEYANCE, EGLIN AIR FORCE BASE, FLORIDA.

(a) RELEASE OF EXCEPTIONS, LIMITATIONS, AND CONDITIONS IN DEEDS.—With respect to approximately 126 acres of real property in Okaloosa County, Florida, more particularly described in subsection (b), which were conveyed by the United States to the Air Force Enlisted Mens' Widows and Dependents Home Foundation, Incorporated ("Air Force Enlisted Village"), the Secretary of the Air Force may release, without consideration, any and all exceptions, limitations, and conditions specified by the United States in the deeds conveying such real property.

(b) PROPERTY DESCRIBED.—The real property subject to subsection (a) was part of Eglin Air Force, Florida, and consists of all parcels conveyed in exchange for fair market value cash payment by the Air Force Enlisted Village pursuant to section 809(c) of the Military Construction Authorization Act, 1979 (Public Law 95–356; 92 Stat. 587), as amended by section 2826 of the Military Construction Authorization Act, 1989 (Public Law 100–456; 102 Stat. 2123), and section 2861 of the Military Construction Authorization Act for Fiscal Year 1999 (Public Law 105–261; 112 Stat. 2223).

(c) INSTRUMENT OF RELEASE AND DESCRIPTION OF PROPERTY.—The Secretary may execute and record in the appropriate office a deed of release, amended deed, or other appropriate instrument reflecting the release of exceptions, limitations, and conditions under subsection (a).

(d) PAYMENT OF ADMINISTRATIVE COSTS.—

(1) PAYMENT REQUIRED.—The Secretary may require the Air Force Enlisted Village to pay for any costs to be incurred by the Secretary, or to reimburse the Secretary for costs incurred by the Secretary, to carry out the release under subsection (a), including survey costs, costs related to environmental documentation, and other administrative costs related to the release. If amounts paid to the Secretary in advance exceed the costs actually incurred by the Secretary to carry out the release, the Secretary shall refund the excess amount to the Air Force Enlisted Village.

(2) TREATMENT OF AMOUNTS RECEIVED.—Amounts received under paragraph (1) as reimbursement for costs incurred by the Secretary to carry out the release under subsection (a) shall be credited and made available to the Secretary as provided in section 2695(c) of title 10, United States Code.

(e) ADDITIONAL TERMS AND CONDITIONS.—The Secretary may require such additional terms and conditions in connection with the release of exceptions, limitations, and conditions under subsection (a) as the Secretary considers appropriate to protect the interests of the United States.

SEC. 2827. LAND EXCHANGE, FORT HOOD, TEXAS.

(a) EXCHANGE AUTHORIZED.—The Secretary of the Army may convey to the City of Copperas Cove, Texas (in this section referred to as the "City"), all right, title, and interest of the United States in and to a parcel of real property, including any improvements thereon, consisting of approximately 437 acres at Fort Hood, Texas, for the purpose of permitting the City to improve arterial transportation routes in the vicinity of Fort Hood and to promote economic development in the area of the City and Fort Hood.

(b) CONSIDERATION.—As consideration for the conveyance under subsection (a), the City shall convey to the Secretary of the Army all right, title, and interest of the City in and to one or more parcels of real property that are acceptable to the Secretary. The fair market value of the real property acquired by the Secretary under this subsection shall be at least equal to the fair market value of the real property conveyed under subsection (a), as determined by appraisals acceptable to the Secretary.

(c) DESCRIPTION OF PROPERTY.—The exact acreage and legal description of the real property to be exchanged under this section shall be determined by surveys satisfactory to the Secretary of the Army.

(d) PAYMENT OF COSTS OF CONVEYANCES.—

(1) PAYMENT REQUIRED.—The Secretary of the Army shall require the City to cover costs to be incurred by the Secretary, or to reimburse the Secretary for costs incurred by the Secretary, to carry out the conveyances under this section, including survey costs related to the conveyances. If amounts are collected from the City in advance of the Secretary incurring the actual costs, and the amount collected exceeds the costs actually incurred by the Secretary to carry out the conveyances, the Secretary shall refund the excess amount to the City.

(2) TREATMENT OF AMOUNTS RECEIVED.—Amounts received under paragraph (1) as reimbursement for costs incurred by the Secretary to carry out the conveyances under this section shall be credited to the fund or account that was used to cover the costs incurred by the Secretary in carrying out the conveyances. Amounts so credited shall be merged with amounts in such fund or account and shall be available for the same purposes, and subject to the same conditions and limitations, as amounts in such fund or account.

(e) ADDITIONAL TERMS AND CONDITIONS.—The Secretary of the Army may require such additional terms and conditions in connection with the conveyances under this section as the Secretary considers appropriate to protect the interests of the United States.

SEC. 2828. LAND CONVEYANCE, P-36 WAREHOUSE, COLBERN UNITED STATES ARMY RESERVE CENTER, LAREDO, TEXAS.

(a) CONVEYANCE AUTHORIZED.—The Secretary of the Army may convey, without consideration, to the Laredo Community College (in this section referred to as the "LCC") all right, title, and interest of the United States in and to a parcel of real property consisting of approximately 0.077 acres, including the approximately 725 sq. ft. Historic Building, P-36 Warehouse, and other improvements thereon, at Colbern United States Army Reserve Center, Laredo, Texas, for the purposes of educational use and historic preservation.

(b) PAYMENT OF COSTS OF CONVEYANCE.—

(1) PAYMENT REQUIRED.—The Secretary of the Army shall require the LCC to cover costs (except costs for environmental remediation of the property) to be incurred by the Secretary, or to reimburse the Secretary for such costs incurred by the Secretary, to carry out the conveyance under subsection (a), including survey costs, costs for environmental documentation, and any

other administrative costs related to the conveyance. If amounts are collected from the LCC in advance of the Secretary incurring the actual costs, and the amount collected exceeds the costs actually incurred by the Secretary to carry out the conveyance, the Secretary shall refund the excess amount to the LCC.

(2) TREATMENT OF AMOUNTS RECEIVED.—Amounts received as reimbursement under paragraph (1) shall be credited to the fund or account that was used to cover those costs incurred by the Secretary in carrying out the conveyance. Amounts so credited shall be merged with amounts in such fund or account, and shall be available for the same purposes, and subject to the same conditions and limitations, as amounts in such fund or account.

(c) DESCRIPTION OF PROPERTY.—The exact acreage and legal description of the property to be conveyed under subsection (a) shall be determined by a survey satisfactory to the Secretary of the Army.

(d) REVERSIONARY INTEREST.—

(1) REVERSION.—If the Secretary of the Army determines at any time that the property conveyed under subsection (a) is not being used in accordance with the purpose of the conveyance specified in subsection (a), all right, title, and interest in and to such property, including any improvements thereto, shall, at the option of the Secretary, revert to and become the property of the United States, and the United States shall have the right of immediate entry onto such property. A determination by the Secretary under this paragraph shall be made on the record after an opportunity for a hearing.

(2) PAYMENT OF CONSIDERATION IN LIEU OF REVERSION.—In lieu of exercising the right of reversion retained under paragraph (1) with respect to the property conveyed under subsection (a), the Secretary may require the LCC to pay to the United States an amount equal to the fair market value of the property conveyed, as determined by the Secretary.

(3) TREATMENT OF CASH CONSIDERATION.—Any cash payment received by the United States under paragraph (2) shall be deposited in the special account in the Treasury established under subsection (b) of section 572 of title 40, United States Code, and shall be available in accordance with paragraph (5)(B) of such subsection.

(e) ADDITIONAL TERMS.—The Secretary of the Army may require such additional terms and conditions in connection with the conveyance under subsection (a) as the Secretary considers appropriate to protect the interests of the United States.

SEC. 2829. LAND CONVEYANCE, ST. GEORGE NATIONAL GUARD ARMORY, ST. GEORGE, UTAH.

(a) LAND CONVEYANCE AUTHORIZED.—The Secretary of the Interior may convey, without consideration, to the State of Utah all right, title, and interest of the United States in and to a parcel of public land in St. George, Utah, comprising approximately 70 acres, as described in Public Land Order 6840 published in the Federal Register on March 29, 1991 (56 Fed. Reg. 13081), and containing the St. George National Guard Armory for the purpose of permitting the Utah National Guard to use the conveyed land for military purposes.

(b) TERMINATION OF PRIOR ADMINISTRATIVE ACTION.—The Public Land Order described in subsection (a), which provided for a 20-year withdrawal of the public land described in the Public Land Order, is withdrawn upon conveyance of the land under this section.

(c) DESCRIPTION OF PROPERTY.—The exact acreage and legal description of the property to be conveyed under this section shall be determined by a survey satisfactory to the Secretary of the Interior.

(d) CONVEYANCE AGREEMENT.—The conveyance under this section shall be accomplished using a quitclaim deed or other legal instrument and upon terms and conditions mutually satisfactory to the Secretary of the Interior and the State of Utah, including such additional terms and conditions as the Secretary considers appropriate to protect the interests of the United States.

(e) REVERSIONARY INTEREST.—If the Secretary of the Interior determines at any time that the property conveyed under subsection (a) is not being used in accordance with the purpose of the conveyance specified in subsection (a), all right, title, and interest in and to such property, including any improvements thereto, shall, at the option of the Secretary, revert to and become the property of the United States, and the United States shall have the right of immediate entry onto such property. A determination by the Secretary under this paragraph shall be made on the record after an opportunity for a hearing.

SEC. 2829A. LAND ACQUISITIONS, ARLINGTON COUNTY, VIRGINIA.

(a) ACQUISITION AUTHORIZED.—

(1) IN GENERAL.—The Secretary of the Army may acquire by purchase, exchange, donation, or by other means, including condemnation, which the Secretary determines is sufficient for the expansion of Arlington National Cemetery for purposes of ensuring maximization of interment sites and compatible use of adjacent properties, including any appropriate cemetery or memorial parking, all right, title, and interest in and to land—

(A) from Arlington County (in this section referred to as the "County"), one or more parcels of real property in the area known as the Southgate Road right-of-way, Columbia Pike right-of-way, and South Joyce Street right-of-way located in Arlington County, Virginia; and

(B) from the Commonwealth of Virginia (in this section referred to as the "Commonwealth"), one or more parcels of property in the area known as the Columbia Pike right-of-way, including the Washington Boulevard-Columbia Pike interchange, but excluding the Virginia Department of Transportation Maintenance and Operations Facility.

(2) SELECTION OF PROPERTY FOR ACQUISITION.—The Memorandum of Understanding between the Department of the Army and Arlington County signed in January 2013 shall be used as a guide in determining the properties to be acquired under this section to expand Arlington National Cemetery to the maximum extent practicable. After consultation with the Commonwealth and the County, the Secretary shall determine the exact parcels to be acquired, and such determination shall be final. In selecting the properties to be acquired under paragraph (1), the Secretary shall seek—

(A) to remove existing barriers to the expansion of Arlington National Cemetery north of Columbia Pike through a realignment of Southgate Road to the western boundary of the former Navy Annex site; and

(B) to support the realignment and straightening of Columbia Pike and redesign of the Washington Boulevard-Columbia Pike interchange.

(3) CONSIDERATION.—The Secretary is authorized to expend amounts up to fair market value consideration for the interests in land acquired under this subsection.

(b) EXCHANGE AUTHORIZED.—

(1) EXCHANGE.—In carrying out the acquisition authorized in subsection (a), in lieu of the consideration authorized under subsection (a)(3), the Secretary may convey through land exchange—

(A) to the County, all right, title, and interest of the United States in and to one or more parcels of real property, together with any improvements thereon, located south of current Columbia Pike and west of South Joyce Street in Arlington County, Virginia;

(B) to the Commonwealth, all right, title, and interest of the United States in and to one or more parcels of property east of Joyce Street in Arlington County, Virginia, necessary for the realignment of Columbia Pike and the Washington Boulevard-Columbia Pike interchange, as well as for future improvements to Interstate 395 ramps; and

(C) to either the County or the Commonwealth, other real property under control of the Secretary determined by the Secretary to be excess to the needs of the Army.

(2) EXCHANGE VALUE.—

(A) MINIMUM VALUE.—The Secretary shall obtain no less than fair market value consideration for any property conveyed under this subsection.

(B) CASH EQUALIZATION.—Where the value of property to be exchanged is greater than the value of property to be acquired by the Secretary, the Secretary may accept cash equalization payments.

(C) TREATMENT OF CASH CONSIDERATION RECEIVED.—Any cash payment received by the United States as consideration for the conveyance under subparagraph (B) shall be deposited in the special account in the Treasury established under subsection (b) of section 572 of title 40, United States Code, and shall be available in accordance with paragraph (5)(B) of such subsection or, in the case of conveyance of excess property located on a military installation closed under the Defense Base Closure and Realignment Act of 1990 (part A of title XXIX of Public Law 101–510; 10 U.S.C. 2687 note), shall be deposited in the special account established under section 2906 of such Act.

(c) APPRAISALS.—The value of property to be acquired or conveyed under this section shall be determined by appraisals acceptable to the Secretary.

(d) DESCRIPTION OF PROPERTY.—The exact acreage and legal description of the real property to be acquired or conveyed under this section shall be determined by surveys satisfactory to the Secretary, in consultation with the Commonwealth and the County where practicable.

(e) ADDITIONAL TERMS AND CONDITIONS.—The Secretary may require such additional terms and conditions in connection with transactions authorized under this section as is considered appropriate to protect the interests of the United States.

(f) REPEAL OF AUTHORITY.—Section 2841 of the Military Construction Authorization Act for Fiscal Year 2015 (division B of Public Law 113–291; 128 Stat. 3712) is repealed.

SEC. 2829B. RELEASE OF RESTRICTIONS, RICHLAND INNOVATION CENTER, RICHLAND, WASHINGTON.

(a) RELEASE AUTHORIZED.—The Secretary of Transportation, acting through the Maritime Administrator and in consultation with the Administrator of General Services, may, upon receipt of full consideration as provided in subsection (b), release all remaining right, title, and interest of the United States in and to a parcel of real property, including any improvements thereon, in Richland, Washington, consisting as of the date of the enactment of this Act of approximately 71.5 acres and containing personal and real property, to the Port of Benton (hereafter in this section referred to as the "Port").

(b) CONSIDERATION.—

(1) CONSIDERATION REQUIRED.—As consideration for the release under subsection (a), the Port shall provide an amount that is acceptable to the Secretary of Transportation, whether by cash payment, in-kind consideration as described under paragraph (2), or a combination thereof, at such time as the Secretary may require. The Secretary may determine the level of acceptable consideration under this paragraph on the basis of the value of the restrictions released under subsection (a), but only if the value of such restrictions is determined without regard to any improvements made by the Port.

(2) IN-KIND CONSIDERATION.—In-kind consideration provided by the Port under paragraph (1) may include the acquisition, construction, provision, improvement, maintenance, repair, or restoration (including environmental restoration), or combination thereof, of any facility or infrastructure under the jurisdiction of any office of the Federal Government.

(3) TREATMENT OF CONSIDERATION RECEIVED.—Consideration in the form of cash payment received by the Secretary under paragraph (1) shall be deposited in the separate fund in the Treasury described in section 572(a)(1) of title 40, United States Code.

(c) PAYMENT OF COST OF RELEASE.—

(1) PAYMENT REQUIRED.—The Secretary of Transportation shall require the Port to cover costs to be incurred by the Secretary, or to reimburse the Secretary for such costs incurred by the Secretary, to carry out the release under subsection (a), including survey costs, costs for environmental documentation related to the release, and any other administrative costs related to the release. If amounts are collected from the Port in advance of the Secretary incurring the actual costs, and the amount collected exceeds the costs actually incurred by the Secretary to carry out the release, the Secretary shall refund the excess amount to the Port.

(2) TREATMENT OF AMOUNTS RECEIVED.—Amounts received as reimbursement under paragraph (1) shall be credited to the fund or account that was used to cover the costs incurred by the Secretary in carrying out the release under subsection (a) or, if the period of availability of obligations for that appropriation has expired, to the appropriations of fund that is currently available to the Secretary for the same purpose. Amounts so credited shall be merged with amounts in such fund or account and shall be available for the same purposes, and subject to the same conditions and limitations, as amounts in such fund or account.

(d) DESCRIPTION OF PROPERTY.—The exact acreage and legal description of the real property which is the subject of the release under subsection (a) shall be determined by a survey satisfactory to the Secretary of Transportation.

(e) ADDITIONAL TERMS AND CONDITIONS.—The Secretary of Transportation may require such additional terms and conditions in connection with the release under subsection (a) as the Secretary, in consultation with the Administrator of General Services, considers appropriate to protect the interests of the United States.

SEC. 2829C. MODIFICATION OF LAND CONVEYANCE, ROCKY MOUNTAIN ARSENAL NATIONAL WILDLIFE REFUGE.

Section 5(d)(1) of the Rocky Mountain Arsenal National Wildlife Refuge Act of 1992 (Public Law 102–402; 16 U.S.C. 668dd note) is amended by adding at the end the following new subparagraph:

"(C)(i) Notwithstanding clause (i) of subparagraph (A), the restriction attached to any deed to any real property designated for disposal under this section that prohibits the use of the property for residential or industrial purposes may be modified or removed if a determination is made that the property will be protective of human health and the environment for the proposed use with an adequate margin of safety following the modification or removal of the restriction.

"(ii) The determination described in clause (i) shall be made after—

"(I) the performance of a risk assessment pursuant to the Comprehensive Environmental Response, Compensation, and Liability Act of 1980 (42 U.S.C. 9601 et seq.); and

"(II) the completion of response actions that are necessary to protect human health and the environment to allow for the proposed use.

"(iii) The Secretary of the Army shall not be responsible or liable for any of the following:

"(I) The cost of the risk assessment performed under subclause (I) of clause (ii) or any response actions described in subclause (II) of clause (ii).

"(II) Any damages attributable to the use of property for residential or industrial purposes as the result of the modification or removal of a deed restriction pursuant to clause (i), or the costs of any actions taken in response to such damages.".

SEC. 2829D. CLOSURE OF ST. MARYS AIRPORT.

(a) RELEASE OF RESTRICTIONS.—Subject to subsection (b), the United States, acting through the Administrator of the Federal Aviation Administration, shall release the city of St. Marys, Georgia, from all restrictions, conditions, and limitations on the use, encumbrance, conveyance, and closure of the St. Marys Airport, to the extent such restrictions, conditions, and limitations are enforceable by the Administrator.

(b) REQUIREMENTS FOR RELEASE OF RESTRICTIONS.—The Administrator shall execute the release under subsection (a) once all of the following occurs:

(1) The Secretary of the Navy transfers to the Georgia Department of Transportation the amounts described in subsection (c) and requires as an enforceable condition on such transfer that all funds transferred shall be used only for airport development (as defined in section 47102 of title 49, United States Code) of a general aviation airport in Georgia, consistent with planning efforts conducted by the Administrator and the Georgia Department of Transportation.

(2) The city of St. Marys, for consideration as provided for in this section, grants to the United States, under the administrative jurisdiction of the Secretary, a restrictive use easement in the real property used for the St. Marys Airport, as determined acceptable by the Secretary, under such terms and conditions as the Secretary considers necessary to protect the interests of the United States and prohibiting the future use of such property for all aviation-related purposes and any other purposes deemed by the Secretary to be incompatible with the operations, functions, and missions of Naval Submarine Base, Kings Bay, Georgia.

(3) The Secretary obtains an appraisal to determine the fair market value of the real property used for the St. Marys Airport in the manner described in subsection (c)(1).

(4) The Administrator fulfills the obligations under the National Environmental Policy Act of 1969 (42 U.S.C. 4321 et seq.) in connection with the release under subsection (a). In carrying out such obligations—

(A) the Administrator shall not assume or consider any potential or proposed future redevelopment of the current St. Marys airport property;

(B) any potential new general aviation airport in Georgia shall be deemed to be not connected with the release noted in subsection (a) nor the closure of St. Marys Airport; and

(C) any environmental review under the National Environmental Policy Act of 1969 (42 U.S.C. 4321 et seq.) for a potential general aviation airport in Georgia shall be considered through an environmental review process separate and apart from the environmental review made a condition of release by this section.

(c) TRANSFER OF AMOUNTS DESCRIBED.—The amounts described in this subsection are the following:

(1) An amount equal to the fair market value of the real property of the St. Marys Airport, as determined by the Secretary and concurred in by the Administrator, based on an appraisal report and title documentation that—

(A) is prepared or adopted by the Secretary, and concurred in by the Administrator, not more than 180 days prior to the transfer described in subsection (b)(1); and

(B) meets all requirements of Federal law and the appraisal and documentation standards applicable to the acquisition and disposal of real property interests of the United States.

(2) An amount equal to the unamortized portion of any Federal development grants (including grants available under a State block grant program established pursuant to section 47128 of title 49, United States Code), other than used for the acquisition of land, paid to the city of St. Marys for use as the St. Marys Airport.

(3) An amount equal to the airport revenues remaining in the airport account for the St. Marys Airport as of the date of the enactment of this Act and as otherwise due to or received by the city of St. Marys after such date of enactment pursuant to sections 47107(b) and 47133 of title 49, United States Code.

(d) AUTHORIZATION FOR TRANSFER OF FUNDS.—Using funds available to the Department of the Navy for operation and maintenance, the Secretary may pay the amounts described in subsection (c) to the Georgia Department of Transportation, conditioned as described in subsection (b)(1).

(e) ADDITIONAL REQUIREMENTS.—

(1) SURVEY.—The exact acreage and legal description of St. Marys Airport shall be determined by a survey satisfactory to the Secretary and concurred in by the Administrator.

(2) PLANNING OF GENERAL AVIATION AIRPORT.—Any planning effort for the development of a new general aviation airport in southeast Georgia using the amounts described in subsection (c) shall be conducted in coordination with the Secretary, and shall ensure that any such airport does not encroach on the operations, functions, and missions of Naval Submarine Base, Kings Bay, Georgia.

(f) RULE OF CONSTRUCTION.—Nothing in this section may be construed to limit the applicability of—

(1) the requirements and processes under section 46319 of title 49, United States Code;

(2) the requirements and processes under part 157 of title 14, Code of Federal Regulations; or

(3) the public notice requirements under section 47107(h)(2) of title 49, United States Code.

SEC. 2829E. TRANSFER OF FORT BELVOIR MARK CENTER CAMPUS FROM THE SECRETARY OF THE ARMY TO THE SECRETARY OF DEFENSE AND APPLICABILITY OF CERTAIN PROVISIONS OF LAW RELATING TO THE PENTAGON RESERVATION.

(a) INCLUSION OF MARK CENTER CAMPUS UNDER PENTAGON RESERVATION AUTHORITIES.—

(1) DEFINITION OF PENTAGON RESERVATION.—Paragraph (1) of subsection (f) of section 2674 of title 10, United States Code, is amended to read as follows:

"(1) The term 'Pentagon Reservation' means the Pentagon, the Mark Center Campus, and the Raven Rock Mountain Complex.".

(2) OTHER DEFINITIONS.—Such subsection is further amended by adding at the end the following new paragraphs:

"(3) The term 'Pentagon' means that area of land (consisting of approximately 227 acres) and improvements thereon, including parking areas, located in Arlington County, Virginia, containing the Pentagon Office Building and its supporting facilities.

"(4) The term 'Mark Center Campus' means that area of land (consisting of approximately 16 acres) and improvements thereon, including

parking areas, located in Alexandria, Virginia, and known on the day before the date of the enactment of this paragraph as the Fort Belvoir Mark Center Campus.

"(5) The term 'Raven Rock Mountain Complex' means that area of land (consisting of approximately 720 acres) and improvements thereon, including parking areas, at the Raven Rock Mountain Complex and its supporting facilities located in Maryland and Pennsylvania.".

(3) CONFORMING AMENDMENT RELATING TO LAW ENFORCEMENT AUTHORITY.—Subsection (b)(1) of such section is amended by inserting "for the Pentagon Reservation and" after "law enforcement and security functions".

(4) CONFORMING AMENDMENT RELATING TO DEFINITIONS.—Subsection (g) of such section is repealed.

(b) UPDATE TO REFERENCE TO SECRETARY OF DEFENSE AUTHORITY.—Subsection (a) of such section is amended—

(1) by striking "jurisdiction" and inserting "The Secretary of Defense has jurisdiction"; and

(2) by striking "is transferred to the Secretary of Defense".

(c) REPEAL OF OBSOLETE REPORTING REQUIREMENT.—Such subsection is further amended—

(1) by striking "(1)" after "(a)"; and

(2) by striking paragraphs (2) and (3).

(d) SUBSECTION CAPTIONS.—Such section is further amended—

(1) in subsection (a), as amended by subsection (c) of this section, by inserting "PENTAGON RESERVATION.—" after "(a)";

(2) in subsection (b), by striking "(b)(1)" and inserting "(b) LAW ENFORCEMENT AUTHORITIES AND PERSONNEL.—(1)";

(3) in subsection (c), by striking "(c)(1)" and inserting "(c) REGULATIONS AND ENFORCEMENT.—(1)";

(4) in subsection (d), by inserting "AUTHORITY TO CHARGE FOR PROVISION OF CERTAIN SERVICES AND FACILITIES.—" after "(d)";

(5) in subsection (e), by striking "(e)(1)" and inserting "(e) PENTAGON RESERVATION MAINTENANCE REVOLVING FUND.—(1)"; and

(6) in subsection (f), by inserting "DEFINITIONS.—" after "(f)".

SEC. 2829F. RETURN OF CERTAIN LANDS AT FORT WINGATE, NEW MEXICO, TO THE ORIGINAL INHABITANTS.

(a) DIVISION AND TREATMENT OF LANDS OF FORMER FORT WINGATE DEPOT ACTIVITY, NEW MEXICO, TO BENEFIT THE ZUNI TRIBE AND NAVAJO NATION.—

(1) IMMEDIATE TRUST ON BEHALF OF ZUNI TRIBE; EXCEPTION.—Subject to valid existing rights and to easements reserved pursuant to subsection (b), all right, title, and interest of the United States in and to the lands of Former Fort Wingate Depot Activity depicted in dark blue on the map titled "The Fort Wingate Depot Activity Negotiated Property Division April 2016" (in this section referred to as the "Map") and transferred to the Secretary of the Interior are to be held in trust by the Secretary of the Interior for the Zuni Tribe as part of the Zuni Reservation, unless the Zuni Tribe otherwise elects under clause (ii) of paragraph (3)(C) to have the parcel conveyed to it in Restricted Fee Status.

(2) IMMEDIATE TRUST ON BEHALF OF THE NAVAJO NATION; EXCEPTION.—Subject to valid existing rights and to easements reserved pursuant to subsection (b), all right, title, and interest of the United States in and to the lands of Former Fort Wingate Depot Activity depicted in dark green on the Map and transferred to the Secretary of the Interior are to be held in trust by the Secretary of the Interior for the Navajo Nation as part of the Navajo Reservation, unless the Navajo Nation otherwise elects under clause (ii) of paragraph (3)(C) to have the parcel conveyed to it in Restricted Fee Status.

(3) SUBSEQUENT TRANSFER AND TRUST; RESTRICTED FEE STATUS ALTERNATIVE.—

(A) TRANSFER UPON COMPLETION OF REMEDIATION.—Not later than 60 days after the date on which the Secretary of the Army, with the concurrence of the New Mexico Environment Department, notifies the Secretary of the Interior that remediation of a parcel of land of Former Fort Wingate Depot Activity has been completed consistent with subsection (c), the Secretary of the Army shall transfer administrative jurisdiction over the parcel to the Secretary of the Interior.

(B) NOTIFICATION OF TRANSFER.—Not later than 30 days after the date on which the Secretary of the Army transfers administrative jurisdiction over a parcel of land of Former Fort Wingate Depot Activity under subparagraph (A), the Secretary of the Interior shall notify the Zuni Tribe and Navajo Nation of the transfer of administrative jurisdiction over the parcel.

(C) TRUST OR RESTRICTED FEE STATUS.—

(i) TRUST.—Except as provided in clause (ii), the Secretary of the Interior shall hold each parcel of land of Former Fort Wingate Depot Activity transferred under subparagraph (A) in trust—

(I) for the Zuni Tribe, in the case of land depicted in blue on the Map; or

(II) for the Navajo Nation, in the case of land depicted in green on the Map.

(ii) RESTRICTED FEE STATUS.—In lieu of having a parcel of land held in trust under clause (i), the Zuni Tribe, with respect to land depicted in blue on the Map, and the Navajo Nation, with respect to land depicted in green on the Map, may elect to have the Secretary of the Interior convey the parcel or any portion of the parcel to it in restricted fee status.

(iii) NOTIFICATION OF ELECTION.—Not later than 45 days after the date on which the Zuni Tribe or the Navajo Nation receives notice under subparagraph (B) of the transfer of administrative jurisdiction over a parcel of land of Former Fort Wingate Depot Activity, the Zuni Tribe or the Navajo Nation shall notify the Secretary of the Interior of an election under clause (ii) for conveyance of the parcel or any portion of the parcel in restricted fee status.

(iv) CONVEYANCE.—As soon as practicable after receipt of a notice from the Zuni Tribe or the Navajo Nation under clause (iii), but in no case later than 6 months after receipt of the notice, the Secretary of the Interior shall convey, in restricted fee status, the parcel of land of Former Fort Wingate Depot Activity covered by the notice to the Zuni Tribe or the Navajo Nation, as the case may be.

(v) RESTRICTED FEE STATUS DEFINED.—For purposes of this section only, the term "restricted fee status", with respect to land conveyed under clause (iv), means that the land so conveyed—

(I) shall be owned in fee by the Indian tribe to whom the land is conveyed;

(II) shall be part of the Indian tribe's Reservation and expressly made subject to the jurisdiction of the Indian tribe;

(III) shall not be sold by the Indian tribe without the consent of Congress;

(IV) shall not be subject to taxation by a State or local government other than the government of the Indian tribe; and

(V) shall not be subject to any provision of law providing for the review or approval by the Secretary of the Interior before an Indian tribe may use the land for any purpose, directly or through agreement with another party.

(4) SURVEY AND BOUNDARY REQUIREMENTS.—

(A) IN GENERAL.—The Secretary of the Interior shall—

(i) provide for the survey of lands of Former Fort Wingate Depot Activity taken into trust for the Zuni Tribe or the Navajo Nation or conveyed in restricted fee status for the Zuni Tribe

or the Navajo Nation under paragraph (1), (2), or (3); and

(ii) establish legal boundaries based on the Map as parcels are taken into trust or conveyed in restricted fee status.

(B) CONSULTATION.—Not later than 90 days after the date of the enactment of this section, the Secretary of the Interior shall consult with the Zuni Tribe and the Navajo Nation to determine their priorities regarding the order in which parcels should be surveyed and, to the greatest extent feasible, the Secretary shall follow these priorities.

(5) RELATION TO CERTAIN REGULATIONS.—Part 151 of title 25, Code of Federal Regulations, shall not apply to taking lands of Former Fort Wingate Depot Activity into trust under paragraph (1), (2), or (3).

(6) FORT WINGATE LAUNCH COMPLEX LAND STATUS.—Upon certification by the Secretary of Defense that the area generally depicted as "Fort Wingate Launch Complex" on the Map is no longer required for military purposes and can be transferred to the Secretary of the Interior—

(A) the areas generally depicted as "FWLC A" and "FWLC B" on the Map shall be held in trust by the Secretary of the Interior for the Zuni Tribe in accordance with this subsection; and

(B) the areas generally depicted as "FWLC C" and "FWLC D" on the Map shall be held in trust by the Secretary of the Interior for the Navajo Nation in accordance with this subsection.

(b) TEMPORARY RETENTION OF NECESSARY EASEMENTS AND ACCESS.—

(1) TREATMENT OF EXISTING EASEMENTS, PERMIT RIGHTS, AND RIGHTS-OF-WAY.—

(A) IN GENERAL.—The lands of Former Fort Wingate Depot Activity held in trust or conveyed in restricted fee status pursuant to subsection (a) shall be held in trust with easements, permit rights, and rights-of-way, and access associated with such easements, permit rights, and rights-of-way, of any applicable utility service provider in existence or for which an application is pending for existing facilities at the time of the conveyance or change to trust status, including the right to upgrade applicable utility services recognized and preserved, for a period of 40 years beginning on the date of the conveyance or change to trust status and without the right of revocation during such period (except as provided in subparagraph (B)).

(B) TERMINATION.—During the 40-year period referred to in subparagraph (A), an easement, permit right, or right-of-way recognized and preserved under subparagraph (A) shall terminate only—

(i) on the relocation of an applicable utility service referred to in subparagraph (A), but only with respect to that portion of the utility facilities that are relocated; or

(ii) with the consent of the holder of the easement, permit right, or right-of-way.

(C) ADDITIONAL EASEMENTS.—During the 40-year period referred to in subparagraph (A), the Secretary of the Interior shall grant to a utility service provider, without consideration, such additional easements across lands held in trust or conveyed in restricted fee status pursuant to subsection (a) as the Secretary considers necessary to accommodate the relocation or reconnection of a utility service existing on the date of enactment of this section.

(2) ACCESS FOR ENVIRONMENTAL RESPONSE ACTIONS.—The lands of Former Fort Wingate Depot Activity held in trust or conveyed in restricted fee status pursuant to subsection (a) shall be subject to reserved access by the United States as the Secretary of the Army and the Secretary of the Interior determine are reasonably required to permit access to lands of Former Fort Wingate Depot Activity for administrative

and environmental response purposes. The Secretary of the Army shall provide to the governments of the Zuni Tribe and the Navajo Nation written copies of all access reservations under this subsection.

(3) SHARED ACCESS.—

(A) PARCEL 1 SHARED CULTURAL AND RELIGIOUS ACCESS.—In the case of the lands of Former Fort Wingate Depot Activity depicted as Parcel 1 on the Map, the lands shall be held in trust subject to a shared easement for cultural and religious purposes only. Both the Zuni Tribe and the Navajo Nation shall have unhindered access to their respective cultural and religious sites within Parcel 1. Within 1 year after the date of the enactment of this section, the Zuni Tribe and the Navajo Nation shall exchange detailed information to document the existence of cultural and religious sites within Parcel 1 for the purpose of carrying out this subparagraph. The information shall also be provided to the Secretary of the Interior.

(B) OTHER SHARED ACCESS.—Subject to the written consent of both the Zuni Tribe and the Navajo Nation, the Secretary of the Interior may facilitate shared access to other lands held in trust or restricted fee status pursuant to subsection (a), including, but not limited to, religious and cultural sites.

(4) I–40 FRONTAGE ROAD ENTRANCE.—The access road for the Former Fort Wingate Depot Activity, which originates at the frontage road for Interstate 40 and leads to the parcel of the Former Fort Wingate Depot Activity depicted as "administration area" on the Map, shall be held in common by the Zuni Tribe and Navajo Nation to provide for equal access to Former Fort Wingate Depot Activity.

(5) COMPATIBILITY WITH DEFENSE ACTIVITIES.—The lands of Former Fort Wingate Depot Activity held in trust or conveyed in restricted fee status pursuant to subsection (a) shall be subject to reservations by the United States as the Secretary of Defense determines are reasonably required to permit access to lands of the Fort Wingate launch complex for administrative, test operations, and launch operations purposes. The Secretary of Defense shall provide the governments of the Zuni Tribe and the Navajo Nation written copies of all reservations under this paragraph.

(c) ENVIRONMENTAL REMEDIATION.—Nothing in this section shall be construed as alleviating, altering, or affecting the responsibility of the United States for cleanup and remediation of Former Fort Wingate Depot Activity in accordance with the Comprehensive Environmental Response, Compensation, and Liability Act of 1980.

(d) PROHIBITION ON GAMING.—Any real property of the Former Fort Wingate Depot Activity and all other real property subject to this section shall not be eligible, or used, for any gaming activity carried out under the Indian Gaming Regulatory Act (25 U.S.C. 2701 et seq.).

Subtitle D—Military Memorials, Monuments, and Museums

SEC. 2831. CYBER CENTER FOR EDUCATION AND INNOVATION-HOME OF THE NATIONAL CRYPTOLOGIC MUSEUM.

(a) AUTHORITY TO ESTABLISH AND OPERATE CENTER.—Chapter 449 of title 10, United States Code, is amended by adding at the end the following new section:

"§ 4781. Cyber Center for Education and Innovation-Home of the National Cryptologic Museum

"(a) ESTABLISHMENT.—The Secretary of Defense may establish at a publicly accessible location at Fort George G. Meade the 'Cyber Center for Education and Innovation-Home of the National Cryptologic Museum' (in this section referred to as the 'Center'). The Center may be used for the identification, curation, storage,

and public viewing of materials relating to the activities of the National Security Agency, its predecessor or successor organizations, and the history of cryptology. The Center may contain meeting, conference, and classroom facilities that will be used to support such education, training, public outreach, and other purposes as the Secretary considers appropriate.

"(b) DESIGN, CONSTRUCTION, AND OPERATION.—The Secretary may enter into an agreement with the National Cryptologic Museum Foundation (in this section referred to as the 'Foundation'), a nonprofit organization, for the design, construction, and operation of the Center.

"(c) ACCEPTANCE AUTHORITY.—

"(1) ACCEPTANCE OF FACILITY.—If the Foundation constructs the Center pursuant to an agreement with the Foundation under subsection (b), upon satisfactory completion of the Center's construction or any phase thereof, as determined by the Secretary, and upon full satisfaction by the Foundation of any other obligations pursuant to such agreement, the Secretary may accept the Center (or any phase thereof) from the Foundation, and all right, title, and interest in the Center or such phase shall vest in the United States.

"(2) ACCEPTANCE OF SERVICES.—Notwithstanding section 1342 of title 31, the Secretary may accept services from the Foundation in connection with the design, construction, and operation of the Center. For purposes of this section and any other provision of law, employees or personnel of the Foundation shall not be considered to be employees of the United States.

"(d) FEES AND USER CHARGES.—

"(1) AUTHORITY TO ASSESS FEES AND USER CHARGES.—The Secretary may assess fees and user charges sufficient to cover the cost of the use of Center facilities and property, including rental, user, conference, and concession fees.

"(2) USE OF FUNDS.—Amounts received by the Secretary under paragraph (1) shall be deposited into the Fund established under subsection (e).

"(e) FUND.—

"(1) ESTABLISHMENT.—Upon the Secretary's acceptance of the Center under subsection (c)(1), there is established in the Treasury a fund to be known as the Cyber Center for Education and Innovation-Home of the National Cryptologic Museum Fund (in this section referred to as the 'Fund').

"(2) CONTENTS.—The Fund shall consist of the following amounts:

"(A) Fees and user charges deposited by the Secretary under subsection (d).

"(B) Any other amounts received by the Secretary which are attributable to the operation of the Center.

"(3) USE OF FUND.—Amounts in the Fund shall be available to the Secretary for the benefit and operation of the Center, including the costs of operation and the acquisition of books, manuscripts, works of art, historical artifacts, drawings, plans, models, and condemned or obsolete combat materiel.

"(4) CONTINUING AVAILABILITY OF AMOUNTS.—Amounts in the Fund shall be available without fiscal year limitation.".

(b) CLERICAL AMENDMENT.—The table of sections at the beginning of such chapter is amended by adding at the end the following new item:

"4781. Cyber Center for Education and Innovation-Home of the National Cryptologic Museum.".

SEC. 2832. RENAMING SITE OF THE DAYTON AVIATION HERITAGE NATIONAL HISTORICAL PARK, OHIO.

Section 101(b)(5) of the Dayton Aviation Heritage Preservation Act of 1992 (16 U.S.C. 410ww(b)(5)) is amended by striking "Aviation Center" and inserting "National Museum".

SEC. 2833. WOMEN'S MILITARY SERVICE MEMORIALS AND MUSEUMS.

(a) AUTHORIZATION.—The Secretary of Defense may provide not more than $5,000,000 in financial support for the acquisition, installation, and maintenance of exhibits, facilities, historical displays, and programs at military service memorials and museums that highlight the role of women in the military. The Secretary may enter into a contract with a nonprofit organization for the purpose of performing such acquisition, installation, and maintenance.

(b) OFFSET.—Of the funds authorized to be appropriated by section 301 for operation and maintenance, Army, and available for the National Museum of the United States Army, not more than $5,000,000 shall be provided, at the discretion of the Secretary of Defense, to carry out activities under subsection (a).

SEC. 2834. PETERSBURG NATIONAL BATTLEFIELD BOUNDARY MODIFICATION.

(a) IN GENERAL.—The boundary of the Petersburg National Battlefield is modified to include the land and interests in land as generally depicted on the map titled "Petersburg National Battlefield Proposed Boundary Expansion", numbered 325/80,080, and dated June 2007/March 2016. The map shall be on file and available for public inspection in the appropriate offices of the National Park Service.

(b) ACQUISITION OF PROPERTIES.—

(1) AUTHORITY.—The Secretary of the Interior (referred to in this section as the "Secretary") is authorized to acquire the land and interests in land described in subsection (a) from willing sellers only, by donation, purchase with donated or appropriated funds, exchange, or transfer.

(2) TECHNICAL CORRECTION.—Section 313(a) of the National Parks and Recreation Act of 1978 (Public Law 95–625; 92 Stat. 3479) is amended by striking "twenty-one" and inserting "23".

(c) ADMINISTRATION.—The Secretary shall administer any land or interests in land acquired under subsection (b) as part of the Petersburg National Battlefield in accordance with applicable laws and regulations.

(d) ADMINISTRATIVE JURISDICTION TRANSFER.—

(1) IN GENERAL.—There is transferred—

(A) from the Secretary to the Secretary of the Army administrative jurisdiction over the approximately 1.170-acre parcel of land depicted as "Area to be transferred to Fort Lee Military Reservation" on the map described in paragraph (2); and

(B) from the Secretary of the Army to the Secretary administrative jurisdiction over the approximately 1.171-acre parcel of land depicted as "Area to be transferred to Petersburg National Battlefield" on the map described in paragraph (2).

(2) MAP.—The parcels of land described in paragraph (1) are depicted on the map titled "Petersburg National Battlefield Proposed Transfer of Administrative Jurisdiction", numbered 325/80,801A, dated May 2011/March 2016. The map shall be on file and available for public inspection in the appropriate offices of the National Park Service.

(3) CONDITIONS OF TRANSFER.—The transfer of administrative jurisdiction under paragraph (1) is subject to the following conditions:

(A) NO REIMBURSEMENT OR CONSIDERATION.—The transfer shall be without reimbursement or consideration.

(B) MANAGEMENT.—

(i) LAND TRANSFERRED TO THE SECRETARY OF THE ARMY.—The land transferred to the Secretary of the Army under paragraph (1)(A) shall be excluded from the boundary of the Petersburg National Battlefield.

(ii) LAND TRANSFERRED TO THE SECRETARY.—The land transferred to the Secretary under paragraph (1)(B)—

(I) shall be included within the boundary of the Petersburg National Battlefield; and

(II) shall be administered as part of Petersburg National Battlefield in accordance with applicable laws and regulations.

Subtitle E—Designations and Other Matters

SEC. 2841. DESIGNATION OF PORTION OF MOFFETT FEDERAL AIRFIELD, CALIFORNIA, AS MOFFETT AIR NATIONAL GUARD BASE.

(a) DESIGNATION.—The 111-acre cantonment area at Moffett Federal Airfield, California, utilized by the 129th Rescue Wing of the California Air National Guard shall be known and designated as "Moffett Air National Guard Base".

(b) REFERENCES.—Any reference in any law, regulation, map, document, paper, or other record of the United States to the cantonment area at Moffett Federal Airfield described in subsection (a) shall be considered to be a reference to Moffett Air National Guard Base.

SEC. 2842. REDESIGNATION OF MIKE O'CALLAGHAN FEDERAL MEDICAL CENTER.

Section 2867 of the Military Construction Authorization Act for Fiscal Year 1997 (division B of Public Law 104–201; 110 Stat. 2806), as amended by section 8135(a) of the Department of Defense Appropriations Act, 1997 (section 101(b) of division A of the Omnibus Consolidated Appropriations Act, 1997 (Public Law 104–208; 110 Stat. 3009–118)), and as amended by section 2862 of the Military Construction Authorization Act for Fiscal Year 2012 (division B of Public Law 112–81; 125 Stat. 1701), is further amended—

(1) by striking "Mike O'Callaghan Federal Medical Center" each place it appears and inserting "Mike O'Callaghan Military Medical Center"; and

(2) in the heading, by striking "**MIKE O'CALLAGHAN**" and all that follows and inserting "**MIKE O'CALLAGHAN MILITARY MEDICAL CENTER.**".

SEC. 2843. REPLENISHMENT OF SIERRA VISTA SUBWATERSHED REGIONAL AQUIFER, ARIZONA.

The Secretary of the Army or the Secretary of the Interior may enter into agreements with the Cochise Conservation Recharge Network, Arizona, in support of water conservation, recharge, and reuse efforts for the regional aquifer identified under section 321(g) of the National Defense Authorization Act for Fiscal Year 2004 (Public Law 108–136; 117 Stat. 1439).

SEC. 2844. LIMITED EXCEPTIONS TO RESTRICTION ON DEVELOPMENT OF PUBLIC INFRASTRUCTURE IN CONNECTION WITH REALIGNMENT OF MARINE CORPS FORCES IN ASIA-PACIFIC REGION.

(a) REVISION.—Notwithstanding section 2821(b) of the Military Construction Authorization Act for Fiscal Year 2015 (division B of Public Law 113–291; 128 Stat. 3701), the Secretary of Defense may proceed with a public infrastructure project on Guam which is described in subsection (b) if—

(1) the project was identified in the report prepared by the Secretary of Defense under section 2822(d)(2) of the Military Construction Authorization Act for Fiscal Year 2014 (division B of Public Law 113–66; 127 Stat. 1017); and

(2) amounts have been appropriated or made available to be expended by the Department of Defense for the project.

(b) PROJECTS DESCRIBED.—A project described in this subsection is any of the following:

(1) A project intended to improve water and wastewater systems.

(2) A project intended to improve curation of archeological and cultural artifacts.

(c) REPEAL OF SUPERSEDED LAW.—Section 2821 of the Military Construction Authorization Act for Fiscal Year 2016 (division B of Public Law 114–92; 129 Stat. 1177) is repealed.

SEC. 2845. DURATION OF WITHDRAWAL AND RESERVATION OF PUBLIC LAND, NAVAL AIR WEAPONS STATION CHINA LAKE, CALIFORNIA.

Section 2979 of the Military Construction Authorization Act for Fiscal Year 2014 (division B of Public Law 113–66; 127 Stat. 1047) is amended by striking "March 31, 2039" and inserting "March 31, 2064".

TITLE XXIX—OVERSEAS CONTINGENCY OPERATIONS MILITARY CONSTRUCTION

Sec. 2901. Authorized Navy construction and land acquisition projects.
Sec. 2902. Authorized Air Force construction and land acquisition projects.
Sec. 2903. Authorization of appropriations.

SEC. 2901. AUTHORIZED NAVY CONSTRUCTION AND LAND ACQUISITION PROJECTS.

The Secretary of the Navy may acquire real property and carry out the military construction projects for the installations outside the United States, and in the amounts, set forth in the following table:

Navy: Outside the United States

Country	Installation	Amount
Djibouti	Camp Lemonier	$37,409,000
Iceland	Keflavik	$19,600,000

SEC. 2902. AUTHORIZED AIR FORCE CONSTRUCTION AND LAND ACQUISITION PROJECTS.

The Secretary of the Air Force may acquire real property and carry out the military construction projects for the installations outside the United States, and in the amounts, set forth in the following table:

Air Force: Outside the United States

Country	Installation	Amount
Bulgaria	Graf Ignatievo	$13,400,000
Djibouti	Chabelley Airfield	$10,500,000
Estonia	Amari Air Base	$6,500,000
Germany	Spangdahlem Air Base	$18,700,000
Lithuania	Siauliai	$3,000,000
Poland	Powidz Air Base	$4,100,000
	Lask Air Base	$4,100,000
Romania	Campia Turzii	$18,500,000

SEC. 2903. AUTHORIZATION OF APPROPRIATIONS.

Funds are hereby authorized to be appropriated for fiscal years beginning after September 30, 2016, for the military construction projects outside the United States authorized by this title as specified in the funding table in section 4602 and 4603.

TITLE XXX—UTAH TEST AND TRAINING RANGE AND RELATED MATTERS

Subtitle A—Authorization for Temporary Closure of Certain Public Land Adjacent to the Utah Test and Training Range

Sec. 3001. Definitions.
Sec. 3002. Memorandum of agreement.
Sec. 3003. Temporary closures.
Sec. 3004. Liability.
Sec. 3005. Community resource advisory group.
Sec. 3006. Savings clauses.

Subtitle B—Bureau of Land Management Land Exchange With State of Utah

Sec. 3011. Definitions.
Sec. 3012. Exchange of Federal land and non-Federal land.
Sec. 3013. Status and management of non-Federal land acquired by the United States.
Sec. 3014. Hazardous substances.

Subtitle A—Authorization for Temporary Closure of Certain Public Land Adjacent to the Utah Test and Training Range

SEC. 3001. DEFINITIONS.

In this subtitle:

(1) BLM LAND.—The term "BLM land" means certain public land administered by the Bureau of Land Management in the State comprising approximately 703,621 acres, as generally depicted on the map entitled "Utah Test and Training Range Enhancement/West Desert Land Exchange" and dated July 21, 2016.

(2) SECRETARY.—The term "Secretary" means the Secretary of the Interior.

(3) STATE.—The term "State" means the State of Utah.

(4) UTAH TEST AND TRAINING RANGE.—The term "Utah Test and Training Range" means the portions of the military land and airspace operating area of the Utah Test and Training Area that are located in the State, including the Dugway Proving Ground.

SEC. 3002. MEMORANDUM OF AGREEMENT.

(a) MEMORANDUM OF AGREEMENT.—

(1) IN GENERAL.—Not later than 1 year after the date of enactment of this Act, the Secretary and the Secretary of the Air Force shall enter into a memorandum of agreement to authorize the Secretary of the Air Force, in consultation with the Secretary, to impose limited closures of the BLM land for military operations and national security and public safety purposes, as provided in this subtitle.

(2) DRAFT.—

(A) IN GENERAL.—Not later than 180 days after the date of enactment of this Act, the Secretary and the Secretary of the Air Force shall complete a draft of the memorandum of agreement required under paragraph (1).

(B) PUBLIC COMMENT PERIOD.—During the 30-day period beginning on the date on which the draft memorandum of agreement is completed under subparagraph (A), there shall be an opportunity for public comment on the draft memorandum of agreement, including an opportunity for the Utah Test and Training Range Community Resource Advisory Group established under section 3005 to provide comments on the draft memorandum of agreement.

(3) MANAGEMENT BY SECRETARY.—The memorandum of agreement entered into under paragraph (1) shall provide that the Secretary shall continue to manage the BLM land in accordance with the Federal Land Policy and Management Act of 1976 (43 U.S.C. 1701 et seq.) and applicable land use plans, while allowing for the temporary closure of the BLM land in accordance with this subtitle.

(4) PERMITS AND RIGHTS-OF-WAY.—

(A) IN GENERAL.—The Secretary shall consult with the Secretary of the Air Force regarding Utah Test and Training Range mission requirements before issuing new use permits or rights-of-way on the BLM land.

(B) FRAMEWORK.—The Secretary and the Secretary of the Air Force shall establish within the memorandum of agreement entered into under paragraph (1) a framework agreed to by the Secretary and the Secretary of the Air Force for resolving any disagreement on the issuance of permits or rights-of-way on the BLM land.

(5) TERMINATION.—

(A) IN GENERAL.—The memorandum of agreement entered into under paragraph (1) shall be for a term to be determined by the Secretary and the Secretary of the Air Force, not to exceed 25 years.

(B) EARLY TERMINATION.—The memorandum of agreement may be terminated before the date determined under subparagraph (A) if the Secretary of the Air Force determines that the temporary closure of the BLM land is no longer necessary to fulfill Utah Test and Training Range mission requirements.

(b) MAP.—The Secretary may correct any minor errors in the map described in section 3001(1).

(c) LAND SAFETY.—If decontamination of the BLM land is necessary due to an action of the Air Force, the Secretary of the Air Force shall—

(1) render the BLM land safe for public use; and

(2) appropriately communicate the safety of the land to the Secretary on the date on which the BLM land is rendered safe for public use under paragraph (1).

(d) CONSULTATION.—The Secretary shall consult with any federally recognized Indian tribe in the vicinity of the BLM land before entering into any agreement under this subtitle.

(e) GRAZING.—

(1) EFFECT.—Nothing in this subtitle affects the management of grazing on the BLM land.

(2) CONTINUATION OF GRAZING MANAGEMENT.—The Secretary shall continue grazing management on the BLM land pursuant to the Federal Land Policy and Management Act of 1976 (43 U.S.C. 1701 et seq.) and applicable resource management plans.

(f) MEMORANDUM OF UNDERSTANDING ON EMERGENCY ACCESS AND RESPONSE.—Nothing in this section precludes the continuation of the memorandum of understanding between the Department of the Interior and the Department of the Air Force with respect to emergency access and response, as in existence on the date of enactment of this Act.

(g) WITHDRAWAL.—Subject to valid existing rights, the BLM land is withdrawn from all forms of appropriation under the public land laws, including the mining laws, the mineral leasing laws, and the geothermal leasing laws.

SEC. 3003. TEMPORARY CLOSURES.

(a) IN GENERAL.—If the Secretary of the Air Force determines that military operations (including operations relating to the fulfillment of the mission of the Utah Test and Training Range), public safety, or national security require the temporary closure to public use of any road, trail, or other portion of the BLM land, the Secretary of the Air Force may take such action as the Secretary of the Air Force, in consultation with the Secretary, determines necessary to carry out the temporary closure.

(b) LIMITATIONS.—Any temporary closure under subsection (a)—

(1) shall be limited to the minimum areas and periods that the Secretary of the Air Force determines are required to carry out a closure under this section;

(2) shall not occur on a State or Federal holiday, unless notice is provided in accordance with subsection (c)(1)(B);

(3) shall not occur on a Friday, Saturday, or Sunday, unless notice is provided in accordance with subsection (c)(1)(B); and

(4)(A) if practicable, shall be for not longer than a 3-hour period per day;

(B) shall only be for longer than a 3-hour period per day—

(i) for mission essential reasons; and

(ii) as infrequently as practicable and in no case for more than 10 days per year; and

(C) shall in no case be for longer than a 6-hour period per day.

(c) NOTICE.—

(1) IN GENERAL.—Except as provided in paragraph (2), the Secretary of the Air Force shall—

(A) keep appropriate warning notices posted before and during any temporary closure; and

(B) provide notice to the Secretary, public, and relevant stakeholders concerning the temporary closure—

(i) at least 30 days before the date on which the temporary closure goes into effect;

(ii) in the case of a closure during the period beginning on March 1 and ending on May 31, at least 60 days before the date on which the closure goes into effect; or

(iii) in the case of a closure described in paragraph (3) or (4) of subsection (b), at least 90 days before the date on which the closure goes into effect.

(2) SPECIAL NOTIFICATION PROCEDURES.—In each case for which a mission-unique security requirement does not allow for the notifications described in paragraph (1)(B), the Secretary of the Air Force shall work with the Secretary to achieve a mutually agreeable timeline for notification.

(d) MAXIMUM ANNUAL CLOSURES.—The total cumulative hours of temporary closures authorized under this section with respect to the BLM land shall not exceed 100 hours annually.

(e) PROHIBITION ON CERTAIN TEMPORARY CLOSURES.—The northernmost area identified as "Newfoundland's" on the map described in section 3001(1) shall not be subject to any temporary closure between August 21 and February 28, in accordance with the lawful hunting seasons of the State of Utah.

(f) EMERGENCY GROUND RESPONSE.—A temporary closure of a portion of the BLM land shall not affect the conduct of emergency response activities on the BLM land during the temporary closure.

(g) LIVESTOCK.—Livestock authorized by a Federal grazing permit shall be allowed to remain on the BLM land during a temporary closure of the BLM land under this section.

(h) LAW ENFORCEMENT AND SECURITY.—The Secretary and the Secretary of the Air Force may enter into cooperative agreements with State and local law enforcement officials with respect to lawful procedures and protocols to be used in promoting public safety and operation security on or near the BLM land during noticed test and training periods.

SEC. 3004. LIABILITY.

The United States (including all departments, agencies, officers, and employees of the United States) shall be held harmless and shall not be liable for any injury or damage to any individual or property suffered in the course of any mining, mineral, or geothermal activity, or any other authorized nondefense-related activity, conducted on the BLM land.

SEC. 3005. COMMUNITY RESOURCE ADVISORY GROUP.

(a) ESTABLISHMENT.—Not later than 90 days after the date of enactment of this Act, there shall be established the Utah Test and Training Range Community Resource Advisory Group (referred to in this section as the "Community Group") to provide regular and continuing input to the Secretary and the Secretary of the Air Force on matters involving public access to, use of, and overall management of the BLM land.

(b) MEMBERSHIP.—

(1) IN GENERAL.—The Secretary shall appoint members to the Community Group, including—

(A) 1 representative of Indian tribes in the vicinity of the BLM land, to be nominated by a majority vote conducted among the Indian tribes in the vicinity of the BLM land;

(B) not more than 1 county commissioner from each of Box Elder, Tooele, and Juab Counties, Utah;

(C) 2 representatives of off-road and highway use, hunting, or other recreational users of the BLM land;

(D) 2 representatives of livestock permittees on public land located within the BLM land;

(E) 1 representative of the Utah Department of Agriculture and Food; and

(F) not more than 3 representatives of State or Federal offices or agencies, or private groups or individuals, if the Secretary determines that such representatives would further the goals and objectives of the Community Group.

(2) CHAIRPERSON.—The members described in paragraph (1) shall elect from among the members of the Community Group—

(A) 1 member to serve as Chairperson of the Community Group; and

(B) 1 member to serve as Vice-Chairperson of the Community Group.

(3) AIR FORCE PERSONNEL.—The Secretary of the Air Force shall appoint appropriate operational and land management personnel of the Air Force to serve as a liaison to the Community Group.

(c) CONDITIONS AND TERMS OF APPOINTMENT.—

(1) IN GENERAL.—Each member of the Community Group shall serve voluntarily and without compensation.

(2) TERM OF APPOINTMENT.—

(A) IN GENERAL.—Each member of the Community Group shall be appointed for a term of 4 years.

(B) ORIGINAL MEMBERS.—Notwithstanding subparagraph (A), the Secretary shall select ½ of the original members of the Community Group to serve for a term of 4 years and the other ½ of the original members of the Community Group to serve for a term of 2 years, to ensure the replacement of members shall be staggered from year to year.

(C) REAPPOINTMENT AND REPLACEMENT.—The Secretary may reappoint or replace a member of the Community Group appointed under subsection (b)(1), if—

(i) the term of the member has expired;

(ii) the member has resigned; or

(iii) the position held by the member described in subparagraph (A) through (F) of paragraph (1) has changed to the extent that the ability of the member to represent the group or entity that the member represents has been significantly affected.

(d) MEETINGS.—

(1) IN GENERAL.—The Community Group shall meet not less than once per year, and at such other frequencies as determined by 5 or more of the members of the Community Group.

(2) RESPONSIBILITIES OF COMMUNITY GROUP.—The Community Group shall be responsible for determining appropriate schedules for, details of, and actions for meetings of the Community Group.

(3) NOTICE.—The Chairperson shall provide notice to each member of the Community Group not less than 10 business days before the date of a scheduled meeting.

(4) EXEMPT FROM FEDERAL ADVISORY COMMITTEE ACT.—The Federal Advisory Committee Act (5 U.S.C. App.) shall not apply to meetings of the Community Group.

(e) RECOMMENDATIONS OF COMMUNITY GROUP.—The Secretary and Secretary of the Air Force, consistent with existing laws (including regulations), shall take under consideration recommendations from the Community Group.

(f) TERMINATION OF AUTHORITY.—

(1) IN GENERAL.—The Community Group shall terminate on the date that is seven years after the date of enactment of this Act.

(2) EARLY TERMINATION.—The Secretary and the Community Group, acting jointly, may elect to terminate the Community Group before the date provided in subsection (a).

SEC. 3006. SAVINGS CLAUSES.

(a) EFFECT ON WEAPON IMPACT AREA.—Nothing in this subtitle expands the boundaries of the weapon impact area of the Utah Test and Training Range.

(b) EFFECT ON SPECIAL USE AIRSPACE AND TRAINING ROUTES.—Nothing in this subtitle precludes—

(1) the designation of new units of special use airspace; or

(2) the expansion of existing units of special use airspace.

(c) EFFECT ON EXISTING MILITARY SPECIAL USE AIRSPACE AGREEMENT.—Nothing in this subtitle limits or alters the Military Operating Areas of Airspace Use Agreement between the Federal Aviation Administration and the Air Force in effect on the date of enactment of this Act.

(d) EFFECT ON EXISTING RIGHTS AND AGREEMENTS.—Except as otherwise provided in section 3003, nothing in this subtitle limits or alters any existing right or right of access to—

(1) the Knolls Special Recreation Management Area; or

(2)(A) the Bureau of Land Management Community Pits Central Grayback and South Grayback; and

(B) any other county or community pit located within close proximity to the BLM land.

(e) INTERSTATE 80.—Nothing in this subtitle authorizes any additional authority or right to the Secretary or the Secretary of the Air Force to temporarily close Interstate 80.

(f) EFFECT ON LIMITATION ON AMENDMENTS TO CERTAIN INDIVIDUAL RESOURCE MANAGEMENT PLANS.—Nothing in this subtitle affects the limitation established under section 2815(d) of the National Defense Authorization Act for Fiscal Year 2000 (Public Law 106–65; 113 Stat. 852).

(g) EFFECT ON PREVIOUS MEMORANDUM OF UNDERSTANDING.—Nothing in this subtitle affects the memorandum of understanding entered into by the Air Force, the Bureau of Land Management, the Utah Department of Natural Resources, and the Utah Division of Wildlife Resources relating to the reestablishment of bighorn sheep in the Newfoundland Mountains and signed by the parties to the memorandum of understanding during the period beginning on January 24, 2000, and ending on February 4, 2000.

(h) EFFECT ON FEDERALLY RECOGNIZED INDIAN TRIBES.—Nothing in this subtitle alters any right reserved by treaty or Federal law for a Federally recognized Indian tribe for tribal use.

(i) PAYMENTS IN LIEU OF TAXES.—Nothing in this subtitle diminishes, enhances, or otherwise affects any other right or entitlement of the counties in which the BLM land is situated to payments in lieu of taxes based on the BLM land, under section 6901 of title 31, United States Code.

(j) WILDLIFE IMPROVEMENTS.—The Secretary and the Utah Division of Wildlife Resources shall continue the management of wildlife improvements, including guzzlers, in existence as of the date of enactment of this Act on the BLM land.

Subtitle B—Bureau of Land Management Land Exchange With State of Utah

SEC. 3011. DEFINITIONS.

In this subtitle:

(1) EXCHANGE MAP.—The term "Exchange Map" means the map prepared by the Bureau of Land Management entitled "Utah Test and Training Range Enhancement/West Desert Land Exchange" and dated July 21, 2016.

(2) FEDERAL LAND.—The term "Federal land" means the Bureau of Land Management land located in Box Elder, Millard, Juab, Tooele, and Beaver Counties, Utah, that is identified on the Exchange Map as "BLM Lands Proposed for Transfer to State Trust Lands".

(3) NON-FEDERAL LAND.—The term "non-Federal land" means the land owned by the State in Box Elder, Tooele, and Juab Counties, Utah, that is identified on the Exchange Map as—

(A) "State Trust Land Proposed for Transfer to BLM"; and

(B) "State Trust Minerals Proposed for Transfer to BLM".

(4) SECRETARY.—The term "Secretary" means the Secretary of the Interior.

(5) STATE.—The term "State" means the State of Utah, acting through the School and Institutional Trust Lands Administration.

SEC. 3012. EXCHANGE OF FEDERAL LAND AND NON-FEDERAL LAND.

(a) IN GENERAL.—If the State offers to convey to the United States title to the non-Federal land, the Secretary shall—

(1) accept the offer; and

(2) on receipt of all right, title, and interest in and to the non-Federal land, convey to the State (or a designee) all right, title, and interest of the United States in and to the Federal land.

(b) APPLICABLE LAW.—

(1) IN GENERAL.—The land exchange shall be subject to section 206 of the Federal Land Policy and Management Act of 1976 (43 U.S.C. 1716) and other applicable law.

(2) EFFECT OF STUDY.—The Secretary shall carry out the land exchange under this subtitle notwithstanding section 2815(d) of the National Defense Authorization Act for Fiscal Year 2000 (Public Law 106–65; 113 Stat. 852).

(3) LAND USE PLANNING.—The Secretary shall not be required to undertake any additional land use planning under section 202 of the Federal Land Policy and Management Act of 1976 (43 U.S.C. 1712) before the conveyance of the Federal land under this subtitle.

(c) VALID EXISTING RIGHTS.—The exchange authorized under subsection (a) shall be subject to valid existing rights.

(d) TITLE APPROVAL.—Title to the Federal land and non-Federal land to be exchanged under this subtitle shall be in a format acceptable to the Secretary and the State.

(e) APPRAISALS.—

(1) IN GENERAL.—The value of the Federal land and the non-Federal land to be exchanged under this subtitle shall be determined by appraisals conducted by 1 or more independent and qualified appraisers.

(2) STATE APPRAISER.—The Secretary and the State may agree to use an independent and qualified appraiser retained by the State, with the consent of the Secretary.

(3) APPLICABLE LAW.—The appraisals under paragraph (1) shall be conducted in accordance with nationally recognized appraisal standards, including, as appropriate, the Uniform Appraisal Standards for Federal Land Acquisitions and the Uniform Standards of Professional Appraisal Practice.

(4) MINERALS.—

(A) MINERAL REPORTS.—The appraisals under paragraph (1) may take into account mineral and technical reports provided by the Secretary and the State in the evaluation of minerals in the Federal land and non-Federal land.

(B) MINING CLAIMS.—Federal land that is encumbered by a mining or millsite claim located under sections 2318 through 2352 of the Revised Statutes (commonly known as the "Mining Law of 1872") (30 U.S.C. 21 et seq.) shall be appraised in accordance with standard appraisal practices, including, as appropriate, the Uniform Appraisal Standards for Federal Land Acquisition.

(C) VALIDITY EXAMINATION.—Nothing in this subtitle requires the Secretary to conduct a mineral examination for any mining claim on the Federal land.

(5) APPROVAL.—An appraisal conducted under paragraph (1) shall be submitted to the Secretary and the State for approval.

(6) DURATION.—An appraisal conducted under paragraph (1) shall remain valid for 3 years after the date on which the appraisal is approved by the Secretary and the State.

(7) COST OF APPRAISAL.—

(A) IN GENERAL.—The cost of an appraisal conducted under paragraph (1) shall be paid equally by the Secretary and the State.

(B) REIMBURSEMENT BY SECRETARY.—If the State retains an appraiser in accordance with paragraph (2), the Secretary shall reimburse the State in an amount equal to 50 percent of the costs incurred by the State.

(f) CONVEYANCE OF TITLE.—It is the intent of Congress that the land exchange authorized under this subtitle shall be completed not later than 1 year after the date of final approval by the Secretary and the State of the appraisals conducted under subsection (e).

(g) PUBLIC INSPECTION AND NOTICE.—

(1) PUBLIC INSPECTION.—At least 30 days before the date of conveyance of the Federal land and non-Federal land, all final appraisals and appraisal reviews for the Federal land and non-Federal land to be exchanged under this subtitle shall be available for public review at the office of the State Director of the Bureau of Land Management in the State.

(2) NOTICE.—The Secretary or the State, as applicable, shall publish in a newspaper of general circulation in Salt Lake County, Utah, a notice that the appraisals conducted under subsection (e) are available for public inspection.

(h) CONSULTATION WITH INDIAN TRIBES.—The Secretary shall consult with any federally recognized Indian tribe in the vicinity of the Federal land and non-Federal land to be exchanged under this subtitle before the completion of the land exchange.

(i) EQUAL VALUE EXCHANGE.—

(1) IN GENERAL.—The value of the Federal land and non-Federal land to be exchanged under this subtitle—

(A) shall be equal; or

(B) shall be made equal in accordance with paragraph (2).

(2) EQUALIZATION.—

(A) SURPLUS OF FEDERAL LAND.—

(i) IN GENERAL.—If the value of the Federal land exceeds the value of the non-Federal land, the value of the Federal land and non-Federal land shall be equalized by the State conveying to the Secretary, as necessary to equalize the value of the Federal land and non-Federal land—

(I) State trust land parcel 1, as described in the assessment entitled "Bureau of Land Management Environmental Assessment UT–100–06–EA", numbered UTU–82090, and dated March 2008; or

(II) State trust land located within any of the wilderness areas or national conservation areas in Washington County, Utah, established under subtitle O of title I of the Omnibus Public Land Management Act of 2009 (Public Law 111–11; 123 Stat. 1075).

(ii) ORDER OF CONVEYANCES.—Any non-Federal land required to be conveyed to the Secretary under clause (i) shall be conveyed until the value of the Federal land and non-Federal land is equalized.

(B) SURPLUS OF NON-FEDERAL LAND.—If the value of the non-Federal land exceeds the value of the Federal land, the value of the Federal land and the non-Federal land shall be equalized—

(i) by the Secretary making a cash equalization payment to the State, in accordance with section 206(b) of the Federal Land Policy and Management Act of 1976 (43 U.S.C. 1716(b)); or

(ii) by removing non-Federal land from the exchange.

(j) GRAZING PERMITS.—

(1) IN GENERAL.—If the Federal land or non-Federal land exchanged under this subtitle is subject to a lease, permit, or contract for the grazing of domestic livestock in effect on the date of acquisition, the Secretary and the State shall allow the grazing to continue for the remainder of the term of the lease, permit, or contract, subject to the related terms and conditions of user agreements, including permitted stocking rates, grazing fee levels, access rights, and ownership and use of range improvements.

(2) RENEWAL.—To the extent allowed by Federal or State law, on expiration of any grazing lease, permit, or contract described in paragraph (1), the holder of the lease, permit, or contract shall be entitled to a preference right to renew the lease, permit, or contract.

(3) CANCELLATION.—

(A) IN GENERAL.—Nothing in this subtitle prevents the Secretary or the State from canceling or modifying a grazing permit, lease, or contract if the Federal land or non-Federal land subject to the permit, lease, or contract is sold, conveyed, transferred, or leased for non-grazing purposes by the Secretary or the State.

(B) LIMITATION.—Except to the extent reasonably necessary to accommodate surface operations in support of mineral development, the Secretary or the State shall not cancel or modify a grazing permit, lease, or contract because the land subject to the permit, lease, or contract has been leased for mineral development.

(4) BASE PROPERTIES.—If non-Federal land conveyed by the State under this subtitle is used by a grazing permittee or lessee to meet the base property requirements for a Federal grazing permit or lease, the land shall continue to qualify as a base property for—

(A) the remaining term of the lease or permit; and

(B) the term of any renewal or extension of the lease or permit.

(k) WITHDRAWAL OF FEDERAL LAND FROM MINERAL ENTRY PRIOR TO EXCHANGE.—Subject to valid existing rights, the Federal land to be conveyed to the State under this subtitle is withdrawn from mineral location, entry, and patent under the mining laws pending conveyance of the Federal land to the State.

SEC. 3013. STATUS AND MANAGEMENT OF NON-FEDERAL LAND ACQUIRED BY THE UNITED STATES.

(a) IN GENERAL.—On conveyance to the United States under this subtitle, the non-Federal land shall be managed by the Secretary in accordance with the Federal Land Policy and Management Act of 1976 (43 U.S.C. 1701 et seq.) and applicable land use plans.

(b) NON-FEDERAL LAND WITHIN CEDAR MOUNTAINS WILDERNESS.—On conveyance to the Secretary under this subtitle, the non-Federal land located within the Cedar Mountains Wilderness shall, in accordance with section 206(c) of the Federal Land Policy Act of 1976 (43 U.S.C. 1716(c)), be added to, and administered as part of, the Cedar Mountains Wilderness.

(c) NON-FEDERAL LAND WITHIN WILDERNESS AREAS OR NATIONAL CONSERVATION AREAS.—On conveyance to the Secretary under this subtitle, non-Federal land located in a national wilderness area or national conservation area shall be managed in accordance with the applicable provisions of subtitle O of title I of the Omnibus Public Land Management Act of 2009 (Public Law 111–11).

SEC. 3014. HAZARDOUS SUBSTANCES.

(a) COSTS.—Except as provided in subsection (b), the costs of remedial actions relating to hazardous substances on land acquired under this subtitle shall be paid by those entities responsible for the costs under applicable law.

(b) REMEDIATION OF PRIOR TESTING AND TRAINING ACTIVITY.—The Secretary of the Air Force shall bear all costs of remediation required as a result of the previous testing of military weapons systems and the training of military forces on non-Federal land to be conveyed to the United States under this subtitle.

DIVISION C—DEPARTMENT OF ENERGY NATIONAL SECURITY AUTHORIZATIONS AND OTHER AUTHORIZATIONS

TITLE XXXI—DEPARTMENT OF ENERGY NATIONAL SECURITY PROGRAMS

Subtitle A—National Security Programs and Authorizations

Sec. 3101. National Nuclear Security Administration.
Sec. 3102. Defense environmental cleanup.
Sec. 3103. Other defense activities.
Sec. 3104. Nuclear energy.

Subtitle B—Program Authorizations, Restrictions, and Limitations

Sec. 3111. Independent acquisition project reviews of capital assets acquisition projects.
Sec. 3112. Protection of certain nuclear facilities and assets from unmanned aircraft.
Sec. 3113. Common financial reporting system for the nuclear security enterprise.
Sec. 3114. Rough estimate of total life cycle cost of tank waste cleanup at Hanford Nuclear Reservation.

Sec. 3115. Annual certification of shipments to Waste Isolation Pilot Plant.

Sec. 3116. Disposition of weapons-usable plutonium.

Sec. 3117. Design basis threat.

Sec. 3118. Industry best practices in operations at National Nuclear Security Administration facilities and sites.

Sec. 3119. Pilot program on unavailability for overhead costs of amounts specified for laboratory-directed research and development.

Sec. 3120. Research and development of advanced naval nuclear fuel system based on low-enriched uranium.

Sec. 3121. Increase in certain limitations applicable to funds for conceptual and construction design of the Department of Energy.

Sec. 3122. Prohibition on availability of funds for programs in Russian Federation.

Sec. 3123. Limitation on availability of funds for Federal salaries and expenses.

Sec. 3124. Limitation on availability of funds for defense environmental cleanup program direction.

Sec. 3125. Limitation on availability of funds for acceleration of nuclear weapons dismantlement.

Subtitle C—Plans and Reports

Sec. 3131. Independent assessment of technology development under defense environmental cleanup program.

Sec. 3132. Updated plan for verification and monitoring of proliferation of nuclear weapons and fissile material.

Sec. 3133. Report on the use of highly-enriched uranium for naval reactors.

Sec. 3134. Analysis of approaches for supplemental treatment of low-activity waste at Hanford Nuclear Reservation.

Sec. 3135. Clarification of annual report and certification on status of security of atomic energy defense facilities.

Sec. 3136. Report on service support contracts and authority for appointment of certain personnel.

Sec. 3137. Elimination of certain reporting requirements.

Sec. 3138. Report on United States nuclear deterrence.

Subtitle A—National Security Programs and Authorizations

SEC. 3101. NATIONAL NUCLEAR SECURITY ADMINISTRATION.

(a) AUTHORIZATION OF APPROPRIATIONS.—Funds are hereby authorized to be appropriated to the Department of Energy for fiscal year 2017 for the activities of the National Nuclear Security Administration in carrying out programs as specified in the funding table in section 4701.

(b) AUTHORIZATION OF NEW PLANT PROJECTS.—From funds referred to in subsection (a) that are available for carrying out plant projects, the Secretary of Energy may carry out new plant projects for the National Nuclear Security Administration as follows:

Project 17–D–630, Expand Electrical Distribution System, Lawrence Livermore National Laboratory, Livermore, California, $25,000,000.

Project 17–D–640, U1a Complex Enhancements Project, Nevada National Security Site, Mercury, Nevada, $11,500,000.

Project 17–D–911, BL Fire System Upgrade, Bettis Atomic Power Laboratory, West Mifflin, Pennsylvania, $1,400,000.

SEC. 3102. DEFENSE ENVIRONMENTAL CLEANUP.

(a) AUTHORIZATION OF APPROPRIATIONS.—Funds are hereby authorized to be appropriated to the Department of Energy for fiscal year 2017 for defense environmental cleanup activities in carrying out programs as specified in the funding table in section 4701.

(b) AUTHORIZATION OF NEW PLANT PROJECTS.—From funds referred to in subsection (a) that are available for carrying out plant projects, the Secretary of Energy may carry out, for defense environmental cleanup activities, the following new plant project:

Project 17–D–401, Saltstone Disposal Unit #7, Savannah River Site, Aiken, South Carolina, $9,729,000.

SEC. 3103. OTHER DEFENSE ACTIVITIES.

Funds are hereby authorized to be appropriated to the Department of Energy for fiscal year 2017 for other defense activities in carrying out programs as specified in the funding table in section 4701.

SEC. 3104. NUCLEAR ENERGY.

Funds are hereby authorized to be appropriated to the Department of Energy for fiscal year 2017 for nuclear energy as specified in the funding table in section 4701.

Subtitle B—Program Authorizations, Restrictions, and Limitations

SEC. 3111. INDEPENDENT ACQUISITION PROJECT REVIEWS OF CAPITAL ASSETS ACQUISITION PROJECTS.

(a) IN GENERAL.—Subtitle C of title XLVII of the Atomic Energy Defense Act (50 U.S.C. 2772) is amended by inserting after section 4732 the following new section:

"SEC. 4733. INDEPENDENT ACQUISITION PROJECT REVIEWS OF CAPITAL ASSETS ACQUISITION PROJECTS.

"(a) REVIEWS.—The appropriate head shall ensure that an independent entity conducts reviews of each capital assets acquisition project as the project moves toward the approval of each of critical decision 0, critical decision 1, and critical decision 2 in the acquisition process.

"(b) PRE-CRITICAL DECISION 1 REVIEWS.—In addition to any other matters, with respect to each review of a capital assets acquisition project under subsection (a) that has not reached critical decision 1 approval in the acquisition process, such review shall include—

"(1) a review using best practices of the analysis of alternatives for the project; and

"(2) identification of any deficiencies in such analysis of alternatives for the appropriate head to address.

"(c) INDEPENDENT ENTITIES.—The appropriate head shall ensure that each review of a capital assets acquisition project under subsection (a) is conducted by an independent entity with the appropriate expertise with respect to the project and the stage in the acquisition process of the project.

"(d) DEFINITIONS.—In this section:

"(1) The term 'acquisition process' means the acquisition process for a project, as defined in Department of Energy Order 413.3B (relating to project management and project management for the acquisition of capital assets), or a successor order.

"(2) The term 'appropriate head' means—

"(A) the Administrator, with respect to capital assets acquisition projects of the Administration; and

"(B) the Assistant Secretary of Energy for Environmental Management, with respect to capital assets acquisition projects of the Office of Environmental Management.

"(3) The term 'capital assets acquisition project' means a project—

"(A) the total project cost of which is more than $500,000,000; and

"(B) that is covered by Department of Energy Order 413.3, or a successor order, for the acquisition of capital assets for atomic energy defense activities.".

(b) CLERICAL AMENDMENT.—The table of contents for such Act is amended by inserting after the item relating to section 4732 the following new item:

"Sec. 4733. Independent acquisition project reviews of capital assets acquisition projects.".

SEC. 3112. PROTECTION OF CERTAIN NUCLEAR FACILITIES AND ASSETS FROM UNMANNED AIRCRAFT.

(a) IN GENERAL.—Subtitle A of title XLV of the Atomic Energy Defense Act (50 U.S.C. 2651 et seq.) is amended by adding at the end the following new section:

"SEC. 4510. PROTECTION OF CERTAIN NUCLEAR FACILITIES AND ASSETS FROM UNMANNED AIRCRAFT.

"(a) AUTHORITY.—Notwithstanding any provision of title 18, United States Code, the Secretary of Energy may take such actions described in subsection (b)(1) that are necessary to mitigate the threat (as defined by the Secretary of Energy, in consultation with the Secretary of Transportation) that an unmanned aircraft system or unmanned aircraft poses to the safety or security of a covered facility or asset.

"(b) ACTIONS DESCRIBED.—(1) The actions described in this paragraph are the following:

"(A) Detect, identify, monitor, and track the unmanned aircraft system or unmanned aircraft, without prior consent, including by means of intercept or other access of a wire, oral, or electronic communication used to control the unmanned aircraft system or unmanned aircraft.

"(B) Warn the operator of the unmanned aircraft system or unmanned aircraft, including by passive or active, and direct or indirect physical, electronic, radio, and electromagnetic means.

"(C) Disrupt control of the unmanned aircraft system or unmanned aircraft, without prior consent, including by disabling the unmanned aircraft system or unmanned aircraft by intercepting, interfering, or causing interference with wire, oral, electronic, or radio communications used to control the unmanned aircraft system or unmanned aircraft.

"(D) Seize or exercise control of the unmanned aircraft system or unmanned aircraft.

"(E) Seize or otherwise confiscate the unmanned aircraft system or unmanned aircraft.

"(F) Use reasonable force to disable, damage, or destroy the unmanned aircraft system or unmanned aircraft.

"(2) The Secretary of Energy shall develop the actions described in paragraph (1) in coordination with the Secretary of Transportation.

"(c) FORFEITURE.—Any unmanned aircraft system or unmanned aircraft described in subsection (a) that is seized by the Secretary of Energy is subject to forfeiture to the United States.

"(d) REGULATIONS.—The Secretary of Energy and the Secretary of Transportation may prescribe regulations and shall issue guidance in the respective areas of each Secretary to carry out this section.

"(e) DEFINITIONS.—In this section:

"(1) The term 'covered facility or asset' means any facility or asset that is—

"(A) identified by the Secretary of Energy for purposes of this section;

"(B) located in the United States (including the territories and possessions of the United States); and

"(C) owned by the United States or contracted to the United States, to store or use special nuclear material.

"(2) The terms 'unmanned aircraft' and 'unmanned aircraft system' have the meanings given those terms in section 331 of the FAA Modernization and Reform Act of 2012 (Public Law 112–95; 49 U.S.C. 40101 note).".

(b) CLERICAL AMENDMENT.—The table of contents for such Act is amended by inserting after the item relating to section 4509 the following new item:

"Sec. 4510. *Protection of certain nuclear facilities and assets from unmanned aircraft.*".

SEC. 3113. COMMON FINANCIAL REPORTING SYSTEM FOR THE NUCLEAR SECURITY ENTERPRISE.

(a) IN GENERAL.—By not later than four years after the date of the enactment of this Act, the Administrator for Nuclear Security shall, in consultation with the National Nuclear Security Administration Council established by section 4102(b) of the Atomic Energy Defense Act (50 U.S.C. 2512(b)), complete, to the extent practicable, the implementation of a common financial reporting system for the nuclear security enterprise.

(b) ELEMENTS.—The common financial reporting system implemented pursuant to subsection (a) shall include the following:

(1) Common data reporting requirements for work performed using funds of the National Nuclear Security Administration, including reporting of financial data by standardized labor categories, labor hours, functional elements, and cost elements.

(2) A common work breakdown structure for the Administration that aligns contractor work breakdown structures with the budget structure of the Administration.

(3) Definitions and methodologies for identifying and reporting costs for programs of records and base capabilities within the Administration.

(4) A capability to leverage, where appropriate, the Defense Cost Analysis Resource Center of the Office of Cost Assessment and Program Evaluation of the Department of Defense using historical costing data by the Administration.

(c) REPORTS.—

(1) IN GENERAL.—Not later than March 1, 2017, and annually thereafter, the Administrator shall, in consultation with the National Nuclear Security Administration Council, submit to the congressional defense committees a report on progress of the Administration toward implementing a common financial reporting system for the nuclear security enterprise as required by subsection (a).

(2) REPORT.—Each report under this subsection shall include the following:

(A) A summary of activities, accomplishments, challenges, benefits, and costs related to the implementation of a common financial reporting system for the nuclear security enterprise during the year preceding the year in which such report is submitted.

(B) A summary of planned activities in connection with the implementation of a common financial reporting system for the nuclear security enterprise in the year in which such report is submitted.

(C) A description of any anticipated modifications to the schedule for implementing a common financial reporting system for the nuclear security enterprise, including an update on possible risks, challenges, and costs related to such implementation.

(3) TERMINATION.—No report is required under this subsection after the completion of the implementation of a common financial reporting system for the nuclear security enterprise.

(d) NUCLEAR SECURITY ENTERPRISE DEFINED.—In this section, the term "nuclear security enterprise" has the meaning given that term in section 4002 of the Atomic Energy Defense Act (50 U.S.C. 2501).

SEC. 3114. ROUGH ESTIMATE OF TOTAL LIFE CYCLE COST OF TANK WASTE CLEANUP AT HANFORD NUCLEAR RESERVATION.

(a) IN GENERAL.—Not later than two years after the date of the enactment of this Act, the Secretary of Energy shall submit to the congressional defense committees a rough estimate of the total life cycle cost of the cleanup of tank waste at Hanford Nuclear Reservation, Richland, Washington.

(b) ELEMENTS.—The rough estimate of the total life cycle cost required by subsection (a) shall include cost estimates for the following:

(1) The Waste Treatment and Immobilization Plant, assuming a hot start occurs in 2033 and initial plant operations commence in 2036.

(2) Operations of the Waste Treatment and Immobilization Plant, assuming operations continue through 2061.

(3) Tank waste management and treatment, assuming operations of the Waste Treatment and Immobilization Plant continue through 2061.

(4) Anticipated increases in the volume of waste in the double shell tanks resulting from tank waste management activities.

(5) High-level waste canister temporary storage and preparation for permanent disposal.

(6) Any additional facilities, including additional evaporative capacity, that may be needed to treat tank waste at Hanford Nuclear Reservation.

(c) COST ESTIMATING BEST PRACTICES.—To the maximum extent practicable, the rough estimate of the total life cycle cost required by subsection (a) shall be developed in accordance with the cost estimating best practices of the Government Accountability Office.

(d) SUBMISSION OF ADDITIONAL INDEPENDENT COST ESTIMATES.—The Secretary shall submit to the congressional defense committees, as part of the rough estimate of the total life cycle cost required by subsection (a), any other independent cost estimates for the Waste Treatment and Immobilization Plant or related facilities conducted before the date on which the rough estimate of the total life cycle cost is required to be submitted under that subsection.

SEC. 3115. ANNUAL CERTIFICATION OF SHIPMENTS TO WASTE ISOLATION PILOT PLANT.

(a) IN GENERAL.—In order to ensure that waste shipments to the Waste Isolation Pilot Plant, Carlsbad, New Mexico (in this section referred to as "WIPP") are packaged and handled properly to prevent the release of radiation or contamination above regulatory limits, the Secretary of Energy shall submit to the congressional defense committees, not later than February 1 of each year during the five-year period beginning on the date of the enactment of this Act, a written certification that—

(1) the Secretary knew of the contents of such shipments during the 12-month period preceding the date of the certification and has ensured that the Secretary will know of the contents of such shipments planned during the 12-month period following the date of the certification; and

(2) such shipments made during the 12-month period preceding the date of the certification were sufficiently safe and secure for transportation and disposal and the Secretary has ensured that such shipments planned during the 12-month period following the date of the certification will be sufficiently safe and secure for transportation and disposal.

(b) ADDITIONAL ASSURANCES.—The Secretary shall submit to the congressional defense committees, with the certification required by subsection (a), assurances that—

(1) the Carlsbad Field Office of the Department of Energy has certified that—

(A) the contents of each shipment of waste that arrived at WIPP during 12-month period preceding the date of the certification met the criteria for accepting waste at WIPP; and

(B) the Office will ensure that the waste destined for WIPP during the 12-month period following the date of the certification is packaged according to the criteria for accepting waste at WIPP;

(2) the Assistant Secretary of Energy for Environmental Management has reviewed and accepted the certification of the Carlsbad Field Office under paragraph (1); and

(3) the Administrator for Nuclear Security has ensured that waste destined for WIPP that was packaged at facilities of the National Nuclear Security Administration during the 12-month period preceding the date of the certification, and waste planned to be packaged at such facilities during the 12-month period following the date of the certification, and for which the Administration is responsible, meets the criteria for accepting waste at WIPP.

SEC. 3116. DISPOSITION OF WEAPONS-USABLE PLUTONIUM.

(a) CONSTRUCTION AND PROJECT SUPPORT ACTIVITIES AT MOX FACILITY.—

(1) IN GENERAL.—Using funds described in paragraph (2), the Secretary of Energy shall carry out construction and project support activities relating to the MOX facility.

(2) FUNDS DESCRIBED.—The funds described in this paragraph are the following:

(A) Funds authorized to be appropriated by this Act or otherwise made available for fiscal year 2017 for the National Nuclear Security Administration for the MOX facility for construction and project support activities.

(B) Funds authorized to be appropriated for a fiscal year prior to fiscal year 2017 for the National Nuclear Security Administration for the MOX facility for construction and project support activities that are unobligated as of the date of the enactment of this Act.

(b) ASSESSMENT OF THE MOX FACILITY CONTRACT BY OWNER'S AGENT.—

(1) ARRANGEMENT WITH OWNER'S AGENT.—Not later than 30 days after the date of the enactment of this Act, the Secretary of Energy shall enter into an arrangement pursuant to sections 1535 and 1536 of title 31, United States Code, with the Chief of Engineers to act as an owner's agent with respect to preparing the report required by paragraph (2).

(2) REPORT OF OWNER'S AGENT.—

(A) IN GENERAL.—The Chief of Engineers shall prepare a report on the contract for the construction, management and operations of the MOX facility, as in effect on the date of the enactment of this Act, that includes the following:

(i) An assessment of the contractual, technical, and managerial risks for the Department of Energy and the contractor.

(ii) An assessment of what elements of the contract can be changed to—

(I) a fixed price provision;

(II) a fixed price incentive fee provision; or

(III) another contractual mechanism designed to minimize risk to the Department of Energy while reducing cost.

(iii) An assessment of the options under clause (ii), including milestones, cost, schedules, and any damage fees for those options.

(iv) Recommendations on changes to the contract, based on the assessments described in clauses (i), (ii), and (iii), to reduce risk and cost to the Department of Energy while preserving a fair and reasonable contract.

(v) For each element of the contract that the Chief of Engineers does not recommend be changed pursuant to clause (iv), an assessment of the risks and costs associated with that element and a description of why that element is not appropriate for the provision types described in clause (ii).

(B) CONSULTATIONS.—In preparing the report required by subparagraph (A), the Chief of Engineers shall consult with the Secretary, the contractor referred to in subparagraph (A)(i), and other knowledgeable parties, as the Chief of Engineers considers appropriate.

(C) SUBMISSION TO SECRETARY.—Not later than 30 days after entering into the arrangement under paragraph (1), the Chief of Engineers shall submit to the Secretary the report required by subparagraph (A).

(3) SUBMISSIONS BY DEPARTMENT OF ENERGY.— Not later than 60 days after receiving the report required by paragraph (2), the Secretary shall transmit to the congressional defense committees and the Comptroller General of the United States—

(A) the report;

(B) any comments of the Secretary with respect to the report;

(C) a determination of whether the contractor referred to in paragraph (2)(A)(i) will or will not agree to the revisions to the contract recommended by the Chief of Engineers and offered by the Secretary to the contractor;

(D) if the contractor will not agree to such revisions, a description of the reasons given for not agreeing to such revisions; and

(E) any other materials relating to the potential modification of the contract that the Secretary considers appropriate.

(4) BRIEFING BY GOVERNMENT ACCOUNTABILITY OFFICE.—Not later than 30 days after receiving the report and other matters under paragraph (3), the Comptroller General of the United States shall brief the congressional defense committees on the actions taken by the Secretary under this subsection, to be followed by a written report not later than 120 days after the briefing is provided to Congress.

(c) DEFINITIONS.—In this section:

(1) MOX FACILITY.—The term "MOX facility" means the mixed-oxide fuel fabrication facility at the Savannah River Site, Aiken, South Carolina.

(2) PROJECT SUPPORT ACTIVITIES.—The term "project support activities" means activities that support the design, long-lead equipment procurement, and site preparation of the MOX facility.

SEC. 3117. DESIGN BASIS THREAT.

(a) UPDATE TO ORDER.—Not later than 30 days after the date of the enactment of this Act, the Secretary of Energy shall update Department of Energy Order 470.3B relating to the design basis threat for protecting nuclear weapons, special nuclear material, and other critical assets in the custody of the Department of Energy.

(b) SENSE OF CONGRESS.—It is the sense of Congress that—

(1) the intelligence community (as defined in section 3(4) of the National Security Act of 1947 (50 U.S.C. 3003(4))) should promulgate regular, biannual updates to the Nuclear Security Threat Capabilities Assessment to better inform nuclear security postures within the Department of Defense and the Department of Energy;

(2) the Department of Defense and the Department of Energy should closely, and in real-time, track and assess national, regional, and local threats to the defense nuclear facilities of the respective Departments; and

(3) the Department of Defense and the Department of Energy should regularly review assessments and other input provided by activities described in paragraphs (1) and (2) and adjust security postures accordingly.

SEC. 3118. INDUSTRY BEST PRACTICES IN OPERATIONS AT NATIONAL NUCLEAR SECURITY ADMINISTRATION FACILITIES AND SITES.

(a) COMMITTEE ON INDUSTRY BEST PRACTICES IN OPERATIONS.—The Administrator for Nuclear Security shall establish within the National Nuclear Security Administration a committee (in this section referred to as the "committee") to identify and oversee the implementation of best practices of industry in the operations of the facilities and sites of the Administration for the purposes of—

(1) improving mission performance and effectiveness;

(2) lowering costs and administrative burdens; and

(3) also both—

(A) maintaining or reducing risks; and

(B) preserving and protecting health, safety, and security.

(b) MEMBERSHIP.—The committee shall be composed of personnel of the Administration assigned by the Administrator to the committee as follows:

(1) The Principal Deputy Administrator for Nuclear Security, who shall serve as chair of the committee.

(2) Government personnel representing the headquarters of the Administration.

(3) Government personnel representing offices of facilities and sites of the Administration.

(4) Contractor personnel representing the national security laboratories and the nuclear weapons production facilities (as those terms are defined in section 4002 of the Atomic Energy Defense Act (50 U.S.C. 2501)).

(5) Such other personnel as the Administrator considers appropriate.

(c) DUTIES.—The duties of the committee shall include the following:

(1) To identify and oversee the implementation of best practices of industry in the operations of the facilities and sites of the Administration for the purposes described in subsection (a).

(2) To conduct surveys of the facilities and sites of the Administration in order to assess the adoption, implementation, and use by such facilities and sites of best practices of industry described in subsection (a).

(3) To carry out such other activities consistent with the duties of the committee under this subsection as the Administrator may specify for purposes of this section.

(d) ANNUAL REPORT.—

(1) IN GENERAL.—Not later than 60 days after the date on which the budget of the President for a fiscal year after fiscal year 2017 is submitted to Congress pursuant to section 1105(a) of title 31, United States Code, the Administrator shall submit to the appropriate congressional committees a report on the activities of the committee under this section during the preceding calendar year.

(2) ELEMENTS.—Each report under this subsection shall include, for the calendar year covered by such report, the following:

(A) A description of the activities of the committee.

(B) The results of the surveys undertaken pursuant to subsection (c)(2).

(C) As a result of the surveys, recommendations for modifications to the scope or applicability of regulations and orders of the Department of Energy to particular facilities and sites of the Administration in order to implement best practices of industry in the operation of such facilities and sites, including—

(i) a list of the facilities and sites at which such regulations and orders could be so modified; and

(ii) for each such facility and site, the manner in which the scope or applicability of such regulations and orders could be so modified.

(D) An assessment of the progress of the Administration in implementing best practices of industry in the operations of the facilities and sites of the Administration.

(E) An estimate of the costs to be saved as a result of the best practices of industry implemented by the Administration at the facilities and sites of the Administration, set forth by fiscal year.

(3) APPROPRIATE CONGRESSIONAL COMMITTEES DEFINED.—In this subsection, the term "appropriate congressional committees" means—

(A) the congressional defense committees; and

(B) the Committee on Energy and Natural Resources of the Senate and the Committee on Energy and Commerce of the House of Representatives.

(e) TERMINATION.—The committee shall terminate after the submittal under subsection (d) of the report required by that subsection that covers 2021.

SEC. 3119. PILOT PROGRAM ON UNAVAILABILITY FOR OVERHEAD COSTS OF AMOUNTS SPECIFIED FOR LABORATORY-DIRECTED RESEARCH AND DEVELOPMENT.

(a) IN GENERAL.—The Secretary of Energy shall establish a pilot program under which each national security laboratory (as defined in section 4002 of the Atomic Energy Defense Act (50 U.S.C. 2501)) is prohibited from using funds described in subsection (b) to cover the costs of general and administrative overhead for the laboratory.

(b) FUNDS DESCRIBED.—The funds described in this subsection are funds made available for a national security laboratory under section 4811(c) of the Atomic Energy Defense Act (50 U.S.C. 2791(c)) for laboratory-directed research and development.

(c) DURATION.—The pilot program required by subsection (a) shall—

(1) take effect on the first day of the first fiscal year beginning after the date of the enactment of this Act; and

(2) terminate on the date that is three years after the day described in paragraph (1).

(d) REPORT REQUIRED.—Before the termination under subsection (c)(2) of the pilot program required by subsection (a), the Administrator for Nuclear Security shall submit to the congressional defense committees a report that assesses the costs, benefits, risks, and other effects of the pilot program.

SEC. 3120. RESEARCH AND DEVELOPMENT OF ADVANCED NAVAL NUCLEAR FUEL SYSTEM BASED ON LOW-ENRICHED URANIUM.

(a) PROHIBITION.—Except as provided in subsection (b), none of the funds authorized to be appropriated by this Act or otherwise made available for fiscal year 2017 for the Department of Energy may be obligated or expended to plan or carry out research and development of an advanced naval nuclear fuel system based on low-enriched uranium.

(b) EXCEPTION.—Of the funds authorized to be appropriated by this Act or otherwise made available for fiscal year 2017 for defense nuclear nonproliferation, as specified in the funding table in division D, not more than $5,000,000 shall be made available to the Deputy Administrator for Naval Reactors of the National Nuclear Security Administration for initial planning and early research and development of an advanced naval nuclear fuel system based on low-enriched uranium.

(c) BUDGET MATTERS.—Section 3118 of the National Defense Authorization Act for Fiscal Year 2016 (Public Law 114–92; 129 Stat. 1196) is amended—

(1) in subsection (c), by striking paragraph (2) and inserting the following new paragraph:

"(2) BUDGET REQUESTS.—If the Secretaries determine under paragraph (1) that research and development of an advanced naval nuclear fuel system based on low-enriched uranium should continue, the Secretaries shall ensure that each budget of the President submitted to Congress under section 1105(a) of title 31, United States Code, for fiscal year 2018 and each fiscal year thereafter in which such research and development is carried out includes in the budget line item for the 'Defense Nuclear Nonproliferation' account amounts necessary to carry out the conceptual plan under subsection (b)."; and

(2) in subsection (d), by striking "for material management and minimization".

SEC. 3121. INCREASE IN CERTAIN LIMITATIONS APPLICABLE TO FUNDS FOR CONCEPTUAL AND CONSTRUCTION DESIGN OF THE DEPARTMENT OF ENERGY.

(a) REQUESTS FOR CONCEPTUAL DESIGN FUNDS.—Subsection (a)(2) of section 4706 of the Atomic Energy Defense Act (50 U.S.C. 2746) is amended by striking "$3,000,000" and inserting "$5,000,000".

(b) CONSTRUCTION DESIGN.—Subsection (b) of such section is amended by striking "$1,000,000" each place it appears and inserting "$2,000,000".

SEC. 3122. PROHIBITION ON AVAILABILITY OF FUNDS FOR PROGRAMS IN RUSSIAN FEDERATION.

(a) PROHIBITION.—

(1) IN GENERAL.—None of the funds described in paragraph (2) may be obligated or expended to enter into a contract with, or otherwise provide assistance to, the Russian Federation.

(2) FUNDS DESCRIBED.—The funds described in this paragraph are the following:

(A) Funds authorized to be appropriated by this Act or otherwise made available for fiscal year 2017 for atomic energy defense activities.

(B) Funds authorized to be appropriated or otherwise made available for a fiscal year prior to fiscal year 2017 for atomic energy defense activities that are unobligated or unexpended as of the date of the enactment of this Act.

(b) WAIVER.—The Secretary of Energy, without delegation, may waive the prohibition in subsection (a)(1) only if—

(1) the Secretary determines, in writing, that a nuclear-related threat arising in the Russian Federation must be addressed urgently and it is necessary to waive the prohibition to address that threat;

(2) the Secretary of State and the Secretary of Defense concur in the determination under paragraph (1);

(3) the Secretary of Energy submits to the appropriate congressional committees a report containing—

(A) a notification that the waiver is in the national security interest of the United States;

(B) justification for the waiver, including the determination under paragraph (1); and

(C) a description of the activities to be carried out pursuant to the waiver, including the expected cost and timeframe for such activities; and

(4) a period of 15 days elapses following the date on which the Secretary submits the report under paragraph (3).

(c) EXCEPTION.—The prohibition under subsection (a)(1) and the requirements under subsection (b) to waive that prohibition shall not apply to an amount, not to exceed $3,000,000, that the Secretary may make available for the Department of Energy Russian Health Studies Program.

(d) APPROPRIATE CONGRESSIONAL COMMITTEES DEFINED.—In this section, the term "appropriate congressional committees" means the following:

(1) The congressional defense committees.

(2) The Committee on Foreign Relations of the Senate and the Committee on Foreign Affairs of the House of Representatives.

SEC. 3123. LIMITATION ON AVAILABILITY OF FUNDS FOR FEDERAL SALARIES AND EXPENSES.

(a) IN GENERAL.—Of the funds authorized to be appropriated by this Act or otherwise made available for fiscal year 2017 for the National Nuclear Security Administration for defense-related Federal salaries and expenses, not more than 90 percent may be obligated or expended until the date on which the Secretary of Energy submits to the congressional defense committees and the congressional intelligence committees the following:

(1) The updated plan on the designing and building of prototypes of nuclear weapons that is required—

(A) by paragraph (2) of section 4509(a) of the Atomic Energy Defense Act (50 U.S.C. 2660(a)), to be developed by not later than the date on which the budget of the President for fiscal year 2018 is submitted to Congress; and

(B) by paragraph (3)(B) of such section, to be submitted to the congressional defense committees and the congressional intelligence committees.

(2) A description of the determination of the Secretary under paragraph (4)(B) of such section with respect to the manner in which the designing and building of prototypes of nuclear weapons is carried out under such updated plan.

(b) CONGRESSIONAL INTELLIGENCE COMMITTEES DEFINED.—In this section, the term "congressional intelligence committees" means the Select Committee on Intelligence of the Senate and the Permanent Select Committee on Intelligence of the House of Representatives.

SEC. 3124. LIMITATION ON AVAILABILITY OF FUNDS FOR DEFENSE ENVIRONMENTAL CLEANUP PROGRAM DIRECTION.

Of the funds authorized to be appropriated by this Act or otherwise made available for fiscal year 2017 for defense environmental cleanup for program direction, not more than 90 percent may be obligated or expended until the date on which the Secretary of Energy submits to Congress the future-years defense environmental cleanup plan required to be submitted during 2017 under section 4402A of the Atomic Energy Defense Act (50 U.S.C. 2582a).

SEC. 3125. LIMITATION ON AVAILABILITY OF FUNDS FOR ACCELERATION OF NUCLEAR WEAPONS DISMANTLEMENT.

(a) LIMITATION ON MAXIMUM AMOUNT FOR DISMANTLEMENT.—Of the funds authorized to be appropriated by this Act or otherwise made available for any of fiscal years 2017 through 2021 for the National Nuclear Security Administration, not more than $56,000,000 may be obligated or expended in each such fiscal year to carry out the nuclear weapons dismantlement and disposition activities of the Administration.

(b) LIMITATION ON ACCELERATION OF DISMANTLEMENT ACTIVITIES.—Except as provided by subsection (c), none of the funds authorized to be appropriated by this Act or otherwise made available for any of fiscal years 2017 through 2021 for the National Nuclear Security Administration may be obligated or expended to accelerate the nuclear weapons dismantlement activities of the United States to a rate that exceeds the rate described in the Stockpile Stewardship and Management Plan schedule.

(c) EXCEPTION.—The limitation in subsection (b) shall not apply to the following:

(1) The dismantlement of a nuclear weapon not covered by the Stockpile Stewardship and Management Plan schedule if the Administrator for Nuclear Security certifies, in writing, to the congressional defense committees that—

(A) the components of the nuclear weapon are directly required for the purposes of a current life extension program; or

(B) such dismantlement is necessary to conduct maintenance or surveillance of the nuclear weapons stockpile or to ensure the safety or reliability of the nuclear weapons stockpile.

(2) The dismantlement of a nuclear weapon if the President certifies, in writing, to the congressional defense committees that—

(A) such dismantlement is being carried out pursuant to a nuclear arms reduction treaty or similar international agreement that requires such dismantlement; and

(B) such treaty or similar international agreement—

(i) has entered into force after the date of the enactment of this Act; and

(ii) was approved—

(I) with the advice and consent of the Senate pursuant to clause 2 of section 2 of Article II of the Constitution of the United States after the date of the enactment of this Act; or

(II) by an Act of Congress, as described in section 303(b) of the Arms Control and Disarmament Act (22 U.S.C. 2573(b)).

(d) STOCKPILE STEWARDSHIP AND MANAGEMENT PLAN SCHEDULE DEFINED.—In this section, the term "Stockpile Stewardship and Management Plan schedule" means the schedule described in table 2–7 of the annex of the report titled "Fiscal Year 2016 Stockpile Stewardship and Management Plan" submitted in March 2015 by the Administrator for Nuclear Security to the congressional defense committees under section 4203(b)(2) of the Atomic Energy Defense Act (50 U.S.C. 2523(b)(2)).

Subtitle C—Plans and Reports

SEC. 3131. INDEPENDENT ASSESSMENT OF TECHNOLOGY DEVELOPMENT UNDER DEFENSE ENVIRONMENTAL CLEANUP PROGRAM.

(a) ASSESSMENT.—Not later than 60 days after the date of the enactment of this Act, the Secretary of Energy shall seek to enter into an agreement with the National Academy of Sciences to conduct an independent assessment of the technology development efforts of the defense environmental cleanup program of the Department of Energy.

(b) ELEMENTS.—The assessment under subsection (a) shall include the following:

(1) A review of the technology development efforts of the defense environmental cleanup program of the Department of Energy, including an assessment of the process by which the Secretary identifies and chooses technologies to pursue under the program.

(2) A comprehensive review and assessment of technologies or alternative approaches to defense environmental cleanup efforts that could—

(A) reduce the long-term costs of such efforts;

(B) accelerate schedules for carrying out such efforts;

(C) mitigate uncertainties, vulnerabilities, or risks relating to such efforts; or

(D) otherwise significantly improve the defense environmental cleanup program.

(c) SUBMISSION.—Not later than the date that is 18 months after the date of the enactment of this Act, the National Academy of Sciences shall submit to the congressional defense committees and the Secretary a report on the assessment under subsection (a).

SEC. 3132. UPDATED PLAN FOR VERIFICATION AND MONITORING OF PROLIFERATION OF NUCLEAR WEAPONS AND FISSILE MATERIAL.

(a) UPDATED PLAN.—

(1) TRANSMISSION.—Not later than 90 days after the date of the enactment of this Act, the President shall transmit to the appropriate congressional committees a comprehensive and detailed update to the plan developed under section 3133(a) of the Carl Levin and Howard P. "Buck" McKeon National Defense Authorization Act for Fiscal Year 2015 (Public Law 113–291; 128 Stat. 3896) with respect to verification and monitoring relating to the potential proliferation of nuclear weapons, components of such weapons, and fissile material.

(2) FORM.—The updated plan under paragraph (1) shall be transmitted in unclassified form, but may include a classified annex.

(b) LIMITATION.—Of the funds authorized to be appropriated by this Act or otherwise made available for fiscal year 2017 for the Department of Defense for supporting the Executive Office of the President, $10,000,000 may not be obligated or expended until the date on which the President transmits to the appropriate congressional committees the updated plan under subsection (a)(1).

(c) BRIEFING.—Not later than 30 days after the date of the enactment of this Act, the President shall provide to the Committees on Armed

Services of the Senate and House of Representatives (and any other appropriate congressional committee upon request) an interim briefing on the updated plan under subsection (a)(1).

(d) APPROPRIATE CONGRESSIONAL COMMITTEES DEFINED.—In this section, the term "appropriate congressional committees" means the following:

(1) The congressional defense committees.

(2) The Select Committee on Intelligence of the Senate and the Permanent Select Committee on Intelligence of the House of Representatives.

(3) The Committee on Foreign Relations of the Senate and the Committee on Foreign Affairs of the House of Representatives.

(4) The Committee on Homeland Security and Governmental Affairs of the Senate and the Committee on Homeland Security of the House of Representatives.

(5) The Committee on Commerce, Science, and Transportation of the Senate and the Committee on Energy and Commerce of the House of Representatives.

SEC. 3133. REPORT ON THE USE OF HIGHLY-ENRICHED URANIUM FOR NAVAL REACTORS.

(a) REPORT.—Not later than 120 days after the date of the enactment of this Act, the Director of National Intelligence, in consultation with the Secretary of Defense, the Secretary of Energy, and the Secretary of State, shall, in accordance with the protection of sources and methods, submit to the appropriate congressional committees a report that includes the following:

(1) An assessment on the current and anticipated intentions of countries producing or using highly-enriched uranium in naval reactors or considering the development of naval reactors.

(2) An evaluation of the security measures each country producing or using highly-enriched uranium in naval reactors has in place.

(3) An evaluation of the potential effects on nuclear nonproliferation efforts and the naval reactor programs and related actions of other countries if the United States pursued the development of an advanced low-enriched uranium fuel for certain United States naval reactors as described in the report of the Director of Naval Reactors to Congress, dated July 2016 and entitled "Conceptual Research and Development Plan for Low-Enriched Uranium Naval Fuel".

(4) Such other information or updates as the Director of National Intelligence, the Secretary of Defense, the Secretary of Energy, and the Secretary of State consider appropriate.

(b) FORM.—The report required by subsection (a) shall be submitted in unclassified form, but may include a classified annex.

(c) APPROPRIATE CONGRESSIONAL COMMITTEES DEFINED.—In this section, the term "appropriate congressional committees" means—

(1) the congressional defense committees;

(2) the Select Committee on Intelligence of the Senate and the Permanent Select Committee on Intelligence of the House of Representatives; and

(3) the Committee on Foreign Relations of the Senate and the Committee on Foreign Affairs of the House of Representatives.

SEC. 3134. ANALYSIS OF APPROACHES FOR SUPPLEMENTAL TREATMENT OF LOW-ACTIVITY WASTE AT HANFORD NUCLEAR RESERVATION.

(a) IN GENERAL.—Not later than 60 days after the date of the enactment of this Act, the Secretary of Energy shall enter into an arrangement with a federally funded research and development center to conduct an analysis of approaches for treating the portion of low-activity waste at the Hanford Nuclear Reservation, Richland, Washington, that, as of such date of enactment, is intended for supplemental treatment.

(b) ELEMENTS.—The analysis required by subsection (a) shall include the following:

(1) An analysis of, at a minimum, the following approaches for treating the low-activity waste described in subsection (a):

(A) Further processing of the low-activity waste to remove long-lived radioactive constituents, particularly technetium-99 and iodine-129, for immobilization with high-level waste.

(B) Vitrification, grouting, and steam reforming, and other alternative approaches identified by the Department of Energy for immobilizing the low-activity waste.

(2) An analysis of the following:

(A) The risks of the approaches described in paragraph (1) relating to treatment and final disposition.

(B) The benefits and costs of such approaches.

(C) Anticipated schedules for such approaches, including the time needed to complete necessary construction and to begin treatment operations.

(D) The compliance of such approaches with applicable technical standards associated with and contained in regulations prescribed pursuant to the Comprehensive Environmental Response, Compensation, and Liability Act of 1980 (42 U.S.C. 9601 et seq.), the Solid Waste Disposal Act (42 U.S.C. 6901 et seq.) (commonly referred to as the "Resource Conservation and Recovery Act of 1976"), the Federal Water Pollution Control Act (33 U.S.C. 1251 et seq.) (commonly referred to as the "Clean Water Act"), and the Clean Air Act (42 U.S.C. 7401 et seq.).

(E) Any obstacles that would inhibit the ability of the Department of Energy to pursue such approaches.

(c) REVIEW OF ANALYSIS.—

(1) IN GENERAL.—Concurrent with entering into an arrangement with a federally funded research and development center under subsection (a), the Secretary shall enter into an arrangement with the National Academies of Sciences, Engineering, and Medicine to conduct a review of the analysis conducted by the federally funded research and development center.

(2) METHOD OF REVIEW.—The review required by paragraph (1) shall be conducted concurrent with the analysis required by subsection (a), and in a manner that is parallel to that analysis, so that the results of the review may be used to improve the quality of the analysis.

(3) PUBLIC REVIEW.—In conducting the review required paragraph (1), the National Academies of Sciences, Engineering, and Medicine shall provide an opportunity for public comment, with sufficient notice, to inform and improve the quality of the review.

(d) CONSULTATION WITH STATE.—Prior to the submission in accordance with subsection (e)(2) of the analysis required by subsection (a) and the review of the analysis required by subsection (c), the federally funded research and development center and the National Academies of Sciences, Engineering, and Medicine shall provide to the State of Washington—

(1) the analysis and review in draft form; and

(2) an opportunity to comment on the analysis and review for a period of not less than 60 days.

(e) SUBMISSION TO CONGRESS.—

(1) BRIEFINGS ON PROGRESS.—Not later than 180 days after the date of the enactment of this Act, and every 180 days thereafter until the materials described in paragraph (2) are submitted in accordance with that paragraph, the Secretary shall provide to the congressional defense committees a briefing on the progress being made on the analysis required by subsection (a) and the review of the analysis required by subsection (c).

(2) COMPLETED ANALYSIS AND REVIEW.—Not later than two years after the date of the enactment of this Act, the Secretary shall submit to the congressional defense committees the analysis required by subsection (a), the review of the analysis required by subsection (c), any com-

ments of the State of Washington under subsection (d)(2), and any comments of the Secretary on the analysis or the review of the analysis.

(f) LIMITATIONS.—

(1) SECRETARY OF ENERGY.—This section does not conflict with or impair the obligation of the Secretary to comply with any requirement of—

(A) the amended consent decree in Washington v. Moniz, No. 2:08-CV-5085-RMP (E.D. Wash.); or

(B) the Hanford Federal Facility Agreement and Consent Order.

(2) STATE OF WASHINGTON.—This section does not conflict with or impair the regulatory authority of the State of Washington under the Solid Waste Disposal Act (42 U.S.C. 6901 et seq.) (commonly referred to as the "Resource Conservation and Recovery Act of 1976") and any corresponding State law.

SEC. 3135. CLARIFICATION OF ANNUAL REPORT AND CERTIFICATION ON STATUS OF SECURITY OF ATOMIC ENERGY DEFENSE FACILITIES.

Section 4506(b)(1)(B) of the Atomic Energy Defense Act (50 U.S.C. 2657(b)(1)(B)) is amended to read as follows:

"(B) written certification that such facilities are secure and that the security measures at such facilities meet the security standards and requirements of the Department of Energy.".

SEC. 3136. REPORT ON SERVICE SUPPORT CONTRACTS AND AUTHORITY FOR APPOINTMENT OF CERTAIN PERSONNEL.

(a) ANNUAL REPORT ON SERVICE SUPPORT CONTRACTS.—Section 3241A(f) of the National Nuclear Security Administration Act (50 U.S.C. 2441a(f)) is amended by adding at the end the following new paragraph:

"(5) With respect to each contract identified under paragraph (2)—

"(A) the cost of the contract; and

"(B) identification of the program or program direction accounts that support the contract.".

(b) EXTENSION OF AUTHORITY FOR APPOINTMENT OF CERTAIN PERSONNEL.—Section 4601(c)(1) of the Atomic Energy Defense Act (50 U.S.C. 2701(c)(1)) is amended by striking "2016" and inserting "2020".

SEC. 3137. ELIMINATION OF CERTAIN REPORTING REQUIREMENTS.

(a) REPORTS ON PLAN TO PROTECT AGAINST INADVERTENT RELEASE OF RESTRICTED DATA AND FORMERLY RESTRICTED DATA.—Section 4522 of the Atomic Energy Defense Act (50 U.S.C. 2672) is amended—

(1) by striking subsection (e); and

(2) by redesignating subsection (f) as subsection (e).

(b) GAO REPORT ON PROGRAM ON SCIENTIFIC ENGAGEMENT FOR NONPROLIFERATION.—Section 3122 of the National Defense Authorization Act for Fiscal Year 2013 (Public Law 112–239; 50 U.S.C. 2571 note) is amended—

(1) in subsection (b)(1), by striking ", and to the Comptroller General of the United States,";

(2) by striking subsection (e); and

(3) by redesignating subsections (f) and (g) as subsections (e) and (f), respectively.

(c) GAO STUDY ON ADEQUACY OF BUDGET REQUESTS WITH RESPECT TO MODERNIZATION AND REFURBISHMENT OF NUCLEAR WEAPONS STOCKPILE.—Section 3255 of the National Nuclear Security Administration Act (50 U.S.C. 2455) is amended—

(1) by redesignating subsection (b) as subsection (c); and

(2) by inserting after subsection (a) the following new subsection (b):

"(b) TEMPORARY SUSPENSION.—The requirements of subsection (a) shall not apply with respect to the nuclear security budget materials submitted for fiscal year 2018 or 2019.".

(d) STRATEGY ON RISKS TO NONPROLIFERATION CAUSED BY ADDITIVE MANUFACTURING.—Section

3139(b) of the National Defense Authorization Act for Fiscal Year 2016 (Public Law 114–92; 129 Stat. 1215; 50 U.S.C. 2367 note) is amended to read as follows:

"(b) BRIEFINGS.—

"(1) IN GENERAL.—Not later than March 31, 2016, and annually thereafter through 2019, the President shall provide to the appropriate congressional committees a briefing on the strategy developed under subsection (a).

"(2) INTERIM BRIEFINGS.—In addition to the briefings required by paragraph (1), the President shall provide to the appropriate congressional committees a notification or briefing if there is a development in additive manufacture technology, or increased use of additive manufacture technology, that could pose an increased risk to the United States from nuclear proliferation.".

SEC. 3138. REPORT ON UNITED STATES NUCLEAR DETERRENCE.

(a) IN GENERAL.—Not later than 15 days after the date of the enactment of this Act, the Secretary of Energy shall, consistent with the protection of sources and methods, submit to the appropriate congressional committees the full, unredacted report, and any related materials, titled "U.S. Nuclear Deterrence in the Coming Decades", dated August 15, 2014.

(b) COVER LETTER.—The Secretary may submit to the appropriate congressional committees, with the report submitted under subsection (a), a cover letter containing any views or perspectives of the Secretary on the report or related matters.

(c) APPROPRIATE CONGRESSIONAL COMMITTEES DEFINED.—In this section, the term "appropriate congressional committees" means—

(1) the congressional defense committees; and

(2) the Select Committee on Intelligence of the Senate and the Permanent Select Committee on Intelligence of the House of Representatives.

TITLE XXXII—DEFENSE NUCLEAR FACILITIES SAFETY BOARD

Sec. 3201. Authorization.

SEC. 3201. AUTHORIZATION.

There are authorized to be appropriated for fiscal year 2017, $31,000,000 for the operation of the Defense Nuclear Facilities Safety Board under chapter 21 of the Atomic Energy Act of 1954 (42 U.S.C. 2286 et seq.).

TITLE XXXIV—NAVAL PETROLEUM RESERVES

Sec. 3401. Authorization of appropriations.

SEC. 3401. AUTHORIZATION OF APPROPRIATIONS.

(a) AMOUNT.—There are hereby authorized to be appropriated to the Secretary of Energy $14,950,000 for fiscal year 2017 for the purpose of carrying out activities under chapter 641 of title 10, United States Code, relating to the naval petroleum reserves.

(b) PERIOD OF AVAILABILITY.—Funds appropriated pursuant to the authorization of appropriations in subsection (a) shall remain available until expended.

TITLE XXXV—MARITIME MATTERS

Subtitle A—Maritime Administration, Coast Guard, and Shipping Matters

Sec. 3501. Authorization of the Maritime Administration.

Sec. 3502. Authority to extend certain age restrictions relating to vessels in the Maritime Security Fleet.

Sec. 3503. Corrections to provisions enacted by Coast Guard Authorization Acts.

Sec. 3504. Status of National Defense Reserve Fleet vessels.

Sec. 3505. NDRF national security multi-mission vessel.

Sec. 3506. Superintendent of United States Merchant Marine Academy.

Sec. 3507. Use of National Defense Reserve Fleet scrapping proceeds.

Sec. 3508. Floating dry docks.

Sec. 3509. Transportation worker identification credentials for individuals undergoing separation, discharge, or release from the Armed Forces.

Sec. 3510. Actions to address sexual harassment and sexual assault at the United States Merchant Marine Academy.

Sec. 3511. Sexual assault response coordinators and sexual assault victim advocates.

Sec. 3512. Report from the Department of Transportation Inspector General.

Sec. 3513. Sexual assault prevention and response working group.

Sec. 3514. Sea Year compliance.

Sec. 3515. State maritime academy physical standards and reporting.

Sec. 3516. Appointments.

Sec. 3517. Maritime workforce working group.

Sec. 3518. Maritime extreme weather task force.

Sec. 3519. Workforce plans and onboarding policies.

Sec. 3520. Drug and alcohol policy.

Sec. 3521. Vessel transfers.

Sec. 3522. Clarifying amendment; continuation boards.

Sec. 3523. Polar icebreaker recapitalization plan.

Sec. 3524. GAO report on icebreaking capability in United States.

Subtitle B—Pribilof Islands Transition Completion

Sec. 3531. Short title.

Sec. 3532. Conveyance of property.

Sec. 3533. Transfer, use, and disposal of tract 43.

Subtitle C—Sexual Harassment and Assault Prevention at the National Oceanic and Atmospheric Administration

Sec. 3541. Actions to address sexual harassment at National Oceanic and Atmospheric Administration.

Sec. 3542. Actions to address sexual assault at National Oceanic and Atmospheric Administration.

Sec. 3543. Rights of the victim of a sexual assault.

Sec. 3544. Change of station.

Sec. 3545. Applicability of policies to crews of vessels secured by National Oceanic and Atmospheric Administration under contract.

Sec. 3546. Annual report on sexual assaults in the National Oceanic and Atmospheric Administration.

Sec. 3547. Sexual assault defined.

Subtitle A—Maritime Administration, Coast Guard, and Shipping Matters

SEC. 3501. AUTHORIZATION OF THE MARITIME ADMINISTRATION.

There are authorized to be appropriated to the Department of Transportation for fiscal year 2017, to be available without fiscal year limitation if so provided in appropriations Acts, for programs associated with maintaining the United States merchant marine, the following amounts:

(1) For expenses necessary for operations of the United States Merchant Marine Academy, $99,902,000, of which—

(A) $74,851,000 shall be for Academy operations; and

(B) $25,051,000 shall remain available until expended for capital asset management at the Academy.

(2) For expenses necessary to support the State maritime academies, $29,550,000, of which—

(A) $2,400,000 shall remain available until September 30, 2018, for the Student Incentive Program;

(B) $3,000,000 shall remain available until expended for direct payments to such academies;

(C) $22,000,000 shall remain available until expended for maintenance and repair of State maritime academy training vessels;

(D) $1,800,000 shall remain available until expended for training ship fuel assistance; and

(E) $350,000 shall remain available until expended for expenses to improve the monitoring of the service obligations of graduates.

(3) For expenses necessary to support the National Security Multi-Mission Vessel Program, $36,000,000, which shall remain available until expended.

(4) For expenses necessary to support Maritime Administration operations and programs, $58,694,000.

(5) For expenses necessary to dispose of vessels in the National Defense Reserve Fleet, $20,000,000, which shall remain available until expended.

(6) For expenses necessary to maintain and preserve a United States flag merchant marine to serve the national security needs of the United States under chapter 531 of title 46, United States Code, $299,997,000.

(7) For expenses necessary to provide assistance for small shipyards and maritime communities under section 54101 of title 46, United States Code, $30,000,000, of which—

(A) $5,000,000 shall remain available until expended for training grants; and

(B) $25,000,000 shall remain available until expended for capital and related improvements.

(8) For administrative expenses associated with the program authorized by chapter 537 of title 46, United States Code, $3,000,000, which shall remain available until expended.

SEC. 3502. AUTHORITY TO EXTEND CERTAIN AGE RESTRICTIONS RELATING TO VESSELS IN THE MARITIME SECURITY FLEET.

(a) AUTHORITY.—

(1) IN GENERAL.—Section 53102 of title 46, United States Code, is amended by adding at the end the following:

"(g) AUTHORITY TO EXTEND MAXIMUM SERVICE AGE FOR VESSEL.—The Secretary of Defense, in conjunction with the Secretary of Transportation, may, for a particular participating fleet vessel, treat the ages specified in section 53101(5)(A)(ii) and section 53106(c)(3) as increased by up to 5 years if the Secretaries jointly determine that it is in the national interest to do so.".

(2) CONFORMING AMENDMENT.—The heading of subsection (f) of such section is amended to read as follows: "AUTHORITY TO WAIVE AGE RESTRICTION FOR ELIGIBILITY OF A VESSEL TO BE INCLUDED IN FLEET.—".

(b) REPEAL OF REDUNDANT AGE LIMITATION.—Section 53106(c)(3) of such title is amended—

(1) in subparagraph (A), by striking "or (C);" and inserting "; or";

(2) in subparagraph (B), by striking "; or" and inserting a period; and

(3) by striking subparagraph (C).

SEC. 3503. CORRECTIONS TO PROVISIONS ENACTED BY COAST GUARD AUTHORIZATION ACTS.

(a) SHORT TITLE CORRECTION.—The Coast Guard Authorization Act of 2015 (Public Law 114–120) is amended by striking "Coast Guard Authorization Act of 2015" each place it appears (including in quoted material) and inserting "Coast Guard Authorization Act of 2016".

(b) TITLE 46, UNITED STATES CODE.—

(1) EXAM REVIEW.—Section 7510(c) of title 46, United States Code, is amended—

(A) in paragraph (1)(D), by striking "engine" and inserting "engineer"; and

(B) in paragraph (9), by inserting a period after "App".

(2) VESSEL CERTIFICATION.—Section 4503(f)(2) of title 46, United States Code, is amended by striking ", that" and inserting ", then".

(c) PROVISIONS RELATING TO THE PRIBILOF IS-LANDS.—Section 521 of the Coast Guard Authorization Act of 2016 (Public Law 114–120), as amended by subsection (a), is amended by striking "2015" and inserting "2016".

(d) TITLE 14, UNITED STATES CODE.—

(1) REDISTRIBUTION OF AUTHORIZATIONS OF APPROPRIATIONS.—Section 2702 of title 14, United States Code, is amended—

(A) in paragraph (1)(B), by striking "$6,981,036,000" and inserting "$6,986,815,000"; and

(B) in paragraph (3)(B), by striking "$140,016,000" and inserting "$134,237,000".

(2) CLERICAL AMENDMENT.—The analysis at the beginning of part III of title 14, United States Code, is amended by striking the period at the end of the item relating to chapter 29.

(e) EFFECTIVE DATE.—The amendments made by this section shall take effect as if included in the enactment of Public Law 114–120.

SEC. 3504. STATUS OF NATIONAL DEFENSE RE-SERVE FLEET VESSELS.

Section 11 of the Merchant Ship Sales Act of 1946 (50 U.S.C. 4405) is amended—

(1) in subsection (a), by adding at the end the following: "Vessels in the National Defense Reserve Fleet, including vessels loaned to State maritime academies, shall be considered public vessels of the United States."; and

(2) by adding at the end the following:

"(g) VESSEL STATUS.—A vessel in the National Defense Reserve Fleet determined by the Maritime Administration to be of insufficient value to remain in the National Defense Reserve Fleet shall remain a vessel within the meaning of that term in section 3 of title 1, United States Code, and subject to the rights and responsibilities of a vessel under admiralty law at least until such time as the vessel is delivered to a dismantling facility or is disposed of otherwise from the National Defense Reserve Fleet.".

SEC. 3505. NDRF NATIONAL SECURITY MULTI-MIS-SION VESSEL.

(a) IN GENERAL.—The Secretary of Transportation, in consultation with the Chief of Naval Operations and the Commandant of the Coast Guard, shall ensure that the Maritime Administrator takes all necessary actions—

(1) to complete the design of a national security multi-mission vessel for the National Defense Reserve Fleet to allow for the construction of such vessel to begin in fiscal year 2018; and

(2) subject to the availability of appropriations, to have an entity enter into a contract for the construction of such vessel in accordance with this section.

(b) USE OF VESSEL.—A vessel constructed pursuant to this section shall be for use—

(1) as a training vessel that can be provided to State maritime academies under section 51504(b) of title 46, United States Code; and

(2) in conducting humanitarian assistance, disaster response, domestic and foreign emergency contingency operations, and other authorized uses of vessels of the National Defense Reserve Fleet.

(c) CONSTRUCTION AND DOCUMENTATION RE-QUIREMENTS.—A vessel constructed pursuant to this section shall meet the requirements for and be issued a certificate of documentation and a coastwise endorsement under chapter 121 of title 46, United States Code.

(d) DESIGN STANDARDS AND CONSTRUCTION PRACTICES.—Subject to subsection (c), a vessel constructed pursuant to this section shall be constructed using commercial design standards and commercial construction practices that are consistent with the best interests of the Federal Government.

(e) CONSULTATION WITH OTHER FEDERAL EN-TITIES.—The Maritime Administrator may consult and coordinate with the Secretary of the Navy regarding the vessel described in sub-section (a) and activities associated with such vessel.

(f) CONTRACTING.—The Maritime Administrator shall provide for an entity other than the Maritime Administration to contract for the construction of the vessel described in subsection (a).

(g) REPEAL OF PLAN APPROVAL REQUIRE-MENT.—Section 109(j)(3) of title 49, United States Code, is repealed.

SEC. 3506. SUPERINTENDENT OF UNITED STATES MERCHANT MARINE ACADEMY.

(a) IN GENERAL.—Section 51301 of title 46, United States Code, is amended by adding at the end the following:

"(c) SUPERINTENDENT.—

"(1) IN GENERAL.—The immediate command of the United States Merchant Marine Academy shall be in the Superintendent of the Academy, subject to the direction of the Maritime Administrator under the general supervision of the Secretary of Transportation.

"(2) APPOINTMENT.—The Secretary of Transportation shall appoint as the Superintendent—

"(A) an individual who has—

"(i) attained a general or flag officer rank in the Navy, Army, Air Force, Marine Corps, Coast Guard, or National Oceanic and Atmospheric Administration; and

"(ii) served at sea in any rank;

"(B) an individual who has—

"(i)(I) served at sea in the Navy, Army, Air Force, Marine Corps, Coast Guard, or National Oceanic and Atmospheric Administration; or

"(II) held a valid Coast Guard merchant mariner credential; and

"(ii) demonstrated exemplary leadership in the education of individuals in the Armed Forces or United States merchant marine; or

"(C) if a qualified individual described in sub-paragraph (A) or (B) does not apply for the position, an individual who has—

"(i) attained the grade of captain or above in the Navy, Coast Guard, or National Oceanic and Atmospheric Administration or colonel or above in the Army, Air Force, or Marine Corps; and

"(ii) served at sea in any grade.

"(3) RULE OF CONSTRUCTION.—Notwithstanding paragraph (2), the Secretary of Transportation may appoint an individual who is the best qualified candidate, even if such individual does not fully meet the criteria described in paragraph (2).".

(b) SAVINGS CLAUSE.—Nothing in this section may be construed to require any change to the current leadership of the United States Merchant Marine Academy.

SEC. 3507. USE OF NATIONAL DEFENSE RESERVE FLEET SCRAPPING PROCEEDS.

(a) FUNDING ALLOCATION.—Section 308704 of title 54, United States Code, is amended—

(1) in subsection (a)(1), by amending subparagraph (C) to read as follows:

"(C) The remainder shall be available to the Secretary to carry out the Program, as provided in subsection (b)."; and

(2) in subsection (b), by amending paragraph (1) to read as follows:

"(1) ALLOCATION.—

"(A) IN GENERAL.—Except as provided in subparagraph (B) and paragraph (2), of the amounts available each fiscal year for the Program under subsection (a)(1)(C)—

"(i) 50 percent shall be used for grants under section 308703(b); and

"(ii) 50 percent shall be used for grants under section 308703(c).

"(B) SET ASIDE.—

"(i) IN GENERAL.—Not less than 25 percent of the amounts available each fiscal year for the Program under subsection (a)(1)(C) shall be used for the preservation and presentation to the public of the maritime heritage property of the Maritime Administration.

"(ii) DIRECT TRANSFERS.—The Secretary may provide amounts used for the preservation and presentation to the public of the maritime heritage property of the Maritime Administration through direct transfers to the Maritime Administration.

"(iii) WAIVER.—The Maritime Administrator may waive the application of clause (i) for any fiscal year.".

(b) CONFORMING AMENDMENT.—Section 308703(c)(1) of title 54, United States Code, is amended by striking "under section 308704(b)(1)(B)" and inserting "under section 308704(b)(1)(A)".

(c) REPORTING REQUIREMENT.—Section 308703(j) of title 54, United States Code, is amended—

(1) in the matter preceding paragraph (1), by striking "Congress" and inserting "the Committee on Commerce, Science, and Transportation of the Senate, the Committee on Energy and Natural Resources of the Senate, the Committee on Natural Resources of the House of Representatives, the Committee on Armed Services of the House of Representatives, and the Committee on Transportation and Infrastructure of the House of Representatives";

(2) by redesignating paragraphs (1), (2), and (3) as paragraphs (2), (3), and (4), respectively;

(3) by inserting before paragraph (2), as redesignated, the following:

"(1) the total number of grant applications submitted and approved under the Program in the period covered by the report;"; and

(4) in paragraph (2), as redesignated, by inserting "detailed" before "description".

(d) ANNUAL REPORT BY THE MARITIME ADMIN-ISTRATION.—

(1) IN GENERAL.—Not later than January 1 of each year, the Maritime Administrator shall submit to the Committee on Commerce, Science, and Transportation of the Senate and the Committee on Armed Services and the Committee on Transportation and Infrastructure of the House of Representatives a report on the management of the Ship Disposal program of the Maritime Administration.

(2) CONTENTS.—Each report under paragraph (1) shall include—

(A) the total amount of funds, attributable to the Ship Disposal program of the Maritime Administration, credited in the most recently completed fiscal year to—

(i) the Vessel Operations Revolving Fund established by section 50301(a) of title 46, United States Code; and

(ii) any other account;

(B) the balance of funds available at the end of that fiscal year in—

(i) the Vessel Operations Revolving Fund; and

(ii) any other account for which a credited amount was included under subparagraph (A)(ii);

(C) a detailed description of the funds credited to and distributions from the Vessel Operations Revolving Fund in that fiscal year; and

(D) a summary of each maritime heritage project selected by the Maritime Administrator, for preservation and presentation to the public of the Maritime Administration's maritime heritage property, for which funds from the Vessel Operations Revolving Fund were expended in that fiscal year.

(e) ASSESSMENTS BY THE MARITIME ADMINIS-TRATION.—

(1) IN GENERAL.—Not later than 1 year after the date of the enactment of this Act, and biennially thereafter, the Maritime Administrator shall complete an assessment of the Ship Disposal program of the Maritime Administration.

(2) CONTENTS.—Each assessment under paragraph (1) shall include—

(A) an inventory of each vessel, subject to a disposal agreement or a memorandum of agreement with another Federal agency relating to

the disposal of the vessel, for which the Maritime Administration is acting as the disposal agency, including—

(i) the age of the vessel; and

(ii) the name of the Federal agency that has or had custody over the vessel prior to any disposal agreement or memorandum of agreement with the Maritime Administration;

(B) an inventory of each vessel of a Federal agency that may meet the criteria for the Maritime Administration to act as the disposal agency, including—

(i) the age of the vessel;

(ii) the name of the applicable Federal agency; and

(iii) whether the vessel is expected to be declared obsolete and dismantled in the next 5 years;

(C) a plan to serve as the disposal agency, as appropriate, for the vessels described in subparagraph (B);

(D) a plan for the timely distribution of the proceeds that the Maritime Administration currently has in ship disposal accounts;

(E) a projection of future distributions of such proceeds; and

(F) any other assessment related to the Ship Disposal program that the Maritime Administrator determines appropriate.

(3) INCLUSION IN THE ANNUAL REPORT.—A detailed description of the results of each assessment under paragraph (1) shall be included in the annual report under subsection (d) for the year in which the assessment was completed.

(f) CESSATION OF EFFECTIVENESS.—Subsections (d) and (e) of this section shall cease to be effective on the date that is 5 years and 1 day after the date of the enactment of this Act.

SEC. 3508. FLOATING DRY DOCKS.

Section 55122 of title 46, United States Code, is amended—

(1) by redesignating subsection (b) as subsection (c); and

(2) by inserting after subsection (a) the following:

"(b) DRY DOCKS FOR CONSTRUCTION OF CERTAIN NAVAL VESSELS.—

"(1) IN GENERAL.—In applying subsection (a) to a floating dry dock used for the construction of naval vessels in a shipyard located in the United States, the ownership and operation requirement in paragraph (1)(B) of that subsection shall be treated as satisfied and 'December 19, 2017' shall be substituted for the date referred to in paragraph (1)(C) of that subsection if the Secretary of the Navy determines that—

"(A) such dry dock is necessary for the timely completion of such construction; and

"(B) such dry dock—

"(i) is owned and operated by—

"(I) a shipyard located in the United States that is an eligible owner specified under section 12103(b); or

"(II) an affiliate of such a shipyard; or

"(ii) is—

"(I) owned by the State in which the shipyard is located or a political subdivision of that State; and

"(II) operated by a shipyard located in the United States that is an eligible owner specified under section 12103(b).

"(2) NOTICE TO CONGRESS.—Not later than 30 days after making a determination under paragraph (1), the Secretary of the Navy shall notify the Committee on Armed Services and the Committee on Transportation and Infrastructure of the House of Representatives and the Committee on Armed Services and the Committee on Commerce, Science, and Transportation of the Senate of such determination.".

SEC. 3509. TRANSPORTATION WORKER IDENTIFICATION CREDENTIALS FOR INDIVIDUALS UNDERGOING SEPARATION, DISCHARGE, OR RELEASE FROM THE ARMED FORCES.

(a) IN GENERAL.—Section 70105 of title 46, United States Code, is amended—

(1) in subsection (b)(2), by striking "and" after the semicolon at the end of subparagraph (F), by redesignating subparagraph (G) as subparagraph (H), and by inserting after subparagraph (F) the following:

"(G) a member of the Armed Forces who—

"(i) is undergoing separation, discharge, or release from the Armed Forces under honorable conditions;

"(ii) applies for a transportation security card; and

"(iii) is otherwise eligible for such a card; and"; and

(2) by amending subsection (j) to read as follows:

"(j) PRIORITY PROCESSING FOR SEPARATING SERVICE MEMBERS.—(1) The Secretary and the Secretary of Defense shall enter into a memorandum of understanding regarding the submission and processing of applications for transportation security cards under subsection (b)(2)(G).

"(2) Not later than 30 days after the submission of such an application by an individual who is eligible to submit such an application, the Secretary shall process and approve or deny the application unless an appeal or waiver applies or further application documentation is necessary.".

(b) DEADLINE FOR MEMORANDUM.—The Secretary of the department in which the Coast Guard is operating and the Secretary of Defense shall enter into the memorandum of understanding required by the amendment made by subsection (a)(2) by not later than 180 days after the date of the enactment of this Act.

(c) APPLICATION OF PROCESSING DEADLINE.—Section 70105(j)(2) of title 46, United States Code, as amended by this section, shall apply to applications for transportation security cards submitted after the expiration of the 180-day period beginning on the date of the enactment of this Act.

(d) REPORTS.—

(1) INITIAL REPORT.—

(A) REQUIREMENT.—Not later than 1 year after the date of the enactment of this Act, the Secretary of Defense and the Secretary of Homeland Security shall jointly submit a report described in subparagraph (B) to the Committee on Armed Services, the Committee on Commerce, Science, and Transportation, and the Committee on Homeland Security and Governmental Affairs of the Senate and the Committee on Armed Services, the Committee on Homeland Security, and the Committee on Transportation and Infrastructure of the House of Representatives.

(B) CONTENTS.—The report under subparagraph (A) shall include the following:

(i) The memorandum of understanding required by section 70105(j)(1) of title 46, United States Code, as amended by this section.

(ii) The number of individuals eligible to apply for a transportation security card under section 70105(b)(2)(G) of title 46, United States Code, as amended by this section, the number of such individuals who applied for such a card, and the number of such individuals who have been issued such a card, as of the date of the report.

(iii) If the Secretary failed to process and approve or deny any applications received from individuals eligible to apply for such a card under such section before the deadline specified in section 70105(j)(2) of such title, as amended by this section, a description of the reasons for the failure and of the actions being taken to assure that future applications are processed and issued or denied within such deadline.

(2) SUBSEQUENT REPORT.—Not later than 2 years after the date of enactment of this Act, the Secretary of Defense and the Secretary of Homeland Security shall jointly submit a report to such Committees containing the information described in clauses (ii) and (iii) of paragraph (1)(B).

SEC. 3510. ACTIONS TO ADDRESS SEXUAL HARASSMENT AND SEXUAL ASSAULT AT THE UNITED STATES MERCHANT MARINE ACADEMY.

(a) POLICY.—Chapter 513 of title 46, United States Code, is amended by adding at the end the following:

"§ 51318. Policy on sexual harassment and sexual assault

"(a) REQUIRED POLICY.—

"(1) IN GENERAL.—The Secretary of Transportation shall direct the Superintendent of the United States Merchant Marine Academy to prescribe a policy on sexual harassment and sexual assault applicable to the cadets and other personnel of the Academy.

"(2) MATTERS TO BE SPECIFIED IN POLICY.—The policy on sexual harassment and sexual assault prescribed under this subsection shall include—

"(A) a program to promote awareness of the incidence of rape, acquaintance rape, and other sexual offenses of a criminal nature that involve cadets or other Academy personnel;

"(B) procedures that a cadet or other Academy personnel should follow in the case of an occurrence of sexual harassment or sexual assault, including—

"(i) specifying the person or persons to whom an alleged occurrence of sexual harassment or sexual assault should be reported by the victim and the options for confidential reporting;

"(ii) specifying any other person whom the victim should contact; and

"(iii) procedures on the preservation of evidence potentially necessary for proof of criminal sexual assault;

"(C) a procedure for disciplinary action in cases of alleged criminal sexual assault involving a cadet or other Academy personnel;

"(D) any other sanction authorized to be imposed in a substantiated case of sexual harassment or sexual assault involving a cadet or other Academy personnel in rape, acquaintance rape, or any other criminal sexual offense, whether forcible or nonforcible;

"(E) procedures through which—

"(i) questions regarding sexual harassment or sexual assault can be confidentially asked and confidentially answered;

"(ii) victims can report incidents of sexual assault confidentially; and

"(iii) the privacy of victims of sexual harassment and sexual assault will be protected; and

"(F) required training on the policy for all cadets and other Academy personnel, including the specific training required for personnel who process allegations of sexual harassment or sexual assault involving Academy personnel.

"(3) AVAILABILITY OF POLICY.—The Secretary shall ensure that the policy developed under this subsection is available to—

"(A) all cadets and employees of the Academy; and

"(B) the public.

"(4) CONSULTATION AND ASSISTANCE.—In developing the policy under this subsection, the Secretary may consult with or receive assistance from such Federal, State, local, and national organizations and subject matter experts as the Secretary considers appropriate.

"(b) DEVELOPMENT PROGRAM.—

"(1) IN GENERAL.—The Secretary shall ensure that the development program of the Academy includes a section that—

"(A) describes the relationship between honor, respect, and character development and the prevention of sexual harassment and sexual assault at the Academy;

"(B) includes a brief history of the problem of sexual harassment and sexual assault in the merchant marine, in the Armed Forces, and at the Academy; and

"(C) includes information relating to reporting sexual harassment and sexual assault, victims' rights, and dismissal for offenders.

"(2) MINIMUM TRAINING REQUIREMENTS.—The Superintendent shall ensure that all cadets receive training on the sexual harassment and sexual assault prevention and response sections of the development program of the Academy, as described in paragraph (1), as follows:

"(A) An initial training session, which shall occur not later than 7 days after a cadet's initial arrival at the Academy.

"(B) Additional training sessions, which shall occur biannually following the cadet's initial training session until the cadet graduates or leaves the Academy.

"(c) ANNUAL ASSESSMENT.—

"(1) IN GENERAL.—The Secretary, in cooperation with the Superintendent, shall conduct an assessment at the Academy, during each Academy program year, to determine the effectiveness of the policies, procedures, and training program of the Academy with respect to sexual harassment and sexual assault involving cadets or other Academy personnel.

"(2) BIENNIAL SURVEY.—For each assessment of the Academy under paragraph (1) during an Academy program year that begins in an odd-numbered calendar year, the Secretary shall conduct a survey of cadets and other Academy personnel—

"(A) to measure—

"(i) the incidence, during that program year, of sexual harassment and sexual assault events involving cadets or other Academy personnel, on or off the Academy campus, that have been reported to officials of the Academy; and

"(ii) the incidence, during that program year, of sexual harassment and sexual assault events involving cadets or other Academy personnel, on or off the Academy campus, that have not been reported to officials of the Academy; and

"(B) to assess the perceptions of cadets and other Academy personnel on—

"(i) the policies, procedures, and training programs of the Academy on sexual harassment and sexual assault involving cadets or other Academy personnel;

"(ii) the enforcement of the policies described in clause (i);

"(iii) the incidence of sexual harassment and sexual assault involving cadets or other Academy personnel; and

"(iv) any other issues relating to sexual harassment and sexual assault involving cadets or other Academy personnel.

"(3) FOCUS GROUPS FOR YEARS WHEN SURVEY NOT REQUIRED.—In any year in which the Secretary is not required to conduct the survey described in paragraph (2), the Secretary shall conduct focus groups at the Academy for the purposes of ascertaining information relating to sexual assault and sexual harassment issues at the Academy.

"(d) ANNUAL REPORT.—

"(1) IN GENERAL.—For each Academy program year, the Superintendent shall submit to the Secretary a report that provides information about sexual harassment and sexual assault involving cadets or other Academy personnel.

"(2) CONTENTS.—Each report submitted under paragraph (1) shall include, for the Academy program year covered by the report—

"(A) the number of sexual assaults, rapes, and other sexual offenses involving cadets or other Academy personnel that have been reported to Academy officials;

"(B) the number of the reported cases described in subparagraph (A) that have been substantiated;

"(C) the policies, procedures, and training implemented by the Superintendent and the leadership of the Academy in response to incidents of sexual harassment and sexual assault involving cadets and other Academy personnel; and

"(D) a plan for the actions that will be taken in the following Academy program year regard-

ing prevention of, and response to, incidents of sexual harassment and sexual assault involving cadets and other Academy personnel.

"(3) SURVEY AND FOCUS GROUP RESULTS.—

"(A) SURVEY RESULTS.—Each report under paragraph (1) for an Academy program year that begins in an odd-numbered calendar year shall include the results of the survey conducted in that program year under subsection (c)(2).

"(B) FOCUS GROUP RESULTS.—Each report under paragraph (1) for an Academy program year in which the Secretary is not required to conduct the survey described in subsection (c)(2) shall include the results of the focus group conducted in that program year under subsection (c)(3).

"(4) REPORTING REQUIREMENT.—

"(A) BY THE SUPERINTENDENT.—For each incident of sexual harassment or sexual assault reported to the Superintendent, the Superintendent shall provide to the Secretary and the Board of Visitors of the Academy a report that includes—

"(i) the facts surrounding the incident, except for any details that would reveal the identities of the people involved; and

"(ii) the Academy's response to the incident.

"(B) BY THE SECRETARY.—The Secretary shall submit a copy of each report received under subparagraph (A) and the Secretary's comments on the report to the Committee on Commerce, Science, and Transportation of the Senate and the Committee on Transportation and Infrastructure of the House of Representatives.".

(b) CLERICAL AMENDMENT.—The table of sections for chapter 513 of title 46, United States Code, is amended by adding at the end the following:

"51318. Policy on sexual harassment and sexual assault.".

SEC. 3511. SEXUAL ASSAULT RESPONSE COORDINATORS AND SEXUAL ASSAULT VICTIM ADVOCATES.

(a) COORDINATORS AND ADVOCATES.—Chapter 513 of title 46, United States Code, as amended by this Act, is further amended by adding at the end the following:

"§ 51319. Sexual assault response coordinators and sexual assault victim advocates

"(a) SEXUAL ASSAULT RESPONSE COORDINATORS.—The United States Merchant Marine Academy shall employ or contract with at least 1 full-time sexual assault response coordinator who shall reside at or near the Academy. The Secretary of Transportation may assign additional full-time or part-time sexual assault response coordinators at the Academy as necessary.

"(b) VOLUNTEER SEXUAL ASSAULT VICTIM ADVOCATES.—

"(1) IN GENERAL.—The Secretary, acting through the Superintendent of the Academy, shall designate from among volunteers 1 or more permanent employees of the Academy to serve as advocates for victims of sexual assaults involving cadets of the Academy or other Academy personnel.

"(2) TRAINING; OTHER DUTIES.—Each victim advocate designated under this subsection shall—

"(A) have or receive training in matters relating to sexual assault and the comprehensive policy developed under section 51318; and

"(B) serve as a victim advocate voluntarily, in addition to the individual's other duties as an employee of the Academy.

"(3) PRIMARY DUTIES.—While performing the duties of a victim advocate under this subsection, a designated employee shall—

"(A) support victims of sexual assault by informing them of the rights and resources available to them as victims;

"(B) identify additional resources to ensure the safety of victims of sexual assault; and

"(C) connect victims of sexual assault to companions, as described in paragraph (4).

"(4) COMPANIONS.—

"(A) IN GENERAL.—At least 1 victim advocate designated under this subsection, or a sexual assault response coordinator designated under subsection (a), while performing the duties of a victim advocate, shall act as a companion to a victim described in paragraph (1) in navigating investigative, medical, mental, and emotional health, and recovery processes relating to sexual assault.

"(B) ALTERNATE VICTIM ADVOCATES.—If requested by the victim, an alternate victim advocate shall be designated under this subsection to act as a companion to the victim, as described in subparagraph (A).

"(5) HOTLINE.—The Secretary shall establish a 24-hour hotline through which the victim of a sexual assault described in paragraph (1) can receive victim support services.

"(6) FORMAL RELATIONSHIPS WITH OTHER ENTITIES.—The Secretary may enter into formal relationships with other entities to make available additional victim advocates or to implement paragraphs (3), (4), and (5).".

(b) CLERICAL AMENDMENT.—The table of sections for chapter 513 of title 46, United States Code, as amended by this Act, is further amended by adding at the end the following:

"51319. Sexual assault response coordinators and sexual assault victim advocates.".

SEC. 3512. REPORT FROM THE DEPARTMENT OF TRANSPORTATION INSPECTOR GENERAL.

(a) IN GENERAL.—Not later than March 31, 2018, the Inspector General of the Department of Transportation shall submit to the Committee on Commerce, Science, and Transportation of the Senate and the Committee on Transportation and Infrastructure of the House of Representatives a report that describes the effectiveness of the sexual harassment and sexual assault prevention and response program at the United States Merchant Marine Academy.

(b) CONTENTS.—The report required under subsection (a) shall—

(1) assess progress toward addressing any outstanding recommendations;

(2) include any recommendations to reduce the number of sexual assaults involving members of the Academy, whether a member is the victim, the alleged assailant, or both; and

(3) include any recommendations to improve the response of the Department and the Academy to reports of sexual assaults involving members of the Academy, whether a member is the victim, a member is the alleged assailant, or both.

(c) EXPERTISE.—In compiling the report required under this section, the Inspector General shall—

(1) include on the inspection teams acting under the direction of the Inspector General at least 1 member with expertise and knowledge of sexual assault prevention and response policies; or

(2) consult with subject matter experts in the prevention of and response to sexual assaults.

SEC. 3513. SEXUAL ASSAULT PREVENTION AND RESPONSE WORKING GROUP.

(a) IN GENERAL.—Not later than 21 days after the date of the enactment of this Act, the Maritime Administrator shall convene a working group to examine methods to improve the prevention of, and response to, any sexual harassment, sexual assault, or other inappropriate conduct, as well as methods to improve the shipboard climate, that occurs during a cadet's Sea Year experience with the United States Merchant Marine Academy.

(b) MEMBERSHIP.—The working group shall be composed of members designated by the Maritime Administrator as follows:

(1) A representative of the Maritime Administration, who shall serve as the chair of the working group.

(2) The Superintendent of the Academy (or the Superintendent's designee).

(3) A sexual assault response coordinator appointed under section 51319 of title 46, United States Code, as added by this Act.

(4) A subject matter expert from the Coast Guard.

(5) A subject matter expert from the Military Sealift Command.

(6) A subject matter expert from the National Oceanic and Atmospheric Administration.

(7) At least 1 representative from each State maritime academy.

(8) At least 1 representative from each private contracting party participating in the maritime security program.

(9) At least 1 representative from each nonprofit labor organization representing a class or craft of employees employed on vessels in the Maritime Security Fleet.

(10) At least 2 representatives from approved maritime training institutions.

(11) At least 1 representative from companies that—

(A) participate in sea training of Academy cadets; and

(B) do not participate in the maritime security program.

(12) Such additional individuals as the Maritime Administrator may designate.

(c) NO QUORUM REQUIREMENT.—The chair may convene the working group without all members present.

(d) RESPONSIBILITIES.—The working group shall—

(1) evaluate options that could promote a climate of honor and respect, and a culture that is intolerant of sexual harassment, sexual assault, or other inappropriate conduct and those who commit it, with operators of vessels of the United States;

(2) raise awareness of sexual harassment, sexual assault, or other inappropriate conduct with operators of vessels of the United States;

(3) assess options that could be implemented by the operators of vessels of the United States that would remove any barriers to the reporting of sexual harassment, sexual assault, or other inappropriate conduct that occurs during a cadet's Sea Year experience and protect the victim's confidentiality;

(4) assess a potential program or policy to improve the prevention of, and response to, incidents of sexual harassment, sexual assault, or other inappropriate conduct;

(5) assess a potential program or policy requiring crews to complete a sexual harassment and sexual assault prevention and response training program before the cadet's Sea Year that includes—

(A) fostering a shipboard climate—

(i) that does not tolerate sexual harassment, sexual assault, or other inappropriate conduct;

(ii) in which persons assigned to vessel crews are encouraged to intervene to prevent such potential incidents; and

(iii) that encourages victims to report any incident of sexual harassment, sexual assault, or other inappropriate conduct; and

(B) promoting an understanding of the needs of, and the resources available to, a victim after an incident of sexual harassment, sexual assault, or other inappropriate conduct;

(6) assess all other feasible changes to Sea Year training at the Academy, and corresponding changes to curricula, to improve prevention of and response to incidents of sexual harassment, sexual assault, and other inappropriate conduct; and

(7) assess how vessel operators could ensure the confidentiality of a report of sexual harassment, sexual assault, or other inappropriate conduct in order to protect the victim and prevent retribution.

(e) REPORT.—Not later than 9 months after the date of the enactment of this Act, the working group shall submit to the Committee on Commerce, Science, and Transportation of the Senate and the Committee on Transportation and Infrastructure of the House of Representatives a report that includes—

(1) recommendations on each of the working group's responsibilities described in subsection (d);

(2) a description of the trade-offs, opportunities, and challenges associated with the recommendations described in paragraph (1);

(3) a description of administrative actions taken as result of the recommendations described in paragraph (1); and

(4) any other information the working group determines appropriate.

SEC. 3514. SEA YEAR COMPLIANCE.

Not later than 90 days after the date of the enactment of this Act, the Maritime Administrator, in consultation with operators of commercial vessels of the United States, shall establish—

(1) criteria that vessel operators must meet in order to participate in the Sea Year program of the United States Merchant Marine Academy that addresses sexual harassment, sexual assault, and other inappropriate conduct; and

(2) a process for verifying compliance with the criteria.

SEC. 3515. STATE MARITIME ACADEMY PHYSICAL STANDARDS AND REPORTING.

Section 51506 of title 46, United States Code, is amended—

(1) in subsection (a)—

(A) in the matter preceding paragraph (1), by striking "must" and inserting "shall";

(B) in paragraph (2), by striking "and" at the end;

(C) in paragraph (3), by striking the period at the end and inserting "; and"; and

(D) by adding at the end the following:

"(4) agree that any individual enrolled at such State maritime academy in a merchant marine officer preparation program—

"(A) shall, not later than 9 months after such individual's date of enrollment, pass an examination in form and substance satisfactory to the Secretary that demonstrates that such individual meets the medical and physical requirements—

"(i) required for the issuance of an original license under section 7101; or

"(ii) set by the Coast Guard for issuing merchant mariners' documentation under section 7302, with no limit to the individual's operational authority;

"(B) following passage of the examination under subparagraph (A), shall continue to meet the requirements described in subparagraph (A) throughout the remainder of the individual's enrollment at the State maritime academy; and

"(C) if the individual has a medical or physical condition that disqualifies the individual from meeting the requirements referred to in subparagraph (A), shall be transferred to a program other than a merchant marine officer preparation program, or otherwise appropriately disenrolled from such State maritime academy, until the individual demonstrates to the Secretary that the individual meets such requirements."; and

(2) by adding at the end the following:

"(c) SECRETARIAL WAIVER AUTHORITY.—The Secretary may modify or waive any of the terms set forth in subsection (a)(4) with respect to any individual or State maritime academy.".

SEC. 3516. APPOINTMENTS.

(a) IN GENERAL.—Section 51303 of title 46, United States Code, is amended by striking "40" and inserting "50".

(b) CLASS PROFILES.—

(1) IN GENERAL.—Not later than August 31 of each year, the Superintendent of the United States Merchant Marine Academy shall post on the Academy's public website a profile of each class at the Academy.

(2) CONTENTS.—Each profile posted under paragraph (1) shall include, for the incoming class of the Academy and for the 4 classes that preceded that class at the Academy, the number and percentage of students by—

(A) State;

(B) country;

(C) gender;

(D) race and ethnicity; and

(E) prior military service.

SEC. 3517. MARITIME WORKFORCE WORKING GROUP.

(a) IN GENERAL.—Not later than 120 days after the date of the enactment of this Act, the Maritime Administrator, in consultation with the Coast Guard Merchant Marine Personnel Advisory Committee and the Committee on the Marine Transportation System, shall convene a working group to examine and assess the size of the pool of United States citizen mariners necessary to support the United States flag fleet in times of national emergency.

(b) MEMBERSHIP.—The Maritime Administrator shall designate individuals to serve as members of the working group convened under subsection (a). The working group shall include, at a minimum, at least 1 representative from each of—

(1) the Maritime Administration, who shall serve as chairperson of the working group;

(2) the United States Merchant Marine Academy;

(3) the Coast Guard;

(4) the Military Sealift Command;

(5) the Navy;

(6) the State maritime academies;

(7) a nonprofit labor organization representing a class of licensed employees who are employed on vessels operating in the United States flag fleet;

(8) a nonprofit labor organization representing a class of unlicensed employees who are employed on vessels operating in the United States flag fleet;

(9) the pool of owners of vessels operating in the United States flag fleet, or their private contracting parties, that are primarily operating in coastwise trades; and

(10) the pool of owners of vessels operating in the United States flag fleet, or their private contracting parties, that are primarily operating in international transportation.

(c) NO QUORUM REQUIREMENT.—The Maritime Administrator may convene the working group virtually and without all members present.

(d) RESPONSIBILITIES.—The working group shall—

(1) identify the number of United States citizen mariners—

(A) in total;

(B) that have a valid Coast Guard merchant mariner credential with the necessary endorsements for service on unlimited tonnage vessels that are subject to the International Convention on Standards of Training, Certification and Watchkeeping for Seafarers, 1978, as amended;

(C) that are involved in Federal programs that support the United States merchant marine and the United States flag fleet;

(D) that are available to crew the United States flag fleet and the surge sealift fleet in times of a national emergency;

(E) that are full-time mariners;

(F) that have sailed in the prior 18 months;

(G) that are primarily operating in noncontiguous or coastwise trades; and

(H) that are merchant mariner credentialed officers in the United States Navy Reserve;

(2) *assess the impact on the United States merchant marine and United States Merchant Marine Academy if graduates from State maritime academies and the United States Merchant Marine Academy were assigned to, or required to fulfill, certain maritime positions based on the overall needs of the United States merchant marine;*

(3) *assess the Coast Guard Merchant Mariner Licensing and Documentation System and its accessibility and value to the Maritime Administration for the purposes of evaluating the pool of United States citizen mariners; and*

(4) *make recommendations to enhance the availability and quality of interagency data, including data from the United States Transportation Command, the Coast Guard, the Navy, and the Bureau of Transportation Statistics, for use by the Maritime Administration for evaluating the pool of United States citizen mariners.*

(e) REPORT.—*Not later than 1 year after the date of the enactment of this Act, the Secretary of Transportation shall submit a report to the Committee on Commerce, Science, and Transportation of the Senate, the Committee on Armed Services of the House of Representatives, and the Committee on Transportation and Infrastructure of the House of Representatives that contains the results of the study conducted under this section, including—*

(1) *the number of United States citizen mariners identified for each category described in subparagraphs (A) through (H) of subsection (d)(1);*

(2) *the results of the assessments conducted under paragraphs (2) and (3) of subsection (d); and*

(3) *the recommendations made under subsection (d)(4).*

(f) INCLUSION OF MERCHANT MARINE-CREDENTIALED OFFICERS IN THE NAVY RESERVE.—*For the purposes of this section, the term "United States citizen mariners" includes, but is not limited to, officers in the United States Navy Reserve who are holders of merchant mariner credentials, as determined by the Secretary of the Navy.*

(g) SUNSET.—*The Maritime Administrator may disband the working group upon submission of the report under subsection (e).*

SEC. 3518. MARITIME EXTREME WEATHER TASK FORCE.

(a) ESTABLISHMENT OF TASK FORCE.—*Not later than 15 days after the date of the enactment of this Act, the Secretary of Transportation shall establish a task force to analyze the impact of extreme weather events, such as in the maritime environment (referred to in this section as the "Task Force").*

(b) MEMBERSHIP.—*The Task Force shall be composed of—*

(1) *the Secretary or the Secretary's designee; and*

(2) *a representative of—*

(A) *the Coast Guard;*

(B) *the National Oceanic and Atmospheric Administration; and*

(C) *such other Federal agency or independent commission as the Secretary considers appropriate.*

(c) REPORT.—

(1) IN GENERAL.—*Except as provided in paragraph (4), not later than 180 days after the date it is established under subsection (a), the Task Force shall submit to the Committee on Commerce, Science, and Transportation of the Senate and the Committee on Transportation and Infrastructure of the House of Representatives a report on the analysis under subsection (a).*

(2) CONTENTS.—*The report under paragraph (1) shall include—*

(A) *an identification of available weather prediction, monitoring, and routing technology resources;*

(B) *an identification of industry best practices relating to response to, and prevention of marine casualties from, extreme weather events;*

(C) *a description of how the resources described in subparagraph (A) are used in the various maritime sectors, including by passenger and cargo vessels;*

(D) *recommendations for improving maritime response operations to extreme weather events and preventing marine casualties from extreme weather events, such as promoting the use of risk communications and the technologies identified under subparagraph (A); and*

(E) *recommendations for any legislative or regulatory actions for improving maritime response operations to extreme weather events and preventing marine casualties from extreme weather events.*

(3) PUBLICATION.—*The Secretary shall make the report under paragraph (1) and any notification under paragraph (4) publicly accessible in an electronic format.*

(4) IMMINENT THREATS.—*The Task Force shall immediately notify the Secretary of any finding or recommendations that could protect the safety of an individual on a vessel from an imminent threat of extreme weather.*

SEC. 3519. WORKFORCE PLANS AND ONBOARDING POLICIES.

(a) WORKFORCE PLANS.—*Not later than 9 months after the date of the enactment of this Act, the Maritime Administrator shall review the Maritime Administration's workforce plans, including its Strategic Human Capital Plan and Leadership Succession Plan, and fully implement competency models for mission-critical occupations, including—*

(1) *leadership positions;*

(2) *human resources positions; and*

(3) *transportation specialist positions.*

(b) ONBOARDING POLICIES.—*Not later than 9 months after the date of the enactment of this Act, the Maritime Administrator shall—*

(1) *review the Maritime Administration's policies related to new hire orientation, training, and misconduct;*

(2) *align the onboarding policies and procedures at headquarters and the field offices to ensure consistent implementation and provision of critical information across the Maritime Administration; and*

(3) *update the Maritime Administration's training policies and training systems to include controls that ensure that all completed training is tracked in a standardized training repository.*

(c) REPORT.—*Not later than 1 year after the date of the enactment of this Act, the Maritime Administrator shall submit a report to the Committee on Commerce, Science, and Transportation of the Senate and the Committee on Armed Services and the Committee on Transportation and Infrastructure of the House of Representatives that describes the Maritime Administration's compliance with the requirements under this section.*

SEC. 3520. DRUG AND ALCOHOL POLICY.

(a) REVIEW.—*Not later than 9 months after the date of the enactment of this Act, the Maritime Administrator shall—*

(1) *review the Maritime Administration's drug and alcohol policies, procedures, and training practices;*

(2) *ensure that all fleet managers have received training on the Department of Transportation's drug and alcohol policy, including the testing procedures used by the Department and the Maritime Administration in cases of reasonable suspicion; and*

(3) *institute a system for tracking all drug and alcohol policy training conducted under paragraph (2) in a standardized training repository.*

(b) REPORT.—*Not later than 1 year after the date of the enactment of this Act, the Maritime Administrator shall submit a report to the Com-*

mittee on Commerce, Science, and Transportation of the Senate and the Committee on Armed Services and the Committee on Transportation and Infrastructure of the House of Representatives that describes the Maritime Administration's compliance with the requirements under this section.

SEC. 3521. VESSEL TRANSFERS.

Not later than 9 months after the date of the enactment of this Act, the Maritime Administrator shall submit a report to the Committee on Commerce, Science, and Transportation of the Senate and the Committee on Armed Services and the Committee on Transportation and Infrastructure of the House of Representatives that describes the Maritime Administration policies and procedures for vessel transfer, including—

(1) *a summary of the actions taken to update the Vessel Transfer Office procedures manual to reflect the current range of program responsibilities and processes; and*

(2) *a copy of the updated Vessel Transfer Office procedures to process vessel transfer applications.*

SEC. 3522. CLARIFYING AMENDMENT; CONTINUATION BOARDS.

Section 290(a) of title 14, United States Code, is amended by striking "five officers serving in the grade of vice admiral" and inserting "5 officers (other than the Commandant) serving in the grade of admiral or vice admiral".

SEC. 3523. POLAR ICEBREAKER RECAPITALIZATION PLAN.

(a) REQUIREMENT.—*Not later than 120 days after the date of the enactment of this Act, the Secretary, in consultation with the Secretary of the Navy, shall submit to the appropriate committees of Congress a detailed recapitalization plan to address the 2013 Department of Homeland Security Mission Need Statement with respect to icebreaking.*

(b) CONTENTS.—*The plan required under subsection (a) shall—*

(1) *detail the number of heavy and medium polar icebreakers required to meet Coast Guard statutory missions in the polar regions;*

(2) *identify the vessel specifications, capabilities, systems, equipment, and other details required for the design of heavy polar icebreakers capable of fulfilling the mission requirements of the Coast Guard and the Navy, and the requirements of other agencies and departments of the United States, as the Secretary determines appropriate;*

(3) *list the specific appropriations required for the acquisition of each icebreaker, for each fiscal year, until the full fleet is recapitalized;*

(4) *describe the potential savings of serial acquisition for new polar class icebreakers, including specific schedule and acquisition requirements needed to realize such savings;*

(5) *describe any polar icebreaking capacity gaps that may arise based on the current fleet and current procurement outlook; and*

(6) *describe any additional polar icebreaking capability gaps that may arise due to any further delay in procurement schedules.*

(c) DEFINITIONS.—*In this section, the following definitions apply:*

(1) APPROPRIATE COMMITTEES OF CONGRESS.—*The term "appropriate committees of Congress" means the Committee on Commerce, Science, and Transportation of the Senate and the Committee on Transportation and Infrastructure of the House of Representatives.*

(2) SECRETARY.—*Except as otherwise specifically provided, the term "Secretary" means the Secretary of the department in which the Coast Guard is operating.*

SEC. 3524. GAO REPORT ON ICEBREAKING CAPABILITY IN UNITED STATES.

(a) REQUIREMENT.—*Not later than 180 days after the date of the enactment of this Act, the*

Comptroller General of the United States shall submit to the appropriate committees of Congress a report on the current state of the United States Federal icebreaking fleet.

(b) CONTENTS.—The report required under subsection (a) shall include—

(1) an analysis of the icebreaking assets in operation in the United States and a description of the missions completed by such assets;

(2) an analysis of how such assets and the capabilities of such assets are consistent, or inconsistent, with the icebreaking mission requirements described in the 2013 Department of Homeland Security Mission Need Statement, the Naval Operations Concept 2010, and other military and civilian governmental missions in the United States;

(3) an analysis of the gaps in icebreaking capability of the United States based on the expected service life of the fleet of United States icebreaking assets;

(4) a list of countries that are allies of the United States that have the icebreaking capacity to exercise missions during any identified gap in United States icebreaking capacity; and

(5) a description of the policy, financial, and other barriers that have prevented timely recapitalization of the Coast Guard icebreaking fleet and recommendations to overcome such barriers, including potential international fee-based models used to compensate governments for icebreaking escorts or maintenance of maritime routes.

(c) APPROPRIATE COMMITTEES OF CONGRESS.—In this section, the term "appropriate committees of Congress" means the Committee on Commerce, Science, and Transportation of the Senate and the Committee on Transportation and Infrastructure of the House of Representatives.

Subtitle B—Pribilof Islands Transition Completion

SEC. 3531. SHORT TITLE.

This subtitle may be cited as the "Pribilof Islands Transition Completion Amendments Act of 2016".

SEC. 3532. CONVEYANCE OF PROPERTY.

(a) CONVEYANCE.—Subsection (a) of section 522 of the Pribilof Island Transition Completion Act of 2016 (Public Law 114–120, as amended by this Act) is amended to read as follows:

"(a) CONVEYANCE.—In partial settlement of land claims under the Alaska Native Claims Settlement Act (43 U.S.C. 1601 et seq.), and not later than 30 days after the date of enactment of the Pribilof Islands Transition Completion Amendments Act of 2016, the Secretary of Commerce shall, notwithstanding section 105(a) of the Pribilof Islands Transition Act (16 U.S.C. 1161 note; Public Law 106–562), convey to the Alaska Native Village Corporation for St. Paul Island all right, title, and interest of the United States in and to the following property, including improvements on such property:

"(1) Lots 4, 5, and 6A, Block 18, Tract A, U.S. Survey 4943, Alaska, the plat of which was Officially Filed on January 20, 2004, aggregating 13,006 square feet (0.30 acres).

"(2) T. 35 S., R. 131 W., Seward Meridian, Alaska, Tract 39, the plat of which was Officially Filed on May 14, 1986, containing 0.90 acres.".

(b) CONFORMING AMENDMENTS; EASEMENT.—Section 522 of such Act, as amended by subsection (a), is further amended—

(1) by striking subsection (b);

(2) by redesignating subsection (c) as subsection (b); and

(3) by adding at the end the following:

"(c) EASEMENT.—As part of the conveyance under subsection (a), the Secretary of Commerce, in cooperation with the Alaska Native Village Corporation for St. Paul Island, shall provide an easement to the Secretary of Transportation to maintain a non-directional beacon on the property described in subsection (a)(2).".

SEC. 3533. TRANSFER, USE, AND DISPOSAL OF TRACT 43.

(a) IN GENERAL.—Section 524 of the Pribilof Island Transition Completion Act of 2016 (Public Law 114–120, as amended by this Act) is amended to read as follows:

"SEC. 524. TRANSFER, USE, AND DISPOSAL OF TRACT 43.

"(a) TRANSFER.—Not later than 30 days after the date of the enactment of the Pribilof Islands Transition Completion Amendments Act of 2016, the Secretary of Commerce shall—

"(1) terminate the license; and

"(2) transfer tract 43 to the Secretary of the department in which the Coast Guard is operating.

"(b) DETERMINATION, TRANSFER, AND CONVEYANCE.—

"(1) IN GENERAL.—Not later than the end of the 90-day period beginning on the date of the transfer required under subsection (a)(2), the Secretary shall submit to the Committee on Transportation and Infrastructure of the House of Representatives and the Committee on Commerce, Science, and Transportation of the Senate a determination of—

"(A) lands and improvements in tract 43 that are not necessary to carry out Coast Guard communications and search and rescue activities; and

"(B) the smallest practicable tract enclosing lands and improvements in tract 43 that are necessary to carry out such communications and activities.

"(2) SURVEYS, MAPS, DESCRIPTIONS, AND PLAN.—

"(A) LANDS AND IMPROVEMENTS NOT NECESSARY TO COAST GUARD ACTIVITIES.—The determination under paragraph (1)(A) shall include a metes-and-bounds survey, map, and legal description of the lands and improvements to which the determination applies. Such survey, map, and legal description shall have the same force and effect as if included in this section, except that the Secretary may correct clerical and typographical errors in the survey, map, and legal description.

"(B) LANDS AND IMPROVEMENTS NECESSARY TO COAST GUARD ACTIVITIES.—The determination under paragraph (1)(B) shall include with respect to the lands and improvements to which the determination applies—

"(i) a metes-and-bounds survey, map, and legal description of such lands and improvements, which shall have the same force and effect as if included in this section, except that the Secretary may correct clerical and typographical errors in the survey, map, and legal description;

"(ii) a description of Coast Guard actual use and occupancy of such lands and improvements intended to occur within 3 years after the date of the enactment of the Pribilof Islands Transition Completion Amendments Act of 2016; and

"(iii) a plan to maintain existing facilities in useable condition, or demolish or replace those facilities, including a cost estimate for carrying out such plan.

"(3) CONVEYANCE.—In partial settlement of land claims under the Alaska Native Claims Settlement Act (43 U.S.C. 1601 et seq.), and not later than 60 days after the submission of the determination under paragraph (1)(A), the Secretary shall convey to the Alaska Native Village Corporation for St. Paul Island all right, title, and interest of the United States in and to the land and improvements depicted on the metes-and-bounds survey, map, and legal description of the lands and improvements to which the determination under paragraph (1)(A) applies.

"(4) FAILURE TO PROVIDE DETERMINATION.—If a determination under paragraph (1) is not provided within the period specified in that paragraph, in partial settlement of land claims

under the Alaska Native Claims Settlement Act (43 U.S.C. 1601 et seq.) the Secretary shall, by not later than 30 days after the end of that period, convey all right, title, and interest of the United States in and to tract 43 to the Alaska Native Village Corporation for St. Paul Island.

"(5) FAILURE TO IMPLEMENT USE AND OCCUPANCY.—If the use and occupancy described in paragraph (2)(B)(ii) have not been fully implemented within 5 years after the date of enactment of the Pribilof Islands Transition Completion Amendments Act of 2016, in partial settlement of land claims under the Alaska Native Claims Settlement Act (43 U.S.C. 1601 et seq.) the Secretary shall convey to the Alaska Native Village Corporation for St. Paul Island all right, title, and interest of the United States in and to such portions of the lands and improvements to which the determination under paragraph (1)(B) applies and for which such implementation has not occurred.

"(c) FURTHER DETERMINATION AND CONVEYANCE.—

"(1) IN GENERAL.—Not later than 5 years after the date of the enactment of the Pribilof Islands Transition Completion Amendments Act of 2016, and not less than once every 5 years thereafter, the Secretary shall—

"(A) review the determination made under subsection (b)(1)(B); and

"(B) determine if the lands and improvements to which the determination applies are in excess of the smallest practicable tract enclosing the lands and improvements needed to carry out Coast Guard missions.

"(2) REPORT OF DETERMINATION.—When a determination is made under paragraph (1), the Secretary shall report the determination to—

"(A) the Committee on Transportation and Infrastructure of the House of Representatives;

"(B) the Committee on Commerce, Science, and Transportation of the Senate; and

"(C) the Alaska Native Village Corporation for St. Paul Island.

"(3) ELECTION TO RECEIVE.—Not later than 60 days after the date it receives a determination under paragraph (1), the Alaska Native Village Corporation for St. Paul Island shall notify the Secretary in writing whether the Alaska Native Village Corporation elects to receive all right, title, and interest of the United States in and to any lands and improvements or a portion of any lands and improvements determined to be in excess of those needed to carry out Coast Guard missions in partial settlement of land claims under the Alaska Native Claims Settlement Act (43 U.S.C. 1601 et seq.).

"(4) CONVEYANCE.—If such Alaska Native Village Corporation provides notice under paragraph (3) that the Alaska Native Village Corporation elects to receive all right, title, and interest of the United States in and to any lands and improvements or a portion of any lands and improvements, in partial settlement of land claims under the Alaska Native Claims Settlement Act (43 U.S.C. 1601 et seq.) the Secretary shall convey all right, title, and interest of the United States in and to the lands and improvements or portion thereof to such Alaska Native Village Corporation.

"(5) OTHER DISPOSAL.—If such Alaska Native Village Corporation does not provide notice under paragraph (3) that the Alaska Native Village Corporation elects to receive all right, title, and interest of the United States in and to any lands and improvements or a portion of any lands and improvements, the Secretary may dispose of the lands and improvements in accordance with other applicable law.

"(d) CERCLA NOT AFFECTED.—No transfer or conveyance of property under this section shall be construed to affect or limit the application of section 120(h) of the Comprehensive Environmental Response, Compensation, and Liability Act of 1980 (42 U.S.C. 9620(h)).

''(e) REPORTS.—

''(1) REMEDIATION OF CONTAMINATED SOIL.— Not later than 2 years after the date of the enactment of the Pribilof Islands Transition Completion Amendments Act of 2016 and not less than once every 2 years thereafter, the Secretary shall submit to the Committee on Transportation and Infrastructure of the House of Representatives and the Committee on Commerce, Science, and Transportation of the Senate a report on—

''(A) efforts taken to remediate contaminated soils on tract 43 and tract 39; and

''(B) a schedule for the completion of remediation of contaminated soils on tract 43 and tract 39.

''(2) NUMBER OF COAST GUARD PERSONNEL WHO CARRIED OUT COAST GUARD MISSIONS.—On the 15th day of each month, the Commandant of the Coast Guard shall submit to the Committee on Transportation and Infrastructure of the House of Representatives and the Committee on Commerce, Science, and Transportation of the Senate a notice detailing the number of Coast Guard personnel who carried out Coast Guard missions on tract 43 during the previous month and what Coast Guard missions were carried out by such personnel.

''(f) REDUNDANT CAPABILITY.—

''(1) RULE OF CONSTRUCTION.—Except as provided in paragraph (2), section 681 of title 14, United States Code, shall not be construed to prohibit any conveyance of lands or improvements under this subtitle or any actions that involve the dismantling or disposal of infrastructure that supported the former LORAN system that are associated with the conveyance of lands or improvements under this subtitle.

''(2) REDUNDANT CAPABILITY.—If, within the 5-year period beginning on the date of the enactment of the Pribilof Islands Transition Completion Amendments Act of 2016, the Secretary determines that communication equipment, including towers, antennae, and transmitters, on property conveyed in accordance with this subtitle is subsequently required to provide a positioning, navigation, and timing system to provide redundant capability in the event GPS signals are disrupted, the Secretary may—

''(A) operate, maintain, keep, locate, inspect, repair, and replace such equipment; and

''(B) in carrying out the activities described in subparagraph (A), enter, at any time, a facility without notice, to the extent that it is not possible to provide advance notice, for as long as such equipment is needed to provide such capability.

''(g) FEDERAL USE.—In addition to entry under subsection (f)(2)(B), the Secretary may enter property conveyed in accordance with this subtitle for purposes of environmental compliance and remediation after providing advance notice to the property owner to the extent that it is possible to provide such notice.

''(h) HIGH FREQUENCY COMMUNICATIONS.—

''(1) RESTRICTION.—Except as provided in paragraph (2), on property contained within the boundaries of tract 43 as in effect on the date of enactment of the Pribilof Islands Transition Completion Amendments Act of 2016, no person may operate or maintain—

''(A) radio frequency transmitting equipment that produces a signal that exceeds 5 microvolts per meter field intensity, other than such equipment that was in use on the site before the date of the enactment of such Act; or

''(B) electric welding equipment, electric generating equipment, a diathermy machine, electric motors of any kind having greater than 5 horsepower, or any other machinery, engine, or equipment that causes any electromagnetic interference.

''(2) EXCEPTION.—A person may engage in operations or maintenance otherwise prohibited by paragraph (1) with the concurrence of the Secretary.

''(i) DEFINITIONS.—For purposes of this section:

''(1) LICENSE.—The term 'license' means the agreement dated January 9, 2006, entitled 'License Agreement Between The Department of Homeland Security, United States Coast Guard, and The Department of Commerce, National Oceanic and Atmospheric Administration'.

''(2) TRACT 39.—The term 'tract 39' means T. 35 S., R. 131 W., Seward Meridian, Alaska, Tract 39, the plat of which was Officially Filed on May 14, 1986, containing 0.90 acres.

''(3) TRACT 43.—The term 'tract 43' means T. 35 S., R. 131 W., Seward Meridian, Alaska, Tract 43, the plat of which was Officially Filed on May 14, 1986, containing 84.88 acres, and any improvements on such tract.

''(4) SECRETARY.—The term 'Secretary' means the Secretary of the department in which the Coast Guard is operating.''.

(b) CHARGEABILITY FOR LANDS CONVEYED.— The Secretary of the Interior shall charge against the remaining entitlement of the Alaska Native Village Corporation for St. Paul Island under the Alaska Native Claims Settlement Act (43 U.S.C. 1601 et seq.) any conveyance of land to such corporation under this subtitle, including the amendments made by this subtitle.

(c) CLERICAL AMENDMENT.—The table of contents in section 2 of the Coast Guard Authorization Act of 2016 (Public Law 114–120, as amended by this Act) is amended by striking the item relating to section 524 and inserting the following:

''Sec. 524. Transfer, use, and disposal of tract 43.''.

(d) CONFORMING AMENDMENTS.—Section 105 of the Pribilof Islands Transition Act (16 U.S.C. 1161 note; Public Law 106–562) is amended—

(1) in subsection (e)(1), by striking ''or section 522 of the Pribilof Island Transition Completion Act of 2015'' and inserting ''or section 522 of the Pribilof Island Transition Completion Act of 2016, or transferred to the Secretary of the department in which the Coast Guard is operating under section 524 of such Act,''; and

(2) in subsection (f)(1), by striking ''and not transferred'' and inserting ''and not transferred to the Secretary of the department in which the Coast Guard is operating under section 524 of the Pribilof Island Transition Completion Act of 2016 or''.

(e) SAVINGS CLAUSE.—The Memorandum of Understanding among the Tanadgusix Corporation, St. Paul Island, Alaska, the Tanaq Corporation, St. George Island, Alaska, and the National Marine Fisheries Service of the National Oceanic and Atmospheric Administration of the Department of Commerce, dated December 22, 1976, regarding Pribilof Islands Land Selections and the establishment and operation of a Joint Management Board, shall remain in effect with respect to land selections and conveyances until all obligations for conveyances under that agreement have been met, and the obligation to maintain a Joint Management Board remains in effect.

Subtitle C—Sexual Harassment and Assault Prevention at the National Oceanic and Atmospheric Administration

SEC. 3541. ACTIONS TO ADDRESS SEXUAL HARASSMENT AT NATIONAL OCEANIC AND ATMOSPHERIC ADMINISTRATION.

(a) REQUIRED POLICY.—Not later than 1 year after the date of the enactment of this Act, the Secretary of Commerce shall, acting through the Under Secretary for Oceans and Atmosphere, develop a policy on the prevention of and response to sexual harassment involving employees of the National Oceanic and Atmospheric Administration, members of the commissioned officer corps of the Administration, and individuals who work with or conduct business on behalf of the Administration.

(b) MATTERS TO BE SPECIFIED IN POLICY.— The policy developed under subsection (a) shall include—

(1) establishment of a program to promote awareness of the incidence of sexual harassment;

(2) clear procedures an individual should follow in the case of an occurrence of sexual harassment, including—

(A) a specification of the person or persons to whom an alleged occurrence of sexual harassment should be reported by an individual and options for confidential reporting, including—

(i) options and contact information for after-hours contact; and

(ii) a procedure for obtaining assistance and reporting sexual harassment while working in a remote scientific field camp, at sea, or in another field status; and

(B) a specification of any other person whom the victim should contact;

(3) establishment of a mechanism by which—

(A) questions regarding sexual harassment can be confidentially asked and confidentially answered; and

(B) incidents of sexual harassment can be confidentially reported; and

(4) a prohibition on retaliation and consequences for retaliatory actions.

(c) CONSULTATION AND ASSISTANCE.—In developing the policy required by subsection (a), the Secretary may consult or receive assistance from such State, local, and national organizations and subject matter experts as the Secretary considers appropriate.

(d) AVAILABILITY OF POLICY.—The Secretary shall ensure that the policy developed under subsection (a) is available to—

(1) all employees of the Administration and members of the commissioned officer corps of the Administration, including those employees and members who conduct field work for the Administration; and

(2) the public.

(e) GEOGRAPHIC DISTRIBUTION OF EQUAL EMPLOYMENT OPPORTUNITY PERSONNEL.—The Secretary shall designate out of existing staff at least 1 employee of the Administration who is tasked with handling matters relating to equal employment opportunity or sexual harassment at each marine and aviation center of the Administration.

(f) QUARTERLY REPORTS.—

(1) IN GENERAL.—Not less frequently than 4 times each year, the Director of the Civil Rights Office of the Administration shall submit to the Under Secretary a report on sexual harassment in the Administration.

(2) CONTENTS.—Each report submitted under paragraph (1) shall include the following:

(A) The number of sexual harassment cases, both actionable and non-actionable, involving individuals covered by the policy developed under subsection (a).

(B) The number of open actionable sexual harassment cases and how long the cases have been open.

(C) Such trends or region-specific issues as the Director may have discovered with respect to sexual harassment in the Administration.

(D) Such recommendations as the Director may have with respect to sexual harassment in the Administration.

SEC. 3542. ACTIONS TO ADDRESS SEXUAL ASSAULT AT NATIONAL OCEANIC AND ATMOSPHERIC ADMINISTRATION.

(a) COMPREHENSIVE POLICY ON PREVENTION OF AND RESPONSE TO SEXUAL ASSAULTS.—Not later than 1 year after the date of the enactment of this Act, the Secretary of Commerce shall, acting through the Under Secretary for Oceans and Atmosphere, develop a comprehensive policy on the prevention of and response to sexual assaults involving employees of the National Oceanic and Atmospheric Administration, members of the commissioned officer corps of the Administration, and individuals who work with or conduct business on behalf of the Administration.

(b) ELEMENTS OF COMPREHENSIVE POLICY.— The comprehensive policy developed under subsection (a) shall, at minimum, address the following matters:

(1) Prevention measures.

(2) Education and training on prevention and response.

(3) A list of support resources an individual may use in the occurrence of sexual assault, including—

(A) options and contact information for after-hours contact; and

(B) a procedure for obtaining assistance and reporting sexual assault while working in a remote scientific field camp, at sea, or in another field status.

(4) Easy and ready availability of information described in paragraph (3).

(5) Establishing a mechanism by which—

(A) questions regarding sexual assault can be confidentially asked and confidentially answered; and

(B) incidents of sexual assault can be confidentially reported.

(6) Protocols for the investigation of complaints by command and law enforcement personnel.

(7) Prohibiting retaliation and consequences for retaliatory actions against someone who reports a sexual assault.

(8) Oversight by the Under Secretary of administrative and disciplinary actions in response to substantiated incidents of sexual assault.

(9) Victim advocacy, including establishment of and the responsibilities and training requirements for victim advocates as described in subsection (c).

(10) Availability of resources for victims of sexual assault within other Federal agencies and State, local, and national organizations.

(c) VICTIM ADVOCACY.—

(1) IN GENERAL.—The Secretary, acting through the Under Secretary, shall establish victim advocates to advocate for victims of sexual assaults involving employees of the Administration, members of the commissioned officer corps of the Administration, and individuals who work with or conduct business on behalf of the Administration.

(2) VICTIM ADVOCATES.—For purposes of this subsection, a victim advocate is an existing permanent employee of the Administration who—

(A) is trained in matters relating to sexual assault and the comprehensive policy developed under subsection (a); and

(B) serves as a victim advocate voluntarily and in addition to the employee's other duties as an employee of the Administration.

(3) PRIMARY DUTIES.—The primary duties of a victim advocate established under paragraph (1) shall include the following:

(A) Supporting victims of sexual assault and informing them of their rights and the resources available to them as victims.

(B) Acting as a companion in navigating investigative, medical, mental and emotional health, and recovery processes relating to sexual assault.

(C) Helping to identify resources to ensure the safety of victims of sexual assault.

(4) LOCATION.—The Secretary shall ensure that at least 1 victim advocate established under paragraph (1) is stationed—

(A) in each region in which the Administration conducts operations; and

(B) in each marine and aviation center of the Administration.

(5) HOTLINE.—

(A) IN GENERAL.—In carrying out this subsection, the Secretary shall provide a telephone number at which a victim of a sexual assault can contact a victim advocate.

(B) 24-HOUR ACCESS.—The Secretary shall ensure that the telephone number established under subparagraph (A) is monitored at all times.

(C) PARTNERSHIP.—The Secretary shall, where possible, use established hotlines for purposes of this paragraph.

(6) FORMAL RELATIONSHIPS WITH OTHER ENTITIES.—The Secretary may enter into formal relationships with other entities to make available additional victim advocates.

(d) AVAILABILITY OF POLICY.—The Secretary shall ensure that the policy developed under subsection (a) is available to—

(1) all employees of the Administration and members of the commissioned officer corps of the Administration, including those employees and members who conduct field work for the Administration; and

(2) the public.

(e) CONSULTATION AND ASSISTANCE.—In developing the policy required by subsection (a), the Secretary may consult or receive assistance from such State, local, and national organizations and subject matter experts as the Secretary considers appropriate.

SEC. 3543. RIGHTS OF THE VICTIM OF A SEXUAL ASSAULT.

A victim of a sexual assault covered by the comprehensive policy developed under section 3542(a) has the right to be reasonably protected from the accused.

SEC. 3544. CHANGE OF STATION.

(a) CHANGE OF STATION, UNIT TRANSFER, OR CHANGE OF WORK LOCATION OF VICTIMS.—

(1) TIMELY CONSIDERATION AND ACTION UPON REQUEST.—The Secretary of Commerce, acting through the Under Secretary for Oceans and Atmosphere, shall—

(A) in the case of a member of the commissioned officer corps of the National Oceanic and Atmospheric Administration who was a victim of a sexual assault, in order to reduce the possibility of retaliation or further sexual assault, provide for timely determination and action on an application submitted by the victim for consideration of a change of station or unit transfer of the victim; and

(B) in the case of an employee of the Administration who was a victim of a sexual assault, to the degree practicable and in order to reduce the possibility of retaliation against the employee for reporting the sexual assault, accommodate a request for a change of work location of the victim.

(2) PROCEDURES.—

(A) PERIOD FOR APPROVAL AND DISAPPROVAL.—The Secretary, acting through the Under Secretary, shall ensure that an application or request submitted under paragraph (1) for a change of station, unit transfer, or change of work location is approved or denied within 72 hours of the submission of the application or request.

(B) REVIEW.—If an application or request submitted under paragraph (1) by a victim of a sexual assault for a change of station, unit transfer, or change of work location of the victim is denied—

(i) the victim may request the Secretary to review the denial; and

(ii) the Secretary, acting through the Under Secretary, shall, not later than 72 hours after receiving such request, affirm or overturn the denial.

(b) CHANGE OF STATION, UNIT TRANSFER, AND CHANGE OF WORK LOCATION OF ALLEGED PERPETRATORS.—

(1) IN GENERAL.—The Secretary, acting through the Under Secretary, shall develop a policy for the protection of victims of sexual assault described in subsection (a)(1) by providing the alleged perpetrator of the sexual assault with a change of station, unit transfer, or change of work location, as the case may be, if the alleged perpetrator is a member of the commissioned officer corps of the Administration or an employee of the Administration.

(2) POLICY REQUIREMENTS.—The policy required by paragraph (1) shall include the following:

(A) A means to control access to the victim.

(B) Due process for the victim and the alleged perpetrator.

(c) REGULATIONS.—

(1) IN GENERAL.—The Secretary shall promulgate regulations to carry out this section.

(2) CONSISTENCY.—When practicable, the Secretary shall make regulations promulgated under this section consistent with similar regulations promulgated by the Secretary of Defense.

SEC. 3545. APPLICABILITY OF POLICIES TO CREWS OF VESSELS SECURED BY NATIONAL OCEANIC AND ATMOSPHERIC ADMINISTRATION UNDER CONTRACT.

The Under Secretary for Oceans and Atmosphere shall ensure that each contract into which the Under Secretary enters for the use of a vessel by the National Oceanic and Atmospheric Administration that covers the crew of the vessel, if any, shall include as a condition of the contract a provision that subjects such crew to the policy developed under section 3541(a) and the comprehensive policy developed under section 3542(a).

SEC. 3546. ANNUAL REPORT ON SEXUAL ASSAULTS IN THE NATIONAL OCEANIC AND ATMOSPHERIC ADMINISTRATION.

(a) IN GENERAL.—Not later than January 15 of each year, the Secretary of Commerce shall submit to the Committee on Commerce, Science, and Transportation of the Senate and the Committee on Natural Resources of the House of Representatives a report on the sexual assaults involving employees of the National Oceanic and Atmospheric Administration, members of the commissioned officer corps of the Administration, and individuals who work with or conduct business on behalf of the Administration.

(b) CONTENTS.—Each report submitted under subsection (a) shall include, with respect to the previous calendar year, the following:

(1) The number of alleged sexual assaults involving employees, members, and individuals described in subsection (a).

(2) A synopsis of each case and the disciplinary action taken, if any, in each case.

(3) The policies, procedures, and processes implemented by the Secretary, and any updates or revisions to such policies, procedures, and processes.

(4) A summary of the reports received by the Under Secretary for Oceans and Atmosphere under section 3541(f).

(c) PRIVACY PROTECTION.—In preparing and submitting a report under subsection (a), the Secretary shall ensure that no individual involved in an alleged sexual assault can be identified by the contents of the report.

SEC. 3547. SEXUAL ASSAULT DEFINED.

In this subtitle, the term "sexual assault" shall have the meaning given such term in section 40002(a) of the Violence Against Women Act of 1994 (42 U.S.C. 13925(a)).

DIVISION D—FUNDING TABLES

Sec. 4001. Authorization of amounts in funding tables.

TITLE XLI—PROCUREMENT

Sec. 4101. Procurement.

Sec. 4102. Procurement for overseas contingency operations.

Sec. 4103. Procurement for overseas contingency operations for base requirements.

TITLE XLII—RESEARCH, DEVELOPMENT, TEST, AND EVALUATION

Sec. 4201. Research, development, test, and evaluation.
Sec. 4202. Research, development, test, and evaluation for overseas contingency operations.
Sec. 4203. Research, development, test, and evaluation for overseas contingency operations for base requirements.

TITLE XLIII—OPERATION AND MAINTENANCE

Sec. 4301. Operation and maintenance.
Sec. 4302. Operation and maintenance for overseas contingency operations.
Sec. 4303. Operation and maintenance for overseas contingency operations for base requirements.

TITLE XLIV—MILITARY PERSONNEL

Sec. 4401. Military personnel.
Sec. 4402. Military personnel for overseas contingency operations.
Sec. 4403. Military personnel for overseas contingency operations for base requirements.

TITLE XLV—OTHER AUTHORIZATIONS

Sec. 4501. Other authorizations.

Sec. 4502. Other authorizations for overseas contingency operations.
Sec. 4503. Other authorizations for overseas contingency operations for base requirements.

TITLE XLVI—MILITARY CONSTRUCTION

Sec. 4601. Military construction.
Sec. 4602. Military construction for overseas contingency operations.
Sec. 4603. Military construction for overseas contingency operations for base requirements.

TITLE XLVII—DEPARTMENT OF ENERGY NATIONAL SECURITY PROGRAMS

Sec. 4701. Department of Energy national security programs.

SEC. 4001. AUTHORIZATION OF AMOUNTS IN FUNDING TABLES.

(a) IN GENERAL.—Whenever a funding table in this division specifies a dollar amount authorized for a project, program, or activity, the obligation and expenditure of the specified dollar amount for the project, program, or activity is hereby authorized, subject to the availability of appropriations.

(b) MERIT-BASED DECISIONS.—A decision to commit, obligate, or expend funds with or to a specific entity on the basis of a dollar amount authorized pursuant to subsection (a) shall—

(1) be based on merit-based selection procedures in accordance with the requirements of sections 2304(k) and 2374 of title 10, United States Code, or on competitive procedures; and

(2) comply with other applicable provisions of law.

(c) RELATIONSHIP TO TRANSFER AND PROGRAMMING AUTHORITY.—An amount specified in the funding tables in this division may be transferred or reprogrammed under a transfer or reprogramming authority provided by another provision of this Act or by other law. The transfer or reprogramming of an amount specified in such funding tables shall not count against a ceiling on such transfers or reprogrammings under section 1001 or section 1522 of this Act or any other provision of law, unless such transfer or reprogramming would move funds between appropriation accounts.

(d) APPLICABILITY TO CLASSIFIED ANNEX.—This section applies to any classified annex that accompanies this Act.

(e) ORAL AND WRITTEN COMMUNICATIONS.—No oral or written communication concerning any amount specified in the funding tables in this division shall supersede the requirements of this section.

TITLE XLI—PROCUREMENT

SEC. 4101. PROCUREMENT.

SEC. 4101. PROCUREMENT.
(In Thousands of Dollars)

Line	Item	FY 2017 Request	Conference Authorized
	AIRCRAFT PROCUREMENT, ARMY		
	FIXED WING		
001	UTILITY F/W AIRCRAFT	57,529	57,529
003	MQ–1 UAV	55,388	55,388
	ROTARY		
006	AH–64 APACHE BLOCK IIIA REMAN	803,084	803,084
007	ADVANCE PROCUREMENT (CY)	185,160	185,160
008	UH–60 BLACKHAWK M MODEL (MYP)	755,146	755,146
009	ADVANCE PROCUREMENT (CY)	174,107	174,107
010	UH–60 BLACK HAWK A AND L MODELS	46,173	46,173
011	CH–47 HELICOPTER	556,257	556,257
012	ADVANCE PROCUREMENT (CY)	8,707	8,707
	MODIFICATION OF AIRCRAFT		
013	MQ–1 PAYLOAD (MIP)	43,735	43,735
015	MULTI SENSOR ABN RECON (MIP)	94,527	94,527
016	AH–64 MODS	137,883	137,883
017	CH–47 CARGO HELICOPTER MODS (MYP)	102,943	102,943
018	GRCS SEMA MODS (MIP)	4,055	4,055
019	ARL SEMA MODS (MIP)	6,793	6,793
020	EMARSS SEMA MODS (MIP)	13,197	13,197
021	UTILITY/CARGO AIRPLANE MODS	17,526	17,526
022	UTILITY HELICOPTER MODS	10,807	10,807
023	NETWORK AND MISSION PLAN	74,752	74,752
024	COMMS, NAV SURVEILLANCE	69,960	69,960
025	GATM ROLLUP	45,302	45,302
026	RQ–7 UAV MODS	71,169	71,169
027	UAS MODS	21,804	21,804
	GROUND SUPPORT AVIONICS		
028	AIRCRAFT SURVIVABILITY EQUIPMENT	67,377	67,377
029	SURVIVABILITY CM	9,565	9,565
030	CMWS	41,626	41,626
	OTHER SUPPORT		
032	AVIONICS SUPPORT EQUIPMENT	7,007	7,007
033	COMMON GROUND EQUIPMENT	48,234	48,234
034	AIRCREW INTEGRATED SYSTEMS	30,297	30,297
035	AIR TRAFFIC CONTROL	50,405	50,405
036	INDUSTRIAL FACILITIES	1,217	1,217
037	LAUNCHER, 2.75 ROCKET	3,055	3,055
	TOTAL AIRCRAFT PROCUREMENT, ARMY	**3,614,787**	**3,614,787**
	MISSILE PROCUREMENT, ARMY		
	SURFACE-TO-AIR MISSILE SYSTEM		
001	LOWER TIER AIR AND MISSILE DEFENSE (AMD)	126,470	126,470
002	MSE MISSILE	423,201	423,201
003	ADVANCE PROCUREMENT (CY)	19,319	19,319
	AIR-TO-SURFACE MISSILE SYSTEM		
004	HELLFIRE SYS SUMMARY	42,013	42,013
005	JOINT AIR-TO-GROUND MSLS (JAGM)	64,751	64,751

SEC. 4101. PROCUREMENT
(In Thousands of Dollars)

Line	Item	FY 2017 Request	Conference Authorized
006	ADVANCE PROCUREMENT (CY)	37,100	37,100
	ANTI-TANK/ASSAULT MISSILE SYS		
007	JAVELIN (AAWS-M) SYSTEM SUMMARY	73,508	72,904
	Engineering services cost growth		*[-604]*
008	TOW 2 SYSTEM SUMMARY	64,922	64,922
009	ADVANCE PROCUREMENT (CY)	19,949	10,716
	Advance procurement cost growth		*[-9,233]*
010	GUIDED MLRS ROCKET (GMLRS)	172,088	172,088
011	MLRS REDUCED RANGE PRACTICE ROCKETS (RRPR)	18,004	18,004
	MODIFICATIONS		
013	PATRIOT MODS	197,107	197,107
014	ATACMS MODS	150,043	150,043
015	GMLRS MOD	395	395
017	AVENGER MODS	33,606	33,606
018	ITAS/TOW MODS	383	383
019	MLRS MODS	34,704	34,704
020	HIMARS MODIFICATIONS	1,847	1,847
	SPARES AND REPAIR PARTS		
021	SPARES AND REPAIR PARTS	34,487	34,487
	SUPPORT EQUIPMENT & FACILITIES		
022	AIR DEFENSE TARGETS	4,915	4,915
024	PRODUCTION BASE SUPPORT	1,154	1,154
	TOTAL MISSILE PROCUREMENT, ARMY	**1,519,966**	**1,510,129**
	PROCUREMENT OF W&TCV, ARMY		
	TRACKED COMBAT VEHICLES		
001	STRYKER VEHICLE	71,680	71,680
	MODIFICATION OF TRACKED COMBAT VEHICLES		
002	STRYKER (MOD)	74,348	74,348
003	STRYKER UPGRADE	444,561	433,561
	Early to need		*[-11,000]*
005	BRADLEY PROGRAM (MOD)	276,433	273,333
	Excess program management growth		*[-3,100]*
006	HOWITZER, MED SP FT 155MM M109A6 (MOD)	63,138	63,138
007	PALADIN INTEGRATED MANAGEMENT (PIM)	469,305	469,305
008	IMPROVED RECOVERY VEHICLE (M88A2 HERCULES)	91,963	91,963
009	ASSAULT BRIDGE (MOD)	3,465	3,465
010	ASSAULT BREACHER VEHICLE	2,928	2,928
011	M88 FOV MODS	8,685	8,685
012	JOINT ASSAULT BRIDGE	64,752	64,752
013	M1 ABRAMS TANK (MOD)	480,166	480,166
014	ABRAMS UPGRADE PROGRAM		100,000
	Realign APS Unit Set Requirements from OCO		*[100,000]*
	WEAPONS & OTHER COMBAT VEHICLES		
016	INTEGRATED AIR BURST WEAPON SYSTEM FAMILY	9,764	9,764
017	MORTAR SYSTEMS	8,332	8,332
018	XM320 GRENADE LAUNCHER MODULE (GLM)	3,062	3,062
019	COMPACT SEMI-AUTOMATIC SNIPER SYSTEM	992	992
020	CARBINE	40,493	40,493
021	COMMON REMOTELY OPERATED WEAPONS STATION	25,164	25,164
	MOD OF WEAPONS AND OTHER COMBAT VEH		
022	MK-19 GRENADE MACHINE GUN MODS	4,959	4,959
023	M777 MODS	11,913	11,913
024	M4 CARBINE MODS	29,752	29,752
025	M2 50 CAL MACHINE GUN MODS	48,582	48,582
026	M249 SAW MACHINE GUN MODS	1,179	1,179
027	M240 MEDIUM MACHINE GUN MODS	1,784	1,784
028	SNIPER RIFLES MODIFICATIONS	971	971
029	M119 MODIFICATIONS	6,045	6,045
030	MORTAR MODIFICATION	12,118	12,118
031	MODIFICATIONS LESS THAN $5.0M (WOCV-WTCV)	3,157	3,157
	SUPPORT EQUIPMENT & FACILITIES		
032	ITEMS LESS THAN $5.0M (WOCV-WTCV)	2,331	2,331
035	SMALL ARMS EQUIPMENT (SOLDIER ENH PROG)	3,155	3,155
	TOTAL PROCUREMENT OF W&TCV, ARMY	**2,265,177**	**2,351,077**
	PROCUREMENT OF AMMUNITION, ARMY		
	SMALL/MEDIUM CAL AMMUNITION		
001	CTG, 5.56MM, ALL TYPES	40,296	40,296
002	CTG, 7.62MM, ALL TYPES	39,237	39,237
003	CTG, HANDGUN, ALL TYPES	5,193	5,193
004	CTG, .50 CAL, ALL TYPES	46,693	46,693
005	CTG, 20MM, ALL TYPES	7,000	7,000
006	CTG, 25MM, ALL TYPES	7,753	6,453
	Program reduction		*[-1,300]*
007	CTG, 30MM, ALL TYPES	47,000	47,000
008	CTG, 40MM, ALL TYPES	118,178	111,824
	Early to need		*[-6,354]*
	MORTAR AMMUNITION		

SEC. 4101. PROCUREMENT
(In Thousands of Dollars)

Line	Item	FY 2017 Request	Conference Authorized
009	60MM MORTAR, ALL TYPES	69,784	69,784
010	81MM MORTAR, ALL TYPES	36,125	36,125
011	120MM MORTAR, ALL TYPES	69,133	69,133
	TANK AMMUNITION		
012	CARTRIDGES, TANK, 105MM AND 120MM, ALL TYPES	120,668	117,868
	Early to need		[−2,800]
	ARTILLERY AMMUNITION		
013	ARTILLERY CARTRIDGES, 75MM & 105MM, ALL TYPES	64,800	61,300
	75mm blanks early to need		[−3,500]
014	ARTILLERY PROJECTILE, 155MM, ALL TYPES	109,515	109,515
015	PROJ 155MM EXTENDED RANGE M982	39,200	39,200
016	ARTILLERY PROPELLANTS, FUZES AND PRIMERS, ALL	70,881	70,881
	ROCKETS		
019	SHOULDER LAUNCHED MUNITIONS, ALL TYPES	38,000	38,000
020	ROCKET, HYDRA 70, ALL TYPES	87,213	87,213
	OTHER AMMUNITION		
021	CAD/PAD, ALL TYPES	4,914	4,914
022	DEMOLITION MUNITIONS, ALL TYPES	6,380	6,380
023	GRENADES, ALL TYPES	22,760	22,760
024	SIGNALS, ALL TYPES	10,666	10,666
025	SIMULATORS, ALL TYPES	7,412	7,412
	MISCELLANEOUS		
026	AMMO COMPONENTS, ALL TYPES	12,726	12,726
027	NON-LETHAL AMMUNITION, ALL TYPES	6,100	5,900
	Early to need		[−200]
028	ITEMS LESS THAN $5 MILLION (AMMO)	10,006	9,506
	Early to need		[−500]
029	AMMUNITION PECULIAR EQUIPMENT	17,275	13,575
	Early to need		[−3,700]
030	FIRST DESTINATION TRANSPORTATION (AMMO)	14,951	14,951
	PRODUCTION BASE SUPPORT		
032	INDUSTRIAL FACILITIES	222,269	242,269
	Program increase		[20,000]
033	CONVENTIONAL MUNITIONS DEMILITARIZATION	157,383	157,383
034	ARMS INITIATIVE	3,646	3,646
	TOTAL PROCUREMENT OF AMMUNITION, ARMY	**1,513,157**	**1,514,803**
	OTHER PROCUREMENT, ARMY		
	TACTICAL VEHICLES		
001	TACTICAL TRAILERS/DOLLY SETS	3,733	3,733
002	SEMITRAILERS, FLATBED:	3,716	3,716
003	HI MOB MULTI-PURP WHLD VEH (HMMWV)		50,000
	HMMWV M997A3 ambulance recapitalization for Active Component		[50,000]
004	GROUND MOBILITY VEHICLES (GMV)	4,907	4,907
006	JOINT LIGHT TACTICAL VEHICLE	587,514	587,514
007	TRUCK, DUMP, 20T (CCE)	3,927	3,927
008	FAMILY OF MEDIUM TACTICAL VEH (FMTV)	53,293	53,293
009	FIRETRUCKS & ASSOCIATED FIREFIGHTING EQUIP	7,460	7,460
010	FAMILY OF HEAVY TACTICAL VEHICLES (FHTV)	39,564	39,564
011	PLS ESP	11,856	11,856
013	TACTICAL WHEELED VEHICLE PROTECTION KITS	49,751	49,751
014	MODIFICATION OF IN SVC EQUIP	64,000	54,000
	Program reduction		[−10,000]
015	MINE-RESISTANT AMBUSH-PROTECTED (MRAP) MODS	10,611	10,611
	NON-TACTICAL VEHICLES		
016	HEAVY ARMORED SEDAN	394	394
018	NONTACTICAL VEHICLES, OTHER	1,755	1,755
	COMM—JOINT COMMUNICATIONS		
019	WIN-T—GROUND FORCES TACTICAL NETWORK	427,598	427,598
020	SIGNAL MODERNIZATION PROGRAM	58,250	58,250
021	JOINT INCIDENT SITE COMMUNICATIONS CAPABILITY	5,749	5,749
022	JCSE EQUIPMENT (USREDCOM)	5,068	5,068
	COMM—SATELLITE COMMUNICATIONS		
023	DEFENSE ENTERPRISE WIDEBAND SATCOM SYSTEMS	143,805	143,805
024	TRANSPORTABLE TACTICAL COMMAND COMMUNICATIONS	36,580	36,580
025	SHF TERM	1,985	1,985
027	SMART-T (SPACE)	9,165	9,165
	COMM—C3 SYSTEM		
031	ARMY GLOBAL CMD & CONTROL SYS (AGCCS)	2,530	2,530
	COMM—COMBAT COMMUNICATIONS		
033	HANDHELD MANPACK SMALL FORM FIT (HMS)	273,645	273,645
034	MID-TIER NETWORKING VEHICULAR RADIO (MNVR)	25,017	25,017
035	RADIO TERMINAL SET, MIDS LVT(2)	12,326	12,326
037	TRACTOR DESK	2,034	2,034
038	TRACTOR RIDE	2,334	2,334
039	SPIDER APLA REMOTE CONTROL UNIT	1,985	1,985
040	SPIDER FAMILY OF NETWORKED MUNITIONS INCR	10,796	10,796
042	TACTICAL COMMUNICATIONS AND PROTECTIVE SYSTEM	3,607	3,607
043	UNIFIED COMMAND SUITE	14,295	14,295

SEC. 4101. PROCUREMENT
(In Thousands of Dollars)

Line	Item	FY 2017 Request	Conference Authorized
045	FAMILY OF MED COMM FOR COMBAT CASUALTY CARE	19,893	19,893
	COMM—INTELLIGENCE COMM		
047	CI AUTOMATION ARCHITECTURE	1,388	1,388
048	ARMY CA/MISO GPF EQUIPMENT	5,494	5,494
	INFORMATION SECURITY		
049	FAMILY OF BIOMETRICS	2,978	2,978
051	COMMUNICATIONS SECURITY (COMSEC)	131,356	131,356
052	DEFENSIVE CYBER OPERATIONS	15,132	15,132
	COMM—LONG HAUL COMMUNICATIONS		
053	BASE SUPPORT COMMUNICATIONS	27,452	27,452
	COMM—BASE COMMUNICATIONS		
054	INFORMATION SYSTEMS	122,055	122,055
055	EMERGENCY MANAGEMENT MODERNIZATION PROGRAM	4,286	4,286
056	INSTALLATION INFO INFRASTRUCTURE MOD PROGRAM	131,794	131,794
	ELECT EQUIP—TACT INT REL ACT (TIARA)		
059	JTT/CIBS-M	5,337	5,337
062	DCGS-A (MIP)	242,514	217,814
	Program reduction		[–24,700]
063	JOINT TACTICAL GROUND STATION (JTAGS)	4,417	4,417
064	TROJAN (MIP)	17,455	17,455
065	MOD OF IN-SVC EQUIP (INTEL SPT) (MIP)	44,965	44,965
066	CI HUMINT AUTO REPRTING AND COLL(CHARCS)	7,658	7,658
067	CLOSE ACCESS TARGET RECONNAISSANCE (CATR)	7,970	7,970
068	MACHINE FOREIGN LANGUAGE TRANSLATION SYSTEM-M	545	545
	ELECT EQUIP—ELECTRONIC WARFARE (EW)		
070	LIGHTWEIGHT COUNTER MORTAR RADAR	74,038	68,453
	Unit cost growth		[–5,585]
071	EW PLANNING & MANAGEMENT TOOLS (EWPMT)	3,235	3,235
072	AIR VIGILANCE (AV)	733	733
074	FAMILY OF PERSISTENT SURVEILLANCE CAPABILITIE	1,740	1,740
075	COUNTERINTELLIGENCE/SECURITY COUNTERMEASURES	455	455
076	CI MODERNIZATION	176	176
	ELECT EQUIP—TACTICAL SURV. (TAC SURV)		
077	SENTINEL MODS	40,171	40,171
078	NIGHT VISION DEVICES	163,029	163,029
079	SMALL TACTICAL OPTICAL RIFLE MOUNTED MLRF	15,885	15,885
080	INDIRECT FIRE PROTECTION FAMILY OF SYSTEMS	48,427	48,427
081	FAMILY OF WEAPON SIGHTS (FWS)	55,536	55,536
082	ARTILLERY ACCURACY EQUIP	4,187	4,187
085	JOINT BATTLE COMMAND—PLATFORM (JBC-P)	137,501	137,501
086	JOINT EFFECTS TARGETING SYSTEM (JETS)	50,726	50,726
087	MOD OF IN-SVC EQUIP (LLDR)	28,058	28,058
088	COMPUTER BALLISTICS: LHMBC XM32	5,924	5,924
089	MORTAR FIRE CONTROL SYSTEM	22,331	22,331
090	COUNTERFIRE RADARS	314,509	281,509
	Unit cost savings		[–33,000]
	ELECT EQUIP—TACTICAL C2 SYSTEMS		
091	FIRE SUPPORT C2 FAMILY	8,660	8,660
092	AIR & MSL DEFENSE PLANNING & CONTROL SYS	54,376	54,376
093	IAMD BATTLE COMMAND SYSTEM	204,969	204,969
094	LIFE CYCLE SOFTWARE SUPPORT (LCSS)	4,718	4,718
095	NETWORK MANAGEMENT INITIALIZATION AND SERVICE	11,063	11,063
096	MANEUVER CONTROL SYSTEM (MCS)	151,318	151,318
097	GLOBAL COMBAT SUPPORT SYSTEM-ARMY (GCSS-A)	155,660	155,660
098	INTEGRATED PERSONNEL AND PAY SYSTEM-ARMY (IPP	4,214	4,214
099	RECONNAISSANCE AND SURVEYING INSTRUMENT SET	16,185	16,185
100	MOD OF IN-SVC EQUIPMENT (ENFIRE)	1,565	1,565
	ELECT EQUIP—AUTOMATION		
101	ARMY TRAINING MODERNIZATION	17,693	17,693
102	AUTOMATED DATA PROCESSING EQUIP	107,960	107,960
103	GENERAL FUND ENTERPRISE BUSINESS SYSTEMS FAM	6,416	6,416
104	HIGH PERF COMPUTING MOD PGM (HPCMP)	58,614	58,614
105	CONTRACT WRITING SYSTEM	986	986
106	RESERVE COMPONENT AUTOMATION SYS (RCAS)	23,828	23,828
	ELECT EQUIP—AUDIO VISUAL SYS (A/V)		
107	TACTICAL DIGITAL MEDIA	1,191	1,191
108	ITEMS LESS THAN $5M (SURVEYING EQUIPMENT)	1,995	1,995
	ELECT EQUIP—SUPPORT		
109	PRODUCTION BASE SUPPORT (C-E)	403	403
	CLASSIFIED PROGRAMS		
110A	CLASSIFIED PROGRAMS	4,436	4,436
	CHEMICAL DEFENSIVE EQUIPMENT		
111	PROTECTIVE SYSTEMS	2,966	2,966
112	FAMILY OF NON-LETHAL EQUIPMENT (FNLE)	9,795	9,795
114	CBRN DEFENSE	17,922	17,922
	BRIDGING EQUIPMENT		
115	TACTICAL BRIDGING	13,553	13,553
116	TACTICAL BRIDGE, FLOAT-RIBBON	25,244	25,244
117	BRIDGE SUPPLEMENTAL SET	983	983

SEC. 4101. PROCUREMENT
(In Thousands of Dollars)

Line	Item	FY 2017 Request	Conference Authorized
118	COMMON BRIDGE TRANSPORTER (CBT) RECAP	25,176	25,176
	ENGINEER (NON-CONSTRUCTION) EQUIPMENT		
119	GRND STANDOFF MINE DETECTN SYSM (GSTAMIDS)	39,350	39,350
120	AREA MINE DETECTION SYSTEM (AMDS)	10,500	10,500
121	HUSKY MOUNTED DETECTION SYSTEM (HMDS)	274	274
122	ROBOTIC COMBAT SUPPORT SYSTEM (RCSS)	2,951	2,951
123	EOD ROBOTICS SYSTEMS RECAPITALIZATION	1,949	1,949
124	ROBOTICS AND APPLIQUE SYSTEMS	5,203	5,203
125	EXPLOSIVE ORDNANCE DISPOSAL EQPMT (EOD EQPMT)	5,570	5,570
126	REMOTE DEMOLITION SYSTEMS	6,238	6,238
127	< $5M, COUNTERMINE EQUIPMENT	836	836
128	FAMILY OF BOATS AND MOTORS	3,171	3,171
	COMBAT SERVICE SUPPORT EQUIPMENT		
129	HEATERS AND ECU'S	18,707	18,707
130	SOLDIER ENHANCEMENT	2,112	2,112
131	PERSONNEL RECOVERY SUPPORT SYSTEM (PRSS)	10,856	10,856
132	GROUND SOLDIER SYSTEM	32,419	32,419
133	MOBILE SOLDIER POWER	30,014	30,014
135	FIELD FEEDING EQUIPMENT	12,544	12,544
136	CARGO AERIAL DEL & PERSONNEL PARACHUTE SYSTEM	18,509	18,509
137	FAMILY OF ENGR COMBAT AND CONSTRUCTION SETS	29,384	29,384
	PETROLEUM EQUIPMENT		
139	QUALITY SURVEILLANCE EQUIPMENT	4,487	4,487
140	DISTRIBUTION SYSTEMS, PETROLEUM & WATER	42,656	35,656
	Program decrease		[–7,000]
	MEDICAL EQUIPMENT		
141	COMBAT SUPPORT MEDICAL	59,761	59,761
	MAINTENANCE EQUIPMENT		
142	MOBILE MAINTENANCE EQUIPMENT SYSTEMS	35,694	32,194
	Program reduction		[–3,500]
143	ITEMS LESS THAN $5.0M (MAINT EQ)	2,716	2,716
	CONSTRUCTION EQUIPMENT		
144	GRADER, ROAD MTZD, HVY, 6X4 (CCE)	1,742	1,742
145	SCRAPERS, EARTHMOVING	26,233	26,233
147	HYDRAULIC EXCAVATOR	1,123	1,123
149	ALL TERRAIN CRANES	65,285	65,285
151	HIGH MOBILITY ENGINEER EXCAVATOR (HMEE)	1,743	1,743
152	ENHANCED RAPID AIRFIELD CONSTRUCTION CAPAP	2,779	2,779
154	CONST EQUIP ESP	26,712	22,212
	Program reduction		[–4,500]
155	ITEMS LESS THAN $5.0M (CONST EQUIP)	6,649	6,649
	RAIL FLOAT CONTAINERIZATION EQUIPMENT		
156	ARMY WATERCRAFT ESP	21,860	21,860
157	ITEMS LESS THAN $5.0M (FLOAT/RAIL)	1,967	1,967
	GENERATORS		
158	GENERATORS AND ASSOCIATED EQUIP	113,266	113,266
159	TACTICAL ELECTRIC POWER RECAPITALIZATION	7,867	7,867
	MATERIAL HANDLING EQUIPMENT		
160	FAMILY OF FORKLIFTS	2,307	2,307
	TRAINING EQUIPMENT		
161	COMBAT TRAINING CENTERS SUPPORT	75,359	75,359
162	TRAINING DEVICES, NONSYSTEM	253,050	253,050
163	CLOSE COMBAT TACTICAL TRAINER	48,271	48,271
164	AVIATION COMBINED ARMS TACTICAL TRAINER	40,000	40,000
165	GAMING TECHNOLOGY IN SUPPORT OF ARMY TRAINING	11,543	11,543
	TEST MEASURE AND DIG EQUIPMENT (TMD)		
166	CALIBRATION SETS EQUIPMENT	4,963	4,963
167	INTEGRATED FAMILY OF TEST EQUIPMENT (IFTE)	29,781	29,781
168	TEST EQUIPMENT MODERNIZATION (TEMOD)	6,342	6,342
	OTHER SUPPORT EQUIPMENT		
169	M25 STABILIZED BINOCULAR	3,149	3,149
170	RAPID EQUIPPING SOLDIER SUPPORT EQUIPMENT	18,003	18,003
171	PHYSICAL SECURITY SYSTEMS (OPA3)	44,082	44,082
172	BASE LEVEL COMMON EQUIPMENT	2,168	2,168
173	MODIFICATION OF IN-SVC EQUIPMENT (OPA–3)	67,367	67,367
174	PRODUCTION BASE SUPPORT (OTH)	1,528	1,528
175	SPECIAL EQUIPMENT FOR USER TESTING	8,289	8,289
177	TRACTOR YARD	6,888	6,888
	OPA2		
179	INITIAL SPARES—C&E	27,243	27,243
	TOTAL OTHER PROCUREMENT, ARMY	**5,873,949**	**5,835,664**
	AIRCRAFT PROCUREMENT, NAVY		
	COMBAT AIRCRAFT		
003	JOINT STRIKE FIGHTER CV	890,650	890,650
004	ADVANCE PROCUREMENT (CY)	80,908	80,908
005	JSF STOVL	2,037,768	2,037,768
006	ADVANCE PROCUREMENT (CY)	233,648	233,648
007	CH–53K (HEAVY LIFT)	348,615	348,615

SEC. 4101. PROCUREMENT
(In Thousands of Dollars)

Line	Item	FY 2017 Request	Conference Authorized
008	ADVANCE PROCUREMENT (CY)	88,365	88,365
009	V–22 (MEDIUM LIFT)	1,264,134	1,249,134
	Support cost growth		[–15,000]
010	ADVANCE PROCUREMENT (CY)	19,674	19,674
011	H–1 UPGRADES (UH–1Y/AH–1Z)	759,778	756,586
	Airframe unit cost growth		[–3,192]
012	ADVANCE PROCUREMENT (CY)	57,232	57,232
014	MH–60R (MYP)	61,177	53,177
	Line shutdown costs—early to need		[–8,000]
016	P–8A POSEIDON	1,940,238	1,863,238
	Airframe unit cost growth		[–77,000]
017	ADVANCE PROCUREMENT (CY)	123,140	123,140
018	E–2D ADV HAWKEYE	916,483	916,483
019	ADVANCE PROCUREMENT (CY)	125,042	125,042
	TRAINER AIRCRAFT		
020	JPATS	5,849	5,849
	OTHER AIRCRAFT		
021	KC–130J	128,870	128,870
022	ADVANCE PROCUREMENT (CY)	24,848	24,848
023	MQ–4 TRITON	409,005	396,125
	Unit cost savings		[–12,880]
024	ADVANCE PROCUREMENT (CY)	55,652	55,652
025	MQ–8 UAV	72,435	72,435
	MODIFICATION OF AIRCRAFT		
029	AEA SYSTEMS	51,900	51,900
030	AV–8 SERIES	60,818	60,818
031	ADVERSARY	5,191	5,191
032	F–18 SERIES	1,023,492	986,192
	Unobligated balances		[–37,300]
034	H–53 SERIES	46,095	46,095
035	SH–60 SERIES	108,328	108,328
036	H–1 SERIES	46,333	46,333
037	EP–3 SERIES	14,681	14,681
038	P–3 SERIES	2,781	2,781
039	E–2 SERIES	32,949	32,949
040	TRAINER A/C SERIES	13,199	13,199
041	C–2A	19,066	19,066
042	C–130 SERIES	61,788	59,788
	Training equipment unjustified growth (OSIP 022–07)		[–2,000]
043	FEWSG	618	618
044	CARGO/TRANSPORT A/C SERIES	9,822	9,822
045	E–6 SERIES	222,077	222,077
046	EXECUTIVE HELICOPTERS SERIES	66,835	66,835
047	SPECIAL PROJECT AIRCRAFT	16,497	16,497
048	T–45 SERIES	114,887	114,887
049	POWER PLANT CHANGES	16,893	14,893
	Excess support growth		[–2,000]
050	JPATS SERIES	17,401	17,401
051	COMMON ECM EQUIPMENT	143,773	143,773
052	COMMON AVIONICS CHANGES	164,839	164,839
053	COMMON DEFENSIVE WEAPON SYSTEM	4,403	4,403
054	ID SYSTEMS	45,768	45,768
055	P–8 SERIES	18,836	18,836
056	MAGTF EW FOR AVIATION	5,676	5,676
057	MQ–8 SERIES	19,003	19,003
058	RQ–7 SERIES	3,534	3,534
059	V–22 (TILT/ROTOR ACFT) OSPREY	141,545	141,545
060	F–35 STOVL SERIES	34,928	34,928
061	F–35 CV SERIES	26,004	26,004
062	QRC	5,476	5,476
	AIRCRAFT SPARES AND REPAIR PARTS		
063	SPARES AND REPAIR PARTS	1,407,626	1,407,626
	AIRCRAFT SUPPORT EQUIP & FACILITIES		
064	COMMON GROUND EQUIPMENT	390,103	390,103
065	AIRCRAFT INDUSTRIAL FACILITIES	23,194	23,194
066	WAR CONSUMABLES	40,613	40,613
067	OTHER PRODUCTION CHARGES	860	860
068	SPECIAL SUPPORT EQUIPMENT	36,282	36,282
069	FIRST DESTINATION TRANSPORTATION	1,523	1,523
	TOTAL AIRCRAFT PROCUREMENT, NAVY	**14,109,148**	**13,951,776**
	WEAPONS PROCUREMENT, NAVY		
	MODIFICATION OF MISSILES		
001	TRIDENT II MODS	1,103,086	1,103,086
	SUPPORT EQUIPMENT & FACILITIES		
002	MISSILE INDUSTRIAL FACILITIES	6,776	6,776
	STRATEGIC MISSILES		
003	TOMAHAWK	186,905	179,905
	Tomahawk unit cost growth		[–7,000]

SEC. 4101. PROCUREMENT
(In Thousands of Dollars)

Line	Item	FY 2017 Request	Conference Authorized
	TACTICAL MISSILES		
004	AMRAAM	204,697	197,447
	Unit cost growth		[−7,250]
005	SIDEWINDER	70,912	70,912
006	JSOW	2,232	2,232
007	STANDARD MISSILE	501,212	497,968
	Diminishing manufacturing sources excess growth		[−3,244]
008	RAM	71,557	71,557
009	JOINT AIR GROUND MISSILE (JAGM)	26,200	21,922
	Unit cost savings		[−4,278]
012	STAND OFF PRECISION GUIDED MUNITIONS (SOPGM)	3,316	3,316
013	AERIAL TARGETS	137,484	137,484
014	OTHER MISSILE SUPPORT	3,248	3,248
015	LRASM	29,643	29,643
	MODIFICATION OF MISSILES		
016	ESSM	52,935	52,935
018	HARM MODS	178,213	178,213
019	STANDARD MISSILES MODS	8,164	8,164
	SUPPORT EQUIPMENT & FACILITIES		
020	WEAPONS INDUSTRIAL FACILITIES	1,964	1,964
021	FLEET SATELLITE COMM FOLLOW-ON	36,723	36,723
	ORDNANCE SUPPORT EQUIPMENT		
022	ORDNANCE SUPPORT EQUIPMENT	59,096	59,096
	TORPEDOES AND RELATED EQUIP		
023	SSTD	5,910	5,910
024	MK–48 TORPEDO	44,537	44,537
025	ASW TARGETS	9,302	9,302
	MOD OF TORPEDOES AND RELATED EQUIP		
026	MK–54 TORPEDO MODS	98,092	98,092
027	MK–48 TORPEDO ADCAP MODS	46,139	46,139
028	QUICKSTRIKE MINE	1,236	1,236
	SUPPORT EQUIPMENT		
029	TORPEDO SUPPORT EQUIPMENT	60,061	60,061
030	ASW RANGE SUPPORT	3,706	3,706
	DESTINATION TRANSPORTATION		
031	FIRST DESTINATION TRANSPORTATION	3,804	3,804
	GUNS AND GUN MOUNTS		
032	SMALL ARMS AND WEAPONS	18,002	18,002
	MODIFICATION OF GUNS AND GUN MOUNTS		
033	CIWS MODS	50,900	50,900
034	COAST GUARD WEAPONS	25,295	25,295
035	GUN MOUNT MODS	77,003	77,003
036	LCS MODULE WEAPONS	2,776	2,776
038	AIRBORNE MINE NEUTRALIZATION SYSTEMS	15,753	15,753
	SPARES AND REPAIR PARTS		
040	SPARES AND REPAIR PARTS	62,383	62,383
	TOTAL WEAPONS PROCUREMENT, NAVY	**3,209,262**	**3,187,490**
	PROCUREMENT OF AMMO, NAVY & MC		
	NAVY AMMUNITION		
001	GENERAL PURPOSE BOMBS	91,659	91,659
002	AIRBORNE ROCKETS, ALL TYPES	65,759	65,759
003	MACHINE GUN AMMUNITION	8,152	8,152
004	PRACTICE BOMBS	41,873	41,873
005	CARTRIDGES & CART ACTUATED DEVICES	54,002	54,002
006	AIR EXPENDABLE COUNTERMEASURES	57,034	57,034
007	JATOS	2,735	2,735
009	5 INCH/54 GUN AMMUNITION	19,220	19,220
010	INTERMEDIATE CALIBER GUN AMMUNITION	30,196	30,196
011	OTHER SHIP GUN AMMUNITION	39,009	39,009
012	SMALL ARMS & LANDING PARTY AMMO	46,727	46,727
013	PYROTECHNIC AND DEMOLITION	9,806	9,806
014	AMMUNITION LESS THAN $5 MILLION	2,900	2,900
	MARINE CORPS AMMUNITION		
015	SMALL ARMS AMMUNITION	27,958	27,958
017	40 MM, ALL TYPES	14,758	14,758
018	60MM, ALL TYPES	992	992
020	120MM, ALL TYPES	16,757	12,157
	120mm early to need		[−4,600]
021	GRENADES, ALL TYPES	972	972
022	ROCKETS, ALL TYPES	14,186	14,186
023	ARTILLERY, ALL TYPES	68,656	68,656
024	DEMOLITION MUNITIONS, ALL TYPES	1,700	1,700
025	FUZE, ALL TYPES	26,088	26,088
027	AMMO MODERNIZATION	14,660	14,660
028	ITEMS LESS THAN $5 MILLION	8,569	6,069
	Early to need		[−2,500]
	TOTAL PROCUREMENT OF AMMO, NAVY & MC	**664,368**	**657,268**

SEC. 4101. PROCUREMENT
(In Thousands of Dollars)

Line	Item	FY 2017 Request	Conference Authorized
	SHIPBUILDING AND CONVERSION, NAVY		
	FLEET BALLISTIC MISSILE SHIPS		
001	OHIO REPLACEMENT SUBMARINE ADVANCE PROCUREMENT	773,138	773,138
	OTHER WARSHIPS		
002	CARRIER REPLACEMENT PROGRAM	1,291,783	1,291,783
003	ADVANCE PROCUREMENT (CY)	1,370,784	1,370,784
004	VIRGINIA CLASS SUBMARINE	3,187,985	3,187,985
005	ADVANCE PROCUREMENT (CY)	1,767,234	1,852,234
	Long-lead Time Materiel Orders for Virginia Class		[85,000]
006	CVN REFUELING OVERHAULS	1,743,220	1,743,220
007	ADVANCE PROCUREMENT (CY)	248,599	248,599
008	DDG 1000	271,756	271,756
009	DDG–51	3,211,292	3,261,092
	Fund additional FY16 destroyer		[49,800]
011	LITTORAL COMBAT SHIP	1,125,625	1,097,625
	Unjustified growth		[–28,000]
	AMPHIBIOUS SHIPS		
012 A	AMPHIBIOUS SHIP REPLACEMENT LX(R)		440,000
	Procurement of LPD–29 or LX (R)		[440,000]
016	LHA REPLACEMENT	1,623,024	1,623,024
	AUXILIARIES, CRAFT AND PRIOR YR PROGRAM COST		
020	ADVANCE PROCUREMENT (CY)	73,079	73,079
022	MOORED TRAINING SHIP	624,527	624,527
025	OUTFITTING	666,158	645,054
	Outfitting and post delivery funds early to need		[–21,104]
026	SHIP TO SHORE CONNECTOR	128,067	128,067
027	SERVICE CRAFT	65,192	65,192
028	LCAC SLEP	1,774	1,774
029	YP CRAFT MAINTENANCE/ROH/SLEP	21,363	21,363
030	COMPLETION OF PY SHIPBUILDING PROGRAMS	160,274	160,274
	TOTAL SHIPBUILDING AND CONVERSION, NAVY	**18,354,874**	**18,880,570**
	OTHER PROCUREMENT, NAVY		
	SHIP PROPULSION EQUIPMENT		
003	SURFACE POWER EQUIPMENT	15,514	15,514
004	HYBRID ELECTRIC DRIVE (HED)	40,132	39,282
	Installation early to need		[–850]
	GENERATORS		
005	SURFACE COMBATANT HM&E	29,974	29,974
	NAVIGATION EQUIPMENT		
006	OTHER NAVIGATION EQUIPMENT	63,942	63,942
	OTHER SHIPBOARD EQUIPMENT		
008	SUB PERISCOPE, IMAGING AND SUPT EQUIP PROG	136,421	136,421
009	DDG MOD	367,766	367,766
010	FIREFIGHTING EQUIPMENT	14,743	14,743
011	COMMAND AND CONTROL SWITCHBOARD	2,140	2,140
012	LHA/LHD MIDLIFE	24,939	24,939
014	POLLUTION CONTROL EQUIPMENT	20,191	19,342
	HF062 lightering systems unit cost growth		[–849]
015	SUBMARINE SUPPORT EQUIPMENT	8,995	8,995
016	VIRGINIA CLASS SUPPORT EQUIPMENT	66,838	66,838
017	LCS CLASS SUPPORT EQUIPMENT	54,823	54,823
018	SUBMARINE BATTERIES	23,359	23,359
019	LPD CLASS SUPPORT EQUIPMENT	40,321	40,321
020	DDG 1000 CLASS SUPPORT EQUIPMENT	33,404	33,404
021	STRATEGIC PLATFORM SUPPORT EQUIP	15,836	15,836
022	DSSP EQUIPMENT	806	806
024	LCAC	3,090	3,090
025	UNDERWATER EOD PROGRAMS	24,350	24,350
026	ITEMS LESS THAN $5 MILLION	88,719	86,899
	LSD boat davit kit cost growth		[–993]
	Propellers and shafts unit cost growth		[–827]
027	CHEMICAL WARFARE DETECTORS	2,873	2,873
028	SUBMARINE LIFE SUPPORT SYSTEM	6,043	6,043
	REACTOR PLANT EQUIPMENT		
030	REACTOR COMPONENTS	342,158	342,158
	OCEAN ENGINEERING		
031	DIVING AND SALVAGE EQUIPMENT	8,973	8,973
	SMALL BOATS		
032	STANDARD BOATS	43,684	43,684
	PRODUCTION FACILITIES EQUIPMENT		
034	OPERATING FORCES IPE	75,421	75,421
	OTHER SHIP SUPPORT		
035	NUCLEAR ALTERATIONS	172,718	172,718
036	LCS COMMON MISSION MODULES EQUIPMENT	27,840	17,840
	RMMV program restructure		[–10,000]
037	LCS MCM MISSION MODULES	57,146	57,146
038	LCS ASW MISSION MODULES	31,952	21,952
	Early to need		[–10,000]

SEC. 4101. PROCUREMENT
(In Thousands of Dollars)

Line	Item	FY 2017 Request	Conference Authorized
039	LCS SUW MISSION MODULES	22,466	21,064
	MK–46 gun weapon system contract delays		[–1,402]
	LOGISTIC SUPPORT		
041	LSD MIDLIFE	10,813	10,813
	SHIP SONARS		
042	SPQ–9B RADAR	14,363	14,363
043	AN/SQQ–89 SURF ASW COMBAT SYSTEM	90,029	90,029
045	SSN ACOUSTIC EQUIPMENT	248,765	248,765
046	UNDERSEA WARFARE SUPPORT EQUIPMENT	7,163	7,163
	ASW ELECTRONIC EQUIPMENT		
048	SUBMARINE ACOUSTIC WARFARE SYSTEM	21,291	21,291
049	SSTD	6,893	6,893
050	FIXED SURVEILLANCE SYSTEM	145,701	145,701
051	SURTASS	36,136	36,136
	ELECTRONIC WARFARE EQUIPMENT		
053	AN/SLQ–32	274,892	266,641
	Block 3 excess support		[–4,270]
	Block 3T excess support		[–1,000]
	Block 3T installation prior year carryover		[–2,981]
	RECONNAISSANCE EQUIPMENT		
054	SHIPBOARD IW EXPLOIT	170,733	170,733
055	AUTOMATED IDENTIFICATION SYSTEM (AIS)	958	958
	OTHER SHIP ELECTRONIC EQUIPMENT		
057	COOPERATIVE ENGAGEMENT CAPABILITY	22,034	22,034
059	NAVAL TACTICAL COMMAND SUPPORT SYSTEM (NTCSS)	12,336	12,336
060	ATDLS	30,105	30,105
061	NAVY COMMAND AND CONTROL SYSTEM (NCCS)	4,556	4,556
062	MINESWEEPING SYSTEM REPLACEMENT	56,675	32,198
	Ahead of need		[–24,477]
063	SHALLOW WATER MCM	8,875	8,875
064	NAVSTAR GPS RECEIVERS (SPACE)	12,752	12,752
065	AMERICAN FORCES RADIO AND TV SERVICE	4,577	4,577
066	STRATEGIC PLATFORM SUPPORT EQUIP	8,972	8,972
	AVIATION ELECTRONIC EQUIPMENT		
069	ASHORE ATC EQUIPMENT	75,068	75,068
070	AFLOAT ATC EQUIPMENT	33,484	33,484
076	ID SYSTEMS	22,177	22,177
077	NAVAL MISSION PLANNING SYSTEMS	14,273	14,273
	OTHER SHORE ELECTRONIC EQUIPMENT		
080	TACTICAL/MOBILE C4I SYSTEMS	27,927	27,927
081	DCGS–N	12,676	12,676
082	CANES	212,030	212,030
083	RADIAC	8,092	8,092
084	CANES-INTELL	36,013	36,013
085	GPETE	6,428	6,428
087	INTEG COMBAT SYSTEM TEST FACILITY	8,376	8,376
088	EMI CONTROL INSTRUMENTATION	3,971	3,971
089	ITEMS LESS THAN $5 MILLION	58,721	58,721
	SHIPBOARD COMMUNICATIONS		
090	SHIPBOARD TACTICAL COMMUNICATIONS	17,366	17,366
091	SHIP COMMUNICATIONS AUTOMATION	102,479	102,479
092	COMMUNICATIONS ITEMS UNDER $5M	10,403	10,403
	SUBMARINE COMMUNICATIONS		
093	SUBMARINE BROADCAST SUPPORT	34,151	34,151
094	SUBMARINE COMMUNICATION EQUIPMENT	64,529	64,529
	SATELLITE COMMUNICATIONS		
095	SATELLITE COMMUNICATIONS SYSTEMS	14,414	14,414
096	NAVY MULTIBAND TERMINAL (NMT)	38,365	38,365
	SHORE COMMUNICATIONS		
097	JCS COMMUNICATIONS EQUIPMENT	4,156	4,156
	CRYPTOGRAPHIC EQUIPMENT		
099	INFO SYSTEMS SECURITY PROGRAM (ISSP)	85,694	85,694
100	MIO INTEL EXPLOITATION TEAM	920	920
	CRYPTOLOGIC EQUIPMENT		
101	CRYPTOLOGIC COMMUNICATIONS EQUIP	21,098	21,098
	OTHER ELECTRONIC SUPPORT		
102	COAST GUARD EQUIPMENT	32,291	32,291
	SONOBUOYS		
103	SONOBUOYS—ALL TYPES	162,588	159,541
	Excess unit cost growth		[–3,047]
	AIRCRAFT SUPPORT EQUIPMENT		
104	WEAPONS RANGE SUPPORT EQUIPMENT	58,116	58,116
105	AIRCRAFT SUPPORT EQUIPMENT	120,324	120,324
106	METEOROLOGICAL EQUIPMENT	29,253	29,253
107	DCRS/DPL	632	632
108	AIRBORNE MINE COUNTERMEASURES	29,097	29,097
109	AVIATION SUPPORT EQUIPMENT	39,099	39,099
	SHIP GUN SYSTEM EQUIPMENT		
110	SHIP GUN SYSTEMS EQUIPMENT	6,191	6,191

SEC. 4101. PROCUREMENT
(In Thousands of Dollars)

Line	Item	FY 2017 Request	Conference Authorized
	SHIP MISSILE SYSTEMS EQUIPMENT		
111	SHIP MISSILE SUPPORT EQUIPMENT	320,446	310,946
	Program execution		[–9,500]
112	TOMAHAWK SUPPORT EQUIPMENT	71,046	71,046
	FBM SUPPORT EQUIPMENT		
113	STRATEGIC MISSILE SYSTEMS EQUIP	215,138	215,138
	ASW SUPPORT EQUIPMENT		
114	SSN COMBAT CONTROL SYSTEMS	130,715	130,715
115	ASW SUPPORT EQUIPMENT	26,431	26,431
	OTHER ORDNANCE SUPPORT EQUIPMENT		
116	EXPLOSIVE ORDNANCE DISPOSAL EQUIP	11,821	11,821
117	ITEMS LESS THAN $5 MILLION	6,243	6,243
	OTHER EXPENDABLE ORDNANCE		
118	SUBMARINE TRAINING DEVICE MODS	48,020	48,020
120	SURFACE TRAINING EQUIPMENT	97,514	94,979
	Unjustified growth		[–2,535]
	CIVIL ENGINEERING SUPPORT EQUIPMENT		
121	PASSENGER CARRYING VEHICLES	8,853	8,853
122	GENERAL PURPOSE TRUCKS	4,928	4,928
123	CONSTRUCTION & MAINTENANCE EQUIP	18,527	18,527
124	FIRE FIGHTING EQUIPMENT	13,569	13,569
125	TACTICAL VEHICLES	14,917	14,917
126	AMPHIBIOUS EQUIPMENT	7,676	7,676
127	POLLUTION CONTROL EQUIPMENT	2,321	2,321
128	ITEMS UNDER $5 MILLION	12,459	12,459
129	PHYSICAL SECURITY VEHICLES	1,095	1,095
	SUPPLY SUPPORT EQUIPMENT		
131	SUPPLY EQUIPMENT	16,023	16,023
133	FIRST DESTINATION TRANSPORTATION	5,115	5,115
134	SPECIAL PURPOSE SUPPLY SYSTEMS	295,471	295,471
	TRAINING DEVICES		
136	TRAINING AND EDUCATION EQUIPMENT	9,504	9,504
	COMMAND SUPPORT EQUIPMENT		
137	COMMAND SUPPORT EQUIPMENT	37,180	29,980
	CNIC building control systems unjustified request		[–7,200]
139	MEDICAL SUPPORT EQUIPMENT	4,128	4,128
141	NAVAL MIP SUPPORT EQUIPMENT	1,925	1,925
142	OPERATING FORCES SUPPORT EQUIPMENT	4,777	4,777
143	C4ISR EQUIPMENT	9,073	9,073
144	ENVIRONMENTAL SUPPORT EQUIPMENT	21,107	21,107
145	PHYSICAL SECURITY EQUIPMENT	100,906	100,906
146	ENTERPRISE INFORMATION TECHNOLOGY	67,544	67,544
	OTHER		
150	NEXT GENERATION ENTERPRISE SERVICE	98,216	98,216
	CLASSIFIED PROGRAMS		
150A	CLASSIFIED PROGRAMS	9,915	9,915
	SPARES AND REPAIR PARTS		
151	SPARES AND REPAIR PARTS	199,660	199,660
	TOTAL OTHER PROCUREMENT, NAVY	**6,338,861**	**6,258,930**
	PROCUREMENT, MARINE CORPS		
	TRACKED COMBAT VEHICLES		
001	AAV7A1 PIP	73,785	71,785
	Production engineering support excess growth		[–2,000]
002	LAV PIP	53,423	53,423
	ARTILLERY AND OTHER WEAPONS		
003	EXPEDITIONARY FIRE SUPPORT SYSTEM	3,360	3,360
004	155MM LIGHTWEIGHT TOWED HOWITZER	3,318	3,318
005	HIGH MOBILITY ARTILLERY ROCKET SYSTEM	33,725	33,725
006	WEAPONS AND COMBAT VEHICLES UNDER $5 MILLION	8,181	8,181
	OTHER SUPPORT		
007	MODIFICATION KITS	15,250	15,250
	GUIDED MISSILES		
009	GROUND BASED AIR DEFENSE	9,170	9,170
010	JAVELIN	1,009	1,009
011	FOLLOW ON TO SMAW	24,666	24,666
012	ANTI-ARMOR WEAPONS SYSTEM-HEAVY (AAWS-H)	17,080	17,080
	COMMAND AND CONTROL SYSTEMS		
015	COMMON AVIATION COMMAND AND CONTROL SYSTEM (C	47,312	47,312
	REPAIR AND TEST EQUIPMENT		
016	REPAIR AND TEST EQUIPMENT	16,469	16,469
	COMMAND AND CONTROL SYSTEM (NON-TEL)		
019	ITEMS UNDER $5 MILLION (COMM & ELEC)	7,433	7,433
020	AIR OPERATIONS C2 SYSTEMS	15,917	15,917
	RADAR + EQUIPMENT (NON-TEL)		
021	RADAR SYSTEMS	17,772	17,772
022	GROUND/AIR TASK ORIENTED RADAR (G/ATOR)	123,758	123,758
023	RQ–21 UAS	80,217	80,217
	INTELL/COMM EQUIPMENT (NON-TEL)		

SEC. 4101. PROCUREMENT
(In Thousands of Dollars)

Line	Item	FY 2017 Request	Conference Authorized
024	GCSS-MC	1,089	1,089
025	FIRE SUPPORT SYSTEM	13,258	13,258
026	INTELLIGENCE SUPPORT EQUIPMENT	56,379	56,379
029	RQ–11 UAV	1,976	1,976
031	DCGS-MC	1,149	1,149
032	UAS PAYLOADS	2,971	2,971
	OTHER SUPPORT (NON-TEL)		
034	NEXT GENERATION ENTERPRISE NETWORK (NGEN)	76,302	76,302
035	COMMON COMPUTER RESOURCES	41,802	39,477
	Prior year carryover		[–2,325]
036	COMMAND POST SYSTEMS	90,924	90,924
037	RADIO SYSTEMS	43,714	43,714
038	COMM SWITCHING & CONTROL SYSTEMS	66,383	66,383
039	COMM & ELEC INFRASTRUCTURE SUPPORT	30,229	30,229
	CLASSIFIED PROGRAMS		
039A	CLASSIFIED PROGRAMS	2,738	2,738
	ADMINISTRATIVE VEHICLES		
041	COMMERCIAL CARGO VEHICLES	88,312	88,312
	TACTICAL VEHICLES		
043	MOTOR TRANSPORT MODIFICATIONS	13,292	13,292
045	JOINT LIGHT TACTICAL VEHICLE	113,230	113,230
046	FAMILY OF TACTICAL TRAILERS	2,691	2,691
	ENGINEER AND OTHER EQUIPMENT		
048	ENVIRONMENTAL CONTROL EQUIP ASSORT	18	18
050	TACTICAL FUEL SYSTEMS	78	78
051	POWER EQUIPMENT ASSORTED	17,973	17,973
052	AMPHIBIOUS SUPPORT EQUIPMENT	7,371	7,371
053	EOD SYSTEMS	14,021	14,021
	MATERIALS HANDLING EQUIPMENT		
054	PHYSICAL SECURITY EQUIPMENT	31,523	31,523
	GENERAL PROPERTY		
058	TRAINING DEVICES	33,658	33,658
060	FAMILY OF CONSTRUCTION EQUIPMENT	21,315	21,315
061	FAMILY OF INTERNALLY TRANSPORTABLE VEH (ITV)	9,654	9,654
	OTHER SUPPORT		
062	ITEMS LESS THAN $5 MILLION	6,026	6,026
	SPARES AND REPAIR PARTS		
064	SPARES AND REPAIR PARTS	22,848	22,848
	TOTAL PROCUREMENT, MARINE CORPS	**1,362,769**	**1,358,444**
	AIRCRAFT PROCUREMENT, AIR FORCE		
	TACTICAL FORCES		
001	F–35	4,401,894	4,188,894
	Program efficiencies		[–213,000]
002	ADVANCE PROCUREMENT (CY)	404,500	404,500
	TACTICAL AIRLIFT		
003	KC–46A TANKER	2,884,591	2,884,591
	OTHER AIRLIFT		
004	C–130J	145,655	145,655
006	HC–130J	317,576	317,576
007	ADVANCE PROCUREMENT (CY)	20,000	20,000
008	MC–130J	548,358	548,358
009	ADVANCE PROCUREMENT (CY)	50,000	50,000
	HELICOPTERS		
010	UH–1N REPLACEMENT	18,337	18,337
	MISSION SUPPORT AIRCRAFT		
012	CIVIL AIR PATROL A/C	2,637	2,637
	OTHER AIRCRAFT		
013	TARGET DRONES	114,656	114,656
014	RQ–4	12,966	12,966
015	MQ–9	122,522	122,522
	STRATEGIC AIRCRAFT		
016	B–2A	46,729	46,729
017	B–1B	116,319	116,319
018	B–52	109,020	109,020
	TACTICAL AIRCRAFT		
020	A–10	1,289	1,289
021	F–15	105,685	105,685
022	F–16	97,331	114,331
	Active missile warning system		[12,000]
	Anti-jam global positioning system (GPS) upgrade		[5,000]
023	F–22A	163,008	163,008
024	F–35 MODIFICATIONS	175,811	175,811
025	INCREMENT 3.2B	76,410	76,410
026	ADVANCE PROCUREMENT (CY)	2,000	2,000
	AIRLIFT AIRCRAFT		
027	C–5	24,192	24,192
029	C–17A	21,555	21,555
030	C–21	5,439	5,439

SEC. 4101. PROCUREMENT
(In Thousands of Dollars)

Line	Item	FY 2017 Request	Conference Authorized
031	C–32A	35,235	35,235
032	C–37A	5,004	5,004
	TRAINER AIRCRAFT		
033	GLIDER MODS	394	394
034	T–6	12,765	12,765
035	T–1	25,073	17,073
	Production schedule slip		[–8,000]
036	T–38	45,090	45,090
	OTHER AIRCRAFT		
037	U–2 MODS	36,074	36,074
038	KC–10A (ATCA)	4,570	4,570
039	C–12	1,995	1,995
040	VC–25A MOD	102,670	102,670
041	C–40	13,984	13,984
042	C–130	9,168	81,668
	8–Bladed Propellers		[16,000]
	Electronic Propeller Control Systems		[13,500]
	In-flight Propeller Balancing System Certification		[1,500]
	T56 3.5 Engine Upgrade Kits		[41,500]
043	C–130J MODS	89,424	89,424
044	C–135	64,161	64,161
045	COMPASS CALL MODS	130,257	59,857
	Compass Call Program Restructure		[–70,400]
046	RC–135	211,438	211,438
047	E–3	82,786	82,786
048	E–4	53,348	53,348
049	E–8	6,244	6,244
050	AIRBORNE WARNING AND CONTROL SYSTEM	223,427	223,427
051	FAMILY OF BEYOND LINE-OF-SIGHT TERMINALS	4,673	4,673
052	H–1	9,007	9,007
054	H–60	91,357	91,357
055	RQ–4 MODS	32,045	32,045
056	HC/MC–130 MODIFICATIONS	30,767	30,767
057	OTHER AIRCRAFT	33,886	33,886
059	MQ–9 MODS	141,929	141,929
060	CV–22 MODS	63,395	63,395
	AIRCRAFT SPARES AND REPAIR PARTS		
061	INITIAL SPARES/REPAIR PARTS	686,491	673,291
	Compass Call Program Restructure		[–13,200]
	COMMON SUPPORT EQUIPMENT		
062	AIRCRAFT REPLACEMENT SUPPORT EQUIP	121,935	121,935
	POST PRODUCTION SUPPORT		
063	B–2A	154	154
064	B–2A	43,330	43,330
065	B–52	28,125	28,125
066	C–17A	23,559	23,559
069	F–15	2,980	2,980
070	F–16	15,155	39,955
	Additional mission trainers		[24,800]
071	F–22A	48,505	48,505
074	RQ–4 POST PRODUCTION CHARGES	99	99
	INDUSTRIAL PREPAREDNESS		
075	INDUSTRIAL RESPONSIVENESS	14,126	14,126
	WAR CONSUMABLES		
076	WAR CONSUMABLES	120,036	120,036
	OTHER PRODUCTION CHARGES		
077	OTHER PRODUCTION CHARGES	1,252,824	1,252,824
	CLASSIFIED PROGRAMS		
077A	CLASSIFIED PROGRAMS	16,952	119,952
	Compass Call Program Restructure		[103,000]
	TOTAL AIRCRAFT PROCUREMENT, AIR FORCE	**13,922,917**	**13,835,617**
	MISSILE PROCUREMENT, AIR FORCE		
	MISSILE REPLACEMENT EQUIPMENT—BALLISTIC		
001	MISSILE REPLACEMENT EQ-BALLISTIC	70,247	70,247
	TACTICAL		
002	JOINT AIR-SURFACE STANDOFF MISSILE	431,645	431,645
003	LRASM0	59,511	59,511
004	SIDEWINDER (AIM-9X)	127,438	127,438
005	AMRAAM	350,144	339,392
	Pricing adjustment		[–10,752]
006	PREDATOR HELLFIRE MISSILE	33,955	33,955
007	SMALL DIAMETER BOMB	92,361	92,361
	INDUSTRIAL FACILITIES		
008	INDUSTR'L PREPAREDNS/POL PREVENTION	977	977
	CLASS IV		
009	ICBM FUZE MOD	17,095	17,095
010	MM III MODIFICATIONS	68,692	68,692
011	AGM–65D MAVERICK	282	282

SEC. 4101. PROCUREMENT
(In Thousands of Dollars)

Line	Item	FY 2017 Request	Conference Authorized
013	AIR LAUNCH CRUISE MISSILE (ALCM)	21,762	21,762
014	SMALL DIAMETER BOMB	15,349	15,349
	MISSILE SPARES AND REPAIR PARTS		
015	INITIAL SPARES/REPAIR PARTS	81,607	81,607
	SPECIAL PROGRAMS		
030	SPECIAL UPDATE PROGRAMS	46,125	46,125
	CLASSIFIED PROGRAMS		
030A	CLASSIFIED PROGRAMS	1,009,431	1,009,431
	TOTAL MISSILE PROCUREMENT, AIR FORCE	**2,426,621**	**2,415,869**
	SPACE PROCUREMENT, AIR FORCE		
	SPACE PROGRAMS		
001	ADVANCED EHF	645,569	645,569
002	AF SATELLITE COMM SYSTEM	42,375	42,375
003	COUNTERSPACE SYSTEMS	26,984	26,984
004	FAMILY OF BEYOND LINE-OF-SIGHT TERMINALS	88,963	88,963
005	WIDEBAND GAPFILLER SATELLITES(SPACE)	86,272	86,272
006	GPS III SPACE SEGMENT	34,059	34,059
007	GLOBAL POSTIONING (SPACE)	2,169	2,169
008	SPACEBORNE EQUIP (COMSEC)	46,708	46,708
009	GLOBAL POSITIONING (SPACE)	13,171	10,271
	Excess to Need		[−2,900]
010	MILSATCOM	41,799	41,799
011	EVOLVED EXPENDABLE LAUNCH CAPABILITY	768,586	742,586
	Early to need		[−26,000]
012	EVOLVED EXPENDABLE LAUNCH VEH(SPACE)	737,853	536,853
	Early to need		[−201,000]
013	SBIR HIGH (SPACE)	362,504	362,504
014	NUDET DETECTION SYSTEM	4,395	4,395
015	SPACE MODS	8,642	8,642
016	SPACELIFT RANGE SYSTEM SPACE	123,088	123,088
	SSPARES		
017	INITIAL SPARES/REPAIR PARTS	22,606	22,606
	TOTAL SPACE PROCUREMENT, AIR FORCE	**3,055,743**	**2,825,843**
	PROCUREMENT OF AMMUNITION, AIR FORCE		
	ROCKETS		
001	ROCKETS	18,734	18,734
	CARTRIDGES		
002	CARTRIDGES	220,237	220,237
	BOMBS		
003	PRACTICE BOMBS	97,106	97,106
004	GENERAL PURPOSE BOMBS	581,561	581,561
005	MASSIVE ORDNANCE PENETRATOR (MOP)	3,600	3,600
006	JOINT DIRECT ATTACK MUNITION	303,988	297,988
	Pricing adjustment for increased quantity		[−6,000]
	OTHER ITEMS		
007	CAD/PAD	38,890	38,890
008	EXPLOSIVE ORDNANCE DISPOSAL (EOD)	5,714	5,714
009	SPARES AND REPAIR PARTS	740	740
010	MODIFICATIONS	573	573
011	ITEMS LESS THAN $5 MILLION	5,156	5,156
	FLARES		
012	FLARES	134,709	134,709
	FUZES		
013	FUZES	229,252	229,252
	SMALL ARMS		
014	SMALL ARMS	37,459	37,459
	TOTAL PROCUREMENT OF AMMUNITION, AIR FORCE	**1,677,719**	**1,671,719**
	OTHER PROCUREMENT, AIR FORCE		
	PASSENGER CARRYING VEHICLES		
001	PASSENGER CARRYING VEHICLES	14,437	14,437
	CARGO AND UTILITY VEHICLES		
002	MEDIUM TACTICAL VEHICLE	24,812	24,812
003	CAP VEHICLES	984	984
004	ITEMS LESS THAN $5 MILLION	11,191	11,191
	SPECIAL PURPOSE VEHICLES		
005	SECURITY AND TACTICAL VEHICLES	5,361	5,361
006	ITEMS LESS THAN $5 MILLION	4,623	4,623
	FIRE FIGHTING EQUIPMENT		
007	FIRE FIGHTING/CRASH RESCUE VEHICLES	12,451	12,451
	MATERIALS HANDLING EQUIPMENT		
008	ITEMS LESS THAN $5 MILLION	18,114	18,114
	BASE MAINTENANCE SUPPORT		
009	RUNWAY SNOW REMOV & CLEANING EQUIP	2,310	2,310
010	ITEMS LESS THAN $5 MILLION	46,868	46,868
	COMM SECURITY EQUIPMENT(COMSEC)		
012	COMSEC EQUIPMENT	72,359	72,359

SEC. 4101. PROCUREMENT
(In Thousands of Dollars)

Line	Item	FY 2017 Request	Conference Authorized
	INTELLIGENCE PROGRAMS		
014	INTELLIGENCE TRAINING EQUIPMENT	6,982	6,982
015	INTELLIGENCE COMM EQUIPMENT	30,504	30,504
	ELECTRONICS PROGRAMS		
016	AIR TRAFFIC CONTROL & LANDING SYS	55,803	55,803
017	NATIONAL AIRSPACE SYSTEM	2,673	2,673
018	BATTLE CONTROL SYSTEM—FIXED	5,677	5,677
019	THEATER AIR CONTROL SYS IMPROVEMENTS	1,163	1,163
020	WEATHER OBSERVATION FORECAST	21,667	21,667
021	STRATEGIC COMMAND AND CONTROL	39,803	39,803
022	CHEYENNE MOUNTAIN COMPLEX	24,618	24,618
023	MISSION PLANNING SYSTEMS	15,868	15,868
025	INTEGRATED STRAT PLAN & ANALY NETWORK (ISPAN)	9,331	9,331
	SPCL COMM-ELECTRONICS PROJECTS		
026	GENERAL INFORMATION TECHNOLOGY	41,779	41,779
027	AF GLOBAL COMMAND & CONTROL SYS	15,729	15,729
028	MOBILITY COMMAND AND CONTROL	9,814	9,814
029	AIR FORCE PHYSICAL SECURITY SYSTEM	99,460	99,460
030	COMBAT TRAINING RANGES	34,850	34,850
031	MINIMUM ESSENTIAL EMERGENCY COMM N	198,925	198,925
032	WIDE AREA SURVEILLANCE (WAS)	6,943	6,943
033	C3 COUNTERMEASURES	19,580	19,580
034	GCSS-AF FOS	1,743	1,743
036	THEATER BATTLE MGT C2 SYSTEM	9,659	9,659
037	AIR & SPACE OPERATIONS CTR-WPN SYS	15,474	15,474
038	AIR OPERATIONS CENTER (AOC) 10.2	30,623	15,323
	Fielding		[−15,300]
	AIR FORCE COMMUNICATIONS		
039	INFORMATION TRANSPORT SYSTEMS	40,043	40,043
040	AFNET	146,897	146,897
041	JOINT COMMUNICATIONS SUPPORT ELEMENT (JCSE)	5,182	5,182
042	USCENTCOM	13,418	13,418
	ORGANIZATION AND BASE		
052	TACTICAL C-E EQUIPMENT	109,836	109,836
053	RADIO EQUIPMENT	16,266	16,266
054	CCTV/AUDIOVISUAL EQUIPMENT	7,449	7,449
055	BASE COMM INFRASTRUCTURE	109,215	109,215
	MODIFICATIONS		
056	COMM ELECT MODS	65,700	65,700
	PERSONAL SAFETY & RESCUE EQUIP		
058	ITEMS LESS THAN $5 MILLION	54,416	54,416
	DEPOT PLANT+MTRLS HANDLING EQ		
059	MECHANIZED MATERIAL HANDLING EQUIP	7,344	7,344
	BASE SUPPORT EQUIPMENT		
060	BASE PROCURED EQUIPMENT	6,852	6,852
063	MOBILITY EQUIPMENT	8,146	8,146
064	ITEMS LESS THAN $5 MILLION	28,427	28,427
	SPECIAL SUPPORT PROJECTS		
066	DARP RC135	25,287	25,287
067	DCGS-AF	169,201	169,201
069	SPECIAL UPDATE PROGRAM	576,710	576,710
	CLASSIFIED PROGRAMS		
070A	CLASSIFIED PROGRAMS	15,119,705	15,119,705
	SPARES AND REPAIR PARTS		
072	SPARES AND REPAIR PARTS	15,784	15,784
	TOTAL OTHER PROCUREMENT, AIR FORCE	**17,438,056**	**17,422,756**
	PROCUREMENT, DEFENSE-WIDE		
	MAJOR EQUIPMENT, WHS		
037	MAJOR EQUIPMENT, OSD	29,211	29,211
	MAJOR EQUIPMENT, NSA		
036	INFORMATION SYSTEMS SECURITY PROGRAM (ISSP)	4,399	4,399
	MAJOR EQUIPMENT, WHS		
040	MAJOR EQUIPMENT, WHS	24,979	24,979
	MAJOR EQUIPMENT, DISA		
006	INFORMATION SYSTEMS SECURITY	21,347	21,347
007	TELEPORT PROGRAM	50,597	50,597
008	ITEMS LESS THAN $5 MILLION	10,420	10,420
009	NET CENTRIC ENTERPRISE SERVICES (NCES)	1,634	1,634
010	DEFENSE INFORMATION SYSTEM NETWORK	87,235	87,235
011	CYBER SECURITY INITIATIVE	4,528	4,528
012	WHITE HOUSE COMMUNICATION AGENCY	36,846	36,846
013	SENIOR LEADERSHIP ENTERPRISE	599,391	599,391
015	JOINT REGIONAL SECURITY STACKS (JRSS)	150,221	150,221
	MAJOR EQUIPMENT, DLA		
017	MAJOR EQUIPMENT	2,055	2,055
	MAJOR EQUIPMENT, DSS		
020	MAJOR EQUIPMENT	1,057	1,057
	MAJOR EQUIPMENT, DCAA		

SEC. 4101. PROCUREMENT
(In Thousands of Dollars)

Line	Item	FY 2017 Request	Conference Authorized
001	ITEMS LESS THAN $5 MILLION	2,964	2,964
	MAJOR EQUIPMENT, TJS		
038	MAJOR EQUIPMENT, TJS	7,988	7,988
	MAJOR EQUIPMENT, MISSILE DEFENSE AGENCY		
023	THAAD	369,608	369,608
024	AEGIS BMD	463,801	528,801
	Increasing BMD capability for Aegis Ships		[65,000]
025	BMDS AN/TPY-2 RADARS	5,503	5,503
026	ARROW UPPER TIER		120,000
	Increase for Arrow 3 Coproduction subject to Title XVI		[120,000]
027	DAVID'S SLING		150,000
	Increase for DSWS Coproduction subject to Title XVI		[150,000]
028	AEGIS ASHORE PHASE III	57,493	57,493
029	IRON DOME	42,000	62,000
	Increase for Coproduction of Iron Dome Tamir Interceptors subject to Title XVI		[20,000]
030	AEGIS BMD HARDWARE AND SOFTWARE	50,098	50,098
	MAJOR EQUIPMENT, DHRA		
003	PERSONNEL ADMINISTRATION	14,232	14,232
	MAJOR EQUIPMENT, DEFENSE THREAT REDUCTION AGENCY		
021	VEHICLES	200	200
022	OTHER MAJOR EQUIPMENT	6,437	6,437
	MAJOR EQUIPMENT, DODEA		
019	AUTOMATION/EDUCATIONAL SUPPORT & LOGISTICS	288	288
	MAJOR EQUIPMENT, DCMA		
002	MAJOR EQUIPMENT	92	92
	MAJOR EQUIPMENT, DMACT		
018	MAJOR EQUIPMENT	8,060	8,060
	CLASSIFIED PROGRAMS		
040A	CLASSIFIED PROGRAMS	568,864	568,864
	AVIATION PROGRAMS		
042	ROTARY WING UPGRADES AND SUSTAINMENT	150,396	150,396
043	UNMANNED ISR	21,190	21,190
045	NON-STANDARD AVIATION	4,905	4,905
046	U-28	3,970	3,970
047	MH-47 CHINOOK	25,022	25,022
049	CV-22 MODIFICATION	19,008	19,008
051	MQ-9 UNMANNED AERIAL VEHICLE	10,598	10,598
053	PRECISION STRIKE PACKAGE	213,122	200,072
	SOCOM requested transfer		[-13,050]
054	AC/MC-130J	73,548	86,598
	SOCOM requested transfer		[13,050]
055	C-130 MODIFICATIONS	32,970	32,970
	SHIPBUILDING		
056	UNDERWATER SYSTEMS	37,098	37,098
	AMMUNITION PROGRAMS		
057	ORDNANCE ITEMS <$5M	105,267	105,267
	OTHER PROCUREMENT PROGRAMS		
058	INTELLIGENCE SYSTEMS	79,963	79,963
059	DISTRIBUTED COMMON GROUND/SURFACE SYSTEMS	13,432	13,432
060	OTHER ITEMS <$5M	66,436	66,436
061	COMBATANT CRAFT SYSTEMS	55,820	55,820
062	SPECIAL PROGRAMS	107,432	107,432
063	TACTICAL VEHICLES	67,849	67,849
064	WARRIOR SYSTEMS <$5M	245,781	245,781
065	COMBAT MISSION REQUIREMENTS	19,566	19,566
066	GLOBAL VIDEO SURVEILLANCE ACTIVITIES	3,437	3,437
067	OPERATIONAL ENHANCEMENTS INTELLIGENCE	17,299	17,299
069	OPERATIONAL ENHANCEMENTS	219,945	219,945
	CBDP		
070	CHEMICAL BIOLOGICAL SITUATIONAL AWARENESS	148,203	148,203
071	CB PROTECTION & HAZARD MITIGATION	161,113	161,113
	TOTAL PROCUREMENT, DEFENSE-WIDE	**4,524,918**	**4,879,918**
	JOINT URGENT OPERATIONAL NEEDS FUND		
	JOINT URGENT OPERATIONAL NEEDS FUND		
001	JOINT URGENT OPERATIONAL NEEDS FUND	99,300	0
	Program decrease		[-99,300]
	TOTAL JOINT URGENT OPERATIONAL NEEDS FUND	**99,300**	**0**
	NATIONAL GUARD AND RESERVE EQUIPMENT		
	UNDISTRIBUTED		
007	MISCELLANEOUS EQUIPMENT		250,000
	Program increase		[250,000]
	TOTAL NATIONAL GUARD AND RESERVE EQUIPMENT		**250,000**
	TOTAL PROCUREMENT	**101,971,592**	**102,422,660**

SEC. 4102. PROCUREMENT FOR OVERSEAS CON-
   TINGENCY OPERATIONS.

SEC. 4102. PROCUREMENT FOR OVERSEAS CONTINGENCY OPERATIONS
(In Thousands of Dollars)

Line	Item	FY 2017 Request	Conference Authorized
	AIRCRAFT PROCUREMENT, ARMY		
	MODIFICATION OF AIRCRAFT		
015	MULTI SENSOR ABN RECON (MIP)	21,400	21,400
020	EMARSS SEMA MODS (MIP)	42,700	42,700
026	RQ–7 UAV MODS	1,775	1,775
027	UAS MODS	4,420	4,420
	GROUND SUPPORT AVIONICS		
030	CMWS	56,115	56,115
031	CIRCM	108,721	108,721
	TOTAL AIRCRAFT PROCUREMENT, ARMY	235,131	235,131
	MISSILE PROCUREMENT, ARMY		
	AIR-TO-SURFACE MISSILE SYSTEM		
004	HELLFIRE SYS SUMMARY	305,830	305,830
	ANTI-TANK/ASSAULT MISSILE SYS		
007	JAVELIN (AAWS-M) SYSTEM SUMMARY	15,567	15,567
008	TOW 2 SYSTEM SUMMARY	80,652	80,652
010	GUIDED MLRS ROCKET (GMLRS)	75,991	75,991
012	LETHAL MINIATURE AERIAL MISSILE SYSTEM (LMAMS	51,277	51,277
	TOTAL MISSILE PROCUREMENT, ARMY	529,317	529,317
	PROCUREMENT OF W&TCV, ARMY		
	MODIFICATION OF TRACKED COMBAT VEHICLES		
007	PALADIN INTEGRATED MANAGEMENT (PIM)	125,184	125,184
009	ASSAULT BRIDGE (MOD)	5,950	5,950
014	ABRAMS UPGRADE PROGRAM		72,000
	Army requested realignment (ERI)		[172,000]
	Realign APS Unit Set Requirements to Base		[–100,000]
	WEAPONS & OTHER COMBAT VEHICLES		
017	MORTAR SYSTEMS	22,410	22,410
	SUPPORT EQUIPMENT & FACILITIES		
036	BRADLEY PROGRAM		72,800
	Army requested realignment (ERI)		[72,800]
	TOTAL PROCUREMENT OF W&TCV, ARMY	153,544	298,344
	PROCUREMENT OF AMMUNITION, ARMY		
	SMALL/MEDIUM CAL AMMUNITION		
002	CTG, 7.62MM, ALL TYPES	9,642	9,642
004	CTG, .50 CAL, ALL TYPES	6,607	6,607
005	CTG, 20MM, ALL TYPES	1,077	1,077
006	CTG, 25MM, ALL TYPES	28,534	28,534
007	CTG, 30MM, ALL TYPES	20,000	20,000
008	CTG, 40MM, ALL TYPES	7,423	7,423
	MORTAR AMMUNITION		
009	60MM MORTAR, ALL TYPES	10,000	10,000
010	81MM MORTAR, ALL TYPES	2,677	2,677
	TANK AMMUNITION		
012	CARTRIDGES, TANK, 105MM AND 120MM, ALL TYPES	8,999	8,999
	ARTILLERY AMMUNITION		
014	ARTILLERY PROJECTILE, 155MM, ALL TYPES	30,348	30,348
015	PROJ 155MM EXTENDED RANGE M982	140	140
016	ARTILLERY PROPELLANTS, FUZES AND PRIMERS, ALL	29,655	29,655
	MINES		
017	MINES & CLEARING CHARGES, ALL TYPES	16,866	16,866
	NETWORKED MUNITIONS		
018	SPIDER NETWORK MUNITIONS, ALL TYPES	10,353	10,353
	ROCKETS		
019	SHOULDER LAUNCHED MUNITIONS, ALL TYPES	63,210	63,210
020	ROCKET, HYDRA 70, ALL TYPES	42,851	42,851
	OTHER AMMUNITION		
022	DEMOLITION MUNITIONS, ALL TYPES	6,373	6,373
023	GRENADES, ALL TYPES	4,143	4,143
024	SIGNALS, ALL TYPES	1,852	1,852
	MISCELLANEOUS		
027	NON-LETHAL AMMUNITION, ALL TYPES	773	773
	TOTAL PROCUREMENT OF AMMUNITION, ARMY	301,523	301,523
	OTHER PROCUREMENT, ARMY		
	TACTICAL VEHICLES		
002	SEMITRAILERS, FLATBED:	4,180	4,180
008	FAMILY OF MEDIUM TACTICAL VEH (FMTV)	147,476	147,476
010	FAMILY OF HEAVY TACTICAL VEHICLES (FHTV)	6,122	6,122
011	PLS ESP	106,358	106,358
012	HVY EXPANDED MOBILE TACTICAL TRUCK EXT SERV	203,766	203,766
013	TACTICAL WHEELED VEHICLE PROTECTION KITS	101,154	101,154
014	MODIFICATION OF IN SVC EQUIP	155,456	155,456

SEC. 4102. PROCUREMENT FOR OVERSEAS CONTINGENCY OPERATIONS
(In Thousands of Dollars)

Line	Item	FY 2017 Request	Conference Authorized
	COMM—JOINT COMMUNICATIONS		
019	*WIN-T—GROUND FORCES TACTICAL NETWORK*	9,572	9,572
	COMM—SATELLITE COMMUNICATIONS		
025	*SHF TERM*	24,000	24,000
	COMM—INTELLIGENCE COMM		
047	*CI AUTOMATION ARCHITECTURE*	1,550	1,550
	INFORMATION SECURITY		
051	*COMMUNICATIONS SECURITY (COMSEC)*	1,928	1,928
052	*DEFENSIVE CYBER OPERATIONS*	26,500	26,500
	COMM—BASE COMMUNICATIONS		
056	*INSTALLATION INFO INFRASTRUCTURE MOD PROGRAM*	20,510	20,510
	ELECT EQUIP—TACT INT REL ACT (TIARA)		
062	*DCGS-A (MIP)*	33,032	33,032
064	*TROJAN (MIP)*	3,305	3,305
066	*CI HUMINT AUTO REPRTING AND COLL(CHARCS)*	7,233	7,233
069	*BIOMETRIC TACTICAL COLLECTION DEVICES (MIP)*	5,670	5,670
	ELECT EQUIP—ELECTRONIC WARFARE (EW)		
070	*LIGHTWEIGHT COUNTER MORTAR RADAR*	25,892	25,892
074	*FAMILY OF PERSISTENT SURVEILLANCE CAPABILITIE*	11,610	11,610
075	*COUNTERINTELLIGENCE/SECURITY COUNTERMEASURES*	23,890	23,890
	ELECT EQUIP—TACTICAL SURV. (TAC SURV)		
080	*INDIRECT FIRE PROTECTION FAMILY OF SYSTEMS*	76,270	76,270
089	*MORTAR FIRE CONTROL SYSTEM*	2,572	2,572
	ELECT EQUIP—TACTICAL C2 SYSTEMS		
092	*AIR & MSL DEFENSE PLANNING & CONTROL SYS*	69,958	69,958
	ELECT EQUIP—AUTOMATION		
102	*AUTOMATED DATA PROCESSING EQUIP*	9,900	9,900
	ELECT EQUIP—AUDIO VISUAL SYS (A/V)		
108	*ITEMS LESS THAN $5M (SURVEYING EQUIPMENT)*	96	96
	CHEMICAL DEFENSIVE EQUIPMENT		
114	*CBRN DEFENSE*	1,841	1,841
	BRIDGING EQUIPMENT		
115	*TACTICAL BRIDGING*	26,000	26,000
	ENGINEER (NON-CONSTRUCTION) EQUIPMENT		
124	*ROBOTICS AND APPLIQUE SYSTEMS*	268	268
128	*FAMILY OF BOATS AND MOTORS*	280	280
	COMBAT SERVICE SUPPORT EQUIPMENT		
129	*HEATERS AND ECU'S*	894	894
134	*FORCE PROVIDER*	53,800	53,800
135	*FIELD FEEDING EQUIPMENT*	2,665	2,665
136	*CARGO AERIAL DEL & PERSONNEL PARACHUTE SYSTEM*	2,400	2,400
137	*FAMILY OF ENGR COMBAT AND CONSTRUCTION SETS*	9,789	9,789
138	*ITEMS LESS THAN $5M (ENG SPT)*	300	300
	PETROLEUM EQUIPMENT		
139	*QUALITY SURVEILLANCE EQUIPMENT*	4,800	4,800
140	*DISTRIBUTION SYSTEMS, PETROLEUM & WATER*	78,240	78,240
	MEDICAL EQUIPMENT		
141	*COMBAT SUPPORT MEDICAL*	5,763	5,763
	MAINTENANCE EQUIPMENT		
142	*MOBILE MAINTENANCE EQUIPMENT SYSTEMS*	1,609	1,609
143	*ITEMS LESS THAN $5.0M (MAINT EQ)*	145	145
	CONSTRUCTION EQUIPMENT		
144	*GRADER, ROAD MTZD, HVY, 6X4 (CCE)*	3,047	3,047
148	*TRACTOR, FULL TRACKED*	4,426	4,426
151	*HIGH MOBILITY ENGINEER EXCAVATOR (HMEE)*	2,900	2,900
155	*ITEMS LESS THAN $5.0M (CONST EQUIP)*	96	96
	GENERATORS		
158	*GENERATORS AND ASSOCIATED EQUIP*	21,861	21,861
	MATERIAL HANDLING EQUIPMENT		
160	*FAMILY OF FORKLIFTS*	846	846
	TEST MEASURE AND DIG EQUIPMENT (TMD)		
168	*TEST EQUIPMENT MODERNIZATION (TEMOD)*	1,140	1,140
	OTHER SUPPORT EQUIPMENT		
170	*RAPID EQUIPPING SOLDIER SUPPORT EQUIPMENT*	8,500	8,500
	TOTAL OTHER PROCUREMENT, ARMY	**1,309,610**	**1,309,610**
	JOINT IMPROVISED-THREAT DEFEAT FUND		
	NETWORK ATTACK		
001	*RAPID ACQUISITION AND THREAT RESPONSE*	332,000	332,000
	STAFF AND INFRASTRUCTURE		
002	*MISSION ENABLERS*	62,800	62,800
	TOTAL JOINT IMPROVISED-THREAT DEFEAT FUND	**394,800**	**394,800**
	AIRCRAFT PROCUREMENT, NAVY		
	COMBAT AIRCRAFT		
002	*F/A–18E/F (FIGHTER) HORNET*	184,912	184,912
	OTHER AIRCRAFT		
026	*STUASL0 UAV*	70,000	70,000
	MODIFICATION OF AIRCRAFT		

SEC. 4102. PROCUREMENT FOR OVERSEAS CONTINGENCY OPERATIONS
(In Thousands of Dollars)

Line	Item	FY 2017 Request	Conference Authorized
037	EP–3 SERIES	7,505	7,505
047	SPECIAL PROJECT AIRCRAFT	14,869	14,869
051	COMMON ECM EQUIPMENT	70,780	70,780
059	V–22 (TILT/ROTOR ACFT) OSPREY	8,740	8,740
	AIRCRAFT SPARES AND REPAIR PARTS		
063	SPARES AND REPAIR PARTS	1,500	1,500
	AIRCRAFT SUPPORT EQUIP & FACILITIES		
065	AIRCRAFT INDUSTRIAL FACILITIES	524	524
	TOTAL AIRCRAFT PROCUREMENT, NAVY	**358,830**	**358,830**
	WEAPONS PROCUREMENT, NAVY		
	TACTICAL MISSILES		
010	HELLFIRE	8,600	8,600
	TOTAL WEAPONS PROCUREMENT, NAVY	**8,600**	**8,600**
	PROCUREMENT OF AMMO, NAVY & MC		
	NAVY AMMUNITION		
001	GENERAL PURPOSE BOMBS	40,366	40,366
002	AIRBORNE ROCKETS, ALL TYPES	8,860	8,860
006	AIR EXPENDABLE COUNTERMEASURES	7,060	7,060
013	PYROTECHNIC AND DEMOLITION	1,122	1,122
014	AMMUNITION LESS THAN $5 MILLION	3,495	3,495
	MARINE CORPS AMMUNITION		
015	SMALL ARMS AMMUNITION	1,205	1,205
017	40 MM, ALL TYPES	539	539
018	60MM, ALL TYPES	909	909
020	120MM, ALL TYPES	530	530
022	ROCKETS, ALL TYPES	469	469
023	ARTILLERY, ALL TYPES	1,196	1,196
024	DEMOLITION MUNITIONS, ALL TYPES	261	261
025	FUZE, ALL TYPES	217	217
	TOTAL PROCUREMENT OF AMMO, NAVY & MC	**66,229**	**66,229**
	OTHER PROCUREMENT, NAVY		
	OTHER SHORE ELECTRONIC EQUIPMENT		
081	DCGS-N	12,000	12,000
	OTHER ORDNANCE SUPPORT EQUIPMENT		
116	EXPLOSIVE ORDNANCE DISPOSAL EQUIP	40,000	40,000
	CIVIL ENGINEERING SUPPORT EQUIPMENT		
124	FIRE FIGHTING EQUIPMENT	630	630
	SUPPLY SUPPORT EQUIPMENT		
133	FIRST DESTINATION TRANSPORTATION	25	25
	COMMAND SUPPORT EQUIPMENT		
137	COMMAND SUPPORT EQUIPMENT	10,562	10,562
139	MEDICAL SUPPORT EQUIPMENT	5,000	5,000
	CLASSIFIED PROGRAMS		
150A	CLASSIFIED PROGRAMS	1,660	1,660
	TOTAL OTHER PROCUREMENT, NAVY	**69,877**	**69,877**
	PROCUREMENT, MARINE CORPS		
	ARTILLERY AND OTHER WEAPONS		
006	WEAPONS AND COMBAT VEHICLES UNDER $5 MILLION	572	572
	GUIDED MISSILES		
010	JAVELIN	1,606	1,606
	OTHER SUPPORT (TEL)		
018	MODIFICATION KITS	2,600	2,600
	COMMAND AND CONTROL SYSTEM (NON-TEL)		
019	ITEMS UNDER $5 MILLION (COMM & ELEC)	2,200	2,200
	INTELL/COMM EQUIPMENT (NON-TEL)		
026	INTELLIGENCE SUPPORT EQUIPMENT	20,981	20,981
029	RQ–11 UAV	3,817	3,817
	OTHER SUPPORT (NON-TEL)		
035	COMMON COMPUTER RESOURCES	2,600	2,600
037	RADIO SYSTEMS	9,563	9,563
	ENGINEER AND OTHER EQUIPMENT		
053	EOD SYSTEMS	75,000	75,000
	TOTAL PROCUREMENT, MARINE CORPS	**118,939**	**118,939**
	AIRCRAFT PROCUREMENT, AIR FORCE		
	OTHER AIRLIFT		
004	C–130J	73,000	73,000
	OTHER AIRCRAFT		
015	MQ–9	273,600	186,600
	Air Force requested transfer to line 61 for spares		[–87,000]
	STRATEGIC AIRCRAFT		
019	LARGE AIRCRAFT INFRARED COUNTERMEASURES	135,801	135,801
	TACTICAL AIRCRAFT		
020	A–10	23,850	23,850
	OTHER AIRCRAFT		

SEC. 4102. PROCUREMENT FOR OVERSEAS CONTINGENCY OPERATIONS
(In Thousands of Dollars)

Line	Item	FY 2017 Request	Conference Authorized
047	E–3	6,600	6,600
056	HC/MC–130 MODIFICATIONS	13,550	13,550
057	OTHER AIRCRAFT	7,500	7,500
059	MQ–9 MODS	112,068	112,068
	AIRCRAFT SPARES AND REPAIR PARTS		
061	INITIAL SPARES/REPAIR PARTS	25,600	87,000
	Air Force requested transfer from line 15 for spares		[87,000]
	Compass Call Program Restructure		[–25,600]
	OTHER PRODUCTION CHARGES		
077	OTHER PRODUCTION CHARGES	8,400	8,400
	TOTAL AIRCRAFT PROCUREMENT, AIR FORCE	**679,969**	**654,369**
	MISSILE PROCUREMENT, AIR FORCE		
	TACTICAL		
006	PREDATOR HELLFIRE MISSILE	145,125	145,125
	CLASS IV		
011	AGM–65D MAVERICK	9,720	9,720
	TOTAL MISSILE PROCUREMENT, AIR FORCE	**154,845**	**154,845**
	PROCUREMENT OF AMMUNITION, AIR FORCE		
	CARTRIDGES		
002	CARTRIDGES	9,830	9,830
	BOMBS		
004	GENERAL PURPOSE BOMBS	7,921	7,921
006	JOINT DIRECT ATTACK MUNITION	140,126	130,876
	Pricing adjustment		[–9,250]
	FLARES		
012	FLARES	6,531	6,531
	TOTAL PROCUREMENT OF AMMUNITION, AIR FORCE	**164,408**	**155,158**
	OTHER PROCUREMENT, AIR FORCE		
	PASSENGER CARRYING VEHICLES		
001	PASSENGER CARRYING VEHICLES	2,003	2,003
	CARGO AND UTILITY VEHICLES		
002	MEDIUM TACTICAL VEHICLE	9,066	9,066
004	ITEMS LESS THAN $5 MILLION	12,264	12,264
	SPECIAL PURPOSE VEHICLES		
006	ITEMS LESS THAN $5 MILLION	16,789	16,789
	FIRE FIGHTING EQUIPMENT		
007	FIRE FIGHTING/CRASH RESCUE VEHICLES	48,590	48,590
	MATERIALS HANDLING EQUIPMENT		
008	ITEMS LESS THAN $5 MILLION	2,366	2,366
	BASE MAINTENANCE SUPPORT		
009	RUNWAY SNOW REMOV & CLEANING EQUIP	6,468	6,468
010	ITEMS LESS THAN $5 MILLION	9,271	9,271
	ELECTRONICS PROGRAMS		
016	AIR TRAFFIC CONTROL & LANDING SYS	42,650	42,650
	SPCL COMM-ELECTRONICS PROJECTS		
029	AIR FORCE PHYSICAL SECURITY SYSTEM	7,500	7,500
033	C3 COUNTERMEASURES	620	620
	ORGANIZATION AND BASE		
052	TACTICAL C-E EQUIPMENT	8,100	8,100
	MODIFICATIONS		
056	COMM ELECT MODS	3,800	3,800
	BASE SUPPORT EQUIPMENT		
061	ENGINEERING AND EOD EQUIPMENT	53,900	53,900
	SPECIAL SUPPORT PROJECTS		
067	DCGS-AF	800	800
	CLASSIFIED PROGRAMS		
070A	CLASSIFIED PROGRAMS	3,609,978	3,609,978
	TOTAL OTHER PROCUREMENT, AIR FORCE	**3,834,165**	**3,834,165**
	PROCUREMENT, DEFENSE-WIDE		
	MAJOR EQUIPMENT, DISA		
007	TELEPORT PROGRAM	1,900	1,900
	CLASSIFIED PROGRAMS		
040A	CLASSIFIED PROGRAMS	32,482	32,482
	AVIATION PROGRAMS		
041	MC–12	5,000	5,000
043	UNMANNED ISR	11,880	11,880
046	U–28	38,283	38,283
	AMMUNITION PROGRAMS		
057	ORDNANCE ITEMS <$5M	52,504	52,504
	OTHER PROCUREMENT PROGRAMS		
058	INTELLIGENCE SYSTEMS	22,000	22,000
060	OTHER ITEMS <$5M	11,580	11,580
062	SPECIAL PROGRAMS	13,549	13,549
063	TACTICAL VEHICLES	3,200	3,200
069	OPERATIONAL ENHANCEMENTS	42,056	22,806

SEC. 4102. PROCUREMENT FOR OVERSEAS CONTINGENCY OPERATIONS
(In Thousands of Dollars)

Line	Item	FY 2017 Request	Conference Authorized
	Classified adjustment		[–19,250]
	TOTAL PROCUREMENT, DEFENSE-WIDE	**234,434**	**215,184**
	TOTAL PROCUREMENT	**8,614,221**	**8,704,921**

SEC. 4103. PROCUREMENT FOR OVERSEAS CONTINGENCY OPERATIONS FOR BASE REQUIREMENTS.

SEC. 4103. PROCUREMENT FOR OVERSEAS CONTINGENCY OPERATIONS FOR BASE REQUIREMENTS
(In Thousands of Dollars)

Line	Item	FY 2017 Request	Conference Authorized
	AIRCRAFT PROCUREMENT, ARMY		
	ROTARY		
006	AH–64 APACHE BLOCK IIIA REMAN	78,040	78,040
	TOTAL AIRCRAFT PROCUREMENT, ARMY	**78,040**	**78,040**
	MISSILE PROCUREMENT, ARMY		
	AIR-TO-SURFACE MISSILE SYSTEM		
004	HELLFIRE SYS SUMMARY	150,000	150,000
	ANTI-TANK/ASSAULT MISSILE SYS		
007	JAVELIN (AAWS-M) SYSTEM SUMMARY		104,200
	Army unfunded requirement		[104,200]
010	GUIDED MLRS ROCKET (GMLRS)		76,000
	Army unfunded requirement		[76,000]
	MODIFICATIONS		
014	ATACMS MODS		15,900
	Army unfunded requirement		[15,900]
	TOTAL MISSILE PROCUREMENT, ARMY	**150,000**	**346,100**
	PROCUREMENT OF AMMUNITION, ARMY		
	SMALL/MEDIUM CAL AMMUNITION		
001	CTG, 5.56MM, ALL TYPES		4,000
	Army unfunded requirement		[4,000]
002	CTG, 7.62MM, ALL TYPES		14,000
	Army unfunded requirement		[14,000]
003	CTG, HANDGUN, ALL TYPES		9,000
	Army unfunded requirement		[9,000]
004	CTG, .50 CAL, ALL TYPES		20,000
	Army unfunded requirement		[20,000]
005	CTG, 20MM, ALL TYPES		14,000
	Army unfunded requirement		[14,000]
007	CTG, 30MM, ALL TYPES		8,200
	Army unfunded requirement		[8,200]
	MORTAR AMMUNITION		
011	120MM MORTAR, ALL TYPES		30,000
	Army unfunded requirement		[30,000]
	TANK AMMUNITION		
012	CARTRIDGES, TANK, 105MM AND 120MM, ALL TYPES		35,000
	Army unfunded requirement		[35,000]
	ARTILLERY AMMUNITION		
015	PROJ 155MM EXTENDED RANGE M982		23,500
	Army unfunded requirement		[23,500]
016	ARTILLERY PROPELLANTS, FUZES AND PRIMERS, ALL		10,000
	Army unfunded requirement		[10,000]
	ROCKETS		
019	SHOULDER LAUNCHED MUNITIONS, ALL TYPES		30,000
	Army unfunded requirement		[30,000]
020	ROCKET, HYDRA 70, ALL TYPES		42,500
	Army unfunded requirement		[27,500]
	Army unfunded requirement- guided hydra rockets		[15,000]
	TOTAL PROCUREMENT OF AMMUNITION, ARMY		**240,200**
	OTHER PROCUREMENT, ARMY		
	TACTICAL VEHICLES		
008	FAMILY OF MEDIUM TACTICAL VEH (FMTV)	152,000	152,000
	GENERATORS		
158	GENERATORS AND ASSOCIATED EQUIP	9,900	9,900
	TOTAL OTHER PROCUREMENT, ARMY	**161,900**	**161,900**
	JOINT IMPROVISED-THREAT DEFEAT FUND		
	NETWORK ATTACK		
001	RAPID ACQUISITION AND THREAT RESPONSE	113,272	113,272
	TOTAL JOINT IMPROVISED-THREAT DEFEAT FUND	**113,272**	**113,272**

AIRCRAFT PROCUREMENT, NAVY

SEC. 4103. PROCUREMENT FOR OVERSEAS CONTINGENCY OPERATIONS FOR BASE REQUIREMENTS
(In Thousands of Dollars)

Line	Item	FY 2017 Request	Conference Authorized
	MODIFICATION OF AIRCRAFT		
035	SH–60 SERIES	3,000	3,000
036	H–1 SERIES	3,740	3,740
051	COMMON ECM EQUIPMENT	27,460	27,460
	TOTAL AIRCRAFT PROCUREMENT, NAVY	**34,200**	**34,200**
	WEAPONS PROCUREMENT, NAVY		
	STRATEGIC MISSILES		
003	TOMAHAWK		84,200
	Scope Increase		[84,200]
	TACTICAL MISSILES		
005	SIDEWINDER		33,000
	Navy unfunded requirement		[33,000]
	TOTAL WEAPONS PROCUREMENT, NAVY		**117,200**
	PROCUREMENT OF AMMO, NAVY & MC		
	NAVY AMMUNITION		
001	GENERAL PURPOSE BOMBS		58,000
	Navy unfunded requirement—JDAM components		[58,000]
	MARINE CORPS AMMUNITION		
023	ARTILLERY, ALL TYPES		19,200
	Marine Corps unfunded requirement- GMLRS AW munitions		[19,200]
	TOTAL PROCUREMENT OF AMMO, NAVY & MC		**77,200**
	OTHER PROCUREMENT, NAVY		
	OTHER ORDNANCE SUPPORT EQUIPMENT		
116	EXPLOSIVE ORDNANCE DISPOSAL EQUIP	59,329	59,329
	TOTAL OTHER PROCUREMENT, NAVY	**59,329**	**59,329**
	AIRCRAFT PROCUREMENT, AIR FORCE		
	OTHER AIRCRAFT		
015	MQ–9	179,430	179,430
	TOTAL AIRCRAFT PROCUREMENT, AIR FORCE	**179,430**	**179,430**
	MISSILE PROCUREMENT, AIR FORCE		
	TACTICAL		
007	SMALL DIAMETER BOMB	167,800	167,800
	CLASS IV		
011	AGM–65D MAVERICK	16,900	16,900
	TOTAL MISSILE PROCUREMENT, AIR FORCE	**184,700**	**184,700**
	PROCUREMENT OF AMMUNITION, AIR FORCE		
	ROCKETS		
001	ROCKETS	60,000	60,000
	BOMBS		
006	JOINT DIRECT ATTACK MUNITION	263,000	263,000
	TOTAL PROCUREMENT OF AMMUNITION, AIR FORCE	**323,000**	**323,000**
	PROCUREMENT, DEFENSE-WIDE		
	MAJOR EQUIPMENT, DISA		
007	TELEPORT PROGRAM	2,000	2,000
016	DEFENSE INFORMATION SYSTEMS NETWORK	2,000	2,000
	TOTAL PROCUREMENT, DEFENSE-WIDE	**4,000**	**4,000**
	TOTAL PROCUREMENT	**1,287,871**	**1,918,571**

TITLE XLII—RESEARCH, DEVELOPMENT, TEST, AND EVALUATION

SEC. 4201. RESEARCH, DEVELOPMENT, TEST, AND EVALUATION.

SEC. 4201. RESEARCH, DEVELOPMENT, TEST, AND EVALUATION
(In Thousands of Dollars)

Line	Program Element	Item	FY 2017 Request	Conference Authorized
		RESEARCH, DEVELOPMENT, TEST & EVAL, ARMY		
		BASIC RESEARCH		
001	0601101A	IN-HOUSE LABORATORY INDEPENDENT RESEARCH	12,381	12,381
002	0601102A	DEFENSE RESEARCH SCIENCES	253,116	253,116
003	0601103A	UNIVERSITY RESEARCH INITIATIVES	69,166	69,166
004	0601104A	UNIVERSITY AND INDUSTRY RESEARCH CENTERS	94,280	94,280
		SUBTOTAL BASIC RESEARCH	**428,943**	**428,943**
		APPLIED RESEARCH		
005	0602105A	MATERIALS TECHNOLOGY	31,533	37,033
		Ground vehicle coating system		[5,500]

SEC. 4201. RESEARCH, DEVELOPMENT, TEST, AND EVALUATION
(In Thousands of Dollars)

Line	Program Element	Item	FY 2017 Request	Conference Authorized
006	0602120A	SENSORS AND ELECTRONIC SURVIVABILITY	36,109	38,109
		Program increase		[2,000]
007	0602122A	TRACTOR HIP	6,995	6,995
008	0602211A	AVIATION TECHNOLOGY	65,914	65,914
009	0602270A	ELECTRONIC WARFARE TECHNOLOGY	25,466	25,466
010	0602303A	MISSILE TECHNOLOGY	44,313	44,313
011	0602307A	ADVANCED WEAPONS TECHNOLOGY	28,803	28,803
012	0602308A	ADVANCED CONCEPTS AND SIMULATION	27,688	27,688
013	0602601A	COMBAT VEHICLE AND AUTOMOTIVE TECHNOLOGY	67,959	67,959
014	0602618A	BALLISTICS TECHNOLOGY	85,436	85,436
015	0602622A	CHEMICAL, SMOKE AND EQUIPMENT DEFEATING TECHNOLOGY	3,923	3,923
016	0602623A	JOINT SERVICE SMALL ARMS PROGRAM	5,545	5,545
017	0602624A	WEAPONS AND MUNITIONS TECHNOLOGY	53,581	53,581
018	0602705A	ELECTRONICS AND ELECTRONIC DEVICES	56,322	56,322
019	0602709A	NIGHT VISION TECHNOLOGY	36,079	36,079
020	0602712A	COUNTERMINE SYSTEMS	26,497	26,497
021	0602716A	HUMAN FACTORS ENGINEERING TECHNOLOGY	23,671	23,671
022	0602720A	ENVIRONMENTAL QUALITY TECHNOLOGY	22,151	22,151
023	0602782A	COMMAND, CONTROL, COMMUNICATIONS TECHNOLOGY	37,803	37,803
024	0602783A	COMPUTER AND SOFTWARE TECHNOLOGY	13,811	13,811
025	0602784A	MILITARY ENGINEERING TECHNOLOGY	67,416	67,416
026	0602785A	MANPOWER/PERSONNEL/TRAINING TECHNOLOGY	26,045	26,045
027	0602786A	WARFIGHTER TECHNOLOGY	37,403	42,403
		Program Increase		[5,000]
028	0602787A	MEDICAL TECHNOLOGY	77,111	77,111
		SUBTOTAL APPLIED RESEARCH	**907,574**	**920,074**
		ADVANCED TECHNOLOGY DEVELOPMENT		
029	0603001A	WARFIGHTER ADVANCED TECHNOLOGY	38,831	38,831
030	0603002A	MEDICAL ADVANCED TECHNOLOGY	68,365	68,365
031	0603003A	AVIATION ADVANCED TECHNOLOGY	94,280	94,280
032	0603004A	WEAPONS AND MUNITIONS ADVANCED TECHNOLOGY	68,714	68,714
033	0603005A	COMBAT VEHICLE AND AUTOMOTIVE ADVANCED TECHNOLOGY	122,132	152,132
		Emerging requirement		[30,000]
034	0603006A	SPACE APPLICATION ADVANCED TECHNOLOGY	3,904	3,904
035	0603007A	MANPOWER, PERSONNEL AND TRAINING ADVANCED TECHNOLOGY	14,417	14,417
037	0603009A	TRACTOR HIKE	8,074	21,374
		Classified adjustment		[13,300]
038	0603015A	NEXT GENERATION TRAINING & SIMULATION SYSTEMS	18,969	18,969
039	0603020A	TRACTOR ROSE	11,910	11,910
040	0603125A	COMBATING TERRORISM—TECHNOLOGY DEVELOPMENT	27,686	27,686
041	0603130A	TRACTOR NAIL	2,340	2,340
042	0603131A	TRACTOR EGGS	2,470	2,470
043	0603270A	ELECTRONIC WARFARE TECHNOLOGY	27,893	27,893
044	0603313A	MISSILE AND ROCKET ADVANCED TECHNOLOGY	52,190	52,190
045	0603322A	TRACTOR CAGE	11,107	11,107
046	0603461A	HIGH PERFORMANCE COMPUTING MODERNIZATION PROGRAM	177,190	179,190
		Program increase		[2,000]
047	0603606A	LANDMINE WARFARE AND BARRIER ADVANCED TECHNOLOGY	17,451	17,451
048	0603607A	JOINT SERVICE SMALL ARMS PROGRAM	5,839	5,839
049	0603710A	NIGHT VISION ADVANCED TECHNOLOGY	44,468	44,468
050	0603728A	ENVIRONMENTAL QUALITY TECHNOLOGY DEMONSTRATIONS	11,137	11,137
051	0603734A	MILITARY ENGINEERING ADVANCED TECHNOLOGY	20,684	20,684
052	0603772A	ADVANCED TACTICAL COMPUTER SCIENCE AND SENSOR TECHNOLOGY	44,239	44,239
053	0603794A	C3 ADVANCED TECHNOLOGY	35,775	35,775
		SUBTOTAL ADVANCED TECHNOLOGY DEVELOPMENT	**930,065**	**975,365**
		ADVANCED COMPONENT DEVELOPMENT & PROTOTYPES		
054	0603305A	ARMY MISSILE DEFENSE SYSTEMS INTEGRATION	9,433	9,433
055	0603308A	ARMY SPACE SYSTEMS INTEGRATION	23,056	23,056
056	0603619A	LANDMINE WARFARE AND BARRIER—ADV DEV	72,117	72,117
057	0603627A	SMOKE, OBSCURANT AND TARGET DEFEATING SYS-ADV DEV	28,244	28,244
058	0603639A	TANK AND MEDIUM CALIBER AMMUNITION	40,096	40,096
059	0603747A	SOLDIER SUPPORT AND SURVIVABILITY	10,506	10,506
060	0603766A	TACTICAL ELECTRONIC SURVEILLANCE SYSTEM—ADV DEV	15,730	15,730
061	0603774A	NIGHT VISION SYSTEMS ADVANCED DEVELOPMENT	10,321	10,321
062	0603779A	ENVIRONMENTAL QUALITY TECHNOLOGY—DEM/VAL	7,785	7,785
063	0603790A	NATO RESEARCH AND DEVELOPMENT	2,300	2,300
064	0603801A	AVIATION—ADV DEV	10,014	10,014
065	0603804A	LOGISTICS AND ENGINEER EQUIPMENT—ADV DEV	20,834	20,834
066	0603807A	MEDICAL SYSTEMS—ADV DEV	33,503	33,503
067	0603827A	SOLDIER SYSTEMS—ADVANCED DEVELOPMENT	31,120	40,520
		Accelerate small arms improvement		[9,400]
068	0604100A	ANALYSIS OF ALTERNATIVES	6,608	6,608
069	0604114A	LOWER TIER AIR MISSILE DEFENSE (LTAMD) SENSOR	35,132	35,132
070	0604115A	TECHNOLOGY MATURATION INITIATIVES	70,047	61,038
		Excess growth		[-9,009]
071	0604120A	ASSURED POSITIONING, NAVIGATION AND TIMING (PNT)	83,279	83,279
073	0305251A	CYBERSPACE OPERATIONS FORCES AND FORCE SUPPORT	40,510	30,510

SEC. 4201. RESEARCH, DEVELOPMENT, TEST, AND EVALUATION
(In Thousands of Dollars)

Line	Program Element	Item	FY 2017 Request	Conference Authorized
		Inadequate justification		[–10,000]
		SUBTOTAL ADVANCED COMPONENT DEVELOPMENT & PROTOTYPES	550,635	541,026
		SYSTEM DEVELOPMENT & DEMONSTRATION		
074	0604201A	AIRCRAFT AVIONICS	83,248	83,248
075	0604270A	ELECTRONIC WARFARE DEVELOPMENT	34,642	34,642
077	0604290A	MID-TIER NETWORKING VEHICULAR RADIO (MNVR)	12,172	12,172
078	0604321A	ALL SOURCE ANALYSIS SYSTEM	3,958	3,958
079	0604328A	TRACTOR CAGE	12,525	12,525
080	0604601A	INFANTRY SUPPORT WEAPONS	66,943	66,943
082	0604611A	JAVELIN	20,011	20,011
083	0604622A	FAMILY OF HEAVY TACTICAL VEHICLES	11,429	11,429
084	0604633A	AIR TRAFFIC CONTROL	3,421	3,421
085	0604641A	TACTICAL UNMANNED GROUND VEHICLE (TUGV)	39,282	39,282
086	0604642A	LIGHT TACTICAL WHEELED VEHICLES	494	494
087	0604645A	ARMORED SYSTEMS MODERNIZATION (ASM)—ENG DEV	9,678	9,678
088	0604710A	NIGHT VISION SYSTEMS—ENG DEV	84,519	84,519
089	0604713A	COMBAT FEEDING, CLOTHING, AND EQUIPMENT	2,054	2,054
090	0604715A	NON-SYSTEM TRAINING DEVICES—ENG DEV	30,774	30,774
091	0604741A	AIR DEFENSE COMMAND, CONTROL AND INTELLIGENCE—ENG DEV	53,332	61,332
		Program increase- all digital radar technology for CRAM		[8,000]
092	0604742A	CONSTRUCTIVE SIMULATION SYSTEMS DEVELOPMENT	17,887	17,887
093	0604746A	AUTOMATIC TEST EQUIPMENT DEVELOPMENT	8,813	8,813
094	0604760A	DISTRIBUTIVE INTERACTIVE SIMULATIONS (DIS)—ENG DEV	10,487	10,487
095	0604780A	COMBINED ARMS TACTICAL TRAINER (CATT) CORE	15,068	15,068
096	0604798A	BRIGADE ANALYSIS, INTEGRATION AND EVALUATION	89,716	89,716
097	0604802A	WEAPONS AND MUNITIONS—ENG DEV	80,365	80,365
098	0604804A	LOGISTICS AND ENGINEER EQUIPMENT—ENG DEV	75,098	86,198
		Program Increase- next generation signature management		[11,100]
099	0604805A	COMMAND, CONTROL, COMMUNICATIONS SYSTEMS—ENG DEV	4,245	4,245
100	0604807A	MEDICAL MATERIEL/MEDICAL BIOLOGICAL DEFENSE EQUIPMENT—ENG DEV	41,124	41,124
101	0604808A	LANDMINE WARFARE/BARRIER—ENG DEV	39,630	39,630
102	0604818A	ARMY TACTICAL COMMAND & CONTROL HARDWARE & SOFTWARE	205,590	205,590
103	0604820A	RADAR DEVELOPMENT	15,983	15,983
104	0604822A	GENERAL FUND ENTERPRISE BUSINESS SYSTEM (GFEBS)	6,805	6,805
105	0604823A	FIREFINDER	9,235	9,235
106	0604827A	SOLDIER SYSTEMS—WARRIOR DEM/VAL	12,393	12,393
107	0604854A	ARTILLERY SYSTEMS—EMD	1,756	1,756
108	0605013A	INFORMATION TECHNOLOGY DEVELOPMENT	74,236	74,236
109	0605018A	INTEGRATED PERSONNEL AND PAY SYSTEM-ARMY (IPPS-A)	155,584	144,584
		Unjustified growth		[–11,000]
110	0605028A	ARMORED MULTI-PURPOSE VEHICLE (AMPV)	184,221	184,221
111	0605029A	INTEGRATED GROUND SECURITY SURVEILLANCE RESPONSE CAPABILITY (IGSSR-C)	4,980	4,980
112	0605030A	JOINT TACTICAL NETWORK CENTER (JTNC)	15,041	15,041
113	0605031A	JOINT TACTICAL NETWORK (JTN)	16,014	16,014
114	0605032A	TRACTOR TIRE	27,254	27,254
115	0605033A	GROUND-BASED OPERATIONAL SURVEILLANCE SYSTEM—EXPEDITIONARY (GBOSS-E)	5,032	5,032
116	0605034A	TACTICAL SECURITY SYSTEM (TSS)	2,904	2,904
117	0605035A	COMMON INFRARED COUNTERMEASURES (CIRCM)	96,977	96,977
118	0605036A	COMBATING WEAPONS OF MASS DESTRUCTION (CWMD)	2,089	2,089
119	0605041A	DEFENSIVE CYBER TOOL DEVELOPMENT	33,836	33,836
120	0605042A	TACTICAL NETWORK RADIO SYSTEMS (LOW-TIER)	18,824	18,824
121	0605047A	CONTRACT WRITING SYSTEM	20,663	20,663
122	0605051A	AIRCRAFT SURVIVABILITY DEVELOPMENT	41,133	41,133
123	0605052A	INDIRECT FIRE PROTECTION CAPABILITY INC 2—BLOCK 1	83,995	83,995
125	0605380A	AMF JOINT TACTICAL RADIO SYSTEM (JTRS)	5,028	5,028
126	0605450A	JOINT AIR-TO-GROUND MISSILE (JAGM)	42,972	42,972
128	0605457A	ARMY INTEGRATED AIR AND MISSILE DEFENSE (AIAMD)	252,811	252,811
131	0605766A	NATIONAL CAPABILITIES INTEGRATION (MIP)	4,955	4,955
132	0605812A	JOINT LIGHT TACTICAL VEHICLE (JLTV) ENGINEERING AND MANUFACTURING DEVELOPMENT PH.	11,530	11,530
133	0605830A	AVIATION GROUND SUPPORT EQUIPMENT	2,142	2,142
134	0210609A	PALADIN INTEGRATED MANAGEMENT (PIM)	41,498	41,498
135	0303032A	TROJAN—RH12	4,273	4,273
136	0304270A	ELECTRONIC WARFARE DEVELOPMENT	14,425	14,425
		SUBTOTAL SYSTEM DEVELOPMENT & DEMONSTRATION	**2,265,094**	**2,273,194**
		RDT&E MANAGEMENT SUPPORT		
137	0604256A	THREAT SIMULATOR DEVELOPMENT	25,675	25,675
138	0604258A	TARGET SYSTEMS DEVELOPMENT	19,122	19,122
139	0604759A	MAJOR T&E INVESTMENT	84,777	84,777
140	0605103A	RAND ARROYO CENTER	20,658	20,658
141	0605301A	ARMY KWAJALEIN ATOLL	236,648	236,648
142	0605326A	CONCEPTS EXPERIMENTATION PROGRAM	25,596	25,596
144	0605601A	ARMY TEST RANGES AND FACILITIES	293,748	293,748
145	0605602A	ARMY TECHNICAL TEST INSTRUMENTATION AND TARGETS	52,404	52,404
146	0605604A	SURVIVABILITY/LETHALITY ANALYSIS	38,571	38,571
147	0605606A	AIRCRAFT CERTIFICATION	4,665	4,665
148	0605702A	METEOROLOGICAL SUPPORT TO RDT&E ACTIVITIES	6,925	6,925

SEC. 4201. RESEARCH, DEVELOPMENT, TEST, AND EVALUATION
(In Thousands of Dollars)

Line	Program Element	Item	FY 2017 Request	Conference Authorized
149	0605706A	MATERIEL SYSTEMS ANALYSIS	21,677	21,677
150	0605709A	EXPLOITATION OF FOREIGN ITEMS	12,415	12,415
151	0605712A	SUPPORT OF OPERATIONAL TESTING	49,684	49,684
152	0605716A	ARMY EVALUATION CENTER	55,905	55,905
153	0605718A	ARMY MODELING & SIM X-CMD COLLABORATION & INTEG	7,959	7,959
154	0605801A	PROGRAMWIDE ACTIVITIES	51,822	51,822
155	0605803A	TECHNICAL INFORMATION ACTIVITIES	33,323	33,323
156	0605805A	MUNITIONS STANDARDIZATION, EFFECTIVENESS AND SAFETY	40,545	40,545
157	0605857A	ENVIRONMENTAL QUALITY TECHNOLOGY MGMT SUPPORT	2,130	2,130
158	0605898A	MANAGEMENT HQ—R&D	49,885	49,885
159	0303260A	DEFENSE MILITARY DECEPTION INITIATIVE	2,000	2,000
		SUBTOTAL RDT&E MANAGEMENT SUPPORT	**1,136,134**	**1,136,134**
		OPERATIONAL SYSTEMS DEVELOPMENT		
161	0603778A	MLRS PRODUCT IMPROVEMENT PROGRAM	9,663	9,663
162	0603813A	TRACTOR PULL	3,960	3,960
163	0605024A	ANTI-TAMPER TECHNOLOGY SUPPORT	3,638	3,638
164	0607131A	WEAPONS AND MUNITIONS PRODUCT IMPROVEMENT PROGRAMS	14,517	14,517
165	0607133A	TRACTOR SMOKE	4,479	4,479
166	0607134A	LONG RANGE PRECISION FIRES (LRPF)	39,275	39,275
167	0607135A	APACHE PRODUCT IMPROVEMENT PROGRAM	66,441	66,441
168	0607136A	BLACKHAWK PRODUCT IMPROVEMENT PROGRAM	46,765	46,765
169	0607137A	CHINOOK PRODUCT IMPROVEMENT PROGRAM	91,848	91,848
170	0607138A	FIXED WING PRODUCT IMPROVEMENT PROGRAM	796	796
171	0607139A	IMPROVED TURBINE ENGINE PROGRAM	126,105	126,105
172	0607140A	EMERGING TECHNOLOGIES FROM NIE	2,369	2,369
173	0607141A	LOGISTICS AUTOMATION	4,563	4,563
174	0607665A	FAMILY OF BIOMETRICS	12,098	12,098
175	0607865A	PATRIOT PRODUCT IMPROVEMENT	49,482	49,482
176	0202429A	AEROSTAT JOINT PROJECT—COCOM EXERCISE	45,482	2,482
		Program reduction		[−43,000]
178	0203728A	JOINT AUTOMATED DEEP OPERATION COORDINATION SYSTEM (JADOCS)	30,455	30,455
179	0203735A	COMBAT VEHICLE IMPROVEMENT PROGRAMS	316,857	316,857
180	0203740A	MANEUVER CONTROL SYSTEM	4,031	4,031
181	0203744A	AIRCRAFT MODIFICATIONS/PRODUCT IMPROVEMENT PROGRAMS	35,793	35,793
182	0203752A	AIRCRAFT ENGINE COMPONENT IMPROVEMENT PROGRAM	259	259
183	0203758A	DIGITIZATION	6,483	6,483
184	0203801A	MISSILE/AIR DEFENSE PRODUCT IMPROVEMENT PROGRAM	5,122	5,122
185	0203802A	OTHER MISSILE PRODUCT IMPROVEMENT PROGRAMS	7,491	7,491
186	0203808A	TRACTOR CARD	20,333	20,333
188	0205410A	MATERIALS HANDLING EQUIPMENT	124	124
190	0205456A	LOWER TIER AIR AND MISSILE DEFENSE (AMD) SYSTEM	69,417	69,417
191	0205778A	GUIDED MULTIPLE-LAUNCH ROCKET SYSTEM (GMLRS)	22,044	22,044
192	0208053A	JOINT TACTICAL GROUND SYSTEM	12,649	12,649
194	0303028A	SECURITY AND INTELLIGENCE ACTIVITIES	11,619	11,619
195	0303140A	INFORMATION SYSTEMS SECURITY PROGRAM	38,280	38,280
196	0303141A	GLOBAL COMBAT SUPPORT SYSTEM	27,223	27,223
197	0303142A	SATCOM GROUND ENVIRONMENT (SPACE)	18,815	18,815
198	0303150A	WWMCCS/GLOBAL COMMAND AND CONTROL SYSTEM	4,718	4,718
202	0305204A	TACTICAL UNMANNED AERIAL VEHICLES	8,218	8,218
203	0305206A	AIRBORNE RECONNAISSANCE SYSTEMS	11,799	11,799
204	0305208A	DISTRIBUTED COMMON GROUND/SURFACE SYSTEMS	32,284	32,284
205	0305219A	MQ–1C GRAY EAGLE UAS	13,470	13,470
206	0305232A	RQ–11 UAV	1,613	1,613
207	0305233A	RQ–7 UAV	4,597	4,597
209	0310349A	WIN-T INCREMENT 2—INITIAL NETWORKING	4,867	4,867
210	0708045A	END ITEM INDUSTRIAL PREPAREDNESS ACTIVITIES	62,287	62,287
210A	9999999999	CLASSIFIED PROGRAMS	4,625	4,625
		SUBTOTAL OPERATIONAL SYSTEMS DEVELOPMENT	**1,296,954**	**1,253,954**
		TOTAL RESEARCH, DEVELOPMENT, TEST & EVAL, ARMY	**7,515,399**	**7,528,690**
		RESEARCH, DEVELOPMENT, TEST & EVAL, NAVY		
		BASIC RESEARCH		
001	0601103N	UNIVERSITY RESEARCH INITIATIVES	101,714	121,714
		Program increase		[20,000]
002	0601152N	IN-HOUSE LABORATORY INDEPENDENT RESEARCH	18,508	18,508
003	0601153N	DEFENSE RESEARCH SCIENCES	422,748	422,748
		SUBTOTAL BASIC RESEARCH	**542,970**	**562,970**
		APPLIED RESEARCH		
004	0602114N	POWER PROJECTION APPLIED RESEARCH	41,371	41,371
005	0602123N	FORCE PROTECTION APPLIED RESEARCH	158,745	158,745
006	0602131M	MARINE CORPS LANDING FORCE TECHNOLOGY	51,590	51,590
007	0602235N	COMMON PICTURE APPLIED RESEARCH	41,185	41,185
008	0602236N	WARFIGHTER SUSTAINMENT APPLIED RESEARCH	45,467	45,467
009	0602271N	ELECTROMAGNETIC SYSTEMS APPLIED RESEARCH	118,941	118,941
010	0602435N	OCEAN WARFIGHTING ENVIRONMENT APPLIED RESEARCH	42,618	72,618
		Service Life Extension Program—AGOR		[30,000]

SEC. 4201. RESEARCH, DEVELOPMENT, TEST, AND EVALUATION
(In Thousands of Dollars)

Line	Program Element	Item	FY 2017 Request	Conference Authorized
011	0602651M	JOINT NON-LETHAL WEAPONS APPLIED RESEARCH	6,327	6,327
012	0602747N	UNDERSEA WARFARE APPLIED RESEARCH	126,313	126,313
013	0602750N	FUTURE NAVAL CAPABILITIES APPLIED RESEARCH	165,103	165,103
014	0602782N	MINE AND EXPEDITIONARY WARFARE APPLIED RESEARCH	33,916	33,916
015	0602898N	SCIENCE AND TECHNOLOGY MANAGEMENT—ONR HEADQUARTERS	29,575	29,575
		SUBTOTAL APPLIED RESEARCH	861,151	891,151
		ADVANCED TECHNOLOGY DEVELOPMENT		
016	0603114N	POWER PROJECTION ADVANCED TECHNOLOGY	96,406	96,406
017	0603123N	FORCE PROTECTION ADVANCED TECHNOLOGY	48,438	48,438
018	0603271N	ELECTROMAGNETIC SYSTEMS ADVANCED TECHNOLOGY	26,421	26,421
019	0603640M	USMC ADVANCED TECHNOLOGY DEMONSTRATION (ATD)	140,416	140,416
020	0603651M	JOINT NON-LETHAL WEAPONS TECHNOLOGY DEVELOPMENT	13,117	13,117
021	0603673N	FUTURE NAVAL CAPABILITIES ADVANCED TECHNOLOGY DEVELOPMENT	249,092	247,092
		Capable manpower, and power and energy		*[−2,000]*
022	0603680N	MANUFACTURING TECHNOLOGY PROGRAM	56,712	56,712
023	0603729N	WARFIGHTER PROTECTION ADVANCED TECHNOLOGY	4,789	4,789
024	0603747N	UNDERSEA WARFARE ADVANCED TECHNOLOGY	25,880	25,880
025	0603758N	NAVY WARFIGHTING EXPERIMENTS AND DEMONSTRATIONS	60,550	60,550
026	0603782N	MINE AND EXPEDITIONARY WARFARE ADVANCED TECHNOLOGY	15,167	15,167
		SUBTOTAL ADVANCED TECHNOLOGY DEVELOPMENT	736,988	734,988
		ADVANCED COMPONENT DEVELOPMENT & PROTOTYPES		
027	0603207N	AIR/OCEAN TACTICAL APPLICATIONS	48,536	48,536
028	0603216N	AVIATION SURVIVABILITY	5,239	5,239
030	0603251N	AIRCRAFT SYSTEMS	1,519	1,519
031	0603254N	ASW SYSTEMS DEVELOPMENT	7,041	7,041
032	0603261N	TACTICAL AIRBORNE RECONNAISSANCE	3,274	3,274
033	0603382N	ADVANCED COMBAT SYSTEMS TECHNOLOGY	57,034	15,496
		Rapid prototype development excess growth		*[−30,267]*
		Unmanned rapid prototype development excess growth		*[−11,271]*
034	0603502N	SURFACE AND SHALLOW WATER MINE COUNTERMEASURES	165,775	143,548
		Excess prior year funds		*[−1,500]*
		LDUUV product development excess growth		*[−13,800]*
		USV with AQS–20 product development excess growth		*[−5,750]*
		USV with AQS–20 support excess growth		*[−1,177]*
035	0603506N	SURFACE SHIP TORPEDO DEFENSE	87,066	87,066
036	0603512N	CARRIER SYSTEMS DEVELOPMENT	7,605	7,605
037	0603525N	PILOT FISH	132,068	132,068
038	0603527N	RETRACT LARCH	14,546	14,546
039	0603536N	RETRACT JUNIPER	115,435	115,435
040	0603542N	RADIOLOGICAL CONTROL	702	702
041	0603553N	SURFACE ASW	1,081	1,081
042	0603561N	ADVANCED SUBMARINE SYSTEM DEVELOPMENT	100,565	100,565
043	0603562N	SUBMARINE TACTICAL WARFARE SYSTEMS	8,782	8,782
044	0603563N	SHIP CONCEPT ADVANCED DESIGN	14,590	14,590
045	0603564N	SHIP PRELIMINARY DESIGN & FEASIBILITY STUDIES	15,805	15,805
046	0603570N	ADVANCED NUCLEAR POWER SYSTEMS	453,313	453,313
047	0603573N	ADVANCED SURFACE MACHINERY SYSTEMS	36,655	36,655
048	0603576N	CHALK EAGLE	367,016	367,016
049	0603581N	LITTORAL COMBAT SHIP (LCS)	51,630	51,630
050	0603582N	COMBAT SYSTEM INTEGRATION	23,530	23,530
051	0603595N	OHIO REPLACEMENT	700,811	700,811
052	0603596N	LCS MISSION MODULES	160,058	129,187
		Program Restructure		*[−30,871]*
053	0603597N	AUTOMATED TEST AND ANALYSIS		8,000
		Program increase		*[8,000]*
054	0603599N	FRIGATE DEVELOPMENT	84,900	84,900
055	0603609N	CONVENTIONAL MUNITIONS	8,342	8,342
056	0603611M	MARINE CORPS ASSAULT VEHICLES	158,682	138,762
		Product development prior year carryover		*[−19,920]*
057	0603635M	MARINE CORPS GROUND COMBAT/SUPPORT SYSTEM	1,303	1,303
058	0603654N	JOINT SERVICE EXPLOSIVE ORDNANCE DEVELOPMENT	46,911	46,911
060	0603713N	OCEAN ENGINEERING TECHNOLOGY DEVELOPMENT	4,556	4,556
061	0603721N	ENVIRONMENTAL PROTECTION	20,343	20,343
062	0603724N	NAVY ENERGY PROGRAM	52,479	52,479
063	0603725N	FACILITIES IMPROVEMENT	5,458	5,458
064	0603734N	CHALK CORAL	245,860	245,860
065	0603739N	NAVY LOGISTIC PRODUCTIVITY	3,089	3,089
066	0603746N	RETRACT MAPLE	323,526	323,526
067	0603748N	LINK PLUMERIA	318,497	318,497
068	0603751N	RETRACT ELM	52,834	52,834
069	0603764N	LINK EVERGREEN	48,116	48,116
070	0603787N	SPECIAL PROCESSES	13,619	13,619
071	0603790N	NATO RESEARCH AND DEVELOPMENT	9,867	9,867
072	0603795N	LAND ATTACK TECHNOLOGY	6,015	6,015
073	0603851M	JOINT NON-LETHAL WEAPONS TESTING	27,904	27,904
074	0603860N	JOINT PRECISION APPROACH AND LANDING SYSTEMS—DEM/VAL	104,144	102,722
		UCLASS test support unjustified request		*[−1,422]*

SEC. 4201. RESEARCH, DEVELOPMENT, TEST, AND EVALUATION
(In Thousands of Dollars)

Line	Program Element	Item	FY 2017 Request	Conference Authorized
075	0603925N	DIRECTED ENERGY AND ELECTRIC WEAPON SYSTEMS	32,700	32,700
076	0604112N	GERALD R. FORD CLASS NUCLEAR AIRCRAFT CARRIER (CVN 78—80)	70,528	70,528
077	0604122N	REMOTE MINEHUNTING SYSTEM (RMS)	3,001	3,001
078	0604272N	TACTICAL AIR DIRECTIONAL INFRARED COUNTERMEASURES (TADIRCM)	34,920	34,920
080	0604292N	MH-XX	1,620	1,620
081	0604454N	LX (R)	6,354	6,354
082	0604536N	ADVANCED UNDERSEA PROTOTYPING	78,589	44,189
		Ahead of need		*[−34,400]*
084	0604659N	PRECISION STRIKE WEAPONS DEVELOPMENT PROGRAM	9,910	9,910
085	0604707N	SPACE AND ELECTRONIC WARFARE (SEW) ARCHITECTURE/ENGINEERING SUPPORT	23,971	23,971
086	0604786N	OFFENSIVE ANTI-SURFACE WARFARE WEAPON DEVELOPMENT	252,409	250,371
		Increment II early to need		*[−2,038]*
087	0605812M	JOINT LIGHT TACTICAL VEHICLE (JLTV) ENGINEERING AND MANUFACTURING DEVELOPMENT PH.	23,197	23,197
088	0303354N	ASW SYSTEMS DEVELOPMENT—MIP	9,110	9,110
089	0304270N	ELECTRONIC WARFARE DEVELOPMENT—MIP	437	437
		SUBTOTAL ADVANCED COMPONENT DEVELOPMENT & PROTOTYPES	**4,662,867**	**4,518,451**
		SYSTEM DEVELOPMENT & DEMONSTRATION		
090	0603208N	TRAINING SYSTEM AIRCRAFT	19,938	19,938
091	0604212N	OTHER HELO DEVELOPMENT	6,268	6,268
092	0604214N	AV-8B AIRCRAFT—ENG DEV	33,664	33,664
093	0604215N	STANDARDS DEVELOPMENT	1,300	1,300
094	0604216N	MULTI-MISSION HELICOPTER UPGRADE DEVELOPMENT	5,275	5,275
095	0604218N	AIR/OCEAN EQUIPMENT ENGINEERING	3,875	3,875
096	0604221N	P-3 MODERNIZATION PROGRAM	1,909	1,909
097	0604230N	WARFARE SUPPORT SYSTEM	13,237	13,237
098	0604231N	TACTICAL COMMAND SYSTEM	36,323	36,323
099	0604234N	ADVANCED HAWKEYE	363,792	363,792
100	0604245N	H-1 UPGRADES	27,441	27,441
101	0604261N	ACOUSTIC SEARCH SENSORS	34,525	34,525
102	0604262N	V-22A	174,423	157,698
		Hardware development airframe excess growth		*[−8,474]*
		Refueling system development excess growth		*[−8,251]*
103	0604264N	AIR CREW SYSTEMS DEVELOPMENT	13,577	13,577
104	0604269N	EA-18	116,761	116,761
105	0604270N	ELECTRONIC WARFARE DEVELOPMENT	48,766	48,766
106	0604273N	EXECUTIVE HELO DEVELOPMENT	338,357	338,357
107	0604274N	NEXT GENERATION JAMMER (NGJ)	577,822	577,822
108	0604280N	JOINT TACTICAL RADIO SYSTEM—NAVY (JTRS-NAVY)	2,365	2,365
109	0604282N	NEXT GENERATION JAMMER (NGJ) INCREMENT II	52,065	42,065
		Program growth		*[−10,000]*
110	0604307N	SURFACE COMBATANT COMBAT SYSTEM ENGINEERING	282,764	282,764
111	0604311N	LPD-17 CLASS SYSTEMS INTEGRATION	580	580
112	0604329N	SMALL DIAMETER BOMB (SDB)	97,622	97,622
113	0604366N	STANDARD MISSILE IMPROVEMENTS	120,561	120,561
114	0604373N	AIRBORNE MCM	45,622	45,622
116	0604378N	NAVAL INTEGRATED FIRE CONTROL—COUNTER AIR SYSTEMS ENGINEERING	25,750	25,750
118	0604501N	ADVANCED ABOVE WATER SENSORS	85,868	85,868
119	0604503N	SSN-688 AND TRIDENT MODERNIZATION	117,476	117,476
120	0604504N	AIR CONTROL	47,404	47,404
121	0604512N	SHIPBOARD AVIATION SYSTEMS	112,158	112,158
122	0604518N	COMBAT INFORMATION CENTER CONVERSION	6,283	6,283
123	0604522N	AIR AND MISSILE DEFENSE RADAR (AMDR) SYSTEM	144,395	144,395
124	0604558N	NEW DESIGN SSN	113,013	113,013
125	0604562N	SUBMARINE TACTICAL WARFARE SYSTEM	43,160	43,160
126	0604567N	SHIP CONTRACT DESIGN/ LIVE FIRE T&E	65,002	85,002
		CVN Design		*[20,000]*
127	0604574N	NAVY TACTICAL COMPUTER RESOURCES	3,098	3,098
128	0604580N	VIRGINIA PAYLOAD MODULE (VPM)	97,920	97,920
129	0604601N	MINE DEVELOPMENT	10,490	10,490
130	0604610N	LIGHTWEIGHT TORPEDO DEVELOPMENT	20,178	20,178
131	0604654N	JOINT SERVICE EXPLOSIVE ORDNANCE DEVELOPMENT	7,369	7,369
132	0604703N	PERSONNEL, TRAINING, SIMULATION, AND HUMAN FACTORS	4,995	4,995
133	0604727N	JOINT STANDOFF WEAPON SYSTEMS	412	412
134	0604755N	SHIP SELF DEFENSE (DETECT & CONTROL)	134,619	134,619
135	0604756N	SHIP SELF DEFENSE (ENGAGE: HARD KILL)	114,475	105,475
		Program Execution		*[−9,000]*
136	0604757N	SHIP SELF DEFENSE (ENGAGE: SOFT KILL/EW)	114,211	111,211
		Decoy development effort unjustified growth		*[−3,000]*
137	0604761N	INTELLIGENCE ENGINEERING	11,029	11,029
138	0604771N	MEDICAL DEVELOPMENT	9,220	9,220
139	0604777N	NAVIGATION/ID SYSTEM	42,723	42,723
140	0604800M	JOINT STRIKE FIGHTER (JSF)—EMD	531,426	531,426
141	0604800N	JOINT STRIKE FIGHTER (JSF)—EMD	528,716	528,716
142	0604810M	JOINT STRIKE FIGHTER FOLLOW ON DEVELOPMENT—MARINE CORPS	74,227	71,977
		Follow-on development excess funds		*[−2,250]*
143	0604810N	JOINT STRIKE FIGHTER FOLLOW ON DEVELOPMENT—NAVY	63,387	61,137
		Follow-on development excess funds		*[−2,250]*

SEC. 4201. RESEARCH, DEVELOPMENT, TEST, AND EVALUATION
(In Thousands of Dollars)

Line	Program Element	Item	FY 2017 Request	Conference Authorized
144	0605013M	INFORMATION TECHNOLOGY DEVELOPMENT	4,856	4,856
145	0605013N	INFORMATION TECHNOLOGY DEVELOPMENT	97,066	97,066
146	0605024N	ANTI-TAMPER TECHNOLOGY SUPPORT	2,500	2,500
147	0605212N	CH–53K RDTE	404,810	373,297
		Program delay		[–31,513]
148	0605215N	MISSION PLANNING	33,570	33,570
149	0605217N	COMMON AVIONICS	51,599	51,599
150	0605220N	SHIP TO SHORE CONNECTOR (SSC)	11,088	11,088
151	0605327N	T-AO (X)	1,095	1,095
152	0605414N	MQ-XX	89,000	77,000
		Excess Obligation		[–12,000]
153	0605450N	JOINT AIR-TO-GROUND MISSILE (JAGM)	17,880	17,880
154	0605500N	MULTI-MISSION MARITIME AIRCRAFT (MMA)	59,126	59,126
155	0605504N	MULTI-MISSION MARITIME (MMA) INCREMENT III	182,220	152,220
		Program execution		[–30,000]
156	0204202N	DDG–1000	45,642	45,642
159	0304231N	TACTICAL COMMAND SYSTEM—MIP	676	676
160	0304785N	TACTICAL CRYPTOLOGIC SYSTEMS	36,747	36,747
161	0305124N	SPECIAL APPLICATIONS PROGRAM	35,002	35,002
162	0306250M	CYBER OPERATIONS TECHNOLOGY DEVELOPMENT	4,942	4,942
		SUBTOTAL SYSTEM DEVELOPMENT & DEMONSTRATION	**6,025,655**	**5,928,917**
		MANAGEMENT SUPPORT		
163	0604256N	THREAT SIMULATOR DEVELOPMENT	16,633	16,633
164	0604258N	TARGET SYSTEMS DEVELOPMENT	36,662	36,662
165	0604759N	MAJOR T&E INVESTMENT	42,109	42,109
166	0605126N	JOINT THEATER AIR AND MISSILE DEFENSE ORGANIZATION	2,998	2,998
167	0605152N	STUDIES AND ANALYSIS SUPPORT—NAVY	3,931	3,931
168	0605154N	CENTER FOR NAVAL ANALYSES	46,634	46,634
169	0605285N	NEXT GENERATION FIGHTER	1,200	1,200
171	0605804N	TECHNICAL INFORMATION SERVICES	903	903
172	0605853N	MANAGEMENT, TECHNICAL & INTERNATIONAL SUPPORT	87,077	87,077
173	0605856N	STRATEGIC TECHNICAL SUPPORT	3,597	3,597
174	0605861N	RDT&E SCIENCE AND TECHNOLOGY MANAGEMENT	62,811	62,811
175	0605863N	RDT&E SHIP AND AIRCRAFT SUPPORT	106,093	106,093
176	0605864N	TEST AND EVALUATION SUPPORT	349,146	349,146
177	0605865N	OPERATIONAL TEST AND EVALUATION CAPABILITY	18,160	18,160
178	0605866N	NAVY SPACE AND ELECTRONIC WARFARE (SEW) SUPPORT	9,658	9,658
179	0605867N	SEW SURVEILLANCE/RECONNAISSANCE SUPPORT	6,500	6,500
180	0605873M	MARINE CORPS PROGRAM WIDE SUPPORT	22,247	22,247
181	0605898N	MANAGEMENT HQ—R&D	16,254	16,254
182	0606355N	WARFARE INNOVATION MANAGEMENT	21,123	21,123
		SUBTOTAL MANAGEMENT SUPPORT	**853,736**	**853,736**
		OPERATIONAL SYSTEMS DEVELOPMENT		
188	0607658N	COOPERATIVE ENGAGEMENT CAPABILITY (CEC)	84,501	84,501
189	0607700N	DEPLOYABLE JOINT COMMAND AND CONTROL	2,970	2,970
190	0101221N	STRATEGIC SUB & WEAPONS SYSTEM SUPPORT	136,556	136,556
191	0101224N	SSBN SECURITY TECHNOLOGY PROGRAM	33,845	33,845
192	0101226N	SUBMARINE ACOUSTIC WARFARE DEVELOPMENT	9,329	9,329
193	0101402N	NAVY STRATEGIC COMMUNICATIONS	17,218	17,218
195	0204136N	F/A–18 SQUADRONS	189,125	189,125
196	0204163N	FLEET TELECOMMUNICATIONS (TACTICAL)	48,225	48,225
197	0204228N	SURFACE SUPPORT	21,156	21,156
198	0204229N	TOMAHAWK AND TOMAHAWK MISSION PLANNING CENTER (TMPC)	71,355	71,355
199	0204311N	INTEGRATED SURVEILLANCE SYSTEM	58,542	57,058
		TASW prototypes excess growth		[–1,484]
200	0204413N	AMPHIBIOUS TACTICAL SUPPORT UNITS (DISPLACEMENT CRAFT)	13,929	13,929
201	0204460M	GROUND/AIR TASK ORIENTED RADAR (G/ATOR)	83,538	83,538
202	0204571N	CONSOLIDATED TRAINING SYSTEMS DEVELOPMENT	38,593	38,593
203	0204574N	CRYPTOLOGIC DIRECT SUPPORT	1,122	1,122
204	0204575N	ELECTRONIC WARFARE (EW) READINESS SUPPORT	99,998	99,998
205	0205601N	HARM IMPROVEMENT	48,635	48,635
206	0205604N	TACTICAL DATA LINKS	124,785	124,785
207	0205620N	SURFACE ASW COMBAT SYSTEM INTEGRATION	24,583	24,583
208	0205632N	MK–48 ADCAP	39,134	39,134
209	0205633N	AVIATION IMPROVEMENTS	120,861	120,861
210	0205675N	OPERATIONAL NUCLEAR POWER SYSTEMS	101,786	101,786
211	0206313M	MARINE CORPS COMMUNICATIONS SYSTEMS	82,159	82,159
212	0206335M	COMMON AVIATION COMMAND AND CONTROL SYSTEM (CAC2S)	11,850	11,850
213	0206623M	MARINE CORPS GROUND COMBAT/SUPPORTING ARMS SYSTEMS	47,877	47,877
214	0206624M	MARINE CORPS COMBAT SERVICES SUPPORT	13,194	13,194
215	0206625M	USMC INTELLIGENCE/ELECTRONIC WARFARE SYSTEMS (MIP)	17,171	17,171
216	0206629M	AMPHIBIOUS ASSAULT VEHICLE	38,020	38,020
217	0207161N	TACTICAL AIM MISSILES	56,285	56,285
218	0207163N	ADVANCED MEDIUM RANGE AIR-TO-AIR MISSILE (AMRAAM)	40,350	40,350
219	0219902M	GLOBAL COMBAT SUPPORT SYSTEM—MARINE CORPS (GCSS-MC)	9,128	9,128
223	0303109N	SATELLITE COMMUNICATIONS (SPACE)	37,372	37,372
224	0303138N	CONSOLIDATED AFLOAT NETWORK ENTERPRISE SERVICES (CANES)	23,541	23,541

SEC. 4201. RESEARCH, DEVELOPMENT, TEST, AND EVALUATION
(In Thousands of Dollars)

Line	Program Element	Item	FY 2017 Request	Conference Authorized
225	0303140N	INFORMATION SYSTEMS SECURITY PROGRAM	38,510	38,510
228	0305192N	MILITARY INTELLIGENCE PROGRAM (MIP) ACTIVITIES	6,019	6,019
229	0305204N	TACTICAL UNMANNED AERIAL VEHICLES	8,436	8,436
230	0305205N	UAS INTEGRATION AND INTEROPERABILITY	36,509	33,509
		Prior year carryover		[–3,000]
231	0305208M	DISTRIBUTED COMMON GROUND/SURFACE SYSTEMS	2,100	2,100
232	0305208N	DISTRIBUTED COMMON GROUND/SURFACE SYSTEMS	44,571	44,571
233	0305220N	MQ–4C TRITON	111,729	111,729
234	0305231N	MQ–8 UAV	26,518	26,518
235	0305232M	RQ–11 UAV	418	418
236	0305233N	RQ–7 UAV	716	716
237	0305234N	SMALL (LEVEL 0) TACTICAL UAS (STUASL0)	5,071	5,071
238	0305239M	RQ–21A	9,497	9,497
239	0305241N	MULTI-INTELLIGENCE SENSOR DEVELOPMENT	77,965	77,965
240	0305242N	UNMANNED AERIAL SYSTEMS (UAS) PAYLOADS (MIP)	11,181	11,181
241	0305421N	RQ–4 MODERNIZATION	181,266	181,266
242	0308601N	MODELING AND SIMULATION SUPPORT	4,709	4,709
243	0702207N	DEPOT MAINTENANCE (NON-IF)	49,322	49,322
245	0708730N	MARITIME TECHNOLOGY (MARITECH)	3,204	3,204
245A	9999999999	CLASSIFIED PROGRAMS	1,228,460	1,228,460
		SUBTOTAL OPERATIONAL SYSTEMS DEVELOPMENT	**3,592,934**	**3,588,450**
		TOTAL RESEARCH, DEVELOPMENT, TEST & EVAL, NAVY	**17,276,301**	**17,078,663**
		RESEARCH, DEVELOPMENT, TEST & EVAL, AF		
		BASIC RESEARCH		
001	0601102F	DEFENSE RESEARCH SCIENCES	340,812	340,812
002	0601103F	UNIVERSITY RESEARCH INITIATIVES	145,044	145,044
003	0601108F	HIGH ENERGY LASER RESEARCH INITIATIVES	14,168	14,168
		SUBTOTAL BASIC RESEARCH	**500,024**	**500,024**
		APPLIED RESEARCH		
004	0602102F	MATERIALS	126,152	131,152
		Precision measuring tools		[5,000]
005	0602201F	AEROSPACE VEHICLE TECHNOLOGIES	122,831	127,831
		Reusable Hypersonic vehicle structures development		[5,000]
006	0602202F	HUMAN EFFECTIVENESS APPLIED RESEARCH	111,647	111,647
007	0602203F	AEROSPACE PROPULSION	185,671	190,671
		Program increase		[5,000]
008	0602204F	AEROSPACE SENSORS	155,174	155,174
009	0602601F	SPACE TECHNOLOGY	117,915	117,915
010	0602602F	CONVENTIONAL MUNITIONS	109,649	109,649
011	0602605F	DIRECTED ENERGY TECHNOLOGY	127,163	127,163
012	0602788F	DOMINANT INFORMATION SCIENCES AND METHODS	161,650	161,650
013	0602890F	HIGH ENERGY LASER RESEARCH	42,300	42,300
		SUBTOTAL APPLIED RESEARCH	**1,260,152**	**1,275,152**
		ADVANCED TECHNOLOGY DEVELOPMENT		
014	0603112F	ADVANCED MATERIALS FOR WEAPON SYSTEMS	35,137	45,137
		Metals Affordability Initiative		[10,000]
015	0603199F	SUSTAINMENT SCIENCE AND TECHNOLOGY (S&T)	20,636	20,636
016	0603203F	ADVANCED AEROSPACE SENSORS	40,945	40,945
017	0603211F	AEROSPACE TECHNOLOGY DEV/DEMO	130,950	130,950
018	0603216F	AEROSPACE PROPULSION AND POWER TECHNOLOGY	94,594	99,594
		Silicon Carbide for aerospace power application		[5,000]
019	0603270F	ELECTRONIC COMBAT TECHNOLOGY	58,250	58,250
020	0603401F	ADVANCED SPACECRAFT TECHNOLOGY	61,593	61,593
021	0603444F	MAUI SPACE SURVEILLANCE SYSTEM (MSSS)	11,681	11,681
022	0603456F	HUMAN EFFECTIVENESS ADVANCED TECHNOLOGY DEVELOPMENT	26,492	26,492
023	0603601F	CONVENTIONAL WEAPONS TECHNOLOGY	102,009	102,009
024	0603605F	ADVANCED WEAPONS TECHNOLOGY	39,064	39,064
025	0603680F	MANUFACTURING TECHNOLOGY PROGRAM	46,344	46,344
026	0603788F	BATTLESPACE KNOWLEDGE DEVELOPMENT AND DEMONSTRATION	58,110	58,110
		SUBTOTAL ADVANCED TECHNOLOGY DEVELOPMENT	**725,805**	**740,805**
		ADVANCED COMPONENT DEVELOPMENT & PROTOTYPES		
027	0603260F	INTELLIGENCE ADVANCED DEVELOPMENT	5,598	5,598
028	0603438F	SPACE CONTROL TECHNOLOGY	7,534	7,534
029	0603742F	COMBAT IDENTIFICATION TECHNOLOGY	24,418	24,418
030	0603790F	NATO RESEARCH AND DEVELOPMENT	4,333	4,333
032	0603830F	SPACE SECURITY AND DEFENSE PROGRAM	32,399	32,399
033	0603851F	INTERCONTINENTAL BALLISTIC MISSILE—DEM/VAL	108,663	108,663
035	0604015F	LONG RANGE STRIKE—BOMBER	1,358,309	1,358,309
036	0604257F	ADVANCED TECHNOLOGY AND SENSORS	34,818	34,818
037	0604317F	TECHNOLOGY TRANSFER	3,368	3,368
038	0604327F	HARD AND DEEPLY BURIED TARGET DEFEAT SYSTEM (HDBTDS) PROGRAM	74,308	74,308
039	0604422F	WEATHER SYSTEM FOLLOW-ON	118,953	113,953
		Transfer Cloud Characterization and Theater Weather Imagery to NRO		[–5,000]
040	0604425F	SPACE SITUATION AWARENESS SYSTEMS	9,901	9,901

SEC. 4201. RESEARCH, DEVELOPMENT, TEST, AND EVALUATION
(In Thousands of Dollars)

Line	Program Element	Item	FY 2017 Request	Conference Authorized
041	0604776F	DEPLOYMENT & DISTRIBUTION ENTERPRISE R&D	25,890	25,890
042	0604857F	OPERATIONALLY RESPONSIVE SPACE	7,921	18,421
		Program increase		[10,500]
043	0604858F	TECH TRANSITION PROGRAM	347,304	347,304
044	0605230F	GROUND BASED STRATEGIC DETERRENT	113,919	113,919
046	0207110F	NEXT GENERATION AIR DOMINANCE	20,595	20,595
047	0207455F	THREE DIMENSIONAL LONG-RANGE RADAR (3DELRR)	49,491	49,491
048	0305164F	NAVSTAR GLOBAL POSITIONING SYSTEM (USER EQUIPMENT) (SPACE)	278,147	278,147
049	0305236F	COMMON DATA LINK EXECUTIVE AGENT (CDL EA)	42,338	42,338
050	0306250F	CYBER OPERATIONS TECHNOLOGY DEVELOPMENT	158,002	158,002
051	0306415F	ENABLED CYBER ACTIVITIES	15,842	15,842
052	0901410F	CONTRACTING INFORMATION TECHNOLOGY SYSTEM	5,782	5,782
		SUBTOTAL ADVANCED COMPONENT DEVELOPMENT & PROTOTYPES	**2,847,833**	**2,853,333**
		SYSTEM DEVELOPMENT & DEMONSTRATION		
054	0604270F	ELECTRONIC WARFARE DEVELOPMENT	12,476	9,176
		Improved GPS		[-3,300]
055	0604281F	TACTICAL DATA NETWORKS ENTERPRISE	82,380	82,380
056	0604287F	PHYSICAL SECURITY EQUIPMENT	8,458	8,458
057	0604329F	SMALL DIAMETER BOMB (SDB)—EMD	54,838	47,038
		Improved GPS		[-7,800]
058	0604421F	COUNTERSPACE SYSTEMS	34,394	34,394
059	0604425F	SPACE SITUATION AWARENESS SYSTEMS	23,945	23,945
060	0604426F	SPACE FENCE	168,364	168,364
061	0604429F	AIRBORNE ELECTRONIC ATTACK	9,187	9,187
062	0604441F	SPACE BASED INFRARED SYSTEM (SBIRS) HIGH EMD	181,966	181,966
063	0604602F	ARMAMENT/ORDNANCE DEVELOPMENT	20,312	20,312
064	0604604F	SUBMUNITIONS	2,503	2,503
065	0604617F	AGILE COMBAT SUPPORT	53,680	53,680
066	0604618F	JOINT DIRECT ATTACK MUNITION	9,901	9,901
067	0604706F	LIFE SUPPORT SYSTEMS	7,520	7,520
068	0604735F	COMBAT TRAINING RANGES	77,409	77,409
069	0604800F	F-35—EMD	450,467	450,467
070	0604853F	EVOLVED EXPENDABLE LAUNCH VEHICLE PROGRAM (SPACE)—EMD	296,572	160,000
		Launch System Development		[160,000]
		Next Generation Launch System Investment		[-296,572]
070A	0604XXXF	ROCKET PROPULSION SYSTEM		220,000
		Rocket Propulsion System Replacement of RD-180		[220,000]
071	0604932F	LONG RANGE STANDOFF WEAPON	95,604	95,604
072	0604933F	ICBM FUZE MODERNIZATION	189,751	189,751
073	0605030F	JOINT TACTICAL NETWORK CENTER (JTNC)	1,131	1,131
074	0605213F	F-22 MODERNIZATION INCREMENT 3.2B	70,290	70,290
075	0605214F	GROUND ATTACK WEAPONS FUZE DEVELOPMENT	937	937
076	0605221F	KC-46	261,724	121,724
		Scope Reduction		[-140,000]
077	0605223F	ADVANCED PILOT TRAINING	12,377	7,377
		Early to need		[-5,000]
078	0605229F	CSAR HH-60 RECAPITALIZATION	319,331	304,331
		Forward financing		[-15,000]
080	0605431F	ADVANCED EHF MILSATCOM (SPACE)	259,131	229,131
		Delayed analysis of alternatives		[-30,000]
081	0605432F	POLAR MILSATCOM (SPACE)	50,815	50,815
082	0605433F	WIDEBAND GLOBAL SATCOM (SPACE)	41,632	51,632
		COMSATCOM pilot program		[10,000]
083	0605458F	AIR & SPACE OPS CENTER 10.2 RDT&E	28,911	28,911
084	0605931F	B-2 DEFENSIVE MANAGEMENT SYSTEM	315,615	288,915
		Scope Reduction		[-26,700]
085	0101125F	NUCLEAR WEAPONS MODERNIZATION	137,909	137,909
086	0207171F	F-15 EPAWSS	256,669	256,669
087	0207701F	FULL COMBAT MISSION TRAINING	12,051	12,051
088	0305176F	COMBAT SURVIVOR EVADER LOCATOR	29,253	29,253
089	0307581F	JSTARS RECAP	128,019	128,019
090	0401319F	PRESIDENTIAL AIRCRAFT REPLACEMENT (PAR)	351,220	351,220
091	0701212F	AUTOMATED TEST SYSTEMS	19,062	19,062
		SUBTOTAL SYSTEM DEVELOPMENT & DEMONSTRATION	**4,075,804**	**3,941,432**
		MANAGEMENT SUPPORT		
092	0604256F	THREAT SIMULATOR DEVELOPMENT	21,630	21,630
093	0604759F	MAJOR T&E INVESTMENT	66,385	66,385
094	0605101F	RAND PROJECT AIR FORCE	34,641	34,641
096	0605712F	INITIAL OPERATIONAL TEST & EVALUATION	11,529	11,529
097	0605807F	TEST AND EVALUATION SUPPORT	661,417	661,417
098	0605860F	ROCKET SYSTEMS LAUNCH PROGRAM (SPACE)	11,198	11,198
099	0605864F	SPACE TEST PROGRAM (STP)	27,070	27,070
100	0605976F	FACILITIES RESTORATION AND MODERNIZATION—TEST AND EVALUATION SUPPORT	134,111	134,111
101	0605978F	FACILITIES SUSTAINMENT—TEST AND EVALUATION SUPPORT	28,091	28,091
102	0606017F	REQUIREMENTS ANALYSIS AND MATURATION	29,100	29,100
103	0606116F	SPACE TEST AND TRAINING RANGE DEVELOPMENT	18,528	18,528
104	0606392F	SPACE AND MISSILE CENTER (SMC) CIVILIAN WORKFORCE	176,666	176,666

SEC. 4201. RESEARCH, DEVELOPMENT, TEST, AND EVALUATION
(In Thousands of Dollars)

Line	Program Element	Item	FY 2017 Request	Conference Authorized
105	0308602F	ENTEPRISE INFORMATION SERVICES (EIS)	4,410	4,410
106	0702806F	ACQUISITION AND MANAGEMENT SUPPORT	14,613	14,613
107	0804731F	GENERAL SKILL TRAINING	1,404	1,404
109	1001004F	INTERNATIONAL ACTIVITIES	4,784	4,784
		SUBTOTAL MANAGEMENT SUPPORT	**1,245,577**	**1,245,577**
		OPERATIONAL SYSTEMS DEVELOPMENT		
110	0603423F	GLOBAL POSITIONING SYSTEM III—OPERATIONAL CONTROL SEGMENT	393,268	393,268
111	0604233F	SPECIALIZED UNDERGRADUATE FLIGHT TRAINING	15,427	15,427
112	0604445F	WIDE AREA SURVEILLANCE	46,695	46,695
115	0605018F	AF INTEGRATED PERSONNEL AND PAY SYSTEM (AF-IPPS)	10,368	10,368
116	0605024F	ANTI-TAMPER TECHNOLOGY EXECUTIVE AGENCY	31,952	31,952
117	0605117F	FOREIGN MATERIEL ACQUISITION AND EXPLOITATION	42,960	42,960
118	0605278F	HC/MC–130 RECAP RDT&E	13,987	13,987
119	0101113F	B–52 SQUADRONS	78,267	78,267
120	0101122F	AIR-LAUNCHED CRUISE MISSILE (ALCM)	453	453
121	0101126F	B–1B SQUADRONS	5,830	5,830
122	0101127F	B–2 SQUADRONS	152,458	152,458
123	0101213F	MINUTEMAN SQUADRONS	182,958	182,958
124	0101313F	STRAT WAR PLANNING SYSTEM—USSTRATCOM	39,148	39,148
126	0101316F	WORLDWIDE JOINT STRATEGIC COMMUNICATIONS	6,042	6,042
128	0102110F	UH–1N REPLACEMENT PROGRAM	14,116	14,116
129	0102326F	REGION/SECTOR OPERATION CONTROL CENTER MODERNIZATION PROGRAM	10,868	10,868
130	0105921F	SERVICE SUPPORT TO STRATCOM—SPACE ACTIVITIES	8,674	8,674
131	0205219F	MQ–9 UAV	151,373	161,373
		Auto take-off and landing capability		[10,000]
133	0207131F	A–10 SQUADRONS	14,853	14,853
134	0207133F	F–16 SQUADRONS	132,795	132,795
135	0207134F	F–15E SQUADRONS	356,717	356,717
136	0207136F	MANNED DESTRUCTIVE SUPPRESSION	14,773	14,773
137	0207138F	F–22A SQUADRONS	387,564	379,464
		Improved GPS		[–8,100]
138	0207142F	F–35 SQUADRONS	153,045	147,545
		Follow-on development—excess funds		[–5,500]
139	0207161F	TACTICAL AIM MISSILES	52,898	52,898
140	0207163F	ADVANCED MEDIUM RANGE AIR-TO-AIR MISSILE (AMRAAM)	62,470	62,470
143	0207227F	COMBAT RESCUE—PARARESCUE	362	362
144	0207247F	AF TENCAP	28,413	28,413
145	0207249F	PRECISION ATTACK SYSTEMS PROCUREMENT	649	649
146	0207253F	COMPASS CALL	13,723	50,823
		Compass Call Program Restructure		[37,100]
147	0207268F	AIRCRAFT ENGINE COMPONENT IMPROVEMENT PROGRAM	109,859	109,859
148	0207325F	JOINT AIR-TO-SURFACE STANDOFF MISSILE (JASSM)	30,002	30,002
149	0207410F	AIR & SPACE OPERATIONS CENTER (AOC)	37,621	25,343
		Weapon system modification		[–12,278]
150	0207412F	CONTROL AND REPORTING CENTER (CRC)	13,292	13,292
151	0207417F	AIRBORNE WARNING AND CONTROL SYSTEM (AWACS)	86,644	86,644
152	0207418F	TACTICAL AIRBORNE CONTROL SYSTEMS	2,442	2,442
154	0207431F	COMBAT AIR INTELLIGENCE SYSTEM ACTIVITIES	10,911	15,911
		Geospatial software development		[5,000]
155	0207444F	TACTICAL AIR CONTROL PARTY-MOD	11,843	11,843
156	0207448F	C2ISR TACTICAL DATA LINK	1,515	1,515
157	0207452F	DCAPES	14,979	14,979
158	0207590F	SEEK EAGLE	25,308	25,308
159	0207601F	USAF MODELING AND SIMULATION	16,666	16,666
160	0207605F	WARGAMING AND SIMULATION CENTERS	4,245	4,245
161	0207697F	DISTRIBUTED TRAINING AND EXERCISES	3,886	3,886
162	0208006F	MISSION PLANNING SYSTEMS	71,785	71,785
164	0208087F	AF OFFENSIVE CYBERSPACE OPERATIONS	25,025	25,025
165	0208088F	AF DEFENSIVE CYBERSPACE OPERATIONS	29,439	29,439
168	0301017F	GLOBAL SENSOR INTEGRATED ON NETWORK (GSIN)	3,470	3,470
169	0301112F	NUCLEAR PLANNING AND EXECUTION SYSTEM (NPES)	4,060	4,060
175	0301400F	SPACE SUPERIORITY INTELLIGENCE	13,880	13,880
176	0302015F	E–4B NATIONAL AIRBORNE OPERATIONS CENTER (NAOC)	30,948	30,948
177	0303001F	FAMILY OF ADVANCED BLOS TERMINALS (FAB-T)	42,378	42,378
178	0303131F	MINIMUM ESSENTIAL EMERGENCY COMMUNICATIONS NETWORK (MEECN)	47,471	47,471
179	0303140F	INFORMATION SYSTEMS SECURITY PROGRAM	46,388	46,388
180	0303141F	GLOBAL COMBAT SUPPORT SYSTEM	52	52
181	0303142F	GLOBAL FORCE MANAGEMENT—DATA INITIATIVE	2,099	2,099
184	0304260F	AIRBORNE SIGINT ENTERPRISE	90,762	90,762
187	0305099F	GLOBAL AIR TRAFFIC MANAGEMENT (GATM)	4,354	4,354
188	0305110F	SATELLITE CONTROL NETWORK (SPACE)	15,624	15,624
189	0305111F	WEATHER SERVICE	19,974	22,974
		Commercial Weather Pilot Program		[3,000]
190	0305114F	AIR TRAFFIC CONTROL, APPROACH, AND LANDING SYSTEM (ATCALS)	9,770	9,770
191	0305116F	AERIAL TARGETS	3,051	3,051
194	0305128F	SECURITY AND INVESTIGATIVE ACTIVITIES	405	405
195	0305145F	ARMS CONTROL IMPLEMENTATION	4,844	4,844
196	0305146F	DEFENSE JOINT COUNTERINTELLIGENCE ACTIVITIES	339	339

SEC. 4201. RESEARCH, DEVELOPMENT, TEST, AND EVALUATION
(In Thousands of Dollars)

Line	Program Element	Item	FY 2017 Request	Conference Authorized
199	0305173F	SPACE AND MISSILE TEST AND EVALUATION CENTER	3,989	3,989
200	0305174F	SPACE INNOVATION, INTEGRATION AND RAPID TECHNOLOGY DEVELOPMENT	3,070	3,070
201	0305179F	INTEGRATED BROADCAST SERVICE (IBS)	8,833	8,833
202	0305182F	SPACELIFT RANGE SYSTEM (SPACE)	11,867	11,867
203	0305202F	DRAGON U–2	37,217	37,217
205	0305206F	AIRBORNE RECONNAISSANCE SYSTEMS	3,841	18,841
		Wide area motion imagery		[15,000]
206	0305207F	MANNED RECONNAISSANCE SYSTEMS	20,975	20,975
207	0305208F	DISTRIBUTED COMMON GROUND/SURFACE SYSTEMS	18,902	18,902
208	0305220F	RQ–4 UAV	256,307	256,307
209	0305221F	NETWORK-CENTRIC COLLABORATIVE TARGETING	22,610	22,610
211	0305238F	NATO AGS	38,904	38,904
212	0305240F	SUPPORT TO DCGS ENTERPRISE	23,084	23,084
213	0305258F	ADVANCED EVALUATION PROGRAM	116,143	116,143
214	0305265F	GPS III SPACE SEGMENT	141,888	141,888
215	0305600F	INTERNATIONAL INTELLIGENCE TECHNOLOGY AND ARCHITECTURES	2,360	2,360
216	0305614F	JSPOC MISSION SYSTEM	72,889	72,889
217	0305881F	RAPID CYBER ACQUISITION	4,280	4,280
218	0305906F	NCMC—TW/AA SYSTEM	4,951	4,951
219	0305913F	NUDET DETECTION SYSTEM (SPACE)	21,093	21,093
220	0305940F	SPACE SITUATION AWARENESS OPERATIONS	35,002	35,002
222	0308699F	SHARED EARLY WARNING (SEW)	6,366	6,366
223	0401115F	C–130 AIRLIFT SQUADRON	15,599	15,599
224	0401119F	C–5 AIRLIFT SQUADRONS (IF)	66,146	66,146
225	0401130F	C–17 AIRCRAFT (IF)	12,430	12,430
226	0401132F	C–130J PROGRAM	16,776	16,776
227	0401134F	LARGE AIRCRAFT IR COUNTERMEASURES (LAIRCM)	5,166	5,166
229	0401314F	OPERATIONAL SUPPORT AIRLIFT	13,817	13,817
230	0401318F	CV–22	16,702	16,702
231	0408011F	SPECIAL TACTICS / COMBAT CONTROL	7,164	7,164
232	0702207F	DEPOT MAINTENANCE (NON-IF)	1,518	1,518
233	0708610F	LOGISTICS INFORMATION TECHNOLOGY (LOGIT)	61,676	61,676
234	0708611F	SUPPORT SYSTEMS DEVELOPMENT	9,128	9,128
235	0804743F	OTHER FLIGHT TRAINING	1,653	1,653
236	0808716F	OTHER PERSONNEL ACTIVITIES	57	57
237	0901202F	JOINT PERSONNEL RECOVERY AGENCY	3,663	3,663
238	0901218F	CIVILIAN COMPENSATION PROGRAM	3,735	3,735
239	0901220F	PERSONNEL ADMINISTRATION	5,157	5,157
240	0901226F	AIR FORCE STUDIES AND ANALYSIS AGENCY	1,523	1,523
242	0901538F	FINANCIAL MANAGEMENT INFORMATION SYSTEMS DEVELOPMENT	10,581	10,581
242A	9999999999	CLASSIFIED PROGRAMS	13,091,557	13,091,557
		SUBTOTAL OPERATIONAL SYSTEMS DEVELOPMENT	**17,457,056**	**17,501,278**
		TOTAL RESEARCH, DEVELOPMENT, TEST & EVAL, AF	**28,112,251**	**28,057,601**
		RESEARCH, DEVELOPMENT, TEST & EVAL, DW **BASIC RESEARCH**		
001	0601000BR	DTRA BASIC RESEARCH INITIATIVE	35,436	35,436
002	0601101E	DEFENSE RESEARCH SCIENCES	362,297	362,297
003	0601110D8Z	BASIC RESEARCH INITIATIVES	36,654	36,654
004	0601117E	BASIC OPERATIONAL MEDICAL RESEARCH SCIENCE	57,791	57,791
005	0601120D8Z	NATIONAL DEFENSE EDUCATION PROGRAM	69,345	79,345
		K–12 STEM program increase		[10,000]
006	0601228D8Z	HISTORICALLY BLACK COLLEGES AND UNIVERSITIES/MINORITY INSTITUTIONS	23,572	33,572
		Program increase		[10,000]
007	0601384BP	CHEMICAL AND BIOLOGICAL DEFENSE PROGRAM	44,800	44,800
		SUBTOTAL BASIC RESEARCH	**629,895**	**649,895**
		APPLIED RESEARCH		
008	0602000D8Z	JOINT MUNITIONS TECHNOLOGY	17,745	17,745
009	0602115E	BIOMEDICAL TECHNOLOGY	115,213	115,213
010	0602230D8Z	DEFENSE TECHNOLOGY INNOVATION	30,000	0
		Program decrease		[–30,000]
011	0602234D8Z	LINCOLN LABORATORY RESEARCH PROGRAM	48,269	48,269
012	0602251D8Z	APPLIED RESEARCH FOR THE ADVANCEMENT OF S&T PRIORITIES	42,206	42,206
013	0602303E	INFORMATION & COMMUNICATIONS TECHNOLOGY	353,635	353,635
014	0602383E	BIOLOGICAL WARFARE DEFENSE	21,250	21,250
015	0602384BP	CHEMICAL AND BIOLOGICAL DEFENSE PROGRAM	188,715	188,715
016	0602668D8Z	CYBER SECURITY RESEARCH	12,183	12,183
017	0602702E	TACTICAL TECHNOLOGY	313,843	313,843
018	0602715E	MATERIALS AND BIOLOGICAL TECHNOLOGY	220,456	214,456
		Program reduction		[–6,000]
019	0602716E	ELECTRONICS TECHNOLOGY	221,911	221,911
020	0602718BR	WEAPONS OF MASS DESTRUCTION DEFEAT TECHNOLOGIES	154,857	154,857
021	0602751D8Z	SOFTWARE ENGINEERING INSTITUTE (SEI) APPLIED RESEARCH	8,420	8,420
022	1160401BB	SOF TECHNOLOGY DEVELOPMENT	37,820	37,820
		SUBTOTAL APPLIED RESEARCH	**1,786,523**	**1,750,523**

ADVANCED TECHNOLOGY DEVELOPMENT

SEC. 4201. RESEARCH, DEVELOPMENT, TEST, AND EVALUATION
(In Thousands of Dollars)

Line	Program Element	Item	FY 2017 Request	Conference Authorized
023	0603000D8Z	JOINT MUNITIONS ADVANCED TECHNOLOGY	23,902	23,902
025	0603122D8Z	COMBATING TERRORISM TECHNOLOGY SUPPORT	73,002	73,002
026	0603133D8Z	FOREIGN COMPARATIVE TESTING	19,343	29,343
		Anti-tunnel defense systems		[10,000]
027	0603160BR	COUNTERPROLIFERATION INITIATIVES—PROLIFERATION PREVENTION AND DEFEAT	266,444	266,444
028	0603176C	ADVANCED CONCEPTS AND PERFORMANCE ASSESSMENT	17,880	17,880
030	0603178C	WEAPONS TECHNOLOGY	71,843	71,843
031	0603179C	ADVANCED C4ISR	3,626	3,626
032	0603180C	ADVANCED RESEARCH	23,433	23,433
033	0603225D8Z	JOINT DOD-DOE MUNITIONS TECHNOLOGY DEVELOPMENT	17,256	17,256
035	0603274C	SPECIAL PROGRAM—MDA TECHNOLOGY	83,745	11,795
		Program reduction		[−71,950]
036	0603286E	ADVANCED AEROSPACE SYSTEMS	182,327	182,327
037	0603287E	SPACE PROGRAMS AND TECHNOLOGY	175,240	165,240
		Program reduction		[−10,000]
038	0603288D8Z	ANALYTIC ASSESSMENTS	12,048	12,048
039	0603289D8Z	ADVANCED INNOVATIVE ANALYSIS AND CONCEPTS	57,020	57,020
041	0603375D8Z	TECHNOLOGY INNOVATION	39,923	19,923
		Program decrease		[−20,000]
042	0603384BP	CHEMICAL AND BIOLOGICAL DEFENSE PROGRAM—ADVANCED DEVELOPMENT	127,941	127,941
043	0603527D8Z	RETRACT LARCH	181,977	181,977
044	0603618D8Z	JOINT ELECTRONIC ADVANCED TECHNOLOGY	22,030	22,030
045	0603648D8Z	JOINT CAPABILITY TECHNOLOGY DEMONSTRATIONS	148,184	132,184
		Program decrease		[−16,000]
046	0603662D8Z	NETWORKED COMMUNICATIONS CAPABILITIES	9,331	9,331
047	0603680D8Z	DEFENSE-WIDE MANUFACTURING SCIENCE AND TECHNOLOGY PROGRAM	158,398	158,398
048	0603680S	MANUFACTURING TECHNOLOGY PROGRAM	31,259	31,259
049	0603699D8Z	EMERGING CAPABILITIES TECHNOLOGY DEVELOPMENT	49,895	49,895
050	0603712S	GENERIC LOGISTICS R&D TECHNOLOGY DEMONSTRATIONS	11,011	11,011
052	0603716D8Z	STRATEGIC ENVIRONMENTAL RESEARCH PROGRAM	65,078	65,078
053	0603720S	MICROELECTRONICS TECHNOLOGY DEVELOPMENT AND SUPPORT	97,826	97,826
054	0603727D8Z	JOINT WARFIGHTING PROGRAM	7,848	5,348
		Prior year carryover		[−2,500]
055	0603739E	ADVANCED ELECTRONICS TECHNOLOGIES	49,807	49,807
056	0603760E	COMMAND, CONTROL AND COMMUNICATIONS SYSTEMS	155,081	155,081
057	0603766E	NETWORK-CENTRIC WARFARE TECHNOLOGY	428,894	428,894
058	0603767E	SENSOR TECHNOLOGY	241,288	241,288
060	0603781D8Z	SOFTWARE ENGINEERING INSTITUTE	14,264	14,264
061	0603826D8Z	QUICK REACTION SPECIAL PROJECTS	74,943	72,943
		QRSP		[−2,000]
063	0603833D8Z	ENGINEERING SCIENCE & TECHNOLOGY	17,659	17,659
064	0603941D8Z	TEST & EVALUATION SCIENCE & TECHNOLOGY	87,135	87,135
065	0604055D8Z	OPERATIONAL ENERGY CAPABILITY IMPROVEMENT	37,329	41,329
		Competitive technology investment		[4,000]
066	0303310D8Z	CWMD SYSTEMS	44,836	21,236
		Constellation program reduction		[−23,600]
067	1160402BB	SOF ADVANCED TECHNOLOGY DEVELOPMENT	61,620	61,620
		SUBTOTAL ADVANCED TECHNOLOGY DEVELOPMENT	**3,190,666**	**3,058,616**

ADVANCED COMPONENT DEVELOPMENT & PROTOTYPES
ADVANCED COMPONENT DEVELOPMENT AND PROTOTYPES

Line	Program Element	Item	FY 2017 Request	Conference Authorized
068	0603161D8Z	NUCLEAR AND CONVENTIONAL PHYSICAL SECURITY EQUIPMENT RDT&E ADC&P	28,498	28,498
069	0603600D8Z	WALKOFF	89,643	89,643
071	0603821D8Z	ACQUISITION ENTERPRISE DATA & INFORMATION SERVICES	2,136	2,136
072	0603851D8Z	ENVIRONMENTAL SECURITY TECHNICAL CERTIFICATION PROGRAM	52,491	52,491
073	0603881C	BALLISTIC MISSILE DEFENSE TERMINAL DEFENSE SEGMENT	206,834	206,834
074	0603882C	BALLISTIC MISSILE DEFENSE MIDCOURSE DEFENSE SEGMENT	862,080	862,080
075	0603884BP	CHEMICAL AND BIOLOGICAL DEFENSE PROGRAM—DEM/VAL	138,187	138,187
076	0603884C	BALLISTIC MISSILE DEFENSE SENSORS	230,077	230,077
077	0603890C	BMD ENABLING PROGRAMS	401,594	401,594
078	0603891C	SPECIAL PROGRAMS—MDA	321,607	304,707
		Program reduction		[−16,900]
079	0603892C	AEGIS BMD	959,066	939,066
		SM-3 IIA development excess growth		[−20,000]
080	0603893C	SPACE TRACKING & SURVEILLANCE SYSTEM	32,129	32,129
081	0603895C	BALLISTIC MISSILE DEFENSE SYSTEM SPACE PROGRAMS	20,690	20,690
082	0603896C	BALLISTIC MISSILE DEFENSE COMMAND AND CONTROL, BATTLE MANAGEMENT AND COMMUNICATI.	439,617	443,517
		Post Intercept Assessment Acceleration		[3,900]
083	0603898C	BALLISTIC MISSILE DEFENSE JOINT WARFIGHTER SUPPORT	47,776	47,776
084	0603904C	MISSILE DEFENSE INTEGRATION & OPERATIONS CENTER (MDIOC)	54,750	54,750
085	0603906C	REGARDING TRENCH	8,785	8,785
086	0603907C	SEA BASED X-BAND RADAR (SBX)	68,787	68,787
087	0603913C	ISRAELI COOPERATIVE PROGRAMS	103,835	268,735
		Increase for Cooperative Development Programs subject to Title XVI		[164,900]
088	0603914C	BALLISTIC MISSILE DEFENSE TEST	293,441	293,441
089	0603915C	BALLISTIC MISSILE DEFENSE TARGETS	563,576	563,576
090	0603920D8Z	HUMANITARIAN DEMINING	10,007	10,007
091	0603923D8Z	COALITION WARFARE	10,126	10,126

SEC. 4201. RESEARCH, DEVELOPMENT, TEST, AND EVALUATION
(In Thousands of Dollars)

Line	Program Element	Item	FY 2017 Request	Conference Authorized
092	0604016D8Z	DEPARTMENT OF DEFENSE CORROSION PROGRAM	3,893	8,893
		Corrosion prevention		[5,000]
093	0604115C	TECHNOLOGY MATURATION INITIATIVES	90,266	90,266
094	0604132D8Z	MISSILE DEFEAT PROJECT	45,000	45,000
095	0604250D8Z	ADVANCED INNOVATIVE TECHNOLOGIES	844,870	829,870
		SCO		[−15,000]
097	0604400D8Z	DEPARTMENT OF DEFENSE (DOD) UNMANNED SYSTEM COMMON DEVELOPMENT	3,320	3,320
099	0604682D8Z	WARGAMING AND SUPPORT FOR STRATEGIC ANALYSIS (SSA)	4,000	4,000
102	0604826J	JOINT C5 CAPABILITY DEVELOPMENT, INTEGRATION AND INTEROPERABILITY ASSESSMENTS.	23,642	23,642
104	0604873C	LONG RANGE DISCRIMINATION RADAR (LRDR)	162,012	162,012
105	0604874C	IMPROVED HOMELAND DEFENSE INTERCEPTORS	274,148	274,148
106	0604876C	BALLISTIC MISSILE DEFENSE TERMINAL DEFENSE SEGMENT TEST	63,444	63,444
107	0604878C	AEGIS BMD TEST	95,012	95,012
108	0604879C	BALLISTIC MISSILE DEFENSE SENSOR TEST	83,250	83,250
109	0604880C	LAND-BASED SM–3 (LBSM3)	43,293	43,293
110	0604881C	AEGIS SM–3 BLOCK IIA CO-DEVELOPMENT	106,038	106,038
111	0604887C	BALLISTIC MISSILE DEFENSE MIDCOURSE SEGMENT TEST	56,481	56,481
112	0604894C	MULTI-OBJECT KILL VEHICLE	71,513	71,513
114	0303191D8Z	JOINT ELECTROMAGNETIC TECHNOLOGY (JET) PROGRAM	2,636	2,636
115	0305103C	CYBER SECURITY INITIATIVE	969	969
		SUBTOTAL ADVANCED COMPONENT DEVELOPMENT AND PROTOTYPES	**6,919,519**	**7,041,419**
115A	0604XXXD	WEATHER SYSTEM FOLLOW-ON		5,000
		Transfer Cloud Characterization and Theater Weather Imagery from USAF		[5,000]
		SUBTOTAL ADVANCED COMPONENT DEVELOPMENT & PROTOTYPES	**0**	**5,000**

SYSTEM DEVELOPMENT AND DEMONSTRATION

Line	Program Element	Item	FY 2017 Request	Conference Authorized
116	0604161D8Z	NUCLEAR AND CONVENTIONAL PHYSICAL SECURITY EQUIPMENT RDT&E SDD	10,324	10,324
117	0604165D8Z	PROMPT GLOBAL STRIKE CAPABILITY DEVELOPMENT	181,303	181,303
118	0604384BP	CHEMICAL AND BIOLOGICAL DEFENSE PROGRAM—EMD	266,231	266,231
120	0604771D8Z	JOINT TACTICAL INFORMATION DISTRIBUTION SYSTEM (JTIDS)	16,288	16,288
121	0605000BR	WEAPONS OF MASS DESTRUCTION DEFEAT CAPABILITIES	4,568	4,568
122	0605013BL	INFORMATION TECHNOLOGY DEVELOPMENT	11,505	11,505
123	0605021SE	HOMELAND PERSONNEL SECURITY INITIATIVE	1,658	1,658
124	0605022D8Z	DEFENSE EXPORTABILITY PROGRAM	2,920	2,920
126	0605070S	DOD ENTERPRISE SYSTEMS DEVELOPMENT AND DEMONSTRATION	12,631	12,631
128	0605080S	DEFENSE AGENCY INTIATIVES (DAI)—FINANCIAL SYSTEM	26,657	26,657
129	0605090S	DEFENSE RETIRED AND ANNUITANT PAY SYSTEM (DRAS)	4,949	4,949
130	0605140D8Z	TRUSTED FOUNDRY	69,000	69,000
131	0605210D8Z	DEFENSE-WIDE ELECTRONIC PROCUREMENT CAPABILITIES	9,881	9,881
132	0303141K	GLOBAL COMBAT SUPPORT SYSTEM	7,600	7,600
133	0305304D8Z	DOD ENTERPRISE ENERGY INFORMATION MANAGEMENT (EEIM)	2,703	2,703
		SUBTOTAL SYSTEM DEVELOPMENT AND DEMONSTRATION	**628,218**	**628,218**

MANAGEMENT SUPPORT

Line	Program Element	Item	FY 2017 Request	Conference Authorized
134	0604774D8Z	DEFENSE READINESS REPORTING SYSTEM (DRRS)	4,678	4,678
135	0604875D8Z	JOINT SYSTEMS ARCHITECTURE DEVELOPMENT	4,499	4,499
136	0604940D8Z	CENTRAL TEST AND EVALUATION INVESTMENT DEVELOPMENT (CTEIP)	219,199	219,199
137	0604942D8Z	ASSESSMENTS AND EVALUATIONS	28,706	28,706
138	0605001E	MISSION SUPPORT	69,244	69,244
139	0605100D8Z	JOINT MISSION ENVIRONMENT TEST CAPABILITY (JMETC)	87,080	67,080
		Prior year carryover and minimize growth		[−20,000]
140	0605104D8Z	TECHNICAL STUDIES, SUPPORT AND ANALYSIS	23,069	23,069
142	0605126J	JOINT INTEGRATED AIR AND MISSILE DEFENSE ORGANIZATION (JIAMDO)	32,759	32,759
144	0605142D8Z	SYSTEMS ENGINEERING	32,429	32,429
145	0605151D8Z	STUDIES AND ANALYSIS SUPPORT—OSD	3,797	3,797
146	0605161D8Z	NUCLEAR MATTERS-PHYSICAL SECURITY	5,302	5,302
147	0605170D8Z	SUPPORT TO NETWORKS AND INFORMATION INTEGRATION	7,246	7,246
148	0605200D8Z	GENERAL SUPPORT TO USD (INTELLIGENCE)	1,874	1,874
149	0605384BP	CHEMICAL AND BIOLOGICAL DEFENSE PROGRAM	85,754	85,754
158	0605790D8Z	SMALL BUSINESS INNOVATION RESEARCH (SBIR)/ SMALL BUSINESS TECHNOLOGY TRANSFER.	2,187	2,187
159	0605798D8Z	DEFENSE TECHNOLOGY ANALYSIS	22,650	22,650
160	0605801KA	DEFENSE TECHNICAL INFORMATION CENTER (DTIC)	43,834	43,834
161	0605803SE	R&D IN SUPPORT OF DOD ENLISTMENT, TESTING AND EVALUATION	22,240	22,240
162	0605804D8Z	DEVELOPMENT TEST AND EVALUATION	19,541	23,541
		Program increase		[4,000]
163	0605898E	MANAGEMENT HQ—R&D	4,759	4,759
164	0605998KA	MANAGEMENT HQ—DEFENSE TECHNICAL INFORMATION CENTER (DTIC)	4,400	4,400
165	0606100D8Z	BUDGET AND PROGRAM ASSESSMENTS	4,014	4,014
166	0203345D8Z	DEFENSE OPERATIONS SECURITY INITIATIVE (DOSI)	2,072	2,072
167	0204571J	JOINT STAFF ANALYTICAL SUPPORT	7,464	7,464
170	0303166J	SUPPORT TO INFORMATION OPERATIONS (IO) CAPABILITIES	857	857
171	0303260D8Z	DEFENSE MILITARY DECEPTION PROGRAM OFFICE (DMDPO)	916	916
172	0305172K	COMBINED ADVANCED APPLICATIONS	15,336	15,336
173	0305193D8Z	CYBER INTELLIGENCE	18,523	13,523
		Program decrease		[−5,000]
175	0804767D8Z	COCOM EXERCISE ENGAGEMENT AND TRAINING TRANSFORMATION (CE2T2)—MHA	34,384	34,384
176	0901598C	MANAGEMENT HQ—MDA	31,160	31,160

SEC. 4201. RESEARCH, DEVELOPMENT, TEST, AND EVALUATION
(In Thousands of Dollars)

Line	Program Element	Item	FY 2017 Request	Conference Authorized
179	0903235D8W	JOINT SERVICE PROVIDER (JSP)	827	827
180A	9999999999	CLASSIFIED PROGRAMS	56,799	56,799
		SUBTOTAL MANAGEMENT SUPPORT	897,599	876,599
		OPERATIONAL SYSTEM DEVELOPMENT		
181	0604130V	ENTERPRISE SECURITY SYSTEM (ESS)	4,241	4,241
182	0605127T	REGIONAL INTERNATIONAL OUTREACH (RIO) AND PARTNERSHIP FOR PEACE INFORMATION MANA.	1,424	1,424
183	0605147T	OVERSEAS HUMANITARIAN ASSISTANCE SHARED INFORMATION SYSTEM (OHASIS)	287	287
184	0607210D8Z	INDUSTRIAL BASE ANALYSIS AND SUSTAINMENT SUPPORT	16,195	16,195
185	0607310D8Z	CWMD SYSTEMS: OPERATIONAL SYSTEMS DEVELOPMENT	4,194	4,194
186	0607327T	GLOBAL THEATER SECURITY COOPERATION MANAGEMENT INFORMATION SYSTEMS (G-TSCMIS).	7,861	7,861
187	0607384BP	CHEMICAL AND BIOLOGICAL DEFENSE (OPERATIONAL SYSTEMS DEVELOPMENT)	33,361	33,361
189	0208043J	PLANNING AND DECISION AID SYSTEM (PDAS)	3,038	3,038
190	0208045K	C4I INTEROPERABILITY	57,501	57,501
192	0301144K	JOINT/ALLIED COALITION INFORMATION SHARING	5,935	5,935
196	0302016K	NATIONAL MILITARY COMMAND SYSTEM-WIDE SUPPORT	575	575
197	0302019K	DEFENSE INFO INFRASTRUCTURE ENGINEERING AND INTEGRATION	18,041	18,041
198	0303126K	LONG-HAUL COMMUNICATIONS—DCS	13,994	13,994
199	0303131K	MINIMUM ESSENTIAL EMERGENCY COMMUNICATIONS NETWORK (MEECN)	12,206	12,206
200	0303135G	PUBLIC KEY INFRASTRUCTURE (PKI)	34,314	34,314
201	0303136G	KEY MANAGEMENT INFRASTRUCTURE (KMI)	36,602	36,602
202	0303140D8Z	INFORMATION SYSTEMS SECURITY PROGRAM	8,876	8,876
203	0303140G	INFORMATION SYSTEMS SECURITY PROGRAM	159,068	161,068
		SHARKSEER Program Increase		[2,000]
204	0303150K	GLOBAL COMMAND AND CONTROL SYSTEM	24,438	24,438
205	0303153K	DEFENSE SPECTRUM ORGANIZATION	13,197	13,197
207	0303228K	JOINT INFORMATION ENVIRONMENT (JIE)	2,789	2,789
209	0303430K	FEDERAL INVESTIGATIVE SERVICES INFORMATION TECHNOLOGY	75,000	75,000
210	0303610K	TELEPORT PROGRAM	657	657
215	0305103K	CYBER SECURITY INITIATIVE	1,553	1,553
220	0305186D8Z	POLICY R&D PROGRAMS	6,204	4,204
		Program decrease		[–2,000]
221	0305199D8Z	NET CENTRICITY	17,971	17,971
223	0305208BB	DISTRIBUTED COMMON GROUND/SURFACE SYSTEMS	5,415	5,415
226	0305208K	DISTRIBUTED COMMON GROUND/SURFACE SYSTEMS	3,030	3,030
229	0305327V	INSIDER THREAT	5,034	5,034
230	0305387D8Z	HOMELAND DEFENSE TECHNOLOGY TRANSFER PROGRAM	2,037	2,037
236	0307577D8Z	INTELLIGENCE MISSION DATA (IMD)	13,800	13,800
238	0708012S	PACIFIC DISASTER CENTERS	1,754	1,754
239	0708047S	DEFENSE PROPERTY ACCOUNTABILITY SYSTEM	2,154	2,154
240	0902298J	MANAGEMENT HQ—OJCS	826	826
241	1105219BB	MQ–9 UAV	17,804	17,804
244	1160403BB	AVIATION SYSTEMS	159,143	159,143
245	1160405BB	INTELLIGENCE SYSTEMS DEVELOPMENT	7,958	7,958
246	1160408BB	OPERATIONAL ENHANCEMENTS	64,895	64,895
247	1160431BB	WARRIOR SYSTEMS	44,885	44,885
248	1160432BB	SPECIAL PROGRAMS	1,949	1,949
249	1160434BB	UNMANNED ISR	22,117	22,117
250	1160480BB	SOF TACTICAL VEHICLES	3,316	3,316
251	1160483BB	MARITIME SYSTEMS	54,577	54,577
252	1160488BB	GLOBAL VIDEO SURVEILLANCE ACTIVITIES	3,841	3,841
253	1160490BB	OPERATIONAL ENHANCEMENTS INTELLIGENCE	11,834	11,834
253A	9999999999	CLASSIFIED PROGRAMS	3,270,515	3,270,515
		SUBTOTAL OPERATIONAL SYSTEM DEVELOPMENT	4,256,406	4,256,406
		TOTAL RESEARCH, DEVELOPMENT, TEST & EVAL, DW	18,308,826	18,266,676
		OPERATIONAL TEST & EVAL, DEFENSE MANAGEMENT SUPPORT		
001	0605118OTE	OPERATIONAL TEST AND EVALUATION	78,047	78,047
002	0605131OTE	LIVE FIRE TEST AND EVALUATION	48,316	48,316
003	0605814OTE	OPERATIONAL TEST ACTIVITIES AND ANALYSES	52,631	52,631
		SUBTOTAL MANAGEMENT SUPPORT	178,994	178,994
		TOTAL OPERATIONAL TEST & EVAL, DEFENSE	178,994	178,994
		TOTAL RDT&E	71,391,771	71,110,624

SEC. 4202. RESEARCH, DEVELOPMENT, TEST, AND EVALUATION FOR OVERSEAS CONTINGENCY OPERATIONS.

SEC. 4202. RESEARCH, DEVELOPMENT, TEST, AND EVALUATION FOR OVERSEAS CONTINGENCY OPERATIONS
(In Thousands of Dollars)

Line	Program Element	Item	FY 2017 Request	Conference Authorized
		ADVANCED COMPONENT DEVELOPMENT & PROTOTYPES		
055	0603308A	ARMY SPACE SYSTEMS INTEGRATION	9,375	9,375
		SUBTOTAL ADVANCED COMPONENT DEVELOPMENT & PROTOTYPES	**9,375**	**9,375**
		SYSTEM DEVELOPMENT & DEMONSTRATION		
091	0604741A	AIR DEFENSE COMMAND, CONTROL AND INTELLIGENCE—ENG DEV	78,700	78,700
114	0605032A	TRACTOR TIRE	10,000	10,000
117	0605035A	COMMON INFRARED COUNTERMEASURES (CIRCM)	10,900	10,900
119	0605041A	DEFENSIVE CYBER TOOL DEVELOPMENT	50,500	50,500
122	0605051A	AIRCRAFT SURVIVABILITY DEVELOPMENT	73,110	73,110
		SUBTOTAL SYSTEM DEVELOPMENT & DEMONSTRATION	**223,210**	**223,210**
		OPERATIONAL SYSTEMS DEVELOPMENT		
208	0307665A	BIOMETRICS ENABLED INTELLIGENCE	7,104	7,104
		SUBTOTAL OPERATIONAL SYSTEMS DEVELOPMENT	**7,104**	**7,104**
		TOTAL RESEARCH, DEVELOPMENT, TEST & EVAL, ARMY	**239,689**	**239,689**
		ADVANCED COMPONENT DEVELOPMENT & PROTOTYPES		
038	0603527N	RETRACT LARCH	3,907	3,907
		SUBTOTAL ADVANCED COMPONENT DEVELOPMENT & PROTOTYPES	**3,907**	**3,907**
		OPERATIONAL SYSTEMS DEVELOPMENT		
245A	9999999999	CLASSIFIED PROGRAMS	36,426	36,426
		SUBTOTAL OPERATIONAL SYSTEMS DEVELOPMENT	**36,426**	**36,426**
		TOTAL RESEARCH, DEVELOPMENT, TEST & EVAL, NAVY	**40,333**	**40,333**
		SYSTEM DEVELOPMENT & DEMONSTRATION		
058	0604421F	COUNTERSPACE SYSTEMS	425	425
		SUBTOTAL SYSTEM DEVELOPMENT & DEMONSTRATION	**425**	**425**
		OPERATIONAL SYSTEMS DEVELOPMENT		
200	0305174F	SPACE INNOVATION, INTEGRATION AND RAPID TECHNOLOGY DEVELOPMENT	4,715	4,715
242A	9999999999	CLASSIFIED PROGRAMS	27,765	27,765
		SUBTOTAL OPERATIONAL SYSTEMS DEVELOPMENT	**32,480**	**32,480**
		TOTAL RESEARCH, DEVELOPMENT, TEST & EVAL, AF	**32,905**	**32,905**
		OPERATIONAL SYSTEM DEVELOPMENT		
253A	9999999999	CLASSIFIED PROGRAMS	165,419	165,419
		SUBTOTAL OPERATIONAL SYSTEM DEVELOPMENT	**165,419**	**165,419**
		TOTAL RESEARCH, DEVELOPMENT, TEST & EVAL, DW	**165,419**	**165,419**
		TOTAL RDT&E	**478,346**	**478,346**

SEC. 4203. RESEARCH, DEVELOPMENT, TEST, AND EVALUATION FOR OVERSEAS CONTINGENCY OPERATIONS FOR BASE REQUIREMENTS.

SEC. 4203. RESEARCH, DEVELOPMENT, TEST, AND EVALUATION FOR OVERSEAS CONTINGENCY OPERATIONS FOR BASE OPERATIONS
(In Thousands of Dollars)

Line	Program Element	Item	FY 2017 Request	Conference Authorized
		RESEARCH, DEVELOPMENT, TEST & EVAL, ARMY		
		SYSTEM DEVELOPMENT & DEMONSTRATION		
090	0604715A	NON-SYSTEM TRAINING DEVICES—ENG DEV	33	33
		SUBTOTAL SYSTEM DEVELOPMENT & DEMONSTRATION	**33**	**33**
		TOTAL RESEARCH, DEVELOPMENT, TEST & EVAL, ARMY	**33**	**33**
		RESEARCH, DEVELOPMENT, TEST & EVAL, NAVY		
		ADVANCED COMPONENT DEVELOPMENT & PROTOTYPES		
078	0604272N	TACTICAL AIR DIRECTIONAL INFRARED COUNTERMEASURES (TADIRCM)	37,990	37,990
		SUBTOTAL ADVANCED COMPONENT DEVELOPMENT & PROTOTYPES	**37,990**	**37,990**
		TOTAL RESEARCH, DEVELOPMENT, TEST & EVAL, NAVY	**37,990**	**37,990**
		TOTAL RDT&E	**38,023**	**38,023**

TITLE XLIII—OPERATION AND MAINTENANCE
SEC. 4301. OPERATION AND MAINTENANCE.

SEC. 4301. OPERATION AND MAINTENANCE
(In Thousands of Dollars)

Line	Item	FY 2017 Request	Conference Authorized
	OPERATION & MAINTENANCE, ARMY		
	OPERATING FORCES		
010	MANEUVER UNITS	791,450	841,450
	Home station training unfunded requirement		[50,000]
020	MODULAR SUPPORT BRIGADES	68,373	68,373
030	ECHELONS ABOVE BRIGADE	438,823	438,823
040	THEATER LEVEL ASSETS	660,258	660,258
050	LAND FORCES OPERATIONS SUPPORT	863,928	863,928
060	AVIATION ASSETS	1,360,597	1,461,097
	Eleventh CAB		[32,500]
	Flying hour program unfunded requirement		[68,000]
070	FORCE READINESS OPERATIONS SUPPORT	3,086,443	3,086,443
080	LAND FORCES SYSTEMS READINESS	439,488	439,488
090	LAND FORCES DEPOT MAINTENANCE	1,013,452	1,032,852
	Depot maintenance unfunded requirement		[19,400]
100	BASE OPERATIONS SUPPORT	7,816,343	7,838,443
	Eleventh CAB Support		[22,100]
110	FACILITIES SUSTAINMENT, RESTORATION & MODERNIZATION	2,234,546	2,319,946
	Restore Sustainment shortfalls		[85,400]
120	MANAGEMENT AND OPERATIONAL HEADQUARTERS	452,105	452,105
130	COMBATANT COMMANDERS CORE OPERATIONS	155,658	155,658
170	COMBATANT COMMANDS DIRECT MISSION SUPPORT	441,143	441,143
	SUBTOTAL OPERATING FORCES	**19,822,607**	**20,100,007**
	MOBILIZATION		
180	STRATEGIC MOBILITY	336,329	336,329
190	ARMY PREPOSITIONED STOCKS	390,848	415,848
	Program increase		[25,000]
200	INDUSTRIAL PREPAREDNESS	7,401	7,401
	SUBTOTAL MOBILIZATION	**734,578**	**759,578**
	TRAINING AND RECRUITING		
210	OFFICER ACQUISITION	131,942	131,942
220	RECRUIT TRAINING	47,846	47,846
230	ONE STATION UNIT TRAINING	45,419	45,419
240	SENIOR RESERVE OFFICERS TRAINING CORPS	482,747	482,747
250	SPECIALIZED SKILL TRAINING	921,025	927,525
	Defense Foreign Language Program		[6,500]
260	FLIGHT TRAINING	902,845	945,779
	Graduate pilot training unfunded requirement		[5,405]
	School Air OPTEMPO unfunded requirement		[31,125]
	Train full ARPINT load of 990		[6,404]
270	PROFESSIONAL DEVELOPMENT EDUCATION	216,583	248,183
	Military Training and PME		[31,600]
280	TRAINING SUPPORT	607,534	607,534
290	RECRUITING AND ADVERTISING	550,599	525,599
	Unjustified program growth		[-25,000]
300	EXAMINING	187,263	187,263
310	OFF-DUTY AND VOLUNTARY EDUCATION	189,556	189,556
320	CIVILIAN EDUCATION AND TRAINING	182,835	182,835
330	JUNIOR RESERVE OFFICER TRAINING CORPS	171,167	171,167
	SUBTOTAL TRAINING AND RECRUITING	**4,637,361**	**4,693,395**
	ADMIN & SRVWIDE ACTIVITIES		
350	SERVICEWIDE TRANSPORTATION	230,739	295,739
	Restore cricital shortfalls		[65,000]
360	CENTRAL SUPPLY ACTIVITIES	850,060	850,060
370	LOGISTIC SUPPORT ACTIVITIES	778,757	778,757
380	AMMUNITION MANAGEMENT	370,010	370,010
390	ADMINISTRATION	451,556	451,556
400	SERVICEWIDE COMMUNICATIONS	1,888,123	1,888,123
410	MANPOWER MANAGEMENT	276,403	276,403
420	OTHER PERSONNEL SUPPORT	369,443	369,443
430	OTHER SERVICE SUPPORT	1,096,074	1,096,074
440	ARMY CLAIMS ACTIVITIES	207,800	207,800
450	REAL ESTATE MANAGEMENT	240,641	240,641
460	FINANCIAL MANAGEMENT AND AUDIT READINESS	250,612	250,612
470	INTERNATIONAL MILITARY HEADQUARTERS	416,587	416,587
480	MISC. SUPPORT OF OTHER NATIONS	36,666	36,666
530	CLASSIFIED PROGRAMS	1,151,023	1,151,023
	SUBTOTAL ADMIN & SRVWIDE ACTIVITIES	**8,614,494**	**8,679,494**
	UNDISTRIBUTED		
540	UNDISTRIBUTED		-400,200
	Excessive standard price for fuel		[-56,100]
	Foreign Currency adjustments		[-194,100]
	Working Capital Fund Carryover Above Allowable Ceiling		[-150,000]
	SUBTOTAL UNDISTRIBUTED		**-400,200**

SEC. 4301. OPERATION AND MAINTENANCE
(In Thousands of Dollars)

Line	Item	FY 2017 Request	Conference Authorized
	TOTAL OPERATION & MAINTENANCE, ARMY	33,809,040	33,832,274
	OPERATION & MAINTENANCE, ARMY RES		
	OPERATING FORCES		
010	MODULAR SUPPORT BRIGADES	11,435	11,435
020	ECHELONS ABOVE BRIGADE	491,772	511,772
	Home station training unfunded requirement		[20,000]
030	THEATER LEVEL ASSETS	116,163	116,163
040	LAND FORCES OPERATIONS SUPPORT	563,524	563,524
050	AVIATION ASSETS	91,162	91,162
060	FORCE READINESS OPERATIONS SUPPORT	347,459	347,459
	Defense Language Program		[200]
070	LAND FORCES SYSTEMS READINESS	101,926	101,926
080	LAND FORCES DEPOT MAINTENANCE	56,219	56,219
090	BASE OPERATIONS SUPPORT	573,843	573,843
100	FACILITIES SUSTAINMENT, RESTORATION & MODERNIZATION	214,955	223,055
	Restore Sustainment shortfalls		[8,100]
110	MANAGEMENT AND OPERATIONAL HEADQUARTERS	37,620	37,620
	SUBTOTAL OPERATING FORCES	2,606,078	2,634,378
	ADMIN & SRVWD ACTIVITIES		
120	SERVICEWIDE TRANSPORTATION	11,027	11,027
130	ADMINISTRATION	16,749	16,749
140	SERVICEWIDE COMMUNICATIONS	17,825	17,825
150	MANPOWER MANAGEMENT	6,177	6,177
160	RECRUITING AND ADVERTISING	54,475	54,475
	SUBTOTAL ADMIN & SRVWD ACTIVITIES	106,253	106,253
	UNDISTRIBUTED		
180	UNDISTRIBUTED		−6,800
	Excessive standard price for fuel		[−6,800]
	SUBTOTAL UNDISTRIBUTED		**−6,800**
	TOTAL OPERATION & MAINTENANCE, ARMY RES	2,712,331	2,733,831
	OPERATION & MAINTENANCE, ARNG		
	OPERATING FORCES		
010	MANEUVER UNITS	708,251	758,251
	Home station training unfunded requirement		[50,000]
020	MODULAR SUPPORT BRIGADES	197,251	197,251
030	ECHELONS ABOVE BRIGADE	792,271	792,271
040	THEATER LEVEL ASSETS	80,341	80,341
050	LAND FORCES OPERATIONS SUPPORT	37,138	37,138
060	AVIATION ASSETS	887,625	884,825
	Unjustified program growth		[−2,800]
070	FORCE READINESS OPERATIONS SUPPORT	696,267	690,152
	Defense Language Program		[200]
	Unjustified program growth		[−6,315]
080	LAND FORCES SYSTEMS READINESS	61,240	61,240
090	LAND FORCES DEPOT MAINTENANCE	219,948	219,948
100	BASE OPERATIONS SUPPORT	1,040,012	1,040,012
110	FACILITIES SUSTAINMENT, RESTORATION & MODERNIZATION	676,715	691,115
	Restore Sustainment shortfalls		[14,400]
120	MANAGEMENT AND OPERATIONAL HEADQUARTERS	1,021,144	1,021,144
	SUBTOTAL OPERATING FORCES	6,418,203	6,473,688
	ADMIN & SRVWD ACTIVITIES		
130	SERVICEWIDE TRANSPORTATION	6,396	6,396
140	ADMINISTRATION	68,528	69,678
	State Partnership Program		[1,150]
150	SERVICEWIDE COMMUNICATIONS	76,524	76,524
160	MANPOWER MANAGEMENT	7,712	7,712
170	OTHER PERSONNEL SUPPORT	245,046	245,046
180	REAL ESTATE MANAGEMENT	2,961	2,961
	SUBTOTAL ADMIN & SRVWD ACTIVITIES	407,167	408,317
	UNDISTRIBUTED		
190	UNDISTRIBUTED		−29,000
	Excessive standard price for fuel		[−29,000]
	SUBTOTAL UNDISTRIBUTED		**−29,000**
	TOTAL OPERATION & MAINTENANCE, ARNG	6,825,370	6,853,005
	OPERATION & MAINTENANCE, NAVY		
	OPERATING FORCES		
010	MISSION AND OTHER FLIGHT OPERATIONS	4,094,765	4,094,765
020	FLEET AIR TRAINING	1,722,473	1,722,473
030	AVIATION TECHNICAL DATA & ENGINEERING SERVICES	52,670	52,670
040	AIR OPERATIONS AND SAFETY SUPPORT	97,584	97,584

SEC. 4301. OPERATION AND MAINTENANCE
(In Thousands of Dollars)

Line	Item	FY 2017 Request	Conference Authorized
050	AIR SYSTEMS SUPPORT	446,733	453,233
	Marine Corps unfunded requirement—accelerate readiness - H–1		[5,300]
	Marine Corps unfunded requirement—accelerate readiness - MV–22B		[1,200]
060	AIRCRAFT DEPOT MAINTENANCE	1,007,681	1,071,681
	AC Depot maintenance unfunded requirement		[34,000]
	Navy unfunded requirement—Improve Afloat Readiness		[30,000]
070	AIRCRAFT DEPOT OPERATIONS SUPPORT	38,248	38,248
080	AVIATION LOGISTICS	564,720	598,220
	E–6B and F–35 sustainment unfunded requirement		[16,000]
	Marine Corps unfunded requirement—accelerate readiness - KC–130J		[6,800]
	Marine Corps unfunded requirement—accelerate readiness - MV–22B		[10,700]
090	MISSION AND OTHER SHIP OPERATIONS	3,513,083	3,861,283
	Cruiser Modernization		[90,200]
	Navy unfunded requirement—Improve Afloat Readiness		[158,000]
	Navy unfunded requirement—Restore 3 CG Deployments		[41,000]
	Navy unfunded requirement—Reverse PONCE (LPD–15) Inactivation		[59,000]
100	SHIP OPERATIONS SUPPORT & TRAINING	743,765	763,465
	Navy unfunded requirement—Restore Fleet Training		[19,700]
110	SHIP DEPOT MAINTENANCE	5,168,273	5,486,873
	Cruiser Modernization		[71,100]
	Navy unfunded requirement—Ship Depot Wholeness		[238,000]
	Program increase		[9,500]
120	SHIP DEPOT OPERATIONS SUPPORT	1,575,578	1,654,578
	Navy unfunded requirement—Increase Alfoat Readiness		[79,000]
130	COMBAT COMMUNICATIONS	558,727	558,727
140	ELECTRONIC WARFARE	105,680	105,680
150	SPACE SYSTEMS AND SURVEILLANCE	180,406	180,406
160	WARFARE TACTICS	470,032	470,032
170	OPERATIONAL METEOROLOGY AND OCEANOGRAPHY	346,703	346,703
180	COMBAT SUPPORT FORCES	1,158,688	1,158,688
190	EQUIPMENT MAINTENANCE	113,692	113,692
200	DEPOT OPERATIONS SUPPORT	2,509	2,509
210	COMBATANT COMMANDERS CORE OPERATIONS	91,019	91,019
220	COMBATANT COMMANDERS DIRECT MISSION SUPPORT	74,780	74,780
230	CRUISE MISSILE	106,030	106,030
240	FLEET BALLISTIC MISSILE	1,233,805	1,233,805
250	IN-SERVICE WEAPONS SYSTEMS SUPPORT	163,025	163,025
260	WEAPONS MAINTENANCE	553,269	553,269
270	OTHER WEAPON SYSTEMS SUPPORT	350,010	350,010
280	ENTERPRISE INFORMATION	790,685	790,685
290	SUSTAINMENT, RESTORATION AND MODERNIZATION	1,642,742	1,697,842
	Restore Sustainment shortfalls		[55,100]
300	BASE OPERATING SUPPORT	4,206,136	4,206,136
	SUBTOTAL OPERATING FORCES	**31,173,511**	**32,098,111**
	MOBILIZATION		
310	SHIP PREPOSITIONING AND SURGE	893,517	893,517
320	READY RESERVE FORCE	274,524	274,524
330	AIRCRAFT ACTIVATIONS/INACTIVATIONS	6,727	6,727
340	SHIP ACTIVATIONS/INACTIVATIONS	288,154	288,154
350	EXPEDITIONARY HEALTH SERVICES SYSTEMS	95,720	95,720
360	INDUSTRIAL READINESS	2,109	2,109
370	COAST GUARD SUPPORT	21,114	21,114
	SUBTOTAL MOBILIZATION	**1,581,865**	**1,581,865**
	TRAINING AND RECRUITING		
380	OFFICER ACQUISITION	143,815	143,815
390	RECRUIT TRAINING	8,519	8,519
400	RESERVE OFFICERS TRAINING CORPS	143,445	143,445
410	SPECIALIZED SKILL TRAINING	699,214	699,214
420	FLIGHT TRAINING	5,310	5,310
430	PROFESSIONAL DEVELOPMENT EDUCATION	172,852	172,852
440	TRAINING SUPPORT	222,728	222,728
450	RECRUITING AND ADVERTISING	225,647	225,647
460	OFF-DUTY AND VOLUNTARY EDUCATION	130,569	130,569
470	CIVILIAN EDUCATION AND TRAINING	73,730	73,730
480	JUNIOR ROTC	50,400	50,400
	SUBTOTAL TRAINING AND RECRUITING	**1,876,229**	**1,876,229**
	ADMIN & SRVWD ACTIVITIES		
490	ADMINISTRATION	917,453	917,453
500	EXTERNAL RELATIONS	14,570	14,570
510	CIVILIAN MANPOWER AND PERSONNEL MANAGEMENT	124,070	124,070
520	MILITARY MANPOWER AND PERSONNEL MANAGEMENT	369,767	369,767
530	OTHER PERSONNEL SUPPORT	285,927	285,927
540	SERVICEWIDE COMMUNICATIONS	319,908	319,908
570	SERVICEWIDE TRANSPORTATION	171,659	171,659
590	PLANNING, ENGINEERING AND DESIGN	270,863	270,863
600	ACQUISITION AND PROGRAM MANAGEMENT	1,112,766	1,112,766

SEC. 4301. OPERATION AND MAINTENANCE
(In Thousands of Dollars)

Line	Item	FY 2017 Request	Conference Authorized
610	HULL, MECHANICAL AND ELECTRICAL SUPPORT	49,078	49,078
620	COMBAT/WEAPONS SYSTEMS	24,989	24,989
630	SPACE AND ELECTRONIC WARFARE SYSTEMS	72,966	72,966
640	NAVAL INVESTIGATIVE SERVICE	595,711	595,711
700	INTERNATIONAL HEADQUARTERS AND AGENCIES	4,809	4,809
730	CLASSIFIED PROGRAMS	517,440	517,440
	SUBTOTAL ADMIN & SRVWD ACTIVITIES	**4,851,976**	**4,851,976**
	UNDISTRIBUTED		
740	UNDISTRIBUTED		−416,900
	Excessive standard price for fuel		*[−390,500]*
	Foreign Currency adjustments		*[−26,400]*
	SUBTOTAL UNDISTRIBUTED		**−416,900**
	TOTAL OPERATION & MAINTENANCE, NAVY	**39,483,581**	**39,991,281**
	OPERATION & MAINTENANCE, MARINE CORPS		
	OPERATING FORCES		
010	OPERATIONAL FORCES	674,613	760,313
	Enterprise network defense unfunded requirement		*[5,700]*
	Exercise program unfunded requirement		*[58,000]*
	Marine Corps unfunded requirement- enhanced combat helmets		*[22,000]*
020	FIELD LOGISTICS	947,424	983,674
	Critical/ no fail EOD unfunded requirement		*[600]*
	Marine Corps unfunded requirement- rifle combat optic modernization		*[13,200]*
	Marine Corps unfunded requirement- SPMAGTF—C4 UUNS		*[8,250]*
	Nano/VTOL unfunded requirement		*[14,200]*
030	DEPOT MAINTENANCE	206,783	214,583
	Depot maintenance unfunded requirement		*[7,800]*
040	MARITIME PREPOSITIONING	85,276	85,276
050	SUSTAINMENT, RESTORATION & MODERNIZATION	632,673	694,673
	Facility demolition unfunded requirement		*[39,200]*
	Restore Sustainment shortfalls		*[22,800]*
060	BASE OPERATING SUPPORT	2,136,626	2,136,626
	SUBTOTAL OPERATING FORCES	**4,683,395**	**4,875,145**
	TRAINING AND RECRUITING		
070	RECRUIT TRAINING	15,946	15,946
080	OFFICER ACQUISITION	935	935
090	SPECIALIZED SKILL TRAINING	99,305	99,305
100	PROFESSIONAL DEVELOPMENT EDUCATION	45,495	45,495
110	TRAINING SUPPORT	369,979	369,979
120	RECRUITING AND ADVERTISING	165,566	165,566
130	OFF-DUTY AND VOLUNTARY EDUCATION	35,133	35,133
140	JUNIOR ROTC	23,622	23,622
	SUBTOTAL TRAINING AND RECRUITING	**755,981**	**755,981**
	ADMIN & SRVWD ACTIVITIES		
150	SERVICEWIDE TRANSPORTATION	34,534	34,534
160	ADMINISTRATION	355,932	355,932
180	ACQUISITION AND PROGRAM MANAGEMENT	76,896	76,896
200	CLASSIFIED PROGRAMS	47,520	47,520
	SUBTOTAL ADMIN & SRVWD ACTIVITIES	**514,882**	**514,882**
	UNDISTRIBUTED		
210	UNDISTRIBUTED		−6,400
	Excessive standard price for fuel		*[−4,900]*
	Foreign Currency adjustments		*[−1,500]*
	SUBTOTAL UNDISTRIBUTED		**−6,400**
	TOTAL OPERATION & MAINTENANCE, MARINE CORPS	**5,954,258**	**6,139,608**
	OPERATION & MAINTENANCE, NAVY RES		
	OPERATING FORCES		
010	MISSION AND OTHER FLIGHT OPERATIONS	526,190	526,190
020	INTERMEDIATE MAINTENANCE	6,714	6,714
030	AIRCRAFT DEPOT MAINTENANCE	86,209	90,209
	Navy unfunded requirement—Improve Afloat Readiness		*[4,000]*
040	AIRCRAFT DEPOT OPERATIONS SUPPORT	389	389
050	AVIATION LOGISTICS	10,189	10,189
070	SHIP OPERATIONS SUPPORT & TRAINING	560	860
	Navy unfunded requirement—Restore Fleet Training		*[300]*
090	COMBAT COMMUNICATIONS	13,173	13,173
100	COMBAT SUPPORT FORCES	109,053	109,053
120	ENTERPRISE INFORMATION	27,226	27,226
130	SUSTAINMENT, RESTORATION AND MODERNIZATION	27,571	28,671
	Restore Sustainment shortfalls		*[1,100]*
140	BASE OPERATING SUPPORT	99,166	99,166
	SUBTOTAL OPERATING FORCES	**906,440**	**911,840**

SEC. 4301. OPERATION AND MAINTENANCE
(In Thousands of Dollars)

Line	Item	FY 2017 Request	Conference Authorized
	ADMIN & SRVWD ACTIVITIES		
150	ADMINISTRATION	1,351	1,351
160	MILITARY MANPOWER AND PERSONNEL MANAGEMENT	13,251	13,251
170	SERVICEWIDE COMMUNICATIONS	3,445	3,445
180	ACQUISITION AND PROGRAM MANAGEMENT	3,169	3,169
	SUBTOTAL ADMIN & SRVWD ACTIVITIES	21,216	21,216
	UNDISTRIBUTED		
200	UNDISTRIBUTED		−26,600
	Excessive standard price for fuel		[−26,600]
	SUBTOTAL UNDISTRIBUTED		−26,600
	TOTAL OPERATION & MAINTENANCE, NAVY RES	927,656	906,456
	OPERATION & MAINTENANCE, MC RESERVE		
	OPERATING FORCES		
010	OPERATING FORCES	94,154	94,154
020	DEPOT MAINTENANCE	18,594	18,594
030	SUSTAINMENT, RESTORATION AND MODERNIZATION	25,470	26,170
	Restore Sustainment shortfalls		[700]
040	BASE OPERATING SUPPORT	111,550	111,550
	SUBTOTAL OPERATING FORCES	249,768	250,468
	ADMIN & SRVWD ACTIVITIES		
050	SERVICEWIDE TRANSPORTATION	902	902
060	ADMINISTRATION	11,130	11,130
070	RECRUITING AND ADVERTISING	8,833	8,833
	SUBTOTAL ADMIN & SRVWD ACTIVITIES	20,865	20,865
	UNDISTRIBUTED		
090	UNDISTRIBUTED		−800
	Excessive standard price for fuel		[−800]
	SUBTOTAL UNDISTRIBUTED		−800
	TOTAL OPERATION & MAINTENANCE, MC RESERVE	270,633	270,533
	OPERATION & MAINTENANCE, AIR FORCE		
	OPERATING FORCES		
010	PRIMARY COMBAT FORCES	3,294,124	3,294,124
020	COMBAT ENHANCEMENT FORCES	1,682,045	1,684,845
	HH-60 unfunded requirement		[2,800]
030	AIR OPERATIONS TRAINING (OJT, MAINTAIN SKILLS)	1,730,757	1,730,757
040	DEPOT MAINTENANCE	7,042,988	7,156,064
	Compass Call Program Restructure		[−56,500]
	Weapon system sustainment unfunded requirement		[169,576]
050	FACILITIES SUSTAINMENT, RESTORATION & MODERNIZATION	1,657,019	1,710,019
	Restore Sustainment shortfalls		[53,000]
060	BASE SUPPORT	2,787,216	2,787,216
070	GLOBAL C3I AND EARLY WARNING	887,831	927,831
	Air Force unfunded requirement—Ground Based Radars		[40,000]
080	OTHER COMBAT OPS SPT PROGRAMS	1,070,178	1,070,178
100	LAUNCH FACILITIES	208,582	208,582
110	SPACE CONTROL SYSTEMS	362,250	362,250
120	COMBATANT COMMANDERS DIRECT MISSION SUPPORT	907,245	907,245
130	COMBATANT COMMANDERS CORE OPERATIONS	199,171	199,171
135	CLASSIFIED PROGRAMS	930,757	930,757
	SUBTOTAL OPERATING FORCES	22,760,163	22,969,039
	MOBILIZATION		
140	AIRLIFT OPERATIONS	1,703,059	1,703,059
150	MOBILIZATION PREPAREDNESS	138,899	138,899
160	DEPOT MAINTENANCE	1,553,439	1,619,863
	Weapon system sustainment unfunded requirement		[66,424]
170	FACILITIES SUSTAINMENT, RESTORATION & MODERNIZATION	258,328	266,628
	Restore Sustainment shortfalls		[8,300]
180	BASE SUPPORT	722,756	722,756
	SUBTOTAL MOBILIZATION	4,376,481	4,451,205
	TRAINING AND RECRUITING		
190	OFFICER ACQUISITION	120,886	120,886
200	RECRUIT TRAINING	23,782	23,782
210	RESERVE OFFICERS TRAINING CORPS (ROTC)	77,692	77,692
220	FACILITIES SUSTAINMENT, RESTORATION & MODERNIZATION	236,254	243,854
	Restore Sustainment shortfalls		[7,600]
230	BASE SUPPORT	819,915	819,915
240	SPECIALIZED SKILL TRAINING	387,446	387,446
250	FLIGHT TRAINING	725,134	725,134
260	PROFESSIONAL DEVELOPMENT EDUCATION	264,213	264,213

SEC. 4301. OPERATION AND MAINTENANCE
(In Thousands of Dollars)

Line	Item	FY 2017 Request	Conference Authorized
270	TRAINING SUPPORT	86,681	86,681
280	DEPOT MAINTENANCE	305,004	305,004
290	RECRUITING AND ADVERTISING	104,754	104,754
300	EXAMINING	3,944	3,944
310	OFF-DUTY AND VOLUNTARY EDUCATION	184,841	184,841
320	CIVILIAN EDUCATION AND TRAINING	173,583	173,583
330	JUNIOR ROTC	58,877	58,877
	SUBTOTAL TRAINING AND RECRUITING	**3,573,006**	**3,580,606**
	ADMIN & SRVWD ACTIVITIES		
340	LOGISTICS OPERATIONS	1,107,846	1,107,846
350	TECHNICAL SUPPORT ACTIVITIES	924,185	924,185
360	DEPOT MAINTENANCE	48,778	48,778
370	FACILITIES SUSTAINMENT, RESTORATION & MODERNIZATION	321,013	331,313
	Restore Sustainment shortfalls		*[10,300]*
380	BASE SUPPORT	1,115,910	1,115,910
390	ADMINISTRATION	811,650	811,650
400	SERVICEWIDE COMMUNICATIONS	269,809	269,809
410	OTHER SERVICEWIDE ACTIVITIES	961,304	961,304
420	CIVIL AIR PATROL	25,735	28,535
	Civil Air Patrol O&M Support		*[2,800]*
450	INTERNATIONAL SUPPORT	90,573	90,573
460	CLASSIFIED PROGRAMS	1,131,603	1,131,603
	SUBTOTAL ADMIN & SRVWD ACTIVITIES	**6,808,406**	**6,821,506**
	UNDISTRIBUTED		
470	UNDISTRIBUTED		−484,700
	Excessive standard price for fuel		*[−368,000]*
	Foreign Currency adjustments		*[−116,700]*
	SUBTOTAL UNDISTRIBUTED		**−484,700**
	TOTAL OPERATION & MAINTENANCE, AIR FORCE	**37,518,056**	**37,337,656**
	OPERATION & MAINTENANCE, AF RESERVE		
	OPERATING FORCES		
010	PRIMARY COMBAT FORCES	1,707,882	1,707,882
020	MISSION SUPPORT OPERATIONS	230,016	230,016
030	DEPOT MAINTENANCE	541,743	541,743
040	FACILITIES SUSTAINMENT, RESTORATION & MODERNIZATION	113,470	116,170
	Restore Sustainment shortfalls		*[2,700]*
050	BASE SUPPORT	384,832	384,832
	SUBTOTAL OPERATING FORCES	**2,977,943**	**2,980,643**
	ADMINISTRATION AND SERVICEWIDE ACTIVITIES		
060	ADMINISTRATION	54,939	54,939
070	RECRUITING AND ADVERTISING	14,754	14,754
080	MILITARY MANPOWER AND PERS MGMT (ARPC)	12,707	12,707
090	OTHER PERS SUPPORT (DISABILITY COMP)	7,210	7,210
100	AUDIOVISUAL	376	376
	SUBTOTAL ADMINISTRATION AND SERVICEWIDE ACTIVITIES	**89,986**	**89,986**
	UNDISTRIBUTED		
110	UNDISTRIBUTED		−59,700
	Excessive standard price for fuel		*[−59,700]*
	SUBTOTAL UNDISTRIBUTED		**−59,700**
	TOTAL OPERATION & MAINTENANCE, AF RESERVE	**3,067,929**	**3,010,929**
	OPERATION & MAINTENANCE, ANG		
	OPERATING FORCES		
010	AIRCRAFT OPERATIONS	3,282,238	3,278,238
	Unjustifed growth		*[−4,000]*
020	MISSION SUPPORT OPERATIONS	723,062	723,062
030	DEPOT MAINTENANCE	1,824,329	1,867,529
	Weapon system sustainment engines unfunded requirement		*[3,200]*
	Weapon system sustainment unfunded requirement		*[40,000]*
040	FACILITIES SUSTAINMENT, RESTORATION & MODERNIZATION	245,840	254,940
	Restore Sustainment shortfalls		*[9,100]*
050	BASE SUPPORT	575,548	575,548
	SUBTOTAL OPERATING FORCES	**6,651,017**	**6,699,317**
	ADMINISTRATION AND SERVICE-WIDE ACTIVITIES		
060	ADMINISTRATION	23,715	23,715
070	RECRUITING AND ADVERTISING	28,846	28,846
	SUBTOTAL ADMINISTRATION AND SERVICE-WIDE ACTIVITIES	**52,561**	**52,561**
	UNDISTRIBUTED		
080	UNDISTRIBUTED		−117,700
	Excessive standard price for fuel		*[−117,700]*

SEC. 4301. OPERATION AND MAINTENANCE
(In Thousands of Dollars)

Line	Item	FY 2017 Request	Conference Authorized
	SUBTOTAL UNDISTRIBUTED		−117,700
	TOTAL OPERATION & MAINTENANCE, ANG	6,703,578	6,634,178
	OPERATION & MAINTENANCE, DEFENSE-WIDE		
	OPERATING FORCES		
010	JOINT CHIEFS OF STAFF	506,113	506,113
020	OFFICE OF THE SECRETARY OF DEFENSE	524,439	524,439
030	SPECIAL OPERATIONS COMMAND/OPERATING FORCES	4,898,159	4,889,359
	Unjustified growth in total civilian compensation		[−8,800]
	SUBTOTAL OPERATING FORCES	5,928,711	5,919,911
	TRAINING AND RECRUITING		
040	DEFENSE ACQUISITION UNIVERSITY	138,658	138,658
050	JOINT CHIEFS OF STAFF	85,701	85,701
070	SPECIAL OPERATIONS COMMAND/TRAINING AND RECRUITING	365,349	365,349
	SUBTOTAL TRAINING AND RECRUITING	589,708	589,708
	ADMINISTRATION AND SERVICEWIDE ACTIVITIES		
080	CIVIL MILITARY PROGRAMS	160,480	195,819
	National Guard Youth Challenge Program		[10,339]
	STARBASE		[25,000]
100	DEFENSE CONTRACT AUDIT AGENCY	630,925	630,925
110	DEFENSE CONTRACT MANAGEMENT AGENCY	1,356,380	1,356,380
120	DEFENSE HUMAN RESOURCES ACTIVITY	683,620	683,620
130	DEFENSE INFORMATION SYSTEMS AGENCY	1,439,891	1,439,891
150	DEFENSE LEGAL SERVICES AGENCY	24,984	24,984
160	DEFENSE LOGISTICS AGENCY	357,964	352,164
	Price Comparability Office unjustified growth		[−5,800]
170	DEFENSE MEDIA ACTIVITY	223,422	223,422
180	DEFENSE PERSONNEL ACCOUNTING AGENCY	112,681	112,681
190	DEFENSE SECURITY COOPERATION AGENCY	496,754	621,754
	Transfer from Drug Interdiction and Counter-Drug Activities		[125,000]
200	DEFENSE SECURITY SERVICE	538,711	538,711
230	DEFENSE TECHNOLOGY SECURITY ADMINISTRATION	35,417	35,417
240	DEFENSE THREAT REDUCTION AGENCY	448,146	448,146
260	DEPARTMENT OF DEFENSE EDUCATION ACTIVITY	2,671,143	2,701,143
	Impact Aid		[25,000]
	Impact Aid severe disabilities		[5,000]
270	MISSILE DEFENSE AGENCY	446,975	446,975
290	OFFICE OF ECONOMIC ADJUSTMENT	155,399	136,199
	Guam public health lab		[−19,200]
300	OFFICE OF THE SECRETARY OF DEFENSE	1,481,643	1,487,293
	BRAC 2017 Round Planning and Analyses		[−3,530]
	CWMD Sustainment: Constellation program reduction		[−3,800]
	DOD rewards early to need		[−1,000]
	Intelligence Management—program reduction		[−1,000]
	Reeadiness environmental protection initiative		[14,980]
310	SPECIAL OPERATIONS COMMAND/ADMIN & SVC-WIDE ACTIVITIES	89,429	89,429
320	WASHINGTON HEADQUARTERS SERVICES	629,874	629,874
330	CLASSIFIED PROGRAMS	14,069,333	14,069,333
	SUBTOTAL ADMINISTRATION AND SERVICEWIDE ACTIVITIES	26,053,171	26,224,160
	UNDISTRIBUTED		
340	UNDISTRIBUTED		−47,100
	Excessive standard price for fuel		[−17,800]
	Foreign Currency adjustments		[−34,300]
	Temporary Duty Assignment Per Diem Rate Waiver		[5,000]
	SUBTOTAL UNDISTRIBUTED		−47,100
	TOTAL OPERATION & MAINTENANCE, DEFENSE-WIDE	32,571,590	32,686,679
	MISCELLANEOUS APPROPRIATIONS		
	MISCELLANEOUS APPROPRIATIONS		
010	US COURT OF APPEALS FOR THE ARMED FORCES, DEFENSE	14,194	14,194
020	OVERSEAS HUMANITARIAN, DISASTER AND CIVIC AID	105,125	105,125
030	COOPERATIVE THREAT REDUCTION	325,604	325,604
050	ENVIRONMENTAL RESTORATION, ARMY	170,167	170,167
060	ENVIRONMENTAL RESTORATION, NAVY	281,762	281,762
070	ENVIRONMENTAL RESTORATION, AIR FORCE	371,521	371,521
080	ENVIRONMENTAL RESTORATION, DEFENSE	9,009	9,009
090	ENVIRONMENTAL RESTORATION FORMERLY USED SITES	197,084	197,084
	SUBTOTAL MISCELLANEOUS APPROPRIATIONS	1,474,466	1,474,466
	TOTAL MISCELLANEOUS APPROPRIATIONS	1,474,466	1,474,466
	TOTAL OPERATION & MAINTENANCE	171,318,488	171,870,896

SEC. 4302. OPERATION AND MAINTENANCE FOR OVERSEAS CONTINGENCY OPER-ATIONS.

SEC. 4302. OPERATION AND MAINTENANCE FOR OVERSEAS CONTINGENCY OPERATIONS
(In Thousands of Dollars)

Line	Item	FY 2017 Request	Conference Authorized
	OPERATION & MAINTENANCE, ARMY		
	OPERATING FORCES		
010	MANEUVER UNITS	427,063	416,263
	Army requested realignment (ERI)		[−10,800]
040	THEATER LEVEL ASSETS	1,834,423	1,834,423
050	LAND FORCES OPERATIONS SUPPORT	558,086	426,086
	Army requested realignment (ERI)		[−132,000]
060	AVIATION ASSETS	58,620	58,620
070	FORCE READINESS OPERATIONS SUPPORT	1,552,468	1,550,468
	Army requested realignment (ERI)		[−2,000]
080	LAND FORCES SYSTEMS READINESS	476,853	476,853
100	BASE OPERATIONS SUPPORT	45,749	45,749
140	ADDITIONAL ACTIVITIES	8,234,566	8,234,566
150	COMMANDERS EMERGENCY RESPONSE PROGRAM	5,000	5,000
160	RESET	1,100,722	1,100,722
170	COMBATANT COMMANDS DIRECT MISSION SUPPORT	79,568	79,568
	SUBTOTAL OPERATING FORCES	**14,373,118**	**14,228,318**
	MOBILIZATION		
190	ARMY PREPOSITIONED STOCKS	350,200	130,000
	Army requested realignment (ERI)		[−220,200]
	SUBTOTAL MOBILIZATION	**350,200**	**130,000**
	ADMIN & SRVWIDE ACTIVITIES		
350	SERVICEWIDE TRANSPORTATION	720,399	840,399
	Army requested realignment (ERI)		[120,000]
380	AMMUNITION MANAGEMENT	13,974	13,974
420	OTHER PERSONNEL SUPPORT	105,508	105,508
450	REAL ESTATE MANAGEMENT	185,904	185,904
530	CLASSIFIED PROGRAMS	909,278	909,278
	SUBTOTAL ADMIN & SRVWIDE ACTIVITIES	**1,935,063**	**2,055,063**
	TOTAL OPERATION & MAINTENANCE, ARMY	**16,658,381**	**16,413,381**
	OPERATION & MAINTENANCE, ARMY RES		
	OPERATING FORCES		
020	ECHELONS ABOVE BRIGADE	6,252	6,252
040	LAND FORCES OPERATIONS SUPPORT	2,075	2,075
060	FORCE READINESS OPERATIONS SUPPORT	1,140	1,140
090	BASE OPERATIONS SUPPORT	14,653	14,653
	SUBTOTAL OPERATING FORCES	**24,120**	**24,120**
	TOTAL OPERATION & MAINTENANCE, ARMY RES	**24,120**	**24,120**
	OPERATION & MAINTENANCE, ARNG		
	OPERATING FORCES		
010	MANEUVER UNITS	10,564	10,564
020	MODULAR SUPPORT BRIGADES	748	748
030	ECHELONS ABOVE BRIGADE	5,751	5,751
040	THEATER LEVEL ASSETS	200	200
060	AVIATION ASSETS	27,183	27,183
070	FORCE READINESS OPERATIONS SUPPORT	2,741	2,741
100	BASE OPERATIONS SUPPORT	18,800	18,800
120	MANAGEMENT AND OPERATIONAL HEADQUARTERS	920	920
	SUBTOTAL OPERATING FORCES	**66,907**	**66,907**
	TOTAL OPERATION & MAINTENANCE, ARNG	**66,907**	**66,907**
	AFGHANISTAN SECURITY FORCES FUND		
	MINISTRY OF DEFENSE		
010	SUSTAINMENT	2,173,341	2,173,341
020	INFRASTRUCTURE	48,262	48,262
030	EQUIPMENT AND TRANSPORTATION	821,716	821,716
040	TRAINING AND OPERATIONS	289,139	289,139
	SUBTOTAL MINISTRY OF DEFENSE	**3,332,458**	**3,332,458**
	MINISTRY OF INTERIOR		
050	SUSTAINMENT	860,441	860,441
060	INFRASTRUCTURE	20,837	20,837
070	EQUIPMENT AND TRANSPORTATION	8,153	8,153
080	TRAINING AND OPERATIONS	41,326	41,326
	SUBTOTAL MINISTRY OF INTERIOR	**930,757**	**930,757**
	TOTAL AFGHANISTAN SECURITY FORCES FUND	**4,263,215**	**4,263,215**

SEC. 4302. OPERATION AND MAINTENANCE FOR OVERSEAS CONTINGENCY OPERATIONS
(In Thousands of Dollars)

Line	Item	FY 2017 Request	Conference Authorized
	IRAQ TRAIN AND EQUIP FUND		
	IRAQ TRAIN AND EQUIP FUND		
010	IRAQ TRAIN AND EQUIP FUND	919,500	0
	Transfer to Counter-ISIL Fund		[−919,500]
	SUBTOTAL IRAQ TRAIN AND EQUIP FUND	**919,500**	**0**
	TOTAL IRAQ TRAIN AND EQUIP FUND	**919,500**	**0**
	SYRIA TRAIN AND EQUIP FUND		
	SYRIA TRAIN AND EQUIP FUND		
010	SYRIA TRAIN AND EQUIP FUND	250,000	0
	Transfer to Counter-ISIL Fund		[−250,000]
	SUBTOTAL SYRIA TRAIN AND EQUIP FUND	**250,000**	**0**
	TOTAL SYRIA TRAIN AND EQUIP FUND	**250,000**	**0**
	COUNTER-ISIL FUND		
	COUNTER-ISIL FUND		
010	COUNTER-ISIL FUND		1,169,500
	Transfer from Iraq Train and Equip		[919,500]
	Transfer from Syria Train and Equip		[250,000]
	SUBTOTAL COUNTER-ISIL FUND		**1,169,500**
	TOTAL COUNTER-ISIL FUND		**1,169,500**
	OPERATION & MAINTENANCE, NAVY		
	OPERATING FORCES		
010	MISSION AND OTHER FLIGHT OPERATIONS	427,452	427,452
040	AIR OPERATIONS AND SAFETY SUPPORT	4,603	4,603
050	AIR SYSTEMS SUPPORT	159,049	159,049
060	AIRCRAFT DEPOT MAINTENANCE	113,994	113,994
070	AIRCRAFT DEPOT OPERATIONS SUPPORT	1,840	1,840
080	AVIATION LOGISTICS	35,529	35,529
090	MISSION AND OTHER SHIP OPERATIONS	1,073,080	1,073,080
100	SHIP OPERATIONS SUPPORT & TRAINING	17,306	17,306
110	SHIP DEPOT MAINTENANCE	2,128,431	2,128,431
130	COMBAT COMMUNICATIONS	21,257	21,257
160	WARFARE TACTICS	22,603	22,603
170	OPERATIONAL METEOROLOGY AND OCEANOGRAPHY	22,934	22,934
180	COMBAT SUPPORT FORCES	575,305	575,305
190	EQUIPMENT MAINTENANCE	11,358	11,358
250	IN-SERVICE WEAPONS SYSTEMS SUPPORT	61,000	61,000
260	WEAPONS MAINTENANCE	309,045	309,045
270	OTHER WEAPON SYSTEMS SUPPORT	8,000	8,000
290	SUSTAINMENT, RESTORATION AND MODERNIZATION	7,819	7,819
300	BASE OPERATING SUPPORT	61,493	61,493
	SUBTOTAL OPERATING FORCES	**5,062,098**	**5,062,098**
	MOBILIZATION		
330	AIRCRAFT ACTIVATIONS/INACTIVATIONS	1,530	1,530
350	EXPEDITIONARY HEALTH SERVICES SYSTEMS	6,713	6,713
370	COAST GUARD SUPPORT	162,692	162,692
	SUBTOTAL MOBILIZATION	**170,935**	**170,935**
	TRAINING AND RECRUITING		
410	SPECIALIZED SKILL TRAINING	43,365	43,365
	SUBTOTAL TRAINING AND RECRUITING	**43,365**	**43,365**
	ADMIN & SRVWD ACTIVITIES		
490	ADMINISTRATION	3,764	3,764
500	EXTERNAL RELATIONS	515	515
520	MILITARY MANPOWER AND PERSONNEL MANAGEMENT	5,409	5,409
530	OTHER PERSONNEL SUPPORT	1,578	1,578
570	SERVICEWIDE TRANSPORTATION	126,700	126,700
600	ACQUISITION AND PROGRAM MANAGEMENT	9,261	9,261
640	NAVAL INVESTIGATIVE SERVICE	1,501	1,501
730	CLASSIFIED PROGRAMS	16,280	16,280
	SUBTOTAL ADMIN & SRVWD ACTIVITIES	**165,008**	**165,008**
	TOTAL OPERATION & MAINTENANCE, NAVY	**5,441,406**	**5,441,406**
	OPERATION & MAINTENANCE, MARINE CORPS		
	OPERATING FORCES		
010	OPERATIONAL FORCES	571,935	571,935
020	FIELD LOGISTICS	266,094	266,094
030	DEPOT MAINTENANCE	147,000	147,000
060	BASE OPERATING SUPPORT	18,576	18,576
	SUBTOTAL OPERATING FORCES	**1,003,605**	**1,003,605**

SEC. 4302. OPERATION AND MAINTENANCE FOR OVERSEAS CONTINGENCY OPERATIONS
(In Thousands of Dollars)

Line	Item	FY 2017 Request	Conference Authorized
	TRAINING AND RECRUITING		
110	TRAINING SUPPORT	31,750	31,750
	SUBTOTAL TRAINING AND RECRUITING	**31,750**	**31,750**
	ADMIN & SRVWD ACTIVITIES		
150	SERVICEWIDE TRANSPORTATION	73,800	73,800
200	CLASSIFIED PROGRAMS	3,650	3,650
	SUBTOTAL ADMIN & SRVWD ACTIVITIES	**77,450**	**77,450**
	TOTAL OPERATION & MAINTENANCE, MARINE CORPS	**1,112,805**	**1,112,805**
	OPERATION & MAINTENANCE, NAVY RES		
	OPERATING FORCES		
030	AIRCRAFT DEPOT MAINTENANCE	16,500	16,500
050	AVIATION LOGISTICS	2,522	2,522
100	COMBAT SUPPORT FORCES	7,243	7,243
	SUBTOTAL OPERATING FORCES	**26,265**	**26,265**
	TOTAL OPERATION & MAINTENANCE, NAVY RES	**26,265**	**26,265**
	OPERATION & MAINTENANCE, MC RESERVE		
	OPERATING FORCES		
010	OPERATING FORCES	2,500	2,500
040	BASE OPERATING SUPPORT	804	804
	SUBTOTAL OPERATING FORCES	**3,304**	**3,304**
	TOTAL OPERATION & MAINTENANCE, MC RESERVE	**3,304**	**3,304**
	OPERATION & MAINTENANCE, AIR FORCE		
	OPERATING FORCES		
010	PRIMARY COMBAT FORCES	1,852,159	1,890,159
	Enhancing readiness levels of DCA aircraft		[10,000]
	ERI nuclear readiness		[28,000]
020	COMBAT ENHANCEMENT FORCES	1,127,319	1,127,319
030	AIR OPERATIONS TRAINING (OJT, MAINTAIN SKILLS)	152,278	152,278
040	DEPOT MAINTENANCE	1,061,506	1,087,106
	Compass Call Program Restructure		[25,600]
050	FACILITIES SUSTAINMENT, RESTORATION & MODERNIZATION	56,700	56,700
060	BASE SUPPORT	941,714	941,714
070	GLOBAL C3I AND EARLY WARNING	30,219	30,219
080	OTHER COMBAT OPS SPT PROGRAMS	213,696	218,696
	Promoting additional DCA burden sharing		[5,000]
100	LAUNCH FACILITIES	869	869
110	SPACE CONTROL SYSTEMS	5,008	5,008
120	COMBATANT COMMANDERS DIRECT MISSION SUPPORT	100,081	100,081
135	CLASSIFIED PROGRAMS	79,893	79,893
	SUBTOTAL OPERATING FORCES	**5,621,442**	**5,690,042**
	MOBILIZATION		
140	AIRLIFT OPERATIONS	2,606,729	2,606,729
150	MOBILIZATION PREPAREDNESS	108,163	108,163
160	DEPOT MAINTENANCE	891,102	891,102
180	BASE SUPPORT	3,686	3,686
	SUBTOTAL MOBILIZATION	**3,609,680**	**3,609,680**
	TRAINING AND RECRUITING		
230	BASE SUPPORT	52,740	52,740
240	SPECIALIZED SKILL TRAINING	4,500	4,500
	SUBTOTAL TRAINING AND RECRUITING	**57,240**	**57,240**
	ADMIN & SRVWD ACTIVITIES		
340	LOGISTICS OPERATIONS	86,716	86,716
380	BASE SUPPORT	59,133	59,133
400	SERVICEWIDE COMMUNICATIONS	165,348	165,348
410	OTHER SERVICEWIDE ACTIVITIES	141,883	116,825
	Program reduction		[−25,058]
450	INTERNATIONAL SUPPORT	61	61
460	CLASSIFIED PROGRAMS	15,823	15,823
	SUBTOTAL ADMIN & SRVWD ACTIVITIES	**468,964**	**443,906**
	TOTAL OPERATION & MAINTENANCE, AIR FORCE	**9,757,326**	**9,800,868**
	OPERATION & MAINTENANCE, AF RESERVE		
	OPERATING FORCES		
030	DEPOT MAINTENANCE	51,086	51,086
050	BASE SUPPORT	6,500	6,500
	SUBTOTAL OPERATING FORCES	**57,586**	**57,586**
	TOTAL OPERATION & MAINTENANCE, AF RESERVE	**57,586**	**57,586**

SEC. 4302. OPERATION AND MAINTENANCE FOR OVERSEAS CONTINGENCY OPERATIONS
(In Thousands of Dollars)

Line	Item	FY 2017 Request	Conference Authorized
	OPERATION & MAINTENANCE, ANG		
	OPERATING FORCES		
020	MISSION SUPPORT OPERATIONS	3,400	3,400
050	BASE SUPPORT	16,600	16,600
	SUBTOTAL OPERATING FORCES	**20,000**	**20,000**
	TOTAL OPERATION & MAINTENANCE, ANG	**20,000**	**20,000**
	OPERATION & MAINTENANCE, DEFENSE-WIDE		
	OPERATING FORCES		
010	JOINT CHIEFS OF STAFF		10,000
	Enhancing exercise of DCA aircraft		*[10,000]*
030	SPECIAL OPERATIONS COMMAND/OPERATING FORCES	2,853,363	2,853,363
	SUBTOTAL OPERATING FORCES	**2,853,363**	**2,863,363**
	ADMINISTRATION AND SERVICEWIDE ACTIVITIES		
100	DEFENSE CONTRACT AUDIT AGENCY	13,436	13,436
110	DEFENSE CONTRACT MANAGEMENT AGENCY	13,564	13,564
130	DEFENSE INFORMATION SYSTEMS AGENCY	34,299	34,299
150	DEFENSE LEGAL SERVICES AGENCY	111,986	111,986
170	DEFENSE MEDIA ACTIVITY	13,317	13,317
190	DEFENSE SECURITY COOPERATION AGENCY	1,412,000	2,162,000
	Transfer from Counterterrorism Partnership Fund		*[750,000]*
260	DEPARTMENT OF DEFENSE EDUCATION ACTIVITY	67,000	67,000
300	OFFICE OF THE SECRETARY OF DEFENSE	31,106	31,106
320	WASHINGTON HEADQUARTERS SERVICES	3,137	3,137
330	CLASSIFIED PROGRAMS	1,803,880	1,803,880
	SUBTOTAL ADMINISTRATION AND SERVICEWIDE ACTIVITIES	**3,503,725**	**4,253,725**
	TOTAL OPERATION & MAINTENANCE, DEFENSE-WIDE	**6,357,088**	**7,117,088**
	TOTAL OPERATION & MAINTENANCE	**44,957,903**	**45,516,445**

SEC. 4303. OPERATION AND MAINTENANCE FOR OVERSEAS CONTINGENCY OPERATIONS FOR BASE REQUIREMENTS.

SEC. 4303. OPERATION AND MAINTENANCE FOR OVERSEAS CONTINGENCY OPERATIONS FOR BASE REQUIREMENTS
(In Thousands of Dollars)

Line	Item	FY 2017 Request	Conference Authorized
	OPERATION & MAINTENANCE, ARMY		
	OPERATING FORCES		
010	MANEUVER UNITS	317,093	317,093
020	MODULAR SUPPORT BRIGADES	5,904	5,904
030	ECHELONS ABOVE BRIGADE	38,614	38,614
040	THEATER LEVEL ASSETS	8,361	8,361
050	LAND FORCES OPERATIONS SUPPORT	279,072	279,072
060	AVIATION ASSETS	106,424	106,424
070	FORCE READINESS OPERATIONS SUPPORT	253,533	253,533
090	LAND FORCES DEPOT MAINTENANCE	350,000	350,000
110	FACILITIES SUSTAINMENT, RESTORATION & MODERNIZATION		113,800
	Increase Restoration & Modernization funding		*[113,800]*
140	ADDITIONAL ACTIVITIES	11,200	11,200
	SUBTOTAL OPERATING FORCES	**1,370,201**	**1,484,001**
	TRAINING AND RECRUITING		
250	SPECIALIZED SKILL TRAINING	3,565	3,565
270	PROFESSIONAL DEVELOPMENT EDUCATION	9,021	9,021
280	TRAINING SUPPORT	2,434	2,434
290	RECRUITING AND ADVERTISING		284,800
	Recruiting and Advertising Add		*[284,800]*
320	CIVILIAN EDUCATION AND TRAINING	1,254	1,254
	SUBTOTAL TRAINING AND RECRUITING	**16,274**	**301,074**
	ADMIN & SRVWIDE ACTIVITIES		
350	SERVICEWIDE TRANSPORTATION	200,000	200,000
	SUBTOTAL ADMIN & SRVWIDE ACTIVITIES	**200,000**	**200,000**
	UNDISTRIBUTED		
540	UNDISTRIBUTED		563,400
	Additional funding to support increase in Army end strength		*[563,400]*
	SUBTOTAL UNDISTRIBUTED		**563,400**
	TOTAL OPERATION & MAINTENANCE, ARMY	**1,586,475**	**2,548,475**

SEC. 4303. OPERATION AND MAINTENANCE FOR OVERSEAS CONTINGENCY OPERATIONS FOR BASE REQUIREMENTS
(In Thousands of Dollars)

Line	Item	FY 2017 Request	Conference Authorized
	OPERATION & MAINTENANCE, ARMY RES		
	OPERATING FORCES		
010	MODULAR SUPPORT BRIGADES	708	708
020	ECHELONS ABOVE BRIGADE	8,570	8,570
030	THEATER LEVEL ASSETS	375	375
040	LAND FORCES OPERATIONS SUPPORT	13	13
050	AVIATION ASSETS	608	608
060	FORCE READINESS OPERATIONS SUPPORT	4,285	4,285
100	FACILITIES SUSTAINMENT, RESTORATION & MODERNIZATION		13,100
	Increase Restoration & Modernization funding		*[13,100]*
	SUBTOTAL OPERATING FORCES	**14,559**	**27,659**
	UNDISTRIBUTED		
180	UNDISTRIBUTED		82,700
	Additional funding to support increase in Army Reserve end strength		*[82,700]*
	SUBTOTAL UNDISTRIBUTED		**82,700**
	TOTAL OPERATION & MAINTENANCE, ARMY RES	**14,559**	**110,359**
	OPERATION & MAINTENANCE, ARNG		
	OPERATING FORCES		
010	MANEUVER UNITS	5,585	5,585
030	ECHELONS ABOVE BRIGADE	28,956	28,956
040	THEATER LEVEL ASSETS	10,272	10,272
060	AVIATION ASSETS	5,621	5,621
070	FORCE READINESS OPERATIONS SUPPORT	9,694	9,694
110	FACILITIES SUSTAINMENT, RESTORATION & MODERNIZATION		1,500
	Increase Restoration & Modernization funding		*[1,500]*
	SUBTOTAL OPERATING FORCES	**60,128**	**61,628**
	UNDISTRIBUTED		
190	UNDISTRIBUTED		127,300
	Additional funding to support increase in Army National Guard end strength		*[127,300]*
	SUBTOTAL UNDISTRIBUTED		**127,300**
	TOTAL OPERATION & MAINTENANCE, ARNG	**60,128**	**188,928**
	OPERATION & MAINTENANCE, NAVY		
	OPERATING FORCES		
010	MISSION AND OTHER FLIGHT OPERATIONS	500,000	500,000
110	SHIP DEPOT MAINTENANCE	775,000	775,000
290	SUSTAINMENT, RESTORATION AND MODERNIZATION	19,270	45,370
	Increase Restoration & Modernization funding		*[26,100]*
300	BASE OPERATING SUPPORT	158,032	158,032
	SUBTOTAL OPERATING FORCES	**1,452,302**	**1,478,402**
	MOBILIZATION		
350	EXPEDITIONARY HEALTH SERVICES SYSTEMS	3,597	3,597
	SUBTOTAL MOBILIZATION	**3,597**	**3,597**
	ADMIN & SRVWD ACTIVITIES		
540	SERVICEWIDE COMMUNICATIONS	25,617	25,617
	SUBTOTAL ADMIN & SRVWD ACTIVITIES	**25,617**	**25,617**
	TOTAL OPERATION & MAINTENANCE, NAVY	**1,481,516**	**1,507,616**
	OPERATION & MAINTENANCE, MARINE CORPS		
	OPERATING FORCES		
010	OPERATIONAL FORCES	300,000	300,000
050	SUSTAINMENT, RESTORATION & MODERNIZATION		7,200
	Increase Restoration & Modernization funding		*[7,200]*
	SUBTOTAL OPERATING FORCES	**300,000**	**307,200**
	TOTAL OPERATION & MAINTENANCE, MARINE CORPS	**300,000**	**307,200**
	OPERATION & MAINTENANCE, NAVY RES		
	OPERATING FORCES		
130	SUSTAINMENT, RESTORATION AND MODERNIZATION		500
	Increase Restoration & Modernization funding		*[500]*
	SUBTOTAL OPERATING FORCES		**500**
	TOTAL OPERATION & MAINTENANCE, NAVY RES		**500**
	OPERATION & MAINTENANCE, MC RESERVE		
	OPERATING FORCES		
030	SUSTAINMENT, RESTORATION AND MODERNIZATION		1,000
	Increase Restoration & Modernization funding		*[1,000]*
	SUBTOTAL OPERATING FORCES		**1,000**

SEC. 4303. OPERATION AND MAINTENANCE FOR OVERSEAS CONTINGENCY OPERATIONS FOR BASE REQUIREMENTS
(In Thousands of Dollars)

Line	Item	FY 2017 Request	Conference Authorized
	TOTAL OPERATION & MAINTENANCE, MC RESERVE		*1,000*
	OPERATION & MAINTENANCE, AIR FORCE		
	OPERATING FORCES		
040	DEPOT MAINTENANCE	124,000	124,000
050	FACILITIES SUSTAINMENT, RESTORATION & MODERNIZATION		32,900
	Increase Restoration & Modernization funding		[32,900]
	SUBTOTAL OPERATING FORCES	124,000	156,900
	MOBILIZATION		
170	FACILITIES SUSTAINMENT, RESTORATION & MODERNIZATION		5,100
	Increase Restoration & Modernization funding		[5,100]
	SUBTOTAL MOBILIZATION		5,100
	TRAINING AND RECRUITING		
220	FACILITIES SUSTAINMENT, RESTORATION & MODERNIZATION		4,700
	Increase Restoration & Modernization funding		[4,700]
	SUBTOTAL TRAINING AND RECRUITING		4,700
	ADMIN & SRVWD ACTIVITIES		
370	FACILITIES SUSTAINMENT, RESTORATION & MODERNIZATION		6,400
	Increase Restoration & Modernization funding		[6,400]
	SUBTOTAL ADMIN & SRVWD ACTIVITIES		6,400
	TOTAL OPERATION & MAINTENANCE, AIR FORCE	124,000	173,100
	OPERATION & MAINTENANCE, AF RESERVE		
	OPERATING FORCES		
040	FACILITIES SUSTAINMENT, RESTORATION & MODERNIZATION		1,600
	Increase Restoration & Modernization funding		[1,600]
	SUBTOTAL OPERATING FORCES		1,600
	TOTAL OPERATION & MAINTENANCE, AF RESERVE		1,600
	OPERATION & MAINTENANCE, ANG		
	OPERATING FORCES		
040	FACILITIES SUSTAINMENT, RESTORATION & MODERNIZATION		4,300
	Increase Restoration & Modernization funding		[4,300]
	SUBTOTAL OPERATING FORCES		4,300
	TOTAL OPERATION & MAINTENANCE, ANG		4,300
	OPERATION & MAINTENANCE, DEFENSE-WIDE		
	OPERATING FORCES		
030	SPECIAL OPERATIONS COMMAND/OPERATING FORCES	14,344	14,344
	SUBTOTAL OPERATING FORCES	14,344	14,344
	ADMINISTRATION AND SERVICEWIDE ACTIVITIES		
130	DEFENSE INFORMATION SYSTEMS AGENCY	14,700	14,700
330	CLASSIFIED PROGRAMS	9,000	9,000
	SUBTOTAL ADMINISTRATION AND SERVICEWIDE ACTIVITIES	23,700	23,700
	TOTAL OPERATION & MAINTENANCE, DEFENSE-WIDE	38,044	38,044
	TOTAL OPERATION & MAINTENANCE	3,604,722	4,881,122

TITLE XLIV—MILITARY PERSONNEL
SEC. 4401. MILITARY PERSONNEL.

SEC. 4401. MILITARY PERSONNEL
(In Thousands of Dollars)

Item	FY 2017 Request	Conference Authorized
Military Personnel Appropriations	128,902,332	128,202,564
Military Personnel Pay Raise		[330,000]
Marine Corps—Bonus Pay/PCS Resotral/Foreign Language Bonus		[49,000]
Foreign currency adjustments		[−200,400]
Historical unobligated balances		[−880,050]
National Guard State Partnership Program, Army, Special Training		[841]
National Guard State Partnership Program, Air Force, Special Training		[841]
Medicare-Eligible Retiree Health Fund Contributions	6,366,908	6,366,908
Total, Military Personnel	135,269,240	134,569,472

SEC. 4402. MILITARY PERSONNEL FOR OVERSEAS
CONTINGENCY OPERATIONS.

SEC. 4402. MILITARY PERSONNEL FOR OVERSEAS CONTINGENCY OPERATIONS
(In Thousands of Dollars)

Item	FY 2017 Request	Conference Authorized
Military Personnel Appropriations	3,644,161	3,644,161
Total, Military Personnel Appropriations	3,644,161	3,644,161

SEC. 4403. MILITARY PERSONNEL FOR OVERSEAS
CONTINGENCY OPERATIONS FOR
BASE REQUIREMENTS.

SEC. 4403. MILITARY PERSONNEL FOR OVERSEAS CONTINGENCY OPERATIONS FOR BASE REQUIREMENTS
(In Thousands of Dollars)

Item	FY 2017 Request	Conference Authorized
Military Personnel Appropriations	62,965	1,350,465
Fund Active Army End Strength to 476k		[719,000]
Fund Army National Guard End Strength to 343k		[129,600]
Fund Army Reserves End Strength to 199k		[53,300]
Fund Active Navy End Strength to 323.9k		[29,600]
Fund Active Air Force End Strength to 321k		[116,000]
Fund Active Marine Corps End Strength to 185k		[240,000]
Total, Military Personnel	62,965	1,350,465

TITLE XLV—OTHER AUTHORIZATIONS
SEC. 4501. OTHER AUTHORIZATIONS.

SEC. 4501. OTHER AUTHORIZATIONS
(In Thousands of Dollars)

Program Title	FY 2017 Request	Conference Authorized
WORKING CAPITAL FUND, ARMY		
SUPPLY MANAGEMENT—ARMY	56,469	56,469
TOTAL WORKING CAPITAL FUND, ARMY	**56,469**	**56,469**
WORKING CAPITAL FUND, AIR FORCE		
SUPPLIES AND MATERIALS	63,967	63,967
TOTAL WORKING CAPITAL FUND, AIR FORCE	**63,967**	**63,967**
WORKING CAPITAL FUND, DEFENSE-WIDE		
SUPPLY CHAIN MANAGEMENT—DEF	37,132	37,132
TOTAL WORKING CAPITAL FUND, DEFENSE-WIDE	**37,132**	**37,132**
WORKING CAPITAL FUND, DECA		
COMMISSARY	1,214,045	1,214,045
TOTAL WORKING CAPITAL FUND, DECA	**1,214,045**	**1,214,045**
CHEM AGENTS & MUNITIONS DESTRUCTION		
OPERATION & MAINTENANCE	147,282	147,282
RDT&E	388,609	388,609
PROCUREMENT	15,132	15,132
TOTAL CHEM AGENTS & MUNITIONS DESTRUCTION	**551,023**	**551,023**
DRUG INTERDICTION & CTR-DRUG ACTIVITIES, DEF		
DRUG INTERDICTION AND COUNTER-DRUG ACTIVITIES, DEFENSE	730,087	605,087
Transfer to Defense Security Cooperation Agency		[−125,000]
DRUG DEMAND REDUCTION PROGRAM	114,713	114,713
TOTAL DRUG INTERDICTION & CTR-DRUG ACTIVITIES, DEF	**844,800**	**719,800**
OFFICE OF THE INSPECTOR GENERAL		
OPERATION AND MAINTENANCE	318,882	318,882
RDT&E	3,153	3,153
TOTAL OFFICE OF THE INSPECTOR GENERAL	**322,035**	**322,035**
DEFENSE HEALTH PROGRAM		
OPERATION & MAINTENANCE		
IN-HOUSE CARE	9,240,160	9,240,160
PRIVATE SECTOR CARE	15,738,759	15,738,759
CONSOLIDATED HEALTH SUPPORT	2,367,759	2,367,759
INFORMATION MANAGEMENT	1,743,749	1,743,749
MANAGEMENT ACTIVITIES	311,380	311,380
EDUCATION AND TRAINING	743,231	743,231
BASE OPERATIONS/COMMUNICATIONS	2,086,352	2,086,352
SUBTOTAL OPERATION & MAINTENANCE	**32,231,390**	**32,231,390**

SEC. 4501. OTHER AUTHORIZATIONS
(In Thousands of Dollars)

Program Title	FY 2017 Request	Conference Authorized
RDT&E		
RESEARCH	9,097	9,097
EXPLORATRY DEVELOPMENT	58,517	58,517
ADVANCED DEVELOPMENT	221,226	221,226
DEMONSTRATION/VALIDATION	96,602	96,602
ENGINEERING DEVELOPMENT	364,057	364,057
MANAGEMENT AND SUPPORT	58,410	58,410
CAPABILITIES ENHANCEMENT	14,998	14,998
SUBTOTAL RDT&E	**822,907**	**822,907**
PROCUREMENT		
INITIAL OUTFITTING	20,611	20,611
REPLACEMENT & MODERNIZATION	360,727	360,727
JOINT OPERATIONAL MEDICINE INFORMATION SYSTEM	2,413	2,413
DOD HEALTHCARE MANAGEMENT SYSTEM MODERNIZATION	29,468	29,468
SUBTOTAL PROCUREMENT	**413,219**	**413,219**
UNDISTRIBUTED		
Historical unobligated balances		[–399,100]
Reduction for unjustified travel expenses		[–6,500]
Reimbursement rates for Comprehensive Autism Care Demonstration program		[32,000]
SUBTOTAL UNDISTRIBUTED		**–373,600**
TOTAL DEFENSE HEALTH PROGRAM	**33,467,516**	**33,093,916**
TOTAL OTHER AUTHORIZATIONS	**36,556,987**	**36,058,387**

SEC. 4502. OTHER AUTHORIZATIONS FOR OVER-
SEAS CONTINGENCY OPERATIONS.

SEC. 4502. OTHER AUTHORIZATIONS FOR OVERSEAS CONTINGENCY OPERATIONS
(In Thousands of Dollars)

Program Title	FY 2017 Request	Conference Authorized
WORKING CAPITAL FUND, ARMY		
INDUSTRIAL OPERATIONS		
SUPPLY MANAGEMENT—ARMY	46,833	46,833
TOTAL WORKING CAPITAL FUND, ARMY	**46,833**	**46,833**
WORKING CAPITAL FUND, DEFENSE-WIDE		
DEFENSE LOGISTICS AGENCY (DLA)	93,800	93,800
TOTAL WORKING CAPITAL FUND, DEFENSE-WIDE	**93,800**	**93,800**
DRUG INTERDICTION & CTR-DRUG ACTIVITIES, DEF		
DRUG INTERDICTION AND COUNTER-DRUG ACTIVITIES, DEFENSE	191,533	191,533
TOTAL DRUG INTERDICTION & CTR-DRUG ACTIVITIES, DEF	**191,533**	**191,533**
OFFICE OF THE INSPECTOR GENERAL		
OPERATION AND MAINTENANCE	22,062	22,062
TOTAL OFFICE OF THE INSPECTOR GENERAL	**22,062**	**22,062**
DEFENSE HEALTH PROGRAM		
OPERATION AND MAINTENANCE		
IN-HOUSE CARE	95,366	95,366
PRIVATE SECTOR CARE	235,620	235,620
CONSOLIDATED HEALTH SUPPORT	3,325	3,325
SUBTOTAL OPERATION AND MAINTENANCE	**334,311**	**334,311**
TOTAL DEFENSE HEALTH PROGRAM	**334,311**	**334,311**
UKRAINE SECURITY ASSISTANCE		
UKRAINE SECURITY ASSISTANCE		350,000
Program increase		[350,000]
TOTAL UKRAINE SECURITY ASSISTANCE		**350,000**
COUNTERTERRORISM PARTNERSHIPS FUND		
COUNTERTERRORISM PARTNERSHIPS FUND	1,000,000	0
Program decrease		[–250,000]
Transfer to Counter-ISIL Fund		[–750,000]
TOTAL COUNTERTERRORISM PARTNERSHIPS FUND	**1,000,000**	**0**
TOTAL OTHER AUTHORIZATIONS	**1,688,539**	**1,038,539**

SEC. 4503. OTHER AUTHORIZATIONS FOR OVER-
SEAS CONTINGENCY OPERATIONS
FOR BASE REQUIREMENTS.

SEC. 4503. OTHER AUTHORIZATIONS FOR OVERSEAS CONTINGENCY OPERATIONS FOR BASE REQUIREMENTS
(In Thousands of Dollars)

Program Title	FY 2017 Request	Conference Authorized
DRUG INTERDICTION & CTR-DRUG ACTIVITIES, DEF		
DRUG INTERDICTION AND COUNTER-DRUG ACTIVITIES, DEFENSE	*23,800*	*23,800*
TOTAL DRUG INTERDICTION & CTR-DRUG ACTIVITIES, DEF	**23,800**	**23,800**
TOTAL OTHER AUTHORIZATIONS	**23,800**	**23,800**

TITLE XLVI—MILITARY CONSTRUCTION
SEC. 4601. MILITARY CONSTRUCTION.

SEC. 4601. MILITARY CONSTRUCTION
(In Thousands of Dollars)

Account	State/Country and Installation	Project Title	FY 2017 Request	Conference Authorized
	Alaska			
Army	Fort Wainwright	Unmanned Aerial Vehicle Hangar	47,000	47,000
	California			
Army	Concord	Access Control Point	12,600	12,600
	Colorado			
Army	Fort Carson	Automated Infantry Platoon Battle Course	8,100	8,100
Army	Fort Carson	Unmanned Aerial Vehicle Hangar	5,000	5,000
	Cuba			
Army	Guantanamo Bay	Guantanamo Bay Naval Station Migration Complex	33,000	33,000
	Georgia			
Army	Fort Gordon	Access Control Point	0	0
Army	Fort Gordon	Company Operations Facility	0	10,600
Army	Fort Gordon	Cyber Protection Team Ops Facility	90,000	90,000
Army	Fort Stewart	Automated Qualification/Training Range	14,800	14,800
	Germany			
Army	East Camp Grafenwoehr	Training Support Center	22,000	22,000
Army	Garmisch	Dining Facility	9,600	9,600
Army	Wiesbaden Army Airfield	Controlled Humidity Warehouse	16,500	16,500
Army	Wiesbaden Army Airfield	Hazardous Material Storage Building	2,700	2,700
	Hawaii			
Army	Fort Shafter	Command and Control Facility, Incr 2	40,000	40,000
	Missouri			
Army	Fort Leonard Wood	Fire Station	0	6,900
	Texas			
Army	Fort Hood	Automated Infantry Platoon Battle Course	7,600	7,600
	Utah			
Army	Camp Williams	Live Fire Exercise Shoothouse	7,400	7,400
	Virginia			
Army	Fort Belvoir	Secure Admin/Operations Facility, Incr 2	64,000	64,000
Army	Fort Belvoir	Vehicle Maintenance Shop	0	23,000
	Worldwide Unspecified			
Army	Unspecified Worldwide Locations	Host Nation Support FY17	18,000	18,000
Army	Unspecified Worldwide Locations	Minor Construction FY17	25,000	35,000
Army	Unspecified Worldwide Locations	Planning and Design FY17	80,159	80,159
	Military Construction, Army Total		**503,459**	**553,959**
	Arizona			
Navy	Yuma	VMX–22 Maintenance Hangar	48,355	48,355
	California			
Navy	Coronado	Coastal Campus Entry Control Point	13,044	13,044
Navy	Coronado	Coastal Campus Utilities Infrastructure	81,104	81,104
Navy	Coronado	Grace Hopper Data Center Power Upgrades	10,353	10,353
Navy	Lemoore	F–35C Engine Repair Facility	26,723	26,723
Navy	Miramar	Aircraft Maintenance Hangar, Incr 1	0	79,399
Navy	Miramar	Communications Complex & Infrastructure Upgrade	0	34,700
Navy	Miramar	F–35 Aircraft Parking Apron	0	40,000
Navy	San Diego	Energy Security Hospital Microgrid	6,183	0
Navy	Seal Beach	Missile Magazines	21,007	21,007
	Florida			
Navy	Eglin AFB	WMD Field Training Facilities	20,489	20,489
Navy	Mayport NS	Advanced Wastewater Treatment Plant	0	0
Navy	Pensacola	A-School Dormitory	0	0
	Guam			
Navy	Joint Region Marianas	Hardening of Guam POL Infrastructure	26,975	26,975
Navy	Joint Region Marianas	Power Upgrade—Harmon	62,210	62,210
	Hawaii			
Navy	Barking Sands	Upgrade Power Plant & Electrical Distrib Sys	43,384	43,384
Navy	Kaneohe Bay	Regimental Consolidated Comm/Elec Facility	72,565	72,565
	Japan			

SEC. 4601. MILITARY CONSTRUCTION
(In Thousands of Dollars)

Account	State/Country and Installation	Project Title	FY 2017 Request	Conference Authorized
Navy	Kadena AB	Aircraft Maintenance Complex	26,489	26,489
Navy	Sasebo	Shore Power (Juliet Pier)	16,420	16,420
	Maine			
Navy	Kittery	Unaccompanied Housing	17,773	17,773
Navy	Kittery	Utility Improvements for Nuclear Platforms	30,119	30,119
	Maryland			
Navy	Patuxent River	UCLASS RDT&E Hangar	40,576	40,576
	Nevada			
Navy	Fallon	Air Wing Simulator Facility	13,523	13,523
	North Carolina			
Navy	Camp Lejeune	Range Facilities Safety Improvements	18,482	18,482
Navy	Cherry Point	Central Heating Plant Conversion	12,515	12,515
	South Carolina			
Navy	Beaufort	Aircraft Maintenance Hangar	83,490	83,490
Navy	Parris Island	Recruit Reconditioning Center & Barracks	29,882	29,882
	Spain			
Navy	Rota	Communication Station	23,607	23,607
	Virginia			
Navy	Norfolk	Chambers Field Magazine Recap Ph I	0	27,000
	Washington			
Navy	Bangor	SEAWOLF Class Service Pier	0	73,000
Navy	Bangor	Service Pier Electrical Upgrades	18,939	18,939
Navy	Bangor	Submarine Refit Maint Support Facility	21,476	21,476
Navy	Bremerton	Nuclear Repair Facility	6,704	6,704
Navy	Whidbey Island	EA–18G Maintenance Hangar	45,501	45,501
Navy	Whidbey Island	Triton Mission Control Facility	30,475	30,475
	Worldwide Unspecified			
Navy	Unspecified Worldwide Locations	Planning and Design	88,230	88,230
Navy	Unspecified Worldwide Locations	Unspecified Minor Construction	29,790	29,790
Navy	Various Worldwide Locations	Triton Forward Operating Base Hangar	41,380	41,380
Military Construction, Navy Total			**1,027,763**	**1,275,679**
	Alabama			
AF	Maxwell AFB	Jag School Expansion	0	15,500
	Alaska			
AF	Clear AFS	Fire Station	20,000	20,000
AF	Eielson AFB	F–35A ADAL Field Training Detachment Fac	22,100	22,100
AF	Eielson AFB	F–35A Aircraft Weather Shelter (Sqd 2)	82,300	82,300
AF	Eielson AFB	F–35A Aircraft Weather Shelters (Sqd 1)	79,500	79,500
AF	Eielson AFB	F–35A Earth Covered Magazines	11,300	11,300
AF	Eielson AFB	F–35A Hangar/Propulsion MX/Dispatch	44,900	44,900
AF	Eielson AFB	F–35A Hangar/Squad Ops/AMU Sq #2	42,700	42,700
AF	Eielson AFB	F–35A Missile Maintenance Facility	12,800	12,800
AF	Joint Base Elmendorf-Richardson	Add/Alter AWACS Alert Hangar	29,000	29,000
	Arizona			
AF	Luke AFB	F–35A Squad Ops/Aircraft Maint Unit #5	20,000	20,000
	Australia			
AF	Darwin	APR—Aircraft MX Support Facility	1,800	1,800
AF	Darwin	APR—Expand Parking Apron	28,600	28,600
	California			
AF	Edwards AFB	Flightline Fire Station	24,000	24,000
	Colorado			
AF	Buckley AFB	Small Arms Range Complex	13,500	13,500
	Delaware			
AF	Dover AFB	Aircraft Maintenance Hangar	39,000	39,000
	Florida			
AF	Eglin AFB	Advanced Munitions Technology Complex	75,000	75,000
AF	Eglin AFB	Dormitories (288 rooms)	0	35,000
AF	Eglin AFB	Flightline Fire Station	13,600	13,600
AF	Patrick AFB	Fire/Crash Rescue Station	13,500	13,500
	Georgia			
AF	Moody AFB	Personnel Recovery 4-Bay Hangar/Helo MX Unit	30,900	30,900
	Germany			
AF	Ramstein AB	37 AS Squadron Operations/Aircraft Maint Unit	13,437	13,437
AF	Spangdahlem AB	EIC—Site Development and Infrastructure	43,465	43,465
	Guam			
AF	Joint Region Marianas	APR—Munitions Storage Igloos, Ph 2	35,300	35,300
AF	Joint Region Marianas	APR—SATCOM C4I Facility	14,200	14,200
AF	Joint Region Marianas	Block 40 Maintenance Hangar	31,158	31,158
	Illinois			
AF	Scott AFB	Consolidated Corrosion Facility add/alter	0	41,000
	Japan			
AF	Kadena AB	APR—Replace Munitions Structures	19,815	19,815
AF	Yokota AB	C–130J Corrosion Control Hangar	23,777	23,777
AF	Yokota AB	Construct Combat Arms Training & Maint Fac	8,243	8,243
	Kansas			
AF	McConnell AFB	Air Traffic Control Tower	11,200	11,200
AF	McConnell AFB	KC–46A ADAL Taxiway Delta	5,600	5,600

SEC. 4601. MILITARY CONSTRUCTION
(In Thousands of Dollars)

Account	State/Country and Installation	Project Title	FY 2017 Request	Conference Authorized
AF	McConnell AFB	KC–46A Alter Flight Simulator Bldgs	3,000	3,000
	Louisiana			
AF	Barksdale AFB	Consolidated Communication Facility	21,000	21,000
	Mariana Islands			
AF	Unspecified Location	APR—Land Acquisition	9,000	9,000
	Maryland			
AF	Joint Base Andrews	21 Points Enclosed Firing Range	13,000	13,000
AF	Joint Base Andrews	Consolidated Communications Center	0	50,000
AF	Joint Base Andrews	PAR Relocate JADOC Satellite Site	3,500	3,500
	Massachusetts			
AF	Hanscom AFB	Construct Vandenberg Gate Complex	0	10,965
AF	Hanscom AFB	System Management Engineering Facility	20,000	20,000
	Montana			
AF	Malmstrom AFB	Missile Maintenance Facility	14,600	14,600
	Nevada			
AF	Nellis AFB	F–35A POL Fill Stand Addition	10,600	10,600
	New Mexico			
AF	Cannon AFB	North Fitness Center	21,000	21,000
AF	Holloman AFB	Hazardous Cargo Pad and Taxiway	10,600	10,600
AF	Kirtland AFB	Combat Rescue Helicopter Simulator	7,300	7,300
	Ohio			
AF	Wright-Patterson AFB	Relocated Entry Control Facility 26A	12,600	12,600
	Oklahoma			
AF	Altus AFB	KC–46A FTU/FTC Simulator Facility Ph 2	11,600	11,600
AF	Tinker AFB	E–3G Mission and Flight Simulator Training Facility	0	26,000
AF	Tinker AFB	KC–46A Depot System Integration Laboratory	17,000	17,000
	South Carolina			
AF	Joint Base Charleston	Fire & Rescue Station	0	17,000
	Texas			
AF	Joint Base San Antonio	BMT Recruit Dormitory 6	67,300	67,300
	Turkey			
AF	Incirlik AB	Airfield Fire/Crash Rescue Station	13,449	13,449
	United Arab Emirates			
AF	Al Dhafra	Large Aircraft Maintenance Hangar	35,400	35,400
	United Kingdom			
AF	RAF Croughton	JIAC Consolidation—Ph 3	53,082	53,082
AF	RAF Croughton	Main Gate Complex	16,500	16,500
	Utah			
AF	Hill AFB	649 MUNS Munitions Storage Magazines	6,600	6,600
AF	Hill AFB	649 MUNS Precision Guided Missile MX Facility	8,700	8,700
AF	Hill AFB	649 MUNS STAMP/Maint & Inspection Facility	12,000	12,000
AF	Hill AFB	Composite Aircraft Antenna Calibration Fac	7,100	7,100
AF	Hill AFB	F–35A Munitions Maintenance Complex	10,100	10,100
	Virginia			
AF	Joint Base Langley-Eustis	Air Force Targeting Center	45,000	45,000
AF	Joint Base Langley-Eustis	Fuel System Maintenance Dock	14,200	14,200
	Washington			
AF	Fairchild AFB	Pipeline Dorm, USAF SERE School (150 RM)	27,000	27,000
	Worldwide Unspecified			
AF	Various Worldwide Locations	Planning & Design	143,582	143,582
AF	Various Worldwide Locations	Unspecified Minor Military Construction	30,000	40,000
	Wyoming			
AF	F. E. Warren AFB	Missile Transfer Facility Bldg 4331	5,550	5,550
Military Construction, Air Force Total			**1,481,058**	**1,686,523**
	Alaska			
Def-Wide	Clear AFS	Long Range Discrim Radar Sys Complex Ph 1	155,000	155,000
Def-Wide	Fort Greely	Missile Defense Complex Switchgear Facility	9,560	9,560
Def-Wide	Joint Base Elmendorf-Richardson	Construct Truck Offload Facility	4,900	4,900
	Arizona			
Def-Wide	Fort Huachuca	JITC Building 52110 Renovation	4,493	4,493
	California			
Def-Wide	Coronado	SOF Human Performance Training Center	15,578	15,578
Def-Wide	Coronado	SOF Seal Team Ops Facility	47,290	47,290
Def-Wide	Coronado	SOF Seal Team Ops Facility	47,290	47,290
Def-Wide	Coronado	SOF Special RECON Team ONE Operations Fac	20,949	20,949
Def-Wide	Coronado	SOF Training Detachment ONE Ops Facility	44,305	44,305
Def-Wide	Travis AFB	Replace Hydrant Fuel System	26,500	26,500
	Delaware			
Def-Wide	Dover AFB	Welch ES/Dover MS Replacement	44,115	44,115
	Diego Garcia			
Def-Wide	Diego Garcia	Improve Wharf Refueling Capability	30,000	30,000
	Florida			
Def-Wide	Patrick AFB	Replace Fuel Tanks	10,100	10,100
	Georgia			
Def-Wide	Fort Benning	SOF Tactical Unmanned Aerial Vehicle Hangar	4,820	4,820
Def-Wide	Fort Gordon	Medical Clinic Replacement	25,000	25,000
	Germany			

SEC. 4601. MILITARY CONSTRUCTION
(In Thousands of Dollars)

Account	State/Country and Installation	Project Title	FY 2017 Request	Conference Authorized
Def-Wide	Kaiserlautern AB	Sembach Elementary/Middle School Replacement	45,221	45,221
Def-Wide	Rhine Ordnance Barracks	Medical Center Replacement Incr 6	58,063	58,063
	Japan			
Def-Wide	Iwakuni	Construct Truck Offload & Loading Facilities	6,664	6,664
Def-Wide	Kadena AB	Kadena Elementary School Replacement	84,918	84,918
Def-Wide	Kadena AB	Medical Materiel Warehouse	20,881	20,881
Def-Wide	Kadena AB	SOF Maintenance Hangar	42,823	42,823
Def-Wide	Kadena AB	SOF Simulator Facility (MC-130)	12,602	12,602
Def-Wide	Yokota AB	Airfield Apron	41,294	41,294
Def-Wide	Yokota AB	Hangar/AMU	39,466	39,466
Def-Wide	Yokota AB	Operations and Warehouse Facilities	26,710	26,710
Def-Wide	Yokota AB	Simulator Facility	6,261	6,261
	Kwajalein			
Def-Wide	Kwajalein Atoll	Replace Fuel Storage Tanks	85,500	85,500
	Maine			
Def-Wide	Kittery	Medical/Dental Clinic Replacement	27,100	27,100
	Maryland			
Def-Wide	Bethesda Naval Hospital	MEDCEN Addition/Alteration Incr 1	50,000	50,000
Def-Wide	Fort Meade	Access Control Facility	21,000	21,000
Def-Wide	Fort Meade	NSAW Campus Feeders Phase 3	17,000	17,000
Def-Wide	Fort Meade	NSAW Recapitalize Building #2 Incr 2	195,000	195,000
	Missouri			
Def-Wide	St. Louis	Land Acquisition—Next NGA West Campus	801	801
	North Carolina			
Def-Wide	Camp Lejeune	Dental Clinic Replacement	31,000	31,000
Def-Wide	Fort Bragg	SOF Combat Medic Training Facility	10,905	10,905
Def-Wide	Fort Bragg	SOF Parachute Rigging Facility	21,420	21,420
Def-Wide	Fort Bragg	SOF Special Tactics Facility (Ph 3)	30,670	30,670
Def-Wide	Fort Bragg	SOF Tactical Equipment Maintenance Facility	23,598	23,598
	South Carolina			
Def-Wide	Joint Base Charleston	Construct Hydrant Fuel System	17,000	17,000
	Texas			
Def-Wide	Red River Army Depot	Construct Warehouse & Open Storage	44,700	44,700
Def-Wide	Sheppard AFB	Medical/Dental Clinic Replacement	91,910	91,910
	United Kingdom			
Def-Wide	RAF Croughton	Croughton Elem/Middle/High School Replacement	71,424	71,424
Def-Wide	RAF Lakenheath	Construct Hydrant Fuel System	13,500	13,500
	Virginia			
Def-Wide	Pentagon	Pentagon Metro Entrance Facility	12,111	12,111
Def-Wide	Pentagon	Upgrade IT Facilities Infrastructure—RRMC	8,105	8,105
	Wake Island			
Def-Wide	Wake Island	Test Support Facility	11,670	11,670
	Worldwide Unspecified			
Def-Wide	Unspecified Worldwide Locations	Battalion Complex	0	0
Def-Wide	Unspecified Worldwide Locations	Contingency Construction	10,000	0
Def-Wide	Unspecified Worldwide Locations	Energy Conservation Investment Program Design	10,000	0
Def-Wide	Unspecified Worldwide Locations	Energy Conservation Investment Program	150,000	150,000
Def-Wide	Unspecified Worldwide Locations	Exercise Related Minor Construction	8,631	8,631
Def-Wide	Unspecified Worldwide Locations	Planning and Design, Defense Wide	13,450	23,450
Def-Wide	Unspecified Worldwide Locations	Planning and Design, DODEA	23,585	23,585
Def-Wide	Unspecified Worldwide Locations	Planning and Design, NGA	71,647	36,000
Def-Wide	Unspecified Worldwide Locations	Planning and Design, NSA	24,000	24,000
Def-Wide	Unspecified Worldwide Locations	Planning and Design, WHS	3,427	3,427
Def-Wide	Unspecified Worldwide Locations	Unspecified Minor Construction	3,000	3,000
Def-Wide	Unspecified Worldwide Locations	Unspecified Minor Construction	3,000	3,000
Def-Wide	Unspecified Worldwide Locations	Unspecified Minor Construction	5,994	5,994
Def-Wide	Unspecified Worldwide Locations	Unspecified Minor Construction	8,500	8,500
Def-Wide	Unspecified Worldwide Locations	Unspecified Minor Milcon	3,913	3,913
Def-Wide	Unspecified Worldwide Locations	Worldwide Unspecified Minor Construction	2,414	2,414
Def-Wide	Various Worldwide Locations	Planning & Design, DLA	27,660	27,660
Def-Wide	Various Worldwide Locations	Planning and Design, SOCOM	27,653	27,653
	Worldwide Unspecified Locations			
Def-Wide	Unspecified Worldwide Locations	Planning & Design, MDA	0	15,000
	Military Construction, Defense-Wide Total		**2,056,091**	**2,025,444**
	Worldwide Unspecified			
NATO	NATO Security Investment Program	NATO Security Investment Program	177,932	177,932
	NATO Security Investment Program Total		**177,932**	**177,932**
	Colorado			
Army NG	Fort Carson	National Guard Readiness Center	0	16,500
	Hawaii			
Army NG	Hilo	Combined Support Maintenance Shop	31,000	31,000
	Iowa			
Army NG	Davenport	National Guard Readiness Center	23,000	23,000
	Kansas			

SEC. 4601. MILITARY CONSTRUCTION
(In Thousands of Dollars)

Account	State/Country and Installation	Project Title	FY 2017 Request	Conference Authorized
Army NG	Fort Leavenworth	National Guard Readiness Center	29,000	29,000
	New Hampshire			
Army NG	Hooksett	National Guard Vehicle Maintenance Shop	11,000	11,000
Army NG	Rochester	National Guard Vehicle Maintenance Shop	8,900	8,900
	Oklahoma			
Army NG	Ardmore	National Guard Readiness Center	22,000	22,000
	Pennsylvania			
Army NG	Fort Indiantown Gap	Access Control Buildings	0	20,000
Army NG	York	National Guard Readiness Center	9,300	9,300
	Rhode Island			
Army NG	East Greenwich	National Guard/Reserve Center Building (JFHQ)	20,000	20,000
	Utah			
Army NG	Camp Williams	National Guard Readiness Center	37,000	37,000
	Worldwide Unspecified			
Army NG	Unspecified Worldwide Locations	Planning and Design	8,729	8,729
Army NG	Unspecified Worldwide Locations	Unspecified Minor Construction	12,001	12,001
	Wyoming			
Army NG	Camp Guernsey	General Instruction Building	0	31,000
Army NG	Laramie	National Guard Readiness Center	21,000	21,000
Military Construction, Army National Guard Total			**232,930**	**300,430**
	Arizona			
Army Res	Phoenix	Army Reserve Center	0	30,000
	California			
Army Res	Barstow	Equipment Concentration Site	0	0
Army Res	Camp Parks	Transient Training Barracks	19,000	19,000
Army Res	Fort Hunter Liggett	Emergency Services Center	21,500	21,500
	Virginia			
Army Res	Dublin	Organizational Maintenance Shop/AMSA	6,000	6,000
	Washington			
Army Res	Joint Base Lewis-McChord	Army Reserve Center	0	0
	Wisconsin			
Army Res	Fort McCoy	AT/MOB Dining Facility	11,400	11,400
	Worldwide Unspecified			
Army Res	Unspecified Worldwide Locations	Planning and Design	7,500	7,500
Army Res	Unspecified Worldwide Locations	Unspecified Minor Construction	2,830	2,830
Military Construction, Army Reserve Total			**68,230**	**98,230**
	Louisiana			
N/MC Res	New Orleans	Joint Reserve Intelligence Center	11,207	11,207
	New York			
N/MC Res	Brooklyn	Electric Feeder Ductbank	1,964	1,964
N/MC Res	Syracuse	Marine Corps Reserve Center	13,229	13,229
	Texas			
N/MC Res	Galveston	Reserve Center Annex	8,414	8,414
	Worldwide Unspecified			
N/MC Res	Unspecified Worldwide Locations	MCNR Planning & Design	3,783	3,783
Military Construction, Naval Reserve Total			**38,597**	**38,597**
	Connecticut			
Air NG	Bradley IAP	Construct Small Air Terminal	6,300	6,300
	Florida			
Air NG	Jacksonville IAP	Replace Fire Crash/Rescue Station	9,000	9,000
	Hawaii			
Air NG	Joint Base Pearl Harbor-Hickam	F–22 Composite Repair Facility	11,000	11,000
	Iowa			
Air NG	Sioux Gateway Airport	Construct Consolidated Support Functions	12,600	12,600
	Maryland			
Air NG	Joint Base Andrews	Munitions Load Crew Trng/Corrosion Cntrl Facility	0	5,000
	Minnesota			
Air NG	Duluth IAP	Load Crew Training/Weapon Shops	7,600	7,600
	New Hampshire			
Air NG	Pease International Trade Port	KC–46A Install Fuselage Trainer Bldg 251	1,500	1,500
	North Carolina			
Air NG	Charlotte/Douglas IAP	C–17 Corrosion Control/Fuel Cell Hangar	29,600	29,600
Air NG	Charlotte/Douglas IAP	C–17 Type III Hydrant Refueling System	21,000	21,000
	Ohio			
Air NG	Toledo Express Airport	Indoor Small Arms Range	0	6,000
	South Carolina			
Air NG	McEntire ANGS	Replace Operations and Training Facility	8,400	8,400
	Texas			
Air NG	Ellington Field	Consolidate Crew Readiness Facility	4,500	4,500
	Vermont			
Air NG	Burlington IAP	F–35 Beddown 4-Bay Flight Simulator	4,500	4,500
	Worldwide Unspecified			
Air NG	Unspecified Worldwide Locations	Unspecified Minor Construction	17,495	17,495

SEC. 4601. MILITARY CONSTRUCTION
(In Thousands of Dollars)

Account	State/Country and Installation	Project Title	FY 2017 Request	Conference Authorized
Air NG	Various Worldwide Locations	Planning and Design	10,462	10,462
Military Construction, Air National Guard Total			**143,957**	**154,957**
	Guam			
AF Res	Andersen AFB	Reserve Medical Training Facility	0	0
	Massachusetts			
AF Res	Westover ARB	Indoor Small Arms Range	0	0
	North Carolina			
AF Res	Seymour Johnson AFB	KC–46A ADAL Bldg for AGE/Fuselage Training	5,700	5,700
AF Res	Seymour Johnson AFB	KC–46A ADAL Squadron Operations Facilities	2,250	2,250
AF Res	Seymour Johnson AFB	KC–46A Two Bay Corrosion/Fuel Cell Hangar	90,000	90,000
	Pennsylvania			
AF Res	Pittsburgh IAP	C–17 ADAL Fuel Hydrant System	22,800	22,800
AF Res	Pittsburgh IAP	C–17 Const/Overlay Taxiway and Apron	8,200	8,200
AF Res	Pittsburgh IAP	C–17 Construct Two Bay Corrosion/Fuel Hangar	54,000	54,000
	Utah			
AF Res	Hill AFB	ADAL Life Support Facility	0	0
	Worldwide Unspecified			
AF Res	Unspecified Worldwide Locations	Planning & Design	4,500	4,500
AF Res	Unspecified Worldwide Locations	Unspecified Minor Construction	1,500	1,500
Military Construction, Air Force Reserve Total			**188,950**	**188,950**
	Korea			
FH Con Army	Camp Humphreys	Family Housing New Construction, Incr 1	143,563	100,000
FH Con Army	Camp Walker	Family Housing New Construction	54,554	54,554
	Worldwide Unspecified			
FH Con Army	Unspecified Worldwide Locations	Planning & Design	2,618	2,618
Family Housing Construction, Army Total			**200,735**	**157,172**
	Worldwide Unspecified			
FH Ops Army	Unspecified Worldwide Locations	Furnishings	10,178	10,178
FH Ops Army	Unspecified Worldwide Locations	Housing Privatization Support	19,146	19,146
FH Ops Army	Unspecified Worldwide Locations	Leasing	131,761	131,761
FH Ops Army	Unspecified Worldwide Locations	Maintenance	60,745	60,745
FH Ops Army	Unspecified Worldwide Locations	Management	40,344	40,344
FH Ops Army	Unspecified Worldwide Locations	Miscellaneous	400	400
FH Ops Army	Unspecified Worldwide Locations	Services	7,993	7,993
FH Ops Army	Unspecified Worldwide Locations	Utilities	55,428	55,428
Family Housing Operation And Maintenance, Army Total			**325,995**	**325,995**
	Mariana Islands			
FH Con Navy	Guam	Replace Andersen Housing Ph I	78,815	78,815
	Worldwide Unspecified			
FH Con Navy	Unspecified Worldwide Locations	Construction Improvements	11,047	11,047
FH Con Navy	Unspecified Worldwide Locations	Planning & Design	4,149	4,149
Family Housing Construction, Navy And Marine Corps Total			**94,011**	**94,011**
	Worldwide Unspecified			
FH Ops Navy	Unspecified Worldwide Locations	Furnishings	17,457	17,457
FH Ops Navy	Unspecified Worldwide Locations	Housing Privatization Support	26,320	26,320
FH Ops Navy	Unspecified Worldwide Locations	Leasing	54,689	54,689
FH Ops Navy	Unspecified Worldwide Locations	Maintenance	81,254	81,254
FH Ops Navy	Unspecified Worldwide Locations	Management	51,291	51,291
FH Ops Navy	Unspecified Worldwide Locations	Miscellaneous	364	364

SEC. 4601. MILITARY CONSTRUCTION
(In Thousands of Dollars)

Account	State/Country and Installation	Project Title	FY 2017 Request	Conference Authorized
FH Ops Navy	Unspecified Worldwide Locations	Services	12,855	12,855
FH Ops Navy	Unspecified Worldwide Locations	Utilities	56,685	56,685
Family Housing Operation And Maintenance, Navy And Marine Corps Total			**300,915**	**300,915**
	Worldwide Unspecified			
FH Con AF	Unspecified Worldwide Locations	Construction Improvements	56,984	56,984
FH Con AF	Unspecified Worldwide Locations	Planning & Design	4,368	4,368
Family Housing Construction, Air Force Total			**61,352**	**61,352**
	Worldwide Unspecified			
FH Ops AF	Unspecified Worldwide Locations	Furnishings	31,690	31,690
FH Ops AF	Unspecified Worldwide Locations	Housing Privatization Support	41,809	41,809
FH Ops AF	Unspecified Worldwide Locations	Leasing	20,530	20,530
FH Ops AF	Unspecified Worldwide Locations	Maintenance	85,469	85,469
FH Ops AF	Unspecified Worldwide Locations	Management	42,919	42,919
FH Ops AF	Unspecified Worldwide Locations	Miscellaneous	1,745	1,745
FH Ops AF	Unspecified Worldwide Locations	Services	13,026	13,026
FH Ops AF	Unspecified Worldwide Locations	Utilities	37,241	37,241
Family Housing Operation And Maintenance, Air Force Total			**274,429**	**274,429**
	Worldwide Unspecified			
FH Ops DW	Unspecified Worldwide Locations	Furnishings	20	20
FH Ops DW	Unspecified Worldwide Locations	Furnishings	500	500
FH Ops DW	Unspecified Worldwide Locations	Furnishings	399	399
FH Ops DW	Unspecified Worldwide Locations	Leasing	40,984	40,984
FH Ops DW	Unspecified Worldwide Locations	Leasing	11,044	11,044
FH Ops DW	Unspecified Worldwide Locations	Maintenance	349	349
FH Ops DW	Unspecified Worldwide Locations	Maintenance	800	800
FH Ops DW	Unspecified Worldwide Locations	Management	388	388
FH Ops DW	Unspecified Worldwide Locations	Services	32	32
FH Ops DW	Unspecified Worldwide Locations	Utilities	4,100	4,100
FH Ops DW	Unspecified Worldwide Locations	Utilities	174	174
FH Ops DW	Unspecified Worldwide Locations	Utilities	367	367
Family Housing Operation And Maintenance, Defense-Wide Total			**59,157**	**59,157**
	Worldwide Unspecified			
FHIF	Unspecified Worldwide Locations	Program Expenses	3,258	3,258
DoD Family Housing Improvement Fund Total			**3,258**	**3,258**
	Worldwide Unspecified			
BRAC	Base Realignment & Closure, Army	Base Realignment and Closure	14,499	24,499
Base Realignment and Closure—Army Total			**14,499**	**24,499**
	Worldwide Unspecified			
BRAC	Base Realignment & Closure, Navy	Base Realignment & Closure	110,606	135,606
BRAC	Unspecified Worldwide Locations	DON–100: Planning, Design and Management	4,604	4,604
BRAC	Unspecified Worldwide Locations	DON–101: Various Locations	10,461	10,461
BRAC	Unspecified Worldwide Locations	DON–138: NAS Brunswick, ME	557	557
BRAC	Unspecified Worldwide Locations	DON–157: MCSA Kansas City, MO	100	100
BRAC	Unspecified Worldwide Locations	DON–172: NWS Seal Beach, Concord, CA	4,648	4,648
BRAC	Unspecified Worldwide Locations	DON–84: JRB Willow Grove & Cambria Reg AP	3,397	3,397
Base Realignment and Closure—Navy Total			**134,373**	**159,373**
	Worldwide Unspecified			
BRAC	Unspecified Worldwide Locations	DoD BRAC Activities—Air Force	56,365	56,365
Base Realignment and Closure—Air Force Total			**56,365**	**56,365**
	Worldwide Unspecified			
PYS	Unspecified Worldwide Locations	Planning and Design, Defense Wide	0	−30,000
PYS	Worldwide	Air Force	0	−51,460
PYS	Worldwide	Army	0	−29,602
PYS	Worldwide	Defense-Wide	0	−141,600
PYS	Worldwide	Navy	0	0
	Worldwide Unspecified Locations			
PYS	Worldwide	HAP	0	−25,000
PYS	Worldwide	NSIP	0	−30,000

SEC. 4601. MILITARY CONSTRUCTION
(In Thousands of Dollars)

Account	State/Country and Installation	Project Title	FY 2017 Request	Conference Authorized
Prior Year Savings Total			0	–307,662
Total, Military Construction			7,444,056	7,709,565

**SEC. 4602. MILITARY CONSTRUCTION FOR OVER-
SEAS CONTINGENCY OPERATIONS.**

SEC. 4602. MILITARY CONSTRUCTION FOR OVERSEAS CONTINGENCY OPERATIONS
(In Thousands of Dollars)

Account	State/Country and Installation	Project Title	FY 2017 Request	Conference Authorized
	Worldwide Unspecified			
Army	Unspecified Worldwide Locations	ERI: Planning and Design	18,900	18,900
Military Construction, Army Total			**18,900**	**18,900**
	Iceland			
Navy	Keflavik	ERI: P–8A Aircraft Rinse Rack	5,000	5,000
Navy	Keflavik	ERI: P–8A Hangar Upgrade	14,600	14,600
	Worldwide Unspecified			
Navy	Unspecified Worldwide Locations	ERI: Planning and Design	1,800	1,800
Military Construction, Navy Total			**21,400**	**21,400**
	Bulgaria			
AF	Graf Ignatievo	ERI: Construct Sq Ops/Operational Alert Fac	3,800	3,800
AF	Graf Ignatievo	ERI: Fighter Ramp Extension	7,000	7,000
AF	Graf Ignatievo	ERI: Upgrade Munitions Storage Area	2,600	2,600
	Djibouti			
AF	Chabelley Airfield	OCO: Construct Chabelley Access Road	3,600	3,600
AF	Chabelley Airfield	OCO: Construct Parking Apron and Taxiway	6,900	6,900
	Estonia			
AF	Amari AB	ERI: Construct Bulk Fuel Storage	6,500	6,500
	Germany			
AF	Spangdahlem AB	ERI: Construct High Cap Trim Pad & Hush House	1,000	1,000
AF	Spangdahlem AB	ERI: F/A–22 Low Observable/Comp Repair Fac	12,000	12,000
AF	Spangdahlem AB	ERI: F/A–22 Upgrade Infrastructure/Comm/Util	1,600	1,600
AF	Spangdahlem AB	ERI: Upgrade Hardened Aircraft Shelters	2,700	2,700
AF	Spangdahlem AB	ERI: Upgrade Munitions Storage Doors	1,400	1,400
	Lithuania			
AF	Siauliai	ERI: Munitions Storage	3,000	3,000
	Poland			
AF	Lask AB	ERI: Construct Squadron Operations Facility	4,100	4,100
AF	Powidz AB	ERI: Construct Squadron Operations Facility	4,100	4,100
	Romania			
AF	Campia Turzii	ERI: Construct Munitions Storage Area	3,000	3,000
AF	Campia Turzii	ERI: Construct Squadron Operations Facility	3,400	3,400
AF	Campia Turzii	ERI: Construct Two-Bay Hangar	6,100	6,100
AF	Campia Turzii	ERI: Extend Parking Aprons	6,000	6,000
	Worldwide Unspecified			
AF	Unspecified Worldwide Locations	CTP: Planning and Design	9,000	8,551
AF	Unspecified Worldwide Locations	OCO: Planning and Design	940	940
Military Construction, Air Force Total			**88,740**	**88,291**
	Worldwide Unspecified			
Def-Wide	Unspecified Worldwide Locations	ERI: Unspecified Minor Construction	5,000	5,000
Military Construction, Defense-Wide Total			**5,000**	**5,000**
Total, Military Construction			**134,040**	**133,591**

**SEC. 4603. MILITARY CONSTRUCTION FOR OVER-
SEAS CONTINGENCY OPERATIONS
FOR BASE REQUIREMENTS.**

SEC. 4603. MILITARY CONSTRUCTION FOR OVERSEAS CONTINGENCY OPERATIONS FOR BASE REQUIREMENTS
(In Thousands of Dollars)

Service	State/Country and Installation	Project	FY 2017 Request	Conference Authorized
	Djibouti			
Navy	Camp Lemonier	OCO: Medical/Dental Facility	37,409	37,409
	Worldwide Unspecified			
Navy	Unspecified Worldwide Locations	Planning and Design	1,000	1,000

SEC. 4603. MILITARY CONSTRUCTION FOR OVERSEAS CONTINGENCY OPERATIONS FOR BASE REQUIREMENTS
(In Thousands of Dollars)

Service	State/Country and Installation	Project	FY 2017 Request	Conference Authorized
Military Construction, Navy Total			*38,409*	*38,409*
Total, Military Construction			*38,409*	*38,409*

TITLE XLVII—DEPARTMENT OF ENERGY NATIONAL SECURITY PROGRAMS

SEC. 4701. DEPARTMENT OF ENERGY NATIONAL SECURITY PROGRAMS.

SEC. 4701. DEPARTMENT OF ENERGY NATIONAL SECURITY PROGRAMS
(In Thousands of Dollars)

Program	FY 2017 Request	Conference Authorized
Discretionary Summary By Appropriation		
Energy And Water Development, And Related Agencies		
Appropriation Summary:		
Energy Programs		
Nuclear Energy	*151,876*	*136,616*
Atomic Energy Defense Activities		
National nuclear security administration:		
Weapons activities	*9,243,147*	*9,429,029*
Defense nuclear nonproliferation	*1,807,916*	*1,886,916*
Naval reactors	*1,420,120*	*1,417,620*
Federal salaries and expenses	*412,817*	*395,517*
Total, National nuclear security administration	*12,884,000*	*13,129,082*
Environmental and other defense activities:		
Defense environmental cleanup	*5,382,050*	*5,273,558*
Other defense activities	*791,552*	*789,552*
Total, Environmental & other defense activities	*6,173,602*	*6,063,110*
Total, Atomic Energy Defense Activities	*19,057,602*	*19,192,192*
Total, Discretionary Funding	*19,209,478*	*19,328,808*
Nuclear Energy		
Idaho sitewide safeguards and security	*129,303*	*129,303*
Idaho operations and maintenance	*7,313*	*7,313*
Consent Based Siting	*15,260*	*0*
Denial of funds for defense-only repository		*[–15,260]*
Total, Nuclear Energy	*151,876*	*136,616*
Weapons Activities		
Directed stockpile work		
Life extension programs		
B61 Life extension program	*616,079*	*616,079*
W76 Life extension program	*222,880*	*222,880*
W88 Alt 370	*281,129*	*281,129*
W80–4 Life extension program	*220,253*	*220,253*
Total, Life extension programs	*1,340,341*	*1,340,341*
Stockpile systems		
B61 Stockpile systems	*57,313*	*57,313*
W76 Stockpile systems	*38,604*	*38,604*
W78 Stockpile systems	*56,413*	*56,413*
W80 Stockpile systems	*64,631*	*64,631*
B83 Stockpile systems	*41,659*	*41,659*
W87 Stockpile systems	*81,982*	*81,982*
W88 Stockpile systems	*103,074*	*103,074*
Total, Stockpile systems	*443,676*	*443,676*
Weapons dismantlement and disposition		
Operations and maintenance	*68,984*	*56,000*
Denial of dismantlement acceleration		*[–12,984]*
Stockpile services		
Production support	*457,043*	*457,043*
Research and development support	*34,187*	*34,187*
R&D certification and safety	*156,481*	*156,481*
Management, technology, and production	*251,978*	*251,978*
Total, Stockpile services	*899,689*	*899,689*
Nuclear material commodities		
Uranium sustainment	*20,988*	*20,988*
Plutonium sustainment	*184,970*	*184,970*
Tritium sustainment	*109,787*	*109,787*

SEC. 4701. DEPARTMENT OF ENERGY NATIONAL SECURITY PROGRAMS
(In Thousands of Dollars)

Program	FY 2017 Request	Conference Authorized
Domestic uranium enrichment	50,000	50,000
Strategic materials sustainment	212,092	212,092
Total, Nuclear material commodities	**577,837**	**577,837**
Total, Directed stockpile work	**3,330,527**	**3,317,543**
Research, development, test and evaluation (RDT&E)		
Science		
Advanced certification	58,000	58,000
Primary assessment technologies	99,000	99,000
Dynamic materials properties	106,000	106,000
Advanced radiography	50,500	50,500
Secondary assessment technologies	76,000	76,000
Academic alliances and partnerships	52,484	52,484
Total, Science	**441,984**	**441,984**
Engineering		
Enhanced surety	37,196	37,196
Weapon systems engineering assessment technology	16,958	16,958
Nuclear survivability	43,105	43,105
Enhanced surveillance	42,228	42,228
Total, Engineering	**139,487**	**139,487**
Inertial confinement fusion ignition and high yield		
Ignition	75,432	75,432
Support of other stockpile programs	23,363	23,363
Diagnostics, cryogenics and experimental support	68,696	68,696
Pulsed power inertial confinement fusion	5,616	5,616
Joint program in high energy density laboratory plasmas	9,492	9,492
Facility operations and target production	340,360	340,360
Total, Inertial confinement fusion and high yield	**522,959**	**522,959**
Advanced simulation and computing	663,184	656,184
Program decrease		[–7,000]
Stockpile Responsiveness Program	0	40,000
Program increase		[40,000]
Advanced manufacturing		
Additive manufacturing	12,000	12,000
Component manufacturing development	46,583	46,583
Processing technology development	28,522	28,522
Total, Advanced manufacturing	**87,105**	**87,105**
Total, RDT&E	**1,854,719**	**1,887,719**
Infrastructure and operations (formerly RTBF)		
Operating		
Operations of facilities		
Kansas City Plant	101,000	101,000
Lawrence Livermore National Laboratory	70,500	70,500
Los Alamos National Laboratory	196,500	196,500
Nevada Test Site	92,500	92,500
Pantex	55,000	55,000
Sandia National Laboratory	118,000	118,000
Savannah River Site	83,500	83,500
Y–12 National security complex	107,000	107,000
Total, Operations of facilities	**824,000**	**824,000**
Safety and environmental operations	110,000	110,000
Maintenance and repair of facilities	294,000	324,000
Address high-priority preventative maintenance		[30,000]
Recapitalization:		
Infrastructure and safety	554,643	630,509
Address high-priority deferred maintenance		[75,866]
Capability based investment	112,639	112,639
Total, Recapitalization	**667,282**	**743,148**
Construction:		
17–D–640 U1a Complex Enhancements Project, NNSS	11,500	11,500
17–D–630 Electrical Infrastructure Upgrades, LLNL	25,000	25,000
16–D–515 Albuquerque complex upgrades project	15,047	15,047
15–D–613 Emergency Operations Center, Y–12	2,000	2,000
15–D–302 TA–55 Reinvestment project, Phase 3, LANL	21,455	21,455
07–D–220–04 Transuranic liquid waste facility, LANL	17,053	17,053
06–D–141 PED/Construction, UPF Y–12, Oak Ridge, TN	575,000	575,000
04–D–125–04 RLUOB equipment installation	159,615	159,615
Total, Construction	**826,670**	**826,670**
Total, Infrastructure and operations	**2,721,952**	**2,827,818**

SEC. 4701. DEPARTMENT OF ENERGY NATIONAL SECURITY PROGRAMS
(In Thousands of Dollars)

Program	FY 2017 Request	Conference Authorized
Secure transportation asset		
Operations and equipment	179,132	179,132
Program direction	103,600	103,600
Total, Secure transportation asset	**282,732**	**282,732**
Defense nuclear security		
Operations and maintenance	657,133	693,133
Support to physical security infrastructure recapitalization and CSTART		[36,000]
Construction:		
14–D–710 Device assembly facility argus installation project, NV	13,000	13,000
17–D–710 West end protected area reduction project, Y–12	0	24,000
Total, Defense nuclear security	**670,133**	**730,133**
Information technology and cybersecurity	176,592	176,592
Legacy contractor pensions	248,492	248,492
Rescission of prior year balances	−42,000	−42,000
Total, Weapons Activities	**9,243,147**	**9,429,029**
Defense Nuclear Nonproliferation		
Defense Nuclear Nonproliferation Programs		
Defense Nuclear Nonproliferation R&D		
Global material security	337,108	337,108
Material management and minimization	341,094	321,094
Program decrease		[−20,000]
Nonproliferation and arms control	124,703	124,703
Defense Nuclear Nonproliferation R&D	393,922	417,922
Acceleration of low-yield detection experiments		[4,000]
Nuclear detection technology and new challenges such as 3D printing		[20,000]
Low Enriched Uranium R&D for Naval Reactors	0	5,000
Low Enriched Uranium R&D for Naval Reactors		[5,000]
Nonproliferation Construction:		
99–D–143 Mixed Oxide (MOX) Fuel Fabrication Facility, SRS	270,000	340,000
Increase to support construction		[70,000]
Total, Nonproliferation construction	**270,000**	**340,000**
Total, Defense Nuclear Nonproliferation Programs	**1,466,827**	**1,545,827**
Legacy contractor pensions	83,208	83,208
Nuclear counterterrorism and incident response program	271,881	271,881
Rescission of prior year balances	−14,000	−14,000
Total, Defense Nuclear Nonproliferation	**1,807,916**	**1,886,916**
Naval Reactors		
Naval reactors operations and infrastructure	449,682	447,182
Naval reactors development	437,338	437,338
Ohio replacement reactor systems development	213,700	213,700
S8G Prototype refueling	124,000	124,000
Program direction	47,100	47,100
Construction:		
17–D–911, BL Fire System Upgrade	1,400	1,400
15–D–904 NRF Overpack Storage Expansion 3	700	700
15–D–902 KS Engineroom team trainer facility	33,300	33,300
14–D–901 Spent fuel handling recapitalization project, NRF	100,000	100,000
10–D–903, Security upgrades, KAPL	12,900	12,900
Total, Construction	**148,300**	**148,300**
Total, Naval Reactors	**1,420,120**	**1,417,620**
Federal Salaries And Expenses		
Program direction	412,817	395,517
Program decrease		[−17,300]
Total, Office Of The Administrator	**412,817**	**395,517**
Defense Environmental Cleanup		
Closure sites:		
Closure sites administration	9,389	9,389
Hanford site:		
River corridor and other cleanup operations	69,755	114,755
Acceleration of priority programs		[45,000]
Central plateau remediation	620,869	644,369
Acceleration of priority programs		[23,500]
Richland community and regulatory support	14,701	14,701
Construction:		
15–D–401 Containerized sludge removal annex, RL	11,486	11,486

SEC. 4701. DEPARTMENT OF ENERGY NATIONAL SECURITY PROGRAMS
(In Thousands of Dollars)

Program	FY 2017 Request	Conference Authorized
Total, Hanford site	**716,811**	**785,311**
Idaho National Laboratory:		
Idaho cleanup and waste disposition	359,088	359,088
Idaho community and regulatory support	3,000	3,000
Total, Idaho National Laboratory	**362,088**	**362,088**
Los Alamos National Laboratory		
EMLA cleanup activities	185,606	195,606
Program Increase		[10,000]
EMLA community and regulatory support	3,394	3,394
Total, Los Alamos National Laboratory	**189,000**	**199,000**
NNSA sites		
Lawrence Livermore National Laboratory	1,396	1,396
Separations Process Research Unit	3,685	3,685
Nevada	62,176	62,176
Sandia National Laboratories	4,130	4,130
Total, NNSA sites and Nevada off-sites	**71,387**	**71,387**
Oak Ridge Reservation:		
OR Nuclear facility D & D		
OR Nuclear facility D & D	93,851	93,851
Construction:		
14–D–403 Outfall 200 Mercury Treatment Facility	5,100	5,100
Total, OR Nuclear facility D & D	**98,951**	**98,951**
U233 Disposition Program	37,311	37,311
OR cleanup and disposition	54,557	54,557
OR reservation community and regulatory support	4,400	4,400
Oak Ridge technology development	3,000	3,000
Total, Oak Ridge Reservation	**198,219**	**198,219**
Office of River Protection:		
Waste treatment and immobilization plant		
WTP operations	3,000	3,000
15–D–409 Low activity waste pretreatment system, ORP	73,000	73,000
01–D–416 A–D/ORP–0060 / Major construction	690,000	690,000
Total, Waste treatment and immobilization plant	**766,000**	**766,000**
Tank farm activities		
Rad liquid tank waste stabilization and disposition	721,456	721,456
Total, Tank farm activities	**721,456**	**721,456**
Total, Office of River protection	**1,487,456**	**1,487,456**
Savannah River sites:		
Nuclear Material Management	311,062	311,062
Environmental Cleanup	152,504	152,504
SR community and regulatory support	11,249	11,249
Radioactive liquid tank waste:		
Radioactive liquid tank waste stabilization and disposition	645,332	645,332
Construction:		
15–D–402—Saltstone Disposal Unit #6, SRS	7,577	7,577
17–D–401—Saltstone Disposal Unit #7	9,729	9,729
05–D–405 Salt waste processing facility, Savannah River Site	160,000	160,000
Total, Construction	**177,306**	**177,306**
Total, Radioactive liquid tank waste	**822,638**	**822,638**
Total, Savannah River site	**1,297,453**	**1,297,453**
Waste Isolation Pilot Plant		
Operations and maintenance	257,188	267,188
Program increase		[10,000]
Construction:		
15–D–411 Safety significant confinement ventilation system, WIPP	2,532	2,532
15–D–412 Exhaust shaft, WIPP	2,533	2,533
Total, Construction	**5,065**	**5,065**
Total, Waste Isolation Pilot Plant	**262,253**	**272,253**
Program direction	290,050	290,050
Program support	14,979	14,979
Safeguards and Security	255,973	255,973
Technology development	30,000	30,000
Infrastructure recapitalization	41,892	0
Defense Uranium enrichment D&D	155,100	0
Ahead of need		[–155,100]
Subtotal, Defense environmental cleanup	**5,382,050**	**5,273,558**
Total, Defense Environmental Cleanup	**5,382,050**	**5,273,558**

SEC. 4701. DEPARTMENT OF ENERGY NATIONAL SECURITY PROGRAMS
(In Thousands of Dollars)

Program	FY 2017 Request	Conference Authorized
Other Defense Activities		
Environment, health, safety and security		
Environment, health, safety and security	130,693	128,693
Program direction	66,519	66,519
Total, Environment, health, safety and security	**197,212**	**195,212**
Independent enterprise assessments		
Independent enterprise assessments	24,580	24,580
Program direction	51,893	51,893
Total, Independent enterprise assessments	**76,473**	**76,473**
Specialized security activities	237,912	237,912
Office of Legacy Management		
Legacy management	140,306	140,306
Program direction	14,014	14,014
Total, Office of Legacy Management	**154,320**	**154,320**
Defense-related activities		
Defense related administrative support		
Chief financial officer	23,642	23,642
Chief information officer	93,074	93,074
Project management oversight and assessments	3,000	3,000
Total, Defense related administrative support	**119,716**	**116,716**
Office of hearings and appeals	5,919	5,919
Subtotal, Other defense activities	**791,552**	**789,552**
Total, Other Defense Activities	**791,552**	**789,552**

DIVISION E—UNIFORM CODE OF MILITARY JUSTICE REFORM

SEC. 5001. SHORT TITLE.

This division may be cited as the "Military Justice Act of 2016".

TITLE LI—GENERAL PROVISIONS

Sec. 5101. Definitions.
Sec. 5102. Clarification of persons subject to UCMJ while on inactive-duty training.
Sec. 5103. Staff judge advocate disqualification due to prior involvement in case.
Sec. 5104. Conforming amendment relating to military magistrates.
Sec. 5105. Rights of victim.

SEC. 5101. DEFINITIONS.

(a) MILITARY JUDGE.—Paragraph (10) of section 801 of title 10, United States Code (article 1 of the Uniform Code of Military Justice), is amended to read as follows:

"(10) The term 'military judge' means a judge advocate designated under section 826(c) of this title (article 26(c)) who is detailed under section 826(a) or section 830a of this title (article 26(a) or 30a).".

(b) JUDGE ADVOCATE.—Paragraph (13) of such section (article) is amended—

(1) in subparagraph (A), by striking "the Army or the Navy" and inserting "the Army, the Navy, or the Air Force"; and

(2) in subparagraph (B), by striking "the Air Force or".

SEC. 5102. CLARIFICATION OF PERSONS SUBJECT TO UCMJ WHILE ON INACTIVE-DUTY TRAINING.

Paragraph (3) of section 802(a) of title 10, United States Code (article 2(a) of the Uniform Code of Military Justice), is amended to read as follows:

"(3)(A) While on inactive-duty training and during any of the periods specified in subparagraph (B)—

"(i) members of a reserve component; and

"(ii) members of the Army National Guard of the United States or the Air National Guard of the United States, but only when in Federal service.

"(B) The periods referred to in subparagraph (A) are the following:

"(i) Travel to and from the inactive-duty training site of the member, pursuant to orders or regulations.

"(ii) Intervals between consecutive periods of inactive-duty training on the same day, pursuant to orders or regulations.

"(iii) Intervals between inactive-duty training on consecutive days, pursuant to orders or regulations.".

SEC. 5103. STAFF JUDGE ADVOCATE DISQUALI-FICATION DUE TO PRIOR INVOLVE-MENT IN CASE.

Subsection (c) of section 806 of title 10, United States Code (article 6 of the Uniform Code of Military Justice), is amended to read as follows:

"(c)(1) No person who, with respect to a case, serves in a capacity specified in paragraph (2) may later serve as a staff judge advocate or legal officer to any reviewing or convening authority upon the same case.

"(2) The capacities referred to in paragraph (1) are, with respect to the case involved, any of the following:

"(A) Preliminary hearing officer, court member, military judge, military magistrate, or appellate judge.

"(B) Counsel who have acted in the same case or appeared in any proceeding before a military judge, military magistrate, preliminary hearing officer, or appellate court.".

SEC. 5104. CONFORMING AMENDMENT RELATING TO MILITARY MAGISTRATES.

The first sentence of section 806a(a) of title 10, United States Code (article 6a(a) of the Uniform Code of Military Justice), is amended by striking "military judge" and all that follows through the end of the sentence and inserting "military appellate judge, military judge, or military magistrate to perform the duties of the position involved.".

SEC. 5105. RIGHTS OF VICTIM.

(a) DESIGNATION OF REPRESENTATIVE.—Subsection (c) of section 806b of title 10, United States Code (article 6b of the Uniform Code of Military Justice), is amended in the first sentence by striking "the military judge" and all that follows through the end of the sentence and inserting the following: "the legal guardians of the victim or the representatives of the victim's estate, family members, or any other person designated as suitable by the military judge, may assume the rights of the victim under this section.".

(b) RULE OF CONSTRUCTION.—Subsection (d) of such section (article) is amended—

(1) in paragraph (1), by striking "or" at the end;

(2) in paragraph (2), by striking the period at the end and inserting "; or"; and

(3) by adding at the end the following new paragraph:

"(3) to impair the exercise of discretion under sections 830 and 834 of this title (articles 30 and 34).".

(c) INTERVIEW OF VICTIM.—Such section (article) is amended by adding at the end the following new subsection:

"(f) COUNSEL FOR ACCUSED INTERVIEW OF VICTIM OF ALLEGED OFFENSE.—(1) Upon notice by counsel for the Government to counsel for the accused of the name of an alleged victim of an offense under this chapter who counsel for the Government intends to call as a witness at a proceeding under this chapter, counsel for the accused shall make any request to interview the victim through the Special Victims' Counsel or other counsel for the victim, if applicable.

"(2) If requested by an alleged victim who is subject to a request for interview under paragraph (1), any interview of the victim by counsel for the accused shall take place only in the presence of the counsel for the Government, a counsel for the victim, or, if applicable, a victim advocate.".

TITLE LII—APPREHENSION AND RESTRAINT

Sec. 5121. Restraint of persons charged.
Sec. 5122. Modification of prohibition of confinement of members of the Armed Forces with enemy prisoners and certain others.

SEC. 5121. RESTRAINT OF PERSONS CHARGED.

Section 810 of title 10, United States Code (article 10 of the Uniform Code of Military Justice), is amended to read as follows:

"§810. Art. 10. Restraint of persons charged

"(a) IN GENERAL.—(1) Subject to paragraph (2), any person subject to this chapter who is charged with an offense under this chapter may be ordered into arrest or confinement as the circumstances require.

"(2) When a person subject to this chapter is charged only with an offense that is normally tried by summary court-martial, the person ordinarily shall not be ordered into confinement.

"(b) NOTIFICATION TO ACCUSED AND RELATED PROCEDURES.—(1) When a person subject to this chapter is ordered into arrest or confinement before trial, immediate steps shall be taken—

"(A) to inform the person of the specific offense of which the person is accused; and

"(B) to try the person or to dismiss the charges and release the person.

"(2) To facilitate compliance with paragraph (1), the President shall prescribe regulations setting forth procedures relating to referral for trial, including procedures for prompt forwarding of the charges and specifications and, if applicable, the preliminary hearing report submitted under section 832 of this title (article 32).".

SEC. 5122. MODIFICATION OF PROHIBITION OF CONFINEMENT OF MEMBERS OF THE ARMED FORCES WITH ENEMY PRISONERS AND CERTAIN OTHERS.

Section 812 of title 10, United States Code (article 12 of the Uniform Code of Military Justice), is amended to read as follows:

"§812. Art. 12. Prohibition of confinement of members of the armed forces with enemy prisoners and certain others

"No member of the armed forces may be placed in confinement in immediate association with—

"(1) enemy prisoners; or

"(2) other individuals—

"(A) who are detained under the law of war and are foreign nationals; and

"(B) who are not members of the armed forces.".

TITLE LIII—NON-JUDICIAL PUNISHMENT

Sec. 5141. Modification of confinement as non-judicial punishment.

SEC. 5141. MODIFICATION OF CONFINEMENT AS NON-JUDICIAL PUNISHMENT.

Section 815 of title 10, United States Code (article 15 of the Uniform Code of Military Justice), is amended—

(1) in subsection (b)—

(A) in paragraph (2)(A), by striking "on bread and water or diminished rations"; and

(B) in the undesignated matter after paragraph (2), by striking "on bread and water or diminished rations" in the sentence beginning "No two or more"; and

(2) in subsection (d), by striking "on bread and water or diminished rations" in paragraphs (2) and (3).

TITLE LIV—COURT-MARTIAL JURISDICTION

Sec. 5161. Courts-martial classified.
Sec. 5162. Jurisdiction of general courts-martial.
Sec. 5163. Jurisdiction of special courts-martial.
Sec. 5164. Summary court-martial as non-criminal forum.

SEC. 5161. COURTS-MARTIAL CLASSIFIED.

Section 816 of title 10, United States Code (article 16 of the Uniform Code of Military Justice), is amended to read as follows:

"§816. Art 16. Courts-martial classified

"(a) IN GENERAL.—The three kinds of courts-martial in each of the armed forces are the following:

"(1) General courts-martial, as described in subsection (b).

"(2) Special courts-martial, as described in subsection (c).

"(3) Summary courts-martial, as described in subsection (d).

"(b) GENERAL COURTS-MARTIAL.—General courts-martial are of the following three types:

"(1) A general court-martial consisting of a military judge and eight members, subject to sections 825(d)(3) and 829 of this title (articles 25(d)(3) and 29).

"(2) In a capital case, a general court-martial consisting of a military judge and the number of members determined under section 825a of this title (article 25a), subject to sections 825(d)(3) and 829 of this title (articles 25(d)(3) and 29).

"(3) A general court-martial consisting of a military judge alone, if, before the court is assembled, the accused, knowing the identity of the military judge and after consultation with defense counsel, requests, orally on the record or in writing, a court composed of a military judge alone and the military judge approves the request.

"(c) SPECIAL COURTS-MARTIAL.—Special courts-martial are of the following two types:

"(1) A special court-martial consisting of a military judge and four members, subject to sections 825(d)(3) and 829 of this title (articles 25(d)(3) and 29).

"(2) A special court-martial consisting of a military judge alone—

"(A) if the case is so referred by the convening authority, subject to section 819 of this title (article 19) and such limitations as the President may prescribe by regulation; or

"(B) if the case is referred under paragraph (1) and, before the court is assembled, the accused, knowing the identity of the military judge and after consultation with defense counsel, requests, orally on the record or in writing, a court composed of a military judge alone and the military judge approves the request.

"(d) SUMMARY COURT-MARTIAL.—A summary court-martial consists of one commissioned officer.".

SEC. 5162. JURISDICTION OF GENERAL COURTS-MARTIAL.

Section 818 of title 10, United States Code (article 18 of the Uniform Code of Military Justice), is amended—

(1) in subsection (b), by striking "section 816(1)(B) of this title (article 16(1)(B))" and inserting "section 816(b)(3) of this title (article 16(b)(3))"; and

(2) by striking subsection (c) and inserting the following new subsection (c):

"(c) Consistent with sections 819 and 820 of this title (articles 19 and 20), only general courts-martial have jurisdiction over the following offenses:

"(1) A violation of subsection (a) or (b) of section 920 of this title (article 120).

"(2) A violation of subsection (a) or (b) of section 920b of this title (article 120b).

"(3) An attempt to commit an offense specified in paragraph (1) or (2) that is punishable under section 880 of this title (article 80).".

SEC. 5163. JURISDICTION OF SPECIAL COURTS-MARTIAL.

Section 819 of title 10, United States Code (article 19 of the Uniform Code of Military Justice), is amended—

(1) by striking "Subject to" in the first sentence and inserting the following:

"(a) IN GENERAL.—Subject to";

(2) by striking "A bad-conduct discharge" and all that follows through the end; and

(3) by adding after subsection (a), as designated by paragraph (1), the following new subsections:

"(b) ADDITIONAL LIMITATION.—Neither a bad-conduct discharge, nor confinement for more than six months, nor forfeiture of pay for more than six months may be adjudged if charges and specifications are referred to a special court-martial consisting of a military judge alone under section 816(c)(2)(A) of this title (article 16(c)(2)(A)).

"(c) MILITARY MAGISTRATE.—If charges and specifications are referred to a special court-martial consisting of a military judge alone under section 816(c)(2)(A) of this title (article 16(c)(2)(A)), the military judge, with the consent of the parties, may designate a military magistrate to preside over the special court-martial.".

SEC. 5164. SUMMARY COURT-MARTIAL AS NON-CRIMINAL FORUM.

Section 820 of title 10, United States Code (article 20 of the Uniform Code of Military Justice), is amended—

(1) by inserting "(a) IN GENERAL.—" before "Subject to"; and

(2) by adding at the end the following new subsection:

"(b) NON-CRIMINAL FORUM.—A summary court-martial is a non-criminal forum. A finding of guilty at a summary court-martial does not constitute a criminal conviction.".

TITLE LV—COMPOSITION OF COURTS-MARTIAL

Sec. 5181. Technical amendment relating to persons authorized to convene general courts-martial.
Sec. 5182. Who may serve on courts-martial and related matters.
Sec. 5183. Number of court-martial members in capital cases.
Sec. 5184. Detailing, qualifications, and other matters relating to military judges.
Sec. 5185. Military magistrates.
Sec. 5186. Qualifications of trial counsel and defense counsel.
Sec. 5187. Assembly and impaneling of members and related matters.

SEC. 5181. TECHNICAL AMENDMENT RELATING TO PERSONS AUTHORIZED TO CONVENE GENERAL COURTS-MARTIAL.

Section 822(a)(6) of title 10, United States Code (article 22(a)(6) of the Uniform Code of Military Justice), is amended by striking "in chief".

SEC. 5182. WHO MAY SERVE ON COURTS-MARTIAL AND RELATED MATTERS.

(a) WHO MAY SERVE ON COURTS-MARTIAL.—Subsection (c) of section 825 of title 10, United States Code (article 25 of the Uniform Code of Military Justice), is amended to read as follows:

"(c)(1) Any enlisted member on active duty is eligible to serve on a general or special court-martial for the trial of any other enlisted member.

"(2) Before a court-martial with a military judge and members is assembled for trial, an enlisted member who is an accused may personally request, orally on the record or in writing, that—

"(A) the membership of the court-martial be comprised entirely of officers; or

"(B) enlisted members comprise at least one-third of the membership of the court-martial, regardless of whether enlisted members have been detailed to the court-martial.

"(3) Except as provided in paragraph (4), after such a request, the accused may not be tried by a general or special court-martial if the membership of the court-martial is inconsistent with the request.

"(4) If, because of physical conditions or military exigencies, a sufficient number of eligible officers or enlisted members, as the case may be, is not available to carry out paragraph (2), the trial may nevertheless be held. In that event, the convening authority shall make a detailed written statement of the reasons for nonavailability. The statement shall be appended to the record.".

(b) WHO MAY SENTENCE.—Such section (article) is further amended—

(1) by redesignating subsections (d) and (e) as subsections (e) and (f), respectively; and

(2) by inserting after subsection (c) the following new subsection (d):

"(d)(1) Except as provided in paragraph (2) for capital offenses, the accused in a court-martial with a military judge and members may, after the findings are announced and before any matter is presented in the sentencing phase, request, orally on the record or in writing, sentencing by members.

"(2) In a capital case, the accused shall be sentenced by the members for all offenses for which the court-martial may sentence the accused to death in accordance with section 853(c) of this title (article 53(c)).

"(3) In a capital case, if the accused is convicted of a non-capital offense, the accused shall be sentenced for such non-capital offense in accordance with section 853(b) of this title (article 53(b)), regardless of whether the accused is convicted of an offense for which the court-martial may sentence the accused to death.".

(c) DETAIL OF MEMBERS.—Subsection (e) of such section (article), as redesignated by subsection (b)(1) of this section, is amended by adding at the end the following new paragraph:

"(3) The convening authority shall detail not less than the number of members necessary to impanel the court-martial under section 829 of this title (article 29).".

SEC. 5183. NUMBER OF COURT-MARTIAL MEMBERS IN CAPITAL CASES.

Section 825a of title 10, United States Code (article 25a of the Uniform Code of Military Justice), is amended to read as follows:

"§ 825a. Art. 25a. Number of court-martial members in capital cases

"(a) IN GENERAL.—In a case in which the accused may be sentenced to death, the number of members shall be 12.

"(b) CASE NO LONGER CAPITAL.—Subject to section 829 of this title (article 29)—

"(1) if a case is referred for trial as a capital case and, before the members are impaneled, the accused may no longer be sentenced to death, the number of members shall be eight; and

"(2) if a case is referred for trial as a capital case and, after the members are impaneled, the accused may no longer be sentenced to death, the number of members shall remain 12.".

SEC. 5184. DETAILING, QUALIFICATIONS, AND OTHER MATTERS RELATING TO MILITARY JUDGES.

(a) DETAIL TO SPECIAL COURTS-MARTIAL.—Subsection (a) of section 826 of title 10, United States Code (article 26 of the Uniform Code of Military Justice), is amended—

(1) in the first sentence, by inserting after "each general" the following: "and special"; and

(2) by striking the second sentence.

(b) QUALIFICATIONS.—Subsection (b) of such section (article) is amended by striking "qualified for duty" and inserting "qualified, by reason of education, training, experience, and judicial temperament, for duty".

(c) DETAIL AND ASSIGNMENT.—Subsection (c) of such section (article) is amended to read as follows:

"(c)(1) In accordance with regulations prescribed under subsection (a), a military judge of a general or special court-martial shall be designated for detail by the Judge Advocate General of the armed force of which the military judge is a member.

"(2) Neither the convening authority nor any member of the staff of the convening authority shall prepare or review any report concerning the effectiveness, fitness, or efficiency of the military judge so detailed, which relates to the military judge's performance of duty as a military judge.

"(3) A commissioned officer who is certified to be qualified for duty as a military judge of a general court-martial—

"(A) may perform such duties only when the officer is assigned and directly responsible to the Judge Advocate General of the armed force of which the military judge is a member; and

"(B) may perform duties of a judicial or nonjudicial nature other than those relating to the officer's primary duty as a military judge of a general court-martial when such duties are assigned to the officer by or with the approval of that Judge Advocate General.

"(4) In accordance with regulations prescribed by the President, assignments of military judges under this section (article) shall be for appropriate minimum periods, subject to such exceptions as may be authorized in the regulations.".

(d) DETAIL TO A DIFFERENT ARMED FORCE.—Such section (article) is further amended by adding at the end the following new subsection:

"(f) A military judge may be detailed under subsection (a) to a court-martial or a proceeding under section 830a of this title (article 30a) that is convened in a different armed force, when so permitted by the Judge Advocate General of the armed force of which the military judge is a member.".

(e) CHIEF TRIAL JUDGES.—Such section (article), as amended by subsection (d), is further amended by adding at the end the following new subsection:

"(g) In accordance with regulations prescribed by the President, each Judge Advocate General shall designate a chief trial judge from among the members of the applicable trial judiciary.".

SEC. 5185. MILITARY MAGISTRATES.

Subchapter V of chapter 47 of title 10, United States Code, is amended by inserting after section 826 (article 26 of the Uniform Code of Military Justice) the following new section (article):

"§ 826a. Art. 26a. Military magistrates

"(a) QUALIFICATIONS.—A military magistrate shall be a commissioned officer of the armed forces who—

"(1) is a member of the bar of a Federal court or a member of the bar of the highest court of a State; and

"(2) is certified to be qualified, by reason of education, training, experience, and judicial temperament, for duty as a military magistrate by the Judge Advocate General of the armed force of which the officer is a member.

"(b) DUTIES.—In accordance with regulations prescribed by the Secretary concerned, in addition to duties when designated under section 819 or 830a of this title (article 19 or 30a), a military magistrate may be assigned to perform other duties of a nonjudicial nature.".

SEC. 5186. QUALIFICATIONS OF TRIAL COUNSEL AND DEFENSE COUNSEL.

Section 827 of title 10, United States Code (article 27 of the Uniform Code of Military Justice), is amended—

(1) in the first sentence of paragraph (2) of subsection (a), by striking "No person" and all that follows through "trial counsel," the first place it appears and inserting "No person who, with respect to a case, has served as a preliminary hearing officer, court member, military judge, military magistrate, or appellate judge, may later serve as trial counsel,";

(2) in the first sentence of subsection (b), by striking "Trial counsel or defense counsel" and inserting "Trial counsel, defense counsel, or assistant defense counsel"; and

(3) by striking subsection (c) and inserting the following new subsections:

"(c)(1) Defense counsel and assistant defense counsel detailed for a special court-martial shall have the qualifications set forth in subsection (b).

"(2) Trial counsel and assistant trial counsel detailed for a special court-martial and assist-

ant trial counsel detailed for a general court-martial must be determined to be competent to perform such duties by the Judge Advocate General, under such rules as the President may prescribe.

"(d) To the greatest extent practicable, in any capital case, at least one defense counsel shall, as determined by the Judge Advocate General, be learned in the law applicable to such cases. If necessary, this counsel may be a civilian and, if so, may be compensated in accordance with regulations prescribed by the Secretary of Defense.".

SEC. 5187. ASSEMBLY AND IMPANELING OF MEMBERS AND RELATED MATTERS.

Section 829 of title 10, United States Code (article 29 of the Uniform Code of Military Justice), is amended to read as follows:

"§ 829. Art 29. Assembly and impaneling of members; detail of new members and military judges

"(a) ASSEMBLY.—The military judge shall announce the assembly of a general or special court-martial with members. After such a court-martial is assembled, no member may be absent, unless the member is excused—

"(1) as a result of a challenge;

"(2) under subsection (b)(1)(B); or

"(3) by order of the military judge or the convening authority for disability or other good cause.

"(b) IMPANELING.—(1) Under rules prescribed by the President, the military judge of a general or special court-martial with members shall—

"(A) after determination of challenges, impanel the court-martial; and

"(B) excuse the members who, having been assembled, are not impaneled.

"(2) In a general court-martial, the military judge shall impanel—

"(A) 12 members in a capital case; and

"(B) eight members in a noncapital case.

"(3) In a special court-martial, the military judge shall impanel four members.

"(c) ALTERNATE MEMBERS.—In addition to members under subsection (b), the military judge shall impanel alternate members, if the convening authority authorizes alternate members.

"(d) DETAIL OF NEW MEMBERS.—(1) If, after members are impaneled, the membership of the court-martial is reduced to—

"(A) fewer than 12 members with respect to a general court-martial in a capital case;

"(B) fewer than six members with respect to a general court-martial in a noncapital case; or

"(C) fewer than four members with respect to a special court-martial;

the trial may not proceed unless the convening authority details new members and, from among the members so detailed, the military judge impanels new members sufficient in number to provide the membership specified in paragraph (2).

"(2) The membership referred to in paragraph (1) is as follows:

"(A) 12 members with respect to a general court-martial in a capital case.

"(B) At least six but not more than eight members with respect to a general court-martial in a noncapital case.

"(C) Four members with respect to a special court-martial.

"(e) DETAIL OF NEW MILITARY JUDGE.—If the military judge is unable to proceed with the trial because of disability or otherwise, a new military judge shall be detailed to the court-martial.

"(f) EVIDENCE.—(1) In the case of new members under subsection (d), the trial may proceed with the new members present after the evidence previously introduced is read or, in the case of audiotape, videotape, or similar recording, is played, in the presence of the new members, the military judge, the accused, and counsel for both sides.

"(2) In the case of a new military judge under subsection (e), the trial shall proceed as if no

evidence had been introduced, unless the evidence previously introduced is read or, in the case of audiotape, videotape, or similar recording, is played, in the presence of the new military judge, the accused, and counsel for both sides.''.

TITLE LVI—PRE-TRIAL PROCEDURE

Sec. 5201. Charges and specifications.
Sec. 5202. Certain proceedings conducted before referral.
Sec. 5203. Preliminary hearing required before referral to general court-martial.
Sec. 5204. Disposition guidance.
Sec. 5205. Advice to convening authority before referral for trial.
Sec. 5206. Service of charges and commencement of trial.

SEC. 5201. CHARGES AND SPECIFICATIONS.

Section 830 of title 10, United States Code (article 30 of the Uniform Code of Military Justice), is amended to read as follows:

"§ 830. Art 30. Charges and specifications

"(a) IN GENERAL.—Charges and specifications—

"(1) may be preferred only by a person subject to this chapter; and

"(2) shall be preferred by presentment in writing, signed under oath before a commissioned officer of the armed forces who is authorized to administer oaths.

"(b) REQUIRED CONTENT.—The writing under subsection (a) shall state that—

"(1) the signer has personal knowledge of, or has investigated, the matters set forth in the charges and specifications; and

"(2) the matters set forth in the charges and specifications are true, to the best of the knowledge and belief of the signer.

"(c) DUTY OF PROPER AUTHORITY.—When charges and specifications are preferred under subsection (a), the proper authority shall, as soon as practicable—

"(1) inform the person accused of the charges and specifications; and

"(2) determine what disposition should be made of the charges and specifications in the interest of justice and discipline.''.

SEC. 5202. CERTAIN PROCEEDINGS CONDUCTED BEFORE REFERRAL.

Subchapter VI of chapter 47 of title 10, United States Code, is amended by inserting after section 830 (article 30 of the Uniform Code of Military Justice) the following new section (article):

"§ 830a. Art. 30a. Certain proceedings conducted before referral

"(a) IN GENERAL.—(1) Proceedings may be conducted to review the following matters before referral of charges and specifications to court-martial for trial in accordance with regulations prescribed by the President:

"(A) Pre-referral investigative subpoenas.

"(B) Pre-referral warrants or orders for electronic communications.

"(C) Pre-referral matters referred by an appellate court.

"(2) The regulations prescribed under paragraph (1) shall—

"(A) include procedures for the review of such rulings that may be ordered under this section as the President considers appropriate; and

"(B) provide such limitations on the relief that may be ordered under this section as the President considers appropriate.

"(3) If any matter in a proceeding under this section becomes a subject at issue with respect to charges that have been referred to a general or special court-martial, the matter shall be transferred to the military judge detailed to the court-martial.

"(b) DETAIL OF MILITARY JUDGE.—The Secretary concerned shall prescribe regulations providing for the manner in which military judges are detailed to proceedings under subsection (a)(1).

"(c) DISCRETION TO DESIGNATE MAGISTRATE TO PRESIDE.—In accordance with regulations prescribed by the Secretary concerned, a military judge detailed to a proceeding under subsection (a)(1), other than a proceeding described in subparagraph (B) of that subsection, may designate a military magistrate to preside over the proceeding.''.

SEC. 5203. PRELIMINARY HEARING REQUIRED BEFORE REFERRAL TO GENERAL COURT-MARTIAL.

(a) IN GENERAL.—Section 832 of title 10, United States Code (article 32 of the Uniform Code of Military Justice), is amended by striking the section heading and subsections (a), (b), and (c) and inserting the following:

"§ 832. Art. 32. Preliminary hearing required before referral to general court-martial

"(a) IN GENERAL.—(1)(A) Except as provided in subparagraph (B), a preliminary hearing shall be held before referral of charges and specifications for trial by general court-martial. The preliminary hearing shall be conducted by an impartial hearing officer, detailed by the convening authority in accordance with subsection (b).

"(B) Under regulations prescribed by the President, a preliminary hearing need not be held if the accused submits a written waiver to the convening authority and the convening authority determines that a hearing is not required.

"(2) The purpose of the preliminary hearing shall be limited to determining the following:

"(A) Whether or not the specification alleges an offense under this chapter.

"(B) Whether or not there is probable cause to believe that the accused committed the offense charged.

"(C) Whether or not the convening authority has court-martial jurisdiction over the accused and over the offense.

"(D) A recommendation as to the disposition that should be made of the case.

"(b) HEARING OFFICER.—(1) A preliminary hearing under this section shall be conducted by an impartial hearing officer, who—

"(A) whenever practicable, shall be a judge advocate who is certified under section 827(b)(2) of this title (article 27(b)(2)); or

"(B) when it is not practicable to appoint a judge advocate because of exceptional circumstances, is not a judge advocate so certified.

"(2) In the case of a hearing officer under paragraph (1)(B), a judge advocate who is certified under section 827(b)(2) of this title (article 27(b)(2)) shall be available to provide legal advice to the hearing officer.

"(3) Whenever practicable, the hearing officer shall be equal in grade or senior in grade to military counsel who are detailed to represent the accused or the Government at the preliminary hearing.

"(c) REPORT TO CONVENING AUTHORITY.—After a preliminary hearing under this section, the hearing officer shall submit to the convening authority a written report (accompanied by a recording of the preliminary hearing under subsection (e)) that includes the following:

"(1) For each specification, a statement of the reasoning and conclusions of the hearing officer with respect to determinations under subsection (a)(2), including a summary of relevant witness testimony and documentary evidence presented at the hearing and any observations of the hearing officer concerning the testimony of witnesses and the availability and admissibility of evidence at trial.

"(2) Recommendations for any necessary modifications to the form of the charges or specifications.

"(3) An analysis of any additional information submitted after the hearing by the parties or by a victim of an offense, that, under such rules as the President may prescribe, is relevant to disposition under sections 830 and 834 of this title (articles 30 and 34).

"(4) A statement of action taken on evidence adduced with respect to uncharged offenses, as described in subsection (f).''.

(b) SUNDRY AMENDMENTS.—Subsection (d) of such section (article) is amended—

"(1) in paragraph (1), by striking "subsection (a)" in the first sentence and inserting "this section";

(2) in paragraph (2), by striking "in defense" and all that follows through the end and inserting "that is relevant to the issues for determination under subsection (a)(2).";

(3) in paragraph (3), by adding at the end the following new sentence: "A declination under this paragraph shall not serve as the sole basis for ordering a deposition under section 849 of this title (article 49)."; and

(4) in paragraph (4), by striking "the limited purposes of the hearing, as provided in subsection (a)(2)" and inserting "determinations under subsection (a)(2)".

(c) REFERENCE TO MCM.—Subsection (e) of such section (article) is amended by striking "as prescribed by the Manual for Courts-Martial" in the second sentence and inserting "under such rules as the President may prescribe".

(d) EFFECT OF VIOLATION.—Subsection (g) of such section (article) is amended by adding at the end the following new sentence: "A defect in a report under subsection (c) is not a basis for relief if the report is in substantial compliance with that subsection.''.

(e) CONFORMING AMENDMENTS.—The following provisions are each amended by striking "investigating officer" and inserting "preliminary hearing officer":

(1) Section 806b(a)(3) of title 10, United States Code (article 6b(a)(3) of the Uniform Code of Military Justice).

(2) Section 825(d)(2) of such title (article 25(d)(2) of the Uniform Code of Military Justice).

(3) Section 826(d) of such title (article 26(d) of the Uniform Code of Military Justice).

SEC. 5204. DISPOSITION GUIDANCE.

Section 833 of title 10, United States Code (article 33 of the Uniform Code of Military Justice), is amended to read as follows:

"§ 833. Art 33. Disposition guidance

"The President shall direct the Secretary of Defense to issue, in consultation with the Secretary of the department in which the Coast Guard is operating when it is not operating as a service in the Navy, non-binding guidance regarding factors that commanders, convening authorities, staff judge advocates, and judge advocates should take into account when exercising their duties with respect to disposition of charges and specifications in the interest of justice and discipline under sections 830 and 834 of this title (articles 30 and 34). Such guidance shall take into account, with appropriate consideration of military requirements, the principles contained in official guidance of the Attorney General to attorneys for the Government with respect to disposition of Federal criminal cases in accordance with the principle of fair and evenhanded administration of Federal criminal law.''.

SEC. 5205. ADVICE TO CONVENING AUTHORITY BEFORE REFERRAL FOR TRIAL.

Section 834 of title 10, United States Code (article 34 of the Uniform Code of Military Justice), is amended to read as follows:

"§ 834. Art. 34. Advice to convening authority before referral for trial

"(a) GENERAL COURT-MARTIAL.—

"(1) STAFF JUDGE ADVOCATE ADVICE REQUIRED BEFORE REFERRAL.—Before referral of charges and specifications to a general court-martial for trial, the convening authority shall submit the matter to the staff judge advocate for advice, which the staff judge advocate shall provide to the convening authority in writing. The convening authority may not refer a specification under a charge to a general court-martial unless the staff judge advocate advises the convening authority in writing that—

"(A) the specification alleges an offense under this chapter;

"(B) there is probable cause to believe that the accused committed the offense charged; and

"(C) a court-martial would have jurisdiction over the accused and the offense.

"(2) STAFF JUDGE ADVOCATE RECOMMENDATION AS TO DISPOSITION.—Together with the written advice provided under paragraph (1), the staff judge advocate shall provide a written recommendation to the convening authority as to the disposition that should be made of the specification in the interest of justice and discipline.

"(3) STAFF JUDGE ADVOCATE ADVICE AND RECOMMENDATION TO ACCOMPANY REFERRAL.—When a convening authority makes a referral for trial by general court-martial, the written advice of the staff judge advocate under paragraph (1) and the written recommendation of the staff judge advocate under paragraph (2) with respect to each specification shall accompany the referral.

"(b) SPECIAL COURT-MARTIAL; CONVENING AUTHORITY CONSULTATION WITH JUDGE ADVOCATE.—Before referral of charges and specifications to a special court-martial for trial, the convening authority shall consult a judge advocate on relevant legal issues.

"(c) GENERAL AND SPECIAL COURTS-MARTIAL; CORRECTION OF CHARGES AND SPECIFICATIONS BEFORE REFERRAL.—Before referral for trial by general court-martial or special court-martial, changes may be made to charges and specifications—

"(1) to correct errors in form; and

"(2) when applicable, to conform to the substance of the evidence contained in a report under section 832(c) of this title (article 32(c)).

"(d) REFERRAL DEFINED.—In this section, the term 'referral' means the order of a convening authority that charges and specifications against an accused be tried by a specified court-martial.".

SEC. 5206. SERVICE OF CHARGES AND COMMENCEMENT OF TRIAL.

Section 835 of title 10, United States Code (article 35 of the Uniform Code of Military Justice), is amended to read as follows:

"§ 835. Art. 35. Service of charges; commencement of trial

"(a) IN GENERAL.—Trial counsel detailed for a court-martial under section 827 of this title (article 27) shall cause to be served upon the accused a copy of the charges and specifications referred for trial.

"(b) COMMENCEMENT OF TRIAL.—(1) Subject to paragraphs (2) and (3), no trial or other proceeding of a general court-martial or a special court-martial (including any session under section 839(a) of this title (article 39(a)) may be held over the objection of the accused—

"(A) with respect to a general court-martial, from the time of service through the fifth day after the date of service; or

"(B) with respect to a special court-martial, from the time of service through the third day after the date of service.

"(2) An objection under paragraph (1) may be raised only at the first session of the trial or other proceeding and only if the first session occurs before the end of the applicable period under paragraph (1)(A) or (1)(B). If the first session occurs before the end of the applicable period, the military judge shall, at that session, inquire as to whether the defense objects under this subsection.

"(3) This subsection shall not apply in time of war.".

TITLE LVII—TRIAL PROCEDURE

Sec. 5221. Duties of assistant defense counsel.
Sec. 5222. Sessions.
Sec. 5223. Technical amendment relating to continuances.
Sec. 5224. Conforming amendments relating to challenges.
Sec. 5225. Statute of limitations.
Sec. 5226. Former jeopardy.
Sec. 5227. Pleas of the accused.
Sec. 5228. Subpoena and other process.
Sec. 5229. Refusal of person not subject to UCMJ to appear, testify, or produce evidence.
Sec. 5230. Contempt.
Sec. 5231. Depositions.
Sec. 5232. Admissibility of sworn testimony by audiotape or videotape from records of courts of inquiry.
Sec. 5233. Conforming amendment relating to defense of lack of mental responsibility.
Sec. 5234. Voting and rulings.
Sec. 5235. Votes required for conviction, sentencing, and other matters.
Sec. 5236. Findings and sentencing.
Sec. 5237. Plea agreements.
Sec. 5238. Record of trial.

SEC. 5221. DUTIES OF ASSISTANT DEFENSE COUNSEL.

Section 838(e) of title 10, United States Code (article 38(e) of the Uniform Code of Military Justice), is amended by striking ", under the direction" and all that follows through "(article 27),".

SEC. 5222. SESSIONS.

Section 839 of title 10, United States Code (article 39 of the Uniform Code of Military Justice), is amended—

(1) in subsection (a)—

(A) in paragraph (3)—

(i) by striking "if permitted by regulations of the Secretary concerned,"; and

(ii) by striking "and" at the end;

(B) by redesignating paragraph (4) as paragraph (5); and

(C) by inserting after paragraph (3) the following new paragraph (4):

"(4) conducting a sentencing proceeding and sentencing the accused in non-capital cases unless the accused requests sentencing by members under section 825 of this title (article 25); and"; and

(2) in the second sentence of subsection (c), by striking ", in cases in which a military judge has been detailed to the court,".

SEC. 5223. TECHNICAL AMENDMENT RELATING TO CONTINUANCES.

Section 840 of title 10, United States Code (article 40 of the Uniform Code of Military Justice), is amended by striking "court-martial without a military judge" and inserting "summary court-martial".

SEC. 5224. CONFORMING AMENDMENTS RELATING TO CHALLENGES.

Section 841 of title 10, United States Code (article 41 of the Uniform Code of Military Justice), is amended—

(1) in subsection (a)(1), by striking ", or, if none, the court," in the second sentence;

(2) in subsection (a)(2), by striking "minimum" in the first sentence; and

(3) in subsection (b)(2), by striking "minimum".

SEC. 5225. STATUTE OF LIMITATIONS.

(a) INCREASE IN PERIOD FOR CHILD ABUSE OFFENSES.—Subsection (b)(2)(A) of section 843 of title 10, United States Code (article 43 of the Uniform Code of Military Justice), is amended by striking "five years" and inserting "ten years".

(b) INCREASE IN PERIOD FOR FRAUDULENT ENLISTMENT OR APPOINTMENT OFFENSES.—Such section (article) is further amended by adding at the end the following new subsection:

"(h) FRAUDULENT ENLISTMENT OR APPOINTMENT.—A person charged with fraudulent enlistment or fraudulent appointment under section 904a(1) of this title (article 104a(1)) may be tried by court-martial if the sworn charges and specifications are received by an officer exercising summary court-martial jurisdiction with respect to that person, as follows:

"(1) In the case of an enlisted member, during the period of the enlistment or five years, whichever provides a longer period.

"(2) In the case of an officer, during the period of the appointment or five years, whichever provides a longer period.".

(c) DNA EVIDENCE.—Such section (article), as amended by subsection (b) of this section, is further amended by adding at the end the following new subsection:

"(i) DNA EVIDENCE.—If DNA testing implicates an identified person in the commission of an offense punishable by confinement for more than one year, no statute of limitations that would otherwise preclude prosecution of the offense shall preclude such prosecution until a period of time following the implication of the person by DNA testing has elapsed that is equal to the otherwise applicable limitation period.".

(d) CONFORMING AMENDMENTS.—Subsection (b)(2)(B) of such section (article) is amended by striking clauses (i) through (v) and inserting the following new clauses:

"(i) Any offense in violation of section 920, 920a, 920b, 920c, or 930 of this title (article 120, 120a, 120b, 120c, or 130), unless the offense is covered by subsection (a).

"(ii) Maiming in violation of section 928a of this title (article 128a).

"(iii) Aggravated assault, assault consummated by a battery, or assault with intent to commit specified offenses in violation of section 928 of this title (article 128).

"(iv) Kidnapping in violation of section 925 of this title (article 125).".

(e) SUBSECTION HEADING AMENDMENTS FOR STYLISTIC CONSISTENCY.—Such section (article) is further amended—

(1) in subsection (a), by inserting "NO LIMITATION FOR CERTAIN OFFENSES.—" after "(a)";

(2) in subsection (b), by inserting "FIVE-YEAR LIMITATION FOR TRIAL BY COURT-MARTIAL.—" after "(b)";

(3) in subsection (c), by inserting "TOLLING FOR ABSENCE WITHOUT LEAVE OR FLIGHT FROM JUSTICE.—" after "(c)";

(4) in subsection (d), by inserting "TOLLING FOR ABSENCE FROM US OR MILITARY JURISDICTION.—" after "(d)";

(5) in subsection (e), by inserting "EXTENSION FOR OFFENSES IN TIME OF WAR DETRIMENTAL TO PROSECUTION OF WAR.—" after "(e)";

(6) in subsection (f), by inserting "EXTENSION FOR OTHER OFFENSES IN TIME OF WAR.—" after "(f)"; and

(7) in subsection (g), by inserting "DEFECTIVE OR INSUFFICIENT CHARGES.—" after "(g)".

(f) APPLICATION.—The amendments made by subsections (a), (b), (c), and (d) shall apply to the prosecution of any offense committed before, on, or after the date of the enactment of this subsection if the applicable limitation period has not yet expired.

SEC. 5226. FORMER JEOPARDY.

Subsection (c) of section 844 of title 10, United States Code (article 44 of the Uniform Code of Military Justice), is amended to read as follows:

"(c)(1) A court-martial with a military judge alone is a trial in the sense of this section (article) if, without fault of the accused—

"(A) after introduction of evidence; and

"(B) before announcement of findings under section 853 of this title (article 53);

the case is dismissed or terminated by the convening authority or on motion of the prosecution for failure of available evidence or witnesses.

"(2) A court-martial with a military judge and members is a trial in the sense of this section (article) if, without fault of the accused—

"(A) after the members, having taken an oath as members under section 842 of this title (article 42) and after completion of challenges under section 841 of this title (article 41), are impaneled; and

"(B) before announcement of findings under section 853 of this title (article 53);

the case is dismissed or terminated by the convening authority or on motion of the prosecution for failure of available evidence or witnesses.".

SEC. 5227. PLEAS OF THE ACCUSED.

(a) PLEAS OF GUILTY.—Subsection (b) of section 845 of title 10, United States Code (article 45 of the Uniform Code of Military Justice), is amended—

(1) in the first sentence, by striking "may be adjudged" and inserting "is mandatory"; and

(2) in the second sentence—

(A) by striking "or by a court-martial without a military judge"; and

(B) by striking ", if permitted by regulations of the Secretary concerned,".

(b) HARMLESS ERROR.—Such section (article) is further amended by adding at the end the following new subsection:

"(c) HARMLESS ERROR.—A variance from the requirements of this article is harmless error if the variance does not materially prejudice the substantial rights of the accused.".

(c) SUBSECTION HEADING AMENDMENTS FOR STYLISTIC CONSISTENCY.—Such section (article) is further amended—

(1) in subsection (a), by inserting "IRREGULAR AND SIMILAR PLEAS.—" after "(a)"; and

(2) in subsection (b), by inserting "PLEAS OF GUILTY.—" after "(b)".

SEC. 5228. SUBPOENA AND OTHER PROCESS.

(a) AMENDMENTS TO UCMJ ARTICLE.—

(1) IN GENERAL.—Subsection (a) of section 846 of title 10, United States Code (article 46 of the Uniform Code of Military Justice), is amended by striking "The counsel for the Government, the counsel for the accused," and inserting "In a case referred for trial by court-martial, the trial counsel, the defense counsel,".

(2) SUBPOENA AND OTHER PROCESS GENERALLY.—Subsection (b) of such section (article) is amended to read as follows:

"(b) SUBPOENA AND OTHER PROCESS GENERALLY.—Any subpoena or other process issued under this section (article)—

"(1) shall be similar to that which courts of the United States having criminal jurisdiction may issue;

"(2) shall be executed in accordance with regulations prescribed by the President; and

"(3) shall run to any part of the United States and to the Commonwealths and possessions of the United States.".

(3) SUBPOENA AND OTHER PROCESS FOR WITNESSES.—Subsection (c) of such section (article) is amended to read as follows:

"(c) SUBPOENA AND OTHER PROCESS FOR WITNESSES.—A subpoena or other process may be issued to compel a witness to appear and testify—

"(1) before a court-martial, military commission, or court of inquiry;

"(2) at a deposition under section 849 of this title (article 49); or

"(3) as otherwise authorized under this chapter.".

(4) OTHER MATTERS.—Such section (article) is further amended by adding at the end the following new subsections:

"(d) SUBPOENA AND OTHER PROCESS FOR EVIDENCE.—

"(1) IN GENERAL.—A subpoena or other process may be issued to compel the production of evidence—

"(A) for a court-martial, military commission, or court of inquiry;

"(B) for a deposition under section 849 of this title (article 49);

"(C) for an investigation of an offense under this chapter; or

"(D) as otherwise authorized under this chapter.

"(2) INVESTIGATIVE SUBPOENA.—An investigative subpoena under paragraph (1)(C) may be issued before referral of charges to a court-martial only if a general court-martial convening authority has authorized counsel for the Government to issue such a subpoena or a military judge issues such a subpoena pursuant to section 830a of this title (article 30a).

"(3) WARRANT OR ORDER FOR WIRE OR ELECTRONIC COMMUNICATIONS.—With respect to an investigation of an offense under this chapter, a military judge detailed in accordance with section 826 or 830a of this title (article 26 or 30a) may issue warrants or court orders for the contents of, and records concerning, wire or electronic communications in the same manner as such warrants and orders may be issued by a district court of the United States under chapter 121 of title 18, subject to such limitations as the President may prescribe by regulation.

"(e) REQUEST FOR RELIEF FROM SUBPOENA OR OTHER PROCESS.—If a person requests relief from a subpoena or other process under this section (article) on grounds that compliance is unreasonable or oppressive or is prohibited by law, a military judge detailed in accordance with section 826 or 830a of this title (article 26 or 30a) shall review the request and shall—

"(1) order that the subpoena or other process be modified or withdrawn, as appropriate; or

"(2) order the person to comply with the subpoena or other process.".

(5) SECTION HEADING.—The heading of such section (article) is amended to read as follows:

"§846. Art. 46. Opportunity to obtain witnesses and other evidence in trials by court-martial".

(b) CONFORMING AMENDMENTS TO TITLE 18, UNITED STATES CODE.—

(1) Section 2703 of title 18, United States Code, is amended—

(A) in the first sentence of subsection (a);

(B) in subsection (b)(1)(A); and

(C) in subsection (c)(1)(A);

by inserting after "warrant procedures" the following: "and, in the case of a court-martial or other proceeding under chapter 47 of title 10 (the Uniform Code of Military Justice), issued under section 846 of that title, in accordance with regulations prescribed by the President".

(2) Section 2711(3) of title 18, United States Code, is amended—

(A) in subparagraph (A), by striking "or" at the end;

(B) in subparagraph (B), by striking "and" at the end and inserting "or"; and

(C) by adding at the end the following new subparagraph:

"(C) a court-martial or other proceeding under chapter 47 of title 10 (the Uniform Code of Military Justice) to which a military judge has been detailed; and".

SEC. 5229. REFUSAL OF PERSON NOT SUBJECT TO UCMJ TO APPEAR, TESTIFY, OR PRODUCE EVIDENCE.

(a) IN GENERAL.—Subsection (a) of section 847 of title 10, United States Code (article 47 of the Uniform Code of Military Justice), is amended to read as follows:

"(a) IN GENERAL.—(1) Any person described in paragraph (2) who—

"(A) willfully neglects or refuses to appear; or

"(B) willfully refuses to qualify as a witness or to testify or to produce any evidence which that person is required to produce;

is guilty of an offense against the United States.

"(2) The persons referred to in paragraph (1) are the following:

"(A) Any person not subject to this chapter who—

"(i) is issued a subpoena or other process described in subsection (c) of section 846 of this title (article 46); and

"(ii) is provided a means for reimbursement from the Government for fees and mileage at the rates allowed to witnesses attending the courts of the United States or, in the case of extraordinary hardship, is advanced such fees and mileage.

"(B) Any person not subject to this chapter who is issued a subpoena or other process described in subsection (d) of section 846 of this title (article 46).".

(b) SECTION HEADING.—The heading of such section (article) is amended to read as follows:

"§847. Art. 47. Refusal of person not subject to chapter to appear, testify, or produce evidence".

SEC. 5230. CONTEMPT.

(a) AUTHORITY TO PUNISH.—Subsection (a) of section 848 of title 10, United States Code (article 48 of the Uniform Code of Military Justice), is amended to read as follows:

"(a) AUTHORITY TO PUNISH.—(1) With respect to any proceeding under this chapter, a judicial officer specified in paragraph (2) may punish for contempt any person who—

"(A) uses any menacing word, sign, or gesture in the presence of the judicial officer during the proceeding;

"(B) disturbs the proceeding by any riot or disorder; or

"(C) willfully disobeys a lawful writ, process, order, rule, decree, or command issued with respect to the proceeding.

"(2) A judicial officer referred to in paragraph (1) is any of the following:

"(A) Any judge of the Court of Appeals for the Armed Forces and any judge of a Court of Criminal Appeals under section 866 of this title (article 66).

"(B) Any military judge detailed to a court-martial, a provost court, a military commission, or any other proceeding under this chapter.

"(C) Any military magistrate designated to preside under section 819 of this title (article 19).

"(D) The president of a court of inquiry.".

(b) REVIEW.—Such section (article) is further amended—

(1) by redesignating subsection (c) as subsection (d); and

(2) by inserting after subsection (b) the following new subsection (c):

"(c) REVIEW.—A punishment under this section—

"(1) if imposed by a military judge or military magistrate, may be reviewed by the Court of Criminal Appeals in accordance with the uniform rules of procedure for the Courts of Criminal Appeals under section 866(g) of this title (article 66(g));

"(2) if imposed by a judge of the Court of Appeals for the Armed Forces or a judge of a Court of Criminal Appeals, shall constitute a judgment of the court, subject to review under the applicable provisions of section 867 or 867a of this title (article 67 or 67a); and

"(3) if imposed by a court of inquiry, shall be subject to review by the convening authority in accordance with rules prescribed by the President.".

(c) SECTION HEADING.—The heading of such section (article) is amended to read as follows:

"§848. Art. 48. Contempt".

SEC. 5231. DEPOSITIONS.

Section 849 of title 10, United States Code (article 49 of the Uniform Code of Military Justice), is amended to read as follows:

"§ 849. Art. 49. Depositions

"(a) IN GENERAL.—(1) Subject to paragraph (2), a convening authority or a military judge may order depositions at the request of any party.

"(2) A deposition may be ordered under paragraph (1) only if the requesting party demonstrates that, due to exceptional circumstances, it is in the interest of justice that the testimony of a prospective witness be preserved for use at a court-martial, military commission, court of inquiry, or other military court or board.

"(3) A party who requests a deposition under this section shall give to every other party reasonable written notice of the time and place for the deposition.

"(4) A deposition under this section shall be taken before, and authenticated by, an impartial officer, as follows:

"(A) Whenever practicable, by an impartial judge advocate certified under section 827(b) of this title (article 27(b)).

"(B) In exceptional circumstances, by an impartial military or civil officer authorized to administer oaths by (i) the laws of the United States or (ii) the laws of the place where the deposition is taken.

"(b) REPRESENTATION BY COUNSEL.—Representation of the parties with respect to a deposition shall be by counsel detailed in the same manner as trial counsel and defense counsel are detailed under section 827 of this title (article 27). In addition, the accused shall have the right to be represented by civilian or military counsel in the same manner as such counsel are provided for in section 838(b) of this title (article 38(b)).

"(c) ADMISSIBILITY AND USE AS EVIDENCE.—A deposition order under subsection (a) does not control the admissibility of the deposition in a court-martial or other proceeding under this chapter. Except as provided by subsection (d), a party may use all or part of a deposition as provided by the rules of evidence.

"(d) CAPITAL CASES.—Testimony by deposition may be presented in capital cases only by the defense.".

SEC. 5232. ADMISSIBILITY OF SWORN TESTIMONY BY AUDIOTAPE OR VIDEOTAPE FROM RECORDS OF COURTS OF INQUIRY.

(a) IN GENERAL.—Section 850 of title 10, United States Code (article 50 of the Uniform Code of Military Justice), is amended by adding at the end the following new subsection:

"(d) AUDIOTAPE OR VIDEOTAPE.—Sworn testimony that—

"(1) is recorded by audiotape, videotape, or similar method; and

"(2) is contained in the duly authenticated record of proceedings of a court of inquiry;

is admissible before a court-martial, military commission, court of inquiry, or military board, to the same extent as sworn testimony may be read in evidence before any such body under subsection (a), (b), or (c).".

(b) SECTION HEADING.—The heading of such section (article) is amended to read as follows:

"§ 850. Art. 50. Admissibility of sworn testimony from records of courts of inquiry".

(c) SUBSECTION HEADING AMENDMENTS FOR STYLISTIC CONSISTENCY.—Such section (article) is further amended—

(1) in subsection (a), by inserting "USE AS EVIDENCE BY ANY PARTY.—" after "(a)";

(2) in subsection (b), by inserting "USE AS EVIDENCE BY DEFENSE.—" after "(b)"; and

(3) in subsection (c), by inserting "USE IN COURTS OF INQUIRY AND MILITARY BOARDS.—" after "(c)".

SEC. 5233. CONFORMING AMENDMENT RELATING TO DEFENSE OF LACK OF MENTAL RESPONSIBILITY.

Section 850a(c) of title 10, United States Code (article 50a(c) of the Uniform Code of Military

Justice), is amended by striking ", or the president of a court-martial without a military judge,".

SEC. 5234. VOTING AND RULINGS.

Section 851 of title 10, United States Code (article 51 of the Uniform Code of Military Justice), is amended—

(1) in subsection (a), by striking ", and by members of a court-martial without a military judge upon questions of challenge," in the first sentence;

(2) in subsection (b)—

(A) in the first sentence, by striking "and, except for questions of challenge, the president of a court-martial without a military judge"; and

(B) in the second sentence, by striking ", or by the president" and all that follows through the end of the subsection and inserting "is final and constitutes the ruling of the court, except that the military judge may change a ruling at any time during trial."; and

(3) in subsection (c), by striking "or the president of a court-martial without a military judge" in the matter before paragraph (1).

SEC. 5235. VOTES REQUIRED FOR CONVICTION, SENTENCING, AND OTHER MATTERS.

Section 852 of title 10, United States Code (article 52 of the Uniform Code of Military Justice), is amended to read as follows:

"§ 852. Art. 52. Votes required for conviction, sentencing, and other matters

"(a) IN GENERAL.—No person may be convicted of an offense in a general or special court-martial, other than—

"(1) after a plea of guilty under section 845(b) of this title (article 45(b));

"(2) by a military judge in a court-martial with a military judge alone, under section 816 of this title (article 16); or

"(3) in a court-martial with members under section 816 of this title (article 16), by the concurrence of at least three-fourths of the members present when the vote is taken.

"(b) LEVEL OF CONCURRENCE REQUIRED.—

"(1) IN GENERAL.—Except as provided in subsection (a) and in paragraph (2), all matters to be decided by members of a general or special court-martial shall be determined by a majority vote, but a reconsideration of a finding of guilty or reconsideration of a sentence, with a view toward decreasing the sentence, may be made by any lesser vote which indicates that the reconsideration is not opposed by the number of votes required for that finding or sentence.

"(2) SENTENCING.—A sentence of death requires (A) a unanimous finding of guilty of an offense in this chapter expressly made punishable by death and (B) a unanimous determination by the members that the sentence for that offense shall include death. All other sentences imposed by members shall be determined by the concurrence of at least three-fourths of the members present when the vote is taken.".

SEC. 5236. FINDINGS AND SENTENCING.

Section 853 of title 10, United States Code (article 53 of the Uniform Code of Military Justice), is amended to read as follows:

"§ 853. Art. 53. Findings and sentencing

"(a) ANNOUNCEMENT.—A court-martial shall announce its findings and sentence to the parties as soon as determined.

"(b) SENTENCING GENERALLY.—

"(1) GENERAL AND SPECIAL COURTS-MARTIAL.—

"(A) SENTENCING BY MILITARY JUDGE.—Except as provided in subparagraph (B), and in subsection (c) for capital offenses, if the accused is convicted of an offense in a trial by general or special court-martial, the military judge shall sentence the accused.

"(B) SENTENCING BY MEMBERS.—If the accused is convicted of an offense in a trial by general or special court-martial consisting of a military judge and members and the accused

elects sentencing by members under section 825 of this title (article 25), the members shall sentence the accused.

"(C) SENTENCE OF THE ACCUSED.—The sentence determined pursuant to this paragraph constitutes the sentence of the accused.

"(2) SUMMARY COURTS-MARTIAL.—If the accused is convicted of an offense in a trial by summary court-martial, the court-martial shall sentence the accused.

"(c) SENTENCING FOR CAPITAL OFFENSES.—

"(1) IN GENERAL.—In a capital case, if the accused is convicted of an offense for which the court-martial may sentence the accused to death, the members shall determine whether the sentence for that offense shall be death or a lesser authorized punishment.

"(2) LESSER AUTHORIZED PUNISHMENTS.—In accordance with regulations prescribed by the President, the court-martial may include in any sentence to death or life in prison without eligibility for parole other lesser punishments authorized under this chapter.

"(3) OTHER NON-CAPITAL OFFENSES.—In a capital case, if the accused is convicted of a non-capital offense, the accused shall be sentenced for such non-capital offense in accordance with subsection (b), regardless of whether the accused is convicted of an offense for which the court-martial may sentence the accused to death.".

SEC. 5237. PLEA AGREEMENTS.

Subchapter VII of chapter 47 of title 10, United States Code, is amended by inserting after section 853 (article 53 of the Uniform Code of Military Justice), as amended by section 5236 of this Act, the following new section (article):

"§ 853a. Art. 53a. Plea agreements

"(a) IN GENERAL.—(1) At any time before the announcement of findings under section 853 of this title (article 53), the convening authority and the accused may enter into a plea agreement with respect to such matters as—

"(A) the manner in which the convening authority will dispose of one or more charges and specifications; and

"(B) limitations on the sentence that may be adjudged for one or more charges and specifications.

"(2) The military judge of a general or special court-martial may not participate in discussions between the parties concerning prospective terms and conditions of a plea agreement.

"(b) LIMITATION ON ACCEPTANCE OF PLEA AGREEMENTS.—The military judge of a general or special court-martial shall reject a plea agreement that—

"(1) contains a provision that has not been accepted by both parties;

"(2) contains a provision that is not understood by the accused; or

"(3) except as provided in subsection (c), contains a provision for a sentence that is less than the mandatory minimum sentence applicable to an offense referred to in section 856(b)(2) of this title (article 56(b)(2)).

"(c) LIMITED CONDITIONS FOR ACCEPTANCE OF PLEA AGREEMENT FOR SENTENCE BELOW MANDATORY MINIMUM FOR CERTAIN OFFENSES.—With respect to an offense referred to in section 856(b)(2) of this title (article 56(b)(2))—

"(1) the military judge may accept a plea agreement that provides for a sentence of bad conduct discharge; and

"(2) upon recommendation of the trial counsel, in exchange for substantial assistance by the accused in the investigation or prosecution of another person who has committed an offense, the military judge may accept a plea agreement that provides for a sentence that is less than the mandatory minimum sentence for the offense charged.

"(d) BINDING EFFECT OF PLEA AGREEMENT.—Upon acceptance by the military judge of a general or special court-martial, a plea agreement shall bind the parties and the military judge.".

SEC. 5238. RECORD OF TRIAL.

Section 854 of title 10, United States Code (article 54 of the Uniform Code of Military Justice), is amended—

(1) by striking subsection (a) and inserting the following new subsection (a):

"(a) GENERAL AND SPECIAL COURTS-MARTIAL.—Each general or special court-martial shall keep a separate record of the proceedings in each case brought before it. The record shall be certified by a court-reporter, except that in the case of death, disability, or absence of a court reporter, the record shall be certified by an official selected as the President may prescribe by regulation.";

(2) in subsection (b)—

(A) by striking "(b) Each special and summary court-martial" and inserting "(b) SUMMARY COURTS-MARTIAL.—Each summary court-martial"; and

(B) by striking "authenticated" and inserting "certified";

(3) by striking subsection (c) and inserting the following new subsection (c):

"(c) CONTENTS OF RECORD.—(1) Except as provided in paragraph (2), the record shall contain such matters as the President may prescribe by regulation.

"(2) In accordance with regulations prescribed by the President, a complete record of proceedings and testimony shall be prepared in any case of a sentence of death, dismissal, discharge, confinement for more than six months, or forfeiture of pay for more than six months.";

(4) in subsection (d)—

(A) by striking "(d) A copy" and inserting "(d) COPY TO ACCUSED.—A copy"; and

(B) by striking "authenticated" and inserting "certified"; and

(5) in subsection (e)—

(A) by striking "(e) In the case" and inserting "(e) COPY TO VICTIM.—In the case";

(B) by striking "involving a sexual assault or other offense covered by section 920 of this title (article 120)," in the first sentence and inserting ", upon request,"; and

(C) by striking "authenticated" in the second sentence and inserting "certified".

TITLE LVIII—SENTENCES

Sec. 5301. Sentencing.
Sec. 5302. Effective date of sentences.
Sec. 5303. Sentence of reduction in enlisted grade.

SEC. 5301. SENTENCING.

(a) IN GENERAL.—Section 856 of title 10, United States Code (article 56 of the Uniform Code of Military Justice), is amended to read as follows:

"§ 856. Art. 56. Sentencing

"(a) SENTENCE MAXIMUMS.—The punishment which a court-martial may direct for an offense may not exceed such limits as the President may prescribe for that offense.

"(b) SENTENCE MINIMUMS FOR CERTAIN OFFENSES.—(1) Except as provided in subsection (d) of section 853a of this title (article 53a), punishment for any offense specified in paragraph (2) shall include dismissal or dishonorable discharge, as applicable.

"(2) The offenses referred to in paragraph (1) are as follows:

"(A) Rape under subsection (a) of section 920 of this title (article 120).

"(B) Sexual assault under subsection (b) of such section (article).

"(C) Rape of a child under subsection (a) of section 920b of this title (article 120b).

"(D) Sexual assault of a child under subsection (b) of such section (article).

"(E) An attempt to commit an offense specified in subparagraph (A), (B), (C), or (D) that is punishable under section 880 of this title (article 80).

"(F) Conspiracy to commit an offense specified in subparagraph (A), (B), (C), or (D) that is punishable under section 881 of this title (article 81).

"(c) IMPOSITION OF SENTENCE.—

"(1) IN GENERAL.—In sentencing an accused under section 853 of this title (article 53), a court-martial shall impose punishment that is sufficient, but not greater than necessary, to promote justice and to maintain good order and discipline in the armed forces, taking into consideration—

"(A) the nature and circumstances of the offense and the history and characteristics of the accused;

"(B) the impact of the offense on—

"(i) the financial, social, psychological, or medical well-being of any victim of the offense; and

"(ii) the mission, discipline, or efficiency of the command of the accused and any victim of the offense;

"(C) the need for the sentence—

"(i) to reflect the seriousness of the offense;

"(ii) to promote respect for the law;

"(iii) to provide just punishment for the offense;

"(iv) to promote adequate deterrence of misconduct;

"(v) to protect others from further crimes by the accused;

"(vi) to rehabilitate the accused; and

"(vii) to provide, in appropriate cases, the opportunity for retraining and return to duty to meet the needs of the service; and

"(D) the sentences available under this chapter.

"(2) SENTENCING BY MILITARY JUDGE.—In announcing the sentence in a general or special court-martial in which the accused is sentenced by a military judge alone under section 853 of this title (article 53), the military judge shall, with respect to each offense of which the accused is found guilty, specify the term of confinement, if any, and the amount of the fine, if any. If the accused is sentenced to confinement for more than one offense, the military judge shall specify whether the terms of confinement are to run consecutively or concurrently.

"(3) SENTENCING BY MEMBERS.—In a general or special court-martial in which the accused has elected sentencing by members, the court-martial shall announce a single sentence for all of the offenses of which the accused was found guilty.

"(4) SENTENCE OF CONFINEMENT FOR LIFE WITHOUT ELIGIBILITY FOR PAROLE.—(A) If an offense is subject to a sentence of confinement for life, a court-martial may impose a sentence of confinement for life without eligibility for parole.

"(B) An accused who is sentenced to confinement for life without eligibility for parole shall be confined for the remainder of the accused's life unless—

"(i) the sentence is set aside or otherwise modified as a result of—

"(I) action taken by the convening authority or the Secretary concerned; or

"(II) any other action taken during post-trial procedure and review under any other provision of subchapter IX of this chapter;

"(ii) the sentence is set aside or otherwise modified as a result of action taken by a Court of Criminal Appeals, the Court of Appeals for the Armed Forces, or the Supreme Court; or

"(iii) the accused is pardoned.

"(d) APPEAL OF SENTENCE BY THE UNITED STATES.—(1) With the approval of the Judge Advocate General concerned, the Government may appeal a sentence to the Court of Criminal Appeals, on the grounds that—

"(A) the sentence violates the law; or

"(B) the sentence is plainly unreasonable.

"(2) An appeal under this subsection must be filed within 60 days after the date on which the judgment of a court-martial is entered into the record under section 860c of this title (article 60c).".

(b) CONFORMING AMENDMENT.—Section 856a of title 10, United States Code (article 56a of the Uniform Code of Military Justice), is repealed.

SEC. 5302. EFFECTIVE DATE OF SENTENCES.

(a) IN GENERAL.—Section 857 of title 10, United States Code (article 57 of the Uniform Code of Military Justice), is amended to read as follows:

"§ 857. Art. 57. Effective date of sentences

"(a) EXECUTION OF SENTENCES.—A court-martial sentence shall be executed and take effect as follows:

"(1) FORFEITURE AND REDUCTION.—A forfeiture of pay or allowances shall be applicable to pay and allowances accruing on and after the date on which the sentence takes effect. Any forfeiture of pay or allowances or reduction in grade that is included in a sentence of a court-martial takes effect on the earlier of—

"(A) the date that is 14 days after the date on which the sentence is adjudged; or

"(B) in the case of a summary court-martial, the date on which the sentence is approved by the convening authority.

"(2) CONFINEMENT.—Any period of confinement included in a sentence of a court-martial begins to run from the date the sentence is adjudged by the court-martial, but periods during which the sentence to confinement is suspended or deferred shall be excluded in computing the service of the term of confinement.

"(3) APPROVAL OF SENTENCE OF DEATH.—If the sentence of the court-martial extends to death, that part of the sentence providing for death may not be executed until approved by the President. In such a case, the President may commute, remit, or suspend the sentence, or any part thereof, as the President sees fit. That part of the sentence providing for death may not be suspended.

"(4) APPROVAL OF DISMISSAL.—If in the case of a commissioned officer, cadet, or midshipman, the sentence of a court-martial extends to dismissal, that part of the sentence providing for dismissal may not be executed until approved by the Secretary concerned or such Under Secretary or Assistant Secretary as may be designated by the Secretary concerned. In such a case, the Secretary, Under Secretary, or Assistant Secretary, as the case may be, may commute, remit, or suspend the sentence, or any part of the sentence, as the Secretary sees fit. In time of war or national emergency he may commute a sentence of dismissal to reduction to any enlisted grade. A person so reduced may be required to serve for the duration of the war or emergency and six months thereafter.

"(5) COMPLETION OF APPELLATE REVIEW.—If a sentence extends to death, dismissal, or a dishonorable or bad-conduct discharge, that part of the sentence extending to death, dismissal, or a dishonorable or bad-conduct discharge may be executed, in accordance with service regulations, after completion of appellate review (and, with respect to death or dismissal, approval under paragraph (3) or (4), as appropriate).

"(6) OTHER SENTENCES.—Except as otherwise provided in this subsection, a general or special court-martial sentence is effective upon entry of judgment and a summary court-martial sentence is effective when the convening authority acts on the sentence.

"(b) DEFERRAL OF SENTENCES.—

"(1) IN GENERAL.—On application by an accused, the convening authority or, if the accused is no longer under his or her jurisdiction, the officer exercising general court-martial jurisdiction over the command to which the accused is currently assigned, may, in his or her sole discretion, defer the effective date of a sentence of confinement, reduction, or forfeiture. The deferment shall terminate upon entry of judgment or, in the case of a summary court-martial, when the convening authority acts on the sentence. The deferment may be rescinded at any time by the officer who granted it or, if the accused is no longer under his jurisdiction, by the officer exercising general court-martial jurisdiction over the command to which the accused is currently assigned.

"(2) DEFERRAL OF CERTAIN PERSONS SENTENCED TO CONFINEMENT.—In any case in which a court-martial sentences a person referred to in paragraph (3) to confinement, the convening authority may defer the service of the sentence to confinement, without the consent of that person, until after the person has been permanently released to the armed forces by a State or foreign country referred to in that paragraph.

"(3) COVERED PERSONS.—Paragraph (2) applies to a person subject to this chapter who—

"(A) while in the custody of a State or foreign country is temporarily returned by that State or foreign country to the armed forces for trial by court-martial; and

"(B) after the court-martial, is returned to that State or foreign country under the authority of a mutual agreement or treaty, as the case may be.

"(4) STATE DEFINED.—In this subsection, the term 'State' includes the District of Columbia and any Commonwealth, territory, or possession of the United States.

"(5) DEFERRAL WHILE REVIEW PENDING.—In any case in which a court-martial sentences a person to confinement, but in which review of the case under section 867(a)(2) of this title (article 67(a)(2)) is pending, the Secretary concerned may defer further service of the sentence to confinement while that review is pending.

"(c) APPELLATE REVIEW.—

"(1) COMPLETION OF APPELLATE REVIEW.—Appellate review is complete under this section when—

"(A) a review under section 865 of this title (article 65) is completed; or

"(B) a review under section 866 of this title (article 66) is completed by a Court of Criminal Appeals and—

"(i) the time for the accused to file a petition for review by the Court of Appeals for the Armed Forces has expired and the accused has not filed a timely petition for such review and the case is not otherwise under review by that Court;

"(ii) such a petition is rejected by the Court of Appeals for the Armed Forces; or

"(iii) review is completed in accordance with the judgment of the Court of Appeals for the Armed Forces and—

"(I) a petition for a writ of certiorari is not filed within the time limits prescribed by the Supreme Court;

"(II) such a petition is rejected by the Supreme Court; or

"(III) review is otherwise completed in accordance with the judgment of the Supreme Court.

"(2) COMPLETION AS FINAL JUDGMENT OF LEGALITY OF PROCEEDINGS.—The completion of appellate review shall constitute a final judgment as to the legality of the proceedings.".

(b) CONFORMING AMENDMENTS.—

(1) Subchapter VIII of chapter 47 of title 10, United States Code, is amended by striking section 857a (article 57a of the Uniform Code of Military Justice).

(2) Subchapter IX of chapter 47 of title 10, United States Code, is amended by striking section 871 (article 71 of the Uniform Code of Military Justice).

(3) The second sentence of subsection (a)(1) of section 858b of title 10, United States Code (article 58b of the Uniform Code of Military Justice), is amended by striking "section 857(a) of this

title (article 57(a))" and inserting "section 857 of this title (article 57)".

SEC. 5303. SENTENCE OF REDUCTION IN ENLISTED GRADE.

Section 858a of title 10, United States Code (article 58a of the Uniform Code of Military Justice), is amended—

(1) in subsection (a)—

(A) by striking "Unless otherwise provided in regulations to be prescribed by the Secretary concerned, a" and inserting "A";

(B) by striking "as approved by the convening authority" and inserting "as set forth in the judgment of the court-martial entered into the record under section 860c of this title (article 60c)"; and

(C) in the matter after paragraph (3), by striking "of that approval" and inserting "on which the judgment is so entered"; and

(2) in subsection (b), by striking "disapproved, or, as finally approved" and inserting "reduced, or, as finally affirmed".

TITLE LIX—POST-TRIAL PROCEDURE AND REVIEW OF COURTS-MARTIAL

Sec. 5321. Post-trial processing in general and special courts-martial.
Sec. 5322. Limited authority to act on sentence in specified post-trial circumstances.
Sec. 5323. Post-trial actions in summary courts-martial and certain general and special courts-martial.
Sec. 5324. Entry of judgment.
Sec. 5325. Waiver of right to appeal and withdrawal of appeal.
Sec. 5326. Appeal by the United States.
Sec. 5327. Rehearings.
Sec. 5328. Judge advocate review of finding of guilty in summary court-martial.
Sec. 5329. Transmittal and review of records.
Sec. 5330. Courts of Criminal Appeals.
Sec. 5331. Review by Court of Appeals for the Armed Forces.
Sec. 5332. Supreme Court review.
Sec. 5333. Review by Judge Advocate General.
Sec. 5334. Appellate defense counsel in death penalty cases.
Sec. 5335. Authority for hearing on vacation of suspension of sentence to be conducted by qualified judge advocate.
Sec. 5336. Extension of time for petition for new trial.
Sec. 5337. Restoration.
Sec. 5338. Leave requirements pending review of certain court-martial convictions.

SEC. 5321. POST-TRIAL PROCESSING IN GENERAL AND SPECIAL COURTS-MARTIAL.

Section 860 of title 10, United States Code (article 60 of the Uniform Code of Military Justice), is amended to read as follows:

"§ 860. Art 60. Post-trial processing in general and special courts-martial

"(a) STATEMENT OF TRIAL RESULTS.—(1) The military judge of a general or special court-martial shall enter into the record of trial a document entitled 'Statement of Trial Results', which shall set forth—

"(A) each plea and finding;

"(B) the sentence, if any; and

"(C) such other information as the President may prescribe by regulation.

"(2) Copies of the Statement of Trial Results shall be provided promptly to the convening authority, the accused, and any victim of the offense.

"(b) POST-TRIAL MOTIONS.—In accordance with regulations prescribed by the President, the military judge in a general or special court-martial shall address all post-trial motions and other post-trial matters that—

"(1) may affect a plea, a finding, the sentence, the Statement of Trial Results, the record

of trial, or any post-trial action by the convening authority; and

"(2) are subject to resolution by the military judge before entry of judgment.".

SEC. 5322. LIMITED AUTHORITY TO ACT ON SENTENCE IN SPECIFIED POST-TRIAL CIRCUMSTANCES.

Subchapter IX of chapter 47 of title 10, United States Code, is amended by inserting after section 860 (article 60 of the Uniform Code of Military Justice), as amended by section 5321 of this Act, the following new section (article):

"§ 860a. Art. 60a. Limited authority to act on sentence in specified post-trial circumstances

"(a) IN GENERAL.—(1) The convening authority of a general or special court-martial described in paragraph (2)—

"(A) may act on the sentence of the court-martial only as provided in subsection (b), (c), or (d); and

"(B) may not act on the findings of the court-martial.

"(2) The courts-martial referred to in paragraph (1) are the following:

"(A) A general or special court-martial in which the maximum sentence of confinement established under subsection (a) of section 856 of this title (article 56) for any offense of which the accused is found guilty is more than two years.

"(B) A general or special court-martial in which the total of the sentences of confinement imposed, running consecutively, is more than six months.

"(C) A general or special court-martial in which the sentence imposed includes a dismissal, dishonorable discharge, or bad-conduct discharge.

"(D) A general or special court-martial in which the accused is found guilty of a violation of subsection (a) or (b) of section 920 of this title (article 120), section 920b of this title (article 120b), or such other offense as the Secretary of Defense may specify by regulation.

"(3) Except as provided in subsection (d), the convening authority may act under this section only before entry of judgment.

"(4) Under regulations prescribed by the Secretary concerned, a commissioned officer commanding for the time being, a successor in command, or any person exercising general court-martial jurisdiction may act under this section in place of the convening authority.

"(b) REDUCTION, COMMUTATION, AND SUSPENSION OF SENTENCES GENERALLY.—(1) Except as provided in subsection (c) or (d), the convening authority may not reduce, commute, or suspend any of the following sentences:

"(A) A sentence of confinement, if the total period of confinement imposed for all offenses involved, running consecutively, is greater than six months.

"(B) A sentence of dismissal, dishonorable discharge, or bad-conduct discharge.

"(C) A sentence of death.

"(2) The convening authority may reduce, commute, or suspend any sentence not specified in paragraph (1).

"(c) SUSPENSION OF CERTAIN SENTENCES UPON RECOMMENDATION OF MILITARY JUDGE.—(1) Upon recommendation of the military judge, as included in the Statement of Trial Results, together with an explanation of the facts supporting the recommendation, the convening authority may suspend—

"(A) a sentence of confinement, in whole or in part; or

"(B) a sentence of dismissal, dishonorable discharge, or bad-conduct discharge.

"(2) The convening authority may not, under paragraph (1)—

"(A) suspend a mandatory minimum sentence; or

"(B) suspend a sentence to an extent in excess of the suspension recommended by the military judge.

"*(d) REDUCTION OF SENTENCE FOR SUBSTANTIAL ASSISTANCE BY ACCUSED.—(1) Upon a recommendation by the trial counsel, if the accused, after sentencing and before entry of judgment, provides substantial assistance in the investigation or prosecution of another person, the convening authority may reduce, commute, or suspend a sentence, in whole or in part, including any mandatory minimum sentence.*

"*(2) Upon a recommendation by a trial counsel, designated in accordance with rules prescribed by the President, if the accused, after entry of judgment, provides substantial assistance in the investigation or prosecution of another person, a convening authority, designated under such regulations, may reduce, commute, or suspend a sentence, in whole or in part, including any mandatory minimum sentence.*

"*(3) In evaluating whether the accused has provided substantial assistance under this subsection, the convening authority may consider the presentence assistance of the accused.*

"*(e) SUBMISSIONS BY ACCUSED AND VICTIM.— (1) In accordance with rules prescribed by the President, in determining whether to act under this section, the convening authority shall consider matters submitted in writing by the accused or any victim of an offense. Such rules shall include—*

"*(A) procedures for notice of the opportunity to make such submissions;*

"*(B) the deadlines for such submissions; and*

"*(C) procedures for providing the accused and any victim of an offense with a copy of the recording of any open sessions of the court-martial and copies of, or access to, any admitted, unsealed exhibits.*

"*(2) The convening authority shall not consider under this section any submitted matters that relate to the character of a victim unless such matters were presented as evidence at trial and not excluded at trial.*

"*(f) DECISION OF CONVENING AUTHORITY.—(1) The decision of the convening authority under this section shall be forwarded to the military judge, with copies provided to the accused and to any victim of the offense.*

"*(2) If, under this section, the convening authority reduces, commutes, or suspends the sentence, the decision of the convening authority shall include a written explanation of the reasons for such action.*

"*(3) If, under subsection (d)(2), the convening authority reduces, commutes, or suspends the sentence, the decision of the convening authority shall be forwarded to the chief trial judge for appropriate modification of the entry of judgment, which shall be transmitted to the Judge Advocate General for appropriate action.*".

SEC. 5323. POST-TRIAL ACTIONS IN SUMMARY COURTS-MARTIAL AND CERTAIN GENERAL AND SPECIAL COURTS-MARTIAL.

Subchapter IX of chapter 47 of title 10, United States Code, is amended by inserting after section 860a (article 60a of the Uniform Code of Military Justice), as added by section 5322 of this Act, the following new section (article):

"§ 860b. Art. 60b. Post-trial actions in summary courts-martial and certain general and special courts-martial

"*(a) IN GENERAL.—(1) In a court-martial not specified in section 860a(a)(2) of this title (article 60a(a)(2)), the convening authority may—*

"*(A) dismiss any charge or specification by setting aside the finding of guilty;*

"*(B) change a finding of guilty to a charge or specification to a finding of guilty to a lesser included offense;*

"*(C) disapprove the findings and the sentence and dismiss the charges and specifications;*

"*(D) disapprove the findings and the sentence and order a rehearing as to the findings and the sentence;*

"*(E) disapprove, commute, or suspend the sentence, in whole or in part; or*

"*(F) disapprove the sentence and order a rehearing as to the sentence.*

"*(2) In a summary court-martial, the convening authority shall approve the sentence or take other action on the sentence under paragraph (1).*

"*(3) Except as provided in paragraph (4), the convening authority may act under this section only before entry of judgment.*

"*(4) The convening authority may act under this section after entry of judgment in a general or special court-martial in the same manner as the convening authority may act under section 860a(d)(2) of this title (article 60a(d)(2)). Such action shall be forwarded to the chief trial judge, who shall ensure appropriate modification to the entry of judgment and shall transmit the entry of judgment to the Judge Advocate General for appropriate action.*

"*(5) Under regulations prescribed by the Secretary concerned, a commissioned officer commanding for the time being, a successor in command, or any person exercising general court-martial jurisdiction may act under this section in place of the convening authority.*

"*(b) LIMITATIONS ON REHEARINGS.—The convening authority may not order a rehearing under this section—*

"*(1) as to the findings, if there is insufficient evidence in the record to support the findings;*

"*(2) to reconsider a finding of not guilty of any specification or a ruling which amounts to a finding of not guilty; or*

"*(3) to reconsider a finding of not guilty of any charge, unless there has been a finding of guilty under a specification laid under that charge, which sufficiently alleges a violation of some article of this chapter.*

"*(c) SUBMISSIONS BY ACCUSED AND VICTIM.— In accordance with rules prescribed by the President, in determining whether to act under this section, the convening authority shall consider matters submitted in writing by the accused or any victim of the offense. Such rules shall include the matter required by section 860a(e) of this title (article 60a(e)).*

"*(d) DECISION OF CONVENING AUTHORITY.—(1) In a general or special court-martial, the decision of the convening authority under this section shall be forwarded to the military judge, with copies provided to the accused and to any victim of the offense.*

"*(2) If the convening authority acts on the findings or the sentence under subsection (a)(1), the decision of the convening authority shall include a written explanation of the reasons for such action.*".

SEC. 5324. ENTRY OF JUDGMENT.

Subchapter IX of chapter 47 of title 10, United States Code, is amended by inserting after section 860b (article 60b of the Uniform Code of Military Justice), as added by section 5323 of this Act, the following new section (article):

"§ 860c. Art. 60c. Entry of judgment

"*(a) ENTRY OF JUDGMENT OF GENERAL OR SPECIAL COURT-MARTIAL.—(1) In accordance with rules prescribed by the President, in a general or special court-martial, the military judge shall enter into the record of trial the judgment of the court. The judgment of the court shall consist of the following:*

"*(A) The Statement of Trial Results under section 860 of this title (article 60).*

"*(B) Any modifications of, or supplements to, the Statement of Trial Results by reason of—*

"*(i) any post-trial action by the convening authority; or*

"*(ii) any ruling, order, or other determination of the military judge that affects a plea, a finding, or the sentence.*

"*(2) Under rules prescribed by the President, the judgment under paragraph (1) shall be—*

"*(A) provided to the accused and to any victim of the offense; and*

"*(B) made available to the public.*

"*(b) SUMMARY COURT-MARTIAL JUDGMENT.— The findings and sentence of a summary court-martial, as modified by any post-trial action by the convening authority under section 860b of this title (article 60b), constitutes the judgment of the court-martial and shall be recorded and distributed under rules prescribed by the President.*".

SEC. 5325. WAIVER OF RIGHT TO APPEAL AND WITHDRAWAL OF APPEAL.

Section 861 of title 10, United States Code (article 61 of the Uniform Code of Military Justice), is amended to read as follows:

"§ 861. Art. 61. Waiver of right to appeal; withdrawal of appeal

"*(a) WAIVER OF RIGHT TO APPEAL.—After entry of judgment in a general or special court-martial, under procedures prescribed by the Secretary concerned, the accused may waive the right to appellate review in each case subject to such review under section 866 of this title (article 66). Such a waiver shall be—*

"*(1) signed by the accused and by defense counsel; and*

"*(2) attached to the record of trial.*

"*(b) WITHDRAWAL OF APPEAL.—In a general or special court-martial, the accused may withdraw an appeal at any time.*

"*(c) DEATH PENALTY CASE EXCEPTION.—Notwithstanding subsections (a) and (b), an accused may not waive the right to appeal or withdraw an appeal with respect to a judgment that includes a sentence of death.*

"*(d) WAIVER OR WITHDRAWAL AS BAR.—A waiver or withdrawal under this section bars review under section 866 of this title (article 66).*".

SEC. 5326. APPEAL BY THE UNITED STATES.

Section 862 of title 10, United States Code (article 62 of the Uniform Code of Military Justice), is amended—

(1) in paragraph (1) of subsection (a)—

(A) in the matter before subparagraph (A), by striking "court-martial" and all that follows through the colon at the end and inserting "general or special court-martial, or in a pretrial proceeding under section 830a of this title (article 30a), the United States may appeal the following:"; and

(B) by adding at the end the following new subparagraph:

"*(G) An order or ruling of the military judge entering a finding of not guilty with respect to a charge or specification following the return of a finding of guilty by the members.*";

(2) in paragraph (2) of subsection (a)—

(A) by striking "(2)" and inserting "(2)(A)"; and

(B) by adding at the end the following new subparagraph:

"*(B) An appeal of an order or ruling may not be taken when prohibited by section 844 of this title (article 44).*"; and

(3) by adding at the end the following:

"*(d) The United States may appeal a ruling or order of a military magistrate in the same manner as had the ruling or order been made by a military judge, except that the issue shall first be presented to the military judge who designated the military magistrate or to a military judge detailed to hear the issue.*

"*(e) The provisions of this section shall be liberally construed to effect its purposes.*".

SEC. 5327. REHEARINGS.

Section 863 of title 10, United States Code (article 63 of the Uniform Code of Military Justice), is amended—

(1) by inserting "(a)" before "Each rehearing";

(2) in the second sentence, by striking "may be approved" and inserting "may be adjudged";

(3) by striking the third sentence; and

(4) by adding at the end the following new subsections:

"(b) If the sentence adjudged by the first court-martial was in accordance with a plea agreement under section 853a of this title (article 53a) and the accused at the rehearing does not comply with the agreement, or if a plea of guilty was entered for an offense at the first court-martial and a plea of not guilty was entered at the rehearing, the sentence as to those charges or specifications may include any punishment not in excess of that which could have been adjudged at the first court-martial.

"(c) If, after appeal by the Government under section 856(d) of this title (article 56(d)), the sentence adjudged is set aside and a rehearing on sentence is ordered by the Court of Criminal Appeals or Court of Appeals for the Armed Forces, the court-martial may impose any sentence that is in accordance with the order or ruling setting aside the adjudged sentence, subject to such limitations as the President may prescribe by regulation.".

SEC. 5328. JUDGE ADVOCATE REVIEW OF FINDING OF GUILTY IN SUMMARY COURT-MARTIAL.

(a) IN GENERAL.—Subsection (a) of section 864 of title 10, United States Code (article 64 of the Uniform Code of Military Justice), is amended by striking the first two sentences and inserting the following:

"(a) IN GENERAL.—Under regulations prescribed by the Secretary concerned, each summary court-martial in which there is a finding of guilty shall be reviewed by a judge advocate. A judge advocate may not review a case under this subsection if the judge advocate has acted in the same case as an accuser, preliminary hearing officer, member of the court, military judge, or counsel or has otherwise acted on behalf of the prosecution or defense.".

(b) TECHNICAL AND CONFORMING AMENDMENTS.—

(1) The heading of such section (article) is amended to read as follows:

"§ 864. Art. 64. Judge advocate review of finding of guilty in summary court-martial".

(2) Subsection (b) of such section (article) is amended—

(A) by striking "(b) The record" and inserting "(b) RECORD.—The record";

(B) in paragraph (1), by adding "or" at the end;

(C) by striking paragraph (2); and

(D) by redesignating paragraph (3) as paragraph (2).

(3) Subsection (c)(3) of such section (article) is amended by striking "section 869(b) of this title (article 69(b))." and inserting "section 869 of this title (article 69).".

SEC. 5329. TRANSMITTAL AND REVIEW OF RECORDS.

Section 865 of title 10, United States Code (article 65 of the Uniform Code of Military Justice), is amended to read as follows:

"§ 865. Art. 65. Transmittal and review of records

"(a) TRANSMITTAL OF RECORDS.—

"(1) FINDING OF GUILTY IN GENERAL OR SPECIAL COURT-MARTIAL.—If the judgment of a general or special court-martial entered under section 860c of this title (article 60c) includes a finding of guilty, the record shall be transmitted to the Judge Advocate General.

"(2) OTHER CASES.—In all other cases, records of trial by court-martial and related documents shall be transmitted and disposed of as the Secretary concerned may prescribe by regulation.

"(b) CASES FOR DIRECT APPEAL.—

"(1) AUTOMATIC REVIEW.—If the judgment includes a sentence of death, dismissal of a commissioned officer, cadet, or midshipman, dishon-

orable discharge or bad-conduct discharge, or confinement for 2 years or more, the Judge Advocate General shall forward the record of trial to the Court of Criminal Appeals for review under section 866(b)(2) of this title (article 66(b)(2)).

"(2) CASES ELIGIBLE FOR DIRECT APPEAL REVIEW.—

"(A) IN GENERAL.—If the case is eligible for direct review under section 866(b)(1) of this title (article 66(b)(1)), the Judge Advocate General shall—

"(i) forward a copy of the record of trial to an appellate defense counsel who shall be detailed to review the case and, upon request of the accused, to represent the accused before the Court of Criminal Appeals; and

"(ii) upon written request of the accused, forward a copy of the record of trial to civilian counsel provided by the accused.

"(B) INAPPLICABILITY.—Subparagraph (A) shall not apply if the accused—

"(i) waives the right to appeal under section 861 of this title (article 61); or

"(ii) declines in writing the detailing of appellate defense counsel under subparagraph (A)(i).

"(c) NOTICE OF RIGHT TO APPEAL.—

"(1) IN GENERAL.—The Judge Advocate General shall provide notice to the accused of the right to file an appeal under section 866(b)(1) of this title (article 66(b)(1)) by means of depositing in the United States mails for delivery by first class certified mail to the accused at an address provided by the accused or, if no such address has been provided by the accused, at the latest address listed for the accused in the official service record of the accused.

"(2) INAPPLICABILITY UPON WAIVER OF APPEAL.—Paragraph (1) shall not apply if the accused waives the right to appeal under section 861 of this title (article 61).

"(d) REVIEW BY JUDGE ADVOCATE GENERAL.—

"(1) BY WHOM.—A review conducted under this subsection may be conducted by an attorney within the Office of the Judge Advocate General or another attorney designated under regulations prescribed by the Secretary concerned.

"(2) REVIEW OF CASES NOT ELIGIBLE FOR DIRECT APPEAL.—

"(A) IN GENERAL.—A review under subparagraph (B) shall be completed in each general and special court-martial that is not eligible for direct appeal under paragraph (1) or (3) of section 866(b) of this title (article 66(b)).

"(B) SCOPE OF REVIEW.—A review referred to in subparagraph (A) shall include a written decision providing each of the following:

"(i) A conclusion as to whether the court had jurisdiction over the accused and the offense.

"(ii) A conclusion as to whether the charge and specification stated an offense.

"(iii) A conclusion as to whether the sentence was within the limits prescribed as a matter of law.

"(iv) A response to each allegation of error made in writing by the accused.

"(3) REVIEW WHEN DIRECT APPEAL IS WAIVED, WITHDRAWN, OR NOT FILED.—

"(A) IN GENERAL.—A review under subparagraph (B) shall be completed in each general and special court-martial if—

"(i) the accused waives the right to appeal or withdraws appeal under section 861 of this title (article 61); or

"(ii) the accused does not file a timely appeal in a case eligible for direct appeal under subparagraph (A), (B), or (C) of section 866(b)(1) of this title (article 66(b)(1)).

"(B) SCOPE OF REVIEW.—A review referred to in subparagraph (A) shall include a written decision limited to providing conclusions on the matters specified in clauses (i), (ii), and (iii) of paragraph (2)(B).

"(e) REMEDY.—

"(1) IN GENERAL.—If after a review of a record under subsection (d), the attorney conducting the review believes corrective action may be required, the record shall be forwarded to the Judge Advocate General, who may set aside the findings or sentence, in whole or in part.

"(2) REHEARING.—In setting aside findings or sentence, the Judge Advocate General may order a rehearing, except that a rehearing may not be ordered in violation of section 844 of this title (article 44).

"(3) REMEDY WITHOUT REHEARING.—

"(A) DISMISSAL WHEN NO REHEARING ORDERED.—If the Judge Advocate General sets aside findings and sentence and does not order a rehearing, the Judge Advocate General shall dismiss the charges.

"(B) DISMISSAL WHEN REHEARING IMPRACTICAL.—If the Judge Advocate General sets aside findings and orders a rehearing and the convening authority determines that a rehearing would be impractical, the convening authority shall dismiss the charges.".

SEC. 5330. COURTS OF CRIMINAL APPEALS.

(a) APPELLATE MILITARY JUDGES.—Subsection (a) of section 866 of title 10, United States Code (article 66 of the Uniform Code of Military Justice), is amended—

(1) in the second sentence, by striking "subsection (f)" and inserting "subsection (h)";

(2) in the fourth sentence, by inserting after "highest court of a State" the following: "and must be certified by the Judge Advocate General as qualified, by reason of education, training, experience, and judicial temperament, for duty as an appellate military judge"; and

(3) by adding at the end the following new sentence: "In accordance with regulations prescribed by the President, assignments of appellate military judges under this section (article) shall be for appropriate minimum periods, subject to such exceptions as may be authorized in the regulations.".

(b) REVISION OF APPELLATE PROCEDURES.—Such section (article) is further amended—

(1) by redesignating subsections (e), (f), (g), and (h) as subsections (g), (h), (i), and (j), respectively; and

(2) by striking subsections (b), (c), and (d) and inserting the following new subsections:

"(b) REVIEW.—

"(1) APPEALS BY ACCUSED.—A Court of Criminal Appeals shall have jurisdiction over a timely appeal from the judgment of a court-martial, entered into the record under section 860c of this title (article 60c), as follows:

"(A) On appeal by the accused in a case in which the sentence extends to confinement for more than six months and the case is not subject to automatic review under paragraph (3).

"(B) On appeal by the accused in a case in which the Government previously filed an appeal under section 862 of this title (article 62).

"(C) On appeal by the accused in a case that the Judge Advocate General has sent to the Court of Criminal Appeals for review of the sentence under section 856(d) of this title (article 56(d)).

"(D) In a case in which the accused filed an application for review with the Court under section 869(d)(1)(B) of this title (article 69(d)(1)(B)) and the application has been granted by the Court.

"(2) REVIEW OF CERTAIN SENTENCES.—A Court of Criminal Appeals shall have jurisdiction over all cases that the Judge Advocate General orders sent to the Court for review under section 856(d) of this title (article 56(d)).

"(3) AUTOMATIC REVIEW.—A Court of Criminal Appeals shall have jurisdiction over a court-martial in which the judgment entered into the record under section 860c of this title (article 60c) includes a sentence of death, dismissal of a

commissioned officer, cadet, or midshipman, dishonorable discharge or bad-conduct discharge, or confinement for 2 years or more.

"(c) TIMELINESS.—An appeal under subsection (b)(1) is timely if it is filed as follows:

"(1) In the case of an appeal by the accused under subsection (b)(1)(A) or (b)(1)(B), if filed before the later of—

"(A) the end of the 90-day period beginning on the date the accused is provided notice of appellate rights under section 865(c) of this title (article 65(c)); or

"(B) the date set by the Court of Criminal Appeals by rule or order.

"(2) In the case of an appeal by the accused under subsection (b)(1)(C), if filed before the later of—

"(A) the end of the 90-day period beginning on the date the accused is notified that the application for review has been granted by letter placed in the United States mails for delivery by first class certified mail to the accused at an address provided by the accused or, if no such address has been provided by the accused, at the latest address listed for the accused in his official service record; or

"(B) the date set by the Court of Criminal Appeals by rule or order.

"(d) DUTIES.—

"(1) CASES APPEALED BY ACCUSED.—In any case before the Court of Criminal Appeals under subsection (b), the Court may act only with respect to the findings and sentence as entered into the record under section 860c of this title (article 60c). The Court may affirm only such findings of guilty and, the sentence or such part or amount of the sentence, as the Court finds correct in law and fact and determines, on the basis of the entire record, should be approved. In considering the record, the Court may weigh the evidence, judge the credibility of witnesses, and determine controverted questions of fact, recognizing that the trial court saw and heard the witnesses.

"(2) ERROR OR EXCESSIVE DELAY.—In any case before the Court of Criminal Appeals under subsection (b), the Court may provide appropriate relief if the accused demonstrates error or excessive delay in the processing of the court-martial after the judgment was entered into the record under section 860c of this title (article 60c).

"(e) CONSIDERATION OF APPEAL OF SENTENCE BY THE UNITED STATES.—

"(1) IN GENERAL.—In considering a sentence on appeal or review as provided in section 856(d) of this title (article 56(d)), the Court of Criminal Appeals may consider—

"(A) whether the sentence violates the law; and

"(B) whether the sentence is plainly unreasonable.

"(2) RECORD ON APPEAL OR REVIEW.—In an appeal or review under this subsection or section 856(d) of this title (article 56(d)), the record on appeal or review shall consist of—

"(A) any portion of the record in the case that is designated as pertinent by either of the parties;

"(B) the information submitted during the sentencing proceeding; and

"(C) any information required by rule or order of the Court of Criminal Appeals.

"(f) LIMITS OF AUTHORITY.—

"(1) SET ASIDE OF FINDINGS.—

"(A) IN GENERAL.—If the Court of Criminal Appeals sets aside the findings, the Court—

"(i) may affirm any lesser included offense; and

"(ii) may, except when prohibited by section 844 of this title (article 44), order a rehearing.

"(B) DISMISSAL WHEN NO REHEARING ORDERED.—If the Court of Criminal Appeals sets aside the findings and does not order a rehearing, the Court shall order that the charges be dismissed.

"(C) DISMISSAL WHEN REHEARING IMPRACTICABLE.—If the Court of Criminal Appeals orders a rehearing on a charge and the convening authority finds a rehearing impracticable, the convening authority may dismiss the charge.

"(2) SET ASIDE OF SENTENCE.—If the Court of Criminal Appeals sets aside the sentence, the Court may—

"(A) modify the sentence to a lesser sentence; or

"(B) order a rehearing.

"(3) ADDITIONAL PROCEEDINGS.—If the Court determines that additional proceedings are warranted, the Court may order a hearing as may be necessary to address a substantial issue, subject to such limitations as the Court may direct and under such regulations as the President may prescribe.".

(c) ACTION WHEN REHEARING IMPRACTICABLE AFTER REHEARING ORDER.—Subsection (g) of such section (article), as redesignated by subsection (b)(1) of this section, is amended—

(1) in the first sentence, by striking "convening authority" and inserting "appropriate authority"; and

(2) by striking the last sentence.

(d) SECTION HEADING.—The heading of such section (article) is amended to read as follows:

"§866. Art. 66. Courts of Criminal Appeals".

(e) SUBSECTION HEADING AMENDMENTS FOR STYLISTIC CONSISTENCY.—Such section (article) is further amended—

(1) in subsection (a), by inserting "COURTS OF CRIMINAL APPEALS.—" after "(a)";

(2) in subsection (g), as redesignated by subsection (b)(1) of this section, by inserting "ACTION IN ACCORDANCE WITH DECISIONS OF COURTS.—" after "(g)";

(3) in subsection (h), as so redesignated, by inserting "RULES OF PROCEDURE.—" after "(h)";

(4) in subsection (i), as so redesignated, by inserting "PROHIBITION ON EVALUATION OF OTHER MEMBERS OF COURTS.—" after "(i)"; and

(5) in subsection (j), as so redesignated, by inserting "INELIGIBILITY OF MEMBERS OF COURTS TO REVIEW RECORDS OF CASES INVOLVING CERTAIN PRIOR MEMBER SERVICE.—" after "(j)".

SEC. 5331. REVIEW BY COURT OF APPEALS FOR THE ARMED FORCES.

(a) JAG NOTIFICATION.—Subsection (a)(2) of section 867 of title 10, United States Code (article 67 of the Uniform Code of Military Justice), is amended by inserting after "the Judge Advocate General" the following: ", after appropriate notification to the other Judge Advocates General and the Staff Judge Advocate to the Commandant of the Marine Corps,".

(b) BASIS FOR REVIEW.—Subsection (c) of such section (article) is amended—

(1) by inserting "(1)" after "(c)";

(2) by designating the second sentence as paragraph (2);

(3) by designating the third sentence as paragraph (3);

(4) by designating the fourth sentence as paragraph (4); and

(5) in paragraph (1), as designated by paragraph (1) of this subsection, by striking "only with respect to" and all that follows through the end of the sentence and inserting "only with respect to—

"(A) the findings and sentence set forth in the entry of judgment, as affirmed or set aside as incorrect in law by the Court of Criminal Appeals; or

"(B) a decision, judgment, or order by a military judge, as affirmed or set aside as incorrect in law by the Court of Criminal Appeals.".

SEC. 5332. SUPREME COURT REVIEW.

The second sentence of section 867a(a) of title 10, United States Code (article 67a(a) of the Uniform Code of Military Justice), is amended by inserting before "Court of Appeals" the following: "United States".

SEC. 5333. REVIEW BY JUDGE ADVOCATE GENERAL.

Section 869 of title 10, United States Code (article 69 of the Uniform Code of Military Justice), is amended to read as follows:

"§869. Art. 69. Review by Judge Advocate General

"(a) IN GENERAL.—Upon application by the accused and subject to subsections (b), (c), and (d), the Judge Advocate General may modify or set aside, in whole or in part, the findings and sentence in a court-martial that is not reviewed under section 866 of this title (article 66).

"(b) TIMING.—To qualify for consideration, an application under subsection (a) must be submitted to the Judge Advocate General not later than one year after the date of completion of review under section 864 or 865 of this title (article 64 or 65), as the case may be. The Judge Advocate General may, for good cause shown, extend the period for submission of an application, but may not consider an application submitted more than three years after such completion date.

"(c) SCOPE.—(1)(A) In a case reviewed under section 864 or 865(b) of this title (article 64 or 65(b)), the Judge Advocate General may set aside the findings or sentence, in whole or in part on the grounds of newly discovered evidence, fraud on the court, lack of jurisdiction over the accused or the offense, error prejudicial to the substantial rights of the accused, or the appropriateness of the sentence.

"(B) In setting aside findings or sentence, the Judge Advocate General may order a rehearing, except that a rehearing may not be ordered in violation of section 844 of this title (article 44).

"(C) If the Judge Advocate General sets aside findings and sentence and does not order a rehearing, the Judge Advocate General shall dismiss the charges.

"(D) If the Judge Advocate General sets aside findings and orders a rehearing and the convening authority determines that a rehearing would be impractical, the convening authority shall dismiss the charges.

"(2) In a case reviewed under section 865(b) of this title (article 65(b)), review under this section is limited to the issue of whether the waiver or withdrawal of an appeal was invalid under the law. If the Judge Advocate General determines that the waiver or withdrawal of an appeal was invalid, the Judge Advocate General shall order appropriate corrective action under rules prescribed by the President.

"(d) COURT OF CRIMINAL APPEALS.—(1) A Court of Criminal Appeals may review the action taken by the Judge Advocate General under subsection (c)—

"(A) in a case sent to the Court of Criminal Appeals by order of the Judge Advocate General; or

"(B) in a case submitted to the Court of Criminal Appeals by the accused in an application for review.

"(2) The Court of Criminal Appeals may grant an application under paragraph (1)(B) only if—

"(A) the application demonstrates a substantial basis for concluding that the action on review under subsection (c) constituted prejudicial error; and

"(B) the application is filed not later than the earlier of—

"(i) 60 days after the date on which the accused is notified of the decision of the Judge Advocate General; or

"(ii) 60 days after the date on which a copy of the decision of the Judge Advocate General is deposited in the United States mails for delivery by first-class certified mail to the accused at an address provided by the accused or, if no such address has been provided by the accused, at the latest address listed for the accused in his official service record.

"(3) The submission of an application for review under this subsection does not constitute a proceeding before the Court of Criminal Appeals for purposes of section 870(c)(1) of this title (article 70(c)(1)).

"(e) ACTION ONLY ON MATTERS OF LAW.—Notwithstanding section 866 of this title (article 66), in any case reviewed by a Court of Criminal Appeals under subsection (d), the Court may take action only with respect to matters of law.".

SEC. 5334. APPELLATE DEFENSE COUNSEL IN DEATH PENALTY CASES.

Section 870 of title 10, United States Code (article 70 of the Uniform Code of Military Justice), is amended by adding at the end the following new subsection:

"(f) To the greatest extent practicable, in any capital case, at least one defense counsel under subsection (c) shall, as determined by the Judge Advocate General, be learned in the law applicable to such cases. If necessary, this counsel may be a civilian and, if so, may be compensated in accordance with regulations prescribed by the Secretary of Defense.".

SEC. 5335. AUTHORITY FOR HEARING ON VACATION OF SUSPENSION OF SENTENCE TO BE CONDUCTED BY QUALIFIED JUDGE ADVOCATE.

(a) IN GENERAL.—Subsection (a) of section 872 of title 10, United States Code (article 72 of the Uniform Code of Military Justice), is amended by inserting after the first sentence the following new sentence: "The special court-martial convening authority may detail a judge advocate, who is certified under section 827(b) of this title (article 27(b)), to conduct the hearing.".

(b) TECHNICAL AMENDMENTS.—Such section (article) is further amended—

(1) in the last sentence of subsection (a), by striking "if he so desires" and inserting "if the probationer so desires"; and

(2) in the second sentence of subsection (b)—

(A) by striking "If he" and inserting "If the officer exercising general court-martial jurisdiction"; and

(B) by striking "section 871(c) of this title (article 71(c))" and inserting "section 857 of this title (article 57)".

SEC. 5336. EXTENSION OF TIME FOR PETITION FOR NEW TRIAL.

The first sentence of section 873 of title 10, United States Code (article 73 of the Uniform Code of Military Justice), is amended by striking "two years after approval by the convening authority of a court-martial sentence" and inserting "three years after the date of the entry of judgment under section 860c of this title (article 60c)".

SEC. 5337. RESTORATION.

Section 875 of title 10, United States Code (article 75 of the Uniform Code of Military Justice), is amended by adding at the end the following new subsection:

"(d) The President shall prescribe regulations, with such limitations as the President considers appropriate, governing eligibility for pay and allowances for the period after the date on which an executed part of a court-martial sentence is set aside.".

SEC. 5338. LEAVE REQUIREMENTS PENDING REVIEW OF CERTAIN COURT-MARTIAL CONVICTIONS.

Section 876a of title 10, United States Code (article 76a of the Uniform Code of Military Justice), is amended—

(1) in the first sentence, by striking ", as approved under section 860 of this title (article 60),"; and

(2) in the second sentence, by striking "on which the sentence is approved under section 860 of this title (article 60)" and inserting "of the entry of judgment under section 860c of this title (article 60c)".

TITLE LX—PUNITIVE ARTICLES

Sec. 5401. Reorganization of punitive articles.
Sec. 5402. Conviction of offense charged, lesser included offenses, and attempts.
Sec. 5403. Soliciting commission of offenses.
Sec. 5404. Malingering.
Sec. 5405. Breach of medical quarantine.
Sec. 5406. Missing movement; jumping from vessel.
Sec. 5407. Offenses against correctional custody and restriction.
Sec. 5408. Disrespect toward superior commissioned officer; assault of superior commissioned officer.
Sec. 5409. Willfully disobeying superior commissioned officer.
Sec. 5410. Prohibited activities with military recruit or trainee by person in position of special trust.
Sec. 5411. Offenses by sentinel or lookout.
Sec. 5412. Disrespect toward sentinel or lookout.
Sec. 5413. Release of prisoner without authority; drinking with prisoner.
Sec. 5414. Penalty for acting as a spy.
Sec. 5415. Public records offenses.
Sec. 5416. False or unauthorized pass offenses.
Sec. 5417. Impersonation offenses.
Sec. 5418. Insignia offenses.
Sec. 5419. False official statements; false swearing.
Sec. 5420. Parole violation.
Sec. 5421. Wrongful taking, opening, etc. of mail matter.
Sec. 5422. Improper hazarding of vessel or aircraft.
Sec. 5423. Leaving scene of vehicle accident.
Sec. 5424. Drunkenness and other incapacitation offenses.
Sec. 5425. Lower blood alcohol content limits for conviction of drunken or reckless operation of vehicle, aircraft, or vessel.
Sec. 5426. Endangerment offenses.
Sec. 5427. Communicating threats.
Sec. 5428. Technical amendment relating to murder.
Sec. 5429. Child endangerment.
Sec. 5430. Rape and sexual assault offenses.
Sec. 5431. Deposit of obscene matter in the mail.
Sec. 5432. Fraudulent use of credit cards, debit cards, and other access devices.
Sec. 5433. False pretenses to obtain services.
Sec. 5434. Robbery.
Sec. 5435. Receiving stolen property.
Sec. 5436. Offenses concerning Government computers.
Sec. 5437. Bribery.
Sec. 5438. Graft.
Sec. 5439. Kidnapping.
Sec. 5440. Arson; burning property with intent to defraud.
Sec. 5441. Assault.
Sec. 5442. Burglary and unlawful entry.
Sec. 5443. Stalking.
Sec. 5444. Subornation of perjury.
Sec. 5445. Obstructing justice.
Sec. 5446. Misprision of serious offense.
Sec. 5447. Wrongful refusal to testify.
Sec. 5448. Prevention of authorized seizure of property.
Sec. 5449. Wrongful interference with adverse administrative proceeding.
Sec. 5450. Retaliation.
Sec. 5451. Extraterritorial application of certain offenses.
Sec. 5452. Table of sections.

SEC. 5401. REORGANIZATION OF PUNITIVE ARTICLES.

Sections of subchapter X of chapter 47 of title 10, United States Code (articles of the Uniform Code of Military Justice), are transferred within subchapter X and redesignated as follows:

(1) ENLISTMENT AND SEPARATION.—Sections 883 and 884 (articles 83 and 84) are transferred so as to appear (in that order) after section 904 (article 104) and are redesignated as sections 904a and 904b (articles 104a and 104b), respectively.

(2) RESISTANCE, FLIGHT, BREACH OF ARREST, AND ESCAPE.—Section 895 (article 95) is transferred so as to appear after section 887 (article 87) and is redesignated as section 887a (article 87a).

(3) NONCOMPLIANCE WITH PROCEDURAL RULES.—Section 898 (article 98) is transferred so as to appear after section 931 (article 131) and is redesignated as section 931f (article 131f).

(4) CAPTURED OR ABANDONED PROPERTY.—Section 903 (article 103) is transferred so as to appear after section 908 (article 108) and is redesignated as section 908a (article 108a).

(5) AIDING THE ENEMY.—Section 904 (article 104) is redesignated as section 903b (article 103b).

(6) MISCONDUCT AS PRISONER.—Section 905 (article 105) is transferred so as to appear after section 897 (article 97) and is redesignated as section 898 (article 98).

(7) SPIES; ESPIONAGE.—Sections 906 and 906a (articles 106 and 106a) are transferred so as to appear (in that order) after section 902 (article 102) and are redesignated as sections 903 and 903a (articles 103 and 103a), respectively.

(8) MISBEHAVIOR OF SENTINEL.—Section 913 (article 113) is transferred so as to appear after section 894 (article 94) and is redesignated as section 895 (article 95).

(9) DRUNKEN OR RECKLESS OPERATION OF A VEHICLE, AIRCRAFT, OR VESSEL.—Section 911 (article 111) is transferred so as to appear after section 912a (article 912a) and is redesignated as section 913 (article 113).

(10) HOUSEBREAKING.—Section 930 (article 130) is redesignated as section 929a (article 129a).

(11) STALKING.—Section 920a (article 120a) is transferred so as to appear after section 929a (article 129a), as redesignated by paragraph (10), and is redesignated as section 930 (article 130).

(12) FORGERY.—Section 923 (article 123) is transferred so as to appear after section 904b (article 104b), as transferred and redesignated by paragraph (1), and is redesignated as section 905 (article 105).

(13) MAIMING.—

(A) IN GENERAL.—Section 924 (article 124) is transferred so as to appear after section 928 (article 128) and is redesignated as section 928a (article 128a).

(B) CONFORMING AMENDMENTS.—Section 919a(b) (article 919a(b)) is amended—

(i) by striking "924," and inserting "928a,"; and

(ii) by striking "124," and inserting "128a".

(14) FRAUDS AGAINST THE UNITED STATES.—Section 932 of (article 132) is transferred so as to appear after section 923a (article 123a) and is redesignated as section 924 (article 124).

SEC. 5402. CONVICTION OF OFFENSE CHARGED, LESSER INCLUDED OFFENSES, AND ATTEMPTS.

Section 879 of title 10, United States Code (article 79 of the Uniform Code of Military Justice), is amended to read as follows:

"§ 879. Art. 79. Conviction of offense charged, lesser included offenses, and attempts

"(a) IN GENERAL.—An accused may be found guilty of any of the following:

"(1) The offense charged.

"(2) A lesser included offense.

"(3) An attempt to commit the offense charged.

"(4) An attempt to commit a lesser included offense, if the attempt is an offense in its own right.

"(b) LESSER INCLUDED OFFENSE DEFINED.—In this section (article), the term 'lesser included offense' means—

"(1) an offense that is necessarily included in the offense charged; and

"(2) any lesser included offense so designated by regulation prescribed by the President.

"(c) REGULATORY AUTHORITY.—Any designation of a lesser included offense in a regulation referred to in subsection (b) shall be reasonably included in the greater offense.".

SEC. 5403. SOLICITING COMMISSION OF OFFENSES.

Section 882 of title 10, United States Code (article 82 of the Uniform Code of Military Justice), is amended to read as follows:

"§ 882. Art. 82. Soliciting commission of offenses

"(a) SOLICITING COMMISSION OF OFFENSES GENERALLY.—Any person subject to this chapter who solicits or advises another to commit an offense under this chapter (other than an offense specified in subsection (b)) shall be punished as a court-martial may direct.

"(b) SOLICITING DESERTION, MUTINY, SEDITION, OR MISBEHAVIOR BEFORE THE ENEMY.—Any person subject to this chapter who solicits or advises another to violate section 885 of this title (article 85), section 894 of this title (article 94), or section 99 of this title (article 99)—

"(1) if the offense solicited or advised is attempted or is committed, shall be punished with the punishment provided for the commission of the offense; and

"(2) if the offense solicited or advised is not attempted or committed, shall be punished as a court-martial may direct.".

SEC. 5404. MALINGERING.

Subchapter X of chapter 47 of title 10, United States Code, is amended by inserting after section 882 (article 82 of the Uniform Code of Military Justice), as amended by section 5403 of this Act, the following new section (article):

"§ 883. Art. 83. Malingering

"Any person subject to this chapter who, with the intent to avoid work, duty, or service—

"(1) feigns illness, physical disablement, mental lapse, or mental derangement; or

"(2) intentionally inflicts self-injury; shall be punished as a court-martial may direct.".

SEC. 5405. BREACH OF MEDICAL QUARANTINE.

Subchapter X of chapter 47 of title 10, United States Code, is amended by inserting after section 883 (article 83 of the Uniform Code of Military Justice), as added by section 5404 of this Act, the following new section (article):

"§ 884. Art. 84. Breach of medical quarantine

"Any person subject to this chapter—

"(1) who is ordered into medical quarantine by a person authorized to issue such order; and

"(2) who, with knowledge of the quarantine and the limits of the quarantine, goes beyond those limits before being released from the quarantine by proper authority; shall be punished as a court-martial may direct.".

SEC. 5406. MISSING MOVEMENT; JUMPING FROM VESSEL.

Section 887 of title 10, United States Code (article 87 of the Uniform Code of Military Justice), is amended to read as follows:

"§ 887. Art. 87. Missing movement; jumping from vessel

"(a) MISSING MOVEMENT.—Any person subject to this chapter who, through neglect or design, misses the movement of a ship, aircraft, or unit with which the person is required in the course of duty to move shall be punished as a court-martial may direct.

"(b) JUMPING FROM VESSEL INTO THE WATER.—Any person subject to this chapter who wrongfully and intentionally jumps into the water from a vessel in use by the armed forces shall be punished as a court-martial may direct.".

SEC. 5407. OFFENSES AGAINST CORRECTIONAL CUSTODY AND RESTRICTION.

Subchapter X of chapter 47 of title 10, United States Code, is amended by inserting after section 887a (article 87a of the Uniform Code of Military Justice), as transferred and redesignated by section 5401(2) of this Act, the following new section (article):

"§ 887b. Art. 87b. Offenses against correctional custody and restriction

"(a) ESCAPE FROM CORRECTIONAL CUSTODY.—Any person subject to this chapter—

"(1) who is placed in correctional custody by a person authorized to do so;

"(2) who, while in correctional custody, is under physical restraint; and

"(3) who escapes from the physical restraint before being released from the physical restraint by proper authority; shall be punished as a court-martial may direct.

"(b) BREACH OF CORRECTIONAL CUSTODY.—Any person subject to this chapter—

"(1) who is placed in correctional custody by a person authorized to do so;

"(2) who, while in correctional custody, is under restraint other than physical restraint; and

"(3) who goes beyond the limits of the restraint before being released from the correctional custody or relieved of the restraint by proper authority; shall be punished as a court-martial may direct.

"(c) BREACH OF RESTRICTION.—Any person subject to this chapter—

"(1) who is ordered to be restricted to certain limits by a person authorized to do so; and

"(2) who, with knowledge of the limits of the restriction, goes beyond those limits before being released by proper authority; shall be punished as a court-martial may direct.".

SEC. 5408. DISRESPECT TOWARD SUPERIOR COMMISSIONED OFFICER; ASSAULT OF SUPERIOR COMMISSIONED OFFICER.

Section 889 of title 10, United States Code (article 89 of the Uniform Code of Military Justice), is amended to read as follows:

"§ 889. Art. 89. Disrespect toward superior commissioned officer; assault of superior commissioned officer

"(a) DISRESPECT.—Any person subject to this chapter who behaves with disrespect toward that person's superior commissioned officer shall be punished as a court-martial may direct.

"(b) ASSAULT.—Any person subject to this chapter who strikes that person's superior commissioned officer or draws or lifts up any weapon or offers any violence against that officer while the officer is in the execution of the officer's office shall be punished—

"(1) if the offense is committed in time of war, by death or such other punishment as a court-martial may direct; and

"(2) if the offense is committed at any other time, by such punishment, other than death, as a court-martial may direct.".

SEC. 5409. WILLFULLY DISOBEYING SUPERIOR COMMISSIONED OFFICER.

Section 890 of title 10, United States Code (article 90 of the Uniform Code of Military Justice), is amended to read as follows:

"§ 890. Art. 90. Willfully disobeying superior commissioned officer

"Any person subject to this chapter who willfully disobeys a lawful command of that person's superior commissioned officer shall be punished—

"(1) if the offense is committed in time of war, by death or such other punishment as a court-martial may direct; and

"(2) if the offense is committed at any other time, by such punishment, other than death, as a court-martial may direct.".

SEC. 5410. PROHIBITED ACTIVITIES WITH MILITARY RECRUIT OR TRAINEE BY PERSON IN POSITION OF SPECIAL TRUST.

Subchapter X of chapter 47 of title 10, United States Code, is amended by inserting after section 893 (article 93 of the Uniform Code of Military Justice), the following new section (article):

"§ 893a. Art. 93a. Prohibited activities with military recruit or trainee by person in position of special trust

"(a) ABUSE OF TRAINING LEADERSHIP POSITION.—Any person subject to this chapter—

"(1) who is an officer, a noncommissioned officer, or a petty officer;

"(2) who is in a training leadership position with respect to a specially protected junior member of the armed forces; and

"(3) who engages in prohibited sexual activity with such specially protected junior member of the armed forces; shall be punished as a court-martial may direct.

"(b) ABUSE OF POSITION AS MILITARY RECRUITER.—Any person subject to this chapter—

"(1) who is a military recruiter and engages in prohibited sexual activity with an applicant for military service; or

"(2) who is a military recruiter and engages in prohibited sexual activity with a specially protected junior member of the armed forces who is enlisted under a delayed entry program; shall be punished as a court-martial may direct.

"(c) CONSENT.—Consent is not a defense for any conduct at issue in a prosecution under this section (article).

"(d) DEFINITIONS.—In this section (article):

"(1) SPECIALLY PROTECTED JUNIOR MEMBER OF THE ARMED FORCES.—The term 'specially protected junior member of the armed forces' means—

"(A) a member of the armed forces who is assigned to, or is awaiting assignment to, basic training or other initial active duty for training, including a member who is enlisted under a delayed entry program;

"(B) a member of the armed forces who is a cadet, a midshipman, an officer candidate, or a student in any other officer qualification program; and

"(C) a member of the armed forces in any program that, by regulation prescribed by the Secretary concerned, is identified as a training program for initial career qualification.

"(2) TRAINING LEADERSHIP POSITION.—The term 'training leadership position' means, with respect to a specially protected junior member of the armed forces, any of the following:

"(A) Any drill instructor position or other leadership position in a basic training program, an officer candidate school, a reserve officers' training corps unit, a training program for entry into the armed forces, or any program that, by regulation prescribed by the Secretary concerned, is identified as a training program for initial career qualification.

"(B) Faculty and staff of the United States Military Academy, the United States Naval Academy, the United States Air Force Academy, and the United States Coast Guard Academy.

"(3) APPLICANT FOR MILITARY SERVICE.—The term 'applicant for military service' means a person who, under regulations prescribed by the Secretary concerned, is an applicant for original enlistment or appointment in the armed forces.

"(4) MILITARY RECRUITER.—The term 'military recruiter' means a person who, under regulations prescribed by the Secretary concerned, has the primary duty to recruit persons for military service.

"(5) PROHIBITED SEXUAL ACTIVITY.—The term 'prohibited sexual activity' means, as specified in regulations prescribed by the Secretary concerned, inappropriate physical intimacy under circumstances described in such regulations.".

SEC. 5411. OFFENSES BY SENTINEL OR LOOKOUT.

Section 895 of title 10, United States Code (article 95 of the Uniform Code of Military Justice), as transferred and redesignated by section 5401(8) of this Act, is amended to read as follows:

"§ 895. Art. 95. Offenses by sentinel or lookout

"(a) DRUNK OR SLEEPING ON POST, OR LEAVING POST BEFORE BEING RELIEVED.—Any sentinel or lookout who is drunk on post, who sleeps on post, or who leaves post before being regularly relieved, shall be punished—

"(1) if the offense is committed in time of war, by death or such other punishment as a court-martial may direct; and

"(2) if the offense is committed other than in time of war, by such punishment, other than death, as a court-martial may direct.

"(b) LOITERING OR WRONGFULLY SITTING ON POST.—Any sentinel or lookout who loiters or wrongfully sits down on post shall be punished as a court-martial may direct.".

SEC. 5412. DISRESPECT TOWARD SENTINEL OR LOOKOUT.

Subchapter X of chapter 47 of title 10, United States Code, is amended by inserting after section 895 (article 95 of the Uniform Code of Military Justice), as amended by section 5411 of this Act, the following new section (article):

"§ 895a. Art. 95a. Disrespect toward sentinel or lookout

"(a) DISRESPECTFUL LANGUAGE TOWARD SENTINEL OR LOOKOUT.—Any person subject to this chapter who, knowing that another person is a sentinel or lookout, uses wrongful and disrespectful language that is directed toward and within the hearing of the sentinel or lookout, who is in the execution of duties as a sentinel or lookout, shall be punished as a court-martial may direct.

"(b) DISRESPECTFUL BEHAVIOR TOWARD SENTINEL OR LOOKOUT.—Any person subject to this chapter who, knowing that another person is a sentinel or lookout, behaves in a wrongful and disrespectful manner that is directed toward and within the sight of the sentinel or lookout, who is in the execution of duties as a sentinel or lookout, shall be punished as a court-martial may direct.".

SEC. 5413. RELEASE OF PRISONER WITHOUT AUTHORITY; DRINKING WITH PRISONER.

Section 896 of title 10, United States Code (article 96 of the Uniform Code of Military Justice), is amended to read as follows:

"§ 896. Art. 96. Release of prisoner without authority; drinking with prisoner

"(a) RELEASE OF PRISONER WITHOUT AUTHORITY.—Any person subject to this chapter—

"(1) who, without authority to do so, releases a prisoner; or

"(2) who, through neglect or design, allows a prisoner to escape;
shall be punished as a court-martial may direct, whether or not the prisoner was committed in strict compliance with the law.

"(b) DRINKING WITH PRISONER.—Any person subject to this chapter who unlawfully drinks any alcoholic beverage with a prisoner shall be punished as a court-martial may direct.".

SEC. 5414. PENALTY FOR ACTING AS A SPY.

Section 903 of title 10, United States Code (article 103 of the Uniform Code of Military Justice), as transferred and redesignated by section 5401(7) of this Act, is amended by inserting before the period at the end of the first sentence the following: "or such other punishment as a court-martial or a military commission may direct".

SEC. 5415. PUBLIC RECORDS OFFENSES.

Subchapter X of chapter 47 of title 10, United States Code, is amended by inserting after section 903b (article 103b of the Uniform Code of Military Justice), as redesignated by section 5401(5) of this Act, the following new section (article):

"§ 904. Art. 104. Public records offenses

"Any person subject to this chapter who, willfully and unlawfully—

"(1) alters, conceals, removes, mutilates, obliterates, or destroys a public record; or

"(2) takes a public record with the intent to alter, conceal, remove, mutilate, obliterate, or destroy the public record;
shall be punished as a court-martial may direct.".

SEC. 5416. FALSE OR UNAUTHORIZED PASS OFFENSES.

Subchapter X of chapter 47 of title 10, United States Code, is amended by inserting after section 905 (article 105 of the Uniform Code of Military Justice), as transferred and redesignated by section 5401(12) of this Act, the following new section (article):

"§ 905a. Art. 105a. False or unauthorized pass offenses

"(a) WRONGFUL MAKING, ALTERING, ETC.—Any person subject to this chapter who, wrongfully and falsely, makes, alters, counterfeits, or tampers with a military or official pass, permit, discharge certificate, or identification card shall be punished as a court-martial may direct.

"(b) WRONGFUL SALE, ETC.—Any person subject to this chapter who wrongfully sells, gives, lends, or disposes of a false or unauthorized military or official pass, permit, discharge certificate, or identification card, knowing that the pass, permit, discharge certificate, or identification card is false or unauthorized, shall be punished as a court-martial may direct.

"(c) WRONGFUL USE OR POSSESSION.—Any person subject to this chapter who wrongfully uses or possesses a false or unauthorized military or official pass, permit, discharge certificate, or identification card, knowing that the pass, permit, discharge certificate, or identification card is false or unauthorized, shall be punished as a court-martial may direct.".

SEC. 5417. IMPERSONATION OFFENSES.

Subchapter X of chapter 47 of title 10, United States Code, is amended by inserting after section 905a (article 105a of the Uniform Code of Military Justice), as added by section 5416 of this Act, the following new section (article):

"§ 906. Art. 106. Impersonation of officer, noncommissioned or petty officer, or agent or official

"(a) IN GENERAL.—Any person subject to this chapter who, wrongfully and willfully, impersonates—

"(1) an officer, a noncommissioned officer, or a petty officer;

"(2) an agent of superior authority of one of the armed forces; or

"(3) an official of a government;
shall be punished as a court-martial may direct.

"(b) IMPERSONATION WITH INTENT TO DEFRAUD.—Any person subject to this chapter who, wrongfully, willfully, and with intent to defraud, impersonates any person referred to in paragraph (1), (2), or (3) of subsection (a) shall be punished as a court-martial may direct.

"(c) IMPERSONATION OF GOVERNMENT OFFICIAL WITHOUT INTENT TO DEFRAUD.—Any person subject to this chapter who, wrongfully, willfully, and without intent to defraud, impersonates an official of a government by committing an act that exercises or asserts the authority of the office that the person claims to have shall be punished as a court-martial may direct.".

SEC. 5418. INSIGNIA OFFENSES.

Subchapter X of chapter 47 of title 10, United States Code, is amended by inserting after section 906 (article 106 of the Uniform Code of Military Justice), as added by section 5417 of this Act, the following new section (article):

"§ 906a. Art. 106a. Wearing unauthorized insignia, decoration, badge, ribbon, device, or lapel button

"Any person subject to this chapter—

"(1) who is not authorized to wear an insignia, decoration, badge, ribbon, device, or lapel button; or

"(2) who wrongfully wears such insignia, decoration, badge, ribbon, device, or lapel button upon the person's uniform or civilian clothing;
shall be punished as a court-martial may direct.".

SEC. 5419. FALSE OFFICIAL STATEMENTS; FALSE SWEARING.

Section 907 of title 10, United States Code (article 107 of the Uniform Code of Military Justice), is amended to read as follows:

"§ 907. Art. 107. False official statements; false swearing

"(a) FALSE OFFICIAL STATEMENTS.—Any person subject to this chapter who, with intent to deceive—

"(1) signs any false record, return, regulation, order, or other official document, knowing it to be false; or

"(2) makes any other false official statement knowing it to be false;
shall be punished as a court-martial may direct.

"(b) FALSE SWEARING.—Any person subject to this chapter—

"(1) who takes an oath that—

"(A) is administered in a matter in which such oath is required or authorized by law; and

"(B) is administered by a person with authority to do so; and

"(2) who, upon such oath, makes or subscribes to a statement;
if the statement is false and at the time of taking the oath, the person does not believe the statement to be true, shall be punished as a court-martial may direct.".

SEC. 5420. PAROLE VIOLATION.

Subchapter X of chapter 47 of title 10, United States Code, is amended by inserting after section 907 (article 107 of the Uniform Code of Military Justice), as amended by section 5419 of this Act, the following new section (article):

"§ 907a. Art. 107a. Parole violation

"Any person subject to this chapter—

"(1) who, having been a prisoner as the result of a court-martial conviction or other criminal proceeding, is on parole with conditions; and

"(2) who violates the conditions of parole;
shall be punished as a court-martial may direct.".

SEC. 5421. WRONGFUL TAKING, OPENING, ETC. OF MAIL MATTER.

Subchapter X of chapter 47 of title 10, United States Code, is amended by inserting after section 909 (article 109 of the Uniform Code of Military Justice), the following new section (article):

"§ 909a. Art. 109a. Mail matter: wrongful taking, opening, etc.

"(a) TAKING.—Any person subject to this chapter who, with the intent to obstruct the correspondence of, or to pry into the business or secrets of, any person or organization, wrongfully takes mail matter before the mail matter is delivered to or received by the addressee shall be punished as a court-martial may direct.

"(b) OPENING, SECRETING, DESTROYING, STEALING.—Any person subject to this chapter who wrongfully opens, secretes, destroys, or steals mail matter before the mail matter is delivered to or received by the addressee shall be punished as a court-martial may direct.".

SEC. 5422. IMPROPER HAZARDING OF VESSEL OR AIRCRAFT.

Section 910 of title 10, United States Code (article 110 of the Uniform Code of Military Justice), is amended to read as follows:

"§ 910. Art. 110. Improper hazarding of vessel or aircraft

"(a) WILLFUL AND WRONGFUL HAZARDING.—Any person subject to this chapter who, willfully and wrongfully, hazards or suffers to be hazarded any vessel or aircraft of the armed forces shall be punished by death or such other punishment as a court-martial may direct.

"(b) NEGLIGENT HAZARDING.—Any person subject to this chapter who negligently hazards or suffers to be hazarded any vessel or aircraft of the armed forces shall be punished as a court-martial may direct.".

SEC. 5423. LEAVING SCENE OF VEHICLE ACCIDENT.

Subchapter X of chapter 47 of title 10, United States Code, is amended by inserting after section 910 (article 110 of the Uniform Code of Military Justice), as amended by section 5422 of this Act, the following new section (article):

"§911. Art. 111. Leaving scene of vehicle accident

"(a) DRIVER.—Any person subject to this chapter—

"(1) who is the driver of a vehicle that is involved in an accident that results in personal injury or property damage; and

"(2) who wrongfully leaves the scene of the accident—

"(A) without providing assistance to an injured person; or

"(B) without providing personal identification to others involved in the accident or to appropriate authorities;

shall be punished as a court-martial may direct.

"(b) SENIOR PASSENGER.—Any person subject to this chapter—

"(1) who is a passenger in a vehicle that is involved in an accident that results in personal injury or property damage;

"(2) who is the superior commissioned or noncommissioned officer of the driver of the vehicle or is the commander of the vehicle; and

"(3) who wrongfully and unlawfully orders, causes, or permits the driver to leave the scene of the accident—

"(A) without providing assistance to an injured person; or

"(B) without providing personal identification to others involved in the accident or to appropriate authorities;

shall be punished as a court-martial may direct.".

SEC. 5424. DRUNKENNESS AND OTHER INCAPACITATION OFFENSES.

Section 912 of title 10, United States Code (article 112 of the Uniform Code of Military Justice), is amended to read as follows:

"§912. Art. 112. Drunkenness and other incapacitation offenses

"(a) DRUNK ON DUTY.—Any person subject to this chapter who is drunk on duty shall be punished as a court-martial may direct.

"(b) INCAPACITATION FOR DUTY FROM DRUNKENNESS OR DRUG USE.—Any person subject to this chapter who, as a result of indulgence in any alcoholic beverage or any drug, is incapacitated for the proper performance of duty shall be punished as a court-martial may direct.

"(c) DRUNK PRISONER.—Any person subject to this chapter who is a prisoner and, while in such status, is drunk shall be punished as a court-martial may direct.".

SEC. 5425. LOWER BLOOD ALCOHOL CONTENT LIMITS FOR CONVICTION OF DRUNKEN OR RECKLESS OPERATION OF VEHICLE, AIRCRAFT, OR VESSEL.

Subsection (b)(3) of section 913 of title 10, United States Code (article 113 of the Uniform Code of Military Justice), as transferred and redesignated by section 5401(9) of this Act, is amended—

(1) by striking "0.10 grams" both places it appears and inserting "0.08 grams"; and

(2) by adding at the end the following new sentence: "The Secretary may by regulation prescribe limits that are lower than the limits specified in the preceding sentence, if such lower lim-

its are based on scientific developments, as reflected in Federal law of general applicability.".

SEC. 5426. ENDANGERMENT OFFENSES.

Section 914 of title 10, United States Code (article 114 of the Uniform Code of Military Justice), is amended to read as follows:

"§914. Art. 114. Endangerment offenses

"(a) RECKLESS ENDANGERMENT.—Any person subject to this chapter who engages in conduct that—

"(1) is wrongful and reckless or is wanton; and

"(2) is likely to produce death or grievous bodily harm to another person;

shall be punished as a court-martial may direct.

"(b) DUELING.—Any person subject to this chapter—

"(1) who fights or promotes, or is concerned in or connives at fighting, a duel; or

"(2) who, having knowledge of a challenge sent or about to be sent, fails to report the facts promptly to the proper authority;

shall be punished as a court-martial may direct.

"(c) FIREARM DISCHARGE, ENDANGERING HUMAN LIFE.—Any person subject to this chapter who, willfully and wrongly, discharges a firearm, under circumstances such as to endanger human life shall be punished as a court-martial may direct.

"(d) CARRYING CONCEALED WEAPON.—Any person subject to this chapter who unlawfully carries a dangerous weapon concealed on or about his person shall be punished as a court-martial may direct.".

SEC. 5427. COMMUNICATING THREATS.

Section 915 of title 10, United States Code (article 115 of the Uniform Code of Military Justice), is amended to read as follows:

"§915. Art. 115. Communicating threats

"(a) COMMUNICATING THREATS GENERALLY.—Any person subject to this chapter who wrongfully communicates a threat to injure the person, property, or reputation of another shall be punished as a court-martial may direct.

"(b) COMMUNICATING THREAT TO USE EXPLOSIVE, ETC.—Any person subject to this chapter who wrongfully communicates a threat to injure the person or property of another by use of (1) an explosive, (2) a weapon of mass destruction, (3) a biological or chemical agent, substance, or weapon, or (4) a hazardous material, shall be punished as a court-martial may direct.

"(c) COMMUNICATING FALSE THREAT CONCERNING USE OF EXPLOSIVE, ETC.—Any person subject to this chapter who maliciously communicates a false threat concerning injury to the person or property of another by use of (1) an explosive, (2) a weapon of mass destruction, (3) a biological or chemical agent, substance, or weapon, or (4) a hazardous material, shall be punished as a court-martial may direct. As used in the preceding sentence, the term 'false threat' means a threat that, at the time the threat is communicated, is known to be false by the person communicating the threat.".

SEC. 5428. TECHNICAL AMENDMENT RELATING TO MURDER.

Section 918(4) of title 10, United States Code (article 118(4) of the Uniform Code of Military Justice), is amended by striking "forcible sodomy,".

SEC. 5429. CHILD ENDANGERMENT.

Subchapter X of chapter 47 of title 10, United States Code, is amended by inserting after section 919a (article 119a of the Uniform Code of Military Justice), the following new section (article):

"§919b. Art. 119b. Child endangerment

"Any person subject to this chapter—

"(1) who has a duty for the care of a child under the age of 16 years; and

"(2) who, through design or culpable negligence, endangers the child's mental or physical health, safety, or welfare;

shall be punished as a court-martial may direct.".

SEC. 5430. RAPE AND SEXUAL ASSAULT OFFENSES.

(a) OFFENSE OF SEXUAL ASSAULT.—Subsection (b) of section 920 of title 10, United States Code (article 120 of the Uniform Code of Military Justice), is amended—

(1) in paragraph (1)—

(A) by striking subparagraph (B); and

(B) by redesignating subparagraphs (C) and (D) as subparagraphs (B) and (C), respectively; and

(2) in paragraph (2)—

(A) by striking "another person when" and inserting "another person—

"(B) when"; and

(B) by inserting before subparagraph (B), as added by subparagraph (A) of this paragraph, the following new subparagraph:

"(A) without the consent of the other person; or".

(b) DEFINITIONS.—

(1) SEXUAL ACT.—Paragraph (1) of subsection (g) of such section (article) is amended to read as follows:

"(1) SEXUAL ACT.—The term 'sexual act' means—

"(A) the penetration, however slight, of the penis into the vulva or anus or mouth;

"(B) contact between the mouth and the penis, vulva, scrotum, or anus; or

"(C) the penetration, however slight, of the vulva or penis or anus of another by any part of the body or any object, with an intent to abuse, humiliate, harass, or degrade any person or to arouse or gratify the sexual desire of any person.".

(2) SEXUAL CONTACT.—Paragraph (2) of such subsection is amended to read as follows:

"(2) SEXUAL CONTACT.—The term 'sexual contact' means touching, or causing another person to touch, either directly or through the clothing, the vulva, penis, scrotum, anus, groin, brest, inner thigh, or buttocks of any person, with an intent to abuse, humiliate, harass, or degrade any person or to arouse or gratify the sexual desire of any person. Touching may be accomplished by any part of the body or an object.".

(3) REPEAL OF DEFINITION OF BODILY HARM.—Such subsection is further amended—

(A) by striking paragraph (3); and

(B) by redesignating paragraphs (4) through (8) as paragraphs (3) through (7), respectively.

(4) CONSENT.—Paragraph (7) of such subsection, as redesignated by paragraph (3)(B) of this subsection, is further amended—

(A) in subparagraph (A)—

(i) in the second sentence, by striking "or submission resulting from the use of force, threat of force, or placing another in fear";

(ii) by inserting after the second sentence, as amended by clause (i) of this subparagraph the following new sentence: "Submission resulting from the use of force, threat of force, or placing another person in fear also does not constitute consent."; and

(iii) in the last sentence, by striking "shall not" and inserting "does not";

(B) in subparagraph (B), by striking "subparagraph (B) or (D)" and inserting "subparagraph (B) or (C)"; and

(C) in subparagraph (C)—

(i) by striking the first sentence; and

(ii) in the last sentence, by striking ", or whether" and all that follows and inserting a period.

(5) INCAPABLE OF CONSENTING.—Such subsection is further amended by adding at the end the following new paragraph (8):

"(8) INCAPABLE OF CONSENTING.—The term 'incapable of consenting' means the person is—

"(A) incapable of appraising the nature of the conduct at issue; or

"(B) physically incapable of declining participation in, or communicating unwillingess to engage in, the sexual act at issue.''.

"(c) RAPE AND SEXUAL ASSAULT OF A CHILD.—Subsection (h)(1) of section 920b of title 10, United States Code (article 120b of the Uniform Code of Military Justice), is amended by inserting before the period at the end the following: '', except that the term 'sexual act' also includes the intentional touching, not through the clothing, of the genitalia of another person who has not attained the age of 16 years with an intent to abuse, humiliate, harass, degrade, or arouse or gratify the sexual desire of any person''.

SEC. 5431. DEPOSIT OF OBSCENE MATTER IN THE MAIL.

Subchapter X of chapter 47 of title 10, United States Code, is amended by inserting after section 920 (article 120 of the Uniform Code of Military Justice), the following new section (article):

"§920a. Art. 120a. Mails: deposit of obscene matter

"Any person subject to this chapter who, wrongfully and knowingly, deposits obscene matter for mailing and delivery shall be punished as a court-martial may direct.''.

SEC. 5432. FRAUDULENT USE OF CREDIT CARDS, DEBIT CARDS, AND OTHER ACCESS DEVICES.

Subchapter X of chapter 47 of title 10, United States Code, is amended by inserting after section 921 (article 121 of the Uniform Code of Military Justice), the following new section (article):

"§921a. Art. 121a. Fraudulent use of credit cards, debit cards, and other access devices

"(a) IN GENERAL.—Any person subject to this chapter who, knowingly and with intent to defraud, uses—

"(1) a stolen credit card, debit card, or other access device;

"(2) a revoked, cancelled, or otherwise invalid credit card, debit card, or other access device; or

"(3) a credit card, debit card, or other access device without the authorization of a person whose authorization is required for such use;

to obtain money, property, services, or anything else of value shall be punished as a court-martial may direct.

"(b) ACCESS DEVICE DEFINED.—In this section (article), the term 'access device' has the meaning given that term in section 1029 of title 18.''.

SEC. 5433. FALSE PRETENSES TO OBTAIN SERVICES.

Subchapter X of chapter 47 of title 10, United States Code, is amended by inserting after section 921a (article 121a of the Uniform Code of Military Justice), as added by section 5432 of this Act, the following new section (article):

"§921b. Art. 121b. False pretenses to obtain services

"Any person subject to this chapter who, with intent to defraud, knowingly uses false pretenses to obtain services shall be punished as a court-martial may direct.''.

SEC. 5434. ROBBERY.

Section 922 of title 10, United States Code (article 122 of the Uniform Code of Military Justice), is amended to read as follows:

"§922. Art. 122. Robbery

"Any person subject to this chapter who takes anything of value from the person or in the presence of another, against his will, by means of force or violence or fear of immediate or future injury to his person or property or to the person or property of a relative or member of his family or of anyone in his company at the time of the robbery, is guilty of robbery and shall be punished as a court-martial may direct.''.

SEC. 5435. RECEIVING STOLEN PROPERTY.

Subchapter X of chapter 47 of title 10, United States Code, is amended by inserting after section 922 (article 122 of the Uniform Code of Mili-

tary Justice), as amended by section 5434 of this Act, the following new section (article):

"§922a. Art. 122a. Receiving stolen property

"Any person subject to this chapter who wrongfully receives, buys, or conceals stolen property, knowing the property to be stolen property, shall be punished as a court-martial may direct.''.

SEC. 5436. OFFENSES CONCERNING GOVERNMENT COMPUTERS.

Subchapter X of chapter 47 of title 10, United States Code, is amended by inserting after section 922a (article 122a of the Uniform Code of Military Justice), as added by section 5435 of this Act, the following new section (article):

"§923. Art. 123. Offenses concerning Government computers

"(a) IN GENERAL.—Any person subject to this chapter who—

"(1) knowingly accesses a Government computer, with an unauthorized purpose, and by doing so obtains classified information, with reason to believe such information could be used to the injury of the United States, or to the advantage of any foreign nation, and intentionally communicates, delivers, transmits, or causes to be communicated, delivered, or transmitted such information to any person not entitled to receive it;

"(2) intentionally accesses a Government computer, with an unauthorized purpose, and thereby obtains classified or other protected information from any Government computer; or

"(3) knowingly causes the transmission of a program, information, code, or command, and as a result of such conduct, intentionally causes damage without authorization to a Government computer;

shall be punished as a court-martial may direct.

"(b) DEFINITIONS.—In this section:

"(1) The term 'computer' has the meaning given that term in section 1030 of title 18.

"(2) The term 'Government computer' means a computer owned or operated by or on behalf of the United States Government.

"(3) The term 'damage' has the meaning given that term in section 1030 of title 18.''.

SEC. 5437. BRIBERY.

Subchapter X of chapter 47 of title 10, United States Code, is amended by inserting after section 924 (article 124 of the Uniform Code of Military Justice), as transferred and redesignated by section 5401(14) of this Act, the following new section (article):

"§924a. Art. 124a. Bribery

"(a) ASKING, ACCEPTING, OR RECEIVING THING OF VALUE.—Any person subject to this chapter—

"(1) who occupies an official position or who has official duties; and

"(2) who wrongfully asks, accepts, or receives a thing of value with the intent to have the person's decision or action influenced with respect to an official matter in which the United States is interested;

shall be punished as a court-martial may direct.

"(b) PROMISING, OFFERING, OR GIVING THING OF VALUE.—Any person subject to this chapter who wrongfully promises, offers, or gives a thing of value to another person, who occupies an official position or who has official duties, with the intent to influence the decision or action of the other person with respect to an official matter in which the United States is interested, shall be punished as a court-martial may direct.''.

SEC. 5438. GRAFT.

Subchapter X of chapter 47 of title 10, United States Code, is amended by inserting after section 924a (article 124a of the Uniform Code of Military Justice), as added by section 5437 of this Act, the following new section (article):

"§924b. Art. 124b. Graft

"(a) ASKING, ACCEPTING, OR RECEIVING THING OF VALUE.—Any person subject to this chapter—

"(1) who occupies an official position or who has official duties; and

"(2) who wrongfully asks, accepts, or receives a thing of value as compensation for or in recognition of services rendered or to be rendered by the person with respect to an official matter in which the United States is interested;

shall be punished as a court-martial may direct.

"(b) PROMISING, OFFERING, OR GIVING THING OF VALUE.—Any person subject to this chapter who wrongfully promises, offers, or gives a thing of value to another person, who occupies an official position or who has official duties, as compensation for or in recognition of services rendered or to be rendered by the other person with respect to an official matter in which the United States is interested, shall be punished as a court-martial may direct.''.

SEC. 5439. KIDNAPPING.

Section 925 of title 10, United States Code (article 125 of the Uniform Code of Military Justice), is amended to read as follows:

"§925. Art. 125. Kidnapping

"Any person subject to this chapter who wrongfully—

"(1) seizes, confines, inveigles, decoys, or carries away another person; and

"(2) holds the other person against that person's will;

shall be punished as a court-martial may direct.''.

SEC. 5440. ARSON; BURNING PROPERTY WITH INTENT TO DEFRAUD.

Section 926 of title 10, United States Code (article 126 of the Uniform Code of Military Justice), is amended to read as follows:

"§926. Art. 126. Arson; burning property with intent to defraud

"(a) AGGRAVATED ARSON.—Any person subject to this chapter who, willfully and maliciously, burns or sets on fire an inhabited dwelling, or any other structure, movable or immovable, wherein, to the knowledge of that person, there is at the time a human being, is guilty of aggravated arson and shall be punished as a court-martial may direct.

"(b) SIMPLE ARSON.—Any person subject to this chapter who, willfully and maliciously, burns or sets fire to the property of another is guilty of simple arson and shall be punished as a court-martial may direct.

"(c) BURNING PROPERTY WITH INTENT TO DEFRAUD.—Any person subject to this chapter who, willfully, maliciously, and with intent to defraud, burns or sets fire to any property shall be punished as a court-martial may direct.''.

SEC. 5441. ASSAULT.

Section 928 of title 10, United States Code (article 128 of the Uniform Code of Military Justice), is amended to read as follows:

"§928. Art. 128. Assault

"(a) ASSAULT.—Any person subject to this chapter who, unlawfully and with force or violence—

"(1) attempts to do bodily harm to another person;

"(2) offers to do bodily harm to another person; or

"(3) does bodily harm to another person;

is guilty of assault and shall be punished as a court-martial may direct.

"(b) AGGRAVATED ASSAULT.—Any person subject to this chapter—

"(1) who, with the intent to do bodily harm, offers to do bodily harm with a dangerous weapon; or

"(2) who, in committing an assault, inflicts substantial bodily harm, or grievous bodily harm on another person;

is guilty of aggravated assault and shall be punished as a court-martial may direct.

"(c) ASSAULT WITH INTENT TO COMMIT SPECIFIED OFFENSES.—

"(1) IN GENERAL.—Any person subject to this chapter who commits assault with intent to commit an offense specified in paragraph (2) shall be punished as a court-martial may direct.

"(2) OFFENSES SPECIFIED.—The offenses referred to in paragraph (1) are murder, voluntary manslaughter, rape, sexual assault, rape of a child, sexual assault of a child, robbery, arson, burglary, and kidnapping.".

SEC. 5442. BURGLARY AND UNLAWFUL ENTRY.

Section 929 of title 10, United States Code (article 129 of the Uniform Code of Military Justice), and section 929a of such title (article 129a), as redesignated by section 5401(10) of this Act, are amended to read as follows:

"§ 929. Art. 129. Burglary; unlawful entry

"(a) BURGLARY.—Any person subject to this chapter who, with intent to commit an offense under this chapter, breaks and enters the building or structure of another shall be punished as a court-martial may direct.

"(b) UNLAWFUL ENTRY.—Any person subject to this chapter who unlawfully enters—

"(1) the real property of another; or

"(2) the personal property of another which amounts to a structure usually used for habitation or storage;

shall be punished as a court-martial may direct.".

SEC. 5443. STALKING.

Section 930 of title 10, United States Code (article 130 of the Uniform Code of Military Justice), as transferred and redesignated by section 5401(11) of this Act, is amended to read as follows:

"§ 930. Art. 130. Stalking

"(a) IN GENERAL.—Any person subject to this chapter—

"(1) who wrongfully engages in a course of conduct directed at a specific person that would cause a reasonable person to fear death or bodily harm, including sexual assault, to himself or herself, to a member of his or her immediate family, or to his or her intimate partner;

"(2) who has knowledge, or should have knowledge, that the specific person will be placed in reasonable fear of death or bodily harm, including sexual assault, to himself or herself, to a member of his or her immediate family, or to his or her intimate partner; and

"(3) whose conduct induces reasonable fear in the specific person of death or bodily harm, including sexual assault, to himself or herself, to a member of his or her immediate family, or to his or her intimate partner;

is guilty of stalking and shall be punished as a court-martial may direct.

"(b) DEFINITIONS.—In this section:

"(1) The term 'conduct' means conduct of any kind, including use of surveillance, the mails, an interactive computer service, an electronic communication service, or an electronic communication system.

"(2) The term 'course of conduct' means—

"(A) a repeated maintenance of visual or physical proximity to a specific person;

"(B) a repeated conveyance of verbal threat, written threats, or threats implied by conduct, or a combination of such threats, directed at or toward a specific person; or

"(C) a pattern of conduct composed of repeated acts evidencing a continuity of purpose.

"(3) The term 'repeated', with respect to conduct, means two or more occasions of such conduct.

"(4) The term 'immediate family', in the case of a specific person, means—

"(A) that person's spouse, parent, brother or sister, child, or other person to whom he or she stands in loco parentis; or

"(B) any other person living in his or her household and related to him or her by blood or marriage.

"(5) The term 'intimate partner', in the case of a specific person, means—

"(A) a former spouse of the specific person, a person who shares a child in common with the specific person, or a person who cohabits with or has cohabited as a spouse with the specific person; or

"(B) a person who has been in a social relationship of a romantic or intimate nature with the specific person, as determined by the length of the relationship, the type of relationship, and the frequency of interaction between the persons involved in the relationship.".

SEC. 5444. SUBORNATION OF PERJURY.

Subchapter X of chapter 47 of title 10, United States Code, is amended by inserting after section 931 (article 131 of the Uniform Code of Military Justice), the following new section (article):

"§ 931a. Art. 131a. Subornation of perjury

"(a) IN GENERAL.—Any person subject to this chapter who induces and procures another person—

"(1) to take an oath; and

"(2) to falsely testify, depose, or state upon such oath;

shall, if the conditions specified in subsection (b) are satisfied, be punished as a court-martial may direct.

"(b) CONDITIONS.—The conditions referred to in subsection (a) are the following:

"(1) The oath is administered with respect to a matter for which such oath is required or authorized by law.

"(2) The oath is administered by a person having authority to do so.

"(3) Upon the oath, the other person willfully makes or subscribes a statement.

"(4) The statement is material.

"(5) The statement is false.

"(6) When the statement is made or subscribed, the person subject to this chapter and the other person do not believe that the statement is true.".

SEC. 5445. OBSTRUCTING JUSTICE.

Subchapter X of chapter 47 of title 10, United States Code, is amended by inserting after section 931a (article 131a of the Uniform Code of Military Justice), as added by section 5444 of this Act, the following new section (article):

"§ 931b. Art. 131b. Obstructing justice

"Any person subject to this chapter who engages in conduct in the case of a certain person against whom the accused had reason to believe there were or would be criminal or disciplinary proceedings pending, with intent to influence, impede, or otherwise obstruct the due administration of justice shall be punished as a court-martial may direct.".

SEC. 5446. MISPRISION OF SERIOUS OFFENSE.

Subchapter X of chapter 47 of title 10, United States Code, is amended by inserting after section 931b (article 131b of the Uniform Code of Military Justice), as added by section 5445 of this Act, the following new section (article):

"§ 931c. Art. 131c. Misprision of serious offense

"Any person subject to this chapter—

"(1) who knows that another person has committed a serious offense; and

"(2) wrongfully conceals the commission of the offense and fails to make the commission of the offense known to civilian or military authorities as soon as possible;

shall be punished as a court-martial may direct.".

SEC. 5447. WRONGFUL REFUSAL TO TESTIFY.

Subchapter X of chapter 47 of title 10, United States Code, is amended by inserting after section 931c (article 131c of the Uniform Code of Military Justice), as added by section 5446 of this Act, the following new section (article):

"§ 931d. Art. 131d. Wrongful refusal to testify

"Any person subject to this chapter who, in the presence of a court-martial, a board of officers, a military commission, a court of inquiry, a preliminary hearing, or an officer taking a deposition, of or for the United States, wrongfully refuses to qualify as a witness or to answer a question after having been directed to do so by the person presiding shall be punished as a court-martial may direct.".

SEC. 5448. PREVENTION OF AUTHORIZED SEIZURE OF PROPERTY.

Subchapter X of chapter 47 of title 10, United States Code, is amended by inserting after section 931d (article 131d of the Uniform Code of Military Justice), as added by section 5447 of this Act, the following new section (article):

"§ 931e. Art. 131e. Prevention of authorized seizure of property

"Any person subject to this chapter who, knowing that one or more persons authorized to make searches and seizures are seizing, are about to seize, or are endeavoring to seize property, destroys, removes, or otherwise disposes of the property with intent to prevent the seizure thereof shall be punished as a court-martial may direct.".

SEC. 5449. WRONGFUL INTERFERENCE WITH ADVERSE ADMINISTRATIVE PROCEEDING.

Subchapter X of chapter 47 of title 10, United States Code, is amended by inserting after section 931f (article 131f of the Uniform Code of Military Justice), as transferred and redesignated by section 5401(3) of this Act, the following new section (article):

"§ 931g. Art. 131g. Wrongful interference with adverse administrative proceeding

"Any person subject to this chapter who, having reason to believe that an adverse administrative proceeding is pending against any person subject to this chapter, wrongfully acts with the intent—

"(1) to influence, impede, or obstruct the conduct of the proceeding; or

"(2) otherwise to obstruct the due administration of justice;

shall be punished as a court-martial may direct.".

SEC. 5450. RETALIATION.

Subchapter X of chapter 47 of title 10, United States Code, is amended by inserting after section 931g (article 131g of the Uniform Code of Military Justice), as added by section 5449 of this Act, the following new section (article):

"§ 932. Art. 132. Retaliation

"(a) IN GENERAL.—Any person subject to this chapter who, with the intent to retaliate against any person for reporting or planning to report a criminal offense, or making or planning to make a protected communication, or with the intent to discourage any person from reporting a criminal offense or making or planning to make a protected communication—

"(1) wrongfully takes or threatens to take an adverse personnel action against any person; or

"(2) wrongfully withholds or threatens to withhold a favorable personnel action with respect to any person;

shall be punished as a court-martial may direct.

"(b) DEFINITIONS.—In this section:

"(1) The term 'protected communication' means the following:

"(A) A lawful communication to a Member of Congress or an Inspector General.

"(B) A communication to a covered individual or organization in which a member of the armed forces complains of, or discloses information that the member reasonably believes constitutes evidence of, any of the following:

"(i) A violation of law or regulation, including a law or regulation prohibiting sexual harassment or unlawful discrimination.

''(ii) Gross mismanagement, a gross waste of funds, an abuse of authority, or a substantial and specific danger to public health or safety.

''(2) The term 'Inspector General' has the meaning given that term in section 1034(h) of this title.

''(3) The term 'covered individual or organization' means any recipient of a communication specified in clauses (i) through (v) of section 1034(b)(1)(B) of this title.

''(4) The term 'unlawful discrimination' means discrimination on the basis of race, color, religion, sex, or national origin.''.

SEC. 5451. EXTRATERRITORIAL APPLICATION OF CERTAIN OFFENSES.

Section 934 of title 10, United States Code (article 134 of the Uniform Code of Military Justice), is amended by adding at the end the following new sentence: ''As used in the preceding sentence, the term 'crimes and offenses not capital' includes any conduct engaged in outside the United States, as defined in section 5 of title 18, that would constitute a crime or offense not capital if the conduct had been engaged in within the special maritime and territorial jurisdiction of the United States, as defined in section 7 of title 18.''.

SEC. 5452. TABLE OF SECTIONS.

The table of sections at the beginning of subchapter X of chapter 47 of title 10, United States Code (the Uniform Code of Military Justice), is amended to read as follows:

''SUBCHAPTER X—PUNITIVE ARTICLES

''Sec. Art.
''877. Art. 77. Principals.
''878. Art. 78. Accessory after the fact.
''879. Art. 79. Conviction of offense charged, lesser included offenses, and attempts.
''880. Art. 80. Attempts.
''881. Art. 81. Conspiracy.
''882. Art. 82. Soliciting commission of offenses.
''883. Art. 83. Malingering.
''884. Art. 84. Breach of medical quarantine.
''885. Art. 85. Desertion.
''886. Art. 86. Absence without leave.
''887. Art. 87. Missing movement; jumping from vessel.
''887a. Art. 87a. Resistence, flight, breach of arrest, and escape.
''887b. Art. 87b. Offenses against correctional custody and restriction.
''888. Art. 88. Contempt toward officials.
''889. Art. 89. Disrespect toward superior commissioned officer; assault of superior commissioned officer.
''890. Art. 90. Willfully disobeying superior commissioned officer.
''891. Art. 91. Insubordinate conduct toward warrant officer, noncommissioned officer, or petty officer.
''892. Art. 92. Failure to obey order or regulation.
''893. Art. 93. Cruelty and maltreatment.
''893a. Art. 93a. Prohibited activities with military recruit or trainee by person in position of special trust.
''894. Art. 94. Mutiny or sedition.
''895. Art. 95. Offenses by sentinel or lookout.
''895a. Art. 95a. Disrespect toward sentinel or lookout.
''896. Art. 96. Release of prisoner without authority; drinking with prisoner.
''897. Art. 97. Unlawful detention.
''898. Art. 98. Misconduct as prisoner.
''899. Art. 99. Misbehavior before the enemy.
''900. Art. 100. Subordinate compelling surrender.
''901. Art. 101. Improper use of countersign.
''902. Art. 102. Forcing a safeguard.
''903. Art. 103. Spies.
''903a. Art. 103a. Espionage.
''903b. Art. 103b. Aiding the enemy.
''904. Art. 104. Public records offenses.
''904a. Art. 104a. Fraudulent enlistment, appointment, or separation.
''904b. Art. 104b. Unlawful enlistment, appointment, or separation.
''905. Art. 105. Forgery.
''905a. Art. 105a. False or unauthorized pass offenses.
''906. Art. 106. Impersonation of officer, noncommissioned or petty officer, or agent or official.
''906a. Art. 106a. Wearing unauthorized insignia, decoration, badge, ribbon, device, or lapel button.
''907. Art. 107. False official statements; false swearing.
''907a. Art. 107a. Parole violation.
''908. Art. 108. Military property of the United States—Loss damage, destruction, or wrongful disposition.
''908a. Art. 108a. Captured or abandoned property.
''909. Art. 109. Property other than military property of the United States—Waste, spoilage, or destruction.
''909a. Art. 109a. Mail matter: wrongful taking, opening, etc..
''910. Art. 110. Improper hazarding of vessel or aircraft.
''911. Art. 111. Leaving scene of vehicle accident.
''912. Art. 112. Drunkenness and other incapacitation offenses.
''912a. Art. 112a. Wrongful use, possession, etc., of controlled substances.
''913. Art. 113. Drunken or reckless operation of a vehicle, aircraft, or vessel.
''914. Art. 114. Endangerment offenses.
''915. Art. 115. Communicating threats.
''916. Art. 116. Riot or breach of peace.
''917. Art. 117. Provoking speeches or gestures.
''918. Art. 118. Murder.
''919. Art. 119. Manslaughter.
''919a. Art. 119a. Death or injury of an unborn child.
''919b. Art. 119b. Child endangerment.
''920. Art. 120. Rape and sexual assault generally.
''920a. Art. 120a. Mails: deposit of obscene matter.
''920b. Art. 120b. Rape and sexual assault of a child.
''920c. Art. 120c. Other sexual misconduct.
''921. Art. 121. Larceny and wrongful appropriation.
''921a. Art. 121a. Fraudulent use of credit cards, debit cards, and other access devices.
''921b. Art. 121b. False pretenses to obtain services.
''922. Art. 122. Robbery.
''922a. Art. 122a. Receiving stolen property.
''923. Art. 123. Offenses concerning Government computers.
''923a. Art. 123a. Making, drawing, or uttering check, draft, or order without sufficient funds.
''924. Art. 124. Frauds against the United States.
''924a. Art. 124a. Bribery.
''924b. Art. 124b. Graft.
''925. Art. 125. Kidnapping.
''926. Art. 126. Arson; burning property with intent to defraud.
''927. Art. 127. Extortion.
''928. Art. 128. Assault.
''928a. Art 128a. Maiming.
''929. Art. 129. Burglary; unlawful entry.
''930. Art. 130. Stalking.
''931. Art. 131. Perjury.
''931a. Art. 131a. Subornation of perjury.
''931b. Art. 131b. Obstructing justice.
''931c. Art. 131c. Misprision of serious offense.
''931d. Art. 131d. Wrongful refusal to testify.
''931e. Art. 131e. Prevention of authorized seizure of property.
''931f. Art. 131f. Noncompliance with procedural rules.
''931g. Art. 131g. Wrongful interference with adverse administrative proceeding.
''932. Art. 132. Retaliation.
''933. Art. 133. Conduct unbecoming an officer and a gentleman.
''934. Art. 134. General article.''.

TITLE LXI—MISCELLANEOUS PROVISIONS

Sec. 5501. Technical amendments relating to courts of inquiry.
Sec. 5502. Technical amendment to Article 136.
Sec. 5503. Articles of Uniform Code of Military Justice to be explained to officers upon commissioning.
Sec. 5504. Military justice case management; data collection and accessibility.

SEC. 5501. TECHNICAL AMENDMENTS RELATING TO COURTS OF INQUIRY.

Section 935(c) of title 10, United States Code (article 135(c) of the Uniform Code of Military Justice), is amended—

(1) by striking ''(c) Any person'' and inserting ''(c)(1) Any person'';

(2) by designating the second and third sentences as paragraphs (2) and (3), respectively; and

(3) in paragraph (2), as so designated, by striking ''subject to this chapter or employed by the Department of Defense'' and inserting ''who is (A) subject to this chapter, (B) employed by the Department of Defense, or (C) with respect to the Coast Guard, employed by the department in which the Coast Guard is operating when it is not operating as a service in the Navy, and''.

SEC. 5502. TECHNICAL AMENDMENT TO ARTICLE 136.

Section 936 of title 10, United States Code (article 136 of the Uniform Code of Military Justice), is amended by striking the last five words in the section heading.

SEC. 5503. ARTICLES OF UNIFORM CODE OF MILITARY JUSTICE TO BE EXPLAINED TO OFFICERS UPON COMMISSIONING.

Section 937 of title 10, United States Code (article 137 of the Uniform Code of Military Justice), is amended—

(1) in subsection (a), by striking ''(a)(1) The sections of this title (articles of the Uniform Code of Military Justice)'' and inserting ''(a) ENLISTED MEMBERS.—(1) The sections (articles) of this chapter (the Uniform Code of Military Justice)'';

(2) by striking subsection (b); and

(3) by adding after subsection (a) the following new subsections:

''(b) OFFICERS.—(1) The sections (articles) of this chapter (the Uniform Code of Military Justice) specified in paragraph (2) shall be carefully explained to each officer at the time of (or within six months after)—

''(A) the initial entrance of the officer on active duty as an officer; or

''(B) the initial commissioning of the officer in a reserve component.

''(2) This subsection applies with respect to the sections (articles) specified in subsection (a)(3) and such other sections (articles) as the Secretary concerned may prescribe by regulation.

''(c) TRAINING FOR CERTAIN OFFICERS.—Under regulations prescribed by the Secretary concerned, officers with the authority to convene courts-martial or to impose non-judicial punishment shall receive periodic training regarding the purposes and administration of this chapter. Under regulations prescribed by the Secretary of Defense, officers assigned to duty in a joint command or a combatant command, who have such authority, shall receive additional specialized training regarding the purposes and administration of this chapter with respect to joint commands and the combatant commands.

''(d) AVAILABILITY AND MAINTENANCE OF TEXT.—The text of this chapter (the Uniform Code of Military Justice) and the text of the regulations prescribed by the President under this chapter shall be—

"(1) made available to a member on active duty or to a member of a reserve component, upon request by the member, for the member's personal examination; and

"(2) maintained by the Secretary of Defense in electronic formats that are updated periodically and made available on the Internet.".

SEC. 5504. MILITARY JUSTICE CASE MANAGEMENT; DATA COLLECTION AND ACCESSIBILITY.

(a) IN GENERAL.—Subchapter XI of chapter 47 of title 10, United States Code (the Uniform Code of Military Justice), is amended by adding at the end the following new section (article):

"§940a. Art. 140a. Case management; data collection and accessibility

"The Secretary of Defense shall prescribe uniform standards and criteria for conduct of each of the following functions at all stages of the military justice system, including pretrial, trial, post-trial, and appellate processes, using, insofar as practicable, the best practices of Federal and State courts:

"(1) Collection and analysis of data concerning substantive offenses and procedural matters in a manner that facilitates case management and decision making within the military justice system, and that enhances the quality of periodic reviews under section 946 of this title (article 146).

"(2) Case processing and management.

"(3) Timely, efficient, and accurate production and distribution of records of trial within the military justice system.

"(4) Facilitation of access to docket information, filings, and records, taking into consideration restrictions appropriate to judicial proceedings and military records.".

(b) EFFECTIVE DATES.—

(1) IN GENERAL.—Not later than 2 years after the date of the enactment of this Act, the Secretary of Defense shall carry out section 940a of title 10, United States Code (article 140a of the Uniform Code of Military Justice), as added by subsection (a).

(2) STANDARDS AND CRITERIA.—Not later than 4 years after the date of the enactment of this Act, the standards and criteria under section 940a of title 10, United States Code (article 140a of the Uniform Code of Military Justice), as added by subsection (a), shall take effect.

TITLE LXII—MILITARY JUSTICE REVIEW PANEL AND ANNUAL REPORTS

Sec. 5521. Military Justice Review Panel.
Sec. 5522. Annual reports.

SEC. 5521. MILITARY JUSTICE REVIEW PANEL.

Section 946 of title 10, United States Code (article 146 of the Uniform Code of Military Justice), is amended to read as follows:

"§946. Art. 146. Military Justice Review Panel

"(a) ESTABLISHMENT.—The Secretary of Defense shall establish a panel to conduct independent periodic reviews and assessments of the operation of this chapter. The panel shall be known as the 'Military Justice Review Panel' (in this section referred to as the 'Panel').

"(b) MEMBERS.—

"(1) NUMBER OF MEMBERS.—The Panel shall be composed of thirteen members.

"(2) APPOINTMENT OF CERTAIN MEMBERS.—Each of the following shall appoint one member of the Panel:

"(A) The Secretary of Defense (in consultation with the Secretary of the department in which the Coast Guard is operating when it is not operating as a service in the Navy).

"(B) The Attorney General.

"(C) The Judge Advocates General of the Army, Navy, Air Force, and Coast Guard, and the Staff Judge Advocate to the Commandant of the Marine Corps.

"(3) APPOINTMENT OF REMAINING MEMBERS BY SECRETARY OF DEFENSE.—The Secretary of Defense shall appoint the remaining members of the Panel, taking into consideration recommendations made by each of the following:

"(A) The chairman and ranking minority member of the Committee on Armed Services of the Senate and the Committee on Armed Services of the House of Representatives.

"(B) The Chief Justice of the United States.

"(C) The Chief Judge of the United States Court of Appeals for the Armed Forces.

"(c) QUALIFICATIONS OF MEMBERS.—The members of the Panel shall be appointed from among private United States citizens with expertise in criminal law, as well as appropriate and diverse experience in investigation, prosecution, defense, victim representation, or adjudication with respect to courts-martial, Federal civilian courts, or State courts.

"(d) CHAIR.—The Secretary of Defense shall select the chair of the Panel from among the members.

"(e) TERM; VACANCIES.—Each member shall be appointed for a term of eight years, and no member may serve more than one term. Any vacancy shall be filled in the same manner as the original appointment.

"(f) REVIEWS AND REPORTS.—

"(1) INITIAL REVIEW OF RECENT AMENDMENTS TO UCMJ.—During fiscal year 2020, the Panel shall conduct an initial review and assessment of the implementation of the amendments made to this chapter during the preceding five years. In conducting the initial review and assessment, the Panel may review such other aspects of the operation of this chapter as the Panel considers appropriate.

"(2) SENTENCING DATA COLLECTION AND REPORT.—During fiscal year 2020, the Panel shall gather and analyze sentencing data collected from each of the armed forces from general and special courts-martial applying offense-based sentencing under section 856 of this title (article 56). The sentencing data shall include the number of accused who request member sentencing and the number who request sentencing by military judge alone, the offenses which the accused were convicted of, and the resulting sentence for each offense in each case. The Judge Advocates General and the Staff Judge Advocate to the Commandant of the Marine Corps shall provide the sentencing data in the format and for the duration established by the chair of the Panel. Not later than October 31, 2020, the Panel shall submit to the Committees on Armed Services of the Senate and the House of Representatives through the Secretary of Defense a report setting forth the Panel's findings and recommendations on the need for sentencing reform.

"(3) PERIODIC COMPREHENSIVE REVIEWS.—During fiscal year 2024 and every eight years thereafter, the Panel shall conduct a comprehensive review and assessment of the operation of this chapter.

"(4) PERIODIC INTERIM REVIEWS.—During fiscal year 2028 and every eight years thereafter, the Panel shall conduct an interim review and assessment of such other aspects of the operation of this chapter as the Panel considers appropriate. In addition, at the request of the Secretary of Defense, the Panel may, at any time, review and assess other specific matters relating to the operation of this chapter.

"(5) REPORTS.—Not later than December 31 of each year during which the Panel conducts a review and assessment under this subsection, the Panel shall submit to the Committees on Armed Services of the Senate and the House of Representatives a report setting forth the results of such review and assessment, including the Panel's findings and recommendations.

"(g) HEARINGS.—The Panel may hold such hearings, sit and act at such times and places, take such testimony, and receive such evidence as the Panel considers appropriate to carry out its duties under this section.

"(h) INFORMATION FROM FEDERAL AGENCIES.—Upon request of the chair of the Panel, a department or agency of the Federal Government shall provide information that the Panel considers necessary to carry out its duties under this section.

"(i) ADMINISTRATIVE MATTERS.—

"(1) MEMBERS TO SERVE WITHOUT PAY.—Members of the Panel shall serve without pay, but shall be allowed travel expenses, including per diem in lieu of subsistence, at rates authorized for employees of agencies under subchapter I of chapter 57 of title 5, while away from their homes or regular places of business in the performance of services for the Panel.

"(2) STAFFING AND RESOURCES.—The Secretary of Defense shall provide staffing and resources to support the Panel.

"(j) FEDERAL ADVISORY COMMITTEE ACT.—The Federal Advisory Committee Act (5 U.S.C. App.) shall not apply to the Panel.".

SEC. 5522. ANNUAL REPORTS.

Subchapter XII of chapter 47 of title 10, United States Code (the Uniform Code of Military Justice), is amended by adding at the end the following new section (article):

"§946a. Art. 146a. Annual reports

"(a) COURT OF APPEALS FOR THE ARMED FORCES.—Not later than December 31 each year, the Court of Appeals for the Armed Forces shall submit a report that, with respect to the previous fiscal year, provides information on the number and status of completed and pending cases before the Court, and such other matters as the Court considers appropriate regarding the operation of this chapter.

"(b) SERVICE REPORTS.—Not later than December 31 each year, the Judge Advocates General and the Staff Judge Advocate to the Commandant of the Marine Corps shall each submit a report, with respect to the preceding fiscal year, containing the following:

"(1) Data on the number and status of pending cases.

"(2) Information on the appellate review process, including—

"(A) information on compliance with processing time goals;

"(B) descriptions of the circumstances surrounding cases in which general or special court-martial convictions were (i) reversed because of command influence or denial of the right to speedy review or (ii) otherwise remitted because of loss of records of trial or other administrative deficiencies; and

"(C) an analysis of each case in which a provision of this chapter was held unconstitutional.

"(3)(A) An explanation of measures implemented by the armed force concerned to ensure the ability of judge advocates—

"(i) to participate competently as trial counsel and defense counsel in cases under this chapter;

"(ii) to preside as military judges in cases under this chapter; and

"(iii) to perform the duties of Special Victims' Counsel, when so designated under section 1044e of this title.

"(B) The explanation under subparagraph (A) shall specifically identify the measures that focus on capital cases, national security cases, sexual assault cases, and proceedings of military commissions.

"(4) The independent views of each Judge Advocate General and of the Staff Judge Advocate to the Commandant of the Marine Corps as to the sufficiency of resources available within the respective armed forces, including total workforce, funding, training, and officer and enlisted grade structure, to capably perform military justice functions.

"(5) Such other matters regarding the operation of this chapter as may be appropriate.

"(c) SUBMISSION.—Each report under this section shall be submitted—

"(1) to the Committee on Armed Services of the Senate and the Committee on Armed Services of the House of Representatives; and

"(2) to the Secretary of Defense, the Secretaries of the military departments, and the Secretary of the department in which the Coast Guard is operating when it is not operating as a service in the Navy.".

TITLE LXIII—CONFORMING AMENDMENTS AND EFFECTIVE DATES

Sec. 5541. Amendments to UCMJ subchapter tables of sections.
Sec. 5542. Effective dates.

SEC. 5541. AMENDMENTS TO UCMJ SUBCHAPTER TABLES OF SECTIONS.

The tables of sections for the specified subchapters of chapter 47 of title 10, United States Code (the Uniform Code of Military Justice), are amended as follows:

(1) SUBCHAPTER II; APPREHENSION AND RESTRAINT.—The table of sections at the beginning of subchapter II is amended—

(A) by striking the item relating to section 810 (article 10) and inserting the following new item:

"810. Art. 10. Restraint of persons charged."; and

(B) by striking the item relating to section 812 (article 12) and inserting the following new item:

"812. Art. 12. Prohibition of confinement of members of the armed forces with enemy prisoners and certain others.".

(2) SUBCHAPTER V; COMPOSITION OF COURTS-MARTIAL.—The table of sections at the beginning of subchapter V is amended—

(A) by striking the item relating to section 825a (article 25a) and inserting the following new item:

"825. Art. 25a. Number of court-martial members in capital cases.";

(B) by inserting after the item relating to section 826 (article 26) the following new item:

"826a. Art. 26a. Military magistrates."; and

(C) by striking the item relating to section 829 (article 29) and inserting the following new item:

"829. Art. 29. Assembly and impaneling of members; detail of new members and military judges.".

(3) SUBCHAPTER VI; PRE-TRIAL PROCEDURE.—The table of sections at the beginning of subchapter VI is amended—

(A) by inserting after the item relating to section 830 (article 30) the following new item:

"830. Art. 30a. Certain proceedings conducted before referral."; and

(B) by striking the items relating to sections 832 through 835 (articles 32 through 35) and inserting the following new items:

"832. Art. 32. Preliminary hearing required before referral to general court-martial.
"833. Art. 33. Disposition guidance.
"834. Art. 34. Advice to convening authority before referral for trial.
"835. Art. 35. Service of charges; commencement of trial.".

(4) SUBCHAPTER VII; TRIAL PROCEDURE.—The table of sections at the beginning of subchapter VII is amended—

(A) by striking the items relating to sections 846 through 848 (articles 46 through 48) and inserting the following new items:

"846. Art. 46. Opportunity to obtain witnesses and other evidence in trials by court-martial.
"847. Art. 47. Refusal of person not subject to chapter to appear, testify, or produce evidence.
"848. Art. 48. Contempt.";

(B) by striking the item relating to section 850 (article 50) and inserting the following new item:

"850. Art. 50. Admissibility of sworn testimony from records of courts of inquiry.";

(C) by striking the items relating to section 852 (article 52) and inserting the following new item:

"852. Art. 52. Votes required for conviction, sentencing, and other matters."; and

(D) by striking the item relating to section 853 (article 53) and inserting the following new items:

"853. Art. 53. Findings and sentencing.
"853a. Art. 53a. Plea agreements.".

(5) SUBCHAPTER VIII; SENTENCES.—The table of sections at the beginning of subchapter VIII is amended—

(A) by striking the item relating to section 856 (article 56) and inserting the following new item:

"856. Art. 56. Sentencing."; and

(B) by striking the items relating to sections 856a and 857a (articles 56a and 57a).

(6) SUBCHAPTER IX; POST-TRIAL PROCEDURE.—The table of sections at the beginning of subchapter IX is amended—

(A) by striking the items relating to sections 860 and 61 (articles 60 and 61) and inserting the following new items:

"860. Art. 60. Post-trial processing in general and special courts-martial.
"860a. Art. 60a. Limited authority to act on sentence in specified post-trial circumstances.
"860b. Art. 60b. Post-trial actions in summary courts-martial and certain general and special courts-martial.
"860c. Art. 60c. Entry of judgment.
"861. Art. 61. Waiver of right to appeal; withdrawal of appeal.";

(B) by striking the items relating to sections 864 through 866 (articles 64 through 66) and inserting the following new items:

"864. Art. 64. Judge advocate review of finding of guilty in summary court-martial.
"865. Art. 65. Transmittal and review of records.
"866. Art. 66. Courts of Criminal Appeals.";

(C) by striking the item relating to section 869 (article 69) and inserting the following new item:

"869. Art. 69. Review by Judge Advocate General."; and

(D) by striking the item relating to section 871 (article 71).

(7) SUBCHAPTER XI; MISCELLANEOUS PROVISIONS.—The table of sections at the beginning of subchapter XI is amended—

(A) by striking the item relating to section 936 (article 136) and inserting the following new item:

"936. Art. 136. Authority to administer oaths."; and

(B) by inserting after the item relating to section 940 (article 140) the following new item:

"940a. Art. 140a. Case management; data collection and accessibility.".

(8) SUBCHAPTER XII; UNITED STATES COURT OF APPEALS FOR THE ARMED FORCES.—The table of sections at the beginning of subchapter XII is amended by striking the item relating to section 946 (article 146) and inserting the following new items:

"946. Art. 146. Military Justice Review Panel.
"946a. Art. 146a. Annual reports.".

SEC. 5542. EFFECTIVE DATES.

(a) IN GENERAL.—Except as otherwise provided in this division, the amendments made by this division shall take effect on the date designated by the President, which date shall be not later than the first day of the first calendar month that begins two years after the date of the enactment of this Act.

(b) IMPLEMENTING REGULATIONS.—The President shall prescribe regulations implementing this division and the amendments made by this division by not later than one year after the date of the enactment of this Act, except as otherwise provided in this division.

(c) APPLICABILITY.—

(1) IN GENERAL.—Subject to the provisions of this division and the amendments made by this division, the President shall prescribe in regulations whether, and to what extent, the amendments made by this division shall apply to a case in which one or more actions under chapter 47 of title 10, United States Code (the Uniform Code of Military Justice), have been taken before the effective date of such amendments.

(2) INAPPLICABILITY TO CASES IN WHICH CHARGES ALREADY REFERRED TO TRIAL ON EFFECTIVE DATE.—Except as otherwise provided in this division or the amendments made by this division, the amendments made by this division shall not apply to any case in which charges are referred to trial by court-martial before the effective date of such amendments. Proceedings in any such case shall be held in the same manner and with the same effect as if such amendments had not been enacted.

(3) PUNITIVE ARTICLE AMENDMENTS.—

(A) IN GENERAL.—The amendments made by title LX shall not apply to any offense committed before the effective date of such amendments.

(B) CONSTRUCTION.—Nothing in subparagraph (A) shall be construed to invalidate the prosecution of any offense committed before the effective date of such amendments.

(4) SENTENCING AMENDMENTS.—The regulations prescribing the authorized punishments for any offense committed before the effective date of the amendments made by title LVIII shall apply to the authorized punishments for the offense, as in effect at the time the offense is committed.

And the House agree to the same.
From the Committee on Armed Services, for consideration of the Senate bill and the House amendment, and modifications committed to conference:

MAC THORNBERRY,
J. RANDY FORBES,
JEFF MILLER of Florida,
JOE WILSON of South Carolina,
FRANK A. LOBIONDO,
MICHAEL R. TURNER,
JOHN KLINE,
MIKE ROGERS of Alabama,
TRENT FRANKS of Arizona,
K. MICHAEL CONAWAY,
DOUG LAMBORN,
ROBERT J. WITTMAN,
CHRISTOPHER P. GIBSON,
VICKY HARTZLER,
JOSEPH J. HECK of Nevada,
ELISE M. STEFANIK,
ADAM SMITH of Washington,
LORETTA SANCHEZ,
SUSAN A. DAVIS of California,
JAMES R. LANGEVIN,
RICK LARSEN of Washington,
JIM COOPER,
MADELEINE Z. BORDALLO,
JOE COURTNEY,
NIKI TSONGAS,
JOHN GARAMENDI,
HENRY C. "HANK" JOHNSON, JR.
JACKIE SPEIER,

SCOTT H. PETERS,
From the Permanent Select Committee on Intelligence, for consideration of matters within the jurisdiction of that committee under clause 11 of rule X:
DEVIN NUNES,
MIKE POMPEO,
From the Committee on Education and the Workforce, for consideration of secs. 571–74 and 578 of the Senate bill, and secs. 571, 573, 1098E, and 3512 of the House amendment, and modifications committed to conference:
TIM WALBERG,
BRETT GUTHRIE,
ROBERT C. "BOBBY" SCOTT,
From the Committee on Energy and Commerce, for consideration of secs. 3112 and 3123 of the Senate bill, and secs. 346, 601, 749, 1045, 1090, 1095, 1673, 3119A, and 3119C of the House amendment, and modifications committed to conference:
ROBERT E. LATTA,
BILL JOHNSON of Ohio,
From the Committee on Foreign Affairs, for consideration of secs. 828, 1006, 1007, 1050, 1056, 1089, 1204, 1211, 1221–23, 1231, 1232, 1242, 1243, 1247, 1252, 1253, 1255–58, 1260, 1263, 1264, 1271–73, 1276, 1283, 1301, 1302, 1531–33, and 1662 of the Senate bill, and secs. 926, 1011, 1013, 1083, 1084, 1098K, 1099B, 1099C, 1201, 1203, 1214, 1221–23, 1227, 1229, 1233, 1235, 1236, 1245, 1246, 1250, 1259A–59E, 1259J, 1259L, 1259P, 1259Q, 1259U, 1261, 1262, 1301–03, 1510, 1531–33, 1645, 1653, and 2804 of the House amendment, and modifications committed to conference:
EDWARD R. ROYCE,
LEE M. ZELDIN,
From the Committee on Homeland Security, for consideration of secs. 564 and 1091 of the Senate bill, and secs. 1097, 1869, 1869A, and 3510 of the House amendment, and modifications committed to conference:
MICHAEL T. MCCAUL,
DANIEL M. DONOVAN, Jr.,
BENNIE G. THOMPSON,
From the Committee on the Judiciary, for consideration of secs. 829J, 829K, 944, 963, 1006, 1023–25, 1053, 1093, 1283, 3303, and 3304 of the Senate bill, and secs. 598, 1090, 1098H, 1216,1261, and 3608 of the House amendment, and modifications committed to conference:
BOB GOODLATTE,
DARRELL E. ISSA,
From the Committee on Natural Resources, for consideration of secs. 601, 2825, subtitle D of title XXVIII, and sec. 2852 of the Senate bill, and secs. 312, 601, 1090, 1098H, 2837, 2839, 2839A, subtitle E of title XXVIII, secs. 2852, 2854, 2855, 2864–66, title XXX, secs. 3508, 7005, and title LXXIII of the House amendment, and modifications committed to conference:
PAUL COOK,
CRESENT HARDY,
From the Committee on Oversight and Government Reform, for consideration of secs. 339, 703, 819, 821, 829H, 829I, 861, 944, 1048, 1054, 1097, 1103–07, 1109–13, 1121, 1124, 1131–33, 1135 and 1136 of the Senate bill, and secs. 574, 603, 807, 832, 1048, 1088, 1095, 1098L, 1101,1102, 1104–06, 1108–11, 1113, 1259C, and 1631 of the House amendment, and modifications committed to conference:
JASON CHAFFETZ,
STEVE RUSSELL,
From the Committee on Science, Space, and Technology, for consideration of sec. 874 of the Senate bill and secs. 1605, 1673, and title XXXIII of the House amendment, and modifications committed to conference:
EDDIE BERNICE JOHNSON of Texas,
From the Committee on Small Business, for consideration of secs. 818, 838, 874, and 898 of the Senate bill, and title XVIII of the House amendment, and modifications committed to conference:
STEVE CHABOT,
STEPHEN KNIGHT,
From the Committee on Transportation and Infrastructure, for consideration of secs. 541, 562, 601, 961, 3302–07, 3501, and 3502 of the Senate bill, and secs. 343, 601, 731, 835, 1043, 1671, 3119C, 3501, 3504, 3509, 3512, and title XXXVI of the House amendment, and modifications committed to conference:
DUNCAN HUNTER,
DAVID ROUZER,
SEAN PATRICK MALONEY of New York,
From the Committee on Veterans' Affairs, for consideration of secs. 706, 755, and 1431 of the Senate bill, and secs. 741, 1421, and 1864 of the House amendment, and modifications committed to conference:
DAVID P. ROE of Tennessee,
MIKE BOST,
From the Committee on Ways and Means, for consideration of sec. 1271 of the Senate bill, and modifications committed to conference:
KEVIN BRADY of Texas,
DAVID G.REICHERT,
Managers on the Part of the House.

JOHN MCCAIN,
JAMES M. INHOFE,
JEFF SESSION,
ROGER F. WICKER,
KELLY AYOTTE,
DEB FISCHER,
TOM COTTON,
MIKE ROUNDS,
JONI ERNST,
THOM TILLIS,
DAN SULLIVAN,
LINDSEY GRAHAM,
TED CRUZ,
JACK REED,
BILL NELSON,
CLAIRE MCCASKILL,
JOE MANCHIN III,
JEANNE SHAHEEN,
RICHARD BLUMENTHAL,
JOE DONNELLY,
MAZIE K. HIRONO,
TIM KAINE,
ANGUS S. KING, Jr.
MARTIN HEINRICH,
Managers on the Part of the Senate.

JOINT EXPLANATORY STATEMENT OF THE COMMITTEE OF CONFERENCE

The managers on the part of the House and the Senate at the conference on the disagreeing votes of the two Houses on the amendment of the House to the bill (S. 2943), to authorize appropriations for fiscal year 2017 for military activities of the Department of Defense, for military construction, and for defense activities of the Department of Energy, to prescribe military personnel strengths for such fiscal year, and for other purposes, submit the following joint statement to the House and the Senate in explanation of the effect of the action agreed upon by the managers and recommended in the accompanying conference report:

The House amendment struck all of the Senate bill after the enacting clause and inserted a substitute text.

The Senate recedes from its disagreement to the amendment of the House with an amendment that is a substitute for the Senate bill and the House amendment. The differences between the Senate bill, the House amendment, and the substitute agreed to in conference are noted below, except for clerical corrections, conforming changes made necessary by agreements reached by the conferees, and minor drafting and clarifying changes.

Compliance with rules of the House of Representatives and Senate regarding earmarks and congressionally directed spending items

Pursuant to clause 9 of rule XXI of the Rules of the House of Representatives and Rule XLIV (3) of the Standing Rules of the Senate, neither this conference report nor the accompanying joint statement of managers contains any congressional earmarks, congressionally directed spending items, limited tax benefits, or limited tariff benefits, as defined in such rules.

Summary of discretionary authorizations and budget authority implication

The budget request for national defense discretionary programs within the jurisdiction of the Committees on Armed Services of the Senate and the House of Representatives for fiscal year 2017 was $608.0 billion. Of this amount, $524.0 billion was requested for base Department of Defense programs, $64.6 billion was requested for overseas contingency operations of which $5.1 billion was for base requirements, $19.2 billion was requested for national security programs in the Department of Energy and the Defense Nuclear Facilities Safety Board, and $0.2 billion for the Maritime Security Program.

The conference agreement would authorize $611.2 billion in fiscal year 2017, including $523.7 billion for base Department of Defense programs, $67.8 billion for overseas contingency operations of which $8.3 billion was for base requirements, $19.4 billion for national security programs in the Department of Energy and the Defense Nuclear Facilities Safety Board, and $0.3 billion for the Maritime Security Program.

The two tables preceding the detailed program adjustments in Division D of the accompanying joint statement of managers summarize the discretionary authorizations in the agreement and the equivalent budget authority levels for fiscal year 2017 defense programs.

Budgetary effects of this Act (sec. 4)

The Senate bill contained a provision (sec. 4) that would require that the budgetary effects of this Act be determined in accordance with the procedures established in the Statutory Pay-As-You-Go Act of 2010 (title I of Public Law 111–139).

The House amendment contained no similar provision.

The House recedes.

DIVISION A—DEPARTMENT OF DEFENSE AUTHORIZATIONS

TITLE I—PROCUREMENT

Subtitle A—Authorization of Appropriations

Authorization of appropriations (sec. 101)

The Senate bill contained a provision (sec. 101) that would authorize appropriations for procurement at the levels identified in section 4101 of division D of this Act.

The House amendment contained an identical provision (sec. 101).

The conference agreement includes this provision.

Subtitle B—Army Programs

Multiyear procurement authority for AH–64E Apache helicopters (sec. 111)

The Senate bill contained a provision (sec. 113) that would authorize the Secretary of the Army to enter into a multiyear contract for AH–64E Apache helicopters for fiscal years 2017 through 2021.

The House amendment contained an identical provision (sec. 111).

The conference agreement includes this provision.

Multiyear procurement authority for UH–60M and HH–60M Black Hawk helicopters (sec. 112)

The Senate bill contained a provision (sec. 112) that would authorize the Secretary of the Army to enter into a multiyear contract for UH–60M/HH–60M Black Hawk helicopters for fiscal years 2017 through 2021.

The House amendment contained a similar provision (sec. 111) that would authorize the Secretary of the Army to enter into one or more multiyear contracts for UH–60M and HH–60M Black Hawk helicopters beginning in fiscal year 2017, in accordance with section 2306b of title 10, United States Code.

The Senate recedes.

Distributed Common Ground System—Army increment 1 (sec. 113)

The Senate bill contained a provision (sec. 111) that would require the Secretary of the Army to improve and tailor training for units equipped with the Distributed Common Ground System—Army Increment 1. The provision would also require the Secretary of the Army to rapidly identify and field a commercially available capability that meets tactical requirements, can integrate at the tactical unit level, is substantially easier for personnel to use, and requires less training.

The House amendment contained no similar provision.

The House recedes with an amendment that would allow the Secretary of Defense to waive limitations if any adversely affect ongoing operational activities.

Assessment of certain capabilities of the Department of the Army (sec. 114)

The House amendment contained a provision (Sec. 113) that would require the Secretary of Defense, in consultation with the Secretary of the Army and the Chief of Staff of the Army, to provide an assessment to the congressional defense committees by April 1, 2017, of the ways, and associated costs, to reduce or eliminate shortfalls in responsiveness and capacity of the following capabilities:

(1) AH–64-equipped Attack Reconnaissance Battalion capacity to meet future needs;

(2) Air defense artillery (ADA) capacity, responsiveness, and the capability of short range ADA to meet existing and emerging threats (including unmanned aerial systems, cruise missiles, and manned aircraft), including an assessment of the potential for commercial-off-the-shelf solutions;

(3) Chemical, biological, radiological, and nuclear capabilities and modernization;

(4) Field artillery capabilities and the changes in doctrine and war plans resulting from the memorandum of the Secretary of Defense dated June 19, 2008, regarding the Department of Defense policy on cluster munitions and unintended harm to civilians, as well as required modernization or munition inventory shortfalls;

(5) Fuel distribution and water purification capacity and responsiveness;

(6) Army watercraft and port opening capabilities and responsiveness;

(7) Transportation (fuel, water, and cargo) capacity and responsiveness;

(8) Military police capacity; and

(9) Tactical mobility and tactical wheeled vehicle capacity and capability, to include adequacy of heavy equipment prime movers.

The Senate bill contained no similar provision.

The Senate recedes.

Subtitle C—Navy Programs

Determination of vessel delivery dates (sec. 121)

The Senate bill contained a provision (sec. 123) that would require the Secretary of the

Navy to deem ship delivery to occur at the completion of the final phase of construction.

The House amendment contained no similar provision.

The House recedes with an amendment that would clarify the determination of vessel delivery dates and include such determination in title 10, United States Code.

Incremental funding for detail design and construction of LHA replacement ship designated LHA 8 (sec. 122)

The Senate bill contained a provision (sec. 121) that would allow the Secretary of the Navy to enter into and incrementally fund a contract for detail design and construction of the LHA Replacement ship, designated LHA–8. Subject to the availability of appropriations, funds for payments under the contract may be provided from amounts authorized to be appropriated for the Department of Defense for Shipbuilding and Conversion, Navy, for fiscal years 2017 and 2018.

The House amendment contained a similar provision (sec. 123).

The House recedes.

Littoral Combat Ship (sec. 123)

The Senate bill contained a provision (sec. 122) that would require an annual report on Littoral Combat Ship (LCS) mission packages, a certification on the acquisition inventory objective of LCS mission packages, a limitation on the use of funds to revise or deviate from revision three of the LCS acquisition strategy, and a repeal of a reporting requirement related to LCS mission modules.

The House amendment contained a similar provision (sec. 126).

The House recedes with an amendment that would:

(1) Replace the limitation on the use of funds to revise or deviate from revision three of the LCS acquisition strategy with a requirement that the Secretary of Defense provide a certification to the congressional defense committees prior to a revision or deviation from revision three of the LCS acquisition strategy. The conferees' intent is this subsection be limited to those revisions or deviations that would result in a change to: the acquisition inventory objective of 40 ships, annual procurement quantities through fiscal year 2021, or the planned down-select to a single LCS prime contractor no later than fiscal year 2019; and

(2) Prohibit the Secretary of Defense from selecting a single contractor for the LCS or frigate program unless such selection is conducted using competitive procedures, performed for the purpose of constructing a frigate class ship, and occurs only after a frigate design has reached sufficient maturity and completeness.

Limitation on use of sole-source shipbuilding contracts for certain vessels (sec. 124)

The Senate bill contained a provision (sec. 124) that would prohibit funds from being used to enter into or prepare to enter into sole source contracts for one or more Joint High Speed Vessels (JHSV) or Expeditionary Fast Transports (EPF) unless the Secretary of the Navy submits to the congressional defense committees a certification and a report.

The House amendment contained no similar provision.

The House recedes.

Limitation on availability of funds for the Advanced Arresting Gear Program (sec. 125)

The Senate bill contained a provision (sec. 125) that would limit funds for the Advanced

Arresting Gear (AAG) to be installed on USS Enterprise (CVN–80) until the Secretary of Defense submits to the congressional defense committees the report described under section 2433a(c)(2) of title 10, United States Code, for the AAG program.

The provision would also direct the Secretary of Defense to deem the 2009 AAG acquisition program baseline as the original baseline estimate and to execute the requirements of sections 2433 and 2433a of title 10, United States Code, as though the Department had submitted a Selected Acquisition Report with this baseline estimate included. This action would provide clarity on the original baseline estimate, which is a necessary element of a Nunn-McCurdy review.

The House amendment contained no similar provision.

The House recedes with an amendment that would:

(1) Require the Navy to report on the AAG program in accordance with section 2432 of title 10, United States Code, which deals with Selected Acquisition Reports, instead of reporting in accordance with section 2433a(c) (2) which deals with critical cost growth in major defense acquisition programs;

(2) Add a limitation of funds for the AAG to be installed on USS John F. Kennedy (CVN–79) unless the Milestone Decision Authority (MDA) determines that AAG should be installed on that ship, and the MDA submits notification of such determination to the congressional defense committees;

(3) Establish the original baseline estimate for the AAG program and require the Secretary of Defense to execute the requirements of sections 2433 and 2433a of title 10, United States Code, but exempt the Department from having to rescind the milestone decision approval for the AAG program during the review required by those provisions; and

(4) During the review required by section 2433a of title 10, United States Code, allow the Secretary of Defense to approve contract action or actions to enter a new contract, exercise an option under an existing contract, or otherwise extend the scope of an existing contract under the AAG program for CVN–80 only if the MDA, on a non-delegable basis, were to determine that such action would be needed to appropriately restructure the program as intended by the Secretary of Defense.

The conferees note that, although the AAG program is now being managed as a Major Defense Acquisition Program, it began more than 10 years ago as an Acquisition Category II program, which limited transparency and insight of the Navy's acquisition and contract management. In 2015, the Comptroller General reported that the Department of Defense needed a better approach to manage Acquisition Category II programs, particularly those programs that have the potential to become Major Defense Acquisition Programs.

Therefore, the conferees direct the Comptroller General to review no fewer than five Navy aircraft launch and recovery equipment (ALRE) Acquisition Category II programs to determine:

(1) The roles and responsibilities for acquiring ALRE systems for major ship programs, and the relationship of these programs to the Navy's overall acquisition of the ship platform;

(2) How the acquisition and contracting practices for these programs compare to guidance, regulations, and best practices for acquisition management;

(3) How the Navy manages cost, schedule, and performance to meet ship delivery

schedules, and what mechanisms, if any, are in place to periodically reassess assignment of such programs to a particular acquisition category;

(4) Recommendations to improve the Navy's performance in managing ALRE and other Acquisition Category II programs; and

(5) Any other observations of the Comptroller General.

The conferees request a briefing to the congressional defense committees no later than June 1, 2017, to be followed by a report.

Limitation on availability of funds for procurement of U.S.S. Enterprise (CVN–80) (sec. 126)

The Senate bill contained a provision (sec. 126) that would limit more than 25 percent of funds authorized to be appropriated by this Act or otherwise made available for fiscal year 2017 for advance procurement or procurement of USS John F. Kennedy (CVN–79) or USS Enterprise (CVN–80) from being obligated or expended until the Secretary of the Navy and Chief of Naval Operations submit a report to the congressional defense committees.

The House amendment contained no similar provision.

The House recedes with an amendment that would remove the limitation of funds on CVN–79 and terminate this section on September 30, 2021.

Sense of Congress on aircraft carrier procurement schedules (sec. 127)

The House amendment contained a provision (sec. 122) that would provide the sense of Congress that the Secretary of the Navy's schedule to procure 1 aircraft carrier every 5 years will reduce the overall aircraft carrier inventory to 10 aircraft carriers, a level insufficient to meet peacetime and war plan requirements. The section would also recommend that the Secretary begin construction for the Ford-class aircraft carrier designated CVN–81 in fiscal year 2022 and align advance procurement activities with this accelerated programming.

The Senate bill contained no similar provision.

The Senate recedes with an amendment that would remove the reference to CVN–81.

Report on P–8 Poseidon aircraft (sec. 128)

The House amendment contained a provision that would require the Secretary of the Navy to submit to the congressional defense committees a report regarding future capabilities for the P–8 Poseidon aircraft.

The Senate bill contained no similar provision.

The Senate recedes.

Design and construction of replacement dock landing ship designated LX(R) or amphibious transport dock designated LPD–29 (sec. 129)

The House amendment contained a provision (sec. 124) that would authorize the Secretary of the Navy to enter into and incrementally fund a contract for design and construction of the replacement dock landing ship designated LX(R) or the amphibious transport dock designated LPD–29.

The Senate bill contained no similar provision.

The Senate recedes.

Subtitle D—Air Force Programs

EC–130H Compass Call recapitalization program (sec. 131)

The Senate bill contained a provision (Sec. 145) that would prohibit the availability of funds for the Air Force EC–130H Compass Call recapitalization program unless the Air Force conducts a full and open competition to acquire the replacement aircraft platform.

The House amendment contained no similar provision.

The House recedes with an amendment that strikes the full and open competition requirement, and authorizes the Secretary of the Air Force to obligate and expend fiscal year 2017 funds for the purpose of re-hosting the primary mission equipment of the current EC–130H Compass Call aircraft fleet on to a more operationally effective and survivable airborne platform to meet combatant commander requirements. The amendment limits procurement to the first two aircraft of the planned ten aircraft fleet until the Secretary determines there is a high likelihood the program will meet the requirements of the combatant commands.

The conferees agree the restructured EC–130H Compass Call program shall be implemented consistent with existing authorities, including Federal Acquisition Regulation Part 6.3 and Department of Defense Instruction 5000.02, "Operation of the Defense Acquisition System."

The conferees note the fiscal year 2017 funding adjustments to allow the Secretary of the Air Force to proceed with the program are outlined in Division D.

Repeal of requirement to preserve certain retired C–5 aircraft (sec. 132)

The Senate bill contained a provision (Sec. 143) that would repeal the requirement in Section 141 of the National Defense Authorization Act for Fiscal Year 2013 (Public Law 112–239) for the Secretary of the Air Force to preserve certain retired C–5 aircraft.

The House amendment contained a similar provision (Sec. 132).

The Senate recedes.

Repeal of requirement to preserve F–117 aircraft in recallable condition (sec. 133)

The Senate bill contained a provision (Sec. 144) that would repeal the requirement in Section 136 of the John Warner National Defense Authorization Act for Fiscal Year 2007 (Public Law 109–364; 120 Stat. 2114) to preserve F–117 aircraft in recallable condition.

The House amendment contained a similar provision (Sec. 133).

The House recedes.

Prohibition on availability of funds for retirement of A–10 aircraft (sec. 134)

The Senate bill contained a provision (Sec. 141) that would amend section 142 of the National Defense Authorization Act for Fiscal Year 2016 (Public Law 114–92) by extending the prohibition on obligation or expenditure of funds to retire or prepare to retire A–10 aircraft until the Secretary of the Air Force and Chief of Staff of the Air Force submit a report to the congressional defense committees describing their views on the results of an F–35A initial operational test and evaluation (IOT&E). The provision would also ensure the F–35A IOT&E includes comparison tests and evaluation of the F–35A and A–10C in conducting close air support, combat search and rescue, and airborne forward air controller missions. The provision would also require the Comptroller General of the United States to provide an independent assessment of the report from the Secretary and Chief of Staff.

The House amendment contained a similar provision (Sec. 134) that would prevent retirements of A–10 aircraft, but would allow the Secretary of the Air Force to transition the A–10 unit at Fort Wayne Air National Guard Base, Indiana, to an F–16 unit in fiscal year 2018, as the Secretary had proposed in the budget of the President for fiscal year 2017.

The Senate recedes.

The conferees agree that section (f)(2) of the House provision explicitly prevents the divestment of any A–10 aircraft if the special rule were to be invoked.

The conferees also agree the Comptroller General of the United States shall assess the conclusions and assertions contained in the Secretary's and Chief of Staff's report on the F–35A IOT&E, and submit a report to the congressional defense committees of such assessment not later than 90 days after the Secretary's and Chief of Staff's report is submitted.

The conferees also agree the Comptroller General's report shall include the following:

(1) An assessment of whether the conclusions and assertions included in the report submitted by the Secretary and Chief of Staff are comprehensive, fully supported, and sufficiently detailed; and

(2) An identification of any shortcomings, limitations, or other matters that affect the quality of the report's findings or conclusions.

Limitation on availability of funds for destruction of A–10 aircraft in storage status (sec. 135)

The Senate bill contained a provision (Sec. 142) that would prohibit the availability of funds authorized to be appropriated by this Act or otherwise made available for the Air Force to be obligated for the purpose of scrapping, destroying, or otherwise disposing of any A–10 aircraft in any storage status in the Aerospace Maintenance and Regeneration Group (AMARG) that have serviceable wings or other components that could be used to prevent total active inventory A–10 aircraft from being permanently removed from flyable status due to unserviceable wings or other components.

The House amendment contained no similar provision.

The House recedes with minor technical corrections.

The conferees agree the provision does not prevent the Air Force from reclaiming any usable parts or components on A–10 aircraft in any storage status for the purpose of keeping active inventory A–10 aircraft in flyable and mission capable condition.

Prohibition on availability of funds for retirement of Joint Surveillance Target Attack Radar System aircraft (sec. 136)

The House amendment contained a provision (Sec. 135) that would prohibit the availability of funds for retirement of Joint Surveillance Target Attack Radar System aircraft in fiscal year 2018.

The Senate bill contained no similar provision.

The Senate recedes.

Elimination of annual report on aircraft inventory (sec. 137)

The House amendment contained a provision (Sec. 131) that would strike the requirement in Section 231a of title 10, United States Code, for the Secretary of Defense to deliver an annual report on the military services' aircraft inventory to the congressional defense committees.

The Senate bill contained no similar provision.

The Senate recedes.

Subtitle E—Defense-Wide, Joint, and Multiservice Matters

Standardization of 5.56mm rifle ammunition (sec. 141)

The House amendment contained a provision (sec. 146) that would require the Secretary of Defense to ensure that the Army and the Marine Corps are using in combat one standard type of enhanced 5.56mm rifle ammunition not later than one year after the date of the enactment of this Act with exceptions that require the Secretary of Defense to certify to the congressional defense committees the reasons why there are different 5.56mm rounds being used in combat.

The Senate bill contained no similar provision.

The Senate recedes.

Fire suppressant and fuel containment standards for certain vehicles (sec. 142)

The House amendment contained a provision (Sec. 142) that would require the Secretary of the Army, or his designee, and the Secretary of the Navy, or his designee, to establish and maintain policy guidance regarding the establishment of, and updates to, fire suppressant and fuel containment standards that meet survivability requirements across various classes of vehicles, including light tactical vehicles, medium tactical vehicles, heavy tactical vehicles, and ground combat vehicles for the Army and Marine Corps. This section would also require the Secretary of the Army and the Secretary of the Navy to provide a report to the congressional defense committees, not later than 180 days after the date of the enactment of this Act, that contains policy guidance for each class of vehicle including armor, fire suppression systems, self-sealing material and containment technologies, and any other information as determined by the Secretaries.

The Senate bill contained no similar provision.

The Senate recedes.

Limitation on availability of funds for destruction of certain cluster munitions (sec. 143)

The Senate bill contained a provision (section 152) that would limit the funds available for the destruction of cluster munitions until the Secretary of Defense submits a report on the Department's policy on, and plan for, cluster munitions.

The House amendment contained no similar provision.

The House recedes with an amendment that would limit the funds for the destruction of serviceable cluster munitions, but would allow the demilitarization of cluster munitions determined to be unserviceable due to a significant failure to meet performance or logistics requirements. Cluster munitions categorized as unserviceable solely due to current or amended Department of Defense policy related to cluster munitions would not meet this definition of unserviceable and would be subject to the limitation in this provision.

Report on Department of Defense munitions strategy for the combatant commands (sec. 144)

The House amendment contained a provision that would require the Secretary of Defense to submit to the congressional defense committees a report on the munitions strategy of the combatant commands.

The Senate bill contained no similar provision.

The Senate recedes with an amendment that would reduce the time horizon for the strategy and modify the elements of the required report.

Modifications to reporting on use of combat mission requirements funds (sec. 145)

The House amendment contained a provision (sec. 141) that would amend the quarterly report requirement in section 123 of the Ike Skelton National Defense Authorization Act for Fiscal Year 2011 (Public Law 111–383),

to sunset the requirement for such reports on September 30, 2018.

The Senate bill contained no similar provision.

The Senate recedes with an amendment that would change from quarterly to annually the requirement for the commander of U.S. Special Operations Command to submit a report on use of Combat Mission Requirements funds.

Report on alternative management structures for the F–35 joint strike fighter program (sec. 146)

The Senate bill contained a provision that would disestablish the F–35 Joint Program Office (JPO) and devolve relevant responsibilities to the Air Force and the Navy.

The House amendment contained no similar provision.

The House recedes with an amendment that would remove the requirement to disestablish the JPO and require the Secretary of Defense, no later than March 31, 2017, to submit to the congressional defense committees a report on potential options for the future management of the Joint Strike Fighter program.

Comptroller General review of F–35 Lightning II aircraft sustainment support (sec. 147)

The House amendment contained a provision (Sec. 144) that would direct the Comptroller General of the United States to conduct an analysis of the sustainment support strategy for the F–35 Joint Strike Fighter program.

The Senate bill contained no similar provision.

The Senate recedes.

Briefing on acquisition strategy for Ground Mobility Vehicle (sec. 148)

The House amendment contained a provision (Sec. 145) that would direct the Under Secretary of Defense for Acquisition, Technology, and Logistics, in consultation with the Secretary of the Army, to provide a briefing to the congressional defense committees on the acquisition strategy for the ground mobility vehicle.

The Senate bill contained no similar provision.

The Senate recedes.

Study and report on optimal mix of aircraft capabilities for the Armed Forces (sec. 149)

The Senate bill contained a provision (Sec. 151) that would direct the Secretary of Defense to obtain an independent study on the future mix of aircraft platforms for the Armed Forces.

The House amendment contained no similar provision.

The House recedes with an amendment changing the study to be conducted by the Secretary of Defense rather than by an independent entity, adds the congressional intelligence committees as recipients of the study report, and includes other minor technical corrections.

LEGISLATIVE PROVISIONS NOT ADOPTED

Funding for surface-to-air missile system

The House amendment contained a provision (Section 114) that would authorize an increase in funding for Missile Procurement, Army line 002, MSE missile, by $84.2 million and decrease funding for Defense Nuclear Nonproliferation Research and Development, material management and minimization, by an equal $84.2 million.

The Senate bill contained no similar provision.

The House recedes.

The outcome is reflected in sections 4101 and 4701 of the Act.

Procurement authority for aircraft carrier programs

The House amendment contained a provision (sec. 121) that would provide economic order quantity authority for the construction of two Ford-class aircraft carriers and incremental funding authority for the nuclear refueling and complex overhaul of five *Nimitz*-class aircraft carriers.

The Senate bill contained no similar provision.

The House recedes.

Ship to shore connector program

The House amendment contained a provision (sec. 125) that would authorize the Secretary of the Navy to enter into a contract for the procurement of up to 45 Ship to Shore Connector vessels.

The Senate bill contained no similar provision.

The House recedes.

Limitation on availability of funds for Tactical Combat Training System Increment II

The Senate bill contained a provision (sec. 127) that would limit the obligation or expenditure of 25 percent of funds for the Tactical Combat Training Systems (TCTS) Increment II program until 60 days after the Secretary of the Navy submitted the report required by section 235 of the National Defense Authorization Act for Fiscal Year 2016 (Public Law 114–92).

The House amendment contained a similar provision (sec. 218) that would limit the obligation or expenditure of 20 percent of the funds for TCTS Increment II until the Secretary of the Navy and Secretary of the Air Force provided the required report.

The conference agreement includes neither provision. Because the Secretary of the Navy submitted the required report in May 2016, the limitation on availability of funds within these provisions is no longer applicable.

However, the conferees remain concerned about training gaps, both in live and simulated environments, for pilots in fourth and fifth-generation aircraft. Pilots will have to operate these aircraft with advanced weapon systems in highly complex anti-access, area denial environments. The conferees recognize the importance of developing higher fidelity interoperable training for combat pilots using live-virtual-constructive (LVC) exercises. Such exercises should allow the Department to simulate a broader range of threat system capabilities that enable training aircraft pilots under more realistic combat conditions.

Therefore, the conferees expect the Department of Defense to apply the necessary focus and resources to develop and support LVC training as soon as possible.

Prohibition on availability of funds for retirement of U–2 aircraft

The House amendment contained a provision (Sec. 137) that would prohibit the availability of funds for the retirement of U–2 aircraft.

The Senate bill contained no similar provision.

The House recedes. Section 133 of the National Defense Authorization Act for Fiscal Year 2012 (Public Law 112–81) prohibits the Secretary of the Air Force from taking any action that would prevent the Air Force from maintaining the U–2 aircraft fleet in its current configuration and capability beyond fiscal year 2016. The conferees agree that this provision remains in full force and effect.

Medium Altitude Intelligence, Surveillance, and Reconnaissance aircraft

The Senate bill contained a provision (sec. 153) that would prohibit the obligation or expenditure of funds for the acquisition of Medium Altitude Intelligence, Surveillance, and Reconnaissance (MAISR) aircraft in fiscal year 2017 until the Assistant Secretary of Defense for Special Operations and Low Intensity Conflict (ASD SOLIC), in consultation with the Commander of U.S. Special Operations Command (SOCOM), provides the congressional defense committees with a report on the manned ISR requirements of the command and how such an acquisition aligns with the SOCOM ISR Roadmap.

The House amendment contained no similar provision.

The Senate recedes.

The conferees understand that a SOCOM analysis determined that the cost avoidance of acquiring versus leasing MAISR aircraft is approximately $1.3 million per month with a break even return on investment of approximately 11 months. However, the conferees believe that procurement of ISR aircraft should not be ad hoc, but instead be a deliberate acquisition informed by an analysis of alternatives that fully considers changing requirements, threats, capabilities, tactics, and resource constraints. Therefore, the conferees direct ASD SOLIC and SOCOM to provide an interim briefing on the scope, methodology and timeline for the Next Generation Manned ISR Study and Analysis of Alternatives no later than 90 days after enactment of this Act.

TITLE II—RESEARCH, DEVELOPMENT, TEST, AND EVALUATION

Subtitle A—Authorization of Appropriations

Authorization of appropriations (sec. 201)

The Senate bill contained a provision (sec. 201) that would authorize appropriations for Research, Development, Test, and Evaluation at the levels identified in section 4201 of division D of this Act.

The House amendment contained an identical provision (sec. 201).

The conference agreement includes this provision.

Subtitle B—Program Requirements, Restrictions, and Limitations

Laboratory quality enhancement program (sec. 211)

The House amendment contained a provision (sec. 211) that would require the establishment of a Laboratory Quality Enhancement Program to support the analysis and implementation of current policies, as well as make recommendations for new initiatives to support the improvement and enhancement of the Department of Defense's Science and Technology Reinvention Laboratories. The House provision would also align management of the laboratory demonstration program with the Assistant Secretary of Defense for Research and Engineering.

The Senate bill contained a provision (sec. 1126) that would align management of the laboratory demonstration program with the Under Secretary of Defense for Acquisition, Technology, and Logistics.

The Senate recedes with an amendment to adjust the membership of the panel and to emphasize that the goal of the laboratory personnel system should be to support the efficient operations of those institutions.

Modification of mechanisms to provide funds for defense laboratories for research and development of technologies for military missions (sec. 212)

The Senate bill contained a provision (sec. 211) that would raise the limit of funds authorized under Section 219 of the Duncan Hunter National Defense Authorization Act for Fiscal Year 2009 (Public Law 110–417) up to four percent of all funds available to a laboratory. The provision would also eliminate the sunset date for authorization of this authority.

The House amendment contained a similar provision (sec. 212) that would set the level of funding at three percent, eliminate the sunset date, and allow certain federally funded research and development centers to use this authority.

The House recedes with an amendment that would set the level of Section 219 funding at between two and four percent.

Making permanent authority for defense research and development rapid innovation program (sec. 213)

The Senate bill contained a provision (sec. 212) that would repeal the sunset provision of the Rapid Innovation Program and make the authorization of the program permanent.

The House amendment contained no similar provision.

The House recedes.

Authorization for National Defense University and Defense Acquisition University to enter into cooperative research and development agreements (sec. 214)

The Senate bill contained a provision (sec. 213) that would authorize the Defense Acquisition University and the National Defense University to enter into cooperative agreements, which involve the provision of grant money, and cooperative research and development agreements with universities, not-for-profit institutions, and other entities to support their designated missions.

The House amendment contained no similar provision.

The House recedes.

Manufacturing engineering education grant program (sec. 215)

The Senate bill contained a provision (sec. 214) that would allow the Department of Defense to provide grants to institutions of higher education, including technical and community colleges, for the purposes of enhancing education in manufacturing engineering.

The House amendment contained no similar provision.

The House recedes with technical amendments to clarify several aspects of the grant program.

Notification requirement for certain rapid prototyping, experimentation, and demonstration activities (sec. 216)

The House amendment contained a provision (sec. 213) that would require the Secretary of the Navy to provide written notification to the congressional defense committees within 10 days before initiating a rapid prototyping, experimentation, or demonstration activity using funds from PE 63382N (Navy Advanced Combat Systems Technology).

The Senate bill contained no similar provision.

The Senate recedes.

Increased micro-purchase threshold for research programs and entities (sec. 217)

The Senate bill contained a provision (sec. 215) that would increase the micro-purchase threshold in Department of Defense research and laboratories activities from $3,000 to $10,000. In raising the limit, this provision would allow appropriate organizations, such as universities, defense labs, and other performers, to facilitate easy and administratively efficient purchasing of small dollar items.

The House amendment contained no similar provision.

The House recedes with an amendment to extend the increase in micro-purchase threshold to all research activities government-wide.

Improved biosafety for handling of select agents and toxins (sec. 218)

The House amendment contained a provision (sec. 214) that would direct the Department of Defense to implement several improvements for handling of select agents and toxins, as recommended from an Army 15–6 investigative report on the individual and institutional accountability for the shipment of viable Bacillus Anthracis from Dugway Proving Ground. This section would require the Department to implement a quality assurance and quality control program for any facility producing biological select agents and toxins, and for the Secretary of Defense to submit a report to the congressional defense committees by February 1, 2017, on the potential consolidation of facilities that work with biological select agents and toxins. This section would also require the Comptroller General of the United States to submit a report to the congressional defense committees by September 1, 2017, on the effectiveness and completeness of the Department of Defense's actions taken to address the findings and recommendations of the Army 15–6 investigation.

The Senate bill contained no similar provision.

The Senate recedes with a technical amendment.

Designation of Department of Defense senior official with principal responsibility for directed energy weapons (sec. 219)

The Senate bill contained a provision (sec. 216) that would grant rapid acquisition authorities for directed energy weapons systems to accelerate the development and fielding of directed energy technology and to help offset the gains of potential adversaries. The Senate provision would also establish a joint directed energy program office at the Department of Defense.

The House amendment contained a provision (sec. 220) that would require the Secretary of Defense to designate a senior official already serving within the Department of Defense as a senior official with principal responsibility for the development and demonstration of directed energy weapons for the Department.

The Senate recedes with an amendment that would require the senior designated official to develop a strategic roadmap for the development and fielding of directed energy technology and to accelerate such development and fielding. The amendment would also rename the joint technology office for high energy lasers to the joint directed energy transition office, and would expand its mission to work with the senior designated official to push the demonstration and transition of directed energy systems, as well as the development of key technologies.

The conferees expect and encourage the Department of Defense to use rapid acquisition authorities authorized to the department in Section 806 of the Bob Stump National Defense Authorization Act for Fiscal Year 2003 (Public Law 107–314; 10 U.S.C. 2302 note) to speed the development and deployment of operational directed energy capabilities. The committee believes that this provision allows the Secretary of Defense to better use the range of acquisition authorities already at the disposal of the department for the purposes of directed energy weapons system acquisition, including:

(1) Rapid acquisition authority provided under Section 806;

(2) Use of other transactions authority provided under section 2371 of Title 10, United States Code;

(3) Simplified acquisition procedures for the acquisition of commercial items; and

(4) Authority for procurement for experimental purposes provided under section 2373 of Title 10, United States Code.

Restructuring of the distributed common ground system of the Army (sec. 220)

The House amendment contained a provision (sec. 219) that would require the Secretary of the Army to restructure versions of the distributed common ground system of the Army after Increment 1. The Secretary of the Army shall discontinue development of new software code of any component of the system for which there is commercial, open source, or Government off the shelf software that is capable of fulfilling at least 80 percent of the system requirements; and conduct a review of the acquisition strategy for the program to ensure that procurement of commercial software is the preferred method of meeting program requirements. The Secretary of the Army shall not award any contract for the development of a new component software capability if such a capability is already a commercial item.

The Senate bill contained no similar provision.

The Senate recedes with an amendment.

The conferees expect the Secretary of the Army to rapidly execute this acquisition so as to quickly improve the field performance of the existing distributed common ground system for the Army, which we do not believe is adequately serving the needs of units at division, brigade and battalion levels.

Limitation on availability of funds for countering weapons of mass destruction system Constellation (sec. 221)

The House amendment contained a provision (sec. 216) that would prohibit the Department of Defense from obligating or expending any funds in fiscal year 2017 for research, development, and prototyping of the countering weapons of mass destruction situational awareness information system, known as "Constellation."

The Senate bill contained no similar provision.

The Senate recedes with an amendment that would limit half the funds available for Constellation until the Secretary of Defense provides an independent review and assessment of the requirements and implementation plan for this system. In addition congressional defense committees shall receive periodic updates prior to the completion of the review.

Limitation on availability of funds for Defense Innovation Unit Experimental (sec. 222)

The House amendment contained a provision (sec. 217) that would limit the amount of authorized funds available to be obligated or expended for the Defense Innovation Unit Experimental (DIUx) to no more than 80 percent until the Secretary of Defense provides a report to the congressional defense committees on the charter for and the use of funds to establish and expand DIUx.

The Senate bill contained no similar provision.

The Senate recedes with an amendment that would alter the amount of funds subject to limitation and add additional specificity to the reporting requirement.

The conferees remain cautiously optimistic that the changes to the organizational structure and functions of DIUx could become important tools for the Department of Defense (DoD) to engage with new and non-traditional commercial sources of innovation, as well as rapidly identify and integrate new technologies into defense systems.

The conferees believe that outreach to commercial companies, small businesses and other non-traditional defense contractors, in Silicon Valley and across the nation, will be a key element in all efforts at modernizing defense systems and pursuing offsetting technology strategies. However, the conferees are concerned that investments made by DIUx to-date were not focused on rapid delivery of much needed game-changing technologies. Additionally, DIUx's customer base is not as diverse as expected and includes organizations, such as U.S. Special Operations Command, with their own acquisition authority and entity established to leverage innovation. Although the conferees are not opposed to any organization partnering with DIUx, the conferees encourage DIUx to establish relationships with services and other Department of Defense organizations that do not have their own funding, authorities, and innovation hubs.

Additionally, the conferees remain concerned that in the Department's rush to try something new, defense leaders have not taken the time to determine how effective recent organizational and management changes are before seeking a rapid expansion of resources. Nor do the conferees believe that the Department has postured DIUx to be successful in the innovation ecosystem with partners across the Department, finding ways to multiply the effectiveness and networking potential of DIUx by leveraging the personnel, expertise, authorities, and resources of existing successful research, development, innovation, and tech transfer mechanisms. These existing mechanisms include the Small Business Innovative Research and Small Business Technology Transition programs, the Department of Defense research laboratories, and other entities that look at technology in classified settings.

Additionally, the conferees are concerned that the Department has found useful mechanisms to identify and engage with new commercial entities, without making demonstrable progress in reducing the acquisition and contractual barriers of entry for these non-traditional providers, as well as all commercial entities wishing to do business with the Department. Without such progress, the conferees are concerned that these non-traditional vendors will become frustrated over time, as has happened in the past, and will revert back to a posture that, at best, reluctantly partners in defense work, and at worst, actively rejects all work with the Department of Defense because the acquisition system is too burdensome and bureaucratic.

Limitation on availability of funds for Joint Surveillance Target Attack Radar System (JSTARS) recapitalization program (sec. 223)

The Senate bill contained a provision (Sec. 146) that would limit the availability of fiscal year 2017 and beyond funds for the Joint Surveillance Target Attack Radar System recapitalization program unless the contract for engineering and manufacturing development uses a firm fixed price contract structure.

The House amendment contained no similar provision.

The House recedes with an amendment that provides the Secretary of Defense with authority to waive the limitation in the provision if the Secretary determines the waiver is in the national security interests of the United States, and includes other minor technical corrections.

The conferees note that to ensure the integrity of the full and open competition nature of this program, they caution the Air

Force to guard against the potential prejudicing of this source selection by other Air Force recapitalization programs.

Acquisition program baseline and annual reports on follow-on modernization program for F–35 Joint Strike Fighter (sec. 224)

The Senate bill contained a provision (sec. 1087) that would require the Department of Defense to treat the F–35 Follow-on Modernization program as a separate Major Defense Acquisition Program (MDAP).

The House amendment contained no similar provision.

The House recedes with an amendment that would remove the requirement to treat the Follow-on Modernization program as a separate MDAP and require the Secretary of Defense, not later than March 31, 2017, to submit to the congressional defense committees a report that contains the basic elements of an acquisition program baseline for Block 4 modernization.

Subtitle C—Reports and Other Matters

Strategy for assured access to trusted microelectronics (sec. 231)

The House amendment contained a provision (sec. 231) that would require the Secretary of Defense to develop and implement a strategy for developing and acquiring trusted microelectronics from various sources by 2020. The House provision would further require the Secretary of Defense to certify by September 30, 2020, that the Department has implemented the recommendations of the strategy, and has created an assured means of accessing sufficient supply of trusted microelectronics.

The Senate bill contained no similar provision.

The Senate recedes with an amendment that would add additional elements to the required strategy.

Pilot program on evaluation of commercial information technology (sec. 232)

The House amendment contained a provision (sec. 232) that would require the Defense Information Systems Agency to establish a pilot program to evaluate commercially available information technology tools to better understand and characterize their potential impact on Department of Defense networks and computing environments through prototyping, experimentation, operational demonstration, military user assessment, or other means to get quantitative and qualitative feedback on the commercial item.

The Senate bill contained no similar provision.

The Senate recedes with a clarifying amendment.

Pilot program for the enhancement of the research, development, test, and evaluation centers of the Department of Defense (sec. 233)

The Senate bill contained a provision (sec. 948) that would allow directors of Department of Defense research and development laboratories, as well as the director of the Defense Advanced Research Projects Agency to waive on a temporary basis regulations, instructions, publications, policies, and procedures of the Department of Defense as the director believes appropriate.

The House amendment contained a similar provision (sec. 233) that would allow the services to demonstrate methods for the more effective development of research, development, test, and evaluation functions.

The Senate recedes with an amendment that would combine features of both provisions and create a pilot program open to research and development laboratories, test and evaluation centers, and the Defense Advanced Research Projects Agency. The amended provision would allow directors of these entities to waive on a temporary basis any regulation, restriction, requirement, guidance, policy, procedure, or departmental instruction that would generate greater value and efficiencies in research and development activities, enable more efficient and effective operations, and enable more rapid deployment of warfighter capabilities.

In this provision, the conferees expect the secretaries of the services to ensure that participation in the program includes at least five science and technology reinvention laboratories and at least five test and evaluation centers from each service with the highest likelihood to use innovatively the authority for this new management flexibility to demonstrate the value for the entire Department.

In addition, the conferees expect that the assistant secretaries of the services will work with their appropriate counterparts within the services to complete evaluation of waiver requests in a timely and responsive manner.

Pilot program on modernization and fielding of electromagnetic spectrum warfare systems and electronic warfare capabilities (sec. 234)

The Senate bill contained a provision (sec. 897) that would stipulate that funds for electromagnetic spectrum warfare systems and EW systems may be used for the development and fielding of such systems. The provision would also amend section 806(c)(1) of the Bob Stump National Defense Authorization Act for Fiscal Year 2003 (Public Law 107–314) to add a new subparagraph addressing the rapid acquisition of electronic warfare capabilities.

The House amendment contained a provision (sec. 234) that would authorize the Secretary of Defense to carry out a pilot program on the modernization of electromagnetic spectrum warfare systems and electronic warfare (EW) systems. The House provision would direct the Electronic Warfare Executive Committee (EWEC) to select a total of five such systems currently in sustainment for modernization under the pilot program.

The Senate recedes with an amendment that would including fielding of EW systems, increases the number of systems to be selected for the pilot program from 5 to 10, adds a termination date of September 30, 2023 to the pilot program, and authorizes appropriated electromagnetic spectrum warfare and electronic warfare funds to be used for the development and fielding of electromagnetic spectrum warfare systems and electronic warfare capabilities.

Pilot program on disclosure of certain sensitive information to federally funded research and development centers (sec. 235)

The Senate bill contained a provision (sec. 218) that would permit the Department of Defense to provide personnel of a Defense federally-funded research and development center with access to sensitive information necessary to carry out their assigned duties and functions.

The House amendment contained no similar provision.

The House recedes with an amendment to clarify certain elements of the program and further prevent any unauthorized disclosure of sensitive information.

Pilot program on enhanced interaction between the Defense Advanced Research Projects Agency and the service academies (sec. 236)

The Senate bill contained a provision (sec. 219) that would authorize the Secretary of Defense to establish a pilot program to assess the feasibility and advisability of enhanced interaction between the Defense Advanced Research Projects Agency and the military service academies.

The House amendment contained no similar provision.

The House recedes with technical amendments to streamline the pilot program.

Independent review of F/A–18 physiological episodes and corrective actions (sec. 237)

The House amendment contained a provision that would require the Secretary of the Navy to establish an independent review team to review the Navy's data on, and mitigation efforts related to, the increase in F/A–18 physiological events since January 1, 2009 and submit a report on the findings of said review team.

The Senate bill contained no similar provision.

The Senate recedes.

B–21 bomber development program accountability matrices (sec. 238)

The Senate bill contained a provision (sec. 844) that would establish specific cost growth thresholds and cost controls for the Air Force's B–21 bomber program, directs the Secretary of the Air Force to provide quarterly program performance data to the Comptroller General of the United States, and directs the transfer of the difference between the Department of Defense's annual program budget funding amount and the contract award value to the Defense Rapid Prototyping Fund for each budget year submission.

The House amendment contained no similar provision.

The House recedes with an amendment that strikes the cost growth thresholds and cost controls, and strikes the requirement to transfer funds into the Defense Rapid Prototyping Fund. The amendment also changes the program performance data submission from a quarterly to semi-annual reporting frequency, and includes other minor technical corrections.

Study on helicopter crash prevention and mitigation technology (sec. 239)

The House amendment contained a provision (Sec. 236) that would require the Secretary of Defense to enter into a contract with a federally funded research and development center to conduct a study on technologies with the potential to prevent and mitigate helicopter crashes.

The Senate bill contained no similar provision.

The Senate recedes.

Strategy for improving electronic and electromagnetic spectrum warfare capabilities (sec. 240)

The House amendment contained a provision (sec. 237) that would require the Under Secretary of Defense for Acquisition, Technology, and Logistics, acting through the Electronic Warfare Executive Committee, to submit to the congressional defense committees a report by April 1, 2017, on future electronic warfare concepts and technologies.

The Senate bill contained no similar provision.

The Senate recedes with an amendment that would require a strategy for improving electronic and electromagnetic spectrum warfare capabilities.

Sense of Congress on development and fielding of fifth generation airborne systems (sec. 241)

The Senate bill contained a provision (Sec. 1057) that would express the sense of the Senate on the definition of and need for continued prioritization, development, and fielding of fifth-generation airborne capabilities.

The House amendment contained no similar provision.

The House recedes with an amendment that replaces the term "the Senate" with "Congress" in each instance where it occurs in the title and body of the provision, and includes other minor technical corrections.

LEGISLATIVE PROVISIONS NOT ADOPTED

Report on cost of B–21 aircraft

The Senate bill contained a provision (Sec. 217) that would limit the funds authorized to be appropriated by this Act or otherwise made available for fiscal year 2017 to be made available for the B–21 Engineering and Manufacturing Development (EMD) program until the Air Force releases the value of the B–21 EMD contract award made on October 27, 2015, to the congressional defense committees.

The House amendment contained a similar provision (Sec. 136) that would require the Secretary of Defense to submit to the congressional defense committees a report on the cost of the B–21 aircraft.

The Senate recedes.

The House recedes.

Neither provision was adopted.

TITLE III—OPERATION AND MAINTENANCE

Subtitle A—Authorization of Appropriations

Authorization of appropriations (sec. 301)

The Senate bill contained a provision (sec. 301) that would authorize appropriations for operation and maintenance activities at the levels identified in section 4301 of division D of this Act.

The House amendment contained an identical provision (sec. 301).

The conference agreement includes this provision.

Subtitle B—Energy and the Environment

Modified reporting requirement related to installations energy management (sec. 311)

The Senate bill contained a provision (sec. 302) that would amend subsection (a) of section 2925 of title 10, United States Code, by significantly reducing the contents of the Department of Defense's Annual Energy Management Report.

The House amendment contained a similar provision (sec. 331) that would modify subsection (a) and (b) of section 2925 of title 10, United States Code, to modify and extend, with a sunset date of January 31, 2021, the "Annual Report Related to Installations Energy Management" and the "Annual Report Related to Operational Energy."

The House recedes with a technical amendment.

Waiver authority for alternative fuel procurement requirement (sec. 312)

The House amendment contained a provision (sec. 311) that would amend section 526 of the Energy Independence and Security Act of 2007 (Public Law 110–140) to clarify that this section shall not be construed as a constraint on any conventional or unconventional fuel procurement necessary for military operations.

The Senate bill contained no similar provision.

The Senate recedes with an amendment that would allow the Secretary of Defense to waive section 526 of the Energy Independence and Security Act of 2007 if in the interest of national security.

Utility data management for military facilities (sec. 313)

The Senate bill contained a provision (sec. 304) that would direct the Department of Defense, in consultation with the Department of Energy, to develop a pilot program to investigate the utilization of utility data management services to perform utility bill aggregation, analysis, third-party payment, storage and distribution.

The House amendment contained no similar provision.

The House recedes with an amendment that would provide permissive authority to the Secretary of Defense to develop a utility data management program with a funding cap of $250,000.

Alternative technologies for munitions disposal (sec. 314)

The House amendment contained a provision (sec. 313) that authorizes the Secretary of the Army to consider using cost-competitive technologies that minimize waste generation and air emissions as alternatives to disposal of conventional munitions by open burning, open detonation, direct contact combustion, and incineration.

The Senate bill contained no similar provision.

The Senate recedes.

Report on efforts to reduce high energy costs at military installations (sec. 315)

The Senate bill contained a provision (sec. 303) that would require the Under Secretary of Defense for Acquisition, Technology, and Logistics, in consultation with the assistant secretaries responsible for energy installations and environment for the military services and the Defense Logistics Agency, to conduct an assessment of the efforts to achieve cost savings at military installations with high energy costs.

The House amendment contained no similar provision.

The House recedes with an amendment to clarify the focus on installations with high levels of energy intensity.

Sense of Congress on funding decisions relating to climate change (sec. 316)

The House amendment contained a provision (sec. 315) that would prohibit the Department of Defense from obligating or expending any funds in fiscal year 2017 to carry out sections 2, 3, 4, 5, 6(b) (iii), and 6(c) of Executive Order 13653 and sections 2, 3, 7, 8, 9, 10, 11, 12, 13, 14, and 15(b) of Executive Order 13693.

The Senate bill contained no similar provision.

The Senate recedes with an amendment that would provide the Sense of Congress that Fiscal Year 2017 funding decisions for the Department should be based on supporting and increasing combat capability, in addition to constantly seeking efficiency and efficacy. Additionally, the Department's programs should allocate funds in a manner that best serves our national security interests. Accordingly, the conferees believe that the collective issues regarding energy efficiency, energy use, and climate change should adhere to these principles.

Subtitle C—Logistics and Sustainment

Revision of deployability rating system and planning reform (sec. 321)

The Senate bill contained a provision (sec. 311) that would amend Chapter 1003 of title 10, United States Code, requiring the Secretary of the Army to maintain a system for identifying the priority of deployment for units of all components of the Army.

The House amendment contained an identical provision (sec. 523).

The conference agreement includes this provision.

Revision of guidance related to corrosion control and prevention executives (sec. 322)

The Senate bill contained a provision (sec. 312) that would require the Under Secretary of Defense for Acquisition, Technology, and Logistics, in coordination with the Director of Corrosion Policy and Oversight, to revise corrosion-related guidance to clearly define the role of the corrosion control and prevention executives of the military departments in assisting the Office of Corrosion Policy and Oversight.

The House amendment contained no similar provision.

The House recedes.

Pilot program for inclusion of certain industrial plants in the Armament Retooling and Manufacturing Support Initiative (sec. 323)

The House amendment contained a provision (sec. 321) that would establish a pilot program for a period of five years requiring the Secretary of Defense to treat all government-owned, contractor-operated (GOCO) industrial plants of the Department of the Army as an eligible facility under section 4551(2) of title 10, United States Code.

The Senate bill contained no similar provision.

The Senate recedes with a technical amendment that would provide permissive authority to the Secretary of Defense to consider all government-owned, contractor operated industrial plants for all military services within the Department of Defense as an eligible facility under section 4551(2) of title 10, United States Code, as part of a pilot program for a period of five years.

The conferees note this provision does not authorize GOCO industrial plants' use of Army Working Capital Funds.

Repair, recapitalization, and certification of dry docks at naval shipyards (sec. 324)

The Senate bill contained a provision (sec. 313) that would authorize amounts available as foreign currency fluctuation savings as specified in the funding table in section 4301 to be authorized to be appropriated for fiscal year 2017 by section 301 for operation and maintenance to be made available for the repair, recapitalization, and certification of dry docks at government-owned and government-operated naval shipyards.

The House amendment contained no similar provision.

The House recedes with a technical amendment that would authorize the Secretary of Defense to transfer up to $250 million of authorizations made available in this Act to the Department of Defense towards the repair, recapitalization, and certification of dry docks at government-owned and government-operated naval shipyards and if such a transfer occurs, the Secretary of Defense shall promptly notify Congress of the transfer.

Private sector port loading assessment (sec. 325)

The House amendment contained a provision (sec. 322) that would require the Secretary of the Navy to conduct quarterly assessments of naval ship maintenance and loading activities carried out by private sector entities at each covered port.

The Senate bill contained no similar provision.

The Senate recedes with a technical amendment that would remove the Sense of Congress.

Strategy on revitalizing Army organic industrial base (sec. 326)

The House amendment contained a provision (sec. 332) that would require the Secretary of Defense to provide a report on certain equipment purchased from foreign entities with an assessment of how that work could be performed by the Army arsenals and establish a pilot program for the period of two years to allow the Army arsenals to adjust their labor rates through the fiscal year.

The Senate bill contained no similar provision.

The Senate recedes with a technical amendment that would expand the report to include the Department of Defense organic industrial base in its entirety and strike the pilot program for adjustable labor rates.

Subtitle D—Reports

Modifications to Quarterly Readiness Report to Congress (sec. 331)

The Senate bill contained a provision (sec. 321) that would amend subsection (a) of section 482 of title 10, United States Code, modifying the Department of Defense's requirements for the Quarterly Readiness Report to Congress.

The House amendment contained no similar provision.

The House recedes.

Report on average travel costs of members of the reserve components (sec. 332)

The House amendment contained a provisions (sec. 333) that would require the Secretary of Defense to submit a report to the congressional defense committees on the travel expenses of members of the reserve components performing certain service, to include the average annual cost for all travel expenses for a member of a reserve component.

The Senate bill contained no similar provision.

The Senate recedes with an amendment that would require the report be executed by the Comptroller General of the United States.

Report on HH–60G sustainment and Combat Rescue Helicopter program (sec. 333)

The Senate bill contained a provision (sec. 322) that would require the Secretary of Defense to report to the congressional defense committees a plan to modernize, train, and maintain the HH–60 fleet.

The House amendment contained no similar provision.

The House recedes.

Subtitle E—Other Matters

Air navigation matters (sec. 341)

The Senate bill contained a provision (sec. 333) that would amend Section 358 of the National Defense Authorization Act for fiscal year 2011 (Public Law 111–383) to ensure that due diligence and proper assessment is given so energy projects do not interfere with operational training of the military services.

The House amendment contained a similar provision (sec. 343) that would amend section 44718 of title 49, United States Code, to authorize the Secretary of Transportation to include the interests of national security, as determined by the Secretary of Defense, in the Secretary's aeronautical studies and reports required under this statute.

The Senate recedes with an amendment that would include the due diligence and proper assessment to ensure energy projects do not interfere with operational training, and would amend title 49, United States Code, to require the Secretary of Transportation to review flight path changes at civilian airports to determine if recent adjustments have had an impact on local communities.

Contract working dogs (sec. 342)

The Senate bill contained a provision (sec. 337) that would amend Section 2583(h) of title 10, United States Code, and require each future contract with a provider of tactical explosive detection dogs to include a provision requiring the contractor to transfer the dog to the 341st Training Squadron after the animal's service life.

The House amendment contained no similar provision.

The House recedes with a technical amendment that would include the terminology a working dog that is "trained and kenneled by an entity that provides such a dog pursuant to such a contract."

Plan, funding documents, and management review relating to explosive ordnance disposal (sec. 343)

The House amendment contained a provision (sec. 342) that would establish a joint Explosive Ordnance Disposal (EOD) program, with the Navy as executive agent for the Department of Defense, to coordinate and integrate research, development, and procurement for EOD defense programs. This section would also require the Secretary of Defense to conduct a review of the management structure of the program and to brief the results of the review to the Committees on Armed Services of the Senate and the House of Representatives by May 1, 2018.

The Senate bill contained no similar provision.

The Senate recedes with an amendment that would direct the Secretary of Defense to develop a plan to create an EOD program, in addition to requiring the Secretary of Defense to identify EOD funding documents in all military services and to conduct an EOD management review. The amendment also requires the Secretary of Defense to brief both the results of the management review and the details of the plan to the Committees on Armed Services of the Senate and the House of Representatives by March 1, 2017.

Process for communicating availability of surplus ammunition (sec. 344)

The House amendment contained a provision (sec. 351) that would require the Secretary of Defense to implement a formal process for communicating to other Federal Government agencies the availability of surplus, serviceable ammunition from the Department of Defense.

The Senate bill contained no similar provision.

The Senate recedes.

Mitigation of risks posed by window coverings with accessible cords in certain military housing units (sec. 345)

The Senate bill contained a provision (sec. 336) that would direct the Secretary of Defense to remove and replace window coverings with accessible cords from military housing units in which children under the age of 9 reside and require housing contractors to phase out window coverings with accessible cords.

The House amendment contained no similar provision.

The House recedes with an amendment that would ensure that the requirement would be applied to contracts for housing units going forward and would not violate existing contract terms.

Access to military installations by transportation companies (sec. 346)

The Senate bill contained a provision (sec. 339) that would require the Secretary of Defense to establish policies, terms, and conditions under which online transportation networks and their drivers shall be permitted access to military installations to serve base personnel.

The House amendment contained no similar provision.

The House recedes with an amendment that would require the Secretary of Defense,

within one year of enactment, to establish policies under which covered drivers may be authorized to access military installations.

Access to wireless high-speed Internet and network connections for certain members of the Armed Forces (sec. 347)

The House amendment contained a provision (sec. 350) that would encourage the Secretary of Defense to provide members of the Armed Forces who are deployed overseas at any United States military facility access to high-speed internet and network connections without charge.

The Senate bill contained no similar provision.

The Senate recedes.

Limitation on availability of funds for Office of the Under Secretary of Defense for Intelligence (sec. 348)

The House amendment contained a provision (sec. 347) that would limit the obligation or expenditure of 15 percent of the funds authorized to be appropriated for Operation and Maintenance, Defense-Wide, for the Office of the Under Secretary of Defense for Policy for fiscal year 2017, until the Secretary of Defense establishes and implements a process by which members of the Armed Forces may carry an appropriate firearm on a military installation, as required by section 526 of the National Defense Authorization Act for Fiscal Year 2016 (Public Law 114–92).

The Senate bill contained no similar provision.

The Senate recedes with an amendment that would limit the obligation or expenditure of 10 percent of the funds authorized to be appropriated for Operation and Maintenance, Defense-Wide, for the Office of the Under Secretary of Defense for Intelligence for fiscal year 2017, until the Secretary of Defense issues guidance on the process by which members of the Armed Forces may carry an appropriate firearm on a military installation, as required by section 526 of the National Defense Authorization Act for Fiscal Year 2016. The conferees note that the Under Secretary of Defense for Intelligence is the official responsible to provide the Secretary of Defense recommendations for the policy and regulations implementing the process required under section 526 of the National Defense Authorization Act for Fiscal Year 2016.

Limitation on development and fielding of new camouflage and utility uniforms (sec. 349)

The Senate bill contained a provision (sec. 332) that would restrict funds to be obligated or expended for the development or fielding of new camouflage or utility uniforms or families of uniforms until one year after the Secretary of Defense notifies the congressional defense committees of the proposed development or fielding.

The House amendment contained no similar provision.

The House recedes.

Plan for improved dedicated adversary air training enterprise of the Air Force (sec. 350)

The Senate bill contained a provision (Sec. 334) that would direct the Chief of Staff of the Air Force to submit to the Committees on Armed Services of the Senate and the House of Representatives, not later than March 3, 2017, a resource ready and executable plan and briefing for developing and emplacing a modernized dedicated adversary air training enterprise to support the full spectrum air combat readiness of the United States Air Force.

The House amendment contained no similar provision.

The House recedes with minor technical corrections.

Independent review and assessment of the Ready Aircrew Program of the Air Force (sec. 351)

The Senate bill contained a provision (Sec. 335) that would direct the Secretary of the Air Force to commission an independent review and assessment of the assumptions underlying the Air Force's annual continuation training requirements, and the efficacy of the overall Ready Aircrew Program in the management of the Air Force's aircrew training requirements.

The House amendment contained no similar provision.

The House recedes with minor technical corrections.

Study on space-available travel system of the Department of Defense (sec. 352)

The House amendment contained a provision (sec. 345) that would require the Secretary of Defense to conduct a study of the space-available travel system and to provide the result of the study to the congressional defense committees within 180 days after entering into a contract with a federally funded research and development center to conduct the study.

The Senate bill contained no similar provision.

The Senate recedes with an amendment that would require the study to consider the feasibility and the impact on the space-available system of extending eligibility for space-available travel to members or former members of the armed forces with a disability rated as total, on the same basis as such transportation is provided to members of the Armed Forces entitled to retired or retainer pay.

Evaluation of motor carrier safety performance and safety technology (sec. 353)

The House amendment contained a provision (sec. 348) that would require the Secretary of Defense to evaluate the need for proven safety technology such as electronic logging devices, roll stability control, forward collision avoidance, lane departure warning systems, and speed limiters in vehicles transporting Transportation Protective Services shipments.

The Senate bill contained no similar position.

The Senate recedes with a clarifying amendment that would strike the Sense of Congress but still include the findings of the Government Accountability Office (GAO) report, GAO 16–82.

LEGISLATIVE PROVISIONS NOT ADOPTED

Increase in funding for civil military programs

The House amendment contained a provision (sec. 302) that would increase funding for the National Guard Youth Challenge Program by $15.0 million by taking a reduction from Defense-wide Operations and Maintenance funding.

The Senate bill contained no similar provision.

The House recedes.

The conferees note that the National Guard Youth Challenge program is fully funded in the conference agreement at the President's budget request level.

Linear LED lamps

The Senate bill contained a provision (sec. 305) that would amend section 2–4.1.1.2 of the Department of Defense's Unified Facilities Criteria to allow linear light emitting diode lamps for facilities and installation retrofits.

The House amendment contained no similar provision.

The Senate recedes.

The conferees note that the Department of the Navy has safely adopted the use of linear light emitting diode lamps for facilities and installation retrofits. The conferees encourage all of the military services to do so in a safe and effective manner, in order to consume less energy and realize life-cycle cost savings.

Production and use of natural gas at Fort Knox

The House amendment contained a provision (sec. 312) that would amend chapter 449 of title 10, United States Code, to grant the Secretary of the Army authority to provide for the production and management of natural gas located under Fort Knox, Kentucky.

The Senate bill contained no similar provision.

The House recedes.

Sense of Congress on perfluorinated chemicals

The House amendment contained a provision (sec. 314) that would express the sense of Congress that the Department of Defense should work with State and local health officials to prevent human exposure to perfluorinated chemicals.

The Senate bill contained no similar provision.

The House recedes.

Limitation on availability of funds for Defense Contract Management Agency

The House amendment contained a provision (sec. 323) that would limit funding for the Defense Contract Management Agency (DCMA) until the DCMA Director provides a briefing to the Committees on Armed Services of the Senate and the House of Representatives on the agency's plan to foster the adoption, implementation, and verification of the Department of Defense's revised Item Unique Identification policy across the Department and the defense industrial base.

The Senate bill contained no similar provision.

The House recedes.

The conferees note the importance of use of Item Unique Identification within the Department of Defense and direct the Secretary of Defense to provide a briefing to the Committees on Armed Services of the Senate and the House of Representatives on the agency's plan to foster the adoption, implementation, and verification of the Department of Defense's revised Item Unique Identification policy no later than 45 days after enactment of this Act.

Repurposing and reuse of surplus military firearms

The Senate bill contained a provision (sec. 331) that would require the Secretary of the Army to transfer all excess firearms, related spare parts and components, small arms ammunition, and ammunition components currently stored at Defense Distribution Depot, Anniston, Alabama to Rock Island Arsenal to be melted and repurposed for military use for re-forging of new firearms or related components and force protection barriers and security bollards. The provision would also authorize the Secretary of the Navy to

transfer M–1 Garand and caliber .22 rimfire rifles held within the inventories of the United States Navy and the United States Marine Corps and stored at Defense Distribution Depot, Anniston, Alabama, or Naval Surface Warfare Center, Crane, Indiana to the Corporation for the Promotion of Rifle Practice and Firearms Safety to be used as awards for competitors in marksmanship competitions held by the United States Marine Corps or United States Navy.

The House amendment contained no similar provision.

The Senate recedes.

STARBASE Program

The Senate bill contained a provision (sec. 338) that would express a sense of Congress on the importance of the Starbase program.

The House amendment contained no similar provision.

The Senate recedes.

The conferees agree to continue funding for the Starbase program and to include an appropriate funding level in the budget tables of this bill.

Explosive Ordnance Disposal Corps

The House amendment contained a provision (sec. 341) that would amend section 3063 of title 10, United States Code, to add Explosive Ordnance Disposal Corps to the list of Army branches.

The Senate bill contained no similar provision.

The House recedes.

Development of personal protective equipment for female Marines and soldiers

The House amendment contained a provision (sec. 344) that would require the Secretary of the Navy and the Commandant of the Marine Corps to work in coordination with the Secretary of the Army to develop a joint acquisition strategy to provide more effective personal protective equipment and organizational clothing and equipment to meet the specific and unique requirements for female Marines and soldiers.

The Senate bill contained no similar provision.

The House recedes.

The conferees note that both the committee report (H. Rept. 114–537) accompanying the National Defense Authorization Act for Fiscal Year 2017 and the committee report (S. Rept. 114–255) accompanying the National Defense Authorization Act for Fiscal Year 2017 contained directive report language requiring the Secretary of Defense to report on the plans for programming, budgeting, requirements, and procurement of female specific equipment including helmets, combat clothing, body armor, footwear, and other critical safety item equipment categories. The conferees remained concerned that currently available items of personal protective equipment (PPE) and organizational clothing and individual equipment (OCIE) may not meet the specific and unique requirements for female combat troops. The conferees expect the Secretary of Defense to consider development and use of joint acquisition strategies for this equipment as part of the two reporting requirements.

Supply of specialty motors from certain manufacturers

The House amendment contained a provision (sec. 346) that would exempt certain small business manufacturers of specialty motors from the requirements of section 431.25 of title 10, Code of Federal Regulations, regarding energy conservation standards.

The Senate bill contained no similar provision.

The House recedes.

Briefing on well-drilling capabilities of active duty and reserve components

The House amendment contained a provision (sec. 349) that would require the Secretary of Defense to provide a briefing on the well-drilling capabilities of active and reserve components, including details on training requirements and locations.

The Senate bill contained no similar provision.

The House recedes.

The conferees direct the Secretary of Defense, not later than March 1, 2017, to provide the congressional defense committees with a briefing on the well drilling capabilities of active duty and reserve forces. The briefing should include a description of the training requirements of active and reserve units with well-drilling capabilities, the locations at which such units conduct training related to well-drilling, and the cost of feasibility of rotating training locations of such units to areas in the United States that are affected by drought conditions.

Increase in funding for National Guard counter-drug programs

The House amendment contained a provision (sec. 352) that would increase funding to support the National Guard counter-drug program by $30 million.

The Senate bill contained no similar provision.

The House recedes.

TITLE IV—MILITARY PERSONNEL AUTHORIZATIONS

Subtitle A—Active Forces

End strength for active forces (sec. 401)

The Senate bill contained a provision (sec. 401) that would authorize active-duty end strengths for fiscal year 2017 as follows: Army 460,000; Navy 322,900; Marine Corps 182,000; Air Force 317,000.

The House amendment contained a provision (sec. 401) that would authorize active-duty end strengths for fiscal year 2017 as follows: Army 480,000; Navy 324,615; Marine Corps 185,000; Air Force 321,000.

The Senate recedes with an amendment that would authorize active-duty end strengths for fiscal year 2017 as follows: Army 476,000; Navy 323,900; Marine Corps 185,000; Air Force 321,000.

The committee recommends a provision that would authorize active-duty end strengths for fiscal year 2017, as shown below:

Service	FY 2016 Authorized	FY 2017		Change from	
		Request	Recommendation	FY 2017 Request	FY 2016 Authorized
Army	475,000	460,000	476,000	+16,000	+1,000
Navy	329,200	322,900	323,900	+1,000	−5,300
Marine Corps	184,000	182,000	185,000	+3,000	+1,000
Air Force	320,715	317,000	321,000	+4,000	+285
DOD Total	1,308,915	1,281,900	1,305,900	+24,000	−3,015

Revisions in permanent active duty end strength minimum levels (sec. 402)

The House amendment contained a provision (sec. 402) that would establish new minimum active-duty end strengths for the Army, Navy, Marine Corps, and Air Force as of September 30, 2017.

The Senate bill contained no similar provision.

The Senate recedes.

Subtitle B—Reserve Forces

End strengths for Selected Reserve (sec. 411)

The Senate bill contained a provision (sec. 411) that would authorize the following end strengths for Selected Reserve personnel of the Armed Forces as of September 30, 2017: the Army National Guard, 335,000; the Army Reserve, 195,000; the Navy Reserve, 58,000; the Marine Corps Reserve, 38,500; the Air National Guard of the United States, 105,700; the Air Force Reserve, 69,000; and the Coast Guard Reserve, 7,000.

The House amendment contained a provision (sec. 411) that would authorize the following end strengths for Selected Reserve personnel of the Armed Forces as of September 30, 2017: the Army National Guard, 350,000; the Army Reserve, 205,000; the Navy Reserve, 58,000; the Marine Corps Reserve, 38,500; the Air National Guard of the United States, 105,700; the Air Force Reserve, 69,000; and the Coast Guard Reserve, 7,000.

The Senate recedes with an amendment that would authorize the following end strengths for Selected Reserve personnel of the Armed Forces as of September 30, 2017: the Army National Guard, 343,000; the Army Reserve, 199,000; the Navy Reserve, 58,000; the Marine Corps Reserve, 38,500; the Air National Guard of the United States, 105,700; the Air Force Reserve, 69,000; and the Coast Guard Reserve, 7,000.

The committee recommends a provision that would authorize Selected Reserve end strengths for fiscal year 2017, as shown below:

| Service | FY 2016 Authorized | FY 2017 | | Change from | |
		Request	Recommendation	FY 2017 Authorized	FY 2016 Authorized
Army National Guard	342,000	335,000	343,000	+8,000	+1,000
Army Reserve	198,000	195,000	199,000	+4,000	+1,000
Navy Reserve	57,400	58,000	58,000	0	+600
Marine Corps Reserve	38,900	38,500	38,500	0	−400
Air National Guard	105,500	105,700	105,700	0	+200
Air Force Reserve	69,200	69,000	69,000	0	−200
DOD Total	811,000	801,200	813,200	+12,000	+2,200
Coast Guard Reserve	7,000	7,000	7,000	0	0

End strengths for Reserves on active duty in support of the reserves (sec. 412)

The Senate bill contained a provision (sec. 412) that would authorize the following end strengths for Reserves on Active Duty in support of the reserve components as of September 30, 2017: the Army National Guard of the United States, 30,155; the Army Reserve, 16,261; The Navy Reserve, 9,955; the Marine Corps Reserve, 2,261; the Air National Guard of the United States, 14,764; and the Air Force Reserve, 2,955.

The House amendment contained an identical provision (sec. 412).

The conference agreement includes this provision.

End strength levels for the reserves on active duty in support of the reserves for fiscal year 2017 are set forth in the following table:

| Service | FY 2016 Authorized | FY 2017 | | Change from | |
		Request	Recommendation	FY 2017 Request	FY 2016 Authorized
Army National Guard	30,770	30,155	30,155	0	−615
Army Reserve	16,261	16,261	16,261	0	0
Navy Reserve	9,934	9,955	9,955	0	+21
Marine Corps Reserve	2,260	2,261	2,261	0	+1
Air National Guard	14,748	14,764	14,764	0	+16
Air Force Reserve	3,032	2,955	2,955	0	−77
DOD Total	77,005	76,351	76,351	0	−654

End strengths for military technicians (dual status) (sec. 413)

The House amendment contained a provision (sec. 413) that would authorize the following end strengths for military technicians (dual status) as of September 30, 2017: the Army National Guard of the United States, 25,507; the Army Reserve, 7,570; the Air National Guard of the United States, 22,103; and the Air Force Reserve, 10,061.

The Senate bill contained a similar provision (sec. 413) that would authorize variance from the end strengths described above in accordance with the variance authorities found in subsections (f)(1) and (g)(1)(B) of section 115 of title 10, United States Code.

The House recedes.

End strength levels for military technicians (dual status) for fiscal year 2017 are set forth in the following table:

| Service | FY 2016 Authorized | FY 2017 | | Change from | |
		Request	Recommendation	FY 2017 Request	FY 2016 Authorized
Army National Guard	26,099	25,507	25,507	0	−592
Army Reserve	7,395	7,570	7,570	0	+175
Air National Guard	22,104	22,103	22,103	0	−1
Air Force Reserve	9,814	10,061	10,061	0	+247
DOD Total	65,412	65,241	65,241	0	−171

Fiscal year 2017 limitation on number of non-dual status technicians (sec. 414)

The Senate bill contained a provision (sec. 414) that would authorize the following personnel limits for the reserve components of the Army and Air Force for non-dual status technicians as of September 30, 2017: the Army National Guard of the United States, 1,600; the Air National Guard of the United States, 350; the Army Reserve, 595; and the Air Force Reserve, 90.

The House amendment contained an identical provision (sec. 414).

The conference agreement includes this provision.

End strength levels for the non-dual status technicians for fiscal year 2017 are set forth in the following table:

| Service | FY 2016 Authorized | FY 2017 | | Change from | |
		Request	Recommendation	FY 2017 Request	FY 2016 Authorized
Army National Guard	1,600	1,600	1,600	0	0
Air National Guard	350	350	350	0	0
Army Reserve	595	420	420	0	−175
Air Force Reserve	90	90	90	0	0

Service	FY 2016 Authorized	FY 2017		Change from	
		Request	Recommendation	FY 2017 Request	FY 2016 Authorized
DOD Total	2,635	2,460	2,460	0	−175

Maximum number of reserve personnel authorized to be on active duty for operational support (sec. 415)

The Senate bill contained a provision (sec. 415) that would authorize the maximum number of reserve component personnel who may be on Active Duty or full-time National Guard duty under section 115(b) of title 10, United States Code, during fiscal year 2017 to provide operational support.

The House amendment contained an identical provision (sec. 415).

The conference agreement includes this provision.

End strength levels for reserve personnel authorized to be on Active Duty for operational support for fiscal year 2017 are set forth in the following table:

Service	FY 2016 Authorized	FY 2017		Change from	
		Request	Recommendation	FY 2017 Request	FY 2016 Authorized
Army National Guard	17,000	17,000	17,000	0	0
Army Reserve	13,000	13,000	13,000	0	0
Navy Reserve	6,200	6,200	6,200	0	0
Marine Corps Reserve	3,000	3,000	3,000	0	0
Air National Guard	16,000	16,000	16,000	0	0
Air Force Reserve	14,000	14,000	14,000	0	0
DOD Total	69,200	69,200	69,200	0	0

Technical corrections to annual authorization for personnel strengths (sec. 416)

The Senate bill contained a provision (sec. 416) that would make a technical correction to section 115 of title 10, United States Code.

The House amendment contained an identical provision (sec. 521).

The conference agreement includes this provision.

Subtitle C—Authorization of Appropriations

Military personnel (sec. 421)

The Senate bill contained a provision (sec. 421) that would authorize appropriations for military personnel at the levels identified in the funding table in section 4401 of this Act.

The House amendment contained an identical provision (sec. 421).

The conference agreement includes this provision.

LEGISLATIVE PROVISIONS NOT ADOPTED

Sense of Congress on full-time support for the Army National Guard

The House amendment contained a provision (sec. 416) that would express a sense of Congress that an adequately supported, full-time support force consisting of active and reserve personnel and military technicians for the Army National Guard is essential to maintaining the readiness of the Army National Guard.

The Senate bill contained no similar provision.

The House recedes.

TITLE V—MILITARY PERSONNEL POLICY

Subtitle A—Officer Personnel Policy

Reduction in number of general and flag officers on active duty and authorized end strength after December 31, 2022, of such general and flag officers (sec. 501)

The Senate bill contained a provision (sec. 501) that would add a new section 525a to title 10, United States Code, to establish the authorized distribution of general and flag officers for the Army, Navy, Marine Corps, and Air Force and to require a 25 percent reduction in the number of general and flag officers in the military departments. The provision would also sunset the authorized distribution of general and flag officers in section 525 of title 10, after December 31, 2017.

The amendment would add a new section 526a to title 10, United States Code, to limit the number of general and flag officers on Active Duty in the military departments and to exclude from those limits the specified number of general and flag officers serving in joint duty assignments and to require a 25 percent reduction in the number of general and flag officers in the military departments and the joint pool. The provision would also sunset the authorized distribution of general and flag officers in section 526 of title 10, after December 31, 2017.

The amendment would add a new section 12004a to title 10 United States Code, to require a 25 percent reduction in the number of general and flag officers in active status in the reserve component, including general officers of the National Guard of the States and territories and general officers serving in the National Guard Bureau, but excluding officers serving as adjutants general or assistant adjutants general of a state. The provision would also sunset the authorized distribution of general and flag officers in section 12004 of title 10, after December 31, 2017.

The House amendment included a provision (sec. 910) that would amend section 164(e) of title 10, United States Code, to specify that the grade of an officer serving as commander of a service or functional component command shall be no higher than lieutenant general or vice admiral. The provision would further require that the total number of officers in the grade of general or admiral on active duty be reduced by five positions, and to require a report to the congressional defense committees on the Department's plan to implement those reductions.

The House recedes with an amendment that would create a new section 526a of title 10, United States Code, to establish authorized end strength of general and flag officers, to reflect a reduction of 110 general and flag officers on active duty by not later than December 31, 2022, and to redistribute authorized general and flag officers across the military departments and the joint pool.

The amendment would require the Secretary of Defense to conduct a study of general and flag officer requirements with a goal of identifying and justifying each general or flag officer position in terms of overall force structure, scope of responsibility, command and control requirements, and force readiness execution and to identify an additional 10 percent reduction in the number of general and flag officers above the reduction of 110 billets. The results of the study shall be submitted to the Committees on Armed Services of the Senate and the House of Representatives no later than April 1, 2017. If practicable, an interim report shall be submitted to the Committees on Armed Forces of the Senate and the House of Representatives on the progress of the completion of the study and recommendations for achieving the additional 10% reductions in the number of general and flag officer positions.

The provision would also require the Secretary of Defense to submit to Congress with the budget for the Department of Defense for fiscal year 2019 a plan to achieve the reduction of 110 general and flag officers and the proposed distribution of authorized general and flag officer positions by prescribed levels by December 31, 2022. Progress reports on implementing the required plan for reductions would be required with the budget of the Department of Defense for fiscal years 2020, 2021, and 2022. The provision would require the Secretary of Defense to revise applicable guidance of the Department of Defense on general and flag officer authorizations not later than 120 days after completion of the plan to ensure that the reductions required under this provision are incorporated into the planning for executing promotions by the military departments, to ensure that resulting grades for general and flag officers are uniformly applied to positions of similar duties and responsibilities across the military departments and the joint pool, and that planning achieves a reduction in headquarters functions and administrative and support activities and staff of the Department of Defense and the military departments.

The provision would provide for an orderly transition for officers recently assigned to positions that would be eliminated and to require notification to Congress for any affected officer who, by December 31, 2022, has not completed 24 months in a position to be eliminated who may be allowed to complete at least 24 months in such position. The provision would also require certification to accompany all nominations of officers to a grade above O-6, forwarded by the President to the Senate for appointment, by and with advice and consent of the Senate, that the appointment will not interfere with achieving the reduction of 110 general and flag officers required by the provision.

The conferees note that despite two decades of Congressional concern the Department of Defense and the military departments have not demonstrated the willingness to implement even the reduction in the number of general and flag officer positions directed by the Secretary of Defense's Track Four Efficiencies Initiatives decision of

March 14, 2011. In the context of the Department of Defense's continued requests to reduce military end strength, especially in the Army and the Marine Corps, reductions that Congress has cautiously considered and authorized, the time has come for the Department to rigorously evaluate and validate every general and flag officer position. The conferees believe that an additional 10% reduction in the number of general and flag officer positions may be appropriate by downgrading or eliminating positions in addition to the 110 positions required to be eliminated under this provision are achieved. The conferees expect that the Department of Defense and the military departments will improve efficiency by eliminating bloated headquarters and staffs while preserving the necessary number and grades of positions for general and flag officers who are responsible to train and lead our Nation's forces in battle and to bring them safely home again. The conferees expect that the leadership of the Department of Defense and the military departments will approach this effort with the seriousness of conviction that our men and women in uniform, and the American people deserve.

Repeal of statutory specification of general or flag officer grade for various positions in the Armed Forces (sec. 502)

The Senate bill contained a provision (sec. 502) that would amend or repeal various statutory specifications in title 10, United States Code, to remove the requirement that an officer serving must hold a specified general or flag officer grade for certain positions in the Armed Forces.

The House amendment contained no similar provision.

The House recedes with an amendment that would remove the statutory general officer grade requirement associated with the Surgeon General of the Navy and the Surgeon General of the Air Force to conform with the elimination of the grade requirements for the Surgeon General of the Army. The amendment would also remove the entitlement of the Assistant Judge Advocate Generals of the Navy to receive retired pay for the grade of rear admiral (lower half) unless the officer is authorized the pay under another provision of law.

The conferees note that the provision would not affect the grade of an officer currently serving in the positions and would not prohibit the positions from being filled by an officer with the same, or a higher, or lower grade than the law currently requires.

Number of Marine Corps general officers (sec. 503)

The House amendment contained a provision (sec. 501) that would amend sections 525 and 526 of title 10, United States Code, to authorize an increase in the number of general officers in the grade above major general from 15 to 17, decrease the number of general officers in the grade of major general from 23 to 22, and increase the number of deputy commandants within the Marine Corps from 6 to 7.

The Senate bill contained no similar provision.

The Senate recedes.

Promotion eligibility period for officers whose confirmation of appointment is delayed due to nonavailability to the Senate of probative information under control of non-Department of Defense agencies (sec. 504)

The Senate bill contained a provision (sec. 506) that would amend section 629(c) of title 10, United States Code, to provide that the period for promotion eligibility of an officer

would not expire during the period when the Senate is unable to obtain information necessary to give its advice and consent to the appointment concerned because the information is under control of a department or agency of the Federal Government other than the Department of Defense.

The House amendment contained no similar provision.

The House recedes.

Continuation of certain officers on active duty without regard to requirement for retirement for years of service (sec. 505)

The Senate bill contained a provision (sec. 509) that would amend chapter 36 of title 10, United States Code, to authorize service secretaries to allow officers in a grade above O–4 who are serving in military occupational specialties designated by the secretary to remain on Active Duty for up to 40 years of active service.

The House amendment contained no similar provision.

The House recedes.

Equal consideration of officers for early retirement or discharge (sec. 506)

The House amendment contained a provision (sec. 502) that would amend section 638a of title 10, United States Code, to authorize the secretaries of the military departments to convene boards to consider officers for involuntary separation below the grade of lieutenant colonel or commander as a single, consolidated year group without distinctions based on retirement eligibility and to align separation boards for such officers with the practices for promotion selection boards.

The Senate bill contained no similar provision.

The Senate recedes.

Modification of authority to drop from rolls a commissioned officer (sec. 507)

The House amendment contained a provision (sec. 503) that would amend section 1161(b) of title 10, United States Code, to authorize the Secretary of Defense, or the Secretary of the department in which the Coast Guard is operating when it is not operating in the Navy, to drop from the rolls of any armed force any commissioned officer (1) who has been absent without authority for at least three months, (2) who may be separated under section 1167 of title 10, United States Code, by reason of a sentence to confinement adjudged by a court-martial, or (3) who is sentenced to confinement in a Federal or State penitentiary or correctional institution after having been found guilty of an offense by a court other than a court-martial or other military court, and whose sentence has become final.

The Senate bill contained no similar provision.

The Senate recedes.

Extension of force management authorities allowing enhanced flexibility for officer personnel management (sec. 508)

The Senate bill contained a provision (sec. 510) that would:

(a) amend section 4403(i) of the National Defense Authorization Act for Fiscal Year 1993 (Public Law 102–484) to extend Temporary Early Retirement Authority through December 31, 2025;

(b) amend section 638a(a)(2) of title 10, United States Code, to extend through December 31, 2025 authority for service secretaries to manage authorized officer personnel strength by shortening the period of continuation of service by officers on Active Duty, to authorize involuntary early retirement for certain officers on Active Duty, and

to consider officers for involuntary discharge who are not eligible for retirement;

(c) amend section 1175a(k)(1) of title 10, United States Code to extend through December 31, 2025 authority to provide voluntary separation pay and benefits; and

(d) amend section 1370(a)(2)(F) of title 10, United States Code to extend through fiscal year 2025, authority for early retirement of up to 4 percent of the authorized Active-Duty strength of officers in the grades of O–5 and O–6 without reduction in grade in each fiscal year.

The House amendment contained no similar provision.

The House recedes.

Pilot programs on direct commissions to cyber positions (sec. 509)

The House amendment contained a provision (sec. 1635) that would require the Secretaries of the Army and the Air Force to carry out a pilot program to improve the ability of the Army and Air Force to recruit cyber professionals.

The Senate bill contained no similar provision.

The Senate recedes with an amendment that would authorize the secretaries of the military departments to conduct pilot programs to recruit and confer original appointments to qualified individuals as commissioned officers in a cyber specialty. Pilot programs established under this provision may commence on or after January 1, 2017, and shall terminate no later than December 31, 2022. Each Secretary of a military department who conducts a pilot program under this provision shall provide a report to the Committees on Armed Services of the Senate and of the House of Representatives, not later than January 1, 2020, evaluating the success of the program in obtaining skilled cyber personnel for the Armed Forces.

Length of joint duty assignments (sec. 510)

The Senate bill contained a provision (sec. 507) that would amend section 664 of title 10, United States Code, to modify the qualifying period for joint duty assignments from 3 years to not less than 2 years. The proposal would repeal the average tour length requirement and repeal the authority for shorter tour lengths for officers initially assigned to critical occupational specialties.

The House amendment contained a similar provision (sec. 912).

The House recedes.

Revision of definitions used for joint officer management (sec. 510A)

The Senate bill contained a provision (sec. 508) that would amend section 668 of title 10, United States Code, to update the definitions of joint matters and joint duty assignment for the purpose of joint officer management. The provision would also repeal the definition of critical occupational specialty.

The House amendment contained a similar provision (sec. 913).

The Senate recedes.

Subtitle B—Reserve Component Management

Authority for temporary waiver of limitation on term of service of Vice Chief of the National Guard Bureau (sec. 511)

The Senate bill contained a provision (sec. 521) that would amend section 10505(a)(4) of title 10, United States Code, to authorize the Secretary of Defense to extend the term of office of the Vice Chief of the National Guard Bureau for up to 90 days to provide for the orderly transition of officers appointed to the positions of the Chief and the Vice Chief of the National Guard Bureau.

The House amendment contained no similar provision.

The House recedes.

Rights and protections available to military technicians (sec. 512)

The Senate bill contained a provision (sec. 523) that would amend section 709 of title 32, United States Code, to clarify the employment rights and protections of military technicians.

The House amendment contained no such provision.

The House recedes with an amendment that would clarify that military technicians, under certain conditions, may appeal adverse employment actions to the Merit Systems Protection Board and Equal Employment Opportunity Commission.

Inapplicability of certain laws to National Guard technicians performing Active Guard and Reserve duty (sec. 513)

The Senate bill contained a provision (sec. 525) that would amend section 709 of title 32, United States Code, to clarify that the provision that grants military leave to individuals appointed to the civil service does not apply to members of the Active Guard and Reserve, just as it does not apply to members on Active Duty.

The House amendment contained no similar provision.

The House recedes.

Extension of removal of restrictions on the transfer of officers between the active and inactive National Guard (sec. 514)

The House amendment contained a provision (sec. 511) that would extend through December 31, 2019, the temporary authority for the Secretary of the Army and Secretary of the Air Force to transfer officers of the Army and Air National Guard from the Selected Reserve to the inactive National Guard and from the inactive National guard to the Selected reserve.

The Senate bill contained no similar provision.

The Senate recedes.

Extension of temporary authority to use Air Force reserve component personnel to provide training and instruction regarding pilot training (sec. 515)

The House amendment contained a provision (sec. 512) that would amend section 514(a)(1) of the National Defense Authorization Act for Fiscal Year 2016 (Public Law 114–92) to extend for 1 year the current temporary authority for the Air Force to allow no more than 50 Active Guard and Reserve (AGR) personnel and dual status military technicians to instruct and train Active Duty and members of foreign military forces in the United States, the Commonwealth of Puerto Rico, or possessions of the United States as a primary duty.

The Senate bill contained no similar provision.

The Senate recedes.

The conferees expect the Air Force to devise a solution to this issue that does not include amending the underlying statutory authorities for AGRs and technicians. The conferees urge the Air Force to consider solutions as part of the ongoing duty status review.

Expansion of eligibility for deputy commander of combatant command having United States among geographic area of responsibility to include officers of the Reserves (sec. 516)

The Senate bill contained a provision (sec. 925) that would amend section 164 of title 10, United States Code, to require that at least one deputy commander of the combatant command of the geographic area of responsibility which includes the United States be a member of a reserve component of the Armed Forces, unless a reserve component officer is serving as commander of that combatant command.

The House amendment contained no similar provision.

The House recedes.

Subtitle C—General Service Authorities

Matters relating to provision of leave for members of the Armed Forces, including prohibition on leave not expressly authorized by law (sec. 521)

The Senate bill contained a provision (sec. 532) that would modify section 701 of title 10, United States Code, to authorize up to 12 weeks of leave to be allowed in the case of a servicemember who is the primary caregiver in the case of the birth of a child or the adoption of a child. In the case of leave taken following the birth of a child, the availability of primary caregiver leave would commence after completion of medical convalescent leave resulting from the birth of such child. The provision would also increase the amount of uncharged leave authorized for a secondary caregiver in the case of the birth of a child or the adoption of child. The provision would authorize 21 days of uncharged leave for a birth parent or an adoptive parent who is the secondary caregiver. The provision would repeal subsections of section 701 relating to spouse and adoption leave as obsolete. The provision would require the Secretary of Defense to prescribe in regulation definitions of eligible primary and secondary caregivers for the purposes of this benefit, and to establish regulations for requesting and approving uncharged leave associated with births to a military family, and with adoptions by a military family, and would allow a military member to accept a 1-week extension of a servicemember's military service obligation for every week of such leave approved and taken. The implementing regulations would authorize the secretary concerned to waive service obligation extensions related to this leave as an incentive for re-enlistments.

The provision would also create a new section 704a of title 10, United States Code, which would prohibit leave to be authorized, granted or assigned, including uncharged leave, unless expressly authorized by law. The committee considers this provision necessary to clarify that military leave is established by law and may not be created without express congressional authority.

The House amendment contained a provision (sec. 529) that would amend chapter 40 of title 10, United States Code, by adding a new section 701a which would authorize 14 days of leave to a member of the Armed Forces who becomes a parent when that member's spouse gives birth. The provision would also amend section 701 of title 10, United States Code, to authorize 36 days of leave, to be shared between two members of the Armed Forces who are married to each other and adopt a child.

The House amendment contained a provision (sec. 522) that would amend section 701(i) of title 10, United States Code, to provide one servicemember up to 21 days of leave and another servicemember up to 14 days of leave for the adoption of a child for dual-military couples of the Armed Forces.

The House recedes with an amendment that would authorize up to 12 weeks of total leave, including up to six weeks of medical convalescent leave, to be used by a servicemember who is the primary caregiver in connection with the birth of a child. The provision would authorize additional medical convalescent leave when specifically recommended, in writing, by the medical provider of the servicemember to address a diagnosed medical condition and when approved by the servicemember's commander. The provision would authorize up to six weeks of leave for the primary caregiver in the case of the adoption of a child, to be used in connection with the adoption. The provision would authorize up to 21 days of leave for the secondary caregiver in the case of the birth of a child or adoption. The provision would require the Secretary of Defense to prescribe in regulation definitions of eligible primary and secondary caregivers for the purposes of this benefit, and to establish regulations for requesting and approving uncharged leave associated with births to a military family, and with adoptions by a military family, and would allow a military member to accept a 1-week extension of a servicemember's military service obligation for every week of such leave approved and taken. The implementing regulations would authorize the secretary concerned to waive service obligation extensions related to this leave as an incentive for re-enlistments. The provision would also create a new section 704a of title 10, United States Code, that would prohibit leave to be authorized, granted, or assigned, including uncharged leave, unless expressly authorized by law.

Transfer of provision relating to expenses incurred in connection with leave canceled due to contingency operations (sec. 522)

The Senate bill contained a provision (sec. 533) that would relocate the authority to reimburse members of the Armed Forces for expenses incurred in connection with leave cancelled due to contingency operations from section 453 of title 37, United States Code, to title 10, United States Code.

The House amendment contained no similar provision.

The House recedes.

Expansion of authority to execute certain military instruments (sec. 523)

The Senate bill contained a provision (sec. 552) that would amend section 1044d of title 10, United States Code, to authorize a person authorized to act as a notary under section 1044a of title 10, United States Code, or a state-licensed notary employed by a military department or the Coast Guard, who is supervised by a military legal assistance counsel, to notarize military testamentary instruments. The provision would also amend section 1044a(b) to authorize all civilian paralegals serving at military legal assistance offices, supervised by a military legal assistance counsel, to act as a notary.

The House amendment contained a similar provision (sec. 524).

The House recedes with a technical amendment.

Medical examination before administrative separation for members with post-traumatic stress disorder or traumatic brain injury in connection with sexual assault (sec. 524)

The Senate bill contained a provision (sec. 554) that would amend section 1177(a)(1) of title 10, United States Code, to require that a member of the Armed Forces who was sexually assaulted within 24 months prior to a proposed administrative separation under conditions other than honorable, including an administrative separation in lieu of court-martial, and who is diagnosed with post-traumatic stress disorder or traumatic brain injury by a physician, clinical psychologist, psychiatrist, licensed clinical social worker, or psychiatric advanced practice registered nurse as experiencing post-traumatic stress disorder or traumatic brain injury or who otherwise reasonably alleges, based on the service of the member sexually assaulted, the influence of such a condition, may not be separated until the results of the medical examination have been reviewed by appropriate authorities responsible for evaluating, reviewing, and approving the separation case, as determined by the Secretary concerned.

The House amendment contained no similar provision.

The House recedes.

Reduction of tenure on the temporary disability retired list (sec. 525)

The Senate bill contained a provision (sec. 534) that would amend section 1210 of title 10, United States Code, to reduce the maximum tenure for servicemembers placed on the Temporary Disability Retired List (TDRL), due to an injury or illness eligible for disability retirement, from 5 years to 3 years. The committee notes that this provision addresses a recommendation from the Government Accountability Office in 2009 for Congress to shorten the maximum tenure for placement on the TDRL.

The House amendment contained no similar provision.

The House recedes.

Technical correction to voluntary separation pay and benefits (sec. 526)

The House amendment contained a provision (sec. 525) that would amend section 1175a of title 10, United States Code, by updating the references to section 502(f) of title 32, United States Code, and the list of involuntary mobilization authorities.

The Senate bill contained no similar provision.

The Senate recedes.

Consolidation of Army marketing and pilot program on consolidated Army recruiting (sec. 527)

The Senate bill contained a provision (sec. 1092) that would require the Secretary of the Army to consolidate within the Army Marketing Research Group all functions relating to the marketing of the Army and each of the components of the Army in order to assure unity of effort and cost effectiveness in the marketing of the Army and each of the components of the Army.

The House amendment contained a related provision (sec. 527) that would require the Secretary of the Army to establish a pilot program to consolidate the recruiting efforts of the Regular Army, Army Reserve, and Army National Guard under which a recruiter in one of the components participating in the pilot program may recruit individuals to enlist in any of the components regardless of the funding source of the recruiting activity.

The Senate recedes with a clarifying amendment that would combine both provisions.

Subtitle D—Member Whistleblower Protections and Correction of Military Records

Improvements to whistleblower protection procedures (sec. 531)

The Senate bill contained a provision (sec. 961) that would make numerous amendments to section 1034 of title 10, United States Code, to clarify and expand the types of adverse personnel actions prohibited under the military whistleblower protection program, to include retaliatory investigations and failures of superiors to respond to retaliatory actions in certain circumstances, as

prohibited personnel actions reviewable under that statute. The provision would also require inspectors general (IG) to notify the secretary concerned if, during the IG's preliminary investigation, the IG determined there were reasonable grounds to believe that a prohibited personnel action occurred, and that the action would result in an immediate hardship to the service member, and would authorize the secretary concerned to take action, as appropriate, in such cases. The provision would require an IG to provide periodic updates to whistleblowers on the progress of investigations, to include an estimate of the time remaining until an investigation was complete. Finally, the provision would require the Department of Defense Inspector General, within 1 year of enactment of this Act, to prescribe uniform standards for the conduct of military whistleblower investigations and for the training of staffs conducting such investigations.

The House amendment contained no similar provision.

The House recedes with a clarifying amendment.

Modification of whistleblower protection authorities to restrict contrary findings of prohibited personnel action by the Secretary concerned (sec. 532)

The Senate bill contained a provision (sec. 962) that would amend section 1034 of title 10, United States Code, to clarify that when the secretary of the military department concerned receives a report from an inspector general that substantiates that a prohibited personnel action occurred, the secretary may consider whether to take corrective action but may not make a determination in such cases that a prohibited personnel action did not occur.

The House amendment contained no similar provision.

The House recedes.

Availability of certain correction of military records and discharge review board information through the Internet (sec. 533)

The Senate bill contained a provision (sec. 536) that would amend section 1552 of title 10, United States Code, to require that a board convened to consider a claim for correction of military records by a former servicemember (1) who had been deployed in support of contingency operation and who was subsequently diagnosed as experiencing post-traumatic stress disorder (PTSD) or traumatic brain injury (TBI), or (2) who was diagnosed while serving in the military as experiencing a mental health disorder include a clinical psychologist or psychiatrist, or a physician with training on mental health issues connected with PTSD or TBI. The proposal would require the military department concerned, or the Department of Homeland Security, to make available to the public on an Internet website information regarding claims considered by the service board for correction of military records in a calendar quarter.

The Senate bill would also modify section 1553 of title 10, United States Code, to require similar information be made available to the public on an Internet website information regarding claims considered by the service discharge review boards in a calendar quarter.

The House amendment contained no similar provision.

The House recedes with an amendment that would remove the requirement that boards for correction of military records considering dismissal or discharge of an individual who was diagnosed while serving in

the military as experiencing a mental health disorder include a clinical psychologist or psychiatrist, or a physician with training on mental health issues connected with PTSD or TBI, and would modify the information required to be made available to the public on an Internet website.

The conferees note that section 1552(g) of title 10, United States Code, already requires that any medical advisory opinion issued with respect to a member or former member of the armed forces who was diagnosed while serving in the armed forces as experiencing a mental health disorder shall include the opinion of a clinical psychologist or psychiatrist if the request for correction of records concerned relates to a mental health disorder.

Improvements to authorities and procedures for the correction of military records (sec. 534)

The Senate bill contained a provision (sec. 963) that would amend section 1552(a) of title 10, United States Code, to require that boards for correction of military records (BCMRs) notify claimants of what specific information or documents are needed to make their claim reviewable by the board, if such information or documents are missing, and would require the BCMR to make reasonable efforts to obtain missing records when they cannot be obtained by a claimant. The provision would require the BCMR to consider any request for reconsideration of a determination of a BCMR when new information is provided by a claimant, not previously considered. The provision would reaffirm that claimants may seek judicial review of BCMR decisions, and would require BCMRs to publish final decisions with personally identifiable information redacted. The provision would require each secretary concerned to develop, within 1 year of enactment of this Act, a comprehensive training curriculum for members of BCMRs, and would require the Secretary of Defense and Secretary of Homeland Security to ensure such curricula are uniform. Finally, the provision would require each secretary concerned to submit to Congress within 18 months of enactment a report setting forth the training curriculum established under this section.

The House amendment contained no similar provision.

The House recedes with an amendment that does not include the provision on judicial review of BCMR decisions.

Treatment by discharge review boards of claims asserting post-traumatic stress disorder or traumatic brain injury in connection with combat or sexual trauma as a basis for review of discharge (sec. 535)

The Senate bill contained a provision (sec. 536A) that would amend section 1553(d) of title 10, United States Code, to require discharge review boards to review medical evidence of the Secretary of Veterans Affairs or a civilian health care provider presented by a former member of the Armed Forces, and to grant liberal consideration to claims by a former member of the Armed Forces that post-traumatic stress disorder or traumatic brain injury potentially contributed to the circumstances resulting in a less favorable characterization of discharge. An application for relief that may be reviewed under this provision includes matters relating to post-traumatic stress disorder or traumatic brain injury related to combat or military sexual trauma, as determined by the Secretary concerned.

The House amendment contained no similar provision.

The House recedes.

Comptroller General of the United States review of integrity of Department of Defense whistleblower program (sec. 536)

The Senate bill contained a provision (sec. 964) that would require the Comptroller General of the United States to conduct an assessment of the integrity of the Department of Defense (DOD) whistleblower program, to include an assessment of the extent to which the DOD whistleblower program meets executive branch policies and goals for whistleblower protections, the adequacy of procedures to address whistleblower complaints submitted by employees of the Office of the Inspector General of the Department of Defense (OIG), the extent to which there have been violations of confidentiality standards, the extent to which there have been retaliatory investigations within OIG, the extent to which whistleblower complaints against Senate-confirmed civilian officials of DOD have been substantiated and reported to Congress in the past 10 years, and the ability of the inspectors general of DOD and the military services to access agency information necessary to the execution of their duties, including classified and other sensitive information, and of the adequacy of security procedures to safeguard such information. The provision would require the Comptroller General to report to the Committees on Armed Services of the Senate and House of Representatives within 1 year of enactment of this Act on the results of this review.

The House amendment contained no similar provision.

The House recedes with an amendment that would require the Comptroller General to submit the report within 18 months from enactment of this Act.

Subtitle E—Military Justice and Legal Assistance Matters

United States Court of Appeals for the Armed Forces (sec. 541)

The Senate bill contained a provision (sec. 553) that would amend sections 942 and 936 of title 10, United States Code (Articles 142 and 136 of the Uniform Code of Military Justice) to modify the terms of two civilian judges of the United States Court of Appeals for the Armed Forces ("the court") to avoid disruption that may occur to the operations of the court when two judicial vacancies occur simultaneously. The provision would modify the daily rate of compensation for senior judges performing judicial duties with the court so that they would be paid the difference between the pay of a judge of the court and their federal retired pay, consistent with the process employed by the United States Court of Appeals for the District of Columbia and the United States Bankruptcy Courts. The provision would authorize the judges of the court to administer oaths in a similar manner as other federal judges. The provision would repeal the provision in article 142(b)(3) that precludes more than three judges of the court from being from the same political party.

The House amendment contained no similar provision.

The House recedes with technical and clarifying amendments.

Effective prosecution and defense in courts-martial and pilot programs on professional military justice development for judge advocates (sec. 542)

The Senate bill contained a provision (sec. 548) that would require the service secretaries to carry out a program to ensure that trial and defense counsel detailed to prosecute or defend a court-martial have suffi-

cient experience and knowledge to effectively prosecute or defend the case, or that there is adequate supervision and oversight of the trial counsel and the defense counsel to ensure effective prosecution and defense in the court-martial. The provision would also require service secretaries to establish and use a system of skill identifiers to identify judge advocates with skill and experience in military justice proceedings to identify judge advocates to provide supervision and oversight of less experienced judge advocates prosecuting and defending in military courts-martial.

The Senate bill also contained a provision (sec. 549) that would require the secretary of each military department to conduct a 5 year pilot program to assess the feasibility and advisability of a career military justice litigation track for judge advocates in the Armed Forces. The pilot programs would include a military justice career track that leads to senior judge advocates with military justice expertise in prosecuting and defending complex cases in military courts-martial. The provision would use authority provided elsewhere in this Act to suspend limitations on the number of certain senior commissioned officers on active duty, under section 532(a) of title 10, United States Code. The provision would require the use of skill identifiers to identify judge advocates participating in the pilot programs. The provision would also require promotion boards to give the same opportunity for promotion as all other judge advocates being considered for promotion. The provision would require the Secretary of Defense to submit reports on the pilot programs not later than 4 years after the date of enactment of this Act.

The House amendment contained a provision (sec. 547) that would require the secretary of each military department to establish a career military justice litigation track for judge advocates. The military justice career litigation track would provide for assignment and advancement of qualified judge advocates to serve in specified billets in military justice trial and defense counsel, as military trial and appellate judges, military justice instructors, positions in the criminal law offices or divisions of the Armed Forces, Special Victims Prosecutors, Victims' Legal Counsel, Special Victims' Counsel, and other positions as the secretary of the military department shall specify. The provision would prohibit a judge advocate participating in the military justice litigation career track from serving more than four years of duty outside of the litigation track. The provision would prohibit any adverse assessment of a judge advocate by reason of participating in the litigation track. The provision would require the secretary of each military department to implement the career litigation track not later than 18 months after enactment. It would require a report from the secretaries of the military departments to the Committees on Armed Services of the Senate and the House of Representatives on the progress in implementing the career litigation track.

The House receded with an amendment that would require the service secretaries to establish programs for deliberate professional developmental programs to ensure effective prosecution and defense in all courts-martial. The amendment requires the service secretaries to establish and use a system of military justice experience designators or skill identifiers. The amendment requires the service secretaries to carry out a pilot program to assess the feasibility and advisability of establishing a deliberate profes-

sional development process for judge advocates that leads to military justice practitioners capable of prosecuting and defending complex cases in military courts-martial. Pilot programs established under this provision would be for a period of five years. Not later than four years after the date of enactment of this Act, the secretaries concerned shall submit a report to the Committees on Armed Services of the Senate and of the House of Representatives providing a description and assessment of the pilot programs and providing such recommendations as the secretary considers appropriate.

Inclusion in annual reports on sexual assault prevention and response efforts of the Armed Forces of information on complaints of retaliation in connection with reports of sexual assault in the Armed Forces (sec. 543)

The Senate bill contained a provision (sec. 543) that would amend section 1631(b) of the Ike Skelton National Defense Authorization Act for Fiscal Year 2011 (10 U.S.C. 1561 note) to require the annual report on sexual assault and response efforts to include information on complaints of retaliation in connection with reports of sexual assault in the Armed Forces.

The House amendment contained no similar provision.

The House recedes.

Extension of the requirement for annual report regarding sexual assaults and coordination with release of Family Advocacy Program report (sec. 544)

The Senate bill contained a provision (sec. 551) that would amend section 1631 of the Ike Skelton National Defense Authorization Act for Fiscal Year 2011 (Public Law 111–383) that would extend the requirement for the annual report on sexual assault in the military under that section through February, 2025, and require the reports to be submitted to the Committees on Armed Services of the Senate and the House of Representatives not later than March 31 each year. The provision would also clarify the scope of sexual assaults covered by the report to include all reported sexual assaults, regardless of the age of the offender or victim or the relationship status between the offender and victim, including, at a minimum, all sexual assault reports received by the Sexual Assault Prevention and Response Program, or equivalent, and the Family Advocacy Program, or equivalent, of each Armed Force.

The House amendment contained a provision (sec. 542) that would extend the requirement for the annual report through January 31, 2021. The provision would also require release of the report to coincide with the release of the Family Advocacy Program report, as required elsewhere in this Act.

The Senate recedes with an amendment that would establish the date by which the annual report would be provided to be not later than April 30th.

Metrics for evaluating the efforts of the Armed Forces to prevent and respond to retaliation in connection with reports of sexual assault in the Armed Forces (sec. 545)

The Senate bill contained a provision (sec. 544) that would require the Sexual Assault Prevention and Response Office of the Department of Defense to establish and issue metrics to be used by the military departments to evaluate the efforts of the Armed Forces to prevent and respond to retaliation in connection with reports of sexual assault in the Armed Forces.

The House amendment contained no similar provision.

The House recedes.

Training for Department of Defense personnel who investigate claims of retaliation (sec. 546)

The Senate bill contained a provision (sec. 542) that would require the Secretary of Defense to prescribe training to individuals in the Department of Defense who investigate claims of retaliation on the nature and consequences of retaliation and, in cases involving reports of sexual assault, the nature and consequences of sexual assault trauma.

The House amendment contained a similar provision (sec. 546).

The House recedes with a clarifying amendment.

Notification to complainants of resolution of investigations into retaliation (sec. 547)

The Senate bill contained a provision (sec. 541) that would require the Secretary of Defense to prescribe regulations that would require that the results of an investigation of a retaliation complaint by a member of the Armed Forces be reported to the member who initiated the complaint. The report would inform the member whether the complaint was substantiated, unsubstantiated, or dismissed. The provision would also require the Secretary of Homeland Security to prescribe similar regulations to report on retaliation complaints by a member of the Coast Guard.

The House amendment contained no similar provision.

The House recedes with an amendment that would require that the results of the investigation be reported in writing to the member who initiated the complaint.

Modification of definition of sexual harassment for purposes of investigations by commanding officers of complaints of harassment (sec. 548)

The Senate bill contained a provision (sec. 550) that would amend section 1561(i) of title 10, United States Code, to modify the definition of sexual harassment. The committee is concerned that the existing definition of sexual harassment has caused the military services to consider sexual harassment as a violation of equal opportunity policy instead of an adverse behavior that data have demonstrated is on the spectrum of behavior that can contribute to an increase in the incidence of sexual assault.

The House amendment contained no similar provision.

The House recedes with a technical amendment that would clarify that the provision would amend section 1561(e) of title 10, United States Code.

Improved Department of Defense prevention and response to hazing in the Armed Forces (sec. 549)

The House amendment contained a provision (sec. 544) that would require the Secretary of Defense to establish a system for collection of reports of hazing involving a member of the Armed Forces. The provision would also require the secretaries of the military departments, in consultation with the Chief of Staff of each armed force, to improve training to assist members to better recognize, prevent, and respond to hazing. The amendment would also require an annual survey on hazing and annual reports on hazing that include a description of efforts to prevent and respond to hazing incidents, to track and encourage reporting hazing incidents, and to ensure consistent implementation of anti-hazing policies. The reports required under this section would also address elements prescribed for anti-hazing reports in section 534 of the national Defense Authorization Act for Fiscal Year 2013 (P.L. 112–239).

The Senate bill contained no similar provision.

The Senate recedes with an amendment that would remove the requirement that service secretaries conduct an annual survey on hazing.

The conferees are concerned that the extent of hazing incidents in the armed forces is not fully known. Therefore, the conferees direct that the Department of Defense include questions in existing surveys of members of the Armed Forces to assist in determining the prevalence of hazing incidents in the Armed Forces, to assess the effectiveness of training in recognizing and preventing hazing, and to determine the extent to which members of the Armed Forces are aware of options to report hazing incidents, including anonymous report options.

Subtitle F—National Commission on Military, National, and Public Service

Purpose, scope, and definitions (sec. 551)

The Senate bill contained a series of provisions (sec. 1066–1073) that would create an independent National Commission on Military, National, and Public Service, including a provision (sec. 1066) to establish the purpose and scope of this Commission to consider: (1) the need for a military selective service process, including a continuing need for a mechanism to draft large numbers of replacement combat troops; (2) the means by which to foster a greater attitude and ethos of service among United States youth, including an increased propensity for military service; (3) the feasibility of modifying the military selective service process to obtain for military, national, and public service individuals with skills for which the Nation has a critical need, without regard to age or gender; and (4) the feasibility of including in the military selective service process, as so modified, an eligibility for one or more Federal benefits to incentivize the necessary education, training, and service to fulfill such critical needs.

The House amendment contained no similar provision.

The House recedes.

Preliminary report on purpose and utility of registration system under Military Selective Service Act (sec. 552)

The House amendment contained a provision (sec. 528) that would require the Secretary of Defense to submit, not later than July 1, 2017, a report to the Committees on Armed Services of the Senate and the House of Representatives, on the current and future need for a centralized registration system under the Military Selective Service Act, chapter 49 of title 50, United States Code, and provide a briefing on the results of the report not later than July 1, 2017.

The Senate bill contained no similar provision.

The Senate recedes with an amendment that would require the report to also be provided to the National Commission on Military, National, and Public Service created under this Act.

National Commission on Military, National, and Public Service (sec. 553)

The Senate bill contained a provision (sec. 1067) that would establish the National Commission on Military, National, and Public Service as an independent commission. The provision would prescribe the manner and timing in which the Commission would be appointed, its composition, pay rates for members and staff, and would provide sundry other authorities attending to the operation of the Commission as an independent entity.

The Senate bill contained a provision (sec. 1073) that would require that of the amounts authorized to be appropriated for the Department of Defense for fiscal year 2017, $15.0 million be available to the National Commission on Military, National, and Public Service until expended to carry out its duties under this subtitle.

The House amendment contained no similar provisions.

The House recedes.

Commission hearings and meetings (sec. 554)

The Senate bill contained a provision (sec. 1068) that would require the National Commission on Military, National, and Public Service to conduct public hearings (except classified hearings) on recommendations under consideration, and that such hearings be noticed on a public website at least 14 days in advance. The provision would require the Commission to hold its first meeting within 30 days after all members have been appointment.

The House amendment contained no similar provision.

The House recedes.

Principles and procedure for Commission recommendations (sec. 555)

The Senate bill contained a provision (sec. 1069) that would require the President, within 3 months after the establishment date of the National Commission on Military, National, and Public Service, to establish and transmit to the Commission and Congress principles for reform of the military selective service process, including the means by which to best acquire skills to meet the military, national, and public service requirements of the country. The provision would require these Presidential principles to address: (1) whether, in light of the current global security environment, there continues to be a need for a selective service process designed to produce large quantities of combat troops, and if so, whether that system should include mandatory registration by citizens and residents regardless of gender; (2) the need, and how best to meet the need, of the Nation, the military, the Federal civilian sector, and the private sector (including the non-profit sector) for individuals possessing certain critical skills and abilities, and how to best employ individuals with those skills and abilities; (3) how to foster within the nation, particularly among the nation's youth, an increased sense of service and civic responsibility to enhance the acquisition of critically needed skills through education and training, and how best to acquire those skills for military, national, and public service; (4) how to increase propensity among the nation's youth for service in the military, or alternatively in national or public service, including how to increase the pool of qualified applicants for military service; (5) the need in government to increase interest, education, and employment in certain critical fields, including particularly science, technology, engineering, and mathematics, national security, cyber, linguistics and foreign language, education, health care, and the medical professions; and (6) how military national, and public service may be incentivized, including through educational benefits, grants, Federally-insured loans, Federal or State hiring preferences, or other mechanisms the President considers appropriate. The provision would require certain cabinet officials and other officials or experts to transmit to the Commission and Congress recommendations for the reform of the military selective service process, and military, national, and public service in connection with that process.

The Senate bill contained a provision (sec. 1071) that would preclude the actions of the

President, cabinet officials and other individuals required to provide recommendations under this subtitle, and the Commission on Military, National, and Public Service from judicial review of their actions taken under this subtitle.

The House amendment contained no similar provisions.

The House recedes.

Executive Director and staff (sec. 556)

The Senate bill contained a provision (sec. 1070) that would authorize the National Commission on Military, National, and Public Service to appoint, and fix the rate of pay of, an Executive Director and staff. The provision would limit detailees from Executive Branch agencies to no more than one-third of the personnel employed by the Commission, and would prohibit the detail of executive branch employees to the Commission who in the year prior to the detail were substantially involved with the development of recommendations provided to the Commission.

The House amendment contained no similar provision.

The House recedes.

Termination of Commission (sec. 557)

The Senate bill contained a provision (sec. 1072) that would provide for the termination of the National Commission on Military, National, and Public Service no later than 36 months after the Commission establishment date.

The House amendment contained no similar provision.

The House recedes.

Subtitle G—Member Education, Training, Resilience, and Transition

Modification of program to assist members of the Armed Forces in obtaining professional credentials (sec. 561)

The Senate bill contained a provision (sec. 562) that would amend section 2015 of title 10, United States Code, to include within the program to assist members in obtaining professional credentials those credentials that were acquired during military service but which were not necessarily obtained incident to the performance of their military duties. The provision would also eliminate the requirement that credentialing programs be accredited by third party accreditation bodies, and instead would require that credentialing programs meet certain other quality assurance benchmarks.

The House amendment contained a similar provision (sec. 561).

The House recedes with a technical amendment.

Inclusion of alcohol, prescription drug, opioid, and other substance abuse counseling as part of required preseparation counseling (sec. 562)

The House amendment contained a provision (sec. 569) that would amend section 1142(b)(11) of title 10, United States Code, to include alcohol, prescription drug, opioid, and other substance abuse counseling as part of required preseparation counseling.

The Senate bill contained no similar provision.

The Senate recedes.

Inclusion of information in Transition Assistance Program regarding effect of receipt of both veteran disability compensation and voluntary separation pay (sec. 563)

The House amendment contained a provision (sec. 569A) that would amend section 1144(b) of title 10, United States Code, to require information be provided in the course of the Transition Assistance Program re-

garding the required deduction of disability compensation paid by the Secretary of Veterans Affairs by the amount of voluntary separation pay received by the member.

The Senate bill contained no similar provision.

The Senate recedes with a technical amendment.

Training under Transition Assistance Program on employment opportunities associated with transportation security cards (sec. 564)

The House amendment contained a provision (sec. 3511) that would require the Transition Assistance Program to provide information on career opportunities for employment available to members with transportation security cards issued under section 70105 of title 46, United States Code, within 180 days after the date of enactment.

The Senate bill contained no similar provision.

The Senate recedes with a technical amendment.

Extension of suicide prevention and resilience program (sec. 565)

The Senate bill contained a provision (sec. 524) that would amend section 10219(g) of title 10, United States Code, to extend the authority for suicide prevention and resilience programs for the National Guard and Reserves until October 1, 2022.

The House amendment contained a provision (sec. 599G) that would amend section 10219(g) of title 10, United States Code, to extend the authority for suicide prevention and resilience programs for the National Guard and Reserves until October 1, 2018.

The Senate recedes.

Congressional notification in advance of appointments to service academies (sec. 566)

The House amendment contained a provision (sec. 569C) that would amend sections 4342, 6954, and 9342 of title 10, United States Code, and section 51302 of title 46, United States Code, to require the United States Military Academy, the United States Naval Academy, the United States Air Force Academy, and the United States Merchant Marine Academy to notify a Senator, Representative, or Delegate of the appointment of a cadet or midshipman nominated by that member of Congress at least 48 hours in advance of the official notification or announcement of the appointment. The advance notification requirement would be effective for classes entering these service academies after January 1, 2018.

The Senate bill contained no similar provision.

The Senate recedes.

Report and guidance regarding Job Training, Employment Skills Training, Apprenticeships, and Internships and SkillBridge initiatives for members of the Armed Forces who are being separated (sec. 567)

The House amendment contained a provision (sec. 569B) that would require the Under Secretary of Defense for Personnel and Readiness to submit to the Committees on Armed Services of the Senate and the House of Representatives a detailed report evaluating the success of the Job Training, Employment Skills Training, Apprenticeships, and Internships (known as JTEST–AI) and SkillBridge initiatives.

The Senate bill contained no similar provision.

The Senate recedes with an amendment that would extend the completion date for the report from 90 days to 180 days and narrow the scope of the report.

Military-to-mariner transition (sec. 568)

The House amendment contained a provision (sec. 563) that would require a report

from the Secretary of Defense and the Secretary of Homeland Security to the Committees on Armed Services of the Senate and House of Representatives, the Committee on Transportation and Infrastructure of the House of Representatives, and the Committee on Commerce, Science, and Transportation of the Senate on the efforts to ensure military service, training and qualifications are creditable towards merchant marine licenses and certifications.

The Senate bill contained no similar provision.

The Senate recedes.

Subtitle H—Defense Dependents' Education and Military Family Readiness Matters

Continuation of authority to assist local educational agencies that benefit dependents of members of the Armed Forces and Department of Defense civilian employees (sec. 571)

The Senate bill contained a provision (sec. 571) that would authorize $25.0 million in Operation and Maintenance, Defense-wide, for continuation of the Department of Defense (DOD) assistance program to local educational agencies impacted by enrollment of dependent children of military members and DOD civilian employees.

The Senate bill also contained a provision (sec. 572) that would authorize $5.0 million in Operation and Maintenance, Defense-wide, for impact aid payments for children with disabilities (as enacted by Public Law 106–398; 114 Stat. 1654A–77; 20 U.S.C. 7703a) using the formula set forth in section 363 of the Floyd D. Spence National Defense Authorization Act for Fiscal Year 2001 (Public Law 106–398), for continuation of Department of Defense assistance to local educational agencies that benefit eligible dependents with severe disabilities.

The House amendment contained a provision (sec. 571) that would authorize $30.0 million in Operation and Maintenance, Defense-wide, for continuation of the DOD assistance program to local educational agencies impacted by enrollment of dependent children of military members and DOD civilian employees.

The Senate recedes with an amendment that would authorize $30.0 million in supplemental impact aid, and $5.0 million for impact aid for children with severe disabilities.

One-year extension of authorities relating to the transition and support of military dependent students to local educational agencies (sec. 572)

The Senate bill contained a provision (sec. 574) that would amend section 547(c)(3) of the John Warner National Defense Authorization Act for Fiscal Year 2007 (20 U.S.C. 7703b note) to extend the authorities relating to transition and support of military dependent students to local educational agencies from September 30, 2016, to September 30, 2017. The provision would also require the administration to submit detailed budget justification information with any annual budget request that includes a request for the future extension of these authorities.

The House amendment contained no similar provision.

The House recedes with a technical amendment to correct the statutory citation of the amended section.

Annual notice to members of the Armed Forces regarding child custody protections guaranteed by the Servicemembers Civil Relief Act (sec. 573)

The House amendment contained a provision (sec. 526) that would require the secretaries of the military departments to ensure that each member of the Armed Forces with dependents receives annually, and prior to each deployment, notice of the child custody protections afforded to members of the Armed Forces under the Servicemembers Civil Relief Act (50 U.S.C. 3901 et seq.).

The Senate bill contained no similar provision.

The Senate recedes.

Requirement for annual Family Advocacy Program report regarding child abuse and domestic violence (sec. 574)

The House amendment contained a provision (sec. 543) that would require the Secretary of Defense to provide to the Committees on Armed Services of the Senate and of the House of Representatives an annual report, beginning not later than January 31, 2017 and continuing through January 31, 2012, on the child abuse and domestic abuse incident data contained in the Department of Defense Family Advocacy Program central registry for the previous year, and an analysis of the effectiveness of the Family Advocacy Program.

The Senate bill amendment contained no similar provision.

The Senate recedes with an amendment that would establish the date by which the annual report would be provided to be not later than April 30, 2017, and annually thereafter through April 30, 2021.

Reporting on allegations of child abuse in military families and homes (sec. 575)

The Senate bill contained a provision (sec. 577) that would require the Secretary of Defense and the Secretary of Homeland Security to prescribe regulations to ensure that the family advocacy program office at a military installation to which a member of the Armed Forces is assigned is provided an immediate report of credible information obtained by any individual in the chain of command of the servicemember, that a child in the family or home of the servicemember has suffered an incident of child abuse. The provision would require a similar report by any member of the Armed Forces in a profession described by subsection 226(b) of the Victims of Child Abuse Act of 1990 (42 U.S.C. 13031) who has reason to suspect that a child in the family or home of a servicemember has suffered an incident of child abuse.

The House amendment contained a similar provision (sec. 541).

The House recedes with a technical amendment.

Repeal of Advisory Council on Dependents' Education (sec. 576)

The Senate bill contained a provision (sec. 581) that would repeal section 1411 of the Defense Dependents' Education Act of 1978 to abolish the Advisory Council on Dependents' Education.

The House amendment contained no similar provision.

The House recedes.

Support for programs providing camp experience for children of military families (sec. 577)

The Senate bill contained a provision (sec. 579) that would authorize the Secretary of Defense to provide financial or non-monetary support to qualified non-profit organizations to assist those organizations in carrying out programs to support attendance at a camp or camp-like setting for children of military families.

The House amendment contained a similar provision (sec. 572).

The Senate recedes with an amendment that would remove the requirement that the Secretary accord a preference in the approval of applications submitted by certain organizations.

Comptroller General of the United States assessment and report on Exceptional Family Member Programs (sec. 578)

The Senate bill contained a provision (sec. 580) that would require the Comptroller General of the United States to submit a report to the Committees on Armed Services of the Senate and the House of Representatives on the effectiveness of each Exceptional Family Member Program of the Armed Forces.

The House amendment contained no similar provision.

The House recedes with an amendment that would require the Comptroller General of the United States to conduct an assessment on the effectiveness of each Exceptional Family Member Program of the Armed Forces and to provide a report to the Committees on Armed Services of the Senate and the House of Representatives by December 31, 2017.

Impact aid amendments (sec. 579)

The Senate bill contained a provision (sec. 573) that would amend sections 7003(b)(2)(B)(i)(I), 7003(b)(2)(B)(i)(II)(bb), and 7003(b)(2)(B)(i)(IV) of the Elementary and Secondary Education Act of 1965 (most recently amended by Public Law 114–95) to: 1) make a technical correction to the current statute to prevent the inadvertent disqualification of some local school districts from the Impact Aid heavily impacted program whose boundaries are within the perimeter of military installations; 2) provide additional time to collect data on the effects to the Impact Aid heavily impacted program; and 3) adjust eligibility criteria to meet congressional intent.

The House amendment contained a provision (sec. 573) that would amend section 8003(a)(5)(A) of the Elementary and Secondary Education Act of 1965 (most recently amended by Public Law 114–95) to authorize a provision that counts all military-connected students living in military housing equally to take effect immediately.

The Senate recedes with an amendment that would combine these provisions.

The conferees intend that if a local educational agency is eligible to receive a basic support payment under subclause (IV) of section 7003(b)(2)(B)(i) as amended by this section and the Every Student Succeeds Act then subclause (IV) takes priority over other subclauses. The conferees further intend that if a local educational agency is not eligible for a basic support payment under subclause (IV) of section 7003(b)(2)(B) (i) as amended by this section and the Every Student Succeeds Act but is eligible under section 7003(b)(2) then the local educational agency may apply under that section.

Subtitle I—Decorations and Awards

Posthumous advancement of Colonel George E. "Bud" Day, United States Air Force, on the retired list (sec. 581)

The Senate bill contained a provision (sec. 589) that would posthumously advance Colonel George E. "Bud" Day, United States Air Force, to the rank of brigadier general on the retired list of the United States Air Force. Colonel Day's benefits would not be affected by this action.

The House amendment contained no similar provision.

The House recedes.

Authorization for award of medals for acts of valor during certain contingency operations (sec. 582)

The House amendment contained a provision (section 582) that would waive the time limitations prescribed in various sections of title 10, United States Code, to authorize the President to award certain valor awards, including the Congressional Medal of Honor, to a member or former member of the Armed Forces for service in Operation Enduring Freedom, Operation Iraqi Freedom, Operation New Dawn, Operation Freedom's Sentinel, and Operation Inherent Resolve, resulting from a review of valor award nominations directed by the Secretary of Defense on January 7, 2016. The time waiver provided under the House amendment would expire on December 31, 2019.

The Senate bill had no similar provision.

The Senate recedes with a technical amendment.

Authorization for award of the Medal of Honor to Gary M. Rose and James C. McCloughan for acts of valor during the Vietnam War (sec. 583)

The Senate bill contained a provision (sec. 587) that would waive the time limitations specified in section 3744 of title 10, United States Code, to authorize the President to award the Medal of Honor to Gary M. Rose for acts of valor from September 11 through 14, 1970, during the Vietnam War, while a member of the United States Army, Military Assistance Command Vietnam—Studies and Observation Group (MACVSOG).

The House amendment contained an identical provision (sec. 583).

The conference agreement includes the provision with an amendment that would waive the time limitations specified in section 3744 of title 10, United States Code, to authorize the President to award the Medal of Honor to James C. McCloughan for acts of valor during combat operations between May 13, 1969 and May 15, 1969, during the Vietnam War, while serving as a combat medic with Company C, 3d Battalion, 21st Infantry, 196th Light Infantry Brigade, American Division, Republic of Vietnam.

Authorization for award of Distinguished Service Cross to First Lieutenant Melvin M. Spruiell for acts of valor during World War II (sec. 584)

The House amendment contained a provision (sec. 585) that would authorize the Secretary of the Army to award the Distinguished Service Cross to First Lieutenant Melvin M. Spruiell for acts of valor while a member of the Army serving in France with the 377th Parachute Field Artillery, 101st Airborne Division, from June 10 to 11, 1944.

The Senate bill contained no similar provision.

The Senate recedes.

Authorization for award of the Distinguished Service Cross to Chaplain (First Lieutenant) Joseph Verbis LaFleur for acts of valor during World War II (sec. 585)

The Senate bill contained a provision (sec. 588) that would authorize the Secretary of the Army to award the Distinguished Service Cross to Chaplain (First Lieutenant) Joseph Verbis LaFleur for acts of valor while interned as a prisoner of war by Japan, from December 30, 1941 to September 7, 1944.

The House amendment contained no similar provision.

The House recedes.

Review regarding award of Medal of Honor to certain Asian American and Native American Pacific Islander War Veterans (sec. 586)

The House amendment contained a provision (sec. 581) that would require the Secretaries of the military departments to review the service records of certain Asian American and Native American Pacific Islander veterans from the Korean war and Vietnam war veterans to determine if the award of the Medal of Honor is appropriate. The House provision would require the services to review the records of veterans who were previously awarded the Distinguished Service Cross, the Navy Cross, and the Air Force Cross, and in those cases where the Secretary concerned determines that the service records of those veterans support the award of the Medal of Honor, this section would also waive the statutory time limitations for award of the Medal of Honor.

The Senate bill contained no similar provision.

The Senate recedes with an amendment that would require the Secretaries of the military departments to review the service records of former members of the Armed Forces whose service records identify them as an Asian American or Native American Pacific Islander war veteran who was previously awarded the Distinguished Service Cross, the Navy Cross, and the Air Force Cross and in those cases where the Secretary concerned determines that the service records of those veterans support the award of the Medal of Honor, this section would also waive the statutory time limitations for award of the Medal of Honor.

Subtitle J—Miscellaneous Reports and Other Matters

Repeal of requirement for a chaplain at the United States Air Force Academy appointed by the President (sec. 591)

The Senate bill contained a provision (sec. 595) that would repeal section 9337 of title 10, United States Code, that requires a chaplain at the United States Air Force Academy appointed by the President. The section is not required because the Air Force and the other military departments already assign chaplains to the service academies under existing service personnel assignment procedures.

The House amendment contained no similar provision.

The House recedes.

Extension of limitation on reduction in number of military and civilian personnel assigned to duty with service review agencies (sec. 592)

The Senate bill contained a provision (sec. 596) that would amend section 1559 of title 10, United States Code, to extend the limitation on reducing the number of military and civilian personnel assigned to duty with the service review agencies through December 31, 2019.

The House amendment contained no similar provision.

The House recedes.

Annual reports on progress of the Army and the Marine Corps in integrating women into military occupational specialties and units recently opened to women (sec. 593)

The Senate bill contained a provision (sec. 593) that would require a report to be delivered to the Committees on Armed Services of the Senate and the House of Representatives by the Chief of Staff of the Army, the Commandant of the Marine Corps, and the Commander of the United States Special Operations Command annually on April 1, 2017, and each year thereafter through 2021 on the progress of integrating women into military occupational specialties and units recently opened to women.

The House amendment contained no similar provision.

The House recedes with an amendment that would narrow the scope of the report and change the final report date to 2020.

Report on feasibility of electronic tracking of operational active-duty service performed by members of the Ready Reserve of the Armed Forces (sec. 594)

The House amendment contained a provision (sec. 515) that would require the Secretary of Defense to establish electronic means for reserve component members to track qualifying operational active-duty service that would enable early receipt of reserve retired pay under section 12731(f) of title 10, United States Code.

The Senate bill contained no similar provision.

The Senate recedes with an amendment that would require the Secretary to assess the feasibility of such an electronic tracking system, and to provide a report to the Committees on Armed Services of the Senate and House of Representatives by no later than May 1, 2017.

Report on discharge by warrant officers of pilot and other flight officer positions in the Navy, Marine Corps, and Air Force currently discharged by commissioned officers (sec. 595)

The Senate bill contained a provision (sec. 597) that would require the secretaries of the Navy and the Air Force to submit a report to the Committees on Armed Services of the Senate and of the House of Representatives, not later than 180 days after enactment, on the feasibility and advisability of having warrant officers discharge the duties of pilots and other flight officer positions currently discharged by commissioned officers.

The House amendment contained no similar provision.

The House recedes.

Body mass index test (sec. 596)

The House amendment contained a provision (sec. 593) that would require the Secretary of Defense to review the current body mass index test procedure used by the Armed Forces and to determine the best methods to assess body fat percentages to improve the accuracy of body fat measurements.

The Senate bill contained no similar provision.

The Senate recedes with an amendment that would require the service secretaries to conduct the review of current body mass index test procedures and other methods to measure body fat with a more holistic health and wellness approach.

Report on career progression tracks of the Armed Forces for women in combat arms units (sec. 597)

The Senate bill contained a provision (sec. 594) that would require the Secretary of Defense to submit a description of the career progression track for entry level and laterally moved female service members, both officer and enlisted, of each Armed Force for positions that have been opened as a result of the December 3, 2015, decision by the Secretary to open all previously closed military occupations to women.

The House amendment contained no similar provision.

The House recedes.

LEGISLATIVE PROVISIONS NOT ADOPTED

Temporary suspension of officer grade strength tables

The Senate bill contained a provision (sec. 503) that would amend sections 523 (a) and 12011(a) of title 10, United States Code, to remove the limitations on the total number of commissioned officers authorized to serve on Active Duty or on full-time reserve component duty in the pay grades of O–4 through O–6 as of the end of the fiscal year for fiscal years 2017 through 2021.

The House amendment contained no similar provision.

The Senate recedes.

The conferees believe that providing relief from statutory caps on the numbers of officers of the active and reserve components serving in pay grades from O–4 to O–6, for an appropriate trial period, may allow the secretaries of the military departments to adjust the shape of their officer corps to affect talent management-based promotion systems and more quickly adapt to changing war fighting requirements and available talent supply. The conferees are concerned that such statutory flexibility must be exercised in a manner that would promote lean, efficient, and highly effective officer corps and must not result in bloated senior officer ranks that impede the proper administration of the officer personnel management system. Therefore, the conferees modify the reporting requirement directed in the Senate report accompanying section 503 of S.2943 (S. Rept. 114–255) to require the Secretary of Defense to submit a report to the Committees on Armed Services of the Senate and the House of Representatives, not later than March 1, 2017, describing how the military departments would propose to use the authority described in section 503 of the Senate-passed bill, a description of the specific categories of adjustments in control grades and the number and percentages of such adjustments desired, and an assessment of the impact of the authority, if implemented, on the desired officer grade composition of the military departments. The report shall specifically address the proposed use of this authority for military intelligence officers, foreign area specialists, judge advocates with a military justice skill identifier, and officers with expertise in cyber matters.

Enhanced authority for service credit for experience or advanced education upon original appointment as a commissioned officer

The Senate bill contained a provision (sec. 504) that would amend section 533 of title 10, United States Code, to authorize service secretaries to credit an applicant for an original appointment in a commissioned grade with an amount of constructive credit limited to the amount required for an original appointment in the grade of colonel in the Army, Air Force, or Marine Corps, or in the grade of captain in the Navy. The provision would authorize the secretary concerned to award constructive credit for leadership experience, professional credentials, and technical expertise to directly commission officers up to the grade of O–6.

The House amendment contained no similar provision.

The Senate recedes.

The conferees note that another provision of this Act would authorize the military departments to conduct pilot programs to commission cyber professionals. The conferees recognize that the use of similar authorities to commission professionals such as doctors, lawyers, and chaplains continues to have great utility in providing trained professionals for the military departments. It may be useful to extend such authorities to branches, career fields, and occupational specialties that may be designated by the services as having technical or warfighter status. The conferees encourage the Department of Defense to provide detailed information to the Committees on Armed Services of the Senate and of the House of Representatives on how the expanded use of such authorities may be utilized.

Authority of promotion boards to recommend officers of particular merit be placed at the top of the promotion list

The Senate bill contained a provision (sec. 505) that would amend section 616 of title 10, United States Code, to authorize an officer promotion board to recommend Active-Duty officers of particular merit to be placed at the top of the promotion list.

The House amendment contained no similar provision.

The Senate recedes.

The conferees remind the Department of Defense that the Joint Explanatory Statement accompanying the National Defense Authorization Act for Fiscal Year 2016 (P.L. 114–92) identified the need to review and modernize procedures to select officers for promotion. The Department of Defense was encouraged to develop recommendations to enhance the flexibility of selection boards to identify and select officers of particular merit for early promotion, using procedures that all stakeholders would view as objective and fair. Despite the Department's much-touted Force of the Future studies, the last year saw no recommendations to Congress that would provide the flexibility the Department claims to need to recruit, commission, promote, and retain the high quality all-volunteer force the Nation requires.

Limitations on ordering selected reserve to active duty for preplanned missions in support of the combatant commands

The House amendment contained a provision (sec. 513) that would amend section 12304(b) of title 10, United States Code, to authorize the Secretary of Defense to order any unit of the Selected Reserve to Active Duty during the year of execution if the Secretary identifies manpower and associated costs as an emerging requirement in the year of execution and provides a 30-day notice to the congressional defense committees.

The Senate bill contained no similar provision.

The House recedes.

The conferees note that the authority to order Selected Reserve units to Active Duty under section 12304(b) of title 10, United States Code, is designed to incentivize deliberate planning for the use of the Selective Reserve as part of the operational force by requiring missions to be planned in advance and included in annual budget submissions. Other provisions of title 10, United States Code, provide authority to order members and units of the reserve components to Active Duty to address emerging requirements arising during the year of execution.

Exemption of military technicians (dual status) from civilian employee furloughs

The House amendment contained a provision (sec. 514) that would amend section 10216(b)(3) of title 10, United States Code, to exempt military dual-status technicians from civilian employee furloughs.

The Senate bill contained no similar provision.

The House recedes.

Authority to designate certain Reserve officers as not to be considered for selection for promotion

The Senate bill contained a provision (sec. 522) that would amend section 14301 of title 10, United States Code, to authorize the secretaries of the military departments to defer promotion consideration for reserve component officers in a non-participatory (membership points only) status.

The House amendment contained no similar provision.

The Senate recedes.

Responsibility of Chiefs of Staff of the Armed Forces for standards and qualifications for military specialties within the Armed Forces

The Senate bill contained a provision (sec. 531) that would vest in the Chief of Staff of each of the Armed Forces the responsibility for establishing, approving, and modifying the criteria, standards, and qualifications for military specialty codes within that Armed Force. The Secretary of Defense would retain oversight authority.

The House amendment contained no similar provision.

The Senate recedes.

The conferees expect service secretaries to consult with and receive the advice of the Chiefs of Staff of each of the Armed Forces when making decisions on military standards and qualifications.

Reconciliation of contradictory provisions relating to qualifications for enlistment in the reserve components of the Armed Forces

The Senate bill contained a provision (sec. 537) that would amend section 12102(b) of title 10, United States Code, to align the requirements for enlistment in the reserve components of the Armed Forces with the requirements for enlistment in the active components.

The House amendment contained no similar provision.

The Senate recedes.

Burdens of proof applicable to investigations and reviews related to protected communications of members of the armed forces and prohibited retaliatory actions

The House amendment contained a provision (sec. 545) that would amend section 1034 of title 10, United States Code, to establish the burden of proof under this section for military retaliation investigations to be the same as the burden of proof applicable to retaliation investigations under section 1221(e) of title 5, United States Code.

The Senate bill contained no similar provision.

The House recedes.

The conferees included a number of provisions in this Act that will provide necessary tools to allow military victims of retaliation to be provided full, fair, and expeditious investigation and relief, when appropriate, in response to alleged retaliation. The conferees are mindful however that the requirements, hardships, and sacrifices of military service are unique and unlike those of the federal civilian workplace that section 1221(e) of title 5 is intended to address. We consider the burden of proof standards under section 1221(e) to be properly tailored to the federal civilian workforce. However, the conferees concluded that the burden of proof standards that properly apply in a civilian context are not amenable to the unique demands of military service. The conferees remain concerned about reports from military personnel who indicate they have been subjected to retaliation after making protected communications. The conferees intend to remain seized of this issue and will assess the impact of the provisions in this bill to reducing the prevalence of retaliation in the military.

Discretionary authority for military judges to designate an individual to assume the rights of the victim of an offense under the Uniform Code of Military Justice when the victim is a minor, incompetent, incapacitated, or deceased

The Senate bill contained a provision (sec. 546) that would amend section 806b(c) of title 10, United States Code (Article 6b(c), Uniform Code of Military Justice (UCMJ)) to au-

thorize military judges to decide on a case-by-case basis whether it is appropriate to appoint an individual to assume the victim's rights in all cases under the UCMJ in which the victim of an offense is under 18 years of age (unless the victim is a member of the Armed Forces) or is incompetent, incapacitated, or deceased.

The House amendment contained no similar provision.

The Senate recedes.

The conferees note that a similar provision is included in the Military Justice Act of 2016 which is enacted elsewhere in this Act.

Appellate standing of victims in enforcing rights of victims under the Uniform Code of Military Justice

The Senate bill contained a provision (sec. 547) that would amend section 806b of title 10, United States Code (article 6b of the Uniform Code of Military Justice (UCMJ)) to authorize victims to file pleadings as a real party in interest when the Government files appellate pleadings implicating the victim's rights relating to Military Rule of Evidence (MRE) 412, relating to the admission of evidence regarding a victim's sexual background; MRE 513, relating to the psychotherapist-patient privilege; or MRE 514, relating to the victim advocate-patient privilege. The provision would also amend section 806b of title 10, United States Code (article 6b of the UCMJ) to afford a victim with the right to reasonable, accurate, and timely notice of any appellate matters.

The House contained no similar provision.

The Senate recedes.

The conferees understand that the Judicial Proceedings Panel (JPP) established by section 576 of the National Defense Authorization Act for Fiscal Year 2013 (Public Law 112–239) will receive testimony and address this issue in future public meetings of the JPP. The conferees will reconsider this issue after receipt of the JPP recommendations.

Limitation on tuition assistance for off-duty training or education

The Senate bill contained a provision (sec. 561) that would amend section 2007 of title 10, United States Code, to limit the tuition assistant program for off-duty training and education to education programs likely to contribute to the professional development of the servicemember.

The House amendment contained no similar provision.

The Senate recedes.

The conferees support Department of Defense and military service efforts over the past several years to ensure the integrity of the tuition assistance program, and the educational success of servicemembers utilizing the benefit, through implementation of common-sense restrictions on premature use by servicemembers still adjusting to military life and who are still learning their military occupations, as well as restrictions on those who would inappropriately use the benefit to acquire additional degrees at the same level of attainment.

Establishment of ROTC cyber institutes at senior military colleges

The House amendment contained a provision (sec. 562) that would amend chapter 103 of title 10, United States Code, to authorize the Secretary of Defense to carry out a program to establish ROTC Cyber Institutes at the six Senior Military Colleges for purposes of accelerating the development of foundational expertise in critical cyber operational skills for future military and civilian leaders of the Armed Forces and Department of Defense, to include such leaders of the Reserve Components.

The Senate bill contained no similar provision.

The House recedes.

The conferees note that many ROTC programs are beginning to implement cyber training for critical cyber operational skills. The conferees encourage these and other ROTC programs to continue building and teaching a cyber framework for future military and civilian leaders of the Armed Forces and Department of Defense.

Access to Department of Defense installations of institutions of higher education providing certain advising and student support services

The Senate bill contained a provision (sec. 563) that would amend chapter 101 of title 10, United States Code, to require the Secretary of Defense to grant access to all Department of Defense installations any institution of higher education that has a Voluntary Education Partnership Memorandum of Understanding with the Department for the purposes of student advising and support services.

The House amendment contained no similar provision.

The Senate recedes.

Employment authority for civilian faculty at certain military department schools

The House amendment contained a provision (sec. 564) that would amend section 4021 of title 10, United States Code, to authorize the Secretary concerned to hire staff for professional military education courses regardless of course length.

The Senate bill contained no similar provision.

The House recedes.

Revision of name on military service record to reflect change in name of a member of the Army, Navy, Air Force, or Marine Corps, after separation from the Armed Forces

The House amendment contained a provision (sec. 565) that would amend section 1551 of title 10, United States Code, to allow persons who legally change their name to reflect their gender identity after separation from the Armed Forces to receive a new certificate of discharge or acceptance of resignation order under that new name.

The Senate bill contained no similar provision.

The House recedes.

The conferees note that former service members currently have a process to request their name be changed on official service discharge documents to reflect a legal name change, by submitting a request to the appropriate service board for correction of military or naval records. Effective October 1, 2016, the Department of Defense (DoD) and the Military Departments will implement DoD Instruction 1300.28, that requires the services to provide servicemembers a process by which, while serving, they may change their gender. The conferees expect the Department to make the necessary changes to regulations to provide former members a simplified process to reflect a name change in military personnel records due to change in gender identity or other lawful purpose.

Direct employment pilot program for members of the National Guard and Reserve

The House amendment contained a provision (sec. 566) that would authorize the Secretary of Defense to carry out a pilot program to enhance efforts of the Department of Defense to provide job placement assistance and related employment services directly to members of the National Guard and Reserves. This section would also require the

Secretary to submit a report on the program to the Committees on Armed Services of the Senate and the House of Representatives by January 31, 2021.

The Senate bill contained no similar provision.

The House recedes.

The conferees note that the South Carolina and California National Guards conduct state employment programs that have seen success in recent years and serve as a model for other states and territories to set up similar state employment programs. The conferees note the numerous employment assistance programs for transitioning servicemembers coordinated by the military services, the Department of Defense, the Department of Labor, and the Department of Veterans Affairs, such as the Department of Labor's Veterans' Employment and Training Service and the Department of Veterans Affairs' VA for Vets program and Feds Hire Vets employment tool. The conferees encourage the Chief of the National Guard Bureau to work with the Secretary of Defense to coordinate with the Secretary of Labor and the Secretary of Veterans Affairs to leverage these preexisting Federal employment programs.

Prohibition on establishment, maintenance, or support of Senior Reserve Officers' Training Corps units at educational institutions that display the Confederate battle flag

The House amendment contained a provision (sec. 567) that would amend section 2102 of title 10, United States Code, to prohibit the secretary concerned from establishing, maintaining, or supporting a Senior Reserve Officers' Training Corps unit at an educational institution that displays the Confederate battle flag except where the board of visitors has voted to take down the flag described.

The Senate bill contained no similar provision.

The House recedes.

Report on composition of service academies

The House amendment contained a provision (sec. 568) that would require the Comptroller General of the United States to submit a report on the demographic composition of the service academies.

The Senate bill contained no similar provision.

The House recedes.

Enhanced flexibility in provision of relocation assistance to members of the Armed Forces and their families

The Senate bill contained a provision (sec. 576) that would amend section 1056 of title 10, United States Code, to permit enhanced flexibility in giving relocation assistance to members of the Armed Forces and their families. The provision would allow the Department of Defense to adapt the delivery of relocation assistance to meet the evolving needs of military servicemembers and their families by leveraging technology to improve access, efficiency, and responsiveness of the relocation assistance program, especially in situations where servicemembers reside overseas or away from a military installation with a relocation assistance program. Finally, the provision would establish the position of Program Manager of Military Relocation Assistance in the office of the Assistant Secretary of Defense for Manpower and Reserve Affairs.

The House amendment contained no similar provision.

The Senate recedes.

Background checks for employees of agencies and schools providing elementary and secondary education for Department of Defense dependents

The Senate bill contained a provision (sec. 578) that would require certain local educational agencies receiving impact aid under subchapter VII of chapter 70 of title 20, United States Code, and each Department of Defense (DOD) domestic dependent elementary and secondary school, within 2 years of enactment of this Act, to establish policies and procedures requiring a criminal background check for each school employee of the agency or school.

The House amendment contained no similar provision.

The Senate recedes.

The conferees believe the protection of school children from would-be predators is of paramount importance. Children of military personnel, who by virtue of a parent's military service are more transient with fewer community ties and relationships, may be more vulnerable to such predators. The conferees believe it is important that appropriate criminal background checks be conducted of school employees in Department of Defense (DOD) schools and local educational activities that educate military family members. Despite the requirement in every state that background checks be conducted, and recently-enacted prohibitions in the Every Student Succeeds Act that restrict the movement and reemployment of predators in other states, there were still 496 arrests of school employees in the United States last year for sexual misconduct with children, according to press reports. Clearly, the problem of child predation and abuse remains in our local school systems. The conferees note that DOD schools conduct thorough criminal background checks on their employees, and the conferees are committed to subjecting DOD schools to the oversight required to ensure that they conduct thorough criminal background checks on their employees. Given the critical importance of this issue and the defense authorizing committees' continuing concern that children at risk are adequately protected, the conferees strongly urge DOD to work as closely as possible with local school districts that educate military family members to share best practices to help those districts develop and improve comprehensive employment screening policies to ensure the safety of military children. The conferees direct the Department to provide a report to the Committees on Armed Services of the Senate and the House of Representatives, not later than 1 year after the date of enactment of this Act, on the Department's efforts to: 1) identify, to the extent practicable, any shortfalls in employee screening processes in local school districts educating military family members; and 2) provide recommendations to help address those shortfalls in the future.

Authorization for award of the Medal of Honor to Charles S. Kettles for acts of valor during the Vietnam war

The Senate bill contained a provision (sec. 586) that would waive the time limitations specified in section 3744 of title 10, United States Code, to authorize the President to award the Medal of Honor to Charles S. Kettles, for acts of valor on May 15, 1967, during the Vietnam War, while serving as Flight Commander in the United States Army, 176th Aviation Company, 14th Aviation Battalion, Task Force Oregon, Republic of Vietnam.

The House amendment contained a similar provision (sec. 584).

The conference agreement does not include this provision.

The conferees note the authority to waive the time limitations for award of the Medal of Honor were included in the Consolidated Appropriations Act of 2016 (P.L. 114–113). The President awarded Mr. Kettles the Medal of Honor in a ceremony at the White House on July 18, 2016.

Burial of cremated remains in Arlington National Cemetery of certain persons whose service is deemed to be active service.

The House amendment contained a provision (sec. 591) that would amend section 2410 of title 38, United States Code, to require the Secretary of the Army to ensure that the cremated remains of certain individuals whose service has been determined to be active duty service are eligible for inurnment with military honors in Arlington National Cemetery.

The Senate bill contained no similar provision.

The House recedes.

The conferees note that on May 20, 2016 the President signed into law the Women Airforce Service Pilot Arlington Inurnment Restoration Act (P.L. 114–158), which provided the authority contained in section 591 of the House amendment.

Applicability of Military Selective Service Act to female citizens and persons

The Senate bill contained a provision (sec. 591) that would amend the Selective Service Act (Public Law 65–12) to include women in the requirement to register for selective service, to the same extent men are currently required, beginning January 1, 2018.

The House amendment contained no similar provision.

The Senate recedes.

Representation from member of the Armed Forces on boards, councils, and committees making recommendations relating to military personnel issues

The House amendment contained a provision (sec. 592) that would require that enlisted or retired enlisted members of the armed forces be represented on all boards, panels, commissions, or task forces established under chapter 7 of title 10, United States Code, to render a recommendation on any aspect of personnel policy directly affecting enlisted personnel.

The Senate bill contained no similar provision.

The House recedes.

The conferees believe it is essential that the views of enlisted members must be considered by boards charged with developing informed and effective military personnel policy. The conferees expect that the Secretary of Defense, the secretaries of the military departments, the Chairman of the Joint Chiefs of Staff, the service chiefs, and their senior enlisted advisers will ensure that enlisted representation is included in such boards to the maximum extent practicable.

Preseparation counseling regarding options for donating brain tissue at time of death for research

The House amendment contained a provision (sec. 594) that would require servicemembers to receive information during transition separation counseling concerning options for donating brain tissue at the time of death of the servicemember for chronic traumatic encephalopathy research.

The Senate bill contained no similar provision.

The House recedes.

Recognition of the expanded service opportunities available to female members of the Armed Forces and the long service of women in the Armed Forces

The House amendment contained a provision (sec. 595) that would express Congress' recognition of women who have served and are currently serving in the Armed Forces.

The Senate bill contained no similar provision.

The House recedes.

The conferees note that female members of the Armed Forces are invaluable and integral to the Armed Forces and that the United States must continue to encourage and support female members of the Armed Forces as they serve our Nation.

Sense of Congress regarding plight of male victims of military sexual assault

The House amendment contained a provision (sec. 596) that would express the sense of Congress that the Secretary of Defense should enhance access to intensive medical and mental health treatment of male victims of sexual assault, look for opportunities to use male victims as presenters at prevention training, and ensure medical and mental health providers are trained to meet the needs of male victims.

The Senate bill contained no similar provision.

The House recedes.

The conferees remain concerned that more must be done to address the unique issues and concerns affecting male victims of sexual assault. For that reason, section 538 of the National Defense Authorization Act for Fiscal Year 2016 (P.L. 114–92) requires the Secretary of Defense, in collaboration with the secretaries of the military departments, to develop a comprehensive plan to improve Department of Defense prevention and response to sexual assaults in which the victim is a male member of the armed forces. The conferees look forward to receiving the plan from the Secretary of Defense and intend to monitor the efficacy of the plan.

Sense of Congress regarding section 504 of title 10, United States Code, on existing authority of the Department of Defense to enlist individuals, not otherwise eligible for enlistment, whose enlistment is vital to the national interest

The House amendment contained a provision (sec. 597) that would express the sense of Congress that section 504 of title 10, United States Code, authorizes the Department of Defense to enlist individuals, not otherwise eligible for enlistment, whose enlistment is vital to the national interest.

The Senate bill contained no similar provision.

The House recedes.

Protection of Second Amendment rights of military families

The House amendment contained a provision (sec. 598) that would amend section 921(b) of title 18, United States Code, to provide that the residence of the spouse of a military member for the purpose of federal firearms laws, is the State of the permanent duty station of the member.

The Senate bill contained no similar provision.

The House recedes.

The conferees note that the residence of a spouse of a military member is the State in which that spouse resides, which is the State of the permanent duty station of the member, or such other State as the spouse may reside.

Pilot program on advanced technology for alcohol abuse prevention

The House amendment contained a provision (sec. 599) that would require the Sec-

retary of Defense, within 90 days of enactment of this Act, to consult with the service secretaries and establish a pilot program to demonstrate the feasibility of using portable, disposable alcohol breathalyzers and a cloud-based server platform to collect data and monitor the progress of alcohol abuse programs through digital applications. The provision would require the Secretary to conduct the pilot program for a minimum of 6 months, and the program would terminate by September 30, 2018. The Secretary would submit a report to the Committees on Armed Services of the Senate and the House of Representatives on implementation of the program within 120 days after implementation and then submit a final report to the committees within 1 year of implementation.

The Senate bill contained no similar provision.

The House recedes.

Report on availability of college credit for skills acquired during military service

The House amendment contained a provision (sec. 599A) that would require the Secretary of Defense, in consultation with the Secretaries of Veterans Affairs, Education, and Labor, to submit a report on the transfer of skills into equivalent college credits or technical certifications for members of the Armed Forces leaving the military.

The Senate bill contained no similar provision.

The House recedes.

Atomic veterans service medal

The House amendment contained a provision (sec. 599B) that would require the Secretary of Defense to design, produce, and distribute a military service medal to honor retired and former members of the Armed Forces who are radiation-exposed veterans.

The Senate bill contained no similar provision.

The House recedes.

Report on extending protections for student loans for active duty borrowers

The House amendment contained a provision (sec. 599C) that would require the Secretary of Defense, in consultation with the Secretary of Education, to submit a report detailing the information, assistance, and efforts to support and inform active duty members of the Armed Forces with respect to the rights and resources available under the Servicemembers Civil Relief Act.

The Senate bill contained no similar provision.

The House recedes.

Exclusion of certain reimbursements of medical expenses and other payments from determination of annual income with respect to pensions for veterans and surviving spouses and children of veterans

The House amendment contained a provision (sec. 599D) that would amend section 1503(a) of title 38, United States Code, to exclude payments regarding reimbursements of medical expenses from the determination of annual income with respect to pensions.

The Senate bill contained no similar provision.

The House recedes.

Sense of Congress on desirability of service-wide adoption of Gold Star installation access card

The House amendment contained a provision (sec. 599E) that would express the sense of Congress that the secretaries of the military departments and the Secretary of the department in which the Coast Guard is operating should work jointly to develop, issue, and ensure acceptance of a Gold Star installation access card for family members who are the survivors of deceased members of the Armed Forces in order to expedite the ability of a Gold Star family member to gain unescorted access to military installations for the purpose of obtaining on-base services and benefits for which the Gold Star family member is entitled or eligible.

The Senate bill contained no similar provision.

The House recedes.

Servicemembers' Group Life Insurance

The House amendment contained a provision (sec. 599F) that would amend section 1967(f)(4) of title 38, United States Code, by striking the second sentence.

The Senate bill contained no similar provision.

The House recedes.

TITLE VI—COMPENSATION AND OTHER PERSONNEL BENEFITS

Subtitle A—Pay and Allowances

Fiscal year 2017 increase in military basic pay (sec. 601)

The Senate bill contained a provision (sec. 601) that would authorize a pay raise of 1.6 percent for all members of the uniformed services effective January 1, 2017.

The House amendment contained a provision (sec. 601) that would direct that the rates of basic pay under section 203(a) of title 37, United States Code, be increased in accordance with section 1009 of title 37, United States Code, notwithstanding a determination made by the President under subsection (e) of such section 1009.

The Senate recedes.

Publication by Department of Defense of actual rates of basic pay payable to members of the Armed Forces by pay grade for annual or other pay periods (sec. 602)

The Senate bill contained a provision (sec. 602) that would direct the Department of Defense to ensure that pay tables of basic pay for members of the uniformed services published by the Department reflect the operation of the pay cap contained in section 203(a)(2) of title 37, United States Code, to more accurately reflect the rates of basic pay that may actually be received by service members whose basic pay is affected by that cap.

The House amendment contained no similar provision.

The House recedes.

Extension of authority to provide temporary increase in rates of basic allowance for housing under certain circumstances (sec. 603)

The Senate bill contained a provision (sec. 603) that would extend for 1 year the authority of the Secretary of Defense to temporarily increase the rate of basic allowance for housing in areas impacted by natural disasters or experiencing a sudden influx of personnel.

The House amendment contained an identical provision (sec. 602).

The conference agreement includes this provision.

Reports on a new single-salary pay system for members of the Armed Forces (sec. 604)

The Senate bill contained a provision (sec. 604) that would reform the basic allowance for housing (BAH) benefit for members of the uniformed services, applicable January 1, 2018. The provision would require a system that utilizes actual costs up to a maximum allowable amount. No service member will see a change in their allowance until such time as they undergo a permanent change of duty station outside their military housing area after January 1, 2018.

The House amendment contained no similar provision.

The Senate recedes with an amendment that would require the Department of Defense to report back with revised pay tables and a plan to transition to a salary system by no later than January 1, 2018. An initial assessment and progress report will be due to the Committees on Armed Services of the Senate and the House of Representatives no later than March 1, 2017, to contain the military pay tables as of January 1, 2017, that reflect the Regular Military Compensation of members of the Armed Forces as of that date in the range of grades, dependency statuses, and assignment locations.

The conferees note that the BAH, as an entitlement, and the perception of BAH among servicemembers, has evolved over the past 20 years. BAH, and the iterations of the benefit that came before, was intended to provide a housing benefit for service members to offset the cost of housing in high cost housing areas where adequate government-provided quarters was not available and in recognition of the transient nature of military service and the impact it has on military members and their families. Indeed, that the housing allowance was and is intended as primarily a housing benefit is demonstrated by its tax-free nature, the differentiation based on dependency status, and the fact that junior enlisted personnel required to reside in barracks or on a ship are ineligible to receive BAH. Accordingly, the conferees direct the Secretary of Defense to begin planning for a transition to a salary system that better aligns the payment of the allowance with the Department's use of the housing allowance as compensation rather than its intended purpose as an allowance.

Subtitle B—Bonuses and Special and Incentive Pays

One-year extension of certain bonus and special pay authorities for reserve forces (sec. 611)

The Senate bill contained a provision (sec. 611) that would extend for 1 year the authority to pay the Selected Reserve reenlistment bonus, the Selected Reserve affiliation or enlistment bonus, special pay for enlisted members assigned to certain high-priority units, the Ready Reserve enlistment bonus for persons without prior service, the Ready Reserve enlistment and reenlistment bonus for persons with prior service, the Selected Reserve enlistment and reenlistment bonus for persons with prior service, travel expenses for certain inactive-duty training, and income replacement for reserve component members experiencing extended and frequent mobilization for Active-Duty service.

The House amendment contained an identical provision (sec. 611).

The conference agreement includes this provision.

One-year extension of certain bonus and special pay authorities for health care professionals (sec. 612)

The Senate bill contained a provision (sec. 612) that would extend for 1 year the authority to pay the nurse officer candidate accession bonus, education loan repayment for certain health professionals who serve in the Selected Reserve, accession and retention bonuses for psychologists, the accession bonus for registered nurses, incentive special pay for nurse anesthetists, special pay for Selected Reserve health professionals in critically short wartime specialties, the accession bonus for dental officers, the accession bonus for pharmacy officers, the accession bonus for medical officers in critically short wartime specialties, and the accession bonus for dental specialist officers in critically short wartime specialties.

The House amendment contained an identical provision (sec. 612).

The conference agreement includes this provision.

One-year extension of special pay and bonus authorities for nuclear officers (sec. 613)

The Senate bill contained a provision (sec. 613) that would extend for 1 year the authority to pay the special pay for nuclear-qualified officers extending period of active service, the nuclear career accession bonus, and the nuclear career annual incentive bonus.

The House amendment contained an identical provision (sec. 613).

The conference agreement includes this provision.

One-year extension of authorities relating to title 37 consolidated special pay, incentive pay, and bonus authorities (sec. 614)

The Senate bill contained a provision (sec. 614) that would extend for 1 year the general bonus authority for enlisted members, the general bonus authority for officers, special bonus and incentive pay authorities for nuclear officers, special aviation incentive pay and bonus authorities for officers, and special bonus and incentive pay authorities for officers in health professions, and contracting bonus for cadets and midshipmen enrolled in the Senior Officers' Training Corps. The provision would also extend for 1 year the authority to pay hazardous duty pay, assignment or special duty pay, skill incentive pay or proficiency bonus, and retention incentives for members qualified in critical military skills or assigned to high priority units.

The House amendment contained an identical provision (sec. 614).

The conference agreement includes this provision.

One-year extension of authorities relating to payment of other title 37 bonuses and special pays (sec. 615)

The Senate bill contained a provision (sec. 615) that would extend for 1 year the authority to pay the aviation officer retention bonus, assignment incentive pay, the reenlistment bonus for active members, the enlistment bonus, precommissioning incentive pay for foreign language proficiency, the accession bonus for new officers in critical skills, the incentive bonus for conversion to military occupational specialty to ease personnel shortage, the incentive bonus for transfer between Armed Forces, and the accession bonus for officer candidates.

The House amendment contained an identical provision (sec. 615).

The conference agreement includes this provision.

Aviation incentive pay and bonus matters (sec. 616)

The House amendment contained a provision (sec. 616) that would amend section 334(c)(1) of title 37, United States Code, to increase the statutory limits for the aviation incentive pay and retention bonus to $1,000 per month and $60,000 per year, respectively, and would allow the Secretary concerned the flexibility to increase the aviation incentive pay limit set forth in regulations issued by the Secretary of Defense under section 374 of title 37, United States Code.

The Senate bill contained no similar provision.

The Senate recedes with an amendment that would authorize a maximum aviation bonus of $35,000 for each 12-month period of obligated service, and requires the appropriate Service Secretary to submit a justification with each fiscal year's budget request for the aviation bonus amounts by aircraft type category, the business case supporting the amount requested, and a description by the Secretary concerned on how they will address manning shortfalls by non-monetary means.

The conferees note the current Chief of Staff of the Air Force stated in response to advance policy questions in preparation for his confirmation hearing, "We will tailor any potential bonus based upon specific platform and overall Air Force requirements. The requested increase is not a set amount. If approved, this will give us the flexibility to tailor bonus amounts and contract terms by platform." The conferees strongly agree with targeting aviation bonuses toward the most critical manning shortfalls by aircraft type category as a way to incentivize retention behavior, and strongly support this method for use across the Department of Defense.

The conferees also expect the Services to continue developing and implementing policies to tackle non-monetary reasons for low aviator retention rates, and to use these incentive and bonus authorities to incentivize needed retention levels using a business case rather than as a reward or entitlement, to correct both the undermanning of certain aircraft type categories and the overmanning of others.

Conforming amendment to consolidation of special pay, incentive pay, and bonus authorities (sec. 617)

The Senate bill contained a provision (sec. 616) that would amend section 332 of title 10, United States Code, to correct an inequity that will exist when the Department transitions to a general bonus authority on October 1, 2017. This amendment will increase the maximum bonus authority under the new general bonus authority to $20,000 to match the maximum bonus level under the old authority. Maintaining the current bonus level will enable the Services to retain the ability to recruit and retain reserve component officers.

The House amendment contained an identical provision (sec. 617).

The conference agreement includes this provision.

Technical amendments relating to 2008 consolidation of certain special pay authorities (sec. 618)

The House amendment contained a provision (sec. 618) that would make technical and clerical corrections to titles 10, 20, 24, 36, 37, and 42, United States Code, as well as section 586 of the National Defense Authorization Act for Fiscal Year 2008 (Public Law 110–181), section 362 of the John Warner National Defense Authorization Act for Fiscal Year 2007 (Public Law 109–364), and section 112(c)(5)(B) of the Internal Revenue Code of 1986, as part of the Department of Defense's transition to the consolidated authorities in sections 661 and 662 of the National Defense Authorization Act for Fiscal Year 2008 (Public Law 110–181), which consolidated statutory special and incentive pay authorities for members of the uniformed services. This section is consistent with the purpose and intent of the consolidated special and incentive pay reform contained in the 2008 defense bill.

The Senate bill contained no similar provision.

The Senate recedes.

Subtitle C—Travel and Transportation Allowances

Maximum reimbursement amount for travel expenses of members of the Reserves attending inactive duty training outside of normal commuting distances (sec. 621)

The House amendment contained a provision (sec. 641) that would amend section 478a(c) of title 37, United States Code, to allow for a higher reimbursement amount on a case-by-case basis for certain members of the Reserve component traveling to attend inactive duty training outside of normal committing distances.

The Senate bill contained a similar provision (sec. 621).

The Senate recedes.

Subtitle D—Disability Pay, Retired Pay, and Survivor Benefits

Part I—Amendments in Connection with Retired Pay Reform

Election period for members in the service academies and inactive Reserves to participate in the modernized retirement system (sec. 631)

The Senate bill contained a provision (sec. 631) that would amend section 1409 of title 10, United States Code, to clarify the timing for cadets and midshipmen at the service academies to opt-in to the new military retirement system enacted in the National Defense Authorization Act for Fiscal Year 2016 (Public Law 114–92). The provision would also clarify the timing of such elections for reservists who are on Inactive Duty during the election period otherwise provided for under the new retirement system.

The House amendment contained no similar provision.

The House recedes.

Effect of separation of members from the uniformed services on participation in the Thrift Savings Plan (sec. 632)

The Senate bill contained a provision (sec. 632) that would repeal paragraph (2) of section 632(c) of the National Defense Authorization Act for Fiscal Year 2016 (Public Law 114–92). This amendment makes a technical correction for the new military retirement plan enacted in that Act relative to defining separation from service under the Thrift Savings Plan.

The House amendment contained a similar provision (sec. 621).

The House recedes.

Continuation pay for full Thrift Savings Plan members who have completed 8 to 12 years of service (sec. 633)

The House amendment contained a provision (sec. 622) that would amend section 356 of title 37, United States Code, to modify the continuation pay for members under the new military retirement system enacted in the National Defense Authorization Act for Fiscal Year 2016 (Public Law 114–92) to provide the Secretary of Defense with the flexibility to offer continuation pay in the window between 8 and 12 years of service in exchange for a 3 years of service or greater commitment as the Secretary deems appropriate for retention.

The Senate bill contained a similar provision (sec. 633).

The Senate recedes with a technical amendment.

Combat-related special compensation coordinating amendment (sec. 634)

The House amendment contained a provision (sec. 619) that would amend section 1413a of title 10, United States Code, to make a technical and conforming amendment to Combat-Related Special Compensation, to

bring that authority in line with the new military retirement system enacted in the National Defense Authorization Act for Fiscal Year 2016 (Public Law 114–92).

The Senate bill contained a similar provision (sec. 634).

The House recedes.

Part II—Other Matters

Use of member's current pay grade and years of service and retired pay cost-of-living adjustments, rather than final retirement pay grade and years of service, in a division of property involving disposable retired pay (sec. 641)

The Senate bill contained a provision (sec. 642) that would amend section 1408 of title 10, United States Code, to modify the division of military retired pay in a divorce decree to the amount the member would be entitled based upon the member's pay grade and years of service at the time of the divorce rather than at the time of retirement with the spousal share of the retired pay computed on the retired pay as adjusted by the annual increases in military pay.

The House amendment contained a similar provision (sec. 625) that would amend section 1408 of title 10, United States Code, to modify the division of military retired pay in a divorce decree to the amount the member would be entitled based upon the member's pay grade and years of service at the time of the divorce.

The House recedes with an amendment that would modify the division of military retired pay in a divorce decree to the amount the member would be entitled based upon the member's pay grade and years of service at the time of the divorce as adjusted by the annual retired pay cost-of-living adjustments between the date of the divorce decree and the date of retirement. The conferees note that this provision is prospective only and would not affect existing divorce settlements.

Equal benefits under Survivor Benefit Plan for survivors of reserve component members who die in the line of duty during inactive-duty training (sec. 642)

The House amendment contained a provision (sec. 624) that would amend section 1451(c)(1)(A) of title 10, United States Code, to eliminate the different treatment under the Survivor Benefit Plan accorded members of the reserve component who die from an injury or illness incurred or aggravated in the line of duty during inactive-duty training, as compared to the treatment of members of the Armed Forces who die in the line of duty while on Active Duty.

The Senate bill contained no similar provision.

The Senate recedes.

Authority to deduct Survivor Benefit Plan premiums from combat-related special compensation when retired pay not sufficient (sec. 643)

The Senate bill contained a provision (sec. 644) that would amend section 1452 of title 10, United States Code, to authorize the deduction of Survivor Benefit Plan (SBP) premiums from monthly combat related special compensation (CRSC) when retired pay is insufficient to cover the premiums.

The House amendment contained no similar provision.

The House recedes.

Extension of allowance covering monthly premium for Servicemembers' Group Life Insurance while in certain overseas areas to cover members in any combat zone or overseas direct support area (sec. 644)

The Senate bill contained a provision (sec. 641) that would amend section 437 of title 37,

United States Code, to expand the areas eligible for the allowance for covering monthly premiums for the Servicemembers' Group Life Insurance to include any designated combat zone or an area directly supporting a designated combat zone.

The House amendment contained no similar provision.

The House recedes.

Authority for payment of pay and allowances and retired and retainer pay pursuant to power of attorney (sec. 645)

The Senate bill contained a provision (sec. 672) that would amend section 602 of title 37, United States Code, to authorize payment of certain pay and allowances of a servicemember or retired servicemember to an individual to whom the member has granted authority to manage these funds pursuant to a valid and legally executed durable power of attorney. This proposal would enable members to responsibly and proactively plan their personal affairs in the event of their incapacitation, and to allow those durable powers of attorney to be recognized by the military departments and the Department of Defense.

The House amendment contained no similar provision.

The House recedes.

Extension of authority to pay special survivor indemnity allowance under Survivor Benefit Plan (sec. 646)

The Senate bill contained a provision (sec. 643) that would amend section 1450 of title 10, United States Code, to permanently extend the authority to pay the Special Survivor Indemnity Allowance (SSIA).

The House amendment contained a provision (sec. 623) that would extend the authority to pay the SSIA for one year.

The Senate recedes with an amendment that would extend the authority to pay the SSIA until May 31, 2018.

Repeal of obsolete authority for combat-related injury rehabilitation pay (sec. 647)

The Senate bill contained a provision (sec. 605) that would repeal section 328 of title 10, United States Code, relating to an obsolete authority for combat-related injury rehabilitation pay.

The House amendment contained no similar provision.

The House recedes.

Independent assessment of the Survivor Benefit Plan (sec. 648)

The Senate bill contained a provision (sec. 646) that would require the Secretary of Defense to provide for an independent assessment of the Department of Defense Survivor Benefit Plan (SBP) by a federally-funded research and development center (FFRDC).

The House amendment contained no similar provision.

The House recedes.

Subtitle E—Commissary and Non-Appropriated Fund Instrumentality Benefits and Operations

Protection and enhancement of access to and savings at commissaries and exchanges (sec. 661)

The Senate bill contained a provision (sec. 661) that would amend sections 2481, 2483, 2484, and 2487 of title 10, United States Code, to require the Secretary of Defense to develop and implement a comprehensive strategy to optimize management practices across the defense commissary system and the exchange system that reduces their reliance on appropriated funding without reducing benefits to commissary patrons or revenues generated by non-appropriated fund en-

tities. This provision would authorize the Secretary to carry out an alternative pricing program, evaluated against specific, measurable benchmarks and a documented baseline level of savings, within the defense commissary system to establish prices for goods and services in response to market conditions and customer demand. Furthermore, the provision would authorize the Secretary to convert the commissary system to a non-appropriated fund entity or instrumentality if the Secretary determines that the alternative pricing program met established benchmarks for success for a period of at least 6 months. If conversion to a non-appropriated fund entity or instrumentality occurs, the Secretary would ensure that no employee of the defense commissary system, as of the date of enactment of this Act, would incur a loss or decrease in pay resulting from the conversion. This provision would also authorize the Secretary of Defense to establish common business processes, practices, and systems to optimize the operations of the entire defense resale system, including authorizing the use of appropriated and non-appropriated funds on contracts or agreements for the acquisition of common systems. Finally, the provision would authorize the Secretary to supplement appropriated funds for defense commissary system operations with additional funds derived from improved management practices and the alternative pricing program.

The House amendment contained a provision (sec. 631) that would amend sections 2481(a) and (c), 2483(c), 2484, 2485, and 2487 of title 10, United States Code, to authorize the Secretary of Defense to develop and implement a comprehensive strategy to: 1) optimize practices across the commissary and exchange systems to reduce the reliance of those systems on appropriated funds without reducing benefits to patrons or any revenues generated by non-appropriated fund entities or instrumentalities of the Department for the morale, welfare, and recreation of servicemembers; 2) authorize use of additional funds derived from improved management practices to supplement appropriated funds for commissary operations; 3) authorize a variable pricing program whereby commissary prices may be established in response to market conditions and customer demand; 4) authorize conversion of the commissary system to a non-appropriated fund entity or instrumentality if the Secretary determines that the variable pricing program meets established benchmarks for success for a period of at least 6 months; and 5) authorize the Secretary to contract with an entity to obtain expert commercial advice, assistance, or other services not otherwise carried out by the Defense Commissary Agency.

The Senate recedes.

The conferees believe this provision will significantly improve the business operations of the commissary system and lead to greater efficiency in the delivery of high quality grocery products and services to commissary patrons without diminishing the current level of patron savings. The conferees remain concerned, however, that the current senior management of the Defense Commissary Agency may lack the necessary talent and skills to transform the commissary system into an efficient, high-performing purveyor of grocery products and services. The conferees strongly urge the Department to engage experts in the commercial grocery industry to assist the Defense Commissary Agency in the transformation of the commissary system into a high-performing grocery operation.

Acceptance of Military Star Card at commissaries (sec. 662)

The House amendment contained a provision (sec. 632) that would require the Secretary of Defense to ensure that commissary stores accept the Military Star Card as payment for goods and services. Under this provision, the Army and Air Force Exchange Service would assume any financial liability of the United States relating to acceptance of the Military Star Card as payment for goods and services at commissary stores.

The Senate bill contained no similar provision.

The Senate recedes.

Subtitle F—Other Matters

Recovery of amounts owed to the United States by members of the uniformed services (sec. 671)

The House amendment contained a provision (sec. 642) that would amend section 1007(c)(3) of title 37, United States Code, to establish a 10-year statute of limitations on the authority of the government to collect an indebtedness to the government owed by a servicemember if the indebtedness occurred through no fault of the member. The statute of limitations established under this provision would apply to indebtedness incurred on or after October 1, 2027. The provision would require the Director of the Defense Finance and Accounting Service to provide an annual report, commencing on January 1, 2017 and each year through 2027, on cases in which recovery of indebtedness commenced after the end of the 10-year period beginning on the date when the indebtedness was incurred, or in which the member was not notified of the indebtedness during such 10-year period.

The Senate bill contained no similar provision.

The Senate recedes with an amendment that would direct the Secretary of Defense to conduct a review of all bonus pays, special pays, student loan repayments, and similar special payments paid to members of the California National Guard between January 1, 2004 and December 31, 2015. The review is required to be completed by July 30, 2017. The provision requires a board of review designated by the Secretary of Defense to determine whether the special pay to these members and former members was unwarranted and, if so, to recommend to the Secretary concerned whether to recoup the payment, waive the recoupment, or in the case of recoupments that were previously collected but were unwarranted by the evidence, to recommend whether the payments should be repaid to the member or former member. The provision would authorize the Secretary concerned to waive collection of overpayments or to repay previously recouped payments that were unwarranted. The provision would require the Secretary concerned to notify consumer credit reporting agencies if the review determines that an indebtedness previously reported to the credit reporting agency was invalid. The funding for activities associated with the review, including repayments to members and former members, shall be paid from amounts available for the National Guard of the United States for the State of California. The provision requires the Secretary of Defense to submit a report on the results of the review to the Committees on Armed Services of the Senate and of the House of Representatives not later than August 1, 2017. The provision also requires the Comptroller General of the United States to report, not later than one year after the date of enactment of this Act, on the actions of the National Guard of the State of California related to the bonus pays, special pays, student loan repayments, and other special pays from 2004 through 2015.

Modification of flat rate per diem requirement for personnel on long-term temporary duty assignments (sec. 672)

The Senate bill contained a provision (sec. 1151) that would require the Secretary of Defense to take such action as may be necessary to provide that, to the extent that regulations implementing travel and transportation authorities for military and civilian personnel of the Department of Defense impose a flat rate per diem for meals and incidental expenses for authorized travelers on long term temporary duty (TDY) assignments that is at a reduced rate compared to the per diem rate otherwise applicable, the Service Secretary concerned may waive the applicability of such reduced rate and pay such travelers actual expenses up to the full per diem rate for such travel in any case when the Secretary concerned determines that the reduced flat rate per diem for meals and incidental expenses is not sufficient under the circumstances of the TDY assignment.

The House amendment contained a provision (sec. 603) that would prohibit the Secretary concerned from altering the per diem allowance for the duration of a temporary duty assignment of a member of the Armed Forces or an employee of the Department of Defense.

The House recedes with a clarifying amendment.

LEGISLATIVE PROVISIONS NOT ADOPTED

Sense of the Congress on Roth contributions as default contributions of members of the Armed Forces participating in the Thrift Savings Plan under retired pay reform

The Senate bill contained a provision (sec. 635) that would state the sense of the Congress that the Department of Defense should explore making the default contributions of a full Thrift Savings Plan member under the new military retirement plan enacted in the National Defense Authorization Act for Fiscal Year 2016 (Public Law 114–92) to be designated as Roth contributions until the member elects not to designate such contributions as Roth contributions.

The House amendment contained no similar provision.

The Senate recedes.

Sense of the Congress on options for members of the Armed Forces to designate payment of the death gratuity to a trust for a special needs individual

The Senate bill contained a provision (sec. 645) that would express the Sense of the Congress that the Department of Defense should explore options to allow servicemembers to designate that, upon their death, the death gratuity may be paid to a trust that is legally established under any federal, state, or territorial law.

The House amendment contained no similar provision.

The Senate recedes.

Period for relocation of spouses and dependents of certain members of the Armed Forces undergoing a permanent change of station

The Senate bill contained a provision (sec. 622) that would add a new section 1784b of title 10, United States Code, to provide greater flexibility for families to determine the sequencing of permanent change of station moves under certain circumstances.

The House amendment contained no similar provision.

The Senate recedes.

The conferees direct the Secretary of Defense to submit a report to the Committees on Armed Services of the Senate and the House of Representatives no later than six months after the date of enactment of this Act on actions taken by the Department of Defense to enhance the stability of military families undergoing a permanent change of station (PCS). The report shall include an analysis of the current extent of family disruption associated with PCS moves of members of the Armed Forces, a description of the actions taken by the Department of Defense to minimize such disruptions, and further actions recommended by the Secretary of Defense to alleviate family disruption associated with a PCS move.

TITLE VII—HEALTH CARE PROVISIONS

Subtitle A—Reform of Tricare and Military Health System

TRICARE Select and other TRICARE Reform (sec. 701)

The Senate bill contained a provision (sec. 701) that would amend chapter 55 of title 10, United States Code, to reform health care plans available under the TRICARE program. The provision would establish three health plan choices for families of Active-Duty servicemembers, and retired military members and their families: 1) TRICARE Prime, a managed care option; 2) TRICARE Choice, a self-managed option; and 3) TRICARE Supplemental, an option for retired members and their families, other than TRICARE–For-Life beneficiaries, who have other health insurance. Beneficiaries would be required to enroll in one of the TRICARE options during an annual open enrollment period in order to obtain care through the TRICARE Program.

Under this provision, the Department would offer TRICARE Prime in areas near military treatment facilities (MTFs). Active-Duty family members would be authorized to enroll in TRICARE Prime, and there would be no cost shares. Retirees and their family members would be authorized to enroll in TRICARE Prime in areas where an MTF has a significant number of health care providers, including specialty providers, and sufficient capability to support efficient operations of the MTF. A TRICARE Prime enrollee would be required to obtain a referral for care from a designated primary care manager prior to obtaining care under the TRICARE program. A referral to network providers for specialty care services would not require a beneficiary to obtain a pre-authorization. The provision would require the Secretary to ensure that beneficiaries have the same level of access to care within timelines that meet or exceed those of high-performing health systems in the private sector. The provision would establish TRICARE Choice in other locations in the country, and beneficiaries may receive care from any health care provider selected by the member subject to any restrictions established by the Secretary.

This provision would include a cost-share table for calendar year 2018 for both TRICARE Prime and TRICARE Choice that would establish rates for annual enrollment fees, annual deductibles, annual catastrophic caps, and co-payments for inpatient visits, outpatient visits, and other services. The provision would gradually increase the annual enrollment fee for military retirees and their families under TRICARE Choice over a period of 5 years through 2023. Subsequently, annual enrollment fees for military retirees and their families in TRICARE Choice after

2023, and for military retirees and their families under TRICARE Prime after 2018, would increase by the annual percent of the Consumer Price Index for Health Care Services, published by the Bureau of Labor Statistics. Additionally, the provision would increase the deductible, co-payment, and annual catastrophic cap amounts after 2018, by the annual cost of living adjustment for military retired pay. The provision would authorize the Secretary to adopt special coverage and reimbursement methods, amounts, and procedures to encourage the use of high-value services and products and to discourage the use of low-value services and products.

Under this provision, retirees and their family members with other health insurance would be authorized to enroll in the TRICARE Supplemental option. The provision would establish an annual enrollment fee that would be one-half of the fee for the TRICARE Choice option. Under TRICARE Supplemental, TRICARE would pay the deductible and co-payment amounts under the beneficiary's primary health plan, not to exceed the amount TRICARE would have paid as primary payer to an out-of-network provider.

A number of existing TRICARE programs would remain unchanged under this provision: 1) Extended Health Care Option Program; 2) TRICARE Reserve Select; 3) TRICARE Retired Reserve; 4) TRICARE Dental Program; and 5) the Continued Health Care Benefits Program. This provision would not affect the required cost-shares under the TRICARE Pharmacy Benefits Program, but the annual enrollment fee, annual deductible, and annual catastrophic cap established in this section would apply to the pharmacy program. With this provision, the cost-share requirements for remote area dependents would be the same as those established under the TRICARE Prime Option but without a referral requirement.

The House amendment contained a provision (sec. 701) that would amend chapter 55 of title 10, United States Code, to establish TRICARE Preferred as the self-managed, preferred provider option in the TRICARE program, replacing TRICARE Standard and Extra. The provision would establish annual enrollment fees and fixed dollar co-payments for Active-Duty family members and retirees who join the Armed Services on or after January 1, 2018, and enroll in TRICARE Preferred or TRICARE Prime, the managed care option. In addition, the provision would authorize an annual enrollment fee for TRICARE Preferred for beneficiaries who were in either the Active-Duty or retired beneficiary categories prior to January 1, 2018. However, the provision would prohibit the Secretary from establishing this annual enrollment fee until 90 days after the Comptroller General of the United States submits a report, not later than February 1, 2020, to the Committees on Armed Services of the Senate and the House of Representatives on access to care, network adequacy, and beneficiary satisfaction under TRICARE Preferred. The provision would also require the Comptroller General, not later than September 1, 2017, to submit to the committees a report on the assessment of network adequacy and beneficiaries' access to care under the TRICARE health care provider network. Finally, the provision would require the Secretary to submit an implementation plan, not later than June 1, 2017, to the committees to improve access for TRICARE beneficiaries. The Comptroller General would be required to submit to the committees, not later than December 1, 2017, a review of the implementation plan submitted by the Secretary.

The Senate recedes with an amendment that would: 1) rename the TRICARE Preferred health plan option to TRICARE Select; 2) modify the tables prescribing enrollment fees, deductibles, catastrophic caps, and co-payments for beneficiaries in the retired category who join the military on or after January 1, 2018, and to establish a calendar year enrollment period for those fees; 3) require the Secretary to establish an open enrollment period, with a grace period during the first year of open enrollment, and to allow enrollment for qualifying events for annual participation in either TRICARE Prime or TRICARE Select; 4) prescribe certain requirements for pre-authorization for referrals under TRICARE Prime; and 5) require a pilot program on incorporation of value-based health care methodology in the purchased care component of the TRICARE program.

Reform of administration of the Defense Health Agency and military medical treatment facilities (sec. 702)

The Senate bill contained a provision (sec. 721) that would require the Secretary of Defense to disestablish the medical departments of the Armed Forces and consolidate all activities of those departments into the Defense Health Agency. The Secretary could not undertake this action until 60 days after submission of the Department's consolidation plan to the Committees on Armed Services of the Senate and the House of Representatives. The provision would also require the Comptroller General of the United States to review the consolidation plan and submit that review to the Committees on Armed Services of the Senate and the House of Representatives within 180 days after the Secretary submits the plan to the committees. Under this provision, the Defense Health Agency would be led by an officer of the Armed Forces holding the grade of lieutenant general or vice admiral and be responsible for the medical operations of the Department of Defense. The resultant Defense Health Agency would consist of four subordinate organizations: 1) an organization responsible for all military medical treatment facilities (MTFs); 2) an organization responsible for medical professional recruitment and retention activities, medical education and training, research and development activities, and executive agencies for medical operations or activities; 3) an organization responsible for activities and duties of the current Defense Health Agency; and 4) an organization responsible for activities and duties to improve and maintain operational medical force readiness capabilities and to ensure sustainment of combat casualty care and trauma readiness of military health care providers. A major general or rear admiral upper half would serve as head of each subordinate organization. The provision would give broad authorities to the Director of the Defense Health Agency, under the supervision and control of the Assistant Secretary of Defense for Health Affairs, to conduct the medical operations functions of the Department. In addition, the provision would amend sections 3036, 5137, and 8036 of title 10, United States Code, to establish the duties and responsibilities of the Surgeons General of the Services as principal adviser to the service secretary and service chief as well as chief medical adviser of that service to the Defense Health Agency. Finally, the provision would require the Secretary of Defense to submit a report on consolidation, by January 1, 2017, to the Committees on Armed Services of the Senate and the House of Representatives.

The House amendment contained a provision (sec. 702) that would amend chapter 55 of title 10, United States Code, to require the Defense Health Agency to become responsible for management of MTFs throughout the Department of Defense, while preserving the responsibility of MTF commanders for ensuring the readiness of members of the Armed Forces and civilian employees at MTFs and for providing health care services at MTFs. In carrying out this provision, the Defense Health Agency would establish an executive-level management office consisting of professional health care administrators to manage health care operations, finance and budget, information technology, and medical affairs across all MTFs. This provision would direct the Secretary of Defense to submit an interim report to the congressional defense committees by March 1, 2017, on the preliminary plan to implement these changes, and a final report by March 1, 2018. Finally, this provision would require the Comptroller General of the United States to review each of the Department's plans and to submit an assessment of those plans to the congressional defense committees by September 1, 2017, and September 1, 2018, respectively.

The Senate recedes with an amendment that would require the Director of the Defense Health Agency, beginning October 1, 2018, to take responsibility for the administration of each MTF, including all matters with respect to: 1) budget; 2) information technology; 3) health care administration and management; 4) administrative policy and procedure; 5) military medical construction and 6) any other matters the Secretary determines appropriate. The amendment would require the establishment of a professional staff within the Defense Health Agency to provide policy, oversight, and direction of all matters related to the administration of MTFs. In addition, the amendment would codify the roles and responsibilities of the Services' Surgeons General. The amendment would require the Secretary to develop an implementation plan and to submit: 1) an interim report providing a preliminary draft of the plan to the Committees on Armed Services of the Senate and the House of Representatives by March 1, 2017; and 2) a final report to the committees by March 1, 2018, containing a final version of the plan. Finally, the amendment would require the Comptroller General of the United States to submit to the committees a review of the Department's preliminary draft of the plan by September 1, 2017, and a review of the final version of the plan by September 1, 2018.

After careful study and deliberation, the conferees conclude that a single agency responsible for the administration of all MTFs would best improve and sustain operational medical force readiness and the medical readiness of the Armed Forces, improve beneficiaries' access to care and the experience of care, improve health outcomes, and lower the total management cost of the military health system. The conferees believe that the current organizational structure of the military health system—essentially three separate health systems each managed by one of the three Services—paralyzes rapid decision-making and stifles innovation in producing a modern health care delivery system that would better serve all beneficiaries. A streamlined military health system management structure would eliminate redundancy and generate greater efficiency, yielding monetary savings to the Department

while leading to true reform of the military health system and improving the experience of care for beneficiaries.

Military medical treatment facilities (sec. 703)

The Senate bill contained a provision (sec. 725) that would authorize the secretary of a military department to realign the infrastructure of or modify the health care services provided by a military treatment facility (MTF) if a realignment or modification would better: 1) ensure the delivery of safe, high quality health care services; 2) adapt the delivery of health care in a facility to rapid changes in private sector health care delivery models; or 3) maintain the medical force readiness skills and core competencies of health care providers in a facility. Before taking any action under this provision, the Secretary of Defense would be required to submit a report to the Committees on Armed Services of the Senate and the House of Representatives on proposed realignments of infrastructure or modifications of health care services at MTFs. Within 60 days after the Secretary submits a report under this provision, the Comptroller General of the United States would submit a review of such report to the Committees on Armed Services of the Senate and the House of Representatives.

The Senate bill also contained a provision (sec. 729) that would require the Secretary of Defense to establish regional centers of excellence for the provision of specialty care to covered beneficiaries at major medical centers of the Department of Defense. The provision would authorize the Secretary to establish satellite centers, when and where appropriate, particularly to provide specialty care for post-traumatic stress and traumatic brain injury. Furthermore, the provision would specify the types of centers of excellence that the Secretary could establish while allowing for the establishment of additional centers when appropriate. The centers of excellence established under this provision would serve as the primary sources for specialty care within the direct care health system, and health care providers throughout the system would refer beneficiaries to those facilities. The provision would require the Secretary to submit a report to the Committees on Armed Services of the Senate and the House of Representatives, within 180 days of the date of enactment of this Act, which provides a plan to establish specialty care centers of excellence in the military health system.

The House amendment contained a provision (sec. 703) that would amend chapter 55 of title 10, United States Code, to establish the requirements for the types of MTFs needed to support the medical readiness of the Armed Forces and the readiness of medical personnel. The provision would require the Secretary of Defense, in collaboration with the secretaries of the military departments, to submit an updated Military Health System Modernization Study report to the congressional defense committees within 270 days after the date of enactment of this Act. In addition, the provision would require the Secretary to submit, within 2 years after the date of enactment of this Act, an implementation plan to restructure or realign the MTFs in accordance with section 1079d of title 10, United States Code.

The Senate recedes with an amendment that would combine these provisions.

Access to urgent and primary care under TRICARE program (sec. 704)

The House amendment contained a provision (sec. 704) that would amend chapter 55 of title 10, United States Code, to require the

Secretary of Defense, within 1 year of the date of enactment of this Act, to improve access to urgent care services in both military medical treatment facilities (MTFs) and the private sector. The provision would ensure that covered beneficiaries have access to urgent care services through the health care provider network under the TRICARE program, without the need for preauthorization, in areas where no MTFs exist for those services. Finally, this provision would require the Secretary of Defense to ensure that the nurse advice line of the Department directs covered beneficiaries seeking access to health care services to the most appropriate level of care required to treat medical conditions of beneficiaries, including urgent care services.

The House amendment also contained a provision (sec. 705) that would amend section 1077a of title 10, United States Code, to require the Secretary of Defense, within 180 days of the date of enactment of this Act, to ensure the availability of primary care services for members of the Armed Forces and covered beneficiaries during expanded business hours on weekdays and weekends, based on the needs of the MTF to meet access standards under the TRICARE Prime program and the primary care utilization patterns at the MTF.

The Senate bill contained no similar provisions.

The Senate recedes with an amendment that would combine these provisions.

Value-based purchasing and acquisition of managed care support contracts for TRICARE program (sec. 705)

The Senate bill contained a provision (sec. 726) that would require the Secretary of Defense to conduct a new competition of all medical support contracts, except the overseas medical support contract, with private sector entities under the TRICARE program by January 1, 2018, upon expiration of each such contract. New contracts would be competitively procured and automatically renewable for a period of not more than 10 years unless notice for termination is provided by either party not later than 180 days before contract termination. The Department would award contracts with a combination of local, regional and national private sector entities to develop individual and institutional networks of high-performing health care providers. The Secretary could not exercise an option to extend an existing medical support contract with a private sector entity that would delay the award of a new contract. Within 1 year of the award of new medical support contracts, the Secretary would be required to issue an open broad agency announcement to allow potential contractors to propose innovative ideas and solutions to meet the medical support contract needs of the Department. A medical support contract awarded through the open broad agency announcement would be deemed to meet the requirements under section 2304 of title 10, United States Code, relating to use of competitive procedures to procure services. For new medical support contracts, the Department would be required to include, to the extent practicable: 1) maximum flexibility in network design and development; 2) integrated medical management between military medical treatment facilities and network providers; 3) maximum use of the full range of telehealth services; 4) use of value-based reimbursement methods that transfer financial risk to health care providers and medical support contractors; 5) use of prevention and wellness incentives to encourage bene-

ficiaries to seek health care services from high-value providers; 6) a streamlined enrollment process and timely assignment of primary care managers; 7) elimination of the requirement to seek authorization of referrals for specialty care services; 8) the use of incentives to encourage certain beneficiaries to engage in medical and lifestyle intervention programs; and 9) the use of financial incentives for contractors and health care providers to receive an equitable share in cost savings resulting from improvement in health outcomes and the experience of care for beneficiaries. In establishing new medical support contracts, the provision would require the Secretary to: 1) assess the unique characteristics of providing health care services in rural, remote, or isolated locations, such as Alaska, Hawaii, and locations in the contiguous 48 states; 2) consider the various challenges inherent in developing robust provider networks in those locations; and 3) develop a provider reimbursement rate structure in those locations that ensures timely access to care, high quality primary and specialty care, and improvement in health outcomes. Additionally, the Secretary could not modify existing medical support contracts or enter into new contracts in rural, remote, or isolated locations until the Secretary certifies to the Committees on Armed Services of the Senate and the House of Representatives that those contracts would ensure timely access to care, high quality care, better health outcomes, and a better experience of care. The provision would also require the Comptroller General of the United States to submit a report, by January 1, 2019, that assesses the compliance of the Secretary with the requirements of this section.

The Senate bill contained another provision (sec. 727) that would authorize the Secretary of Defense to enter into contracts to provide health care, including behavioral health care, to covered beneficiaries under the TRICARE program with any of the following: 1) the Department of Veterans Affairs; 2) an Indian tribe or tribal organization that is party to the Alaska Native Health Compact with the Indian Health Service; and 3) an Indian tribe or tribal organization that has entered into a contract with the Indian Health Service to provide health care in rural Alaska or other locations in the United States.

The House amendment contained a provision (sec. 706) that would authorize the Secretary of Defense to develop and implement value-based incentive programs as part of TRICARE contracts to encourage health care providers under the TRICARE program to improve the quality of care and the experience of care for covered beneficiaries. The provision would require the Secretary to brief the Committees on Armed Services of the Senate and the House of Representatives on the implementation plan not later than 60 days before the Secretary modifies a TRICARE contract to implement a value-based incentive program. Furthermore, the provision would require the Secretary to brief the committees, and any other appropriate congressional committees, within 1 year after implementation and annually through 2022, on the quality performance metrics and expenditures related to the incentive program.

The House recedes with an amendment that would require the Secretary of Defense to develop and implement value-based incentive programs as part of any contract awarded under chapter 55 of title 10, United States Code, for the provision of health care services to covered beneficiaries. The amend-

ment would transfer contracting responsibility for the acquisition of managed care support contracts under the TRICARE program, initiated after the date of enactment of this Act, from the Defense Health Agency to the Under Secretary of Defense for Acquisition, Technology, and Logistics. The amendment would require the Secretary to develop and implement, by January 1, 2018, a new acquisition strategy for managed care support contracts under the TRICARE program and to modify contracts existing prior to implementation of this strategy to ensure consistency with the strategy.

The conferees remain concerned about the current acquisition strategy for managed care support contracts under the TRICARE program. The Department's current contract strategy results in routine bid protests, implementation delays, high management costs, and costly contract extensions. Under those contracts, the Department remains solely at risk for the cost of all healthcare services provided, and the adherence to fee-for-service provider reimbursement fails to encourage individual and institutional network providers to provide higher quality care, better access to care, and higher patient satisfaction at lower costs to the Department. As a result, the conferees believe it is necessary to transfer contracting responsibility for the acquisition of managed care support contracts under the TRICARE program to the Under Secretary of Defense for Acquisition, Technology, and Logistics.

Establishment of high performance military-civilian integrated health delivery systems (sec. 706)

The Senate bill contained a provision (sec. 736) that would require the Secretary of Defense, by January 1, 2018, to establish high performance military-civilian integrated health delivery systems through partnerships with other health systems, including local or regional health systems in the private sector, and the Veterans Health Administration. The Department of Defense would accomplish these partnerships either through memoranda of understanding or contracts between military treatment facilities and private sector health systems, such as health maintenance organizations, regional health organizations, integrated health systems, and health care centers of excellence, or the Veterans Health Administration. Under this provision, covered beneficiaries would be eligible to enroll in and receive medical services in the private sector component of established military-civilian integrated health networks. The Secretary of Defense would be required to incorporate value-based reimbursement methodologies into any memoranda of understanding or contracts to reimburse private sector entities for medical services provided to covered beneficiaries.

The House amendment contained a provision (sec. 707) that would amend section 1096 of title 10, United States Code, to authorize the Secretary of Defense to enter into partnership agreements between military treatment facilities and local or regional health care systems to deliver health care to beneficiaries in a more effective, efficient, or economical manner and provide members of the Armed Forces with additional training opportunities to maintain operational medical force readiness.

The House recedes with a clarifying amendment.

Joint Trauma System (sec. 707)

The House amendment contained a provision (sec. 708) that would require the Secretary of Defense to submit an implementation plan, within 180 days of enactment of this Act, to the Committees on Armed Services of the Senate and the House of Representatives to establish a Joint Trauma System within the Defense Health Agency that promotes improved trauma care to members of the Armed Forces and other individuals eligible for trauma care at a military medical treatment facility (MTF). The Secretary would not implement this plan until a 90-day period has elapsed following the date that the Comptroller General of the United States provides a review of the plan to the committees. The Comptroller General would have 120 days to review the plan. Under this provision, the Joint Trauma System would: 1) serve as the reference body for all trauma care provided across the military health system; 2) establish standards of care for trauma services provided at MTFs; 3) coordinate the translation of research from centers of excellence of the Department into clinical trauma care standards; and 4) coordinate the incorporation of lessons learned from military-civilian trauma education and training partnerships into clinical practice. The provision would also authorize the Secretary to seek to enter into an agreement with a nongovernmental entity to conduct a system-wide review of the military trauma system.

The Senate bill contained no similar provision.

The Senate recedes with a clarifying amendment.

Joint Trauma Education and Training Directorate (sec. 708)

The Senate bill contained a provision (sec. 734) that would require the Secretary of Defense to implement measures to improve and maintain the combat casualty care and trauma care skills for health care providers of the Department of Defense by January 1, 2018. The provision would require the Secretary to: 1) conduct a comprehensive review of combat casualty care and wartime trauma systems from January 1, 2001, to the present time; 2) expand military-civilian trauma training sites to provide enhanced training for integrated combat trauma teams; 3) establish a personnel management plan for important wartime medical specialties; 4) develop standardized tactical combat casualty care instructions and training for all servicemembers; 5) develop a comprehensive trauma care registry; 6) develop quality of care outcome measures for combat casualty care; and 7) conduct research to understand better the causes of morbidity and mortality of servicemembers in combat.

The House amendment contained a provision (Sec. 709) that would require the Secretary of Defense to establish a Joint Trauma Education and Training Directorate to ensure military traumatologists maintain readiness skills and can be rapidly deployed in future armed conflicts. Under this provision, the Secretary would establish enduring partnerships with civilian academic medical centers and large metropolitan teaching hospitals with level one trauma centers to embed combat casualty care teams, led by military traumatologists, within trauma centers of medical centers and hospitals. The provision would require the Secretary to conduct an analysis to determine the number of military traumatologists, by specialty, that the Department of Defense needs to meet combatant commander requirements. Finally, this provision would require the Secretary to submit an implementation plan to the Committees on Armed Services of the Senate and the House of Representatives by July 1, 2017.

The Senate recedes with an amendment that would combine these two provisions.

Standardized system for scheduling medical appointments at military treatment facilities (sec. 709)

The Senate bill contained a provision (sec. 732) that would require the Secretary of Defense to implement, by January 1, 2018, a standardized medical appointment scheduling system at military treatment facilities (MTFs) throughout the military health system. Under this provision, no MTF would have the authority to use an appointment scheduling system other than the standardized system. Each MTF would make available a centralized appointment system that allows beneficiaries to make appointments, either by telephone or by an internet-connected device, including by smartphone application, through an online scheduling system available 24 hours per day, 7 days per week. The online appointment system would be able to send automated email and text message reminders to patients.

The House amendment contained a provision (sec. 710) that would require the Secretary of Defense to ensure that military treatment facilities implement: 1) first call resolution for beneficiaries contacting the facility by telephone; 2) standardized appointment scheduling that includes capabilities to schedule follow-up appointments within a 6-month period or longer from the date of the appointment request and to remind beneficiaries of future appointments; 3) increased provider productivity standards to improve access to care and medical readiness requirements; and 4) maximum use of telehealth and secure messaging between beneficiaries and health care providers. This provision would require the Secretary to implement the requirements by February 1, 2017, and provide a briefing on implementation to the Committees on Armed Services of the Senate and the House of Representatives by March 1, 2017.

The House recedes with an amendment that would require the Secretary of Defense to: 1) implement a standardized appointment system in the military health system by January 1, 2018, and provide to the Committees on Armed Services of the Senate and the House of Representatives, by January 1, 2017, a comprehensive plan to implement the system; 2) implement standards for productivity of health care providers at MTFs; and 3) submit a report to the committees, by March 1 of each year, on the total number of missed appointments at MTFs for which a covered beneficiary failed to appear without prior notification during the 1-year period preceding the submission of the report. Additionally, the provision would require the Secretary to brief the committees on implementation of the standardized appointment system and health care provider productivity standards by February 1, 2018.

Subtitle B—Other Health Care Benefits

Extended TRICARE program coverage for certain members of the National Guard and dependents during certain disaster response duty (sec. 711)

The House amendment contained a provision (sec. 722) that would amend chapter 55 of title 10, United States Code, to extend TRICARE program coverage for certain members of the National Guard and dependents performing certain disaster response duty if the period immediately follows a period of full-time National Guard duty. Under this provision, a member would not receive extended TRICARE program coverage if a governor of a state or the mayor of the District of Columbia (DC) determines that such coverage is not in the best interest of the member, state, or DC. This provision would authorize the Secretary of Defense to charge a state or DC for the costs of providing extended TRICARE program coverage to members of the National Guard and their dependents.

The Senate bill contained no similar provision.

The Senate recedes with an amendment that provides discretionary authority to extend TRICARE program coverage for certain members of the National Guard and dependents performing certain disaster response duty if the period immediately follows a period of full-time National Guard duty. Additionally, the amendment would require the Secretary of Defense to charge a state or DC for the costs of providing extended TRICARE program coverage to members of the National Guard and their dependents if such coverage is extended.

Continuity of health care coverage for reserve components (sec. 712)

The Senate bill contained a provision (sec. 707) that would authorize the Secretary of Defense to carry out a pilot program jointly with the Director of the Office of Personnel Management (Director), of at least 5 years duration, to provide commercial health insurance coverage to eligible reserve component members who enroll for either individual, self plus one, or self and family coverage. If the Secretary and the Director determine that a pilot program is feasible, the Director would contract with qualified health insurance carriers to provide eligible beneficiaries with a variety of high quality health benefits plans, which could vary by plan design, covered benefits, geography, and price. Reserve component members and their family members would not be eligible to enroll in a health plan in the pilot program if they are eligible to enroll in a health benefits plan under the Federal Employees Health Benefits Program.

Under the pilot program, the Secretary could contract with qualified health insurance carriers to provide coverage for health care services provided at military treatment facilities to pilot program participants, and the Department would receive payment from those carriers for any services provided at those facilities. Family members of an eligible reserve component member could remain covered under the pilot program even when the reserve component member became ineligible for coverage while serving on Active Duty for a period greater than 30 days.

In addition, an eligible reserve component member would be responsible for payment of all cost sharing amounts applicable to the health benefits plan plus an annual premium amount equal to 28 percent of the total annual amount of the premium under the plan. During a period in which a reserve component member served on Active Duty for more than 30 days, the premium amount and cost shares would be zero for eligible family members.

In consultation with the Secretary of Homeland Security, the Secretary would provide recommendations and data to the Director on matters regarding military treatment facilities, matters unique to eligible reserve component members and their families, and any other guidance necessary to administer the pilot program. The Secretary and the Director would jointly establish a funding mechanism for the pilot program, and the Secretary would make funds available to the Director, without fiscal year limitation, for payment of health plan costs and administrative expenses.

The House amendment contained a provision (sec. 712) that would require the Secretary of Defense to study options for providing health care coverage to certain current and former members of the Selected Reserve and to submit a report of the findings and recommendations to the congressional defense committees within 180 days of the date of enactment of this Act.

The Senate recedes with an amendment that would combine these provisions. The resultant provision would require the Director to submit to the Secretary of Defense, on an annual basis during each year the pilot program may be conducted, information on the use of health care benefits under the pilot program. The provision would also require the Secretary to submit an initial and a final report on the pilot program to the Committees on Armed Services of the Senate and the House of Representatives. Finally, the provision would clarify the elements required in the study of options for providing health care coverage that improves the continuity of health care provided to certain current and former members of the Selected Reserve.

Provision of hearing aids to dependents of retired members (sec. 713)

The House amendment contained a provision (sec. 721) that would amend section 1077 of title 10, United States Code, to authorize the Secretary of Defense to sell hearing aids to dependents of retired members of the uniformed services.

The Senate bill contained no similar provision.

The Senate recedes.

Coverage of medically necessary food and vitamins for certain conditions under the TRICARE program (sec. 714)

The Senate bill contained a provision (sec. 704) that would amend section 1077 of title 10, United States Code, to provide TRICARE program coverage for medically necessary food, including the equipment and supplies necessary to administer that food, and vitamins for digestive disorders and inherited metabolic disorders.

The House amendment contained no similar provision.

The House recedes with a clarifying amendment.

Eligibility of certain beneficiaries under the TRICARE program for participation in the Federal Employees Dental and Vision Insurance Program (sec. 715)

The Senate bill contained a provision (sec. 703) that would amend sections 8951 and 8981 of title 5, United States Code, to require the Secretary of Defense to enter into an agreement with the Director of the Office of Personnel Management to offer eligible beneficiaries the opportunity to purchase dental and vision insurance currently available to federal employees under the Federal Employees Dental and Vision Insurance Program.

The House amendment contained no similar provision.

The House recedes with an amendment that would make this provision effective on or after January 1, 2018.

Applied behavior analysis (sec. 716)

The Senate bill contained a provision (sec. 758) that would require the Secretary of Defense, on the date of enactment of this Act, to reinstate the reimbursement rates in effect on March 1, 2016, for the provision of applied behavior analysis therapy and to preserve those rates throughout the duration of the Comprehensive Autism Care Demonstration program conducted under section 705 of the National Defense Authorization Act for Fiscal Year 2013 (Public Law 112–239; 10 U.S.C. 1092 note), as extended and modified by the Secretary.

The House amendment contained a provision (sec. 734) that would require the Secretary to ensure that the reimbursement rates for providers of applied behavior analysis are not less than the rates in effect on March 31, 2016. The provision would require the Assistant Secretary of Defense for Health Affairs, upon completion of the demonstration, to conduct an analysis of the program and to submit a report to the Committees on Armed Services of the Senate and the House of Representatives.

The Senate recedes with an amendment that would require the analysis to include a determination of whether the use of applied behavioral analysis under the demonstration improved outcomes for beneficiaries with autism spectrum disorder.

Evaluation and treatment of veterans and civilians at military treatment facilities (sec. 717)

The Senate bill contained a provision (sec. 706) that would authorize a veteran or civilian to be evaluated and treated at a military treatment facility (MTF) if the Secretary of Defense determines that: 1) the evaluation and treatment of the individual is necessary to maintain the medical readiness skills and competencies of health care providers at the facility; 2) health care providers at the facility have the competencies, skills, and abilities to treat the individual; and 3) the facility has available space, equipment, and materials. The provision would authorize an MTF to bill and accept reimbursement for services provided to a civilian patient. Under this provision, the Secretary of Defense would be required to enter into a memorandum of understanding with the Secretary of Veterans Affairs whereby the Secretary of Veterans Affairs would reimburse an MTF for the costs of any health care services provided to individuals eligible for health care services from the Department of Veterans Affairs (VA).

The House amendment contained no similar provision.

The House recedes with an amendment that would: 1) prioritize the evaluation and treatment of covered beneficiaries in MTFs ahead of the evaluation and treatment of veterans and civilians in those facilities; 2) require an MTF to bill and to accept reimbursement from a civilian or a third-party payer on behalf of the individual for the costs of health care services provided to the individual; and 3) require the Secretary of Defense to enter into a memorandum of agreement with the Secretary of Veterans Affairs under which the Secretary of Veterans Affairs would reimburse an MTF, using a prospective payment methodology, for the costs of any health care services provided to an individual eligible for health care services from the VA.

Enhancement of use of telehealth services in military health system (sec. 718)

The Senate bill contained a provision (sec. 705) that would require the Secretary of Defense, within 1 year of the date of enactment of this Act, to incorporate the use of telehealth services throughout the direct and purchased care components of the military health system. The provision would require the Department to make telehealth services available to: 1) improve access to primary care, urgent care, behavioral health care, and specialty care; 2) perform health assessments; 3) provide diagnoses, treatments, interventions, and supervision; 4) monitor individual health outcomes of covered beneficiaries with chronic diseases or conditions; 5) improve communication between health care providers and patients; and 6) reduce health care costs for beneficiaries and the Department of Defense.

The provision would require the Secretary to establish standardized payment methods to reimburse health care providers for telehealth services provided to covered beneficiaries in the purchased care component of the TRICARE program to incentivize the provision of telehealth services. The provision would also require the Secretary to reduce or eliminate co-payments or cost-shares for covered beneficiaries for receipt of telehealth services.

The provision would require the Secretary to submit an initial report, within 180 days of the date of enactment of this Act, to the Committees on Armed Services of the Senate and the House of Representatives, describing the full range of telehealth services to be available in the direct and purchased care components of the military health system. Within 3 years after the date of incorporation of telehealth services throughout the military health system, the Secretary would be required to submit a final report to the committees describing the impact made by use of telehealth services in the direct and purchased care components of the military health system.

The House amendment contained no similar provision.

The House recedes with a clarifying amendment that would require the implementation of the use of telehealth services throughout the direct and purchased care components of the military health system not later than 18 months after the date of enactment of this Act and would delete the requirement that the location of the provider be considered to be the location of care.

Authorization of reimbursement by Department of Defense to entities carrying out state vaccination programs for costs of vaccines provided to covered beneficiaries (sec. 719)

The Senate bill contained a provision (sec. 757) that would authorize the Secretary of Defense to reimburse an entity carrying out a state vaccination program for the cost of providing vaccines to covered beneficiaries. Under this provision, the amount of reimbursement could not exceed the amount that the Department would reimburse an entity for providing vaccines to covered beneficiaries under the TRICARE program.

The House amendment contained no similar provision.

The House recedes with a clarifying amendment.

Subtitle C—Health Care Administration

Authority to convert military medical and dental positions to civilian medical and dental positions (sec. 721)

The Senate bill contained a provision (sec. 724) that would amend chapter 49 of title 10, United States Code, to authorize the Department of Defense to convert military medical and dental positions to civilian positions if: 1) conversion would not result in a loss of a military-essential position; 2) conversion would not result in degradation of medical care or the medical readiness of the Armed Forces; and 3) conversion to a civilian position would be more cost effective.

The House amendment contained no similar provision.

The House recedes with an amendment that would require the Secretary of Defense, in collaboration with the service secretaries, to establish a process to define military medical and dental personnel requirements necessary to meet operational medical force readiness requirements. The amendment would authorize conversion of a military medical or dental position to a civilian medical or dental position if the Secretary determines that the position is unnecessary to meet operational medical force readiness requirements. Additionally, the amendment would require the Secretary to convert an applicable military position to a civilian position with a level of compensation commensurate with the skills and experience necessary to conduct the duties of the civilian position. The Secretary would not be authorized to place any limitation on the grade or level to which the military position would be converted. Finally, the amendment would require the Secretary to submit a report, within 90 days of enactment of this Act, to the Committees on Armed Services of the Senate and the House of Representatives that: 1) describes the process established to define military medical and dental personnel requirements necessary to meet operational medical force readiness requirements; and 2) provides a complete list, by position, of the military medical and dental requirements necessary to meet operational medical force readiness requirements. The amendment would not authorize conversions of military medical or dental positions to civilian positions until 180 days after the date on which the Secretary submits the report to the committees.

Prospective payment of funds necessary to provide medical care for the Coast Guard (sec. 722)

The House amendment contained a provision (sec. 731) that would amend chapter 13 of title 14, United States Code, to require the Secretary of Homeland Security to make a prospective payment to the Secretary of Defense of an amount that represents the actuarial valuation of medical treatment or care provided to members of the Coast Guard, former members of the Coast Guard, and their dependents at facilities under the jurisdiction of the Department of Defense except during any period in which the Coast Guard operates as a service in the Navy.

The Senate bill contained no similar provision.

The Senate recedes.

Reduction of administrative requirements relating to automatic renewal of enrollments in TRICARE Prime (sec. 723)

The Senate bill contained a provision (sec. 739) that would eliminate an annual requirement that the managed care support contractors under the TRICARE program generate and mail an enrollment renewal letter to all beneficiaries enrolled in TRICARE Prime.

The House amendment contained no similar provision.

The House recedes.

Modification of authority of Uniformed Services University of the Health Sciences to include undergraduate and other medical education and training programs (sec. 724)

The Senate bill contained a provision (sec. 753) that would amend sections 2112(a) and 2113 of title 10, United States Code, to authorize the Uniformed Services University of the Health Sciences to grant certificates, certification, and undergraduate degree programs in addition to advanced degrees.

The House amendment contained no similar provision.

The House recedes.

Adjustment of medical services, personnel authorized strengths, and infrastructure in military health system to maintain readiness and core competencies of health care providers (sec. 725)

The Senate bill contained a provision (sec. 735) that would require the Secretary of Defense to implement measures, within 180 days of the date of enactment of this Act, to maintain the critical wartime medical readiness skills and core competencies of health care providers within the Armed Forces. The provision would require the Secretary to implement a measure to ensure the Services do not substitute a medical specialty required for medical force readiness with another medical specialty. Additionally, the provision would require the Secretary to: 1) modify medical services; 2) reduce authorized strengths of military and civilian personnel; and 3) reduce or eliminate unnecessary infrastructure in the military health system such that military treatment facilities would provide only those services required to maintain the critical wartime medical skills and core competencies of health care providers and to ensure the medical readiness of the Armed Forces. Moreover, this provision would require the Comptroller General of the United States to provide a report, within 18 months of the date of enactment of this Act, which assesses the Department's implementation of this provision, to the Committees on Armed Services of the Senate and the House of Representatives.

The House amendment contained no similar provision.

The House recedes with an amendment that would require the Secretary to implement measures, within 1 year of the date of enactment of this Act, to maintain the critical wartime medical readiness skills and core competencies of health care providers within the Armed Forces. In implementing those measures, the Secretary must ensure that the medical services provided in military medical treatment facilities (MTFs), the authorized strengths of military and civilian personnel working in MTFs, and the infrastructure of MTFs maintain the critical wartime medical readiness skills and core competencies of health care providers within the Armed Forces. The amendment would not require the Secretary to implement any of these measures at MTFs located in a foreign country if the Secretary determines that beneficiaries in that country would not have access to medical services in that country similar to access to medical services for covered beneficiaries in the United States.

Program to eliminate variability in health outcomes and improve quality of health care services delivered in military medical treatment facilities (sec. 726)

The Senate bill contained a provision (sec. 730) that would require the Secretary of Defense to conduct a program, beginning not later than January 1, 2018, to: 1) establish best practices for the delivery of health care services for certain diseases or conditions at military treatment facilities (MTFs); 2) incorporate those best practices into the daily operations of MTFs participating in the program; and 3) eliminate variability in health outcomes and improve the quality of health care services delivered at MTFs. Under this provision, the Secretary would conduct the program in three phases and be required to complete each phase within 180 days following initiation of that phase. The initiation of phases two and three would immediately follow completion of the previous phase. The provision would require the Secretary, during the conduct of the program,

to continuously monitor and adjust the health care services delivered at MTFs and the number of patients enrolled at those facilities to ensure: 1) a high degree of safety and quality in the delivery of health care at those facilities; and 2) the delivery of only those health care services critical for maintaining operational medical force readiness and the medical readiness of the Armed Forces.

The House amendment contained no similar provision.

The House recedes with an amendment that would require the Secretary, by January 1, 2018, to implement a program to establish best practices for the delivery of health care services for certain diseases or conditions at MTFs, as selected by the Secretary, and to incorporate those best practices into the daily operations of MTFs to eliminate variability in health outcomes and to improve the quality of care at MTFs. In conducting this program, the Secretary shall develop, implement, monitor, and update clinical practice guidelines reflecting best practices for the delivery of health care services. The amendment would require the Secretary to monitor the implementation of the clinical practice guidelines and to update those guidelines periodically through a process of continual assessment of evidence-based best practices within the direct care component of the military health system and the private sector.

Acquisition strategy for health care professional staffing services (sec. 727)

The Senate bill contained a provision (sec. 738) that would amend section 725(a) of the Carl Levin and Howard P. "Buck" McKeon National Defense Authorization Act for Fiscal Year 2015 (Public Law 113–291), to require the Department of Defense to implement a performance-based, strategic sourcing contract for acquiring health care professional staffing services for the military health system. The provision would require all components of the military health system to use the contract, and the Department would be required to develop a process for obtaining a waiver, based on documented rationale, to use another contract or acquisition approach.

The Senate bill also contained a provision (sec. 737) that would require the Secretary of Defense to enter into centrally-managed, performance-based contracts with private sector entities to augment the delivery of health care services at military treatment facilities (MTFs) with limited or restricted ability to provide services such as primary care or expanded-hours urgent care. Under this provision, contracts would be designed to purchase improvement in health outcomes for covered beneficiaries seeking health care services in MTFs. This provision would require the Secretary to submit a plan to the Committees on Armed Services of the Senate and the House of Representatives, within 180 days of enactment of this Act, that includes: 1) a description of the number and types of contracts the Secretary intends to procure; and 2) a description of the performance measures used in procuring performance-based contracts.

The House amendment contained no similar provisions.

The House recedes with an amendment that would combine these provisions. The amendment would require the Secretary of Defense to develop and carry out a performance-based, strategic sourcing acquisition strategy for health care professional services at MTFs located in a state. The new acquisition strategy, as developed by the Secretary, would require all MTFs to use the contracts awarded under the strategy, but it would provide a process for an MTF to obtain a waiver of this requirement to use another acquisition strategy. The amendment would require the Secretary to submit a report to the Committees on Armed Services of the Senate and the House of Representatives, by July 1, 2017, on the status of implementing the new acquisition strategy. Finally, the amendment would repeal section 725 of the Carl Levin and Howard P. "Buck" McKeon National Defense Authorization Act for Fiscal Year 2015 (Public Law 113–291; 10 U.S.C. 1091 note).

Adoption of core quality performance metrics (sec. 728)

The House amendment contained a provision (sec. 711) that would require the Secretary of Defense to adopt the core quality performance measures agreed upon by a collaborative group of federal agencies, private sector health insurance plans, national physician organizations, employers, and health care consumers. These core quality performance measures would be used to evaluate the performance of the direct care and purchased care components of the military health system.

The Senate bill contained no similar provision.

The Senate recedes with an amendment that would include in the core quality metrics such other sets of core quality performance metrics released by the Core Quality Measures Collaborative as the Secretary considers appropriate. The amendment would amend section 1073b of title 10, United States Code, to require the Secretary to include the core quality performance metrics mandated under this section in those metrics publicly available on an Internet website of the Department of Defense.

Improvement of health outcomes and control of costs of health care under TRICARE program through programs to involve covered beneficiaries (sec. 729)

The Senate bill contained a provision (sec. 728) that would require the Secretary of Defense, by January 1, 2018, to implement programs to increase involvement of covered beneficiaries in making health care decisions and to encourage beneficiaries to share more responsibility for the improvement in their health outcomes through participation in medical and lifestyle intervention programs. This provision would incentivize those beneficiaries with chronic diseases or conditions, such as diabetes, asthma, or depression, or those exhibiting unhealthy behaviors, such as tobacco use or obesity, to participate in comprehensive medical or lifestyle intervention programs designed to improve beneficiaries' health outcomes and functional status while controlling health care costs for those beneficiaries and the Department. This provision would also authorize the Secretary to charge and collect a fee from a covered beneficiary, other than an Active-Duty servicemember, for failure to notify a military treatment facility, within 24 hours of a scheduled appointment with a health care provider, that the beneficiary will be unable to attend the appointment. The Secretary of Defense would be required to submit a report to the Committees on Armed Services of the Senate and the House of Representatives, by January 1, 2020, that describes implementation of the programs mandated under this provision.

The House amendment contained no similar provision.

The House recedes with an amendment that would also require the Secretary to es-

tablish a program to incentivize the maintenance of a healthy lifestyle, such as exercise and weight management, among covered beneficiaries. The amendment would not authorize the Secretary to charge and collect a fee from a covered beneficiary, other than an Active-Duty servicemember, for failure to notify a military treatment facility, within 24 hours of a scheduled appointment with a health care provider, that the beneficiary will be unable to attend the appointment.

The conferees are concerned, however, about the high number of failed medical appointments in the military health system. From October 2014 through September 2015, there were over 1.6 million scheduled appointments missed by all categories of beneficiaries. The large number of failed appointments negatively affects access to care for all beneficiaries. The conferees strongly urge the Secretary to implement programs to minimize the number of failed appointments in military hospitals and clinics.

Accountability for the performance of the military health system of certain leaders within the system (sec. 730)

The Senate bill contained a provision (sec. 722) that would require the Secretary of Defense and the secretaries of the military departments, within 180 days of the date of enactment of this Act, to incorporate performance accountability measures into the annual performance reviews of certain leadership positions in the military health care system. The provision would prohibit payment of a performance bonus to a civilian employee of the Department of Defense occupying a position, specified in the provision, unless the operations of the military health care system met or exceeded performance measures during the period of the employee's annual performance review. The Secretary of Defense would submit a report to the Committees on Armed Services of the Senate and the House of Representatives, within 180 days of enactment of this Act, which describes the incorporation of performance accountability measures in the annual performance reviews of leadership positions in the military health care system.

The House amendment contained no similar provision.

The House recedes with an amendment that would require the Secretary of Defense to determine which military and civilian leaders in the military health system would be required to have measures of accountability incorporated into their performance reviews and would delete the prohibition on performance bonuses for civilian employees who do not meet or exceed performance measures.

Establishment of advisory committees for military treatment facilities (sec. 731)

The Senate bill contained a provision (sec. 731) that would require the Secretary of Defense to establish an advisory committee for each military medical treatment facility (MTF). Each advisory committee would include six beneficiaries eligible for health care services in the military health system: 1) two Active-Duty servicemembers; 2) two Active-Duty family members; and 3) two military retirees.

The House amendment contained no similar provision.

The House recedes with an amendment that would not prescribe the composition of members of an advisory committee established by the Secretary. The amendment would also clarify that each advisory committee shall provide advice to the commanding officer or director of a MTF on the

administration and activities of the facility as it relates to the experience of care for beneficiaries.

Subtitle D—Reports and Other Matters

Extension of authority for joint Department of Defense-Department of Veterans Affairs Medical Facility Demonstration Fund and report on implementation of information technology capabilities (sec. 741)

The Senate bill contained a provision (sec. 755) that would extend the authority for the joint Department of Defense-Department of Veterans Affairs demonstration fund from September 30, 2017, to September 30, 2018.

The House amendment contained no similar provision.

The House recedes with an amendment that would require the Secretary of Defense to submit a report, not later than March 30, 2017, to the Committees on Armed Services of the Senate and the House of Representatives on plans to implement all information technology capabilities required by the executive agreement entered into under section 1701(a) of the National Defense Authorization Act for fiscal year 2010 (Public Law 111–84) that remain unimplemented as of the date of the report.

Pilot program on expansion of use of physician assistants to provide mental health care to members of the Armed Forces (sec. 742)

The Senate bill contained a provision (sec. 751) that would require the Secretary of Defense to commence a physician assistant psychiatric fellowship pilot program, within 1 year of the date of enactment of this Act, to assess the feasibility and advisability of expanding the use of physician assistants specializing in psychiatric medicine. The pilot program would consist of two rounds with each round taking a maximum of 2 years to complete. Under this provision, the Secretary would select a least five individuals to participate in the pilot program for each round. Within 180 days after the date the Secretary completes the first round of the psychiatric fellowship pilot program, the Secretary would submit an initial report to the Committees on Armed Services of the Senate and the House of Representatives on the program. Subsequently, the Secretary would submit a final report that updates the initial report within 90 days after termination of the pilot program. The authority for the pilot program would terminate upon completion of the second round of the psychiatric fellowship program.

The House amendment contained no similar provision.

The House recedes with an amendment that would authorize the Secretary to conduct a pilot program to assess the feasibility and advisability of expanding the use of physician assistants specializing in psychiatric medicine at medical facilities of the Department of Defense. If the Secretary conducts the pilot program, the Secretary would submit a report to the Committees on Armed Services of the Senate and the House of Representatives on the pilot program within 90 days of completion of the program.

Pilot program for prescription drug acquisition cost parity in the TRICARE pharmacy benefits program (sec. 743)

The House amendment contained a provision (sec. 745) that would authorize the Secretary of Defense to conduct a pilot program to evaluate whether extending additional discounts for prescription drugs filled at TRICARE retail network pharmacies would either maintain or reduce prescription drug costs for the Department of Defense. If the Secretary decides to conduct the pilot program, the Secretary would submit to the congressional defense committees: 1) an initial report, within 90 days of enactment of this Act, containing an implementation plan for the pilot program; 2) an interim report within 180 days after the pilot program begins; and 3) a final report, within 90 days of the end of the pilot program, describing the results of the program.

The Senate bill contained no similar provision.

The Senate recedes with an amendment that would authorize the Secretary, in conducting the pilot program, to allow any TRICARE beneficiaries, other than Medicare-eligible beneficiaries, to participate in the pilot program.

The amendment would also modify the requirements for the final report.

Pilot program on display of wait times at urgent care clinics and pharmacies of military medical treatment facilities (sec. 744)

The Senate bill contained a provision (sec. 733) that would require the commander or director of a military treatment facility, by January 1, 2018, to display in a conspicuous location at each urgent care clinic, emergency department, and pharmacy in a military treatment facility (MTF) an electronic sign that displays the current average wait time either to be seen by a qualified medical provider or to receive a filled prescription for a pharmaceutical agent. The provision would prescribe how the commander or director should determine the average wait times for beneficiaries at urgent care clinics, emergency departments, and pharmacies in military treatment facilities.

The House amendment contained a provision (sec. 746) that would require the Secretary of Defense to study the feasibility of displaying average wait times at urgent care clinics, pharmacies, and emergency departments of MTFs and to submit a report, which includes the estimated costs for displaying wait times, to the Committees on Armed Services of the Senate and the House of Representatives by March 1, 2017.

The Senate recedes with an amendment that would require the Secretary of Defense to conduct a pilot program, not later than 1 year after the date of enactment of this Act, for the display of wait times in urgent care clinics and pharmacies of MTFs. The provision would require the Secretary to submit a report to the Committees on Armed Services of the Senate and the House of Representatives within 90 days of completion of the pilot program that would include, among the report elements, a determination of the feasibility of expanding the posting of wait times in emergency departments in MTFs.

Requirement to review and monitor prescribing practices at military treatment facilities of pharmaceutical agents for treatment of post-traumatic stress (sec. 745)

The Senate bill contained a provision (sec. 761) that would require the Secretary of Defense, within 180 days of enactment of this Act, to: 1) conduct a comprehensive review of the prescribing practices at military treatment facilities of pharmaceutical agents for the treatment of post-traumatic stress (PTS); 2) implement a process or processes to monitor the prescribing practices at military treatment facilities of pharmaceutical agents discouraged from use under the clinical practice guideline for management for PTS published by the Department of Defense (DOD) and the Department of Veterans Affairs (VA); 3) implement a plan to address any deviations from that guideline in the prescribing practices of pharmaceutical agents for management of PTS; and 4) implement a plan to address any instances where benzodiazepines and opioids are concurrently prescribed.

The House amendment contained a similar provision (sec. 732)

The Senate recedes.

Department of Defense study on preventing the diversion of opioid medications (sec. 746)

The House amendment contained a provision (sec. 750) that would require the Secretary of Defense to conduct a study on the feasibility and effectiveness in preventing the diversion of opioid medications by requiring opioid medications to be dispensed in vials designed to prevent unauthorized access to those medications and by educating patients and family members, with special emphasis on adolescents, on the risks associated with opioid medications.

The Senate bill contained no similar provision.

The Senate recedes with a clarifying amendment.

Incorporation into survey by Department of Defense of questions on experiences of members of the Armed Forces with family planning services and counseling (sec. 747)

The Senate bill contained a provision (sec. 759) that would require the Secretary of Defense, within 90 days after the date of enactment of this Act, to begin action to integrate into certain surveys administered by the Department of Defense questions designed to obtain information on the experiences of service women with family planning and counseling.

The House amendment contained no similar provision.

The House recedes with an amendment that would require the Secretary of Defense, within 90 days of enactment of this Act, to initiate action to integrate into the the Health Related Behavior Survey of Active-Duty Military Personnel questions designed to obtain information on the experiences of servicemembers with family planning and counseling.

Assessment of transition to TRICARE program by families of members of reserve components called to Active Duty and elimination of certain charges for such families (sec. 748)

The Senate bill contained a provision (sec. 760) that would require the Secretary of Defense, within 180 days of enactment of this Act, to complete an assessment of the extent to which families of members of the reserve components of the Armed Forces serving on Active Duty, pursuant to a call to or order to Active Duty for a period of more than 30 days, experience difficulties in transitioning from health care arrangements relied upon when the member is not in such an Active-Duty status to health benefits under the TRICARE program. Within 180 days after completing the assessment, the Secretary shall submit a report detailing the results of the assessment to the Committees on Armed Services of the Senate and the House of Representatives. This provision would also amend section 1079(h)(4)(C)(ii) of title 10, United States Code, to expand the authority of the Secretary to eliminate balance billing for families of members of the reserve components of the Armed Forces serving on Active Duty.

The House amendment contained no similar provision.

The House recedes with a clarifying amendment.

Oversight of graduate medical education programs of military departments (sec. 749)

The Senate bill contained a provision (sec. 752) that would require the Secretary of Defense to implement a phased plan, within 1 year of the date of enactment of this Act, to eliminate those graduate medical education programs of the Department that do not directly support the medical force readiness requirements for health care providers within the Armed Forces. The Secretary would provide a report, within 180 days of the date of enactment of this Act, which provides the Department's plan to eliminate graduate medical education programs non-essential for medical force readiness.

The House amendment contained no similar provision.

The House recedes with an amendment that would require the Secretary of Defense, within 1 year of the date of enactment of this Act, to establish and implement a process to provide oversight of the graduate medical education programs of the military departments to ensure that those programs fully support the operational medical force readiness requirements for health care providers of the Armed Forces and the medical readiness of the Armed Forces. The amendment would require the Secretary, within 30 days of the establishment of the oversight process, to submit a report to the Committees on Armed Services of the Senate and the House of Representatives that describes the process. In addition, the amendment would require the Comptroller General of the United States to conduct a review of the oversight process and to provide a report to the committees within 180 days after the date that the Secretary submits the Department's report to the committees.

Study on health of helicopter and tiltrotor pilots (sec. 750)

The House amendment contained a provision (sec. 744) that would require the Secretary of Defense to conduct a long-term study of helicopter and tiltrotor pilots to assess the acute and chronic medical conditions of those pilots. The provision would also require the Secretary to brief the Committees on Armed Services of the Senate and the House of Representatives on the results of the study.

The Senate bill contained no similar provision.

The Senate recedes with an amendment that would require the Secretary to submit a report to the Committees on Armed Services of the Senate and the House of Representatives not later than 30 days after completion of the study.

Comptroller General reports on health care delivery and waste in military health system (sec. 751)

The Senate bill contained a provision (sec. 763) that would require the Comptroller General of the United States, within 1 year after the date of enactment of this Act, and at least annually thereafter for 4 years, to submit to the Committees on Armed Services of the Senate and the House of Representatives, a report assessing and identifying potential waste and inefficiency relating to the delivery of health care within the military health system.

The House amendment contained no similar provision.

The House recedes with a clarifying amendment.

LEGISLATIVE PROVISIONS NOT ADOPTED

Modifications of cost-sharing requirements for the TRICARE pharmacy benefits program and treatment of certain pharmaceutical agents

The Senate bill contained a provision (sec. 702) that would modify cost-sharing amounts for the TRICARE pharmacy benefits program for years 2017 through 2025. After 2025, the Department could establish cost-sharing amounts equal to the cost-sharing amounts for the previous year adjusted by an amount, if any, to reflect increases in costs of pharmaceutical agents and pharmacy dispensing fees. With this provision, beneficiaries would continue to receive pharmaceuticals at no cost in military medical treatment facilities. Under this provision, there would be no changes to cost-sharing amounts for survivors of members who died on Active Duty or for disabled retirees and their family members. The provision would authorize the Secretary of Defense, upon recommendation from the Pharmacy and Therapeutics Committee and review by the Uniform Formulary Beneficiary Advisory Panel, to exclude from the pharmacy benefits program any pharmaceutical agent that the Secretary determines provides little or no value to covered beneficiaries and the Department. Additionally, the Secretary would give preferential status to any non-generic pharmaceutical agent on the uniform formulary by treating it, for the purposes of cost-sharing, as a generic product under the TRICARE retail pharmacy and mail order programs. Finally, the provision would authorize the Secretary to adopt special reimbursement methods, amounts, and procedures in medical contracts to encourage physicians to use high-value pharmaceutical agents and to discourage use of low-value agents.

The House amendment contained no similar provision.

The Senate recedes.

Pilot program on treatment of members of the Armed Forces for post-traumatic stress disorder related to military sexual trauma

The Senate bill contained a provision (sec. 708) that would authorize the Secretary of Defense to conduct a pilot program, of not more than 3 years duration, to award competitive grants to community partners to provide intensive outpatient programs to treat members of the Armed Forces suffering from post-traumatic stress disorder resulting from military sexual trauma, including treatment for substance use disorder, depression, and other issues related to those conditions.

The House amendment contained no similar provision.

The Senate recedes.

Selection of commanders and directors of military treatment facilities and tours of duty of commanders of such facilities

The Senate bill contained a provision (sec. 723) that would require the Secretary of Defense to develop common qualifications and core competencies required for selection of commanders or directors of military medical treatment facilities. The provision would also establish a minimum length of 4 years for tours of duty, with limited exceptions, for those commanders or directors to ensure greater stability in health system executive management at each facility and throughout the military health system.

The House amendment contained no similar provision.

The Senate recedes.

Use of mefloquine for malaria

The House amendment contained a provision (sec. 733) that would: 1) limit the use of mefloquine for malaria prophylaxis to servicemembers with intolerance or contraindications to other chemoprophylaxis agents; 2) require licensed medical providers to prescribe mefloquine on an individual basis; and 3) require medical providers to counsel servicemembers on the potential side effects of the drug and to provide written patient information required by the Food and Drug Administration.

The Senate bill contained no similar provision.

The House recedes.

The conferees note that mefloquine is one of several drugs recommended by the Centers for Disease Control to prevent malaria and to treat certain forms of the disease. The conferees are concerned, however, that mefloquine may produce serious neuropsychiatric side effects such as depression, auditory and visual hallucinations, anxiety, and suicidal ideation. The conferees urge the Department of Defense to limit the prescription of mefloquine to those servicemembers who may be unable to take other first-line anti-malarial drugs. If medical providers must prescribe mefloquine to certain servicemembers, providers must ensure that those servicemembers understand the potential adverse effects of the drug.

Mental health resources for members of the military services at high risk of suicide

The House amendment contained a provision (sec. 741) that would require the Secretary of Defense to: 1) develop a methodology that identifies servicemembers and military units at high risk of suicide; and 2) provide additional preventative and mental health treatment resources for servicemembers.

The Senate bill contained no similar provision.

The House recedes.

Research of chronic traumatic encephalopathy

The House amendment contained a provision (sec. 742) that would provide that not more than $25 million of the funds available for advanced development for research, development, test, and evaluation for the Defense Health Program for fiscal year 2017 may be used to award grants to medical researchers and universities to support research into early detection of chronic traumatic encephalopathy.

The Senate bill contained no similar provision.

The House recedes.

Active oscillating negative pressure treatment

The House amendment contained a provision (sec. 743) that would require the Secretary of Defense to consider using noninvasive technologies, such as active oscillating negative pressure, to treat servicemembers who have incurred injuries from blast-related events.

The Senate bill contained no similar provision.

The House recedes.

Report on feasibility of including acupuncture and chiropractic services for retirees under TRICARE program

The House amendment contained a provision (sec. 747) that would require the Secretary of Defense to submit a report to the congressional defense committees on the feasibility of providing acupuncture and chiropractic services under the TRICARE program to beneficiaries who are retired members of the uniformed Services.

The Senate bill contained no similar provision.

The House recedes.

Clarification of submission of reports on longitudinal study on traumatic brain injury

The House amendment contained a provision (sec. 748) that would clarify that section 1080 of the National Defense Authorization Act for Fiscal Year 2016 (Public Law 114–92; 129 Stat. 1000; 10 U.S.C. 111 note) should not apply to reports submitted by the Secretary of Defense to Congress under section 721 of the John Warner National Defense Authorization Act for Fiscal Year 2007 (Public Law 109–364; 120 Stat. 2294).

The Senate bill contained no similar provision.

The House recedes.

Increased collaboration with NIH to combat triple negative breast cancer

The House amendment contained a provision (sec. 749) that would require the Department of Defense to: 1) collaborate with the National Institutes of Health to identify genetic and molecular targets and biomarkers for triple negative breast cancer; and 2) provide information in biomarker selection, drug discovery, and clinical trials design to enable early identification of this form of breast cancer and development of multiple targeted therapies for the disease.

The Senate bill contained no similar provision.

The House recedes.

Memoranda of agreement with institutions of higher education that offer degrees in allopathic or osteopathic medicine

The Senate bill contained a provision (sec. 754) that would require the Secretary of Defense to enter into memoranda of agreement with local or regional allopathic or osteopathic schools of medicine to establish military treatment facilities as affiliate teaching hospitals.

The House amendment contained no similar provision.

The Senate recedes.

The conferees note that the Department of Defense has existing authority to enter into agreements with medical schools to establish military treatment facilities as affiliate teaching hospitals, and the conferees strongly urge the Department to expand those affiliations. By sharing training facilities, staffing, and material resources, the conferees believe these new academic affiliations could help improve and sustain operational medical force readiness and serve as productive recruiting grounds for new military physicians.

Prohibition on conduct of certain medical research and development projects

The Senate bill contained a provision (sec. 756) that would prohibit the Secretary of Defense and each service secretary from funding or conducting a medical research and development project unless the secretary concerned determines that the project would protect, enhance, or restore the health and safety of members of the Armed Forces.

The House amendment contained no similar provision.

The Senate recedes.

The conferees express concern regarding the amount of congressional funding for medical research in the Department of Defense's (DOD) Congressionally Directed Medical Research Program. Since 1992, Congress has appropriated almost $10 billion for medical research—most of it outside of DOD's core medical research mission and not requested in the Department's annual budget requests.

Report on plan to improve pediatric care and related services for children of members of the Armed Forces

The Senate bill contained a provision (sec. 762) that would require the Secretary of Defense to submit to the Committees on Armed Services of the Senate and the House of Representatives a report setting forth a plan of the Department to improve pediatric care and related services for children of members of the Armed Forces.

The House amendment contained no similar provision.

The Senate recedes.

Treatment of certain provisions relating to limitations, transparency, and oversight regarding medical research conducted by the Department of Defense

The Senate bill contained a provision (sec. 764) that would require sections 756 and 898 of the Senate bill relating to limitations, transparency, and oversight regarding medical research conducted by the Department of Defense to have no force or effect.

The House amendment contained no similar provision.

The Senate recedes.

TITLE VIII—ACQUISITION POLICY, ACQUISITION MANAGEMENT, AND RELATED MATTERS

Subtitle A—Acquisition Policy and Management

Rapid acquisition authority amendments (sec. 801)

The Senate bill contained a provision (sec. 801) that would amend section 806 of the Bob Stump National Defense Authorization Act for Fiscal Year 2003 (Public Law 107–314) to better integrate and conform the provision with the rapid acquisition authorities established in section 804 of the National Defense Authorization Act for Fiscal Year 2016 (Public Law 114–92).

The House amendment contained no similar provision.

The House recedes.

Authority for temporary service of Principal Military Deputies to the Assistant Secretaries of the military departments for acquisition as Acting Assistant Secretaries (sec. 802)

The Senate bill contained a provision (sec. 802) that would amend sections 3016(b)(5)(B), 5016(b)(4)(B), and 8016(b)(4)(B) of title 10, United States Code, to allow Principal Military Deputies to serve in an acting capacity if there is a vacancy in the position of the Service Acquisition Executive.

The House amendment contained no similar provision.

The House recedes.

Modernization of services acquisition (sec. 803)

The Senate bill contained a provision (sec. 804) that would require the Secretary of Defense to revise the Department of Defense Instruction 5000.74, dated January 6, 2016.

The House amendment contained no similar provision.

The House recedes with an amendment that would require the Secretary of Defense to review and, if necessary, revise Department of Defense Instruction 5000.74, dated January 5, 2016, and other guidance pertaining to the acquisition of services not later than 180 days after the date of the enactment of this Act. The amendment also would expand, from the acquisition workforce to all Department of Defense employees engaged in the procurement of services, the workforce to be developed and trained on the acquisition of services.

Defense Modernization Account amendments (sec. 804)

The Senate bill contained a provision (sec. 899B) that would amend section 2216 of title 10, United States Code, to clarify authorizations for the Defense Modernization Account.

The House amendment contained no similar provision.

The House recedes with an amendment that would exclude the transfer of funds that support installations and facilities to the De-

fense Modernization Account. The amendment would set a $1.0 billion limit on the total balance of the account and require that an acquisition program milestone decision authority approve the use of funds in the account. The amendment would also require that subaccounts be established for each of the military departments and defense agencies that deposit and use funds in the account.

Subtitle B—Department of Defense Acquisition Agility

Modular open system approach in development of major weapon systems (sec. 805)

The House amendment contained a provision (sec. 1701) that would require all major defense acquisition programs (MDAPs) initiated after January 1, 2019, to be designed and developed with a modular open system approach (MOSA), to the maximum extent practicable.

The Senate bill contained no similar provision.

The Senate recedes with an amendment that would clarify when programs are required to start using MOSA. The amendment also would modify the definition of a major system interface to include characterization of the form, function, and content that flows across the interface. The amendment would require the acquisition strategy for a program that uses MOSA to also describe the approach to systems integration and configuration management.

Development, prototyping, and deployment of weapon system components or technology (sec. 806)

The House amendment contained a provision (sec. 1702) that would require a major defense acquisition program (MDAP) initiated after January 1, 2019, to include only technical development that the milestone decision authority determines, with a high degree of confidence, would not delay fielding target for the program. Concurrent technology maturation and system development would remain authorized, but only for technologies for which there is high confidence that concurrency would not postpone fielding. For higher risk technologies, the milestone decision authority would use the new authorities provided in this section, or other available authorities, to mature and demonstrate technologies prior to initiating or separate from a program of record. This section also would provide the military services with new funding and acquisition flexibility to experiment with, prototype, and rapidly deploy weapon system components and other technologies.

The Senate bill contained no similar provision.

The Senate recedes with an amendment that would expand the considerations for planning and conducting prototype projects to include existing commercial technologies and opportunities to reduce operation and support costs of major weapon systems. The amendment would clarify that the military services can use an existing oversight board, if one exists, to carry out the prototyping oversight requirements of this provision. The amendment would require prototyping projects to develop a plan for transition into a fielded system or operational use. The amendment also would reduce the duration of a project to 2 years and would clarify that the rapid prototyping process established by section 804 of the Fiscal Year 2016 National Defense Authorization Act (Public Law 114–92) should be pursued if projects exceed the duration and funding limits of this provision.

Cost, schedule, and performance of major defense acquisition programs (sec. 807)

The House amendment contained a provision (sec. 1703) that would require the Secretary of Defense, or his designee, to assign program cost and fielding targets when major defense acquisition programs (MDAPs) are initiated.

The Senate bill contained no similar provision.

The Senate recedes with an amendment that would clarify that cost and fielding targets should be established before funds are obligated for technology development, system development, or production of a major defense acquisition program. The amendment would modify the definition of the cost target to include the program procurement unit cost and sustainment cost. The amendment would remove the list of elements that should be considered in establishing the program goals because such elements are generally known and are included in existing acquisition policy guidance. The amendment would modify the delegation of authority for establishing program targets only to the Deputy Secretary of Defense. The amendment also would clarify that the required independent technical risk assessments conducted prior to program milestone approvals should identify any manufacturing processes that need to be matured.

Transparency in major defense acquisition programs (sec. 808)

The House amendment contained a provision (sec. 1704) that would require the milestone decision authority for a major defense acquisition program to provide a new "acquisition scorecard" report to the congressional defense committees and, when appropriate, to congressional intelligence committees at each milestone decision point of each program.

The Senate bill contained no similar provision.

The Senate recedes with an amendment that would modify the information required in the program summary reports, to include the major cost contributors identified at Milestone A that could affect the life-cycle costs of the program and any manufacturing risks identified at Milestone A or B that are associated with the program.

Amendments relating to technical data rights (sec. 809)

The House amendment contained a provision (sec. 1705) that would make several amendments to technical data rights conferred in section 2320 of title 10, United States Code. Among other things, the provision would delineate types of interfaces and specify the rights provided to the U.S. Government in such interfaces. It would require the U.S. Government and Department of Defense contractors to negotiate for data rights when items or processes are developed with a mix of Federal and private funds. The provision also would limit deferred ordering of technical data to 6 years after delivery of the last item on a contract and to technical data generated, not utilized, in the performance of the contract.

The Senate bill contained no similar provision.

The Senate recedes with an amendment that would allow the Secretary of Defense to negotiate for rights other than government purpose rights for technical data relating to major system interfaces if it would be in the best interest of the United States. The amendment would require the Department of Defense to identify major system interfaces in contract solicitations and contracts. For major system interfaces developed exclusively at private expense, the amendment would clarify that the Secretary shall negotiate with the developer appropriate compensation for the technical data. The conferees understand that section 2320 sets forth various rights in technical data, and that the price for acquiring technical data to which the U.S. Government is entitled is determined through negotiations between the Department and contractors. The conferees believe that in the case of privately funded major system interfaces for which the Department asserts government purpose rights it is necessary to explicitly require negotiation for compensation. Notwithstanding this amendment, the conferees expect the standard practice of negotiating prices for technical data to continue for all other categories of rights and circumstances set forth in section 2320.

The amendment also would specify the U.S. Government's rights to technical data pertaining to privately funded general interfaces necessary for the segregation and reintegration of an item or process. Finally, the amendment would extend the duration of the government-industry advisory panel established in section 813 of the National Defense Authorization Act for Fiscal Year 2016 (Public Law 114–92) and require the advisory panel to consider the technical data rights necessary to support the modular open system approach (MOSA) required elsewhere in this Act. The conferees are aware that the advisory panel has not yet completed its review of sections 2320 and 2321 of title 10, United States Code. The conferees recognize there are many issues in technical data rights that this conference agreement does not address, and are encouraged that the panel's comprehensive and thoughtful analysis thus far will yield promising recommendations.

Additionally, the conferees understand that successful implementation of MOSA necessitates the allocation of technical data rights in major system interfaces, a new concept under MOSA. The use of MOSA relies upon the ability of major system components to be added, removed, or replaced as needed throughout the life cycle of the major weapon system due to evolving technology, threats, sustainment, and other factors. Therefore, major system interfaces that share a boundary between major system components and major system platforms are critical, and it is imperative that the government have appropriate access to the technical data of such interfaces. The conferees understand the importance of technical precision in establishing clear delineation of major system platforms, major system interfaces, and major system components. As such, the conferees urge the Department to carefully consider and take input from the advisory panel and industry on the meanings and implications of these key terms. The conferees expect the Department to include this consideration in its review of the MOSA authorities and its briefing on the implementation of MOSA required in the House report accompanying H.R. 4909 (H. Rept. 114–537) of the National Defense Authorization Act for Fiscal Year 2017.

The conferees also note that the Department recently issued a proposed rule that would implement amendments to section 2320 of title 10, United States Code, enacted in section 815 of the National Defense Authorization Act for Fiscal Year 2012 (Public Law 112–81). Various representatives of industry have expressed concern about the effects on defense acquisition of the amend-

ments made in Public Law 112–81 and the Department's implementation of such amendments. Therefore, the conferees believe the amendments to technical data rights included in this conference agreement are necessary at this time.

Subtitle C—Amendments to General Contracting Authorities, Procedures, and Limitations

Modified restrictions on undefinitized contractual actions (sec. 811)

The Senate bill contained a provision (sec. 816) that would amend section 2326 of title 10, United States Code, to revise policies regarding undefinitized contractual actions (UCAs). Over the past decade the use of UCAs by the services and defense agencies has grown significantly while the speed at which these UCAs are definitized has lagged. To address this situation, the provision would: (1) require a written determination by senior officials to extend a UCA beyond 90 days; (2) require UCAs to be awarded on a fixed-price level-of-effort basis; and (3) extend the 180 day definitization requirement to contracts in support of Foreign Military Sales cases.

The House amendment contained a similar provision (sec. 802).

The House recedes with an amendment that would eliminate the requirement that undefinitized contractual actions be awarded on a fixed-price basis, ensure that allowable profit reflects the cost risk at the time that a contractor submits a qualifying proposal to definitize a contract, and specify that such a proposal contain the information necessary to conduct a meaningful audit of the proposal.

Amendments relating to inventory and tracking of purchases of services (sec. 812)

The Senate bill contained a provision (sec. 820) that would amend section 2330a of title 10, United States Code, to clarify the applicability of the contractor inventory requirement to staff augmentation contracts and to reduce data collection and unnecessary reporting requirements.

The House amendment contained a provision (sec. 803) that would amend section 2330a of title 10, United States Code, to revise the current requirement related to how the Department of Defense accounts for and reports contracts for services.

The Senate recedes with an amendment that would set the inventory collection threshold at contracts for services in excess of $3.0 million and would narrow the focus of the inventory collection requirement to staff augmentation contracts as informed by the specified Service Acquisition Portfolio Groups. Rather than providing the inventory itself to the Congress, the amendment would require the Secretary of Defense to provide to Congress an annual summary of the inventory activities performed during the past year pursuant to staff augmentation contracts as defined in the amendment. Additionally, the amendment removes the Department of Defense Office of the Inspector General reporting requirement and reduces the annual Comptroller General reporting requirement to a one-time review in 2018 that would cover the changes implemented by this Act.

In performing the review and planning requirements in (d), the conferees direct the Secretary of the military department or the head of the Defense Agency to focus on the 17 Product Service Codes identified by the Office of Federal Procurement Policy and the Government Accountability Office in report GAO–16–46 as high risk for including services that are closely associated with inherently governmental functions.

The conferees direct the Secretary of Defense to brief the Committees on Armed Services of the Senate and House of Representatives, no later than February 1, 2017, on the plan to implement the inventory and reporting changes required by this Act, particularly implementation of the inventory of Product Service Codes and staff augmentation contracts. The briefing shall include information on differences in the number and value of contracts captured before and after the changes made by this Act.

Use of lowest price technically acceptable source selection process (sec. 813)

The Senate bill contained a provision (sec. 825) that would require the Department of Defense to revise the Defense Federal Acquisition Regulation Supplement (DFARS) to limit the use of lowest price technically acceptable (LPTA) source selection criteria in circumstances that would potentially deny the Department the benefits of cost and technical tradeoffs in the source selection process. The Department would be required to only use LPTA criteria in specified circumstances and avoid them to the maximum extent practicable for the procurement of knowledge-based professional services such as information technology services.S0634

The House amendment contained a similar provision (sec. 847).

The House recedes with an amendment that would require justification of LPTA evaluation methodologies in each contract file, require determination that lowest price reflects full life-cycle costs, and expand restrictions on the use of LPTA evaluation methodologies to include advanced electronic testing and knowledge-based, training, or logistics services in overseas contingency operations. The amendment would also limit LPTA reporting to only contracts that exceed $10.0 million.

Procurement of personal protective equipment (sec. 814)

The Senate bill contained a provision (sec. 829D) that would prohibit the use of reverse auctions and lowest price technically acceptable (LPTA) contracting methods for the procurement of personal protective equipment where the level of quality needed or the failure of the item could result in combat casualties.

The House amendment contained a similar provision (sec. 804) that would amend section 884 of the National Defense Authorization Act for Fiscal Year 2016 (Public Law 114–92) to clarify source selection criteria to be used in the procurement of personal protective equipment or critical safety items.

The House recedes.

The conferees understand that, in some cases, both LPTA and reverse auctions are appropriate contracting methods and price discovery methods. However, the conferees do not believe that such methods are appropriate for equipment that provides personal protection to members of the Armed Services.

Amendments related to detection and avoidance of counterfeit electronic parts (sec. 815)

The House amendment contained a provision (sec. 806) that would modify section 818 of the National Defense Authorization Act for Fiscal Year 2012 (Public Law 112–81) by replacing the term "trusted suppliers" with the term "suppliers that meet anticounterfeiting requirements", as well as related conforming amendments. This provision would clear up confusion about the term, which refers to the specific category of microelectronics supplies that have been accredited by the Defense Microelectronics Activity.

The Senate bill contained no similar provision.

The Senate recedes.

Amendments to special emergency procurement authority (sec. 816)

The House amendment contained a provision (sec. 807) that would amend section 1903 of title 41, United States Code, to expand the permissible uses of special emergency procurement authorities to include support of international disaster assistance and support of a national emergency or natural disaster relief efforts in the United States as defined by the Robert T. Stafford Disaster Relief and Emergency Assistance Act.

The Senate recedes.

The conferees direct the Comptroller General, not later than 4 years after the date of enactment of this Act, to submit to the Committees on Armed Services of the Senate and House of Representatives a review of all procurement activities conducted under the authorities provided by this provision.

The conferees direct any agency making use of this expanded authority to closely consult with the Congress on its use, especially its use over extended periods of time; the establishment of mechanisms to ensure proper oversight over its use; and the monitoring of its impact on industry, especially small and disadvantaged businesses.

Compliance with domestic source requirements for footwear furnished to enlisted members of the Armed Forces upon their initial entry into the Armed Forces (sec. 817)

The Senate bill contained a provision (sec. 671) that would require the Secretary of Defense to furnish athletic footwear directly to members of the Army, Navy, Air Force, and Marine Corps instead of providing a cash allowance. Such footwear must comply with section 2533a of title 10, United States Code.

The House amendment contained a similar provision (sec. 808).

The House recedes with an amendment that would authorize the Department of Defense, for two years, to purchase additional footwear that is necessary to provide sufficient choices to minimize the incidence of athletic injuries in initial entry training. During those two years, the conferees expect the Secretary, to the maximum extent practicable, to furnish footwear from domestic sources while taking appropriate steps to minimize the incidence of athletic injuries. The conferees direct the Secretary of Defense to develop a plan and schedule to fully implement this provision, and brief that plan and schedule to the Committees on Armed Services of the Senate and the House of Representatives no later than six months following the date of enactment of this Act.

The conferees are aware that a number of scientific studies have been and are being conducted to evaluate variances in foot structures, related causes of athletic foot injuries, and appropriate footwear to reduce the incidence of such injuries. The conferees direct the Secretary of Defense to brief the results of those studies to the Committees on Armed Services of the Senate and the House of Representatives no later than 18 months following the date of enactment of this Act. The briefing shall include recommendations for reducing injuries in recruits, including modifying initial entry training methods, medically evaluating the foot types of members of the Armed Forces in initial entry training, furnishing appropriate footwear to such members in initial entry training, and domestic sourcing of such footwear.

Extension of authority for enhanced transfer of technology developed at Department of Defense laboratories (sec. 818)

The Senate bill contained a provision (sec. 899) that would extend until 2020 the authorization granted to the Secretary of Defense and military service secretaries to license Department of Defense-owned intellectual property.

The House amendment contained a similar provision (sec. 809B) to extend the authorization until 2021.

The Senate recedes.

Modified notification requirement for exercise of waiver authority to acquire vital national security capabilities (sec. 819)

The Senate bill contained a provision (sec. 805) that would amend subsection (d) of section 806 of the National Defense Authorization Act for Fiscal Year 2016 (Public Law 114–92) to provide for a notification to Congress not later than ten days after the use of the waiver authority to acquire vital national security capabilities outlined earlier in section 806.

The House amendment contained no similar provision.

The House recedes.

Defense cost accounting standards (sec. 820)

The Senate bill contained a provision (sec. 811) that would amend chapter 7 of title 10, United States Code, and establish an independent board chaired by the Chief Financial Officer of the Department of Defense to prescribe, amend, and rescind cost accounting standards as they affect operations at the Department of Defense. The provision also requires that cost accounting standards developed shall to the maximum extent practicable align with Generally Accepted Accounting Principles (GAAP), thereby minimizing the requirement for government-unique cost accounting systems. The provision would also ensure that managerial cost accounting and activity-based accounting structures derived from cost accounting standards are applied to the financial operations of the Department of Defense.

The House amendment contained no similar provision.

The House recedes with an amendment that would modify sections 1501 and 1502 of title 41, United States Code, to improve the government-wide Cost Accounting Standards Board (CASB) and require that Federal Cost Accounting Standards (CAS) be reconciled, to the extent possible, with U.S. Generally Accepted Accounting Principles. The amendment also would require the CASB to hire an executive director and meet at least quarterly to reduce inconsistencies between CAS and GAAP, as well as address problems identified by cases presented to the Armed Services Board of Contract Appeals and Civilian Board of Contract Appeals. Additionally, the amendment would allow the head of a Federal agency to waive the application of the CAS for contracts valued at less than $100.0 million. The amendment also would retain the Senate proposal to create a Defense Cost Accounting Standards Board, but would authorize the new board to advise the CASB, oversee implementation of CAS within the Department of Defense, and ensure that managerial cost accounting is appropriately implemented for commercial functions performed by employees of the Department. The conferees also encourage the Director, Defense Contract Audit Agency (DCAA) to examine the potential for electronic quality management systems to improve the ability of DCAA to conduct thorough and timely audits.

Increased micro-purchase threshold applicable to Department of Defense procurements (sec. 821)

The Senate bill contained a provision (sec. 812) that would amend chapter 137 of title 10, United States Code, to establish the micro-purchase threshold for Department of Defense activities at $5,000.

The House amendment contained no similar provision.

The House recedes.

Enhanced competition requirements (sec. 822)

The Senate bill contained a provision (sec. 813) that would amend section 2306a of title 10, United States Code, to clarify the definition of competition and the role of the prime contractor in determining whether a subcontract meets the competitive or commercial test under the section.

The House amendment contained no similar provision.

The House recedes.

The conferees recognize that the government retains the right to review determinations made by prime contractors.

Revision to effective date of senior executive benchmark compensation for allowable cost limitations (sec. 823)

The House amendment contained a provision (sec. 805) that would remove the retroactive application requirement of section 803 of the National Defense Authorization Act for Fiscal Year 2012 (Public Law 112–81), which implemented a cap on the allowable compensation of contractor employees. As a result of this revision, section 803 would apply to compensation costs incurred after January 1, 2012, under contracts entered into on or after December 31, 2011.

The Senate bill contained no similar provision.

The Senate recedes.

Treatment of independent research and development costs on certain contracts (sec. 824)

The Senate bill contained a provision (sec. 814) that would amend section 2372 of title 10, United States Code, to clarify in what circumstances independent research and development costs are considered fair, reasonable, and allowable expenses on Department of Defense contracts.

The House amendment contained no similar provision.

The House recedes with an amendment that would create a new section 2372a of title 10, United States Code, that would specify that bid and proposal expenses considered as allowable indirect costs on cost-reimbursement contracts should be reported independently of independent research and development costs under section 2372 of title 10, United States Code. The amendment would establish for the Department of Defense a goal that Department-wide bid and proposal costs should not exceed one percent of the amount of contractor sales to the Department. The conferees do not intend for the Department to achieve this goal by arbitrarily limiting the amount of bid and proposal costs contractors may have reimbursed, but to instead address the factors driving bid and proposal costs. The amendment would also require the Department to contract with an outside, independent entity to study the laws, regulations, and practices driving bid and proposal costs and provide recommendations to the Department on how to reduce these costs. If, in any year the Department fails to meet the one percent goal, the amendment would require that an advisory panel pursuant to the Federal Advisory Committees Act (5 U.S.C. app) be established to provide recommendations on changes to statute, regulation, and practice to reduce bid and proposal costs. The amendment also would require the Department to report on bid and proposal costs and independent research and development costs as part of the report required under 2313a of title 10, United States Code.

Exception to requirement to include cost or price to the Government as a factor in the evaluation of proposals for certain multiple-award task or delivery order contracts (sec. 825)

The Senate bill contained a provision (sec. 815) that would amend section 2305(a)(3) of title 10, United States Code, to provide an exception to the existing statutory requirement to include cost or price to the Federal Government as an evaluation factor that must be considered in the evaluation of proposals for all contracts. The provision would only apply to multiple award task or delivery order contracts to buy services and the Department would then appropriately focus on price when individual task orders are issued and competed.

The House amendment contained no similar provision.

The House recedes with an amendment that would allow task or delivery orders to be awarded on a sole-source basis when a standalone contract could be awarded on a sole-source basis. The amendment also would preclude the award of multiple award contracts without cost or pricing data in cases where task orders are expected to be awarded as sole source contracts to small businesses under section 8(a) of the Small Business Act (Public Law 85–536) because price competition at the time of task or delivery order award would not be expected.

Extension of program for comprehensive small business contracting plans (sec. 826)

The Senate bill contained a provision (sec. 818) that would amend chapter 137 of title 10, United States Code, to add a new section that would codify the authority to conduct small business subcontracting plans. The Government Accountability Office (GAO) recently reported to the committee that the Test Program for Negotiation of Comprehensive Small Business Subcontracting Plans has resulted in the avoidance of millions of dollars in administrative costs and recommended that the program be made permanent. This provision would implement GAO's recommendation.

The House amendment contained no similar provision.

The House recedes with an amendment that would extend the current pilot program through the end of fiscal year 2027.

Treatment of side-by-side testing of certain equipment, munitions, and technologies manufactured and developed under cooperative research and development agreements as use of competitive procedures (sec. 827)

The Senate bill contained a provision (sec. 823) that would amend section 2350a(g) of title 10, Untied States Code, to add a new paragraph to clarify that the general solicitation and testing competitive procedures used under the program are competitive procedures under chapter 137 of title 10, United States Code.

The House amendment contained no similar provision.

The House recedes with an amendment that would make discretionary the use of side-by-side testing to fulfill competitive procedures for follow-on procurements and that would set a time limit within which such follow-on procurements could be conducted. The conferees expect that, prior to procuring any items under this provision,

market research will be conducted to determine that comparable items are not available.

Defense Acquisition Challenge Program amendments (sec. 828)

The Senate bill contained a provision (sec. 824) that would amend section 2359b(a)(2) of title 10, United States Code, to expand the scope of the defense acquisition challenge program to include alternatives to existing acquisition programs and to clarify that the general solicitation competitive procedures used under the program are competitive procedures under chapter 137 of title 10, United States Code.

The House amendment contained no similar provision.

The House recedes.

Preference for fixed-price contracts (sec. 829)

The Senate bill contained a provision (sec. 827) that would revise the Defense Federal Acquisition Regulation Supplement to establish a preference for fixed-price contracts, including fixed-price incentive fee contracts, in the determination of contract type and establish an approval mechanism for the use of cost-type contracts over $5.0 million in value.

The House amendment contained no similar provision.

The House recedes with an amendment that would expand the number of Department of Defense officials who can approve a cost-type contract and that would increase the contractual dollar threshold that require such approvals.

Requirement to use firm fixed-price contracts for foreign military sales (sec. 830)

The Senate bill contained a provision (sec. 828) that would require the Secretary of Defense to prescribe regulations to require the use of firm fixed-price contracts for foreign military sales not later than 180 days after the enactment of this Act. Additionally, this provision would grant the Secretary waiver authority if the Secretary determines that a different type of contract is in the best interest of the United States taxpayers.

The House amendment contained no similar provision.

The House recedes with an amendment that would clarify that foreign countries that are counterparties to foreign military sales may select a contracting vehicle that is not firm fixed-price. The conferees direct the Secretary of Defense to develop a process to determine the contracting preferences of foreign counterparties and to brief the Committees on Armed Services of the Senate and House of Representatives on the elements of the process no later than 6 months after enactment of this Act. The conferees further expect that the Secretary shall waive the requirement for firm fixed-price contracts only in exceptional cases. The conferees expect that the Department of Defense will not interfere in the process of the host nation selecting a contract type. If a contract type other than firm fixed-price is selected at the request of a country, the Secretary of Defense shall be prepared to notify Congress that the Department of Defense did not encourage the country in the decision to pursue that contract type. The amendment also would establish a pilot program to accelerate contracting of foreign military sales by allowing the Department of Defense to base price reasonableness determinations on actual cost and pricing data for purchases of the same product for the Department.

Preference for performance-based contractual payments (sec. 831)

The Senate bill contained a provision (sec. 829) that would amend section 2307(b) of title

10, United States Code, to establish a preference for performance-based payments to contractors and would re-establish the policy objective laid out in Federal Acquisition Regulation 32.1001, which established performance-based payments as the preferred Government financing mechanism.

The House amendment contained no similar provision.

The House recedes with an amendment that would clarify that nothing in the provision authorizes the Defense Contract Audit Agency to perform audits of a contractor's compliance with Generally Accepted Accounting Principles.

Contractor incentives to achieve savings and improve mission performance (sec. 832)

The Senate bill contained a provision (sec. 829A) that would amend section 2332 of title 10, United States Code, to require the Defense Acquisition University to develop and implement a training program for Department of Defense acquisition personnel on share-in-savings contracts not later than 180 days after the enactment of this Act.

The House amendment contained no similar provision.

The House recedes with an amendment that would require the Defense Acquisition University to provide training on the use of contracting authorities that incentivize contractors to deliver additional savings to the government.

Sunset and repeal of certain contracting provisions (sec. 833)

The Senate bill contained a provision (sec. 829F) that would: (1) amend title 10, United States Code, to sunset sections 2212, 2220, 2228, 2304e, 2421 by September 30, 2018;(2) amend title 10, United States Code, to sunset section 1706 by September 30, 2019; and (3) repeal sections 2245a, 2225, 2302c, 2378, 2387 of title 10, United States Code.

The House amendment contained no similar provision.

The House recedes with an amendment that would retain the reporting requirement in section 2212 of title 10, United States Code, which provides budget information on service contracting, as well as section 1706 of title 10, United States Code, which provides the Department of Defense with a list of acquisition positions considered inherently governmental.

Flexibility in contracting award program (sec. 834)

The Senate bill contained a provision (sec. 829G) that would establish an award to recognize defense acquisition programs and acquisition professionals that make the best use of flexibilities and those authorities granted in the Federal Acquisition Regulation and Department of Defense Instruction 5000.02 (Operation of the Defense Acquisition System) meant to increase the efficiency of programs.

The House amendment contained no similar provision.

The House recedes with an amendment that would reduce the administrative burdens associated with the awards program.

Protection of task order competition (sec. 835)

The Senate bill contained a provision (sec. 819) that would amend section 2304c(e) of title 10, United States Code, that would prohibit task and delivery order protests if the Secretary of Defense has appointed an ombudsman in accordance with section 2304c(f) of title 10, United States Code, to review complaints related to task and delivery order contracts.

The House amendment contained a similar provision (sec. 1862) that would amend section 4106(f) of title 41, United States Code, to maintain a consistent approach to task-order protests between civilian and defense agencies.

The House recedes with an amendment that would permanently authorize protests of task and delivery orders with values exceeding $10.0 million at civilian agencies. For protests of task and delivery orders of the Department of Defense, the amendment modifies section 2304c(e)(1)(B) of title 10, United States Code, to increase the minimum value of a task or delivery order that may be protested from $10.0 million to $25.0 million.

Contract closeout authority (sec. 836)

The Senate bill contained a provision (sec. 829J) that would grant the Secretary of Defense the authority to close out contracts entered into prior to fiscal year 2000 without completing further reconciliation audits other than those described in this section.

The House amendment contained no similar provision.

The House recedes with an amendment that would make a series of technical corrections to conform the language of this provision to similar provisions in this bill.

Closeout of old Department of the Navy contracts (sec. 837)

The Senate bill contained a provision (sec. 829K) that would grant the Secretary of the Navy authority to close out contracts entered into between fiscal years 1974 and 1998 to design, construct, repair, or support the construction or repair of Navy submarines without completing further reconciliation audits other than those described in this section.

The House amendment contained a similar provision (sec. 837).

The House recedes with an amendment that would make a series of technical corrections to conform the language of this provision to similar provisions in this bill.

Subtitle D—Provisions Relating to Major Defense Acquisition Programs

Change in date of submission to Congress of Selected Acquisition Reports (sec. 841)

The House amendment contained a provision (sec. 811) that would amend section 2342(f) of title 10, United States Code, by changing, from 45 to 10, the number of days after the President's budget request transmittal that comprehensive annual Selected Acquisition Reports are due to Congress.

The Senate bill contained no similar provision.

The Senate recedes with an amendment that would modify the date when Selected Acquisition Reports are due to Congress.

Amendments relating to independent cost estimation and cost analysis (sec. 842)

The Senate bill contained a provision (sec. 803) that would amend section 2334 of title 10, United States Code, and would repeal section 2434 of title 10, United States Code, in order to remove the ambiguity concerning the roles and responsibilities for the conduct of independent cost estimates (ICEs) by designating the Director of Cost Assessment and Program Evaluation (CAPE) to ensure standards are met. The Senate bill also contained a provision (sec. 836) that would amend subsection (d) of section 2334 of title 10, United States Code, to remove the requirement for disclosure of confidence levels for baseline estimates of major defense acquisition programs.

The House amendment contained a similar provision (sec. 812) that would amend sections 2334 and 2434 of title 10, United States Code, to make clear that CAPE conducts or approves ICEs for all major defense acquisition programs and major automated information systems.

The Senate recedes with an amendment that would require an ICE for the technology maturation and risk reduction phase of a major defense acquisition program or major subprogram that identifies the key contributors to the life-cycle costs of the program or subprogram. The conferees expect that the procedures to be developed for collecting cost data from acquisition program contractors are cost effective and make use of existing sources of data, to the best extent practicable.

Revisions to Milestone B determinations (sec. 843)

The Senate bill contained a provision (sec. 835) that would amend section 2366b(a)(3) of title 10, United States Code to eliminate the need for waivers that are regularly submitted to the committee for programs that are executed at the beginning of the fiscal year but before the Future Years Defense Program (FYDP) has been submitted, and should receive Milestone B certification as long as there is funding in the current FYDP. This provision would reduce the number of required waivers and therefore reduce unnecessary staff burden.

The House amendment contained a similar provision (sec. 813).

The Senate recedes.

Review and report on sustainment planning in the acquisition process (sec. 844)

The House amendment contained a provision (sec. 814) that would require the Secretary of Defense to enter into a contract with an independent entity with appropriate expertise to conduct an assessment of the extent to which sustainment matters are considered in decisions related to requirements, acquisition, cost estimating, and programming and budgeting for major defense acquisition programs.

The Senate bill contained no similar provision.

The Senate recedes with an amendment that would extend and include additional elements in the review, such as an evaluation of how well life-cycle sustainment strategies required under section 2337 of title 10, United States Code, are incorporated into the acquisition strategy required by section 2431a of title 10, United States Code, and other acquisition planning.

Revision to distribution of annual report on operational test and evaluation (sec. 845)

The House amendment contained a provision (sec. 815) that would amend section 139 of title 10, United States Code, by including the Secretaries of the military departments in the list of people who receive the annual report of the Director of Operational Test and Evaluation (DOTE). The section would also extend the annual report through January 31, 2021.

The Senate bill contained no similar provision.

The Senate recedes.

The conferees recognize the importance in having an independent report each year on operational test and evaluation activities in the Department of Defense, but encourage the Director of Operational Test and Evaluation to seek and consider input from other Department test organizations in developing such reports. Further, the conferees believe that more rigorous developmental testing, realistic requirements, and disciplined systems engineering will likely improve operational test outcomes. The conferees expect program offices to take the necessary steps to improve operational test outcomes and adopt lessons learned and best practices that are identified in the DOTE annual report. The conferees note that these reports are public documents and available electronically to all interested parties.

Repeal of major automated information systems provisions (sec. 846)

The Senate bill contained a provision (sec. 831) that would repeal chapter 144A of title 10, United States Code.

The House amendment contained no similar provision.

The House recedes with an amendment that would sunset the requirements chapter 144A of title 10, United States Code, on September 30, 2017.

Revisions to definition of major defense acquisition program (sec. 847)

The Senate bill contained a provision (sec. 832) that would amend section 2430 of title 10, United States Code, and revise the definition of a major defense acquisition program to exclude fixed-price prototypes not planned as part of an existing major defense acquisition program and those programs or projects developed under the rapid fielding or rapid prototyping acquisition pathway authorized under section 804 of the National Defense Authorization Act for Fiscal Year 2016 (Public Law 114–92).

The House amendment contained no similar provision.

The House recedes with an amendment that would specify that major defense acquisition program costs exclude acquisition programs or projects that are carried out using the rapid fielding or rapid prototyping acquisition pathway under section 804 of the National Defense Authorization Act for Fiscal Year 2016 (Public Law 114–92).

Acquisition strategy (sec. 848)

The Senate bill contained a provision (sec. 833) that would amend section 2431a of title 10, United States Code, to make technical changes and require that the acquisition strategy for each major defense acquisition program must also consider a comprehensive sustainment strategy that includes all aspects of the total life-cycle management of the weapon system, including product support, logistics, product support engineering, supply chain integration, maintenance, acquisition logistics, and all aspects of software sustainment.

The House amendment contained no similar provision.

The House recedes with an amendment that would remove the requirement to include a sustainment strategy within the acquisition strategy required under section 2431a of title 10, United States Code. The conferees note that section 2431a of title 10, United States Code, requires logistics, maintenance, and sustainment issues to be considered in acquisition strategies, and that a life-cycle sustainment strategy is mandated under section 2337 of title 10, United States Code. Another provision in this Act requires an evaluation of the existing life-cycle sustainment strategy and an assessment of how well its elements are incorporated into the acquisition strategy in section 2431a of title 10, United States Code.

Improved life-cycle cost control (sec. 849)

The Senate bill contained a provision (sec. 834) that would make several amendments to improve life-cycle cost controls. First, this provision would amend section 804(c)(3) of the National Defense Authorization Act for Fiscal Year 2016 (Public Law 114–92), to require rapid fielding guidance from the Under

Secretary of Defense for Acquisition, Technology, and Logistics to include direction on a process for identifying and exploiting opportunities to use the rapid fielding pathway to reduce total ownership costs. Secondly, this provision would amend section 805(2) of the National Defense Authorization Act for Fiscal Year 2016 (NDAA) to include life-cycle cost management as a procedure that the Secretary of Defense should establish for alternative acquisition pathways to meet national security needs. Thirdly, this provision would amend section 833(e) of the NDAA for Fiscal Year 2016 to require the Secretary to also issue guidance on policies to maximize the use of fixed-price contracts and the ability to implement tradeoffs in total cost of ownership, schedule, and performance. Fourthly, this provision would add a new section to chapter 144 of title 10, United States Code, which would require sustainment reviews of acquisition programs 5 years after initial operational capability—unless the program has failed to maintain its availability or reliability threshold or has breached its affordability cap before that time. Additionally, this provision would require the Secretary of Defense to establish a commercial operational and support savings initiative to insert existing commercial items or technology into military legacy programs through rapid development and fielding of prototypes in order to improve readiness and reduce operations and support costs.

The House amendment contained no similar provision.

The House recedes with an amendment that would require the military departments to conduct a sustainment review five years after declaration of initial operational capability of a major defense acquisition program and throughout the system's life cycle, using availability and reliability thresholds and cost estimates as the triggers that prompt such a review. The amendment also would clarify that sustainment reviews would be conducted in coordination with the requirements of section 2337 of title 10, United States Code, and section 832 of the National Defense Authorization Act for Fiscal Year 2012 (Public Law 112–81). The amendment also would authorize a commercial operational and support savings initiative.

Authority to designate increments or blocks of items delivered under major defense acquisition programs as major subprograms for purposes of acquisition reporting (sec. 850)

The Senate bill contained a provision (sec. 837) that would amend section 2430a(1)(B) of title 10, United States Code, to expand the authority to designate increments or blocks of items delivered under major defense acquisition programs as major subprograms.

The House amendment contained no similar provision.

The House recedes.

Reporting of small business participation on Department of Defense programs (sec. 851)

The Senate bill contained a provision (sec. 838) that would amend chapter 137 of title 10, United States Code, to include a new section to include first and second tier subcontracts awarded by the Department of Defense under major defense acquisition programs in the Department's overall count of small business goals.

The House amendment contained no similar provision.

The House recedes with an amendment that would require the Department of Defense to annually report on its attainment of the small business prime contracting goals and subcontracting goals as required by section 15(h) of the Small Business Act (15 United States Code 644(h)) and to report separately on its small business use after excluding certain types of contracts that may not be suitable for award to small businesses.

Waiver of congressional notification for acquisition of tactical missiles and munitions greater than quantity specified in law (sec. 852)

The Senate bill contained a provision (sec. 840) that would amend section 2308(c) of title 10, United States Code, to waive the requirement for the head of an agency to notify congressional defense committees of the decision to acquire a higher quantity of an end item for tactical missiles and munitions annual procurements.

The House amendment contained a similar provision (sec. 836) that would waive the requirement for the Secretary of Defense to notify the congressional defense committees of a decision, not later than 30 days after the date of the decision, to acquire a higher quantity of an end item (for tactical missiles and munitions annual procurements only) than is specified in law.

The Senate recedes.

Multiple program multiyear contract pilot demonstration program (sec. 853)

The Senate bill contained a provision (sec. 841) that would grant the Secretary of Defense the authority to conduct a multiyear contract for multiple defense programs that are produced at common facilities at a high rate, and which maximize commonality, efficiencies, and quality, in order to provide maximum benefit and significant savings to the Department of Defense.

The House amendment contained no similar provision.

The House recedes.

Key performance parameter reduction pilot program (sec. 854)

The Senate bill contained a provision (sec. 842) that would require the Secretary of Defense to enact a pilot program aimed at decreasing the number of Key Performance Parameters (KPPs) on acquisition programs. The Secretary would be required to select one acquisition program from each of the services to determine if limiting the number of KPPs to three, at the most, leads to operational or programmatic improvements of outcomes.

The House amendment contained no similar provision.

The House recedes with an amendment that would clarify the types of key performance parameters that may be reduced in the pilot program.

Mission integration management (sec. 855)

The Senate bill contained a provision (sec. 843) that would further enhance the Department of Defense's (DOD) efforts to adopt an open systems approach to defense acquisition. The provision would require the Secretary of Defense to implement modular open systems architecture in acquisition programs in specified mission areas when implementing section 801 of the Carl Levin and Howard P. "Buck" McKeon National Defense Authorization Act for Fiscal Year 2015 (Public Law 113–291). The provision would require each multi-service and multi-program mission outlined in the provision to have a mission integration manager to act as the principal substantive advisor to the Deputy Secretary of Defense and the Vice Chairman of the Joint Chiefs of Staff for all aspects of capability integration for the mission area.

The House amendment contained no similar provision.

The House recedes with an amendment that would incorporate into another section of this Act the requirement of the Senate provision (sec. 843) for the Department to ensure that external facing interfaces are identified and clearly and publicly characterized in terms of form, function, and the content that flows across to enable the creation of interoperable "systems of systems." The conferees urge the Department to ensure that the standards bodies and processes, which are established to support modular open systems approaches, promote interfaces that are dynamically managed, flexible, and extensible to enable technological innovation and performance growth.

The amendment also would modify the Senate provision to provide flexibility to the Department of Defense in implementing mission integration activities, and to provide an alternative funding source for mission integration activities. The conferees urge the Department of Defense to propose its own funding mechanism in future budget requests.

Subtitle E—Provisions Relating to Acquisition Workforce

Project management (sec. 861)

The Senate bill contained a provision (sec. 851) that would outline the responsibilities of the Department of Defense under chapter 87 of title 10, United States Code, for improving program and project management. This provision would require that not later than 1 year after the enactment of this Act that the Secretary of Defense develop Department-wide standards, policies, and guidelines for program and project management.

The Senate bill also contained a provision (sec. 1097) that would amend section 503 of title 31, United States Code, and Chapter 11 of title 31, United States Code, to improve Federal program and project management in the Department of Defense.

The House amendment contained a similar provision (sec. 1098L).

The Senate recedes with an amendment that would clarify that all members of the Program Management Policy Council must be officers or employees of the Federal government or the armed services. This obviates the need to address the application of the Federal Advisory Committee (5 U.S.C. App.).

Authority to waive tenure requirement for program managers for program definition and program execution periods (sec. 862)

The Senate bill contained a provision (sec. 852) that would amend sections 826(e) and 827(e) of the National Defense Authorization Act for Fiscal Year 2016 (Public Law 114–92) to harmonize the waiver authorities granted in these sections to the Service Acquisition Executive or the Under Secretary of Defense for Acquisition, Technology, and Logistics.

The House amendment contained no similar provision.

The House recedes.

Purposes for which the Department of Defense Acquisition Workforce Development Fund may be used; advisory panel amendments (sec. 863)

The Senate bill contained a provision (sec. 854) that would amend section 1705 of title 10, United States Code, to expand the use of the Department of Defense Acquisition Workforce Development Fund. The provision would clarify that the fund could be used for the development of acquisition tools and methodologies and the undertaking of research and development of activities that could lead to acquisition policies and practices that will improve the efficiency and effectiveness of defense acquisition efforts.

The House amendment contained no similar provision.

The House recedes with an amendment that would clarify that the advisory panel on streamlining and codifying acquisition regulations that was established in section 809 of the National Defense Authorization Act for Fiscal Year 2016 (Public Law 114–92) is an independent advisory panel to be supported by the Defense Acquisition University and the National Defense University. The amendment would further clarify that, as an independent advisory panel, the panel has the hiring authorities provided in section 3161 of title 5, United States Code. The amendment also would limit the amount of funds that may be used in fiscal year 2017 for acquisition tools and methodologies and the undertaking of research and development to $35.0 million.

Department of Defense Acquisition Workforce Development Fund determination adjustment (sec. 864)

The House amendment contained a provision (sec. 839) that would amend section 1705 of title 10, United States Code, to allow the Secretary of Defense to reduce the threshold amount that must be credited to the Defense Acquisition Workforce Development Fund during fiscal year 2017 from $400.0 million to $0. This section addresses an overfunding of the fund that has resulted from carryovers from prior years.

The Senate bill contained no similar provision.

The Senate recedes with an amendment that would require the Department of Defense to transfer $225.0 million from the Defense Acquisition Workforce Development Fund (DAWDF) in fiscal year 2017 to the Department's Rapid Prototyping Fund. The conferees also direct the Secretary of Defense to brief the Committees on Armed Services of the Senate and the House of Representatives, not later than March 15, 2017, on the extent to which DAWDF funding is sufficient to meet acquisition workforce development requirements and on steps the Department has taken to improve the management and implementation of the DAWDF to avoid carryover funding. The conferees encourage the Department to make use of the expanded authorities for the use of the DAWDF to address workforce training and development of acquisition tools and practices to improve acquisition practice and outcomes.

It is the opinion of the conferees per section 1705 of title 10, United States Code, that the amounts transferred into the DAWDF from unobligated balances, as described in subsection 3, does not have a maximum limit each year. The $500,000,000 limitation only applies to subsection 2 relating to credits for contract services. The conferees direct the Secretary of Defense to establish waivers to procedures regarding obligation and expenditure rates, applicability of standard financial management regulations, and other financial management procedures, as necessary, to ensure the most efficient and effective execution of projects supported by the Rapid Prototyping Fund. Specifically, the conferees direct the Secretary to establish procedures that provide relief from strict obligation and expenditure benchmarks and flexibility in using amounts in the Fund consistent with a broad range of efforts under research, development, test and evaluation budget activities. The conferees believe that strict adherence to standard Department financial management procedures may negatively impact program execution and not enable the program to achieve its

goals. The conferees direct the Secretary to notify the congressional defense committees within 30 days after any such procedures are waived.

Limitations on funds used for staff augmentation contracts at management headquarters of the Department of Defense and the military departments (sec. 865)

The Senate bill contained a provision (sec. 905) that would limit the amount of funds available for staff augmentation contracts at the Office of the Secretary of Defense and the headquarters of the military departments for fiscal years 2017 and 2018 to not more than the amount expended for those contracts in fiscal year 2016. The provision would further require a 25 percent reduction to the fiscal year 2016 funding for those contracts after fiscal year 2018.

The House amendment contained a provision (sec. 809A) that would extend the limitation on the aggregate annual amount available to the Department of Defense for contract services through fiscal year 2017.

The House recedes with an amendment that would limit the amount of funds available for staff augmentation contracts, as defined in the amendment, at the Office of the Secretary of Defense and the headquarters of the military departments for fiscal years 2017 and 2018 to not more than the amount expended for those contracts in fiscal year 2016 and would further require a 25 percent reduction to the fiscal year 2016 funding for those contracts in fiscal years 2018 through fiscal year 2022.

The conferees direct the Secretary of Defense to brief the Committees on Armed Services of the Senate and the House of Representatives, no later than February 1, 2017, on the plan to implement the requirements of this provision.

Senior Military Acquisition Advisors in the Defense Acquisition Corps (sec. 866)

The Senate bill contained a provision (sec. 592) that would add a new section 1725 to title 10, United States Code, to authorize the Secretary of Defense to establish in the Defense Acquisition Corps positions to be known as "Senior Military Acquisition Advisors". Senior Military Acquisition Advisors would be appointed by the President, by and with the advice and consent of the Senate. Eligible officers include officers in the grade of colonel or captain in the Navy, with extensive defense acquisition experience, and who are eligible for retirement. Senior Military Acquisition Advisors would be authorized to remain in service in support of their Service Acquisition Executive and be assigned as an adjunct professor at the Defense Acquisition University.

Senior Military Acquisition Advisors would be competitively selected and would provide senior level acquisition expertise to the Service Acquisition Executive of their military department for the remainder of their career. An officer who is continued on active duty under this program is not eligible for consideration for selection for promotion. A Senior Military Acquisition Advisor will serve no longer than a 5-year term. When a Senior Military Acquisition Advisor retires with a minimum of 3 years of service, the officer may, at the discretion of the President, be retired as a brigadier general or rear admiral (lower half), but without increase in retired pay or other compensation by reason of retirement of an officer in the grade of brigadier general or rear admiral (lower half).

The House amendment contained no similar provision.

The House recedes.

Authority of the Secretary of Defense under the acquisition demonstration project (sec. 867)

The Senate bill contained a provision (sec. 1104) that would repeal section 1762 of title 10, United States Code, and create a new section 1763 of title 10, United States Code, to provide a permanent authority that would allow the Secretary of Defense to establish and adjust a special system of personnel programs for employees in the Department of Defense civilian acquisition workforce and supporting personnel assigned to work directly with that workforce.

The House amendment contained no similar provision.

The House recedes with an amendment that moves the administration of the Department of Defense acquisition workforce demonstration project from the Office of Personnel Management to the Department of Defense.

Subtitle F—Provisions Related to Commercial Items

Market research for determination of price reasonableness in acquisition of commercial items (sec. 871)

The House amendment contained a provision (sec. 822) that would amend section 2377 of title 10, United States Code, relating to the preference for acquisition of commercial items by adding a new subsection that would require procurement officials of the Department of Defense to conduct or obtain market research when determining price reasonableness for commercial items.

The Senate bill contained no similar provision.

The Senate recedes.

Value analysis for the determination of price reasonableness (sec. 872)

The House amendment contained a provision (sec. 823) that would amend section 2379(d) of title 10, United States Code, by adding a new paragraph that would allow contractors to submit information or analysis pertaining to the value of a commercial item when responding to solicitations. This section would also allow contracting officers to consider value analysis, in addition to historic pricing data, when determining price reasonableness for commercial items.

The Senate bill contained no similar provision.

The Senate recedes.

Clarification of requirements relating to commercial item determinations (sec. 873)

The House amendment contained a provision (sec. 824) that would amend section 2380 of title 10, United States Code, to expand Department of Defense centralized records relating to commercial item determinations to include market research and price reasonableness analysis. This section would also eliminate the requirement that such records be publicly accessible.

The Senate bill contained no similar provision.

The Senate recedes.

Inapplicability of certain laws and regulations to the acquisition of commercial items and commercially available off-the-shelf items (sec. 874)

The Senate bill contained a provision (sec. 861) that would amend section 2375 of title 10, United States Code, to require the establishment of a list in the Defense Federal Acquisition Regulation Supplement of inapplicable defense-unique statutes applicable to contracts for commercial items and commercially available off-the-shelf items.

The House amendment contained no similar provision.

The House recedes with an amendment that would exclude sections 2533a and 2533b of title 10, United States Code, from the applicability of this section.

Use of commercial or non-Government standards in lieu of military specifications and standards (sec. 875)

The Senate bill contained a provision (sec. 863) that would require the Secretary of Defense to ensure that the Department of Defense uses performance and commercial specifications and standards in lieu of military specifications and standards, including for procuring new systems, major modifications, upgrades to current systems, non-developmental and commercial items, and programs in all acquisition categories, unless no practical alternative exists to meet user needs.

The House amendment contained no similar provision.

The House recedes with an amendment that would clarify that commercial or non-governmental specifications and standards should be used in lieu of military specifications and standards. The amendment also would require the Department of Defense to maintain an inventory of commercial and non-governmental standards licenses.

Preference for commercial services (sec. 876)

The Senate bill contained a provision (sec. 864) that would require the Secretary of Defense to issue guidance pursuant to section 855 of the National Defense Authorization Act for Fiscal Year 2016 (Public Law 114–92). This provision would ensure that no head of an agency would enter into a contract in excess of the simplified acquisition threshold for specified services that are not commercial services unless the head of the agency determines in writing that no commercial services are suitable to meet the agency's needs as provided in section 2377(c)(2) of title 10, United States Code.

The House amendment contained no similar provision.

The House recedes with an amendment that would require written determination that market research has been conducted prior to awarding a contract for facilities-related services, knowledge-based services (except engineering services), construction services, medical services, or transportation services that are not commercial services. For contracts over $10 million, the service acquisition executive, the head of a defense agency, the combatant commander, or the Under Secretary of Defense for Acquisition, Technology, and Logistics shall provide the written determination. For contracts valued between the simplified acquisition threshold and $10 million, the contracting officer shall provide the written determination.

The conferees direct the contracting officer to retain a copy of each written determination required by this provision in the relevant contract file.

Treatment of commingled items purchased by contractors as commercial items (sec. 877)

The Senate bill contained a provision (sec. 865) that would add a new section to chapter 140 of title 10, United States Code, to treat the purchase of items valued at less than $10,000 prior to the release of a government request for proposal as a commercial item.

The House amendment contained no similar provision.

The House recedes with an amendment that would clarify that items procured by any contractor for use in the performance of multiple contracts with the Department of Defense and other parties and are not identifiable to any particular contract should be treated as commercial items.

Treatment of services provided by nontraditional contractors as commercial items (sec. 878)

The Senate bill contained a provision (sec. 866) that would amend section 2380A of title 10, United States Code, to treat business units of nontraditional contractors that offer services as a commercial item, if the business unit uses the same personnel and similar pricing as offered to commercial customers.

The House amendment contained no similar provision.

The House recedes.

Defense pilot program for authority to acquire innovative commercial items, technologies, and services using general solicitation competitive procedures (sec. 879)

The Senate bill contained a provision (sec. 868) that would grant the Secretary of Defense the authority to carry out a pilot program to acquire innovative commercial items on a fixed-price basis using general solicitation competitive procedures and a peer review of such proposals.

The House amendment contained no similar provision.

The House recedes with an amendment that would require the Secretary of Defense to issue public guidance for the implementation of the pilot provision, require congressional notification for the award of any contract exceeding $100.0 million using the authority, and modifies the definition of "innovative".

Pilot programs for authority to acquire innovative commercial items using general solicitation competitive procedures (sec. 880)

The House amendment contained a provision (sec. 825) that would allow the Secretary of Defense to carry out a pilot program under which innovative commercial items may be acquired through a competitive selection of proposals, resulting from a general solicitation and the peer review of such proposals.

The Senate bill contained no similar provision.

The Senate recedes with an amendment that would change the authority to apply to the Department of Homeland Security and the General Services Administration, add a total annual limitation to the authority, reduce the reporting required to the congressional committees, modifies the definition of "innovative", and extends the termination date of the authority to September 30, 2022.

Subtitle G—Industrial Base Matters

Greater integration of the national technology industrial base (sec. 881)

The Senate bill contained a provision (sec. 871) that would require the Secretary of Defense to develop a plan to reduce the barriers to the seamless integration between the persons and organizations that comprise the National Technology Industrial Base and expand the definition in section 2500(1) of title 10, United States Code to include the United Kingdom and Australia.

The House amendment contained no similar provision.

The House recedes with an amendment that would make technical changes.

Integration of civil and military roles in attaining national technology and industrial base objectives (sec. 882)

The Senate bill contained a provision (sec. 872) that would amend section 2501(b) of title 10, United States Code, to ensure that the Secretary of Defense when meeting the national security strategy for the national technology and industrial base shall engage

in acquisition reform efforts that: (1) rely, to the maximum extent practicable, upon the commercial national technology and industrial base that is required to meet the national security needs of the United States; (2) reduce the reliance of the Department of Defense on technology and industrial base sectors that are economically dependent on Department of Defense business; and (3) reduce Federal Government barriers to the use of commercial products, processes, and standards.

The House amendment contained no similar provision.

The House recedes.

Pilot program for distribution support and services for weapon systems contractors (sec. 883)

The Senate bill contained a provision (sec. 873) that would grant permissive authority to the Secretary of Defense to make available storage and distribution services support to a contractor in support of the performance by the contractor of a contract for the production, modification, maintenance, or repair of a weapon system that is entered into by an official of the Department of Defense.

The House amendment contained no similar provision.

The House recedes with a clarifying amendment that would remove the permanent authority and grant permissive authority to the Secretary of Defense to establish a six-year pilot program with a report to be delivered in the fourth year of the pilot program outlining the cost effectiveness for both government and industry as well as any performance enhancements, and recommendations on whether to make the authority permanent, and a review to be conducted by the Comptroller General of the United States during the fifth year to inform the potential extension or permanent authorization of the program.

Nontraditional and small contractor innovation prototyping program (sec. 884)

The Senate bill contained a provision (sec. 876) that would establish a pilot program for nontraditional contractors and small businesses to prototype disruptive solutions that demonstrate new capabilities that could provide alternatives to existing acquisition programs and assets.

The House amendment contained no similar provision.

The House recedes with an amendment that would add the Missile Defense Agency and protection against hypersonic weapons to the pilot program.

Subtitle H—Other Matters

Report on bid protests (sec. 885)

The Senate bill contained a provision (sec. 821) that would amend chapter 137 of title 10, United States Code, to add a new section to outline the role of the Government Accountability Office (GAO) in bid protests on certain contracts with the Department of Defense. The provision would require a large contractor filing a bid protest on a defense contract with GAO to cover the cost of processing the protest if all of the elements in the protest are denied in an opinion issued by GAO. The provision would also impose a withhold on payments above incurred costs on any bridge or temporary contract to an incumbent contractor who submits a protest and that protest results in the issuance of a bridge or temporary contract. The distribution of this withhold would be dependent on the outcome of the protest.

The House amendment contained a similar provision (sec. 831) that would require the

Secretary of Defense to enter into a contract with an independent entity with appropriate expertise to conduct a review of the bid protest process related to major defense acquisition programs.

The Senate recedes with an amendment that expands the scope of the report to look at ways that the possibility of bid protests may influence behavior by contracting officers and by contractors. The report shall be due 1 year after the date of enactment of this Act.

Review and report on indefinite delivery contracts (sec. 886)

The House amendment contained a provision (sec. 832) that would require the Comptroller General of the United States to review the use of indefinite delivery type contracts by the Department of Defense during fiscal years 2015, 2016, and 2017.

The Senate bill contained no similar provision.

The Senate recedes with an amendment that would require the review to include an assessment of Department of Defense guidance for entering into indefinite delivery contracts and for the number of vendors that should receive multiple award contracts, as well as the number and value of indefinite delivery contracts entered into with a single vendor.

Review and report on contractual flow-down provisions (sec. 887)

The House amendment contained a provision (sec. 833) that would require the Secretary of Defense to enter into a contract with an independent entity with appropriate expertise to conduct a review of contractual flow-down provisions related to major defense acquisition programs.

The Senate bill contained no similar provision.

The Senate recedes with an amendment that would expand the types of contractors and suppliers to be included in the required review. The conferees direct the Secretary of Defense or his designee to brief the Committees on Armed Services of the Senate and the House of Representatives on the interim findings and initial recommendations from the review not later than April 1, 2017.

Requirement and review relating to use of brand names or brand-name or equivalent descriptions in solicitations (sec. 888)

The Senate bill contained a provision (sec. 829E) that would require the Secretary of Defense to ensure that Department of Defense contract language does not specify a brand name in solicitations unless justification for such a specification is provided and approved in accordance with section 2304(f) of title 10, United States Code.

The House amendment contained a similar provision (sec. 834) that would require a review of specifications in information technology acquisitions to increase competition and a review of brand names and specifications for acquisitions of goods and services.

The House recedes with an amendment that would add a review of the policy, guidance, regulations, and training related to specifications included in information technology acquisitions to ensure current policies eliminate the unjustified use of potentially anti-competitive specifications.

Inclusion of information on common grounds for sustaining bid protests in annual Government Accountability Office reports to Congress (sec. 889)

The House amendment contained a provision (sec. 845) that would require the Comptroller General of the United States to include in his annual report to Congress on the Government Accountability Office each year a list of the most common grounds for sustaining protests relating to bids for contracts during the preceding year.

The Senate bill contained no similar provision.

The Senate recedes.

Study and report on contracts awarded to minority-owned and women-owned businesses (sec. 890)

The House amendment contained a provision (sec. 848) that would require the Comptroller General of the United States to perform a study on the number and types of contracts for the procurement of goods or services for the Department of Defense awarded to minority-owned and women-owned businesses during fiscal years 2010 through 2015. The report would be due to the congressional defense committees no later than 1 year after the enactment date of this Act.

The Senate bill contained no similar provision.

The Senate recedes.

Authority to provide reimbursable auditing services to certain non-Defense Agencies (sec. 891)

The Senate bill contained a provision (sec. 892) that would amend section 893 of the National Defense Authorization Act for Fiscal Year 2016 (Public Law 114–92) to provide an exception for the Defense Contract Audit Agency to provide audit support to the National Nuclear Security Administration on a reimbursable basis.

The House amendment contained a similar provision (sec. 840).

The House recedes.

Selection of service providers for auditing services and audit readiness services (sec. 892)

The House amendment contained a provision that would require the Department of Defense to select service providers for auditing services and audit readiness services based on the best value to the Department rather than based on the lowest price technically acceptable service provider.

The Senate bill contained no similar provision.

The Senate recedes.

Amendments to contractor business system requirements (sec. 893)

The Senate bill contained a provision (sec. 891) that would amend chapter 137 of title 10, United States Code, to add a new section that would require the Secretary of Defense to develop and initiate a program to improve contractor business systems. The provision would clarify that this program would only apply to those contractors that do more than 30 percent of their business with the federal government and more than 1 percent of their business under cost-type contracts.

The House amendment contained no similar provision.

The House recedes with an amendment that would require the Department of Defense to identify and make public clear business system requirements, allow contractors to submit certification from their third-party independent auditors that their business systems conform to the Department's business system requirements, and allow a milestone decision authority to require further auditing of business systems to manage contractual risk. The amendment would also specify that business system requirements only apply to contractors that have covered contracts with the United States Government accounting for greater than 1 percent of their total gross revenue and that are not subject to full cost accounting standards pursuant to either section 1502 of title 41, United States Code, or regulations implementing section 1502 of title 41, United States Code.

Improved management practices to reduce cost and improve performance of certain Department of Defense organizations (sec. 894)

The Senate bill contained a provision (sec. 893) that would require all Department of Defense entities, with the exception of the Centers of Industrial and Technical Excellence designated pursuant to section 2474 of title 10, United States Code, which conduct commercial or non-inherently governmental work to establish cost baselines for their operations and begin to adopt best commercial and business management practices to reduce costs and improve the performance of such organizations.

The House amendment contained no similar provision.

The House recedes.

Exemption from requirement for capital planning and investment control for information technology equipment included as integral part of a weapon or weapon system (sec. 895)

The Senate bill contained a provision (sec. 895) that would require that the milestone decision authority shall only apply the requirements of paragraphs (2) through (5) of section 11312(b) of title 40, United States Code, to national security systems upon a written determination that the application of these requirements is appropriate and in the best interests of the Department of Defense.

The House amendment contained no similar provision.

The House recedes.

Modifications to pilot program for streamlining awards for innovative technology projects (sec. 896)

The Senate bill contained a provision (sec. 896) that would amend section 873 of the National Defense Authorization Act for Fiscal Year 2016 (Public Law 114–92) to clarify that the use of a technical, merit-based selection procedure or the Small Business Innovation Research Program or Small Business Technology Transfer Program for the pilot program under this section are competitive procedures for the purposes of chapter 137 of title 10, United States Code. The provision would also direct the Secretary of Defense to establish procedures under which a small business or a nontraditional contractor may engage an independent certified public accountant for the review and certification of its accounting system for the purposes of any audits required by this section.

The House amendment contained no similar provision.

The House recedes with an amendment that would include auditing officials in the list of personnel who are provided guidance and training on the flexible use and tailoring of authorities under the pilot program.

Rapid prototyping funds for the military departments (sec. 897)

The Senate bill contained a provision (sec. 899A) that would amend section 804(d) of the National Defense Authorization Act for Fiscal Year 2016 (Public Law 114–92) to authorize the Secretary of the Army, Navy, and Air Force each to establish service-specific funds for acquisition programs under the rapid fielding and prototyping pathways established in this section.

The House amendment contained no similar provision.

The House recedes.

Establishment of Panel on Department of Defense and AbilityOne Contracting Oversight, Accountability, and Integrity; Defense Acquisition University training (sec. 898)

The Senate bill contained a provision (sec. 829H) that would prohibit the Secretary of Defense from arranging contracts through AbilityOne, or its central non-profit agency, SourceAmerica, and instead require the Secretary to contract directly with qualified nonprofit agencies for the severely disabled until the Department of Defense (DOD) Inspector General conducted a review and certified the effectiveness of the internal controls and financial management of AbilityOne and SourceAmerica.

The House amendment contained no similar provision.

The House recedes with an amendment that would establish a panel on DOD and AbilityOne contracting oversight, accountability, and integrity to review and address the effectiveness and internal controls of the program related to DOD contracts.

Coast Guard major acquisition programs (sec. 899)

The House amendment contained a provision (sec. 835) that would amend section 56(c) of title 14, United States Code, to direct the Chief Acquisitions Officer of the Coast Guard to inform the Commandant of developments in major acquisition programs that have new or revisited trade-offs between costs, scheduling, feasibility, and performance. This section also would amend chapter 15 of title 14, United States Code, to clarify the role of the Acquisition Directorate in ensuring that the needs of customers in major acquisition programs are met in the most cost-effective manner practicable. The Vice Commandant of the Coast Guard would be responsible for representing the operating field units and would serve an advisory role to the Commandant for major acquisition programs. The customer of a major acquisition program would be specified as the operating field unit that would field the acquired system and "major acquisition program" would be defined as a program with a life-cycle cost estimate of $300.0 million or more.

This section also would prohibit the Commandant of the Coast Guard from awarding a contract for the design of an unmanned aerial system (UAS) for use by the Coast Guard, and would require the Commandant to use and operate only UASs that have already been acquired by either the Department of Defense or the Department of Homeland Security.

This section also would allow the Coast Guard to extend major acquisition program contracts if the Comptroller General of the United States finds that extending a current contract would be more cost effective than awarding a new contract. The Comptroller General would determine the costs for acquiring additional vessels under an existing contract, as well as the incurred costs due to schedule delays and asset design changes that would result from awarding a new contract.

This section also would require the Commandant to review all authorities provided under chapter 15 of title 14, United States Code, and other relevant statutes and deliver a report to the Committee on Commerce, Science, and Transportation of the Senate and the Committee on Transportation and Infrastructure of the House of Representatives on how the Commandant can play a more appropriate role in the acquisition process with regard to policies, requirements, and implementing a more customer-oriented acquisition system.

This section also would require the Secretary for the department in which the Coast Guard is operating to submit a report to the Committee on Commerce, Science, and Transportation of the Senate and the Committee on Transportation and Infrastructure of the House of Representatives on an analysis of multiyear procurement authorities for the procurement of at least five Fast Response Cutters (beginning with hull 43) and Offshore Patrol Cutters (beginning with hull 5). The report would include an assessment of costs and benefits, impact on delivery times, and whether acquisitions would meet the four-part test under section 2306b of title 10, United States Code.

The Senate bill contained no similar provision.

The Senate recedes with an amendment that would allow the Coast Guard to acquire unmanned aerial systems that have been previously funded by the Departments of Defense or Homeland Security. The amendment would also require the Cost Analysis Division of the Department of Homeland Security to determine if contracts for procurement of additional units under an existing Coast Guard major acquisition program contract would be cost effective.

Enhanced authority to acquire products and services produced in Africa in support of covered activities (sec. 899A)

The Senate bill contained a provision (sec. 885) that would grant the Secretary of Defense authority to make a determination to limit competition or provide a preference for products and services produced in areas where the United States has long-term agreements with host nations in the African region.

The House amendment contained no similar provision.

The House recedes with an amendment that would provide for an exemption from preferred local procurement for items included on the procurement list described in section 8503(a) of title 41, United States Code, if such a good can be produced and delivered by a qualified non-profit agency for the blind or a non-profit agency for other severely disabled in a timely fashion to support mission requirements.

LEGISLATIVE PROVISIONS NOT ADOPTED

Revision to authorities relating to Department of Defense Test Resource Management Center

The House amendment contained a provision (sec. 801) that would limit application of existing law to the Major Range and Test Facility Base and those test and evaluation facilities that are used to support the acquisition programs of the Department of Defense. The provision would align the statute to the original enactment of the law and would prevent reporting requirements from being broadened to small laboratory and educational test and evaluation facilities. The provision would also define the term "significant change" in test and evaluation facilities.

The Senate bill contained no similar provision.

The House recedes.

Repeal of temporary suspension of public-private competitions for conversion of Department of Defense functions to performance by contractors

The Senate bill contained a provision (sec. 806) that would repeal section 325 of the National Defense Authorization Act for Fiscal Year 2010 (Public Law 111-84).

The House amendment contained no similar provision.

The Senate recedes.

Requirement for policies and standard checklist in procurement of services

The House amendment contained a provision (sec. 809) that would establish a procurement policy checklist to ensure accountability in the acquisition of services.

The Senate bill contained no similar provision.

The House recedes.

Non-traditional contractor definition

The Senate bill contained a provision (sec. 817) that would amend section 2302(9) of title 10, United States Code, to clarify the definition of a non-traditional contractor.

The House amendment contained no similar provision.

The Senate recedes.

Revision to definition of commercial item

The House amendment contained a provision (sec. 821) that would amend section 103 of title 41, United States Code, to expand the types of nondevelopmental items that may be considered commercial items to include items that the procuring agency determines were developed at private expense and sold in substantial quantities on a competitive basis to foreign governments.

The Senate bill contained no similar provision.

The House recedes.

Government Accountability Office bid protest reforms

The Senate bill contained a provision (sec. 821) that would amend chapter 137 of title 10, United States Code, to add a new section to outline the role of the Government Accountability Office in bid protests on certain contracts with the Department of Defense.

The House amendment contained no similar provision.

The Senate recedes.

Penalties for the use of cost-type contracts

The Senate bill contained a provision (sec. 826) that would require the secretary of each military department and the head of each of the defense agencies to pay a penalty for the use of cost-type contracts in certain cases that are awarded in fiscal year 2018 through fiscal year 2021.

The House amendment contained no similar provision.

The Senate recedes.

Nonapplicability of certain executive order to Department of Defense and National Nuclear Security Administration

The Senate bill contained a provision (sec. 829I) that would limit the application of the acquisition regulations mandated by Executive Order 13673 to contractors or subcontractors of the Department of Defense that have been suspended or debarred as a result of the federal labor law violations referenced in the Executive Order in effect on May 28, 2015.

The House amendment contained a similar provision (sec. 1095) that would exempt the Department of Defense and the National Nuclear Security Administration from implementation of Executive Order 13673.

The conference agreement does not include either provision.

Requirement that certain ship components be manufactured in the national technology and industrial base

The House amendment contained a provision (sec. 838) that would amend section 2534 of title 10, United States Code, and would require certain auxiliary ship components to be procured from a manufacturer in the national technology and industrial base.

The Senate bill contained no similar provision.

The House recedes.

Use of economy-wide inflation index to calculate percentage increase in unit costs

The Senate bill contained a provision (sec. 839) that would amend section 2433(f) of title 10, United States Code, to require that unit costs be calculated in constant dollars with an economy-wide inflation index, such as the Gross Domestic Product Price Index.

The House amendment contained no similar provision.

The Senate recedes.

Modifications to the justification and approval process for certain sole-source contracts for small business concerns

The House amendment contained a provision (sec. 842) that would repeal section 811 of the National Defense Authorization Act for Fiscal Year 2010 (Public Law 111–84) and establish a standard justification and approval process for sole-source contracts valued at $20.0 million or greater.

The Senate bill contained no similar provision.

The House recedes.

Briefing on design-build construction process for defense contracts

The House amendment contained a provision (sec. 843) that would require the Secretary of Defense to provide the Committee on Armed Services of the House of Representatives with a briefing on the use and implementation of the two-phase design-build selection procedures. The briefing would include: plans to implement the updates to the Federal Acquisition Regulation that amended section 2305a, title 10, United States Code; a list of awards for design-build contracts pursuant to 2305a of title 10, United States Code, that had more than five finalists; feedback from industry; and any challenges to the implementation of this amended statute.

The Senate bill contained no similar provision.

The House recedes.

The conferees direct the Secretary of Defense, not later than March 1, 2017, to provide the congressional defense committees with a briefing on the use and implementation of the two-phase design-build selection procedures. The briefing should include how the Department of Defense continues to implement the updates to the Federal Acquisition Regulation that implemented the 2015 amendments to section 2305a, title 10, United States Code, a list of instances in which the Department awarded a design-build contract pursuant to section 2305a of title 10, United States Code, that had more than five finalists for phase-two requests for proposals during fiscal year 2016, and the list of design-build requests for proposals that used a one-step process, any feedback the Department has received from industry on the Department's design-build selection procedure, and any challenges to the implementation of this statute.

Assessment of outreach for small business concerns owned and controlled by women and minorities required before conversion of certain functions to contractor performance

The House amendment contained a provision (sec. 844) that would prohibit any Department of Defense functions performed by civilian employees tied to a military base to be converted to performance by contractors until an assessment is conducted to determine if the Department has sufficiently carried out outreach programs to assist small business concerns owned and controlled by women or socially and economically disadvantaged individuals located near a military base.

The Senate bill contained no similar provision.

The House recedes.

Enhanced use of data analytics to improve acquisition program outcomes

The Senate bill contained a provision (sec. 853) that that would mandate the establishment of activities to promote the use of data analytics and other evaluation-related methods to support acquisition decision-making and enhance organizational learning.

The House amendment contained no similar provision.

The Senate recedes.

The conferees note a widespread recognition that the Department of Defense (DOD) does not sufficiently incorporate data into its acquisition-related learning and decision-making. Many major policy decisions are made without the benefit of being informed by substantive data. These policies are sometimes based on assumptions, and program reviews do not always sufficiently incorporate relevant data against which to evaluate success. The conferees note that the Government Accountability Office reported in 2015 that DOD officials responsible for acquisitions and developing requirements lacked access to data and the analytical tools necessary to conduct effective reviews.

The conferees believe that data analysis and other evaluation-related methods are a critical element in making well-informed acquisition decisions and managing programs. As the Congressional Research Service noted, a lack of data or effective data analyses can lead to incorrect or misleading conclusions. The result may be policies that squander resources, waste taxpayer dollars, and undermine the effectiveness of government programs or military operations.

The conferees believe that one important aspect of enhancing the use of data analytics in acquisitions is for DOD to improve data sharing both within its programs and organizations, and where appropriate outside the Department. Sharing data externally includes publishing, to the maximum extent practicable, and in a manner that protects classified and proprietary information, data collected by the Department that is related to acquisition program costs and activities. Effectively sharing such data would allow industry, academia, think tanks, and the public to develop analyses of trends, lessons learned, best practices, and new analytical methods and tools for decision-making. To this end, the conferees encourage the Department to fund intramural and extramural research and development activities to develop and implement data analytics capabilities in support of improved acquisition outcomes, possibly through leveraging the authorities of the Defense Acquisition Workforce Development Fund.

Therefore, the conferees direct the Secretary of Defense, acting through the Under Secretary of Defense for Acquisition, Technology, and Logistics, the Deputy Chief Management Officer, and the Chief Information Officer, and in coordination with the military services, to assess the effectiveness of current activities and policies related to the use of data analysis, measurement, and other evaluation-related methods to the planning, implementation, and management of acquisition programs and the improvement of acquisition outcomes in the Department of Defense. The activities to be assessed should include data analytics capabilities and organizations within the military services; capabilities in Department of Defense laboratories, test centers, and Federally Funded Research and Development Centers to provide technical support for data analytics; and the use of existing analytical capabilities available to acquisition programs and offices to support improved acquisition outcomes.

Further, the Secretary of Defense, acting through the Under Secretary of Defense for Acquisition, Technology, and Logistics, shall conduct a review of the curriculum taught at the National Defense University, the Defense Acquisition University, and appropriate private-sector academic institutions to determine the extent to which the curricula includes appropriate courses on data analytics and other evaluation-related methods and their application to defense acquisitions, and how these efforts can be used by the acquisition workforce to perform their missions.

The conferees direct the Secretary of Defense, not later than 1 year after the date of the enactment of this Act, to brief the Armed Services Committees of the Senate and House of Representatives on the use of data analysis, measurement, and other evaluation-related methods in DOD acquisition programs. The briefing shall address the extent to which data analytics capabilities have been implemented within the military services, DOD laboratories, test centers, and Federally Funded Research and Development Centers to provide technical support for acquisition program management; the potential to increase the use of analytical capabilities for acquisition programs and offices to improve acquisition outcomes; the amount of funding for intramural and extramural research and development activities to develop and implement data analytics capabilities in support of improved acquisition outcomes; any potential improvements, based on private-sector best practices, in the efficiency of current data collection and analysis processes that could minimize collection and delivery of data by, from, and to government organizations; steps being taken to appropriately expose acquisition data in an anonymized fashion to researchers and analysts; and an assessment of whether the curriculum at the National Defense University, the Defense Acquisition University, and appropriate private-sector academic institutions includes appropriate courses on data analytics and other evaluation-related methods and their application to defense acquisitions.

Department of Defense exemptions from certain regulations

The Senate bill contained a provision (sec. 862) that would exempt purchases of commercial off-the-shelf items by the Department of Defense from certain Executive Orders and give the Secretary of Defense waiver authority for other purchases.

The House amendment contained no similar provision.

The Senate recedes.

Use of non-cost type contracts to acquire commercial items

The Senate bill contained a provision (sec. 867) that would amend section 2377 of title 10, United States Code, to require that the Defense Federal Acquisition Regulation Supplement include guidance that firm fixed-priced contracts, fixed-price incentive contracts, or fixed-price with economic price adjustment contracts be used to the maximum extent practicable for the acquisition of commercial items. Additionally, this provision would prohibit the use of cost-type contracts for commercial items.

The House amendment contained no similar provision.

The Senate recedes.

Modified requirements for distribution of assistance under procurement technical assistance cooperative agreements

The Senate bill contained a provision (sec. 875) that would amend section 2413(c) of title 10, United States Code, to conform the Procurement Technical Assistance Program with the Defense Logistics Agency current practice of using states as the geographic basis for cooperative agreement awards.

The House amendment contained no similar provision.

The Senate recedes.

The conferees agree that the current formula for distribution of grants to procurement technical assistance centers (PTACs) should be adjusted to address that the Department of Defense has consolidated its contract administration services districts, which are currently the basis for grant distribution pursuant to section 2413 of title 10, United States Code. However, the conferees believe that a successful funding formula should consider factors such as avoiding the discontinuation of services to existing clients of PTACs, the desirability of adding new PTACs or expanding the client base of existing PTACs, the population density, geographic accessibility of PTACs, duplication of services, the level of success obtained by particular grant recipients, the availability of funds, and other possible factors. Therefore, the conferees direct the Department to provide recommendations on appropriate factors and a funding formula. To develop these recommendations, the Department shall, at a minimum, work in consultation with current grantees and their representatives and examine comparable grant programs operated by other agencies. Such programs could include the Small Business Development Centers, Women's Business Centers, and Veterans Business Outreach Centers of the Small Business Administration or the Business Centers of the Minority Business Development Agency of the Department of Commerce. The Department's recommendations shall be provided no later than March 1, 2017.

Working capital fund for precision guided munitions exports in support of contingency operations

The Senate bill contained a provision (sec. 882) that would authorize the Secretary of Defense to establish a working capital fund to finance inventories of supplies of precision guided munitions in advance of partner and allied forces requirements to enhance the effectiveness of overseas contingency operations conducted or supported by the United States.

The House amendment contained no similar provision.

The Senate recedes.

Director of Developmental Test and Evaluation

The Senate bill contained a provision (sec. 894) that would amend section 139 of title 10, United States Code, and section 196(g) of title 10, United States Code, that would refine the role of the Director of Operational Test and Evaluation.

The House amendment contained no similar provision.

The Senate recedes.

The conferees note that Congress re-established a developmental test and evaluation organization within the defense research and

engineering enterprise in 2009. Since that time, the conferees have become concerned that the Department has not established a reasonable balance of investment between developmental and operational test activities. The conferees believe it is necessary to examine the functions and resources of the organizations of the Deputy Assistant Secretary of Defense for Developmental Test and Evaluation (DT&E) and the Director of Operational Test and Evaluation to better understand if the Department has struck the right balance between these activities. To improve test and evaluation results for the Department's acquisition programs in the most efficient manner, the Department's leadership must ensure sufficient resources to support testing and oversight activities.

The conferees note that, over time, the resources and influence of the Office of the Secretary of Defense and the Service developmental test and evaluation organizations have declined, adversely impacting the successful outcomes of acquisition efforts. However, the conferees believe that this decline should be re-examined in light of the need for stronger developmental test organizations to support department-wide efforts to promote technical innovation and re-establish battlefield technological superiority. As a result, the conferees believe it would be useful for the Department of Defense to review the resources allocated to developmental and operational test and evaluation organizations to address a number of issues and questions.

The conferees direct the Secretary of Defense to form an independent study panel, unaffiliated with a Federally Funded Research and Development Center, to review the appropriate roles, responsibilities, and level of resources for both developmental and operational test and evaluation activities required to execute statutory and regulatory responsibilities within the Office of the Secretary of Defense. The panel will develop such recommendations as it believes appropriate for optimal resources and authorities to support developmental and operational test missions. The review and report should be completed no later than 1 year after the enactment of this Act.

The committee recommends that the panel address the following questions:

(a) How can the Director of Operational Test and Evaluation and the Deputy Assistant Secretary of Defense for Developmental Test and Evaluation (DASD DT&E) at the Office of the Secretary of Defense approach oversight within the system development cycle to avoid overlap but be mutually supporting without sacrificing the independence of either organization?

(b) Does participation with and assessment of program progress during phases prior to operational test and evaluation bias the independent objectivity of the operational test and evaluation organization?

(c) Are there specific test and evaluation activities that should be realigned for management within OSD or the services to promote effectiveness and efficiency of those programs?

(d) Overall are the developmental and operational test and evaluation organizations effectively carrying out the missions as described in title 10, United States Code, and are there impediments to meeting those responsibilities? In addition, are they engaged in activities outside their mission areas?

(e) Are the activities of the test and evaluation organizations constructive, not duplicative or disruptive, to support the acquisition goals of the military departments and defense agencies?

(f) What staffing authorities and other resources are needed to support effective and efficient oversight of both the developmental and operational phases of testing commensurate with the effort to each relative to the portion of the programs that their oversight entails?

Improved transparency and oversight over Department of Defense research, development, test, and evaluation efforts and procurement activities related to medical research

The Senate bill contained a provision (sec. 898) that would prohibit the Secretary of Defense from entering into a contract, grant, or cooperative agreement for congressional special interest medical research programs under the congressionally directed medical research program of the Department of Defense unless additional cost accounting and other specified requirements were implemented.

The House amendment contained no similar provision.

The Senate recedes.

TITLE IX—DEPARTMENT OF DEFENSE ORGANIZATION AND MANAGEMENT

Subtitle A—Office of the Secretary of Defense and Related Matters

Organization of the Office of the Secretary of Defense (sec. 901)

The Senate bill contained a provision (sec. 901) that would amend section 133 of title 10, United States Code, to establish the position of the Under Secretary of Defense for Research and Engineering, amend section 138 of title 10, United States Code, to establish and consolidate certain Assistant Secretary of Defense positions, and make other conforming changes. The provision would also amend section 132a of title 10, United States Code, to redesignate the Under Secretary of Defense for Business Management and Information as the Under Secretary of Defense for Management and Support.

The House amendment contained a provision (sec. 846) that would revise the effective date for amendments relating to the conversion of the position of the Deputy Chief Management Officer to the position of the Under Secretary of Defense for Business Management and Information.

The House recedes with an amendment that would amend chapter 4 of title 10, United States Code, to establish an Under Secretary of Defense for Research and Engineering, an Under Secretary of Defense for Acquisition and Sustainment, and a chief management officer within the Department of Defense, effective on February 1, 2018. The amendment would make other modifying and conforming changes, and require the Secretary of Defense to conduct a review and submit a report to the congressional defense committees on the organizational and management structure for the Department.

Three broad priorities framed the conference discussions: (1) elevate the mission of advancing technology and innovation within the Department; (2) foster distinct technology and acquisition cultures to better deliver superior capabilities for the armed forces; and (3) provide greater oversight and management of the Department's Fourth Estate. The conferees believe that separating the "chief technology officer" and "chief acquisition officer" responsibilities currently residing with the Under Secretary of Defense for Acquisition, Technology, and Logistics, as well as establishing a "chief management officer" within the Department, addresses these priorities and better postures the Office of the Secretary of Defense organizationally to meet future national security challenges.

The conferees believe the technology and acquisition missions and cultures are distinct. The conferees expect that the Under Secretary of Defense for Research and Engineering would take risks, press the technology envelope, test and experiment, and have the latitude to fail, as appropriate. Whereas the conferees would expect the Under Secretary of Defense for Acquisition and Sustainment to focus on timely, cost-effective delivery and sustainment of products and services, and thus seek to minimize any risks to that objective.

Some will argue that the agreement exacerbates the technology "valley of death." The conferees acknowledge that there will be seams in any organizational construct, but also believe that this seam creates a healthy tension that can be mitigated through effective leadership and management. As an Under Secretary, third in precedence, the conferees expect that the "chief technology officer" would have the stature and resources to drive innovation throughout the Department, including as needed through development and implementation of innovative policies and practices. At the same time, the conferees would expect the Under Secretary of Defense for Acquisition and Sustainment to challenge any advanced technology ideas that the Under Secretary cannot confidently deliver on within cost, schedule, and performance objectives, and shape those efforts appropriately.

The conferees recognize that the implementation of this provision will require further examination and analysis, to include a deeper review of authorities, responsibilities, resource implications, and the appropriate allocation of subordinate positions and organizations. As such, the provision provides policy guidance on roles and responsibilities for each of the three senior leadership positions and repeals requirements in statute for specific subordinate assistant and deputy assistant secretaries of defense to provide flexibility to the Department to allocate such subordinate positions to best meet congressional policy guidance.

The conferees believe a review of authorities is particularly important, especially as they relate to any direction and supervisory authorities vested in the three senior leadership positions, to allow those senior leaders to effectively oversee and manage activities and resources within their portfolios at the direction of the Secretary of Defense. Similarly, the conferees believe an in-depth examination of the placement within the Department and the responsibilities of the chief management officer is also warranted, as they believe such an officer could provide greater oversight and management of the non-homogenous organizations that comprise the Department's Fourth Estate. The conferees also believe an examination of the potential for the establishment of a Chief Innovation Officer position, informed by best private sector practices, is warranted.

The conferees set a date of February 1, 2018, for the implementation of the three senior leadership positions, to provide the Department with time to conduct the required review, to engage the congressional defense committees, and to provide its recommendations on an organization and management structure for the Department. However, the conferees encourage the President to move out earlier on nominations for these senior leadership positions.

Lastly, while the focus of this provision is on the Office of the Secretary of Defense, the conferees also recognize that the Department as a whole must be examined to provide the organizational and management agility and adaptability necessary to address longer-term national security challenges.

Responsibilities and reporting of the Chief Information Officer of the Department of Defense (sec. 902)

The Senate bill contained a provision (sec. 903) that would amend paragraph 8 of section 132(b) of title 10, United States Code, to establish the position of the Assistant Secretary of Defense for Information.

The House amendment contained no similar provision.

The House recedes with an amendment that would clarify in sections 131 and 142 of title 10, United States Code, the responsibilities of the Chief Information Officer of the Department of Defense.

The conferees direct the Secretary of Defense to develop a plan within 180 days after the enactment of this Act to implement a more optimized organizational structure and processes to support information management and cyber operations to include the policy, direction, oversight and acquisition functions performed by the Deputy Chief Management Officer, the Chief Information Officer, the Under Secretary of Defense for Acquisition, Technology and Logistics, the Under Secretary for Policy, and the Under Secretary for Intelligence and any other relevant entity in the Department of Defense. This plan should include both business systems and national security systems and explore the responsibilities for cyber and space policy, information network defense, and the development of policies and standards governing information technology systems and related information security activities of the Department. This plan should also assess the effectiveness and utility of the cross functional team supporting the Principal Cyber Advisor established by section 932(c)(3) of the National Defense Authorization Act for Fiscal Year 2014 (Public Law 113–66).

Maximum number of personnel in Office of the Secretary of Defense and other Department of Defense headquarters offices (sec. 903)

The Senate bill contained a provision (sec. 904) that would:

(1) amend section 143 of title 10, United States Code, to limit the number of civilian and detailed individuals authorized to be assigned to the Office of the Secretary of Defense to 3,767;

(2) amend section 155 of title 10, to limit the number of personnel on the Joint Staff to 1,930 including not more than 1,500 Active-Duty service members;

(3) amend section 3014 of title 10, to limit the total number of members of the Armed Forces and civilian employees of the Department of the Army assigned or detailed to permanent duty in the Office of the Secretary of the Army and on the Army staff to 3,105; and to reduce the total number of general officers assigned or detailed to permanent duty in the Office of the Secretary of the Army and on the Army staff from 67 to 50.

(4) amend section 5014 of title 10, to limit the total number of members of the Armed Forces and civilian employees of the Department of the Navy assigned or detailed to permanent duty in the Office of the Secretary of the Navy and on the Navy staff to 2,866; and to reduce the total number of flag officers assigned or detailed to permanent duty in the Office of the Secretary of the Navy and on the Navy staff from 67 to 50.

(5) amend section 8014 of title 10, to limit the total number of members of the Armed Forces and civilian employees of the Department of the Air Force assigned or detailed to permanent duty in the Office of the Secretary of the Air Force and on the Air Force staff to 2,639; and to reduce the total number of general officers assigned or detailed to permanent duty in the Office of the Secretary of the Air Force and on the Air Force staff from 60 to 45.

The provision would further clarify the exceptions to the personnel limits. It would allow the limits to be increased by 15 percent during a national emergency.

The House amendment contained no similar provision.

The House recedes with an amendment that would limit the number of civilians assigned or detailed to the headquarters operations, establish a 2,069 personnel limit for the Joint Staff, and clarify that the exceptions to the personnel limits allow an additional 15 percent during national emergencies.

Repeal of Financial Management Modernization Executive Committee (sec. 904)

The Senate bill contained a provision that would repeal section 185 of title 10, United States Code, regarding the Department of Defense Financial Management Modernization Executive Committee.

The House amendment contained no similar provision.

The House recedes.

Subtitle B—Organization and Management of the Department of Defense Generally

Organizational Strategy for the Department of Defense (sec. 911)

The Senate bill contained a provision (sec. 941) that would require the Secretary of Defense to develop and implement an organizational strategy for the Department of Defense (DOD).

The House bill contained no similar provision.

The House recedes with an amendment that would: (1) streamline and condense the organizational strategy required from the Secretary; (2) substantially enhance the requirement for an independent study of private sector and government experience with cross-functional teams (CFTs), and the use of cross-functional groups by the Department of Defense, to inform the Secretary's implementation of CFTs and the cultural changes needed for their success; (3) lengthen and rationalize the timelines for the next Secretary of Defense to accomplish the changes mandated by the Senate provision; and (4) provide additional discretion to the Secretary regarding the number, characteristics, and application of mandated CFTs.

The intention of the conferees in adopting this provision is to provide the Secretary of Defense with a valuable tool for improving the performance of even the most elite organizations. Recognizing that the civilian and military employees of the Department of Defense are committed to the mission of protecting and defending the United States, the conferees believe that CFTs will provide the Secretary, and therefore the DOD workforce, a tool to more-effectively achieve their shared mission. The conferees believe that CFTs will enable the Secretary to more rapidly and effectively develop solutions and strategies for complex critical objectives and other organizational outputs of the Department of Defense by harnessing and integrating the expertise and ingenuity resident in the Department's functional organizations.

Successful CFTs require that DOD develop a more collaborative culture, just as the Goldwater-Nichols Act reforms required a cultural change to instill "jointness" among the military services to better support integrated operations for the combatant commands. The conferees recognize that it is difficult to legislate cultural change, but note that cultural change mandated by Goldwater-Nichols was achieved, and that this section promotes a more collaborative culture by such practical steps as training, directives and guidance, and performance reviews. However, the views and expectations of the Secretary and his principal staff advisers will be critical to success.

DOD officials have expressed the concern that the CFTs mandated under this section will undermine the authority of the Secretary of Defense and confuse lines of responsibility. The conferees emphasize that the authority of the CFTs, which will be established and directed by the Secretary and will support the Secretary, derives from the authority of the Secretary. Any authority being exercised is the delegated authority of the Secretary and is to be applied to cross-cutting objectives and other organizational issues that are not under the authority of any officials other than the Secretary and Deputy Secretary of Defense.

The conferees note that DOD has established CFTs in the past that were highly effective, including teams to improve care for wounded warriors, dramatically increase intelligence support to counter-terrorism forces, and rapidly build thousands of life-saving armored vehicles to protect forces facing dire threats from improvised explosive devices. The attributes of these successful teams, and the manner in which they were managed, as well as the collective experience of the private sector and other government organizations, are reflected in the provision adopted by the conferees.

The conferees hope and expect that the good-faith implementation of this provision will demonstrate the value of properly constructed CFTs, which will spur the use of such teams across the Department, supporting officials and decision-making at all levels of the enterprise.

Policy, organization, and management goals and priorities of the Secretary of Defense for the Department of Defense (sec. 912)

The Senate bill contained a provision (sec. 942) that would require a series of management directives for the next Secretary of Defense.

The House amendment contained no similar provision.

The House recedes with an amendment that would scope the management overview to focus on policy goals, organizational management, and delayering of Department of Defense organizations and require updates in the form of a briefing on February 1 of each year through 2022 after the initial written report is submitted by April 1, 2017.

The Conferees note that the Secretary of Defense is expected to utilize the delivery unit authorized in this Act to assist with the execution and tracking of goals set under this provision.

Secretary of Defense delivery unit (sec. 913)

The Senate bill contained a provision (sec. 906) that would provide the Secretary of Defense with the authority to establish a delivery unit that would report directly to the Secretary in order to provide expertise and support on key reform and business transformation priorities across the Department for no more than four years beginning February 1, 2017. Such delivery unit may utilize the public-private talent exchange authorities available to the Secretary and consist of no more than 30 professionals with deep experience in management consulting, organization transformation, and data analytics.

The House amendment contained no similar provision.

The House recedes with an amendment that would expand the role of the delivery unit beyond the business transformation process to also include the authority to identify and recommend resolutions to obstacles impeding the implementation of the Secretary's policies. The amendment also moves the establishment date of the delivery unit to March 1, 2017.

Performance of civilian functions by military personnel (sec. 914)

The House amendment contained a provision (H. 923) that would prohibit the conversion of positions performed by civilian personnel to performance by military personnel in most cases.

The Senate bill contained no similar provision.

The Senate recedes with an amendment that would further clarify that functions performed by civilian personnel should not be performed by military personnel except to meet mission requirements, as determined by the Secretary of a military department, or to address critical staffing needs for no more than one year resulting from congressional reductions in personnel or budgetary resources.

Repeal of requirements relating to efficiencies plan for the civilian personnel workforce and service contractor workforce of the Department of Defense (sec. 915)

The Senate bill contained a provision (sec. 1084) that would repeal section 955 of the National Defense Authorization Act for Fiscal Year 2013 (Public Law 112–239).

The House amendment contained no similar provision.

The House recedes.

Subtitle C—Joint Chiefs of Staff and Combatant Command Matters

Joint Chiefs of Staff and related combatant command matters (sec. 921)

The Senate bill contained a provision (sec. 921) that would amend sections 151 and 153 of title 10, United States Code, to clarify the role of the Chairman of the Joint Chiefs of Staff and the key duties that this officer must perform on behalf of the joint force, specifically: providing advice on the military elements of defense strategy and the global integration of military activities; advocating for the joint warfighter of today and tomorrow, especially with respect to developing joint capabilities; ensuring comprehensive joint readiness; and fostering joint force development. This provision seeks to clarify the role of the Chairman and thereby set an expectation that the preponderance of any Chairman's time should be devoted to the key strategic, global, and joint duties that are the Chairman's unique purview within the military.

The provision would also enhance the role of the other members of the Joint Chiefs, and the Joint Chiefs of Staff as a corporate body, to provide military advice to civilian leaders, including on the military elements of strategy. Current law provides the Chairman discretion with regard to how much to consult with the other Joint Chiefs and whether to inform civilian leaders of alternative military advice. This provision would seek to better enable the Chairman to act as the principal military adviser to civilian leaders.

The House amendment contained two similar provisions (sec. 907 and sec. 908). The first provision in the House amendment (sec. 907) would amend section 152(a) of title 10, United States Code, to extend the term of office of the Chairman of the Joint Chiefs of Staff from 2 years to 4 years. This section would also limit the reappointment of the Chairman to additional terms only in a time of war, and limit the combined period of service of an officer serving as Chairman or Vice Chairman of the Joint Chiefs of Staff to 8 years.

The second provision (sec. 908) in the House amendment would amend section 153(a) of title 10, United States Code, which sets forth the functions of the Chairman of the Joint Chiefs of Staff, by codifying the Chairman's responsibility to provide advice to the President and the Secretary of Defense on ongoing military operations and to provide advice to the Secretary on the allocation and transfer of forces among combatant commands.

The House recedes with an amendment that would make certain changes to enhance the position of the other members of the Joint Chiefs as military advisors, extend the terms of the Chairman and the Vice Chairman to 4 years and ensure that such terms are staggered, outline the Chairman's role in planning, advice, global military integration, and ensure open communication between the combatant commands and the Chairman.

Organization of the Department of Defense for management of special operations forces and special operations (sec. 922)

The Senate bill contained a provision (sec. 923) that would amend sections 138 and 167 of title 10, United States Code, to modify the roles and responsibilities of the Assistant Secretary of Defense for Special Operations and Low Intensity Conflict (ASD SOLIC) and the Commander of U.S. Special Operations Command (SOCOM).

The House amendment contained no similar provision.

The House recedes with an amendment that would make clarifying changes.

The conferees note that in recent years SOCOM has undergone significant change and the capabilities of special operations forces (SOF) have taken on critical importance for addressing the threat posed by violent extremist groups and other security challenges facing our nation. Since 2001, SOCOM's personnel numbers (civilian and military) have nearly doubled, its budget nearly tripled, and overseas deployments of SOF nearly quadrupled.

Under provisions included in the National Defense Authorization Act for Fiscal Year 1987 (Public Law 99–661), commonly referred to as the "Nunn-Cohen Amendment," the ASD SOLIC is tasked with the responsibility to provide "the overall supervision (including oversight of policy and resources) of special operations activities" and is identified as "the principal civilian advisor to the Secretary of Defense on special operations and low intensity conflict matters."

The provisions described above were intended to empower the ASD SOLIC to serve a hybrid role as: 1) the Department's lead civilian policy official for matters related to special operations and low intensity conflict; and 2) the "service secretary-like" civilian with responsibility for the oversight and advocacy of SOCOM and the organization, training, and equipping of SOF. However, the conferees believe the ASD SOLIC has been challenged in fulfilling their "service secretary-like" responsibilities for a number of reasons. For example, the ASD SOLIC's organizational location within the office of the Undersecretary of Defense for Policy (USD(P)) has resulted in the ASD SOLIC dedicating a preponderance of their time and resources to policy and operational issues, at the expense of their "service secretary-like" responsibilities. Additionally, other civilian offices with greater seniority within the Department exercise related and, at times, overlapping responsibilities for aspects of SOF oversight, thereby complicating the ASD SOLIC's primacy in such matters. Furthermore, the conferees understand that studies directed by the Department when the ASD SOLIC was created determined that appropriate staffing levels for the organization would require between 95 and 110 personnel. However, the office of the ASD SOLIC is currently only staffed by approximately 60 military and civilian personnel, only 6 of whom are focused on tasks related to the oversight and advocacy of the organization, training, and equipping of SOF. Furthermore, the addition of responsibilities for the counter-narcotics programs, building partner capacity initiatives, and humanitarian and disaster relief efforts of the DOD have further stretched the resources available to the office since its creation.

The conferees intend for this provision to clarify and strengthen the original mandate provided by the Nunn-Cohen Amendment that established the ASD SOLIC. The provision is intended to facilitate the unique "service secretary-like" responsibilities of the ASD SOLIC by mirroring the administrative chain of command relationship between the service secretaries and the military services for issues impacting the special operations-peculiar (commonly referred to as Major Force Program–11) administration and support of SOCOM, including the readiness and organization of SOF, resources (including program planning, allocation, and execution) and equipment, and relevant civilian personnel matters. The provision shall not impact the operational chain of command for SOF activities or the "service-common" responsibilities of the military services including personnel and other matters that are not special operations-peculiar.

The conferees are mindful of the congressionally-directed reductions to headquarters staff, but believe that the "service secretary-like" mission of the ASD SOLIC should be more robustly resourced in order to rebalance the ASD SOLIC's lines of effort and fulfill its mandate under title 10, United States Code. The conferees also expect the codification of the Special Operations Policy and Oversight Council under this provision to improve the oversight and advocacy of SOF by integrating the efforts of the various functional offices with direct or tangential responsibilities for SOF issues, thereby partially mitigating the need for significant numbers of additional personnel.

Additionally, the conferees note that the President approved the transfer of the mission for synchronizing global Department of Defense operations for countering weapons of mass destruction (CWMD) from United States Strategic Command (STRATCOM) to United States Special Operations Command on August 4, 2016. According to the Secretary of Defense "Expediting the transfer of CWMD responsibilities will allow USSOCOM to assume leadership for synchronization of Department of Defense (DoD) efforts in this critical mission, which will include updating the DoD CWMD Campaign Plan and instituting a comprehensive mission assessment process. I recommend this course of action to

best ensure consistent, focused, and strengthened CWMD efforts across the Department and with our interagency and international partners." The conferees support the transfer of the CWMD global synchronization mission to SOCOM because it may ensure appropriate DOD and interagency attention for this critical mission, facilitate synchronization with counterterrorism and other transregional efforts, and strengthen the preparedness of U.S. Special Operations Forces to counter these threats. However, the conferees are concerned that the requirements to successfully implement this mission change may not be fully defined and understood at this time. The conferees believe that it is important to clearly define requirements for this mission transfer to ensure that resources needed by SOCOM to adequately carry out this mission are appropriately transferred and provided for across the future years defense program.

Therefore, not later than 90 days after enactment of this Act, the conferees direct the Secretary of Defense to submit to the congressional defense committees the implementation plan for the transfer of the CWMD global synchronization mission. The report should include: an identification of resources, authorities, personnel or capabilities needed for this mission, and plans to implement those in the future years defense program; identification of the responsibilities, organizations, personnel and capabilities to be transferred from Strategic Command, including those at the Defense Threat Reduction Agency, to SOCOM to support the mission; oversight responsibilities within the Office of the Secretary of Defense; dates and criteria for the initial operating capability and full operating capability milestones.

Establishment of Unified Combatant Command for Cyber Operations (sec. 923)

The House amendment contained a provision (sec. 911) that would establish a unified combatant command for cyber operations with the primary function to prepare cyber operations forces to carry out assigned missions.

The Senate bill contained no similar provision.

The Senate recedes with a clarifying amendment.

The conferees note transparency of U.S. Cyber Command operations, forces, and other activities is critical to oversight of the command by Congress. The conferees expect the quarterly cyber operations briefings, mandated by Title 10, United States Code, Section 484, to continue to serve as a forum for providing information to Congress on all offensive and significant defensive military operations in cyberspace carried out by the unified combatant command in the preceding quarter and serve as mechanism for informing Congress of other activities of the command.

In establishing the unified combatant command for cyber operations, the conferees also expect the Secretary of Defense, in conjunction with the relevant agencies and entities within the Department of Defense, to establish formal procedures for notification to Congress of significant operations in cyberspace on a timely basis. The conferees also expect the Secretary to establish formal procedures for notification to Congress of other significant command activities, such as delegation of new authorities to the United States Cyber Command Commander for cyberspace operations by the Secretary of Defense and relevant policy and internal oversight decisions affecting activities of the command.

Assigned forces of the combatant commands (sec. 924)

The Senate bill contained a provision (sec. 1041) that would amend section 162 of title 10, United States Code, to require the secretaries of the military departments, at the direction of the Secretary of Defense, to assign forces under the jurisdiction of the secretaries concerned to the combatant commands to perform missions assigned to the combatant commands. Forces that are not so assigned shall remain under the direction and control of the respective military department secretaries for purposes of carrying out the secretaries' responsibilities under sections 3013, 5013, and 8013 including organizing, training, and mobilizing of all United States military forces.

The House amendment contained a similar provision (sec. 909).

The House recedes.

Modifications to the requirements process (sec. 925)

The Senate bill contained a provision (sec. 943) that would amend Section 181 of title 10, United States Code, to clarify and modify the joint and service-specific requirements process. This provision would ensure that the service chief of the relevant military service is responsible for all service-specific requirements, and Joint Requirements Oversight Council (JROC) validation is not required before commencing a service-specific acquisition program, except for a major defense acquisition program or a service-specific program designated for JROC oversight by the Chairman of the Joint Chiefs of Staff. Additionally, this provision would require the Chairman to determine whether a major defense acquisition program meets joint requirements before the program or subprogram receives Milestone A approval or is otherwise initiated prior to Milestone B. The provision also would make the Vice Chairman of the Joint Chiefs of Staff the principal adviser to the Chairman on requirements.

The House amendment contained no similar provision.

The House recedes with an amendment that would modify the responsibilities of the JROC to focus on critical joint warfighting needs by: (1) determining gaps in joint military capabilities; (2) validating that proposed capabilities fulfill a gap; and (3) approving only joint performance requirements, such as interoperability or those involving more than one military service. The amendment would retain language from section 181 of title 10, United States Code, to clarify that the mission of the JROC shall include other matters assigned to it by the President or Secretary of Defense, and that the Chairman of the Joint Chiefs of Staff shall appoint members to the JROC who are recommended by the Secretaries of the military departments. The amendment would retain the Under Secretary of Defense (Comptroller) as an advisor to the JROC and broaden the base of analytic support that shall assist the JROC to include organizations within the Department that have operations research, systems analysis, and cost estimation expertise. The amendment also would modify definitions of joint military capabilities and performance requirements.

The amendment also would provide the JROC with authority to review performance requirements for other proposed or existing capabilities that the Chairman determines should be reviewed by the JROC. The conferees expect that this authority would be used only in limited situations, such as the review of proposed capabilities that may affect the joint force or an existing materiel capability solution that may no longer satisfy a previously identified gap. This authority should not supersede any other existing statutory or regulatory authority that pertains to the review and approval of requirements by other entities, such as the Missile Defense Agency or the authority to validate requirements provided to the Special Operations Command in Section 167 of title 10, United States Code.

Additionally, the amendment requires that the Secretary of Defense establish an investment review process, to be co-chaired by the Deputy Secretary of Defense and the Vice Chairman of the Joint Chiefs of Staff, to establish cost and fielding targets for new programs pursuant to section 2448a of this Act. To support establishment of cost and fielding targets, the amendment transfers from the JROC to the new investment review process the review of trade-offs among life-cycle cost, schedule, and performance objectives. The conferees direct the Secretary to develop a plan for implementing this investment review process and to brief the defense committees on the elements of the plan no later than 6 months after enactment of the Act. In developing the plan, the conferees direct the Secretary to evaluate the Department's Analysis of Alternatives process for determining trade-offs and weapon system solutions in acquisition programs.

Assessments of combatant command structure (sec. 926)

The Senate bill contained a provision (sec. 924) that would direct the Secretary of Defense to initiate a pilot program on the organization of a unified combatant command by organizing the subordinate commands of such unified combatant command in the form of joint task forces.

The House amendment contained a similar provision (sec. 914) that would require the Secretary of Defense to enter into a contract with an independent entity to conduct an assessment on the combatant command structure and to provide recommendations for improving the overall effectiveness of combatant command structures.

The Senate recedes with an amendment clarifying that the Secretary of Defense shall conduct an assessment of the organization of the combatant commands and provide recommendations for changes to improve the effectiveness of such commands as well as enter into a contract for an independent assessment of the organization of the combatant commands.

The conferees expect the assessments to address any deficiencies in the current organization of the combatant commands; to review the growth in the size of staffs of the unified combatant commands and whether such growth inhibits an effective and efficient performance; to determine whether the combatant commands are best aligned to address persistent, trans-regional, cross-functional, and multi-domain threats; and to assess whether the current structure encourages the unified combatant commands to be overly focused on mission support activities and not sufficiently focused on operational missions of the combatant commands.

Subtitle D—Organization and Management of Other Department of Defense Offices and Elements

Qualifications for appointment of the Secretaries of the military departments (sec. 931)

The Senate bill contained a provision (sec. 902) that would amend sections 3013, 5013, 8013 of title 10, United States Code, to prescribe management experience of large and complex organizations as qualification required for individuals to serve as the Secretaries of the Army, Navy, and Air Force, respectively.

The House amendment contained no similar provision.

The House recedes with an amendment that would establish that service secretaries shall, to the greatest extent practicable, be appointed from among persons most highly qualified for the position by reason of background and experience, including persons with appropriate management or leadership experience.

Enhanced personnel management authorities for the Chief of the National Guard Bureau (sec. 932)

The Senate bill contained a provision (sec. 944) that would amend section 1058 of title 10, United States Code, to enhance the personnel management authority of the Chief of the National Guard Bureau by authorizing the Chief to program for, appoint, employ, administer, detail, and assign federal civilian employees to provide full-time support to the non-federalized National Guard. This provision clarifies that state adjutants general will continue to exercise their authority to hire, employ, and supervise the federal civilian employees providing full-time support to their state.

The House amendment contained no similar provision.

The House recedes.

Reorganization and redesignation of Office of Family Policy and Office of Community Support for Military Families with Special Needs (sec. 933)

The Senate bill contained a provision (sec. 947) that would amend sections 1781 (a) and 1781 (c) of title 10, United States Code, to reorganize and redesignate the Office of Family Policy into the Office of Military Family Readiness Policy and the Office of Community Support for Military Families with Special Needs into the Office of Special Needs. The provision would reorganize the Office of Special Needs under the Office of Military Family Readiness Policy. The provision would also require the director of the Office of Military Family Readiness Policy to be a member of the Senior Executive Service or a general or flag officer.

The House amendment contained no similar provision.

The House recedes with an amendment that would repeal the requirement for the head of the office to be a member of the Senior Executive Service or a general or flag officer.

Redesignation of Assistant Secretary of the Air Force for Acquisition as Assistant Secretary of the Air Force for Acquisition, Technology, and Logistics (sec. 934)

The Senate bill contained a provision (sec. 949) that would amend section 8016(b)(4) (A) of title 10, United States Code, to redesignate the title of "Assistant Secretary of the Air Force for Acquisition" to read "Assistant Secretary of the Air Force for Acquisition, Technology, and Logistics" in this and all other laws.

The House amendment contained no similar provision.

The House recedes.

Subtitle E—Strategies, Reports, and Related Matters

National Defense Strategy (sec. 941)

The Senate bill contained a provision (sec. 1096) that would require the Secretary of Defense to provide the congressional defense committees a national defense strategy that addresses the highest priority missions for the Department of Defense, the most critical and enduring threats to the national security of the United States and its allies, and the strategies that the Department will use to counter those threats.

The House amendment contained a similar provision (sec. 904).

The House recedes with amendments clarifying the form and frequency of the national defense strategy and making other technical changes.

Commission on the National Defense Strategy for the United States (sec. 942)

The House amendment contained a provision (sec. 903) that would establish a commission to be known as the "Commission on the National Defense Strategy for the United States" to examine and make recommendations with respect to national defense strategy for the United States.

The Senate bill contained a similar provision (sec. 1078).

The Senate recedes with amendments addressing threat assessments and force structure and making other technical changes.

The commission would replace the National Defense Panel and precede the development of the National Defense Strategy, required elsewhere in this Act. The conferees believe that such an independent effort to provide recommendations and identify key issues and areas of focus, would improve the Secretary's development of strategy. Furthermore, the conferees believe that such a bipartisan effort could help build national consensus on how to address complex and challenging national security issues.

Reform of the national military strategy (sec. 943)

The Senate bill contained a provision (sec. 921(c)) that would revise the requirements of the national military strategy.

The House amendment contained a similar provision (sec. 905).

The Senate recedes with technical amendments that include language from the Senate provision.

Form of annual national security strategy report (sec. 944)

The Senate bill contained a provision (Sec. 1090) that would amend Section 108(c) of the National Security Act of 1947 (50 U.S.C. 3043(c)) by requiring the national security strategy report to be delivered in classified form, but it may include an unclassified summary.

The House amendment contained no similar provision.

The Senate recedes with technical amendment that clarifies the report should be delivered to Congress.

Modification to independent study of national security strategy formulation process (sec. 945)

The House amendment contained a provision (sec. 906) that would amend section 1064 of the National Defense Authorization Act for Fiscal Year 2016 (Public Law 114–92), which requires an independent study of the national security strategy formulation process, by adding a requirement for the study to address the workforce responsible for conducting strategic planning and to examine how Congress fits into the strategy formulation process.

The Senate bill contained no similar provision.

The Senate recedes.

Subtitle F—Other Matters

Enhanced security programs for Department of Defense personnel and innovation initiatives (sec. 951)

The Senate bill contained a provision (sec. 973) that would require the Secretary of Defense to take actions to allow the Defense Security Service to conduct before October 1, 2017, all personnel background and security investigations adjudicated by the Consolidated Adjudication Facility of the Department of Defense. This provision would also strengthen insider threat detection programs by streamlining requirements for the collection, storage, and retention of information and would allow the Department to seek solutions from commercial companies and improve the process for the reciprocity of security clearances.

The House amendment contained a similar provision (sec. 215) that would require the Secretary of Defense to develop and sustain a new security clearance information technology architecture to replace the legacy system of the Office of Personnel Management. Further, this section would require the Secretary of Defense, Director of National Intelligence, and Director of the Office of Personnel Management to issue a governance charter to delineate responsibilities between organizations, as well as to review and revise as necessary the executive orders, statutes, and other authorities related to personnel security. This section would also require quarterly notifications to designated congressional committees until September 30, 2019.

The House recedes with an amendment that would require the Department to prepare a plan to potentially transfer personal background and security clearance investigations back to the Department of Defense, include requirements for developing the information technology systems to support background investigations, and provide authority to waive some statutory deadlines related to the timelines for background investigations.

Modification of authority of the Secretary of Defense relating to protection of the Pentagon Reservation and other Department of Defense facilities in the National Capital Region (sec. 952)

The Senate bill contained a provision (S. 972) that would amend section 2674 of title 10, United States Code, to update the authority of the Secretary of Defense to appoint law enforcement personnel to protect the Pentagon reservation and Department of Defense activities in the National Capital Region, and to set the rates of basic pay for law enforcement and security personnel whose permanent duty station is the Pentagon reservation.

The House amendment contained no similar provision.

The House recedes.

Modifications to requirements for accounting for members of the Armed Forces and Department of Defense civilian employees listed as missing (sec. 953)

The Senate bill contained a provision (sec. 971) that would amend sections 1501, 1505, and 1513 of title 10, United States Code, to elevate oversight of recovery policy and operations for current conflicts from the Defense POW/MIA Accounting Agency (DPAA) to the Secretary of Defense, and to clarify that the DPAA director retains authority to establish policy and execute recovery operations for missing persons from past conflicts. In addition, this provision would clarify that the Department is required to account for missing persons only to the extent practicable upon discovery of remains of missing personnel.

The House amendment contained a similar provision (sec. 925).

The Senate recedes.

Modifications to corrosion report (sec. 954)

The House amendment contained a provision (sec. 921) that would amend section 2228(e)

(1) of title 10, United States Code, to modify Department of Defense corrosion reporting requirements.

The Senate bill contained no similar provision.

The Senate recedes.

Legislative Provisions Not Adopted

Sense of Congress on Goldwater-Nichols Reform

The House amendment contained a provision (sec. 901) that would express the sense of Congress that certain principles should be adhered to in any reform of the Goldwater-Nichols Department of Defense Reorganization Act of 1986 (Public Law 99–433).

The Senate bill contained no similar provision.

The House recedes.

Authority to employ civilian faculty members at Joint Special Operations University

The House amendment contained a provisions (sec. 922) that would amend section 1595(c) of title 10, United States Code, to provide the Joint Special Operations University the flexibility to hire civilians as professors, instructors, and lecturers.

The Senate bill contained no similar provision.

The House recedes.

Public release by inspectors general of reports of misconduct

The House amendment contained a provision (sec. 924) that would amend sections 141, 3020, 5020, and 8020 of title 10, United States Code, to require the Department of Defense Inspector General and the service inspectors general to publicly release reports of administrative investigations that substantiate misconduct of members of the Senior Executive Service, schedule C employees, or commissioned officers in pay grade O–6 promotable and above.

The Senate bill contained no similar provision.

The House recedes.

The conferees believe the public is entitled to appropriate access to investigations that substantiate misconduct by senior officials of the Department of Defense and the military departments. The conferees note that the Department of Defense Inspector General's on-line FOIA Reading Room currently includes reports concerning those senior officials.

Redesignation of the Department of the Navy as the Department of the Navy and Marine Corps

The House amendment contained a provision (sec. 931) that would redesignate the Department of the Navy as the Department of the Navy and Marine Corps. The House amendment contained additional provisions (sections 932, 933, and 934) that would provide technical and conforming amendments to other provisions of the law consistent with the redesignation proposed under section 931.

The Senate bill contained no similar provision.

The House recedes.

Title X—General Provisions
Subtitle A—Financial Matters
General transfer authority (sec. 1001)

The Senate bill contained a provision (sec. 1001) that would allow the Secretary of Defense to transfer up to $4.0 billion of fiscal year 2017 funds authorized in division A of this Act to unforeseen higher priority needs in accordance with normal reprogramming procedures. Transfers of funds between military personnel authorizations would not be counted toward the dollar limitation in this provision.

The House amendment contained a similar provision (sec. 1001) that would allow the Secretary of Defense, with certain limitations, to make transfers between amounts authorized for fiscal year 2017 in division A of this Act. This section would limit the total amount transferred under this authority to $5.0 billion. This section would also require prompt notification to Congress of each transfer made.

The Senate recedes with an amendment that would allow the Secretary of Defense to transfer up to $4.5 billion of fiscal year 2017 funds authorized in division A of this Act to unforeseen higher priority needs in accordance with normal reprogramming procedures.

Report on auditable financial statements (sec. 1002)

The House amendment contained a provision that would require the Secretary of Defense to submit to the congressional defense committees, not later than 30 days after enactment, a report ranking all military departments and Defense Agencies in order of how advanced they are in achieving auditable financial statements as required by law.

The Senate bill contained no similar provision.

The Senate recedes with an amendment that would change the deadline for the report to 90 days after enactment.

Increased use of commercial data integration and analysis products for the purpose of preparing financial statement audits (sec. 1003)

The Senate bill contained a provision that would require the Department of Defense to procure information technology services, data analysis, and data integration platforms to improve the preparation of Department of Defense financial statements.

The House amendment contained no similar provision.

The House recedes with a clarifying amendment.

Sense of Congress on sequestration (sec. 1004)

The Senate bill contained a provision (sec. 1003) that would express the sense of the Senate that the statutory budget caps imposed by the Budget Control Act of 2011 (BCA) remain an unreasonable and inadequate budgeting tool to address the Nation's fiscal challenges. The Senate remains concerned about the harmful impacts of sequestration on our national defense, to include non-defense agencies that contribute to our national security. This provision acknowledges that relief from the BCA should include both defense and non-defense spending.

The House amendment contained no similar provision.

The House recedes with an amendment that would express the sense of the congress that sequestration is an unreasonable and inadequate budgeting tool, imposes unacceptable limitations on the budget and increased risk to national security, and that the caps in the budget control act should be modified through a bipartisan legislative agreement.

Requirement to transfer funds from Department of Defense Acquisition Workforce Development Fund to the Treasury (sec. 1005)

The House amendment contained a provision (sec. 1002) that would reduce the unobligated balance of the Defense Acquisition

Workforce Development Fund by $475.0 million due to excess funds.

The Senate bill contained no similar provision.

The Senate recedes.

Subtitle B—Counter–Drug Activities

Codification and modification of authority to provide support for counter-drug activities and activities to counter transnational organized crime of civilian law enforcement agencies (sec. 1011)

The Senate bill contained a provision (sec. 1006) that would establish a new section in title 10, United States Code, to codify section 1004 of the National Defense Authorization Act for Fiscal Year 1991 (Public Law 101–510), as most recently amended by section 1012 of the Carl Levin and Howard P. 'Buck' McKeon National Defense Authorization Act for Fiscal Year 2015 (Public Law 113–291). The provision would also make modifications to the types of support that may be provided with respect to foreign law enforcement.

The House amendment contained no similar provision.

The House recedes with an amendment that would codify and make modifications to the authority of the Department of Defense to provide support for counter-drug activities and activities to counter transnational organized crime of civilian law enforcement agencies. The provision would also require coordination with the Secretary of State for support for foreign law enforcement agencies under the authority.

The conferees are concerned about the threat posed by the production and trafficking of heroin, fentanyl (and precursor chemicals), and other illicit drugs. Consistent with the Department's authorities and missions, the conferees direct the Department to ensure appropriate resources are allocated to efforts to combat this threat.

Secretary of Defense review of curricula and program structures of National Guard counterdrug schools (sec. 1012)

The House amendment contained a provision (sec. 1012) that would amend section 901 of the Office of National Drug Control Policy Reauthorization Act of 2006 (Public Law 109–469) to authorize the Secretary of Defense to review and approve the curriculum and program structure of each of the National Guard counterdrug schools.

The Senate bill contained no similar provision.

The Senate recedes with a clarifying amendment.

The conferees note the importance of the National Guard counterdrug schools in the development, training, and maintenance of skills for Federal, State, local, and foreign government officials to combat illicit trafficking. The committee supports increased oversight of these schools by the Secretary to improve the alignment of curriculum to defense priorities and the allocation of limited resources.

Extension of authority to support unified counterdrug and counterterrorism campaign in Colombia (sec. 1013)

The Senate bill contained a provision (sec. 1007) that would extend by 4 years the authority to support the unified counterdrug and counterterrorism campaign in the Republic of Colombia originally authorized by section 1021 of the Ronald W. Reagan National Defense Authorization Act for Fiscal Year 2005 (Public Law 108–375), and most recently amended by section 1011 of the National Defense Authorization Act for Fiscal Year 2016 (Public Law 114–92).

The House amendment contained a similar provision (sec. 1013) that would extend by 1

year the authority to support the unified counterdrug and counterterrorism campaign in the Republic of Colombia authorized by section 1021 of the Ronald W. Reagan National Defense Authorization Act for Fiscal Year 2005 (Public Law 108–375), and most recently amended by section 1011 of the National Defense Authorization Act for Fiscal Year 2016 (Public Law 114–92).

The House recedes with an amendment that would extend the authority for 2 years.

The conferees strongly support the vital partnership between the United States and Colombia and note the remarkable security gains the Government of Colombia has achieved over the last 15 years. The conferees believe that an enduring security relationship between the U.S. and Colombia is essential to sustaining and building upon these gains and urge the Department of Defense, in coordination with the interagency, to ensure its security cooperation programs and authorities reflect the evolving security environment in Colombia and the region.

Enhancement of information sharing and coordination of military training between Department of Homeland Security and Department of Defense (sec. 1014)

The Senate bill contained a provision (sec. 1051) that would require the Secretary of Homeland Security to ensure that the information needs of the Department of Homeland Security (DHS) relating to civilian law enforcement activities in proximity to the borders of the United States are identified and communicated to the Secretary of Defense for the purposes of planning and executing military training. The provision would require the Secretary of Defense to ensure that such military training conducted in proximity to the borders of the U.S. is coordinated with DHS. Further, the provision would require the Secretary of Homeland Security and the Secretary of Defense to create joint guidance to ensure information relevant to drug interdiction or other civilian law enforcement matters that is collected by the U.S. military during the normal course of military training or operations is provided promptly to civilian law enforcement officials in accordance with section 371 of title 10, United States Code.

The House amendment contained a similar provision (sec. 1014) that would require the Secretary of Defense to coordinate unmanned aerial systems training missions along the southern border of the United States in order to support the Department of Homeland Security's counter-narcotic trafficking efforts.

The House recedes with a technical amendment.

Subtitle C—Naval Vessels and Shipyards

Definition of short-term work with respect to overhaul, repair, or maintenance of naval vessels (sec. 1021)

The House amendment contained a provision (sec. 1021) that would amend section 7299a of title 10, United States Code, and expand the homeport limitation of an overhaul, repair, or maintenance ship availability from six months to ten months.

The Senate bill contained no similar provision.

The Senate recedes.

Warranty requirements for shipbuilding contracts (sec. 1022)

The House amendment contained a provision (sec. 1022) that would require shipbuilding contracts to include warranty of work for a period of at least 1 year. A contracting officer may waive this requirement if a limited liability of warranted work is in the best interest of the government.

The Senate bill contained no similar provision.

The Senate recedes with an amendment that would limit this provision to new construction contracts in the Shipbuilding and Conversion, Navy account, as well as establish the effective date of this provision as the date of the enactment of the National Defense Authorization for Fiscal Year 2018 or September 30, 2017, whichever occurs later.

The conferees direct the Secretary of the Navy to submit two reports to the congressional defense committees:

(1) A report describing the status of the Department of the Navy policy being developed to implement this provision shall be submitted not later than March 30, 2017; and

(2) A report describing the final or draft Department of the Navy policy to implement this provision shall be submitted not later than June 30, 2017.

National Sea-Based Deterrence Fund (sec. 1023)

The House amendment contained a provision (sec. 1023) that would:

(1) Expand the Fund's transfer authority provided by section 1022(b)(1) of the National Defense Authorization Act for Fiscal Year 2015 (Public Law 113–291) to include fiscal year 2018;

(2) Amend section 2218a of title 10, United States Code, relating to the National Sea-Based Deterrence Fund to include authority for multiyear procurement of critical components to support continuous production;

(3) Clarify the definition of a national sea-based deterrence vessel.

The Senate bill contained no similar provision.

The Senate recedes with an amendment that would delete the transfer authority expansion and limit the use of multiyear procurement authority to that needed to support continuous production of the common missile compartment.

The conferees expect the Navy to continue reviewing production approaches for the *Ohio* Replacement Program to achieve additional efficiencies. The conferees would be willing to consider expanding multiyear production authority if the Navy is able to demonstrate savings or greater efficiencies could be achievable through such use.

Availability of funds for retirement or inactivation of Ticonderoga-class cruisers or dock landing ships (sec. 1024)

The House amendment contained a provision (sec. 1024) that would prohibit the Secretary of the Navy from using funds authorized to be appropriated by this Act to retire a cruiser or dock landing ship or to place in a modernization status more than six cruisers and one dock landing ship. Furthermore, the Secretary of Defense would be prohibited from obligating more than 75 percent of the funds made available for the Office of the Secretary of Defense until the Secretary of the Navy enters into a contract for the modernization of four cruisers and one dock landing ship and enters into a contract for the procurement of combat systems upgrades associated with six such cruisers.

The Senate bill contained a similar provision (sec. 1011).

The Senate recedes with an amendment that would prohibit the retirement, preparation for retirement, inactivation, or placement in storage of any *Ticonderoga*-class cruisers or *Whidbey Island*-class amphibious ships, except to allow the modernization and upgrades for those ships to continue in accordance with section 1026 of the Carl Levin and Howard P. "Buck" McKeon National Defense Authorization Act for Fiscal Year 2015 (Public Law 113—291).

The conferees continue to support a cruiser modernization plan consistent with the "2-4-6" plan that allows the Secretary of the Navy to induct two cruisers per year into a modernization period of up to four years with no more than six cruisers in this prolonged modernization status at any one time.

Subtitle D—Counterterrorism

Frequency of counterterrorism operations briefings (sec. 1031)

The House amendment contained a provision (sec. 1031) that would amend section 485 of title 10, United States Code, to require the Secretary of Defense to provide monthly counterterrorism operations briefings to the congressional defense committees.

The Senate bill contained no similar provision.

The Senate recedes.

Prohibition on use of funds for transfer or release of individuals detained at United States Naval Station, Guantanamo Bay, Cuba to the United States (sec. 1032)

The Senate bill contained a provision (sec. 1021) that would extend until December 31, 2017, the prohibition on the use of funds provided to the Department of Defense to transfer or release individuals detained at United States Naval Station, Guantanamo Bay, Cuba, to the United States.

The House amendment contained a similar provision (sec. 1032).

The Senate recedes.

Prohibition on use of funds to construct or modify facilities in the United States to house detainees transferred from United States Naval Station, Guantanamo Bay, Cuba (sec. 1033)

The Senate bill contained a provision (sec. 1022) that would extend until December 31, 2017, the prohibition on the use of funds provided to the Department of Defense to construct or modify facilities in the United States to house detainees transferred from United States Naval Station, Guantanamo Bay, Cuba.

The House amendment contained a similar provision (sec. 1033).

The Senate recedes.

Prohibition on use of funds for transfer or release to certain countries of individuals detained at United States Naval Station, Guantanamo Bay, Cuba (sec. 1034)

The Senate bill contained a provision (sec. 1026) that would extend until December 31, 2017, the prohibition on the use of funds provided to the Department of Defense to transfer or release individuals detained at United States Naval Station, Guantanamo Bay, Cuba, to Libya, Somalia, Syria, or Yemen.

The House amendment contained a similar provision (sec. 1034).

The Senate recedes.

Prohibition on use of funds for realignment of forces at or closure of United States Naval Station, Guantanamo Bay, Cuba. (sec. 1035)

The Senate bill contained a provision (sec. 1030) that would extend until December 31, 2017, the prohibition on the use of funds to close or abandon United States Naval Station, Guantanamo Bay, Cuba, to relinquish control of Guantanamo Bay to the Republic of Cuba, or to implement a material modification to the Treaty between the United States of America and Cuba signed at Washington, D.C. on May 29, 1934, that constructively closes United States Naval Station, Guantanamo Bay.

The House amendment contained a similar provision (sec. 1035).

The Senate recedes.

Subtitle E—Miscellaneous Authorities and Limitations

Expanded authority for transportation by the Department of Defense of non-Department of Defense personnel and cargo (sec. 1041)

The House amendment contained a provision (sec. 1041) that would amend section 2649 of title 10, United States Code, to expand the authority for transportation by the Department of Defense of non-Department of Defense personnel and cargo as well as allowing the Secretary of Defense the ability to enter into a contract or other arrangement with one or more commercial providers to make insurance products available to non-Department of Defense shippers using the Defense Transportation System to insure against the loss or damage of the shipper's cargo.

The Senate bill contained no similar provision.

The Senate recedes.

Reduction in minimum number of Navy carrier air wings and carrier air wing headquarters required to be maintained (sec. 1042)

The Senate bill contained a provision (sec. 1088) that would amend section 5062 of title 10, United States Code, to reduce the number of air wings required to be maintained and fully staffed from 10 to 9.

The House amendment contained a similar provision (sec. 1072) that would require the Secretary of Defense to submit a report to Congress on the impact of changes to the existing carrier air wing force structure.

The House recedes with an amendment that would reduce the minimum number of carrier air wings to be maintained to nine until additional deployable aircraft carriers can fully support a tenth carrier air wing, or October 1, 2025, whichever comes first, at which time the Secretary of the Navy shall maintain a minimum of ten carrier air wings.

Modification to support for non-Federal development and testing of material for chemical agent defense (sec. 1043)

The House amendment contained a provision (sec. 1082) that would modify subsection (d) and subsection (e) of section 1034 of the National Defense Authorization Act for Fiscal Year 2008 (Public Law 110–181), to modify and extend, with a sunset date of January 31, 2021, the "Support for Non-Federal Development and Testing of Material for Chemical Agent Defense" report to include reporting on any instance where the Department provides biological select agents or toxins to a non-Federal entity for development of biological defenses. This amendment would supersede section 1080 of the Defense Authorization Act for Fiscal Year 2016 (Public Law 114–92).

The Senate bill contained no similar provision.

The Senate recedes.

Protection of certain Federal spectrum operations (sec. 1044)

The House amendment contained a provision (sec. 1045) that would amend section 1004 of the Bipartisan Budget Act of 2015 (Public Law 114–74; 47 U.S.C. 921 note) by adding protections of certain Federal spectrum operations.

The Senate bill contained no similar provision.

The Senate recedes.

Prohibition on use of funds for retirement of legacy maritime mine countermeasures platforms (sec. 1045)

The Senate bill contained a provision (sec. 1012) that would prohibit funds from being used to retire, prepare to retire, transfer, or place in storage any *Avenger*-class mine countermeasures ship, MH–53 *Sea Dragon* helicopter, or associated equipment, as well as make any reductions to the manning levels of any *Avenger*-class mine countermeasures ship or *Sea Dragon* squadron or detachment. The Secretary of the Navy may waive this prohibition by making the prescribed certification to the congressional defense committees.

The House amendment contained a similar provision (sec. 1042).

The House recedes.

Extension of authority of Secretary of Transportation to issue non-premium aviation insurance (sec. 1046)

The House amendment contained a provision (sec. 1043) that would amend Section 44310(b) of title 49, United States Code, to extend the authority of the Secretary of Transportation to provide aviation insurance and reinsurance upon the request of another U.S. Government agency.

The Senate bill contained no similar provision.

The Senate recedes.

Evaluation of Navy alternate combination cover and unisex combination cover (sec. 1047)

The House amendment contained a provision (sec. 1044) that would change the Department of the Navy's mandatory wear date of the alternate combination cover from October 31, 2016, to October 31, 2020, and prohibit the Secretary of the Navy from implementing any future changes or enforce any current changes to female service dress uniforms until the Secretary submits a report to the Committees on Armed Services of the Senate and House of Representatives on the evaluation of the Navy female service dress uniform.

The Senate bill contained no similar provision.

The Senate recedes with a technical amendment that would remove the prohibition on the Secretary of the Navy to make changes to uniforms, lower the delayed implementation of existing changes from five to three years, and add a requirement for the Secretary of the Navy to submit a report to the Committees on Armed Services of the Senate and House of Representatives no later than February 1, 2017, on the survey results regarding the new covers or any other uniform changes.

Independent evaluation of Department of Defense excess property program (sec. 1048)

The Senate bill contained a provision (sec. 1053) that would amend section 2576a of title 10, United States Code to modify the availability of defense items eligible for transfer and notification requirements.

The House amendment contained a similar provision (sec. 1049) that would amend section 2576a of title 10, United States Code to modify the preference for certain purposes for the transfer of excess Department of Defense equipment to Federal and State agencies.

The House recedes with an amendment that would require the Secretary of Defense to enter into an agreement with a federally funded research and development center, or another independent entity, with relevant expertise to conduct an evaluation of the Department of Defense excess property program under section 2576a of title 10, United States Code.

The conferees note that section 1051 of the National Defense Authorization Act for Fiscal Year 2016 (Public Law 114–92) required the Secretary of Defense to enter into an agreement with a federally funded research and development center for the conduct of an assessment of the excess property program, to include an evaluation of the policies and controls governing the determination of the suitability of recipients of controlled property transferred under the program and an analysis of reported statistics on controlled property transfers, and other related matters.

The conferees intend for the evaluation required in this Act to be part of an ongoing review of the Department of Defense excess property program.

Waiver of certain polygraph examination requirements (sec. 1049)

The House amendment contained a provision (sec. 1097) that would authorize the Commissioner of U.S. Customs and Border Protection to waive polygraph examination requirements for certain veterans.

The Senate bill contained no similar provision.

The Senate recedes.

Use of transportation worker identification credential to gain access at Department of Defense installations (sec. 1050)

The House amendment contained a provision (sec. 1098) that would require the Secretary of Defense, to the maximum extent practicable, to ensure that the Transportation Worker Identification Credential (TWIC) be accepted as a valid credential for unescorted access to Department of Defense installations by transportation workers. The provision would also exempt TWIC-carrying transportation workers with a current secret clearance issued by the Department of Defense from further vetting when seeking unescorted access to Department of Defense facilities provided that installation access personnel shall verify the person's security clearance in a timely manner. The provision would also require the Secretary of Defense to document and report each instance when a TWIC-carrying transportation worker is denied access to a military installation in designated locations, together with a reason for such denial, and the amount of time the TWIC-carrying person was required to wait for access. The report would be required not later than 90 days after enactment of this Act and annually until the Department completes fielding of Identity Management Enterprise Services Architecture and electronic access control systems are fielded.

The Senate bill included no similar provision.

The Senate recedes with an amendment that does not include the reporting requirement in the House amendment.

Limitation on availability of funds for destruction of certain landmines and briefing on development of replacement anti-personnel landmine munitions (sec. 1051)

The House amendment contained a provision that would limit the funds available for the destruction of anti-personnel landmine munitions until the Secretary of Defense submits to Congress a report on the assessment of the current state of research into operational alternatives to anti-personnel landmines.

The Senate bill contained no similar provision.

The Senate recedes with an amendment that would limit the funds available for the destruction of anti-personnel landmines until the Secretary of Defense submits to Congress the report required by section 1058 of the National Defense Authorization Act for Fiscal Year 2016 (Public Law 114–92), instead of a new report. The amendment would also require a briefing on the current state of

research and development into operational alternatives to anti-personnel landmines.

Transition of Air Force to operation of remotely piloted aircraft by enlisted personnel (sec. 1052)

The Senate bill contained a provision (Sec. 1046) that would require the Air Force, by September 30, 2019, to transition all remotely piloted aircraft (RPA) operations to an organizational model that uses enlisted personnel for the preponderance of RPA operators.

The House amendment contained no similar provision.

The House recedes with an amendment that changes "preponderance" to "a significant number of enlisted personnel," changes the required transition date to September 30, 2020, for the active duty component, and adds September 30, 2023, as the required date for transition by the Air Force Reserve and Air National Guard. The amendment also includes other minor technical corrections.

Prohibition on divestment of Marine Corps Search and Rescue Units (sec. 1053)

The Senate bill contained a provision (sec. 1047) that does not authorize appropriated amounts to retire, prepare to retire, transfer or place in storage any Marine Corps Search and Rescue Unit or to make any changes to manning levels to the same.

The House amendment contained no similar provision.

The House recedes.

Support for the Associate Director of Central Intelligence for Military Affairs (sec. 1054)

The Senate bill contained a provision (sec. 1049) that would direct the Secretary of Defense and the Under Secretary of Defense for Intelligence to ensure that the Associate Director for Military Affairs of the Central Intelligence Agency (ADMA) has access to, and support from, offices, agencies, and programs of the Department necessary for the ADMA to achieve its intended function.

The House amendment contained no similar provision.

The House recedes with amendments that clarify that the intent of the provision is to encourage effective use of the position, and to remove a requirement that any officer nominated to the position have significant interaction with the CIA within the five years prior to appointment. The conferees learned that such a requirement might impede—rather than encourage—nominees from outside of the special operations community. Therefore, the conferees believe that the relationship between the CIA and the Department's conventional forces should be encouraged, especially given the evolving and complex global threats faced by the United States.

Notification on the provision of defense sensitive support (sec. 1055)

The Senate bill contained a provision (sec. 1052) that would require the Secretary of Defense, prior to the provision of defense sensitive support to non-Department of Defense departments and agencies, to determine and notify the congressional defense committees that the support does not interfere with the mission and functions of the Department, or if it does so interfere, that it is in the national security interest of the United States.

The House amendment contained no similar provision.

The House recedes with a clarifying amendment.

Prohibition on enforcement of military commission rulings preventing members of the Armed Forces from carrying out otherwise lawful duties based on member sex (sec. 1056)

The Senate bill contained a provision (sec. 535) that would prohibit a military commission established under chapter 47A of title 10, United States Code, from acting by order, ruling, finding, or otherwise that a member of the Armed Forces may not perform duties otherwise lawfully assigned if the prohibition is based solely on the gender of the servicemember. The provision would also vacate any such order issued before the date of enactment of this Act.

The House amendment contained a similar provision (sec. 1039).

The House recedes with an amendment that would prohibit any order or other determination of a military commission that would restrict a member of the Armed Forces from carrying out otherwise lawfully assigned duties where the basis for such prohibition or restriction is the sex of the member. Upon enactment, the rule of prohibition established under this provision would apply to a military commission upon a motion to reconsider any such determination that was issued prior to enactment of this Act.

Congressional notification requirements for sensitive military operations (sec. 1057)

The Senate bill contained a provision (sec. 1044) that would amend section 130f in title 10, United States Code.

The House amendment contained a similar provision (sec. 1036).

The Senate recedes with clarifying amendment.

Subtitle F—Studies and Reports

Temporary continuation of certain Department of Defense reporting requirements (sec. 1061)

The Senate bill contained a provision (sec. 1082) that would repeal the requirements for several reports that are mandated by an annual National Defense Authorization Act and by other public laws.

The Senate bill also contained a provision (sec. 1083) that would repeal several requirements for the Department of Defense to provide reports that have been added by an annual National Defense Authorization Act.

The House amendment contained a similar provision (1061) that would repeal several reporting requirements as well.

The Senate recedes with an amendment that would provide for the repeal of those reporting requirements agreed to by both the House and Senate as listed in the final bill.

Reports on programs managed under alternative compensatory control measures in the Department of Defense (sec. 1062)

The Senate bill contained a provision (sec. 1080) that would require the Department of Defense (DOD) to provide certain reports and notifications regarding programs that DOD manages under alternative compensatory control measures (ACCM).

The House amendment contained no similar provision.

The House recedes.

The Department of Defense typically uses the ACCM system to manage programs of lesser sensitivity or programs with a less enduring life than the programs that it manages under special access (SAP) program channels. The conferees believe that DOD needs to provide more rigorous oversight of and reporting on ACCM programs to the congressional defense committees. Despite several directions from Congress to the DOD to produce better information and inventories of these programs, DOD has failed to do so. Therefore, the conferees see no alternative but to include legislation on the matter, and note that failure to use and report ACCMs accordingly will jeopardize future reauthorizations.

Matters for inclusion in report on designation of countries for which rewards may be paid under Department of Defense rewards program (sec. 1063)

The House amendment contained a provision (sec. 1062) that would modify section 127b(h) of title 10, United States Code, relating to the Department of Defense rewards program.

The Senate bill contained no similar provision.

The Senate recedes.

Annual reports on unfunded priorities of the Armed Forces and the combatant commands and annual report on combatant command requirements (sec. 1064)

The Senate bill contained a provision (sec. 1076) that would require the Chief of Staff of the Army, Chief of Naval Operations, Chief of Staff of the Air Force, Commandant of the Marine Corps, and commanders of the combatant commands (COCOM) to submit to the Secretary of Defense, Chairman of the Joint Chiefs of Staff, and congressional defense committees a report on the unfunded priorities no later than 25 days after the date on which the President submits the annual budget request.

The House amendment contained no similar provision.

The House recedes with a technical amendment that would change the due date for the report from 25 days to 10 days after the budget request is submitted to Congress and amends section 153(c)(1) of title 10, United States Code to require the Chairman of the Joint Chiefs of Staff to submit an annual report on COCOM requirements no later than 25 days after the date on which the President submits the budget request to Congress.

The conferees note that the COCOM commanders can satisfy the requirement regarding unfunded priorities, as set forth by this provision through their submission of the integrated priority lists (IPL), provided that the IPLs contain sufficient detail on the commands' requirements shortfalls and any relevant or appropriate funding recommendations.

Management and reviews of electromagnetic spectrum (sec. 1065)

The House amendment contained a provision (sec. 1068) that would direct the Secretary of Defense and the Chairman of the Joint Chiefs of Staff to conduct a comprehensive review of all uses by the Department of Defense of spectrum.

The Senate bill contained no similar provision.

The Senate recedes with an amendment that would amend 10 U.S.C. 488 by directing the Secretary of Defense to ensure the effective organization and management of electromagnetic spectrum used by the Department of Defense and establish an enduring review process that considers all requirements relating to such spectrum and ensures that all uses of such spectrum, regardless of the classification of such uses, are involved in the decision-making process of the Department concerning the potential sharing, reassigning, or relocating of such spectrum, of the relocation of the uses by the Department of such spectrum.

Requirement for notice and reporting to Committees on Armed Services of certain expenditures of funds by Defense Intelligence Agency (sec. 1066)

The Senate bill contained a provision (sec. 1081) that would add the Armed Services Committees of the Senate and the House of Representatives to a reporting requirement under 50 U.S.C. 3038(c) that allows the Defense Intelligence Agency to use a percentage of its funds without regard to the provisions of law or regulation relating to the expenditure of U.S. government funds.

The House amendment contained no similar provision.

The House recedes.

Congressional notification of biological select agent and toxin theft, loss, or release involving the Department of Defense (sec. 1067)

The House amendment contained a provision (sec. 1063) that would direct the Secretary of Defense to provide notification to the congressional defense committees within 15 days of notifying the Centers for Disease Control and Prevention and/or the Animal and Plant Health Inspection Service of any theft, loss, or release of biological select agents or toxins.

The Senate bill contained no similar provision.

The Senate recedes.

Report on service-provided support and enabling capabilities to United States special operations forces (sec. 1068)

The House amendment contained a provision (sec. 1064) that would require the Secretary of Defense to submit to the congressional defense committees not later than 180 days after enactment of this Act on support contributed from each of the military services towards special operations forces for each of the fiscal years 2018 through 2020.

The Senate bill contained no similar provision.

The Senate recedes with a clarifying amendment.

Report on citizen security responsibilities in the Northern Triangle of Central America (sec. 1069)

The House amendment contained a provision (sec. 1065) that would require the Secretary of Defense and the Secretary of State to jointly submit a report to specified congressional committees not later than 180 days after enactment of this Act on the military units that have been assigned to policing or citizen security responsibilities in the Republic of Guatemala, the Republic of Honduras, and the Republic of El Salvador.

The Senate bill contained no similar provision.

The Senate recedes.

Report on counterproliferation activities and programs (sec. 1070)

The House amendment contained a provision (sec. 1066) that would require the Secretary of Defense to submit to the congressional defense committees a report on the counterproliferation activities and programs of the Department of Defense.

The Senate bill contained no similar provision.

The Senate recedes with an amendment that would require a single report no later than July 1, 2017.

Report on testing and integration of minehunting sonar systems to improve Littoral Combat Ship minehunting capabilities (sec. 1071)

The House amendment contained a provision (sec. 1071) that would require a report on testing and integration of minehunting sonar systems to improve Littoral Combat Ship minehunting capabilities.

The Senate bill contained no similar provision.

The Senate recedes.

Quarterly reports on parachute jumps conducted at Fort Bragg and Pope Army Airfield and Air Force support for such jumps (sec. 1072)

The House amendment contained a provision (Sec. 1073) that would direct the Secretary of the Air Force and the Secretary of the Army to submit to the Committees on Armed Services of the House of Representatives and the Senate quarterly reports that contain information regarding parachute drop requirements for the XVIII Airborne Corps, the 82nd Airborne Division, and the United States Army Special Operations Command.

The Senate bill contained no similar provision.

The Senate recedes with an amendment that adjusts the end date of the reporting period and clarifies the elements required in the reports.

Study on military helicopter noise (sec. 1073)

The House amendment contained a provision (Sec. 1098D) that would require the Secretary of Defense, in coordination with the Administrator of the Federal Aviation Administration to conduct a study on the effects of and provide recommendations for the reduction of military helicopter noise on the National Capital Region.

The Senate bill contained no similar provision.

The Senate recedes.

Independent review of United States military strategy and force posture in the United States Pacific Command area of responsibility (sec. 1074)

The Senate bill contained a provision (sec. 1042) that would require an independent review of United States military strategy and force posture in the United States Pacific Command area of responsibility be submit to Congress beginning in 2018 and recurring every four years thereafter.

The House amendment contained no similar provision.

The House recedes with an amendment that would require one independent review to be completed by September 1, 2018.

Assessment of the joint ground forces of the Armed Forces (sec. 1075)

The Senate bill contained a provision (Sec. 1077) that would require the Secretary of Defense and Chairman of the Joint Chiefs of Staff to oversee a comprehensive assessment of the joint ground forces and provide a report on the assessment's findings no later than one year after the enactment of this act.

The House amendment contained no similar provision.

The House recedes with an amendment that would require the Secretary of Defense, in consultation with the Chairman of the Joint Chiefs of Staff, the Chief of Staff of the Army, and the Commandant of the Marine Corps, to oversee an assessment of the joint ground forces of the Armed Forces, and provide a report on the assessment's findings to the Committees on Armed Services of the Senate and the House of Representatives not later than one year after the enactment of this Act. The report shall include an assessment by the Chief of Staff of the Army and the Commandant of the Marine Corps of any specific gaps in the capability and capacity of the Army and Marine Corps, respectively, that threaten the successful execution of decisive operational maneuver.

Subtitle G—Other Matters

Technical and clerical amendments (sec. 1081)

The Senate bill contained a provision (sec. 1058) that would make technical and clerical corrections to title 10, United States Code, and various National Defense Authorization Acts.

The House amendment contained a similar provision (sec. 1081).

The Senate recedes with an amendment making additional technical and clerical amendments.

Increase in maximum amount available for equipment, services, and supplies provided for humanitarian demining assistance (sec. 1082)

The House amendment contained a provision (sec. 1083) that would raise the monetary cap in section 407 of title 10, United States Code, for the cost of equipment, services, and supplies for humanitarian demining assistance and stockpiled conventional munitions assistance provided by the Department of Defense, from $10.0 million to $15.0 million in any fiscal year.

The Senate bill contained no similar provision.

The Senate recedes.

Liquidation of unpaid credits accrued as a result of transactions under a cross-servicing agreement (sec. 1083)

The House amendment contained a provision (sec. 1084) that would amend section 2345 of title 10, United States Code, to provide the Secretary of Defense with the discretionary authority to liquidate unpaid debts owed to the United States by a foreign government or international organization as a result of the Department of Defense providing logistic support, supplies, or services to that foreign government or international organization.

The Senate bill contained no similar provision.

The Senate recedes.

Modification of requirements relating to management of military technicians (sec. 1084)

The House amendment contained a provision (sec. 1088) that would delay the implementation date of section 1053 of the National Defense Authorization Act for Fiscal Year 2016 (Public Law 114–92) until October 1, 2017 and align the date of conversion for military technicians (non-dual status) with military technicians (dual status).

The Senate bill contained a similar provision (sec. 1048).

The Senate recedes with an amendment that would clarify that the Secretary of Defense will continue to play a role in the conversion of positions.

Streamlining of the National Security Council (sec. 1085)

The Senate bill contained a provision (sec. 1089) that would streamline the statutory requirements for the National Security Council (NSC) and limit the size of the NSC's professional staff to 150, to include detailees and assignees from other agencies and Departments and contractors.

The House amendment contained a similar provision (sec. 926).

The House recedes with an amendment to increase the cap to 200 professional personnel, to include a transition period for the personnel cap of 18 months, and to make other technical changes.

National biodefense strategy (sec. 1086)

The House amendment contained a provision (sec. 1086) that would require the Sec-

retary of Defense, the Secretary of Health and Human Services, the Secretary of Homeland Security, and the Secretary of Agriculture to jointly develop and submit to the appropriate congressional committees, within 275 days after the date of the enactment of this Act, a national bio defense strategy and implementation plan. This section would also require the Secretary of Defense, the Secretary of Health and Human Services, the Secretary of Homeland Security, and the Secretary of Agriculture to provide a joint briefing to the appropriate congressional committees annually, starting March 1, 2017, and ending March 1, 2019, on the strategy and status of its implementation. This section would also require the Comptroller General of the United States to submit a report to the appropriate congressional committees, within 180 days of submission of the national biodefense strategy, on a gap analysis of the national biodefense strategy and its implementation plan.

The Senate bill contained no similar provision.

The Senate recedes.

Global Cultural Knowledge Network (sec. 1087)

The House amendment contained a provision (Sec. 1087) that would require the Secretary of the Army to support the socio-cultural understanding needs of the Department of the Army, to be known as the Global Cultural Knowledge Network.

The Senate bill contained no similar provision.

The Senate recedes with amendment.

Sense of Congress regarding Connecticut's Submarine Century (sec. 1088)

The House amendment contained a provision (sec. 1089) that would express the sense of Congress commending the dedication and contributions of the people of Connecticut to the Navy and the submarine force.

The Senate bill contained no similar provision.

The Senate recedes with a clarifying amendment.

Sense of Congress regarding the reporting of the MV–22 mishap in Marana, Arizona, on April 8, 2000 (sec. 1089)

The House amendment contained a provision (Sec. 1091) that would state that the Deputy Secretary of Defense did an excellent job reviewing the investigation of this mishap.

The Senate bill contained no similar provision.

The Senate recedes.

Cost of wars (sec. 1090)

The House amendment contained a provision (sec. 1098G) that would require the Secretary of Defense, in consultation with the Commissioner of the Internal Revenue Service and the Director of the Bureau of Economic Analysis, to post the costs, including legacy costs, to the American taxpayers of the wars in Afghanistan, Iraq, and Syria.

The Senate bill contained no similar provision.

The Senate recedes with an amendment that would remove the requirement to provide the legacy costs of the wars.

Reconnaissance Strike Group matters (sec. 1091)

The Senate bill contained a provision (sec. 1045) that would require the Secretary of Defense and Chairman of the Joint Chiefs of Staff to oversee the modeling of an alternative Army design and operational concept for the Reconnaissance Strike Group (RSG), and require a report no later than one year after the enactment of this Act that explicitly addresses the value of a follow-on pilot

program to test further any promising alternative force designs and concept of operation. The provision would also require the Secretary of Defense to direct an appropriate combatant commander to establish an office for the testing, evaluation, development and validation of the RSG's joint warfighting concepts, required platforms and structure.

The House amendment contained no similar provision.

The House recedes with an amendment that would require the Chairman of the Joint Chiefs of Staff and the Chief of Staff of the Army, in consultation with the Commanding General, U.S. European Command, to each conduct a separate analysis of RSG organizational design and operational concepts and provide a report to the Committees on Armed Services of the Senate and House of Representatives on the results of these analysis. The amendment would also require a Federally Funded Research and Development Center or 501(c)(3) to review and evaluate the reports.

Border security metrics (sec. 1092)

The Senate bill contained a provision (sec. 1091) that would require the Secretary of Homeland Security to develop metrics to measure the effectiveness of security at ports of entry, between ports of entry, and in the maritime environment not later than 120 days after the enactment of this Act.

The House amendment contained no similar provision.

The House recedes with a clarifying amendment.

Program to commemorate the 100th anniversary of the Tomb of the Unknown Soldier (sec. 1093)

The Senate bill contained a provision (sec. 1094) that would require the Secretary of Defense to conduct a program to commemorate the 100th anniversary of the Tomb of the Unknown Soldier.

The House amendment contained no similar provision.

The House recedes.

Sense of Congress regarding the OCONUS basing of the KC–46A aircraft (sec. 1094)

The Senate bill contained a provision (Sec. 1095) that would express the sense of the Congress regarding the basing of KC–46A tanker aircraft outside of the continental United States.

The House amendment contained no similar provision.

The House recedes.

Designation of a Department of Defense Strategic Arctic Port (sec. 1095)

The Senate bill contained a provision (sec. 1043) that would require not later than 180 days after enactment of this Act, the Secretary of Defense, in consultation with the Chairman of the Joint Chiefs of Staff, the Commanding General of the United States Army Corps of Engineers, the Commandant of the Coast Guard, and the Administrator of the Maritime Administration, to submit a report to the congressional defense committees assessing the future security requirements for one or more strategic ports in the Arctic. The provision would further require the Secretary to establish designation criteria for a Department of Defense "Strategic Arctic Port" and submit recommendations for the designation of one or more' such ports, including estimated costs for sufficient construction to initiate and sustain expected operations.

The House amendment contained no similar provision.

The House recedes with a technical amendment.

Recovery of Excess Rifles, Ammunition, and Parts Granted to Foreign Countries and Transfer to Certain Persons (sec. 1096)

The Senate bill contained a provision (sec. 1056) that would authorize the Secretary of the Army to acquire from any person any rifle, ammunition, repair parts, or other supplies provided to any country on a grant basis under the conditions imposed by section 505 of the Foreign Assistance Act of 1961 and have become excess to the needs of such country. The Secretary of the Army may not acquire items if the United States would incur any cost for such acquisition. Rifles, ammunition, repair parts, or supplies shall be available for transfer to persons who are licensed manufacturers, importers, or dealers pursuant to section 923(a) of title 18 or uses an Army ammunition depot.

The House amendment contained a similar provision (sec. 1098K)

The Senate recedes with an amendment that would allow the Secretary of the Army to recover items so long as the Army receives fair market value and the items are transferred in accordance with the Arms Export Control Act. The Secretary of the Army is directed to provide a report, not later than 180 days after the enactment of the Act, to the Committees on Armed Services of the Senate and House of Representatives, the Committee on Foreign Relations of the Senate, and the Committee on Foreign Affairs of the House of Representatives, on the acquisition and transfer of excess rifles, ammunition, repair parts, other supplies eligible for transfer.

LEGISLATIVE PROVISIONS NOT ADOPTED

Delegation to Chairman of Joint Chiefs of Staff of authority to direct transfer of forces

The Senate bill contained a provision (sec. 922) that would amend section 113 of title 10, United States Code, to allow the Secretary of Defense to delegate some authority to the Chairman of the Joint Chiefs of Staff for the worldwide reallocation of limited military assets on a short-term basis, consistent with the Secretary's policy guidance and the national defense strategy.

The House amendment contained no similar provision.

The Senate recedes.

Management of Defense clandestine human intelligence collection

The Senate bill contained a provision (sec. 945) that would require the Secretary of Defense, in coordination with the Director of National Intelligence, to carry out a pilot program to assess the feasibility and advisability of establishing a military division within the Directorate of Operations of the Central Intelligence Agency.

The House amendment contained no similar provision.

The Senate recedes.

Extension of authority to provide additional support for counter-drug activities of foreign governments

The House amendment contained a provision (sec. 1011) that would amend section 1033 of the National Defense Authorization Act for Fiscal Year 1998 (Public Law 105–85), as most recently amended by section 1012 of the National Defense Authorization Act for Fiscal Year 2016 (Public Law 114–92), by extending the authority to provide additional support for counter-drug activities of foreign governments to September 30, 2019.

The Senate bill contained no similar provision.

The House recedes.

The conferees note that elsewhere in this Act is a provision that would consolidate multiple authorities to build the capacity of friendly foreign nations to conduct specified operations, to include counter-drug and counter-transnational organized crime operations. The conferees intend for activities conducted to date under section 1033 of the National Defense Authorization Act for Fiscal Year 1998 (Public Law 105–85), as most recently amended by section 1012 of the National Defense Authorization Act for Fiscal Year 2016 (Public Law 114–92) to be conducted under the new building partnership capacity authority.

Funding for counter narcotics operations

The House amendment contained a provision (sec. 1015) that would increase the amount authorized to be appropriated for drug interdiction and counterdrug activities by $3 million.

The Senate bill contained no similar provision.

The House recedes.

Report on efforts of United States Southern Command to detect and monitor drug trafficking

The House amendment contained a provision (sec. 1016) that would require the Secretary of Defense to submit to Congress a report on the effectiveness of efforts by United States Southern Command to limit threats to the national security of the United States by detecting and monitoring drug trafficking, specifically heroin and fentanyl.

The Senate bill contained no similar provision.

The House recedes.

The conferees remain concerned about the trafficking of illicit drugs into the United States, particularly heroin and fentanyl, and the devastating impact these substances are having on communities. The conferees urge the Department of Defense, in coordination with the interagency, to continue efforts to combat the flow of drugs into the United States.

Prohibition on reprogramming requests for funds for transfer or release, or construction for transfer or release, of individuals detained at United States Naval Station, Guantanamo Bay, Cuba

The Senate bill contained a provision (sec. 1022A) that would prohibit the Department of Defense from submitting reprogramming requests to Congress for funds for transfer or release, or construction for transfer or release, of individuals detained at United States Naval Station, Guantanamo Bay, Cuba.

The House amendment contained no similar provision.

The Senate recedes.

Designing and planning related to construction of certain facilities in the United States

The Senate bill contained a provision (sec. 1023) that would authorize the Secretary of Defense to use amounts authorized to be appropriated for the Department of Defense for designing and planning related to the construction or modification of facilities in the United States to house individuals detained at United States Naval Station, Guantanamo Bay, Cuba.

The House amendment contained no similar provision.

The Senate recedes.

Authority to transfer individuals detained at United States Naval Station, Guantanamo Bay, Cuba, to the United States temporarily for emergency or critical medical treatment

The Senate bill contained a provision (sec. 1024) that would authorize the temporary transfer of individuals detained at United States Naval Station, Guantanamo Bay, Cuba to the United States for necessary medical treatment that is not available at Guantanamo.

The House amendment contained no similar provision.

The Senate recedes.

Authority for Article III judges to take certain actions relating to individuals detained at United States Naval Station, Guantanamo Bay, Cuba

The Senate bill contained a provision (sec. 1025) that would authorize a judge of the United States District Court to have jurisdiction to use video teleconferencing to arraign, accept a plea to a charge from, and enter a judgment of conviction and sentencing against individuals held at United States Naval Station, Guantanamo Bay, Cuba.

The House amendment contained no similar provision.

The Senate recedes.

Requirement for Memorandum of Understanding Regarding Transfer of Detainees

The Senate bill contained a provision (sec. 1027) that would require any certification by the Secretary of Defense provided pursuant to Section 1034(b) of the National Defense Authorization Act of Fiscal Year 2016 (Public Law 114–92; 10 U.S.C. 801 note) to include a requirement that the United States and the foreign government of transfer have entered into a written memorandum of understanding regarding the transfer of the individual and the memorandum of understanding has been provided to the appropriate congressional committees.

The House amendment contained a similar provision (sec. 1098B).

The conference agreement does not contain this provision.

Limitation on transfer of detainees at United States Naval Station, Guantanamo Bay, Cuba, pending a report on their terrorist actions and affiliations

The Senate bill contained a provision (sec. 1028) that would require, prior to transferring any individual detained at United States Naval Station, Guantanamo Bay, Cuba to any foreign government or entity, that the Secretary of Defense submit to appropriate committees of Congress a report on the individuals' previous terrorist activities.

The House amendment contained no similar provision.

The Senate recedes.

Prohibition on use of funds for transfer or release of individuals detained at United States Naval Station, Guantanamo Bay, Cuba, to countries covered by Department of State travel warnings

The Senate bill contained a provision (sec. 1029) that would prohibit the use of funds to transfer any individual held at United States Naval Station, Guantanamo Bay, Cuba, to a foreign country that is the subject of a State Department travel warning with certain exceptions.

The House amendment contained no similar provision.

The Senate recedes.

Restrictions on the overhaul and repair of vessels in foreign shipyards

The House amendment contained a provision (sec. 1025) that would amend section 7310(b)

(1) of title 10, United States Code, to prohibit the Department of the Navy from performing any overhaul, repair, or maintenance work that takes longer than six months in foreign shipyards.

The Senate bill contained no similar provision.

The House recedes.

Restrictions on use of rocket engines from the Russian Federation for space launch of national security satellites

The Senate bill contained a provision (sec. 1036) that would prohibit the Secretary of Defense from launching any national security satellite with a launch vehicle requiring a rocket engine designed or manufactured in the Russian Federation.

The House amendment contained no similar provision.

The Senate recedes.

Limitations on use of rocket engines from the Russian Federation to achieve assured access to space

The Senate bill contained a provision (sec. 1037) that would amend section 2273(b) of title 10, United States Code, to require that assured access to space be achieved without the use of rocket engines designed or manufactured in the Russian Federation.

The House amendment contained no similar provision.

The Senate recedes.

Transportation on military aircraft on a space-available basis for members and former members of the Armed Forces with disabilities rated as total

The House amendment contained a provision (sec. 1046) that would amend section 2641b of title 10, United States Code, to authorize space-available travel for disabled veterans with a service-connected, permanent disability rated as total by the Department of Defense.

The Senate bill contained no similar provision.

The House recedes.

The conferees direct the Secretary of Defense to submit to the Committees on Armed Services of the Senate and the House of Representatives, by not later than March 1, 2017, a report clarifying the retirement and benefit eligibility status of certain disabled veterans. The report will identify with particularity any differences in the "retired" status, or benefit eligibility status, for servicemembers who otherwise meet the current statutory standards for disability retirement, but who may not be retired owing to the timing of the enactment of disability retirement changes, particularly the enactment of sections 534 of the National Defense Authorization Act for Fiscal Year 1997 (Public Law 104–201) and 513 of the National Defense Authorization Act for Fiscal Year 1998 (Public Law 105–85) which redefined disability and retirement eligibility under section 1204 of title 10, United States Code. The conferees are aware that at least in some cases, veterans may have been separated for disability who now meet disability retirement eligibility.

The report shall describe all available processes or procedures by which a veteran who believes they should be designated as "retired" may seek redesignation by appeal to the boards for correction of military or naval records or through some other process. Finally, the Secretary of Defense will identify the number of individuals who may be eligible for redesignation under the processes or procedures so identified.

The conferees are committed to ensuring every veteran is afforded all the rights and benefits to which they are entitled under the law, especially those who are disabled with a service-connected, permanent disability.

National Guard flyovers of public events

The House amendment contained a provision (sec. 1047) that would prohibit all National Guard flyovers of public events in support of community relations activities unless flown as part of an approved training mission.

The Senate bill contained no similar provision.

The House recedes.

Application of Freedom of Information Act to the National Security Council

The House amendment contained a provision (sec. 1048) that would apply the Freedom of Information Act (5 U.S.C. 552) to the National Security Council in certain circumstances.

The Senate bill contained no similar provision.

The House recedes.

Exemption of information on military tactics, techniques, and procedures from release under Freedom of Information Act

The Senate bill contained a provision (sec. 1054) that would amend section 130e of title 10, United States Code, to authorize the Secretary of Defense to exempt information related to military tactics, techniques, and procedures from public disclosure if the information could reasonably be expected to risk impairment of the effective operation of the Department of Defense by providing an advantage to an adversary or potential adversary, and the public interest consideration in the disclosure of such information does not outweigh preventing the disclosure of such information.

The House amendment contained no similar provision.

The Senate recedes.

Annual report on personnel, training, and equipment requirements for the non-federalized National Guard to support civilian authorities in prevention and response to domestic disasters

The House amendment contained a provision (sec. 1069) that would modify the reporting requirement of section 10504 of title 10, United States Code, to include a report on non-federalized National Guard personnel, training, and equipment requirements.

The Senate bill contained no similar provision.

The House recedes.

Briefing on criteria for determining locations of Air Force Installation and Mission Support Center headquarters

The House amendment contained a provision (sec. 1070) that would require the Secretary of the Air Force to brief the congressional defense committees on the Air Force's process and reasoning for using proximity to primary medium commercial hub airports as part of the mission criteria for the Air Force Installation and Mission Support Center headquarters strategic basing process.

The Senate bill contained no similar provision.

The House recedes.

The conferees direct the Secretary of the Air Force to provide the congressional defense committees with a briefing by March 1, 2017 on the criteria used for determining locations of Air Force Installation and Mission Support Center headquarters, specifically the reasoning for using proximity to primary medium commercial hub airports as part of the mission criteria.

Briefing on real property inventory

The House amendment contained a provision (sec. 1074) that would require the Secretary of Defense to brief the Committee on Armed Services of the House of Representatives on the status of the Installation Geospatial Information Services of the Department of Defense as it relates to the real property inventory of the Department.

The Senate bill contained no similar provision.

The House recedes.

The conferees direct the Secretary of Defense to provide a briefing by March 1, 2017 on the status of the Installation Geospatial Information Services of the Department of Defense as it relates to the real property inventory of the Department

Report on adjustment and diversification assistance

The House amendment contained a provision (sec. 1075) that would require the Secretary of Defense to provide a briefing on the adjustment and diversification assistance authorized by subsections (b) and (c) of section 2391 of title 10, United States Code.

The Senate bill contained no similar provision.

The House recedes.

The conferees direct the Secretary of Defense to provide to the Committee on Armed Services of the House of Representatives a briefing on the adjustment and diversification assistance authorized by subsections (b) and (c) of section 2391 of title 10, United States Code. Such briefing shall be provided not later than 90 days after the date of the enactment of this Act and shall include each of the following:

(1) A description of the activities and programs currently being conducted under subsections (b)(1) and (c) of such section, including a list of the recipients of grants, and amount received by each recipient, of such activities and programs in each of the five most recent fiscal years.

(2) For each of the five fiscal years preceding the fiscal year during which the briefing is conducted, separate estimates of the funding the Department of Defense has directed to activities under each of clauses (A) through (E) of paragraph (1) of subsection (b) and under subsection (c) of such section and the recipients of such funding.

Briefing on the protection of personally identifying information of members of the Armed Forces

The House amendment contained a provision (sec. 1076) that would require the Secretary of Defense to provide the congressional defense committees a briefing on the efforts of the Department of Defense to protect the personally identifiable information of members of the Armed Forces and their families.

The Senate bill contained no similar provision.

The House recedes.

The conferees are concerned about the impact of recent, significant disclosures of personally identifiable information of service members, government civilians and their families as a result of lax information security practices at the Office of Personnel Management. Coupled with similar breeches occurring in the private sector that have resulted in sensitive personal information, including credit information and medical records, being released to unknown parties, the conferees recognize that such breaches have the potential to jeopardize both the financial security as well as the physical security of these individuals. The conferees urge the Department of Defense to continue to strengthen ongoing initiatives and to develop and implement new initiatives to protect the personally identifiable information of members of the Armed Forces, government civilians, and their families. Further, the conferees expect the Department to keep the Committees on Armed Services of the Senate and the House of Representatives informed of any challenges associated with these initiatives, as well as any trends related to fraudulent or suspicious activity that targets the personally identifiable information of members of the Armed Forces, government civilians, and their families.

Report on priorities for bed downs, basing criteria, and special mission units for C–130J aircraft of the Air Force

The Senate bill contained a provision (Sec. 1085) that would direct the Secretary of the Air Force to submit a report to the congressional defense committees on the overall prioritization, bed downs, basing criteria, and unit conversion priorities for C–130J aircraft and special mission units of the Air Force Reserve Command, Air National Guard, and the regular Air Force.

The House amendment contained no similar provision.

The Senate recedes.

The conferees direct the Secretary of the Air Force, not later than February 1, 2017, to submit to the congressional defense committees a report on the following:

(1) The overall prioritization scheme of the Air Force for future C–130J aircraft unit bed downs;

(2) The strategic basing criteria of the Air Force for C–130J aircraft unit conversions;

(3) The unit conversion priorities for special mission units of the Air Force Reserve Command, the Air National Guard, and the regular Air Force, and the manner which considerations such as age of airframes factor into such priorities; and,

(4) Such other information relating to C–130J aircraft unit conversions and bed downs as the Secretary considers appropriate.

Clarification of contracts covered by airlift service provision

The House amendment contained a provision (sec. 1085) that would amend section 9516 of title 10, United States Code, to define "contract for airlift service" to include any contract or subcontract that may be utilized in the performance of airlift service or transportation services.

The Senate bill contained no similar provision.

The House recedes.

LNG permitting certainty and transparency

The House amendment contained a provision (sec. 1090) that would require the Department of Energy to issue a final decision on any application for the authorization to export natural gas not later than 30 days after completing an environmental review or the date of enactment of this Act.

The Senate bill contained no similar provision.

The House recedes.

Transfer of surplus firearms to Corporation for the Promotion of Rifle Practice and Firearms Safety

The House amendment contained a provision (sec. 1092) that would amend section 40728(h) of title 26, United States Code, by changing the authority of the Secretary of the Army from permissive to directive and striking the limitation of 10,000 .45 caliber M1911/M1911A1 pistols.

The Senate bill contained no similar provision.

The House recedes.

Sense of Congress regarding the importance of Panama City, Florida, to the history and future of the Armed Forces

The House amendment contained a provision (sec. 1093) that would express the Sense of Congress on the role of Panama City, Florida to the Armed Forces of the United States.

The Senate bill contained no similar provision.

The House recedes.

The conferees note that Panama City, Florida has long played an important role in the development and support of the United States armed forces.

Protection against misuse of Naval Special Warfare Command insignia

The Senate bill contained a provision (sec. 1093) that would add a new section 7882 to title 10, United States Code, to prohibit a person from using any covered Naval Special Warfare insignia in connection with any promotion, service or other commercial activity when a particular use would be likely to suggest a false affiliation, connection, or association with, endorsement by, or approval of, the United States, the Department of Defense, or the Department of the Navy, and to authorize the Attorney General to initiate civil proceedings to prevent unauthorized use of such insignia.

The House amendment contained no similar provision.

The Senate recedes.

Protections relating to civil rights and disabilities

The House amendment contained a provision (sec. 1094) that would require any branch or agency of the federal government to provide the protection and exemptions consistent with sections 702(a) and 703(e)(2) of the Civil Rights Act of 1964 (sections 2000e–1(a) and 2000e–2(e) of title 42, United States Code) and section 103(d) of the Americans with Disabilities Act of 1990 (section 12113(d) of title 42, United States Code) with respect to any religious corporation, religious association, religious educational institution, or religious society that is a recipient of or offeror for a federal government contract, grant or similar arrangement.

The Senate bill contained no similar provision.

The House recedes.

Determination and disclosure of transportation costs incurred by Secretary of Defense for congressional trips outside the United States

The House amendment contained a provision (sec. 1096) that would require the Secretary of Defense to determine and disclose the transportation costs incurred by the Department of Defense for certain congressional trips outside the United States.

The Senate bill contained no similar provision.

The House recedes.

The conferees continue to support public disclosure of official travel by Members, officers, and employees of the Senate and the House of Representatives. To this end, the conferees note that section 1754(b) of title 22, United States Code, contains reporting and disclosure requirements for congressional travel outside the United States, including a requirement for reports to be open to public inspection and published in the Congressional Record. The conferees recognize that there are circumstances under which transportation provided by the Department of Defense best meets the needs of congressional delegations, ranging from protecting the safety and security of the delegations, expediency, and accessing destinations that have little or no commercial air service. The conferees further note that the Committees on Armed Services of the Senate and the House of Representatives each maintain policies and processes to provide further oversight of travel requests by members and employees of the committees.

Sense of Congress regarding American veterans disabled for life

The House amendment contained a provision (sec. 1098C) that would express the sense of Congress regarding American veterans disabled for life.

The Senate bill contained no similar provision.

The House recedes.

Maritime Occupational Safety and Health Advisory Committee

The House amendment contained a provision (sec. 1098E) that would establish a Maritime Occupational Safety and Health Advisory Committee.

The Senate bill contained no similar provision.

The House recedes.

Sense of Congress regarding United States Northern Command Preparedness

The House amendment contained a provision (sec. 1098F) that would express the sense of the Congress related to the preparedness of United States Northern Command.

The Senate bill contained no similar provision.

The House recedes.

The conferees note the important role of United States Northern Command in domestic disaster relief and consequence management operations. The conferees encourage United States Northern Command to build on current efforts and leverage, where possible, existing training and management expertise within the Department and other available resources to support this important mission.

Workforce issues for relocation of marines to Guam

The House amendment contained a provision (sec. 1098H) that would grant the U.S. Citizenship Immigration Services flexibility to approve H–2B visa application renewals for contractors performing work on Guam for the duration of the construction plans supporting the realignment of U.S. Marines to Guam.

The Senate bill contained no similar provision.

The House recedes.

The conferees direct the Secretary of the Navy to submit a report to the Committees on Armed Services of the Senate and the House of Representatives and the Committees on the Judiciary of the Senate and the House of Representatives no later than April 1, 2017, regarding the impacts the current H–2B visa program and renewal process have on the relocation of U.S. Marine forces to Guam. At minimum, the report should include the following elements:

(1) A description of the impacts to the cost and schedule of the relocation of U.S. Marine forces to Guam;

(2) A description of the impacts to U.S. bilateral and multilateral relations and agreements in the Pacific;

(3) A description of the specific impacts for the military construction program required to support the relocation of U.S. Marine forces to Guam;

(4) A description of the specific impacts on the delivery of healthcare to support the relocation of U.S. Marine forces to Guam as well as challenges to providing health care on Guam as identified in the supplemental environmental impact statement;

(5) Any other such information as the Secretary believes is relevant to workforce issues for the relocation of U.S. Marines to Guam; and

(6) If the Secretary believes that changes to the statute governing the non-immigrant worker program described above are necessary in order to mitigate adverse impacts to the cost or schedule of the military construction program, or the delivery of healthcare, required to support the relocation of U.S. Marine forces to Guam, the Secretary, in coordination with the Director of U.S. Citizenship and Immigration Services, is encouraged to include a legislative proposal that would mitigate the impacts described in the report.

Review of Department of Defense debt collection regulations

The House amendment contained a provision (sec. 1098I) that would require the Secretary of Defense to review and update Department of Defense regulations to ensure such regulations comply with Federal consumer protection law with respect to the collection of debt.

The Senate bill contained no similar provision.

The House recedes.

Importance of role played by women in World War II

The House amendment contained a provision (sec. 1098J) that would express the sense of Congress in acknowledging the important role played by women in World War II.

The Senate bill contained no similar provision.

The House recedes.

The conferees note, with gratitude, the enduring legacy and example of patriotic service by those women who worked and volunteered on the home front in support of the military overseas.

Prohibition on modification, abrogation, or other related actions with respect to United States jurisdiction and control over United States Naval Station, Guantanamo Bay, Cuba, without congressional action

The House amendment contained provisions (secs. 1099, 1099A–C) that prohibit action to modify, abrogate, or replace the stipulations, agreements, and commitments in the Guantanamo Lease Agreements, or to impair or abandon the jurisdiction of the United States over United States Naval Station, Guantanamo Bay, Cuba, without congressional action.

The Senate bill contained no similar provision.

The House recedes.

Pilot's Bill of Rights 2

The Senate bill contained a series of provisions (sec. 3301, 3302, 3303, 3304, 3305, 3306, and 3307) that would establish Federal Aviation Administration third class medical reform and general aviation pilot protections, "The Pilots Bill of Rights 2".

The House amendment contained no similar provisions.

The Senate recedes on these provisions.

Comprehensive strategy for detention of certain individuals

The House amendment contained a provision that would require the Secretary of Defense, in consultation with the Attorney General and the Director of National Intelligence, to submit a report to the appropriate congressional committees by July 19, 2017, setting forth the details of a comprehensive strategy for the detention of individuals captured and held pursuant to the Authorization of the Use of Military Force (Public Law 107–40) pending the end of hostilities.

The Senate bill contained no similar provision.

The House recedes.

Declassification of information on past terrorist activities of detainees transferred from United States Naval Station, Guantanamo Bay, Cuba

The House amendment contained a provision that would require the Director of National Intelligence to complete a declassification review of intelligence reports prepared by the National Counterterrorism Center prior to Periodic Review Board sessions or detainee transfers on the past terrorist activities of individuals detained at United States Naval Station, Guantanamo Bay, Cuba, who were transferred or released from United States Naval Station, Guantanamo Bay, Cuba, and make any information declassified available to the public.

The Senate bill contained no similar provision.

The House recedes.

TITLE XI—CIVILIAN PERSONNEL MATTERS

Subtitle A—Department of Defense Matters Generally

Civilian personnel management (sec. 1101)

The Senate bill contained a provision (sec. 1101) that would modify Section 129 of title 10, United States Code to remove restrictions on managing civilian personnel within the Department of Defense on the basis of man years, end strength, full-time equivalent positions, or maximum number of employees. The provision would add a new section requiring a report no later than February 1 of each year from the Secretary of Defense to the congressional defense committees on the management of the civilian workforce of the Office of the Secretary of Defense and the Defense Agencies and Field Activities. The provision would require the Secretary of each military department to submit a report on the management of the civilian workforce under the jurisdiction of each Secretary which provides for the projected size of the civilian workforce in the current year and for each year in the future-years defense program to include a justification of any projected increases.

The House amendment contained no similar provision.

The House recedes.

Repeal of requirement for annual strategic workforce plan for the Department of Defense (sec. 1102)

The Senate bill contained a provision (sec. 1102) that would repeal the reporting requirement for the Department of Defense to submit a biennial strategic workforce plan, as contained in section 115b of title 10, United States Code.

The House amendment contained no similar provision.

The House recedes.

Training for employment personnel of Department of Defense on matters relating to authorities for recruitment and retention at United States Cyber Command (sec. 1103)

The Senate bill contained a provision (sec. 1108) that would require training for employment and human resources personnel at the Department of Defense on special recruitment, hiring, special pays, and retention authorities for positions at United States Cyber Command. In addition to training, written guidance would also be required to inform such employees of the Department of Defense on which authorities are available and how to use those authorities.

The House amendment contained no similar provision.

The House recedes with a technical amendment.

Public-private talent exchange (sec. 1104)

The Senate bill contained a provision (sec. 1107) that would allow Department of Defense employees to work in the private sector and private industry employees to work within the Department of Defense. Exchanges would encourage Department of Defense employees to gain skills that align with functional communities or occupational specialties.

The House amendment contained a similar provision (sec. 1113).

The Senate recedes with an amendment that would clarify the conditions under which a temporary assignment of an employee of the Department of Defense may be made and the terms and conditions for private-sector employees assigned to a Department of Defense organization.

The conferees note that as this authority would build on programs like the Intergovernmental Personnel Act (IPA), the committee understands that the Department of Defense has established procedures for monitoring and controlling salaries and expenses for the IPA program, including a limitation on salaries that may be paid or reimbursed for IPAs, and expects that such constraints will be applied to the pilot authorized by this provision.

Temporary and term appointments in the competitive service in the Department of Defense (sec. 1105)

The Senate bill contained a provision (sec. 1103) that would allow non-competitive appointments to Department of Defense temporary and term positions for no more than 18 months without the possibility of extension.

The House amendment contained no similar provision.

The House recedes.

Direct-hire authority for the Department of Defense for post-secondary students and recent graduates (sec. 1106)

The Senate bill contained a provision (sec. 1106) that would establish a Department of Defense (DoD) civilian on-campus recruiting authority under title 10 as an alternative to the federal government-wide Pathways program (established by Executive Order 13562) and other Title 5 hiring authorities. This proposal would facilitate DoD recruiters' efforts to recruit students directly to civilian positions using a new hiring authority expressly designed for this purpose. Hiring managers and recruiters, who already travel to specific schools with programs they want to target, would be able to involve candidates in a rigorous interview process, and make conditional offers on the spot. This would allow DoD to compete for highly qualified students and recent graduates. This authority would be limited to no more than 15 percent of the total number of hires made into professional and administrative occupations of the Department at the GS–11 level and below annually and would sunset four years after the date on which the Secretary first appoints a recent graduate or current post-secondary student to a position under this section.

The House amendment contained no similar provision.

The House recedes with an amendment that would sunset the provision on September 30, 2021 and require the Secretary of Defense, to the extent practical, to provide public notice and advertising of positions offered under this authority.

Temporary increase in maximum amount of voluntary separation incentive pay authorized for civilian employees of the Department of Defense (sec. 1107)

The Senate bill contained a provision (sec. 1109) that would increase the maximum amount of separation pay authorized for Voluntary Separation Incentive Pay (VSIP) from the current ceiling of $25,000 to $40,000 for civilian employees of the Department of Defense. This increased maximum amount would adjust for inflation from when VSIP was first authorized for the Department of Defense in 1993. The Chief Human Capital Officers Act of 2002 (Public Law 107–296) provided government-wide authority to provide VSIP. The maximum payable amount has not been adjusted since VSIP was first authorized.

The House amendment contained no similar provision.

The House recedes with an amendment that would sunset the provision on September 30, 2018.

Extension of the rate of overtime pay for Department of the Navy employees performing work aboard or dockside in support of the nuclear-powered aircraft carrier forward deployed in Japan (sec. 1108)

The Senate bill contains a provision (sec. 1136) that would amend sections 5542 and 5544 of title 5, United States Code, to allow overtime pay equal to one and one-half times the hourly rate of basic pay for nonexempt Federal civilian employees assigned to temporary duty travel in exempt areas as defined by the Fair Labor Standards Act of 1938.

The House amendment contains no similar provision.

The House recedes with an amendment that would extend the authority to pay overtime to Department of the Navy employees performing work aboard or dockside in support of the nuclear-powered aircraft carrier forward deployed in Japan through September 30, 2018.

Limitation on number of DOD SES positions (sec. 1109)

The Senate bill contained a provision (sec. 1112) that would limit the number of employees at the Department of Defense who are in the Senior Executive Service (SES). The limitation in this provision would reduce by 25 percent the number of covered SES employees of the Department, which were employed on December 31, 2015. The reduction required by this provision would be effective on January 1, 2019. Covered SES employees would not include "Highly Qualified Experts," which the provision limits to 200. The limitation would not apply to those employees of the Department who are appointed by the President and confirmed by the Senate.

The House amendment contained no similar provision.

The House recedes with an amendment that would limit the number of senior executives authorized for the Department of Defense to 1,260, and Highly Qualified Experts to 200.

Direct hire authority for financial management experts into the Department of Defense workforce (sec. 1110)

The Senate bill contained a provision (sec. 1105) that would provide each secretary of a military department with the authority to appoint qualified candidates possessing a finance, accounting, management, or actuarial science degree to financial management, accounting, auditing, and actuarial positions within the Department of Defense workforce. The authority would be limited to 10 percent of the total number of finance, accounting, management, actuarial science, or financial management positions within each military department that are filled as of the close of the fiscal year last ending before the start of such calendar year. The authority would expire on January 1, 2023.

The House amendment contained no similar provision.

The House recedes with an amendment that would include within this direct appointment authority those possessing a degree or related experience with business administration.

Repeal of certain basis for appointment of a retired member of the Armed Forces to Department of Defense position within 180 days of retirement (sec. 1111)

The Senate bill contained a provision (sec. 1110) that would amend section 3326 of title 5, United States Code, to repeal subsection (b)(3) which allows the Secretary concerned to waive the restriction on the appointment of retired members of the armed forces to positions in the civil service in the Department of Defense within 180 days of their retirement based on a state of national emergency.

The House amendment contained no similar provision.

The House recedes.

Subtitle B—Department of Defense Science and Technology Laboratories and Related Matters

Permanent personnel management authority for the Department of Defense for experts in science and engineering (sec. 1121)

The Senate bill contained a provision (sec. 1121) that would support efforts by the Defense Advanced Research Projects Agency to attract, recruit, and employ world-class scientific, technical, and engineering talent to manage and oversee the innovative research and technology development programs of the agency. The provision would make permanent and codify the current experimental personnel authority that the agency has quite successfully employed, as well as preserve the agency's ability to compete with the private sector for technical talent through flexibility in setting compensation levels.

The House amendment contained a similar provision (sec. 1105) that would remove the sunset date and annual reporting requirement for these authorities and codify them in chapter 81 of title 10, United States Code.

The House recedes with a technical amendment.

Codification and modification of certain authorities for certain positions at Department of Defense research and engineering laboratories (sec. 1122)

The Senate bill contained a provision (sec. 1122) that would increase the limit from 3 percent to 10 percent on the total number of student employees eligible for direct hire by the directors of the Department of Defense science and technology reinvention laboratories. The provision would also make this authority permanent.

The House amendment contained no similar provision.

The House recedes with an amendment to codify this authority in chapter 139 of Title 10, United States Code.

Modification to information technology personnel exchange program (sec. 1123)

The Senate bill contained a provision (sec. 1124) that would make the Department of Defense's Information Technology Exchange Program permanent.

The House amendment contained a similar provision (sec. 1106) that would expand the scope of the program to include cyber operations personnel, and increase the number of personnel that could be exchanged from 10 to 50.

The Senate recedes with an amendment to extend the sunset of the program from 2018 to 2022.

Pilot program on enhanced pay authority for certain research and technology positions in the science and technology reinvention laboratories of the Department of Defense (sec. 1124)

The Senate bill contained a provision (sec. 1125) that would give Department of Defense science and technology laboratories the authority to offer compensation for certain positions requiring extremely high levels of experience above the maximum amount normally allowed by the executive schedule.

The House amendment contained no similar provision.

The House recedes.

Temporary direct hire authority for domestic defense industrial base facilities, the Major Range and Test Facilities Base, and the Office of the Director of Operational Test and Evaluation (sec. 1125)

The Senate bill contained a provision (sec. 1123) that would give the directors of Department of Defense test and evaluations facilities the same direct hire authorities already provided to the directors of the Department's science and technology laboratories.

The House amendment contained a similar provision (sec. 1101) that would provide direct hire authority for Department of Defense industrial base facilities located in the United States, as well as the Major Range and Test Facilities Base.

The Senate recedes with an amendment to clarify and enhance several aspects of the authorities.

The conferees direct the Secretary of Defense to provide a briefing to the House and Senate Armed Services Committees as well as the House Committee on Oversight and Government Reform and the Senate Homeland Security and Governmental Affairs Committee, not later than 60 days after the end of fiscal year 2018 and again each year until the temporary authorities expire, on the effectiveness of all direct hire authorities granted in this Act in fulfilling the civilian manpower needs of the Department.

Subtitle C—Government-Wide Matters

Elimination of two-year eligibility limitation for noncompetitive appointment of spouses of members of the Armed Forces (sec. 1131)

The House amendment contained a provision (sec. 574) that would specify that there is no time limitation on a relocating spouse's eligibility for noncompetitive appointment from the date of the servicemember's permanent change of station orders to the spouse's permanent appointment per duty station.

The Senate bill contained a similar provision (sec. 1113).

The Senate recedes.

Temporary personnel flexibilities for domestic defense industrial base facilities and Major Range and Test Facilities Base civilian personnel (sec. 1132)

The House amendment contained a provision (sec. 1102) that would allow Department of Defense industrial base facilities located in the United States and Major Range and Test Facilities Base centers to hire temporary employees into permanent positions outside of the requirements of the competitive services.

The Senate bill contained no similar provision.

The Senate recedes with an amendment to clarify the benefits available to such personnel.

One-year extension of temporary authority to grant allowances, benefits, and gratuities to civilian personnel on official duty in a combat zone (sec. 1133)

The House amendment contained a provision (sec. 1103) that would extend by 1 year the discretionary authority of the head of a federal agency to provide allowances, benefits, and gratuities comparable to those provided to members of the Foreign Service to an agency's civilian employees on official duty in a combat zone.

The Senate bill contained a similar provision (sec. 1152).

The Senate recedes.

Advance payments for employees relocating within the United States and its territories (sec. 1134)

The Senate bill contained a provision (sec. 1135) that would authorize the use of advance payment of basic pay for current employees who relocate within the United States and its territories to a location outside the employee's current commuting area. Advance payment of basic pay under this provision would be limited in amount to not more than two pay periods.

The House amendment contained a similar provision (sec. 1104) that would limit the amount to not more than six pay periods.

The Senate recedes with an amendment that would limit the amount to not more than four pay periods.

Eligibility of employees in a time-limited appointment to compete for a permanent appointment at any Federal agency (sec. 1135)

The House amendment contained a provision (sec. 1108) that would modify section 9602 of title 5, United States Code, to clarify the eligibility of employees of a land management agency in a time-limited appointment to compete for a permanent appointment at any Federal agency.

The Senate bill contained a similar provision (sec. 1131).

The Senate recedes.

Review of official personnel file of former Federal employee before rehiring (sec. 1136)

The House amendment contained an amendment (sec. 1111) that would require an appointing authority to review and consider the information relating to a prospective employee's former government service in the candidate's official personnel record file prior to making any determination with respect to the appointment or reinstatement of the employee to such a person.

The Senate bill contained no similar provision.

The Senate recedes with an amendment that would clarify which types of information an appointing authority should review.

One-year extension of authority to waive annual limitation on premium pay and aggregate limitation on pay for Federal civilian employees working overseas (sec. 1137)

The Senate bill contained a provision (sec. 1137) that would amend section 1101 of the Duncan Hunter National Defense Authorization Act for Fiscal Year 2009 (Public Law 110–417), as most recently amended by section 1108 of the National Defense Authorization Act for Fiscal Year 2016 (Public Law 114–92), to extend through 2017 the authority of heads of executive agencies to waive limitation on the aggregate of basic and premium pay of employ-

ees who perform work in an overseas location that is in the area of responsibility of the commander, U.S. Central Command (CENTCOM), or a location that was formerly in CENTCOM but has been moved to an area of responsibility for the Commander, U.S. Africa Command, in support of a military operation or an operation in response to a declared emergency.

The House amendment contained no similar provision.

The House recedes.

Administrative leave (sec. 1138)

The House amendment contained a provision (sec. 1109) that would provide that a Federal employee may not be placed on administrative leave, or other paid non-duty status without charging leave, for more than 14 total days for reasons relating to misconduct or performance.

The Senate bill contained no similar provision.

The Senate recedes with an amendment that would provide that a Federal employee may not be placed on administrative leave for more than 10 work days in any calendar year, and authorize additional periods of administrative leave only for employees under investigation or in a notice period, subject to agency determination that the continued presence of the employee in the workplace poses a threat to other employees, evidence relevant to a pending investigation, Government property, or legitimate Government interests.

Direct hiring for Federal wage schedule employees (sec. 1139)

The Senate bill contained a provision (sec. 1132) that would direct the Director of the Office of Personnel Management to permit certain agencies to use the direct-hire authority of permanent and non-permanent positions in the competitive service for prevailing rate employees when there is a severe shortage of candidates or a critical hiring need for such positions.

The House amendment contained no similar provision.

The House recedes.

Record of investigation of personnel action in separated employee's official personnel file (sec. 1140)

The House amendment contained a provision (sec. 1110) that would require the head of an agency to make a permanent notation in an individual's personnel file if the individual resigns from government employment while the subject of a personnel investigation and an adverse finding against the individual is made as a result of the investigation.

The Senate bill contained no similar amendment.

The Senate recedes.

LEGISLATIVE PROVISIONS NOT ADOPTED

Treatment of certain localities for calculation of per diem allowances

The House amendment contained a provision (sec. 1107) that would consolidate per diem localities in the Dayton, Ohio, area.

The Senate bill contained no similar provision.

The House recedes.

Pilot programs on career sabbaticals for Department of Defense civilian employees

The Senate bill contained a provision (sec. 1111) that would create a pilot program on career sabbaticals for Department of Defense civilian employees.

The House amendment contained no similar provision.

The Senate recedes.

Report on Department of Defense civilian workforce personnel and contractors

The House amendment contained a provision (sec. 1112) that would require the Secretary of Defense to submit a detailed report on the structure and number of the civilian workforce and contractors of the Department of Defense.

The Senate bill contained no similar amendment.

The House recedes.

Appointment authority for uniquely qualified prevailing rate employees

The Senate bill contained a provision (sec. 1133) that would allow the head of an agency to appoint an individual to a prevailing rate position at such a rate of basic pay above the minimum rate of the appropriate grade in cases where there is an unusually large shortage of qualified candidates for employment, unique qualifications of a candidate of employment, or a special need of the Government for the services of a candidate for employment.

The House amendment contained no similar provision.

The Senate recedes.

Limitation on preference eligible hiring preferences for permanent employees in the competitive service

The Senate bill contained a provision (sec. 1134) that would limit the application of points for preference eligible hiring to the first appointment of a preference eligible candidate in a permanent position in the competitive service.

The House amendment contained no similar provision.

The Senate recedes.

The conferees remain concerned that the Department of Defense has difficulty accessing highly skilled non-veterans into its civilian labor force due to strict preference eligible hiring requirements, and believes that a detailed examination of Department of Defense preference eligible hiring practices is overdue. Therefore, the conferees direct the Secretary of Defense, in coordination with the Secretary of Labor, Secretary of Veterans Affairs, and the Director of the Office of Personnel Management to submit a report no later than May 1, 2017, to the Committees on Armed Services of the Senate and House of Representatives, the Committee on Homeland Security and Governmental Affairs of the Senate, and the Committee on Oversight and Government Reform of the House of Representatives. Such report shall consist of a coordinated overview of the Veterans preference process in Federal hiring and shall contain the following elements: (1) an analysis of how the current process of applying preference eligible points works in practice, including initial hires and the process as employees move and advance into new positions; (2) a review of positive impacts realized in the past five years of preference eligible hiring; (3) an analysis of the impact of preference eligible hiring on agencies' ability to hire qualified non-veteran applicants; (4) an analysis of the impact of preference eligible hiring on agencies' ability to hire qualified non-veteran recent graduates and young talent needed to build the future workforce; (5) a review of challenges identified in the past five years of preference eligible hiring; (6) an analysis of the impact of preference eligible hiring on science, technology, engineering and math positions; and (7) proposals from the reviewing agencies to improve the current preference eligible hiring process.

TITLE XII—MATTERS RELATING TO FOREIGN NATIONS

Subtitle A—Assistance and Training

One-year extension of logistical support for coalition forces supporting certain United States military operations (sec. 1201)

The House amendment contained a provision (sec. 1201) that would amend section 1234 of the National Defense Authorization Act for Fiscal Year 2008 (Public Law 110–181), as most recently amended by section 1201 of the National Defense Authorization Act for Fiscal Year 2016 (Public Law 114–92), by authorizing the Secretary of Defense to provide supplies, services, transportation, and other logistical support to coalition forces supporting U.S. operations in the Republic of Iraq and the Islamic Republic of Afghanistan during fiscal year 2017.

The Senate bill contained no similar provision.

The Senate recedes.

Special Defense Acquisition Fund matters (sec. 1202)

The Senate bill contained a provision (sec. 1202) that would increase the obligation authority for the Special Defense Acquisition Fund.

The House amendment contained no similar provision.

The House recedes with an amendment that would require quarterly spending plans and annual inventories to ensure more regular and routine oversight and alignment of the use of such funds with security assistance priorities and national security objectives.

The amendment also requires that $500.0 million of the Special Defense Acquisition Fund may only be used to procure and stock precision guided munitions that may be required by partner and allied forces to enhance the effectiveness of their contribution to overseas contingency operations conducted or supported by the United States. If necessary, the conferees understand that nothing in this provision would preclude the Secretary of Defense from using precision guided munitions that have been procured and stocked using the Special Defense Acquisition Fund to meet immediate United States military requirements.

Codification of authority for support of special operations to combat terrorism (sec. 1203)

The Senate bill contained a provision (sec. 1203) that would establish a new section 127e in title 10, United States Code, to codify section 1208 of the Ronald W. Reagan National Defense Authorization Act for Fiscal Year 2005 (Public Law 108–375), as most recently amended by section 1274 of the National Defense Authorization Act for Fiscal Year 2016 (Public Law 114–92). The provision would increase the annual cap on the authority from $85.0 million to $100.0 million and would limit the amount available to support any particular military operation under the authority to $10.0 million in a fiscal year as well as modify notification requirements.

The House amendment contained a similar provision that would modify and extend section 1208 of Public Law 108–375, as amended, for 3 years.

The House recedes with an amendment that would eliminate the limitation of $10.0 million on support to any particular military operation in a fiscal year and make other clarifying changes to the reporting requirements associated with this authority.

The conferees express strong support for "section 1208" authority and its importance in countering threats posed by violent extremist groups. The conferees believe that

the maturity of the authority, the need for predictability when working with foreign partner forces, and the enduring nature of the threats facing our nation support the codification of this authority. The conferees believe that an increase of the annual cap to $100.0 million will provide for stability and sufficient flexibility to address unforeseen contingencies in future years.

The conferees expect the Department to exercise judicious use of the authority and conduct appropriate planning to preserve the flexibility afforded by the codification and expansion of this authority.

Furthermore, the conferees expect the Department to appropriately scope support provided under this authority to address operational requirements in support of defined counterterrorism missions. This authority should not be used solely for the purpose of building the capacity of or engagement with foreign partner forces. When operational requirements no longer require the use of this tailored authority, support for foreign partner forces should be expeditiously terminated or transitioned to other authorities and funding sources that are more appropriately designed for longer-term, sustained capacity-building efforts.

Independent evaluation of Strategic Framework for Department of Defense security cooperation (sec. 1204)

The House amendment contained a provision (sec. 1206) that would require the Secretary of Defense to enter into an agreement with a federally funded research and development center, or another appropriate independent entity, with expertise in security cooperation to conduct an assessment of the Strategic Framework for Department of Defense Security Cooperation and submit a report to the congressional defense committees, the Committee on Foreign Relations of the Senate, and the Committee on Foreign Affairs of the House of Representatives not later than November 1, 2017, containing the assessment.

The Senate bill contained no similar provision.

The Senate recedes with a technical amendment.

Sense of Congress regarding an assessment, monitoring, and evaluation framework for security cooperation (sec. 1205)

The House amendment contained a provision (sec. 1207) that would express the sense of Congress that the Secretary of Defense should develop and maintain an assessment, monitoring, and evaluation framework for security cooperation with foreign countries to ensure accountability and foster implementation of best practices.

The Senate bill contained no similar provision.

The Senate recedes.

Subtitle B—Matters Relating to Afghanistan and Pakistan

Extension and modification of Commanders' Emergency Response Program (sec. 1211)

The Senate bill contained a provision (sec. 1201) that would extend through fiscal year 2019 the Commanders' Emergency Response Program (CERP) in Afghanistan under section 1201 of the National Defense Authorization Act for Fiscal Year 2012 (Public Law 112–81) as amended. The provision would also expand the authorization to make certain payments to redress injury and loss in Iraq in accordance with section 1211 of the National Defense Authorization Act for Fiscal Year 2016 to Afghanistan and Syria.

The House amendment contained a similar provision (sec. 1211).

The Senate recedes with a technical amendment.

Extension of authority to acquire products and services produced in countries along a major route of supply to Afghanistan (sec. 1212)

The Senate bill contained a provision (sec. 883) that would amend section 801(f) of the National Defense Authorization Act for Fiscal Year 2010 (Public Law 111–84) to extend by 2 years the authority to acquire products and services produced in countries along the major route of supply to Afghanistan.

The House amendment contained a similar provision (sec. 1213) that would extend the authority by 1 year.

The House recedes.

Extension and modification of authority to transfer defense articles and provide defense services to the military and security forces of Afghanistan (sec. 1213)

The Senate bill contained a provision (sec. 1211) that would extend through December 31, 2017, the authority under section 1222 of the National Defense Authorization Act for Fiscal Year 2013 (Public Law 112–239) to transfer defense articles being drawn down in Afghanistan, and to provide defense services in connection with such transfers, to the military and security forces of Afghanistan. The provision would also extend through fiscal year 2017 the exemption for excess defense articles (EDA) transferred from Department of Defense stocks in Afghanistan from counting toward the annual limitation on the aggregate value of EDA transferred under section 516 of the Foreign Assistance Act of 1961 (Public Law 87–195). The provision would also convert certain quarterly reports into an annual report.

The House amendment contained a similar provision (sec. 1241).

The House recedes.

Special immigrant status for certain Afghans (sec. 1214)

The House amendment contained a provision (sec. 1216) that would extend the authorization for the Afghan Special Immigrant Visa (SIV) program for one year and narrow the eligibility requirements for Afghan SIV candidates.

The Senate bill contained no similar provision.

The Senate recedes with a technical amendment that would modify eligibility requirements for applicants to include those that perform sensitive and trusted activities for the United States Government in Afghanistan; extend the underlying SIV program for four additional years; and provide an additional 1,500 visas. The conferees believe that any Afghan performing sensitive and trusted activities for or on the behalf of the United States Government should be eligible for the Special Immigrant Visa program.

Modification to semiannual report on enhancing security and stability in Afghanistan (sec. 1215)

The House amendment contained a provision (sec. 1217) that would add the requirement for an assessment of the implementation of the Afghan Personnel and Pay System to the report on enhancing the strategic partnership between the United States and Afghanistan.

The Senate bill contained no similar provision.

The Senate recedes with a technical amendment.

Prohibition on use of funds for certain programs and projects of the Department of Defense in Afghanistan that cannot be safely accessed by United States Government personnel (sec. 1216)

The Senate bill contained a provision (sec. 1213) that would prohibit the obligation or expenditure of amounts available to the Department of Defense for a construction or other infrastructure program or project in Afghanistan unless certain conditions are met. The provision also provides for certain waivers.

The House amendment contained no similar provision.

The House recedes with an amendment that would provide for an additional waiver by the Commander of the Combined Security Transition Command—Afghanistan for projects greater than $1.0 million, but less than $20.0 million.

Improvement of oversight of United States Government efforts in Afghanistan (sec. 1217)

The Senate bill contained a provision (sec. 1215) that would require the Lead Inspector General for Operation Freedom's Sentinel, in coordination with certain other inspectors general, to submit a report on oversight activities in Afghanistan to optimize the utilization of oversight resources through planning, coordination, and reduction of redundancies in oversight activities.

The House amendment contained no similar provision.

The House recedes with an amendment that would add the requirement to report on the professional standards used by inspectors general to ensure the accuracy, precision, and overall quality of the products they publish regarding Afghanistan.

The conferees note that inspectors general play a crucial role in helping to ensure appropriate oversight and efficient use of federal resources in challenging environments, including Afghanistan. The conferees believe the Inspectors General operating in Afghanistan should work together to ensure appropriate oversight occurs at all levels, with minimal burden to U.S. military operations, diplomatic efforts and developmental projects. The conferees urge additional efforts to optimize coordination and to maximize the use of professional standards among inspectors general in Afghanistan to ensure the most efficient and effective use of oversight resources.

Extension and modification of authority for reimbursement of certain coalition nations for support provided to United States military operations (sec. 1218)

The Senate bill contained a provision (sec. 1214) that would provide the Secretary of Defense the authority to reimburse Pakistan up to $800.0 million in fiscal year 2017 for certain activities that enhance the security situation in the northwest regions of Pakistan and along the Afghanistan-Pakistan border. The provision would also make $300.0 million of this amount contingent upon a certification from the Secretary of Defense that Pakistan is taking demonstrable steps against the Haqqani Network in Pakistan. The Senate bill also contained a companion provision (sec. 1212) that would extend and modify the authority for reimbursement of coalition nations in support of U.S. operations in Iraq and Afghanistan to include Syria.

The House amendment contained a similar provision (sec. 1212) that would extend the authority for reimbursement of coalition nations for support provided to the United States for military operations in Iraq and

Afghanistan through December 31, 2017. The provision would make $1.1 billion in funding available for the overall coalition support funds program, including up to $900.0 million for reimbursement of Pakistan. The provision would also make $450.0 million of this amount contingent upon a certification from the Secretary of Defense that Pakistan is taking demonstrable steps against the Haqqani Network in Pakistan.

The Senate recedes with an amendment to merge the three provisions into one provision. The revised provision would extend the authorization of the coalition support funds program for reimbursement of nations in support of U.S. operations in Iraq and Afghanistan. The provision would expand the authorization to include support for operations in Syria and would retain the authority to provide such reimbursement to Pakistan. In addition, the provision would include a modified list of security enhancement activities for which Pakistan would be eligible for reimbursement.

The provision authorizes $1.1 billion for the overall coalition support funds program, including up to $900.0 million for Pakistan. Of this amount, the provision would make $400.0 million contingent upon a certification from the Secretary of Defense that Pakistan is taking demonstrable steps against the Haqqani Network in Pakistani territory.

The conferees remain concerned about the persecution of groups seeking political or religious freedom in Pakistan, including the Balochi, Sindhi, and Hazara ethnic groups, as well as religious groups, including Christian, Hindu, and Ahmadiyya Muslim. Consequently, the conferees believe that the Secretary of Defense should continue to closely monitor the provision of U.S. security assistance to Pakistan and ensure that Pakistan is not using its military or any assistance provided by the United States to persecute minority groups.

In addition, the conferees note that the renewed authority allows for reimbursement of Pakistan for security activities along the Afghanistan-Pakistan border, including providing training and equipment for the Pakistan Frontier Corps Khyber Pakhtunkhwa. However, the conferees are concerned that Pakistan continues to delay or deny visas for U.S. personnel that could assist with the provision of such training. Given this situation, the conferees recommend that the Department of Defense condition reimbursements for training and equipment with appropriate access by U.S. personnel.

The conferees note that while the pilot program for stability activities in the Federally Administered Tribal Areas that was authorized under Section 1212 of the National Defense Authorization Act for Fiscal Year 2016 (P.L.114-92) would not be specifically reauthorized by this provision, the activities covered by the pilot program would be eligible for reimbursement under the modifications made by this provision. The conferees also note that coalition support funds appropriated by the Consolidated Appropriations Act of 2016 (P.L.114-113) remain eligible for obligation for two fiscal years. As a result, the conferees expect that the Department of Defense will continue activities under the pilot program through the end of fiscal year 2017.

Subtitle C—Matters Relating to Syria, Iraq, and Iran

Modification and extension of authority to provide assistance to the vetted Syrian opposition (sec. 1221)

The Senate bill contained a provision (sec. 1221) that would extend and modify the au-

thority under section 1209 of the Carl Levin and Howard P. 'Buck' McKeon National Defense Authorization Act for Fiscal Year 2015 (Public Law 113-291; 128 Stat. 3541) to assist the vetted elements of the Syrian opposition for certain purposes to December 31, 2019, as well as strike the prior approval reprogramming requirement and replace it with a notification requirement before carrying out new initiatives.

The House amendment contained a similar provision (sec. 1221) that would extend the authority for one year and add certain certification requirements.

The Senate recedes with an amendment that would extend the authority through December 31, 2018, maintain the reprogramming requirement, and strike the certification requirements.

Modification and extension of authority to provide assistance to counter the Islamic State of Iraq and the Levant (sec. 1222)

The Senate bill contained a provision (sec. 1222) that would extend the authority under section 1236 of the Carl Levin and Howard P. "Buck" McKeon National Defense Authorization Act for Fiscal Year 2015 (Public Law 113-291; 128 Stat. 3559) to military and other security forces of or associated with the Government of Iraq, including Kurdish and tribal security forces, with a national mission, to counter the Islamic State in Iraq and the Levant (ISIL) to December 31, 2019.

The House amendment contained a similar provision (sec. 1222) that would extend the authority to December 31, 2017.

The House recedes with an amendment that would extend the authority through December 31, 2018.

The conferees direct the Secretary of Defense in coordination with the Secretary of State to brief the congressional defense committees, the Senate Foreign Relations Committee, and the House Foreign Affairs Committee, not later than 90 days after the enactment of this Act, on the campaign to liberate Mosul, Iraq from the control of ISIL. The briefing on the campaign to liberate Mosul shall also contain the plan to hold Mosul after liberation and include a detailed blueprint on how humanitarian, reconstruction, and stabilization assistance will be provided to support a follow on governance structure.

The conferees note the importance of the provision of up to $480 million in stipends and sustainment through the Government of Iraq to the Iraqi Kurdish Peshmerga and urge the Secretary of Defense, in coordination with the Secretary of State, to provide such assistance through the Government of Iraq to Sunni tribal security forces and other local security forces with a national security mission. The conferees remind the Secretaries that local security forces with a national security mission may include, in addition to Sunni tribal elements, local security forces that are committed to protecting highly vulnerable ethnic and religious communities, such as Yazidi, Christian, Assyrian, and Turkoman communities, against the ISIL threat.

Extension and modification of authority to support operations and activities of the Office of Security Cooperation in Iraq (sec. 1223)

The Senate bill contained a provision (sec. 1223) that would extend through fiscal year 2017 the authority under section 1215 of the National Defense Authorization Act for Fiscal Year 2012 (Public Law 112-81) as amended, for the Secretary of Defense to support the operations and activities of the Office of Security Cooperation in Iraq (OSC-I).

The House amendment contained a similar provision (sec. 1223) that would extend the authority for OSC–I for one year through fiscal year 2017 and authorize the Secretary of Defense to conduct training with the Iraqi Border Police.

The Senate recedes with an amendment that would extend the authority through fiscal year 2017.

The conferees direct the Secretary of Defense and the Secretary of State to submit to the congressional defense committees, the Senate Foreign Relations Committee, and the House Foreign Affairs Committee, a plan to transition the activities conducted by OSC–I but funded by the Department of Defense to another entity or transition the funding of such activities to another source not later than the end of fiscal year 2018.

Limitation on provision of man-portable air defense systems to the vetted Syrian opposition during fiscal year 2017 (sec. 1224)

The House amendment contained a provision (sec. 1229) that would prohibit the funds authorized to be appropriated or otherwise made available for the Department of Defense for fiscal year 2017 to be obligated or expended to transfer or facilitate the transfer of man-portable air defense systems (MANPADs) to any entity in Syria.

The Senate bill contained no similar provision.

The Senate recedes with an amendment that would require the Secretary of Defense and Secretary of State to notify the congressional defense committees, the Senate Foreign Relations Committee, and the House Foreign Affairs Committee should a determination be made to provide MANPADs to elements of the appropriately vetted Syrian opposition. The conferees expect that should such a determination be made, the requirement for the provision of such a capability and the decision to provide it would be thoroughly vetted by and receive broad support from the interagency.

Modification of annual report on military power of Iran (sec. 1225)

The Senate bill contained a provision (sec. 1226) that would add additional elements concerning cyber capabilities to the annual report on the military power of Iran required under section 1245 of the National Defense Authorization Act for Fiscal Year 2010 (Public Law 111–84).

The House amendment contained a similar provision (sec. 1253).

The Senate recedes with a technical amendment.

Quarterly report on confirmed ballistic missile launches from Iran (sec. 1226)

The House amendment contained a provision (sec. 1259S) that would require the President to notify Congress within 48 hours of a suspected ballistic missile launch, including a test, by Iran. The President shall further notify Congress of the entities involved in the launch and a description of the steps the President will take in response to the launch, including diplomatic efforts and the imposition of unilateral sanctions.

The Senate bill contained no similar provision.

The Senate recedes with an amendment that would replace the house provision with the requirement for a quarterly report to Congress by the Director of National Intelligence describing any confirmed ballistic missile launches by Iran. An additional quarterly report to Congress from the Secretary of State and the Secretary of Treasury is required setting forth a description of the efforts, if any, to impose unilateral sanctions

against entities or individuals in connection with a confirmed ballistic missile launch from Iran and any diplomatic efforts to impose multilateral sanctions.

Subtitle D—Matters Relating to the Russian Federation

Military response options to Russian Federation violation of INF Treaty (sec. 1231)

The House amendment contained a provision (sec. 1232) that would withhold $10.0 million of funding for the Department of Defense to provide support services to the Executive Office of the President until the Secretary of Defense submits to the appropriate congressional committees a plan for the development of military capabilities in response to the Russian Federation non-compliance with its obligations under the INF Treaty, as required by section 1243(d) of the National Defense Authorization Act for Fiscal Year 2016 (Public Law 114–92; 129 Stat. 1062).

The Senate bill contained no similar provision.

The Senate recedes with an amendment that would drop section (a)(1) from the House provision. The conferees note that the plan contained in the report previously submitted to Congress, pursuant to the above Public Law, was insufficient and failed to address adequately the military response options that were outlined in congressional testimony presented by Mr. Brian McKeon, Deputy Under Secretary of Defense for Policy. For example, in testimony to the House Armed Services Committee on December 10, 2014, Mr. McKeon stated: "The range of options we are looking at in the military sphere fall into three broad categories: Active defenses to counter intermediate-range ground-launched cruise missiles; counterforce capabilities to prevent intermediate-range ground-launched cruise missile attacks; and countervailing strike capabilities to enhance U.S. or allied forces." The conferees note that nothing in this provision is intended to direct testing or deployment of systems that would cause the United States to violate the INF Treaty.

Limitation on military cooperation between the United States and the Russian Federation (sec. 1232)

The House amendment contained a provision (sec. 1233) that would prohibit funds authorized to be appropriated or otherwise made available by this Act through fiscal year 2017 from being used for bilateral military-to-military contact between the United States and the Russian Federation without certain certifications by the Secretary of Defense, in consultation with the Secretary of State, or unless certain waiver conditions are met.

The Senate bill contained no similar provision.

The Senate recedes.

Extension and modification of authority on training for Eastern European national military forces in the course of multilateral exercises (sec. 1233)

The Senate bill contained a provision (sec. 1232) that would extend through fiscal year 2019 the authority under section 1251 of the National Defense Authorization Act for Fiscal Year 2016 (Public Law 114–92) for the Secretary of Defense to provide multilateral or regional training, and pay the incremental expenses of participating in such training, for countries in Eastern Europe that are a signatory to the Partnership for Peace Framework Documents but not a member of the North Atlantic Treaty Organization (NATO) or became a NATO member after

January 1, 1999. The provision would also add the authority to utilize under this section amounts authorized to be appropriated for certain purposes under the European Deterrence Initiative.

The House amendment contained no similar provision.

The House recedes with an amendment that would extend the authority through fiscal year 2018 and pay the incremental expenses incurred by a country as a result of national security forces participation in certain types of training. The conferees note that the purpose of such training is to promote interoperability, improve the ability of participating countries to respond to external threats including from hybrid warfare, and increase the ability of NATO to take collective action when required.

The conferees note the importance of regular updates on the status and effectiveness of the implementation and planned use of the authority and direct the Secretary of Defense to brief, not later than 120 days after the enactment of this Act, the Committees on Armed Services of the Senate and the House of Representatives on the overall strategy to increase capabilities and develop key participants' skills under this authority, the expenditure of funds under this authority to date, and planned future activities, including the types of national security forces trained or planned to be trained under this authority.

Prohibition on availability of funds relating to sovereignty of the Russian Federation over Crimea (sec. 1234)

The House amendment contained a provision (sec. 1236) that would prohibit funds authorized to be appropriated or made available by this Act through fiscal year 2017 for the Department of Defense to implement any activity that recognizes the sovereignty of the Russian Federation over Crimea. The provision included a waiver if the Secretary of Defense, with the concurrence of the Secretary of State, determines that to do so would be in the national security interest of the United States and submits a notification of the waiver to certain Congressional committees.

The Senate bill contained no similar provision.

The Senate recedes.

Annual report on military and security developments involving the Russian Federation (sec. 1235)

The Senate bill contained a provision (sec. 1233) that would add additional elements to the annual report on Russian military and security developments required under section 1245 of the Carl Levin and Howard P. "Buck" McKeon National Defense Authorization Act for Fiscal Year 2015 (Public Law 113–291) including an assessment of Russian operations in Ukraine and an analysis of the nuclear strategy and associated doctrine of Russia.

The House amendment contained a similar provision that would require reporting on the Russian Federation's foreign military deployments.

The House recedes with an amendment that would add the Russian Federation's foreign military deployments, including significant deployments of naval vessels to foreign countries, to the annual report.

Limitation on use of funds to vote to approve or otherwise adopt any implementing decision of the Open Skies Consultative Commission and related requirements (sec. 1236)

The Senate bill contained a provision (sec. 1079) that would require the Secretary of Defense to submit to the appropriate committees of Congress, an annual report on observation flights over the United States under the Open Skies Treaty during the previous year.

The House amendment contained a similar provision (sec. 1231) that would limit funds that may be used to approve or permit approval of a request by the Russian Federation to carry out observation flights with an aircraft that has installed an upgraded sensor with infrared or synthetic aperture radar capability over the United States or the territory covered in the Open Skies Treaty, unless the administration can certify certain conditions.

The Senate recedes with an amendment that would limit funding that may be used to vote to approve or otherwise adopt any implementing decision of the Open Skies Consultative Commission to authorize approval of requests by state parties to the Treaty of infrared or synthetic aperture radars, pursuant to the Open Skies Treaty, unless and until the Secretary of Defense, jointly with the relevant U.S. government officials, submits to the appropriate congressional committees a certification that such implementing decision would not be detrimental or otherwise harmful to the national security of the United States, and submits a report.

Further, not later than 90 days prior to when the U.S. votes to approve or otherwise adopt any implementing decision, the Secretary of State shall submit to Congress certain certifications. If the Secretary is unable to make these certifications, the Secretary must submit a report to Congress explaining why it is in the national interest of the U.S. to vote to approve or otherwise adopt such implementing decision.

The amendment also requires a quarterly report by certain government officials evaluating Open Skies Treaty overflights of the United States by the Russian Federation.

The amendment further states that not more than 65–percent of the funds authorized for fiscal year 2017 may be used to carry out any activities to implement the Open Skies Treaty until the Director of National Intelligence and the Director of the National Geospatial-Intelligence Agency submit an evaluation of whether it is possible, consistent with U.S. national security interests, to substitute commercial imagery or other phenomenologies for such data generated by Treaty overflights. The amendment further limits the funding until the Secretary of State submits a report on cost of implementing the Open Skies Treaty and on impact on participation and contributions by covered state parties and relationships among covered state parties.

Extension and enhancement of Ukraine Security Assistance Initiative (sec. 1237)

The Senate bill contained a provision (sec. 1231) that would extend through fiscal year 2019 the authority under section 1250 of the National Defense Authorization Act for Fiscal Year 2016 (Public Law 114–92) for the Secretary of Defense, in coordination with the Secretary of State, to provide security assistance and intelligence support to military and other security forces of the government of Ukraine. The provision would authorize the use of up to $500.0 million in fiscal year 2017 to provide security assistance to Ukraine. The provision would prohibit the obligation or expenditure of half of the funds authorized to be appropriated in fiscal year 2017 under this authority until the Secretary of Defense, in coordination with the Secretary of State, certifies that Ukraine has taken substantial action to make defense institutional reforms and outlines areas where further work may remain.

The House amendment contained a similar provision (sec. 1235) that would make conforming changes of a non-substantive nature to section 1250 of the National Defense Authorization Act for Fiscal Year 2016 (Public Law 114–92).

The House recedes with an amendment that would extend the authority through December 31, 2018, and authorize the use of up to $350 million in fiscal year 2017 to provide security assistance to Ukraine. The provision would limit the obligation or expenditure of funds to $175 million of the funds authorized to be appropriated in fiscal year 2017 until a certification is made that Ukraine has taken substantial action on defense institutional reforms.

The conferees remain deeply concerned by the continuing aggression of Russia and Russian-backed separatists that violate ceasefire agreements and as such, continue to emphasize the fundamental importance of providing security assistance and intelligence support, including lethal military assistance, to the Government of Ukraine to build its capacity to defend its territory and sovereignty.

The conferees are concerned that progress in the area of defense institutional reform has been slow and uneven and note that such reforms are critical to sustaining capabilities developed using security assistance. Such reforms are critical to the long-term stability and security of Ukraine. The conferees welcome the signing of the Partner Concept document between the United States and Ukraine as well as the appointment of a senior advisor to the Ukrainian government and encourage further progress on institutional reform efforts.

Subtitle E—Reform of Department of Defense Security Cooperation

Enactment of new chapter for defense security cooperation (sec. 1241)

The Senate bill contained a provision (sec. 1252) that would create a new chapter in title 10, United States Code, on security cooperation, and would transfer, modify, and codify security cooperation-related provisions from elsewhere in title 10 and public law to this new chapter.

The House amendment contained a similar provision (sec. 1261).

The House recedes with amendments that would make several modifications, including to: 1) narrow the scope of the authority for the Department to provide assistance to build the capacity of a friendly foreign nation to conduct specified military operations, modify the availability of funds for such purposes, and change notification requirements; 2) preserve the existing authority for the Department of Defense (DOD) to operate five Regional Centers for Security Studies; 3) require the Secretary of Defense to designate an individual and office at the Under Secretary of Defense-level or below with responsibility for oversight of strategic policy and guidance and responsibility for overall resource allocation for security cooperation programs and activities of the Department; and 4) authorize the Department to provide support to other departments and agencies of the United States Government for the purpose of implementing or supporting foreign assistance programs and activities that advance security cooperation objectives.

The conferees note that over the last 15 years, the Department of Defense's engagement with national security forces of friendly foreign countries has expanded in response to changing strategic requirements. Correspondingly, the number and complexity of authorities and associated funding provided to the Department to conduct security cooperation programs has expanded, resulting in security cooperation authorities being dispersed throughout title 10 and public law. This architecture has led to a confusing and unwieldy security cooperation enterprise that undermines the ability of the Department—particularly its senior civilian and military leaders—to prioritize, plan, synchronize, execute, allocate resources, and oversee activities. The current situation has also resulted in frequent changes for the security cooperation professionals attempting to implement security cooperation programs and activities. This has contributed to suboptimal outcomes and missed opportunities. Further, the conferees believe the complex patchwork of authorities and sources of funding hinders appropriate congressional and public transparency and complicates robust congressional oversight of a key mission for the Department.

As such, the conferees believe that consolidating the various security cooperation authorities under a single security cooperation chapter in title 10 will provide greater clarity and consistency about the nature and scope of DOD's security cooperation programs and activities to those who plan, manage, implement, and conduct oversight of these programs. The conferees note that the functional areas in which the Department is authorized to provide assistance under this provision are consistent with existing focus areas of the Department's 'train and equip' programs. The conferees also note that authority to provide assistance to build the capacity of friendly foreign countries to conduct military intelligence operations already exists, because the Department's existing authorities include support functions, and intelligence operations frequently act in that capacity. The inclusion of intelligence operations is intended solely to clarify that the Department may conduct such activities either as a supporting activity for other operations or as a stand-alone operation, and it is not meant to suggest that other activities that support or enable programs providing training and equipment to foreign forces (such as logistics or communications activities) are not permitted under existing authorities.

Additionally, for the purposes of executing programs and activities in the new security cooperation chapter in title 10, funds available to DOD for security cooperation may be used prior to the submission of a consolidated security cooperation budget as required by section 1249 of this subtitle.

Moreover, consolidation of a single 'train and equip' authority will ensure that the Department has flexibility to meet its evolving strategic objectives, without being forced to bend its strategy to meet the contours of available tailored authorities. The conferees do not intend for the consolidation to create a DOD mission that competes with security assistance overseen by the Department of State. Rather, a consolidated 'train and equip' authority should enable the Department to meet its own defense-specific objectives in support of broader defense strategy and plans, as well as to better integrate title

10 security cooperation activities into the broader United States Government approach to security sector assistance. To that end, the conferees note that the provision would increase coordination between the Department of Defense and the Department of State in the planning and implementation of security sector assistance programs by requiring the Secretary of Defense and the Secretary of State to jointly develop and plan 'train and equip' programs as well as to coordinate the implementation of such programs and ensure robust end-use monitoring of provided assistance. The conferees believe that the Department of Defense and the Department of State should have greater visibility into the planning, programming, and execution of each organization's security sector assistance programs and activities and urge both Departments to enhance visibility and collaboration on such programs early in the planning process and through execution so as to avoid unnecessary duplication and enhance overall unity of effort.

Additionally, the conferees are concerned that the existing process for coordination between the two Departments on security sector assistance programs is too ad-hoc in nature and often elevates responsibility for such coordination, particularly those activities requiring concurrence, to the seniormost echelons of the respective organizations—to include the Deputy Secretary or Secretary level—resulting in a cumbersome and time-intensive process. Therefore, the provision would require the Secretary of Defense and the Secretary of State to designate individuals at the lowest possible level in their respective organizations with responsibility for such coordination.

The conferees note that the Department's security cooperation activities over the last 15 years have emphasized building the capacity of partner forces at the tactical and operational level. However, the conferees are concerned that insufficient attention and resources have been provided for building institutional capacity at higher echelons, particularly the generating force (e.g. those with 'man, train, and equip' responsibilities) and at the strategic level (e.g. ministerial and general staff levels). The conferees expect the Department to increase its emphasis on strengthening the defense institutions of friendly foreign nations as it builds security cooperation programs and activities and expects proposals submitted to Congress to include a robust defense institution building component. Moreover, the conferees expect the Department to take advantage of the simplified framework of security cooperation authorities adopted in this section to develop security cooperation programs that integrate activities to simultaneously engage partners and build capacity at each of these levels—tactical, operational, and strategic.

Additionally, the conferees note the importance of sustaining capabilities provided to friendly foreign nations, particularly equipment, to the long-term success of DOD's security cooperation programs and activities. As such, the conferees expect that there is a plan to transition sustainment support from DOD to other sources of funding, such as foreign countries' national funds, will be part of each security cooperation program.

In addition to the cumbersome, confusing, and complex patchwork of authorities and funding sources, the Department's organizational structure for the security cooperation enterprise has undermined the ability of senior Department officials to adequately oversee, prioritize, and synchronize security cooperation programs and activities to support strategic priorities. Currently, there is no individual or office below the Deputy Secretary of Defense with responsibility to oversee strategic policy and resource allocation for the security cooperation enterprise. Instead, such responsibility spans multiple components and offices at the level of Under Secretary. Therefore, the provision would require the Secretary to assign responsibility for the oversight of strategic policy and guidance and responsibility for overall resource allocation for security cooperation programs and activities of the Department of Defense to a single official and office in the Office of the Secretary of Defense at the level of Under Secretary or below. The conferees intend for this individual and office to better synchronize planning and programs across the regional and functional components of the Department and ensure that such activities and resources are appropriately aligned with strategic priorities. Further, the conferees expect that this arrangement will empower the Department to prioritize resources and consider trade-offs across the full range of security cooperation programs and funding sources. Additionally, the provision would assign responsibility for the execution and administration of all security cooperation programs and activities of the Department of Defense involving the provision of defense articles, military training, and other defense-related services by grant, loan, cash sale, or lease to the Director of the Defense Security Cooperation Agency. This assignment of responsibility is meant to help the Department overcome the distortions, lack of coordination, and duplication that occurs across the Department's security cooperation enterprise, arising from narrowly-focused program offices found throughout the Office of the Secretary of Defense, the Joint Staff, Military Departments, Combatant Commands, and the defense agencies.

The provision would preserve the five Department of Defense Regional Centers for Security Studies. The provision would also require the Secretary to review, on an annual basis, the program and structure of each Regional Center in order to ensure that they are appropriately aligned with the strategic priorities of the Department. The conferees intend for the Regional Centers to more closely align activities with the requirements of DOD, and to serve as an effective tool to advance clearly defined security cooperation objectives in direct support of defense strategy.

The conferees note that, despite the marked increase in DOD security cooperation programs and activities over the last 15 years, the Department has not applied sufficient emphasis and resources to develop a comprehensive framework to assess, monitor, and evaluate its security cooperation programs and activities from inception to completion. Instead, the conferees believe that the Department has focused on assessments of partner nation capability gaps at the beginning of assistance programs rather than over the life cycle of the program, which has undermined the Department's ability to measure outcomes against objectives. Sufficient attention must be given to the implementation of programs with continuous robust evaluation to gauge whether programs and activities are meeting or have met defined objectives. The conferees expect the Department to allocate sufficient resources to its assessment, monitoring, and evaluation program, and to apply lessons learned from the program to improve and reshape security cooperation programs and activities to maximize effectiveness and efficiency.

Further, in this context, the conferees believe the Department's security cooperation data systems should provide an enterprisewide view of security cooperation activities to facilitate best practices and enable strategic decision-making. In addition to basic data about security cooperation programs, the system should support the distribution of lessons-learned, including the activities' goals and history of development, and inform future activities and resource allocation. The conferees note the current limitations of the Global Theater Security Cooperation Management information Systems (G–TSCMIS) program and encourage the Department to review the use and functionality of G–TSCMIS at all user levels. The Department should further consider measures to promote more wide-spread and regular use of G–TSCMIS and ensure that processes and system functionality appropriately collects, stores, integrates, and distributes information Department-wide.

Military-to-military exchanges (sec. 1242)

The Senate bill contained a provision (sec. 1253) that would combine existing security cooperation authorities permitting the exchange of military and defense personnel with allies of the United States and other friendly foreign countries.

The House amendment contained no similar provision.

The House recedes with a clarifying amendment.

The conferees encourage the Department to make more effective use of exchanges of military and defense personnel as important elements of broader security cooperation efforts, particularly with regard to building partner operational capacity or strengthening the management functions of partner defense institutions. Such exchanges offer opportunities for U.S. military and civilian personnel to mentor foreign counterparts, share relevant operational concepts, and assess how well previous assistance has been employed and sustained. Meanwhile, foreign exchange officers can obtain valuable on-the-job training working among their U.S. counterparts and improve their understanding of U.S. military organizations and operations, contributing to deeper interoperability. Such exchanges should be planned with these advantages in mind, in integration with other security cooperation activities and authorities.

Consolidation and revision of authorities for payment of personnel expenses necessary for theater security cooperation (sec. 1243)

The Senate bill contained a provision (sec. 1254) that would consolidate and modify similar authorities permitting the payment of personnel expenses of allied or partner countries during theater security cooperation activities.

The House amendment contained no similar provision.

The House recedes with a technical amendment.

Transfer and revision of certain authorities on payment of expenses of training and exercises with friendly foreign forces (sec. 1244)

The Senate bill contained a provision (sec. 1255) that would combine and modify similar authorities for paying for the expenses of partner nations when conducting training with U.S. Armed Forces and for the expenses of developing countries when participating in exercises.

The House amendment contained a similar provision (sec. 1202) that would extend the authority in section 1203 of the National Defense Authorization Act for Fiscal Year 2014 (Public Law 113–66) for training of general purpose forces of the United States Armed Forces with military and other security forces of friendly foreign countries to December 31, 2019.

The House recedes with an amendment that would combine and modify similar authorities for paying for the expenses of partner nations when conducting training with U.S. Armed Forces and for the expenses of developing countries when participating in exercises. The provision would also transfer section 2011 of title 10, United States Code to the new chapter 16 on security cooperation created elsewhere in this Act.

The conferees note that the transfer of section 2011 of title 10, United States Code to the new chapter 16 is part of a broader effort to consolidate and simplify authorities related to security cooperation. The conferees do not intend for this transfer to negatively impact administration of Special Operations Forces Joint Combined Exchange and Training Program by the Commander, United States Special Operations Command, which remains a standalone authority within the new chapter.

Transfer and revision of authority to provide operational support to forces of friendly foreign countries (sec. 1245)

The Senate bill contained a provision (sec. 1256) that would consolidate and modify section 127d of title 10, United States Code, section 1207 of the National Defense Authorization Act for Fiscal Year 2016 (Public Law 114–92), and section 1234 of the National Defense Authorization Act for Fiscal Year 2008 (Public Law 110–181), as amended, relating to the provision of operational support to partners and allies in combined operations with U.S. Armed Forces, in military operations that support U.S. national security interests, or in support of U.S. operations in Iraq and Afghanistan.

The House amendment contained no similar provision.

The House recedes with technical amendment.

Department of Defense State Partnership Program (sec. 1246)

The Senate bill contained a provision (sec. 1257) that would codify the Department of Defense State Partnership Program (section 1205 of the National Defense Authorization Act for Fiscal Year 2014 (Public Law 113–66), as amended by section 1203 of the National Defense Authorization Act for Fiscal Year 2016 (Public Law 114–92)).

The House amendment contained no similar provision.

The House recedes with a clarifying amendment.

Transfer of authority on regional defense combating terrorism fellowship program (sec. 1247)

The Senate bill contained a provision (sec. 1258) that would transfer to the new chapter 16 on security cooperation in title 10, United States Code, the regional combating terrorism fellowship program (section 2249c of title 10, United States Code) and modify the program to authorize the Secretary of Defense to carry out a program under which the Secretary may pay costs associated with the education and training of national-level security officials of friendly foreign nations.

The House amendment contained no similar provision.

The House recedes with an amendment that would transfer the underlying authority for the regional combating terrorism fellow-

ship program to the new chapter 16 on security cooperation and would make a technical modification to the reporting requirement.

Consolidation of authorities for service academy international engagement (sec. 1248)

The Senate bill contained a provision (sec. 1259) that would amend Chapter 16 of title 10, United States Code, to consolidate international engagement authorities for the service academies of the Army, Navy, and Air Force.

The House amendment contained no similar provision.

The House recedes.

The conferees note that under current law, there are nine separate authorities that determine the selection of, funding for, and conditions for international students attending the service academies of the Army, Navy, or Air Force. The conferees believe consolidating these authorities would provide consistency by creating a single, common authority for use by the service academies to select international students and conduct exchange programs with foreign military academies.

Consolidated annual budget for security cooperation programs and activities of the Department of Defense (sec. 1249)

The Senate bill contained a provision (sec. 1262) that would require the budget of the President for each fiscal year after fiscal year 2018, as submitted to Congress by the President pursuant to section 1105 of title 31, United States Code, to include as a separate item the amounts requested for the Department of Defense (including those funds in the budgets of the military departments) for such fiscal year for all security cooperation programs and activities of the Department, including the specific amounts, if any, and the specific country or region, to the maximum extent practicable, for such programs and activities.

The House amendment contained no similar provision.

The House recedes with a technical amendment.

Consistent with the creation of the new chapter 16 on security cooperation and the consolidation of the Department of Defense's security cooperation funding and related authorities, this provision is intended to enhance the ability of the congressional defense committees to conduct oversight of the Department's security cooperation programs and activities, including those undertaken by the military services; to understand better how the Department plans, programs, and prioritizes its security cooperation programs and activities to fill gaps in its contingency plans; to enable foreign partners against a common threat or enemy; and to align resources with the Department's strategic objectives. This approach is also intended to better enable public transparency.

Department of Defense security cooperation workforce development (sec. 1250)

The Senate bill contained a provision (sec. 1263) that would direct the Secretary of Defense to create a Department of Defense security cooperation workforce development program to oversee the development and management of a professional workforce supporting security cooperation programs of the Department of Defense as well as the execution of security assistance programs and activities under the Foreign Assistance Act and the Arms Control Act by the Department of Defense.

The House amendment contained no similar provision.

The House recedes with a clarifying amendment.

Despite the increasing emphasis on security cooperation to further its strategic objectives, the conferees are concerned that the Department of Defense—whether in implementing State Department programs or its own programs—has not devoted sufficient attention and resources to the development, management, and sustainment of the Department's security cooperation workforce to ensure effective assessment, planning, monitoring, execution, evaluation, and administration of security cooperation programs and initiatives. As a result of this inattention, security cooperation initiatives are not always planned and implemented in such a way as to most effectively advance national security objectives, and the Military Departments are left to pursue their unique service objectives, which may not always align with broader foreign policy objectives or integrate with Department of Defense efforts. The conferees are also concerned about the lack of standardization in the organization of the security cooperation workforce within the Military Departments.

Finally, the conferees believe that security cooperation outcomes would improve if the security cooperation planning workforce, including within Embassy country teams and at Geographic Combatant Commands, was able to draw upon not just the foreign area officer specialty, but also upon other relevant specialties such as force planning, logistics, and acquisition.

The conferees believe that building security capabilities of a partner nation and deepening interoperability through security cooperation requires a specialized set of skills, and the current system neither develops those skills among its workforce nor rationally assigns its workforce to match appropriate skills with requirements. The conferees believe increased attention and resourcing must be focused on the recruitment, training, certification, assignment, and career development of the security cooperation workforce. The conferees expect the Department to implement this authority expansively in order to address shortfalls in the security cooperation workforce throughout the enterprise.

Specifically, implementation of this authority should (1) ensure the development and rational allocation of qualified and experienced personnel in order to support high-priority security cooperation initiatives and partners; (2) ensure the appropriate sizing, organization, and chain-of-command for the security cooperation workforce within the Military Departments; (3) ensure the appropriate skills and capabilities are developed within the workforce and that there are standard and viable career paths; and (4) ensure sufficient size of the Title 10 workforce to enhance program management and administration, as well as to strike a more appropriate balance with the Title 22 workforce. The conferees expect that the Department will allocate necessary resources, from available Title 10 security cooperation program resources and other appropriate sources, sufficient to achieve these objectives, and reflect these costs in its annual security cooperation budget submission.

The conferees note that effectiveness and efficiency of security cooperation implementation will depend on a workforce that is integrated across the enterprise and responsive to clear strategic direction in support of Department priorities.

Reporting requirements (sec. 1251)

The Senate bill contained a provision (sec. 1261) to consolidate and standardize the Department's reporting on security cooperation authorities and programs in an annual report.

The House amendment contained a similar provision (sec. 1205).

The Senate recedes with a technical amendment.

The conferees note that this Act retains nearly all of the notification requirements with respect to the Department's security cooperation activities. Coupled with the requirement for an annual budget submission that appears elsewhere in this Act, this approach relieves the Department of an overly burdensome reporting regime while maintaining the transparency and accountability required for appropriate oversight and real-time monitoring of the Department's new programs. The conferees expect that the level of detail contained in the annual report should be equal to or greater than the existing individual reports. Any degradation in the quality of the reporting on the Department's security cooperation program and activities would be inconsistent with the intent of the conferees in undertaking this broader reform initiative.

Quadrennial Review of Security Sector Assistance Program and Authorities of the United States Government (sec. 1252)

The conference agreement includes a provision that would require the President to conduct a quadrennial review of all U.S. Government security sector assistance programs, policies, authorities, and resources.

Other conforming amendments and authority for administration (sec. 1253)

The Senate bill contained a provision (sec. 1265) that would repeal superseded, obsolete, or duplicate statutes relating to security cooperation as part of its efforts to streamline and rationalize the authorities of the Department to conduct security cooperation.

The House amendment contained no similar provision.

The House recedes with a technical amendment.

Subtitle F—Human Rights Sanctions

Global Magnitsky Human Rights Accountability Act (secs. 1261–1265)

The Senate bill contained provisions (secs. 1281–1284) that would authorize the President to impose sanctions with respect to any foreign person that the President determines is responsible for gross human rights violations or acts of significant corruption.

The House amendment contained no similar provision.

The House recedes with amendments which would sunset the provision six years after enactment, modify the congressional referral mechanism, and revise the waiver threshold for the termination of sanctions, as well as several technical amendments.

Subtitle G—Miscellaneous Reports

Modification of annual report on military and security developments involving the People's Republic of China (sec. 1271)

The House amendment contained a provision (sec. 1242) that would require a summary of the order of battle of the People's Liberation Army, including anti-ship ballistic missiles, theater ballistic missiles, and land attack cruise missile inventory and a description of the People's Republic of China's military and nonmilitary activities in the South China Sea to be added to the Annual Report on Military and Security Developments Involving the People's Republic of China.

The Senate bill contained no similar provision.

The Senate recedes.

Monitoring and evaluation of overseas humanitarian, disaster, and civic aid programs of the Department of Defense (sec. 1272)

The House amendment contained a provision (sec. 1245) that would authorize the Secretary of Defense to use up to 5 percent of the amounts authorized to be appropriated by this Act for Overseas Humanitarian, Disaster, and Civic Aid (OHDACA) for fiscal year 2017, to conduct monitoring and evaluation of the OHDACA programs of the Department of Defense. This section would also require the Secretary of Defense to provide a briefing to the specified committees not later than 90 days after the date of the enactment of this Act on mechanisms to evaluate OHDACA programs.

The Senate bill contained no similar provision.

The Senate recedes with an amendment that would extend the authorization to fiscal year 2018.

Strategy for United States defense interests in Africa (sec. 1273)

The House amendment contained a provision (sec. 1249) that would require the Secretary of Defense to submit a report not later than 1 year after the date of the enactment of this Act to the congressional defense committees that contains a strategy for United States defense interests in Africa.

The Senate bill contained no similar provision.

The Senate recedes with a technical amendment.

Report on the potential for cooperation between the United States and Israel on directed energy capabilities (sec. 1274)

The House amendment contained a provision (sec. 1250) that would allow the Secretary of Defense to carry out research, development, test and evaluation activities, on a joint basis with Israel to establish directed energy capabilities to detect and defeat ballistic missiles, cruise missiles, unmanned aerial vehicles, mortars, and improvised explosive devices that threaten the United States, deployed forced of the United States, or Israel.

The Senate bill contained no similar provision.

The Senate recedes with an amendment that would replace the House provision with the requirement for a report on the potential for United States and Israeli directed energy cooperation to defeat ballistic missiles, cruise missiles, unmanned aerial vehicles, mortars, and improvised explosive devices. The report is due to the congressional defense and foreign relations committees not later than 180 days after enactment of this act.

Annual update of Department of Defense Freedom of Navigation Report (sec. 1275)

The Senate bill contained a provision (sec. 1241) that directs the Secretary of Defense to submit an annual report to the Committees on Armed Services of the Senate and the House of Representatives setting forth an update on the most current Freedom of Navigation Report under the Freedom of Navigation Operations (FONOPS) program.

The House amendment contained a similar provision (sec. 1255) that directs the Secretary of Defense to submit a quarterly report to the congressional defense committees on any excessive territorial claims of foreign countries that were challenged by freedom of navigation operations and flights carried out by the armed forces during such fiscal quarter.

The House recedes with an amendment that would terminate the report on September 30, 2021.

Reports on INF Treaty and Open Skies Treaty (sec. 1276)

The House amendment contained a provision (sec. 1259H) that would require the Chairman of the Joint Chiefs of Staff to submit to the appropriate congressional committees a report on the Open Skies Treaty that assesses possible non-compliance of the treaty by the Russian Federation, and whether the treaty remains in the national security interest of the United States. It would also require a report on the INF Treaty of whether and why the Treaty remains in the national security interests of the United States and a specific plan to remedy the Russian violation of the INF Treaty.

The Senate bill contained no similar provision.

The Senate recedes with an amendment that would add the House Permanent Select Committee on Intelligence and the Senate Select Committee on Intelligence to the list of congressional committees to receive the reports.

Assessment of proliferation of certain remotely piloted aircraft systems (sec. 1277)

The Senate bill contained a provision (sec. 1275) that would require an independent assessment directed by the Chairman of the Joint Chiefs of Staff to report on the impact to United States national security interests of the proliferation of certain remotely piloted aircraft. The assessment would include an analysis of the threat posed to the United States as a result of the proliferation of such aircraft to adversaries, the impact of such proliferation on the combat capabilities of and interoperability with partners and allies of the United States, and the potential benefits and risks of continuing to limit exports of such aircraft.

The House amendment contained no similar provision.

The House recedes.

The conferees note that the proliferation of remotely piloted aircraft has significantly altered the context of the international security environment since the origination of the Missile Technology Control Regime that proscribes a "strong presumption of denial" for the export of such aircraft.

Subtitle H—Other Matters

Enhancement of interagency support during contingency operations and transition periods (sec. 1281)

The Senate bill contained a provision (sec. 1050) that would authorize the Secretary of Defense and the Secretary of State to enter into an agreement allowing each Secretary to provide support, supplies, and services on a reimbursement basis, or by exchange of support, supplies, and services, to the other Secretary during a contingency operation and related transition period.

The House amendment contained a similar provision (sec. 1246).

The Senate recedes with a technical amendment.

Two-year extension and modification of authorization of non-conventional assisted recovery capabilities (sec. 1282)

The Senate bill contained a provision (sec. 1274) that would extend the authority of the Department of Defense to establish, develop, and maintain non-conventional assisted recovery (NAR) capabilities for three additional years and modify the eligibility of personnel for whom such support may be provided.

The House amendment contained a similar provision that would modify section 943 of the Duncan Hunter National Defense Authorization Act for Fiscal Year 2009 (Public

Law 110–417), as most recently amended by section 1271 of the National Defense Authorization Act for Fiscal Year 2016 (Public Law 114–92), to permit the recovery of individuals identified by the Secretary of Defense when a non-conventional assisted recovery capability is already in place and would extend the authority through 2020.

The Senate recedes with a technical amendment.

The conferees direct the Department to ensure that the planning, initiation, sustainment, and utilization of NAR capabilities are fully coordinated and de-conflicted with other U.S. departments and agencies who may also play a role in the recovery of designated individuals overseas. (The conferees also note that non-conventional assisted recovery is a traditional military activity and the authority modified and extended by this provision does not authorize the conduct of intelligence activities.)

Authority to destroy certain specified World War II-era United States-origin chemical munitions located on San Jose Island, Republic of Panama (sec. 1283)

The House amendment contained a provision (sec. 1248) that would authorize the Secretary of Defense to destroy eight chemical munitions on San Jose Island, Panama. The use of these funds shall not take effect until there is an agreement between the United States and Panama that such munitions are termed "old chemical weapons" and not "abandoned chemical weapons" and that per the prior lease agreement, the United States is under no legal obligation to destroy any additional chemical munitions, munitions constituents, and associated debris that may be located on San Jose Island as a result of research, development, and testing activities conducted on San Jose Island during the period of 1943 through 1947. This provision is not applicable to agreements with or obligations to countries other than Panama.

The Senate bill contained a similar provision (sec. 1421).

The Senate recedes.

Sense of Congress on military exchanges between the United States and Taiwan (sec. 1284)

The Senate bill contained a provision (sec. 1243) that directed the Secretary of Defense to carry out a program of exchanges of senior military officers and senior officials between the United States and Taiwan, both in the United States and Taiwan, designed to improve military to military relations between the United States and Taiwan.

The House amendment contained a similar provision (sec. 1254) that expressed a sense of the congress that that the Secretary of Defense should conduct a program of senior military exchanges between the United States and Taiwan, both in the United States and Taiwan, that have the objective of improving military-to-military relations and defense cooperation between the United States and Taiwan.

The House recedes with an amendment that the Secretary of Defense should carry out such a program of exchanges, both in the United States and Taiwan.

Limitation on availability of funds to implement the Arms Trade Treaty (sec. 1285)

The House amendment contained a provision (sec. 1259A) that would prohibit the use of funds to implement the Arms Trade Treaty unless the Treaty has received the advice and consent of the Senate and has been the subject of implementing legislation. The National Defense Authorization Act for Fiscal Year 2016 (Public Law 114–92; 10 U.S.C. 801 note) contained a similar provision.

The Senate bill contained no similar provision.

The Senate recedes with a technical amendment.

Prohibition on use of funds to invite, assist, or otherwise assure the participation of Cuba in certain joint or multilateral exercises (sec. 1286)

The Senate bill contained a provision (sec. 1204) that would prohibit the Secretary of Defense from using any funds to invite, assist, or otherwise assure the participation of the Government of Cuba in any joint or multilateral exercise or related security conference between the United States and Cuba until the Secretary, in coordination with the Director of National Intelligence, submits to Congress certain assurances. The provision would provide an exception to the prohibition for any joint or multilateral exercise or operation related to humanitarian assistance or disaster response.

The House amendment contained a similar provision (sec. 1259B) that would prohibit the use of funds authorized to be appropriated or otherwise made available to the Department of Defense for any bilateral military-to-military contact or cooperation between the Governments of the United States and Cuba until the Secretary of Defense and the Secretary of State, in consultation with the Director of National Intelligence, certify to the appropriate congressional committees that the Government of Cuba has taken specified actions.

The Senate recedes with an amendment that would prohibit the Secretary of Defense from using any funds authorized to be appropriated or otherwise made available for fiscal year 2017 for the Department of Defense unless the Secretary of Defense and the Secretary of State, in consultation with the Director of National Intelligence, certify to the appropriate congressional committees that the Government of Cuba has taken specified actions, with certain exceptions.

It is the intent of the conferees that the exception contained in subsection (b)(1) of this section includes periodic contact between appropriate officials of the Governments of the United States and Cuba concerning the security and management of personnel and facilities at Naval Station Guantanamo Bay, commonly referred to as "fence-line talks," which have been a routine and ongoing activity for many years and have proven important to ensuring the safety of U.S. personnel serving at Naval Station Guantanamo Bay.

Global Engagement Center (sec. 1287)

The House amendment contained a provision (sec. 1259C) that would direct the Secretary of State in coordination with the Secretary of Defense (and relevant federal departments and agencies and partner nations) to establish a Global Engagement Center (GEC) within 6 months of enactment. The GEC's general purpose would be to discover, expose and counter foreign government information warfare efforts (to include foreign propaganda and disinformation efforts) and proactively advance fact-based narratives that support US allies and interests. The GEC would terminate 5 years after enactment.

The Senate bill contained no similar provision.

The Senate recedes with an amendment that included changes to the purpose and functions of the GEC, further specified the appointment, delegation and scope and responsibility and authority of the head of the GEC, modified the authority to transfer funds for the GEC, added a reporting requirement to the appropriate congressional committees, and extended the termination of the GEC to 8 years after enactment.

Modification of United States International Broadcasting Act of 1994 (sec. 1288)

The House amendment contained a provision (sec. 1259D) that would amend Section 304 of P.L. 103–236 (22 USC 6203) to permanently establish the Chief Executive Officer (CEO) position as head of the Broadcasting Board of Governors (BBG), the federal agency that oversees all U.S.-funded non-military international broadcasting, while removing the nine-member bipartisan Board that currently heads the agency. It would also provide certain new flexibilities in the BBG CEO's authorities, including expanded authority to allow the BBG CEO to direct appropriated funds and to hire certain personnel. The House amendment also contained a provision (sec. 1259E) that would authorize the BBG CEO to consolidate the current U.S. international broadcasters that receive federal grants as independent non-profit corporations (Radio Free Europe/Radio Liberty, Radio Free Asia, and the Middle East Broadcasting Networks) into one grantee broadcaster, with certain related expanded supervisory roles and authorities vested in the BBG CEO. This provision would also authorize the BBG CEO to establish a similar non-federal broadcasting corporation, receiving a federal operating grant, to assume the broadcasting responsibilities of the Voice of America (VOA, the federal government broadcaster operating within the BBG), and abolish VOA as a federal entity.

The Senate bill contained no similar provision.

The Senate recedes with an amendment that would eliminate the timing requirement for nomination of the BBG CEO, add a notification requirement for redirection of funds, establish the international broadcasting advisory board, add a mission definition for the consolidated broadcast entities, and deleted specific discussion of Voice of America.

Redesignation of South China Sea Initiative (sec. 1289)

The Senate bill contained a provision (sec. 1246) that would redesignate the South China Sea Initiative (Public Law 114–92; 129 Stat. 1073; U.S.C. 2282 note) as the Southeast Asia Maritime Security Initiative.

The House amendment contained a similar provision (sec. 1259F).

The Senate recedes.

The conferees believe that the United States should continue supporting the efforts of countries participating in the Southeast Asia Maritime Security Initiative to strengthen their maritime security capacity, domain awareness, and integration of their capabilities.

Measures against persons involved in activities that violate arms control treaties or agreements with the United States (sec. 1290)

The House amendment contained a provision (sec. 1259L) that would require the President to impose certain measures on a person the President determines has engaged in any activity that contributed to the President's or Secretary of State's determination that such a country is not in full compliance with its obligations undertaken in all arms control, on proliferation, and disarmament agreements to which the United States is participating state. Certain measures, exceptions, remedies, and waivers are included in the provision, including an exception for sanctions that would impact contracts related to major routes of supply; a waiver on a case-by-case if the person or entity engaging in, or supporting, an activity that contributed to a country not being in full compliance did not knowingly engage in such activity, and such waiver is in the interest of the national security of the United States; and termination of sanctions when the country concerned is no longer in violation.

The Senate bill contained no similar provision.

The Senate recedes with an amendment that would direct the Secretary of the Treasury to produce a list of persons (including an entity or entities) involved in sanctionable activity under this section not later than 30 days after the annual report on Adherence to and Compliance with Arms Control, Nonproliferation, and Disarmament Agreements and Commitments (required by 22 U.S.C. 2593a) has been submitted. Such person(s) would be subject to immediate sanction.

Additionally, the Senate amendment narrows the scope of the new sanction only to those countries who are not determined to be closely cooperating with the United States by the Director of National Intelligence.

The Senate amendment also required the waiver tied to a knowing violation include a requirement that such conduct has been terminated or that verifiable assurances that the person will terminate such activity have been provided.

The Senate amendment further provides waiver authority if the President determines on a case-by-case basis that the imposition of a sanction under this section would jeopardize an intelligence source or method. The conferees expect this waiver to be used only when there is a clear and specific risk that sources and methods would be compromised or exposed. Detailed information on such risk will be reported to the specified congressional committees.

The Senate amendment also provides measures to delay the immediate imposition of sanctions if the President determines the government of the country concerned has taken specific and effective actions, including penalties as appropriate, to terminate the involvement of a domiciled person in the activity that triggered sanctions. This delay includes up to 120 days if the President initiates consultations with the government of the country concerned and an additional 120 days if such government is in the process of taking specific and effective actions to terminate the involvement of a domiciled entity in the activity that triggered sanctions.

The Senate amendment contains additional measures for termination if the person has ceased the activity contributing to a country's violation.

Agreements with foreign governments to develop land-based water resources in support of and in preparation for contingency operations (sec. 1291)

The House amendment contained a provision (sec. 1259Q) that would authorize the Secretary of Defense, with the concurrence of the Secretary of State, to enter into agreements with foreign nations to develop land-based water resources in support of contingency operations.

The Senate bill contained no similar provision.

The Senate recedes with an amendment that would require the Secretary of Defense to notify the appropriate congressional committees 30 days after entering into an agreement.

Enhancing defense and security cooperation with India (sec. 1292)

The Senate bill contained a provision (sec. 1247) that would enhance military coopera-

tion between the United States and India by recommending the Secretary of Defense take certain steps regarding exchanges between senior military officers and senior civilian defense officials of the Government of India and the United States Government.

The House amendment contained a similar provision (sec. 1262) that would require certain actions by the Secretary of Defense and the Secretary of State to enhance defense and security cooperation between India and the United States.

The Senate recedes with an amendment.

Coordination of efforts to develop free trade agreements with sub-Saharan African countries (sec. 1293)

The Senate bill contained a provision (sec. 1271) that would amend section 116 of the African Growth and Opportunity Act (19 U.S.C. 3723).

The House amendment contained no similar provision.

The House recedes with a technical amendment.

Extension and expansion of authority to support border security operations of certain foreign countries (sec. 1294)

The Senate bill contained a provision (sec. 1272) that would expand the authority under section 1226 of the National Defense Authorization Act for Fiscal Year 2016 (Public Law 114–92; 129 Stat. 1056; 22 U.S.C. 2551 note) to provide assistance to the Governments of Jordan and Lebanon to support efforts to enhance security along borders with Syria and/or Iraq to also provide assistance to the Governments of Tunisia and Egypt to support efforts to enhance security along borders with Libya.

The House amendment contained no similar provision.

The House recedes with a technical amendment.

Should funds from the Counter Islamic State of Iraq and the Levant Fund be utilized to conduct activities pursuant to this authority, the conferees direct the Secretary of Defense to submit to the congressional defense committees a notification not later than 15 days before providing such support.

Modification and clarification of United States-Israel anti-tunnel cooperation authority (sec. 1295)

The Senate bill contained a provision (sec. 1273) that would increase the annual limitation of the authority under section 1279 of the National Defense Authorization Act for Fiscal Year 2016 (P.L. 114–92) for the Secretary of Defense, in consultation with the Secretary of State, to carry out research, development, test, and evaluation, on a joint basis with Israel to establish anti-tunnel defense capabilities to detect, map, and neutralize underground tunnels.

The House amendment contained no similar provision.

The House recedes.

Maintenance of prohibition on procurement by Department of Defense of People's Republic of China-origin items that meet the definition of goods and services controlled as munitions items when moved to the "600 series" of the Commerce Control List (sec. 1296)

The Senate bill contained a provision (sec. 886) that would amend section 1211 of the National Defense Authorization Act for Fiscal Year 2006 (Public Law 109–163) to maintain the prohibition on procuring military items from China.

The House amendment contained no similar provision.

The House recedes.

International sales process improvements (sec. 1297)

The Senate bill contained a provision (sec. 881) that would require the Secretary of Defense to develop a plan to improve the management and use of fees collected on the transfer of defense articles and services under programs in which the Defense Security Cooperation Agency has administrative responsibilities.

The House amendment contained no similar provision.

The House recedes with an amendment that would clarify requirements to be addressed in the plan and require that the plan be submitted to the congressional defense committees no later than 180 days after the date of enactment of this Act.

Efforts to end modern slavery (sec. 1298)

The Senate bill contained a provision (sec. 1276) that would require the Secretary of Defense to implement policies and procedures to ensure Armed Forces personnel engaged in partnership activities with foreign nations receive education and training on human slavery, and to ensure the United States Armed Forces maximize efforts to appropriately assist in combatting trafficking in persons. The provision would authorize grants to support transformational programs and projects that seek to achieve a measurable and substantial reduction of the prevalence of modern slavery in target populations within partner countries.

The House amendment contained no similar provision.

The House recedes with a technical amendment.

LEGISLATIVE PROVISIONS NOT ADOPTED

Modification and extension of authority to conduct activities to enhance the capability of foreign countries to respond to incidents involving weapons of mass destruction

The House amendment contained a provision (sec. 1203) that would modify section 1204 of the National Defense Authorization Act for Fiscal Year 2014 (Public Law 113–66) to include a 48-hour congressional notification when assistance expected to exceed $4.0 million is provided to certain foreign countries, to cap the funds available at $20.0 million, and extend the authority 1 year, through September 30, 2020.

The Senate bill contained no similar provision.

The House recedes.

The conferees note that elsewhere in this Act is a provision that would consolidate multiple authorities to build the capacity of friendly foreign nations to conduct specified operations, to include counter-weapons of mass destruction operations. The conferees intend for activities conducted to date under section 1204 of the National Defense Authorization Act for Fiscal Year 2014 (Public Law 113–66) to be conducted under the new building partnership capacity in the new chapter 16 on security cooperation without disruption. Further, the conferees intend that such activities to build the capacity of friendly foreign nations to conduct counter-weapons of mass destruction operations will continue to be administered by the Director of the Defense Threat Reduction Agency.

Report on the prohibition on use of funds for assistance to units of foreign security forces that have committed a gross violation of human rights

The House amendment included a provision (sec. 1208) that would require the Secretary of Defense to submit to the congressional defense committees a report on the implementation of section 294 of title 10, United States Code (relating to prohibition on use of funds for assistance to units of foreign security forces that have committed a gross violation of human rights).

The Senate bill included no similar provision.

The House recedes.

The conferees direct the Secretary of Defense, no later than 180 days after the enactment of this Act, to submit to the congressional defense committees a report on the implementation of section 294 of title 10, United States Code (relating to prohibition on use of funds for assistance to units of foreign security forces that have committed a gross violation of human rights). The report shall include (1) A detailed description of the policies and procedures governing the manner in which Department of Defense personnel identify and report information on gross violations of human rights and how such information is shared with personnel responsible for implementing the prohibition in subsection (a)(1) of section 294 of title 10, United States Code; (2) The funding expended in fiscal years 2015 and 2016 for purposes of implementing section 294 of title 10, United States Code, including any relevant training of personnel, and a description of the titles, roles, and responsibilities of the personnel responsible for reviewing credible information relating to human rights violations and the personnel responsible for making decisions regarding the implementation of the prohibition in subsection (a)(1) of such section 294; (3) An addendum that includes any findings or recommendations included in any report issued by a Federal Inspector General related to the implementation of section 294 of title 10, United States Code, and, as appropriate, the Department of Defense's response to such findings or recommendations; (4) implementation of section 1206 of the Carl Levin and Howard P. ''Buck'' McKeon National Defense Authorization Act for Fiscal Year 2015; and (5) Any other matters the Secretary determines is appropriate.

Sense of Congress on United States policy and strategy in Afghanistan

The House amendment contained a provision (sec. 1215) that would express the sense of Congress that the President should authorize a certain number of United States troops for missions in Afghanistan and provide the appropriate authorities, capabilities, and resources to ensure both mission success and adequate force protection for United State forces.

The Senate bill contained no similar provision.

The House recedes.

The conferees note that the United States continues to have vital national security interests in ensuring that Afghanistan is a stable, sovereign country and that stability and security in Afghanistan reinforces stability and security in the region. The conferees urge the President to ensure that the commander in Afghanistan has the required resources, authorities, and capabilities to protect U.S. and Coalition troops and to enable their counterterrorism and train, advise and assist missions. Further, the conferees believe that the United States should continue to provide the required support to the Afghan National Defense and Security Forces to secure Afghanistan.

Sense of Congress relating to Dr. Shakil Afridi

The House amendment contained a provision (sec. 1218) that would establish findings and a sense of Congress regarding the continued detention of Dr. Shakil Afridi by the Pakistani government.

The Senate bill contained no similar provision.

The House recedes.

The conferees note the contributions of Dr. Afridi to efforts to locate Osama bin Laden, remain concerned about Dr. Afridi's continuing incarceration, and urge the Government of Pakistan to release him immediately.

Report on access to financial records of the Government of Afghanistan to audit the use of funds for assistance for Afghanistan

The House amendment contained a provision (sec. 1219) that would require the Secretary of Defense to submit a report to Congress on the extent to which the Combined Security Transition Command-Afghanistan has adequate access to financial records of the Government of Afghanistan to audit the use of funds authorized to be appropriated by this Act or otherwise made available for fiscal year 2017 for assistance for Afghanistan.

The Senate bill contained no similar provision.

The House recedes.

The conferees direct the Secretary of Defense to provide a briefing to the congressional defense committees not later than 90 days after the enactment of this Act on the extent to which the Department of Defense has adequate access, for accountability purposes, to financial records of the Government of Afghanistan associated with the use of funds authorized to be appropriated by this act or otherwise made available for fiscal year 2017 for security assistance for Afghanistan.

Report on prevention of future terrorist organizations in Iraq and Syria

The House amendment contained a provision (sec. 1224) that would require the Secretary of Defense to submit a report that describes the political, economic, and security conditions in Iraq and Syria that would be necessary and sufficient to prevent the formation of future terrorist organizations in Iraq and Syria that may present a danger to the United States, its allies, and the stability of Iraq, Syria, and the rest of the Middle East region.

The Senate bill contained no similar provision.

The House recedes.

The conferees direct the Secretary of Defense and Secretary of State to jointly provide a report to the congressional defense committees, the Senate Foreign Relations Committee, and the House Foreign Affairs Committee not later than one year after the date of the enactment of this Act on the political and military strategies to defeat the Islamic State in Iraq and the Levant (ISIL), and on the political, economic, and security conditions in Iraq and Syria that would be necessary and sufficient to prevent the formation of future terrorist organizations in Iraq and Syria. At a minimum, the briefing should include a description of: (1) the military conditions that must be met for ISIL to be considered defeated; (2) the plan for achieving a political transition in Syria; (3) a plan for Iraqi political reform and reconciliation among ethnic groups and political parties; (4) an assessment of the required future size and structure of the Iraqi Security Forces, including irregular forces; and (5) a description of the roles and responsibilities of U.S. allies and partners and other countries in the region in establishing regional stability.

The conferees also direct the Comptroller General of the United States to submit to the congressional defense committees, the Senate Foreign Relations Committee, and the House Foreign Affairs Committee, not later than one year after the date of the enactment of this Act, a report on the United States' and the Government of Iraq's capacities to apply transparency and anti-fraud mechanisms, accounting and internal controls standards, and other financial management and accountability measures to transfers of cash and other forms of assistance provided to the Iraqi Security Forces, including irregular forces, and other recipients through the Iraq Train and Equip Fund.

Semiannual report on integration of political and military strategies against ISIL

The House amendment contained a provision (sec. 1225) that would require the Secretary of Defense and Secretary of State to jointly submit a semi-annual report on the political and military strategies to defeat the Islamic State in Iraq and the Levant. The provision would also require the Comptroller General of the United States to review certain financial management and accountability measures relating to assistance provided through the Iraq Train and Equip Fund.

The Senate bill contained no similar provision.

The House recedes.

The conferees note that matters raised by the House provision are addressed elsewhere in this report.

Sense of Congress condemning continuing attacks on medical facilities in Syria

The House amendment contained a provision (sec. 1226) that would express the sense of Congress that the United States Government should condemn and call for an immediate end to attacks on medical facilities and medical providers in Syria and encourage the United States Government to support efforts to meet urgent humanitarian needs where appropriate.

The Senate bill contained no similar provision.

The House recedes.

The conferees note with deep concern continued attacks on civilians, medical personnel, and medical facilities in Syria. These attacks constitute violations of international humanitarian law. The conferees urge the Department of Defense to ensure these violations are documented and further encourage the Department of Defense to support, where appropriate, international efforts to meet humanitarian and medical needs in Syria.

Sense of Congress on business practices of the Islamic State of Iraq and Syria

The House amendment contained a provision (sec. 1228) that would express the sense of Congress that the United States should focus all necessary efforts in the Middle East to disrupt the financing of the Islamic State of Iraq and the Levant (ISIL) through oil production and sale.

The Senate bill contained no similar provision.

The House recedes.

The conferees remain prepared to provide U.S. military forces engaged in Operation Inherent Resolve and other counterterrorism operations across the globe with the resources and authorities necessary to defeat the Islamic State in Iraq and the Levant, al Qaeda, and forces associated with these groups, including the resources and authorities necessary to disrupt the financing of those groups through oil production and sale.

Statement of policy on United States efforts in Europe to reassure United States partners and allies and deter aggression by the Government of the Russian Federation

The House amendment contained a provision (sec. 1234) that would express a statement that it is the policy of the United States to reassure U.S. partners and allies in Europe and to deter aggression by the Government of the Russian Federation in order to enhance regional and global security and stability.

The Senate bill contained no similar provision.

The House recedes.

The conferees remain concerned about the evolving security situation throughout the European continent. A revanchist Russian Federation, rising incidents of terrorism, and unprecedented refugee and migrant flows are among the issues that continue to present significant security challenges to the region. The conferees recognize the North Atlantic Treaty Organization (NATO) as the cornerstone of transatlantic security cooperation and the guarantor of peace and stability in Europe. The conferees believe that NATO members must continue to review defense spending to ensure sufficient funding is obligated to meet security needs, as well as providing adequate NATO contributions. The fulfillment of NATO members' commitments to allocate a minimum of two percent of Gross Domestic Product (GDP) for defense expenditures and 20 percent of defense expenditures on major equipment, is of vital importance to the health of the NATO alliance. The conferees remain committed to supporting and upholding the policies enumerated in the NATO 2012 Wales Summit and the NATO 2016 Warsaw Summit including full realization of the Readiness Action Plan, fulfillment of defense spending commitments, and timely implementation of an enhanced forward military presence.

The conferees support U.S. efforts to increase presence in the European theater and commend the work of the Department of Defense thus far to reassure U.S. allies and partners in the region, increase NATO interoperability, provide critical training and assistance to European allies and partners, and deter Russian aggression. The conferees view the fiscal year 2017 President's Budget Request of $3.42 billion for the European Deterrence Initiative (EDI) as an important step to support the stability and security of the region and deter further Russian antagonism and aggression. EDI will continue to serve as an important tool to bolster U.S. force presence in the region, train and equip the security forces of European partners and allies, enhance indications and warning mechanisms, and improve U.S. agility and flexibility through strategic infrastructure investments. The conferees believe additional emphasis is necessary on developing capabilities for countering unconventional methods of warfare such as cyber warfare, economic coercion, information operations, and intelligence operations. The conferees encourage the Department of Defense to include EDI resources and programs in the base budget in order to ensure persistent funding support as well as the ability to plan for long-term investments towards the security and stability of the European continent.

European investment in security and stability

The Senate bill contained a provision (sec. 1234) that would express the sense of Congress that North Atlantic Treaty Organization (NATO) allies and European partners are indispensable to addressing global security challenges and that their investment in

developing and employing robust security capabilities in Europe should meet or exceed U.S. efforts in this regard and would require an accounting by the Secretary of Defense of current and planned security investments by NATO allies and European partners.

The House amendment contained no similar provision.

The Senate recedes.

The conferees direct the Secretary of Defense, not later than 60 days after the date of the enactment of this Act, to present to the congressional defense committees, the Senate Foreign Relations Committee, and the House Foreign Affairs Committee an accounting of European investment in security capabilities including current and planned efforts to contribute to global security operations. The presentation should include a summary of major outcomes from recent NATO summits, as well as a detailed accounting of initiatives by other NATO members and European partners to: a.) deter security challenges posed by Russia, b.) increase capabilities to respond to unconventional or hybrid warfare tactics, c.) enhance security in Europe in ways that match or compliment United States contributions to conventional deterrence in the region, d.) contribute to the campaign to counter the Islamic State of Iraq and the Levant and the NATO-led mission in Afghanistan, and e.) counter terrorism in Europe and Africa, as well as any other matters the Secretary of Defense considers appropriate.

Sense of Senate on European Deterrence Initiative

The Senate Bill contained a provision (sec. 1235) that would express the sense of the Senate that the European Deterrence Initiative will bolster efforts to deter further Russian aggression, enhance the capability to defend territorial integrity and preserve regional stability, and improve the agility and flexibility of military forces to address threats across the full spectrum of warfighting requirements and diverse geographic locations. The provision would also express the sense of the Senate that such efforts as the European Deterrence Initiative should be in the base budget of the Department of Defense to address long-term stability on the European continent.

The House amendment contained no similar provision.

The Senate recedes.

The conferees note that support for the European Deterrence Initiative and its importance to the stability and security of the region and deterring further Russian antagonism and aggression is addressed elsewhere in this report.

Modification and extension of report on military assistance to Ukraine

The House amendment contained a provision (sec. 1237) that would express the sense of Congress that the United States should continue to support the Government of Ukraine's efforts to provide and maintain security in Ukraine including support to the Ukrainian military, the Ukrainian National Guard, and the State Border Guard Service of Ukraine.

The Senate bill contained no similar provision.

The House recedes.

The conferees remain deeply concerned about the ongoing threats to the sovereignty and territorial integrity of Ukraine, including the continued violations of ceasefire agreements by Russia and Russian-backed separatists. The conferees urge the Department of Defense to continue to provide ro-

bust support to the Government of Ukraine, including through lethal assistance, to help defend against such aggression. The conferees note that authorization to provide assistance to the State Border Guard Service of Ukraine is included in another provision of this Act.

Sense of Congress on malign activities of the Government of Iran

The House amendment contained a provision (sec. 1241) that would express the sense of Congress that the United States should increase efforts to counter the continued expansion of malign activities of the Government of Iran in the Middle East.

The Senate bill contained no similar provision.

The House recedes.

The conferees urge the Secretary of Defense to increase efforts to counter the Government of Iran's malign activities, including by maintaining a robust U.S. military presence forward deployed in the United States Central Command area of responsibility and by further enhancing regional ballistic missile defense capabilities and cooperation.

Inclusion of the Philippines among allied countries with whom United States may enter into cooperative military airlift agreements

The Senate bill contained a provision (sec. 1242) that would include the Philippines among allied countries that the United States can enter into a cooperative military airlift agreement with.

The House amendment contained no similar provision.

The Senate recedes.

Sense of Congress on trilateral cooperation between Japan, South Korea, and the United States

The House amendment contained a provision (sec. 1243) that expressed a sense of the Congress that Japan and the Republic of Korea (South Korea) are both treaty allies and critically important security partners of the United States.

The Senate bill contained no similar provision.

The House recedes.

The conferees recognize the continued importance of trilateral cooperation among the United States, Japan, and the Republic of Korea. More specifically, the conferees believe the United States should continue to support defense cooperation between Japan and the Republic of Korea on the full range of issues related to North Korea as well as other security challenges in the Asia-Pacific region.

Sense of Congress on cooperation between Singapore and the United States

The House amendment contained a provision (sec. 1244) that expressed a sense of the Congress regarding continued cooperation between the United States and the Republic of Singapore.

The Senate bill contained no similar provision.

The House recedes.

The conferees recognize the continued role Singapore has played as a security partner in Southeast Asia, including its recent decision to host rotational P-8 Poseidon deployments.

United States policy on Taiwan

The Senate bill contained a provision (sec. 1244) that expressed a sense of the Senate that the United States should strengthen and enhance its long-standing partnership and strategic cooperation with Taiwan, with the objective of reinforcing its commitment to the Taiwan Relations Act and the "Six Assurances."

The House amendment contained a similar provision (sec. 1259) that directs the Secretary of Defense and the Secretary of State to jointly submit to the appropriate committees of Congress a report that contains a description of the steps the United States has taken, plans to take, and will take to provide Taiwan with arms of a defensive character in accordance with the Taiwan Relations Act (Public Law 96–8; 22 U.S.C. 3301 et seq.) no later than February 15, 2017.

The legislative provisions were not adopted.

The conferees direct the Secretary of Defense and the Secretary of State to provide a briefing to the congressional defense committees on the steps the United States has taken, plans to take, and will take to provide Taiwan with arms of a defensive character in accordance with the Taiwan Relations Act (Public Law 96–8; 22 U.S.C. 3301 et seq.) no later than September 1, 2017.

The conferees believe the United States should conduct regular transfers of defense articles and defense services with the government of Taiwan, support the efforts of Taiwan to integrate innovative and asymmetric capabilities, including undersea warfare capabilities optimized for the defense of the Taiwan Strait, assist Taiwan in building an effective air defense capability consisting of a balance of fighters and mobile air defense systems, and permit Taiwan to participate in bilateral training activities hosted by the United States that increase the credible deterrent capabilities of Taiwan.

Sense of Congress on military relations between Vietnam and the United States

The Senate bill contained a provision (sec. 1245) that expressed a sense of the Senate that removing the prohibition on the sale of lethal military equipment to the Government of Vietnam would further United States national security interests, that any future arms sales by the United States to Vietnam should be monitored to ensure that Vietnam continues to make progress on human rights and that arms sold in the future are not being used by Vietnam in ways that violate the human rights and freedom of civilians in Vietnam.

The House amendment contained a similar provision (sec. 1259V) that expressed a sense of the Congress that the United States Government should review its policy on the transfer of lethal weapons to Vietnam and that it should evaluate certain human rights benchmarks when providing military assistance to Vietnam.

The legislative provisions were not adopted.

The conferees support the decision to fully lift the ban on the sale of lethal military equipment to Vietnam and believe that the United States Government must continue to monitor Vietnam's human rights record in the context of providing Vietnam with lethal military equipment in the future.

Annual report on foreign military sales to Taiwan

The House amendment contained a provision (sec. 1256) that directs the Secretary of Defense to submit to the Committees on Armed Services and Foreign Relations of the Senate and the Committees on Armed Services and Foreign Affairs of the House of Representatives a report that lists each request received from Taiwan and each letter of offer to sell any defense articles or services under this Act to Taiwan during such fiscal year.

The Senate bill contained no similar provision.

The House recedes.

Elsewhere in this report, the conferees note that the United States should conduct regular transfers of defense articles and defense services with the government of Taiwan.

Sense of Congress in support of a denuclearized Korean peninsula

The House amendment contained a provision (sec. 1259K) that expressed a sense of the Congress that United States foreign policy should support a denuclearized Korean peninsula.

The Senate bill contained no similar provision.

The House recedes.

The conferees express their strong support for the decision to deploy the Terminal High Altitude Area Defense (THAAD) missile defense system to the Republic of Korea. The conferees regard this deployment as benefiting the United States and the Republic of Korea by further protecting the citizens of both countries against the threat of missile attack on the Korean Peninsula.

Authority to grant observer status to the military forces of Taiwan at RIMPAC exercises

The House amendment contained a provision (sec. 1259P) that authorized the Secretary of Defense to grant observer status to the military forces of Taiwan in the maritime exercise known as the Rim of the Pacific Exercise.

The Senate bill contained no similar provision.

The House recedes.

The conferees note that the Secretary of Defense has the authority to invite Taiwan to the Rim of the Pacific exercise.

Sense of Congress on commitment to the Republic of Palau

The Senate bill contained a provision (sec. 1277) that would express a sense of the Congress that Congress and the President should promptly enact the Compact Review Agreement signed by the United States and Palau in 2010.

The House amendment contained no similar provision.

The Senate recedes.

The conferees believe that enacting the Compact Review Agreement is important to United States' national security interests and, as such, believe that the President should include the Compact Review Agreement in the Fiscal Year 2018 budget request.

Sense of Congress on support for Estonia, Latvia, and Lithuania

The House amendment contained a provision (sec. 1251) that would express the sense of the Congress on support for the Republic of Estonia, the Republic of Latvia, and the Republic of Lithuania, including support for their sovereignty.

The Senate bill contained no similar provision.

The House recedes.

The conferees note that support for allies and partners in Europe is addressed elsewhere in this report.

Sense of Congress on security sector assistance

The Senate bill contained a provision (sec. 1251) that would express the Sense of the Congress on the security cooperation programs and activities of the Department of Defense, as well as the broader security sector assistance activities of the U.S. government.

The House amendment contained no similar provision.

The Senate recedes.

Sense of Congress on support for Georgia

The House amendment contained a provision (sec. 1252) that would express the sense of the Congress on support for Georgia's sovereignty and territorial integrity as well as support for continued cooperation between the United States and Georgia.

The Senate bill contained no similar provision.

The House recedes.

The conferees note that support for allies and partners in Europe is addressed elsewhere in this report.

Sense of Congress regarding on July 2016 NATO Summit in Warsaw, Poland

The House amendment contained a provision (sec. 1257) that would express the sense of the Congress on supporting certain outcomes of the July 2016 North Atlantic Treaty Organization (NATO) Summit in Warsaw, Poland.

The Senate bill contained no similar provision.

The House recedes.

The conferees note that support for certain outcomes of the NATO Summit is addressed elsewhere in this report.

Report on violence and cartel activity in Mexico

The House amendment contained a provision (sec. 1258) that would require the Secretary of Defense to submit to the congressional defense committees a report on violence and cartel activity in Mexico and the impact on the national security of the United States.

The Senate bill contained no similar provision.

The House recedes.

The conferees note that the ongoing violence associated with transnational organized crime poses a threat to the security interests of Mexico and the United States. The conferees recognize the shared commitment of the United States and Mexico to combat this threat and expect the Secretary of Defense to update periodically the Committees on Armed Services of the House of Representatives and the Senate on the Department's security cooperation activities with the Government of Mexico.

Opportunities to equip certain foreign military entities

The House amendment contained a provision (sec. 1259G) that would add the requirement for a report that describes efforts to make United States manufacturers aware of opportunities to equip foreign military forces approved to receive assistance from the United States and any new plans to raise awareness of such opportunities.

The Senate bill contained no similar provision.

The House recedes.

The conferees direct the Secretary of Defense and the Secretary of State to jointly provide a briefing to the congressional defense committees, the Senate Foreign Relations Committee, and the House Foreign Affairs Committee, within 180 days of the enactment of this act, on efforts to make United States manufacturers aware of procurement opportunities related to equipping foreign security forces approved to purchase or receive equipment from United States manufacturers.

Sense of Congress regarding the role of the United States in the North Atlantic Treaty Organization

The House amendment contained a provision (sec. 1259I) that would express the sense of the Congress that continued United States leadership in the North Atlantic Treaty Organization is critical to the national security of the United States.

The Senate bill contained no similar provision.

The House recedes.

The conferees note that the importance of continued United States leadership in the North Atlantic Treaty Organization is addressed elsewhere in this report.

Authorization of United States assistance to Israel

The House amendment contained a provision (sec. 1259J) that would authorize the President to provide assistance to Israel to improve maritime security and maritime domain awareness.

The Senate bill contained no similar provision.

The House recedes.

The conferees note that maritime security and maritime domain awareness in the Eastern Mediterranean Sea are critical not only to the security of Israel but also to U.S. national security interests and encourage the Department of Defense to continue efforts to develop and improve capabilities in these areas.

Department of Defense report on cooperation between Iran and the Russian Federation

The House amendment contained a provision (sec. 1259M) that would require a report on cooperation between Iran and the Russian Federation.

The Senate bill contained no similar provision.

The House recedes.

The conferees direct the Secretary of Defense and Secretary of State to jointly provide a briefing to the congressional defense committees, the Senate Foreign Relations Committee, and the House Foreign Affairs Committee not later than 180 days after the date of the enactment of this Act, on cooperation between Iran and the Russian Federation. The briefing shall, at a minimum, include (1) how such cooperation affects the national security interests of the United States; (2) cooperation relating to the conflict in Syria; (3) weapons, if any, transferred from Russia to Iran; (4) cooperation, if any, in space and to what extent those capabilities can be applied to Iran's ballistic missile program; and (5) naval cooperation in the Eastern Mediterranean Sea and Arabian Gulf.

Report on maintenance by Israel of a robust independent capability to remove existential security threats

The House amendment contained a provision (sec. 1259N) that would express the sense of Congress that Israel should be able to defend its vital national interests and protect its territory and population against existential threats. The provision would also require a report to certain committees of Congress that would identify capabilities and platforms requested by the Government of Israel that would contribute to the maintenance of Israel's defensive capability, assess the availability for sale or transfer of such items, and describe what steps the President is taking to transfer those items.

The Senate bill contained no similar provision.

The House recedes.

Report on use by the Government of Iran of commercial aircraft and related services for illicit military or other activities

The House amendment contained a provision (sec. 1259O) that would require a report to certain committees of Congress on the use by the Government of Iran of commercial aircraft and related services for illicit military and other activities for the past five years.

The Senate bill contained no similar provision.

The House recedes.

The conferees direct that not later than 180 days after the date of the enactment of this Act, the Secretary of Defense and the Secretary of State shall provide a briefing to the congressional defense committees and the Committee on Foreign Relations of the Senate and the Committee on Foreign Affairs of the House of Representatives on the use of the commercial entities by the Government of Iran for illicit military or other activities during the 5-year period ending on the date of enactment of this Act. The briefing, at a minimum, should include a description of the extent to which: (1) the Government of Iran has used commercial entities to facilitate the shipment of illicit cargo; (2) the commercial sector of Iran has provided financial, material, and technological support to the Islamic Revolutionary Guard Corps (IRGC); and (3) foreign governments and persons have facilitated such activities, including allowing the use of airports, services, or other resources.

Extension of reporting requirements on the use of certain Iranian seaports by foreign vessels and use of foreign airports by sanctioned Iranian air carriers

The House amendment contained a provision (sec. 1259R) that would amend section 1252(a) of the National Defense Authorization Act for Fiscal Year 2013 (22 U.S.C. 8808(a)).

The Senate bill contained no similar provision.

The House recedes.

Sense of Congress on integrated ballistic missile defense system for GCC partner countries, Jordan, Egypt and Israel

The House amendment contained a provision (sec. 1259T) that would express the sense of Congress that to assist in preventing an attack by Iran, the United States should encourage and enable as appropriate an integrated ballistic missile defense system that links GCC partner countries, Jordan, Egypt, and Israel.

The Senate bill contained no similar provision.

The House recedes.

The conferees encourage the United States Government to continue to work towards a ballistic missile defense system that integrates the capabilities of Gulf Cooperation Council partner nations.

Authority to provide assistance and training to increase maritime security and domain awareness of foreign countries bordering the Persian Gulf, Arabian Sea, or Mediterranean Sea

The House amendment contained a provision (sec. 1259U) that would authorize assistance and training to increase maritime security and domain awareness of foreign countries bordering the Persian Gulf, the Arabian Sea, or the Mediterranean Sea in order to deter and counter illicit smuggling and related maritime activity by Iran, including illicit Iranian weapons shipments.

The Senate bill contained no similar provision.

The House recedes.

The conferees note that this provision would be duplicative of provisions included elsewhere in this Act. The conferees further note that the stated purpose of this provision is indeed an important matter—maritime security in the Arabian Sea, Arabian Gulf, and Mediterranean Sea are critical to U.S. national security interests and the global marketplace.

Report on efforts to combat Boko Haram in Nigeria and the Lake Chad Basin

The House amendment contained a provision (sec. 1259W) that would express a sense of Congress and require the Secretary of Defense, the Secretary of State, and the Attorney General to jointly submit to Congress a report on efforts to combat Boko Haram against the people of Nigeria and the Lake Chad Basin.

The Senate bill contained no similar provision.

The House recedes.

The conferees note that the ongoing violence and abhorrent human rights violations perpetrated by the terrorist group Boko Haram against the people of the Lake Chad Basin region of Africa poses a threat to the regional stability and to the security interests of the United States associated with ongoing violence and the gross human rights violations against the people of the Lake Chad Basin carried out by Boko Haram and the need to investigate and prosecute such violations. The conferees also note the need to bring to justice those responsible for such atrocities should be brought to justice. The conferees recognize the shared commitment of the United States and countries of the Lake Chad Basin to combat Boko Haram and expect the Secretary of Defense to update the Committees on Armed Services of the House of Representatives and the Senate periodically on the Department's activities in this regard.

Security cooperation enhancement fund

The Senate bill contained a provision (sec. 1260) that would create a central fund for the security cooperation programs and activities of the Department of Defense.

The House amendment contained no similar provision.

The Senate recedes.

Coordination between Department of Defense and Department of State on certain security cooperation and security assistance programs and activities

The Senate bill contained a provision (sec. 1264) that would require the Secretary of Defense and the Secretary of State not later than 90 days after enactment of this Act to establish interim regulations and, not later than 270 days after enactment of this Act, final regulations, to establish a formal process for the two Departments on all matters relating to the policy, planning, and implementation of security cooperation programs and activities as specified in the Act.

The House amendment contained no similar provision.

The Senate recedes.

United Nations processing center in Erbil, Iraqi Kurdistan, to assist internationally-displaced communities

The House amendment contained a provision (sec. 1227) that would seek the establishment of a United Nations processing center in Erbil, Iraqi Kurdistan, to assist internationally-displaced communities through the voice and vote of the United States at the United Nations.

The Senate bill contained no similar provision.

The House recedes.

TITLE XIII—COOPERATIVE THREAT REDUCTION

Specification of Cooperative Threat Reduction funds (sec. 1301)

The Senate bill contained a provision (sec. 1301) that would authorize funds to be appropriated by the Department of Defense for the Cooperative Threat Reduction Program.

The House amendment contained an identical provision (sec. 1301).

The conference agreement includes this provision.

Funding allocations (sec. 1302)

The Senate bill contained a provision (sec. 1302) that would allocate funding for the Cooperative Threat Reduction program from within the overall $325.6 million that the committee would authorize for the CTR Program. The allocation under this section reflects the amount of the budget request for fiscal year 2017.

The House amendment contained a similar provision (sec. 1302) that would allocate funding for the Cooperative Threat Reduction program at $325.6 million, including for certain specific purposes. In addition, the House amendment would also extend certain notification requirements, which would allow the committee to enhance its oversight of proposed CTR projects. Further, it would require a new determination as to whether other authorities are also available to the Secretary of Defense, and other Secretaries as applicable, and if they exist, an explanation for why the Secretaries were not able to use them for a specific proposed project.

The Senate recedes.

Limitation on availability of funds for Cooperative Threat Reduction in People's Republic of China (sec. 1303)

The House amendment contained a provision (sec. 1303) that would ensure Cooperative Threat Reduction funds are obligated or expended in quarterly installments. The provision would further require that the Secretary of Defense not obligate or expend funds for CTR activities in China unless he has submitted to the specific congressional committees a certification regarding certain nonproliferation benchmarks (including the arrest of Li Fangwei, also known as "Karl Lee") with respect to China.

The Senate bill contained no similar provision.

The Senate recedes with an amendment that requires obligation or expenditure of such funds in semiannual installments. The amendment further requires that 15 days before funds are obligated, the Secretary of Defense shall submit to the congressional defense committees, the House Foreign Affairs Committee and the Senate Committee on Foreign Affairs the report on such activities as required by section 50 United States Code 3711(g). In addition to the matters required by 50 United States Code 3711(g), each report shall include in coordination with the Secretary of State whether China has taken material steps to disrupt proliferation activities of Li Fangwei; and arrest Li Fangwei pursuant to an indictment charged in the United States District Court of New York on April 29, 2014; and whether China has proliferated to any non-nuclear weapons state or any nuclear weapons state in violation of the Treaty on Non-Proliferation of Nuclear Weapons including any item that contributes to a ballistic missile as well as the number and type of demarches with respect to the above matters.

TITLE XIV—OTHER AUTHORIZATIONS

Subtitle A—Military Programs

Working Capital Funds (sec. 1401)

The Senate bill contained a provision (sec. 1401) that would authorize appropriations for Defense Working Capital Funds at the levels identified in section 4501 of division D of this Act.

The House amendment contained an identical provision (sec. 1401).

The conference agreement includes this provision.

Chemical Agents and Munitions Destruction, Defense (sec. 1402)

The Senate bill contained a provision (sec. 1402) that would authorize the appropriations for Chemical Agents and Munitions Destruction, Defense, at levels identified in section 4501 of division D of this Act.

The House amendment contained an identical provision (sec. 1403).

The conference agreement includes this provision.

Drug Interdiction and Counter-Drug Activities, Defense-Wide (sec. 1403)

The Senate bill contained a provision (sec. 1403) that would authorize appropriations for Drug Interdiction and Counter-Drug Activities, Defense-Wide at the levels identified in section 4501 of division D of this Act.

The House amendment contained an identical provision (sec. 1404).

The conference agreement includes this provision.

Defense Inspector General (sec. 1404)

The Senate bill contained a provision (sec. 1404) that would authorize appropriations for the Office of the Inspector General at the levels identified in section 4501 of division D of this Act.

The House amendment contained an identical provision (sec. 1405).

The conference agreement includes this provision.

Defense Health Program (sec. 1405)

The Senate bill contained a provision (sec. 1405) that would authorize appropriations for the Defense Health Program activities at the levels identified in section 4501 of division D of this Act.

The House amendment contained an identical provision (sec. 1406).

The conference agreement includes this provision.

Subtitle B—National Defense Stockpile

Authority to dispose of certain materials from and to acquire additional materials for the National Defense Stockpile (sec. 1411)

The Senate bill contained a provision (sec. 1412) that would require the National Defense Stockpile (NDS) Manager to dispose of specific rare earth elements (REE) while also allowing funds available in the National Defense Stockpile Transaction Fund to be used for the acquisition of other materials.

The House amendment contained a similar provision (sec. 1411) that would grant permissive authority to the NDS Manager to dispose of specific REE while also allowing funds available in the NDS Transaction Fund to be used for the acquisition of other materials.

The Senate recedes.

The conferees note that REE acquisitions would alleviate some defense supply chain vulnerability as well as mitigate some risk of foreign reliance for REE and critical materials.

National Defense Stockpile matters (sec. 1412)

The Senate bill contained a provision (sec. 1411) that would amend section 4 of the Strategic and Critical Materials Stock Piling Act, title 50 United States Code, to provide the authority to recover, acquire, recycle, and manage the disposal of excess and recyclable strategic and critical materials containing rare earth elements (REE) from other federal agencies, including the Department of Defense. The provision would also enable the National Defense Stockpile (NDS) Manager to fund the qualification of domestically-produced strategic materials and REE, which could provide significant cost savings to DOD compared to foreign REE.

The House amendment contained a similar provision (sec. 1412).

The House recedes.

The conferees strongly believe that enabling the NDS to qualify domestic materials and create substitutions could provide a significant risk mitigation for DOD's supply chain and reduce the reliance upon foreign-sourced REE, along with cost-effective domestic and strategic alternatives.

Additionally, the conferees strongly encourage DOD to use its authority to recycle previously discarded items such as unclassified electronic waste, fluorescent lamps, batteries, magnets, and thermal barrier coatings in order to extract, reclaim, and reuse critical materials and REE to address DOD requirements.

Subtitle C—Chemical Demilitarization Matters

National Academies of Sciences study on conventional munitions demilitarization alternative technologies (sec. 1421)

The Senate bill contained a provision (sec. 1422) that would require the Secretary of the Army in concurrence with the Board on Army Science and Technology of the National Academies of Sciences, Engineering, and Medicine to conduct a study of the conventional munitions demilitarization program of the Department of Defense.

The House amendment contained no similar provision.

The House recedes.

Subtitle D—Other Matters

Authority for transfer of funds to Joint Department of Defense-Department of Veterans Affairs Medical Facility Demonstration Fund for Captain James A. Lovell Health Care Center, Illinois (sec. 1431)

The Senate bill contained a provision (sec. 1431) that would authorize the Secretary of Defense to transfer $122.4 million to the Joint Department of Defense-Department of Veterans Affairs Medical Facility Demonstration Fund for operations of the Captain James A. Lovell Federal Health Care Center, consisting of the North Chicago Veterans Affairs Medical Center, the Navy Ambulatory Care Center, and supporting facilities.

The House amendment contained a similar provision (sec. 1421).

The Senate recedes.

Authorization of appropriations for Armed Forces Retirement Home (sec. 1432)

The Senate bill contained a provision (sec. 1432) that would authorize appropriations of $64.3 million for the Armed Forces Retirement Home for fiscal year 2017.

The House amendment contained an identical provision (sec. 1422).

The conference agreement includes this provision.

LEGISLATIVE PROVISIONS NOT ADOPTED

National Defense Sealift Fund

The House amendment contained a provision (sec. 1402) that would authorize appropriations for the National Defense Sealift Fund at the levels identified in section 4501 of the House amendment.

The Senate bill contained no similar provision.

The House recedes.

National Sea-Based Deterrence Fund

The House amendment contained a provision (sec. 1407) that would authorize appropriations for the National Sea-Based Deterrence Fund at the levels identified in section 4501 of the House amendment.

The Senate bill contained no similar provision.

The House recedes.

Security Cooperation Enhancement Fund

The Senate bill contained a provision (sec. 1406) that authorized appropriations for the Security Cooperation Enhancement Fund activities at the levels identified in section 4501 of division D of this Act.

The House amendment contained no similar provision.

The Senate recedes.

TITLE XV—AUTHORIZATION OF ADDITIONAL APPROPRIATIONS FOR OVERSEAS CONTINGENCY OPERATIONS

Subtitle A—Authorization of Appropriations

Purpose and treatment of certain authorizations of appropriations (sec. 1501)

The Senate bill contained a provision (sec. 1501) that would establish this title and make authorization of appropriations available upon enactment of this Act for the Department of Defense, in addition to amounts otherwise authorized in this Act.

The House amendment contained a similar provision (sec. 1501).

The Senate recedes.

Procurement (sec. 1502)

The Senate bill contained a provision (sec. 1503) that would authorize additional appropriations for Procurement at the levels identified in section 4102 of division D of this Act.

The House amendment contained a similar provision (sec. 1502).

The Senate recedes.

Research, development, test, and evaluation (sec. 1503)

The Senate bill contained a provision (sec. 1504) that would authorize additional appropriations for Research, Development, Test, and Evaluation at the levels identified in section 4202 of division D of this Act.

The House amendment contained a similar provision (sec. 1503).

The Senate recedes.

Operation and maintenance (sec. 1504)

The Senate bill contained a provision (sec. 1505) that would authorize the additional appropriations for operation and maintenance activities.

The House amendment contained a similar provision (sec. 1504) that would authorize additional appropriations for operation and maintenance programs at the levels identified in section 4302 and section 4303 of division D of the amendment. This section would limit the appropriations for operation and maintenance identified in section 4302 to only be available for obligation until April 30, 2017.

The Senate recedes with an amendment that would allow funds to be available through the entirety of the fiscal year.

Military personnel (sec. 1505)

The Senate bill contained a provision (sec. 1506) that would authorize the additional appropriations for military personnel activities.

The House amendment contained a similar provision (sec. 1505) would authorize additional appropriations for military personnel programs at the levels identified in section 4402 and section 4403 of division D of the amendment. This section would limit the appropriations for military personnel activities identified in section 4402 to only be available for obligation until April 30, 2017.

The Senate recedes with an amendment that would allow funds to be available through the entirety of the fiscal year.

Working capital funds (sec. 1506)

The Senate bill contained a provision (sec. 1507) that would authorize the additional appropriations for the Defense Working Capital Funds.

The House amendment contained a similar provision (sec. 1506) would authorize additional appropriations for Defense Working Capital Funds at the levels identified in section 4502 of division D of the amendment. This section would limit the appropriations for the Defense Working Capital Funds to only be available for obligation until April 30, 2017.

The House recedes.

Drug Interdiction and Counter-Drug Activities, Defense-wide (sec. 1507)

The Senate bill contained a provision (sec. 1508) that would authorize additional appropriations for Drug Interdiction and Counterdrug Activities, Defense-Wide at the levels identified in section 4502 of division D of this Act.

The House amendment contained a similar provision (sec. 1507).

The Senate recedes.

Defense Inspector General (sec. 1508)

The Senate bill contained a provision (sec. 1509) that would authorize additional appropriations for the Office of the Inspector General at the levels identified in section 4502 of division D of this Act.

The House amendment contained an identical provision (sec. 1508).

The conference agreement includes this provision.

Defense Health program (sec. 1509)

The Senate bill contained a provision (sec. 1510) that would authorize additional appropriations for the Defense Health Program.

The House amendment contained a similar provision (sec. 1509) would authorize additional appropriations for the Defense Health Program at the levels identified in section 4502 of division D of the amendment. This section would limit the appropriations for the Defense Health Program to only be available for obligation until April 30, 2017.

The House recedes.

Subtitle B—Financial Matters

Treatment as additional authorizations (sec. 1511)

The Senate bill contained a provision (sec. 1521) that would state that amounts authorized to be appropriated by this title are in addition to amounts otherwise authorized to be appropriated by this Act.

The House amendment contained an identical provision (sec. 1521).

The conference agreement includes this provision.

Special transfer authority (sec. 1512)

The Senate bill contained a provision (sec. 1522) that would allow the Secretary of Defense to transfer up to $3.5 billion of overseas contingency operation funding authorized for fiscal year 2017 in this title to unforeseen higher priority needs in accordance with normal reprogramming procedures.

The House amendment contained a similar provision (sec. 1522) that would authorize the transfer of up to $4.5 billion of additional war-related funding authorizations in this title among the accounts in this title.

The Senate recedes with an amendment that would allow the Secretary of Defense to transfer up to $3.5 billion of overseas contingency operation funding authorized for fiscal year 2017 in this title to unforeseen higher priority needs in accordance with normal reprogramming procedures.

Subtitle C—Limitations, Reports, and Other Matters

Afghanistan Security Forces Fund (sec. 1521)

The Senate bill contained a provision (sec. 1533) that would require that amounts authorized for the Afghanistan Security Forces Fund (ASFF) for fiscal year 2017 continue to be subject to the conditions specified in subsections (b) through (g) of section 1513 of the Carl Levin and Howard P. "Buck" McKeon National Defense Authorization Act for Fiscal Year 2008 Public Law 110–181), as amended. The provision would extend the authority under subsection 1532(b) of the National Defense Authorization Act for Fiscal Year 2015 (Public Law 113–291) to accept certain equipment procured using ASFF funds and to treat such equipment as Department of Defense stocks as well as the goal of using $25.0 million to support to the extent practicable the efforts of the Government of Afghanistan to promote the security of Afghan women and girls and report on a plan to promote the security of Afghan women as required by section 1531 of the National Defense Authorization Act of 2016.

The House amendment contained a similar provision (sec. 1531).

The House recedes with a technical amendment.

Joint Improvised Explosive Device Defeat Fund (sec. 1522)

The House amendment contained a provision (sec. 1532) that would modify subsection 1532(a) of the National Defense Authorization Act for Fiscal Year 2016 (Public Law 114–92) to extend the use and transfer authority for the Joint Improvised Explosive Device Defeat Fund (JIEDDF) through fiscal year 2017. It would also modify section 1532(c) of the National Defense Authorization Act for Fiscal Year 2013 (Public Law 112–239) to expand the foreign governments to whom assistance may be provided in order to counter the flow of improvised explosive device (IED) precursor chemicals.

The Senate bill contained a similar provision (sec. 1531) that would extend the use and transfer authority for the JIEDDF for one year.

The Senate recedes with an amendment to modify and expand the reporting requirements under section 1532(c).

The conferees expect the expanded IED precursor chemical authority to be focused on efforts to counter the Islamic State of Iraq and the Levant. The conferees direct the Secretary of Defense to brief the congressional defense committees, not later than 90 days after enactment of this Act, regarding utilization of the IED precursor chemical authority to date, the plans for future employment of the authority, and a discussion of additional authorities that would be useful to the efforts to stem the flow of IED precursor chemicals and components.

Furthermore, the conferees note that Section 1532(c) of the National Defense Authorization Act for Fiscal Year 2016 (Public Law 114–92), required a plan for transition of the Joint Improvised-Threat Defeat Agency (JIDA) activities, functions, and resources to an existing military department or Defense Agency. On January 29, 2016, the congressional defense committees were notified by the Under Secretary of Defense for Acquisition, Technology and Logistics that the entirety of activities, functions, and resources of JIDA would transition under the authority, direction, and control of the Defense Threat Reduction Agency (DTRA) not later than September 30, 2016 as the Joint Improvised-Threat Defeat Organization (JIDO).

The conferees support the transition of JIDA as JIDO under the authority, direction, and control of DTRA. Integration of the roles, mission, and activities of JIDA under DTRA should result in reduced overhead management costs while maintaining core competencies of each entity in order to respond to warfighter needs. The conferees commend the identification of potential areas to reduce overhead costs and achieve efficiencies in the transition plan submitted on August 21, 2016. However, the conferees note the lack of detail regarding the processes used to integrate cost reduction efforts into the ongoing transition plan needed to realize savings and efficiencies.

The conferees recognize the transition will impact both DTRA's and JIDA's organizational construct. The conferees also recognize that the transition and associated efficiencies may warrant changes in JIDA's leadership construct and associated billets as JIDA becomes an organization under the authority, direction, and control of DTRA.

Therefore, the conferees direct the Under Secretary of Defense for Acquisition, Technology and Logistics to brief the congressional defense committees, not later than 60 days after enactment of this act, on the implementation of the transition of JIDA to DTRA as JIDO. The briefing shall include a progress report on the overhead cost reductions and efficiencies as well as cost reduction processes identified in the transition plan, an identification of efficiencies expected to be achieved in addition to those identified in the initial transition plan, the organizational and command and control constructs of DTRA and JIDO, an overview of the combined budget estimations across the Future Years Defense Program, and a description of how the core competencies of both DTRA and JIDO are being retained in order to fulfill designated missions and respond to warfighter needs.

Extension of authority to use Joint Improvised Explosive Device Defeat Fund for training of foreign security forces to defeat improvised explosive devices (sec. 1523)

The House amendment contained a provision (sec. 1533) that would modify section 1533(e) of the National Defense Authorization Act for Fiscal Year 2016 (Public Law 114–92) by extending the Authority to use the Joint Improvised Explosive Device Defeat Fund for training of foreign security forces to defeat improvised explosive devices and precursor chemicals from September 30, 2018, to September 30, 2020.

The Senate bill contained no similar provision.

The Senate recedes.

Overseas contingency operations (sec. 1524)

The Senate bill contained a provision (sec. 1502) that would designate authorization of appropriations in this section as overseas contingency operations.

The House amendment contained no similar provision.

The House recedes.

Extension and modification of authorities on Counterterrorism Partnerships Fund (sec. 1525)

The Senate bill contained a provision (sec. 1532) that would modify and extend for 1 fiscal year section 1534 of the National Defense Authorization Act for Fiscal Year 2015 (Public Law 113–291).

The House amendment contained no similar provision.

The House recedes.

Legislative Provisions Not Adopted

Counterterrorism Partnerships Fund

The House amendment included a provision (sec. 1510) that would authorize additional appropriations for the Counterterrorism Partnerships Fund (CTPF).

The Senate bill included no similar provision.

The House recedes.

The conferees note that elsewhere in this Act, funding requested by the Department of Defense for the CTPF was transferred to Operations and Maintenance, Defense-Wide, Defense Security Cooperation Agency, consistent with the reform of the Department of Defense's security cooperation programs and associated funding. It is the intent of the conferees that the CTPF funding transferred to the Defense Security Cooperation Agency be available for the purposes authorized in chapter 16 of title 10, United States Code as added elsewhere in this Act.

Security Cooperation Enhancement Fund

The Senate bill contained a provision (sec. 1511) that authorized appropriations for the Security Cooperation Enhancement Fund activities at the levels identified in section 4502 of division D of this Act.

The House bill contained no similar provision.

The Senate recedes.

Codification of Office of Management and Budget criteria

The House amendment contained a provision (sec. 1523) that would delineate guidance for the Secretary of Defense when submitting requests for overseas contingency operations.

The Senate bill contained no similar provision.

The House recedes.

TITLE XVI—STRATEGIC PROGRAMS, CYBER, AND INTELLIGENCE MATTERS

Subtitle A—Space Activities

Repeal of provision permitting the use of rocket engines from the Russian Federation for the evolved expendable launch vehicle program (sec. 1601)

The Senate bill contained a provision (sec. 1038) that would repeal section 8048 of the Department of Defense Appropriations Act, Fiscal Year 2016 (division C, Public Law 114–113; 129 Stat. 2363).

The House amendment contained no similar provision.

The House recedes.

Exception to the prohibition on contracting with Russian suppliers of rocket engines for the evolved expendable launch vehicle program (sec. 1602)

The House amendment contained a provision (sec. 1602) that would modify section 1608 of the Carl Levin and Howard P. "Buck" McKeon National Defense Authorization Act for Fiscal Year 2015 (Public Law 113–291), as amended by section 1607 of the National Defense Authorization Act for Fiscal Year 2016 (Public Law 114–92) by striking subsection (c) and inserting a new subsection. The new subsection would state that the prohibition would not apply to either the placement of orders or exercise of options under the contract numbered FA8811–13–C–0003 and awarded on December 18, 2013, or contracts that are awarded for the procurement of property or services for space launch activities that include the use of a total of 18 rocket engines designed or manufactured in the Russian Federation in addition to the Russian-designed or manufactured engines to which paragraph (1) applies.

The Senate bill contained a similar provision (sec. 829B) that would allow until December 31, 2022, the Secretary of Defense to award contracts to launch providers of launch services that intends to use any certified launch vehicle in its inventory without regard to the country of origin of the rocket engine that will be used on that launch vehicle. The provision would limit the total number of rocket engines designed or manufactured in the Russian Federation to not more than eighteen.

The Senate recedes with an amendment that would adopt the House language and prohibit the award of a contract requiring a rocket engine designed or manufactured in the Russian Federation after December 31, 2022.

Rocket propulsion system to replace RD–180 (sec. 1603)

The House amendment contained a provision (sec. 1601) that would modify section 1604 of the Carl Levin and Howard P. "Buck" McKeon National Defense Authorization Act for Fiscal Year 2015 (Public Law 113–291), as amended by section 1606 of the National Defense Authorization Act for Fiscal Year 2016 (Public Law 114–92).

The Senate bill contained no similar provision.

The Senate recedes with a clarifying amendment.

Plan for use of allied launch vehicles (sec. 1604)

The Senate bill contained a provision (sec. 1602) that would require the Commander of the Air Force Space Command to develop a contingency plan for using allied space launch vehicles to meet assured access to space requirements should the Department of Defense not be able to meet those requirements, for a limited period of time, using only United States launch vehicles.

The House amendment contained no similar provision.

The House recedes with an amendment that would require the Secretary of Defense to coordinate the required plan with the Director of National Intelligence. The amendment would require the required plan assess the relevant laws, regulations, and policies governing the launch of national security satellites and whether any legislative, regulatory, or policy actions (including with respect to waivers) would be necessary to allow for the launch of a national security satellite on an allied launch vehicle. The amendment also requires an assessment of the certification requirements for using allied launch vehicles pursuant to the plan and the estimated cost, schedule, and actions that would be necessary to certify allied launch vehicles.

The conferees note that the term "allied launch vehicle" explicitly prohibits the consideration of space launch vehicles from Russia, China, Iran, and North Korea.

The conferees expect that the Secretary and Director take into consideration the findings of the related study of options for a backup plan for assured access to space as identified in the Fiscal Year 2016 National Defense Authorization Act Joint Explanatory Statement.

Analysis of alternatives for wide-band communications (sec. 1605)

The House amendment contained a provision (sec. 1603) that would amend section 1611 of the National Defense Authorization Act for Fiscal Year 2016 (Public Law 114–92) by striking subsection (b) and would insert a requirement for the Secretary of Defense to develop study guidance for the analysis of alternatives for wide-band communications to consider the full range of military and commercial satellite communications capabilities, acquisition processes, and service delivery models. The provision would also require the Secretary to ensure that any cost assessments of military or commercial satellite communications systems include detailed full life cycle costs, as applicable, including but not limited to military personnel, military construction, military infrastructure operation, maintenance costs, and ground and user terminal impacts; and to also identify any considerations relating to the use of military versus commercial systems for wide-band satellite communications. The provision would also direct the Comptroller General the United States to assess the sufficiency of the study.

The Senate bill contained a similar provision (sec. 1608) that would require the Comptroller General to assess the types of analyses the Department of Defense has conducted to understand the costs and benefits of the use of KA-band commercial satellite communications by the department.

The Senate recedes with an amendment that would combine the Senate and House provisions.

Modification to pilot program for acquisition of commercial satellite communications services (sec. 1606)

The Senate bill contained a provision (sec. 1601) that would amend section 1605 of the Carl Levin and Howard P. "Buck" McKeon National Defense Authorization Act for Fiscal Year 2015 (Public Law 113–291) to prohibit the obligation or expenditure of any funding made available until the Secretary of Defense submits to the congressional defense committees a plan to demonstrate that the pilot program will achieve order-of-magnitude improvements in satellite communications capability.

The House amendment contained a similar provision (sec. 1604) that would also amend section 1605 of the Carl Levin and Howard P. "Buck" McKeon National Defense Authorization Act for Fiscal Year 2015 (Public Law 113–291), as amended by section 1612 of the National Defense Authorization Act for Fiscal Year 2016 (Public Law 114–92), by adding a requirement that in developing and carrying out the pilot program, the Secretary shall take actions to begin the implementation of each specified goal by not later than September 30, 2017.

The House recedes with an amendment that would merge the two provisions and prohibit the obligation or expenditure of 5 percent of the funds authorized to be appropriated by this Act or otherwise made available for fiscal year 2017 for the headquarters of Air Force Space Command until the Secretary of Defense submits a plan to demonstrate that the pilot program will achieve order-of-magnitude improvements in satellite communications capability.

The conferees agree that the pilot program and pathfinders are separate but complementary efforts. The conferees direct the Secretary of Defense to provide a briefing to the Congressional Defense committees by December 1, 2016 on the status of the pilot program and pathfinder activities, including an implementation timeline and an identification of any implementation challenges and options to address them.

Space-based environmental monitoring (sec. 1607)

The House amendment contained a provision (sec. 1605) that would direct the Secretary of Defense and the Director of the National Oceanic and Atmospheric Administration (NOAA) to establish mechanisms to collaborate and coordinate in defining the roles and responsibilities of the Department of Defense and NOAA with regards to carrying out space-based environmental monitoring and planning for future non-governmental space-based environmental monitoring capabilities.

The Senate bill contained no similar provision.

The Senate recedes with a technical amendment.

The conferees note that this is not an authorization for a joint satellite program of the Department of Defense and NOAA.

Prohibition on use of certain non-allied positioning, navigation, and timing systems (sec. 1608)

The House amendment contained a provision (sec. 1606) that would require that, not later than 60 days after the date of the enactment of this Act, the Secretary of Defense shall ensure that the Armed Forces and each element of the Department of Defense do not use a non-allied positioning, navigation, and timing system or a service provided by such a system. This requirement would sunset on September 30, 2018.

The provision would also provide that the Secretary of Defense may waive the prohibition if the Secretary determines it is in the national security interest of the United States and is necessary to mitigate exigent operational concerns, and notifies the appropriate congressional committees in writing and a period of 30 days has elapsed from the date of such notification.

The provision would further require the Secretary of Defense, Chairman of the Joint Chiefs of Staff, and the Director of National Intelligence to submit to the congressional defense committees and the congressional intelligence committees not later than 120 days after the date of the enactment of this Act an assessment of the risks to national security and to the operations and plans of the Department of Defense from using a non-allied positioning, navigation, and timing system or service provided by such a system.

The Senate bill contained no similar provision.

The Senate recedes.

Limitation of availability of funds for the Joint Space Operations Center Mission System (sec. 1609)

The House amendment contained a provision (sec. 1607) that would limit 75 percent of the funds authorized to be appropriated by this Act or otherwise made available for fiscal year 2017 for increment 3 of the Joint Space Operations Center Mission System program, until the Secretary of the Air Force, in coordination with the Commander of the U.S. Strategic Command, submits to the congressional defense committees a report on such increment.

The Senate bill contained a similar provision (sec. 1609) that would limit the use of funds for increment 3 of the Joint Space Operations Center Mission System until the Secretary of the Air Force submits to the congressional defense committees a report setting forth a strategy for acquiring a common software and hardware framework for battle management, communication, and control.

The Senate recedes with an amendment that would combine the conditions of both provisions into one reporting requirement.

The conferees do not expect to restrict the study activities to develop the plan for the JMS increment 3 space battle management, communications, and control.

Limitation on availability of funds for the Global Positioning System Next Generation Operational Control System (sec. 1610)

The Senate bill contained a provision (sec. 1610) that would restrict the obligation or expenditure of amounts authorized to be appropriated for fiscal year 2017 and available for the current product development contract for the Global Positioning System Next Generation Operational Control System (GPS-OCX) until the Secretary of Defense submits to Congress the certification required under section 2433a(c)(2), title 10, United States Code, commonly referred to as a Nunn-McCurdy certification.

The House amendment contained no similar provision.

The House recedes with an amendment that would impose spending limitations subject to certain certifications and briefings to Congress.

Availability of funds for certain secure voice conferencing capabilities (sec. 1611)

The Senate bill contained a provision (sec. 1612) that would authorize up to $10.2 million in Air Force research, development, test, and evaluation funds from fiscal year 2015 or 2016 for the Presidential and National Voice Conferencing Program and the Advanced Extremely High Frequency Extended Data Rate, worldwide, secure, survivable voice conferencing capability for the President and national leaders.

The House amendment contained no similar provision.

The House recedes with a technical amendment.

The conferees direct the Co-Chairmen of the Council on Oversight of the National Leadership Command, Control, and Communications System to provide a report to the congressional defense committees, not later than 180 days after the date of the enactment of this Act, on the requirements and gaps, if any, for manpower to operate and sustain and to modernize the national leadership communications system. Such report shall detail the requirements and gaps, if any, by each agency comprising the national leadership communications system; the plan to close those gaps including through the use of existing hiring and retention authorities; the related estimated costs of such plan; the requirements and gaps broken down by job activity and geographic region. The report required should explicitly detail any recommendations or requirements for new hiring and retention authorities that may be required to assist the Department in closing any gaps identified by the Council. The co-chairmen of the Council shall provide a briefing to the congressional defense committees on their preliminary findings and recommendations not later than 90 days after the date of the enactment of this Act.

Space-based infrared system and advanced extremely high frequency program (sec. 1612)

The House amendment contained a provision (sec. 1608) that would restrict the Secretary of Defense from developing or acquiring an alternative to the space-based infrared system program of record, as well as developing or acquiring an alternative to the advanced extremely high frequency program of record, until the Commander of U.S. Strategic Command and the Director of the Space Security and Defense Program, in coordination with the Defense Intelligence Officer for Science and Technology of the Defense Intelligence Agency, jointly submit an assessment to the appropriate congressional committees of the resilience and mission assurance of each alternative considered for the respective programs.

The Senate bill contained no similar provision.

The Senate recedes with a technical amendment.

Pilot program on commercial weather data (sec. 1613)

The House amendment contained a provision (sec. 1610) that would direct the Secretary of Defense to establish a pilot program to assess the viability of commercial satellite weather data to support requirements of the Department of Defense.

The Senate bill contained no similar provision.

The Senate recedes with a technical amendment.

Plans on transfer of acquisition and funding authority of certain weather missions to National Reconnaissance Office (sec. 1614)

The House amendment contained a provision (sec. 1609) that would limit 50 percent of the funding for the weather satellite follow-on program until the Secretary of the Air Force submits to the appropriate committees a plan for the Air Force to transfer, beginning with fiscal year 2018, the acquisition authority and the funding authority for certain space-based environmental monitoring missions from the Air Force to the National Reconnaissance Office (NRO), including a description of the amount of funds that would be necessary to be transferred from the Air Force to the NRO during fiscal years 2018 through 2022 to carry out such plan.

The provision would direct the Director of the NRO to develop a plan to carry out certain space-based environmental monitoring missions. The provision would also require the Director of the Cost Assessment Improvement Group of the Office of the Director of National Intelligence, in coordination with the Director of the Cost Assessment and Program Evaluation of the Office of the Secretary of Defense, to certify the funding identified by the Secretary of the Air Force and the Director of the NRO is sufficient.

The Senate bill contained no similar provision.

The Senate recedes with an amendment that would allow the Secretary of the Air Force and the Director of the NRO to waive the limitation and requirement for a plan if the Under Secretary of Defense for Acquisition, Technology, and Logistics and the Chairman of the Joint Chiefs of Staff jointly certify that the Secretary of the Air Force is carrying out a formal acquisition program that has received milestone A approval to address the cloud characterization and theater weather imagery requirements of the Department of Defense.

Five-year plan for Joint Interagency Combined Space Operations Center (sec. 1615)

The Senate bill contained a provision (sec. 1604) that would require the Secretary of Defense to submit a 5-year plan for the Joint Interagency Combined Space Operations Center.

The House amendment contained no similar provision.

The Senate recedes with an amendment that would require the Secretary of Defense to coordinate the required plan with the Director of National Intelligence. The amendment would also require that the plan be provided to the appropriate congressional committees within 90 days and that it include a description of the command and control of the related operations of the Joint Interagency Combined Space Operations Center.

Organization and management of national security space activities of the Department of Defense (sec. 1616)

The House amendment contained a provision (sec. 1611) that would state findings and the sense of Congress on the organization and management of the national security space activities of the Department of Defense. The provision would also direct the Secretary of Defense and the Director of the Office of Management and Budget to each separately submit a report to the appropriate committees not later than 180 days after the date of the enactment of this Act on the recommendations to strengthen the leadership, management, and organization of the Department of Defense with respect to the national security space activities of the Department.

The Senate bill contained no similar provision.

The Senate recedes with an amendment that would require the reports required address the findings covered in the report of the Comptroller General of the United States numbered GAO–16–592R regarding space acquisition and oversight of the Department of Defense.

Review of charter of Operationally Responsive Space Program Office (sec. 1617)

The House amendment contained a provision (sec. 1612) that would direct the Secretary of Defense to conduct a review of the Operationally Responsive Space Program Office and submit a report to the congressional defense committees not later than 180 days after the date of the enactment of this Act.

The Senate bill contained no similar provision.

The Senate recedes.

Backup and complementary positioning, navigation, and timing capabilities of Global Positioning System (sec. 1618)

The House amendment contained a provision (sec. 1613) that would direct the Secretary of Defense, Secretary of Transportation, and Secretary of Homeland Security to jointly conduct a study to assess and identify the technology-neutral requirements to backup and complement the positioning, navigation, and timing (PNT) capabilities of the Global Positioning System for national security and critical infrastructure. The provision would also direct the Secretary of Defense, Secretary of Transportation, and Secretary of Homeland Security to submit a report to the appropriate congressional committees not later than 1 year after the date of the enactment of this Act on the study.

The Senate bill contained no similar provision.

The Senate recedes with an amendment that would expand upon the analysis of alternative requirements.

The conferees assert that each Department should only fund activities which meet their own respective requirements.

Report on use of spacecraft assets of the space-based infrared system wide-field-of-view program (sec. 1619)

The House amendment contained a provision (sec. 1614) that would direct the Secretary of Defense, in coordination with the Director of National Intelligence, to submit a report on the feasibility of using available spacecraft assets of the space-based infrared system wide-field-of-view program to satisfy other mission requirements of the Department of Defense or the intelligence community.

The Senate bill contained no similar provision.

The Senate recedes with a technical amendment.

Provision of certain information to Government Accountability Office by National Reconnaissance Office (sec. 1620)

The Senate bill contained a provision (sec. 1606) that would require the Comptroller General of the United States to conduct an assessment, for calendar year 2017 and each calendar year thereafter, of the cost, schedule, and performance of each program of the National Reconnaissance Office (NRO) for developing, acquiring, launching, and deploying satellites or overhead reconnaissance systems that receive funding from the Military Intelligence Program or is supported by personnel of the Department of Defense. The provision would also direct the director of the NRO to provide the Comptroller General access, in a timely manner, to the information the Comptroller General requires to conduct the assessment.

The House amendment contained no similar provision.

The House recedes with an amendment that would require the Director of the NRO provide access to the Comptroller General of the United States, in a timely manner, to the cost, schedule, and performance information the Comptroller General requires to conduct assessments, as required by any of the appropriate congressional committees, of programs of the NRO.

The conferees note that the committees of jurisdiction recognize the unique security requirements associated with classified and compartmented programs and activities. Access by the Comptroller General to such programs of the NRO will be carefully reviewed, similar to the manner of such access to such programs of the Department of Defense. Such access will be considered by the committees on a case-by-case basis.

Cost-benefit analysis of commercial use of excess ballistic missile solid rocket motors (sec. 1621)

The Senate bill contained a provision (sec. 1607) that would require the Comptroller General of the United States to conduct an analysis of the cost and benefits of allowing the use of excess ballistic missile solid rocket motors for commercial space launch purposes. The analysis would include an evaluation of the effect of allowing such use on national security, the Department of Defense, the solid rocket motor industrial base, the commercial space launch market, and any other areas the Comptroller General considers appropriate.

The House amendment contained no similar provision.

The House recedes with an amendment that would require the Comptroller General to provide an interim briefing on March 17, 2017 and a final briefing not later than 180 days after the date of enactment of this Act.

Independent assessment of Global Positioning System Next Generation Operational Control System (sec. 1622)

The Senate bill contained a provision (sec. 1605) that would require the Secretary of Defense to enter into an agreement with a federally funded research and development center to review the acquisition strategy for the Next Generation Operational Control System for the Global Positioning System.

The House amendment contained no similar provision.

The House recedes with an amendment that would require the Secretary of Defense, not later than 60 days after the date of the enactment of this act, to enter into an arrangement with a federally funded research and development center, or other appropriate independent entity to review the acquisition strategy for the Next Generation Operational Control System for the Global Positioning System. The amendment would also add a requirement that the independent assessment evaluate the ability of alternative systems to satisfy the requirements of the Department of Defense.

Subtitle B—Defense Intelligence and
Intelligence-Related Activities

Report on United States Central Command Intelligence Fusion Center (sec. 1631)

The House amendment contained a provision (sec. 1622) that would limit funding until the Commander of the United States Central Command submits to the appropriate committees reports on the steps taken by the Commander to formalize and disseminate procedures for the Intelligence Fusion Center of the United States Central Command and on the steps taken by the Commander to address the findings of the final report of the Inspector General of the Department of Defense (IG).

The Senate bill contained no similar provision.

The Senate recedes with an amendment to remove the funding limitations and the requirement to provide a report on the findings of the final report of the Inspector General of the Department of Defense.

The conferees urge the Inspector General of the Department of Defense to finalize its investigation into the Directorate for Intelligence at United States Central Command and, if related allegations are substantiated, provide recommendations on any corrective measures that should be undertaken. The conferees also direct the Secretary of Defense to provide the appropriate congressional committees a briefing on the Department's views of the final IG report within 60 days of the report's completion.

Prohibition on availability of funds for certain relocation activities for NATO Intelligence Fusion Cell (sec. 1632)

The House amendment contained a provision (sec. 1623) that would limit 15 percent of the increase in spending for manpower for the Joint Intelligence Analysis Complex until the Secretary of Defense provides a revised analysis of alternatives to the congressional defense committees and the Permanent Select Committee on Intelligence of the House of Representatives for the basing of a new complex. The new analysis should be based on operational requirements and costs and informed by the findings of the report of the Comptroller General of the United States on the Joint Intelligence Analysis Complex cost estimating and basing decision process.

The Senate bill contained no similar provision.

The Senate recedes with an amendment that would prohibit funds authorized to be appropriated by this Act or otherwise made available for fiscal year 2017 for operation and maintenance to be obligated or expended for the procurement of certain supplies and equipment for the relocation of the NATO Intelligence Fusion Cell (NIFC) to Royal Air Force Base Croughton, United Kingdom, and would also require the Secretary of Defense in coordination with the Director of National Intelligence to submit a report on the requirements and costs associated with such a relocation.

Survey and review of Defense Intelligence Enterprise (sec. 1633)

The Senate bill contained a provision (sec. 1671) that would require the Chairman of the Joint Chiefs of Staff to conduct a review of the Defense Intelligence Enterprise, including the defense intelligence agencies and intelligence elements of the combatant commands and military departments, to assess the capabilities and capacity of such Enterprise to meet present and future defense intelligence requirements and to report to appropriate congressional committees.

The House amendment contained no similar provision.

The House recedes with a clarifying amendment.

Subtitle C—Cyberspace-Related Matters

Special emergency procurement authority to facilitate the defense against or recovery from a cyber attack (sec. 1641)

The House amendment contained a provision (sec. 1631) that would modify the current special procurement authority in section 1903(a)(2) of title 41, United States Code, to include use of such authority for recovery from or defense against cyber attacks.

The Senate bill contained a similar provision (sec. 829C) to provide special emergency procurement authority in title 10, United States Code.

The Senate recedes.

Limitation on termination of dual-hat arrangement for Command of the United States Cyber Command (sec. 1642)

The Senate bill contained a provision (sec. 1633) that would express the sense of Congress that the arrangement (commonly referred to as a "dual-hat arrangement") under which the Commander of the United States Cyber Command (CYBERCOM) also serves as the Director of the National Security Agency is in the national security interests of the United States. The provision would also prohibit the Secretary of Defense from taking action to end the "dual-hat arrangement" until the Secretary and the Chairman of the Joint Chiefs of Staff jointly determine and certify to the appropriate committees of Congress that ending that arrangement will not pose unacceptable risks to the military effectiveness of CYBERCOM. The provision would also require the establishment of conditions-based criteria for assessing the need to sustain the "dual-hat arrangement."

The House amendment contained no similar provision.

The House recedes with a clarifying amendment.

Cyber mission forces matters (sec. 1643)

The Senate bill contained a provision (sec. 1632) that would provide interim authorities to the Secretary of Defense to enhance the Department's ability to hire and retain civilian personnel with the high-level of skill and aptitude necessary to provide critical technical support to the Cyber Mission Teams that are now nearing full operational capability. The provision also would direct the Principal Cyber Advisor to (1) supervise the development of training standards and capacity to train civilian cyber personnel to develop tools and weapons for the Cyber Mission Forces and (2) ensure that sufficient priority exists for the timely completion of security clearance investigations and adjudications for such personnel.

The House amendment contained no similar provision.

The House recedes with a technical amendment.

Requirement to enter into agreements relating to use of cyber opposition forces (sec. 1644)

The House amendment contained a provision (sec. 1633) that would require the Secretary of Defense to enter into agreements with each combatant command relating to the use of cyber opposition forces by September 30, 2017. This section would also require the development of a joint certification and training standard for cyber opposition forces by March 31, 2017.

The Senate bill contained no similar provision.

The Senate recedes with an amendment that would include an additional requirement for the Secretary of Defense to issue a joint training and certification standard by June 30, 2017 for the protection of control systems for use by all cyber operations forces within the Department of Defense.

Cyber protection support for Department of Defense personnel in positions highly vulnerable to cyber attack (sec. 1645)

The Senate bill contained a provision (sec. 1631) that would authorize the Secretary of Defense to provide cyber protection support to personnel who are determined by the Secretary to be of highest risk of vulnerability to cyber attacks on their personal devices, networks, and persons.

The House amendment contained no similar provision.

The House recedes with an amendment that would clarify that the providing of cyber protection support is at the discretion of the Secretary of Defense and that nothing in the provision should be construed to encourage personnel of the Department of Defense to use personal technology devices for official business or to authorize cyber protection team support for senior Department personnel using personal devices and networks in an official capacity.

Limitation on full deployment of joint regional security stacks (sec. 1646)

The House amendment contained a provision (sec. 1634) that would limit the amount of authorized funds available to be obligated or expended in fiscal year 2017 for cryptographic systems and key management infrastructure until the Secretary of Defense, in coordination with the Director of the National Security Agency, provides a report on the integration of the cryptographic modernization and key management infrastructure programs of the military departments, including a description of how the military departments have implemented stronger leadership, increased integration, and reduced redundancy with respect to such modernization and programs.

The Senate bill contained no similar provision.

The Senate recedes with an amendment that would prohibit any Department of Defense service or agency from declaring full operational capability for deployment of joint regional security stacks until such time as the service or agency has completed operational test and evaluation activities to determine the effectiveness, suitability, and survivability of the system. The provision would allow this requirement to be waived under certain circumstances.

The conferees direct the Department of Defense to provide a briefing to the Armed Services Committee of the Senate and House of Representatives, as well as the House Permanent Select Committee on Intelligence, no later than 60 days after the enactment of this Act, on the progress and activities of the Communications Security Review and Advisory Board. The conferees recognize the importance of cryptographic modernization and key management programs with the Department in providing critical encryption and communications security capabilities for the Department, and remain focused on ensuring such activities are coordinated and managed across the military services and Defense Agencies in a reasonable manner. The conferees encourage the Department to strengthen mechanisms like the Communications Security Review and Advisory Board in order to maintain oversight across the Department and deliver those capabilities in a timely and cost effective manner.

Advisory committee on industrial security and industrial base policy (sec. 1647)

The House amendment contained a provision (sec. 1637) that would require the Secretary of Defense to: (1) assess the sufficiency of the Department of Defense's regulatory mechanisms for secure defense information held by cleared defense contractors to determine whether there are any gaps that may undermine the protection of such information; and (2) prescribe regulations to improve security of such information.

The Senate bill contained no similar provision.

The Senate recedes with an amendment that would establish an advisory committee to review, assess, and make recommendations with respect to industrial security and industrial base policy. The committee should meet at least annually until its termination on September 30, 2022.

Change in name of National Defense University's Information Resources Management College to College of Information and Cyberspace (sec. 1648)

The House amendment contained a provision (sec. 1632) that would modify section 2165 of title 10, United States Code, to change the name of the Information Resources Management College to the College of Information and Cyberspace.

The Senate bill contained no similar provision.

The Senate recedes with a technical amendment.

Evaluation of cyber vulnerabilities of F–35 aircraft and support systems (sec. 1649)

The Senate bill contained a provision (sec. 1635) that would modify a provision from the National Defense Authorization Act for Fiscal Year 2016 (Public Law 114–92), requiring the Secretary of Defense to evaluate the cyber vulnerabilities of every major Department of Defense weapons system by not later than December 31, 2019. The provision would do so by requiring that a complete evaluation of the F–35 aircraft and its support systems, such as the Autonomic Logistics Information System, be completed before February 1, 2017. The provision would require the Secretary of Defense to submit a report on the F–35 cyber vulnerability evaluation to the congressional defense committees no later than February 28, 2017. The provision would also allow for funding to be used for the development of tools that improve cyber vulnerability assessments, non-recurring engineering for the design of mitigation solutions, and Department-wide information repositories to share assessment findings and mitigation solutions.

The House amendment contained no similar provision.

The House recedes with an amendment that would require the evaluation of cyber vulnerabilities of the F–35 and support systems not later than 120 days after the date of enactment of this act. The amendment would also require the report on the evaluation completed to be submitted to the congressional defense committees not later than 180 days after the date of enactment.

Evaluation of cyber vulnerabilities of Department of Defense critical infrastructure (sec. 1650)

The Senate bill contained a provision (sec. 1637) that would require the Secretary of Defense to evaluate the cyber vulnerabilities of Department of Defense critical infrastructure by not later than December 31, 2020.

The Senate bill also contained a provision (sec. 1634) that would authorize the Secretary of Defense to carry out a Pilot program on application of consequence-driven, cyber-informed engineering to mitigate against cyber-security threats.

The House amendment contained no similar provision.

The House recedes with an amendment that would combine the two Senate provisions.

Strategy to incorporate Army reserve component cyber protection teams into Department of Defense cyber mission force (sec. 1651)

The House amendment contained a provision (sec. 1639) that would require the Secretary of the Army to provide a briefing on a strategy for incorporating Army National Guard protection teams into the cyber mission force of the Department of Defense.

The Senate bill contained no similar provision.

The Senate recedes with an amendment that would expand the scope of the strategy to include both the Army National Guard and the other reserve components of the Army.

Strategic plan for the Defense Information Systems Agency (sec. 1652)

The Senate bill contained a provision (sec. 1636) that would require the Director of the Defense Information Systems Agency (DISA) to develop a technology strategy.

The House amendment contained no similar provision.

The House recedes with an amendment that requires the Director of DISA to develop strategic plan that reviews the requirements and missions of the agency, and assesses the adequacy of the technology strategy, workforce, and facilities to meet those requirements.

The conferees note that the Secretary of Defense is making efforts to increase the department's use of and exposure to innovative commercial information technologies and increase outreach to innovative small businesses in locations including Silicon Valley. Many of the technologies and systems of interest are within the mission area of DISA.

However, the conferees note with acute concern that at the same time this trend is occurring to seek out and exploit new commercial innovation, DISA appears to be reducing its support for research and technology innovation, and has limited connectivity and coordination with other science and technology activities of the Department of Defense. The conferees believe that for a technology organization to eliminate its funding for flexible exploration of new technology is short-sighted and detrimental to the long term health of the organization. The conferees are concerned that DISA has not adequately built its research and technology needs in a way to support the overall missions of the Agency, which has repercussions on the workforce it is able to attract, and the quality of support it is able to provide the warfighter. To use one example, the conferees believe that such behavior has impacted the ability of the Agency to fully realize the benefits, as well as the operational challenges and potentialities of emerging technologies like cloud and mobile computing, cyber defense and big data analytics. That impacts interactions with industry, but the conferees also believe that DISA has not adequately leveraged potential relationships with DOD labs and other innovative research activities. The conferees believe that through the process of developing a regular strategic plan, the Director of DISA should be taking the opportunity to develop closer coordination with appropriate research and development organizations in the Office of the Secretary of Defense and the Military Services to improve DISA's innovative capacity, strengthen its R&D programs, and improve DOD's ability to adopt the best commercial and other information technologies to support defense missions.

Plan for information security continuous monitoring capability and comply-to-connect policy; limitation on software licensing (sec. 1653)

The Senate bill contained a provision (sec. 1638) that would require the Chief Information Officer of the Department of Defense and the Commander of United States Cyber Command, in coordination with the Principal Cyber Adviser, to jointly develop a plan for a modernized, enterprise-wide information security continuous monitoring capability and a comply-to-connect policy.

The House amendment contained no similar provision.

The House recedes with a technical amendment.

Reports on deterrence of adversaries in cyberspace (sec. 1654)

The Senate bill contained a provision (sec. 1639) that would require the Secretary of Defense to submit a report to the congressional defense committees specifying in detail the authorities that have been delegated by the President to the Secretary for conducting cyber operations. The report would require the Secretary to detail the standing authorities and limitations that authorize or limit the Secretary in conducting cyber operations and how those authorities compare to the authorities delegated to the Secretary for activities in non-cyber domains.

The Senate bill also contained a provision (sec. 1640) that would require the Chairman of the Joint Chiefs of Staff to submit to the President and the congressional defense committees a report on the military and nonmilitary options available to the United States to deter Russia, China, Iran, North Korea, and terrorist organizations in cyberspace. The provision would require the report to include an assessment of the effectiveness of the deterrence options available. It also would require the Chairman provide an integrated priorities list of cyber deterrence capabilities of the Department of Defense that identify, at a minimum, high priority capability needs prioritized across armed forces and functional lines, risk areas, and long-term strategic planning issues. The provision would also require within 60 days of receiving the report from the Chairman of the Joint Chiefs of Staff, that the President submit to the congressional defense committees a separate report identifying when an action carried out in cyberspace constitutes an act of war against the United States. The report would include (1) identification of what actions carried out in cyberspace constitute an act of war against the United States; (2) identification of how the law of war applies to the cyber operations of the Department of Defense; (3) identification of the circumstances required for responding to a cyber attack against the United States; and (4) a declaratory policy on the use of cyber weapons by the United States.

The House amendment contained a related provision (sec. 1636) that would require the Secretary of Defense submit a report to the congressional defense committees on the policies, doctrine, procedures, and authorities governing Department of Defense activities in response to malicious cyber activities carried out against the United States or United States persons by foreign states or non-state actors.

The House recedes with an amendment that would combine the three related provisions.

The conferees note that in preparing the report required by the provision the President shall consider (1) what severity of cyber attack would elicit a military response; (2) The ways in which the effects of a cyber attack may be equivalent to effects of an attack using conventional kinetic weapons, including with respect to physical destruction or casualties; (3) intangible effects of significant scope, intensity, or duration; and (4) how the law of neutrality applies, how the utilization or exploitation of communications infrastructure in neutral States applies, and what limitations, if any, apply in exercising the right of the United States to act in self-defense through a cyber-operation.

Sense of Congress on cyber resiliency of the networks and communications systems of the National Guard (sec. 1655)

The House amendment contained a provision (sec. 1638) that would assert the sense of Congress concerning cyber resiliency of the networks and communications systems of the National Guard.

The Senate bill contained no similar provision.

The Senate recedes with an amendment that encourages the National Guard to budget within National Guard resources.

Subtitle D—Nuclear Forces

Improvements to Council on Oversight of National Leadership Command, Control, and Communications System (sec. 1661)

The Senate bill contained a provision (sec. 1652) that would modify an existing report and add an assessment of the readiness of the command, control, and communications system for the national leadership of the United States.

The House amendment contained a similar provision (sec. 1641) that would require a report on space architecture development and limits funding to make changes to the command, control, and communications system in a manner that reduces warning time provided to the national leadership of the United States with respect to a warning of a strategic missile attack on the United States.

The conference agreement includes both the House and Senate provisions.

The General Accountability Office (GAO) in its report titled Nuclear Command, Control, and Communications: DOD Has Taken Steps to Address Sustainment and Maintenance Challenges for Critical Satellite Systems but Could Better Identify Risks and Mitigation Actions, GAO–16–370C (May 26, 2016). In that report the GAO highlighted a number of concerns regarding critical satellite systems used for nuclear command, control, and communications and recommended the Department of Defense take action to improve the identification of risks and mitigation actions. DOD, in its official response to GAO's report, disagreed with GAO's recommendation. The department stated that it understood the concerns that GAO raised in respect to risks to these systems, but stated that DOD has a strong governance and oversight structure. The department asserted that it believes the actions taken to date address risk at an acceptable level with the transition of these satellite systems to their replacement systems.

Given the concerns raised by the GAO in its report, the conferees direct the Council on Oversight of the National Leadership Command, Control, and Communications System to provide a written assessment to the congressional defense committees that details (1) the actions the department has taken to identify the risks associated with the transition of these critical satellite systems, (2) information about the department's evaluation of the acceptability of each of the identified risks, and (3) information regarding actions the department has identified to mitigate these risks. The committee directs the Council to provide its written assessment to the congressional defense committees no later than February 28, 2017.

Treatment of certain sensitive information by State and local governments (sec. 1662)

The Senate bill contained a provision (sec. 1055) that would authorize the Secretary of Defense to designate information as being Department of Defense critical infrastructure security information to ensure that such information is not disseminated without authorization.

The House amendment contained a similar provision (sec. 1642).

House recedes with technical and conforming amendments.

Procurement authority for certain parts of intercontinental ballistic missile fuzes (sec. 1663)

The Senate bill contained a provision (sec. 1651) that would give the Department of Defense the authority to buy intercontinental ballistic missile fuze parts.

The House amendment contained an identical provision (sec. 1643).

The conference agreement includes this provision.

Prohibition on availability of funds for mobile variant of ground-based strategic deterrent missile (sec. 1664)

The House amendment contained a provision (sec. 1644) that would prohibit funds authorized to be appropriated to retain the option for, or develop, a mobile variant of the ground-based strategic deterrent missile.

The Senate bill contained no similar provision.

The Senate recedes.

Limitation on availability of funds for extension of New START Treaty (sec. 1665)

The House amendment contained a provision (sec. 1645) that would limit authorized funds to be appropriated for the Department of Defense to extend the New Start Treaty under certain circumstances.

The Senate bill contained no similar provision.

The Senate recedes with an amendment that would change the reporting period from 180 days to 120 days following the submission of both the report required by the provision and the National Intelligence Estimate.

Certifications regarding integrated tactical warning and attack assessment mission of the Air Force (sec. 1666)

The House amendment contained a provision (sec. 1646) that would require the Secretary of the Air Force to consolidate under a major command, commanded by a single general officer, the responsibility, authority, accountability, and resources for carrying out the nuclear command, control, and communications functions of the Air Force by March 31, 2017. This consolidation would be required to include, at a minimum, all terrestrial and aerial components of the nuclear command and control system that are survivable and endurable, as well as all terrestrial and aerial components of the integrated tactical warning and attack assessment (ITW/AA) system that are survivable and endurable.

The Senate bill contained no similar provision.

The Senate recedes with an amendment that would require that, not later than March 31, 2017 and each year through 2020, the Commander of the U.S. Strategic Command certify to the Secretary of Defense and the congressional defense committees that the Air Force is organized, staffed, trained and equipped to carry out the portions of the ITW/AA system assigned to the Air Force that are survivable and endurable. The Commander would further be required to certify that the programs and plans of the Air Force for sustaining, modernizing, training and exercising capabilities relating to such missions are sufficient for mission success. If the Commander of the U.S. Strategic Command does not make such a certification, the Secretary of the Air Force would be required to immediately consolidate the terrestrial and aerial components of the ITW/AA system that are survivable and enduring under the Air Force Global Strike Command. The amendment also contains a rule of construction that this section may not be construed to affect any responsibilities relating to the ITW/AA system in effect on the date of enactment of this Act pursuant to certain agreements between the United States and Canada.

Matters relating to intercontinental ballistic missiles (sec. 1667)

The House amendment contained a provision (sec. 1649A) that would state the policy of the United States to maintain and modernize a responsive and alert intercontinental ballistic missile force and prohibit (1) funding for reducing the responsiveness or alert level of the intercontinental ballistic missiles of the United States and (2) reducing the quantity of deployed intercontinental ballistic missiles of the United States to less than 400.

The Senate bill contained no similar provision.

The Senate recedes with an amendment that would drop the policy statement and add an element on cost to the reporting requirement.

Requests for forces to meet security requirements for land-based nuclear forces (sec. 1668)

The Senate bill contained a provision (sec. 1655) that would require the Secretary of Defense and the Chairman of the Joint Chiefs of Staff to decide if the land-based missile fields using UH–1N helicopters meet security requirements and if there are any shortfalls or gaps in meeting such requirements.

The House amendment contained a similar provision (sec. 1649) that would require the Chairman of the Joint Chiefs of Staff to certify to the congressional defense committees that the Chairman has approved any requests for forces of a commander of a combatant command to meet the security requirements of land-based nuclear forces.

The Senate recedes with an amendment that would combine the two provisions while eliminating the certification required under the House provision. The provision includes a restriction of 25 percent on travel and representational expenses of the Under Secretary of Defense for Acquisition, Technology, and Logistics until the Under Secretary certifies that there is an acquisition process in place to ensure that a UH–1N replacement aircraft is under contract in fiscal year 2018.

Report on Russian and Chinese political and military leadership survivability, command and control, and continuity of government programs and activities (sec. 1669)

The House amendment contained a provision (sec. 1647) that would require the Director of National Intelligence to submit to the appropriate congressional committees, a report on the leadership survivability, command and control, and continuity of government programs and activities with respect to the People's Republic of China and the Russian Federation.

The Senate bill contained no similar provision.

The Senate recedes.

Review by the Comptroller General of the United States of recommendations relating to nuclear enterprise of Department of Defense (sec. 1670)

The Senate bill contained a provision (sec. 1653) that would require the Comptroller General to review the Department of Defense's nuclear enterprise review process to ascertain whether recommendations are adequately being implemented.

The House amendment contained no similar provision.

The House recedes.

Sense of Congress on nuclear deterrence (sec. 1671)

The Senate bill contained a provision (sec. 1654) that would state the sense of Congress that the nuclear forces of the United States continue to play a fundamental role in deterring aggression against the interests of the United States and its allies. It also states that the prevention of war through effective deterrence requires survivable and flexible nuclear forces that are well exercised and ready to respond to nuclear escalation if necessary.

The House amendment contained no similar provision.

The House recedes with an amendment that would update the provision to take into account the July 2016 NATO Warsaw Summit communique.

Sense of Congress on importance of independent nuclear deterrent of United Kingdom (sec. 1672)

The House amendment contained a provision (sec. 1648) that would express the sense of Congress that the United States believes that the independent nuclear deterrent and decision-making of the United Kingdom provides a crucial contribution to international stability, the North Atlantic Treaty Organization alliance, and the national security of the United States.

The Senate bill contained no similar provision.

The Senate recedes.

Subtitle E—Missile Defense Programs

National missile defense policy (sec. 1681)

The Senate bill contained a provision (sec. 1665) that would remove the word "limited" from Section 2 of the National Missile Defense Act of 1999 (Public Law 106–38; 10 U.S.C. 2431 note).

The House amendment contained a similar provision (sec. 1665) that would replace the National Missile Defense Act of 1999 with new policy language to the effect that the United States should maintain and improve a robust layered missile defense system capable of defending the territory of the United States and its allies against the developing and increasingly complex ballistic missile threat.

The Senate recedes with an amendment that would add to the House provision language making it clear that the United States should deploy effective missile defense systems.

The conferees note, nothing in this legislative provision requires or directs the development of missile defenses against any country or its strategic nuclear forces.

Extensions of prohibitions relating to missile defense information and systems (sec. 1682)

The Senate bill contained a provision (sec. 1666) that would extend prohibitions relating to missile defense information and systems as described in section 130h(d) of title 10, United States Code, to 2018.

The House amendment contained a provision (sec. 1651) that would prohibit funds to integrate a missile defense system of the Russian Federation or a missile defense system of the People's Republic of China into any missile defense system of the United States, and which would extend this prohibition, and a prohibition on sharing certain missile defense information with Russia, to 2027.

The Senate recedes with an amendment that would extend the current prohibitions by two years to January 1, 2019.

Non-terrestrial missile defense intercept and defeat capability for the ballistic missile defense system (sec. 1683)

The Senate bill contained a provision (sec. 1663) that would amend section 1685 of the National Defense Authorization Act for Fiscal Year 2016 by adding at the end a new subsection stating that no later than 60 days after the submittal of the report required, the Director may commence coordination and activities associated with research, development, test, and evaluation on the programs described.

The House amendment contained a similar provision (sec. 1656) that would require the Director of the Missile Defense Agency to commence the planning for concept definition, design, research, development, engineering evaluation, and test of a space-based ballistic missile intercept and defeat layer to the ballistic missile defense system, including with respect to a space test bed for a missile interceptor capability, and submit a detailed budget and development plan for these activities with the budget of the president submitted for fiscal year 2018.

The House recedes.

The conferees note that while the United States enjoys a measure of protection against ballistic missiles of all ranges, the ballistic missile threat—including to the U.S. homeland—continues to grow. The 2010 Ballistic Missile Defense Review noted, "It is difficult to predict precisely how the threat to the U.S. homeland will evolve, but it is certain that it will do so." The conferees agree and received testimony that the threat from ballistic missiles has continued to grow in numbers and in range and countermeasures, making missiles more complex, survivable, reliable, and accurate.

Likewise, the conferees observe that United States space assets are under increasing threat. Director of National Intelligence, James Clapper, testified before the Senate Armed Services Committee on February 9, 2016 that "Threats to our use of military, civil, and commercial space systems will increase in the next few years as Russia and China progress in developing counterspace weapon systems to deny, degrade, or disrupt U.S. space systems." And that "Russia and China continue to pursue weapons systems capable of destroying satellites on orbit, placing U.S. satellites at greater risk in the next few years. China has probably made progress on the antisatellite missile system that it tested in July 2014."

All of this is to suggest that the United States cannot stop exploring new and more effective means for protecting our homeland and forces against ballistic missile threats and for guarding our critical civilian and military space assets. This provision encourages the Department of Defense to examine the feasibility of defeating such threats with a new generation of missile defense capabilities based in space.

Review of the missile defeat policy and strategy of the United States (sec. 1684)

The Senate bill contained a provision (sec. 1664) that would require the Secretary of Defense and the Chairman of the Joint Chiefs of Staff to conduct a review of the strategy, programs and capabilities to counter cruise and ballistic missiles prior to launch using the full range of active, passive, kinetic, and non-kinetic defense measures.

The House amendment contained a provision (sec. 1652) that required the Secretary of Defense and the Chairman of the Joint Chiefs of Staff to conduct a new review of the missile defeat capability, policy, and strategy of the United States with respect to left and right of launch ballistic missile defense, for both regional and homeland missile defense, incorporating the full range of active, passive, kinetic and non-kinetic defense measures, and integrating offensive and defensive forces for the defeat of ballistic and cruise missiles.

The House amendment also contained a provision (sec. 1662) that required the Secretary of Defense and the Chairman of the Joint Chiefs of Staff to submit to the congressional defense committees the classified and unclassified declaratory policy of the United States regarding the use of the left-of-launch capability of the United States and how the Secretary and Chairman intend to ensure such capability is a deterrent to attacks by adversaries.

The Senate recedes with an amendment that combines the three provisions into a single provision with technical changes to the former House provision (sec. 1652). The new provision reduces the prohibition on acquisition changes to the Missile Defense Agency to two years, rather than the indefinite period included in the original House provision.

Maximizing Aegis Ashore capability and developing medium range discrimination radar (sec. 1685)

The House amendment contained a provision (sec. 1654) that would require the Secretary of Defense to conduct a complete evaluation of the optimal anti-air warfare capability for each current Aegis Ashore site and as part of any future deployment by the United States of an Aegis Ashore site. The provision also required the Director of the Missile Defense Agency to notify Congress whether the preferred location for fielding a medium range ballistic missile defense radar for the defense of Hawaii would require an updated environmental impact statement. The Department would also be required to conduct an assessment of the ballistic and air threat against Hawaii and the efficacy of making the Aegis Ashore site at the Pacific Missile Range Facility operational and deploying the preferred alternative for fielding a medium range ballistic missile defense sensor for the defense of Hawaii.

The Senate bill contained no similar provision.

The Senate recedes with an amendment that would require the Secretary of Defense to continue the development, procurement, and deployment of anti-air warfare capabilities at each Aegis Ashore site in Romania and Poland.

The provision also requires the Director of the Missile Defense Agency, if he determines that an updated environmental impact statement is required for fielding a medium range ballistic missile defense sensor for the defense of Hawaii, to commence such action not later than 60 days after the date of notification.

With respect to the requirement for an evaluation of the ballistic and air threat to Hawaii and the efficacy of various defensive measures, the conferees note that the Department has already submitted reports addressing the various alternatives and therefore expect the Department only to provide an update.

Technical authority for integrated air and missile defense activities and programs (sec. 1686)

The House amendment contained a provision (sec. 1655) that would allow the Director of the Missile Defense Agency to seek to have staff detailed to the Missile Defense Agency from the Joint Functional Component Command for Integrated Missile Defense and the Joint Integrated Air and Missile Defense Organization in a number the Director determines necessary.

The Senate bill contained no similar provision.

The Senate recedes.

Hypersonic defense capability development (sec. 1687)

The House amendment contained a provision (sec. 1657) that would require the Director of the Missile Defense Agency to establish a program of record in the ballistic missile defense system to develop and field a defensive system to defeat hypersonic boost-glide and maneuvering ballistic missiles. A limitation was placed on funding for certain headquarters operations in the Office of the Secretary of Defense until such a program of record is created. A report to Congress on the Missile Technology Control Regime (MTCR) was also required.

The Senate bill contained no similar provision.

The Senate recedes with an amendment that would direct that the Director of the Missile Defense Agency serve as the executive agent for the Department of Defense for the development of a capability to counter hypersonic boost-glide vehicle capabilities and conventional prompt global strike capabilities that may be employed against the U.S., its allies, and U.S. deployed forces, and establish a program of record for such capability not later than September 30, 2017. Reports to Congress must be provided on the architecture and sensors needed to detect hypersonic threats and on the military capabilities and capability gaps related to the threat posed by hypersonic boost-glide vehicles and maneuvering ballistic missiles. The limitation on funds and the MTCR report were removed.

Conventional Prompt Global Strike weapons system (sec. 1688)

The Senate bill contained a provision (sec. 1672) that would require the Secretary of Defense to make a Milestone A decision for Conventional Prompt Global Strike no later than September 30, 2020, or 8 months after the successful completion of the Intermediate Range Flight 2 test.

The House amendment contained a similar provision (sec. 1659) that would make no more than 75 percent of funds be obligated or expended for research, development, test, and evaluation, for the conventional prompt global strike until the Chairman of the Joint Chiefs of Staff submits to the congressional defense committees a report on warfighter requirements and whether the program schedule supports such requirements.

The Senate recedes with an amendment that would combine the two provisions,

merging the Senate provision into the House amendment.

Required testing by Missile Defense Agency of ground-based midcourse defense element of ballistic missile defense system (sec. 1689)

The Senate bill contained a provision (sec. 1661) that would require the Director of the Missile Defense Agency to administer a flight test of the ground-based mid-course defense element of the ballistic missile defense system not less frequently than once each fiscal year and allows certain exceptions.

The House amendment contained no similar provision.

The House recedes with a clarifying amendment.

Iron Dome short-range rocket defense system and Israeli cooperative missile defense program codevelopment and coproduction (sec. 1690)

The Senate bill contained a provision (sec. 1662) that would authorize not more than $42.0 million for the Missile Defense Agency to provide to the Government of Israel to procure Tamir interceptors for the Iron Dome short-range rocket defense system through co-production of such interceptors in the United States, including certain conditions.

The House amendment contained a similar provision (sec. 1653) that would authorize not more than $62.0 million for the Missile Defense Agency to provide to the Government of Israel to procure Tamir interceptors for the Iron Dome short-range rocket defense system through coproduction of such interceptors in the United States by industry of the United States, including certain conditions. The House provision would also authorize not more than $150.0 million to procure the David's Sling weapon system and not more than $120.0 million for the Arrow 3 Upper Tier interceptor program, including for coproduction of parts and components in the United States, subject to certain certifications.

The House recedes with an amendment that would combine the two provisions with certain technical corrections and clarifications. The certification concerning the requirement for a bilateral international agreement required by the provision may be waived if the Under Secretary certifies that the funds specified for the David's Sling weapon system and for the Arrow 3 Upper Tier interceptor program are provided to Israel solely for funding the procurement of long-lead components and critical hardware in accordance with a production plan and funding profile detailing Israeli contributions and if the long-lead procurement will be conducted in a manner that does not incur nonrecurring engineering activity or additional cost to United States suppliers. The agreement authorizes $62.0 million to procure Tamir interceptors, the amount prescribed in the House amendment.

Limitations on availability of funds for lower-tier air and missile defense capability of the Army (sec. 1691)

The House amendment contained a provision that would limit the obligation or expenditure of fifty percent of the amount authorized to be appropriated in fiscal year 2017 for the Patriot Lower Tier Air and Missile Defense (LTAMDS) capability of the Army until certain conditions are met.

The Senate bill contained no similar provision.

The Senate recedes with an amendment that would reduce the limitation to twenty-five percent of the funds authorized to be ap-

propriated for LTAMDS Research, Development, Test and Evaluation (RDT&E). The amendment would also amend the conditions the Department of Defense would need to meet to lift the limitation on funds.

The conferees note that the amended provision would not require either a Capabilities Development Document in 2017 or Low Rate Initial Production earlier than 2021, nor is it the conferees intent to mandate such actions.

The conferees agree on the vital importance of the expeditious fielding of a lower tier air and missile defense capability that meets the needs of our warfighters and seamlessly integrates with the nation's other deployed, or planned to be deployed, air and missile defense capabilities.

The conferees also note the Government Accountability Office's (GAO) recent report on the Army's strategy for modernizing the Patriot missile defense system found that throughput limitations under the Army's current maintenance schedule present an elevated risk of equipment failure. The conferees are concerned that potential delays in modernizing Patriot systems, components, and software will amplify these risks as units continue to train, deploy, and operate legacy Patriot equipment at a high tempo over an extended period.

Therefore, the conferees direct GAO to assess the Army's Patriot maintenance and recapitalization plans to ensure that operational needs are met. As part of its assessment, the conferees direct the GAO to review whether Patriot units are undergoing sufficient maintenance in between deployments, and the extent to which the Army has identified and assessed options for increasing its maintenance throughput, including associated costs and impacts on Patriot training and operations. The GAO also should assess whether and how the Army plans to mitigate the risk of equipment failure should Patriot modernization efforts be delayed. The GAO shall complete its review and report to congressional defense committees at an agreed upon date.

Pilot program on loss of unclassified, controlled technical information (sec. 1692)

The House amendment contained a provision (sec. 1660) that would require the Director of the Missile Defense Agency to carry out a pilot program to implement improvements to the data protection options in the programs of the Missile Defense Agency, particularly with respect to unclassified, controlled technical information and controlled unclassified information.

The Senate bill contained no similar provision.

The Senate recedes.

Plan for procurement of medium-range discrimination radar to improve homeland missile defense (sec. 1693)

The House amendment contained a provision (sec. 1663) that would require the Director of the Missile Defense Agency to plan to procure a medium range discrimination radar or equivalent sensor to improve homeland missile defense of Hawaii, and to issue a request for proposals for the medium-range discrimination radar no later than October 1, 2017.

The Senate bill contained no similar provision.

The Senate recedes with an amendment that would clarify that the Missile Defense Agency shall develop a plan to procure a medium-range discrimination radar or equivalent sensor to improve homeland missile defense for Hawaii and to field such radar or equivalent sensor by not later than December 31, 2021, and that the Director shall submit the plan to the congressional defense committees not later than 60 days after enactment.

Review of Missile Defense Agency budget submissions for ground-based midcourse defense and evaluation of alternative ground-based interceptor deployments (sec. 1694)

The House amendment contained a provision (sec. 1661) that would require the Director of Cost Assessment and Program Evaluation to submit to the congressional defense committees a report on the modernization requirements for the ground-based midcourse defense system. The provision would also require the Commander of United States Northern Command to certify the level of funding for the ground-based midcourse defense system, and an evaluation of transportable ground-based interceptors by the Director of the Missile Defense Agency.

The Senate bill contained no similar provision.

The Senate recedes with an amendment that would strike the certification required by the Commander of United States Northern Command, and make it clear that the industrial base requirements required by the report be those requirements generally understood by the Missile Defense Agency.

Semiannual notifications on missile defense tests and costs (sec. 1695)

The House amendment contained a provision (sec. 1664) that would require the Director of the Missile Defense Agency to submit to the congressional defense committees a notification on certain matters related to each planned flight test, including intercept tests.

The Senate bill contained no similar provision.

The Senate recedes.

Reports on unfunded priorities of the Missile Defense Agency (sec. 1696)

The House amendment contained a provision (sec. 1067) that would require the inclusion of ballistic missile defense information in the annual reports on requirements of the combatant commanders and the prioritized capabilities list for ballistic missile defense developed by the commander of the United States Strategic Command.

The Senate bill contained no similar provision.

The Senate recedes with an amendment that would modify the House provision with a requirement that not later than 10 days after the budget of the President for fiscal years 2018 and 2019 are submitted to Congress, the Director of the Missile Defense Agency shall submit to the Secretary of Defense and the Chairman of the Joint Chiefs of Staff, and to the congressional defense committees, a report on the unfunded priorities of the Missile Defense Agency.

Subtitle F—Other Matters

Protection of certain facilities and assets from unmanned aircraft (sec. 1697)

The House amendment contained a provision (sec. 1671) that would authorize the Secretary of Defense, and allow the Secretary to authorize the armed forces, to take actions that are necessary to mitigate the threat of an unmanned aircraft system or unmanned aircraft that poses an imminent threat to the safety or security of a covered facility or asset that is: (1) identified by the Secretary; (2) located in the United States; and (3) related to the nuclear deterrence mission of the Department of Defense (including nuclear command and control, integrated tactical warning and attack assessment, and continuity of government), the missile defense mission of the Department; or the national security space mission of the Department.

The Senate bill contained no similar provision.

The Senate recedes with an amendment that would authorize the Secretary, notwithstanding title 18 of the United States Code, to take actions that are necessary to mitigate the threat (as defined by the Secretary of Defense, in consultation with the Secretary of Transportation) that an unmanned aircraft system or unmanned aircraft poses to the safety or security of a covered facility or asset. The amendment would also clarify the actions that would be authorized.

Harmful interference to Department of Defense Global Positioning System (sec. 1698)

The House amendment contained a provision (sec. 1673) that would amend the Federal Communications Commission (FCC) conditions on commercial terrestrial operations (47 U.S.C. 301 et seq.) by adding that the FCC shall not permit commercial terrestrial operations in the 1525–1559 megahertz band or the 1626.5–1660.5 megahertz band until 90 days after the FCC resolves concerns of widespread harmful interference by such operations in such band to Department of Defense Global Positioning System (GPS) devices. The provision would also require the Secretary of Defense to conduct a review of harmful interference of Department of Defense GPS devices and to notify congress if the Secretary determines the existence of widespread harmful interference.

The Senate bill contained no similar provision.

The Senate recedes with a technical amendment.

LEGISLATIVE PROVISIONS NOT ADOPTED

Availability of certain amounts to meet requirements in connection with United States policy on assured access to space

The Senate bill contained a provision (sec. 1611) that would allow for up to half of the funds made available for a replacement space launch propulsion system or new launch vehicle in fiscal years 2016, 2017, or any future fiscal year, be made available for meeting the requirements in connection with United States policy on assured access to space (section 2273(b), title 10, United States Code).

The House amendment contained no similar provision.

The Senate recedes.

Department of Defense-wide requirements for security clearances for military intelligence officers

The Senate bill contained a provision (sec. 1621) that would require the Secretary of Defense to ensure that each military intelligence officer serving as a unit or service intelligence officer, or in command of an intelligence unit or activity, has an active security clearance.

The House amendment contained no similar provision.

The Senate recedes.

The conferees note with displeasure the recent situation in which an officer serving as the Deputy Chief of Naval Operations for Information Warfare, N2/N6, Office of the Chief of Naval Operations, and Director of Naval Intelligence, was unable to fully perform the duties of the office to which he was appointed, with the advice and consent of the Senate, because his access to classified information was suspended. The conferees expect that in the future every officer serving as a unit or service intelligence officer, or in command of an intelligence unit or activity will have an active security clearance.

Limitation on availability of funds for intelligence management

The House amendment contained a provision (sec. 1621) that would limit the amount of authorized funds available to be obligated or expended for intelligence management until the Under Secretary of Defense for Intelligence provides a report to the appropriate congressional committees on counterintelligence activities described in the classified annex accompanying this Act.

The Senate bill contained no similar provision.

The House recedes.

Sense of Congress on initial operating capability of phase 2 of European Phased Adaptive Approach to missile defense

The House amendment contained a provision (sec. 1666) that would express the Sense of Congress that the United States is committed to the defense of deployed members of the Armed Forces of the United States and to the defense of the European allies of the United States by increasing the ballistic missile defense capability of the North Atlantic Treaty Organization.

The Senate bill contained no similar provision.

The conferees note that on July 9, 2016, the Heads of State and Government participating in the meeting of the North Atlantic Council in Warsaw, Poland, issued the "Warsaw Summit Communique." In that document, the Heads of State and Government stated that:

"At our Summit in Chicago in 2012, we declared the achievement of an Interim NATO BMD Capability as an operationally significant first step. At the Wales Summit, we welcomed the forward deployment of BMD-capable Aegis ships to Rota, Spain that could be made available to NATO. Today a new milestone in the development of NATO BMD has been reached and we are pleased to declare the achievement of the NATO BMD Initial Operational Capability. This is a significant step toward the aim of NATO BMD that offers a stronger capability to defend our populations, territory, and forces across southern NATO Europe against a potential ballistic missile attack. The Aegis Ashore site in Deveselu, Romania represents a significant portion of this increase in capability, and the command and control (C2) of the Aegis Ashore site is being transferred to NATO. We also welcome that Turkey hosts a forward-based early-warning BMD radar at Kürecik and that Poland will be hosting an Aegis Ashore site at the Redzikowo military base. We are also pleased that additional voluntary national contributions have been offered by Allies, and we encourage further voluntary contributions, all of which will add robustness to the capability."

The Communique further stated that, "NATO missile defence is not directed against Russia and will not undermine Russia's strategic deterrence capabilities. NATO missile defence is intended to defend against potential threats emanating from outside the Euro-Atlantic area."

The House recedes.

Pilot program on application of consequence-driven, cyber-informed engineering to mitigate against cyber-security threats

The Senate bill contained a provision (sec. 1634) that would authorize the Secretary of Defense, in coordination with the secretaries of the military departments, to carry out a pilot program to assess the feasibility and advisability of applying consequence-driven, cyber-informed engineering methodologies to military installation operating technologies, including industrial control systems, to increase resilience against cybersecurity threats.

The House amendment contained no similar provision.

The Senate recedes.

The conferees note that elsewhere in the conference agreement there is a requirement for the Secretary of Defense to conduct a pilot program to assess the feasibility and advisability of applying, innovative methodologies or engineering approaches to improve the defense of control systems against cyber attacks in order to increase the resilience of military installations against cybersecurity threats and prevent or mitigate the potential for high-consequence cyberattacks, and to inform future requirements development for such systems.

TITLE XVII—GUAM WORLD WAR II LOYALTY RECOGNITION ACT

Guam World War II Loyalty Recognition Act (secs. 1701–1707)

The House amendment contained a number of provisions (sec. 7301–7306) that would honor the suffering and loyalty of the residents of Guam during its occupation by Imperial Japanese forces during the Second World War and direct the federal government to adjudicate and facilitate the claims of compensable Guam victims and survivors of compensable Guam decedents.

Specifically, the House amendment contained a provision (sec. 7302) that would express the eternal gratitude of the United States to the residents of Guam for their loyalty and courage under threat of death and great bodily harm at the hands of occupying forces. It also contained a provision that would direct the Secretary of the Treasury to establish a special fund for the payment of claims to compensable Guam victims and their survivors (sec. 7303), a provision that would require the Secretary of the Treasury to compensate compensable victims and survivors of compensable Guam decedents following certification from the Foreign Claims Settlement Commission (sec. 7304), and a provision that would direct the Foreign Claims Settlement Commission to adjudicate claims and to determine eligibility for claims under the aforementioned section 7304 (sec. 7305). Finally, it contained a provision that would direct the Secretary of the Interior to establish a grant program designed to educate and to memorialize the occupation of Guam while honoring the loyalty of its inhabitants (sec. 7306) and a provision that would authorize appropriations for the aforementioned sections 7304 and 7305 for any fiscal year beginning after the date of the enactment, with $5,000,000 authorized per fiscal year for section 7306 (sec. 7307).

The Senate bill contained no similar provisions.

The Senate recedes.

TITLE XVIII—MATTERS RELATING TO SMALL BUSINESS PROCUREMENT

Subtitle A—Improving Transparency and Clarity for Small Businesses

Plain language rewrite of requirements for small business procurements (sec. 1801)

The House amendment contained a provision (sec. 1801) that would amend section 15(a) of the Small Business Act (15 U.S.C. 644(a)) to revise existing statute by better organizing the section and modernizing the terms consistent with those in titles 10 and 41, United States Code.

The Senate bill contained no similar provision.

The Senate recedes.

Transparency in small business goals (sec. 1802)

The House amendment contained a provision (sec. 1803) that would amend section 15(h) of the Small Business Act (15 U.S.C. 644(h)) to require the Administrator of the General Services Administration to issue an annual report on the share of total contract value awarded to small businesses.

The Senate bill contained no similar provision.

The Senate recedes.

Subtitle B—Clarifying the Roles of Small Business Advocates

Scope of review by procurement center representatives (sec. 1811)

The Senate bill contained a provision (sec. 884) that would codify for Department of Defense contracts the longstanding exemption contained in Federal Acquisition Regulation 19.000(b) that small business set-asides are not applied to overseas contracts.

The House amendment contained a similar provision (sec. 1811) that would amend section 15(l) of the Small Business Act (15 U.S.C. 644(l)) to reverse a regulatory change made by the Small Business Administration during enactment of the Small Business Jobs Act of 2010 (Public Law 111–240) and to ensure that procurement center representatives review consolidated contracts or task orders that are fully or partially set aside or reserved for small business.

The Senate recedes with an amendment that would clarify that procurement center representatives of the Small Business Administration shall not review contracts awarded pursuant to status of forces agreements or contracts of the Department of Defense awarded and performed overseas. The amendment also would stipulate that contracts excluded from procurement center representative review shall not be included in any calculation of the Department's attainment of the small business goals established in 15(g) of the Small Business Act (15 USC 644(g)).

Duties of the Office of Small and Disadvantaged Business Utilization (sec. 1812)

The House amendment contained a provision (sec. 1813) that would amend section 15(k) of the Small Business Act (15 U.S.C. 644(k)) to revise the duties of the Offices of Small and Disadvantaged Business Utilization in Federal agencies. The offices would be authorized to provide assistance to service-disabled veteran-owned small businesses and participants in the Historically Underutilized Business Zone program which are not included in the current list of small business programs. The offices also would review annual summaries of Government credit card purchases to ensure compliance with the Small Business Act.

The Senate bill contained no similar provision.

The Senate recedes.

Improving contractor compliance (sec. 1813)

The House amendment contained a provision (sec. 1814) that would amend sections 15 and 45 of the Small Business Act (15 U.S.C. 644 and 15 U.S.C. 657r), and section 831(e)1(1) of the National Defense Authorization Act for Fiscal Year 1991 (Public Law 101–510), to promote the availability of existing programs that assist small contractors attempting to comply with Federal regulations. The Small Business Administration would develop a list of no-cost compliance assistance programs for small contractors which would be distributed through the Small Business Administration and Federal agency small-

business offices to small contractors. This section would also require that any mentor-protégé agreement approved by the Small Business Administration or the Department of Defense address the provision of compliance assistance to the protégé firm.

The Senate bill contained no similar provision.

The Senate recedes.

Improving education on small business regulations (sec. 1814)

The House amendment contained a provision (sec. 1861) that would amend section 15 of the Small Business Act (15 U.S.C. 644) to require the Small Business Administration to annually share a list of regulatory changes affecting small-business contracting with entities responsible for training acquisition personnel, such as the Federal Acquisition Institute and the Defense Acquisition University, and to entities providing technical assistance to small contractors. This section would also require that the applicable entities periodically update training materials.

The Senate bill contained no similar provision.

The Senate recedes.

Subtitle C—Strengthening Opportunities for Competition in Subcontracting

Good faith in subcontracting (sec. 1821)

The House amendment contained a provision (sec. 1821) that would amend section 8(d) of the Small Business Act (15 U.S.C. 637(d)) to improve compliance with subcontracting requirements.

The Senate bill contained no similar provision.

The Senate recedes.

Pilot program to provide opportunities for qualified subcontractors to obtain past performance ratings (sec. 1822)

The House amendment contained a provision (sec. 1822) that would establish a 3-year pilot program in which small, first-tier subcontractors could obtain past performance credit from the Small Business Administration.

The Senate bill contained no similar provision.

The Senate recedes with an amendment that would establish a deadline by which small business concerns must submit requests for a past performance rating.

The conferees direct the Secretary of Defense to ensure that the Department of Defense, its components, and the Services are providing timely evaluations of past performance and giving due credit to the evaluations previously conducted, even those conducted by a different component, Service, or agency, consistent with current law and regulation. No later than 60 days after enactment of the National Defense Authorization for Fiscal Year 2017, the conferees direct the Secretary to provide a briefing to the Committees on Armed Services of the Senate and the House of Representatives on the Department's progress meeting these objectives.

Amendments to the Mentor-Protege Program of the Department of Defense (sec. 1823)

The House amendment contained a provision (sec. 1831) that would amend section 831 of the National Defense Authorization Act for Fiscal Year 1991 (Public Law 101–510), to require the Small Business Administration to determine whether a prospective protege firm is affiliated with its proposed mentor prior to approval of a mentor-protege agreement. The same requirement would be removed from the Department of Defense.

The Senate bill contained no similar provision.

The Senate recedes with a technical amendment that would better organize the eligibility requirements. The conferees note that the changes in this provision will allow for determinations of small business status to be made in the same manner as such determinations are for purposes of federal contracting. The change does not alter the Department's control of its mentor-protege program, nor the statutory provision that prohibits the Small Business Administration from considering support provided by a mentor to a protege firm under this program as evidence of affiliation. However, the provision would prevent instances of confusion, and the potential for fraud, by preventing competing determinations of small business status.

Subtitle D—Miscellaneous Provisions

Improvements to size standards for small agricultural producers (sec. 1831)

The House amendment contained a provision (sec. 1863) that would amend section 18(b) of the Small Business Act (15 U.S.C. 647(b)) to revise the definition of an agricultural enterprise. This section would also amend section 3(a) of the Small Business Act (15 U.S.C. 632(a)) to authorize the Small Business Administration to establish different size standards for various types of agricultural enterprises. Size standards would be established according to the existing method and appeals process by which the Small Business Administration establishes other size standards.

The Senate bill contained no similar provision.

The Senate recedes.

Uniformity in service-disabled veteran definitions (sec. 1832)

The House amendment contained a provision (sec. 1864) that would amend section 3(q) of the Small Business Act (15 U.S.C. 632(q)) and section 8127 of title 38, United States Code, to standardize definitions for veteran-owned small businesses (VOSBs) and service-disabled veteran-owned small businesses (SDVOSBs). This section would also require the Secretary of Veterans Affairs to use the regulations established by the Small Business Administration for establishing ownership and control of VOSBs and SDVOSBs. The Secretary would continue to determine whether individuals are veterans or service-disabled veterans and would be responsible for verification of applicant firms. Challenges to the status of a VOSB or SDVOSB based upon issues of ownership or control would be decided by the administrative judges at the Office of Hearings and Appeals of the Small Business Administration. This section would not affect the Department of Defense.

The Senate bill contained no similar provision.

The Senate recedes.

Office of Hearings and Appeals (sec. 1833)

The House amendment contained a provision (sec. 1866) that would amend sections 3(a) and 5(i) of the Small Business Act (15 U.S.C. 632(a) and 15 U.S.C. 634(i)) to clarify that the Office of Hearings and Appeals will not hear appeals on programs not found in the Small Business Act. This section also would allow a grace period for appeals that occur before the Small Business Administration implements the requirements of this section.

The Senate bill contained no similar provision.

The Senate recedes.

Extension of SBIR and STTR programs (sec. 1834)

The Senate bill contained a provision (sec. 874) that would amend sections 9(m) and 9(n)(1) of the Small Business Act (15 U.S.C. 638(m)) in order to make the Small Business Innovation Research (SBIR) program and the Small Business Technology Transfer (STTR) program at the Department of Defense permanent.

The House amendment contained no similar provision.

The House recedes with an amendment that would extend the programs government-wide for an additional 5 years.

Issuance of guidance on small business matters (sec. 1835)

The House amendment contained a provision (sec. 1867) that would require the Administrator of the Small Business Administration to issue guidance with respect to the changes to the Small Business Act made in this title.

The Senate bill contained no similar provision.

The Senate recedes with a technical amendment that would provide a timeline for implementing guidance by the Department of Veterans Affairs.

Subtitle E—Improving Cyber Preparedness for Small Businesses

Small Business Development Center Cyber Strategy and outreach (sec. 1841)

The House amendment contained a provision (sec. 1869A) that would amend section 227 of the Homeland Security Act of 2002 (6 U.S.C. 148) to grant the Secretary of Homeland Security authority to provide assistance to small business development centers in the form of training and dissemination of information on cybersecurity, as outlined elsewhere in this Act.

The Senate bill contained no similar provision.

The Senate recedes with a technical amendment that would maintain consistency in the use of terms such as cyber threat awareness.

Role of small business development centers in cybersecurity and preparedness (sec. 1842)

The House amendment contained a provision (sec. 1868) that would amend section 21 of the Small Business Act (15 U.S.C. 648) to define the role of the Small Business Development Center Cyber Strategy, which was established elsewhere in this Act.

The Senate bill contained no similar provision.

The Senate recedes.

Additional cybersecurity assistance for small business development centers (sec. 1843)

The House amendment contained a provision (sec. 1869) that would amend section 21(a) of the Small Business Act (15 U.S.C. 648) to give the Department of Homeland Security the authority to provide cybersecurity assistance, in the form of trainings and other outreach, to small business development centers to enhance security and awareness.

The Senate bill contained no similar provision.

The Senate recedes.

Prohibition on additional funds (sec. 1844)

The House amendment contained a provision (sec. 1869C) that would prohibit the use of additional funds to be appropriated to carry out the previous sections, other than those already appropriated within these sections.

The Senate bill contained no similar provision.

The Senate recedes.

Improving reporting on small business goals

The House amendment contained a provision (sec. 1802) that would amend section 15(h) of the Small Business Act (15 U.S.C. 644(h)) to require the Small Business Administration, using data already required to be collected from contractors, to track companies that outgrow or no longer qualify for a small business program, as well as identify how prime contracting goals are met.

The Senate bill contained no similar provision.

The House recedes.

Uniformity in procurement terminology

The House amendment contained a provision (sec. 1804) that would amend section 3(m) of the Small Business Act (15 U.S.C. 632(m)) and section 15(j) of the Small Business Act (15 U.S.C. 644(j)) to update procurement terminology consistent with the Federal Acquisition Regulation and with terminology used in titles 10 and 41, United States Code.

The Senate bill contained no similar provision.

The House recedes.

Responsibilities of Commercial Market Representatives

The House amendment contained a provision (sec. 1812) that would amend section 4(h) of the Small Business Act (15 U.S.C. 633(h)), to provide a definition of the duties and responsibilities of the commercial market representatives employed by the Small Business Administration.

The Senate bill contained no similar provision.

The House recedes.

Responsibilities of Business Opportunity Specialists

The House amendment contained a provision (sec. 1815) that would amend section 4(g) of the Small Business Act (15 U.S.C. 633(g)) to add a job description and reporting hierarchy for business opportunity specialists of the Small Business Administration.

The Senate bill contained no similar provision.

The House recedes.

Improving cooperation between the mentor-protege programs of the Small Business Administration and the Department of Defense

The House amendment contained a provision (sec. 1832) that would amend section 45(b) of the Small Business Act (15 U.S.C. 657r(b)) to require the Department of Defense to obtain approval from the Administrator of the Small Business Administration prior to carrying out a mentor-protege program.

The Senate bill contained no similar provision.

The House recedes.

Office of Women's Business Ownership

The House amendment contained a provision (sec. 1841) that would amend section 29(g) of the Small Business Act (15 U.S.C. 656(g)) to clarify the duties of the Small Business Administration's Office of Women's Business Ownership, and to require that the office establish an accreditation program for its grant recipients.

The Senate bill contained no similar provision.

The House recedes.

Women's Business Center Program

The House amendment contained a provision (sec. 1842) that would amend section 29 of the Small Business Act (15 U.S.C. 656), relating to the Women's Business Center Program.

The Senate bill contained no similar provision.

The House recedes.

Matching requirements under Women's Business Center Program

The House amendment contained a provision (sec. 1843) that would amend section 29 of the Small Business Act (15 U.S.C. 656), relating to the Women's Business Center Program, to limit the ability of the Administrator to waive the requirement for matching funds by grant recipients, and to provide that excess non-Federal dollars obtained by a grant recipient will not be subject to part 200 of title 2, Code of Federal Regulations, or any successor regulations.

The Senate bill contained no similar provision.

The House recedes.

SCORE reauthorization

The House amendment contained a provision (sec. 1851) that would amend section 20 of the Small Business Act (15 U.S.C. 631 note) to authorize the SCORE program through fiscal year 2018, and to permit the current level of appropriations to extend through that period.

The Senate bill contained no similar provision.

The House recedes.

SCORE program

The House amendment contained a provision (sec. 1852) that would amend sections 8(b) and 8(c) of the Small Business Act (15 U.S.C. 637(b)–(c)) to rename the Service Corps of Retired Executives program, the "SCORE" program.

The Senate bill contained no similar provision.

The House recedes.

Online component

The House amendment contained a provision (sec. 1853) that would amend section 8(c) of the Small Business Act (15 U.S.C. 637(c)) to create an online component for the SCORE Association to utilize.

The Senate bill contained no similar provision.

The House recedes.

Study and report on the future role of the SCORE program

The House amendment contained a provision (sec. 1854) that would require the SCORE Association to conduct a study and develop a plan for how the SCORE program will evolve to meet the needs of small business concerns.

The Senate bill contained no similar provision.

The House recedes.

Technical and conforming amendments

The House amendment contained a provision (sec. 1855) that would make technical and conforming amendments to various places in law which reference the program that SCORE would replace.

The Senate bill contained no similar provision.

The House recedes.

Required reports pertaining to capital planning and investment control

The House amendment contained a provision (sec. 1865) that would require the Small Business Administration to provide information regarding certain Federal major information technology investments to the Small Business and Entrepreneurship Committee of the Senate and the Small Business Committee of the House of Representatives.

The Senate bill contained no similar provision.

The House recedes.

GAO study on small business cyber support services and small business development center cyber strategy

The House amendment contained a provision (sec. 1869B) that would require the Comptroller General of the United States to conduct a review of current cybersecurity resources at the Federal level aimed at assisting small business concerns with developing or enhancing cybersecurity infrastructure, cyber threat awareness, or cyber training programs for employees.

The Senate bill contained no similar provision.

The House recedes.

Short title

The House amendment contained a provision (sec. 1871) that would cite this subtitle as the "Small Business Development Centers Improvement Act of 2016".

The Senate bill contained no similar provision.

The House recedes.

Use of authorized entrepreneurial development programs

The House amendment contained a provision (sec. 1872) that would amend the Small Business Act (15 U.S.C. 631 et seq.) to add a new section that would expand the use of entrepreneurial development programs.

The Senate bill contained no similar provision.

The House recedes.

Marketing of services

The House amendment contained a provision (sec. 1873) that would amend section 21 of the Small Business Act (15 U.S.C. 648) to ensure that the Administrator will not prohibit applicants who have received grants under the Small Business Development Center program from marketing and advertising their services to individuals and small business concerns.

The Senate bill contained no similar provision.

The House recedes.

Data collection

The House amendment contained a provision (sec. 1874) that would amend section 21 of the Small Business Act (15 U.S.C. 648) to ensure that data collection regarding grant applicants is improved.

The Senate bill contained no similar provision.

The House recedes.

Fees from private partnerships and cosponsorships

The House amendment contained a provision (sec. 1875) that would amend section 21(a)(3) of the Small Business Act (15 U.S.C. 648(a)(3)(C)) that would ensure that small business development centers participating in private partnerships and cosponsorships with the Administration are not limited from collecting fees or other income related to the operation of such partnerships.

The Senate bill contained no similar provision.

The House recedes.

Equity for small business development centers

The House amendment contained a provision (sec. 1876) that would amend subclause (I) of section 21(a)(4)(C)(v) of the Small Business Act (15 U.S.C. 648(a)(4)(C)(v)) to increase the threshold allowed to the Administrator to pay expenses related to the development program from $500,000 to $600,000.

The Senate bill contained no similar provision.

The House recedes.

Confidentiality requirements

The House amendment contained a provision (sec. 1877) that would amend Section 21(a)(7)(A) of the Small Business Act (15 U.S.C. 648(a)(7)(A)) to clarify that certain information regarding small business participation in this program would not be disclosed without the consent of the individual or small business concern to any State, local or Federal agency, or third party.

The Senate bill contained no similar provision.

The House recedes.

Limitation on award of grants to small business development centers

The House amendment contained a provision (sec. 1878) that would amend section 21 of the Small Business Act (15 U.S.C. 648) to limit the award of grants.

The Senate bill contained no similar provision.

The House recedes.

TITLE XIX—DEPARTMENT OF HOMELAND SECURITY STRATEGY FOR INTERNATIONAL PROGRAMS

Department of Homeland Security Strategy for International Programs (secs. 1901–1913)

The conference agreement includes a subtitle that would make various authorizations and modifications with respect to the Department of Homeland Security.

DIVISION B—MILITARY CONSTRUCTION AUTHORIZATIONS

Summary and explanation of funding tables

Division B of this Act authorizes funding for military construction projects of the Department of Defense. It includes funding authorizations for the construction and operation of military family housing as well as military construction for the reserve components, the defense agencies, and the North Atlantic Treaty Organization Security Investment Program. It also provides authorization for the base closure accounts that fund military construction, environmental cleanup, and other activities required to implement the decisions in base closure rounds.

The tables contained in this Act provide the project-level authorizations for the military construction funding authorized in Division B of this Act and summarize that funding by account.

Short title (sec. 2001)

The Senate bill contained a provision (sec. 2001) that would designate division B of this Act as the "Military Construction Authorization Act for Fiscal Year 2017."

The House amendment contained an identical provision (sec. 2001).

The conference agreement includes this provision.

Expiration of authorizations and amounts required to be specified by law (sec. 2002)

The Senate bill contained a provision (sec. 2002) that would establish the expiration date for authorizations in this Act for military construction projects, land acquisition, family housing projects, and contributions to the North Atlantic Treaty Organization Security Investment Program as of October 1, 2019, or the date of enactment of an act authorizing funds for military construction for fiscal year 2020, whichever is later.

The House amendment contained a similar provision (sec. 2002).

The Senate recedes.

Effective date (sec. 2003)

The Senate bill contained a provision (sec. 2003) that would provide an effective date for titles XXI through XXVII of October 1, 2016 or the date of enactment of this Act.

The House amendment contained a similar provision (sec. 2003).

The Senate recedes.

TITLE XXI—ARMY MILITARY CONSTRUCTION

Summary

The budget request included authorization of appropriations of $503.5 million for military construction and $526.7 million for family housing for the Army in fiscal year 2017.

The conference agreement includes authorization of appropriations of $553.9 million for military construction and $483.2 million for family housing for the Army in fiscal year 2017.

The agreement includes authorization for three projects from the Army's unfunded requirements list: $10.6 million for a Company Operations Facility at Fort Gordon, Georgia; $6.9 million for a Fire Station at Fort Leonard Wood, Missouri; and $23.0 million for a Vehicle Maintenance Shop at Fort Belvoir, Virginia.

The conferees note that the budget request included $143.6 million for Family Housing New Construction at Camp Humphries, Republic of Korea. Furthermore, the conferees are aware that this is the first phase of proposed military family housing construction at Camp Humphries, with a $153.0 million second phase planned for fiscal year 2019. Given the requirements that have been established by the Commander of U.S. Forces Korea to house command sponsored families on installation and the timelines for the relocation of U.S. Forces Korea and Eighth Army to Camp Humphries, the conferees believe that combining the two phases into a single project will result in efficiencies in terms of the financial cost of the project and the construction timeline. Therefore, the agreement recommends a total authorization of $297.0 million for Family Housing New Construction at Camp Humphries, Republic of Korea. However, the conferees support the authorization of appropriations for fiscal year 2017 only in an amount equivalent to the ability of the military department to execute in the year of authorization of appropriations. Therefore, the agreement recommends $100.0 million, a reduction of $43.6 million, for this project in fiscal year 2017.

In addition, the conference agreement authorizes $35.0 million for the Army's unspecified minor construction program, an increase of $10.0 million above the budget request.

Authorized Army construction and land acquisition projects (sec. 2101)

The Senate bill contained a provision (sec. 2101) that would contain the list of authorized Army construction projects for fiscal year 2017. The authorized amounts are listed on an installation-by-installation basis. The state list contained in this Act is intended to be the binding list of the specific projects authorized at each location.

The House amendment contained a similar provision (sec. 2101).

The Senate recedes.

Family housing (sec. 2102)

The Senate bill contained a provision (sec. 2102) that would authorize new construction and planning and design of family housing units for the Army for fiscal year 2017.

The House amendment contained a similar provision (sec. 2102).

The Senate recedes.

Authorization of appropriations, Army (sec. 2103)

The Senate bill contained a provision (sec. 2103) that would authorize appropriations for the active component military construction and family housing projects of the Army authorized for construction for fiscal year 2017. This provision would also provide an overall limit on the amount authorized for military construction and family housing projects for the active component of the Army.

The House amendment contained an identical provision (sec. 2103).

The conference agreement includes this provision.

Modification of authority to carry out certain fiscal year 2014 project (sec. 2104)

The Senate bill contained a provision (sec. 2104) that would modify the authorization contained in section 2101(a) of the Military Construction Authorization Act for Fiscal Year 2014 (division B of Public Law 113–66) for construction of an aircraft maintenance hangar at Joint Base Lewis-McChord, Washington to include an aircraft washing apron.

The House amendment contained an identical provision (sec. 2104).

The conference agreement includes this provision.

Extension of authorizations of certain fiscal year 2013 projects (sec. 2105)

The Senate bill contained a provision (sec. 2105) that would extend the authorization contained in section 2101 of the Military Construction Authorization Act for Fiscal Year 2013 (division B of Public Law 112–239) for two projects until October 1, 2017, or the date of the enactment of an Act authorizing funds for military construction for fiscal year 2018, whichever is later.

The House amendment contained a similar provision (sec. 2105).

The Senate recedes.

Extension of authorizations of certain fiscal year 2014 projects (sec. 2106)

The Senate bill contained a provision (sec. 2106) that would extend the authorization contained in section 2101 of the Military Construction Authorization Act for Fiscal Year 2014 (division B of Public Law 113–66) for three projects until October 1, 2017, or the date of the enactment of an Act authorizing funds for military construction for fiscal year 2018, whichever is later.

The House amendment contained a similar provision (sec. 2106).

The House recedes.

TITLE XXII—NAVY MILITARY CONSTRUCTION

Summary

The budget request included authorization of appropriations of $1.03 billion for military construction and $394.9 million for family housing for the Navy and Marine Corps in fiscal year 2017.

The conference agreement includes authorization of appropriations of $1.2 billion for military construction and $394.9 million for family housing for the Navy and Marine Corps in fiscal year 2017.

The conference agreement includes authorization for two projects from the Navy's unfunded requirements list unfunded requirements list: $27.0 million for Chambers Field Magazine Recap Phase 1 at Norfolk, Virginia, and $73.0 million for *SEAWOLF* Class Service Pier at Bangor, Washington.

The agreement includes authorization for three projects from the Marine Corp's unfunded requirements list: $118.9 million for an Aircraft Maintenance Hangar Increment 1 at Miramar, California; $34.7 million for a Communication Complex & Infrastructure Upgrade at Miramar, California; $40.0 million for F–35 Parking Apron at Miramar, California. With respect to the Aircraft Maintenance Hangar, we support the authorization for appropriations in an amount equivalent to the ability of the military department to execute in the year of the authorization for appropriations. For this project, the conferees believe that the Department of the Navy has exceeded its ability to fully expend the funding requested for fiscal year 2017. As such, the agreement recommends incremental funding with an authorization of appropriations in the amount of $79.4 million, a reduction of $39.5 million, for this project. Furthermore, the conferees note that these three projects at Miramar were included in the Marine Corps' unfunded requirements list due to a late development and the need to align F–35C squadron operational dates with plans to stand up the first F–35C compatible aircraft carrier on the west coast of the United States.

Authorized Navy construction and land acquisition projects (sec. 2201)

The Senate bill contained a provision (sec. 2201) that would authorize Navy and Marine Corps military construction projects for fiscal year 2017. The authorized amounts are listed on an installation-by-installation basis.

The House amendment contained a similar provision (sec. 2201).

The Senate recedes with a technical amendment.

Family housing (sec. 2202)

The Senate bill contained a provision (sec. 2202) that would authorize new construction, planning, and design of family housing units for the Navy for fiscal year 2017. This provision would also authorize funds for facilities that support family housing, including housing management offices, housing maintenance, and storage facilities.

The House amendment contained an identical provision (sec. 2202).

The conference agreement includes this provision.

Improvements to military family housing units (sec. 2203)

The Senate bill contained a provision (sec. 2203) that would authorize the Secretary of the Navy to improve existing family housing units of the Department of the Navy in an amount not to exceed $11.1 million.

The House amendment contained an identical provision (sec. 2203).

The conference agreement includes this provision.

Authorization of appropriations, Navy (sec. 2204)

The Senate bill contained a provision (sec. 2204) that would authorize appropriations for the active component military construction and family housing projects of the Department of the Navy authorized for construction for fiscal year 2017. This provision would also provide an overall limit on the amount authorized for military construction and family housing projects for the active components of the Navy and the Marine Corps. The state list contained in this report is the binding list of the specific projects authorized at each location.

The House amendment contained an identical provision (sec. 2204).

The conference agreement includes this provision.

Modification of authority to carry out certain fiscal year 2014 project (sec. 2205)

The Senate bill contained a provision (sec. 2205) that would modify the authorization contained in section 2201 of the Military Construction Authorization Act for Fiscal Year 2014 (division B of Public Law 113–66) for construction of a water transmission line at Pearl City, Hawaii to include a 591-meter long, 16-inch diameter water transmission line as part of the network required to provide the main water supply to Joint Base Pearl Harbor-Hickam, Hawaii.

The House amendment contained an identical provision (sec. 2205).

The conference agreement includes this provision.

Extension of authorizations of certain fiscal year 2013 projects (sec. 2206)

The Senate bill contained a provision (sec. 2206) that would extend the authorization contained in section 2201 of the Military Construction Authorization Act for Fiscal Year 2013 (division B of Public Law 112–239), for various projects until October 1, 2017, or the date of the enactment of an Act authorizing funds for military construction for fiscal year 2018, whichever is later.

The House amendment contained a similar provision (sec. 2206).

The Senate recedes.

Extension of authorizations of certain fiscal year 2014 projects (sec. 2207)

The Senate bill contained a provision (sec. 2207) that would modify the authorization contained in section 2201 of the Military Construction Authorization Act for Fiscal Year 2014 (division B of Public Law 113–66), for seven projects until October 1, 2017, or the date of the enactment of an Act authorizing funds for military construction for fiscal year 2018, whichever is later.

The House amendment contained an identical provision (sec. 2207).

The conference agreements includes this provision.

Status of "net negative" policy regarding Navy acreage on Guam (sec. 2208)

The House amendment included a provision (Sec. 2208) that would require the Secretary of the Navy to submit a report to the congressional defense committees not later than 6 months after the date of the enactment of this Act regarding the status of the implementation of the "Net Negative" policy regarding the total number of acres of real property controlled by the Department of the Navy on the Territory of Guam.

The Senate bill contained no similar provision.

The Senate recedes with an amendment.

The conferees are concerned that the Department of the Navy has not adequately defined the scope of lands that will be returned to the Government of Guam pursuant to the Net Negative policy announced in 2011, or the process that will be used to identify and transfer such lands. Specifically, the conferees are concerned by the ambiguity regarding the status of lands identified for return prior to the announcement of the Net Negative policy, such as Guam Land Use Plan of 1977, which were not originally identified for inclusion in the calculation of lands under the Net Negative policy.

TITLE XXIII—AIR FORCE MILITARY CONSTRUCTION

Summary

The budget request included authorization of appropriations of $1.5 billion for military construction and $335.7 million for family housing for the Air Force in fiscal year 2017.

The conference agreement includes authorization of appropriations of $1.7 billion for military construction and $335.7 million for family housing for the Air Force in fiscal year 2017.

The conference agreement includes authorization for seven projects on the Air Force's unfunded requirements list: $15.5 million for a JAG School Expansion at Maxwell Air

Force Base, Alabama; $36.0 million for Dormitories (288 rooms) at Eglin Air Force Base, Florida; $41.0 million for Consolidated Corrosion Facility Add/Alt at Scott Air Force Base, Illinois; $50.0 million for Consolidated Communications Center at Joint Base Andrews, Maryland; $10.9 million to Construction Vandenberg Gate Complex at Hanscom Air Force Base, Massachusetts; $26.0 million for E–3G Mission and Flight Simulator Training Facility at Tinker Air Force Base, Oklahoma; and $17.0 million for Fire & Rescue Station at Joint Base Charleston, South Carolina.

In addition, the conference agreement authorizes $40.0 million for the Air Force's unspecified minor construction program, an increase of $10.0 million above the budget request.

Authorized Air Force construction and land acquisition projects (sec. 2301)

The Senate bill contained a provision (sec. 2301) that would authorize Air Force military construction projects for fiscal year 2017. The authorized amounts are listed on an installation-by-installation basis.

The House amendment contained a similar provision (sec. 2301).

The Senate recedes with a technical amendment.

Family housing (sec. 2302)

The Senate bill contained a provision (sec. 2302) that would authorize new construction, planning, and design of family housing units for the Air Force for fiscal year 2017. This provision would also authorize funds for facilities that support family housing, including housing management offices, housing maintenance, and storage facilities.

The House amendment contained an identical provision (sec. 2302).

The conference agreement includes this provision.

Improvements to military family housing units (sec. 2303)

The Senate bill contained a provision (sec. 2303) that would authorize the Secretary of the Air Force to improve existing family housing units of the Department of the Air Force in an amount not to exceed $150.7 million.

The House amendment contained an identical provision (sec. 2303).

The conference agreement includes this provision.

Authorization of appropriations, Air Force (sec. 2304)

The Senate bill contained a provision (sec. 2304) that would authorize appropriations for the active component military construction and family housing projects of the Air Force authorized for construction for fiscal year 2017. This provision would also provide an overall limit on the amount authorized for military construction and family housing projects for the active component of the Air Force. The state list contained in this report is the binding list of the specific projects authorized at each location.

The House amendment contained an identical provision (sec. 2304).

The conference agreement includes this provision.

Modification of authority to carry out certain fiscal year 2016 project (sec. 2305)

The Senate bill contained a provision (sec. 2305) that would modify the authorization contained in section 2301 of the National Defense Authorization Act for Fiscal Year 2016 (Public Law 114–92) for a tactical response force alert facility at Malstrom Air Force Base, Montana to include the construction of an emergency power generator system.

The House amendment contained an identical provision (sec. 2305).

The conference agreement includes this provision.

Extension of authorization of certain fiscal year 2013 project (sec. 2306)

The House amendment contained a provision (sec. 2306) that would extend the authorization listed, originally provided by section 2301 of the Military Construction Authorization Act for Fiscal Year 2013 (division B of Public Law 112–239), and previously extended by section 2309 of the Military Construction Authorization Act for Fiscal Year 2016 (Public Law 114–92), until October 1, 2017, or the date of the enactment of an act authorizing funds for military construction for fiscal year 2018, whichever is later.

The Senate bill contained no similar provision.

The Senate recedes.

Extension of authorization of certain fiscal year 2014 project (sec. 2307)

The Senate bill contained a provision (sec. 2306) that would extend the authorization contained in section 2301 of the Military Construction Act for Fiscal Year 2014 (division B of Public Law 113–66) for various projects until October 1, 2017, or the date of the enactment of an act authorizing funds for military construction for fiscal year 2018, whichever is later.

The House amendment contained a similar provision (sec. 2307).

The Senate recedes.

Restriction on acquisition of property in Northern Mariana Islands (sec. 2308)

The House amendment contained a provision (sec. 2308) that would prohibit the Secretary of the Air Force from using any of the amounts authorized to be appropriated to acquire property or interests in property at an unspecified location in the Commonwealth of the Northern Mariana Islands until the congressional defense committees have received a report from the Secretary that provides the specific location of the property or interest in property to be acquired, the total cost, scope and location of military construction projects for divert activities and exercises at the location, and an analysis of any alternative locations considered, including other locations or interests within the Commonwealth of the Northern Mariana Islands or the Freely Associated States.

The Senate bill contained no similar provision.

The Senate recedes.

TITLE XXIV—DEFENSE AGENCIES MILITARY CONSTRUCTION

Summary

The budget request included authorization of appropriations of $2.06 billion for military construction and $62.4 million for family housing for the defense agencies in fiscal year 2017.

The conference agreement includes authorization of appropriations of $2.03 billion for military construction and $62.4 million for family housing for the defense agencies in fiscal year 2017.

The budget request included $10.0 million for contingency construction at various world-wide locations. The conferees note that the Department of Defense has not requested a military construction project using funds from this account since 2008. As such, the agreement recommends no funds, a reduction of $10.0 million for this program.

The budget request included $10.0 million for the Energy Conservation Investment Program's Planning and Design activities. The conferees recommend that this program be carried out as part of the Defense-Wide Military Construction program. Therefore, the agreement recommends no funding for the Energy Conservation Investment Program's Planning and Design activities, a reduction of $10.0 million, and $23.5 million for Defense Wide Military Construction Planning and Design activities, an increase of $10.0 million, to reflect the inclusion of the Energy Conservation Investment Program as part of the Defense Wide Military Construction program.

The budget request included $71.6 million for the National Geospatial Intelligence Agency Military Construction Planning and Design activities. The conferees understand that the National Geospatial Intelligence Agency would be unable to execute the full amount requested for Military Construction Planning and Design activities in fiscal year 2017. Therefore, the agreement recommends $36.0 million, a reduction of $35.6 million, for this program.

In addition, the agreement recommends an increase of funding for a military construction project not included in the budget request, $15.0 million for the Missile Defense Agency Military Construction Planning and Design activities for an East Coast site for homeland missile defense.

Authorized Defense Agencies construction and land acquisition projects (sec. 2401)

The Senate bill contained a provision (sec. 2401) that would revise the list of authorized defense agencies' construction projects for fiscal year 2017. The authorized amounts are listed on an installation-by-installation basis. The state list contained in this Act is intended to be the binding list of the specific projects authorized at each location.

The House amendment contained a similar provision (sec. 2401).

The Senate recedes with a technical amendment.

Authorized energy conservation projects (sec. 2402)

The House amendment contained a provision (sec. 2402) that would authorize the Secretary of Defense to carry out energy conservation projects valued at a cost greater than $3.0 million at the amounts authorized for each project at a specific location. This section would also authorize the sum total of projects across various locations, each project of which is less than $3.0 million.

The Senate bill contained a similar provision (sec. 2402).

The Senate recedes.

Authorization of appropriations, Defense Agencies (sec. 2403)

The Senate bill contained a provision (sec. 2403) that would authorize appropriations for the military construction and family housing projects of the defense agencies authorized for construction for fiscal year 2017. This provision would also provide an overall limit on the amount authorized for military construction and family housing projects for the defense agencies.

The House amendment contained an identical provision (sec. 2403).

The conference agreement includes this provision.

Modification of authority to carry out certain fiscal year 2014 project (sec. 2404)

The Senate bill contained a provision (sec. 2404) that would modify the authority contained in section 2401 of the Military Construction Authorization Act for Fiscal Year 2014 (division B of Public Law 113–66) for the construction of a high school at Royal Air Force Base Lakenheath, United Kingdom to allow the construction of a combined middle/high school.

The House amendment contained an identical provision (sec. 2404).

The conference agreement includes this provision.

Extension of authorizations of certain fiscal year 2013 projects (sec. 2405)

The Senate bill contained a provision (sec. 2405) that would extend the authorization contained in section 2401 of the Military Construction Authorization Act for Fiscal Year 2013 (division B of Public Law 112–239) for two projects until October 1, 2017, or the date of the enactment of an act authorizing funds for military construction for fiscal year 2018, whichever is later.

The House amendment contained an identical provision (sec. 2405).

The conference agreement includes this provision.

Extension of authorizations of certain fiscal year 2014 projects (sec. 2406)

The Senate bill contained a provision (sec. 2406) that would extend the authorization contained in section 2401 of the Military Construction Authorization Act for Fiscal Year 2014 (division B of Public Law 113–66) for ten projects until October 1, 2017, or the date of enactment of an act authorizing funds for the military construction for fiscal year 2018, whichever is later.

The House amendment contained an identical provision (sec. 2406).

The conference agreement includes this provision.

TITLE XXV—INTERNATIONAL PROGRAMS

Summary

The budget request included authorization of appropriations of $177.9 million for military construction in fiscal year 2017 for the North Atlantic Treaty Organization (NATO) Security Investment Program. In addition, pursuant to agreement with the Republic of Korea, the budget request included a list of $618.6 million in military construction projects to be funded as in-kind contributions by the Republic of Korea.

The conference agreement includes this amount for the NATO projects and the authorization to accept the military construction projects funded by the Republic of Korea.

Subtitle A—North Atlantic Treaty Organization Security Investment Program

Authorized NATO construction and land acquisition projects (sec. 2501)

The Senate bill contained a provision (sec. 2501) that would authorize the Secretary of Defense to make contributions to the North Atlantic Treaty Organization Security Investment Program in an amount equal to the sum of the amount specifically authorized in section 2502 of this title and the amount of recoupment due to the United States for construction previously financed by the United States.

The House amendment contained an identical provision (sec. 2501).

The conference agreement includes this provision.

Authorization of appropriations, NATO (sec. 2502)

The Senate bill contained a provision (sec. 2502) that would authorize appropriations of $177.9 million for the U.S. contribution to the North Atlantic Treaty Organization Security Investment Program for fiscal year 2017.

The House amendment contained an identical provision (sec. 2502).

The conference agreement includes this provision.

Subtitle B—Host Country In-Kind Contributions

Republic of Korea funded construction projects (sec. 2511)

The Senate bill contained a provision (sec. 2511) that would authorize the Secretary of Defense to accept 19 military construction projects totaling $684.1 million from the Republic of Korea as in-kind contributions.

The House amendment contained no similar provision.

The House recedes with a technical amendment.

TITLE XXVI—GUARD AND RESERVE FORCES FACILITIES

Summary

The budget request included $672.7 million for military construction for National Guard and Reserve facilities for fiscal year 2017.

The conference agreement includes authorization of appropriations of $781.2 million for military construction for National Guard and Reserve facilities in fiscal year 2017.

The agreement includes authorization for three projects from the Army National Guard's unfunded requirements list: $16.5 million for National Guard Readiness Center at Fort Carson, Colorado; $20.0 million for Access Control Buildings at Fort Indiantown Gap, Pennsylvania; and $31.0 million for a General Instruction Building at Camp Guernsey, Wyoming.

The agreement includes authorization for one project from the Army Reserves unfunded requirements list: $30.0 million for an Army Reserve Center in Phoenix, Arizona.

The agreement includes authorization for two projects from the Air National Guard's unfunded requirements list: $5.0 million for Munitions Load Crew Training/Corrosion Control Facility at Joint Base Andrews, Maryland and $6.0 million for Indoor Small Arms Range at Toledo Express Airport, Ohio.

Subtitle A—Project Authorizations and Authorizations of Appropriations

Authorized Army National Guard construction and land acquisition projects (sec. 2601)

The Senate bill contained a provision (sec. 2601) that would authorize military construction projects for the Army National Guard for fiscal year 2017. The authorized amounts are listed on an installation-by-installation basis.

The House amendment contained a similar provision (sec. 2601).

The Senate recedes with a technical amendment.

Authorized Army Reserve construction and land acquisition projects (sec. 2602)

The Senate bill contained a provision (sec. 2602) that would authorize military construction projects for the Army Reserve for fiscal year 2017. The authorized amounts are listed on an installation-by-installation basis.

The House amendment contained a similar provision (sec. 2602).

The House recedes.

Authorized Navy Reserve and Marine Corps Reserve construction and land acquisition projects (sec. 2603)

The Senate bill contained a provision (sec. 2603) that would contain the list of authorized Navy Reserve and Marine Corps Reserve construction projects for fiscal year 2017.

The House amendment contained an identical provision (sec. 2603).

The conference agreement includes this provision.

Authorized Air National Guard construction and land acquisition projects (sec. 2604)

The Senate bill contained a provision (sec. 2604) that would authorize military construction projects for the Air National Guard for fiscal year 2017. The authorized amounts are listed on an installation-by-installation basis.

The House amendment contained a similar provision (sec. 2604).

The Senate recedes.

Authorized Air Force Reserve construction and land acquisition projects (sec. 2605)

The Senate bill contained a provision (sec. 2605) that would authorize military construction projects for the Air Force Reserve for fiscal year 2017. The authorized amounts are listed on an installation-by-installation basis.

The House amendment contained a similar provision (sec. 2605).

The House recedes.

Authorization of appropriations, National Guard and Reserve (sec. 2606)

The Senate bill contained a provision (sec. 2606) that would authorize appropriations for the reserve component military construction projects authorized for construction for fiscal year 2017 in this Act. This provision would also provide an overall limit on the amount authorized for military construction projects for each of the reserve components of the military departments. The state list contained in this report is the binding list of the specific projects authorized at each location.

The House amendment contained an identical provision (sec. 2606).

The conference agreement includes this provision.

Subtitle B—Other Matters

Modification of authority to carry out certain fiscal year 2014 project (sec. 2611)

The Senate bill contained a provision (sec. 2611) that would modify the authorization contained in section 2602 of the Military Construction Authorization Act for Fiscal Year 2014 (division B of Public Law 113–66) for construction of a new Army Reserve Center at Bullville, New York to allow the Secretary of the Army to add to or alter the existing Army Reserve Center at that location.

The House amendment contained an identical provision (sec. 2611).

The conference agreement includes this provision.

Modification of authority to carry out certain fiscal year 2015 project (sec. 2612)

The Senate bill contained a provision (sec. 2612) that would modify the authorizations contained in section 2603 of the Military Construction Authorization Act for Fiscal Year 2015 (division B of Public Law 113–291), for construction of a Reserve Training Center in Pittsburgh, Pennsylvania to allow the acquisition of approximately 8.5 acres of adjacent land necessary to construct road improvements and associated supporting facilities to provide required access to that site.

The House amendment contained an identical provision (sec. 2612).

The conference agreement includes this provision.

Modification of authority to carry out certain fiscal year 2016 project (sec. 2613)

The House amendment contained a provision (sec. 2613) that would modify the authority provided by section 2602 of the Military Construction Authorization Act for Fiscal Year 2016 (division B of Public Law 114–92) to authorize the Secretary of the Army to

make certain modifications to the scope of a previously authorized construction project.

The Senate bill contained no similar provision.

The Senate recedes.

Extension of authorization of certain fiscal year 2013 project (sec. 2614)

The Senate bill contained a provision (sec. 2613) that would extend the authorization contained in section 2603 of the Military Construction Authorization Act for Fiscal Year 2013 (division B of Public Law 112–239) for one project until October 1, 2017, or the date of the enactment of an act authorizing funds for military construction for fiscal year 2018, whichever is later.

The House amendment contained an identical provision (sec. 2614).

The conference agreement includes this provision.

Extension of authorizations of certain fiscal year 2014 projects (sec. 2615)

The Senate bill contained a provision (sec. 2614) that would extend the authorization contained in sections 2602, 2603, 2604, and 2605 of the Military Construction Authorization Act for Fiscal Year 2014 (division B of Public Law 113–66) for six projects until October 1, 2017, or the date of the enactment of an act authorizing funds for military construction for fiscal year 2018, whichever is later.

The House amendment contained an identical provision (sec. 2615).

The conference agreement includes this provision.

LEGISLATIVE PROVISIONS NOT ADOPTED

Report on replacement of security forces and communications training facility at Frances S. Gabreski Air National Guard Base, New York

The Senate bill contained a provision (sec. 2615) that would require the Secretary of the Air Force to submit a report to the congressional defense committees assessing the need to replace security forces and communication facilities at Frances S. Gabreski Air National Guard Base, New York.

The House amendment contained no similar provision.

The Senate recedes.

The conferees direct the Secretary of the Air Force to provide the congressional defense committees, by April 1, 2017, a report detailing an assessment of the need to replace security forces and communication facilities at Frances S. Gabreski Air National Guard Base, New York.

TITLE XXVII—BASE REALIGNMENT AND CLOSURE ACTIVITIES

Summary

The budget request included authorization of appropriations of $205.2 million for the ongoing cost of environmental remediation and other activities necessary to continue implementation of the 1988, 1991, 1993, 1995, and 2005 Base Realignment and Closure (BRAC) rounds.

The conference agreement includes authorization of appropriations of $240.7 million for activities related to BRAC activities from previous rounds. This includes $24.5 million, an increase of $10.0 million, for the Army, $159.4 million, an increase of $25.0 million, for the Navy, and $56.4 million, as included in the budget request, for the Air Force.

Extension of authorizations of certain fiscal year 2014 projects (sec. 2701)

The Senate bill contained a provision (sec. 2701) that would authorize appropriations for fiscal year 2017 for ongoing activities that are required to implement the decisions of

the 1988, 1991, 1993, 1995, and 2005 Base Realignment and Closure rounds.

The House amendment contained an identical provision (sec. 2701).

The conference agreement includes this provision.

Prohibition on conducting additional base realignment and closure (BRAC) round (sec. 2702)

The Senate bill contained a provision (sec. 2702) that would make clear that nothing in this Act shall be construed to authorize a future Base Realignment and Closure (BRAC) round. Elsewhere in the Act, the Senate recommended a reduction of $4.0 million for BRAC planning activities.

The House amendment contained a similar provision (sec. 2701).

The House recedes.

The conferees remain concerned that the Secretary of Defense has yet to provide the force structure plan, the infrastructure inventory, and the assessment of infrastructure necessary to support the force structure that were required to be prepared under section 2815 of the National Defense Authorization Act for Fiscal Year 2016 (Public Law 114–92; 129 Stat. 1175). The conferees believe this congressionally directed report is necessary in order to evaluate the Department's need, and request for a new base realignment and closure round.

TITLE XXVIII—MILITARY CONSTRUCTION GENERAL PROVISIONS

Subtitle A—Military Construction Program and Military Family Housing Changes

Modification of criteria for treatment of laboratory revitalization projects as minor military construction projects (sec. 2801)

The Senate bill contained a provision (sec. 220) that would modify the authority to use minor military construction to revitalize antiquated laboratories and to increase the scope of the projects that are allowed under this provision to $6.0 million. Additionally, this provision would extend the authorization to 2025.

The House amendment contained a similar provision (sec. 2801).

The Senate recedes with an amendment that includes the extension of the authorization through 2025.

Classification of facility conversion projects as repair projects (sec. 2802)

The House amendment contained a provision (sec. 2802) that would amend section 2811 of title 10, United States Code, to re-classify facility conversion as repair, thereby allowing all work within the existing dimensions of a facility to be considered repair.

The Senate bill contained no similar provision.

The Senate recedes.

Limited authority for scope of work increase (sec. 2803)

The Senate bill contained a provision (sec. 2802) that would allow the Department of Defense to increase the scope of military construction projects by up to 10 percent above the amount authorized by Congress after notifying the appropriate congressional committees.

The House amendment contained no similar provision.

The House recedes.

Extension of temporary, limited authority to use operation and maintenance funds for construction projects in certain areas outside the United States (sec. 2804)

The Senate bill contained a provision (sec. 2801) that would reauthorize contingency construction authority in certain areas outside the United States for an additional year.

The House amendment contained a similar provision (sec. 2803) that would provide continued authority for the Secretary of Defense to use funds appropriated for Operation and Maintenance for military construction to meet temporary operational requirements during a time of declared war, national emergency, or contingency operation through the end of fiscal year 2017.

The Senate recedes.

Authority to expand energy conservation construction program to include energy resiliency projects (sec. 2805)

The House amendment contained a provision (sec. 2805) that would amend section 2914 of title 10, United States Code, to address gaps in the information contained in congressional notifications submitted by the Secretary of Defense for the Energy Conservation Investment Program. This section would also add an annual reporting requirement on the status of projects being executed under the program beginning with fiscal year 2017 and ending with fiscal year 2020.

The Senate bill contained a related provision (sec. 2811) that would allow the Energy Conservation Investment Program to invest in projects relating to resiliency and security.

The Senate recedes with an amendment to expand the authority of the Energy Conservation Investment Program to include resiliency projects.

Additional entities eligible for participation in defense laboratory modernization pilot program (sec. 2806)

The House amendment contained a provision (sec. 2806) that would expand the defense laboratory modernization pilot program to include a Department of Defense research, development, test, and evaluation facility that is not designated as a Science and Technology Reinvention Laboratory, but nonetheless is involved with developmental test and evaluation.

The Senate bill contained no similar provision.

The Senate recedes.

Extension of temporary authority for acceptance and use of contributions for certain construction, maintenance, and repair projects mutually beneficial to the Department of Defense and Kuwait military forces (sec. 2807)

The Senate bill contained a provision (sec. 2803) that would make permanent the authority to accept contributions from the Government of Kuwait for certain infrastructure projects that are mutually beneficial to the Department of Defense and Kuwait Military Forces.

The House amendment contained a similar provision (sec. 2804) that would extend for 5 years the temporary project authority for acceptance and use of contributions for construction, maintenance, and repair projects mutually beneficial to the Department of Defense and Kuwait military forces from September 30, 2020, to September 30, 2025.

The House recedes with an amendment that would extend the temporary project authority for 10 years.

Subtitle B—Real Property and Facilities Administration

Acceptance of military construction projects as payments in-kind and in-kind contributions (sec. 2811)

The House amendment contained a provision (sec. 2811) that would establish a notification requirement for payment in-kind and in-kind contributions used for overseas military construction projects and repeal the authorization requirement established for such projects in section 2803 of the Carl Levin and Howard P. "Buck" McKeon National Defense Authorization Act for Fiscal Year 2015 (Public Law 113–291).

The Senate bill contained no similar provision.

The Senate recedes with a technical amendment.

Allotment of space and provision of services to WIC offices operating on military installations (sec. 2812)

The House amendment contained a provision (sec. 2813) that would authorize the Secretary of a military department to allot space and services on military installations to local agencies administering WIC programs to service members and their families.

The Senate bill contained no similar provision.

The Senate recedes.

Sense of Congress regarding inclusion of stormwater systems and components within the meaning of "wastewater system" under the Department of Defense authority for conveyance of utility systems (sec. 2813)

The House amendment contained a provision (sec. 2815) that would express the sense of Congress that stormwater systems and components are included within the meaning of "wastewater system" under the Department of Defense authority for conveyance of utility systems in section 2688 of title 10, United States Code.

The Senate bill contained no similar provision.

The Senate recedes.

Assessment of public schools on Department of Defense installations (sec. 2814)

The Senate bill contained a provision (sec. 575) that would require the Comptroller General of the United States to submit a report, within 1 year after the date of enactment of this Act, which provides an analysis of the condition and capacity of public schools on military installations. The provision would require the analysis to include schools omitted from the July 2011 Department of Defense analysis of such schools.

The House amendment contained a provision (sec. 2816) that would require the Secretary of Defense, within 1 year of the date of enactment of this Act, to submit a report to the congressional defense committees, which includes an update to the July 2011 assessment on the condition and capacity of elementary and secondary public schools on military installations.

The Senate recedes with an amendment that would require the Secretary to submit additional information in the report required under this provision on the status of funds appropriated and the schedule for completion of projects approved for funding. Additionally, the provision would require the Comptroller General of the United States to submit a report to the congressional defense committees, within 180 days after the date of submission of the report by the Secretary, providing an evaluation of the accuracy and analytical sufficiency of the updated assessment conducted by the Department of Defense.

Prior certification required for use of Department of Defense facilities by other Federal agencies for temporary housing support (sec. 2815)

The House amendment contained a provision (sec. 2812) that would prohibit any military installation, not including those installations located outside of the United States, from being used to house unaccompanied alien children.

The Senate bill contained no similar provision.

The Senate recedes with an amendment that would require the Secretary of Defense to certify that the use of federal facilities by another agency would not negatively affect military training, operations, readiness, or other military requirements.

Subtitle C—Land Conveyances

Land conveyances, High Frequency Active Auroral Research Program facility and adjacent property, Gakona, Alaska (sec. 2821)

The Senate bill contained a provision (sec. 2823) that would authorize the Secretary of the Air Force to convey a portion of the property that was used for the High Frequency Active Auroral Research Program near the Gulkana Village to the University of Alaska for consideration that the Secretary determines is appropriate. The provision would authorize the Secretary of the Air Force to convey another portion of the property, for consideration, to the Ahtna Alaska Native Corporation from which the property was purchased by the Secretary.

The House amendment contained a similar provision (sec. 2831).

The House recedes.

Land conveyance, Campion Air Force Radar Station, Galena, Alaska (sec. 2822)

The Senate bill contained a provision (sec. 2822) that would authorize the Secretary of the Air Force to convey the former Campion Air Force station to the town of Galena, Alaska.

The House amendment contained a similar provision (sec. 2832).

The House recedes.

Lease, Joint Base Elmendorf-Richardson, Alaska (sec. 2823)

The Senate bill contained a provision (sec. 2826) that would authorize the Secretary of the Air Force to lease certain property at Joint Base Elmendorf-Richardson to the Municipality of Anchorage, Alaska and Mountain View Loins Club.

The House amendment contained no similar provision.

The House recedes.

Transfer of administrative jurisdictions, Navajo Army Depot, Arizona (sec. 2824)

The Senate bill contained a provision (sec. 2825) that would provide for the transfer of administrative jurisdiction of property at Navajo Army Depot, Arizona, to the Department of the Army for the purposes of continued military operations.

The House amendment contained no similar provision.

The House recedes with a technical amendment.

Exchange of property interests, San Diego Unified Port District, California (sec. 2825)

The House amendment contained a provision (sec. 2833) that would authorize the Secretary of the Navy to exchange approximately 0.33 acres in San Diego, California that contains 48 parking spaces, with the San Diego Unified Port District in return for property of equal value, and without encumbrances, that provides the rights to an equivalent number of parking spaces.

The Senate bill contained no similar provision.

The Senate recedes.

Release of property interests retained in connection with land conveyance, Eglin Air Force Base, Florida (sec. 2826)

The House amendment contained a provision (sec. 2834) that would authorize the Secretary of the Air Force to release any and all exceptions, limitations, and conditions specified by the United States in the deeds conveying approximately 126 acres of real property in Okaloosa County, Florida, which were conveyed to the Air Force Enlisted Men's Widows and Dependents Home Foundations, Incorporated.

The Senate bill contained no similar provision.

The Senate recedes with a technical amendment.

Land exchange, Fort Hood, Texas (sec. 2827)

The House amendment contained a provision (sec. 2835) that would authorize the Secretary of the Army to exchange land at Fort Hood, Texas, with the City of Copperas Cove, Texas, to support the city's efforts to improve arterial transportation routes in the vicinity of Fort Hood and to promote economic development.

The Senate bill contained no similar provision.

The Senate recedes.

Land conveyance, P–36 Warehouse, Colbern United States Army Reserve Center, Laredo, Texas (sec. 2828)

The House amendment contained a provision (sec. 2836) that would authorize the Secretary of the Army to convey, without consideration, to the Laredo Community College all right, title, and interest of the United States in and to the approximately 725 square foot Historic Building, P–36 Quartermaster Warehouse, at Colbern United States Army Reserve Center, Laredo, Texas.

The Senate bill contained no similar provision.

The Senate recedes with a technical amendment.

Land conveyance, St. George National Guard Armory, St. George, Utah (sec. 2829)

The House amendment contained a provision (sec. 2837) that would authorize the Secretary of the Interior to covey, without consideration, to the State of Utah all right, title, and interest of the United States in and to a parcel of public land in St. George, Utah, comprising approximately 70 acres, for the purpose of permitting the Utah National Guard to use the conveyed land for military purposes.

The Senate bill contained no similar provision.

The Senate recedes with an amendment that would include a reversionary clause.

Land acquisitions, Arlington County, Virginia (sec. 2829A)

The Senate bill contained a provision (sec. 2821) that would authorize the Secretary of the Army to acquire by whatever means the Secretary determines is sufficient for the expansion of Arlington National Cemetery in order to maximize the number of interment sites and the compatible use of adjacent properties.

The House amendment contained no similar provision.

The House recedes with a technical amendment.

Release of restrictions, Richland Innovation Center, Richland, Washington (sec. 2829B)

The House amendment contained a provision (sec. 2838) that would authorize the Secretary of Transportation, acting through the Maritime Administrator and in consultation with the Administrator of General Services, to release, for consideration, to the Port of Benton all remaining right, title, and interest of the United States in and to a parcel of real property consisting of approximately 71.5 acres, including any improvements thereon, in Richland, Washington.

The Senate bill contained no similar provision.

The Senate recedes.

Modification of land conveyance, Rocky Mountain Arsenal National Wildlife Refuge (sec. 2829C)

The House amendment contained a provision (sec. 2839) that would amend section 5(d)(1) of the Rocky Mountain Arsenal National Wildlife Refuge Act of 1992 (Public Law 102–402), to stipulate that any real property designated for disposal under this section that prohibits the use of the property for residential or industrial purposes may be modified or removed if it is determined, through a risk assessment, that the property is protective for the proposed use.

The Senate bill contained no similar provision.

The Senate recedes with an amendment that would allow property to be used if a determination is made that the property will be protective of human health and the environment for the proposed use with an adequate margin of safety following the modification or removal of the restriction. The provision would further state that the Secretary of the Army is not responsible for the cost of risk assessment, any damages attributable to the use as a result of any modification to the original deed restriction, or costs of any actions taken in response to such damages.

Closure of St. Marys Airport (sec. 2829D)

The House amendment contained a provision (sec. 2839A) that would provide for the release of the City of St. Marys, Georgia, from its obligations to the Federal Aviation Administration (FAA) associated with operation of an airport and for the Secretary of the Navy to pay for certain costs owed by the City of St. Marys to FAA associated with the release. This would then lead to the closure of the airport.

The Senate bill contained no similar provision.

The Senate recedes.

Transfer of Fort Belvoir Mark Center Campus from the Secretary of the Army to the Secretary of Defense and applicability of certain provisions of law relating to the Pentagon Reservation (sec. 2829E)

The Senate bill contained a provision (sec. 2824) that would transfer the administrative jurisdiction of the Fort Belvoir Mark Center, where the Washington Headquarters Service is located, from the Secretary of the Army to the Secretary of Defense.

The House amendment contained no similar provision.

The House recedes.

Return of certain lands at Fort Wingate to the original inhabitants (sec. 2829F)

The House amendment contained a provision (sec. 7005) that would incorporate the Return of Certain Lands at Fort Wingate to The Original Inhabitants Act into this Act. This Act would require all U.S. interest in and to specified lands of the former Fort Wingate Depot Activity in McKinley County, New Mexico, transferred to the Department of the Interior to be held in trust for: (1) the Zuni Tribe as part of the Zuni Reservation; and (2) the Navajo Nation as part of the Navajo Reservation.

The Senate bill contained no similar provision.

The Senate recedes with an amendment that would limit the term of the utility easements.

Subtitle D—Military Memorials, Monuments, and Museums

Cyber Center for Education and Innovation— Home of the National Cryptological Museum (sec. 2831)

The Senate bill contained a provision (sec. 1673) that would authorize the Secretary of Defense to establish a Cyber Center for Education and Innovation and National Cryptologic Museum at Fort George G. Meade, and to enter into an agreement with a non-profit organization to design, construct, and operate the Center.

The House amendment contained a similar provision (sec. 2851).

The Senate recedes with technical amendment.

Renaming site of the Dayton Aviation Heritage National Historical Park, Ohio (sec. 2832)

The House amendment contained a provision (sec. 2852) that would modify the name of the John W. Berry, Sr. Wright Brothers Aviation Center, Dayton, Ohio, to the John W. Berry, Sr. Wright Brothers National Museum, Dayton, Ohio.

The Senate bill contained no similar provision.

The Senate recedes.

Women's military service memorials and museums (sec. 2833)

The Senate bill contained a provision (sec. 340) that would provide permissive authority to the Secretary of Defense to enter into a contract, or contracts, valued at no more than $5,000,000, with a non-profit organization for the acquisition, installation, and maintenance of exhibits, facilities, historical displays, and programs at military service memorials and museums that highlight the role of women in the military.

The House amendment contained a similar provision (sec. 2853).

The House recedes.

The conferees note the important role of women in the military history of the United States and directs the Secretary of Defense to notify the congressional defense committees upon funding being used to honor the service and sacrifice of these women.

Petersburg National Battlefield boundary modification (sec. 2834)

The House amendment contained a provision (sec. 2854) that would authorize the Secretary of the Interior to acquire the land and interest in land, only from willing sellers and without use of condemnation, to expand the boundary of the Petersburg National Battlefield. This section would also authorize a land swap of approximately 1.170-acres between the Secretary of the Interior and the Secretary of the Army.

The Senate bill contained no similar provision.

The Senate recedes with a technical amendment.

Subtitle E—Designations and Other Matters

Designation of portion of Moffett Federal Airfield, California, as Moffett Air National Guard Base (sec. 2841)

The House amendment contained a provision (sec. 2861) that would designate the 111-acre cantonment area at Moffett Federal Airfield, California, utilized by the California Air National Guard as "Moffett Air National Guard Base."

The Senate bill contained no similar provision.

The Senate recedes.

Redesignation of Mike O'Callaghan Federal Medical Center (sec. 2842)

The House amendment contained a provision (sec. 2862) that would rename the Mike

O'Callaghan Federal Medical Center to the Mike O'Callaghan Military Medical Center by amending the Military Construction Authorization Act for Fiscal Year 1997 (division B of Public Law 104–201), as amended by section 8135(a) of the Department of Defense Appropriations Act, 1997 (section 101(b) of division A of the Omnibus Consolidated Appropriations Act, 1997 (Public Law 104–208), and as amended by section 2862 of the Military Construction Authorization Act for Fiscal Year 2012 (division B of Public Law 112–81).

The Senate bill contained no similar provision.

The Senate recedes.

Replenishment of Sierra Vista subwatershed regional aquifer, Arizona (sec. 2843)

The Senate bill contained a provision that would allow the Secretary of the Army or the Secretary of the Interior to enter into a cooperative agreement with the Cochise Conservation Recharge Network, Arizona, in support of efforts to replenish the regional aquifer identified under Section 321(g) of the National Defense Authorization Act for Fiscal Year 2004 (Public Law 108–136).

The House amendment contained no similar provision.

The House recedes.

Limited exceptions to restriction on development of public infrastructure in connection with realignment of Marine Corps forces in Asia-Pacific region (sec. 2844)

The House amendment contained a provision (sec. 2821) that would amend restrictions placed on the development of civilian infrastructure on Guam to support the realignment of Marine Corps Forces in the Asia-Pacific region to allow the use of funds for infrastructure projects that are identified in the report of the Economic Adjustment Committee required by section 2822(d) of the National Defense Authorization Act for Fiscal Year 2014 (Public Law 113–66).

The Senate bill contained no similar provision.

The Senate recedes with an amendment that would lift the restriction for the cultural repository facility where artifacts discovered during military construction projects would be stored.

Permanent withdrawal or transfer of administrative jurisdiction of public land, Naval Air Weapons Station China Lake, California (sec. 2845)

The House amendment contained a provision (sec. 2842) that would amend section 2979 of the Military Construction Authorization Act for Fiscal Year 2014 (division B of Public Law 113–66) to make permanent or authorize transfer of administrative jurisdiction of the public land withdrawal for Naval Air Weapons China Lake, California.

The Senate bill contained no similar provision.

The Senate recedes with an amendment that would provide for a 50 year withdrawal of the land.

LEGISLATIVE PROVISIONS NOT ADOPTED

Sense of Congress on maximizing number of veterans employed on military construction projects

The House amendment contained a provision (sec. 2807) that would express the sense of Congress that the Department of Defense should seek ways to employ veterans on military construction projects.

The Senate bill contained no similar provision.

The House recedes.

Authority of the Secretary concerned to accept lessee improvements at Government-owned/contractor-operated industrial plants or facilities

The Senate bill contained a provision (sec. 2812) that would amend section 2535 of title 10, United States Code, to allow a service secretary to accept facility improvements of the leased plant or facility if necessary for the development or production of military weapon systems, munitions, components, or supplies. Upon completion of the improvement the Department of Defense would assume ownership.

The House amendment contained no similar provision.

The Senate recedes.

Treatment of insured depository institutions operating on land leased from military installations

The Senate bill contained a provision (sec. 2813) that would amend section 2667 of title 10, United States Code, to authorize the Secretary concerned to treat all Federal or State chartered insured depository institutions to be treated equally with regard to certain financial arrangements.

The House amendment contained no similar provision.

The Senate recedes.

Sense of Congress regarding need to consult with State and local officials prior to acquisitions of real property

The House amendment contained a provision (sec. 2814) that would express the sense of Congress regarding the need for the Department of Defense to consult with state and local officials prior to acquisitions of real property.

The Senate bill contained no similar provision.

The House recedes.

Improved process for disposal of Department of Defense surplus real property located overseas

The House amendment contained a provision (sec. 2817) that would amend section 2687a of title 10, United States Code, to require the Secretary of Defense to establish a process for foreign governments to petition to transfer surplus real estate property in the foreign country.

The Senate bill contained no similar provision.

The House recedes.

Prohibition on transfer of administrative jurisdiction, portion of Organ Mountains Area, Fillmore Canyon, New Mexico

The House amendment contained a provision (sec. 2839B) that would prohibit the Secretary of Defense from transferring the administrative jurisdiction over the parcel of Federal land depicted as "Parcel D" on the map entitled "Organ Mountains Area—Fillmore Canyon" and dated April 19, 2016 from the Department of Defense to the Secretary of the Interior.

The Senate bill contained no similar provision.

The House recedes.

Bureau of Land Management withdrawn military lands under Military Lands Withdrawal Act of 1999

The House amendment contained a provision (sec. 2841) that would extend the public lands withdrawn for military purposes listed in the Military Lands Withdrawal Act of 1999 (title 30 of Public Law 106–65) until the Secretary of a military department determines a military purpose does not exist, or the Secretary of Interior permanently transfers the administrative jurisdiction to the Secretary of the military department concerned.

The Senate bill contained no similar provision.

The House recedes.

Certification of optimal location for 4th and 5th generation combat aircraft basing and for rotation of forces at Naval Air Station El Centro or Marine Corps Air Station Kaneohe Bay

The Senate bill contained a provision (sec. 2851) that would prohibit the expenditure of any funds for the construction of hangars, housing, maintenance or related facilities to support any current or future F/A–18 or F–35 squadrons at Naval Air Station Lemoore until an analysis of operational requirements confirms that Naval Air Station Lemoore is the optimal location for those squadrons.

The House amendment contained no similar provision.

The Senate recedes.

Amendments to the National Historic Preservation Act

The House amendment contained a provision (sec. 2855) that would prohibit the designation of Federal property as a National Historic Landmark or for nomination to the World Heritage List if the head of the agency managing the Federal property objects to such inclusion or designation for reasons of national security. This section would also authorize the expedited removal of Federal property listed on the National Register of Historic Places if the managing agency of that Federal property submits a request to the Secretary of Interior for such removal for reasons of national security.

The Senate bill contained no similar provision.

The House recedes.

Recognition of the National Museum of World War II Aviation

The House amendment contained a provision (sec. 2856) that would require a certification by the Secretary of the Air Force, Secretary of the Navy, and Secretary of the Army to allow recognition of the National Museum of World War II Aviation in Colorado Springs, Colorado, as America's National World War II Aviation Museum.

The Senate bill contained no similar provision.

The House recedes.

Battleship preservation grant program

The House amendment contained a provision (sec. 2857) that would create a grant program for the Department of the Interior for the preservation of United States' most historic battleships.

The Senate bill contained no similar provision.

The House recedes.

Implementation of lesser prairie-chicken range-wide conservation plan and other conservation measures

The House amendment contained a provision (sec. 2865) that would prohibit the Secretary of Interior from treating the Lesser Prairie Chicken as a threatened or endangered species under the Endangered Species Act of 1973 before December 31, 2022.

The Senate bill contained no similar provision.

The House recedes.

Transfer of certain items of the Omar Bradley Foundation to the descendants of General Omar Bradley

The House amendment contained a provision (sec. 2863) that would authorize the transfer of certain items of the Omar Bradley estate under the control of the Omar

Bradley Foundation to the descendants of General Omar Bradley.

The Senate bill contained no similar provision.

The House recedes.

Protection and recovery of Greater Sage Grouse

The House amendment contained a provision (sec. 2864) would delay any finding by the Secretary of the Interior with respect to the Greater Sage Grouse under clause (i), (ii), or (iii) of section 4(b)(3)(B) of the Endangered Species Act of 1973 (16 U.S.C. 1533(b)(3)(B)) through September 30, 2025. In an effort to foster greater coordination between the States and the Federal Government regarding management plans for the Greater Sage Grouse, this section would prohibit the Secretary of the Interior and the Secretary of Agriculture from amending any Federal resource management plan applicable to Federal lands in a State in which the Governor of the State has notified the Secretaries concerned that the State has a State management plan in place. Lastly, this section would also require the Secretary of the Interior and the Secretary of Agriculture to jointly submit an annual report to the Committee on Natural Resources of the House of Representatives through 2026 on the effectiveness of the systems to monitor the status of Greater Sage Grouse on Federal lands under their jurisdiction.

The Senate bill contained no similar provision.

The House recedes.

Removal of endangered species status for American burying beetle

The House amendment contained a provision (sec. 2866) would remove the endangered species status for the American Burying Beetle.

The Senate bill contained no similar provision.

The House recedes.

Report on documentation for acquisition of certain properties along Columbia River, Washington, by Corps of Engineers

The House amendment contained a provision (sec. 2867) that would require a report from the Secretary of the Army on the process by which the Corps of Engineers acquired certain properties along the Columbia River in Washington.

The Senate bill contained no similar provision.

The House recedes.

The conferees direct the Secretary of the Army to provide a report to the congressional defense committees by March 1, 2017 on the process by which the Corps of Engineers acquired certain properties along the Columbia River in Washington as described in paragraph (2) of section 501(i) of the Water Resources Development Act of 1996 (Public Law 104–303; 110 Stat. 3752), and shall include in the report the specific legal documentation pursuant to which the properties were acquired.

TITLE XXIX—OVERSEAS CONTINGENCY OPERATIONS MILITARY CONSTRUCTION

Authorized Navy construction and land acquisition projects (sec. 2901)

The Senate bill contained a provision (sec. 2901) that would authorize Navy and Marine Corps military construction projects for fiscal year 2017 for overseas contingency operations. The authorized amounts are listed on an installation-by-installation basis.

The House amendment contained an identical provision (sec. 2901).

The conference agreement includes this provision.

Authorized Air Force construction and land acquisition projects (sec. 2902)

The Senate bill contained a provision (sec. 2902) that would authorize Air Force military construction projects for fiscal year 2017 for overseas contingency operations. The authorized amounts are listed on an installation-by-installation basis.

The House amendment contained an identical provision (sec. 2902).

The conference agreement includes this provision.

Authorization of appropriations (sec. 2903)

The Senate bill contained a provision (sec. 2903) that would authorize appropriations for military construction for the specified projects in the overseas contingency operations account for fiscal year 2017.

The House amendment contained a similar provision (sec. 2903).

The Senate recedes.

TITLE XXX—UTAH TEST AND TRAINING RANGE AND RELATED MATTERS

Subtitle A—Authorization for Temporary Closure of Certain Public Land Adjacent to the Utah Test and Training Range

Definitions (sec. 3001)

The Senate bill contained a provision (sec. 2832) that would define the terms Exchange Map, Federal Land, Non-Federal Land, Secretary, and State.

The House amendment contained a similar provision (sec. 3001).

The House recedes with a technical edit.

Memorandum of agreement (sec. 3002)

The Senate bill contained a provision (sec. 2833) that would require the Secretary of the Air Force and the Secretary of the Interior to enter into a memorandum of agreement that authorizes the Secretary of the Air Force, in consultation with the Secretary of the Interior, to impose limited closures of specific Bureau of Land Management land for military operations and national security and public safety purposes at the Utah Test and Training Range.

The House amendment contained a similar provision (sec. 3011).

The House recedes with a technical edit.

Temporary closures (sec. 3003)

The Senate bill contained a provision (sec. 2834) that would allow the Secretary of the Air Force, in consultation with the Secretary of the Interior, to determine necessary temporary closures related to the military operations, public safety, or national security.

The House amendment contained a similar provision (sec. 3012).

The House recedes with a technical edit.

Liability (sec. 3004)

The Senate bill contained a provision (sec. 2835) that would hold harmless the United States, including all departments, agencies, officers, and employees and not be liable for any injury or damage to any individual or property suffered in the course of any mining, mineral, or geothermal activity, or any other authorized non defense-related activity conducted on BLM Land.

The House amendment contained an identical provision (sec. 3014).

The conference agreement includes this provision.

Community resource advisory group (sec. 3005)

The Senate bill contained a provision (sec. 2836) that would require the establishment of the Utah Test and Training Range Community Relations Advisory Group not later than 90 days after enactment of this Act.

The House amendment contained a similar provision (sec. 3013).

The House recedes with an amendment to change the termination period for the advisory group from 10 to 7 years, and authorize the group, acting jointly with Secretary of Interior, to elect to terminate the group earlier.

Savings clauses (sec. 3006)

The Senate bill contained a provision (sec. 2837) that would outline the limitations of this act on current agreements.

The House amendment contained a similar provision (sec. 3015).

The House recedes.

Subtitle B—Bureau of Land Management Land Exchange with State of Utah

Definitions (sec. 3011)

The Senate bill contained a provision (sec. 2841) that would provide for definitions for BLM Land, Secretary of the Interior, the State of Utah, and the Utah Test and Training Range.

The House amendment contained a similar provision (sec. 3022).

The House recedes with a technical edit.

Exchange of Federal land and non-Federal land (sec. 3012)

The Senate bill contained a provision (sec. 2842) that would outline the manner in which the exchange of federal land and non-federal land would take place.

The House amendment contained a similar provision (sec. 3023).

The House recedes.

Status and management of non-Federal land acquired by the United States (sec. 3013)

The Senate bill contained a provision (sec. 2843) that would stipulate the management of non-federal land acquired by the United States.

The House amendment contained a similar provision (sec. 3024).

The House recedes.

Hazardous substances (sec. 3014)

The Senate bill contained a provision (sec. 2844) that would stipulate the responsible party for any costs related to the cleanup of hazardous materials.

The House amendment contained a similar provision (sec. 3025).

The House recedes with a technical edit.

LEGISLATIVE PROVISIONS NOT ADOPTED

Short title

The Senate bill contained a provision (sec. 2831) that would allow for the section to be cited as the "Utah Test and Training Range Encroachment Prevention and Temporary Closure Act."

The House amendment contained no similar provision.

The Senate recedes.

Findings and purpose

The House amendment contained a provision (sec. 3021) that would state the key findings and define the purpose for the Land Exchange of certain Federal land and non-Federal land between the United States and the State of Utah.

The Senate bill contained no similar provision.

The House recedes.

Recognition and transfer of certain highway rights-of-way

The House amendment contained a provision (sec. 3031) that would recognize the existence and validity of certain highway rights-of-way and authorize the Secretary with administrative jurisdiction to convey, without consideration, to certain counties and the State of Utah as joint tenants, easements for motorized travel rights-of-way across Federal land for all highways as shown and described in the official transportation maps, but excludes any class D road located within the boundaries of Cedar Mountain Wilderness Area or any wilderness study area designated in law or by administrative action in any of the counties.

The Senate bill contained no similar provision.

The House recedes.

DIVISION C—DEPARTMENT OF ENERGY NATIONAL SECURITY AUTHORIZATIONS AND OTHER AUTHORIZATIONS

TITLE XXXI—DEPARTMENT OF ENERGY NATIONAL SECURITY PROGRAMS

Subtitle A—National Security Programs Authorizations

National Nuclear Security Administration (sec. 3101)

The Senate bill contained a provision (sec. 3101) that would authorize a total of $12.9 billion for the Department of Energy in fiscal year 2017 for the National Nuclear Security Administration to carry out programs necessary to national security.

The House amendment contained a similar provision (sec. 3101) that would authorize appropriations for the National Nuclear Security Administration for fiscal year 2017 and would also authorize new plant projects for the National Nuclear Security Administration.

The Senate recedes.

The Department of Energy's (DOE) National Nuclear Security Administration (NNSA) is pursuing a revised strategy for its Chemistry and Metallurgy Research Replacement (CMRR) project after spending $500.0 million on the design of the original project and cancelling the Nuclear Facility subproject in 2014. The revised project, which is now broken down into 4 subprojects, includes renovating two existing facilities, the RLUOB and the PF-4 facility, at NNSA's Los Alamos site and installing plutonium research equipment in those facilities to support NNSA's plutonium pit production and defense plutonium work in the near term. NNSA is also studying the possibility that, in the future, it may need to expand the capacity for plutonium chemistry and research beyond that provided by the 4 subprojects. In addition, NNSA is looking at a modular approach of constructing one or more identical buildings to support future plutonium pit manufacturing requirements beyond what can be currently produced in PF-4. In accordance with DOE Order 413.3B and the Secretary's guidance on project management, NNSA is currently conducting an analysis of alternatives for the proposed modular approach.

The conferees are pleased that NNSA has adopted a strategy that maximizes the space within existing facilities to the greatest extent practicable while continuing to examine options to support future work. However, while the conferees recognize the complexity and importance of the CMRR project and defense-related plutonium activities in general, the conferees remain concerned that NNSA has not adequately estimated the cost and schedule, nor properly specified project requirements, for either the CMRR project or the proposed modular approach to ensure that the two projects together will provide the capabilities needed to support NNSA's plutonium strategy, including legislatively directed pit production levels.

To enable the conferees to monitor any future cost increases and schedule delays associated with these projects, the conferees direct NNSA to brief the congressional defense committees, no later than October 1, 2017, on the status of its actions taken to address the recommendations contained within a recent Government Accountability Office report numbered GAO–16–585 and titled "DOE Project Management: NNSA Needs to Clarify Requirements for Its Plutonium Analysis Project at Los Alamos". This briefing should be accompanied by a written briefing document.

This briefing should clarify the relationship between the requirements for the CMRR project and the proposed modular approach and NNSA's plutonium strategy. The briefing should identify any gaps between the capabilities these projects will deliver and the requirements of the plutonium strategy and provide information on NNSA plans to address any such gaps. The briefing should also address the degree to which these projects can provide plutonium capabilities to support other DOE activities outside of the Office of Defense Programs. Finally, the briefing should provide an update on the analysis of alternatives for the proposed modular approach, including the specific requirements identified, the analysis conducted for each alternative identified, and the proposed path forward, if known.

Defense environmental cleanup (sec. 3102)

The Senate bill contained a provision (sec. 3102) that would authorize appropriations for defense environmental cleanup activities for fiscal year 2017.

The House amendment contained a similar provision (sec. 3102).

The Senate recedes.

Other defense activities (sec. 3103)

The Senate bill contained a provision (sec. 3103) that would authorize appropriations for other defense activities for the Department of Energy for fiscal year 2017.

The House amendment contained an identical provision (sec. 3103).

The conference agreement includes this provision.

Nuclear energy (sec. 3104)

The Senate bill contained a provision (sec. 3104) that would authorize appropriations for certain nuclear energy programs for the Department of Energy for fiscal year 2017.

The House amendment contained an identical provision (sec. 3104).

The conference agreement includes this provision.

Subtitle B—Program Authorizations, Restrictions, and Limitations

Independent acquisition project reviews of capital assets acquisition projects (sec. 3111)

The House amendment contained a provision (sec. 3111) that would ensure that an independent entity conducts reviews of each capital asset acquisition project as the project moves toward the approval of each critical decision, 0, 1 and 2 in the acquisition process.

The Senate bill contained no similar provision.

The Senate recedes.

Protection of certain nuclear facilities and assets from unmanned aircraft (sec. 3112)

The House amendment contained a provision (sec. 3119C) that would authorize the Secretary of Energy to take actions that are necessary to mitigate the threat of an unmanned aircraft system or unmanned aircraft that poses an imminent threat to the safety or security of a covered facility or asset that is identified by the Secretary of Energy, is located in the United States, and is owned by the United States, or contracted to the United States, to store or use special nuclear material.

The Senate bill contained no similar provision.

The Senate recedes with an amendment that would authorize the Secretary, notwithstanding title 18 of the United States Code, to take actions that are necessary to mitigate the threat (as defined by the Secretary of Energy, in consultation with the Secretary of Transportation) that an unmanned aircraft system or unmanned aircraft poses to the safety or security of a covered facility or asset. The amendment would also clarify the actions that would be authorized.

Common financial reporting system for the nuclear security enterprise (sec. 3113)

The Senate Bill contained a provision (sec. 3111) that would require the Administrator of the National Nuclear Security Administration (NNSA) to complete implementation of a common financial system for the nuclear security enterprise no later than 3 years after the date of enactment of this Act.

The House amendment contained no similar provision. The House recedes with an amendment that would adjust the timeline for implementation to four years; require the Administrator to work in consultation with NNSA Council; clarify that implementation of a common system should be to the extent practicable; that such system should be for common financial reporting system rather than a common financial system; while leveraging CAPE where appropriate; and ensure the reports required on progress of implementation include discussion of benefits, costs and challenges related to implementation.

The conferees note that the intention of this provision is not to enforce a single financial accounting system upon the various management and operating contractors of the nuclear security enterprise. Instead, this provision seeks, to the extent practicable, commonality and consistency in the way the contractors report data up to NNSA to better enable NNSA to manage and track programs across the enterprise.

Rough estimate of total life cycle cost of tank waste cleanup at Hanford Nuclear Reservation (sec. 3114)

The Senate bill contained a provision (sec. 3121) that would require Department of Energy's Office of Environmental Management to provide a rough order-of-magnitude estimate of the total lifecycle cost of the Waste Treatment and Immobilization Plant (WTP) project and tank waste management and treatment operations.

The House amendment contained no similar provision.

The House recedes with an amendment that would make technical corrections to the life cycle cost estimation dates as well as changing life-cycle cost to a rough estimation of life cycle cost.

Annual certification of shipments to Waste Isolation Pilot Plant (sec. 3115)

The House amendment contained a provision (sec. 3119) that would require the Secretary of Energy to certify to the congressional defense committees that the covered contractors are aware of the contents of each container shipped to the Waste Isolation Pilot Plant and that the Administrator is aware of the contents of each container shipped to the Waste Isolation Pilot Plant.

The Senate bill contained no similar provision.

The Senate recedes with an amendment that would make technical corrections. The conferees note that the certification includes the WIPP Waste Acceptance Criteria as well as pertinent regulatory requirements for transportation, which are consistent with Waste Isolation Pilot Plant Land Withdrawal Act, P.L. 102–579, as amended.

Disposition of weapons-usable plutonium (sec. 3116)

The Senate bill contained a provision (sec. 3114) that would require the Secretary of Energy to enter into an arrangement with the Chief of Engineers to act as an owner's agent for the Secretary with respect to the MOX facility. The Chief would assess the MOX facility contract and report to the Secretary on recommended contract changes to reduce risk and cost to the Department of Energy.

The House amendment contained a provision (sec. 3113) that would direct the Secretary of Energy to carry out construction and project support activities relating to the MOX facility. The Secretary would be able to waive this requirement if certain conditions are satisfied.

The House recedes with an amendment that makes certain technical and conforming amendments to the Senate provision and that directs the Secretary of Energy to carry out construction and project support activities relating to the MOX facility.

Design basis threat (sec. 3117)

The House amendment contained a provision (sec. 3114) that would require the Secretary of Energy to update Department of Energy Order 470.3 billion relating to the design basis threat for protecting nuclear weapons, special nuclear material, and other critical assets in the custody of the Department of Energy.

The Senate bill contained no similar provision.

The Senate recedes with an amendment that would modify the due date to 30 days after the date of enactment of this act.

Industry best practices in operations at National Nuclear Security Administration facilities and sites (sec. 3118)

The Senate bill contained a provision (sec. 3112) that would require the National Nuclear Security Administration to review how to implement industry best practices at its sites consistent with maintaining or reducing risks and preserving and protecting health, safety, and security.

The House amendment contained no similar provision.

The House recedes with an amendment that would include improving mission performance and effectiveness in the purposes of the committee established by this section; modify the termination date for the committee to 2021; and make other technical conforming changes. The conferees note that industry best practices may not always be applicable, especially in the case of high-hazard and nuclear operations, and do not intend any changes that would reduce or undermine health, safety or security at National Nuclear Security Administration sites.

Pilot program on unavailability for overhead costs of amounts specified for laboratory-directed research and development (sec. 3119)

The Senate bill contained a provision (sec. 3115) that would remove the overhead burden on National Nuclear Security Administration (NNSA) laboratories for Laboratory Directed Research and Development (LDRD).

The House amendment contained a similar provision (sec. 3119B) that would express the Sense of Congress that the Secretary of Energy should ensure that each laboratory operating contractor or plant or site manager of a NNSA facility adopt generally accepted and consistent accounting practices for lab-oratory, plant, or site directed research and development.

The House recedes with an amendment that would create a 3-year pilot program for the exemption of LDRD at national security laboratories from overhead changes and require the Administrator to submit a report to the congressional defense committees before the end of the pilot program that assesses the costs, benefits, risks, and other effects of the pilot program.

Research and development of advanced naval nuclear fuel system based on low-enriched uranium (sec. 3120)

The House amendment contained a provision (sec. 3112) that would prohibit authorized funds to be appropriated for the Department of Energy to plan or carry out research and development of an advanced naval nuclear fuel system based on low-enriched uranium.

The Senate bill contained no similar provision.

The Senate recedes with an amendment that makes technical and conforming changes.

Increase in certain limitations applicable to funds for conceptual and construction design of the Department of Energy (sec. 3121)

The Senate bill contained a provision (sec. 3116) that would update older statutory ceilings for construction design that require authorization.

The House amendment contained no similar provision.

The House recedes.

Prohibition on availability of funds for programs in Russian Federation (sec. 3122)

The House amendment contained a provision (sec. 3115) that would prohibit funding to enter into a contract with, or otherwise provide assistance to, the Russian Federation.

The Senate bill contained no similar provision.

The Senate recedes with an amendment that would adjust the Secretary of Energy waiver for urgent circumstances and include an exception for not more than $3.0 million that may be spent on the Department of Energy's Russian Health Study Program.

Limitation on availability of funds for Federal salaries and expenses (sec. 3123)

The House amendment contained a provision (sec. 3116) that would require not more than 90 percent of the National Nuclear Security Administration defense related Federal salaries may be obligated or expended until the date on which the Secretary of Energy submits to the congressional defense committees and the congressional intelligence committees an updated plan on the designing and building of prototypes of nuclear weapons, and a description of the determination of the Secretary with respect to the manner in which the designing and building of prototypes of nuclear weapons is carried out under such an updated plan.

The Senate bill contained no similar provision.

The Senate recedes with an amendment containing technical conforming changes as well as clarifying the definition of congressional intelligence committees.

Limitation on availability of funds for defense environmental cleanup program direction (sec. 3124)

The House amendment contained a provision (sec. 3117) that would require no more than 90 percent of funds authorized to be appropriated for defense environmental cleanup for program direction may be expended until the Secretary of Energy submits to Congress the future-years defense environmental cleanup plan.

The Senate bill contained no similar provision.

The Senate recedes.

Limitation on availability of funds for acceleration of nuclear weapons dismantlement (sec. 3125)

The Senate bill contained a provision (sec. 3113) that would limit the rate at which the National Nuclear Security Agency is authorized to dismantle weapons to the schedule and funding profile put forth in the fiscal year 2016 stockpile stewardship and management plan but which provided for an exception if the budget request included a certain amount of funding for nuclear weapons modernization.

The House amendment contained a similar provision (sec. 3118) that would limit funding to be obligated or expended in fiscal years 2017 to 2021 to carry out the nuclear weapons dismantlement and disposition activities of the National Nuclear Security Administration.

The Senate recedes with an amendment that would strike the prohibition on the dismantlement of the W84 warhead.

Subtitle C—Plans and Reports

Independent assessment of technology development under defense environmental cleanup program (sec. 3131)

The House amendment contained a provision (sec. 3124) that would require the Secretary of Energy, in association with the National Academy of Sciences, to conduct an independent assessment of the technology development efforts of the defense environmental cleanup program at the Department of Energy.

The Senate bill contained no similar provision.

The Senate recedes with an amendment that would change the due date of the assessment to 18 months after the date of enactment.

Updated plan for verification and monitoring of proliferation of nuclear weapons and fissile material (sec. 3132)

The House amendment contained a provision (sec. 3125) that would require the President to submit to the appropriate congressional committees, a comprehensive and detailed update to the plan developed under section 3133(a) of the Carl Levin and Howard P. "Buck" McKeon national Defense Authorization Act for Fiscal Year 2015.

The Senate bill contained no similar provision.

The Senate recedes.

Report on the use of highly-enriched uranium for naval reactors (sec. 3133)

The House amendment contained a provision (sec. 3126) that would require the Secretary of Defense, the Secretary of Energy, and the Secretary of State to provide a briefing to the appropriate congressional committees on the feasibility and potential benefits of a dialogue between the United States and France on the use of low-enriched uranium in naval reactors.

The Senate bill contained no similar provision.

The Senate recedes with an amendment that would require a report by the Director of National Intelligence on various matters related to the impact of using low-enriched uranium in naval reactor fuel. The conferees do not intend this provision to indicate concurrence with all aspects of the proposal contained in the Naval Reactors report dated

July 2016, and do not intend to indicate a presumption of whether or how such a program should be implemented. In addition, the conferees note that the Secretary of the Navy and the Secretary of Energy have not yet submitted to the defense committees their determination as to whether the United States should continue to pursue such a program.

Analysis of approaches for supplemental treatment of low-activity waste at Hanford Nuclear Reservation (sec. 3134)

The Senate bill contained a provision (sec. 3122) that would require the Secretary of Energy to enter into an agreement with a federally funded research and development center (FFRDC) to conduct an analysis of supplemental waste treatment options at the Hanford site.

The House amendment contained no similar provision.

The House recedes with an amendment that would require the review of the National Academies of Science, Engineering, and Medicine to provide an opportunity for public comment, with sufficient notice, to inform and improve the quality of the review. In addition, the briefings on progress to be made to the congressional defense committees every 180 days shall terminate upon submission of the materials required in subsection (f) paragraph (2). The National Academies shall provide to the State of Washington both the analysis and the review in draft form, with an opportunity to comment on them for a period of not less than 60 days, and comments of the State of Washington shall be included in the Secretary's submission to the congressional defense committees of the analysis, review, and Secretary's comments. This section shall not conflict with or impair the obligation of the Secretary to comply with the amended consent decree in Washington v. Moniz, No. 2:08–CV–5085–RMP (E.D. Wash.) or the Hanford Federal Facility Agreement and Consent Order, nor shall this section conflict with or impair the regulatory authority of the State of Washington under the Solid Waste Disposal Act (42 U.S.C. 6901 et seq.) and any corresponding State law. The amendment removes the requirement of a specific analytical approach. However, the conferees note that section 3161 of the National Defense Authorization Act for Fiscal Year 2013 (Public Law 112–239) directs the use of national international standards and nuclear industry best practices, including probabilistic or quantitative risk assessment if sufficient data exist, while maintaining adequate health and safety protection, at facilities of the Office of Environmental Management of the Department of Energy. The conferees therefore expect that, to the extent practicable and appropriate, the analysis shall be conducted using state-of-the-art risk assessment practices such as probabilistic risk assessment.

Clarification of annual report and certification on status of security of atomic energy defense facilities (sec. 3135)

The House amendment contained a provision (sec. 3121) that would clarify Section 4506(b)(1)(B) of the Atomic Energy Defense Act that such facilities are secure and that the security measures at such facilities meet the security standards and requirements of the Department of Energy.

The Senate bill contained no similar provision.

The Senate recedes.

Report on service support contracts and authority for appointment of certain personnel (sec. 3136)

The House amendment contained a provision (sec. 3122) that would add to the annual reporting requirements, the cost of the contract and identification of the program or program direction accounts that support the contract.

The Senate bill contained no similar provision.

The Senate recedes with an amendment extending Section 4601(c) of the Atomic Energy Defense Act (50 U.S.C.(c)(1)) from September 30, 2016 to September 30, 2020.

Elimination of certain reporting requirements (sec. 3137)

The Senate bill contained a provision (sec. 3125 and 3124) that would repeal a reporting requirement by the Comptroller General as the underlying program has been terminated and eliminate duplicate reviews of the National Nuclear Security Administration's budget.

The House amendment contained a similar provision (sec. 3123).

The House recedes with an amendment that would combine the repeals described in Senate bill sections 3124 and 3125 with the House amendment section 3123; add a subsection (d) that would modify the requirement for a briefing on additive manufacturing technologies contained in section 3139(c) of the National Defense Authorization Act for Fiscal Year 2016 (Public Law 114–92) and make certain technical and conforming changes.

Report on United States nuclear deterrence (sec. 3138)

The House amendment contained a provision (sec. 3119A) that would limit funds for the Department of Energy and require the Secretary of Energy to submit to the appropriate congressional committees the report entitled "U.S. Nuclear Deterrence in the Coming Decades" no later than 15 days after the date of enactment.

The Senate bill contained no similar provision.

The Senate recedes with an amendment that would drop the fence on funding and add that the Secretary may state his views in the cover letter to the report.

LEGISLATIVE PROVISIONS NOT ADOPTED

Analyses of options for disposal of high-level radioactive waste

The Senate bill contained a provision (sec. 3123) that would require the Secretary of Energy to enter into an arrangement with a federally funded research and development center to conduct analyses of options referenced in the Department's October 2014 report. These analyses shall include comprehensive system life cycle cost and schedule estimates conducted using Government Accountability Office (GAO) best practices and covering all phases of work, from site selection and characterization to site closure and monitoring.

The House amendment contained no similar provision.

The Senate recedes, the provision was not adopted.

TITLE XXXII—DEFENSE NUCLEAR FACILITIES SAFETY BOARD

Authorization (sec. 3201)

The Senate bill contained a provision (sec. 3201) that would authorize funding for the Defense Facilities Nuclear Safety Board at $31.0 million consistent with the budget request.

The House amendment contained an identical provision (sec. 3201).

The conference agreement includes this provision.

TITLE XXXIII—FEDERAL AVIATION ADMINISTRATION THIRD CLASS MEDICAL REFORM AND GENERAL AVIATION PILOT PROTECTIONS

LEGISLATIVE PROVISIONS NOT ADOPTED

Pilot's Bill of Rights 2

The Senate bill contained a series of provisions (sec. 3301, 3302, 3303, 3304, 3305, 3306, and 3307) that would establish Federal Aviation Administration third class medical reform and general aviation pilot protections, "The Pilots Bill of Rights 2".

The House amendment contained no similar provisions.

The Senate recedes on these provisions.

TITLE XXXIV—NAVAL PETROLEUM RESERVES

Authorization of appropriations (sec. 3401)

The House amendment contained a provision (sec. 3401) that would authorize $14,950,000 for fiscal year 2017 for operation and maintenance of the Naval Petroleum Reserves.

The Senate bill contained no similar provision.

The Senate recedes.

TITLE XXXV—MARITIME MATTERS

SUBTITLE A—MARITIME ADMINISTRATION, COAST GUARD, AND SHIPPING MATTERS

Authorization of the Maritime Administration (sec. 3501)

The House amendment contained a provision (sec. 3501) that would authorize appropriations for the national security aspects of the merchant marine for fiscal year 2017.

The Maritime Administration Authorization and Enhancement Act for Fiscal Year 2017 (S.2829) contained a similar provision (sec. 101).

The Senate recedes with an amendment that would include greater specificity within program authorizations and authorize funding for the National Security Multi-Mission Vessel.

Authority to extend certain age restrictions relating to vessels in the Maritime Security Fleet (sec. 3502)

The House amendment contained a provision (sec. 3503) that would amend section 53102 of title 46, United States Code, to provide authority to the Secretary of Defense, in conjunction with the Secretary of Transportation, to extend the age restriction for vessels in the Maritime Security Fleet by five years if the Secretaries jointly determine it is in the national interest to do so.

The Maritime Administration Authorization and Enhancement Act for Fiscal Year 2017 (S.2829) contained a similar provision (sec. 304).

The Senate recedes.

Corrections to provisions enacted by Coast Guard Authorization Acts (sec. 3503)

The House amendment contained a provision (sec. 3504) that would make technical and conforming corrections to provisions of the Coast Guard Authorization Act of 2015 (Public Law 114–120).

The Maritime Administration Authorization and Enhancement Act for Fiscal Year 2017 (S.2829) contained a similar provision (sec. 503).

The Senate recedes with a technical amendment.

Status of National Defense Reserve Fleet vessels (sec. 3504)

The House amendment contained a provision (sec. 3505) that would clarify that National Defense Reserve Fleet (NDRF) vessels, including the U.S. Maritime Administration's training vessels, are public vessels of the United States. This provision would also clarify that a NDRF vessel remains a "vessel" within the meaning of section 3 of title 1, United States Code, until it is delivered to a dismantling facility.

The Maritime Administration Authorization and Enhancement Act for Fiscal Year 2017 (S.2829) contained a similar provision (sec. 301).

The Senate recedes.

NDRF National Security Multi-Mission Vessel (sec. 3505)

The House amendment contained a provision (sec. 3506) that would authorize the Maritime Administrator to enter into a contract for a National Security Multi-Mission Vessel. The provision would also require the Maritime Administrator to enter into a contract or agreement with the Secretary of the Navy under which the Navy would serve as the general agent for the Maritime Administration for the purposes of the construction of the ship.

The Senate bill and Maritime Administration Authorization and Enhancement Act for Fiscal Year 2017 (S.2829) contained no similar provision.

The Senate recedes with an amendment that would require the Secretary of Transportation, in consultation with the Chief of Naval Operations and the Commandant of the Coast Guard, to ensure the Maritime Administrator has completed the design of the National Security Multi-Mission Vessel that will allow for the start of construction in fiscal year 2018. The amendment would also require the Maritime Administrator to provide for an entity other than the Maritime Administration to contract for the construction of the vessel. The conferees believe that the Maritime Administrator should leverage the ship construction expertise of the Department of the Navy, the Coast Guard or a commercial operator when contracting for the construction of the vessel.

The conferees direct the Maritime Administrator to submit to the Committees on Armed Services of the House and Senate, the Committee on Commerce, Science and Transportation of the Senate, and the Committee on Transportation and Infrastructure of the House the acquisition strategy for the National Security Multi-Mission Vessel concurrent with the budget submission in which the request for construction funding is included. This acquisition strategy shall address each of the elements described in paragraphs 6.a(1) through 6.a(4) of enclosure 2 to Department of Defense Instruction 5000.02.

Superintendent of United States Merchant Marine Academy (sec. 3506)

The House amendment contained a provision (sec. 3507) that would require the Secretary of Transportation to appoint as Superintendent of U.S. Merchant Marine Academy an individual from the senior ranks of the United States merchant marine, maritime industry, or from the retired list of flag-rank Navy or Coast Guard officers who possess significant merchant marine experience.

The Senate bill and Maritime Administration Authorization and Enhancement Act for Fiscal Year 2017 (S.2829) contained no similar provision.

The Senate recedes with amendment that would also allow the appointment of an individual who has served at sea and who has achieved general officer rank in other branches of the Armed Forces or has exemplary educational leadership experience. It also would allow for the selection of the best qualified candidate that may not fully meet all criteria defined in this provision.

Use of National Defense Reserve Fleet scrapping proceeds (sec. 3507)

The House amendment contained a provision (sec. 3508) that would increase the apportionment of National Defense Reserve Fleet (NDRF) scrapping proceeds to the National Maritime Heritage Grant Program.

The Maritime Administration Authorization and Enhancement Act for Fiscal Year 2017 (S.2829) contained a provision (sec. 308) that would require the U.S. Maritime Administration to submit an annual report to Congress on the management of NDRF scrapping proceeds and the National Heritage Grant Program and conduct a biennial assessment of the vessel disposal program.

The Senate recedes with an amendment that would combine the House and Senate provisions, better align reporting requirements with agency responsibilities, and reserve a portion of the National Maritime Grant Program apportionment for the U.S. Maritime Administration.

Floating dry docks (sec. 3508)

The House amendment contained a provision (sec. 3509) that would amend section 55122 of title 46, United States Code, to exempt certain floating dry docks from limitations imposed by such section 55122.

The Senate bill contained a similar provision (sec. 3502).

The Senate recedes with a technical amendment.

Transportation worker identification credentials for individuals undergoing separation, discharge, or release from the Armed Forces (sec. 3509)

The Senate bill contained a provision (sec. 564) that would require the Secretary of Defense to consult, and enter into a memorandum of understanding, with the Secretary of Homeland Security to afford a priority in the processing of applications for Transportation Worker Identification Credentials (TWIC) by members of the Armed Forces who are undergoing separation, discharge or release from the Armed forces. The provision would require adjudication of such applications not later than 14 days after the application is submitted, unless an appeal or waiver applies, or if other documentation is required. The priority for separating servicemembers shall commence not later than 180 days after enactment of this Act. The provision also requires a report on the implementation of this provision one year after enactment of this Act.

The House amendment contained a provision (sec. 3510) that would amend section 70105 of title 46, United States Code, to require the Secretary of Homeland Security to provide priority processing of applications from, and to issue TWIC for members of the Armed Forces who are undergoing separation, discharge or release from the Armed forces. The provision would require adjudication of such applications by such transitioning members of the Armed Forces not later than 13 days after the application is submitted, unless an appeal or waiver applies, or if other documentation is required.

The Senate recedes with an amendment that would require adjudication of applications not later than 30 days after the application is submitted, unless an appeal or waiver applies, or if other documentation is required. The processing deadline would apply to applications for TWIC submitted after the end of the 180 day period beginning on the date of enactment of this Act. The amendment requires the Secretary of Homeland Defense and the Secretary of Defense to enter into a memorandum of understanding

within 180 days after the date of enactment of this Act regarding the submission and processing of applications for TWIC by transitioning service members. The amendment also requires a report on the implementation of this provision one year after enactment of this Act.

Actions to address sexual harassment and sexual assault at the United States Merchant Marine Academy (sec. 3510)

The Maritime Administration Authorization and Enhancement Act for Fiscal Year 2017 (S.2829) contained a provision (sec. 201) that would set minimum training requirements and comprehensive policies for sexual harassment and sexual assault prevention and response at the United States Merchant Marine Academy. The provision would also expand existing requirements for an annual assessment of sexual assault and harassment policies to include a biennial focus group.

The House amendment contained no similar provision.

The House recedes with an amendment that would add confidentiality procedures to the comprehensive policy requirement.

Sexual assault response coordinators and sexual assault victim advocates (sec. 3511)

The Maritime Administration Authorization and Enhancement Act for Fiscal Year 2017 (S.2829) contained a provision (sec. 202) that would require the U.S. Merchant Marine Academy to employ or contract with at least one full-time sexual assault response coordinator, maintain a program for volunteer sexual assault victim advocates, and maintain a 24-hour hotline through which a victim of a sexual assault can receive victim support services.

The House amendment contained no similar provision.

The House recedes with an amendment that would clarify a victim's discretion in selecting a victim advocate and make a conforming change concerning confidentiality requirements.

Report from the Department of Transportation Inspector General (sec. 3512)

The Maritime Administration Authorization and Enhancement Act for Fiscal Year 2017 (S.2829) contained a provision (sec. 203) that would require the Department of Transportation Inspector General to submit a report to Congress that describes the effectiveness of the sexual harassment and sexual assault prevention and response program at the U.S. Merchant Marine Academy.

The House amendment contained no similar provision.

The House recedes with a technical amendment.

Sexual assault prevention and response working group (sec. 3513)

The Maritime Administration Authorization and Enhancement Act for Fiscal Year 2017 (S.2829) contained a provision (sec. 204) that would require the Maritime Administrator to convene a working group to examine methods to improve the prevention of, and response to, any sexual harassment or sexual assault that occurs during a cadet's Sea Year experience with the U.S. Merchant Marine Academy. This provision would require the working group to submit a report containing actionable recommendations to Congress.

The House amendment contained no similar provision.

The House recedes with amendment that would make technical changes and would separate as a new section a requirement that the Maritime Administrator establish certain criteria for vessel operators to participate in U.S. Merchant Marine Academy Sea Year program.

Sea Year compliance (sec. 3514)

The Maritime Administration Authorization and Enhancement Act for Fiscal Year 2017 (S.2829) contained a provision (sec. 204) that would require the Maritime Administrator to convene a working group to examine methods to improve the prevention of, and response to, any sexual harassment or sexual assault that occurs during a cadet's Sea Year experience with the U.S. Merchant Marine Academy. This provision would require the working group to submit a report containing actionable recommendations to Congress.

The House amendment contained no similar provision.

The House recedes with an amendment that would create a new section to require that the Maritime Administrator establish certain criteria for vessel operators to participate in U.S. Merchant Marine Academy Sea Year program. This provision is the new section.

State maritime academy physical standards and reporting (sec. 3515)

The Maritime Administration Authorization and Enhancement Act for Fiscal Year 2017 (S.2829) contained a provision (sec. 303) that would require any individual enrolled at a State maritime academy in a merchant marine officer program to meet, throughout enrollment at the academy, the medical and physical requirements required to obtain a mariner's license or merchant mariner documentation.

The House amendment contained no similar provision.

The House recedes with a technical amendment.

Appointments (sec. 3516)

The Maritime Administration Authorization and Enhancement Act for Fiscal Year 2017 (S.2829) contained a provision (sec. 305) that would increase from 40 to 50 the number of potential appointments to the U.S. Merchant Marine Academy for individuals the Secretary considers to be of special value, including factors such as prior military experience and whether the individual is the first in their family to attend college.

The House amendment contained no similar provision.

The House recedes with a technical amendment.

Maritime workforce working group (sec. 3517)

The Maritime Administration Authorization and Enhancement Act for Fiscal Year 2017 (S.2829) contained a provision (sec. 307) that would require the Secretary of Transportation to convene a working group to assess the pool of citizen mariners necessary to support the United States flag fleet, especially in times of emergency, and report to Congress on the assessment and recommendations for improving the quality of interagency data.

The House amendment contained no similar provision.

The House recedes with an amendment that would add the Committee on Armed Services of the House of Representatives as a report recipient, add the U.S. Navy to the working group, and add a sunset clause.

Maritime extreme weather task force (sec. 3518)

The Maritime Administration Authorization and Enhancement Act for Fiscal Year 2017 (S.2829) contained a provision (sec. 309) that would require the Secretary of Transportation to create an extreme weather task force to analyze the impact of extreme weather events on the maritime environment and to report to Congress on best practices and recommendations.

The House amendment contained no similar provision.

The House recedes with an amendment that would remove the Federal Maritime Commission from the task force and remove the authorization of appropriations.

Workforce plans and onboarding policies (sec. 3519)

The Maritime Administration Authorization and Enhancement Act for Fiscal Year 2017 (S.2829) contained a provision (sec. 401) that would require the Maritime Administrator to review and update the U.S. Maritime Administration's workforce and onboarding policies to fully implement competency models for mission-critical occupations, align training programs and systems, and report to Congress on actions taken.

The House amendment contained no similar provision.

The House recedes with amendment that would add the Committee on Armed Services of the House of Representatives as a report recipient.

Drug and alcohol policy (sec. 3520)

The Maritime Administration Authorization and Enhancement Act for Fiscal Year 2017 (S.2829) contained a provision (sec. 402) that would require the Maritime Administrator to ensure that all fleet managers have received applicable training on the Department of Transportation's drug and alcohol policy, institute a system for tracking all drug and alcohol policy training in a standardized repository, and report to Congress on actions taken.

The House amendment contained no similar provision.

The House recedes with an amendment that would add the Committee on Armed Services of the House of Representatives as a report recipient.

Vessel transfers (sec. 3521)

The Maritime Administration Authorization and Enhancement Act for Fiscal Year 2017 (S.2829) contained a provision (sec. 403) that would require the Maritime Administrator to submit a report to Congress that describes the policies and procedures for vessel transfer at the U.S. Maritime Administration, including updated Vessel Transfer Office procedures to process vessel transfer applications.

The House amendment contained no similar provision.

The House recedes with an amendment that would add the Committee on Armed Services of the House of Representatives as a report recipient.

Clarifying amendment; continuation boards (sec. 3522)

The Maritime Administration Authorization and Enhancement Act for Fiscal Year 2017 (S.2829) contained a provision (sec. 501) that would make a clarifying amendment concerning the continuation board convened for the U.S. Coast Guard.

The House amendment contained no similar provision.

The House recedes.

Polar icebreaker recapitalization plan (sec. 3523)

The Maritime Administration Authorization and Enhancement Act for Fiscal Year 2017 (S.2829) contained a provision (sec. 603) that would require the Secretary of Homeland Security, in consultation with the Secretary of the Navy, to submit to Congress a detailed recapitalization plan that meets the 2013 Department of Homeland Security Mission Need Statement.

The House amendment contained no similar provision.

The House recedes with a technical amendment.

GAO report on icebreaking capability in the United States (sec. 3524)

The Maritime Administration Authorization and Enhancement Act for Fiscal Year 2017 (S.2829) contained a provision (sec. 604) that would require the Comptroller General to submit a report to Congress on the current state of the United States Federal icebreaking fleet, including analysis of the icebreaking assets and gaps in icebreaking capabilities.

The House amendment contained no similar provision.

The House recedes with amendment that would define the appropriate report recipients and would clarify the applicability of the report to all icebreaking assets.

Subtitle B—Pribilof Islands Transition Completion

Pribilof Islands Transition Completion (secs. 3531–3533)

The Maritime Administration Authorization and Enhancement Act for Fiscal Year 2017 (S.2829) contained a provision (sec. 504) that would require the U.S. Coast Guard to report to Congress on the Coast Guard's use of certain tracts of land on St. Paul Island, planned use of those tracts of land, and planned use of other facilities on St. Paul Island.

The House amendment contained no similar provision.

The House recedes with an amendment that would make changes to Coast Guard access to certain specified tracts of land.

Subtitle C—Sexual Harassment and Assault Prevention at the National Oceanic and Atmospheric Administration

Actions to address sexual harassment at National Oceanic and Atmospheric Administration (sec. 3541)

The Maritime Administration Authorization and Enhancement Act for Fiscal Year 2017 (S.2829) contained a provision (sec. 711) that would require the Secretary of Commerce to develop a policy on the prevention and response to sexual harassment involving NOAA employees, NOAA Corps members, and all individuals who work with or conduct business on behalf of the Administration. The Administration would also be required to create a process for after-hours reporting and ensure that Equal Employment Opportunity personnel are distributed in each region of operations and at the marine and aviation centers.

The House amendment contained no similar provision.

The House recedes with an amendment that would reduce the number of personnel required to implement this section.

Actions to address sexual assault at National Oceanic and Atmospheric Administration (sec. 3542)

The Maritime Administration Authorization and Enhancement Act for Fiscal Year 2017 (S.2829) contained a provision (sec. 712) that would require the Secretary of Commerce to develop a policy on the prevention and response to sexual assault involving NOAA employees, NOAA Corps members, and all individuals who work with or conduct business on behalf of the Administration (wage mariners, scientists, students, interns, volunteers, etc.). The Secretary would be required to establish victim advocates and create a process for 24-hour reporting.

The House amendment contained no similar provision.

The House recedes with an amendment that would reduce the number of personnel required to implement this section.

Rights of the victim of a sexual assault (sec. 3543)

The Maritime Administration Authorization and Enhancement Act for Fiscal Year 2017 (S.2829) contained a provision (sec. 713) that would provide the victim of a sexual assault the right to be reasonably protected from the accused.

The House amendment contained no similar provision.

The House recedes.

Change of station (sec. 3544)

The Maritime Administration Authorization and Enhancement Act for Fiscal Year 2017 (S.2829) contained a provision (sec. 714) that would require timely consideration of a unit transfer or work location change to accommodate the victim of a sexual assault.

The House amendment contained no similar provision.

The House recedes.

Applicability of policies to crews of vessels secured by National Oceanic and Atmospheric Administration under contract (sec. 3545)

The Maritime Administration Authorization and Enhancement Act for Fiscal Year 2017 (S.2829) contained a provision (sec. 715) that would require any contract into which the NOAA enters for use of a vessel (ship, small boat, aircraft) to include as a condition that any personnel attached to the vessel are subject to the policies developed under section 711(a) and 712(a) of S.2829.

The House amendment contained no similar provision.

The House recedes.

Annual report on sexual assaults in the National Oceanic and Atmospheric Administration (sec. 3546)

The Maritime Administration Authorization and Enhancement Act for Fiscal Year 2017 (S.2829) contained a provision (sec. 716) that would require the Secretary of Commerce to submit an annual report to Congress that includes the number of sexual assaults, a synopsis of each case, and the disciplinary actions taken.

The House amendment contained no similar provision.

The House recedes.

Sexual assault defined (sec. 3547)

The Maritime Administration Authorization and Enhancement Act for Fiscal Year 2017 (S.2829) contained a provision (sec. 717) that would define the term "sexual assault".

The House amendment contained no similar provision.

The House recedes.

LEGISLATIVE PROVISIONS NOT ADOPTED

Short title

The Maritime Administration Authorization and Enhancement Act for Fiscal Year 2017 (S.2829) contained a provision (sec. 1) that would allow the bill to be cited as the "Maritime Administration Authorization and Enhancement Act for Fiscal Year 2017."

The House amendment contained no similar provision.

The Senate recedes.

Maritime Administration authorization request

The Maritime Administration Authorization and Enhancement Act for Fiscal Year 2017 (S.2829) contained a provision (sec. 102) that would require the U.S. Maritime Administration to submit an authorization request to Congress within 30 days of the date the President's budget is submitted to Congress.

The House amendment contained no similar provision.

The House recedes.

Port infrastructure development

The Maritime Administration Authorization and Enhancement Act for Fiscal Year 2017 (S.2829) contained a provision (sec. 302) that would allow the Maritime Administrator to use not more than three percent of port infrastructure development program funds for administrative expenses of the program.

The House amendment contained no similar provision.

The Senate recedes.

High-speed craft classification services

The Maritime Administration Authorization and Enhancement Act for Fiscal Year 2017 (S.2829) contained a provision (sec. 306) that would allow the Secretary of the Navy to select, under certain conditions, a classification society recognized and authorized by the Secretary to provide a classification for high-speed craft.

The House amendment contained no similar provision.

The Senate recedes.

Short title

The Maritime Administration Authorization and Enhancement Act for Fiscal Year 2017 (S.2829) contained a provision (sec. 601) that would allow the title to be cited as the "Polar Icebreaker Fleet Recapitalization Transparency Act."

The House amendment contained no similar provision.

The Senate recedes.

Definitions

The Maritime Administration Authorization and Enhancement Act for Fiscal Year 2017 (S.2829) contained a provision (sec. 602) that would define certain terms in the "Polar Icebreaker Fleet Recapitalization Transparency Act."

The House amendment contained no similar provision.

The Senate recedes.

Short title

The Maritime Administration Authorization and Enhancement Act for Fiscal Year 2017 (S.2829) contained a provision (sec. 701) that would allow the title to be cited as the "National Oceanic and Atmospheric Administration Sexual Harassment and Assault Prevention Act".

The House amendment contained no similar provision.

The Senate recedes.

Reauthorization of Hydrographic Services Improvement Act of 1998

The Maritime Administration Authorization and Enhancement Act for Fiscal Year 2017 (S.2829) contained a provision (sec. 771) that would reauthorize the Hydrographic Services Improvement Act of 1998.

The House amendment contained no similar provision.

The Senate recedes.

Maritime Administration

The Senate bill contained a provision (sec. 3501) that would re-authorize certain aspects of the Maritime Administration.

The House amendment contained no similar provision.

The Senate recedes.

Authority to make pro rata annual payments under operating agreements for vessels participating in Maritime Security Fleet

The House amendment contained a provision (sec. 3502) that would amend subsection (d) of section 53106 of title 46, United States Code, to permit the Secretary of Transportation to make a pro rata reduction in the amounts paid to vessel owners or operators under operating agreements under chapter 531 of that title if appropriations are insufficient to make full payment of the amounts authorized and agreed to under subsection (a) of section 53106.

The Senate bill and Maritime Administration Authorization and Enhancement Act for Fiscal Year 2017 (S.2829) contained no similar provision.

The House recedes.

Application of law

The House amendment contained a provision (sec. 3512) that would amend section 4301 of title 46, United States Code, to deem, for the purposes of any Federal law except the Federal Water Pollution Control Act, any vessel being repaired or dismantled as a recreational vessel if that vessel shares elements of design and construction of traditional recreational vessels and, when operating, is not normally engaged in a military, commercial, or traditionally commercial undertaking.

The Senate bill and Maritime Administration Authorization and Enhancement Act for Fiscal Year 2017 (S.2829) contained no similar provision.

The House recedes.

Commissioned officer corps of the National Oceanic and Atmospheric Administration

The Maritime Administration Authorization and Enhancement Act for Fiscal Year 2017 (S.2829) contained a subtitle (subtitle B of title VII) that would provide authorities for the commissioned officer corps of the National Oceanic and Atmospheric Administration.

The House amendment contained no similar provisions.

The Senate recedes.

Ballast water

The House amendment contained a title (title XXXVI) that would enact the Vessel Incident Discharge Act.

The Senate bill and Maritime Administration Authorization and Enhancement Act for Fiscal Year 2017 (S.2829) contained no similar provisions.

The House recedes.

DIVISION D—FUNDING TABLES

Authorization of amounts in funding tables (sec. 4001)

The Senate bill contained a provision (sec. 4001) that would provide for the allocation of funds among programs, projects, and activities in accordance with the tables in division D of this Act, subject to reprogramming in accordance with established procedures.

Consistent with the previously expressed views of the committee, the provision would also require that decisions by an agency head to commit, obligate, or expend funds to a specific entity on the basis of such funding tables be based on authorized, transparent, statutory criteria, or merit-based selection procedures in accordance with the requirements of sections 2304(k) and 2374 of title 10, United States Code, and other applicable provisions of law.

The House amendment contained a similar provision (sec. 4001).

The Senate recedes.

SUMMARY OF NATIONAL DEFENSE AUTHORIZATIONS FOR FISCAL YEAR 2017

(In Thousands of Dollars)

	FY 2017 Request	Conference Change	Conference Authorized

DISCRETIONARY AUTHORIZATIONS WITHIN THE JURISDICTION OF THE ARMED SERVICES COMMITTEE

National Defense Funding, Base Budget Request

Function 051, Department of Defense-Military

Division A: Department of Defense Authorizations

Title I—Procurement

	FY 2017 Request	Conference Change	Conference Authorized
Aircraft Procurement, Army	3,614,787		3,614,787
Missile Procurement, Army	1,519,966	−9,837	1,510,129
Weapons & Tracked Combat Vehicles, Army	2,265,177	85,900	2,351,077
Procurement of Ammunition, Army	1,513,157	1,646	1,514,803
Other Procurement, Army	5,873,949	−38,285	5,835,664
Aircraft Procurement, Navy	14,109,148	−157,372	13,951,776
Weapons Procurement, Navy	3,209,262	−21,772	3,187,490
Procurement of Ammunition, Navy & Marine Corps	664,368	−7,100	657,268
Shipbuilding & Conversion, Navy	18,354,874	525,696	18,880,570
Other Procurement, Navy	6,338,861	−79,931	6,258,930
Procurement, Marine Corps	1,362,769	−4,325	1,358,444
Aircraft Procurement, Air Force	13,922,917	−87,300	13,835,617
Missile Procurement, Air Force	2,426,621	−10,752	2,415,869
Space Procurement, Air Force	3,055,743	−229,900	2,825,843
Procurement of Ammunition, Air Force	1,677,719	−6,000	1,671,719
Other Procurement, Air Force	17,438,056	−15,300	17,422,756
Procurement, Defense-Wide	4,524,918	355,000	4,879,918
Joint Urgent Operational Needs Fund	99,300	−99,300	0
National Guard & Reserve Equipment		250,000	250,000
Subtotal, Title I—Procurement	**101,971,592**	**451,068**	**102,422,660**

Title II—Research, Development, Test and Evaluation

	FY 2017 Request	Conference Change	Conference Authorized
Research, Development, Test & Evaluation, Army	7,515,399	13,291	7,528,690
Research, Development, Test & Evaluation, Navy	17,276,301	−197,638	17,078,663
Research, Development, Test & Evaluation, Air Force	28,112,251	−54,650	28,057,601
Research, Development, Test & Evaluation, Defense-Wide	18,308,826	−42,150	18,266,676
Operational Test & Evaluation, Defense	178,994		178,994
Subtotal, Title II—Research, Development, Test and Evaluation	**71,391,771**	**−281,147**	**71,110,624**

Title III—Operation and Maintenance

	FY 2017 Request	Conference Change	Conference Authorized
Operation & Maintenance, Army	33,809,040	23,234	33,832,274
Operation & Maintenance, Army Reserve	2,712,331	21,500	2,733,831
Operation & Maintenance, Army National Guard	6,825,370	27,635	6,853,005
Operation & Maintenance, Navy	39,483,581	507,700	39,991,281
Operation & Maintenance, Marine Corps	5,954,258	185,350	6,139,608
Operation & Maintenance, Navy Reserve	927,656	−21,200	906,456
Operation & Maintenance, Marine Corps Reserve	270,633	−100	270,533
Operation & Maintenance, Air Force	37,518,056	−180,400	37,337,656
Operation & Maintenance, Air Force Reserve	3,067,929	−57,000	3,010,929
Operation & Maintenance, Air National Guard	6,703,578	−69,400	6,634,178
Operation & Maintenance, Defense-Wide	32,571,590	115,089	32,686,679
US Court of Appeals for the Armed Forces, Defense	14,194		14,194
Overseas Humanitarian, Disaster and Civic Aid	105,125		105,125
Cooperative Threat Reduction	325,604		325,604
Environmental Restoration, Army	170,167		170,167
Environmental Restoration, Navy	281,762		281,762
Environmental Restoration, Air Force	371,521		371,521

SUMMARY OF NATIONAL DEFENSE AUTHORIZATIONS FOR FISCAL YEAR 2017

(In Thousands of Dollars)

	FY 2017 Request	Conference Change	Conference Authorized
Environmental Restoration, Defense	9,009		9,009
Environmental Restoration, Formerly Used Sites	197,084		197,084
Subtotal, Title III—Operation and Maintenance	**171,318,488**	**552,408**	**171,870,896**
Title IV—Military Personnel			
Military Personnel Appropriations	128,902,332	−699,768	128,202,564
Medicare-Eligible Retiree Health Fund Contributions	6,366,908		6,366,908
Subtotal, Title IV—Military Personnel	**135,269,240**	**−699,768**	**134,569,472**
Title XIV—Other Authorizations			
Working Capital Fund, Army	56,469		56,469
Working Capital Fund, Air Force	63,967		63,967
Working Capital Fund, Defense-Wide	37,132		37,132
Working Capital Fund, DECA	1,214,045		1,214,045
Chemical Agents & Munitions Destruction	551,023		551,023
Drug Interdiction and Counter Drug Activities	844,800	−125,000	719,800
Office of the Inspector General	322,035		322,035
Defense Health Program	33,467,516	−373,600	33,093,916
Subtotal, Title XIV—Other Authorizations	**36,556,987**	**−498,600**	**36,058,387**
Total, Division A: Department of Defense Authorizations	**516,508,078**	**−476,039**	**516,032,039**
Division B: Military Construction Authorizations			
Military Construction			
Army	503,459	50,500	553,959
Navy	1,027,763	247,916	1,275,679
Air Force	1,481,058	205,465	1,686,523
Defense-Wide	2,056,091	−30,647	2,025,444
NATO Security Investment Program	177,932		177,932
Army National Guard	232,930	67,500	300,430
Army Reserve	68,230	30,000	98,230
Navy and Marine Corps Reserve	38,597		38,597
Air National Guard	143,957	11,000	154,957
Air Force Reserve	188,950		188,950
Subtotal, Military Construction	**5,918,967**	**581,734**	**6,500,701**
Family Housing			
Construction, Army	200,735	−43,563	157,172
Operation & Maintenance, Army	325,995		325,995
Construction, Navy and Marine Corps	94,011		94,011
Operation & Maintenance, Navy and Marine Corps	300,915		300,915
Construction, Air Force	61,352		61,352
Operation & Maintenance, Air Force	274,429		274,429
Operation & Maintenance, Defense-Wide	59,157		59,157
Improvement Fund	3,258		3,258
Subtotal, Family Housing	**1,319,852**	**−43,563**	**1,276,289**
Base Realignment and Closure			
Base Realignment and Closure—Army	14,499	10,000	24,499
Base Realignment and Closure—Navy	134,373	25,000	159,373
Base Realignment and Closure—Air Force	56,365		56,365
Subtotal, Base Realignment and Closure	**205,237**	**35,000**	**240,237**
Undistributed Adjustments			
Prior Year Savings	0	−307,662	−307,662

SUMMARY OF NATIONAL DEFENSE AUTHORIZATIONS FOR FISCAL YEAR 2017

(In Thousands of Dollars)

	FY 2017 Request	Conference Change	Conference Authorized
Subtotal, Undistributed Adjustments	0	−307,662	−307,662
Total, Division B: Military Construction Authorizations	7,444,056	265,509	7,709,565
Total, 051, Department of Defense-Military	523,952,134	−210,530	523,741,604

Division C: Department of Energy National Security Authorization and Other Authorizations

Function 053, Atomic Energy Defense Activities

Environmental and Other Defense Activities			
Nuclear Energy	151,876	−15,260	136,616
Weapons Activities	9,243,147	185,882	9,429,029
Defense Nuclear Nonproliferation	1,807,916	79,000	1,886,916
Naval Reactors	1,420,120	−2,500	1,417,620
Federal salaries and expenses	412,817	−17,300	395,517
Defense Environmental Cleanup	5,382,050	−108,492	5,273,558
Other Defense Activities	791,552	−2,000	789,552
Subtotal, Environmental and Other Defense Activities	19,209,478	119,330	19,328,808
Independent Federal Agency Authorization			
Defense Nuclear Facilities Safety Board	31,000		31,000
Subtotal, Independent Federal Agency Authorization	31,000	0	31,000
Subtotal, 053, Atomic Energy Defense Activities	19,240,478	119,330	19,359,808

Function 054, Defense-Related Activities

Other Agency Authorizations			
Maritime Security Program	211,000	88,997	299,997
Subtotal, Independent Federal Agency Authorization	211,000	88,997	299,997
Subtotal, 054, Defense-Related Activities	211,000	88,997	299,997
Subtotal, Division C: Department of Energy National Security Authorization and Other Authorizations	19,451,478	208,327	19,659,805
Total, National Defense Funding, Base Budget Request	543,403,612	−2,203	543,401,409

National Defense Funding, Overseas Contingency Operations

National Defense Funding, Overseas Contingency Operations Budget Request

Function 051, Department of Defense-Military

Procurement			
Aircraft Procurement, Army	235,131		235,131
Missile Procurement, Army	529,317		529,317
Weapons & Tracked Combat Vehicles, Army	153,544	144,800	298,344
Procurement of Ammunition, Army	301,523		301,523
Other Procurement, Army	1,309,610		1,309,610
Joint Improvised-Threat Defeat Fund	394,800		394,800
Aircraft Procurement, Navy	358,830		358,830
Weapons Procurement, Navy	8,600		8,600
Procurement of Ammunition, Navy & Marine Corps	66,229		66,229
Other Procurement, Navy	69,877		69,877

SUMMARY OF NATIONAL DEFENSE AUTHORIZATIONS FOR FISCAL YEAR 2017

(In Thousands of Dollars)

	FY 2017 Request	Conference Change	Conference Authorized
Procurement, Marine Corps	118,939		118,939
Aircraft Procurement, Air Force	679,969	−25,600	654,369
Missile Procurement, Air Force	154,845		154,845
Procurement of Ammunition, Air Force	164,408	−9,250	155,158
Other Procurement, Air Force	3,834,165		3,834,165
Procurement, Defense-Wide	234,434	−19,250	215,184
Subtotal, Procurement	**8,614,221**	**90,700**	**8,704,921**
Research, Development, Test and Evaluation			
Research, Development, Test & Evaluation, Army	239,689		239,689
Research, Development, Test & Evaluation, Navy	40,333		40,333
Research, Development, Test & Evaluation, Air Force	32,905		32,905
Research, Development, Test & Evaluation, Defense-Wide	165,419		165,419
Subtotal, Research, Development, Test and Evaluation	**478,346**	**0**	**478,346**
Operation and Maintenance			
Operation & Maintenance, Army	16,658,381	−245,000	16,413,381
Operation & Maintenance, Army Reserve	24,120		24,120
Operation & Maintenance, Army National Guard	66,907		66,907
Afghanistan Security Forces Fund	4,263,215		4,263,215
Iraq Train & Equip Fund	919,500	−919,500	0
Syria Train & Equip Fund	250,000	−250,000	0
Counter-ISIL Fund	0	1,169,500	1,169,500
Operation & Maintenance, Navy	5,441,406		5,441,406
Operation & Maintenance, Marine Corps	1,112,805		1,112,805
Operation & Maintenance, Navy Reserve	26,265		26,265
Operation & Maintenance, Marine Corps Reserve	3,304		3,304
Operation & Maintenance, Air Force	9,757,326	43,542	9,800,868
Operation & Maintenance, Air Force Reserve	57,586		57,586
Operation & Maintenance, Air National Guard	20,000		20,000
Operation & Maintenance, Defense-Wide	6,357,088	760,000	7,117,088
Subtotal, Operation and Maintenance	**44,957,903**	**558,542**	**45,516,445**
Military Personnel			
Military Personnel Appropriations	3,644,161		3,644,161
Subtotal, Military Personnel	**3,644,161**	**0**	**3,644,161**
Other Authorizations			
Working Capital Fund, Army	46,833		46,833
Working Capital Fund, Defense-Wide	93,800		93,800
Drug Interdiction and Counter Drug Activities	191,533		191,533
Office of the Inspector General	22,062		22,062
Defense Health Program	334,311		334,311
Counterterrorism Partnerships Fund	1,000,000	−1,000,000	0
Ukraine Security Assistance		350,000	350,000
Subtotal, Other Authorizations	**1,688,539**	**−650,000**	**1,038,539**
Military Construction			
Army	18,900		18,900
Navy	21,400		21,400
Air Force	88,740	−449	88,291
Defense-Wide	5,000		5,000
Subtotal, Military Construction	**134,040**	**−449**	**133,591**
Subtotal, Overseas Contingency Operations	**59,517,210**	**−1,207**	**59,516,003**

SUMMARY OF NATIONAL DEFENSE AUTHORIZATIONS FOR FISCAL YEAR 2017

(In Thousands of Dollars)

	FY 2017 Request	Conference Change	Conference Authorized
Subtotal, 051, Department of Defense-Military	**59,517,210**	**−1,207**	**59,516,003**
Total, National Defense Funding, Overseas Contingency Operations Budget Request	**59,517,210**	**−1,207**	**59,516,003**

National Defense Funding, Overseas Contingency Operations Funding for Base Requirements

Function 051, Department of Defense-Military

	FY 2017 Request	Conference Change	Conference Authorized
Procurement			
Aircraft Procurement, Army	78,040		78,040
Missile Procurement, Army	150,000	196,100	346,100
Procurement of Ammunition, Army		240,200	240,200
Other Procurement, Army	161,900		161,900
Joint Improvised-Threat Defeat Fund	113,272		113,272
Aircraft Procurement, Navy	34,200		34,200
Weapons Procurement, Navy		117,200	117,200
Procurement of Ammunition, Navy & Marine Corps		77,200	77,200
Other Procurement, Navy	59,329		59,329
Aircraft Procurement, Air Force	179,430		179,430
Missile Procurement, Air Force	184,700		184,700
Procurement of Ammunition, Air Force	323,000		323,000
Procurement, Defense-Wide	4,000		4,000
Subtotal, Procurement	**1,287,871**	**630,700**	**1,918,571**
Research, Development, Test and Evaluation			
Research, Development, Test & Evaluation, Army	33		33
Research, Development, Test & Evaluation, Navy	37,990		37,990
Subtotal, Research, Development, Test and Evaluation	**38,023**	**0**	**38,023**
Operation and Maintenance			
Operation & Maintenance, Army	1,586,475	962,000	2,548,475
Operation & Maintenance, Army Reserve	14,559	95,800	110,359
Operation & Maintenance, Army National Guard	60,128	128,800	188,928
Operation & Maintenance, Navy	1,481,516	26,100	1,507,616
Operation & Maintenance, Marine Corps	300,000	7,200	307,200
Operation & Maintenance, Navy Reserve		500	500
Operation & Maintenance, Marine Corps Reserve		1,000	1,000
Operation & Maintenance, Air Force	124,000	49,100	173,100
Operation & Maintenance, Air Force Reserve		1,600	1,600
Operation & Maintenance, Air National Guard		4,300	4,300
Operation & Maintenance, Defense-Wide	38,044		38,044
Subtotal, Operation and Maintenance	**3,604,722**	**1,276,400**	**4,881,122**
Military Personnel			
Military Personnel Appropriations	62,965	1,287,500	1,350,465
Subtotal, Military Personnel	**62,965**	**1,287,500**	**1,350,465**
Other Authorizations			
Drug Interdiction and Counter Drug Activities	23,800		23,800
Subtotal, Other Authorizations	**23,800**	**0**	**23,800**
Military Construction			
Navy	38,409		38,409
Subtotal, Military Construction	**38,409**	**0**	**38,409**
Subtotal, 051, Department of Defense-Military	**5,055,790**	**3,194,600**	**8,250,390**

SUMMARY OF NATIONAL DEFENSE AUTHORIZATIONS FOR FISCAL YEAR 2017

(In Thousands of Dollars)

	FY 2017 Request	Conference Change	Conference Authorized
Total, National Defense Funding, Overseas Contingency Operations Funding for Base Requirements	5,055,790	3,194,600	8,250,390
Total, National Defense Funding, Overseas Contingency Operations	64,573,000	3,193,393	67,766,393
Total, National Defense	607,976,612	3,191,190	611,167,802
MEMORANDUM: BASE BUDGET REQUIREMENTS			
Base Funding	543,403,612	−2,203	543,401,409
Overseas Contingency Operations Funding for Base Requirements	5,055,790	3,194,600	8,250,390
Total, Base Budget Requirements	548,459,402	3,192,397	551,651,799
MEMORANDUM: NON-DEFENSE AUTHORIZATIONS			
Title XIV—Armed Forces Retirement Home (Function 600)	64,300		64,300
Title XXXIV—Naval Petroleum and Oil Shale Reserves (Function 270)	14,950		14,950
MEMORANDUM: TRANSFER AUTHORITIES (NON-ADD)			
Title X—General Transfer Authority	[5,000,000]	[−500,000]	[4,500,000]
Title XV—Special Transfer Authority	[4,500,000]	[−1,000,000]	[3,500,000]
MEMORANDUM: DEFENSE AUTHORIZATIONS NOT UNDER THE JURISDICTION OF THE ARMED SERVICES COMMITTEE (NON-ADD)			
Defense Production Act	[44,605]		[44,605]

NATIONAL DEFENSE BUDGET AUTHORITY IMPLICATION

(In Thousands of Dollars)

	FY 2017 Request	Conference Change	Conference Authorized
Summary, Discretionary Authorizations Within the Jurisdiction of the Armed Services Committee			
SUBTOTAL, DEPARTMENT OF DEFENSE (051)	523,952,134	−210,530	523,741,604
SUBTOTAL, ATOMIC ENERGY DEFENSE PROGRAMS (053)	19,240,478	119,330	19,359,808
SUBTOTAL, DEFENSE-RELATED ACTIVITIES (054)	211,000	88,997	299,997
TOTAL, NATIONAL DEFENSE (050)—BASE BILL	543,403,612	−2,203	543,401,409
TOTAL, OVERSEAS CONTINGENCY OPERATIONS	64,573,000	3,193,393	67,766,393
GRAND TOTAL, NATIONAL DEFENSE	607,976,612	3,191,190	611,167,802
Base National Defense Discretionary Programs that Are Not In the Jurisdiction of the Armed Services Committee or Do Not Require Additional Authorization			
Defense Production Act Purchases	44,000		44,000
Indefinite Account: Disposal Of DOD Real Property	8,000		8,000
Indefinite Account: Lease Of DOD Real Property	37,000		37,000
Subtotal, Budget Sub-Function 051	89,000		89,000
Formerly Utilized Sites Remedial Action Program	103,000		103,000
Subtotal, Budget Sub-Function 053	103,000		103,000
Other Discretionary Programs	7,750,000		7,750,000
Other Discretionary Programs—proposed rescission (FBI S&E)	−133,000		−133,000
Subtotal, Budget Sub-Function 054	7,617,000		7,617,000
Total Defense Discretionary Adjustments (050)	7,809,000		7,809,000
Budget Authority Implication, National Defense Discretionary			
Department of Defense--Military (051)	588,614,134	2,982,863	591,596,997
Atomic Energy Defense Activities (053)	19,343,478	119,330	19,462,808
Defense-Related Activities (054)	7,828,000	88,997	7,916,997

NATIONAL DEFENSE BUDGET AUTHORITY IMPLICATION

(In Thousands of Dollars)

	FY 2017 Request	Conference Change	Conference Authorized
Total BA Implication, National Defense Discretionary	615,785,612	3,191,190	618,976,802
National Defense Mandatory Programs, Current Law (CBO Estimates)			
Concurrent receipt accrual payments to the Military Retirement Fund	6,769,000		6,769,000
Revolving, trust and other DOD Mandatory	1,463,000		1,463,000
Offsetting receipts	−1,856,000		−1,856,000
Subtotal, Budget Sub-Function 051	**6,376,000**		**6,376,000**
Energy employees occupational illness compensation programs and other	1,169,000		1,169,000
Subtotal, Budget Sub-Function 053	**1,169,000**		**1,169,000**
Radiation exposure compensation trust fund	62,000		62,000
Payment to CIA retirement fund and other	514,000		514,000
Subtotal, Budget Sub-Function 054	**576,000**		**576,000**
Total National Defense Mandatory (050)	**8,121,000**		**8,121,000**
Budget Authority Implication, National Defense Discretionary and Mandatory			
Department of Defense--Military (051)	594,990,134	2,982,863	597,972,997
Atomic Energy Defense Activities (053)	20,512,478	119,330	20,631,808
Defense-Related Activities (054)	8,404,000	88,997	8,492,997
Total BA Implication, National Defense Discretionary and Mandatory	**623,906,612**	**3,191,190**	**627,097,802**

TITLE XLI—PROCUREMENT

SEC. 4101. PROCUREMENT.

SEC. 4101. PROCUREMENT
(In Thousands of Dollars)

Line	Item	FY 2017 Request Qty	FY 2017 Request Cost	House Authorized Qty	House Authorized Cost	Senate Authorized Qty	Senate Authorized Cost	Conference Change Qty	Conference Change Cost	Conference Authorized Qty	Conference Authorized Cost
	AIRCRAFT PROCUREMENT, ARMY										
	FIXED WING										
001	UTILITY F/W AIRCRAFT	3	57,529	3	57,529	3	57,529			3	57,529
003	MQ–1 UAV		55,388		84,988		55,388				55,388
	Ground Mounted Airspace Deconfliction Radar.				[29,600]						
	ROTARY										
006	AH–64 APACHE BLOCK IIIA REMAN	48	803,084	48	803,084	48	803,084			48	803,084
007	ADVANCE PROCUREMENT (CY)		185,160		185,160		185,160				185,160
008	UH–60 BLACKHAWK M MODEL (MYP)	36	755,146	36	755,146	36	755,146			36	755,146
009	ADVANCE PROCUREMENT (CY)		174,107		174,107		174,107				174,107
010	UH–60 BLACK HAWK A AND L MODELS	38	46,173	38	46,173	38	46,173			38	46,173
011	CH–47 HELICOPTER	22	556,257	22	556,257	22	556,257			22	556,257
012	ADVANCE PROCUREMENT (CY)		8,707		8,707		8,707				8,707
	MODIFICATION OF AIRCRAFT										
013	MQ–1 PAYLOAD (MIP)		43,735		43,735		43,735				43,735
015	MULTI SENSOR ABN RECON (MIP)		94,527		94,527		94,527				94,527
016	AH–64 MODS		137,883		137,883		137,883				137,883
017	CH–47 CARGO HELICOPTER MODS (MYP)		102,943		102,943		102,943				102,943
018	GRCS SEMA MODS (MIP)		4,055		4,055		4,055				4,055
019	ARL SEMA MODS (MIP)		6,793		6,793		6,793				6,793
020	EMARSS SEMA MODS (MIP)		13,197		13,197		13,197				13,197
021	UTILITY/CARGO AIRPLANE MODS		17,526		17,526		17,526				17,526
022	UTILITY HELICOPTER MODS		10,807		10,807		10,807				10,807
023	NETWORK AND MISSION PLAN		74,752		74,752		74,752				74,752
024	COMMS, NAV SURVEILLANCE		69,960		69,960		69,960				69,960
025	GATM ROLLUP		45,302		45,302		45,302				45,302
026	RQ–7 UAV MODS		71,169		71,169		71,169				71,169
027	UAS MODS		21,804		26,224		21,804				21,804
	Realign APS Unit Set Requirements from OCO.				[4,420]						
	GROUND SUPPORT AVIONICS										
028	AIRCRAFT SURVIVABILITY EQUIPMENT		67,377		67,377		67,377				67,377
029	SURVIVABILITY CM		9,565		9,565		35,565				9,565

SEC. 4101. PROCUREMENT
(In Thousands of Dollars)

Line	Item	FY 2017 Request Qty	Cost	House Authorized Qty	Cost	Senate Authorized Qty	Cost	Conference Change Qty	Cost	Conference Authorized Qty	Cost
	ASE PNT unfunded requirement						[26,000]				
030	CMWS		41,626		41,626		41,626				41,626
	OTHER SUPPORT										
032	AVIONICS SUPPORT EQUIPMENT		7,007		7,007		7,007				7,007
033	COMMON GROUND EQUIPMENT		48,234		48,234		48,234				48,234
034	AIRCREW INTEGRATED SYSTEMS		30,297		30,297		30,297				30,297
035	AIR TRAFFIC CONTROL		50,405		50,405		50,405				50,405
036	INDUSTRIAL FACILITIES		1,217		1,217		1,217				1,217
037	LAUNCHER, 2.75 ROCKET		3,055		3,055		3,055				3,055
	TOTAL AIRCRAFT PROCUREMENT, ARMY.	147	3,614,787	147	3,648,807	147	3,640,787			147	3,614,787
	MISSILE PROCUREMENT, ARMY										
	SURFACE-TO-AIR MISSILE SYSTEM										
001	LOWER TIER AIR AND MISSILE DEFENSE (AMD).		126,470		126,470		126,470				126,470
002	MSE MISSILE	85	423,201	85	505,601	85	423,201			85	423,201
	Program increase				[82,400]						
003	ADVANCE PROCUREMENT (CY)		19,319		19,319		19,319				19,319
	AIR-TO-SURFACE MISSILE SYSTEM										
004	HELLFIRE SYS SUMMARY	155	42,013	155	42,013	155	42,013			155	42,013
005	JOINT AIR-TO-GROUND MSLS (JAGM)	324	64,751	324	64,751	324	64,751			324	64,751
006	ADVANCE PROCUREMENT (CY)		37,100		37,100		37,100				37,100
	ANTI-TANK/ASSAULT MISSILE SYS										
007	JAVELIN (AAWS-M) SYSTEM SUMMARY ...	309	73,508	309	89,075	309	73,508		−604	309	72,904
	Engineering services cost growth								[−604]		
	Realign APS Unit Set Requirements from OCO.				[15,567]						
008	TOW 2 SYSTEM SUMMARY	595	64,922	595	145,574	595	64,922			595	64,922
	Realign APS Unit Set Requirements from OCO.				[80,652]						
009	ADVANCE PROCUREMENT (CY)		19,949		19,949		19,949		−9,233		10,716
	Advance procurement cost growth								[−9,233]		
010	GUIDED MLRS ROCKET (GMLRS)	1,068	172,088	1,068	248,079	1,068	172,088			1,068	172,088
	Realign APS Unit Set Requirements from OCO.				[75,991]						
011	MLRS REDUCED RANGE PRACTICE ROCKETS (RRPR).	1,704	18,004	1,704	18,004	1,704	18,004			1,704	18,004
	MODIFICATIONS										
013	PATRIOT MODS		197,107		197,107		197,107				197,107
014	ATACMS MODS		150,043		150,043		150,043				150,043
015	GMLRS MOD		395		395		395				395
017	AVENGER MODS		33,606		33,606		33,606				33,606
018	ITAS/TOW MODS		383		383		383				383
019	MLRS MODS		34,704		34,704		34,704				34,704
020	HIMARS MODIFICATIONS		1,847		1,847		1,847				1,847
	SPARES AND REPAIR PARTS										
021	SPARES AND REPAIR PARTS		34,487		34,487		34,487				34,487
	SUPPORT EQUIPMENT & FACILITIES										
022	AIR DEFENSE TARGETS		4,915		4,915		4,915				4,915
024	PRODUCTION BASE SUPPORT		1,154		1,154		1,154				1,154
	TOTAL MISSILE PROCUREMENT, ARMY.	4,240	1,519,966	4,240	1,774,576	4,240	1,519,966		−9,837	4,240	1,510,129
	PROCUREMENT OF W&TCV, ARMY										
	TRACKED COMBAT VEHICLES										
001	STRYKER VEHICLE		71,680		71,680		71,680				71,680
	MODIFICATION OF TRACKED COMBAT VEHICLES										
002	STRYKER (MOD)		74,348		74,348		74,348				74,348
003	STRYKER UPGRADE		444,561		444,561		433,561		−11,000		433,561
	Early to need						[−11,000]		[−11,000]		
005	BRADLEY PROGRAM (MOD)		276,433		276,433		276,433		−3,100		273,333
	Excess program management growth.								[−3,100]		
006	HOWITZER, MED SP FT 155MM M109A6 (MOD).		63,138		63,138		63,138				63,138
007	PALADIN INTEGRATED MANAGEMENT (PIM).	36	469,305	36	594,489	36	469,305			36	469,305

SEC. 4101. PROCUREMENT
(In Thousands of Dollars)

Line	Item	FY 2017 Request		House Authorized		Senate Authorized		Conference Change		Conference Authorized	
		Qty	Cost	Qty	Cost	Qty	Cost	Qty	Cost	Qty	Cost
	Realign APS Unit Set Requirements from OCO.				[125,184]						
008	IMPROVED RECOVERY VEHICLE (M88A2 HERCULES).	22	91,963	22	91,963	22	91,963			22	91,963
009	ASSAULT BRIDGE (MOD)		3,465		9,415		3,465				3,465
	Realign APS Unit Set Requirements from OCO.				[5,950]						
010	ASSAULT BREACHER VEHICLE		2,928		2,928		2,928				2,928
011	M88 FOV MODS		8,685		8,685		8,685				8,685
012	JOINT ASSAULT BRIDGE	9	64,752	9	64,752	9	64,752			9	64,752
013	M1 ABRAMS TANK (MOD)		480,166		480,166		620,166				480,166
	APS Unfunded requirement						[82,000]				
	M1 industrial base Unfunded requirement.						[58,000]				
014	ABRAMS UPGRADE PROGRAM				172,200				100,000		100,000
	Realign APS Unit Set Requirements from OCO.				[172,200]				[100,000]		
	WEAPONS & OTHER COMBAT VEHICLES										
016	INTEGRATED AIR BURST WEAPON SYSTEM FAMILY.		9,764		9,764		9,764				9,764
017	MORTAR SYSTEMS		8,332		8,332		8,332				8,332
018	XM320 GRENADE LAUNCHER MODULE (GLM).		3,062		3,062		3,062				3,062
019	COMPACT SEMI-AUTOMATIC SNIPER SYSTEM.		992		992		992				992
020	CARBINE		40,493		40,493		40,493				40,493
021	COMMON REMOTELY OPERATED WEAPONS STATION.		25,164		25,164		25,164				25,164
	MOD OF WEAPONS AND OTHER COMBAT VEH										
022	MK–19 GRENADE MACHINE GUN MODS		4,959		4,959		4,959				4,959
023	M777 MODS		11,913		11,913		11,913				11,913
024	M4 CARBINE MODS		29,752		29,752		28,752				29,752
	Program decrease						[–1,000]				
025	M2 50 CAL MACHINE GUN MODS		48,582		48,582		48,582				48,582
026	M249 SAW MACHINE GUN MODS		1,179		1,179		1,179				1,179
027	M240 MEDIUM MACHINE GUN MODS		1,784		1,784		1,784				1,784
028	SNIPER RIFLES MODIFICATIONS		971		971		971				971
029	M119 MODIFICATIONS		6,045		6,045		6,045				6,045
030	MORTAR MODIFICATION		12,118		12,118		12,118				12,118
031	MODIFICATIONS LESS THAN $5.0M (WOCV-WTCV).		3,157		3,157		3,157				3,157
	SUPPORT EQUIPMENT & FACILITIES										
032	ITEMS LESS THAN $5.0M (WOCV-WTCV)		2,331		2,331		2,331				2,331
035	SMALL ARMS EQUIPMENT (SOLDIER ENH PROG).		3,155		3,155		3,155				3,155
036	BRADLEY PROGRAM				72,800		1,000				
	Program increase for Modular Handgun System.						[1,000]				
	Realign APS Unit Set Requirements from OCO.				[72,800]						
	TOTAL PROCUREMENT OF W&TCV, ARMY.	67	2,265,177	67	2,641,311	67	2,394,177		85,900	67	2,351,077
	PROCUREMENT OF AMMUNITION, ARMY										
	SMALL/MEDIUM CAL AMMUNITION										
001	CTG, 5.56MM, ALL TYPES		40,296		40,296		37,696				40,296
	Early to need						[–2,600]				
002	CTG, 7.62MM, ALL TYPES		39,237		48,879		38,937				39,237
	Early to need						[–300]				
	Realign APS Unit Set Requirements from OCO.				[9,642]						
003	CTG, HANDGUN, ALL TYPES		5,193		5,193		3,893				5,193
	Early to need						[–1,300]				
004	CTG, .50 CAL, ALL TYPES		46,693		52,691		41,993				46,693
	Early to need						[–4,700]				
	Realign APS Unit Set Requirements from OCO.				[5,998]						
005	CTG, 20MM, ALL TYPES		7,000		8,077		7,000				7,000
	Realign APS Unit Set Requirements from OCO.				[1,077]						

SEC. 4101. PROCUREMENT
(In Thousands of Dollars)

Line	Item	FY 2017 Request		House Authorized		Senate Authorized		Conference Change		Conference Authorized	
		Qty	Cost	Qty	Cost	Qty	Cost	Qty	Cost	Qty	Cost
006	CTG, 25MM, ALL TYPES		7,753		34,987		6,453		−1,300		6,453
	Program reduction				[−1,300]		[−1,300]		[−1,300]		
	Realign APS Unit Set Requirements from OCO.				[28,534]						
007	CTG, 30MM, ALL TYPES		47,000		47,000		47,000				47,000
008	CTG, 40MM, ALL TYPES		118,178		115,501		111,878		−6,354		111,824
	Early to need								[−6,300]		[−6,354]
	Realign APS Unit Set Requirements from OCO.				[7,423]						
	Unobligated balances				[−10,100]						
	MORTAR AMMUNITION										
009	60MM MORTAR, ALL TYPES		69,784		69,784		69,784				69,784
010	81MM MORTAR, ALL TYPES		36,125		38,802		36,125				36,125
	Realign APS Unit Set Requirements from OCO.				[2,677]						
011	120MM MORTAR, ALL TYPES		69,133		69,133		69,133				69,133
	TANK AMMUNITION										
012	CARTRIDGES, TANK, 105MM AND 120MM, ALL TYPES.		120,668		129,667		117,868		−2,800		117,868
	Early to need						[−2,800]		[−2,800]		
	Realign APS Unit Set Requirements from OCO.				[8,999]						
	ARTILLERY AMMUNITION										
013	ARTILLERY CARTRIDGES, 75MM & 105MM, ALL TYPES.		64,800		64,800		60,800		−3,500		61,300
	75mm blanks early to need						[−4,000]		[−3,500]		
014	ARTILLERY PROJECTILE, 155MM, ALL TYPES.		109,515		129,863		109,515				109,515
	Realign APS Unit Set Requirements from OCO.				[20,348]						
015	PROJ 155MM EXTENDED RANGE M982		39,200		39,340		39,200				39,200
	Realign APS Unit Set Requirements from OCO.				[140]						
016	ARTILLERY PROPELLANTS, FUZES AND PRIMERS, ALL.		70,881		95,536		70,881				70,881
	Realign APS Unit Set Requirements from OCO.				[24,655]						
	MINES										
017	MINES & CLEARING CHARGES, ALL TYPES.				16,866						
	Realign APS Unit Set Requirements from OCO.				[16,866]						
	NETWORKED MUNITIONS										
018	SPIDER NETWORK MUNITIONS, ALL TYPES.				10,353						
	Realign APS Unit Set Requirements from OCO.				[10,353]						
	ROCKETS										
019	SHOULDER LAUNCHED MUNITIONS, ALL TYPES.		38,000		101,210		38,000				38,000
	Realign APS Unit Set Requirements from OCO.				[63,210]						
020	ROCKET, HYDRA 70, ALL TYPES		87,213		87,213		87,213				87,213
	OTHER AMMUNITION										
021	CAD/PAD, ALL TYPES		4,914		4,914		4,914				4,914
022	DEMOLITION MUNITIONS, ALL TYPES		6,380		12,753		6,380				6,380
	Realign APS Unit Set Requirements from OCO.				[6,373]						
023	GRENADES, ALL TYPES		22,760		26,903		22,760				22,760
	Realign APS Unit Set Requirements from OCO.				[4,143]						
024	SIGNALS, ALL TYPES		10,666		12,518		10,666				10,666
	Realign APS Unit Set Requirements from OCO.				[1,852]						
025	SIMULATORS, ALL TYPES		7,412		7,412		7,412				7,412
	MISCELLANEOUS										
026	AMMO COMPONENTS, ALL TYPES		12,726		12,726		12,726				12,726
027	NON-LETHAL AMMUNITION, ALL TYPES		6,100		6,873		5,900		−200		5,900
	Early to need						[−200]		[−200]		
	Realign APS Unit Set Requirements from OCO.				[773]						

SEC. 4101. PROCUREMENT
(In Thousands of Dollars)

Line	Item	FY 2017 Request Qty	Cost	House Authorized Qty	Cost	Senate Authorized Qty	Cost	Conference Change Qty	Cost	Conference Authorized Qty	Cost
028	ITEMS LESS THAN $5 MILLION (AMMO) ..		10,006		10,006		9,506		−500		9,506
	Early to need						[−500]		[−500]		
029	AMMUNITION PECULIAR EQUIPMENT		17,275		13,575		13,575		−3,700		13,575
	Early to need				[−3,700]		[−3,700]		[−3,700]		
030	FIRST DESTINATION TRANSPORTATION (AMMO).		14,951		14,951		14,951				14,951
	PRODUCTION BASE SUPPORT										
032	INDUSTRIAL FACILITIES		222,269		242,269		222,269		20,000		242,269
	Program increase				[20,000]				[20,000]		
033	CONVENTIONAL MUNITIONS DEMILITARIZATION.		157,383		157,383		157,383				157,383
034	ARMS INITIATIVE		3,646		3,646		3,646				3,646
	TOTAL PROCUREMENT OF AMMUNITION, ARMY.		**1,513,157**		**1,731,120**		**1,485,457**		**1,646**		**1,514,803**
	OTHER PROCUREMENT, ARMY										
	TACTICAL VEHICLES										
001	TACTICAL TRAILERS/DOLLY SETS		3,733		3,733		3,733				3,733
002	SEMITRAILERS, FLATBED:		3,716		7,896		3,716				3,716
	Realign APS Unit Set Requirements from OCO.				[4,180]						
003	HI MOB MULTI-PURP WHLD VEH (HMMWV).				50,000		21,000		50,000		50,000
	HMMWV M997A3 ambulance recapitalization for Active Component.				[50,000]		[21,000]		[50,000]		
004	GROUND MOBILITY VEHICLES (GMV)		4,907		4,907		4,907				4,907
006	JOINT LIGHT TACTICAL VEHICLE	1,828	587,514	1,828	587,514	1,828	587,514			1,828	587,514
007	TRUCK, DUMP, 20T (CCE)		3,927		3,927		3,927				3,927
008	FAMILY OF MEDIUM TACTICAL VEH (FMTV).	8	53,293	8	200,769	8	53,293			8	53,293
	Realign APS Unit Set Requirements from OCO.				[147,476]						
009	FIRETRUCKS & ASSOCIATED FIREFIGHTING EQUIP.		7,460		7,460		7,460				7,460
010	FAMILY OF HEAVY TACTICAL VEHICLES (FHTV).	430	39,564	430	45,686	430	39,564			430	39,564
	Realign APS Unit Set Requirements from OCO.				[6,122]						
011	PLS ESP		11,856		118,214		11,856				11,856
	Realign APS Unit Set Requirements from OCO.				[106,358]						
012	HVY EXPANDED MOBILE TACTICAL TRUCK EXT SERV.				76,561						
	Realign APS Unit Set Requirements from OCO.				[76,561]						
013	TACTICAL WHEELED VEHICLE PROTECTION KITS.		49,751		76,870		49,751				49,751
	Realign APS Unit Set Requirements from OCO.				[27,119]						
014	MODIFICATION OF IN SVC EQUIP		64,000		57,456		52,000		−10,000		54,000
	Program reduction				[−10,000]		[−12,000]		[−10,000]		
	Realign APS Unit Set Requirements from OCO.				[3,456]						
015	MINE-RESISTANT AMBUSH-PROTECTED (MRAP) MODS.		10,611		10,611		10,611				10,611
	NON-TACTICAL VEHICLES										
016	HEAVY ARMORED SEDAN		394		394		394				394
018	NONTACTICAL VEHICLES, OTHER		1,755		1,755		1,755				1,755
	COMM—JOINT COMMUNICATIONS										
019	WIN-T—GROUND FORCES TACTICAL NETWORK.		427,598		434,170		327,598				427,598
	Ahead of need						[−100,000]				
	Realign APS Unit Set Requirements from OCO.				[6,572]						
020	SIGNAL MODERNIZATION PROGRAM		58,250		58,250		58,250				58,250
021	JOINT INCIDENT SITE COMMUNICATIONS CAPABILITY.		5,749		5,749		5,749				5,749
022	JCSE EQUIPMENT (USREDCOM)		5,068		5,068		5,068				5,068
	COMM—SATELLITE COMMUNICATIONS										

SEC. 4101. PROCUREMENT
(In Thousands of Dollars)

Line	Item	FY 2017 Request		House Authorized		Senate Authorized		Conference Change		Conference Authorized	
		Qty	Cost	Qty	Cost	Qty	Cost	Qty	Cost	Qty	Cost
023	DEFENSE ENTERPRISE WIDEBAND SATCOM SYSTEMS.		143,805		143,805		143,805				143,805
024	TRANSPORTABLE TACTICAL COMMAND COMMUNICATIONS.		36,580		36,580		36,580				36,580
025	SHF TERM		1,985		25,985		1,985				1,985
	Realign APS Unit Set Requirements from OCO.				[24,000]						
027	SMART-T (SPACE)		9,165		9,165		9,165				9,165
	COMM—C3 SYSTEM										
031	ARMY GLOBAL CMD & CONTROL SYS (AGCCS).		2,530		2,530		2,530				2,530
	COMM—COMBAT COMMUNICATIONS										
033	HANDHELD MANPACK SMALL FORM FIT (HMS).	5,656	273,645	5,656	273,645	5,656	273,645			5,656	273,645
034	MID-TIER NETWORKING VEHICULAR RADIO (MNVR).		25,017		25,017		25,017				25,017
035	RADIO TERMINAL SET, MIDS LVT(2)		12,326		12,326		12,326				12,326
037	TRACTOR DESK		2,034		2,034		2,034				2,034
038	TRACTOR RIDE		2,334		2,334		2,334				2,334
039	SPIDER APLA REMOTE CONTROL UNIT ...		1,985		1,985		1,985				1,985
040	SPIDER FAMILY OF NETWORKED MUNITIONS INCR.		10,796		10,796		10,796				10,796
042	TACTICAL COMMUNICATIONS AND PROTECTIVE SYSTEM.		3,607		3,607		3,607				3,607
043	UNIFIED COMMAND SUITE		14,295		14,295		14,295				14,295
045	FAMILY OF MED COMM FOR COMBAT CASUALTY CARE.		19,893		19,893		19,893				19,893
	COMM—INTELLIGENCE COMM										
047	CI AUTOMATION ARCHITECTURE		1,388		1,388		1,388				1,388
048	ARMY CA/MISO GPF EQUIPMENT		5,494		5,494		5,494				5,494
	INFORMATION SECURITY										
049	FAMILY OF BIOMETRICS		2,978		2,978		2,978				2,978
051	COMMUNICATIONS SECURITY (COMSEC)		131,356		133,284		131,356				131,356
	Realign APS Unit Set Requirements from OCO.				[1,928]						
052	DEFENSIVE CYBER OPERATIONS		15,132		15,132		15,132				15,132
	COMM—LONG HAUL COMMUNICATIONS										
053	BASE SUPPORT COMMUNICATIONS		27,452		27,452		27,452				27,452
	COMM—BASE COMMUNICATIONS										
054	INFORMATION SYSTEMS		122,055		122,055		122,055				122,055
055	EMERGENCY MANAGEMENT MODERNIZATION PROGRAM.	1	4,286	1	4,286	1	4,286			1	4,286
056	INSTALLATION INFO INFRASTRUCTURE MOD PROGRAM.		131,794		131,794		131,794				131,794
	ELECT EQUIP—TACT INT REL ACT (TIARA)										
059	JTT/CIBS-M		5,337		5,337		5,337				5,337
062	DCGS-A (MIP)		242,514		242,514		149,514		−24,700		217,814
	Program reduction						[−93,000]		[−24,700]		
063	JOINT TACTICAL GROUND STATION (JTAGS).		4,417		4,417		4,417				4,417
064	TROJAN (MIP)		17,455		17,615		17,455				17,455
	Realign APS Unit Set Requirements from OCO.				[160]						
065	MOD OF IN-SVC EQUIP (INTEL SPT) (MIP).		44,965		44,965		44,965				44,965
066	CI HUMINT AUTO REPRTING AND COLL(CHARCS).		7,658		7,658		7,658				7,658
067	CLOSE ACCESS TARGET RECONNAISSANCE (CATR).		7,970		7,970		7,970				7,970
068	MACHINE FOREIGN LANGUAGE TRANSLATION SYSTEM-M.		545		545		545				545
	ELECT EQUIP—ELECTRONIC WARFARE (EW)										
070	LIGHTWEIGHT COUNTER MORTAR RADAR		74,038		99,930		61,538		−5,585		68,453
	Realign APS Unit Set Requirements from OCO.				[25,892]						
	Unit cost growth						[−12,500]		[−5,585]		
071	EW PLANNING & MANAGEMENT TOOLS (EWPMT).		3,235		3,235		3,235				3,235
072	AIR VIGILANCE (AV)		733		733		733				733

SEC. 4101. PROCUREMENT
(In Thousands of Dollars)

Line	Item	FY 2017 Request		House Authorized		Senate Authorized		Conference Change		Conference Authorized	
		Qty	Cost	Qty	Cost	Qty	Cost	Qty	Cost	Qty	Cost
074	FAMILY OF PERSISTENT SURVEILLANCE CAPABILITIE.		1,740		1,740		1,740				1,740
075	COUNTERINTELLIGENCE/SECURITY COUNTERMEASURES.		455		455		455				455
076	CI MODERNIZATION		176		176		176				176
	ELECT EQUIP—TACTICAL SURV. (TAC SURV)										
077	SENTINEL MODS		40,171		40,171		40,171				40,171
078	NIGHT VISION DEVICES		163,029		163,029		163,029				163,029
079	SMALL TACTICAL OPTICAL RIFLE MOUNTED MLRF.		15,885		15,885		15,885				15,885
080	INDIRECT FIRE PROTECTION FAMILY OF SYSTEMS.		48,427		52,697		48,427				48,427
	Realign APS Unit Set Requirements from OCO.				[4,270]						
081	FAMILY OF WEAPON SIGHTS (FWS)		55,536		55,536		55,536				55,536
082	ARTILLERY ACCURACY EQUIP		4,187		4,187		4,187				4,187
085	JOINT BATTLE COMMAND—PLATFORM (JBC-P).		137,501		137,501		137,501				137,501
086	JOINT EFFECTS TARGETING SYSTEM (JETS).		50,726		50,726		50,726				50,726
087	MOD OF IN-SVC EQUIP (LLDR)		28,058		28,058		21,558				28,058
	Reduce to FY16 levels						[−6,500]				
088	COMPUTER BALLISTICS: LHMBC XM32 ...		5,924		5,924		5,924				5,924
089	MORTAR FIRE CONTROL SYSTEM		22,331		22,621		22,331				22,331
	Realign APS Unit Set Requirements from OCO.				[290]						
090	COUNTERFIRE RADARS		314,509		281,509		278,509		−33,000		281,509
	Unit cost savings				[−33,000]		[−36,000]		[−33,000]		
	ELECT EQUIP—TACTICAL C2 SYSTEMS										
091	FIRE SUPPORT C2 FAMILY		8,660		8,660		8,660				8,660
092	AIR & MSL DEFENSE PLANNING & CONTROL SYS.		54,376		124,334		54,376				54,376
	Realign APS Unit Set Requirements from OCO.				[69,958]						
093	IAMD BATTLE COMMAND SYSTEM		204,969		204,969		204,969				204,969
094	LIFE CYCLE SOFTWARE SUPPORT (LCSS)		4,718		4,718		4,718				4,718
095	NETWORK MANAGEMENT INITIALIZATION AND SERVICE.		11,063		11,063		11,063				11,063
096	MANEUVER CONTROL SYSTEM (MCS)		151,318		151,318		124,318				151,318
	Reduce to FY16 level						[−27,000]				
097	GLOBAL COMBAT SUPPORT SYSTEM-ARMY (GCSS-A).		155,660		155,660		155,660				155,660
098	INTEGRATED PERSONNEL AND PAY SYSTEM-ARMY (IPP.		4,214		4,214		4,214				4,214
099	RECONNAISSANCE AND SURVEYING INSTRUMENT SET.		16,185		16,185		16,185				16,185
100	MOD OF IN-SVC EQUIPMENT (ENFIRE) ...		1,565		1,565		1,565				1,565
	ELECT EQUIP—AUTOMATION										
101	ARMY TRAINING MODERNIZATION		17,693		17,693		17,693				17,693
102	AUTOMATED DATA PROCESSING EQUIP ..		107,960		107,960		98,560				107,960
	Program reduction						[−9,400]				
103	GENERAL FUND ENTERPRISE BUSINESS SYSTEMS FAM.		6,416		6,416		6,416				6,416
104	HIGH PERF COMPUTING MOD PGM (HPCMP).		58,614		58,614		58,614				58,614
105	CONTRACT WRITING SYSTEM		986		986						986
	Contract writing unjustified requirement.						[−986]				
106	RESERVE COMPONENT AUTOMATION SYS (RCAS).		23,828		23,828		23,828				23,828
	ELECT EQUIP—AUDIO VISUAL SYS (A/V)										
107	TACTICAL DIGITAL MEDIA		1,191		1,191		1,191				1,191
108	ITEMS LESS THAN $5M (SURVEYING EQUIPMENT).		1,995		2,091		1,995				1,995
	Realign APS Unit Set Requirements from OCO.				[96]						
	ELECT EQUIP—SUPPORT										
109	PRODUCTION BASE SUPPORT (C-E)		403		403		403				403
	CLASSIFIED PROGRAMS										
110A	CLASSIFIED PROGRAMS		4,436		4,436		4,436				4,436

SEC. 4101. PROCUREMENT
(In Thousands of Dollars)

Line	Item	FY 2017 Request		House Authorized		Senate Authorized		Conference Change		Conference Authorized	
		Qty	Cost	Qty	Cost	Qty	Cost	Qty	Cost	Qty	Cost
	CHEMICAL DEFENSIVE EQUIPMENT										
111	PROTECTIVE SYSTEMS		2,966		2,966		2,966				2,966
112	FAMILY OF NON-LETHAL EQUIPMENT (FNLE).		9,795		9,795		9,795				9,795
114	CBRN DEFENSE		17,922		19,763		17,922				17,922
	Realign APS Unit Set Requirements from OCO.				[1,841]						
	BRIDGING EQUIPMENT										
115	TACTICAL BRIDGING		13,553		39,553		13,553				13,553
	Realign APS Unit Set Requirements from OCO.				[26,000]						
116	TACTICAL BRIDGE, FLOAT-RIBBON		25,244		25,244		25,244				25,244
117	BRIDGE SUPPLEMENTAL SET		983		983		983				983
118	COMMON BRIDGE TRANSPORTER (CBT) RECAP.		25,176		25,176		25,176				25,176
	ENGINEER (NON-CONSTRUCTION) EQUIPMENT										
119	GRND STANDOFF MINE DETECTN SYSM (GSTAMIDS).		39,350		39,350		39,350				39,350
120	AREA MINE DETECTION SYSTEM (AMDS)		10,500		10,500		10,500				10,500
121	HUSKY MOUNTED DETECTION SYSTEM (HMDS).		274		274		274				274
122	ROBOTIC COMBAT SUPPORT SYSTEM (RCSS).		2,951		2,951		2,951				2,951
123	EOD ROBOTICS SYSTEMS RECAPITALIZATION.		1,949		1,949		1,949				1,949
124	ROBOTICS AND APPLIQUE SYSTEMS		5,203		5,471		5,203				5,203
	Realign APS Unit Set Requirements from OCO.				[268]						
125	EXPLOSIVE ORDNANCE DISPOSAL EQPMT (EOD EQPMT).		5,570		5,570		5,570				5,570
126	REMOTE DEMOLITION SYSTEMS		6,238		6,238		6,238				6,238
127	< $5M, COUNTERMINE EQUIPMENT		836		836		836				836
128	FAMILY OF BOATS AND MOTORS		3,171		3,451		3,171				3,171
	Realign APS Unit Set Requirements from OCO.				[280]						
	COMBAT SERVICE SUPPORT EQUIPMENT										
129	HEATERS AND ECU'S		18,707		19,601		18,707				18,707
	Realign APS Unit Set Requirements from OCO.				[894]						
130	SOLDIER ENHANCEMENT		2,112		2,112		2,112				2,112
131	PERSONNEL RECOVERY SUPPORT SYSTEM (PRSS).		10,856		10,856		10,856				10,856
132	GROUND SOLDIER SYSTEM		32,419		32,419		32,419				32,419
133	MOBILE SOLDIER POWER		30,014		30,014		30,014				30,014
135	FIELD FEEDING EQUIPMENT		12,544		15,209		12,544				12,544
	Realign APS Unit Set Requirements from OCO.				[2,665]						
136	CARGO AERIAL DEL & PERSONNEL PARACHUTE SYSTEM.		18,509		18,509		18,509				18,509
137	FAMILY OF ENGR COMBAT AND CONSTRUCTION SETS.		29,384		39,173		29,384				29,384
	Realign APS Unit Set Requirements from OCO.				[9,789]						
138	ITEMS LESS THAN $5M (ENG SPT)				300						
	Realign APS Unit Set Requirements from OCO.				[300]						
	PETROLEUM EQUIPMENT										
139	QUALITY SURVEILLANCE EQUIPMENT		4,487		9,287		4,487				4,487
	Realign APS Unit Set Requirements from OCO.				[4,800]						
140	DISTRIBUTION SYSTEMS, PETROLEUM & WATER.		42,656		63,476		32,656		−7,000		35,656
	Program decrease						[−10,000]		[−7,000]		
	Realign APS Unit Set Requirements from OCO.				[20,820]						
	MEDICAL EQUIPMENT										
141	COMBAT SUPPORT MEDICAL		59,761		65,524		59,761				59,761
	Realign APS Unit Set Requirements from OCO.				[5,763]						
	MAINTENANCE EQUIPMENT										

SEC. 4101. PROCUREMENT
(In Thousands of Dollars)

Line	Item	FY 2017 Request		House Authorized		Senate Authorized		Conference Change		Conference Authorized	
		Qty	Cost	Qty	Cost	Qty	Cost	Qty	Cost	Qty	Cost
142	MOBILE MAINTENANCE EQUIPMENT SYSTEMS.		35,694		33,803		30,694		−3,500		32,194
	Program reduction				[−3,500]		[−5,000]		[−3,500]		
	Realign APS Unit Set Requirements from OCO.				[1,609]						
143	ITEMS LESS THAN $5.0M (MAINT EQ)		2,716		2,861		2,716				2,716
	Realign APS Unit Set Requirements from OCO.				[145]						
	CONSTRUCTION EQUIPMENT										
144	GRADER, ROAD MTZD, HVY, 6X4 (CCE)		1,742		4,789		1,742				1,742
	Realign APS Unit Set Requirements from OCO.				[3,047]						
145	SCRAPERS, EARTHMOVING		26,233		26,233		26,233				26,233
147	HYDRAULIC EXCAVATOR		1,123		1,123		1,123				1,123
148	TRACTOR, FULL TRACKED				4,426						
	Realign APS Unit Set Requirements from OCO.				[4,426]						
149	ALL TERRAIN CRANES		65,285		65,285		65,285				65,285
151	HIGH MOBILITY ENGINEER EXCAVATOR (HMEE).		1,743		4,643		1,743				1,743
	Realign APS Unit Set Requirements from OCO.				[2,900]						
152	ENHANCED RAPID AIRFIELD CONSTRUCTION CAPAP.		2,779		2,779		2,779				2,779
154	CONST EQUIP ESP		26,712		23,212		22,212		−4,500		22,212
	Program reduction				[−3,500]		[−4,500]		[−4,500]		
155	ITEMS LESS THAN $5.0M (CONST EQUIP)		6,649		6,745		6,649				6,649
	Realign APS Unit Set Requirements from OCO.				[96]						
	RAIL FLOAT CONTAINERIZATION EQUIPMENT										
156	ARMY WATERCRAFT ESP		21,860		16,860		10,860				21,860
	Program reduction				[−5,000]		[−11,000]				
157	ITEMS LESS THAN $5.0M (FLOAT/RAIL)		1,967		1,967		1,967				1,967
	GENERATORS										
158	GENERATORS AND ASSOCIATED EQUIP		113,266		125,727		113,266				113,266
	Program decrease				[−7,500]						
	Realign APS Unit Set Requirements from OCO.				[19,961]						
159	TACTICAL ELECTRIC POWER RECAPITALIZATION.		7,867		7,867		7,867				7,867
	MATERIAL HANDLING EQUIPMENT										
160	FAMILY OF FORKLIFTS		2,307		3,153		2,307				2,307
	Realign APS Unit Set Requirements from OCO.				[846]						
	TRAINING EQUIPMENT										
161	COMBAT TRAINING CENTERS SUPPORT		75,359		75,359		75,359				75,359
162	TRAINING DEVICES, NONSYSTEM		253,050		253,050		253,050				253,050
163	CLOSE COMBAT TACTICAL TRAINER		48,271		48,271		48,271				48,271
164	AVIATION COMBINED ARMS TACTICAL TRAINER.		40,000		40,000		40,000				40,000
165	GAMING TECHNOLOGY IN SUPPORT OF ARMY TRAINING.		11,543		11,543		11,543				11,543
	TEST MEASURE AND DIG EQUIPMENT (TMD)										
166	CALIBRATION SETS EQUIPMENT		4,963		4,963		4,963				4,963
167	INTEGRATED FAMILY OF TEST EQUIPMENT (IFTE).		29,781		29,781		29,781				29,781
168	TEST EQUIPMENT MODERNIZATION (TEMOD).		6,342		7,482		6,342				6,342
	Realign APS Unit Set Requirements from OCO.				[1,140]						
	OTHER SUPPORT EQUIPMENT										
169	M25 STABILIZED BINOCULAR		3,149		3,149		3,149				3,149
170	RAPID EQUIPPING SOLDIER SUPPORT EQUIPMENT.		18,003		18,003		18,003				18,003
171	PHYSICAL SECURITY SYSTEMS (OPA3)		44,082		44,082		44,082				44,082
172	BASE LEVEL COMMON EQUIPMENT		2,168		2,168		2,168				2,168
173	MODIFICATION OF IN-SVC EQUIPMENT (OPA-3).		67,367		67,367		62,367				67,367
	Reduce to FY16 level						[−5,000]				

SEC. 4101. PROCUREMENT
(In Thousands of Dollars)

Line	Item	FY 2017 Request		House Authorized		Senate Authorized		Conference Change		Conference Authorized	
		Qty	Cost	Qty	Cost	Qty	Cost	Qty	Cost	Qty	Cost
174	PRODUCTION BASE SUPPORT (OTH)		1,528		1,528		1,528				1,528
175	SPECIAL EQUIPMENT FOR USER TESTING		8,289		8,289		8,289				8,289
177	TRACTOR YARD		6,888		6,888		6,888				6,888
	OPA2										
179	INITIAL SPARES—C&E		27,243		27,243		27,243				27,243
	TOTAL OTHER PROCUREMENT, ARMY.	7,923	5,873,949	7,923	6,473,477	7,923	5,562,063		−38,285	7,923	5,835,664
	AIRCRAFT PROCUREMENT, NAVY										
	COMBAT AIRCRAFT										
003	JOINT STRIKE FIGHTER CV	4	890,650	4	890,650	4	890,650			4	890,650
004	ADVANCE PROCUREMENT (CY)		80,908		80,908		80,908				80,908
005	JSF STOVL	16	2,037,768	16	2,037,768	16	2,037,768			16	2,037,768
006	ADVANCE PROCUREMENT (CY)		233,648		233,648		233,648				233,648
007	CH–53K (HEAVY LIFT)	2	348,615	2	348,615	2	348,615			2	348,615
008	ADVANCE PROCUREMENT (CY)		88,365		88,365		88,365				88,365
009	V–22 (MEDIUM LIFT)	16	1,264,134	16	1,264,134	16	1,264,134		−15,000	16	1,249,134
	Support cost growth								[−15,000]		
010	ADVANCE PROCUREMENT (CY)		19,674		19,674		19,674				19,674
011	H–1 UPGRADES (UH–1Y/AH–1Z)	24	759,778	24	759,778	24	759,778		−3,192	24	756,586
	Airframe unit cost growth								[−3,192]		
012	ADVANCE PROCUREMENT (CY)		57,232		57,232		57,232				57,232
014	MH–60R (MYP)		61,177		26,177		61,177		−8,000		53,177
	Line shutdown costs—early to need.				[−35,000]				[−8,000]		
016	P–8A POSEIDON	11	1,940,238	11	1,940,238	11	1,940,238		−77,000	11	1,863,238
	Airframe unit cost growth								[−77,000]		
017	ADVANCE PROCUREMENT (CY)		123,140		123,140		123,140				123,140
018	E–2D ADV HAWKEYE	6	916,483	6	916,483	6	916,483			6	916,483
019	ADVANCE PROCUREMENT (CY)		125,042		125,042		125,042				125,042
	TRAINER AIRCRAFT										
020	JPATS		5,849		5,849		5,849				5,849
	OTHER AIRCRAFT										
021	KC–130J	2	128,870	2	128,870	2	128,870			2	128,870
022	ADVANCE PROCUREMENT (CY)		24,848		24,848		24,848				24,848
023	MQ–4 TRITON	2	409,005	2	409,005	2	409,005		−12,880	2	396,125
	Unit cost savings								[−12,880]		
024	ADVANCE PROCUREMENT (CY)		55,652		55,652		55,652				55,652
025	MQ–8 UAV	1	72,435	1	72,435	1	72,435			1	72,435
	MODIFICATION OF AIRCRAFT										
029	AEA SYSTEMS		51,900		51,900		51,900				51,900
030	AV–8 SERIES		60,818		60,818		60,818				60,818
031	ADVERSARY		5,191		5,191		5,191				5,191
032	F–18 SERIES		1,023,492		986,192		1,023,492		−37,300		986,192
	Unobligated balances				[−37,300]				[−37,300]		
034	H–53 SERIES		46,095		46,095		46,095				46,095
035	SH–60 SERIES		108,328		108,328		108,328				108,328
036	H–1 SERIES		46,333		46,333		46,333				46,333
037	EP–3 SERIES		14,681		14,681		14,681				14,681
038	P–3 SERIES		2,781		2,781		2,781				2,781
039	E–2 SERIES		32,949		32,949		32,949				32,949
040	TRAINER A/C SERIES		13,199		13,199		13,199				13,199
041	C–2A		19,066		19,066		19,066				19,066
042	C–130 SERIES		61,788		61,788		61,788		−2,000		59,788
	Training equipment unjustified growth (OSIP 022–07).								[−2,000]		
043	FEWSG		618		618		618				618
044	CARGO/TRANSPORT A/C SERIES		9,822		9,822		9,822				9,822
045	E–6 SERIES		222,077		222,077		222,077				222,077
046	EXECUTIVE HELICOPTERS SERIES		66,835		66,835		66,835				66,835
047	SPECIAL PROJECT AIRCRAFT		16,497		16,497		16,497				16,497
048	T–45 SERIES		114,887		114,887		114,887				114,887
049	POWER PLANT CHANGES		16,893		16,893		16,893		−2,000		14,893
	Excess support growth								[−2,000]		
050	JPATS SERIES		17,401		17,401		17,401				17,401
051	COMMON ECM EQUIPMENT		143,773		143,773		143,773				143,773
052	COMMON AVIONICS CHANGES		164,839		164,839		164,839				164,839
053	COMMON DEFENSIVE WEAPON SYSTEM		4,403		4,403		4,403				4,403
054	ID SYSTEMS		45,768		45,768		45,768				45,768

SEC. 4101. PROCUREMENT
(In Thousands of Dollars)

Line	Item	FY 2017 Request		House Authorized		Senate Authorized		Conference Change		Conference Authorized	
		Qty	Cost	Qty	Cost	Qty	Cost	Qty	Cost	Qty	Cost
055	P–8 SERIES		18,836		18,836		18,836				18,836
056	MAGTF EW FOR AVIATION		5,676		5,676		5,676				5,676
057	MQ–8 SERIES		19,003		19,003		19,003				19,003
058	RQ–7 SERIES		3,534		3,534		3,534				3,534
059	V–22 (TILT/ROTOR ACFT) OSPREY		141,545		141,545		141,545				141,545
060	F–35 STOVL SERIES		34,928		34,928		34,928				34,928
061	F–35 CV SERIFS		26,004		26,004		26,004				26,004
062	QRC		5,476		5,476		5,476				5,476
	AIRCRAFT SPARES AND REPAIR PARTS										
063	SPARES AND REPAIR PARTS		1,407,626		1,407,626		1,458,426				1,407,626
	F–35B spares unfunded requirement.						[50,800]				
	AIRCRAFT SUPPORT EQUIP & FACILITIES										
064	COMMON GROUND EQUIPMENT		390,103		370,103		390,103				390,103
	Program decrease				[–20,000]						
065	AIRCRAFT INDUSTRIAL FACILITIES		23,194		23,194		23,194				23,194
066	WAR CONSUMABLES		40,613		40,613		40,613				40,613
067	OTHER PRODUCTION CHARGES		860		860		860				860
068	SPECIAL SUPPORT EQUIPMENT		36,282		36,282		36,282				36,282
069	FIRST DESTINATION TRANSPORTATION		1,523		1,523		1,523				1,523
	TOTAL AIRCRAFT PROCUREMENT, NAVY.	84	**14,109,148**	84	**14,016,848**	84	**14,159,948**		**–157,372**	84	**13,951,776**
	WEAPONS PROCUREMENT, NAVY										
	MODIFICATION OF MISSILES										
001	TRIDENT II MODS		1,103,086		1,103,086		1,103,086				1,103,086
	SUPPORT EQUIPMENT & FACILITIES										
002	MISSILE INDUSTRIAL FACILITIES		6,776		6,776		6,776				6,776
	STRATEGIC MISSILES										
003	TOMAHAWK	100	186,905	100	186,905	196	271,105		–7,000	100	179,905
	Program increase					[96]	[84,200]				
	Tomahawk unit cost growth								[–7,000]		
	TACTICAL MISSILES										
004	AMRAAM	163	204,697	163	204,697	163	204,697		–7,250	163	197,447
	Unit cost growth								[–7,250]		
005	SIDEWINDER	152	70,912	152	70,912	152	70,912			152	70,912
006	JSOW		2,232		2,232		2,232				2,232
007	STANDARD MISSILE	125	501,212	125	501,212	125	501,212		–3,244	125	497,968
	Diminishing manufacturing sources excess growth.								[–3,244]		
008	RAM	90	71,557	90	71,557	90	71,557			90	71,557
009	JOINT AIR GROUND MISSILE (JAGM)	96	26,200	96	26,200	96	26,200		–4,278	96	21,922
	Unit cost savings								[–4,278]		
012	STAND OFF PRECISION GUIDED MUNITIONS (SOPGM).	24	3,316	24	3,316	24	3,316			24	3,316
013	AERIAL TARGETS		137,484		137,484		137,484				137,484
014	OTHER MISSILE SUPPORT		3,248		3,248		3,248				3,248
015	LRASM	10	29,643	10	29,643	10	29,643			10	29,643
	MODIFICATION OF MISSILES										
016	ESSM	75	52,935	75	52,935	75	52,935			75	52,935
018	HARM MODS		178,213		178,213		148,213				178,213
	Advanced Anti-Radiation Guided Missile production issues.						[–30,000]				
019	STANDARD MISSILES MODS		8,164		8,164		8,164				8,164
	SUPPORT EQUIPMENT & FACILITIES										
020	WEAPONS INDUSTRIAL FACILITIES		1,964		1,964		1,964				1,964
021	FLEET SATELLITE COMM FOLLOW-ON		36,723		36,723		36,723				36,723
	ORDNANCE SUPPORT EQUIPMENT										
022	ORDNANCE SUPPORT EQUIPMENT		59,096		59,096		66,066				59,096
	Program increase						[6,970]				
	TORPEDOES AND RELATED EQUIP										
023	SSTD		5,910		5,910		5,910				5,910
024	MK–48 TORPEDO	11	44,537	11	44,537	11	44,537			11	44,537
025	ASW TARGETS		9,302		9,302		9,302				9,302
	MOD OF TORPEDOES AND RELATED EQUIP										
026	MK–54 TORPEDO MODS		98,092		98,092		98,092				98,092
027	MK–48 TORPEDO ADCAP MODS		46,139		46,139		46,139				46,139

SEC. 4101. PROCUREMENT
(In Thousands of Dollars)

Line	Item	FY 2017 Request		House Authorized		Senate Authorized		Conference Change		Conference Authorized	
		Qty	Cost	Qty	Cost	Qty	Cost	Qty	Cost	Qty	Cost
028	QUICKSTRIKE MINE		1,236		1,236		1,236				1,236
	SUPPORT EQUIPMENT										
029	TORPEDO SUPPORT EQUIPMENT		60,061		60,061		60,061				60,061
030	ASW RANGE SUPPORT		3,706		3,706		3,706				3,706
	DESTINATION TRANSPORTATION										
031	FIRST DESTINATION TRANSPORTATION		3,804		3,804		3,804				3,804
	GUNS AND GUN MOUNTS										
032	SMALL ARMS AND WEAPONS		18,002		18,002		18,002				18,002
	MODIFICATION OF GUNS AND GUN MOUNTS										
033	CIWS MODS		50,900		50,900		50,900				50,900
034	COAST GUARD WEAPONS		25,295		25,295		25,295				25,295
035	GUN MOUNT MODS		77,003		77,003		77,003				77,003
036	LCS MODULE WEAPONS	24	2,776	24	2,776	24	2,776			24	2,776
038	AIRBORNE MINE NEUTRALIZATION SYSTEMS.		15,753		15,753		15,753				15,753
	SPARES AND REPAIR PARTS										
040	SPARES AND REPAIR PARTS		62,383		62,383		62,383				62,383
	TOTAL WEAPONS PROCUREMENT, NAVY.	870	3,209,262	870	3,209,262	966	3,270,432		−21,772	870	3,187,490
	PROCUREMENT OF AMMO, NAVY & MC										
	NAVY AMMUNITION										
001	GENERAL PURPOSE BOMBS		91,659		91,659		91,659				91,659
002	AIRBORNE ROCKETS, ALL TYPES		65,759		65,759		65,759				65,759
003	MACHINE GUN AMMUNITION		8,152		8,152		8,152				8,152
004	PRACTICE BOMBS		41,873		41,873		41,873				41,873
005	CARTRIDGES & CART ACTUATED DEVICES.		54,002		54,002		54,002				54,002
006	AIR EXPENDABLE COUNTERMEASURES		57,034		57,034		57,034				57,034
007	JATOS		2,735		2,735		2,735				2,735
009	5 INCH/54 GUN AMMUNITION		19,220		19,220		19,220				19,220
010	INTERMEDIATE CALIBER GUN AMMUNITION.		30,196		30,196		30,196				30,196
011	OTHER SHIP GUN AMMUNITION		39,009		39,009		39,009				39,009
012	SMALL ARMS & LANDING PARTY AMMO		46,727		46,727		46,727				46,727
013	PYROTECHNIC AND DEMOLITION		9,806		9,806		9,806				9,806
014	AMMUNITION LESS THAN $5 MILLION		2,900		2,900		2,900				2,900
	MARINE CORPS AMMUNITION										
015	SMALL ARMS AMMUNITION		27,958		27,958		27,958				27,958
017	40 MM, ALL TYPES		14,758		14,758		14,758				14,758
018	60MM, ALL TYPES		992		992		992				992
020	120MM, ALL TYPES		16,757		16,757		12,757		−4,600		12,157
	120mm early to need						[−4,000]		[−4,600]		
021	GRENADES, ALL TYPES		972		972		972				972
022	ROCKETS, ALL TYPES		14,186		14,186		14,186				14,186
023	ARTILLERY, ALL TYPES		68,656		68,656		68,656				68,656
024	DEMOLITION MUNITIONS, ALL TYPES		1,700		1,700		1,700				1,700
025	FUZE, ALL TYPES		26,088		26,088		26,088				26,088
027	AMMO MODERNIZATION		14,660		14,660		14,660				14,660
028	ITEMS LESS THAN $5 MILLION		8,569		8,569		6,069		−2,500		6,069
	Early to need						[−2,500]		[−2,500]		
	TOTAL PROCUREMENT OF AMMO, NAVY & MC.		664,368		664,368		657,868		−7,100		657,268
	SHIPBUILDING AND CONVERSION, NAVY										
	FLEET BALLISTIC MISSILE SHIPS										
001	OHIO REPLACEMENT SUBMARINE ADVANCE PROCUREMENT.		773,138				773,138				773,138
	Transfer to Title XIV National Sea-Based Deterrence Fund.				[−773,138]						
	OTHER WARSHIPS										
002	CARRIER REPLACEMENT PROGRAM		1,291,783		1,291,783		1,291,783				1,291,783
003	ADVANCE PROCUREMENT (CY)		1,370,784		1,370,784		1,370,784				1,370,784
004	VIRGINIA CLASS SUBMARINE	2	3,187,985	2	3,187,985	2	3,187,985			2	3,187,985
005	ADVANCE PROCUREMENT (CY)		1,767,234		1,767,234		1,767,234		85,000		1,852,234
	Long-lead Time Materiel Orders for Virginia Class.								[85,000]		
006	CVN REFUELING OVERHAULS		1,743,220		1,743,220		1,743,220				1,743,220
007	ADVANCE PROCUREMENT (CY)		248,599		248,599		248,599				248,599

SEC. 4101. PROCUREMENT
(In Thousands of Dollars)

Line	Item	FY 2017 Request		House Authorized		Senate Authorized		Conference Change		Conference Authorized	
		Qty	Cost	Qty	Cost	Qty	Cost	Qty	Cost	Qty	Cost
008	DDG 1000		271,756		271,756		271,756				271,756
009	DDG–51	2	3,211,292	2	3,211,292	2	3,261,092		49,800	2	3,261,092
	Fund additional FY16 destroyer						[49,800]		[49,800]		
011	LITTORAL COMBAT SHIP	2	1,125,625	2	1,125,625	2	1,097,625		–28,000	2	1,097,625
	Unjustified growth						[–28,000]		[–28,000]		
	AMPHIBIOUS SHIPS										
012A	AMPHIBIOUS SHIP REPLACEMENT LX(R)								440,000		440,000
	Procurement of LPD–29 or LX (R)								[440,000]		
013	AMPHIBIOUS SHIP REPLACEMENT LX(R) ADVANCE PROCUREMENT.						50,000				
	Advanced procurement for LX (R)						[50,000]				
016	LHA REPLACEMENT	1	1,623,024	1	1,623,024	1	1,623,024			1	1,623,024
	AUXILIARIES, CRAFT AND PRIOR YR PROGRAM COST										
020	ADVANCE PROCUREMENT (CY)		73,079		73,079		73,079				73,079
022	MOORED TRAINING SHIP	1	624,527	1	624,527	1	624,527			1	624,527
025	OUTFITTING		666,158		666,158		666,158		–21,104		645,054
	Outfitting and post delivery funds early to need.								[–21,104]		
026	SHIP TO SHORE CONNECTOR	2	128,067	2	128,067	2	128,067			2	128,067
027	SERVICE CRAFT		65,192		65,192		65,192				65,192
028	LCAC SLEP		1,774		1,774		1,774				1,774
029	YP CRAFT MAINTENANCE/ROH/SLEP		21,363		21,363		21,363				21,363
030	COMPLETION OF PY SHIPBUILDING PROGRAMS.		160,274		160,274		160,274				160,274
	TOTAL SHIPBUILDING AND CONVERSION, NAVY.	**10**	**18,354,874**	**10**	**17,581,736**	**10**	**18,426,674**		**525,696**	**10**	**18,880,570**
	OTHER PROCUREMENT, NAVY										
	SHIP PROPULSION EQUIPMENT										
003	SURFACE POWER EQUIPMENT		15,514		15,514		15,514				15,514
004	HYBRID ELECTRIC DRIVE (HED)		40,132		40,132		40,132		–850		39,282
	Installation early to need								[–850]		
	GENERATORS										
005	SURFACE COMBATANT HM&E		29,974		29,974		29,974				29,974
	NAVIGATION EQUIPMENT										
006	OTHER NAVIGATION EQUIPMENT		63,942		63,942		63,942				63,942
	OTHER SHIPBOARD EQUIPMENT										
008	SUB PERISCOPE, IMAGING AND SUPT EQUIP PROG.		136,421		136,421		136,421				136,421
009	DDG MOD		367,766		367,766		432,766				367,766
	BMD upgrade unfunded requirement.						[65,000]				
010	FIREFIGHTING EQUIPMENT		14,743		14,743		14,743				14,743
011	COMMAND AND CONTROL SWITCHBOARD		2,140		2,140		2,140				2,140
012	LHA/LHD MIDLIFE		24,939		24,939		24,939				24,939
014	POLLUTION CONTROL EQUIPMENT		20,191		20,191		20,191		–849		19,342
	HF062 lightering systems unit cost growth.								[–849]		
015	SUBMARINE SUPPORT EQUIPMENT		8,995		8,995		8,995				8,995
016	VIRGINIA CLASS SUPPORT EQUIPMENT ...		66,838		66,838		66,838				66,838
017	LCS CLASS SUPPORT EQUIPMENT		54,823		54,823		54,823				54,823
018	SUBMARINE BATTERIES		23,359		23,359		23,359				23,359
019	LPD CLASS SUPPORT EQUIPMENT		40,321		40,321		40,321				40,321
020	DDG 1000 CLASS SUPPORT EQUIPMENT		33,404		33,404		33,404				33,404
021	STRATEGIC PLATFORM SUPPORT EQUIP		15,836		15,836		15,836				15,836
022	DSSP EQUIPMENT		806		806		806				806
024	LCAC		3,090		3,090		3,090				3,090
025	UNDERWATER EOD PROGRAMS		24,350		24,350		24,350				24,350
026	ITEMS LESS THAN $5 MILLION		88,719		88,719		88,719		–1,820		86,899
	LSD boat davit kit cost growth								[–993]		
	Propellers and shafts unit cost growth.								[–827]		
027	CHEMICAL WARFARE DETECTORS		2,873		2,873		2,873				2,873
028	SUBMARINE LIFE SUPPORT SYSTEM		6,043		6,043		6,043				6,043
	REACTOR PLANT EQUIPMENT										
030	REACTOR COMPONENTS		342,158		342,158		342,158				342,158
	OCEAN ENGINEERING										
031	DIVING AND SALVAGE EQUIPMENT		8,973		8,973		8,973				8,973
	SMALL BOATS										

SEC. 4101. PROCUREMENT
(In Thousands of Dollars)

Line	Item	FY 2017 Request		House Authorized		Senate Authorized		Conference Change		Conference Authorized	
		Qty	Cost	Qty	Cost	Qty	Cost	Qty	Cost	Qty	Cost
032	STANDARD BOATS		43,684		43,684		43,684				43,684
	PRODUCTION FACILITIES EQUIPMENT										
034	OPERATING FORCES IPE		75,421		75,421		75,421				75,421
	OTHER SHIP SUPPORT										
035	NUCLEAR ALTERATIONS		172,718		172,718		172,718				172,718
036	LCS COMMON MISSION MODULES EQUIPMENT.		27,840		17,840		24,140		−10,000		17,840
	RMMV program restructure				[−10,000]		[−3,700]		[−10,000]		
037	LCS MCM MISSION MODULES		57,146		20,746		57,146				57,146
	RMMV program restructure				[−36,400]						
038	LCS ASW MISSION MODULES		31,952		21,952		31,952		−10,000		21,952
	Early to need				[−10,000]				[−10,000]		
039	LCS SUW MISSION MODULES		22,466		22,466		22,466		−1,402		21,064
	MK–46 gun weapon system contract delays.								[−1,402]		
	LOGISTIC SUPPORT										
041	LSD MIDLIFE		10,813		10,813		10,813				10,813
	SHIP SONARS										
042	SPQ–9B RADAR		14,363		14,363		14,363				14,363
043	AN/SQQ–89 SURF ASW COMBAT SYSTEM		90,029		90,029		90,029				90,029
045	SSN ACOUSTIC EQUIPMENT		248,765		248,765		248,765				248,765
046	UNDERSEA WARFARE SUPPORT EQUIPMENT.		7,163		7,163		7,163				7,163
	ASW ELECTRONIC EQUIPMENT										
048	SUBMARINE ACOUSTIC WARFARE SYSTEM.		21,291		21,291		21,291				21,291
049	SSTD		6,893		6,893		6,893				6,893
050	FIXED SURVEILLANCE SYSTEM		145,701		145,701		145,701				145,701
051	SURTASS		36,136		36,136	1	46,136				36,136
	Additional SURTASS array unfunded requirement.					[1]	[10,000]				
	ELECTRONIC WARFARE EQUIPMENT										
053	AN/SLQ–32		274,892		274,892	1	297,892		−8,251		266,641
	Additional SEWIP Blk 3 unfunded requirement.					[1]	[23,000]				
	Block 3 excess support								[−4,270]		
	Block 3T excess support								[−1,000]		
	Block 3T installation prior year carryover.								[−2,981]		
	RECONNAISSANCE EQUIPMENT										
054	SHIPBOARD IW EXPLOIT		170,733		170,733		170,733				170,733
055	AUTOMATED IDENTIFICATION SYSTEM (AIS).		958		958		958				958
	OTHER SHIP ELECTRONIC EQUIPMENT										
057	COOPERATIVE ENGAGEMENT CAPABILITY		22,034		22,034		22,034				22,034
059	NAVAL TACTICAL COMMAND SUPPORT SYSTEM (NTCSS).		12,336		12,336		12,336				12,336
060	ATDLS		30,105		30,105		30,105				30,105
061	NAVY COMMAND AND CONTROL SYSTEM (NCCS).		4,556		4,556		4,556				4,556
062	MINESWEEPING SYSTEM REPLACEMENT		56,675		56,675		32,175		−24,477		32,198
	Ahead of need						[−24,500]		[−24,477]		
063	SHALLOW WATER MCM		8,875		8,875		8,875				8,875
064	NAVSTAR GPS RECEIVERS (SPACE)		12,752		12,752		12,752				12,752
065	AMERICAN FORCES RADIO AND TV SERVICE.		4,577		4,577		4,577				4,577
066	STRATEGIC PLATFORM SUPPORT EQUIP		8,972		8,972		8,972				8,972
	AVIATION ELECTRONIC EQUIPMENT										
069	ASHORE ATC EQUIPMENT		75,068		75,068		75,068				75,068
070	AFLOAT ATC EQUIPMENT		33,484		33,484		33,484				33,484
076	ID SYSTEMS		22,177		22,177		22,177				22,177
077	NAVAL MISSION PLANNING SYSTEMS		14,273		14,273		14,273				14,273
	OTHER SHORE ELECTRONIC EQUIPMENT										
080	TACTICAL/MOBILE C4I SYSTEMS		27,927		27,927		27,927				27,927
081	DCGS–N		12,676		12,676		12,676				12,676
082	CANES		212,030		212,030		212,030				212,030
083	RADIAC		8,092		8,092		8,092				8,092
084	CANES–INTELL		36,013		36,013		36,013				36,013
085	GPETE		6,428		6,428		6,428				6,428
087	INTEG COMBAT SYSTEM TEST FACILITY		8,376		8,376		8,376				8,376

SEC. 4101. PROCUREMENT
(In Thousands of Dollars)

Line	Item	FY 2017 Request Qty	FY 2017 Request Cost	House Authorized Qty	House Authorized Cost	Senate Authorized Qty	Senate Authorized Cost	Conference Change Qty	Conference Change Cost	Conference Authorized Qty	Conference Authorized Cost
088	EMI CONTROL INSTRUMENTATION		3,971		3,971		3,971				3,971
089	ITEMS LESS THAN $5 MILLION		58,721		58,721		58,721				58,721
	SHIPBOARD COMMUNICATIONS										
090	SHIPBOARD TACTICAL COMMUNICATIONS		17,366		17,366		17,366				17,366
091	SHIP COMMUNICATIONS AUTOMATION		102,479		102,479		102,479				102,479
092	COMMUNICATIONS ITEMS UNDER $5M ...		10,403		10,403		10,403				10,403
	SUBMARINE COMMUNICATIONS										
093	SUBMARINE BROADCAST SUPPORT		34,151		34,151		34,151				34,151
094	SUBMARINE COMMUNICATION EQUIPMENT.		64,529		64,529		64,529				64,529
	SATELLITE COMMUNICATIONS										
095	SATELLITE COMMUNICATIONS SYSTEMS		14,414		14,414		14,414				14,414
096	NAVY MULTIBAND TERMINAL (NMT)		38,365		38,365		38,365				38,365
	SHORE COMMUNICATIONS										
097	JCS COMMUNICATIONS EQUIPMENT		4,156		4,156		4,156				4,156
	CRYPTOGRAPHIC EQUIPMENT										
099	INFO SYSTEMS SECURITY PROGRAM (ISSP).		85,694		85,694		85,694				85,694
100	MIO INTEL EXPLOITATION TEAM		920		920		920				920
	CRYPTOLOGIC EQUIPMENT										
101	CRYPTOLOGIC COMMUNICATIONS EQUIP		21,098		21,098		21,098				21,098
	OTHER ELECTRONIC SUPPORT										
102	COAST GUARD EQUIPMENT		32,291		32,291		32,291				32,291
	SONOBUOYS										
103	SONOBUOYS—ALL TYPES		162,588		162,588		162,588		−3,047		159,541
	Excess unit cost growth								[−3,047]		
	AIRCRAFT SUPPORT EQUIPMENT										
104	WEAPONS RANGE SUPPORT EQUIPMENT		58,116		58,116		58,116				58,116
105	AIRCRAFT SUPPORT EQUIPMENT		120,324		120,324		120,324				120,324
106	METEOROLOGICAL EQUIPMENT		29,253		29,253		29,253				29,253
107	DCRS/DPL		632		632		632				632
108	AIRBORNE MINE COUNTERMEASURES		29,097		29,097		29,097				29,097
109	AVIATION SUPPORT EQUIPMENT		39,099		39,099		39,099				39,099
	SHIP GUN SYSTEM EQUIPMENT										
110	SHIP GUN SYSTEMS EQUIPMENT		6,191		6,191		6,191				6,191
	SHIP MISSILE SYSTEMS EQUIPMENT										
111	SHIP MISSILE SUPPORT EQUIPMENT		320,446		310,946		320,446		−9,500		310,946
	Program execution				[−9,500]				[−9,500]		
112	TOMAHAWK SUPPORT EQUIPMENT		71,046		71,046		71,046				71,046
	FBM SUPPORT EQUIPMENT										
113	STRATEGIC MISSILE SYSTEMS EQUIP		215,138		215,138		215,138				215,138
	ASW SUPPORT EQUIPMENT										
114	SSN COMBAT CONTROL SYSTEMS		130,715		130,715		130,715				130,715
115	ASW SUPPORT EQUIPMENT		26,431		26,431		26,431				26,431
	OTHER ORDNANCE SUPPORT EQUIPMENT										
116	EXPLOSIVE ORDNANCE DISPOSAL EQUIP		11,821		11,821		11,821				11,821
117	ITEMS LESS THAN $5 MILLION		6,243		6,243		6,243				6,243
	OTHER EXPENDABLE ORDNANCE										
118	SUBMARINE TRAINING DEVICE MODS		48,020		48,020		48,020				48,020
120	SURFACE TRAINING EQUIPMENT		97,514		97,514		97,514		−2,535		94,979
	Unjustified growth								[−2,535]		
	CIVIL ENGINEERING SUPPORT EQUIPMENT										
121	PASSENGER CARRYING VEHICLES		8,853		8,853		8,853				8,853
122	GENERAL PURPOSE TRUCKS		4,928		4,928		4,928				4,928
123	CONSTRUCTION & MAINTENANCE EQUIP		18,527		18,527		18,527				18,527
124	FIRE FIGHTING EQUIPMENT		13,569		13,569		13,569				13,569
125	TACTICAL VEHICLES		14,917		14,917		14,917				14,917
126	AMPHIBIOUS EQUIPMENT		7,676		7,676		7,676				7,676
127	POLLUTION CONTROL EQUIPMENT		2,321		2,321		2,321				2,321
128	ITEMS UNDER $5 MILLION		12,459		12,459		12,459				12,459
129	PHYSICAL SECURITY VEHICLES		1,095		1,095		1,095				1,095
	SUPPLY SUPPORT EQUIPMENT										
131	SUPPLY EQUIPMENT		16,023		16,023		16,023				16,023
133	FIRST DESTINATION TRANSPORTATION		5,115		5,115		5,115				5,115
134	SPECIAL PURPOSE SUPPLY SYSTEMS		295,471		295,471		295,471				295,471
	TRAINING DEVICES										
136	TRAINING AND EDUCATION EQUIPMENT ..		9,504		9,504		9,504				9,504

SEC. 4101. PROCUREMENT
(In Thousands of Dollars)

Line	Item	FY 2017 Request		House Authorized		Senate Authorized		Conference Change		Conference Authorized	
		Qty	Cost	Qty	Cost	Qty	Cost	Qty	Cost	Qty	Cost
	COMMAND SUPPORT EQUIPMENT										
137	COMMAND SUPPORT EQUIPMENT		37,180		37,180		37,180		−7,200 [−7,200]		29,980
	CNIC building control systems un-justified request.										
139	MEDICAL SUPPORT EQUIPMENT		4,128		4,128		4,128				4,128
141	NAVAL MIP SUPPORT EQUIPMENT		1,925		1,925		1,925				1,925
142	OPERATING FORCES SUPPORT EQUIPMENT.		4,777		4,777		4,777				4,777
143	C4ISR EQUIPMENT		9,073		9,073		9,073				9,073
144	ENVIRONMENTAL SUPPORT EQUIPMENT		21,107		21,107		21,107				21,107
145	PHYSICAL SECURITY EQUIPMENT		100,906		100,906		100,906				100,906
146	ENTERPRISE INFORMATION TECHNOLOGY		67,544		67,544		67,544				67,544
	OTHER										
150	NEXT GENERATION ENTERPRISE SERVICE		98,216		98,216		98,216				98,216
	CLASSIFIED PROGRAMS										
150A	CLASSIFIED PROGRAMS		9,915		9,915		9,915				9,915
	SPARES AND REPAIR PARTS										
151	SPARES AND REPAIR PARTS		199,660		199,660		199,660				199,660
	TOTAL OTHER PROCUREMENT, NAVY.		**6,338,861**		**6,272,961**	2	**6,408,661**		**−79,931**		**6,258,930**
	PROCUREMENT, MARINE CORPS										
	TRACKED COMBAT VEHICLES										
001	AAV7A1 PIP		73,785		73,785		73,785		−2,000 [−2,000]		71,785
	Production engineering support excess growth.										
002	LAV PIP		53,423		53,423		53,423				53,423
	ARTILLERY AND OTHER WEAPONS										
003	EXPEDITIONARY FIRE SUPPORT SYSTEM		3,360		3,360		3,360				3,360
004	155MM LIGHTWEIGHT TOWED HOWITZER		3,318		3,318		3,318				3,318
005	HIGH MOBILITY ARTILLERY ROCKET SYSTEM.		33,725		33,725		33,725				33,725
006	WEAPONS AND COMBAT VEHICLES UNDER $5 MILLION.		8,181		8,181		8,181				8,181
	OTHER SUPPORT										
007	MODIFICATION KITS		15,250		15,250		15,250				15,250
	GUIDED MISSILES										
009	GROUND BASED AIR DEFENSE		9,170		9,170		9,170				9,170
010	JAVELIN		1,009		1,009		1,009				1,009
011	FOLLOW ON TO SMAW		24,666		24,666		24,666				24,666
012	ANTI-ARMOR WEAPONS SYSTEM-HEAVY (AAWS-H).		17,080		17,080		17,080				17,080
	COMMAND AND CONTROL SYSTEMS										
015	COMMON AVIATION COMMAND AND CONTROL SYSTEM (C.		47,312		47,312		47,312				47,312
	REPAIR AND TEST EQUIPMENT										
016	REPAIR AND TEST EQUIPMENT		16,469		16,469		16,469				16,469
	COMMAND AND CONTROL SYSTEM (NON-TEL)										
019	ITEMS UNDER $5 MILLION (COMM & ELEC).		7,433		7,433		7,433				7,433
020	AIR OPERATIONS C2 SYSTEMS		15,917		15,917		15,917				15,917
	RADAR + EQUIPMENT (NON-TEL)										
021	RADAR SYSTEMS		17,772		17,772		17,772				17,772
022	GROUND/AIR TASK ORIENTED RADAR (G/ATOR).	3	123,758	3	123,758	3	123,758			3	123,758
023	RQ–21 UAS	4	80,217	4	80,217	4	80,217			4	80,217
	INTELL/COMM EQUIPMENT (NON-TEL)										
024	GCSS-MC		1,089		1,089		1,089				1,089
025	FIRE SUPPORT SYSTEM		13,258		13,258		13,258				13,258
026	INTELLIGENCE SUPPORT EQUIPMENT		56,379		56,379		56,379				56,379
029	RQ–11 UAV		1,976		1,976		1,976				1,976
031	DCGS-MC		1,149		1,149		1,149				1,149
032	UAS PAYLOADS		2,971		2,971		2,971				2,971
	OTHER SUPPORT (NON-TEL)										
034	NEXT GENERATION ENTERPRISE NETWORK (NGEN).		76,302		76,302		76,302				76,302
035	COMMON COMPUTER RESOURCES		41,802		41,802		41,802		−2,325 [−2,325]		39,477
	Prior year carryover										
036	COMMAND POST SYSTEMS		90,924		90,924		90,924				90,924

SEC. 4101. PROCUREMENT
(In Thousands of Dollars)

Line	Item	FY 2017 Request		House Authorized		Senate Authorized		Conference Change		Conference Authorized	
		Qty	Cost	Qty	Cost	Qty	Cost	Qty	Cost	Qty	Cost
037	RADIO SYSTEMS		43,714		43,714		43,714				43,714
038	COMM SWITCHING & CONTROL SYSTEMS		66,383		66,383		66,383				66,383
039	COMM & ELEC INFRASTRUCTURE SUPPORT.		30,229		30,229		30,229				30,229
	CLASSIFIED PROGRAMS										
039A	CLASSIFIED PROGRAMS		2,738		2,738		2,738				2,738
	ADMINISTRATIVE VEHICLES										
041	COMMERCIAL CARGO VEHICLES		88,312		88,312		88,312				88,312
	TACTICAL VEHICLES										
043	MOTOR TRANSPORT MODIFICATIONS		13,292		13,292		13,292				13,292
045	JOINT LIGHT TACTICAL VEHICLE	192	113,230	192	113,230	192	113,230			192	113,230
046	FAMILY OF TACTICAL TRAILERS		2,691		2,691		2,691				2,691
	ENGINEER AND OTHER EQUIPMENT										
048	ENVIRONMENTAL CONTROL EQUIP ASSORT.		18		18		18				18
050	TACTICAL FUEL SYSTEMS		78		78		78				78
051	POWER EQUIPMENT ASSORTED		17,973		17,973		17,973				17,973
052	AMPHIBIOUS SUPPORT EQUIPMENT		7,371		7,371		7,371				7,371
053	EOD SYSTEMS		14,021		14,021		14,021				14,021
	MATERIALS HANDLING EQUIPMENT										
054	PHYSICAL SECURITY EQUIPMENT		31,523		31,523		31,523				31,523
	GENERAL PROPERTY										
058	TRAINING DEVICES		33,658		33,658		33,658				33,658
060	FAMILY OF CONSTRUCTION EQUIPMENT		21,315		21,315		21,315				21,315
061	FAMILY OF INTERNALLY TRANSPORTABLE VEH (ITV).		9,654		9,654		9,654				9,654
	OTHER SUPPORT										
062	ITEMS LESS THAN $5 MILLION		6,026		6,026		6,026				6,026
	SPARES AND REPAIR PARTS										
064	SPARES AND REPAIR PARTS		22,848		22,848		22,848				22,848
	TOTAL PROCUREMENT, MARINE CORPS.	199	1,362,769	199	1,362,769	199	1,362,769		−4,325	199	1,358,444
	AIRCRAFT PROCUREMENT, AIR FORCE										
	TACTICAL FORCES										
001	F–35	43	4,401,894	43	4,401,894	43	4,401,894		−213,000	43	4,188,894
	Program efficiencies								[−213,000]		
002	ADVANCE PROCUREMENT (CY)		404,500		404,500		404,500				404,500
	TACTICAL AIRLIFT										
003	KC–46A TANKER	15	2,884,591	15	2,884,591	15	2,884,591			15	2,884,591
	OTHER AIRLIFT										
004	C–130J	2	145,655	2	145,655	2	145,655			2	145,655
006	HC–130J	4	317,576	4	317,576	4	317,576			4	317,576
007	ADVANCE PROCUREMENT (CY)		20,000		20,000		20,000				20,000
008	MC–130J	6	548,358	6	548,358	6	548,358			6	548,358
009	ADVANCE PROCUREMENT (CY)		50,000		50,000		50,000				50,000
	HELICOPTERS										
010	UH–1N REPLACEMENT		18,337		18,337	8	320,637				18,337
	HH–60 Blackhawks, initial spares, and support equipment.					[8]	[302,300]				
	MISSION SUPPORT AIRCRAFT										
012	CIVIL AIR PATROL A/C	6	2,637	6	2,637	6	2,637			6	2,637
	OTHER AIRCRAFT										
013	TARGET DRONES	41	114,656	41	114,656	41	114,656			41	114,656
014	RQ–4		12,966		12,966		12,966				12,966
015	MQ–9		122,522		122,522		35,522				122,522
	Air Force requested realignment ...						[−87,000]				
	STRATEGIC AIRCRAFT										
016	B–2A		46,729		46,729		46,729				46,729
017	B–1B		116,319		116,319		116,319				116,319
018	B–52		109,020		109,020		109,020				109,020
	TACTICAL AIRCRAFT										
020	A–10		1,289		1,289		1,289				1,289
021	F–15		105,685		105,685		105,685				105,685
022	F–16		97,331		97,331		185,631		17,000		114,331
	Active missile warning system						[12,000]		[12,000]		
	Anti-jam global positioning system (GPS) upgrade.						[5,000]		[5,000]		
	Digital radar warning system						[23,000]				

SEC. 4101. PROCUREMENT
(In Thousands of Dollars)

Line	Item	FY 2017 Request		House Authorized		Senate Authorized		Conference Change		Conference Authorized	
		Qty	Cost	Qty	Cost	Qty	Cost	Qty	Cost	Qty	Cost
	Multi-mission computer and MIDS-JTRS.						[48,300]				
023	F–22A		163,008		163,008		163,008				163,008
024	F–35 MODIFICATIONS		175,811		175,811		175,811				175,811
025	INCREMENT 3.2B		76,410		76,410		76,410				76,410
026	ADVANCE PROCUREMENT (CY)		2,000		2,000		2,000				2,000
	AIRLIFT AIRCRAFT										
027	C–5		24,192		24,192		24,192				24,192
029	C–17A		21,555		21,555		21,555				21,555
030	C–21		5,439		5,439		5,439				5,439
031	C–32A		35,235		35,235		35,235				35,235
032	C–37A		5,004		5,004		5,004				5,004
	TRAINER AIRCRAFT										
033	GLIDER MODS		394		394		394				394
034	T–6		12,765		12,765		12,765				12,765
035	T–1		25,073		25,073		25,073		–8,000		17,073
	Production schedule slip								[–8,000]		
036	T–38		45,090		45,090		45,090				45,090
	OTHER AIRCRAFT										
037	U–2 MODS		36,074		36,074		36,074				36,074
038	KC–10A (ATCA)		4,570		4,570		4,570				4,570
039	C–12		1,995		1,995		1,995				1,995
040	VC–25A MOD		102,670		102,670		102,670				102,670
041	C–40		13,984		13,984		13,984				13,984
042	C–130		9,168	50	81,668		9,168	50	72,500	50	81,668
	8–Bladed Propellers				[16,000]				[16,000]		
	Electronic Propeller Control Systems.				[13,500]				[13,500]		
	In-flight Propeller Balancing System Certification.				[1,500]				[1,500]		
	T56 3.5 Engine Upgrade Kits			[50]	[41,500]			[50]	[41,500]		
043	C–130J MODS		89,424		89,424		89,424				89,424
044	C–135		64,161		64,161		64,161				64,161
045	COMPASS CALL MODS		130,257		59,857		155,857		–70,400		59,857
	Air Force requested realignment from Initial Spares.						[25,600]				
	Compass Call Program Restructure.				[–70,400]				[–70,400]		
046	RC–135		211,438		211,438		211,438				211,438
047	E–3		82,786		82,786		82,786				82,786
048	E–4		53,348		53,348		53,348				53,348
049	E–8		6,244		6,244		6,244				6,244
050	AIRBORNE WARNING AND CONTROL SYSTEM.		223,427		223,427		223,427				223,427
051	FAMILY OF BEYOND LINE-OF-SIGHT TERMINALS.	3	4,673	3	4,673	3	4,673			3	4,673
052	H–1		9,007		9,007		9,007				9,007
054	H–60		91,357		91,357		91,357				91,357
055	RQ–4 MODS		32,045		32,045		32,045				32,045
056	HC/MC–130 MODIFICATIONS		30,767		30,767		30,767				30,767
057	OTHER AIRCRAFT		33,886		33,886		33,886				33,886
059	MQ–9 MODS		141,929		141,929		141,929				141,929
060	CV–22 MODS		63,395		63,395		63,395				63,395
	AIRCRAFT SPARES AND REPAIR PARTS										
061	INITIAL SPARES/REPAIR PARTS		686,491		673,291		747,891		–13,200		673,291
	Air Force requested realignment ...						[–25,600]				
	Air Force requested realignment from MQ–9.						[87,000]				
	Compass Call Program Restructure.				[–13,200]				[–13,200]		
	COMMON SUPPORT EQUIPMENT										
062	AIRCRAFT REPLACEMENT SUPPORT EQUIP.		121,935		121,935		121,935				121,935
	POST PRODUCTION SUPPORT										
063	B–2A		154		154		154				154
064	B–2A		43,330		43,330		43,330				43,330
065	B–52		28,125		28,125		28,125				28,125
066	C–17A		23,559		23,559		23,559				23,559
069	F–15		2,980		2,980		2,980				2,980
070	F–16		15,155		39,955		15,155		24,800		39,955

SEC. 4101. PROCUREMENT
(In Thousands of Dollars)

Line	Item	FY 2017 Request Qty	FY 2017 Request Cost	House Authorized Qty	House Authorized Cost	Senate Authorized Qty	Senate Authorized Cost	Conference Change Qty	Conference Change Cost	Conference Authorized Qty	Conference Authorized Cost
	Additional mission trainers				[24,800]				[24,800]		
071	F–22A		48,505		48,505		48,505				48,505
074	RQ–4 POST PRODUCTION CHARGES		99		99		99				99
	INDUSTRIAL PREPAREDNESS										
075	INDUSTRIAL RESPONSIVENESS		14,126		14,126		14,126				14,126
	WAR CONSUMABLES										
076	WAR CONSUMABLES		120,036		120,036		120,036				120,036
	OTHER PRODUCTION CHARGES										
077	OTHER PRODUCTION CHARGES		1,252,824		1,252,824		1,252,824				1,252,824
	CLASSIFIED PROGRAMS										
077A	CLASSIFIED PROGRAMS		16,952		16,952		16,952		103,000		119,952
	Compass Call Program Restructure.								[103,000]		
	TOTAL AIRCRAFT PROCUREMENT, AIR FORCE.	120	13,922,917	170	13,936,617	128	14,313,517	50	−87,300	170	13,835,617
	MISSILE PROCUREMENT, AIR FORCE										
	MISSILE REPLACEMENT EQUIPMENT—BALLISTIC										
001	MISSILE REPLACEMENT EQ-BALLISTIC		70,247		70,247		70,247				70,247
	TACTICAL										
002	JOINT AIR-SURFACE STANDOFF MISSILE	360	431,645	360	431,645	360	431,645			360	431,645
003	LRASMO	20	59,511	20	59,511	20	59,511			20	59,511
004	SIDEWINDER (AIM–9X)	287	127,438	287	127,438	287	127,438			287	127,438
005	AMRAAM	256	350,144	256	350,144	256	350,144		−10,752	256	339,392
	Pricing adjustment								[−10,752]		
006	PREDATOR HELLFIRE MISSILE	284	33,955	284	33,955	284	33,955			284	33,955
007	SMALL DIAMETER BOMB	312	92,361	312	92,361	312	92,361			312	92,361
	INDUSTRIAL FACILITIES										
008	INDUSTR'L PREPAREDNS/POL PREVENTION.		977		977		977				977
	CLASS IV										
009	ICBM FUZE MOD		17,095		17,095		17,095				17,095
010	MM III MODIFICATIONS		68,692		68,692		68,692				68,692
011	AGM–65D MAVERICK		282		282		282				282
013	AIR LAUNCH CRUISE MISSILE (ALCM)		21,762		21,762		21,762				21,762
014	SMALL DIAMETER BOMB		15,349		15,349		15,349				15,349
	MISSILE SPARES AND REPAIR PARTS										
015	INITIAL SPARES/REPAIR PARTS		81,607		81,607		81,607				81,607
	SPECIAL PROGRAMS										
030	SPECIAL UPDATE PROGRAMS		46,125		46,125		46,125				46,125
	CLASSIFIED PROGRAMS										
030A	CLASSIFIED PROGRAMS		1,009,431		1,009,431		1,009,431				1,009,431
	TOTAL MISSILE PROCUREMENT, AIR FORCE.	1,519	2,426,621	1,519	2,426,621	1,519	2,426,621		−10,752	1,519	2,415,869
	SPACE PROCUREMENT, AIR FORCE										
	SPACE PROGRAMS										
001	ADVANCED EHF		645,569		645,569		645,569				645,569
002	AF SATELLITE COMM SYSTEM		42,375		42,375		42,375				42,375
003	COUNTERSPACE SYSTEMS		26,984		26,984		26,984				26,984
004	FAMILY OF BEYOND LINE-OF-SIGHT TERMINALS.	16	88,963	16	88,963	16	88,963			16	88,963
005	WIDEBAND GAPFILLER SATELLITES(SPACE).		86,272		116,272		86,272				86,272
	Pilot Program				[30,000]						
006	GPS III SPACE SEGMENT		34,059		34,059		34,059				34,059
007	GLOBAL POSITIONING (SPACE)		2,169		2,169		2,169				2,169
008	SPACEBORNE EQUIP (COMSEC)		46,708		46,708		46,708				46,708
009	GLOBAL POSITIONING (SPACE)		13,171		10,271		13,171		−2,900		10,271
	Excess to Need				[−2,900]				[−2,900]		
010	MILSATCOM		41,799		41,799		41,799				41,799
011	EVOLVED EXPENDABLE LAUNCH CAPABILITY.		768,586		768,586		768,586		−26,000		742,586
	Early to need								[−26,000]		
012	EVOLVED EXPENDABLE LAUNCH VEH(SPACE).	5	737,853	5	737,853	5	737,853		−201,000	5	536,853
	Early to need								[−201,000]		
013	SBIR HIGH (SPACE)		362,504		362,504		362,504				362,504
014	NUDET DETECTION SYSTEM		4,395		4,395		4,395				4,395

SEC. 4101. PROCUREMENT
(In Thousands of Dollars)

Line	Item	FY 2017 Request		House Authorized		Senate Authorized		Conference Change		Conference Authorized	
		Qty	Cost	Qty	Cost	Qty	Cost	Qty	Cost	Qty	Cost
015	SPACE MODS		8,642		8,642		8,642				8,642
016	SPACELIFT RANGE SYSTEM SPACE		123,088		123,088		123,088				123,088
	SSPARES										
017	INITIAL SPARES/REPAIR PARTS		22,606		22,606		22,606				22,606
	TOTAL SPACE PROCUREMENT, AIR FORCE.	21	3,055,743	21	3,082,843	21	3,055,743		−229,900	21	2,825,843
	PROCUREMENT OF AMMUNITION, AIR FORCE										
	ROCKETS										
001	ROCKETS		18,734		18,734		18,734				18,734
	CARTRIDGES										
002	CARTRIDGES		220,237		220,237		220,237				220,237
	BOMBS										
003	PRACTICE BOMBS		97,106		97,106		97,106				97,106
004	GENERAL PURPOSE BOMBS		581,561		581,561		581,561				581,561
005	MASSIVE ORDNANCE PENETRATOR (MOP).		3,600		3,600		3,600				3,600
006	JOINT DIRECT ATTACK MUNITION	12,133	303,988	12,133	303,988	12,133	303,988		−6,000	12,133	297,988
	Pricing adjustment for increased quantity.								[−6,000]		
	OTHER ITEMS										
007	CAD/PAD		38,890		38,890		38,890				38,890
008	EXPLOSIVE ORDNANCE DISPOSAL (EOD)		5,714		5,714		5,714				5,714
009	SPARES AND REPAIR PARTS		740		740		740				740
010	MODIFICATIONS		573		573		573				573
011	ITEMS LESS THAN $5 MILLION		5,156		5,156		5,156				5,156
	FLARES										
012	FLARES		134,709		134,709		134,709				134,709
	FUZES										
013	FUZES		229,252		229,252		229,252				229,252
	SMALL ARMS										
014	SMALL ARMS		37,459		37,459		37,459				37,459
	TOTAL PROCUREMENT OF AMMUNITION, AIR FORCE.	12,133	1,677,719	12,133	1,677,719	12,133	1,677,719		−6,000	12,133	1,671,719
	OTHER PROCUREMENT, AIR FORCE										
	PASSENGER CARRYING VEHICLES										
001	PASSENGER CARRYING VEHICLES		14,437		14,437		14,437				14,437
	CARGO AND UTILITY VEHICLES										
002	MEDIUM TACTICAL VEHICLE		24,812		24,812		24,812				24,812
003	CAP VEHICLES		984		984		984				984
004	ITEMS LESS THAN $5 MILLION		11,191		11,191		11,191				11,191
	SPECIAL PURPOSE VEHICLES										
005	SECURITY AND TACTICAL VEHICLES		5,361		5,361		5,361				5,361
006	ITEMS LESS THAN $5 MILLION		4,623		4,623		4,623				4,623
	FIRE FIGHTING EQUIPMENT										
007	FIRE FIGHTING/CRASH RESCUE VEHICLES.		12,451		7,451		12,451				12,451
	Program reduction				[−5,000]						
	MATERIALS HANDLING EQUIPMENT										
008	ITEMS LESS THAN $5 MILLION		18,114		18,114		18,114				18,114
	BASE MAINTENANCE SUPPORT										
009	RUNWAY SNOW REMOV & CLEANING EQUIP.		2,310		2,310		2,310				2,310
010	ITEMS LESS THAN $5 MILLION		46,868		46,868		46,868				46,868
	COMM SECURITY EQUIPMENT(COMSEC)										
012	COMSEC EQUIPMENT		72,359		72,359		72,359				72,359
	INTELLIGENCE PROGRAMS										
014	INTELLIGENCE TRAINING EQUIPMENT		6,982		6,982		6,982				6,982
015	INTELLIGENCE COMM EQUIPMENT		30,504		30,504		35,604				30,504
	Air Force requested realignment from AFNET.						[5,100]				
	ELECTRONICS PROGRAMS										
016	AIR TRAFFIC CONTROL & LANDING SYS		55,803		55,803		55,803				55,803
017	NATIONAL AIRSPACE SYSTEM		2,673		2,673		2,673				2,673
018	BATTLE CONTROL SYSTEM—FIXED		5,677		5,677		5,677				5,677
019	THEATER AIR CONTROL SYS IMPROVEMENTS.		1,163		1,163		1,163				1,163
020	WEATHER OBSERVATION FORECAST		21,667		21,667		21,667				21,667

SEC. 4101. PROCUREMENT
(In Thousands of Dollars)

Line	Item	FY 2017 Request		House Authorized		Senate Authorized		Conference Change		Conference Authorized	
		Qty	Cost	Qty	Cost	Qty	Cost	Qty	Cost	Qty	Cost
021	STRATEGIC COMMAND AND CONTROL		39,803		39,803		39,803				39,803
022	CHEYENNE MOUNTAIN COMPLEX		24,618		24,618		24,618				24,618
023	MISSION PLANNING SYSTEMS		15,868		15,868		15,868				15,868
025	INTEGRATED STRAT PLAN & ANALY NETWORK (ISPAN).		9,331		9,331		9,331				9,331
	SPCL COMM-ELECTRONICS PROJECTS										
026	GENERAL INFORMATION TECHNOLOGY		41,779		41,779		41,779				41,779
027	AF GLOBAL COMMAND & CONTROL SYS		15,729		15,729		15,729				15,729
028	MOBILITY COMMAND AND CONTROL		9,814		9,814		9,814				9,814
029	AIR FORCE PHYSICAL SECURITY SYSTEM		99,460		99,460		99,460				99,460
030	COMBAT TRAINING RANGES		34,850		34,850		34,850				34,850
031	MINIMUM ESSENTIAL EMERGENCY COMM N.		198,925		198,925		198,925				198,925
032	WIDE AREA SURVEILLANCE (WAS)		6,943		6,943		6,943				6,943
033	C3 COUNTERMEASURES		19,580		19,580		19,580				19,580
034	GCSS-AF FOS		1,743		1,743		1,743				1,743
036	THEATER BATTLE MGT C2 SYSTEM		9,659		9,659		9,659				9,659
037	AIR & SPACE OPERATIONS CTR-WPN SYS.		15,474		15,474		15,474				15,474
038	AIR OPERATIONS CENTER (AOC) 10.2		30,623		30,623		30,623		−15,300		15,323
	Fielding								[−15,300]		
	AIR FORCE COMMUNICATIONS										
039	INFORMATION TRANSPORT SYSTEMS		40,043		40,043		40,043				40,043
040	AFNET		146,897		146,897		141,797				146,897
	Air Force requested realignment ...						[−5,100]				
041	JOINT COMMUNICATIONS SUPPORT ELEMENT (JCSE).		5,182		5,182		5,182				5,182
042	USCENTCOM		13,418		13,418		13,418				13,418
	ORGANIZATION AND BASE										
052	TACTICAL C-E EQUIPMENT		109,836		109,836		109,836				109,836
053	RADIO EQUIPMENT		16,266		16,266		16,266				16,266
054	CCTV/AUDIOVISUAL EQUIPMENT		7,449		7,449		7,449				7,449
055	BASE COMM INFRASTRUCTURE		109,215		109,215		109,215				109,215
	MODIFICATIONS										
056	COMM ELECT MODS		65,700		65,700		65,700				65,700
	PERSONAL SAFETY & RESCUE EQUIP										
058	ITEMS LESS THAN $5 MILLION		54,416		54,416		54,416				54,416
	DEPOT PLANT+MTRLS HANDLING EQ										
059	MECHANIZED MATERIAL HANDLING EQUIP.		7,344		7,344		7,344				7,344
	BASE SUPPORT EQUIPMENT										
060	BASE PROCURED EQUIPMENT		6,852		11,852		6,852				6,852
	Program increase				[5,000]						
063	MOBILITY EQUIPMENT		8,146		8,146		8,146				8,146
064	ITEMS LESS THAN $5 MILLION		28,427		28,427		28,427				28,427
	SPECIAL SUPPORT PROJECTS										
066	DARP RC135		25,287		25,287		25,287				25,287
067	DCGS-AF		169,201		169,201		169,201				169,201
069	SPECIAL UPDATE PROGRAM		576,710		576,710		576,710				576,710
	CLASSIFIED PROGRAMS										
070A	CLASSIFIED PROGRAMS		15,119,705		15,119,705		15,119,705				15,119,705
	SPARES AND REPAIR PARTS										
072	SPARES AND REPAIR PARTS		15,784		15,784		15,784				15,784
	TOTAL OTHER PROCUREMENT, AIR FORCE.		**17,438,056**		**17,438,056**		**17,438,056**		**−15,300**		**17,422,756**
	PROCUREMENT, DEFENSE-WIDE										
	MAJOR EQUIPMENT, WHS										
037	MAJOR EQUIPMENT, OSD	39	29,211	39	29,211	39	6,111			39	29,211
	Mentor Protégé						[−23,100]				
	MAJOR EQUIPMENT, NSA										
036	INFORMATION SYSTEMS SECURITY PROGRAM (ISSP).		4,399		4,399		4,399				4,399
	MAJOR EQUIPMENT, WHS										
040	MAJOR EQUIPMENT, WHS		24,979		24,979		24,979				24,979
	MAJOR EQUIPMENT, DISA										
006	INFORMATION SYSTEMS SECURITY		21,347		21,347		21,347				21,347
007	TELEPORT PROGRAM		50,597		50,597		50,597				50,597
008	ITEMS LESS THAN $5 MILLION		10,420		10,420		10,420				10,420

SEC. 4101. PROCUREMENT
(In Thousands of Dollars)

Line	Item	FY 2017 Request		House Authorized		Senate Authorized		Conference Change		Conference Authorized	
		Qty	Cost	Qty	Cost	Qty	Cost	Qty	Cost	Qty	Cost
009	NET CENTRIC ENTERPRISE SERVICES (NCES).		1,634		1,634		1,634				1,634
010	DEFENSE INFORMATION SYSTEM NETWORK.		87,235		87,235		87,235				87,235
011	CYBER SECURITY INITIATIVE		4,528		4,528		4,528				4,528
012	WHITE HOUSE COMMUNICATION AGENCY		36,846		36,846		36,846				36,846
013	SENIOR LEADERSHIP ENTERPRISE		599,391		599,391		599,391				599,391
015	JOINT REGIONAL SECURITY STACKS (JRSS).		150,221		150,221		150,221				150,221
	MAJOR EQUIPMENT, DLA										
017	MAJOR EQUIPMENT		2,055		2,055		2,055				2,055
	MAJOR EQUIPMENT, DSS										
020	MAJOR EQUIPMENT		1,057		1,057		1,057				1,057
	MAJOR EQUIPMENT, DCAA										
001	ITEMS LESS THAN $5 MILLION		2,964		2,964		2,964				2,964
	MAJOR EQUIPMENT, TJS										
038	MAJOR EQUIPMENT, TJS		7,988		7,988		7,988				7,988
	MAJOR EQUIPMENT, MISSILE DEFENSE AGENCY										
023	THAAD	24	369,608	24	369,608	24	369,608			24	369,608
024	AEGIS BMD	35	463,801	35	528,801	35	463,801		65,000	35	528,801
	Increasing BMD capability for Aegis Ships.				[65,000]				[65,000]		
025	BMDS AN/TPY–2 RADARS		5,503		5,503		5,503				5,503
026	ARROW UPPER TIER				120,000				120,000		120,000
	Increase for Arrow 3 Coproduction subject to Title XVI.				[120,000]				[120,000]		
027	DAVID'S SLING				150,000				150,000		150,000
	Increase for DSWS Coproduction subject to Title XVI.				[150,000]				[150,000]		
028	AEGIS ASHORE PHASE III		57,493		82,493		57,493				57,493
	Classified adjustment				[25,000]						
029	IRON DOME		42,000		62,000		42,000		20,000		62,000
	Increase for Coproduction of Iron Dome Tamir Interceptors subject to Title XVI.				[20,000]				[20,000]		
030	AEGIS BMD HARDWARE AND SOFTWARE	6	50,098	6	50,098	6	50,098			6	50,098
	MAJOR EQUIPMENT, DHRA										
003	PERSONNEL ADMINISTRATION		14,232		14,232		14,232				14,232
	MAJOR EQUIPMENT, DEFENSE THREAT REDUCTION AGENCY										
021	VEHICLES		200		200		200				200
022	OTHER MAJOR EQUIPMENT		6,437		6,437		6,437				6,437
	MAJOR EQUIPMENT, DODEA										
019	AUTOMATION/EDUCATIONAL SUPPORT & LOGISTICS.		288		288		288				288
	MAJOR EQUIPMENT, DCMA										
002	MAJOR EQUIPMENT		92		92		92				92
	MAJOR EQUIPMENT, DMACT										
018	MAJOR EQUIPMENT	4	8,060	4	8,060	4	8,060			4	8,060
	CLASSIFIED PROGRAMS										
040A	CLASSIFIED PROGRAMS		568,864		568,864		568,864				568,864
	AVIATION PROGRAMS										
042	ROTARY WING UPGRADES AND SUSTAINMENT.		150,396		168,996		168,996				150,396
	Program increase				[18,600]		[18,600]				
043	UNMANNED ISR		21,190		21,190		21,190				21,190
045	NON-STANDARD AVIATION		4,905		4,905		4,905				4,905
046	U–28		3,970		3,970		3,970				3,970
047	MH–47 CHINOOK		25,022		25,022		25,022				25,022
049	CV–22 MODIFICATION		19,008		19,008		19,008				19,008
051	MQ–9 UNMANNED AERIAL VEHICLE		10,598		10,598		25,398				10,598
	MQ–9 capability enhancements						[14,800]				
053	PRECISION STRIKE PACKAGE		213,122		213,122		200,022		–13,050		200,072
	SOCOM requested transfer						[–13,100]		[–13,050]		
054	AC/MC–130J		73,548		85,648		86,648		13,050		86,598
	SOCOM requested transfer				[12,100]		[13,100]		[13,050]		
055	C–130 MODIFICATIONS		32,970		32,970		32,970				32,970
	SHIPBUILDING										
056	UNDERWATER SYSTEMS		37,098		37,098		37,098				37,098

SEC. 4101. PROCUREMENT
(In Thousands of Dollars)

Line	Item	FY 2017 Request		House Authorized		Senate Authorized		Conference Change		Conference Authorized	
		Qty	Cost	Qty	Cost	Qty	Cost	Qty	Cost	Qty	Cost
	AMMUNITION PROGRAMS										
057	ORDNANCE ITEMS <$5M		105,267		105,267		105,267				105,267
	OTHER PROCUREMENT PROGRAMS										
058	INTELLIGENCE SYSTEMS		79,963		79,963		79,963				79,963
059	DISTRIBUTED COMMON GROUND/SURFACE SYSTEMS.		13,432		13,432		13,432				13,432
060	OTHER ITEMS <$5M		66,436		66,436		66,436				66,436
061	COMBATANT CRAFT SYSTEMS		55,820		55,820		55,820				55,820
062	SPECIAL PROGRAMS		107,432		107,432		107,432				107,432
063	TACTICAL VEHICLES		67,849		67,849		67,849				67,849
064	WARRIOR SYSTEMS <$5M		245,781		245,781		245,781				245,781
065	COMBAT MISSION REQUIREMENTS		19,566		19,566		19,566				19,566
066	GLOBAL VIDEO SURVEILLANCE ACTIVITIES.		3,437		3,437		3,437				3,437
067	OPERATIONAL ENHANCEMENTS INTELLIGENCE.		17,299		17,299		17,299				17,299
069	OPERATIONAL ENHANCEMENTS		219,945		219,945		219,945				219,945
	CBDP										
070	CHEMICAL BIOLOGICAL SITUATIONAL AWARENESS.		148,203		148,203		148,203				148,203
071	CB PROTECTION & HAZARD MITIGATION		161,113		161,113		161,113				161,113
	TOTAL PROCUREMENT, DEFENSE-WIDE.	108	4,524,918	108	4,935,618	108	4,535,218		355,000	108	4,879,918
	JOINT URGENT OPERATIONAL NEEDS FUND										
	JOINT URGENT OPERATIONAL NEEDS FUND										
001	JOINT URGENT OPERATIONAL NEEDS FUND.		99,300				99,300		−99,300		
	Program decrease				[−99,300]				[−99,300]		
	TOTAL JOINT URGENT OPERATIONAL NEEDS FUND.		99,300				99,300		−99,300		
	NATIONAL GUARD AND RESERVE EQUIPMENT										
	UNDISTRIBUTED										
007	MISCELLANEOUS EQUIPMENT				250,000				250,000		250,000
	Program increase				[250,000]				[250,000]		
	TOTAL NATIONAL GUARD AND RESERVE EQUIPMENT.				250,000				250,000		250,000
	TOTAL PROCUREMENT	27,441	101,971,592	27,491	103,124,709	27,547	102,434,976	50	451,068	27,491	102,422,660

SEC. 4102. PROCUREMENT FOR OVERSEAS CONTINGENCY OPERATIONS.

SEC. 4102. PROCUREMENT FOR OVERSEAS CONTINGENCY OPERATIONS
(In Thousands of Dollars)

Line	Item	FY 2017 Request		House Authorized		Senate Authorized		Conference Change		Conference Authorized	
		Qty	Cost	Qty	Cost	Qty	Cost	Qty	Cost	Qty	Cost
	AIRCRAFT PROCUREMENT, ARMY										
	MODIFICATION OF AIRCRAFT										
015	MULTI SENSOR ABN RECON (MIP)		21,400		21,400		21,400				21,400
020	EMARSS SEMA MODS (MIP)	2	42,700	2	42,700	2	42,700			2	42,700
026	RQ–7 UAV MODS		1,775		1,775		1,775				1,775
027	UAS MODS		4,420				4,420				4,420
	Realign APS Unit Set Requirements to Base				[−4,420]						
	GROUND SUPPORT AVIONICS										
030	CMWS		56,115		56,115		56,115				56,115
031	CIRCM		108,721		108,721		108,721				108,721
	TOTAL AIRCRAFT PROCUREMENT, ARMY	2	235,131	2	230,711	2	235,131			2	235,131
	MISSILE PROCUREMENT, ARMY										
	AIR-TO-SURFACE MISSILE SYSTEM										
004	HELLFIRE SYS SUMMARY	2,570	305,830	2,570	305,830	2,570	305,830			2,570	305,830
	ANTI-TANK/ASSAULT MISSILE SYS										
007	JAVELIN (AAWS-M) SYSTEM SUMMARY	83	15,567	83		83	15,567			83	15,567
	Realign APS Unit Set Requirements to Base				[−15,567]						

SEC. 4102. PROCUREMENT FOR OVERSEAS CONTINGENCY OPERATIONS
(In Thousands of Dollars)

Line	Item	FY 2017 Request		House Authorized		Senate Authorized		Conference Change		Conference Authorized	
		Qty	Cost	Qty	Cost	Qty	Cost	Qty	Cost	Qty	Cost
008	TOW 2 SYSTEM SUMMARY	815	80,652	815		815	80,652			815	80,652
	Realign APS Unit Set Requirements to Base				[−80,652]						
010	GUIDED MLRS ROCKET (GMLRS)	698	75,991	698		698	75,991			698	75,991
	Realign APS Unit Set Requirements to Base				[−75,991]						
012	LETHAL MINIATURE AERIAL MISSILE SYSTEM (LMAMS	545	51,277	545	51,277	545	51,277			545	51,277
	TOTAL MISSILE PROCUREMENT, ARMY	4,711	529,317	4,711	357,107	4,711	529,317			4,711	529,317
	PROCUREMENT OF W&TCV, ARMY										
	MODIFICATION OF TRACKED COMBAT VEHICLES										
007	PALADIN INTEGRATED MANAGEMENT (PIM)	12	125,184	12		12	125,184			12	125,184
	Realign APS Unit Set Requirements to Base				[−125,184]						
009	ASSAULT BRIDGE (MOD)		5,950				5,950				5,950
	Realign APS Unit Set Requirements to Base				[−5,950]						
014	ABRAMS UPGRADE PROGRAM								72,000		72,000
	Army requested realignment (ERI)				[172,200]				[172,000]		
	Realign APS Unit Set Requirements to Base				[−172,200]				[−100,000]		
	WEAPONS & OTHER COMBAT VEHICLES										
017	MORTAR SYSTEMS		22,410		22,410		22,410				22,410
	SUPPORT EQUIPMENT & FACILITIES										
036	BRADLEY PROGRAM								72,800		72,800
	Army requested realignment (ERI)				[72,800]				[72,800]		
	Realign APS Unit Set Requirements to Base				[−72,800]						
	TOTAL PROCUREMENT OF W&TCV, ARMY	12	153,544	12	22,410	12	153,544		144,800	12	298,344
	PROCUREMENT OF AMMUNITION, ARMY										
	SMALL/MEDIUM CAL AMMUNITION										
002	CTG, 7.62MM, ALL TYPES		9,642				9,642				9,642
	Realign APS Unit Set Requirements to Base				[−9,642]						
004	CTG, .50 CAL, ALL TYPES		6,607		609		6,607				6,607
	Realign APS Unit Set Requirements to Base				[−5,998]						
005	CTG, 20MM, ALL TYPES		1,077				1,077				1,077
	Realign APS Unit Set Requirements to Base				[−1,077]						
006	CTG, 25MM, ALL TYPES		28,534				28,534				28,534
	Realign APS Unit Set Requirements to Base				[−28,534]						
007	CTG, 30MM, ALL TYPES		20,000		20,000		20,000				20,000
008	CTG, 40MM, ALL TYPES		7,423				7,423				7,423
	Realign APS Unit Set Requirements to Base				[−7,423]						
	MORTAR AMMUNITION										
009	60MM MORTAR, ALL TYPES		10,000		10,000		10,000				10,000
010	81MM MORTAR, ALL TYPES		2,677				2,677				2,677
	Realign APS Unit Set Requirements to Base				[−2,677]						
	TANK AMMUNITION										
012	CARTRIDGES, TANK, 105MM AND 120MM, ALL TYPES		8,999				8,999				8,999
	Realign APS Unit Set Requirements to Base				[−8,999]						
	ARTILLERY AMMUNITION										
014	ARTILLERY PROJECTILE, 155MM, ALL TYPES		30,348		10,000		30,348				30,348
	Realign APS Unit Set Requirements to Base				[−20,348]						
015	PROJ 155MM EXTENDED RANGE M982		140				140				140
	Realign APS Unit Set Requirements to Base				[−140]						
016	ARTILLERY PROPELLANTS, FUZES AND PRIMERS, ALL		29,655		5,000		29,655				29,655
	Realign APS Unit Set Requirements to Base				[−24,655]						
	MINES										
017	MINES & CLEARING CHARGES, ALL TYPES		16,866				16,866				16,866
	Realign APS Unit Set Requirements to Base				[−16,866]						
	NETWORKED MUNITIONS										
018	SPIDER NETWORK MUNITIONS, ALL TYPES		10,353								10,353
	Early to need						[−10,353]				
	Realign APS Unit Set Requirements to Base				[−10,353]						
	ROCKETS										
019	SHOULDER LAUNCHED MUNITIONS, ALL TYPES		63,210				63,210				63,210
	Realign APS Unit Set Requirements to Base				[−63,210]						
020	ROCKET, HYDRA 70, ALL TYPES		42,851		42,851		42,851				42,851
	OTHER AMMUNITION										
022	DEMOLITION MUNITIONS, ALL TYPES		6,373				6,373				6,373
	Realign APS Unit Set Requirements to Base				[−6,373]						
023	GRENADES, ALL TYPES		4,143				4,143				4,143
	Realign APS Unit Set Requirements to Base				[−4,143]						
024	SIGNALS, ALL TYPES		1,852				1,852				1,852
	Realign APS Unit Set Requirements to Base				[−1,852]						

SEC. 4102. PROCUREMENT FOR OVERSEAS CONTINGENCY OPERATIONS
(In Thousands of Dollars)

Line	Item	FY 2017 Request		House Authorized		Senate Authorized		Conference Change		Conference Authorized	
		Qty	Cost	Qty	Cost	Qty	Cost	Qty	Cost	Qty	Cost
	MISCELLANEOUS										
027	NON-LETHAL AMMUNITION, ALL TYPES		773				773				773
	Realign APS Unit Set Requirements to Base				[–773]						
	TOTAL PROCUREMENT OF AMMUNITION, ARMY		301,523		88,460		291,170				301,523
	OTHER PROCUREMENT, ARMY										
	TACTICAL VEHICLES										
002	SEMITRAILERS, FLATBED:		4,180				4,180				4,180
	Realign APS Unit Set Requirements to Base				[–4,180]						
008	FAMILY OF MEDIUM TACTICAL VEH (FMTV)	643	147,476	643		643	147,476			643	147,476
	Realign APS Unit Set Requirements to Base				[–147,476]						
010	FAMILY OF HEAVY TACTICAL VEHICLES (FHTV)	51	6,122	51		51	6,122			51	6,122
	Realign APS Unit Set Requirements to Base				[–6,122]						
011	PLS ESP		106,358				106,358				106,358
	Realign APS Unit Set Requirements to Base				[–106,358]						
012	HVY EXPANDED MOBILE TACTICAL TRUCK EXT SERV		203,766		127,205		203,766				203,766
	Realign APS Unit Set Requirements to Base				[–76,561]						
013	TACTICAL WHEELED VEHICLE PROTECTION KITS		101,154		74,035		101,154				101,154
	Realign APS Unit Set Requirements to Base				[–27,119]						
014	MODIFICATION OF IN SVC EQUIP		155,456		152,000		155,456				155,456
	Realign APS Unit Set Requirements to Base				[–3,456]						
	COMM—JOINT COMMUNICATIONS										
019	WIN-T—GROUND FORCES TACTICAL NETWORK		9,572		3,000		9,572				9,572
	Realign APS Unit Set Requirements to Base				[–6,572]						
	COMM—SATELLITE COMMUNICATIONS										
025	SHF TERM		24,000				24,000				24,000
	Realign APS Unit Set Requirements to Base				[–24,000]						
	COMM—INTELLIGENCE COMM										
047	CI AUTOMATION ARCHITECTURE		1,550		1,550		1,550				1,550
	INFORMATION SECURITY										
051	COMMUNICATIONS SECURITY (COMSEC)		1,928				1,928				1,928
	Realign APS Unit Set Requirements to Base				[–1,928]						
052	DEFENSIVE CYBER OPERATIONS		26,500		26,500		26,500				26,500
	COMM—BASE COMMUNICATIONS										
056	INSTALLATION INFO INFRASTRUCTURE MOD PROGRAM		20,510		20,510		20,510				20,510
	ELECT EQUIP—TACT INT REL ACT (TIARA)										
062	DCGS-A (MIP)		33,032		33,032		33,032				33,032
064	TROJAN (MIP)		3,305		3,145		3,305				3,305
	Realign APS Unit Set Requirements to Base				[–160]						
066	CI HUMINT AUTO REPRTING AND COLL(CHARCS)		7,233		7,233		7,233				7,233
069	BIOMETRIC TACTICAL COLLECTION DEVICES (MIP)		5,670		5,670		5,670				5,670
	ELECT EQUIP—ELECTRONIC WARFARE (EW)										
070	LIGHTWEIGHT COUNTER MORTAR RADAR		25,892				25,892				25,892
	Realign APS Unit Set Requirements to Base				[–25,892]						
074	FAMILY OF PERSISTENT SURVEILLANCE CAPABILITIE		11,610		11,610		11,610				11,610
075	COUNTERINTELLIGENCE/SECURITY COUNTERMEASURES		23,890		23,890		23,890				23,890
	ELECT EQUIP—TACTICAL SURV. (TAC SURV)										
080	INDIRECT FIRE PROTECTION FAMILY OF SYSTEMS		76,270		72,000		76,270				76,270
	Realign APS Unit Set Requirements to Base				[–4,270]						
089	MORTAR FIRE CONTROL SYSTEM		2,572		2,282		2,572				2,572
	Realign APS Unit Set Requirements to Base				[–290]						
	ELECT EQUIP—TACTICAL C2 SYSTEMS										
092	AIR & MSL DEFENSE PLANNING & CONTROL SYS	31	69,958	31		31	69,958			31	69,958
	Realign APS Unit Set Requirements to Base				[–69,958]						
	ELECT EQUIP—AUTOMATION										
102	AUTOMATED DATA PROCESSING EQUIP		9,900		9,900		9,900				9,900
	ELECT EQUIP—AUDIO VISUAL SYS (A/V)										
108	ITEMS LESS THAN $5M (SURVEYING EQUIPMENT)		96				96				96
	Realign APS Unit Set Requirements to Base				[–96]						
	CHEMICAL DEFENSIVE EQUIPMENT										
114	CBRN DEFENSE		1,841				1,841				1,841
	Realign APS Unit Set Requirements to Base				[–1,841]						
	BRIDGING EQUIPMENT										
115	TACTICAL BRIDGING		26,000				26,000				26,000
	Realign APS Unit Set Requirements to Base				[–26,000]						
	ENGINEER (NON-CONSTRUCTION) EQUIPMENT										
124	ROBOTICS AND APPLIQUE SYSTEMS		268				268				268
	Realign APS Unit Set Requirements to Base				[–268]						
128	FAMILY OF BOATS AND MOTORS		280				280				280

SEC. 4102. PROCUREMENT FOR OVERSEAS CONTINGENCY OPERATIONS
(In Thousands of Dollars)

Line	Item	FY 2017 Request		House Authorized		Senate Authorized		Conference Change		Conference Authorized	
		Qty	Cost	Qty	Cost	Qty	Cost	Qty	Cost	Qty	Cost
	Realign APS Unit Set Requirements to Base				[−280]						
	COMBAT SERVICE SUPPORT EQUIPMENT										
129	HEATERS AND ECU'S		894				894				894
	Realign APS Unit Set Requirements to Base				[−894]						
134	FORCE PROVIDER		53,800		53,800		53,800				53,800
135	FIELD FEEDING EQUIPMENT		2,665				2,665				2,665
	Realign APS Unit Set Requirements to Base				[−2,665]						
136	CARGO AERIAL DEL & PERSONNEL PARACHUTE SYSTEM		2,400		2,400		2,400				2,400
137	FAMILY OF ENGR COMBAT AND CONSTRUCTION SETS		9,789				9,789				9,789
	Realign APS Unit Set Requirements to Base				[−9,789]						
138	ITEMS LESS THAN $5M (ENG SPT)		300				300				300
	Realign APS Unit Set Requirements to Base				[−300]						
	PETROLEUM EQUIPMENT										
139	QUALITY SURVEILLANCE EQUIPMENT		4,800				4,800				4,800
	Realign APS Unit Set Requirements to Base				[−4,800]						
140	DISTRIBUTION SYSTEMS, PETROLEUM & WATER	174	78,240	174	57,420	174	78,240			174	78,240
	Realign APS Unit Set Requirements to Base				[−20,820]						
	MEDICAL EQUIPMENT										
141	COMBAT SUPPORT MEDICAL		5,763				5,763				5,763
	Realign APS Unit Set Requirements to Base				[−5,763]						
	MAINTENANCE EQUIPMENT										
142	MOBILE MAINTENANCE EQUIPMENT SYSTEMS		1,609				1,609				1,609
	Realign APS Unit Set Requirements to Base				[−1,609]						
143	ITEMS LESS THAN $5.0M (MAINT EQ)		145				145				145
	Realign APS Unit Set Requirements to Base				[−145]						
	CONSTRUCTION EQUIPMENT										
144	GRADER, ROAD MTZD, HVY, 6X4 (CCE)		3,047				3,047				3,047
	Realign APS Unit Set Requirements to Base				[−3,047]						
148	TRACTOR, FULL TRACKED		4,426				4,426				4,426
	Realign APS Unit Set Requirements to Base				[−4,426]						
151	HIGH MOBILITY ENGINEER EXCAVATOR (HMEE)		2,900				2,900				2,900
	Realign APS Unit Set Requirements to Base				[−2,900]						
155	ITEMS LESS THAN $5.0M (CONST EQUIP)		96				96				96
	Realign APS Unit Set Requirements to Base				[−96]						
	GENERATORS										
158	GENERATORS AND ASSOCIATED EQUIP		21,861		1,900		21,861				21,861
	Realign APS Unit Set Requirements to Base				[−19,961]						
	MATERIAL HANDLING EQUIPMENT										
160	FAMILY OF FORKLIFTS		846				846				846
	Realign APS Unit Set Requirements to Base				[−846]						
	TEST MEASURE AND DIG EQUIPMENT (TMD)										
168	TEST EQUIPMENT MODERNIZATION (TEMOD)		1,140				1,140				1,140
	Realign APS Unit Set Requirements to Base				[−1,140]						
	OTHER SUPPORT EQUIPMENT										
170	RAPID EQUIPPING SOLDIER SUPPORT EQUIPMENT		8,500		8,500		8,500				8,500
	TOTAL OTHER PROCUREMENT, ARMY	899	1,309,610	899	697,582	899	1,309,610			899	1,309,610
	JOINT IMPROVISED-THREAT DEFEAT FUND										
	NETWORK ATTACK										
001	RAPID ACQUISITION AND THREAT RESPONSE		332,000		307,000		332,000				332,000
	Program decrease				[−25,000]						
	STAFF AND INFRASTRUCTURE										
002	MISSION ENABLERS		62,800		62,800		62,800				62,800
	TOTAL JOINT IMPROVISED-THREAT DEFEAT FUND		394,800		369,800		394,800				394,800
	AIRCRAFT PROCUREMENT, NAVY										
	COMBAT AIRCRAFT										
002	F/A−18E/F (FIGHTER) HORNET	2	184,912	2	184,912	2	184,912			2	184,912
	OTHER AIRCRAFT										
026	STUASLO UAV	4	70,000	4	70,000	4	70,000			4	70,000
	MODIFICATION OF AIRCRAFT										
037	EP−3 SERIES		7,505		7,505		7,505				7,505
047	SPECIAL PROJECT AIRCRAFT		14,869		14,869		14,869				14,869
051	COMMON ECM EQUIPMENT		70,780		70,780		70,780				70,780
059	V−22 (TILT/ROTOR ACFT) OSPREY		8,740		8,740		8,740				8,740
	AIRCRAFT SPARES AND REPAIR PARTS										
063	SPARES AND REPAIR PARTS		1,500		1,500		1,500				1,500
	AIRCRAFT SUPPORT EQUIP & FACILITIES										
065	AIRCRAFT INDUSTRIAL FACILITIES		524		524		524				524

SEC. 4102. PROCUREMENT FOR OVERSEAS CONTINGENCY OPERATIONS
(In Thousands of Dollars)

Line	Item	FY 2017 Request		House Authorized		Senate Authorized		Conference Change		Conference Authorized	
		Qty	Cost	Qty	Cost	Qty	Cost	Qty	Cost	Qty	Cost
	TOTAL AIRCRAFT PROCUREMENT, NAVY	6	358,830	6	358,830	6	358,830			6	358,830
	WEAPONS PROCUREMENT, NAVY										
	TACTICAL MISSILES										
010	HELLFIRE	100	8,600	100	8,600	100	8,600			100	8,600
	TOTAL WEAPONS PROCUREMENT, NAVY	100	8,600	100	8,600	100	8,600			100	8,600
	PROCUREMENT OF AMMO, NAVY & MC										
	NAVY AMMUNITION										
001	GENERAL PURPOSE BOMBS		40,366		40,366		40,366				40,366
002	AIRBORNE ROCKETS, ALL TYPES		8,860		8,860		8,860				8,860
006	AIR EXPENDABLE COUNTERMEASURES		7,060		7,060		7,060				7,060
013	PYROTECHNIC AND DEMOLITION		1,122		1,122		1,122				1,122
014	AMMUNITION LESS THAN $5 MILLION		3,495		3,495		3,495				3,495
	MARINE CORPS AMMUNITION										
015	SMALL ARMS AMMUNITION		1,205		1,205		1,205				1,205
017	40 MM, ALL TYPES		539		539		539				539
018	60MM, ALL TYPES		909		909		909				909
020	120MM, ALL TYPES		530		530		530				530
022	ROCKETS, ALL TYPES		469		469		469				469
023	ARTILLERY, ALL TYPES		1,196		1,196		1,196				1,196
024	DEMOLITION MUNITIONS, ALL TYPES		261		261		261				261
025	FUZE, ALL TYPES		217		217		217				217
	TOTAL PROCUREMENT OF AMMO, NAVY & MC		66,229		66,229		66,229				66,229
	OTHER PROCUREMENT, NAVY										
	OTHER SHORE ELECTRONIC EQUIPMENT										
081	DCGS-N		12,000		12,000		12,000				12,000
	OTHER ORDNANCE SUPPORT EQUIPMENT										
116	EXPLOSIVE ORDNANCE DISPOSAL EQUIP		40,000		40,000		40,000				40,000
	CIVIL ENGINEERING SUPPORT EQUIPMENT										
124	FIRE FIGHTING EQUIPMENT		630		630		630				630
	SUPPLY SUPPORT EQUIPMENT										
133	FIRST DESTINATION TRANSPORTATION		25		25		25				25
	COMMAND SUPPORT EQUIPMENT										
137	COMMAND SUPPORT EQUIPMENT		10,562		10,562		10,562				10,562
139	MEDICAL SUPPORT EQUIPMENT		5,000		5,000		5,000				5,000
	CLASSIFIED PROGRAMS										
150A	CLASSIFIED PROGRAMS		1,660		1,660		1,660				1,660
	TOTAL OTHER PROCUREMENT, NAVY		69,877		69,877		69,877				69,877
	PROCUREMENT, MARINE CORPS										
	ARTILLERY AND OTHER WEAPONS										
006	WEAPONS AND COMBAT VEHICLES UNDER $5 MILLION		572		572		572				572
	GUIDED MISSILES										
010	JAVELIN	9	1,606	9	1,606	9	1,606			9	1,606
	OTHER SUPPORT (TEL)										
018	MODIFICATION KITS		2,600		2,600		2,600				2,600
	COMMAND AND CONTROL SYSTEM (NON-TEL)										
019	ITEMS UNDER $5 MILLION (COMM & ELEC)		2,200		2,200		2,200				2,200
	INTELL/COMM EQUIPMENT (NON-TEL)										
026	INTELLIGENCE SUPPORT EQUIPMENT		20,981		20,981		20,981				20,981
029	RQ-11 UAV		3,817		3,817		3,817				3,817
	OTHER SUPPORT (NON-TEL)										
035	COMMON COMPUTER RESOURCES		2,600		2,600		2,600				2,600
037	RADIO SYSTEMS		9,563		9,563		9,563				9,563
	ENGINEER AND OTHER EQUIPMENT										
053	EOD SYSTEMS		75,000		75,000		75,000				75,000
	TOTAL PROCUREMENT, MARINE CORPS	9	118,939	9	118,939	9	118,939			9	118,939
	AIRCRAFT PROCUREMENT, AIR FORCE										
	OTHER AIRLIFT										
004	C-130J	1	73,000	1	73,000	1	73,000			1	73,000
	OTHER AIRCRAFT										
015	MQ-9	12	273,600	12	273,600	12	273,600		−87,000 [−87,000]	12	186,600
	Air Force requested transfer to line 61 for spares										
	STRATEGIC AIRCRAFT										
019	LARGE AIRCRAFT INFRARED COUNTERMEASURES		135,801		135,801		135,801				135,801
	TACTICAL AIRCRAFT										

SEC. 4102. PROCUREMENT FOR OVERSEAS CONTINGENCY OPERATIONS
(In Thousands of Dollars)

Line	Item	FY 2017 Request		House Authorized		Senate Authorized		Conference Change		Conference Authorized	
		Qty	Cost	Qty	Cost	Qty	Cost	Qty	Cost	Qty	Cost
020	A–10		23,850		23,850		23,850				23,850
	OTHER AIRCRAFT										
047	E–3		6,600		6,600		6,600				6,600
056	HC/MC–130 MODIFICATIONS		13,550		13,550		13,550				13,550
057	OTHER AIRCRAFT		7,500		7,500		7,500				7,500
059	MQ–9 MODS		112,068		112,068		112,068				112,068
	AIRCRAFT SPARES AND REPAIR PARTS										
061	INITIAL SPARES/REPAIR PARTS		25,600				25,600		61,400		87,000
	Air Force requested transfer from line 15 for spares								[87,000]		
	Compass Call Program Restructure				[–25,600]				[–25,600]		
	OTHER PRODUCTION CHARGES										
077	OTHER PRODUCTION CHARGES		8,400		8,400		8,400				8,400
	TOTAL AIRCRAFT PROCUREMENT, AIR FORCE	13	679,969	13	654,369	13	679,969		–25,600	13	654,369
	MISSILE PROCUREMENT, AIR FORCE										
	TACTICAL										
006	PREDATOR HELLFIRE MISSILE	1,252	145,125	1,252	145,125	1,252	145,125			1,252	145,125
	CLASS IV										
011	AGM–65D MAVERICK		9,720		9,720		9,720				9,720
	TOTAL MISSILE PROCUREMENT, AIR FORCE	1,252	154,845	1,252	154,845	1,252	154,845			1,252	154,845
	PROCUREMENT OF AMMUNITION, AIR FORCE										
	CARTRIDGES										
002	CARTRIDGES		9,830		9,830		9,830				9,830
	BOMBS										
004	GENERAL PURPOSE BOMBS		7,921		7,921		7,921				7,921
006	JOINT DIRECT ATTACK MUNITION	6,033	140,126	6,033	140,126	6,033	140,126		–9,250	6,033	130,876
	Pricing adjustment								[–9,250]		
	FLARES										
012	FLARES		6,531		6,531		6,531				6,531
	TOTAL PROCUREMENT OF AMMUNITION, AIR FORCE.	6,033	164,408	6,033	164,408	6,033	164,408		–9,250	6,033	155,158
	OTHER PROCUREMENT, AIR FORCE										
	PASSENGER CARRYING VEHICLES										
001	PASSENGER CARRYING VEHICLES		2,003		2,003		2,003				2,003
	CARGO AND UTILITY VEHICLES										
002	MEDIUM TACTICAL VEHICLE		9,066		9,066		9,066				9,066
004	ITEMS LESS THAN $5 MILLION		12,264		12,264		12,264				12,264
	SPECIAL PURPOSE VEHICLES										
006	ITEMS LESS THAN $5 MILLION		16,789		16,789		16,789				16,789
	FIRE FIGHTING EQUIPMENT										
007	FIRE FIGHTING/CRASH RESCUE VEHICLES		48,590		48,590		48,590				48,590
	MATERIALS HANDLING EQUIPMENT										
008	ITEMS LESS THAN $5 MILLION		2,366		2,366		2,366				2,366
	BASE MAINTENANCE SUPPORT										
009	RUNWAY SNOW REMOV & CLEANING EQUIP		6,468		6,468		6,468				6,468
010	ITEMS LESS THAN $5 MILLION		9,271		9,271		9,271				9,271
	ELECTRONICS PROGRAMS										
016	AIR TRAFFIC CONTROL & LANDING SYS		42,650		42,650		42,650				42,650
	SPCL COMM-ELECTRONICS PROJECTS										
029	AIR FORCE PHYSICAL SECURITY SYSTEM		7,500		7,500		7,500				7,500
033	C3 COUNTERMEASURES		620		620		620				620
	ORGANIZATION AND BASE										
052	TACTICAL C-E EQUIPMENT		8,100		8,100		8,100				8,100
	MODIFICATIONS										
056	COMM ELECT MODS		3,800		3,800		3,800				3,800
	BASE SUPPORT EQUIPMENT										
061	ENGINEERING AND EOD EQUIPMENT		53,900		53,900		53,900				53,900
	SPECIAL SUPPORT PROJECTS										
067	DCGS-AF		800		800		800				800
	CLASSIFIED PROGRAMS										
070A	CLASSIFIED PROGRAMS		3,609,978		3,609,978		3,609,978				3,609,978
	TOTAL OTHER PROCUREMENT, AIR FORCE		3,834,165		3,834,165		3,834,165				3,834,165
	PROCUREMENT, DEFENSE-WIDE										
	MAJOR EQUIPMENT, DISA										
007	TELEPORT PROGRAM		1,900		1,900		1,900				1,900
	CLASSIFIED PROGRAMS										

SEC. 4102. PROCUREMENT FOR OVERSEAS CONTINGENCY OPERATIONS
(In Thousands of Dollars)

Line	Item	FY 2017 Request Qty	FY 2017 Request Cost	House Authorized Qty	House Authorized Cost	Senate Authorized Qty	Senate Authorized Cost	Conference Change Qty	Conference Change Cost	Conference Authorized Qty	Conference Authorized Cost
040A	CLASSIFIED PROGRAMS		32,482		32,482		32,482				32,482
	AVIATION PROGRAMS										
041	MC–12		5,000		5,000		5,000				5,000
043	UNMANNED ISR		11,880		11,880		11,880				11,880
046	U–28		38,283		38,283		38,283				38,283
	AMMUNITION PROGRAMS										
057	ORDNANCE ITEMS <$5M		52,504		52,504		52,504				52,504
	OTHER PROCUREMENT PROGRAMS										
058	INTELLIGENCE SYSTEMS		22,000		22,000		22,000				22,000
060	OTHER ITEMS <$5M		11,580		11,580		11,580				11,580
062	SPECIAL PROGRAMS		13,549		13,549		13,549				13,549
063	TACTICAL VEHICLES		3,200		3,200		3,200				3,200
069	OPERATIONAL ENHANCEMENTS		42,056		42,056		42,056		−19,250		22,806
	Classified adjustment								[−19,250]		
	TOTAL PROCUREMENT, DEFENSE-WIDE		234,434		234,434		234,434		−19,250		215,184
	TOTAL PROCUREMENT	13,037	8,614,221	13,037	7,430,766	13,037	8,603,868		90,700	13,037	8,704,921

SEC. 4103. PROCUREMENT FOR OVERSEAS CONTINGENCY OPERATIONS FOR BASE REQUIREMENTS.

SEC. 4103. PROCUREMENT FOR OVERSEAS CONTINGENCY OPERATIONS FOR BASE REQUIREMENTS
(In Thousands of Dollars)

Line	Item	FY 2017 Request Qty	FY 2017 Request Cost	House Authorized Qty	House Authorized Cost	Senate Authorized Qty	Senate Authorized Cost	Conference Change Qty	Conference Change Cost	Conference Authorized Qty	Conference Authorized Cost
	AIRCRAFT PROCUREMENT, ARMY										
	FIXED WING										
003	MQ–1 UAV				95,100						
	Army unfunded requirement				[95,100]						
	ROTARY										
005	HELICOPTER, LIGHT UTILITY (LUH)			17	110,000						
	Army unfunded requirement (ARI)			[17]	[110,000]						
006	AH–64 APACHE BLOCK IIIA REMAN	4	78,040	4	78,040	4	78,040			4	78,040
007	ADVANCE PROCUREMENT (CY)			10	72,900						
	Army unfunded requirement (ARI)			[10]	[72,900]						
007A	AH–64 APACHE BLOCK IIIA NEW BUILD			5	190,000						
	Army unfunded requirement (ARI)			[5]	[190,000]						
008	UH–60 BLACKHAWK M MODEL (MYP)			36	440,200						
	Army unfunded requirement (ARI)			[36]	[440,200]						
	MODIFICATION OF AIRCRAFT										
017	CH–47 CARGO HELICOPTER MODS (MYP)				102,000						
	Army unfunded requirement (ARI)				[102,000]						
	GROUND SUPPORT AVIONICS										
028	AIRCRAFT SURVIVABILITY EQUIPMENT				22,000						
	Army unfunded requirement-modernized warning system (ARI).				[22,000]						
029	SURVIVABILITY CM				28,000						
	Army unfunded requirement-assured PNT (ARI)				[28,000]						
	TOTAL AIRCRAFT PROCUREMENT, ARMY	4	78,040	72	1,138,240	4	78,040			4	78,040
	MISSILE PROCUREMENT, ARMY										
	AIR-TO-SURFACE MISSILE SYSTEM										
004	HELLFIRE SYS SUMMARY	1,485	150,000	1,485	150,000	1,485	150,000			1,485	150,000
	ANTI-TANK/ASSAULT MISSILE SYS										
007	JAVELIN (AAWS-M) SYSTEM SUMMARY			591	104,200				104,200		104,200
	Army unfunded requirement			[591]	[104,200]				[104,200]		
010	GUIDED MLRS ROCKET (GMLRS)			1,158	76,000				76,000		76,000
	Army unfunded requirement			[1,158]	[76,000]				[76,000]		
	MODIFICATIONS										
014	ATACMS MODS			17	15,900				15,900		15,900
	Army unfunded requirement			[17]	[15,900]				[15,900]		
	TOTAL MISSILE PROCUREMENT, ARMY	1,485	150,000	3,251	346,100	1,485	150,000		196,100	1,485	346,100
	PROCUREMENT OF W&TCV, ARMY										
	MODIFICATION OF TRACKED COMBAT VEHICLES										
008	IMPROVED RECOVERY VEHICLE (M88A2 HERCULES)			16	72,000						
	Army unfunded requirement			[16]	[72,000]						
013	M1 ABRAMS TANK (MOD)				140,000						

SEC. 4103. PROCUREMENT FOR OVERSEAS CONTINGENCY OPERATIONS FOR BASE REQUIREMENTS
(In Thousands of Dollars)

Line	Item	FY 2017 Request		House Authorized		Senate Authorized		Conference Change		Conference Authorized	
		Qty	Cost	Qty	Cost	Qty	Cost	Qty	Cost	Qty	Cost
	Army unfunded requirement—Industrial base risk mitigation.				[60,000]						
	Army unfunded requirement—Vehicle APS				[80,000]						
	UNDISTRIBUTED										
036A	UNDISTRIBUTED				55,100						
	Additional funding to support increase in Army end strength.				[55,100]						
	TOTAL PROCUREMENT OF W&TCV, ARMY			16	267,100						
	PROCUREMENT OF AMMUNITION, ARMY										
	SMALL/MEDIUM CAL AMMUNITION										
001	CTG, 5.56MM, ALL TYPES				4,000				4,000		4,000
	Army unfunded requirement				[4,000]				[4,000]		
002	CTG, 7.62MM, ALL TYPES				14,000				14,000		14,000
	Army unfunded requirement				[14,000]				[14,000]		
003	CTG, HANDGUN, ALL TYPES				9,000				9,000		9,000
	Army unfunded requirement				[9,000]				[9,000]		
004	CTG, .50 CAL, ALL TYPES				21,000				20,000		20,000
	Army unfunded requirement				[21,000]				[20,000]		
005	CTG, 20MM, ALL TYPES				14,000				14,000		14,000
	Army unfunded requirement				[14,000]				[14,000]		
007	CTG, 30MM, ALL TYPES				8,200				8,200		8,200
	Army unfunded requirement				[8,200]				[8,200]		
	MORTAR AMMUNITION										
011	120MM MORTAR, ALL TYPES				30,000				30,000		30,000
	Army unfunded requirement				[30,000]				[30,000]		
	TANK AMMUNITION										
012	CARTRIDGES, TANK, 105MM AND 120MM, ALL TYPES				35,000				35,000		35,000
	Army unfunded requirement				[35,000]				[35,000]		
	ARTILLERY AMMUNITION										
015	PROJ 155MM EXTENDED RANGE M982			332	23,500			332	23,500	332	23,500
	Army unfunded requirement			[332]	[23,500]			[332]	[23,500]		
016	ARTILLERY PROPELLANTS, FUZES AND PRIMERS, ALL				10,000				10,000		10,000
	Army unfunded requirement				[10,000]				[10,000]		
	ROCKETS										
019	SHOULDER LAUNCHED MUNITIONS, ALL TYPES				30,000				30,000		30,000
	Army unfunded requirement				[30,000]				[30,000]		
020	ROCKET, HYDRA 70, ALL TYPES			44,606	42,500			44606	42,500	44,606	42,500
	Army unfunded requirement			[44,106]	[27,500]			[44,106]	[27,500]		
	Army unfunded requirement- guided hydra rockets			[500]	[15,000]			[500]	[15,000]		
	UNDISTRIBUTED										
034A	UNDISTRIBUTED				46,500						
	Additional funding to support increase in Army end strength.				[46,500]						
	TOTAL PROCUREMENT OF AMMUNITION, ARMY			44,938	287,700			44,938	240,200	44,938	240,200
	OTHER PROCUREMENT, ARMY										
	TACTICAL VEHICLES										
008	FAMILY OF MEDIUM TACTICAL VEH (FMTV)	449	152,000	449	152,000	449	152,000			449	152,000
	COMM—JOINT COMMUNICATIONS										
019	WIN-T—GROUND FORCES TACTICAL NETWORK				80,000						
	BBA Restoration—2BCTs - Increment 2				[80,000]						
	ELECT EQUIP—TACTICAL SURV. (TAC SURV)										
080	INDIRECT FIRE PROTECTION FAMILY OF SYSTEMS				8,400						
	Army unfunded requirement- CRAM Upgrades and MODS.				[8,400]						
	GENERATORS										
158	GENERATORS AND ASSOCIATED EQUIP		9,900		9,900		9,900				9,900
	UNDISTRIBUTED										
180	UNDISTRIBUTED				18,400						
	Additional funding to support increase in Army end strength.				[18,400]						
	TOTAL OTHER PROCUREMENT, ARMY	449	161,900	449	268,700	449	161,900			449	161,900
	JOINT IMPROVISED-THREAT DEFEAT FUND										
	NETWORK ATTACK										
001	RAPID ACQUISITION AND THREAT RESPONSE		113,272		113,272		113,272				113,272
	TOTAL JOINT IMPROVISED-THREAT DEFEAT FUND		113,272		113,272		113,272				113,272

SEC. 4103. PROCUREMENT FOR OVERSEAS CONTINGENCY OPERATIONS FOR BASE REQUIREMENTS
(In Thousands of Dollars)

Line	Item	FY 2017 Request		House Authorized		Senate Authorized		Conference Change		Conference Authorized	
		Qty	Cost	Qty	Cost	Qty	Cost	Qty	Cost	Qty	Cost
	AIRCRAFT PROCUREMENT, NAVY										
	COMBAT AIRCRAFT										
002	F/A–18E/F (FIGHTER) HORNET			14	1,400,000						
	Navy unfunded requirement			[14]	[1,400,000]						
003	JOINT STRIKE FIGHTER CV			4	540,000						
	Marine Corps unfunded requirement			[2]	[270,000]						
	Navy unfunded requirement			[2]	[270,000]						
005	JSF STOVL			2	254,200						
	Marine Corps unfunded requirement			[2]	[254,200]						
009	V–22 (MEDIUM LIFT)			2	150,000						
	Marine Corps unfunded requirement			[2]	[150,000]						
011	H–1 UPGRADES (UH–1Y/AH–1Z)			2	57,000						
	Marine Corps unfunded requirement- AH–1Zs			[2]	[57,000]						
	AIRLIFT AIRCRAFT										
019A	C–40A			4	415,000						
	Marine Corps unfunded requirement			[2]	[207,500]						
	Navy unfunded requirement			[2]	[207,500]						
	OTHER AIRCRAFT										
023	MQ–4 TRITON			1	95,000						
	Additional system—ISR shortfalls			[1]	[95,000]						
025	MQ–8 UAV			4	47,500						
	Scope Increase			[4]	[47,500]						
	MODIFICATION OF AIRCRAFT										
034	H–53 SERIES				16,100						
	Accelerate readiness improvement				[2,800]						
	Marine Corps unfunded requirement- degraded visual environment.				[13,300]						
035	SH–60 SERIES		3,000		3,000		3,000				3,000
036	H–1 SERIES		3,740		27,140		3,740				3,740
	Accelerate readiness improvement				[23,400]						
051	COMMON ECM EQUIPMENT		27,460		27,460		27,460				27,460
059	V–22 (TILT/ROTOR ACFT) OSPREY				39,300						
	Marine Corps unfunded requirement- SPMAGTF- C4 UUNS.				[39,300]						
	AIRCRAFT SPARES AND REPAIR PARTS										
063	SPARES AND REPAIR PARTS				140,300						
	KC–130J spares				[36,000]						
	Marine Corps unfunded requirement- F35 B spares				[91,000]						
	Marine Corps unfunded requirement- F35 C spares				[13,300]						
	TOTAL AIRCRAFT PROCUREMENT, NAVY		34,200	33	3,212,000		34,200				34,200
	WEAPONS PROCUREMENT, NAVY										
	STRATEGIC MISSILES										
003	TOMAHAWK			98	76,000				84,200		84,200
	Scope Increase			[98]	[76,000]				[84,200]		
	TACTICAL MISSILES										
005	SIDEWINDER			75	33,000			75	33,000	75	33,000
	Navy unfunded requirement			[75]	[33,000]			[75]	[33,000]		
015A	LCS OVER-THE-HORIZON MISSILE			8	18,100						
	Navy unfunded requirement			[8]	[18,100]						
	TOTAL WEAPONS PROCUREMENT, NAVY			181	127,100			75	117,200	75	117,200
	PROCUREMENT OF AMMO, NAVY & MC										
	NAVY AMMUNITION										
001	GENERAL PURPOSE BOMBS				58,000				58,000		58,000
	Navy unfunded requirement—JDAM components				[58,000]				[58,000]		
	MARINE CORPS AMMUNITION										
023	ARTILLERY, ALL TYPES								19,200		19,200
	Marine Corps unfunded requirement- GMLRS AW munitions.								[19,200]		
	TOTAL PROCUREMENT OF AMMO, NAVY & MC				58,000				77,200		77,200
	SHIPBUILDING AND CONVERSION, NAVY										
	OTHER WARSHIPS										
003	ADVANCE PROCUREMENT (CY)				263,000						
	Advance Procurement for CVN–81				[263,000]						
005	ADVANCE PROCUREMENT (CY)				85,000						
	Long-lead Time Materiel Orders				[85,000]						
009	DDG–51			1	433,000						

SEC. 4103. PROCUREMENT FOR OVERSEAS CONTINGENCY OPERATIONS FOR BASE REQUIREMENTS
(In Thousands of Dollars)

Line	Item	FY 2017 Request		House Authorized		Senate Authorized		Conference Change		Conference Authorized	
		Qty	Cost	Qty	Cost	Qty	Cost	Qty	Cost	Qty	Cost
	Scope Increase			[1]	[433,000]						
011	LITTORAL COMBAT SHIP			1	384,700						
	Scope Increase			[1]	[384,700]						
	AMPHIBIOUS SHIPS										
012A	AMPHIBIOUS SHIP REPLACEMENT LX(R)			1	856,000						
	Procurement of LPD–29 or LX (R)			[1]	[856,000]						
	AUXILIARIES, CRAFT AND PRIOR YR PROGRAM COST										
026	SHIP TO SHORE CONNECTOR			3	165,000						
	Scope Increase			[3]	[165,000]						
028	LCAC SLEP			4	80,300						
	Scope Increase			[4]	[80,300]						
	TOTAL SHIPBUILDING AND CONVERSION, NAVY			10	2,267,000						
	OTHER PROCUREMENT, NAVY										
	OTHER SHIPBOARD EQUIPMENT										
009	DDG MOD			1	65,000						
	Scope Increase			[1]	[65,000]						
	SMALL BOATS										
032	STANDARD BOATS				20,000						
	Program Acceleration				[20,000]						
	OTHER SHIP SUPPORT										
039A	LCS LAUNCHER			2	24,900						
	Navy unfunded requirement			[2]	[24,900]						
	AIRCRAFT SUPPORT EQUIPMENT										
104	WEAPONS RANGE SUPPORT EQUIPMENT				9,000						
	Navy unfunded requirement—Barking Sands Tactical Underwater Range.				[9,000]						
	OTHER ORDNANCE SUPPORT EQUIPMENT										
116	EXPLOSIVE ORDNANCE DISPOSAL EQUIP		59,329		59,329		59,329				59,329
	TOTAL OTHER PROCUREMENT, NAVY		59,329	3	178,229		59,329				59,329
	PROCUREMENT, MARINE CORPS										
	ARTILLERY AND OTHER WEAPONS										
004	155MM LIGHTWEIGHT TOWED HOWITZER				14,000						
	Marine Corps unfunded requirement- chrome tubes				[14,000]						
005	HIGH MOBILITY ARTILLERY ROCKET SYSTEM				19,200						
	Program Increase- 148 additional GMLRS				[19,200]						
	OTHER SUPPORT (NON-TEL)										
036	COMMAND POST SYSTEMS				40,800						
	Marine Corps unfunded requirement- SPMAGTF—C4 UUNS.				[40,800]						
	TOTAL PROCUREMENT, MARINE CORPS				74,000						
	AIRCRAFT PROCUREMENT, AIR FORCE										
	TACTICAL FORCES										
001	F–35			5	690,500						
	Air Force unfunded requirement			[5]	[690,500]						
	OTHER AIRLIFT										
004	C–130J			3	271,500						
	Scope Increase			[3]	[271,500]						
	HELICOPTERS										
010	UH–1N REPLACEMENT				80,000						
	Program increase to address urgent need				[80,000]						
	OTHER AIRCRAFT										
015	MQ–9	12	179,430	12	179,430	12	179,430			12	179,430
015A	EC–130H			1	103,000						
	Scope increase			[1]	[103,000]						
	TACTICAL AIRCRAFT										
020	A–10				218,500						
	A–10 wing upgrades				[120,000]						
	Air Force unfunded requirement- A–10 antijam GPS				[10,300]						
	Air Force unfunded requirement- A–10 situation awareness upgrade kits.				[23,200]						
	Air Force unfunded requirement- ASE radar warning receiver upgrades.				[65,000]						
021	F–15				60,400						
	Air Force unfunded requirement- ASE radar warning receiver upgrades.				[60,400]						
022	F–16				187,500						

SEC. 4103. PROCUREMENT FOR OVERSEAS CONTINGENCY OPERATIONS FOR BASE REQUIREMENTS
(In Thousands of Dollars)

Line	Item	FY 2017 Request		House Authorized		Senate Authorized		Conference Change		Conference Authorized	
		Qty	Cost	Qty	Cost	Qty	Cost	Qty	Cost	Qty	Cost
	Air Force unfunded requirement- antijam GPS				[5,000]						
	Air Force unfunded requirement- missile warning system.				[12,000]						
	Air Force unfunded requirement- radar warning receiver upgrades.				[170,500]						
	OTHER AIRCRAFT										
049	E–8			2	17,500						
	Additional 2 PME-DMS kits			[2]	[17,500]						
054	H–60				70,700						
	Air Force unfunded requirement- ASE radar warning receivers.				[70,700]						
	TOTAL AIRCRAFT PROCUREMENT, AIR FORCE	12	179,430	23	1,879,030	12	179,430			12	179,430
	MISSILE PROCUREMENT, AIR FORCE										
	TACTICAL										
007	SMALL DIAMETER BOMB	4,195	167,800	4,195	167,800	4,195	167,800			4,195	167,800
	CLASS IV										
011	AGM–65D MAVERICK		16,900		16,900		16,900				16,900
	TOTAL MISSILE PROCUREMENT, AIR FORCE	4,195	184,700	4,195	184,700	4,195	184,700			4,195	184,700
	PROCUREMENT OF AMMUNITION, AIR FORCE										
	ROCKETS										
001	ROCKETS		60,000		60,000		60,000				60,000
	BOMBS										
006	JOINT DIRECT ATTACK MUNITION	12,498	263,000	12,498	263,000	12,498	263,000			12,498	263,000
	TOTAL PROCUREMENT OF AMMUNITION, AIR FORCE.	12,498	323,000	12,498	323,000	12,498	323,000			12,498	323,000
	PROCUREMENT, DEFENSE-WIDE										
	MAJOR EQUIPMENT, DISA										
007	TELEPORT PROGRAM		2,000		2,000		2,000				2,000
016	DEFENSE INFORMATION SYSTEMS NETWORK		2,000		2,000		2,000				2,000
	TOTAL PROCUREMENT, DEFENSE-WIDE		4,000		4,000		4,000				4,000
	TOTAL PROCUREMENT	18,643	1,287,871	65,669	10,728,171	18,643	1,287,871	45,013	630,700	63,656	1,918,571

TITLE XLII—RESEARCH, DEVELOPMENT, TEST, AND EVALUATION

SEC. 4201. RESEARCH, DEVELOPMENT, TEST, AND EVALUATION.

SEC. 4201. RESEARCH, DEVELOPMENT, TEST, AND EVALUATION
(In Thousands of Dollars)

Line	Program Element	Item	FY 2017 Request	House Authorized	Senate Authorized	Conference Change	Conference Authorized
		RESEARCH, DEVELOPMENT, TEST & EVAL, ARMY					
		BASIC RESEARCH					
001	0601101A	IN-HOUSE LABORATORY INDEPENDENT RESEARCH	12,381	12,381	12,381		12,381
002	0601102A	DEFENSE RESEARCH SCIENCES	253,116	253,116	253,116		253,116
003	0601103A	UNIVERSITY RESEARCH INITIATIVES	69,166	69,166	69,166		69,166
004	0601104A	UNIVERSITY AND INDUSTRY RESEARCH CENTERS	94,280	94,280	94,280		94,280
		SUBTOTAL BASIC RESEARCH	428,943	428,943	428,943		428,943
		APPLIED RESEARCH					
005	0602105A	MATERIALS TECHNOLOGY	31,533	31,533	37,033	5,500	37,033
		Ground vehicle coating system			[5,500]	[5,500]	
006	0602120A	SENSORS AND ELECTRONIC SURVIVABILITY	36,109	36,109	38,109	2,000	38,109
		Program increase			[2,000]	[2,000]	
007	0602122A	TRACTOR HIP	6,995	6,995	6,995		6,995
008	0602211A	AVIATION TECHNOLOGY	65,914	65,914	65,914		65,914
009	0602270A	ELECTRONIC WARFARE TECHNOLOGY	25,466	25,466	25,466		25,466
010	0602303A	MISSILE TECHNOLOGY	44,313	44,313	44,313		44,313
011	0602307A	ADVANCED WEAPONS TECHNOLOGY	28,803	28,803	28,803		28,803
012	0602308A	ADVANCED CONCEPTS AND SIMULATION	27,688	27,688	27,688		27,688

SEC. 4201. RESEARCH, DEVELOPMENT, TEST, AND EVALUATION
(In Thousands of Dollars)

Line	Program Element	Item	FY 2017 Request	House Authorized	Senate Authorized	Conference Change	Conference Authorized
013	0602601A	COMBAT VEHICLE AND AUTOMOTIVE TECHNOLOGY	67,959	67,959	67,959		67,959
014	0602618A	BALLISTICS TECHNOLOGY	85,436	85,436	85,436		85,436
015	0602622A	CHEMICAL, SMOKE AND EQUIPMENT DEFEATING TECHNOLOGY	3,923	3,923	3,923		3,923
016	0602623A	JOINT SERVICE SMALL ARMS PROGRAM	5,545	5,545	5,545		5,545
017	0602624A	WEAPONS AND MUNITIONS TECHNOLOGY	53,581	53,581	53,581		53,581
018	0602705A	ELECTRONICS AND ELECTRONIC DEVICES	56,322	56,322	56,322		56,322
019	0602709A	NIGHT VISION TECHNOLOGY	36,079	36,079	36,079		36,079
020	0602712A	COUNTERMINE SYSTEMS	26,497	26,497	26,497		26,497
021	0602716A	HUMAN FACTORS ENGINEERING TECHNOLOGY	23,671	23,671	23,671		23,671
022	0602720A	ENVIRONMENTAL QUALITY TECHNOLOGY	22,151	22,151	22,151		22,151
023	0602782A	COMMAND, CONTROL, COMMUNICATIONS TECHNOLOGY	37,803	37,803	37,803		37,803
024	0602783A	COMPUTER AND SOFTWARE TECHNOLOGY	13,811	13,811	13,811		13,811
025	0602784A	MILITARY ENGINEERING TECHNOLOGY	67,416	67,416	67,416		67,416
026	0602785A	MANPOWER/PERSONNEL/TRAINING TECHNOLOGY	26,045	26,045	21,045		26,045
		Decrease for social science research			[−5,000]		
027	0602786A	WARFIGHTER TECHNOLOGY	37,403	42,403	37,403	5,000	42,403
		Program Increase		[5,000]		[5,000]	
028	0602787A	MEDICAL TECHNOLOGY	77,111	77,111	77,111		77,111
		SUBTOTAL APPLIED RESEARCH	**907,574**	**912,574**	**910,074**	**12,500**	**920,074**
		ADVANCED TECHNOLOGY DEVELOPMENT					
029	0603001A	WARFIGHTER ADVANCED TECHNOLOGY	38,831	38,831	38,831		38,831
030	0603002A	MEDICAL ADVANCED TECHNOLOGY	68,365	68,365	68,365		68,365
031	0603003A	AVIATION ADVANCED TECHNOLOGY	94,280	94,280	94,280		94,280
032	0603004A	WEAPONS AND MUNITIONS ADVANCED TECHNOLOGY	68,714	68,714	68,714		68,714
033	0603005A	COMBAT VEHICLE AND AUTOMOTIVE ADVANCED TECHNOLOGY	122,132	122,132	172,132	30,000	152,132
		Emerging requirement			[50,000]	[30,000]	
034	0603006A	SPACE APPLICATION ADVANCED TECHNOLOGY	3,904	3,904	3,904		3,904
035	0603007A	MANPOWER, PERSONNEL AND TRAINING ADVANCED TECHNOLOGY	14,417	14,417	14,417		14,417
037	0603009A	TRACTOR HIKE	8,074	21,374	8,074	13,300	21,374
		Classified adjustment		[13,300]		[13,300]	
038	0603015A	NEXT GENERATION TRAINING & SIMULATION SYSTEMS	18,969	18,969	18,969		18,969
039	0603020A	TRACTOR ROSE	11,910	11,910	11,910		11,910
040	0603125A	COMBATING TERRORISM—TECHNOLOGY DEVELOPMENT	27,686	27,686	27,686		27,686
041	0603130A	TRACTOR NAIL	2,340	2,340	2,340		2,340
042	0603131A	TRACTOR EGGS	2,470	2,470	2,470		2,470
043	0603270A	ELECTRONIC WARFARE TECHNOLOGY	27,893	27,893	22,893		27,893
		General decrease			[−5,000]		
044	0603313A	MISSILE AND ROCKET ADVANCED TECHNOLOGY	52,190	52,190	52,190		52,190
045	0603322A	TRACTOR CAGE	11,107	11,107	11,107		11,107
046	0603461A	HIGH PERFORMANCE COMPUTING MODERNIZATION PROGRAM	177,190	179,190	177,190	2,000	179,190
		Program increase		[2,000]		[2,000]	
047	0603606A	LANDMINE WARFARE AND BARRIER ADVANCED TECHNOLOGY	17,451	17,451	17,451		17,451
048	0603607A	JOINT SERVICE SMALL ARMS PROGRAM	5,839	5,839	5,839		5,839
049	0603710A	NIGHT VISION ADVANCED TECHNOLOGY	44,468	44,468	44,468		44,468
050	0603728A	ENVIRONMENTAL QUALITY TECHNOLOGY DEMONSTRATIONS	11,137	11,137	11,137		11,137
051	0603734A	MILITARY ENGINEERING ADVANCED TECHNOLOGY	20,684	20,684	20,684		20,684
052	0603772A	ADVANCED TACTICAL COMPUTER SCIENCE AND SENSOR TECHNOLOGY	44,239	44,239	39,239		44,239
		General program decrease			[−5,000]		
053	0603794A	C3 ADVANCED TECHNOLOGY	35,775	35,775	35,775		35,775
		SUBTOTAL ADVANCED TECHNOLOGY DEVELOPMENT	**930,065**	**945,365**	**970,065**	**45,300**	**975,365**
		ADVANCED COMPONENT DEVELOPMENT & PROTOTYPES					
054	0603305A	ARMY MISSILE DEFENSE SYSTEMS INTEGRATION	9,433	9,433	9,433		9,433
055	0603308A	ARMY SPACE SYSTEMS INTEGRATION	23,056	23,056	23,056		23,056
056	0603619A	LANDMINE WARFARE AND BARRIER—ADV DEV	72,117	72,117	72,117		72,117
057	0603627A	SMOKE, OBSCURANT AND TARGET DEFEATING SYS-ADV DEV	28,244	28,244	28,244		28,244

SEC. 4201. RESEARCH, DEVELOPMENT, TEST, AND EVALUATION
(In Thousands of Dollars)

Line	Program Element	Item	FY 2017 Request	House Authorized	Senate Authorized	Conference Change	Conference Authorized
058	0603639A	TANK AND MEDIUM CALIBER AMMUNITION	40,096	40,096	40,096		40,096
059	0603747A	SOLDIER SUPPORT AND SURVIVABILITY	10,506	10,506	10,506		10,506
060	0603766A	TACTICAL ELECTRONIC SURVEILLANCE SYSTEM—ADV DEV	15,730	15,730	15,730		15,730
061	0603774A	NIGHT VISION SYSTEMS ADVANCED DEVELOPMENT	10,321	10,321	10,321		10,321
062	0603779A	ENVIRONMENTAL QUALITY TECHNOLOGY—DEM/VAL	7,785	7,785	7,785		7,785
063	0603790A	NATO RESEARCH AND DEVELOPMENT	2,300	2,300	2,300		2,300
064	0603801A	AVIATION—ADV DEV	10,014	10,014	10,014		10,014
065	0603804A	LOGISTICS AND ENGINEER EQUIPMENT—ADV DEV	20,834	20,834	20,834		20,834
066	0603807A	MEDICAL SYSTEMS—ADV DEV	33,503	41,003	33,503		33,503
		Program increase		[7,500]			
067	0603827A	SOLDIER SYSTEMS—ADVANCED DEVELOPMENT	31,120	31,120	40,520	9,400	40,520
		Accelerate small arms improvement			[9,400]	[9,400]	
068	0604100A	ANALYSIS OF ALTERNATIVES	6,608	6,608	6,608		6,608
069	0604114A	LOWER TIER AIR MISSILE DEFENSE (LTAMD) SENSOR	35,132	35,132	35,132		35,132
070	0604115A	TECHNOLOGY MATURATION INITIATIVES	70,047	70,047	70,047	−9,009	61,038
		Excess growth				[−9,009]	
071	0604120A	ASSURED POSITIONING, NAVIGATION AND TIMING (PNT)	83,279	83,279	83,279		83,279
073	0305251A	CYBERSPACE OPERATIONS FORCES AND FORCE SUPPORT	40,510	40,510	40,510	−10,000	30,510
		Inadequate justification				[−10,000]	
		SUBTOTAL ADVANCED COMPONENT DEVELOPMENT & PROTOTYPES	**550,635**	**558,135**	**560,035**	**−9,609**	**541,026**
		SYSTEM DEVELOPMENT & DEMONSTRATION					
074	0604201A	AIRCRAFT AVIONICS	83,248	83,248	83,248		83,248
075	0604270A	ELECTRONIC WARFARE DEVELOPMENT	34,642	34,642	34,642		34,642
077	0604290A	MID-TIER NETWORKING VEHICULAR RADIO (MNVR)	12,172	12,172	12,172		12,172
078	0604321A	ALL SOURCE ANALYSIS SYSTEM	3,958	3,958	3,958		3,958
079	0604328A	TRACTOR CAGE	12,525	12,525	12,525		12,525
080	0604601A	INFANTRY SUPPORT WEAPONS	66,943	66,943	66,943		66,943
082	0604611A	JAVELIN	20,011	20,011	20,011		20,011
083	0604622A	FAMILY OF HEAVY TACTICAL VEHICLES	11,429	11,429	11,429		11,429
084	0604633A	AIR TRAFFIC CONTROL	3,421	3,421	3,421		3,421
085	0604641A	TACTICAL UNMANNED GROUND VEHICLE (TUGV)	39,282	39,282	39,282		39,282
086	0604642A	LIGHT TACTICAL WHEELED VEHICLES	494	494	494		494
087	0604645A	ARMORED SYSTEMS MODERNIZATION (ASM)—ENG DEV	9,678	9,678	9,678		9,678
088	0604710A	NIGHT VISION SYSTEMS—ENG DEV	84,519	84,519	84,519		84,519
089	0604713A	COMBAT FEEDING, CLOTHING, AND EQUIPMENT	2,054	2,054	2,054		2,054
090	0604715A	NON-SYSTEM TRAINING DEVICES—ENG DEV	30,774	30,774	30,774		30,774
091	0604741A	AIR DEFENSE COMMAND, CONTROL AND INTELLIGENCE—ENG DEV	53,332	61,332	53,332	8,000	61,332
		Program increase- all digital radar technology for CRAM		[8,000]		[8,000]	
092	0604742A	CONSTRUCTIVE SIMULATION SYSTEMS DEVELOPMENT	17,887	17,887	17,887		17,887
093	0604746A	AUTOMATIC TEST EQUIPMENT DEVELOPMENT	8,813	8,813	8,813		8,813
094	0604760A	DISTRIBUTIVE INTERACTIVE SIMULATIONS (DIS)—ENG DEV	10,487	10,487	10,487		10,487
095	0604780A	COMBINED ARMS TACTICAL TRAINER (CATT) CORE	15,068	15,068	15,068		15,068
096	0604798A	BRIGADE ANALYSIS, INTEGRATION AND EVALUATION	89,716	89,716	89,716		89,716
097	0604802A	WEAPONS AND MUNITIONS—ENG DEV	80,365	80,365	80,365		80,365
098	0604804A	LOGISTICS AND ENGINEER EQUIPMENT—ENG DEV	75,098	86,198	75,098	11,100	86,198
		Program Increase- next generation signature management		[11,100]		[11,100]	
099	0604805A	COMMAND, CONTROL, COMMUNICATIONS SYSTEMS—ENG DEV	4,245	4,245	4,245		4,245
100	0604807A	MEDICAL MATERIEL/MEDICAL BIOLOGICAL DEFENSE EQUIPMENT—ENG DEV.	41,124	41,124	41,124		41,124
101	0604808A	LANDMINE WARFARE/BARRIER—ENG DEV	39,630	39,630	39,630		39,630
102	0604818A	ARMY TACTICAL COMMAND & CONTROL HARDWARE & SOFTWARE	205,590	205,590	205,590		205,590
103	0604820A	RADAR DEVELOPMENT	15,983	15,983	15,983		15,983
104	0604822A	GENERAL FUND ENTERPRISE BUSINESS SYSTEM (GFEBS)	6,805	6,805	6,805		6,805
105	0604823A	FIREFINDER	9,235	9,235	9,235		9,235
106	0604827A	SOLDIER SYSTEMS—WARRIOR DEM/VAL	12,393	12,393	12,393		12,393
107	0604854A	ARTILLERY SYSTEMS—EMD	1,756	1,756	1,756		1,756
108	0605013A	INFORMATION TECHNOLOGY DEVELOPMENT	74,236	74,236	74,236		74,236

SEC. 4201. RESEARCH, DEVELOPMENT, TEST, AND EVALUATION
(In Thousands of Dollars)

Line	Program Element	Item	FY 2017 Request	House Authorized	Senate Authorized	Conference Change	Conference Authorized
109	0605018A	INTEGRATED PERSONNEL AND PAY SYSTEM-ARMY (IPPS-A)	155,584	155,584	135,584	−11,000	144,584
		Unjustified growth			[−20,000]	[−11,000]	
110	0605028A	ARMORED MULTI-PURPOSE VEHICLE (AMPV)	184,221	184,221	184,221		184,221
111	0605029A	INTEGRATED GROUND SECURITY SURVEILLANCE RESPONSE CAPABILITY (IGSSR-C).	4,980	4,980	4,980		4,980
112	0605030A	JOINT TACTICAL NETWORK CENTER (JTNC)	15,041	15,041	15,041		15,041
113	0605031A	JOINT TACTICAL NETWORK (JTN)	16,014	16,014	16,014		16,014
114	0605032A	TRACTOR TIRE	27,254	27,254	27,254		27,254
115	0605033A	GROUND-BASED OPERATIONAL SURVEILLANCE SYSTEM—EXPEDITIONARY (GBOSS-E).	5,032	5,032	5,032		5,032
116	0605034A	TACTICAL SECURITY SYSTEM (TSS)	2,904	2,904	2,904		2,904
117	0605035A	COMMON INFRARED COUNTERMEASURES (CIRCM)	96,977	96,977	96,977		96,977
118	0605036A	COMBATING WEAPONS OF MASS DESTRUCTION (CWMD)	2,089	2,089	2,089		2,089
119	0605041A	DEFENSIVE CYBER TOOL DEVELOPMENT	33,836	33,836	33,836		33,836
120	0605042A	TACTICAL NETWORK RADIO SYSTEMS (LOW-TIER)	18,824	18,824	18,824		18,824
121	0605047A	CONTRACT WRITING SYSTEM	20,663	20,663			20,663
		Unjustified request			[−20,663]		
122	0605051A	AIRCRAFT SURVIVABILITY DEVELOPMENT	41,133	41,133	54,133		41,133
		ASE unfunded requirement			[13,000]		
123	0605052A	INDIRECT FIRE PROTECTION CAPABILITY INC 2—BLOCK 1	83,995	83,995	83,995		83,995
125	0605380A	AMF JOINT TACTICAL RADIO SYSTEM (JTRS)	5,028	5,028	5,028		5,028
126	0605450A	JOINT AIR-TO-GROUND MISSILE (JAGM)	42,972	42,972	42,972		42,972
128	0605457A	ARMY INTEGRATED AIR AND MISSILE DEFENSE (AIAMD)	252,811	252,811	252,811		252,811
131	0605766A	NATIONAL CAPABILITIES INTEGRATION (MIP)	4,955	4,955	4,955		4,955
132	0605812A	JOINT LIGHT TACTICAL VEHICLE (JLTV) ENGINEERING AND MANUFACTURING DEVELOPMENT PH.	11,530	11,530	11,530		11,530
133	0605830A	AVIATION GROUND SUPPORT EQUIPMENT	2,142	2,142	2,142		2,142
134	0210609A	PALADIN INTEGRATED MANAGEMENT (PIM)	41,498	41,498	41,498		41,498
135	0303032A	TROJAN—RH12	4,273	4,273	4,273		4,273
136	0304270A	ELECTRONIC WARFARE DEVELOPMENT	14,425	14,425	14,425		14,425
		SUBTOTAL SYSTEM DEVELOPMENT & DEMONSTRATION	**2,265,094**	**2,284,194**	**2,237,431**	**8,100**	**2,273,194**
		RDT&E MANAGEMENT SUPPORT					
137	0604256A	THREAT SIMULATOR DEVELOPMENT	25,675	25,675	25,675		25,675
138	0604258A	TARGET SYSTEMS DEVELOPMENT	19,122	19,122	19,122		19,122
139	0604759A	MAJOR T&E INVESTMENT	84,777	84,777	84,777		84,777
140	0605103A	RAND ARROYO CENTER	20,658	20,658	20,658		20,658
141	0605301A	ARMY KWAJALEIN ATOLL	236,648	236,648	236,648		236,648
142	0605326A	CONCEPTS EXPERIMENTATION PROGRAM	25,596	25,596	25,596		25,596
144	0605601A	ARMY TEST RANGES AND FACILITIES	293,748	293,748	293,748		293,748
145	0605602A	ARMY TECHNICAL TEST INSTRUMENTATION AND TARGETS	52,404	52,404	52,404		52,404
146	0605604A	SURVIVABILITY/LETHALITY ANALYSIS	38,571	38,571	38,571		38,571
147	0605606A	AIRCRAFT CERTIFICATION	4,665	4,665	4,665		4,665
148	0605702A	METEOROLOGICAL SUPPORT TO RDT&E ACTIVITIES	6,925	6,925	6,925		6,925
149	0605706A	MATERIEL SYSTEMS ANALYSIS	21,677	21,677	21,677		21,677
150	0605709A	EXPLOITATION OF FOREIGN ITEMS	12,415	12,415	12,415		12,415
151	0605712A	SUPPORT OF OPERATIONAL TESTING	49,684	49,684	49,684		49,684
152	0605716A	ARMY EVALUATION CENTER	55,905	55,905	55,905		55,905
153	0605718A	ARMY MODELING & SIM X-CMD COLLABORATION & INTEG	7,959	7,959	7,959		7,959
154	0605801A	PROGRAMWIDE ACTIVITIES	51,822	51,822	51,822		51,822
155	0605803A	TECHNICAL INFORMATION ACTIVITIES	33,323	33,323	35,823		33,323
		Program increase Geospatial			[2,500]		
156	0605805A	MUNITIONS STANDARDIZATION, EFFECTIVENESS AND SAFETY	40,545	40,545	40,545		40,545
157	0605857A	ENVIRONMENTAL QUALITY TECHNOLOGY MGMT SUPPORT	2,130	2,130	2,130		2,130
158	0605898A	MANAGEMENT HQ—R&D	49,885	49,885	49,885		49,885
159	0303260A	DEFENSE MILITARY DECEPTION INITIATIVE	2,000	2,000	2,000		2,000
		SUBTOTAL RDT&E MANAGEMENT SUPPORT	**1,136,134**	**1,136,134**	**1,138,634**		**1,136,134**

SEC. 4201. RESEARCH, DEVELOPMENT, TEST, AND EVALUATION
(In Thousands of Dollars)

Line	Program Element	Item	FY 2017 Request	House Authorized	Senate Authorized	Conference Change	Conference Authorized
		OPERATIONAL SYSTEMS DEVELOPMENT					
161	0603778A	MLRS PRODUCT IMPROVEMENT PROGRAM	9,663	9,663	9,663		9,663
162	0603813A	TRACTOR PULL	3,960	3,960	3,960		3,960
163	0605024A	ANTI-TAMPER TECHNOLOGY SUPPORT	3,638	3,638	3,638		3,638
164	0607131A	WEAPONS AND MUNITIONS PRODUCT IMPROVEMENT PROGRAMS	14,517	14,517	14,517		14,517
165	0607133A	TRACTOR SMOKE	4,479	4,479	4,479		4,479
166	0607134A	LONG RANGE PRECISION FIRES (LRPF)	39,275	39,275	39,275		39,275
167	0607135A	APACHE PRODUCT IMPROVEMENT PROGRAM	66,441	66,441	66,441		66,441
168	0607136A	BLACKHAWK PRODUCT IMPROVEMENT PROGRAM	46,765	46,765	46,765		46,765
169	0607137A	CHINOOK PRODUCT IMPROVEMENT PROGRAM	91,848	91,848	91,848		91,848
170	0607138A	FIXED WING PRODUCT IMPROVEMENT PROGRAM	796	796	796		796
171	0607139A	IMPROVED TURBINE ENGINE PROGRAM	126,105	126,105	126,105		126,105
172	0607140A	EMERGING TECHNOLOGIES FROM NIE	2,369	2,369	2,369		2,369
173	0607141A	LOGISTICS AUTOMATION	4,563	4,563	4,563		4,563
174	0607665A	FAMILY OF BIOMETRICS	12,098	12,098	12,098		12,098
175	0607865A	PATRIOT PRODUCT IMPROVEMENT	49,482	49,482	49,482		49,482
176	0202429A	AEROSTAT JOINT PROJECT—COCOM EXERCISE	45,482	2,482	4,482	−43,000	2,482
		Program reduction		[−43,000]	[−41,000]	[−43,000]	
178	0203728A	JOINT AUTOMATED DEEP OPERATION COORDINATION SYSTEM (JADOCS).	30,455	30,455	30,455		30,455
179	0203735A	COMBAT VEHICLE IMPROVEMENT PROGRAMS	316,857	316,857	328,857		316,857
		APS unfunded requirement			[12,000]		
180	0203740A	MANEUVER CONTROL SYSTEM	4,031	4,031	4,031		4,031
181	0203744A	AIRCRAFT MODIFICATIONS/PRODUCT IMPROVEMENT PROGRAMS	35,793	35,793	35,793		35,793
182	0203752A	AIRCRAFT ENGINE COMPONENT IMPROVEMENT PROGRAM	259	259	259		259
183	0203758A	DIGITIZATION	6,483	6,483	6,483		6,483
184	0203801A	MISSILE/AIR DEFENSE PRODUCT IMPROVEMENT PROGRAM	5,122	5,122	5,122		5,122
185	0203802A	OTHER MISSILE PRODUCT IMPROVEMENT PROGRAMS	7,491	7,491	7,491		7,491
186	0203808A	TRACTOR CARD	20,333	20,333	20,333		20,333
188	0205410A	MATERIALS HANDLING EQUIPMENT	124	124	124		124
190	0205456A	LOWER TIER AIR AND MISSILE DEFENSE (AMD) SYSTEM	69,417	69,417	69,417		69,417
191	0205778A	GUIDED MULTIPLE-LAUNCH ROCKET SYSTEM (GMLRS)	22,044	22,044	22,044		22,044
192	0208053A	JOINT TACTICAL GROUND SYSTEM	12,649	12,649	12,649		12,649
194	0303028A	SECURITY AND INTELLIGENCE ACTIVITIES	11,619	11,619	11,619		11,619
195	0303140A	INFORMATION SYSTEMS SECURITY PROGRAM	38,280	38,280	38,280		38,280
196	0303141A	GLOBAL COMBAT SUPPORT SYSTEM	27,223	27,223	2,023		27,223
		GCSS unjustified request			[−25,200]		
197	0303142A	SATCOM GROUND ENVIRONMENT (SPACE)	18,815	18,815	18,815		18,815
198	0303150A	WWMCCS/GLOBAL COMMAND AND CONTROL SYSTEM	4,718	4,718	4,718		4,718
202	0305204A	TACTICAL UNMANNED AERIAL VEHICLES	8,218	8,218	8,218		8,218
203	0305206A	AIRBORNE RECONNAISSANCE SYSTEMS	11,799	11,799	11,799		11,799
204	0305208A	DISTRIBUTED COMMON GROUND/SURFACE SYSTEMS	32,284	32,284	284		32,284
		Change in tactical requirements			[−32,000]		
205	0305219A	MQ–1C GRAY EAGLE UAS	13,470	13,470	13,470		13,470
206	0305232A	RQ–11 UAV	1,613	1,613	1,613		1,613
207	0305233A	RQ–7 UAV	4,597	4,597	4,597		4,597
209	0310349A	WIN–T INCREMENT 2—INITIAL NETWORKING	4,867	4,867	4,867		4,867
210	0708045A	END ITEM INDUSTRIAL PREPAREDNESS ACTIVITIES	62,287	62,287	62,287		62,287
210A	9999999999	CLASSIFIED PROGRAMS	4,625	4,625	4,625		4,625
		SUBTOTAL OPERATIONAL SYSTEMS DEVELOPMENT	**1,296,954**	**1,253,954**	**1,210,754**	**−43,000**	**1,253,954**
		TOTAL RESEARCH, DEVELOPMENT, TEST & EVAL, ARMY	**7,515,399**	**7,519,299**	**7,455,936**	**13,291**	**7,528,690**
		RESEARCH, DEVELOPMENT, TEST & EVAL, NAVY					
		BASIC RESEARCH					
001	0601103N	UNIVERSITY RESEARCH INITIATIVES	101,714	121,714	101,714	20,000	121,714
		Program increase		[20,000]		[20,000]	
002	0601152N	IN-HOUSE LABORATORY INDEPENDENT RESEARCH	18,508	18,508	18,508		18,508

SEC. 4201. RESEARCH, DEVELOPMENT, TEST, AND EVALUATION
(In Thousands of Dollars)

Line	Program Element	Item	FY 2017 Request	House Authorized	Senate Authorized	Conference Change	Conference Authorized
003	0601153N	DEFENSE RESEARCH SCIENCES	422,748	422,748	422,748		422,748
		SUBTOTAL BASIC RESEARCH	**542,970**	**562,970**	**542,970**	**20,000**	**562,970**
		APPLIED RESEARCH					
004	0602114N	POWER PROJECTION APPLIED RESEARCH	41,371	41,371	41,371		41,371
005	0602123N	FORCE PROTECTION APPLIED RESEARCH	158,745	158,745	158,745		158,745
006	0602131M	MARINE CORPS LANDING FORCE TECHNOLOGY	51,590	51,590	51,590		51,590
007	0602235N	COMMON PICTURE APPLIED RESEARCH	41,185	41,185	41,185		41,185
008	0602236N	WARFIGHTER SUSTAINMENT APPLIED RESEARCH	45,467	45,467	45,467		45,467
009	0602271N	ELECTROMAGNETIC SYSTEMS APPLIED RESEARCH	118,941	118,941	118,941		118,941
010	0602435N	OCEAN WARFIGHTING ENVIRONMENT APPLIED RESEARCH	42,618	74,618	42,618	30,000	72,618
		Service Life Extension Program—AGOR		[32,000]		[30,000]	
011	0602651M	JOINT NON-LETHAL WEAPONS APPLIED RESEARCH	6,327	6,327	6,327		6,327
012	0602747N	UNDERSEA WARFARE APPLIED RESEARCH	126,313	126,313	136,313		126,313
		Program increase			[10,000]		
013	0602750N	FUTURE NAVAL CAPABILITIES APPLIED RESEARCH	165,103	165,103	165,103		165,103
014	0602782N	MINE AND EXPEDITIONARY WARFARE APPLIED RESEARCH	33,916	33,916	33,916		33,916
015	0602898N	SCIENCE AND TECHNOLOGY MANAGEMENT—ONR HEADQUARTERS	29,575	29,575	29,575		29,575
		SUBTOTAL APPLIED RESEARCH	**861,151**	**893,151**	**871,151**	**30,000**	**891,151**
		ADVANCED TECHNOLOGY DEVELOPMENT					
016	0603114N	POWER PROJECTION ADVANCED TECHNOLOGY	96,406	106,406	81,406		96,406
		General decrease			[−15,000]		
		Program increase for common mount		[10,000]			
017	0603123N	FORCE PROTECTION ADVANCED TECHNOLOGY	48,438	48,438	48,438		48,438
018	0603271N	ELECTROMAGNETIC SYSTEMS ADVANCED TECHNOLOGY	26,421	26,421	26,421		26,421
019	0603640M	USMC ADVANCED TECHNOLOGY DEMONSTRATION (ATD)	140,416	140,416	140,416		140,416
020	0603651M	JOINT NON-LETHAL WEAPONS TECHNOLOGY DEVELOPMENT	13,117	13,117	13,117		13,117
021	0603673N	FUTURE NAVAL CAPABILITIES ADVANCED TECHNOLOGY DEVELOPMENT	249,092	249,092	239,092	−2,000	247,092
		Capable manpower, and power and energy			[−10,000]	[−2,000]	
022	0603680N	MANUFACTURING TECHNOLOGY PROGRAM	56,712	56,712	56,712		56,712
023	0603729N	WARFIGHTER PROTECTION ADVANCED TECHNOLOGY	4,789	4,789	4,789		4,789
024	0603747N	UNDERSEA WARFARE ADVANCED TECHNOLOGY	25,880	25,880	25,880		25,880
025	0603758N	NAVY WARFIGHTING EXPERIMENTS AND DEMONSTRATIONS	60,550	65,550	60,550		60,550
		Program Increase		[5,000]			
026	0603782N	MINE AND EXPEDITIONARY WARFARE ADVANCED TECHNOLOGY	15,167	15,167	15,167		15,167
		SUBTOTAL ADVANCED TECHNOLOGY DEVELOPMENT	**736,988**	**751,988**	**711,988**	**−2,000**	**734,988**
		ADVANCED COMPONENT DEVELOPMENT & PROTOTYPES					
027	0603207N	AIR/OCEAN TACTICAL APPLICATIONS	48,536	48,536	48,536		48,536
028	0603216N	AVIATION SURVIVABILITY	5,239	5,239	5,239		5,239
030	0603251N	AIRCRAFT SYSTEMS	1,519	1,519	1,519		1,519
031	0603254N	ASW SYSTEMS DEVELOPMENT	7,041	7,041	7,041		7,041
032	0603261N	TACTICAL AIRBORNE RECONNAISSANCE	3,274	3,274	3,274		3,274
033	0603382N	ADVANCED COMBAT SYSTEMS TECHNOLOGY	57,034	72,034	57,034	−41,538	15,496
		Program Increase		[15,000]			
		Rapid prototype development excess growth				[−30,267]	
		Unmanned rapid prototype development excess growth				[−11,271]	
034	0603502N	SURFACE AND SHALLOW WATER MINE COUNTERMEASURES	165,775	165,775	164,275	−22,227	143,548
		Excess prior year funds			[−1,500]	[−1,500]	
		LDUUV product development excess growth				[−13,800]	
		USV with AQS−20 product development excess growth				[−5,750]	
		USV with AQS−20 support excess growth				[−1,177]	
035	0603506N	SURFACE SHIP TORPEDO DEFENSE	87,066	87,066	87,066		87,066
036	0603512N	CARRIER SYSTEMS DEVELOPMENT	7,605	7,605	7,605		7,605
037	0603525N	PILOT FISH	132,068	132,068	132,068		132,068
038	0603527N	RETRACT LARCH	14,546	14,546	14,546		14,546

SEC. 4201. RESEARCH, DEVELOPMENT, TEST, AND EVALUATION
(In Thousands of Dollars)

Line	Program Element	Item	FY 2017 Request	House Authorized	Senate Authorized	Conference Change	Conference Authorized
039	0603536N	RETRACT JUNIPER	115,435	115,435	115,435		115,435
040	0603542N	RADIOLOGICAL CONTROL	702	702	702		702
041	0603553N	SURFACE ASW	1,081	1,081	1,081		1,081
042	0603561N	ADVANCED SUBMARINE SYSTEM DEVELOPMENT	100,565	100,565	100,565		100,565
043	0603562N	SUBMARINE TACTICAL WARFARE SYSTEMS	8,782	8,782	8,782		8,782
044	0603563N	SHIP CONCEPT ADVANCED DESIGN	14,590	14,590	14,590		14,590
045	0603564N	SHIP PRELIMINARY DESIGN & FEASIBILITY STUDIES	15,805	15,805	15,805		15,805
046	0603570N	ADVANCED NUCLEAR POWER SYSTEMS	453,313	453,313	453,313		453,313
047	0603573N	ADVANCED SURFACE MACHINERY SYSTEMS	36,655	36,655	36,655		36,655
048	0603576N	CHALK EAGLE	367,016	367,016	367,016		367,016
049	0603581N	LITTORAL COMBAT SHIP (LCS)	51,630	51,630	51,630		51,630
050	0603582N	COMBAT SYSTEM INTEGRATION	23,530	23,530	23,530		23,530
051	0603595N	OHIO REPLACEMENT	700,811	700,811	700,811		700,811
052	0603596N	LCS MISSION MODULES	160,058	129,158	129,158	−30,871	129,187
		Program Restructure		[−30,900]	[−30,900]	[−30,871]	
053	0603597N	AUTOMATED TEST AND ANALYSIS		8,000		8,000	8,000
		Program increase		[8,000]		[8,000]	
054	0603599N	FRIGATE DEVELOPMENT	84,900	84,900	84,900		84,900
055	0603609N	CONVENTIONAL MUNITIONS	8,342	8,342	8,342		8,342
056	0603611M	MARINE CORPS ASSAULT VEHICLES	158,682	158,682	158,682	−19,920	138,762
		Product development prior year carryover				[−19,920]	
057	0603635M	MARINE CORPS GROUND COMBAT/SUPPORT SYSTEM	1,303	1,303	1,303		1,303
058	0603654N	JOINT SERVICE EXPLOSIVE ORDNANCE DEVELOPMENT	46,911	46,911	46,911		46,911
060	0603713N	OCEAN ENGINEERING TECHNOLOGY DEVELOPMENT	4,556	4,556	4,556		4,556
061	0603721N	ENVIRONMENTAL PROTECTION	20,343	20,343	20,343		20,343
062	0603724N	NAVY ENERGY PROGRAM	52,479	52,479	52,479		52,479
063	0603725N	FACILITIES IMPROVEMENT	5,458	5,458	5,458		5,458
064	0603734N	CHALK CORAL	245,860	245,860	245,860		245,860
065	0603739N	NAVY LOGISTIC PRODUCTIVITY	3,089	3,089	3,089		3,089
066	0603746N	RETRACT MAPLE	323,526	323,526	323,526		323,526
067	0603748N	LINK PLUMERIA	318,497	318,497	318,497		318,497
068	0603751N	RETRACT ELM	52,834	52,834	52,834		52,834
069	0603764N	LINK EVERGREEN	48,116	48,116	48,116		48,116
070	0603787N	SPECIAL PROCESSES	13,619	13,619	13,619		13,619
071	0603790N	NATO RESEARCH AND DEVELOPMENT	9,867	9,867	9,867		9,867
072	0603795N	LAND ATTACK TECHNOLOGY	6,015	6,015	6,015		6,015
073	0603851M	JOINT NON-LETHAL WEAPONS TESTING	27,904	27,904	27,904		27,904
074	0603860N	JOINT PRECISION APPROACH AND LANDING SYSTEMS—DEM/VAL	104,144	104,144	104,144	−1,422	102,722
		UCLASS test support unjustified request				[−1,422]	
075	0603925N	DIRECTED ENERGY AND ELECTRIC WEAPON SYSTEMS	32,700	32,700	32,700		32,700
076	0604112N	GERALD R. FORD CLASS NUCLEAR AIRCRAFT CARRIER (CVN 78—80)	70,528	70,528	70,528		70,528
077	0604122N	REMOTE MINEHUNTING SYSTEM (RMS)	3,001	3,001	3,001		3,001
078	0604272N	TACTICAL AIR DIRECTIONAL INFRARED COUNTERMEASURES (TADIRCM).	34,920	34,920	34,920		34,920
080	0604292N	MH-XX	1,620	1,620	1,620		1,620
081	0604454N	LX (R)	6,354	6,354	25,354		6,354
		Needed to maintain schedule			[19,000]		
082	0604536N	ADVANCED UNDERSEA PROTOTYPING	78,589	78,589	44,189	−34,400	44,189
		Ahead of need			[−34,400]	[−34,400]	
084	0604659N	PRECISION STRIKE WEAPONS DEVELOPMENT PROGRAM	9,910	9,910	9,910		9,910
085	0604707N	SPACE AND ELECTRONIC WARFARE (SEW) ARCHITECTURE/ENGINEERING SUPPORT.	23,971	23,971	23,971		23,971
086	0604786N	OFFENSIVE ANTI-SURFACE WARFARE WEAPON DEVELOPMENT	252,409	252,409	252,409	−2,038	250,371
		Increment II early to need				[−2,038]	
087	0605812M	JOINT LIGHT TACTICAL VEHICLE (JLTV) ENGINEERING AND MANUFACTURING DEVELOPMENT PH.	23,197	23,197	23,197		23,197
088	0303354N	ASW SYSTEMS DEVELOPMENT—MIP	9,110	9,110	9,110		9,110
089	0304270N	ELECTRONIC WARFARE DEVELOPMENT—MIP	437	437	437		437

SEC. 4201. RESEARCH, DEVELOPMENT, TEST, AND EVALUATION
(In Thousands of Dollars)

Line	Program Element	Item	FY 2017 Request	House Authorized	Senate Authorized	Conference Change	Conference Authorized
		SUBTOTAL ADVANCED COMPONENT DEVELOPMENT & PROTOTYPES	4,662,867	4,654,967	4,615,067	−144,416	4,518,451
		SYSTEM DEVELOPMENT & DEMONSTRATION					
090	0603208N	TRAINING SYSTEM AIRCRAFT	19,938	19,938	19,938		19,938
091	0604212N	OTHER HELO DEVELOPMENT	6,268	6,268	6,268		6,268
092	0604214N	AV–8B AIRCRAFT—ENG DEV	33,664	33,664	33,664		33,664
093	0604215N	STANDARDS DEVELOPMENT	1,300	1,300	1,300		1,300
094	0604216N	MULTI-MISSION HELICOPTER UPGRADE DEVELOPMENT	5,275	5,275	5,275		5,275
095	0604218N	AIR/OCEAN EQUIPMENT ENGINEERING	3,875	3,875	3,875		3,875
096	0604221N	P–3 MODERNIZATION PROGRAM	1,909	1,909	1,909		1,909
097	0604230N	WARFARE SUPPORT SYSTEM	13,237	13,237	13,237		13,237
098	0604231N	TACTICAL COMMAND SYSTEM	36,323	36,323	36,323		36,323
099	0604234N	ADVANCED HAWKEYE	363,792	363,792	363,792		363,792
100	0604245N	H–1 UPGRADES	27,441	27,441	27,441		27,441
101	0604261N	ACOUSTIC SEARCH SENSORS	34,525	34,525	34,525		34,525
102	0604262N	V–22A	174,423	174,423	174,423	−16,725	157,698
		Hardware development airframe excess growth				[−8,474]	
		Refueling system development excess growth				[−8,251]	
103	0604264N	AIR CREW SYSTEMS DEVELOPMENT	13,577	13,577	13,577		13,577
104	0604269N	EA–18	116,761	116,761	116,761		116,761
105	0604270N	ELECTRONIC WARFARE DEVELOPMENT	48,766	48,766	48,766		48,766
106	0604273N	EXECUTIVE HELO DEVELOPMENT	338,357	338,357	338,357		338,357
107	0604274N	NEXT GENERATION JAMMER (NGJ)	577,822	577,822	577,822		577,822
108	0604280N	JOINT TACTICAL RADIO SYSTEM—NAVY (JTRS-NAVY)	2,365	2,365	2,365		2,365
109	0604282N	NEXT GENERATION JAMMER (NGJ) INCREMENT II	52,065	52,065	52,065	−10,000	42,065
		Program growth				[−10,000]	
110	0604307N	SURFACE COMBATANT COMBAT SYSTEM ENGINEERING	282,764	282,764	282,764		282,764
111	0604311N	LPD–17 CLASS SYSTEMS INTEGRATION	580	580	580		580
112	0604329N	SMALL DIAMETER BOMB (SDB)	97,622	97,622	97,622		97,622
113	0604366N	STANDARD MISSILE IMPROVEMENTS	120,561	120,561	120,561		120,561
114	0604373N	AIRBORNE MCM	45,622	45,622	45,622		45,622
116	0604378N	NAVAL INTEGRATED FIRE CONTROL—COUNTER AIR SYSTEMS ENGINEERING.	25,750	25,750	25,750		25,750
118	0604501N	ADVANCED ABOVE WATER SENSORS	85,868	85,868	85,868		85,868
119	0604503N	SSN–688 AND TRIDENT MODERNIZATION	117,476	117,476	117,476		117,476
120	0604504N	AIR CONTROL	47,404	47,404	47,404		47,404
121	0604512N	SHIPBOARD AVIATION SYSTEMS	112,158	112,158	112,158		112,158
122	0604518N	COMBAT INFORMATION CENTER CONVERSION	6,283	6,283	6,283		6,283
123	0604522N	AIR AND MISSILE DEFENSE RADAR (AMDR) SYSTEM	144,395	144,395	144,395		144,395
124	0604558N	NEW DESIGN SSN	113,013	113,013	113,013		113,013
125	0604562N	SUBMARINE TACTICAL WARFARE SYSTEM	43,160	43,160	43,160		43,160
126	0604567N	SHIP CONTRACT DESIGN/ LIVE FIRE T&E	65,002	85,002	65,002	20,000	85,002
		CVN Design		[20,000]		[20,000]	
127	0604574N	NAVY TACTICAL COMPUTER RESOURCES	3,098	3,098	3,098		3,098
128	0604580N	VIRGINIA PAYLOAD MODULE (VPM)	97,920	97,920	97,920		97,920
129	0604601N	MINE DEVELOPMENT	10,490	10,490	10,490		10,490
130	0604610N	LIGHTWEIGHT TORPEDO DEVELOPMENT	20,178	20,178	20,178		20,178
131	0604654N	JOINT SERVICE EXPLOSIVE ORDNANCE DEVELOPMENT	7,369	7,369	7,369		7,369
132	0604703N	PERSONNEL, TRAINING, SIMULATION, AND HUMAN FACTORS	4,995	4,995	4,995		4,995
133	0604727N	JOINT STANDOFF WEAPON SYSTEMS	412	412	412		412
134	0604755N	SHIP SELF DEFENSE (DETECT & CONTROL)	134,619	134,619	134,619		134,619
135	0604756N	SHIP SELF DEFENSE (ENGAGE: HARD KILL)	114,475	105,475	114,475	−9,000	105,475
		Program Execution		[−9,000]		[−9,000]	
136	0604757N	SHIP SELF DEFENSE (ENGAGE: SOFT KILL/EW)	114,211	114,211	114,211	−3,000	111,211
		Decoy development effort unjustified growth				[−3,000]	
137	0604761N	INTELLIGENCE ENGINEERING	11,029	11,029	11,029		11,029
138	0604771N	MEDICAL DEVELOPMENT	9,220	9,220	9,220		9,220
139	0604777N	NAVIGATION/ID SYSTEM	42,723	42,723	42,723		42,723

SEC. 4201. RESEARCH, DEVELOPMENT, TEST, AND EVALUATION
(In Thousands of Dollars)

Line	Program Element	Item	FY 2017 Request	House Authorized	Senate Authorized	Conference Change	Conference Authorized
140	0604800M	JOINT STRIKE FIGHTER (JSF)—EMD	531,426	531,426	531,426		531,426
141	0604800N	JOINT STRIKE FIGHTER (JSF)—EMD	528,716	528,716	528,716		528,716
142	0604810M	JOINT STRIKE FIGHTER FOLLOW ON DEVELOPMENT—MARINE CORPS	74,227	74,227	74,227	−2,250	71,977
		Follow-on development excess funds				[−2,250]	
143	0604810N	JOINT STRIKE FIGHTER FOLLOW ON DEVELOPMENT—NAVY	63,387	63,387	63,387	−2,250	61,137
		Follow-on development excess funds				[−2,250]	
144	0605013M	INFORMATION TECHNOLOGY DEVELOPMENT	4,856	4,856	4,856		4,856
145	0605013N	INFORMATION TECHNOLOGY DEVELOPMENT	97,066	97,066	97,066		97,066
146	0605024N	ANTI-TAMPER TECHNOLOGY SUPPORT	2,500	2,500	2,500		2,500
147	0605212N	CH–53K RDTE	404,810	404,810	404,810	−31,513	373,297
		Program delay				[−31,513]	
148	0605215N	MISSION PLANNING	33,570	33,570	33,570		33,570
149	0605217N	COMMON AVIONICS	51,599	51,599	51,599		51,599
150	0605220N	SHIP TO SHORE CONNECTOR (SSC)	11,088	11,088	11,088		11,088
151	0605327N	T-AO (X)	1,095	1,095	1,095		1,095
152	0605414N	MQ-XX	89,000	77,000	89,000	−12,000	77,000
		Excess Obligation		[−12,000]		[−12,000]	
153	0605450N	JOINT AIR-TO-GROUND MISSILE (JAGM)	17,880	17,880	17,880		17,880
154	0605500N	MULTI-MISSION MARITIME AIRCRAFT (MMA)	59,126	59,126	59,126		59,126
155	0605504N	MULTI-MISSION MARITIME (MMA) INCREMENT III	182,220	182,220	182,220	−30,000	152,220
		Program execution				[−30,000]	
156	0204202N	DDG–1000	45,642	45,642	45,642		45,642
159	0304231N	TACTICAL COMMAND SYSTEM—MIP	676	676	676		676
160	0304785N	TACTICAL CRYPTOLOGIC SYSTEMS	36,747	36,747	36,747		36,747
161	0305124N	SPECIAL APPLICATIONS PROGRAM	35,002	35,002	35,002		35,002
162	0306250M	CYBER OPERATIONS TECHNOLOGY DEVELOPMENT	4,942	4,942	6,726		4,942
		Full spectrum cyber operations unfunded requirement			[1,784]		
		SUBTOTAL SYSTEM DEVELOPMENT & DEMONSTRATION	**6,025,655**	**6,024,655**	**6,027,439**	**−96,738**	**5,928,917**
		MANAGEMENT SUPPORT					
163	0604256N	THREAT SIMULATOR DEVELOPMENT	16,633	16,633	16,633		16,633
164	0604258N	TARGET SYSTEMS DEVELOPMENT	36,662	36,662	36,662		36,662
165	0604759N	MAJOR T&E INVESTMENT	42,109	42,109	42,109		42,109
166	0605126N	JOINT THEATER AIR AND MISSILE DEFENSE ORGANIZATION	2,998	2,998	2,998		2,998
167	0605152N	STUDIES AND ANALYSIS SUPPORT—NAVY	3,931	3,931	3,931		3,931
168	0605154N	CENTER FOR NAVAL ANALYSES	46,634	46,634	46,634		46,634
169	0605285N	NEXT GENERATION FIGHTER	1,200	1,200	1,200		1,200
171	0605804N	TECHNICAL INFORMATION SERVICES	903	903	903		903
172	0605853N	MANAGEMENT, TECHNICAL & INTERNATIONAL SUPPORT	87,077	87,077	76,277		87,077
		Unjustified growth			[−10,800]		
173	0605856N	STRATEGIC TECHNICAL SUPPORT	3,597	3,597	3,597		3,597
174	0605861N	RDT&E SCIENCE AND TECHNOLOGY MANAGEMENT	62,811	62,811	62,811		62,811
175	0605863N	RDT&E SHIP AND AIRCRAFT SUPPORT	106,093	106,093	106,093		106,093
176	0605864N	TEST AND EVALUATION SUPPORT	349,146	349,146	349,146		349,146
177	0605865N	OPERATIONAL TEST AND EVALUATION CAPABILITY	18,160	18,160	18,160		18,160
178	0605866N	NAVY SPACE AND ELECTRONIC WARFARE (SEW) SUPPORT	9,658	9,658	9,658		9,658
179	0605867N	SEW SURVEILLANCE/RECONNAISSANCE SUPPORT	6,500	6,500	6,500		6,500
180	0605873M	MARINE CORPS PROGRAM WIDE SUPPORT	22,247	22,247	22,247		22,247
181	0605898N	MANAGEMENT HQ—R&D	16,254	16,254	16,254		16,254
182	0606355N	WARFARE INNOVATION MANAGEMENT	21,123	21,123	21,123		21,123
		SUBTOTAL MANAGEMENT SUPPORT	**853,736**	**853,736**	**842,936**		**853,736**
		OPERATIONAL SYSTEMS DEVELOPMENT					
188	0607658N	COOPERATIVE ENGAGEMENT CAPABILITY (CEC)	84,501	84,501	84,501		84,501
189	0607700N	DEPLOYABLE JOINT COMMAND AND CONTROL	2,970	2,970	2,970		2,970
190	0101221N	STRATEGIC SUB & WEAPONS SYSTEM SUPPORT	136,556	136,556	136,556		136,556
191	0101224N	SSBN SECURITY TECHNOLOGY PROGRAM	33,845	33,845	33,845		33,845

SEC. 4201. RESEARCH, DEVELOPMENT, TEST, AND EVALUATION
(In Thousands of Dollars)

Line	Program Element	Item	FY 2017 Request	House Authorized	Senate Authorized	Conference Change	Conference Authorized
192	0101226N	SUBMARINE ACOUSTIC WARFARE DEVELOPMENT	9,329	9,329	9,329		9,329
193	0101402N	NAVY STRATEGIC COMMUNICATIONS	17,218	17,218	17,218		17,218
195	0204136N	F/A–18 SQUADRONS	189,125	189,125	189,125		189,125
196	0204163N	FLEET TELECOMMUNICATIONS (TACTICAL)	48,225	48,225	48,225		48,225
197	0204228N	SURFACE SUPPORT	21,156	21,156	21,156		21,156
198	0204229N	TOMAHAWK AND TOMAHAWK MISSION PLANNING CENTER (TMPC)	71,355	71,355	71,355		71,355
199	0204311N	INTEGRATED SURVEILLANCE SYSTEM	58,542	58,542	58,542	−1,484	57,058
		TASW prototypes excess growth				[−1,484]	
200	0204413N	AMPHIBIOUS TACTICAL SUPPORT UNITS (DISPLACEMENT CRAFT)	13,929	13,929	13,929		13,929
201	0204460M	GROUND/AIR TASK ORIENTED RADAR (G/ATOR)	83,538	83,538	83,538		83,538
202	0204571N	CONSOLIDATED TRAINING SYSTEMS DEVELOPMENT	38,593	38,593	38,593		38,593
203	0204574N	CRYPTOLOGIC DIRECT SUPPORT	1,122	1,122	1,122		1,122
204	0204575N	ELECTRONIC WARFARE (EW) READINESS SUPPORT	99,998	99,998	99,998		99,998
205	0205601N	HARM IMPROVEMENT	48,635	48,635	48,635		48,635
206	0205604N	TACTICAL DATA LINKS	124,785	124,785	124,785		124,785
207	0205620N	SURFACE ASW COMBAT SYSTEM INTEGRATION	24,583	24,583	24,583		24,583
208	0205632N	MK–48 ADCAP	39,134	39,134	39,134		39,134
209	0205633N	AVIATION IMPROVEMENTS	120,861	120,861	120,861		120,861
210	0205675N	OPERATIONAL NUCLEAR POWER SYSTEMS	101,786	101,786	101,786		101,786
211	0206313M	MARINE CORPS COMMUNICATIONS SYSTEMS	82,159	82,159	82,159		82,159
212	0206335M	COMMON AVIATION COMMAND AND CONTROL SYSTEM (CAC2S)	11,850	11,850	11,850		11,850
213	0206623M	MARINE CORPS GROUND COMBAT/SUPPORTING ARMS SYSTEMS	47,877	47,877	47,877		47,877
214	0206624M	MARINE CORPS COMBAT SERVICES SUPPORT	13,194	13,194	13,194		13,194
215	0206625M	USMC INTELLIGENCE/ELECTRONIC WARFARE SYSTEMS (MIP)	17,171	17,171	17,171		17,171
216	0206629M	AMPHIBIOUS ASSAULT VEHICLE	38,020	38,020	38,020		38,020
217	0207161N	TACTICAL AIM MISSILES	56,285	56,285	56,285		56,285
218	0207163N	ADVANCED MEDIUM RANGE AIR-TO-AIR MISSILE (AMRAAM)	40,350	40,350	40,350		40,350
219	0219902M	GLOBAL COMBAT SUPPORT SYSTEM—MARINE CORPS (GCSS-MC)	9,128	9,128	9,128		9,128
223	0303109N	SATELLITE COMMUNICATIONS (SPACE)	37,372	37,372	37,372		37,372
224	0303138N	CONSOLIDATED AFLOAT NETWORK ENTERPRISE SERVICES (CANES)	23,541	23,541	23,541		23,541
225	0303140N	INFORMATION SYSTEMS SECURITY PROGRAM	38,510	38,510	38,510		38,510
228	0305192N	MILITARY INTELLIGENCE PROGRAM (MIP) ACTIVITIES	6,019	6,019	6,019		6,019
229	0305204N	TACTICAL UNMANNED AERIAL VEHICLES	8,436	8,436	8,436		8,436
230	0305205N	UAS INTEGRATION AND INTEROPERABILITY	36,509	36,509	36,509	−3,000	33,509
		Prior year carryover				[−3,000]	
231	0305208M	DISTRIBUTED COMMON GROUND/SURFACE SYSTEMS	2,100	2,100	2,100		2,100
232	0305208N	DISTRIBUTED COMMON GROUND/SURFACE SYSTEMS	44,571	44,571	44,571		44,571
233	0305220N	MQ–4C TRITON	111,729	111,729	111,729		111,729
234	0305231N	MQ–8 UAV	26,518	26,518	26,518		26,518
235	0305232M	RQ–11 UAV	418	418	418		418
236	0305233N	RQ–7 UAV	716	716	716		716
237	0305234N	SMALL (LEVEL 0) TACTICAL UAS (STUASLO)	5,071	5,071	5,071		5,071
238	0305239M	RQ–21A	9,497	9,497	9,497		9,497
239	0305241N	MULTI-INTELLIGENCE SENSOR DEVELOPMENT	77,965	77,965	77,965		77,965
240	0305242M	UNMANNED AERIAL SYSTEMS (UAS) PAYLOADS (MIP)	11,181	11,181	11,181		11,181
241	0305421N	RQ–4 MODERNIZATION	181,266	181,266	181,266		181,266
242	0308601N	MODELING AND SIMULATION SUPPORT	4,709	4,709	4,709		4,709
243	0702207N	DEPOT MAINTENANCE (NON-IF)	49,322	54,322	49,322		49,322
		MH–60 Fleet Mid-Life Upgrades		[5,000]			
245	0708730N	MARITIME TECHNOLOGY (MARITECH)	3,204	3,204	3,204		3,204
245A	9999999999	CLASSIFIED PROGRAMS	1,228,460	1,228,460	1,228,460		1,228,460
		SUBTOTAL OPERATIONAL SYSTEMS DEVELOPMENT	**3,592,934**	**3,597,934**	**3,592,934**	**−4,484**	**3,588,450**
		TOTAL RESEARCH, DEVELOPMENT, TEST & EVAL, NAVY	**17,276,301**	**17,339,401**	**17,204,485**	**−197,638**	**17,078,663**

RESEARCH, DEVELOPMENT, TEST & EVAL, AF
BASIC RESEARCH

SEC. 4201. RESEARCH, DEVELOPMENT, TEST, AND EVALUATION
(In Thousands of Dollars)

Line	Program Element	Item	FY 2017 Request	House Authorized	Senate Authorized	Conference Change	Conference Authorized
001	0601102F	DEFENSE RESEARCH SCIENCES	340,812	340,812	340,812		340,812
002	0601103F	UNIVERSITY RESEARCH INITIATIVES	145,044	145,044	145,044		145,044
003	0601108F	HIGH ENERGY LASER RESEARCH INITIATIVES	14,168	14,168	14,168		14,168
		SUBTOTAL BASIC RESEARCH	**500,024**	**500,024**	**500,024**		**500,024**
		APPLIED RESEARCH					
004	0602102F	MATERIALS	126,152	131,152	126,152	5,000	131,152
		Precision measuring tools		[5,000]		[5,000]	
005	0602201F	AEROSPACE VEHICLE TECHNOLOGIES	122,831	127,831	122,831	5,000	127,831
		Reusable Hypersonic vehicle structures development		[5,000]		[5,000]	
006	0602202F	HUMAN EFFECTIVENESS APPLIED RESEARCH	111,647	116,647	111,647		111,647
		Human-Machine Teaming		[5,000]			
007	0602203F	AEROSPACE PROPULSION	185,671	185,671	190,671	5,000	190,671
		Program increase			[5,000]	[5,000]	
008	0602204F	AEROSPACE SENSORS	155,174	155,174	155,174		155,174
009	0602601F	SPACE TECHNOLOGY	117,915	117,915	117,915		117,915
010	0602602F	CONVENTIONAL MUNITIONS	109,649	109,649	109,649		109,649
011	0602605F	DIRECTED ENERGY TECHNOLOGY	127,163	127,163	127,163		127,163
012	0602788F	DOMINANT INFORMATION SCIENCES AND METHODS	161,650	161,650	161,650		161,650
013	0602890F	HIGH ENERGY LASER RESEARCH	42,300	42,300	47,300		42,300
		Joint technology office			[5,000]		
		SUBTOTAL APPLIED RESEARCH	**1,260,152**	**1,275,152**	**1,270,152**	**15,000**	**1,275,152**
		ADVANCED TECHNOLOGY DEVELOPMENT					
014	0603112F	ADVANCED MATERIALS FOR WEAPON SYSTEMS	35,137	45,137	35,137	10,000	45,137
		Metals Affordability Initiative		[10,000]		[10,000]	
015	0603199F	SUSTAINMENT SCIENCE AND TECHNOLOGY (S&T)	20,636	20,636	20,636		20,636
016	0603203F	ADVANCED AEROSPACE SENSORS	40,945	40,945	40,945		40,945
017	0603211F	AEROSPACE TECHNOLOGY DEV/DEMO	130,950	130,950	130,950		130,950
018	0603216F	AEROSPACE PROPULSION AND POWER TECHNOLOGY	94,594	99,594	99,594	5,000	99,594
		Silicon Carbide for aerospace power application		[5,000]	[5,000]	[5,000]	
019	0603270F	ELECTRONIC COMBAT TECHNOLOGY	58,250	58,250	53,250		58,250
		General decrease			[−5,000]		
020	0603401F	ADVANCED SPACECRAFT TECHNOLOGY	61,593	61,593	61,593		61,593
021	0603444F	MAUI SPACE SURVEILLANCE SYSTEM (MSSS)	11,681	11,681	11,681		11,681
022	0603456F	HUMAN EFFECTIVENESS ADVANCED TECHNOLOGY DEVELOPMENT	26,492	26,492	26,492		26,492
023	0603601F	CONVENTIONAL WEAPONS TECHNOLOGY	102,009	102,009	102,009		102,009
024	0603605F	ADVANCED WEAPONS TECHNOLOGY	39,064	39,064	39,064		39,064
025	0603680F	MANUFACTURING TECHNOLOGY PROGRAM	46,344	46,344	46,344		46,344
026	0603788F	BATTLESPACE KNOWLEDGE DEVELOPMENT AND DEMONSTRATION	58,110	58,110	48,110		58,110
		Unjustified increase			[−10,000]		
		SUBTOTAL ADVANCED TECHNOLOGY DEVELOPMENT	**725,805**	**740,805**	**715,805**	**15,000**	**740,805**
		ADVANCED COMPONENT DEVELOPMENT & PROTOTYPES					
027	0603260F	INTELLIGENCE ADVANCED DEVELOPMENT	5,598	5,598	5,598		5,598
028	0603438F	SPACE CONTROL TECHNOLOGY	7,534	7,534	7,534		7,534
029	0603742F	COMBAT IDENTIFICATION TECHNOLOGY	24,418	24,418	24,418		24,418
030	0603790F	NATO RESEARCH AND DEVELOPMENT	4,333	4,333	4,333		4,333
032	0603830F	SPACE SECURITY AND DEFENSE PROGRAM	32,399	32,399	32,399		32,399
033	0603851F	INTERCONTINENTAL BALLISTIC MISSILE—DEM/VAL	108,663	108,663	108,663		108,663
035	0604015F	LONG RANGE STRIKE—BOMBER	1,358,309	1,358,309	1,056,009		1,358,309
		Excess to contract award			[−302,300]		
036	0604257F	ADVANCED TECHNOLOGY AND SENSORS	34,818	34,818	34,818		34,818
037	0604317F	TECHNOLOGY TRANSFER	3,368	3,368	3,368		3,368
038	0604327F	HARD AND DEEPLY BURIED TARGET DEFEAT SYSTEM (HDBTDS) PROGRAM.	74,308	74,308	74,308		74,308
039	0604422F	WEATHER SYSTEM FOLLOW-ON	118,953	113,953	118,953	−5,000	113,953

SEC. 4201. RESEARCH, DEVELOPMENT, TEST, AND EVALUATION
(In Thousands of Dollars)

Line	Program Element	Item	FY 2017 Request	House Authorized	Senate Authorized	Conference Change	Conference Authorized
		Transfer Cloud Characterization and Theater Weather Imagery to NRO.		[−5,000]		[−5,000]	
040	0604425F	SPACE SITUATION AWARENESS SYSTEMS	9,901	9,901	9,901		9,901
041	0604776F	DEPLOYMENT & DISTRIBUTION ENTERPRISE R&D	25,890	25,890	25,890		25,890
042	0604857F	OPERATIONALLY RESPONSIVE SPACE	7,921	27,921	17,921	10,500	18,421
		Program increase		[20,000]	[10,000]	[10,500]	
043	0604858F	TECH TRANSITION PROGRAM	347,304	347,304	347,304		347,304
044	0605230F	GROUND BASED STRATEGIC DETERRENT	113,919	113,919	113,919		113,919
046	0207110F	NEXT GENERATION AIR DOMINANCE	20,595	15,595	20,595		20,595
		Program reduction		[−5,000]			
047	0207455F	THREE DIMENSIONAL LONG-RANGE RADAR (3DELRR)	49,491	39,491	49,491		49,491
		Excess funding to need		[−10,000]			
048	0305164F	NAVSTAR GLOBAL POSITIONING SYSTEM (USER EQUIPMENT) (SPACE)	278,147	278,147	278,147		278,147
049	0305236F	COMMON DATA LINK EXECUTIVE AGENT (CDL EA)	42,338	42,338	42,338		42,338
050	0306250F	CYBER OPERATIONS TECHNOLOGY DEVELOPMENT	158,002	158,002	158,002		158,002
051	0306415F	ENABLED CYBER ACTIVITIES	15,842	15,842	15,842		15,842
052	0901410F	CONTRACTING INFORMATION TECHNOLOGY SYSTEM	5,782	5,782	5,782		5,782
		SUBTOTAL ADVANCED COMPONENT DEVELOPMENT & PROTOTYPES	**2,847,833**	**2,847,833**	**2,555,533**	**5,500**	**2,853,333**
		SYSTEM DEVELOPMENT & DEMONSTRATION					
054	0604270F	ELECTRONIC WARFARE DEVELOPMENT	12,476	12,476	12,476	−3,300	9,176
		Improved GPS				[−3,300]	
055	0604281F	TACTICAL DATA NETWORKS ENTERPRISE	82,380	82,380	82,380		82,380
056	0604287F	PHYSICAL SECURITY EQUIPMENT	8,458	8,458	8,458		8,458
057	0604329F	SMALL DIAMETER BOMB (SDB)—EMD	54,838	54,838	54,838	−7,800	47,038
		Improved GPS				[−7,800]	
058	0604421F	COUNTERSPACE SYSTEMS	34,394	34,394	34,394		34,394
059	0604425F	SPACE SITUATION AWARENESS SYSTEMS	23,945	23,945	23,945		23,945
060	0604426F	SPACE FENCE	168,364	168,364	168,364		168,364
061	0604429F	AIRBORNE ELECTRONIC ATTACK	9,187	9,187	9,187		9,187
062	0604441F	SPACE BASED INFRARED SYSTEM (SBIRS) HIGH EMD	181,966	181,966	181,966		181,966
063	0604602F	ARMAMENT/ORDNANCE DEVELOPMENT	20,312	20,312	20,312		20,312
064	0604604F	SUBMUNITIONS	2,503	2,503	2,503		2,503
065	0604617F	AGILE COMBAT SUPPORT	53,680	53,680	53,680		53,680
066	0604618F	JOINT DIRECT ATTACK MUNITION	9,901	9,901	9,901		9,901
067	0604706F	LIFE SUPPORT SYSTEMS	7,520	7,520	7,520		7,520
068	0604735F	COMBAT TRAINING RANGES	77,409	77,409	77,409		77,409
069	0604800F	F–35—EMD	450,467	450,467	450,467		450,467
070	0604853F	EVOLVED EXPENDABLE LAUNCH VEHICLE PROGRAM (SPACE)—EMD	296,572	100,000	296,572	−136,572	160,000
		Launch System Development		[100,000]		[160,000]	
		Next Generation Launch System Investment		[−296,572]		[−296,572]	
070A	0604XXXF	ROCKET PROPULSION SYSTEM		220,000		220,000	220,000
		Rocket Propulsion System Replacement of RD–180		[220,000]		[220,000]	
071	0604932F	LONG RANGE STANDOFF WEAPON	95,604	95,604	95,604		95,604
072	0604933F	ICBM FUZE MODERNIZATION	189,751	189,751	189,751		189,751
073	0605030F	JOINT TACTICAL NETWORK CENTER (JTNC)	1,131	1,131	1,131		1,131
074	0605213F	F–22 MODERNIZATION INCREMENT 3.2B	70,290	70,290	70,290		70,290
075	0605214F	GROUND ATTACK WEAPONS FUZE DEVELOPMENT	937	937	937		937
076	0605221F	KC–46	261,724	121,724	121,724	−140,000	121,724
		Scope Reduction		[−140,000]	[−140,000]	[−140,000]	
077	0605223F	ADVANCED PILOT TRAINING	12,377	12,377	4,477	−5,000	7,377
		Early to need			[−7,900]	[−5,000]	
078	0605229F	CSAR HH–60 RECAPITALIZATION	319,331	319,331	319,331	−15,000	304,331
		Forward financing				[−15,000]	
080	0605431F	ADVANCED EHF MILSATCOM (SPACE)	259,131	259,131	229,131	−30,000	229,131
		Delayed analysis of alternatives			[−30,000]	[−30,000]	
081	0605432F	POLAR MILSATCOM (SPACE)	50,815	50,815	50,815		50,815
082	0605433F	WIDEBAND GLOBAL SATCOM (SPACE)	41,632	41,632	41,632	10,000	51,632

SEC. 4201. RESEARCH, DEVELOPMENT, TEST, AND EVALUATION
(In Thousands of Dollars)

Line	Program Element	Item	FY 2017 Request	House Authorized	Senate Authorized	Conference Change	Conference Authorized
		COMSATCOM pilot program				[10,000]	
083	0605458F	AIR & SPACE OPS CENTER 10.2 RDT&E	28,911	28,911	28,911		28,911
084	0605931F	B–2 DEFENSIVE MANAGEMENT SYSTEM	315,615	288,957	288,915	–26,700	288,915
		Scope Reduction		[–26,658]	[–26,700]	[–26,700]	
085	0101125F	NUCLEAR WEAPONS MODERNIZATION	137,909	137,909	137,909		137,909
086	0207171F	F–15 EPAWSS	256,669	256,669	256,669		256,669
087	0207701F	FULL COMBAT MISSION TRAINING	12,051	12,051	12,051		12,051
088	0305176F	COMBAT SURVIVOR EVADER LOCATOR	29,253	29,253	29,253		29,253
089	0307581F	JSTARS RECAP	128,019	128,019	128,019		128,019
090	0401319F	PRESIDENTIAL AIRCRAFT REPLACEMENT (PAR)	351,220	351,220	351,220		351,220
091	0701212F	AUTOMATED TEST SYSTEMS	19,062	19,062	19,062		19,062
		SUBTOTAL SYSTEM DEVELOPMENT & DEMONSTRATION	**4,075,804**	**3,932,574**	**3,871,204**	**–134,372**	**3,941,432**
		MANAGEMENT SUPPORT					
092	0604256F	THREAT SIMULATOR DEVELOPMENT	21,630	21,630	21,630		21,630
093	0604759F	MAJOR T&E INVESTMENT	66,385	66,385	66,385		66,385
094	0605101F	RAND PROJECT AIR FORCE	34,641	34,641	34,641		34,641
096	0605712F	INITIAL OPERATIONAL TEST & EVALUATION	11,529	11,529	11,529		11,529
097	0605807F	TEST AND EVALUATION SUPPORT	661,417	661,417	661,417		661,417
098	0605860F	ROCKET SYSTEMS LAUNCH PROGRAM (SPACE)	11,198	11,198	11,198		11,198
099	0605864F	SPACE TEST PROGRAM (STP)	27,070	27,070	27,070		27,070
100	0605976F	FACILITIES RESTORATION AND MODERNIZATION—TEST AND EVALUATION SUPPORT.	134,111	134,111	134,111		134,111
101	0605978F	FACILITIES SUSTAINMENT—TEST AND EVALUATION SUPPORT	28,091	28,091	28,091		28,091
102	0606017F	REQUIREMENTS ANALYSIS AND MATURATION	29,100	29,100	29,100		29,100
103	0606116F	SPACE TEST AND TRAINING RANGE DEVELOPMENT	18,528	18,528	18,528		18,528
104	0606392F	SPACE AND MISSILE CENTER (SMC) CIVILIAN WORKFORCE	176,666	176,666	176,666		176,666
105	0308602F	ENTEPRISE INFORMATION SERVICES (EIS)	4,410	4,410	4,410		4,410
106	0702806F	ACQUISITION AND MANAGEMENT SUPPORT	14,613	14,613	14,613		14,613
107	0804731F	GENERAL SKILL TRAINING	1,404	1,404	1,404		1,404
109	1001004F	INTERNATIONAL ACTIVITIES	4,784	4,784	4,784		4,784
		SUBTOTAL MANAGEMENT SUPPORT	**1,245,577**	**1,245,577**	**1,245,577**		**1,245,577**
		OPERATIONAL SYSTEMS DEVELOPMENT					
110	0603423F	GLOBAL POSITIONING SYSTEM III—OPERATIONAL CONTROL SEGMENT	393,268	393,268	393,268		393,268
111	0604233F	SPECIALIZED UNDERGRADUATE FLIGHT TRAINING	15,427	15,427	15,427		15,427
112	0604445F	WIDE AREA SURVEILLANCE	46,695	46,695	46,695		46,695
115	0605018F	AF INTEGRATED PERSONNEL AND PAY SYSTEM (AF-IPPS)	10,368	10,368	10,368		10,368
116	0605024F	ANTI-TAMPER TECHNOLOGY EXECUTIVE AGENCY	31,952	31,952	31,952		31,952
117	0605117F	FOREIGN MATERIEL ACQUISITION AND EXPLOITATION	42,960	42,960	42,960		42,960
118	0605278F	HC/MC-130 RECAP RDT&E	13,987	13,987	13,987		13,987
119	0101113F	B–52 SQUADRONS	78,267	78,267	78,267		78,267
120	0101122F	AIR-LAUNCHED CRUISE MISSILE (ALCM)	453	453	453		453
121	0101126F	B–1B SQUADRONS	5,830	5,830	5,830		5,830
122	0101127F	B–2 SQUADRONS	152,458	152,458	152,458		152,458
123	0101213F	MINUTEMAN SQUADRONS	182,958	182,958	182,958		182,958
124	0101313F	STRAT WAR PLANNING SYSTEM—USSTRATCOM	39,148	39,148	39,148		39,148
126	0101316F	WORLDWIDE JOINT STRATEGIC COMMUNICATIONS	6,042	6,042	6,042		6,042
128	0102110F	UH–1N REPLACEMENT PROGRAM	14,116	14,116	14,116		14,116
129	0102326F	REGION/SECTOR OPERATION CONTROL CENTER MODERNIZATION PROGRAM.	10,868	10,868	10,868		10,868
130	0105921F	SERVICE SUPPORT TO STRATCOM—SPACE ACTIVITIES	8,674	8,674	8,674		8,674
131	0205219F	MQ–9 UAV	151,373	200,373	186,473	10,000	161,373
		Auto take-off and landing capability		[35,000]	[35,100]	[10,000]	
		Tactical Datalink Integration		[14,000]			
133	0207131F	A–10 SQUADRONS	14,853	14,853	14,853		14,853
134	0207133F	F–16 SQUADRONS	132,795	132,795	132,795		132,795
135	0207134F	F–15E SQUADRONS	356,717	356,717	356,717		356,717

SEC. 4201. RESEARCH, DEVELOPMENT, TEST, AND EVALUATION
(In Thousands of Dollars)

Line	Program Element	Item	FY 2017 Request	House Authorized	Senate Authorized	Conference Change	Conference Authorized
136	0207136F	MANNED DESTRUCTIVE SUPPRESSION	14,773	14,773	14,773		14,773
137	0207138F	F–22A SQUADRONS	387,564	387,564	387,564	–8,100	379,464
		Improved GPS				[–8,100]	
138	0207142F	F–35 SQUADRONS	153,045	153,045	153,045	–5,500	147,545
		Follow-on development—excess funds				[–5,500]	
139	0207161F	TACTICAL AIM MISSILES	52,898	52,898	52,898		52,898
140	0207163F	ADVANCED MEDIUM RANGE AIR-TO-AIR MISSILE (AMRAAM)	62,470	62,470	62,470		62,470
143	0207227F	COMBAT RESCUE—PARARESCUE	362	362	362		362
144	0207247F	AF TENCAP	28,413	31,613	28,413		28,413
		Restore FY16 level		[3,200]			
145	0207249F	PRECISION ATTACK SYSTEMS PROCUREMENT	649	649	649		649
146	0207253F	COMPASS CALL	13,723	50,823	13,723	37,100	50,823
		Compass Call Program Restructure		[37,100]		[37,100]	
147	0207268F	AIRCRAFT ENGINE COMPONENT IMPROVEMENT PROGRAM	109,859	109,859	109,859		109,859
148	0207325F	JOINT AIR-TO-SURFACE STANDOFF MISSILE (JASSM)	30,002	30,002	30,002		30,002
149	0207410F	AIR & SPACE OPERATIONS CENTER (AOC)	37,621	37,621	37,621	–12,278	25,343
		Weapon system modification				[–12,278]	
150	0207412F	CONTROL AND REPORTING CENTER (CRC)	13,292	13,292	13,292		13,292
151	0207417F	AIRBORNE WARNING AND CONTROL SYSTEM (AWACS)	86,644	86,644	86,644		86,644
152	0207418F	TACTICAL AIRBORNE CONTROL SYSTEMS	2,442	2,442	2,442		2,442
154	0207431F	COMBAT AIR INTELLIGENCE SYSTEM ACTIVITIES	10,911	15,911	10,911	5,000	15,911
		Geospatial software development		[5,000]		[5,000]	
155	0207444F	TACTICAL AIR CONTROL PARTY-MOD	11,843	11,843	11,843		11,843
156	0207448F	C2ISR TACTICAL DATA LINK	1,515	1,515	1,515		1,515
157	0207452F	DCAPES	14,979	14,979	14,979		14,979
158	0207590F	SEEK EAGLE	25,308	25,308	25,308		25,308
159	0207601F	USAF MODELING AND SIMULATION	16,666	16,666	16,666		16,666
160	0207605F	WARGAMING AND SIMULATION CENTERS	4,245	4,245	4,245		4,245
161	0207697F	DISTRIBUTED TRAINING AND EXERCISES	3,886	3,886	3,886		3,886
162	0208006F	MISSION PLANNING SYSTEMS	71,785	71,785	71,785		71,785
164	0208087F	AF OFFENSIVE CYBERSPACE OPERATIONS	25,025	25,025	25,025		25,025
165	0208088F	AF DEFENSIVE CYBERSPACE OPERATIONS	29,439	29,439	29,439		29,439
168	0301017F	GLOBAL SENSOR INTEGRATED ON NETWORK (GSIN)	3,470	3,470	3,470		3,470
169	0301112F	NUCLEAR PLANNING AND EXECUTION SYSTEM (NPES)	4,060	4,060	4,060		4,060
175	0301400F	SPACE SUPERIORITY INTELLIGENCE	13,880	13,880	13,880		13,880
176	0302015F	E–4B NATIONAL AIRBORNE OPERATIONS CENTER (NAOC)	30,948	30,948	30,948		30,948
177	0303001F	FAMILY OF ADVANCED BLOS TERMINALS (FAB-T)	42,378	42,378	42,378		42,378
178	0303131F	MINIMUM ESSENTIAL EMERGENCY COMMUNICATIONS NETWORK (MEECN).	47,471	47,471	47,471		47,471
179	0303140F	INFORMATION SYSTEMS SECURITY PROGRAM	46,388	46,388	46,388		46,388
180	0303141F	GLOBAL COMBAT SUPPORT SYSTEM	52	52	52		52
181	0303142F	GLOBAL FORCE MANAGEMENT—DATA INITIATIVE	2,099	2,099	2,099		2,099
184	0304260F	AIRBORNE SIGINT ENTERPRISE	90,762	90,762	90,762		90,762
187	0305099F	GLOBAL AIR TRAFFIC MANAGEMENT (GATM)	4,354	4,354	4,354		4,354
188	0305110F	SATELLITE CONTROL NETWORK (SPACE)	15,624	15,624	15,624		15,624
189	0305111F	WEATHER SERVICE	19,974	22,974	19,974	3,000	22,974
		Commercial Weather Pilot Program		[3,000]		[3,000]	
190	0305114F	AIR TRAFFIC CONTROL, APPROACH, AND LANDING SYSTEM (ATCALS)	9,770	9,770	9,770		9,770
191	0305116F	AERIAL TARGETS	3,051	3,051	3,051		3,051
194	0305128F	SECURITY AND INVESTIGATIVE ACTIVITIES	405	405	405		405
195	0305145F	ARMS CONTROL IMPLEMENTATION	4,844	4,844	4,844		4,844
196	0305146F	DEFENSE JOINT COUNTERINTELLIGENCE ACTIVITIES	339	339	339		339
199	0305173F	SPACE AND MISSILE TEST AND EVALUATION CENTER	3,989	3,989	3,989		3,989
200	0305174F	SPACE INNOVATION, INTEGRATION AND RAPID TECHNOLOGY DEVELOPMENT.	3,070	3,070	3,070		3,070
201	0305179F	INTEGRATED BROADCAST SERVICE (IBS)	8,833	8,833	8,833		8,833
202	0305182F	SPACELIFT RANGE SYSTEM (SPACE)	11,867	11,867	11,867		11,867
203	0305202F	DRAGON U–2	37,217	37,217	37,217		37,217

SEC. 4201. RESEARCH, DEVELOPMENT, TEST, AND EVALUATION
(In Thousands of Dollars)

Line	Program Element	Item	FY 2017 Request	House Authorized	Senate Authorized	Conference Change	Conference Authorized
205	0305206F	AIRBORNE RECONNAISSANCE SYSTEMS	3,841	18,841	3,841	15,000	18,841
		Wide area motion imagery		[15,000]		[15,000]	
206	0305207F	MANNED RECONNAISSANCE SYSTEMS	20,975	20,975	20,975		20,975
207	0305208F	DISTRIBUTED COMMON GROUND/SURFACE SYSTEMS	18,902	18,902	18,902		18,902
208	0305220F	RQ–4 UAV	256,307	256,307	256,307		256,307
209	0305221F	NETWORK-CENTRIC COLLABORATIVE TARGETING	22,610	16,310	22,610		22,610
		Program reduction		[–6,300]			
211	0305238F	NATO AGS	38,904	38,904	38,904		38,904
212	0305240F	SUPPORT TO DCGS ENTERPRISE	23,084	23,084	23,084		23,084
213	0305258F	ADVANCED EVALUATION PROGRAM	116,143	116,143	116,143		116,143
214	0305265F	GPS III SPACE SEGMENT	141,888	141,888	141,888		141,888
215	0305600F	INTERNATIONAL INTELLIGENCE TECHNOLOGY AND ARCHITECTURES	2,360	2,360	2,360		2,360
216	0305614F	JSPOC MISSION SYSTEM	72,889	72,889	72,889		72,889
217	0305881F	RAPID CYBER ACQUISITION	4,280	4,280	4,280		4,280
218	0305906F	NCMC—TW/AA SYSTEM	4,951	4,951	4,951		4,951
219	0305913F	NUDET DETECTION SYSTEM (SPACE)	21,093	21,093	21,093		21,093
220	0305940F	SPACE SITUATION AWARENESS OPERATIONS	35,002	35,002	35,002		35,002
222	0308699F	SHARED EARLY WARNING (SEW)	6,366	6,366	6,366		6,366
223	0401115F	C–130 AIRLIFT SQUADRON	15,599	15,599	15,599		15,599
224	0401119F	C–5 AIRLIFT SQUADRONS (IF)	66,146	66,146	66,146		66,146
225	0401130F	C–17 AIRCRAFT (IF)	12,430	12,430	12,430		12,430
226	0401132F	C–130J PROGRAM	16,776	16,776	16,776		16,776
227	0401134F	LARGE AIRCRAFT IR COUNTERMEASURES (LAIRCM)	5,166	5,166	5,166		5,166
229	0401314F	OPERATIONAL SUPPORT AIRLIFT	13,817	13,817	13,817		13,817
230	0401318F	CV–22	16,702	16,702	16,702		16,702
231	0408011F	SPECIAL TACTICS / COMBAT CONTROL	7,164	7,164	7,164		7,164
232	0702207F	DEPOT MAINTENANCE (NON-IF)	1,518	1,518	1,518		1,518
233	0708610F	LOGISTICS INFORMATION TECHNOLOGY (LOGIT)	61,676	61,676	61,676		61,676
234	0708611F	SUPPORT SYSTEMS DEVELOPMENT	9,128	9,128	9,128		9,128
235	0804743F	OTHER FLIGHT TRAINING	1,653	1,653	1,653		1,653
236	0808716F	OTHER PERSONNEL ACTIVITIES	57	57	57		57
237	0901202F	JOINT PERSONNEL RECOVERY AGENCY	3,663	3,663	3,663		3,663
238	0901218F	CIVILIAN COMPENSATION PROGRAM	3,735	3,735	3,735		3,735
239	0901220F	PERSONNEL ADMINISTRATION	5,157	5,157	5,157		5,157
240	0901226F	AIR FORCE STUDIES AND ANALYSIS AGENCY	1,523	1,523	1,523		1,523
242	0901538F	FINANCIAL MANAGEMENT INFORMATION SYSTEMS DEVELOPMENT	10,581	10,581	3,781		10,581
		Cost estimating unjustified request			[–4,900]		
		PBES unjustified request			[–1,900]		
242A	9999999999	CLASSIFIED PROGRAMS	13,091,557	13,091,557	13,091,557		13,091,557
		SUBTOTAL OPERATIONAL SYSTEMS DEVELOPMENT	**17,457,056**	**17,563,056**	**17,485,356**	**44,222**	**17,501,278**
		TOTAL RESEARCH, DEVELOPMENT, TEST & EVAL, AF	**28,112,251**	**28,105,021**	**27,643,651**	**–54,650**	**28,057,601**
		RESEARCH, DEVELOPMENT, TEST & EVAL, DW					
		BASIC RESEARCH					
001	0601000BR	DTRA BASIC RESEARCH INITIATIVE	35,436	35,436	35,436		35,436
002	0601101E	DEFENSE RESEARCH SCIENCES	362,297	352,297	362,297		362,297
		Program reduction		[–10,000]			
003	0601110D8Z	BASIC RESEARCH INITIATIVES	36,654	36,654	36,654		36,654
004	0601117E	BASIC OPERATIONAL MEDICAL RESEARCH SCIENCE	57,791	57,791	57,791		57,791
005	0601120D8Z	NATIONAL DEFENSE EDUCATION PROGRAM	69,345	79,345	69,345	10,000	79,345
		K–12 STEM program increase		[10,000]		[10,000]	
006	0601228D8Z	HISTORICALLY BLACK COLLEGES AND UNIVERSITIES/MINORITY INSTITUTIONS.	23,572	33,572	23,572	10,000	33,572
		Program increase		[10,000]		[10,000]	
007	0601384BP	CHEMICAL AND BIOLOGICAL DEFENSE PROGRAM	44,800	44,800	44,800		44,800
		SUBTOTAL BASIC RESEARCH	**629,895**	**639,895**	**629,895**	**20,000**	**649,895**

SEC. 4201. RESEARCH, DEVELOPMENT, TEST, AND EVALUATION
(In Thousands of Dollars)

Line	Program Element	Item	FY 2017 Request	House Authorized	Senate Authorized	Conference Change	Conference Authorized
		APPLIED RESEARCH					
008	0602000D8Z	JOINT MUNITIONS TECHNOLOGY	17,745	17,745	17,745		17,745
009	0602115E	BIOMEDICAL TECHNOLOGY	115,213	105,213	115,213		115,213
		Program reduction		[−10,000]			
010	0602230D8Z	DEFENSE TECHNOLOGY INNOVATION	30,000		30,000	−30,000	0
		Program decrease		[−30,000]		[−30,000]	
011	0602234D8Z	LINCOLN LABORATORY RESEARCH PROGRAM	48,269	48,269	48,269		48,269
012	0602251D8Z	APPLIED RESEARCH FOR THE ADVANCEMENT OF S&T PRIORITIES	42,206	42,206	42,206		42,206
013	0602303E	INFORMATION & COMMUNICATIONS TECHNOLOGY	353,635	348,635	353,635		353,635
		Program reduction		[−5,000]			
014	0602383E	BIOLOGICAL WARFARE DEFENSE	21,250	21,250	21,250		21,250
015	0602384BP	CHEMICAL AND BIOLOGICAL DEFENSE PROGRAM	188,715	188,715	188,715		188,715
016	0602668D8Z	CYBER SECURITY RESEARCH	12,183	12,183	12,183		12,183
017	0602702E	TACTICAL TECHNOLOGY	313,843	313,843	313,843		313,843
018	0602715E	MATERIALS AND BIOLOGICAL TECHNOLOGY	220,456	210,456	220,456	−6,000	214,456
		Program reduction		[−10,000]		[−6,000]	
019	0602716E	ELECTRONICS TECHNOLOGY	221,911	221,911	221,911		221,911
020	0602718BR	WEAPONS OF MASS DESTRUCTION DEFEAT TECHNOLOGIES	154,857	154,857	154,857		154,857
021	0602751D8Z	SOFTWARE ENGINEERING INSTITUTE (SEI) APPLIED RESEARCH	8,420	8,420	8,420		8,420
022	1160401BB	SOF TECHNOLOGY DEVELOPMENT	37,820	37,820	37,820		37,820
		SUBTOTAL APPLIED RESEARCH	**1,786,523**	**1,731,523**	**1,786,523**	**−36,000**	**1,750,523**
		ADVANCED TECHNOLOGY DEVELOPMENT					
023	0603000D8Z	JOINT MUNITIONS ADVANCED TECHNOLOGY	23,902	23,902	23,902		23,902
025	0603122D8Z	COMBATING TERRORISM TECHNOLOGY SUPPORT	73,002	100,002	73,002		73,002
		Additional EOD equipment for Conventional Units		[12,000]			
		Program increase for DOD CT and C-UAS		[15,000]			
026	0603133D8Z	FOREIGN COMPARATIVE TESTING	19,343	29,343	19,343	10,000	29,343
		Anti-tunnel defense systems		[10,000]		[10,000]	
027	0603160BR	COUNTERPROLIFERATION INITIATIVES—PROLIFERATION PREVENTION AND DEFEAT.	266,444	266,444	266,444		266,444
028	0603176C	ADVANCED CONCEPTS AND PERFORMANCE ASSESSMENT	17,880	17,880	17,880		17,880
030	0603178C	WEAPONS TECHNOLOGY	71,843	71,843	71,843		71,843
031	0603179C	ADVANCED C4ISR	3,626	3,626	3,626		3,626
032	0603180C	ADVANCED RESEARCH	23,433	23,433	23,433		23,433
033	0603225D8Z	JOINT DOD-DOE MUNITIONS TECHNOLOGY DEVELOPMENT	17,256	17,256	17,256		17,256
035	0603274C	SPECIAL PROGRAM—MDA TECHNOLOGY	83,745	108,745	83,745	−71,950	11,795
		Classified Annex		[25,000]			
		Program reduction				[−71,950]	
036	0603286E	ADVANCED AEROSPACE SYSTEMS	182,327	177,327	182,327		182,327
		Program reduction		[−5,000]			
037	0603287E	SPACE PROGRAMS AND TECHNOLOGY	175,240	165,240	175,240	−10,000	165,240
		Program reduction		[−10,000]		[−10,000]	
038	0603288D8Z	ANALYTIC ASSESSMENTS	12,048	12,048	12,048		12,048
039	0603289D8Z	ADVANCED INNOVATIVE ANALYSIS AND CONCEPTS	57,020	57,020	57,020		57,020
041	0603375D8Z	TECHNOLOGY INNOVATION	39,923	19,923	39,923	−20,000	19,923
		Program decrease		[−20,000]		[−20,000]	
042	0603384BP	CHEMICAL AND BIOLOGICAL DEFENSE PROGRAM—ADVANCED DEVELOPMENT.	127,941	127,941	127,941		127,941
043	0603527D8Z	RETRACT LARCH	181,977	181,977	181,977		181,977
044	0603618D8Z	JOINT ELECTRONIC ADVANCED TECHNOLOGY	22,030	22,030	22,030		22,030
045	0603648D8Z	JOINT CAPABILITY TECHNOLOGY DEMONSTRATIONS	148,184	158,184	148,184	−16,000	132,184
		Program decrease				[−16,000]	
		Social Medial Analysis Cell		[10,000]			
046	0603662D8Z	NETWORKED COMMUNICATIONS CAPABILITIES	9,331	9,331	9,331		9,331
047	0603680D8Z	DEFENSE-WIDE MANUFACTURING SCIENCE AND TECHNOLOGY PROGRAM.	158,398	148,398	158,398		158,398
		Program decrease		[−10,000]			

SEC. 4201. RESEARCH, DEVELOPMENT, TEST, AND EVALUATION
(In Thousands of Dollars)

Line	Program Element	Item	FY 2017 Request	House Authorized	Senate Authorized	Conference Change	Conference Authorized
048	0603680S	MANUFACTURING TECHNOLOGY PROGRAM	31,259	31,259	31,259		31,259
049	0603699D8Z	EMERGING CAPABILITIES TECHNOLOGY DEVELOPMENT	49,895	49,895	49,895		49,895
050	0603712S	GENERIC LOGISTICS R&D TECHNOLOGY DEMONSTRATIONS	11,011	11,011	11,011		11,011
052	0603716D8Z	STRATEGIC ENVIRONMENTAL RESEARCH PROGRAM	65,078	65,078	65,078		65,078
053	0603720S	MICROELECTRONICS TECHNOLOGY DEVELOPMENT AND SUPPORT	97,826	97,826	97,826		97,826
054	0603727D8Z	JOINT WARFIGHTING PROGRAM	7,848	7,848	7,848	−2,500	5,348
		Prior year carryover				[−2,500]	
055	0603739E	ADVANCED ELECTRONICS TECHNOLOGIES	49,807	49,807	49,807		49,807
056	0603760E	COMMAND, CONTROL AND COMMUNICATIONS SYSTEMS	155,081	155,081	155,081		155,081
057	0603766E	NETWORK-CENTRIC WARFARE TECHNOLOGY	428,894	428,894	428,894		428,894
058	0603767E	SENSOR TECHNOLOGY	241,288	241,288	241,288		241,288
060	0603781D8Z	SOFTWARE ENGINEERING INSTITUTE	14,264	14,264	14,264		14,264
061	0603826D8Z	QUICK REACTION SPECIAL PROJECTS	74,943	72,943	74,943	−2,000	72,943
		QRSP		[−2,000]		[−2,000]	
063	0603833D8Z	ENGINEERING SCIENCE & TECHNOLOGY	17,659	17,659	17,659		17,659
064	0603941D8Z	TEST & EVALUATION SCIENCE & TECHNOLOGY	87,135	87,135	87,135		87,135
065	0604055D8Z	OPERATIONAL ENERGY CAPABILITY IMPROVEMENT	37,329	37,329	41,329	4,000	41,329
		Competitive technology investment				[4,000]	[4,000]
066	0303310D8Z	CWMD SYSTEMS	44,836	21,236	44,836	−23,600	21,236
		Constellation program reduction		[−23,600]		[−23,600]	
067	1160402BB	SOF ADVANCED TECHNOLOGY DEVELOPMENT	61,620	61,620	61,620		61,620
		SUBTOTAL ADVANCED TECHNOLOGY DEVELOPMENT	**3,190,666**	**3,192,066**	**3,194,666**	**−132,050**	**3,058,616**
		ADVANCED COMPONENT DEVELOPMENT & PROTOTYPES					
		ADVANCED COMPONENT DEVELOPMENT AND PROTOTYPES					
068	0603161D8Z	NUCLEAR AND CONVENTIONAL PHYSICAL SECURITY EQUIPMENT RDT&E ADC&P.	28,498	28,498	28,498		28,498
069	0603600D8Z	WALKOFF	89,643	89,643	89,643		89,643
071	0603821D8Z	ACQUISITION ENTERPRISE DATA & INFORMATION SERVICES	2,136	2,136	2,136		2,136
072	0603851D8Z	ENVIRONMENTAL SECURITY TECHNICAL CERTIFICATION PROGRAM	52,491	52,491	52,491		52,491
073	0603881C	BALLISTIC MISSILE DEFENSE TERMINAL DEFENSE SEGMENT	206,834	206,834	206,834		206,834
074	0603882C	BALLISTIC MISSILE DEFENSE MIDCOURSE DEFENSE SEGMENT	862,080	862,080	862,080		862,080
075	0603884BP	CHEMICAL AND BIOLOGICAL DEFENSE PROGRAM—DEM/VAL	138,187	138,187	138,187		138,187
076	0603884C	BALLISTIC MISSILE DEFENSE SENSORS	230,077	230,077	230,077		230,077
077	0603890C	BMD ENABLING PROGRAMS	401,594	401,594	401,594		401,594
078	0603891C	SPECIAL PROGRAMS—MDA	321,607	321,607	321,607	−16,900	304,707
		Program reduction				[−16,900]	
079	0603892C	AEGIS BMD	959,066	959,066	959,066	−20,000	939,066
		SM–3 IIA development excess growth				[−20,000]	
080	0603893C	SPACE TRACKING & SURVEILLANCE SYSTEM	32,129	32,129	32,129		32,129
081	0603895C	BALLISTIC MISSILE DEFENSE SYSTEM SPACE PROGRAMS	20,690	20,690	20,690		20,690
082	0603896C	BALLISTIC MISSILE DEFENSE COMMAND AND CONTROL, BATTLE MANAGEMENT AND COMMUNICATI.	439,617	439,617	449,617	3,900	443,517
		Post Intercept Assessment Acceleration			[10,000]	[3,900]	
083	0603898C	BALLISTIC MISSILE DEFENSE JOINT WARFIGHTER SUPPORT	47,776	47,776	47,776		47,776
084	0603904C	MISSILE DEFENSE INTEGRATION & OPERATIONS CENTER (MDIOC)	54,750	54,750	54,750		54,750
085	0603906C	REGARDING TRENCH	8,785	8,785	8,785		8,785
086	0603907C	SEA BASED X-BAND RADAR (SBX)	68,787	68,787	68,787		68,787
087	0603913C	ISRAELI COOPERATIVE PROGRAMS	103,835	293,835	238,835	164,900	268,735
		Directed Energy Cooperation through MDA		[25,000]			
		Increase for Cooperative Development Programs subject to Title XVI.		[165,000]	[135,000]	[164,900]	
088	0603914C	BALLISTIC MISSILE DEFENSE TEST	293,441	293,441	293,441		293,441
089	0603915C	BALLISTIC MISSILE DEFENSE TARGETS	563,576	563,576	563,576		563,576
090	0603920D8Z	HUMANITARIAN DEMINING	10,007	10,007	10,007		10,007
091	0603923D8Z	COALITION WARFARE	10,126	10,126	11,126		10,126
		Long Endurance UAS			[1,000]		
092	0604016D8Z	DEPARTMENT OF DEFENSE CORROSION PROGRAM	3,893	3,893	8,893	5,000	8,893

SEC. 4201. RESEARCH, DEVELOPMENT, TEST, AND EVALUATION
(In Thousands of Dollars)

Line	Program Element	Item	FY 2017 Request	House Authorized	Senate Authorized	Conference Change	Conference Authorized
		Corrosion prevention			[5,000]	[5,000]	
093	0604115C	TECHNOLOGY MATURATION INITIATIVES	90,266	105,266	90,266		90,266
		Directed Energy Acceleration—Low Power Laser Demonstrator - to reclaim schdule slippage.		[15,000]			
094	0604132D8Z	MISSILE DEFEAT PROJECT	45,000	45,000	45,000		45,000
095	0604250D8Z	ADVANCED INNOVATIVE TECHNOLOGIES	844,870	794,870	844,870	−15,000	829,870
		SCO		[−50,000]		[−15,000]	
096	0604342D8Z	DEFENSE TECHNOLOGY OFFSET			25,000		
		Directed energy systems prototyping			[25,000]		
097	0604400D8Z	DEPARTMENT OF DEFENSE (DOD) UNMANNED SYSTEM COMMON DEVELOPMENT.	3,320	3,320	3,320		3,320
099	0604682D8Z	WARGAMING AND SUPPORT FOR STRATEGIC ANALYSIS (SSA)	4,000	4,000	4,000		4,000
102	0604826J	JOINT C5 CAPABILITY DEVELOPMENT, INTEGRATION AND INTEROPERABILITY ASSESSMENTS.	23,642	23,642	23,642		23,642
104	0604873C	LONG RANGE DISCRIMINATION RADAR (LRDR)	162,012	162,012	162,012		162,012
105	0604874C	IMPROVED HOMELAND DEFENSE INTERCEPTORS	274,148	274,148	329,148		274,148
		GBI Booster Acceleration			[30,000]		
		RKV Risk Reduction			[25,000]		
106	0604876C	BALLISTIC MISSILE DEFENSE TERMINAL DEFENSE SEGMENT TEST	63,444	63,444	63,444		63,444
107	0604878C	AEGIS BMD TEST	95,012	95,012	95,012		95,012
108	0604879C	BALLISTIC MISSILE DEFENSE SENSOR TEST	83,250	83,250	83,250		83,250
109	0604880C	LAND-BASED SM-3 (LBSM3)	43,293	43,293	43,293		43,293
110	0604881C	AEGIS SM-3 BLOCK IIA CO-DEVELOPMENT	106,038	106,038	106,038		106,038
111	0604887C	BALLISTIC MISSILE DEFENSE MIDCOURSE SEGMENT TEST	56,481	56,481	56,481		56,481
112	0604894C	MULTI-OBJECT KILL VEHICLE	71,513	71,513	121,513		71,513
		Technology maturation			[50,000]		
114	0303191D8Z	JOINT ELECTROMAGNETIC TECHNOLOGY (JET) PROGRAM	2,636	2,636	2,636		2,636
115	0305103C	CYBER SECURITY INITIATIVE	969	969	969		969
		SUBTOTAL ADVANCED COMPONENT DEVELOPMENT AND PROTOTYPES.	**6,919,519**	**7,074,519**	**7,200,519**	**121,900**	**7,041,419**
115A	0604XXXD	WEATHER SYSTEM FOLLOW-ON		5,000		5,000	5,000
		Transfer Cloud Characterization and Theater Weather Imagery from USAF.		[5,000]		[5,000]	
		SUBTOTAL ADVANCED COMPONENT DEVELOPMENT & PROTOTYPES		**5,000**		**5,000**	**5,000**
		SYSTEM DEVELOPMENT AND DEMONSTRATION					
116	0604161D8Z	NUCLEAR AND CONVENTIONAL PHYSICAL SECURITY EQUIPMENT RDT&E SDD.	10,324	10,324	10,324		10,324
117	0604165D8Z	PROMPT GLOBAL STRIKE CAPABILITY DEVELOPMENT	181,303	186,303	181,303		181,303
		Examination of Army land-attack and anti-ship capability		[5,000]			
118	0604384BP	CHEMICAL AND BIOLOGICAL DEFENSE PROGRAM—EMD	266,231	266,231	266,231		266,231
119	0604764K	ADVANCED IT SERVICES JOINT PROGRAM OFFICE (AITS-JPO)		15,000			
		Commercial IT Eval Program		[15,000]			
120	0604771D8Z	JOINT TACTICAL INFORMATION DISTRIBUTION SYSTEM (JTIDS)	16,288	16,288	16,288		16,288
121	0605000BR	WEAPONS OF MASS DESTRUCTION DEFEAT CAPABILITIES	4,568	4,568	4,568		4,568
122	0605013BL	INFORMATION TECHNOLOGY DEVELOPMENT	11,505	11,505	11,505		11,505
123	0605021SE	HOMELAND PERSONNEL SECURITY INITIATIVE	1,658	1,658	1,658		1,658
124	0605022D8Z	DEFENSE EXPORTABILITY PROGRAM	2,920	2,920	2,920		2,920
126	0605070S	DOD ENTERPRISE SYSTEMS DEVELOPMENT AND DEMONSTRATION	12,631	12,631	12,631		12,631
128	0605080S	DEFENSE AGENCY INTIATIVES (DAI)—FINANCIAL SYSTEM	26,657	26,657	26,657		26,657
129	0605090S	DEFENSE RETIRED AND ANNUITANT PAY SYSTEM (DRAS)	4,949	4,949	4,949		4,949
130	0605140D8Z	TRUSTED FOUNDRY	69,000	69,000	69,000		69,000
131	0605210D8Z	DEFENSE-WIDE ELECTRONIC PROCUREMENT CAPABILITIES	9,881	9,881	9,881		9,881
132	0303141K	GLOBAL COMBAT SUPPORT SYSTEM	7,600	7,600	7,600		7,600
133	0305304D8Z	DOD ENTERPRISE ENERGY INFORMATION MANAGEMENT (EEIM)	2,703	2,703	2,703		2,703
		SUBTOTAL SYSTEM DEVELOPMENT AND DEMONSTRATION	**628,218**	**648,218**	**628,218**		**628,218**

MANAGEMENT SUPPORT

SEC. 4201. RESEARCH, DEVELOPMENT, TEST, AND EVALUATION
(In Thousands of Dollars)

Line	Program Element	Item	FY 2017 Request	House Authorized	Senate Authorized	Conference Change	Conference Authorized
134	0604774D8Z	DEFENSE READINESS REPORTING SYSTEM (DRRS)	4,678	4,678	4,678		4,678
135	0604875D8Z	JOINT SYSTEMS ARCHITECTURE DEVELOPMENT	4,499	4,499	4,499		4,499
136	0604940D8Z	CENTRAL TEST AND EVALUATION INVESTMENT DEVELOPMENT (CTEIP)	219,199	219,199	219,199		219,199
137	0604942D8Z	ASSESSMENTS AND EVALUATIONS	28,706	28,706	128,706		28,706
		Classified assessment			[100,000]		
138	0605001E	MISSION SUPPORT	69,244	69,244	69,244		69,244
139	0605100D8Z	JOINT MISSION ENVIRONMENT TEST CAPABILITY (JMETC)	87,080	87,080	87,080	−20,000	67,080
		Prior year carryover and minimize growth				[−20,000]	
140	0605104D8Z	TECHNICAL STUDIES, SUPPORT AND ANALYSIS	23,069	23,069	23,069		23,069
142	0605126J	JOINT INTEGRATED AIR AND MISSILE DEFENSE ORGANIZATION (JIAMDO).	32,759	32,759	32,759		32,759
144	0605142D8Z	SYSTEMS ENGINEERING	32,429	32,429	32,429		32,429
145	0605151D8Z	STUDIES AND ANALYSIS SUPPORT—OSD	3,797	3,797	3,797		3,797
146	0605161D8Z	NUCLEAR MATTERS-PHYSICAL SECURITY	5,302	5,302	5,302		5,302
147	0605170D8Z	SUPPORT TO NETWORKS AND INFORMATION INTEGRATION	7,246	7,246	7,246		7,246
148	0605200D8Z	GENERAL SUPPORT TO USD (INTELLIGENCE)	1,874	1,874	1,874		1,874
149	0605384BP	CHEMICAL AND BIOLOGICAL DEFENSE PROGRAM	85,754	85,754	85,754		85,754
158	0605790D8Z	SMALL BUSINESS INNOVATION RESEARCH (SBIR)/ SMALL BUSINESS TECHNOLOGY TRANSFER.	2,187	2,187	2,187		2,187
159	0605798D8Z	DEFENSE TECHNOLOGY ANALYSIS	22,650	22,650	22,650		22,650
160	0605801KA	DEFENSE TECHNICAL INFORMATION CENTER (DTIC)	43,834	43,834	43,834		43,834
161	0605803SE	R&D IN SUPPORT OF DOD ENLISTMENT, TESTING AND EVALUATION	22,240	22,240	22,240		22,240
162	0605804D8Z	DEVELOPMENT TEST AND EVALUATION	19,541	23,541	24,541	4,000	23,541
		Program increase		[4,000]	[5,000]	[4,000]	
163	0605898E	MANAGEMENT HQ—R&D	4,759	4,759	4,759		4,759
164	0605998KA	MANAGEMENT HQ—DEFENSE TECHNICAL INFORMATION CENTER (DTIC).	4,400	4,400	4,400		4,400
165	0606100D8Z	BUDGET AND PROGRAM ASSESSMENTS	4,014	4,014	4,014		4,014
166	0203345D8Z	DEFENSE OPERATIONS SECURITY INITIATIVE (DOSI)	2,072	2,072	2,072		2,072
167	0204571J	JOINT STAFF ANALYTICAL SUPPORT	7,464	7,464	7,464		7,464
170	0303166J	SUPPORT TO INFORMATION OPERATIONS (IO) CAPABILITIES	857	857	857		857
171	0303260D8Z	DEFENSE MILITARY DECEPTION PROGRAM OFFICE (DMDPO)	916	916	916		916
172	0305172K	COMBINED ADVANCED APPLICATIONS	15,336	15,336	15,336		15,336
173	0305193D8Z	CYBER INTELLIGENCE	18,523	18,523	18,523	−5,000	13,523
		Program decrease				[−5,000]	
175	0804767D8Z	COCOM EXERCISE ENGAGEMENT AND TRAINING TRANSFORMATION (CE2T2)—MHA.	34,384	34,384	34,384		34,384
176	0901598C	MANAGEMENT HQ—MDA	31,160	56,160	31,160		31,160
		Cyber Improvements Acceleration		[25,000]			
179	0903235D8W	JOINT SERVICE PROVIDER (JSP)	827	827	827		827
180A	9999999999	CLASSIFIED PROGRAMS	56,799	56,799	56,799		56,799
		SUBTOTAL MANAGEMENT SUPPORT	**897,599**	**926,599**	**1,002,599**	**−21,000**	**876,599**
		OPERATIONAL SYSTEM DEVELOPMENT					
181	0604130V	ENTERPRISE SECURITY SYSTEM (ESS)	4,241	4,241	4,241		4,241
182	0605127T	REGIONAL INTERNATIONAL OUTREACH (RIO) AND PARTNERSHIP FOR PEACE INFORMATION MANA.	1,424	1,424	1,424		1,424
183	0605147T	OVERSEAS HUMANITARIAN ASSISTANCE SHARED INFORMATION SYSTEM (OHASIS).	287	287	287		287
184	0607210D8Z	INDUSTRIAL BASE ANALYSIS AND SUSTAINMENT SUPPORT	16,195	16,195	16,195		16,195
185	0607310D8Z	CWMD SYSTEMS: OPERATIONAL SYSTEMS DEVELOPMENT	4,194	4,194	4,194		4,194
186	0607327T	GLOBAL THEATER SECURITY COOPERATION MANAGEMENT INFORMATION SYSTEMS (G-TSCMIS).	7,861	7,861	7,861		7,861
187	0607384BP	CHEMICAL AND BIOLOGICAL DEFENSE (OPERATIONAL SYSTEMS DEVELOPMENT).	33,361	33,361	33,361		33,361
189	0208043J	PLANNING AND DECISION AID SYSTEM (PDAS)	3,038	3,038	3,038		3,038
190	0208045K	C4I INTEROPERABILITY	57,501	57,501	57,501		57,501
192	0301144K	JOINT/ALLIED COALITION INFORMATION SHARING	5,935	5,935	5,935		5,935

SEC. 4201. RESEARCH, DEVELOPMENT, TEST, AND EVALUATION
(In Thousands of Dollars)

Line	Program Element	Item	FY 2017 Request	House Authorized	Senate Authorized	Conference Change	Conference Authorized
196	0302016K	NATIONAL MILITARY COMMAND SYSTEM-WIDE SUPPORT	575	575	575		575
197	0302019K	DEFENSE INFO INFRASTRUCTURE ENGINEERING AND INTEGRATION	18,041	18,041	18,041		18,041
198	0303126K	LONG-HAUL COMMUNICATIONS—DCS	13,994	18,994	13,994		13,994
		Secure cellular communications for senior leaders		[5,000]			
199	0303131K	MINIMUM ESSENTIAL EMERGENCY COMMUNICATIONS NETWORK (MEECN).	12,206	12,206	12,206		12,206
200	0303135G	PUBLIC KEY INFRASTRUCTURE (PKI)	34,314	34,314	34,314		34,314
201	0303136G	KEY MANAGEMENT INFRASTRUCTURE (KMI)	36,602	36,602	36,602		36,602
202	0303140D8Z	INFORMATION SYSTEMS SECURITY PROGRAM	8,876	8,876	8,876		8,876
203	0303140G	INFORMATION SYSTEMS SECURITY PROGRAM	159,068	161,068	172,068	2,000	161,068
		Cross Domain Solutions			[5,000]		
		Reduction to NSA Information Systems and Security Programs			[−8,000]		
		SHARKSEER Program Increase		[2,000]	[16,000]	[2,000]	
204	0303150K	GLOBAL COMMAND AND CONTROL SYSTEM	24,438	24,438	24,438		24,438
205	0303153K	DEFENSE SPECTRUM ORGANIZATION	13,197	13,197	13,197		13,197
207	0303228K	JOINT INFORMATION ENVIRONMENT (JIE)	2,789	2,789	2,789		2,789
209	0303430K	FEDERAL INVESTIGATIVE SERVICES INFORMATION TECHNOLOGY	75,000	75,000	75,000		75,000
210	0303610K	TELEPORT PROGRAM	657	657	657		657
215	0305103K	CYBER SECURITY INITIATIVE	1,553	1,553	1,553		1,553
220	0305186D8Z	POLICY R&D PROGRAMS	6,204	4,204	6,204	−2,000	4,204
		Program decrease		[−2,000]		[−2,000]	
221	0305199D8Z	NET CENTRICITY	17,971	17,971	17,971		17,971
223	0305208BB	DISTRIBUTED COMMON GROUND/SURFACE SYSTEMS	5,415	5,415	5,415		5,415
226	0305208K	DISTRIBUTED COMMON GROUND/SURFACE SYSTEMS	3,030	3,030	3,030		3,030
229	0305327V	INSIDER THREAT	5,034	5,034	5,034		5,034
230	0305387D8Z	HOMELAND DEFENSE TECHNOLOGY TRANSFER PROGRAM	2,037	2,037	2,037		2,037
236	0307577D8Z	INTELLIGENCE MISSION DATA (IMD)	13,800	13,800	13,800		13,800
238	0708012S	PACIFIC DISASTER CENTERS	1,754	1,754	1,754		1,754
239	0708047S	DEFENSE PROPERTY ACCOUNTABILITY SYSTEM	2,154	2,154	2,154		2,154
240	0902298J	MANAGEMENT HQ—OJCS	826	826	826		826
241	1105219BB	MQ–9 UAV	17,804	17,804	29,804		17,804
		MQ–9 capability enhancements			[12,000]		
244	1160403BB	AVIATION SYSTEMS	159,143	147,043	159,143		159,143
		AC–130 Precision Strike		[−12,100]			
245	1160405BB	INTELLIGENCE SYSTEMS DEVELOPMENT	7,958	7,958	7,958		7,958
246	1160408BB	OPERATIONAL ENHANCEMENTS	64,895	64,895	64,895		64,895
247	1160431BB	WARRIOR SYSTEMS	44,885	44,885	44,885		44,885
248	1160432BB	SPECIAL PROGRAMS	1,949	1,949	1,949		1,949
249	1160434BB	UNMANNED ISR	22,117	22,117	22,117		22,117
250	1160480BB	SOF TACTICAL VEHICLES	3,316	3,316	3,316		3,316
251	1160483BB	MARITIME SYSTEMS	54,577	54,577	54,577		54,577
252	1160489BB	GLOBAL VIDEO SURVEILLANCE ACTIVITIES	3,841	3,841	3,841		3,841
253	1160490BB	OPERATIONAL ENHANCEMENTS INTELLIGENCE	11,834	11,834	11,834		11,834
253A	9999999999	CLASSIFIED PROGRAMS	3,270,515	3,270,515	3,270,515		3,270,515
255	0303140K	INFORMATION SYSTEMS SECURITY PROGRAM			16,300		
		Sharkseer email protection			[16,300]		
		SUBTOTAL OPERATIONAL SYSTEM DEVELOPMENT	**4,256,406**	**4,249,306**	**4,297,706**		**4,256,406**
		TOTAL RESEARCH, DEVELOPMENT, TEST & EVAL, DW	**18,308,826**	**18,467,126**	**18,740,126**	**−42,150**	**18,266,676**

OPERATIONAL TEST & EVAL, DEFENSE
MANAGEMENT SUPPORT

Line	Program Element	Item	FY 2017 Request	House Authorized	Senate Authorized	Conference Change	Conference Authorized
001	06051180TE	OPERATIONAL TEST AND EVALUATION	78,047	88,047	78,047		78,047
		DOT&E Cybersecurity Exercises		[10,000]			
002	06051310TE	LIVE FIRE TEST AND EVALUATION	48,316	48,316	48,316		48,316
003	06058140TE	OPERATIONAL TEST ACTIVITIES AND ANALYSES	52,631	52,631	52,631		52,631
		SUBTOTAL MANAGEMENT SUPPORT	**178,994**	**188,994**	**178,994**		**178,994**

SEC. 4201. RESEARCH, DEVELOPMENT, TEST, AND EVALUATION
(In Thousands of Dollars)

Line	Program Element	Item	FY 2017 Request	House Authorized	Senate Authorized	Conference Change	Conference Authorized
		TOTAL OPERATIONAL TEST & EVAL, DEFENSE	178,994	188,994	178,994		178,994
		UNDISTRIBUTED GENERAL PROVISIONS					
		UNDISTRIBUTED GENERAL PROVISIONS					
010	9999999999	UNDISTRIBUTED GENERAL PROVISIONS			4,000		
		Cyber pilot program for installations			[4,000]		
		SUBTOTAL UNDISTRIBUTED GENERAL PROVISIONS			4,000		
		TOTAL UNDISTRIBUTED GENERAL PROVISIONS			4,000		
		TOTAL RDT&E	71,391,771	71,619,841	71,227,192	−281,147	71,110,624

SEC. 4202. RESEARCH, DEVELOPMENT, TEST, AND EVALUATION FOR OVERSEAS CONTINGENCY OPERATIONS.

SEC. 4202. RESEARCH, DEVELOPMENT, TEST, AND EVALUATION FOR OVERSEAS CONTINGENCY OPERATIONS
(In Thousands of Dollars)

Line	Program Element	Item	FY 2017 Request	House Authorized	Senate Authorized	Conference Change	Conference Authorized
		ADVANCED COMPONENT DEVELOPMENT & PROTOTYPES					
055	0603308A	ARMY SPACE SYSTEMS INTEGRATION	9,375	9,375	9,375		9,375
		SUBTOTAL ADVANCED COMPONENT DEVELOPMENT & PROTO-TYPES.	9,375	9,375	9,375		9,375
		SYSTEM DEVELOPMENT & DEMONSTRATION					
091	0604741A	AIR DEFENSE COMMAND, CONTROL AND INTELLIGENCE—ENG DEV	78,700	78,700	78,700		78,700
114	0605032A	TRACTOR TIRE	10,000	10,000	10,000		10,000
117	0605035A	COMMON INFRARED COUNTERMEASURES (CIRCM)	10,900	10,900	10,900		10,900
119	0605041A	DEFENSIVE CYBER TOOL DEVELOPMENT	50,500	50,500	50,500		50,500
122	0605051A	AIRCRAFT SURVIVABILITY DEVELOPMENT	73,110	73,110	73,110		73,110
		SUBTOTAL SYSTEM DEVELOPMENT & DEMONSTRATION	223,210	223,210	223,210		223,210
		OPERATIONAL SYSTEMS DEVELOPMENT					
208	0307665A	BIOMETRICS ENABLED INTELLIGENCE	7,104	7,104	7,104		7,104
		SUBTOTAL OPERATIONAL SYSTEMS DEVELOPMENT	7,104	7,104	7,104		7,104
		TOTAL RESEARCH, DEVELOPMENT, TEST & EVAL, ARMY	239,689	239,689	239,689		239,689
		ADVANCED COMPONENT DEVELOPMENT & PROTOTYPES					
038	0603527N	RETRACT LARCH	3,907	3,907	3,907		3,907
		SUBTOTAL ADVANCED COMPONENT DEVELOPMENT & PROTO-TYPES.	3,907	3,907	3,907		3,907
		OPERATIONAL SYSTEMS DEVELOPMENT					
245A	9999999999	CLASSIFIED PROGRAMS	36,426	36,426	36,426		36,426
		SUBTOTAL OPERATIONAL SYSTEMS DEVELOPMENT	36,426	36,426	36,426		36,426
		TOTAL RESEARCH, DEVELOPMENT, TEST & EVAL, NAVY	40,333	40,333	40,333		40,333
		SYSTEM DEVELOPMENT & DEMONSTRATION					
058	0604421F	COUNTERSPACE SYSTEMS	425	425	425		425
		SUBTOTAL SYSTEM DEVELOPMENT & DEMONSTRATION	425	425	425		425
		OPERATIONAL SYSTEMS DEVELOPMENT					
200	0305174F	SPACE INNOVATION, INTEGRATION AND RAPID TECHNOLOGY DEVELOPMENT.	4,715	4,715	4,715		4,715
242A	9999999999	CLASSIFIED PROGRAMS	27,765	27,765	27,765		27,765
		SUBTOTAL OPERATIONAL SYSTEMS DEVELOPMENT	32,480	32,480	32,480		32,480

SEC. 4202. RESEARCH, DEVELOPMENT, TEST, AND EVALUATION FOR OVERSEAS CONTINGENCY OPERATIONS
(In Thousands of Dollars)

Line	Program Element	Item	FY 2017 Request	House Authorized	Senate Authorized	Conference Change	Conference Authorized
		TOTAL RESEARCH, DEVELOPMENT, TEST & EVAL, AF	32,905	32,905	32,905		32,905
		OPERATIONAL SYSTEM DEVELOPMENT					
253A	9999999999	CLASSIFIED PROGRAMS	165,419	165,419	165,419		165,419
		SUBTOTAL OPERATIONAL SYSTEM DEVELOPMENT	165,419	165,419	165,419		165,419
		TOTAL RESEARCH, DEVELOPMENT, TEST & EVAL, DW	165,419	165,419	165,419		165,419
		TOTAL RDT&E	478,346	478,346	478,346		478,346

SEC. 4203. RESEARCH, DEVELOPMENT, TEST, AND EVALUATION FOR OVERSEAS CONTINGENCY OPERATIONS FOR BASE REQUIREMENTS.

SEC. 4203. RESEARCH, DEVELOPMENT, TEST, AND EVALUATION FOR OVERSEAS CONTINGENCY OPERATIONS FOR BASE REQUIREMENTS
(In Thousands of Dollars)

Line	Program Element	Item	FY 2017 Request	House Authorized	Senate Authorized	Conference Change	Conference Authorized
		RESEARCH, DEVELOPMENT, TEST & EVAL, ARMY					
		SYSTEM DEVELOPMENT & DEMONSTRATION					
090	0604715A	NON-SYSTEM TRAINING DEVICES—ENG DEV	33	33	33		33
122	0605051A	AIRCRAFT SURVIVABILITY DEVELOPMENT		10,000			
		Army unfunded requirement—modernized warning system		[10,000]			
		SUBTOTAL SYSTEM DEVELOPMENT & DEMONSTRATION	33	10,033	33		33
		OPERATIONAL SYSTEMS DEVELOPMENT					
161	0603778A	MLRS PRODUCT IMPROVEMENT PROGRAM		16,000			
		Army unfunded requirement—GMLRS M-code upgrade		[16,000]			
166	0607134A	LONG RANGE PRECISION FIRES (LRPF)		27,700			
		Army unfunded requirement		[27,700]			
179	0203735A	COMBAT VEHICLE IMPROVEMENT PROGRAMS		10,000			
		Army unfunded requirement—Vehicle APS		[10,000]			
		SUBTOTAL OPERATIONAL SYSTEMS DEVELOPMENT		53,700			
		TOTAL RESEARCH, DEVELOPMENT, TEST & EVAL, ARMY	33	63,733	33		33
		RESEARCH, DEVELOPMENT, TEST & EVAL, NAVY					
		ADVANCED COMPONENT DEVELOPMENT & PROTOTYPES					
078	0604272N	TACTICAL AIR DIRECTIONAL INFRARED COUNTERMEASURES (TADIRCM).	37,990	37,990	37,990		37,990
081	0604454N	LX (R)		19,000			
		LX (R) Design		[19,000]			
		SUBTOTAL ADVANCED COMPONENT DEVELOPMENT & PROTOTYPES.	37,990	56,990	37,990		37,990
		SYSTEM DEVELOPMENT & DEMONSTRATION					
102	0604262N	V–22A		11,400			
		Accelerate Readiness Improvement—Swashplate actuator redesign.		[11,400]			
118	0604501N	ADVANCED ABOVE WATER SENSORS		20,000			
		Aegis Radar Solid State Improvements		[20,000]			
		SUBTOTAL SYSTEM DEVELOPMENT & DEMONSTRATION		31,400			
		TOTAL RESEARCH, DEVELOPMENT, TEST & EVAL, NAVY	37,990	88,390	37,990		37,990
		RESEARCH, DEVELOPMENT, TEST & EVAL, DW					
		ADVANCED COMPONENT DEVELOPMENT AND PROTOTYPES					
074	0603882C	BALLISTIC MISSILE DEFENSE MIDCOURSE DEFENSE SEGMENT		65,000			
		Ground System Communications Modernization & Upgrades to Enable Full RKV Capabilities.		[65,000]			

SEC. 4203. RESEARCH, DEVELOPMENT, TEST, AND EVALUATION FOR OVERSEAS CONTINGENCY OPERATIONS FOR BASE REQUIREMENTS
(In Thousands of Dollars)

Line	Program Element	Item	FY 2017 Request	House Authorized	Senate Authorized	Conference Change	Conference Authorized
076	0603884C	BALLISTIC MISSILE DEFENSE SENSORS		45,000			
		Electronic Protection Acceleration for Sensors		[25,000]			
		RFPs for Hawaii & East Coast Radars		[20,000]			
077	0603890C	BMD ENABLING PROGRAMS		10,000			
		Modeling and Simulation Improvements		[10,000]			
079	0603892C	AEGIS BMD		10,000			
		Aegis BMD Integration with AMDR		[10,000]			
082	0603896C	BALLISTIC MISSILE DEFENSE COMMAND AND CONTROL, BATTLE MANAGEMENT AND COMMUNICATI.		30,000			
		C2BMC Acceleration		[20,000]			
		Post-Intercept Assessment Acceleration		[10,000]			
088	0603914C	BALLISTIC MISSILE DEFENSE TEST		10,000			
		Test Infrastructure		[10,000]			
105	0604874C	IMPROVED HOMELAND DEFENSE INTERCEPTORS		75,000			
		Modernized Booster Acceleration		[50,000]			
		RKV risk reduction		[25,000]			
112	0604894C	MULTI-OBJECT KILL VEHICLE		55,000			
		MOKV Technology Maturation		[55,000]			
		SUBTOTAL ADVANCED COMPONENT DEVELOPMENT AND PROTOTYPES		300,000			
		TOTAL RESEARCH, DEVELOPMENT, TEST & EVAL, DW		300,000			
		TOTAL RDT&E	38,023	452,123	38,023		38,023

TITLE XLIII—OPERATION AND MAINTENANCE

SEC. 4301. OPERATION AND MAINTENANCE.

SEC. 4301. OPERATION AND MAINTENANCE
(In Thousands of Dollars)

Line	Item	FY 2017 Request	House Authorized	Senate Authorized	Conference Change	Conference Authorized
	OPERATION & MAINTENANCE, ARMY					
	OPERATING FORCES					
010	MANEUVER UNITS	791,450	791,450	841,450	50,000	841,450
	Home station training unfunded requirement			[50,000]	[50,000]	
020	MODULAR SUPPORT BRIGADES	68,373	68,373	68,373		68,373
030	ECHELONS ABOVE BRIGADE	438,823	438,823	438,823		438,823
040	THEATER LEVEL ASSETS	660,258	660,258	660,258		660,258
050	LAND FORCES OPERATIONS SUPPORT	863,928	1,198,828	863,928		863,928
	Realign APS Unit Set Requirements from OCO		[334,900]			
060	AVIATION ASSETS	1,360,597	1,360,597	1,428,597	100,500	1,461,097
	Eleventh CAB				[32,500]	
	Flying hour program unfunded requirement			[68,000]	[68,000]	
070	FORCE READINESS OPERATIONS SUPPORT	3,086,443	3,094,443	3,086,443		3,086,443
	Additional cyber protection teams		[3,000]			
	Public-private cyber training partnership		[5,000]			
080	LAND FORCES SYSTEMS READINESS	439,488	439,488	439,488		439,488
090	LAND FORCES DEPOT MAINTENANCE	1,013,452	1,026,052	1,032,852	19,400	1,032,852
	Depot maintenance unfunded requirement			[19,400]	[19,400]	
	Realign APS Unit Set Requirements from OCO		[12,600]			
100	BASE OPERATIONS SUPPORT	7,816,343	7,831,343	7,816,343	22,100	7,838,443
	Eleventh CAB Support				[22,100]	
	Realign APS Unit Set Requirements from OCO		[15,000]			
110	FACILITIES SUSTAINMENT, RESTORATION & MODERNIZATION	2,234,546	2,234,546	2,588,946	85,400	2,319,946
	Restore Sustainment shortfalls			[354,400]	[85,400]	
120	MANAGEMENT AND OPERATIONAL HEADQUARTERS	452,105	452,105	452,105		452,105
130	COMBATANT COMMANDERS CORE OPERATIONS	155,658	155,658	155,658		155,658

SEC. 4301. OPERATION AND MAINTENANCE
(In Thousands of Dollars)

Line	Item	FY 2017 Request	House Authorized	Senate Authorized	Conference Change	Conference Authorized
170	COMBATANT COMMANDS DIRECT MISSION SUPPORT	441,143	441,143	447,843		441,143
	SOUTHCOM LIDAR unfunded requirement			[6,700]		
	SUBTOTAL OPERATING FORCES	**19,822,607**	**20,193,107**	**20,321,107**	**277,400**	**20,100,007**
	MOBILIZATION					
180	STRATEGIC MOBILITY	336,329	336,329	336,329		336,329
190	ARMY PREPOSITIONED STOCKS	390,848	574,848	415,848	25,000	415,848
	Program increase			[25,000]	[25,000]	
	Realign APS Unit Set Requirements from OCO		[184,000]			
200	INDUSTRIAL PREPAREDNESS	7,401	7,401	7,401		7,401
	SUBTOTAL MOBILIZATION	**734,578**	**918,578**	**759,578**	**25,000**	**759,578**
	TRAINING AND RECRUITING					
210	OFFICER ACQUISITION	131,942	131,942	131,942		131,942
220	RECRUIT TRAINING	47,846	47,846	47,846		47,846
230	ONE STATION UNIT TRAINING	45,419	45,419	45,419		45,419
240	SENIOR RESERVE OFFICERS TRAINING CORPS	482,747	482,747	482,747		482,747
250	SPECIALIZED SKILL TRAINING	921,025	927,525	921,025	6,500	927,525
	Defense Foreign Language Program		[6,500]		[6,500]	
260	FLIGHT TRAINING	902,845	902,845	939,445	42,934	945,779
	Graduate pilot training unfunded requirement			[5,400]	[5,405]	
	School Air OPTEMPO unfunded requirement			[31,200]	[31,125]	
	Train full ARPINT load of 990				[6,404]	
270	PROFESSIONAL DEVELOPMENT EDUCATION	216,583	216,583	216,583	31,600	248,183
	Military Training and PME				[31,600]	
280	TRAINING SUPPORT	607,534	607,534	607,534		607,534
290	RECRUITING AND ADVERTISING	550,599	550,599	515,599	−25,000	525,599
	Unjustified program growth			[−35,000]	[−25,000]	
300	EXAMINING	187,263	187,263	187,263		187,263
310	OFF-DUTY AND VOLUNTARY EDUCATION	189,556	189,556	189,556		189,556
320	CIVILIAN EDUCATION AND TRAINING	182,835	182,835	182,835		182,835
330	JUNIOR RESERVE OFFICER TRAINING CORPS	171,167	171,167	171,167		171,167
	SUBTOTAL TRAINING AND RECRUITING	**4,637,361**	**4,643,861**	**4,638,961**	**56,034**	**4,693,395**
	ADMIN & SRVWIDE ACTIVITIES					
350	SERVICEWIDE TRANSPORTATION	230,739	350,739	230,739	65,000	295,739
	Realign APS Unit Set Requirements from OCO		[120,000]			
	Restore crictial shortfalls				[65,000]	
360	CENTRAL SUPPLY ACTIVITIES	850,060	850,060	850,060		850,060
370	LOGISTIC SUPPORT ACTIVITIES	778,757	778,757	782,757		778,757
	Corrosion oil assistance unfunded requirement			[4,000]		
380	AMMUNITION MANAGEMENT	370,010	370,010	370,010		370,010
390	ADMINISTRATION	451,556	451,556	451,556		451,556
400	SERVICEWIDE COMMUNICATIONS	1,888,123	1,888,123	1,888,123		1,888,123
410	MANPOWER MANAGEMENT	276,403	276,403	276,403		276,403
420	OTHER PERSONNEL SUPPORT	369,443	369,443	369,443		369,443
430	OTHER SERVICE SUPPORT	1,096,074	1,096,074	1,066,574		1,096,074
	Army museum early to need			[−29,500]		
440	ARMY CLAIMS ACTIVITIES	207,800	207,800	207,800		207,800
450	REAL ESTATE MANAGEMENT	240,641	240,641	240,641		240,641
460	FINANCIAL MANAGEMENT AND AUDIT READINESS	250,612	250,612	250,612		250,612
470	INTERNATIONAL MILITARY HEADQUARTERS	416,587	416,587	416,587		416,587
480	MISC. SUPPORT OF OTHER NATIONS	36,666	36,666	36,666		36,666
530	CLASSIFIED PROGRAMS	1,151,023	1,151,023	1,157,023		1,151,023
	SOUTHCOM unfunded requirement			[6,000]		
	SUBTOTAL ADMIN & SRVWIDE ACTIVITIES	**8,614,494**	**8,734,494**	**8,594,994**	**65,000**	**8,679,494**

SEC. 4301. OPERATION AND MAINTENANCE
(In Thousands of Dollars)

Line	Item	FY 2017 Request	House Authorized	Senate Authorized	Conference Change	Conference Authorized
	UNDISTRIBUTED					
540	UNDISTRIBUTED		−654,600	−279,780	−400,200	−400,200
	15% printing reduction			[−34,300]		
	DCGS-A undistributed reduction			[−63,000]		
	Excessive standard price for fuel		[−56,100]	[−123,300]	[−56,100]	
	Foreign Currency adjustments		[−229,900]	[−59,180]	[−194,100]	
	Historical unobligated balances		[−376,300]			
	Prohibition on Per Diem Allowance Reduction		[7,700]			
	Working Capital Fund Carryover Above Allowable Ceiling				[−150,000]	
	SUBTOTAL UNDISTRIBUTED		**−654,600**	**−279,780**	**−400,200**	**−400,200**
	TOTAL OPERATION & MAINTENANCE, ARMY	**33,809,040**	**33,835,440**	**34,034,860**	**23,234**	**33,832,274**
	OPERATION & MAINTENANCE, ARMY RES					
	OPERATING FORCES					
010	MODULAR SUPPORT BRIGADES	11,435	11,435	11,435		11,435
020	ECHELONS ABOVE BRIGADE	491,772	491,772	537,772	20,000	511,772
	Home station training unfunded requirement			[20,000]	[20,000]	
	Lodging in kind unfunded requirement			[26,000]		
030	THEATER LEVEL ASSETS	116,163	116,163	116,163		116,163
040	LAND FORCES OPERATIONS SUPPORT	563,524	563,524	563,524		563,524
050	AVIATION ASSETS	91,162	91,162	91,162		91,162
060	FORCE READINESS OPERATIONS SUPPORT	347,459	347,659	347,759	200	347,659
	Defense Language Program		[200]		[200]	
	Range increase unfunded requirement			[300]		
070	LAND FORCES SYSTEMS READINESS	101,926	101,926	101,926		101,926
080	LAND FORCES DEPOT MAINTENANCE	56,219	56,219	56,219		56,219
090	BASE OPERATIONS SUPPORT	573,843	573,843	573,843		573,843
100	FACILITIES SUSTAINMENT, RESTORATION & MODERNIZATION	214,955	214,955	236,455	8,100	223,055
	Restore Sustainment shortfalls			[21,500]	[8,100]	
110	MANAGEMENT AND OPERATIONAL HEADQUARTERS	37,620	37,620	37,620		37,620
	SUBTOTAL OPERATING FORCES	**2,606,078**	**2,606,278**	**2,673,878**	**28,300**	**2,634,378**
	ADMIN & SRVWD ACTIVITIES					
120	SERVICEWIDE TRANSPORTATION	11,027	11,027	11,027		11,027
130	ADMINISTRATION	16,749	16,749	16,749		16,749
140	SERVICEWIDE COMMUNICATIONS	17,825	17,825	17,825		17,825
150	MANPOWER MANAGEMENT	6,177	6,177	6,177		6,177
160	RECRUITING AND ADVERTISING	54,475	54,475	54,475		54,475
	SUBTOTAL ADMIN & SRVWD ACTIVITIES	**106,253**	**106,253**	**106,253**		**106,253**
	UNDISTRIBUTED					
180	UNDISTRIBUTED		−6,800		−6,800	−6,800
	Excessive standard price for fuel		[−6,800]		[−6,800]	
	SUBTOTAL UNDISTRIBUTED		**−6,800**		**−6,800**	**−6,800**
	TOTAL OPERATION & MAINTENANCE, ARMY RES	**2,712,331**	**2,705,731**	**2,780,131**	**21,500**	**2,733,831**
	OPERATION & MAINTENANCE, ARNG					
	OPERATING FORCES					
010	MANEUVER UNITS	708,251	708,251	778,251	50,000	758,251
	Home station training unfunded requirement			[70,000]	[50,000]	
020	MODULAR SUPPORT BRIGADES	197,251	197,251	197,251		197,251
030	ECHELONS ABOVE BRIGADE	792,271	792,271	792,271		792,271
040	THEATER LEVEL ASSETS	80,341	80,341	80,341		80,341
050	LAND FORCES OPERATIONS SUPPORT	37,138	37,138	39,538		37,138
	Range increase unfunded requirement			[2,400]		

SEC. 4301. OPERATION AND MAINTENANCE
(In Thousands of Dollars)

Line	Item	FY 2017 Request	House Authorized	Senate Authorized	Conference Change	Conference Authorized
060	AVIATION ASSETS	887,625	887,625	887,625	−2,800	884,825
	Unjustified program growth				[−2,800]	
070	FORCE READINESS OPERATIONS SUPPORT	696,267	696,467	696,267	−6,115	690,152
	Defense Language Program		[200]		[200]	
	Unjustified program growth				[−6,315]	
080	LAND FORCES SYSTEMS READINESS	61,240	61,240	61,240		61,240
090	LAND FORCES DEPOT MAINTENANCE	219,948	219,948	274,548		219,948
	Depot maintenance unfunded requirement			[42,300]		
	TWV depot maintenance unfunded requirement			[12,300]		
100	BASE OPERATIONS SUPPORT	1,040,012	1,040,012	1,040,012		1,040,012
110	FACILITIES SUSTAINMENT, RESTORATION & MODERNIZATION	676,715	676,715	708,815	14,400	691,115
	Restore Sustainment shortfalls			[32,100]	[14,400]	
120	MANAGEMENT AND OPERATIONAL HEADQUARTERS	1,021,144	1,021,144	1,021,144		1,021,144
	SUBTOTAL OPERATING FORCES	**6,418,203**	**6,418,403**	**6,577,303**	**55,485**	**6,473,688**
	ADMIN & SRVWD ACTIVITIES					
130	SERVICEWIDE TRANSPORTATION	6,396	6,396	6,396		6,396
140	ADMINISTRATION	68,528	71,052	68,528	1,150	69,678
	National Guard State Partnership Program		[2,524]			
	State Partnership Program				[1,150]	
150	SERVICEWIDE COMMUNICATIONS	76,524	76,524	76,524		76,524
160	MANPOWER MANAGEMENT	7,712	7,712	7,712		7,712
170	OTHER PERSONNEL SUPPORT	245,046	245,046	249,546		245,046
	Director of Psychological Health (DPH) Positions			[9,500]		
	Program decrease			[−5,000]		
180	REAL ESTATE MANAGEMENT	2,961	2,961	2,961		2,961
	SUBTOTAL ADMIN & SRVWD ACTIVITIES	**407,167**	**409,691**	**411,667**	**1,150**	**408,317**
	UNDISTRIBUTED					
190	UNDISTRIBUTED		−29,000		−29,000	−29,000
	Excessive standard price for fuel		[−29,000]		[−29,000]	
	SUBTOTAL UNDISTRIBUTED		**−29,000**		**−29,000**	**−29,000**
	TOTAL OPERATION & MAINTENANCE, ARNG	**6,825,370**	**6,799,094**	**6,988,970**	**27,635**	**6,853,005**
	OPERATION & MAINTENANCE, NAVY					
	OPERATING FORCES					
010	MISSION AND OTHER FLIGHT OPERATIONS	4,094,765	4,094,765	4,094,765		4,094,765
020	FLEET AIR TRAINING	1,722,473	1,722,473	1,722,473		1,722,473
030	AVIATION TECHNICAL DATA & ENGINEERING SERVICES	52,670	52,670	52,670		52,670
040	AIR OPERATIONS AND SAFETY SUPPORT	97,584	97,584	97,584		97,584
050	AIR SYSTEMS SUPPORT	446,733	446,733	446,733	6,500	453,233
	Marine Corps unfunded requirement—accelerate readiness - H–1				[5,300]	
	Marine Corps unfunded requirement—accelerate readiness - MV–22B				[1,200]	
060	AIRCRAFT DEPOT MAINTENANCE	1,007,681	1,007,681	1,041,681	64,000	1,071,681
	AC Depot maintenance unfunded requirement			[34,000]	[34,000]	
	Navy unfunded requirement—Improve Afloat Readiness				[30,000]	
070	AIRCRAFT DEPOT OPERATIONS SUPPORT	38,248	38,248	38,248		38,248
080	AVIATION LOGISTICS	564,720	564,720	586,120	33,500	598,220
	E–6B and F–35 sustainment unfunded requirement			[16,000]	[16,000]	
	Marine Corps unfunded requirement—accelerate readiness - KC–130J				[6,800]	
	Marine Corps unfunded requirement—accelerate readiness - MV–22B				[10,700]	
	MV–22 JPBL unfunded requirement			[5,400]		
090	MISSION AND OTHER SHIP OPERATIONS	3,513,083	3,513,083	3,513,083	348,200	3,861,283
	Cruiser Modernization				[90,200]	
	Navy unfunded requirement—Improve Afloat Readiness				[158,000]	
	Navy unfunded requirement—Restore 3 CG Deployments				[41,000]	

SEC. 4301. OPERATION AND MAINTENANCE
(In Thousands of Dollars)

Line	Item	FY 2017 Request	House Authorized	Senate Authorized	Conference Change	Conference Authorized
	Navy unfunded requirement—Reverse PONCE (LPD–15) Inactivation				[59,000]	
100	SHIP OPERATIONS SUPPORT & TRAINING	743,765	743,765	743,765	19,700	763,465
	Navy unfunded requirement—Restore Fleet Training				[19,700]	
110	SHIP DEPOT MAINTENANCE	5,168,273	5,177,773	5,168,273	318,600	5,486,873
	Cruiser Modernization				[71,100]	
	Navy unfunded requirement—Ship Depot Wholeness				[238,000]	
	Program increase		[9,500]		[9,500]	
120	SHIP DEPOT OPERATIONS SUPPORT	1,575,578	1,575,578	1,575,578	79,000	1,654,578
	Navy unfunded requirement—Increase Alfoat Readiness				[79,000]	
130	COMBAT COMMUNICATIONS	558,727	558,727	558,727		558,727
140	ELECTRONIC WARFARE	105,680	105,680	105,680		105,680
150	SPACE SYSTEMS AND SURVEILLANCE	180,406	180,406	180,406		180,406
160	WARFARE TACTICS	470,032	470,032	470,032		470,032
170	OPERATIONAL METEOROLOGY AND OCEANOGRAPHY	346,703	346,703	346,703		346,703
180	COMBAT SUPPORT FORCES	1,158,688	1,158,688	1,158,688		1,158,688
190	EQUIPMENT MAINTENANCE	113,692	113,692	113,692		113,692
200	DEPOT OPERATIONS SUPPORT	2,509	2,509	2,509		2,509
210	COMBATANT COMMANDERS CORE OPERATIONS	91,019	91,019	91,019		91,019
220	COMBATANT COMMANDERS DIRECT MISSION SUPPORT	74,780	74,780	74,780		74,780
230	CRUISE MISSILE	106,030	106,030	106,030		106,030
240	FLEET BALLISTIC MISSILE	1,233,805	1,241,305	1,233,805		1,233,805
	Engineering and Technical Services, Project 934		[7,500]			
250	IN-SERVICE WEAPONS SYSTEMS SUPPORT	163,025	163,025	163,025		163,025
260	WEAPONS MAINTENANCE	553,269	551,469	553,269		553,269
	Heavy Weight Torpedo Program Execution		[−1,500]			
	Light Weight Torpedo Program Execution		[−300]			
270	OTHER WEAPON SYSTEMS SUPPORT	350,010	350,010	350,010		350,010
280	ENTERPRISE INFORMATION	790,685	790,685	736,385		790,685
	Underexecution			[−54,300]		
290	SUSTAINMENT, RESTORATION AND MODERNIZATION	1,642,742	1,642,742	1,803,642	55,100	1,697,842
	Restore Sustainment shortfalls			[160,900]	[55,100]	
300	BASE OPERATING SUPPORT	4,206,136	4,206,136	4,206,136		4,206,136
	SUBTOTAL OPERATING FORCES	**31,173,511**	**31,188,711**	**31,335,511**	**924,600**	**32,098,111**
	MOBILIZATION					
310	SHIP PREPOSITIONING AND SURGE	893,517	893,517	893,517		893,517
320	READY RESERVE FORCE	274,524	274,524	274,524		274,524
330	AIRCRAFT ACTIVATIONS/INACTIVATIONS	6,727	6,727	6,727		6,727
340	SHIP ACTIVATIONS/INACTIVATIONS	288,154	288,154	288,154		288,154
350	EXPEDITIONARY HEALTH SERVICES SYSTEMS	95,720	95,720	95,720		95,720
360	INDUSTRIAL READINESS	2,109	2,109	2,109		2,109
370	COAST GUARD SUPPORT	21,114	21,114	21,114		21,114
	SUBTOTAL MOBILIZATION	**1,581,865**	**1,581,865**	**1,581,865**		**1,581,865**
	TRAINING AND RECRUITING					
380	OFFICER ACQUISITION	143,815	143,815	143,815		143,815
390	RECRUIT TRAINING	8,519	8,519	8,519		8,519
400	RESERVE OFFICERS TRAINING CORPS	143,445	143,445	143,445		143,445
410	SPECIALIZED SKILL TRAINING	699,214	699,214	699,214		699,214
420	FLIGHT TRAINING	5,310	5,310	5,310		5,310
430	PROFESSIONAL DEVELOPMENT EDUCATION	172,852	174,052	172,852		172,852
	Naval Sea Cadets		[1,200]			
440	TRAINING SUPPORT	222,728	222,728	222,728		222,728
450	RECRUITING AND ADVERTISING	225,647	225,647	225,647		225,647
460	OFF-DUTY AND VOLUNTARY EDUCATION	130,569	130,569	130,569		130,569
470	CIVILIAN EDUCATION AND TRAINING	73,730	73,730	73,730		73,730
480	JUNIOR ROTC	50,400	50,400	50,400		50,400

SEC. 4301. OPERATION AND MAINTENANCE
(In Thousands of Dollars)

Line	Item	FY 2017 Request	House Authorized	Senate Authorized	Conference Change	Conference Authorized
	SUBTOTAL TRAINING AND RECRUITING	1,876,229	1,877,429	1,876,229		1,876,229
	ADMIN & SRVWD ACTIVITIES					
490	ADMINISTRATION	917,453	917,453	917,453		917,453
500	EXTERNAL RELATIONS	14,570	14,570	14,570		14,570
510	CIVILIAN MANPOWER AND PERSONNEL MANAGEMENT	124,070	124,070	124,070		124,070
520	MILITARY MANPOWER AND PERSONNEL MANAGEMENT	369,767	369,767	369,767		369,767
530	OTHER PERSONNEL SUPPORT	285,927	285,927	281,927		285,927
	NHHC unjustified growth			[−4,000]		
540	SERVICEWIDE COMMUNICATIONS	319,908	319,908	319,908		319,908
570	SERVICEWIDE TRANSPORTATION	171,659	171,659	171,659		171,659
580	ENVIRONMENTAL PROGRAMS			18,000		
	Environmental program shortfall unfunded requirement			[18,000]		
590	PLANNING, ENGINEERING AND DESIGN	270,863	270,863	270,863		270,863
600	ACQUISITION AND PROGRAM MANAGEMENT	1,112,766	1,112,766	1,112,766		1,112,766
610	HULL, MECHANICAL AND ELECTRICAL SUPPORT	49,078	49,078	49,078		49,078
620	COMBAT/WEAPONS SYSTEMS	24,989	24,989	24,989		24,989
630	SPACE AND ELECTRONIC WARFARE SYSTEMS	72,966	72,966	72,966		72,966
640	NAVAL INVESTIGATIVE SERVICE	595,711	595,711	595,711		595,711
700	INTERNATIONAL HEADQUARTERS AND AGENCIES	4,809	4,809	4,809		4,809
730	CLASSIFIED PROGRAMS	517,440	517,440	517,440		517,440
	SUBTOTAL ADMIN & SRVWD ACTIVITIES	4,851,976	4,851,976	4,865,976		4,851,976
	UNDISTRIBUTED					
740	UNDISTRIBUTED		−585,600	−260,290	−416,900	−416,900
	15% printing reduction			[−7,300]		
	Excessive standard price for fuel		[−390,500]	[−238,380]	[−390,500]	
	Foreign Currency adjustments		[−26,400]	[−14,610]	[−26,400]	
	Historical unobligated balances		[−174,100]			
	Prohibition on Per Diem Allowance Reduction		[5,400]			
	SUBTOTAL UNDISTRIBUTED		−585,600	−260,290	−416,900	−416,900
	TOTAL OPERATION & MAINTENANCE, NAVY	39,483,581	38,914,381	39,399,291	507,700	39,991,281
	OPERATION & MAINTENANCE, MARINE CORPS					
	OPERATING FORCES					
010	OPERATIONAL FORCES	674,613	674,613	738,313	85,700	760,313
	Enterprise network defense unfunded requirement			[5,700]	[5,700]	
	Exercise program unfunded requirement			[58,000]	[58,000]	
	Marine Corps unfunded requirement- enhanced combat helmets				[22,000]	
020	FIELD LOGISTICS	947,424	947,424	975,524	36,250	983,674
	Critical/ no fail EOD unfunded requirement			[600]	[600]	
	Marine Corps unfunded requirement- rifle combat optic modernization			[13,300]	[13,200]	
	Marine Corps unfunded requirement- SPMAGTF—C4 UUNS				[8,250]	
	Nano/VTOL unfunded requirement			[14,200]	[14,200]	
030	DEPOT MAINTENANCE	206,783	206,783	214,583	7,800	214,583
	Depot maintenance unfunded requirement			[7,800]	[7,800]	
040	MARITIME PREPOSITIONING	85,276	85,276	85,276		85,276
050	SUSTAINMENT, RESTORATION & MODERNIZATION	632,673	632,673	711,173	62,000	694,673
	Facility demolition unfunded requirement			[39,200]	[39,200]	
	Restore Sustainment shortfalls			[39,300]	[22,800]	
060	BASE OPERATING SUPPORT	2,136,626	2,136,626	2,136,626		2,136,626
	SUBTOTAL OPERATING FORCES	4,683,395	4,683,395	4,861,495	191,750	4,875,145
	TRAINING AND RECRUITING					
070	RECRUIT TRAINING	15,946	15,946	15,946		15,946
080	OFFICER ACQUISITION	935	935	935		935

SEC. 4301. OPERATION AND MAINTENANCE
(In Thousands of Dollars)

Line	Item	FY 2017 Request	House Authorized	Senate Authorized	Conference Change	Conference Authorized
090	SPECIALIZED SKILL TRAINING	99,305	99,305	99,305		99,305
100	PROFESSIONAL DEVELOPMENT EDUCATION	45,495	45,995	45,495		45,495
	MOS-to-Degree Program		[500]			
110	TRAINING SUPPORT	369,979	369,979	369,979		369,979
120	RECRUITING AND ADVERTISING	165,566	165,566	165,566		165,566
130	OFF-DUTY AND VOLUNTARY EDUCATION	35,133	35,133	35,133		35,133
140	JUNIOR ROTC	23,622	23,622	23,622		23,622
	SUBTOTAL TRAINING AND RECRUITING	**755,981**	**756,481**	**755,981**		**755,981**
	ADMIN & SRVWD ACTIVITIES					
150	SERVICEWIDE TRANSPORTATION	34,534	34,534	34,534		34,534
160	ADMINISTRATION	355,932	355,932	355,932		355,932
180	ACQUISITION AND PROGRAM MANAGEMENT	76,896	76,896	76,896		76,896
200	CLASSIFIED PROGRAMS	47,520	47,520	47,520		47,520
	SUBTOTAL ADMIN & SRVWD ACTIVITIES	**514,882**	**514,882**	**514,882**		**514,882**
	UNDISTRIBUTED					
210	UNDISTRIBUTED		−37,700	−41,830	−6,400	−6,400
	15% printing reduction			[−14,300]		
	Excessive standard price for fuel		[−4,900]	[−24,660]	[−4,900]	
	Foreign Currency adjustments		[−1,500]	[−2,870]	[−1,500]	
	Historical unobligated balances		[−33,100]			
	Prohibition on Per Diem Allowance Reduction		[1,800]			
	SUBTOTAL UNDISTRIBUTED		**−37,700**	**−41,830**	**−6,400**	**−6,400**
	TOTAL OPERATION & MAINTENANCE, MARINE CORPS	**5,954,258**	**5,917,058**	**6,090,528**	**185,350**	**6,139,608**
	OPERATION & MAINTENANCE, NAVY RES					
	OPERATING FORCES					
010	MISSION AND OTHER FLIGHT OPERATIONS	526,190	526,190	526,190		526,190
020	INTERMEDIATE MAINTENANCE	6,714	6,714	6,714		6,714
030	AIRCRAFT DEPOT MAINTENANCE	86,209	86,209	86,209	4,000	90,209
	Navy unfunded requirement—Improve Afloat Readiness				[4,000]	
040	AIRCRAFT DEPOT OPERATIONS SUPPORT	389	389	389		389
050	AVIATION LOGISTICS	10,189	10,189	10,189		10,189
070	SHIP OPERATIONS SUPPORT & TRAINING	560	560	560	300	860
	Navy unfunded requirement—Restore Fleet Training				[300]	
090	COMBAT COMMUNICATIONS	13,173	13,173	13,173		13,173
100	COMBAT SUPPORT FORCES	109,053	109,053	109,053		109,053
120	ENTERPRISE INFORMATION	27,226	27,226	27,226		27,226
130	SUSTAINMENT, RESTORATION AND MODERNIZATION	27,571	27,571	33,371	1,100	28,671
	Restore Sustainment shortfalls			[5,800]	[1,100]	
140	BASE OPERATING SUPPORT	99,166	99,166	99,166		99,166
	SUBTOTAL OPERATING FORCES	**906,440**	**906,440**	**912,240**	**5,400**	**911,840**
	ADMIN & SRVWD ACTIVITIES					
150	ADMINISTRATION	1,351	1,351	1,351		1,351
160	MILITARY MANPOWER AND PERSONNEL MANAGEMENT	13,251	13,251	13,251		13,251
170	SERVICEWIDE COMMUNICATIONS	3,445	3,445	3,445		3,445
180	ACQUISITION AND PROGRAM MANAGEMENT	3,169	3,169	3,169		3,169
	SUBTOTAL ADMIN & SRVWD ACTIVITIES	**21,216**	**21,216**	**21,216**		**21,216**
	UNDISTRIBUTED					
200	UNDISTRIBUTED		−26,600		−26,600	−26,600
	Excessive standard price for fuel		[−26,600]		[−26,600]	
	SUBTOTAL UNDISTRIBUTED		**−26,600**		**−26,600**	**−26,600**

SEC. 4301. OPERATION AND MAINTENANCE
(In Thousands of Dollars)

Line	Item	FY 2017 Request	House Authorized	Senate Authorized	Conference Change	Conference Authorized
	TOTAL OPERATION & MAINTENANCE, NAVY RES	927,656	901,056	933,456	−21,200	906,456
	OPERATION & MAINTENANCE, MC RESERVE					
	OPERATING FORCES					
010	OPERATING FORCES	94,154	94,154	94,154		94,154
020	DEPOT MAINTENANCE	18,594	18,594	18,594		18,594
030	SUSTAINMENT, RESTORATION AND MODERNIZATION	25,470	25,470	30,970	700	26,170
	Restore Sustainment shortfalls			[5,500]	[700]	
040	BASE OPERATING SUPPORT	111,550	111,550	111,550		111,550
	SUBTOTAL OPERATING FORCES	**249,768**	**249,768**	**255,268**	**700**	**250,468**
	ADMIN & SRVWD ACTIVITIES					
050	SERVICEWIDE TRANSPORTATION	902	902	902		902
060	ADMINISTRATION	11,130	11,130	11,130		11,130
070	RECRUITING AND ADVERTISING	8,833	8,833	8,833		8,833
	SUBTOTAL ADMIN & SRVWD ACTIVITIES	**20,865**	**20,865**	**20,865**		**20,865**
	UNDISTRIBUTED					
090	UNDISTRIBUTED		−800		−800	−800
	Excessive standard price for fuel		[−800]		[−800]	
	SUBTOTAL UNDISTRIBUTED		**−800**		**−800**	**−800**
	TOTAL OPERATION & MAINTENANCE, MC RESERVE	270,633	269,833	276,133	−100	270,533
	OPERATION & MAINTENANCE, AIR FORCE					
	OPERATING FORCES					
010	PRIMARY COMBAT FORCES	3,294,124	3,294,124	3,294,124		3,294,124
020	COMBAT ENHANCEMENT FORCES	1,682,045	1,682,045	1,684,845	2,800	1,684,845
	HH–60 unfunded requirement			[2,800]	[2,800]	
030	AIR OPERATIONS TRAINING (OJT, MAINTAIN SKILLS)	1,730,757	1,730,757	1,730,757		1,730,757
040	DEPOT MAINTENANCE	7,042,988	6,986,488	7,193,388	113,076	7,156,064
	Compass Call Program Restructure		[−56,500]		[−56,500]	
	Weapon system sustainment unfunded requirement			[150,400]	[169,576]	
050	FACILITIES SUSTAINMENT, RESTORATION & MODERNIZATION	1,657,019	1,657,019	1,657,019	53,000	1,710,019
	Restore Sustainment shortfalls				[53,000]	
060	BASE SUPPORT	2,787,216	2,787,216	2,787,216		2,787,216
070	GLOBAL C3I AND EARLY WARNING	887,831	887,831	887,831	40,000	927,831
	Air Force unfunded requirement—Ground Based Radars				[40,000]	
080	OTHER COMBAT OPS SPT PROGRAMS	1,070,178	1,070,178	1,070,178		1,070,178
100	LAUNCH FACILITIES	208,582	208,582	208,582		208,582
110	SPACE CONTROL SYSTEMS	362,250	362,250	362,250		362,250
120	COMBATANT COMMANDERS DIRECT MISSION SUPPORT	907,245	907,245	907,245		907,245
130	COMBATANT COMMANDERS CORE OPERATIONS	199,171	199,171	199,171		199,171
135	CLASSIFIED PROGRAMS	930,757	930,757	930,757		930,757
	SUBTOTAL OPERATING FORCES	**22,760,163**	**22,703,663**	**22,913,363**	**208,876**	**22,969,039**
	MOBILIZATION					
140	AIRLIFT OPERATIONS	1,703,059	1,703,059	1,703,059		1,703,059
150	MOBILIZATION PREPAREDNESS	138,899	138,899	138,899		138,899
160	DEPOT MAINTENANCE	1,553,439	1,553,439	1,619,839	66,424	1,619,863
	Weapon system sustainment unfunded requirement			[66,400]	[66,424]	
170	FACILITIES SUSTAINMENT, RESTORATION & MODERNIZATION	258,328	258,328	258,328	8,300	266,628
	Restore Sustainment shortfalls				[8,300]	
180	BASE SUPPORT	722,756	722,756	722,756		722,756
	SUBTOTAL MOBILIZATION	**4,376,481**	**4,376,481**	**4,442,881**	**74,724**	**4,451,205**

TRAINING AND RECRUITING

SEC. 4301. OPERATION AND MAINTENANCE
(In Thousands of Dollars)

Line	Item	FY 2017 Request	House Authorized	Senate Authorized	Conference Change	Conference Authorized
190	OFFICER ACQUISITION	120,886	120,886	120,886		120,886
200	RECRUIT TRAINING	23,782	23,782	23,782		23,782
210	RESERVE OFFICERS TRAINING CORPS (ROTC)	77,692	77,692	77,692		77,692
220	FACILITIES SUSTAINMENT, RESTORATION & MODERNIZATION	236,254	236,254	393,954	7,600	243,854
	Restore Sustainment shortfalls			[157,700]	[7,600]	
230	BASE SUPPORT	819,915	819,915	819,915		819,915
240	SPECIALIZED SKILL TRAINING	387,446	387,446	387,446		387,446
250	FLIGHT TRAINING	725,134	725,134	725,134		725,134
260	PROFESSIONAL DEVELOPMENT EDUCATION	264,213	264,213	264,213		264,213
270	TRAINING SUPPORT	86,681	86,681	86,681		86,681
280	DEPOT MAINTENANCE	305,004	305,004	305,004		305,004
290	RECRUITING AND ADVERTISING	104,754	104,754	77,754		104,754
	Advertising unjustified growth			[−27,000]		
300	EXAMINING	3,944	3,944	3,944		3,944
310	OFF-DUTY AND VOLUNTARY EDUCATION	184,841	184,841	184,841		184,841
320	CIVILIAN EDUCATION AND TRAINING	173,583	173,583	173,583		173,583
330	JUNIOR ROTC	58,877	58,877	58,877		58,877
	SUBTOTAL TRAINING AND RECRUITING	**3,573,006**	**3,573,006**	**3,703,706**	**7,600**	**3,580,606**
	ADMIN & SRVWD ACTIVITIES					
340	LOGISTICS OPERATIONS	1,107,846	1,107,846	1,107,846		1,107,846
350	TECHNICAL SUPPORT ACTIVITIES	924,185	924,185	924,185		924,185
360	DEPOT MAINTENANCE	48,778	48,778	48,778		48,778
370	FACILITIES SUSTAINMENT, RESTORATION & MODERNIZATION	321,013	321,013	321,013	10,300	331,313
	Restore Sustainment shortfalls				[10,300]	
380	BASE SUPPORT	1,115,910	1,115,910	1,115,910		1,115,910
390	ADMINISTRATION	811,650	811,650	811,650		811,650
400	SERVICEWIDE COMMUNICATIONS	269,809	269,809	269,809		269,809
410	OTHER SERVICEWIDE ACTIVITIES	961,304	961,304	961,304		961,304
420	CIVIL AIR PATROL	25,735	30,500	25,735	2,800	28,535
	Civil Air Patrol O&M Support		[4,765]		[2,800]	
450	INTERNATIONAL SUPPORT	90,573	90,573	90,573		90,573
460	CLASSIFIED PROGRAMS	1,131,603	1,131,603	1,131,603		1,131,603
	SUBTOTAL ADMIN & SRVWD ACTIVITIES	**6,808,406**	**6,813,171**	**6,808,406**	**13,100**	**6,821,506**
	UNDISTRIBUTED					
470	UNDISTRIBUTED		−765,900	−436,910	−484,700	−484,700
	15% printing reduction			[−8,900]		
	Excessive standard price for fuel		[−368,000]	[−394,560]	[−368,000]	
	Foreign Currency adjustments		[−116,700]	[−33,450]	[−116,700]	
	Historical unobligated balances		[−288,000]			
	Prohibition on Per Diem Allowance Reduction		[6,800]			
	SUBTOTAL UNDISTRIBUTED		**−765,900**	**−436,910**	**−484,700**	**−484,700**
	TOTAL OPERATION & MAINTENANCE, AIR FORCE	**37,518,056**	**36,700,421**	**37,431,446**	**−180,400**	**37,337,656**
	OPERATION & MAINTENANCE, AF RESERVE					
	OPERATING FORCES					
010	PRIMARY COMBAT FORCES	1,707,882	1,707,882	1,707,882		1,707,882
020	MISSION SUPPORT OPERATIONS	230,016	230,016	259,016		230,016
	Lodging in kind unfunded requirement			[29,000]		
030	DEPOT MAINTENANCE	541,743	541,743	541,743		541,743
040	FACILITIES SUSTAINMENT, RESTORATION & MODERNIZATION	113,470	113,470	125,170	2,700	116,170
	Restore Sustainment shortfalls			[11,700]	[2,700]	
050	BASE SUPPORT	384,832	384,832	384,832		384,832
	SUBTOTAL OPERATING FORCES	**2,977,943**	**2,977,943**	**3,018,643**	**2,700**	**2,980,643**

SEC. 4301. OPERATION AND MAINTENANCE
(In Thousands of Dollars)

Line	Item	FY 2017 Request	House Authorized	Senate Authorized	Conference Change	Conference Authorized
	ADMINISTRATION AND SERVICEWIDE ACTIVITIES					
060	ADMINISTRATION	54,939	54,939	54,939		54,939
070	RECRUITING AND ADVERTISING	14,754	14,754	14,754		14,754
080	MILITARY MANPOWER AND PERS MGMT (ARPC)	12,707	12,707	12,707		12,707
090	OTHER PERS SUPPORT (DISABILITY COMP)	7,210	7,210	7,210		7,210
100	AUDIOVISUAL	376	376	376		376
	SUBTOTAL ADMINISTRATION AND SERVICEWIDE ACTIVITIES	**89,986**	**89,986**	**89,986**		**89,986**
	UNDISTRIBUTED					
110	UNDISTRIBUTED		−59,700		−59,700	−59,700
	Excessive standard price for fuel		[−59,700]		[−59,700]	
	SUBTOTAL UNDISTRIBUTED		**−59,700**		**−59,700**	**−59,700**
	TOTAL OPERATION & MAINTENANCE, AF RESERVE	**3,067,929**	**3,008,229**	**3,108,629**	**−57,000**	**3,010,929**
	OPERATION & MAINTENANCE, ANG					
	OPERATING FORCES					
010	AIRCRAFT OPERATIONS	3,282,238	3,282,238	3,282,238	−4,000	3,278,238
	Unjustifed growth				[−4,000]	
020	MISSION SUPPORT OPERATIONS	723,062	723,062	723,062		723,062
030	DEPOT MAINTENANCE	1,824,329	1,824,329	1,867,529	43,200	1,867,529
	Weapon system sustainment engines unfunded requirement			[3,200]	[3,200]	
	Weapon system sustainment unfunded requirement			[40,000]	[40,000]	
040	FACILITIES SUSTAINMENT, RESTORATION & MODERNIZATION	245,840	245,840	259,840	9,100	254,940
	Restore Sustainment shortfalls			[14,000]	[9,100]	
050	BASE SUPPORT	575,548	575,548	575,548		575,548
	SUBTOTAL OPERATING FORCES	**6,651,017**	**6,651,017**	**6,708,217**	**48,300**	**6,699,317**
	ADMINISTRATION AND SERVICE-WIDE ACTIVITIES					
060	ADMINISTRATION	23,715	26,239	23,715		23,715
	National Guard State Partnership Program		[2,524]			
070	RECRUITING AND ADVERTISING	28,846	28,846	28,846		28,846
	SUBTOTAL ADMINISTRATION AND SERVICE-WIDE ACTIVITIES	**52,561**	**55,085**	**52,561**		**52,561**
	UNDISTRIBUTED					
080	UNDISTRIBUTED		−117,700		−117,700	−117,700
	Excessive standard price for fuel		[−117,700]		[−117,700]	
	SUBTOTAL UNDISTRIBUTED			**−117,700**	**−117,700**	**−117,700**
	TOTAL OPERATION & MAINTENANCE, ANG	**6,703,578**	**6,588,402**	**6,760,778**	**−69,400**	**6,634,178**
	OPERATION & MAINTENANCE, DEFENSE-WIDE					
	OPERATING FORCES					
010	JOINT CHIEFS OF STAFF	506,113	506,113	506,113		506,113
020	OFFICE OF THE SECRETARY OF DEFENSE	524,439	519,439	524,439		524,439
	Program decrease		[−5,000]			
030	SPECIAL OPERATIONS COMMAND/OPERATING FORCES	4,898,159	4,898,159	4,852,859	−8,800	4,889,359
	Unjustified growth in total civilian compensation			[−45,300]	[−8,800]	
	SUBTOTAL OPERATING FORCES	**5,928,711**	**5,923,711**	**5,883,411**	**−8,800**	**5,919,911**
	TRAINING AND RECRUITING					
040	DEFENSE ACQUISITION UNIVERSITY	138,658	138,658	138,658		138,658
050	JOINT CHIEFS OF STAFF	85,701	85,701	95,701		85,701
	Model alternative design of reconaissance strike group			[10,000]		
070	SPECIAL OPERATIONS COMMAND/TRAINING AND RECRUITING	365,349	365,349	365,349		365,349
	SUBTOTAL TRAINING AND RECRUITING	**589,708**	**589,708**	**599,708**		**589,708**

SEC. 4301. OPERATION AND MAINTENANCE
(In Thousands of Dollars)

Line	Item	FY 2017 Request	House Authorized	Senate Authorized	Conference Change	Conference Authorized
	ADMINISTRATION AND SERVICEWIDE ACTIVITIES					
080	CIVIL MILITARY PROGRAMS	160,480	195,480	185,480	35,339	195,819
	National Guard Youth Challenge Program		[15,000]		[10,339]	
	STARBASE		[20,000]	[25,000]	[25,000]	
100	DEFENSE CONTRACT AUDIT AGENCY	630,925	630,925	630,925		630,925
110	DEFENSE CONTRACT MANAGEMENT AGENCY	1,356,380	1,356,380	1,356,380		1,356,380
120	DEFENSE HUMAN RESOURCES ACTIVITY	683,620	683,620	683,620		683,620
130	DEFENSE INFORMATION SYSTEMS AGENCY	1,439,891	1,439,891	1,439,891		1,439,891
150	DEFENSE LEGAL SERVICES AGENCY	24,984	24,984	24,984		24,984
160	DEFENSE LOGISTICS AGENCY	357,964	354,964	352,164	−5,800	352,164
	Price Comparability Office unjustified growth		[−3,000]	[−5,800]	[−5,800]	
170	DEFENSE MEDIA ACTIVITY	223,422	213,422	223,422		223,422
	Program decrease		[−10,000]			
180	DEFENSE PERSONNEL ACCOUNTING AGENCY	112,681	112,681	112,681		112,681
190	DEFENSE SECURITY COOPERATION AGENCY	496,754	496,754	81,954	125,000	621,754
	Transfer Combatting Terrorism Fellowship to to Security Cooperation Enhancement Fund			[−26,800]		
	Transfer Defense Institute of International Legal Studies to Security Cooperation Enhancement Fund			[−2,600]		
	Transfer Defense Institution Reform Initiative to to Security Cooperation Enhancement Fund			[−25,600]		
	Transfer from Drug Interdiction and Counter-Drug Activities				[125,000]	
	Transfer Global Train and Equip to Security Cooperation Enhancement Fund			[−270,200]		
	Transfer Ministry of Defense Advisors to to Security Cooperation Enhancement Fund			[−9,200]		
	Transfer Regional Centers to Security Cooperation Enhancement Fund			[−58,600]		
	Transfer Wales initaitive Fund/Partnership for Peace to Security Cooperation Enhancement Fund			[−21,800]		
200	DEFENSE SECURITY SERVICE	538,711	538,711	538,711		538,711
230	DEFENSE TECHNOLOGY SECURITY ADMINISTRATION	35,417	35,417	35,417		35,417
240	DEFENSE THREAT REDUCTION AGENCY	448,146	448,146	448,146		448,146
260	DEPARTMENT OF DEFENSE EDUCATION ACTIVITY	2,671,143	2,701,143	2,701,143	30,000	2,701,143
	Impact Aid		[30,000]	[25,000]	[25,000]	
	Impact Aid severe disabilities			[5,000]	[5,000]	
270	MISSILE DEFENSE AGENCY	446,975	446,975	446,975		446,975
290	OFFICE OF ECONOMIC ADJUSTMENT	155,399	155,399	123,199	−19,200	136,199
	Guam public health lab			[−32,200]	[−19,200]	
300	OFFICE OF THE SECRETARY OF DEFENSE	1,481,643	1,406,713	1,502,643	5,650	1,487,293
	Alcohol Abuse Prevention Program		[1,000]			
	BRAC 2017 Round Planning and Analyses		[−3,530]	[−4,000]	[−3,530]	
	CWMD Sustainment: Constellation program reduction		[−3,800]		[−3,800]	
	DOD rewards early to need			[−5,000]	[−1,000]	
	Intelligence Management—program reduction				[−1,000]	
	Program decrease		[−84,428]			
	Reeadiness environmental protection initiative		[15,828]		[14,980]	
	Secretary of Defense Delivery Unit			[30,000]		
310	SPECIAL OPERATIONS COMMAND/ADMIN & SVC-WIDE ACTIVITIES	89,429	70,829	89,429		89,429
	SOCOM MH–60 Block Upgrades / MH–60M Replacement		[−18,600]			
320	WASHINGTON HEADQUARTERS SERVICES	629,874	619,874	629,874		629,874
	Program decrease		[−10,000]			
330	CLASSIFIED PROGRAMS	14,069,333	14,071,333	14,054,033		14,069,333
	Classified adjustment		[2,000]			
	Reduction to NSA Information Systems and Security Program (4GT4)			[−27,000]		
	Sharkseer email protection			[11,700]		
	SUBTOTAL ADMINISTRATION AND SERVICEWIDE ACTIVITIES	**26,053,171**	**26,003,641**	**25,661,071**	**170,989**	**26,224,160**

UNDISTRIBUTED

SEC. 4301. OPERATION AND MAINTENANCE
(In Thousands of Dollars)

Line	Item	FY 2017 Request	House Authorized	Senate Authorized	Conference Change	Conference Authorized
340	UNDISTRIBUTED		−308,900	−33,080	−47,100	−47,100
	15% printing reduction			[−1,400]		
	Commission on Military, National, and Public Service			[15,000]		
	Excessive standard price for fuel		[−17,800]	[−41,100]	[−17,800]	
	Foreign Currency adjustments		[−34,300]	[−10,580]	[−34,300]	
	Historical unobligated balances		[−248,100]			
	Program decrease		[−15,000]			
	Prohibition on Per Diem Allowance Reduction		[6,300]			
	Temporary Duty Assignment Per Diem Rate Waiver			[5,000]	[5,000]	
	SUBTOTAL UNDISTRIBUTED		**−308,900**	**−33,080**	**−47,100**	**−47,100**
	TOTAL OPERATION & MAINTENANCE, DEFENSE-WIDE	**32,571,590**	**32,208,160**	**32,111,110**	**115,089**	**32,686,679**
	MISCELLANEOUS APPROPRIATIONS					
	MISCELLANEOUS APPROPRIATIONS					
010	US COURT OF APPEALS FOR THE ARMED FORCES, DEFENSE	14,194	14,194	14,194		14,194
020	OVERSEAS HUMANITARIAN, DISASTER AND CIVIC AID	105,125	105,125	105,125		105,125
030	COOPERATIVE THREAT REDUCTION	325,604	325,604	325,604		325,604
050	ENVIRONMENTAL RESTORATION, ARMY	170,167	170,167	170,167		170,167
060	ENVIRONMENTAL RESTORATION, NAVY	281,762	281,762	281,762		281,762
070	ENVIRONMENTAL RESTORATION, AIR FORCE	371,521	371,521	371,521		371,521
080	ENVIRONMENTAL RESTORATION, DEFENSE	9,009	9,009	9,009		9,009
090	ENVIRONMENTAL RESTORATION FORMERLY USED SITES	197,084	197,084	197,084		197,084
	SUBTOTAL MISCELLANEOUS APPROPRIATIONS	**1,474,466**	**1,474,466**	**1,474,466**		**1,474,466**
	TOTAL MISCELLANEOUS APPROPRIATIONS	**1,474,466**	**1,474,466**	**1,474,466**		**1,474,466**
	TOTAL OPERATION & MAINTENANCE	**171,318,488**	**169,322,271**	**171,389,798**	**552,408**	**171,870,896**

SEC. 4302. OPERATION AND MAINTENANCE FOR OVERSEAS CONTINGENCY OPERATIONS.

SEC. 4302. OPERATION AND MAINTENANCE FOR OVERSEAS CONTINGENCY OPERATIONS
(In Thousands of Dollars)

Line	Item	FY 2017 Request	House Authorized	Senate Authorized	Conference Change	Conference Authorized
	OPERATION & MAINTENANCE, ARMY					
	OPERATING FORCES					
010	MANEUVER UNITS	427,063	416,263	427,063	−10,800	416,263
	Army requested realignment (ERI)		[−10,800]		[−10,800]	
040	THEATER LEVEL ASSETS	1,834,423	1,904,523	1,834,423		1,834,423
	Operational support for deployed end strength of 9,800 in Afghanistan		[70,100]			
050	LAND FORCES OPERATIONS SUPPORT	558,086	158,386	558,086	−132,000	426,086
	Army requested realignment (ERI)		[−132,000]		[−132,000]	
	Operational support for deployed end strength of 9,800 in Afghanistan		[67,200]			
	Realign APS Unit Set Requirements to Base		[−334,900]			
060	AVIATION ASSETS	58,620	90,120	58,620		58,620
	Operational support for deployed end strength of 9,800 in Afghanistan		[31,500]			
070	FORCE READINESS OPERATIONS SUPPORT	1,552,468	1,725,968	1,552,468	−2,000	1,550,468
	Army requested realignment (ERI)		[−2,000]		[−2,000]	
	Operational support for deployed end strength of 9,800 in Afghanistan		[175,500]			
080	LAND FORCES SYSTEMS READINESS	476,853	486,853	476,853		476,853
	Operational support for deployed end strength of 9,800 in Afghanistan		[10,000]			
100	BASE OPERATIONS SUPPORT	45,749	30,749	45,749		45,749
	Realign APS Unit Set Requirements to Base		[−15,000]			
140	ADDITIONAL ACTIVITIES	8,234,566	9,315,166	8,234,566		8,234,566
	Operational support for deployed end strength of 9,800 in Afghanistan		[1,093,200]			
	Realign APS Unit Set Requirements to Base		[−12,600]			
150	COMMANDERS EMERGENCY RESPONSE PROGRAM	5,000	5,000	5,000		5,000

SEC. 4302. OPERATION AND MAINTENANCE FOR OVERSEAS CONTINGENCY OPERATIONS
(In Thousands of Dollars)

Line	Item	FY 2017 Request	House Authorized	Senate Authorized	Conference Change	Conference Authorized
160	RESET	1,100,722	1,100,722	1,100,722		1,100,722
170	COMBATANT COMMANDS DIRECT MISSION SUPPORT	79,568	79,568	79,568		79,568
	SUBTOTAL OPERATING FORCES	**14,373,118**	**15,313,318**	**14,373,118**	**−144,800**	**14,228,318**
	MOBILIZATION					
190	ARMY PREPOSITIONED STOCKS	350,200	130,000	350,200	−220,200	130,000
	Army requested realignment (ERI)		[−220,200]		[−220,200]	
	SUBTOTAL MOBILIZATION	**350,200**	**130,000**	**350,200**	**−220,200**	**130,000**
	ADMIN & SRVWIDE ACTIVITIES					
350	SERVICEWIDE TRANSPORTATION	720,399	739,499	720,399	120,000	840,399
	Army requested realignment (ERI)		[120,000]		[120,000]	
	Operational support for deployed end strength of 9,800 in Afghanistan		[203,100]			
	Realign APS Unit Set Requirements to Base		[−304,000]			
380	AMMUNITION MANAGEMENT	13,974	49,074	13,974		13,974
	Operational support for deployed end strength of 9,800 in Afghanistan		[35,100]			
420	OTHER PERSONNEL SUPPORT	105,508	105,508	105,508		105,508
450	REAL ESTATE MANAGEMENT	185,904	283,404	185,904		185,904
	Operational support for deployed end strength of 9,800 in Afghanistan		[97,500]			
530	CLASSIFIED PROGRAMS	909,278	923,578	909,278		909,278
	Operational support for deployed end strength of 9,800 in Afghanistan		[14,300]			
	SUBTOTAL ADMIN & SRVWIDE ACTIVITIES	**1,935,063**	**2,101,063**	**1,935,063**	**120,000**	**2,055,063**
	UNDISTRIBUTED					
540	UNDISTRIBUTED		−6,083,330			
	Excessive standard price for fuel		[−138,600]			
	Historical unobligated balances		[−188,500]			
	Prorated OCO allocation in support of base readiness requirements		[−5,756,230]			
	SUBTOTAL UNDISTRIBUTED		**−6,083,330**			
	TOTAL OPERATION & MAINTENANCE, ARMY	**16,658,381**	**11,461,051**	**16,658,381**	**−245,000**	**16,413,381**
	OPERATION & MAINTENANCE, ARMY RES					
	OPERATING FORCES					
020	ECHELONS ABOVE BRIGADE	6,252	9,252	6,252		6,252
	Operational support for deployed end strength of 9,800 in Afghanistan		[3,000]			
040	LAND FORCES OPERATIONS SUPPORT	2,075	3,075	2,075		2,075
	Operational support for deployed end strength of 9,800 in Afghanistan		[1,000]			
060	FORCE READINESS OPERATIONS SUPPORT	1,140	1,440	1,140		1,140
	Operational support for deployed end strength of 9,800 in Afghanistan		[300]			
090	BASE OPERATIONS SUPPORT	14,653	15,153	14,653		14,653
	Operational support for deployed end strength of 9,800 in Afghanistan		[500]			
	SUBTOTAL OPERATING FORCES	**24,120**	**28,920**	**24,120**		**24,120**
	UNDISTRIBUTED					
180	UNDISTRIBUTED		−11,394			
	Prorated OCO allocation in support of base readiness requirements		[−11,394]			
	SUBTOTAL UNDISTRIBUTED		**−11,394**			
	TOTAL OPERATION & MAINTENANCE, ARMY RES	**24,120**	**17,526**	**24,120**		**24,120**
	OPERATION & MAINTENANCE, ARNG					
	OPERATING FORCES					
010	MANEUVER UNITS	10,564	16,564	10,564		10,564
	Operational support for deployed end strength of 9,800 in Afghanistan		[6,000]			
020	MODULAR SUPPORT BRIGADES	748	748	748		748
030	ECHELONS ABOVE BRIGADE	5,751	7,451	5,751		5,751

SEC. 4302. OPERATION AND MAINTENANCE FOR OVERSEAS CONTINGENCY OPERATIONS
(In Thousands of Dollars)

Line	Item	FY 2017 Request	House Authorized	Senate Authorized	Conference Change	Conference Authorized
	Operational support for deployed end strength of 9,800 in Afghanistan		[1,700]			
040	THEATER LEVEL ASSETS	200	200	200		200
060	AVIATION ASSETS	27,183	30,983	27,183		27,183
	Operational support for deployed end strength of 9,800 in Afghanistan		[3,800]			
070	FORCE READINESS OPERATIONS SUPPORT	2,741	2,741	2,741		2,741
100	BASE OPERATIONS SUPPORT	18,800	18,800	18,800		18,800
120	MANAGEMENT AND OPERATIONAL HEADQUARTERS	920	920	920		920
	SUBTOTAL OPERATING FORCES	**66,907**	**78,407**	**66,907**		**66,907**
	UNDISTRIBUTED					
190	UNDISTRIBUTED		−30,892			
	Prorated OCO allocation in support of base readiness requirements		[−30,892]			
	SUBTOTAL UNDISTRIBUTED		**−30,892**			
	TOTAL OPERATION & MAINTENANCE, ARNG	**66,907**	**47,515**	**66,907**		**66,907**
	AFGHANISTAN SECURITY FORCES FUND					
	MINISTRY OF DEFENSE					
010	SUSTAINMENT	2,173,341	2,173,341	2,173,341		2,173,341
020	INFRASTRUCTURE	48,262	48,262	48,262		48,262
030	EQUIPMENT AND TRANSPORTATION	821,716	921,547	821,716		821,716
	Maintain security forces at fiscal year 2016 levels		[99,831]			
040	TRAINING AND OPERATIONS	289,139	350,555	289,139		289,139
	Maintain security forces at fiscal year 2016 levels		[61,416]			
	SUBTOTAL MINISTRY OF DEFENSE	**3,332,458**	**3,493,705**	**3,332,458**		**3,332,458**
	MINISTRY OF INTERIOR					
050	SUSTAINMENT	860,441	880,300	860,441		860,441
	Maintain security forces at fiscal year 2016 levels		[19,859]			
060	INFRASTRUCTURE	20,837	20,837	20,837		20,837
070	EQUIPMENT AND TRANSPORTATION	8,153	116,573	8,153		8,153
	Maintain security forces at fiscal year 2016 levels		[108,420]			
080	TRAINING AND OPERATIONS	41,326	65,342	41,326		41,326
	Maintain security forces at fiscal year 2016 levels		[24,016]			
	SUBTOTAL MINISTRY OF INTERIOR	**930,757**	**1,083,052**	**930,757**		**930,757**
	UNDISTRIBUTED					
110	UNDISTRIBUTED		−1,482,289			
	Prorated OCO allocation in support of base readiness requirements		[−1,482,289]			
	SUBTOTAL UNDISTRIBUTED		**−1,482,289**			
	TOTAL AFGHANISTAN SECURITY FORCES FUND	**4,263,215**	**3,094,468**	**4,263,215**		**4,263,215**
	IRAQ TRAIN AND EQUIP FUND					
	IRAQ TRAIN AND EQUIP FUND					
010	IRAQ TRAIN AND EQUIP FUND	919,500	969,500	1,549,500	−919,500	0
	Support to Kurdish and Sunni tribal security forces for operations in Mosul, Iraq		[50,000]			
	Transfer from Coalition Support Fund			[180,000]		
	Transfer from Counterterrorism Partnership Fund			[200,000]		
	Transfer from Syria Train and Equip Fund			[250,000]		
	Transfer to Counter-ISIL Fund				[−919,500]	
	SUBTOTAL IRAQ TRAIN AND EQUIP FUND	**919,500**	**969,500**	**1,549,500**	**−919,500**	**0**
	UNDISTRIBUTED					
020	UNDISTRIBUTED		−267,913			
	Prorated OCO allocation in support of base readiness requirements		[−267,913]			
	SUBTOTAL UNDISTRIBUTED		**−267,913**			

SEC. 4302. OPERATION AND MAINTENANCE FOR OVERSEAS CONTINGENCY OPERATIONS
(In Thousands of Dollars)

Line	Item	FY 2017 Request	House Authorized	Senate Authorized	Conference Change	Conference Authorized
	TOTAL IRAQ TRAIN AND EQUIP FUND	919,500	701,587	1,549,500	−919,500	0
	SYRIA TRAIN AND EQUIP FUND					
	SYRIA TRAIN AND EQUIP FUND					
010	SYRIA TRAIN AND EQUIP FUND	250,000	250,000		−250,000	0
	Transfer to Counter-ISIL Fund			[−250,000]	[−250,000]	
	SUBTOTAL SYRIA TRAIN AND EQUIP FUND	250,000	250,000		−250,000	0
	UNDISTRIBUTED					
020	UNDISTRIBUTED		−98,497			
	Prorated OCO allocation in support of base readiness requirements		[−98,497]			
	SUBTOTAL UNDISTRIBUTED		−98,497			
	TOTAL SYRIA TRAIN AND EQUIP FUND	250,000	151,503		−250,000	0
	COUNTER-ISIL FUND					
	COUNTER-ISIL FUND					
010	COUNTER-ISIL FUND				1,169,500	1,169,500
	Transfer from Iraq Train and Equip				[919,500]	
	Transfer from Syria Train and Equip				[250,000]	
	SUBTOTAL COUNTER-ISIL FUND				1,169,500	1,169,500
	TOTAL COUNTER-ISIL FUND				1,169,500	1,169,500
	OPERATION & MAINTENANCE, NAVY					
	OPERATING FORCES					
010	MISSION AND OTHER FLIGHT OPERATIONS	427,452	427,452	427,452		427,452
040	AIR OPERATIONS AND SAFETY SUPPORT	4,603	4,603	4,603		4,603
050	AIR SYSTEMS SUPPORT	159,049	159,049	159,049		159,049
060	AIRCRAFT DEPOT MAINTENANCE	113,994	113,994	113,994		113,994
070	AIRCRAFT DEPOT OPERATIONS SUPPORT	1,840	1,840	1,840		1,840
080	AVIATION LOGISTICS	35,529	35,529	35,529		35,529
090	MISSION AND OTHER SHIP OPERATIONS	1,073,080	1,073,080	1,073,080		1,073,080
100	SHIP OPERATIONS SUPPORT & TRAINING	17,306	17,306	17,306		17,306
110	SHIP DEPOT MAINTENANCE	2,128,431	2,128,431	2,128,431		2,128,431
130	COMBAT COMMUNICATIONS	21,257	21,257	21,257		21,257
160	WARFARE TACTICS	22,603	22,603	22,603		22,603
170	OPERATIONAL METEOROLOGY AND OCEANOGRAPHY	22,934	22,934	22,934		22,934
180	COMBAT SUPPORT FORCES	575,305	575,305	575,305		575,305
190	EQUIPMENT MAINTENANCE	11,358	11,358	11,358		11,358
250	IN-SERVICE WEAPONS SYSTEMS SUPPORT	61,000	61,000	61,000		61,000
260	WEAPONS MAINTENANCE	309,045	309,045	309,045		309,045
270	OTHER WEAPON SYSTEMS SUPPORT	8,000	8,000	8,000		8,000
290	SUSTAINMENT, RESTORATION AND MODERNIZATION	7,819	7,819	7,819		7,819
300	BASE OPERATING SUPPORT	61,493	61,493	61,493		61,493
	SUBTOTAL OPERATING FORCES	5,062,098	5,062,098	5,062,098		5,062,098
	MOBILIZATION					
330	AIRCRAFT ACTIVATIONS/INACTIVATIONS	1,530	1,530	1,530		1,530
350	EXPEDITIONARY HEALTH SERVICES SYSTEMS	6,713	6,713	6,713		6,713
370	COAST GUARD SUPPORT	162,692	162,692	162,692		162,692
	SUBTOTAL MOBILIZATION	170,935	170,935	170,935		170,935
	TRAINING AND RECRUITING					
410	SPECIALIZED SKILL TRAINING	43,365	43,365	43,365		43,365
	SUBTOTAL TRAINING AND RECRUITING	43,365	43,365	43,365		43,365

SEC. 4302. OPERATION AND MAINTENANCE FOR OVERSEAS CONTINGENCY OPERATIONS
(In Thousands of Dollars)

Line	Item	FY 2017 Request	House Authorized	Senate Authorized	Conference Change	Conference Authorized
	ADMIN & SRVWD ACTIVITIES					
490	ADMINISTRATION	3,764	3,764	3,764		3,764
500	EXTERNAL RELATIONS	515	515	515		515
520	MILITARY MANPOWER AND PERSONNEL MANAGEMENT	5,409	5,409	5,409		5,409
530	OTHER PERSONNEL SUPPORT	1,578	1,578	1,578		1,578
570	SERVICEWIDE TRANSPORTATION	126,700	126,700	126,700		126,700
600	ACQUISITION AND PROGRAM MANAGEMENT	9,261	9,261	9,261		9,261
640	NAVAL INVESTIGATIVE SERVICE	1,501	1,501	1,501		1,501
730	CLASSIFIED PROGRAMS	16,280	16,280	16,280		16,280
	SUBTOTAL ADMIN & SRVWD ACTIVITIES	**165,008**	**165,008**	**165,008**		**165,008**
	UNDISTRIBUTED					
740	UNDISTRIBUTED		−2,226,518			
	Excessive standard price for fuel		[−120,300]			
	Prorated OCO allocation in support of base readiness requirements		[−2,106,218]			
	SUBTOTAL UNDISTRIBUTED		**−2,226,518**			
	TOTAL OPERATION & MAINTENANCE, NAVY	**5,441,406**	**3,214,888**	**5,441,406**		**5,441,406**
	OPERATION & MAINTENANCE, MARINE CORPS					
	OPERATING FORCES					
010	OPERATIONAL FORCES	571,935	638,235	571,935		571,935
	Operational support for deployed end strength of 9,800 in Afghanistan		[66,300]			
020	FIELD LOGISTICS	266,094	266,094	266,094		266,094
030	DEPOT MAINTENANCE	147,000	147,000	147,000		147,000
060	BASE OPERATING SUPPORT	18,576	18,576	18,576		18,576
	SUBTOTAL OPERATING FORCES	**1,003,605**	**1,069,905**	**1,003,605**		**1,003,605**
	TRAINING AND RECRUITING					
110	TRAINING SUPPORT	31,750	31,750	31,750		31,750
	SUBTOTAL TRAINING AND RECRUITING	**31,750**	**31,750**	**31,750**		**31,750**
	ADMIN & SRVWD ACTIVITIES					
150	SERVICEWIDE TRANSPORTATION	73,800	89,800	73,800		73,800
	Operational support for deployed end strength of 9,800 in Afghanistan		[16,000]			
200	CLASSIFIED PROGRAMS	3,650	3,650	3,650		3,650
	SUBTOTAL ADMIN & SRVWD ACTIVITIES	**77,450**	**93,450**	**77,450**		**77,450**
	UNDISTRIBUTED					
210	UNDISTRIBUTED		−413,593			
	Excessive standard price for fuel		[−9,100]			
	Prorated OCO allocation in support of base readiness requirements		[−404,493]			
	SUBTOTAL UNDISTRIBUTED		**−413,593**			
	TOTAL OPERATION & MAINTENANCE, MARINE CORPS	**1,112,805**	**781,512**	**1,112,805**		**1,112,805**
	OPERATION & MAINTENANCE, NAVY RES					
	OPERATING FORCES					
030	AIRCRAFT DEPOT MAINTENANCE	16,500	16,500	16,500		16,500
050	AVIATION LOGISTICS	2,522	2,522	2,522		2,522
100	COMBAT SUPPORT FORCES	7,243	7,243	7,243		7,243
	SUBTOTAL OPERATING FORCES	**26,265**	**26,265**	**26,265**		**26,265**
	UNDISTRIBUTED					
200	UNDISTRIBUTED		−10,448			
	Excessive standard price for fuel		[−100]			

SEC. 4302. OPERATION AND MAINTENANCE FOR OVERSEAS CONTINGENCY OPERATIONS
(In Thousands of Dollars)

Line	Item	FY 2017 Request	House Authorized	Senate Authorized	Conference Change	Conference Authorized
	Prorated OCO allocation in support of base readiness requirements		[−10,348]			
	SUBTOTAL UNDISTRIBUTED		**−10,448**			
	TOTAL OPERATION & MAINTENANCE, NAVY RES	**26,265**	**15,817**	**26,265**		**26,265**
	OPERATION & MAINTENANCE, MC RESERVE					
	OPERATING FORCES					
010	OPERATING FORCES	2,500	2,500	2,500		2,500
040	BASE OPERATING SUPPORT	804	804	804		804
	SUBTOTAL OPERATING FORCES	**3,304**	**3,304**	**3,304**		**3,304**
	UNDISTRIBUTED					
090	UNDISTRIBUTED		−1,302			
	Prorated OCO allocation in support of base readiness requirements		[−1,302]			
	SUBTOTAL UNDISTRIBUTED		**−1,302**			
	TOTAL OPERATION & MAINTENANCE, MC RESERVE	**3,304**	**2,002**	**3,304**		**3,304**
	OPERATION & MAINTENANCE, AIR FORCE					
	OPERATING FORCES					
010	PRIMARY COMBAT FORCES	1,852,159	1,883,059	1,880,159	38,000	1,890,159
	Enhancing readiness levels of DCA aircraft		[10,000]		[10,000]	
	ERI nuclear readiness			[28,000]	[28,000]	
	Operational support for deployed end strength of 9,800 in Afghanistan		[20,900]			
020	COMBAT ENHANCEMENT FORCES	1,127,319	1,148,219	1,127,319		1,127,319
	Operational support for deployed end strength of 9,800 in Afghanistan		[20,900]			
030	AIR OPERATIONS TRAINING (OJT, MAINTAIN SKILLS)	152,278	152,278	152,278		152,278
040	DEPOT MAINTENANCE	1,061,506	1,087,106	1,061,506	25,600	1,087,106
	Compass Call Program Restructure		[25,600]		[25,600]	
050	FACILITIES SUSTAINMENT, RESTORATION & MODERNIZATION	56,700	56,700	56,700		56,700
060	BASE SUPPORT	941,714	941,714	941,714		941,714
070	GLOBAL C3I AND EARLY WARNING	30,219	30,219	30,219		30,219
080	OTHER COMBAT OPS SPT PROGRAMS	213,696	223,696	213,696	5,000	218,696
	Promoting additional DCA burden sharing		[5,000]		[5,000]	
	Supporting DCA dispersal CONOP development		[5,000]			
100	LAUNCH FACILITIES	869	869	869		869
110	SPACE CONTROL SYSTEMS	5,008	5,008	5,008		5,008
120	COMBATANT COMMANDERS DIRECT MISSION SUPPORT	100,081	100,081	100,081		100,081
135	CLASSIFIED PROGRAMS	79,893	79,893	79,893		79,893
	SUBTOTAL OPERATING FORCES	**5,621,442**	**5,708,842**	**5,649,442**	**68,600**	**5,690,042**
	MOBILIZATION					
140	AIRLIFT OPERATIONS	2,606,729	2,704,429	2,606,729		2,606,729
	Operational support for deployed end strength of 9,800 in Afghanistan		[97,700]			
150	MOBILIZATION PREPAREDNESS	108,163	108,163	108,163		108,163
160	DEPOT MAINTENANCE	891,102	891,102	891,102		891,102
180	BASE SUPPORT	3,686	3,686	3,686		3,686
	SUBTOTAL MOBILIZATION	**3,609,680**	**3,707,380**	**3,609,680**		**3,609,680**
	TRAINING AND RECRUITING					
230	BASE SUPPORT	52,740	52,740	52,740		52,740
240	SPECIALIZED SKILL TRAINING	4,500	4,500	4,500		4,500
	SUBTOTAL TRAINING AND RECRUITING	**57,240**	**57,240**	**57,240**		**57,240**
	ADMIN & SRVWD ACTIVITIES					
340	LOGISTICS OPERATIONS	86,716	86,716	86,716		86,716
380	BASE SUPPORT	59,133	59,133	59,133		59,133

SEC. 4302. OPERATION AND MAINTENANCE FOR OVERSEAS CONTINGENCY OPERATIONS
(In Thousands of Dollars)

Line	Item	FY 2017 Request	House Authorized	Senate Authorized	Conference Change	Conference Authorized
400	SERVICEWIDE COMMUNICATIONS	165,348	165,348	165,348		165,348
410	OTHER SERVICEWIDE ACTIVITIES	141,883	141,883	116,783	−25,058	116,825
	Program reduction			[−25,100]	[−25,058]	
450	INTERNATIONAL SUPPORT	61	61	61		61
460	CLASSIFIED PROGRAMS	15,823	15,823	15,823		15,823
	SUBTOTAL ADMIN & SRVWD ACTIVITIES	**468,964**	**468,964**	**443,864**	**−25,058**	**443,906**
	UNDISTRIBUTED					
470	UNDISTRIBUTED		−3,868,111			
	Excessive standard price for fuel		[−101,600]			
	Prorated OCO allocation in support of base readiness requirements		[−3,766,511]			
	SUBTOTAL UNDISTRIBUTED		**−3,868,111**			
	TOTAL OPERATION & MAINTENANCE, AIR FORCE	**9,757,326**	**6,074,315**	**9,760,226**	**43,542**	**9,800,868**
	OPERATION & MAINTENANCE, AF RESERVE					
	OPERATING FORCES					
030	DEPOT MAINTENANCE	51,086	51,086	51,086		51,086
050	BASE SUPPORT	6,500	6,500	6,500		6,500
	SUBTOTAL OPERATING FORCES	**57,586**	**57,586**	**57,586**		**57,586**
	UNDISTRIBUTED					
110	UNDISTRIBUTED		−22,788			
	Excessive standard price for fuel		[−100]			
	Prorated OCO allocation in support of base readiness requirements		[−22,688]			
	SUBTOTAL UNDISTRIBUTED		**−22,788**			
	TOTAL OPERATION & MAINTENANCE, AF RESERVE	**57,586**	**34,798**	**57,586**		**57,586**
	OPERATION & MAINTENANCE, ANG					
	OPERATING FORCES					
020	MISSION SUPPORT OPERATIONS	3,400	3,400	3,400		3,400
050	BASE SUPPORT	16,600	16,600	16,600		16,600
	SUBTOTAL OPERATING FORCES	**20,000**	**20,000**	**20,000**		**20,000**
	UNDISTRIBUTED					
080	UNDISTRIBUTED		−7,880			
	Prorated OCO allocation in support of base readiness requirements		[−7,880]			
	SUBTOTAL UNDISTRIBUTED		**−7,880**			
	TOTAL OPERATION & MAINTENANCE, ANG	**20,000**	**12,120**	**20,000**		**20,000**
	OPERATION & MAINTENANCE, DEFENSE-WIDE					
	OPERATING FORCES					
010	JOINT CHIEFS OF STAFF		10,000		10,000	10,000
	Enhancing exercise of DCA aircraft		[10,000]		[10,000]	
030	SPECIAL OPERATIONS COMMAND/OPERATING FORCES	2,853,363	3,022,963	2,853,363		2,853,363
	Operational support for deployed end strength of 9,800 in Afghanistan		[169,600]			
	SUBTOTAL OPERATING FORCES	**2,853,363**	**3,032,963**	**2,853,363**	**10,000**	**2,863,363**
	ADMINISTRATION AND SERVICEWIDE ACTIVITIES					
100	DEFENSE CONTRACT AUDIT AGENCY	13,436	13,436	13,436		13,436
110	DEFENSE CONTRACT MANAGEMENT AGENCY	13,564	13,564	13,564		13,564
130	DEFENSE INFORMATION SYSTEMS AGENCY	34,299	34,299	34,299		34,299
150	DEFENSE LEGAL SERVICES AGENCY	111,986	111,986	111,986		111,986
170	DEFENSE MEDIA ACTIVITY	13,317	13,317	13,317		13,317
190	DEFENSE SECURITY COOPERATION AGENCY	1,412,000	1,412,000	312,000	750,000	2,162,000

SEC. 4302. OPERATION AND MAINTENANCE FOR OVERSEAS CONTINGENCY OPERATIONS
(In Thousands of Dollars)

Line	Item	FY 2017 Request	House Authorized	Senate Authorized	Conference Change	Conference Authorized
	Reduction to Coalition Support Funds			[−100,000]		
	Transfer from Counterterrorism Partnership Fund				[750,000]	
	Transfer to Counter-ISIL Fund			[−180,000]		
	Transfer to Security Cooperation Enhancement Fund			[−820,000]		
260	DEPARTMENT OF DEFENSE EDUCATION ACTIVITY	67,000	67,000	67,000		67,000
300	OFFICE OF THE SECRETARY OF DEFENSE	31,106	31,106	31,106		31,106
320	WASHINGTON HEADQUARTERS SERVICES	3,137	3,137	3,137		3,137
330	CLASSIFIED PROGRAMS	1,803,880	1,803,880	1,803,880		1,803,880
	SUBTOTAL ADMINISTRATION AND SERVICEWIDE ACTIVITIES	**3,503,725**	**3,503,725**	**2,403,725**	**750,000**	**4,253,725**
	UNDISTRIBUTED					
340	UNDISTRIBUTED		−2,418,878			
	Excessive standard price for fuel		[−6,800]			
	Operational support for deployed end strength of 9,800 in Afghanistan		[1,000]			
	Prorated OCO allocation in support of base readiness requirements		[−2,413,078]			
	SUBTOTAL UNDISTRIBUTED		**−2,418,878**			
	TOTAL OPERATION & MAINTENANCE, DEFENSE-WIDE	**6,357,088**	**4,117,810**	**5,257,088**	**760,000**	**7,117,088**
	TOTAL OPERATION & MAINTENANCE	**44,957,903**	**29,726,912**	**44,240,803**	**558,542**	**45,516,445**

SEC. 4303. OPERATION AND MAINTENANCE FOR OVERSEAS CONTINGENCY OPERATIONS FOR BASE REQUIREMENTS.

SEC. 4303. OPERATION AND MAINTENANCE FOR OVERSEAS CONTINGENCY OPERATIONS FOR BASE REQUIREMENTS
(In Thousands of Dollars)

Line	Item	FY 2017 Request	House Authorized	Senate Authorized	Conference Change	Conference Authorized
	OPERATION & MAINTENANCE, ARMY					
	OPERATING FORCES					
010	MANEUVER UNITS	317,093	367,093	317,093		317,093
	Army unfunded requirement—Improve training from BN+ to BCT-		[50,000]			
020	MODULAR SUPPORT BRIGADES	5,904	5,904	5,904		5,904
030	ECHELONS ABOVE BRIGADE	38,614	38,614	38,614		38,614
040	THEATER LEVEL ASSETS	8,361	8,361	8,361		8,361
050	LAND FORCES OPERATIONS SUPPORT	279,072	279,072	279,072		279,072
060	AVIATION ASSETS	106,424	206,924	106,424		106,424
	Army unfunded requirement—Meet air readiness targets		[68,000]			
	Increase to support ARI—Eleventh CAB		[32,500]			
070	FORCE READINESS OPERATIONS SUPPORT	253,533	253,533	253,533		253,533
090	LAND FORCES DEPOT MAINTENANCE	350,000	350,000	350,000		350,000
100	BASE OPERATIONS SUPPORT		22,100			0
	Increase to support ARI—Eleventh CAB		[22,100]			
110	FACILITIES SUSTAINMENT, RESTORATION & MODERNIZATION		922,000		113,800	113,800
	Increase Restoration & Modernization funding		[494,900]		[113,800]	
	Restore Sustainment shortfalls		[427,100]			
140	ADDITIONAL ACTIVITIES	11,200	11,200	11,200		11,200
	SUBTOTAL OPERATING FORCES	**1,370,201**	**2,464,801**	**1,370,201**	**113,800**	**1,484,001**
	TRAINING AND RECRUITING					
250	SPECIALIZED SKILL TRAINING	3,565	3,565	3,565		3,565
260	FLIGHT TRAINING		42,934			0
	Army unfunded requirement—Ensure AVN restructure initiative execution		[5,405]			
	Army unfunded requirement—Increase student workload for additional warrant officers		[31,125]			
	Army unfunded requirement—Train full ARPINT load of 990		[6,404]			
270	PROFESSIONAL DEVELOPMENT EDUCATION	9,021	40,621	9,021		9,021

SEC. 4303. OPERATION AND MAINTENANCE FOR OVERSEAS CONTINGENCY OPERATIONS FOR BASE REQUIREMENTS
(In Thousands of Dollars)

Line	Item	FY 2017 Request	House Authorized	Senate Authorized	Conference Change	Conference Authorized
	Military Training and PME		[31,600]			
280	TRAINING SUPPORT	2,434	2,434	2,434		2,434
290	RECRUITING AND ADVERTISING		356,500		284,800	284,800
	Recruiting and Advertising Add		[356,500]		[284,800]	
320	CIVILIAN EDUCATION AND TRAINING	1,254	1,254	1,254		1,254
	SUBTOTAL TRAINING AND RECRUITING	**16,274**	**447,308**	**16,274**	**284,800**	**301,074**
	ADMIN & SRVWIDE ACTIVITIES					
350	SERVICEWIDE TRANSPORTATION	200,000	265,000	200,000		200,000
	Army unfunded requirement—Restore cricital shortfalls		[65,000]			
	SUBTOTAL ADMIN & SRVWIDE ACTIVITIES	**200,000**	**265,000**	**200,000**		**200,000**
	UNDISTRIBUTED					
540	UNDISTRIBUTED		704,300		563,400	563,400
	Additional funding to support increase in Army end strength		[704,300]		[563,400]	
	SUBTOTAL UNDISTRIBUTED		**704,300**		**563,400**	**563,400**
	TOTAL OPERATION & MAINTENANCE, ARMY	**1,586,475**	**3,881,409**	**1,586,475**	**962,000**	**2,548,475**
	OPERATION & MAINTENANCE, ARMY RES					
	OPERATING FORCES					
010	MODULAR SUPPORT BRIGADES	708	708	708		708
020	ECHELONS ABOVE BRIGADE	8,570	28,570	8,570		8,570
	Army unfunded requirement—Improve training from PLT to CO proficiency		[20,000]			
030	THEATER LEVEL ASSETS	375	375	375		375
040	LAND FORCES OPERATIONS SUPPORT	13	13	13		13
050	AVIATION ASSETS	608	608	608		608
060	FORCE READINESS OPERATIONS SUPPORT	4,285	4,285	4,285		4,285
100	FACILITIES SUSTAINMENT, RESTORATION & MODERNIZATION		97,500		13,100	13,100
	Increase Restoration & Modernization funding		[57,100]		[13,100]	
	Restore Sustainment shortfalls		[40,400]			
	SUBTOTAL OPERATING FORCES	**14,559**	**132,059**	**14,559**	**13,100**	**27,659**
	UNDISTRIBUTED					
180	UNDISTRIBUTED		103,400		82,700	82,700
	Additional funding to support increase in Army Reserve end strength		[103,400]		[82,700]	
	SUBTOTAL UNDISTRIBUTED		**103,400**		**82,700**	**82,700**
	TOTAL OPERATION & MAINTENANCE, ARMY RES	**14,559**	**235,459**	**14,559**	**95,800**	**110,359**
	OPERATION & MAINTENANCE, ARNG					
	OPERATING FORCES					
010	MANEUVER UNITS	5,585	5,585	5,585		5,585
030	ECHELONS ABOVE BRIGADE	28,956	28,956	28,956		28,956
040	THEATER LEVEL ASSETS	10,272	10,272	10,272		10,272
060	AVIATION ASSETS	5,621	51,621	5,621		5,621
	Increase to support ARI		[46,000]			
070	FORCE READINESS OPERATIONS SUPPORT	9,694	9,694	9,694		9,694
110	FACILITIES SUSTAINMENT, RESTORATION & MODERNIZATION		121,000		1,500	1,500
	Increase Restoration & Modernization funding		[16,800]		[1,500]	
	Restore Sustainment shortfalls		[104,200]			
	SUBTOTAL OPERATING FORCES	**60,128**	**227,128**	**60,128**	**1,500**	**61,628**
	UNDISTRIBUTED					
190	UNDISTRIBUTED		159,100		127,300	127,300

SEC. 4303. OPERATION AND MAINTENANCE FOR OVERSEAS CONTINGENCY OPERATIONS FOR BASE REQUIREMENTS
(In Thousands of Dollars)

Line	Item	FY 2017 Request	House Authorized	Senate Authorized	Conference Change	Conference Authorized
	Additional funding to support increase in Army National Guard end strength		[159,100]		[127,300]	
	SUBTOTAL UNDISTRIBUTED		159,100		127,300	127,300
	TOTAL OPERATION & MAINTENANCE, ARNG	**60,128**	**386,228**	**60,128**	**128,800**	**188,928**
	OPERATION & MAINTENANCE, NAVY					
	OPERATING FORCES					
010	MISSION AND OTHER FLIGHT OPERATIONS	500,000	556,520	500,000		500,000
	Carrier Air Wing Restoration		[56,520]			
020	FLEET AIR TRAINING		23,020			0
	Carrier Air Wing Restoration		[23,020]			
050	AIR SYSTEMS SUPPORT		6,500			0
	Marine Corps unfunded requirement—accelerate readiness - H–1		[5,300]			
	Marine Corps unfunded requirement—accelerate readiness - MV–22B		[1,200]			
060	AIRCRAFT DEPOT MAINTENANCE		36,000			0
	Carrier Air Wing Restoration		[6,000]			
	Navy unfunded requirement—Improve Afloat Readiness		[30,000]			
080	AVIATION LOGISTICS		33,500			0
	Marine Corps unfunded requirement—accelerate readiness - KC–130J		[6,800]			
	Marine Corps unfunded requirement—accelerate readiness - MV–22B		[10,700]			
	Navy unfunded requirement—Improve Afloat Readiness		[16,000]			
090	MISSION AND OTHER SHIP OPERATIONS		348,200			0
	Cruiser Modernization		[90,200]			
	Navy unfunded requirement—Improve Afloat Readiness		[158,000]			
	Navy unfunded requirement—Restore 3 CG Deployments		[41,000]			
	Navy unfunded requirement—Reverse PONCE (LPD–15) In-activation		[59,000]			
100	SHIP OPERATIONS SUPPORT & TRAINING		19,700			0
	Navy unfunded requirement—Restore Fleet Training		[19,700]			
110	SHIP DEPOT MAINTENANCE	775,000	1,084,100	775,000		775,000
	Cruiser Modernization		[71,100]			
	Navy unfunded requirement—Ship Depot Wholeness		[238,000]			
120	SHIP DEPOT OPERATIONS SUPPORT		79,000			0
	Navy unfunded requirement—Increase Alfoat Readiness		[79,000]			
290	SUSTAINMENT, RESTORATION AND MODERNIZATION	19,270	408,470	19,270	26,100	45,370
	Increase Restoration & Modernization funding		[113,600]		[26,100]	
	Restore Sustainment shortfalls		[275,600]			
300	BASE OPERATING SUPPORT	158,032	158,032	158,032		158,032
	SUBTOTAL OPERATING FORCES	1,452,302	2,753,042	1,452,302	26,100	1,478,402
	MOBILIZATION					
350	EXPEDITIONARY HEALTH SERVICES SYSTEMS	3,597	3,597	3,597		3,597
	SUBTOTAL MOBILIZATION	3,597	3,597	3,597		3,597
	ADMIN & SRVWD ACTIVITIES					
540	SERVICEWIDE COMMUNICATIONS	25,617	25,617	25,617		25,617
	SUBTOTAL ADMIN & SRVWD ACTIVITIES	25,617	25,617	25,617		25,617
	TOTAL OPERATION & MAINTENANCE, NAVY	**1,481,516**	**2,782,256**	**1,481,516**	**26,100**	**1,507,616**
	OPERATION & MAINTENANCE, MARINE CORPS					
	OPERATING FORCES					
010	OPERATIONAL FORCES	300,000	322,000	300,000		300,000

SEC. 4303. OPERATION AND MAINTENANCE FOR OVERSEAS CONTINGENCY OPERATIONS FOR BASE REQUIREMENTS
(In Thousands of Dollars)

Line	Item	FY 2017 Request	House Authorized	Senate Authorized	Conference Change	Conference Authorized
	Marine Corps unfunded requirement- enhanced combat helmets		[22,000]			
020	FIELD LOGISTICS		21,450			0
	Marine Corps unfunded requirement- rifle combat optic modernization		[13,200]			
	Marine Corps unfunded requirement- SPMAGTF—C4 UUNS		[8,250]			
050	SUSTAINMENT, RESTORATION & MODERNIZATION		145,600		7,200	7,200
	Increase Restoration & Modernization funding		[31,400]		[7,200]	
	Restore Sustainment shortfalls		[114,200]			
	SUBTOTAL OPERATING FORCES	**300,000**	**489,050**	**300,000**	**7,200**	**307,200**
	TOTAL OPERATION & MAINTENANCE, MARINE CORPS	**300,000**	**489,050**	**300,000**	**7,200**	**307,200**
	OPERATION & MAINTENANCE, NAVY RES **OPERATING FORCES**					
030	AIRCRAFT DEPOT MAINTENANCE		4,000			0
	Navy unfunded requirement—Improve Afloat Readiness		[4,000]			
070	SHIP OPERATIONS SUPPORT & TRAINING		300			0
	Navy unfunded requirement—Restore Fleet Training		[300]			
130	SUSTAINMENT, RESTORATION AND MODERNIZATION		7,800		500	500
	Increase Restoration & Modernization funding		[2,100]		[500]	
	Restore Sustainment shortfalls		[5,700]			
	SUBTOTAL OPERATING FORCES		**12,100**		**500**	**500**
	TOTAL OPERATION & MAINTENANCE, NAVY RES		**12,100**		**500**	**500**
	OPERATION & MAINTENANCE, MC RESERVE **OPERATING FORCES**					
030	SUSTAINMENT, RESTORATION AND MODERNIZATION		7,700		1,000	1,000
	Increase Restoration & Modernization funding		[4,300]		[1,000]	
	Restore Sustainment shortfalls		[3,400]			
	SUBTOTAL OPERATING FORCES		**7,700**		**1,000**	**1,000**
	TOTAL OPERATION & MAINTENANCE, MC RESERVE		**7,700**		**1,000**	**1,000**
	OPERATION & MAINTENANCE, AIR FORCE **OPERATING FORCES**					
040	DEPOT MAINTENANCE	124,000	447,576	124,000		124,000
	Air Force unfunded requirement—Weapons System Sustainment		[323,576]			
050	FACILITIES SUSTAINMENT, RESTORATION & MODERNIZATION		407,900		32,900	32,900
	Increase Restoration & Modernization funding		[142,900]		[32,900]	
	Restore Sustainment shortfalls		[265,000]			
070	GLOBAL C3I AND EARLY WARNING		40,000			0
	Air Force unfunded requirement—Ground Based Radars		[40,000]			
	SUBTOTAL OPERATING FORCES	**124,000**	**895,476**	**124,000**	**32,900**	**156,900**
	MOBILIZATION					
160	DEPOT MAINTENANCE		66,424			0
	Air Force unfunded requirement—Weapons System Sustainment		[66,424]			
170	FACILITIES SUSTAINMENT, RESTORATION & MODERNIZATION		63,600		5,100	5,100
	Increase Restoration & Modernization funding		[22,300]		[5,100]	
	Restore Sustainment shortfalls		[41,300]			
	SUBTOTAL MOBILIZATION		**130,024**		**5,100**	**5,100**
	TRAINING AND RECRUITING					
220	FACILITIES SUSTAINMENT, RESTORATION & MODERNIZATION		58,200		4,700	4,700

SEC. 4303. OPERATION AND MAINTENANCE FOR OVERSEAS CONTINGENCY OPERATIONS FOR BASE REQUIREMENTS
(In Thousands of Dollars)

Line	Item	FY 2017 Request	House Authorized	Senate Authorized	Conference Change	Conference Authorized
	Increase Restoration & Modernization funding		[20,400]		[4,700]	
	Restore Sustainment shortfalls		[37,800]			
	SUBTOTAL TRAINING AND RECRUITING		**58,200**		**4,700**	**4,700**
	ADMIN & SRVWD ACTIVITIES					
370	FACILITIES SUSTAINMENT, RESTORATION & MODERNIZATION		79,000		6,400	6,400
	Increase Restoration & Modernization funding		[27,700]		[6,400]	
	Restore Sustainment shortfalls		[51,300]			
	SUBTOTAL ADMIN & SRVWD ACTIVITIES		**79,000**		**6,400**	**6,400**
	TOTAL OPERATION & MAINTENANCE, AIR FORCE	**124,000**	**1,162,700**	**124,000**	**49,100**	**173,100**
	OPERATION & MAINTENANCE, AF RESERVE					
	OPERATING FORCES					
040	FACILITIES SUSTAINMENT, RESTORATION & MODERNIZATION		20,500		1,600	1,600
	Increase Restoration & Modernization funding		[7,100]		[1,600]	
	Restore Sustainment shortfalls		[13,400]			
	SUBTOTAL OPERATING FORCES		**20,500**		**1,600**	**1,600**
	TOTAL OPERATION & MAINTENANCE, AF RESERVE		**20,500**		**1,600**	**1,600**
	OPERATION & MAINTENANCE, ANG					
	OPERATING FORCES					
030	DEPOT MAINTENANCE		40,000			0
	Air Force unfunded requirement—Weapons System Sustainment		[40,000]			
040	FACILITIES SUSTAINMENT, RESTORATION & MODERNIZATION		64,500		4,300	4,300
	Increase Restoration & Modernization funding		[18,900]		[4,300]	
	Restore Sustainment shortfalls		[45,600]			
	SUBTOTAL OPERATING FORCES		**104,500**		**4,300**	**4,300**
	ADMINISTRATION AND SERVICE-WIDE ACTIVITIES					
070	RECRUITING AND ADVERTISING		67,000			0
	Air Force unfunded requirement		[67,000]			
	SUBTOTAL ADMINISTRATION AND SERVICE-WIDE ACTIVITIES		**67,000**			**0**
	TOTAL OPERATION & MAINTENANCE, ANG		**171,500**		**4,300**	**4,300**
	OPERATION & MAINTENANCE, DEFENSE-WIDE					
	OPERATING FORCES					
030	SPECIAL OPERATIONS COMMAND/OPERATING FORCES	14,344	14,344	14,344		14,344
	SUBTOTAL OPERATING FORCES	**14,344**	**14,344**	**14,344**		**14,344**
	ADMINISTRATION AND SERVICEWIDE ACTIVITIES					
130	DEFENSE INFORMATION SYSTEMS AGENCY	14,700	14,700	14,700		14,700
330	CLASSIFIED PROGRAMS	9,000	9,000	9,000		9,000
	SUBTOTAL ADMINISTRATION AND SERVICEWIDE ACTIVITIES ..	**23,700**	**23,700**	**23,700**		**23,700**
	TOTAL OPERATION & MAINTENANCE, DEFENSE-WIDE	**38,044**	**38,044**	**38,044**		**38,044**
	TOTAL OPERATION & MAINTENANCE	**3,604,722**	**9,186,946**	**3,604,722**	**1,276,400**	**4,881,122**

TITLE XLIV—MILITARY PERSONNEL

SEC. 4401. MILITARY PERSONNEL.

SEC. 4401. MILITARY PERSONNEL
(In Thousands of Dollars)

Item	FY 2017 Request	House Authorized	Senate Authorized	Conference Change	Conference Authorized
Military Personnel Appropriations	128,902,332	−419,418	−1,250,890	−699,768	128,202,564
Military Personnel Pay Raise				[330,000]	
Marine Corps—Bonus Pay/PCS Resotral/Foreign Language Bonus				[49,000]	
Foreign currency adjustments		[−200,400]	[−72,940]	[−200,400]	
Historical unobligated balances		[−248,700]	[−880,450]	[−880,050]	
National Guard State Partnership Program, Army, Special Training		[841]		[841]	
National Guard State Partnership Program, Air Force, Special Training		[841]		[841]	
Prohibition on Per Diem Allowance Reduction		[28,000]			
Defense Officer Personnel Management Act reforms			[100,000]		
Non-adoption of Air Force Pilot Bonus Increase			[−2,500]		
Non-adoption of DOD retirement reforms			[−400,000]		
Rural Guard Act			[5,000]		
Medicare-Eligible Retiree Health Fund Contributions	6,366,908	0	0	0	6,366,908
Total, Military Personnel	135,269,240	−419,418	−1,250,890	−699,768	134,569,472

SEC. 4402. MILITARY PERSONNEL FOR OVERSEAS CONTINGENCY OPERATIONS.

SEC. 4402. MILITARY PERSONNEL FOR OVERSEAS CONTINGENCY OPERATIONS
(In Thousands of Dollars)

Item	FY 2017 Request	House Authorized	Senate Authorized	Conference Change	Conference Authorized
Military Personnel Appropriations	3,644,161	−1,299,721	0	0	3,644,161
Maintain end strength of 9,800 in Afghanistan		[130,300]			
Prorated OCO allocation in support of base readiness requirements		[−1,430,021]			
Total, Military Personnel Appropriations	3,644,161	−1,299,721	0	0	3,644,161

SEC. 4403. MILITARY PERSONNEL FOR OVERSEAS CONTINGENCY OPERATIONS FOR BASE REQUIREMENTS.

SEC. 4403. MILITARY PERSONNEL FOR OVERSEAS CONTINGENCY OPERATIONS FOR BASE REQUIREMENTS
(In Thousands of Dollars)

Item	FY 2017 Request	House Authorized	Senate Authorized	Conference Change	Conference Authorized
Military Personnel Appropriations	62,965	2,509,750	0	1,287,500	1,350,465
Fund Active Army End Strength to 476k		[1,123,500]		[719,000]	
Fund Army National Guard End Strength to 343k		[303,700]		[129,600]	
Fund Army Reserves End Strength to 199k		[166,650]		[53,300]	
Fund Active Navy End Strength to 323.9k		[65,300]		[29,600]	
Fund Active Air Force End Strength to 321k		[145,000]		[116,000]	
Fund Active Marine Corps End Strength to 185k		[300,000]		[240,000]	
Military Personnel Pay Raise		[330,000]			
Marine Corps—Bonus Pay/PCS Resotral/Foreign Language Bonus		[75,600]			
Medicare-Eligible Retiree Health Fund Contributions	0	49,900	0	0	0
Increase associated with additional end strength		[49,900]			
Total, Military Personnel	62,965	2,559,650	0	1,287,500	1,350,465

TITLE XLV—OTHER AUTHORIZATIONS

SEC. 4501. OTHER AUTHORIZATIONS.

SEC. 4501. OTHER AUTHORIZATIONS
(In Thousands of Dollars)

Program Title	FY 2017 Request	House Authorized	Senate Authorized	Conference Change	Conference Authorized
WORKING CAPITAL FUND, ARMY					
SUPPLY MANAGEMENT—ARMY	56,469	56,469	56,469		56,469
TOTAL WORKING CAPITAL FUND, ARMY	**56,469**	**56,469**	**56,469**		**56,469**
WORKING CAPITAL FUND, AIR FORCE					
SUPPLIES AND MATERIALS	63,967	63,967	63,967		63,967
TOTAL WORKING CAPITAL FUND, AIR FORCE	**63,967**	**63,967**	**63,967**		**63,967**
WORKING CAPITAL FUND, DEFENSE-WIDE					
SUPPLY CHAIN MANAGEMENT—DEF	37,132	37,132	37,132		37,132
TOTAL WORKING CAPITAL FUND, DEFENSE-WIDE	**37,132**	**37,132**	**37,132**		**37,132**
WORKING CAPITAL FUND, DECA					
COMMISSARY	1,214,045	1,214,045	1,214,045		1,214,045
TOTAL WORKING CAPITAL FUND, DECA	**1,214,045**	**1,214,045**	**1,214,045**		**1,214,045**
NATIONAL DEFENSE SEALIFT FUND					
NATIONAL DEF SEALIFT VESSEL		85,000			
National Security Multi-Mission Vehicle		[85,000]			
TOTAL NATIONAL DEFENSE SEALIFT FUND		**85,000**			
NATIONAL SEA-BASED DETERRENCE FUND					
DEVELOPMENT		773,138			
Realignment of funds to the National Sea-Based Deterrence Fund		[773,138]			
TOTAL NATIONAL SEA-BASED DETERRENCE FUND		**773,138**			
CHEM AGENTS & MUNITIONS DESTRUCTION					
OPERATION & MAINTENANCE	147,282	147,282	147,282		147,282
RDT&E	388,609	388,609	388,609		388,609
PROCUREMENT	15,132	15,132	15,132		15,132
TOTAL CHEM AGENTS & MUNITIONS DESTRUCTION	**551,023**	**551,023**	**551,023**		**551,023**
DRUG INTERDICTION & CTR-DRUG ACTIVITIES, DEF					
DRUG INTERDICTION AND COUNTER-DRUG ACTIVITIES, DEFENSE	730,087	793,087	471,787	−125,000	605,087
Counter narcotics operations		[3,000]			
National Guard counter-drug programs		[30,000]			
SOUTHCOM Operational Support		[30,000]			
Transfer to Defense Security Cooperation Agency			[−258,300]	[−125,000]	
DRUG DEMAND REDUCTION PROGRAM	114,713	114,713	114,713		114,713
TOTAL DRUG INTERDICTION & CTR-DRUG ACTIVITIES, DEF	**844,800**	**907,800**	**586,500**	**−125,000**	**719,800**
OFFICE OF THE INSPECTOR GENERAL					
OPERATION AND MAINTENANCE	318,882	318,882	311,582		318,882
Audit FTE unjustified growth			[−7,300]		
RDT&E	3,153	3,153	3,153		3,153
TOTAL OFFICE OF THE INSPECTOR GENERAL	**322,035**	**322,035**	**314,735**		**322,035**
DEFENSE HEALTH PROGRAM					
OPERATION & MAINTENANCE					
IN-HOUSE CARE	9,240,160	9,240,160	9,240,160		9,240,160
PRIVATE SECTOR CARE	15,738,759	15,738,759	15,738,759		15,738,759
CONSOLIDATED HEALTH SUPPORT	2,367,759	2,367,759	2,367,759		2,367,759
INFORMATION MANAGEMENT	1,743,749	1,743,749	1,743,749		1,743,749
MANAGEMENT ACTIVITIES	311,380	311,380	311,380		311,380
EDUCATION AND TRAINING	743,231	743,231	743,231		743,231
BASE OPERATIONS/COMMUNICATIONS	2,086,352	2,086,352	2,086,352		2,086,352
SUBTOTAL OPERATION & MAINTENANCE	**32,231,390**	**32,231,390**	**32,231,390**		**32,231,390**

SEC. 4501. OTHER AUTHORIZATIONS
(In Thousands of Dollars)

Program Title	FY 2017 Request	House Authorized	Senate Authorized	Conference Change	Conference Authorized
RDT&E					
RESEARCH	9,097	9,097	9,097		9,097
EXPLORATRY DEVELOPMENT	58,517	58,517	58,517		58,517
ADVANCED DEVELOPMENT	221,226	221,226	221,226		221,226
DEMONSTRATION/VALIDATION	96,602	96,602	96,602		96,602
ENGINEERING DEVELOPMENT	364,057	364,057	364,057		364,057
MANAGEMENT AND SUPPORT	58,410	58,410	58,410		58,410
CAPABILITIES ENHANCEMENT	14,998	14,998	14,998		14,998
SUBTOTAL RDT&E	**822,907**	**822,907**	**822,907**		**822,907**
PROCUREMENT					
INITIAL OUTFITTING	20,611	20,611	20,611		20,611
REPLACEMENT & MODERNIZATION	360,727	360,727	360,727		360,727
JOINT OPERATIONAL MEDICINE INFORMATION SYSTEM	2,413	2,413	2,413		2,413
DOD HEALTHCARE MANAGEMENT SYSTEM MODERNIZATION	29,468	29,468	29,468		29,468
SUBTOTAL PROCUREMENT	**413,219**	**413,219**	**413,219**		**413,219**
UNDISTRIBUTED					
Foreign Currency adjustments		[−20,400]	[−6,470]		
Historical unobligated balances		[−399,100]		[−399,100]	
Incorporation of value-based health care into TRICARE program			[24,500]		
Pilot program on health insurance for reserve component members			[20,000]		
Reduction for unauthorized fertility treatment benefits			[−38,000]		
Reduction for unjustified travel expenses			[−6,500]	[−6,500]	
Reimbursement rates for Comprehensive Autism Care Demonstration program			[40,000]	[32,000]	
TRICARE reform implementation			[400,000]		
SUBTOTAL UNDISTRIBUTED		**−419,500**	**433,530**	**−373,600**	**−373,600**
TOTAL DEFENSE HEALTH PROGRAM	33,467,516	33,048,016	33,901,046	−373,600	33,093,916
SECURITY COOPERATION ENHANCEMENT FUND (SCEF)					
Transfer from Drug Interdiction and Counter-Drug Activities			[258,300]		
Transfer of Combatting Terrorism Fellowship Program			[26,800]		
Transfer of Defense Institute of International Legal Studies			[2,600]		
Transfer of Defense Institution Reform Initiative			[25,600]		
Transfer of Global Train and Equip Program			[270,200]		
Transfer of Ministry of Defense Advisors			[9,200]		
Transfer of Regional Centers			[58,600]		
Transfer of Wales Initaitive Fund/Partnership for Peace			[21,800]		
TOTAL SECURITY COOPERATION ENHANCEMENT FUND (SCEF)			**673,100**		
TOTAL OTHER AUTHORIZATIONS	36,556,987	37,058,625	37,398,017	−498,600	36,058,387

SEC. 4502. OTHER AUTHORIZATIONS FOR OVERSEAS CONTINGENCY OPERATIONS.

SEC. 4502. OTHER AUTHORIZATIONS FOR OVERSEAS CONTINGENCY OPERATIONS
(In Thousands of Dollars)

Program Title	FY 2017 Request	House Authorized	Senate Authorized	Conference Change	Conference Authorized
WORKING CAPITAL FUND, ARMY					
INDUSTRIAL OPERATIONS					
SUPPLY MANAGEMENT—ARMY	46,833	46,833	46,833		46,833
UNDISTRIBUTED		−18,452			
Prorated OCO allocation in support of base readiness requirements		[−18,452]			
TOTAL WORKING CAPITAL FUND, ARMY	46,833	28,381	46,833		46,833

SEC. 4502. OTHER AUTHORIZATIONS FOR OVERSEAS CONTINGENCY OPERATIONS
(In Thousands of Dollars)

Program Title	FY 2017 Request	House Authorized	Senate Authorized	Conference Change	Conference Authorized
WORKING CAPITAL FUND, DEFENSE-WIDE					
DEFENSE LOGISTICS AGENCY (DLA)	93,800	93,800	93,800		93,800
UNDISTRIBUTED		−36,956			
Prorated OCO allocation in support of base readiness requirements		[−36,956]			
TOTAL WORKING CAPITAL FUND, DEFENSE-WIDE	**93,800**	**56,844**	**93,800**		**93,800**
DRUG INTERDICTION & CTR-DRUG ACTIVITIES, DEF					
DRUG INTERDICTION AND COUNTER-DRUG ACTIVITIES, DEFENSE	191,533	191,533	191,533		191,533
TOTAL DRUG INTERDICTION & CTR-DRUG ACTIVITIES, DEF	**191,533**	**191,533**	**191,533**		**191,533**
OFFICE OF THE INSPECTOR GENERAL					
OPERATION AND MAINTENANCE	22,062	22,062	22,062		22,062
TOTAL OFFICE OF THE INSPECTOR GENERAL	**22,062**	**22,062**	**22,062**		**22,062**
DEFENSE HEALTH PROGRAM					
OPERATION AND MAINTENANCE					
IN-HOUSE CARE	95,366	95,366	95,366		95,366
PRIVATE SECTOR CARE	235,620	235,620	235,620		235,620
CONSOLIDATED HEALTH SUPPORT	3,325	3,325	3,325		3,325
SUBTOTAL OPERATION AND MAINTENANCE	**334,311**	**334,311**	**334,311**		**334,311**
UNDISTRIBUTED					
Prorated OCO allocation in support of base readiness requirements		[−130,711]			
SUBTOTAL UNDISTRIBUTED		**−130,711**			
TOTAL DEFENSE HEALTH PROGRAM	**334,311**	**203,600**	**334,311**		**334,311**
UKRAINE SECURITY ASSISTANCE					
UKRAINE SECURITY ASSISTANCE		150,000	350,000	350,000	350,000
Program increase		[150,000]	[350,000]	[350,000]	
TOTAL UKRAINE SECURITY ASSISTANCE		**150,000**	**350,000**	**350,000**	**350,000**
COUNTERTERRORISM PARTNERSHIPS FUND					
COUNTERTERRORISM PARTNERSHIPS FUND	1,000,000	750,000		−1,000,000	
Ahead of need			[−150,000]		
Program decrease		[−250,000]		[−250,000]	
Transfer to Counter-ISIL Fund			[−200,000]	[−750,000]	
Transfer to Security Cooperation Enhancement Fund			[−650,000]		
TOTAL COUNTERTERRORISM PARTNERSHIPS FUND	**1,000,000**	**750,000**		**−1,000,000**	
SECURITY COOPERATION ENHANCEMENT FUND (SCEF)					
SECURITY COOPERATION ENHANCEMENT FUND (SCEF)			1,470,000		
Transfer from Coalition Support Fund			[820,000]		
Transfer from Counterterrorism Partnership Fund			[650,000]		
TOTAL SECURITY COOPERATION ENHANCEMENT FUND (SCEF)			**1,470,000**		
TOTAL OTHER AUTHORIZATIONS	**1,688,539**	**1,402,420**	**2,508,539**	**−650,000**	**1,038,539**

SEC. 4503. OTHER AUTHORIZATIONS FOR OVERSEAS CONTINGENCY OPERATIONS FOR BASE REQUIREMENTS.

SEC. 4503. OTHER AUTHORIZATIONS FOR OVERSEAS CONTINGENCY OPERATIONS FOR BASE REQUIREMENTS
(In Thousands of Dollars)

Program Title	FY 2017 Request	House Authorized	Senate Authorized	Conference Change	Conference Authorized
DRUG INTERDICTION & CTR-DRUG ACTIVITIES, DEF					
DRUG INTERDICTION AND COUNTER-DRUG ACTIVITIES, DEFENSE	23,800	23,800	23,800		23,800

SEC. 4503. OTHER AUTHORIZATIONS FOR OVERSEAS CONTINGENCY OPERATIONS FOR BASE REQUIREMENTS
(In Thousands of Dollars)

Program Title	FY 2017 Request	House Authorized	Senate Authorized	Conference Change	Conference Authorized
TOTAL DRUG INTERDICTION & CTR-DRUG ACTIVITIES, DEF	23,800	23,800	23,800		23,800
TOTAL OTHER AUTHORIZATIONS	23,800	23,800	23,800		23,800

TITLE XLVI—MILITARY CONSTRUCTION

SEC. 4601. MILITARY CONSTRUCTION.

SEC. 4601. MILITARY CONSTRUCTION
(In Thousands of Dollars)

Account	State/ Country	Installation	Project Title	FY 2017 Request	House Authorized	Senate Authorized	Conference Change	Conference Authorized
Army	ALASKA	Fort Wainwright	Unmanned Aerial Vehicle Hangar	47,000	47,000	47,000		47,000
Army	CALIFORNIA	Concord	Access Control Point	12,600	12,600	12,600		12,600
Army	COLORADO	Fort Carson	Automated Infantry Platoon Battle Course	8,100	8,100	8,100		8,100
Army	COLORADO	Fort Carson	Unmanned Aerial Vehicle Hangar	5,000	5,000	5,000		5,000
Army	CUBA	Guantanamo Bay	Guantanamo Bay Naval Station Migration Complex	33,000	33,000	0		33,000
Army	GEORGIA	Fort Gordon	Access Control Point	0	29,000	0		0
Army	GEORGIA	Fort Gordon	Company Operations Facility	0	10,600	10,600	10,600	10,600
Army	GEORGIA	Fort Gordon	Cyber Protection Team Ops Facility	90,000	90,000	90,000		90,000
Army	GEORGIA	Fort Stewart	Automated Qualification/Training Range	14,800	14,800	14,800		14,800
Army	GERMANY	East Camp Grafenwoehr	Training Support Center	22,000	22,000	22,000		22,000
Army	GERMANY	Garmisch	Dining Facility	9,600	9,600	9,600		9,600
Army	GERMANY	Wiesbaden Army Airfield	Controlled Humidity Warehouse	16,500	16,500	16,500		16,500
Army	GERMANY	Wiesbaden Army Airfield	Hazardous Material Storage Building	2,700	2,700	2,700		2,700
Army	HAWAII	Fort Shafter	Command and Control Facility, Incr 2	40,000	40,000	40,000		40,000
Army	MISSOURI	Fort Leonard Wood	Fire Station	0	6,900	0	6,900	6,900
Army	TEXAS	Fort Hood	Automated Infantry Platoon Battle Course	7,600	7,600	7,600		7,600
Army	UTAH	Camp Williams	Live Fire Exercise Shoothouse	7,400	7,400	7,400		7,400
Army	VIRGINIA	Fort Belvoir	Secure Admin/Operations Facility, Incr 2	64,000	64,000	64,000		64,000
Army	VIRGINIA	Fort Belvoir	Vehicle Maintenance Shop	0	23,000	0	23,000	23,000
Army	WORLDWIDE UN-SPECIFIED	Unspecified Worldwide Locations	Host Nation Support FY17	18,000	18,000	18,000		18,000
Army	WORLDWIDE UN-SPECIFIED	Unspecified Worldwide Locations	Minor Construction FY17	25,000	25,000	25,000	10,000	35,000
Army	WORLDWIDE UN-SPECIFIED	Unspecified Worldwide Locations	Planning and Design FY17	80,159	80,159	80,159		80,159
Military Construction, Army Total				**503,459**	**572,959**	**481,059**	**50,500**	**553,959**
Navy	ARIZONA	Yuma	VMX–22 Maintenance Hangar	48,355	48,355	48,355		48,355
Navy	CALIFORNIA	Coronado	Coastal Campus Entry Control Point	13,044	13,044	13,044		13,044
Navy	CALIFORNIA	Coronado	Coastal Campus Utilities Infrastructure	81,104	81,104	81,104		81,104
Navy	CALIFORNIA	Coronado	Grace Hopper Data Center Power Upgrades	10,353	10,353	10,353		10,353
Navy	CALIFORNIA	Lemoore	F–35C Engine Repair Facility	26,723	26,723	26,723		26,723
Navy	CALIFORNIA	Miramar	Aircraft Maintenance Hangar, Incr 1	0	79,399	0	79,399	79,399
Navy	CALIFORNIA	Miramar	Communications Complex & Infrastructure Upgrade	0	34,700	34,700	34,700	34,700
Navy	CALIFORNIA	Miramar	F–35 Aircraft Parking Apron	0	40,000	40,000	40,000	40,000
Navy	CALIFORNIA	San Diego	Energy Security Hospital Microgrid	6,183	0	0	–6,183	0
Navy	CALIFORNIA	Seal Beach	Missile Magazines	21,007	21,007	21,007		21,007
Navy	FLORIDA	Eglin AFB	WMD Field Training Facilities	20,489	20,489	20,489		20,489
Navy	FLORIDA	Mayport NS	Advanced Wastewater Treatment Plant	0	66,000	0		0
Navy	FLORIDA	Pensacola	A-School Dormitory	0	53,000	0		0
Navy	GUAM	Joint Region Marianas	Hardening of Guam POL Infrastructure	26,975	26,975	26,975		26,975
Navy	GUAM	Joint Region Marianas	Power Upgrade—Harmon	62,210	62,210	62,210		62,210
Navy	HAWAII	Barking Sands	Upgrade Power Plant & Electrical Distrib Sys	43,384	43,384	43,384		43,384
Navy	HAWAII	Kaneohe Bay	Regimental Consolidated Comm/Elec Facility	72,565	72,565	72,565		72,565
Navy	JAPAN	Kadena AB	Aircraft Maintenance Complex	26,489	26,489	26,489		26,489
Navy	JAPAN	Sasebo	Shore Power (Juliet Pier)	16,420	16,420	16,420		16,420
Navy	MAINE	Kittery	Unaccompanied Housing	17,773	17,773	17,773		17,773

SEC. 4601. MILITARY CONSTRUCTION
(In Thousands of Dollars)

Account	State/Country	Installation	Project Title	FY 2017 Request	House Authorized	Senate Authorized	Conference Change	Conference Authorized
Navy	MAINE	Kittery	Utility Improvements for Nuclear Platforms	30,119	30,119	30,119		30,119
Navy	MARYLAND	Patuxent River	UCLASS RDT&E Hangar	40,576	40,576	40,576		40,576
Navy	NEVADA	Fallon	Air Wing Simulator Facility	13,523	13,523	13,523		13,523
Navy	NORTH CAROLINA	Camp Lejeune	Range Facilities Safety Improvements	18,482	18,482	18,482		18,482
Navy	NORTH CAROLINA	Cherry Point	Central Heating Plant Conversion	12,515	12,515	12,515		12,515
Navy	SOUTH CAROLINA	Beaufort	Aircraft Maintenance Hangar	83,490	83,490	83,490		83,490
Navy	SOUTH CAROLINA	Parris Island	Recruit Reconditioning Center & Barracks	29,882	29,882	29,882		29,882
Navy	SPAIN	Rota	Communication Station	23,607	23,607	23,607		23,607
Navy	VIRGINIA	Norfolk	Chambers Field Magazine Recap Ph I	0	27,000	27,000	27,000	27,000
Navy	WASHINGTON	Bangor	SEAWOLF Class Service Pier	0	73,000	0	73,000	73,000
Navy	WASHINGTON	Bangor	Service Pier Electrical Upgrades	18,939	18,939	18,939		18,939
Navy	WASHINGTON	Bangor	Submarine Refit Maint Support Facility	21,476	21,476	21,476		21,476
Navy	WASHINGTON	Bremerton	Nuclear Repair Facility	6,704	6,704	6,704		6,704
Navy	WASHINGTON	Whidbey Island	EA–18G Maintenance Hangar	45,501	45,501	45,501		45,501
Navy	WASHINGTON	Whidbey Island	Triton Mission Control Facility	30,475	30,475	30,475		30,475
Navy	WORLDWIDE UN-SPECIFIED	Unspecified Worldwide Locations	Planning and Design	88,230	88,230	88,230		88,230
Navy	WORLDWIDE UN-SPECIFIED	Unspecified Worldwide Locations	Unspecified Minor Construction	29,790	29,790	29,790		29,790
Navy	WORLDWIDE UN-SPECIFIED	Various Worldwide Locations	Triton Forward Operating Base Hangar	41,380	41,380	41,380		41,380
Military Construction, Navy Total				**1,027,763**	**1,394,679**	**1,123,280**	**247,916**	**1,275,679**
AF	ALABAMA	Maxwell AFB	JAG School Expansion	0	0	0	15,500	15,500
AF	ALASKA	Clear AFS	Fire Station	20,000	20,000	20,000		20,000
AF	ALASKA	Eielson AFB	F–35A ADAL Field Training Detachment Fac	22,100	22,100	22,100		22,100
AF	ALASKA	Eielson AFB	F–35A Aircraft Weather Shelter (Sqd 2)	82,300	0	82,300		82,300
AF	ALASKA	Eielson AFB	F–35A Aircraft Weather Shelters (Sqd 1)	79,500	79,500	79,500		79,500
AF	ALASKA	Eielson AFB	F–35A Earth Covered Magazines	11,300	11,300	11,300		11,300
AF	ALASKA	Eielson AFB	F–35A Hangar/Propulsion MX/Dispatch	44,900	44,900	44,900		44,900
AF	ALASKA	Eielson AFB	F–35A Hangar/Squad Ops/AMU Sq #2	42,700	42,700	42,700		42,700
AF	ALASKA	Eielson AFB	F–35A Missile Maintenance Facility	12,800	12,800	12,800		12,800
AF	ALASKA	Joint Base Elmendorf-Richardson	Add/Alter AWACS Alert Hangar	29,000	29,000	29,000		29,000
AF	ARIZONA	Luke AFB	F–35A Squad Ops/Aircraft Maint Unit #5	20,000	20,000	20,000		20,000
AF	AUSTRALIA	Darwin	APR—Aircraft MX Support Facility	1,800	1,800	1,800		1,800
AF	AUSTRALIA	Darwin	APR—Expand Parking Apron	28,600	28,600	28,600		28,600
AF	CALIFORNIA	Edwards AFB	Flightline Fire Station	24,000	24,000	24,000		24,000
AF	COLORADO	Buckley AFB	Small Arms Range Complex	13,500	13,500	13,500		13,500
AF	DELAWARE	Dover AFB	Aircraft Maintenance Hangar	39,000	39,000	39,000		39,000
AF	FLORIDA	Eglin AFB	Advanced Munitions Technology Complex	75,000	75,000	75,000		75,000
AF	FLORIDA	Egiin AFB	Dormitories (288 rooms)	0	0	0	35,000	35,000
AF	FLORIDA	Eglin AFB	Flightline Fire Station	13,600	13,600	13,600		13,600
AF	FLORIDA	Patrick AFB	Fire/Crash Rescue Station	13,500	13,500	13,500		13,500
AF	GEORGIA	Moody AFB	Personnel Recovery 4-Bay Hangar/Helo MX Unit	30,900	30,900	30,900		30,900
AF	GERMANY	Ramstein AB	37 AS Squadron Operations/Aircraft Maint Unit	13,437	13,437	13,437		13,437
AF	GERMANY	Spangdahlem AB	EIC—Site Development and Infrastructure	43,465	43,465	43,465		43,465
AF	GUAM	Joint Region Marianas	APR—Munitions Storage Igloos, Ph 2	35,300	35,300	35,300		35,300
AF	GUAM	Joint Region Marianas	APR—SATCOM C4I Facility	14,200	14,200	14,200		14,200
AF	GUAM	Joint Region Marianas	Block 40 Maintenance Hangar	31,158	31,158	31,158		31,158
AF	ILLINOIS	Scott AFB	Consolidated Corrosion Facility add/alter	0	0	0	41,000	41,000
AF	JAPAN	Kadena AB	APR—Replace Munitions Structures	19,815	19,815	19,815		19,815
AF	JAPAN	Yokota AB	C–130J Corrosion Control Hangar	23,777	23,777	23,777		23,777
AF	JAPAN	Yokota AB	Construct Combat Arms Training & Maint Fac	8,243	8,243	8,243		8,243
AF	KANSAS	McConnell AFB	Air Traffic Control Tower	11,200	11,200	11,200		11,200
AF	KANSAS	McConnell AFB	KC–46A ADAL Taxiway Delta	5,600	5,600	5,600		5,600
AF	KANSAS	McConnell AFB	KC–46A Alter Flight Simulator Bldgs	3,000	3,000	3,000		3,000
AF	LOUISIANA	Barksdale AFB	Consolidated Communication Facility	21,000	21,000	21,000		21,000
AF	MARIANA ISLANDS	Unspecified Location	APR—Land Acquisition	9,000	9,000	9,000		9,000
AF	MARYLAND	Joint Base Andrews	21 Points Enclosed Firing Range	13,000	13,000	13,000		13,000
AF	MARYLAND	Joint Base Andrews	Consolidated Communications Center	0	50,000	50,000	50,000	50,000
AF	MARYLAND	Joint Base Andrews	PAR Relocate JADOC Satellite Site	3,500	3,500	3,500		3,500
AF	MASSACHUSETTS	Hanscom AFB	Construct Vandenberg Gate Complex	0	10,965	0	10,965	10,965
AF	MASSACHUSETTS	Hanscom AFB	System Management Engineering Facility	20,000	20,000	20,000		20,000

SEC. 4601. MILITARY CONSTRUCTION
(In Thousands of Dollars)

Account	State/Country	Installation	Project Title	FY 2017 Request	House Authorized	Senate Authorized	Conference Change	Conference Authorized
AF	MONTANA	Malmstrom AFB	Missile Maintenance Facility	14,600	14,600	14,600		14,600
AF	NEVADA	Nellis AFB	F–35A POL Fill Stand Addition	10,600	10,600	10,600		10,600
AF	NEW MEXICO	Cannon AFB	North Fitness Center	21,000	21,000	21,000		21,000
AF	NEW MEXICO	Holloman AFB	Hazardous Cargo Pad and Taxiway	10,600	10,600	10,600		10,600
AF	NEW MEXICO	Kirtland AFB	Combat Rescue Helicopter Simulator	7,300	7,300	7,300		7,300
AF	OHIO	Wright-Patterson AFB	Relocated Entry Control Facility 26A	12,600	12,600	12,600		12,600
AF	OKLAHOMA	Altus AFB	KC–46A FTU/FTC Simulator Facility Ph 2	11,600	11,600	11,600		11,600
AF	OKLAHOMA	Tinker AFB	E–3G Mission and Flight Simulator Training Facility	0	26,000	26,000	26,000	26,000
AF	OKLAHOMA	Tinker AFB	KC–46A Depot System Integration Laboratory	17,000	17,000	17,000		17,000
AF	SOUTH CAROLINA	Joint Base Charleston	Fire & Rescue Station	0	17,000	0	17,000	17,000
AF	TEXAS	Joint Base San Antonio	BMT Recruit Dormitory 6	67,300	67,300	67,300		67,300
AF	TURKEY	Incirlik AB	Airfield Fire/Crash Rescue Station	13,449	13,449	13,449		13,449
AF	UNITED ARAB EMIRATES	Al Dhafra	Large Aircraft Maintenance Hangar	35,400	35,400	35,400		35,400
AF	UNITED KINGDOM	RAF Croughton	JIAC Consolidation—Ph 3	53,082	0	53,082		53,082
AF	UNITED KINGDOM	RAF Croughton	Main Gate Complex	16,500	16,500	16,500		16,500
AF	UTAH	Hill AFB	649 MUNS Munitions Storage Magazines	6,600	6,600	6,600		6,600
AF	UTAH	Hill AFB	649 MUNS Precision Guided Missile MX Facility	8,700	8,700	8,700		8,700
AF	UTAH	Hill AFB	649 MUNS STAMP/Maint & Inspection Facility	12,000	12,000	12,000		12,000
AF	UTAH	Hill AFB	Composite Aircraft Antenna Calibration Fac	7,100	7,100	7,100		7,100
AF	UTAH	Hill AFB	F–35A Munitions Maintenance Complex	10,100	10,100	10,100		10,100
AF	VIRGINIA	Joint Base Langley-Eustis	Air Force Targeting Center	45,000	45,000	45,000		45,000
AF	VIRGINIA	Joint Base Langley-Eustis	Fuel System Maintenance Dock	14,200	14,200	14,200		14,200
AF	WASHINGTON	Fairchild AFB	Pipeline Dorm, USAF SERE School (150 RM)	27,000	27,000	27,000		27,000
AF	WORLDWIDE UN-SPECIFIED	Various Worldwide Locations	Planning & Design	143,582	163,582	143,582		143,582
AF	WORLDWIDE UN-SPECIFIED	Various Worldwide Locations	Unspecified Minor Military Construction	30,000	63,082	30,000	10,000	40,000
AF	WYOMING	F. E. Warren AFB	Missile Transfer Facility Bldg 4331	5,550	5,550	5,550		5,550
Military Construction, Air Force Total				**1,481,058**	**1,502,723**	**1,557,058**	**205,465**	**1,686,523**
Def-Wide	ALASKA	Clear AFS	Long Range Discrim Radar Sys Complex Ph 1	155,000	100,000	155,000		155,000
Def-Wide	ALASKA	Fort Greely	Missile Defense Complex Switchgear Facility	9,560	9,560	9,560		9,560
Def-Wide	ALASKA	Joint Base Elmendorf-Richardson	Construct Truck Offload Facility	4,900	4,900	4,900		4,900
Def-Wide	ARIZONA	Fort Huachuca	JITC Building 52110 Renovation	4,493	4,493	4,493		4,493
Def-Wide	CALIFORNIA	Coronado	SOF Human Performance Training Center	15,578	15,578	15,578		15,578
Def-Wide	CALIFORNIA	Coronado	SOF Seal Team Ops Facility	47,290	47,290	47,290		47,290
Def-Wide	CALIFORNIA	Coronado	SOF Seal Team Ops Facility	47,290	47,290	47,290		47,290
Def-Wide	CALIFORNIA	Coronado	SOF Special RECON Team ONE Operations Fac	20,949	20,949	20,949		20,949
Def-Wide	CALIFORNIA	Coronado	SOF Training Detachment ONE Ops Facility	44,305	44,305	44,305		44,305
Def-Wide	CALIFORNIA	Travis AFB	Replace Hydrant Fuel System	26,500	26,500	26,500		26,500
Def-Wide	DELAWARE	Dover AFB	Welch ES/Dover MS Replacement	44,115	44,115	44,115		44,115
Def-Wide	DIEGO GARCIA	Diego Garcia	Improve Wharf Refueling Capability	30,000	30,000	30,000		30,000
Def-Wide	FLORIDA	Patrick AFB	Replace Fuel Tanks	10,100	10,100	10,100		10,100
Def-Wide	GEORGIA	Fort Benning	SOF Tactical Unmanned Aerial Vehicle Hangar	4,820	4,820	4,820		4,820
Def-Wide	GEORGIA	Fort Gordon	Medical Clinic Replacement	25,000	25,000	25,000		25,000
Def-Wide	GERMANY	Kaiserlautern AB	Sembach Elementary/Middle School Replacement	45,221	45,221	45,221		45,221
Def-Wide	GERMANY	Rhine Ordnance Barracks	Medical Center Replacement Incr 6	58,063	58,063	58,063		58,063
Def-Wide	JAPAN	Iwakuni	Construct Truck Offload & Loading Facilities	6,664	6,664	6,664		6,664
Def-Wide	JAPAN	Kadena AB	Kadena Elementary School Replacement	84,918	84,918	84,918		84,918
Def-Wide	JAPAN	Kadena AB	Medical Materiel Warehouse	20,881	20,881	20,881		20,881
Def-Wide	JAPAN	Kadena AB	SOF Maintenance Hangar	42,823	42,823	42,823		42,823
Def-Wide	JAPAN	Kadena AB	SOF Simulator Facility (MC–130)	12,602	12,602	12,602		12,602
Def-Wide	JAPAN	Yokota AB	Airfield Apron	41,294	41,294	41,294		41,294
Def-Wide	JAPAN	Yokota AB	Hangar/AMU	39,466	39,466	39,466		39,466
Def-Wide	JAPAN	Yokota AB	Operations and Warehouse Facilities	26,710	26,710	26,710		26,710
Def-Wide	JAPAN	Yokota AB	Simulator Facility	6,261	6,261	6,261		6,261
Def-Wide	KWAJALEIN	Kwajalein Atoll	Replace Fuel Storage Tanks	85,500	85,500	85,500		85,500

SEC. 4601. MILITARY CONSTRUCTION
(In Thousands of Dollars)

Account	State/Country	Installation	Project Title	FY 2017 Request	House Authorized	Senate Authorized	Conference Change	Conference Authorized
Def-Wide	MAINE	Kittery	Medical/Dental Clinic Replacement	27,100	27,100	27,100		27,100
Def-Wide	MARYLAND	Bethesda Naval Hospital	MEDCEN Addition/Alteration Incr 1	50,000	50,000	50,000		50,000
Def-Wide	MARYLAND	Fort Meade	Access Control Facility	21,000	21,000	21,000		21,000
Def-Wide	MARYLAND	Fort Meade	NSAW Campus Feeders Phase 3	17,000	17,000	17,000		17,000
Def-Wide	MARYLAND	Fort Meade	NSAW Recapitalize Building #2 Incr 2	195,000	145,000	195,000		195,000
Def-Wide	MISSOURI	St. Louis	Land Acquisition—Next NGA West Campus	801	0	801		801
Def-Wide	NORTH CAROLINA	Camp Lejeune	Dental Clinic Replacement	31,000	31,000	31,000		31,000
Def-Wide	NORTH CAROLINA	Fort Bragg	SOF Combat Medic Training Facility	10,905	10,905	10,905		10,905
Def-Wide	NORTH CAROLINA	Fort Bragg	SOF Parachute Rigging Facility	21,420	21,420	21,420		21,420
Def-Wide	NORTH CAROLINA	Fort Bragg	SOF Special Tactics Facility (Ph 3)	30,670	30,670	30,670		30,670
Def-Wide	NORTH CAROLINA	Fort Bragg	SOF Tactical Equipment Maintenance Facility	23,598	23,598	23,598		23,598
Def-Wide	SOUTH CAROLINA	Joint Base Charleston	Construct Hydrant Fuel System	17,000	17,000	17,000		17,000
Def-Wide	TEXAS	Red River Army Depot	Construct Warehouse & Open Storage	44,700	44,700	44,700		44,700
Def-Wide	TEXAS	Sheppard AFB	Medical/Dental Clinic Replacement	91,910	91,910	91,910		91,910
Def-Wide	UNITED KINGDOM	RAF Croughton	Croughton Elem/Middle/High School Replacement	71,424	71,424	71,424		71,424
Def-Wide	UNITED KINGDOM	RAF Lakenheath	Construct Hydrant Fuel System	13,500	13,500	13,500		13,500
Def-Wide	VIRGINIA	Pentagon	Pentagon Metro Entrance Facility	12,111	12,111	0		12,111
Def-Wide	VIRGINIA	Pentagon	Upgrade IT Facilities Infrastructure—RRMC	8,105	8,105	8,105		8,105
Def-Wide	WAKE ISLAND	Wake Island	Test Support Facility	11,670	11,670	11,670		11,670
Def-Wide	WORLDWIDE UNSPECIFIED	Unspecified Worldwide Locations	Battalion Complex	0	0	64,400		0
Def-Wide	WORLDWIDE UNSPECIFIED	Unspecified Worldwide Locations	Contingency Construction	10,000	10,000	10,000	−10,000	0
Def-Wide	WORLDWIDE UNSPECIFIED	Unspecified Worldwide Locations	Energy Conservation Investment Program Design	10,000	0	10,000	−10,000	0
Def-Wide	WORLDWIDE UNSPECIFIED	Unspecified Worldwide Locations	Energy Conservation Investment Program	150,000	150,000	150,000		150,000
Def-Wide	WORLDWIDE UNSPECIFIED	Unspecified Worldwide Locations	Exercise Related Minor Construction	8,631	8,631	8,631		8,631
Def-Wide	WORLDWIDE UNSPECIFIED	Unspecified Worldwide Locations	Planning and Design, Defense Wide	13,450	23,450	13,450	10,000	23,450
Def-Wide	WORLDWIDE UNSPECIFIED	Unspecified Worldwide Locations	Planning and Design, DODEA	23,585	23,585	23,585		23,585
Def-Wide	WORLDWIDE UNSPECIFIED	Unspecified Worldwide Locations	Planning and Design, NGA	71,647	36,000	71,647	−35,647	36,000
Def-Wide	WORLDWIDE UNSPECIFIED	Unspecified Worldwide Locations	Planning and Design, NSA	24,000	24,000	24,000		24,000
Def-Wide	WORLDWIDE UNSPECIFIED	Unspecified Worldwide Locations	Planning and Design, WHS	3,427	3,427	3,427		3,427
Def-Wide	WORLDWIDE UNSPECIFIED	Unspecified Worldwide Locations	Unspecified Minor Construction	3,000	3,000	3,000		3,000
Def-Wide	WORLDWIDE UNSPECIFIED	Unspecified Worldwide Locations	Unspecified Minor Construction	3,000	3,000	3,000		3,000
Def-Wide	WORLDWIDE UNSPECIFIED	Unspecified Worldwide Locations	Unspecified Minor Construction	5,994	5,994	5,994		5,994
Def-Wide	WORLDWIDE UNSPECIFIED	Unspecified Worldwide Locations	Unspecified Minor Construction	8,500	8,500	8,500		8,500
Def-Wide	WORLDWIDE UNSPECIFIED	Unspecified Worldwide Locations	Unspecified Minor Milcon	3,913	3,913	3,913		3,913
Def-Wide	WORLDWIDE UNSPECIFIED	Unspecified Worldwide Locations	Worldwide Unspecified Minor Construction	2,414	2,414	2,414		2,414
Def-Wide	WORLDWIDE UNSPECIFIED	Various Worldwide Locations	Planning & Design, DLA	27,660	27,660	27,660		27,660
Def-Wide	WORLDWIDE UNSPECIFIED	Various Worldwide Locations	Planning and Design, SOCOM	27,653	27,653	27,653		27,653
Def-Wide	WORLDWIDE UNSPECIFIED LOCATIONS	Unspecified Worldwide Locations	Planning & Design, MDA	0	15,000	0	15,000	15,000
Military Construction, Defense-Wide Total				**2,056,091**	**1,929,643**	**2,108,380**	**−30,647**	**2,025,444**
NATO	WORLDWIDE UNSPECIFIED	NATO Security Investment Program	NATO Security Investment Program	177,932	177,932	177,932		177,932
NATO Security Investment Program Total				**177,932**	**177,932**	**177,932**	**0**	**177,932**

SEC. 4601. MILITARY CONSTRUCTION
(In Thousands of Dollars)

Account	State/Country	Installation	Project Title	FY 2017 Request	House Authorized	Senate Authorized	Conference Change	Conference Authorized
Army NG	COLORADO	Fort Carson	National Guard Readiness Center	0	16,500	16,500	16,500	16,500
Army NG	HAWAII	Hilo	Combined Support Maintenance Shop	31,000	31,000	31,000		31,000
Army NG	IOWA	Davenport	National Guard Readiness Center	23,000	23,000	23,000		23,000
Army NG	KANSAS	Fort Leavenworth	National Guard Readiness Center	29,000	29,000	29,000		29,000
Army NG	NEW HAMPSHIRE	Hooksett	National Guard Vehicle Maintenance Shop	11,000	11,000	11,000		11,000
Army NG	NEW HAMPSHIRE	Rochester	National Guard Vehicle Maintenance Shop	8,900	8,900	8,900		8,900
Army NG	OKLAHOMA	Ardmore	National Guard Readiness Center	22,000	22,000	22,000		22,000
Army NG	PENNSYLVANIA	Fort Indiantown Gap	Access Control Buildings	0	20,000	0	20,000	20,000
Army NG	PENNSYLVANIA	York	National Guard Readiness Center	9,300	9,300	9,300		9,300
Army NG	RHODE ISLAND	East Greenwich	National Guard/Reserve Center Building (JFHQ)	20,000	20,000	20,000		20,000
Army NG	UTAH	Camp Williams	National Guard Readiness Center	37,000	37,000	37,000		37,000
Army NG	WORLDWIDE UNSPECIFIED	Unspecified Worldwide Locations	Planning and Design	8,729	8,729	8,729		8,729
Army NG	WORLDWIDE UNSPECIFIED	Unspecified Worldwide Locations	Unspecified Minor Construction	12,001	12,001	12,001		12,001
Army NG	WYOMING	Camp Guernsey	General Instruction Building	0	31,000	0	31,000	31,000
Army NG	WYOMING	Laramie	National Guard Readiness Center	21,000	21,000	21,000		21,000
Military Construction, Army National Guard Total				**232,930**	**300,430**	**249,430**	**67,500**	**300,430**
Army Res	ARIZONA	Phoenix	Army Reserve Center	0	30,000	30,000	30,000	30,000
Army Res	CALIFORNIA	Barstow	Equipment Concentration Site	0	29,000	0		0
Army Res	CALIFORNIA	Camp Parks	Transient Training Barracks	19,000	19,000	19,000		19,000
Army Res	CALIFORNIA	Fort Hunter Liggett	Emergency Services Center	21,500	21,500	21,500		21,500
Army Res	VIRGINIA	Dublin	Organizational Maintenance Shop/AMSA	6,000	6,000	6,000		6,000
Army Res	WASHINGTON	Joint Base Lewis-McChord	Army Reserve Center	0	27,500	0		0
Army Res	WISCONSIN	Fort McCoy	AT/MOB Dining Facility	11,400	11,400	11,400		11,400
Army Res	WORLDWIDE UNSPECIFIED	Unspecified Worldwide Locations	Planning and Design	7,500	7,500	7,500		7,500
Army Res	WORLDWIDE UNSPECIFIED	Unspecified Worldwide Locations	Unspecified Minor Construction	2,830	2,830	2,830		2,830
Military Construction, Army Reserve Total				**68,230**	**154,730**	**98,230**	**30,000**	**98,230**
N/MC Res	LOUISIANA	New Orleans	Joint Reserve Intelligence Center	11,207	11,207	11,207		11,207
N/MC Res	NEW YORK	Brooklyn	Electric Feeder Ductbank	1,964	1,964	1,964		1,964
N/MC Res	NEW YORK	Syracuse	Marine Corps Reserve Center	13,229	13,229	13,229		13,229
N/MC Res	TEXAS	Galveston	Reserve Center Annex	8,414	8,414	8,414		8,414
N/MC Res	WORLDWIDE UNSPECIFIED	Unspecified Worldwide Locations	MCNR Planning & Design	3,783	3,783	3,783		3,783
Military Construction, Naval Reserve Total				**38,597**	**38,597**	**38,597**	**0**	**38,597**
Air NG	CONNECTICUT	Bradley IAP	Construct Small Air Terminal	6,300	6,300	6,300		6,300
Air NG	FLORIDA	Jacksonville IAP	Replace Fire Crash/Rescue Station	9,000	9,000	9,000		9,000
Air NG	HAWAII	Joint Base Pearl Harbor-Hickam	F–22 Composite Repair Facility	11,000	11,000	11,000		11,000
Air NG	IOWA	Sioux Gateway Airport	Construct Consolidated Support Functions	12,600	12,600	12,600		12,600
Air NG	MARYLAND	Joint Base Andrews	Munitions Load Crew Trng/Corrosion Cntrl Facility	0	5,000	0	5,000	5,000
Air NG	MINNESOTA	Duluth IAP	Load Crew Training/Weapon Shops	7,600	7,600	7,600		7,600
Air NG	NEW HAMPSHIRE	Pease International Trade Port	KC–46A Install Fuselage Trainer Bldg 251	1,500	1,500	1,500		1,500
Air NG	NORTH CAROLINA	Charlotte/Douglas IAP	C–17 Corrosion Control/Fuel Cell Hangar	29,600	29,600	29,600		29,600
Air NG	NORTH CAROLINA	Charlotte/Douglas IAP	C–17 Type III Hydrant Refueling System	21,000	21,000	21,000		21,000
Air NG	OHIO	Toledo Express Airport	Indoor Small Arms Range	0	6,000	0	6,000	6,000
Air NG	SOUTH CAROLINA	McEntire ANGS	Replace Operations and Training Facility	8,400	8,400	8,400		8,400
Air NG	TEXAS	Ellington Field	Consolidate Crew Readiness Facility	4,500	4,500	4,500		4,500
Air NG	VERMONT	Burlington IAP	F–35 Beddown 4-Bay Flight Simulator	4,500	4,500	4,500		4,500
Air NG	WORLDWIDE UNSPECIFIED	Unspecified Worldwide Locations	Unspecified Minor Construction	17,495	29,495	17,495		17,495
Air NG	WORLDWIDE UNSPECIFIED	Various Worldwide Locations	Planning and Design	10,462	10,462	10,462		10,462
Military Construction, Air National Guard Total				**143,957**	**166,957**	**143,957**	**11,000**	**154,957**

SEC. 4601. MILITARY CONSTRUCTION
(In Thousands of Dollars)

Account	State/ Country	Installation	Project Title	FY 2017 Request	House Authorized	Senate Authorized	Conference Change	Conference Authorized
AF Res	GUAM	Andersen AFB	Reserve Medical Training Facility	0	5,200	0		0
AF Res	MASSACHUSETTS	Westover ARB	Indoor Small Arms Range	0	9,200	0		0
AF Res	NORTH CAROLINA	Seymour Johnson AFB	KC–46A ADAL Bldg for AGE/Fuselage Training	5,700	5,700	5,700		5,700
AF Res	NORTH CAROLINA	Seymour Johnson AFB	KC–46A ADAL Squadron Operations Facilities	2,250	2,250	2,250		2,250
AF Res	NORTH CAROLINA	Seymour Johnson AFB	KC–46A Two Bay Corrosion/Fuel Cell Hangar	90,000	90,000	90,000		90,000
AF Res	PENNSYLVANIA	Pittsburgh IAP	C–17 ADAL Fuel Hydrant System	22,800	22,800	22,800		22,800
AF Res	PENNSYLVANIA	Pittsburgh IAP	C–17 Const/OverlayTaxiway and Apron	8,200	8,200	8,200		8,200
AF Res	PENNSYLVANIA	Pittsburgh IAP	C–17 Construct Two Bay Corrosion/Fuel Hangar	54,000	54,000	54,000		54,000
AF Res	UTAH	Hill AFB	ADAL Life Support Facility	0	3,050	0		0
AF Res	WORLDWIDE UNSPECIFIED	Unspecified Worldwide Locations	Planning & Design	4,500	4,500	4,500		4,500
AF Res	WORLDWIDE UNSPECIFIED	Unspecified Worldwide Locations	Unspecified Minor Construction	1,500	1,500	1,500		1,500
Military Construction, Air Force Reserve Total				**188,950**	**206,400**	**188,950**	**0**	**188,950**
FH Con Army	KOREA	Camp Humphreys	Family Housing New Construction, Incr 1	143,563	100,000	143,563	–43,563	100,000
FH Con Army	KOREA	Camp Walker	Family Housing New Construction	54,554	54,554	54,554		54,554
FH Con Army	WORLDWIDE UNSPECIFIED	Unspecified Worldwide Locations	Planning & Design	2,618	2,618	2,618		2,618
Family Housing Construction, Army Total				**200,735**	**157,172**	**200,735**	**–43,563**	**157,172**
FH Ops Army	WORLDWIDE UNSPECIFIED	Unspecified Worldwide Locations	Furnishings	10,178	10,178	10,178		10,178
FH Ops Army	WORLDWIDE UNSPECIFIED	Unspecified Worldwide Locations	Housing Privatization Support	19,146	19,146	19,146		19,146
FH Ops Army	WORLDWIDE UNSPECIFIED	Unspecified Worldwide Locations	Leasing	131,761	131,761	131,761		131,761
FH Ops Army	WORLDWIDE UNSPECIFIED	Unspecified Worldwide Locations	Maintenance	60,745	60,745	60,745		60,745
FH Ops Army	WORLDWIDE UNSPECIFIED	Unspecified Worldwide Locations	Management	40,344	40,344	40,344		40,344
FH Ops Army	WORLDWIDE UNSPECIFIED	Unspecified Worldwide Locations	Miscellaneous	400	400	400		400
FH Ops Army	WORLDWIDE UNSPECIFIED	Unspecified Worldwide Locations	Services	7,993	7,993	7,993		7,993
FH Ops Army	WORLDWIDE UNSPECIFIED	Unspecified Worldwide Locations	Utilities	55,428	55,428	55,428		55,428
Family Housing Operation And Maintenance, Army Total				**325,995**	**325,995**	**325,995**	**0**	**325,995**
FH Con Navy	MARIANA ISLANDS	Guam	Replace Andersen Housing Ph I	78,815	78,815	78,815		78,815
FH Con Navy	WORLDWIDE UNSPECIFIED	Unspecified Worldwide Locations	Construction Improvements	11,047	11,047	11,047		11,047
FH Con Navy	WORLDWIDE UNSPECIFIED	Unspecified Worldwide Locations	Planning & Design	4,149	4,149	4,149		4,149
Family Housing Construction, Navy And Marine Corps Total				**94,011**	**94,011**	**94,011**	**0**	**94,011**
FH Ops Navy	WORLDWIDE UNSPECIFIED	Unspecified Worldwide Locations	Furnishings	17,457	17,457	17,457		17,457
FH Ops Navy	WORLDWIDE UNSPECIFIED	Unspecified Worldwide Locations	Housing Privatization Support	26,320	26,320	26,320		26,320
FH Ops Navy	WORLDWIDE UNSPECIFIED	Unspecified Worldwide Locations	Leasing	54,689	54,689	54,689		54,689
FH Ops Navy	WORLDWIDE UNSPECIFIED	Unspecified Worldwide Locations	Maintenance	81,254	81,254	81,254		81,254
FH Ops Navy	WORLDWIDE UNSPECIFIED	Unspecified Worldwide Locations	Management	51,291	51,291	51,291		51,291
FH Ops Navy	WORLDWIDE UNSPECIFIED	Unspecified Worldwide Locations	Miscellaneous	364	364	364		364
FH Ops Navy	WORLDWIDE UNSPECIFIED	Unspecified Worldwide Locations	Services	12,855	12,855	12,855		12,855
FH Ops Navy	WORLDWIDE UNSPECIFIED	Unspecified Worldwide Locations	Utilities	56,685	56,685	56,685		56,685
Family Housing Operation And Maintenance, Navy And Marine Corps Total				**300,915**	**300,915**	**300,915**	**0**	**300,915**

SEC. 4601. MILITARY CONSTRUCTION
(In Thousands of Dollars)

Account	State/Country	Installation	Project Title	FY 2017 Request	House Authorized	Senate Authorized	Conference Change	Conference Authorized
FH Con AF	WORLDWIDE UN-SPECIFIED	Unspecified Worldwide Locations	Construction Improvements	56,984	56,984	56,984		56,984
FH Con AF	WORLDWIDE UN-SPECIFIED	Unspecified Worldwide Locations	Planning & Design	4,368	4,368	4,368		4,368
Family Housing Construction, Air Force Total				**61,352**	**61,352**	**61,352**	**0**	**61,352**
FH Ops AF	WORLDWIDE UN-SPECIFIED	Unspecified Worldwide Locations	Furnishings	31,690	31,690	31,690		31,690
FH Ops AF	WORLDWIDE UN-SPECIFIED	Unspecified Worldwide Locations	Housing Privatization Support	41,809	41,809	41,809		41,809
FH Ops AF	WORLDWIDE UN-SPECIFIED	Unspecified Worldwide Locations	Leasing	20,530	20,530	20,530		20,530
FH Ops AF	WORLDWIDE UN-SPECIFIED	Unspecified Worldwide Locations	Maintenance	85,469	85,469	85,469		85,469
FH Ops AF	WORLDWIDE UN-SPECIFIED	Unspecified Worldwide Locations	Management	42,919	42,919	42,919		42,919
FH Ops AF	WORLDWIDE UN-SPECIFIED	Unspecified Worldwide Locations	Miscellaneous	1,745	1,745	1,745		1,745
FH Ops AF	WORLDWIDE UN-SPECIFIED	Unspecified Worldwide Locations	Services	13,026	13,026	13,026		13,026
FH Ops AF	WORLDWIDE UN-SPECIFIED	Unspecified Worldwide Locations	Utilities	37,241	37,241	37,241		37,241
Family Housing Operation And Maintenance, Air Force Total				**274,429**	**274,429**	**274,429**	**0**	**274,429**
FH Ops DW	WORLDWIDE UN-SPECIFIED	Unspecified Worldwide Locations	Furnishings	20	20	20		20
FH Ops DW	WORLDWIDE UN-SPECIFIED	Unspecified Worldwide Locations	Furnishings	500	500	500		500
FH Ops DW	WORLDWIDE UN-SPECIFIED	Unspecified Worldwide Locations	Furnishings	399	399	399		399
FH Ops DW	WORLDWIDE UN-SPECIFIED	Unspecified Worldwide Locations	Leasing	40,984	40,984	40,984		40,984
FH Ops DW	WORLDWIDE UN-SPECIFIED	Unspecified Worldwide Locations	Leasing	11,044	11,044	11,044		11,044
FH Ops DW	WORLDWIDE UN-SPECIFIED	Unspecified Worldwide Locations	Maintenance	349	349	349		349
FH Ops DW	WORLDWIDE UN-SPECIFIED	Unspecified Worldwide Locations	Maintenance	800	800	800		800
FH Ops DW	WORLDWIDE UN-SPECIFIED	Unspecified Worldwide Locations	Management	388	388	388		388
FH Ops DW	WORLDWIDE UN-SPECIFIED	Unspecified Worldwide Locations	Services	32	32	32		32
FH Ops DW	WORLDWIDE UN-SPECIFIED	Unspecified Worldwide Locations	Utilities	4,100	4,100	4,100		4,100
FH Ops DW	WORLDWIDE UN-SPECIFIED	Unspecified Worldwide Locations	Utilities	174	174	174		174
FH Ops DW	WORLDWIDE UN-SPECIFIED	Unspecified Worldwide Locations	Utilities	367	367	367		367
Family Housing Operation And Maintenance, Defense-Wide Total				**59,157**	**59,157**	**59,157**	**0**	**59,157**
FHIF	WORLDWIDE UN-SPECIFIED	Unspecified Worldwide Locations	Program Expenses	3,258	3,258	3,258		3,258
DoD Family Housing Improvement Fund Total				**3,258**	**3,258**	**3,258**	**0**	**3,258**
BRAC	WORLDWIDE UN-SPECIFIED	Base Realignment & Closure, Army	Base Realignment and Closure	14,499	24,499	14,499	10,000	24,499
Base Realignment and Closure—Army Total				**14,499**	**24,499**	**14,499**	**10,000**	**24,499**
BRAC	WORLDWIDE UN-SPECIFIED	Base Realignment & Closure, Navy	Base Realignment & Closure	110,606	125,606	110,606	25,000	135,606
BRAC	WORLDWIDE UN-SPECIFIED	Unspecified Worldwide Locations	DON–100: Planning, Design and Management	4,604	4,604	4,604		4,604
BRAC	WORLDWIDE UN-SPECIFIED	Unspecified Worldwide Locations	DON–101: Various Locations	10,461	10,461	10,461		10,461
BRAC	WORLDWIDE UN-SPECIFIED	Unspecified Worldwide Locations	DON–138: NAS Brunswick, ME	557	557	557		557

SEC. 4601. MILITARY CONSTRUCTION
(In Thousands of Dollars)

Account	State/ Country	Installation	Project Title	FY 2017 Request	House Authorized	Senate Authorized	Conference Change	Conference Authorized
BRAC	WORLDWIDE UN-SPECIFIED	Unspecified Worldwide Locations	DON–157: MCSA Kansas City, MO	100	100	100		100
BRAC	WORLDWIDE UN-SPECIFIED	Unspecified Worldwide Locations	DON–172: NWS Seal Beach, Concord, CA	4,648	4,648	4,648		4,648
BRAC	WORLDWIDE UN-SPECIFIED	Unspecified Worldwide Locations	DON–84: JRB Willow Grove & Cambria Reg AP	3,397	3,397	3,397		3,397
	Base Realignment and Closure—Navy Total			134,373	149,373	134,373	25,000	159,373
BRAC	WORLDWIDE UN-SPECIFIED	Unspecified Worldwide Locations	DoD BRAC Activities—Air Force	56,365	56,365	56,365		56,365
	Base Realignment and Closure—Air Force Total			56,365	56,365	56,365	0	56,365
PYS	WORLDWIDE UN-SPECIFIED	Unspecified Worldwide Locations	Planning and Design, Defense Wide	0	0	0	−30,000	−30,000
PYS	WORLDWIDE UN-SPECIFIED	Worldwide	Air Force	0	−29,300	−22,300	−51,460	−51,460
PYS	WORLDWIDE UN-SPECIFIED	Worldwide	Army	0	−25,000	−30,000	−29,602	−29,602
PYS	WORLDWIDE UN-SPECIFIED	Worldwide	Defense-Wide	0	−60,577	−132,200	−141,600	−141,600
PYS	WORLDWIDE UN-SPECIFIED	Worldwide	Navy	0	−87,699	0		0
PYS	WORLDWIDE UN-SPECIFIED LO-CATIONS	Worldwide	HAP	0	−25,000	0	−25,000	−25,000
PYS	WORLDWIDE UN-SPECIFIED LO-CATIONS	Worldwide	NSIP	0	−30,000	−30,000	−30,000	−30,000
	Prior Year Savings Total			0	−257,576	−214,500	−307,662	−307,662
	Total, Military Construction			7,444,056	7,694,000	7,477,462	265,509	7,709,565

SEC. 4602. MILITARY CONSTRUCTION FOR OVERSEAS CONTINGENCY OPERATIONS.

SEC. 4602. MILITARY CONSTRUCTION FOR OVERSEAS CONTINGENCY OPERATIONS
(In Thousands of Dollars)

Account	State/ Country	Installation	Project Title	FY 2017 Request	House Authorized	Senate Authorized	Conference Change	Conference Authorized
Army	WORLDWIDE UN-SPECIFIED	Unspecified Worldwide Locations	ERI: Planning and Design	18,900	18,900	18,900		18,900
	Military Construction, Army Total			18,900	18,900	18,900	0	18,900
Navy	ICELAND	Keflavik	ERI: P–8A Aircraft Rinse Rack	5,000	5,000	5,000		5,000
Navy	ICELAND	Keflavik	ERI: P–8A Hangar Upgrade	14,600	14,600	14,600		14,600
Navy	WORLDWIDE UN-SPECIFIED	Unspecified Worldwide Locations	ERI: Planning and Design	1,800	1,800	1,800		1,800
	Military Construction, Navy Total			21,400	21,400	21,400	0	21,400
AF	BULGARIA	Graf Ignatievo	ERI: Construct Sq Ops/Operational Alert Fac	3,800	3,800	3,800		3,800
AF	BULGARIA	Graf Ignatievo	ERI: Fighter Ramp Extension	7,000	7,000	7,000		7,000
AF	BULGARIA	Graf Ignatievo	ERI: Upgrade Munitions Storage Area	2,600	2,600	2,600		2,600
AF	DJIBOUTI	Chabelley Airfield	OCO: Construct Chabelley Access Road	3,600	3,600	3,600		3,600
AF	DJIBOUTI	Chabelley Airfield	OCO: Construct Parking Apron and Taxiway	6,900	6,900	6,900		6,900
AF	ESTONIA	Amari AB	ERI: Construct Bulk Fuel Storage	6,500	6,500	6,500		6,500
AF	GERMANY	Spangdahlem AB	ERI: Construct High Cap Trim Pad & Hush House	1,000	1,000	1,000		1,000
AF	GERMANY	Spangdahlem AB	ERI: F/A–22 Low Observable/Comp Repair Fac	12,000	12,000	12,000		12,000
AF	GERMANY	Spangdahlem AB	ERI: F/A–22 Upgrade Infrastructure/Comm/Util	1,600	1,600	1,600		1,600
AF	GERMANY	Spangdahlem AB	ERI: Upgrade Hardened Aircraft Shelters	2,700	2,700	2,700		2,700
AF	GERMANY	Spangdahlem AB	ERI: Upgrade Munitions Storage Doors	1,400	1,400	1,400		1,400
AF	LITHUANIA	Siauliai	ERI: Munitions Storage	3,000	3,000	3,000		3,000
AF	POLAND	Lask AB	ERI: Construct Squadron Operations Facility	4,100	4,100	4,100		4,100
AF	POLAND	Powidz AB	ERI: Construct Squadron Operations Facility	4,100	4,100	4,100		4,100
AF	ROMANIA	Campia Turzii	ERI: Construct Munitions Storage Area	3,000	3,000	3,000		3,000
AF	ROMANIA	Campia Turzii	ERI: Construct Squadron Operations Facility	3,400	3,400	3,400		3,400

SEC. 4602. MILITARY CONSTRUCTION FOR OVERSEAS CONTINGENCY OPERATIONS
(In Thousands of Dollars)

Account	State/ Country	Installation	Project Title	FY 2017 Request	House Authorized	Senate Authorized	Conference Change	Conference Authorized
AF	ROMANIA	Campia Turzii	ERI: Construct Two-Bay Hangar	6,100	6,100	6,100		6,100
AF	ROMANIA	Campia Turzii	ERI: Extend Parking Aprons	6,000	6,000	6,000		6,000
AF	WORLDWIDE UN-SPECIFIED	Unspecified Worldwide Locations	CTP: Planning and Design	9,000	8,551	9,000	−449	8,551
AF	WORLDWIDE UN-SPECIFIED	Unspecified Worldwide Locations	OCO: Planning and Design	940	940	940		940
Military Construction, Air Force Total				**88,740**	**88,291**	**88,740**	**−449**	**88,291**
Def-Wide	WORLDWIDE UN-SPECIFIED	Unspecified Worldwide Locations	ERI: Unspecified Minor Construction	5,000	5,000	5,000		5,000
Military Construction, Defense-Wide Total				**5,000**	**5,000**	**5,000**	**0**	**5,000**
Total, Military Construction				**134,040**	**133,591**	**134,040**	**−449**	**133,591**

SEC. 4603. MILITARY CONSTRUCTION FOR OVERSEAS CONTINGENCY OPERATIONS FOR BASE REQUIREMENTS.

SEC. 4603. MILITARY CONSTRUCTION FOR OVERSEAS CONTINGENCY OPERATIONS FOR BASE REQUIREMENTS
(In Thousands of Dollars)

Account	State/ Country	Installation	Project Title	FY 2017 Request	House Authorized	Senate Authorized	Conference Change	Conference Authorized
Navy	DJIBOUTI	Camp Lemonier	OCO: Medical/Dental Facility	37,409	0	0	0	37,409
Navy	WORLDWIDE UN-SPECIFIED	Unspecified Worldwide Locations	Planning and Design	1,000	0	0	0	1,000
Military Construction, Navy Total				**38,409**	**0**	**0**	**0**	**38,409**
Total, Military Construction				**38,409**	**0**	**0**	**0**	**38,409**

TITLE XLVII—DEPARTMENT OF ENERGY NATIONAL SECURITY PROGRAMS

SEC. 4701. DEPARTMENT OF ENERGY NATIONAL SECURITY PROGRAMS.

SEC. 4701. DEPARTMENT OF ENERGY NATIONAL SECURITY PROGRAMS
(In Thousands of Dollars)

Program	FY 2017 Request	House Authorized	Senate Authorized	Conference Change	Conference Authorized
Discretionary Summary By Appropriation					
Energy And Water Development, And Related Agencies					
Appropriation Summary:					
Energy Programs					
Nuclear Energy	151,876	−15,260	0	−15,260	136,616
Atomic Energy Defense Activities					
National nuclear security administration:					
Weapons activities	9,243,147	316,000	−7,750	185,882	9,429,029
Defense nuclear nonproliferation	1,807,916	11,600	70,000	79,000	1,886,916
Naval reactors	1,420,120	0	0	−2,500	1,417,620
Federal salaries and expenses	412,817	−40,000	0	−17,300	395,517
Total, National nuclear security administration	**12,884,000**	**287,600**	**62,250**	**245,082**	**13,129,082**
Environmental and other defense activities:					
Defense environmental cleanup	5,382,050	−92,100	−135,100	−108,492	5,273,558
Other defense activities	791,552	9,000	0	−2,000	789,552
Total, Environmental & other defense activities	**6,173,602**	**−83,100**	**−135,100**	**−110,492**	**6,063,110**
Total, Atomic Energy Defense Activities	**19,057,602**	**204,500**	**−72,850**	**134,590**	**19,192,192**
Total, Discretionary Funding	**19,209,478**	**189,240**	**−72,850**	**119,330**	**19,328,808**
Nuclear Energy					
Idaho sitewide safeguards and security	129,303				129,303
Idaho operations and maintenance	7,313				7,313
Consent Based Siting	15,260	−15,260		−15,260	0

SEC. 4701. DEPARTMENT OF ENERGY NATIONAL SECURITY PROGRAMS
(In Thousands of Dollars)

Program	FY 2017 Request	House Authorized	Senate Authorized	Conference Change	Conference Authorized
Denial of funds for defense-only repository		[−15,260]		[−15,260]	
Total, Nuclear Energy	**151,876**	**−15,260**	**0**	**−15,260**	**136,616**
Weapons Activities					
Directed stockpile work					
Life extension programs					
B61 Life extension program	616,079				616,079
W76 Life extension program	222,880				222,880
W88 Alt 370	281,129				281,129
W80–4 Life extension program	220,253	21,000			220,253
Mitigation of schedule risk		[21,000]			
Total, Life extension programs	**1,340,341**	**21,000**	**0**	**0**	**1,340,341**
Stockpile systems					
B61 Stockpile systems	57,313				57,313
W76 Stockpile systems	38,604				38,604
W78 Stockpile systems	56,413				56,413
W80 Stockpile systems	64,631				64,631
B83 Stockpile systems	41,659				41,659
W87 Stockpile systems	81,982				81,982
W88 Stockpile systems	103,074				103,074
Total, Stockpile systems	**443,676**	**0**	**0**	**0**	**443,676**
Weapons dismantlement and disposition					
Operations and maintenance	68,984	−14,000	−12,750	−12,984	56,000
Denial of dismantlement acceleration		[−14,000]		[−12,984]	
Program Reduction			[−12,750]		
Stockpile services					
Production support	457,043				457,043
Research and development support	34,187				34,187
R&D certification and safety	156,481	46,000			156,481
Stockpile Responsiveness Program and technology maturation efforts		[46,000]			
Management, technology, and production	251,978				251,978
Total, Stockpile services	**899,689**	**46,000**	**0**	**0**	**899,689**
Nuclear material commodities					
Uranium sustainment	20,988				20,988
Plutonium sustainment	184,970	6,000			184,970
Mitigation of schedule risk for meeting statutory pit production requirements		[6,000]			
Tritium sustainment	109,787				109,787
Domestic uranium enrichment	50,000				50,000
Strategic materials sustainment	212,092				212,092
Total, Nuclear material commodities	**577,837**	**6,000**	**0**	**0**	**577,837**
Total, Directed stockpile work	**3,330,527**	**59,000**	**−12,750**	**−12,984**	**3,317,543**
Research, development, test and evaluation (RDT&E)					
Science					
Advanced certification	58,000				58,000
Primary assessment technologies	99,000	12,000			99,000
Support to Prototype Nuclear Weapons for Intelligence Estimates program		[12,000]			
Dynamic materials properties	106,000				106,000
Advanced radiography	50,500				50,500
Secondary assessment technologies	76,000				76,000
Academic alliances and partnerships	52,484				52,484
Total, Science	**441,984**	**12,000**	**0**	**0**	**441,984**

SEC. 4701. DEPARTMENT OF ENERGY NATIONAL SECURITY PROGRAMS
(In Thousands of Dollars)

Program	FY 2017 Request	House Authorized	Senate Authorized	Conference Change	Conference Authorized
Engineering					
Enhanced surety	37,196	16,000			37,196
Stockpile Responsiveness Program and technology maturation efforts		[16,000]			
Weapon systems engineering assessment technology	16,958				16,958
Nuclear survivability	43,105	4,000			43,105
Improve planning and coordination on strategic radiation-hardened micro-systems		[4,000]			
Enhanced surveillance	42,228				42,228
Total, Engineering	**139,487**	**20,000**	**0**	**0**	**139,487**
Inertial confinement fusion ignition and high yield					
Ignition	75,432	−5,000			75,432
Program decrease		[−5,000]			
Support of other stockpile programs	23,363				23,363
Diagnostics, cryogenics and experimental support	68,696				68,696
Pulsed power inertial confinement fusion	5,616				5,616
Joint program in high energy density laboratory plasmas	9,492				9,492
Facility operations and target production	340,360	−4,000			340,360
Program decrease		[−4,000]			
Total, Inertial confinement fusion and high yield	**522,959**	**−9,000**	**0**	**0**	**522,959**
Advanced simulation and computing	663,184	−7,000		−7,000	656,184
Program decrease		[−7,000]		[−7,000]	
Stockpile Responsiveness Program	0		5,000	40,000	40,000
Program increase			[5,000]	[40,000]	
Advanced manufacturing					
Additive manufacturing	12,000				12,000
Component manufacturing development	46,583	31,000			46,583
Stockpile Responsiveness Program and technology maturation efforts		[31,000]			
Processing technology development	28,522				28,522
Total, Advanced manufacturing	**87,105**	**31,000**	**0**	**0**	**87,105**
Total, RDT&E	**1,854,719**	**47,000**	**5,000**	**33,000**	**1,887,719**
Infrastructure and operations (formerly RTBF)					
Operating					
Operations of facilities					
Kansas City Plant	101,000				101,000
Lawrence Livermore National Laboratory	70,500				70,500
Los Alamos National Laboratory	196,500				196,500
Nevada Test Site	92,500				92,500
Pantex	55,000				55,000
Sandia National Laboratory	118,000				118,000
Savannah River Site	83,500				83,500
Y–12 National security complex	107,000				107,000
Total, Operations of facilities	**824,000**	**0**	**0**	**0**	**824,000**
Safety and environmental operations	110,000				110,000
Maintenance and repair of facilities	294,000	30,000		30,000	324,000
Address high-priority preventative maintenance		[30,000]		[30,000]	
Recapitalization:					
Infrastructure and safety	554,643	120,000		75,866	630,509
Address high-priority deferred maintenance		[120,000]		[75,866]	
Capability based investment	112,639				112,639
Total, Recapitalization	**667,282**	**120,000**	**0**	**75,866**	**743,148**

SEC. 4701. DEPARTMENT OF ENERGY NATIONAL SECURITY PROGRAMS
(In Thousands of Dollars)

Program	FY 2017 Request	House Authorized	Senate Authorized	Conference Change	Conference Authorized
Construction:					
17–D–640 U1a Complex Enhancements Project, NNSS	11,500				11,500
17–D–630 Electrical Infrastructure Upgrades, LLNL	25,000				25,000
16–D–515 Albuquerque complex upgrades project	15,047				15,047
15–D–613 Emergency Operations Center, Y–12	2,000				2,000
15–D–302 TA–55 Reinvestment project, Phase 3, LANL	21,455				21,455
07–D–220–04 Transuranic liquid waste facility, LANL	17,053				17,053
06–D–141 PED/Construction, UPF Y–12, Oak Ridge, TN	575,000				575,000
04–D–125–04 RLUOB equipment installation	159,615				159,615
Total, Construction	**826,670**	**0**	**0**	**0**	**826,670**
Total, Infrastructure and operations	**2,721,952**	**150,000**	**0**	**105,866**	**2,827,818**
Secure transportation asset					
Operations and equipment	179,132				179,132
Program direction	103,600				103,600
Total, Secure transportation asset	**282,732**	**0**	**0**	**0**	**282,732**
Defense nuclear security					
Operations and maintenance	657,133	60,000		36,000	693,133
Support to physical security infrastructure recapitalization and CSTART		[60,000]		[36,000]	
Construction:					
14–D–710 Device assembly facility argus installation project, NV	13,000				13,000
17–D–710 West end protected area reduction project, Y–12	0			24,000	24,000
Total, Defense nuclear security	**670,133**	**60,000**	**0**	**60,000**	**730,133**
Information technology and cybersecurity	176,592				176,592
Legacy contractor pensions	248,492				248,492
Rescission of prior year balances	–42,000				–42,000
Total, Weapons Activities	**9,243,147**	**316,000**	**–7,750**	**185,882**	**9,429,029**
Defense Nuclear Nonproliferation					
Defense Nuclear Nonproliferation Programs					
Defense Nuclear Nonproliferation R&D					
Global material security	337,108	–5,000			337,108
Program decrease		[–5,000]			
Material management and minimization	341,094	–82,400		–20,000	321,094
Program decrease		[–82,400]		[–20,000]	
Nonproliferation and arms control	124,703				124,703
Defense Nuclear Nonproliferation R&D	393,922	24,000		24,000	417,922
Acceleration of low-yield detection experiments		[4,000]		[4,000]	
Nuclear detection technology and new challenges such as 3D printing		[20,000]		[20,000]	
Low Enriched Uranium R&D for Naval Reactors	0	5,000		5,000	5,000
Low Enriched Uranium R&D for Naval Reactors		[5,000]		[5,000]	
Nonproliferation Construction:					
99–D–143 Mixed Oxide (MOX) Fuel Fabrication Facility, SRS	270,000	70,000	70,000	70,000	340,000
Increase to support construction		[70,000]	[70,000]	[70,000]	
Total, Nonproliferation construction	**270,000**	**70,000**	**70,000**	**70,000**	**340,000**
Total, Defense Nuclear Nonproliferation Programs	**1,466,827**	**11,600**	**70,000**	**79,000**	**1,545,827**
Legacy contractor pensions	83,208				83,208
Nuclear counterterrorism and incident response program	271,881				271,881
Rescission of prior year balances	–14,000				–14,000
Total, Defense Nuclear Nonproliferation	**1,807,916**	**11,600**	**70,000**	**79,000**	**1,886,916**

SEC. 4701. DEPARTMENT OF ENERGY NATIONAL SECURITY PROGRAMS
(In Thousands of Dollars)

Program	FY 2017 Request	House Authorized	Senate Authorized	Conference Change	Conference Authorized
Naval Reactors					
Naval reactors operations and infrastructure	449,682			−2,500	447,182
Naval reactors development	437,338				437,338
Ohio replacement reactor systems development	213,700				213,700
S8G Prototype refueling	124,000				124,000
Program direction	47,100				47,100
Construction:					
17–D–911, BL Fire System Upgrade	1,400				1,400
15–D–904 NRF Overpack Storage Expansion 3	700				700
15–D–902 KS Engineroom team trainer facility	33,300				33,300
14–D–901 Spent fuel handling recapitalization project, NRF	100,000				100,000
10–D–903, Security upgrades, KAPL	12,900				12,900
Total, Construction	**148,300**	**0**	**0**	**0**	**148,300**
Total, Naval Reactors	**1,420,120**	**0**	**0**	**−2,500**	**1,417,620**
Federal Salaries And Expenses					
Program direction	412,817	−40,000		−17,300	395,517
Program decrease		[−40,000]		[−17,300]	
Total, Office Of The Administrator	**412,817**	**−40,000**	**0**	**−17,300**	**395,517**
Defense Environmental Cleanup					
Closure sites:					
Closure sites administration	9,389				9,389
Hanford site:					
River corridor and other cleanup operations	69,755	45,000		45,000	114,755
Acceleration of priority programs		[45,000]		[45,000]	
Central plateau remediation	620,869	8,000		23,500	644,369
Acceleration of priority programs		[8,000]		[23,500]	
Richland community and regulatory support	14,701				14,701
Construction:					
15–D–401 Containerized sludge removal annex, RL	11,486				11,486
Total, Hanford site	**716,811**	**53,000**	**0**	**68,500**	**785,311**
Idaho National Laboratory:					
Idaho cleanup and waste disposition	359,088				359,088
Idaho community and regulatory support	3,000				3,000
Total, Idaho National Laboratory	**362,088**	**0**	**0**	**0**	**362,088**
Los Alamos National Laboratory					
EMLA cleanup activities	185,606		10,000	10,000	195,606
Program Increase			[10,000]	[10,000]	
EMLA community and regulatory support	3,394				3,394
Total, Los Alamos National Laboratory	**189,000**	**0**	**10,000**	**10,000**	**199,000**
NNSA sites					
Lawrence Livermore National Laboratory	1,396				1,396
Separations Process Research Unit	3,685				3,685
Nevada	62,176				62,176
Sandia National Laboratories	4,130				4,130
Total, NNSA sites and Nevada off-sites	**71,387**	**0**	**0**	**0**	**71,387**
Oak Ridge Reservation:					
OR Nuclear facility D & D					

SEC. 4701. DEPARTMENT OF ENERGY NATIONAL SECURITY PROGRAMS
(In Thousands of Dollars)

Program	FY 2017 Request	House Authorized	Senate Authorized	Conference Change	Conference Authorized
OR Nuclear facility D & D	93,851				93,851
Construction:					
14–D–403 Outfall 200 Mercury Treatment Facility	5,100				5,100
Total, OR Nuclear facility D & D	98,951	0	0	0	98,951
U233 Disposition Program	37,311				37,311
OR cleanup and disposition	54,557				54,557
OR reservation community and regulatory support	4,400				4,400
Oak Ridge technology development	3,000				3,000
Total, Oak Ridge Reservation	198,219	0	0	0	198,219
Office of River Protection:					
Waste treatment and immobilization plant					
WTP operations	3,000				3,000
15–D–409 Low activity waste pretreatment system, ORP	73,000				73,000
01–D–416 A–D/ORP–0060 / Major construction	690,000				690,000
Total, Waste treatment and immobilization plant	766,000	0	0	0	766,000
Tank farm activities					
Rad liquid tank waste stabilization and disposition	721,456				721,456
Total, Tank farm activities	721,456	0	0	0	721,456
Total, Office of River protection	1,487,456	0	0	0	1,487,456
Savannah River sites:					
Nuclear Material Management	311,062				311,062
Environmental Cleanup	152,504				152,504
SR community and regulatory support	11,249				11,249
Radioactive liquid tank waste:					
Radioactive liquid tank waste stabilization and disposition	645,332				645,332
Construction:					
15–D–402—Saltstone Disposal Unit #6, SRS	7,577				7,577
17–D–401—Saltstone Disposal Unit #7	9,729				9,729
05–D–405 Salt waste processing facility, Savannah River Site	160,000				160,000
Total, Construction	177,306	0	0	0	177,306
Total, Radioactive liquid tank waste	822,638	0	0	0	822,638
Total, Savannah River site	1,297,453	0	0	0	1,297,453
Waste Isolation Pilot Plant					
Operations and maintenance	257,188		10,000	10,000	267,188
Program increase			[10,000]	[10,000]	
Construction:					
15–D–411 Safety significant confinement ventilation system, WIPP	2,532				2,532
15–D–412 Exhaust shaft, WIPP	2,533				2,533
Total, Construction	5,065	0	0	0	5,065
Total, Waste Isolation Pilot Plant	262,253	0	10,000	10,000	272,253
Program direction	290,050				290,050
Program support	14,979				14,979
Safeguards and Security	255,973				255,973
Technology development	30,000	10,000			30,000
NAS study on technology development, acceleration of priority efforts		[10,000]			
Infrastructure recapitalization	41,892			–41,892	0
Defense Uranium enrichment D&D	155,100	–155,100	–155,100	–155,100	0
Ahead of need		[–155,100]	[–155,100]	[–155,100]	
Subtotal, Defense environmental cleanup	5,382,050	–92,100	–135,100	–108,492	5,273,558

SEC. 4701. DEPARTMENT OF ENERGY NATIONAL SECURITY PROGRAMS
(In Thousands of Dollars)

Program	FY 2017 Request	House Authorized	Senate Authorized	Conference Change	Conference Authorized
Total, Defense Environmental Cleanup	5,382,050	−92,100	−135,100	−108,492	5,273,558
Other Defense Activities					
Environment, health, safety and security					
Environment, health, safety and security	130,693			−2,000	128,693
Program direction	66,519				66,519
Total, Environment, health, safety and security	197,212	0	0	−2,000	195,212
Independent enterprise assessments					
Independent enterprise assessments	24,580				24,580
Program direction	51,893				51,893
Total, Independent enterprise assessments	76,473	0	0	0	76,473
Specialized security activities	237,912	9,000			237,912
IT infrastructure and red teaming		[9,000]			
Office of Legacy Management					
Legacy management	140,306				140,306
Program direction	14,014				14,014
Total, Office of Legacy Management	154,320	0	0	0	154,320
Defense-related activities					
Defense related administrative support					
Chief financial officer	23,642				23,642
Chief information officer	93,074				93,074
Project management oversight and assessments	3,000				3,000
Total, Defense related administrative support	119,716	0	0	0	116,716
Office of hearings and appeals	5,919				5,919
Subtotal, Other defense activities	791,552	9,000	0	−2,000	789,552
Total, Other Defense Activities	791,552	9,000	0	−2,000	789,552

DIVISION E—UNIFORM CODE OF MILITARY JUSTICE REFORM

Short title (sec. 5001)

The Senate bill contained a provision (sec. 5001) that would provide that the short title for this division may be cited as the "Military Justice Act of 2016".

The House amendment contained an identical provision (sec. 6000).

The conference agreement includes this provision.

TITLE LI—GENERAL PROVISIONS

Definitions (sec. 5101)

The Senate bill contained a provision (sec. 5101) that would amend section 801 of title 10, United States Code, (Article 1, Uniform Code of Military Justice (UCMJ)) to amend the definition of "judge advocate"; to reflect the change within the Department of the Air Force from the "Judge Advocate General's Department" to the "Judge Advocate General's Corps"; and to amend the definition of "military judge" to conform to the proposed changes in Article 30a of the Uniform Code of Military Justice (10 U.S.C. 830a) allowing military judges to address certain matters prior to referral of charges.

The House amendment contained a similar provision (sec. 6101).

The House recedes.

Clarification of persons subject to UCMJ while on inactive-duty training (sec. 5102)

The Senate bill contained a provision (sec. 5102) that would amend section 802 of title 10, United States Code, (Article 2, Uniform Code of Military Justice (UCMJ)) that would clarify jurisdiction for reserve component members during time periods incidental to Inactive-Duty Training (IDT).

The House amendment contained an identical provision (sec. 6002).

The conference agreement includes this provision.

Staff judge advocate disqualification due to prior involvement in case (sec. 5103)

The Senate bill contained a provision (sec. 5103) that would amend section 806 of title 10, United States Code, (Article 6, Uniform Code of Military Justice (UCMJ)) to include appellate judges and counsel, including special victims' counsel, who have acted in the same case or in any proceeding before a military judge, preliminary hearing officer, or appellate court, in those disqualified to serve as a staff judge advocate or legal officer to any reviewing or convening authority on the same case.

The House amendment contained an identical provision (sec. 6003).

The conference agreement includes this provision.

Conforming amendment relating to military magistrates (sec. 5104)

The Senate bill contained a provision (sec. 5104) that would amend section 806a of title 10, United States Code, (Article 6a, Uniform Code of Military Justice (UCMJ)) to conform Article 6a, UCMJ, with the provision to allow the detailing of military magistrates to proceedings under Article 30a and to add "military magistrates" to the list of officials whose fitness to perform duties shall be subject to investigation and disposition under regulations prescribed by the President.

The House amendment contained an identical provision (sec. 6004).

The conference agreement includes this provision.

Rights of victim (sec. 5105)

The Senate bill contained a provision (sec. 5104) that would amend section 806b(c) of title 10, United States Code (Article 6b(c), Uniform Code of Military Justice (UCMJ)) to authorize military judges to decide on a case-by-case basis whether it is appropriate to appoint an individual to assume the victim's rights in all cases under the UCMJ in which the victim of an offense is under 18 years of age (unless the victim is a member of the Armed Forces) or is incompetent, incapacitated, or deceased.

The Senate bill also contained a provision (sec. 5105) that would amend section 806b of title 10, United States Code, (Article 6b, UCMJ), to clarify the relationship between the rights of victims and the disposition of offenses, as well as the procedures for judicial appointment of individuals to assume the rights of certain victims. The provision would also modify Article 6b, UCMJ, to incorporate procedures on defense counsel interviews of victims of sex-related offenses into Article 6b, UCMJ, and would extend those procedures to victims of all offenses, consistent with related victims' rights provisions.

The House amendment contained a provision (sec. 6005) that is identical to the Senate provision (sec. 5105).

The conference agreement includes the identical provisions.

TITLE LII—APPREHENSION AND RESTRAINT

Restraint of persons charged (sec. 5121)

The Senate bill contained a provision (sec. 5121) that would amend section 810 of title 10, United States Code, (Article 10, Uniform Code of Military Justice (UCMJ)) to conform the language of the section to reflect current military justice practice regarding the arrest or confinement of an individual who is charged with an offense under the UCMJ. Additionally, it would amend Article 10 to require forwarding of charges and, when applicable, the preliminary hearing report, whenever a person is ordered into arrest or confinement before trial.

The House amendment contained an identical provision (sec. 6101).

The conference agreement includes this provision.

Modification of prohibition of confinement of members of the Armed Forces with enemy prisoners and certain others (sec. 5122)

The Senate bill contained a provision (sec. 5122) that would amend section 812 of title 10, United States Code, (Article 12, Uniform Code of Military Justice (UCMJ)) to limit the prohibition on confining military members with foreign nationals to situations where the foreign nationals are not members of the U.S. Armed Forces and are detained under the law of war.

The House amendment contained an identical provision (sec. 6102).

The conference agreement includes this provision.

TITLE LIII—NON-JUDICIAL PUNISHMENT

Modification of confinement as non-judicial punishment (sec. 5141)

The Senate bill contained a provision (sec. 5141) that would amend section 815 of title 10, United States Code, (Article 15, Uniform Code of Military Justice (UCMJ)) to remove punishment in the form of confinement on a diet limited to bread and water from the list of authorized punishments.

The House amendment contained an identical provision (sec. 6201).

The conference agreement includes this provision.

TITLE LIV—COURT-MARTIAL JURISDICTION

Courts-martial classified (sec. 5161)

The Senate bill contained a provision (sec. 5161) that would amend section 816 of title 10, United States Code, (Article 16, Uniform Code of Military Justice (UCMJ)) to establish standard panel sizes in all courts-martial: 8 members in a general court-martial (subject to the requirements of Article 25a in capital cases), and 4 members in a special court-martial. The provision would require a military judge to be detailed to all special courts-martial and would provide the mili-

tary justice system with an option for a judge-alone trial by special court-martial, with confinement limited to 6 months or less, as reflected in the proposed changes to Article 19, UCMJ.

The House amendment contained an identical provision (sec. 6301).

The conference agreement includes this provision.

Jurisdiction of general courts-martial (sec. 5162)

The Senate bill contained a provision (sec. 5162) that would amend section 818 of title 10, United States Code, (Article 18, Uniform Code of Military Justice (UCMJ)) to conform Article 18 to the proposed changes to Article 16 concerning the types of general courts-martial and the proposed changes to Article 56 concerning sex-related offenses.

The House amendment contained a similar provision (sec. 6302).

The House recedes.

Jurisdiction of special courts-martial (sec. 5163)

The Senate bill contained a provision (sec. 5163) that would amend section 819 of title 10, United States Code, (Article 19, Uniform Code of Military Justice (UCMJ)) to conform to the proposal in Article 16, UCMJ, that would authorize special courts-martial to be referred for trial by military judge-alone, and to authorize a military judge to designate a military magistrate to preside over trials, and to conform to current practice requiring a military judge, qualified defense counsel, and a recorder at every special court-martial.

The House amendment contained an identical provision (sec. 6303).

The conference agreement includes this provision.

Summary court-martial as non-criminal forum (sec. 5164)

The Senate bill contained a provision (sec. 5164) that would amend section 820 of title 10, United States Code, (Article 20, Uniform Code of Military Justice (UCMJ)) by adding a new subsection defining the summary court-martial as a non-criminal forum and clarifying that a finding of guilty at a summary court-martial does not constitute a criminal conviction.

The House amendment contained an identical provision (sec. 6304).

The conference agreement includes this provision.

TITLE LV—COMPOSITION OF COURTS-MARTIAL

Technical amendment relating to persons authorized to convene general courts-martial (sec. 5181)

The Senate bill contained a provision (sec. 5181) that would amend section 822 of title 10, United States Code, (Article 22, Uniform Code of Military Justice (UCMJ)) by removing the words "in chief" to reflect the current terminology for the commander of a naval fleet.

The House amendment contained an identical provision (sec. 6401).

The conference agreement includes this provision.

Who may serve on courts-martial and related matters (sec. 5182)

The Senate bill contained a provision (sec. 5182) that would amend section 825 of title 10, United States Code, (Article 25, Uniform Code of Military Justice (UCMJ)) to permit convening authorities to detail enlisted personnel to court-martial panels, subject to the accused's ability to specifically elect an all-officer panel, under the same rules and procedures with which an accused may elect one-third enlisted panel membership; to remove the statutory prohibition against de-

tailing enlisted members to courts-martial who are from the same unit as an enlisted accused; and to conform to the proposed amendments to Article 29, UCMJ, concerning impaneling of members.

The House amendment contained a similar provision (sec. 6402).

The House recedes with an amendment that would establish that sentencing in courts-martial in which members convict the accused for any offense would be by military judge alone unless, after the findings are announced and before any matter is presented in the sentencing phase, the accused requests sentencing by members. The amendment retains the requirement for sentencing by members in capital cases for which the court-martial may sentence the accused to death.

The Department of Defense Military Justice Review Group recommended that sentencing should be by military judge alone in all cases except in capital cases for which the court-martial may sentence the accused to death. There may be non-capital cases in which an accused prefers that his or her sentence should be determined by members. The conferees determined that it would be appropriate to allow an accused found guilty by a court-martial with a military judge and members the option to select members for sentencing. The conferees further direct that the Military Justice Review Panel established elsewhere in this Act shall gather and analyze data on the frequency and sentencing outcomes in non-capital cases in which an accused requests sentencing by members and to include this information in the report to the Committees on Armed Services of the Senate and the House of Representatives required under this Act.

Number of court-martial members in capital cases (sec. 5183)

The Senate bill contained a provision (sec. 5183) that would amend section 825a of title 10, United States Code, (Article 25a, Uniform Code of Military Justice (UCMJ)) to require a fixed-size panel of twelve members in capital cases.

The House amendment contained an identical provision (sec. 6403).

The conference agreement includes this provision.

Detailing, qualifications, and other matters relating to military judges (sec. 5184)

The Senate bill contained a provision (sec. 5184) that would amend section 826 of title 10, United States Code, (Article 26, Uniform Code of Military Justice (UCMJ)) to conform the section to the current practice of detailing a military judge to every general and special court-martial; to provide for cross-service detailing of military judges; to require a chief trial judge in each armed force; and to provide appropriate criteria for service as a military judge. The provision would also authorize the President to establish uniform regulations concerning minimum tour lengths for military judges with provisions for early reassignment as necessary.

The House amendment contained a similar provision (sec. 6404).

The House recedes.

Military magistrates (sec. 5185)

The Senate bill contained a provision (sec. 5178) that would amend chapter 47 of title 10, United States Code, to add a new section 826a (Article 26a of the Uniform Code of Military Justice (UCMJ)) to establish the minimum qualifications for military magistrates, and to provide that military magistrates may be assigned under service regulations to perform duties other than those described under Articles 19 and 30a.

The House amendment contained a similar provision.

The House recedes (sec. 6407).

Qualifications of trial counsel and defense counsel (sec. 5186)

The Senate bill contained a provision (sec. 5185) that would amend section 827 of title 10, United States Code, (Article 27, Uniform Code of Military Justice (UCMJ)) to provide that an individual who has served as a preliminary hearing officer, court member, military judge, military magistrate, or appellate judge on a case may not later serve as trial counsel on that case. The provision would require that all defense counsel detailed to general or special courts-martial must be qualified under Article 27(b), and all trial counsel and assistant trial counsel detailed to special courts-martial, and all assistant trial counsel detailed to general courts-martial, must be determined to be competent to perform such duties under regulations prescribed by the President. The provision would also require, to the greatest extent practicable, at least one defense counsel detailed for a court-martial in a case in which the death penalty may be adjudged shall be learned in the law applicable to capital cases.

The House amendment contained a similar provision (sec. 6405).

The House recedes.

Assembly and impaneling of members and related matters (sec. 5187)

The Senate bill contained a provision (sec. 5186) that would amend section 829 of title 10, United States Code, (Article 29, Uniform Code of Military Justice (UCMJ)) to clarify the function of assembly and impanelment in general and special courts-martial with members, and the limited situations in which members may be absent from the court-martial after assembly; to provide for the impaneling of 12 members in a capital general court-martial, 8 members in a non-capital general court-martial, and 4 members in a special court-martial; to authorize (but not require) the convening authority to direct the use of alternate members; and to authorize non-capital general courts-martial to proceed with a minimum of 6 members if one or more members are excused for good cause after the members have been impaneled. It would further amend Article 29 to clarify that a newly-detailed court-martial member or military judge may consider the record of previously admitted evidence through the use of an electronic or other similar recording.

The House amendment contained a similar provision (sec. 6406).

The House recedes.

TITLE LVI—PRE-TRIAL PROCEDURE

Charges and specifications (sec. 5201)

The Senate bill contained a provision (sec. 5201) that would amend section 830 of title 10, United States Code, (Article 30, Uniform Code of Military Justice (UCMJ)) to reorganize the section into three subsections: (a) to provide the mode of preferring charges and specifications and the oath requirement; (b) to provide the required statement of the person who signs the charges; and (c) to prescribe the duty of a proper authority to notify the accused of the charges and to dispose of them in the interest of justice and discipline. The provision would amend Article 30 to clarify the sequence of the notification and disposition requirements and to require that both actions take place as soon as practicable.

The House amendment contained an identical provision (sec. 6501).

The conference agreement includes this provision.

Certain proceedings conducted before referral (sec. 5202)

The Senate bill contained a provision (sec. 5202) that would amend chapter 47 of title 10, United States Code, to add a new section 830a (Article 30a of the Uniform Code of Military Justice (UCMJ)) to provide statutory authority for military judges or magistrates to provide timely review, prior to referral of charges, of certain matters currently subject to judicial review only on a delayed basis at trial.

The House amendment contained no similar provision.

The House recedes with an amendment that would limit the matters which may be reviewed prior to referral of charges to pre-referral investigative subpoenas, pre-referral warrants or orders for electronic communications, and pre-referral matters referred by an appellate court.

Preliminary hearing required before referral to general court-martial (sec. 5203)

The Senate bill contained a provision (sec. 5203) that would amend section 832 of title 10, United States Code, (Article 32, Uniform Code of Military Justice (UCMJ)) to require the preliminary hearing officer to provide an analysis of information that will be useful in fulfilling the statutory responsibilities of the staff judge advocate, in providing legal determinations and a disposition recommendation to the convening authority under Article 34; and to assist the convening authority, in disposing of the charges and specifications in the interest of justice and discipline.

The House amendment contained a similar provision (sec. 6502).

The House recedes with an amendment that would include as a purpose of the preliminary hearing a recommendation as to the disposition that should be made of the case.

Disposition guidance (sec. 5204)

The Senate bill contained a provision (sec. 5204) that would amend section 833 of title 10, United States Code, (Article 33, Uniform Code of Military Justice (UCMJ)) to move the requirement for prompt forwarding of charges in cases involving pretrial arrest or confinement from Article 33 to Article 10. The provision would require the Secretary of Defense, in consultation with the Secretary of Homeland Security, to establish non-binding guidance regarding factors that commanders, convening authorities, staff judge advocates, and judge advocates may take into account when exercising their duties with respect to disposition of charges and specifications in the interest of justice and discipline.

The House amendment contained a similar provision (sec. 6503).

The Senate recedes.

Advice to convening authority before referral for trial (sec. 5205)

The Senate bill contained a provision (sec. 5205) that would amend section 834 of title 10, United States Code, (Article 34, Uniform Code of Military Justice (UCMJ)) to clarify the relationship between the staff judge advocate's advice under Article 34 and the general standard for disposition of charges and specifications under Article 30. The provision would require the convening authority to consult with a judge advocate before referral of charges to special courts-martial. The provision would clarify that formal corrections to the charges and specifications may be made before referral for trial in special courts-martial as well as in general courts-martial.

The House amendment contained a similar provision (sec. 6504).

The House recedes.

Service of charges and commencement of trial (sec. 5206)

The Senate bill contained a provision (sec. 5206) that would amend section 835 of title 10, United States Code, (Article 35, Uniform Code of Military Justice (UCMJ)) to conform procedures for service of charges and waiting period requirements to current practice and other UCMJ articles.

The House amendment contained an identical provision (sec. 6505).

The conference agreement includes this provision.

TITLE LVII—TRIAL PROCEDURE

Duties of assistant defense counsel (sec. 5221)

The Senate bill contained a provision (sec. 5221) that would amend section 838 of title 10, United States Code, (Article 38, Uniform Code of Military Justice (UCMJ)) to require all defense counsel, including assistant defense counsel, to be qualified under Article 27(b), UCMJ.

The House amendment contained an identical provision (sec. 6601).

The conference agreement includes this provision.

Sessions (sec. 5222)

The Senate bill contained a provision (sec. 5222) that would amend section 839 of title 10, United States Code, (Article 39, Uniform Code of Military Justice (UCMJ)) to establish uniform requirements for arraignment by a military judge and to eliminate references to courts-martial without a military judge, and to conform to the provision under Article 53 to authorize judicial sentencing in all non-capital general courts-martial and all special courts-martial.

The House amendment contained a similar provision (sec. 6602).

The Senate recedes with an amendment to conform to the provision under Article 25, UCMJ, as amended in a separate provision in this Act, that would provide an accused the option to request sentencing by members.

Technical amendment relating to continuances (sec. 5223)

The Senate bill contained a provision (sec. 5223) that would amend section 840 of title 10, United States Code, (Article 40, Uniform Code of Military Justice (UCMJ)) to eliminate references to courts-martial without a military judge, and to clarify that the authority to grant continuances extends to summary courts-martial.

The House amendment contained an identical provision (sec. 6603).

The conference agreement includes this provision.

Conforming amendments relating to challenges (sec. 5224)

The Senate bill contained a provision (sec. 5224) that would amend section 841 of title 10, United States Code, (Article 41, Uniform Code of Military Justice (UCMJ)) to conform the section with changes proposed to amend Article 16 concerning fixed panel sizes and to eliminate special courts-martial without a military judge.

The House amendment contained a similar provision (sec. 6604).

The Senate recedes with a technical amendment.

Statute of limitations (sec. 5225)

The Senate bill contained a provision (sec. 5225) that would amend section 843 of title 10,

United States Code, (Article 43, Uniform Code of Military Justice (UCMJ)) to extend the statute of limitations applicable to child abuse offenses from the current 5 years or the life of the child, whichever is longer, to 10 years or life of the child, whichever is longer. The provision would extend the statute of limitations for Article 83 fraudulent enlistment cases from 5 years to: (1) the length of the enlistment, in the case of enlisted members; (2) the length of the appointment, in the case of officers; or (3) 5 years, whichever is longer. The provision would extend the statute of limitations when DNA testing implicates an identified person in the commission of an offense by excluding periods prior to the DNA identification in computing the period of limitations.

The House amendment contained a similar provision (sec. 6605).

The House recedes with a technical amendment.

Former jeopardy (sec. 5226)

The Senate bill contained a provision (sec. 5226) that would amend section 844 of title 10, United States Code, (Article 44, Uniform Code of Military Justice (UCMJ)) to more closely align double jeopardy protections under the UCMJ with federal civilian practice.

The House amendment contained an identical provision (sec. 6606).

The conference agreement includes this provision.

Pleas of the accused (sec. 5227)

The Senate bill contained a provision (sec. 5227) that would amend section 845 of title 10, United States Code, (Article 45, Uniform Code of Military Justice (UCMJ)) to permit an accused to plead guilty in capital cases where a sentence of death is not mandatory. The provision would delete the reference to a court-martial without a military judge. The provision would eliminate the need for separate service regulations authorizing entry of findings upon acceptance of a guilty plea. The provision would add a new subsection to provide for harmless error review in guilty plea cases.

The House amendment contained a similar provision (sec. 6607).

The House recedes.

Subpoena and other process (sec. 5228)

The Senate bill contained a provision (sec. 5228) that would amend section 846 of title 10, United States Code, (Article 46, Uniform Code of Military Justice (UCMJ)) to clarify the authority to issue and enforce subpoenas for witnesses and other evidence, to allow subpoenas duces tecum to be issued for investigations of offenses under the UCMJ when authorized by a general court-martial convening authority, and to authorize military judges to issue warrants and orders for the production of stored electronic communications under the Stored Communications Act (sections 2701–2712 of chapter 121, title 18, United States Code).

The House amendment contained no similar provision.

The House recedes with an amendment that would authorize a military judge to issue an investigative subpoena before referral of charges to a court-martial.

Refusal of person not subject to UCMJ to appear, testify, or produce evidence (sec. 5229)

The Senate bill contained a provision (sec. 5229) that would amend section 847 of title 10, United States Code, (Article 47, Uniform Code of Military Justice (UCMJ)) to provide that a person not subject to the UCMJ who fails to comply with military subpoenas issued under Article 46, UCMJ, is guilty of an offense against the United States.

The House amendment contained no similar provision.

The House recedes.

Contempt (sec. 5230)

The Senate bill contained a provision (sec. 5230) that would amend section 848 of title 10, United States Code, (Article 48, Uniform Code of Military Justice (UCMJ)) to authorize the contempt power for military judges and military magistrates detailed to pre-referral proceedings under the proposed Article 30a. The provision would also clarify that judges on the United States Court of Appeals for the Armed Forces and the service courts of criminal appeals do not have to be detailed to cases or proceedings in order to exercise the contempt power under this article. The provision would clarify that the president (as opposed to the judge) of a court of inquiry is vested with the contempt power, and would provide for appellate review of contempt punishments consistent with the review of other orders and judgments under the UCMJ.

The House amendment contained a similar provision (sec. 6608).

The House recedes with an amendment that would exclude commissioned officers detailed as a summary court-martial from the officials authorized to punish a person for contempt.

Depositions (sec. 5231)

The Senate bill contained a provision (sec. 5231) that would amend section 849 of title 10, United States Code, (Article 49, Uniform Code of Military Justice (UCMJ)) to conform the UCMJ with the language and function of Federal Rule of Criminal Procedure 15(a)(1), and to move the procedural aspects of Article 49 to Rules for Courts-Martial 702. The provision would clarify that a convening authority or a military judge may order depositions only if the requesting party demonstrates that, due to exceptional circumstances, it is in the interest of justice that the testimony of a prospective witness be preserved for use at a court-martial, military commission, court of inquiry, or other military court or board. The provision would clarify parties who may request a deposition, and require that, whenever practicable, depositions be taken before an impartial judge advocate. The provision would provide that: (1) representation of the parties with respect to a deposition shall be by counsel detailed in the same manner as trial counsel and defense counsel are detailed under Article 27; and (2) the accused shall have the right to be represented by civilian or military counsel in the same manner as such counsel are provided for in Article 38(b). The provision would clarify situations in which depositions may be used in military proceedings with a more direct reference to the military rules of evidence. The provision would amend the section to provide that testimony by deposition may be presented in capital cases only by the defense.

The House amendment contained an identical provision (sec. 6609).

The conference agreement includes this provision.

Admissibility of sworn testimony by audiotape or videotape from records of courts of inquiry (sec. 5232)

The Senate bill contained a provision (sec. 5232) that would amend section 850 of title 10, United States Code, (Article 50, Uniform Code of Military Justice (UCMJ)) to authorize sworn testimony from a court of inquiry to be played, in addition to read, into evidence in courts-martial and military commissions not established under section 948a, et seq., of title 10, United States Code, when it is otherwise admissible under the rules of evidence.

The House amendment contained a similar provision (sec. 6610).

The House recedes.

Conforming amendment relating to defense of lack of mental responsibility (sec. 5233)

The Senate bill contained a provision (sec. 5233) that would amend section 850a of title 10, United States Code, (Article 50a, Uniform Code of Military Justice (UCMJ)) to delete provisions pertaining to courts-martial without a military judge.

The House amendment contained an identical provision (sec. 6611).

The conference agreement includes this provision.

Voting and rulings (sec. 5234)

The Senate bill contained a provision (sec. 5234) that would amend section 851 of title 10, United States Code, (Article 51, Uniform Code of Military Justice (UCMJ)) to delete references pertaining to courts-martial without a military judge.

The House amendment contained an identical provision (sec. 6612).

The conference agreement includes this provision.

Votes required for conviction, sentencing, and other matters (sec. 5235)

The Senate bill contained a provision (sec. 5235) that would amend section 852 of title 10, United States Code, (Article 52, Uniform Code of Military Justice (UCMJ)) to require concurrence of at least three-fourths of the members present, and to require concurrence of at least three-fourths of the members present on offenses in a case referred for trial as a capital case where there was not a unanimous finding of guilty. The provision would eliminate the language concerning tie votes on challenges, motions, and other questions, which is applicable only to special courts-martial without a military judge, and which would no longer be necessary given the provision in Article 16, UCMJ, that would eliminate these members-only courts-martial.

The House amendment contained an identical provision (sec. 6613).

The conference agreement includes this provision.

Findings and sentencing (sec. 5236)

The Senate bill contained a provision (sec. 5236) that would amend section 853 of title 10, United States Code, (Article 53, Uniform Code of Military Justice (UCMJ)) to require sentencing by a military judge in all non-capital general and special courts-martial. The provision would require that, in cases where the accused may be sentenced to death, the members shall participate in the sentence determination.

The House amendment contained no similar provision.

The House recedes with an amendment to conform to the provision under Article 25, UCMJ, as amended in a separate provision in this Act, that would provide an accused an option to request sentencing by members.

Plea agreements (sec. 5237)

The Senate bill contained a provision (sec. 5237) that would amend chapter 47 of title 10, United States Code to add a new section 853a (Article 53a, Uniform Code of Military Justice (UCMJ)) that would authorize: (1) construction and negotiation of charge and sentence agreements; (2) military judges to determine whether to accept a proposed plea agreement; and (3) the operation of sentence agreements with respect to the military judge's sentencing authority. The new Article 53a would provide that the military judge shall accept any lawful sentence agreement submitted by the parties, except that: (1) in the case of an offense with a sentencing parameter under Article 56, the military judge may reject the agreement only if it proposes a sentence that is both outside the sentencing parameter and plainly unreasonable; and (2) in the case of an offense without a sentencing parameter, the military judge may reject the agreement only if it proposes a sentence that is plainly unreasonable.

The House amendment contained a similar provision (sec. 6614) that did not include the authority for the military judge to reject a sentencing provision that the military judge determines is plainly unreasonable.

The Senate recedes.

Record of trial (sec. 5238)

The Senate bill contained a provision (sec. 5238) that would amend section 854 of title 10, United States Code, (Article 54, Uniform Code of Military Justice (UCMJ)) to require certification of the record by a court reporter. The provision would require a complete record in any general or special court-martial if the sentence includes death, dismissal, discharge, or confinement or forfeitures of pay for more than 6 months. The provision would provide all victims who testify at a court-martial with access to records of trial.

The House amendment contained a similar provision (sec. 6615).

The House recedes with a technical amendment.

TITLE LVIII—SENTENCES

Sentencing (sec. 5301)

The Senate bill contained a provision (sec. 5261) that would amend section 856 of title 10, United States Code, (Article 56, Uniform Code of Military Justice (UCMJ)) to replace the court-martial practice of "unitary" sentencing with "segmented" sentencing where, if confinement is adjudged for guilty findings, the amount of confinement for each guilty finding would be determined separately. The provision would also authorize segmented sentencing for fines. The provision would authorize sentencing parameters and criteria to provide guidance to military judges in determining an appropriate sentence and would authorize the United States to appeal a sentence to the Court of Criminal Appeals. The provision would incorporate Article 56a, authorizing a sentence of confinement for life without the eligibility of parole any time a life sentence is authorized, into Article 56, UCMJ, without substantive change.

The House amendment contained a similar provision (sec. 6701) that did not include sentencing parameters.

The Senate recedes with an amendment to conform to the provision under Article 25, UCMJ, as amended in a separate provision in this Act, that would provide an accused the option to request sentencing by members. In cases in which the accused has elected sentencing by members the court-martial will announce a single sentence for all the offenses for which an accused was found guilty.

Effective date of sentences (sec. 5302)

The Senate bill contained a provision (sec. 5262) that would amend section 857 of title 10, United States Code, (Article 57, Uniform Code of Military Justice (UCMJ)) to consolidate portions of Article 57 and 57a that govern deferment of sentences, and portions of Articles 57 and 71 that govern when sen-

tences become effective into Article 57, as modified. The provision would make a conforming change to remove from Article 71 the authority for a convening authority to suspend a sentence under Article 71(d). The provision would strike Articles 57a and 71, because the authorities in those two Articles would be included in Article 57, as modified.

The House amendment contained a similar provision (sec. 6702).

The Senate recedes with a technical amendment.

Sentence of reduction in enlisted grade (sec. 5303)

The Senate bill contained a provision (sec. 5263) that would amend section 858a of title 10, United States Code, (Article 58a, Uniform Code of Military Justice (UCMJ)) to authorize reduction of enlisted members to the grade of E–1 whenever the approved sentence of a court-martial includes a punitive discharge, confinement, or hard labor without confinement.

The House amendment contained a similar provision (sec. 6703).

The Senate recedes.

TITLE LIX—POST-TRIAL PROCEDURE AND REVIEW OF COURTS-MARTIAL

Post-trial processing in general and special courts-martial (sec. 5321)

The Senate bill contained a provision (sec. 5281) that would amend section 860 of title 10, United States Code, (Article 60, Uniform Code of Military Justice (UCMJ)) to provide for the distribution of the trial results and to authorize post-trial motions to be filed with the military judge in general and special courts-martial.

The House amendment contained an identical provision (sec. 6801).

The conference agreement includes this provision.

Limited authority to act on sentence in specified post-trial circumstances (sec. 5322)

The Senate bill contained a provision (sec. 5282) that would amend chapter 47 of title 10, United States Code, to add a new section 860a (Article 60a, Uniform Code of Military Justice (UCMJ)) to consolidate current limitations on the convening authority's post-trial authority in most general and special courts-martial, subject to a narrowly limited suspension authority and a revised authority to adjust an adjudged sentence in cases where an accused provides substantial assistance in the investigation or prosecution of another person.

The provision would retain and clarify existing limitations on the convening authority's post-trial actions in general and special courts-martial in which: (1) the maximum sentence of confinement for any offense is more than 2 years; (2) adjudged confinement exceeds 6 months; (3) the sentence includes dismissal or discharge; or (4) the accused is found guilty of designated sex-related offenses. Under current law, the convening authority in such cases is prohibited from modifying the findings of the court-martial, or reducing, commuting, or suspending a punishment of death, confinement of more than 6 months, or a punitive discharge.

The provision would provide a limited suspension authority in specified circumstances. For the convening authority to exercise this authority, the military judge would be required to make a specific suspension recommendation in the Statement of Trial Results. The suspension authority would be limited to punishments of confinement in excess of 6 months and punitive discharges. The provision would retain, with

clarifying amendments, the key features of current law with respect to the convening authority's power to reduce the sentence of an accused who assists in the prosecution or investigation of another person. As amended, the provision would authorize the President to prescribe rules providing for a convening authority to exercise this power after entry of judgment. This provision would allow for the reduction of a sentence of an accused who provides substantial assistance in the prosecution of another person, even well after his own trial is over and appellate review is complete.

The provision would allow the accused and a victim of the offense to submit matters to the convening authority for consideration.

The provision would require the decision of the convening authority to be forwarded to the military judge. If the convening authority modified the sentence of the court-martial, the convening authority would be required to explain the reasons for the modification. An explanation for the convening authority's decision would only be required when the convening authority modifies the sentence. No approval of the findings or sentence would be required. The decision of the convening authority would be forwarded to the military judge, who would incorporate any change in the sentence into the entry of judgment. In a case where the accused provides substantial assistance and a designated convening authority reduces the sentence of the accused after entry of judgment, the convening authority's action would be forwarded to the chief trial judge, who would be responsible for ensuring appropriate modification of the entry of judgment. Because a modification might happen during or after the completion of appellate review, the modified entry of judgment would be forwarded to the Judge Advocate General for appropriate action.

The House amendment contained a similar provision (sec. 6802).

The Senate recedes with a technical amendment.

Post-trial actions in summary courts-martial and certain general and special courts-martial (sec. 5323)

The Senate bill contained a provision (sec. 5283) that would amend chapter 47 of title 10, United States Code, to add a new section 860b (Article 60b of the Uniform Code of Military Justice (UCMJ)) that would clarify the convening authority's post-trial authorities and responsibilities with respect to the findings and sentence of summary courts-martial and a limited number of general and special courts-martial which, because of the offenses charged and the sentence adjudged, would not be covered under Article 60a, UCMJ. Consistent with existing law, the convening authority in such cases would be authorized to act on the findings and the sentence, and could order rehearings, subject to certain limitations. The procedural requirements under Article 60b, including consideration of matters submitted by the accused and victim, would be the same as provided in Article 60a. In summary courts-martial, the convening authority would be required to act on the sentence, and would have discretion to act on the findings, as under current law.

The House amendment contained a similar provision (sec. 6803).

The House recedes.

Entry of judgment (sec. 5324)

The Senate bill contained a provision (sec. 5284) that would amend chapter 47 of title 10, United States Code, to create a new section 860c (Article 60c of the Uniform Code of Military Justice (UCMJ)) that would require the military judge to enter the judgment of the court-martial into the record in all general and special courts-martial, and would mark the conclusion of trial proceedings. The judgment would reflect the Statement of Trial Results, any action by the convening authority on the findings or sentence, and any post-trial rulings by the military judge. The judgment also would indicate the time when the accused's case becomes eligible for direct appeal to a service court of criminal appeals under Article 66, or for review by the Judge Advocate General under Article 65. This requirement for an entry of judgment is modeled after Federal Rules of Criminal Procedure 32(k). The findings and sentence of a summary court-martial, as modified by any post-trial action by the convening authority under Article 60b, would constitute the judgment of the court-martial.

The House amendment contained a similar provision (sec. 6804).

The House recedes with a technical amendment.

Waiver of right to appeal and withdrawal of appeal (sec. 5325)

The Senate bill contained a provision (sec. 5285) that would amend section 861 of title 10, United States Code, (Article 61, Uniform Code of Military Justice (UCMJ)) to conform the section with proposed amendments to Articles 60, 65, and 69 concerning post-trial processing.

The House amendment contained a similar provision (sec. 6805).

The Senate recedes.

Appeal by the United States (sec. 5326)

The Senate bill contained a provision (sec. 5386) that would amend section 862 of title 10, United States Code, (Article 62, Uniform Code of Military Justice (UCMJ)) to authorize the government to appeal a decision when, upon defense motion, the military judge sets aside a panel's finding of guilty because of legally insufficient evidence, except in cases where such an appeal would violate Article 44's prohibitions on double jeopardy. The provision would align the rule of construction with the similar rule applicable to interlocutory appeals in federal civilian courts. The provision would amend Article 62 to conform to the proposed revisions to the review and appeal provisions under Articles 66 and 69.

The House amendment contained a similar provision (sec. 6806).

The Senate recedes with a technical amendment.

Rehearings (sec. 5327)

The Senate bill contained a provision (sec. 5287) that would amend section 863 of title 10, United States Code, (Article 63, Uniform Code of Military Justice (UCMJ)) to remove the sentence limitation at a rehearing in cases in which an accused changes a plea from guilty to not guilty, or otherwise fails to comply with the terms of a pretrial agreement, or after a sentence is set aside based on a government appeal.

The House amendment contained a similar provision (sec. 6807).

The Senate recedes.

Judge advocate review of finding of guilty in summary court-martial (sec. 5328)

The Senate bill contained a provision (sec. 5288) that would amend section 864 of title 10, United States Code, (Article 64, Uniform Code of Military Justice (UCMJ)) to apply only to the initial review of summary courts-martial. Article 65, UCMJ, as amended, would provide for review of general and special courts-martial that do not qualify for

direct review by the service courts of criminal appeals.

The House amendment contained a similar provision (sec. 6808).

The House recedes with a technical amendment.

Transmittal and review of records (sec. 5329)

The Senate bill contained a provision (sec. 5289) that would amend section 865 of title 10, United States Code, (Article 65, Uniform Code of Military Justice (UCMJ)) to require that the record of trial be forwarded to appellate defense counsel for review whenever the case is eligible for an appeal under Article 66, and to require a review by the Judge Advocate General of all general and special court-martial cases not eligible for direct appeal under Article 66. The provision would require the Judge Advocate General to forward cases to the Court of Criminal Appeals for mandatory review if the judgment includes a sentence of death. The provision would require a review of all general and special courts-martial cases that are eligible for an appeal under Article 66, but where appeal has been waived, withdrawn, or not filed.

The House amendment contained a similar provision (sec. 6809) that did not include requirements regarding cases eligible for direct appeal.

The Senate recedes with an amendment that would provide for an automatic appeal in all cases in which the adjudged sentence includes death, dismissal, dishonorable discharge, or bad-conduct discharge, or confinement for 2 years or more.

Courts of Criminal Appeals (sec. 5330)

The Senate bill contained a provision (sec. 5290) that would amend section 866 of title 10, United States Code, (Article 66, Uniform Code of Military Justice (UCMJ)) to establish an appeal as of right in non-capital cases under the UCMJ, similar to the federal civilian appellate courts, and expand the opportunity for direct review of courts-martial convictions by the service courts of criminal appeals. The provision would provide statutory standards for factual sufficiency review, sentence appropriateness review, and review of excessive post-trial delay. The provision would provide the courts of criminal appeals with express authority to order a hearing, rehearing or remand for further proceedings as may be necessary to address a substantial issue.

The House amendment contained a similar provision (sec. 6810).

The Senate recedes with a clarifying amendment. The provision would establish appeal as of right in non-capital cases in which the sentence adjudged includes a confinement for more than six months and the case is not subject to automatic review. The provision would also provide for automatic review in cases in which the sentence adjudged includes death, dismissal, a dishonorable or bad-conduct discharge, or confinement for two years or more. The provision would also provide for consideration of appeal of a sentence by the United States.

Review by Court of Appeals for the Armed Forces (sec. 5331)

The Senate bill contained a provision (sec. 5291) that would amend section 867 of title 10, United States Code, (Article 67, Uniform Code of Military Justice (UCMJ)) to conform the section with proposed creation of an "entry of judgment" in Article 60c, UCMJ, and related amendments to Articles 60 and 66, UCMJ. The provision would require the Judge Advocate General to notify the other Judge Advocates General prior to certifying a case for review by the Court of Appeals for the Armed Forces.

The House amendment contained a similar provision (sec. 6811).

The House recedes with a technical amendment.

Supreme Court review (sec. 5332)

The Senate bill contained a provision (sec. 5292) that would make a technical amendment to section 867a of title 10, United States Code, (Article 67a, Uniform Code of Military Justice (UCMJ)).

The House amendment contained an identical provision (sec. 6812).

The conference agreement includes this provision.

Review by Judge Advocate General (sec. 5333)

The Senate bill contained a provision (sec. 5293) that would amend section 869 of title 10, United States Code, (Article 69, Uniform Code of Military Justice (UCMJ)) to authorize an accused, after a decision is issued by the Office of the Judge Advocate General under Article 69, UCMJ, to apply for discretionary review by the Court of Criminal Appeals under Article 66, UCMJ. The Judge Advocates General would retain authority to certify cases for review by the appellate courts.

The House amendment contained a similar provision (sec. 6813).

The Senate recedes with a technical amendment.

Appellate defense counsel in death penalty cases (sec. 5334)

The Senate bill contained a provision (sec. 5294) that would amend section 870 of title 10, United States Code, (Article 70, Uniform Code of Military Justice (UCMJ)) to require, to the greatest extent practicable, that in appeals of courts-martial in which the death penalty has been adjudged, at least one appellate defense counsel representing an accused must be learned in the law applicable to capital cases.

The House amendment contained an identical provision (sec. 6814).

The conference agreement includes this provision.

Authority for hearing on vacation of suspension of sentence to be conducted by qualified judge advocate (sec. 5335)

The Senate bill contained a provision (sec. 5295) that would amend section 872 of title 10, United States Code, (Article 72, Uniform Code of Military Justice (UCMJ)) to authorize a special court-martial convening authority to detail a judge advocate to conduct a hearing on the vacation of a suspended sentence.

The House amendment contained an identical provision (sec. 6815).

The conference agreement includes this provision.

Extension of time for petition for new trial (sec. 5336)

The Senate bill contained a provision (sec. 5296) that would amend section 873 of title 10, United States Code, (Article 73, Uniform Code of Military Justice (UCMJ)) to extend the time to file a petition for a new trial from 2 years to 3 years.

The House amendment contained an identical provision (sec. 6816).

The conference agreement includes this provision.

Restoration (sec. 5337)

The Senate bill contained a provision (sec. 5297) that would amend section 875 of title 10, United States Code, (Article 75, Uniform Code of Military Justice (UCMJ)) to require the President to establish rules governing the eligibility for pay and allowances during the period after a court-martial sentence is set aside or disapproved.

The House amendment contained an identical provision (sec. 6817).

The conference agreement includes this provision.

Leave requirements pending review of certain court-martial convictions (sec. 5338)

The Senate bill contained a provision (sec. 5298) that would amend section 876a of title 10, United States Code, (Article 76a, Uniform Code of Military Justice (UCMJ)) to conform Article 76a with proposed changes in Article 60 and the proposed new Article 60c, with no substantive changes. Article 76a currently authorizes the services, at their discretion, to place an accused on involuntarily leave if the accused has been sentenced to an unsuspended punitive discharge or dismissal that has been approved by the convening authority.

The House amendment contained an identical provision (sec. 6818).

The conference agreement includes this provision.

TITLE LX—PUNITIVE ARTICLES

Reorganization of punitive articles (sec. 5401)

The Senate bill contained a provision (sec. 5301) that would transfer and redesignate certain articles of the Uniform Code of Military Justice within subchapter X of chapter 10 of title 10, United States Code.

The House amendment contained an identical provision (sec. 6901).

The conference agreement includes this provision.

Conviction of offense charged, lesser included offenses, and attempts (sec. 5402)

The Senate bill contained a provision (sec. 5302) that would amend section 879 of title 10, United States Code, (Article 79, Uniform Code of Military Justice (UCMJ)) to authorize the President to designate an authoritative, but non-exhaustive, list of lesser included offenses for each punitive article of the UCMJ in addition to judicially-determined lesser included offenses.

The House amendment contained a similar provision (sec. 6902).

The House recedes.

Soliciting commission of offenses (sec. 5403)

The Senate bill contained a provision (sec. 5303) that would amend section 882 of title 10, United States Code, (Article 82, Uniform Code of Military Justice (UCMJ)) to consolidate the general solicitation offense under Article 134, the general article, with specific solicitation offenses under Article 82.

The House amendment contained an identical provision (sec. 6903).

The conference agreement includes this provision.

Malingering (sec. 5404)

The Senate bill contained a provision (sec. 5304) that would add a new section 883 to chapter 47 of title 10, United States Code, (Article 83, Uniform Code of Military Justice (UCMJ)) to establish the offense of malingering.

The House amendment contained an identical provision (sec. 6904).

The conference agreement includes this provision.

Breach of medical quarantine (sec. 5405)

The Senate bill contained a provision (sec. 5305) that would add a new section 884 to chapter 47 of title 10, United States Code, (Article 84, Uniform Code of Military Justice (UCMJ)) to establish the offense of breaking a medical quarantine.

The House amendment contained an identical provision (sec. 6905).

The conference agreement includes this provision.

Missing movement; jumping from vessel (sec. 5406)

The Senate bill contained a provision (sec. 5306) that would amend section 887 of title 10, United States Code, (Article 87, Uniform Code of Military Justice (UCMJ)) to include the offense of jumping from a vessel into the water.

The House amendment contained an identical provision (sec. 6906).

The conference agreement includes this provision.

Offenses against correctional custody and restriction (sec. 5407)

The Senate bill contained a provision (sec. 5307) that would add a new section 887b to chapter 47 of title 10, United States Code, (Article 87b, Uniform Code of Military Justice (UCMJ)) to establish the offense of violating various forms of custody and breaking restriction.

The House amendment contained a similar provision (sec. 6907).

The House recedes.

Disrespect toward superior commissioned officer; assault of superior commissioned officer (sec. 5408)

The Senate bill contained a provision (sec. 5308) that would amend section 889 of title 10, United States Code, (Article 89, Uniform Code of Military Justice (UCMJ)) to include the offense of assaulting a superior commissioned officer.

The House amendment contained an identical provision (sec. 6908).

The conference agreement includes this provision.

Willfully disobeying superior commissioned officer (sec. 5409)

The Senate bill contained a provision (sec. 5309) that would amend section 890 of title 10, United States Code, (Article 90, Uniform Code of Military Justice (UCMJ)) to remove the offense of assaulting a superior commissioned officer, which will be transferred to Article 89, UCMJ.

The House amendment contained an identical provision (sec. 6909).

The conference agreement includes this provision.

Prohibited activities with military recruit or trainee by person in position of special trust (sec. 5410)

The Senate bill contained a provision (sec. 5310) that would add a new section 893a to title 10, United States Code, (Article 93a, Uniform Code of Military Justice (UCMJ)) that would provide specific accountability for sexual misconduct committed by recruiters and trainers during the various phases within the recruiting and basic military training environments. Because of the unique nature of military training and the initial training environments among the services, the statute would authorize the service secretaries to publish regulations designating the types of physical intimacy that would constitute "prohibited sexual activity" under the new article. Article 93a would apply to military recruiters and trainers who knowingly engage in prohibited sexual activity with prospective recruits or junior members of the Armed Forces in initial training environments. Consent would not be a defense to this offense. Article 93a would address specific conduct and would not supersede or preempt service regulations governing professional conduct by staff involved in recruiting, entry level training, or other follow-on training programs. The Secretary

concerned may prescribe by regulation any additional initial career qualification training programs related to servicemembers that would be covered under this statute.

The House amendment contained a similar provision (sec. 6910).

The Senate recedes.

Offenses by sentinel or lookout (sec. 5411)

The Senate bill contained a provision (sec. 5311) that would amend section 895 of title 10, United States Code, (Article 95, Uniform Code of Military Justice (UCMJ)) to include the offense of loitering by sentinels or lookouts.

The House amendment contained a similar provision (sec. 6911).

The House recedes.

Disrespect toward sentinel or lookout (sec. 5412)

The Senate bill contained a provision (sec. 5312) that would add a new section 895a to chapter 47 of title 10, United States Code, (Article 95a, Uniform Code of Military Justice (UCMJ)) to establish the offense of disrespect toward sentinels or lookouts.

The House amendment contained a similar provision (sec. 6912).

The House recedes.

Release of prisoner without authority; drinking with prisoner (sec. 5413)

The Senate bill contained a provision (sec. 5313) that would amend section 896 of title 10, United States Code, (Article 96, Uniform Code of Military Justice (UCMJ)) to include the offense of drinking liquor with a prisoner.

The House amendment contained an identical provision (sec. 6913).

The conference agreement includes this provision.

Penalty for acting as a spy (sec. 5414)

The Senate bill contained a provision (sec. 5314) that would amend section 903 of title 10, United States Code, (Article 103, Uniform Code of Military Justice (UCMJ)) to redesignate Article 106, UCMJ, as Article 103, UCMJ, and replace the mandatory death penalty currently prescribed with a discretionary death penalty similar to that authorized under existing Article 106a, UCMJ, (Espionage) and for all other capital offenses under the Uniform Code of Military Justice.

The House amendment contained a similar provision (sec. 6914).

The House recedes.

Public records offenses (sec. 5415)

The Senate bill contained a provision (sec. 5315) that would add a new section 904 to chapter 47 of title 10, United States Code, (Article 104, Uniform Code of Military Justice (UCMJ)) to establish the offense of altering, concealing, removing, mutilating, obliterating, or destroying a public record.

The House amendment contained a similar provision (sec. 6915).

The House recedes.

False or unauthorized pass offenses (sec. 5416)

The Senate bill contained a provision (sec. 5316) that would add a new section 905a to chapter 47 of title 10, United States Code, (Article 105a, Uniform Code of Military Justice (UCMJ)) to establish false or unauthorized pass offenses.

The House amendment contained a similar provision (sec. 6916).

The House recedes.

Impersonation offenses (sec. 5417)

The Senate bill contained a provision (sec. 5317) that would add a new section 906 to chapter 47 of title 10, United States Code, (Article 106, Uniform Code of Military Justice (UCMJ)) to establish the offense of impersonating a commissioned, warrant, noncommissioned or petty officer, or an agent or official, and conform the article to the definition of "officer" in section 101(1) of title 10, United States Code.

The House amendment contained a similar provision (sec. 6917).

The House recedes.

Insignia offenses (sec. 5418)

The Senate bill contained a provision (sec. 5318) that would add a new section 906a to chapter 47 of title 10, United States Code, (Article 106a, Uniform Code of Military Justice (UCMJ)) to establish the offense of wearing unauthorized insignia, decoration, badge, ribbon, device, or lapel button.

The House amendment contained a similar provision (sec. 6918).

The House recedes.

False official statements; false swearing (sec. 5419)

The Senate bill contained a provision (sec. 5319) that would amend section 907 of title 10, United States Code, (Article 107, Uniform Code of Military Justice (UCMJ)) to include the offense of false swearing.

The House amendment contained an identical provision (sec. 6919).

The conference agreement includes this provision.

Parole violation (sec. 5420)

The Senate bill contained a provision (sec. 5320) that would add a new section 907a to chapter 47 of title 10, United States Code, (Article 107a, Uniform Code of Military Justice (UCMJ)) to establish the offense of violating parole.

The House amendment contained a similar provision (sec. 6920).

The House recedes.

Wrongful taking, opening, etc. of mail matter (sec. 5421)

The Senate bill contained a provision (sec. 5321) that would add a new section 909a to chapter 47 of title 10, United States Code, (Article 109a, Uniform Code of Military Justice (UCMJ)) to establish the offense of wrongfully taking, opening, secreting, destroying, or stealing mail.

The House amendment contained an identical provision (sec. 6921).

The conference agreement includes this provision.

Improper hazarding of vessel or aircraft (sec. 5422)

The Senate bill contained a provision (sec. 5322) that would amend section 910, title 10, United States Code, (Article 110, Uniform Code of Military Justice (UCMJ)) to include the offense of improper hazarding of an aircraft.

The House amendment contained an identical provision (sec. 6922).

The conference agreement includes this provision.

Leaving scene of vehicle accident (sec. 5423)

The Senate bill contained a provision (sec. 5323) that would add a new section 911 to chapter 47 of title 10, United States Code, (Article 111, Uniform Code of Military Justice (UCMJ)) to establish the offense of fleeing the scene of an accident.

The House amendment contained a similar provision (sec. 6923).

The House recedes.

Drunkenness and other incapacitation offenses (sec. 5424)

The Senate bill contained a provision (sec. 5324) that would amend section 912 of title 10, United States Code, (Article 112, Uniform Code of Military Justice (UCMJ)) to include the offense of incapacitation for duty from drunkenness or drug use and drunk prisoner.

The House amendment contained an identical provision (sec. 6924).

The conference agreement includes this provision.

Lower blood alcohol content limits for conviction of drunken or reckless operation of vehicle, aircraft, or vessel (sec. 5425)

The Senate bill contained a provision (sec. 5325) that would amend section 913 of title 10, United States Code, (Article 113, Uniform Code of Military Justice (UCMJ)) to lower the blood alcohol standard for conviction of drunken or reckless operation of a vehicle, aircraft, or vessel from 0.10 grams to 0.08 grams of alcohol per 100 milliliters of blood, and to allow service secretaries to prescribe lower levels of blood alcohol to convict if such lower limits are based on scientific developments, as reflected in federal law of general applicability.

The House amendment contained a similar provision (sec. 6925).

The House recedes.

Endangerment offenses (sec. 5426)

The Senate bill contained a provision (sec. 5326) that would amend section 914 of title 10, United States Code, (Article 114, Uniform Code of Military Justice (UCMJ)) to include the offense of reckless endangerment, discharge of firearm/endangering human life, and carrying of a concealed weapon.

The House amendment contained an identical provision (sec. 6926).

The conference agreement includes this provision.

Communicating threats (sec. 5427)

The Senate bill contained a provision (sec. 5327) that would amend section 915 of title 10, United States Code, (Article 115, Uniform Code of Military Justice (UCMJ)) to include the offense of communicating a threat.

The House amendment contained an identical provision (sec. 6927).

The conference agreement includes this provision.

Technical amendment relating to murder (sec. 5428)

The Senate bill contained a provision (sec. 5328) that would amend section 918 of title 10, United States Code, (Article 118, Uniform Code of Military Justice (UCMJ)) to strike the words "forcible sodomy" which has the effect of clarifying that forcible sodomy is included within the sexual offenses punishable under Article 120, UCMJ.

The House amendment contained an identical provision (sec. 6928).

The conference agreement includes this provision.

Child endangerment (sec. 5429)

The Senate bill contained a provision (sec. 5329) that would add a new section 919b to chapter 47 of title 10, United States Code, (Article 119b, Uniform Code of Military Justice (UCMJ)) to establish the offense of child endangerment.

The House amendment contained an identical provision (sec. 6929).

The conference agreement includes this provision.

Rape and sexual assault offenses (sec. 5430)

The Senate bill contained a provision (sec. 5330) that would amend section 920 of title 10, United States Code, (Article 120, Uniform Code of Military Justice (UCMJ)) to amend the definition of "sexual act" in both Article 120 (rape and sexual assault generally) and Article 120b (rape and sexual assault of a child) to conform to the definition of that term in federal criminal law in the civilian sector, under section 2246(2)(A)–(C) of title 18, United States Code.

The House amendment contained no similar provision.

The House recedes with an amendment that would remove the element of committing a sexual act upon another person by wrongfully using position, rank, or authority to coerce the acquiescence of the other person in the sexual act. The conferees note that this conduct is prohibited in section 893a of title 10, United States Code, (Article 93a, UCMJ), added elsewhere in this Act.

Deposit of obscene matter in the mail (sec. 5431)

The Senate bill contained a provision (sec. 5331) that would add a new section 920a to chapter 47 of title 10, United States Code, (Article 120a, Uniform Code of Military Justice (UCMJ)) to establish the offense of depositing, or causing to be deposited, obscene materials in the mails.

The House amendment contained an identical provision (sec. 6930).

The conference agreement includes this provision.

Fraudulent use of credit cards, debit cards, and other access devices (sec. 5432)

The Senate bill contained a provision (sec. 5332) that would add a new section 921a to chapter 47 of title 10, United States Code, (Article 121a, Uniform Code of Military Justice (UCMJ)) to establish the offense of misuse of credit cards, debit cards, and other electronic payment technology, also known as "access devices."

The House amendment contained a similar provision (sec. 6931).

The House recedes.

False pretenses to obtain services (sec. 5433)

The Senate bill contained a provision (sec. 5333) that would add a new section 921b to chapter 47 of title 10, United States Code, (Article 121b, Uniform Code of Military Justice (UCMJ)) to establish the offense of obtaining services under false pretenses.

The House amendment contained a similar provision (sec. 6932).

The House recedes.

Robbery (sec. 5434)

The Senate bill contained a provision (sec. 5334) that would amend section 922 of title 10, United States Code, (Article 122, Uniform Code of Military Justice (UCMJ)) by removing the words "with the intent to steal" from the section, eliminating the requirement to prove that the accused intended to permanently deprive the victim of his property.

The House amendment contained an identical provision (sec. 6933).

The conference agreement includes this provision.

Receiving stolen property (sec. 5435)

The Senate bill contained a provision (sec. 5335) that would add a new section 922a to chapter 47 of title 10, United States Code, (Article 122a, Uniform Code of Military Justice (UCMJ)) to establish the offense of knowingly receiving, buying, or concealing stolen property.

The House amendment contained a similar provision (sec. 6934).

The House recedes.

Offenses concerning Government computers (sec. 5436)

The Senate bill contained a provision (sec. 5336) that would add a new section 923 to chapter 47 of title 10, United States Code, (Article 123, Uniform Code of Military Justice (UCMJ)) to prohibit certain actions directed at U.S. Government computers and U.S. Government protected information.

The House amendment contained a similar provision (sec. 6935).

The House recedes with a technical amendment.

Bribery (sec. 5437)

The Senate bill contained a provision (sec. 5337) that would add a new section 924a to chapter 47 of title 10, United States Code, (Article 124a, Uniform Code of Military Justice (UCMJ)) to establish the offense of bribery.

The House amendment contained a similar provision (sec. 6936).

The House recedes.

Graft (sec. 5438)

The Senate bill contained a provision (sec. 5338) that would add a new section 924b to chapter 47 of title 10, United States Code, (Article 124b, Uniform Code of Military Justice (UCMJ)) to establish the offense of graft.

The House amendment contained a similar provision (sec. 6937).

The House recedes.

Kidnapping (sec. 5439)

The Senate bill contained a provision (sec. 5339) that would add a new section 925 to chapter 47 of title 10, United States Code, (Article 125, Uniform Code of Military Justice (UCMJ)) to establish the offense of kidnapping.

The House amendment contained an identical provision (sec. 6938).

The conference agreement includes this provision.

Arson; burning property with intent to defraud (sec. 5440)

The Senate bill contained a provision (sec. 5340) that would amend section 926 of title 10, United States Code, (Article 126, Uniform Code of Military Justice (UCMJ)) to include the offense of burning with intent to defraud.

The House amendment contained an identical provision (sec. 6939).

The conference agreement includes this provision.

Assault (sec. 5441)

The Senate bill contained a provision (sec. 5341) that would amend section 928 of title 10, United States Code, (Article 128, Uniform Code of Military Justice (UCMJ)) to prescribe a standard that focuses on the malicious intent of the accused rather than the "likelihood" of the activity actually resulting in harm. The provision would also amend this section to include the offense of assault with intent to commit murder, voluntary manslaughter, rape, robbery, sodomy, arson, burglary, or housebreaking.

The House amendment contained an identical provision (sec. 6940).

The conference agreement includes this provision.

Burglary and unlawful entry (sec. 5442)

The Senate bill contained a provision (sec. 5342) that would amend section 929 of title 10, United States Code, (Article 129, Uniform Code of Military Justice (UCMJ)) that would remove the "private dwelling" and "nighttime" elements of the offense, and to establish the offense of unlawful entry.

The House amendment contained a similar provision (sec. 6941).

The House recedes.

Stalking (sec. 5443)

The Senate bill contained a provision (sec. 5343) that would amend section 930 of title 10, United States Code, (Article 130, Uniform Code of Military Justice (UCMJ)) to establish the offenses of cyberstalking and threats to intimate partners. The provision would continue to address stalking activity involving a broad range of misconduct including,

but not limited to, sex-related offenses. The redesignated stalking offense would not preempt service regulations that specify additional types of misconduct that may be punishable at court-martial, including under Article 92 (failure to obey order or regulation), nor would it preempt other forms of misconduct from being prosecuted under other appropriate Articles, such as under Article 134, the general article. These uniquely military offenses are available to address similar misconduct that causes, for example, substantial emotional distress or targets professional reputation.

The House amendment contained a similar provision (sec. 6942).

The House recedes with a technical amendment.

Subornation of perjury (sec. 5444)

The Senate bill contained a provision (sec. 5344) that would add a new section 931a to chapter 47 of title 10, United States Code, (Article 131a, Uniform Code of Military Justice (UCMJ)) to establish the offense of subornation of perjury.

The House amendment contained an identical provision (sec. 6943).

The conference agreement includes this provision.

Obstructing justice (sec. 5445)

The Senate bill contained a provision (sec. 5345) that would add a new section 931b to chapter 47 of title 10, United States Code, (Article 131b, Uniform Code of Military Justice (UCMJ)) to establish the offense of obstructing justice.

The House amendment contained a similar provision (sec. 6944).

The House recedes.

Misprision of serious offense (sec. 5446)

The Senate bill contained a provision (sec. 5346) that would add a new section 931c to chapter 47 of title 10, United States Code, (Article 131c, Uniform Code of Military Justice (UCMJ)) to establish the offense of misprision of serious offense.

The House amendment contained a similar provision (sec. 6945).

The House recedes.

Wrongful refusal to testify (sec. 5447)

The Senate bill contained a provision (sec. 5347) that would add a new section 931d to chapter 47 of title 10, United States Code, (Article 131d, Uniform Code of Military Justice (UCMJ)) to establish the offense of wrongful refusal to testify.

The House amendment contained a similar provision (sec. 6946).

The House recedes with a technical amendment.

Prevention of authorized seizure of property (sec. 5448)

The Senate bill contained a provision (sec. 5348) that would add a new section 931e to chapter 47 of title 10, United States Code, (Article 131e, Uniform Code of Military Justice (UCMJ)) to establish the offense of prevention of authorized seizure of property.

The House amendment contained a similar provision (sec. 6947).

The House recedes.

Wrongful interference with adverse administrative proceeding (sec. 5449)

The Senate bill contained a provision (sec. 5349) that would add a new section 931g to chapter 47 of title 10, United States Code, (Article 131g, Uniform Code of Military Justice (UCMJ)) to establish the offense of wrongful interference with adverse administrative proceeding. The proceedings covered by this offense would include any administrative proceeding or action initiated

against a servicemember that could lead to discharge, loss of special or incentive pay, administrative reduction in grade, loss of a security clearance, bar to reenlistment, or reclassification.

The House amendment contained a similar provision (sec. 6948).

The House recedes.

Retaliation (sec. 5450)

The Senate bill contained a provision (sec. 5350) that would add a new section 932 to chapter 47 of title 10, United States Code, (Article 132, Uniform Code of Military Justice (UCMJ)) that would prohibit retaliation against witnesses, victims, or persons who report or plan to report a criminal offense to law enforcement or military authority or a protected communication to appropriate authority. Article 132 would not preempt service regulations that specify additional types of retaliatory conduct that may be punishable at court-martial under Article 92 (failure to obey order or regulation), nor would it preempt other forms of retaliatory conduct from being prosecuted under other appropriate Articles, such as Article 109 (destruction of property), Article 93 (cruelty and maltreatment), Article 128 (Assault), Article 131b (obstructing justice), Article 130 (stalking), or Article 134, the General article.

The House amendment contained a similar provision (sec. 6949).

The House recedes.

Extraterritorial application of certain offenses (sec. 5451)

The Senate bill contained a provision (sec. 5351) that would amend section 934 of title 10, United States Code, (Article 134, Uniform Code of Military Justice (UCMJ)) to authorize prosecution under clause 3 of Article 134, UCMJ, of all non-capital federal crimes of general applicability, regardless of where the federal crime is committed. This change would make military practice uniform throughout the world and would align it with the Military Extraterritorial Jurisdiction Act, section 3261 of title 18, United States Code.

The House amendment contained an identical provision (sec. 6950).

The conference agreement includes this provision.

Table of sections (sec. 5452)

The Senate bill contained a provision (sec. 5352) that would amend the table of sections at the beginning of subchapter X of chapter 47 of title 10, United States Code.

The House amendment contained a similar provision (sec. 6951).

The House recedes.

TITLE LXI—MISCELLANEOUS PROVISIONS

Technical amendments relating to courts of inquiry (sec. 5501)

The Senate bill contained a provision (sec. 5401) that would amend section 935 of title 10, United States Code, (Article 135, Uniform Code of Military Justice (UCMJ)) to provide individuals employed by the Department of Homeland Security, the department under which the Coast Guard operates, the right to be designated as parties in interest when they have a direct interest in the subject of a court of inquiry convened under Article 135. This change would align the rights of employees of the Department of Homeland Security with the rights of employees of the Department of Defense, ensuring consistent application of this statute for all military services.

The House amendment contained a similar provision (sec. 7001).

The Senate recedes.

Technical amendment to Article 136 (sec. 5502)

The Senate bill contained a provision (sec. 5402) that would amend section 936 of title 10, United States Code, (Article 136, Uniform Code of Military Justice (UCMJ)) to remove, from the section heading, the authority to act as a notary which is not provided for in the text of the section.

The House amendment contained a similar provision (sec. 7002).

The Senate recedes.

Articles of Uniform Code of Military Justice to be explained to officers upon commissioning (sec. 5503)

The Senate bill contained a provision (sec. 5403) that would amend section 937 of title 10, United States Code, (Article 137, Uniform Code of Military Justice (UCMJ)) to require that officers, in addition to enlisted personnel, receive training on the UCMJ upon entry to service, and periodically thereafter. The amendment would require specific military justice training for military commanders and convening authorities, and would require the Secretary of Defense to prescribe regulations for additional specialized training on the UCMJ for combatant commanders and commanders of combined commands. The provision would also require the Secretary of Defense to maintain an electronic version of the UCMJ and the Manual for Courts-Martial that would be updated periodically and made available on the Internet for review by servicemembers and the public.

The House amendment contained a similar provision (sec. 7003).

The House recedes.

Military justice case management; data collection and accessibility (sec. 5504)

The Senate bill contained a provision (sec. 5404) that would add a new section 940a to title 10, United States Code, (Article 140a, Uniform Code of Military Justice (UCMJ)) that would require the Secretary of Defense to prescribe uniform standards and criteria for case processing and management, military justice data collection, production and distribution of records of trial, and access to case information. The purpose of this section is to enhance the management of military justice cases, to standardize the collection of data necessary for evaluation and analysis, and to provide appropriate public access to military justice information at all stages of court-martial proceedings. At a minimum, the system developed for implementation should permit timely and appropriate access to filings, objections, instructions, and judicial rulings at the trial and appellate level, and to actions at trial and in subsequent proceedings concerning the findings and sentences of courts-martial.

The provision would require promulgation of standards by the Secretary of Defense not later than 2 years after enactment of this Act, with an effective date for such standards not later than 4 years after enactment.

The House amendment contained a similar provision (sec. 7004).

The Senate recedes with a technical amendment.

TITLE LXII—MILITARY JUSTICE REVIEW PANEL AND ANNUAL REPORTS

Military Justice Review Panel (sec. 5521)

The Senate bill contained a provision (sec. 5421) that would amend section 946 of title 10, United States Code, (Article 146, Uniform Code of Military Justice (UCMJ)) and retitle the section as "Military Justice Review Panel." The Military Justice Review Panel (Panel) would replace the Code Committee

and would be an independent, blue ribbon panel of experts tasked to conduct a periodic review and assessment of the operation of the UCMJ on a regular basis, thereby enhancing the efficiency and effectiveness of the UCMJ and the Code's implementing regulations.

The House amendment contained a similar provision (sec. 7101).

The House recedes with an amendment that would require the Panel to gather and analyze sentencing data and submit a report to the Committees on Armed Services of the Senate and the House of Representatives not later than October 31, 2020, setting forth the Panel's findings and recommendations on the need for sentencing reform.

Annual reports (sec. 5522)

The Senate bill contained a provision (sec. 5422) that would add a new section 946a to title 10, United States Code, (Article 146a, Uniform Code of Military Justice (UCMJ)) that would retain the valuable informational aspects of the annual reports issued individually by the Court of Appeals for the Armed Forces, the Judge Advocates General, and the Staff Judge Advocate to the Commandant of the Marine Corps.

The House amendment contained a similar provision (sec. 7102).

The House recedes with a technical amendment.

TITLE LXIII—CONFORMING AMENDMENTS AND EFFECTIVE DATES

Amendments to UCMJ subchapter tables of sections (sec. 5541)

The Senate bill contained a provision (sec. 5441) that would make conforming amendments to the tables of sections for specified subchapters of chapter 47 of title 10, United Stated Code (the Uniform Code of Military Justice).

The House amendment contained a similar provision (sec. 7201).

The House recedes with a technical amendment.

Effective dates (sec. 5542)

The Senate bill contained a provision (sec. 5442) that would require that the amendments made by this title shall take effect not later than the first day of the first calendar month that begins 2 years after the date of enactment of this Act.

The House amendment contained a similar provision (sec. 7202).

The House recedes.

LEGISLATIVE PROVISIONS NOT ADOPTED

Repeal of sentence reduction provision when interim guidance takes effect

The Senate bill contained a provision (sec. 5264) that would sunset section 856a of title 10, United States Code, (Article 56a, Uniform Code of Military Justice (UCMJ)) after sentencing parameters and criteria were established under Article 56.

The House amendment contained no similar provision.

The Senate recedes.

The conference agreement does not include a provision requiring interim guidance on sentencing parameters and criteria.

Minimum confinement period required for conviction of certain sex-related offenses committed by members of the Armed Forces

The House amendment contained a provision (sec. 6701A) that would amend section 856 of title 10, United States Code (Article 56, Uniform Code of Military Justice), to increase the minimum punishment for certain sex-related offenses from a dismissal or dishonorable discharge, to a dismissal or dis-

honorable discharge and confinement for two years.

The Senate bill contained no similar provision.

The House recedes.

The conferees note that the military justice reforms included in this Act will retain the existing minimum sentences under Article 56.

From the Committee on Armed Services, for consideration of the Senate bill and the House amendment, and modifications committed to conference:

MAC THORNBERRY,
J. RANDY FORBES,
JEFF MILLER of Florida,
JOE WILSON of South Carolina,
FRANK A. LOBIONDO,
MICHAEL R. TURNER,
JOHN KLINE,
MIKE ROGERS of Alabama,
TRENT FRANKS of Arizona,
K. MICHAEL CONAWAY,
DOUG LAMBORN,
ROBERT J. WITTMAN,
CHRISTOPHER P. GIBSON,
VICKY HARTZLER,
JOSEPH J. HECK of Nevada,
ELISE M. STEFANIK,
ADAM SMITH of Washington,
LORETTA SANCHEZ,
SUSAN A. DAVIS of California,
JAMES R. LANGEVIN,
RICK LARSEN of Washington,
JIM COOPER,
MADELEINE Z. BORDALLO,
JOE COURTNEY,
NIKI TSONGAS,
JOHN GARAMENDI,
HENRY C. "HANK" JOHNSON,
JACKIE SPEIER,
SCOTT H. PETERS,

From the Permanent Select Committee on Intelligence, for consideration of matters within the jurisdiction of that committee under clause 11 of rule X:

DEVIN NUNES,
MIKE POMPEO,

From the Committee on Education and the Workforce, for consideration of secs. 571–74 and 578 of the Senate bill, and secs. 571, 573, 1098E, and 3512 of the House amendment, and modifications committee to conference:

TIM WALBERG,
BRETT GUTHRIE,
ROBERT C. "BOBBY" SCOTT,

From the Committee on Energy and Commerce, for consideration of secs. 3112 and 3123 of the Senate bill, and secs. 346, 601, 749, 1045, 1090, 1095, 1673, 3119A and 3119C of the House amendment, and modifications committee to conference:

ROBERT E. LATTA,
BILL JOHNSON of Ohio,

From the Committee on Foreign Affairs, for consideration of secs. 828, 1006, 1007, 1050, 1056, 1089, 1204, 1211, 1221–23, 1231, 1232, 1242, 1243, 1247, 1252, 1253, 1255–58, 1260, 1263, 1264, 1271–73, 1276, 1283, 1301, 1302, 1531–33, and 1662 of the Senate bill, and secs 926, 1011, 1013, 1083, 1084, 1098K, 1099B, 1099C, 1201, 1203, 1214, 1221–23, 1227, 1229, 1233, 1235, 1236, 1245, 1246, 1250, 1259A–59E, 1259J, 1259L, 1259P, 1259Q, 1259U, 1261, 1262, 1301–03, 1510, 1531–33, 1645, 1653, and 2804 of the House amendment, and modifications committed to conference:

EDWARD R. ROYCE,
LEE M. ZELDIN,

From the Committee on Homeland Security, for consideration of secs. 564 and 1091 of the

Senate bill, and secs. 1097, 1869, 1869A, and 3510 of the House amendment, and modifications committee to conference:

MICHAEL T. MCCAUL,
DANIEL M. DONOVAN, JR.
BENNIE G. THOMPSON,

From the Committee on the Judiciary, for consideration of secs. 829J, 829K, 944, 963, 1006, 1023–25, 1053, 1093, 1283, 3303, and 3304 of the Senate bill, and secs. 598, 1090, 1098H, 1216, 1261, and 3608 of the House amendment, and modifications committee to conference:

BOB GOODLATTE,
DARRELL E. ISSA,

From the Committee on Natural Resources, for consideration of secs. 601, 2825, subtitle D of title XXVIII, and sec. 2852 of the Senate bill, and secs. 312, 601, 1090, 1098H, 2837, 2839, 2839A, subtitle E of title XXVIII, secs. 2852, 2854, 2855, 2864–66, title XXX, secs. 3508, 7005, and title LXXIII of the House amendment, and modifications committee to conference:

PAUL COOK,
CRESENT HARDY,

From the Committee on Oversight and Government Reform, for consideration of secs. 339, 703, 819, 821, 829H, 829I, 861, 944, 1048, 1054, 1097, 1103–07, 1109–13, 1121, 1124, 1131–33, 1135, and 1136 of the Senate bill, and secs. 574, 603, 807, 821, 1048, 1088, 1095, 1098L, 1101, 1102, 1104–06, 1108–11, 1113, 1259C, and 1631 of the House amendment, and modifications committee to conference:

JASON CHAFFETZ,
STEVE RUSSELL,

From the Committee on Science, Space, and Technology, for consideration of sec. 874 of the Senate bill and secs. 1605, 1673, and title XXXIII of the House amendment, and modifications committee to conference:

EDDIE BERNICE JOHNSON of Texas,

From the Committee on Small Business, for consideration of secs. 818, 838, 874, and 898 of the Senate bill, and title XVIII of the House amendment, and modifications committed to conference:

STEVE CHABOT,
STEPHEN KNIGHT,

From the Committee on Transportation and Infrastructure, for consideration of secs. 541, 562, 601, 961, 3302–07, 3501, and 3502 of the Senate bill, and secs. 343, 601, 731, 835, 1043, 1671, 3119C, 3501, 3504, 3509, 3512, and title XXXVI of the House amendment, and modifications committed to conference:

DUNCAN HUNTER,
DAVID ROUZER,
SEAN PATRICK MALONEY of New York,

From the Committee on Veterans' Affairs, for consideration of secs. 706, 755, and 1431 of the Senate bill, and secs. 741, 1421, and 1864 of the House amendment, and modifications committee to conference:

DAVID P. ROE of Tennessee,
MIKE BOST,

From the Committee on Ways and Means, for consideration of sec. 1271 of the Senate bill, and modifications committed to conference:

KEVIN BRADY of Texas,
DAVID G. REICHERT,
Managers on the Part of the House.

JOHN MCCAIN,
JAMES M. INHOFE,
JEFF SESSIONS,
ROGER F. WICKER,
KELLY AYOTTE,
DEB FISCHER,
TOM COTTON,
MIKE ROUNDS,
JONI ERNST,
THOM TILLIS,
DAN SULLIVAN,

LINDSEY GRAHAM,
TED CRUZ,
JACK REED,
BILL NELSON,
CLAIRE MCCASKILL,
JOE MANCHIN III,
JEANNE SHAHEEN,
RICHARD BLUMENTHAL,
JOE DONNELLY,
MAZIE K. HIRONO,
TIM KAINE,
ANGUS S. KING, JR.
MARTIN HEINRICH,
Managers on the Part of the Senate.

PROVIDING FOR CONSIDERATION OF SENATE AMENDMENT TO H.R. 34, TSUNAMI WARNING, EDUCATION, AND RESEARCH ACT OF 2015, AND PROVIDING FOR CONSIDERATION OF H.R. 6392, SYSTEMIC RISK DESIGNATION IMPROVEMENT ACT OF 2016

Mr. BURGESS. Mr. Speaker, by the direction of the Committee on Rules, I call up House Resolution 934 and ask for its immediate consideration.

The Clerk read the resolution, as follows:

H. RES. 934

Resolved, That upon adoption of this resolution it shall be in order to take from the Speaker's table the bill (H.R. 34) to authorize and strengthen the tsunami detection, forecast, warning, research, and mitigation program of the National Oceanic and Atmospheric Administration, and for other purposes, with the Senate amendment thereto, and to consider in the House, without intervention of any point of order, a motion offered by the chair of the Committee on Energy and Commerce or his designee that the House concur in the Senate amendment with an amendment consisting of the text of Rules Committee Print 114-67 modified by the amendment printed in part A of the report of the Committee on Rules accompanying this resolution. The Senate amendment and the motion shall be considered as read. The motion shall be debatable for 80 minutes, with 60 minutes equally divided and controlled by the chair and ranking minority member of the Committee on Energy and Commerce and 20 minutes equally divided and controlled by the chair and ranking minority member of the Committee on Ways and Means. The previous question shall be considered as ordered on the motion to its adoption without intervening motion.

SEC. 2. Upon adoption of this resolution it shall be in order to consider in the House the bill (H.R. 6392) to amend the Dodd-Frank Wall Street Reform and Consumer Protection Act to specify when bank holding companies may be subject to certain enhanced supervision, and for other purposes. All points of order against consideration of the bill are waived. The bill shall be considered as read. All points of order against provisions in the bill are waived. The previous question shall be considered as ordered on the bill and on any amendment thereto to final passage without intervening motion except: (1) one hour of debate equally divided and controlled by the chair and ranking minority member of the Committee on Financial Services; (2) the amendment printed in part B of the report of the Committee on Rules accompanying this resolution, if offered by the Member designated in the report, which shall be in order without inter-

vention of any point of order, shall be considered as read, shall be separately debatable for the time specified in the report equally divided and controlled by the proponent and an opponent, and shall not be subject to a demand for a division of the question; and (3) one motion to recommit with or without instructions.

The SPEAKER pro tempore. The gentleman from Texas (Mr. BURGESS) is recognized for 1 hour.

Mr. BURGESS. Mr. Speaker, for the purpose of debate only, I yield the customary 30 minutes to the gentleman from Colorado (Mr. POLIS), pending which I yield myself such time as I may consume. During consideration of this resolution, all time yielded is for the purpose of debate only.

GENERAL LEAVE

Mr. BURGESS. Mr. Speaker, I ask unanimous consent that all Members may have 5 legislative days to revise and extend their remarks.

The SPEAKER pro tempore. Is there objection to the request of the gentleman from Texas?

There was no objection.

Mr. BURGESS. Mr. Speaker, House Resolution 934 provides for a rule to consider a critical bill that will help millions of Americans and their families who are suffering from diseases. The rule provides 80 minutes of debate, with 1 hour being provided to the Energy and Commerce Committee, and 20 minutes given to the Committee on Ways and Means. The rule provides for a motion to concur with the Senate amendment to H.R. 34, placing the base text of the 21st Century Cures into the bill. The rule further incorporates the manager's amendment into the base text of the Cures bill, reflecting the bipartisan and bicameral negotiations which took place to get us to where we are today with the legislation.

Second, the resolution before us today provides for a rule to consider H.R. 6392, the Systemic Risk Designation Improvement Act of 2016, an important bill to remove onerous Federal regulations imposed on small and community banks by the ill-conceived Dodd-Frank Act by replacing current and arbitrary SIFI designation standards with a more effective activity-based standard. The rule provides for 1 hour of debate, equally divided between the majority and minority of the Committee on Financial Services. Further, the rule makes one amendment in order and provides the minority with the standard motion to recommit.

I am pleased that the House is considering both of these pieces of legislation today.

The Energy and Commerce Committee has spent 4 years working to bring our healthcare innovation infrastructure into the 21st century.

Today, there are 10,000 known diseases or conditions, but the bad news is we have cures and treatments for only 500.

There is a gap between innovation and therapy. There are problems with how we regulate our therapies. It is not unheard of to have a company take over 14 years and $2 billion to bring a new drug to market.

□ 1230

Members held 20 roundtables, discussions, hearings, field hearings, and events around the country to ensure that we involved our patients, their advocates, researchers, innovators, financiers—all who have firsthand experience and who understand the gaps in our current system.

The House amendment to H.R. 34 includes two bipartisan bills that have been developed over the course of several years by the Committee on Energy and Commerce and its members to meet some of our country's most pressing healthcare needs. The mental health reforms that are based on the Helping Families in Mental Health Crisis Act, authored by Representative TIM MURPHY, passed the House in July by a vote of 422–2. This legislative effort represents the most significant reforms in the mental health system in over a decade.

The 21st Century Cures Act title in the bill is the result of a unified Energy and Commerce Committee effort, championed by Chairman FRED UPTON of Michigan and Representative DIANA DEGETTE of Colorado over the course of multiple Congresses, to bring our laws into a modern era of medicine. The House passed the 21st Century Cures Act in July of 2015 by a vote of 344–77. Our commitment to this transformational bill has not and must not waver until it is across the finish line and signed into law. We owe it to the patients, their families, medical providers, advocates, scientists, and researchers to see this through.

Our country is a global leader in medical innovation, but even in recognizing that, there is progress that we can make. With 10,000 known diseases and with 10,000 known conditions, and with cures and treatments for only 500, we must do more to alleviate that gap which is causing so much human suffering. Advances in science and technology over the past decade have the potential to revolutionize medical innovation; yet the way drugs and devices are approved is back in the horse-and-buggy days. It is largely unchanged.

In recognizing the growing divide between innovation and regulation, the House Committee on Energy and Commerce launched the 21st Century Cures Initiative in the 113th Congress—that was a Congress ago—to examine the state of discovery, development, and delivery of medical therapies in America. The ensuing process by which the Cures legislation was developed should serve as a model for policy development long into the future.

Members of the committee convened hearings, forums, and roundtables in Washington, DC, and in centers and locations around the Nation. These forums brought together the leading scientists, the medical experts, patient and disease group advocates, and researchers and innovators across multiple sectors. The objective of these events was to uncover opportunities and to strengthen and streamline the process by which cures are discovered and made available to patients.

Based on what we have learned, Representatives worked across the aisle—across the dais—on comprehensive legislation that would make the government an ally rather than an obstacle in the cycle of medical innovation. The 21st Century Cures Act touches each step of the process through which new treatments and cures come to market: the discovery, the development, the delivery.

To accelerate discovery, the House amendment to H.R. 34 includes provisions that facilitate collaboration and increase access to health data. It invests billions of dollars in research through the National Institutes of Health, and it incentivizes the exploration of the most rare and challenging conditions. To modernize the development, among other things, the 21st Century Cures Act establishes a review pathway at the Food and Drug Administration for biomarkers and other drug development tools that can be used to help shorten drug development time while, at the same time, maintaining the safety standard that the public demands and that we have all come to expect from the agency.

The very confused regulation of combination products by the very different centers at the Food and Drug Administration will be improved to cut down on inefficiencies and to reduce the cost of development. The Food and Drug Administration will be required to work with stakeholders and the National Institute of Standards and Technology to establish a regulatory framework for the development, evaluation, and review of drugs that are classified as regenerative medicine and advanced therapies.

A number of provisions seek to empower patients to engage in their health care and to engage in their treatment decisions with their doctors, to contribute health information to scientific research, and to participate in the drug and device approval process. The Food and Drug Administration is required to engage in a range of activities that will establish a framework for the consideration of patient experience data when weighing the benefits of a new treatment. Individuals will have the opportunity to share health data with the global research community through platforms, such as the Precision Medicine Initiative and a new National Neurological Diseases Surveillance System. Multiple measures ensure patients will have better access to secure, up-to-date information through their electronic health records, and they ensure that this health information technology will continue to be developed with patient needs and patient safety and privacy as a priority.

I am grateful to have had the opportunity to work directly on several provisions in the bill. This includes the creation of a national surveillance system for neurologic diseases and conditions which may then be used to help us further understand these devastating diseases. Thousands of Americans are affected—multiple sclerosis, Parkinson's, Alzheimer's, other neurologic diseases—but there is very little accurate information that exists today to assist those who research, treat, and provide care for individuals who suffer from these diseases.

I have also worked on a provision that will improve patient access to pharmaceutical companies' compassionate use policies for drugs that treat serious or life-threatening conditions. To increase the efficiency and foster robust data collection analysis, the Food and Drug Administration will be required to evaluate the use of real-world evidence and summary-level review where an application is submitted for a new indication for an already approved drug. To help insurers and formulary committees make informed coverage decisions, a provision in the 21st Century Cures Act clarifies how medical product manufacturers can communicate economic information about therapies and technologies.

I am particularly happy that the House amendment to H.R. 34 includes multiple provisions that will make meaningful progress toward achieving an interoperable health system. Increasingly, electronic health system interoperability is critical to achieving the promises of the 21st Century Cures and to scaling up the benefits of health reform more broadly. While we have seen the widespread adoption of electronic health records, our Nation continues to maintain a fragmented system, which makes it difficult to ensure the continuity of evidence-based care for patients.

The 21st Century Cures Act would finally set us on a path towards achieving a nationwide interoperable health system that puts the needs of patients and that puts the needs of providers first. Federal advisory committees are streamlined and directed to prioritize interoperability. Preference is directed to utilizing the existing standards of implementation rather than of recreating them.

In addition to increasing the transparency and accountability for providers and patients, enforcement mechanisms will arm the Office of Inspector General with the authority necessary to punish bad actors for improperly impeding the flow of information. Data blocking will stop. The provisions in this bill will expedite the interoperability of electronic health record systems to make good on the $30 billion taxpayer investment in order to benefit patients, doctors, and researchers.

As I have referenced, developing the 21st Century Cures Act was a process that brought everyone to the table. No one is getting everything that he wanted. I would note my disappointment that this bill does not include an important clarification to the Physician Payments Sunshine Act that was part of the House-passed version of this bill and was supported by over 200 supporting organizations.

Certified continuing medical education, peer-reviewed medical textbooks, and journal reprints play a vital role in improving patient outcomes. They play a role in facilitating medical innovation, keeping our Nation's medical professionals up to date with the rapid pace of scientific discoveries. These materials and activities should not be confused with improper payments from pharmaceutical manufacturers to physicians. These materials were always intended to be excluded from the reporting requirements in the physician sunshine law, but, unfortunately, the Centers for Medicare & Medicaid Services' interpretation of the exemption has been inconsistent and unreliable. The narrowly constructed language in the 21st Century Cures Act was carefully drafted to maintain the transparency originally intended in the sunshine law while it ensured robust access to medical education.

Mr. Speaker, I think it goes without saying that we all want our doctors to be smart, that we want them to be informed, and that we want them to be up to date. Certainly, that is a priority that I will continue to pursue going forward.

Groundbreaking discoveries rely on a robust and reliable investment in basic research. The House amendment to H.R. 34 provides the National Institutes of Health with almost $5 billion in funding, including almost $2 billion for the Cancer Moonshot and $1.5 billion for the BRAIN Initiative. It also includes $500 million for the Food and Drug Administration and $1 billion in grants to four States in order to address the growing and burgeoning opioid crisis that continues to claim so many lives across our country. This approach provides dedicated funding through 2026 while it ensures spending is subject to review and oversight in the annual appropriations process. In addition to fully offsetting all of the authorized funds, H.R. 34 will actually reduce the deficit by almost $6 billion over the next 10 years.

Federal regulation, Federal policy, and Federal investment have been outpaced by science, medicine, and technology. The bipartisan 21st Century Cures Act will make needed changes to bring our laws into a modern era of medicine and to keep the Nation at the forefront of healthcare innovation. The 21st Century Cures Act not only delivers hope to millions of patients who are living with untreatable diseases, but it also helps modernize and helps streamline the regulation in America's healthcare system.

I encourage all of my colleagues to vote "yes" on the rule and "yes" on the two underlying bills. The 21st Century Cures Act will not only deliver hope to millions of people who are living with untreatable disease, but it will also help modernize and streamline America's healthcare system.

Mr. Speaker, I reserve the balance of my time.

Mr. POLIS. Mr. Speaker, I yield myself such time as I may consume.

I thank the gentleman for yielding me the customary time, but I have to say that I think that this somewhat breaks with the custom of this body not to delay floor proceedings during the reorganization of the Democratic Caucus. I know that, when the Democrats were in the majority, we routinely gave deference to the Republican Conference's plan for retreats and for caucus reorganizations. We have before us several contested races. Of course, the Nation's business comes first, which is why we are here making the case on these bills.

I would like to add that I hope that this is not the tone we are going to be setting for the next Congress. I think it is very important that, despite our differences on policies, both conferences are respectful of the responsibilities that Members have not only within the institution of Congress but within their respective conferences and caucuses. On our side, we will be brief because we do have additional responsibilities, as I mentioned.

Mr. Speaker, I yield 2½ minutes to the gentlewoman from Oregon (Ms. BONAMICI).

Ms. BONAMICI. I thank the gentleman for yielding.

Mr. Speaker, I rise in opposition to the rule on H.R. 34, which is now the vehicle for the 21st Century Cures Act.

Although I understand the detailed rules of our Chamber, I am deeply disappointed that the underlying bill, the Tsunami Warning, Education, and Research Act, was completely stripped out and replaced with unrelated language. The Tsunami Warning, Education, and Research Act is bipartisan. It was passed by a voice vote on January 7 of 2015, and a similar version has passed the Senate. We have worked out our differences, and this legislation is ready to be signed into law, and it is vital for our West Coast communities.

My constituents on the Oregon coast know that it is a matter of when, not if, our community will face a Cascadia subduction zone earthquake and tsunami. Most of the city of Seaside, including all of its public schools, is located in the tsunami inundation zone. It is some of my youngest constituents—the students of Seaside—who have been the most vocal about keeping their communities safe. Recently, I met with the students there at the high school. They have spoken all over the State about the dangers they face from tsunami. Their presentation was very strong. They made a case for moving their schools out of the tsunami zone.

□ 1245

It helped the community pass a bond measure earlier this month to move the schools. That is a positive step for Seaside, but there is so much more to be done.

I have an app on my phone. Almost every day, there is an earthquake off the coast of Alaska or Hawaii. Two days ago there were two earthquakes off the coast of Oregon. When there is a near-shore tsunami, the warning time is about 15 minutes. That is all.

The Tsunami Warning, Education, and Research Act would help communities up and down the entire coast by strengthening the warning system, providing more assistance to local communities like Seaside to prepare for that disaster, coordinating government agencies to make sure they're sharing information and working together, and supporting community outreach and education programs.

This is not just about Oregonians. Millions of people in Alaska, Hawaii, Washington State, California also face significant risk. We are overdue for the really big one.

Now, I understand that the Cures Act may save lives, but I am very disappointed that the provisions of the tsunami bill, which is also lifesaving policy, was not retained in the underlying bill.

Mr. Speaker, again, I urge my colleagues to oppose this rule so we can immediately consider swift passage of the Tsunami Warning, Education, and Research Act. Our West Coast communities are counting on us to keep them safe.

Mr. BURGESS. Mr. Speaker, I yield 3 minutes to the gentleman from Pennsylvania (Mr. MURPHY), the author of the mental health portion of this bill.

Mr. MURPHY of Pennsylvania. Mr. Speaker, this bill includes in it elements of H.R. 2646, the Helping Families in Mental Health Crisis Act, which is the most revolutionary change to mental health since the Community Mental Health Act of 1963.

It includes fundamental changes in how we think about, talk about, and treat serious mental illness. It establishes an assistant secretary for mental health and substance use to disseminate evidence-based practices, ensure grants meet objective outcome measures, conduct ongoing oversight of grantees, and collaborates with other Federal departments on mental health.

It creates an interagency coordinating committee to evaluate Federal programs related to mental illness and provide recommendations to better coordinate those programs. It authorizes a national mental health and substance use policy laboratory to promote evidence-based models of care and further develop, expand, replicate, or scale those programs. It provides funding for treatment and recovery for homeless individuals with mental health and substance use disorder services.

It authorizes for the first time in law the National Suicide Prevention Lifeline program and the Minority Fellowship Program. It awards grants to develop, maintain, and enhance online psychiatric bed registries.

It funds programs for telehealth so that people in rural communities and primary care physicians can have ready access to mental health services so sorely needed for their patients. It reauthorizes the Garrett Lee Smith Suicide Prevention program, increases funding for assisted outpatient treatment and, for the first time, provides Federal grants for assertive community treatment.

It increases access to medical residencies and fellowships in psychiatry and addiction medicine in underserved, community-based settings for nurse practitioners, physician assistants, health service psychologists, and social workers. It removes barriers for providing volunteering at community health centers.

It updates the National Child Traumatic Stress Initiative, which supports a national network of child trauma centers, including university, hospital, and community-based centers.

It requires the Secretary of HHS to clarify how healthcare providers can communicate with the caregiver of an adult with a mental health or substance use disorder. It clarifies the coverage of eating disorder benefits, including residential treatment under existing mental parity requirements.

It allows Federal grants to local law enforcement to be used for crisis intervention teams to roll back the tragedies of violence that occur when a mentally ill person encounters a policeman. It provides funding to develop school-based mental health crisis intervention teams. And this list goes on.

I am pleased that this has all been merged into one bill here so that we can move forward on this. This truly will provide many lifesaving measures and bring mental health treatment out of the shadows.

I encourage my colleagues to support this bill as we move forward and provide help because where there is help, there is hope.

Mr. POLIS. Mr. Speaker, I just want to note that this rule contains two completely different bills. The first is the 21st Century Cures Act, which would help address many of the health crises that we face. The other bill is H.R. 6392, the Systemic Risk Designation Improvement Act, that would weaken many of the protections that were put in place in the Dodd-Frank Wall Street reform bill. So there are two very different bills here under one rule, a very closed process which the Democrats will be opposing.

Mr. Speaker, I yield 3 minutes to the gentleman from Oregon (Mr. BLUMENAUER).

Mr. BLUMENAUER. Mr. Speaker, it is a pleasure to follow my friend from Pennsylvania, acknowledging his hard work in the mental health sphere. I do think that this is setting the platform for the most significant initiative in the next half century. There are some good things in this bill, but I hope it is just the beginning. I know the gentleman has a number of other initiatives that he is working on in a bipartisan way, and I am hopeful that this Bill serves as a springboard.

On a personal note, the Garrett Smith Suicide Prevention Act, was created by our former colleague, Senator Gordon Smith from Oregon, who took a personal tragedy in his family and moved forward with important legislation that other families may be spared by that effort.

There are a number of things here that matter in another context. In terms of what happens dealing with the opioid crisis that we have now, America has been too slow to respond. I am hopeful that these resources will help us move in the right direction. Again, I must, I suppose, note with a certain amount of irony that there are other alternatives available to deal with the epidemic of opioid overdose deaths.

I would note that it is interesting that States that actually utilize medical marijuana prescribe fewer pills. There is an opportunity here for us to do something that is less expensive, less addictive, and not deadly. But the provisions in this bill, I think, are a step in the right direction.

It also is important to note the investments in neuroscience. We have created a Neuroscience Caucus in Congress because this is an area that has stubbornly resisted being able to have the progress that we have seen in other areas, like cancer and cardiac health, and building on an initiative that the administration has developed the BRAIN Initiative, which is modest but potentially very significant to accelerate the understanding of the human brain, leading to new ways to treat and cure neurological disorders.

Everybody in this Chamber knows a variety of people who suffer—everything from Alzheimer's, multiple sclerosis, addiction problem—and being able to double down those investments in a more systematic way will pay dividends that are incalculable.

Already, mental and behavioral disorders are among the leading causes of disability around the world. The impact is greater than heart disease and cancer combined. As I mentioned, where we have actually made some progress.

Last but not least, there is a technical fix that matters in my community and others around the country, which is bringing fairness to hospitals. When Congress changed the hospital payment rules last November, there were hospitals like Oregon Health & Science University that were caught unfairly in the middle of payment changes. We did not provide any exceptions for hospital outpatient departments that were under development at that time.

The SPEAKER pro tempore. The time of the gentleman has expired.

Mr. POLIS. Mr. Speaker, I yield an additional 1 minute to the gentleman from Oregon.

Mr. BLUMENAUER. Mr. Speaker, this means that hospitals like Oregon Health & Science University, who made significant investments in building offsite departments under one set of Medicare rules, suddenly faced a new set of rules that were changed by Congress midstream. I am pleased that this will prevent pulling the rug out from underneath them.

So, in sum, Mr. Speaker, this technical fix, which is important, support for the BRAIN Initiative, the important work in mental health, and dealing with the opioid crisis are reasons that I think this bill is worthy of support, although I share the concerns of the gentlewoman from Oregon (Ms. BONAMICI), whose underlying, bipartisan, very important bill somehow is a casualty of this legislation. That is unfortunate.

I hope the rule is defeated so we can fix that and get on with business.

Mr. BURGESS. Mr. Speaker, I yield 2 minutes to the gentleman from Oklahoma (Mr. COLE).

Mr. COLE. Mr. Speaker, I rise for the purpose of supporting the rule and the underlying legislation.

I want to begin by congratulating Chairman UPTON and the members of the Energy and Commerce Committee on both sides of the aisle for crafting what is genuinely a bipartisan piece of legislation in a very divisive era and working it for years and bringing it to a successful conclusion. They have given all of us an opportunity to vote for something really, really important to every single American.

Now, a lot of focus will be put on the money aspect of this bill. Certainly, $6-plus billion is a nice chunk of change and will be very, very gratefully received. But in that same multiple-year period, in 5 years, if we didn't increase appropriations by a dime, we would spend $160 billion dollars at NIH. And over a 10-year period, if we didn't increase annual appropriations by a dime, we would spend $320 billion.

So the real genius of the bill is not the money. It is actually the three things that have been mentioned by multiple speakers before me. First is the regulatory reform that, at the FDA and at the NIH, will literally save billions of dollars and thousands of lives over the next decade.

Second is the opioid initiative. We all know the crisis. It touches all of our districts. To direct money there and then to build on that through the appropriations process is extraordinarily important, and I congratulate the Energy and Commerce Committee for taking a lead here.

Finally, the mental health legislation that is wound up in this that the gentleman from Pennsylvania (Mr. MURPHY) provided is just absolutely spectacular in terms of its long-term importance.

We can all disagree about this or that or some technicality in the rule. The reality is this is important legislation. If it doesn't pass now, it won't pass and we will be missing an opportunity.

So I want to urge my friends on both sides of the aisle—I don't expect my friends to vote for the rule. They shouldn't. They never do. I wouldn't if I were in the minority. But I hope they will vote for the underlying legislation because that legislation is worthy of passage. It is a bipartisan compromise, and it will improve the life of every single American.

Mr. POLIS. Mr. Speaker, there is a lot of bipartisan support for the 21st Century Cures Act. I commend Chairman UPTON, Ranking Member PALLONE, Ranking Member DEGETTE, Ranking Member GENE GREEN, and so many others who worked hard on this legislation that will save lives by improving the access that Americans have to potentially lifesaving drugs and devices, helping to keep people healthy and independent and out of the hospital.

I plan to support this legislation. I think we also all know that it is a starting point. We have additional work to do to make prescription drugs more affordable, to make the approval process more streamlined for both prescription drugs and medical devices, regenerative medicines safe, and, of course, funding levels for research.

Mr. Speaker, I would like to inquire if there are any speakers remaining on the other side?

Mr. BURGESS. Mr. Speaker, I have two additional speakers and myself to close.

Mr. POLIS. Mr. Speaker, I reserve the balance of my time.

Mr. BURGESS. Mr. Speaker, I yield 2 minutes to the gentleman from Pennsylvania (Mr. PITTS), the chairman of the Subcommittee on Health that played a vital role in getting the 21st Century Cures bill across the finish line.

Mr. PITTS. Mr. Speaker, I rise in strong support of the rule for the 21st Century Cures Act, a momentous innovation package which will help advance the discovery, development, and delivery of new treatments and cures for patients and will foster private-sector innovation here in the United States.

Additionally, the package includes provisions of H.R. 2646, the Helping Families in Mental Health Crisis Act, as well as provisions to increase choice, access, and quality health care for Americans.

Arriving here today has been a long journey full of lots of steps and twists and turns along the way. I especially want to thank legislative counsel for their tireless efforts in helping translate our legislative aims into legislative language. Together with our health team staff, they worked nights and weekends and were consummate professionals throughout the process.

Additionally, I want to thank the healthcare staff of the Congressional Budget Office for all of their help in recent months. In addition to their role in estimating the budgetary effects of numerous policies in the bill, they were instrumental in helping us shape a number of proposals the committee considered.

I would be remiss if I did not thank again the outstanding team on Energy and Commerce and most especially the health team led by Chief Health Counsel Paul Edattel, supported by Josh Trent, John Stone, Carly McWilliams, J.P. Paluskiewicz, Adrianna Simonelli, Adam Buckalew, Sophie Trainor, and Jay Gulshen; and Heidi Stirrup and Monica Valenti on my staff, without whose expertise, wisdom, and counsel this legislative work would not be possible.

□ 1300

This landmark medical innovation package includes provisions designed to help almost every American family, whether it is leading to the discovery, development, and delivery of new treatments and cures, or advancing the President's Precision Medicine Initiative or the Vice President's Cancer Moonshot, or the BRAIN Initiative to advance Alzheimer's research. This package is an innovation game changer and will truly bring our health innovation into the 21st century. I urge support for this bipartisan effort.

Mr. POLIS. Mr. Speaker, I reserve the balance of my time.

Mr. BURGESS. Mr. Speaker, I yield 2 minutes to the gentleman from Michigan (Mr. WALBERG).

Mr. WALBERG. Mr. Speaker, I stand in support of the rule and the underlying bill. Why? Well, the 21st Century Cures Act is a transformational piece of legislation that will allow us to discover and develop new lifesaving cures and treatments for some of the worst diseases.

This act will offer hope to millions of patients and families, including Gale, a constituent of mine from Newport, who has been affected and afflicted with pancreatic cancer. Or Brandon, a boy from Rives Junction, who has been on a clinical trial for 8 years as he battles Duchenne muscular dystrophy.

In addition to streamlining the FDA approval process and boosting NIH funding, the Cures Act includes significant provisions to update our mental health system and help States fight opioid addiction.

I congratulate my good friend and colleague Chairman FRED UPTON for his vision in tackling this challenge and for his tireless efforts to get this bill to the floor. The Cures Act is innovative; it is bipartisan; it is fully paid for and life changing for my constituents in Michigan and many others around this great country.

I ask my colleagues to vote in support of the rule and the underlying bill.

Mr. POLIS. Is the gentleman prepared to close?

Mr. BURGESS. I am prepared to close.

Mr. POLIS. Mr. Speaker, I yield myself such time as I may consume.

Again, I do want to point out, in breaking with custom, there were many other Democrats who wanted to discuss this bill; but, as we speak, the Democratic Caucus is having elections for the vice chair position. While we were on the floor, we had elections for the whip position and the assistant leader position, both of which I was unable to participate in because, of course, I had to conduct the business of the Nation.

But, again, I would hope that both parties are respectful of the scheduling requirements that are incumbent upon being a member of one of the two major parties of this body. In the past, we have always been able to work in when Republican Conference has a retreat or a reorganization meeting. I think that is important to this body because, while, of course, as Americans and Representatives we have responsibilities to the institution of Congress, as elected officials of the Democratic or Republican Party, we do have a responsibility to select our leaders and establish our rules.

I don't think that the amount of time that either party spends doing that is unreasonable, but I think that it is very important that both parties and leadership of this body, the Speaker and the majority leader, are respectful of that while, of course, understanding we have important people's business to conduct. There were, of course, many other options. This House could have come to order and gotten this work done at 8 in the morning or they could do it later in the afternoon. There are a number of different ways we could have worked around the previously scheduled reorganization of the Democratic Caucus.

Frankly, I am disappointed not just for myself having been unable to participate in those party functions, but also on behalf of other members of the Democratic Caucus who were unable to come and speak on these very important issues because of playing active roles in running for or supporting or speaking on behalf of various candidates for party positions, which is occurring as I speak.

This bill has two completely unrelated bills that are in it. Again, the 21st Century Cures Act has strong bipartisan support. I add my voice to those who have praised this legislation, and hopefully it will challenge the next Congress to continue to move forward with facilitating the approval process.

I have often heard the approval process, for instance, for a new drug for inception to market can often be in excess of $1 billion or $2 billion. We hear a number of different figures tossed around. I think sometimes it is in the high hundreds of millions. Sometimes it is as high as 1.5 or 2 billion. Regardless, that is one of the reasons that there is an upward pressure on prices for proprietary prescription drugs. It is also one of the reasons that lifesaving prescription drugs are often unavailable here even while they are on the market in Europe and other areas. Of course, without compromising safety—and Democrats and Republicans agree on that—there needs to be a way that we can facilitate, particularly in the realm of personalized medicine, bringing new lifesaving products to market in an affordable way.

An excellent model for that that has saved hundreds of thousands of lives was put in place during the first administration of the first George Bush, which provided an expedited route for HIV drugs. Thanks to that route that was used for many of the HIV drugs, some of which are still in use today, hundreds of thousands of people affected by HIV, including many LGBT Americans, are still alive today because of that effort. I am also confident, because of today's effort with the 21st Century Cures Act, it will save the lives of many more Americans. Again, it is a starting point. We have room to go.

The other bill would, for some reason—it is not something I hear from constituents, but apparently it is something Republicans want to do—exempt some of the very biggest banks from some of the requirements under Dodd-Frank regarding ensuring their stability and preventing them from failing. It is my understanding it only affects a few dozen banks, the very largest banks, banks that are worth tens or hundreds of billions of dollars. I am sure they like it. It probably reduces their ability to have to comply.

But there is a reason those requirements were put in place for those very big banks. We are worried that the failure of any one or certainly multiple banks could create a systemic risk and lead to future bailouts. So I strongly believe that this bill before us today on the banking regulations, if it were to become the law, it would increase the likelihood of future bailouts, which surprises me because many of us have been traditionally opposed to those very kinds of bailouts.

It is my understanding there is one remaining speaker on the other side, so I reserve the balance of my time to allow that speaker to speak.

Mr. BURGESS. Mr. Speaker, I thank the gentleman for the accommodation. I am pleased to yield 2 minutes to the gentleman from Oregon (Mr. WALDEN).

Mr. WALDEN. Mr. Speaker, I want to thank my colleagues on both sides of the aisle and especially for the courtesy to spend a minute or two talking about not only this rule, but also the legislation that will be coming to the floor soon. I want to thank especially Chairman FRED UPTON, who has put his whole heart and soul into the 21st Century Cures Act, joined by DIANA DEGETTE, certainly Dr. BURGESS, Congressman MURPHY, and others who have really played a key role in trying to find cures to diseases that don't exist today, find treatments for those in order to bring better health to all Americans, both physical health and, certainly in the case of Dr. Murphy, mental health as well.

This really means a lot. This will make a difference in real people's lives back home in our communities. I have heard from those people, like Carol Fulkerson in Bend, who has MS. She is ecstatic about this. She said it is a great step toward making it possible to find a cure to MS. Can you imagine what that means in a person's life?

There are critical reforms and improvements on mental health and substance abuse programs, as we have heard. These changes will help people all across America, and certainly in Oregon. A Medford resident, Justin, overcame his own battle with addiction through a dual diagnosis treatment program that dealt with the underlying issues fueling addiction instead of just sort of a Band-Aid approach to his symptoms. These are the kinds of ideas coming from our folks back home that are now incorporated in legislation.

I heard from a clinical lab owner in rural Oregon, Judy Kennedy, who voiced her support for the provisions in Cures that provide precise diagnostic testing services to rural and other underserved communities across the country. We are going to do so much to improve the health, both mental and physical, in the lives of people we represent when this legislation becomes law.

Mr. Speaker, I am just delighted to support this bill. I think it is an enormous step forward in so many ways, and I commend Chairman UPTON and all those who have been involved in this in its writing. I urge passage of the rule so we can get on to this legislation.

Mr. POLIS. Is the gentleman prepared to close?

Mr. BURGESS. Once again.

Mr. POLIS. Mr. Speaker, I yield myself the balance of my time.

So, again, I think there is some good and some bad in this. The 21st Century Cures Act is very important, and I hope that this body sees it as a starting point, not an ending point. There are some important reforms in there that will save lives and also help remove some of the upward pressure on prescription drug prices, something we hear about very often from constituents.

There is another bill in there which most Democrats will be voting against with regard to making it potentially more likely that larger banks can fail us or need bailouts, and that is not something that most of us have an appetite for. Of course, the closed nature of the bill is not consistent with the expressed desire of the Speaker to have an open process. The Committee on Rules yesterday shut down a number of excellent ideas and amendments that were offered, and they are not allowed to be debated here on the floor.

Of course the timing of this bill, particularly for a bipartisan bill, to bring it up in a way, in a manner and a time that conflicts with the previously noticed meeting that happens to include all of the members of one of the two political parties is not the best way to foster the type of bipartisan cooperation that is important to get things done around here.

So Democrats will not be supporting the rule. Many of us will, thanks to the work of Chairman UPTON, Ranking Member PALLONE, Ranking Member DEGETTE, Ranking Member GENE GREEN, and others, be proud to hopefully send to the President's desk the 21st Century Cures Act as an excellent starting point in helping to save lives.

I urge a "no" vote on the rule.

Mr. Speaker, I yield back the balance of my time.

Mr. BURGESS. I yield myself the balance of my time.

Mr. Speaker, today's rule provides for the consideration of two important bills: a bill that will transform and advance the discovery, the development, the delivery of treatments and cures; and a bill that will help our small and community banks, institutions that, in turn, can further assist small and local businesses and help our communities grow.

I want to thank all of the Members who did put a lot of effort into the final package on the Cures bill, as well as the staff on both sides of the aisle, all members of the Committee on Energy and Commerce, and the House as a whole, who were asked to bring their ideas to the table, and we worked to include as many of those as we could.

I would also like to express my thanks to the great attorneys at the

Legislative Counsel who sometimes worked around the clock to get this bill ready for both the committee and floor activity. I want to thank Chairman UPTON, Representative DEGETTE, as well as Chairman PITTS and Ranking Member PALLONE and Ranking Member GENE GREEN for their leadership throughout.

It has already been mentioned, but I also want to thank the staff, both in our personal offices and at the committee staff, who have worked so hard on this over the past 4 years. This was truly all hands on deck. There is not one staffer on the Subcommittee on Health of the Committee on Energy and Commerce who does not have their fingerprints all over this bill.

Mr. Speaker, I yield back the balance of my time, and I move the previous question on the resolution.

The previous question was ordered.

Mr. DESAULNIER. Madam Speaker, I rise today in support of H.R. 34, the 21st Century Cures Act. It is vital that we ensure that the National Institutes of Health (NIH) have the resources they need to continue to advance biomedical and mental health research, and improve access to innovative treatments for some of the most debilitating illnesses.

The additional $4.8 billion authorized for the NIH to improve biomedical research and treatment innovations is commendable, particularly the $1.8 billion for the Vice President's Cancer Moonshot, in line with the President's budget request, that will advance critical life-saving research. I fully support the Cancer Moonshot's mission to speed up the advancement of other treatments that will help individuals and families who are fighting diseases or disorders. As a Cancer survivor, I know all too well the value of these investments and how many lives can be saved as a result.

Additionally, the allocation of $1 billion to step up federal efforts combating the growing opioid and heroin epidemic is a positive step towards better treatment of addicted individuals. Every day, families across California and the nation are torn apart by a loved one or neighbor abusing opioids. Hopefully our Republican colleagues consider this the first of many steps to advance meaningful policies designed to erode the strong grip these drugs have on so many Americans.

Unfortunately, key aspects of this legislation fall short and are clearly designed to benefit Big Pharma over American consumers, patients, and doctors. I am deeply troubled by the Majority's decision to drastically reduce new NIH funding in the legislation compared to H.R. 6, stifling new research and vital progress. Additionally, it is disappointing that an amendment I authored, which would have helped to improve doctor-patient communication around the diagnosis and treatment of severe or chronic illnesses, was not included in this legislation. This oversight shows the lack of understanding of the importance of communication between patients and doctors in a patient's treatment and recovery.

The SPEAKER pro tempore. The question is on the resolution.

The question was taken; and the Speaker pro tempore announced that the ayes appeared to have it.

Mr. POLIS. Mr. Speaker, on that I demand the yeas and nays.

The yeas and nays were ordered.

The SPEAKER pro tempore. Pursuant to clause 8 of rule XX, this 15-minute vote on adopting House Resolution 934 will be followed by a 5-minute vote on suspending the rules and passing H.R. 5047.

The vote was taken by electronic device, and there were—yeas 230, nays 180, not voting 24, as follows:

[Roll No. 590]

YEAS—230

Abraham	Graves (LA)	Palmer
Aderholt	Graves (MO)	Paulsen
Allen	Griffith	Pearce
Amash	Grothman	Perry
Amodei	Guinta	Pittenger
Babin	Guthrie	Pitts
Barr	Hanna	Poliquin
Barton	Hardy	Pompeo
Benishek	Harper	Posey
Bilirakis	Harris	Price, Tom
Bishop (MI)	Hartzler	Ratcliffe
Bishop (UT)	Heck (NV)	Reed
Black	Herrera Beutler	Reichert
Blackburn	Hice, Jody B.	Ribble
Blum	Hill	Rice (SC)
Bost	Holding	Rigell
Boustany	Hudson	Roby
Brady (TX)	Huelskamp	Roe (TN)
Brat	Huizenga (MI)	Rogers (AL)
Bridenstine	Hultgren	Rogers (KY)
Brooks (AL)	Hunter	Rohrabacher
Brooks (IN)	Hurd (TX)	Rokita
Buchanan	Issa	Rooney (FL)
Buck	Jenkins (KS)	Ros-Lehtinen
Bucshon	Jenkins (WV)	Roskam
Burgess	Johnson (OH)	Ross
Byrne	Johnson, Sam	Rothfus
Calvert	Jordan	Rouzer
Carter (GA)	Joyce	Royce
Carter (TX)	Katko	Russell
Chabot	Kelly (MS)	Salmon
Chaffetz	Kelly (PA)	Sanford
Coffman	King (IA)	Scalise
Cole	King (NY)	Schweikert
Collins (GA)	Kinzinger (IL)	Scott, Austin
Collins (NY)	Kline	Sensenbrenner
Comer	Knight	Sessions
Comstock	Labrador	Shimkus
Conaway	LaHood	Simpson
Cook	LaMalfa	Sinema
Costello (PA)	Lamborn	Smith (MO)
Cramer	Lance	Smith (NE)
Crawford	Latta	Smith (NJ)
Culberson	LoBiondo	Smith (TX)
Curbelo (FL)	Long	Stefanik
Davidson	Loudermilk	Stewart
Davis, Rodney	Lucas	Stivers
Denham	Luetkemeyer	Stutzman
Dent	Lummis	Thompson (PA)
DeSantis	MacArthur	Thornberry
DesJarlais	Marchant	Tiberi
Diaz-Balart	Marino	Tipton
Dold	Massie	Trott
Donovan	McCarthy	Turner
Duffy	McClintock	Upton
Duncan (SC)	McHenry	Valadao
Duncan (TN)	McKinley	Wagner
Emmer (MN)	McMorris	Walberg
Farenthold	Rodgers	Walden
Fitzpatrick	McSally	Walker
Fleischmann	Meadows	Walorski
Fleming	Meehan	Walters, Mimi
Flores	Messer	Weber (TX)
Forbes	Mica	Webster (FL)
Fortenberry	Miller (FL)	Wenstrup
Foxx	Miller (MI)	Westerman
Franks (AZ)	Moolenaar	Wilson (SC)
Frelinghuysen	Mooney (WV)	Wittman
Garrett	Mullin	Womack
Gibbs	Mulvaney	Woodall
Gibson	Murphy (PA)	Yoder
Gohmert	Neugebauer	Yoho
Goodlatte	Newhouse	Young (AK)
Gosar	Noem	Young (IA)
Gowdy	Nunes	Young (IN)
Granger	Olson	Zeldin
Graves (GA)	Palazzo	Zinke

NAYS—180

Adams	Fudge	Nolan
Aguilar	Gabbard	Norcross
Ashford	Gallego	O'Rourke
Bass	Garamendi	Pallone
Beatty	Graham	Pascrell
Becerra	Grayson	Payne
Bera	Green, Al	Pelosi
Beyer	Green, Gene	Perlmutter
Bishop (GA)	Grijalva	Peters
Blumenauer	Gutiérrez	Peterson
Bonamici	Hanabusa	Pingree
Boyle, Brendan	Hastings	Pocan
F.	Heck (WA)	Polis
Brady (PA)	Higgins	Price (NC)
Brownley (CA)	Himes	Quigley
Bustos	Hinojosa	Rangel
Butterfield	Honda	Rice (NY)
Capps	Hoyer	Richmond
Capuano	Huffman	Roybal-Allard
Cárdenas	Israel	Ruiz
Carney	Jackson Lee	Ruppersberger
Carson (IN)	Jeffries	Rush
Cartwright	Johnson (GA)	Ryan (OH)
Castor (FL)	Johnson, E. B.	Sánchez, Linda
Castro (TX)	Kaptur	T.
Chu, Judy	Keating	Sanchez, Loretta
Cicilline	Kelly (IL)	Sarbanes
Clark (MA)	Kennedy	Schakowsky
Clarke (NY)	Kildee	Schiff
Clay	Kilmer	Schrader
Cleaver	Kind	Scott (VA)
Clyburn	Kuster	Scott, David
Cohen	Langevin	Serrano
Connolly	Larsen (WA)	Sewell (AL)
Conyers	Larson (CT)	Sherman
Cooper	Lawrence	Sires
Costa	Lee	Slaughter
Courtney	Levin	Smith (WA)
Crowley	Lewis	Speier
Cuellar	Lieu, Ted	Swalwell (CA)
Cummings	Lipinski	Takano
Davis (CA)	Loebsack	Thompson (CA)
Davis, Danny	Lofgren	Thompson (MS)
DeFazio	Lowenthal	Titus
DeGette	Lowey	Tonko
Delaney	Lujan Grisham	Torres
DeLauro	(NM)	Tsongas
DelBene	Luján, Ben Ray	Van Hollen
DeSaulnier	(NM)	Vargas
Deutch	Lynch	Veasey
Dingell	Maloney,	Vela
Doggett	Carolyn	Velázquez
Doyle, Michael	Maloney, Sean	Visclosky
F.	Matsui	Walz
Duckworth	McCollum	Wasserman
Edwards	McGovern	Schultz
Ellison	McNerney	Waters, Maxine
Engel	Meeks	Watson Coleman
Eshoo	Meng	Welch
Esty	Moulton	Wilson (FL)
Evans	Nadler	Yarmuth
Foster	Napolitano	
Frankel (FL)	Neal	

NOT VOTING—24

Barletta	Hensarling	Moore
Brown (FL)	Hurt (VA)	Murphy (FL)
Clawson (FL)	Jolly	Nugent
Crenshaw	Jones	Poe (TX)
Ellmers (NC)	Kirkpatrick	Renacci
Farr	Love	Shuster
Fincher	McCaul	Westmoreland
Hahn	McDermott	Williams

☐ 1333

Mr. HONDA changed his vote from "yea" to "nay."

So the resolution was agreed to.

The result of the vote was announced as above recorded.

A motion to reconsider was laid on the table.

PROTECTING VETERANS' EDUCATIONAL CHOICE ACT OF 2016

The SPEAKER pro tempore (Mr. HULTGREN). The unfinished business is the vote on the motion to suspend the rules and pass the bill (H.R. 5047) to direct the Secretary of Veterans Affairs and the Secretary of Labor to provide information to veterans and members of the Armed Forces about articulation agreements between institutions of higher learning, and for other purposes, on which the yeas and nays were ordered.

The Clerk read the title of the bill.

The SPEAKER pro tempore. The question is on the motion offered by the gentleman from Florida (Mr. MILLER) that the House suspend the rules and pass the bill.

This is a 5-minute vote.

The vote was taken by electronic device, and there were—yeas 411, nays 3, not voting 20, as follows:

[Roll No. 591]

YEAS—411

Abraham	Comer	Gibbs
Adams	Comstock	Gibson
Aderholt	Conaway	Gohmert
Aguilar	Connolly	Goodlatte
Allen	Conyers	Gosar
Amash	Cook	Gowdy
Amodei	Cooper	Graham
Ashford	Costa	Granger
Babin	Costello (PA)	Graves (GA)
Barr	Courtney	Graves (LA)
Barton	Cramer	Graves (MO)
Beatty	Crawford	Grayson
Becerra	Crowley	Green, Al
Benishek	Cuellar	Green, Gene
Bera	Culberson	Griffith
Beyer	Cummings	Grijalva
Bilirakis	Curbelo (FL)	Grothman
Bishop (GA)	Davidson	Guinta
Bishop (MI)	Davis (CA)	Guthrie
Bishop (UT)	Davis, Danny	Gutiérrez
Black	Davis, Rodney	Hanabusa
Blackburn	DeFazio	Hanna
Blum	DeGette	Hardy
Blumenauer	Delaney	Harper
Bonamici	DeLauro	Harris
Bost	DelBene	Hartzler
Boustany	Denham	Hastings
Boyle, Brendan	Dent	Heck (NV)
F.	DeSantis	Heck (WA)
Brady (PA)	DeSaulnier	Hensarling
Brady (TX)	DesJarlais	Herrera Beutler
Brat	Deutch	Hice, Jody B.
Bridenstine	Diaz-Balart	Higgins
Brooks (AL)	Dingell	Hill
Brooks (IN)	Doggett	Himes
Brownley (CA)	Dold	Hinojosa
Buchanan	Donovan	Holding
Buck	Doyle, Michael	Honda
Bucshon	F.	Hoyer
Burgess	Duckworth	Hudson
Bustos	Duffy	Huelskamp
Butterfield	Duncan (SC)	Huffman
Byrne	Duncan (TN)	Huizenga (MI)
Calvert	Edwards	Hultgren
Capps	Ellison	Hunter
Capuano	Ellmers (NC)	Hurd (TX)
Cárdenas	Emmer (MN)	Israel
Carney	Engel	Issa
Carson (IN)	Eshoo	Jackson Lee
Carter (GA)	Esty	Jeffries
Carter (TX)	Evans	Jenkins (KS)
Cartwright	Farenthold	Jenkins (WV)
Castor (FL)	Fitzpatrick	Johnson (GA)
Castro (TX)	Fleischmann	Johnson (OH)
Chabot	Fleming	Johnson, E. B.
Chaffetz	Flores	Johnson, Sam
Chu, Judy	Forbes	Jordan
Cicilline	Fortenberry	Joyce
Clark (MA)	Foster	Kaptur
Clarke (NY)	Foxx	Katko
Clay	Frankel (FL)	Keating
Cleaver	Franks (AZ)	Kelly (IL)
Clyburn	Frelinghuysen	Kelly (MS)
Coffman	Fudge	Kelly (PA)
Cohen	Gabbard	Kennedy
Cole	Gallego	Kildee
Collins (GA)	Garamendi	Kilmer
Collins (NY)	Garrett	Kind
King (IA)	Napolitano	Scott, David
King (NY)	Neal	Sensenbrenner
Kinzinger (IL)	Neugebauer	Serrano
Kline	Newhouse	Sessions
Knight	Noem	Sewell (AL)
Kuster	Norcross	Sherman
Labrador	Nunes	Shimkus
LaHood	O'Rourke	Shuster
LaMalfa	Olson	Simpson
Lamborn	Palazzo	Sinema
Lance	Pallone	Sires
Langevin	Palmer	Slaughter
Larsen (WA)	Pascrell	Smith (MO)
Larson (CT)	Paulsen	Smith (NE)
Latta	Payne	Smith (NJ)
Lawrence	Pearce	Smith (TX)
Lee	Pelosi	Speier
Levin	Perry	Stefanik
Lewis	Peters	Stewart
Lieu, Ted	Peterson	Stivers
Lipinski	Pingree	Stutzman
LoBiondo	Pittenger	Swalwell (CA)
Loebsack	Pitts	Takano
Lofgren	Pocan	Thompson (CA)
Long	Poliquin	Thompson (MS)
Loudermilk	Polis	Thompson (PA)
Love	Pompeo	Thornberry
Lowenthal	Posey	Tiberi
Lowey	Price (NC)	Tipton
Lucas	Price, Tom	Titus
Luetkemeyer	Quigley	Tonko
Lujan Grisham	Rangel	Torres
(NM)	Ratcliffe	Trott
Luján, Ben Ray	Reed	Tsongas
(NM)	Reichert	Turner
Lummis	Ribble	Upton
Lynch	Rice (NY)	Valadao
MacArthur	Rice (SC)	Vargas
Maloney,	Richmond	Veasey
Carolyn	Rigell	Vela
Maloney, Sean	Roby	Velázquez
Marchant	Roe (TN)	Visclosky
Marino	Rogers (AL)	Wagner
Massie	Rogers (KY)	Walberg
Matsui	Rohrabacher	Walden
McCarthy	Rokita	Walker
McClintock	Rooney (FL)	Walorski
McCollum	Ros-Lehtinen	Walters, Mimi
McGovern	Roskam	Walz
McHenry	Ross	Wasserman
McKinley	Rothfus	Schultz
McMorris	Rouzer	Waters, Maxine
Rodgers	Roybal-Allard	Watson Coleman
McNerney	Royce	Weber (TX)
McSally	Ruiz	Webster (FL)
Meadows	Ruppersberger	Welch
Meehan	Rush	Wenstrup
Meeks	Russell	Westerman
Meng	Ryan (OH)	Wilson (FL)
Messer	Salmon	Wilson (SC)
Mica	Sánchez, Linda	Wittman
Miller (FL)	T.	Womack
Miller (MI)	Sanchez, Loretta	Woodall
Moolenaar	Sanford	Yarmuth
Mooney (WV)	Sarbanes	Yoder
Moore	Scalise	Yoho
Moulton	Schakowsky	Young (AK)
Mullin	Schiff	Young (IA)
Mulvaney	Schrader	Young (IN)
Murphy (FL)	Schweikert	Zeldin
Murphy (PA)	Scott (VA)	Zinke
Nadler	Scott, Austin	

NAYS—3

Bass	Perlmutter	Smith (WA)

NOT VOTING—20

Barletta	Hurt (VA)	Nugent
Brown (FL)	Jolly	Poe (TX)
Clawson (FL)	Jones	Renacci
Crenshaw	Kirkpatrick	Van Hollen
Farr	McCaul	Westmoreland
Fincher	McDermott	Williams
Hahn	Nolan	

□ 1340

So (two-thirds being in the affirmative) the rules were suspended and the bill was passed.

The result of the vote was announced as above recorded.

A motion to reconsider was laid on the table.

Mr. RENACCI. Mr. Speaker, I was unavoidably detained on rollcalls 590 and 591. Had I been present, I would have voted "yea" on rollcall No. 590 and "yea" on rollcall No. 591.

PERMISSION TO POSTPONE PROCEEDINGS ON MOTION TO CONCUR ON SENATE AMENDMENT TO H.R. 34, TSUNAMI WARNING, EDUCATION, AND RESEARCH ACT OF 2015

Mr. UPTON. Mr. Speaker, I ask unanimous consent that the question of adopting a motion to concur in the Senate amendment to H.R. 34 with an amendment may be subject to postponement as though under clause 8 of rule XX.

The SPEAKER pro tempore. Is there objection to the request of the gentleman from Michigan?

There was no objection.

TSUNAMI WARNING, EDUCATION, AND RESEARCH ACT OF 2015

Mr. UPTON. Mr. Speaker, pursuant to House Resolution 934, I call up the bill (H.R. 34) to authorize and strengthen the tsunami detection, forecast, warning, research, and mitigation program of the National Oceanic and Atmospheric Administration, and for other purposes, with the Senate amendment thereto, and ask for its immediate consideration.

The Clerk read the title of the bill.

The SPEAKER pro tempore. The Clerk will designate the Senate amendment.

Senate amendment:

In lieu of the matter proposed to be inserted, add the following:

SECTION 1. SHORT TITLE.

This Act may be cited as the "Tsunami Warning, Education, and Research Act of 2015".

SEC. 2. REFERENCES TO THE TSUNAMI WARNING AND EDUCATION ACT.

Except as otherwise expressly provided, whenever in this Act an amendment or repeal is expressed in terms of an amendment to, or repeal of, a section or other provision, the reference shall be considered to be made to a section or other provision of the Tsunami Warning and Education Act (Public Law 109–424; 33 U.S.C. 3201 et seq.).

SEC. 3. EXPANSION OF PURPOSES OF TSUNAMI WARNING AND EDUCATION ACT.

Section 3 (33 U.S.C. 3202) is amended—

(1) in paragraph (1), by inserting "research," after "warnings,";

(2) by amending paragraph (2) to read as follows:

"(2) to enhance and modernize the existing United States Tsunami Warning System to increase the accuracy of forecasts and warnings, to ensure full coverage of tsunami threats to the United States with a network of detection assets, and to reduce false alarms;";

(3) by amending paragraph (3) to read as follows:

"(3) to improve and develop standards and guidelines for mapping, modeling, and assessment efforts to improve tsunami detection, forecasting, warnings, notification, mitigation, resiliency, response, outreach, and recovery;";

(4) by redesignating paragraphs (4), (5), and (6) as paragraphs (5), (6), and (8), respectively;

(5) by inserting after paragraph (3) the following:

"(4) to improve research efforts related to improving tsunami detection, forecasting, warnings, notification, mitigation, resiliency, response, outreach, and recovery;";

(6) in paragraph (5), as redesignated—

(A) by striking "and increase" and inserting ", increase, and develop uniform standards and guidelines for"; and

(B) by inserting ", including the warning signs of locally generated tsunami" after "approaching";

(7) in paragraph (6), as redesignated, by striking ", including the Indian Ocean; and" and inserting a semicolon; and

(8) by inserting after paragraph (6), as redesignated, the following:

"(7) to foster resilient communities in the face of tsunami and other similar coastal hazards; and".

SEC. 4. MODIFICATION OF TSUNAMI FORECASTING AND WARNING PROGRAM.

(a) IN GENERAL.—Subsection (a) of section 4 (33 U.S.C. 3203(a)) is amended by striking "Atlantic Ocean, Caribbean Sea, and Gulf of Mexico region" and inserting "Atlantic Ocean region, including the Caribbean Sea and the Gulf of Mexico".

(b) COMPONENTS.—Subsection (b) of section 4 (33 U.S.C. 3203(b)) is amended—

(1) in paragraph (1), by striking "established" and inserting "supported or maintained";

(2) by redesignating paragraphs (7) through (9) as paragraphs (8) through (10), respectively;

(3) by redesignating paragraphs (2) through (6) as paragraphs (3) through (7), respectively;

(4) by inserting after paragraph (1) the following:

"(2) to the degree practicable, maintain not less than 80 percent of the Deep-ocean Assessment and Reporting of Tsunamis buoy array at operational capacity to optimize data reliability;".

(5) by amending paragraph (5), as redesignated by paragraph (3), to read as follows:

"(5) provide tsunami forecasting capability based on models and measurements, including tsunami inundation models and maps for use in increasing the preparedness of communities and safeguarding port and harbor operations, that incorporate inputs, including—

"(A) the United States and global ocean and coastal observing system;

"(B) the global Earth observing system;

"(C) the global seismic network;

"(D) the Advanced National Seismic system;

"(E) tsunami model validation using historical and paleotsunami data;

"(F) digital elevation models and bathymetry;

"(G) newly developing tsunami detection methodologies using satellites and airborne remote sensing; and

"(H) any other data the Administrator determines is necessary;";

(6) by amending paragraph (7), as redesignated by paragraph (3), to read as follows:

"(7) include a cooperative effort among the Administration, the United States Geological Survey, and the National Science Foundation under which the Director of the United States Geological Survey and the Director of the National Science Foundation shall—

"(A) provide rapid and reliable seismic information to the Administrator from international and domestic seismic networks; and

"(B) support seismic stations installed before the date of the enactment of the Tsunami Warning, Education, and Research Act of 2015 to supplement coverage in areas of sparse instrumentation;";

(7) in paragraph (8), as redesignated by paragraph (2)—

(A) by inserting ", including graphical warning products," after "warnings";

(B) by inserting ", territories," after "States"; and

(C) by inserting "and Wireless Emergency Alerts" after "Hazards Program"; and

(8) in paragraph (9), as redesignated by paragraph (2)—

(A) by inserting "provide and" before "allow"; and

(B) by inserting "and commercial and Federal undersea communications cables" after "observing technologies".

(c) TSUNAMI WARNING SYSTEM.—Subsection (c) of section 4 (33 U.S.C. 3203(c)) is amended to read as follows:

"(c) TSUNAMI WARNING SYSTEM.—The program under this section shall operate a tsunami warning system that—

"(1) is capable of forecasting tsunami, including forecasting tsunami arrival time and inundation estimates, anywhere in the Pacific and Arctic Ocean regions and providing adequate warnings;

"(2) is capable of forecasting and providing adequate warnings, including tsunami arrival time and inundation models where applicable, in areas of the Atlantic Ocean, including the Caribbean Sea and Gulf of Mexico, that are determined—

"(A) to be geologically active, or to have significant potential for geological activity; and

"(B) to pose significant risks of tsunami for States along the coastal areas of the Atlantic Ocean, Caribbean Sea, or Gulf of Mexico; and

"(3) supports other international tsunami forecasting and warning efforts.".

(d) TSUNAMI WARNING CENTERS.—Subsection (d) of section 4 (33 U.S.C. 3203(d)) is amended to read as follows:

"(d) TSUNAMI WARNING CENTERS.—

"(1) IN GENERAL.—The Administrator shall support or maintain centers to support the tsunami warning system required by subsection (c). The Centers shall include—

"(A) the National Tsunami Warning Center, located in Alaska, which is primarily responsible for Alaska and the continental United States;

"(B) the Pacific Tsunami Warning Center, located in Hawaii, which is primarily responsible for Hawaii, the Caribbean, and other areas of the Pacific not covered by the National Center; and

"(C) any additional forecast and warning centers determined by the National Weather Service to be necessary.

"(2) RESPONSIBILITIES.—The responsibilities of the centers supported or maintained under paragraph (1) shall include the following:

"(A) Continuously monitoring data from seismological, deep ocean, coastal sea level, and tidal monitoring stations and other data sources as may be developed and deployed.

"(B) Evaluating earthquakes, landslides, and volcanic eruptions that have the potential to generate tsunami.

"(C) Evaluating deep ocean buoy data and tidal monitoring stations for indications of tsunami resulting from earthquakes and other sources.

"(D) To the extent practicable, utilizing a range of models, including ensemble models, to predict tsunami, including arrival times, flooding estimates, coastal and harbor currents, and duration.

"(E) Using data from the Integrated Ocean Observing System of the Administration in coordination with regional associations to calculate new inundation estimates and periodically update existing inundation estimates.

"(F) Disseminating forecasts and tsunami warning bulletins to Federal, State, tribal, and local government officials and the public.

"(G) Coordinating with the tsunami hazard mitigation program conducted under section 5 to

ensure ongoing sharing of information between forecasters and emergency management officials.

"(H) In coordination with the Coast Guard, evaluating and recommending procedures for ports and harbors at risk of tsunami inundation, including review of readiness, response, and communication strategies, and data sharing policies.

"(I) Making data gathered under this Act and post-warning analyses conducted by the National Weather Service or other relevant Administration offices available to the public.

"(J) Integrating and modernizing the program operated under this section with advances in tsunami science to improve performance without compromising service.

"(3) FAIL-SAFE WARNING CAPABILITY.—The tsunami warning centers supported or maintained under paragraph (1) shall maintain a fail-safe warning capability and perform backup duties for each other.

"(4) COORDINATION WITH NATIONAL WEATHER SERVICE.—The Administrator shall coordinate with the forecast offices of the National Weather Service, the centers supported or maintained under paragraph (1), and such program offices of the Administration as the Administrator or the coordinating committee, as established in section 5(d), consider appropriate to ensure that regional and local forecast offices—

"(A) have the technical knowledge and capability to disseminate tsunami warnings for the communities they serve;

"(B) leverage connections with local emergency management officials for optimally disseminating tsunami warnings and forecasts; and

"(C) implement mass communication tools in effect on the day before the date of the enactment of the Tsunami Warning, Education, and Research Act of 2015 used by the National Weather Service on such date and newer mass communication technologies as they are developed as a part of the Weather-Ready Nation program of the Administration, or otherwise, for the purpose of timely and effective delivery of tsunami warnings.

"(5) UNIFORM OPERATING PROCEDURES.—The Administrator shall—

"(A) develop uniform operational procedures for the centers supported or maintained under paragraph (1), including the use of software applications, checklists, decision support tools, and tsunami warning products that have been standardized across the program supported under this section;

"(B) ensure that processes and products of the warning system operated under subsection (c)—

"(i) reflect industry best practices when practicable;

"(ii) conform to the maximum extent practicable with internationally recognized standards for information technology; and

"(iii) conform to the maximum extent practicable with other warning products and practices of the National Weather Service;

"(C) ensure that future adjustments to operational protocols, processes, and warning products—

"(i) are made consistently across the warning system operated under subsection (c); and

"(ii) are applied in a uniform manner across such warning system;

"(D) establish a systematic method for information technology product development to improve long-term technology planning efforts; and

"(E) disseminate guidelines and metrics for evaluating and improving tsunami forecast models.

"(6) AVAILABLE RESOURCES.—The Administrator, through the National Weather Service, shall ensure that resources are available to fulfill the obligations of this Act. This includes ensuring supercomputing resources are available

to run, as rapidly as possible, such computer models as are needed for purposes of the tsunami warning system operated under subsection (c).''.

(e) TRANSFER OF TECHNOLOGY; MAINTENANCE AND UPGRADES.—Subsection (e) of section 4 (33 U.S.C. 3203(e)) is amended to read as follows:

''*(e) TRANSFER OF TECHNOLOGY; MAINTENANCE AND UPGRADES.*—In carrying out this section, the Administrator shall—

''*(1)* develop requirements for the equipment used to forecast tsunami, including—

''*(A)* provisions for multipurpose detection platforms;

''*(B)* reliability and performance metrics; and

''*(C)* to the maximum extent practicable, requirements for the integration of equipment with other United States and global ocean and coastal observation systems, the global Earth observing system of systems, the global seismic networks, and the Advanced National Seismic System;

''*(2)* develop and execute a plan for the transfer of technology from ongoing research conducted as part of the program supported or maintained under section 6 into the program under this section; and

''*(3)* ensure that the Administration's operational tsunami detection equipment is properly maintained.''.

(f) FEDERAL COOPERATION.—Subsection (f) of section 4 (33 U.S.C. 3203(f)) is amended to read as follows:

''*(f) FEDERAL COOPERATION.*—When deploying and maintaining tsunami detection technologies under the program under this section, the Administrator shall—

''*(1)* identify which assets of other Federal agencies are necessary to support such program; and

''*(2)* work with each agency identified under paragraph (1)—

''*(A)* to acquire the agency's assistance; and

''*(B)* to prioritize the necessary assets in support of the tsunami forecast and warning program.''.

(g) UNNECESSARY PROVISIONS.—Section 4 (33 U.S.C. 3203) is further amended—

(1) by striking subsection (g);

(2) by striking subsections (i) through (k); and

(3) by redesignating subsection (h) as subsection (g).

(h) CONGRESSIONAL NOTIFICATIONS.—Subsection (g) of section 4 (33 U.S.C. 3203(g)), as redesignated by subsection (g)(3), is amended—

(1) in the matter before paragraph (1), by striking ''30'' and inserting ''90'';

(2) by redesignating paragraphs (1) and (2) as subparagraphs (A) and (B), respectively, and moving such subparagraphs 2 ems to the right;

(3) in the matter before subparagraph (A), as redesignated by paragraph (2), by striking ''The Administrator'' and inserting the following:

''*(1) IN GENERAL.*—The Administrator'';

(4) in paragraph (1), as redesignated by paragraph (3)—

(A) in subparagraph (A), as redesignated by paragraph (2), by striking ''and'' at the end;

(B) in subparagraph (B), as redesignated by paragraph (2), by striking the period at the end and inserting ''; and''; and

(C) by adding at the end the following:

''*(C)* the occurrence of a significant tsunami warning.''; and

(5) by adding at the end the following:

''*(2) CONTENTS.*—In a case in which notice is submitted under paragraph (1) within 90 days of a significant tsunami warning described in subparagraph (C) of such paragraph, such notice shall include, as appropriate, brief information and analysis of—

''*(A)* the accuracy of the tsunami model used; and

''*(B)* the specific deep ocean or other monitoring equipment that detected the incident, as well as the deep ocean or other monitoring equipment that did not detect the incident due to malfunction or other reasons;

''*(C)* the effectiveness of the warning communication, including the dissemination of warnings with State, territory, local, and tribal partners in the affected area under the jurisdiction of the National Weather Service; and

''*(D)* such other findings as the Administrator considers appropriate.''.

SEC. 5. MODIFICATION OF NATIONAL TSUNAMI HAZARD MITIGATION PROGRAM.

(a) IN GENERAL.—Section 5 (33 U.S.C. 3204) is amended by striking subsections (a) through (d) and inserting the following:

''*(a) PROGRAM REQUIRED.*—The Administrator, in coordination with the Administrator of the Federal Emergency Management Agency and the heads of such other agencies as the Administrator considers relevant, shall conduct a community-based tsunami hazard mitigation program to improve tsunami preparedness and resiliency of at-risk areas in the United States and the territories of the United States.

''*(b) PROGRAM COMPONENTS.*—The Program conducted under subsection (a) shall include the following:

''*(1)* Technical and financial assistance to coastal States, territories, tribes, and local governments to develop and implement activities under this section.

''*(2)* Integration of tsunami preparedness and mitigation programs into ongoing State-based hazard warning, resilience planning, and risk management activities, including predisaster planning, emergency response, evacuation planning, disaster recovery, hazard mitigation, and community development and redevelopment planning programs in affected areas.

''*(3)* Activities to promote the adoption of tsunami resilience, preparedness, warning, and mitigation measures by Federal, State, territorial, tribal, and local governments and nongovernmental entities, including educational and risk communication programs to discourage development in high-risk areas.

''*(4)* Activities to support the development of regional tsunami hazard and risk assessments. Such regional risk assessments may include the following:

''*(A)* The sources, sizes, and other relevant historical data of tsunami in the region, including paleotsunami data.

''*(B)* Inundation models and maps of critical infrastructure and socioeconomic vulnerability in areas subject to tsunami inundation.

''*(C)* Maps of evacuation areas and evacuation routes, including, when appropriate, traffic studies that evaluate the viability of evacuation routes.

''*(D)* Evaluations of the size of populations that will require evacuation, including populations with special evacuation needs.

''*(E)* Evaluations and technical assistance for vertical evacuation structure planning for communities where models indicate limited or no ability for timely evacuation, especially in areas at risk of near shore generated tsunami.

''*(F)* Evaluation of at-risk ports and harbors.

''*(G)* Evaluation of the effect of tsunami currents on the foundations of closely-spaced, coastal high-rise structures.

''*(5)* Activities to promote preparedness in at-risk ports and harbors, including the following:

''*(A)* Evaluation and recommendation of procedures for ports and harbors in the event of a distant or near-field tsunami.

''*(B)* A review of readiness, response, and communication strategies to ensure coordination and data sharing with the Coast Guard.

''*(6)* Activities to support the development of community-based outreach and education programs to ensure community readiness and resilience, including the following:

''*(A)* The development, implementation, and assessment of technical training and public education programs, including education programs that address unique characteristics of distant and near-field tsunami.

''*(B)* The development of decision support tools.

''*(C)* The incorporation of social science research into community readiness and resilience efforts.

''*(D)* The development of evidence-based education guidelines.

''*(7)* Dissemination of guidelines and standards for community planning, education, and training products, programs, and tools, including—

''*(A)* standards for—

''*(i)* mapping products;

''*(ii)* inundation models; and

''*(iii)* effective emergency exercises; and

''*(B)* recommended guidance for at-risk port and harbor tsunami warning, evacuation, and response procedures in coordination with the Coast Guard.

''*(c) AUTHORIZED ACTIVITIES.*—In addition to activities conducted under subsection (b), the program conducted under subsection (a) may include the following:

''*(1)* Multidisciplinary vulnerability assessment research, education, and training to help integrate risk management and resilience objectives with community development planning and policies.

''*(2)* Risk management training for local officials and community organizations to enhance understanding and preparedness.

''*(3)* Interagency, Federal, State, tribal, and territorial intergovernmental tsunami response exercise planning and implementation in high risk areas.

''*(4)* Development of practical applications for existing or emerging technologies, such as modeling, remote sensing, geospatial technology, engineering, and observing systems, including the integration of tsunami sensors into Federal and commercial submarine telecommunication cables if practicable.

''*(5)* Risk management, risk assessment, and resilience data and information services, including—

''*(A)* access to data and products derived from observing and detection systems; and

''*(B)* development and maintenance of new integrated data products to support risk management, risk assessment, and resilience programs.

''*(6)* Risk notification systems that coordinate with and build upon existing systems and actively engage decisionmakers, State, local, tribal, and territorial governments and agencies, business communities, nongovernmental organizations, and the media.

''*(d) COORDINATING COMMITTEE.*—

''*(1) IN GENERAL.*—The Administrator shall maintain a coordinating committee to assist the Administrator in the conduct of the program required by subsection (a).

''*(2) COMPOSITION.*—The coordinating committee shall be composed of members as follows:

''*(A)* Representatives from each of the States and territories most at risk from tsunami, including Alaska, Washington, Oregon, California, Hawaii, Puerto Rico, Guam, American Samoa, and the Northern Marianas Islands.

''*(B)* Such other members as the Administrator considers appropriate to represent Federal, State, tribal, territorial, and local governments.

''*(3) SUBCOMMITTEES.*—The Administrator may approve the formation of subcommittees to address specific program components or regional issues.

''*(4) RESPONSIBILITIES.*—The coordinating committee shall—

''*(A)* provide feedback on how funds should be prioritized to carry out the program required by subsection (a);

"(B) ensure that areas described in section 4(c) in the United States and its territories have the opportunity to participate in the program;

"(C) provide recommendations to the Administrator on how to improve and continuously advance the TsunamiReady program of the National Weather Service, particularly on ways to make communities more tsunami resilient through the use of inundation maps and models and other hazard mitigation practices;

"(D) ensure that all components of the program required by subsection (a) are integrated with ongoing State based hazard warning, risk management, and resilience activities, including—

"(i) integrating activities with emergency response plans, disaster recovery, hazard mitigation, and community development programs in affected areas; and

"(ii) integrating information to assist in tsunami evacuation route planning.

"(5) EXEMPTION FROM FACA.—The provisions of the Federal Advisory Committee Act (5 U.S.C. App.) shall not apply to the committee established and maintained under paragraph (1).

"(e) NO PREEMPTION WITH RESPECT TO DESIGNATION OF AT-RISK AREAS.—The establishment of national standards for inundation models under this section shall not prevent States, territories, tribes, and local governments from designating additional areas as being at risk based on knowledge of local conditions.

"(f) NO NEW REGULATORY AUTHORITY.—Nothing in this Act may be construed as establishing new regulatory authority for any Federal agency.".

(b)   REPORT   ON   ACCREDITATION   OF TSUNAMIREADY PROGRAM.—Not later than 180 days after the date of enactment of this Act, the Administrator of the National Oceanic and Atmospheric Administration shall submit to the Committee on Commerce, Science, and Transportation of the Senate and the Committee on Science, Space, and Technology of the House of Representatives a report on which authorities and activities would be needed to have the TsunamiReady program of the National Weather Service accredited by the Emergency Management Accreditation Program.

SEC. 6. MODIFICATION OF TSUNAMI RESEARCH PROGRAM.

Section 6 (33 U.S.C. 3205) is amended—

(1) in the matter before paragraph (1), by striking "The Administrator shall" and all that follows through "establish or maintain" and inserting the following:

"(a) IN GENERAL.—The Administrator shall, in consultation with such other Federal agencies, State, tribal, and territorial governments, and academic institutions as the Administrator considers appropriate, the coordinating committee under section 5(d), and the panel under section 8(a), support or maintain";

(2) in subsection (a), as designated by paragraph (1), by striking "and assessment for tsunami tracking and numerical forecast modeling. Such research program shall—" and inserting the following: "assessment for tsunami tracking and numerical forecast modeling, and standards development.

"(b) RESPONSIBILITIES.—The research program supported or maintained under subsection (a) shall—"; and

(3) in subsection (b), as designated by paragraph (2)—

(A) by amending paragraph (1) to read as follows:

"(1) consider other appropriate and cost effective solutions to mitigate the impact of tsunami, including the improvement of near-field and distant tsunami detection and forecasting capabilities, which may include use of a new generation of the Deep-ocean Assessment and Reporting of Tsunamis array, integration of tsunami sensors

into commercial and Federal telecommunications cables, and other real-time tsunami monitoring systems and supercomputer capacity of the Administration to develop a rapid tsunami forecast for all United States coastlines;";

(B) in paragraph (3)—

(i) by striking "include" and inserting "conduct"; and

(ii) by striking "and" at the end;

(C) by redesignating paragraph (4) as paragraph (5);

(D) by inserting after paragraph (3) the following:

"(4) develop the technical basis for validation of tsunami maps, numerical tsunami models, digital elevation models, and forecasts; and"; and

(E) in paragraph (5), as redesignated by subparagraph (C), by striking "to the scientific community" and inserting "to the public and the scientific community".

SEC. 7. GLOBAL TSUNAMI WARNING AND MITIGATION NETWORK.

Section 7 (33 U.S.C. 3206) is amended—

(1) by amending subsection (a) to read as follows:

"(a) SUPPORT FOR DEVELOPMENT OF AN INTERNATIONAL TSUNAMI WARNING SYSTEM.—The Administrator shall, in coordination with the Secretary of State and in consultation with such other agencies as the Administrator considers relevant, provide technical assistance, operational support, and training to the Intergovernmental Oceanographic Commission of the United Nations Educational, Scientific, and Cultural Organization, the World Meteorological Organization of the United Nations, and such other international entities as the Administrator considers appropriate, as part of the international efforts to develop a fully functional global tsunami forecast and warning system comprised of regional tsunami warning networks.";

(2) in subsection (b), by striking "shall" each place it appears and inserting "may"; and

(3) in subsection (c)—

(A) in paragraph (1), by striking "establishing" and inserting "supporting"; and

(B) in paragraph (2)—

(i) by striking "establish" and inserting "support"; and

(ii) by striking "establishing" and inserting "supporting".

SEC. 8. TSUNAMI SCIENCE AND TECHNOLOGY ADVISORY PANEL.

(a) IN GENERAL.—The Act is further amended—

(1) by redesignating section 8 (33 U.S.C. 3207) as section 9; and

(2) by inserting after section 7 (33 U.S.C. 3206) the following:

"SEC. 8. TSUNAMI SCIENCE AND TECHNOLOGY ADVISORY PANEL.

"(a) DESIGNATION.—The Administrator shall designate an existing working group within the Science Advisory Board of the Administration to manage the Tsunami Science and Technology Advisory Panel to provide advice to the Administrator on matters regarding tsunami science, technology, and regional preparedness.

"(b) MEMBERSHIP.—

"(1) COMPOSITION.—The Panel shall be composed of no fewer than 7 members selected by the Administrator from among individuals from academia or State agencies who have academic or practical expertise in physical sciences, social sciences, information technology, coastal resilience, emergency management, or such other disciplines as the Administrator considers appropriate.

"(2) FEDERAL EMPLOYMENT.—No member of the Panel may be a Federal employee.

"(c) RESPONSIBILITIES.—Not less frequently than once every 4 years, the Panel shall—

"(1) review the activities of the Administration, and other Federal activities as appropriate, relating to tsunami research, detection, forecasting, warning, mitigation, resiliency, and preparation; and

"(2) submit to the Administrator and such others as the Administrator considers appropriate—

"(A) the findings of the working group with respect to the most recent review conducted under paragraph (1); and

"(B) such recommendations for legislative or administrative action as the working group considers appropriate to improve Federal tsunami research, detection, forecasting, warning, mitigation, resiliency, and preparation.

"(d) REPORTS TO CONGRESS.—Not less frequently than once every 4 years, the Administrator shall submit to the Committee on Commerce, Science, and Transportation of the Senate, and the Committee on Science, Space, and Technology of the House of Representatives a report on the findings and recommendations received by the Administrator under subsection (c)(2).".

SEC. 9. REPORTS.

(a) REPORT ON IMPLEMENTATION OF TSUNAMI WARNING AND EDUCATION ACT.—

(1) IN GENERAL.—Not later than 1 year after the date of the enactment of this Act, the Administrator of the National Oceanic and Atmospheric Administration shall submit to Congress a report on the implementation of the Tsunami Warning and Education Act (33 U.S.C. 3201 et seq.).

(2) ELEMENTS.—The report required by paragraph (1) shall include the following:

(A) A detailed description of the progress made in implementing sections 4(d)(6), 5(b)(6), and 6(b)(4) of the Tsunami Warning and Education Act.

(B) A description of the ways that tsunami warnings and warning products issued by the Tsunami Forecasting and Warning Program established under section 4 of the Tsunami Warning and Education Act (33 U.S.C. 3203) can be standardized and streamlined with warnings and warning products for hurricanes, coastal storms, and other coastal flooding events.

(b) REPORT ON NATIONAL EFFORTS THAT SUPPORT RAPID RESPONSE FOLLOWING NEAR-SHORE TSUNAMI EVENTS.—

(1) IN GENERAL.—Not later than 1 year after the date of the enactment of this Act, the Administrator and the Secretary of Homeland Security shall jointly, in coordination with the Director of the United States Geological Survey, Administrator of the Federal Emergency Management Agency, the Chief of the National Guard Bureau, and the heads of such other Federal agencies as the Administrator considers appropriate, submit to the appropriate committees of Congress a report on the national efforts in effect on the day before the date of the enactment of this Act that support and facilitate rapid emergency response following a domestic near-shore tsunami event to better understand domestic effects of earthquake derived tsunami on people, infrastructure, and communities in the United States.

(2) ELEMENTS.—The report required by paragraph (1) shall include the following:

(A) A description of scientific or other measurements collected on the day before the date of the enactment of this Act to quickly identify and quantify lost or degraded infrastructure or terrestrial formations.

(B) A description of scientific or other measurements that would be necessary to collect to quickly identify and quantify lost or degraded infrastructure or terrestrial formations.

(C) Identification and evaluation of Federal, State, local, tribal, territorial, and military first responder and search and rescue operation centers, bases, and other facilities as well as other *critical response assets and infrastructure, including search and rescue aircraft, located within near-shore and distant tsunami inundation areas on the day before the date of the enactment of this Act.*

(D) An evaluation of near-shore tsunami response plans in areas described in subparagraph (C) in effect on the day before the date of the enactment of this Act, and how those response plans would be affected by the loss of search and rescue and first responder infrastructure described in such subparagraph.

(E) A description of redevelopment plans and reports in effect on the day before the date of the enactment of this Act for communities in areas that are at high-risk for near-shore tsunami, as well identification of States or communities that do not have redevelopment plans.

(F) Recommendations to enhance near-shore tsunami preparedness and response plans, including recommended responder exercises, predisaster planning, and mitigation needs.

(G) Such other data and analysis information as the Administrator and the Secretary of Homeland Security consider appropriate.

(3) APPROPRIATE COMMITTEES OF CONGRESS.—In this subsection, the term "appropriate committees of Congress" means—

(A) the Committee on Commerce, Science, and Transportation and the Committee on Homeland Security and Governmental Affairs of the Senate; and

(B) the Committee on Science, Space, and Technology and the Committee on Homeland Security of the House of Representatives.

SEC. 10. AUTHORIZATION OF APPROPRIATIONS.

Section 9 of the Act, as redesignated by section 8(a)(1) of this Act, is amended—

(1) in paragraph (4)(B), by striking "and" at the end;

(2) in paragraph (5)(B), by striking the period at the end and inserting "; and"; and

(3) by adding at the end the following:

"(6) $27,000,000 for each of fiscal years 2016 through 2021, of which—

"(A) not less than 27 percent of the amount appropriated for each fiscal year shall be for activities conducted at the State level under the tsunami hazard mitigation program under section 5; and

"(B) not less than 8 percent of the amount appropriated shall be for the tsunami research program under section 6.".

SEC. 11. OUTREACH RESPONSIBILITIES.

The Administrator of the National Oceanic and Atmospheric Administration, in coordination with State and local emergency managers, shall develop and carry out formal outreach activities to improve tsunami education and awareness and foster the development of resilient communities. Outreach activities may include—

(1) the development of outreach plans to ensure the close integration of tsunami warning centers supported or maintained under section 4(d) of the Tsunami Warning and Education Act (33 U.S.C. 3203(d)) with local Weather Forecast Offices of the National Weather Service and emergency managers;

(2) working with appropriate local Weather Forecast Offices to ensure they have the technical knowledge and capability to disseminate tsunami warnings to the communities they serve; and

(3) evaluating the effectiveness of warnings and of coordination with local Weather Forecast Offices after significant tsunami events.

SEC. 12. MODIFICATION OF COASTAL OCEAN PROGRAM.

Section 201(c) of the National Oceanic and Atmospheric Administration Authorization Act of 1992 (Public Law 102–567; 106 Stat. 4280) is amended—

(1) by inserting "(1) IN GENERAL.—" before "Of the sums" and indenting appropriately; and

(2) by adding at the end the following:

"(2) REGIONAL COASTAL RISK MANAGEMENT COALITIONS.—The Administrator of the National Oceanic and Atmospheric Administration may form regional coastal risk management coalitions comprised of representatives of Federal, State, local, and tribal governments, community groups, academic institutions, and nongovernmental groups to advance the goals of this section for communities facing common coastal hazards and risks. Such coalitions may enter into an agreement with an organization described in section 501(c)(3) of the Internal Revenue Code of 1986 to establish a nonprofit foundation in order to accept gifts and donations to support the goals of this subsection.".

SEC. 13. REPEAL OF DUPLICATE PROVISIONS OF LAW.

(a) REPEAL.—The Magnuson-Stevens Fishery Conservation and Management Reauthorization Act of 2006 (Public Law 109–479) is amended by striking title VIII (relating to tsunami warning and education).

(b) CONSTRUCTION.—Nothing in this section shall be construed to repeal, or affect in any way, Public Law 109–424.

MOTION OFFERED BY MR. UPTON

Mr. UPTON. Mr. Speaker, I have a motion at the desk.

The SPEAKER pro tempore. The Clerk will designate the motion.

The text of the motion is as follows:

Mr. Upton moves that the House concur in the Senate amendment to H.R. 34 with an amendment inserting the text of Rules Committee Print 114–67, modified by the amendment printed in part A of House Report 114–839, in lieu of the matter proposed to be added by the Senate.

The text of the House amendment to the Senate amendment to the text is as follows:

SECTION 1. SHORT TITLE; TABLE OF CONTENTS.

(a) SHORT TITLE.—This Act may be cited as the "21st Century Cures Act".

(b) TABLE OF CONTENTS.—The table of contents for this Act is as follows:

Sec. 1. Short title; table of contents.

DIVISION A—21ST CENTURY CURES

Sec. 1000. Short title.

TITLE I—INNOVATION PROJECTS AND STATE RESPONSES TO OPIOID ABUSE

Sec. 1001. NIH innovation projects.
Sec. 1002. FDA innovation projects.
Sec. 1003. Account for the state response to the opioid abuse crisis.
Sec. 1004. Budgetary treatment.

TITLE II—DISCOVERY

Subtitle A—National Institutes of Health Reauthorization

Sec. 2001. National Institutes of Health Reauthorization.
Sec. 2002. EUREKA prize competitions.

Subtitle B—Advancing Precision Medicine

Sec. 2011. Precision Medicine Initiative.
Sec. 2012. Privacy protection for human research subjects.
Sec. 2013. Protection of identifiable and sensitive information.
Sec. 2014. Data sharing.

Subtitle C—Supporting Young Emerging Scientists

Sec. 2021. Investing in the next generation of researchers.
Sec. 2022. Improvement of loan repayment program.

Subtitle D—National Institutes of Health Planning and Administration

Sec. 2031. National Institutes of Health strategic plan.

Sec. 2032. Triennial reports.
Sec. 2033. Increasing accountability at the National Institutes of Health.
Sec. 2034. Reducing administrative burden for researchers.
Sec. 2035. Exemption for the National Institutes of Health from the Paperwork Reduction Act requirements.
Sec. 2036. High-risk, high-reward research.
Sec. 2037. National Center for Advancing Translational Sciences.
Sec. 2038. Collaboration and coordination to enhance research.
Sec. 2039. Enhancing the rigor and reproducibility of scientific research.
Sec. 2040. Improving medical rehabilitation research at the National Institutes of Health.
Sec. 2041. Task force on research specific to pregnant women and lactating women.
Sec. 2042. Streamlining National Institutes of Health reporting requirements.
Sec. 2043. Reimbursement for research substances and living organisms.
Sec. 2044. Sense of Congress on increased inclusion of underrepresented populations in clinical trials.

Subtitle E—Advancement of the National Institutes of Health Research and Data Access

Sec. 2051. Technical updates to clinical trials database.
Sec. 2052. Compliance activities reports.
Sec. 2053. Updates to policies to improve data.
Sec. 2054. Consultation.

Subtitle F—Facilitating Collaborative Research

Sec. 2061. National neurological conditions surveillance system.
Sec. 2062. Tick-borne diseases.
Sec. 2063. Accessing, sharing, and using health data for research purposes.

Subtitle G—Promoting Pediatric Research

Sec. 2071. National pediatric research network.
Sec. 2072. Global pediatric clinical study network.

TITLE III—DEVELOPMENT

Subtitle A—Patient-Focused Drug Development

Sec. 3001. Patient experience data.
Sec. 3002. Patient-focused drug development guidance.
Sec. 3003. Streamlining patient input.
Sec. 3004. Report on patient experience drug development.

Subtitle B—Advancing New Drug Therapies

Sec. 3011. Qualification of drug development tools.
Sec. 3012. Targeted drugs for rare diseases.
Sec. 3013. Reauthorization of program to encourage treatments for rare pediatric diseases.
Sec. 3014. GAO study of priority review voucher programs.
Sec. 3015. Amendments to the Orphan Drug grants.
Sec. 3016. Grants for studying continuous drug manufacturing.

Subtitle C—Modern Trial Design and Evidence Development

Sec. 3021. Novel clinical trial designs.
Sec. 3022. Real world evidence.
Sec. 3023. Protection of human research subjects.
Sec. 3024. Informed consent waiver or alteration for clinical investigations.

Subtitle D—Patient Access to Therapies and Information

Sec. 3031. Summary level review.
Sec. 3032. Expanded access policy.
Sec. 3033. Accelerated approval for regenerative advanced therapies.
Sec. 3034. Guidance regarding devices used in the recovery, isolation, or delivery of regenerative advanced therapies.

Sec. 3035. Report on regenerative advanced therapies.
Sec. 3036. Standards for regenerative medicine and regenerative advanced therapies.
Sec. 3037. Health care economic information.
Sec. 3038. Combination product innovation.

Subtitle E—Antimicrobial Innovation and Stewardship

Sec. 3041. Antimicrobial resistance monitoring.
Sec. 3042. Limited population pathway.
Sec. 3043. Prescribing authority.
Sec. 3044. Susceptibility test interpretive criteria for microorganisms; antimicrobial susceptibility testing devices.

Subtitle F—Medical Device Innovations

Sec. 3051. Breakthrough devices.
Sec. 3052. Humanitarian device exemption.
Sec. 3053. Recognition of standards.
Sec. 3054. Certain class I and class II devices.
Sec. 3055. Classification panels.
Sec. 3056. Institutional review board flexibility.
Sec. 3057. CLIA waiver improvements.
Sec. 3058. Least burdensome device review.
Sec. 3059. Cleaning instructions and validation data requirement.
Sec. 3060. Clarifying medical software regulation.

Subtitle G—Improving Scientific Expertise and Outreach at FDA

Sec. 3071. Silvio O. Conte Senior Biomedical Research and Biomedical Product Assessment Service.
Sec. 3072. Hiring authority for scientific, technical, and professional personnel.
Sec. 3073. Establishment of Food and Drug Administration Intercenter Institutes.
Sec. 3074. Scientific engagement.
Sec. 3075. Drug surveillance.
Sec. 3076. Reagan-Udall Foundation for the Food and Drug Administration.

Subtitle H—Medical Countermeasures Innovation

Sec. 3081. Medical countermeasure guidelines.
Sec. 3082. Clarifying BARDA contracting authority.
Sec. 3083. Countermeasure budget plan.
Sec. 3084. Medical countermeasures innovation.
Sec. 3085. Streamlining Project BioShield procurement.
Sec. 3086. Encouraging treatments for agents that present a national security threat.
Sec. 3087. Paperwork Reduction Act waiver during a public health emergency.
Sec. 3088. Clarifying Food and Drug Administration emergency use authorization.

Subtitle I—Vaccine Access, Certainty, and Innovation

Sec. 3091. Predictable review timelines of vaccines by the Advisory Committee on Immunization Practices.
Sec. 3092. Review of processes and consistency of Advisory Committee on Immunization Practices recommendations.
Sec. 3093. Encouraging vaccine innovation.

Subtitle J—Technical Corrections

Sec. 3101. Technical corrections.
Sec. 3102. Completed studies.

TITLE IV—DELIVERY

Sec. 4001. Assisting doctors and hospitals in improving quality of care for patients.
Sec. 4002. Transparent reporting on usability, security, and functionality.
Sec. 4003. Interoperability.
Sec. 4004. Information blocking.
Sec. 4005. Leveraging electronic health records to improve patient care.

Sec. 4006. Empowering patients and improving patient access to their electronic health information.
Sec. 4007. GAO study on patient matching.
Sec. 4008. GAO study on patient access to health information.
Sec. 4009. Streamlining transfers used for educational purposes.
Sec. 4010. Improving Medicare local coverage determinations.
Sec. 4011. Medicare pharmaceutical and technology ombudsman.
Sec. 4012. Medicare site-of-service price transparency.
Sec. 4013. Telehealth services in Medicare.

TITLE V—SAVINGS

Sec. 5001. Savings in the Medicare Improvement Fund.
Sec. 5002. Medicaid reimbursement to States for durable medical equipment.
Sec. 5003. Penalties for violations of grants, contracts, and other agreements.
Sec. 5004. Reducing overpayments of infusion drugs.
Sec. 5005. Increasing oversight of termination of Medicaid providers.
Sec. 5006. Requiring publication of fee-for-service provider directory.
Sec. 5007. Fairness in Medicaid supplemental needs trusts.
Sec. 5008. Eliminating Federal financial participation with respect to expenditures under Medicaid for agents used for cosmetic purposes or hair growth.
Sec. 5009. Amendment to the Prevention and Public Health Fund.
Sec. 5010. Strategic Petroleum Reserve drawdown.
Sec. 5011. Rescission of portion of ACA territory funding.
Sec. 5012. Medicare coverage of home infusion therapy.

DIVISION B—HELPING FAMILIES IN MENTAL HEALTH CRISIS

Sec. 6000. Short title.

TITLE VI—STRENGTHENING LEADERSHIP AND ACCOUNTABILITY

Subtitle A—Leadership

Sec. 6001. Assistant Secretary for Mental Health and Substance Use.
Sec. 6002. Strengthening the leadership of the Substance Abuse and Mental Health Services Administration.
Sec. 6003. Chief Medical Officer.
Sec. 6004. Improving the quality of behavioral health programs.
Sec. 6005. Strategic plan.
Sec. 6006. Biennial report concerning activities and progress.
Sec. 6007. Authorities of centers for mental health services, substance abuse prevention, and substance abuse treatment.
Sec. 6008. Advisory councils.
Sec. 6009. Peer review.

Subtitle B—Oversight and Accountability

Sec. 6021. Improving oversight of mental and substance use disorders programs through the Assistant Secretary for Planning and Evaluation.
Sec. 6022. Reporting for protection and advocacy organizations.
Sec. 6023. GAO study.

Subtitle C—Interdepartmental Serious Mental Illness Coordinating Committee

Sec. 6031. Interdepartmental Serious Mental Illness Coordinating Committee.

TITLE VII—ENSURING MENTAL AND SUBSTANCE USE DISORDERS PREVENTION, TREATMENT, AND RECOVERY PROGRAMS KEEP PACE WITH SCIENCE AND TECHNOLOGY

Sec. 7001. Encouraging innovation and evidence-based programs.
Sec. 7002. Promoting access to information on evidence-based programs and practices.
Sec. 7003. Priority mental health needs of regional and national significance.
Sec. 7004. Priority substance use disorder treatment needs of regional and national significance.
Sec. 7005. Priority substance use disorder prevention needs of regional and national significance.

TITLE VIII—SUPPORTING STATE PREVENTION ACTIVITIES AND RESPONSES TO MENTAL HEALTH AND SUBSTANCE USE DISORDER NEEDS

Sec. 8001. Community mental health services block grant.
Sec. 8002. Substance abuse prevention and treatment block grant.
Sec. 8003. Additional provisions related to the block grants.
Sec. 8004. Study of distribution of funds under the substance abuse prevention and treatment block grant and the community mental health services block grant.

TITLE IX—PROMOTING ACCESS TO MENTAL HEALTH AND SUBSTANCE USE DISORDER CARE

Subtitle A—Helping Individuals and Families

Sec. 9001. Grants for treatment and recovery for homeless individuals.
Sec. 9002. Grants for jail diversion programs.
Sec. 9003. Promoting integration of primary and behavioral health care.
Sec. 9004. Projects for assistance in transition from homelessness.
Sec. 9005. National Suicide Prevention Lifeline Program.
Sec. 9006. Connecting individuals and families with care.
Sec. 9007. Strengthening community crisis response systems.
Sec. 9008. Garrett Lee Smith Memorial Act reauthorization.
Sec. 9009. Adult suicide prevention.
Sec. 9010. Mental health awareness training grants.
Sec. 9011. Sense of Congress on prioritizing American Indians and Alaska Native youth within suicide prevention programs.
Sec. 9012. Evidence-based practices for older adults.
Sec. 9013. National violent death reporting system.
Sec. 9014. Assisted outpatient treatment.
Sec. 9015. Assertive community treatment grant program.
Sec. 9016. Sober truth on preventing underage drinking reauthorization.
Sec. 9017. Center and program repeals.

Subtitle B—Strengthening the Health Care Workforce

Sec. 9021. Mental and behavioral health education and training grants.
Sec. 9022. Strengthening the mental and substance use disorders workforce.
Sec. 9023. Clarification on current eligibility for loan repayment programs.
Sec. 9024. Minority fellowship program.
Sec. 9025. Liability protections for health professional volunteers at community health centers.
Sec. 9026. Reports.

Subtitle C—Mental Health on Campus Improvement

Sec. 9031. *Mental health and substance use disorder services on campus.*
Sec. 9032. *Interagency Working Group on College Mental Health.*
Sec. 9033. *Improving mental health on college campuses.*

TITLE X—STRENGTHENING MENTAL AND SUBSTANCE USE DISORDER CARE FOR CHILDREN AND ADOLESCENTS

Sec. 10001. *Programs for children with a serious emotional disturbance.*
Sec. 10002. *Increasing access to pediatric mental health care.*
Sec. 10003. *Substance use disorder treatment and early intervention services for children and adolescents.*
Sec. 10004. *Children's recovery from trauma.*
Sec. 10005. *Screening and treatment for maternal depression.*
Sec. 10006. *Infant and early childhood mental health promotion, intervention, and treatment.*

TITLE XI—COMPASSIONATE COMMUNICATION ON HIPAA

Sec. 11001. *Sense of Congress.*
Sec. 11002. *Confidentiality of records.*
Sec. 11003. *Clarification on permitted uses and disclosures of protected health information.*
Sec. 11004. *Development and dissemination of model training programs.*

TITLE XII—MEDICAID MENTAL HEALTH COVERAGE

Sec. 12001. *Rule of construction related to Medicaid coverage of mental health services and primary care services furnished on the same day.*
Sec. 12002. *Study and report related to Medicaid managed care regulation.*
Sec. 12003. *Guidance on opportunities for innovation.*
Sec. 12004. *Study and report on Medicaid emergency psychiatric demonstration project.*
Sec. 12005. *Providing EPSDT services to children in IMDs.*
Sec. 12006. *Electronic visit verification system required for personal care services and home health care services under Medicaid.*

TITLE XIII—MENTAL HEALTH PARITY

Sec. 13001. *Enhanced compliance with mental health and substance use disorder coverage requirements.*
Sec. 13002. *Action plan for enhanced enforcement of mental health and substance use disorder coverage.*
Sec. 13003. *Report on investigations regarding parity in mental health and substance use disorder benefits.*
Sec. 13004. *GAO study on parity in mental health and substance use disorder benefits.*
Sec. 13005. *Information and awareness on eating disorders.*
Sec. 13006. *Education and training on eating disorders.*
Sec. 13007. *Clarification of existing parity rules.*

TITLE XIV—MENTAL HEALTH AND SAFE COMMUNITIES

Subtitle A—Mental Health and Safe Communities

Sec. 14001. *Law enforcement grants for crisis intervention teams, mental health purposes.*
Sec. 14002. *Assisted outpatient treatment programs.*
Sec. 14003. *Federal drug and mental health courts.*

Sec. 14004. *Mental health in the judicial system.*
Sec. 14005. *Forensic assertive community treatment initiatives.*
Sec. 14006. *Assistance for individuals transitioning out of systems.*
Sec. 14007. *Co-occurring substance abuse and mental health challenges in drug courts.*
Sec. 14008. *Mental health training for Federal uniformed services.*
Sec. 14009. *Advancing mental health as part of offender reentry.*
Sec. 14010. *School mental health crisis intervention teams.*
Sec. 14011. *Active-shooter training for law enforcement.*
Sec. 14012. *Co-occurring substance abuse and mental health challenges in residential substance abuse treatment programs.*
Sec. 14013. *Mental health and drug treatment alternatives to incarceration programs.*
Sec. 14014. *National criminal justice and mental health training and technical assistance.*
Sec. 14015. *Improving Department of Justice data collection on mental illness involved in crime.*
Sec. 14016. *Reports on the number of mentally ill offenders in prison.*
Sec. 14017. *Department of Veterans Affairs patients' rights.*
Sec. 14018. *Reauthorization of appropriations.*

Subtitle B—Comprehensive Justice and Mental Health

Sec. 14021. *Sequential intercept model.*
Sec. 14022. *Prison and jails.*
Sec. 14023. *Allowable uses.*
Sec. 14024. *Law enforcement training.*
Sec. 14025. *Federal law enforcement training.*
Sec. 14026. *GAO report.*
Sec. 14027. *Evidence based practices.*
Sec. 14028. *Transparency, program accountability, and enhancement of local authority.*
Sec. 14029. *Grant accountability.*

DIVISION C—INCREASING CHOICE, ACCESS, AND QUALITY IN HEALTH CARE FOR AMERICANS

Sec. 15000. *Short title.*

TITLE XV—PROVISIONS RELATING TO MEDICARE PART A

Sec. 15001. *Development of Medicare HCPCS version of MS–DRG codes for similar hospital services.*
Sec. 15002. *Establishing beneficiary equity in the Medicare hospital readmission program.*
Sec. 15003. *Five-year extension of the rural community hospital demonstration program.*
Sec. 15004. *Regulatory relief for LTCHs.*
Sec. 15005. *Savings from IPPS MACRA pay-for through not applying documentation and coding adjustments.*
Sec. 15006. *Extension of certain LTCH Medicare payment rules.*
Sec. 15007. *Application of rules on the calculation of hospital length of stay to all LTCHs.*
Sec. 15008. *Change in Medicare classification for certain hospitals.*
Sec. 15009. *Temporary exception to the application of the Medicare LTCH site neutral provisions for certain spinal cord specialty hospitals.*
Sec. 15010. *Temporary extension to the application of the Medicare LTCH site neutral provisions for certain discharges with severe wounds.*

TITLE XVI—PROVISIONS RELATING TO MEDICARE PART B

Sec. 16001. *Continuing Medicare payment under HOPD prospective payment system for services furnished by mid-build off-campus outpatient departments of providers.*
Sec. 16002. *Treatment of cancer hospitals in off-campus outpatient department of a provider policy.*
Sec. 16003. *Treatment of eligible professionals in ambulatory surgical centers for meaningful use and MIPS.*
Sec. 16004. *Continuing Access to Hospitals Act of 2016.*
Sec. 16005. *Delay of implementation of Medicare fee schedule adjustments for wheelchair accessories and seating systems when used in conjunction with complex rehabilitation technology (CRT) wheelchairs.*
Sec. 16006. *Allowing physical therapists to utilize locum tenens arrangements under Medicare.*
Sec. 16007. *Extension of the transition to new payment rates for durable medical equipment under the Medicare program.*
Sec. 16008. *Requirements in determining adjustments using information from competitive bidding programs.*

TITLE XVII—OTHER MEDICARE PROVISIONS

Sec. 17001. *Delay in authority to terminate contracts for Medicare Advantage plans failing to achieve minimum quality ratings.*
Sec. 17002. *Requirement for enrollment data reporting for Medicare.*
Sec. 17003. *Updating the Welcome to Medicare package.*
Sec. 17004. *No payment for items and services furnished by newly enrolled providers or suppliers within a temporary moratorium area.*
Sec. 17005. *Preservation of Medicare beneficiary choice under Medicare Advantage.*
Sec. 17006. *Allowing end-stage renal disease beneficiaries to choose a Medicare Advantage plan.*
Sec. 17007. *Improvements to the assignment of beneficiaries under the Medicare Shared Savings Program.*

TITLE XVIII—OTHER PROVISIONS

Sec. 18001. *Exception from group health plan requirements for qualified small employer health reimbursement arrangements.*

DIVISION D—CHILD AND FAMILY SERVICES AND SUPPORT

Sec. 19000. *Short title.*

TITLE XIX—INVESTING IN PREVENTION AND FAMILY SERVICES

Sec. 19001. *Purpose.*

Subtitle A—Prevention Activities Under Title IV–E

Sec. 19011. *Foster care prevention services and programs.*
Sec. 19012. *Foster care maintenance payments for children with parents in a licensed residential family-based treatment facility for substance abuse.*
Sec. 19013. *Title IV–E payments for evidence-based kinship navigator programs.*

Subtitle B—Enhanced Support Under Title IV–B

Sec. 19021. Elimination of time limit for family reunification services while in foster care and permitting time-limited family reunification services when a child returns home from foster care.

Sec. 19022. Reducing bureaucracy and unnecessary delays when placing children in homes across State lines.

Sec. 19023. Enhancements to grants to improve well-being of families affected by substance abuse.

Subtitle C—Miscellaneous

Sec. 19031. Reviewing and improving licensing standards for placement in a relative foster family home.

Sec. 19032. Development of a statewide plan to prevent child abuse and neglect fatalities.

Sec. 19033. Modernizing the title and purpose of title IV–E.

Sec. 19034. Effective dates.

TITLE XX—ENSURING THE NECESSITY OF A PLACEMENT THAT IS NOT IN A FOSTER FAMILY HOME

Sec. 20001. Limitation on Federal financial participation for placements that are not in foster family homes.

Sec. 20002. Assessment and documentation of the need for placement in a qualified residential treatment program.

Sec. 20003. Protocols to prevent inappropriate diagnoses.

Sec. 20004. Additional data and reports regarding children placed in a setting that is not a foster family home.

Sec. 20005. Effective dates; application to waivers.

TITLE XXI—CONTINUING SUPPORT FOR CHILD AND FAMILY SERVICES

Sec. 21001. Supporting and retaining foster families for children.

Sec. 21002. Extension of child and family services programs.

Sec. 21003. Improvements to the John H. Chafee foster care independence program and related provisions.

TITLE XXII—CONTINUING INCENTIVES TO STATES TO PROMOTE ADOPTION AND LEGAL GUARDIANSHIP

Sec. 22001. Reauthorizing adoption and legal guardianship incentive programs.

TITLE XXIII—TECHNICAL CORRECTIONS

Sec. 23001. Technical corrections to data exchange standards to improve program coordination.

Sec. 23002. Technical corrections to State requirement to address the developmental needs of young children.

TITLE XXIV—ENSURING STATES REINVEST SAVINGS RESULTING FROM INCREASE IN ADOPTION ASSISTANCE

Sec. 24001. Delay of adoption assistance phase-in.

Sec. 24002. GAO study and report on State reinvestment of savings resulting from increase in adoption assistance.

TITLE XXV—SOCIAL IMPACT PARTNERSHIPS TO PAY FOR RESULTS

Sec. 25001. Short title.

Sec. 25002. Social Impact Partnerships to Pay for Results.

Sec. 25003. Extension of TANF program.

Sec. 25004. Strengthening welfare research and evaluation and development of a What Works Clearinghouse.

Sec. 25005. Technical corrections to data exchange standards to improve program coordination.

DIVISION A—21ST CENTURY CURES

SEC. 1000. SHORT TITLE.

This Division may be cited as the "21st Century Cures Act".

TITLE I—INNOVATION PROJECTS AND STATE RESPONSES TO OPIOID ABUSE

SEC. 1001. NIH INNOVATION PROJECTS.

(a) IN GENERAL.—The Director of the National Institutes of Health (referred to in this section as the "Director of NIH") shall use any funds appropriated pursuant to the authorization of appropriations in subsection (b)(3) to carry out the National Institutes of Health innovation projects described in subsection (b)(4) (referred to in this section as the "NIH Innovation Projects").

(b) NATIONAL INSTITUTES OF HEALTH INNOVATION ACCOUNT.—

(1) ESTABLISHMENT OF NIH INNOVATION ACCOUNT.—There is established in the Treasury an account, to be known as the "NIH Innovation Account" (referred to in this subsection as the "Account"), for purposes of carrying out the NIH Innovation Projects described in paragraph (4).

(2) TRANSFER OF DIRECT SPENDING SAVINGS.—

(A) IN GENERAL.—The following amounts shall be transferred to the Account from the general fund of the Treasury:

(i) For fiscal year 2017, $352,000,000.

(ii) For fiscal year 2018, $496,000,000.

(iii) For fiscal year 2019, $711,000,000.

(iv) For fiscal year 2020, $492,000,000.

(v) For fiscal year 2021, $404,000,000.

(vi) For fiscal year 2022, $496,000,000.

(vii) For fiscal year 2023, $1,085,000,000.

(viii) For fiscal year 2024, $407,000,000.

(ix) For fiscal year 2025, $194,000,000.

(x) For fiscal year 2026, $226,000,000.

(B) AMOUNTS DEPOSITED.—Any amounts transferred under subparagraph (A) shall remain unavailable in the Account until such amounts are appropriated pursuant to paragraph (3).

(3) APPROPRIATIONS.—

(A) AUTHORIZATION OF APPROPRIATIONS.—For each of the fiscal years 2017 through 2026, there is authorized to be appropriated from the Account to the Director of NIH, for the purpose of carrying out the NIH Innovation Projects, an amount not to exceed the total amount transferred to the Account under paragraph (2)(A), to remain available until expended.

(B) OFFSETTING FUTURE APPROPRIATIONS.—For any of fiscal years 2017 through 2026, for any discretionary appropriation under the heading "NIH Innovation Account" provided to the Director of NIH pursuant to the authorization of appropriations under subparagraph (A) for the purpose of carrying out the NIH Innovation Projects, the total amount of such appropriations for the applicable fiscal year (not to exceed the total amount remaining in the Account) shall be subtracted from the estimate of discretionary budget authority and the resulting outlays for any estimate under the Congressional Budget and Impoundment Control Act of 1974 or the Balanced Budget and Emergency Deficit Control Act of 1985, and the amount transferred to the Account shall be reduced by the same amount.

(4) NIH INNOVATION PROJECTS.—NIH Innovation Projects authorized to be funded under this section shall consist of the following and, of the total amounts authorized to be appropriated under paragraph (3), there are authorized to be appropriated to each such project a total amount not to exceed the following, over the period of fiscal years 2017 through 2026:

(A) For the Precision Medicine Initiative, including for the advancement of a cohort of individuals to support the goals of the Precision Medicine Initiative, not to exceed a total of $1,455,000,000, as follows:

(i) For fiscal year 2017, $40,000,000.

(ii) For fiscal year 2018, $100,000,000.

(iii) For fiscal year 2019, $186,000,000.

(iv) For fiscal year 2020, $149,000,000.

(v) For fiscal year 2021, $109,000,000.

(vi) For fiscal year 2022, $150,000,000.

(vii) For fiscal year 2023, $419,000,000.

(viii) For fiscal year 2024, $235,000,000.

(ix) For fiscal year 2025, $36,000,000.

(x) For fiscal year 2026, $31,000,000.

(B) For the Brain Research through Advancing Innovative Neurotechnologies Initiative (known as the "BRAIN Initiative"), not to exceed a total of $1,511,000,000, as follows:

(i) For fiscal year 2017, $10,000,000.

(ii) For fiscal year 2018, $86,000,000.

(iii) For fiscal year 2019, $115,000,000.

(iv) For fiscal year 2020, $140,000,000.

(v) For fiscal year 2021, $100,000,000.

(vi) For fiscal year 2022, $152,000,000.

(vii) For fiscal year 2023, $450,000,000.

(viii) For fiscal year 2024, $172,000,000.

(ix) For fiscal year 2025, $91,000,000.

(x) For fiscal year 2026, $195,000,000.

(C) To support cancer research, such as the development of cancer vaccines, the development of more sensitive diagnostic tests for cancer, immunotherapy and the development of combination therapies, and research that has the potential to transform the scientific field, that has inherently higher risk, and that seeks to address major challenges related to cancer, not to exceed a total of $1,800,000,000, as follows:

(i) For fiscal year 2017, $300,000,000.

(ii) For fiscal year 2018, $300,000,000.

(iii) For fiscal year 2019, $400,000,000.

(iv) For fiscal year 2020, $195,000,000.

(v) For fiscal year 2021, $195,000,000.

(vi) For fiscal year 2022, $194,000,000.

(vii) For fiscal year 2023, $216,000,000.

(D) For the National Institutes of Health, in coordination with the Food and Drug Administration, to award grants and contracts for clinical research to further the field of regenerative medicine using adult stem cells, including autologous stem cells, for which grants and contracts shall be contingent upon the recipient making available non-Federal contributions toward the costs of such research in an amount not less than $1 for each $1 of Federal funds provided in the award, not to exceed a total of $30,000,000, as follows:

(i) For fiscal year 2017, $2,000,000.

(ii) For each of fiscal years 2018 and 2019, $10,000,000.

(iii) For fiscal year 2020, $8,000,000.

(iv) For each of fiscal years 2021 through 2026, $0.

(c) ACCOUNTABILITY AND OVERSIGHT.—

(1) WORK PLAN.—

(A) IN GENERAL.—Not later than 180 days after the date of enactment of this Act, the Director of NIH shall submit to the Committee on Health, Education, Labor, and Pensions and the Committee on Appropriations of the Senate and the Committee on Energy and Commerce and the Committee on Appropriations of the House of Representatives, a work plan including the proposed allocation of funds authorized to be appropriated pursuant to subsection (b)(3) for each of fiscal years 2017 through 2026 for the NIH Innovation Projects and the contents described in subparagraph (B).

(B) CONTENTS.—The work plan submitted under subparagraph (A) shall include—

(i) recommendations from the Advisory Committee described in subparagraph (C);

(ii) the amount of money to be obligated or expended in each fiscal year for each NIH Innovation Project;

(iii) a description and justification of each such project; and

(iv) a description of how each such project supports the strategic research priorities identified in the NIH Strategic Plan under subsection

(m) of section 402 of the Public Health Service Act (42 U.S.C. 282), as added by section 2031.

(C) RECOMMENDATIONS.—Prior to submitting the work plan under this paragraph, the Director of NIH shall seek recommendations from the Advisory Committee to the Director of NIH appointed under section 222 of the Public Health Service Act (42 U.S.C. 217a) on—

(i) the allocations of funds appropriated pursuant to the authorization of appropriations under subsection (b)(3) for each of fiscal years 2017 through 2026; and

(ii) on the contents of the proposed work plan.

(2) REPORTS.—

(A) ANNUAL REPORTS.—Not later than October 1 of each of fiscal years 2018 through 2027, the Director of NIH shall submit to the Committee on Health, Education, Labor, and Pensions and the Committee on Appropriations of the Senate and the Committee on Energy and Commerce and the Committee on Appropriations of the House of Representatives, a report including—

(i) the amount of money obligated or expended in the prior fiscal year for each NIH Innovation Project;

(ii) a description of any such project using funds provided pursuant to the authorization of appropriations under subsection (b)(3); and

(iii) whether such projects are advancing the strategic research priorities identified in the NIH Strategic Plan under subsection (m) of section 402 of the Public Health Service Act (42 U.S.C. 282), as added by section 2031.

(B) ADDITIONAL REPORTS.—At the request of the Committee on Health, Education, Labor, and Pensions or the Committee on Appropriations of the Senate, or the Committee on Energy and Commerce or the Committee on Appropriations of the House of Representatives, the Director of NIH shall provide an update in the form of testimony and any additional reports to the respective congressional committee regarding the allocation of funding under this section or the description of the NIH Innovation Projects.

(d) LIMITATIONS.—Notwithstanding any transfer authority authorized by this Act or any appropriations Act, any funds made available pursuant to the authorization of appropriations under subsection (b)(3) may not be used for any purpose other than a NIH Innovation Project.

(e) SUNSET.—This section shall expire on September 30, 2026.

SEC. 1002. FDA INNOVATION PROJECTS.

(a) IN GENERAL.—The Commissioner of Food and Drugs (referred to in this section as the "Commissioner") shall use any funds appropriated pursuant to the authorization of appropriations under subsection (b)(3) to carry out the activities described in subsection (b)(4).

(b) FDA INNOVATION ACCOUNT.—

(1) ESTABLISHMENT OF FDA INNOVATION ACCOUNT.—There is established in the Treasury an account, to be known as the "FDA Innovation Account" (referred to in this subsection as the "Account"), for purposes of carrying out the activities described in paragraph (4).

(2) TRANSFER OF DIRECT SPENDING SAVINGS.—

(A) IN GENERAL.—For each of fiscal years 2017 through 2025, the following amounts shall be transferred to the Account from the general fund of the Treasury:

(i) For fiscal year 2017, $20,000,000.

(ii) For fiscal year 2018, $60,000,000.

(iii) For fiscal year 2019, $70,000,000.

(iv) For fiscal year 2020, $75,000,000.

(v) For fiscal year 2021, $70,000,000.

(vi) For fiscal year 2022, $50,000,000.

(vii) For fiscal year 2023, $50,000,000.

(viii) For fiscal year 2024, $50,000,000.

(ix) For fiscal year 2025, $55,000,000.

(B) AMOUNTS DEPOSITED.—Any amounts transferred under subparagraph (A) shall remain unavailable in the Account until such amounts are appropriated pursuant to paragraph (3).

(3) APPROPRIATIONS.—

(A) AUTHORIZATION OF APPROPRIATIONS.—For each of the fiscal years 2017 through 2025, there is authorized to be appropriated from the Account to the Commissioner, for the purpose of carrying out the activities described in paragraph (5), an amount not to exceed the total amount transferred to the Account under paragraph (2)(A), to remain available until expended.

(B) OFFSETTING FUTURE APPROPRIATIONS.—For any fiscal years 2017 through 2025, for any discretionary appropriation under the heading "FDA Innovation Account" provided to the Commissioner pursuant to the authorization of appropriations under subparagraph (A) for the purpose of carrying out the projects activities described in paragraph (4), the total amount of such appropriations in the applicable fiscal year (not to exceed the total amount remaining in the Account) shall be subtracted from the estimate of discretionary budget authority and the resulting outlays for any estimate under the Congressional Budget and Impoundment Control Act of 1974 or the Balanced Budget and Emergency Deficit Control Act of 1985, and the amount transferred to the Account shall be reduced by the same amount.

(4) FDA ACTIVITIES.—The activities authorized to be funded under this section are the activities under subtitles A through F (including the amendments made by such subtitles) of title III of this Act and section 1014 of the Federal Food, Drug, and Cosmetic Act, as added by section 3073 of this Act.

(c) ACCOUNTABILITY AND OVERSIGHT.—

(1) WORK PLAN.—

(A) IN GENERAL.—Not later than 180 days after the date of enactment of this Act, the Commissioner shall submit to the Committee on Health, Education, Labor, and Pensions and the Committee on Appropriations of the Senate and the Committee on Energy and Commerce and the Committee on Appropriations of the House of Representatives, a work plan including the proposed allocation of funds appropriated pursuant to the authorization of appropriations under subsection (b)(3) for each of fiscal years 2017 through 2025 and the contents described in subparagraph (B).

(B) CONTENTS.—The work plan submitted under subparagraph (A) shall include—

(i) recommendations from the Advisory Committee described in subparagraph (C);

(ii) the amount of money to be obligated or expended in each fiscal year for each activity described in subsection (b)(4); and

(iii) a description and justification of each such project activity.

(C) RECOMMENDATIONS.—Prior to submitting the work plan under this paragraph, the Commissioner shall seek recommendations from the Science Board to the Food and Drug Administration, on the proposed allocation of funds appropriated pursuant to the authorization of appropriations under subsection (b)(3) for each of fiscal years 2017 through 2025 and on the contents of the proposed work plan.

(2) REPORTS.—

(A) ANNUAL REPORTS.—Not later than October 1 of each of fiscal years 2018 through 2026, the Commissioner shall submit to the Committee on Health, Education, Labor, and Pensions and the Committee on Appropriations of the Senate and the Committee on Energy and Commerce and the Committee on Appropriations of the House of Representatives, a report including—

(i) the amount of money obligated or expended in the prior fiscal year for each activity described in subsection (b)(4);

(ii) a description of all such activities using funds provided pursuant to the authorization of appropriations under subsection (b)(3); and

(iii) how the activities are advancing public health.

(B) ADDITIONAL REPORTS.—At the request of the Committee on Health, Education, Labor, and Pensions or the Committee on Appropriations of the Senate, or the Committee on Energy and Commerce or the Committee on Appropriations of the House of Representatives, the Commissioner shall provide an update in the form of testimony and any additional reports to the respective congressional committee regarding the allocation of funding under this section or the description of the activities undertaken with such funding.

(d) LIMITATIONS.—Notwithstanding any transfer authority authorized by this Act or any appropriations Act, any funds made available pursuant to the authorization of appropriations in subsection (b)(3) shall not be used for any purpose other than an activity described in subsection (b)(4).

(e) SUNSET.—This section shall expire on September 30, 2025.

SEC. 1003. ACCOUNT FOR THE STATE RESPONSE TO THE OPIOID ABUSE CRISIS.

(a) IN GENERAL.—The Secretary of Health and Human Services (referred to in this section as the "Secretary") shall use any funds appropriated pursuant to the authorization of appropriations under subsection (b) to carry out the grant program described in subsection (c) for purposes of addressing the opioid abuse crisis within the States.

(b) ACCOUNT FOR THE STATE RESPONSE TO THE OPIOID ABUSE CRISIS.—

(1) ESTABLISHMENT.—There is established in the Treasury an account, to be known as the "Account For the State Response to the Opioid Abuse Crisis" (referred to in this subsection as the "Account"), to carry out the opioid grant program described in subsection (c).

(2) TRANSFER OF DIRECT SPENDING SAVINGS.—

(A) IN GENERAL.—The following amounts shall be transferred to the Account from the general fund of the Treasury:

(i) For fiscal year 2017, $500,000,000.

(ii) For fiscal year 2018, $500,000,000.

(B) AMOUNTS DEPOSITED.—Any amounts transferred under subparagraph (A) shall remain unavailable in the Account until such amounts are appropriated pursuant to paragraph (3).

(3) APPROPRIATIONS.—

(A) AUTHORIZATION OF APPROPRIATIONS.—In each of the fiscal years 2017 and 2018, there is authorized to be appropriated from the Account to the Secretary, for the grant program described in subsection (c), an amount not to exceed the total amount transferred to the Account under paragraph (2)(A), to remain available until expended.

(B) OFFSETTING FUTURE APPROPRIATIONS.—In each of fiscal years 2017 and 2018, for any discretionary appropriation under the heading "Account For the State Response to the Opioid Abuse Crisis" for the grant program described in subsection (c), the total amount of such appropriations in the applicable fiscal year (not to exceed the total amount remaining in the Account) shall be subtracted from the estimate of discretionary budget authority and the resulting outlays for any estimate under the Congressional Budget and Impoundment Control Act of 1974 or the Balanced Budget and Emergency Deficit Control Act of 1985, and the amount transferred to the Account shall be reduced by the same amount.

(c) OPIOID GRANT PROGRAM.—

(1) STATE RESPONSE TO THE OPIOID ABUSE CRISIS.—Subject to the availability of appropriations, the Secretary shall award grants to States for the purpose of addressing the opioid abuse crisis within such States, in accordance with subparagraph (B). In awarding such grants, the Secretary shall give preference to States with an incidence or prevalence of opioid use disorders

that is substantially higher relative to other States.

(2) OPIOID GRANTS.—Grants awarded to a State under this subsection shall be used for carrying out activities that supplement activities pertaining to opioids undertaken by the State agency responsible for administering the substance abuse prevention and treatment block grant under subpart II of part B of title XIX of the Public Health Service Act (42 U.S.C. 300x–21 et seq.), which may include public health-related activities such as the following:

(A) Improving State prescription drug monitoring programs.

(B) Implementing prevention activities, and evaluating such activities to identify effective strategies to prevent opioid abuse.

(C) Training for health care practitioners, such as best practices for prescribing opioids, pain management, recognizing potential cases of substance abuse, referral of patients to treatment programs, and overdose prevention.

(D) Supporting access to health care services, including those services provided by Federally certified opioid treatment programs or other appropriate health care providers to treat substance use disorders.

(E) Other public health-related activities, as the State determines appropriate, related to addressing the opioid abuse crisis within the State.

(d) ACCOUNTABILITY AND OVERSIGHT.—A State receiving a grant under subsection (c) shall include in a report related to substance abuse submitted to the Secretary pursuant to section 1942 of the Public Health Service Act (42 U.S.C. 300x–52), a description of—

(1) the purposes for which the grant funds received by the State under such subsection for the preceding fiscal year were expended and a description of the activities of the State under the program; and

(2) the ultimate recipients of amounts provided to the State in the grant.

(e) LIMITATIONS.—Any funds made available pursuant to the authorization of appropriations under subsection (b)—

(1) notwithstanding any transfer authority in any appropriations Act, shall not be used for any purpose other than the grant program in subsection (c); and

(2) shall be subject to the same requirements as substance abuse prevention and treatment programs under titles V and XIX of the Public Health Service Act (42 U.S.C. 290aa et seq., 300w et seq.).

(f) SUNSET.—This section shall expire on September 30, 2026.

SEC. 1004. BUDGETARY TREATMENT.

(a) STATUTORY PAYGO SCORECARDS.—The budgetary effects of division A of this Act shall not be entered on either PAYGO scorecard maintained pursuant to section 4(d) of the Statutory Pay-As-You-Go Act of 2010.

(b) SENATE PAYGO SCORECARDS.—The budgetary effects of division A of this Act shall not be entered on any PAYGO scorecard maintained for purposes of section 201 of S. Con. Res. 21 (110th Congress).

(c) RESERVATION OF SAVINGS.—None of the funds in the NIH Innovation Account, the FDA Innovation Account, or the Account For the State Response to the Opioid Abuse Crisis established by this title shall be made available except to the extent provided in advance in appropriations Acts, and legislation or an Act that rescinds or reduces amounts in such accounts shall not be estimated as a reduction in direct spending under the Congressional Budget and Impoundment Control Act of 1974 or the Balanced Budget and Emergency Deficit Control Act of 1985.

TITLE II—DISCOVERY
Subtitle A—National Institutes of Health Reauthorization

SEC. 2001. NATIONAL INSTITUTES OF HEALTH RE-AUTHORIZATION.

Section 402A(a)(1) of the Public Health Service Act (42 U.S.C. 282a(a)(1)) is amended—

(1) in subparagraph (B), by striking "and" at the end;

(2) in subparagraph (C), by striking the period at the end and inserting a semicolon; and

(3) by adding at the end the following new subparagraphs:

"(D) $34,851,000,000 for fiscal year 2018;

"(E) $35,585,871,000 for fiscal year 2019; and

"(F) $36,472,442,775 for fiscal year 2020.".

SEC. 2002. EUREKA PRIZE COMPETITIONS.

(a) IN GENERAL.—Pursuant to the authorities and processes established under section 24 of the Stevenson-Wydler Technology Innovation Act of 1980 (15 U.S.C. 3719), the Director of the National Institutes of Health shall support prize competitions for one or both of the following goals:

(1) Identifying and funding areas of biomedical science that could realize significant advancements through a prize competition.

(2) Improving health outcomes, particularly with respect to human diseases and conditions—

(A) for which public and private investment in research is disproportionately small relative to Federal Government expenditures on prevention and treatment activities with respect to such diseases and conditions, such that Federal expenditures on health programs would be reduced;

(B) that are serious and represent a significant disease burden in the United States; or

(C) for which there is potential for significant return on investment to the United States.

(b) TRACKING; REPORTING.—The Director of the National Institutes of Health shall—

(1) collect information on—

(A) the effect of innovations funded through the prize competitions under this section in advancing biomedical science or improving health outcomes pursuant to subsection (a); and

(B) the effect of the innovations on Federal expenditures; and

(2) include the information collected under paragraph (1) in the triennial report under section 403 of the Public Health Service Act (42 U.S.C. 283) (as amended by section 2032).

Subtitle B—Advancing Precision Medicine

SEC. 2011. PRECISION MEDICINE INITIATIVE.

Part H of title IV of the Public Health Service Act (42 U.S.C. 289 et seq.) is amended by adding at the end the following:

"SEC. 498E. PRECISION MEDICINE INITIATIVE.

"(a) IN GENERAL.—The Secretary is encouraged to establish and carry out an initiative, to be known as the 'Precision Medicine Initiative' (in this section referred to as the 'Initiative'), to augment efforts to address disease prevention, diagnosis, and treatment.

"(b) COMPONENTS.—The Initiative described under subsection (a) may include—

"(1) developing a network of scientists to assist in carrying out the purposes of the Initiative;

"(2) developing new approaches for addressing scientific, medical, public health, and regulatory science issues;

"(3) applying genomic technologies, such as whole genomic sequencing, to provide data on the molecular basis of disease;

"(4) collecting information voluntarily provided by a diverse cohort of individuals that can be used to better understand health and disease; and

"(5) other activities to advance the goals of the Initiative, as the Secretary determines appropriate.

"(c) AUTHORITY OF THE SECRETARY.—In carrying out this section, the Secretary may—

"(1) coordinate with the Secretary of Energy, private industry, and others, as the Secretary determines appropriate, to identify and address the advanced supercomputing and other advanced technology needs for the Initiative;

"(2) develop and utilize public-private partnerships; and

"(3) leverage existing data sources.

"(d) REQUIREMENTS.—In the implementation of the Initiative under subsection (a), the Secretary shall—

"(1) ensure the collaboration of the National Institutes of Health, the Food and Drug Administration, the Office of the National Coordinator for Health Information Technology, and the Office for Civil Rights of the Department of Health and Human Services;

"(2) comply with existing laws and regulations for the protection of human subjects involved in research, including the protection of participant privacy;

"(3) implement policies and mechanisms for appropriate secure data sharing across systems that include protections for privacy and security of data;

"(4) consider the diversity of the cohort to ensure inclusion of a broad range of participants, including consideration of biological, social, and other determinants of health that contribute to health disparities;

"(5) ensure that only authorized individuals may access controlled or sensitive, identifiable biological material and associated information collected or stored in connection with the Initiative; and

"(6) on the appropriate Internet website of the Department of Health and Human Services, identify any entities with access to such information and provide information with respect to the purpose of such access, a summary of the research project for which such access is granted, as applicable, and a description of the biological material and associated information to which the entity has access.

"(e) REPORT.—Not later than 1 year after the date of enactment of the 21st Century Cures Act, the Secretary shall submit a report on the relevant data access policies and procedures to the Committee on Health, Education, Labor, and Pensions of the Senate and the Committee on Energy and Commerce of the House of Representatives. Such report shall include steps the Secretary has taken to consult with experts or other heads of departments or agencies of the Federal Government in the development of such policies.".

SEC. 2012. PRIVACY PROTECTION FOR HUMAN RE-SEARCH SUBJECTS.

(a) IN GENERAL.—Subsection (d) of section 301 of the Public Health Service Act (42 U.S.C. 241) is amended to read as follows:

"(d)(1)(A) If a person is engaged in biomedical, behavioral, clinical, or other research, in which identifiable, sensitive information is collected (including research on mental health and research on the use and effect of alcohol and other psychoactive drugs), the Secretary, in coordination with other agencies, as applicable—

"(i) shall issue to such person a certificate of confidentiality to protect the privacy of individuals who are the subjects of such research if the research is funded wholly or in part by the Federal Government; and

"(ii) may, upon application by a person engaged in research, issue to such person a certificate of confidentiality to protect the privacy of such individuals if the research is not so funded.

"(B) Except as provided in subparagraph (C), any person to whom a certificate is issued under subparagraph (A) to protect the privacy of individuals described in such subparagraph shall not disclose or provide to any other person not connected with the research the name of such an individual or any information, document, or biospecimen that contains identifiable, sensitive information about such an individual and that was created or compiled for purposes of the research.

"(C) The disclosure prohibition in subparagraph (B) shall not apply to disclosure or use that is—

"(i) required by Federal, State, or local laws, excluding instances described in subparagraph (D);

"(ii) necessary for the medical treatment of the individual to whom the information, document, or biospecimen pertains and made with the consent of such individual;

"(iii) made with the consent of the individual to whom the information, document, or biospecimen pertains; or

"(iv) made for the purposes of other scientific research that is in compliance with applicable Federal regulations governing the protection of human subjects in research.

"(D) Any person to whom a certificate is issued under subparagraph (A) to protect the privacy of an individual described in such subparagraph shall not, in any Federal, State, or local civil, criminal, administrative, legislative, or other proceeding, disclose or provide the name of such individual or any such information, document, or biospecimen that contains identifiable, sensitive information about the individual and that was created or compiled for purposes of the research, except in the circumstance described in subparagraph (C)(iii).

"(E) Identifiable, sensitive information protected under subparagraph (A), and all copies thereof, shall be immune from the legal process, and shall not, without the consent of the individual to whom the information pertains, be admissible as evidence or used for any purpose in any action, suit, or other judicial, legislative, or administrative proceeding.

"(F) Identifiable, sensitive information collected by a person to whom a certificate has been issued under subparagraph (A), and all copies thereof, shall be subject to the protections afforded by this section for perpetuity.

"(G) The Secretary shall take steps to minimize the burden to researchers, streamline the process, and reduce the time it takes to comply with the requirements of this subsection.

"(2) The Secretary shall coordinate with the heads of other applicable Federal agencies to ensure that such departments have policies in place with respect to the issuance of a certificate of confidentiality pursuant to paragraph (1) and other requirements of this subsection.

"(3) Nothing in this subsection shall be construed to limit the access of an individual who is a subject of research to information about himself or herself collected during such individual's participation in the research.

"(4) For purposes of this subsection, the term 'identifiable, sensitive information' means information that is about an individual and that is gathered or used during the course of research described in paragraph (1)(A) and—

"(A) through which an individual is identified; or

"(B) for which there is at least a very small risk, as determined by current scientific practices or statistical methods, that some combination of the information, a request for the information, and other available data sources could be used to deduce the identity of an individual.".

(b) APPLICABILITY.—Beginning 180 days after the date of enactment of this Act, all persons engaged in research and authorized by the Secretary of Health and Human Services to protect information under section 301(d) of the Public Health Service Act (42 U.S.C. 241(d)) prior to the date of enactment of this Act shall be subject to the requirements of such section (as amended by this Act).

SEC. 2013. PROTECTION OF IDENTIFIABLE AND SENSITIVE INFORMATION.

Section 301 of the Public Health Service Act (42 U.S.C. 241) is amended by adding at the end the following:

"(f)(1) The Secretary may exempt from disclosure under section 552(b)(3) of title 5, United States Code, biomedical information that is about an individual and that is gathered or used during the course of biomedical research if—

"(A) an individual is identified; or

"(B) there is at least a very small risk, as determined by current scientific practices or statistical methods, that some combination of the information, the request, and other available data sources could be used to deduce the identity of an individual.

"(2)(A) Each determination of the Secretary under paragraph (1) to exempt information from disclosure shall be made in writing and accompanied by a statement of the basis for the determination.

"(B) Each such determination and statement of basis shall be available to the public, upon request, through the Office of the Chief FOIA Officer of the Department of Health and Human Services.

"(3) Nothing in this subsection shall be construed to limit a research participant's access to information about such participant collected during the participant's participation in the research.".

SEC. 2014. DATA SHARING.

(a) IN GENERAL.—Section 402(b) of the Public Health Service Act (42 U.S.C. 282(b)) is amended—

(1) in paragraph (23), by striking "and" at the end;

(2) in paragraph (24), by striking the period and inserting "; and"; and

(3) by inserting after paragraph (24) the following:

"(25) may require recipients of National Institutes of Health awards to share scientific data, to the extent feasible, generated from such National Institutes of Health awards in a manner that is consistent with all applicable Federal laws and regulations, including such laws and regulations for the protection of—

"(A) human research participants, including with respect to privacy, security, informed consent, and protected health information; and

"(B) proprietary interests, confidential commercial information, and the intellectual property rights of the funding recipient.".

(b) CONFIDENTIALITY.—Nothing in the amendments made by subsection (a) authorizes the Secretary of Health and Human Services to disclose any information that is a trade secret, or other privileged or confidential information, described in section 552(b)(4) of title 5, United States Code, or section 1905 of title 18, United States Code, or be construed to require recipients of grants or cooperative agreements through the National Institutes of Health to share such information.

Subtitle C—Supporting Young Emerging Scientists

SEC. 2021. INVESTING IN THE NEXT GENERATION OF RESEARCHERS.

(a) IN GENERAL.—Part A of title IV of the Public Health Service Act (42 U.S.C. 281 et seq.) is amended by adding at the end the following:

"SEC. 404M. NEXT GENERATION OF RESEARCHERS.

"(a) NEXT GENERATION OF RESEARCHERS INITIATIVE.—There shall be established within the Office of the Director of the National Institutes of Health, the Next Generation of Researchers Initiative (referred to in this section as the 'Initiative'), through which the Director shall coordinate all policies and programs within the National Institutes of Health that are focused on promoting and providing opportunities for new researchers and earlier research independence.

"(b) ACTIVITIES.—The Director of the National Institutes of Health, through the Initiative shall—

"(1) promote policies and programs within the National Institutes of Health that are focused on improving opportunities for new researchers and promoting earlier research independence, including existing policies and programs, as appropriate;

"(2) develop, modify, or prioritize policies, as needed, within the National Institutes of Health to promote opportunities for new researchers and earlier research independence, such as policies to increase opportunities for new researchers to receive funding, enhance training and mentorship programs for researchers, and enhance workforce diversity;

"(3) coordinate, as appropriate, with relevant agencies, professional and academic associations, academic institutions, and others, to improve and update existing information on the biomedical research workforce in order to inform programs related to the training, recruitment, and retention of biomedical researchers; and

"(4) carry out other activities, including evaluation and oversight of existing programs, as appropriate, to promote the development of the next generation of researchers and earlier research independence.".

(b) CONSIDERATION OF RECOMMENDATIONS.—In carrying out activities under section 404M(b) of the Public Health Service Act, the Director of the National Institutes of Health shall take into consideration the recommendations made by the National Academies of Sciences, Engineering, and Medicine as part of the comprehensive study on policies affecting the next generation of researchers under the Department of Health and Human Services Appropriations Act, 2016 (Public Law 114–113), and submit a report to the Committee on Health, Education, Labor, and Pensions and the Committee on Appropriations of the Senate, and the Committee on Energy and Commerce and the Committee on Appropriations of the House of Representatives, with respect to any actions taken by the National Institutes of Health based on the recommendations not later than 2 years after the completion of the study required pursuant to the Department of Health and Human Services Appropriations Act, 2016.

SEC. 2022. IMPROVEMENT OF LOAN REPAYMENT PROGRAM.

(a) INTRAMURAL LOAN REPAYMENT PROGRAM.—Section 487A of the Public Health Service Act (42 U.S.C. 288–1) is amended—

(1) by amending the section heading to read as follows: "**INTRAMURAL LOAN REPAYMENT PROGRAM**";

(2) in subsection (a)—

(A) by striking "The Secretary shall carry out a program" and inserting "The Director of the National Institutes of Health shall, as appropriate and based on workforce and scientific priorities, carry out a program through the subcategories listed in subsection (b)(1) (or modified subcategories as provided for in subsection (b)(2))";

(B) by striking "conduct" and inserting "conduct research";

(C) by striking "research with respect to acquired immune deficiency syndrome"; and

(D) by striking "$35,000" and inserting "$50,000";

(3) by redesignating subsection (b) as subsection (d);

(4) by inserting after subsection (a), the following:

"*(b) SUBCATEGORIES OF RESEARCH.—*

"*(1) IN GENERAL.—In carrying out the program under subsection (a), the Director of the National Institutes of Health—*

"*(A) shall continue to focus on—*

"*(i) general research;*

"*(ii) research on acquired immune deficiency syndrome; and*

"*(iii) clinical research conducted by appropriately qualified health professional who are from disadvantaged backgrounds; and*

"*(B) may focus on an area of emerging scientific or workforce need.*

"*(2) ELIMINATION OR ESTABLISHMENT OF SUBCATEGORIES.—The Director of the National Institutes of Health may eliminate one or more subcategories provided for in paragraph (1) due to changes in workforce or scientific needs related to biomedical research. The Director may establish other subcategory areas based on workforce and scientific priorities if the total number of subcategories does not exceed the number of subcategories listed in paragraph (1).*

"*(c) LIMITATION.—The Director of the National Institutes of Health may not enter into a contract with a health professional pursuant to subsection (a) unless such professional has a substantial amount of education loans relative to income (as determined pursuant to guidelines issued by the Director).''; and*

(5) by adding at the end the following:

"*(e) AVAILABILITY OF APPROPRIATIONS.— Amounts available for carrying out this section shall remain available until the expiration of the second fiscal year beginning after the fiscal year for which such amounts are made available.''.*

(b) EXTRAMURAL LOAN REPAYMENT PROGRAM.—Section 487B of the Public Health Service Act (42 U.S.C. 288–2) is amended—

(1) by amending the section heading to read as follows: "**EXTRAMURAL LOAN REPAYMENT PROGRAM**'';

(2) in subsection (a)—

(A) by striking "The Secretary, in consultation with the Director of the Eunice Kennedy Shriver National Institute of Child Health and Human Development, shall establish a program'' and inserting "IN GENERAL.—The Director of the National Institutes of Health shall, as appropriate and based on workforce and scientific priorities, carry out a program through the subcategories listed in subsection (b)(1) (or modified subcategories as provided for in subsection (b)(2)),'';

(B) by striking "(including graduate students)'';

(C) by striking "with respect to contraception, or with respect to infertility,''; and

(D) by striking "service, not more than $35,000'' and inserting "research, not more than $50,000'';

(3) by redesignating subsections (b) and (c) as subsections (d) and (e), respectively;

(4) by inserting after subsection (a), the following:

"*(b) SUBCATEGORIES OF RESEARCH.—*

"*(1) IN GENERAL.—In carrying out the program under subsection (a), the Director of the National Institutes of Health—*

"*(A) shall continue to focus on—*

"*(i) contraception or infertility research;*

"*(ii) pediatric research, including pediatric pharmacological research;*

"*(iii) minority health disparities research;*

"*(iv) clinical research; and*

"*(v) clinical research conducted by appropriately qualified health professional who are from disadvantaged backgrounds; and*

"*(B) may focus on an area of emerging scientific or workforce need.*

"*(2) ELIMINATION OR ESTABLISHMENT OF SUBCATEGORIES.—The Director of the National Institutes of Health may eliminate one or more*

subcategories provided for in paragraph (1) due to changes in workforce or scientific needs related to biomedical research. The Director may establish other subcategory areas based on workforce and scientific priorities if the total number of subcategories does not exceed the number of subcategories listed in paragraph (1).

"*(c) LIMITATION.—The Director of the National Institutes of Health may not enter into a contract with a health professional pursuant to subsection (a) unless such professional has a substantial amount of education loans relative to income (as determined pursuant to guidelines issued by the Director).'';*

(5) in subsection (d) (as so redesignated), by striking "The provisions'' and inserting "APPLICABILITY OF CERTAIN PROVISIONS REGARDING OBLIGATED SERVICE.—The provisions''; and

(6) in subsection (e) (as so redesignated), by striking "Amounts'' and inserting "AVAILABILITY OF APPROPRIATIONS.—Amounts''.

(c) TECHNICAL AND CONFORMING AMENDMENTS.—Title IV of the Public Health Service Act is amended—

(1) by striking section 464z–5 (42 U.S.C. 285t–2);

(2) by striking section 487C (42 U.S.C. 288–3);

(3) by striking section 487E (42 U.S.C. 288–5);

(4) by striking section 487F (42 U.S.C. 288–5a), as added by section 205 of Public Law 106–505, relating to loan repayment for clinical researchers; and

(5) by striking section 487F (42 U.S.C. 288–6), as added by section 1002(b) of Public Law 106–310 relating to pediatric research loan repayment.

(d) GAO REPORT.—Not later than 18 months after the date of enactment of this Act, the Comptroller General of the United States shall submit to Congress a report on the efforts of the National Institutes of Health to attract, retain, and develop emerging scientists, including underrepresented individuals in the sciences, such as women, racial and ethnic minorities, and other groups. Such report shall include an analysis of the impact of the additional authority provided to the Secretary of Health and Human Services under this Act to address workforce shortages and gaps in priority research areas, including which centers and research areas offered loan repayment program participants the increased award amount.

Subtitle D—National Institutes of Health Planning and Administration

SEC. 2031. NATIONAL INSTITUTES OF HEALTH STRATEGIC PLAN.

(a) STRATEGIC PLAN.—Section 402 of the Public Health Service Act (42 U.S.C. 282) is amended—

(1) in subsection (b)(5), by inserting before the semicolon the following: ", and through the development, implementation, and updating of the strategic plan developed under subsection (m)''; and

(2) by adding at the end the following:

"*(m) NATIONAL INSTITUTES OF HEALTH STRATEGIC PLAN.—*

"*(1) IN GENERAL.—Not later than 2 years after the date of enactment of the 21st Century Cures Act, and at least every 6 years thereafter, the Director of the National Institutes of Health shall develop and submit to the appropriate committees of Congress and post on the Internet website of the National Institutes of Health, a coordinated strategy (to be known as the 'National Institutes of Health Strategic Plan') to provide direction to the biomedical research investments made by the National Institutes of Health, to facilitate collaboration across the institutes and centers, to leverage scientific opportunity, and to advance biomedicine.*

"*(2) REQUIREMENTS.—The strategy under paragraph (1) shall—*

"*(A) identify strategic research priorities and objectives across biomedical research, including—*

"*(i) an assessment of the state of biomedical and behavioral research, including areas of opportunity with respect to basic, clinical, and translational research;*

"*(ii) priorities and objectives to advance the treatment, cure, and prevention of health conditions;*

"*(iii) emerging scientific opportunities, rising public health challenges, and scientific knowledge gaps; and*

"*(iv) the identification of near-, mid-, and long-term scientific needs;*

"*(B) consider, in carrying out subparagraph (A)—*

"*(i) disease burden in the United States and the potential for return on investment to the United States;*

"*(ii) rare diseases and conditions;*

"*(iii) biological, social, and other determinants of health that contribute to health disparities; and*

"*(iv) other factors the Director of National Institutes of Health determines appropriate;*

"*(C) include multi-institute priorities, including coordination of research among institutes and centers;*

"*(D) include strategic priorities for funding research through the Common Fund, in accordance with section 402A(c)(1)(C);*

"*(E) address the National Institutes of Health's proposed and ongoing activities related to training and the biomedical workforce; and*

"*(F) describe opportunities for collaboration with other agencies and departments, as appropriate.*

"*(3) USE OF PLANS.—Strategic plans developed and updated by the national research institutes and national centers of the National Institutes of Health shall be prepared regularly and in such manner that such plans will be informed by the strategic plans developed and updated under this subsection. Such plans developed by and updated by the national research institutes and national centers shall have a common template.*

"*(4) CONSULTATION.—The Director of National Institutes of Health shall develop the strategic plan under paragraph (1) in consultation with the directors of the national research institutes and national centers, researchers, patient advocacy groups, and industry leaders.''.*

(b) CONFORMING AMENDMENT.—Section 402A(c)(1)(C) of the Public Health Service Act (42 U.S.C. 282a(c)(1)(C)) is amended by striking "Not later than June 1, 2007, and every 2 years thereafter,'' and inserting "As part of the National Institutes of Health Strategic Plan required under section 402(m),''.

(c) STRATEGIC PLAN.—Section 492B(a) of the Public Health Service Act (42 U.S.C. 289a–2(a)) is amended by adding at the end the following:

"*(3) STRATEGIC PLANNING.—*

"*(A) IN GENERAL.—The directors of the national institutes and national centers shall consult at least once annually with the Director of the National Institute on Minority Health and Health Disparities and the Director of the Office of Research on Women's Health regarding objectives of the national institutes and national centers to ensure that future activities by such institutes and centers take into account women and minorities and are focused on reducing health disparities.*

"*(B) STRATEGIC PLANS.—Any strategic plan issued by a national institute or national center shall include details on the objectives described in subparagraph (A).''.*

SEC. 2032. TRIENNIAL REPORTS.

Section 403 of the Public Health Service Act (42 U.S.C. 283) is amended—

(1) in the section heading, by striking "**BIENNIAL**'' *and inserting* "**TRIENNIAL**''*; and*

(2) in subsection (a)—

(A) in the matter preceding paragraph (1), by striking "biennial'' and inserting "triennial'';

(B) by amending paragraph (3) to read as follows:

"(3) A description of intra-National Institutes of Health activities, including—

"(A) identification of the percentage of funds made available by each national research institute and national center with respect to each applicable fiscal year for conducting or supporting research that involves collaboration between the institute or center and 1 or more other national research institutes or national centers; and

"(B) recommendations for promoting coordination of information among the centers of excellence.";

(C) in paragraph (4)—

(i) in subparagraph (B), by striking "demographic variables and other variables" and inserting "demographic variables, including biological and social variables and relevant age categories (such as pediatric subgroups), and determinants of health,"; and

(ii) in subparagraph (C)(v)—

(I) by striking "demographic variables and such" and inserting "demographic variables, including relevant age categories (such as pediatric subgroups), information submitted by each national research institute and national center to the Director of National Institutes of Health under section 492B(f), and such"; and

(II) by striking "(regarding inclusion of women and minorities in clinical research)" and inserting "and other applicable requirements regarding inclusion of demographic groups"; and

(D) in paragraph (6)—

(i) in the matter preceding subparagraph (A), by striking "the following:" and inserting "the following—";

(ii) in subparagraph (A)—

(I) by striking "An evaluation" and inserting "an evaluation"; and

(II) by striking the period and inserting "; and";

(iii) by striking subparagraphs (B) and (D);

(iv) by redesignating subparagraph (C) as subparagraph (B); and

(v) in subparagraph (B), as redesignated by clause (iv), by striking "Recommendations" and inserting "recommendations".

SEC. 2033. INCREASING ACCOUNTABILITY AT THE NATIONAL INSTITUTES OF HEALTH.

(a) APPOINTMENT AND TERMS OF DIRECTORS OF NATIONAL RESEARCH INSTITUTES AND NATIONAL CENTERS.—Subsection (a) of section 405 of the Public Health Service Act (42 U.S.C. 284) is amended to read as follows:

"(a) APPOINTMENT.—

"(1) IN GENERAL.—The Director of the National Cancer Institute shall be appointed by the President, and the Directors of the other national research institutes and national centers shall be appointed by the Secretary, acting through the Director of National Institutes of Health. Each Director of a national research institute or national center shall report directly to the Director of National Institutes of Health.

"(2) APPOINTMENT.—

"(A) TERM.—A Director of a national research institute or national center who is appointed by the Secretary, acting through the Director of National Institutes of Health, shall be appointed for 5 years.

"(B) REAPPOINTMENT.—At the end of the term of a Director of a national research institute or national center, the Director may be reappointed in accordance with standards applicable to the relevant appointment mechanism. There shall be no limit on the number of terms that a Director may serve.

"(C) VACANCIES.—If the office of a Director of a national research institute or national center becomes vacant before the end of such Director's term, the Director appointed to fill the vacancy shall be appointed for a 5-year term starting on the date of such appointment.

"(D) CURRENT DIRECTORS.—Each Director of a national research institute or national center who is serving on the date of enactment of the 21st Century Cures Act shall be deemed to be appointed for a 5-year term under this subsection beginning on such date of enactment.

"(E) RULE OF CONSTRUCTION.—Nothing in this subsection shall be construed to limit the authority of the Secretary or the Director of National Institutes of Health to terminate the appointment of a director referred to in subparagraph (A) before the expiration of such director's 5-year term.

"(F) NATURE OF APPOINTMENT.—Appointments and reappointments under this subsection shall be made on the basis of ability and experience as it relates to the mission of the National Institutes of Health and its components, including compliance with any legal requirement that the Secretary or Director of National Institutes of Health determines relevant.

"(3) NONAPPLICATION OF CERTAIN PROVISION.—The restrictions contained in section 202 of the Departments of Labor, Health and Human Services, and Education, and Related Agencies Appropriations Act, 1993 (Public Law 102–394; 42 U.S.C. 238f note) related to consultants and individual scientists appointed for limited periods of time shall not apply to Directors appointed under this subsection.".

(b) REVIEW OF CERTAIN AWARDS BY DIRECTORS.—Section 405(b) of the Public Health Service Act (42 U.S.C. 284(b)) is amended by adding at the end the following:

"(3) Before an award is made by a national research institute or by a national center for a grant for a research program or project (commonly referred to as an 'R-series grant'), other than an award constituting a noncompetitive renewal of such a grant, or a noncompetitive administrative supplement to such a grant, the Director of such national research institute or national center shall, consistent with the peer review process—

"(A) review and make the final decision with respect to making the award; and

"(B) take into consideration, as appropriate—

"(i) the mission of the national research institute or national center and the scientific priorities identified in the strategic plan under section 402(m);

"(ii) programs or projects funded by other agencies on similar research topics; and

"(iii) advice by staff and the advisory council or board of such national research institute or national center.".

(c) REPORT ON DUPLICATION IN FEDERAL BIOMEDICAL RESEARCH.—The Secretary of Health and Human Services (referred to in this subsection as the "Secretary"), shall, not later than 2 years after the date of enactment of this Act, submit a report to Congress on efforts to prevent and eliminate duplicative biomedical research that is not necessary for scientific purposes. Such report shall—

(1) describe the procedures in place to identify such duplicative research, including procedures for monitoring research applications and funded research awards to prevent unnecessary duplication;

(2) describe the steps taken to improve the procedures described in paragraph (1), in response to relevant recommendations made by the Comptroller General of the United States;

(3) describe how the Secretary operationally distinguishes necessary and appropriate scientific replication from unnecessary duplication; and

(4) provide examples of instances where the Secretary has identified unnecessarily duplicative research and the steps taken to eliminate the unnecessary duplication.

SEC. 2034. REDUCING ADMINISTRATIVE BURDEN FOR RESEARCHERS.

(a) PLAN PREPARATION AND IMPLEMENTATION OF MEASURES TO REDUCE ADMINISTRATIVE BURDENS.—

(1) IN GENERAL.—Not later than 2 years after the date of enactment of this Act, the Secretary of Health and Human Services (referred to in this section as the "Secretary") shall—

(A) lead a review by research funding agencies of all regulations and policies related to the disclosure of financial conflicts of interest, including the minimum threshold for reporting financial conflicts of interest;

(B) make revisions, as appropriate, to harmonize existing policies and reduce administrative burden on researchers while maintaining the integrity and credibility of research findings and protections of human participants; and

(C) confer with the Office of the Inspector General about the activities of such office related to financial conflicts of interest involving research funding agencies.

(2) CONSIDERATIONS.—In updating policies under paragraph (1)(B), the Secretary shall consider—

(A) modifying the timelines for the reporting of financial conflicts of interest to just-in-time information by institutions receiving grant or cooperative agreement funding from the National Institutes of Health;

(B) ensuring that financial interest disclosure reporting requirements are appropriate for, and relevant to, awards that will directly fund research, which may include modification of the definition of the term "investigator" for purposes of the regulations and policies described in subparagraphs (A) and (B) of paragraph (1); and

(C) updating any applicable training modules of the National Institutes of Health related to Federal financial interest disclosure.

(b) MONITORING OF SUBRECIPIENTS OF FUNDING FROM THE NATIONAL INSTITUTES OF HEALTH.—The Director of the National Institutes of Health (referred to in this section as the "Director of National Institutes of Health") shall implement measures to reduce the administrative burdens related to monitoring of subrecipients of grants by primary awardees of funding from the National Institutes of Health, which may incorporate findings and recommendations from existing and ongoing activities. Such measures may include, as appropriate—

(1) an exemption from subrecipient monitoring requirements, upon request from the primary awardees, provided that—

(A) the subrecipient is subject to Federal audit requirements pursuant to the Uniform Guidance of the Office of Management and Budget;

(B) the primary awardee conducts, pursuant to guidance of the National Institutes of Health, a pre-award evaluation of each subrecipient's risk of noncompliance with Federal statutes and regulations, the conditions of the subaward, and any recurring audit findings; and

(C) such exemption does not absolve the primary awardee of liability for misconduct by subrecipients; and

(2) the implementation of alternative grant structures that obviate the need for subrecipient monitoring, which may include collaborative grant models allowing for multiple primary awardees.

(c) REPORTING OF FINANCIAL EXPENDITURES.—The Secretary, in consultation with the Director of National Institutes of Health, shall evaluate financial expenditure reporting procedures and requirements for recipients of funding from the National Institutes of Health and take action, as appropriate, to avoid duplication between department and agency procedures and requirements and minimize burden to funding recipients.

(d) ANIMAL CARE AND USE IN RESEARCH.—Not later than 2 years after the date of enactment of this Act, the Director of National Institutes of Health, in collaboration with the Secretary of Agriculture and the Commissioner of Food and Drugs, shall complete a review of applicable regulations and policies for the care and use of laboratory animals and make revisions, as appropriate, to reduce administrative burden on investigators while maintaining the integrity and credibility of research findings and protection of research animals. In carrying out this effort, the Director of the National Institutes of Health shall seek the input of experts, as appropriate. The Director of the National Institutes of Health shall—

(1) identify ways to ensure such regulations and policies are not inconsistent, overlapping, or unnecessarily duplicative, including with respect to inspection and review requirements by Federal agencies and accrediting associations;

(2) take steps to eliminate or reduce identified inconsistencies, overlap, or duplication among such regulations and policies; and

(3) take other actions, as appropriate, to improve the coordination of regulations and policies with respect to research with laboratory animals.

(e) DOCUMENTATION OF PERSONNEL EXPENSES.—The Secretary shall clarify the applicability of the requirements under the Office of Management and Budget Uniform Guidance for management and certification systems adopted by entities receiving Federal research grants through the Department of Health and Human Services regarding documentation of personnel expenses, including clarification of the extent to which any flexibility to such requirements specified in such Uniform Guidance applies to entities receiving grants through the Department of Health and Human Services.

(f) RESEARCH POLICY BOARD.—

(1) ESTABLISHMENT.—Not later than 1 year after the date of enactment of this Act, the Director of the Office of Management and Budget shall establish an advisory committee, to be known as the "Research Policy Board" (referred to in this subsection as the "Board"), to provide Federal Government officials with information on the effects of regulations related to Federal research requirements.

(2) MEMBERSHIP.—

(A) IN GENERAL.—The Board shall include not more than 10 Federal members, including each of the following Federal members or their designees:

(i) The Administrator of the Office of Information and Regulatory Affairs of the Office of Management and Budget.

(ii) The Director of the Office of Science and Technology Policy.

(iii) The Secretary of Health and Human Services.

(iv) The Director of the National Science Foundation.

(v) The secretaries and directors of other departments and agencies that support or regulate scientific research, as determined by the Director of the Office of Management and Budget.

(B) NON-FEDERAL MEMBERS.—The Board shall be comprised of not less than 9 and not more than 12 representatives of academic research institutions, other private, nonprofit research institutions, or other nonprofit organizations with relevant expertise. Such members shall be appointed by a formal process, to be established by the Director of the Office of Management and Budget, in consultation with the Federal membership, and that incorporates—

(i) nomination by members of the nonprofit scientific research community, including academic research institutions; and

(ii) procedures to fill membership positions vacated before the end of a member's term.

(3) PURPOSE AND RESPONSIBILITIES.—The Board shall make recommendations regarding the modification and harmonization of regulations and policies having similar purposes across research funding agencies to ensure that the administrative burden of such research policy and regulation is minimized to the greatest extent possible and consistent with maintaining responsible oversight of federally funded research. Activities of the Board may include—

(A) providing thorough and informed analysis of regulations and policies;

(B) identifying negative or adverse consequences of existing policies and making actionable recommendations regarding possible improvement of such policies;

(C) making recommendations with respect to efforts within the Federal Government to improve coordination of regulation and policy related to research;

(D) creating a forum for the discussion of research policy or regulatory gaps, challenges, clarification, or harmonization of such policies or regulation, and best practices; and

(E) conducting ongoing assessment and evaluation of regulatory burden, including development of metrics, periodic measurement, and identification of process improvements and policy changes.

(4) EXPERT SUBCOMMITTEES.—The Board may form temporary expert subcommittees, as appropriate, to develop timely analysis on pressing issues and assist the Board in anticipating future regulatory challenges, including challenges emerging from new scientific advances.

(5) REPORTING REQUIREMENTS.—Not later than 2 years after the date of enactment of this Act, and once thereafter, the Board shall submit a report to the Director of the Office of Management and Budget, the Administrator of the Office of Information and Regulatory Affairs of the Office of Management and Budget, the Director of the Office of Science and Technology Policy, the heads of relevant Federal departments and agencies, the Committee on Health, Education, Labor, and Pensions of the Senate, and the Committee on Energy and Commerce of the House of Representatives containing formal recommendations on the conceptualization, development, harmonization, and reconsideration of scientific research policy, including the regulatory benefits and burdens.

(6) SUNSET.—The Board shall terminate on September 30, 2021.

(7) GAO REPORT.—Not later than 4 years after the date of enactment of this Act, the Comptroller General of the United States shall conduct an independent evaluation of the activities carried out by the Board pursuant to this subsection and submit to the appropriate committees of Congress a report regarding the results of the independent evaluation. Such report shall review and assess the Board's activities with respect to the responsibilities described in paragraph (3).

SEC. 2035. EXEMPTION FOR THE NATIONAL INSTITUTES OF HEALTH FROM THE PAPERWORK REDUCTION ACT REQUIREMENTS.

Section 301 of the Public Health Service Act (42 U.S.C. 241), as amended by section 2013, is further amended by adding at the end the following:

"(g) Subchapter I of chapter 35 of title 44, United States Code, shall not apply to the voluntary collection of information during the conduct of research by the National Institutes of Health.".

SEC. 2036. HIGH-RISK, HIGH-REWARD RESEARCH.

(a) IN GENERAL.—Section 402 of the Public Health Service Act (42 U.S.C. 282), as amended by section 2031, is further amended by adding at the end the following:

"(n) UNIQUE RESEARCH INITIATIVES.—

"(1) IN GENERAL.—The Director of NIH may approve, after consideration of a proposal under paragraph (2)(A), requests by the national research institutes and centers, or program officers within the Office of the Director to engage in transactions other than a contract, grant, or cooperative agreement with respect to projects that carry out—

"(A) the Precision Medicine Initiative under section 498E; or

"(B) section 402(b)(7), except that not more than 50 percent of the funds available for a fiscal year through the Common Fund under section 402A(c)(1) for purposes of carrying out such section 402(b)(7) may be used to engage in such other transactions.

"(2) REQUIREMENTS.—The authority provided under this subsection may be used to conduct or support high impact cutting-edge research described in paragraph (1) using the other transactions authority described in such paragraph if the institute, center, or office—

"(A) submits a proposal to the Director of NIH for the use of such authority before conducting or supporting the research, including why the use of such authority is essential to promoting the success of the project;

"(B) receives approval for the use of such authority from the Director of NIH; and

"(C) for each year in which the institute, center, or office has used such authority in accordance with this subsection, submits a report to the Director of NIH on the activities of the institute, center, or office relating to such research.".

(b) REPORT TO CONGRESS.—Not later than September 30, 2020, the Secretary of Health and Human Services, acting through the Director of the National Institutes of Health, shall conduct an evaluation of the activities under subsection (n) of section 402 of the Public Health Service Act (42 U.S.C. 282), as added by subsection (a), and submit a report to the Committee on Health, Education, Labor, and Pensions of the Senate and the Committee on Energy and Commerce of the House of Representatives on the results of such evaluation.

(c) DUTIES OF DIRECTORS OF INSTITUTES.—Section 405(b)(1) of the Public Health Service Act (42 U.S.C. 284(b)(1)) is amended—

(1) by redesignating subparagraphs (C) through (L) as subparagraphs (D) through (M), respectively; and

(2) by inserting after subparagraph (B), the following:

"(C) shall, as appropriate, conduct and support research that has the potential to transform the scientific field, has inherently higher risk, and that seeks to address major current challenges;".

SEC. 2037. NATIONAL CENTER FOR ADVANCING TRANSLATIONAL SCIENCES.

(a) IN GENERAL.—Section 479(b) of the Public Health Service Act (42 U.S.C. 287(b)) is amended—

(1) in paragraph (1), by striking "phase IIA" and inserting "phase IIB"; and

(2) in paragraph (2)—

(A) in the matter preceding subparagraph (A), by striking "phase IIB" and inserting "phase III";

(B) in subparagraph (A), by striking "phase IIB" and inserting "phase III";

(C) in subparagraph (B), by striking "phase IIA" and inserting "phase IIB"; and

(D) in subparagraph (C), by striking "phase IIB" and inserting "phase III".

(b) INCREASED TRANSPARENCY.—Section 479 of the Public Health Service Act (42 U.S.C. 287) is amended—

(1) in subsection (c)—

(A) in paragraph (4)(D), by striking "and" at the end;

(B) in paragraph (5), by striking the period and inserting a semicolon; and

(C) by adding at the end the following:

"(6) the methods and tools, if any, that have been developed since the last biennial report was prepared; and

"(7) the methods and tools, if any, that have been developed and are being utilized by the Food and Drug Administration to support medical product reviews."; and

(2) by adding at the end the following:

"(d) INCLUSION OF LIST.—The first biennial report submitted under this section after the date of enactment of the 21st Century Cures Act shall include a complete list of all of the methods and tools, if any, which have been developed by research supported by the Center.

"(e) RULE OF CONSTRUCTION.—Nothing in this section shall be construed as authorizing the Secretary to disclose any information that is a trade secret, or other privileged or confidential information subject to section 552(b)(4) of title 5, United States Code, or section 1905 of title 18, United States Code.".

SEC. 2038. COLLABORATION AND COORDINATION TO ENHANCE RESEARCH.

(a) RESEARCH PRIORITIES; COLLABORATIVE RESEARCH PROJECTS.—Section 402(b) of the Public Health Service Act (42 U.S.C. 282(b)) is amended—

(1) by amending paragraph (4) to read as follows:

"(4) shall assemble accurate data to be used to assess research priorities, including—

"(A) information to better evaluate scientific opportunity, public health burdens, and progress in reducing health disparities; and

"(B) data on study populations of clinical research, funded by or conducted at each national research institute and national center, which—

"(i) specifies the inclusion of—

"(I) women;

"(II) members of minority groups;

"(III) relevant age categories, including pediatric subgroups; and

"(IV) other demographic variables as the Director of the National Institutes of Health determines appropriate;

"(ii) is disaggregated by research area, condition, and disease categories; and

"(iii) is to be made publicly available on the Internet website of the National Institutes of Health;"; and

(2) in paragraph (8)—

(A) in subparagraph (A), by striking "and" at the end; and

(B) by adding at the end the following:

"(C) foster collaboration between clinical research projects funded by the respective national research institutes and national centers that—

"(i) conduct research involving human subjects; and

"(ii) collect similar data; and

"(D) encourage the collaboration described in subparagraph (C) to—

"(i) allow for an increase in the number of subjects studied; and

"(ii) utilize diverse study populations, with special consideration to biological, social, and other determinants of health that contribute to health disparities;".

(b) REPORTING.—Section 492B(f) of the Public Health Service Act (42 U.S.C. 289a-2(f)) is amended—

(1) by striking "biennial" each place such term appears and inserting "triennial";

(2) by striking "The advisory council" and inserting the following:

"(1) IN GENERAL.—The advisory council"; and

(3) by adding at the end the following:

"(2) CONTENTS.—Each triennial report prepared by an advisory council of each national research institute as described in paragraph (1) shall include each of the following:

"(A) The number of women included as subjects, and the proportion of subjects that are women, in any project of clinical research conducted during the applicable reporting period, disaggregated by categories of research area, condition, or disease, and accounting for single-sex studies.

"(B) The number of members of minority groups included as subjects, and the proportion of subjects that are members of minority groups, in any project of clinical research conducted during the applicable reporting period, disaggregated by categories of research area, condition, or disease and accounting for single-race and single-ethnicity studies.

"(C) For the applicable reporting period, the number of projects of clinical research that include women and members of minority groups and that—

"(i) have been completed during such reporting period; and

"(ii) are being carried out during such reporting period and have not been completed.

"(D) The number of studies completed during the applicable reporting period for which reporting has been submitted in accordance with subsection (c)(2)(A).".

(c) COORDINATION.—Section 486(c)(2) of the Public Health Service Act (42 U.S.C. 287d(c)(2)) is amended by striking "designees" and inserting "senior-level staff designees".

(d) IN GENERAL.—Part A of title IV of the Public Health Service Act (42 U.S.C. 281 et seq.), as amended by section 2021, is further amended by adding at the end the following:

"SEC. 404N. POPULATION FOCUSED RESEARCH.

"The Director of the National Institutes of Health shall, as appropriate, encourage efforts to improve research related to the health of sexual and gender minority populations, including by—

"(1) facilitating increased participation of sexual and gender minority populations in clinical research supported by the National Institutes of Health, and reporting on such participation, as applicable;

"(2) facilitating the development of valid and reliable methods for research relevant to sexual and gender minority populations; and

"(3) addressing methodological challenges.".

(e) REPORTING.—

(1) IN GENERAL.—The Secretary, in collaboration with the Director of the National Institutes of Health, shall as appropriate—

(A) continue to support research for the development of appropriate measures related to reporting health information about sexual and gender minority populations; and

(B) not later than 2 years after the date of enactment of this Act, disseminate and make public such measures.

(2) NATIONAL ACADEMY OF MEDICINE RECOMMENDATIONS.—In developing the measures described in paragraph (1)(A), the Secretary shall take into account recommendations made by the National Academy of Medicine.

(f) IMPROVING COORDINATION RELATED TO MINORITY HEALTH AND HEALTH DISPARITIES.—Section 464z-3 of the Public Health Service Act (42 U.S.C. 285t) is amended—

(1) by redesignating subsection (h), relating to interagency coordination, that follows subsection (j) as subsection (k); and

(2) in subsection (k) (as so redesignated)—

(A) in the subsection heading, by striking "INTERAGENCY" and inserting "INTRA-NATIONAL INSTITUTES OF HEALTH";

(B) by striking "as the primary Federal officials" and inserting "as the primary Federal official";

(C) by inserting a comma after "review";

(D) by striking "Institutes and Centers of the National Institutes of Health" and inserting "national research institutes and national centers"; and

(E) by adding at the end the following: "The Director of the Institute may foster partnerships between the national research institutes and national centers and may encourage the funding of collaborative research projects to achieve the goals of the National Institutes of Health that are related to minority health and health disparities.".

(g) BASIC RESEARCH.—

(1) DEVELOPING POLICIES.—Not later than 2 years after the date of enactment of this Act, the Director of the National Institutes of Health (referred to in this section as the "Director of the National Institutes of Health"), taking into consideration the recommendations developed under section 2039, shall develop policies for projects of basic research funded by National Institutes of Health to assess—

(A) relevant biological variables including sex, as appropriate; and

(B) how differences between male and female cells, tissues, or animals may be examined and analyzed.

(2) REVISING POLICIES.—The Director of the National Institutes of Health may update or revise the policies developed under paragraph (1) as appropriate.

(3) CONSULTATION AND OUTREACH.—In developing, updating, or revising the policies under this section, the Director of the National Institutes of Health shall—

(A) consult with—

(i) the Office of Research on Women's Health;

(ii) the Office of Laboratory Animal Welfare; and

(iii) appropriate members of the scientific and academic communities; and

(B) conduct outreach to solicit feedback from members of the scientific and academic communities on the influence of sex as a variable in basic research, including feedback on when it is appropriate for projects of basic research involving cells, tissues, or animals to include both male and female cells, tissues, or animals.

(4) ADDITIONAL REQUIREMENTS.—The Director of the National Institutes of Health shall—

(A) ensure that projects of basic research funded by the National Institutes of Health are conducted in accordance with the policies developed, updated, or revised under this section, as applicable; and

(B) encourage that the results of such research, when published or reported, be disaggregated as appropriate with respect to the analysis of any sex differences.

(h) CLINICAL RESEARCH.—

(1) IN GENERAL.—Not later than 1 year after the date of enactment of this Act, the Director of the National Institutes of Health, in consultation with the Director of the Office of Research on Women's Health and the Director of the National Institute on Minority Health and Health Disparities, shall update the guidelines established under section 492B(d) of Public Health Service Act (42 U.S.C. 289a-2(d)) in accordance with paragraph (2).

(2) REQUIREMENTS.—The updated guidelines described in paragraph (1) shall—

(A) reflect the science regarding sex differences;

(B) improve adherence to the requirements under section 492B of the Public Health Service Act (42 U.S.C. 289a-2), including the reporting requirements under subsection (f) of such section; and

(C) clarify the circumstances under which studies should be designed to support the conduct of analyses to detect significant differences in the intervention effect due to demographic factors related to section 492B of the Public Health Service Act, including in the absence of prior studies that demonstrate a difference in study outcomes on the basis of such factors and considering the effects of the absence of such analyses on the availability of data related to demographic differences.

(i) APPROPRIATE AGE GROUPINGS IN CLINICAL RESEARCH.—

(1) INPUT FROM EXPERTS.—Not later than 180 days after the date of enactment of this Act, the Director of the National Institutes of Health shall convene a workshop of experts on pediatric and older populations to provide input on—

(A) appropriate age groups to be included in research studies involving human subjects; and

(B) acceptable justifications for excluding participants from a range of age groups from human subjects research studies.

(2) POLICY UPDATES.—Not later than 180 days after the conclusion of the workshop under paragraph (1), the Director of the National Institutes of Health shall make a determination with respect to whether the policies of the National Institutes of Health on the inclusion of relevant age groups in clinical studies need to be updated, and shall update such policies as appropriate. In making the determination, the Director of the National Institutes of Health shall take into consideration whether such policies—

(A) address the consideration of age as an inclusion variable in research involving human subjects; and

(B) identify the criteria for justification for any age-related exclusions in such research.

(3) PUBLIC AVAILABILITY OF FINDINGS AND CONCLUSIONS.—The Director of the National Institutes of Health shall—

(A) make the findings and conclusions resulting from the workshop under paragraph (1) and updates to policies in accordance with paragraph (2), as applicable, available to the public on the Internet website of the National Institutes of Health; and

(B) ensure that age-related data reported in the triennial report under section 403 of the Public Health Service Act (42 U.S.C. 283) (as amended by section 2032) are made available to the public on the Internet website of the National Institutes of Health.

SEC. 2039. ENHANCING THE RIGOR AND REPRODUCIBILITY OF SCIENTIFIC RESEARCH.

(a) ESTABLISHMENT.—Not later than 1 year after the date of enactment of this Act, the Secretary of Health and Human Services, acting through the Director of the National Institutes of Health, shall convene a working group under the Advisory Committee to the Director of the National Institutes of Health (referred to in this section as the "Advisory Committee"), appointed under section 222 of the Public Health Service Act (42 U.S.C. 217a), to develop and issue recommendations through the Advisory Committee for a formal policy, which may incorporate or be informed by relevant existing and ongoing activities, to enhance rigor and reproducibility of scientific research funded by the National Institutes of Health.

(b) CONSIDERATIONS.—In developing and issuing recommendations through the Advisory Committee under subsection (a), the working group established under such subsection shall consider, as appropriate—

(1) preclinical experiment design, including analysis of sex as a biological variable;

(2) clinical experiment design, including—

(A) the diversity of populations studied for clinical research, with respect to biological, social, and other determinants of health that contribute to health disparities;

(B) the circumstances under which summary information regarding biological, social, and other factors that contribute to health disparities should be reported; and

(C) the circumstances under which clinical studies, including clinical trials, should conduct an analysis of the data collected during the study on the basis of biological, social, and other factors that contribute to health disparities;

(3) applicable levels of rigor in statistical methods, methodology, and analysis;

(4) data and information sharing in accordance with applicable privacy laws and regulations; and

(5) any other matter the working group determines relevant.

(c) POLICIES.—Not later than 18 months after the date of enactment of this Act, the Director of the National Institutes of Health shall consider the recommendations developed by the working group and issued by the Advisory Committee under subsection (a) and develop or update policies as appropriate.

(d) REPORT.—Not later than 2 years after the date of enactment of this Act, the Director of the National Institutes of Health shall issue a report to the Secretary of Health and Human Services, the Committee on Health, Education, Labor, and Pensions of the Senate, and the Committee on Energy and Commerce of the House of Representatives regarding recommendations developed under subsection (a) and any subsequent policy changes implemented, to enhance rigor and reproducibility in scientific research funded by the National Institutes of Health.

(e) CONFIDENTIALITY.—Nothing in this section authorizes the Secretary of Health and Human Services to disclose any information that is a trade secret, or other privileged or confidential information, described in section 552(b)(4) of title 5, United States Code, or section 1905 of title 18, United States Code.

SEC. 2040. IMPROVING MEDICAL REHABILITATION RESEARCH AT THE NATIONAL INSTITUTES OF HEALTH.

(a) IN GENERAL.—Section 452 of the Public Health Service Act (42 U.S.C. 285g–4) is amended—

(1) in subsection (b), by striking "conduct and support" and inserting "conduct, support, and coordination";

(2) in subsection (c)(1)(C), by striking "of the Center" and inserting "within the Center";

(3) in subsection (d)—

(A) by striking "(d)(1) In consultation" and all that follows through the end of paragraph (1) and inserting the following:

"(d)(1) The Director of the Center, in consultation with the Director of the Institute, the coordinating committee established under subsection (e), and the advisory board established under subsection (f), shall develop a comprehensive plan (referred to in this section as the 'Research Plan') for the conduct, support, and coordination of medical rehabilitation research.";

(B) in paragraph (2)—

(i) in subparagraph (A), by striking "; and" and inserting a semicolon;

(ii) in subparagraph (B), by striking the period and inserting "; and"; and

(iii) by adding at the end the following:

"(C) include goals and objectives for conducting, supporting, and coordinating medical rehabilitation research, consistent with the purpose described in subsection (b).";

(C) by striking paragraph (4) and inserting the following:

"(4) The Director of the Center, in consultation with the Director of the Institute, the coordinating committee established under subsection (e), and the advisory board established under subsection (f), shall revise and update the Research Plan periodically, as appropriate, or not less than every 5 years. Not later than 30 days after the Research Plan is so revised and updated, the Director of the Center shall transmit the revised and updated Research Plan to the President, the Committee on Health, Education, Labor, and Pensions of the Senate, and the Committee on Energy and Commerce of the House of Representatives."; and

(D) by adding at the end the following:

"(5) The Director of the Center, in consultation with the Director of the Institute, shall, prior to revising and updating the Research Plan, prepare a report for the coordinating committee established under subsection (e) and the advisory board established under subsection (f) that describes and analyzes the progress during the preceding fiscal year in achieving the goals and objectives described in paragraph (2)(C) and includes expenditures for rehabilitation research at the National Institutes of Health. The report shall include recommendations for revising and updating the Research Plan, and such initiatives as the Director of the Center and the Director of the Institute determine appropriate. In preparing the report, the Director of the Center and the Director of the Institute shall consult with the Director of the National Institutes of Health.";

(4) in subsection (e)—

(A) in paragraph (2), by inserting "periodically host a scientific conference or workshop on medical rehabilitation research and" after "The Coordinating Committee shall"; and

(B) in paragraph (3), by inserting "the Director of the Division of Program Coordination, Planning, and Strategic Initiatives within the Office of the Director of the National Institutes of Health," after "shall be composed of";

(5) in subsection (f)(3)(B)—

(A) by redesignating clauses (ix) through (xi) as clauses (x) through (xii), respectively; and

(B) by inserting after clause (viii) the following:

"(ix) The Director of the Division of Program Coordination, Planning, and Strategic Initiatives."; and

(6) by adding at the end the following:

"(g)(1) The Secretary and the heads of other Federal agencies shall jointly review the programs carried out (or proposed to be carried out) by each such official with respect to medical rehabilitation research and, as appropriate, enter into agreements preventing duplication among such programs.

"(2) The Secretary shall, as appropriate, enter into interagency agreements relating to the coordination of medical rehabilitation research conducted by agencies of the National Institutes of Health and other agencies of the Federal Government.

"(h) For purposes of this section, the term 'medical rehabilitation research' means the science of mechanisms and interventions that prevent, improve, restore, or replace lost, underdeveloped, or deteriorating function.".

(b) CONFORMING AMENDMENT.—Section 3 of the National Institutes of Health Amendments of 1990 (42 U.S.C. 285g–4 note) is amended—

(1) in subsection (a), by striking "IN GENERAL.—"; and

(2) by striking subsection (b).

SEC. 2041. TASK FORCE ON RESEARCH SPECIFIC TO PREGNANT WOMEN AND LACTATING WOMEN.

(a) TASK FORCE ON RESEARCH SPECIFIC TO PREGNANT WOMEN AND LACTATING WOMEN.—

(1) ESTABLISHMENT.—Not later than 90 days after the date of enactment of this Act, the Secretary of Health and Human Services (referred to in this section as the "Secretary") shall establish a task force, in accordance with the Federal Advisory Committee Act (5 U.S.C. App.), to be known as the "Task Force on Research Specific to Pregnant Women and Lactating Women" (in this section referred to as the "Task Force").

(2) DUTIES.—The Task Force shall provide advice and guidance to the Secretary regarding Federal activities related to identifying and addressing gaps in knowledge and research regarding safe and effective therapies for pregnant women and lactating women, including the development of such therapies and the collaboration on and coordination of such activities.

(3) MEMBERSHIP.—

(A) FEDERAL MEMBERS.—The Task Force shall be composed of each of the following Federal members, or the designees of such members:

(i) The Director of the Centers for Disease Control and Prevention.

(ii) The Director of the National Institutes of Health, the Director of the Eunice Kennedy Shriver National Institute of Child Health and Human Development, and the directors of such other appropriate national research institutes.

(iii) The Commissioner of Food and Drugs.

(iv) The Director of the Office on Women's Health.

(v) The Director of the National Vaccine Program Office.

(vi) The head of any other research-related agency or department not described in clauses (i) through (v) that the Secretary determines appropriate, which may include the Department of Veterans Affairs and the Department of Defense.

(B) NON-FEDERAL MEMBERS.—The Task Force shall be composed of each of the following non-Federal members, including—

(i) representatives from relevant medical societies with subject matter expertise on pregnant women, lactating women, or children;

(ii) nonprofit organizations with expertise related to the health of women and children;

(iii) relevant industry representatives; and

(iv) other representatives, as appropriate.

(C) LIMITATIONS.—The non-Federal members described in subparagraph (B) shall—

(i) compose not more than one-half, and not less than one-third, of the total membership of the Task Force; and

(ii) be appointed by the Secretary.

(4) TERMINATION.—

(A) IN GENERAL.—Subject to subparagraph (B), the Task Force shall terminate on the date that is 2 years after the date on which the Task Force is established under paragraph (1).

(B) EXTENSION.—The Secretary may extend the operation of the Task Force for one additional 2-year period following the 2-year period described in subparagraph (A), if the Secretary determines that the extension is appropriate for carrying out the purpose of this section.

(5) MEETINGS.—The Task Force shall meet not less than 2 times each year and shall convene public meetings, as appropriate, to fulfill its duties under paragraph (2).

(6) TASK FORCE REPORT TO CONGRESS.—Not later than 18 months after the date on which the Task Force is established under paragraph (1), the Task Force shall prepare and submit to the Secretary, the Committee on Health, Education, Labor, and Pensions of the Senate, and the Committee on Energy and Commerce of the House of Representatives a report that includes each of the following:

(A) A plan to identify and address gaps in knowledge and research regarding safe and effective therapies for pregnant women and lactating women, including the development of such therapies.

(B) Ethical issues surrounding the inclusion of pregnant women and lactating women in clinical research.

(C) Effective communication strategies with health care providers and the public on information relevant to pregnant women and lactating women.

(D) Identification of Federal activities, including—

(i) the state of research on pregnancy and lactation;

(ii) recommendations for the coordination of, and collaboration on research related to pregnant women and lactating women;

(iii) dissemination of research findings and information relevant to pregnant women and lactating women to providers and the public; and

(iv) existing Federal efforts and programs to improve the scientific understanding of the health impacts on pregnant women, lactating women, and related birth and pediatric outcomes, including with respect to pharmacokinetics, pharmacodynamics, and toxicities.

(E) Recommendations to improve the development of safe and effective therapies for pregnant women and lactating women.

(b) CONFIDENTIALITY.—Nothing in this section shall authorize the Secretary of Health and Human Services to disclose any information that is a trade secret, or other privileged or confidential information, described in section 552(b)(4) of title 5, United States Code, or section 1905 of title 18, United States Code.

(c) UPDATING PROTECTIONS FOR PREGNANT WOMEN AND LACTATING WOMEN IN RESEARCH.—

(1) IN GENERAL.—Not later than 2 years after the date of enactment of this Act, the Secretary, considering any recommendations of the Task Force available at such time and in consultation with the heads of relevant agencies of the Department of Health and Human Services, shall, as appropriate, update regulations and guidance, as applicable, regarding the inclusion of pregnant women and lactating women in clinical research.

(2) CRITERIA FOR EXCLUDING PREGNANT OR LACTATING WOMEN.—In updating any regulations or guidance described in paragraph (1), the Secretary shall consider any appropriate criteria to be used by institutional review boards and individuals reviewing grant proposals for excluding pregnant women or lactating women as a study population requiring additional protections from participating in human subject research.

SEC. 2042. STREAMLINING NATIONAL INSTITUTES OF HEALTH REPORTING REQUIREMENTS.

(a) TRANS-NATIONAL INSTITUTES OF HEALTH RESEARCH REPORTING.—Section 402A(c)(2) of the Public Health Service Act (42 U.S.C. 282a(c)(2)) is amended—

(1) by amending subparagraph (B) to read as follows:

"(B) REPORTING.—Not later than 2 years after the date of enactment of 21st Century Cures Act, the head of each national research institute or national center shall submit to the Director of the National Institutes of Health a report, to be included in the triennial report under section 403, on the amount made available by the institute or center for conducting or supporting research that involves collaboration between the institute or center and 1 or more other national research institutes or national centers."; and

(2) in subparagraphs (D) and (E) by striking "(B)(i)" each place it appears and inserting "(B)".

(b) FRAUD AND ABUSE REPORTING.—Section 403B of the Public Health Service Act (42 U.S.C. 283a–1) is amended—

(1) by striking subsection (b);

(2) by redesignating subsection (c) as subsection (b); and

(3) in subsection (b) (as so redesignated), by striking "subsections (a) and (b)" and inserting "subsection (a)".

(c) DOCTORAL DEGREES REPORTING.—Section 403C(a)(2) of the Public Health Service Act (42 U.S.C. 283a–2(a)(2)) is amended by striking "(not including any leaves of absence)".

(d) VACCINE REPORTING.—Section 404B of the Public Health Service Act (42 U.S.C. 283d) is amended—

(1) by striking subsection (b); and

(2) by striking "(a) DEVELOPMENT OF NEW VACCINES.—The Secretary" and inserting "The Secretary".

(e) NATIONAL CENTER FOR ADVANCING TRANSLATIONAL SCIENCES.—Section 479(c) of the Public Health Service Act (42 U.S.C. 287(c)) is amended—

(1) in the subsection heading, by striking "ANNUAL" and inserting "BIENNIAL"; and

(2) in the matter preceding paragraph (1), by striking "an annual report" and inserting "a report on a biennial basis".

(f) REVIEW OF CENTERS OF EXCELLENCE.—

(1) REPEAL.—Section 404H of the Public Health Service Act (42 U.S.C. 283j) is repealed.

(2) CONFORMING AMENDMENT.—Section 399EE(c) of the Public Health Service Act (42 U.S.C. 280–4(c)) is amended by striking "399CC, 404H," and inserting "399CC".

(g) RAPID HIV TEST REPORT.—Section 502(a) of the Ryan White CARE Act Amendments of 2000 (42 U.S.C. 300cc note) is amended—

(1) by striking paragraph (2); and

(2) by redesignating paragraph (3) as paragraph (2).

(h) NATIONAL INSTITUTE OF NURSING RESEARCH.—

(1) REPEAL.—Section 464Y of the Public Health Service Act (42 U.S.C. 285q–3) is repealed.

(2) CONFORMING AMENDMENT.—Section 464X(g) of the Public Health Service Act (42 U.S.C. 285q–2(g)) is amended by striking "biennial report made under section 464Y," and inserting "triennial report made under section 403".

SEC. 2043. REIMBURSEMENT FOR RESEARCH SUBSTANCES AND LIVING ORGANISMS.

Section 301 of the Public Health Service Act (42 U.S.C. 241), as amended by section 2035, is further amended—

(1) in the flush matter at the end of subsection (a)—

(A) by redesignating such matter as subsection (h)(1); and

(B) by moving such matter so as to appear at the end of such section; and

(2) in subsection (h) (as so redesignated), by adding at the end the following:

"(2) Where research substances and living organisms are made available under paragraph (1) through contractors, the Secretary may direct such contractors to collect payments on behalf of the Secretary for the costs incurred to make available such substances and organisms and to forward amounts so collected to the Secretary, in the time and manner specified by the Secretary.

"(3) Amounts collected under paragraph (2) shall be credited to the appropriations accounts that incurred the costs to make available the research substances and living organisms involved, and shall remain available until expended for carrying out activities under such accounts.".

SEC. 2044. SENSE OF CONGRESS ON INCREASED INCLUSION OF UNDERREPRESENTED POPULATIONS IN CLINICAL TRIALS.

It is the sense of Congress that the National Institute on Minority Health and Health Disparities should include within its strategic plan under section 402(m) of the Public Health Service Act (42 U.S.C. 282(m)) ways to increase representation of underrepresented populations in clinical trials.

Subtitle E—Advancement of the National Institutes of Health Research and Data Access

SEC. 2051. TECHNICAL UPDATES TO CLINICAL TRIALS DATABASE.

Section 402(j)(2)(D) of the Public Health Service Act (42 U.S.C. 282(j)(2)(D)) is amended—

(1) in clause (ii)(I), by inserting before the semicolon ", unless the responsible party affirmatively requests that the Director of the National Institutes of Health publicly post such clinical trial information for an applicable device clinical trial prior to such date of clearance or approval"; and

(2) by adding at the end the following:

"(iii) OPTION TO MAKE CERTAIN CLINICAL TRIAL INFORMATION AVAILABLE EARLIER.—The

Director of the National Institutes of Health shall inform responsible parties of the option to request that clinical trial information for an applicable device clinical trial be publicly posted prior to the date of clearance or approval, in accordance with clause (ii)(I).

"(iv) COMBINATION PRODUCTS.—An applicable clinical trial for a product that is a combination of drug, device, or biological product shall be considered—

"(I) an applicable drug clinical trial, if the Secretary determines under section 503(g) of the Federal Food, Drug, and Cosmetic Act that the primary mode of action of such product is that of a drug or biological product; or

"(II) an applicable device clinical trial, if the Secretary determines under such section that the primary mode of action of such product is that of a device.".

SEC. 2052. COMPLIANCE ACTIVITIES REPORTS.

(a) DEFINITIONS.—In this section:

(1) APPLICABLE CLINICAL TRIAL.—The term "applicable clinical trial" has the meaning given the term in section 402(j) of the Public Health Service Act (42 U.S.C. 282(j)).

(2) SECRETARY.—The term "Secretary" means the Secretary of Health and Human Services.

(b) REPORT ON ACTIVITIES TO ENCOURAGE COMPLIANCE.—Not later than 2 years after the date of enactment of this Act, the Secretary, acting through the Director of the National Institutes of Health and in collaboration with the Commissioner of Food and Drugs, shall submit to the Committee on Health, Education, Labor, and Pensions of the Senate and the Committee on Energy and Commerce of the House of Representatives, a report that describes education and outreach, guidance, enforcement, and other activities undertaken to encourage compliance with section 402(j) of the Public Health Service Act (42 U.S.C. 282(j)).

(c) REPORTS ON CLINICAL TRIALS.—

(1) IN GENERAL.—Not later than 2 years after the final compliance date under the final rule implementing section 402(j) of the Public Health Service Act, and every 2 years thereafter for the next 4 years, the Secretary, acting through the Director of the National Institutes of Health and in collaboration with the Commissioner of Food and Drugs, shall submit to the Committee on Health, Education, Labor, and Pensions of the Senate and the Committee on Energy and Commerce of the House of Representatives, a report describing—

(A) the total number of applicable clinical trials with complete data bank registration information registered during the period for which the report is being prepared (broken down by each year of such reporting period);

(B) the total number of applicable clinical trials registered during the period for which the report is being prepared for which results have been submitted to the data bank (broken down by each year of such reporting period);

(C) the activities undertaken by the Secretary to educate responsible persons about data bank registration and results submission requirements, including through issuance of guidance documents, informational meetings, and training sessions; and

(D) the activities described in the report submitted under subsection (b).

(2) ACTIONS TO ENFORCE COMPLIANCE.—After the Secretary has undertaken the educational activities described in paragraph (1)(C), the Secretary shall include in subsequent reports submitted under paragraph (1) the number of actions taken by the Secretary during the period for which the report is being prepared to enforce compliance with data bank registration and results submission requirements.

SEC. 2053. UPDATES TO POLICIES TO IMPROVE DATA.

Section 492B(c) of the Public Health Service Act (42 U.S.C. 289a–2(c)) is amended—

(1) by striking "In the case" and inserting the following:

"(1) IN GENERAL.—In the case"; and

(2) by adding at the end the following:

"(2) REPORTING REQUIREMENTS.—For any new and competing project of clinical research subject to the requirements under this section that receives a grant award 1 year after the date of enactment of the 21st Century Cures Act, or any date thereafter, for which a valid analysis is provided under paragraph (1)—

"(A) and which is an applicable clinical trial as defined in section 402(j), the entity conducting such clinical research shall submit the results of such valid analysis to the clinical trial registry data bank expanded under section 402(j)(3), and the Director of the National Institutes of Health shall, as appropriate, consider whether such entity has complied with the reporting requirement described in this subparagraph in awarding any future grant to such entity, including pursuant to section 402(j)(5)(A)(ii) when applicable; and

"(B) the Director of the National Institutes of Health shall encourage the reporting of the results of such valid analysis described in paragraph (1) through any additional means determined appropriate by the Director.".

SEC. 2054. CONSULTATION.

Not later than 90 days after the date of enactment of this Act, the Secretary of Health and Human Services shall consult with relevant Federal agencies, including the Food and Drug Administration, the Office of the National Coordinator for Health Information Technology, and the National Institutes of Health, as well as other stakeholders (including patients, researchers, physicians, industry representatives, and developers of health information technology) to receive recommendations with respect to enhancements to the clinical trial registry data bank under section 402(j) of the Public Health Service Act (42 U.S.C. 282(j)), including with respect to usability, functionality, and search capability.

Subtitle F—Facilitating Collaborative Research

SEC. 2061. NATIONAL NEUROLOGICAL CONDITIONS SURVEILLANCE SYSTEM.

Part P of title III of the Public Health Service Act (42 U.S.C. 280g et seq.) is amended by inserting after section 399S the following:

"SEC. 399S–1. SURVEILLANCE OF NEUROLOGICAL DISEASES.

"(a) IN GENERAL.—The Secretary, acting through the Director of the Centers for Disease Control and Prevention and in coordination with other agencies as the Secretary determines, shall, as appropriate—

"(1) enhance and expand infrastructure and activities to track the epidemiology of neurological diseases; and

"(2) incorporate information obtained through such activities into an integrated surveillance system, which may consist of or include a registry, to be known as the National Neurological Conditions Surveillance System.

"(b) RESEARCH.—The Secretary shall ensure that the National Neurological Conditions Surveillance System is designed in a manner that facilitates further research on neurological diseases.

"(c) CONTENT.—In carrying out subsection (a), the Secretary—

"(1) shall provide for the collection and storage of information on the incidence and prevalence of neurological diseases in the United States;

"(2) to the extent practicable, shall provide for the collection and storage of other available information on neurological diseases, including information related to persons living with neurological diseases who choose to participate, such as—

"(A) demographics, such as age, race, ethnicity, sex, geographic location, family history, and other information, as appropriate;

"(B) risk factors that may be associated with neurological diseases, such as genetic and environmental risk factors and other information, as appropriate; and

"(C) diagnosis and progression markers;

"(3) may provide for the collection and storage of information relevant to analysis on neurological diseases, such as information concerning—

"(A) the natural history of the diseases;

"(B) the prevention of the diseases;

"(C) the detection, management, and treatment approaches for the diseases; and

"(D) the development of outcomes measures;

"(4) may address issues identified during the consultation process under subsection (d); and

"(5) initially may address a limited number of neurological diseases.

"(d) CONSULTATION.—In carrying out this section, the Secretary shall consult with individuals with appropriate expertise, which may include—

"(1) epidemiologists with experience in disease surveillance or registries;

"(2) representatives of national voluntary health associations that—

"(A) focus on neurological diseases; and

"(B) have demonstrated experience in research, care, or patient services;

"(3) health information technology experts or other information management specialists;

"(4) clinicians with expertise in neurological diseases; and

"(5) research scientists with experience conducting translational research or utilizing surveillance systems for scientific research purposes.

"(e) GRANTS.—The Secretary may award grants to, or enter into contracts or cooperative agreements with, public or private nonprofit entities to carry out activities under this section.

"(f) COORDINATION WITH OTHER FEDERAL, STATE, AND LOCAL AGENCIES.—Subject to subsection (h), the Secretary shall—

"(1) make information and analysis in the National Neurological Conditions Surveillance System available, as appropriate—

"(A) to Federal departments and agencies, such as the National Institutes of Health and the Department of Veterans Affairs; and

"(B) to State and local agencies; and

"(2) identify, build upon, leverage, and coordinate among existing data and surveillance systems, surveys, registries, and other Federal public health infrastructure, wherever practicable.

"(g) PUBLIC ACCESS.—Subject to subsection (h), the Secretary shall ensure that information and analysis in the National Neurological Conditions Surveillance System are available, as appropriate, to the public, including researchers.

"(h) PRIVACY.—The Secretary shall ensure that information and analysis in the National Neurological Conditions Surveillance System are made available only to the extent permitted by applicable Federal and State law, and in a manner that protects personal privacy, to the extent required by applicable Federal and State privacy law, at a minimum.

"(i) REPORTS.—

"(1) REPORT ON INFORMATION AND ANALYSES.—Not later than 1 year after the date on which any system is established under this section, the Secretary shall submit an interim report to the Committee on Health, Education, Labor, and Pensions of the Senate and the Committee on Energy and Commerce of the House of Representatives regarding aggregate information collected pursuant to this section and epidemiological analyses, as appropriate. Such report shall be posted on the Internet website of the Department of Health and Human Services and shall be updated biennially.

"(2) IMPLEMENTATION REPORT.—Not later than 4 years after the date of the enactment of this section, the Secretary shall submit a report to the Congress concerning the implementation of this section. Such report shall include information on—

"(A) the development and maintenance of the National Neurological Conditions Surveillance System;

"(B) the type of information collected and stored in the surveillance system;

"(C) the use and availability of such information, including guidelines for such use; and

"(D) the use and coordination of databases that collect or maintain information on neurological diseases.

"(j) DEFINITION.—In this section, the term 'national voluntary health association' means a national nonprofit organization with chapters, other affiliated organizations, or networks in States throughout the United States with experience serving the population of individuals with neurological disease and have demonstrated experience in neurological disease research, care, and patient services.

"(k) AUTHORIZATION OF APPROPRIATIONS.—To carry out this section, there is authorized to be appropriated $5,000,000 for each of fiscal years 2018 through 2022.".

SEC. 2062. TICK-BORNE DISEASES.

(a) IN GENERAL.—The Secretary of Health and Human Services (referred to in this section as "the Secretary") shall continue to conduct or support epidemiological, basic, translational, and clinical research related to vector-borne diseases, including tick-borne diseases.

(b) REPORTS.—The Secretary shall ensure that each triennial report under section 403 of the Public Health Service Act (42 U.S.C. 283) (as amended by section 2032) includes information on actions undertaken by the National Institutes of Health to carry out subsection (a) with respect to tick-borne diseases.

(c) TICK-BORNE DISEASES WORKING GROUP.—

(1) ESTABLISHMENT.—The Secretary shall establish a working group, to be known as the Tick-Borne Disease Working Group (referred to in this section as the "Working Group"), comprised of representatives of appropriate Federal agencies and other non-Federal entities, to provide expertise and to review all efforts within the Department of Health and Human Services related to all tick-borne diseases, to help ensure interagency coordination and minimize overlap, and to examine research priorities.

(2) RESPONSIBILITIES.—The working group shall—

(A) not later than 2 years after the date of enactment of this Act, develop or update a summary of—

(i) ongoing tick-borne disease research, including research related to causes, prevention, treatment, surveillance, diagnosis, diagnostics, duration of illness, and intervention for individuals with tick-borne diseases;

(ii) advances made pursuant to such research;

(iii) Federal activities related to tick-borne diseases, including—

(I) epidemiological activities related to tick-borne diseases; and

(II) basic, clinical, and translational tick-borne disease research related to the pathogenesis, prevention, diagnosis, and treatment of tick-borne diseases;

(iv) gaps in tick-borne disease research described in clause (iii)(II);

(v) the Working Group's meetings required under paragraph (4); and

(vi) the comments received by the Working Group;

(B) make recommendations to the Secretary regarding any appropriate changes or improvements to such activities and research; and

(C) solicit input from States, localities, and nongovernmental entities, including organizations representing patients, health care providers, researchers, and industry regarding scientific advances, research questions, surveillance activities, and emerging strains in species of pathogenic organisms.

(3) MEMBERSHIP.—The members of the working group shall represent a diversity of scientific disciplines and views and shall be composed of the following members:

(A) FEDERAL MEMBERS.—Seven Federal members, consisting of one of more representatives of each of the following:

(i) The Office of the Assistant Secretary for Health.

(ii) The Food and Drug Administration.

(iii) The Centers for Disease Control and Prevention.

(iv) The National Institutes of Health.

(v) Such other agencies and offices of the Department of Health and Human Services as the Secretary determines appropriate.

(B) NON-FEDERAL PUBLIC MEMBERS.—Seven non-Federal public members, consisting of representatives of the following categories:

(i) Physicians and other medical providers with experience in diagnosing and treating tick-borne diseases.

(ii) Scientists or researchers with expertise.

(iii) Patients and their family members.

(iv) Nonprofit organizations that advocate for patients with respect to tick-borne diseases.

(v) Other individuals whose expertise is determined by the Secretary to be beneficial to the functioning of the Working Group.

(4) MEETINGS.—The Working Group shall meet not less than twice each year.

(5) REPORTING.—Not later than 2 years after the date of enactment of this Act, and every 2 years thereafter until termination of the Working Group pursuant to paragraph (7), the Working Group shall—

(A) submit a report on its activities under paragraph (2)(A) and any recommendations under paragraph (2)(B) to the Secretary, the Committee on Energy and Commerce of the House of Representatives, and the Committee on Health, Education, Labor, and Pensions of the Senate; and

(B) make such report publicly available on the Internet website of the Department of Health and Human Services.

(6) APPLICABILITY OF FACA.—The Working Group shall be treated as an advisory committee subject to the Federal Advisory Committee Act (5 U.S.C. App.).

(7) SUNSET.—The Working Group under this section shall terminate 6 years after the date of enactment of this Act.

SEC. 2063. ACCESSING, SHARING, AND USING HEALTH DATA FOR RESEARCH PURPOSES.

(a) GUIDANCE RELATED TO REMOTE ACCESS.—Not later than 1 year after the date of enactment of this Act, the Secretary of Health and Human Services (referred to in this section as the "Secretary") shall issue guidance clarifying that subparagraph (B) of section 164.512(i)(1)(ii) of part 164 of the Rule (prohibiting the removal of protected health information by a researcher) does not prohibit remote access to health information by a researcher for such purposes as described in section 164.512(i)(1)(ii) of part 164 of the Rule so long as—

(1) at a minimum, security and privacy safeguards, consistent with the requirements of the Rule, are maintained by the covered entity and the researcher; and

(2) the protected health information is not copied or otherwise retained by the researcher.

(b) GUIDANCE RELATED TO STREAMLINING AUTHORIZATION.—Not later than 1 year after the date of enactment of this Act, the Secretary shall issue guidance on the following:

(1) AUTHORIZATION FOR USE AND DISCLOSURE OF HEALTH INFORMATION.—Clarification of the circumstances under which the authorization for the use or disclosure of protected health information, with respect to an individual, for future research purposes contains a sufficient description of the purpose of the use or disclosure, such as if the authorization—

(A) sufficiently describes the purposes such that it would be reasonable for the individual to expect that the protected health information could be used or disclosed for such future research;

(B) either—

(i) states that the authorization will expire on a particular date or on the occurrence of a particular event; or

(ii) states that the authorization will remain valid unless and until it is revoked by the individual; and

(C) provides instruction to the individual on how to revoke such authorization at any time.

(2) REMINDER OF THE RIGHT TO REVOKE.—Clarification of the circumstances under which it is appropriate to provide an individual with an annual notice or reminder that the individual has the right to revoke such authorization.

(3) REVOCATION OF AUTHORIZATION.—Clarification of appropriate mechanisms by which an individual may revoke an authorization for future research purposes, such as described in paragraph (1)(C).

(c) WORKING GROUP ON PROTECTED HEALTH INFORMATION FOR RESEARCH.—

(1) ESTABLISHMENT.—Not later than 1 year after the date of enactment of this Act, the Secretary shall convene a working group to study and report on the uses and disclosures of protected health information for research purposes, under the Health Insurance Portability and Accountability Act of 1996 (Public Law 104–191).

(2) MEMBERS.—The working group shall include representatives of—

(A) relevant Federal agencies, including the National Institutes of Health, the Centers for Disease Control and Prevention, the Food and Drug Administration, and the Office for Civil Rights;

(B) the research community;

(C) patients;

(D) experts in civil rights, such as privacy rights;

(E) developers of health information technology;

(F) experts in data privacy and security;

(G) health care providers;

(H) bioethicists; and

(I) other experts and entities, as the Secretary determines appropriate.

(3) REPORT.—Not later than 1 year after the date on which the working group is convened under paragraph (1), the working group shall conduct a review and submit a report to the Secretary containing recommendations on whether the uses and disclosures of protected health information for research purposes should be modified to allow protected health information to be available, as appropriate, for research purposes, including studies to obtain generalizable knowledge, while protecting individuals' privacy rights. In conducting the review and making recommendations, the working group shall—

(A) address, at a minimum—

(i) the appropriate manner and timing of authorization, including whether additional notification to the individual should be required when the individual's protected health information will be used or disclosed for such research;

(ii) opportunities for individuals to set preferences on the manner in which their protected health information is used in research;

(iii) opportunities for patients to revoke authorization;

(iv) notification to individuals of a breach in privacy;

(v) existing gaps in statute, regulation, or policy related to protecting the privacy of individuals, and

(vi) existing barriers to research related to the current restrictions on the uses and disclosures of protected health information; and

(B) consider, at a minimum—

(i) expectations and preferences on how an individual's protected health information is shared and used;

(ii) issues related to specific subgroups of people, such as children, incarcerated individuals, and individuals with a cognitive or intellectual disability impacting capacity to consent;

(iii) relevant Federal and State laws;

(iv) models of facilitating data access and levels of data access, including data segmentation, where applicable;

(v) potential impacts of disclosure and nondisclosure of protected health information on access to health care services; and

(vi) the potential uses of such data.

(4) REPORT SUBMISSION.—The Secretary shall submit the report under paragraph (3) to the Committee on Health, Education, Labor, and Pensions of the Senate and the Committee on Energy and Commerce of the House of Representatives, and shall post such report on the appropriate Internet website of the Department of Health and Human Services.

(5) TERMINATION.—The working group convened under paragraph (1) shall terminate the day after the report under paragraph (3) is submitted to Congress and made public in accordance with paragraph (4).

(d) DEFINITIONS.—In this section:

(1) THE RULE.—References to "the Rule" refer to part 160 or part 164, as appropriate, of title 45, Code of Federal Regulations (or any successor regulation).

(2) PART 164.—References to a specified section of "part 164", refer to such specified section of part 164 of title 45, Code of Federal Regulations (or any successor section).

Subtitle G—Promoting Pediatric Research

SEC. 2071. NATIONAL PEDIATRIC RESEARCH NETWORK.

Section 409D(d) of the Public Health Service Act (42 U.S.C. 284h(d)) is amended—

(1) in paragraph (1), by striking "in consultation with the Director of the Eunice Kennedy Shriver National Institute of Child Health and Human Development and in collaboration with other appropriate national research institutes and national centers that carry out activities involving pediatric research, may provide for the establishment of" and inserting "in collaboration with the national research institutes and national centers that carry out activities involving pediatric research, shall support"; and

(2) in paragraph (2)(A) and the first sentence of paragraph (2)(E), by striking "may" each place such term appears and inserting "shall".

SEC. 2072. GLOBAL PEDIATRIC CLINICAL STUDY NETWORK.

It is the sense of Congress that—

(1) the National Institutes of Health should encourage a global pediatric clinical study network by providing grants, contracts, or cooperative agreements to support new and early stage investigators who participate in the global pediatric clinical study network;

(2) the Secretary of Health and Human Services (referred to in this section as the "Secretary") should engage with clinical investigators and appropriate authorities outside of the United States, including authorities in the European Union, during the formation of the global pediatric clinical study network to encourage the participation of such investigator and authorities; and

(3) once a global pediatric clinical study network is established and becomes operational, the

---

Secretary should continue to encourage and facilitate the participation of clinical investigators and appropriate authorities outside of the United States, including in the European Union, to participate in the network with the goal of enhancing the global reach of the network.

TITLE III—DEVELOPMENT

Subtitle A—Patient-Focused Drug Development

SEC. 3001. PATIENT EXPERIENCE DATA.

Section 569C of the Federal Food, Drug, and Cosmetic Act (21 U.S.C. 360bbb–8c) is amended—

(1) in subsection (a)—

(A) in the subsection heading, by striking "IN GENERAL" and inserting "PATIENT ENGAGEMENT IN DRUGS AND DEVICES";

(B) by redesignating paragraphs (1) and (2) as subparagraphs (A) and (B), respectively, and moving such subparagraphs 2 ems to the right; and

(C) by striking "The Secretary" and inserting the following:

"(1) IN GENERAL.—The Secretary";

(2) by redesignating subsections (b) through (e) as paragraphs (2) through (5), respectively, and moving such paragraphs 2 ems to the right; and

(3) by adding at the end the following:

"(b) STATEMENT OF PATIENT EXPERIENCE.—

"(1) IN GENERAL.—Following the approval of an application that was submitted under section 505(b) of this Act or section 351(a) of the Public Health Service Act at least 180 days after the date of enactment of the 21st Century Cures Act, the Secretary shall make public a brief statement regarding the patient experience data and related information, if any, submitted and reviewed as part of such application.

"(2) DATA AND INFORMATION.—The data and information referred to in paragraph (1) are—

"(A) patient experience data;

"(B) information on patient-focused drug development tools; and

"(C) other relevant information, as determined by the Secretary.

"(c) PATIENT EXPERIENCE DATA.—For purposes of this section, the term 'patient experience data' includes data that—

"(1) are collected by any persons (including patients, family members and caregivers of patients, patient advocacy organizations, disease research foundations, researchers, and drug manufacturers); and

"(2) are intended to provide information about patients' experiences with a disease or condition, including—

"(A) the impact of such disease or condition, or a related therapy, on patients' lives; and

"(B) patient preferences with respect to treatment of such disease or condition.".

SEC. 3002. PATIENT-FOCUSED DRUG DEVELOPMENT GUIDANCE.

(a) PUBLICATION OF GUIDANCE DOCUMENTS.—Not later than 180 days after the date of enactment of this Act, the Secretary of Health and Human Services (referred to in this section as the "Secretary"), acting through the Commissioner of Food and Drugs, shall develop a plan to issue draft and final versions of one or more guidance documents, over a period of 5 years, regarding the collection of patient experience data, and the use of such data and related information in drug development. Not later than 18 months after the date of enactment of this Act, the Secretary shall issue a draft version of at least one such guidance document. Not later than 18 months after the public comment period on the draft guidance ends, the Secretary shall issue a revised draft guidance or final guidance.

(b) PATIENT EXPERIENCE DATA.—For purposes of this section, the term "patient experience data" has the meaning given such term in sec-

---

tion 569C of the Federal Food, Drug, and Cosmetic Act (as added by section 3001).

(c) CONTENTS.—The guidance documents described in subsection (a) shall address—

(1) methodological approaches that a person seeking to collect patient experience data for submission to, and proposed use by, the Secretary in regulatory decisionmaking may use, that are relevant and objective and ensure that such data are accurate and representative of the intended population, including methods to collect meaningful patient input throughout the drug development process and methodological considerations for data collection, reporting, management, and analysis;

(2) methodological approaches that may be used to develop and identify what is most important to patients with respect to burden of disease, burden of treatment, and the benefits and risks in the management of the patient's disease;

(3) approaches to identifying and developing methods to measure impacts to patients that will help facilitate collection of patient experience data in clinical trials;

(4) methodologies, standards, and technologies to collect and analyze clinical outcome assessments for purposes of regulatory decisionmaking;

(5) how a person seeking to develop and submit proposed draft guidance relating to patient experience data for consideration by the Secretary may submit such proposed draft guidance to the Secretary;

(6) the format and content required for submissions under this section to the Secretary, including with respect to the information described in paragraph (1);

(7) how the Secretary intends to respond to submissions of information described in paragraph (1), if applicable, including any timeframe for response when such submission is not part of a regulatory application or other submission that has an associated timeframe for response; and

(8) how the Secretary, if appropriate, anticipates using relevant patient experience data and related information, including with respect to the structured risk-benefit assessment framework described in section 505(d) of the Federal Food, Drug, and Cosmetic Act (21 U.S.C. 355(d)), to inform regulatory decisionmaking.

SEC. 3003. STREAMLINING PATIENT INPUT.

Chapter 35 of title 44, United States Code, shall not apply to the collection of information to which a response is voluntary, that is initiated by the Secretary under section 569C of the Federal Food, Drug, and Cosmetic Act (21 U.S.C. 360bbb–8c) (as amended by section 3001) or section 3002.

SEC. 3004. REPORT ON PATIENT EXPERIENCE DRUG DEVELOPMENT.

Not later than June 1 of 2021, 2026, and 2031, the Secretary of Health and Human Services, acting through the Commissioner of Food and Drugs, shall prepare and publish on the Internet website of the Food and Drug Administration a report assessing the use of patient experience data in regulatory decisionmaking, in particular with respect to the review of patient experience data and information on patient-focused drug development tools as part of applications approved under section 505(c) of the Federal Food, Drug, and Cosmetic Act (21 U.S.C. 355(c)) or section 351(a) of the Public Health Service Act (42 U.S.C. 262(a)).

Subtitle B—Advancing New Drug Therapies

SEC. 3011. QUALIFICATION OF DRUG DEVELOPMENT TOOLS.

(a) IN GENERAL.—Chapter V of the Federal Food, Drug, and Cosmetic Act (21 U.S.C. 351 et seq.) is amended by inserting after section 506F the following new section:

"SEC. 507. QUALIFICATION OF DRUG DEVELOPMENT TOOLS.

"(a) PROCESS FOR QUALIFICATION.—

"(1) IN GENERAL.—The Secretary shall establish a process for the qualification of drug development tools for a proposed context of use under which—

"(A)(i) a requestor initiates such process by submitting a letter of intent to the Secretary; and

"(ii) the Secretary accepts or declines to accept such letter of intent;

"(B)(i) if the Secretary accepts the letter of intent, a requestor submits a qualification plan to the Secretary; and

"(ii) the Secretary accepts or declines to accept the qualification plan; and

"(C)(i) if the Secretary accepts the qualification plan, the requestor submits to the Secretary a full qualification package;

"(ii) the Secretary determines whether to accept such qualification package for review; and

"(iii) if the Secretary accepts such qualification package for review, the Secretary conducts such review in accordance with this section.

"(2) ACCEPTANCE AND REVIEW OF SUBMISSIONS.—

"(A) IN GENERAL.—Subparagraphs (B), (C), and (D) shall apply with respect to the treatment of a letter of intent, a qualification plan, or a full qualification package submitted under paragraph (1) (referred to in this paragraph as 'qualification submissions').

"(B) ACCEPTANCE FACTORS; NONACCEPTANCE.—The Secretary shall determine whether to accept a qualification submission based on factors which may include the scientific merit of the qualification submission. A determination not to accept a submission under paragraph (1) shall not be construed as a final determination by the Secretary under this section regarding the qualification of a drug development tool for its proposed context of use.

"(C) PRIORITIZATION OF QUALIFICATION REVIEW.—The Secretary may prioritize the review of a full qualification package submitted under paragraph (1) with respect to a drug development tool, based on factors determined appropriate by the Secretary, including—

"(i) as applicable, the severity, rarity, or prevalence of the disease or condition targeted by the drug development tool and the availability or lack of alternative treatments for such disease or condition; and

"(ii) the identification, by the Secretary or by biomedical research consortia and other expert stakeholders, of such a drug development tool and its proposed context of use as a public health priority.

"(D) ENGAGEMENT OF EXTERNAL EXPERTS.—The Secretary may, for purposes of the review of qualification submissions, through the use of cooperative agreements, grants, or other appropriate mechanisms, consult with biomedical research consortia and may consider the recommendations of such consortia with respect to the review of any qualification plan submitted under paragraph (1) or the review of any full qualification package under paragraph (3).

"(3) REVIEW OF FULL QUALIFICATION PACKAGE.—The Secretary shall—

"(A) conduct a comprehensive review of a full qualification package accepted under paragraph (1)(C); and

"(B) determine whether the drug development tool at issue is qualified for its proposed context of use.

"(4) QUALIFICATION.—The Secretary shall determine whether a drug development tool is qualified for a proposed context of use based on the scientific merit of a full qualification package reviewed under paragraph (3).

"(b) EFFECT OF QUALIFICATION.—

"(1) IN GENERAL.—A drug development tool determined to be qualified under subsection (a)(4) for a proposed context of use specified by the requestor may be used by any person in such

context of use for the purposes described in paragraph (2).

"(2) USE OF A DRUG DEVELOPMENT TOOL.—Subject to paragraph (3), a drug development tool qualified under this section may be used for—

"(A) supporting or obtaining approval or licensure (as applicable) of a drug or biological product (including in accordance with section 506(c)) under section 505 of this Act or section 351 of the Public Health Service Act; or

"(B) supporting the investigational use of a drug or biological product under section 505(i) of this Act or section 351(a)(3) of the Public Health Service Act.

"(3) RESCISSION OR MODIFICATION.—

"(A) IN GENERAL.—The Secretary may rescind or modify a determination under this section to qualify a drug development tool if the Secretary determines that the drug development tool is not appropriate for the proposed context of use specified by the requestor. Such a determination may be based on new information that calls into question the basis for such qualification.

"(B) MEETING FOR REVIEW.—If the Secretary rescinds or modifies under subparagraph (A) a determination to qualify a drug development tool, the requestor involved shall, on request, be granted a meeting with the Secretary to discuss the basis of the Secretary's decision to rescind or modify the determination before the effective date of the rescission or modification.

"(c) TRANSPARENCY.—

"(1) IN GENERAL.—Subject to paragraph (3), the Secretary shall make publicly available, and update on at least a biannual basis, on the Internet website of the Food and Drug Administration the following:

"(A) Information with respect to each qualification submission under the qualification process under subsection (a), including—

"(i) the stage of the review process applicable to the submission;

"(ii) the date of the most recent change in stage status;

"(iii) whether external scientific experts were utilized in the development of a qualification plan or the review of a full qualification package; and

"(iv) submissions from requestors under the qualification process under subsection (a), including any data and evidence contained in such submissions, and any updates to such submissions.

"(B) The Secretary's formal written determinations in response to such qualification submissions.

"(C) Any rescissions or modifications under subsection (b)(3) of a determination to qualify a drug development tool.

"(D) Summary reviews that document conclusions and recommendations for determinations to qualify drug development tools under subsection (a).

"(E) A comprehensive list of—

"(i) all drug development tools qualified under subsection (a); and

"(ii) all surrogate endpoints which were the basis of approval or licensure (as applicable) of a drug or biological product (including in accordance with section 506(c)) under section 505 of this Act or section 351 of the Public Health Service Act.

"(2) RELATION TO TRADE SECRETS ACT.—Information made publicly available by the Secretary under paragraph (1) shall be considered a disclosure authorized by law for purposes of section 1905 of title 18, United States Code.

"(3) APPLICABILITY.—Nothing in this section shall be construed as authorizing the Secretary to disclose any information contained in an application submitted under section 505 of this Act or section 351 of the Public Health Service Act that is confidential commercial or trade secret

information subject to section 552(b)(4) of title 5, United States Code, or section 1905 of title 18, United States Code.

"(d) RULE OF CONSTRUCTION.—Nothing in this section shall be construed—

"(1) to alter the standards of evidence under subsection (c) or (d) of section 505, including the substantial evidence standard in such subsection (d), or under section 351 of the Public Health Service Act (as applicable); or

"(2) to limit the authority of the Secretary to approve or license products under this Act or the Public Health Service Act, as applicable (as in effect before the date of the enactment of the 21st Century Cures Act).

"(e) DEFINITIONS.—In this section:

"(1) BIOMARKER.—The term 'biomarker'—

"(A) means a characteristic (such as a physiologic, pathologic, or anatomic characteristic or measurement) that is objectively measured and evaluated as an indicator of normal biologic processes, pathologic processes, or biological responses to a therapeutic intervention; and

"(B) includes a surrogate endpoint.

"(2) BIOMEDICAL RESEARCH CONSORTIA.—The term 'biomedical research consortia' means collaborative groups that may take the form of public-private partnerships and may include government agencies, institutions of higher education (as defined in section 101(a) of the Higher Education Act of 1965), patient advocacy groups, industry representatives, clinical and scientific experts, and other relevant entities and individuals.

"(3) CLINICAL OUTCOME ASSESSMENT.—The term 'clinical outcome assessment' means—

"(A) a measurement of a patient's symptoms, overall mental state, or the effects of a disease or condition on how the patient functions; and

"(B) includes a patient-reported outcome.

"(4) CONTEXT OF USE.—The term 'context of use' means, with respect to a drug development tool, the circumstances under which the drug development tool is to be used in drug development and regulatory review.

"(5) DRUG DEVELOPMENT TOOL.—The term 'drug development tool' includes—

"(A) a biomarker;

"(B) a clinical outcome assessment; and

"(C) any other method, material, or measure that the Secretary determines aids drug development and regulatory review for purposes of this section.

"(6) PATIENT-REPORTED OUTCOME.—The term 'patient-reported outcome' means a measurement based on a report from a patient regarding the status of the patient's health condition without amendment or interpretation of the patient's report by a clinician or any other person.

"(7) QUALIFICATION.—The terms 'qualification' and 'qualified' mean a determination by the Secretary that a drug development tool and its proposed context of use can be relied upon to have a specific interpretation and application in drug development and regulatory review under this Act.

"(8) REQUESTOR.—The term 'requestor' means an entity or entities, including a drug sponsor or a biomedical research consortia, seeking to qualify a drug development tool for a proposed context of use under this section.

"(9) SURROGATE ENDPOINT.—The term 'surrogate endpoint' means a marker, such as a laboratory measurement, radiographic image, physical sign, or other measure, that is not itself a direct measurement of clinical benefit, and—

"(A) is known to predict clinical benefit and could be used to support traditional approval of a drug or biological product; or

"(B) is reasonably likely to predict clinical benefit and could be used to support the accelerated approval of a drug or biological product in accordance with section 506(c).".

(b) GUIDANCE.—

(1) IN GENERAL.—The Secretary of Health and Human Services (referred to in this section as the "Secretary") shall, in consultation with biomedical research consortia (as defined in subsection (e) of section 507 of the Federal Food, Drug, and Cosmetic Act (as added by subsection (a)) and other interested parties through a collaborative public process, issue guidance to implement such section 507 that—

(A) provides a conceptual framework describing appropriate standards and scientific approaches to support the development of biomarkers delineated under the taxonomy established under paragraph (3);

(B) with respect to the qualification process under such section 507—

(i) describes the requirements that entities seeking to qualify a drug development tool under such section shall observe when engaging in such process;

(ii) outlines reasonable timeframes for the Secretary's review of letters, qualification plans, or full qualification packages submitted under such process; and

(iii) establishes a process by which such entities or the Secretary may consult with biomedical research consortia and other individuals and entities with expert knowledge and insights that may assist the Secretary in the review of qualification plans and full qualification submissions under such section; and

(C) includes such other information as the Secretary determines appropriate.

(2) TIMING.—Not later than 3 years after the date of the enactment of this Act, the Secretary shall issue draft guidance under paragraph (1) on the implementation of section 507 of the Federal Food, Drug, and Cosmetic Act (as added by subsection (a)). The Secretary shall issue final guidance on the implementation of such section not later than 6 months after the date on which the comment period for the draft guidance closes.

(3) TAXONOMY.—

(A) IN GENERAL.—For purposes of informing guidance under this subsection, the Secretary shall, in consultation with biomedical research consortia and other interested parties through a collaborative public process, establish a taxonomy for the classification of biomarkers (and related scientific concepts) for use in drug development.

(B) PUBLIC AVAILABILITY.—Not later than 2 years after the date of the enactment of this Act, the Secretary shall make such taxonomy publicly available in draft form for public comment. The Secretary shall finalize the taxonomy not later than 1 year after the close of the public comment period.

(c) MEETING AND REPORT.—

(1) MEETING.—Not later than 2 years after the date of the enactment of this Act, the Secretary shall convene a public meeting to describe and solicit public input regarding the qualification process under section 507 of the Federal Food, Drug, and Cosmetic Act, as added by subsection (a).

(2) REPORT.—Not later than 5 years after the date of the enactment of this Act, the Secretary shall make publicly available on the Internet website of the Food and Drug Administration a report. Such report shall include, with respect to the qualification process under section 507 of the Federal Food, Drug, and Cosmetic Act, as added by subsection (a), information on—

(A) the number of requests submitted, as a letter of intent, for qualification of a drug development tool (as defined in subsection (e) of such section 507);

(B) the number of such requests accepted and determined to be eligible for submission of a qualification plan or full qualification package (as such terms are defined in subsection (e) of such section 507), respectively;

(C) the number of such requests for which external scientific experts were utilized in the development of a qualification plan or review of a full qualification package;

(D) the number of qualification plans and full qualification packages, respectively, submitted to the Secretary; and

(E) the drug development tools qualified through such qualification process, specified by type of tool, such as a biomarker or clinical outcome assessment (as such terms are defined in subsection (e) of such section 507).

SEC. 3012. TARGETED DRUGS FOR RARE DISEASES.

Subchapter B of chapter V of the Federal Food, Drug, and Cosmetic Act (21 U.S.C. 360aa et seq.) is amended by inserting after section 529 the following:

"SEC. 529A. TARGETED DRUGS FOR RARE DISEASES.

"(a) PURPOSE.—The purpose of this section, through the approach provided for in subsection (b), is to—

"(1) facilitate the development, review, and approval of genetically targeted drugs and variant protein targeted drugs to address an unmet medical need in one or more patient subgroups, including subgroups of patients with different mutations of a gene, with respect to rare diseases or conditions that are serious or life-threatening; and

"(2) maximize the use of scientific tools or methods, including surrogate endpoints and other biomarkers, for such purposes.

"(b) LEVERAGING OF DATA FROM PREVIOUSLY APPROVED DRUG APPLICATION OR APPLICATIONS.—The Secretary may, consistent with applicable standards for approval under this Act or section 351(a) of the Public Health Service Act, allow the sponsor of an application under section 505(b)(1) of this Act or section 351(a) of the Public Health Service Act for a genetically targeted drug or a variant protein targeted drug to rely upon data and information—

"(1) previously developed by the same sponsor (or another sponsor that has provided the sponsor with a contractual right of reference to such data and information); and

"(2) submitted by a sponsor described in paragraph (1) in support of one or more previously approved applications that were submitted under section 505(b)(1) of this Act or section 351(a) of the Public Health Service Act,

for a drug that incorporates or utilizes the same or similar genetically targeted technology as the drug or drugs that are the subject of an application or applications described in paragraph (2) or for a variant protein targeted drug that is the same or incorporates or utilizes the same variant protein targeted drug, as the drug or drugs that are the subject of an application or applications described in paragraph (2).

"(c) DEFINITIONS.—For purposes of this section—

"(1) the term 'genetically targeted drug' means a drug that—

"(A) is the subject of an application under section 505(b)(1) of this Act or section 351(a) of the Public Health Service Act for the treatment of a rare disease or condition (as such term is defined in section 526) that is serious or life-threatening;

"(B) may result in the modulation (including suppression, up-regulation, or activation) of the function of a gene or its associated gene product; and

"(C) incorporates or utilizes a genetically targeted technology;

"(2) the term 'genetically targeted technology' means a technology comprising non-replicating nucleic acid or analogous compounds with a common or similar chemistry that is intended to treat one or more patient subgroups, including subgroups of patients with different mutations

of a gene, with the same disease or condition, including a disease or condition due to other variants in the same gene; and

"(3) the term 'variant protein targeted drug' means a drug that—

"(A) is the subject of an application under section 505(b)(1) of this Act or section 351(a) of the Public Health Service Act for the treatment of a rare disease or condition (as such term is defined in section 526) that is serious or life-threatening;

"(B) modulates the function of a product of a mutated gene where such mutation is responsible in whole or in part for a given disease or condition; and

"(C) is intended to treat one or more patient subgroups, including subgroups of patients with different mutations of a gene, with the same disease or condition.

"(d) RULE OF CONSTRUCTION.—Nothing in this section shall be construed to—

"(1) alter the authority of the Secretary to approve drugs pursuant to this Act or section 351 of the Public Health Service Act (as authorized prior to the date of enactment of the 21st Century Cures Act), including the standards of evidence, and applicable conditions, for approval under such applicable Act; or

"(2) confer any new rights, beyond those authorized under this Act or the Public Health Service Act prior to enactment of this section, with respect to the permissibility of a sponsor referencing information contained in another application submitted under section 505(b)(1) of this Act or section 351(a) of the Public Health Service Act.".

SEC. 3013. REAUTHORIZATION OF PROGRAM TO ENCOURAGE TREATMENTS FOR RARE PEDIATRIC DISEASES.

(a) IN GENERAL.—Section 529(b) of the Federal Food, Drug, and Cosmetic Act (21 U.S.C. 360ff(b)) is amended by striking paragraph (5) and inserting the following:

"(5) TERMINATION OF AUTHORITY.—The Secretary may not award any priority review vouchers under paragraph (1) after September 30, 2020, unless the rare pediatric disease product application—

"(A) is for a drug that, not later than September 30, 2020, is designated under subsection (d) as a drug for a rare pediatric disease; and

"(B) is, not later than September 30, 2022, approved under section 505(b)(1) of this Act or section 351(a) of the Public Health Service Act.".

(b) REPORT.—The Advancing Hope Act of 2016 (Public Law 114–229) is amended by striking section 3.

SEC. 3014. GAO STUDY OF PRIORITY REVIEW VOUCHER PROGRAMS.

(a) STUDY.—The Comptroller General of the United States (referred to in this section as the "Comptroller General") shall conduct a study addressing the effectiveness and overall impact of the following priority review voucher programs, including any such programs amended or established by this Act:

(1) The neglected tropical disease priority review voucher program under section 524 of the Federal Food, Drug, and Cosmetic Act (21 U.S.C. 360n).

(2) The rare pediatric disease priority review voucher program under section 529 of the Federal Food, Drug, and Cosmetic Act (21 U.S.C. 360ff).

(3) The medical countermeasure priority review voucher program under section 565A of the Federal Food, Drug, and Cosmetic Act, as added by section 3086.

(b) ISSUANCE OF REPORT.—Not later than January 31, 2020, the Comptroller General shall submit to the Committee on Health, Education, Labor, and Pensions of the Senate and the Committee on Energy and Commerce of the House of Representatives a report containing the results of the study under subsection (a).

(c) CONTENTS OF REPORTS.—The report submitted under subsection (b) shall address—

(1) for each drug for which a priority review voucher has been awarded as of initiation of the study—

(A) the indications for which the drug is approved under section 505(c) of the Federal Food, Drug, and Cosmetic Act (21 U.S.C. 355(c)), pursuant to an application under section 505(b)(1) of such Act, or licensed under section 351(a) of the Public Health Service Act (42 U.S.C. 262(a));

(B) whether, and to what extent, the voucher impacted the sponsor's decision to develop the drug; and

(C) whether, and to what extent, the approval or licensure of the drug, as applicable and appropriate—

(i) addressed a global unmet need related to the treatment or prevention of a neglected tropical disease, including whether the sponsor of a drug coordinated with international development organizations;

(ii) addressed an unmet need related to the treatment of a rare pediatric disease; or

(iii) affected the Nation's preparedness against a chemical, biological, radiological, or nuclear threat, including naturally occurring threats;

(2) for each drug for which a priority review voucher has been used—

(A) the indications for which such drug is approved under section 505(c) of the Federal Food, Drug, and Cosmetic Act (21 U.S.C. 355(c)), pursuant to an application under section 505(b)(1) of such Act, or licensed under section 351(a) of the Public Health Service Act (42 U.S.C. 262);

(B) the value of the voucher, if transferred; and

(C) the length of time between the date on which the voucher was awarded and the date on which the voucher was used; and

(3) an analysis of the priority review voucher programs described in subsection (a), including—

(A) the resources used by the Food and Drug Administration in reviewing drugs for which vouchers were used, including the effect of the programs on the Food and Drug Administration's review of drugs for which priority review vouchers were not awarded or used;

(B) whether any improvements to such programs are necessary to appropriately target incentives for the development of drugs that would likely not otherwise be developed, or developed in as timely a manner, and, as applicable and appropriate—

(i) address global unmet needs related to the treatment or prevention of neglected tropical diseases, including in countries in which neglected tropical diseases are endemic; or

(ii) address unmet needs related to the treatment of rare pediatric diseases; and

(C) whether the sunset of the rare pediatric disease program and medical countermeasure program has had an impact on the program, including any potential unintended consequences.

(d) PROTECTION OF NATIONAL SECURITY.—The Comptroller General shall conduct the study and issue reports under this section in a manner that does not compromise national security.

SEC. 3015. AMENDMENTS TO THE ORPHAN DRUG GRANTS.

Section 5 of the Orphan Drug Act (21 U.S.C. 360ee) is amended—

(1) in subsection (a), by striking paragraph (1) and inserting the following: "(1) defraying the costs of developing drugs for rare diseases or conditions, including qualified testing expenses,"; and

(2) in subsection (b)(1)—

(A) in subparagraph (A)(ii), by striking "and" after the semicolon;

(B) in subparagraph (B), by striking the period and inserting "; and"; and

(C) by adding at the end the following:

"(C) prospectively planned and designed observational studies and other analyses conducted to assist in the understanding of the natural history of a rare disease or condition and in the development of a therapy, including studies and analyses to—

"(i) develop or validate a drug development tool related to a rare disease or condition; or

"(ii) understand the full spectrum of the disease manifestations, including describing genotypic and phenotypic variability and identifying and defining distinct subpopulations affected by a rare disease or condition.".

SEC. 3016. GRANTS FOR STUDYING CONTINUOUS DRUG MANUFACTURING.

(a) IN GENERAL.—The Secretary of Health and Human Services may award grants to institutions of higher education and nonprofit organizations for the purpose of studying and recommending improvements to the process of continuous manufacturing of drugs and biological products and similar innovative monitoring and control techniques.

(b) DEFINITIONS.—In this section—

(1) the term "drug" has the meaning given such term in section 201 of the Federal Food, Drug, and Cosmetic Act (21 U.S.C. 321);

(2) the term "biological product" has the meaning given such term in section 351(i) of the Public Health Service Act (42 U.S.C. 262(i)); and

(3) the term "institution of higher education" has the meaning given such term in section 101(a) of the Higher Education Act of 1965 (20 U.S.C. 1001(a)).

Subtitle C—Modern Trial Design and Evidence Development

SEC. 3021. NOVEL CLINICAL TRIAL DESIGNS.

(a) PROPOSALS FOR USE OF NOVEL CLINICAL TRIAL DESIGNS FOR DRUGS AND BIOLOGICAL PRODUCTS.—For purposes of assisting sponsors in incorporating complex adaptive and other novel trial designs into proposed clinical protocols and applications for new drugs under section 505 of the Federal Food, Drug, and Cosmetic Act (21 U.S.C. 355) and biological products under section 351 of the Public Health Service Act (42 U.S.C. 262), the Secretary of Health and Human Services (referred to in this section as the "Secretary") shall conduct a public meeting and issue guidance in accordance with subsection (b).

(b) GUIDANCE ADDRESSING USE OF NOVEL CLINICAL TRIAL DESIGNS.—

(1) IN GENERAL.—The Secretary, acting through the Commissioner of Food and Drugs, shall update or issue guidance addressing the use of complex adaptive and other novel trial design in the development and regulatory review and approval or licensure for drugs and biological products.

(2) CONTENTS.—The guidance under paragraph (1) shall address—

(A) the use of complex adaptive and other novel trial designs, including how such clinical trials proposed or submitted help to satisfy the substantial evidence standard under section 505(d) of the Federal Food, Drug, and Cosmetic Act (21 U.S.C. 355(d));

(B) how sponsors may obtain feedback from the Secretary on technical issues related to modeling and simulations prior to—

(i) completion of such modeling or simulations; or

(ii) the submission of resulting information to the Secretary;

(C) the types of quantitative and qualitative information that should be submitted for review; and

(D) recommended analysis methodologies.

(3) PUBLIC MEETING.—Prior to updating or issuing the guidance required by paragraph (1), the Secretary shall consult with stakeholders, including representatives of regulated industry, academia, patient advocacy organizations, consumer groups, and disease research foundations, through a public meeting to be held not later than 18 months after the date of enactment of this Act.

(4) TIMING.—The Secretary shall update or issue a draft version of the guidance required by paragraph (1) not later than 18 months after the date of the public meeting required by paragraph (3) and finalize such guidance not later than 1 year after the date on which the public comment period for the draft guidance closes.

SEC. 3022. REAL WORLD EVIDENCE.

Chapter V of the Federal Food, Drug, and Cosmetic Act is amended by inserting after section 505E (21 U.S.C. 355f) the following:

"SEC. 505F. UTILIZING REAL WORLD EVIDENCE.

"(a) IN GENERAL.—The Secretary shall establish a program to evaluate the potential use of real world evidence—

"(1) to help to support the approval of a new indication for a drug approved under section 505(c); and

"(2) to help to support or satisfy postapproval study requirements.

"(b) REAL WORLD EVIDENCE DEFINED.—In this section, the term 'real world evidence' means data regarding the usage, or the potential benefits or risks, of a drug derived from sources other than randomized clinical trials.

"(c) PROGRAM FRAMEWORK.—

"(1) IN GENERAL.—Not later than 2 years after the date of enactment of the 21st Century Cures Act, the Secretary shall establish a draft framework for implementation of the program under this section.

"(2) CONTENTS OF FRAMEWORK.—The framework shall include information describing—

"(A) the sources of real world evidence, including ongoing safety surveillance, observational studies, registries, claims, and patient-centered outcomes research activities;

"(B) the gaps in data collection activities;

"(C) the standards and methodologies for collection and analysis of real world evidence; and

"(D) the priority areas, remaining challenges, and potential pilot opportunities that the program established under this section will address.

"(3) CONSULTATION.—

"(A) IN GENERAL.—In developing the program framework under this subsection, the Secretary shall consult with regulated industry, academia, medical professional organizations, representatives of patient advocacy organizations, consumer organizations, disease research foundations, and other interested parties.

"(B) PROCESS.—The consultation under subparagraph (A) may be carried out through approaches such as—

"(i) a public-private partnership with the entities described in such subparagraph in which the Secretary may participate;

"(ii) a contract, grant, or other arrangement, as the Secretary determines appropriate, with such a partnership or an independent research organization; or

"(iii) public workshops with the entities described in such subparagraph.

"(d) PROGRAM IMPLEMENTATION.—The Secretary shall, not later than 2 years after the date of enactment of the 21st Century Cures Act and in accordance with the framework established under subsection (c), implement the program to evaluate the potential use of real world evidence.

"(e) GUIDANCE FOR INDUSTRY.—The Secretary shall—

"(1) utilize the program established under subsection (a), its activities, and any subsequent pilots or written reports, to inform a guidance for industry on—

"(A) the circumstances under which sponsors of drugs and the Secretary may rely on real world evidence for the purposes described in paragraphs (1) and (2) of subsection (a); and

"(B) the appropriate standards and methodologies for collection and analysis of real world evidence submitted for such purposes;

"(2) not later than 5 years after the date of enactment of the 21st Century Cures Act, issue draft guidance for industry as described in paragraph (1); and

"(3) not later than 18 months after the close of the public comment period for the draft guidance described in paragraph (2), issue revised draft guidance or final guidance.

"(f) RULE OF CONSTRUCTION.—

"(1) IN GENERAL.—Subject to paragraph (2), nothing in this section prohibits the Secretary from using real world evidence for purposes not specified in this section, provided the Secretary determines that sufficient basis exists for any such nonspecified use.

"(2) STANDARDS OF EVIDENCE AND SECRETARY'S AUTHORITY.—This section shall not be construed to alter—

"(A) the standards of evidence under—

"(i) subsection (c) or (d) of section 505, including the substantial evidence standard in such subsection (d); or

"(ii) section 351(a) of the Public Health Service Act; or

"(B) the Secretary's authority to require post-approval studies or clinical trials, or the standards of evidence under which studies or trials are evaluated.".

SEC. 3023. PROTECTION OF HUMAN RESEARCH SUBJECTS.

(a) IN GENERAL.—In order to simplify and facilitate compliance by researchers with applicable regulations for the protection of human subjects in research, the Secretary of Health and Human Services (referred to in this section as the "Secretary") shall, to the extent practicable and consistent with other statutory provisions, harmonize differences between the HHS Human Subject Regulations and the FDA Human Subject Regulations in accordance with subsection (b).

(b) AVOIDING REGULATORY DUPLICATION AND UNNECESSARY DELAYS.—The Secretary shall, as appropriate—

(1) make such modifications to the provisions of the HHS Human Subject Regulations, the FDA Human Subject Regulations, and the vulnerable populations rules as may be necessary—

(A) to reduce regulatory duplication and unnecessary delays;

(B) to modernize such provisions in the context of multisite and cooperative research projects; and

(C) to protect vulnerable populations, incorporate local considerations, and support community engagement through mechanisms such as consultation with local researchers and human research protection programs, in a manner consistent with subparagraph (B); and

(2) ensure that human subject research that is subject to the HHS Human Subject Regulations and to the FDA Human Subject Regulations may—

(A) use joint or shared review;

(B) rely upon the review of—

(i) an independent institutional review board; or

(ii) an institutional review board of an entity other than the sponsor of the research; or

(C) use similar arrangements to avoid duplication of effort.

(c) CONSULTATION.—In harmonizing or modifying regulations or guidance under this section, the Secretary shall consult with stakeholders (including researchers, academic organizations, hospitals, institutional research boards, pharmaceutical, biotechnology, and medical device developers, clinical research organizations, patient groups, and others).

(d) TIMING.—The Secretary shall complete the harmonization described in subsection (a) not later than 3 years after the date of enactment of this Act.

(e) PROGRESS REPORT.—Not later than 2 years after the date of enactment of this Act, the Secretary shall submit to Congress a report on the progress made toward completing such harmonization.

(f) DEFINITIONS.—

(1) HUMAN SUBJECT REGULATIONS.—In this section:

(A) FDA HUMAN SUBJECT REGULATIONS.—The term "FDA Human Subject Regulations" means the provisions of parts 50, 56, 312, and 812 of title 21, Code of Federal Regulations (or any successor regulations).

(B) HHS HUMAN SUBJECT REGULATIONS.—The term "HHS Human Subject Regulations" means the provisions of subpart A of part 46 of title 45, Code of Federal Regulations (or any successor regulations).

(C) VULNERABLE POPULATION RULES.—The term "vulnerable population rules" means—

(i) except in the case of research described in clause (ii), the provisions of subparts B through D of part 46, Code of Federal Regulations (or any successor regulations); and

(ii) in the case of research that is subject to FDA Human Subject Regulations, the provisions applicable to vulnerable populations under part 56 of title 21, Code of Federal Regulations (or any successor regulations) and subpart D of part 50 of such title 21 (or any successor regulations).

(2) INSTITUTIONAL REVIEW BOARD DEFINED.—In this section, the term "institutional review board" has the meaning that applies to the term "institutional review board" under the HHS Human Subject Regulations.

(B) LEAD INSTITUTIONAL REVIEW BOARD.—The term "lead institutional review board" means an institutional review board that otherwise meets the requirements of the HHS Human Subject Regulations and enters into a written agreement with an institution, another institutional review board, a sponsor, or a principal investigator to approve and oversee human subject research that is conducted at multiple locations. References to an institutional review board include an institutional review board that serves a single institution and a lead institutional review board.

SEC. 3024. INFORMED CONSENT WAIVER OR ALTERATION FOR CLINICAL INVESTIGATIONS.

(a) DEVICES.—Section 520(g)(3) of the Federal Food, Drug, and Cosmetic Act (21 U.S.C. 360j(g)(3)) is amended—

(1) in subparagraph (D), by striking "except where subject to such conditions as the Secretary may prescribe, the investigator" and inserting the following: "except where, subject to such conditions as the Secretary may prescribe—

"(i) the proposed clinical testing poses no more than minimal risk to the human subject and includes appropriate safeguards to protect the rights, safety, and welfare of the human subject; or

"(ii) the investigator"; and

(2) in the matter following subparagraph (D), by striking "subparagraph (D)" and inserting "subparagraph (D)(ii)".

(b) DRUGS.—Section 505(i)(4) of the Federal Food, Drug, and Cosmetic Act (21 U.S.C. 355(i)(4)) is amended by striking "except where it is not feasible or it is contrary to the best interests of such human beings" and inserting "except where it is not feasible, it is contrary to the best interests of such human beings, or the proposed clinical testing poses no more than minimal risk to such human beings and includes appropriate safeguards as prescribed to protect the rights, safety, and welfare of such human beings".

Subtitle D—Patient Access to Therapies and Information

SEC. 3031. SUMMARY LEVEL REVIEW.

(a) FFDCA.—Section 505(c) of the Federal Food, Drug, and Cosmetic Act (21 U.S.C. 355(c)) is amended by adding at the end the following:

"(5)(A) The Secretary may rely upon qualified data summaries to support the approval of a supplemental application, with respect to a qualified indication for a drug, submitted under subsection (b), if such supplemental application complies with subparagraph (B).

"(B) A supplemental application is eligible for review as described in subparagraph (A) only if—

"(i) there is existing data available and acceptable to the Secretary demonstrating the safety of the drug; and

"(ii) all data used to develop the qualified data summaries are submitted to the Secretary as part of the supplemental application.

"(C) The Secretary shall post on the Internet website of the Food and Drug Administration and update annually—

"(i) the number of applications reviewed solely under subparagraph (A) or section 351(a)(2)(E) of the Public Health Service Act;

"(ii) the average time for completion of review under subparagraph (A) or section 351(a)(2)(E) of the Public Health Service Act;

"(iii) the average time for review of supplemental applications where the Secretary did not use review flexibility under subparagraph (A) or section 351(a)(2)(E) of the Public Health Service Act; and

"(iv) the number of applications reviewed under subparagraph (A) or section 351(a)(2)(E) of the Public Health Service Act for which the Secretary made use of full data sets in addition to the qualified data summary.

"(D) In this paragraph—

"(i) the term 'qualified indication' means an indication for a drug that the Secretary determines to be appropriate for summary level review under this paragraph; and

"(ii) the term 'qualified data summary' means a summary of clinical data that demonstrates the safety and effectiveness of a drug with respect to a qualified indication.".

(b) PHSA.—Section 351(a)(2) of the Public Health Service Act (42 U.S.C. 262(a)(2)) is amended by adding at the end the following:

"(E)(i) The Secretary may rely upon qualified data summaries to support the approval of a supplemental application, with respect to a qualified indication for a drug, submitted under this subsection, if such supplemental application complies with the requirements of subparagraph (B) of section 505(c)(5) of the Federal Food, Drug, and Cosmetic Act.

"(ii) In this subparagraph, the terms 'qualified indication' and 'qualified data summary' have the meanings given such terms in section 505(c)(5) of the Federal Food, Drug, and Cosmetic Act.".

SEC. 3032. EXPANDED ACCESS POLICY.

Chapter V of the Federal Food, Drug, and Cosmetic Act is amended by inserting after section 561 (21 U.S.C. 360bbb) the following:

"SEC. 561A. EXPANDED ACCESS POLICY REQUIRED FOR INVESTIGATIONAL DRUGS.

"(a) IN GENERAL.—The manufacturer or distributor of one or more investigational drugs for the diagnosis, monitoring, or treatment of one or more serious diseases or conditions shall make available the policy of the manufacturer or distributor on evaluating and responding to requests submitted under section 561(b) for provision of such a drug.

"(b) PUBLIC AVAILABILITY OF EXPANDED ACCESS POLICY.—The policies under subsection (a) shall be made public and readily available, such as by posting such policies on a publicly available Internet website. Such policies may be generally applicable to all investigational drugs of such manufacturer or distributor.

"(c) CONTENT OF POLICY.—A policy described in subsection (a) shall include—

"(1) contact information for the manufacturer or distributor to facilitate communication about requests described in subsection (a);

"(2) procedures for making such requests;

"(3) the general criteria the manufacturer or distributor will use to evaluate such requests for individual patients, and for responses to such requests;

"(4) the length of time the manufacturer or distributor anticipates will be necessary to acknowledge receipt of such requests; and

"(5) a hyperlink or other reference to the clinical trial record containing information about the expanded access for such drug that is required under section 402(j)(2)(A)(ii)(II)(gg) of the Public Health Service Act.

"(d) NO GUARANTEE OF ACCESS.—The posting of policies by manufacturers and distributors under subsection (a) shall not serve as a guarantee of access to any specific investigational drug by any individual patient.

"(e) REVISED POLICY.—Nothing in this section shall prevent a manufacturer or distributor from revising a policy required under this section at any time.

"(f) APPLICATION.—This section shall apply to a manufacturer or distributor with respect to an investigational drug beginning on the later of—

"(1) the date that is 60 calendar days after the date of enactment of the 21st Century Cures Act; or

"(2) the first initiation of a phase 2 or phase 3 study (as such terms are defined in section 312.21(b) and (c) of title 21, Code of Federal Regulations (or any successor regulations)) with respect to such investigational drug.".

SEC. 3033. ACCELERATED APPROVAL FOR REGENERATIVE ADVANCED THERAPIES.

(a) IN GENERAL.—Section 506 of the Federal Food, Drug, and Cosmetic Act (21 U.S.C. 356) is amended—

(1) by transferring subsection (e) (relating to construction) so that it appears before subsection (f) (relating to awareness efforts); and

(2) by adding at the end the following:

"(g) REGENERATIVE ADVANCED THERAPY.—

"(1) IN GENERAL.—The Secretary, at the request of the sponsor of a drug, shall facilitate an efficient development program for, and expedite review of, such drug if the drug qualifies as a regenerative advanced therapy under the criteria described in paragraph (2).

"(2) CRITERIA.—A drug is eligible for designation as a regenerative advanced therapy under this subsection if—

"(A) the drug is a regenerative medicine therapy (as defined in paragraph (8));

"(B) the drug is intended to treat, modify, reverse, or cure a serious or life-threatening disease or condition; and

"(C) preliminary clinical evidence indicates that the drug has the potential to address unmet medical needs for such a disease or condition.

"(3) REQUEST FOR DESIGNATION.—The sponsor of a drug may request the Secretary to designate the drug as a regenerative advanced therapy concurrently with, or at any time after, submission of an application for the investigation of the drug under section 505(i) of this Act or section 351(a)(3) of the Public Health Service Act.

"(4) DESIGNATION.—Not later than 60 calendar days after the receipt of a request under paragraph (3), the Secretary shall determine whether the drug that is the subject of the request meets the criteria described in paragraph (2). If the Secretary determines that the drug meets the criteria, the Secretary shall designate the drug as a regenerative advanced therapy and shall

take such actions as are appropriate under paragraph (1). If the Secretary determines that a drug does not meet the criteria for such designation, the Secretary shall include with the determination a written description of the rationale for such determination.

"(5) ACTIONS.—The sponsor of a regenerative advanced therapy shall be eligible for the actions to expedite development and review of such therapy under subsection (a)(3)(B), including early interactions to discuss any potential surrogate or intermediate endpoint to be used to support the accelerated approval of an application for the product under subsection (c).

"(6) ACCESS TO EXPEDITED APPROVAL PATHWAYS.—An application for a regenerative advanced therapy under section 505(b)(1) of this Act or section 351(a) of the Public Health Service Act may be—

"(A) eligible for priority review, as described in the Manual of Policies and Procedures of the Food and Drug Administration and goals identified in the letters described in section 101(b) of the Prescription Drug User Fee Amendments of 2012; and

"(B) eligible for accelerated approval under subsection (c), as agreed upon pursuant to subsection (a)(3)(B), through, as appropriate—

"(i) surrogate or intermediate endpoints reasonably likely to predict long-term clinical benefit; or

"(ii) reliance upon data obtained from a meaningful number of sites, including through expansion to additional sites, as appropriate.

"(7) POSTAPPROVAL REQUIREMENTS.—The sponsor of a regenerative advanced therapy that is granted accelerated approval and is subject to the postapproval requirements under subsection (c) may, as appropriate, fulfill such requirements, as the Secretary may require, through—

"(A) the submission of clinical evidence, clinical studies, patient registries, or other sources of real world evidence, such as electronic health records;

"(B) the collection of larger confirmatory data sets, as agreed upon pursuant to subsection (a)(3)(B); or

"(C) postapproval monitoring of all patients treated with such therapy prior to approval of the therapy.

"(8) DEFINITION.—For purposes of this section, the term 'regenerative medicine therapy' includes cell therapy, therapeutic tissue engineering products, human cell and tissue products, and combination products using any such therapies or products, except for those regulated solely under section 361 of the Public Health Service Act and part 1271 of title 21, Code of Federal Regulations.".

(b) RULE OF CONSTRUCTION.—Nothing in this section and the amendments made by this section shall be construed to alter the authority of the Secretary of Health and Human Services—

(1) to approve drugs pursuant to the Federal Food, Drug, and Cosmetic Act (21 U.S.C. 301 et seq.) and section 351 of the Public Health Service Act (42 U.S.C. 262) as authorized prior to the date of enactment of the 21st Century Cures Act, including the standards of evidence, and applicable conditions, for approval under such Acts; or

(2) to alter the authority of the Secretary to require postapproval studies pursuant to such Acts, as authorized prior to the date of enactment of the 21st Century Cures Act.

(c) CONFORMING AMENDMENT.—Section 506(e)(1) of the Federal Food, Drug, and Cosmetic Act (21 U.S.C. 356(e)(1)) is amended by inserting "and the 21st Century Cures Act" after "Food and Drug Administration Safety and Innovation Act".

SEC. 3034. GUIDANCE REGARDING DEVICES USED IN THE RECOVERY, ISOLATION, OR DELIVERY OF REGENERATIVE ADVANCED THERAPIES.

(a) DRAFT GUIDANCE.—Not later than 1 year after the date of enactment of the 21st Century Cures Act, the Secretary of Health and Human Services, acting through the Commissioner of Food and Drugs, shall issue draft guidance clarifying how, in the context of regenerative advanced therapies, the Secretary will evaluate devices used in the recovery, isolation, or delivery of regenerative advanced therapies. In doing so, the Secretary shall specifically address—

(1) how the Food and Drug Administration intends to simplify and streamline regulatory requirements for combination device and cell or tissue products;

(2) what, if any, intended uses or specific attributes would result in a device used with a regenerative therapy product to be classified as a class III device;

(3) when the Food and Drug Administration considers it is necessary, if ever, for the intended use of a device to be limited to a specific intended use with only one particular type of cell; and

(4) application of the least burdensome approach to demonstrate how a device may be used with more than one cell type.

(b) FINAL GUIDANCE.—Not later than 12 months after the close of the period for public comment on the draft guidance under subsection (a), the Secretary of Health and Human Services shall finalize such guidance.

SEC. 3035. REPORT ON REGENERATIVE ADVANCED THERAPIES.

(a) REPORT TO CONGRESS.—Before March 1 of each calendar year, the Secretary of Health and Human Services shall, with respect to the previous calendar year, submit a report to the Committee on Health, Education, Labor, and Pensions of the Senate and the Committee on Energy and Commerce of the House of Representatives on—

(1) the number and type of applications for approval of regenerative advanced therapies filed, approved or licensed as applicable, withdrawn, or denied; and

(2) how many of such applications or therapies, as applicable, were granted accelerated approval or priority review.

(b) REGENERATIVE ADVANCED THERAPY.—In this section, the term "regenerative advanced therapy" has the meaning given such term in section 506(g) of the Federal Food, Drug, and Cosmetic Act, as added by section 3033 of this Act.

SEC. 3036. STANDARDS FOR REGENERATIVE MEDICINE AND REGENERATIVE ADVANCED THERAPIES.

Subchapter A of chapter V of the Federal Food, Drug, and Cosmetic Act (21 U.S.C. 351 et seq.) is amended by inserting after section 506F the following:

"SEC. 506G. STANDARDS FOR REGENERATIVE MEDICINE AND REGENERATIVE ADVANCED THERAPIES.

"(a) IN GENERAL.—Not later than 2 years after the date of enactment of the 21st Century Cures Act, the Secretary, in consultation with the National Institute of Standards and Technology and stakeholders (including regenerative medicine and advanced therapies manufacturers and clinical trial sponsors, contract manufacturers, academic institutions, practicing clinicians, regenerative medicine and advanced therapies industry organizations, and standard setting organizations), shall facilitate an effort to coordinate and prioritize the development of standards and consensus definition of terms, through a public process, to support, through regulatory predictability, the development, evaluation, and review of regenerative medicine therapies and regenerative advanced therapies, including with respect to the manufacturing processes and controls of such products.

"*(b) ACTIVITIES.*—

"*(1) IN GENERAL.*—In carrying out this section, the Secretary shall continue to—

"*(A)* identify opportunities to help advance the development of regenerative medicine therapies and regenerative advanced therapies;

"*(B)* identify opportunities for the development of laboratory regulatory science research and documentary standards that the Secretary determines would help support the development, evaluation, and review of regenerative medicine therapies and regenerative advanced therapies through regulatory predictability; and

"*(C)* work with stakeholders, such as those described in subsection *(a)*, as appropriate, in the development of such standards.

"*(2) REGULATIONS AND GUIDANCE.*—Not later than 1 year after the development of standards as described in subsection *(a)*, the Secretary shall review relevant regulations and guidance and, through a public process, update such regulations and guidance as the Secretary determines appropriate.

"*(c) DEFINITIONS.*—For purposes of this section, the terms 'regenerative medicine therapy' and 'regenerative advanced therapy' have the meanings given such terms in section 506(g).".

SEC. 3037. HEALTH CARE ECONOMIC INFORMATION.

Section 502(a) of the Federal Food, Drug, and Cosmetic Act (21 U.S.C. 352(a)) is amended—

(1) by striking "(a) If its" and inserting "(a)(1) If its";

(2) by striking "a formulary committee, or other similar entity, in the course of the committee or the entity carrying out its responsibilities for the selection of drugs for managed care or other similar organizations" and inserting "a payor, formulary committee, or other similar entity with knowledge and expertise in the area of health care economic analysis, carrying out its responsibilities for the selection of drugs for coverage or reimbursement";

(3) by striking "directly relates" and inserting "relates";

(4) by striking "and is based on competent and reliable scientific evidence. The requirements set forth in section 505(a) or in section 351(a) of the Public Health Service Act shall not apply to health care economic information provided to such a committee or entity in accordance with this paragraph" and inserting ", is based on competent and reliable scientific evidence, and includes, where applicable, a conspicuous and prominent statement describing any material differences between the health care economic information and the labeling approved for the drug under section 505 or under section 351 of the Public Health Service Act. The requirements set forth in section 505(a) or in subsections (a) and (k) of section 351 of the Public Health Service Act shall not apply to health care economic information provided to such a payor, committee, or entity in accordance with this paragraph"; and

(5) by striking "In this paragraph, the term" and all that follows and inserting the following:

"(2)(A) For purposes of this paragraph, the term 'health care economic information' means any analysis (including the clinical data, inputs, clinical or other assumptions, methods, results, and other components underlying or comprising the analysis) that identifies, measures, or describes the economic consequences, which may be based on the separate or aggregated clinical consequences of the represented health outcomes, of the use of a drug. Such analysis may be comparative to the use of another drug, to another health care intervention, or to no intervention.

"(B) Such term does not include any analysis that relates only to an indication that is not approved under section 505 or under section 351 of the Public Health Service Act for such drug.".

SEC. 3038. COMBINATION PRODUCT INNOVATION.

(a) IN GENERAL.—Section 503(g) of the Federal Food, Drug, and Cosmetic Act (21 U.S.C. 353(g)) is amended—

(1) by striking paragraph (3);

(2) by redesignating paragraph (2) as paragraph (7);

(3) by redesignating paragraphs (4) and (5) as paragraphs (8) and (9), respectively;

(4) by striking "(g)(1)" and all that follows through the end of paragraph (1) and inserting the following:

"*(g)(1)(A)* The Secretary shall, in accordance with this subsection, assign a primary agency center to regulate products that constitute a combination of a drug, device, or biological product.

"*(B)* The Secretary shall conduct the premarket review of any combination product under a single application, whenever appropriate.

"*(C)* For purposes of this subsection, the term 'primary mode of action' means the single mode of action of a combination product expected to make the greatest contribution to the overall intended therapeutic effects of the combination product.

"*(D)* The Secretary shall determine the primary mode of action of the combination product. If the Secretary determines that the primary mode of action is that of—

"*(i)* a drug (other than a biological product), the agency center charged with premarket review of drugs shall have primary jurisdiction;

"*(ii)* a device, the agency center charged with premarket review of devices shall have primary jurisdiction; or

"*(iii)* a biological product, the agency center charged with premarket review of biological products shall have primary jurisdiction.

"*(E)* In determining the primary mode of action of a combination product, the Secretary shall not determine that the primary mode of action is that of a drug or biological product solely because the combination product has any chemical action within or on the human body.

"*(F)* If a sponsor of a combination product disagrees with the determination under subparagraph *(D)*—

"*(i)* such sponsor may request, and the Secretary shall provide, a substantive rationale to such sponsor that references scientific evidence provided by the sponsor and any other scientific evidence relied upon by the Secretary to support such determination; and

"*(ii)(I)* the sponsor of the combination product may propose one or more studies (which may be nonclinical, clinical, or both) to establish the relevance, if any, of the chemical action in achieving the primary mode of action of such product;

"*(II)* if the sponsor proposes any such studies, the Secretary and the sponsor of such product shall collaborate and seek to reach agreement, within a reasonable time of such proposal, not to exceed 90 calendar days, on the design of such studies; and

"*(III)* if an agreement is reached under subclause *(II)* and the sponsor conducts one or more of such studies, the Secretary shall consider the data resulting from any such study when reevaluating the determination of the primary mode of action of such product, and unless and until such reevaluation has occurred and the Secretary issues a new determination, the determination of the Secretary under subparagraph *(D)* shall remain in effect.

"*(2)(A)(i)* To establish clarity and certainty for the sponsor, the sponsor of a combination product may request a meeting on such combination product. If the Secretary concludes that a determination of the primary mode of action pursuant to paragraph *(1)(D)* is necessary, the sponsor may request such meeting only after the Secretary makes such determination. If the sponsor submits a written meeting request, the Secretary shall, not later than 75 calendar days after receiving such request, meet with the sponsor of such combination product.

"*(ii)* A meeting under clause *(i)* may—

"*(I)* address the standards and requirements for market approval or clearance of the combination product;

"*(II)* address other issues relevant to such combination product, such as requirements related to postmarket modification of such combination product and good manufacturing practices applicable to such combination product; and

"*(III)* identify elements under subclauses *(I)* and *(II)* that may be more appropriate for discussion and agreement with the Secretary at a later date given that scientific or other information is not available, or agreement is otherwise not feasible regarding such elements, at the time a request for such meeting is made.

"*(iii)* Any agreement under this subparagraph shall be in writing and made part of the administrative record by the Secretary.

"*(iv)* Any such agreement shall remain in effect, except—

"*(I)* upon the written agreement of the Secretary and the sponsor or applicant; or

"*(II)* pursuant to a decision by the director of the reviewing division of the primary agency center, or a person more senior than such director, in consultation with consulting centers and the Office, as appropriate, that an issue essential to determining whether the standard for market clearance or other applicable standard under this Act or the Public Health Service Act applicable to the combination product has been identified since the agreement was reached, or that deviating from the agreement is otherwise justifiable based on scientific evidence, for public health reasons.

"*(3)* For purposes of conducting the premarket review of a combination product that contains an approved constituent part described in paragraph *(4)*, the Secretary may require that the sponsor of such combination product submit to the Secretary only data or information that the Secretary determines is necessary to meet the standard for clearance or approval, as applicable, under this Act or the Public Health Service Act, including any incremental risks and benefits posed by such combination product, using a risk-based approach and taking into account any prior finding of safety and effectiveness or substantial equivalence for the approved constituent part relied upon by the applicant in accordance with paragraph *(5)*.

"*(4)* For purposes of paragraph *(3)*, an approved constituent part is—

"*(A)* a drug constituent part of a combination product being reviewed in a single application or request under section 515, 510(k), or 513(f)(2) (submitted in accordance with paragraph *(5)*), that is an approved drug, provided such application or request complies with paragraph *(5)*;

"*(B)* a device constituent part approved under section 515 that is referenced by the sponsor and that is available for use by the Secretary under section 520(h)(4); or

"*(C)* any constituent part that was previously approved, cleared, or classified under section 505, 510(k), 513(f)(2), or 515 of this Act for which the sponsor has a right of reference or any constituent part that is a nonprescription drug, as defined in section 760(a)(2).

"*(5)(A)* If an application is submitted under section 515 or 510(k) or a request is submitted under section 513(f)(2), consistent with any determination made under paragraph *(1)(D)*, for a combination product containing as a constituent part an approved drug—

"(i) the application or request shall include the certification or statement described in section 505(b)(2); and

"(ii) the applicant or requester shall provide notice as described in section 505(b)(3).

"(B) For purposes of this paragraph and paragraph (4), the term 'approved drug' means an active ingredient—

"(i) that was in an application previously approved under section 505(c);

"(ii) where such application is relied upon by the applicant submitting the application or request described in subparagraph (A);

"(iii) for which full reports of investigations that have been made to show whether such drug is safe for use and whether such drug is effective in use were not conducted by or for the applicant submitting the application or request described in subparagraph (A); and

"(iv) for which the applicant submitting the application or request described in subparagraph (A) has not obtained a right of reference or use from the person by or for whom the investigations described in clause (iii) were conducted.

"(C) The following provisions shall apply with respect to an application or request described in subparagraph (A) to the same extent and in the same manner as if such application or request were an application described in section 505(b)(2) that referenced the approved drug:

"(i) Subparagraphs (A), (B), (C), and (D) of section 505(c)(3).

"(ii) Clauses (ii), (iii), and (iv) of section 505(c)(3)(E).

"(iii) Subsections (b) and (c) of section 505A.

"(iv) Section 505E(a).

"(v) Section 527(a).

"(D) Notwithstanding any other provision of this subsection, an application or request for classification for a combination product described in subparagraph (A) shall be considered an application submitted under section 505(b)(2) for purposes of section 271(e)(2)(A) of title 35, United States Code.

"(6) Nothing in this subsection shall be construed as prohibiting a sponsor from submitting separate applications for the constituent parts of a combination product, unless the Secretary determines that a single application is necessary.";

(5) in paragraph (8) (as redesignated by paragraph (3))—

(A) in subparagraph (C)—

(i) by amending clause (i) to read as follows:

"(i) In carrying out this subsection, the Office shall help to ensure timely and effective premarket review that involves more than one agency center by coordinating such reviews, overseeing the timeliness of such reviews, and overseeing the alignment of feedback regarding such reviews.";

(ii) in clause (ii), by inserting "and alignment" after "the timeliness" each place it appears; and

(iii) by adding at the end the following new clauses:

"(iii) The Office shall ensure that, with respect to a combination product, a designated person or persons in the primary agency center is the primary point or points of contact for the sponsor of such combination product. The Office shall also coordinate communications to and from any consulting center involved in such premarket review, if requested by such primary agency center or any such consulting center. Agency communications and commitments, to the extent consistent with other provisions of law and the requirements of all affected agency centers, from the primary agency center shall be considered as communication from the Secretary on behalf of all agency centers involved in the review.

"(iv) The Office shall, with respect to the premarket review of a combination product—

"(I) ensure that any meeting between the Secretary and the sponsor of such product is attended by each agency center involved in the review, as appropriate;

"(II) ensure that each consulting agency center has completed its premarket review and provided the results of such review to the primary agency center in a timely manner; and

"(III) ensure that each consulting center follows the guidance described in clause (vi) and advises, as appropriate, on other relevant regulations, guidances, and policies.

"(v) In seeking agency action with respect to a combination product, the sponsor of such product—

"(I) shall identify the product as a combination product; and

"(II) may request in writing the participation of representatives of the Office in meetings related to such combination product, or to have the Office otherwise engage on such regulatory matters concerning the combination product.

"(vi) Not later than 4 years after the date of enactment of the 21st Century Cures Act, and after a public comment period of not less than 60 calendar days, the Secretary shall issue a final guidance that describes—

"(I) the structured process for managing presubmission interactions with sponsors developing combination products;

"(II) the best practices for ensuring that the feedback in such pre-submission interactions represents the Agency's best advice based on the information provided during such pre-submission interactions;

"(III) the information that is required to be submitted with a meeting request under paragraph (2), how such meetings relate to other types of meetings in the Food and Drug Administration, and the form and content of any agreement reached through a meeting under such paragraph (2);"; and

(B) in subparagraph (G)—

(i) in the matter preceding clause (i), by inserting "(except with respect to clause (iv), beginning not later than one year after the date of the enactment of the 21st Century Cures Act)" after "enactment of this paragraph";

(ii) in clause (ii), by striking "and" at the end;

(iii) in clause (iii), by striking the period at the end and inserting "; and"; and

(iv) by adding at the end the following new clause:

"(iv) identifying the percentage of combination products for which a dispute resolution, with respect to premarket review, was requested by the combination product's sponsor."; and

(6) in paragraph (9) (as redesignated by paragraph (3))—

(A) in subparagraph (C)—

(i) in clause (i), by striking the comma at the end and inserting a semicolon;

(ii) in clause (ii), by striking ", and" at the end and inserting a semicolon;

(iii) in clause (iii), by striking the period at the end and inserting "; and"; and

(iv) by adding at the end the following:

"(iv) de novo classification under section 513(a)(1)."; and

(B) by adding at the end the following:

"(D) The terms 'premarket review' and 'reviews' include all activities of the Food and Drug Administration conducted prior to approval or clearance of an application, notification, or request for classification submitted under section 505, 510(k), 513(f)(2), 515, or 520 of this Act or under section 351 of the Public Health Service Act, including with respect to investigational use of the product.".

(b) INFORMATION FOR APPROVAL OF COMBINATION PRODUCTS.—Section 520(h)(4) of the Federal Food, Drug, and Cosmetic Act (21 U.S.C. 360j(h)(4)) is amended—

(1) in subparagraph (A), by striking "Any information" and inserting "Subject to subparagraph (C), any information"; and

(2) by adding at the end the following new subparagraph:

"(C) No information contained in an application for premarket approval filed with the Secretary pursuant to section 515(c) may be used to approve or clear any application submitted under section 515 or 510(k) or to classify a product under section 513(f)(2) for a combination product containing as a constituent part an approved drug (as defined in section 503(g)(5)(B)) unless—

"(i) the application includes the certification or statement referenced in section 503(g)(5)(A);

"(ii) the applicant provides notice as described in section 503(g)(5)(A); and

"(iii) the Secretary's approval of such application is subject to the provisions in section 503(g)(5)(C).".

(c) VARIATIONS FROM CGMP STREAMLINED APPROACH.—Not later than 18 months after the date of enactment of this Act, the Secretary of Health and Human Services (referred to in this subsection as the "Secretary") shall identify types of combination products and manufacturing processes with respect to which the Secretary proposes that good manufacturing processes may be adopted that vary from the requirements set forth in section 4.4 of title 21, Code of Federal Regulations (or any successor regulations) or that the Secretary proposes can satisfy the requirements in section 4.4 through alternative or streamlined mechanisms. The Secretary shall identify such types, variations from such requirements, and such mechanisms, in a proposed list published in the Federal Register. After a public comment period regarding the appropriate good manufacturing practices for such types, the Secretary shall publish a final list in the Federal Register, notwithstanding section 553 of title 5, United States Code. The Secretary shall evaluate such types, variations, and mechanisms using a risk-based approach. The Secretary shall periodically review such final list.

Subtitle E—Antimicrobial Innovation and Stewardship

SEC. 3041. ANTIMICROBIAL RESISTANCE MONITORING.

(a) IN GENERAL.—Section 319E of the Public Health Service Act (42 U.S.C. 247d–5) is amended—

(1) by redesignating subsections (f) and (g) as subsections (l) and (m), respectively; and

(2) by inserting after subsection (e), the following:

"(f) MONITORING AT FEDERAL HEALTH CARE FACILITIES.—The Secretary shall encourage reporting on aggregate antimicrobial drug use and antimicrobial resistance to antimicrobial drugs and the implementation of antimicrobial stewardship programs by health care facilities of the Department of Defense, the Department of Veterans Affairs, and the Indian Health Service and shall provide technical assistance to the Secretary of Defense and the Secretary of Veterans Affairs, as appropriate and upon request.

"(g) REPORT ON ANTIMICROBIAL RESISTANCE IN HUMANS AND USE OF ANTIMICROBIAL DRUGS.—Not later than 1 year after the date of enactment of the 21st Century Cures Act, and annually thereafter, the Secretary shall prepare and make publicly available data and information concerning—

"(1) aggregate national and regional trends of antimicrobial resistance in humans to antimicrobial drugs, including such drugs approved under section 506(h) of the Federal Food, Drug, and Cosmetic Act;

"(2) antimicrobial stewardship, which may include summaries of State efforts to address antimicrobial resistance in humans to antimicrobial drugs and antimicrobial stewardship; and

"(3) coordination between the Director of the Centers for Disease Control and Prevention and the Commissioner of Food and Drugs with respect to the monitoring of—

"(A) any applicable resistance under paragraph (1); and

"(B) drugs approved under section 506(h) of the Federal Food, Drug, and Cosmetic Act.

"(h) INFORMATION RELATED TO ANTIMICROBIAL STEWARDSHIP PROGRAMS.—The Secretary shall, as appropriate, disseminate guidance, educational materials, or other appropriate materials related to the development and implementation of evidence-based antimicrobial stewardship programs or practices at health care facilities, such as nursing homes and other long-term care facilities, ambulatory surgical centers, dialysis centers, outpatient clinics, and hospitals, including community and rural hospitals.

"(i) SUPPORTING STATE-BASED ACTIVITIES TO COMBAT ANTIMICROBIAL RESISTANCE.—The Secretary shall continue to work with State and local public health departments on statewide or regional programs related to antimicrobial resistance. Such efforts may include activities to related to—

"(1) identifying patterns of bacterial and fungal resistance in humans to antimicrobial drugs;

"(2) preventing the spread of bacterial and fungal infections that are resistant to antimicrobial drugs; and

"(3) promoting antimicrobial stewardship.

"(j) ANTIMICROBIAL RESISTANCE AND STEWARDSHIP ACTIVITIES.—

"(1) IN GENERAL.—For the purposes of supporting stewardship activities, examining changes in antimicrobial resistance, and evaluating the effectiveness of section 506(h) of the Federal Food, Drug, and Cosmetic Act, the Secretary shall—

"(A) provide a mechanism for facilities to report data related to their antimicrobial stewardship activities (including analyzing the outcomes of such activities); and

"(B) evaluate—

"(i) antimicrobial resistance data using a standardized approach; and

"(ii) trends in the utilization of drugs approved under such section 506(h) with respect to patient populations.

"(2) USE OF SYSTEMS.—The Secretary shall use available systems, including the National Healthcare Safety Network or other systems identified by the Secretary, to fulfill the requirements or conduct activities under this section.

"(k) ANTIMICROBIAL.—For purposes of subsections (f) through (j), the term 'antimicrobial' includes any antibacterial or antifungal drugs, and may include drugs that eliminate or inhibit the growth of other microorganisms, as appropriate.".

(b) AVAILABILITY OF DATA.—The Secretary shall make the data collected pursuant to this subsection public. Nothing in this subsection shall be construed as authorizing the Secretary to disclose any information that is a trade secret or confidential information subject to section 552(b)(4) of title 5, United States Code, or section 1905 of title 18, United States Code.

SEC. 3042. LIMITED POPULATION PATHWAY.

Section 506 of the Federal Food, Drug, and Cosmetic Act (21 U.S.C. 356), as amended by section 3033, is further amended by adding at the end the following:

"(h) LIMITED POPULATION PATHWAY FOR ANTIBACTERIAL AND ANTIFUNGAL DRUGS.—

"(1) IN GENERAL.—The Secretary may approve an antibacterial or antifungal drug, alone or in combination with one or more other drugs, as a limited population drug pursuant to this subsection only if—

"(A) the drug is intended to treat a serious or life-threatening infection in a limited population of patients with unmet needs;

"(B) the standards for approval under section 505(c) and (d), or the standards for licensure under section 351 of the Public Health Service Act, as applicable, are met; and

"(C) the Secretary receives a written request from the sponsor to approve the drug as a limited population drug pursuant to this subsection.

"(2) BENEFIT-RISK CONSIDERATION.—The Secretary's determination of safety and effectiveness of an antibacterial or antifungal drug shall reflect the benefit-risk profile of such drug in the intended limited population, taking into account the severity, rarity, or prevalence of the infection the drug is intended to treat and the availability or lack of alternative treatment in such limited population. Such drug may be approved under this subsection notwithstanding a lack of evidence to fully establish a favorable benefit-risk profile in a population that is broader than the intended limited population.

"(3) ADDITIONAL REQUIREMENTS.—A drug approved under this subsection shall be subject to the following requirements, in addition to any other applicable requirements of this Act:

"(A) LABELING.—To indicate that the safety and effectiveness of a drug approved under this subsection has been demonstrated only with respect to a limited population—

"(i) all labeling and advertising of an antibacterial or antifungal drug approved under this subsection shall contain the statement 'Limited Population' in a prominent manner and adjacent to, and not more prominent than—

"(I) the proprietary name of such drug, if any; or

"(II) if there is no proprietary name, the established name of the drug, if any, as defined in section 503(e)(3), or, in the case of a drug that is a biological product, the proper name, as defined by regulation; and

"(ii) the prescribing information for the drug required by section 201.57 of title 21, Code of Federal Regulations (or any successor regulation) shall also include the following statement: 'This drug is indicated for use in a limited and specific population of patients.'.

"(B) PROMOTIONAL MATERIAL.—The sponsor of an antibacterial or antifungal drug subject to this subsection shall submit to the Secretary copies of all promotional materials related to such drug at least 30 calendar days prior to dissemination of the materials.

"(4) OTHER PROGRAMS.—A sponsor of a drug that seeks approval of a drug under this subsection may also seek designation or approval, as applicable, of such drug under other applicable sections or subsections of this Act or the Public Health Service Act.

"(5) GUIDANCE.—Not later than 18 months after the date of enactment of the 21st Century Cures Act, the Secretary shall issue draft guidance describing criteria, processes, and other general considerations for demonstrating the safety and effectiveness of limited population antibacterial and antifungal drugs. The Secretary shall publish final guidance within 18 months of the close of the public comment period on such draft guidance. The Secretary may approve antibacterial and antifungal drugs under this subsection prior to issuing guidance under this paragraph.

"(6) ADVICE.—The Secretary shall provide prompt advice to the sponsor of a drug for which the sponsor seeks approval under this subsection to enable the sponsor to plan a development program to obtain the necessary data for such approval, and to conduct any additional studies that would be required to gain approval of such drug for use in a broader population.

"(7) TERMINATION OF LIMITATIONS.—If, after approval of a drug under this subsection, the Secretary approves a broader indication for such drug under section 505(b) or section 351(a)

of the Public Health Service Act, the Secretary may remove any postmarketing conditions, including requirements with respect to labeling and review of promotional materials under paragraph (3), applicable to the approval of the drug under this subsection.

"(8) RULES OF CONSTRUCTION.—Nothing in this subsection shall be construed to alter the authority of the Secretary to approve drugs pursuant to this Act or section 351 of the Public Health Service Act, including the standards of evidence and applicable conditions for approval under such Acts, the standards of approval of a drug under such Acts, or to alter the authority of the Secretary to monitor drugs pursuant to such Acts.

"(9) REPORTING AND ACCOUNTABILITY.—

"(A) BIENNIAL REPORTING.—The Secretary shall report to Congress not less often than once every 2 years on the number of requests for approval, and the number of approvals, of an antibacterial or antifungal drug under this subsection.

"(B) GAO REPORT.—Not later than December 2021, the Comptroller General of the United States shall submit to the Committee on Energy and Commerce of the House of Representatives and the Committee on Health, Education, Labor and Pensions of the Senate a report on the coordination of activities required under section 319E of the Public Health Service Act. Such report shall include a review of such activities, and the extent to which the use of the pathway established under this subsection has streamlined premarket approval for antibacterial or antifungal drugs for limited populations, if such pathway has functioned as intended, if such pathway has helped provide for safe and effective treatment for patients, if such premarket approval would be appropriate for other categories of drugs, and if the authorities under this subsection have affected antibacterial or antifungal resistance.".

SEC. 3043. PRESCRIBING AUTHORITY.

Nothing in this subtitle, or an amendment made by this subtitle, shall be construed to restrict the prescribing of antimicrobial drugs or other products, including drugs approved under subsection (h) of section 506 of the Federal Food, Drug, and Cosmetic Act (21 U.S.C. 356) (as added by section 3042), by health care professionals, or to limit the practice of health care.

SEC. 3044. SUSCEPTIBILITY TEST INTERPRETIVE CRITERIA FOR MICROORGANISMS; ANTIMICROBIAL SUSCEPTIBILITY TESTING DEVICES.

(a) IN GENERAL.—Subchapter A of chapter V of the Federal Food, Drug, and Cosmetic Act (21 U.S.C. 351 et seq.) is amended by inserting after section 511 the following:

"SEC. 511A. SUSCEPTIBILITY TEST INTERPRETIVE CRITERIA FOR MICROORGANISMS.

"(a) PURPOSE; IDENTIFICATION OF CRITERIA.—

"(1) PURPOSE.—The purpose of this section is to clarify the Secretary's authority to—

"(A) efficiently update susceptibility test interpretive criteria for antimicrobial drugs when necessary for public health, due to, among other things, the constant evolution of microorganisms that leads to the development of resistance to drugs that have been effective in decreasing morbidity and mortality for patients, which warrants unique management of antimicrobial drugs that is inappropriate for most other drugs in order to delay or prevent the development of further resistance to existing therapies;

"(B) provide for public notice of the availability of recognized interpretive criteria and interpretive criteria standards; and

"(C) clear under section 510(k), classify under section 513(f)(2), or approve under section 515, antimicrobial susceptibility testing devices utilizing updated, recognized susceptibility test interpretive criteria to characterize the in vitro

susceptibility of particular bacteria, fungi, or other microorganisms, as applicable, to antimicrobial drugs.

"(2) IDENTIFICATION OF CRITERIA.—The Secretary shall identify appropriate susceptibility test interpretive criteria with respect to antimicrobial drugs—

"(A) if such criteria are available on the date of approval of the drug under section 505 of this Act or licensure of the drug under section 351 of the Public Health Service Act (as applicable), upon such approval or licensure; or

"(B) if such criteria are unavailable on such date, on the date on which such criteria are available for such drug.

"(3) BASES FOR INITIAL IDENTIFICATION.—The Secretary shall identify appropriate susceptibility test interpretive criteria under paragraph (2), based on the Secretary's review of, to the extent available and relevant—

"(A) preclinical and clinical data, including pharmacokinetic, pharmacodynamic, and epidemiological data;

"(B) the relationship of susceptibility test interpretive criteria to morbidity and mortality associated with the disease or condition for which such drug is used; and

"(C) such other evidence and information as the Secretary considers appropriate.

"(b) SUSCEPTIBILITY TEST INTERPRETIVE CRITERIA WEBSITE.—

"(1) IN GENERAL.—Not later than 1 year after the date of the enactment of the 21st Century Cures Act, the Secretary shall establish, and maintain thereafter, on the website of the Food and Drug Administration, a dedicated website that contains a list of any appropriate new or updated susceptibility test interpretive criteria standards and interpretive criteria in accordance with paragraph (2) (referred to in this section as the 'Interpretive Criteria Website').

"(2) LISTING OF SUSCEPTIBILITY TEST INTERPRETIVE CRITERIA STANDARDS AND INTERPRETIVE CRITERIA.—

"(A) IN GENERAL.—The list described in paragraph (1) shall consist of any new or updated susceptibility test interpretive criteria standards that are—

"(i) established by a nationally or internationally recognized standard development organization that—

"(I) establishes and maintains procedures to address potential conflicts of interest and ensure transparent decisionmaking;

"(II) holds open meetings to ensure that there is an opportunity for public input by interested parties, and establishes and maintains processes to ensure that such input is considered in decisionmaking; and

"(III) permits its standards to be made publicly available, through the National Library of Medicine or another similar source acceptable to the Secretary; and

"(ii) recognized in whole, or in part, by the Secretary under subsection (c).

"(B) OTHER LIST.—The Interpretive Criteria Website shall, in addition to the list described in subparagraph (A), include a list of interpretive criteria, if any, that the Secretary has determined to be appropriate with respect to legally marketed antimicrobial drugs, where—

"(i) the Secretary does not recognize, in whole or in part, an interpretive criteria standard described under subparagraph (A) otherwise applicable to such a drug;

"(ii) the Secretary withdraws under subsection (c)(1)(A) recognition of a standard, in whole or in part, otherwise applicable to such a drug;

"(iii) the Secretary approves an application under section 505 of this Act or section 351 of the Public Health Service Act, as applicable, with respect to marketing of such a drug for which there are no relevant interpretive criteria included in a standard recognized by the Secretary under subsection (c); or

"(iv) because the characteristics of such a drug differ from other drugs with the same active ingredient, the interpretive criteria with respect to such drug—

"(I) differ from otherwise applicable interpretive criteria included in a standard listed under subparagraph (A) or interpretive criteria otherwise listed under this subparagraph; and

"(II) are determined by the Secretary to be appropriate for the drug.

"(C) REQUIRED STATEMENTS.—The Interpretive Criteria Website shall include statements conveying—

"(i) that the website provides information about the in vitro susceptibility of bacteria, fungi, or other microorganisms, as applicable to a certain drug (or drugs);

"(ii) that—

"(I) the safety and efficacy of such drugs in treating clinical infections due to such bacteria, fungi, or other microorganisms, as applicable, may or may not have been established in adequate and well-controlled clinical trials in order for the susceptibility information described in clause (i) to be included on the website; and

"(II) the clinical significance of such susceptibility information in such instances is unknown;

"(iii) that the approved product labeling for specific drugs provides the uses for which the Secretary has approved the product; and

"(iv) any other information that the Secretary determines appropriate to adequately convey the meaning of the data supporting the recognition or listing of susceptibility test interpretive criteria standards or susceptibility test interpretive criteria included on the website.

"(3) NOTICE.—Not later than the date on which the Interpretive Criteria Website is established, the Secretary shall publish a notice of that establishment in the Federal Register.

"(4) INAPPLICABILITY OF MISBRANDING PROVISION.—The inclusion in the approved labeling of an antimicrobial drug of a reference or hyperlink to the Interpretive Criteria Website, in and of itself, shall not cause the drug to be misbranded in violation of section 502.

"(5) TRADE SECRETS AND CONFIDENTIAL INFORMATION.—Nothing in this section shall be construed as authorizing the Secretary to disclose any information that is a trade secret or confidential information subject to section 552(b)(4) of title 5, United States Code.

"(c) RECOGNITION OF SUSCEPTIBILITY TEST INTERPRETIVE CRITERIA.—

"(1) EVALUATION AND PUBLICATION.—

"(A) IN GENERAL.—Beginning on the date of the establishment of the Interpretive Criteria Website, and at least every 6 months thereafter, the Secretary shall—

"(i) evaluate any appropriate new or updated susceptibility test interpretive criteria standards established by a nationally or internationally recognized standard development organization described in subsection (b)(2)(A)(i); and

"(ii) publish on the public website of the Food and Drug Administration a notice—

"(I) withdrawing recognition of any different susceptibility test interpretive criteria standard, in whole or in part;

"(II) recognizing the new or updated standards;

"(III) recognizing one or more parts of the new or updated interpretive criteria specified in such a standard and declining to recognize the remainder of such standard; and

"(IV) making any necessary updates to the lists under subsection (b)(2).

"(B) UPON APPROVAL OF A DRUG.—Upon the approval of an initial or supplemental application for an antimicrobial drug under section 505 of this Act or section 351 of the Public Health Service Act, as applicable, where such approval is based on susceptibility test interpretive criteria which differ from those contained in a standard recognized, or from those otherwise listed, by the Secretary pursuant to this subsection, or for which there are no relevant interpretive criteria standards recognized, or interpretive criteria otherwise listed, by the Secretary pursuant to this subsection, the Secretary shall update the lists under subparagraphs (A) and (B) of subsection (b)(2) to include the susceptibility test interpretive criteria upon which such approval was based.

"(2) BASES FOR UPDATING INTERPRETIVE CRITERIA STANDARDS.—In evaluating new or updated susceptibility test interpretive criteria standards under paragraph (1)(A), the Secretary may consider—

"(A) the Secretary's determination that such a standard is not applicable to a particular drug because the characteristics of the drug differ from other drugs with the same active ingredient;

"(B) information provided by interested third parties, including public comment on the annual compilation of notices published under paragraph (3);

"(C) any bases used to identify susceptibility test interpretive criteria under subsection (a)(2); and

"(D) such other information or factors as the Secretary determines appropriate.

"(3) ANNUAL COMPILATION OF NOTICES.—Each year, the Secretary shall compile the notices published under paragraph (1)(A) and publish such compilation in the Federal Register and provide for public comment. If the Secretary receives comments, the Secretary shall review such comments and, if the Secretary determines appropriate, update pursuant to this subsection susceptibility test interpretive criteria standards or criteria—

"(A) recognized by the Secretary under this subsection; or

"(B) otherwise listed on the Interpretive Criteria Website under subsection (b)(2).

"(4) RELATION TO SECTION 514(c).—Any susceptibility test interpretive standard recognized under this subsection or any criteria otherwise listed under subsection (b)(2)(B) shall be deemed to be recognized as a standard by the Secretary under section 514(c)(1).

"(5) VOLUNTARY USE OF INTERPRETIVE CRITERIA.—Nothing in this section prohibits a person from seeking approval or clearance of a drug or device, or changes to the drug or the device, on the basis of susceptibility test interpretive criteria which differ from those contained in a standard recognized, or from those otherwise listed, by the Secretary pursuant to subsection (b)(2).

"(d) ANTIMICROBIAL DRUG LABELING.—

"(1) DRUGS MARKETED PRIOR TO ESTABLISHMENT OF INTERPRETIVE CRITERIA WEBSITE.—

"(A) IN GENERAL.—With respect to an antimicrobial drug lawfully introduced or delivered for introduction into interstate commerce for commercial distribution before the establishment of the Interpretive Criteria Website, a holder of an approved application under section 505 of this Act or section 351 of the Public Health Service Act, as applicable, for each such drug, not later than 1 year after establishment of the Interpretive Criteria Website described in subsection (b)(1), shall remove susceptibility test interpretive criteria, if any, and related information from the approved drug labeling and replace it with a reference to the Interpretive Criteria Website.

"(B) LABELING CHANGES.—The labeling changes required by this section shall be considered a minor change under section 314.70 of title 21, Code of Federal Regulations (or any successor regulations) that may be implemented through documentation in the next applicable annual report.

''(2) DRUGS MARKETED SUBSEQUENT TO ESTAB-LISHMENT OF INTERPRETIVE CRITERIA WEBSITE.—With respect to antimicrobial drugs approved on or after the date of the establishment of the Interpretive Criteria Website described in subsection (b)(1), the labeling for such a drug shall include, in lieu of susceptibility test interpretive criteria and related information, a reference to such Website.

''(e) SPECIAL CONDITION FOR MARKETING OF ANTIMICROBIAL SUSCEPTIBILITY TESTING DEVICES.—

''(1) IN GENERAL.—Notwithstanding sections 501, 502, 505, 510, 513, and 515, if the conditions specified in paragraph (2) are met (in addition to other applicable provisions under this chapter) with respect to an antimicrobial susceptibility testing device described in subsection (f)(1), the Secretary may authorize the marketing of such device for a use described in such subsection.

''(2) CONDITIONS APPLICABLE TO ANTIMICROBIAL SUSCEPTIBILITY TESTING DEVICES.—The conditions specified in this paragraph are the following:

''(A) The device is used to make a determination of susceptibility using susceptibility test interpretive criteria that are—

''(i) included in a standard recognized by the Secretary under subsection (c); or

''(ii) otherwise listed on the Interpretive Criteria Website under subsection (b)(2).

''(B) The labeling of such device includes statements conveying—

''(i) that the device provides information about the in vitro susceptibility of bacteria, fungi, or other microorganisms, as applicable to antimicrobial drugs;

''(ii) that—

''(I) the safety and efficacy of such drugs in treating clinical infections due to such bacteria, fungi, or other microorganisms, as applicable, may or may not have been established in adequate and well-controlled clinical trials in order for the device to report the susceptibility of such bacteria, fungi, or other microorganisms, as applicable, to such drugs; and

''(II) the clinical significance of such susceptibility information in those instances is unknown;

''(iii) that the approved labeling for drugs tested using such a device provides the uses for which the Secretary has approved such drugs; and

''(iv) any other information the Secretary determines appropriate to adequately convey the meaning of the data supporting the recognition or listing of susceptibility test interpretive criteria standards or susceptibility test interpretive criteria described in subparagraph (A).

''(C) The antimicrobial susceptibility testing device meets all other requirements to be cleared under section 510(k), classified under section 513(f)(2), or approved under section 515.

''(f) DEFINITIONS.—In this section:

''(1) The term 'antimicrobial susceptibility testing device' means a device that utilizes susceptibility test interpretive criteria to determine and report the in vitro susceptibility of certain microorganisms to a drug (or drugs).

''(2) The term 'qualified infectious disease product' means a qualified infectious disease product designated under section 505E(d).

''(3) The term 'susceptibility test interpretive criteria' means—

''(A) one or more specific numerical values which characterize the susceptibility of bacteria or other microorganisms to the drug tested; and

''(B) related categorizations of such susceptibility, including categorization of the drug as susceptible, intermediate, resistant, or such other term as the Secretary determines appropriate.

''(4)(A) The term 'antimicrobial drug' means, subject to subparagraph (B), a systemic antibacterial or antifungal drug that—

''(i) is intended for human use in the treatment of a disease or condition caused by a bacterium or fungus;

''(ii) may include a qualified infectious disease product designated under section 505E(d); and

''(iii) is subject to section 503(b)(1).

''(B) If provided by the Secretary through regulations, such term may include—

''(i) drugs other than systemic antibacterial and antifungal drugs; and

''(ii) biological products (as such term is defined in section 351 of the Public Health Service Act) to the extent such products exhibit antimicrobial activity.

''(5) The term 'interpretive criteria standard' means a compilation of susceptibility test interpretive criteria developed by a standard development organization that meets the criteria set forth in subsection (b)(2)(A)(i).

''(g) RULE OF CONSTRUCTION.—Nothing in this section shall be construed to—

''(1) alter the standards of evidence under subsection (c) or (d) of section 505 (including the substantial evidence standard under section 505(d)) or under section 351 of the Public Health Service Act (as applicable); or

''(2) with respect to clearing devices under section 510(k), classifying devices under section 513(f)(2), or approving devices under section 515—

''(A) apply with respect to any drug, device, or biological product, in any context other than an antimicrobial drug and an antimicrobial susceptibility testing device that uses susceptibility test interpretive criteria to characterize and report the susceptibility of certain bacteria, fungi, or other microorganisms, as applicable, to such drug to reflect patient morbidity and mortality in accordance with this section; or

''(B) unless specifically stated, have any effect on authorities provided under other sections of this Act, including any regulations issued under such sections.''.

(b) CONFORMING AMENDMENTS.—

(1) REPEAL OF PRIOR RELATED AUTHORITY.—Section 1111 of the Food and Drug Administration Amendments Act of 2007 (42 U.S.C. 247d-5a), relating to identification of clinically susceptible concentrations of antimicrobials, is repealed.

(2) ADDITION TO CATEGORIES OF MISBRANDED DRUGS.—Section 502 of the Federal Food, Drug, and Cosmetic Act (21 U.S.C. 352) is amended by adding at the end the following:

''(dd) If it is an antimicrobial drug, as defined in section 511A(f), and its labeling fails to conform with the requirements under section 511A(d).''.

(3) RECOGNITION OF INTERPRETIVE CRITERIA STANDARD AS DEVICE STANDARD.—Section 514(c)(1)(A) of the Federal Food, Drug, and Cosmetic Act (21 U.S.C. 360d(c)(1)(A)) is amended by inserting after ''the Secretary shall, by publication in the Federal Register'' the following:

''(or, with respect to a susceptibility test interpretive criteria standard under section 511A, by posting on the Interpretive Criteria Website in accordance with such section)''.

(c) REPORT TO CONGRESS.—Not later than 2 years after the date of enactment of this Act, the Secretary of Health and Human Services shall submit to the Committee on Health, Education, Labor, and Pensions of the Senate and the Committee on Energy and Commerce of the House of Representatives a report on the progress made in implementing section 511A of the Federal Food, Drug, and Cosmetic Act (21 U.S.C. 360a), as added by subsection (a).

(d) REQUESTS FOR UPDATES TO INTERPRETIVE CRITERIA WEBSITE.—Chapter 35 of title 44, United States Code, shall not apply to the collection of information from interested parties regarding updating the lists established under section 511A(b) of the Federal Food, Drug, and

Cosmetic Act and posted on the Interpretive Criteria Website established under section 511A(c) of such Act.

Subtitle F—Medical Device Innovations
SEC. 3051. BREAKTHROUGH DEVICES.

(a) IN GENERAL.—Chapter V of the Federal Food, Drug, and Cosmetic Act (21 U.S.C. 351 et seq.) is amended by inserting after section 515B, as added by section 3034(b), the following:
''SEC. 515C. BREAKTHROUGH DEVICES.

''(a) PURPOSE.—The purpose of this section is to encourage the Secretary, and provide the Secretary with sufficient authority, to apply efficient and flexible approaches to expedite the development of, and prioritize the Food and Drug Administration's review of, devices that represent breakthrough technologies.

''(b) ESTABLISHMENT OF PROGRAM.—The Secretary shall establish a program to expedite the development of, and provide for the priority review for, devices, as determined by the Secretary—

''(1) that provide for more effective treatment or diagnosis of life-threatening or irreversibly debilitating human disease or conditions; and

''(2)(A) that represent breakthrough technologies;

''(B) for which no approved or cleared alternatives exist;

''(C) that offer significant advantages over existing approved or cleared alternatives, including the potential, compared to existing approved alternatives, to reduce or eliminate the need for hospitalization, improve patient quality of life, facilitate patients' ability to manage their own care (such as through self-directed personal assistance), or establish long-term clinical efficiencies; or

''(D) the availability of which is in the best interest of patients.

''(c) REQUEST FOR DESIGNATION.—A sponsor of a device may request that the Secretary designate such device for expedited development and priority review under this section. Any such request for designation may be made at any time prior to the submission of an application under section 515(c), a notification under section 510(k), or a petition for classification under section 513(f)(2).

''(d) DESIGNATION PROCESS.—

''(1) IN GENERAL.—Not later than 60 calendar days after the receipt of a request under subsection (c), the Secretary shall determine whether the device that is the subject of the request meets the criteria described in subsection (b). If the Secretary determines that the device meets the criteria, the Secretary shall designate the device for expedited development and priority review.

''(2) REVIEW.—Review of a request under subsection (c) shall be undertaken by a team that is composed of experienced staff and senior managers of the Food and Drug Administration.

''(3) WITHDRAWAL.—The Secretary may not withdraw a designation granted under this section on the basis of the criteria under subsection (b) no longer applying because of the subsequent clearance or approval of another device that—

''(A) was designated under this section; or

''(B) was given priority review under section 515(d)(5), as in effect prior to the date of enactment of the 21st Century Cures Act.

''(e) EXPEDITED DEVELOPMENT AND PRIORITY REVIEW.—

''(1) ACTIONS.—For purposes of expediting the development and review of devices designated under subsection (d) the Secretary shall—

''(A) assign a team of staff, including a team leader with appropriate subject matter expertise and experience, for each device for which a request is submitted under subsection (c);

''(B) provide for oversight of the team by senior agency personnel to facilitate the efficient development of the device and the efficient review of any submission described in subsection (c) for the device;

"(C) adopt an efficient process for timely dispute resolution;

"(D) provide for interactive and timely communication with the sponsor of the device during the development program and review process;

"(E) expedite the Secretary's review of manufacturing and quality systems compliance, as applicable;

"(F) disclose to the sponsor, not less than 5 business days in advance, the topics of any consultation the Secretary intends to undertake with external experts or an advisory committee concerning the sponsor's device and provide the sponsor the opportunity to recommend such external experts;

"(G) provide for advisory committee input, as the Secretary determines appropriate (including in response to the request of the sponsor) for applications submitted under section 515(c); and

"(H) assign staff to be available within a reasonable time to address questions by institutional review committees concerning the conditions and clinical testing requirements applicable to the investigational use of the device pursuant to an exemption under section 520(g).

"(2) ADDITIONAL ACTIONS.—In addition to the actions described in paragraph (1), for purposes of expediting the development and review of devices designated under subsection (d), the Secretary, in collaboration with the device sponsor, may, as appropriate—

"(A) coordinate with the sponsor regarding early agreement on a data development plan;

"(B) take steps to ensure that the design of clinical trials is as efficient and flexible as practicable, when scientifically appropriate;

"(C) facilitate, when scientifically appropriate, expedited and efficient development and review of the device through utilization of timely postmarket data collection with regard to application for approval under section 515(c); and

"(D) agree in writing to clinical protocols that the Secretary will consider binding on the Secretary and the sponsor, subject to—

"(i) changes to such protocols agreed to in writing by the sponsor and the Secretary; or

"(ii) a decision, made by the director of the office responsible for reviewing the device submission, that a substantial scientific issue essential to determining the safety or effectiveness of such device exists, provided that such decision is in writing, and is made only after the Secretary provides to the device sponsor or applicant an opportunity for a meeting at which the director and the sponsor or applicant are present and at which the director documents the substantial scientific issue.

"(f) PRIORITY REVIEW GUIDANCE.—

"(1) CONTENT.—Not later than 1 year after the date of enactment of the 21st Century Cures Act, the Secretary shall issue guidance on the implementation of this section. Such guidance shall—

"(A) set forth the process by which a person may seek a designation under subsection (d);

"(B) provide a template for requests under subsection (c);

"(C) identify the criteria the Secretary will use in evaluating a request for designation under this section; and

"(D) identify the criteria and processes the Secretary will use to assign a team of staff, including team leaders, to review devices designated for expedited development and priority review, including any training required for such personnel to ensure effective and efficient review.

"(2) PROCESS.—Prior to finalizing the guidance under paragraph (1), the Secretary shall seek public comment on a proposed guidance.

"(g) RULE OF CONSTRUCTION.—Nothing in this section shall be construed to affect—

"(1) the criteria and standards for evaluating an application pursuant to section 515(c), a report and request for classification under section 513(f)(2), or a report under section 510(k), including the recognition of valid scientific evidence as described in section 513(a)(3)(B) and consideration and application of the least burdensome means of evaluating device effectiveness or demonstrating substantial equivalence between devices with differing technological characteristics, as applicable;

"(2) the authority of the Secretary with respect to clinical holds under section 520(g)(8)(A);

"(3) the authority of the Secretary to act on an application pursuant to section 515(d) before completion of an establishment inspection, as the Secretary determines appropriate; or

"(4) the authority of the Secretary with respect to postmarket surveillance under sections 519(h) and 522.".

(b) DOCUMENTATION AND REVIEW OF SIGNIFICANT DECISIONS.—Section 517A(a)(1) of the Federal Food, Drug, and Cosmetic Act (21 U.S.C. 360g–1(a)(1)) is amended by inserting "a request for designation under section 515C," after "application under section 515,".

(c) TERMINATION OF PREVIOUS PROGRAM.—

(1) IN GENERAL.—Section 515(d) of the Federal Food, Drug, and Cosmetic Act (21 U.S.C. 360e(d)) is amended—

(A) by striking paragraph (5); and

(B) by redesignating paragraph (6) as paragraph (5).

(2) CONFORMING AMENDMENT.—Section 737(5) of the Federal Food, Drug, and Cosmetics Act (21 U.S.C. 379i(5)) is amended by striking "515(d)(6)" and inserting "515(d)(5)".

(d) REPORT.—On January 1, 2019, the Secretary of Health and Human Services shall issue a report to the Committee on Health, Education, Labor, and Pensions of the Senate and the Committee on Energy and Commerce of the House of Representatives—

(1) on the program under section 515C of the Federal Food, Drug, and Cosmetic Act, as added by subsection (a), in bringing safe and effective devices included in such program to patients as soon as possible; and

(2) that includes recommendations, if any, to strengthen the program to better meet patient device needs in a manner as timely as possible.

SEC. 3052. HUMANITARIAN DEVICE EXEMPTION.

(a) IN GENERAL.—Section 520(m) of the Federal Food, Drug, and Cosmetic Act (21 U.S.C. 360j) is amended—

(1) in paragraph (1) by striking "fewer than 4,000" and inserting "not more than 8,000";

(2) in paragraph (2)(A) by striking "fewer than 4,000" and inserting "not more than 8,000"; and

(3) in paragraph (6)(A)(ii), by striking "4,000" and inserting "8,000".

(b) GUIDANCE DOCUMENT ON PROBABLE BENEFIT.—Not later than 18 months after the date of enactment of this Act, the Secretary of Health and Human Services, acting through the Commissioner of Food and Drugs, shall publish a draft guidance that defines the criteria for establishing "probable benefit" as that term is used in section 520(m)(2)(C) of the Federal Food, Drug, and Cosmetic Act (21 U.S.C. 360j(m)(2)(C)).

SEC. 3053. RECOGNITION OF STANDARDS.

(a) IN GENERAL.—Section 514(c) of the Federal Food, Drug, and Cosmetic Act (21 U.S.C. 360d(c)) is amended—

(1) in paragraph (1), by inserting after subparagraph (B) the following new subparagraphs:

"(C)(i) Any person may submit a request for recognition under subparagraph (A) of all or part of an appropriate standard established by a nationally or internationally recognized standard organization.

"(ii) Not later than 60 calendar days after the Secretary receives such a request, the Secretary shall—

"(I) make a determination to recognize all, part, or none of the standard that is the subject of the request; and

"(II) issue to the person who submitted such request a response in writing that states the Secretary's rationale for that determination, including the scientific, technical, regulatory, or other basis for such determination.

"(iii) The Secretary shall make a response issued under clause (ii)(II) publicly available, in such a manner as the Secretary determines appropriate.

"(iv) The Secretary shall take such actions as may be necessary to implement all or part of a standard recognized under clause (ii)(I), in accordance with subparagraph (A).

"(D) The Secretary shall make publicly available, in such manner as the Secretary determines appropriate, the rationale for recognition under subparagraph (A) of all, part, or none of a standard, including the scientific, technical, regulatory, or other basis for the decision regarding such recognition."; and

(2) by adding at the end the following:

"(4) The Secretary shall provide to all employees of the Food and Drug Administration who review premarket submissions for devices periodic training on the concept and use of recognized standards for purposes of meeting a premarket submission requirement or other applicable requirement under this Act, including standards relevant to an employee's area of device review.".

(b) GUIDANCE.—The Secretary of Health and Human Services, acting through the Commissioner of Food and Drugs, shall review and update, if necessary, previously published guidance and standard operating procedures identifying the principles for recognizing standards, and for withdrawing the recognition of standards, under section 514(c) of the Federal Food, Drug, and Cosmetic Act (21 U.S.C. 360d(c)), taking into account the experience with and reliance on a standard by foreign regulatory authorities and the device industry, and whether recognition of a standard will promote harmonization among regulatory authorities in the regulation of devices.

SEC. 3054. CERTAIN CLASS I AND CLASS II DEVICES.

(a) CLASS I DEVICES.—Section 510(l) of the Federal Food, Drug, and Cosmetic Act (21 U.S.C. 360(l)) is amended—

(1) by striking "A report under subsection (k)" and inserting "(1) A report under subsection (k)"; and

(2) by adding at the end the following new paragraph:

"(2) Not later than 120 calendar days after the date of enactment of the 21st Century Cures Act and at least once every 5 years thereafter, as the Secretary determines appropriate, the Secretary shall identify, through publication in the Federal Register, any type of class I device that the Secretary determines no longer requires a report under subsection (k) to provide reasonable assurance of safety and effectiveness. Upon such publication—

"(A) each type of class I device so identified shall be exempt from the requirement for a report under subsection (k); and

"(B) the classification regulation applicable to each such type of device shall be deemed amended to incorporate such exemption.".

(b) CLASS II DEVICES.—Section 510(m) of the Federal Food, Drug, and Cosmetic Act (21 U.S.C. 360(m)) is amended—

(1) by striking "(m)(1)" and all that follows through "by the Secretary." and inserting the following:

"(m)(1) The Secretary shall—

"(A) not later than 90 days after the date of enactment of the 21st Century Cures Act and at least once every 5 years thereafter, as the Secretary determines appropriate—

"(i) publish in the Federal Register a notice that contains a list of each type of class II device that the Secretary determines no longer requires a report under subsection (k) to provide reasonable assurance of safety and effectiveness; and

"(ii) provide for a period of not less than 60 calendar days for public comment beginning on the date of the publication of such notice; and

"(B) not later than 210 calendar days after the date of enactment of the 21st Century Cures Act, publish in the Federal Register a list representing the Secretary's final determination with respect to the devices contained in the list published under subparagraph (A)."; and

(2) in paragraph (2)—

(A) by striking "1 day after the date of publication of a list under this subsection," and inserting "1 calendar day after the date of publication of the final list under paragraph (1)(B),"; and

(B) by striking "30-day period" and inserting "60-calendar-day period"; and

(C) by adding at the end the following new paragraph:

"(3) Upon the publication of the final list under paragraph (1)(B)—

"(A) each type of class II device so listed shall be exempt from the requirement for a report under subsection (k); and

"(B) the classification regulation applicable to each such type of device shall be deemed amended to incorporate such exemption.".

SEC. 3055. CLASSIFICATION PANELS.

(a) CLASSIFICATION PANELS.—Paragraph (5) of section 513(b) of the Federal Food, Drug, and Cosmetic Act (21 U.S.C. 360c(b)) is amended—

(1) by striking "(5)" and inserting "(5)(A)"; and

(2) by adding at the end the following:

"(B) When a device is specifically the subject of review by a classification panel, the Secretary shall—

"(i) ensure that adequate expertise is represented on the classification panel to assess—

"(I) the disease or condition which the device is intended to cure, treat, mitigate, prevent, or diagnose; and

"(II) the technology of the device; and

"(ii) provide an opportunity for the person whose device is specifically the subject of panel review to provide recommendations on the expertise needed among the voting members of the panel.

"(C) For purposes of subparagraph (B)(i), the term 'adequate expertise' means that the membership of the classification panel includes—

"(i) two or more voting members, with a specialty or other expertise clinically relevant to the device under review; and

"(ii) at least one voting member who is knowledgeable about the technology of the device.

"(D) The Secretary shall provide an annual opportunity for patients, representatives of patients, and sponsors of medical device submissions to provide recommendations for individuals with appropriate expertise to fill voting member positions on classification panels.".

(b) PANEL REVIEW PROCESS.—Section 513(b)(6) of the Federal Food, Drug, and Cosmetic Act (21 U.S.C. 360c(b)(6)) is amended—

(1) in subparagraph (A)(iii), by inserting before the period at the end ", including, subject to the discretion of the panel chairperson, by designating a representative who will be provided a time during the panel meeting to address the panel for the purpose of correcting misstatements of fact or providing clarifying information, and permitting the person or representative to call on experts within the person's

organization to address such specific issues in the time provided"; and

(2) by striking subparagraph (B) and inserting the following new subparagraph:

"(B)(i) Any meeting of a classification panel with respect to the review of a device shall—

"(I) provide adequate time for initial presentations by the person whose device is specifically the subject of such review and by the Secretary; and

"(II) encourage free and open participation by all interested persons.

"(ii) Following the initial presentations described in clause (i), the panel may—

"(I) pose questions to a designated representative described in subparagraph (A)(iii); and

"(II) consider the responses to such questions in the panel's review of the device.".

SEC. 3056. INSTITUTIONAL REVIEW BOARD FLEXIBILITY.

Section 520 of the Federal Food, Drug, and Cosmetic Act (21 U.S.C. 360j) is amended—

(1) in subsection (g)(3)—

(A) in subparagraph (A)(i)—

(i) by striking "local"; and

(ii) by striking "which has been"; and

(B) in subparagraph (B), by striking "a local institutional" and inserting "an institutional"; and

(2) in subsection (m)(4)—

(A) by striking subparagraph (A) and inserting the following:

"(A) in facilities in which clinical testing of devices is supervised by an institutional review committee established in accordance with the regulations of the Secretary; and";

(B) in subparagraph (B), by striking "a local institutional" and inserting "an institutional"; and

(C) in the matter following subparagraph (B), by striking "local".

SEC. 3057. CLIA WAIVER IMPROVEMENTS.

(a) DRAFT REVISED GUIDANCE.—Not later than 1 year after the date of the enactment of this Act, the Secretary of Health and Human Services, acting through the Commissioner of Food and Drugs, shall publish a draft guidance that—

(1) revises "Section V. Demonstrating Insignificant Risk of an Erroneous Result – Accuracy" of the guidance entitled "Recommendations for Clinical Laboratory Improvement Amendments of 1988 (CLIA) Waiver Applications for Manufacturers of In Vitro Diagnostic Devices" and dated January 30, 2008; and

(2) includes the appropriate use of comparable performance between a waived user and a moderately complex laboratory user to demonstrate accuracy.

(b) FINAL REVISED GUIDANCE.—The Secretary of Health and Human Services, acting through the Commissioner of Food and Drugs, shall finalize the draft guidance published under subsection (a) not later than 1 year after the comment period for such draft guidance closes.

SEC. 3058. LEAST BURDENSOME DEVICE REVIEW.

(a) IN GENERAL.—Section 513 of the Federal Food, Drug, and Cosmetic Act (21 U.S.C. 360c) is amended by adding at the end the following:

"(j) TRAINING AND OVERSIGHT OF LEAST BURDENSOME REQUIREMENTS.—

"(1) The Secretary shall—

"(A) ensure that each employee of the Food and Drug Administration who is involved in the review of premarket submissions, including supervisors, receives training regarding the meaning and implementation of the least burdensome requirements under subsections (a)(3)(D) and (i)(1)(D) of this section and section 515(c)(5); and

"(B) periodically assess the implementation of the least burdensome requirements, including the employee training under subparagraph (A), to ensure that the least burdensome requirements are fully and consistently applied.

"(2) Not later than 18 months after the date of enactment of the 21st Century Cures Act, the ombudsman for any organizational unit of the Food and Drug Administration responsible for the premarket review of devices shall—

"(A) conduct an audit of the training described in paragraph (1)(A), including the effectiveness of such training in implementing the least burdensome requirements;

"(B) include in such audit interviews of persons who are representatives of the device industry regarding their experiences in the device premarket review process, including with respect to the application of least burdensome concepts to premarket review and decisionmaking;

"(C) include in such audit a list of the measurement tools the Secretary uses to assess the implementation of the least burdensome requirements, including under paragraph (1)(B) and section 517A(a)(3), and may also provide feedback on the effectiveness of such tools in the implementation of the least burdensome requirements;

"(D) summarize the findings of such audit in a final audit report; and

"(E) within 30 calendar days of completion of such final audit report, make such final audit report available—

"(i) to the Committee on Health, Education, Labor, and Pensions of the Senate and the Committee on Energy and Commerce of the House of Representatives; and

"(ii) on the Internet website of the Food and Drug Administration.".

(b) PREMARKET APPLICATIONS.—Section 515(c) of the Federal Food, Drug, and Cosmetic Act (21 U.S.C. 360e(c)) is amended by adding at the end the following:

"(5)(A) In requesting additional information with respect to an application under this section, the Secretary shall consider the least burdensome appropriate means necessary to demonstrate a reasonable assurance of device safety and effectiveness.

"(B) For purposes of subparagraph (A), the term 'necessary' means the minimum required information that would support a determination by the Secretary that an application provides a reasonable assurance of the safety and effectiveness of the device.

"(C) For purposes of this paragraph, the Secretary shall consider the role of postmarket information in determining the least burdensome means of demonstrating a reasonable assurance of device safety and effectiveness.

"(D) Nothing in this paragraph alters the standards for premarket approval of a device.".

(c) RATIONALE FOR SIGNIFICANT DECISIONS REGARDING DEVICES.—Section 517A(a) of the Federal Food, Drug, and Cosmetic Act (21 U.S.C. 360g–1(a)) is amended by adding at the end the following:

"(3) APPLICATION OF LEAST BURDENSOME REQUIREMENTS.—The substantive summary required under this subsection shall include a brief statement regarding how the least burdensome requirements were considered and applied consistent with section 513(i)(1)(D), section 513(a)(3)(D), and section 515(c)(5), as applicable.".

SEC. 3059. CLEANING INSTRUCTIONS AND VALIDATION DATA REQUIREMENT.

(a) IN GENERAL.—Section 510 of the Federal Food, Drug, and Cosmetic Act (21 U.S.C. 360) is amended by adding at the end the following:

"(q) REUSABLE MEDICAL DEVICES.—

"(1) IN GENERAL.—Not later than 180 days after the date of enactment of the 21st Century Cures Act, the Secretary shall identify and publish a list of reusable device types for which reports under subsection (k) are required to include—

"(A) instructions for use, which have been validated in a manner specified by the Secretary; and

"(B) validation data, the types of which shall be specified by the Secretary;
regarding cleaning, disinfection, and sterilization, and for which a substantial equivalence determination may be based.

"(2) REVISION OF LIST.—The Secretary shall revise the list under paragraph (2), as the Secretary determines appropriate, with notice in the Federal Register.

"(3) CONTENT OF REPORTS.—Reports under subsection (k) that are submitted after the publication of the list described in paragraph (1), for devices or types of devices included on such list, shall include such instructions for use and validation data.".

(b) DEVICE MODIFICATIONS.—The Secretary of Health and Human Services, acting through the Commissioner of Food and Drugs, shall issue final guidance regarding when a premarket notification under section 510(k) of the Federal Food, Drug, and Cosmetic Act (21 U.S.C. 360(k)) is required to be submitted for a modification or change to a legally marketed device. Such final guidance shall be issued not later than 1 year after the date on which the comment period closes for the draft guidance on such subject.

SEC. 3060. CLARIFYING MEDICAL SOFTWARE REGULATION.

(a) IN GENERAL.—Section 520 of the Federal Food, Drug, and Cosmetic Act (21 U.S.C. 360j) is amended by adding at the end the following:

"(o) REGULATION OF MEDICAL AND CERTAIN DECISIONS SUPPORT SOFTWARE.—

"(1) The term device, as defined in section 201(h), shall not include a software function that is intended—

"(A) for administrative support of a health care facility, including the processing and maintenance of financial records, claims or billing information, appointment schedules, business analytics, information about patient populations, admissions, practice and inventory management, analysis of historical claims data to predict future utilization or cost-effectiveness, determination of health benefit eligibility, population health management, and laboratory workflow;

"(B) for maintaining or encouraging a healthy lifestyle and is unrelated to the diagnosis, cure, mitigation, prevention, or treatment of a disease or condition;

"(C) to serve as electronic patient records, including patient-provided information, to the extent that such records are intended to transfer, store, convert formats, or display the equivalent of a paper medical chart, so long as—

"(i) such records were created, stored, transferred, or reviewed by health care professionals, or by individuals working under supervision of such professionals;

"(ii) such records are part of health information technology that is certified under section 3001(c)(5) of the Public Health Service Act; and

"(iii) such function is not intended to interpret or analyze patient records, including medical image data, for the purpose of the diagnosis, cure, mitigation, prevention, or treatment of a disease or condition;

"(D) for transferring, storing, converting formats, or displaying clinical laboratory test or other device data and results, findings by a health care professional with respect to such data and results, general information about such findings, and general background information about such laboratory test or other device, unless such function is intended to interpret or analyze clinical laboratory test or other device data, results, and findings; or

"(E) unless the function is intended to acquire, process, or analyze a medical image or a signal from an in vitro diagnostic device or a pattern or signal from a signal acquisition system, for the purpose of—

"(i) displaying, analyzing, or printing medical information about a patient or other medical information (such as peer-reviewed clinical studies and clinical practice guidelines);

"(ii) supporting or providing recommendations to a health care professional about prevention, diagnosis, or treatment of a disease or condition; and

"(iii) enabling such health care professional to independently review the basis for such recommendations that such software presents so that it is not the intent that such health care professional rely primarily on any of such recommendations to make a clinical diagnosis or treatment decision regarding an individual patient.

"(2) In the case of a product with multiple functions that contains—

"(A) at least one software function that meets the criteria under paragraph (1) or that otherwise does not meet the definition of device under section 201(h); and .

"(B) at least one function that does not meet the criteria under paragraph (1) and that otherwise meets the definition of a device under section 201(h),

the Secretary shall not regulate the software function of such product described in subparagraph (A) as a device. Notwithstanding the preceding sentence, when assessing the safety and effectiveness of the device function or functions of such product described in subparagraph (B), the Secretary may assess the impact that the software function or functions described in subparagraph (A) have on such device function or functions.

"(3)(A) Notwithstanding paragraph (1), a software function described in subparagraph (C), (D), or (E) of paragraph (1) shall not be excluded from the definition of device under section 201(h) if—

"(i) the Secretary makes a finding that use of such software function would be reasonably likely to have serious adverse health consequences; and

"(ii) the software function has been identified in a final order issued by the Secretary under subparagraph (B).

"(B) Subparagraph (A) shall apply only if the Secretary—

"(i) publishes a notification and proposed order in the Federal Register;

"(ii) includes in such notification the Secretary's finding, including the rationale and identification of the evidence on which such finding was based, as described in subparagraph (A)(i); and

"(iii) provides for a period of not less than 30 calendar days for public comment before issuing a final order or withdrawing such proposed order.

"(C) In making a finding under subparagraph (A)(i) with respect to a software function, the Secretary shall consider—

"(i) the likelihood and severity of patient harm if the software function were to not perform as intended;

"(ii) the extent to which the software function is intended to support the clinical judgment of a health care professional;

"(iii) whether there is a reasonable opportunity for a health care professional to review the basis of the information or treatment recommendation provided by the software function; and

"(iv) the intended user and user environment, such as whether a health care professional will use a software function of a type described in subparagraph (E) of paragraph (1).

"(4) Nothing in this subsection shall be construed as limiting the authority of the Secretary to—

"(A) exercise enforcement discretion as to any device subject to regulation under this Act;

"(B) regulate software used in the manufacture and transfusion of blood and blood components to assist in the prevention of disease in humans; or

"(C) regulate software as a device under this Act if such software meets the criteria under section 513(a)(1)(C).".

(b) REPORTS.—The Secretary of Health and Human Services (referred to in this subsection as the "Secretary"), after consultation with agencies and offices of the Department of Health and Human Services involved in health information technology, shall publish a report, not later than 2 years after the date of enactment of this Act and every 2 years thereafter, that—

(1) includes input from outside experts, such as representatives of patients, consumers, health care providers, startup companies, health plans or other third-party payers, venture capital investors, information technology vendors, health information technology vendors, small businesses, purchasers, employers, and other stakeholders with relevant expertise, as determined by the Secretary;

(2) examines information available to the Secretary on any risks and benefits to health associated with software functions described in section 520(o)(1) of the Federal Food, Drug, and Cosmetic Act (21 U.S.C. 360j) (as amended by subsection (a)); and

(3) summarizes findings regarding the impact of such software functions on patient safety, including best practices to promote safety, education, and competency related to such functions.

(c) CLASSIFICATION OF ACCESSORIES.—Section 513(b) of the Federal Food, Drug, and Cosmetic Act (21 U.S.C. 360c(b)) is amended by adding at the end the following:

"(9) The Secretary shall classify an accessory under this section based on the intended use of the accessory, notwithstanding the classification of any other device with which such accessory is intended to be used.".

(d) CONFORMING AMENDMENT.—Section 201(h) of the Federal Food, Drug, and Cosmetic Act (21 U.S.C. 321(h)) is amended by adding at the end the following: "The term 'device' does not include software functions excluded pursuant to section 520(o).".

Subtitle G—Improving Scientific Expertise and Outreach at FDA

SEC. 3071. SILVIO O. CONTE SENIOR BIOMEDICAL RESEARCH AND BIOMEDICAL PRODUCT ASSESSMENT SERVICE.

(a) HIRING AND RETENTION AUTHORITY.—Section 228 of the Public Health Service Act (42 U.S.C. 237) is amended—

(1) in the section heading, by inserting "**AND BIOMEDICAL PRODUCT ASSESSMENT**" after "**RESEARCH**";

(2) in subsection (a)—

(A) in paragraph (1), by striking "Silvio O. Conte Senior Biomedical Research Service, not to exceed 500 members" and inserting "Silvio O. Conte Senior Biomedical Research and Biomedical Product Assessment Service (in this section referred to as the 'Service'), not to exceed 2,000 members, the purpose of which is to recruit and retain outstanding and qualified scientific and technical experts in the fields of biomedical research, clinical research evaluation, and biomedical product assessment";

(B) by amending paragraph (2) to read as follows:

"(2) The authority established in paragraph (1) may not be construed to require the Secretary to reduce the number of employees serving under any other employment system in order to offset the number of members serving in the Service."; and

(C) by adding at the end the following:

"(3) The Secretary shall assign experts under this section to agencies within the Department of Health and Human Services taking into account the need for the expertise of such expert.";

(3) in subsection (b)—

(A) in the matter preceding paragraph (1), by striking "or clinical research evaluation" and inserting ", clinical research evaluation, or biomedical product assessment"; and

(B) in paragraph (1), by inserting "or a doctoral or master's level degree in engineering, bioinformatics, or a related or emerging field," after the comma;

(4) in subsection (d)(2), by striking "and shall not exceed the rate payable for level I of the Executive Schedule unless approved by the President under section 5377(d)(2) of title 5, United States Code" and inserting "and shall not exceed the amount of annual compensation (excluding expenses) specified in section 102 of title 3, United States Code";

(5) by striking subsection (e); and

(6) by redesignating subsections (f) and (g) as subsections (e) and (f), respectively.

(b) GAO STUDY.—

(1) IN GENERAL.—The Comptroller General of the United States shall conduct a study of the effectiveness of the amendments to section 228 of the Public Health Service Act (42 U.S.C. 237) made by subsection (a) and the impact of such amendments, if any, on all agencies or departments of the Department of Health and Human Services, and, not later than 4 years after the date of enactment of this Act, shall submit a report based on such study to the Committee on Health, Education, Labor, and Pensions of the Senate and the Committee on Energy and Commerce of the House of Representatives.

(2) CONTENT OF STUDY AND REPORT.—The study and report under paragraph (1) shall include an examination of the extent to which recruitment and retention of outstanding and qualified scientific, medical, or technical experts in the fields of biomedical research, clinical research evaluation, and biomedical product assessment have improved or otherwise have been affected by the amendments to section 228 of the Public Health Service Act (42 U.S.C. 237) made by subsection (a), including by determining, during the period between the date of enactment of this Act and the completion of the study—

(A) the total number of members recruited and retained under the Senior Biomedical Research and Biomedical Product Assessment Service under such section 228, and the effect of increasing the number of members eligible for such Service;

(B) the number of members of such Senior Biomedical Research and Biomedical Product Assessment Service hired with a doctoral level degree in biomedicine or a related field, and the number of such members hired with a doctoral or master's level degree in engineering, bioinformatics, or a related or emerging field; and

(C) the number of Senior Biomedical Research and Biomedical Product Assessment Service members that have been hired by each agency or department of the Department of Health and Human Services, and how such Department assigns such members to each agency or department.

SEC. 3072. HIRING AUTHORITY FOR SCIENTIFIC, TECHNICAL, AND PROFESSIONAL PERSONNEL.

(a) IN GENERAL.—The Federal Food, Drug, and Cosmetic Act is amended by inserting after section 714 (21 U.S.C. 379d–3) the following:

"SEC. 714A. HIRING AUTHORITY FOR SCIENTIFIC, TECHNICAL, AND PROFESSIONAL PERSONNEL.

"(a) IN GENERAL.—The Secretary may, notwithstanding title 5, United States Code, governing appointments in the competitive service, appoint outstanding and qualified candidates to scientific, technical, or professional positions that support the development, review, and regulation of medical products. Such positions shall be within the competitive service.

"(b) COMPENSATION.—

"(1) IN GENERAL.—Notwithstanding any other provision of law, including any requirement with respect to General Schedule pay rates under subchapter III of chapter 53 of title 5, United States Code, and consistent with the requirements of paragraph (2), the Commissioner of Food and Drugs may determine and set—

"(A) the annual rate of pay of any individual appointed under subsection (a); and

"(B) for purposes of retaining qualified employees, the annual rate of pay for any qualified scientific, technical, or professional personnel appointed to a position described in subsection (a) before the date of enactment of the 21st Century Cures Act.

"(2) LIMITATION.—The annual rate of pay established pursuant to paragraph (1) may not exceed the amount of annual compensation (excluding expenses) specified in section 102 of title 3, United States Code.

"(3) PUBLIC AVAILABILITY.—The annual rate of pay provided to an individual in accordance with this section shall be publicly available information.

"(c) RULE OF CONSTRUCTION.—The authorities under this section shall not be construed to affect the authority provided under section 714.

"(d) REPORT ON WORKFORCE PLANNING.—

"(1) IN GENERAL.—Not later than 18 months after the date of enactment of the 21st Century Cures Act, the Secretary shall submit a report on workforce planning to the Committee on Health, Education, Labor, and Pensions of the Senate and the Committee on Energy and Commerce of the House of Representatives that examines the extent to which the Food and Drug Administration has a critical need for qualified individuals for scientific, technical, or professional positions, including—

"(A) an analysis of the workforce needs at the Food and Drug Administration and the Secretary's strategic plan for addressing such needs, including through use of the authority under this section; and

"(B) a recruitment and retention plan for hiring qualified scientific, technical, and professional candidates, which may include the use of—

"(i) recruitment through nongovernmental recruitment or placement agencies;

"(ii) recruitment through academic institutions;

"(iii) recruitment or hiring bonuses, if applicable;

"(iv) recruitment using targeted direct hiring authorities; and

"(v) retention of qualified scientific, technical, and professional employees using the authority under this section, or other applicable authorities of the Secretary.

"(2) RECOMMENDATIONS.—The report under paragraph (1) may include the recommendations of the Commissioner of Food and Drugs that would help the Food and Drug Administration to better recruit and retain qualified individuals for scientific, technical, or professional positions at the agency.".

(b) GAO STUDY AND REPORT.—

(1) IN GENERAL.—The Comptroller General of the United States shall conduct a study of the ability of the Food and Drug Administration to hire, train, and retain qualified scientific, technical, and professional staff, not including contractors, necessary to fulfill the mission of the Food and Drug Administration to protect and promote public health. Not later than January 1, 2022, the Comptroller General shall submit a report on such study to the Committee on Health, Education, Labor, and Pensions of the Senate and the Committee on Energy and Commerce of the House of Representatives.

(2) CONTENTS OF STUDY.—The Comptroller General shall include in the study and report under paragraph (1)—

(A) information about the progress of the Food and Drug Administration in recruiting and retaining qualified scientific, technical, and professional staff outstanding in the field of biomedical research, clinical research evaluation, and biomedical product assessment;

(B) the extent to which critical staffing needs exist at the Food and Drug Administration, and barriers to hiring, training, and retaining qualified staff, if any;

(C) an examination of the recruitment and retention strategies of the Food and Drug Administration, including examining any strategic workforce plan, focused on improving scientific, technical, and professional staff recruitment and retention; and

(D) recommendations for potential improvements that would address staffing needs of the Food and Drug Administration.

SEC. 3073. ESTABLISHMENT OF FOOD AND DRUG ADMINISTRATION INTERCENTER INSTITUTES.

(a) IN GENERAL.—Chapter X of the Federal Food, Drug, and Cosmetic Act (21 U.S.C. 391 et seq.) is amended by adding at the end the following:

"SEC. 1014. FOOD AND DRUG ADMINISTRATION INTERCENTER INSTITUTES.

"(a) IN GENERAL.—The Secretary shall establish one or more Intercenter Institutes within the Food and Drug Administration (referred to in this section as an 'Institute') for a major disease area or areas. With respect to the major disease area of focus of an Institute, such Institute shall develop and implement processes for coordination of activities, as applicable to such major disease area or areas, among the Center for Drug Evaluation and Research, the Center for Biologics Evaluation and Research, and the Center for Devices and Radiological Health (for the purposes of this section, referred to as the 'Centers'). Such activities may include—

"(1) coordination of staff from the Centers with diverse product expertise in the diagnosis, cure, mitigation, treatment, or prevention of the specific diseases relevant to the major disease area of focus of the Institute;

"(2) streamlining, where appropriate, the review of medical products to diagnose, cure, mitigate, treat, or prevent the specific diseases relevant to the major disease area of focus of the Institute, applying relevant standards under sections 505, 510(k), 513(f)(2), and 515 of this Act and section 351 of the Public Health Service Act, and other applicable authorities;

"(3) promotion of scientific programs within the Centers related to the major disease area of focus of the Institute;

"(4) development of programs and enhancement of strategies to recruit, train, and provide continuing education opportunities for the personnel of the Centers with expertise related to the major disease area of focus of the Institute;

"(5) enhancement of the interactions of the Centers with patients, sponsors, and the external biomedical community regarding the major disease area of focus of the Institute; and

"(6) facilitation of the collaborative relationships of the Centers with other agencies within the Department of Health and Human Services regarding the major disease area of focus of the Institute.

"(b) PUBLIC PROCESS.—The Secretary shall provide a period for public comment during the time that each Institute is being implemented.

"(c) TIMING.—The Secretary shall establish at least one Institute under subsection (a) before the date that is 1 year after the date of enactment of the 21st Century Cures Act.

"(d) TERMINATION OF INSTITUTES.—The Secretary may terminate any Institute established pursuant to this section if the Secretary determines such Institute is no longer benefitting the public health. Not less than 60 days prior to so

terminating an Institute, the Secretary shall provide public notice, including the rationale for such termination.".

(b) TECHNICAL AMENDMENTS.—Chapter X of the Federal Food, Drug, and Cosmetic Act (21 U.S.C. 391 et seq.) is amended—

(1) by redesignating section 1012 as section 1013; and

(2) by redesignating the second section 1011 (with respect to improving the training of State, local, territorial, and tribal food safety officials), as added by section 209(a) of the FDA Food Safety Modernization Act (Public Law 111–353), as section 1012.

SEC. 3074. SCIENTIFIC ENGAGEMENT.

(a) IN GENERAL.—Scientific meetings that are attended by scientific or medical personnel, or other professionals, of the Department of Health and Human Services for whom attendance at such meeting is directly related to their professional duties and the mission of the Department—

(1) shall not be considered conferences for the purposes of complying with Federal reporting requirements contained in annual appropriations Acts or in this section; and

(2) shall not be considered conferences for purposes of a restriction contained in an annual appropriations Act, based on Office of Management and Budget Memorandum M-12-12 or any other regulation restricting travel to such meeting.

(b) LIMITATION.—Nothing in this section shall be construed to exempt travel for scientific meetings from Federal regulations relating to travel.

(c) REPORTS.—Not later than 90 days after the end of the fiscal year, each operating division of the Department of Health and Human Services shall prepare, and post on an Internet website of the operating division, an annual report on scientific meeting attendance and related travel spending for each fiscal year. Such report shall include—

(1) general information concerning the scientific meeting activities involved;

(2) information concerning the total amount expended for such meetings;

(3) a description of all such meetings that were attended by scientific or medical personnel, or other professionals, of each such operating division where the total amount expended by the operating division associated with each such meeting were in excess of $30,000, including—

(A) the total amount of meeting expenses incurred by the operating division for such meeting;

(B) the location of such meeting;

(C) the date of such meeting;

(D) a brief explanation on how such meeting advanced the mission of the operating division; and

(E) the total number of individuals whose travel expenses or other scientific meeting expenses were paid by the operating division; and

(4) with respect to any such meeting where the total expenses to the operating division exceeded $150,000, a description of the exceptional circumstances that necessitated the expenditure of such amounts.

SEC. 3075. DRUG SURVEILLANCE.

(a) NEW DRUGS.—Section 505(k)(5) of the Federal Food, Drug, and Cosmetic Act (21 U.S.C. 355(k)(5)), as amended by section 2074, is further amended—

(1) in subparagraph (A), by striking ", biweekly screening" and inserting "screenings";

(2) in subparagraph (B), as redesignated by section 2074(1)(C), by striking the period at the end and inserting "; and"; and

(3) by adding at the end the following:

"(C) make available on the Internet website of the Food and Drug Administration—

"(i) guidelines, developed with input from experts qualified by scientific training and experi-

ence to evaluate the safety and effectiveness of drugs, that detail best practices for drug safety surveillance using the Adverse Event Reporting System; and

"(ii) criteria for public posting of adverse event signals.".

(b) FAERS REVISION.—Section 505(r)(2)(D) of the Federal Food, Drug, and Cosmetic Act (21 U.S.C. 355(r)(2)(D)) is amended by striking ", by 18 months" and all that follows through the semicolon at the end of the subparagraph and inserting "and making publicly available on the Internet website established under paragraph (1) best practices for drug safety surveillance activities for drugs approved under this section or section 351 of the Public Health Service Act;".

(c) RISK EVALUATION AND MITIGATION STRATEGIES.—Section 505–1(f)(5) of the Federal Food, Drug, and Cosmetic Act (21 U.S.C. 355–1(f)(5)) is amended—

(1) in the matter preceding subparagraph (A), by inserting "or other advisory committee" after "(or successor committee)"; and

(2) in subparagraph (B), by striking "at least annually," and inserting "periodically".

SEC. 3076. REAGAN-UDALL FOUNDATION FOR THE FOOD AND DRUG ADMINISTRATION.

(a) BOARD OF DIRECTORS.—

(1) COMPOSITION AND SIZE.—Section 770(d)(1)(C) of the Federal Food, Drug, and Cosmetic Act (21 U.S.C. 379dd(d)(1)(C)) is amended—

(A) by redesignating clause (ii) as clause (iii);

(B) by inserting after clause (i) the following:

"(ii) ADDITIONAL MEMBERS.—The Board, through amendments to the bylaws of the Foundation, may provide that the number of voting members of the Board shall be a number (to be specified in such amendment) greater than 14. Any Board positions that are established by any such amendment shall be appointed (by majority vote) by the individuals who, as of the date of such amendment, are voting members of the Board and persons so appointed may represent any of the categories specified in subclauses (I) through (V) of clause (i), so long as no more than 30 percent of the total voting members of the Board (including members whose positions are established by such amendment) are representatives of the general pharmaceutical, device, food, cosmetic, and biotechnology industries."; and

(C) in clause (iii)(I), as redesignated by subparagraph (A), by striking "The ex officio members shall ensure" and inserting "The ex officio members, acting pursuant to clause (i), and the Board, acting pursuant to clause (ii), shall ensure".

(2) FEDERAL EMPLOYEES ALLOWED TO SERVE ON BOARD.—Clause (iii)(II) of section 770(d)(1)(C) of the Federal Food, Drug, and Cosmetic Act (21 U.S.C. 379dd(d)(1)(C)), as redesignated by paragraph (1)(A), is amended by adding at the end the following: "For purposes of this section, the term 'employee of the Federal Government' does not include a special Government employee, as that term is defined in section 202(a) of title 18, United States Code.".

(3) STAGGERED TERMS.—Subparagraph (A) of section 770(d)(3) of the Federal Food, Drug, and Cosmetic Act (21 U.S.C. 379dd(d)(3)) is amended to read as follows:

"(A) TERM.—The term of office of each member of the Board appointed under paragraph (1)(C)(i), and the term of office of any member of the Board whose position is established pursuant to paragraph (1)(C)(ii), shall be 4 years, except that—

"(i) the terms of offices for the members of the Board initially appointed under paragraph (1)(C)(i) shall expire on a staggered basis as determined by the ex officio members; and

"(ii) the terms of office for the persons initially appointed to positions established pursu-

ant to paragraph (1)(C)(ii) may be made to expire on a staggered basis, as determined by the individuals who, as of the date of the amendment establishing such positions, are members of the Board.".

(b) EXECUTIVE DIRECTOR COMPENSATION.—Section 770(g)(2) of the Federal Food, Drug, and Cosmetic Act (21 U.S.C. 379dd(g)(2)) is amended by striking "but shall not be greater than the compensation of the Commissioner".

(c) SEPARATION OF FUNDS.—Section 770(m) of the Federal Food, Drug, and Cosmetic Act (21 U.S.C. 379dd(m)) is amended by striking "are held in separate accounts from funds received from entities under subsection (i)" and inserting "are managed as individual programmatic funds under subsection (i), according to best accounting practices".

Subtitle H—Medical Countermeasures Innovation

SEC. 3081. MEDICAL COUNTERMEASURE GUIDELINES.

Section 319F–2 of the Public Health Service Act (42 U.S.C. 247d–6b) is amended—

(1) in subsection (a), by adding at the end the following:

"(3) UTILIZATION GUIDELINES.—The Secretary shall ensure timely and accurate recommended utilization guidelines for qualified countermeasures (as defined in section 319F–1), qualified pandemic and epidemic products (as defined in section 319F–3), and security countermeasures (as defined in subsection (c)), including for such products in the stockpile."; and

(2) in subsection (g)—

(A) by amending paragraph (4) to read as follows:

"(4) REPORT ON SECURITY COUNTERMEASURE PROCUREMENT.—Not later than March 1 of each year in which the Secretary determines that the amount of funds available for procurement of security countermeasures is less than $1,500,000,000, the Secretary shall submit to the Committee on Appropriations and the Committee on Health, Education, Labor, and Pensions of the Senate and the Committee on Appropriations and the Committee on Energy and Commerce of the House of Representatives a report detailing the amount of such funds available for procurement and the impact such amount of funding will have—

"(A) in meeting the security countermeasure needs identified under this section; and

"(B) on the annual Public Health Emergency Medical Countermeasures Enterprise and Strategy Implementation Plan (pursuant to section 2811(d)).".

SEC. 3082. CLARIFYING BARDA CONTRACTING AUTHORITY.

(a) IN GENERAL.—Section 319F–2(g) of the Public Health Service Act (42 U.S.C. 247d–6b(g)) is amended by adding at the end the following:

"(5) CLARIFICATION ON CONTRACTING AUTHORITY.—The Secretary, acting through the Director of the Biomedical Advanced Research and Development Authority, shall carry out the programs funded by the special reserve fund (for the procurement of security countermeasures under subsection (c) and for carrying out section 319L), including the execution of procurement contracts, grants, and cooperative agreements pursuant to this section and section 319L.".

(b) BARDA CONTRACTING AUTHORITY.—Section 319L(c)(3) of the Public Health Service Act (42 U.S.C. 247d–7c) is amended by inserting ", including the execution of procurement contracts, grants, and cooperative agreements pursuant to this section" before the period.

SEC. 3083. COUNTERMEASURE BUDGET PLAN.

Section 2811(b)(7) of the Public Health Service Act (42 U.S.C. 300hh–10(b)(7)) is amended—

(1) in the matter preceding subparagraph (A), by striking the first sentence and inserting "Develop, and update not later than March 1 of

each year, a coordinated 5-year budget plan based on the medical countermeasure priorities described in subsection (d), including with respect to chemical, biological, radiological, and nuclear agent or agents that may present a threat to the Nation, including such agents that are novel or emerging infectious diseases, and the corresponding efforts to develop qualified countermeasures (as defined in section 319F–1), security countermeasures (as defined in section 319F–2), and qualified pandemic or epidemic products (as defined in section 319F–3) for each such threat.'';

(2) in subparagraph (C), by striking ''; and'' and inserting a semicolon;

(3) in subparagraph (D), by striking ''to the appropriate committees of Congress upon request.'' and inserting '', not later than March 15 of each year, to the Committee on Appropriations and the Committee on Health, Education, Labor, and Pensions of the Senate and the Committee on Appropriations and the Committee on Energy and Commerce of the House of Representatives; and''; and

(4) by adding at the end the following:

''(E) not later than March 15 of each year, be made publicly available in a manner that does not compromise national security.''.

SEC. 3084. MEDICAL COUNTERMEASURES INNOVATION.

Section 319L(c)(4) of the Public Health Service Act (42 U.S.C. 247d–7e(c)(4)) is amended by adding at the end the following:

''(E) MEDICAL COUNTERMEASURES INNOVATION PARTNER.—

''(i) IN GENERAL.—To support the purposes described in paragraph (2), the Secretary, acting through the Director of BARDA, may enter into an agreement (including through the use of grants, contracts, cooperative agreements, or other transactions as described in paragraph (5)) with an independent, nonprofit entity to—

''(I) foster and accelerate the development and innovation of medical countermeasures and technologies that may assist advanced research and the development of qualified countermeasures and qualified pandemic or epidemic products, including through the use of strategic venture capital practices and methods;

''(II) promote the development of new and promising technologies that address urgent medical countermeasure needs, as identified by the Secretary;

''(III) address unmet public health needs that are directly related to medical countermeasure requirements, such as novel antimicrobials for multidrug resistant organisms and multiuse platform technologies for diagnostics, prophylaxis, vaccines, and therapeutics; and

''(IV) provide expert consultation and advice to foster viable medical countermeasure innovators, including helping qualified countermeasure innovators navigate unique industry challenges with respect to developing chemical, biological, radiological, and nuclear countermeasure products.

''(ii) ELIGIBILITY.—

''(I) IN GENERAL.—To be eligible to enter into an agreement under clause (i) an entity shall—

''(aa) be an independent, nonprofit entity;

''(bb) have a demonstrated record of being able to create linkages between innovators and investors and leverage such partnerships and resources for the purpose of addressing identified strategic needs of the Federal Government;

''(cc) have experience in promoting novel technology innovation;

''(dd) be problem-driven and solution-focused based on the needs, requirements, and problems identified by the Secretary under clause (iv);

''(ee) demonstrate the ability, or the potential ability, to promote the development of medical countermeasure products;

''(ff) demonstrate expertise, or the capacity to develop or acquire expertise, related to technical

and regulatory considerations with respect to medical countermeasures; and

''(gg) not be within the Department of Health and Human Services.

''(II) PARTNERING EXPERIENCE.—In selecting an entity with which to enter into an agreement under clause (i), the Secretary shall place a high value on the demonstrated experience of the entity in partnering with the Federal Government to meet identified strategic needs.

''(iii) NOT AGENCY.—An entity that enters into an agreement under clause (i) shall not be deemed to be a Federal agency for any purpose, including for any purpose under title 5, United States Code.

''(iv) DIRECTION.—Pursuant to an agreement entered into under this subparagraph, the Secretary, acting through the Director of BARDA, shall provide direction to the entity that enters into an agreement under clause (i). As part of this agreement the Director of BARDA shall—

''(I) communicate the medical countermeasure needs, requirements, and problems to be addressed by the entity under the agreement;

''(II) develop a description of work to be performed by the entity under the agreement;

''(III) provide technical feedback and appropriate oversight over work carried out by the entity under the agreement, including subsequent development and partnerships consistent with the needs and requirements set forth in this subparagraph;

''(IV) ensure fair consideration of products developed under the agreement in order to maintain competition to the maximum practical extent, as applicable and appropriate under applicable provisions of this section; and

''(V) ensure, as a condition of the agreement that the entity—

''(aa) has in place a comprehensive set of policies that demonstrate a commitment to transparency and accountability;

''(bb) protects against conflicts of interest through a comprehensive set of policies that address potential conflicts of interest, ethics, disclosure, and reporting requirements;

''(cc) provides monthly accounting on the use of funds provided under such agreement; and

''(dd) provides on a quarterly basis, reports regarding the progress made toward meeting the identified needs set forth in the agreement.

''(v) SUPPLEMENT NOT SUPPLANT.—Activities carried out under this subparagraph shall supplement, and not supplant, other activities carried out under this section.

''(vi) NO ESTABLISHMENT OF ENTITY.—To prevent unnecessary duplication and target resources effectively, nothing in this subparagraph shall be construed to authorize the Secretary to establish within the Department of Health and Human Services an entity for the purposes of carrying out this subparagraph.

''(vii) TRANSPARENCY AND OVERSIGHT.—Upon request, the Secretary shall provide to Congress the information provided to the Secretary under clause (iv)(V)(dd).

''(viii) INDEPENDENT EVALUATION.—Not later than 4 years after the date of enactment of the 21st Century Cures Act, the Comptroller General of the United States shall conduct an independent evaluation, and submit to the Secretary and the appropriate committees of Congress a report, concerning the activities conducted under this subparagraph. Such report shall include recommendations with respect to any agreement or activities carried out pursuant to this subparagraph.

''(ix) SUNSET.—This subparagraph shall have no force or effect after September 30, 2022.''.

SEC. 3085. STREAMLINING PROJECT BIOSHIELD PROCUREMENT.

Section 319F–2(c) of the Public Health Service Act (42 U.S.C. 247d–6b(c)) is amended—

(1) in paragraph (4)(A)(ii), by striking ''make a recommendation under paragraph (6) that the

special reserve fund as defined in subsection (h) be made available for the procurement of such countermeasure'' and inserting ''and subject to the availability of appropriations, make available the special reserve fund as defined in subsection (h) for procurement of such countermeasure, as applicable'';

(2) in paragraph (6)—

(A) by striking subparagraphs (A), (B), and (E);

(B) by redesignating subparagraphs (C) and (D) as subparagraphs (A) and (B), respectively;

(C) by amending subparagraph (A), as so redesignated, to read as follows:

''(A) NOTICE TO APPROPRIATE CONGRESSIONAL COMMITTEES.—The Secretary shall notify the Committee on Appropriations and the Committee on Health, Education, Labor, and Pensions of the Senate and the Committee on Appropriations and the Committee on Energy and Commerce of the House of Representatives of each decision to make available the special reserve fund as defined in subsection (h) for procurement of a security countermeasure, including, where available, the number of, the nature of, and other information concerning potential suppliers of such countermeasure, and whether other potential suppliers of the same or similar countermeasures were considered and rejected for procurement under this section and the reasons for each such rejection.''; and

(D) in the heading, by striking ''RECOMMENDATION FOR PRESIDENT'S APPROVAL'' and inserting ''RECOMMENDATIONS FOR PROCUREMENT''; and

(3) in paragraph (7)—

(A) by striking subparagraphs (A) and (B) and inserting the following:

''(A) PAYMENTS FROM SPECIAL RESERVE FUND.—The special reserve fund as defined in subsection (h) shall be available for payments made by the Secretary to a vendor for procurement of a security countermeasure in accordance with the provisions of this paragraph.''; and

(B) by redesignating subparagraph (C) as subparagraph (B).

SEC. 3086. ENCOURAGING TREATMENTS FOR AGENTS THAT PRESENT A NATIONAL SECURITY THREAT.

Subchapter E of chapter V of the Federal Food, Drug, and Cosmetic Act (21 U.S.C. 360bbb et seq.) is amended by inserting after section 565 the following:

''SEC. 565A. PRIORITY REVIEW TO ENCOURAGE TREATMENTS FOR AGENTS THAT PRESENT NATIONAL SECURITY THREATS.

''(a) DEFINITIONS.—In this section:

''(1) HUMAN DRUG APPLICATION.—The term 'human drug application' has the meaning given such term in section 735(1).

''(2) PRIORITY REVIEW.—The term 'priority review', with respect to a human drug application, means review and action by the Secretary on such application not later than 6 months after receipt by the Secretary of such application, as described in the Manual of Policies and Procedures in the Food and Drug Administration and goals identified in the letters described in section 101(b) of the Food and Drug Administration Safety and Innovation Act.

''(3) PRIORITY REVIEW VOUCHER.—The term 'priority review voucher' means a voucher issued by the Secretary to the sponsor of a material threat medical countermeasure application that entitles the holder of such voucher to priority review of a single human drug application submitted under section 505(b)(1) or section 351(a) of the Public Health Service Act after the date of approval of the material threat medical countermeasure application.

''(4) MATERIAL THREAT MEDICAL COUNTERMEASURE APPLICATION.—The term 'material threat medical countermeasure application' means an application that—

"(A) is a human drug application for a drug intended for use—

"(i) to prevent, or treat harm from a biological, chemical, radiological, or nuclear agent identified as a material threat under section 319F–2(c)(2)(A)(ii) of the Public Health Service Act; or

"(ii) to mitigate, prevent, or treat harm from a condition that may result in adverse health consequences or death and may be caused by administering a drug, or biological product against such agent; and

"(B) the Secretary determines eligible for priority review;

"(C) is approved after the date of enactment of the 21st Century Cures Act; and

"(D) is for a human drug, no active ingredient (including any ester or salt of the active ingredient) of which has been approved in any other application under section 505(b)(1) or section 351(a) of the Public Health Service Act.

"(b) PRIORITY REVIEW VOUCHER.—

"(1) IN GENERAL.—The Secretary shall award a priority review voucher to the sponsor of a material threat medical countermeasure application upon approval by the Secretary of such material threat medical countermeasure application.

"(2) TRANSFERABILITY.—The sponsor of a material threat medical countermeasure application that receives a priority review voucher under this section may transfer (including by sale) the entitlement to such voucher to a sponsor of a human drug for which an application under section 505(b)(1) or section 351(a) of the Public Health Service Act will be submitted after the date of the approval of the material threat medical countermeasure application. There is no limit on the number of times a priority review voucher may be transferred before such voucher is used.

"(3) NOTIFICATION.—

"(A) IN GENERAL.—The sponsor of a human drug application shall notify the Secretary not later than 90 calendar days prior to submission of the human drug application that is the subject of a priority review voucher of an intent to submit the human drug application, including the date on which the sponsor intends to submit the application. Such notification shall be a legally binding commitment to pay for the user fee to be assessed in accordance with this section.

"(B) TRANSFER AFTER NOTICE.—The sponsor of a human drug application that provides notification of the intent of such sponsor to use the voucher for the human drug application under subparagraph (A) may transfer the voucher after such notification is provided, if such sponsor has not yet submitted the human drug application described in the notification.

"(c) PRIORITY REVIEW USER FEE.—

"(1) IN GENERAL.—The Secretary shall establish a user fee program under which a sponsor of a human drug application that is the subject of a priority review voucher shall pay to the Secretary a fee determined under paragraph (2). Such fee shall be in addition to any fee required to be submitted by the sponsor under chapter VII.

"(2) FEE AMOUNT.—The amount of the priority review user fee shall be determined each fiscal year by the Secretary and based on the average cost incurred by the agency in the review of a human drug application subject to priority review in the previous fiscal year.

"(3) ANNUAL FEE SETTING.—The Secretary shall establish, before the beginning of each fiscal year beginning after September 30, 2016, for that fiscal year, the amount of the priority review user fee.

"(4) PAYMENT.—

"(A) IN GENERAL.—The priority review user fee required by this subsection shall be due upon the submission of a human drug application under section 505(b)(1) or section 351(a) of the Public Health Service Act for which the priority review voucher is used.

"(B) COMPLETE APPLICATION.—An application described under subparagraph (A) for which the sponsor requests the use of a priority review voucher shall be considered incomplete if the fee required by this subsection and all other applicable user fees are not paid in accordance with the Secretary's procedures for paying such fees.

"(C) NO WAIVERS, EXEMPTIONS, REDUCTIONS, OR REFUNDS.—The Secretary may not grant a waiver, exemption, reduction, or refund of any fees due and payable under this section.

"(5) OFFSETTING COLLECTIONS.—Fees collected pursuant to this subsection for any fiscal year—

"(A) shall be deposited and credited as offsetting collections to the account providing appropriations to the Food and Drug Administration; and

"(6) shall not be collected for any fiscal year except to the extent provided in advance in appropriation Acts.

"(d) NOTICE OF ISSUANCE OF VOUCHER AND APPROVAL OF PRODUCTS UNDER VOUCHER.—The Secretary shall publish a notice in the Federal Register and on the Internet website of the Food and Drug Administration not later than 30 calendar days after the occurrence of each of the following:

"(1) The Secretary issues a priority review voucher under this section.

"(2) The Secretary approves a drug pursuant to an application submitted under section 505(b) of this Act or section 351(a) of the Public Health Service Act for which the sponsor of the application used a priority review voucher issued under this section.

"(e) ELIGIBILITY FOR OTHER PROGRAMS.—Nothing in this section precludes a sponsor who seeks a priority review voucher under this section from participating in any other incentive program, including under this Act, except that no sponsor of a material threat medical countermeasure application may receive more than one priority review voucher issued under any section of this Act with respect to such drug.

"(f) RELATION TO OTHER PROVISIONS.—The provisions of this section shall supplement, not supplant, any other provisions of this Act or the Public Health Service Act that encourage the development of medical countermeasures.

"(g) SUNSET.—The Secretary may not award any priority review vouchers under subsection (b) after October 1, 2023.".

SEC. 3087. PAPERWORK REDUCTION ACT WAIVER DURING A PUBLIC HEALTH EMERGENCY.

Section 319 of the Public Health Service Act (42 U.S.C. 247d) is amended by adding at the end the following:

"(f) DETERMINATION WITH RESPECT TO PAPERWORK REDUCTION ACT WAIVER DURING A PUBLIC HEALTH EMERGENCY.—

"(1) DETERMINATION.—If the Secretary determines, after consultation with such public health officials as may be necessary, that—

"(A)(i) the criteria set forth for a public health emergency under paragraph (1) or (2) of subsection (a) has been met; or

"(ii) a disease or disorder, including a novel and emerging public health threat, is significantly likely to become a public health emergency; and

"(B) the circumstances of such public health emergency, or potential for such significantly likely public health emergency, including the specific preparation for and response to such public health emergency or threat, necessitate a waiver from the requirements of subchapter I of chapter 35 of title 44, United States Code (commonly referred to as the Paperwork Reduction Act),

then the requirements of such subchapter I with respect to voluntary collection of information shall not be applicable during the immediate investigation of, and response to, such public health emergency during the period of such public health emergency or the period of time necessary to determine if a disease or disorder, including a novel and emerging public health threat, will become a public health emergency as provided for in this paragraph. The requirements of such subchapter I with respect to voluntary collection of information shall not be applicable during the immediate postresponse review regarding such public health emergency if such immediate postresponse review does not exceed a reasonable length of time.

"(2) TRANSPARENCY.—If the Secretary determines that a waiver is necessary under paragraph (1), the Secretary shall promptly post on the Internet website of the Department of Health and Human Services a brief justification for such waiver, the anticipated period of time such waiver will be in effect, and the agencies and offices within the Department of Health and Human Services to which such waiver shall apply, and update such information posted on the Internet website of the Department of Health and Human Services, as applicable.

"(3) EFFECTIVENESS OF WAIVER.—Any waiver under this subsection shall take effect on the date on which the Secretary posts information on the Internet website as provided for in this subsection.

"(4) TERMINATION OF WAIVER.—Upon determining that the circumstances necessitating a waiver under paragraph (1) no longer exist, the Secretary shall promptly update the Internet website of the Department of Health and Human Services to reflect the termination of such waiver.

"(5) LIMITATIONS.—

"(A) PERIOD OF WAIVER.—The period of a waiver under paragraph (1) shall not exceed the period of time for the related public health emergency, including a public health emergency declared pursuant to subsection (a), and any immediate postresponse review regarding the public health emergency consistent with the requirements of this subsection.

"(B) SUBSEQUENT COMPLIANCE.—An initiative subject to a waiver under paragraph (1) that is ongoing after the date on which the waiver expires, shall be subject to the requirements of subchapter I of chapter 35 of title 44, United States Code, and the Secretary shall ensure that compliance with such requirements occurs in as timely a manner as possible based on the applicable circumstances, but not to exceed 30 calendar days after the expiration of the applicable waiver.".

SEC. 3088. CLARIFYING FOOD AND DRUG ADMINISTRATION EMERGENCY USE AUTHORIZATION.

(a) AUTHORIZATION FOR MEDICAL PRODUCTS FOR USE IN EMERGENCIES.—Section 564 of the Federal Food, Drug, and Cosmetic Act (21 U.S.C. 360bbb–3) is amended—

(1) in subsection (a)(2)—

(A) in subparagraph (A)—

(i) by striking "or 515" and inserting "512, or 515"; and

(ii) by inserting "or conditionally approved under section 571 of this Act" after "Public Health Service Act"; and

(B) in subparagraph (B), by inserting "conditionally approved under section 571," after "approved," each place the term appears;

(2) in subsection (b)(4), by striking the second comma after "determination";

(3) in subsection (e)(3)(B), by striking "section 503(b)" and inserting "subsection (b) or (f) of section 503 or under section 504";

(4) in subsection (f)(2)—

(A) by inserting ", or an animal to which," after "to a patient to whom"; and

(B) by inserting "or by the veterinarian caring for such animal, as applicable" after "attending physician";

(5) in subsection (g)(1), by inserting "conditional approval under section 571," after "approval,";

(6) in subsection (h)(1), by striking "or section 520(g)"and inserting "512(j), or 520(g)"; and

(7) in subsection (k), by striking "section 520(g),"and inserting "512(j), or 520(g)".

(b) NEW ANIMAL DRUGS.—Section 512(a)(1) of the Federal Food, Drug, and Cosmetic Act (21 U.S.C. 360b(a)(1)) is amended—

(1) in subparagraph (B), by striking "or" at the end;

(2) in subparagraph (C), by striking the period and inserting "; or"; and

(3) by inserting after subparagraph (C) the following:

"(D) there is in effect an authorization pursuant to section 564 with respect to such use or intended use of such drug, and such drug, its labeling, and such use conform to any conditions of such authorization.".

(c) EMERGENCY USE OF MEDICAL PRODUCTS.—Section 564A of the Federal Food, Drug, and Cosmetic Act (21 U.S.C. 360bbb–3a) is amended—

(1) in subsection (a)(1)(A), by inserting ", conditionally approved under section 571," after "chapter"; and

(2) in subsection (d), by striking "sections 503(b) and 520(e)" and inserting "subsections (b) and (f) of section 503, section 504, and section 520(e)".

(d) PRODUCTS HELD FOR EMERGENCY USE.—Section 564B(2) of the Federal Food, Drug, and Cosmetic Act (21 U.S.C. 360bbb–3b(2)) is amended—

(1) in subparagraph (A)—

(A) by inserting "or conditionally approved under section 571 of this Act" after "Public Health Service Act"; and

(B) by striking "or 515" and inserting "512, or 515"; and

(2) in subparagraph (B), by striking "or 520" and inserting "512, or 520".

Subtitle I—Vaccine Access, Certainty, and Innovation

SEC. 3091. PREDICTABLE REVIEW TIMELINES OF VACCINES BY THE ADVISORY COMMITTEE ON IMMUNIZATION PRACTICES.

(a) CONSIDERATION OF NEW VACCINES.—Upon the licensure of any vaccine or any new indication for a vaccine, the Advisory Committee on Immunization Practices (in this section referred to as the "Advisory Committee") shall, as appropriate, consider the use of the vaccine at its next regularly scheduled meeting.

(b) ADDITIONAL INFORMATION.—If the Advisory Committee does not make a recommendation with respect to the use of a vaccine at the Advisory Committee's first regularly scheduled meeting after the licensure of the vaccine or any new indication for the vaccine, the Advisory Committee shall provide an update on the status of such committee's review.

(c) CONSIDERATION FOR BREAKTHROUGH THERAPIES AND FOR POTENTIAL USE DURING PUBLIC HEALTH EMERGENCY.—The Advisory Committee shall make recommendations with respect to the use of certain vaccines in a timely manner, as appropriate, including vaccines that—

(1) are designated as a breakthrough therapy under section 506 of the Federal Food, Drug, and Cosmetic Act (21 U.S.C. 356) and licensed under section 351 of the Public Health Service Act (42 U.S.C. 262); or

(2) could be used in a public health emergency.

(d) DEFINITION.—In this section, the terms "Advisory Committee on Immunization Practices" and "Advisory Committee" mean the Advisory Committee on Immunization Practices established by the Secretary pursuant to section 222 of the Public Health Service Act (42 U.S.C.

217a), acting through the Director of the Centers for Disease Control and Prevention.".

SEC. 3092. REVIEW OF PROCESSES AND CONSISTENCY OF ADVISORY COMMITTEE ON IMMUNIZATION PRACTICES RECOMMENDATIONS.

(a) REVIEW.—The Director of the Centers for Disease Control and Prevention shall conduct a review of the processes used by the Advisory Committee on Immunization Practices in formulating and issuing recommendations pertaining to vaccines, including with respect to consistency.

(b) CONSIDERATIONS.—The review under subsection (a) shall include an assessment of—

(1) the criteria used to evaluate new and existing vaccines, including the identification of any areas for which flexibility in evaluating such criteria is necessary and the reason for such flexibility;

(2) the Grading of Recommendations, Assessment, Development, and Evaluation (GRADE) approach to the review and analysis of scientific and economic data, including the scientific basis for such approach; and

(3) the extent to which the processes used by the work groups of the Advisory Committee on Immunization Practices are consistent among such groups, including the identification of reasons for any variation.

(c) STAKEHOLDERS.—In carrying out the review under subsection (a), the Director of the Centers for Disease Control and Prevention shall solicit input from vaccine stakeholders.

(d) REPORT.—Not later than 18 months after the date of enactment of this Act, the Director of the Centers for Disease Control and Prevention shall submit to the appropriate committees of the Congress, and make publicly available, a report on the results of the review under subsection (a), including any recommendations on improving the consistency of the processes described in such subsection.

(e) DEFINITION.—In this section, the term "Advisory Committee on Immunization Practices" means the Advisory Committee on Immunization Practices established by the Secretary of Health and Human Services pursuant to section 222 of the Public Health Service Act (42 U.S.C. 217a), acting through the Director of the Centers for Disease Control and Prevention.

SEC. 3093. ENCOURAGING VACCINE INNOVATION.

(a) VACCINE MEETINGS.—The Director of the Centers for Disease Control and Prevention shall ensure that appropriate staff within the relevant centers and divisions of the Office of Infectious Diseases, and others, as appropriate, coordinate with respect to the public health needs, epidemiology, and program planning and implementation considerations related to immunization, including with regard to meetings with stakeholders related to such topics.

(b) REPORT ON VACCINE INNOVATION.—

(1) IN GENERAL.—Not later than 1 year after the date of enactment of this Act, the Secretary of Health and Human Services (referred to in this section as the "Secretary"), in collaboration with appropriate agencies or offices within the Department of Health and Human Services, including the National Institutes of Health, the Centers for Disease Control and Prevention, the Food and Drug Administration, and the Biomedical Advanced Research and Development Authority, shall submit to the Committee on Health, Education, Labor, and Pensions of the Senate and the Committee on Energy and Commerce of the House of Representatives, and post publicly on the Internet website of the Department of Health and Human Services, a report on ways to promote innovation in the development of vaccines that minimize the burden of infectious disease.

(2) CONTENTS.—The report described in paragraph (1) shall review the current status of vaccine development and, as appropriate—

(A) consider the optimal process to determine which vaccines would be beneficial to public health and how information on such vaccines is disseminated to key stakeholders;

(B) examine and identify whether obstacles exist that inhibit the development of beneficial vaccines; and

(C) make recommendations about how best to remove any obstacles identified under subparagraph (B) in order to promote and incentivize vaccine innovation and development.

(3) CONSULTATION.—In preparing the report under this subsection, the Secretary may consult with—

(A) representatives of relevant Federal agencies and departments, including the Department of Defense and the Department of Veterans Affairs;

(B) academic researchers;

(C) developers and manufacturers of vaccines;

(D) medical and public health practitioners;

(E) representatives of patient, policy, and advocacy organizations; and

(F) representatives of other entities, as the Secretary determines appropriate.

(c) UPDATES RELATED TO MATERNAL IMMUNIZATION.—

(1) ADDITIONAL VACCINES.—Section 2114(e) of the Public Health Service Act (42 U.S.C. 300aa–14(e)) is amended by adding at the end the following:

"(3) VACCINES RECOMMENDED FOR USE IN PREGNANT WOMEN.—The Secretary shall revise the Vaccine Injury Table included in subsection (a), through the process described in subsection (c), to include vaccines recommended by the Centers for Disease Control and Prevention for routine administration in pregnant women and the information described in subparagraphs (B) and (C) of paragraph (2) with respect to such vaccines.".

(2) PETITION CONTENT.—Section 2111 of the Public Health Service Act (42 U.S.C. 300aa–11) is amended by adding at the end the following:

"(f) MATERNAL IMMUNIZATION.—

"(1) IN GENERAL.—Notwithstanding any other provision of law, for purposes of this subtitle, both a woman who received a covered vaccine while pregnant and any child who was in utero at the time such woman received the vaccine shall be considered persons to whom the covered vaccine was administered and persons who received the covered vaccine.

"(2) DEFINITION.—As used in this subsection, the term 'child' shall have the meaning given that term by subsections (a) and (b) of section 8 of title 1, United States Code, except that, for purposes of this subsection, such section 8 shall be applied as if the term 'include' in subsection (a) of such section were replaced with the term 'mean'.".

(3) PETITIONERS.—Section 2111(b)(2) of the Public Health Service Act (42 U.S.C. 300aa–11(b)(2)) is amended by adding "A covered vaccine administered to a pregnant woman shall constitute more than one administration, one to the mother and one to each child (as such term is defined in subsection (f)(2)) who was in utero at the time such woman was administered the vaccine." at the end.

Subtitle J—Technical Corrections

SEC. 3101. TECHNICAL CORRECTIONS.

(a) FFDCA.—

(1) REFERENCES.—Except as otherwise expressly provided, whenever in this subsection an amendment is expressed in terms of an amendment to a section or other provision, the reference shall be considered to be made to that section or other provision of the Federal Food, Drug, and Cosmetic Act (21 U.S.C. 301 et seq.).

(2) AMENDMENTS.—

(A) PROHIBITED ACTS.—Section 301(r) (21 U.S.C. 331(r)) is amended by inserting ", drug," after "device" each place the term appears.

(B) NEW DRUGS.—*Section 505 (21 U.S.C. 355) is amended—*

(i) in subsection (d), in the last sentence, by striking "premarket approval" and inserting "marketing approval"; and

(ii) in subsection (q)(5)(A), by striking "subsection (b)(2) or (j) of the Act or 351(k)" and inserting "subsection (b)(2) or (j) of this section or section 351(k)".

(C) RISK EVALUATION AND MITIGATION STRATEGIES.—*Section 505–1(h)(21 U.S.C. 355–1(h)) is amended—*

(i) in paragraph (2)(A)(iii)—

(I) in the clause heading, by striking "LABEL" and inserting "LABELING";

(II) by striking "label" each place the term appears and inserting "labeling"; and

(III) by striking "sponsor" and inserting "responsible person"; and

(ii) in paragraph (8), by striking "and (7)." and inserting "and (7)".

(D) PEDIATRIC STUDY PLANS.—*Section 505B (21 U.S.C. 355c) is amended—*

(i) in subsection (e)—

(I) in paragraph (2)—

(aa) in subparagraph (A), by inserting "study" after "initial pediatric" each place the term appears; and

(bb) in subparagraph (B), in the subparagraph heading, by striking "INITIAL PLAN" and inserting "INITIAL PEDIATRIC STUDY PLAN";

(II) in paragraph (5), in the paragraph heading, by inserting "AGREED INITIAL PEDIATRIC STUDY" before "PLAN"; and

(III) in paragraph (6), by striking "agreed initial pediatric plan" and inserting "agreed initial pediatric study plan"; and

(ii) in subsection (f)(1), by inserting "and any significant amendments to such plans," after "agreed initial pediatric study plans,".

(E) DISCONTINUANCE OR INTERRUPTION IN THE PRODUCTION OF LIVE-SAVING DRUGS.—*Section 506C (21 U.S.C. 356c) is amended—*

(i) in subsection (c), by striking "discontinuation" and inserting "discontinuance"; and

(ii) in subsection (g)(1), by striking "section 505(j) that could help" and inserting "section 505(j), that could help".

(F) ANNUAL REPORTING ON DRUG SHORTAGES.—*Section 506C–1(a) (21 U.S.C. 331(a)) is amended, in the matter before paragraph (1)—*

(i) by striking "Not later than the end of calendar year 2013, and not later than the end of each calendar year thereafter," and inserting "Not later than March 31 of each calendar year,"; and

(ii) by inserting ", with respect to the preceding calendar year," after "a report".

(G) DRUG SHORTAGE LIST.—*Section 506E(b)(3)(E) (21 U.S.C. 356e(b)(3)(E)) is amended by striking "discontinuation" and inserting "discontinuance".*

(H) INSPECTIONS OF ESTABLISHMENTS.—*Section 510(h) (21 U.S.C. 360(h)) is amended—*

(i) in paragraph (4), in the matter preceding subparagraph (A), by striking "establishing the risk-based scheduled" and inserting "establishing a risk-based schedule"; and

(ii) in paragraph (6)—

(I) in subparagraph (A), by striking "fiscal" and inserting "calendar" each place the term appears; and

(II) in subparagraph (B), by striking "an active ingredient of a drug, a finished drug product, or an excipient of a drug" and inserting "an active ingredient of a drug or a finished drug product".

(I) CLASSIFICATION OF DEVICES INTENDED FOR HUMAN USE.—*Section 513(f)(2)(A) (21 U.S.C. 360c(f)(2)(A)) is amended—*

(i) in clause (i), by striking "within 30 days"; and

(ii) in clause (iv), by striking "low-moderate" and inserting "low to moderate".

(J) PREMARKET APPROVAL.—*Section 515(a)(1) (21 U.S.C. 360e(a)(1)) is amended by striking "subject to a an order" and inserting "subject to an order".*

(K) PROGRAM TO IMPROVE THE DEVICE RECALL SYSTEM.—*Section 518A (21 U.S.C. 360h–1) is amended—*

(i) by striking subsection (c); and

(ii) by redesignating subsection (d) as subsection (c).

(L) UNIQUE DEVICE IDENTIFIER.—*Section 519(f) (21 U.S.C. 360i(f)) is amended by striking "and life sustaining" and inserting "or life sustaining".*

(M) PRIORITY REVIEW TO ENCOURAGE TREATMENTS FOR TROPICAL DISEASES.—*Section 524(c)(4)(A) of the Federal Food, Drug, and Cosmetic Act (21 U.S.C. 360n(c)(4)(A)) is amended by striking "Services Act" and inserting "Service Act".*

(N) PRIORITY REVIEW FOR QUALIFIED INFECTIOUS DISEASE PRODUCTS.—*Section 524A (21 U.S.C. 360n–1) is amended—*

(i) by striking "If the Secretary" and inserting the following:

"(a) IN GENERAL.—If the Secretary";

(ii) by striking "any" and inserting "the first"; and

(iii) by adding at the end the following:

"(b) CONSTRUCTION.—Nothing in this section shall prohibit the Secretary from giving priority review to a human drug application or efficacy supplement submitted for approval under section 505(b) that otherwise meets the criteria for the Secretary to grant priority review.".

(O) CONSULTATION WITH EXTERNAL EXPERTS ON RARE DISEASES, TARGETED THERAPIES, AND GENETIC TARGETING OF TREATMENTS.—*Section 569(a)(2)(A) (21 U.S.C. 360bbb–8(a)(2)(A)) is amended, in the first sentence, by striking "subsection (c)" and inserting "subsection (b)".*

(P) OPTIMIZING GLOBAL CLINICAL TRIALS.—*Section 569A(c) (21 U.S.C. 360bbb–8a(c)) is amended by inserting "or under the Public Health Service Act" after "this Act".*

(Q) USE OF CLINICAL INVESTIGATION DATA FROM OUTSIDE THE UNITED STATES.—*Section 569B (21 U.S.C. 360bbb–8b) is amended by striking "drug or device" and inserting "drug, biological product, or device" each place the term appears.*

(R) MEDICAL GASES DEFINITIONS.—*Section 575(1)(H) (21 U.S.C. 360ddd(1)(H)) is amended—*

(i) by inserting "for a new drug" after "any period of exclusivity"; and

(ii) by inserting "or any period of exclusivity for a new animal drug under section 512(c)(2)(F)," after "section 505A,".

(S) REGULATION OF MEDICAL GASES.—*Section 576(a) (21 U.S.C. 360ddd–1(a)) is amended—*

(i) in the matter preceding subparagraph (A) of paragraph (1), by inserting "who seeks to initially introduce or deliver for introduction a designated medical gas into interstate commerce" after "any person"; and

(ii) in paragraph (3)—

(I) in subparagraph (A)—

(aa) in clause (i)(VIII), by inserting "for a new drug" after "any period of exclusivity"; and

(bb) in clause (ii), in the matter preceding subclause (I), by inserting "the" before "final use"; and

(II) in subparagraph (B)—

(aa) in clause (i), by inserting "for a new drug" after "any period of exclusivity"; and

(bb) in clause (ii), by inserting a comma after "drug product".

(T) INAPPLICABILITY OF DRUG FEES TO DESIGNATED MEDICAL GASES.—*Section 577 (21 U.S.C. 360ddd–2) is amended by inserting "or 740(a)" after "section 736(a)".*

(U) CONFLICTS OF INTEREST.—*Section 712(e)(1)(B) (21 U.S.C. 379d–1(e)(1)(B)) is amend-*

ed by striking "services" and inserting "service".

(V) AUTHORITY TO ASSESS AND USE BIOSIMILAR BIOLOGICAL PRODUCT FEES.—*Section 744H(a) (21 U.S.C. 379j–52(a)) is amended—*

(i) in paragraph (1)(A)(v), by striking "Biosimilars User Fee Act of 2012" and inserting "Biosimilar User Fee Act of 2012"; and

(ii) in paragraph (2)(B), by striking "Biosimilars User Fee Act of 2012" and inserting "Biosimilar User Fee Act of 2012".

(W) REGISTRATION OF COMMERCIAL IMPORTERS.—

(i) AMENDMENT.—Section 801(s)(2) (21 U.S.C. 381(s)(2)) is amended by adding at the end the following:

"(D) EFFECTIVE DATE.—In establishing the effective date of the regulations under subparagraph (A), the Secretary shall, in consultation with the Secretary of Homeland Security acting through U.S. Customs and Border Protection, as determined appropriate by the Secretary of Health and Human Services, provide a reasonable period of time for an importer of a drug to comply with good importer practices, taking into account differences among importers and types of imports, including based on the level of risk posed by the imported product.".

(ii) CONFORMING AMENDMENT.—Section 714 of the Food and Drug Administration Safety and Innovation Act (Public Law 112–144; 126 Stat. 1074) is amended by striking subsection (d).

(X) RECOGNITION OF FOREIGN GOVERNMENT INSPECTIONS.—*Section 809(a)(2) (21 U.S.C. 384e(a)(2)) is amended by striking "conduction" and inserting "conducting".*

(b) FDASIA.—

(1) FINDINGS RELATING TO DRUG APPROVAL.—*Section 901(a)(1)(A) of the Food and Drug Administration Safety and Innovation Act (Public Law 112–144; 21 U.S.C. 356 note) is amended by striking "serious and life-threatening diseases" and inserting "serious or life-threatening diseases".*

(2) REPORTING OF INCLUSION OF DEMOGRAPHIC SUBGROUPS.—*Section 907 of the Food and Drug Administration Safety and Innovation Act (Public Law 112–144; 126 Stat. 1092, 1093) is amended—*

*(A) in the section heading, by striking "**BIOLOGICS**" in the heading and inserting "**BIOLOGICAL PRODUCTS**"; and*

(B) in subsection (a)(2)(B), by striking "applications for new drug applications" and inserting "new drug applications".

(3) COMBATING PRESCRIPTION DRUG ABUSE.—*Section 1122 of the Food and Drug Administration Safety and Innovation Act (Public Law 112–144; 126 Stat. 1112, 1113) is amended—*

(A) in subsection (a)(2), by striking "dependance" and inserting "dependence"; and

(B) in subsection (c), by striking "promulgate" and inserting "issue".

SEC. 3102. COMPLETED STUDIES.

The Federal Food, Drug, and Cosmetic Act is amended—

(1) in section 505(k)(5) (21 U.S.C. 355(k)(5))—

(A) in subparagraph (A), by inserting "and" after the semicolon;

(B) by striking subparagraph (B); and

(C) by redesignating subparagraph (C) as subparagraph (B);

(2) in section 505A (21 U.S.C. 355a), by striking subsection (p);

(3) in section 505B (21 U.S.C. 355c)—

(A) by striking subsection (l); and

(B) by redesignating subsection (m) as subsection (l); and

(4) in section 523 (21 U.S.C. 360m), by striking subsection (d).

TITLE IV—DELIVERY

SEC. 4001. ASSISTING DOCTORS AND HOSPITALS IN IMPROVING QUALITY OF CARE FOR PATIENTS.

(a) IN GENERAL.—The Health Information Technology for Economic and Clinical Health

Act (title XIII of division A of Public Law 111–5) is amended—

(1) by adding at the end of part 1 of subtitle A the following:

"SEC. 13103. ASSISTING DOCTORS AND HOSPITALS IN IMPROVING QUALITY OF CARE FOR PATIENTS.

"(a) REDUCTION IN BURDENS GOAL.—The Secretary of Health and Human Services (referred to in this section as the 'Secretary'), in consultation with providers of health services, health care suppliers of services, health care payers, health professional societies, health information technology developers, health care quality organizations, health care accreditation organizations, public health entities, States, and other appropriate entities, shall, in accordance with subsection (b)—

"(1) establish a goal with respect to the reduction of regulatory or administrative burdens (such as documentation requirements) relating to the use of electronic health records;

"(2) develop a strategy for meeting the goal established under paragraph (1); and

"(3) develop recommendations for meeting the goal established under paragraph (1).

"(b) STRATEGY AND RECOMMENDATIONS.—

"(1) IN GENERAL.—To achieve the goal established under subsection (a)(1), the Secretary, in consultation with the entities described in such subsection, shall, not later than 1 year after the date of enactment of the 21st Century Cures Act, develop a strategy and recommendations to meet the goal in accordance with this subsection.

"(2) STRATEGY.—The strategy developed under paragraph (1) shall address the regulatory and administrative burdens (such as documentation requirements) relating to the use of electronic health records. Such strategy shall include broad public comment and shall prioritize—

"(A)(i) incentives for meaningful use of certified EHR technology for eligible professionals and hospitals under sections 1848(a)(7) and 1886(b)(3)(B)(ix), respectively, of the Social Security Act (42 U.S.C. 1395w–4(a)(7), 1395ww(b)(3)(B)(ix));

"(ii) the program for making payments under section 1903(a)(3)(F) of the Social Security Act (42 U.S.C. 1396b(a)(3)(F)) to encourage the adoption and use of certified EHR technology by Medicaid providers;

"(iii) the Merit-based Incentive Payment System under section 1848(q) of the Social Security Act (42 U.S.C. 1395w–4(q));

"(iv) alternative payment models (as defined in section 1833(z)(3)(C) of the Social Security Act (42 U.S.C. 1395l(z)(3)(C));

"(v) the Hospital Value-Based Purchasing Program under section 1886(o) of the Social Security Act (42 U.S.C. 1395ww(o)); and

"(vi) other value-based payment programs, as the Secretary determines appropriate;

"(B) health information technology certification;

"(C) standards and implementation specifications, as appropriate;

"(D) activities that provide individuals access to their electronic health information;

"(E) activities related to protecting the privacy of electronic health information;

"(F) activities related to protecting the security of electronic health information;

"(G) activities related to facilitating health and clinical research;

"(H) activities related to public health;

"(I) activities related to aligning and simplifying quality measures across Federal programs and other payers;

"(J) activities related to reporting clinical data for administrative purposes; and

"(K) other areas, as the Secretary determines appropriate.

"(3) RECOMMENDATIONS.—The recommendations developed under paragraph (1) shall address—

"(A) actions that improve the clinical documentation experience;

"(B) actions that improve patient care;

"(C) actions to be taken by the Secretary and by other entities; and

"(D) other areas, as the Secretary determines appropriate, to reduce the reporting burden required of health care providers.

"(4) FACA.—The Federal Advisory Committee Act (5 U.S.C. App.) shall not apply to the development of the goal, strategies, or recommendations described in this section.

"(c) APPLICATION OF CERTAIN REGULATORY REQUIREMENTS.—A physician (as defined in section 1861(r)(1) of the Social Security Act), to the extent consistent with applicable State law, may delegate electronic medical record documentation requirements specified in regulations promulgated by the Centers for Medicare & Medicaid Services to a person performing a scribe function who is not such physician if such physician has signed and verified the documentation."; and

(2) in the table of contents in section 13001(b), by inserting after the item relating to section 13102 the following:

"13103. Assisting doctors and hospitals in improving the quality and care for patients.".

(b) CERTIFICATION OF HEALTH INFORMATION TECHNOLOGY FOR MEDICAL SPECIALTIES AND SITES OF SERVICE.—Section 3001(c)(5) of the Public Health Service Act (42 U.S.C. 300jj–11(c)(5)) is amended by adding at the end the following:

"(C) HEALTH INFORMATION TECHNOLOGY FOR MEDICAL SPECIALTIES AND SITES OF SERVICE.—

"(i) IN GENERAL.—The National Coordinator shall encourage, keep, or recognize, through existing authorities, the voluntary certification of health information technology under the program developed under subparagraph (A) for use in medical specialties and sites of service for which no such technology is available or where more technological advancement or integration is needed.

"(ii) SPECIFIC MEDICAL SPECIALTIES.—The Secretary shall accept public comment on specific medical specialties and sites of service, in addition to those described in clause (i), for the purpose of selecting additional specialties and sites of service as necessary.

"(iii) HEALTH INFORMATION TECHNOLOGY FOR PEDIATRICS.—Not later than 18 months after the date of enactment of the 21st Century Cures Act, the Secretary, in consultation with relevant stakeholders, shall make recommendations for the voluntary certification of health information technology for use by pediatric health providers to support the health care of children. Not later than 2 years after the date of enactment of the 21st Century Cures Act, the Secretary shall adopt certification criteria under section 3004 to support the voluntary certification of health information technology for use by pediatric health providers to support the health care of children.".

(c) MEANINGFUL USE STATISTICS.—

(1) IN GENERAL.—Not later than 6 months after the date of enactment of this Act, the Secretary of Health and Human Services shall submit to the HIT Advisory Committee of the Office of the National Coordinator for Health Information Technology, a report concerning attestation statistics for the Medicare and Medicaid EHR Meaningful Use Incentive programs to assist in informing standards adoption and related practices. Such statistics shall include attestation information delineated by State, including, to the extent practicable, the number of providers who did not meet the minimum criteria necessary to attest for the Medicare and Medicaid EHR Meaningful Use Incentive programs for a calendar year, and shall be made publicly available

on the Internet website of the Secretary on at least a quarterly basis.

(2) AUTHORITY TO ALTER FORMAT.—The Secretary of Health and Human Services may alter the format of the reports on the attestation of eligible health care professionals following the first performance year of the Merit-based Incentive Payment System to account for changes arising from the implementation of such payment system.

SEC. 4002. TRANSPARENT REPORTING ON USABILITY, SECURITY, AND FUNCTIONALITY.

(a) ENHANCEMENTS TO CERTIFICATION.—Section 3001(c)(5) of the Public Health Service Act (42 U.S.C. 300jj–11), as amended by section 4001(b), is further amended by adding at the end the following:

"(D) CONDITIONS OF CERTIFICATION.—Not later than 1 year after the date of enactment of the 21st Century Cures Act, the Secretary, through notice and comment rulemaking, shall require, as a condition of certification and maintenance of certification for programs maintained or recognized under this paragraph, consistent with other conditions and requirements under this title, that the health information technology developer or entity—

"(i) does not take any action that constitutes information blocking as defined in section 3022(a);

"(ii) provides assurances satisfactory to the Secretary that such developer or entity, unless for legitimate purposes specified by the Secretary, will not take any action described in clause (i) or any other action that may inhibit the appropriate exchange, access, and use of electronic health information;

"(iii) does not prohibit or restrict communication regarding—

"(I) the usability of the health information technology;

"(II) the interoperability of the health information technology;

"(III) the security of the health information technology;

"(IV) relevant information regarding users' experiences when using the health information technology;

"(V) the business practices of developers of health information technology related to exchanging electronic health information; and

"(VI) the manner in which a user of the health information technology has used such technology;

"(iv) has published application programming interfaces and allows health information from such technology to be accessed, exchanged, and used without special effort through the use of application programming interfaces or successor technology or standards, as provided for under applicable law, including providing access to all data elements of a patient's electronic health record to the extent permissible under applicable privacy laws;

"(v) has successfully tested the real world use of the technology for interoperability (as defined in section 3000) in the type of setting in which such technology would be marketed;

"(vi) provides to the Secretary an attestation that the developer or entity—

"(I) has not engaged in any of the conduct described in clause (i);

"(II) has provided assurances satisfactory to the Secretary in accordance with clause (ii);

"(III) does not prohibit or restrict communication as described in clause (iii);

"(IV) has published information in accordance with clause (iv);

"(V) ensures that its technology allows for health information to be exchanged, accessed, and used, in the manner described in clause (iv); and

"(VI) has undertaken real world testing as described in clause (v); and "(vii) submits reporting criteria in accordance with section 3009A(b).".

"(E) COMPLIANCE WITH CONDITIONS OF CERTIFICATION.—The Secretary may encourage compliance with the conditions of certification described in subparagraph (D) and take action to discourage noncompliance, as appropriate.".

(b) EHR SIGNIFICANT HARDSHIP EXCEPTION.—

(1) APPLICATION TO ELIGIBLE PROFESSIONALS.—

(A) IN CASE OF DECERTIFICATION.—Section 1848(a)(7)(B) of the Social Security Act (42 U.S.C. 1395w–4(a)(7)(B)) is amended by inserting after the first sentence the following new sentence: "The Secretary shall exempt an eligible professional from the application of the payment adjustment under subparagraph (A) with respect to a year, subject to annual renewal, if the Secretary determines that compliance with the requirement for being a meaningful EHR user is not possible because the certified EHR technology used by such professional has been decertified under a program kept or recognized pursuant to section 3001(c)(5) of the Public Health Service Act.".

(B) CONTINUED APPLICATION UNDER MIPS.—Section 1848(o)(2)(D) of the Social Security Act (42 U.S.C. 1395w–4(o)(2)(D)) is amended by adding at the end the following new sentence: "The provisions of subparagraphs (B) and (D) of subsection (a)(7), shall apply to assessments of MIPS eligible professionals under subsection (q) with respect to the performance category described in subsection (q)(2)(A)(iv) in an appropriate manner which may be similar to the manner in which such provisions apply with respect to payment adjustments made under subsection (a)(7)(A).".

(2) APPLICATION TO ELIGIBLE HOSPITALS.—Section 1886(b)(3)(B)(ix)(II) of the Social Security Act (42 U.S.C. 1395ww(b)(3)(B)(ix)(II)) is amended by inserting after the first sentence the following new sentence: "The Secretary shall exempt an eligible hospital from the application of the payment adjustment under subclause (I) with respect to a fiscal year, subject to annual renewal, if the Secretary determines that compliance with the requirement for being a meaningful EHR user is not possible because the certified EHR technology used by such hospital is decertified under a program kept or recognized pursuant to section 3001(c)(5) of the Public Health Service Act.".

(c) ELECTRONIC HEALTH RECORD REPORTING PROGRAM.—Subtitle A of title XXX of the Public Health Service Act (42 U.S.C. 300jj–11 et seq.) is amended by adding at the end the following:

"SEC. 3009A. ELECTRONIC HEALTH RECORD REPORTING PROGRAM.

"(a) REPORTING CRITERIA.—

"(1) CONVENING OF STAKEHOLDERS.—Not later than 1 year after the date of enactment of the 21st Century Cures Act, the Secretary shall convene stakeholders, as described in paragraph (2), for the purpose of developing the reporting criteria in accordance with paragraph (3).

"(2) DEVELOPMENT OF REPORTING CRITERIA.—The reporting criteria under this subsection shall be developed through a public, transparent process that reflects input from relevant stakeholders, including—

"(A) health care providers, including primary care and specialty care health care professionals;

"(B) hospitals and hospital systems;

"(C) health information technology developers;

"(D) patients, consumers, and their advocates;

"(E) data sharing networks, such as health information exchanges;

"(F) authorized certification bodies and testing laboratories;

"(G) security experts;

"(H) relevant manufacturers of medical devices;

"(I) experts in health information technology market economics;

"(J) public and private entities engaged in the evaluation of health information technology performance;

"(K) quality organizations, including the consensus based entity described in section 1890 of the Social Security Act;

"(L) experts in human factors engineering and the measurement of user-centered design; and

"(M) other entities or individuals, as the Secretary determines appropriate.

"(3) CONSIDERATIONS FOR REPORTING CRITERIA.—The reporting criteria developed under this subsection—

"(A) shall include measures that reflect categories including—

"(i) security;

"(ii) usability and user-centered design;

"(iii) interoperability;

"(iv) conformance to certification testing; and

"(v) other categories, as appropriate to measure the performance of electronic health record technology;

"(B) may include categories such as—

"(i) enabling the user to order and view the results of laboratory tests, imaging tests, and other diagnostic tests;

"(ii) submitting, editing, and retrieving data from registries such as clinician-led clinical data registries;

"(iii) accessing and exchanging information and data from and through health information exchanges;

"(iv) accessing and exchanging information and data from medical devices;

"(v) accessing and exchanging information and data held by Federal, State, and local agencies and other applicable entities useful to a health care provider or other applicable user in the furtherance of patient care;

"(vi) accessing and exchanging information from other health care providers or applicable users;

"(vii) accessing and exchanging patient generated information;

"(viii) providing the patient or an authorized designee with a complete copy of their health information from an electronic record in a computable format;

"(ix) providing accurate patient information for the correct patient, including exchanging such information, and avoiding the duplication of patients records; and

"(x) other categories regarding performance, accessibility, as the Secretary determines appropriate; and

"(C) shall be designed to ensure that small and startup health information technology developers are not unduly disadvantaged by the reporting criteria.

"(4) MODIFICATIONS.—After the reporting criteria have been developed under paragraph (3), the Secretary may convene stakeholders and conduct a public comment period for the purpose of modifying the reporting criteria developed under such paragraph.

"(b) PARTICIPATION.—As a condition of maintaining certification under section 3001(c)(5)(D), a developer of certified electronic health records shall submit to an appropriate recipient of a grant, contract, or agreement under subsection (c)(1) responses to the criteria developed under subsection (a), with respect to all certified technology offered by such developer.

"(c) REPORTING PROGRAM.—

"(1) IN GENERAL.—Not later than 1 year after the date of enactment of the 21st Century Cures Act, the Secretary shall award grants, contracts, or agreements to independent entities on a competitive basis to support the convening of

stakeholders as described in subsection (a)(2), collect the information required to be reported in accordance with the criteria established as described subsection (a)(3), and develop and implement a process in accordance with paragraph (5) and report such information to the Secretary.

"(2) APPLICATIONS.—An independent entity that seeks a grant, contract, or agreement under this subsection shall submit an application to the Secretary at such time, in such manner, and containing such information as the Secretary may reasonably require, including a description of—

"(A) the proposed method for reviewing and summarizing information gathered based on reporting criteria established under subsection (a);

"(B) if applicable, the intended focus on a specific subset of certified electronic health record technology users, such as health care providers, including primary care, specialty care, and care provided in rural settings; hospitals and hospital systems; and patients, consumers, and patients and consumer advocates;

"(C) the plan for widely distributing reports described in paragraph (6);

"(D) the period for which the grant, contract, or agreement is requested, which may be up to 2 years; and

"(E) the budget for reporting program participation, and whether the eligible independent entity intends to continue participation after the period of the grant, contract, or agreement.

"(3) CONSIDERATIONS FOR INDEPENDENT ENTITIES.—In awarding grants, contracts, and agreements under paragraph (1), the Secretary shall give priority to independent entities with appropriate expertise in health information technology usability, interoperability, and security (especially entities with such expertise in electronic health records) with respect to—

"(A) health care providers, including primary care, specialty care, and care provided in rural settings;

"(B) hospitals and hospital systems; and

"(C) patients, consumers, and patient and consumer advocates.

"(4) LIMITATIONS.—

"(A) ASSESSMENT AND REDETERMINATION.—Not later than 4 years after the date of enactment of the 21st Century Cures Act and every 2 years thereafter, the Secretary, in consultation with stakeholders, shall—

"(i) assess performance of the recipients of the grants, contracts, and agreements under paragraph (1) based on quality and usability of reports described in paragraph (6); and

"(ii) re-determine grants, contracts, and agreements as necessary.

"(B) PROHIBITIONS ON PARTICIPATION.—The Secretary may not award a grant, contract, or cooperative agreement under paragraph (1) to—

"(i) a proprietor of certified health information technology or a business affiliate of such a proprietor;

"(ii) a developer of certified health information technology; or

"(iii) a State or local government agency.

"(5) FEEDBACK.—Based on reporting criteria established under subsection (a), the recipients of grants, contracts, and agreements under paragraph (1) shall develop and implement a process to collect and verify confidential feedback on such criteria from—

"(A) health care providers, patients, and other users of certified electronic health record technology; and

"(B) developers of certified electronic health record technology.

"(6) REPORTS.—

"(A) DEVELOPMENT OF REPORTS.—Each recipient of a grant, contract, or agreement under paragraph (1) shall report on the information reported to such recipient pursuant to subsection (a) and the user feedback collected under paragraph (5) by preparing summary reports and detailed reports of such information.

"(B) DISTRIBUTION OF REPORTS.—Each recipient of a grant, contract, or agreement under paragraph (1) shall submit the reports prepared under subparagraph (A) to the Secretary for public distribution in accordance with subsection (d).

"(d) PUBLICATION.—The Secretary shall distribute widely, as appropriate, and publish, on the Internet website of the Office of the National Coordinator—

"(1) the reporting criteria developed under subsection (a); and

"(2) the summary and detailed reports under subsection (c)(6).

"(e) REVIEW.—Each recipient of a grant, contract, or agreement under paragraph (1) shall develop and implement a process through which participating electronic health record technology developers may review and recommend changes to the reports created under subsection (c)(6) for products developed by such developer prior to the publication of such report under subsection (d).

"(f) ADDITIONAL RESOURCES.—The Secretary may provide additional resources on the Internet website of the Office of the National Coordinator to better inform consumers of health information technology. Such reports may be carried out through partnerships with private organizations with appropriate expertise.".

(d) AUTHORIZATION OF APPROPRIATIONS.—There is authorized to be appropriated $15,000,000 for purposes of carrying out subparagraph (D) of section 3001(c)(5) of the Public Health Service Act (42 U.S.C. 300jj–11) (as added by subsection (a)) and section 3009A of the Public Health Service Act (as added by subsection (b)), including for purposes of administering any contracts, grants, or agreements, to remain available until expended.

SEC. 4003. INTEROPERABILITY.

(a) DEFINITION.—Section 3000 of the Public Health Service Act (42 U.S.C. 300jj) is amended—

(1) by redesignating paragraphs (10) through (14), as paragraphs (11) through (15), respectively; and

(2) by inserting after paragraph (9) the following:

"(10) INTEROPERABILITY.—The term 'interoperability', with respect to health information technology, means such health information technology that—

"(A) enables the secure exchange of electronic health information with, and use of electronic health information from, other health information technology without special effort on the part of the user;

"(B) allows for complete access, exchange, and use of all electronically accessible health information for authorized use under applicable State or Federal law; and

"(C) does not constitute information blocking as defined in section 3022(a).".

(b) SUPPORT FOR INTEROPERABLE NETWORK EXCHANGE.—Section 3001(c) of the Public Health Service Act (42 U.S.C. 300jj–11(c)) is amended by adding at the end the following:

"(9) SUPPORT FOR INTEROPERABLE NETWORKS EXCHANGE.—

"(A) IN GENERAL.—The National Coordinator shall, in collaboration with the National Institute of Standards and Technology and other relevant agencies within the Department of Health and Human Services, for the purpose of ensuring full network-to-network exchange of health information, convene public-private and public-public partnerships to build consensus and develop or support a trusted exchange framework, including a common agreement among health information networks nationally. Such convention may occur at a frequency determined appropriate by the Secretary.

"(B) ESTABLISHING A TRUSTED EXCHANGE FRAMEWORK.—

"(i) IN GENERAL.—Not later than 6 months after the date of enactment of the 21st Century Cures Act, the National Coordinator shall convene appropriate public and private stakeholders to develop or support a trusted exchange framework for trust policies and practices and for a common agreement for exchange between health information networks. The common agreement may include—

"(I) a common method for authenticating trusted health information network participants;

"(II) a common set of rules for trusted exchange;

"(III) organizational and operational policies to enable the exchange of health information among networks, including minimum conditions for such exchange to occur; and

"(IV) a process for filing and adjudicating noncompliance with the terms of the common agreement.

"(ii) TECHNICAL ASSISTANCE.—The National Coordinator, in collaboration with the National Institute of Standards and Technology, shall provide technical assistance on how to implement the trusted exchange framework and common agreement under this paragraph.

"(iii) PILOT TESTING.—The National Coordinator, in consultation with the National Institute of Standards and Technology, shall provide for the pilot testing of the trusted exchange framework and common agreement established or supported under this subsection (as authorized under section 13201 of the Health Information Technology for Economic and Clinical Health Act). The National Coordinator, in consultation with the National Institute of Standards and Technology, may delegate pilot testing activities under this clause to independent entities with appropriate expertise.

"(C) PUBLICATION OF A TRUSTED EXCHANGE FRAMEWORK AND COMMON AGREEMENT.—Not later than 1 year after convening stakeholders under subparagraph (A), the National Coordinator shall publish on its public Internet website, and in the Federal register, the trusted exchange framework and common agreement developed or supported under subparagraph (B). Such trusted exchange framework and common agreement shall be published in a manner that protects proprietary and security information, including trade secrets and any other protected intellectual property.

"(D) DIRECTORY OF PARTICIPATING HEALTH INFORMATION NETWORKS.—

"(i) IN GENERAL.—Not later than 2 years after convening stakeholders under subparagraph (A), and annually thereafter, the National Coordinator shall publish on its public Internet website a list of the health information networks that have adopted the common agreement and are capable of trusted exchange pursuant to the common agreement developed or supported under paragraph (B).

"(ii) PROCESS.—The Secretary shall, through notice and comment rulemaking, establish a process for health information networks that voluntarily elect to adopt the trusted exchange framework and common agreement to attest to such adoption of the framework and agreement.

"(E) APPLICATION OF THE TRUSTED EXCHANGE FRAMEWORK AND COMMON AGREEMENT.—As appropriate, Federal agencies contracting or entering into agreements with health information exchange networks may require that as each such network upgrades health information technology or trust and operational practices, such network may adopt, where available, the trusted exchange framework and common agreement published under subparagraph (C).

"(F) RULE OF CONSTRUCTION.—

"(i) GENERAL ADOPTION.—Nothing in this paragraph shall be construed to require a health

information network to adopt the trusted exchange framework or common agreement.

"(ii) ADOPTION WHEN EXCHANGE OF INFORMATION IS WITHIN NETWORK.—Nothing in this paragraph shall be construed to require a health information network to adopt the trusted exchange framework or common agreement for the exchange of electronic health information between participants of the same network.

"(iii) EXISTING FRAMEWORKS AND AGREEMENTS.—The trusted exchange framework and common agreement published under subparagraph (C) shall take into account existing trusted exchange frameworks and agreements used by health information networks to avoid the disruption of existing exchanges between participants of health information networks.

"(iv) APPLICATION BY FEDERAL AGENCIES.—Notwithstanding clauses (i), (ii), and (iii), Federal agencies may require the adoption of the trusted exchange framework and common agreement published under subparagraph (C) for health information exchanges contracting with or entering into agreements pursuant to subparagraph (E).

"(v) CONSIDERATION OF ONGOING WORK.—In carrying out this paragraph, the Secretary shall ensure the consideration of activities carried out by public and private organizations related to exchange between health information exchanges to avoid duplication of efforts.".

(c) PROVIDER DIGITAL CONTACT INFORMATION INDEX.—

(1) IN GENERAL.—Not later than 3 years after the date of enactment of this Act, the Secretary of Health and Human Services (referred to in this subsection as the "Secretary") shall, directly or through a partnership with a private entity, establish a provider digital contact information index to provide digital contact information for health professionals and health facilities.

(2) USE OF EXISTING INDEX.—In establishing the initial index under paragraph (1), the Secretary may utilize an existing provider directory to make such digital contact information available.

(3) CONTACT INFORMATION.—An index established under this subsection shall ensure that contact information is available at the individual health care provider level and at the health facility or practice level.

(4) RULE OF CONSTRUCTION.—

(A) IN GENERAL.—The purpose of this subsection is to encourage the exchange of electronic health information by providing the most useful, reliable, and comprehensive index of providers possible. In furthering such purpose, the Secretary shall include all health professionals and health facilities applicable to provide a useful, reliable, and comprehensive index for use in the exchange of health information.

(B) LIMITATION.—In no case shall exclusion from the index of providers be used as a measure to achieve objectives other the objectives described in subparagraph (A).

(d) STANDARDS DEVELOPMENT ORGANIZATIONS.—Section 3004 of the Public Health Service Act (42 U.S.C. 300jj–14) is amended by adding at the end the following:

"(c) DEFERENCE TO STANDARDS DEVELOPMENT ORGANIZATIONS.—In adopting and implementing standards under this section, the Secretary shall give deference to standards published by standards development organizations and voluntary consensus-based standards bodies.".

(e) HEALTH INFORMATION TECHNOLOGY ADVISORY COMMITTEE.—

(1) IN GENERAL.—Title XXX of the Public Health Service Act (42 U.S.C. 300jj et seq.) is amended by striking sections 3002 (42 U.S.C. 300jj–12) and 3003 (42 U.S.C. 300jj–13) and inserting the following:

"SEC. 3002. HEALTH INFORMATION TECHNOLOGY ADVISORY COMMITTEE.

"(a) ESTABLISHMENT.—There is established a Health Information Technology Advisory Committee (referred to in this section as the 'HIT Advisory Committee') to recommend to the National Coordinator, consistent with the implementation of the strategic plan described in section 3001(c)(3), policies, and, for purposes of adoption under section 3004, standards, implementation specifications, and certification criteria, relating to the implementation of a health information technology infrastructure, nationally and locally, that advances the electronic access, exchange, and use of health information. Such Committee shall serve to unify the roles of, and replace, the HIT Policy Committee and the HIT Standards Committee, as in existence before the date of the enactment of the 21st Century Cures Act.

"(b) DUTIES.—

"(1) RECOMMENDATIONS ON POLICY FRAMEWORK TO ADVANCE AN INTEROPERABLE HEALTH INFORMATION TECHNOLOGY INFRASTRUCTURE.—

"(A) IN GENERAL.—The HIT Advisory Committee shall recommend to the National Coordinator a policy framework for adoption by the Secretary consistent with the strategic plan under section 3001(c)(3) for advancing the target areas described in this subsection. Such policy framework shall seek to prioritize achieving advancements in the target areas specified in subparagraph (B) of paragraph (2) and may, to the extent consistent with this section, incorporate policy recommendations made by the HIT Policy Committee, as in existence before the date of the enactment of the 21st Century Cures Act.

"(B) UPDATES.—The HIT Advisory Committee shall propose updates to such recommendations to the policy framework and make new recommendations, as appropriate.

"(2) GENERAL DUTIES AND TARGET AREAS.—

"(A) IN GENERAL.—The HIT Advisory Committee shall recommend to the National Coordinator for purposes of adoption under section 3004, standards, implementation specifications, and certification criteria and an order of priority for the development, harmonization, and recognition of such standards, specifications, and certification criteria. Such recommendations shall include recommended standards, architectures, and software schemes for access to electronic individually identifiable health information across disparate systems including user vetting, authentication, privilege management, and access control.

"(B) PRIORITY TARGET AREAS.—For purposes of this section, the HIT Advisory Committee shall make recommendations under subparagraph (A) with respect to at least each of the following target areas:

"(i) Achieving a health information technology infrastructure, nationally and locally, that allows for the electronic access, exchange, and use of health information, including through technology that provides accurate patient information for the correct patient, including exchanging such information, and avoids the duplication of patient records.

"(ii) The promotion and protection of privacy and security of health information in health information technology, including technologies that allow for an accounting of disclosures and protections against disclosures of individually identifiable health information made by a covered entity for purposes of treatment, payment, and health care operations (as such terms are defined for purposes of the regulation promulgated under section 264(c) of the Health Insurance Portability and Accountability Act of 1996), including for the segmentation and protection from disclosure of specific and sensitive individually identifiable health information with the goal of minimizing the reluctance of patients to seek care.

"(iii) The facilitation of secure access by an individual to such individual's protected health information and access to such information by a family member, caregiver, or guardian acting on behalf of a patient, including due to age-related and other disability, cognitive impairment, or dementia.

"(iv) Subject to subparagraph (D), any other target area that the HIT Advisory Committee identifies as an appropriate target area to be considered under this subparagraph.

"(C) ADDITIONAL TARGET AREAS.—For purposes of this section, the HIT Advisory Committee may make recommendations under subparagraph (A), in addition to areas described in subparagraph (B), with respect to any of the following areas:

"(i) The use of health information technology to improve the quality of health care, such as by promoting the coordination of health care and improving continuity of health care among health care providers, reducing medical errors, improving population health, reducing chronic disease, and advancing research and education.

"(ii) The use of technologies that address the needs of children and other vulnerable populations.

"(iii) The use of electronic systems to ensure the comprehensive collection of patient demographic data, including at a minimum, race, ethnicity, primary language, and gender information.

"(iv) The use of self-service, telemedicine, home health care, and remote monitoring technologies.

"(v) The use of technologies that meet the needs of diverse populations.

"(vi) The use of technologies that support—

"(I) data for use in quality and public reporting programs;

"(II) public health; or

"(III) drug safety.

"(vii) The use of technologies that allow individually identifiable health information to be rendered unusable, unreadable, or indecipherable to unauthorized individuals when such information is transmitted in a health information network or transported outside of the secure facilities or systems where the disclosing covered entity is responsible for security conditions.

"(viii) The use of a certified health information technology for each individual in the United States.

"(D) AUTHORITY FOR TEMPORARY ADDITIONAL PRIORITY TARGET AREAS.—For purposes of subparagraph (B)(iv), the HIT Advisory Committee may identify an area to be considered for purposes of recommendations under this subsection as a target area described in subparagraph (B) if—

"(i) the area is so identified for purposes of responding to new circumstances that have arisen in the health information technology community that affect the interoperability, privacy, or security of health information, or affect patient safety; and

"(ii) at least 30 days prior to treating such area as if it were a target area described in subparagraph (B), the National Coordinator provides adequate notice to Congress of the intent to treat such area as so described.

"(E) FOCUS OF COMMITTEE WORK.—It is the sense of Congress that the HIT Advisory Committee shall focus its work on the priority areas described in subparagraph (B) before proceeding to other work under subparagraph (C).

"(3) RULES RELATING TO RECOMMENDATIONS FOR STANDARDS, IMPLEMENTATION SPECIFICATIONS, AND CERTIFICATION CRITERIA.—

"(A) IN GENERAL.—The HIT Advisory Committee shall recommend to the National Coordinator standards, implementation specifications, and certification criteria described in subsection (a), which may include standards, implementa-

tion specifications, and certification criteria that have been developed, harmonized, or recognized by the HIT Advisory Committee or predecessor committee. The HIT Advisory Committee shall update such recommendations and make new recommendations as appropriate, including in response to a notification sent under section 3004(a)(2)(B). Such recommendations shall be consistent with the latest recommendations made by the Committee.

"(B) HARMONIZATION.—The HIT Advisory Committee may recognize harmonized or updated standards from an entity or entities for the purpose of harmonizing or updating standards and implementation specifications in order to achieve uniform and consistent implementation of the standards and implementation specification.

"(C) PILOT TESTING OF STANDARDS AND IMPLEMENTATION SPECIFICATIONS.—In the development, harmonization, or recognition of standards and implementation specifications, the HIT Advisory Committee for purposes of recommendations under paragraph (2)(B), shall, as appropriate, provide for the testing of such standards and specifications by the National Institute for Standards and Technology under section 13201(a) of the Health Information Technology for Economic and Clinical Health Act.

"(D) CONSISTENCY.—The standards, implementation specifications, and certification criteria recommended under paragraph (2)(B) shall be consistent with the standards for information transactions and data elements adopted pursuant to section 1173 of the Social Security Act.

"(E) SPECIAL RULE RELATED TO INTEROPERABILITY.—Any recommendation made by the HIT Advisory Committee after the date of the enactment of this subparagraph with respect to interoperability of health information technology shall be consistent with interoperability as described in section 3000.

"(4) FORUM.—The HIT Advisory Committee shall serve as a forum for the participation of a broad range of stakeholders with specific expertise in policies, including technical expertise, relating to the matters described in paragraphs (1), (2), and (3) to provide input on the development, harmonization, and recognition of standards, implementation specifications, and certification criteria necessary for the development and adoption of health information technology infrastructure nationally and locally that allows for the electronic access, exchange, and use of health information.

"(5) SCHEDULE.—Not later than 30 days after the date on which the HIT Advisory Committee first meets, such HIT Advisory Committee shall develop a schedule for the assessment of policy recommendations developed under paragraph (1). The HIT Advisory Committee shall update such schedule annually. The Secretary shall publish such schedule in the Federal Register.

"(6) PUBLIC INPUT.—The HIT Advisory Committee shall conduct open public meetings and develop a process to allow for public comment on the schedule described in paragraph (5) and recommendations described in this subsection. Under such process comments shall be submitted in a timely manner after the date of publication of a recommendation under this subsection.

"(c) MEASURED PROGRESS IN ADVANCING PRIORITY AREAS.—

"(1) IN GENERAL.—For purposes of this section, the National Coordinator, in collaboration with the Secretary, shall establish, and update as appropriate, objectives and benchmarks for advancing and measuring the advancement of the priority target areas described in subsection (b)(2)(B).

"(2) ANNUAL PROGRESS REPORTS ON ADVANCING INTEROPERABILITY.—

"(A) IN GENERAL.—The HIT Advisory Committee, in consultation with the National Coordinator, shall annually submit to the Secretary and Congress a report on the progress made during the preceding fiscal year in—

"(i) achieving a health information technology infrastructure, nationally and locally, that allows for the electronic access, exchange, and use of health information; and

"(ii) meeting the objectives and benchmarks described in paragraph (1).

"(B) CONTENT.—Each such report shall include, for a fiscal year—

"(i) a description of the work conducted by the HIT Advisory Committee during the preceding fiscal year with respect to the areas described in subsection (b)(2)(B);

"(ii) an assessment of the status of the infrastructure described in subparagraph (A), including the extent to which electronic health information is appropriately and readily available to enhance the access, exchange, and the use of electronic health information between users and across technology offered by different developers;

"(iii) the extent to which advancements have been achieved with respect to areas described in subsection (b)(2)(B);

"(iv) an analysis identifying existing gaps in policies and resources for—

"(I) achieving the objectives and benchmarks established under paragraph (1); and

"(II) furthering interoperability throughout the health information technology infrastructure;

"(v) recommendations for addressing the gaps identified in clause (iii); and

"(vi) a description of additional initiatives as the HIT Advisory Committee and National Coordinator determine appropriate.

"(3) SIGNIFICANT ADVANCEMENT DETERMINATION.—The Secretary shall periodically, based on the reports submitted under this subsection, review the target areas described in subsection (b)(2)(B), and, based on the objectives and benchmarks established under paragraph (1), the Secretary shall determine if significant advancement has been achieved with respect to such an area. Such determination shall be taken into consideration by the HIT Advisory Committee when determining to what extent the Committee makes recommendations for an area other than an area described in subsection (b)(2)(B).

"(d) MEMBERSHIP AND OPERATIONS.—

"(1) IN GENERAL.—The National Coordinator shall take a leading position in the establishment and operations of the HIT Advisory Committee.

"(2) MEMBERSHIP.—The membership of the HIT Advisory Committee shall—

"(A) include at least 25 members, of which—

"(i) no fewer than 2 members are advocates for patients or consumers of health information technology;

"(ii) 3 members are appointed by the Secretary, 1 of whom shall be appointed to represent the Department of Health and Human Services and 1 of whom shall be a public health official;

"(iii) 2 members are appointed by the majority leader of the Senate;

"(iv) 2 members are appointed by the minority leader of the Senate;

"(v) 2 members are appointed by the Speaker of the House of Representatives;

"(vi) 2 members are appointed by the minority leader of the House of Representatives; and

"(vii) such other members are appointed by the Comptroller General of the United States; and

"(B) at least reflect providers, ancillary health care workers, consumers, purchasers, health plans, health information technology developers, researchers, patients, relevant Federal agencies, and individuals with technical expertise on health care quality, system functions,

privacy, security, and on the electronic exchange and use of health information, including the use standards for such activity.

"(3) PARTICIPATION.—The members of the HIT Advisory Committee shall represent a balance among various sectors of the health care system so that no single sector unduly influences the recommendations of the Committee.

"(4) TERMS.—

"(A) IN GENERAL.—The terms of the members of the HIT Advisory Committee shall be for 3 years, except that the Secretary shall designate staggered terms of the members first appointed.

"(B) VACANCIES.—Any member appointed to fill a vacancy in the membership of the HIT Advisory Committee that occurs prior to the expiration of the term for which the member's predecessor was appointed shall be appointed only for the remainder of that term. A member may serve after the expiration of that member's term until a successor has been appointed. A vacancy in the HIT Advisory Committee shall be filled in the manner in which the original appointment was made.

"(C) LIMITS.—Members of the HIT Advisory Committee shall be limited to two 3-year terms, for a total of not to exceed 6 years of service on the Committee.

"(5) OUTSIDE INVOLVEMENT.—The HIT Advisory Committee shall ensure an opportunity for the participation in activities of the Committee of outside advisors, including individuals with expertise in the development of policies and standards for the electronic exchange and use of health information, including in the areas of health information privacy and security.

"(6) QUORUM.—A majority of the members of the HIT Advisory Committee shall constitute a quorum for purposes of voting, but a lesser number of members may meet and hold hearings.

"(7) CONSIDERATION.—The National Coordinator shall ensure that the relevant and available recommendations and comments from the National Committee on Vital and Health Statistics are considered in the development of policies.

"(8) ASSISTANCE.—For the purposes of carrying out this section, the Secretary may provide or ensure that financial assistance is provided by the HIT Advisory Committee to defray in whole or in part any membership fees or dues charged by such Committee to those consumer advocacy groups and not-for-profit entities that work in the public interest as a party of their mission.

"(e) APPLICATION OF FACA.—The Federal Advisory Committee Act (5 U.S.C. App.), other than section 14 of such Act, shall apply to the HIT Advisory Committee.

"(f) PUBLICATION.—The Secretary shall provide for publication in the Federal Register and the posting on the Internet website of the Office of the National Coordinator for Health Information Technology of all policy recommendations made by the HIT Advisory Committee under this section.".

(2) TECHNICAL AND CONFORMING AMENDMENTS.—Title XXX of the Public Health Service Act (42 U.S.C. 300jj et seq.) is amended—

(A) by striking—

(i) "HIT Policy Committee" and "HIT Standards Committee" each place that such terms appear (other than within the term "HIT Policy Committee and the HIT Standards Committee" or within the term "HIT Policy Committee or the HIT Standards Committee") and inserting "HIT Advisory Committee";

(ii) "HIT Policy Committee and the HIT Standards Committee" each place that such term appears and inserting "HIT Advisory Committee"; and

(iii) "HIT Policy Committee or the HIT Standards Committee" each place that such term appears and inserting "HIT Advisory Committee";

(B) in section 3000 (42 U.S.C. 300jj)—

(i) by striking paragraphs (7) and (8) and redesignating paragraphs (9) through (14) as paragraphs (8) through (13), respectively; and

(ii) by inserting after paragraph (6) the following paragraph:

"(7) HIT ADVISORY COMMITTEE.—The term 'HIT Advisory Committee' means such Committee established under section 3002(a).";

(C) in section 3001(c) (42 U.S.C. 300jj–11(c))—

(i) in paragraph (1)(A), by striking "under section 3003" and inserting "under section 3002";

(ii) in paragraph (2), by striking subparagraph (B) and inserting the following:

"(B) HIT ADVISORY COMMITTEE.—The National Coordinator shall be a leading member in the establishment and operations of the HIT Advisory Committee and shall serve as a liaison between that Committee and the Federal Government.";

(D) in section 3004(b)(3) (42 U.S.C. 300jj–14(b)(3)), by striking "3003(b)(2)" and inserting "3002(b)(4)";

(E) in section 3007(b) (42 U.S.C. 300jj–17(b)), by striking "3003(a)" and inserting "3002(a)(2)"; and

(F) in section 3008 (42 U.S.C. 300jj–18)—

(i) in subsection (b), by striking "or 3003"; and

(ii) in subsection (c), by striking "3003(b)(1)(A)" and inserting "3002(b)(2)".

(3) TRANSITION TO THE HIT ADVISORY COMMITTEE.—The Secretary of Health and Human Services shall provide for an orderly and timely transition to the HIT Advisory Committee established under amendments made by this section.

(f) PRIORITIES FOR ADOPTION OF STANDARDS, IMPLEMENTATION SPECIFICATIONS, AND CERTIFICATION CRITERIA.—Title XXX of the Public Health Service Act (42 U.S.C. 300jj et seq.), as amended by subsection (e), is further amended by inserting after section 3002 the following:

"SEC. 3003. SETTING PRIORITIES FOR STANDARDS ADOPTION.

"(a) IDENTIFYING PRIORITIES.—

"(1) IN GENERAL.—Not later than 6 months after the date on which the HIT Advisory Committee first meets, the National Coordinator shall periodically convene the HIT Advisory Committee to—

"(A) identify priority uses of health information technology, focusing on priorities—

"(i) arising from the implementation of the incentive programs for the meaningful use of certified EHR technology, the Merit-based Incentive Payment System, Alternative Payment Models, the Hospital Value-Based Purchasing Program, and any other value-based payment program determined appropriate by the Secretary;

"(ii) related to the quality of patient care;

"(iii) related to public health;

"(iv) related to clinical research;

"(v) related to the privacy and security of electronic health information;

"(vi) related to innovation in the field of health information technology;

"(vii) related to patient safety;

"(viii) related to the usability of health information technology;

"(ix) related to individuals' access to electronic health information; and

"(x) other priorities determined appropriate by the Secretary;

"(B) identify existing standards and implementation specifications that support the use and exchange of electronic health information needed to meet the priorities identified in subparagraph (A); and

"(C) publish a report summarizing the findings of the analysis conducted under subparagraphs (A) and (B) and make appropriate recommendations.

"(2) PRIORITIZATION.—In identifying such standards and implementation specifications under paragraph (1)(B), the HIT Advisory Committee shall prioritize standards and implementation specifications developed by consensus-based standards development organizations.

"(3) GUIDELINES FOR REVIEW OF EXISTING STANDARDS AND SPECIFICATIONS.—In consultation with the consensus-based entity described in section 1890 of the Social Security Act and other appropriate Federal agencies, the analysis of existing standards under paragraph (1)(B) shall include an evaluation of the need for a core set of common data elements and associated value sets to enhance the ability of certified health information technology to capture, use, and exchange structured electronic health information.

"(b) REVIEW OF ADOPTED STANDARDS.—

"(1) IN GENERAL.—Beginning 5 years after the date of enactment of the 21st Century Cures Act and every 3 years thereafter, the National Coordinator shall convene stakeholders to review the existing set of adopted standards and implementation specifications and make recommendations with respect to whether to—

"(A) maintain the use of such standards and implementation specifications; or

"(B) phase out such standards and implementation specifications.

"(2) PRIORITIES.—The HIT Advisory Committee, in collaboration with the National Institute for Standards and Technology, shall annually and through the use of public input, review and publish priorities for the use of health information technology, standards, and implementation specifications to support those priorities.

"(c) RULE OF CONSTRUCTION.—Nothing in this section shall be construed to prevent the use or adoption of novel standards that improve upon the existing health information technology infrastructure and facilitate the secure exchange of health information.".

SEC. 4004. INFORMATION BLOCKING.

Subtitle C of title XXX of the Public Health Service Act (42 U.S.C. 300jj–51 et seq.) is amended by adding at the end the following:

"SEC. 3022. INFORMATION BLOCKING.

"(a) DEFINITION.—

"(1) IN GENERAL.—In this section, the term 'information blocking' means a practice that—

"(A) except as required by law or specified by the Secretary pursuant to rulemaking under paragraph (3), is likely to interfere with, prevent, or materially discourage access, exchange, or use of electronic health information; and

"(B)(i) if conducted by a health information technology developer, exchange, or network, such developer, exchange, or network knows, or should know, that such practice is likely to interfere with, prevent, or materially discourage the access, exchange, or use of electronic health information; or

"(ii) if conducted by a health care provider, such provider knows that such practice is unreasonable and is likely to interfere with, prevent, or materially discourage access, exchange, or use of electronic health information.

"(2) PRACTICES DESCRIBED.—The information blocking practices described in paragraph (1) may include—

"(A) practices that restrict authorized access, exchange, or use under applicable State or Federal law of such information for treatment and other permitted purposes under such applicable law, including transitions between certified health information technologies;

"(B) implementing health information technology in nonstandard ways that are likely to substantially increase the complexity or burden of accessing, exchanging, or using electronic health information; and

"(C) implementing health information technology in ways that are likely to—

"(i) restrict the access, exchange, or use of electronic health information with respect to ex-

porting complete information sets or in transitioning between health information technology systems; or

"(ii) lead to fraud, waste, or abuse, or impede innovations and advancements in health information access, exchange, and use, including care delivery enabled by health information technology.

"(3) RULEMAKING.—The Secretary, through rulemaking, shall identify reasonable and necessary activities that do not constitute information blocking for purposes of paragraph (1).

"(4) NO ENFORCEMENT BEFORE EXCEPTION IDENTIFIED.—The term 'information blocking' does not include any practice or conduct occurring prior to the date that is 30 days after the date of enactment of the 21st Century Cures Act.

"(5) CONSULTATION.—The Secretary may consult with the Federal Trade Commission in promulgating regulations under this subsection, to the extent that such regulations define practices that are necessary to promote competition and consumer welfare.

"(6) APPLICATION.—The term 'information blocking', with respect to an individual or entity, shall not include an act or practice other than an act or practice committed by such individual or entity.

"(7) CLARIFICATION.—In carrying out this section, the Secretary shall ensure that health care providers are not penalized for the failure of developers of health information technology or other entities offering health information technology to such providers to ensure that such technology meets the requirements to be certified under this title.

"(b) INSPECTOR GENERAL AUTHORITY.—

"(1) IN GENERAL.—The inspector general of the Department of Health and Human Services (referred to in this section as the 'Inspector General') may investigate any claim that—

"(A) a health information technology developer of certified health information technology or other entity offering certified health information technology—

"(i) submitted a false attestation under section 3001(c)(5)(D)(vii); or

"(ii) engaged in information blocking;

"(B) a health care provider engaged in information blocking; or

"(C) a health information exchange or network engaged in information blocking.

"(2) PENALTIES.—

"(A) DEVELOPERS, NETWORKS, AND EXCHANGES.—Any individual or entity described in subparagraph (A) or (C) of paragraph (1) that the Inspector General, following an investigation conducted under this subsection, determines to have committed information blocking shall be subject to a civil monetary penalty determined by the Secretary for all such violations identified through such investigation, which may not exceed $1,000,000 per violation. Such determination shall take into account factors such as the nature and extent of the information blocking and harm resulting from such information blocking, including, where applicable, the number of patients affected, the number of providers affected, and the number of days the information blocking persisted.

"(B) PROVIDERS.—Any individual or entity described in subparagraph (B) of paragraph (1) determined by the Inspector General to have committed information blocking shall be referred to the appropriate agency to be subject to appropriate disincentives using authorities under applicable Federal law, as the Secretary sets forth through notice and comment rulemaking.

"(C) PROCEDURE.—The provisions of section 1128A of the Social Security Act (other than subsections (a) and (b) of such section) shall apply to a civil money penalty applied under this paragraph in the same manner as such provisions apply to a civil money penalty or proceeding under such section 1128A(a).

"(D) RECOVERED PENALTY FUNDS.—The amounts recovered under this paragraph shall be allocated as follows:

"(i) ANNUAL OPERATING EXPENSES.—Each year following the establishment of the authority under this subsection, the Office of the Inspector General shall provide to the Secretary an estimate of the costs to carry out investigations under this section. Such estimate may include reasonable reserves to account for variance in annual amounts recovered under this paragraph. There is authorized to be appropriated for purposes of carrying out this section an amount equal to the amount specified in such estimate for the fiscal year.

"(ii) APPLICATION TO OTHER PROGRAMS.—The amounts recovered under this paragraph and remaining after amounts are made available under clause (i) shall be transferred to the Federal Hospital Insurance Trust Fund under section 1817 of the Social Security Act and the Federal Supplementary Medical Insurance Trust Fund under section 1841 of such Act, in such proportion as the Secretary determines appropriate.

"(E) AUTHORIZATION OF APPROPRIATIONS.—There is authorized to be appropriated to the Office of the Inspector General to carry out this section $10,000,000, to remain available until expended.

"(3) RESOLUTION OF CLAIMS.—

"(A) IN GENERAL.—The Office of the Inspector General, if such Office determines that a consultation regarding the health privacy and security rules promulgated under section 264(c) of the Health Insurance Portability and Accountability Act of 1996 (42 U.S.C. 1320d–2 note) will resolve an information blocking claim, may refer such instances of information blocking to the Office for Civil Rights of the Department of Health and Human Services for resolution.

"(B) LIMITATION ON LIABILITY.—If a health care provider or health information technology developer makes information available based on a good faith reliance on consultations with the Office for Civil Rights of the Department of Health and Human Services pursuant to a referral under subparagraph (A), with respect to such information, the health care provider or developer shall not be liable for such disclosure or disclosures made pursuant to subparagraph (A).

"(c) IDENTIFYING BARRIERS TO EXCHANGE OF CERTIFIED HEALTH INFORMATION TECHNOLOGY.—

"(1) TRUSTED EXCHANGE DEFINED.—In this section, the term 'trusted exchange' with respect to certified electronic health records means that the certified electronic health record technology has the technical capability to enable secure health information exchange between users and multiple certified electronic health record technology systems.

"(2) GUIDANCE.—The National Coordinator, in consultation with the Office for Civil Rights of the Department of Health and Human Services, shall issue guidance on common legal, governance, and security barriers that prevent the trusted exchange of electronic health information.

"(3) REFERRAL.—The National Coordinator and the Office for Civil Rights of the Department of Health and Human Services may refer to the Inspector General instances or patterns of refusal to exchange health information with an individual or entity using certified electronic health record technology that is technically capable of trusted exchange and under conditions when exchange is legally permissible.

"(d) ADDITIONAL PROVISIONS.—

"(1) INFORMATION SHARING PROVISIONS.—The National Coordinator may serve as a technical consultant to the Inspector General and the Federal Trade Commission for purposes of carrying out this section. The National Coordinator *may, notwithstanding any other provision of law, share information related to claims or investigations under subsection (b) with the Federal Trade Commission for purposes of such investigations and shall share information with the Inspector General, as required by law.*

"(2) PROTECTION FROM DISCLOSURE OF INFORMATION.—Any information that is received by the National Coordinator in connection with a claim or suggestion of possible information blocking and that could reasonably be expected to facilitate identification of the source of the information—

"(A) shall not be disclosed by the National Coordinator except as may be necessary to carry out the purpose of this section;

"(B) shall be exempt from mandatory disclosure under section 552 of title 5, United States Code, as provided by subsection (b)(3) of such section; and

"(C) may be used by the Inspector General or Federal Trade Commission for reporting purposes to the extent that such information could not reasonably be expected to facilitate identification of the source of such information.

"(3) STANDARDIZED PROCESS.—

"(A) IN GENERAL.—The National Coordinator shall implement a standardized process for the public to submit reports on claims of—

"(i) health information technology products or developers of such products (or other entities offering such products to health care providers) not being interoperable or resulting in information blocking;

"(ii) actions described in subsection (b)(1) that result in information blocking as described in subsection (a); and

"(iii) any other act described in subsection (a).

"(B) COLLECTION OF INFORMATION.—The standardized process implemented under subparagraph (A) shall provide for the collection of such information as the originating institution, location, type of transaction, system and version, timestamp, terminating institution, locations, system and version, failure notice, and other related information.

"(4) NONDUPLICATION OF PENALTY STRUCTURES.—In carrying out this subsection, the Secretary shall, to the extent possible, ensure that penalties do not duplicate penalty structures that would otherwise apply with respect to information blocking and the type of individual or entity involved as of the day before the date of the enactment of this section.".

SEC. 4005. LEVERAGING ELECTRONIC HEALTH RECORDS TO IMPROVE PATIENT CARE.

(a) REQUIREMENT RELATING TO REGISTRIES.—

(1) IN GENERAL.—To be certified in accordance with title XXX of the Public Health Service Act (42 U.S.C. 300jj et seq.), electronic health records shall be capable of transmitting to, and where applicable, receiving and accepting data from, registries in accordance with standards recognized by the Office of the National Coordinator for Health Information Technology, including clinician-led clinical data registries, that are also certified to be technically capable of receiving and accepting from, and where applicable, transmitting data to certified electronic health record technology in accordance with such standards.

(2) RULE OF CONSTRUCTION.—Nothing in this subsection shall be construed to require the certification of registries beyond the technical capability to exchange data in accordance with applicable recognized standards.

(b) DEFINITION.—For purposes of this Act, the term "clinician-led clinical data registry" means a clinical data repository—

(1) that is established and operated by a clinician-led or controlled, tax-exempt (pursuant to section 501(c) of the Internal Revenue Code of

1986), professional society or other similar clinician-led or -controlled organization, or such organization's controlled affiliate, devoted to the care of a population defined by a particular disease, condition, exposure or therapy;

(2) that is designed to collect detailed, standardized data on an ongoing basis for medical procedures, services, or therapies for particular diseases, conditions, or exposures;

(3) that provides feedback to participants who submit reports to the repository;

(4) that meets standards for data quality including—

(A) systematically collecting clinical and other health care data, using standardized data elements and having procedures in place to verify the completeness and validity of those data; and

(B) being subject to regular data checks or audits to verify completeness and validity; and

(5) that provides ongoing participant training and support.

(c) TREATMENT OF HEALTH INFORMATION TECHNOLOGY DEVELOPERS WITH RESPECT TO PATIENT SAFETY ORGANIZATIONS.—

(1) IN GENERAL.—In applying part C of title IX of the Public Health Service Act (42 U.S.C. 299b–21 et seq.), a health information technology developer shall be treated as a provider (as defined in section 921 of such Act) for purposes of reporting and conducting patient safety activities concerning improving clinical care through the use of health information technology that could result in improved patient safety, health care quality, or health care outcomes.

(2) REPORT.—Not later than 4 years after the date of enactment of this Act, the Secretary of Health and Human Services shall submit to the Committee on Health, Education, Labor, and Pensions of the Senate and the Committee on Energy and Commerce of the House of Representatives, a report concerning best practices and current trends voluntarily provided, without identifying individual providers or disclosing or using protected health information or individually identifiable information, by patient safety organizations to improve the integration of health information technology into clinical practice.

SEC. 4006. EMPOWERING PATIENTS AND IMPROVING PATIENT ACCESS TO THEIR ELECTRONIC HEALTH INFORMATION.

(a) USE OF HEALTH INFORMATION EXCHANGES FOR PATIENT ACCESS.—Section 3009 of the Public Health Service Act (42 U.S.C. 300jj–19) is amended by adding at the end the following:

"(c) PROMOTING PATIENT ACCESS TO ELECTRONIC HEALTH INFORMATION THROUGH HEALTH INFORMATION EXCHANGES.—

"(1) IN GENERAL.—The Secretary shall use existing authorities to encourage partnerships between health information exchange organizations and networks and health care providers, health plans, and other appropriate entities with the goal of offering patients access to their electronic health information in a single, longitudinal format that is easy to understand, secure, and may be updated automatically.

"(2) EDUCATION OF PROVIDERS.—The Secretary, in coordination with the Office for Civil Rights of the Department of Health and Human Services, shall—

"(A) educate health care providers on ways of leveraging the capabilities of health information exchanges (or other relevant platforms) to provide patients with access to their electronic health information;

"(B) clarify misunderstandings by health care providers about using health information exchanges (or other relevant platforms) for patient access to electronic health information; and

"(C) to the extent practicable, educate providers about health information exchanges (or other relevant platforms) that employ some or all of the capabilities described in paragraph (1).

"(3) REQUIREMENTS.—In carrying out paragraph (1), the Secretary, in coordination with the Office for Civil Rights, shall issue guidance to health information exchanges related to best practices to ensure that the electronic health information provided to patients is—

"(A) private and secure;

"(B) accurate;

"(C) verifiable; and

"(D) where a patient's authorization to exchange information is required by law, easily exchanged pursuant to such authorization.

"(4) RULE OF CONSTRUCTION.—Nothing in this subsection shall be construed to preempt State laws applicable to patient consent for the access of information through a health information exchange (or other relevant platform) that provide protections to patients that are greater than the protections otherwise provided for under applicable Federal law.

"(d) EFFORTS TO PROMOTE ACCESS TO HEALTH INFORMATION.—The National Coordinator and the Office for Civil Rights of the Department of Health and Human Services shall jointly promote patient access to health information in a manner that would ensure that such information is available in a form convenient for the patient, in a reasonable manner, without burdening the health care provider involved.

"(e) ACCESSIBILITY OF PATIENT RECORDS.—

"(1) ACCESSIBILITY AND UPDATING OF INFORMATION.—

"(A) IN GENERAL.—The Secretary, in consultation with the National Coordinator, shall promote policies that ensure that a patient's electronic health information is accessible to that patient and the patient's designees, in a manner that facilitates communication with the patient's health care providers and other individuals, including researchers, consistent with such patient's consent.

"(B) UPDATING EDUCATION ON ACCESSING AND EXCHANGING PERSONAL HEALTH INFORMATION.—To promote awareness that an individual has a right of access to inspect, obtain a copy of, and transmit to a third party a copy of such individual's protected health information pursuant to the Health Information Portability and Accountability Act, Privacy Rule (subpart E of part 164 of title 45, Code of Federal Regulations), the Director of the Office for Civil Rights, in consultation with the National Coordinator, shall assist individuals and health care providers in understanding a patient's rights to access and protect personal health information under the Health Insurance Portability and Accountability Act of 1996 (Public Law 104–191), including providing best practices for requesting personal health information in a computable format, including using patient portals or third-party applications and common cases when a provider is permitted to exchange and provide access to health information.".

"(2) CERTIFYING USABILITY FOR PATIENTS.—In carrying out certification programs under section 3001(c)(5), the National Coordinator may require that—

"(A) the certification criteria support—

"(i) patient access to their electronic health information, including in a single longitudinal format that is easy to understand, secure, and may be updated automatically;

"(ii) the patient's ability to electronically communicate patient-reported information (such as family history and medical history); and

"(iii) patient access to their personal electronic health information for research at the option of the patient; and

"(B) the HIT Advisory Committee develop and prioritize standards, implementation specifications, and certification criteria required to help

support patient access to electronic health information, patient usability, and support for technologies that offer patients access to their electronic health information in a single, longitudinal format that is easy to understand, secure, and may be updated automatically.''.

(b) ACCESS TO INFORMATION IN AN ELECTRONIC FORMAT.—Section 13405(e) of the Health Information Technology for Economic and Clinical Health Act (42 U.S.C. 17935) is amended—

(1) in paragraph (1), by striking "and" at the end;

(2) by redesignating paragraph (2) as paragraph (3); and

(3) by inserting after paragraph (1), the following:

"(2) if the individual makes a request to a business associate for access to, or a copy of, protected health information about the individual, or if an individual makes a request to a business associate to grant such access to, or transmit such copy directly to, a person or entity designated by the individual, a business associate may provide the individual with such access or copy, which may be in an electronic form, or grant or transmit such access or copy to such person or entity designated by the individual; and''.

SEC. 4007. GAO STUDY ON PATIENT MATCHING.

(a) IN GENERAL.—Not later than 1 year after the date of enactment of this Act, the Comptroller General of the United States shall conduct a study to—

(1) review the policies and activities of the Office of the National Coordinator for Health Information Technology and other relevant stakeholders, which may include standards development organizations, experts in the technical aspects of health information technology, health information technology developers, providers of health services, health care suppliers, health care payers, health care quality organizations, States, health information technology policy experts, and other appropriate entities, to ensure appropriate patient matching to protect patient privacy and security with respect to electronic health records and the exchange of electronic health information; and

(2) survey ongoing efforts related to the policies and activities described in paragraph (1) and the effectiveness of such efforts occurring in the private sector.

(b) AREAS OF CONCENTRATION.—In conducting the study under subsection (a), the Comptroller General shall—

(1) evaluate current methods used in certified electronic health records for patient matching based on performance related to factors such as—

(A) the privacy of patient information;

(B) the security of patient information;

(C) improving matching rates;

(D) reducing matching errors; and

(E) reducing duplicate records; and

(2) determine whether the Office of the National Coordinator for Health Information Technology could improve patient matching by taking steps including—

(A) defining additional data elements to assist in patient data matching;

(B) agreeing on a required minimum set of elements that need to be collected and exchanged;

(C) requiring electronic health records to have the ability to make certain fields required and use specific standards; and

(D) other options recommended by the relevant stakeholders consulted pursuant to subsection (a).

(c) REPORT.—Not later than 2 years after the date of enactment of this Act, the Comptroller General shall submit to the appropriate committees of Congress a report concerning the findings of the study conducted under subsection (a).

SEC. 4008. GAO STUDY ON PATIENT ACCESS TO HEALTH INFORMATION.

(a) STUDY.—

(1) IN GENERAL.—The Comptroller General of the United States (referred to in this section as the "Comptroller General") shall build on prior Government Accountability Office studies and other literature review and conduct a study to review patient access to their own protected health information, including barriers to such patient access and complications or difficulties providers experience in providing access to patients. In conducting such study, the Comptroller General shall consider the increase in adoption of health information technology and the increasing prevalence of protected health information that is maintained electronically.

(2) AREAS OF CONCENTRATION.—In conducting the review under paragraph (1), the Comptroller General shall consider—

(A) instances when covered entities charge individuals, including patients, third parties, and health care providers, for record requests, including records that are requested in an electronic format;

(B) examples of the amounts and types of fees charged to individuals for record requests, including instances when the record is requested to be transmitted to a third party;

(C) the extent to which covered entities are unable to provide the access requested by individuals in the form and format requested by the individual, including examples of such instances;

(D) instances in which third parties may request protected health information through patients' individual right of access, including instances where such requests may be used to circumvent appropriate fees that may be charged to third parties;

(E) opportunities that permit covered entities to charge appropriate fees to third parties for patient records while providing patients with access to their protected health information at low or no cost;

(F) the ability of providers to distinguish between requests originating from an individual that require limitation to a cost-based fee and requests originating from third parties that may not be limited to cost-based fees; and

(G) other circumstances that may inhibit the ability of providers to provide patients with access to their records, and the ability of patients to gain access to their records.

(b) REPORT.—Not later than 18 months after the date of enactment of this Act, the Comptroller General shall submit a report to Congress on the findings of the study conducted under subsection (a).

SEC. 4009. IMPROVING MEDICARE LOCAL COVERAGE DETERMINATIONS.

(a) IN GENERAL.—Section 1862(l)(5) of the Social Security Act (42 U.S.C. 1395y(l)(5)) is amended by adding at the end the following new subparagraph:

"(D) LOCAL COVERAGE DETERMINATIONS.—The Secretary shall require each Medicare administrative contractor that develops a local coverage determination to make available on the Internet website of such contractor and on the Medicare Internet website, at least 45 days before the effective date of such determination, the following information:

"(i) Such determination in its entirety.

"(ii) Where and when the proposed determination was first made public.

"(iii) Hyperlinks to the proposed determination and a response to comments submitted to the contractor with respect to such proposed determination.

"(iv) A summary of evidence that was considered by the contractor during the development of such determination and a list of the sources of such evidence.

"(v) An explanation of the rationale that supports such determination.''.

(b) EFFECTIVE DATE.—The amendment made by subsection (a) shall apply with respect to local coverage determinations that are proposed or revised on or after the date that is 180 days after the date of enactment of this Act.

SEC. 4010. MEDICARE PHARMACEUTICAL AND TECHNOLOGY OMBUDSMAN.

Section 1808 of the Social Security Act (42 U.S.C. 1395b–9) is amended by adding at the end the following new subsection:

"(d) PHARMACEUTICAL AND TECHNOLOGY OMBUDSMAN.—

"(1) IN GENERAL.—Not later than 12 months after the date of enactment of this paragraph, the Secretary shall provide for a pharmaceutical and technology ombudsman within the Centers for Medicare & Medicaid Services who shall receive and respond to complaints, grievances, and requests that—

"(A) are from entities that manufacture pharmaceutical, biotechnology, medical device, or diagnostic products that are covered or for which coverage is being sought under this title; and

"(B) are with respect to coverage, coding, or payment under this title for such products.

"(2) APPLICATION.—The second sentence of subsection (c)(2) shall apply to the ombudsman under subparagraph (A) in the same manner as such sentence applies to the Medicare Beneficiary Ombudsman under subsection (c).''.

SEC. 4011. MEDICARE SITE-OF-SERVICE PRICE TRANSPARENCY.

Section 1834 of the Social Security Act (42 U.S.C. 1395m) is amended by adding at the end the following new subsection:

"(t) SITE-OF-SERVICE PRICE TRANSPARENCY.—

"(1) IN GENERAL.—In order to facilitate price transparency with respect to items and services for which payment may be made either to a hospital outpatient department or to an ambulatory surgical center under this title, the Secretary shall, for 2018 and each year thereafter, make available to the public via a searchable Internet website, with respect to an appropriate number of such items and services—

"(A) the estimated payment amount for the item or service under the outpatient department fee schedule under subsection (t) of section 1833 and the ambulatory surgical center payment system under subsection (i) of such section; and

"(B) the estimated amount of beneficiary liability applicable to the item or service.

"(2) CALCULATION OF ESTIMATED BENEFICIARY LIABILITY.—For purposes of paragraph (1)(B), the estimated amount of beneficiary liability, with respect to an item or service, is the amount for such item or service for which an individual who does not have coverage under a Medicare supplemental policy certified under section 1882 or any other supplemental insurance coverage is responsible.

"(3) IMPLEMENTATION.—In carrying out this subsection, the Secretary—

"(A) shall include in the notice described in section 1804(a) a notification of the availability of the estimated amounts made available under paragraph (1); and

"(B) may utilize mechanisms in existence on the date of enactment of this subsection, such as the portion of the Internet website of the Centers for Medicare & Medicaid Services on which information comparing physician performance is posted (commonly referred to as the Physician Compare Internet website), to make available such estimated amounts under such paragraph.

"(4) FUNDING.—For purposes of implementing this subsection, the Secretary shall provide for the transfer, from the Federal Supplementary Medical Insurance Trust Fund under section 1841 to the Centers for Medicare & Medicaid Services Program Management Account, of $6,000,000 for fiscal year 2017, to remain available until expended.''.

SEC. 4012. TELEHEALTH SERVICES IN MEDICARE.

(a) PROVISION OF INFORMATION BY CENTERS FOR MEDICARE & MEDICAID SERVICES.—Not later than 1 year after the date of enactment of this Act, the Administrator of the Centers for Medicare & Medicaid Services shall provide to the committees of jurisdiction of the House of Representatives and the Senate information on the following:

(1) The populations of Medicare beneficiaries, such as those who are dually eligible for the Medicare program under title XVIII of the Social Security Act (42 U.S.C. 1395 et seq.) and the Medicaid program under title XIX of such Act (42 U.S.C. 1396 et seq.) and those with chronic conditions, whose care may be improved most in terms of quality and efficiency by the expansion, in a manner that meets or exceeds the existing in-person standard of care under the Medicare program under such title XVIII, of telehealth services under section 1834(m)(4) of such Act (42 U.S.C. 1395m(m)(4)).

(2) Activities by the Center for Medicare and Medicaid Innovation which examine the use of telehealth services in models, projects, or initiatives funded through section 1115A of such Act (42 U.S.C. 1315a).

(3) The types of high-volume services (and related diagnoses) under such title XVIII which might be suitable to be furnished using telehealth.

(4) Barriers that might prevent the expansion of telehealth services under section 1834(m)(4) of the Social Security Act (42 U.S.C. 1395m(m)(4)) beyond such services that are in effect as of the date of enactment of this Act.

(b) PROVISION OF INFORMATION BY MEDPAC.—Not later than March 15, 2018, the Medicare Payment Advisory Commission established under section 1805 of the Social Security Act (42 U.S.C. 1395b–6) shall, using quantitative and qualitative research methods, provide information to the committees of jurisdiction of the House of Representatives and the Senate that identifies—

(1) the telehealth services for which payment can be made, as of the date of enactment of this Act, under the fee-for-service program under parts A and B of title XVIII of such Act;

(2) the telehealth services for which payment can be made, as of such date, under private health insurance plans; and

(3) with respect to services identified under paragraph (2) but not under paragraph (1), ways in which payment for such services might be incorporated into such fee-for-service program (including any recommendations for ways to accomplish this incorporation).

(c) SENSE OF CONGRESS.—It is the sense of Congress that—

(1) eligible originating sites should be expanded beyond those originating sites described in section 1834(m)(4)(C) of the Social Security Act (42 U.S.C. 1395m(m)(4)(C)); and

(2) any expansion of telehealth services under the Medicare program under title XVIII of such Act should—

(A) recognize that telemedicine is the delivery of safe, effective, quality health care services, by a health care provider, using technology as the mode of care delivery;

(B) meet or exceed the conditions of coverage and payment with respect to the Medicare program if the service was furnished in person, including standards of care, unless specifically addressed in subsequent legislation; and

(C) involve clinically appropriate means to furnish such services.

TITLE V—SAVINGS

SEC. 5001. SAVINGS IN THE MEDICARE IMPROVEMENT FUND.

Section 1898(b)(1) of the Social Security Act (42 U.S.C. 1395iii(b)(1)), as amended by section 704(h) of the Comprehensive Addiction and Recovery Act of 2016, is amended by striking "$140,000,000" and inserting "$270,000,000".

SEC. 5002. MEDICAID REIMBURSEMENT TO STATES FOR DURABLE MEDICAL EQUIPMENT.

Section 1903(i)(27) of the Social Security Act (42 U.S.C. 1396b(i)(27)) is amended by striking "January 1, 2019" and inserting "January 1, 2018".

SEC. 5003. PENALTIES FOR VIOLATIONS OF GRANTS, CONTRACTS, AND OTHER AGREEMENTS.

(a) IN GENERAL.—Section 1128A of the Social Security Act (42 U.S.C. 1320a–7a) is amended by adding at the end the following new subsections:

"(o) Any person (including an organization, agency, or other entity, but excluding a program beneficiary, as defined in subsection (q)(4)) that, with respect to a grant, contract, or other agreement for which the Secretary provides funding—

"(1) knowingly presents or causes to be presented a specified claim (as defined in subsection (r)) under such grant, contract, or other agreement that the person knows or should know is false or fraudulent;

"(2) knowingly makes, uses, or causes to be made or used any false statement, omission, or misrepresentation of a material fact in any application, proposal, bid, progress report, or other document that is required to be submitted in order to directly or indirectly receive or retain funds provided in whole or in part by such Secretary pursuant to such grant, contract, or other agreement;

"(3) knowingly makes, uses, or causes to be made or used, a false record or statement material to a false or fraudulent specified claim under such grant, contract, or other agreement;

"(4) knowingly makes, uses, or causes to be made or used, a false record or statement material to an obligation (as defined in subsection (s)) to pay or transmit funds or property to such Secretary with respect to such grant, contract, or other agreement, or knowingly conceals or knowingly and improperly avoids or decreases an obligation to pay or transmit funds or property to such Secretary with respect to such grant, contract, or other agreement; or

"(5) fails to grant timely access, upon reasonable request (as defined by such Secretary in regulations), to the Inspector General of the Department, for the purpose of audits, investigations, evaluations, or other statutory functions of such Inspector General in matters involving such grants, contracts, or other agreements;

shall be subject, in addition to any other penalties that may be prescribed by law, to a civil money penalty in cases under paragraph (1), of not more than $10,000 for each specified claim; in cases under paragraph (2), not more than $50,000 for each false statement, omission, or misrepresentation of a material fact; in cases under paragraph (3), not more than $50,000 for each false record or statement; in cases under paragraph (4), not more than $50,000 for each false record or statement or $10,000 for each day that the person knowingly conceals or knowingly and improperly avoids or decreases an obligation to pay; or in cases under paragraph (5), not more than $15,000 for each day of the failure described in such paragraph. In addition, in cases under paragraphs (1) and (3), such a person shall be subject to an assessment of not more than 3 times the amount claimed in the specified claim described in such paragraph in lieu of damages sustained by the United States or a specified State agency because of such specified claim, and in cases under paragraphs (2) and (4), such a person shall be subject to an assessment of not more than 3 times the total amount of the funds described in paragraph (2) or (4), respectively (or, in the case of an obligation to transmit property to the Secretary described in paragraph (4), of the value of the property described in such paragraph) in lieu of damages sustained by the United States or a specified State agency because of such case. In addition, the Secretary may make a determination in the same proceeding to exclude the person from participation in the Federal health care programs (as defined in section 1128B(f)(1)) and to direct the appropriate State agency to exclude the person from participation in any State health care program.

"(p) The provisions of subsections (c), (d), (g), and (h) shall apply to a civil money penalty or assessment under subsection (o) in the same manner as such provisions apply to a penalty, assessment, or proceeding under subsection (a). In applying subsection (d), each reference to a claim under such subsection shall be treated as including a reference to a specified claim (as defined in subsection (r)).

"(q) For purposes of this subsection and subsections (o) and (p):

"(1) The term 'Department' means the Department of Health and Human Services.

"(2) The term 'material' means having a natural tendency to influence, or be capable of influencing, the payment or receipt of money or property.

"(3) The term 'other agreement' includes a cooperative agreement, scholarship, fellowship, loan, subsidy, payment for a specified use, donation agreement, award, or subaward (regardless of whether one or more of the persons entering into the agreement is a contractor or subcontractor).

"(4) The term 'program beneficiary' means, in the case of a grant, contract, or other agreement designed to accomplish the objective of awarding or otherwise furnishing benefits or assistance to individuals and for which the Secretary provides funding, an individual who applies for, or who receives, such benefits or assistance from such grant, contract, or other agreement. Such term does not include, with respect to such grant, contract, or other agreement, an officer, employee, or agent of a person or entity that receives such grant or that enters into such contract or other agreement.

"(5) The term 'recipient' includes a subrecipient or subcontractor.

"(6) The term 'specified State agency' means an agency of a State government established or designated to administer or supervise the administration of a grant, contract, or other agreement funded in whole or in part by the Secretary.

"(r) For purposes of this section, the term 'specified claim' means any application, request, or demand under a grant, contract, or other agreement for money or property, whether or not the United States or a specified State agency has title to the money or property, that is not a claim (as defined in subsection (i)(2)) and that—

"(1) is presented or caused to be presented to an officer, employee, or agent of the Department or agency thereof, or of any specified State agency; or

"(2) is made to a contractor, grantee, or any other recipient if the money or property is to be spent or used on the Department's behalf or to advance a Department program or interest, and if the Department—

"(A) provides or has provided any portion of the money or property requested or demanded; or

"(B) will reimburse such contractor, grantee, or other recipient for any portion of the money or property which is requested or demanded.

"(s) For purposes of subsection (o), the term 'obligation' means an established duty, whether or not fixed, arising from an express or implied contractual, grantor-grantee, or licensor-licensee relationship, for a fee-based or similar relationship, from statute or regulation, or from the retention of any overpayment.".

(b) CONFORMING AMENDMENTS.—Section 1128A of the Social Security Act (42 U.S.C. 1320a–7a) is amended—

(1) in subsection (e), by inserting "or specified claim" after "claim" in the first sentence; and

(2) in subsection (f)—

(A) in the matter preceding paragraph (1)—

(i) by inserting "or specified claim (as defined in subsection (r))" after "district where the claim"; and

(ii) by inserting "(or, with respect to a person described in subsection (o), the person)" after "claimant"; and

(B) in the matter following paragraph (4), by inserting "(or, in the case of a penalty or assessment under subsection (o), by a specified State agency (as defined in subsection (q)(6)),") after "or a State agency".

SEC. 5004. REDUCING OVERPAYMENTS OF INFUSION DRUGS.

(a) TREATMENT OF INFUSION DRUGS FURNISHED THROUGH DURABLE MEDICAL EQUIPMENT.—Section 1842(o)(1) of the Social Security Act (42 U.S.C. 1395u(o)(1)) is amended—

(1) in subparagraph (C), by inserting "(and including a drug or biological described in subparagraph (D)(i) furnished on or after January 1, 2017)" after "2005"; and

(2) in subparagraph (D)—

(A) by striking "infusion drugs" and inserting "infusion drugs or biologicals" each place it appears; and

(B) in clause (i)—

(i) by striking "2004" and inserting "2004, and before January 1, 2017"; and

(ii) by striking "for such drug".

(b) NONINCLUSION OF DME INFUSION DRUGS UNDER DME COMPETITIVE ACQUISITION PROGRAMS.—

(1) IN GENERAL.—Section 1847(a)(2)(A) of the Social Security Act (42 U.S.C. 1395w–3(a)(2)(A)) is amended—

(A) by striking "and excluding" and inserting ", excluding"; and

(B) by inserting before the period at the end the following: ", and excluding drugs and biologicals described in section 1842(o)(1)(D)".

(2) CONFORMING AMENDMENT.—Section 1842(o)(1)(D)(ii) of the Social Security Act (42 U.S.C. 1395u(o)(1)(D)(ii)) is amended by striking "2007" and inserting "2007, and before the date of the enactment of the 21st Century Cures Act.".

SEC. 5005. INCREASING OVERSIGHT OF TERMINATION OF MEDICAID PROVIDERS.

(a) INCREASED OVERSIGHT AND REPORTING.—

(1) STATE REPORTING REQUIREMENTS.—Section 1902(kk) of the Social Security Act (42 U.S.C. 1396a(kk)) is amended—

(A) by redesignating paragraph (8) as paragraph (9); and

(B) by inserting after paragraph (7) the following new paragraph:

"(8) PROVIDER TERMINATIONS.—

"(A) IN GENERAL.—Beginning on July 1, 2018, in the case of a notification under subsection (a)(41) with respect to a termination for a reason specified in section 455.101 of title 42, Code of Federal Regulations (as in effect on November 1, 2015) or for any other reason specified by the Secretary, of the participation of a provider of services or any other person under the State plan (or under a waiver of the plan), the State, not later than 30 days after the effective date of such termination submits to the Secretary with respect to any such provider or person, as appropriate—

"(i) the name of such provider or person;

"(ii) the provider type of such provider or person;

"(iii) the specialty of such provider's or person's practice;

"(iv) the date of birth, Social Security number, national provider identifier (if applicable), Federal taxpayer identification number, and the State license or certification number of such provider or person (if applicable);

"(v) the reason for the termination;

"(vi) a copy of the notice of termination sent to the provider or person;

"(vii) the date on which such termination is effective, as specified in the notice; and

"(viii) any other information required by the Secretary.

"(B) EFFECTIVE DATE DEFINED.—For purposes of this paragraph, the term 'effective date' means, with respect to a termination described in subparagraph (A), the later of—

"(i) the date on which such termination is effective, as specified in the notice of such termination; or

"(ii) the date on which all appeal rights applicable to such termination have been exhausted or the timeline for any such appeal has expired.".

(2) CONTRACT REQUIREMENT FOR MANAGED CARE ENTITIES.—Section 1932(d) of the Social Security Act (42 U.S.C. 1396u–2(d)) is amended by adding at the end the following new paragraph:

"(5) CONTRACT REQUIREMENT FOR MANAGED CARE ENTITIES.—With respect to any contract with a managed care entity under section 1903(m) or 1905(t)(3) (as applicable), no later than July 1, 2018, such contract shall include a provision that providers of services or persons terminated (as described in section 1902(kk)(8)) from participation under this title, title XVIII, or title XXI shall be terminated from participating under this title as a provider in any network of such entity that serves individuals eligible to receive medical assistance under this title.".

(3) TERMINATION NOTIFICATION DATABASE.—Section 1902 of the Social Security Act (42 U.S.C. 1396a) is amended by adding at the end the following new subsection:

"(ll) TERMINATION NOTIFICATION DATABASE.—In the case of a provider of services or any other person whose participation under this title or title XXI is terminated (as described in subsection (kk)(8)), the Secretary shall, not later than 30 days after the date on which the Secretary is notified of such termination under subsection (a)(41) (as applicable), review such termination and, if the Secretary determines appropriate, include such termination in any database or similar system developed pursuant to section 6401(b)(2) of the Patient Protection and Affordable Care Act (42 U.S.C. 1395cc note; Public Law 111–148).".

(4) NO FEDERAL FUNDS FOR ITEMS AND SERVICES FURNISHED BY TERMINATED PROVIDERS.—Section 1903 of the Social Security Act (42 U.S.C. 1396b) is amended—

(A) in subsection (i)(2)—

(i) in subparagraph (A), by striking the comma at the end and inserting a semicolon;

(ii) in subparagraph (B), by striking "or" at the end; and

(iii) by adding at the end the following new subparagraph:

"(D) beginning on July 1, 2018, under the plan by any provider of services or person whose participation in the State plan is terminated (as described in section 1902(kk)(8)) after the date that is 60 days after the date on which such termination is included in the database or other system under section 1902(ll); or"; and

(B) in subsection (m), by inserting after paragraph (2) the following new paragraph:

"(3) No payment shall be made under this title to a State with respect to expenditures incurred by the State for payment for services provided by a managed care entity (as defined under section 1932(a)(1)) under the State plan under this title (or under a waiver of the plan) unless the State—

"(A) beginning on July 1, 2018, has a contract with such entity that complies with the requirement specified in section 1932(d)(5); and

"(B) beginning on January 1, 2018, complies with the requirement specified in section 1932(d)(6)(A).".

(5) DEVELOPMENT OF UNIFORM TERMINOLOGY FOR REASONS FOR PROVIDER TERMINATION.—Not later than July 1, 2017, the Secretary of Health and Human Services shall, in consultation with the heads of State agencies administering State Medicaid plans (or waivers of such plans), issue regulations establishing uniform terminology to be used with respect to specifying reasons under subparagraph (A)(v) of paragraph (8) of section 1902(kk) of the Social Security Act (42 U.S.C. 1396a(kk)), as added by paragraph (1), for the termination (as described in such paragraph (8)) of the participation of certain providers in the Medicaid program under title XIX of such Act or the Children's Health Insurance Program under title XXI of such Act.

(6) CONFORMING AMENDMENT.—Section 1902(a)(41) of the Social Security Act (42 U.S.C. 1396a(a)(41)) is amended by striking "provide that whenever" and inserting "provide, in accordance with subsection (kk)(8) (as applicable), that whenever".

(b) INCREASING AVAILABILITY OF MEDICAID PROVIDER INFORMATION.—

(1) FFS PROVIDER ENROLLMENT.—Section 1902(a) of the Social Security Act (42 U.S.C. 1396a(a)) is amended by inserting after paragraph (77) the following new paragraph:

"(78) provide that, not later than January 1, 2017, in the case of a State that pursuant to its State plan or waiver of the plan for medical assistance pays for medical assistance on a fee-for-service basis, the State shall require each provider furnishing items and services to, or ordering, prescribing, referring, or certifying eligibility for, services for individuals eligible to receive medical assistance under such plan to enroll with the State agency and provide to the State agency the provider's identifying information, including the name, specialty, date of birth, Social Security number, national provider identifier (if applicable), Federal taxpayer identification number, and the State license or certification number of the provider (if applicable);".

(2) MANAGED CARE PROVIDER ENROLLMENT.—Section 1932(d) of the Social Security Act (42 U.S.C. 1396u–2(d)), as amended by subsection (a)(2), is amended by adding at the end the following new paragraph:

"(6) ENROLLMENT OF PARTICIPATING PROVIDERS.—

"(A) IN GENERAL.—Beginning not later than January 1, 2018, a State shall require that, in order to participate as a provider in the network of a managed care entity that provides services to, or orders, prescribes, refers, or certifies eligibility for services for, individuals who are eligible for medical assistance under the State plan under this title (or under a waiver of the plan) and who are enrolled with the entity, the provider is enrolled consistent with section 1902(kk) with the State agency administering the State plan under this title. Such enrollment shall include providing to the State agency the provider's identifying information, including the name, specialty, date of birth, Social Security number, national provider identifier, Federal taxpayer identification number, and the State license or certification number of the provider.

"(B) RULE OF CONSTRUCTION.—Nothing in subparagraph (A) shall be construed as requiring a provider described in such subparagraph to provide services to individuals who are not enrolled with a managed care entity under this title.".

(c) COORDINATION WITH CHIP.—

(1) IN GENERAL.—Section 2107(e)(1) of the Social Security Act (42 U.S.C. 1397gg(e)(1)) is amended—

(A) by redesignating subparagraphs (B), (C), (D), (E), (F), (G), (H), (I), (J), (K), (L), (M), (N), and (O) as subparagraphs (D), (E), (F), (G), (H), (I), (J), (K), (M), (N), (O), (P), (Q), and (R), respectively;

"(B) by inserting after subparagraph (A) the following new subparagraphs:

"(B) Section 1902(a)(39) (relating to termination of participation of certain providers).

"(C) Section 1902(a)(78) (relating to enrollment of providers participating in State plans providing medical assistance on a fee-for-service basis).";

"(C) by inserting after subparagraph (K) (as redesignated by subparagraph (A)) the following new subparagraph:

"(L) Section 1903(m)(3) (relating to limitation on payment with respect to managed care)."; and

"(D) in subparagraph (P) (as redesignated by subparagraph (A)), by striking "(a)(2)(C) and (h)" and inserting "(a)(2)(C) (relating to Indian enrollment), (d)(5) (relating to contract requirement for managed care entities), (d)(6) (relating to enrollment of providers participating with a managed care entity), and (h) (relating to special rules with respect to Indian enrollees, Indian health care providers, and Indian managed care entities)".

(2) EXCLUDING FROM MEDICAID PROVIDERS EXCLUDED FROM CHIP.—Section 1902(a)(39) of the Social Security Act (42 U.S.C. 1396a(a)(39)) is amended by striking "title XVIII or any other State plan under this title" and inserting "title XVIII, any other State plan under this title (or waiver of the plan), or any State child health plan under title XXI (or waiver of the plan) and such termination is included by the Secretary in any database or similar system developed pursuant to section 6401(b)(2) of the Patient Protection and Affordable Care Act".

(d) RULE OF CONSTRUCTION.—Nothing in this section shall be construed as changing or limiting the appeal rights of providers or the process for appeals of States under the Social Security Act.

(e) OIG REPORT.—Not later than March 31, 2020, the Inspector General of the Department of Health and Human Services shall submit to Congress a report on the implementation of the amendments made by this section. Such report shall include the following:

(1) An assessment of the extent to which providers who are included under subsection (ll) of section 1902 of the Social Security Act (42 U.S.C. 1396a) (as added by subsection (a)(3)) in the database or similar system referred to in such subsection are terminated (as described in paragraph (8) of subsection (kk) of such section, as added by subsection (a)(1)) from participation in all State plans under title XIX of such Act (or waivers of such plans).

(2) Information on the amount of Federal financial participation paid to States under section 1903 of such Act in violation of the limitation on such payment specified in subparagraph (D) of subsection (i)(2) of such section and paragraph (3) of subsection (m) of such section, as added by subsection (a)(4).

(3) An assessment of the extent to which contracts with managed care entities under title XIX of such Act comply with the requirement specified in paragraph (5) of section 1932(d) of such Act, as added by subsection (a)(2).

(4) An assessment of the extent to which providers have been enrolled under section 1902(a)(78) or 1932(d)(6)(A) of such Act (42 U.S.C. 1396a(a)(78), 1396u-2(d)(6)(A)) with State agencies administering State plans under title XIX of such Act (or waivers of such plans).

SEC. 5006. REQUIRING PUBLICATION OF FEE-FOR-SERVICE PROVIDER DIRECTORY.

(a) IN GENERAL.—Section 1902(a) of the Social Security Act (42 U.S.C. 1396a(a)) is amended—

(1) in paragraph (81), by striking "and" at the end;

(2) in paragraph (82), by striking the period at the end and inserting "; and"; and

(3) by inserting after paragraph (82) the following new paragraph:

"(83) provide that, not later than January 1, 2017, in the case of a State plan (or waiver of the plan) that provides medical assistance on a fee-for-service basis or through a primary care case-management system described in section 1915(b)(1) (other than a primary care case management entity (as defined by the Secretary)), the State shall publish (and update on at least an annual basis) on the public website of the State agency administering the State plan, a directory of the physicians described in subsection (mm) and, at State option, other providers described in such subsection that—

"(A) includes—

"(i) with respect to each such physician or provider—

"(I) the name of the physician or provider;

"(II) the specialty of the physician or provider;

"(III) the address at which the physician or provider provides services; and

"(IV) the telephone number of the physician or provider; and

"(ii) with respect to any such physician or provider participating in such a primary care case-management system, information regarding—

"(I) whether the physician or provider is accepting as new patients individuals who receive medical assistance under this title; and

"(II) the physician's or provider's cultural and linguistic capabilities, including the languages spoken by the physician or provider or by the skilled medical interpreter providing interpretation services at the physician's or provider's office; and

"(B) may include, at State option, with respect to each such physician or provider—

"(i) the Internet website of such physician or provider; or

"(ii) whether the physician or provider is accepting as new patients individuals who receive medical assistance under this title.".

(b) DIRECTORY PHYSICIAN OR PROVIDER DESCRIBED.—Section 1902 of the Social Security Act (42 U.S.C. 1396a), as amended by section 5005(a)(3), is further amended by adding at the end the following new subsection:

"(mm) DIRECTORY PHYSICIAN OR PROVIDER DESCRIBED.—A physician or provider described in this subsection is—

"(1) in the case of a physician or provider of a provider type for which the State agency, as a condition on receiving payment for items and services furnished by the physician or provider to individuals eligible to receive medical assistance under the State plan, requires the enrollment of the physician or provider with the State agency, a physician or a provider that—

"(A) is enrolled with the agency as of the date on which the directory is published or updated (as applicable) under subsection (a)(83); and

"(B) received payment under the State plan in the 12-month period preceding such date; and

"(2) in the case of a physician or provider of a provider type for which the State agency does not require such enrollment, a physician or provider that received payment under the State plan (or a waiver of the plan) in the 12-month period preceding the date on which the directory is published or updated (as applicable) under subsection (a)(83).".

(c) RULE OF CONSTRUCTION.—

(1) IN GENERAL.—The amendment made by subsection (a) shall not be construed to apply in the case of a State (as defined for purposes of title XIX of the Social Security Act) in which all the individuals enrolled in the State plan under such title (or under a waiver of such plan), other than individuals described in paragraph

(2), are enrolled with a medicaid managed care organization (as defined in section 1903(m)(1)(A) of such Act (42 U.S.C. 1396b(m)(1)(A))), including prepaid inpatient health plans and prepaid ambulatory health plans (as defined by the Secretary of Health and Human Services).

(2) INDIVIDUALS DESCRIBED.—An individual described in this paragraph is an individual who is an Indian (as defined in section 4 of the Indian Health Care Improvement Act (25 U.S.C. 1603)) or an Alaska Native.

(d) EXCEPTION FOR STATE LEGISLATION.—In the case of a State plan under title XIX of the Social Security Act (42 U.S.C. 1396 et seq.), which the Secretary of Health and Human Services determines requires State legislation in order for the respective plan to meet one or more additional requirements imposed by amendments made by this section, the respective plan shall not be regarded as failing to comply with the requirements of such title solely on the basis of its failure to meet such an additional requirement before the first day of the first calendar quarter beginning after the close of the first regular session of the State legislature that begins after the date of enactment of this Act. For purposes of the previous sentence, in the case of a State that has a 2-year legislative session, each year of the session shall be considered to be a separate regular session of the State legislature.

SEC. 5007. FAIRNESS IN MEDICAID SUPPLEMENTAL NEEDS TRUSTS.

(a) IN GENERAL.—Section 1917(d)(4)(A) of the Social Security Act (42 U.S.C. 1396p(d)(4)(A)) is amended by inserting "the individual," after "for the benefit of such individual by".

(b) EFFECTIVE DATE.—The amendment made by subsection (a) shall apply to trusts established on or after the date of the enactment of this Act.

SEC. 5008. ELIMINATING FEDERAL FINANCIAL PARTICIPATION WITH RESPECT TO EXPENDITURES UNDER MEDICAID FOR AGENTS USED FOR COSMETIC PURPOSES OR HAIR GROWTH.

(a) IN GENERAL.—Section 1903(i)(21) of the Social Security Act (42 U.S.C. 1396b(i)(21)) is amended by inserting "section 1927(d)(2)(C) (relating to drugs when used for cosmetic purposes or hair growth), except where medically necessary, and" after "drugs described in".

(b) EFFECTIVE DATE.—The amendment made by subsection (a) shall apply with respect to calendar quarters beginning on or after the date of the enactment of this Act.

SEC. 5009. AMENDMENT TO THE PREVENTION AND PUBLIC HEALTH FUND.

Section 4002(b) of the Patient Protection and Affordable Care Act (42 U.S.C. 300u-11(b)) is amended—

(1) in paragraph (3), by striking "$1,250,000,000" and inserting "$900,000,000";

(2) in paragraph (4), by striking "$1,500,000,000" and inserting "$1,000,000,000"; and

(3) by striking paragraph (5) and inserting the following:

"(5) for fiscal year 2022, $1,500,000,000;

"(6) for fiscal year 2023, $1,000,000,000;

"(7) for fiscal year 2024, $1,700,000,000; and

"(8) for fiscal year 2025 and each fiscal year thereafter, $2,000,000,000.".

SEC. 5010. STRATEGIC PETROLEUM RESERVE DRAWDOWN.

(a) DRAWDOWN AND SALE.—

(1) IN GENERAL.—Notwithstanding section 161 of the Energy Policy and Conservation Act (42 U.S.C. 6241), except as provided in subsections (b) and (c), the Secretary of Energy shall drawdown and sell from the Strategic Petroleum Reserve—

(A) 10,000,000 barrels of crude oil during fiscal year 2017;

(B) 9,000,000 barrels of crude oil during fiscal year 2018; and

(C) 6,000,000 barrels of crude oil during fiscal year 2019.

(2) DEPOSIT OF AMOUNTS RECEIVED FROM SALE.—Amounts received from a sale under paragraph (1) shall be deposited in the general fund of the Treasury during the fiscal year in which the sale occurs.

(b) EMERGENCY PROTECTION.—The Secretary shall not draw down and sell crude oil under this section in quantities that would limit the authority to sell petroleum products under section 161(h) of the Energy Policy and Conservation Act (42 U.S.C. 6241(h)) in the full quantity authorized by that subsection.

(c) STRATEGIC PETROLEUM DRAWDOWN LIMITATIONS.—Subparagraphs (C) and (D) of section 161(h)(2) of the Energy Policy and Conservation Act (42 U.S.C. 6241(h)(2)(C) and (D)) are both amended by striking "500,000,000" and inserting "450,000,000".

SEC. 5011. RESCISSION OF PORTION OF ACA TERRITORY FUNDING.

Of the unobligated amounts available under section 1323(c)(1) of the Patient Protection and Affordable Care Act (42 U.S.C. 18043(c)(1)), $464,000,000 is rescinded immediately upon the date of the enactment of this Act.

SEC. 5012. MEDICARE COVERAGE OF HOME INFUSION THERAPY.

(a) IN GENERAL.—Section 1861 of the Social Security Act (42 U.S.C. 1395x) is amended—

(1) in subsection (s)(2)—

(A) by striking "and" at the end of subparagraph (EE);

(B) by inserting "and" at the end of subparagraph (FF); and

(C) by inserting at the end the following new subparagraph:

"(GG) home infusion therapy (as defined in subsection (iii)(1));"; and

(2) by adding at the end the following new subsection:

"(iii) HOME INFUSION THERAPY.—(1) The term 'home infusion therapy' means the items and services described in paragraph (2) furnished by a qualified home infusion therapy supplier (as defined in paragraph (3)(D)) which are furnished in the individual's home (as defined in paragraph (3)(B)) to an individual—

"(A) who is under the care of an applicable provider (as defined in paragraph (3)(A)); and

"(B) with respect to whom a plan prescribing the type, amount, and duration of infusion therapy services that are to be furnished such individual has been established by a physician (as defined in subsection (r)(1)) and is periodically reviewed by a physician (as so defined) in coordination with the furnishing of home infusion drugs (as defined in paragraph (3)(C)) under part B.

"(2) The items and services described in this paragraph are the following:

"(A) Professional services, including nursing services, furnished in accordance with the plan.

"(B) Training and education (not otherwise paid for as durable medical equipment (as defined in subsection (n)), remote monitoring, and monitoring services for the provision of home infusion therapy and home infusion drugs furnished by a qualified home infusion therapy supplier.

"(3) For purposes of this subsection:

"(A) The term 'applicable provider' means—

"(i) a physician;

"(ii) a nurse practitioner; and

"(iii) a physician assistant.

"(B) The term 'home' means a place of residence used as the home of an individual (as defined for purposes of subsection (n)).

"(C) The term 'home infusion drug' means a parenteral drug or biological administered intravenously, or subcutaneously for an administration period of 15 minutes or more, in the home of an individual through a pump that is an item

of durable medical equipment (as defined in subsection (n)). Such term does not include the following:

"(i) Insulin pump systems.

"(ii) A self-administered drug or biological on a self-administered drug exclusion list.

"(D)(i) The term 'qualified home infusion therapy supplier' means a pharmacy, physician, or other provider of services or supplier licensed by the State in which the pharmacy, physician, or provider or services or supplier furnishes items or services and that—

"(I) furnishes infusion therapy to individuals with acute or chronic conditions requiring administration of home infusion drugs;

"(II) ensures the safe and effective provision and administration of home infusion therapy on a 7-day-a-week, 24-hour-a-day basis;

"(III) is accredited by an organization designated by the Secretary pursuant to section 1834(u)(5); and

"(IV) meets such other requirements as the Secretary determines appropriate, taking into account the standards of care for home infusion therapy established by Medicare Advantage plans under part C and in the private sector.

"(ii) A qualified home infusion therapy supplier may subcontract with a pharmacy, physician, provider of services, or supplier to meet the requirements of this subparagraph.".

(b) PAYMENT AND RELATED REQUIREMENTS FOR HOME INFUSION THERAPY.—Section 1834 of the Social Security Act (42 U.S.C. 1395m), as amended by section 4011, is further amended by adding at the end the following new subsection:

"(u) PAYMENT AND RELATED REQUIREMENTS FOR HOME INFUSION THERAPY.—

"(1) PAYMENT.—

"(A) SINGLE PAYMENT.—

"(i) IN GENERAL.—Subject to clause (iii) and subparagraphs (B) and (C), the Secretary shall implement a payment system under which a single payment is made under this title to a qualified home infusion therapy supplier for items and services described in subparagraphs (A) and (B) of section 1861(iii)(2)) furnished by a qualified home infusion therapy supplier (as defined in section 1861(iii)(3)(D)) in coordination with the furnishing of home infusion drugs (as defined in section 1861(iii)(3)(C)) under this part.

"(ii) UNIT OF SINGLE PAYMENT.—A unit of single payment under the payment system implemented under this subparagraph is for each infusion drug administration calendar day in the individual's home. The Secretary shall, as appropriate, establish single payment amounts for types of infusion therapy, including to take into account variation in utilization of nursing services by therapy type.

"(iii) LIMITATION.—The single payment amount determined under this subparagraph after application of subparagraph (B) and paragraph (3) shall not exceed the amount determined under the fee schedule under section 1848 for infusion therapy services furnished in a calendar day if furnished in a physician office setting, except such single payment shall not reflect more than 5 hours of infusion for a particular therapy in a calendar day.

"(B) REQUIRED ADJUSTMENTS.—The Secretary shall adjust the single payment amount determined under subparagraph (A) for home infusion therapy services under section 1861(iii)(1) to reflect other factors such as—

"(i) a geographic wage index and other costs that may vary by region; and

"(ii) patient acuity and complexity of drug administration.

"(C) DISCRETIONARY ADJUSTMENTS.—

"(i) IN GENERAL.—Subject to clause (ii), the Secretary may adjust the single payment amount determined under subparagraph (A) (after application of subparagraph (B)) to reflect outlier situations and other factors as the Secretary determines appropriate.

"(ii) REQUIREMENT OF BUDGET NEUTRALITY.—Any adjustment under this subparagraph shall be made in a budget neutral manner.

"(2) CONSIDERATIONS.—In developing the payment system under this subsection, the Secretary may consider the costs of furnishing infusion therapy in the home, consult with home infusion therapy suppliers, consider payment amounts for similar items and services under this part and part A, and consider payment amounts established by Medicare Advantage plans under part C and in the private insurance market for home infusion therapy (including average per treatment day payment amounts by type of home infusion therapy).

"(3) ANNUAL UPDATES.—

"(A) IN GENERAL.—Subject to subparagraph (B), the Secretary shall update the single payment amount under this subsection from year to year beginning in 2022 by increasing the single payment amount from the prior year by the percentage increase in the Consumer Price Index for all urban consumers (United States city average) for the 12-month period ending with June of the preceding year.

"(B) ADJUSTMENT.—For each year, the Secretary shall reduce the percentage increase described in subparagraph (A) by the productivity adjustment described in section 1886(b)(3)(B)(xi)(II). The application of the preceding sentence may result in a percentage being less than 0.0 for a year, and may result in payment being less than such payment rates for the preceding year.

"(4) AUTHORITY TO APPLY PRIOR AUTHORIZATION.—The Secretary may, as determined appropriate by the Secretary, apply prior authorization for home infusion therapy services under section 1861(iii)(1).

"(5) ACCREDITATION OF QUALIFIED HOME INFUSION THERAPY SUPPLIERS.—

"(A) FACTORS FOR DESIGNATION OF ACCREDITATION ORGANIZATIONS.—The Secretary shall consider the following factors in designating accreditation organizations under subparagraph (B) and in reviewing and modifying the list of accreditation organizations designated pursuant to subparagraph (C):

"(i) The ability of the organization to conduct timely reviews of accreditation applications.

"(ii) The ability of the organization to take into account the capacities of suppliers located in a rural area (as defined in section 1886(d)(2)(D)).

"(iii) Whether the organization has established reasonable fees to be charged to suppliers applying for accreditation.

"(iv) Such other factors as the Secretary determines appropriate.

"(B) DESIGNATION.—Not later than January 1, 2021, the Secretary shall designate organizations to accredit suppliers furnishing home infusion therapy. The list of accreditation organizations so designated may be modified pursuant to subparagraph (C).

"(C) REVIEW AND MODIFICATION OF LIST OF ACCREDITATION ORGANIZATIONS.—

"(i) IN GENERAL.—The Secretary shall review the list of accreditation organizations designated under subparagraph (B) taking into account the factors under subparagraph (A). Taking into account the results of such review, the Secretary may, by regulation, modify the list of accreditation organizations designated under subparagraph (B).

"(ii) SPECIAL RULE FOR ACCREDITATIONS DONE PRIOR TO REMOVAL FROM LIST OF DESIGNATED ACCREDITATION ORGANIZATIONS.—In the case where the Secretary removes an organization from the list of accreditation organizations designated under subparagraph (B), any supplier that is accredited by the organization during the period beginning on the date on which the organization is designated as an accreditation

organization under subparagraph (B) and ending on the date on which the organization is removed from such list shall be considered to have been accredited by an organization designated by the Secretary under subparagraph (B) for the remaining period such accreditation is in effect.

"(D) RULE FOR ACCREDITATIONS MADE PRIOR TO DESIGNATION.—In the case of a supplier that is accredited before January 1, 2021, by an accreditation organization designated by the Secretary under subparagraph (B) as of January 1, 2019, such supplier shall be considered to have been accredited by an organization designated by the Secretary under such paragraph as of January 1, 2023, for the remaining period such accreditation is in effect.

"(6) NOTIFICATION OF INFUSION THERAPY OPTIONS AVAILABLE PRIOR TO FURNISHING HOME INFUSION THERAPY.—Prior to the furnishing of home infusion therapy to an individual, the physician who establishes the plan described in section 1861(iii)(1) for the individual shall provide notification (in a form, manner, and frequency determined appropriate by the Secretary) of the options available (such as home, physician's office, hospital outpatient department) for the furnishing of infusion therapy under this part.".

(c) CONFORMING AMENDMENTS.—

(1) PAYMENT REFERENCE.—Section 1833(a)(1) of the Social Security Act (42 U.S.C. 1395l(a)(1)) is amended—

(A) by striking "and" before "(AA)"; and

(B) by inserting before the semicolon at the end the following: ", and (BB) with respect to home infusion therapy, the amount paid shall be an amount equal to 80 percent of the lesser of the actual charge for the services or the amount determined under section 1834(u)".

(2) DIRECT PAYMENT.—The first sentence of section 1842(b)(6) of the Social Security Act (42 U.S.C. 1395u(b)(6)) is amended—

(A) by striking "and" before "(H)"; and

(B) by inserting before the period at the end the following: ", and (I) in the case of home infusion therapy, payment shall be made to the qualified home infusion therapy supplier".

(3) EXCLUSION FROM HOME HEALTH SERVICES.—Section 1861(m) of the Social Security Act (42 U.S.C. 1395x(m)) is amended, in the first sentence, by inserting the following before the period at the end: "and home infusion therapy (as defined in subsection (iii)(i))".

(d) EFFECTIVE DATE.—The amendments made by this section shall apply to items and services furnished on or after January 1, 2021.

DIVISION B—HELPING FAMILIES IN MENTAL HEALTH CRISIS

SEC. 6000. SHORT TITLE.

This division may be cited as the "Helping Families in Mental Health Crisis Reform Act of 2016".

TITLE VI—STRENGTHENING LEADERSHIP AND ACCOUNTABILITY

Subtitle A—Leadership

SEC. 6001. ASSISTANT SECRETARY FOR MENTAL HEALTH AND SUBSTANCE USE.

(a) ASSISTANT SECRETARY.—Section 501(c) of the Public Health Service Act (42 U.S.C. 290aa(c)) is amended to read as follows:

"(c) ASSISTANT SECRETARY AND DEPUTY ASSISTANT SECRETARY.—

"(1) ASSISTANT SECRETARY.—The Administration shall be headed by an official to be known as the Assistant Secretary for Mental Health and Substance Use (hereinafter in this title referred to as the 'Assistant Secretary') who shall be appointed by the President, by and with the advice and consent of the Senate.

"(2) DEPUTY ASSISTANT SECRETARY.—The Assistant Secretary, with the approval of the Secretary, may appoint a Deputy Assistant Secretary and may employ and prescribe the func-

tions of such officers and employees, including attorneys, as are necessary to administer the activities to be carried out through the Administration.".

(b) TRANSFER OF AUTHORITIES.—The Secretary of Health and Human Services shall delegate to the Assistant Secretary for Mental Health and Substance Use all duties and authorities that—

(1) as of the day before the date of enactment of this Act, were vested in the Administrator of the Substance Abuse and Mental Health Services Administration; and

(2) are not terminated by this Act.

(c) CONFORMING AMENDMENTS.—Title V of the Public Health Service Act (42 U.S.C. 290aa et seq.), as amended by the previous provisions of this section, is further amended—

(1) by striking "Administrator of the Substance Abuse and Mental Health Services Administration" each place it appears and inserting "Assistant Secretary for Mental Health and Substance Use"; and

(2) by striking "Administrator" or "ADMINISTRATOR" each place it appears (including in any headings) and inserting "Assistant Secretary" or "ASSISTANT SECRETARY", respectively, except where the term "Administrator" appears—

(A) in each of subsections (e) and (f) of section 501 of such Act (42 U.S.C. 290aa), including the headings of such subsections, within the term "Associate Administrator";

(B) in section 507(b)(6) of such Act (42 U.S.C. 290bb(b)(6)), within the term "Administrator of the Health Resources and Services Administration";

(C) in section 507(b)(6) of such Act (42 U.S.C. 290bb(b)(6)), within the term "Administrator of the Centers for Medicare & Medicaid Services";

(D) in section 519B(c)(1)(B) of such Act (42 U.S.C. 290bb–25b(c)(1)(B)), within the term "Administrator of the National Highway Traffic Safety Administration"; or

(E) in each of sections 519B(c)(1)(B), 520C(a), and 520D(a) of such Act (42 U.S.C. 290bb–25b(c)(1)(B), 290bb–34(a), 290bb–35(a)), within the term "Administrator of the Office of Juvenile Justice and Delinquency Prevention".

(d) REFERENCES.—After executing subsections (a), (b), and (c), any reference in statute, regulation, or guidance to the Administrator of the Substance Abuse and Mental Health Services Administration shall be construed to be a reference to the Assistant Secretary for Mental Health and Substance Use.

SEC. 6002. STRENGTHENING THE LEADERSHIP OF THE SUBSTANCE ABUSE AND MENTAL HEALTH SERVICES ADMINISTRATION.

Section 501 of the Public Health Service Act (42 U.S.C. 290aa), as amended by section 6001, is further amended—

(1) in subsection (b)—

(A) in the subsection heading, by striking "AGENCIES" and inserting "CENTERS"; and

(B) in the matter preceding paragraph (1), by striking "entities" and inserting "Centers";

(2) in subsection (d)—

(A) in paragraph (1)—

(i) by striking "agencies" each place the term appears and inserting "Centers"; and

(ii) by striking "such agency" and inserting "such Center";

(B) in paragraph (2)—

(i) by striking "agencies" and inserting "Centers";

(ii) by striking "with respect to substance abuse" and inserting "with respect to substance use disorders"; and

(iii) by striking "and individuals who are substance abusers" and inserting "and individuals with substance use disorders";

(C) in paragraph (5), by striking "substance abuse" and inserting "substance use disorder";

(D) in paragraph (6)—

(i) by striking "the Centers for Disease Control" and inserting "the Centers for Disease Control and Prevention,";

(ii) by striking "Administration develop" and inserting "Administration, develop";

(iii) by striking "HIV or tuberculosis among substance abusers and individuals with mental illness" and inserting "HIV, hepatitis, tuberculosis, and other communicable diseases among individuals with mental or substance use disorders,"; and

(iv) by striking "illnesses" at the end and inserting "diseases or disorders";

(E) in paragraph (7), by striking "abuse utilizing anti-addiction medications, including methadone" and inserting "use disorders, including services that utilize drugs or devices approved or cleared by the Food and Drug Administration for the treatment of substance use disorders";

(F) in paragraph (8)—

(i) by striking "Agency for Health Care Policy Research" and inserting "Agency for Healthcare Research and Quality"; and

(ii) by striking "treatment and prevention" and inserting "prevention and treatment";

(G) in paragraph (9)—

(i) by inserting "and maintenance" after "development";

(ii) by striking "Agency for Health Care Policy Research" and inserting "Agency for Healthcare Research and Quality"; and

(iii) by striking "treatment and prevention services" and inserting "prevention, treatment, and recovery support services and are appropriately incorporated into programs carried out by the Administration";

(H) in paragraph (10), by striking "abuse" and inserting "use disorder";

(I) by striking paragraph (11) and inserting the following:

"(11) work with relevant agencies of the Department of Health and Human Services on integrating mental health promotion and substance use disorder prevention with general health promotion and disease prevention and integrating mental and substance use disorders treatment services with physical health treatment services;";

(J) in paragraph (13)—

(i) in the matter preceding subparagraph (A), by striking "this title, assure that" and inserting "this title or part B of title XIX, or grant programs otherwise funded by the Administration";

(ii) in subparagraph (A)—

(I) by inserting "require that" before "all grants"; and

(II) by striking "and" at the end;

(iii) by redesignating subparagraph (B) as subparagraph (C);

(iv) by inserting after subparagraph (A) the following:

"(B) ensure that the director of each Center of the Administration consistently documents the application of criteria when awarding grants and the ongoing oversight of grantees after such grants are awarded;";

(v) in subparagraph (C), as so redesignated—

(I) by inserting "require that" before "all grants"; and

(II) in clause (ii), by inserting "and" after the semicolon at the end; and

(vi) by adding at the end the following:

"(D) inform a State when any funds are awarded through such a grant to any entity within such State;";

(K) in paragraph (16), by striking "abuse and mental health information" and inserting "use disorder information, including evidence-based and promising best practices for prevention, treatment, and recovery support services for individuals with mental and substance use disorders,";

(L) in paragraph (17)—

(i) by striking "substance abuse" and inserting "substance use disorder"; and

(ii) by striking "and" at the end;

(M) in paragraph (18), by striking the period and inserting a semicolon; and

(N) by adding at the end the following:

"(19) consult with State, local, and tribal governments, nongovernmental entities, and individuals with mental illness, particularly adults with a serious mental illness, children with a serious emotional disturbance, and the family members of such adults and children, with respect to improving community-based and other mental health services;

"(20) collaborate with the Secretary of Defense and the Secretary of Veterans Affairs to improve the provision of mental and substance use disorder services provided by the Department of Defense and the Department of Veterans Affairs to members of the Armed Forces, veterans, and the family members of such members and veterans, including through the provision of services using the telehealth capabilities of the Department of Defense and the Department of Veterans Affairs;

"(21) collaborate with the heads of relevant Federal agencies and departments, States, communities, and nongovernmental experts to improve mental and substance use disorders services for chronically homeless individuals, including by designing strategies to provide such services in supportive housing;

"(22) work with States and other stakeholders to develop and support activities to recruit and retain a workforce addressing mental and substance use disorders;

"(23) collaborate with the Attorney General and representatives of the criminal justice system to improve mental and substance use disorders services for individuals who have been arrested or incarcerated;

"(24) after providing an opportunity for public input, set standards for grant programs under this title for mental and substance use disorders services and prevention programs, which standards may address—

"(A) the capacity of the grantee to implement the award;

"(B) requirements for the description of the program implementation approach;

"(C) the extent to which the grant plan submitted by the grantee as part of its application must explain how the grantee will reach the population of focus and provide a statement of need, which may include information on how the grantee will increase access to services and a description of measurable objectives for improving outcomes;

"(D) the extent to which the grantee must collect and report on required performance measures; and

"(E) the extent to which the grantee is proposing to use evidence-based practices; and

"(25) advance, through existing programs, the use of performance metrics, including those based on the recommendations on performance metrics from the Assistant Secretary for Planning and Evaluation under section 6021(d) of the Helping Families in Mental Health Crisis Reform Act of 2016."; and

(3) in subsection (m), by adding at the end the following:

"(4) EMERGENCY RESPONSE.—Amounts made available for carrying out this subsection shall remain available through the end of the fiscal year following the fiscal year for which such amounts are appropriated.".

SEC. 6003. CHIEF MEDICAL OFFICER.

Section 501 of the Public Health Service Act (42 U.S.C. 290aa), as amended by sections 6001 and 6002, is further amended—

(1) by redesignating subsections (g) through (j) and subsections (k) through (o) as sub-

sections (h) through (k) and subsections (m) through (q), respectively;

(2) in subsection (e)(3)(C), by striking "subsection (k)" and inserting "subsection (m)";

(3) in subsection (f)(2)(C)(iii), by striking "subsection (k)" and inserting "subsection (m)"; and

(4) by inserting after subsection (f) the following:

"(g) CHIEF MEDICAL OFFICER.—

"(1) IN GENERAL.—The Assistant Secretary, with the approval of the Secretary, shall appoint a Chief Medical Officer to serve within the Administration.

"(2) ELIGIBLE CANDIDATES.—The Assistant Secretary shall select the Chief Medical Officer from among individuals who—

"(A) have a doctoral degree in medicine or osteopathic medicine;

"(B) have experience in the provision of mental or substance use disorder services;

"(C) have experience working with mental or substance use disorder programs;

"(D) have an understanding of biological, psychosocial, and pharmaceutical treatments of mental or substance use disorders; and

"(E) are licensed to practice medicine in one or more States.

"(3) DUTIES.—The Chief Medical Officer shall—

"(A) serve as a liaison between the Administration and providers of mental and substance use disorders prevention, treatment, and recovery services;

"(B) assist the Assistant Secretary in the evaluation, organization, integration, and coordination of programs operated by the Administration;

"(C) promote evidence-based and promising best practices, including culturally and linguistically appropriate practices, as appropriate, for the prevention and treatment of, and recovery from, mental and substance use disorders, including serious mental illness and serious emotional disturbances;

"(D) participate in regular strategic planning with the Administration;

"(E) coordinate with the Assistant Secretary for Planning and Evaluation to assess the use of performance metrics to evaluate activities within the Administration related to mental and substance use disorders; and

"(F) coordinate with the Assistant Secretary to ensure mental and substance use disorders grant programs within the Administration consistently utilize appropriate performance metrics and evaluation designs.".

SEC. 6004. IMPROVING THE QUALITY OF BEHAVIORAL HEALTH PROGRAMS.

Section 505 of the Public Health Service Act (42 U.S.C. 290aa-4), as amended by section 6001(c), is amended—

(1) by striking the section designation and heading and inserting the following:

"SEC. 505. CENTER FOR BEHAVIORAL HEALTH STATISTICS AND QUALITY.";

(2) by redesignating subsections (a) through (d) as subsections (b) through (e), respectively;

(3) before subsection (b), as redesignated by paragraph (2), by inserting the following:

"(a) IN GENERAL.—The Assistant Secretary shall maintain within the Administration a Center for Behavioral Health Statistics and Quality (in this section referred to as the 'Center'). The Center shall be headed by a Director (in this section referred to as the 'Director') appointed by the Secretary from among individuals with extensive experience and academic qualifications in research and analysis in behavioral health care or related fields.";

(4) in subsection (b), as redesignated by paragraph (2)—

(A) by redesignating paragraphs (1) and (2) as subparagraphs (A) and (B), respectively;

(B) by striking "The Secretary, acting" and all that follows through "year on—" and inserting "The Director shall—

"(1) coordinate the Administration's integrated data strategy, including by collecting data each year on—";

(C) in the subparagraph (B), as redesignated by subparagraph (A), by striking "Assistant Secretary" and inserting "Director"; and

(D) by adding at the end the following new paragraphs:

"(2) provide statistical and analytical support for activities of the Administration;

"(3) recommend a core set of performance metrics to evaluate activities supported by the Administration; and

"(4) coordinate with the Assistant Secretary, the Assistant Secretary for Planning and Evaluation, and the Chief Medical Officer appointed under section 501(g), as appropriate, to improve the quality of services provided by programs of the Administration and the evaluation of activities carried out by the Administration.".

(5) in subsection (c), as so redesignated—

(A) by striking "With respect to the activities" and inserting "MENTAL HEALTH.—With respect to the activities";

(B) by striking "Assistant Secretary" each place it appears and inserting "Director"; and

(C) by striking "subsection (a)" and inserting "subsection (b)(1)";

(6) in subsection (d), as so redesignated—

(A) by striking the subsection designation and all that follows through "With respect to the activities" and inserting the following:

"(d) SUBSTANCE ABUSE.—

"(1) IN GENERAL.—With respect to the activities";

(B) in paragraph (1)—

(i) in the matter before subparagraph (A)—

(I) by striking "subsection (a)" and inserting "subsection (b)(1)"; and

(II) by striking "Assistant Secretary" each place it appears and inserting "Director"; and

(ii) in subparagraph (B), by inserting "in coordination with the Centers for Disease Control and Prevention" before the semicolon at the end; and

(C) in paragraph (2), by striking "ANNUAL SURVEYS" and inserting "ANNUAL SURVEYS; PUBLIC AVAILABILITY OF DATA.—Annual surveys"; and

(7) in subsection (e), as so redesignated—

(A) by striking "After consultation" and inserting "CONSULTATION.—After consultation"; and

(B) by striking "Assistant Secretary shall develop" and inserting "Assistant Secretary shall use existing standards and best practices to develop".

SEC. 6005. STRATEGIC PLAN.

Section 501 of the Public Health Service Act (42 U.S.C. 290aa), as amended by sections 6001 through 6003, is further amended by inserting after subsection (k), as redesignated by section 6003, the following:

"(l) STRATEGIC PLAN.—

"(1) IN GENERAL.—Not later than September 30, 2018, and every 4 years thereafter, the Assistant Secretary shall develop and carry out a strategic plan in accordance with this subsection for the planning and operation of activities carried out by the Administration, including evidence-based programs.

"(2) COORDINATION.—In developing and carrying out the strategic plan under this subsection, the Assistant Secretary shall take into consideration the findings and recommendations of the Assistant Secretary for Planning and Evaluation under section 6021(d) of the Helping Families in Mental Health Crisis Reform Act of 2016 and the report of the Interdepartmental Serious Mental Illness Coordinating Committee under section 6031 of such Act.

''*(3) PUBLICATION OF PLAN.*—Not later than September 30, 2018, and every 4 years thereafter, the Assistant Secretary shall—

''*(A)* submit the strategic plan developed under paragraph (1) to the Committee on Energy and Commerce and the Committee on Appropriations of the House of Representatives and the Committee on Health, Education, Labor, and Pensions and the Committee on Appropriations of the Senate; and

''*(B)* post such plan on the Internet website of the Administration.

''*(4) CONTENTS.*—The strategic plan developed under paragraph (1) shall—

''*(A)* identify strategic priorities, goals, and measurable objectives for mental and substance use disorders activities and programs operated and supported by the Administration, including priorities to prevent or eliminate the burden of mental and substance use disorders;

''*(B)* identify ways to improve the quality of services for individuals with mental and substance use disorders, and to reduce homelessness, arrest, incarceration, violence, including self-directed violence, and unnecessary hospitalization of individuals with a mental or substance use disorder, including adults with a serious mental illness or children with a serious emotional disturbance;

''*(C)* ensure that programs provide, as appropriate, access to effective and evidence-based prevention, diagnosis, intervention, treatment, and recovery services, including culturally and linguistically appropriate services, as appropriate, for individuals with a mental or substance use disorder;

''*(D)* identify opportunities to collaborate with the Health Resources and Services Administration to develop or improve—

''*(i)* initiatives to encourage individuals to pursue careers (especially in rural and underserved areas and with rural and underserved populations) as psychiatrists, including child and adolescent psychiatrists, psychologists, psychiatric nurse practitioners, physician assistants, clinical social workers, certified peer support specialists, licensed professional counselors, or other licensed or certified mental health or substance use disorder professionals, including such professionals specializing in the diagnosis, evaluation, or treatment of adults with a serious mental illness or children with a serious emotional disturbance; and

''*(ii)* a strategy to improve the recruitment, training, and retention of a workforce for the treatment of individuals with mental or substance use disorders, or co-occurring disorders;

''*(E)* identify opportunities to improve collaboration with States, local governments, communities, and Indian tribes and tribal organizations (as such terms are defined in section 4 of the Indian Self-Determination and Education Assistance Act); and

''*(F)* specify a strategy to disseminate evidence-based and promising best practices related to prevention, diagnosis, early intervention, treatment, and recovery services related to mental illness, particularly for adults with a serious mental illness and children with a serious emotional disturbance, and for individuals with a substance use disorder.''.

SEC. 6006. BIENNIAL REPORT CONCERNING ACTIVITIES AND PROGRESS.

(a) IN GENERAL.—Section 501 of the Public Health Service Act (42 U.S.C. 290aa), as amended, is further amended by amending subsection (m), as redesignated by section 6003, to read as follows:

''*(m) BIENNIAL REPORT CONCERNING ACTIVITIES AND PROGRESS.*—Not later than September 30, 2020, and every 2 years thereafter, the Assistant Secretary shall prepare and submit to the Committee on Energy and Commerce and the Committee on Appropriations of the House of Representatives and the Committee on Health, Education, Labor, and Pensions and the Committee on Appropriations of the Senate, and post on the Internet website of the Administration, a report containing at a minimum—

''*(1)* a review of activities conducted or supported by the Administration, including progress toward strategic priorities, goals, and objectives identified in the strategic plan developed under subsection (l);

''*(2)* an assessment of programs and activities carried out by the Assistant Secretary, including the extent to which programs and activities under this title and part B of title XIX meet identified goals and performance measures developed for the respective programs and activities;

''*(3)* a description of the progress made in addressing gaps in mental and substance use disorders prevention, treatment, and recovery services and improving outcomes by the Administration, including with respect to serious mental illnesses, serious emotional disturbances, and co-occurring disorders;

''*(4)* a description of the manner in which the Administration coordinates and partners with other Federal agencies and departments related to mental and substance use disorders, including activities related to—

''*(A)* the implementation and dissemination of research findings into improved programs, including with respect to how advances in serious mental illness and serious emotional disturbance research have been incorporated into programs;

''*(B)* the recruitment, training, and retention of a mental and substance use disorders workforce;

''*(C)* the integration of mental disorder services, substance use disorder services, and physical health services;

''*(D)* homelessness; and

''*(E)* veterans;

''*(5)* a description of the manner in which the Administration promotes coordination by grantees under this title, and part B of title XIX, with State or local agencies; and

''*(6)* a description of the activities carried out under section 501A(e), with respect to mental and substance use disorders, including—

''*(A)* the number and a description of grants awarded;

''*(B)* the total amount of funding for grants awarded;

''*(C)* a description of the activities supported through such grants, including outcomes of programs supported; and

''*(D)* information on how the National Mental Health and Substance Use Policy Laboratory is consulting with the Assistant Secretary for Planning and Evaluation and collaborating with the Center for Substance Abuse Treatment, the Center for Substance Abuse Prevention, the Center for Behavioral Health Statistics and Quality, and the Center for Mental Health Services to carry out such activities; and

''*(7)* recommendations made by the Assistant Secretary for Planning and Evaluation under section 6021 of the Helping Families in Mental Health Crisis Reform Act of 2016 to improve programs within the Administration, and actions taken in response to such recommendations to improve programs within the Administration.

The Assistant Secretary may meet reporting requirements established under this title by providing the contents of such reports as an addendum to the biennial report established under this subsection, notwithstanding the timeline of other reporting requirements in this title. Nothing in this subsection shall be construed to alter the content requirements of such reports or authorize the Assistant Secretary to alter the timeline of any such reports to be less frequent than biennially, unless as specified in this title.''.

(b) CONFORMING AMENDMENT.—Section 508(p) of the Public Health Service Act (42 U.S.C. 290bb–1(p)) is amended by striking ''section 501(k)'' and inserting ''section 501(m)''.

SEC. 6007. AUTHORITIES OF CENTERS FOR MENTAL HEALTH SERVICES, SUBSTANCE ABUSE PREVENTION, AND SUBSTANCE ABUSE TREATMENT.

(a) CENTER FOR MENTAL HEALTH SERVICES.—Section 520(b) of the Public Health Service Act (42 U.S.C. 290bb–31(b)) is amended—

(1) by redesignating paragraphs (3) through (15) as paragraphs (4) through (16), respectively;

(2) by inserting after paragraph (2) the following:

''*(3)* collaborate with the Director of the National Institute of Mental Health and the Chief Medical Officer, appointed under section 501(g), to ensure that, as appropriate, programs related to the prevention and treatment of mental illness and the promotion of mental health and recovery support are carried out in a manner that reflects the best available science and evidence-based practices, including culturally and linguistically appropriate services, as appropriate;'';

(3) in paragraph (5), as so redesignated, by inserting '', including through programs that reduce risk and promote resiliency'' before the semicolon;

(4) in paragraph (6), as so redesignated, by inserting ''in collaboration with the Director of the National Institute of Mental Health,'' before ''develop'';

(5) in paragraph (8), as so redesignated, by inserting '', increase meaningful participation of individuals with mental illness in programs and activities of the Administration,'' before ''and protect the legal'';

(6) in paragraph (10), as so redesignated, by striking ''professional and paraprofessional personnel pursuant to section 303'' and inserting ''health paraprofessional personnel and health professionals'';

(7) in paragraph (11), as so redesignated, by inserting ''and tele-mental health'' after ''rural mental health'';

(8) in paragraph (12), as so redesignated, by striking ''establish a clearinghouse for mental health information to assure the widespread dissemination of such information'' and inserting ''disseminate mental health information, including evidence-based practices,'';

(9) in paragraph (15), as so redesignated, by striking ''and'' at the end;

(10) in paragraph (16), as so redesignated, by striking the period and inserting ''; and''; and

(11) by adding at the end the following:

''*(17)* ensure the consistent documentation of the application of criteria when awarding grants and the ongoing oversight of grantees after such grants are awarded.''.

(b) DIRECTOR OF THE CENTER FOR SUBSTANCE ABUSE PREVENTION.—Section 515 of the Public Health Service Act (42 U.S.C. 290bb–21) is amended—

(1) in the section heading, by striking ''OFFICE'' and inserting ''CENTER'';

(2) in subsection (a)—

(A) by striking ''an Office'' and inserting ''a Center''; and

(B) by striking ''The Office'' and inserting ''The Prevention Center''; and

(3) in subsection (b)—

(A) in paragraph (1), by inserting ''through the reduction of risk and the promotion of resiliency'' before the semicolon;

(B) by redesignating paragraphs (3) through (11) as paragraphs (4) through (12), respectively;

(C) by inserting after paragraph (2) the following:

''*(3)* collaborate with the Director of the National Institute on Drug Abuse, the Director of the National Institute on Alcohol Abuse and Alcoholism, and States to promote the study of substance abuse prevention and the dissemination and implementation of research findings that will improve the delivery and effectiveness of substance abuse prevention activities;'';

(D) in paragraph (4), as so redesignated, by striking "literature on the adverse effects of cocaine free base (known as crack)" and inserting "educational information on the effects of drugs abused by individuals, including drugs that are emerging as abused drugs";

(E) in paragraph (6), as so redesignated—

(i) by striking "substance abuse counselors" and inserting "health professionals who provide substance use and misuse prevention and treatment services"; and

(ii) by striking "drug abuse education, prevention," and inserting "illicit drug use education and prevention";

(F) by amending paragraph (7), as so redesignated, to read as follows:

"(7) in cooperation with the Director of the Centers for Disease Control and Prevention, develop and disseminate educational materials to increase awareness for individuals at greatest risk for substance use disorders to prevent the transmission of communicable diseases, such as HIV, hepatitis, tuberculosis, and other communicable diseases;'';

(G) in paragraph (9), as so redesignated—

(i) by striking "to discourage" and inserting "that reduce the risk of"; and

(ii) by inserting before the semicolon "and promote resiliency";

(H) in paragraph (11), as so redesignated, by striking "and" after the semicolon;

(I) in paragraph (12), as so redesignated, by striking the period and inserting a semicolon; and

(J) by adding at the end the following:

"(13) ensure the consistent documentation of the application of criteria when awarding grants and the ongoing oversight of grantees after such grants are awarded; and

"(14) assist and support States in preventing illicit drug use, including emerging illicit drug use issues.''.

(c) DIRECTOR OF THE CENTER FOR SUBSTANCE ABUSE TREATMENT.—Section 507 of the Public Health Service Act (42 U.S.C. 290bb) is amended—

(1) in subsection (a)—

(A) by striking "treatment of substance abuse" and inserting "treatment of substance use disorders"; and

(B) by striking "abuse treatment systems" and inserting "use disorder treatment systems"; and

(2) in subsection (b)—

(A) in paragraph (1), by striking "abuse" and inserting "use disorder";

(B) in paragraph (3), by striking "abuse" and inserting "use disorder";

(C) in paragraph (4), by striking "individuals who abuse drugs" and inserting "individuals who illicitly use drugs";

(D) in paragraph (9), by striking "carried out by the Director";

(E) by striking paragraph (10);

(F) by redesignating paragraphs (11) through (14) as paragraphs (10) through (13), respectively;

(G) in paragraph (12), as so redesignated, by striking "; and" and inserting a semicolon; and

(H) by striking paragraph (13), as so redesignated, and inserting the following:

"(13) ensure the consistent documentation of the application of criteria when awarding grants and the ongoing oversight of grantees after such grants are awarded; and

"(14) work with States, providers, and individuals in recovery, and their families, to promote the expansion of recovery support services and systems of care oriented toward recovery.''.

SEC. 6008. ADVISORY COUNCILS.

Section 502(b) of the Public Health Service Act (42 U.S.C. 290aa–1(b)) is amended—

(1) in paragraph (2)—

(A) in subparagraph (E), by striking "and" after the semicolon;

(B) by redesignating subparagraph (F) as subparagraph (J); and

(C) by inserting after subparagraph (E), the following:

"(F) the Chief Medical Officer, appointed under section 501(g);

"(G) the Director of the National Institute of Mental Health for the advisory councils appointed under subsections (a)(1)(A) and (a)(1)(D);

"(H) the Director of the National Institute on Drug Abuse for the advisory councils appointed under subsections (a)(1)(A), (a)(1)(B), and (a)(1)(C);

"(I) the Director of the National Institute on Alcohol Abuse and Alcoholism for the advisory councils appointed under subsections (a)(1)(A), (a)(1)(B), and (a)(1)(C); and''; and

(2) in paragraph (3), by adding at the end the following:

"(C) Not less than half of the members of the advisory council appointed under subsection (a)(1)(D)—

"(i) shall—

"(I) have a medical degree;

"(II) have a doctoral degree in psychology; or

"(III) have an advanced degree in nursing or social work from an accredited graduate school or be a certified physician assistant; and

"(ii) shall specialize in the mental health field.

"(D) Not less than half of the members of the advisory councils appointed under subsections (a)(1)(B) and (a)(1)(C)—

"(i) shall—

"(I) have a medical degree;

"(II) have a doctoral degree; or

"(III) have an advanced degree in nursing, public health, behavioral or social sciences, or social work from an accredited graduate school or be a certified physician assistant; and

"(ii) shall have experience in the provision of substance use disorder services or the development and implementation of programs to prevent substance misuse.''.

SEC. 6009. PEER REVIEW.

Section 504(b) of the Public Health Service Act (42 U.S.C. 290aa–3(b)) is amended by adding at the end the following: "In the case of any such peer review group that is reviewing a grant, cooperative agreement, or contract related to mental illness treatment, not less than half of the members of such peer review group shall be licensed and experienced professionals in the prevention, diagnosis, or treatment of, or recovery from, mental illness or co-occurring mental illness and substance use disorders and have a medical degree, a doctoral degree in psychology, or an advanced degree in nursing or social work from an accredited program, and the Secretary, in consultation with the Assistant Secretary, shall, to the extent possible, ensure such peer review groups include broad geographic representation, including both urban and rural representatives.''.

Subtitle B—Oversight and Accountability

SEC. 6021. IMPROVING OVERSIGHT OF MENTAL AND SUBSTANCE USE DISORDERS PROGRAMS THROUGH THE ASSISTANT SECRETARY FOR PLANNING AND EVALUATION.

(a) IN GENERAL.—The Secretary of Health and Human Services, acting through the Assistant Secretary for Planning and Evaluation, shall ensure efficient and effective planning and evaluation of mental and substance use disorders prevention and treatment programs and related activities.

(b) EVALUATION STRATEGY.—In carrying out subsection (a), the Assistant Secretary for Planning and Evaluation shall, not later than 180 days after the date of enactment of this Act, develop a strategy for conducting ongoing evaluations that identifies priority programs to be evaluated by the Assistant Secretary for Planning and Evaluation and priority programs to be evaluated by other relevant offices and agencies within the Department of Health and Human Services. The strategy shall—

(1) include a plan for evaluating programs related to mental and substance use disorders, including co-occurring disorders, across agencies, as appropriate, including programs related to—

(A) prevention, intervention, treatment, and recovery support services, including such services for adults with a serious mental illness or children with a serious emotional disturbance;

(B) the reduction of homelessness and incarceration among individuals with a mental or substance use disorder; and

(C) public health and health services; and

(2) include a plan for assessing the use of performance metrics to evaluate activities carried out by entities receiving grants, contracts, or cooperative agreements related to mental and substance use disorders prevention and treatment services under title V or title XIX of the Public Health Service Act (42 U.S.C. 290aa et seq.; 42 U.S.C. 300w et seq.).

(c) CONSULTATION.—In carrying out this section, the Assistant Secretary for Planning and Evaluation shall consult, as appropriate, with the Assistant Secretary for Mental Health and Substance Use, the Chief Medical Officer of the Substance Abuse and Mental Health Services Administration appointed under section 501(g) of the Public Health Service Act (42 U.S.C. 290aa(g)), as amended by section 6003, the Behavioral Health Coordinating Council of the Department of Health and Human Services, other agencies within the Department of Health and Human Services, and other relevant Federal departments and agencies.

(d) RECOMMENDATIONS.—In carrying out this section, the Assistant Secretary for Planning and Evaluation shall provide recommendations to the Secretary of Health and Human Services, the Assistant Secretary for Mental Health and Substance Use, and the Congress on improving the quality of prevention and treatment programs and activities related to mental and substance use disorders, including recommendations for the use of performance metrics. The Assistant Secretary for Mental Health and Substance Use shall include such recommendations in the biennial report required by subsection 501(m) of the Public Health Service Act, as redesignated by section 6003 of this Act.

SEC. 6022. REPORTING FOR PROTECTION AND ADVOCACY ORGANIZATIONS.

(a) PUBLIC AVAILABILITY OF REPORTS.—Section 105(a)(7) of the Protection and Advocacy for Individuals with Mental Illness Act (42 U.S.C. 10805(a)(7)) is amended by striking "is located a report" and inserting "is located, and make publicly available, a report".

(b) DETAILED ACCOUNTING.—Section 114(a) of the Protection and Advocacy for Individuals with Mental Illness Act (42 U.S.C. 10824(a)) is amended—

(1) in paragraph (3), by striking "and" at the end;

(2) in paragraph (4), by striking the period at the end and inserting "; and"; and

(3) by adding at the end the following:

"(5) using data from the existing required annual program progress reports submitted by each system funded under this title, a detailed accounting for each such system of how funds are spent, disaggregated according to whether the funds were received from the Federal Government, the State government, a local government, or a private entity.''.

SEC. 6023. GAO STUDY.

(a) IN GENERAL.—Not later than 18 months after the date of enactment of this Act, the

Comptroller General of the United States, in consultation with the Secretary of Health and Human Services and the Assistant Secretary for Mental Health and Substance Use, shall conduct an independent evaluation, and submit a report, to the Committee on Health, Education, Labor, and Pensions of the Senate and the Committee on Energy and Commerce of the House of Representatives, on programs funded by allotments made under title I of the Protection and Advocacy for Individuals with Mental Illness Act (42 U.S.C. 10801 et seq.).

(b) CONTENTS.—The report and evaluation required under subsection (a) shall include—

(1) a review of the programs described in such subsection that are carried out by State agencies and such programs that are carried out by private, nonprofit organizations; and

(2) a review of the compliance of the programs described in subsection (a) with statutory and regulatory responsibilities, such as—

(A) responsibilities relating to family engagement;

(B) responsibilities relating to the grievance procedure for clients or prospective clients of the system to assure that individuals with mental illness have full access to the services of the system, for individuals who have received or are receiving mental health services, and for family members of such individuals with mental illness, or representatives of such individuals or family members, to assure that the eligible system is operating in compliance with the provisions of the Protection and Advocacy for Individuals with Mental Illness Act, as required to be established by section 105(a)(9) of such Act (42 U.S.C. 10805(a)(9));

(C) investigation of alleged abuse and neglect of persons with mental illness;

(D) availability of adequate medical and behavioral health treatment;

(E) denial of rights for persons with mental illness; and

(F) compliance with the Federal prohibition on lobbying.

Subtitle C—Interdepartmental Serious Mental Illness Coordinating Committee

SEC. 6031. INTERDEPARTMENTAL SERIOUS MENTAL ILLNESS COORDINATING COMMITTEE.

(a) ESTABLISHMENT.—

(1) IN GENERAL.—Not later than 3 months after the date of enactment of this Act, the Secretary of Health and Human Services, or the designee of the Secretary, shall establish a committee to be known as the Interdepartmental Serious Mental Illness Coordinating Committee (in this section referred to as the "Committee").

(2) FEDERAL ADVISORY COMMITTEE ACT.—Except as provided in this section, the provisions of the Federal Advisory Committee Act (5 U.S.C. App.) shall apply to the Committee.

(b) MEETINGS.—The Committee shall meet not fewer than 2 times each year.

(c) RESPONSIBILITIES.—Not later than 1 year after the date of enactment of this Act, and 5 years after such date of enactment, the Committee shall submit to Congress and any other relevant Federal department or agency a report including—

(1) a summary of advances in serious mental illness and serious emotional disturbance research related to the prevention of, diagnosis of, intervention in, and treatment and recovery of serious mental illnesses, serious emotional disturbances, and advances in access to services and support for adults with a serious mental illness or children with a serious emotional disturbance;

(2) an evaluation of the effect Federal programs related to serious mental illness have on public health, including public health outcomes such as—

(A) rates of suicide, suicide attempts, incidence and prevalence of serious mental illnesses,

serious emotional disturbances, and substance use disorders, overdose, overdose deaths, emergency hospitalizations, emergency room boarding, preventable emergency room visits, interaction with the criminal justice system, homelessness, and unemployment;

(B) increased rates of employment and enrollment in educational and vocational programs;

(C) quality of mental and substance use disorders treatment services; or

(D) any other criteria as may be determined by the Secretary; and

(3) specific recommendations for actions that agencies can take to better coordinate the administration of mental health services for adults with a serious mental illness or children with a serious emotional disturbance.

(d) COMMITTEE EXTENSION.—Upon the submission of the second report under subsection (c), the Secretary shall submit a recommendation to Congress on whether to extend the operation of the Committee.

(e) MEMBERSHIP.—

(1) FEDERAL MEMBERS.—The Committee shall be composed of the following Federal representatives, or the designees of such representatives—

(A) the Secretary of Health and Human Services, who shall serve as the Chair of the Committee;

(B) the Assistant Secretary for Mental Health and Substance Use;

(C) the Attorney General;

(D) the Secretary of Veterans Affairs;

(E) the Secretary of Defense;

(F) the Secretary of Housing and Urban Development;

(G) the Secretary of Education;

(H) the Secretary of Labor;

(I) the Administrator of the Centers for Medicare & Medicaid Services; and

(J) the Commissioner of Social Security.

(2) NON-FEDERAL MEMBERS.—The Committee shall also include not less than 14 non-Federal public members appointed by the Secretary of Health and Human Services, of which—

(A) at least 2 members shall be an individual who has received treatment for a diagnosis of a serious mental illness;

(B) at least 1 member shall be a parent or legal guardian of an adult with a history of a serious mental illness or a child with a history of a serious emotional disturbance;

(C) at least 1 member shall be a representative of a leading research, advocacy, or service organization for adults with a serious mental illness;

(D) at least 2 members shall be—

(i) a licensed psychiatrist with experience in treating serious mental illnesses;

(ii) a licensed psychologist with experience in treating serious mental illnesses or serious emotional disturbances;

(iii) a licensed clinical social worker with experience treating serious mental illnesses or serious emotional disturbances; or

(iv) a licensed psychiatric nurse, nurse practitioner, or physician assistant with experience in treating serious mental illnesses or serious emotional disturbances;

(E) at least 1 member shall be a licensed mental health professional with a specialty in treating children and adolescents with a serious emotional disturbance;

(F) at least 1 member shall be a mental health professional who has research or clinical mental health experience in working with minorities;

(G) at least 1 member shall be a mental health professional who has research or clinical mental health experience in working with medically underserved populations;

(H) at least 1 member shall be a State certified mental health peer support specialist;

(I) at least 1 member shall be a judge with experience in adjudicating cases related to criminal justice or serious mental illness;

(J) at least 1 member shall be a law enforcement officer or corrections officer with extensive experience in interfacing with adults with a serious mental illness, children with a serious emotional disturbance, or individuals in a mental health crisis; and

(K) at least 1 member shall have experience providing services for homeless individuals and working with adults with a serious mental illness, children with a serious emotional disturbance, or individuals in a mental health crisis.

(3) TERMS.—A member of the Committee appointed under subsection (e)(2) shall serve for a term of 3 years, and may be reappointed for 1 or more additional 3-year terms. Any member appointed to fill a vacancy for an unexpired term shall be appointed for the remainder of such term. A member may serve after the expiration of the member's term until a successor has been appointed.

(f) WORKING GROUPS.—In carrying out its functions, the Committee may establish working groups. Such working groups shall be composed of Committee members, or their designees, and may hold such meetings as are necessary.

(g) SUNSET.—The Committee shall terminate on the date that is 6 years after the date on which the Committee is established under subsection (a)(1).

TITLE VII—ENSURING MENTAL AND SUBSTANCE USE DISORDERS PREVENTION, TREATMENT, AND RECOVERY PROGRAMS KEEP PACE WITH SCIENCE AND TECHNOLOGY

SEC. 7001. ENCOURAGING INNOVATION AND EVIDENCE-BASED PROGRAMS.

Title V of the Public Health Service Act (42 U.S.C. 290aa et seq.) is amended by inserting after section 501 (42 U.S.C. 290aa) the following:

"**SEC. 501A. NATIONAL MENTAL HEALTH AND SUBSTANCE USE POLICY LABORATORY.**

"(a) IN GENERAL.—There shall be established within the Administration a National Mental Health and Substance Use Policy Laboratory (referred to in this section as the 'Laboratory').

"(b) RESPONSIBILITIES.—The Laboratory shall—

"(1) continue to carry out the authorities and activities that were in effect for the Office of Policy, Planning, and Innovation as such Office existed prior to the date of enactment of the Helping Families in Mental Health Crisis Reform Act of 2016;

"(2) identify, coordinate, and facilitate the implementation of policy changes likely to have a significant effect on mental health, mental illness, recovery supports, and the prevention and treatment of substance use disorder services;

"(3) work with the Center for Behavioral Health Statistics and Quality to collect, as appropriate, information from grantees under programs operated by the Administration in order to evaluate and disseminate information on evidence-based practices, including culturally and linguistically appropriate services, as appropriate, and service delivery models;

"(4) provide leadership in identifying and coordinating policies and programs, including evidence-based programs, related to mental and substance use disorders;

"(5) periodically review programs and activities operated by the Administration relating to the diagnosis or prevention of, treatment for, and recovery from, mental and substance use disorders to—

"(A) identify any such programs or activities that are duplicative;

"(B) identify any such programs or activities that are not evidence-based, effective, or efficient; and

"(C) formulate recommendations for coordinating, eliminating, or improving programs or activities identified under subparagraph (A) or (B) and merging such programs or activities into other successful programs or activities; and

"(6) carry out other activities as deemed necessary to continue to encourage innovation and disseminate evidence-based programs and practices.

"(c) EVIDENCE-BASED PRACTICES AND SERVICE DELIVERY MODELS.—

"(1) IN GENERAL.—In carrying out subsection (b)(3), the Laboratory—

"(A) may give preference to models that improve—

"(i) the coordination between mental health and physical health providers;

"(ii) the coordination among such providers and the justice and corrections system; and

"(iii) the cost effectiveness, quality, effectiveness, and efficiency of health care services furnished to adults with a serious mental illness, children with a serious emotional disturbance, or individuals in a mental health crisis; and

"(B) may include clinical protocols and practices that address the needs of individuals with early serious mental illness.

"(2) CONSULTATION.—In carrying out this section, the Laboratory shall consult with—

"(A) the Chief Medical Officer appointed under section 501(g);

"(B) representatives of the National Institute of Mental Health, the National Institute on Drug Abuse, and the National Institute on Alcohol Abuse and Alcoholism, on an ongoing basis;

"(C) other appropriate Federal agencies;

"(D) clinical and analytical experts with expertise in psychiatric medical care and clinical psychological care, health care management, education, corrections health care, and mental health court systems, as appropriate; and

"(E) other individuals and agencies as determined appropriate by the Assistant Secretary.

"(d) DEADLINE FOR BEGINNING IMPLEMENTATION.—The Laboratory shall begin implementation of this section not later than January 1, 2018.

"(e) PROMOTING INNOVATION.—

"(1) IN GENERAL.—The Assistant Secretary, in coordination with the Laboratory, may award grants to States, local governments, Indian tribes or tribal organizations (as such terms are defined in section 4 of the Indian Self-Determination and Education Assistance Act), educational institutions, and nonprofit organizations to develop evidence-based interventions, including culturally and linguistically appropriate services, as appropriate, for—

"(A) evaluating a model that has been scientifically demonstrated to show promise, but would benefit from further applied development, for—

"(i) enhancing the prevention, diagnosis, intervention, and treatment of, and recovery from, mental illness, serious emotional disturbances, substance use disorders, and co-occurring illness or disorders; or

"(ii) integrating or coordinating physical health services and mental and substance use disorders services; and

"(B) expanding, replicating, or scaling evidence-based programs across a wider area to enhance effective screening, early diagnosis, intervention, and treatment with respect to mental illness, serious mental illness, serious emotional disturbances, and substance use disorders, primarily by—

"(i) applying such evidence-based programs to the delivery of care, including by training staff in effective evidence-based treatments; or

"(ii) integrating such evidence-based programs into models of care across specialties and jurisdictions.

"(2) CONSULTATION.—In awarding grants under this subsection, the Assistant Secretary shall, as appropriate, consult with the Chief Medical Officer, appointed under section 501(g), the advisory councils described in section 502, the National Institute of Mental Health, the Na-

tional Institute on Drug Abuse, and the National Institute on Alcohol Abuse and Alcoholism, as appropriate.

"(3) AUTHORIZATION OF APPROPRIATIONS.— There are authorized to be appropriated—

"(A) to carry out paragraph (1)(A), $7,000,000 for the period of fiscal years 2018 through 2020; and

"(B) to carry out paragraph (1)(B), $7,000,000 for the period of fiscal years 2018 through 2020.".

SEC. 7002. PROMOTING ACCESS TO INFORMATION ON EVIDENCE-BASED PROGRAMS AND PRACTICES.

Part D of title V of the Public Health Service Act (42 U.S.C. 290dd et seq.) is amended by inserting after section 543 of such Act (42 U.S.C. 290dd–2) the following:

"SEC. 543A. PROMOTING ACCESS TO INFORMATION ON EVIDENCE-BASED PROGRAMS AND PRACTICES.

"(a) IN GENERAL.—The Assistant Secretary shall, as appropriate, improve access to reliable and valid information on evidence-based programs and practices, including information on the strength of evidence associated with such programs and practices, related to mental and substance use disorders for States, local communities, nonprofit entities, and other stakeholders, by posting on the Internet website of the Administration information on evidence-based programs and practices that have been reviewed by the Assistant Secretary in accordance with the requirements of this section.

"(b) APPLICATIONS.—

"(1) APPLICATION PERIOD.—In carrying out subsection (a), the Assistant Secretary may establish a period for the submission of applications for evidence-based programs and practices to be posted publicly in accordance with subsection (a).

"(2) NOTICE.—In establishing the application period under paragraph (1), the Assistant Secretary shall provide for the public notice of such application period in the Federal Register. Such notice may solicit applications for evidence-based programs and practices to address gaps in information identified by the Assistant Secretary, the National Mental Health and Substance Use Policy Laboratory established under section 501A, or the Assistant Secretary for Planning and Evaluation, including pursuant to the evaluation and recommendations under section 6021 of the Helping Families in Mental Health Crisis Reform Act of 2016 or priorities identified in the strategic plan under section 501(l).

"(c) REQUIREMENTS.—The Assistant Secretary may establish minimum requirements for the applications submitted under subsection (b), including applications related to the submission of research and evaluation.

"(d) REVIEW AND RATING.—

"(1) IN GENERAL.—The Assistant Secretary shall review applications prior to public posting in accordance with subsection (a), and may prioritize the review of applications for evidence-based programs and practices that are related to topics included in the notice provided under subsection (b)(2).

"(2) SYSTEM.—In carrying out paragraph (1), the Assistant Secretary may utilize a rating and review system, which may include information on the strength of evidence associated with the evidence-based programs and practices and a rating of the methodological rigor of the research supporting the applications.

"(3) PUBLIC ACCESS TO METRICS AND RATING.— The Assistant Secretary shall make the metrics used to evaluate applications under this section, and any resulting ratings of such applications, publicly available.".

SEC. 7003. PRIORITY MENTAL HEALTH NEEDS OF REGIONAL AND NATIONAL SIGNIFICANCE.

Section 520A of the Public Health Service Act (42 U.S.C. 290bb–32) is amended—

(1) in subsection (a)—

(A) in paragraph (4), by inserting before the period ", which may include technical assistance centers"; and

(B) in the flush sentence following paragraph (4)—

(i) by inserting ", contracts," before "or cooperative agreements"; and

(ii) by striking "Indian tribes and tribal organizations" and inserting "Indian tribes or tribal organizations (as such terms are defined in section 4 of the Indian Self-Determination and Education Assistance Act), health facilities, or programs operated by or in accordance with a contract or grant with the Indian Health Service, or"; and

(2) by amending subsection (f) to read as follows:

"(f) AUTHORIZATION OF APPROPRIATIONS.— There are authorized to be appropriated to carry out this section $394,550,000 for each of fiscal years 2018 through 2022.".

SEC. 7004. PRIORITY SUBSTANCE USE DISORDER TREATMENT NEEDS OF REGIONAL AND NATIONAL SIGNIFICANCE.

Section 509 of the Public Health Service Act (42 U.S.C. 290bb–2) is amended—

(1) in subsection (a)—

(A) in the matter preceding paragraph (1), by striking "abuse" and inserting "use disorder";

(B) in paragraph (3), by inserting before the period "that permit States, local governments, communities, and Indian tribes and tribal organizations (as the terms 'Indian tribes' and 'tribal organizations' are defined in section 4 of the Indian Self-Determination and Education Assistance Act) to focus on emerging trends in substance abuse and co-occurrence of substance use disorders with mental illness or other conditions"; and

(C) in the flush sentence following paragraph (3)—

(i) by inserting ", contracts," before "or cooperative agreements"; and

(ii) by striking "Indian tribes and tribal organizations," and inserting "Indian tribes or tribal organizations (as such terms are defined in section 4 of the Indian Self-Determination and Education Assistance Act), health facilities, or programs operated by or in accordance with a contract or grant with the Indian Health Service, or";

(2) in subsection (b)—

(A) in paragraph (1), by striking "abuse" and inserting "use disorder"; and

(B) in paragraph (2), by striking "abuse" and inserting "use disorder";

(3) in subsection (e), by striking "abuse" and inserting "use disorder"; and

(4) in subsection (f), by striking "$300,000,000" and all that follows through the period and inserting "$333,806,000 for each of fiscal years 2018 through 2022.".

SEC. 7005. PRIORITY SUBSTANCE USE DISORDER PREVENTION NEEDS OF REGIONAL AND NATIONAL SIGNIFICANCE.

Section 516 of the Public Health Service Act (42 U.S.C. 290bb–22) is amended—

(1) in the section heading, by striking "**ABUSE**" and inserting "**USE DISORDER**";

(2) in subsection (a)—

(A) in the matter preceding paragraph (1), by striking "abuse" and inserting "use disorder";

(B) in paragraph (3), by inserting before the period ", including such programs that focus on emerging drug abuse issues"; and

(C) in the flush sentence following paragraph (3)—

(i) by inserting ", contracts," before "or cooperative agreements"; and

(ii) by striking "Indian tribes and tribal organizations," and inserting "Indian tribes or tribal organizations (as such terms are defined in section 4 of the Indian Self-Determination and Education Assistance Act), health facilities, or programs operated by or in accordance with a contract or grant with the Indian Health Service,";

(3) in subsection (b)—

(A) in paragraph (1), by striking "abuse" and inserting "use disorder"; and

(B) in paragraph (2)—

(i) in subparagraph (A), by striking "; and" at the end and inserting ";";

(ii) in subparagraph (B)—

(I) by striking "abuse" and inserting "use disorder"; and

(II) by striking the period and inserting "; and"; and

(iii) by adding at the end the following:

"(C) substance use disorder prevention among high-risk groups.";

(4) in subsection (e), by striking "abuse" and inserting "use disorder"; and

(5) in subsection (f), by striking "$300,000,000" and all that follows through the period and inserting "$211,148,000 for each of fiscal years 2018 through 2022.".

TITLE VIII—SUPPORTING STATE PREVENTION ACTIVITIES AND RESPONSES TO MENTAL HEALTH AND SUBSTANCE USE DISORDER NEEDS

SEC. 8001. COMMUNITY MENTAL HEALTH SERVICES BLOCK GRANT.

(a) FORMULA GRANTS.—Section 1911(b) of the Public Health Service Act (42 U.S.C. 300x(b)) is amended—

(1) by redesignating paragraphs (1) through (3) as paragraphs (2) through (4), respectively; and

(2) by inserting before paragraph (2) (as so redesignated) the following:

"(1) providing community mental health services for adults with a serious mental illness and children with a serious emotional disturbance as defined in accordance with section 1912(c);".

(b) STATE PLAN.—Section 1912(b) of the Public Health Service Act (42 U.S.C. 300x–1(b)) is amended—

(1) in paragraph (3), by redesignating subparagraphs (A) through (C) as clauses (i) through (iii), respectively, and realigning the margins accordingly;

(2) by redesignating paragraphs (1) through (5) as subparagraphs (A) through (E), respectively, and realigning the margins accordingly;

(3) in the matter preceding subparagraph (A) (as so redesignated), by striking "With respect to" and all that follows through "are as follows:" and inserting "In accordance with subsection (a), a State shall submit to the Secretary a plan every two years that, at a minimum, includes each of the following:

(4) by inserting before subparagraph (A) (as so redesignated) the following:

"(1) SYSTEM OF CARE.—A description of the State's system of care that contains the following:";

(5) by striking subparagraph (A) (as so redesignated) and inserting the following:

"(A) COMPREHENSIVE COMMUNITY-BASED HEALTH SYSTEMS.—The plan shall—

"(i) identify the single State agency to be responsible for the administration of the program under the grant, including any third party who administers mental health services and is responsible for complying with the requirements of this part with respect to the grant;

"(ii) provide for an organized community-based system of care for individuals with mental illness, and describe available services and resources in a comprehensive system of care, including services for individuals with co-occurring disorders;

(iii) include a description of the manner in which the State and local entities will coordinate services to maximize the efficiency, effectiveness, quality, and cost-effectiveness of services and programs to produce the best possible outcomes (including health services, rehabilitation services, employment services, housing services, educational services, substance use disorder services, legal services, law enforcement services, social services, child welfare services, medical and dental care services, and other support services to be provided with Federal, State, and local public and private resources) with other agencies to enable individuals receiving services to function outside of inpatient or residential institutions, to the maximum extent of their capabilities, including services to be provided by local school systems under the Individuals with Disabilities Education Act;

"(iv) include a description of how the State promotes evidence-based practices, including those evidence-based programs that address the needs of individuals with early serious mental illness regardless of the age of the individual at onset, provide comprehensive individualized treatment, or integrate mental and physical health services;

"(v) include a description of case management services;

"(vi) include a description of activities that seek to engage adults with a serious mental illness or children with a serious emotional disturbance and their caregivers where appropriate in making health care decisions, including activities that enhance communication among individuals, families, caregivers, and treatment providers; and

"(vii) as appropriate to, and reflective of, the uses the State proposes for the block grant funds, include—

"(I) a description of the activities intended to reduce hospitalizations and hospital stays using the block grant funds;

"(II) a description of the activities intended to reduce incidents of suicide using the block grant funds;

"(III) a description of how the State integrates mental health and primary care using the block grant funds, which may include providing, in the case of individuals with co-occurring mental and substance use disorders, both mental and substance use disorders services in primary care settings or arrangements to provide primary and specialty care services in community-based mental and substance use disorders settings; and

"(IV) a description of recovery and recovery support services for adults with a serious mental illness and children with a serious emotional disturbance.";

(6) in subparagraph (B) (as so redesignated)—

(A) by striking "The plan contains" and inserting "The plan shall contain"; and

(B) by striking "presents quantitative targets to be achieved in the implementation of the system described in paragraph (1)" and inserting "present quantitative targets and outcome measures for programs and services provided under this subpart";

(7) in subparagraph (C) (as so redesignated)—

(A) by striking "serious emotional disturbance" in the matter preceding clause (i) (as so redesignated) and all that follows through "substance abuse services" in clause (i) (as so redesignated) and inserting the following: "a serious emotional disturbance (as defined pursuant to subsection (c)), the plan shall provide for a system of integrated social services, educational services, child welfare services, juvenile justice services, law enforcement services, and substance use disorder services";

(B) by striking "Education Act);" and inserting "Education Act).", and

(C) by striking clauses (ii) and (iii) (as so redesignated);

(8) in subparagraph (D) (as so redesignated), by striking "plan describes" and inserting "plan shall describe";

(9) in subparagraph (E) (as so redesignated)—

(A) in the subparagraph heading by striking "SYSTEMS" and inserting "SERVICES";

(B) in the first sentence, by striking "plan describes" and all that follows through "and provides for" and inserting "plan shall describe the financial resources available, the existing mental health workforce, and the workforce trained in treating individuals with co-occurring mental and substance use disorders, and shall provide for"; and

(C) in the second sentence—

(i) by striking "further describes" and inserting "shall further describe"; and

(ii) by striking "involved." and inserting "involved, and the manner in which the State intends to comply with each of the funding agreements in this subpart and subpart III.";

(10) by striking the flush matter at the end; and

(11) by adding at the end the following:

"(2) GOALS AND OBJECTIVES.—The establishment of goals and objectives for the period of the plan, including targets and milestones that are intended to be met, and the activities that will be undertaken to achieve those targets.".

(c) EARLY SERIOUS MENTAL ILLNESS.—Section 1920 of the Public Health Service Act (42 U.S.C. 300x–9) is amended by adding at the end the following:

"(c) EARLY SERIOUS MENTAL ILLNESS.—

"(1) IN GENERAL.—Except as provided in paragraph (2), a State shall expend not less than 10 percent of the amount the State receives for carrying out this section for each fiscal year to support evidence-based programs that address the needs of individuals with early serious mental illness, including psychotic disorders, regardless of the age of the individual at onset.

"(2) STATE FLEXIBILITY.—In lieu of expending 10 percent of the amount the State receives under this section for a fiscal year as required under paragraph (1), a State may elect to expend not less than 20 percent of such amount by the end of such succeeding fiscal year.".

(d) ADDITIONAL PROVISIONS.—Section 1915(b) of the Public Health Service Act (42 U.S.C. 300x–4(b)) is amended—

(1) in paragraph (3)—

(A) by striking "The Secretary" and inserting the following:

"(A) IN GENERAL.—The Secretary";

(B) by striking "paragraph (1) if" and inserting "paragraph (1) in whole or in part if";

(C) by striking "State justify the waiver." and inserting "State in the fiscal year involved or in the previous fiscal year justify the waiver"; and

(D) by adding at the end the following:

"(B) DATE CERTAIN FOR ACTION UPON REQUEST.—The Secretary shall approve or deny a request for a waiver under this paragraph not later than 120 days after the date on which the request is made.

"(C) APPLICABILITY OF WAIVER.—A waiver provided by the Secretary under this paragraph shall be applicable only to the fiscal year involved."; and

(2) in paragraph (4)—

(A) in subparagraph (A)—

(i) by inserting after the subparagraph designation the following: "IN GENERAL.—";

(ii) by striking "In making a grant" and inserting the following:

"(i) DETERMINATION.—In making a grant"; and

(iii) by inserting at the end the following:

"(ii) ALTERNATIVE.—A State that has failed to comply with paragraph (1) and would otherwise be subject to a reduction in the State's allotment under section 1911 may, upon request by the State, in lieu of having the amount of the allotment under section 1911 for the State reduced

for the fiscal year of the grant, agree to comply with a negotiated agreement that is approved by the Secretary and carried out in accordance with guidelines issued by the Secretary. If a State fails to enter into or comply with a negotiated agreement, the Secretary may take action under this paragraph or the terms of the negotiated agreement.''; and

(B) in subparagraph (B)—

(i) by inserting after the subparagraph designation the following: ''SUBMISSION OF INFORMATION TO THE SECRETARY.—''; and

(ii) by striking ''subparagraph (A)'' and inserting ''subparagraph (A)(i)''.

(e) APPLICATION FOR GRANT.—Section 1917(a) of the Public Health Service Act (42 U.S.C. 300x-6(a)) is amended—

(1) in paragraph (1), by striking ''1941'' and inserting ''1942(a)''; and

(2) in paragraph (5), by striking ''1915(b)(3)(B)'' and inserting ''1915(b)''.

(f) FUNDING.—Section 1920 of the Public Health Service Act (42 U.S.C. 300x-9) is amended—

(1) in subsection (a)—

(A) by striking ''section 505'' and inserting ''section 505(c)''; and

(B) by striking ''$450,000,000'' and all that follows through the period and inserting ''$532,571,000 for each of fiscal years 2018 through 2022.''; and

(2) in subsection (b)(2) by striking ''sections 505 and'' and inserting ''sections 505(c) and''.

SEC. 8002. SUBSTANCE ABUSE PREVENTION AND TREATMENT BLOCK GRANT.

(a) FORMULA GRANTS.—Section 1921(b) of the Public Health Service Act (42 U.S.C. 300x-21(b)) is amended—

(1) by inserting ''carrying out the plan developed in accordance with section 1932(b) and for'' after ''for the purpose of''; and

(2) by striking ''abuse'' and inserting ''use disorders''.

(b) OUTREACH TO PERSONS WHO INJECT DRUGS.—Section 1923(b) of the Public Health Service Act (42 U.S.C. 300x-23(b)) is amended—

(1) in the subsection heading, by striking ''REGARDING INTRAVENOUS SUBSTANCE ABUSE'' and inserting ''TO PERSONS WHO INJECT DRUGS''; and

(2) by striking ''for intravenous drug abuse'' and inserting ''for persons who inject drugs''.

(c) REQUIREMENTS REGARDING TUBERCULOSIS AND HUMAN IMMUNODEFICIENCY VIRUS.—Section 1924 of the Public Health Service Act (42 U.S.C. 300x-24) is amended—

(1) in subsection (a)(1)—

(A) in the matter preceding subparagraph (A), by striking ''substance abuse'' and inserting ''substance use disorders''; and

(B) in subparagraph (A), by striking ''such abuse'' and inserting ''such disorders'';

(2) in subsection (b)—

(A) in paragraph (1)(A), by striking ''substance abuse'' and inserting ''substance use disorders'';

(B) in paragraph (2), by inserting ''and Prevention'' after ''Disease Control'';

(C) in paragraph (3)—

(i) in the paragraph heading, by striking ''ABUSE'' and inserting ''USE DISORDERS''; and

(ii) by striking ''substance abuse'' and inserting ''substance use disorders''; and

(D) in paragraph (6)(B), by striking ''substance abuse'' and inserting ''substance use disorders'';

(3) by striking subsection (d); and

(4) by redesignating subsection (e) as subsection (d).

(d) GROUP HOMES.—Section 1925 of the Public Health Service Act (42 U.S.C. 300x-25) is amended—

(1) in the section heading, by striking ''**RECOVERING SUBSTANCE ABUSERS**'' and inserting ''**PER-**

SONS IN RECOVERY FROM SUBSTANCE USE DISORDERS''; and

(2) in subsection (a), in the matter preceding paragraph (1), by striking ''recovering substance abusers'' and inserting ''persons in recovery from substance use disorders''.

(e) ADDITIONAL AGREEMENTS.—Section 1928 of the Public Health Service Act (42 U.S.C. 300x-28) is amended—

(1) in subsection (a), by striking ''(relative to fiscal year 1992)'';

(2) by striking subsection (b) and inserting the following:

''(b) PROFESSIONAL DEVELOPMENT.—A funding agreement for a grant under section 1921 is that the State involved will ensure that prevention, treatment, and recovery personnel operating in the State's substance use disorder prevention, treatment, and recovery systems have an opportunity to receive training, on an ongoing basis, concerning—

''(1) recent trends in substance use disorders in the State;

''(2) improved methods and evidence-based practices for providing substance use disorder prevention and treatment services;

''(3) performance-based accountability;

''(4) data collection and reporting requirements; and

''(5) any other matters that would serve to further improve the delivery of substance use disorder prevention and treatment services within the State.''; and

(3) in subsection (d)(1), by striking ''substance abuse'' and inserting ''substance use disorders''.

(f) REPEAL.—Section 1929 of the Public Health Service Act (42 U.S.C. 300x-29) is repealed.

(g) MAINTENANCE OF EFFORT.—Section 1930 of the Public Health Service Act (42 U.S.C. 300x-30) is amended—

(1) in subsection (c)(1), by striking ''in the State justify the waiver'' and inserting ''exist in the State, or any part of the State, to justify the waiver''; and

(2) in subsection (d), by inserting at the end the following:

''(3) ALTERNATIVE.—A State that has failed to comply with this section and would otherwise be subject to a reduction in the State's allotment under section 1921, may, upon request by the State, in lieu of having the State's allotment under section 1921 reduced, agree to comply with a negotiated agreement that is approved by the Secretary and carried out in accordance with guidelines issued by the Secretary. If a State fails to enter into or comply with a negotiated agreement, the Secretary may take action under this paragraph or the terms of the negotiated agreement.''.

(h) RESTRICTIONS ON EXPENDITURES.—Section 1931(b)(1) of the Public Health Service Act (42 U.S.C. 300x-31(b)(1)) is amended by striking ''substance abuse'' and inserting ''substance use disorders''.

(i) APPLICATION.—Section 1932 of the Public Health Service Act (42 U.S.C. 300x-32) is amended—

(1) in subsection (a)—

(A) in the matter preceding paragraph (1), by striking ''subsections (c) and (d)(2)'' and inserting ''subsection (c)''; and

(B) in paragraph (5), by striking ''the information required in section 1929, the information required in section 1930(c)(2), and'';

(2) in subsection (b)—

(A) by striking paragraph (1) and inserting the following:

''(1) IN GENERAL.—In order for a State to be in compliance with subsection (a)(6), the State shall submit to the Secretary a plan that, at a minimum, includes the following:

''(A) A description of the State's system of care that—

''(i) identifies the single State agency responsible for the administration of the program, in-

cluding any third party who administers substance use disorder services and is responsible for complying with the requirements of the grant;

''(ii) provides information on the need for substance use disorder prevention and treatment services in the State, including estimates on the number of individuals who need treatment, who are pregnant women, women with dependent children, individuals with a co-occurring mental health and substance use disorder, persons who inject drugs, and persons who are experiencing homelessness;

''(iii) provides aggregate information on the number of individuals in treatment within the State, including the number of such individuals who are pregnant women, women with dependent children, individuals with a co-occurring mental health and substance use disorder, persons who inject drugs, and persons who are experiencing homelessness;

''(iv) provides a description of the system that is available to provide services by modality, including the provision of recovery support services;

''(v) provides a description of the State's comprehensive statewide prevention efforts, including the number of individuals being served in the system, target populations, and priority needs, and provides a description of the amount of funds from the prevention set-aside expended on primary prevention;

''(vi) provides a description of the financial resources available;

''(vii) describes the existing substance use disorders workforce and workforce trained in treating co-occurring substance use and mental disorders;

''(viii) includes a description of how the State promotes evidence-based practices; and

''(ix) describes how the State integrates substance use disorder services and primary health care, which in the case of those individuals with co-occurring mental health and substance use disorders may include providing both mental health and substance use disorder services in primary care settings or providing primary and specialty care services in community-based mental health and substance use disorder service settings.

''(B) The establishment of goals and objectives for the period of the plan, including targets and milestones that are intended to be met, and the activities that will be undertaken to achieve those targets.

''(C) A description of how the State will comply with each funding agreement for a grant under section 1921 that is applicable to the State, including a description of the manner in which the State intends to expend grant funds.''; and

(B) in paragraph (2)—

(i) in the paragraph heading, by striking ''AUTHORITY OF SECRETARY REGARDING MODIFICATIONS'' and inserting ''MODIFICATIONS'';

(ii) by striking ''As a condition'' and inserting the following:

''(A) AUTHORITY OF SECRETARY.—As a condition;''; and

(iii) by adding at the end the following:

''(B) STATE REQUEST FOR MODIFICATION.—If the State determines that a modification to such plan is necessary, the State may request the Secretary to approve the modification. Any such modification shall be in accordance with paragraph (1) and section 1941.''; and

(C) in paragraph (3), by inserting, '', including any modification under paragraph (2)'' after ''subsection (a)(6)''; and

(3) in subsection (e)(2), by striking ''section 1922(c)'' and inserting ''section 1922(b)''.

(j) DEFINITIONS.—Section 1934 of the Public Health Service Act (42 U.S.C. 300x-34) is amended—

(1) in paragraph (3), by striking "substance abuse" and inserting "substance use disorders"; and

(2) in paragraph (7), by striking "substance abuse" and inserting "substance use disorders".

(k) FUNDING.—Section 1935 of the Public Health Service Act (42 U.S.C. 300x–35) is amended—

(1) in subsection (a)—

(A) by striking "section 505" and inserting "section 505(d)"; and

(B) by striking "$2,000,000,000 for fiscal year 2001, and such sums as may be necessary for each of the fiscal years 2002 and 2003" and inserting "$1,858,079,000 for each of fiscal years 2018 through 2022."; and

(2) in subsection (b)(1)(B) by striking "sections 505 and" and inserting "sections 505(d) and".

SEC. 8003. ADDITIONAL PROVISIONS RELATED TO THE BLOCK GRANTS.

Subpart III of part B of title XIX of the Public Health Service Act (42 U.S.C. 300x–51 et seq.) is amended—

(1) in section 1943(a)(3) (42 U.S.C. 300x–53(a)(3)), by striking "section 505" and inserting "subsections (c) and (d) of section 505";

(2) in section 1953(b) (42 U.S.C. 300x–63(b)), by striking "substance abuse" and inserting "substance use disorder"; and

(3) by adding at the end the following:

"SEC. 1957. PUBLIC HEALTH EMERGENCIES.

"In the case of a public health emergency (as determined under section 319), the Secretary, on a State by State basis, may, as the circumstances of the emergency reasonably require and for the period of the emergency, grant an extension, or waive application deadlines or compliance with any other requirement, of a grant authorized under section 521, 1911, or 1921 or an allotment authorized under Public Law 99–319 (42 U.S.C. 10801 et seq.).

"SEC. 1958. JOINT APPLICATIONS.

"The Secretary, acting through the Assistant Secretary for Mental Health and Substance Use, shall permit a joint application to be submitted for grants under subpart I and subpart II upon the request of a State. Such application may be jointly reviewed and approved by the Secretary with respect to such subparts, consistent with the purposes and authorized activities of each such grant program. A State submitting such a joint application shall otherwise meet the requirements with respect to each such subpart.".

SEC. 8004. STUDY OF DISTRIBUTION OF FUNDS UNDER THE SUBSTANCE ABUSE PREVENTION AND TREATMENT BLOCK GRANT AND THE COMMUNITY MENTAL HEALTH SERVICES BLOCK GRANT.

(a) IN GENERAL.—The Secretary of Health and Human Services, acting through the Assistant Secretary for Mental Health and Substance Use, shall through a grant or contract, or through an agreement with a third party, conduct a study on the formulas for distribution of funds under the substance abuse prevention and treatment block grant, and the community mental health services block grant, under part B of title XIX of the Public Health Service Act (42 U.S.C. 300x et seq.) and recommend changes if necessary. Such study shall include—

(1) an analysis of whether the distributions under such block grants accurately reflect the need for the services under the grants in the States;

(2) an examination of whether the indices used under the formulas for distribution of funds under such block grants are appropriate, and if not, alternatives recommended by the Secretary;

(3) where recommendations are included under paragraph (2) for the use of different indices, a description of the variables and data

sources that should be used to determine the indices;

(4) an evaluation of the variables and data sources that are being used for each of the indices involved, and whether such variables and data sources accurately represent the need for services, the cost of providing services, and the ability of the States to pay for such services;

(5) the effect that the minimum allotment requirements for each such block grant have on each State's final allotment and the effect of such requirements, if any, on each State's formula-based allotment;

(6) recommendations for modifications to the minimum allotment provisions to ensure an appropriate distribution of funds; and

(7) any other information that the Secretary determines appropriate.

(b) REPORT.—Not later than 2 years after the date of enactment of this Act, the Secretary of Health and Human Services shall submit to the Committee on Health, Education, Labor, and Pensions of the Senate and the Committee on Energy and Commerce of the House of Representatives, a report containing the findings and recommendations of the study conducted under subsection (a) and the study conducted under section 9004(g).

TITLE IX—PROMOTING ACCESS TO MENTAL HEALTH AND SUBSTANCE USE DISORDER CARE

Subtitle A—Helping Individuals and Families

SEC. 9001. GRANTS FOR TREATMENT AND RECOVERY FOR HOMELESS INDIVIDUALS.

Section 506 of the Public Health Service Act (42 U.S.C. 290aa–5) is amended—

(1) in subsection (a), by striking "substance abuse" and inserting "substance use disorder";

(2) in subsection (b)—

(A) in paragraphs (1) and (3), by striking "substance abuse" each place the term appears and inserting "substance use disorder"; and

(B) in paragraph (4), by striking "substance abuse" and inserting "a substance use disorder";

(3) in subsection (c)—

(A) in paragraph (1), by striking "substance abuse disorder" and inserting "substance use disorder"; and

(B) in paragraph (2)—

(i) in subparagraph (A), by striking "substance abuse" and inserting "a substance use disorder"; and

(ii) in subparagraph (B), by striking "substance abuse" and inserting "substance use disorder"; and

(4) in subsection (e), by striking ", $50,000,000 for fiscal year 2001, and such sums as may be necessary for each of the fiscal years 2002 and 2003" and inserting "$41,304,000 for each of fiscal years 2018 through 2022".

SEC. 9002. GRANTS FOR JAIL DIVERSION PROGRAMS.

Section 520G of the Public Health Service Act (42 U.S.C. 290bb–38) is amended—

(1) by striking "substance abuse" each place such term appears and inserting "substance use disorder";

(2) in subsection (a)—

(A) by striking "Indian tribes, and tribal organizations" and inserting "and Indian tribes and tribal organizations (as the terms 'Indian tribes' and 'tribal organizations' are defined in section 4 of the Indian Self-Determination and Education Assistance Act)"; and

(B) by inserting "or a health facility or program operated by or in accordance with a contract or grant with the Indian Health Service," after "entities,";

(3) in subsection (c)(2)(A)(i), by striking "the best known" and inserting "evidence-based";

(4) by redesignating subsections (d) through (i) as subsections (e) through (j), respectively;

(5) by inserting after subsection (c) the following:

"(d) SPECIAL CONSIDERATION REGARDING VETERANS.—In awarding grants under subsection (a), the Secretary shall, as appropriate, give special consideration to entities proposing to use grant funding to support jail diversion services for veterans.";

(6) in subsection (e), as so redesignated—

(A) in paragraph (3), by striking "; and" and inserting a semicolon;

(B) in paragraph (4), by striking the period and inserting "; and"; and

(C) by adding at the end the following:

"(5) develop programs to divert individuals prior to booking or arrest."; and

(7) in subsection (j), as so redesignated, by striking "$10,000,000 for fiscal year 2001, and such sums as may be necessary for fiscal years 2002 through 2003" and inserting "$4,269,000 for each of fiscal years 2018 through 2022".

SEC. 9003. PROMOTING INTEGRATION OF PRIMARY AND BEHAVIORAL HEALTH CARE.

Section 520K of the Public Health Service Act (42 U.S.C. 290bb–42) is amended to read as follows:

"SEC. 520K. INTEGRATION INCENTIVE GRANTS AND COOPERATIVE AGREEMENTS.

"(a) DEFINITIONS.—In this section:

"(1) ELIGIBLE ENTITY.—The term 'eligible entity' means a State, or other appropriate State agency, in collaboration with 1 or more qualified community programs as described in section 1913(b)(1) or 1 or more community health centers as described in section 330.

"(2) INTEGRATED CARE.—The term 'integrated care' means collaborative models or practices offering mental and physical health services, which may include practices that share the same space in the same facility.

"(3) SPECIAL POPULATION.—The term 'special population' means—

"(A) adults with a mental illness who have co-occurring physical health conditions or chronic diseases;

"(B) adults with a serious mental illness who have co-occurring physical health conditions or chronic diseases;

"(C) children and adolescents with a serious emotional disturbance with co-occurring physical health conditions or chronic diseases; or

"(D) individuals with a substance use disorder.

"(b) GRANTS AND COOPERATIVE AGREEMENTS.—

"(1) IN GENERAL.—The Secretary may award grants and cooperative agreements to eligible entities to support the improvement of integrated care for primary care and behavioral health care in accordance with paragraph (2).

"(2) PURPOSES.—A grant or cooperative agreement awarded under this section shall be designed to—

"(A) promote full integration and collaboration in clinical practices between primary and behavioral health care;

"(B) support the improvement of integrated care models for primary care and behavioral health care to improve the overall wellness and physical health status of adults with a serious mental illness or children with a serious emotional disturbance; and

"(C) promote integrated care services related to screening, diagnosis, prevention, and treatment of mental and substance use disorders, and co-occurring physical health conditions and chronic diseases.

"(c) APPLICATIONS.—

"(1) IN GENERAL.—An eligible entity seeking a grant or cooperative agreement under this section shall submit an application to the Secretary at such time, in such manner, and accompanied by such information as the Secretary may require, including the contents described in paragraph (2).

"(2) CONTENTS.—The contents described in this paragraph are—

"(A) a description of a plan to achieve fully collaborative agreements to provide services to special populations;

"(B) a document that summarizes the policies, if any, that serve as barriers to the provision of integrated care, and the specific steps, if applicable, that will be taken to address such barriers;

"(C) a description of partnerships or other arrangements with local health care providers to provide services to special populations;

"(D) an agreement and plan to report to the Secretary performance measures necessary to evaluate patient outcomes and facilitate evaluations across participating projects; and

"(E) a plan for sustainability beyond the grant or cooperative agreement period under subsection (e).

"(d) GRANT AND COOPERATIVE AGREEMENT AMOUNTS.—

"(1) TARGET AMOUNT.—The target amount that an eligible entity may receive for a year through a grant or cooperative agreement under this section shall be $2,000,000.

"(2) ADJUSTMENT PERMITTED.—The Secretary, taking into consideration the quality of the application and the number of eligible entities that received grants under this section prior to the date of enactment of the Helping Families in Mental Health Crisis Reform Act of 2016, may adjust the target amount that an eligible entity may receive for a year through a grant or cooperative agreement under this section.

"(3) LIMITATION.—An eligible entity receiving funding under this section may not allocate more than 10 percent of funds awarded under this section to administrative functions, and the remaining amounts shall be allocated to health facilities that provide integrated care.

"(e) DURATION.—A grant or cooperative agreement under this section shall be for a period not to exceed 5 years.

"(f) REPORT ON PROGRAM OUTCOMES.—An eligible entity receiving a grant or cooperative agreement under this section shall submit an annual report to the Secretary that includes—

"(1) the progress made to reduce barriers to integrated care as described in the entity's application under subsection (c); and

"(2) a description of functional outcomes of special populations, including—

"(A) with respect to adults with a serious mental illness, participation in supportive housing or independent living programs, attendance in social and rehabilitative programs, participation in job training opportunities, satisfactory performance in work settings, attendance at scheduled medical and mental health appointments, and compliance with prescribed medication regimes;

"(B) with respect to individuals with co-occurring mental illness and physical health conditions and chronic diseases, attendance at scheduled medical and mental health appointments, compliance with prescribed medication regimes, and participation in learning opportunities related to improved health and lifestyle practices; and

"(C) with respect to children and adolescents with a serious emotional disturbance who have co-occurring physical health conditions and chronic diseases, attendance at scheduled medical and mental health appointments, compliance with prescribed medication regimes, and participation in learning opportunities at school and extracurricular activities.

"(g) TECHNICAL ASSISTANCE FOR PRIMARY-BEHAVIORAL HEALTH CARE INTEGRATION.—

"(1) IN GENERAL.—The Secretary may provide appropriate information, training, and technical assistance to eligible entities that receive a grant or cooperative agreement under this section, in order to help such entities meet the requirements of this section, including assistance with—

"(A) development and selection of integrated care models;

"(B) dissemination of evidence-based interventions in integrated care;

"(C) establishment of organizational practices to support operational and administrative success; and

"(D) other activities, as the Secretary determines appropriate.

"(2) ADDITIONAL DISSEMINATION OF TECHNICAL INFORMATION.—The information and resources provided by the Secretary under paragraph (1) shall, as appropriate, be made available to States, political subdivisions of States, Indian tribes or tribal organizations (as defined in section 4 of the Indian Self-Determination and Education Assistance Act), outpatient mental health and addiction treatment centers, community mental health centers that meet the criteria under section 1913(c), certified community behavioral health clinics described in section 223 of the Protecting Access to Medicare Act of 2014, primary care organizations such as Federally qualified health centers or rural health clinics as defined in section 1861(aa) of the Social Security Act, other community-based organizations, or other entities engaging in integrated care activities, as the Secretary determines appropriate.

"(h) AUTHORIZATION OF APPROPRIATIONS.—To carry out this section, there are authorized to be appropriated $51,878,000 for each of fiscal years 2018 through 2022.".

SEC. 9004. PROJECTS FOR ASSISTANCE IN TRANSITION FROM HOMELESSNESS.

(a) FORMULA GRANTS TO STATES.—Section 521 of the Public Health Service Act (42 U.S.C. 290cc–21) is amended by striking "1991 through 1994" and inserting "2018 through 2022".

(b) PURPOSE OF GRANTS.—Section 522 of the Public Health Service Act (42 U.S.C. 290cc–22) is amended—

(1) in subsection (a)(1)(B), by striking "substance abuse" and inserting "a substance use disorder";

(2) in subsection (b)(6), by striking "substance abuse" and inserting "substance use disorder";

(3) in subsection (c), by striking "substance abuse" and inserting "a substance use disorder";

(4) in subsection (e)—

(A) in paragraph (1), by striking "substance abuse" and inserting "a substance use disorder"; and

(B) in paragraph (2), by striking "substance abuse" and inserting "substance use disorder";

(5) by striking subsection (g) and redesignating subsections (h) and (i) as (g) and (h), accordingly; and

(6) in subsection (g), as redesignated by paragraph (5), by striking "substance abuse" each place such term appears and inserting "substance use disorder".

(c) DESCRIPTION OF INTENDED EXPENDITURES OF GRANT.—Section 527 of the Public Health Service Act (42 U.S.C. 290cc–27) is amended by striking "substance abuse" each place such term appears and inserting "substance use disorder".

(d) TECHNICAL ASSISTANCE.—Section 530 of the Public Health Service Act (42 U.S.C. 290cc–30) is amended by striking "through the National Institute of Mental Health, the National Institute of Alcohol Abuse and Alcoholism, and the National Institute on Drug Abuse" and inserting "acting through the Assistant Secretary".

(e) DEFINITIONS.—Section 534(4) of the Public Health Service Act (42 U.S.C. 290cc–34(4)) is amended to read as follows:

"(4) SUBSTANCE USE DISORDER SERVICES.—The term 'substance use disorder services' has the meaning given the term 'substance abuse services' in section 330(h)(5)(C).".

(f) FUNDING.—Section 535(a) of the Public Health Service Act (42 U.S.C. 290cc–35(a)) is amended by striking "$75,000,000 for each of the fiscal years 2001 through 2003" and inserting "$64,635,000 for each of fiscal years 2018 through 2022".

(g) STUDY CONCERNING FORMULA.—

(1) IN GENERAL.—Not later than 2 years after the date of enactment of this Act, the Assistant Secretary for Mental Health and Substance Use (referred to in this section as the "Assistant Secretary") shall conduct a study concerning the formula used under section 524 of the Public Health Service Act (42 U.S.C. 290cc–24) for making allotments to States under section 521 of such Act (42 U.S.C. 290cc–21). Such study shall include an evaluation of quality indicators of need for purposes of revising the formula for determining the amount of each allotment for the fiscal years following the submission of the study.

(2) REPORT.—In accordance with section 8004(b), the Assistant Secretary shall submit to the committees of Congress described in such section a report concerning the results of the study conducted under paragraph (1).

SEC. 9005. NATIONAL SUICIDE PREVENTION LIFELINE PROGRAM.

Subpart 3 of part B of title V of the Public Health Service Act (42 U.S.C. 290bb–31 et seq.) is amended by inserting after section 520E–2 (42 U.S.C. 290bb–36b) the following:

"SEC. 520E–3. NATIONAL SUICIDE PREVENTION LIFELINE PROGRAM.

"(a) IN GENERAL.—The Secretary, acting through the Assistant Secretary, shall maintain the National Suicide Prevention Lifeline program (referred to in this section as the 'program'), authorized under section 520A and in effect prior to the date of enactment of the Helping Families in Mental Health Crisis Reform Act of 2016.

"(b) ACTIVITIES.—In maintaining the program, the activities of the Secretary shall include—

"(1) coordinating a network of crisis centers across the United States for providing suicide prevention and crisis intervention services to individuals seeking help at any time, day or night;

"(2) maintaining a suicide prevention hotline to link callers to local emergency, mental health, and social services resources; and

"(3) consulting with the Secretary of Veterans Affairs to ensure that veterans calling the suicide prevention hotline have access to a specialized veterans' suicide prevention hotline.

"(c) AUTHORIZATION OF APPROPRIATIONS.—To carry out this section, there are authorized to be appropriated $7,198,000 for each of fiscal years 2018 through 2022.".

SEC. 9006. CONNECTING INDIVIDUALS AND FAMILIES WITH CARE.

Subpart 3 of part B of title V of the Public Health Service Act (42 U.S.C. 290bb–31 et seq.), as amended by section 9005, is further amended by inserting after section 520E–3 the following:

"SEC. 520E–4. TREATMENT REFERRAL ROUTING SERVICE.

"(a) IN GENERAL.—The Secretary, acting through the Assistant Secretary, shall maintain the National Treatment Referral Routing Service (referred to in this section as the 'Routing Service') to assist individuals and families in locating mental and substance use disorders treatment providers.

"(b) ACTIVITIES OF THE SECRETARY.—To maintain the Routing Service, the activities of the Assistant Secretary shall include administering—

"(1) a nationwide, telephone number providing year-round access to information that is updated on a regular basis regarding local behavioral health providers and community-based organizations in a manner that is confidential, without requiring individuals to identify themselves, is in languages that include at least

English and Spanish, and is at no cost to the individual using the Routing Service; and

"(2) an Internet website to provide a searchable, online treatment services locator of behavioral health treatment providers and community-based organizations, which shall include information on the name, location, contact information, and basic services provided by such providers and organizations.

"(c) *REMOVING PRACTITIONER CONTACT INFORMATION.*—In the event that the Internet website described in subsection (b)(2) contains information on any qualified practitioner that is certified to prescribe medication for opioid dependency under section 303(g)(2)(B) of the Controlled Substances Act, the Assistant Secretary—

"(1) shall provide an opportunity to such practitioner to have the contact information of the practitioner removed from the website at the request of the practitioner; and

"(2) may evaluate other methods to periodically update the information displayed on such website.

"(d) *RULE OF CONSTRUCTION.*—Nothing in this section shall be construed to prevent the Assistant Secretary from using any unobligated amounts otherwise made available to the Administration to maintain the Routing Service.''.

SEC. 9007. STRENGTHENING COMMUNITY CRISIS RESPONSE SYSTEMS.

Section 520F of the Public Health Service Act (42 U.S.C. 290bb–37) is amended to read as follows:

"**SEC. 520F. STRENGTHENING COMMUNITY CRISIS RESPONSE SYSTEMS.**

"(a) *IN GENERAL.*—The Secretary shall award competitive grants to—

"(1) State and local governments and Indian tribes and tribal organizations, to enhance community-based crisis response systems; or

"(2) States to develop, maintain, or enhance a database of beds at inpatient psychiatric facilities, crisis stabilization units, and residential community mental health and residential substance use disorder treatment facilities, for adults with a serious mental illness, children with a serious emotional disturbance, or individuals with a substance use disorder.

"(b) *APPLICATIONS.*—

"(1) *IN GENERAL.*—To receive a grant under subsection (a), an entity shall submit to the Secretary an application, at such time, in such manner, and containing such information as the Secretary may require.

"(2) *COMMUNITY-BASED CRISIS RESPONSE PLAN.*—An application for a grant under subsection (a)(1) shall include a plan for—

"(A) promoting integration and coordination between local public and private entities engaged in crisis response, including first responders, emergency health care providers, primary care providers, law enforcement, court systems, health care payers, social service providers, and behavioral health providers;

"(B) developing memoranda of understanding with public and private entities to implement crisis response services;

"(C) addressing gaps in community resources for crisis intervention and prevention; and

"(D) developing models for minimizing hospital readmissions, including through appropriate discharge planning.

"(3) *BEDS DATABASE PLAN.*—An application for a grant under subsection (a)(2) shall include a plan for developing, maintaining, or enhancing a real-time, Internet-based bed database to collect, aggregate, and display information about beds in inpatient psychiatric facilities and crisis stabilization units, and residential community mental health and residential substance use disorder treatment facilities to facilitate the identification and designation of facilities for the temporary treatment of individuals in mental or substance use disorder crisis.

"(c) *DATABASE REQUIREMENTS.*—A bed database described in this section is a database that—

"(1) includes information on inpatient psychiatric facilities, crisis stabilization units, and residential community mental health and residential substance use disorder facilities in the State involved, including contact information for the facility or unit;

"(2) provides real-time information about the number of beds available at each facility or unit and, for each available bed, the type of patient that may be admitted, the level of security provided, and any other information that may be necessary to allow for the proper identification of appropriate facilities for treatment of individuals in mental or substance use disorder crisis; and

"(3) enables searches of the database to identify available beds that are appropriate for the treatment of individuals in mental or substance use disorder crisis.

"(d) *EVALUATION.*—An entity receiving a grant under subsection (a)(1) shall submit to the Secretary, at such time, in such manner, and containing such information as the Secretary may reasonably require, a report, including an evaluation of the effect of such grant on—

"(1) local crisis response services and measures for individuals receiving crisis planning and early intervention supports;

"(2) individuals reporting improved functional outcomes; and

"(3) individuals receiving regular followup care following a crisis.

"(e) *AUTHORIZATION OF APPROPRIATIONS.*—There are authorized to be appropriated to carry out this section, $12,500,000 for the period of fiscal years 2018 through 2022.''.

SEC. 9008. GARRETT LEE SMITH MEMORIAL ACT REAUTHORIZATION.

(a) *SUICIDE PREVENTION TECHNICAL ASSISTANCE CENTER.*—Section 520C of the Public Health Service Act (42 U.S.C. 290bb–34), as amended by section 6001, is further amended—

(1) in the section heading, by striking "YOUTH INTERAGENCY RESEARCH, TRAINING, AND TECHNICAL ASSISTANCE CENTERS" and inserting "SUICIDE PREVENTION TECHNICAL ASSISTANCE CENTER";

(2) in subsection (a), by striking "acting through the Assistant Secretary for Mental Health and Substance Use" and all that follows through the period at the end of paragraph (2) and inserting "acting through the Assistant Secretary, shall establish a research, training, and technical assistance resource center to provide appropriate information, training, and technical assistance to States, political subdivisions of States, federally recognized Indian tribes, tribal organizations, institutions of higher education, public organizations, or private nonprofit organizations regarding the prevention of suicide among all ages, particularly among groups that are at a high risk for suicide.'';

(3) by striking subsections (b) and (c);

(4) by redesignating subsection (d) as subsection (b);

(5) in subsection (b), as so redesignated—

(A) in the subsection heading, by striking "ADDITIONAL CENTER" and inserting "RESPONSIBILITIES OF THE CENTER";

(B) in the matter preceding paragraph (1), by striking "The additional research" and all that follows through "nonprofit organizations for" and inserting "The center established under subsection (a) shall conduct activities for the purpose of";

(C) by striking "youth suicide" each place such term appears and inserting "suicide";

(D) in paragraph (1)—

(i) by striking "the development or continuation of" and inserting "developing and continuing"; and

(ii) by inserting "for all ages, particularly among groups that are at a high risk for suicide" before the semicolon at the end;

(E) in paragraph (2), by inserting "for all ages, particularly among groups that are at a high risk for suicide" before the semicolon at the end;

(F) in paragraph (3), by inserting "and tribal" after "statewide";

(G) in paragraph (5), by striking "and prevention" after "intervention";

(H) in paragraph (8), by striking "in youth";

(I) in paragraph (9), by striking "and behavioral health" and inserting "health and substance use disorder"; and

(J) in paragraph (10), by inserting "conducting" before "other"; and

(6) by striking subsection (e) and inserting the following:

"(c) *AUTHORIZATION OF APPROPRIATIONS.*—For the purpose of carrying out this section, there are authorized to be appropriated $5,988,000 for each of fiscal years 2018 through 2022.

"(d) *ANNUAL REPORT.*—Not later than 2 years after the date of enactment of this subsection, the Secretary shall submit to Congress a report on the activities carried out by the center established under subsection (a) during the year involved, including the potential effects of such activities, and the States, organizations, and institutions that have worked with the center.''.

(b) *YOUTH SUICIDE EARLY INTERVENTION AND PREVENTION STRATEGIES.*—Section 520E of the Public Health Service Act (42 U.S.C. 290bb–36) is amended—

(1) in paragraph (1) of subsection (a) and in subsection (c), by striking "substance abuse" each place such term appears and inserting "substance use disorder";

(2) in subsection (b)—

(A) in paragraph (2)—

(i) by striking "ensure that each State is awarded only 1 grant or cooperative agreement under this section" and inserting "ensure that a State does not receive more than 1 grant or cooperative agreement under this section at any 1 time"; and

(ii) by striking "been awarded" and inserting "received"; and

(B) by adding after paragraph (2) the following:

"(3) *CONSIDERATION.*—In awarding grants under this section, the Secretary shall take into consideration the extent of the need of the applicant, including the incidence and prevalence of suicide in the State and among the populations of focus, including rates of suicide determined by the Centers for Disease Control and Prevention for the State or population of focus.'';

(3) in subsection (g)(2), by striking "2 years after the date of enactment of this section," and insert "2 years after the date of enactment of Helping Families in Mental Health Crisis Reform Act of 2016,''; and

(4) by striking subsection (m) and inserting the following:

"(m) *AUTHORIZATION OF APPROPRIATIONS.*—For the purpose of carrying out this section, there are authorized to be appropriated $30,000,000 for each of fiscal years 2018 through 2022.''.

SEC. 9009. ADULT SUICIDE PREVENTION.

Subpart 3 of part B of title V of the Public Health Service Act (42 U.S.C. 290bb–31 et seq.) is amended by adding at the end the following:

"**SEC. 520L. ADULT SUICIDE PREVENTION.**

"(a) *GRANTS.*—

"(1) *IN GENERAL.*—The Assistant Secretary shall award grants to eligible entities described in paragraph (2) to implement suicide prevention and intervention programs, for individuals who are 25 years of age or older, that are designed to raise awareness of suicide, establish referral processes, and improve care and outcomes for such individuals who are at risk of suicide.

"(2) ELIGIBLE ENTITIES.—To be eligible to receive a grant under this section, an entity shall be a community-based primary care or behavioral health care setting, an emergency department, a State mental health agency (or State health agency with mental or behavioral health functions), public health agency, a territory of the United States, or an Indian tribe or tribal organization (as the terms 'Indian tribe' and 'tribal organization' are defined in section 4 of the Indian Self-Determination and Education Assistance Act).

"(3) USE OF FUNDS.—The grants awarded under paragraph (1) shall be used to implement programs, in accordance with such paragraph, that include one or more of the following components:

"(A) Screening for suicide risk, suicide intervention services, and services for referral for treatment for individuals at risk for suicide.

"(B) Implementing evidence-based practices to provide treatment for individuals at risk for suicide, including appropriate followup services.

"(C) Raising awareness and reducing stigma of suicide.

"(b) EVALUATIONS AND TECHNICAL ASSISTANCE.—The Assistant Secretary shall—

"(1) evaluate the activities supported by grants awarded under subsection (a), and disseminate, as appropriate, the findings from the evaluation; and

"(2) provide appropriate information, training, and technical assistance, as appropriate, to eligible entities that receive a grant under this section, in order to help such entities to meet the requirements of this section, including assistance with selection and implementation of evidence-based interventions and frameworks to prevent suicide.

"(c) DURATION.—A grant under this section shall be for a period of not more than 5 years.

"(d) AUTHORIZATION OF APPROPRIATIONS.—There are authorized to be appropriated to carry out this section $30,000,000 for the period of fiscal years 2018 through 2022.".

SEC. 9010. MENTAL HEALTH AWARENESS TRAINING GRANTS.

Section 520J of the Public Health Service Act (42 U.S.C. 290bb–41) is amended—

(1) in the section heading, by inserting "**MENTAL HEALTH AWARENESS**" before "**TRAINING**"; and

(2) in subsection (b)—

(A) in the subsection heading, by striking "ILLNESS" and inserting "HEALTH";

(B) in paragraph (1), by inserting "veterans, law enforcement, and other categories of individuals, as determined by the Secretary," after "emergency services personnel";

(C) in paragraph (5)—

(i) in the matter preceding subparagraph (A), by striking "to" and inserting "for evidence-based programs that provide training and education in accordance with paragraph (1) on matters including"; and

(ii) by striking subparagraphs (A) through (C) and inserting the following:

"(A) recognizing the signs and symptoms of mental illness; and

"(B)(i) resources available in the community for individuals with a mental illness and other relevant resources; or

"(ii) safely de-escalating crisis situations involving individuals with a mental illness."; and

(D) in paragraph (7), by striking ", $25,000,000" and all that follows through the period at the end and inserting "$14,693,000 for each of fiscal years 2018 through 2022.".

SEC. 9011. SENSE OF CONGRESS ON PRIORITIZING AMERICAN INDIANS AND ALASKA NATIVE YOUTH WITHIN SUICIDE PREVENTION PROGRAMS.

(a) FINDINGS.—The Congress finds as follows:

(1) Suicide is the eighth leading cause of death among American Indians and Alaska Natives across all ages.

(2) Among American Indians and Alaska Natives who are 10 to 34 years of age, suicide is the second leading cause of death.

(3) The suicide rate among American Indian and Alaska Native adolescents and young adults ages 15 to 34 (17.9 per 100,000) is approximately 1.3 times higher than the national average for that age group (13.3 per 100,000).

(b) SENSE OF CONGRESS.—It is the sense of Congress that the Secretary of Health and Human Services, in carrying out suicide prevention and intervention programs, should prioritize programs and activities for populations with disproportionately high rates of suicide, such as American Indians and Alaska Natives.

SEC. 9012. EVIDENCE-BASED PRACTICES FOR OLDER ADULTS.

Section 520A(e) of the Public Health Service Act (42 U.S.C. 290bb–32(e)) is amended by adding at the end the following:

"(3) GERIATRIC MENTAL DISORDERS.—The Secretary shall, as appropriate, provide technical assistance to grantees regarding evidence-based practices for the prevention and treatment of geriatric mental disorders and co-occurring mental health and substance use disorders among geriatric populations, as well as disseminate information about such evidence-based practices to States and nongrantees throughout the United States.".

SEC. 9013. NATIONAL VIOLENT DEATH REPORTING SYSTEM.

The Secretary of Health and Human Services, acting through the Director of the Centers for Disease Control and Prevention, is encouraged to improve, particularly through the inclusion of additional States, the National Violent Death Reporting System as authorized by title III of the Public Health Service Act (42 U.S.C. 241 et seq.). Participation in the system by the States shall be voluntary.

SEC. 9014. ASSISTED OUTPATIENT TREATMENT.

Section 224 of the Protecting Access to Medicare Act of 2014 (42 U.S.C. 290aa note) is amended—

(1) in subsection (e), by striking "and 2018," and inserting "2018, 2019, 2020, 2021, and 2022,"; and

(2) in subsection (g)—

(A) in paragraph (1), by striking "2018" and inserting "2022"; and

(B) in paragraph (2), by striking "is authorized to be appropriated to carry out this section $15,000,000 for each of fiscal years 2015 through 2018" and inserting "are authorized to be appropriated to carry out this section $15,000,000 for each of fiscal years 2015 through 2017, $20,000,000 for fiscal year 2018, $19,000,000 for each of fiscal years 2019 and 2020, and $18,000,000 for each of fiscal years 2021 and 2022".

SEC. 9015. ASSERTIVE COMMUNITY TREATMENT GRANT PROGRAM.

Part B of title V of the Public Health Service Act (42 U.S.C. 290bb et seq.), as amended by section 9009, is further amended by adding at the end the following:

"SEC. 520M. ASSERTIVE COMMUNITY TREATMENT GRANT PROGRAM.

"(a) IN GENERAL.—The Assistant Secretary shall award grants to eligible entities—

"(1) to establish assertive community treatment programs for adults with a serious mental illness; or

"(2) to maintain or expand such programs.

"(b) ELIGIBLE ENTITIES.—To be eligible to receive a grant under this section, an entity shall be a State, political subdivision of a State, Indian tribe or tribal organization (as such terms are defined in section 4 of the Indian Self-Deter-

mination and Education Assistance Act), mental health system, health care facility, or any other entity the Assistant Secretary deems appropriate.

"(c) SPECIAL CONSIDERATION.—In selecting among applicants for a grant under this section, the Assistant Secretary may give special consideration to the potential of the applicant's program to reduce hospitalization, homelessness, and involvement with the criminal justice system while improving the health and social outcomes of the patient.

"(d) ADDITIONAL ACTIVITIES.—The Assistant Secretary shall—

"(1) not later than the end of fiscal year 2021, submit a report to the appropriate congressional committees on the grant program under this section, including an evaluation of—

"(A) any cost savings and public health outcomes such as mortality, suicide, substance use disorders, hospitalization, and use of services;

"(B) rates of involvement with the criminal justice system of patients;

"(C) rates of homelessness among patients; and

"(D) patient and family satisfaction with program participation; and

"(2) provide appropriate information, training, and technical assistance to grant recipients under this section to help such recipients to establish, maintain, or expand their assertive community treatment programs.

"(e) AUTHORIZATION OF APPROPRIATIONS.—

"(1) IN GENERAL.—To carry out this section, there is authorized to be appropriated $5,000,000 for the period of fiscal years 2018 through 2022.

"(2) USE OF CERTAIN FUNDS.—Of the funds appropriated to carry out this section in any fiscal year, not more than 5 percent shall be available to the Assistant Secretary for carrying out subsection (d).".

SEC. 9016. SOBER TRUTH ON PREVENTING UNDERAGE DRINKING REAUTHORIZATION.

Section 519B of the Public Health Service Act (42 U.S.C. 290bb–25b) is amended—

(1) in subsection (c)(3), by striking "fiscal year 2007" and all that follows through the period at the end and inserting "each of the fiscal years 2018 through 2022.";

(2) in subsection (d)(4), by striking "fiscal year 2007" and all that follows through the period at the end and inserting "each of the fiscal years 2018 through 2022.";

(3) in subsection (e)(1)(I), by striking "fiscal year 2007" and all that follows through the period at the end and inserting "each of the fiscal years 2018 through 2022.";

(4) in subsection (f)(2), by striking "$6,000,000 for fiscal year 2007" and all that follows through the period at the end and inserting "$3,000,000 for each of the fiscal years 2018 through 2022"; and

(5) by adding at the end the following new subsection:

"(g) REDUCING UNDERAGE DRINKING THROUGH SCREENING AND BRIEF INTERVENTION.—

"(1) GRANTS TO PEDIATRIC HEALTH CARE PROVIDERS TO REDUCE UNDERAGE DRINKING.—The Assistant Secretary may make grants to eligible entities to increase implementation of practices for reducing the prevalence of alcohol use among individuals under the age of 21, including college students.

"(2) PURPOSES.—Grants under this subsection shall be made to improve—

"(A) screening children and adolescents for alcohol use;

"(B) offering brief interventions to children and adolescents to discourage such use;

"(C) educating parents about the dangers of, and methods of discouraging, such use;

"(D) diagnosing and treating alcohol use disorders; and

"(E) referring patients, when necessary, to other appropriate care.

"(3) USE OF FUNDS.—An entity receiving a grant under this subsection may use such funding for the purposes identified in paragraph (2) by—

"(A) providing training to health care providers;

"(B) disseminating best practices, including culturally and linguistically appropriate best practices, as appropriate, and developing and distributing materials; and

"(C) supporting other activities, as determined appropriate by the Assistant Secretary.

"(4) APPLICATION.—To be eligible to receive a grant under this subsection, an entity shall submit an application to the Assistant Secretary at such time, and in such manner, and accompanied by such information as the Assistant Secretary may require. Each application shall include—

"(A) a description of the entity;

"(B) a description of activities to be completed;

"(C) a description of how the services specified in paragraphs (2) and (3) will be carried out and the qualifications for providing such services; and

"(D) a timeline for the completion of such activities.

"(5) DEFINITIONS.—For the purpose of this subsection:

"(A) BRIEF INTERVENTION.—The term 'brief intervention' means, after screening a patient, providing the patient with brief advice and other brief motivational enhancement techniques designed to increase the insight of the patient regarding the patient's alcohol use, and any realized or potential consequences of such use, to effect the desired related behavioral change.

"(B) CHILDREN AND ADOLESCENTS.—The term 'children and adolescents' means any person under 21 years of age.

"(C) ELIGIBLE ENTITY.—The term 'eligible entity' means an entity consisting of pediatric health care providers and that is qualified to support or provide the activities identified in paragraph (2).

"(D) PEDIATRIC HEALTH CARE PROVIDER.—The term 'pediatric health care provider' means a provider of primary health care to individuals under the age of 21 years.

"(E) SCREENING.—The term 'screening' means using validated patient interview techniques to identify and assess the existence and extent of alcohol use in a patient.".

SEC. 9017. CENTER AND PROGRAM REPEALS.

Part B of title V of the Public Health Service Act (42 U.S.C. 290bb et seq.) is amended by striking section 506B (42 U.S.C. 290aa–5b), the second section 514 (42 U.S.C. 290bb–9) relating to methamphetamine and amphetamine treatment initiatives, and each of sections 514A, 517, 519A, 519C, 519E, 520B, 520D, and 520H (42 U.S.C. 290bb–8, 290bb–23, 290bb–25a, 290bb–25c, 290bb–25e, 290bb–33, 290bb–35, and 290bb–39).

Subtitle B—Strengthening the Health Care Workforce

SEC. 9021. MENTAL AND BEHAVIORAL HEALTH EDUCATION AND TRAINING GRANTS.

Section 756 of the Public Health Service Act (42 U.S.C. 294e–1) is amended—

(1) in subsection (a)—

(A) in the matter preceding paragraph (1), by striking "of higher education"; and

(B) by striking paragraphs (1) through (4) and inserting the following:

"(1) accredited institutions of higher education or accredited professional training programs that are establishing or expanding internships or other field placement programs in mental health in psychiatry, psychology, school psychology, behavioral pediatrics, psychiatric nursing (which may include master's and doctoral level programs), social work, school social work, substance use disorder prevention and treatment, marriage and family therapy, occupational therapy, school counseling, or professional counseling, including such programs with a focus on child and adolescent mental health and transitional-age youth;

"(2) accredited doctoral, internship, and post-doctoral residency programs of health service psychology (including clinical psychology, counseling, and school psychology) for the development and implementation of interdisciplinary training of psychology graduate students for providing behavioral health services, including substance use disorder prevention and treatment services, as well as the development of faculty in health service psychology;

"(3) accredited master's and doctoral degree programs of social work for the development and implementation of interdisciplinary training of social work graduate students for providing behavioral health services, including substance use disorder prevention and treatment services, and the development of faculty in social work; and

"(4) State-licensed mental health nonprofit and for-profit organizations to enable such organizations to pay for programs for preservice or in-service training in a behavioral health-related paraprofessional field with preference for preservice or in-service training of paraprofessional child and adolescent mental health workers.";

(2) in subsection (b)—

(A) by striking paragraph (5);

(B) by redesignating paragraphs (1) through (4) as paragraphs (2) through (5), respectively;

(C) by inserting before paragraph (2), as so redesignated, the following:

"(1) an ability to recruit and place the students described in subsection (a) in areas with a high need and high demand population;";

(D) in paragraph (3), as so redesignated, by striking "subsection (a)" and inserting "paragraph (2), especially individuals with mental disorder symptoms or diagnoses, particularly children and adolescents, and transitional-age youth";

(E) in paragraph (4), as so redesignated, by striking ";" and inserting "; and"; and

(F) in paragraph (5), as so redesignated, by striking "; and" and inserting a period;

(3) in subsection (c), by striking "authorized under subsection (a)(1)" and inserting "awarded under paragraphs (2) and (3) of subsection (a)";

(4) by amending subsection (d) to read as follows:

"(d) PRIORITY.—In selecting grant recipients under this section, the Secretary shall give priority to—

"(1) programs that have demonstrated the ability to train psychology, psychiatry, and social work professionals to work in integrated care settings for purposes of recipients under paragraphs (1), (2), and (3) of subsection (a); and

"(2) programs for paraprofessionals that emphasize the role of the family and the lived experience of the consumer and family-paraprofessional partnerships for purposes of recipients under subsection (a)(4)."; and

(5) by striking subsection (e) and inserting the following:

"(e) REPORT TO CONGRESS.—Not later than 4 years after the date of enactment of the Helping Families in Mental Health Crisis Reform Act of 2016, the Secretary shall include in the biennial report submitted to Congress under section 501(m) an assessment on the effectiveness of the grants under this section in—

"(1) providing graduate students support for experiential training (internship or field placement);

"(2) recruiting students interested in behavioral health practice;

"(3) recruiting students in accordance with subsection (b)(1);

"(4) developing and implementing interprofessional training and integration within primary care;

"(5) developing and implementing accredited field placements and internships; and

"(6) collecting data on the number of students trained in behavioral health care and the number of available accredited internships and field placements.

"(f) AUTHORIZATION OF APPROPRIATIONS.— For each of fiscal years 2018 through 2022, there are authorized to be appropriated to carry out this section $50,000,000, to be allocated as follows:

"(1) For grants described in subsection (a)(1), $15,000,000.

"(2) For grants described in subsection (a)(2), $15,000,000.

"(3) For grants described in subsection (a)(3), $10,000,000.

"(4) For grants described in subsection (a)(4), $10,000,000.".

SEC. 9022. STRENGTHENING THE MENTAL AND SUBSTANCE USE DISORDERS WORKFORCE.

Part D of title VII of the Public Health Service Act (42 U.S.C. 294 et seq.) is amended by adding at the end the following:

"SEC. 760. TRAINING DEMONSTRATION PROGRAM.

"(a) IN GENERAL.—The Secretary shall establish a training demonstration program to award grants to eligible entities to support—

"(1) training for medical residents and fellows to practice psychiatry and addiction medicine in underserved, community-based settings that integrate primary care with mental and substance use disorders prevention and treatment services;

"(2) training for nurse practitioners, physician assistants, health service psychologists, and social workers to provide mental and substance use disorders services in underserved community-based settings that integrate primary care and mental and substance use disorders services; and

"(3) establishing, maintaining, or improving academic units or programs that—

"(A) provide training for students or faculty, including through clinical experiences and research, to improve the ability to be able to recognize, diagnose, and treat mental and substance use disorders, with a special focus on addiction; or

"(B) develop evidence-based practices or recommendations for the design of the units or programs described in subparagraph (A), including curriculum content standards.

"(b) ACTIVITIES.—

"(1) TRAINING FOR RESIDENTS AND FELLOWS.— A recipient of a grant under subsection (a)(1)—

"(A) shall use the grant funds—

"(i)(I) to plan, develop, and operate a training program for medical psychiatry residents and fellows in addiction medicine practicing in eligible entities described in subsection (c)(1); or

"(II) to train new psychiatric residents and fellows in addiction medicine to provide and expand access to integrated mental and substance use disorders services; and

"(ii) to provide at least 1 training track that is—

"(I) a virtual training track that includes an in-person rotation at a teaching health center or in a community-based setting, followed by a virtual rotation in which the resident or fellow continues to support the care of patients at the teaching health center or in the community-based setting through the use of health information technology and, as appropriate, telehealth services;

"(II) an in-person training track that includes a rotation, during which the resident or fellow

practices at a teaching health center or in a community-based setting; or

"(III) an in-person training track that includes a rotation during which the resident practices in a community-based setting that specializes in the treatment of infants, children, adolescents, or pregnant or postpartum women; and

"(B) may use the grant funds to provide additional support for the administration of the program or to meet the costs of projects to establish, maintain, or improve faculty development, or departments, divisions, or other units necessary to implement such training.

"(2) TRAINING FOR OTHER PROVIDERS.—A recipient of a grant under subsection (a)(2)—

"(A) shall use the grant funds to plan, develop, or operate a training program to provide mental and substance use disorders services in underserved, community-based settings, as appropriate, that integrate primary care and mental and substance use disorders prevention and treatment services; and

"(B) may use the grant funds to provide additional support for the administration of the program or to meet the costs of projects to establish, maintain, or improve faculty development, or departments, divisions, or other units necessary to implement such program.

"(3) ACADEMIC UNITS OR PROGRAMS.—A recipient of a grant under subsection (a)(3) shall enter into a partnership with organizations such as an education accrediting organization (such as the Liaison Committee on Medical Education, the Accreditation Council for Graduate Medical Education, the Commission on Osteopathic College Accreditation, the Accreditation Commission for Education in Nursing, the Commission on Collegiate Nursing Education, the Accreditation Council for Pharmacy Education, the Council on Social Work Education, American Psychological Association Commission on Accreditation, or the Accreditation Review Commission on Education for the Physician Assistant) to carry out activities under subsection (a)(3).

"(c) ELIGIBLE ENTITIES.—

"(1) TRAINING FOR RESIDENTS AND FELLOWS.— To be eligible to receive a grant under subsection (a)(1), an entity shall—

"(A) be a consortium consisting of—

"(i) at least one teaching health center; and

"(ii) the sponsoring institution (or parent institution of the sponsoring institution) of—

"(I) a psychiatry residency program that is accredited by the Accreditation Council of Graduate Medical Education (or the parent institution of such a program); or

"(II) a fellowship in addiction medicine, as determined appropriate by the Secretary; or

"(B) be an entity described in subparagraph (A)(ii) that provides opportunities for residents or fellows to train in community-based settings that integrate primary care with mental and substance use disorders prevention and treatment services.

"(2) TRAINING FOR OTHER PROVIDERS.—To be eligible to receive a grant under subsection (a)(2), an entity shall be—

"(A) a teaching health center (as defined in section 749A(f));

"(B) a Federally qualified health center (as defined in section 1905(l)(2)(B) of the Social Security Act);

"(C) a community mental health center (as defined in section 1861(ff)(3)(B) of the Social Security Act);

"(D) a rural health clinic (as defined in section 1861(aa) of the Social Security Act);

"(E) a health center operated by the Indian Health Service, an Indian tribe, a tribal organization, or an urban Indian organization (as defined in section 4 of the Indian Health Care Improvement Act); or

"(F) an entity with a demonstrated record of success in providing training for nurse practitioners, physician assistants, health service psychologists, and social workers.

"(3) ACADEMIC UNITS OR PROGRAMS.—To be eligible to receive a grant under subsection (a)(3), an entity shall be a school of medicine or osteopathic medicine, a nursing school, a physician assistant training program, a school of pharmacy, a school of social work, an accredited public or nonprofit private hospital, an accredited medical residency program, or a public or private nonprofit entity which the Secretary has determined is capable of carrying out such grant.

"(d) PRIORITY.—

"(1) IN GENERAL.—In awarding grants under subsection (a)(1) or (a)(2), the Secretary shall give priority to eligible entities that—

"(A) demonstrate sufficient size, scope, and capacity to undertake the requisite training of an appropriate number of psychiatric residents, fellows, nurse practitioners, physician assistants, or social workers in addiction medicine per year to meet the needs of the area served;

"(B) demonstrate experience in training providers to practice team-based care that integrates mental and substance use disorder prevention and treatment services with primary care in community-based settings;

"(C) demonstrate experience in using health information technology and, as appropriate, telehealth to support—

"(i) the delivery of mental and substance use disorders services at the eligible entities described in subsections (c)(1) and (c)(2); and

"(ii) community health centers in integrating primary care and mental and substance use disorders treatment; or

"(D) have the capacity to expand access to mental and substance use disorders services in areas with demonstrated need, as determined by the Secretary, such as tribal, rural, or other underserved communities.

"(2) ACADEMIC UNITS OR PROGRAMS.—In awarding grants under subsection (a)(3), the Secretary shall give priority to eligible entities that—

"(A) have a record of training the greatest percentage of mental and substance use disorders providers who enter and remain in these fields or who enter and remain in settings with integrated primary care and mental and substance use disorder prevention and treatment services;

"(B) have a record of training individuals who are from underrepresented minority groups, including native populations, or from a rural or disadvantaged background;

"(C) provide training in the care of vulnerable populations such as infants, children, adolescents, pregnant and postpartum women, older adults, homeless individuals, victims of abuse or trauma, individuals with disabilities, and other groups as defined by the Secretary;

"(D) teach trainees the skills to provide interprofessional, integrated care through collaboration among health professionals; or

"(E) provide training in cultural competency and health literacy.

"(e) DURATION.—Grants awarded under this section shall be for a minimum of 5 years.

"(f) STUDY AND REPORT.—

"(1) STUDY.—

"(A) IN GENERAL.—The Secretary, acting through the Administrator of the Health Resources and Services Administration, shall conduct a study on the results of the demonstration program under this section.

"(B) DATA SUBMISSION.—Not later than 90 days after the completion of the first year of the training program and each subsequent year that the program is in effect, each recipient of a grant under subsection (a) shall submit to the

Secretary such data as the Secretary may require for analysis for the report described in paragraph (2).

"(2) REPORT TO CONGRESS.—Not later than 1 year after receipt of the data described in paragraph (1)(B), the Secretary shall submit to Congress a report that includes—

"(A) an analysis of the effect of the demonstration program under this section on the quality, quantity, and distribution of mental and substance use disorders services;

"(B) an analysis of the effect of the demonstration program on the prevalence of untreated mental and substance use disorders in the surrounding communities of health centers participating in the demonstration; and

"(C) recommendations on whether the demonstration program should be expanded.

"(g) AUTHORIZATION OF APPROPRIATIONS.— There are authorized to be appropriated to carry out this section $10,000,000 for each of fiscal years 2018 through 2022.".

SEC. 9023. CLARIFICATION ON CURRENT ELIGIBILITY FOR LOAN REPAYMENT PROGRAMS.

The Administrator of the Health Resources and Services Administration shall clarify the eligibility pursuant to section 338B(b)(1)(B) of the Public Health Service Act (42 U.S.C. 254l-1(b)(1)(B)) of child and adolescent psychiatrists for the National Health Service Corps Loan Repayment Program under subpart D of part D of title III of such Act (42 U.S.C. 254l et seq.).

SEC. 9024. MINORITY FELLOWSHIP PROGRAM.

Title V of the Public Health Service Act (42 U.S.C. 290aa et seq.) is amended by adding at the end the following:

"PART K—MINORITY FELLOWSHIP PROGRAM

"SEC. 597. FELLOWSHIPS.

"(a) IN GENERAL.—The Secretary shall maintain a program, to be known as the Minority Fellowship Program, under which the Secretary shall award fellowships, which may include stipends, for the purposes of—

"(1) increasing the knowledge of mental and substance use disorders practitioners on issues related to prevention, treatment, and recovery support for individuals who are from racial and ethnic minority populations and who have a mental or substance use disorder;

"(2) improving the quality of mental and substance use disorder prevention and treatment services delivered to racial and ethnic minority populations; and

"(3) increasing the number of culturally competent mental and substance use disorders professionals who teach, administer services, conduct research, and provide direct mental or substance use disorder services to racial and ethnic minority populations.

"(b) TRAINING COVERED.—The fellowships awarded under subsection (a) shall be for postbaccalaureate training (including for master's and doctoral degrees) for mental and substance use disorder treatment professionals, including in the fields of psychiatry, nursing, social work, psychology, marriage and family therapy, mental health counseling, and substance use disorder and addiction counseling.

"(c) AUTHORIZATION OF APPROPRIATIONS.—To carry out this section, there are authorized to be appropriated $12,669,000 for each of fiscal years 2018 through 2022.".

SEC. 9025. LIABILITY PROTECTIONS FOR HEALTH PROFESSIONAL VOLUNTEERS AT COMMUNITY HEALTH CENTERS.

Section 224 of the Public Health Service Act (42 U.S.C. 233) is amended by adding at the end the following:

"(q)(1) For purposes of this section, a health professional volunteer at a deemed entity described in subsection (g)(4) shall, in providing a health professional service eligible for funding

under section 330 to an individual, be deemed to be an employee of the Public Health Service for a calendar year that begins during a fiscal year for which a transfer was made under paragraph (4)(C). The preceding sentence is subject to the provisions of this subsection.

"(2) In providing a health service to an individual, a health care practitioner shall for purposes of this subsection be considered to be a health professional volunteer at an entity described in subsection (g)(4) if the following conditions are met:

"(A) The service is provided to the individual at the facilities of an entity described in subsection (g)(4), or through offsite programs or events carried out by the entity.

"(B) The entity is sponsoring the health care practitioner pursuant to paragraph (3)(B).

"(C) The health care practitioner does not receive any compensation for the service from the individual, the entity described in subsection (g)(4), or any third-party payer (including reimbursement under any insurance policy or health plan, or under any Federal or State health benefits program), except that the health care practitioner may receive repayment from the entity described in subsection (g)(4) for reasonable expenses incurred by the health care practitioner in the provision of the service to the individual, which may include travel expenses to or from the site of services.

"(D) Before the service is provided, the health care practitioner or the entity described in subsection (g)(4) posts a clear and conspicuous notice at the site where the service is provided of the extent to which the legal liability of the health care practitioner is limited pursuant to this subsection.

"(E) At the time the service is provided, the health care practitioner is licensed or certified in accordance with applicable Federal and State laws regarding the provision of the service.

"(F) At the time the service is provided, the entity described in subsection (g)(4) maintains relevant documentation certifying that the health care practitioner meets the requirements of this subsection.

"(3) Subsection (g) (other than paragraphs (3) and (5)) and subsections (h), (i), and (l) apply to a health care practitioner for purposes of this subsection to the same extent and in the same manner as such subsections apply to an officer, governing board member, employee, or contractor of an entity described in subsection (g)(4), subject to paragraph (4), and subject to the following:

"(A) The first sentence of paragraph (1) applies in lieu of the first sentence of subsection (g)(1)(A).

"(B) With respect to an entity described in subsection (g)(4), a health care practitioner is not a health professional volunteer at such entity unless the entity sponsors the health care practitioner. For purposes of this subsection, the entity shall be considered to be sponsoring the health care practitioner if—

"(i) with respect to the health care practitioner, the entity submits to the Secretary an application meeting the requirements of subsection (g)(1)(D); and

"(ii) the Secretary, pursuant to subsection (g)(1)(E), determines that the health care practitioner is deemed to be an employee of the Public Health Service.

"(C) In the case of a health care practitioner who is determined by the Secretary pursuant to subsection (g)(1)(E) to be a health professional volunteer at such entity, this subsection applies to the health care practitioner (with respect to services performed on behalf of the entity sponsoring the health care practitioner pursuant to subparagraph (B)) for any cause of action arising from an act or omission of the health care practitioner occurring on or after the date on which the Secretary makes such determination.

"(D) Subsection (g)(1)(F) applies to a health care practitioner for purposes of this subsection only to the extent that, in providing health services to an individual, each of the conditions specified in paragraph (2) is met.

"(4)(A) Amounts in the fund established under subsection (k)(2) shall be available for transfer under subparagraph (C) for purposes of carrying out this subsection.

"(B)(i) Not later than May 1 of each fiscal year, the Attorney General, in consultation with the Secretary, shall submit to the Congress a report providing an estimate of the amount of claims (together with related fees and expenses of witnesses) that, by reason of the acts or omissions of health professional volunteers, will be paid pursuant to this section during the calendar year that begins in the following fiscal year.

"(ii) Subsection (k)(1)(B) applies to the estimate under clause (i) regarding health professional volunteers to the same extent and in the same manner as such subsection applies to the estimate under such subsection regarding officers, governing board members, employees, and contractors of entities described in subsection (g)(4).

"(iii) The report shall include a summary of the data relied upon for the estimate in clause (i), including the number of claims filed and paid from the previous calendar year.

"(C) Not later than December 31 of each fiscal year, the Secretary shall transfer from the fund under subsection (k)(2) to the appropriate accounts in the Treasury an amount equal to the estimate made under subparagraph (B) for the calendar year beginning in such fiscal year, subject to the extent of amounts in the fund.

"(5)(A) This subsection shall take effect on October 1, 2017, except as provided in subparagraph (B) and paragraph (6).

"(B) Effective on the date of the enactment of this subsection—

"(i) the Secretary may issue regulations for carrying out this subsection, and the Secretary may accept and consider applications submitted pursuant to paragraph (3)(B); and

"(ii) reports under paragraph (4)(B) may be submitted to Congress.

"(6) Beginning on October 1, 2022, this subsection shall cease to have any force or effect.".

SEC. 9026. REPORTS.

(a) WORKFORCE DEVELOPMENT REPORT.—

(1) IN GENERAL.—Not later than 2 years after the date of enactment of this Act, the Administrator of the Health Resources and Services Administration, in consultation with the Assistant Secretary for Mental Health and Substance Use, shall conduct a study and publicly post on the appropriate Internet website of the Department of Health and Human Services a report on the adult and pediatric mental health and substance use disorder workforce in order to inform Federal, State, and local efforts related to workforce enhancement.

(2) CONTENTS.—The report under this subsection shall contain—

(A) national and State-level projections of the supply and demand of the mental health and substance use disorder health workforce, disaggregated by profession;

(B) an assessment of the mental health and substance use disorder workforce capacity, strengths, and weaknesses as of the date of the report, including the extent to which primary care providers are preventing, screening, or referring for mental and substance use disorder services;

(C) information on trends within the mental health and substance use disorder provider workforce, including the number of individuals expected to enter the mental health workforce over the next 5 years; and

(D) any additional information determined by the Administrator of the Health Resources and Services Administration, in consultation with the Assistant Secretary for Mental Health and Substance Use, to be relevant to the mental health and substance use disorder provider workforce.

(b) PEER-SUPPORT SPECIALIST PROGRAMS.—

(1) IN GENERAL.—The Comptroller General of the United States shall conduct a study on peer-support specialist programs in up to 10 States that receive funding from the Substance Abuse and Mental Health Services Administration.

(2) CONTENTS OF STUDY.—In conducting the study under paragraph (1), the Comptroller General of the United States shall examine and identify best practices, in the States selected pursuant to such paragraph, related to training and credential requirements for peer-support specialist programs, such as—

(A) hours of formal work or volunteer experience related to mental and substance use disorders conducted through such programs;

(B) types of peer-support specialist exams required for such programs in the selected States;

(C) codes of ethics used by such programs in the selected States;

(D) required or recommended skill sets for such programs in the selected States; and

(E) requirements for continuing education.

(3) REPORT.—Not later than 2 years after the date of enactment of this Act, the Comptroller General of the United States shall submit to the Committee on Health, Education, Labor, and Pensions of the Senate and the Committee on Energy and Commerce of the House of Representatives a report on the study conducted under paragraph (1).

Subtitle C—Mental Health on Campus Improvement

SEC. 9031. MENTAL HEALTH AND SUBSTANCE USE DISORDER SERVICES ON CAMPUS.

Section 520E–2 of the Public Health Service Act (42 U.S.C. 290bb–36b) is amended—

(1) in the section heading, by striking "AND BEHAVIORAL HEALTH" and inserting "HEALTH AND SUBSTANCE USE DISORDER";

(2) in subsection (a)—

(A) by striking "Services," and inserting "Services and";

(B) by striking "and behavioral health problems" and inserting "health or substance use disorders";

(C) by striking "substance abuse" and inserting "substance use disorders"; and

(D) by adding after, "suicide attempts," the following: "prevent mental and substance use disorders, reduce stigma, and improve the identification and treatment for students at risk,";

(3) in subsection (b)—

(A) in the matter preceding paragraph (1), by striking "for—" and inserting "for one or more of the following:"; and

(B) by striking paragraphs (1) through (6) and inserting the following:

"(1) Educating students, families, faculty, and staff to increase awareness of mental and substance use disorders.

"(2) The operation of hotlines.

"(3) Preparing informational material.

"(4) Providing outreach services to notify students about available mental and substance use disorder services.

"(5) Administering voluntary mental and substance use disorder screenings and assessments.

"(6) Supporting the training of students, faculty, and staff to respond effectively to students with mental and substance use disorders.

"(7) Creating a network infrastructure to link institutions of higher education with health care providers who treat mental and substance use disorders.

"(8) Providing mental and substance use disorders prevention and treatment services to students, which may include recovery support services and programming and early intervention, treatment, and management, including through the use of telehealth services.

"(9) Conducting research through a counseling or health center at the institution of higher education involved regarding improving the behavioral health of students through clinical services, outreach, prevention, or academic success, in a manner that is in compliance with all applicable personal privacy laws.

"(10) Supporting student groups on campus, including athletic teams, that engage in activities to educate students, including activities to reduce stigma surrounding mental and behavioral disorders, and promote mental health.

"(11) Employing appropriately trained staff.

"(12) Developing and supporting evidence-based and emerging best practices, including a focus on culturally and linguistically appropriate best practices.";

(4) in subsection (c)(5), by striking "substance abuse" and inserting "substance use disorder";

(5) in subsection (d)—

(A) in the matter preceding paragraph (1), by striking "An institution of higher education desiring a grant under this section" and inserting "To be eligible to receive a grant under this section, an institution of higher education";

(B) by striking paragraph (1) and inserting—

"(1) A description of the population to be targeted by the program carried out under the grant, including veterans whenever possible and appropriate, and of identified mental and substance use disorder needs of students at the institution of higher education.";

(C) in paragraph (2), by inserting ", which may include, as appropriate and in accordance with subsection (b)(7), a plan to seek input from relevant stakeholders in the community, including appropriate public and private entities, in order to carry out the program under the grant" before the period at the end; and

(D) by adding after paragraph (5) the following new paragraphs:

"(6) An outline of the objectives of the program carried out under the grant.

"(7) For an institution of higher education proposing to use the grant for an activity described in paragraph (8) or (9) of subsection (b), a description of the policies and procedures of the institution of higher education that are related to applicable laws regarding access to, and sharing of, treatment records of students at any campus-based mental health center or partner organization, including the policies and State laws governing when such records can be accessed and shared for non-treatment purposes and a description of the process used by the institution of higher education to notify students of these policies and procedures, including the extent to which written consent is required.

"(8) An assurance that grant funds will be used to supplement and not supplant any other Federal, State, or local funds available to carry out activities of the type carried out under the grant.";

(6) in subsection (e)(1), by striking "and behavioral health problems" and inserting "health and substance use disorders";

(7) in subsection (f)(2)—

(A) by striking "and behavioral health" and inserting "health and substance use disorder"; and

(B) by striking "suicide and substance abuse" and inserting "suicide and substance use disorders";

(8) by redesignating subsection (h) as subsection (i);

(9) by inserting after subsection (g) the following new subsection:

"(h) TECHNICAL ASSISTANCE.—The Secretary may provide technical assistance to grantees in carrying out this section."; and

(10) in subsection (i), as redesignated by paragraph (8), by striking "$5,000,000 for fiscal year

2005" and all that follows through the period at the end and inserting "$7,000,000 for each of fiscal years 2018 through 2022.".

SEC. 9032. INTERAGENCY WORKING GROUP ON COLLEGE MENTAL HEALTH.

(a) PURPOSE.—It is the purpose of this section to provide for the establishment of a College Campus Task Force to discuss mental and behavioral health concerns on campuses of institutions of higher education.

(b) ESTABLISHMENT.—The Secretary of Health and Human Services (referred to in this section as the "Secretary") shall establish a College Campus Task Force (referred to in this section as the "Task Force") to discuss mental and behavioral health concerns on campuses of institutions of higher education.

(c) MEMBERSHIP.—The Task Force shall be composed of a representative from each Federal agency (as appointed by the head of the agency) that has jurisdiction over, or is affected by, mental health and education policies and projects, including—

(1) the Department of Education;

(2) the Department of Health and Human Services;

(3) the Department of Veterans Affairs; and

(4) such other Federal agencies as the Assistant Secretary for Mental Health and Substance Use, in consultation with the Secretary, determines to be appropriate.

(d) DUTIES.—The Task Force shall—

(1) serve as a centralized mechanism to coordinate a national effort to—

(A) discuss and evaluate evidence and knowledge on mental and behavioral health services available to, and the prevalence of mental illness among, the age population of students attending institutions of higher education in the United States;

(B) determine the range of effective, feasible, and comprehensive actions to improve mental and behavioral health on campuses of institutions of higher education;

(C) examine and better address the needs of the age population of students attending institutions of higher education dealing with mental illness;

(D) survey Federal agencies to determine which policies are effective in encouraging, and how best to facilitate outreach without duplicating, efforts relating to mental and behavioral health promotion;

(E) establish specific goals within and across Federal agencies for mental health promotion, including determinations of accountability for reaching those goals;

(F) develop a strategy for allocating responsibilities and ensuring participation in mental and behavioral health promotion, particularly in the case of competing agency priorities;

(G) coordinate plans to communicate research results relating to mental and behavioral health amongst the age population of students attending institutions of higher education to enable reporting and outreach activities to produce more useful and timely information;

(H) provide a description of evidence-based practices, model programs, effective guidelines, and other strategies for promoting mental and behavioral health on campuses of institutions of higher education;

(I) make recommendations to improve Federal efforts relating to mental and behavioral health promotion on campuses of institutions of higher education and to ensure Federal efforts are consistent with available standards, evidence, and other programs in existence as of the date of enactment of this Act;

(J) monitor Federal progress in meeting specific mental and behavioral health promotion goals as they relate to settings of institutions of higher education; and

(K) examine and disseminate best practices related to intracampus sharing of treatment records;

(2) consult with national organizations with expertise in mental and behavioral health, especially those organizations working with the age population of students attending institutions of higher education; and

(3) consult with and seek input from mental health professionals working on campuses of institutions of higher education as appropriate.

(e) MEETINGS.—

(1) IN GENERAL.—The Task Force shall meet not fewer than three times each year.

(2) ANNUAL CONFERENCE.—The Secretary shall sponsor an annual conference on mental and behavioral health in settings of institutions of higher education to enhance coordination, build partnerships, and share best practices in mental and behavioral health promotion, data collection, analysis, and services.

(f) DEFINITION.—In this section, the term "institution of higher education" has the meaning given such term in section 101 of the Higher Education Act of 1965 (20 U.S.C. 1001).

(g) AUTHORIZATION OF APPROPRIATIONS.—To carry out this section, there are authorized to be appropriated $1,000,000 for the period of fiscal years 2018 through 2022.

SEC. 9033. IMPROVING MENTAL HEALTH ON COLLEGE CAMPUSES.

Part D of title V of the Public Health Service Act (42 U.S.C. 290dd et seq.) is amended by adding at the end the following:

"SEC. 549. MENTAL AND BEHAVIORAL HEALTH OUTREACH AND EDUCATION ON COLLEGE CAMPUSES.

"(a) PURPOSE.—It is the purpose of this section to increase access to, and reduce the stigma associated with, mental health services to ensure that students at institutions of higher education have the support necessary to successfully complete their studies.

"(b) NATIONAL PUBLIC EDUCATION CAMPAIGN.—The Secretary, acting through the Assistant Secretary and in collaboration with the Director of the Centers for Disease Control and Prevention, shall convene an interagency, public-private sector working group to plan, establish, and begin coordinating and evaluating a targeted public education campaign that is designed to focus on mental and behavioral health on the campuses of institutions of higher education. Such campaign shall be designed to—

"(1) improve the general understanding of mental health and mental disorders;

"(2) encourage help-seeking behaviors relating to the promotion of mental health, prevention of mental disorders, and treatment of such disorders;

"(3) make the connection between mental and behavioral health and academic success; and

"(4) assist the general public in identifying the early warning signs and reducing the stigma of mental illness.

"(c) COMPOSITION.—The working group convened under subsection (b) shall include—

"(1) mental health consumers, including students and family members;

"(2) representatives of institutions of higher education;

"(3) representatives of national mental and behavioral health associations and associations of institutions of higher education;

"(4) representatives of health promotion and prevention organizations at institutions of higher education;

"(5) representatives of mental health providers, including community mental health centers; and

"(6) representatives of private-sector and public-sector groups with experience in the development of effective public health education campaigns.

"(d) PLAN.—The working group under subsection (b) shall develop a plan that—

"(1) targets promotional and educational efforts to the age population of students at institutions of higher education and individuals who are employed in settings of institutions of higher education, including through the use of roundtables;

"(2) develops and proposes the implementation of research-based public health messages and activities;

"(3) provides support for local efforts to reduce stigma by using the National Health Information Center as a primary point of contact for information, publications, and service program referrals; and

"(4) develops and proposes the implementation of a social marketing campaign that is targeted at the population of students attending institutions of higher education and individuals who are employed in settings of institutions of higher education.

"(e) DEFINITION.—In this section, the term 'institution of higher education' has the meaning given such term in section 101 of the Higher Education Act of 1965 (20 U.S.C. 1001).

"(f) AUTHORIZATION OF APPROPRIATIONS.—To carry out this section, there are authorized to be appropriated $1,000,000 for the period of fiscal years 2018 through 2022.''.

TITLE X—STRENGTHENING MENTAL AND SUBSTANCE USE DISORDER CARE FOR CHILDREN AND ADOLESCENTS

SEC. 10001. PROGRAMS FOR CHILDREN WITH A SERIOUS EMOTIONAL DISTURBANCE.

(a) COMPREHENSIVE COMMUNITY MENTAL HEALTH SERVICES FOR CHILDREN WITH A SERIOUS EMOTIONAL DISTURBANCE.—Section 561(a)(1) of the Public Health Service Act (42 U.S.C. 290ff(a)(1)) is amended by inserting '', which may include efforts to identify and serve children at risk'' before the period.

(b) REQUIREMENTS WITH RESPECT TO CARRYING OUT PURPOSE OF GRANTS.—Section 562(b) of the Public Health Service Act (42 U.S.C. 290ff–1(b)) is amended by striking "will not provide an individual with access to the system if the individual is more than 21 years of age" and inserting "will provide an individual with access to the system through the age of 21 years".

(c) ADDITIONAL PROVISIONS.—Section 564(f) of the Public Health Service Act (42 U.S.C. 290ff–3(f)) is amended by inserting "(and provide a copy to the State involved)" after "to the Secretary".

(d) GENERAL PROVISIONS.—Section 565 of the Public Health Service Act (42 U.S.C. 290ff–4) is amended—

(1) in subsection (b)(1)—

(A) in the matter preceding subparagraph (A), by striking "receiving a grant under section 561(a)" and inserting ", regardless of whether such public entity is receiving a grant under section 561(a)"; and

(B) in subparagraph (B), by striking "pursuant to" and inserting "described in";

(2) in subsection (d)(1), by striking "not more than 21 years of age" and inserting "through the age of 21 years"; and

(3) in subsection (f)(1), by striking "$100,000,000 for fiscal year 2001, and such sums as may be necessary for each of the fiscal years 2002 and 2003" and inserting "$119,026,000 for each of fiscal years 2018 through 2022".

SEC. 10002. INCREASING ACCESS TO PEDIATRIC MENTAL HEALTH CARE.

Title III of the Public Health Service Act is amended by inserting after section 330L of such Act (42 U.S.C. 254c–18) the following new section:

"SEC. 330M PEDIATRIC MENTAL HEALTH CARE ACCESS GRANTS.

"(a) IN GENERAL.—The Secretary, acting through the Administrator of the Health Resources and Services Administration and in coordination with other relevant Federal agencies, shall award grants to States, political subdivisions of States, and Indian tribes and tribal organizations (for purposes of this section, as such

terms are defined in section 4 of the Indian Self-Determination and Education Assistance Act (25 U.S.C. 450b)) to promote behavioral health integration in pediatric primary care by—

"(1) supporting the development of statewide or regional pediatric mental health care telehealth access programs; and

"(2) supporting the improvement of existing statewide or regional pediatric mental health care telehealth access programs.

"(b) PROGRAM REQUIREMENTS.—

"(1) IN GENERAL.—A pediatric mental health care telehealth access program referred to in subsection (a), with respect to which a grant under such subsection may be used, shall—

"(A) be a statewide or regional network of pediatric mental health teams that provide support to pediatric primary care sites as an integrated team;

"(B) support and further develop organized State or regional networks of pediatric mental health teams to provide consultative support to pediatric primary care sites;

"(C) conduct an assessment of critical behavioral consultation needs among pediatric providers and such providers' preferred mechanisms for receiving consultation, training, and technical assistance;

"(D) develop an online database and communication mechanisms, including telehealth, to facilitate consultation support to pediatric practices;

"(E) provide rapid statewide or regional clinical telephone or telehealth consultations when requested between the pediatric mental health teams and pediatric primary care providers;

"(F) conduct training and provide technical assistance to pediatric primary care providers to support the early identification, diagnosis, treatment, and referral of children with behavioral health conditions;

"(G) provide information to pediatric providers about, and assist pediatric providers in accessing, pediatric mental health care providers, including child and adolescent psychiatrists, and licensed mental health professionals, such as psychologists, social workers, or mental health counselors and in scheduling and conducting technical assistance;

"(H) assist with referrals to specialty care and community or behavioral health resources; and

"(I) establish mechanisms for measuring and monitoring increased access to pediatric mental health care services by pediatric primary care providers and expanded capacity of pediatric primary care providers to identify, treat, and refer children with mental health problems.

"(2) PEDIATRIC MENTAL HEALTH TEAMS.—In this subsection, the term 'pediatric mental health team' means a team consisting of at least one case coordinator, at least one child and adolescent psychiatrist, and at least one licensed clinical mental health professional, such as a psychologist, social worker, or mental health counselor. Such a team may be regionally based.

"(c) APPLICATION.—A State, political subdivision of a State, Indian tribe, or tribal organization seeking a grant under this section shall submit an application to the Secretary at such time, in such manner, and containing such information as the Secretary may require, including a plan for the comprehensive evaluation of activities that are carried out with funds received under such grant.

"(d) EVALUATION.—A State, political subdivision of a State, Indian tribe, or tribal organization that receives a grant under this section shall prepare and submit an evaluation of activities that are carried out with funds received under such grant to the Secretary at such time, in such manner, and containing such information as the Secretary may reasonably require, including a process and outcome evaluation.

"(e) ACCESS TO BROADBAND.—In administering grants under this section, the Secretary

may coordinate with other agencies to ensure that funding opportunities are available to support access to reliable, high-speed Internet for providers.

"(f) MATCHING REQUIREMENT.—The Secretary may not award a grant under this section unless the State, political subdivision of a State, Indian tribe, or tribal organization involved agrees, with respect to the costs to be incurred by the State, political subdivision of a State, Indian tribe, or tribal organization in carrying out the purpose described in this section, to make available non-Federal contributions (in cash or in kind) toward such costs in an amount that is not less than 20 percent of Federal funds provided in the grant.

"(g) AUTHORIZATION OF APPROPRIATIONS.—To carry out this section, there are authorized to be appropriated, $9,000,000 for the period of fiscal years 2018 through 2022.''.

SEC. 10003. SUBSTANCE USE DISORDER TREATMENT AND EARLY INTERVENTION SERVICES FOR CHILDREN AND ADOLESCENTS.

The first section 514 of the Public Health Service Act (42 U.S.C. 290bb–7), relating to substance abuse treatment services for children and adolescents, is amended—

(1) in the section heading, by striking "ABUSE TREATMENT" and inserting "USE DISORDER TREATMENT AND EARLY INTERVENTION";

(2) by striking subsection (a) and inserting the following:

"(a) IN GENERAL.—The Secretary shall award grants, contracts, or cooperative agreements to public and private nonprofit entities, including Indian tribes or tribal organizations (as such terms are defined in section 4 of the Indian Self-Determination and Education Assistance Act), or health facilities or programs operated by or in accordance with a contract or grant with the Indian Health Service, for the purpose of—

"(1) providing early identification and services to meet the needs of children and adolescents who are at risk of substance use disorders;

"(2) providing substance use disorder treatment services for children, including children and adolescents with co-occurring mental illness and substance use disorders; and

"(3) providing assistance to pregnant women, and parenting women, with substance use disorders, in obtaining treatment services, linking mothers to community resources to support independent family lives, and staying in recovery so that children are in safe, stable home environments and receive appropriate health care services.";

(3) in subsection (b)—

(A) by striking paragraph (1) and inserting the following:

"(1) apply evidence-based and cost-effective methods;";

(B) in paragraph (2)—

(i) by striking "treatment"; and

(ii) by inserting "substance abuse," after "child welfare,";

(C) in paragraph (3), by striking "substance abuse disorders" and inserting "substance use disorders, including children and adolescents with co-occurring mental illness and substance use disorders,";

(D) in paragraph (5), by striking "treatment;" and inserting "services; and";

(E) in paragraph (6), by striking "substance abuse treatment; and" and inserting "treatment."; and

(F) by striking paragraph (7); and

(4) in subsection (f), by striking "$40,000,000" and all that follows through the period and inserting "$29,605,000 for each of fiscal years 2018 through 2022.''.

SEC. 10004. CHILDREN'S RECOVERY FROM TRAUMA.

The first section 582 of the Public Health Service Act (42 U.S.C. 290hh–1; relating to grants to address the problems of persons who experience violence related stress) is amended—

(1) in subsection (a), by striking "developing programs" and all that follows through the period at the end and inserting the following: "developing and maintaining programs that provide for—

"(1) the continued operation of the National Child Traumatic Stress Initiative (referred to in this section as the 'NCTSI'), which includes a cooperative agreement with a coordinating center, that focuses on the mental, behavioral, and biological aspects of psychological trauma response, prevention of the long-term consequences of child trauma, and early intervention services and treatment to address the long-term consequences of child trauma; and

"(2) the development of knowledge with regard to evidence-based practices for identifying and treating mental, behavioral, and biological disorders of children and youth resulting from witnessing or experiencing a traumatic event.";

(2) in subsection (b)—

(A) by striking "subsection (a) related" and inserting "subsection (a)(2) (related";

(B) by striking "treating disorders associated with psychological trauma" and inserting "treating mental, behavioral, and biological disorders associated with psychological trauma)"; and

(C) by striking "mental health agencies and programs that have established clinical and basic research" and inserting "universities, hospitals, mental health agencies, and other programs that have established clinical expertise and research";

(3) by redesignating subsections (c) through (g) as subsections (g) through (k), respectively;

(4) by inserting after subsection (b), the following:

"(c) CHILD OUTCOME DATA.—The NCTSI coordinating center described in subsection (a)(1) shall collect, analyze, report, and make publicly available, as appropriate, NCTSI-wide child treatment process and outcome data regarding the early identification and delivery of evidence-based treatment and services for children and families served by the NCTSI grantees.

"(d) TRAINING.—The NCTSI coordinating center shall facilitate the coordination of training initiatives in evidence-based and trauma-informed treatments, interventions, and practices offered to NCTSI grantees, providers, and partners.

"(e) DISSEMINATION AND COLLABORATION.—The NCTSI coordinating center shall, as appropriate, collaborate with—

"(1) the Secretary, in the dissemination of evidence-based and trauma-informed interventions, treatments, products, and other resources to appropriate stakeholders; and

"(2) appropriate agencies that conduct or fund research within the Department of Health and Human Services, for purposes of sharing NCTSI expertise, evaluation data, and other activities, as appropriate.

"(f) REVIEW.—The Secretary shall, consistent with the peer-review process, ensure that NCTSI applications are reviewed by appropriate experts in the field as part of a consensus-review process. The Secretary shall include review criteria related to expertise and experience in child trauma and evidence-based practices.";

(5) in subsection (g) (as so redesignated), by striking "with respect to centers of excellence are distributed equitably among the regions of the country" and inserting "are distributed equitably among the regions of the United States";

(6) in subsection (i) (as so redesignated), by striking "recipient may not exceed 5 years" and inserting "recipient shall not be less than 4 years, but shall not exceed 5 years"; and

(7) in subsection (j) (as so redesignated), by striking "$50,000,000" and all that follows

through "2006" and inserting "$46,887,000 for each of fiscal years 2018 through 2022".

SEC. 10005. SCREENING AND TREATMENT FOR MATERNAL DEPRESSION.

Part B of title III of the Public Health Service Act (42 U.S.C. 243 et seq.) is amended by inserting after section 317L (42 U.S.C. 247b–13) the following:

"SEC. 317L–1. SCREENING AND TREATMENT FOR MATERNAL DEPRESSION.

"(a) GRANTS.—The Secretary shall make grants to States to establish, improve, or maintain programs for screening, assessment, and treatment services, including culturally and linguistically appropriate services, as appropriate, for women who are pregnant, or who have given birth within the preceding 12 months, for maternal depression.

"(b) APPLICATION.—To seek a grant under this section, a State shall submit an application to the Secretary at such time, in such manner, and containing such information as the Secretary may require. At a minimum, any such application shall include explanations of—

"(1) how a program, or programs, will increase the percentage of women screened and treated, as appropriate, for maternal depression in 1 or more communities; and

"(2) how a program, or programs, if expanded, would increase access to screening and treatment services for maternal depression.

"(c) PRIORITY.—In awarding grants under this section, the Secretary may give priority to States proposing to improve or enhance access to screening services for maternal depression in primary care settings.

"(d) USE OF FUNDS.—The activities eligible for funding through a grant under subsection (a)—

"(1) shall include—

"(A) providing appropriate training to health care providers; and

"(B) providing information to health care providers, including information on maternal depression screening, treatment, and followup support services, and linkages to community-based resources; and

"(2) may include—

"(A) enabling health care providers (including obstetrician-gynecologists, pediatricians, psychiatrists, mental health care providers, and adult primary care clinicians) to provide or receive real-time psychiatric consultation (in-person or remotely) to aid in the treatment of pregnant and parenting women;

"(B) establishing linkages with and among community-based resources, including mental health resources, primary care resources, and support groups; and

"(C) utilizing telehealth services for rural areas and medically underserved areas (as defined in section 330I(a)).

"(e) AUTHORIZATION OF APPROPRIATIONS.—To carry out this section, there are authorized to be appropriated $5,000,000 for each of fiscal years 2018 through 2022.".

SEC. 10006. INFANT AND EARLY CHILDHOOD MENTAL HEALTH PROMOTION, INTERVENTION, AND TREATMENT.

Part Q of title III of the Public Health Service Act (42 U.S.C. 280h et seq.) is amended by adding at the end the following:

"SEC. 399Z–2. INFANT AND EARLY CHILDHOOD MENTAL HEALTH PROMOTION, INTERVENTION, AND TREATMENT.

"(a) GRANTS.—The Secretary shall—

"(1) award grants to eligible entities to develop, maintain, or enhance infant and early childhood mental health promotion, intervention, and treatment programs, including—

"(A) programs for infants and children at significant risk of developing, showing early signs of, or having been diagnosed with mental illness, including a serious emotional disturbance; and

"(B) multigenerational therapy and other services that support the caregiving relationship; and

"(2) ensure that programs funded through grants under this section are evidence-informed or evidence-based models, practices, and methods that are, as appropriate, culturally and linguistically appropriate, and can be replicated in other appropriate settings.

"(b) ELIGIBLE CHILDREN AND ENTITIES.—In this section:

"(1) ELIGIBLE CHILD.—The term 'eligible child' means a child from birth to not more than 12 years of age who—

"(A) is at risk for, shows early signs of, or has been diagnosed with a mental illness, including a serious emotional disturbance; and

"(B) may benefit from infant and early childhood intervention or treatment programs or specialized preschool or elementary school programs that are evidence-based or that have been scientifically demonstrated to show promise but would benefit from further applied development.

"(2) ELIGIBLE ENTITY.—The term 'eligible entity' means a human services agency or nonprofit institution that—

"(A) employs licensed mental health professionals who have specialized training and experience in infant and early childhood mental health assessment, diagnosis, and treatment, or is accredited or approved by the appropriate State agency, as applicable, to provide for children from infancy to 12 years of age mental health promotion, intervention, or treatment services; and

"(B) provides services or programs described in subsection (a) that are evidence-based or that have been scientifically demonstrated to show promise but would benefit from further applied development.

"(c) APPLICATION.—An eligible entity seeking a grant under subsection (a) shall submit to the Secretary an application at such time, in such manner, and containing such information as the Secretary may require.

"(d) USE OF FUNDS FOR EARLY INTERVENTION AND TREATMENT PROGRAMS.—An eligible entity may use amounts awarded under a grant under subsection (a)(1) to carry out the following:

"(1) Provide age-appropriate mental health promotion and early intervention services or mental illness treatment services, which may include specialized programs, for eligible children at significant risk of developing, showing early signs of, or having been diagnosed with a mental illness, including a serious emotional disturbance. Such services may include social and behavioral services as well as multigenerational therapy and other services that support the caregiving relationship.

"(2) Provide training for health care professionals with expertise in infant and early childhood mental health care with respect to appropriate and relevant integration with other disciplines such as primary care clinicians, early intervention specialists, child welfare staff, home visitors, early care and education providers, and others who work with young children and families.

"(3) Provide mental health consultation to personnel of early care and education programs (including licensed or regulated center-based and home-based child care, home visiting, preschool special education, and early intervention programs) who work with children and families.

"(4) Provide training for mental health clinicians in infant and early childhood in promising and evidence-based practices and models for infant and early childhood mental health treatment and early intervention, including with regard to practices for identifying and treating mental illness and behavioral disorders of infants and children resulting from exposure or repeated exposure to adverse childhood experiences or childhood trauma.

"(5) Provide age-appropriate assessment, diagnostic, and intervention services for eligible children, including early mental health promotion, intervention, and treatment services.

"(e) MATCHING FUNDS.—The Secretary may not award a grant under this section to an eligible entity unless the eligible entity agrees, with respect to the costs to be incurred by the eligible entity in carrying out the activities described in subsection (d), to make available non-Federal contributions (in cash or in kind) toward such costs in an amount that is not less than 10 percent of the total amount of Federal funds provided in the grant.

"(f) AUTHORIZATION OF APPROPRIATIONS.—To carry out this section, there are authorized to be appropriated $20,000,000 for the period of fiscal years 2018 through 2022.".

TITLE XI—COMPASSIONATE COMMUNICATION ON HIPAA

SEC. 11001. SENSE OF CONGRESS.

(a) FINDINGS.—Congress finds the following:

(1) According to the National Survey on Drug Use and Health, in 2015, there were approximately 9,800,000 adults in the United States with serious mental illness.

(2) The Substance Abuse and Mental Health Services Administration defines the term "serious mental illness" as an illness affecting individuals 18 years of age or older as having, at any time in the past year, a diagnosable mental, behavioral, or emotional disorder that results in serious functional impairment and substantially interferes with or limits one or more major life activities.

(3) In reporting on the incidence of serious mental illness, the Substance Abuse and Mental Health Services Administration includes major depression, schizophrenia, bipolar disorder, and other mental disorders that cause serious impairment.

(4) Adults with a serious mental illness are at a higher risk for chronic physical illnesses and premature death.

(5) According to the World Health Organization, adults with a serious mental illness have lifespans that are 10 to 25 years shorter than those without serious mental illness. The vast majority of these deaths are due to chronic physical medical conditions, such as cardiovascular, respiratory, and infectious diseases, as well as diabetes and hypertension.

(6) According to the World Health Organization, the majority of deaths of adults with a serious mental illness that are due to physical medical conditions are preventable.

(7) Supported decision making can facilitate care decisions in areas where serious mental illness may impact the capacity of an individual to determine a course of treatment while still allowing the individual to make decisions independently.

(8) Help should be provided to adults with a serious mental illness to address their acute or chronic physical illnesses, make informed choices about treatment, and understand and follow through with appropriate treatment.

(9) There is confusion in the health care community regarding permissible practices under the regulations promulgated under the Health Insurance Portability and Accountability Act of 1996 (commonly known as "HIPAA"). This confusion may hinder appropriate communication of health care information or treatment preferences with appropriate caregivers.

(b) SENSE OF CONGRESS.—It is the sense of Congress that clarification is needed regarding the privacy rule promulgated under section 264(c) of the Health Insurance Portability and Accountability Act of 1996 (42 U.S.C. 1320d–2 note) regarding existing permitted uses and disclosures of health information by health care professionals to communicate with caregivers of adults with a serious mental illness to facilitate treatment.

SEC. 11002. CONFIDENTIALITY OF RECORDS.

Not later than 1 year after the date on which the Secretary of Health and Human Services (in this title referred to as the "Secretary") first finalizes regulations updating part 2 of title 42, Code of Federal Regulations, relating to confidentiality of alcohol and drug abuse patient records, after the date of enactment of this Act, the Secretary shall convene relevant stakeholders to determine the effect of such regulations on patient care, health outcomes, and patient privacy.

SEC. 11003. CLARIFICATION ON PERMITTED USES AND DISCLOSURES OF PROTECTED HEALTH INFORMATION.

(a) IN GENERAL.—The Secretary, acting through the Director of the Office for Civil Rights, shall ensure that health care providers, professionals, patients and their families, and others involved in mental or substance use disorder treatment have adequate, accessible, and easily comprehensible resources relating to appropriate uses and disclosures of protected health information under the regulations promulgated under section 264(c) of the Health Insurance Portability and Accountability Act of 1996 (42 U.S.C. 1320d–2 note).

(b) GUIDANCE.—

(1) ISSUANCE.—In carrying out subsection (a), not later than 1 year after the date of enactment of this section, the Secretary shall issue guidance clarifying the circumstances under which, consistent with regulations promulgated under section 264(c) of the Health Insurance Portability and Accountability Act of 1996, a health care provider or covered entity may use or disclose protected health information.

(2) CIRCUMSTANCES ADDRESSED.—The guidance issued under this section shall address circumstances including those that—

(A) require the consent of the patient;

(B) require providing the patient with an opportunity to object;

(C) are based on the exercise of professional judgment regarding whether the patient would object when the opportunity to object cannot practicably be provided because of the incapacity of the patient or an emergency treatment circumstance; and

(D) are determined, based on the exercise of professional judgment, to be in the best interest of the patient when the patient is not present or otherwise incapacitated.

(3) COMMUNICATION WITH FAMILY MEMBERS AND CAREGIVERS.—In addressing the circumstances described in paragraph (2), the guidance issued under this section shall clarify permitted uses or disclosures of protected health information for purposes of—

(A) communicating with a family member of the patient, caregiver of the patient, or other individual, to the extent that such family member, caregiver, or individual is involved in the care of the patient;

(B) in the case that the patient is an adult, communicating with a family member of the patient, caregiver of the patient, or other individual involved in the care of the patient;

(C) in the case that the patient is a minor, communicating with the parent or caregiver of the patient;

(D) involving the family members or caregivers of the patient, or others involved in the patient's care or care plan, including facilitating treatment and medication adherence;

(E) listening to the patient, or receiving information with respect to the patient from the family or caregiver of the patient;

(F) communicating with family members of the patient, caregivers of the patient, law enforcement, or others when the patient presents a serious and imminent threat of harm to self or others; and

(G) communicating to law enforcement and family members or caregivers of the patient

about the admission of the patient to receive care at, or the release of a patient from, a facility for an emergency psychiatric hold or involuntary treatment.

SEC. 11004. DEVELOPMENT AND DISSEMINATION OF MODEL TRAINING PROGRAMS.

(a) INITIAL PROGRAMS AND MATERIALS.—Not later than 1 year after the date of the enactment of this Act, the Secretary, in consultation with appropriate experts, shall identify the following model programs and materials, or (in the case that no such programs or materials exist) recognize private or public entities to develop and disseminate each of the following:

(1) Model programs and materials for training health care providers (including physicians, emergency medical personnel, psychiatrists, including child and adolescent psychiatrists, psychologists, counselors, therapists, nurse practitioners, physician assistants, behavioral health facilities and clinics, care managers, and hospitals, including individuals such as general counsels or regulatory compliance staff who are responsible for establishing provider privacy policies) regarding the permitted uses and disclosures, consistent with the standards governing the privacy and security of individually identifiable health information promulgated by the Secretary under part C of title XI of the Social Security Act (42 U.S.C. 1320d et seq.) and regulations promulgated under section 264(c) of the Health Insurance Portability and Accountability Act of 1996 (42 U.S.C. 1320d–2 note) and such part C, of the protected health information of patients seeking or undergoing mental or substance use disorder treatment.

(2) A model program and materials for training patients and their families regarding their rights to protect and obtain information under the standards and regulations specified in paragraph (1).

(b) PERIODIC UPDATES.—The Secretary shall—

(1) periodically review and update the model programs and materials identified or developed under subsection (a); and

(2) disseminate the updated model programs and materials to the individuals described in subsection (a).

(c) COORDINATION.—The Secretary shall carry out this section in coordination with the Director of the Office for Civil Rights within the Department of Health and Human Services, the Assistant Secretary for Mental Health and Substance Use, the Administrator of the Health Resources and Services Administration, and the heads of other relevant agencies within the Department of Health and Human Services.

(d) INPUT OF CERTAIN ENTITIES.—In identifying, reviewing, or updating the model programs and materials under subsections (a) and (b), the Secretary shall solicit the input of relevant national, State, and local associations; medical societies; licensing boards; providers of mental and substance use disorder treatment; organizations with expertise on domestic violence, sexual assault, elder abuse, and child abuse; and organizations representing patients and consumers and the families of patients and consumers.

(e) FUNDING.—There are authorized to be appropriated to carry out this section—

(1) $4,000,000 for fiscal year 2018;

(2) $2,000,000 for each of fiscal years 2019 and 2020; and

(3) $1,000,000 for each of fiscal years 2021 and 2022.

TITLE XII—MEDICAID MENTAL HEALTH COVERAGE

SEC. 12001. RULE OF CONSTRUCTION RELATED TO MEDICAID COVERAGE OF MENTAL HEALTH SERVICES AND PRIMARY CARE SERVICES FURNISHED ON THE SAME DAY.

Nothing in title XIX of the Social Security Act (42 U.S.C. 1396 et seq.) shall be construed as *prohibiting separate payment under the State plan under such title (or under a waiver of the plan) for the provision of a mental health service or primary care service under such plan, with respect to an individual, because such service is—*

(1) a primary care service furnished to the individual by a provider at a facility on the same day a mental health service is furnished to such individual by such provider (or another provider) at the facility; or

(2) a mental health service furnished to the individual by a provider at a facility on the same day a primary care service is furnished to such individual by such provider (or another provider) at the facility.

SEC. 12002. STUDY AND REPORT RELATED TO MEDICAID MANAGED CARE REGULATION.

(a) STUDY.—The Secretary of Health and Human Services, acting through the Administrator of the Centers for Medicare & Medicaid Services, shall conduct a study on coverage under the Medicaid program under title XIX of the Social Security Act (42 U.S.C. 1396 et seq.) of services provided through a medicaid managed care organization (as defined in section 1903(m) of such Act (42 U.S.C. 1396b(m)) or a prepaid inpatient health plan (as defined in section 438.2 of title 42, Code of Federal Regulations (or any successor regulation)) with respect to individuals over the age of 21 and under the age of 65 for the treatment of a mental health disorder in institutions for mental diseases (as defined in section 1905(i) of such Act (42 U.S.C. 1396d(i))). Such study shall include information on the following:

(1) The extent to which States, including the District of Columbia and each territory or possession of the United States, are providing capitated payments to such organizations or plans for enrollees who are receiving services in institutions for mental diseases.

(2) The number of individuals receiving medical assistance under a State plan under such title XIX, or a waiver of such plan, who receive services in institutions for mental diseases through such organizations and plans.

(3) The range of and average number of months, and the length of stay during such months, that such individuals are receiving such services in such institutions.

(4) How such organizations or plans determine when to provide for the furnishing of such services through an institution for mental diseases in lieu of other benefits (including the full range of community-based services) under their contract with the State agency administering the State plan under such title XIX, or a waiver of such plan, to address psychiatric or substance use disorder treatment.

(5) The extent to which the provision of services within such institutions has affected the capitated payments for such organizations or plans.

(b) REPORT.—Not later than 3 years after the date of the enactment of this Act, the Secretary shall submit to Congress a report on the study conducted under subsection (a).

SEC. 12003. GUIDANCE ON OPPORTUNITIES FOR INNOVATION.

Not later than 1 year after the date of the enactment of this Act, the Administrator of the Centers for Medicare & Medicaid Services shall issue a State Medicaid Director letter regarding opportunities to design innovative service delivery systems, including systems for providing community-based services, for adults with a serious mental illness or children with a serious emotional disturbance who are receiving medical assistance under title XIX of the Social Security Act (42 U.S.C. 1396 et seq.). The letter shall include opportunities for demonstration projects under section 1115 of such Act (42 U.S.C. 1315) to improve care for such adults and children.

SEC. 12004. STUDY AND REPORT ON MEDICAID EMERGENCY PSYCHIATRIC DEMONSTRATION PROJECT.

(a) COLLECTION OF INFORMATION.—The Secretary of Health and Human Services, acting through the Administrator of the Centers for Medicare & Medicaid Services, shall, to the extent practical and data is available, with respect to each State that has participated in the demonstration project established under section 2707 of the Patient Protection and Affordable Care Act (42 U.S.C. 1396a note), collect from each such State information on the following:

(1) The number of institutions for mental diseases (as defined in section 1905(i) of the Social Security Act (42 U.S.C. 1396d(i))) and beds in such institutions that received payment for the provision of services to individuals who receive medical assistance under a State plan under the Medicaid program under title XIX of the Social Security Act (42 U.S.C. 1396 et seq.) (or under a waiver of such plan) through the demonstration project in each such State as compared to the total number of institutions for mental diseases and beds in the State.

(2) The extent to which there is a reduction in expenditures under the Medicaid program under title XIX of the Social Security Act (42 U.S.C. 1396 et seq.) or other spending on the full continuum of physical or mental health care for individuals who receive treatment in an institution for mental diseases under the demonstration project, including outpatient, inpatient, emergency, and ambulatory care, that is attributable to such individuals receiving treatment in institutions for mental diseases under the demonstration project.

(3) The number of forensic psychiatric hospitals, the number of beds in such hospitals, and the number of forensic psychiatric beds in other hospitals in such State, based on the most recent data available, to the extent practical, as determined by such Administrator.

(4) The amount of any disproportionate share hospital payments under section 1923 of the Social Security Act (42 U.S.C. 1396r–4) that institutions for mental diseases in the State received during the period beginning on July 1, 2012, and ending on June 30, 2015, and the extent to which the demonstration project reduced the amount of such payments.

(5) The most recent data regarding all facilities or sites in the State in which any adults with a serious mental illness who are receiving medical assistance under a State plan under the Medicaid program under title XIX of the Social Security Act (42 U.S.C. 1396 et seq.) (or under a waiver of such plan) are treated during the period referred to in paragraph (4), to the extent practical, as determined by the Administrator, including—

(A) the types of such facilities or sites (such as an institution for mental diseases, a hospital emergency department, or other inpatient hospital);

(B) the average length of stay in such a facility or site by such an individual, disaggregated by facility type; and

(C) the payment rate under the State plan (or a waivers of such plan) for services furnished to such an individual for that treatment, disaggregated by facility type, during the period in which the demonstration project is in operation.

(6) The extent to which the utilization of hospital emergency departments during the period in which the demonstration project was is in operation differed, with respect to individuals who are receiving medical assistance under a State plan under the Medicaid program under title XIX of the Social Security Act (42 U.S.C. 1396 et seq.) (or under a waiver of such plan), between—

(A) those individuals who received treatment in an institution for mental diseases under the demonstration project;

(B) those individuals who met the eligibility requirements for the demonstration project but who did not receive treatment in an institution for mental diseases under the demonstration project; and

(C) those adults with a serious mental illness who did not meet such eligibility requirements and did not receive treatment for such illness in an institution for mental diseases.

(b) REPORT.—Not later than 2 years after the date of the enactment of this Act, the Secretary of Health and Human Services shall submit to Congress a report that summarizes and analyzes the information collected under subsection (a). Such report may be submitted as part of the report required under section 2707(f) of the Patient Protection and Affordable Care Act (42 U.S.C. 1396a note) or separately.

SEC. 12005. PROVIDING EPSDT SERVICES TO CHILDREN IN IMDS.

(a) IN GENERAL.—Section 1905(a)(16) of the Social Security Act (42 U.S.C. 1396d(a)(16)) is amended—

(1) by striking "effective January 1, 1973" and inserting "(A) effective January 1, 1973"; and

(2) by inserting before the semicolon at the end the following: ", and, (B) for individuals receiving services described in subparagraph (A), early and periodic screening, diagnostic, and treatment services (as defined in subsection (r)), whether or not such screening, diagnostic, and treatment services are furnished by the provider of the services described in such subparagraph".

(b) EFFECTIVE DATE.—The amendments made by subsection (a) shall apply with respect to items and services furnished in calendar quarters beginning on or after January 1, 2019.

SEC. 12006. ELECTRONIC VISIT VERIFICATION SYSTEM REQUIRED FOR PERSONAL CARE SERVICES AND HOME HEALTH CARE SERVICES UNDER MEDICAID.

(a) IN GENERAL.—Section 1903 of the Social Security Act (42 U.S.C. 1396b) is amended by inserting after subsection (k) the following new subsection:

"(l)(1) Subject to paragraphs (3) and (4), with respect to any amount expended for personal care services or home health care services requiring an in-home visit by a provider that are provided under a State plan under this title (or under a waiver of the plan) and furnished in a calendar quarter beginning on or after January 1, 2019 (or, in the case of home health care services, on or after January 1, 2023), unless a State requires the use of an electronic visit verification system for such services furnished in such quarter under the plan or such waiver, the Federal medical assistance percentage shall be reduced—

"(A) in the case of personal care services—

"(i) for calendar quarters in 2019 and 2020, by .25 percentage points;

"(ii) for calendar quarters in 2021, by .5 percentage points;

"(iii) for calendar quarters in 2022, by .75 percentage points; and

"(iv) for calendar quarters in 2023 and each year thereafter, by 1 percentage point; and

"(B) in the case of home health care services—

"(i) for calendar quarters in 2023 and 2024, by .25 percentage points;

"(ii) for calendar quarters in 2025, by .5 percentage points;

"(iii) for calendar quarters in 2026, by .75 percentage points; and

"(iv) for calendar quarters in 2027 and each year thereafter, by 1 percentage point.

"(2) Subject to paragraphs (3) and (4), in implementing the requirement for the use of an electronic visit verification system under paragraph (1), a State shall—

"(A) consult with agencies and entities that provide personal care services, home health care services, or both under the State plan (or under

a waiver of the plan) to ensure that such system—

"(i) is minimally burdensome;

"(ii) takes into account existing best practices and electronic visit verification systems in use in the State; and

"(iii) is conducted in accordance with the requirements of HIPAA privacy and security law (as defined in section 3009 of the Public Health Service Act);

"(B) take into account a stakeholder process that includes input from beneficiaries, family caregivers, individuals who furnish personal care services or home health care services, and other stakeholders, as determined by the State in accordance with guidance from the Secretary; and

"(C) ensure that individuals who furnish personal care services, home health care services, or both under the State plan (or under a waiver of the plan) are provided the opportunity for training on the use of such system.

"(3) Paragraphs (1) and (2) shall not apply in the case of a State that, as of the date of the enactment of this subsection, requires the use of any system for the electronic verification of visits conducted as part of both personal care services and home health care services, so long as the State continues to require the use of such system with respect to the electronic verification of such visits.

"(4)(A) In the case of a State described in subparagraph (B), the reduction under paragraph (1) shall not apply—

"(i) in the case of personal care services, for calendar quarters in 2019; and

"(ii) in the case of home health care services, for calendar quarters in 2023.

"(B) For purposes of subparagraph (A), a State described in this subparagraph is a State that demonstrates to the Secretary that the State—

"(i) has made a good faith effort to comply with the requirements of paragraphs (1) and (2) (including by taking steps to adopt the technology used for an electronic visit verification system); and

"(ii) in implementing such a system, has encountered unavoidable system delays.

"(5) In this subsection:

"(A) The term 'electronic visit verification system' means, with respect to personal care services or home health care services, a system under which visits conducted as part of such services are electronically verified with respect to—

"(i) the type of service performed;

"(ii) the individual receiving the service;

"(iii) the date of the service;

"(iv) the location of service delivery;

"(v) the individual providing the service; and

"(vi) the time the service begins and ends.

"(B) The term 'home health care services' means services described in section 1905(a)(7) provided under a State plan under this title (or under a waiver of the plan).

"(C) The term 'personal care services' means personal care services provided under a State plan under this title (or under a waiver of the plan), including services provided under section 1905(a)(24), 1915(c), 1915(i), 1915(j), or 1915(k) or under a wavier under section 1115.

"(6)(A) In the case in which a State requires personal care service and home health care service providers to utilize an electronic visit verification system operated by the State or a contractor on behalf of the State, the Secretary shall pay to the State, for each quarter, an amount equal to 90 per centum of so much of the sums expended during such quarter as are attributable to the design, development, or installation of such system, and 75 per centum of so much of the sums for the operation and maintenance of such system.

"(B) Subparagraph (A) shall not apply in the case in which a State requires personal care service and home health care service providers to utilize an electronic visit verification system that is not operated by the State or a contractor on behalf of the State.".

(b) COLLECTION AND DISSEMINATION OF BEST PRACTICES.—Not later than January 1, 2018, the Secretary of Health and Human Services shall, with respect to electronic visit verification systems (as defined in subsection (l)(5) of section 1903 of the Social Security Act (42 U.S.C. 1396b), as inserted by subsection (a)), collect and disseminate best practices to State Medicaid Directors with respect to—

(1) training individuals who furnish personal care services, home health care services, or both under the State plan under title XIX of such Act (or under a waiver of the plan) on such systems and the operation of such systems and the prevention of fraud with respect to the provision of personal care services or home health care services (as defined in such subsection (l)(5)); and

(2) the provision of notice and educational materials to family caregivers and beneficiaries with respect to the use of such electronic visit verification systems and other means to prevent such fraud.

(c) RULES OF CONSTRUCTION.—

(1) NO EMPLOYER-EMPLOYEE RELATIONSHIP ESTABLISHED.—Nothing in the amendment made by this section may be construed as establishing an employer-employee relationship between the agency or entity that provides for personal care services or home health care services and the individuals who, under a contract with such an agency or entity, furnish such services for purposes of part 552 of title 29, Code of Federal Regulations (or any successor regulations).

(2) NO PARTICULAR OR UNIFORM ELECTRONIC VISIT VERIFICATION SYSTEM REQUIRED.—Nothing in the amendment made by this section shall be construed to require the use of a particular or uniform electronic visit verification system (as defined in subsection (l)(5) of section 1903 of the Social Security Act (42 U.S.C. 1396b), as inserted by subsection (a)) by all agencies or entities that provide personal care services or home health care under a State plan under title XIX of the Social Security Act (or under a waiver of the plan) (42 U.S.C. 1396 et seq.).

(3) NO LIMITS ON PROVISION OF CARE.—Nothing in the amendment made by this section may be construed to limit, with respect to personal care services or home health care services provided under a State plan under title XIX of the Social Security Act (or under a waiver of the plan) (42 U.S.C. 1396 et seq.), provider selection, constrain beneficiaries' selection of a caregiver, or impede the manner in which care is delivered.

(4) NO PROHIBITION ON STATE QUALITY MEASURES REQUIREMENTS.—Nothing in the amendment made by this section shall be construed as prohibiting a State, in implementing an electronic visit verification system (as defined in subsection (l)(5) of section 1903 of the Social Security Act (42 U.S.C. 1396b), as inserted by subsection (a)), from establishing requirements related to quality measures for such system.

TITLE XIII—MENTAL HEALTH PARITY

SEC. 13001. ENHANCED COMPLIANCE WITH MENTAL HEALTH AND SUBSTANCE USE DISORDER COVERAGE REQUIREMENTS.

(a) COMPLIANCE PROGRAM GUIDANCE DOCUMENT.—Section 2726(a) of the Public Health Service Act (42 U.S.C. 300gg–26(a)) is amended by adding at the end the following:

"(6) COMPLIANCE PROGRAM GUIDANCE DOCUMENT.—

"(A) IN GENERAL.—Not later than 12 months after the date of enactment of the Helping Families in Mental Health Crisis Reform Act of 2016,

the Secretary, the Secretary of Labor, and the Secretary of the Treasury, in consultation with the Inspector General of the Department of Health and Human Services, the Inspector General of the Department of Labor, and the Inspector General of the Department of the Treasury, shall issue a compliance program guidance document to help improve compliance with this section, section 712 of the Employee Retirement Income Security Act of 1974, and section 9812 of the Internal Revenue Code of 1986, as applicable. In carrying out this paragraph, the Secretaries may take into consideration the 2016 publication of the Department of Health and Human Services and the Department of Labor, entitled 'Warning Signs - Plan or Policy Non-Quantitative Treatment Limitations (NQTLs) that Require Additional Analysis to Determine Mental Health Parity Compliance'.

"(B) EXAMPLES ILLUSTRATING COMPLIANCE AND NONCOMPLIANCE.—

"(i) IN GENERAL.—The compliance program guidance document required under this paragraph shall provide illustrative, de-identified examples (that do not disclose any protected health information or individually identifiable information) of previous findings of compliance and noncompliance with this section, section 712 of the Employee Retirement Income Security Act of 1974, or section 9812 of the Internal Revenue Code of 1986, as applicable, based on investigations of violations of such sections, including—

"(I) examples illustrating requirements for information disclosures and nonquantitative treatment limitations; and

"(II) descriptions of the violations uncovered during the course of such investigations.

"(ii) NONQUANTITATIVE TREATMENT LIMITATIONS.—To the extent that any example described in clause (i) involves a finding of compliance or noncompliance with regard to any requirement for nonquantitative treatment limitations, the example shall provide sufficient detail to fully explain such finding, including a full description of the criteria involved for approving medical and surgical benefits and the criteria involved for approving mental health and substance use disorder benefits.

"(iii) ACCESS TO ADDITIONAL INFORMATION REGARDING COMPLIANCE.—In developing and issuing the compliance program guidance document required under this paragraph, the Secretaries specified in subparagraph (A)—

"(I) shall enter into interagency agreements with the Inspector General of the Department of Health and Human Services, the Inspector General of the Department of Labor, and the Inspector General of the Department of the Treasury to share findings of compliance and noncompliance with this section, section 712 of the Employee Retirement Income Security Act of 1974, or section 9812 of the Internal Revenue Code of 1986, as applicable; and

"(II) shall seek to enter into an agreement with a State to share information on findings of compliance and noncompliance with this section, section 712 of the Employee Retirement Income Security Act of 1974, or section 9812 of the Internal Revenue Code of 1986, as applicable.

"(C) RECOMMENDATIONS.—The compliance program guidance document shall include recommendations to advance compliance with this section, section 712 of the Employee Retirement Income Security Act of 1974, or section 9812 of the Internal Revenue Code of 1986, as applicable, and encourage the development and use of internal controls to monitor adherence to applicable statutes, regulations, and program requirements. Such internal controls may include illustrative examples of nonquantitative treatment limitations on mental health and substance use disorder benefits, which may fail to comply with this section, section 712 of the Employee Retirement Income Security Act of 1974, or section 9812 of the Internal Revenue Code of 1986, as applicable, in relation to nonquantitative treatment limitations on medical and surgical benefits.

"*(D) UPDATING THE COMPLIANCE PROGRAM GUIDANCE DOCUMENT.*—The Secretary, the Secretary of Labor, and the Secretary of the Treasury, in consultation with the Inspector General of the Department of Health and Human Services, the Inspector General of the Department of Labor, and the Inspector General of the Department of the Treasury, shall update the compliance program guidance document every 2 years to include illustrative, de-identified examples (that do not disclose any protected health information or individually identifiable information) of previous findings of compliance and noncompliance with this section, section 712 of the Employee Retirement Income Security Act of 1974, or section 9812 of the Internal Revenue Code of 1986, as applicable.".

(b) *ADDITIONAL GUIDANCE.*—Section 2726(a) of the Public Health Service Act (42 U.S.C. 300gg-26(a)), as amended by subsection (a), is further amended by adding at the end the following:

"*(7) ADDITIONAL GUIDANCE.*—

"*(A) IN GENERAL.*—Not later than 12 months after the date of enactment of the Helping Families in Mental Health Crisis Reform Act of 2016, the Secretary, the Secretary of Labor, and the Secretary of the Treasury shall issue guidance to group health plans and health insurance issuers offering group or individual health insurance coverage to assist such plans and issuers in satisfying the requirements of this section, section 712 of the Employee Retirement Income Security Act of 1974, or section 9812 of the Internal Revenue Code of 1986, as applicable.

"*(B) DISCLOSURE.*—

"*(i) GUIDANCE FOR PLANS AND ISSUERS.*—The guidance issued under this paragraph shall include clarifying information and illustrative examples of methods that group health plans and health insurance issuers offering group or individual health insurance coverage may use for disclosing information to ensure compliance with the requirements under this section, section 712 of the Employee Retirement Income Security Act of 1974, or section 9812 of the Internal Revenue Code of 1986, as applicable, (and any regulations promulgated pursuant to such sections, as applicable).

"*(ii) DOCUMENTS FOR PARTICIPANTS, BENEFICIARIES, CONTRACTING PROVIDERS, OR AUTHORIZED REPRESENTATIVES.*—The guidance issued under this paragraph shall include clarifying information and illustrative examples of methods that group health plans and health insurance issuers offering group or individual health insurance coverage may use to provide any participant, beneficiary, contracting provider, or authorized representative, as applicable, with documents containing information that the health plans or issuers are required to disclose to participants, beneficiaries, contracting providers, or authorized representatives to ensure compliance with this section, section 712 of the Employee Retirement Income Security Act of 1974, or section 9812 of the Internal Revenue Code of 1986, as applicable, compliance with any regulation issued pursuant to such respective section, or compliance with any other applicable law or regulation. Such guidance shall include information that is comparative in nature with respect to—

"*(I)* nonquantitative treatment limitations for both medical and surgical benefits and mental health and substance use disorder benefits;

"*(II)* the processes, strategies, evidentiary standards, and other factors used to apply the limitations described in subclause (I); and

"*(III)* the application of the limitations described in subclause (I) to ensure that such limitations are applied in parity with respect to

both medical and surgical benefits and mental health and substance use disorder benefits.

"*(C) NONQUANTITATIVE TREATMENT LIMITATIONS.*—The guidance issued under this paragraph shall include clarifying information and illustrative examples of methods, processes, strategies, evidentiary standards, and other factors that group health plans and health insurance issuers offering group or individual health insurance coverage may use regarding the development and application of nonquantitative treatment limitations to ensure compliance with this section, section 712 of the Employee Retirement Income Security Act of 1974, or section 9812 of the Internal Revenue Code of 1986, as applicable, (and any regulations promulgated pursuant to such respective section), including—

"*(i)* examples of methods of determining appropriate types of nonquantitative treatment limitations with respect to both medical and surgical benefits and mental health and substance use disorder benefits, including nonquantitative treatment limitations pertaining to—

"*(I)* medical management standards based on medical necessity or appropriateness, or whether a treatment is experimental or investigative;

"*(II)* limitations with respect to prescription drug formulary design; and

"*(III)* use of fail-first or step therapy protocols;

"*(ii)* examples of methods of determining—

"*(I)* network admission standards (such as credentialing); and

"*(II)* factors used in provider reimbursement methodologies (such as service type, geographic market, demand for services, and provider supply, practice size, training, experience, and licensure) as such factors apply to network adequacy;

"*(iii)* examples of sources of information that may serve as evidentiary standards for the purposes of making determinations regarding the development and application of nonquantitative treatment limitations;

"*(iv)* examples of specific factors, and the evidentiary standards used to evaluate such factors, used by such plans or issuers in performing a nonquantitative treatment limitation analysis;

"*(v)* examples of how specific evidentiary standards may be used to determine whether treatments are considered experimental or investigative;

"*(vi)* examples of how specific evidentiary standards may be applied to each service category or classification of benefits;

"*(vii)* examples of methods of reaching appropriate coverage determinations for new mental health or substance use disorder treatments, such as evidence-based early intervention programs for individuals with a serious mental illness and types of medical management techniques;

"*(viii)* examples of methods of reaching appropriate coverage determinations for which there is an indirect relationship between the covered mental health or substance use disorder benefit and a traditional covered medical and surgical benefit, such as residential treatment or hospitalizations involving voluntary or involuntary commitment; and

"*(ix)* additional illustrative examples of methods, processes, strategies, evidentiary standards, and other factors for which the Secretary determines that additional guidance is necessary to improve compliance with this section, section 712 of the Employee Retirement Income Security Act of 1974, or section 9812 of the Internal Revenue Code of 1986, as applicable.

"*(D) PUBLIC COMMENT.*—Prior to issuing any final guidance under this paragraph, the Secretary shall provide a public comment period of not less than 60 days during which any member of the public may provide comments on a draft of the guidance.".

(c) *AVAILABILITY OF PLAN INFORMATION.*—

(1) *SOLICITATION OF PUBLIC FEEDBACK.*—Not later than 6 months after the date of enactment of this Act, the Secretary of Health and Human Services, the Secretary of Labor, and the Secretary of the Treasury shall solicit feedback from the public on how the disclosure request process for documents containing information that health plans or health insurance issuers are required under Federal or State law to disclose to participants, beneficiaries, contracting providers, or authorized representatives to ensure compliance with existing mental health parity and addiction equity requirements can be improved while continuing to ensure consumers' rights to access all information required by Federal or State law to be disclosed.

(2) *PUBLIC AVAILABILITY.*—Not later than 12 months after the date of the enactment of this Act, the Secretary of Health and Human Services, the Secretary of Labor, and the Secretary of the Treasury shall make such feedback publicly available.

(3) *NAIC.*—The Secretary of Health and Human Services, the Secretary of Labor, and the Secretary of the Treasury shall share feedback obtained pursuant to paragraph (1) directly with the National Association of Insurance Commissioners to the extent such feedback includes recommendations for the development of simplified information disclosure tools to provide consistent information for consumers. Such feedback may be taken into consideration by the National Association of Insurance Commissioners and other appropriate entities for the voluntary development and voluntary use of common templates and other sample standardized forms to improve consumer access to plan information.

(d) *IMPROVING COMPLIANCE.*—

(1) *IN GENERAL.*—In the case that the Secretary of Health and Human Services, the Secretary of Labor, or the Secretary of the Treasury determines that a group health plan or health insurance issuer offering group or individual health insurance coverage has violated, at least 5 times, section 2726 of the Public Health Service Act (42 U.S.C. 300gg-26), section 712 of the Employee Retirement Income Security Act of 1974 (29 U.S.C. 1185a), or section 9812 of the Internal Revenue Code of 1986, respectively, the appropriate Secretary shall audit plan documents for such health plan or issuer in the plan year following the Secretary's determination in order to help improve compliance with such section.

(2) *RULE OF CONSTRUCTION.*—Nothing in this subsection shall be construed to limit the authority, as in effect on the day before the date of enactment of this Act, of the Secretary of Health and Human Services, the Secretary of Labor, or the Secretary of the Treasury to audit documents of health plans or health insurance issuers.

SEC. 13002. ACTION PLAN FOR ENHANCED ENFORCEMENT OF MENTAL HEALTH AND SUBSTANCE USE DISORDER COVERAGE.

(a) *PUBLIC MEETING.*—

(1) *IN GENERAL.*—Not later than 6 months after the date of enactment of this Act, the Secretary of Health and Human Services shall convene a public meeting of stakeholders described in paragraph (2) to produce an action plan for improved Federal and State coordination related to the enforcement of section 2726 of the Public Health Service Act (42 U.S.C. 300gg-26), section 712 of the Employee Retirement Income Security Act of 1974 (29 U.S.C. 1185a), and section 9812 of the Internal Revenue Code of 1986, and any comparable provisions of State law (in this section such sections and provisions are collectively referred to as "mental health parity and addiction equity requirements").

(2) STAKEHOLDERS.—The stakeholders described in this paragraph shall include each of the following:

(A) The Federal Government, including representatives from—

(i) the Department of Health and Human Services;

(ii) the Department of the Treasury;

(iii) the Department of Labor; and

(iv) the Department of Justice.

(B) State governments, including—

(i) State health insurance commissioners;

(ii) appropriate State agencies, including agencies on public health or mental health; and

(iii) State attorneys general or other representatives of State entities involved in the enforcement of mental health parity and addiction equity requirements.

(C) Representatives from key stakeholder groups, including—

(i) the National Association of Insurance Commissioners;

(ii) health insurance issuers;

(iii) providers of mental health and substance use disorder treatment;

(iv) employers; and

(v) patients or their advocates.

(b) ACTION PLAN.—Not later than 6 months after the conclusion of the public meeting under subsection (a), the Secretary of Health and Human Services shall finalize the action plan described in such subsection and make it plainly available on the Internet website of the Department of Health and Human Services.

(c) CONTENT.—The action plan under this section shall—

(1) take into consideration the recommendations of the Mental Health and Substance Use Disorder Parity Task Force in its final report issued in October of 2016, and any subsequent Federal and State actions in relation to such recommendations;

(2) reflect the input of the stakeholders participating in the public meeting under subsection (a);

(3) identify specific strategic objectives regarding how the various Federal and State agencies charged with enforcement of mental health parity and addiction equity requirements will collaborate to improve enforcement of such requirements;

(4) provide a timeline for implementing the action plan; and

(5) provide specific examples of how such objectives may be met, which may include—

(A) providing common educational information and documents, such as the Consumer Guide to Disclosure Rights, to patients about their rights under mental health parity and addiction equity requirements;

(B) facilitating the centralized collection of, monitoring of, and response to patient complaints or inquiries relating to mental health parity and addiction equity requirements, which may be through the development and administration of—

(i) a single, toll-free telephone number; and

(ii) a new parity website—

(I) to help consumers find the appropriate Federal or State agency to assist with their parity complaints, appeals, and other actions; and

(II) that takes into consideration, but is not duplicative of, the parity beta site being tested, and released for public comment, by the Department of Health and Human Services as of the date of the enactment of this Act;

(C) Federal and State law enforcement agencies entering into memoranda of understanding to better coordinate enforcement responsibilities and information sharing—

(i) including whether such agencies should make the results of enforcement actions related to mental health parity and addiction equity requirements publicly available; and

(ii) which may include State Policy Academies on Parity Implementation for State Officials and other forums to bring together national experts to provide technical assistance to teams of State officials on strategies to advance compliance with mental health parity and addiction equity requirements in both the commercial market, and in the Medicaid program under title XIX of the Social Security Act and the State Children's Health Insurance Program under title XXI of such Act; and

(D) recommendations to the Congress regarding the need for additional legal authority to improve enforcement of mental health parity and addiction equity requirements, including the need for additional legal authority to ensure that nonquantitative treatment limitations are applied, and the extent and frequency of the applications of such limitations, both to medical and surgical benefits and to mental health and substance use disorder benefits in a comparable manner.

SEC. 13003. REPORT ON INVESTIGATIONS REGARDING PARITY IN MENTAL HEALTH AND SUBSTANCE USE DISORDER BENEFITS.

(a) IN GENERAL.—Not later than 1 year after the date of enactment of this Act, and annually thereafter for the subsequent 5 years, the Assistant Secretary of Labor of the Employee Benefits Security Administration, in collaboration with the Administrator of the Centers for Medicare & Medicaid Services and the Secretary of the Treasury, shall submit to the Committee on Energy and Commerce of the House of Representatives and the Committee on Health, Education, Labor, and Pensions of the Senate a report summarizing the results of all closed Federal investigations completed during the preceding 12-month period with findings of any serious violation regarding compliance with mental health and substance use disorder coverage requirements under section 2726 of the Public Health Service Act (42 U.S.C. 300gg–26), section 712 of the Employee Retirement Income Security Act of 1974 (29 U.S.C. 1185a), and section 9812 of the Internal Revenue Code of 1986.

(b) CONTENTS.—Subject to subsection (c), a report under subsection (a) shall, with respect to investigations described in such subsection, include each of the following:

(1) The number of closed Federal investigations conducted during the covered reporting period.

(2) Each benefit classification examined by any such investigation conducted during the covered reporting period.

(3) Each subject matter, including compliance with requirements for quantitative and nonquantitative treatment limitations, of any such investigation conducted during the covered reporting period.

(4) A summary of the basis of the final decision rendered for each closed investigation conducted during the covered reporting period that resulted in a finding of a serious violation.

(c) LIMITATION.—Any individually identifiable information shall be excluded from reports under subsection (a) consistent with protections under the health privacy and security rules promulgated under section 264(c) of the Health Insurance Portability and Accountability Act of 1996 (42 U.S.C. 1320d–2 note).

SEC. 13004. GAO STUDY ON PARITY IN MENTAL HEALTH AND SUBSTANCE USE DISORDER BENEFITS.

Not later than 3 years after the date of enactment of this Act, the Comptroller General of the United States, in consultation with the Secretary of Health and Human Services, the Secretary of Labor, and the Secretary of the Treasury, shall submit to the Committee on Energy and Commerce of the House of Representatives and the Committee on Health, Education, Labor, and Pensions of the Senate a report de-

tailing the extent to which group health plans or health insurance issuers offering group or individual health insurance coverage that provides both medical and surgical benefits and mental health or substance use disorder benefits, medicaid managed care organizations with a contract under section 1903(m) of the Social Security Act (42 U.S.C. 1396b(m)), and health plans provided under the State Children's Health Insurance Program under title XXI of the Social Security Act (42 U.S.C. 1397aa et seq.) comply with section 2726 of the Public Health Service Act (42 U.S.C. 300gg–26), section 712 of the Employee Retirement Income Security Act of 1974 (29 U.S.C. 1185a), and section 9812 of the Internal Revenue Code of 1986, including—*

(1) how nonquantitative treatment limitations, including medical necessity criteria, of such plans or issuers comply with such sections;

(2) how the responsible Federal departments and agencies ensure that such plans or issuers comply with such sections, including an assessment of how the Secretary of Health and Human Services has used its authority to conduct audits of such plans to ensure compliance;

(3) a review of how the various Federal and State agencies responsible for enforcing mental health parity requirements have improved enforcement of such requirements in accordance with the objectives and timeline described in the action plan under section 13002; and

(4) recommendations for how additional enforcement, education, and coordination activities by responsible Federal and State departments and agencies could better ensure compliance with such sections, including recommendations regarding the need for additional legal authority.

SEC. 13005. INFORMATION AND AWARENESS ON EATING DISORDERS.

(a) INFORMATION.—The Secretary of Health and Human Services, acting through the Director of the Office on Women's Health, may—

(1) update information, related fact sheets, and resource lists related to eating disorders that are available on the public Internet website of the National Women's Health Information Center sponsored by the Office on Women's Health, to include—

(A) updated findings and current research related to eating disorders, as appropriate; and

(B) information about eating disorders, including information related to males and females;

(2) incorporate, as appropriate, and in coordination with the Secretary of Education, information from publicly available resources into appropriate obesity prevention programs developed by the Office on Women's Health; and

(3) make publicly available (through a public Internet website or other method) information, related fact sheets, and resource lists, as updated under paragraph (1), and the information incorporated into appropriate obesity prevention programs under paragraph (2).

(b) AWARENESS.—The Secretary of Health and Human Services may advance public awareness on—

(1) the types of eating disorders;

(2) the seriousness of eating disorders, including prevalence, comorbidities, and physical and mental health consequences;

(3) methods to identify, intervene, refer for treatment, and prevent behaviors that may lead to the development of eating disorders;

(4) discrimination and bullying based on body size;

(5) the effects of media on self-esteem and body image; and

(6) the signs and symptoms of eating disorders.

SEC. 13006. EDUCATION AND TRAINING ON EATING DISORDERS.

The Secretary of Health and Human Services may facilitate the identification of model programs and materials for educating and training health professionals in effective strategies to—

(1) identify individuals with eating disorders;

(2) provide early intervention services for individuals with eating disorders;

(3) refer patients with eating disorders for appropriate treatment;

(4) prevent the development of eating disorders; and

(5) provide appropriate treatment services for individuals with eating disorders.

SEC. 13007. CLARIFICATION OF EXISTING PARITY RULES.

If a group health plan or a health insurance issuer offering group or individual health insurance coverage provides coverage for eating disorder benefits, including residential treatment, such group health plan or health insurance issuer shall provide such benefits consistent with the requirements of section 2726 of the Public Health Service Act (42 U.S.C. 300gg–26), section 712 of the Employee Retirement Income Security Act of 1974 (29 U.S.C. 1185a), and section 9812 of the Internal Revenue Code of 1986.

TITLE XIV—MENTAL HEALTH AND SAFE COMMUNITIES

Subtitle A—Mental Health and Safe Communities

SEC. 14001. LAW ENFORCEMENT GRANTS FOR CRISIS INTERVENTION TEAMS, MENTAL HEALTH PURPOSES.

(a) EDWARD BYRNE MEMORIAL JUSTICE ASSISTANCE GRANT PROGRAM.—Section 501(a)(1) of title I of the Omnibus Crime Control and Safe Streets Act of 1968 (42 U.S.C. 3751(a)(1)) is amended by adding at the end the following:

"(H) Mental health programs and related law enforcement and corrections programs, including behavioral programs and crisis intervention teams.".

(b) COMMUNITY ORIENTED POLICING SERVICES PROGRAM.—Section 1701(b) of title I of the Omnibus Crime Control and Safe Streets Act of 1968 (42 U.S.C. 3796dd(b)) is amended—

(1) in paragraph (17), by striking "and" at the end;

(2) by redesignating paragraph (18) as paragraph (22);

(3) by inserting after paragraph (17) the following:

"(18) to provide specialized training to law enforcement officers to—

"(A) recognize individuals who have a mental illness; and

"(B) properly interact with individuals who have a mental illness, including strategies for verbal de-escalation of crises;

"(19) to establish collaborative programs that enhance the ability of law enforcement agencies to address the mental health, behavioral, and substance abuse problems of individuals encountered by law enforcement officers in the line of duty;

"(20) to provide specialized training to corrections officers to recognize individuals who have a mental illness;

"(21) to enhance the ability of corrections officers to address the mental health of individuals under the care and custody of jails and prisons, including specialized training and strategies for verbal de-escalation of crises; and"; and

(4) in paragraph (22), as redesignated, by striking "through (17)" and inserting "through (21)".

(c) MODIFICATIONS TO THE STAFFING FOR ADEQUATE FIRE AND EMERGENCY RESPONSE GRANTS.—Section 34(a)(1)(B) of the Federal Fire Prevention and Control Act of 1974 (15 U.S.C. 2229a(a)(1)(B)) is amended by inserting before the period at the end the following: "and to provide specialized training to paramedics, emergency medical services workers, and other first responders to recognize individuals who have mental illness and how to properly intervene with individuals with mental illness, including strategies for verbal de-escalation of crises".

SEC. 14002. ASSISTED OUTPATIENT TREATMENT PROGRAMS.

(a) IN GENERAL.—Section 2201 of title I of the Omnibus Crime Control and Safe Streets Act of 1968 (42 U.S.C. 3796ii) is amended in paragraph (2)(B), by inserting before the semicolon the following: ", or court-ordered assisted outpatient treatment when the court has determined such treatment to be necessary".

(b) DEFINITIONS.—Section 2202 of title I of the Omnibus Crime Control and Safe Streets Act of 1968 (42 U.S.C. 3796ii—1) is amended—

(1) in paragraph (1), by striking "and" at the end;

(2) in paragraph (2), by striking the period at the end and inserting a semicolon; and

(3) by adding at the end the following:

"(3) the term 'court-ordered assisted outpatient treatment' means a program through which a court may order a treatment plan for an eligible patient that—

"(A) requires such patient to obtain outpatient mental health treatment while the patient is not currently residing in a correctional facility or inpatient treatment facility; and

"(B) is designed to improve access and adherence by such patient to intensive behavioral health services in order to—

"(i) avert relapse, repeated hospitalizations, arrest, incarceration, suicide, property destruction, and violent behavior; and

"(ii) provide such patient with the opportunity to live in a less restrictive alternative to incarceration or involuntary hospitalization; and

"(4) the term 'eligible patient' means an adult, mentally ill person who, as determined by a court—

"(A) has a history of violence, incarceration, or medically unnecessary hospitalizations;

"(B) without supervision and treatment, may be a danger to self or others in the community;

"(C) is substantially unlikely to voluntarily participate in treatment;

"(D) may be unable, for reasons other than indigence, to provide for any of his or her basic needs, such as food, clothing, shelter, health, or safety;

"(E) has a history of mental illness or a condition that is likely to substantially deteriorate if the person is not provided with timely treatment; or

"(F) due to mental illness, lacks capacity to fully understand or lacks judgment to make informed decisions regarding his or her need for treatment, care, or supervision.".

SEC. 14003. FEDERAL DRUG AND MENTAL HEALTH COURTS.

(a) DEFINITIONS.—In this section—

(1) the term "eligible offender" means a person who—

(A)(i) previously or currently has been diagnosed by a qualified mental health professional as having a mental illness, mental retardation, or co-occurring mental illness and substance abuse disorders; or

(ii) manifests obvious signs of mental illness, mental retardation, or co-occurring mental illness and substance abuse disorders during arrest or confinement or before any court;

(B) comes into contact with the criminal justice system or is arrested or charged with an offense that is not—

(i) a crime of violence, as defined under applicable State law or in section 3156 of title 18, United States Code; or

(ii) a serious drug offense, as defined in section 924(e)(2)(A) of title 18, United States Code; and

(C) is determined by a judge to be eligible; and

(2) the term "mental illness" means a diagnosable mental, behavioral, or emotional disorder—

(A) of sufficient duration to meet diagnostic criteria within the most recent edition of the Diagnostic and Statistical Manual of Mental Disorders published by the American Psychiatric Association; and

(B) that has resulted in functional impairment that substantially interferes with or limits 1 or more major life activities.

(b) ESTABLISHMENT OF PROGRAM.—Not later than 1 year after the date of enactment of this Act, the Attorney General shall establish a pilot program to determine the effectiveness of diverting eligible offenders from Federal prosecution, Federal probation, or a Bureau of Prisons facility, and placing such eligible offenders in drug or mental health courts.

(c) PROGRAM SPECIFICATIONS.—The pilot program established under subsection (b) shall involve—

(1) continuing judicial supervision, including periodic review, of program participants who have a substance abuse problem or mental illness; and

(2) the integrated administration of services and sanctions, which shall include—

(A) mandatory periodic testing, as appropriate, for the use of controlled substances or other addictive substances during any period of supervised release or probation for each program participant;

(B) substance abuse treatment for each program participant who requires such services;

(C) diversion, probation, or other supervised release with the possibility of prosecution, confinement, or incarceration based on noncompliance with program requirements or failure to show satisfactory progress toward completing program requirements;

(D) programmatic offender management, including case management, and aftercare services, such as relapse prevention, health care, education, vocational training, job placement, housing placement, and child care or other family support services for each program participant who requires such services;

(E) outpatient or inpatient mental health treatment, as ordered by the court, that carries with it the possibility of dismissal of charges or reduced sentencing upon successful completion of such treatment;

(F) centralized case management, including—

(i) the consolidation of all cases, including violations of probations, of the program participant; and

(ii) coordination of all mental health treatment plans and social services, including life skills and vocational training, housing and job placement, education, health care, and relapse prevention for each program participant who requires such services; and

(G) continuing supervision of treatment plan compliance by the program participant for a term not to exceed the maximum allowable sentence or probation period for the charged or relevant offense and, to the extent practicable, continuity of psychiatric care at the end of the supervised period.

(d) IMPLEMENTATION; DURATION.—The pilot program established under subsection (b) shall be conducted—

(1) in not less than 1 United States judicial district, designated by the Attorney General in consultation with the Director of the Administrative Office of the United States Courts, as appropriate for the pilot program; and

(2) during fiscal year 2017 through fiscal year 2021.

(e) CRITERIA FOR DESIGNATION.—Before making a designation under subsection (d)(1), the Attorney General shall—

(1) obtain the approval, in writing, of the United States Attorney for the United States judicial district being designated;

(2) obtain the approval, in writing, of the chief judge for the United States judicial district being designated; and

(3) determine that the United States judicial district being designated has adequate behavioral health systems for treatment, including substance abuse and mental health treatment.

(f) ASSISTANCE FROM OTHER FEDERAL ENTITIES.—The Administrative Office of the United States Courts and the United States Probation Offices shall provide such assistance and carry out such functions as the Attorney General may request in monitoring, supervising, providing services to, and evaluating eligible offenders placed in a drug or mental health court under this section.

(g) REPORTS.—The Attorney General, in consultation with the Director of the Administrative Office of the United States Courts, shall monitor the drug and mental health courts under this section, and shall submit a report to Congress on the outcomes of the program at the end of the period described in subsection (d)(2).

SEC. 14004. MENTAL HEALTH IN THE JUDICIAL SYSTEM.

Part V of title I of the Omnibus Crime Control and Safe Streets Act of 1968 (42 U.S.C. 3796ii et seq.) is amended by inserting at the end the following:

"SEC. 2209. MENTAL HEALTH RESPONSES IN THE JUDICIAL SYSTEM.

"(a) PRETRIAL SCREENING AND SUPERVISION.—

"(1) IN GENERAL.—The Attorney General may award grants to States, units of local government, territories, Indian Tribes, nonprofit agencies, or any combination thereof, to develop, implement, or expand pretrial services programs to improve the identification and outcomes of individuals with mental illness.

"(2) ALLOWABLE USES.—Grants awarded under this subsection may be may be used for—

"(A) behavioral health needs and risk screening of defendants, including verification of interview information, mental health evaluation, and criminal history screening;

"(B) assessment of risk of pretrial misconduct through objective, statistically validated means, and presentation to the court of recommendations based on such assessment, including services that will reduce the risk of pre-trial misconduct;

"(C) followup review of defendants unable to meet the conditions of pretrial release;

"(D) evaluation of process and results of pretrial service programs;

"(E) supervision of defendants who are on pretrial release, including reminders to defendants of scheduled court dates;

"(F) reporting on process and results of pretrial services programs to relevant public and private mental health stakeholders; and

"(G) data collection and analysis necessary to make available information required for assessment of risk.

"(b) BEHAVIORAL HEALTH ASSESSMENTS AND INTERVENTION.—

"(1) IN GENERAL.—The Attorney General may award grants to States, units of local government, territories, Indian Tribes, nonprofit agencies, or any combination thereof, to develop, implement, or expand a behavioral health screening and assessment program framework for State or local criminal justice systems.

"(2) ALLOWABLE USES.—Grants awarded under this subsection may be used for—

"(A) promotion of the use of validated assessment tools to gauge the criminogenic risk, substance abuse needs, and mental health needs of individuals;

"(B) initiatives to match the risk factors and needs of individuals to programs and practices associated with research-based, positive outcomes;

"(C) implementing methods for identifying and treating individuals who are most likely to benefit from coordinated supervision and treatment strategies, and identifying individuals who can do well with fewer interventions; and

"(D) collaborative decision-making among the heads of criminal justice agencies, mental health systems, judicial systems, substance abuse systems, and other relevant systems or agencies for determining how treatment and intensive supervision services should be allocated in order to maximize benefits, and developing and utilizing capacity accordingly.

"(c) USE OF GRANT FUNDS.—A State, unit of local government, territory, Indian Tribe, or nonprofit agency that receives a grant under this section shall, in accordance with subsection (b)(2), use grant funds for the expenses of a treatment program, including—

"(1) salaries, personnel costs, equipment costs, and other costs directly related to the operation of the program, including costs relating to enforcement;

"(2) payments for treatment providers that are approved by the State or Indian Tribe and licensed, if necessary, to provide needed treatment to program participants, including aftercare supervision, vocational training, education, and job placement; and

"(3) payments to public and nonprofit private entities that are approved by the State or Indian Tribe and licensed, if necessary, to provide alcohol and drug addiction treatment to offenders participating in the program.

"(d) SUPPLEMENT OF NON-FEDERAL FUNDS.—

"(1) IN GENERAL.—Grants awarded under this section shall be used to supplement, and not supplant, non-Federal funds that would otherwise be available for programs described in this section.

"(2) FEDERAL SHARE.—The Federal share of a grant made under this section may not exceed 50 percent of the total costs of the program described in an application under subsection (e).

"(e) APPLICATIONS.—To request a grant under this section, a State, unit of local government, territory, Indian Tribe, or nonprofit agency shall submit an application to the Attorney General in such form and containing such information as the Attorney General may reasonably require.

"(f) GEOGRAPHIC DISTRIBUTION.—The Attorney General shall ensure that, to the extent practicable, the distribution of grants under this section is equitable and includes—

"(1) each State; and

"(2) a unit of local government, territory, Indian Tribe, or nonprofit agency—

"(A) in each State; and

"(B) in rural, suburban, Tribal, and urban jurisdictions.

"(g) REPORTS AND EVALUATIONS.—For each fiscal year, each grantee under this section during that fiscal year shall submit to the Attorney General a report on the effectiveness of activities carried out using such grant. Each report shall include an evaluation in such form and containing such information as the Attorney General may reasonably require. The Attorney General shall specify the dates on which such reports shall be submitted.

"(h) ACCOUNTABILITY.—Grants awarded under this section shall be subject to the following accountability provisions:

"(1) AUDIT REQUIREMENT.—

"(A) DEFINITION.—In this paragraph, the term 'unresolved audit finding' means a finding in the final audit report of the Inspector General of the Department of Justice under subparagraph (C) that the audited grantee has used grant funds for an unauthorized expenditure or otherwise unallowable cost that is not

closed or resolved within 1 year after the date on which final audit report is issued.

"(B) AUDITS.—Beginning in the first fiscal year beginning after the date of enactment of this section, and in each fiscal year thereafter, the Inspector General of the Department of Justice shall conduct audits of grantees under this section to prevent waste, fraud, and abuse of funds by grantees. The Inspector General shall determine the appropriate number of grantees to be audited each year.

"(C) FINAL AUDIT REPORT.—The Inspector General of the Department of Justice shall submit to the Attorney General a final report on each audit conducted under subparagraph (B).

"(D) MANDATORY EXCLUSION.—Grantees under this section about which there is an unresolved audit finding shall not be eligible to receive a grant under this section during the 2 fiscal years beginning after the end of the 1-year period described in subparagraph (A).

"(E) PRIORITY.—In making grants under this section, the Attorney General shall give priority to applicants that did not have an unresolved audit finding during the 3 fiscal years before submitting an application for a grant under this section.

"(F) REIMBURSEMENT.—If an entity receives a grant under this section during the 2-fiscal-year period during which the entity is prohibited from receiving grants under subparagraph (D), the Attorney General shall—

"(i) deposit an amount equal to the amount of the grant that was improperly awarded to the grantee into the General Fund of the Treasury; and

"(ii) seek to recoup the costs of the repayment under clause (i) from the grantee that was erroneously awarded grant funds.

"(2) NONPROFIT AGENCY REQUIREMENTS.—

"(A) DEFINITION.—For purposes of this paragraph and the grant program under this section, the term 'nonprofit agency' means an organization that is described in section 501(c)(3) of the Internal Revenue Code of 1986 (26 U.S.C. 501(c)(3)) and is exempt from taxation under section 501(a) of the Internal Revenue Code of 1986 (26 U.S.C. 501(a)).

"(B) PROHIBITION.—The Attorney General may not award a grant under this section to a nonprofit agency that holds money in an offshore account for the purpose of avoiding paying the tax described in section 511(a) of the Internal Revenue Code of 1986 (26 U.S.C. 511(a)).

"(C) DISCLOSURE.—Each nonprofit agency that is awarded a grant under this section and uses the procedures prescribed in regulations to create a rebuttable presumption of reasonableness for the compensation of its officers, directors, trustees, and key employees, shall disclose to the Attorney General, in the application for the grant, the process for determining such compensation, including the independent persons involved in reviewing and approving such compensation, the comparability data used, and contemporaneous substantiation of the deliberation and decision. Upon request, the Attorney General shall make the information disclosed under this subparagraph available for public inspection.

"(3) CONFERENCE EXPENDITURES.—

"(A) LIMITATION.—Not more than $20,000 of the amounts made available to the Department of Justice to carry out this section may be used by the Attorney General, or by any individual or entity awarded a grant under this section to host, or make any expenditures relating to, a conference unless the Deputy Attorney General provides prior written authorization that the funds may be expended to host the conference or make such expenditure.

"(B) WRITTEN APPROVAL.—Written approval under subparagraph (A) shall include a written

estimate of all costs associated with the conference, including the cost of all food, beverages, audio-visual equipment, honoraria for speakers, and entertainment.

"(C) REPORT.—The Deputy Attorney General shall submit an annual report to the Committee on the Judiciary of the Senate and the Committee on the Judiciary of the House of Representatives on all conference expenditures approved under this paragraph.

"(4) ANNUAL CERTIFICATION.—Beginning in the first fiscal year beginning after the date of enactment of this subsection, the Attorney General shall submit to the Committee on the Judiciary and the Committee on Appropriations of the Senate and the Committee on the Judiciary and the Committee on Appropriations of the House of Representatives an annual certification—

"(A) indicating whether—

"(i) all final audit reports issued by the Office of the Inspector General under paragraph (1) have been completed and reviewed by the appropriate Assistant Attorney General or Director;

"(ii) all mandatory exclusions required under paragraph (1)(D) have been issued; and

"(iii) any reimbursements required under paragraph (1)(F) have been made; and

"(B) that includes a list of any grantees excluded under paragraph (1)(D) from the previous year.

"(i) PREVENTING DUPLICATIVE GRANTS.—

"(1) IN GENERAL.—Before the Attorney General awards a grant to an applicant under this section, the Attorney General shall compare the possible grant with any other grants awarded to the applicant under this Act to determine whether the grants are for the same purpose.

"(2) REPORT.—If the Attorney General awards multiple grants to the same applicant for the same purpose, the Attorney General shall submit to the Committee on the Judiciary of the Senate and the Committee on the Judiciary of the House of Representatives a report that includes—

"(A) a list of all duplicate grants awarded, including the total dollar amount of any such grants awarded; and

"(B) the reason the Attorney General awarded the duplicate grants.".

SEC. 14005. FORENSIC ASSERTIVE COMMUNITY TREATMENT INITIATIVES.

Section 2991 of the Omnibus Crime Control and Safe Streets Act of 1968 (42 U.S.C. 3797aa) is amended by—

(1) redesignating subsection (j) as subsection (o); and

(2) inserting after subsection (i) the following:

"(j) FORENSIC ASSERTIVE COMMUNITY TREATMENT (FACT) INITIATIVE PROGRAM.—

"(1) IN GENERAL.—The Attorney General may make grants to States, units of local government, territories, Indian Tribes, nonprofit agencies, or any combination thereof, to develop, implement, or expand Assertive Community Treatment initiatives to develop forensic assertive community treatment (referred to in this subsection as 'FACT') programs that provide high intensity services in the community for individuals with mental illness with involvement in the criminal justice system to prevent future incarcerations.

"(2) ALLOWABLE USES.—Grant funds awarded under this subsection may be used for—

"(A) multidisciplinary team initiatives for individuals with mental illnesses with criminal justice involvement that address criminal justice involvement as part of treatment protocols;

"(B) FACT programs that involve mental health professionals, criminal justice agencies, chemical dependency specialists, nurses, psychiatrists, vocational specialists, forensic peer specialists, forensic specialists, and dedicated administrative support staff who work together to provide recovery oriented, 24/7 wraparound services;

"(C) services such as integrated evidence-based practices for the treatment of co-occurring mental health and substance-related disorders, assertive outreach and engagement, community-based service provision at participants' residence or in the community, psychiatric rehabilitation, recovery oriented services, services to address criminogenic risk factors, and community tenure;

"(D) payments for treatment providers that are approved by the State or Indian Tribe and licensed, if necessary, to provide needed treatment to eligible offenders participating in the program, including behavioral health services and aftercare supervision; and

"(E) training for all FACT teams to promote high-fidelity practice principles and technical assistance to support effective and continuing integration with criminal justice agency partners.

"(3) SUPPLEMENT AND NOT SUPPLANT.—Grants made under this subsection shall be used to supplement, and not supplant, non-Federal funds that would otherwise be available for programs described in this subsection.

"(4) APPLICATIONS.—To request a grant under this subsection, a State, unit of local government, territory, Indian Tribe, or nonprofit agency shall submit an application to the Attorney General in such form and containing such information as the Attorney General may reasonably require.".

SEC. 14006. ASSISTANCE FOR INDIVIDUALS TRANSITIONING OUT OF SYSTEMS.

Section 2976(f) of title I of the Omnibus Crime Control and Safe Streets Act of 1968 (42 U.S.C. 3797w(f)) is amended—

(1) in paragraph (5), by striking "and" at the end;

(2) in paragraph (6), by striking the period at the end and inserting a semicolon; and

(3) by adding at the end the following:

"(7) provide mental health treatment and transitional services for those with mental illnesses or with co-occurring disorders, including housing placement or assistance; and".

SEC. 14007. CO-OCCURRING SUBSTANCE ABUSE AND MENTAL HEALTH CHALLENGES IN DRUG COURTS.

Part EE of title I of the Omnibus Crime Control and Safe Streets Act of 1968 (42 U.S.C. 3797u et seq.) is amended—

(1) in section 2951(a)(1) (42 U.S.C. 3797u(a)(1)), by inserting ", including co-occurring substance abuse and mental health problems," after "problems"; and

(2) in section 2959(a) (42 U.S.C. 3797u–8(a)), by inserting ", including training for drug court personnel and officials on identifying and addressing co-occurring substance abuse and mental health problems" after "part".

SEC. 14008. MENTAL HEALTH TRAINING FOR FEDERAL UNIFORMED SERVICES.

(a) IN GENERAL.—Not later than 180 days after the date of enactment of this Act, the Secretary of Defense, the Secretary of Homeland Security, the Secretary of Health and Human Services, and the Secretary of Commerce shall provide the following to each of the uniformed services (as that term is defined in section 101 of title 10, United States Code) under their direction:

(1) TRAINING PROGRAMS.—Programs that offer specialized and comprehensive training in procedures to identify and respond appropriately to incidents in which the unique needs of individuals with mental illnesses are involved.

(2) IMPROVED TECHNOLOGY.—Computerized information systems or technological improvements to provide timely information to Federal law enforcement personnel, other branches of the uniformed services, and criminal justice system personnel to improve the Federal response to mentally ill individuals.

(3) COOPERATIVE PROGRAMS.—The establishment and expansion of cooperative efforts to promote public safety through the use of effective intervention with respect to mentally ill individuals encountered by members of the uniformed services.

SEC. 14009. ADVANCING MENTAL HEALTH AS PART OF OFFENDER REENTRY.

(a) REENTRY DEMONSTRATION PROJECTS.—Section 2976(f) of title I of the Omnibus Crime Control and Safe Streets Act of 1968 (42 U.S.C. 3797w(f)), as amended by section 14006, is amended—

(1) in paragraph (3)(C), by inserting "mental health services," before "drug treatment"; and

(2) by adding at the end the following:

"(8) target offenders with histories of homelessness, substance abuse, or mental illness, including a prerelease assessment of the housing status of the offender and behavioral health needs of the offender with clear coordination with mental health, substance abuse, and homelessness services systems to achieve stable and permanent housing outcomes with appropriate support service.".

(b) MENTORING GRANTS.—Section 211(b)(2) of the Second Chance Act of 2007 (42 U.S.C. 17531(b)(2)) is amended by inserting ", including mental health care" after "community".

SEC. 14010. SCHOOL MENTAL HEALTH CRISIS INTERVENTION TEAMS.

Section 2701(b) of title I of the Omnibus Crime Control and Safe Streets Act of 1968 (42 U.S.C. 3797a(b)) is amended—

(1) by redesignating paragraphs (4) and (5) as paragraphs (5) and (6), respectively; and

(2) by inserting after paragraph (3) the following:

"(4) The development and operation of crisis intervention teams that may include coordination with law enforcement agencies and specialized training for school officials in responding to mental health crises.".

SEC. 14011. ACTIVE-SHOOTER TRAINING FOR LAW ENFORCEMENT.

The Attorney General, as part of the Preventing Violence Against Law Enforcement and Ensuring Officer Resilience and Survivability Initiative (VALOR) of the Department of Justice, may provide safety training and technical assistance to local law enforcement agencies, including active-shooter response training.

SEC. 14012. CO-OCCURRING SUBSTANCE ABUSE AND MENTAL HEALTH CHALLENGES IN RESIDENTIAL SUBSTANCE ABUSE TREATMENT PROGRAMS.

Section 1901(a) of title I of the Omnibus Crime Control and Safe Streets Act of 1968 (42 U.S.C. 3796ff(a)) is amended—

(1) in paragraph (1), by striking "and" at the end;

(2) in paragraph (2), by striking the period at the end and inserting "; and"; and

(3) by adding at the end the following:

"(3) developing and implementing specialized residential substance abuse treatment programs that identify and provide appropriate treatment to inmates with co-occurring mental health and substance abuse disorders or challenges.".

SEC. 14013. MENTAL HEALTH AND DRUG TREATMENT ALTERNATIVES TO INCARCERATION PROGRAMS.

Title I of the Omnibus Crime Control and Safe Streets Act of 1968 (42 U.S.C. 3711 et seq.) is amended by striking part CC and inserting the following:

"PART CC—MENTAL HEALTH AND DRUG TREATMENT ALTERNATIVES TO INCARCERATION PROGRAMS

"SEC. 2901. MENTAL HEALTH AND DRUG TREATMENT ALTERNATIVES TO INCARCERATION PROGRAMS.

"(a) DEFINITIONS.—In this section—

"(1) the term 'eligible entity' means a State, unit of local government, Indian tribe, or nonprofit organization; and

''(2) the term 'eligible participant' means an individual who—

''(A) comes into contact with the criminal justice system or is arrested or charged with an offense that is not—

''(i) a crime of violence, as defined under applicable State law or in section 3156 of title 18, United States Code; or

''(ii) a serious drug offense, as defined in section 924(e)(2)(A) of title 18, United States Code;

''(B) has a history of, or a current—

''(i) substance use disorder;

''(ii) mental illness; or

''(iii) co-occurring mental illness and substance use disorder; and

''(C) has been approved for participation in a program funded under this section by the relevant law enforcement agency, prosecuting attorney, defense attorney, probation official, corrections official, judge, representative of a mental health agency, or representative of a substance abuse agency, as required by law.

''(b) PROGRAM AUTHORIZED.—The Attorney General may make grants to eligible entities to develop, implement, or expand a treatment alternative to incarceration program for eligible participants, including—

''(1) pre-booking treatment alternative to incarceration programs, including—

''(A) law enforcement training on substance use disorders, mental illness, and co-occurring mental illness and substance use disorders;

''(B) receiving centers as alternatives to incarceration of eligible participants;

''(C) specialized response units for calls related to substance use disorders, mental illness, or co-occurring mental illness and substance use disorders; and

''(D) other arrest and pre-booking treatment alternatives to incarceration models; or

''(2) post-booking treatment alternative to incarceration programs, including—

''(A) specialized clinical case management;

''(B) pre-trial services related to substances use disorders, mental illness, and co-occurring mental illness and substance use disorders;

''(C) prosecutor and defender based programs;

''(D) specialized probation;

''(E) treatment and rehabilitation programs; and

''(F) problem-solving courts, including mental health courts, drug courts, co-occurring mental health and substance abuse courts, DWI courts, and veterans treatment courts.

''(c) APPLICATION.—

''(1) IN GENERAL.—An eligible entity desiring a grant under this section shall submit an application to the Attorney General—

''(A) that meets the criteria under paragraph (2); and

''(B) at such time, in such manner, and accompanied by such information as the Attorney General may require.

''(2) CRITERIA.—An eligible entity, in submitting an application under paragraph (1), shall—

''(A) provide extensive evidence of collaboration with State and local government agencies overseeing health, community corrections, courts, prosecution, substance abuse, mental health, victims services, and employment services, and with local law enforcement agencies;

''(B) demonstrate consultation with the Single State Authority for Substance Abuse of the State (as that term is defined in section 201(e) of the Second Chance Act of 2007);

''(C) demonstrate that evidence-based treatment practices will be utilized; and

''(D) demonstrate that evidence-based screening and assessment tools will be used to place participants in the treatment alternative to incarceration program.

''(d) REQUIREMENTS.—Each eligible entity awarded a grant for a treatment alternative to incarceration program under this section shall—

''(1) determine the terms and conditions of participation in the program by eligible participants, taking into consideration the collateral consequences of an arrest, prosecution or criminal conviction;

''(2) ensure that each substance abuse and mental health treatment component is licensed and qualified by the relevant jurisdiction;

''(3) for programs described in subsection (b)(2), organize an enforcement unit comprised of appropriately trained law enforcement professionals under the supervision of the State, Tribal, or local criminal justice agency involved, the duties of which shall include—

''(A) the verification of addresses and other contact information of each eligible participant who participates or desires to participate in the program; and

''(B) if necessary, the location, apprehension, arrest, and return to custody of an eligible participant in the program who has absconded from the facility of a treatment provider or has otherwise significantly violated the terms and conditions of the program, consistent with Federal and State confidentiality requirements;

''(4) notify the relevant criminal justice entity if any eligible participant in the program absconds from the facility of the treatment provider or otherwise violates the terms and conditions of the program, consistent with Federal and State confidentiality requirements;

''(5) submit periodic reports on the progress of treatment or other measured outcomes from participation in the program of each eligible participant in the program to the relevant State, Tribal, or local criminal justice agency, including mental health courts, drug courts, co-occurring mental health and substance abuse courts, DWI courts, and veterans treatment courts;

''(6) describe the evidence-based methodology and outcome measurements that will be used to evaluate the program, and specifically explain how such measurements will provide valid measures of the impact of the program; and

''(7) describe how the program could be broadly replicated if demonstrated to be effective.

''(e) USE OF FUNDS.—An eligible entity shall use a grant received under this section for expenses of a treatment alternative to incarceration program, including—

''(1) salaries, personnel costs, equipment costs, and other costs directly related to the operation of the program, including the enforcement unit;

''(2) payments for treatment providers that are approved by the relevant State or Tribal jurisdiction and licensed, if necessary, to provide needed treatment to eligible offenders participating in the program, including aftercare supervision, vocational training, education, and job placement; and

''(3) payments to public and nonprofit private entities that are approved by the State or Tribal jurisdiction and licensed, if necessary, to provide alcohol and drug addiction treatment to eligible offenders participating in the program.

''(f) SUPPLEMENT NOT SUPPLANT.—An eligible entity shall use Federal funds received under this section only to supplement the funds that would, in the absence of those Federal funds, be made available from other Federal and non-Federal sources for the activities described in this section, and not to supplant those funds. The Federal share of a grant made under this section may not exceed 50 percent of the total costs of the program described in an application under subsection (d).

''(g) GEOGRAPHIC DISTRIBUTION.—The Attorney General shall ensure that, to the extent practicable, the geographical distribution of grants under this section is equitable and includes a grant to an eligible entity in—

''(1) each State;

''(2) rural, suburban, and urban areas; and

''(3) Tribal jurisdictions.

''(h) REPORTS AND EVALUATIONS.—Each fiscal year, each recipient of a grant under this section during that fiscal year shall submit to the Attorney General a report on the outcomes of activities carried out using that grant in such form, containing such information, and on such dates as the Attorney General shall specify.

''(i) ACCOUNTABILITY.—All grants awarded by the Attorney General under this section shall be subject to the following accountability provisions:

''(1) AUDIT REQUIREMENT.—

''(A) DEFINITION.—In this paragraph, the term 'unresolved audit finding' means a finding in the final audit report of the Inspector General of the Department of Justice that the audited grantee has utilized grant funds for an unauthorized expenditure or otherwise unallowable cost that is not closed or resolved within 12 months from the date on which the final audit report is issued.

''(B) AUDITS.—Beginning in the first fiscal year beginning after the date of enactment of this subsection, and in each fiscal year thereafter, the Inspector General of the Department of Justice shall conduct audits of recipients of grants under this section to prevent waste, fraud, and abuse of funds by grantees. The Inspector General shall determine the appropriate number of grantees to be audited each year.

''(C) MANDATORY EXCLUSION.—A recipient of grant funds under this section that is found to have an unresolved audit finding shall not be eligible to receive grant funds under this section during the first 2 fiscal years beginning after the end of the 12-month period described in subparagraph (A).

''(D) PRIORITY.—In awarding grants under this section, the Attorney General shall give priority to eligible applicants that did not have an unresolved audit finding during the 3 fiscal years before submitting an application for a grant under this section.

''(E) REIMBURSEMENT.—If an entity is awarded grant funds under this section during the 2-fiscal-year period during which the entity is barred from receiving grants under subparagraph (C), the Attorney General shall—

''(i) deposit an amount equal to the amount of the grant funds that were improperly awarded to the grantee into the General Fund of the Treasury; and

''(ii) seek to recoup the costs of the repayment to the fund from the grant recipient that was erroneously awarded grant funds.

''(2) NONPROFIT ORGANIZATION REQUIREMENTS.—

''(A) DEFINITION.—For purposes of this paragraph and the grant programs under this part, the term 'nonprofit organization' means an organization that is described in section 501(c)(3) of the Internal Revenue Code of 1986 and is exempt from taxation under section 501(a) of such Code.

''(B) PROHIBITION.—The Attorney General may not award a grant under this part to a nonprofit organization that holds money in offshore accounts for the purpose of avoiding paying the tax described in section 511(a) of the Internal Revenue Code of 1986.

''(C) DISCLOSURE.—Each nonprofit organization that is awarded a grant under this section and uses the procedures prescribed in regulations to create a rebuttable presumption of reasonableness for the compensation of its officers, directors, trustees, and key employees, shall disclose to the Attorney General, in the application for the grant, the process for determining such compensation, including the independent persons involved in reviewing and approving such compensation, the comparability data used, and contemporaneous substantiation of the deliberation and decision. Upon request, the Attorney General shall make the information disclosed under this subparagraph available for public inspection.

"*(3) CONFERENCE EXPENDITURES.—*

"*(A) LIMITATION.—No amounts made available to the Department of Justice under this section may be used by the Attorney General, or by any individual or entity awarded discretionary funds through a cooperative agreement under this section, to host or support any expenditure for conferences that uses more than $20,000 in funds made available by the Department of Justice, unless the head of the relevant agency or department, provides prior written authorization that the funds may be expended to host the conference.*

"*(B) WRITTEN APPROVAL.—Written approval under subparagraph (A) shall include a written estimate of all costs associated with the conference, including the cost of all food, beverages, audio-visual equipment, honoraria for speakers, and entertainment.*

"*(C) REPORT.—The Deputy Attorney General shall submit an annual report to the Committee on the Judiciary of the Senate and the Committee on the Judiciary of the House of Representatives on all conference expenditures approved under this paragraph.*

"*(4) ANNUAL CERTIFICATION.—Beginning in the first fiscal year beginning after the date of enactment of this subsection, the Attorney General shall submit, to the Committee on the Judiciary and the Committee on Appropriations of the Senate and the Committee on the Judiciary and the Committee on Appropriations of the House of Representatives, an annual certification—*

"*(A) indicating whether—*

"*(i) all audits issued by the Office of the Inspector General under paragraph (1) have been completed and reviewed by the appropriate Assistant Attorney General or Director;*

"*(ii) all mandatory exclusions required under paragraph (1)(C) have been issued; and*

"*(iii) all reimbursements required under paragraph (1)(E) have been made; and*

"*(B) that includes a list of any grant recipients excluded under paragraph (1) from the previous year.*

"*(5) PREVENTING DUPLICATIVE GRANTS.—*

"*(A) IN GENERAL.—Before the Attorney General awards a grant to an applicant under this section, the Attorney General shall compare potential grant awards with other grants awarded under this Act to determine if duplicate grant awards are awarded for the same purpose.*

"*(B) REPORT.—If the Attorney General awards duplicate grants to the same applicant for the same purpose the Attorney General shall submit to the Committee on the Judiciary of the Senate and the Committee on the Judiciary of the House of Representatives a report that includes—*

"*(i) a list of all duplicate grants awarded, including the total dollar amount of any duplicate grants awarded; and*

"*(ii) the reason the Attorney General awarded the duplicate grants.*".

SEC. 14014. NATIONAL CRIMINAL JUSTICE AND MENTAL HEALTH TRAINING AND TECHNICAL ASSISTANCE.

Part HH of title I of the Omnibus Crime Control and Safe Streets Act of 1968 (42 U.S.C. 3797aa et seq.) is amended by adding at the end the following:

"**SEC. 2992. NATIONAL CRIMINAL JUSTICE AND MENTAL HEALTH TRAINING AND TECHNICAL ASSISTANCE.**

"*(a) AUTHORITY.—The Attorney General may make grants to eligible organizations to provide for the establishment of a National Criminal Justice and Mental Health Training and Technical Assistance Center.*

"*(b) ELIGIBLE ORGANIZATION.—For purposes of subsection (a), the term 'eligible organization'* means a national nonprofit organization that provides technical assistance and training to, and has special expertise and broad, national-level experience in, mental health, crisis intervention, criminal justice systems, law enforcement, translating evidence into practice, training, and research, and education and support of people with mental illness and the families of such individuals.

"*(c) USE OF FUNDS.—Any organization that receives a grant under subsection (a) shall collaborate with other grant recipients to establish and operate a National Criminal Justice and Mental Health Training and Technical Assistance Center to—*

"*(1) provide law enforcement officer training regarding mental health and working with individuals with mental illnesses, with an emphasis on de-escalation of encounters between law enforcement officers and those with mental disorders or in crisis, which shall include support the development of in-person and technical information exchanges between systems and the individuals working in those systems in support of the concepts identified in the training;*

"*(2) provide education, training, and technical assistance for States, Indian tribes, territories, units of local government, service providers, nonprofit organizations, probation or parole officers, prosecutors, defense attorneys, emergency response providers, and corrections institutions to advance practice and knowledge relating to mental health crisis and approaches to mental health and criminal justice across systems;*

"*(3) provide training and best practices to mental health providers and criminal justice agencies relating to diversion initiatives, jail and prison strategies, reentry of individuals with mental illnesses into the community, and dispatch protocols and triage capabilities, including the establishment of learning sites;*

"*(4) develop suicide prevention and crisis intervention training and technical assistance for criminal justice agencies;*

"*(5) develop a receiving center system and pilot strategy that provides, for a jurisdiction, a single point of entry into the mental health and substance abuse system for assessments and appropriate placement of individuals experiencing a crisis;*

"*(6) collect data and best practices in mental health and criminal health and criminal justice initiatives and policies from grantees under this part, other recipients of grants under this section, Federal, State, and local agencies involved in the provision of mental health services, and nongovernmental organizations involved in the provision of mental health services;*

"*(7) develop and disseminate to mental health providers and criminal justice agencies evaluation tools, mechanisms, and measures to better assess and document performance measures and outcomes relating to the provision of mental health services;*

"*(8) disseminate information to States, units of local government, criminal justice agencies, law enforcement agencies, and other relevant entities about best practices, policy standards, and research findings relating to the provision of mental health services; and*

"*(9) provide education and support to individuals with mental illness involved with, or at risk of involvement with, the criminal justice system, including the families of such individuals.*

"*(d) ACCOUNTABILITY.—Grants awarded under this section shall be subject to the following accountability provisions:*

"*(1) AUDIT REQUIREMENT.—*

"*(A) DEFINITION.—In this paragraph, the term 'unresolved audit finding' means a finding in the final audit report of the Inspector General of the Department of Justice under subparagraph (C) that the audited grantee has* used grant funds for an unauthorized expenditure or otherwise unallowable cost that is not closed or resolved within 1 year after the date on which the final audit report is issued.

"*(B) AUDITS.—Beginning in the first fiscal year beginning after the date of enactment of this section, and in each fiscal year thereafter, the Inspector General of the Department of Justice shall conduct audits of grantees under this section to prevent waste, fraud, and abuse of funds by grantees. The Inspector General shall determine the appropriate number of grantees to be audited each year.*

"*(C) FINAL AUDIT REPORT.—The Inspector General of the Department of Justice shall submit to the Attorney General a final report on each audit conducted under subparagraph (B).*

"*(D) MANDATORY EXCLUSION.—Grantees under this section about which there is an unresolved audit finding shall not be eligible to receive a grant under this section during the 2 fiscal years beginning after the end of the 1-year period described in subparagraph (A).*

"*(E) PRIORITY.—In making grants under this section, the Attorney General shall give priority to applicants that did not have an unresolved audit finding during the 3 fiscal years before submitting an application for a grant under this section.*

"*(F) REIMBURSEMENT.—If an entity receives a grant under this section during the 2-fiscal-year period during which the entity is prohibited from receiving grants under subparagraph (D), the Attorney General shall—*

"*(i) deposit an amount equal to the amount of the grant that was improperly awarded to the grantee into the General Fund of the Treasury; and*

"*(ii) seek to recoup the costs of the repayment under clause (i) from the grantee that was erroneously awarded grant funds.*

"*(2) NONPROFIT AGENCY REQUIREMENTS.—*

"*(A) DEFINITION.—For purposes of this paragraph and the grant program under this section, the term 'nonprofit agency' means an organization that is described in section 501(c)(3) of the Internal Revenue Code of 1986 (26 U.S.C. 501(c)(3)) and is exempt from taxation under section 501(a) of the Internal Revenue Code of 1986 (26 U.S.C. 501(a)).*

"*(B) PROHIBITION.—The Attorney General may not award a grant under this section to a nonprofit agency that holds money in an off-shore account for the purpose of avoiding paying the tax described in section 511(a) of the Internal Revenue Code of 1986 (26 U.S.C. 511(a)).*

"*(C) DISCLOSURE.—Each nonprofit agency that is awarded a grant under this section and uses the procedures prescribed in regulations to create a rebuttable presumption of reasonableness for the compensation of its officers, directors, trustees, and key employees, shall disclose to the Attorney General, in the application for the grant, the process for determining such compensation, including the independent persons involved in reviewing and approving such compensation, the comparability data used, and contemporaneous substantiation of the deliberation and decision. Upon request, the Attorney General shall make the information disclosed under this subparagraph available for public inspection.*

"*(3) CONFERENCE EXPENDITURES.—*

"*(A) LIMITATION.—No amounts made available to the Department of Justice under this section may be used by the Attorney General, or by any individual or entity awarded discretionary funds through a cooperative agreement under this section, to host or support any expenditure for conferences that uses more than $20,000 in funds made available by the Department of Justice, unless the head of the relevant agency or department, provides prior written authorization that the funds may be expended to host the conference.*

"(B) WRITTEN APPROVAL.—Written approval under subparagraph (A) shall include a written estimate of all costs associated with the conference, including the cost of all food, beverages, audio-visual equipment, honoraria for speakers, and entertainment.

"(C) REPORT.—The Deputy Attorney General shall submit an annual report to the Committee on the Judiciary of the Senate and the Committee on the Judiciary of the House of Representatives on all conference expenditures approved under this paragraph.

"(4) ANNUAL CERTIFICATION.—Beginning in the first fiscal year beginning after the date of enactment of this subsection, the Attorney General shall submit to the Committee on the Judiciary and the Committee on Appropriations of the Senate and the Committee on the Judiciary and the Committee on Appropriations of the House of Representatives an annual certification—

"(A) indicating whether—

"(i) all final audit reports issued by the Office of the Inspector General under paragraph (1) have been completed and reviewed by the appropriate Assistant Attorney General or Director;

"(ii) all mandatory exclusions required under paragraph (1)(D) have been issued; and

"(iii) any reimbursements required under paragraph (1)(F) have been made; and

"(B) that includes a list of any grantees excluded under paragraph (1)(D) from the previous year.

"(5) PREVENTING DUPLICATIVE GRANTS.—

"(A) IN GENERAL.—Before the Attorney General awards a grant to an applicant under this section, the Attorney General shall compare potential grant awards with other grants awarded under this Act to determine if duplicate grant awards are awarded for the same purpose.

"(B) REPORT.—If the Attorney General awards duplicate grants to the same applicant for the same purpose the Attorney General shall submit to the Committee on the Judiciary of the Senate and the Committee on the Judiciary of the House of Representatives a report that includes—

"(i) a list of all duplicate grants awarded, including the total dollar amount of any duplicate grants awarded; and

"(ii) the reason the Attorney General awarded the duplicate grants.".

SEC. 14015. IMPROVING DEPARTMENT OF JUSTICE DATA COLLECTION ON MENTAL ILLNESS INVOLVED IN CRIME.

(a) IN GENERAL.—Notwithstanding any other provision of law, on or after the date that is 90 days after the date on which the Attorney General promulgates regulations under subsection (b), any data prepared by, or submitted to, the Attorney General or the Director of the Federal Bureau of Investigation with respect to the incidences of homicides, law enforcement officers killed, seriously injured, and assaulted, or individuals killed or seriously injured by law enforcement officers shall include data with respect to the involvement of mental illness in such incidences, if any.

(b) REGULATIONS.—Not later than 90 days after the date of the enactment of this Act, the Attorney General shall promulgate or revise regulations as necessary to carry out subsection (a).

SEC. 14016. REPORTS ON THE NUMBER OF MENTALLY ILL OFFENDERS IN PRISON.

(a) REPORT ON THE COST OF TREATING THE MENTALLY ILL IN THE CRIMINAL JUSTICE SYSTEM.—Not later than 12 months after the date of enactment of this Act, the Comptroller General of the United States shall submit to Congress a report detailing the cost of imprisonment for individuals who have serious mental illness by the Federal Government or a State or unit of local government, which shall include—

(1) the number and type of crimes committed by individuals with serious mental illness each year; and

(2) detail strategies or ideas for preventing crimes by those individuals with serious mental illness from occurring.

(b) DEFINITION.—For purposes of this section, the Attorney General, in consultation with the Assistant Secretary of Mental Health and Substance Use Disorders, shall define "serious mental illness" based on the "Health Care Reform for Americans with Severe Mental Illnesses: Report" of the National Advisory Mental Health Council, American Journal of Psychiatry 1993; 150:1447–1465.

SEC. 14017. CODIFICATION OF DUE PROCESS FOR DETERMINATIONS BY SECRETARY OF VETERANS AFFAIRS OF MENTAL CAPACITY OF BENEFICIARIES.

(a) IN GENERAL.—Chapter 55 of title 38, United States Code, is amended by inserting after section 5501 the following new section:

"§ 5501A. Beneficiaries' rights in mental competence determinations

"The Secretary may not make an adverse determination concerning the mental capacity of a beneficiary to manage monetary benefits paid to or for the beneficiary by the Secretary under this title unless such beneficiary has been provided all of the following, subject to the procedures and timelines prescribed by the Secretary for determinations of incompetency:

"(1) Notice of the proposed adverse determination and the supporting evidence.

"(2) An opportunity to request a hearing.

"(3) An opportunity to present evidence, including an opinion from a medical professional or other person, on the capacity of the beneficiary to manage monetary benefits paid to or for the beneficiary by the Secretary under this title.

"(4) An opportunity to be represented at no expense to the Government (including by counsel) at any such hearing and to bring a medical professional or other person to provide relevant testimony at any such hearing.".

(b) CLERICAL AMENDMENT.—The table of sections at the beginning of such chapter 55 is amended by inserting after the item relating to section 5501 the following new item:

"5501A. Beneficiaries' rights in mental competence determinations".

(c) EFFECTIVE DATE.—Section 5501A of title 38, United States Code, as added by subsection (a), shall apply to determinations made by the Secretary of Veterans Affairs on or after the date of the enactment of this Act.

SEC. 14018. REAUTHORIZATION OF APPROPRIATIONS.

Subsection (o) of section 2991 of the Omnibus Crime Control and Safe Streets Act of 1968 (42 U.S.C. 3797aa), as redesignated by section 14006, is amended—

(1) in paragraph (1)(C), by striking "2009 through 2014" and inserting "2017 through 2021"; and

(2) by adding at the end the following:

"(3) LIMITATION.—Not more than 20 percent of the funds authorized to be appropriated under this section may be used for purposes described in subsection (i) (relating to veterans).".

Subtitle B—Comprehensive Justice and Mental Health

SEC. 14021. SEQUENTIAL INTERCEPT MODEL.

Section 2991 of title I of the Omnibus Crime Control and Safe Streets Act of 1968 (42 U.S.C. 3797aa), as amended by section 14005, is amended by inserting after subsection (j), the following:

"(k) SEQUENTIAL INTERCEPT GRANTS.—

"(1) DEFINITION.—In this subsection, the term 'eligible entity' means a State, unit of local government, Indian tribe, or tribal organization.

"(2) AUTHORIZATION.—The Attorney General may make grants under this subsection to an eligible entity for sequential intercept mapping

and implementation in accordance with paragraph (3).

"(3) SEQUENTIAL INTERCEPT MAPPING; IMPLEMENTATION.—An eligible entity that receives a grant under this subsection may use funds for—

"(A) sequential intercept mapping, which—

"(i) shall consist of—

"(I) convening mental health and criminal justice stakeholders to—

"(aa) develop a shared understanding of the flow of justice-involved individuals with mental illnesses through the criminal justice system; and

"(bb) identify opportunities for improved collaborative responses to the risks and needs of individuals described in item (aa); and

"(II) developing strategies to address gaps in services and bring innovative and effective programs to scale along multiple intercepts, including—

"(aa) emergency and crisis services;

"(bb) specialized police-based responses;

"(cc) court hearings and disposition alternatives;

"(dd) reentry from jails and prisons; and

"(ee) community supervision, treatment and support services; and

"(ii) may serve as a starting point for the development of strategic plans to achieve positive public health and safety outcomes; and

"(B) implementation, which shall—

"(i) be derived from the strategic plans described in subparagraph (A)(ii); and

"(ii) consist of—

"(I) hiring and training personnel;

"(II) identifying the eligible entity's target population;

"(III) providing services and supports to reduce unnecessary penetration into the criminal justice system;

"(IV) reducing recidivism;

"(V) evaluating the impact of the eligible entity's approach; and

"(VI) planning for the sustainability of effective interventions.".

SEC. 14022. PRISON AND JAILS.

Section 2991 of title I of the Omnibus Crime Control and Safe Streets Act of 1968 (42 U.S.C. 3797aa) is amended by inserting after subsection (k), as added by section 14021, the following:

"(l) CORRECTIONAL FACILITIES.—

"(1) DEFINITIONS.—

"(A) CORRECTIONAL FACILITY.—The term 'correctional facility' means a jail, prison, or other detention facility used to house people who have been arrested, detained, held, or convicted by a criminal justice agency or a court.

"(B) ELIGIBLE INMATE.—The term 'eligible inmate' means an individual who—

"(i) is being held, detained, or incarcerated in a correctional facility; and

"(ii) manifests obvious signs of a mental illness or has been diagnosed by a qualified mental health professional as having a mental illness.

"(2) CORRECTIONAL FACILITY GRANTS.—The Attorney General may award grants to applicants to enhance the capabilities of a correctional facility—

"(A) to identify and screen for eligible inmates;

"(B) to plan and provide—

"(i) initial and periodic assessments of the clinical, medical, and social needs of inmates; and

"(ii) appropriate treatment and services that address the mental health and substance abuse needs of inmates;

"(C) to develop, implement, and enhance—

"(i) post-release transition plans for eligible inmates that, in a comprehensive manner, coordinate health, housing, medical, employment, and other appropriate services and public benefits;

"*(ii) the availability of mental health care services and substance abuse treatment services; and*

"*(iii) alternatives to solitary confinement and segregated housing and mental health screening and treatment for inmates placed in solitary confinement or segregated housing; and*

"*(D) to train each employee of the correctional facility to identify and appropriately respond to incidents involving inmates with mental health or co-occurring mental health and substance abuse disorders.*".

SEC. 14023. ALLOWABLE USES.

Section 2991(b)(5)(I) of title I of the Omnibus Crime Control and Safe Streets Act of 1968 (42 U.S.C. 3797aa(b)(5)(I)) is amended by adding at the end the following:

"*(v) TEAMS ADDRESSING FREQUENT USERS OF CRISIS SERVICES.—Multidisciplinary teams that—*

"*(I) coordinate, implement, and administer community-based crisis responses and long-term plans for frequent users of crisis services;*

"*(II) provide training on how to respond appropriately to the unique issues involving frequent users of crisis services for public service personnel, including criminal justice, mental health, substance abuse, emergency room, healthcare, law enforcement, corrections, and housing personnel;*

"*(III) develop or support alternatives to hospital and jail admissions for frequent users of crisis services that provide treatment, stabilization, and other appropriate supports in the least restrictive, yet appropriate, environment; and*

"*(IV) develop protocols and systems among law enforcement, mental health, substance abuse, housing, corrections, and emergency medical service operations to provide coordinated assistance to frequent users of crisis services.*".

SEC. 14024. LAW ENFORCEMENT TRAINING.

Section 2991(h) of title I of the Omnibus Crime Control and Safe Streets Act of 1968 (42 U.S.C. 3797aa(h)) is amended—

(1) in paragraph (1), by adding at the end the following:

"*(F) ACADEMY TRAINING.—To provide support for academy curricula, law enforcement officer orientation programs, continuing education training, and other programs that teach law enforcement personnel how to identify and respond to incidents involving persons with mental health disorders or co-occurring mental health and substance abuse disorders.*"; and*

(2) by adding at the end the following:

"*(4) PRIORITY CONSIDERATION.—The Attorney General, in awarding grants under this subsection, shall give priority to programs that law enforcement personnel and members of the mental health and substance abuse professions develop and administer cooperatively.*".

SEC. 14025. FEDERAL LAW ENFORCEMENT TRAINING.

Not later than 1 year after the date of enactment of this Act, the Attorney General shall provide direction and guidance for the following:

(1) TRAINING PROGRAMS.—Programs that offer specialized and comprehensive training, in procedures to identify and appropriately respond to incidents in which the unique needs of individuals who have a mental illness are involved, to first responders and tactical units of—

(A) Federal law enforcement agencies; and

(B) other Federal criminal justice agencies such as the Bureau of Prisons, the Administrative Office of the United States Courts, and other agencies that the Attorney General determines appropriate.

(2) IMPROVED TECHNOLOGY.—The establishment of, or improvement of existing, computerized information systems to provide timely information to employees of Federal law enforcement

agencies, and Federal criminal justice agencies to improve the response of such employees to situations involving individuals who have a mental illness.

SEC. 14026. GAO REPORT.

No later than 1 year after the date of enactment of this Act, the Comptroller General of the United States, in coordination with the Attorney General, shall submit to Congress a report on—

(1) the practices that Federal first responders, tactical units, and corrections officers are trained to use in responding to individuals with mental illness;

(2) procedures to identify and appropriately respond to incidents in which the unique needs of individuals who have a mental illness are involved, to Federal first responders and tactical units;

(3) the application of evidence-based practices in criminal justice settings to better address individuals with mental illnesses; and

(4) recommendations on how the Department of Justice can expand and improve information sharing and dissemination of best practices.

SEC. 14027. EVIDENCE BASED PRACTICES.

Section 2991(c) of title I of the Omnibus Crime Control and Safe Streets Act of 1968 (42 U.S.C. 3797aa(c)) is amended—

(1) in paragraph (3), by striking "or" at the end;

(2) by redesignating paragraph (4) as paragraph (6); and

(3) by inserting after paragraph (3), the following:

"*(4) propose interventions that have been shown by empirical evidence to reduce recidivism;*

"*(5) when appropriate, use validated assessment tools to target preliminarily qualified offenders with a moderate or high risk of recidivism and a need for treatment and services; or*".

SEC. 14028. TRANSPARENCY, PROGRAM ACCOUNTABILITY, AND ENHANCEMENT OF LOCAL AUTHORITY.

(a) IN GENERAL.—Section 2991(a) of title I of the Omnibus Crime Control and Safe Streets Act of 1968 (42 U.S.C. 3797aa(a)) is amended—

(1) in paragraph (7)—

(A) in the heading, by striking "MENTAL ILLNESS" and inserting "MENTAL ILLNESS; MENTAL HEALTH DISORDER"; and

(B) by striking "term 'mental illness' means" and inserting "terms 'mental illness' and 'mental health disorder' mean"; and

(2) by striking paragraph (9) and inserting the following:

"*(9) PRELIMINARILY QUALIFIED OFFENDER.—*

"*(A) IN GENERAL.—The term 'preliminarily qualified offender' means an adult or juvenile accused of an offense who—*

"*(i)(I) previously or currently has been diagnosed by a qualified mental health professional as having a mental illness or co-occurring mental illness and substance abuse disorders;*

"*(II) manifests obvious signs of mental illness or co-occurring mental illness and substance abuse disorders during arrest or confinement or before any court; or*

"*(III) in the case of a veterans treatment court provided under subsection (i), has been diagnosed with, or manifests obvious signs of, mental illness or a substance abuse disorder or co-occurring mental illness and substance abuse disorder;*

"*(ii) has been unanimously approved for participation in a program funded under this section by, when appropriate—*

"*(I) the relevant—*

"*(aa) prosecuting attorney;*

"*(bb) defense attorney;*

"*(cc) probation or corrections official; and*

"*(dd) judge; and*

"*(II) a representative from the relevant mental health agency described in subsection (b)(5)(B)(i);*

"*(iii) has been determined, by each person described in clause (ii) who is involved in approving the adult or juvenile for participation in a program funded under this section, to not pose a risk of violence to any person in the program, or the public, if selected to participate in the program; and*

"*(iv) has not been charged with or convicted of—*

"*(I) any sex offense (as defined in section 111 of the Sex Offender Registration and Notification Act (42 U.S.C. 16911)) or any offense relating to the sexual exploitation of children; or*

"*(II) murder or assault with intent to commit murder.*

"*(B) DETERMINATION.—In determining whether to designate a defendant as a preliminarily qualified offender, the relevant prosecuting attorney, defense attorney, probation or corrections official, judge, and mental health or substance abuse agency representative shall take into account—*

"*(i) whether the participation of the defendant in the program would pose a substantial risk of violence to the community;*

"*(ii) the criminal history of the defendant and the nature and severity of the offense for which the defendant is charged;*

"*(iii) the views of any relevant victims to the offense;*

"*(iv) the extent to which the defendant would benefit from participation in the program;*

"*(v) the extent to which the community would realize cost savings because of the defendant's participation in the program; and*

"*(vi) whether the defendant satisfies the eligibility criteria for program participation unanimously established by the relevant prosecuting attorney, defense attorney, probation or corrections official, judge and mental health or substance abuse agency representative.*".

(b) TECHNICAL AND CONFORMING AMENDMENT.—Section 2927(2) of title I of the Omnibus Crime Control and Safe Streets Act of 1968 (42 U.S.C. 3797s–6(2)) is amended by striking "has the meaning given that term in section 2991(a)." and inserting "means an offense that—

"*(A) does not have as an element the use, attempted use, or threatened use of physical force against the person or property of another; or*

"*(B) is not a felony that by its nature involves a substantial risk that physical force against the person or property of another may be used in the course of committing the offense.*".

SEC. 14029. GRANT ACCOUNTABILITY.

Section 2991 of title I of the Omnibus Crime Control and Safe Streets Act of 1968 (42 U.S.C. 3797aa) is amended by inserting after subsection (l), as added by section 14022, the following:

"*(m) ACCOUNTABILITY.—All grants awarded by the Attorney General under this section shall be subject to the following accountability provisions:*

"*(1) AUDIT REQUIREMENT.—*

"*(A) DEFINITION.—In this paragraph, the term 'unresolved audit finding' means a finding in the final audit report of the Inspector General of the Department of Justice that the audited grantee has utilized grant funds for an unauthorized expenditure or otherwise unallowable cost that is not closed or resolved within 12 months from the date when the final audit report is issued.*

"*(B) AUDITS.—Beginning in the first fiscal year beginning after the date of enactment of this subsection, and in each fiscal year thereafter, the Inspector General of the Department of Justice shall conduct audits of recipients of grants under this section to prevent waste, fraud, and abuse of funds by grantees. The Inspector General shall determine the appropriate number of grantees to be audited each year.*

"*(C) MANDATORY EXCLUSION.—A recipient of grant funds under this section that is found to* have an unresolved audit finding shall not be eligible to receive grant funds under this section during the first 2 fiscal years beginning after the end of the 12-month period described in subparagraph (A).

"(D) PRIORITY.—In awarding grants under this section, the Attorney General shall give priority to eligible applicants that did not have an unresolved audit finding during the 3 fiscal years before submitting an application for a grant under this section.

"(E) REIMBURSEMENT.—If an entity is awarded grant funds under this section during the 2-fiscal-year period during which the entity is barred from receiving grants under subparagraph (C), the Attorney General shall—

"(i) deposit an amount equal to the amount of the grant funds that were improperly awarded to the grantee into the General Fund of the Treasury; and

"(ii) seek to recoup the costs of the repayment to the fund from the grant recipient that was erroneously awarded grant funds.

"(2) NONPROFIT ORGANIZATION REQUIREMENTS.—

"(A) DEFINITION.—For purposes of this paragraph and the grant programs under this part, the term 'nonprofit organization' means an organization that is described in section 501(c)(3) of the Internal Revenue Code of 1986 and is exempt from taxation under section 501(a) of such Code.

"(B) PROHIBITION.—The Attorney General may not award a grant under this part to a nonprofit organization that holds money in offshore accounts for the purpose of avoiding paying the tax described in section 511(a) of the Internal Revenue Code of 1986.

"(C) DISCLOSURE.—Each nonprofit organization that is awarded a grant under this section and uses the procedures prescribed in regulations to create a rebuttable presumption of reasonableness for the compensation of its officers, directors, trustees, and key employees, shall disclose to the Attorney General, in the application for the grant, the process for determining such compensation, including the independent persons involved in reviewing and approving such compensation, the comparability data used, and contemporaneous substantiation of the deliberation and decision. Upon request, the Attorney General shall make the information disclosed under this subparagraph available for public inspection.

"(3) CONFERENCE EXPENDITURES.—

"(A) LIMITATION.—No amounts made available to the Department of Justice under this section may be used by the Attorney General, or by any individual or entity awarded discretionary funds through a cooperative agreement under this section, to host or support any expenditure for conferences that uses more than $20,000 in funds made available by the Department of Justice, unless the head of the relevant agency or department, provides prior written authorization that the funds may be expended to host the conference.

"(B) WRITTEN APPROVAL.—Written approval under subparagraph (A) shall include a written estimate of all costs associated with the conference, including the cost of all food, beverages, audio-visual equipment, honoraria for speakers, and entertainment.

"(C) REPORT.—The Deputy Attorney General shall submit an annual report to the Committee on the Judiciary of the Senate and the Committee on the Judiciary of the House of Representatives on all conference expenditures approved under this paragraph.

"(4) ANNUAL CERTIFICATION.—Beginning in the first fiscal year beginning after the date of enactment of this subsection, the Attorney General shall submit, to the Committee on the Judiciary and the Committee on Appropriations of

the Senate and the Committee on the Judiciary and the Committee on Appropriations of the House of Representatives, an annual certification—

"(A) indicating whether—

"(i) all audits issued by the Office of the Inspector General under paragraph (1) have been completed and reviewed by the appropriate Assistant Attorney General or Director;

"(ii) all mandatory exclusions required under paragraph (1)(C) have been issued; and

"(iii) all reimbursements required under paragraph (1)(E) have been made; and

"(B) that includes a list of any grant recipients excluded under paragraph (1) from the previous year.

"(n) PREVENTING DUPLICATIVE GRANTS.—

"(1) IN GENERAL.—Before the Attorney General awards a grant to an applicant under this section, the Attorney General shall compare potential grant awards with other grants awarded under this Act to determine if duplicate grant awards are awarded for the same purpose.

"(2) REPORT.—If the Attorney General awards duplicate grants to the same applicant for the same purpose the Attorney General shall submit to the Committee on the Judiciary of the Senate and the Committee on the Judiciary of the House of Representatives a report that includes—

"(A) a list of all duplicate grants awarded, including the total dollar amount of any duplicate grants awarded; and

"(B) the reason the Attorney General awarded the duplicate grants.".

DIVISION C—INCREASING CHOICE, ACCESS, AND QUALITY IN HEALTH CARE FOR AMERICANS

SEC. 15000. SHORT TITLE.

This division may be cited as the "Increasing Choice, Access, and Quality in Health Care for Americans Act".

TITLE XV—PROVISIONS RELATING TO MEDICARE PART A

SEC. 15001. DEVELOPMENT OF MEDICARE HCPCS VERSION OF MS–DRG CODES FOR SIMILAR HOSPITAL SERVICES.

Section 1886 of the Social Security Act (42 U.S.C. 1395ww) is amended by adding at the end the following new subsection:

"(t) RELATING SIMILAR INPATIENT AND OUTPATIENT HOSPITAL SERVICES.—

"(1) DEVELOPMENT OF HCPCS VERSION OF MS–DRG CODES.—Not later than January 1, 2018, the Secretary shall develop HCPCS versions for MS–DRGs that are similar to the ICD–10–PCS for such MS–DRGs such that, to the extent possible, the MS–DRG assignment shall be similar for a claim coded with the HCPCS version as an identical claim coded with a ICD–10–PCS code.

"(2) COVERAGE OF SURGICAL MS–DRGS.—In carrying out paragraph (1), the Secretary shall develop HCPCS versions of MS–DRG codes for not fewer than 10 surgical MS–DRGs.

"(3) PUBLICATION AND DISSEMINATION OF THE HCPCS VERSIONS OF MS–DRGS.—

"(A) IN GENERAL.—The Secretary shall develop a HCPCS MS–DRG definitions manual and software that is similar to the definitions manual and software for ICD–10–PCS codes for such MS–DRGs. The Secretary shall post the HCPCS MS–DRG definitions manual and software on the Internet website of the Centers for Medicare & Medicaid Services. The HCPCS MS–DRG definitions manual and software shall be in the public domain and available for use and redistribution without charge.

"(B) USE OF PREVIOUS ANALYSIS DONE BY MEDPAC.—In developing the HCPCS MS–DRG definitions manual and software under subparagraph (A), the Secretary shall consult with the Medicare Payment Advisory Commission and shall consider the analysis done by such Com-

mission in translating outpatient surgical claims into inpatient surgical MS–DRGs in preparing chapter 7 (relating to hospital short-stay policy issues) of its 'Medicare and the Health Care Delivery System' report submitted to Congress in June 2015.

"(4) DEFINITION AND REFERENCE.—In this subsection:

"(A) HCPCS.—The term 'HCPCS' means, with respect to hospital items and services, the code under the Healthcare Common Procedure Coding System (HCPCS) (or a successor code) for such items and services.

"(B) ICD–10–PCS.—The term 'ICD–10–PCS' means the International Classification of Diseases, 10th Revision, Procedure Coding System, and includes any subsequent revision of such International Classification of Diseases, Procedure Coding System.".

SEC. 15002. ESTABLISHING BENEFICIARY EQUITY IN THE MEDICARE HOSPITAL READMISSION PROGRAM.

(a) TRANSITIONAL ADJUSTMENT FOR DUAL ELIGIBLE POPULATION.—Section 1886(q)(3) of the Social Security Act (42 U.S.C. 1395ww(q)(3)) is amended—

(1) in subparagraph (A), by inserting "subject to subparagraph (D)," after "purposes of paragraph (1),"; and

(2) by adding at the end the following new subparagraph:

"(D) TRANSITIONAL ADJUSTMENT FOR DUAL ELIGIBLES.—

"(i) IN GENERAL.—In determining a hospital's adjustment factor under this paragraph for purposes of making payments for discharges occurring during and after fiscal year 2019, and before the application of clause (i) of subparagraph (E), the Secretary shall assign hospitals to groups (as defined by the Secretary under clause (ii)) and apply the applicable provisions of this subsection using a methodology in a manner that allows for separate comparison of hospitals within each such group, as determined by the Secretary.

"(ii) DEFINING GROUPS.—For purposes of this subparagraph, the Secretary shall define groups of hospitals, based on their overall proportion, of the inpatients who are entitled to, or enrolled for, benefits under part A, and who are full-benefit dual eligible individuals (as defined in section 1935(c)(6)). In defining groups, the Secretary shall consult the Medicare Payment Advisory Commission and may consider the analysis done by such Commission in preparing the portion of its report submitted to Congress in June 2013 relating to readmissions.

"(iii) MINIMIZING REPORTING BURDEN ON HOSPITALS.—In carrying out this subparagraph, the Secretary shall not impose any additional reporting requirements on hospitals.

"(iv) BUDGET NEUTRAL DESIGN METHODOLOGY.—The Secretary shall design the methodology to implement this subparagraph so that the estimated total amount of reductions in payments under this subsection equals the estimated total amount of reductions in payments that would otherwise occur under this subsection if this subparagraph did not apply.".

(b) CHANGES IN RISK ADJUSTMENT.—Section 1886(q)(3) of the Social Security Act (42 U.S.C. 1395ww(q)(3)), as amended by subsection (a), is further amended by adding at the end the following new subparagraph:

"(E) CHANGES IN RISK ADJUSTMENT.—

"(i) CONSIDERATION OF RECOMMENDATIONS IN IMPACT REPORTS.—The Secretary may take into account the studies conducted and the recommendations made by the Secretary under section 2(d)(1) of the IMPACT Act of 2014 (Public Law 113–185; 42 U.S.C. 1395lll note) with respect to the application under this subsection of risk adjustment methodologies. Nothing in this clause shall be construed as precluding consideration of the use of groupings of hospitals.

"(ii) CONSIDERATION OF EXCLUSION OF PATIENT CASES BASED ON V OR OTHER APPROPRIATE CODES.—In promulgating regulations to carry out this subsection with respect to discharges occurring after fiscal year 2018, the Secretary may consider the use of V or other ICD-related codes for removal of a readmission. The Secretary may consider modifying measures under this subsection to incorporate V or other ICD-related codes at the same time as other changes are being made under this subparagraph.

"(iii) REMOVAL OF CERTAIN READMISSIONS.—In promulgating regulations to carry out this subsection, with respect to discharges occurring after fiscal year 2018, the Secretary may consider removal as a readmission of an admission that is classified within one or more of the following: transplants, end-stage renal disease, burns, trauma, psychosis, or substance abuse. The Secretary may consider modifying measures under this subsection to remove readmissions at the same time as other changes are being made under this subparagraph.".

(c) MEDPAC STUDY ON READMISSIONS PROGRAM.—The Medicare Payment Advisory Commission shall conduct a study to review overall hospital readmissions described in section 1886(q)(5)(E) of the Social Security Act (42 U.S.C. 1395ww(q)(5)(E)) and whether such readmissions are related to any changes in outpatient and emergency services furnished. The Commission shall submit to Congress a report on such study in its report to Congress in June 2018.

SEC. 15003. FIVE-YEAR EXTENSION OF THE RURAL COMMUNITY HOSPITAL DEMONSTRATION PROGRAM.

(a) EXTENSION.—Section 410A of the Medicare Prescription Drug, Improvement, and Modernization Act of 2003 (Public Law 108–173; 42 U.S.C. 1395ww note) is amended—

(1) in subsection (a)(5), by striking "5-year extension period" and inserting "10-year extension period"; and

(2) in subsection (g)—

(A) in the subsection heading, by striking "FIVE-YEAR" and inserting "TEN-YEAR";

(B) in paragraph (1), by striking "additional 5-year" and inserting "additional 10-year";

(C) by striking "5-year extension period" and inserting "10-year extension period" each place it appears;

(D) in paragraph (4)(B)—

(i) in the matter preceding clause (i), by inserting "each 5-year period in" after "hospital during"; and

(ii) in clause (i), by inserting "each applicable 5-year period in" after "the first day of"; and

(E) by adding at the end the following new paragraphs:

"(5) OTHER HOSPITALS IN DEMONSTRATION PROGRAM.—During the second 5 years of the 10-year extension period, the Secretary shall apply the provisions of paragraph (4) to rural community hospitals that are not described in paragraph (4) but are participating in the demonstration program under this section as of December 30, 2014, in a similar manner as such provisions apply to rural community hospitals described in paragraph (4).

"(6) EXPANSION OF DEMONSTRATION PROGRAM TO RURAL AREAS IN ANY STATE.—

"(A) IN GENERAL.—The Secretary shall, notwithstanding subsection (a)(2) or paragraph (2) of this subsection, not later than 120 days after the date of the enactment of this paragraph, issue a solicitation for applications to select up to the maximum number of additional rural community hospitals located in any State to participate in the demonstration program under this section for the second 5 years of the 10-year extension period without exceeding the limitation under paragraph (3) of this subsection.

"(B) PRIORITY.—In determining which rural community hospitals that submitted an applica-

tion pursuant to the solicitation under subparagraph (A) to select for participation in the demonstration program, the Secretary—

"(i) shall give priority to rural community hospitals located in one of the 20 States with the lowest population densities (as determined by the Secretary using the 2015 Statistical Abstract of the United States); and

"(ii) may consider—

"(I) closures of hospitals located in rural areas in the State in which the rural community hospital is located during the 5-year period immediately preceding the date of the enactment of this paragraph; and

"(II) the population density of the State in which the rural community hospital is located.".

(b) CHANGE IN TIMING FOR REPORT.—Subsection (e) of such section 410A is amended—

(1) by striking "Not later than 6 months after the completion of the demonstration program under this section" and inserting "Not later than August 1, 2018"; and

(2) by striking "such program" and inserting "the demonstration program under this section".

SEC. 15004. REGULATORY RELIEF FOR LTCHS.

(a) TECHNICAL CHANGE TO THE MEDICARE LONG-TERM CARE HOSPITAL MORATORIUM EXCEPTION.—

(1) IN GENERAL.—Section 114(d)(7) of the Medicare, Medicaid, and SCHIP Extension Act of 2007 (42 U.S.C. 1395ww note), as amended by sections 3106(b) and 10312(b) of Public Law 111–148, section 1206(b)(2) of the Pathway for SGR Reform Act of 2013 (division B of Public Law 113–67), and section 112 of the Protecting Access to Medicare Act of 2014 (Public Law 113–93), is amended by striking "The moratorium under paragraph (1)(A)" and inserting "Any moratorium under paragraph (1)".

(2) EFFECTIVE DATE.—The amendment made by paragraph (1) shall take effect as if included in the enactment of section 112 of the Protecting Access to Medicare Act of 2014.

(b) MODIFICATION TO MEDICARE LONG-TERM CARE HOSPITAL HIGH COST OUTLIER PAYMENTS.—Section 1886(m) of the Social Security Act (42 U.S.C. 1395ww(m)) is amended by adding at the end the following new paragraph:

"(7) TREATMENT OF HIGH COST OUTLIER PAYMENTS.—

"(A) ADJUSTMENT TO THE STANDARD FEDERAL PAYMENT RATE FOR ESTIMATED HIGH COST OUTLIER PAYMENTS.—Under the system described in paragraph (1), for fiscal years beginning on or after October 1, 2017, the Secretary shall reduce the standard Federal payment rate as if the estimated aggregate amount of high cost outlier payments for standard Federal payment rate discharges for each such fiscal year would be equal to 8 percent of estimated aggregate payments for standard Federal payment rate discharges for each such fiscal year.

"(B) LIMITATION ON HIGH COST OUTLIER PAYMENT AMOUNTS.—Notwithstanding subparagraph (A), the Secretary shall set the fixed loss amount for high cost outlier payments such that the estimated aggregate amount of high cost outlier payments made for standard Federal payment rate discharges for fiscal years beginning on or after October 1, 2017, shall be equal to 99.6875 percent of 8 percent of estimated aggregate payments for standard Federal payment rate discharges for each such fiscal year.

"(C) WAIVER OF BUDGET NEUTRALITY.—Any reduction in payments resulting from the application of subparagraph (B) shall not be taken into account in applying any budget neutrality provision under such system.

"(D) NO EFFECT ON SITE NEUTRAL HIGH COST OUTLIER PAYMENT RATE.—This paragraph shall not apply with respect to the computation of the applicable site neutral payment rate under paragraph (6).".

SEC. 15005. SAVINGS FROM IPPS MACRA PAY-FOR THROUGH NOT APPLYING DOCUMENTATION AND CODING ADJUSTMENTS.

Section 7(b)(1)(B) of the TMA, Abstinence Education, and QI Programs Extension Act of 2007 (Public Law 110–90), as amended by section 631(b) of the American Taxpayer Relief Act of 2012 (Public Law 112–240) and section 414(1)(B)(iii) of the Medicare Access and CHIP Reauthorization Act of 2015 (Public Law 114–10), is amended in clause (iii) by striking "an increase of 0.5 percentage points for discharges occurring during each of fiscal years 2018 through 2023" and inserting "an increase of 0.4588 percentage points for discharges occurring during fiscal year 2018 and 0.5 percentage points for discharges occurring during each of fiscal years 2019 through 2023".

SEC. 15006. EXTENSION OF CERTAIN LTCH MEDICARE PAYMENT RULES.

(a) 25–PERCENT PATIENT THRESHOLD PAYMENT ADJUSTMENT.—Section 114(c)(1)(A) of the Medicare, Medicaid, and SCHIP Extension Act of 2007 (42 U.S.C. 1395ww note), as amended by section 4302(a) of division B of the American Recovery and Reinvestment Act (Public Law 111–5), sections 3106(a) and 10312(a) of Public Law 111–148, and section 1206(b)(1)(B) of the Pathway for SGR Reform Act of 2013 (division B of Public Law 113–67), is amended by striking "for a 9-year period" and inserting "through June 30, 2016, and for discharges occurring on or after October 1, 2016, and before October 1, 2017".

(b) PAYMENT FOR HOSPITALS-WITHIN-HOSPITALS.—Section 114(c)(2) of the Medicare, Medicaid, and SCHIP Extension Act of 2007 (42 U.S.C. 1395ww note), as amended by section 4302(a) of division B of the American Recovery and Reinvestment Act (Public Law 111–5), sections 3106(a) and 10312(a) of Public Law 111–148, and section 1206(b)(1)(A) of the Pathway for SGR Reform Act of 2013 (division B of Public Law 113–67), is amended—

(1) in subparagraph (A), by inserting "or any similar provision," after "Regulations,";

(2) in subparagraph (B)—

(A) in clause (i), by inserting "or any similar provision," after "Regulations,"; and

(B) in clause (ii), by inserting ", or any similar provision," after "Regulations"; and

(3) in subparagraph (C), by striking "for a 9-year period" and inserting "through June 30, 2016, and for discharges occurring on or after October 1, 2016, and before October 1, 2017".

SEC. 15007. APPLICATION OF RULES ON THE CALCULATION OF HOSPITAL LENGTH OF STAY TO ALL LTCHS.

(a) IN GENERAL.—Section 1206(a)(3) of the Pathway for SGR Reform Act of 2013 (division B of Public Law 113–67; 42 U.S.C. 1395ww note) is amended—

(1) by striking subparagraph (B);

(2) by striking "SITE NEUTRAL BASIS.—" and all that follows through "For discharges occurring" and inserting "SITE NEUTRAL BASIS.—For discharges occurring";

(3) by striking "subject to subparagraph (B),"; and

(4) by redesignating clauses (i) and (ii) as subparagraphs (A) and (B), respectively, and moving each of such subparagraphs (as so redesignated) 2 ems to the left.

(b) EFFECTIVE DATE.—The amendments made by subsection (a) shall be effective as if included in the enactment of section 1206(a)(3) of the Pathway for SGR Reform Act of 2013 (division B of Public Law 113–67; 42 U.S.C. 1395ww note).

SEC. 15008. CHANGE IN MEDICARE CLASSIFICATION FOR CERTAIN HOSPITALS.

(a) IN GENERAL.—Subsection (d)(1)(B)(iv) of section 1886 of the Social Security Act (42 U.S.C. 1395ww) is amended—

(1) in subclause (I), by striking "or" at the end;

(2) in subclause (II)—

(A) by striking '', or'' at the end and inserting a semicolon;

(B) by redesignating such subclause as clause (vi) and by moving it to immediately follow clause (v); and

(C) in clause (v), by striking the semicolon at the end and inserting '', or''; and

(3) by striking ''(iv)(I) a hospital'' and inserting ''(iv) a hospital''.

(b) CONFORMING PAYMENT REFERENCES.—The second sentence of subsection (d)(1)(B) of such section is amended—

(1) by inserting ''(as in effect as of such date)'' after ''clause (iv)''; and

(2) by inserting ''(or, in the case of a hospital described in clause (iv)(II), as so in effect, shall be classified under clause (vi) on and after the effective date of such clause (vi) and for cost reporting periods beginning on or after January 1, 2015, shall not be subject to subsection (m) as of the date of such classification)'' after ''so classified''.

(c) APPLICATION.—

(1) IN GENERAL.—For cost reporting periods beginning on or after January 1, 2015, in the case of an applicable hospital (as defined in paragraph (3)), the following shall apply:

(A) Payment for inpatient operating costs shall be made on a reasonable cost basis in the manner provided in section 412.526(c)(3) of title 42, Code of Federal Regulations (as in effect on January 1, 2015) and in any subsequent modifications.

(B) Payment for capital costs shall be made in the manner provided by section 412.526(c)(4) of title 42, Code of Federal Regulations (as in effect on such date).

(C) Claims for payment for Medicare beneficiaries who are discharged on or after January 1, 2017, shall be processed as claims which are paid on a reasonable cost basis as described in section 412.526(c) of title 42, Code of Federal Regulations (as in effect on such date).

(2) APPLICABLE HOSPITAL DEFINED.—In this subsection, the term ''applicable hospital'' means a hospital that is classified under clause (iv)(II) of section 1886(d)(1)(B) of the Social Security Act (42 U.S.C. 1395ww(d)(1)(B)) on the day before the date of the enactment of this Act and which is classified under clause (vi) of such section, as redesignated and moved by subsection (a), on or after such date of enactment.

(d) CONFORMING TECHNICAL AMENDMENTS.—

(1) Section 1899B(a)(2)(A)(iv) of the Social Security Act (42 U.S.C. 1395lll(a)(2)(A)(iv)) is amended by striking ''1886(d)(1)(B)(iv)(II)'' and inserting ''1886(d)(1)(B)(vi)''.

(2) Section 1886(m)(5)(F) of such Act (42 U.S.C. 1395ww(m)(5)(F)) is amended in each of clauses (i) and (ii) by striking ''(d)(1)(B)(iv)(II)'' and inserting ''(d)(1)(B)(vi)''.

SEC. 15009. TEMPORARY EXCEPTION TO THE APPLICATION OF THE MEDICARE LTCH SITE NEUTRAL PROVISIONS FOR CERTAIN SPINAL CORD SPECIALTY HOSPITALS.

(a) EXCEPTION.—Section 1886(m)(6) of the Social Security Act (42 U.S.C. 1395ww(m)(6)) is amended—

(1) in subparagraph (A)(i), by striking ''and (E)'' and inserting '', (E), and (F)''; and

(2) by adding at the end the following new subparagraph:

''(F) TEMPORARY EXCEPTION FOR CERTAIN SPINAL CORD SPECIALTY HOSPITALS.—For discharges in cost reporting periods beginning during fiscal years 2018 and 2019, subparagraph (A)(i) shall not apply (and payment shall be made to a long-term care hospital without regard to this paragraph) if such discharge is from a long-term care hospital that meets each of the following requirements:

''(i) NOT-FOR-PROFIT.—The long-term care hospital was a not-for-profit long-term care hos-

pital on June 1, 2014, as determined by cost report data.

''(ii) PRIMARILY PROVIDING TREATMENT FOR CATASTROPHIC SPINAL CORD OR ACQUIRED BRAIN INJURIES OR OTHER PARALYZING NEUROMUSCULAR CONDITIONS.—Of the discharges in calendar year 2013 from the long-term care hospital for which payment was made under this section, at least 50 percent were classified under MS–LTCH–DRGs 28, 29, 52, 57, 551, 573, and 963.

''(iii) SIGNIFICANT OUT-OF-STATE ADMISSIONS.—

''(I) IN GENERAL.—The long-term care hospital discharged inpatients (including both individuals entitled to, or enrolled for, benefits under this title and individuals not so entitled or enrolled) during fiscal year 2014 who had been admitted from at least 20 of the 50 States, determined by the States of residency of such inpatients and based on such data submitted by the hospital to the Secretary as the Secretary may require.

''(II) IMPLEMENTATION.—Notwithstanding any other provision of law, the Secretary may implement subclause (I) by program instruction or otherwise.

''(III) NON-APPLICATION OF PAPERWORK REDUCTION ACT.—Chapter 35 of title 44, United States Code, shall not apply to data collected under this clause.''.

(b) STUDY AND REPORT ON THE STATUS AND VIABILITY OF CERTAIN SPINAL CORD SPECIALTY LONG-TERM CARE HOSPITALS.—

(1) STUDY.—The Comptroller General of the United States shall conduct a study on long-term care hospitals described in section 1886(m)(6)(F) of the Social Security Act, as added by subsection (a). Such report shall include an analysis of the following:

(A) The impact on such hospitals of the classification and facility licensure by State agencies of such hospitals.

(B) The Medicare payment rates for such hospitals.

(C) Data on the number and health care needs of Medicare beneficiaries who have been diagnosed with catastrophic spinal cord or acquired brain injuries or other paralyzing neuromuscular conditions (as described within the discharge classifications specified in clause (ii) of such section) who are receiving services from such hospitals.

(2) REPORT.—Not later than October 1, 2018, the Comptroller General shall submit to Congress a report on the study conducted under paragraph (1), including recommendations for such legislation and administrative action as the Comptroller General determines appropriate.

SEC. 15010. TEMPORARY EXTENSION TO THE APPLICATION OF THE MEDICARE LTCH SITE NEUTRAL PROVISIONS FOR CERTAIN DISCHARGES WITH SEVERE WOUNDS.

(a) IN GENERAL.—Section 1886(m)(6) of the Social Security Act (42 U.S.C. 1395ww(m)(6)), as amended by section 15009, is further amended—

(1) in subparagraph (A)(i) by striking ''and (F)'' and inserting ''(F), and (G)'';

(2) in subparagraph (E)(i)(I)(aa), by striking ''the amendment made'' and all that follows before the semicolon and inserting ''the last sentence of subsection (d)(1)(B)''; and

(3) by adding at the end the following new subparagraph:

''(G) ADDITIONAL TEMPORARY EXCEPTION FOR CERTAIN SEVERE WOUND DISCHARGES FROM CERTAIN LONG-TERM CARE HOSPITALS.—

''(i) IN GENERAL.—For a discharge occurring in a cost reporting period beginning during fiscal year 2018, subparagraph (A)(i) shall not apply (and payment shall be made to a long-term care hospital without regard to this paragraph) if such discharge—

''(I) is from a long-term care hospital identified by the last sentence of subsection (d)(1)(B);

''(II) is classified under MS–LTCH–DRG 602, 603, 539, or 540; and

''(III) is with respect to an individual treated by a long-term care hospital for a severe wound.

''(ii) SEVERE WOUND DEFINED.—In this subparagraph, the term 'severe wound' means a wound which is a stage 3 wound, stage 4 wound, unstageable wound, non-healing surgical wound, or fistula as identified in the claim from the long-term care hospital.

''(iii) WOUND DEFINED.—In this subparagraph, the term 'wound' means an injury involving division of tissue or rupture of the integument or mucous membrane with exposure to the external environment.''.

(c) STUDY AND REPORT TO CONGRESS.—

(1) STUDY.—The Comptroller General of the United States shall, in consultation with relevant stakeholders, conduct a study on the treatment needs of individuals entitled to benefits under part A of title XVIII of the Social Security Act or enrolled under part B of such title who require specialized wound care, and the cost, for such individuals and the Medicare program under such title, of treating severe wounds in rural and urban areas. Such study shall include an assessment of—

(A) access of such individuals to appropriate levels of care for such cases;

(B) the potential impact that section 1886(m)(6)(A)(i) of such Act (42 U.S.C. 1395ww(m)(6)(A)(i)) will have on the access, quality, and cost of care for such individuals; and

(C) how to appropriately pay for such care under the Medicare program under such title.

(2) REPORT.—Not later than October 1, 2020, the Comptroller General shall submit to Congress a report on the study conducted under paragraph (1), including recommendations for such legislation and administrative action as the Comptroller General determines appropriate.

TITLE XVI—PROVISIONS RELATING TO MEDICARE PART B

SEC. 16001. CONTINUING MEDICARE PAYMENT UNDER HOPD PROSPECTIVE PAYMENT SYSTEM FOR SERVICES FURNISHED BY MID-BUILD OFF-CAMPUS OUTPATIENT DEPARTMENTS OF PROVIDERS.

(a) IN GENERAL.—Section 1833(t)(21) of the Social Security Act (42 U.S.C. 1395l(t)(21)) is amended—

(1) in subparagraph (B)—

(A) in clause (i), by striking ''clause (ii)'' and inserting ''the subsequent provisions of this subparagraph''; and

(B) by adding at the end the following new clauses:

''(iii) DEEMED TREATMENT FOR 2017.—For purposes of applying clause (ii) with respect to applicable items and services furnished during 2017, a department of a provider (as so defined) not described in such clause is deemed to be billing under this subsection with respect to covered OPD services furnished prior to November 2, 2015, if the Secretary received from the provider prior to December 2, 2015, an attestation (pursuant to section 413.65(b)(3) of title 42 of the Code of Federal Regulations) that such department was a department of a provider (as so defined).

''(iv) ALTERNATIVE EXCEPTION BEGINNING WITH 2018.—For purposes of paragraph (1)(B)(v) and this paragraph with respect to applicable items and services furnished during 2018 or a subsequent year, the term 'off-campus outpatient department of a provider' also shall not include a department of a provider (as so defined) that is not described in clause (ii) if—

''(I) the Secretary receives from the provider an attestation (pursuant to such section 413.65(b)(3)) not later than December 31, 2016 (or, if later, 60 days after the date of the enactment of this clause), that such department met

the requirements of a department of a provider specified in section 413.65 of title 42 of the Code of Federal Regulations;

"(II) the provider includes such department as part of the provider on its enrollment form in accordance with the enrollment process under section 1866(j); and

"(III) the department met the mid-build requirement of clause (v) and the Secretary receives, not later than 60 days after the date of the enactment of this clause, from the chief executive officer or chief operating officer of the provider a written certification that the department met such requirement.

"(v) MID-BUILD REQUIREMENT DESCRIBED.— The mid-build requirement of this clause is, with respect to a department of a provider, that before November 2, 2015, the provider had a binding written agreement with an outside unrelated party for the actual construction of such department.

"(vii) AUDIT.—Not later than December 31, 2018, the Secretary shall audit the compliance with requirements of clause (iv) with respect to each department of a provider to which such clause applies. If the Secretary finds as a result of an audit under this clause that the applicable requirements were not met with respect to such department, the department shall not be excluded from the term 'off-campus outpatient department of a provider' under such clause.

"(viii) IMPLEMENTATION.—For purposes of implementing clauses (iii) through (vii):

"(I) Notwithstanding any other provision of law, the Secretary may implement such clauses by program instruction or otherwise.

"(II) Subchapter I of chapter 35 of title 44, United States Code, shall not apply.

"(III) For purposes of carrying out this subparagraph with respect to clauses (iii) and (iv) (and clause (vii) insofar as it relates to clause (iv)), $10,000,000 shall be available from the Federal Supplementary Medical Insurance Trust Fund under section 1841, to remain available until December 31, 2018."; and

(2) in subparagraph (E), by adding at the end the following new clause:

"(iv) The determination of an audit under subparagraph (B)(vii)."

(b) EFFECTIVE DATE.—The amendments made by this section shall be effective as if included in the enactment of section 603 of the Bipartisan Budget Act of 2015 (Public Law 114–74).

SEC. 16002. TREATMENT OF CANCER HOSPITALS IN OFF-CAMPUS OUTPATIENT DEPARTMENT OF A PROVIDER POLICY.

(a) IN GENERAL.—Section 1833(t)(21)(B) of the Social Security Act (42 U.S.C. 1395l(t)(21)(B)), as amended by section 16001(a), is amended—

(1) by inserting after clause (v) the following new clause:

"(vi) EXCLUSION FOR CERTAIN CANCER HOSPITALS.—For purposes of paragraph (1)(B)(v) and this paragraph with respect to applicable items and services furnished during 2017 or a subsequent year, the term 'off-campus outpatient department of a provider' also shall not include a department of a provider (as so defined) that is not described in clause (ii) if the provider is a hospital described in section 1886(d)(1)(B)(v) and—

"(I) in the case of a department that met the requirements of section 413.65 of title 42 of the Code of Federal Regulations after November 1, 2015, and before the date of the enactment of this clause, the Secretary receives from the provider an attestation that such department met such requirements not later than 60 days after such date of enactment; or

"(II) in the case of a department that meets such requirements after such date of enactment, the Secretary receives from the provider an attestation that such department meets such requirements not later than 60 days after the date

such requirements are first met with respect to such department.";

(2) in clause (vii), by inserting after the first sentence the following: "Not later than 2 years after the date the Secretary receives an attestation under clause (vi) relating to compliance of a department of a provider with requirements referred to in such clause, the Secretary shall audit the compliance with such requirements with respect to the department."; and

(3) in clause (viii)(III), by adding at the end the following: "For purposes of carrying out this subparagraph with respect to clause (vi) (and clause (vii) insofar as it relates to such clause), $2,000,000 shall be available from the Federal Supplementary Medical Insurance Trust Fund under section 1841, to remain available until expended.".

(b) OFFSETTING SAVINGS.—Section 1833(t)(18) of the Social Security Act (42 U.S.C. 1395l(t)(18)) is amended—

(1) in subparagraph (B), by inserting ", subject to subparagraph (C)," after "shall"; and

(2) by adding at the end the following new subparagraph:

"(C) TARGET PCR ADJUSTMENT.—In applying section 419.43(i) of title 42 of the Code of Federal Regulations to implement the appropriate adjustment under this paragraph for services furnished on or after January 1, 2018, the Secretary shall use a target PCR that is 1.0 percentage points less than the target PCR that would otherwise apply. In addition to the percentage point reduction under the previous sentence, the Secretary may consider making an additional percentage point reduction to such target PCR that takes into account payment rates for applicable items and services described in paragraph (21)(C) other than for services furnished by hospitals described in section 1886(d)(1)(B)(v). In making any budget neutrality adjustments under this subsection for 2018 or a subsequent year, the Secretary shall not take into account the reduced expenditures that result from the application of this subparagraph.".

(c) EFFECTIVE DATE.—The amendments made by this section shall be effective as if included in the enactment of section 603 of the Bipartisan Budget Act of 2015 (Public Law 114–74).

SEC. 16003. TREATMENT OF ELIGIBLE PROFESSIONALS IN AMBULATORY SURGICAL CENTERS FOR MEANINGFUL USE AND MIPS.

Section 1848(a)(7)(D) of the Social Security Act (42 U.S.C. 1395w–4(a)(7)(D)) is amended—

(1) by striking "HOSPITAL-BASED ELIGIBLE PROFESSIONALS" and all that follows through "No payment" and inserting the following: "HOSPITAL-BASED AND AMBULATORY SURGICAL CENTER-BASED ELIGIBLE PROFESSIONALS.—

"(i) HOSPITAL-BASED.—No payment"; and

(2) by adding at the end the following new clauses:

"(ii) AMBULATORY SURGICAL CENTER-BASED.— Subject to clause (iv), no payment adjustment may be made under subparagraph (A) for 2017 and 2018 in the case of an eligible professional with respect to whom substantially all of the covered professional services furnished by such professional are furnished in an ambulatory surgical center.

"(iii) DETERMINATION.—The determination of whether an eligible professional is an eligible professional described in clause (ii) may be made on the basis of—

"(I) the site of service (as defined by the Secretary); or

"(II) an attestation submitted by the eligible professional.

Determinations made under subclauses (I) and (II) shall be made without regard to any employment or billing arrangement between the eligible professional and any other supplier or provider of services.

"(iv) SUNSET.—Clause (ii) shall no longer apply as of the first year that begins more than

3 years after the date on which the Secretary determines, through notice and comment rulemaking, that certified EHR technology applicable to the ambulatory surgical center setting is available.".

SEC. 16004. CONTINUING ACCESS TO HOSPITALS ACT OF 2016.

(a) EXTENSION OF ENFORCEMENT INSTRUCTION ON SUPERVISION REQUIREMENTS FOR OUTPATIENT THERAPEUTIC SERVICES IN CRITICAL ACCESS AND SMALL RURAL HOSPITALS THROUGH 2016.—Section 1 of Public Law 113–198, as amended by section 1 of Public Law 114–112, is amended—

(1) in the heading, by striking "2014 AND 2015" and inserting "2016"; and

(2) by striking "and 2015" and inserting ", 2015, and 2016".

(b) REPORT.—Not later than 1 year after the date of the enactment of this Act, the Medicare Payment Advisory Commission (established under section 1805 of the Social Security Act (42 U.S.C. 1395b–6)) shall submit to Congress a report analyzing the effect of the extension of the enforcement instruction under section 1 of Public Law 113–198, as amended by section 1 of Public Law 114–112 and subsection (a) of this section, on the access to health care by Medicare beneficiaries, on the economic impact and the impact upon hospital staffing needs, and on the quality of health care furnished to such beneficiaries.

SEC. 16005. DELAY OF IMPLEMENTATION OF MEDICARE FEE SCHEDULE ADJUSTMENTS FOR WHEELCHAIR ACCESSORIES AND SEATING SYSTEMS WHEN USED IN CONJUNCTION WITH COMPLEX REHABILITATION TECHNOLOGY (CRT) WHEELCHAIRS.

Section 2(a) of the Patient Access and Medicare Protection Act (42 U.S.C. 1305 note) is amended by striking "January 1, 2017" and inserting "July 1, 2017".

SEC. 16006. ALLOWING PHYSICAL THERAPISTS TO UTILIZE LOCUM TENENS ARRANGEMENTS UNDER MEDICARE.

(a) IN GENERAL.—The first sentence of section 1842(b)(6) of the Social Security Act (42 U.S.C. 1395u(b)(6)), as amended by section 5012, is further amended—

(1) by striking "and" before "(I)"; and

(2) by inserting before the period at the end the following: ", and (J) in the case of outpatient physical therapy services furnished by physical therapists in a health professional shortage area (as defined in section 332(a)(1)(A) of the Public Health Service Act), a medically underserved area (as designated pursuant to section 330(b)(3)(A) of such Act), or a rural area (as defined in section 1886(d)(2)(D)), subparagraph (D) of this sentence shall apply to such services and therapists in the same manner as such subparagraph applies to physicians' services furnished by physicians".

(b) EFFECTIVE DATE; IMPLEMENTATION.—

(1) EFFECTIVE DATE.—The amendments made by subsection (a) shall apply to services furnished beginning not later than six months after the date of the enactment of this Act.

(2) IMPLEMENTATION.—The Secretary of Health and Human Services may implement subparagraph (J) of section 1842(b)(6) of the Social Security Act (42 U.S.C. 1395u(b)(6)), as added by subsection (a)(2), by program instruction or otherwise.

SEC. 16007. EXTENSION OF THE TRANSITION TO NEW PAYMENT RATES FOR DURABLE MEDICAL EQUIPMENT UNDER THE MEDICARE PROGRAM.

(a) IN GENERAL.—The Secretary of Health and Human Services shall extend the transition period described in clause (i) of section 414.210(g)(9) of title 42, Code of Federal Regulations, from June 30, 2016, to December 31, 2016 (with the full implementation described in clause (ii) of such section applying to items and services furnished with dates of service on or after January 1, 2017.

(b) STUDY AND REPORT.—

(1) STUDY.—

(A) IN GENERAL.—The Secretary of Health and Human Services shall conduct a study that examines the impact of applicable payment adjustments upon—

(i) the number of suppliers of durable medical equipment that, on a date that is not before January 1, 2016, and not later than December 31, 2016, ceased to conduct business as such suppliers; and

(ii) the availability of durable medical equipment, during the period beginning on January 1, 2016, and ending on December 31, 2016, to individuals entitled to benefits under part A of title XVIII of the Social Security Act (42 U.S.C. 1395 et seq.) or enrolled under part B of such title.

(B) DEFINITIONS.—For purposes of this subsection, the following definitions apply:

(i) SUPPLIER; DURABLE MEDICAL EQUIPMENT.—The terms "supplier" and "durable medical equipment" have the meanings given such terms by section 1861 of the Social Security Act (42 U.S.C. 1395x).

(ii) APPLICABLE PAYMENT ADJUSTMENT.—The term "applicable payment adjustment" means a payment adjustment described in section 414.210(g) of title 42, Code of Federal Regulations, that is phased in by paragraph (9)(i) of such section. For purposes of the preceding sentence, a payment adjustment that is phased in pursuant to the extension under subsection (a) shall be considered a payment adjustment that is phased in by such paragraph (9)(i).

(2) REPORT.—The Secretary of Health and Human Services shall, not later than January 12, 2017, submit to the Committees on Ways and Means and on Energy and Commerce of the House of Representatives, and to the Committee on Finance of the Senate, a report on the findings of the study conducted under paragraph (1).

SEC. 16008. REQUIREMENTS IN DETERMINING AD-JUSTMENTS USING INFORMATION FROM COMPETITIVE BIDDING PRO-GRAMS.

(a) IN GENERAL.—Section 1834(a)(1)(G) of the Social Security Act (42 U.S.C. 1395m(a)(1)(G)) is amended by adding at the end the following new sentence: "In the case of items and services furnished on or after January 1, 2019, in making any adjustments under clause (ii) or (iii) of subparagraph (F), under subsection (h)(1)(H)(ii), or under section 1842(s)(3)(B), the Secretary shall—

"(i) solicit and take into account stakeholder input; and

"(ii) take into account the highest amount bid by a winning supplier in a competitive acquisition area and a comparison of each of the following with respect to non-competitive acquisition areas and competitive acquisition areas:

"(I) The average travel distance and cost associated with furnishing items and services in the area.

"(II) The average volume of items and services furnished by suppliers in the area.

"(III) The number of suppliers in the area.".

(b) CONFORMING AMENDMENTS.—(1) Section 1834(h)(1)(H)(ii) of the Social Security Act (42 U.S.C. 1395m(h)(1)(H)(ii)) is amended by striking "the Secretary" and inserting "subject to subsection (a)(1)(G), the Secretary".

(2) Section 1842(s)(3)(B) of the Social Security Act (42 U.S.C. 1395m(s)(3)(B)) is amended by striking "the Secretary" and inserting "subject to section 1834(a)(1)(G), the Secretary".

TITLE XVII—OTHER MEDICARE PROVISIONS

SEC. 17001. DELAY IN AUTHORITY TO TERMINATE CONTRACTS FOR MEDICARE ADVAN-TAGE PLANS FAILING TO ACHIEVE MINIMUM QUALITY RATINGS.

(a) FINDINGS.—Consistent with the studies provided under the IMPACT Act of 2014 (Public Law 113–185), it is the intent of Congress—

(1) to continue to study and request input on the effects of socioeconomic status and dual-eligible populations on the Medicare Advantage STARS rating system before reforming such system with the input of stakeholders; and

(2) pending the results of such studies and input, to provide for a temporary delay in authority of the Centers for Medicare & Medicaid Services (CMS) to terminate Medicare Advantage plan contracts solely on the basis of performance of plans under the STARS rating system.

(b) DELAY IN MA CONTRACT TERMINATION AU-THORITY FOR PLANS FAILING TO ACHIEVE MIN-IMUM QUALITY RATINGS.—Section 1857(h) of the Social Security Act (42 U.S.C. 1395w–27(h)) is amended by adding at the end the following new paragraph:

"(3) DELAY IN CONTRACT TERMINATION AU-THORITY FOR PLANS FAILING TO ACHIEVE MIN-IMUM QUALITY RATING.—During the period beginning on the date of the enactment of this paragraph and through the end of plan year 2018, the Secretary may not terminate a contract under this section with respect to the offering of an MA plan by a Medicare Advantage organization solely because the MA plan has failed to achieve a minimum quality rating under the 5-star rating system under section 1853(o)(4).".

SEC. 17002. REQUIREMENT FOR ENROLLMENT DATA REPORTING FOR MEDICARE.

Section 1874 of the Social Security Act (42 U.S.C. 1395kk) is amended by adding at the end the following new subsection:

"(g) REQUIREMENT FOR ENROLLMENT DATA REPORTING.—

"(1) IN GENERAL.—Each year (beginning with 2016), the Secretary shall submit to the Committees on Ways and Means and Energy and Commerce of the House of Representatives and the Committee on Finance of the Senate a report on Medicare enrollment data (and, in the case of part A, on data on individuals receiving benefits under such part) as of a date in such year specified by the Secretary. Such data shall be presented—

"(A) by Congressional district and State; and

"(B) in a manner that provides for such data based on—

"(i) fee-for-service enrollment (as defined in paragraph (2));

"(ii) enrollment under part C (including separate for aggregate enrollment in MA–PD plans and aggregate enrollment in MA plans that are not MA–PD plans); and

"(iii) enrollment under part D.

"(2) FEE-FOR-SERVICE ENROLLMENT DE-FINED.—For purpose of paragraph (1)(B)(i), the term 'fee-for-service enrollment' means aggregate enrollment (including receipt of benefits other than through enrollment) under—

"(A) part A only;

"(B) part B only; and

"(C) both part A and part B.".

SEC. 17003. UPDATING THE WELCOME TO MEDI-CARE PACKAGE.

(a) IN GENERAL.—Not later than 12 months after the last day of the period for the request of information described in subsection (b), the Secretary of Health and Human Services shall, taking into consideration information collected pursuant to subsection (b), update the information included in the Welcome to Medicare package to include information, presented in a clear and simple manner, about options for receiving

benefits under the Medicare program under title XVIII of the Social Security Act (42 U.S.C. 1395 et seq.), including through the original medicare fee-for-service program under parts A and B of such title (42 U.S.C. 1395c et seq., 42 U.S.C. 1395j et seq.), Medicare Advantage plans under part C of such title (42 U.S.C. 1395w–21 et seq.), and prescription drug plans under part D of such title (42 U.S.C. 1395w–101 et seq.)). The Secretary shall make subsequent updates to the information included in the Welcome to Medicare package as appropriate.

(b) REQUEST FOR INFORMATION.—Not later than 6 months after the date of the enactment of this Act, the Secretary of Health and Human Services shall request information, including recommendations, from stakeholders (including patient advocates, issuers, and employers) on information included in the Welcome to Medicare package, including pertinent data and information regarding enrollment and coverage for Medicare eligible individuals.

SEC. 17004. NO PAYMENT FOR ITEMS AND SERV-ICES FURNISHED BY NEWLY EN-ROLLED PROVIDERS OR SUPPLIERS WITHIN A TEMPORARY MORATORIUM AREA.

(a) MEDICARE.—Section 1866(j)(7) of the Social Security Act (42 U.S.C. 1395cc(j)(7)) is amended—

(1) in the paragraph heading, by inserting "; NONPAYMENT" before the period; and

(2) by adding at the end the following new subparagraph:

"(C) NONPAYMENT.—

"(i) IN GENERAL.—No payment may be made under this title or under a program described in subparagraph (A) with respect to an item or service described in clause (ii) furnished on or after October 1, 2017.

"(ii) ITEM OR SERVICE DESCRIBED.—An item or service described in this clause is an item or service furnished—

"(I) within a geographic area with respect to which a temporary moratorium imposed under subparagraph (A) is in effect; and

"(II) by a provider of services or supplier that meets the requirements of clause (iii).

"(iii) REQUIREMENTS.—For purposes of clause (ii), the requirements of this clause are that a provider of services or supplier—

"(I) enrolls under this title on or after the effective date of such temporary moratorium; and

"(II) is within a category of providers of services and suppliers (as described in subparagraph (A)) subject to such temporary moratorium.

"(iv) PROHIBITION ON CHARGES FOR SPECIFIED ITEMS OR SERVICES.—In no case shall a provider of services or supplier described in clause (ii)(II) charge an individual or other person for an item or service described in clause (ii) furnished on or after October 1, 2017, to an individual entitled to benefits under part A or enrolled under part B or an individual under a program specified in subparagraph (A).".

(b) CONFORMING AMENDMENTS.—

(1) MEDICAID.—

(A) IN GENERAL.—Section 1903(i)(2) of the Social Security Act (42 U.S.C. 1396b(i)(2)), as amended by section 5005(a)(4), is further amended—

(i) in subparagraph (C), by striking "or" at the end; and

(ii) by adding at the end the following new subparagraph:

"(E) with respect to any amount expended for such an item or service furnished during calendar quarters beginning on or after October 1, 2017, subject to section 1902(kk)(4)(A)(ii)(II), within a geographic area that is subject to a moratorium imposed under section 1866(j)(7) by a provider or supplier that meets the requirements specified in subparagraph (C)(iii) of such section, during the period of such moratorium; or".

(B) EXCEPTION WITH RESPECT TO ACCESS.—Section 1902(kk)(4)(A)(ii) of the Social Security Act (42 U.S.C. 1396a(kk)(4)(A)(ii)) is amended to read as follows:

"(ii) EXCEPTIONS.—

"(I) COMPLIANCE WITH MORATORIUM.—A State shall not be required to comply with a temporary moratorium described in clause (i) if the State determines that the imposition of such temporary moratorium would adversely impact beneficiaries' access to medical assistance.

"(II) FFP AVAILABLE.—Notwithstanding section 1903(i)(2)(E), payment may be made to a State under this title with respect to amounts expended for items and services described in such section if the Secretary, in consultation with the State agency administering the State plan under this title (or a waiver of the plan), determines that denying payment to the State pursuant to such section would adversely impact beneficiaries' access to medical assistance.".

(C) STATE PLAN REQUIREMENT WITH RESPECT TO LIMITATION ON CHARGES TO BENEFICIARIES.—Section 1902(kk)(4)(A) of the Social Security Act (42 U.S.C. 1396a(kk)(4)(A)) is amended by adding at the end the following new clause:

"(iii) LIMITATION ON CHARGES TO BENEFICIARIES.—With respect to any amount expended for items or services furnished during calendar quarters beginning on or after October 1, 2017, the State prohibits, during the period of a temporary moratorium described in clause (i), a provider meeting the requirements specified in subparagraph (C)(iii) of section 1866(j)(7) from charging an individual or other person eligible to receive medical assistance under the State plan under this title (or a waiver of the plan) for an item or service described in section 1903(i)(2)(E) furnished to such an individual.".

(2) CORRECTING AMENDMENTS TO RELATED PROVISIONS.—

(A) SECTION 1866(J).—Section 1866(j) of the Social Security Act (42 U.S.C. 1395cc(j)) is amended—

(i) in paragraph (1)(A)—

(I) by striking "paragraph (4)" and inserting "paragraph (5)";

(II) by striking "moratoria in accordance with paragraph (5)" and inserting "moratoria in accordance with paragraph (7)"; and

(III) by striking "paragraph (6)" and inserting "paragraph (9)"; and

(ii) by redesignating the second paragraph (8) (redesignated by section 1304(1) of Public Law 111-152) as paragraph (9).

(B) SECTION 1902(KK).—Section 1902(kk) of such Act (42 U.S.C. 1396a(kk)) is amended—

(i) in paragraph (1), by striking "section 1886(j)(2)" and inserting "section 1866(j)(2)";

(ii) in paragraph (2), by striking "section 1886(j)(3)" and inserting "section 1866(j)(3)";

(iii) in paragraph (3), by striking "section 1886(j)(4)" and inserting "section 1866(j)(5)"; and

(iv) in paragraph (4)(A), by striking "section 1886(j)(6)" and inserting "section 1866(j)(7)".

SEC. 17005. PRESERVATION OF MEDICARE BENEFICIARY CHOICE UNDER MEDICARE ADVANTAGE.

Section 1851(e)(2) of the Social Security Act (42 U.S.C. 1395w-21(e)(2)) is amended—

(1) in subparagraph (C)—

(A) in the heading, by inserting "FROM 2011 THROUGH 2018" after "45-DAY PERIOD"; and

(B) by inserting "and ending with 2018" after "beginning with 2011"; and

(2) by adding at the end the following new subparagraph:

"(G) CONTINUOUS OPEN ENROLLMENT AND DISENROLLMENT FOR FIRST 3 MONTHS IN 2016 AND SUBSEQUENT YEARS.—

"(i) IN GENERAL.—Subject to clause (ii) and subparagraph (D)—

"(I) in the case of an MA eligible individual who is enrolled in an MA plan, at any time during the first 3 months of a year (beginning with 2019); or

"(II) in the case of an individual who first becomes an MA eligible individual during a year (beginning with 2019) and enrolls in an MA plan, during the first 3 months during such year in which the individual is an MA eligible individual;

such MA eligible individual may change the election under subsection (a)(1).

"(ii) LIMITATION OF ONE CHANGE DURING OPEN ENROLLMENT PERIOD EACH YEAR.—An individual may change the election pursuant to clause (i) only once during the applicable 3-month period described in such clause in each year. The limitation under this clause shall not apply to changes in elections effected during an annual, coordinated election period under paragraph (3) or during a special enrollment period under paragraph (4).

"(iii) LIMITED APPLICATION TO PART D.—Clauses (i) and (ii) of this subparagraph shall only apply with respect to changes in enrollment in a prescription drug plan under part D in the case of an individual who, previous to such change in enrollment, is enrolled in a Medicare Advantage plan.

"(iv) LIMITATIONS ON MARKETING.—Pursuant to subsection (j), no unsolicited marketing or marketing materials may be sent to an individual described in clause (i) during the continuous open enrollment and disenrollment period established for the individual under such clause, notwithstanding marketing guidelines established by the Centers for Medicare & Medicaid Services.".

SEC. 17006. ALLOWING END-STAGE RENAL DISEASE BENEFICIARIES TO CHOOSE A MEDICARE ADVANTAGE PLAN.

(a) REMOVING PROHIBITION.—

(1) IN GENERAL.—Section 1851(a)(3) of the Social Security Act (42 U.S.C. 1395w-21(a)(3)) is amended—

(A) by striking subparagraph (B); and

(B) by striking "ELIGIBLE INDIVIDUAL" and all that follows through "In this title, subject to subparagraph (B)," and inserting "ELIGIBLE INDIVIDUAL.—In this title,".

(2) CONFORMING AMENDMENTS.—

(A) Section 1852(b)(1) of the Social Security Act (42 U.S.C. 1395w-22(b)(1)) is amended—

(i) by striking subparagraph (B); and

(ii) by striking "BENEFICIARIES" and all that follows through "A Medicare+Choice organization" and inserting "BENEFICIARIES.—A Medicare Advantage organization".

(B) Section 1859(b)(6) of the Social Security Act (42 U.S.C. 1395w-28(b)(6)) is amended, in the last sentence, by striking "may waive" and all that follows through "subparagraph and".

(3) EFFECTIVE DATE.—The amendments made by this subsection shall apply with respect to plan years beginning on or after January 1, 2021.

(b) EXCLUDING COSTS FOR KIDNEY ACQUISITIONS FROM MA BENCHMARK.—Section 1853 of the Social Security Act (42 U.S.C. 1395w-23) is amended—

(1) in subsection (k)—

(A) in paragraph (1)—

(i) in the matter preceding subparagraph (A), by striking "paragraphs (2) and (4)" and inserting "paragraphs (2), (4), and (5)"; and

(ii) in subparagraph (B)(i), by striking "paragraphs (2) and (4)" and inserting "paragraphs (2), (4), and (5)"; and

(B) by adding at the end the following new paragraph:

"(5) EXCLUSION OF COSTS FOR KIDNEY ACQUISITIONS FROM CAPITATION RATES.—After determining the applicable amount for an area for a year under paragraph (1) (beginning with 2021),

the Secretary shall adjust such applicable amount to exclude from such applicable amount the Secretary's estimate of the standardized costs for payments for organ acquisitions for kidney transplants covered under this title (including expenses covered under section 1881(d)) in the area for the year."; and

(2) in subsection (n)(2)—

(A) in subparagraph (A)(i), by inserting "and, for 2021 and subsequent years, the exclusion of payments for organ acquisitions for kidney transplants from the capitation rate as described in subsection (k)(5)" before the semicolon at the end;

(B) in subparagraph (E), in the matter preceding clause (i), by striking "subparagraph (F)" and inserting "subparagraphs (F) and (G)"; and

(C) by adding at the end the following new subparagraph:

"(G) APPLICATION OF KIDNEY ACQUISITIONS ADJUSTMENT.—The base payment amount specified in subparagraph (E) for a year (beginning with 2021) shall be adjusted in the same manner under paragraph (5) of subsection (k) as the applicable amount is adjusted under such subsection.".

(c) FFS COVERAGE OF KIDNEY ACQUISITIONS.—

(1) IN GENERAL.—Section 1852(a)(1)(B)(i) of the Social Security Act (42 U.S.C. 1395w-22(a)(1)(B)(i)) is amended by inserting "or coverage for organ acquisitions for kidney transplants, including as covered under section 1881(d)" after "hospice care".

(2) CONFORMING AMENDMENT.—Section 1851(i) of the Social Security Act (42 U.S.C. 1395w-21(i)) is amended by adding at the end the following new paragraph:

"(3) FFS PAYMENT FOR EXPENSES FOR KIDNEY ACQUISITIONS.—Paragraphs (1) and (2) shall not apply with respect to expenses for organ acquisitions for kidney transplants described in section 1852(a)(1)(B)(i).".

(3) EFFECTIVE DATE.—The amendments made by this subsection shall apply with respect to plan years beginning on or after January 1, 2021.

(d) EVALUATION OF QUALITY.—

(1) IN GENERAL.—The Secretary of Health and Human Services (in this subsection referred to as the "Secretary") shall conduct an evaluation of whether the 5-star rating system based on the data collected under section 1852(e) of the Social Security Act (42 U.S.C. 1395w-22(e)) should include a quality measure specifically related to care for enrollees in Medicare Advantage plans under part C of title XVIII of such Act determined to have end-stage renal disease.

(2) PUBLIC AVAILABILITY.—Not later than April 1, 2020, the Secretary shall post on the Internet website of the Centers for Medicare & Medicaid Services the results of the evaluation under paragraph (1).

(e) REPORT.—Not later than December 31, 2023, the Secretary of Health and Human Services (in this subsection referred to as the "Secretary") shall submit to Congress a report on the impact of the provisions of, and amendments made by, this section with respect to the following:

(1) Spending under—

(A) the original Medicare fee-for-service program under parts A and B of title XVIII of the Social Security Act; and

(B) the Medicare Advantage program under part C of such title.

(2) The number of enrollees determined to have end-stage renal disease—

(A) in the original Medicare fee-for-service program; and

(B) in the Medicare Advantage program.

(3) The sufficiency of the amount of data under the original Medicare fee-for-service program for individuals determined to have end-

stage renal disease for purposes of determining payment rates for end-stage renal disease under the Medicare Advantage program.

(f) IMPROVEMENTS TO RISK ADJUSTMENT UNDER MEDICARE ADVANTAGE.—

(1) IN GENERAL.—Section 1853(a)(1) of the Social Security Act (42 U.S.C. 1395w–23(a)(1)) is amended—

(A) in subparagraph (C)(i), by striking "The Secretary" and inserting "Subject to subparagraph (I), the Secretary"; and

(B) by adding at the end the following new subparagraph:

"(I) IMPROVEMENTS TO RISK ADJUSTMENT FOR 2019 AND SUBSEQUENT YEARS.—

"(i) IN GENERAL.—In order to determine the appropriate adjustment for health status under subparagraph (C)(i), the following shall apply:

"(I) TAKING INTO ACCOUNT TOTAL NUMBER OF DISEASES OR CONDITIONS.—The Secretary shall take into account the total number of diseases or conditions of an individual enrolled in an MA plan. The Secretary shall make an additional adjustment under such subparagraph as the number of diseases or conditions of an individual increases.

"(II) USING AT LEAST 2 YEARS OF DIAGNOSTIC DATA.—The Secretary may use at least 2 years of diagnosis data.

"(III) PROVIDING SEPARATE ADJUSTMENTS FOR DUAL ELIGIBLE INDIVIDUALS.—With respect to individuals who are dually eligible for benefits under this title and title XIX, the Secretary shall make separate adjustments for each of the following:

"(aa) Full-benefit dual eligible individuals (as defined in section 1935(c)(6)).

"(bb) Such individuals not described in item (aa).

"(IV) EVALUATION OF MENTAL HEALTH AND SUBSTANCE USE DISORDERS.—The Secretary shall evaluate the impact of including additional diagnosis codes related to mental health and substance use disorders in the risk adjustment model.

"(V) EVALUATION OF CHRONIC KIDNEY DISEASE.—The Secretary shall evaluate the impact of including the severity of chronic kidney disease in the risk adjustment model.

"(VI) EVALUATION OF PAYMENT RATES FOR END-STAGE RENAL DISEASE.—The Secretary shall evaluate whether other factors (in addition to those described in subparagraph (H)) should be taken into consideration when computing payment rates under such subparagraph.

"(ii) PHASED-IN IMPLEMENTATION.—The Secretary shall phase-in any changes to risk adjustment payment amounts under subparagraph (C)(i) under this subparagraph over a 3-year period, beginning with 2019, with such changes being fully implemented for 2022 and subsequent years.

"(iii) OPPORTUNITY FOR REVIEW AND PUBLIC COMMENT.—The Secretary shall provide an opportunity for review of the proposed changes to such risk adjustment payment amounts under this subparagraph and a public comment period of not less than 60 days before implementing such changes.".

(2) STUDIES AND REPORTS.—

(A) REPORTS ON THE RISK ADJUSTMENT SYSTEM.—

(i) MEDPAC EVALUATION AND REPORT.—

(I) EVALUATION.—The Medicare Payment Advisory Commission shall conduct an evaluation of the impact of the provisions of, and amendments made by, this section on risk scores for enrollees in Medicare Advantage plans under part C of title XVIII of the Social Security Act and payments to Medicare Advantage plans under such part, including the impact of such provisions and amendments on the overall accuracy of risk scores under the Medicare Advantage program.

(II) REPORT.—Not later than July 1, 2020, the Medicare Payment Advisory Commission shall submit to Congress a report on the evaluation under subclause (I), together with recommendations for such legislation and administrative action as the Commission determines appropriate.

(ii) REPORTS BY SECRETARY OF HEALTH AND HUMAN SERVICES.—Not later than December 31, 2018, and every 3 years thereafter, the Secretary of Health and Human Services shall submit to Congress a report on the risk adjustment model and the ESRD risk adjustment model under the Medicare Advantage program under part C of title XVIII of the Social Security Act, including any revisions to either such model since the previous report. Such report shall include information on how such revisions impact the predictive ratios under either such model for groups of enrollees in Medicare Advantage plans, including very high and very low cost enrollees, and groups defined by the number of chronic conditions of enrollees.

(B) STUDY AND REPORT ON FUNCTIONAL STATUS.—

(i) STUDY.—The Comptroller General of the United States (in this subparagraph referred to as the "Comptroller General") shall conduct a study on how to most accurately measure the functional status of enrollees in Medicare Advantage plans and whether the use of such functional status would improve the accuracy of risk adjustment payments under the Medicare Advantage program under part C of title XVIII of the Social Security Act. Such study shall include an analysis of the challenges in collecting and reporting functional status information for Medicare Advantage plans under such part, providers of services and suppliers under the Medicare program, and the Centers for Medicare & Medicaid Services.

(ii) REPORT.—Not later than June 30, 2018, the Comptroller General shall submit to Congress a report containing the results of the study under clause (i), together with recommendations for such legislation and administrative action as the Comptroller General determines appropriate.

SEC. 17007. IMPROVEMENTS TO THE ASSIGNMENT OF BENEFICIARIES UNDER THE MEDICARE SHARED SAVINGS PROGRAM.

Section 1899(c) of the Social Security Act (42 U.S.C. 1395jjj(c)) is amended—

(1) by striking "utilization of primary" and inserting "utilization of—

"(1) in the case of performance years beginning on or after April 1, 2012, primary";

(2) in paragraph (1), as added by paragraph (1) of this section, by striking the period at the end and inserting "; and";

(3) by adding at the end the following new paragraph:

"(2) in the case of performance years beginning on or after January 1, 2019, services provided under this title by a Federally qualified health center or rural health clinic (as those terms are defined in section 1861(aa)), as may be determined by the Secretary.".

TITLE XVIII—OTHER PROVISIONS

SEC. 18001. EXCEPTION FROM GROUP HEALTH PLAN REQUIREMENTS FOR QUALIFIED SMALL EMPLOYER HEALTH REIMBURSEMENT ARRANGEMENTS.

(a) AMENDMENTS TO THE INTERNAL REVENUE CODE OF 1986 AND THE PATIENT PROTECTION AND AFFORDABLE CARE ACT.—

(1) IN GENERAL.—Section 9831 of the Internal Revenue Code of 1986 is amended by adding at the end the following new subsection:

"(d) EXCEPTION FOR QUALIFIED SMALL EMPLOYER HEALTH REIMBURSEMENT ARRANGEMENTS.—

"(1) IN GENERAL.—For purposes of this title (except as provided in section 4980I(f)(4) and notwithstanding any other provision of this

title), the term 'group health plan' shall not include any qualified small employer health reimbursement arrangement.

"(2) QUALIFIED SMALL EMPLOYER HEALTH REIMBURSEMENT ARRANGEMENT.—For purposes of this subsection—

"(A) IN GENERAL.—The term 'qualified small employer health reimbursement arrangement' means an arrangement which—

"(i) is described in subparagraph (B), and

"(ii) is provided on the same terms to all eligible employees of the eligible employer.

"(B) ARRANGEMENT DESCRIBED.—An arrangement is described in this subparagraph if—

"(i) such arrangement is funded solely by an eligible employer and no salary reduction contributions may be made under such arrangement,

"(ii) such arrangement provides, after the employee provides proof of coverage, for the payment of, or reimbursement of, an eligible employee for expenses for medical care (as defined in section 213(d)) incurred by the eligible employee or the eligible employee's family members (as determined under the terms of the arrangement), and

"(iii) the amount of payments and reimbursements described in clause (ii) for any year do not exceed $4,950 ($10,000 in the case of an arrangement that also provides for payments or reimbursements for family members of the employee).

"(C) CERTAIN VARIATION PERMITTED.—For purposes of subparagraph (A)(ii), an arrangement shall not fail to be treated as provided on the same terms to each eligible employee merely because the employee's permitted benefit under such arrangement varies in accordance with the variation in the price of an insurance policy in the relevant individual health insurance market based on—

"(i) the age of the eligible employee (and, in the case of an arrangement which covers medical expenses of the eligible employee's family members, the age of such family members), or

"(ii) the number of family members of the eligible employee the medical expenses of which are covered under such arrangement.

The variation permitted under the preceding sentence shall be determined by reference to the same insurance policy with respect to all eligible employees.

"(D) RULES RELATING TO MAXIMUM DOLLAR LIMITATION.—

"(i) AMOUNT PRORATED IN CERTAIN CASES.—In the case of an individual who is not covered by an arrangement for the entire year, the limitation under subparagraph (B)(iii) for such year shall be an amount which bears the same ratio to the amount which would (but for this clause) be in effect for such individual for such year under subparagraph (B)(iii) as the number of months for which such individual is covered by the arrangement for such year bears to 12.

"(ii) INFLATION ADJUSTMENT.—In the case of any year beginning after 2016, each of the dollar amounts in subparagraph (B)(iii) shall be increased by an amount equal to—

"(I) such dollar amount, multiplied by

"(II) the cost-of-living adjustment determined under section 1(f)(3) for the calendar year in which the taxable year begins, determined by substituting 'calendar year 2015' for 'calendar year 1992' in subparagraph (B) thereof.

If any dollar amount increased under the preceding sentence is not a multiple of $50, such dollar amount shall be rounded to the next lowest multiple of $50.

"(3) OTHER DEFINITIONS.—For purposes of this subsection—

"(A) ELIGIBLE EMPLOYEE.—The term 'eligible employee' means any employee of an eligible employer, except that the terms of the arrangement

may exclude from consideration employees described in any clause of section 105(h)(3)(B) (applied by substituting '90 days' for '3 years' in clause (i) thereof).

"(B) ELIGIBLE EMPLOYER.—The term 'eligible employer' means an employer that—

"(i) is not an applicable large employer as defined in section 4980H(c)(2), and

"(ii) does not offer a group health plan to any of its employees.

"(C) PERMITTED BENEFIT.—The term 'permitted benefit' means, with respect to any eligible employee, the maximum dollar amount of payments and reimbursements which may be made under the terms of the qualified small employer health reimbursement arrangement for the year with respect to such employee.

"(4) NOTICE.—

"(A) IN GENERAL.—An employer funding a qualified small employer health reimbursement arrangement for any year shall, not later than 90 days before the beginning of such year (or, in the case of an employee who is not eligible to participate in the arrangement as of the beginning of such year, the date on which such employee is first so eligible), provide a written notice to each eligible employee which includes the information described in subparagraph (B).

"(B) CONTENTS OF NOTICE.—The notice required under subparagraph (A) shall include each of the following:

"(i) A statement of the amount which would be such eligible employee's permitted benefit under the arrangement for the year.

"(ii) A statement that the eligible employee should provide the information described in clause (i) to any health insurance exchange to which the employee applies for advance payment of the premium assistance tax credit.

"(iii) A statement that if the employee is not covered under minimum essential coverage for any month the employee may be subject to tax under section 5000A for such month and reimbursements under the arrangement may be includible in gross income.".

"(2) LIMITATION ON EXCLUSION FROM GROSS INCOME.—Section 106 of such Code is amended by adding at the end the following:

"(g) QUALIFIED SMALL EMPLOYER HEALTH REIMBURSEMENT ARRANGEMENT.—For purposes of this section and section 105, payments or reimbursements from a qualified small employer health reimbursement arrangement (as defined in section 9831(d)) of an individual for medical care (as defined in section 213(d)) shall not be treated as paid or reimbursed under employer-provided coverage for medical expenses under an accident or health plan if for the month in which such medical care is provided the individual does not have minimum essential coverage (within the meaning of section 5000A(f)).".

"(3) COORDINATION WITH HEALTH INSURANCE PREMIUM CREDIT.—Section 36B(c) of such Code is amended by adding at the end the following new paragraph:

"(4) SPECIAL RULES FOR QUALIFIED SMALL EMPLOYER HEALTH REIMBURSEMENT ARRANGEMENTS.—

"(A) IN GENERAL.—The term 'coverage month' shall not include any month with respect to an employee (or any spouse or dependent of such employee) if for such month the employee is provided a qualified small employer health reimbursement arrangement which constitutes affordable coverage.

"(B) DENIAL OF DOUBLE BENEFIT.—In the case of any employee who is provided a qualified small employer health reimbursement arrangement for any coverage month (determined without regard to subparagraph (A)), the credit otherwise allowable under subsection (a) to the taxpayer for such month shall be reduced (but not below zero) by the amount described in subparagraph (C)(i)(II) for such month.

"(C) AFFORDABLE COVERAGE.—For purposes of subparagraph (A), a qualified small employer health reimbursement arrangement shall be treated as constituting affordable coverage for a month if—

"(i) the excess of—

"(I) the amount that would be paid by the employee as the premium for such month for self-only coverage under the second lowest cost silver plan offered in the relevant individual health insurance market, over

"(II) 1/12 of the employee's permitted benefit (as defined in section 9831(d)(3)(C)) under such arrangement, does not exceed—

"(ii) 1/12 of 9.5 percent of the employee's household income.

"(D) QUALIFIED SMALL EMPLOYER HEALTH REIMBURSEMENT ARRANGEMENT.—For purposes of this paragraph, the term 'qualified small employer health reimbursement arrangement' has the meaning given such term by section 9831(d)(2).

"(E) COVERAGE FOR LESS THAN ENTIRE YEAR.—In the case of an employee who is provided a qualified small employer health reimbursement arrangement for less than an entire year, subparagraph (C)(i)(II) shall be applied by substituting 'the number of months during the year for which such arrangement was provided' for '12'.

"(F) INDEXING.—In the case of plan years beginning in any calendar year after 2014, the Secretary shall adjust the 9.5 percent amount under subparagraph (C)(ii) in the same manner as the percentages are adjusted under subsection (b)(3)(A)(ii).".

(4) APPLICATION OF EXCISE TAX ON HIGH COST EMPLOYER-SPONSORED HEALTH COVERAGE.—

(A) IN GENERAL.—Section 4980I(f)(4) of such Code is amended by adding at the end the following: "Section 9831(d)(1) shall not apply for purposes of this section.".

(B) DETERMINATION OF COST OF COVERAGE.—Section 4980I(d)(2) of such Code is amended by redesignating subparagraph (D) as subparagraph (E) and by inserting after subparagraph (C) the following new subparagraph:

"(D) QUALIFIED SMALL EMPLOYER HEALTH REIMBURSEMENT ARRANGEMENTS.—In the case of applicable employer-sponsored coverage consisting of coverage under any qualified small employer health reimbursement arrangement (as defined in section 9831(d)(2)), the cost of coverage shall be equal to the amount described in section 6051(a)(15).".

(5) ENFORCEMENT OF NOTICE REQUIREMENT.—Section 6652 of such Code is amended by adding at the end the following new subsection:

"(o) FAILURE TO PROVIDE NOTICES WITH RESPECT TO QUALIFIED SMALL EMPLOYER HEALTH REIMBURSEMENT ARRANGEMENTS.—In the case of each failure to provide a written notice as required by section 9831(d)(4) unless it is shown that such failure is due to reasonable cause and not willful neglect, there shall be paid, on notice and demand of the Secretary and in the same manner as tax, by the person failing to provide such written notice, an amount equal to $50 per employee per incident of failure to provide such notice, but the total amount imposed on such person for all such failures during any calendar year shall not exceed $2,500.".

(6) REPORTING.—

(A) W–2 REPORTING.—Section 6051(a) of such Code is amended by striking "and" at the end of paragraph (13), by striking the period at the end of paragraph (14) and inserting ", and", and by inserting after paragraph (14) the following new paragraph:

"(15) the total amount of permitted benefit (as defined in section 9831(d)(3)(C)) for the year under a qualified small employer health reimbursement arrangement (as defined in section 9831(d)(2)) with respect to the employee.".

(B) INFORMATION REQUIRED TO BE PROVIDED BY EXCHANGE SUBSIDY APPLICANTS.—Section 1411(b)(3) of the Patient Protection and Affordable Care Act is amended by redesignating subparagraph (B) as subparagraph (C) and by inserting after subparagraph (A) the following new subparagraph:

"(B) CERTAIN INDIVIDUAL HEALTH INSURANCE POLICIES OBTAINED THROUGH SMALL EMPLOYERS.—The amount of the enrollee's permitted benefit (as defined in section 9831(d)(3)(C) of the Internal Revenue Code of 1986) under a qualified small employer health reimbursement arrangement (as defined in section 9831(d)(2) of such Code).".

(7) EFFECTIVE DATES.—

(A) IN GENERAL.—Except as otherwise provided in this paragraph, the amendments made by this subsection shall apply to years beginning after December 31, 2016.

(B) TRANSITION RELIEF.—The relief under Treasury Notice 2015–17 shall be treated as applying to any plan year beginning on or before December 31, 2016.

(C) COORDINATION WITH HEALTH INSURANCE PREMIUM CREDIT.—The amendments made by paragraph (3) shall apply to taxable years beginning after December 31, 2016.

(D) EMPLOYEE NOTICE.—

(i) IN GENERAL.—The amendments made by paragraph (5) shall apply to notices with respect to years beginning after December 31, 2016.

(ii) TRANSITION RELIEF.—For purposes of section 6652(o) of the Internal Revenue Code of 1986 (as added by this Act), a person shall not be treated as failing to provide a written notice as required by section 9831(d)(4) of such Code if such notice is so provided not later than 90 days after the date of the enactment of this Act.

(E) W–2 REPORTING.—The amendments made by paragraph (6)(A) shall apply to calendar years beginning after December 31, 2016.

(F) INFORMATION PROVIDED BY EXCHANGE SUBSIDY APPLICANTS.—

(i) IN GENERAL.—The amendments made by paragraph (6)(B) shall apply to applications for enrollment made after December 31, 2016.

(ii) VERIFICATION.—Verification under section 1411 of the Patient Protection and Affordable Care Act of information provided under section 1411(b)(3)(B) of such Act shall apply with respect to months beginning after October 2016.

(iii) TRANSITIONAL RELIEF.—In the case of an application for enrollment under section 1411(b) of the Patient Protection and Affordable Care Act made before April 1, 2017, the requirement of section 1411(b)(3)(B) of such Act shall be treated as met if the information described therein is provided not later than 30 days after the date on which the applicant receives the notice described in section 9831(d)(4) of the Internal Revenue Code of 1986.

(8) SUBSTANTIATION REQUIREMENTS.—The Secretary of the Treasury (or his designee) may issue substantiation requirements as necessary to carry out this subsection.

(b) AMENDMENTS TO THE EMPLOYEE RETIREMENT INCOME SECURITY ACT OF 1974.—

(1) IN GENERAL.—Section 733(a)(1) of the Employee Retirement Income Security Act of 1974 (29 U.S.C. 1191b(a)(1)) is amended by adding at the end the following: "Such term shall not include any qualified small employer health reimbursement arrangement (as defined in section 9831(d)(2) of the Internal Revenue Code of 1986).".

(2) EXCEPTION FROM CONTINUATION COVERAGE REQUIREMENTS, ETC.—Section 607(1) of such Act (29 U.S.C. 1167(1)) is amended by adding at the end the following: "Such term shall not include any qualified small employer health reimbursement arrangement (as defined in section 9831(d)(2) of the Internal Revenue Code of 1986).".

(3) EFFECTIVE DATE.—The amendments made by this subsection shall apply to plan years beginning after December 31, 2016.

(c) AMENDMENTS TO THE PUBLIC HEALTH SERVICE ACT.—

(1) IN GENERAL.—Section 2791(a)(1) of the Public Health Service Act (42 U.S.C. 300gg–91(a)(1)) is amended by adding at the end the following: "Except for purposes of part C of title XI of the Social Security Act (42 U.S.C. 1320d et seq.), such term shall not include any qualified small employer health reimbursement arrangement (as defined in section 9831(d)(2) of the Internal Revenue Code of 1986).".

(2) EXCEPTION FROM CONTINUATION COVERAGE REQUIREMENTS.—Section 2208(1) of the Public Health Service Act (42 U.S.C. 300bb–8(1)) is amended by adding at the end the following: "Such term shall not include any qualified small employer health reimbursement arrangement (as defined in section 9831(d)(2) of the Internal Revenue Code of 1986).".

(3) EFFECTIVE DATE.—The amendments made by this subsection shall apply to plan years beginning after December 31, 2016.

TITLE XIX—INVESTING IN PREVENTION AND FAMILY SERVICES

SEC. 19001. PURPOSE.

The purpose of this title is to enable States to use Federal funds available under parts B and E of title IV of the Social Security Act to provide enhanced support to children and families and prevent foster care placements through the provision of mental health and substance abuse prevention and treatment services, in-home parent skill-based programs, and kinship navigator services.

Subtitle A—Prevention Activities Under Title IV–E

SEC. 19011. FOSTER CARE PREVENTION SERVICES AND PROGRAMS.

(a) STATE OPTION.—Section 471 of the Social Security Act (42 U.S.C. 671) is amended—

(1) in subsection (a)(1), by striking "and" and all that follows through the semicolon and inserting ", adoption assistance in accordance with section 473, and, at the option of the State, services or programs specified in subsection (e)(1) of this section for children who are candidates for foster care or who are pregnant or parenting foster youth and the parents or kin caregivers of the children, in accordance with the requirements of that subsection;"; and

(2) by adding at the end the following:

"(e) PREVENTION AND FAMILY SERVICES AND PROGRAMS.—

"(1) IN GENERAL.—Subject to the succeeding provisions of this subsection, the Secretary may make a payment to a State for providing the following services or programs for a child described in paragraph (2) and the parents or kin caregivers of the child when the need of the child, such a parent, or such a caregiver for the services or programs are directly related to the safety, permanence, or well-being of the child or to preventing the child from entering foster care:

"(A) MENTAL HEALTH AND SUBSTANCE ABUSE PREVENTION AND TREATMENT SERVICES.—Mental health and substance abuse prevention and treatment services provided by a qualified clinician for not more than a 12-month period that begins on any date described in paragraph (3) with respect to the child.

"(B) IN-HOME PARENT SKILL-BASED PROGRAMS.—In-home parent skill-based programs for not more than a 12-month period that begins on any date described in paragraph (3) with respect to the child and that include parenting skills training, parent education, and individual and family counseling.

"(2) CHILD DESCRIBED.—For purposes of paragraph (1), a child described in this paragraph is the following:

"(A) A child who is a candidate for foster care (as defined in section 475(13)) but can remain safely at home or in a kinship placement with receipt of services or programs specified in paragraph (1).

"(B) A child in foster care who is a pregnant or parenting foster youth.

"(3) DATE DESCRIBED.—For purposes of paragraph (1), the dates described in this paragraph are the following:

"(A) The date on which a child is identified in a prevention plan maintained under paragraph (4) as a child who is a candidate for foster care (as defined in section 475(13)).

"(B) The date on which a child is identified in a prevention plan maintained under paragraph (4) as a pregnant or parenting foster youth in need of services or programs specified in paragraph (1).

"(4) REQUIREMENTS RELATED TO PROVIDING SERVICES AND PROGRAMS.—Services and programs specified in paragraph (1) may be provided under this subsection only if specified in advance in the child's prevention plan described in subparagraph (A) and the requirements in subparagraphs (B) through (E) are met:

"(A) PREVENTION PLAN.—The State maintains a written prevention plan for the child that meets the following requirements (as applicable):

"(i) CANDIDATES.—In the case of a child who is a candidate for foster care described in paragraph (2)(A), the prevention plan—

"(I) identify the foster care prevention strategy for the child so that the child may remain safely at home, live temporarily with a kin caregiver until reunification can be safely achieved, or live permanently with a kin caregiver;

"(II) list the services or programs to be provided to or on behalf of the child to ensure the success of that prevention strategy; and

"(III) comply with such other requirements as the Secretary shall establish.

"(ii) PREGNANT OR PARENTING FOSTER YOUTH.—In the case of a child who is a pregnant or parenting foster youth described in paragraph (2)(B), the prevention plan shall—

"(I) be included in the child's case plan required under section 475(1);

"(II) list the services or programs to be provided to or on behalf of the youth to ensure that the youth is prepared (in the case of a pregnant foster youth) or able (in the case of a parenting foster youth) to be a parent;

"(III) describe the foster care prevention strategy for any child born to the youth; and

"(IV) comply with such other requirements as the Secretary shall establish.

"(B) TRAUMA-INFORMED.—The services or programs to be provided to or on behalf of a child are provided under an organizational structure and treatment framework that involves understanding, recognizing, and responding to the effects of all types of trauma and in accordance with recognized principles of a trauma-informed approach and trauma-specific interventions to address trauma's consequences and facilitate healing.

"(C) ONLY SERVICES AND PROGRAMS PROVIDED IN ACCORDANCE WITH PROMISING, SUPPORTED, OR WELL-SUPPORTED PRACTICES PERMITTED.—

"(i) IN GENERAL.—Only State expenditures for services or programs specified in subparagraph (A) or (B) of paragraph (1) that are provided in accordance with practices that meet the requirements specified in clause (ii) of this subparagraph and that meet the requirements specified in clause (iii), (iv), or (v), respectively, for being a promising, supported, or well-supported practice, shall be eligible for a Federal matching payment under section 474(a)(6)(A).

"(ii) GENERAL PRACTICE REQUIREMENTS.—The general practice requirements specified in this clause are the following:

"(I) The practice has a book, manual, or other available writings that specify the components of the practice protocol and describe how to administer the practice.

"(II) There is no empirical basis suggesting that, compared to its likely benefits, the practice constitutes a risk of harm to those receiving it.

"(III) If multiple outcome studies have been conducted, the overall weight of evidence supports the benefits of the practice.

"(IV) Outcome measures are reliable and valid, and are administered consistently and accurately across all those receiving the practice.

"(V) There is no case data suggesting a risk of harm that was probably caused by the treatment and that was severe or frequent.

"(iii) PROMISING PRACTICE.—A practice shall be considered to be a 'promising practice' if the practice is superior to an appropriate comparison practice using conventional standards of statistical significance (in terms of demonstrated meaningful improvements in validated measures of important child and parent outcomes, such as mental health, substance abuse, and child safety and well-being), as established by the results or outcomes of at least one study that—

"(I) was rated by an independent systematic review for the quality of the study design and execution and determined to be well-designed and well-executed; and

"(II) utilized some form of control (such as an untreated group, a placebo group, or a wait list study).

"(iv) SUPPORTED PRACTICE.—A practice shall be considered to be a 'supported practice' if—

"(I) the practice is superior to an appropriate comparison practice using conventional standards of statistical significance (in terms of demonstrated meaningful improvements in validated measures of important child and parent outcomes, such as mental health, substance abuse, and child safety and well-being), as established by the results or outcomes of at least one study that—

"(aa) was rated by an independent systematic review for the quality of the study design and execution and determined to be well-designed and well-executed;

"(bb) was a rigorous random-controlled trial (or, if not available, a study using a rigorous quasi-experimental research design); and

"(cc) was carried out in a usual care or practice setting; and

"(II) the study described in subclause (I) established that the practice has a sustained effect (when compared to a control group) for at least 6 months beyond the end of the treatment.

"(v) WELL-SUPPORTED PRACTICE.—A practice shall be considered to be a 'well-supported practice' if—

"(I) the practice is superior to an appropriate comparison practice using conventional standards of statistical significance (in terms of demonstrated meaningful improvements in validated measures of important child and parent outcomes, such as mental health, substance abuse, and child safety and well-being), as established by the results or outcomes of at least two studies that—

"(aa) were rated by an independent systematic review for the quality of the study design and execution and determined to be well-designed and well-executed;

"(bb) were rigorous random-controlled trials (or, if not available, studies using a rigorous quasi-experimental research design); and

"(cc) were carried out in a usual care or practice setting; and

"(II) at least one of the studies described in subclause (I) established that the practice has a sustained effect (when compared to a control group) for at least 1 year beyond the end of treatment.

"(D) GUIDANCE ON PRACTICES CRITERIA AND PRE-APPROVED SERVICES AND PROGRAMS.—

"(i) IN GENERAL.—Not later than October 1, 2018, the Secretary shall issue guidance to States regarding the practices criteria required for services or programs to satisfy the requirements of subparagraph (C). The guidance shall include a pre-approved list of services and programs that satisfy the requirements.

"(ii) UPDATES.—The Secretary shall issue updates to the guidance required by clause (i) as often as the Secretary determines necessary.

"(E) OUTCOME ASSESSMENT AND REPORTING.— The State shall collect and report to the Secretary the following information with respect to each child for whom, or on whose behalf mental health and substance abuse prevention and treatment services or in-home parent skill-based programs are provided during a 12-month period beginning on the date the child is determined by the State to be a child described in paragraph (2):

"(i) The specific services or programs provided and the total expenditures for each of the services or programs.

"(ii) The duration of the services or programs provided.

"(iii) In the case of a child described in paragraph (2)(A), the child's placement status at the beginning, and at the end, of the 1-year period, respectively, and whether the child entered foster care within 2 years after being determined a candidate for foster care.

"(5) STATE PLAN COMPONENT.—

"(A) IN GENERAL.—A State electing to provide services or programs specified in paragraph (1) shall submit as part of the State plan required by subsection (a) a prevention services and programs plan component that meets the requirements of subparagraph (B).

"(B) PREVENTION SERVICES AND PROGRAMS PLAN COMPONENT.—In order to meet the requirements of this subparagraph, a prevention services and programs plan component, with respect to each 5-year period for which the plan component is in operation in the State, shall include the following:

"(i) How providing services and programs specified in paragraph (1) is expected to improve specific outcomes for children and families.

"(ii) How the State will monitor and oversee the safety of children who receive services and programs specified in paragraph (1), including through periodic risk assessments throughout the period in which the services and programs are provided on behalf of a child and reexamination of the prevention plan maintained for the child under paragraph (4) for the provision of the services or programs if the State determines the risk of the child entering foster care remains high despite the provision of the services or programs.

"(iii) With respect to the services and programs specified in subparagraphs (A) and (B) of paragraph (1), information on the specific promising, supported, or well-supported practices the State plans to use to provide the services or programs, including a description of—

"(I) the services or programs and whether the practices used are promising, supported, or well-supported;

"(II) how the State plans to implement the services or programs, including how implementation of the services or programs will be continuously monitored to ensure fidelity to the practice model and to determine outcomes achieved and how information learned from the monitoring will be used to refine and improve practices;

"(III) how the State selected the services or programs;

"(IV) the target population for the services or programs; and

"(V) how each service or program provided will be evaluated through a well-designed and rigorous process, which may consist of an ongoing, cross-site evaluation approved by the Secretary.

"(iv) A description of the consultation that the State agencies responsible for administering the State plans under this part and part B engage in with other State agencies responsible for administering health programs, including mental health and substance abuse prevention and treatment services, and with other public and private agencies with experience in administering child and family services, including community-based organizations, in order to foster a continuum of care for children described in paragraph (2) and their parents or kin caregivers.

"(v) A description of how the State shall assess children and their parents or kin caregivers to determine eligibility for services or programs specified in paragraph (1).

"(vi) A description of how the services or programs specified in paragraph (1) that are provided for or on behalf of a child and the parents or kin caregivers of the child will be coordinated with other child and family services provided to the child and the parents or kin caregivers of the child under the State plan under part B.

"(vii) Descriptions of steps the State is taking to support and enhance a competent, skilled, and professional child welfare workforce to deliver trauma-informed and evidence-based services, including—

"(I) ensuring that staff is qualified to provide services or programs that are consistent with the promising, supported, or well-supported practice models selected; and

"(II) developing appropriate prevention plans, and conducting the risk assessments required under clause (iii).

"(viii) A description of how the State will provide training and support for caseworkers in assessing what children and their families need, connecting to the families served, knowing how to access and deliver the needed trauma-informed and evidence-based services, and overseeing and evaluating the continuing appropriateness of the services.

"(ix) A description of how caseload size and type for prevention caseworkers will be determined, managed, and overseen.

"(x) An assurance that the State will report to the Secretary such information and data as the Secretary may require with respect to the provision of services and programs specified in paragraph (1), including information and data necessary to determine the performance measures for the State under paragraph (6) and compliance with paragraph (7).

"(C) REIMBURSEMENT FOR SERVICES UNDER THE PREVENTION PLAN COMPONENT.—

"(i) LIMITATION.—Except as provided in subclause (ii), a State may not receive a Federal payment under this part for a given promising, supported, or well-supported practice unless (in accordance with subparagraph (B)(iii)(V)) the plan includes a well-designed and rigorous evaluation strategy for that practice.

"(ii) WAIVER OF LIMITATION.—The Secretary may waive the requirement for a well-designed and rigorous evaluation of any well-supported practice if the Secretary deems the evidence of the effectiveness of the practice to be compelling and the State meets the continuous quality improvement requirements included in subparagraph (B)(iii)(II) with regard to the practice.

"(6) PREVENTION SERVICES MEASURES.—

"(A) ESTABLISHMENT; ANNUAL UPDATES.—Beginning with fiscal year 2021, and annually thereafter, the Secretary shall establish the following prevention services measures based on information and data reported by States that elect to provide services and programs specified in paragraph (1):

"(i) PERCENTAGE OF CANDIDATES FOR FOSTER CARE WHO DO NOT ENTER FOSTER CARE.—The percentage of candidates for foster care for whom, or on whose behalf, the services or programs are provided who do not enter foster care, including those placed with a kin caregiver outside of foster care, during the 12-month period in which the services or programs are provided and through the end of the succeeding 12-month-period.

"(ii) PER-CHILD SPENDING.—The total amount of expenditures made for mental health and substance abuse prevention and treatment services or in-home parent skill-based programs, respectively, for, or on behalf of, each child described in paragraph (2).

"(B) DATA.—The Secretary shall establish and annually update the prevention services measures—

"(i) based on the median State values of the information reported under each clause of subparagraph (A) for the 3 then most recent years; and

"(ii) taking into account State differences in the price levels of consumption goods and services using the most recent regional price parities published by the Bureau of Economic Analysis of the Department of Commerce or such other data as the Secretary determines appropriate.

"(C) PUBLICATION OF STATE PREVENTION SERVICES MEASURES.—The Secretary shall annually make available to the public the prevention services measures of each State.

"(7) MAINTENANCE OF EFFORT FOR STATE FOSTER CARE PREVENTION EXPENDITURES.—

"(A) IN GENERAL.—If a State elects to provide services and programs specified in paragraph (1) for a fiscal year, the State foster care prevention expenditures for the fiscal year shall not be less than the amount of the expenditures for fiscal year 2014 (or, at the option of a State described in subparagraph (E), fiscal year 2015 or fiscal year 2016 (whichever the State elects)).

"(B) STATE FOSTER CARE PREVENTION EXPENDITURES.—The term 'State foster care prevention expenditures' means the following:

"(i) TANF; IV–B; SSBG.—State expenditures for foster care prevention services and activities under the State program funded under part A (including from amounts made available by the Federal Government), under the State plan developed under part B (including any such amounts), or under the Social Services Block Grant Programs under subtitle A of title XX (including any such amounts).

"(ii) OTHER STATE PROGRAMS.—State expenditures for foster care prevention services and activities under any State program that is not described in clause (i) (other than any State expenditures for foster care prevention services and activities under the State program under this part (including under a waiver of the program)).

"(C) STATE EXPENDITURES.—The term 'State expenditures' means all State or local funds that are expended by the State or a local agency including State or local funds that are matched or reimbursed by the Federal Government and State or local funds that are not matched or reimbursed by the Federal Government.

"(D) DETERMINATION OF PREVENTION SERVICES AND ACTIVITIES.—The Secretary shall require each State that elects to provide services and programs specified in paragraph (1) to report the expenditures specified in subparagraph (B) for fiscal year 2014 and for such fiscal years thereafter as are necessary to determine whether the State is complying with the maintenance of effort requirement in subparagraph (A). The Secretary shall specify the specific services and activities under each program referred to in subparagraph (B) that are 'prevention services and activities' for purposes of the reports.

"(E) STATE DESCRIBED.—For purposes of subparagraph (A), a State is described in this subparagraph if the population of children in the

State in 2014 was less than 200,000 (as determined by the Bureau of the Census).

"(8) PROHIBITION AGAINST USE OF STATE FOSTER CARE PREVENTION EXPENDITURES AND FEDERAL IV–E PREVENTION FUNDS FOR MATCHING OR EXPENDITURE REQUIREMENT.—*A State that elects to provide services and programs specified in paragraph (1) shall not use any State foster care prevention expenditures for a fiscal year for the State share of expenditures under section 474(a)(6) for a fiscal year.*

"(9) ADMINISTRATIVE COSTS.—*Expenditures described in section 474(a)(6)(B)—*

"(A) *shall not be eligible for payment under subparagraph (A), (B), or (E) of section 474(a)(3); and*

"(B) *shall be eligible for payment under section 474(a)(6)(B) without regard to whether the expenditures are incurred on behalf of a child who is, or is potentially, eligible for foster care maintenance payments under this part.*

"(10) APPLICATION.—

"(A) IN GENERAL.—*The provision of services or programs under this subsection to or on behalf of a child described in paragraph (2) shall not be considered to be receipt of aid or assistance under the State plan under this part for purposes of eligibility for any other program established under this Act.*

"(B) CANDIDATES IN KINSHIP CARE.—*A child described in paragraph (2) for whom such services or programs under this subsection are provided for more than 6 months while in the home of a kin caregiver, and who would satisfy the AFDC eligibility requirement of section 472(a)(3)(A)(ii)(II) but for residing in the home of the caregiver for more than 6 months, is deemed to satisfy that requirement for purposes of determining whether the child is eligible for foster care maintenance payments under section 472.".*

(b) DEFINITION.—*Section 475 of such Act (42 U.S.C. 675) is amended by adding at the end the following:*

"(13) The term 'child who is a candidate for foster care' means, a child who is identified in a prevention plan under section 471(e)(4)(A) as being at imminent risk of entering foster care (without regard to whether the child would be eligible for foster care maintenance payments under section 472 or is or would be eligible for adoption assistance or kinship guardianship assistance payments under section 473) but who can remain safely in the child's home or in a kinship placement as long as services or programs specified in section 471(e)(1) that are necessary to prevent the entry of the child into foster care are provided. The term includes a child whose adoption or guardianship arrangement is at risk of a disruption or dissolution that would result in a foster care placement.".*

(c) PAYMENTS UNDER TITLE IV–E.—*Section 474(a) of such Act (42 U.S.C. 674(a)) is amended—*

(1) *in paragraph (5), by striking the period at the end and inserting "; plus"; and*

(2) *by adding at the end the following:*

"(6) *subject to section 471(e)—*

"(A) *for each quarter—*

"(i) *subject to clause (ii)—*

"(I) *beginning after September 30, 2019, and before October 1, 2025, an amount equal to 50 percent of the total amount expended during the quarter for the provision of services or programs specified in subparagraph (A) or (B) of section 471(e)(1) that are provided in accordance with promising, supported, or well-supported practices that meet the applicable criteria specified for the practices in section 471(e)(4)(C); and*

"(II) *beginning after September 30, 2025, an amount equal to the Federal medical assistance percentage (which shall be as defined in section 1905(b), in the case of a State other than the District of Columbia, or 70 percent, in the case*

of the District of Columbia) of the total amount expended during the quarter for the provision of services or programs specified in subparagraph (A) or (B) of section 471(e)(1) that are provided in accordance with promising, supported, or well-supported practices that meet the applicable criteria specified for the practices in section 471(e)(4)(C) (or, with respect to the payments made during the quarter under a cooperative agreement or contract entered into by the State and an Indian tribe, tribal organization, or tribal consortium for the administration or payment of funds under this part, an amount equal to the Federal medical assistance percentage that would apply under section 479B(d) (in this paragraph referred to as the 'tribal FMAP') if the Indian tribe, tribal organization, or tribal consortium made the payments under a program operated under that section, unless the tribal FMAP is less than the Federal medical assistance percentage that applies to the State); except that

"(ii) *not less than 50 percent of the total amount payable to a State under clause (i) for a fiscal year shall be for the provision of services or programs specified in subparagraph (A) or (B) of section 471(e)(1) that are provided in accordance with well-supported practices; plus*

"(B) *for each quarter specified in subparagraph (A), an amount equal to the sum of the following proportions of the total amount expended during the quarter:*

"(i) *50 percent of so much of the expenditures as are found necessary by the Secretary for the proper and efficient administration of the State plan for the provision of services or programs specified in section 471(e)(1), including expenditures for activities approved by the Secretary that promote the development of necessary processes and procedures to establish and implement the provision of the services and programs for individuals who are eligible for the services and programs and expenditures attributable to data collection and reporting; and*

"(ii) *50 percent of so much of the expenditures with respect to the provision of services and programs specified in section 471(e)(1) as are for training of personnel employed or preparing for employment by the State agency or by the local agency administering the plan in the political subdivision and of the members of the staff of State-licensed or State-approved child welfare agencies providing services to children described in section 471(e)(2) and their parents or kin caregivers, including on how to determine who are individuals eligible for the services or programs, how to identify and provide appropriate services and programs, and how to oversee and evaluate the ongoing appropriateness of the services and programs.".*

(d) TECHNICAL ASSISTANCE AND BEST PRACTICES, CLEARINGHOUSE, AND DATA COLLECTION AND EVALUATIONS.—*Section 476 of such Act (42 U.S.C. 676) is amended by adding at the end the following:*

"(d) TECHNICAL ASSISTANCE AND BEST PRACTICES, CLEARINGHOUSE, DATA COLLECTION, AND EVALUATIONS RELATING TO PREVENTION SERVICES AND PROGRAMS.—

"(1) TECHNICAL ASSISTANCE AND BEST PRACTICES.—*The Secretary shall provide to States and, as applicable, to Indian tribes, tribal organizations, and tribal consortia, technical assistance regarding the provision of services and programs described in section 471(e)(1) and shall disseminate best practices with respect to the provision of the services and programs, including how to plan and implement a well-designed and rigorous evaluation of a promising, supported, or well-supported practice.*

"(2) CLEARINGHOUSE OF PROMISING, SUPPORTED, AND WELL-SUPPORTED PRACTICES.—*The Secretary shall, directly or through grants, contracts, or interagency agreements, evaluate re-*

search on the practices specified in clauses (iii), (iv), and (v), respectively, of section 471(e)(4)(C), and programs that meet the requirements described in section 427(a)(1), including culturally specific, or location- or population-based adaptations of the practices, to identify and establish a public clearinghouse of the practices that satisfy each category described by such clauses. In addition, the clearinghouse shall include information on the specific outcomes associated with each practice, including whether the practice has been shown to prevent child abuse and neglect and reduce the likelihood of foster care placement by supporting birth families and kinship families and improving targeted supports for pregnant and parenting youth and their children.

"(3) DATA COLLECTION AND EVALUATIONS.—*The Secretary, directly or through grants, contracts, or interagency agreements, may collect data and conduct evaluations with respect to the provision of services and programs described in section 471(e)(1) for purposes of assessing the extent to which the provision of the services and programs—*

"(A) *reduces the likelihood of foster care placement;*

"(B) *increases use of kinship care arrangements; or*

"(C) *improves child well-being.*

"(4) REPORTS TO CONGRESS.—

"(A) IN GENERAL.—*The Secretary shall submit to the Committee on Finance of the Senate and the Committee on Ways and Means of the House of Representatives periodic reports based on the provision of services and programs described in section 471(e)(1) and the activities carried out under this subsection.*

"(B) PUBLIC AVAILABILITY.—*The Secretary shall make the reports to Congress submitted under this paragraph publicly available.*

"(5) APPROPRIATION.—*Out of any money in the Treasury of the United States not otherwise appropriated, there is appropriated to the Secretary $1,000,000 for fiscal year 2017 and each fiscal year thereafter to carry out this subsection.".*

(e) APPLICATION TO PROGRAMS OPERATED BY INDIAN TRIBAL ORGANIZATIONS.—

(1) IN GENERAL.—*Section 479B of such Act (42 U.S.C. 679c) is amended—*

(A) *in subsection (c)(1)—*

(i) *in subparagraph (C)(i)—*

(I) *in subclause (II), by striking "and" after the semicolon;*

(II) *in subclause (III), by striking the period at the end and inserting "; and"; and*

(III) *by adding at the end the following:*

"(IV) *at the option of the tribe, organization, or consortium, services and programs specified in section 471(e)(1) to children described in section 471(e)(2) and their parents or kin caregivers, in accordance with section 471(e) and subparagraph (E).*"; and*

(ii) *by adding at the end the following:*

"(E) PREVENTION SERVICES AND PROGRAMS FOR CHILDREN AND THEIR PARENTS AND KIN CAREGIVERS.—

"(i) IN GENERAL.—*In the case of a tribe, organization, or consortium that elects to provide services and programs specified in section 471(e)(1) to children described in section 471(e)(2) and their parents or kin caregivers under the plan, the Secretary shall specify the requirements applicable to the provision of the services and programs. The requirements shall, to the greatest extent practicable, be consistent with the requirements applicable to States under section 471(e) and shall permit the provision of the services and programs in the form of services and programs that are adapted to the culture and context of the tribal communities served.*

"(ii) PERFORMANCE MEASURES.—*The Secretary shall establish specific performance measures for* each tribe, organization, or consortium that elects to provide services and programs specified in section 471(e)(1). The performance measures shall, to the greatest extent practicable, be consistent with the prevention services measures required for States under section 471(e)(6) but shall allow for consideration of factors unique to the provision of the services by tribes, organizations, or consortia.''; and

(B) in subsection (d)(1), by striking ''and (5)'' and inserting ''(5), and (6)(A)''.

(2) CONFORMING AMENDMENT.—The heading for subsection (d) of section 479B of such Act (42 U.S.C. 679c) is amended by striking ''FOR FOSTER CARE MAINTENANCE AND ADOPTION ASSISTANCE PAYMENTS''.

(f) APPLICATION TO PROGRAMS OPERATED BY TERRITORIES.—Section 1108(a)(2) of the Social Security Act (42 U.S.C. 1308(a)(2)) is amended by striking ''or 413(f)'' and inserting ''413(f), or 474(a)(6)''.

SEC. 19012. FOSTER CARE MAINTENANCE PAYMENTS FOR CHILDREN WITH PARENTS IN A LICENSED RESIDENTIAL FAMILY-BASED TREATMENT FACILITY FOR SUBSTANCE ABUSE.

(a) IN GENERAL.—Section 472 of the Social Security Act (42 U.S.C. 672) is amended—

(1) in subsection (a)(2)(C), by striking ''or'' and inserting '', with a parent residing in a licensed residential family-based treatment facility, but only to the extent permitted under subsection (j), or in a''; and

(2) by adding at the end the following:

''(j) CHILDREN PLACED WITH A PARENT RESIDING IN A LICENSED RESIDENTIAL FAMILY-BASED TREATMENT FACILITY FOR SUBSTANCE ABUSE.—

''(1) IN GENERAL.—Notwithstanding the preceding provisions of this section, a child who is eligible for foster care maintenance payments under this section, or who would be eligible for the payments if the eligibility were determined without regard to paragraphs (1)(B) and (3) of subsection (a), shall be eligible for the payments for a period of not more than 12 months during which the child is placed with a parent who is in a licensed residential family-based treatment facility for substance abuse, but only if—

''(A) the recommendation for the placement is specified in the child's case plan before the placement;

''(B) the treatment facility provides, as part of the treatment for substance abuse, parenting skills training, parent education, and individual and family counseling; and

''(C) the substance abuse treatment, parenting skills training, parent education, and individual and family counseling is provided under an organizational structure and treatment framework that involves understanding, recognizing, and responding to the effects of all types of trauma and in accordance with recognized principles of a trauma-informed approach and trauma-specific interventions to address the consequences of trauma and facilitate healing.

''(2) APPLICATION.—With respect to children for whom foster care maintenance payments are made under paragraph (1), only the children who satisfy the requirements of paragraphs (1)(B) and (3) of subsection (a) shall be considered to be children with respect to whom foster care maintenance payments are made under this section for purposes of subsection (h) or section 473(b)(3)(B).''.

(b) CONFORMING AMENDMENT.—Section 474(a)(1) of such Act (42 U.S.C. 674(a)(1)) is amended by inserting ''subject to section 472(j),'' before ''an amount equal to the Federal'' the first place it appears.

SEC. 19013. TITLE IV-E PAYMENTS FOR EVIDENCE-BASED KINSHIP NAVIGATOR PROGRAMS.

Section 474(a) of the Social Security Act (42 U.S.C. 674(a)), as amended by section 19011(c), is amended—

(1) in paragraph (6), by striking the period at the end and inserting ''; plus''; and

(2) by adding at the end the following:

''(7) an amount equal to 50 percent of the amounts expended by the State during the quarter as the Secretary determines are for kinship navigator programs that meet the requirements described in section 427(a)(1) and that the Secretary determines are operated in accordance with promising, supported, or well-supported practices that meet the applicable criteria specified for the practices in section 471(e)(4)(C), without regard to whether the expenditures are incurred on behalf of children who are, or are potentially, eligible for foster care maintenance payments under this part.''.

Subtitle B—Enhanced Support Under Title IV-B

SEC. 19021. ELIMINATION OF TIME LIMIT FOR FAMILY REUNIFICATION SERVICES WHILE IN FOSTER CARE AND PERMITTING TIME-LIMITED FAMILY REUNIFICATION SERVICES WHEN A CHILD RETURNS HOME FROM FOSTER CARE.

(a) IN GENERAL.—Section 431(a)(7) of the Social Security Act (42 U.S.C. 629a(a)(7)) is amended—

(1) in the paragraph heading, by striking ''TIME-LIMITED FAMILY'' and inserting ''FAMILY''; and

(2) in subparagraph (A)—

(A) by striking ''time-limited family'' and inserting ''family'';

(B) by inserting ''or a child who has been returned home'' after ''child care institution''; and

(C) by striking '', but only during the 15-month period that begins on the date that the child, pursuant to section 475(5)(F), is considered to have entered foster care'' and inserting ''and to ensure the strength and stability of the reunification. In the case of a child who has been returned home, the services and activities shall only be provided during the 15-month period that begins on the date that the child returns home''.

(b) CONFORMING AMENDMENTS.—

(1) Section 430 of such Act (42 U.S.C. 629) is amended in the matter preceding paragraph (1), by striking ''time-limited''.

(2) Subsections (a)(4), (a)(5)(A), and (b)(1) of section 432 of such Act (42 U.S.C. 629b) are amended by striking ''time-limited'' each place it appears.

SEC. 19022. REDUCING BUREAUCRACY AND UNNECESSARY DELAYS WHEN PLACING CHILDREN IN HOMES ACROSS STATE LINES.

(a) STATE PLAN REQUIREMENT.—Section 471(a)(25) of the Social Security Act (42 U.S.C. 671(a)(25)) is amended—

(1) by striking ''provide'' and insert ''provides''; and

(2) by inserting '', which, not later than October 1, 2026, shall include the use of an electronic interstate case-processing system'' before the first semicolon.

(b) GRANTS FOR THE DEVELOPMENT OF AN ELECTRONIC INTERSTATE CASE-PROCESSING SYSTEM TO EXPEDITE THE INTERSTATE PLACEMENT OF CHILDREN IN FOSTER CARE OR GUARDIANSHIP, OR FOR ADOPTION.—Section 437 of such Act (42 U.S.C. 629g) is amended by adding at the end the following:

''(g) GRANTS FOR THE DEVELOPMENT OF AN ELECTRONIC INTERSTATE CASE-PROCESSING SYSTEM TO EXPEDITE THE INTERSTATE PLACEMENT OF CHILDREN IN FOSTER CARE OR GUARDIANSHIP, OR FOR ADOPTION.—

''(1) PURPOSE.—The purpose of this subsection is to facilitate the development of an electronic interstate case-processing system for the exchange of data and documents to expedite the placements of children in foster, guardianship, or adoptive homes across State lines.

''(2) APPLICATION REQUIREMENTS.—A State that desires a grant under this subsection shall submit to the Secretary an application containing the following:

''(A) A description of the goals and outcomes to be achieved during the period for which grant funds are sought, which goals and outcomes must result in—

''(i) reducing the time it takes for a child to be provided with a safe and appropriate permanent living arrangement across State lines;

''(ii) improving administrative processes and reducing costs in the foster care system; and

''(iii) the secure exchange of relevant case files and other necessary materials in real time, and timely communications and placement decisions regarding interstate placements of children.

''(B) A description of the activities to be funded in whole or in part with the grant funds, including the sequencing of the activities.

''(C) A description of the strategies for integrating programs and services for children who are placed across State lines.

''(D) Such other information as the Secretary may require.

''(3) GRANT AUTHORITY.—The Secretary may make a grant to a State that complies with paragraph (2).

''(4) USE OF FUNDS.—A State to which a grant is made under this subsection shall use the grant to support the State in connecting with the electronic interstate case-processing system described in paragraph (1).

''(5) EVALUATIONS.—Not later than 1 year after the final year in which grants are awarded under this subsection, the Secretary shall submit to the Congress, and make available to the general public by posting on a website, a report that contains the following information:

''(A) How using the electronic interstate case-processing system developed pursuant to paragraph (4) has changed the time it takes for children to be placed across State lines.

''(B) The number of cases subject to the Interstate Compact on the Placement of Children that were processed through the electronic interstate case-processing system, and the number of interstate child placement cases that were processed outside the electronic interstate case-processing system, by each State in each year.

''(C) The progress made by States in implementing the electronic interstate case-processing system.

''(D) How using the electronic interstate case-processing system has affected various metrics related to child safety and well-being, including the time it takes for children to be placed across State lines.

''(E) How using the electronic interstate case-processing system has affected administrative costs and caseworker time spent on placing children across State lines.

''(6) DATA INTEGRATION.—The Secretary, in consultation with the Secretariat for the Interstate Compact on the Placement of Children and the States, shall assess how the electronic interstate case-processing system developed pursuant to paragraph (4) could be used to better serve and protect children that come to the attention of the child welfare system, by—

''(A) connecting the system with other data systems (such as systems operated by State law enforcement and judicial agencies, systems operated by the Federal Bureau of Investigation for the purposes of the Innocence Lost National Initiative, and other systems);

''(B) simplifying and improving reporting related to paragraphs (34) and (35) of section 471(a) regarding children or youth who have been identified as being a sex trafficking victim or children missing from foster care; and

''(C) improving the ability of States to quickly comply with background check requirements of *section 471(a)(20), including checks of child abuse and neglect registries as required by section 471(a)(20)(B).''.*

(c) RESERVATION OF FUNDS TO IMPROVE THE INTERSTATE PLACEMENT OF CHILDREN.—Section 437(b) of such Act (42 U.S.C. 629g(b)) is amended by adding at the end the following:

"(4) IMPROVING THE INTERSTATE PLACEMENT OF CHILDREN.—The Secretary shall reserve $5,000,000 of the amount made available for fiscal year 2017 for grants under subsection (g), and the amount so reserved shall remain available through fiscal year 2021.''.

SEC. 19023. ENHANCEMENTS TO GRANTS TO IMPROVE WELL-BEING OF FAMILIES AFFECTED BY SUBSTANCE ABUSE.

Section 437(f) of the Social Security Act (42 U.S.C. 629g(f)) is amended—

(1) in the subsection heading, by striking "IN-CREASE THE WELL-BEING OF, AND TO IMPROVE THE PERMANENCY OUTCOMES FOR, CHILDREN AFFECTED BY" and inserting "IMPLEMENT IV–E PREVENTION SERVICES, AND IMPROVE THE WELL-BEING OF, AND IMPROVE PERMANENCY OUTCOMES FOR, CHILDREN AND FAMILIES AFFECTED BY HEROIN, OPIOIDS, AND OTHER";

(2) by striking paragraph (2) and inserting the following:

"(2) REGIONAL PARTNERSHIP DEFINED.—In this subsection, the term 'regional partnership' means a collaborative agreement (which may be established on an interstate, State, or intrastate basis) entered into by the following:

"(A) MANDATORY PARTNERS FOR ALL PARTNER-SHIP GRANTS.—

"(i) The State child welfare agency that is responsible for the administration of the State plan under this part and part E.

"(ii) The State agency responsible for administering the substance abuse prevention and treatment block grant provided under subpart II of part B of title XIX of the Public Health Service Act.

"(B) MANDATORY PARTNERS FOR PARTNERSHIP GRANTS PROPOSING TO SERVE CHILDREN IN OUT-OF-HOME PLACEMENTS.—If the partnership proposes to serve children in out-of-home placements, the Juvenile Court or Administrative Office of the Court that is most appropriate to oversee the administration of court programs in the region to address the population of families who come to the attention of the court due to child abuse or neglect.

"(C) OPTIONAL PARTNERS.—At the option of the partnership, any of the following:

"(i) An Indian tribe or tribal consortium.

"(ii) Nonprofit child welfare service providers.

"(iii) For-profit child welfare service providers.

"(iv) Community health service providers, including substance abuse treatment providers.

"(v) Community mental health providers.

"(vi) Local law enforcement agencies.

"(vii) School personnel.

"(viii) Tribal child welfare agencies (or a consortia of the agencies).

"(ix) Any other providers, agencies, personnel, officials, or entities that are related to the provision of child and family services under a State plan approved under this subpart.

"(D) EXCEPTION FOR REGIONAL PARTNERSHIPS WHERE THE LEAD APPLICANT IS AN INDIAN TRIBE OR TRIBAL CONSORTIA.—If an Indian tribe or tribal consortium enters into a regional partnership for purposes of this subsection, the Indian tribe or tribal consortium—

"(i) may (but is not required to) include the State child welfare agency as a partner in the collaborative agreement;

"(ii) may not enter into a collaborative agreement only with tribal child welfare agencies (or a consortium of the agencies); and

"(iii) if the condition described in paragraph (2)(B) applies, may include tribal court organizations in lieu of other judicial partners.'';

(3) in paragraph (3)—

(A) in subparagraph (A)—

(i) by striking "2012 through 2016" and inserting "2017 through 2021"; and

(ii) by striking "$500,000 and not more than $1,000,000" and inserting "$250,000 and not more than $1,000,000";

(B) in subparagraph (B)—

(i) in the subparagraph heading, by inserting "; PLANNING" after "APPROVAL";

(ii) in clause (i), by striking "clause (ii)" and inserting "clauses (ii) and (iii)"; and

(iii) by adding at the end the following:

"(iii) SUFFICIENT PLANNING.—A grant awarded under this subsection shall be disbursed in two phases: a planning phase (not to exceed 2 years); and an implementation phase. The total disbursement to a grantee for the planning phase may not exceed $250,000, and may not exceed the total anticipated funding for the implementation phase.''; and

(C) by adding at the end the following:

"(D) LIMITATION ON PAYMENT FOR A FISCAL YEAR.—No payment shall be made under subparagraph (A) or (C) for a fiscal year until the Secretary determines that the eligible partnership has made sufficient progress in meeting the goals of the grant and that the members of the eligible partnership are coordinating to a reasonable degree with the other members of the eligible partnership.'';

(4) in paragraph (4)—

(A) in subparagraph (B)—

(i) in clause (i), by inserting ", parents, and families" after "children";

(ii) in clause (ii), by striking "safety and permanence for such children; and" and inserting "safe, permanent caregiving relationships for the children;";

(iii) in clause (iii), by striking "or" and inserting "increase reunification rates for children who have been placed in out of home care, or decrease"; and

(iv) by redesignating clause (iii) as clause (v) and inserting after clause (ii) the following:

"(iii) improve the substance abuse treatment outcomes for parents including retention in treatment and successful completion of treatment;

"(iv) facilitate the implementation, delivery, and effectiveness of prevention services and programs under section 471(e); and";

(B) in subparagraph (D), by striking "where appropriate,"; and

(C) by striking subparagraphs (E) and (F) and inserting the following:

"(E) A description of a plan for sustaining the services provided by or activities funded under the grant after the conclusion of the grant period, including through the use of prevention services and programs under section 471(e) and other funds provided to the State for child welfare and substance abuse prevention and treatment services.

"(F) Additional information needed by the Secretary to determine that the proposed activities and implementation will be consistent with research or evaluations showing which practices and approaches are most effective.'';

(5) in paragraph (5)(A), by striking "abuse treatment" and inserting "use disorder treatment including medication assisted treatment and in-home substance abuse disorder treatment and recovery";

(6) in paragraph (7)—

(A) by striking "and" at the end of subparagraph (C); and

(B) by redesignating subparagraph (D) as subparagraph (E) and inserting after subparagraph (C) the following:

"(D) demonstrate a track record of successful collaboration among child welfare, substance abuse disorder treatment and mental health agencies; and'';

(7) in paragraph (8)—

(A) in subparagraph (A)—

(i) by striking "establish indicators that will be" and inserting "review indicators that are"; and

(ii) by striking "in using funds made available under such grants to achieve the purpose of this subsection" and inserting "and establish a set of core indicators related to child safety, parental recovery, parenting capacity, and family well-being. In developing the core indicators, to the extent possible, indicators shall be made consistent with the outcome measures described in section 471(e)(6)"; and

(B) in subparagraph (B)—

(i) in the matter preceding clause (i), by inserting "base the performance measures on lessons learned from prior rounds of regional partnership grants under this subsection, and" before "consult"; and

(ii) by striking clauses (iii) and (iv) and inserting the following:

"(iii) Other stakeholders or constituencies as determined by the Secretary.";

(8) in paragraph (9)(A), by striking clause (i) and inserting the following:

"(i) SEMIANNUAL REPORTS.—Not later than September 30 of each fiscal year in which a recipient of a grant under this subsection is paid funds under the grant, and every 6 months thereafter, the grant recipient shall submit to the Secretary a report on the services provided and activities carried out during the reporting period, progress made in achieving the goals of the program, the number of children, adults, and families receiving services, and such additional information as the Secretary determines is necessary. The report due not later than September 30 of the last such fiscal year shall include, at a minimum, data on each of the performance indicators included in the evaluation of the regional partnership.''; and

(9) in paragraph (10), by striking "2012 through 2016" and inserting "2017 through 2021".

Subtitle C—Miscellaneous

SEC. 19031. REVIEWING AND IMPROVING LICENSING STANDARDS FOR PLACEMENT IN A RELATIVE FOSTER FAMILY HOME.

(a) IDENTIFICATION OF REPUTABLE MODEL LICENSING STANDARDS.—Not later than October 1, 2017, the Secretary of Health and Human Services shall identify reputable model licensing standards with respect to the licensing of foster family homes (as defined in section 472(c)(1) of the Social Security Act).

(b) STATE PLAN REQUIREMENT.—Section 471(a) of the Social Security Act (42 U.S.C. 671(a)) is amended—

(1) in paragraph (34)(B), by striking "and" after the semicolon;

(2) in paragraph (35)(B), by striking the period at the end and inserting a semicolon; and

(3) by adding at the end the following:

"(36) provides that, not later than April 1, 2018, the State shall submit to the Secretary information addressing—

"(A) whether the State licensing standards are in accord with model standards identified by the Secretary, and if not, the reason for the specific deviation and a description as to why having a standard that is reasonably in accord with the corresponding national model standards is not appropriate for the State;

"(B) whether the State has elected to waive standards established in 471(a)(10)(A) for relative foster family homes (pursuant to waiver authority provided by 471(a)(10)(D)), a description of which standards the State most commonly waives, and if the State has not elected to waive the standards, the reason for not waiving these standards;

"(C) if the State has elected to waive standards specified in subparagraph (B), how caseworkers are trained to use the waiver authority

and whether the State has developed a process or provided tools to assist caseworkers in waiving nonsafety standards per the authority provided in 471(a)(10)(D) to quickly place children with relatives; and

"(D) a description of the steps the State is taking to improve caseworker training or the process, if any; and".

SEC. 19032. DEVELOPMENT OF A STATEWIDE PLAN TO PREVENT CHILD ABUSE AND NEGLECT FATALITIES.

Section 422(b)(19) of the Social Security Act (42 U.S.C. 622(b)(19)) is amended to read as follows:

"(19) document steps taken to track and prevent child maltreatment deaths by including—

"(A) a description of the steps the State is taking to compile complete and accurate information on the deaths required by Federal law to be reported by the State agency referred to in paragraph (1), including gathering relevant information on the deaths from the relevant organizations in the State including entities such as State vital statistics department, child death review teams, law enforcement agencies, offices of medical examiners or coroners; and

"(B) a description of the steps the state is taking to develop and implement of a comprehensive, statewide plan to prevent the fatalities that involves and engages relevant public and private agency partners, including those in public health, law enforcement, and the courts.".

SEC. 19033. MODERNIZING THE TITLE AND PURPOSE OF TITLE IV–E.

(a) PART HEADING.—The heading for part E of title IV of the Social Security Act (42 U.S.C. 670 et seq.) is amended to read as follows:

"PART E—FEDERAL PAYMENTS FOR FOSTER CARE, PREVENTION, AND PERMANENCY".

(b) PURPOSE.—The first sentence of section 470 of such Act (42 U.S.C. 670) is amended—

(1) by striking "1995) and" and inserting "1995),";

(2) by inserting "kinship guardianship assistance, and prevention services or programs specified in section 471(e)(1)," after "needs,"; and

(3) by striking "(commencing with the fiscal year which begins October 1, 1980)".

SEC. 19034. EFFECTIVE DATES.

(a) EFFECTIVE DATES.—

(1) IN GENERAL.—Except as provided in paragraph (2), subject to subsection (b), the amendments made by this title shall take effect on January 1, 2017.

(2) EXCEPTIONS.—The amendments made by sections 19031 and 19033 shall take effect on the date of enactment of this Act.

(b) TRANSITION RULE.—

(1) IN GENERAL.—In the case of a State plan under part B or E of title IV of the Social Security Act which the Secretary of Health and Human Services determines requires State legislation (other than legislation appropriating funds) in order for the plan to meet the additional requirements imposed by the amendments made by this title, the State plan shall not be regarded as failing to comply with the requirements of such part solely on the basis of the failure of the plan to meet such additional requirements before the first day of the first calendar quarter beginning after the close of the first regular session of the State legislature that begins after the date of enactment of this Act. For purposes of the previous sentence, in the case of a State that has a 2-year legislative session, each year of the session shall be deemed to be a separate regular session of the State legislature.

(2) APPLICATION TO PROGRAMS OPERATED BY INDIAN TRIBAL ORGANIZATIONS.—In the case of an Indian tribe, tribal organization, or tribal consortium which the Secretary of Health and Human Services determines requires time to take

action necessary to comply with the additional requirements imposed by the amendments made by this title (whether the tribe, organization, or tribal consortium has a plan under section 479B of the Social Security Act or a cooperative agreement or contract entered into with a State), the Secretary shall provide the tribe, organization, or tribal consortium with such additional time as the Secretary determines is necessary for the tribe, organization, or tribal consortium to take the action to comply with the additional requirements before being regarded as failing to comply with the requirements.

TITLE XX—ENSURING THE NECESSITY OF A PLACEMENT THAT IS NOT IN A FOSTER FAMILY HOME

SEC. 20001. LIMITATION ON FEDERAL FINANCIAL PARTICIPATION FOR PLACEMENTS THAT ARE NOT IN FOSTER FAMILY HOMES.

(a) LIMITATION ON FEDERAL FINANCIAL PARTICIPATION.—

(1) IN GENERAL.—Section 472 of the Social Security Act (42 U.S.C. 672), as amended by section 19012, is amended—

(A) in subsection (a)(2)(C), by inserting ", but only to the extent permitted under subsection (k)" after "institution"; and

(B) by adding at the end the following:

"(k) LIMITATION ON FEDERAL FINANCIAL PARTICIPATION.—

"(1) IN GENERAL.—Beginning with the third week for which foster care maintenance payments are made under this section on behalf of a child placed in a child-care institution, no Federal payment shall be made to the State under section 474(a)(1) for amounts expended for foster care maintenance payments on behalf of the child unless—

"(A) the child is placed in a child-care institution that is a setting specified in paragraph (2) (or is placed in a licensed residential family-based treatment facility consistent with subsection (j)); and

"(B) in the case of a child placed in a qualified residential treatment program (as defined in paragraph (4)), the requirements specified in paragraph (3) and section 475A(c) are met.

"(2) SPECIFIED SETTINGS FOR PLACEMENT.—The settings for placement specified in this paragraph are the following:

"(A) A qualified residential treatment program (as defined in paragraph (4)).

"(B) A setting specializing in providing prenatal, post-partum, or parenting supports for youth.

"(C) In the case of a child who has attained 18 years of age, a supervised setting in which the child is living independently.

"(D) A setting providing high-quality residential care and supportive services to children and youth who have been found to be, or are at risk of becoming, sex trafficking victims, in accordance with section 471(a)(9)(C).

"(3) ASSESSMENT TO DETERMINE APPROPRIATENESS OF PLACEMENT IN A QUALIFIED RESIDENTIAL TREATMENT PROGRAM.—

"(A) DEADLINE FOR ASSESSMENT.—In the case of a child who is placed in a qualified residential treatment program, if the assessment required under section 475A(c)(1) is not completed within 30 days after the placement is made, no Federal payment shall be made to the State under section 474(a)(1) for any amounts expended for foster care maintenance payments on behalf of the child during the placement.

"(B) DEADLINE FOR TRANSITION OUT OF PLACEMENT.—If the assessment required under section 475A(c)(1) determines that the placement of a child in a qualified residential treatment program is not appropriate, a court disapproves such a placement under section 475A(c)(2), or a child who has been in an approved placement in a qualified residential treatment program is

going to return home or be placed with a fit and willing relative, a legal guardian, or an adoptive parent, or in a foster family home, Federal payments shall be made to the State under section 474(a)(1) for amounts expended for foster care maintenance payments on behalf of the child while the child remains in the qualified residential treatment program only during the period necessary for the child to transition home or to such a placement. In no event shall a State receive Federal payments under section 474(a)(1) for amounts expended for foster care maintenance payments on behalf of a child who remains placed in a qualified residential treatment program after the end of the 30-day period that begins on the date a determination is made that the placement is no longer the recommended or approved placement for the child.

"(4) QUALIFIED RESIDENTIAL TREATMENT PROGRAM.—For purposes of this part, the term 'qualified residential treatment program' means a program that—

"(A) has a trauma-informed treatment model that is designed to address the needs, including clinical needs as appropriate, of children with serious emotional or behavioral disorders or disturbances and, with respect to a child, is able to implement the treatment identified for the child by the assessment of the child required under section 475A(c);

"(B) subject to paragraph (5), has registered or licensed nursing staff and other licensed clinical staff who—

"(i) provide care within the scope of their practice as defined by State law;

"(ii) are on-site during business hours; and

"(iii) are available 24 hours a day and 7 days a week;

"(C) to extent appropriate, and in accordance with the child's best interests, facilitates participation of family members in the child's treatment program;

"(D) facilitates outreach to the family members of the child, including siblings, documents how the outreach is made (including contact information), and maintains contact information for any known biological family and fictive kin of the child;

"(E) documents how family members are integrated into the treatment process for the child, including post-discharge, and how sibling connections are maintained;

"(F) provides discharge planning and family-based aftercare support for at least 6 months post-discharge; and

"(G) is licensed in accordance with section 471(a)(10) and is accredited by any of the following independent, not-for-profit organizations:

"(i) The Commission on Accreditation of Rehabilitation Facilities (CARF).

"(ii) The Joint Commission on Accreditation of Healthcare Organizations (JCAHO).

"(iii) The Council on Accreditation (COA).

"(iv) Any other independent, not-for-profit accrediting organization approved by the Secretary.

"(5) FLEXIBILITY IN STAFFING REQUIREMENTS FOR QUALIFIED RESIDENTIAL TREATMENT PROGRAMS.—

"(A) IN GENERAL.—In the case of any State that the Secretary determines is described in subparagraph (B) and satisfies the requirements of subparagraphs (C) and (D), respectively, the State may elect to satisfy the requirement of paragraph (4)(B) that a qualified residential treatment program have registered or licensed nursing staff and other licensed clinical staff with clinical staff which include staff licensed to monitor medications and physical and behavioral health staff with demonstrated training in child development and trauma, in lieu of with registered or licensed nursing staff and other licensed clinical staff.

"(B) STATE DESCRIBED.—Subject to subparagraph (E), a State is described in this subparagraph if for the most recent fiscal year for which data are available—

"(i) the percentage of children in foster care under the responsibility of the State who have been placed in congregate care settings—

"(I) is at or below 5 percent for the fiscal year; or

"(II) has been reduced by at least 20 percent from the preceding fiscal year; and

"(ii) the average length of stay for children in foster care under the responsibility of the State in congregate care settings is at or below 9 months.

"(C) DEMONSTRATION OF CAPACITY AND NEED.—A State described in subparagraph (B) shall be eligible to use the alternative staffing model permitted under subparagraph (A) if the State can demonstrate to the satisfaction of the Secretary that the qualified residential treatment programs utilizing the alternative staffing models permitted under subparagraph (A) have the capacity to serve children and youth whose treatment plans—

"(i) indicate a need for increased supervision based on behavioral history, history of juvenile delinquency, or history of sexual offenses; and

"(ii) require a placement that conforms to the alternative staffing model permitted under subparagraph (A).

"(D) EQUITABLE DISTRIBUTION OF CONGREGATE CARE POPULATION.—A State described in subparagraph (B) shall be eligible to use the alternative staffing model permitted under subparagraph (A) if the State annually demonstrates to the satisfaction of the Secretary that the State is reducing the number of children in foster care under the responsibility of the State who are in congregate care placements on a general statewide basis and without wide disparities between rural, suburban, and urban areas in the rates of such children in congregate care placements.

"(E) ANNUAL DETERMINATION OF STATE ELIGIBILITY BASED ON AFCARS AND OTHER DATA.—The Secretary annually shall make the determinations required under subparagraph (B) with respect to a State and a fiscal year, on the basis of data meeting the requirements of the system established pursuant to section 479, as reported by the State and approved by the Secretary, and, to the extent the Secretary determines necessary, on the basis of such other information reported to the Secretary as the Secretary may require to determine that a State is, or continues to be, a State described in subparagraph (B).

"(F) CONGREGATE CARE SETTINGS.—In this paragraph, the term 'congregate care settings' includes any settings described as 'group homes' or 'institutions' for purposes of data reported in accordance with the requirements of the system established pursuant to section 479 or any similar placement settings reported in accordance with such requirements.

"(6) ADMINISTRATIVE COSTS.—The prohibition in paragraph (1) on Federal payments under section 474(a)(1) shall not be construed as prohibiting Federal payments for administrative expenditures incurred on behalf of a child placed in a child-care institution and for which payment is available under section 474(a)(3).".

(2) CONFORMING AMENDMENT.—Section 474(a)(1) of the Social Security Act (42 U.S.C. 674(a)(1)), as amended by section 19012(b), is amended by striking "section 472(j)" and inserting "subsections (j) and (k) of section 472".

(b) DEFINITION OF FOSTER FAMILY HOME, CHILD-CARE INSTITUTION.—Section 472(c) of such Act (42 U.S.C. 672(c)(1)) is amended to read as follows:

"(c) DEFINITIONS.—For purposes of this part:

"(1) FOSTER FAMILY HOME.—

"(A) IN GENERAL.—The term 'foster family home' means the home of an individual or family—

"(i) that is licensed or approved by the State in which it is situated as a foster family home that meets the standards established for the licensing or approval; and

"(ii) in which a child in foster care has been placed in the care of an individual, who resides with the child and who has been licensed or approved by the State to be a foster parent—

"(I) that the State deems capable of adhering to the reasonable and prudent parent standard;

"(II) that provides 24-hour substitute care for children placed away from their parents or other caretakers; and

"(III) that provides the care for not more than six children in foster care.

"(B) STATE FLEXIBILITY.—The number of foster children that may be cared for in a home under subparagraph (A) may exceed the numerical limitation in subparagraph (A)(ii)(III), at the option of the State, for any of the following reasons:

"(i) To allow a parenting youth in foster care to remain with the child of the parenting youth.

"(ii) To allow siblings to remain together.

"(iii) To allow a child with an established meaningful relationship with the family to remain with the family.

"(iv) To allow a family with special training or skills to provide care to a child who has a severe disability.

"(C) RULE OF CONSTRUCTION.—Subparagraph (A) shall not be construed as prohibiting a foster parent from renting the home in which the parent cares for a foster child placed in the parent's care.

"(2) CHILD-CARE INSTITUTION.—

"(A) IN GENERAL.—The term 'child-care institution' means a private child-care institution, or a public child-care institution which accommodates no more than 25 children, which is licensed by the State in which it is situated or has been approved by the agency of the State responsible for licensing or approval of institutions of this type as meeting the standards established for the licensing.

"(B) SUPERVISED SETTINGS.—In the case of a child who has attained 18 years of age, the term shall include a supervised setting in which the individual is living independently, in accordance with such conditions as the Secretary shall establish in regulations.

"(C) EXCLUSIONS.—The term shall not include detention facilities, forestry camps, training schools, or any other facility operated primarily for the detention of children who are determined to be delinquent.".

(c) TRAINING FOR STATE JUDGES, ATTORNEYS, AND OTHER LEGAL PERSONNEL IN CHILD WELFARE CASES.—Section 438(b)(1) of such Act (42 U.S.C. 629h(b)(1)) is amended in the matter preceding subparagraph (A) by inserting "shall provide for the training of judges, attorneys, and other legal personnel in child welfare cases on Federal child welfare policies and payment limitations with respect to children in foster care who are placed in settings that are not a foster family home," after "with respect to the child,".

(d) ASSURANCE OF NONIMPACT ON JUVENILE JUSTICE SYSTEM.—

(1) STATE PLAN REQUIREMENT.—Section 471(a) of such Act (42 U.S.C. 671(a)), as amended by section 19031, is further amended by adding at the end the following:

"(37) includes a certification that, in response to the limitation imposed under section 472(k) with respect to foster care maintenance payments made on behalf of any child who is placed in a setting that is not a foster family home, the State will not enact or advance policies or practices that would result in a significant increase in the population of youth in the State's juvenile justice system.".

(2) GAO STUDY AND REPORT.—The Comptroller General of the United States shall evaluate the

impact, if any, on State juvenile justice systems of the limitation imposed under section 472(k) of the Social Security Act (as added by section 19001(a)(1)) on foster care maintenance payments made on behalf of any child who is placed in a setting that is not a foster family home, in accordance with the amendments made by subsections (a) and (b) of this section. In particular, the Comptroller General shall evaluate the extent to which children in foster care who also are subject to the juvenile justice system of the State are placed in a facility under the jurisdiction of the juvenile justice system and whether the lack of available congregate care placements under the jurisdiction of the child welfare systems is a contributing factor to that result. Not later than December 31, 2023, the Comptroller General shall submit to Congress a report on the results of the evaluation.

SEC. 20002. ASSESSMENT AND DOCUMENTATION OF THE NEED FOR PLACEMENT IN A QUALIFIED RESIDENTIAL TREATMENT PROGRAM.

Section 475A of the Social Security Act (42 U.S.C. 675a) is amended by adding at the end the following:

"(c) ASSESSMENT, DOCUMENTATION, AND JUDICIAL DETERMINATION REQUIREMENTS FOR PLACEMENT IN A QUALIFIED RESIDENTIAL TREATMENT PROGRAM.—In the case of any child who is placed in a qualified residential treatment program (as defined in section 472(k)(4)), the following requirements shall apply for purposes of approving the case plan for the child and the case system review procedure for the child:

"(1)(A) Within 30 days of the start of each placement in such a setting, a qualified individual (as defined in subparagraph (D)) shall—

"(i) assess the strengths and needs of the child using an age-appropriate, evidence-based, validated, functional assessment tool approved by the Secretary;

"(ii) determine whether the needs of the child can be met with family members or through placement in a foster family home or, if not, which setting from among the settings specified in section 472(k)(2) would provide the most effective and appropriate level of care for the child in the least restrictive environment and be consistent with the short- and long-term goals for the child, as specified in the permanency plan for the child; and

"(iii) develop a list of child-specific short- and long-term mental and behavioral health goals.

"(B)(i) The State shall assemble a family and permanency team for the child in accordance with the requirements of clauses (ii) and (iii). The qualified individual conducting the assessment required under subparagraph (A) shall work in conjunction with the family of, and permanency team for, the child while conducting and making the assessment.

"(ii) The family and permanency team shall consist of all appropriate biological family members, relative, and fictive kin of the child, as well as, as appropriate, professionals who are a resource to the family of the child, such as teachers, medical or mental health providers who have treated the child, or clergy. In the case of a child who has attained age 14, the family and permanency team shall include the members of the permanency planning team for the child that are selected by the child in accordance with section 475(5)(C)(iv).

"(iii) The State shall document in the child's case plan—

"(I) the reasonable and good faith effort of the State to identify and include all such individuals on the family of, and permanency team for, the child;

"(II) all contact information for members of the family and permanency team, as well as contact information for other family members and fictive kin who are not part of the family and permanency team;

"(III) evidence that meetings of the family and permanency team, including meetings relating to the assessment required under subparagraph (A), are held at a time and place convenient for family;

"(IV) if reunification is the goal, evidence demonstrating that the parent from whom the child was removed provided input on the members of the family and permanency team;

"(V) evidence that the assessment required under subparagraph (A) is determined in conjunction with the family and permanency team; and

"(VI) the placement preferences of the family and permanency team relative to the assessment and, if the placement preferences of the family and permanency team and child are not the placement setting recommended by the qualified individual conducting the assessment under subparagraph (A), the reasons why the preferences of the team and of the child were not recommended.

"(C) In the case of a child who the qualified individual conducting the assessment under subparagraph (A) determines should not be placed in a foster family home, the qualified individual shall specify in writing the reasons why the needs of the child cannot be met by the family of the child or in a foster family home. A shortage or lack of foster family homes shall not be an acceptable reason for determining that a needs of the child cannot be met in a foster family home. The qualified individual shall also specify in writing why the recommended placement in a qualified residential treatment program is the setting that will provide the child with the most effective and appropriate level of care in the least restrictive environment and how that placement is consistent with the short- and long-term goals for the child, as specified in the permanency plan for the child.

"(D)(i) Subject to clause (ii), in this subsection, the term 'qualified individual' means a trained professional or licensed clinician who is not an employee of the State agency and who is not connected to, or affiliated with, any placement setting in which children are placed by the State.

"(ii) The Secretary may approve a request of a State to waive any requirement in clause (i) upon a submission by the State, in accordance with criteria established by the Secretary, that certifies that the trained professionals or licensed clinicians with responsibility for performing the assessments described in subparagraph (A) shall maintain objectivity with respect to determining the most effective and appropriate placement for a child.

"(2) Within 60 days of the start of each placement in a qualified residential treatment program, a family or juvenile court or another court (including a tribal court) of competent jurisdiction, or an administrative body appointed or approved by the court, independently, shall—

"(A) consider the assessment, determination, and documentation made by the qualified individual conducting the assessment under paragraph (1);

"(B) determine whether the needs of the child can be met through placement in a foster family home or, if not, whether placement of the child in a qualified residential treatment program provides the most effective and appropriate level of care for the child in the least restrictive environment and whether that placement is consistent with the short- and long-term goals for the child, as specified in the permanency plan for the child; and

"(C) approve or disapprove the placement.

"(3) The written documentation made under paragraph (1)(C) and documentation of the determination and approval or disapproval of the placement in a qualified residential treatment program by a court or administrative body

under paragraph (2) shall be included in and made part of the case plan for the child.

"(4) As long as a child remains placed in a qualified residential treatment program, the State agency shall submit evidence at each status review and each permanency hearing held with respect to the child—

"(A) demonstrating that ongoing assessment of the strengths and needs of the child continues to support the determination that the needs of the child cannot be met through placement in a foster family home, that the placement in a qualified residential treatment program provides the most effective and appropriate level of care for the child in the least restrictive environment, and that the placement is consistent with the short- and long-term goals for the child, as specified in the permanency plan for the child;

"(B) documenting the specific treatment or service needs that will be met for the child in the placement and the length of time the child is expected to need the treatment or services; and

"(C) documenting the efforts made by the State agency to prepare the child to return home or to be placed with a fit and willing relative, a legal guardian, or an adoptive parent, or in a foster family home.

"(5) In the case of any child who is placed in a qualified residential treatment program for more than 12 consecutive months or 18 nonconsecutive months (or, in the case of a child who has not attained age 13, for more than 6 consecutive or nonconsecutive months), the State agency shall submit to the Secretary—

"(A) the most recent versions of the evidence and documentation specified in paragraph (4); and

"(B) the signed approval of the head of the State agency for the continued placement of the child in that setting.".

SEC. 20003. PROTOCOLS TO PREVENT INAPPROPRIATE DIAGNOSES.

(a) STATE PLAN REQUIREMENT.—Section 422(b)(15)(A) of the Social Security Act (42 U.S.C. 622(b)(15)(A)) is amended—

(1) in clause (vi), by striking "and" after the semicolon;

(2) by redesignating clause (vii) as clause (viii); and

(3) by inserting after clause (vi) the following:

"(vii) the procedures and protocols the State has established to ensure that children in foster care placements are not inappropriately diagnosed with mental illness, other emotional or behavioral disorders, medically fragile conditions, or developmental disabilities, and placed in settings that are not foster family homes as a result of the inappropriate diagnoses; and".

(b) EVALUATION.—Section 476 of such Act (42 U.S.C. 676), as previously amended, is further amended by adding at the end the following:

"(e) EVALUATION OF STATE PROCEDURES AND PROTOCOLS TO PREVENT INAPPROPRIATE DIAGNOSES OF MENTAL ILLNESS OR OTHER CONDITIONS.—The Secretary shall conduct an evaluation of the procedures and protocols established by States in accordance with the requirements of section 422(b)(15)(A)(vii). The evaluation shall analyze the extent to which States comply with and enforce the procedures and protocols and the effectiveness of various State procedures and protocols and shall identify best practices. Not later than January 1, 2019, the Secretary shall submit a report on the results of the evaluation to Congress.".

SEC. 20004. ADDITIONAL DATA AND REPORTS REGARDING CHILDREN PLACED IN A SETTING THAT IS NOT A FOSTER FAMILY HOME.

Section 479A(a)(7)(A) of the Social Security Act (42 U.S.C. 679b(a)(7)(A)) is amended by striking clauses (i) through (vi) and inserting the following:

"(i) with respect to each such placement—

"(I) the type of the placement setting, including whether the placement is shelter care, a group home and if so, the range of the child population in the home, a residential treatment facility, a hospital or institution providing medical, rehabilitative, or psychiatric care, a setting specializing in providing prenatal, post-partum or parenting supports, or some other kind of child-care institution and if so, what kind;

"(II) the number of children in the placement setting and the age, race, ethnicity, and gender of each of the children;

"(III) for each child in the placement setting, the length of the placement of the child in the setting, whether the placement of the child in the setting is the first placement of the child and if not, the number and type of previous placements of the child, and whether the child has special needs or another diagnosed mental or physical illness or condition; and

"(IV) the extent of any specialized education, treatment, counseling, or other services provided in the setting; and

"(ii) separately, the number and ages of children in the placements who have a permanency plan of another planned permanent living arrangement; and".

SEC. 20005. EFFECTIVE DATES; APPLICATION TO WAIVERS.

(a) EFFECTIVE DATES.—

(1) IN GENERAL.—Subject to paragraph (2) and subsections (b) and (c), the amendments made by this title shall take effect on January 1, 2017.

(2) TRANSITION RULE.—In the case of a State plan under part B or E of title IV of the Social Security Act which the Secretary of Health and Human Services determines requires State legislation (other than legislation appropriating funds) in order for the plan to meet the additional requirements imposed by the amendments made by this title, the State plan shall not be regarded as failing to comply with the requirements of such part solely on the basis of the failure of the plan to meet the additional requirements before the first day of the first calendar quarter beginning after the close of the first regular session of the State legislature that begins after the date of enactment of this Act. For purposes of the previous sentence, in the case of a State that has a 2-year legislative session, each year of the session shall be deemed to be a separate regular session of the State legislature.

(b) LIMITATION ON FEDERAL FINANCIAL PARTICIPATION FOR PLACEMENTS THAT ARE NOT IN FOSTER FAMILY HOMES AND RELATED PROVISIONS.—

(1) IN GENERAL.—The amendments made by sections 20001(a), 20001(b), 20001(d), and 20002 shall take effect on October 1, 2019.

(2) STATE OPTION TO DELAY EFFECTIVE DATE FOR NOT MORE THAN 2 YEARS.—At the sole discretion of a State and for not more than 2 years, the Secretary of Health and Human Services shall delay the effective date provided for in paragraph (1) with respect to the State. If the effective date is so delayed for a period with respect to a State under the preceding sentence, then—

(A) notwithstanding section 1904, the date that the amendments made by section 19011(c) take effect with respect to the State shall be delayed for the period; and

(B) in applying section 474(a)(6) of the Social Security Act with respect to the State, "on or after the date this paragraph takes effect with respect to the State" is deemed to be substituted for "after September 30, 2019" in subparagraph (A)(i)(I) of such section.

(c) APPLICATION TO STATES WITH WAIVERS.—In the case of a State that, on the date of enactment of this Act, has in effect a waiver approved under section 1130 of the Social Security Act (42 U.S.C. 1320a-9), the amendments made by this title shall not apply with respect to the State before the expiration (determined without regard to any extensions) of the waiver to the extent the amendments are inconsistent with the terms of the waiver.

TITLE XXI—CONTINUING SUPPORT FOR CHILD AND FAMILY SERVICES

SEC. 21001. SUPPORTING AND RETAINING FOSTER FAMILIES FOR CHILDREN.

(a) SUPPORTING AND RETAINING FOSTER PARENTS AS A FAMILY SUPPORT SERVICE.—Section 431(a)(2)(B) of the Social Security Act (42 U.S.C. 631(a)(2)(B)) is amended by redesignating clauses (iii) through (vi) as clauses (iv) through (vii), respectively, and inserting after clause (ii) the following:

"(iii) To support and retain foster families so they can provide quality family-based settings for children in foster care.".

(b) SUPPORT FOR FOSTER FAMILY HOMES.—Section 436 of such Act (42 U.S.C. 629f) is amended by adding at the end the following:

"(c) SUPPORT FOR FOSTER FAMILY HOMES.—Out of any money in the Treasury of the United States not otherwise appropriated, there are appropriated to the Secretary for fiscal year 2018, $8,000,000 for the Secretary to make competitive grants to States, Indian tribes, or tribal consortia to support the recruitment and retention of high-quality foster families to increase their capacity to place more children in family settings, focused on States, Indian tribes, or tribal consortia with the highest percentage of children in non-family settings. The amount appropriated under this subparagraph shall remain available through fiscal year 2022.".

SEC. 21002. EXTENSION OF CHILD AND FAMILY SERVICES PROGRAMS.

(a) EXTENSION OF STEPHANIE TUBBS JONES CHILD WELFARE SERVICES PROGRAM.—Section 425 of the Social Security Act (42 U.S.C. 625) is amended by striking "2012 through 2016" and inserting "2017 through 2021".

(b) EXTENSION OF PROMOTING SAFE AND STABLE FAMILIES PROGRAM AUTHORIZATIONS.—

(1) IN GENERAL.—Section 436(a) of such Act (42 U.S.C. 629f(a)) is amended by striking all that follows "$345,000,000" and inserting "for each of fiscal years 2017 through 2021.".

(2) DISCRETIONARY GRANTS.—Section 437(a) of such Act (42 U.S.C. 629g(a)) is amended by striking "2012 through 2016" and inserting "2017 through 2021".

(c) EXTENSION OF FUNDING RESERVATIONS FOR MONTHLY CASEWORKER VISITS AND REGIONAL PARTNERSHIP GRANTS.—Section 436(b) of such Act (42 U.S.C. 629f(b)) is amended—

(1) in paragraph (4)(A), by striking "2012 through 2016" and inserting "2017 through 2021"; and

(2) in paragraph (5), by striking "2012 through 2016" and inserting "2017 through 2021".

(d) REAUTHORIZATION OF FUNDING FOR STATE COURTS.—

(1) EXTENSION OF PROGRAM.—Section 438(c)(1) of such Act (42 U.S.C. 629h(c)(1)) is amended by striking "2012 through 2016" and inserting "2017 through 2021".

(2) EXTENSION OF FEDERAL SHARE.—Section 438(d) of such Act (42 U.S.C. 629h(d)) is amended by striking "2012 through 2016" and inserting "2017 through 2021".

(e) REPEAL OF EXPIRED PROVISIONS.—Section 438(e) of such Act (42 U.S.C. 629h(e)) is repealed.

SEC. 21003. IMPROVEMENTS TO THE JOHN H. CHAFEE FOSTER CARE INDEPENDENCE PROGRAM AND RELATED PROVISIONS.

(a) AUTHORITY TO SERVE FORMER FOSTER YOUTH UP TO AGE 23.—Section 477 of the Social Security Act (42 U.S.C. 677) is amended—

(1) in subsection (a)(5), by inserting "(or 23 years of age, in the case of a State with a certification under subsection (b)(3)(A)(ii) to provide assistance and services to youths who have aged out of foster care and have not attained such age, in accordance with such subsection)" after "21 years of age";

(2) in subsection (b)(3)(A)—

(A) by inserting "(i)" before "A certification";

(B) by striking "children who have left foster care" and all that follows through the period and inserting "youths who have aged out of foster care and have not attained 21 years of age."; and

(C) by adding at the end the following:

"(ii) If the State has elected under section 475(8)(B) to extend eligibility for foster care to all children who have not attained 21 years of age, or if the Secretary determines that the State agency responsible for administering the State plans under this part and part B uses State funds or any other funds not provided under this part to provide services and assistance for youths who have aged out of foster care that are comparable to the services and assistance the youths would receive if the State had made such an election, the certification required under clause (i) may provide that the State will provide assistance and services to youths who have aged out of foster care and have not attained 23 years of age."; and

(3) in subsection (b)(3)(B), by striking "children who have left foster care" and all that follows through the period and inserting "youths who have aged out of foster care and have not attained 21 years of age (or 23 years of age, in the case of a State with a certification under subparagraph (A)(i) to provide assistance and services to youths who have aged out of foster care and have not attained such age, in accordance with subparagraph (A)(ii)).".

(b) AUTHORITY TO REDISTRIBUTE UNSPENT FUNDS.—Section 477(d) of such Act (42 U.S.C. 677(d)) is amended—

(1) in paragraph (4), by inserting "or does not expend allocated funds within the time period specified under section 477(d)(3)" after "provided by the Secretary"; and

(2) by adding at the end the following:

"(5) REDISTRIBUTION OF UNEXPENDED AMOUNTS.—

"(A) AVAILABILITY OF AMOUNTS.—To the extent that amounts paid to States under this section in a fiscal year remain unexpended by the States at the end of the succeeding fiscal year, the Secretary may make the amounts available for redistribution in the second succeeding fiscal year among the States that apply for additional funds under this section for that second succeeding fiscal year.

"(B) REDISTRIBUTION.—

"(i) IN GENERAL.—The Secretary shall redistribute the amounts made available under subparagraph (A) for a fiscal year among eligible applicant States. In this subparagraph, the term 'eligible applicant State' means a State that has applied for additional funds for the fiscal year under subparagraph (A) if the Secretary determines that the State will use the funds for the purpose for which originally allotted under this section.

"(ii) AMOUNT TO BE REDISTRIBUTED.—The amount to be redistributed to each eligible applicant State shall be the amount so made available multiplied by the State foster care ratio, (as defined in subsection (c)(4), except that, in such subsection, 'all eligible applicant States (as defined in subsection (d)(5)(B)(i))' shall be substituted for 'all States').

"(iii) TREATMENT OF REDISTRIBUTED AMOUNT.—Any amount made available to a State under this paragraph shall be regarded as part of the allotment of the State under this section for the fiscal year in which the redistribution is made.

"(C) TRIBES.—For purposes of this paragraph, the term 'State' includes an Indian tribe, tribal organization, or tribal consortium that receives an allotment under this section.".

(c) EXPANDING AND CLARIFYING THE USE OF EDUCATION AND TRAINING VOUCHERS.—

(1) IN GENERAL.—Section 477(i)(3) of such Act (42 U.S.C. 677(i)(3)) is amended—

(A) by striking "on the date" and all that follows through "23" and inserting "to remain eligible until they attain 26"; and

(B) by inserting ", but in no event may a youth participate in the program for more than 5 years (whether or not consecutive)" before the period.

(2) CONFORMING AMENDMENT.—Section 477(i)(1) of such Act (42 U.S.C. 677(i)(1)) is amended by inserting "who have attained 14 years of age" before the period.

(d) OTHER IMPROVEMENTS.—Section 477 of such Act (42 U.S.C. 677), as amended by subsections (a), (b), and (c), is amended—

(1) in the section heading, by striking "**INDEPENDENCE PROGRAM**" and inserting "**PROGRAM FOR SUCCESSFUL TRANSITION TO ADULTHOOD**";

(2) in subsection (a)—

(A) in paragraph (1)—

(i) by striking "identify children who are likely to remain in foster care until 18 years of age and to help these children make the transition to self-sufficiency by providing services" and inserting "support all youth who have experienced foster care at age 14 or older in their transition to adulthood through transitional services";

(ii) by inserting "and post-secondary education" after "high school diploma"; and

(iii) by striking "training in daily living skills, training in budgeting and financial management skills" and inserting "training and opportunities to practice daily living skills (such as financial literacy training and driving instruction)";

(B) in paragraph (2), by striking "who are likely to remain in foster care until 18 years of age receive the education, training, and services necessary to obtain employment" and inserting "who have experienced foster care at age 14 or older achieve meaningful, permanent connections with a caring adult";

(C) in paragraph (3), by striking "who are likely to remain in foster care until 18 years of age prepare for and enter postsecondary training and education institutions" and inserting "who have experienced foster care at age 14 or older engage in age or developmentally appropriate activities, positive youth development, and experiential learning that reflects what their peers in intact families experience"; and

(D) by striking paragraph (4) and redesignating paragraphs (5) through (8) as paragraphs (4) through (7);

(3) in subsection (b)—

(A) in paragraph (2)(D), by striking "adolescents" and inserting "youth"; and

(B) in paragraph (3)—

(i) in subparagraph (D)—

(I) by inserting "including training on youth development" after "to provide training"; and

(II) by striking "adolescents preparing for independent living" and all that follows through the period and inserting "youth preparing for a successful transition to adulthood and making a permanent connection with a caring adult.";

(ii) in subparagraph (H), by striking "adolescents" each place it appears and inserting "youth"; and

(iii) in subparagraph (K)—

(I) by striking "an adolescent" and inserting "a youth"; and

(II) by striking "the adolescent" each place it appears and inserting "the youth"; and

(4) in subsection (f), by striking paragraph (2) and inserting the following:

"(2) REPORT TO CONGRESS.—Not later than October 1, 2017, the Secretary shall submit to the

Committee on Ways and Means of the House of Representatives and the Committee on Finance of the Senate a report on the National Youth in Transition Database and any other databases in which States report outcome measures relating to children in foster care and children who have aged out of foster care or left foster care for kinship guardianship or adoption. The report shall include the following:

"(A) A description of the reasons for entry into foster care and of the foster care experiences, such as length of stay, number of placement settings, case goal, and discharge reason of 17-year-olds who are surveyed by the National Youth in Transition Database and an analysis of the comparison of that description with the reasons for entry and foster care experiences of children of other ages who exit from foster care before attaining age 17.

"(B) A description of the characteristics of the individuals who report poor outcomes at ages 19 and 21 to the National Youth in Transition Database.

"(C) Benchmarks for determining what constitutes a poor outcome for youth who remain in or have exited from foster care and plans the Executive branch will take to incorporate these benchmarks in efforts to evaluate child welfare agency performance in providing services to children transitioning from foster care.

"(D) An analysis of the association between types of placement, number of overall placements, time spent in foster care, and other factors, and outcomes at ages 19 and 21.

"(E) An analysis of the differences in outcomes for children in and formerly in foster care at age 19 and 21 among States.".

(e) CLARIFYING DOCUMENTATION PROVIDED TO FOSTER YOUTH LEAVING FOSTER CARE.—Section 475(5)(I) of such Act (42 U.S.C. 675(5)(I)) is amended by inserting after "REAL ID Act of 2005" the following: ", and any official documentation necessary to prove that the child was previously in foster care".

TITLE XXII—CONTINUING INCENTIVES TO STATES TO PROMOTE ADOPTION AND LEGAL GUARDIANSHIP

SEC. 22001. REAUTHORIZING ADOPTION AND LEGAL GUARDIANSHIP INCENTIVE PROGRAMS.

Section 473A of the Social Security Act (42 U.S.C. 673b) is amended—

(1) in subsection (b)(4), by striking "2013 through 2015" and inserting "2016 through 2020";

(2) in subsection (h)(1)(D), by striking "2016" and inserting "2021"; and

(3) in subsection (h)(2), by striking "2016" and inserting "2021".

TITLE XXIII—TECHNICAL CORRECTIONS

SEC. 23001. TECHNICAL CORRECTIONS TO DATA EXCHANGE STANDARDS TO IMPROVE PROGRAM COORDINATION.

(a) IN GENERAL.—Section 440 of the Social Security Act (42 U.S.C. 629m) is amended to read as follows:

"SEC. 440. DATA EXCHANGE STANDARDS FOR IMPROVED INTEROPERABILITY.

"(a) DESIGNATION.—The Secretary shall, in consultation with an interagency work group established by the Office of Management and Budget and considering State government perspectives, by rule, designate data exchange standards to govern, under this part and part E—

"(1) necessary categories of information that State agencies operating programs under State plans approved under this part are required under applicable Federal law to electronically exchange with another State agency; and

"(2) Federal reporting and data exchange required under applicable Federal law.

"(b) REQUIREMENTS.—The data exchange standards required by paragraph (1) shall, to the extent practicable—

"(1) incorporate a widely accepted, non-proprietary, searchable, computer-readable format, such as the eXtensible Markup Language;

"(2) contain interoperable standards developed and maintained by intergovernmental partnerships, such as the National Information Exchange Model;

"(3) incorporate interoperable standards developed and maintained by Federal entities with authority over contracting and financial assistance;

"(4) be consistent with and implement applicable accounting principles;

"(5) be implemented in a manner that is cost-effective and improves program efficiency and effectiveness; and

"(6) be capable of being continually upgraded as necessary.

"(c) RULE OF CONSTRUCTION.—Nothing in this subsection shall be construed to require a change to existing data exchange standards found to be effective and efficient.".

(b) EFFECTIVE DATE.—Not later than the date that is 24 months after the date of the enactment of this section, the Secretary of Health and Human Services shall issue a proposed rule that—

(1) identifies federally required data exchanges, include specification and timing of exchanges to be standardized, and address the factors used in determining whether and when to standardize data exchanges; and

(2) specifies State implementation options and describes future milestones.

SEC. 23002. TECHNICAL CORRECTIONS TO STATE REQUIREMENT TO ADDRESS THE DEVELOPMENTAL NEEDS OF YOUNG CHILDREN.

Section 422(b)(18) of the Social Security Act (42 U.S.C. 622(b)(18)) is amended by striking "such children" and inserting "all vulnerable children under 5 years of age".

TITLE XXIV—ENSURING STATES REINVEST SAVINGS RESULTING FROM INCREASE IN ADOPTION ASSISTANCE

SEC. 24001. DELAY OF ADOPTION ASSISTANCE PHASE-IN.

(a) IN GENERAL.—The table in section 473(e)(1)(B) of the Social Security Act (42 U.S.C. 673(e)(1)(B)) is amended—

(1) by striking "2016" and inserting "2016, 2017, 2018, or 2019";

(2) by striking "2017" and inserting "2020"; and

(3) by striking "2018" and inserting "2021".

(b) SPECIAL RULE.—Section 473(e) of the Social Security Act (42 U.S.C. 673(e)) is amended by adding at the end the following new paragraph:

"(3) ADDITIONAL EXCEPTION.—Notwithstanding paragraph (1) of this subsection, during the period that begins on October 1, 2016, and ends on December 31, 2016, such term shall include a child—

"(A) who satisfies the requirements for being considered an applicable child under paragraph (1) (as in effect during that period);

"(B) who meets the requirements of subsection (a)(2)(A)(ii); and

"(C) on whose behalf an adoption assistance agreement is entered into under this section during that period.".

(c) EFFECTIVE DATE.—The amendments made by this section take effect on January 1, 2017.

SEC. 24002. GAO STUDY AND REPORT ON STATE REINVESTMENT OF SAVINGS RESULTING FROM INCREASE IN ADOPTION ASSISTANCE.

(a) STUDY.—The Comptroller General of the United States shall study the extent to which States are complying with the requirements of section 473(a)(8) of the Social Security Act relating to the effects of phasing out the AFDC income eligibility requirements for adoption assist-

ance payments under section 473 of the Social Security Act, as enacted by section 402 of the Fostering Connections to Success and Increasing Adoptions Act of 2008 (Public Law 110–351; 122 Stat. 3975) and amended by section 206 of the Preventing Sex Trafficking and Strengthening Families Act (Public Law 113–183; 128 Stat. 1919). In particular, the Comptroller General shall analyze the extent to which States are complying with the following requirements under section 473(a)(8)(D) of the Social Security Act:

(1) The requirement to spend an amount equal to the amount of the savings (if any) in State expenditures under part E of title IV of the Social Security resulting from phasing out the AFDC income eligibility requirements for adoption assistance payments under section 473 of such Act to provide to children of families any service that may be provided under part B or E of title IV of such Act.

(2) The requirement that a State shall spend not less than 30 percent of the amount of any savings described in subparagraph (A) on post-adoption services, post-guardianship services, and services to support and sustain positive permanent outcomes for children who otherwise might enter into foster care under the responsibility of the State, with at least ⅔ of the spending by the State to comply with the 30 percent requirement being spent on post-adoption and post-guardianship services.

(b) REPORT.—The Comptroller General of the United States shall submit to the Committee on Finance of the Senate, the Committee on Ways and Means of the House of Representatives, and the Secretary of Health and Human Services a report that contains the results of the study required by subsection (a), including recommendations to ensure compliance with laws referred to in subsection (a).

TITLE XXV—SOCIAL IMPACT PARTNERSHIPS TO PAY FOR RESULTS

SEC. 25001. SHORT TITLE.

This title may be cited as the "Social Impact Partnership to Pay for Results Act".

SEC. 25002. SOCIAL IMPACT PARTNERSHIPS TO PAY FOR RESULTS.

Section 403 of the Social Security Act (42 U.S.C. 603) is amended by adding at the end the following:

"(c) SOCIAL IMPACT DEMONSTRATION PROJECTS.—

"(1) PURPOSES.—The purposes of this subsection are the following:

"(A) To improve the lives of families and individuals in need in the United States by funding social programs that achieve real results.

"(B) To redirect funds away from programs that, based on objective data, are ineffective, and into programs that achieve demonstrable, measurable results.

"(C) To ensure Federal funds are used effectively on social services to produce positive outcomes for both service recipients and taxpayers.

"(D) To establish the use of social impact partnerships to address some of our Nation's most pressing problems.

"(E) To facilitate the creation of public-private partnerships that bundle philanthropic or other private resources with existing public spending to scale up effective social interventions already being implemented by private organizations, nonprofits, charitable organizations, and State and local governments across the country.

"(F) To bring pay-for-performance to the social sector, allowing the United States to improve the impact and effectiveness of vital social services programs while redirecting inefficient or duplicative spending.

"(G) To incorporate outcomes measurement and randomized controlled trials or other rigorous methodologies for assessing program impact.

"(2) SOCIAL IMPACT PARTNERSHIP APPLICATION.—

"(A) NOTICE.—Not later than 1 year after the date of the enactment of this subsection, the Secretary of the Treasury, in consultation with the Federal Interagency Council on Social Impact Partnerships, shall publish in the Federal Register a request for proposals from States or local governments for social impact partnership projects in accordance with this paragraph.

"(B) REQUIRED OUTCOMES FOR SOCIAL IMPACT PARTNERSHIP PROJECT.—To qualify as a social impact partnership project under this subsection, a project must produce one or more measurable, clearly defined outcomes that result in social benefit and Federal, State, or local savings through any of the following:

"(i) Increasing work and earnings by individuals in the United States who are unemployed for more than 6 consecutive months.

"(ii) Increasing employment and earnings of individuals who have attained 16 years of age but not 25 years of age.

"(iii) Increasing employment among individuals receiving Federal disability benefits.

"(iv) Reducing the dependence of low-income families on Federal means-tested benefits.

"(v) Improving rates of high school graduation.

"(vi) Reducing teen and unplanned pregnancies.

"(vii) Improving birth outcomes and early childhood health and development among low-income families and individuals.

"(viii) Reducing rates of asthma, diabetes, or other preventable diseases among low-income families and individuals to reduce the utilization of emergency and other high-cost care.

"(ix) Increasing the proportion of children living in two-parent families.

"(x) Reducing incidences and adverse consequences of child abuse and neglect.

"(xi) Reducing the number of youth in foster care by increasing adoptions, permanent guardianship arrangements, reunifications, or placements with a fit and willing relative, or by avoiding placing children in foster care by ensuring they can be cared for safely in their own homes.

"(xii) Reducing the number of children and youth in foster care residing in group homes, child care institutions, agency-operated foster homes, or other non-family foster homes, unless it is determined that it is in the interest of the child's long-term health, safety, or psychological well-being to not be placed in a family foster home.

"(xiii) Reducing the number of children returning to foster care.

"(xiv) Reducing recidivism among juvenile offenders, individuals released from prison, or other high-risk populations.

"(xv) Reducing the rate of homelessness among our most vulnerable populations.

"(xvi) Improving the health and well-being of those with mental, emotional, and behavioral health needs.

"(xvii) Improving the educational outcomes of special-needs or low-income children.

"(xviii) Improving the employment and well-being of returning United States military members.

"(xix) Increasing the financial stability of low-income families.

"(xx) Increasing the independence and employability of individuals who are physically or mentally disabled.

"(xxi) Other measurable outcomes defined by the State or local government that result in positive social outcomes and Federal savings.

"(C) APPLICATION REQUIRED.—The notice described in subparagraph (A) shall require a State or local government to submit an application for the social impact partnership project that addresses the following:

"(i) The outcome goals of the project.

"(ii) A description of each intervention in the project and anticipated outcomes of the intervention.

"(iii) Rigorous evidence demonstrating that the intervention can be expected to produce the desired outcomes.

"(iv) The target population that will be served by the project.

"(v) The expected social benefits to participants who receive the intervention and others who may be impacted.

"(vi) Projected Federal, State, and local government costs and other costs to conduct the project.

"(vii) Projected Federal, State, and local government savings and other savings, including an estimate of the savings to the Federal Government, on a program-by-program basis and in the aggregate, if the project is implemented and the outcomes are achieved as a result of the intervention.

"(viii) If savings resulting from the successful completion of the project are estimated to accrue to the State or local government, the likelihood of the State or local government to realize those savings.

"(ix) A plan for delivering the intervention through a social impact partnership model.

"(x) A description of the expertise of each service provider that will administer the intervention, including a summary of the experience of the service provider in delivering the proposed intervention or a similar intervention, or demonstrating that the service provider has the expertise necessary to deliver the proposed intervention.

"(xi) An explanation of the experience of the State or local government, the intermediary, or the service provider in raising private and philanthropic capital to fund social service investments.

"(xii) The detailed roles and responsibilities of each entity involved in the project, including any State or local government entity, intermediary, service provider, independent evaluator, investor, or other stakeholder.

"(xiii) A summary of the experience of the service provider in delivering the proposed intervention or a similar intervention, or a summary demonstrating the service provider has the expertise necessary to deliver the proposed intervention.

"(xiv) A summary of the unmet need in the area where the intervention will be delivered or among the target population who will receive the intervention.

"(xv) The proposed payment terms, the methodology used to calculate outcome payments, the payment schedule, and performance thresholds.

"(xvi) The project budget.

"(xvii) The project timeline.

"(xviii) The criteria used to determine the eligibility of an individual for the project, including how selected populations will be identified, how they will be referred to the project, and how they will be enrolled in the project.

"(xix) The evaluation design.

"(xx) The metrics that will be used in the evaluation to determine whether the outcomes have been achieved as a result of the intervention and how the metrics will be measured.

"(xxi) An explanation of how the metrics used in the evaluation to determine whether the outcomes achieved as a result of the intervention are independent, objective indicators of impact and are not subject to manipulation by the service provider, intermediary, or investor.

"(xxii) A summary explaining the independence of the evaluator from the other entities involved in the project and the evaluator's experience in conducting rigorous evaluations of program effectiveness including, where available,

well-implemented randomized controlled trials on the intervention or similar interventions.

"(xxiii) The capacity of the service provider to deliver the intervention to the number of participants the State or local government proposes to serve in the project.

"(xxiv) A description of whether and how the State or local government and service providers plan to sustain the intervention, if it is timely and appropriate to do so, to ensure that successful interventions continue to operate after the period of the social impact partnership.

"(D) PROJECT INTERMEDIARY INFORMATION REQUIRED.—The application described in subparagraph (C) shall also contain the following information about any intermediary for the social impact partnership project (whether an intermediary is a service provider or other entity):

"(i) Experience and capacity for providing or facilitating the provision of the type of intervention proposed.

"(ii) The mission and goals.

"(iii) Information on whether the intermediary is already working with service providers that provide this intervention or an explanation of the capacity of the intermediary to begin working with service providers to provide the intervention.

"(iv) Experience working in a collaborative environment across government and nongovernmental entities.

"(v) Previous experience collaborating with public or private entities to implement evidence-based programs.

"(vi) Ability to raise or provide funding to cover operating costs (if applicable to the project).

"(vii) Capacity and infrastructure to track outcomes and measure results, including—

"(I) capacity to track and analyze program performance and assess program impact; and

"(II) experience with performance-based awards or performance-based contracting and achieving project milestones and targets.

"(viii) Role in delivering the intervention.

"(ix) How the intermediary would monitor program success, including a description of the interim benchmarks and outcome measures.

"(E) FEASIBILITY STUDIES FUNDED THROUGH OTHER SOURCES.—The notice described in subparagraph (A) shall permit a State or local government to submit an application for social impact partnership funding that contains information from a feasibility study developed for purposes other than applying for funding under this subsection.

"(3) AWARDING SOCIAL IMPACT PARTNERSHIP AGREEMENTS.—

"(A) TIMELINE IN AWARDING AGREEMENT.—Not later than 6 months after receiving an application in accordance with paragraph (2), the Secretary, in consultation with the Federal Interagency Council on Social Impact Partnerships, shall determine whether to enter into an agreement for a social impact partnership project with a State or local government.

"(B) CONSIDERATIONS IN AWARDING AGREEMENT.—In determining whether to enter into an agreement for a social impact partnership project (the application for which was submitted under paragraph (2)) the Secretary, in consultation with the Federal Interagency Council on Social Impact Partnerships (established by paragraph (6)) and the head of any Federal agency administering a similar intervention or serving a population similar to that served by the project, shall consider each of the following:

"(i) The recommendations made by the Commission on Social Impact Partnerships.

"(ii) The value to the Federal Government of the outcomes expected to be achieved if the outcomes specified in the agreement are achieved as a result of the intervention.

"(iii) The likelihood, based on evidence provided in the application and other evidence, that the State or local government in collaboration with the intermediary and the service providers will achieve the outcomes.

"(iv) The savings to the Federal Government if the outcomes specified in the agreement are achieved as a result of the intervention.

"(v) The savings to the State and local governments if the outcomes specified in the agreement are achieved as a result of the intervention.

"(vi) The expected quality of the evaluation that would be conducted with respect to the agreement.

"(vii) The capacity and commitment of the State or local government to sustain the intervention, if appropriate and timely and if the intervention is successful, beyond the period of the social impact partnership.

"(C) AGREEMENT AUTHORITY.—

"(i) AGREEMENT REQUIREMENTS.—In accordance with this paragraph, the Secretary, in consultation with the Federal Interagency Council on Social Impact Partnerships and the head of any Federal agency administering a similar intervention or serving a population similar to that served by the project, may enter into an agreement for a social impact partnership project with a State or local government if the Secretary, in consultation with the Federal Interagency Council on Social Impact Partnerships, determines that each of the following requirements are met:

"(I) The State or local government agrees to achieve one or more outcomes as a result of the intervention, as specified in the agreement and validated by independent evaluation, in order to receive payment.

"(II) The Federal payment to the State or local government for each specified outcome achieved as a result of the intervention is less than or equal to the value of the outcome to the Federal Government over a period not to exceed 10 years, as determined by the Secretary, in consultation with the State or local government.

"(III) The duration of the project does not exceed 10 years.

"(IV) The State or local government has demonstrated, through the application submitted under paragraph (2), that, based on prior rigorous experimental evaluations or rigorous quasi-experimental studies, the intervention can be expected to achieve each outcome specified in the agreement.

"(V) The State, local government, intermediary, or service provider has experience raising private or philanthropic capital to fund social service investments (if applicable to the project).

"(VI) The State or local government has shown that each service provider has experience delivering the intervention, a similar intervention, or has otherwise demonstrated the expertise necessary to deliver the intervention.

"(ii) PAYMENT.—The Secretary shall pay the State or local government only if the independent evaluator described in paragraph (5) determines that the social impact partnership project has met the requirements specified in the agreement and achieved an outcome as a result of the intervention, as specified in the agreement and validated by independent evaluation.

"(D) NOTICE OF AGREEMENT AWARD.—Not later than 30 days after entering into an agreement under this paragraph, the Secretary shall publish a notice in the Federal Register that includes, with regard to the agreement, the following:

"(i) The outcome goals of the social impact partnership project.

"(ii) A description of each intervention in the project.

"(iii) The target population that will be served by the project.

"(iv) The expected social benefits to participants who receive the intervention and others who may be impacted.

"(v) The detailed roles, responsibilities, and purposes of each Federal, State, or local government entity, intermediary, service provider, independent evaluator, investor, or other stakeholder.

"(vi) The payment terms, the methodology used to calculate outcome payments, the payment schedule, and performance thresholds.

"(vii) The project budget.

"(viii) The project timeline.

"(ix) The project eligibility criteria.

"(x) The evaluation design.

"(xi) The metrics that will be used in the evaluation to determine whether the outcomes have been achieved as a result of each intervention and how these metrics will be measured.

"(xii) The estimate of the savings to the Federal, State, and local government, on a program-by-program basis and in the aggregate, if the agreement is entered into and implemented and the outcomes are achieved as a result of each intervention.

"(E) AUTHORITY TO TRANSFER ADMINISTRATION OF AGREEMENT.—The Secretary may transfer to the head of another Federal agency the authority to administer (including making payments under) an agreement entered into under subparagraph (C), and any funds necessary to do so.

"(F) REQUIREMENT ON FUNDING USED TO BENEFIT CHILDREN.—Not less than 50 percent of all Federal payments made to carry out agreements under this paragraph shall be used for initiatives that directly benefit children.

"(4) FEASIBILITY STUDY FUNDING.—

"(A) REQUESTS FOR FUNDING FOR FEASIBILITY STUDIES.—The Secretary shall reserve a portion of the amount reserved to carry out this subsection to assist States or local governments in developing feasibility studies to apply for social impact partnership funding under paragraph (2). To be eligible to receive funding to assist with completing a feasibility study, a State or local government shall submit an application for feasibility study funding addressing the following:

"(i) A description of the outcome goals of the social impact partnership project.

"(ii) A description of the intervention, including anticipated program design, target population, an estimate regarding the number of individuals to be served, and setting for the intervention.

"(iii) Evidence to support the likelihood that the intervention will produce the desired outcomes.

"(iv) A description of the potential metrics to be used.

"(v) The expected social benefits to participants who receive the intervention and others who may be impacted.

"(vi) Estimated costs to conduct the project.

"(vii) Estimates of Federal, State, and local government savings and other savings if the project is implemented and the outcomes are achieved as a result of each intervention.

"(viii) An estimated timeline for implementation and completion of the project, which shall not exceed 10 years.

"(ix) With respect to a project for which the State or local government selects an intermediary to operate the project, any partnerships needed to successfully execute the project and the ability of the intermediary to foster the partnerships.

"(x) The expected resources needed to complete the feasibility study for the State or local government to apply for social impact partnership funding under paragraph (2).

"(B) FEDERAL SELECTION OF APPLICATIONS FOR FEASIBILITY STUDY.—Not later than 6 months after receiving an application for feasibility study funding under subparagraph (A), the Secretary, in consultation with the Federal

Interagency Council on Social Impact Partnerships and the head of any Federal agency administering a similar intervention or serving a population similar to that served by the project, shall select State or local government feasibility study proposals for funding based on the following:

"(i) The recommendations made by the Commission on Social Impact Partnerships.

"(ii) The likelihood that the proposal will achieve the desired outcomes.

"(iii) The value of the outcomes expected to be achieved as a result of each intervention.

"(iv) The potential savings to the Federal Government if the social impact partnership project is successful.

"(v) The potential savings to the State and local governments if the project is successful.

"(C) PUBLIC DISCLOSURE.—Not later than 30 days after selecting a State or local government for feasibility study funding under this paragraph, the Secretary shall cause to be published on the website of the Federal Interagency Council on Social Impact Partnerships information explaining why a State or local government was granted feasibility study funding.

"(D) FUNDING RESTRICTION.—

"(i) FEASIBILITY STUDY RESTRICTION.—The Secretary may not provide feasibility study funding under this paragraph for more than 50 percent of the estimated total cost of the feasibility study reported in the State or local government application submitted under subparagraph (A).

"(ii) AGGREGATE RESTRICTION.—Of the total amount reserved to carry out this subsection, the Secretary may not use more than $10,000,000 to provide feasibility study funding to States or local governments under this paragraph.

"(iii) NO GUARANTEE OF FUNDING.—The Secretary shall have the option to award no funding under this paragraph.

"(E) SUBMISSION OF FEASIBILITY STUDY REQUIRED.—Not later than 9 months after the receipt of feasibility study funding under this paragraph, a State or local government receiving the funding shall complete the feasibility study and submit the study to the Federal Interagency Council on Social Impact Partnerships.

"(F) DELEGATION OF AUTHORITY.—The Secretary may transfer to the head of another Federal agency the authorities provided in this paragraph and any funds necessary to exercise the authorities.

"(5) EVALUATIONS.—

"(A) AUTHORITY TO ENTER INTO AGREEMENTS.—For each State or local government awarded a social impact partnership project approved by the Secretary under this subsection, the head of the relevant agency, as recommended by the Federal Interagency Council on Social Impact Partnerships and determined by the Secretary, shall enter into an agreement with the State or local government to pay for all or part of the independent evaluation to determine whether the State or local government project has achieved a specific outcome as a result of the intervention in order for the State or local government to receive outcome payments under this subsection.

"(B) EVALUATOR QUALIFICATIONS.—The head of the relevant agency may not enter into an agreement with a State or local government unless the head determines that the evaluator is independent of the other parties to the agreement and has demonstrated substantial experience in conducting rigorous evaluations of program effectiveness including, where available and appropriate, well-implemented randomized controlled trials on the intervention or similar interventions.

"(C) METHODOLOGIES TO BE USED.—The evaluation used to determine whether a State or local government will receive outcome payments under this subsection shall use experimental designs using random assignment or other reliable, evidence-based research methodologies, as certified by the Federal Interagency Council on Social Impact Partnerships, that allow for the strongest possible causal inferences when random assignment is not feasible.

''(D) PROGRESS REPORT.—

''(i) SUBMISSION OF REPORT.—The independent evaluator shall—

''(I) not later than 2 years after a project has been approved by the Secretary and biannually thereafter until the project is concluded, submit to the head of the relevant agency and the Federal Interagency Council on Social Impact Partnerships a written report summarizing the progress that has been made in achieving each outcome specified in the agreement; and

''(II) before the scheduled time of the first outcome payment and before the scheduled time of each subsequent payment, submit to the head of the relevant agency and the Federal Interagency Council on Social Impact Partnerships a written report that includes the results of the evaluation conducted to determine whether an outcome payment should be made along with information on the unique factors that contributed to achieving or failing to achieve the outcome, the challenges faced in attempting to achieve the outcome, and information on the improved future delivery of this or similar interventions.

''(ii) SUBMISSION TO THE SECRETARY AND CONGRESS.—Not later than 30 days after receipt of the written report pursuant to clause (i)(II), the Federal Interagency Council on Social Impact Partnerships shall submit the report to the Secretary and each committee of jurisdiction in the House of Representatives and the Senate.

''(E) FINAL REPORT.—

''(i) SUBMISSION OF REPORT.—Within 6 months after the social impact partnership project is completed, the independent evaluator shall—

''(I) evaluate the effects of the activities undertaken pursuant to the agreement with regard to each outcome specified in the agreement; and

''(II) submit to the head of the relevant agency and the Federal Interagency Council on Social Impact Partnerships a written report that includes the results of the evaluation and the conclusion of the evaluator as to whether the State or local government has fulfilled each obligation of the agreement, along with information on the unique factors that contributed to the success or failure of the project, the challenges faced in attempting to achieve the outcome, and information on the improved future delivery of this or similar interventions.

''(ii) SUBMISSION TO THE SECRETARY AND CONGRESS.—Not later than 30 days after receipt of the written report pursuant to clause (i)(II), the Federal Interagency Council on Social Impact Partnerships shall submit the report to the Secretary and each committee of jurisdiction in the House of Representatives and the Senate.

''(F) LIMITATION ON COST OF EVALUATIONS.—Of the amount reserved under this subsection for social impact partnership projects, the Secretary may not obligate more than 15 percent to evaluate the implementation and outcomes of the projects.

''(G) DELEGATION OF AUTHORITY.—The Secretary may transfer to the head of another Federal agency the authorities provided in this paragraph and any funds necessary to exercise the authorities.

''(6) FEDERAL INTERAGENCY COUNCIL ON SOCIAL IMPACT PARTNERSHIPS.—

''(A) ESTABLISHMENT.—There is established the Federal Interagency Council on Social Impact Partnerships (in this paragraph referred to as the 'Council') to—

''(i) coordinate with the Secretary on the efforts of social impact partnership projects funded under this subsection;

''(ii) advise and assist the Secretary in the development and implementation of the projects;

''(iii) advise the Secretary on specific programmatic and policy matter related to the projects;

''(iv) provide subject-matter expertise to the Secretary with regard to the projects;

''(v) certify to the Secretary that each State or local government that has entered into an agreement with the Secretary for a social impact partnership project under this subsection and each evaluator selected by the head of the relevant agency under paragraph (5) has access to Federal administrative data to assist the State or local government and the evaluator in evaluating the performance and outcomes of the project;

''(vi) address issues that will influence the future of social impact partnership projects in the United States;

''(vii) provide guidance to the executive branch on the future of social impact partnership projects in the United States;

''(viii) prior to approval by the Secretary, certify that each State and local government application for a social impact partnership contains rigorous, independent data and reliable, evidence-based research methodologies to support the conclusion that the project will yield savings to the State or local government or the Federal Government if the project outcomes are achieved;

''(ix) certify to the Secretary, in the case of each approved social impact partnership that is expected to yield savings to the Federal Government, that the project will yield a projected savings to the Federal Government if the project outcomes are achieved, and coordinate with the relevant Federal agency to produce an after-action accounting once the project is complete to determine the actual Federal savings realized, and the extent to which actual savings aligned with projected savings; and

''(x) provide periodic reports to the Secretary and make available reports periodically to Congress and the public on the implementation of this subsection.

''(B) COMPOSITION OF COUNCIL.—The Council shall have 11 members, as follows:

''(i) CHAIR.—The Chair of the Council shall be the Director of the Office of Management and Budget.

''(ii) OTHER MEMBERS.—The head of each of the following entities shall designate one officer or employee of the entity to be a Council member:

''(I) The Department of Labor.

''(II) The Department of Health and Human Services.

''(III) The Social Security Administration.

''(IV) The Department of Agriculture.

''(V) The Department of Justice.

''(VI) The Department of Housing and Urban Development.

''(VII) The Department of Education.

''(VIII) The Department of Veterans Affairs.

''(IX) The Department of the Treasury.

''(X) The Corporation for National and Community Service.

''(7) COMMISSION ON SOCIAL IMPACT PARTNERSHIPS.—

''(A) ESTABLISHMENT.—There is established the Commission on Social Impact Partnerships (in this paragraph referred to as the 'Commission').

''(B) DUTIES.—The duties of the Commission shall be to—

''(i) assist the Secretary and the Federal Interagency Council on Social Impact Partnerships in reviewing applications for funding under this subsection;

''(ii) make recommendations to the Secretary and the Federal Interagency Council on Social Impact Partnerships regarding the funding of

social impact partnership agreements and feasibility studies; and

''(iii) provide other assistance and information as requested by the Secretary or the Federal Interagency Council on Social Impact Partnerships.

''(C) COMPOSITION.—The Commission shall be composed of nine members, of whom—

''(i) one shall be appointed by the President, who will serve as the Chair of the Commission;

''(ii) one shall be appointed by the Majority Leader of the Senate;

''(iii) one shall be appointed by the Minority Leader of the Senate;

''(iv) one shall be appointed by the Speaker of the House of Representatives;

''(v) one shall be appointed by the Minority Leader of the House of Representatives;

''(vi) one shall be appointed by the Chairman of the Committee on Finance of the Senate;

''(vii) one shall be appointed by the ranking member of the Committee on Finance of the Senate;

''(viii) one member shall be appointed by the Chairman of the Committee on Ways and Means of the House of Representatives; and

''(ix) one shall be appointed by the ranking member of the Committee on Ways and Means of the House of Representatives.

''(D) QUALIFICATIONS OF COMMISSION MEMBERS.—The members of the Commission shall—

''(i) be experienced in finance, economics, pay for performance, or program evaluation;

''(ii) have relevant professional or personal experience in a field related to one or more of the outcomes listed in this subsection; or

''(iii) be qualified to review applications for social impact partnership projects to determine whether the proposed metrics and evaluation methodologies are appropriately rigorous and reliant upon independent data and evidence-based research.

''(E) TIMING OF APPOINTMENTS.—The appointments of the members of the Commission shall be made not later than 120 days after the date of the enactment of this subsection, or, in the event of a vacancy, not later than 90 days after the date the vacancy arises. If a member of Congress fails to appoint a member by that date, the President may select a member of the President's choice on behalf of the member of Congress. Notwithstanding the preceding sentence, if not all appointments have been made to the Commission as of that date, the Commission may operate with no fewer than five members until all appointments have been made.

''(F) TERM OF APPOINTMENTS.—

''(i) IN GENERAL.—The members appointed under subparagraph (C) shall serve as follows:

''(I) Three members shall serve for 2 years.

''(II) Three members shall serve for 3 years.

''(III) Three members (one of which shall be Chair of the Commission appointed by the President) shall serve for 4 years.

''(ii) ASSIGNMENT OF TERMS.—The Commission shall designate the term length that each member appointed under subparagraph (C) shall serve by unanimous agreement. In the event that unanimous agreement cannot be reached, term lengths shall be assigned to the members by a random process.

''(G) VACANCIES.—Subject to subparagraph (E), in the event of a vacancy in the Commission, whether due to the resignation of a member, the expiration of a member's term, or any other reason, the vacancy shall be filled in the manner in which the original appointment was made and shall not affect the powers of the Commission.

''(H) APPOINTMENT POWER.—Members of the Commission appointed under subparagraph (C) shall not be subject to confirmation by the Senate.

''(8) LIMITATION ON USE OF FUNDS.—Of the amounts reserved to carry out this subsection, the Secretary may not use more than $2,000,000 in any fiscal year to support the review, approval, and oversight of social impact partnership projects, including activities conducted by—

"(A) the Federal Interagency Council on Social Impact Partnerships; and

"(B) any other agency consulted by the Secretary before approving a social impact partnership project or a feasibility study under paragraph (4).

"(9) NO FEDERAL FUNDING FOR CREDIT ENHANCEMENTS.—No amount reserved to carry out this subsection may be used to provide any insurance, guarantee, or other credit enhancement to a State or local government under which a Federal payment would be made to a State or local government as the result of a State or local government failing to achieve an outcome specified in a contract.

"(10) AVAILABILITY OF FUNDS.—Amounts reserved to carry out this subsection shall remain available until 10 years after the date of the enactment of this subsection.

"(11) WEBSITE.—The Federal Interagency Council on Social Impact Partnerships shall establish and maintain a public website that shall display the following:

"(A) A copy of, or method of accessing, each notice published regarding a social impact partnership project pursuant to this subsection.

"(B) A copy of each feasibility study funded under this subsection.

"(C) For each State or local government that has entered into an agreement with the Secretary for a social impact partnership project, the website shall contain the following information:

"(i) The outcome goals of the project.

"(ii) A description of each intervention in the project.

"(iii) The target population that will be served by the project.

"(iv) The expected social benefits to participants who receive the intervention and others who may be impacted.

"(v) The detailed roles, responsibilities, and purposes of each Federal, State, or local government entity, intermediary, service provider, independent evaluator, investor, or other stakeholder.

"(vi) The payment terms, methodology used to calculate outcome payments, the payment schedule, and performance thresholds.

"(vii) The project budget.

"(viii) The project timeline.

"(ix) The project eligibility criteria.

"(x) The evaluation design.

"(xi) The metrics used to determine whether the proposed outcomes have been achieved and how these metrics are measured.

"(D) A copy of the progress reports and the final reports relating to each social impact partnership project.

"(E) An estimate of the savings to the Federal, State, and local government, on a program-by-program basis and in the aggregate, resulting from the successful completion of the social impact partnership project.

"(12) REGULATIONS.—The Secretary, in consultation with the Federal Interagency Council on Social Impact Partnerships, may issue regulations as necessary to carry out this subsection.

"(13) DEFINITIONS.—In this subsection:

"(A) AGENCY.—The term 'agency' has the meaning given that term in section 551 of title 5, United States Code.

"(B) INTERVENTION.—The term 'intervention' means a specific service delivered to achieve an impact through a social impact partnership project.

"(C) SECRETARY.—The term 'Secretary' means the Secretary of the Treasury.

"(D) SOCIAL IMPACT PARTNERSHIP PROJECT.— The term 'social impact partnership project'

means a project that finances social services using a social impact partnership model.

"(E) SOCIAL IMPACT PARTNERSHIP MODEL.— The term 'social impact partnership model' means a method of financing social services in which—

"(i) Federal funds are awarded to a State or local government only if a State or local government achieves certain outcomes agreed on by the State or local government and the Secretary; and

"(ii) the State or local government coordinates with service providers, investors (if applicable to the project), and (if necessary) an intermediary to identify—

"(I) an intervention expected to produce an outcome;

"(II) a service provider to deliver the intervention to the target population; and

"(III) investors to fund the delivery of the intervention.

"(F) STATE.—The term 'State' means each State of the United States, the District of Columbia, each commonwealth, territory or possession of the United States, and each federally recognized Indian tribe.

"(14) FUNDING.—Of the amounts made available to carry out subsection (b) for fiscal year 2017, the Secretary shall reserve $100,000,000 to carry out this subsection.".

SEC. 25003. EXTENSION OF TANF PROGRAM.

(a) FAMILY ASSISTANCE GRANTS.—Section 403(a)(1) of the Social Security Act (42 U.S.C. 603(a)(1)) is amended in each of subparagraphs (A) and (C), by striking "2012" and inserting "2017".

(b) HEALTHY MARRIAGE PROMOTION AND RESPONSIBLE FATHERHOOD GRANTS.—Section 403(a)(2)(D) of such Act (42 U.S.C. 603(a)(2)(D)) is amended by striking "2012" each place it appears and inserting "2017".

(c) TRIBAL GRANTS.—Section 412(a) of such Act (42 U.S.C. 612(a)) is amended in each of paragraphs (1)(A) and (2)(A) by striking "2012" and inserting "2017".

(d) CHILD CARE ENTITLEMENT.—Section 418(a)(3) of such Act (42 U.S.C. 618(a)(3)) is amended by striking "2012" and inserting "2017".

(e) GRANTS TO THE TERRITORIES.—Section 1108(b)(2) of such Act (42 U.S.C. 1308(b)(2)) is amended by striking "2012" and inserting "2017".

SEC. 25004. STRENGTHENING WELFARE RESEARCH AND EVALUATION AND DEVELOPMENT OF A WHAT WORKS CLEARINGHOUSE.

(a) IN GENERAL.—Section 413 of the Social Security Act (42 U.S.C. 613) is amended to read as follows:

"SEC. 413. EVALUATION OF TEMPORARY ASSISTANCE FOR NEEDY FAMILIES AND RELATED PROGRAMS.

"(a) EVALUATION OF THE IMPACTS OF TANF.— The Secretary shall conduct research on the effect of State programs funded under this part and any other State program funded with qualified State expenditures (as defined in section 409(a)(7)(B)(i)) on employment, self-sufficiency, child well-being, unmarried births, marriage, poverty, economic mobility, and other factors as determined by the Secretary.

"(b) EVALUATION OF GRANTS TO IMPROVE CHILD WELL-BEING BY PROMOTING HEALTHY MARRIAGE AND RESPONSIBLE FATHERHOOD.— The Secretary shall conduct research to determine the effects of the grants made under section 403(a)(2) on child well-being, marriage, family stability, economic mobility, poverty, and other factors as determined by the Secretary.

"(c) DISSEMINATION OF INFORMATION.—The Secretary shall, in consultation with States receiving funds provided under this part, develop methods of disseminating information on any re-

search, evaluation, or study conducted under this section, including facilitating the sharing of information and best practices among States and localities.

"(d) STATE-INITIATED EVALUATIONS.—A State shall be eligible to receive funding to evaluate the State program funded under this part or any other State program funded with qualified State expenditures (as defined in section 409(a)(7)(B)(i)) if—

"(1) the State submits to the Secretary a description of the proposed evaluation;

"(2) the Secretary determines that the design and approach of the proposed evaluation is rigorous and is likely to yield information that is credible and will be useful to other States; and

"(3) unless waived by the Secretary, the State contributes to the cost of the evaluation, from non-Federal sources, an amount equal to at least 25 percent of the cost of the proposed evaluation.

"(e) CENSUS BUREAU RESEARCH.—

"(1) The Bureau of the Census shall implement or enhance household surveys of program participation, in consultation with the Secretary and the Bureau of Labor Statistics and made available to interested parties, to allow for the assessment of the outcomes of continued welfare reform on the economic and child well-being of low-income families with children, including those who received assistance or services from a State program funded under this part or any other State program funded with qualified State expenditures (as defined in section 409(a)(7)(B)(i)). The content of the surveys should include such information as may be necessary to examine the issues of unmarried childbearing, marriage, welfare dependency and compliance with work requirements, the beginning and ending of spells of assistance, work, earnings and employment stability, and the well-being of children.

"(2) To carry out the activities specified in paragraph (1), the Bureau of the Census, the Secretary, and the Bureau of Labor Statistics shall consider ways to improve the surveys and data derived from the surveys to—

"(A) address under reporting of the receipt of means-tested benefits and tax benefits for low-income individuals and families;

"(B) increase understanding of poverty spells and long-term poverty, including by facilitating the matching of information to better understand intergenerational poverty;

"(C) generate a better geographical understanding of poverty such as through State-based estimates and measures of neighborhood poverty;

"(D) increase understanding of the effects of means-tested benefits and tax benefits on the earnings and incomes of low-income families; and

"(E) improve how poverty and economic well-being are measured, including through the use of consumption measures, material deprivation measures, social exclusion measures, and economic and social mobility measures.

"(f) RESEARCH AND EVALUATION CONDUCTED UNDER THIS SECTION.—Research and evaluation conducted under this section designed to determine the effects of a program or policy (other than research conducted under subsection (e)) shall use experimental designs using random assignment or other reliable, evidence-based research methodologies that allow for the strongest possible causal inferences when random assignment is not feasible.

"(g) DEVELOPMENT OF WHAT WORKS CLEARINGHOUSE OF PROVEN AND PROMISING APPROACHES TO MOVE WELFARE RECIPIENTS INTO WORK.—

"(1) IN GENERAL.—The Secretary, in consultation with the Secretary of Labor, shall develop a database (which shall be referred to as the

'What Works Clearinghouse of Proven and Promising Projects to Move Welfare Recipients into Work') of the projects that used a proven approach or a promising approach in moving welfare recipients into work, based on independent, rigorous evaluations of the projects. The database shall include a separate listing of projects that used a developmental approach in delivering services and a further separate listing of the projects with no or negative effects. The Secretary shall add to the What Works Clearinghouse of Proven and Promising Projects to Move Welfare Recipients into Work data about the projects that, based on an independent, well-conducted experimental evaluation of a program or project, using random assignment or other research methodologies that allow for the strongest possible causal inferences, have shown they are proven, promising, developmental, or ineffective approaches.

"(2) *CRITERIA FOR EVIDENCE OF EFFECTIVENESS OF APPROACH.*—The Secretary, in consultation with the Secretary of Labor and organizations with experience in evaluating research on the effectiveness of various approaches in delivering services to move welfare recipients into work, shall—

"(A) establish criteria for evidence of effectiveness; and

"(B) ensure that the process for establishing the criteria—

"(i) is transparent;

"(ii) is consistent across agencies;

"(iii) provides opportunity for public comment; and

"(iv) takes into account efforts of Federal agencies to identify and publicize effective interventions, including efforts at the Department of Health and Human Services, the Department of Education, and the Department of Justice.

"(3) *DEFINITIONS.*—In this subsection:

"(A) *APPROACH.*—The term 'approach' means a process, product, strategy, or practice that is—

"(i) research-based, based on the results of one or more empirical studies, and linked to program-determined outcomes; and

"(ii) evaluated using rigorous research designs.

"(B) *PROVEN APPROACH.*—The term 'proven approach' means an approach that—

"(i) meets the requirements of a promising approach; and

"(ii) has demonstrated significant and substantively important positive outcomes at more than one site in terms of increasing work and earnings of participants, reducing poverty and dependence, improving child well-being, or strengthening families.

"(C) *PROMISING APPROACH.*—The term 'promising approach' means an approach—

"(i) that meets the requirements of subparagraph (D)(i);

"(ii) that has been evaluated using well-designed and rigorous randomized controlled trials (or, if not available, rigorous quasi-experimental research designs);

"(iii) that has demonstrated significant and substantively important positive outcomes at one site in terms of increasing work and earnings of participants, reducing poverty and dependence, improving child well-being, or strengthening families; and

"(iv) under which the benefits of the positive outcomes have exceeded the costs of achieving the outcomes.

"(D) *DEVELOPMENTAL APPROACH.*—The term 'developmental approach' means an approach that—

"(i) is research-based, grounded in relevant empirically-based knowledge, and linked to program-determined outcomes;

"(ii) is evaluated using rigorous research designs; and

"(iii) has yet to demonstrate a significant positive outcome in terms of increasing work and earnings of participants in a cost-effective way.

"(h) *APPROPRIATION.*—

"(1) *IN GENERAL.*—Of the amount appropriated by section 403(a)(1) for each fiscal year, 0.33 percent shall be available for research, technical assistance, and evaluation under this section.

"(2) *ALLOCATION.*—Of the amount made available under paragraph (1) for each fiscal year, the Secretary shall make available $10,000,000 plus such additional amount as the Secretary deems necessary and appropriate, to carry out subsection (e).".

(b) CONFORMING AMENDMENT.—Section 403(a)(1)(B) of such Act (42 U.S.C. 603(a)(1)(B)) is amended by inserting ", reduced by the percentage specified in section 413(h) with respect to the fiscal year," before "as the amount".

SEC. 25005. TECHNICAL CORRECTIONS TO DATA EXCHANGE STANDARDS TO IMPROVE PROGRAM COORDINATION.

(a) *IN GENERAL.*—Section 411(d) of the Social Security Act (42 U.S.C. 611(d)) is amended to read as follows:

"(d) *DATA EXCHANGE STANDARDS FOR IMPROVED INTEROPERABILITY.*—

"(1) *DESIGNATION.*—The Secretary shall, in consultation with an interagency work group established by the Office of Management and Budget and considering State government perspectives, by rule, designate data exchange standards to govern, under this part—

"(A) necessary categories of information that State agencies operating programs under State plans approved under this part are required under applicable Federal law to electronically exchange with another State agency; and

"(B) Federal reporting and data exchange required under applicable Federal law.

"(2) *REQUIREMENTS.*—The data exchange standards required by paragraph (1) shall, to the extent practicable—

"(A) incorporate a widely accepted, non-proprietary, searchable, computer-readable format, such as the eXtensible Markup Language;

"(B) contain interoperable standards developed and maintained by intergovernmental partnerships, such as the National Information Exchange Model;

"(C) incorporate interoperable standards developed and maintained by Federal entities with authority over contracting and financial assistance;

"(D) be consistent with and implement applicable accounting principles;

"(E) be implemented in a manner that is cost-effective and improves program efficiency and effectiveness; and

"(F) be capable of being continually upgraded as necessary.

"(3) *RULE OF CONSTRUCTION.*—Nothing in this subsection shall be construed to require a change to existing data exchange standards found to be effective and efficient.".

(b) *EFFECTIVE DATE.*—Not later than the date that is 24 months after the date of the enactment of this section, the Secretary of Health and Human Services shall issue a proposed rule that—

(1) identifies federally required data exchanges, include specification and timing of exchanges to be standardized, and address the factors used in determining whether and when to standardize data exchanges; and

(2) specifies State implementation options and describes future milestones.

The SPEAKER pro tempore. Pursuant to House Resolution 934, the motion shall be debatable for 80 minutes, with 60 minutes equally divided and controlled by the chair and ranking minority member of the Committee on Energy and Commerce and 20 minutes equally divided and controlled by the chair and ranking minority member of the Committee on Ways and Means.

The gentleman from Michigan (Mr. UPTON) and the gentleman from New Jersey (Mr. PALLONE) each will control 30 minutes. The gentleman from Texas (Mr. BRADY) and the gentleman from Michigan (Mr. LEVIN) each will control 10 minutes.

The Chair recognizes the gentleman from Michigan (Mr. UPTON).

□ 1345

GENERAL LEAVE

Mr. UPTON. Mr. Speaker, I ask unanimous consent that all Members may have 5 legislative days in which to revise and extend their remarks and insert extraneous material on H.R. 34.

The SPEAKER pro tempore. Is there objection to the request of the gentleman from Michigan?

There was no objection.

Mr. UPTON. Mr. Speaker, I yield myself 3 minutes.

Mr. Speaker, there is not a single person in this Chamber or watching at home today who has not been touched by disease in some way. We have all said too many early good-byes to folks that we hold dear—families robbed of a parent who will never get to see their child's milestones, a child born without the gift of a future.

Every day, countless folks living vibrant lives are delivered unexpected diagnoses. It is a cycle that repeats itself over and over in every community. Life changes in an instant, and hope seems out of reach, whether it be Alzheimer's, lupus, MS, cancer, you name it.

No matter where you are from, one thing that binds us all together is that we all want more time with our loved ones. That is why we are here today, because the clock is ticking for patients and their families.

So, Mr. Speaker, this brings us to the 21st Century Cures Act. This bipartisan bill will ensure that our health system can keep pace with the incredible advances in science and technology. In Cures, we have got a medical innovation game-changer that will deliver hope to patients across the country.

We have been here before. In July of 2015, after a series of roundtables, hearings, white papers, and public feedback, the House overwhelmingly voted in support of 21st Century Cures.

Sure, we have encountered a number of detours and obstacles along the path to Cures, but we have taken great inspiration in those patients who have partnered in this effort to persevere, stay positive, and continue forward to get the job done, just like my two little Michigan girls, Brooke and Brielle, who are battling SMA, do every day. Each day, they muster incredible strength and courage, conquering challenges that most folks will never encounter in a lifetime.

So 3 years ago, we had an idea that, yes, we could do better. We needed to do something to transform our health research system to effectively fight disease in this century. Finding cures and boosting research and innovation was absent from any policy to-do list. People didn't seem to care that the gap between biomedical innovation and our regulatory process was widening, or that of the 10,000 known diseases—7,000 of which are rare—there are treatments for only about 500. We needed to change the conversation and restore urgency. And working together, we have.

First, we listened to more than just Brooke and Brielle, but to Barb, Becky, Lisa, Geno, the Dons, the Betsys, little Max, and our own little Steve LaTourette who always sat in the corner. Virtually everyone here had a story to tell and for folks here to listen to.

Science and biomedical innovation have made incredible strides over the last two decades: mapping the human genome, new biomarkers, and personal healthcare apps. Each have offered new opportunities to find new treatment and cures. But the way the FDA and the NIH apply these new innovations to our regulatory process, in fact, has lagged behind.

The SPEAKER pro tempore. The time of the gentleman has expired.

Mr. UPTON. Mr. Speaker, I yield myself an additional 2 minutes.

These agencies and the rules and regs they produce, affecting the discovery, development, and delivery of lifesaving drugs and devices, also need modernization and innovation. They need a game-changer, and now we have it. This legislation breaks down regulatory barriers and expedites the approvals for drugs and devices, coupled with billions more for research.

The former head of the NCI and the FDA, Andy von Eschenbach, has called this the most transformational biomedical legislation in the past 3 years. He is right.

But this package is not just about Cures. No. It also achieves several additional top-line priorities for our Energy and Commerce Committee, including valuable resources to fight the opioid epidemic and delivering landmark mental health reforms spearheaded by Dr. TIM MURPHY to help families in crisis and treat mental illnesses rather than incarceration. This is, without a doubt, the most important and impactful bill that we will enact in this Congress.

Patients aren't interested in debating the timelines. The failure rates, the size and cost of conducting clinical trials, are at an all-time high. They just know that despite the promise of scientific breakthroughs, they can't get the therapy that might save their life. That is why we need this bill.

I want to give a special thanks to my many partners, including especially DIANA DEGETTE, not to mention JOE PITTS, FRANK PALLONE, TIM MURPHY, and LAMAR ALEXANDER, the leadership on both sides of the aisle in both Chambers. I thank my truly brilliant committee and personal staff led by Gary Andres and Joan Hillebrands, Health Counsel Paul Edattel, and, of course, my wife, Amey.

We are on the cusp of something special, a once-in-a-generation opportunity to transform how we treat disease. With this vote, we are taking a giant leap on the path to Cures. Working together, we will deliver Cures now.

Mr. Speaker, I reserve the balance of my time.

Mr. PALLONE. Mr. Speaker, I yield 3 minutes to the gentlewoman from Colorado (Ms. DEGETTE), who is the Democratic sponsor of the bill and who has worked so hard to make this day a reality.

Ms. DEGETTE. Mr. Speaker, I rise today in strong support of the 21st Century Cures Act, knowing that I am far from alone in supporting this bill. More than 700 groups representing patients, healthcare providers, researchers, and others have voiced support for the bill, as has the White House, which provided its enthusiastic endorsement last night.

This is a watershed moment in this country for biomedical research. With this bill, we bring hope to millions of patients who suffer from cancer, Alzheimer's, diabetes, and a host of other ailments.

As my cosponsor and partner in crime, FRED UPTON, just said, we started working on this measure 3 years ago. We traveled the country together to gather information about much-needed reforms, and we had tremendous participation in the process from patient groups, medical professionals, academia, and Federal and State healthcare authorities, not to mention the entire Democratic and Republican membership of the Energy and Commerce Committee who worked so closely together to make this happen.

All of this led to a bill that was passed in July, 2015, by 344–77. We can barely pass the Journal every day by that amount, Mr. Speaker.

Now, this was in the summer of 2015, and we have worked tirelessly in a bipartisan way since then to improve and expand the bill and to make sure it can pass through the Senate and be signed by the White House.

The result will help to overcome obstacles to medical progress from discovery to development to delivery through investing in innovation, incorporating the patient perspective, and modernizing clinical trials.

Among the key provisions, this consensus version of the bill will provide $4.8 billion to the National Institutes of Health, including money for Vice President BIDEN's Cancer Moonshot initiative, including money for Precision Medicine and the BRAIN Initiative. It will provide almost $1 billion in grants to the States to address the urgent opioid crisis in this country.

It removes the silos at the Food and Drug Administration by transitioning it to a disease-centric approach, and it gives $500 million so the FDA can implement these reforms. It includes all-important mental health legislation that we have also worked on so hard for so long, and it will catalyze cutting-edge research by supporting potentially transformative efforts.

Mr. Speaker, at a time of heightened acrimony in Washington and in the wake of one of the most rancorous elections we have ever had, isn't it wonderful that we can come together to find cures that affect millions of Americans?

Disease doesn't discriminate according to political party. It knows nothing of claims and counterclaims. It responds only to carefully developed treatments and cures. What we are doing today is we are voting to put vital innovations in biomedical research within reach, potentially saving countless lives. I urge all of our colleagues to think about the millions of Americans who will be heartened by this bill's progress, and I urge you to vote "yes" on the 21st Century Cures Act.

Mr. UPTON. Mr. Speaker, I yield 1 minute to the gentleman from Texas (Mr. BARTON), who is the former chairman and now chairman emeritus of the Energy and Commerce Committee. My friend, the Honorable JOE BARTON, really helped us push this bill every step of the way.

Mr. BARTON. Mr. Speaker, the Affordable Care Act failed because it was a one-sided, partisan, and close-looped system. This bill, the 21st Century Cures Act, will succeed because it has been done just the opposite.

Chairman UPTON, DIANA DEGETTE, FRANK PALLONE, and many other people have worked together, as they said, for the last 3 years to find the best pathway forward to get new drugs and new therapies to our citizenship more quickly and efficiently. I want to congratulate both of them plus Chairman BRADY, Dr. MURPHY, and the others that have worked on this.

This bill makes it possible for cures to actually be put into practice without all the red tape and regulatory overkill. Let me give you an example. This bill makes possible the use of what is called regenerative medicine which we call stem cell therapy.

My 11-year-old son, Jack, last week played football with Coach Sam Harrell of Ennis, Texas, who 3 years ago could not get out of bed because of his disease. He had to go out of the country twice to get stem cell therapy. He can now act normally.

This bill makes possible those kinds of cures. I rise in strong support and thank Chairman UPTON for his strong work on this.

Mr. PALLONE. Mr. Speaker, I yield myself such time as I may consume.

Mr. Speaker, over the past 2 years, my colleagues and I on the Energy and Commerce Committee have worked to craft the 21st Century Cures Act with the goal of getting new treatments and cures to the people who need them the most. It has been a long journey, and I want to thank my colleagues, Chairman UPTON, Representatives DeGette and GENE GREEN of Texas for their commitment to this important legislation.

This is not a perfect bill, but, after much consideration, I believe the benefits outweigh my concerns, and I fully support its passage. This final bill includes many provisions that my Democratic colleagues and I, as well as the administration, fought hard to have included.

The bill provides new funding for the National Institutes of Health, the President's Precision Medicine Initiative, and the Vice President's Cancer Moonshot initiative. It also provides new resources for the Food and Drug Administration and grants for States currently battling the opioid abuse crisis.

This final legislation also includes important policy changes that break down the research silos that have existed for years. The bill includes data sharing among NIH-supported scientists and increases the number of racial and ethnic minorities and women that are included in NIH-funded clinical trials.

These important changes will allow the entire scientific community to learn lessons from this critical NIH-funded research and will strengthen research for diverse populations.

I am also pleased, Mr. Speaker, that the bill includes a new FDA grant program to study the process of continuous drug manufacturing. This innovative process will allow for more effective drug production without sacrificing quality. The bill also includes important hiring provisions to help the FDA recruit and retain the best and the brightest and policies to move us closer to ensuring we have interoperable electronic health records, which are critical to reducing costs and improving care.

As I said, this is not a perfect bill, and I have some concerns with the final product. I am disappointed that the bill does not contain guaranteed funding. Instead, we must ensure each year that the Appropriations Committee and the Republican majority lives up to the promises they make today, and we will hold them to these promises. The lack of immediate funding for the FDA is a particular concern given the fact that this bill asks the FDA to take on significantly more responsibilities that we know are extremely resource intensive.

I am also concerned that the bill removes certain categories of medical software from FDA oversight. This makes it difficult for FDA, in the future, to bring software that is used to support or sustain human life back under FDA's jurisdiction.

I am also troubled by the new priority review voucher program which will likely require the FDA to issue significantly more PRVs. This could pose a burden on FDA drug reviewers when redeemed and could prevent the FDA from being able to prioritize its review of drugs based on public health priorities.

The bill includes new language added without full consideration by the House or Senate regarding FDA oversight of regenerative medicine products.

□ 1400

While most of the harmful language was taken out, I do remain troubled that the bill creates a new designation process under FDA's accelerated approval pathway.

I am pleased, Mr. Speaker, that this package includes the Helping Families in Mental Health Crisis Act. This is a helpful step towards the more substantial reforms our broken mental health system needs.

I am specifically proud that the bill expands an important set of Medicaid benefits to kids receiving inpatient psychiatric treatment. However, let's be clear, the benefits of the mental health bill will be far outweighed by the catastrophic harm caused by individuals with mental illness if the Republicans move forward with their radical plans to repeal the Affordable Care Act or block grants for Medicaid or cut benefits for low-income individuals.

Again, on balance, this is a good bill. I fully support it. I want to thank all of my committee colleagues and their staff for their hard work on this legislation.

I reserve the balance of my time.

Mr. UPTON. Mr. Speaker, I yield 30 seconds to the gentleman from Illinois (Mr. SHIMKUS), one of the senior subcommittee chairmen on the Energy and Commerce Committee, one that helped lead the fight all across the Nation in support of this bill.

Mr. SHIMKUS. Mr. Speaker, I thank Chairman UPTON, and I congratulate my friend DIANA DeGETTE. Also, I thank FRANK PALLONE for a good job. I thank him for being supportive, especially today, as we move this forward.

Thank you for including six of my bills that I had involved, one that deals with the lack of antibiotics in the market in the pipeline. So that is helpful. Four other bills help innovation to get lifesaving devices to the market.

I encourage all of my colleagues on both sides of the aisle to support this bill.

Mr. PALLONE. Mr. Speaker, I yield 3 minutes to the gentleman from Texas

(Mr. GENE GREEN), the ranking member of the Health Subcommittee, who, again, has been critical, particularly in the last 3 months, in putting this bill together.

Mr. GENE GREEN of Texas. Mr. Speaker, I thank my colleague for providing the time.

I rise to express strong support for the 21st Century Cures Act.

Almost 3 years ago, we set out on a mission to do something positive to boost medical research and innovation and accelerate the discovery, development, and delivery of new cures and treatments.

After countless hours devoted to roundtables, white papers, hearings, and drafts, today, Cures has bipartisan support and endorsements from over 700 organizations representing a full spectrum of stakeholders and the strong support of the administration. My Houston area neighbors, Congressmen PETE OLSON and MIKE BURGESS, and I held a roundtable in the Houston area with the great institutions at our Texas Media Center in the Houston area.

It dedicates $6.3 billion in new investments to support priorities like the Cancer Moonshot and Precision Medicine Initiative within the National Institutes of Health, and to combat prescription drug abuse. This also provides money for the Food and Drug Administration to advance the agency's mission and implement the policies in the underlying bill. This influx of investment will be put towards solving today's complex scientific problems, getting new treatments from the lab table to the bedside, and improving public health.

In addition to this much-needed funding, there are so many provisions in this package worthy of support. From facilitating the development of new antibiotics to fight against superbugs, to advancing the use of modern clinical trial designs, to fostering the next generation of medical researchers, the 21st Century Cures Act will develop hope and new treatments for Americans in need. While some of these provisions are technical in nature, the real-world impact they will have is not abstract. Patients and families deserve to have their elected officials respond to their needs, and this bill does that.

Eighteen months ago, 344 Members supported Cures when it passed the House of Representatives. Since then, we have responded to feedback and tailored the bill, and it now includes additional priorities like improvements to our mental health system and nonpartisan provisions to strengthen Medicare on behalf of beneficiaries.

I want to thank Chairman UPTON, Ranking Member PALLONE, Congresswoman DeGETTE, and Chairman PITTS for their leadership, vision, and determination. I also want to thank our staff, the House Legislative Counsel, and the countless stakeholders without whom we would not be here today.

It was a privilege to be part of this landmark effort. As an original sponsor and coauthor of the 21st Century Cures Act, I urge my colleagues to vote "yes."

Mr. Speaker, the following is my complete statement: I rise to express my strong support for the 21st Century Cures Act.

Almost three years ago, we set out on a mission: do something positive to boost medical research and innovation, and accelerate the discovery, development, and delivery of new cures and treatments.

After countless hours devoted to roundtables, whitepapers, hearings and drafts, today Cures has bipartisan support and endorsements from over 700 organizations representing the full spectrum of stakeholders, and the strong support of the Administration. My Houston area neighbors Congressmen PETE OLSON and MIKE BURGESS held a roundtable with the many great institutions at our Texas Media Center.

It dedicates $6.3 billion in new investments to support priorities like the Cancer Moonshot and Precision Medicine Initiative within the National Institutes of Health (NIH), and to combat prescription drug abuse.

It also provides money to the Food and Drug Administration (FDA) to advance the agency's mission and implement the policies in the underlying bill.

This influx of investment will be put towards solving today's complex scientific problems, getting new treatments from the lab table to the bedside, and improving public health.

In addition to this much needed funding, there are so many provisions in this package worthy of support.

From facilitating the development of new antibiotics to fight against superbugs to advancing the use of modern clinical trial designs to the fostering of the next generation of medical researchers, the 21st Century Cures Act will deliver hope and new treatments to Americans in need.

While some of the provisions are technical in nature, the real-world impact they will have is not abstract.

Patients and families deserve to have their elected officials respond to their needs.

This bill does that.

Eighteen months ago, 344 members supported Cures (H.R. 6) when it passed the House of Representatives.

Since then, we have responded to feedback and tailored the bill, and it now includes additional priorities like improvements to our mental health care system and non-partisan provisions to strengthen Medicare on behalf of beneficiaries.

I want to thank Chairman UPTON, Ranking Member PALLONE, Congresswoman DEGETTE, and Chairman PITTS for their leadership, vision, and determination.

I also want to thank our staff, House Legislative Council, and the countless stakeholders without whom we would not be here today.

I want to particularly thank Tiffany Guarascio, Arielle Woronoff, Rachel Pryor, Kimberlee Trzeciak, Megan Velez, Waverly Gordon, Polly Webster, Kristen O'Neill, Paul Edattel, John Stone, Carly McWilliams, Adriana Simonelli, JP Paluskiewicz, Tim Pataki, Josh Trent and others on the Energy and Commerce Committee staff for all their work.

It was a privilege to be a part of this landmark effort.

As an original sponsor and co-author of the 21st Century Cures Act, I urge my colleagues to vote yes.

Mr. UPTON. Mr. Speaker, I yield 2 minutes to the gentleman from Pennsylvania (Mr. MURPHY), one of the subcommittee chairmen who helped craft the bipartisan Murphy mental health bill, which passed the House 422–2 earlier this year, and is a very valuable member of the committee.

Mr. MURPHY of Pennsylvania. Mr. Speaker, this is a moment of great joy out of a situation of tremendous tragedy.

After the last 4 years, since the time of the terrible tragedy at Sandy Hook Elementary School followed by repeated other ones, our Nation has awoken from a slumber of ignoring the problems of mental illness in America, one that when we closed down our institutions decades ago, we turned our eye to those who lay homeless on the street, who filled our prisons, who filled our cemeteries or lay on a gurney in an emergency room or were sent back home to a family who felt helpless and hopeless.

We have changed now to a situation where we are coming together on a bill that will save lives. This is a new era of health care and the next generation of hope for Americans that really transcends boundaries.

To all of the families who brought their stories out of the shadows, that dared to share their sorrows, their hopes, their shattered dreams, today is a day of joy. And today is only possible, I say to all of those families, because they dared to step forward. There is not time enough to thank all of those involved, but to those families who have helped, I say thank you.

I also want to make sure I thank Chairman UPTON, Speaker RYAN, EDDIE BERNICE JOHNSON, DIANA DEGETTE, FRANK PALLONE, Senators BILL CASSIDY and CHRIS MURPHY, Leader KEVIN MCCARTHY, Whip STEVE SCALISE, and so many others from our committee who have worked so hard to make this happen. And a special shout-out to some of the staff: Scott Dziengelski, Gary Andres, Karen Christian, Paul Edattel, Susan Mosychuk, and so many other staff who worked so hard on this.

We can look back on this moment in history and say today that, although we have much to do and although we didn't get everything we needed, we needed everything that we did get. But this is the moment from this day forward we can say today that we took action to save lives.

Mr. PALLONE. Mr. Speaker, I yield 2 minutes to the gentlewoman from Florida (Ms. CASTOR).

Ms. CASTOR of Florida. Mr. Speaker, I rise today in support of the 21st Century Cures Act legislation and the important investment that it will make in medical research across America.

This legislation supports an additional $4.8 billion for the National Institutes of Health, specifically for President Obama's Precision Medicine Initiative and the BRAIN Initiative so we can tackle the challenge of Alzheimer's. It supports Vice President BIDEN's Cancer Moonshot initiative. Hopefully, it will keep the young scientists on the job at institutions like the Moffitt Cancer Center and the University of South Florida's Alzheimer's Research Institute back home in Tampa.

While additional support for NIH is vital and this is a move in the right direction, I would have much preferred that we put this in the mandatory category as we voted on in H.R. 6 earlier in the year. I know many of you agree with that, that medical research in America today shouldn't be subject to the whims of congressional budget battles or political fights. I will continue to advocate for mandatory funding for NIH so that we can remain on the cutting edge of medical innovation and boost higher wage jobs back home. These initiatives save lives and provide investments that we need to make sure that we are developing the cures of tomorrow.

I am very pleased that legislation I introduced with my colleague Representative HERRERA BEUTLER was included in this package. The Safe Medications for Moms and Babies Act ensures that expectant mothers and doctors have accurate information about medications used during pregnancy and when nursing to facilitate the best health outcomes. Representative HERRERA BEUTLER has been a champion for families, and I am grateful to her for leading this effort to improve the quality of data and information on medication used during pregnancy and breastfeeding.

I also applaud the inclusion of language to improve our mental health system, the $1 billion to address the opioid epidemic. This is very positive. I would like to thank Chairman FRED UPTON for his devotion to the issue, to Congresswoman DEGETTE, and to all of my colleagues on the Energy and Commerce Committee.

The SPEAKER pro tempore. The time of the gentlewoman has expired.

Mr. PALLONE. I yield the gentlewoman an additional 30 seconds.

Ms. CASTOR of Florida. This is the way legislation is supposed to be developed: in a bipartisan way, through studies, through asking, reaching out, and working with experts all across the country, because all of the answers do not emanate from a congressional committee in Washington. It is very important that we tap the expertise all across the country to get something done.

Mr. UPTON. Mr. Speaker, I yield 1 minute to the gentlewoman from Tennessee (Mrs. BLACKBURN), the vice chairman of the Energy and Commerce Committee, who, again, helped so much with the medical community to rally around and provide us the input necessary to move this bill to where it is today.

Mrs. BLACKBURN. Mr. Speaker, I congratulate Chairman UPTON and all of our colleagues on the Energy and Commerce Committee for a job well done, and done in the appropriate manner. It really has, as Ms. DEGETTE said, been so interesting to work across the country and work with patients, with physicians, with researchers, with those who are innovating new concepts, who are delving into delivery systems that are necessary for precision medicine which underpins 21st century health care.

There are three components that I want to bring attention to. First of all, section 3060 is there addressing medical technology and software. This is so important that we get the FDA on the right track and move components of this away so that it does not face FDA approval processes that will slow down access to the marketplace for patients.

Also, section 2038, the Children's Count Act—Mrs. CAPPS and I worked on this—allowing children access to clinical trials, and section 3076, the reauthorization of the Reagan-Udall language.

I congratulate my colleagues.

Mr. PALLONE. Mr. Speaker, I yield 2 minutes to the gentleman from Oregon (Mr. SCHRADER).

Mr. SCHRADER. Mr. Speaker, I rise today in strong support of the 21st Century Cures Act and to thank Chairman UPTON and my friends, Mr. PALLONE, Ms. DEGETTE, and Mr. GREEN, for their leadership and willingness to work across the aisle to produce this quality piece of legislation.

For too long, Congress has been shirking its responsibility when it comes to funding the critical research that will lead to cures and treatments at the NIH. Our scientists, physicians, and medical institutions are getting closer every day to medical breakthroughs that will help families and save lives. In my State alone, the NIH is funding research into new therapeutic avenues to combat cancer, heart disease, and illness born by pollution. It is time to streamline the path for critically needed medical devices and pharmaceuticals for vulnerable populations that can't afford to wait.

This bill takes a giant step forward to help fix the mental health infrastructure of our country. Currently, as a result of the mental health system's inadequacy, our emergency rooms, our prisons, and our homeless shelters are full of people who are having trouble getting the care they need. The status quo is not okay.

This bill moves us in the right direction through innovation and integration of mental health services for the overall healthcare system. The Cures Act enhances the capabilities of our law enforcement and first responders, strengthens our crisis intervention programs, and ensures that our Medicaid program does not deny access to beneficiaries seeking mental health care. It also includes a number of Medicare provisions to make sure seniors aren't left behind by bureaucratic red tape.

Getting to this point wasn't easy. Democrats and Republicans didn't always agree on every provision of this bill, but we were able to work together and find common ground and produce a bill that takes great strides toward producing better healthcare outcomes for Americans.

I hope the President-elect and Members of this body are taking note of this achievement today as we move forward instead of pushing through divisive harmful policies that will reduce access to quality health care. Let's work together and produce better results for all Americans.

☐ 1415

Mr. UPTON. Mr. Speaker, I yield 1 minute to the gentleman from Kentucky (Mr. GUTHRIE), a member of the committee and a leader in pushing this bill forward.

Mr. GUTHRIE. I thank the chairman for yielding.

Mr. Speaker, all of us have families who come to our offices, and they are advocating for research or for cures for diseases to which they have lost a parent or a child, or they have their children with them who have the diseases, and they are just hoping for a move forward.

In being on the Health Subcommittee, at least weekly and sometimes daily, innovators and entrepreneurs come to my office, and they talk about a new procedure or a new product—something that is innovative, that will change the lives of these families—but they are having trouble getting them through the system and getting them approved.

It hurts families, though, like a family in Elizabethtown, who has someone with a degenerative disease. This family is trying to beat the clock because they think there is some kind of help out there. I have a friend of mine from Bowling Green whose son went through a diabetes trial. The first time they said they got any sleep through the night was when their kid was in this trial. Then they called me, crying, saying they were out of the trial and that it may be another year before they get in. So, in taking our entrepreneurs and our innovators and putting together these cures, it is not just about getting these products to market—it is about changing the dynamics of these families who are suffering.

Our chairman and Ms. DEGETTE from Colorado put together this effort to move forward, and I urge support for this bill because it will change families' lives.

Mr. PALLONE. Mr. Speaker, I yield 2 minutes to the gentleman from Tennessee (Mr. COHEN).

Mr. COHEN. I thank the gentleman.

Mr. Speaker, I think everybody has been thanked who should be thanked, but I certainly want to thank Mr. UPTON for all of his work and Mr. PALLONE for his time and his work and Ms. DEGETTE. I also want to thank Senator ROGER WICKER, who worked on a bill that is incorporated into this bill that Congressman DUNCAN and I sponsored, called the EUREKA Act, which will incentivize and reward research on diseases for which there is not great public-private partnerships but for which there is a great handicap and problem for the American public because of the particular disease. It will reward successful treatments through a competition, which I think is a great way to go about encouraging research and then paying for it. ROGER WICKER, I think, came up with the idea, and I sponsored it with JOHN DUNCAN, and it is included in the bill. It was originally aimed at Alzheimer's. It is now for other diseases, but Alzheimer's is one of them.

Alzheimer's is a disease that is going to have a particularly crippling effect on our country economically in the future. Beyond that, it will affect many of us, and it will affect our pocketbooks; so it is important that this bill goes after Alzheimer's and that it deals with the opioid crisis, which is great in my State and across the country. It works against all diseases and it encourages moneys in the National Institutes of Health.

I have long said, while we need to have a strong Defense Department, that my Secretary of Defense is Francis Collins, the head of the NIH, because the true enemy of each and every one of us isn't somebody in South Korea or somebody in Iran or ISIS or one of those folk—it is cancer; it is Alzheimer's; it is AIDS; it is diabetes; it is heart disease; it is Parkinson's. It is all of those diseases—the dreadful, awful, awful diseases for which the NIH is looking for cures. That is our Secretary of Defense, and that is what we need to invest our moneys in. I don't think there is enough money that we can put into the NIH, because it is important and it affects all Americans independent of political party, race, sexual orientation—you name it.

I thank the Members for their work on this, and I am proud to vote for it.

Mr. UPTON. Mr. Speaker, I yield 2 minutes to the gentleman from Florida (Mr. BILIRAKIS), a valuable member of the Health Subcommittee and whose father once chaired that subcommittee.

Mr. BILIRAKIS. I thank the chairman for all of his hard work on this great bill.

Mr. Speaker, I rise to talk about the incredible impact the 21st Century Cures Act would have on so many Americans.

Deadly diseases like cancer, Alzheimer's, ALS, and more affect each and every one of us. Within Cures, one will find the voices of patients, doctors, advocacy groups, and families I have met with from throughout Florida's 12th Congressional District. I am proud to say that a lot of their input is reflected in this final bill.

Samantha Lindsay, from Lutz, Florida, has Alpha-1, which is a rare genetic condition that results in serious lung problems. When we met, she talked about the need to use biomarkers for the faster approval of drugs for rare diseases. We did that. We have a framework for biomarker qualifications in this legislation.

Wayne Taylor, from Hudson, Florida, was a leukemia patient. He talked about the difficulty of participating in the clinical trials that eventually saved his life. This bill has reforms to make clinical trials more patient-focused and input-driven.

Dr. David Morgan, the CEO of the Health Byrd Alzheimer's Institute at the University of South Florida, talked about the need for stable funding for Alzheimer's and about reforming institutional review boards.

This bill invests in the NIH, and it reforms the IRB system. Cures also includes my provisions to reform the FDA's Office of Combination Products in order to streamline the approval of these products; to establish a new Medicare Web site to help seniors price shop; and to allow physical therapists to enter into locum tenens arrangements so they can take maternity leave or sick time without having to turn away patients.

For many families, including my own, the potential impact of 21st Century Cures could change their lives. Let's get this meaningful bill across the finish line.

Mr. PALLONE. Mr. Speaker, I have a few additional speakers on their way; so I reserve the balance of my time.

Mr. UPTON. Mr. Speaker, I yield 1 minute to the gentleman from Ohio (Mr. JOHNSON), a valuable member of our committee who has worked so hard to get this bill to where it is today.

Mr. JOHNSON of Ohio. I thank the chairman.

Mr. Speaker, I rise in support of the 21st Century Cures Act and add my voice to the steady stream of acclaim this legislation has already received.

American families and communities are suffering from rare diseases, and this innovative legislation works to align Federal incentives and regulations with the science and technology that make treatments and cures possible and attainable. I am proud to have supported this bill all along the way.

This package includes mental health reform—work that I am grateful to have been a part of during my time on the Oversight and Investigations Subcommittee with Chairman MURPHY. His tireless efforts will benefit many individuals and families who struggle with mental illness and substance abuse. This bill also includes $1 billion for grants to States to fight opioid abuse. A recent report shows that my home State of Ohio leads the Nation in opioid overdose deaths. This funding is sorely needed to address the issue head on.

I ask my colleagues to support the Cures bill today.

Mr. PALLONE. Mr. Speaker, I reserve the balance of my time.

Mr. UPTON. Mr. Speaker, I yield 1 minute to the gentlewoman from North Carolina (Mrs. ELLMERS), a member of the important Health Subcommittee and a real proponent of this legislation from day one.

Mrs. ELLMERS of North Carolina. I thank Chairman UPTON; Ranking Member PALLONE; Ms. DeGETTE, my good friend; TIM MURPHY from Pennsylvania, who worked so hard on the mental health reforms; and Chairman PITTS, the Health Subcommittee's chairman.

Mr. Speaker, there has been a great deal of effort put into this great piece of legislation, which basically has the goal of bringing our healthcare innovation infrastructure into the 21st Century Cures so that real hope for patients and loved ones can be achieved.

From removing barriers in the mental health system, to ensuring collaboration, to modernizing the clinical trial pathways, to boosting modern medical interventions, 21st Century Cures is a win for everyone. It will accelerate the discovery, development, and delivery of lifesaving therapies in a safe and effective way. It will also empower families to support their loved ones.

In closing, Cures will change lives. I, personally, as a nurse, would like to say that this is one of the most important pieces of legislation we will pass here in the House.

Mr. PALLONE. Mr. Speaker, I yield 2 minutes to the gentleman from Massachusetts (Mr. KENNEDY), who has been such a strong advocate on mental health issues.

Mr. KENNEDY. I thank the ranking member for yielding. I also thank him, as well as Chairman UPTON and Congresswoman DeGETTE, for being tireless throughout the entire process in their advocacy of trying to get this bill as a bipartisan compromise and for creating an environment that allows for our committee's members to raise their voices and shape this legislation.

Mr. Speaker, when we first passed the version of this bill last year, it was as a result of strong, bipartisan compromise and sacrifice. It certainly was not easy, but the legislative process is not intended to be.

While I am disappointed that the funding levels for the NIH were cut even further and that the investment is no longer mandatory, I take my Republican colleagues at their word that it will be appropriated in the years ahead. I am also pleased that this legislation includes language to remove obstacles for children who are covered by Medicaid; but my real concerns with the legislation lie with the mental health reform proposals, which don't go nearly far enough. Mental health parity is already the law, thanks to the Mental Health Parity and Addiction Equity Act and the Affordable Care Act; but each study we read, Mr. Speaker, and each story we hear proves that insurance companies are skirting those rules.

Instead of further guidance or meetings or studies carried out years down the road, we need enforcement and transparency today. We need random audits before there have been violations, not after. We need insurers to publicly disclose the rates and reasons for denials in a way that patients and their families can understand, not in a way that mental health advocates can't even obtain. We need to increase Medicaid reimbursements in order to expand access to care, not to reduce them or roll back expansion; and we need to appreciate the difference the ACA has made for mental health patients, especially for the most vulnerable among us. Until we do, we cannot consider these proposals comprehensive, and we certainly can't pretend that they are nearly enough.

This is an important compromise forged from an awful lot of hard work. I am happy and pleased to support this proposal, and I thank my colleagues on both sides of the aisle for getting it here today.

Mr. UPTON. Mr. Speaker, I yield myself 15 seconds.

I appreciate the gentleman from Massachusetts' statement. He is a very valuable player as we move this legislation on all fronts forward. I look very forward to working with the gentleman and with every Member of this body to make sure that the funding is there as we have laid out in this bill and to work with our colleagues in the Senate to make sure that it happens.

Mr. Speaker, how much time remains on both sides?

The SPEAKER pro tempore. The gentleman from Michigan has 15¼ minutes remaining, and the gentleman from New Jersey has 12 minutes remaining.

Mr. UPTON. Mr. Speaker, I yield 1 minute to the gentleman from New Jersey (Mr. LANCE), another valuable member of the Health Subcommittee and someone who pursued this legislation from the very get-go.

Mr. LANCE. Mr. Speaker, I rise in strong support of the 21st Century Cures legislation.

This bill provides significant investments to accelerate the discovery, development, and delivery of new cures and treatments for millions of Americans. The passage of this legislation will protect and create American jobs and will ensure that the United States remains the global leader in biomedical innovation and discovery. The measure reforms and strengthens the country's mental health system and makes mental health a strong national priority. The legislation includes critical funding for States to prevent opioid abuse and provide the needed treatment for those suffering from this public health crisis.

Reducing bureaucratic redtape, advancing lifesaving research, reforming our broken mental health system, and tackling opioid abuse in our communities will reduce healthcare costs and give many Americans new opportunities to live long, healthy, and productive lives.

I thank Chairman UPTON for his unparalleled leadership on this issue. It is an honor to have worked with him and all of our colleagues on the Energy and Commerce Committee to have crafted this landmark legislation.

Mr. PALLONE. Mr. Speaker, I yield 2 minutes to the gentlewoman from Ohio (Ms. KAPTUR).

Ms. KAPTUR. I thank Ranking Member PALLONE for yielding me the time.

Mr. Speaker, I rise in strong support of the bipartisan 21st Century Cures Act, which dedicates more than $6 billion to implement key health priorities, such as combating the heroin and prescription opioid epidemic across this country and the Vice President's Cancer Moonshot. It also takes steps to improve mental health, including provisions that build on the work of the President's Mental Health and Substance Use Disorder Parity Task Force and policies to further modernize the drug approval process. This will mean so much to the researchers across this country who are trying to unlock the mysteries of the human brain and heal.

□ 1430

The legislation includes $1 billion over 2 years, including $500 million in fiscal year 2017, to combat the prescription opioid and heroin epidemic as well. The legislation dedicates support for other key research initiatives with the goal of helping researchers find new ways to treat, cure, and prevent brain disorders, such as Alzheimer's disease, epilepsy, and traumatic brain injury.

This legislation includes a much-needed renewed emphasis on evidence-based strategies for treating serious mental illness, improved coordination between primary care and behavioral health services, reauthorization of im-

portant programs focused on suicide prevention and other prevention services, and mental health and substance use disorder parity provisions.

I would like to thank Dr. Joseph Calabrese at Case Western Reserve University in Cleveland and my good friend, Representative TIM MURPHY, who came to Ohio and hosted a roundtable on mental health that can be added to this major bill in order to move America forward.

I thank Chairman FRED UPTON, knowing the deep commitment that he has to so many Americans who desperately need the help that this bill will provide. Again, to Congressman FRANK PALLONE of New Jersey, I want to compliment both men for working together to do something great for this country for so many Americans who are desperate to find answers for those who are ill. I want to thank Congresswoman DIANA DEGETTE of Colorado who has shepherded this to this point.

Although not perfect or complete, this legislation offers advances in health that greatly outweigh any concerns we might have. I am proud to add my strong support for 21st Century Cures Act.

Mr. UPTON. Mr. Speaker, I yield 1 minute to the gentleman from Indiana (Mr. BUCSHON), who again hosted a number of roundtables and discussions throughout the country and a very valuable member of the committee.

Mr. BUCSHON. Mr. Speaker, I urge my colleagues to support the Senate amendment to H.R. 34, the 21st Century Cures Act.

Over our country's history, American innovators have proven among the best in the world, especially in the field of drug and device research.

21st Century Cures streamlines the process for American innovators to see their research and development reach patients faster than ever, while maintaining a safe and effective review process.

It also invests in the areas we need it the most, to advance research and testing on the most complex and devastating diseases in our country. It also gives young scientists the support they need to bring new ideas to the scientific community.

The mental health and opioid abuse provisions in this legislation are also critical. As a physician who has relied on medical innovation to care for patients, working to pass the 21st Century Cures Act and ensuring America remains on the forefront of cutting edge research has been one of the highlights of my time in Congress.

I thank Chairman UPTON and Representative DEGETTE for their leadership and commitment to this legislation.

Mr. PALLONE. Mr. Speaker, I yield 2 minutes to the gentlewoman from Connecticut (Ms. DELAURO).

Ms. DELAURO. Mr. Speaker, I rise in opposition to this bill. The 21st Cen-

tury Cures bill aims to promote biomedical innovation and mental health, noble goals that I share. Unfortunately, this bill sets a dangerous precedent and has the potential to do more harm than good for millions of Americans.

In its attempt to speed up the drug and device approval process, this legislation neglects the very people whom clinical trials are meant to help, that is, the patients. Rather than protect those who rely on the healthcare system, it reduces the already weak regulation on medical devices, allows drugs to be approved with only limited evidence of the drug's safety and efficacy, and rushes the use of new and unproven antibiotics.

An example, 13 models of the St. Jude's defibrillators are currently being recalled for sudden battery failure that has been linked to at least two deaths, 10 people fainting, and 37 people feeling dizzy.

When the cost of our prescription drugs is skyrocketing, this bill does nothing to combat excessive prices.

Finally, this bill strips away funding from the public health and prevention fund. While the bill authorizes $4.8 billion to the NIH over the next 10 years—on average, a mere $480 million a year—this is barely a quarter per year of what the House passed last year. Let us not forget that we would need to provide $7 billion a year to keep up where we were in 2003.

There is also no guarantee that the appropriators will follow through and provide funding each year, as we have seen with the public health prevention fund, which has been used to fill appropriations shortfalls.

Illness touches us all. We owe it to the patients who depend on the standards that we set. Unfortunately, I believe the standards in this bill are both weak and dangerous. This legislation is the wrong path forward, and I strongly oppose it.

Mr. UPTON. Mr. Speaker, I yield 2 minutes to the gentleman from New York (Mr. COLLINS), whose personal knowledge of the maze of the regulatory approval process made him a very valuable member of the Health Subcommittee in pushing this legislation forward.

Mr. COLLINS of New York. Mr. Speaker, I thank all the people who worked tirelessly to make this legislation a reality.

Simply stated, the goal of this legislation is to incentivize innovation to defeat disease. Today, the 21st Century Cures Act will do that and much more for patients suffering from currently incurable diseases.

This legislation provides substantial funding to the National Institutes of Health, including $1.8 billion to speed up cancer research, $1.5 billion to improve our understanding of debilitating diseases such as Alzheimer's, and another $1.5 billion to assist in genetic and other individual specific research efforts.

This bill provides funding to fight the opioid addiction crisis, which has been particularly devastating to western New York, and it includes mental health legislation to improve those services nationwide.

I am excited that this final bill contains a few provisions I authored and worked on over the past 2 years. Section 3021 encourages the broader application of innovative clinical trial designs to enhance and accelerate effective clinical trials.

Section 3071 will expedite and improve drug approval processes by increasing the allowable number of senior biomedical researchers the FDA is allowed to hire and making their salary more competitive with the private industry.

Section 9023, which I worked on with Representative JOE COURTNEY, incentivizes child and adolescent psychiatrists to begin their practices in underserved areas like those in rural western New York.

Lastly, Section 5006, which I worked on with Congressman PAUL TONKO, includes the House-passed Medicaid DOC Act, which requires States to publish an online directory of physicians who have billed Medicaid in the past year and indicate whether those physicians are accepting new patients.

None of this would have been possible without the tireless work of Chairman FRED UPTON and the entire staff on Energy and Commerce. I thank them for their tremendous effort and look forward to seeing innovation defeat disease because of this game-changing legislation.

Mr. PALLONE. Mr. Speaker, how much time remains on both sides?

The SPEAKER pro tempore. The gentleman from New Jersey has 8 minutes remaining, and the gentleman from Michigan has 11¼ minutes remaining.

Mr. PALLONE. Mr. Speaker, I yield 3 minutes to the gentleman from New Mexico (Mr. BEN RAY LUJÁN).

Mr. BEN RAY LUJÁN of New Mexico. Mr. Speaker, I begin by thanking Chairman UPTON and Ranking Member PALLONE of the Energy and Commerce Committee, as well as Congresswoman DEGETTE, for their bipartisan cooperation during this long legislative process.

This is a good, if imperfect, bill that will provide vital funding to the National Institutes of Health and the Vice President's Cancer Moonshot while taking steps to strengthen our mental health system. I want to focus my remarks on the critical investments this bill promises to combat the opioid epidemic.

In communities across our country, families are struggling with the pain of addiction to opioids. Earlier this year, Congress took an important step against substance abuse by passing the Comprehensive Addiction and Recovery Act, or CARA.

Unfortunately, congressional Republicans did not support including the necessary funding to CARA's success. This was a missed opportunity. In the months since Congress passed CARA, we have lost parents, siblings, children, and friends—129 people every day.

When I talk to New Mexicans on the front lines of this crisis, the most urgent need is for more resources. That is why I introduced the Opioid and Heroin Abuse Crisis Investment Act. This bill, cosponsored by nearly 100 of my colleagues, sought to advance the President's proposal to combat this epidemic.

This legislation we are considering today—like my bill—promises $1 billion for the opioid crisis. Though we cannot bring back those that we have lost, we owe it to them and their families to pass this bill. This funding will make a real difference in people's lives.

While I am relieved that we will soon be able to get the resources to our communities, I am fearful that some of my colleagues will see this as a mission accomplished instead of what it must be, which is only a first step toward healing our communities.

I can't help but ask my Republican colleagues, who support the advances we are making today for mental health: Why are they preparing to roll back the most important advances we made for mental health in the past 8 years by promising to repeal the Affordable Care Act?

The 21st Century Cures Act shows what we can do and what can happen when we work across the aisle, and I hope we will truly continue to work together to strengthen our Nation's health system.

Mr. UPTON. Mr. Speaker, I yield 1 minute to the gentlewoman from California (Mrs. MIMI WALTERS), an original cosponsor of our bill and great proponent from day one.

Mrs. MIMI WALTERS of California. Mr. Speaker, over the last 2 years, I have worked with organizations in my district, including the Children's Hospital of Orange County, the Juvenile Diabetes Research Foundation, and Alzheimer's Orange County.

During my visits with these groups, I have met with constituents who are suffering from incurable diseases. I have met with parents of children suffering from prescription drug addiction and families struggling to find adequate mental health care for their loved ones.

All of these people have one thing in common. The 21st Century Cures Act would directly improve the care they receive. This innovative legislation will provide them with faster and better cures and treatment.

In passing this legislation, we have the opportunity to accelerate the discovery, development, and delivery of lifesaving and life-improving therapies.

I urge my colleagues to join me in supporting the 21st Century Cures Act. It is time for cures now.

Mr. PALLONE. Mr. Speaker, I yield 3 minutes to the gentlewoman from Colorado (Ms. DEGETTE).

Ms. DEGETTE. Mr. Speaker, I thank Mr. PALLONE for yielding me the time and for being an unerring partner on this quest that we have had.

I just want to take a few minutes to talk about the extraordinary journey that we have had here. When Representative FRED UPTON came up to me on the floor about 3 years ago and asked if I would help him work on a bill to help modernize and update the way we do biomedical research in this country, little did I realize the road that lay ahead. There have been a lot of twists and turns in that road. There have been some very interesting sightings along that road, and it has been an extraordinary effort for all of us. It has really brought the Energy and Commerce Committee together in a bipartisan way, and I am hoping that we can continue those efforts in the next Congress.

So many of my colleagues are right. We still have a lot that we have to do in the area of mental health, in the area of biomedical research, and so much more.

I want to thank a number of people because they really all deserve to be thanked: Of course, Energy and Commerce Committee Chairman UPTON and Ranking Member PALLONE, and Subcommittee on Health Ranking Member GENE GREEN and Chairman JOE PITTS. I want to thank the entire committee, as I said.

I want to thank the patient advocacy community who have been with us unerringly throughout this process. I want to thank the researchers. I want to thank the entrepreneurs who came and talked to us about what they needed. I want to thank the agencies themselves, specifically the FDA and the NIH, for technical assistance, and the entire executive branch.

I want to thank a number of people. First of all, I want to thank Lisa Cohen, my chief of staff, who has been with me for 20 years through thick and thin. I want to thank Polly Webster, my health policy director, who took the bar exam, got married, and actually helped pass this bill all during this process. I want to thank Lynne Weil, my communications director, and Eleanor Bastian, my legislative director. I want to thank Rachel Stauffer, my former health policy director who started this, and Matt Inzeo, who is Lynne's predecessor.

From the Upton staff, I want to thank Gary Andres, Joan Hillebrand, Paul Edattel, John Stone, Carly McWilliams, Adrianna Simonelli, and J.P. Paluskiewicz. All of you guys have worked together as a team with my team.

□ 1445

I want to thank Kristen O'Neill from Mr. GREEN's staff. I don't think I thanked Mr. GREEN. I want to thank Mr. GREEN, who has done such an extraordinary job and who has really been my wingman. I want to thank Wendell Primus, who is Leader PELOSI's senior adviser; and Charlene MacDonald, who is Mr. HOYER's adviser. Finally, I want to thank the entire Pallone team, who has worked as our committee staff tirelessly: Jeff Carroll, Tiffany, Kim, Arielle, Waverly, and Megan. They have been fabulous. We haven't always agreed on everything, but in the end we have all worked together. It really is a great team. I hope we can use this in the next Congress to get to even greater heights.

I urge the House to pass this bill on a strong bipartisan basis, and I urge the other body to take it up.

Mr. UPTON. Mr. Speaker, I yield 1 minute to the gentleman from Georgia (Mr. CARTER), the only pharmacist in the Congress.

Mr. CARTER of Georgia. Mr. Speaker, I rise today in support of H.R. 34, the 21st Century Cures Act. This long-awaited legislation promotes medical innovation by streamlining the discovery, development, and delivery of critical medicines. This bill also helps reform our Nation's deteriorating mental health system to ensure that millions of Americans receive the care they need. Such reforms include the reduction of regulatory red tape that slows prescription drugs' entry to the market, the breaking down of barriers that restrict data sharing, and expediting the review of potentially breakthrough devices.

While some may believe that the resources needed to develop new cures or new devices are too costly and time consuming, the potential savings to the broader healthcare system will be significant. By modernizing the governance surrounding the development of new medicines and treatment, we ensure that the lives of millions—not only here in the U.S., but across the world—will improve.

I want to thank Chairman UPTON and Chairman MURPHY for their unrelenting determination to bring this negotiated piece of legislation to the floor for a vote. I urge my colleagues to support H.R. 34.

Mr. PALLONE. Mr. Speaker, I have no additional speakers other than myself to close, so I am going to continue to reserve the balance of my time.

Mr. UPTON. Mr. Speaker, I have a good number of speakers left, and I will use all of our time.

I yield 1 minute to the gentleman from Pennsylvania (Mr. ROTHFUS).

Mr. ROTHFUS. Mr. Speaker, I rise today in strong support of this important legislation that provides significant investments and reforms to accelerate the discovery of new treatments and cures for Americans. I also applaud the inclusion of a provision I authored that is crucial for our seniors. It would restore the open enrollment period for Medicare Advantage beneficiaries, who until 2011 had the ability to change Medicare Advantage plans during the first 3 months of the year.

Unfortunately, those 3 months of flexibility have been replaced with an annual Medicare Advantage disenrollment period during the first 45 days of the year. Given Medicare Advantage's popularity and history of success, seniors should be given the choice of changing to a plan that addresses their needs. Restoring this 90-day open enrollment window will allow seniors who find that their plan is not working for them to make the change that does work for them.

This bill also contains very important legislation authored by my colleague from Pennsylvania, Representative MURPHY, to help families dealing with a mental health crisis by significantly reforming our mental healthcare system. These reforms are crucial for families, veterans, and all individuals dealing with a mental health crisis and the drug addictions that can often accompany such illnesses.

I commend Chairman UPTON's work in bringing this critical legislation to the floor. I urge its passage.

Mr. UPTON. Mr. Speaker, I yield 1 minute to the gentleman from New Jersey (Mr. SMITH), my dear friend who I have served with all my years here in Congress.

Mr. SMITH of New Jersey. I thank the gentleman for yielding and for his extraordinary leadership on this legislation.

Mr. Speaker, in 1992, 24 years ago, I met—along with a great advocate, Pat Smith—with top officials of NIH and CDC on Federal guidelines that precluded the existence of chronic Lyme disease. Subsequently, every Congress, I would introduce legislation trying to get a diversity of viewpoints so that clinicians, patients, and other advocates could be heard.

Today, CDC estimates there are about 380,000 cases of Lyme disease; and a provision in this bill, an important, game-changing provision, insisted upon by Majority Leader KEVIN MCCARTHY and Chairman UPTON requires that a new working group on tickborne disease includes members with a diversity of viewpoints, including patients, clinicians, and researchers. This working group will make a difference. Those patients—and there are tens of thousands of them—have been told chronic Lyme disease doesn't exist, what you are feeling can be attributable to some other disease, and they don't get better.

I thank the chairman for doing this. Also, as cofounder and co-chairman of both the Alzheimer's Caucus 16 years ago and the Autism Caucus 16 years ago, I am thankful for the great work that this will do for those patients as well.

Mr. UPTON. Mr. Speaker, I yield 1 minute to the gentlewoman from Washington (Ms. HERRERA BEUTLER).

Ms. HERRERA BEUTLER. Mr. Speaker, I am really excited about this bill, and I am excited about an inclusion in the 21st Century bill that we are voting today that is going to help moms and babies. Nearly all of the 400 million women who give birth each year in the U.S. and the 3 million women who breast-feed will take medications or receive a vaccine during their pregnancy or while they are nursing.

This bill that we are voting on, that we hope is going to pass and be signed into law, contains a provision that will reduce the health risks faced by these moms. Here is where the risk lies. Pregnant women are often not included in clinical trials on medications, so we really don't know what the effects are of drugs on a woman and on her pregnancy.

Without reliable information, women and doctors are really just playing a guessing game, trying to figure out the impacts of medication, and that could be on medication that is a prescription for a chronic disease: hypertension, diabetes, or severe depression.

The other undesirable choice for moms is whether or not to choose just not to treat their condition. If they don't know what the impact is, maybe they are just going to forgo their therapy altogether.

Moms should be able to safely manage ongoing conditions throughout their pregnancies and while breast-feeding without playing this guessing game. Fortunately, the Safe Medications for Moms and Babies Act is included in the bill that we are voting on. I urge its support.

Mr. UPTON. Mr. Speaker, I yield 1 minute to the gentleman from Pennsylvania (Mr. COSTELLO), a long-time supporter of this legislation.

Mr. COSTELLO of Pennsylvania. Mr. Speaker, I rise today in support of the 21st Century Cures Act, and I want to thank the chairman and ranking member for their advocacy and leadership to bring this bill to the floor today.

I also congratulate my colleague and neighbor, Congressman JOE PITTS, for his leadership as chairman of the Health Subcommittee. Mr. PITTS and I represent adjoining and very similar districts in Pennsylvania, each including parts of Chester and Berks counties. He has done outstanding work for our constituencies by incorporating the concerns and issues important to southeastern Pennsylvania into the Cures Act.

This bill will make an immediate, long-lasting impact on the families and communities we represent. It supports medical research, helps fight the opioid epidemic, and would improve the delivery of mental health care by putting patients at the center of the review process. In short, this bill includes major priorities that will make our communities healthier and safer.

Mr. UPTON. Mr. Speaker, I yield 1 minute to the gentleman from New York (Mr. GIBSON). This may be his last speech on the House floor, as he announced his retirement some time ago. He is a good Member in support of this legislation. He hounded us from the get-go.

Mr. GIBSON. Mr. Speaker, I rise in strong support of 21st Century Cures. I want to thank the chairman, and I want to thank Majority Leader KEVIN MCCARTHY and my colleague CHRIS SMITH for insisting that we restore original language that deals with chronic Lyme and tickborne diseases. This was critically important to my district and to the Nation. I have so many friends and neighbors who are sick, chronically sick, and they are desperate for cures and solutions. Thanks to this bill, they now have a voice and a fighting chance. I am deeply grateful.

Mr. UPTON. Mr. Speaker, I yield 1 minute to the gentlewoman from Arizona (Ms. MCSALLY), my friend who is, again, a strong advocate of this legislation.

Ms. MCSALLY. Mr. Speaker, I rise in strong support of this important legislation. I want to thank Chairman UPTON for his tireless leadership on the 21st Century Cures Act. The bill is the result of years of hard work and brings hope to countless Americans suffering from incurable diseases in all of our districts around this country.

I also want to recognize the work of Congressman TIM MURPHY, who has served as a leader and a champion on the critical issue of mental health and is the author of legislation included in this bill that will overhaul our mental health system for the first time in 50 years.

Additionally, this legislation includes parts of a bill that I introduced with Senator JOHN CORNYN to improve mental health collaboration between Federal, State, and local justice systems to allow better responses to mental health crises. These provisions will also divert low-level offenders from incarceration to treatment programs, help reduce recidivism and provide support to mentally ill offenders reentering the community.

Many diverse groups came together in support of these bipartisan efforts, including mental health advocates and law enforcement organizations. I urge all of my colleagues to vote in favor of this very important bill. I thank the chairman for his leadership.

Mr. UPTON. Mr. Speaker, I have no further speakers. Therefore, I will let Mr. PALLONE use the balance of his time to close, and then I will use the balance of mine.

I reserve the balance of my time.

Mr. PALLONE. Mr. Speaker, may I inquire how much time remains on each side?

The SPEAKER pro tempore. The gentleman from New Jersey has 2½ minutes remaining. The gentleman from Michigan (Mr. UPTON) has 3½ minutes remaining.

Mr. PALLONE. I yield myself such time as I may consume.

Mr. Speaker, I would like to conclude by referencing the Statement of Administration Policy because I believe it reflects my position for the most part.

If I could just read some sections—I am not reading the whole thing—it says:

"The Administration strongly supports passage of the bipartisan House Amendment to the Senate Amendment to H.R. 34, the 21st Century Cures Act, which dedicates more than $6 billion to implement key priorities such as the President's proposal to combat the heroin and prescription opioid epidemic; the Vice President's Cancer Moonshot; and the President's signature biomedical research initiatives, the Precision Medicine and Brain Research through Advancing Innovative Neurotechnologies (BRAIN) Initiatives. It also takes important steps to improve mental health. . . .

"The Administration is committed to taking immediate action to lay the groundwork to ensure that the funds in the bill would be disbursed quickly and effectively so we can begin to address these important public health challenges. . . .

"There are . . . provisions in the bill that raise concerns, but that have been modified from previous versions to help address those concerns, such as provisions that allow for the marketing of drugs to payers for off-label uses. In addition, a number of effective dates will be challenging to meet, especially without additional administrative funding. . . .

"That said, this legislation offers advances in health that far outweigh these concerns. As such, the Administration strongly supports passage of the House Amendment to the Senate Amendment to H.R. 34, the 21st Century Cures Act."

Let me just say also in conclusion, I believe that this is an important piece of legislation that we need to pass, and I would hope that the Senate would take it up and pass it, and, obviously, the administration or the President will sign it.

From the very beginning, when we passed the 21st Century Cures Act, I thought that it would make important strides in actually dealing with those diseases for which we have not made a lot of progress in terms of advancing and finding cures, but, at the same time, I am happy that this legislation has now become a little more of a catch-all or a lot more of a catch-all, if you will, because it is addressing funding for opioids. Many of us know we passed an opioid package that the President signed in July, but it is not funded. So there will be funding for that bill now.

As far as the mental health reforms, our committee spent a tremendous amount of time over the last 2 years trying to address that legislation. We passed a bill here in the House. Again, I am happy that this is included because the kinds of reforms that were in that bill are now in this bill, and I think they are important strides in terms of addressing some of the mental health concerns that we have in this country.

The same is true for Cancer Moonshot. The President spent a lot of time, the Vice President as well, and this will make at least a down payment on that. So, overall, this is a good bill. I support it. I urge my colleagues to support it as well.

Mr. Speaker, I yield back the balance of my time.

Mr. UPTON. Mr. Speaker, I yield myself the balance of my time.

Mr. Speaker, I just want to thank all the people who have been involved in this Chamber, our staff, our Members, the Senate as well. I want to thank all the people outside the Chamber who brought their message to us because one of the things that we wanted to do from the very start was listen. You tell us what we need to do so we can find these cures for you—name the disease. I will confess that some of us had probably never heard of some of the diseases and some of the disease patient advocacy groups that actually came to us.

We are doing the right thing because, yes, we listened; yes, we knew we needed more research; and as fiscal conservatives—and we all care about the deficit, we all do—we want to make sure that we can actually have the resources and a timeline to spend it in a prudent manner, really outlining the priorities that both sides of the aisle share.

□ 1500

I commend the President. He was personally involved in this issue, not a Johnny-come-lately, coming up this aisle with his last couple of State of the Union Addresses on both Precision Medicine and the Cancer Moonshot. Vice President BIDEN spent weeks of his time and many hours with us helping us draft the legislation that we all care about and is included in this legislation. There are LAMAR ALEXANDER, MITCH MCCONNELL, PATTY MURRAY, CHUCK SCHUMER, and others in the Senate caring about this legislation, knowing its impact on so many millions of people—our researchers, who have devoted their lives, and, again, many of us here.

We traveled to MD Anderson, the Mayo Clinic, Ann Arbor, the Cleveland Clinic, and other great places to do research that actually can save people's lives. And we learned a lot. We learned a lot that, working together, we can get something done, and that is what this bill does.

But I will tell you why this vote is important when we take it at about 5 p.m. or so. We don't want to win by a narrow margin. We want to win by a huge margin. We want to send a message to the Senate that what we did in countless hearings and roundtables has made a difference, that it is a strong bipartisan message, including the mental health legislation, again, which we debated for weeks and months here in the House, not only in the committee, but on the House floor. It is very important. It is important to people like JOE KENNEDY, who spoke on the floor earlier today. The Ways and Means provisions that passed on a voice vote here are included so we can get the job done.

Our leadership on both sides—John Boehner, PAUL RYAN, KEVIN MCCARTHY, STEVE SCALISE, CATHY MCMORRIS RODGERS, NANCY PELOSI, STENY HOYER—have really been outstanding. They knew from the get-go that we needed to get this thing done. Patients can't wait. They cannot wait. We are going to have the cure to get this thing done, and, yes, it will impact millions of lives.

So, in an hour or two, when we vote on this, I would urge all my colleagues on both sides of the aisle to vote "yes" for patients.

Madam Speaker, I yield back the balance of my time.

Mr. BRADY of Texas. Madam Speaker, I yield myself such time as I may consume.

America has always been a leader in developing cutting-edge medical treatments and technologies, breakthroughs that have saved countless lives; but due to outdated and burdensome Federal healthcare policies, medical innovation in our country is failing to keep pace with the 21st century challenges facing doctors and families.

Today, Americans nationwide are being forced to wait for the lifesaving treatments they need while important advancements are held up by unnecessary red tape. Chairman UPTON's 21st Century Cures Act provides an opportunity to put America back at the forefront of medical innovation and the delivery of cutting-edge care.

This legislation will empower America's researchers and doctors with the tools needed to solve the biggest healthcare challenges of our time. It includes many bipartisan solutions that will increase healthcare choice, access, and affordability for the American people.

Thanks to Chairman UPTON's leadership and the hard work of many Members of Congress from multiple committees, the 21st Century Cures Act brings together a variety of solutions that will help Americans throughout the country.

Ten of these patient-focused measures are from the Ways and Means Committee. All 10 are bipartisan. More than 20 of our members crafted and introduced these bills. Many more helped move them forward.

In particular, I would like to recognize the leadership of Congressman PAT TIBERI and JIM MCDERMOTT, the chairman and ranking member of our Health Subcommittee.

Ranking Member MCDERMOTT, by the way, is retiring at the end of this Congress. I want to take this moment to thank him for his years of service and friendship. I want to thank him and Chairman TIBERI for their efforts in support of the 21st Century Cures Act.

The Ways and Means healthcare provisions in the bill will remove harmful regulations on providers to impede the delivery of care. They will increase healthcare options for job creators and families. They will expand access to high-quality, affordable care for America's most vulnerable patients.

I am also excited that this legislation includes a policy by Representative ENGEL and Chairman TIBERI to ensure patients have access to new home infusion benefits. We look forward to working with the Energy and Commerce Committee next year to quickly implement this solution so that more patients have access to this vital service.

In closing, I want to thank all the Members on both sides of the aisle who helped develop the bill before us today. I again want to thank Chairman UPTON for his leadership. This historic legislation has been years in the making. We would not be here today without Chairman UPTON's dedication, vision, and commitment to bipartisan collaboration.

The 21st Century Cures Act is an incredible opportunity to help Americans from all walks of life for generations to come. I urge all my colleagues to join me in supporting its passage.

Madam Speaker, I reserve the balance of my time.

Mr. MCDERMOTT. Madam Speaker, I yield myself such time as I may consume.

This bill is a typical lameduck bill. It has one provision in it that people really want, and that is a giveaway to the pharmaceutical industry.

Every provision that Mr. BRADY has talked about with respect to the Ways and Means Committee has already been passed out of here, and none of them are harmless, but the issue here is reducing the effect of the FDA in protecting the American public. My colleague, Ms. DELAURO from Connecticut, was absolutely right: the weakening of the FDA in protecting the American public is the central part of this bill.

Now, it is wrapped in $4 billion worth of inadequate money for NIH. It would take $7 billion to keep us where we are today. The money that went out of here a few months ago was mandatory, and now it is subject to appropriation. Everybody says: Oh, well, there are commitments made. There are commitments made.

Anybody who believes in the tooth fairy will believe that money is going to go to NIH. But the changes in law in how we push drugs, that is going to be in law.

Now, let me tell you what the problem with that is. If you push drugs out there quickly, there are some side effects and people die and people say, Well, it is too bad; the FDA approved it. We put the FDA in the position of protecting the American public, and then we cut them out at the knees.

Once we have done these cures, we come up with these great drugs, who can afford them? The other thing that is wrong with this bill and that this House has failed to do is deal with the cost of pharmaceuticals in this country. There is not one single thing in this bill.

There is a specialty drug called Sovaldi. It is a treatment for hepatitis C. There are actually several million people in this country who need that drug. One pill costs $1,000. Full treatment costs $84,000. Who can afford it? Who is going to pay for that? Are you going to be willing to put the money into part D of Medicare to pay for it?

The question here is: What are we doing in giving away to the pharmaceutical companies an open door to push any drug out they want or that they can get through the screen, make the screen big so that it is easy to get them out, and then we pick up the pieces for the American people? That is the reason I oppose this bill. I think there are good things in it.

I come from a university that is the number one recipient of research money in this country. The University of Washington is the number one public university. We have so little money at NIH now that you have to be 40 years old until you get a grant from NIH for a research project. It used to be that 17 percent of all the grants were approved. Now we are down to 6 percent. That is because we have been squeezing the life out of NIH. And this $4 billion sounds like a lot of money, but it isn't even the $7 billion to keep us at the present level. That is what is wrong with this bill.

Madam Speaker, I reserve the balance of my time.

Mr. BRADY of Texas. Madam Speaker, I yield 1 minute to the gentleman from Ohio (Mr. TIBERI), the chairman of the Health Subcommittee who shepherded these bills through the House earlier and leads the effort to correct issues so important to our hospitals and cancer hospitals, as well as some new reforms for infusion healthcare patients.

Mr. TIBERI. Madam Speaker, I thank Chairman BRADY for his leadership on this issue.

Madam Speaker, Chairman UPTON unveiled the 21st Century Cures Act back in 2014 to initiate quicker development and pathways to approve treatments and cure diseases. This bipartisan and bicameral bill is another example how the House is delivering on patient-focused solutions for Americans.

I am incredibly pleased that three of my initiatives are included in this final package, the first of which is a bill that provides necessary regulatory relief to providers and fixes a site-neutral policy to hospitals that were in the middle of construction when the policy went into effect.

Second, the 21st Century Cures Act gives relief to long-term care hospitals from the 25 percent rule and common-sense Medicare reforms.

Lastly, the bill includes a provision of a bill I sponsored that provides infusion therapy to Medicare beneficiaries in their home.

I look forward to continuing work on these issues with my colleagues in the next session of Congress. I want to congratulate Chairman UPTON for his incredible work on this. He solicited feedback from stakeholders, Members, patients, and has worked tirelessly to make this bill the best version possible. His accomplishments during his chairmanship are admirable, and I am grateful to call him a close friend.

Let's pass the 21st Century Cures Act on a bipartisan basis, Madam Speaker, and get America back in the driver's seat on medical innovation.

Mr. McDERMOTT. Madam Speaker, I yield 3 minutes to the gentleman from Texas (Mr. DOGGETT).

Mr. DOGGETT. Madam Speaker, while certainly saluting the many Members who have worked so diligently on this measure, I cannot vote for it.

In a wide and endless desert of support for research funding, even getting a few drops of rain is understandably welcomed by the thirsty. Under Republican rule, we have seen a dreadful drought in research funding. This is a bill that attempts to address that shortfall. I voted for the bill when it was on the floor of the House at a previous time. At that point, it promised the hope, after this long drought of almost $10 billion in assured, certain funding, for research so that we might find cures for some of these diseases before we get them ourselves—the concern of so many people.

Now, under this new measure, we have only about a fourth of the funding previously approved in the House, and it is no longer certain money; it is maybe money for the future. So there may be bipartisan agreement, but there is not a bipartisan advancement.

At the same time that research dollars are dramatically cut—the very research dollars that were the reason for having this bill in the first place—Big Pharma got some of its wish list approved. And how very appropriate that this measure and so many other moving parts have been packed into what it calls the Tsunami Warning bill.

If there is one thing we can be sure of this past year, it is that those people who rely on lifesaving drugs and who want to be able to have a prescription that the doctor prescribes have been hit by a real tsunami. They have been buried in one wave after another wave after another giant wave of pharmaceutical price gouging. Whether it is the EpiPen for a child who is might have an allergic reaction, whether it is insulin for someone who is diabetic and relies on that insulin, whether it is an oncology drug that costs over $100,000, it is wave after wave of a tsunami of price gouging.

□ 1515

And what has this Congress done about that?

Absolutely nothing. I must say, the administration has done very little more. They have looked at it. There have been a few speeches about it, but there has not been effective action.

So what we get in this bill are a few things that Big Pharma wants that have been on its wish list for a long time, and consumers, they get nothing to look forward to other than more of those big waves of huge price increases.

I am also concerned that the policy arm that publishes Consumer Reports magazine has expressed deep concerns about additional patient risk as a result of some of the provisions that the pharmaceutical companies and the medical device manufacturers have insisted as the price for getting a little additional research funding.

So I am voting "no," not because this provides some research dollars. It ought to be providing the level of certain research funding we approved already, but because it fails to address this critical health need.

Mr. BRADY of Texas. Madam Speaker, I yield 1 minute to the gentlewoman from Kansas (Ms. JENKINS), one of our key members of the Health Subcommittee who also focuses on rural hospitals and access to care for rural communities.

Ms. JENKINS of Kansas. Madam Speaker, I rise today to support this legislation. It improves access to health care for rural communities through measures I introduced, such as the Continuing Access to Hospitals Act, which stops unjustified regulations from interfering with rural healthcare providers offering quality services; and the Rural ACO Provider Equity Act, which will ensure the work of PAs and nurse practitioners is recognized so that rural hospitals can join

ACOs and afford to remain open and serve our rural communities.

Finally, it will help the 40 million Americans who deal with a mental illness each year through inclusion of my Mental Health First Aid Act. This bipartisan legislation delivers $15 million every year to train police officers, teachers, veterans' advocates, and others to identify and aid those with a mental illness, building a stronger mental health safety net in America that addresses the needs of millions of Americans.

I urge my colleagues to pass this legislation.

Mr. McDERMOTT. Madam Speaker, I reserve the balance of my time.

Mr. BRADY of Texas. Madam Speaker, I yield 1 minute to the gentleman from Minnesota (Mr. PAULSEN), one of our leaders in medical devices innovation and bringing lifesaving cures to the market sooner.

Mr. PAULSEN. Madam Speaker, I rise in strong support of the bipartisan 21st Century Cures Act.

There are more than 10,000 known diseases in the world, and many of them are rare diseases. Yet, there are only 500 of them that have an FDA-approved treatment. Millions of Americans today feel powerless because they have a deadly disease and they have no hope of a cure because there aren't enough resources for research or the regulatory barriers are discouraging innovation.

This bipartisan initiative today gives patients new hope. It supports more NIH research; it streamlines the regulatory approval process; and it gives patients more input in the treatment and delivery process.

I am also pleased today, Madam Speaker, that we are providing important reforms to our mental health system. For too long, patients and families, mental healthcare professionals, and law enforcement have been crying for help. This legislative effort represents the most significant improvement to the mental health system that we have seen in over a decade.

Madam Speaker, this is an innovation game-changer. It is a once-in-a-generation, transformational opportunity to change the way we treat disease. It expedites the discovery, the development, and the delivery of new treatments and cures; and it ensures that America will be a leader in the global fight for medical innovation.

Mr. McDERMOTT. Madam Speaker, I reserve the balance of my time.

Mr. BRADY of Texas. Madam Speaker, I yield 1 minute to the gentleman from Ohio (Mr. RENACCI), who has, among many healthcare issues, led the charge to create much smarter measurements in hospital readmissions.

Mr. RENACCI. Madam Speaker, I rise in support of H.R. 34, the 21st Century Cures Act. At its core, this legislation, while not perfect, ensures our country will continue to be at the forefront of medical innovations and breakthroughs.

Also important is what the bill does for States like Ohio that are fighting the opioid epidemic. Just today it was reported that Ohio has seen more opioid overdose deaths than any other State in the Nation. This bill would especially help Ohio reverse this devastating trend.

I also applaud the inclusion of my bill, H.R. 1343, the Establishing Equity in the Hospital Readmission Program. The Hospital Readmission Program was created due to concerns that too few resources were being spent on reducing acute care hospital readmissions. While reducing acute care hospital readmissions is important, my bill ensures that we are not disproportionately penalizing those who see a large number of our most vulnerable patients.

This is one of the many commonsense, bipartisan reforms to improve our healthcare system included in the 21st Century Cures Act, and I urge all Members to support this bill.

Mr. McDERMOTT. Madam Speaker, I reserve the balance of my time.

Mr. BRADY of Texas. Madam Speaker, I yield 1 minute to the gentleman from Pennsylvania (Mr. MEEHAN), again, another key member of our committee who is focused on health care and, in this case, increasing information to seniors about their Medicare plans in advance, and also improving physical therapy, so critical to so many in health care.

Mr. MEEHAN. Madam Speaker, the 21st Century Cures Act is a historic, bipartisan legislation that will eliminate the barriers standing between us and cures for diseases like Alzheimer's and diabetes, and cancer.

The bill fosters coordination and research related to pediatric diseases and birth defects, and we encourage the NIH and FDA to establish a global pediatric clinical study network with the hope that more collaboration will lead to new treatments, and it will help build our understanding of how treatments geared for adults can help to lead to cures for children.

Just 3 years ago, after a fight with Washington bureaucrats, Sarah Murnaghan, a 10-year-old young woman from my district, received an adult lung transplant. She is now a thriving 14-year-old. And through "Sarah's Heroes," we highlight the stories of other children who are courageously working to overcome challenges presented by cystic fibrosis and lung transplant.

Schizophrenia and mental illness are among other conditions without a cure. The bill improves access to mental health by increasing the number of healthcare professionals trained to treat patients. It also strengthens the requirement that mental health cov-

erage be on par with coverage for physical ailments; many good reasons to continue to support. I urge my colleagues to do so.

Mr. McDERMOTT. Madam Speaker, I reserve the balance of my time.

Mr. BRADY of Texas. Madam Speaker, I yield 1 minute to the gentleman from Illinois (Mr. DOLD), one of our smartest members on the Ways and Means Committee who has really carved out a niche in support of medical innovation, really bringing these breakthroughs to the community and patients quickly.

Mr. DOLD. Madam Speaker, I certainly thank the chairman for his leadership.

I also stand here today in strong support of the 21st Century Cures Act. I want to thank Chairman UPTON for his leadership, and Ranking Member PALLONE, Congresswoman DeGETTE, and Congressman MURPHY for their great work on compiling things that are in this bill.

I have been a longtime advocate for both the 21st Century Cures Act and the Helping Families in Mental Health Crisis Act because I believe it is critically important that we modernize how we treat mental health and how we develop lifesaving cures. This package accomplishes both of these important goals and many more.

Over the next 10 years, we will provide an additional $4.8 billion to the National Institutes of Health in support of groundbreaking medical research and an additional $500 million to the FDA to help bring drugs and devices to patients more quickly.

We will also be providing States with $1 billion in grants over the next 2 years to help combat the opioid epidemic, which is impacting every single community across our Nation.

Finally, we will increase choice, access, and quality in health care by making serious improvements to Medicare.

The SPEAKER pro tempore (Mrs. LUMMIS). The time of the gentleman has expired.

Mr. BRADY of Texas. I yield the gentleman an additional 1½ minutes.

Mr. DOLD. This package is proof that when we are willing to work together, we can improve our healthcare system for all Americans through changes large and small. I encourage all of my colleagues to join me in supporting the 21st Century Cures Act.

I also want to thank, again, Chairman UPTON, Congressman MURPHY, Congresswoman DeGETTE, and all those who helped put this together, and the staff that were so instrumental in making this become a reality today.

Mr. BRADY of Texas. Madam Speaker, I have no further speakers and I am prepared to close if the gentleman would like to close.

I reserve the balance of my time.

Mr. McDERMOTT. Madam Speaker, I yield myself such time as I may con-

sume. I want to thank my colleagues for their interest in children. I hear some of the speakers stand up and say they are really interested in kids, yet they oppose the CHIP program. They talk about cutting back the help to children.

Now, the problem here is that if you are talking about cures, and you are going to create a magnificent cure that costs $80,000, if you don't provide Medicaid, the children who are poor in this country aren't going to get access to that cure. That is a cure for rich people who could pay it out of their clippings on their bonds and their stock.

The EPSDT program, which is the program that covers kids, the President-elect has put in the charge of that a woman from Indiana who testified against it. This is the benefit that ensures sick kids will get cures.

Now, you are setting in motion something here for pharmaceutical companies to find a way to take as much money out of the system as they can with every drug they can put out there, and you are, at the same time, moving in the direction of making it impossible for poor children to be taken care of in this country.

How many States have the Governors said: We don't believe in Medicaid; we don't believe that the government should give Medicaid; we believe the government should stay out of medicine?

So they deny their own people health care, simple, everyday, ordinary health care; and we are talking about cures for disease. As somebody said, there were 50 cases in the United States of it last year. One feels for those 50.

I am a physician. I have listened to those people. I know that it is awful, but you have to keep in balance and say to yourself: Are we going to spend all the money there or are we going to spend it dealing with all the Americans?

That is what is wrong with this bill. The pharmaceutical industry has no control on it whatsoever. When you put in that benefit, in part D, you tied the Secretary of Health and Human Services' hands, and he or she cannot negotiate lower prices. You said: Whatever the pharmaceutical company says the cost is, that is what we are going to pay.

Now, the Veterans Administration—veterans are different than ordinary people in this country. They have an administration that has the right to negotiate changes in prices, and their pharmaceutical prices are down 50, 60 percent from what people pay in Medicare.

Now, as long as you have that kind of giveaway going on to the pharmaceutical companies, this bill is just kind of frosting on the cake, and I guess Members will vote for it. In the short run it will seem like, you know, it didn't make any difference, but you are going to pay down the line.

This is going to be a Fram commercial. You either pay now or you are going to pay later, because if you do not screen those drugs carefully and make sure that they are really doing something, and let the pharmaceutical companies add a Chlorine ion or a Boron or whatever, they are simply putting drugs out on the table that cost too much for the Americans to buy.

I urge a "no" vote.

I yield back the balance of my time.

Mr. BRADY of Texas. Madam Speaker, I yield myself the balance of my time.

There are so many Americans who could be watching today who wonder when that lifesaving drug, that new treatment will be made available to them. They know it is in other countries. They read about it in other places, but they can't get it here in America. The Cures Act changes that. It streamlines it, moves things faster; and when you are in that tough situation, it provides options for health care, experimental drugs never before available to them. This is important to patients and it is important to doing it better in America. I urge its support.

I yield back the balance of my time.

Mr. THOMPSON of California. Madam Speaker, I rise in support of this bill.

H.R. 34, the 21st Century Cures Act, is the product of extensive bipartisan, bicameral collaboration between stakeholders and policy makers.

This bill stands to help us make significant progress when it comes to keeping Americans healthy, and keeping America on the forefront of medical innovation.

Included in the bill text are provisions based on legislation I authored, known as the Small Business Healthcare Relief Act.

These provisions would allow small businesses with fewer than 50 employees to offer tax preferred Health Reimbursement Arrangements, or HRAs, to their workforce.

The HRAs can be used to buy health insurance in the individual market, or pay for qualified health expenses if an individual already has coverage.

This targeted bill seeks not to override those long-standing responsibilities between employers and their employees, nor does it seek to override ERISA protections that existed before the Affordable Care Act was enacted, but to provide small employers an option for coverage in a robust individual market.

Given that this bill will be passed late in the year, it's my hope that the incoming Administration acts promptly to ensure a smooth transition for employers, employees, and the current exchange infrastructure.

Small businesses drive job creation and grow our economy. We should be going out of our way to help them support their employees so that they can focus on what they do best: running their business.

I urge my colleagues to support this bill.

Ms. EDDIE BERNICE JOHNSON of Texas. Madam Speaker, I rise in support of H.R. 34, the 21st Century Cures Act which will encourage innovation in biomedical research and development of new treatments.

The bill contains $6.3 billion in spending over the next ten years. With $4.8 billion in funding over the next ten years delivered to Innovation Funds within the National Institutes of Health and $500 million for the Food and Drug Administration over the next five years, it is clear that Congress is committed to investing in health research. Developing a better system of funding towards high-risk high reward research and research by early stage investigators is crucial to finding better health outcomes. With a better focus on infectious disease, precision medicine, and biomarkers, I strongly believe that we will finally address these areas of unmet medical needs, which are often the most pervasive issues in our health system.

The legislation also includes elements of H.R. 2646, the Helping Families in Mental Health Crisis Act, in order to get mental health reforms across the Senate's finish line. I am proud that this legislation will include many of the provisions that Congressman TIM MURPHY (R–PA) and I worked on for several years. The bill establishes an Assistant Secretary for Mental Health and Substance Use within the Substance Abuse and Mental Health Services Administration; reauthorizes Assisted Outpatient Treatment grant programs; and requires the Secretary to clarify HIPAA rules regarding circumstances when a provider can share information. Among other provisions, these aforementioned are just a few that will benefit patients directly and immediately.

While H.R. 34 contains many provisions regarding the biomedical research workforce, clinical trials, FDA improvements, I strongly believe that the Congress has not placed enough importance on scientific research and this is a way to get us back on track. Investing in innovation will yield high rewards for the medical community, especially patients. I am proud to support H.R. 34, the 21st Century Cures Act and urge my Senate colleagues to pass this legislation swiftly.

Ms. JACKSON LEE. Madam Speaker, I rise in support of the House Amendment to the Senate Amendment to H.R. 34, the "21st Century Cures Act," a bipartisan piece of legislation that is vital to the future and health of our Nation's citizens and ecosystem.

This thoughtful legislation is the culmination of the hard work of my dedicated colleagues who have sought out and engaged in public conversations with patients, innovators, providers, regulators and researchers about how to move advances in science and medicine into new therapies.

This outreach has garnered the critical input and support of more than 370 patient and physician groups, state and local organizations, cancer centers, and research and life sciences.

I am proud to be one of the cosponsors of 21st Century Cures Act, which represents a new national effort to find treatment and cures for thousands of unknown and rare diseases.

Looking to the various policies this legislation aims to address, it is important to highlight the commendable objectives and that will not only accelerate the discovery, development and delivery of new treatments and cures for thousands of serious and rare diseases, but it will also open the doors of innovation and the growth of health care system by enhancing and enriching the medical field for all Americans.

The most ambitious action calls for $6.3 billion in mandatory funding to be delivered over the next ten years to the National Institutes of Health (NIH).

NIH is part of our nation's top ranked educational research institutions in the world.

In order to maintain our global competitiveness in the biomedical field, we must invest in the industries that guarantee economic prosperity for our current and future economies.

It has been estimated that every $1 of NIH funding generates about $2.21 in local economic growth, and, in 2012, NIH-funded research supported an estimated 402,000 jobs all across the U.S.

The bill's funding for NIH would provide for an annual 3 percent increase in the NIH budget, which has been stagnant for the past few years and which desperately needs more funding to capitalize on emerging scientific insights.

This increased funding not only aims to continue the sustainability of our economy but it also supports our President's initiative to provide more resources to the biomedical field.

The 21st Century Cures Act supports the President's Precision Medicine Initiative, which would advance a new model of participant-centered research to accelerate biomedical discoveries and provide clinicians with new tools and therapies tailored to individual patients' needs.

The Obama Administration believes we can build on the progress in improving the drug development and approval process made to date by: Incorporating patients' voices into the Food and Drug Administration (FDA) decision-making; encouraging the development and qualification of reliable biomarkers to accelerate work on important new therapies; and reducing barriers to initiating medical device trials.

In furtherance of this initiative, the legislation before us allows, for the creation of an "Innovation Fund" through the National Institute of Health.

This "Innovation Fund" is a welcome effort because it promotes the maintenance of the best biomedical workforce in the world and help to increase the diversity of the biomedical workforce.

In particular, the $4.8 billion provided for the Innovation Fund, will not only increase the number of the research projects it supports but it also increases the cap for NIH's loan repayment programs.

This would include a repayment program for clinical scientists who do research in health disparities and for clinical scientist from disadvantaged backgrounds, from $35,000 per year to $50,000 per year plus a yearly inflation for adjustment.

With the support of H.R. 34, underrepresented communities and those with disadvantaged backgrounds from across the country can undoubtedly provide the future researchers and workers of the biomedical workforce.

The Journal on STEM Education reported in 2011 that only 8.34 percent of the STEM doctorates awarded in 2006 were given to underrepresented minorities, despite making up approximately 28 percent of the U.S. population.

Furthermore, GAO found noted that while the percentage of underrepresented minorities nationwide increased from 13 percent to 19 percent from 1994 to 2003, the total number of STEM doctorates awarded to the same group dropped during this period from 8,335 to 7,310.

In response, the National Institute of General Medical Sciences (NIGMS) created the Minority Opportunities in Research (MORE) Division and similar academic intervention programs.

The MORE programs are comprised of four primary components: research experience, mentoring and advisement, supplemental instruction and workshops, and financial support.

In 2007, NIGMS' annual budget was $1.9 billion, of which nearly $126 million was spent on its MORE programs.

This amount includes the Minority Biomedical Research Support-Research Initiative for Scientific Enhancement (MBRS-RISE) program, the Minority Access to Research Careers (MARC), Post-baccalaureate Research Education Program (PREP), and the Bridges to the Baccalaureate and Bridges to the PhD programs.

The amount of funds dedicated to these programs reflects the commitment by the science and research community to the goals of the MORE Division in addressing this problem.

Increased funding set forth in H.R. 34 will only strengthen NIH's focus on diversifying the biomedical workforce by requiring NIH to focus on ensuring participation from scientists from underrepresented communities.

In addition to addressing the needs of underrepresented communities, H.R. 34 also calls for specific action to increase representation of racial minorities.

The 21st Century Cures Act acknowledges that there are disturbing statistics on the low numbers of African Americans, Hispanics and Native Americans pursuing academic qualification and participating in scientific research.

Under H.R. 34, the National Institute on Minority Health and Health Disparities will necessarily include strategies for increasing representation of minority communities in its strategic plan.

I am proud that H.R. 34 incorporates the Jackson Lee Amendment which I offered during the initial consideration of the 21st Century Cures Act by the House which will help ensure that the national goals of finding and bringing more cures and treatments to patients and strengthening the biomedical innovation ecosystem in the United States is aided by an expanding pool of diverse and talented medical researchers.

Specifically, the Jackson Lee Amendment instructed the Secretary of Health and Human Services to conduct outreach to historically Black colleges and universities, Hispanic-serving institutions, Native American colleges, and rural colleges to ensure that health professionals from underrepresented populations are aware of research opportunities under this Act.

Many racial health disparities stem from lack of access to effective test, treatments and cures for illnesses that have devastating consequences for African American, Hispanic and Native American populations.

For example:

1. African-Americans (represent 12 percent of the U.S. population but only 5 percent of clinical trial participants.

2. Hispanics make up 16 percent of the population but only 1 percent of clinical trial participants.

3. Women are under-represented in cardiovascular device trials, which have 67 percent male participation.

The most significant barriers limiting clinical participation are race, age, and sex of participants:

1. Women and minority patients are more difficult to recruit.

2. Women and minority physicians have less experience and are relatively more costly to engage.

3. Minority patients with limited English proficiency can require costly translation services.

Physicians are the gateway to the patient. Increasing diversity of those conducting research will have implications on the types of conditions that are researched and the participants in clinical trials that are seeking answers to illnesses like lupus, triple negative breast cancer, and sickle cell disease that can be difficult to detect, treat and cure.

Certain medical illnesses have been known to have higher prevalence in certain demographic groups, including type II diabetes, lupus, sickle cell anemia, and Triple Negative Breast Cancer for which African Americans are more than twice as likely to be diagnosed on average.

Lupus, triple negative breast cancer and sickle cell disease are of particular concern because they are often difficult to diagnose and disproportionately impact persons of color and especially women.

In particular, Lupus is a chronic, complex and prevalent autoimmune disease that affects more than 1.5 million Americans. Yet, Lupus is one of America's least recognized major diseases.

More than 90 percent of lupus sufferers are women, mostly young women between the ages of 15 to 44, and women of color are two to three times more at risk for lupus than Caucasians.

Triple negative breast cancer also disproportionately impacts younger women, African American women, Hispanic/Latina women, and women with a "BRCA1" genetic mutation, which is prevalent in Jewish women.

More than 30 percent of all breast cancer diagnoses in African American are of the triple negative variety, and African American women are far more susceptible to this dangerous subtype than white or Hispanic women.

Additionally, there are about 2 million people who carry the sickle cell trait and with about 100,000 having the disease. According to the Centers for Disease Control and Prevention, sickle cell trait is common among African Americans and occurs in about 1 in 12, and sickle cell disease occurs in about 1 out of every 500 African-American births, compared to about 1 out of every 36,000 Hispanic-American births.

Treatments for Lupus, triple negative breast cancer and sickle cell disease are not progressing as quickly as desired by patients, researchers, and policy makers. We must support the advancement of legislation that will

allow for the remediation and end of health care disparities and the promotion of research parity for diseases such as lupus, triple negative breast cancer, sickle cell disease, and countless other rare and serious diseases.

Race and ethnicity have also been shown to affect the effectiveness of and response to certain drugs, such as anti-hypertensive therapies in the treatment of hypertension in African Americans and anti-depressants in Hispanics.

Increased diversity in research trials could help researchers find better, more precise ways to fight diseases that disproportionately impact certain populations, and may be important for the safe and effective use of new therapies. As one of the most diverse cities in the country, Houston is the 4th largest city in the United States and the 5th most populated metropolitan area in the nation. Houston is home to the largest medical complex in the world—the Texas Medical Center, which provides clinical health care, research and education at its 54 institutions.

The University of Houston, ranked number three out of all other colleges and universities in Texas, is an example of a premier institution that can produce students with advanced STEM degrees who would be able to join a progressing biomedical field.

Another important requirement of H.R. 34 is that it would require National Institute of Health to publically report the number of children by race and gender who participate in NIH funded clinical trials.

This legislation would help ensure that children of all races are adequately represented in clinical trials and that we can determine the safety and effectiveness of drugs on children of all demographic backgrounds.

With 10,000 known diseases, 7,000 of which are rare, and treatments for only 500 of them—clear there is much work to do. Medical research saves lives and improves the quality of life for millions of Americans because the government provides a steady and reliable commitment to basic research into cures for debilitating and deadly diseases.

Given the array of commendable initiatives, H.R. 34 is a necessary piece of legislation that will accelerate the discovery, development, and delivery of promising new treatments and cures for all patients while investing in our nation's ability to maintain the best and most diverse biomedical workforce in the world.

Madam Speaker, I call for the support of all of my colleagues in ensuring the passage of the important legislation.

Mr. LONG. Madam Speaker, I rise today in strong support of the 21st Century Cures Act and to congratulate my friends Chairman FRED UPTON and Congresswoman DIANA DEGETTE for their tireless work on this crucial legislation.

Specifically I would like to discuss Section 3037 of the Act which is modeled after my legislation, H.R. 2452 which would amend the Federal Food, Drug and Cosmetic Act to facilitate better dissemination of health care economic information. This provision serves an important public health purpose—namely, ensuring payors and other population health decision-makers have relevant data to assist them in making informed decisions on behalf of patients.

Relevant scientific information such as that related to quality of life, cost-effectiveness, and treatment outcomes can inform coverage decisions and improve healthcare costs and patient outcomes. By requiring only that such information relates to an approved indication, and by making other changes, this section broadens the scope of information that can be communicated without being considered false or misleading.

In particular, the omission of the word "directly" from the requirement in existing law that information be "directly related" to an approved indication means that information that is consistent with an approved use, but not in the labeling itself, falls within the scope of information that can be communicated to payors and other population health decision-makers.

This provision ensures that information providing valuable insight regarding new medicines can be appropriately communicated under the Federal Food, Drug, and Cosmetic Act, and I thank Chairman UPTON for its ultimate inclusion in this package.

The SPEAKER pro tempore. All time for debate has expired.

Pursuant to House Resolution 934, the previous question is ordered on the motion to concur.

The question is on the motion to concur offered by the gentleman from Michigan (Mr. UPTON).

The question was taken; and the Speaker pro tempore announced that the ayes appeared to have it.

Mr. McDERMOTT. Madam Speaker, I demand a recorded vote.

A recorded vote was ordered.

The SPEAKER pro tempore. Pursuant to clause 8 of rule XX, and the order of the House of today, further proceedings on this question will be postponed.

□ 1530

ANNOUNCEMENT BY THE SPEAKER PRO TEMPORE

The SPEAKER pro tempore (Mr. DOLD). Pursuant to clause 8 of rule XX, the Chair will postpone further proceedings today on motions to suspend the rules on which a recorded vote or the yeas and nays are ordered, or on which the vote incurs objection under clause 6 of rule XX.

Record votes on postponed questions will be taken later.

OVERTIME PAY FOR SECRET SERVICE AGENTS ACT OF 2016

Mr. CHAFFETZ. Mr. Speaker, I move to suspend the rules and pass the bill (H.R. 6302) to provide an increase in premium pay for United States Secret Service agents performing protective services during 2016, and for other purposes.

The Clerk read the title of the bill.

The text of the bill is as follows:

H.R. 6302

Be it enacted by the Senate and House of Representatives of the United States of America in Congress assembled,

SECTION 1. SHORT TITLE.

This Act may be cited as the "Overtime Pay for Secret Service Agents Act of 2016".

SEC. 2. PREMIUM PAY EXCEPTION IN 2016 FOR WORK AUTHORIZED UNDER SECTION 3056 OF TITLE 18.

(a) IN GENERAL.—Notwithstanding any other provision of law, including section 5307 of title 5, United States Code, and subject to subsection (b), during calendar year 2016—

(1) section 5547(a) of such title shall not apply to an employee who performs work authorized by section 3056(a) of title 18, United States Code; and

(2) such an employee may be paid premium pay to the extent that the payment of such pay does not cause the total of basic pay and such premium pay for any pay period for such employee to exceed the annual rate of basic pay payable to level II of the Executive Schedule under section 5313 of title 5, United States Code.

(b) TREATMENT OF ADDITIONAL PAY.—To the extent that subsection (a) results in payment of additional premium pay of a type that is normally creditable as basic pay for retirement or any other purpose, such additional pay shall not be considered to be basic pay for any purpose and shall not be used in computing a lump-sum payment for accumulated and accrued annual leave under section 5551 of title 5, United States Code.

(c) DEFINITION.—In this section, the term "employee" means any special agent of the United States Secret Service that is a law enforcement officer, but does not include—

(1) a member of the United States Secret Service Uniformed Division; or

(2) an officer, employee, agent, or law enforcement officer of any other Federal agency.

(d) CONFORMING AMENDMENT.—Section 118 of the Treasury and General Government Appropriations Act, 2001 (Public Law 106–554) is amended by inserting "and except as provided in section 2 of the Overtime Pay for Secret Service Agents Act of 2016," after "Hereafter,".

The SPEAKER pro tempore. Pursuant to the rule, the gentleman from Utah (Mr. CHAFFETZ) and the gentleman from Massachusetts (Mr. LYNCH) each will control 20 minutes.

The Chair recognizes the gentleman from Utah.

GENERAL LEAVE

Mr. CHAFFETZ. Mr. Speaker, I ask unanimous consent that all Members may have 5 legislative days in which to revise and extend their remarks and include extraneous material on the bill under consideration.

The SPEAKER pro tempore. Is there objection to the request of the gentleman from Utah?

There was no objection.

Mr. CHAFFETZ. Mr. Speaker, I yield myself such time as I may consume.

Mr. Speaker, I rise today in support of my bill, H.R. 6302, the Overtime Pay for Secret Service Agents Act of 2016.

The United States Secret Service has a zero-fail mission to protect the President and other protectees at all costs. The 2016 Presidential campaign year was an especially busy year for the Secret Service. They have done an exceptional job.

I will give you some metrics of what this agency was dealing with. They staffed more than 2,500 candidate trips, 8,580 total protective travel stops, and 62 foreign travel trips with the Presi-

dent and the Vice President. The most recent Presidential election saw Secret Service agents working record hours to fulfill their mission. Incredibly, this was accomplished despite the Secret Service suffering from historic levels of attrition and low staffing levels.

In our December 2015 bipartisan report, the Committee on Oversight and Government Reform found that the Secret Service was "experiencing a staffing crisis that threatens to jeopardize its critical mission."

The Secret Service was at a peak staffing level of 7,024 employees in the year 2011. That number has declined every year until the beginning of this year when the agency had 6,289 employees.

The staffing numbers are beginning to improve, now at 6,500. But the problem is the agency hopes to have between 8,000 and 9,000 employees by the next Presidential election in 2020. It is hard and difficult to hire a Secret Service agent, and once they are hired, you can't simply put them out in front of the White House or next to a candidate or one of the protectees and expect them to simply flip on the switch and do their job.

As a result of the current manpower shortage and the lack of employees, Secret Service agents had to work significant overtime to ensure around-the-clock protection of Presidential candidates. No matter the number of hours worked, Secret Service agents are subject to a title 5 statutory cap on their biweekly pay. As a result, agents were not compensated for overtime hours worked that would have resulted in compensation beyond the cap during any pay period. Within the Secret Service, this became known as a max-out problem.

These so-called max-outs contribute to the agency's low morale and exacerbate attrition. The excessive overtime also negatively impacts protective efforts. The agency needs fresh and energetic agents to fulfill a critical mission, one that they have to be in tune with at every moment while they are on the job. The bill, the Overtime Pay for Secret Service Agents Act of 2016, offers relief for agents who have not received pay due to the so-called max-out problem.

Secret Service agents who worked on the 2016 Presidential campaign would be eligible to receive compensation above normal levels up to the basic pay currently given to members of the Executive Schedule Level II for the calendar year 2016.

Every Secret Service agent with outstanding overtime would receive an additional compensation for 2016 under this bill. This is not a bonus. This is not extra pay. This is simply trying to compensate them for hours that they worked. We heard story after story about Secret Service agents who would literally go weeks on end with no pay and yet continue to do their job.

At the same time, the limitation to the 2016 Presidential election in the bill presents a good balance and encourages Secret Service to fix its current staffing problems instead of relying on excessive and expensive overtime pay in the future.

It is my expectation that the Secret Service meets its staffing goals by the next election cycle and does not have to rely on scheduling excessive overtime. It is also my expectation that the Secret Service will focus its staffing capital away from its increasing nonessential investigative and cyber-related missions which distract from the core mission of protecting the President and other protectees.

There are currently three ongoing studies analyzing the Secret Service's nonessential mission of cyber investigations. By the way, this nonprotective mission usually takes more than half of their time, but certainly during a Presidential election cycle, you can see the demand that was there.

I am very pleased with the bipartisan nature in which the committee came together to make sure that we are supporting the men and women who serve in the Secret Service. They have done so in a very admirable fashion. They have provided a great service to the Nation. But when you hear stories where people would go 43 days without a single day off, when they would work, literally, 100-plus hours in a week and they would go to work knowing that they weren't going to be compensated for that work, that is inexcusable. This bill would provide relief to them. Again, it is not a bonus; it is not extra pay; but it is some compensation for the work that they did protecting our Nation and protecting those protectees. By all accounts, they did an exceptional job without any major incident in this 2016 election cycle.

I urge the passage of this bill. Again, I appreciate the bipartisan nature in which we are doing this.

Mr. Speaker, I reserve the balance of my time.

Mr. LYNCH. Mr. Speaker, I yield myself such time as I may consume.

Mr. Speaker, I rise in support of H.R. 6302, the Overtime Pay for Secret Service Agents Act of 2016, which was approved by our committee unanimously by a voice vote. This legislation would authorize an increase in the current pay cap up to Level II of the Executive Schedule so that Secret Service agents are permitted to receive compensation for the hours of overtime they worked in 2016.

As the chairman has indicated, the Presidential campaign of 2016 has been a year of extraordinary challenges and strain on the Secret Service. The Secret Service has provided information to the committee indicating that more than 1,000 Secret Service agents—one-third of the agents on board—have worked so many hours that they maxed

out their annual overtime and salary. Some agents started working overtime for free as of early June and are exceeding the pay cap by as many as $50,000 to $60,000 per agent. Current law prohibits them from receiving any additional overtime pay, and that is what this bill is intended to fix for calendar year 2016.

These spikes in overtime are a necessary factor in these election campaigns. As we know, there were 16 Republican candidates in the primary, and all received Secret Service protection, as well as several candidates on the Democratic side. There were countless stops across the country over the months of our campaigns, and I don't think there is any way to avoid the need for overtime.

I am glad that this is a bipartisan bill, but every 4 years we have to have agents working without pay. There has got to be a way that we can estimate roughly what the overtime needs will be every 4 years and incorporate something that at least eliminates the need to have Secret Service agents working for free in a very dangerous job. I think we can figure that out.

I had a proposal in committee to make this an every-4-year thing and incorporate that. It did not succeed. But I am hoping that, in a bipartisan manner with the chairman and my Republican colleagues on the committee, we can solve this.

Mr. Speaker, I yield back the balance of my time.

The SPEAKER pro tempore. Without objection, the gentleman from Arizona will control the remainder of the time.

There was no objection.

Mr. GOSAR. Mr. Speaker, I urge adoption of the bill.

I yield back the balance of my time.

Mr. CUMMINGS. Mr. Speaker, I support H.R. 6302, the Overtime Pay for Secret Service Agents Act of 2016. The bill would authorize an increase in the annual salary and overtime limit up to level II of the Executive Schedule so that Secret Service agents would be eligible to receive additional back pay for the considerable hours of overtime they worked in 2016.

Last year, the Committee adopted a bipartisan report concluding that the Secret Service, and I quote, "is experiencing a staffing crisis that threatens to jeopardize its critical mission" due in large part to "significant cuts imposed by the Budget Control Act of 2011." The unanimous report recommended that Congress, quote, "ensure that Secret Service has sufficient funds to restore staffing to required levels." Providing this much-needed relief in the highly demanding 2016 presidential campaign year is a first and essential step towards fulfilling the Committee's recommendation.

I appreciate the efforts that Chairman CHAFFETZ and his staff have made to address this issue, and I believe we are in agreement that we must pay the dedicated men and women of the Secret Service for the overtime they worked in 2016. However, addressing

just this one year retroactively does not go far enough.

The Federal Law Enforcement Officers Association, which represents rank-and-file Secret Service agents, testified before our Committee that there should be a legislative fix to raise the overtime pay cap, and I quote, "at a minimum, during a presidential campaign year." The witness added that although, quote, "this last election season was unprecedented in many respects, we do not believe it will prove to be unique in the years ahead," and he stressed, quote, "the importance of working together to find a permanent solution to the effect that the pay cap has on the USSS."

The demands on Secret Service agents are likely to remain extremely high with the substantial resources needed to provide around-the-clock protective details for all 18 Trump family members—including the First Lady, five children and three of their spouses, and eight grandchildren. The announced plan to split time between the White House and the Trump tower in Manhattan would also add significant challenges and strain the resources of the Secret Service.

That is why all Committee Democrats joined together to introduce H.R. 6318, the Fair Pay for Presidential Protection Act of 2016, to ensure that Secret Service agents are paid not just for the overtime they worked in 2016, but also for the overtime they will work in all future presidential years. Our legislation would also authorize a greater level of overtime compensation than H.R. 6302.

I would also note that the Republican Leadership recently decided to change course and use a continuing resolution to fund the government at last year's spending levels through next March. Passing only this stopgap measure would mean Secret Service agents would not see an additional penny unless Congress includes additional funds in this spending bill. Otherwise, Secret Service agents may have to wait at least another four months without any additional compensation for their work in 2016.

I urge my colleagues to support this bill, but I also hope the Committee will revisit this overtime pay issue next year so that the Secret Service will have a legislative solution in time for the 2020 election season.

Ms. JACKSON LEE. Mr. Speaker, I rise in support of H.R. 6302, "The Overtime Pay For Secret Service Agents Act".

This important legislation will provide an increase in premium pay for United States Secret Service agents performing protective services.

H.R. 6302 will raise the cap on overtime compensation for U.S. Secret Service agents tasked with the responsibility of protecting the president, vice president and major presidential and vice presidential candidates during campaigns.

Under current law, an executive branch employee's premium pay, including overtime combined with basic pay cannot exceed the maximum rate of basic pay for a GS–15 or Level V executive schedule, whichever is greater.

The maximum rate for a GS–15 employee in the Washington, D.C., area is set at $160,300 in 2016, while the pay rate for Level V is set at $150,200 adjusted for the current cost of living.

H.R. 6302 will increase the pay rate cap by nearly $35,000.

The H.R. 6302 will also apply to agents responsible for protecting candidates' spouses, former presidents, their spouses and children, high profile foreign visitors, as well as other government officials.

More than 1,000 agents have exceeded the overtime pay limit this year and can greatly benefit from the prospective adjustments.

Some by as much as $60,000, according to the Federal Law Enforcement Officers Association.

For these reasons I support H.R. 6302.

The SPEAKER pro tempore. The question is on the motion offered by the gentleman from Utah (Mr. CHAFFETZ) that the House suspend the rules and pass the bill, H.R. 6302.

The question was taken; and (two-thirds being in the affirmative) the rules were suspended and the bill was passed.

A motion to reconsider was laid on the table.

POST OFFICE DESIGNATIONS AND ESTABLISHING NEW ZIP CODES

Mr. GOSAR. Mr. Speaker, I move to suspend the rules and pass the bill (H.R. 6303) to designate facilities of the United States Postal Service, to establish new ZIP Codes, and for other purposes.

The Clerk read the title of the bill.

The text of the bill is as follows:

H.R. 6303

Be it enacted by the Senate and House of Representatives of the United States of America in Congress assembled,

SECTION 1. POST OFFICE DESIGNATIONS.

(a) SPECIAL WARFARE OPERATOR MASTER CHIEF PETTY OFFICER (SEAL) LOUIS "LOU" J. LANGLAIS POST OFFICE BUILDING.—

(1) DESIGNATION.—The facility of the United States Postal Service located at 1221 State Street, Suite 12, Santa Barbara, California, shall be known and designated as the "Special Warfare Operator Master Chief Petty Officer (SEAL) Louis 'Lou' J. Langlais Post Office Building".

(2) REFERENCES.—Any reference in a law, map, regulation, document, paper, or other record of the United States to the facility referred to in paragraph (1) shall be deemed to be a reference to the "Special Warfare Operator Master Chief Petty Officer (SEAL) Louis 'Lou' J. Langlais Post Office Building".

(b) RICHARD ALLEN CABLE POST OFFICE.—

(1) DESIGNATION.—The facility of the United States Postal Service located at 23323 Shelby Road in Shelby, Indiana, shall be known and designated as the "Richard Allen Cable Post Office".

(2) REFERENCES.—Any reference in a law, map, regulation, document, paper, or other record of the United States to the facility referred to in paragraph (1) shall be deemed to be a reference to the "Richard Allen Cable Post Office".

(c) LEONARD MONTALTO POST OFFICE BUILDING.—

(1) DESIGNATION.—The facility of the United States Postal Service located at 3031 Veterans Road West in Staten Island, New York, shall be known and designated as the "Leonard Montalto Post Office Building".

(2) REFERENCES.—Any reference in a law, map, regulation, document, paper, or other record of the United States to the facility referred to in paragraph (1) shall be deemed to be a reference to the "Leonard Montalto Post Office Building".

(d) ARMY FIRST LIEUTENANT DONALD C. CARWILE POST OFFICE BUILDING.—

(1) DESIGNATION.—The facility of the United States Postal Service located at 401 McElroy Drive in Oxford, Mississippi, shall be known and designated as the "Army First Lieutenant Donald C. Carwile Post Office Building".

(2) REFERENCES.—Any reference in a law, map, regulation, document, paper, or other record of the United States to the facility referred to in paragraph (1) shall be deemed to be a reference to the "Army First Lieutenant Donald C. Carwile Post Office Building".

(e) E. MARIE YOUNGBLOOD POST OFFICE.—

(1) DESIGNATION.—The facility of the United States Postal Service located at 14231 TX–150 in Coldspring, Texas, shall be known and designated as the "E. Marie Youngblood Post Office".

(2) REFERENCES.—Any reference in a law, map, regulation, document, paper, or other record of the United States to the facility referred to in paragraph (1) shall be deemed to be a reference to the "E. Marie Youngblood Post Office".

(f) ZAPATA VETERANS POST OFFICE.—

(1) DESIGNATION.—The facility of the United States Postal Service located at 810 N. U.S. Highway 83 in Zapata, Texas, shall be known and designated as the "Zapata Veterans Post Office".

(2) REFERENCES.—Any reference in a law, map, regulation, document, paper, or other record of the United States to the facility referred to in paragraph (1) shall be deemed to be a reference to the "Zapata Veterans Post Office".

(g) MARINE LANCE CORPORAL SQUIRE "SKIP" WELLS POST OFFICE BUILDING.—

(1) DESIGNATION.—The facility of the United States Postal Service located at 2886 Sandy Plains Road in Marietta, Georgia, shall be known and designated as the "Marine Lance Corporal Squire 'Skip' Wells Post Office Building".

(2) REFERENCES.—Any reference in a law, map, regulation, document, paper, or other record of the United States to the facility referred to in paragraph (1) shall be deemed to be a reference to the "Marine Lance Corporal Squire 'Skip' Wells Post Office Building".

(h) OFFICER JOSEPH P. CALI POST OFFICE BUILDING.—

(1) DESIGNATION.—The facility of the United States Postal Service located at 6300 N. Northwest Highway in Chicago, Illinois, shall be known and designated as the "Officer Joseph P. Cali Post Office Building".

(2) REFERENCES.—Any reference in a law, map, regulation, document, paper, or other record of the United States to the facility referred to in paragraph (1) shall be deemed to be a reference to the "Officer Joseph P. Cali Post Office Building".

(i) SEGUNDO T. SABLAN AND CNMI FALLEN MILITARY HEROES POST OFFICE BUILDING.—

(1) DESIGNATION.—The facility of the United States Postal Service located at 1 Chalan Kanoa VLG in Saipan, Northern Mariana Islands, shall be known and designated as the "Segundo T. Sablan and CNMI Fallen Military Heroes Post Office Building".

(2) REFERENCES.—Any reference in a law, map, regulation, document, paper, or other record of the United States to the facility referred to in paragraph (1) shall be deemed to be a reference to the "Segundo T. Sablan and CNMI Fallen Military Heroes Post Office Building".

(j) ABNER J. MIKVA POST OFFICE BUILDING.—

(1) DESIGNATION.—The facility of the United States Postal Service located at 1101 Davis Street in Evanston, Illinois, shall be known and designated as the "Abner J. Mikva Post Office Building".

(2) REFERENCES.—Any reference in a law, map, regulation, document, paper, or other record of the United States to the facility referred to in paragraph (1) shall be deemed to be a reference to the "Abner J. Mikva Post Office Building".

SEC. 2. ESTABLISHING NEW ZIP CODES.

Not later than September 30, 2017, the United States Postal Service shall designate a single, unique ZIP code for, as nearly as practicable, each of the following communities:

(1) Miami Lakes, Florida.

(2) Storey County, Nevada.

(3) Flanders, Northampton, and Riverside in the Town of Southampton, New York.

(4) Ocoee, Florida.

(5) Glendale, New York.

The SPEAKER pro tempore. Pursuant to the rule, the gentleman from Arizona (Mr. GOSAR) and the gentleman from Massachusetts (Mr. LYNCH) each will control 20 minutes.

The Chair recognizes the gentleman from Arizona.

GENERAL LEAVE

Mr. GOSAR. Mr. Speaker, I ask unanimous consent that all Members may have 5 legislative days in which to revise and extend their remarks and to include extraneous material on the bill under consideration.

The SPEAKER pro tempore. Is there objection to the request of the gentleman from Arizona?

There was no objection.

Mr. GOSAR. Mr. Speaker, I yield myself such time as I may consume.

Mr. Speaker, I rise today in support of H.R. 6303, introduced by Chairman JASON CHAFFETZ. This straightforward legislation would consolidate 10 postal naming bills and solve important local issues by designating five new ZIP Codes.

The 10 postal naming bills have all been passed by the House already this Congress. The five ZIP Codes designated by the bill will address significant issues faced by those five communities. In each case, the ZIP Code designation is driven by local leaders and strongly supported by the relevant Member of Congress. Local communities are not asking for new postal buildings, and no new construction will be required to accommodate the changes.

In the case of Southampton, New York, Chairman CHAFFETZ personally met with individuals and businesses impacted by delivery problems that could be solved with the addition of a new ZIP Code. I look forward to hearing more about the specifics of that situation from Representative LEE ZELDIN of New York, who is here today.

In another example, the community of Ocoee, Florida, faces a lack of identity due to the six different ZIP Codes serving its citizens. Additionally, some Ocoee residents are forced to pay non-resident rates or are flatly denied services because they are not identified by the correct ZIP Code.

These concerns aren't just limited to mail delivery. Communities without a unique ZIP Code are at higher risk for extended response times when calling 911 due to confusion and similar street names. ZIP Codes are also used to determine the appropriate distribution of tax revenue and insurance funds to local communities. Without the proper ZIP Code designations, some local communities may not receive their fair cut of local tax revenues.

In many situations, local leaders within the new ZIP Code designations have exhausted all options to obtain the requested changes. Some of these communities, such as Ocoee and Miami Lakes, have even offered to pay the Postal Service for the cost of new ZIP Codes but have been rebuffed. This legislation is the last path forward for these communities.

I urge my colleagues to support H.R. 6303.

Mr. Speaker, I reserve the balance of my time.

Mr. LYNCH. Mr. Speaker, I yield myself such time as I may consume.

Mr. Speaker, ZIP Codes are used to organize our country to ensure the effective and efficient delivery of the mail to millions of Americans. The Postal Service has the authority to establish ZIP Codes and to adjust their boundaries based on changes in delivery and volume or operational concerns. However, communities, businesses, and other local entities can also voice their concerns about ZIP Code boundaries and petition for corresponding adjustments.

H.R. 6303 would make such adjustments by requiring the Postal Service to establish new ZIP Codes for five communities that have each requested, and subsequently been denied, ZIP Code changes. These communities have based their ZIP Code requests on delays in mail delivery and emergency service response times, the denial or inconsistent application of services to their communities, and other similar community concerns.

□ 1545

These are important issues and they should be addressed accordingly. The Postal Service has worked with affected communities to find solutions, and I commend those efforts by the Postal Service.

The Oversight and Government Reform Committee has also worked to find solutions to these concerns in its proposed postal reform legislation, and, in fact, most of these would receive unique ZIP Codes as part of that bill. That is why I support H.R. 6303 today.

Finally, I want to highlight my strong support for the language in this bill before us today that would name ten post offices after honorable men and women, all of whom made important contributions to our Nation. Individual legislation allowing for the naming of those postal facilities has already passed the House and is simply awaiting action in the Senate.

Mr. Speaker, I urge my colleagues to support this bill.

I reserve the balance of my time.

Mr. GOSAR. Mr. Speaker, I yield 2 minutes to the gentleman from New York (Mr. ZELDIN).

Mr. ZELDIN. Mr. Speaker, I rise in support of H.R. 6303, which would create a new, unique ZIP Code for the hamlets of Flanders, Riverside, and Northampton in my district.

These three hamlets currently share the same ZIP Code with the nearby town of Riverhead, and there are at least 18 identical street names and 32 similar street names. This causes a number of issues, including delay of mail and packages, which can hold important goods like medications. Shared street names can also delay the response time of emergency and medical personnel in situations where every second counts.

This could all be avoided by assigning a new and unique ZIP Code to Flanders, Northampton, and Riverside, which is why I have been working closely with Chairman CHAFFETZ, even bringing him to Long Island to speak with those impacted in the community firsthand. I thank Chairman CHAFFETZ for his exceptional help with this issue.

For many years, residents, local elected officials, and community organizations have been aware of this issue and the problems it brings. But despite their previous efforts, the issue still serves to be a burden for those in this area of the First Congressional District of New York.

I would also like to thank Ron Fisher, chairman of the Flanders/Riverside/Northampton Citizen Advisory Council and president of the Flanders, Riverside and Northampton Community Association, and all the members of these organizations for continuing this effort over the years. This has been a priority for them for many years, and it is an honor to be their voice in the House.

I know this legislation also includes a new ZIP Code for the area, including Glendale. I have spoken with my colleague, Ms. MENG, who has been a tireless advocate on behalf of those residents in Glendale. I am real thrilled to see that that is included as well.

I thank Mr. GOSAR for his support and his efforts. To the entire staff of the Oversight and Government Reform Committee, Chairman CHAFFETZ is fortunate to have an amazing team working with him.

Mr. LYNCH. Mr. Speaker, I yield such time as she may consume to the gentlewoman from New York (Ms. MENG), one of the other champions of this legislation.

Ms. MENG. Mr. Speaker, I thank my friend, Mr. LYNCH, for yielding.

Mr. Speaker, I rise in support of H.R. 6303, which includes a section to establish a new ZIP Code for the community of Glendale, New York. This section is identical to legislation I introduced last February, H.R. 657.

I thank Oversight and Government Reform Chairman CHAFFETZ for authoring this legislation, and I thank Ranking Member CUMMINGS for his support.

For almost 30 years, the residents of Glendale, New York, have sought to obtain a unique ZIP Code for their community in Queens. They have experienced mail and service-related problems due to sharing a ZIP Code with the neighboring community of Ridgewood. These problems include medications that were spoiled or not received due to mail processing errors, delays in first responder services to residents in need of care, and inaccuracies with GPS devices.

Roughly one-quarter of Glendale's population is eligible to receive Medicare, or will become eligible in the next decade. Many use a mail-order pharmacy to receive their prescription drugs, and many more will use such services in the years to come. A single, unique ZIP Code for Glendale will ensure that mail delivery will be improved in the future.

Creating a new ZIP Code for Glendale has been an ongoing and bipartisan challenge for Members of Congress who previously represented the area. I commend them for their efforts on behalf of the community, especially my predecessor, Representative Bob Turner.

When I took office in the 113th Congress, the only recourse left to address this matter was through legislation. I am grateful to Chairman CHAFFETZ for including Glendale in this legislation. It has been a long fight for the community of Glendale to receive its own ZIP Code.

Mr. Speaker, before I close, I would like to thank the local elected officials, civic associations, and community activists who have voiced their support for this issue over the years. In particular, I would like to thank Queens Borough President Melinda Katz, New York State Senator Joseph Addabbo, New York State Assemblymen Michael Miller and Andrew Hevesi, and New York City Councilwoman Elizabeth Crowley. I would also like to thank Dori Figliola, the Glendale Property Owners Association, Glendale Civic Association, and Citizens for a Better Ridgewood for their advocacy.

Mr. Speaker, I thank you for allowing this legislation to the floor for a vote today, and I urge all of my colleagues to support this important measure.

Mr. LYNCH. Mr. Speaker, having no further speakers, I yield back the balance of my time.

Mr. GOSAR. Mr. Speaker, I yield 2 minutes to the gentleman from Nevada (Mr. AMODEI).

Mr. AMODEI. Mr. Speaker, I thank my colleague from Arizona and the ranking member. I appreciate the fact that the committee has taken this issue.

As the person who represents the only district west of the Mississippi that was fortunate enough to be considered as deserving in this, I just want to make a couple of points. From the earlier talks too, it is like none of these ZIP Codes were ones where people just said: hey, let's go, OGR folks, and create a new one. Without exception, everybody went to the Postal Service and said: here is our stuff. And while the people in my State were good about it, what we got from the folks back here was basically: we kind of don't do that, and if you ask and if you are turned down, you can't ask again for X number of years. It is almost an implied threat for requesting one.

So I can't thank the committee enough for taking a look into the issue. This particular one is actually the largest industrial park in the Nation—the marketing people tell me, so I will assume they are right—and it helps in another area, which is the State tax department that collects sales taxes. When you are building something, there are a lot of sales taxes based on ZIP Codes. So this will make sure that those sales tax dollars are generated and credited to where those materials are actually going.

And I want to also note for the RECORD before I yield back that what you have here, apparently, is the three greatest States in the Nation—New York, Florida, and Nevada—and so the other 47, keep trying.

Mr. GOSAR. Mr. Speaker, I yield 2 minutes to the gentleman from Florida (Mr. DIAZ-BALART).

Mr. DIAZ-BALART. Mr. Speaker, let me first thank the gentleman from Arizona for the time. And I also need to, in particular, thank Chairman CHAFFETZ for introducing this, I think, very important piece of legislation.

We have heard what the issue is. Look, for years now the city of Miami Lakes, which I am privileged to represent, has attempted to receive a unique ZIP Code for all the same reasons that you have already heard. This would help with auto insurance rates, with branding and economic development, and, frankly, would lead to less election and census confusion, Mr. Speaker. So it is a no-brainer.

But, unfortunately, the Postal Service has continued, and continues, to stonewall the city, despite absolutely no opposition from either anyone in Miami Lakes or, frankly, the areas around it. I have had meetings with the mayors from the areas around it, and everybody supports it. This legislation solves the problem and grants Miami Lakes its own ZIP Code.

I really need to, by the way, give credit to then-Vice Mayor, now Mayor-elect of Miami Lakes, Manny Cid. He has made this a priority. He was told "no" time and time again, refused to accept that as an answer, and came to us. It has been a privilege to work with him. Because of his hard work, together, we were able to get the committee, with the chairman and the ranking member and all of the rest of the members of this committee, to get this done through the House.

Again, I want to thank Congressman CHAFFETZ. I want to thank the committee staff. His staff has been great to work with.

Mr. Speaker, I urge the passage of this legislation.

Mr. GOSAR. Mr. Speaker, I urge the adoption of the bill.

I yield back the balance of my time.

The SPEAKER pro tempore. The question is on the motion offered by the gentleman from Arizona (Mr. GOSAR) that the House suspend the rules and pass the bill, H.R. 6303.

The question was taken; and (two-thirds being in the affirmative) the rules were suspended and the bill was passed.

A motion to reconsider was laid on the table.

FEDERAL REGISTER PRINTING SAVINGS ACT OF 2016

Mr. GOSAR. Mr. Speaker, I move to suspend the rules and pass the bill (H.R. 5384) to amend title 44, United States Code, to restrict the distribution of free printed copies of the Federal Register to Members of Congress and other officers and employees of the United States, and for other purposes.

The Clerk read the title of the bill.

The text of the bill is as follows:

H.R. 5384

Be it enacted by the Senate and House of Representatives of the United States of America in Congress assembled,

SECTION 1. SHORT TITLE.

This Act may be cited as the "Federal Register Printing Savings Act of 2016".

SEC. 2. RESTRICTIONS ON DISTRIBUTION OF FREE PRINTED COPIES OF FEDERAL REGISTER TO MEMBERS OF CONGRESS AND FEDERAL EMPLOYEES.

(a) RESTRICTIONS.—Section 1506 of title 44, United States Code, is amended—

(1) by striking "The Administrative Committee" and inserting "(a) COMPOSITION; DUTIES.—The Administrative Committee";

(2) in subsection (a)(4), by striking "the number of copies" and inserting "subject to subsection (b), the number of copies"; and

(3) by adding at the end the following new subsection:

"(b) RESTRICTIONS ON DISTRIBUTION OF FREE PRINTED COPIES TO MEMBERS OF CONGRESS AND OFFICERS AND EMPLOYEES OF THE UNITED STATES.—

"(1) PROHIBITING SUBSCRIPTION TO PRINTED COPIES WITHOUT REQUEST.—Under the regulations prescribed to carry out subsection (a)(4), the Director of the Government Publishing Office may not provide a printed copy of the Federal Register without charge to any Member of Congress or any other office of the United States during a year unless—

"(A) the Member or office requests a printed copy of a specific issue of the Federal Register; or

"(B) during that year or during the previous year, the Member or office requested a subscription to printed copies of the Federal Register for that year, as described in paragraph (2).

"(2) ADMINISTRATION OF SUBSCRIPTIONS.—The regulations prescribed to carry out subsection (a)(4) shall include—

"(A) provisions regarding notifications to offices of Members of Congress and other offices of the United States of the restrictions of paragraph (1);

"(B) provisions describing the process by which Members and other offices may request a specific issue of the Federal Register for purposes of paragraph (1)(A); and

"(C) provisions describing the process by which Members and other offices may request a subscription to the Federal Register for purposes of paragraph (1)(B), except that such regulations shall limit the period for such a subscription to not longer than one year.".

(b) EFFECTIVE DATE.—The amendment made by subsection (a) shall take effect January 1, 2017.

The SPEAKER pro tempore. Pursuant to the rule, the gentleman from Arizona (Mr. GOSAR) and the gentleman from Massachusetts (Mr. LYNCH) each will control 20 minutes.

The Chair recognizes the gentleman from Arizona.

GENERAL LEAVE

Mr. GOSAR. Mr. Speaker, I ask unanimous consent that all Members may have 5 legislative days in which to revise and extend their remarks and include extraneous material on the bill under consideration.

The SPEAKER pro tempore. Is there objection to the request of the gentleman from Arizona?

There was no objection.

Mr. GOSAR. Mr. Speaker, I yield myself such time as I may consume.

I rise today in support of H.R. 5384, the Federal Register Printing Savings Act of 2016, introduced by my colleague on the Oversight and Government Reform Committee, the gentleman from Oklahoma (Mr. RUSSELL).

This commonsense legislation will help curb government waste.

The Federal Register is aptly described as the official newspaper of the Federal Government. Its daily editions include copies of proposed and final regulations, requests for comment, executive orders, and information concerning other government activities.

Today, virtually every Member of Congress, the White House, and many Federal agencies receive printed copies of the Federal Register. It is important to note that Members of Congress do not proactively request, or pay for this service. However, for the public, an annual subscription costs $929 annually.

In the days before the Internet, this paper-based service brought great value to Members, agencies, and the White House, allowing them to keep track of activity across the government. Today, though, the full Federal Register is available online in a completely searchable and downloadable format. As a result, offices on Capitol Hill and across the government throw away the paper version every morning, often unopened, resulting in hundreds of thousands of dollars of waste.

This legislation, H.R. 5384, would change this dynamic by banning automatic subscriptions to the Federal Register by the Federal Government. Instead, Members of Congress and offices across the Federal Government who still want to receive printed copies would be required to request individual copies, or an annual subscription.

This is a simple, good government piece of legislation that will save the American taxpayer potentially hundreds of thousands of dollars every year.

I urge my colleagues to support this legislation.

I reserve the balance of my time.

HOUSE OF REPRESENTATIVES, COMMITTEE ON OVERSIGHT AND GOVERNMENT REFORM,
Washington, DC, November 29, 2016.
Hon. CANDICE S. MILLER,
Chairman, Committee on House Administration, Washington, DC.

DEAR MADAM CHAIRMAN: On November 16, 2016, the Committee on Oversight and Government Reform ordered reported without amendment H.R. 5384, the Federal Register Printing Savings Act of 2016. The bill was referred primarily to the Committee on Oversight and Government Reform, with an additional referral to the Committee on House Administration.

I ask that you allow the Committee on House Administration to be discharged from further consideration of the bill so that it may be scheduled by the Majority Leader. This discharge in no way affects your jurisdiction over the subject matter of the bill, and it will not serve as precedent for future referrals. In addition, should a conference on the bill be necessary, I would support your request to have the Committee on House Administration represented on the conference committee. Finally, I would be pleased to include this letter and any response in the bill report filed by the Committee on Oversight and Government Reform, as well as in the Congressional Record during floor consideration, to memorialize our understanding.

Thank you for your consideration of my request.

Sincerely,
JASON CHAFFETZ,
Chairman.

HOUSE OF REPRESENTATIVES, COMMITTEE ON HOUSE ADMINISTRATION,
Washington, DC, November 29, 2016.
Hon. JASON CHAFFETZ,
Chairman, Committee on Oversight and Government Reform, Washington, DC.

DEAR MR. CHAIRMAN: Thank you for your letter regarding H.R. 5384. As you know, the bill was received in the House of Representatives on June 3, 2016, and referred primarily to the Committee on Oversight and Government Reform and in addition to the Committee on the Committee on House Administration. The bill seeks to restrict the distribution of free printed copies of the Federal Register to Members of Congress and

other officers and employees of the United States. On November 16, 2016 your Committee ordered H.R. 5384 to be reported without amendment.

I realize that discharging the Committee on House Administration from further consideration of H.R. 5384 will serve in the best interest of the House of Representatives and agree to do so. It is the understanding of the Committee on House Administration that forgoing action on H.R. 5384 will not prejudice the Committee with respect to appointment of conferees or any future jurisdictional claim. I request that your letter and this response be included in the bill report filed by your Committee, as well as in the Congressional Record.

Sincerely,
CANDICE S. MILLER,
Chairman.

Mr. LYNCH. Mr. Speaker, I yield myself such time as I may consume.

Mr. Speaker, I rise in support of H.R. 5384, the Federal Register Printing Savings Act of 2016. I agree with the gentleman from Arizona (Mr. GOSAR) that this is a commonsense, good government bill about cutting waste.

This bill would allow the Government Publishing Office to avoid sending printed copies of the Federal Register to Members of Congress and other Federal offices, unless those offices actually want the printed copies. Of course, the Federal Register would continue to be available online.

This bill would be good for the environment and good for taxpayers. The Congressional Budget Office estimates that this bill would save about $1 million a year.

I urge my colleagues to support H.R. 5384.

I yield back the balance of my time.

Mr. GOSAR. Mr. Speaker, I urge the adoption of the bill.

I yield back the balance of my time.

The SPEAKER pro tempore. The question is on the motion offered by the gentleman from Arizona (Mr. GOSAR) that the House suspend the rules and pass the bill, H.R. 5384.

The question was taken; and (two-thirds being in the affirmative) the rules were suspended and the bill was passed.

A motion to reconsider was laid on the table.

☐ 1600

FEDERAL AGENCY MAIL MANAGEMENT ACT OF 2016

Mr. GOSAR. Mr. Speaker, I move to suspend the rules and pass the bill (H.R. 6009) to ensure the effective processing of mail by Federal agencies, and for other purposes.

The Clerk read the title of the bill.

The text of the bill is as follows:

H.R. 6009

Be it enacted by the Senate and House of Representatives of the United States of America in Congress assembled,

SECTION 1. SHORT TITLE.

This Act may be cited as the "Federal Agency Mail Management Act of 2016".

SEC. 2. RECORD MANAGEMENT.

(a) AMENDMENTS.—Section 9 of the Presidential and Federal Records Act Amendments of 2014 (44 U.S.C. 101 note) is amended—

(1) in subsection (a), by amending paragraph (3) to read as follows:

"(3) in paragraph (7), by striking 'the Administrator or the Archivist' and inserting 'the Archivist or the Administrator'.";

(2) in subsection (c)—

(A) by amending paragraph (1) to read as follows:

"(1) by amending subsection (a) to read as follows:

" '(a) The Archivist shall provide guidance and assistance to Federal agencies with respect to ensuring—

" '(1) economical and effective records management;

" '(2) adequate and proper documentation of the policies and transactions of the Federal Government; and

" '(3) proper records disposition.';

(B) by redesignating paragraphs (2) and (3) as paragraphs (3) and (4), respectively;

(C) by inserting after paragraph (1), the following new paragraph:

"(2) in subsection (b), by striking 'effective records management by such agencies' and inserting 'effective processing of mail by Federal agencies';";

(D) in paragraph (3), as so redesignated—

(i) in subparagraph (A)(ii), by striking " 'subsections (a) and (b)' " and inserting " 'subsection (a)' "; and

(ii) in subparagraph (B), by striking "; and" and inserting a semicolon;

(E) in paragraph (4), as so redesignated, by striking the period at the end and inserting "; and"; and

(F) by inserting at the end the following new paragraph:

"(5) by inserting at the end the following new subsection:

" '(e) The Administrator, in carrying out subsection (b), shall have the responsibility to promote economy and efficiency in the selection and utilization of space, staff, equipment, and supplies for processing mail at Federal facilities.'.

(3) in subsection (d)—

(A) in paragraph (1), by striking "; and" at the end and inserting a semicolon;

(B) in paragraph (2), by striking the period at the end and inserting "; and"; and

(C) by inserting at the end the following new paragraph:

"(3) by inserting at the end the following new subsection:

" '(c) The Administrator (or the Administrator's designee) may inspect the mail processing practices and programs of any Federal agency for the purpose of rendering recommendations for the improvement of mail processing practices and programs. Officers and employees of such agencies shall cooperate fully in such inspections of mail processing practices and programs.'.

(4) by striking subsection (f); and

(5) by redesignating subsection (g) as subsection (f).

(b) EFFECTIVE DATE.—The amendments made by this section shall take effect as if included in the Presidential and Federal Records Act Amendments of 2014 (Public Law 113–187).

The SPEAKER pro tempore. Pursuant to the rule, the gentleman from Arizona (Mr. GOSAR) and the gentleman from Massachusetts (Mr. LYNCH) each will control 20 minutes.

The Chair recognizes the gentleman from Arizona.

Mr. GOSAR. Mr. Speaker, I ask unanimous consent that all Members may have 5 legislative days in which to revise and extend their remarks and to include extraneous material on the bill under consideration.

The SPEAKER pro tempore. Is there objection to the request of the gentleman from Arizona?

There was no objection.

Mr. GOSAR. Mr. Speaker, I yield myself such time as I may consume.

I rise in support of H.R. 6009, the Federal Agency Mail Management Act of 2016, introduced by my colleague on the Oversight and Government Reform Committee, Representative STEVE RUSSELL of Oklahoma.

This legislation is intended to make a bipartisan technical correction to the Presidential and Federal Records Act Amendments of 2014, enacted as Public Law 113–187.

Among the provisions of that bipartisan law was language designed to eliminate outdated references to the General Services Administration, or GSA, relating to records management. These changes updated outdated references from a time period when the National Archives was a part of the GSA. Since the National Archives became independent in 1984, these housekeeping changes were long overdue. However, after the bill was enacted, the GSA and the Archives realized that the GSA had relied upon the now altered provisions for its oversight and management authority for Federal agency mail processing and management, which is a function that had not previously been transferred to the Archives. It was never the intent of the Congress to transfer this function.

The Archives and the GSA have been working closely together to ensure the law is being appropriately followed, but both agencies support clarification that this responsibility is properly the GSA's. This legislation provides that exact clarification. Specifically, the bill makes technical corrections to the 2014 law to carve out the responsibility for mailroom management from records management to ensure that the former is properly the GSA's duty and that the latter is the Archives'.

I believe this is a commonsense, good-government bill, and I am pleased to see that my colleague Representative GERALD CONNOLLY is a cosponsor. I urge my colleagues to support this bill, and I hope it will move quickly through the legislative process so that we can properly resolve any lingering uncertainty that has been created regarding Federal mail management.

I reserve the balance of my time.

Mr. LYNCH. Mr. Speaker, I yield myself such time as I may consume.

I support this bipartisan bill, which simply makes a technical correction to clarify that the Administrator of the General Services Administration is responsible for managing mail in the executive branch.

The Administrator of the GSA has historically had this responsibility. When the Federal Records Act was updated in 2014, changes made to the statute made it unclear whether the Administrator's role had changed. This bill makes clear that Congress never intended to take away the GSA Administrator's authority to manage the executive mail.

In closing, I would like to especially thank Representative STEVE RUSSELL from Oklahoma and Representative GERRY CONNOLLY from Virginia for their excellent work that they put into this legislation, and I hope that the Senate will take it up before the end of this Congress.

I yield back the balance of my time.

Mr. GOSAR. Mr. Speaker, I urge the adoption of the bill.

I yield back the balance of my time.

The SPEAKER pro tempore (Mr. SIMPSON). The question is on the motion offered by the gentleman from Arizona (Mr. GOSAR) that the House suspend the rules and pass the bill, H.R. 6009.

The question was taken; and (two-thirds being in the affirmative) the rules were suspended and the bill was passed.

A motion to reconsider was laid on the table.

FOLLOW THE RULES ACT

Mr. GOSAR. Mr. Speaker, I move to suspend the rules and pass the bill (H.R. 6186) to amend title 5, United States Code, to extend certain protections against prohibited personnel practices, and for other purposes.

The Clerk read the title of the bill.

The text of the bill is as follows:

H.R. 6186

Be it enacted by the Senate and House of Representatives of the United States of America in Congress assembled,

SECTION 1. SHORT TITLE.

This Act may be cited as the "Follow the Rules Act".

SEC. 2. PROHIBITED PERSONNEL ACTION BASED ON ORDERING INDIVIDUAL TO VIOLATE RULE OR REGULATION.

(a) IN GENERAL.—Subparagraph (D) of section 2302(b)(9) of title 5, United States Code, is amended by inserting ", rule, or regulation" after "law".

(b) TECHNICAL CORRECTION.—Such subparagraph is further amended by striking "for".

(c) APPLICATION.—The amendment made by subsection (a) shall apply to any personnel action (as that term is defined in section 2302(a)(2)(A) of such title) occurring after the date of enactment of this Act.

The SPEAKER pro tempore. Pursuant to the rule, the gentleman from Arizona (Mr. GOSAR) and the gentleman from Massachusetts (Mr. LYNCH) each will control 20 minutes.

The Chair recognizes the gentleman from Arizona.

Mr. GOSAR. Mr. Speaker, I ask unanimous consent that all Members may have 5 legislative days in which to revise and extend their remarks and to include extraneous material on the bill under consideration.

The SPEAKER pro tempore. Is there objection to the request of the gentleman from Arizona?

There was no objection.

Mr. GOSAR. Mr. Speaker, I yield myself such time as I may consume.

I rise in support of H.R. 6186, the Follow the Rules Act, introduced by Representative SEAN DUFFY. This legislation reiterates Congress' intent that whistleblower protections be broadly construed.

Whistleblowers are the best source of information about waste, fraud, and abuse in the Federal Government. We should do all we can to protect them. Under the Whistleblower Protection Act of 1989, a whistleblower is protected for disclosing violations of laws, rules, or regulations; yet a recent opinion by the U.S. Court of Appeals for the Federal Circuit would limit the scope of those protections. The Federal Circuit held that Federal employees are not protected if they refuse to violate a rule or a regulation. This would mean whistleblowers could be ordered to violate the same rule or regulation whose violation they blew the whistle on. If they refuse, they could be retaliated against, such as being demoted or even fired.

In the case heard by the Federal Circuit, Dr. Timothy Allen Rainey, a contracting officer at the Department of State, was ordered to tell a contractor to rehire a terminated subcontractor. Dr. Rainey refused on the grounds it would violate the Federal Acquisition Regulation—governmentwide contracting standards that have been in place for over 30 years. These contracting standards are exactly the sort of thing the Oversight and Government Reform Committee oversees to ensure compliance. In return for his objections, Dr. Rainey was stripped of his duties as a contracting officer and was given a negative performance rating. The Court of Appeals for the Federal Circuit held that, because Dr. Rainey was refusing to obey an order that would require him to violate a regulation and not a law, he could not be shielded by the Whistleblower Protection Act.

We should protect Federal workers who act in good faith to abide by the rules of their agencies. They shouldn't have to choose between disobeying the order of a supervisor and being disciplined for violating an agency's rules or regulations.

While nearly all Federal laws have implementing regulations, not all regulations have a detailed basis in law. Furthermore, agencies do not always train their employees to know which regulations are based in law. This means Federal workers may have to conduct extensive legal research before deciding on the safest course of action, in this case, whether to apply the very standards their own agencies put into place.

Whether the issue is regulations aimed against whistleblowers or whistleblowers acting to uphold other regulations, the issue is the same: we should incentivize and protect Federal employees for acting as principled civil servants. The Follow the Rules Act would send a clear, consistent message that Federal employees are expected to uphold standards of good government. It would ensure Federal workers are protected if they refuse to obey an order that would require them to violate even just a rule or a regulation.

Mr. Speaker, we are a nation based on the rule of law. We expect agencies to act in a transparent fashion and to be governed by predictable rules. We should provide the same sort of predictability to whistleblowers and protect them when they apply what they have been trained to follow. For that reason, I urge my colleagues to support this legislation.

I reserve the balance of my time.

Mr. LYNCH. Mr. Speaker, I yield myself such time as I may consume.

I rise in strong support of H.R. 6186, the Follow the Rules Act.

I appreciate the hard work done by Representative DUFFY of Wisconsin and by Mr. CONNOLLY of Virginia in taking the lead in introducing this legislation and then in working diligently and in a bipartisan manner to achieve its passage.

This bill would clarify that an employee who refuses to obey an order that would require the employee to violate the law, a rule, or a regulation is protected from retaliation under the Whistleblower Protection Act.

In June 2016, the U.S. Court of Appeals for the Federal Circuit issued a ruling that is contrary to the Whistleblower Protection Act and that is contrary to congressional intent. As Mr. GOSAR of Arizona previously laid out the facts, in Rainey v. MSPB, the court ruled that an employee who refuses to obey an order is protected only if the order would violate a statute but that the employee would not be protected if the order would simply violate a rule or a regulation.

This ruling incorrectly interprets congressional intent. Employees should be protected from retaliation if they do the right thing. That includes refusing to obey orders that would violate an agency's rules and regulations, as well as statutes. It is more critical than ever that we send a message to Federal employees that they have the right to do their jobs free from political pressure to bend or to violate the rules.

I urge my colleagues to support the passage of this legislation today.

I reserve the balance of my time.

Mr. GOSAR. Mr. Speaker, I yield 4 minutes to the gentleman from Wisconsin (Mr. DUFFY).

Mr. DUFFY. I thank the gentleman from Arizona for yielding, and I thank my friends across the aisle for their support of this commonsense piece of legislation that, again, rights a wrong perception from the U.S. Court of Appeals.

Mr. Speaker, many of us in this institution do talk about how we are a nation of laws; but, unfortunately, on June 7, when the U.S. Court of Appeals handed down its decision, it ruled that we are a nation of laws but not a nation of rules and regulations, at least as they apply to Federal workers.

We have had a good discussion about the case. Dr. Timothy Rainey, just to summarize again, is a State Department employee who was asked to violate the Federal Acquisition Regulation, and he didn't want to do it; so he denied, and he invoked his right to disobey under the Whistleblower Protection Act. This was brought to the Merit Systems Protection Board, and it ruled against Dr. Rainey. It went to the U.S. Court of Appeals, and it also found against Dr. Rainey. This exposed a glaring inconsistency in the application of the Whistleblower Protection Act, which, again, is inconsistent with the intent of this institution.

So we ask ourselves: What does this mean?

I chair the Financial Services Committee's Subcommittee on Oversight and Investigation. Federal whistleblowers play an important role in exposing the mismanagement at Federal agencies and in supporting the oversight that all of us do in this Congress. Critical to them is the Whistleblower Protection Act, which provides Federal workers with certain safeguards to disclose information that an employee reasonably believes evidences gross mismanagement, a waste of funds, an abuse of authority, or a violation of law.

This court ruling will take away those protections when Federal employees stand up against bad actors within our Federal workforce. In effect, this ruling will give permission to supervisors in positions of authority to force Federal workers to violate the rules and regulations that Congress, through law, directs the agencies to implement.

For example, at the Treasury Department, one of the agencies that I have the great privilege of overseeing, this would mean that Federal workers could be forced to violate sanctions against Russia for a violation of Ukraine's territorial integrity. Many of those sanctions are enforced through the Code of Federal Regulations pursuant to laws that are passed by this Congress.

Regardless of one's opinion about rules and regulations—and if that were the conversation today, I am sure one would have a debate that was far more disagreeable, but that is not the issue.

No matter what one thinks about rules and regulations, we should not leave exposed Federal workers who simply want to follow those rules and regulations. This bipartisan Follow the Rules Act, which, again, I introduced with my good friend from Virginia (Mr. CONNOLLY), will close the loophole that was created by the court. What we are doing is ensuring that Federal employees aren't just protected under our whistleblower statute for violations of Federal law, but that they are also protected as whistleblowers if there is a violation of a Federal rule or regulation.

This makes sense. It closes a loophole. I think that is why we have seen such bipartisan support from the far right of this institution and the far left of this institution. I think this is a great bill, and I thank my friends for so closely working with me to garner the support.

Mr. LYNCH. Mr. Speaker, I yield such time as he may consume to the gentleman from Virginia (Mr. CONNOLLY), the other champion along with Mr. DUFFY of Wisconsin.

☐ 1615

Mr. CONNOLLY. Mr. Speaker, I thank the gentleman from Massachusetts (Mr. LYNCH). I thank the gentleman from Arizona (Mr. GOSAR). I thank the gentleman from Wisconsin (Mr. DUFFY) for his leadership and collaboration on this important bill that he and I have introduced and is on the floor today, the Follow the Rules Act, H.R. 6186.

I appreciate Representative DUFFY's efforts to work to advance this legislation that falls under the umbrella of good government, which the Oversight and Government Reform Committee usually strives to promote on a bipartisan basis.

I welcome consideration of the bill, the Follow the Rules Act, to extend Congress' commitment to whistleblowers. The Follow the Rules Act upholds the committee's obligation to protect whistleblowers and help identify mismanagement at Federal agencies in supporting the oversight work of Congress.

The bill's language was previously adopted by a voice vote as section 1206 of the House-passed Financial Services and General Government Appropriations Act of 2017, H.R. 5482. The bill closes a loophole in the Whistleblower Protection Act created falsely, in my view, by the ruling in Rainey v. Merit Systems Protection Board, a precedent-setting case decided on June 7 in the U.S. Court of Appeals for the Federal Circuit.

The Whistleblower Protection Act provides Federal workers with legal safeguards to disclose information that an employee reasonably believes is evidence of gross mismanagement of a contract or a grant, gross waste of funds, abuse of authority regarding a contract or grant, or violation of law or rule regarding a contract or grant. That language ought to be fairly clear, but apparently it wasn't to the appellate court.

In Rainey, the right-to-disobey provision of the Whistleblower Protection Act was determined to only provide protection to Federal workers who refuse to obey an order that would require the individual to violate a law, but not to Federal workers who refuse to violate rules and regulations. God knoweth why.

This distinction leaves a gap in protections originally clearly intended for Federal employees by this Congress. In effect, the ruling exposes whistleblowers who refuse to violate the rules and regulations that were promulgated as a result of laws passed by Congress and signed by the President. That is how it flows.

This is a gap in coverage that must be addressed by Congress and clarified in the statute. Though, had the appellate court ruled correctly, it would be unnecessary.

The only way to protect whistleblowers from this court decision is to update the law to ensure that rules and regulations are covered by the right-to-disobey provision of the Whistleblower Protection Act.

I urge my colleagues to continue Congress' longstanding support for whistleblowers and vote in the affirmative for the Follow the Rules Act.

Mr. LYNCH. Mr. Speaker, having no further speakers on our side, I yield back the balance of my time.

Mr. GOSAR. Mr. Speaker, I urge the adoption of the bill.

I yield back the balance of my time.

The SPEAKER pro tempore. The question is on the motion offered by the gentleman from Arizona (Mr. GOSAR) that the House suspend the rules and pass the bill, H.R. 6186.

The question was taken; and (two-thirds being in the affirmative) the rules were suspended and the bill was passed.

A motion to reconsider was laid on the table.

─────────────

ADOLFO "HARPO" CELAYA POST OFFICE

Mr. GOSAR. Mr. Speaker, I move to suspend the rules and pass the bill (H.R. 6304) to designate the facility of the United States Postal Service located at 501 North Main Street in Florence, Arizona, as the "Adolfo 'Harpo' Celaya Post Office".

The Clerk read the title of the bill.

The text of the bill is as follows:

H.R. 6304

Be it enacted by the Senate and House of Representatives of the United States of America in Congress assembled,

SECTION 1. ADOLFO "HARPO" CELAYA POST OFFICE.

(a) DESIGNATION.—The facility of the United States Postal Service located at 501 North Main Street in Florence, Arizona, shall be known and designated as the "Adolfo 'Harpo' Celaya Post Office".

(b) REFERENCES.—Any reference in a law, map, regulation, document, paper, or other record of the United States to the facility referred to in subsection (a) shall be deemed to be a reference to the "Adolfo 'Harpo' Celaya Post Office".

The SPEAKER pro tempore. Pursuant to the rule, the gentleman from Arizona (Mr. GOSAR) and the gentlewoman from the Virgin Islands (Ms. PLASKETT) each will control 20 minutes.

The Chair recognizes the gentleman from Arizona.

GENERAL LEAVE

Mr. GOSAR. Mr. Speaker, I ask unanimous consent that all Members have 5 legislative days to revise and extend their remarks and to include any extraneous material on the bill under consideration.

The SPEAKER pro tempore. Is there objection to the request of the gentleman from Arizona?

There was no objection.

Mr. GOSAR. Mr. Speaker, I yield myself such time as I may consume.

I rise today in support of my bill, H.R. 6304. The bill designates a post office in Florence, Arizona, as the Adolfo "Harpo" Celaya Post Office.

Mr. Speaker, this bill honors a great man and an Arizona hero. He has served his Nation both in combat and with a lifetime of community service. That man is Adolfo "Harpo" Celaya.

The bill being considered here today, H.R. 6304, would designate the United States Postal Service facility in Florence, Arizona, as the Adolfo "Harpo" Celaya Post Office. This is a small gesture to honor a man who has given so much to this Nation and to his community.

By way of background, Harpo Celaya was born in Florence, Arizona, on May 16, 1927. He worked numerous jobs, including picking cotton and working at the local dairy from the time he was only 8 years old. He earned the nickname "Harpo" because he had thick black curls that reminded his friends of Harpo Marx.

When he was just 17 years old, he read a recruitment poster that boasted "Join the Navy, see the world" and he begged his father to let him join. He was assigned to the USS *Indianapolis*, the flagship of the 5th Fleet.

The *Indy* saw many battles during World War II, and Harpo was there with the ship at the battle of Iwo Jima and witnessed the historic flag-raising on the island in February of 1945. He was also aboard when the *Indy* went on a secret mission delivering parts for Little Boy, the atomic bomb that was dropped on Hiroshima.

His experiences on the *Indy* would change his life forever. On the night of July 30, 1945, the *Indy* was on its way back to the Philippines after a secret mission delivering the atomic bomb.

Harpo and many of his mates were sleeping on the deck because it was too hot to sleep in their bunks below. Despite the heat, Harpo covered himself with a blanket, as had been his habit for many years in trying to ward off mosquitoes in the Arizona desert.

Shortly after midnight, a Japanese submarine hit the *Indy* with two torpedoes. Fire tore through the deck, burning Harpo and his mates. Harpo credits his blanket, which was essentially vaporized in the heat, for saving him from being burned more severely.

He was en route to retrieve his life-jacket when he ran into his friend, Santos Pena, who told him that the ship was sinking and they needed to abandon it immediately. The USS *Indianapolis* sank within 12 minutes.

The two friends separated after jumping into the water, and 3 days passed before they found each other again. They continued to endure excruciating conditions with their fellow sailors in the choppy open seas, most slowly succumbing to dehydration, exposure, and shark attacks.

The survivors of the *Indy* were eventually rescued after spending almost 5 harrowing days in the water. Of the 1,196 men aboard, only 317 survived. After this incident, Harpo was medically discharged from the Navy and awarded the Purple Heart.

Still only 17 years of age, he went back to high school in his hometown of Florence, Arizona, and was recruited to play on the Florence Gophers basketball team. Even though none of the players were over 6 feet tall, Harpo led his team to the Arizona State Basketball Championship and was named captain of the first-string all-state team.

Harpo continued his winning streak by playing for and eventually coaching the basketball team at Palo Verde Community College in Blythe, California.

Harpo went on to become a cowboy for a few years and eventually ran his own small business, providing heating and air-conditioning services to his new community of San Jose, California.

Throughout his life, Harpo could often be found coaching or refereeing games for local youth. He knew firsthand of the value of sports and exercise as a means to keep young boys out of trouble.

Harpo's walls are adorned by many plaques and awards honoring his efforts. He is honored in the Arizona Basketball Hall of Fame at Arizona State University, the Florence High School Athletic Hall of Fame, and served as grand marshal for the Florence Junior Parade in November 2009.

Harpo Celaya is a true hero, beloved by his hometown of Florence.

I would like to thank all of the survivors of the USS *Indianapolis* for their sacrifice. Of the 23 survivors still alive today, Harpo is the only Native American. We are humbled to honor him today.

I would like to thank the town of Florence for their support of this bill and for proposing this great honor for Mr. Celaya. Thank you to the Oversight and Government Reform Committee for their expertise and patience in bringing this bill forward.

I urge Members to support my bill.

I reserve the balance of my time.

Ms. PLASKETT. Mr. Speaker, I yield myself such time as I may consume.

I rise today in strong support of H.R. 6304, to designate the facility of the United States Postal Service located at 501 North Main Street in Florence, Arizona, as the Adolfo "Harpo" Celaya Post Office.

Born in 1927, Mr. Celaya overcame a childhood of poverty, neglect, and abuse. At age 17, he joined the Navy and was assigned to the USS *Indianapolis* during World War II. Harpo fought in the battles of Iwo Jima and Okinawa and was aboard the USS *Indianapolis* during its secret mission to deliver the ingredients of the atomic bomb Little Boy to the island of Tinian.

As the ship was returning from this mission, it was hit with two torpedoes from a Japanese submarine. Despite being badly burned, Harpo Celaya jumped from a sinking ship into the water, where he remained for 5 days until rescuers arrived.

Of the 1,196 men aboard the ship that day, Harpo was one of only 317 survivors. He received the Purple Heart and returned to high school in his hometown of Florence, Arizona. There, he led the basketball team to the Arizona State Basketball Championship and was named captain of the all-state team in spite of his combat injuries.

Harpo Celaya attended Palo Verde Community College and again led the basketball team to a championship. He was inducted into the Arizona Basketball Hall of Fame in 1972 and the Florence High School Athletic Hall of Fame in 2008.

Outside of basketball, Harpo led a successful career as a cowboy and then as a small-business owner, but always made time to mentor local youth by coaching or refereeing athletic sports.

Mr. Speaker, we should pass this bill to honor Harpo Celaya for both his valiant military service and his ability to overcome hardship and having a lasting positive impact on his community.

I urge my colleagues to support this bill.

Mr. Speaker, I yield back the balance of my time.

Mr. GOSAR. Mr. Speaker, I ask that Members pass this bill.

I yield back the balance of my time.

The SPEAKER pro tempore. The question is on the motion offered by the gentleman from Arizona (Mr. GOSAR) that the House suspend the rules and pass the bill, H.R. 6304.

The question was taken.

The SPEAKER pro tempore. In the opinion of the Chair, two-thirds being in the affirmative, the ayes have it.

Mr. GOSAR. Mr. Speaker, I object to the vote on the ground that a quorum is not present and make the point of order that a quorum is not present.

The SPEAKER pro tempore. Pursuant to clause 8 of rule XX, further proceedings on this question will be postponed.

The point of no quorum is considered withdrawn.

JONATHAN "J.D." DE GUZMAN POST OFFICE BUILDING

Mr. GOSAR. Mr. Speaker, I move to suspend the rules and pass the bill (H.R. 5948) to designate the facility of the United States Postal Service located at 830 Kuhn Drive in Chula Vista, California, as the "Jonathan 'J.D.' De Guzman Post Office Building".

The Clerk read the title of the bill.

The text of the bill is as follows:

H.R. 5948

Be it enacted by the Senate and House of Representatives of the United States of America in Congress assembled,

SECTION 1. JONATHAN "J.D." DE GUZMAN POST OFFICE BUILDING.

(a) DESIGNATION.—The facility of the United States Postal Service located at 830 Kuhn Drive in Chula Vista, California, shall be known and designated as the "Jonathan 'J.D.' De Guzman Post Office Building".

(b) REFERENCES.—Any reference in a law, map, regulation, document, paper, or other record of the United States to the facility referred to in subsection (a) shall be deemed to be a reference to the "Jonathan 'J.D.' De Guzman Post Office Building".

The SPEAKER pro tempore. Pursuant to the rule, the gentleman from Arizona (Mr. GOSAR) and the gentlewoman from the Virgin Islands (Ms. PLASKETT) each will control 20 minutes.

The Chair recognizes the gentleman from Arizona.

GENERAL LEAVE

Mr. GOSAR. Mr. Speaker, I ask unanimous consent that all Members have 5 legislative days to revise and extend their remarks and to include any extraneous material on the bill under consideration.

The SPEAKER pro tempore. Is there objection to the request of the gentleman from Arizona?

There was no objection.

Mr. GOSAR. Mr. Speaker, I yield myself such time as I may consume.

I rise today in support of H.R. 5948, introduced by my colleague, Representative SUSAN DAVIS of California. The bill designates a post office in Chula Vista, California, as the Jonathan "J.D." De Guzman Post Office Building.

Jonathan De Guzman was born in the Philippines in 1972. He later traveled to the United States and became an American citizen and served as an officer with the San Diego Police Department. Officer De Guzman received the Purple Heart for bravery from the San Diego Police Department in 2003 after

being stabbed in the line of duty. He returned to work, but tragically was killed in the line of duty in July of this year.

I join my colleague, Representative DAVIS of California, in honoring Officer De Guzman.

I urge Members to support the bill.

I reserve the balance of my time.

Ms. PLASKETT. Mr. Speaker, I yield myself such time as I may consume.

Mr. Speaker, I rise today in strong support of H.R. 5948, a bill to designate the facility of the United States Postal Service located at 830 Kuhn Drive in Chula Vista, California, as the Jonathan "J.D." De Guzman Post Office Building.

Jonathan De Guzman emigrated to the U.S. from the Philippines with a strong desire to become a contributor to his new community. His selflessness led him to join the San Diego Police Department, where he served for 16 years.

Officer De Guzman was awarded the San Diego Police Department's Purple Heart in 2003 after surviving a stabbing while on duty. Officer De Guzman was again attacked while on duty in July of 2016. This time, however, he was shot multiple times at pointblank range and tragically did not survive.

Mr. Speaker, we should pass this bill to honor Officer Jonathan De Guzman's courageous life of public service and ensure that the ultimate sacrifice he made is never forgotten.

I urge my colleagues to support H.R. 5948.

I reserve the balance of my time.

☐ 1630

Mr. GOSAR. Mr. Speaker, I have no further speakers. I reserve the balance of my time.

Ms. PLASKETT. Mr. Speaker, I yield such time as she may consume to the gentlewoman from California (Mrs. DAVIS).

Mrs. DAVIS of California. Mr. Speaker, I rise today to ask for support of H.R. 5948 in commemorating the life of a humble role model and a courageous American hero. Officer Jonathan De Guzman, or J.D., as he was better known by family and friends, dedicated his life to protecting and serving the San Diego community that he loved.

Born in the Philippines, J.D. traveled to the United States at the age of 20 with high hopes of achieving the American Dream. Through hard work and perseverance, he achieved this dream as a San Diego law enforcement officer, serving in many different roles within the San Diego Police Department, including serving on the gang suppression unit.

☐ 1630

A devoted public servant, J.D. felt most rewarded by the bonds he created through community engagement. J.D.'s family, his friends, and fellow officers characterized him as a selfless, honorable, and caring warrior. San Diego Police Chief Shelley Zimmerman praised J.D. saying: "He always raised the bar" and "cared deeply for his community."

In 2003, he survived a brutal stabbing from a suspect he had stopped for speeding. A true warrior, indeed, upon recovery, he quickly returned to the force to defend the people of San Diego. In that same year, he was awarded the San Diego Police Department's Purple Heart for bravery in the line of duty. Although he appreciated the gesture, the accolades were not what motivated him to serve. The reactions of the community brought J.D. true fulfillment.

Tragically, on July 28, 2016, Officer De Guzman, a 16-year veteran of the force, was shot multiple times at point-blank range and killed. Prosecutors on the case say the attack happened so quickly that J.D. never had the opportunity to pull his service weapon.

On August 5, thousands—I mean thousands—of fellow officers and private citizens lined the streets of San Diego for J.D.'s funeral procession, tossing flowers along the path, holding signs, and waving American flags. I can assure you, it was really a moving experience. The amount of love and admiration I witnessed that day showed just how deeply he touched the lives of everyone he encountered in a life that was cut much too short.

He was only 43 years old. He was a beloved son to his proud parents, a caring husband to his adoring wife, Mary Jane, and a hero to their beautiful children, Amira and Jonathan, Jr. I had the pleasure of meeting with his family and some of his close friends to offer my deepest condolences. I saw the wound that was left behind, a wound that may never truly be healed, but through loving memories of their time together, combined with the support of the community, his strong family will endure the pain.

While nothing will ever fill the void, we can take action today to ensure that his legacy will never be forgotten. J.D. made the ultimate sacrifice in protecting our community, and this bill will mean that future generations will know and understand the commitment that Officer De Guzman made and our law enforcement officers continue to make every day.

I urge you to vote "yes" on H.R. 5948 to designate the facility of the United States Postal Service located at 830 Kuhn Drive in Chula Vista, California, as the Jonathan "J.D." De Guzman Post Office Building. This post office sits right in the Eastlake community that Officer De Guzman called home and will stand as a lasting remembrance of a true role model and American hero.

Ms. PLASKETT. Mr. Speaker, I yield back the balance of my time.

Mr. GOSAR. Mr. Speaker, I urge the adoption of the bill. I yield back the balance of my time.

Mr. VARGAS. Mr. Speaker, I rise today in support of H.R. 5948—An Act to designate the United States Postal Service facility in Chula Vista as the "Johnathan 'J.D.' De Guzman Post Office Building." This legislation is sponsored by my colleague, the gentlewoman from San Diego, Susan Davis. I urge my colleagues to support this bill, so that we may forever honor the sacrifice that Officer De Guzman made for the San Diego community and our great nation.

San Diego Police Officer Johnathan 'J.D.' De Guzman was a true American hero who was killed in the line of duty. Born in the Philippines on September 17, 1972, Officer De Guzman traveled to the United States at the age of 20 and eventually became an American citizen. He believed deeply in the American Dream and in the importance of public service and community involvement, leading him to join the San Diego Police Department (SDPD) in 2000.

Officer De Guzman was a SDPD 16 year veteran and a member of the department's gang suppression unit. In 2003, he received the SDPD's Purple Heart. Officer De Guzman was characterized as a caring, selfless, honorable, and courageous individual. It wasn't uncommon for him to show up at his children's school and engage students about careers in law enforcement.

Tragically, Officer De Guzman was killed while on patrol on July 28th, 2016. He is survived by his parents, his wife Mary Jane, and his two children Amira and Jonathan De Guzman II.

I urge my colleagues to pass H.R. 5948.

The SPEAKER pro tempore. The question is on the motion offered by the gentleman from Arizona (Mr. GOSAR) that the House suspend the rules and pass the bill, H.R. 5948.

The question was taken; and (two-thirds being in the affirmative) the rules were suspended and the bill was passed.

A motion to reconsider was laid on the table.

U.S. NAVAL CONSTRUCTION BATTALION "SEABEES" FALLEN HEROES POST OFFICE BUILDING

Mr. GOSAR. Mr. Speaker, I move to suspend the rules and pass the bill (H.R. 6138) to designate the facility of the United States Postal Service located at 560 East Pleasant Valley Road, Port Hueneme, California, as the U.S. Naval Construction Battalion "Seabees" Fallen Heroes Post Office Building.

The Clerk read the title of the bill.

The text of the bill is as follows:

H.R. 6138

Be it enacted by the Senate and House of Representatives of the United States of America in Congress assembled,

SECTION 1. U.S. NAVAL CONSTRUCTION BATTALION "SEABEES" FALLEN HEROES POST OFFICE BUILDING.

(a) DESIGNATION.—The facility of the United States Postal Service located at 560 East Pleasant Valley Road, Port Hueneme, California, shall be known and designated as the "U.S. Naval Construction Battalion 'Seabees' Fallen Heroes Post Office Building".

(b) REFERENCES.—Any reference in a law, map, regulation, document, paper, or other record of the United States to the facility referred to in subsection (a) shall be deemed to be a reference to the "U.S. Naval Construction Battalion 'Seabees' Fallen Heroes Post Office Building".

The SPEAKER pro tempore. Pursuant to the rule, the gentleman from Arizona (Mr. GOSAR) and the gentlewoman from the Virgin Islands (Ms. PLASKETT) each will control 20 minutes.

The Chair recognizes the gentleman from Arizona.

GENERAL LEAVE

Mr. GOSAR. Mr. Speaker, I ask unanimous consent that all Members may have 5 legislative days in which to revise and extend their remarks and include extraneous material on the bill under consideration.

The SPEAKER pro tempore. Is there objection to the request of the gentleman from Arizona?

There was no objection.

Mr. GOSAR. I yield myself such time as I may consume.

Mr. Speaker, I rise today in support of H.R. 6138, introduced by the gentlewoman from California (Ms. BROWNLEY). The bill designates a post office in Port Hueneme, California, as the U.S. Naval Construction Battalion "Seabees" Fallen Heroes Post Office Building.

The Seabees were founded during World War II to help complete construction projects, such as airstrips and bridges necessary to help U.S. servicemen win the war. These brave servicemen and -women have since risked their lives in many conflicts to build bases, roadways, airstrips, and other construction projects, often in combat zones while under fire.

I look forward to hearing more about the achievements of the Seabees from the gentlewoman from California (Ms. BROWNLEY). For now, I urge Members to support the bill.

Mr. Speaker, I reserve the balance of my time.

Ms. PLASKETT. I yield myself such time as I may consume.

Mr. Speaker, I rise today in strong support of H.R. 6138, a bill to designate the facility of the United States Postal Service located at 560 East Pleasant Valley Road, Port Hueneme, California, as the U.S. Naval Construction Battalion "Seabees" Fallen Heroes Post Office Building.

For over 70 years, the Seabees have provided critical naval construction capabilities during times of war. They assisted in the Normandy invasion during World War II, cut a mountain in half, and carved through a jungle to build a runway during the Korean war, constructed military facilities during the Vietnam and gulf wars, and supported combat forces in Iraq. Today they continue to build and maintain bases and infrastructure for coalition forces in the global war on terror.

In addition to their military support, the Seabees have also provided vital humanitarian assistance around the world in times of peace. They have helped rebuild after devastating earthquakes, such as the one in Haiti in 2010, and they have led various construction projects in a number of undeveloped countries.

Mr. Speaker, we should pass this bill to honor the brave men and women who have played such an important role in both our military and humanitarian efforts around the globe. I urge my colleagues to support H.R. 6138.

Mr. Speaker, I reserve the balance of my time.

Mr. GOSAR. I reserve the balance of my time.

Ms. PLASKETT. Mr. Speaker, I yield such time as she may consume to the gentlewoman from California (Ms. BROWNLEY).

Ms. BROWNLEY of California. Mr. Speaker, as the very proud representative of Naval Base Ventura County, the West Coast home of the Navy Seabees, I rise today in support of H.R. 6138, which would designate the United States Postal Office in Port Hueneme, California, as the U.S. Naval Construction Battalion "Seabees" Fallen Heroes Post Office Building.

My bill is intended to honor the many brave men and women of the U.S. Naval Construction Battalion, also known as the Seabees, who have made the ultimate sacrifice for our freedom. In their more than 70-year history, the Seabees have diligently and honorably served our great Nation in times of war and peace with their renowned can-do spirit. They say: "The difficult we do immediately. The impossible takes a little longer."

First established in 1942 after the attack on Pearl Harbor, the Seabees were created to meet the demand for capable builders who could also fight. Their motto is "We build, we fight." During World War II, over 250,000 Seabees passed through the Naval Construction Battalion Center at Port Hueneme on their way to or from the Pacific theater.

The Seabees also played vital roles in the Korean war, the Vietnam war, the Persian Gulf war, the Iraq war, and in Afghanistan, moving the immovable and taming the untamable to build bases, roadways, airstrips, and other critical infrastructure necessary for our troops to succeed in their missions.

Although primarily known as builders, many Seabees fought tenaciously throughout these conflicts, side by side with other servicemembers. For instance, Construction Mechanic Third Class Marvin Glenn Shields, who trained at Port Hueneme, battled bravely alongside U.S. Special Forces in the Battle of Dong Xoai in Vietnam despite being badly wounded. Ignoring his wounds, Marvin helped return a wounded special forces second lieuten-

ant back to safety while destroying a Viet Cong machine gun emplacement. His bravery and heroism cost him his life. For his conspicuous gallantry, Marvin was awarded the Medal of Honor after his death.

My bill would honor the contributions of all of our fallen Seabees to our Nation. I am both honored and proud to lead this effort to recognize the heroism of many brave Seabees like Marvin Shields who have paid so dearly for our freedom. We are forever indebted to them for their immense service to our Nation.

Finally, I would like to thank the chair and ranking member of the Committee on Oversight and Government Reform for supporting my bill, as well as my colleagues from California who are all cosponsors of the bill. I urge my colleagues to support H.R. 6138.

Ms. PLASKETT. Mr. Speaker, I yield back the balance of my time.

Mr. GOSAR. Mr. Speaker, I urge the adoption of the bill. I yield back the balance of my time.

The SPEAKER pro tempore. The question is on the motion offered by the gentleman from Arizona (Mr. GOSAR) that the House suspend the rules and pass the bill, H.R. 6138.

The question was taken; and (two-thirds being in the affirmative) the rules were suspended and the bill was passed.

A motion to reconsider was laid on the table.

DR. ROSCOE C. BROWN, JR. POST OFFICE BUILDING

Mr. GOSAR. Mr. Speaker, I move to suspend the rules and pass the bill (H.R. 6282) to designate the facility of the United States Postal Service located at 2024 Jerome Avenue, in Bronx, New York, as the "Dr. Roscoe C. Brown, Jr. Post Office Building".

The Clerk read the title of the bill.

The text of the bill is as follows:

H.R. 6282

Be it enacted by the Senate and House of Representatives of the United States of America in Congress assembled,

SECTION 1. DR. ROSCOE C. BROWN, JR. POST OFFICE BUILDING.

(a) DESIGNATION.—The facility of the United States Postal Service located at 2024 Jerome Avenue, in Bronx, New York, shall be known and designated as the "Dr. Roscoe C. Brown, Jr. Post Office Building".

(b) REFERENCES.—Any reference in a law, map, regulation, document, paper, or other record of the United States to the facility referred to in subsection (a) shall be deemed to be a reference to the "Dr. Roscoe C. Brown, Jr. Post Office Building".

The SPEAKER pro tempore. Pursuant to the rule, the gentleman from Arizona (Mr. GOSAR) and the gentlewoman from the Virgin Islands (Ms. PLASKETT) each will control 20 minutes.

The Chair recognizes the gentleman from Arizona.

Mr. GOSAR. Mr. Speaker, I ask unanimous consent that all Members may have 5 legislative days in which to revise and extend their remarks and include extraneous material on the bill under consideration.

The SPEAKER pro tempore. Is there objection to the request of the gentleman from Arizona?

There was no objection.

Mr. GOSAR. I yield myself such time as I may consume.

Mr. Speaker, I rise today in support of H.R. 6282, introduced by the gentleman from New York (Mr. SERRANO). The bill designates a post office in the Bronx, New York, as the Dr. Roscoe C. Brown, Jr. Post Office Building.

As a member of the Tuskegee Airmen in World War II, Dr. Brown was the first African American fighter pilot to shoot down a German fighter jet. After serving in World War II, Dr. Brown earned his Ph.D. at New York University, where he later taught, and served as the president of Bronx Community College.

His service to the Nation is admirable, and I look forward to learning more about his extraordinary life from my colleague, the gentleman from New York (Mr. SERRANO).

I urge Members to support the bill.

Mr. Speaker, I reserve the balance of my time.

Ms. PLASKETT. Mr. Speaker, I yield myself such time as I may consume.

Mr. Speaker, I rise today in strong support of H.R. 6282, a bill to designate the facility of the United States Postal Service located at 2024 Jerome Avenue, in the Bronx, New York, as the Dr. Roscoe C. Brown, Jr. Post Office Building.

Born in 1922, Dr. Roscoe Brown, Jr. fell in love with aviation after visiting the Smithsonian Institution. During World War II, Dr. Brown joined the Tuskegee Airmen, conducting 68 missions and becoming the first African American fighter pilot to shoot down a German fighter jet. He earned the Distinguished Flying Cross for his service, and, in 2007, Dr. Brown and his fellow remaining Tuskegee Airmen were awarded the Congressional Gold Medal by President George W. Bush.

Following his honorable military service, Dr. Brown earned his Ph.D. at New York University and served as the president of Bronx Community College for 17 years. He also served as an informal adviser to many political leaders in New York City and founded 100 Black Men, an organization dedicated to improving conditions for African Americans.

Mr. Speaker, we should pass H.R. 6282 to commemorate the selflessness exhibited by Dr. Roscoe Brown, Jr.'s military and community service. I urge my colleagues to support this bill.

I reserve the balance of my time.

Mr. GOSAR. Mr. Speaker, I reserve the balance of my time.

Ms. PLASKETT. Mr. Speaker, I yield such time as he may consume to the gentleman from New York (Mr. SERRANO).

Mr. SERRANO. I thank the gentlewoman for yielding me time.

Mr. Speaker, I rise today to urge my colleagues to pass H.R. 6282. This legislation will rename the Morris Heights Post Office in the Bronx, New York, in my district, after a legend. Dr. Roscoe Brown was a giant among men and a revered figure in the Bronx, New York City, and the Nation.

□ 1645

I had the privilege of knowing Dr. Brown for decades and considered him a dear friend. He faced the horrors of segregation early in his life, but he never let that stop him from achieving what he wanted and set out to do.

Dr. Brown was a fearless Tuskegee Airman during World War II, conducting some 68 missions and becoming one of the first fighters to shoot down a German fighter jet. The heroism he displayed paved the way for the desegregation of the Armed Forces and, decades later, earned him and his fellow airmen a Congressional Gold Medal.

After the war, he went on to further his studies at New York University, where he eventually served as a professor and an academic of the highest caliber. For 17 years, Dr. Brown served as president of Bronx Community College, which is located in my district, leading an institution that gave hope of a better life through education to a predominantly minority and nontraditional student population.

Throughout his life, Dr. Brown was a quiet, yet fierce advocate and leader that many turned to during the racial discord that plagued the city of New York in the sixties and seventies. His activism in the civil rights movement led him to start 100 Black Men, a civic organization devoted to improving the treatment of African Americans in New York.

Dr. Brown was also an avid runner and participated in nine New York City Marathons. During his tenure at Bronx Community College, he established the Annual Hall of Fame 5K and 10K races to help benefit the school. His invitation to participate in one of those races inspired me to start running myself, and I have now run that particular race for more than 30 years.

While his accomplishments and contributions are far too numerous to list, it is fair to say that Dr. Brown left the world around him in a much better place than which he found it. He was a unique individual with a great smile, a great sense of humor, and a great sense of history. Above all, he was a coalition builder. No one was too far for him to speak to or to bring close to him.

We will miss him, and I know that he is looking on us today. This is a small but very important tribute for a great man, Dr. Roscoe Brown.

Ms. PLASKETT. Mr. Speaker, I yield back the balance of my time.

Mr. GOSAR. Mr. Speaker, I urge adoption of the bill.

I yield back the balance of my time.

The SPEAKER pro tempore. The question is on the motion offered by the gentleman from Arizona (Mr. GOSAR) that the House suspend the rules and pass the bill, H.R. 6282.

The question was taken; and (two-thirds being in the affirmative) the rules were suspended and the bill was passed.

A motion to reconsider was laid on the table.

─────────

MERCHANT MARINE OF WORLD WAR II CONGRESSIONAL GOLD MEDAL ACT

Mr. HUIZENGA of Michigan. Mr. Speaker, I move to suspend the rules and pass the bill (H.R. 2992) to award a Congressional Gold Medal, collectively, to the U.S. Merchant Marine of World War II, in recognition of their dedicated and vital service during World War II.

The Clerk read the title of the bill.

The text of the bill is as follows:

H.R. 2992

Be it enacted by the Senate and House of Representatives of the United States of America in Congress assembled,

SECTION 1. SHORT TITLE.

This Act may be cited as the "Merchant Marine of World War II Congressional Gold Medal Act".

SEC. 2. FINDINGS.

The Congress finds the following:

(1) 2015 marks the 70th anniversary of the Allied victory in World War II and the restoration of peacetime across the European and Pacific theaters.

(2) The United States Merchant Marine was integral in providing the link between domestic production and the fighting forces overseas, providing combat equipment, fuel, food, commodities, and raw materials to troops stationed overseas.

(3) Fleet Admiral Ernest J. King acknowledged the indispensability of the Merchant Marine to the victory in a 1945 letter stating that without their support, "the Navy could not have accomplished its mission".

(4) President and former Supreme Commander of the Allied Forces, Dwight D. Eisenhower, acknowledged that "through the prompt delivery of supplies and equipment to our armed forces overseas, and of cargoes representing economic and military aid to friendly nations, the American Merchant Marine has effectively helped to strengthen the forces of freedom throughout the world".

(5) Military missions and war planning were contingent upon the availability of resources and that the United States Merchant Marine played a vital role in this regard, ensuring the efficient and reliable transoceanic transport of military equipment as well as both military and civilian personnel.

(6) The United States Merchant Marine provided for the successful transport of resources and personnel despite consistent and ongoing exposure to enemy combatants from both the air and the sea, such as enemy bomber squadrons, submarines, and mines.

(7) The efforts of the United States Merchant Marine were not without sacrifices as they bore a higher per capita casualty rate than any other branch of the military during the war.

(8) The United States Merchant Marine proved to be an instrumental asset on untold occasions, participating in every landing operation by the United States Marine Corps from Guadalcanal to Iwo Jima as well as providing, for instance, the bulk tonnage of material necessary for the invasion of Normandy which "would not have been possible without the Merchant Marine", as a 1944 New York Times article observed.

(9) In also assessing their performance, General Dwight D. Eisenhower stated, "every man in this Allied command is quick to express his admiration for the loyalty, courage, and fortitude of the officers and men of the Merchant Marine. We count upon their efficiency and their utter devotion to duty as we do our own; they have never failed us".

(10) During a September 1944 speech, President Franklin D. Roosevelt stated, the Merchant Marine has "delivered the goods when and where needed in every theater of operations and across every ocean in the biggest, the most difficult, and dangerous transportation job ever undertaken. As time goes on, there will be greater public understanding of our merchant fleet's record during this war.".

(11) The feats and accomplishments of the Merchant Marine are deserving of broader public recognition.

(12) The United States will be forever grateful and indebted to the U.S. Merchant Marine for their effective, reliable, and courageous transport of goods and resources in enemy territory throughout theaters of every variety in World War II; that these goods and resources saved thousands of lives and enabled the Allied Powers to claim victory in World War II.

(13) The Congressional Gold Medal will be an appropriate way to shed further light on the service of the Merchant Marine in World War II and the instrumental role they played in winning World War II.

SEC. 3. CONGRESSIONAL GOLD MEDAL.

(a) AWARD AUTHORIZED.—The Speaker of the House of Representatives and the President pro tempore of the Senate shall make appropriate arrangements for the award, on behalf of the Congress, of a single gold medal of appropriate design to the U.S. Merchant Marine of World War II, in recognition of their dedicated and vital service during World War II.

(b) DESIGN AND STRIKING.—For the purposes of the award referred to in subsection (a), the Secretary of the Treasury (hereafter referred to as the "Secretary") shall strike the gold medal with suitable emblems, devices, and inscriptions, to be determined by the Secretary.

(c) AMERICAN MERCHANT MARINE MUSEUM.—

(1) IN GENERAL.—Following the award of the gold medal in honor of the U.S. Merchant Marine, the gold medal shall be given to the American Merchant Marine Museum, where it will be available for display as appropriate and available for research.

SEC. 4. DUPLICATE MEDALS.

Under such regulations as the Secretary may prescribe, the Secretary may strike and sell duplicates in bronze of the gold medal struck under section 3, at a price sufficient to cover the costs of the medals, including labor, materials, dies, use of machinery, and overhead expenses.

SEC. 5. STATUS OF MEDALS.

(a) NATIONAL MEDALS.—Medals struck pursuant to this Act are national medals for purposes of chapter 51 of title 31, United States Code.

(b) NUMISMATIC ITEMS.—For purposes of section 5134 of title 31, United States Code, all medals struck under this Act shall be considered to be numismatic items.

The SPEAKER pro tempore. Pursuant to the rule, the gentleman from Michigan (Mr. HUIZENGA) and the gentleman from Illinois (Mr. FOSTER) each will control 20 minutes.

The Chair recognizes the gentleman from Michigan.

GENERAL LEAVE

Mr. HUIZENGA of Michigan. Mr. Speaker, I ask unanimous consent that all Members may have 5 legislative days in which to revise and extend their remarks and include extraneous material on the bill.

The SPEAKER pro tempore. Is there objection to the request of the gentleman from Michigan?

There was no objection.

Mr. HUIZENGA of Michigan. Mr. Speaker, merchant mariners act as an auxiliary to the U.S. Navy and are recognized as an integral link between domestic production and forces overseas, delivering combat equipment, food, fuel, raw materials, and commodities to those stationed abroad.

Military success in World War II hinged on the merchant marine delivering these resources and provisions of transport to military and civilian personnel, sailing while exposed to enemy combatants by both air and by sea. During World War II, these merchant mariners suffered the highest per capita casualty rate of any other branch in the U.S. Armed Forces. It is estimated that hundreds of mariner ships and thousands of mariners were lost to enemy combatants as a result of their service during World War II.

Yet, Mr. Speaker, the merchant marine is rarely mentioned when people list the military branches of service during the war. I rise today to help remedy that oversight by supporting H.R. 2992, the Merchant Marine of World War II Congressional Gold Medal Act, introduced by our colleague, Representative SUSAN BROOKS. This bill, which has 312 House cosponsors, would award a single Congressional Gold Medal to the American Merchant Marine of World War II in the recognition of their dedicated and vital service. After the medal is awarded, it will be given to the American Merchant Marine Museum, which is housed within the United States Merchant Marine Academy at Kings Point, New York.

The Treasury Secretary is authorized to make and offer for sale bronze replicas of the medal at a price that will help defray the design and production costs of the actual medal. A companion bill in the Senate, S. 2989, has been introduced by Senator LISA MURKOWSKI.

Mr. Speaker, the merchant marine has contributed greatly to every war in which this country has been involved, beginning with the Revolutionary War and continuing right up until today. Its efforts during peacetime helped carry millions of tons of cargo and countless passengers, but the merchant marines' efforts in lightly guarded ships on the dangerous waters of the Atlantic and Pacific during the Second World War were invaluable to the overall war effort.

President Franklin Roosevelt summed it up succinctly: they delivered the goods.

Now, Mr. Speaker, it is our turn to deliver the goods for those heroes who have so often gone unnoticed. I urge immediate passage of this bill.

Mr. Speaker, I reserve the balance of my time.

Mr. FOSTER. Mr. Speaker, I yield myself such time as I may consume.

Mr. Speaker, I rise in support of H.R. 2992, legislation to honor the dedicated and unwavering service provided by the U.S. Merchant Marine during World War II, a bill that I am proud to cosponsor. I hope that, upon its passage in the House, the Senate will move quickly to take it up and pass this bill before the 114th Congress adjourns.

While many are familiar with the sacrifices made by those who served in the Armed Forces during World War II, less often do we stop and take time to recognize the members of the U.S. Merchant Marine who played an essential role in supplying our troops overseas with the equipment, food, and materials necessary to sustain the fight against the Axis powers.

Despite the unrelenting threat of attack and the risk to their lives, the U.S. Merchant Marine proved to be an invaluable asset on innumerable occasions, participating in every landing operation by the United States Marine Corps during the war.

In speaking of the brave contributions made by the U.S. Merchant Marine, President Franklin Roosevelt said that the Merchant Marine "delivered the goods when and where needed in every theater of operations and across every ocean in the biggest, the most difficult, and dangerous transportation job ever undertaken." President Roosevelt also said that "as time goes on, there will be greater public understanding of our merchant fleet's record during this war."

In fact, during a recent visit to the National World War II Museum in New Orleans, Louisiana, I was pleased and proud to see the proper and impressive display dedicated to the role of the merchant marine in that war. Indeed, more than 70 years after President Roosevelt spoke those words, the House is taking an important step today to honor and to shed light on the contributions of the merchant marines made during World War II.

To further the public's understanding of the role the merchant marines played in securing the defeat of the Axis powers, the legislation will ensure that the Gold Medal will be given to the American Merchant Marine Museum, where it will be available for viewing by the public.

I urge my colleagues to support this legislation before us.

Mr. Speaker, I reserve the balance of my time.

Mr. HUIZENGA of Michigan. Mr. Speaker, I yield such time as she may consume to the gentlewoman from Indiana (Mrs. BROOKS).

Mrs. BROOKS of Indiana. Mr. Speaker, I rise today in support of H.R. 2992, the Merchant Marine of World War II Congressional Gold Medal Act. This measure awards a Congressional Gold Medal to the merchant mariners who served during World War II in appreciation of their dedicated and vital service to our Nation.

I also want to thank my colleague from across the aisle, Congresswoman JANICE HAHN of California's 44th District, who worked with me and other Members here in the House to secure so many cosponsorships of this bill.

The Congressional Gold Medal is the highest honor Congress can bestow upon an individual or group, and these brave servicemen deserve such an honor. The merchant marine was the linchpin connecting the fighting forces overseas with the production forces at home. In the face of certain peril, these brave mariners provided efficient and reliable transport of combat equipment, fuel, food, commodities, personnel, and raw materials that were pivotal in the allied victory.

Oftentimes forgotten, merchant mariners took part in every invasion from Normandy to Okinawa. Never before had the maritime power of America been so effectively utilized. The total cargo lift transported by the mariners totaled over 300 million tons. They transported the great majority of the thousands of military personnel and civilians who traveled overseas during the war and those returning to America after triumphant victories.

Risking their lives to provide the needed supplies for the war, merchant ships faced danger from submarines, mines, armed raiders and destroyers, aircraft, kamikaze attacks, and the elements from Mother Nature.

With an estimated 9,300 total casualties, the merchant marines bore a higher per capita casualty rate than any other branch in the U.S. Armed Forces during World War II. On top of that, about 11,000 mariners were wounded in action and 663 were taken prisoners of war.

Yet, despite these heroic efforts, they were not recognized as veterans until 1988, and they never received the benefits that other World War II veterans received under the GI bill. They came home from the war without recognition for their service and still, to this day, their service is often overlooked.

Today, there are less than 5,000 surviving World War II mariners, and with nearly 500 World War II veterans dying each day, it is more important than ever to recognize these brave achievements today.

Mr. Speaker, the merchant mariners provided the greatest sealift in history and became the difference between victory and defeat. These loyal and brave men put their lives on the line for the cause of freedom and selflessly answered their Nation's call to duty. It is time we give these courageous mariners the recognition they have earned with the Congressional Gold Medal.

I am proud that 312 of my colleagues agreed and are cosponsors of this bill. Now it is time to get it across the finish line, pay respect to these deserving veterans, and recognize the sacrifices and contributions of this brave group. I urge passage of the bill.

Mr. FOSTER. Mr. Speaker, I have no further requests for time, and I urge my colleagues to support this bill.

I yield back the balance of my time.

Ms. JACKSON LEE. Mr. Speaker, I rise to express my strong support for the bipartisan H.R. 2992, the "Merchant Marine of World War II Congressional Gold Medal Act," introduced by my colleague, Congresswoman SUSAN BROOKS of Indiana.

I stand to recognize every service member who has dedicated his or her life to the protection of this nation and the world.

The Merchant Marines of World War II were vital in the collective effort to defeat the Axis powers.

Serving our military as a distributor, Merchant Marine fleets carry imports and exports during peacetime and become a naval auxiliary during wartime, delivering troops and needed war supplies and materials.

Many Merchant Marines have sacrificed their lives, perishing at the highest rate of casualties of any service members, sometimes as high as 1 in 24 in any given mission.

During World War II, a total of 1,554 ships were sunk by German U-boats, including 733 ships weighing over 1,000 gross tons.

One hundred forty Merchant Marines have been awarded the Distinguished Service Medal, the Merchant Marine's highest honor, seven of whom were cadet graduates from the U.S. Merchant Marine Academy.

Mr. Speaker, I support H.R. 2992 which honors those civilians who answered the call to serve our nation in the United States Merchant Marines during World War II.

Mr. HUIZENGA of Michigan. Mr. Speaker, I, too, have no further speakers.

I yield back the balance of my time.

The SPEAKER pro tempore. The question is on the motion offered by the gentleman from Michigan (Mr. HUIZENGA) that the House suspend the rules and pass the bill, H.R. 2992.

The question was taken; and (two-thirds being in the affirmative) the rules were suspended and the bill was passed.

A motion to reconsider was laid on the table.

FILIPINO VETERANS OF WORLD WAR II CONGRESSIONAL GOLD MEDAL ACT OF 2015

Mr. HUIZENGA of Michigan. Mr. Speaker, I move to suspend the rules and pass the bill (S. 1555) to award a Congressional Gold Medal, collectively, to the Filipino veterans of World War II, in recognition of the dedicated service of the veterans during World War II.

The Clerk read the title of the bill.

The text of the bill is as follows:

S. 1555

Be it enacted by the Senate and House of Representatives of the United States of America in Congress assembled,

SECTION 1. SHORT TITLE.

This Act may be cited as the "Filipino Veterans of World War II Congressional Gold Medal Act of 2015".

SEC. 2. FINDINGS.

Congress finds the following:

(1) The First Philippine Republic was founded as a result of the Spanish-American War in which Filipino revolutionaries and the United States Armed Forces fought to overthrow Spanish colonial rule. On June 12, 1898, Filipinos declared the Philippines to be an independent and sovereign nation. The Treaty of Paris negotiated between the United States and Spain ignored this declaration of independence, and the United States paid Spain $20,000,000 to cede control of the Philippines to the United States. Filipino nationalists who sought independence rather than a change in colonial rulers clashed with forces of the United States in the Islands. The Philippine-American War, which officially lasted for 3 years from 1899 to 1902, led to the establishment of the United States civil government in the Philippines.

(2) In 1901, units of Filipino soldiers who fought for the United States against the nationalist insurrection were formally incorporated into the United States Army as the Philippine Scouts.

(3) In 1934, the Philippine Independence Act (Public Law 73–127; 48 Stat. 456) established a timetable for ending colonial rule of the United States. Between 1934 and Philippine independence in 1946, the United States retained sovereignty over Philippine foreign policy and reserved the right to call Filipinos into the service of the United States Armed Forces.

(4) On December 21 1935, President of the Philippine Commonwealth, Manuel Quezon, signed the National Defense Act, passed by the Philippine Assembly. General Douglas MacArthur set upon the task of creating an independent army in the Philippines, consisting of a small regular force, the Philippine Constabulary, a police force created during the colonial period of the United States, and reservists. By July 1941, the Philippine army had 130,000 reservists and 6,000 officers.

(5) On July 26, 1941, as tensions with Japan rose in the Pacific, President Franklin D. Roosevelt used his authority vested in the Constitution of the United States and the Philippine Independence Act to "call into service of the United States . . . all of the organized military forces of the Government of the Philippines." On July 27th, 1941, in accordance with a War Department directive received a day earlier, the United States Forces in the Far East (USAFFE) was established, and Manila was designated as the

command headquarters. Commander of the USAFFE, General Douglas MacArthur, planned to absorb the entire Philippine army into the USAFFE in phases. The first phase, which began on September 1, 1941, included 25,000 men and 4,000 officers.

(6) Filipinos who served in the USAFFE included—

(A) the Philippine Scouts, who comprised half of the 22,532 soldiers in the Philippine Department, or United States Army garrison stationed in the Islands at the start of the war;

(B) the Philippine Commonwealth Army;

(C) the new Philippine Scouts, or Filipinos who volunteered to serve with the United States Army when the United States Armed Forces returned to the island;

(D) Filipino civilians who volunteered to serve in the United States Armed Forces in 1945 and 1946, and who became "attached" to various units of the United States Army; and

(E) the "Guerrilla Services" who had fought behind enemy lines throughout the war.

(7) Even after hostilities ceased, wartime service of the new Philippine Scouts continued as a matter of law until the end of 1946, and the force gradually disbanded until it was disestablished in 1950.

(8) On December 8th, 1941, not even 24 hours after the bombing of Pearl Harbor, Japanese Imperial forces attacked bases of the United States Army in the Philippines.

(9) In the spring of 1942, the Japanese 14th Army overran the Bataan Peninsula, and, after a heroic but futile defense, more than 78,000 members of the United States Armed Forces were captured, specifically 66,000 Filipinos and 12,000 service members from the United States. The Japanese transferred the captured soldiers from Bataan to Camp O'Donnell, in what is now known as the infamous Bataan Death March. Forced to march the 70-mile distance in 1 week, without adequate food, water, or medicine, nearly 700 members of the United States Armed Forces and an estimated 6,000 to 10,000 Filipinos perished during the journey.

(10) After the fall of the Bataan Peninsula, the Japanese Army turned its sights on Corregidor. The estimated forces in defense of Corregidor totaled 13,000, and were comprised of members of the United States Armed Forces and Filipino troops. Of this number, 800 were killed, 1,000 were wounded, and 11,000 were captured and forced to march through the city of Manila, after which the captured troops were distributed to various POW camps. The rest of the captured troops escaped to organize or join an underground guerrilla army.

(11) Even before the fall of Corregidor, Philippine resistance, in the form of guerrilla armies, began to wage warfare on the Japanese invaders. Guerrilla armies, from Northern Luzon to Mindanao—

(A) raided Japanese camps, stealing weapons and supplies;

(B) sabotaged and ambushed Japanese troops on the move; and

(C) with little weaponry, and severely outmatched in numbers, began to extract victories.

(12) Japanese intelligence reports reveal that from the time the Japanese invaded until the return of the United States Armed Forces in the summer of 1944, an estimated 300,000 Filipinos continued to fight against Japanese forces. Filipino resistance against the Japanese was so strong that, in 1942, the Imperial Army formed the Morista Butai, a unit designated to suppress guerrillas.

(13) Because Philippine guerrillas worked to restore communication with United

States forces in the Pacific, General Mac-Arthur was able to use the guerrillas in advance of a conventional operation and provided the headquarters of General MacArthur with valuable information. Guerrillas captured and transmitted to the headquarters of General MacArthur Japanese naval plans for the Central Pacific, including defense plans for the Mariana Islands. Intelligence derived from guerrillas relating to aircraft, ship, and troop movements allowed for Allied forces to attack Japanese supply lines and guerrillas and even directed United States submarines where to land agents and cargo on the Philippine coast.

(14) On December 20, 1941, President Roosevelt signed the Selective Training and Service Amendments Act (Public Law 77–360; 55 Stat. 844) which, among other things, allowed Filipinos in the United States to enlist in the United States Armed Forces. In February 1942, President Roosevelt issued the Second War Powers Act (Public Law 77–507; 56 Stat. 176), promising a simplified naturalization process for Filipinos who served in the United States Armed Forces. Subsequently, 16,000 Filipinos in California alone decided to enlist.

(15) The mobilization of forces included the activation and assumption of command of the First Filipino Infantry Battalion on April 1, 1942, at Camp San Luis Obispo, California. Orders were issued to activate the First Filipino Infantry Regiment and Band at Salinas, California, effective July 13, 1942. The activation of the Second Filipino Infantry Regiment occurred at Fort Ord, California, on November 21, 1942. Nearly 9,000 Filipinos and Filipino Americans fought in the United States Army 1st and 2nd Filipino Infantry Regiments.

(16) Soldiers of the 1st and 2nd Infantry Regiments participated in the bloody combat and mop-up operations at New Guinea, Leyte, Samar, Luzon, and the Southern Philippines. In 1943, 800 men were selected from the 1st and 2nd Regiments and shipped to Australia to receive training in intelligence gathering, sabotage, and demolition. Reorganized as part of the 1st Reconnaissance Battalion, this group was sent to the Philippines to coordinate with major guerrilla armies in the Islands. Members of the 1st Regiment were also attached to the United States 6th Army "Alamo Scouts", a reconnaissance group that traveled 30 miles behind enemy lines to free Allied prisoners from the Cabanatuan death camp on January 30, 1945. In addition, in 1945, according to the 441st Counter Intelligence Unit of the United States Armed Forces, Philippine guerrillas provided "very important information and sketches of enemy positions and installations" for the liberation of the Santo Tomas prisoner of war camp, an event that made front page news across the United States.

(17) In March 1944, members of the 2nd Filipino Infantry Regiment were selected for special assignments, including intelligence missions, and reorganized as the 2nd Filipino Infantry Battalion (Separate). The 2nd Filipino Infantry Battalion (Separate) contributed to mop-up operations as a civil affairs unit.

(18) Filipinos participated in the war out of national pride, as well as out of a commitment to the Allied forces struggle against fascism. 57,000 Filipinos in uniform died in the war effort. Estimates of civilian deaths range from 700,000 to upwards of 1,000,000, or between 4.38 to 6.25 percent of the prewar population of 16,000,000.

(19) Because Filipinos who served in the Commonwealth Army of the Philippines were originally considered a part of the Allied struggle, the military order issued by President Roosevelt on July 26, 1941, stated that Filipinos who served in the Commonwealth Army of the Philippines were entitled to full veterans benefits. The guarantee to pay back the service of Filipinos through veterans benefits was reversed by the Rescission Acts of 1946 (Public Laws 79–301 and 79–391; 60 Stat. 6 and 60 Stat. 221), which deemed that the wartime service of the Commonwealth Army of the Philippines and the new Philippine Scouts was not considered active and, therefore, did not qualify for benefits.

(20) The loyal and valiant Filipino Veterans of World War II fought, suffered, and, in many instances, died in the same manner and under the same commander as other members of the United States Armed Forces during World War II.

(21) The Filipino Veterans of World War II fought alongside, and as an integral part of, the United States Armed Forces. The Philippines remained a territory of the United States for the duration of the war and, accordingly, the United States maintained sovereignty over Philippine foreign relations, including Philippine laws enacted by the Philippine Government. Filipinos who fought in the Philippines were not only defending or fighting for the Philippines, but also defending, and ultimately liberating, sovereign territory held by the United States Government.

(22) The United States remains forever indebted to the bravery, valor, and dedication that the Filipino Veterans of World War II displayed. Their commitment and sacrifice demonstrates a highly uncommon and commendable sense of patriotism and honor.

SEC. 3. DEFINITIONS.
In this Act—
(a) the term "Filipino Veterans of World War II" includes any individual who served—
(1) honorably at any time during the period beginning on July 26, 1941, and ending on December 31, 1946;
(2) in an active-duty status under the command of the United States Armed Forces in the Far East; and
(3)(A) within the Philippine Commonwealth Army, the Philippine Scouts, the Philippine Constabulary, Recognized Guerrilla units, the New Philippine Scouts, the First Filipino Infantry Regiment, the Second Filipino Infantry Battalion (Separate), or the First Reconnaissance Battalion; or
(B) commanding or serving in a unit described in paragraph (3)(A) as a United States military officer or enlisted soldier; and
(b) the term "Secretary" means the Secretary of the Treasury.

SEC. 4. CONGRESSIONAL GOLD MEDAL.
(a) AWARD AUTHORIZED.—The President pro tempore of the Senate and the Speaker of the House of Representatives shall make appropriate arrangements for the award, on behalf of Congress, of a single gold medal of appropriate design to the Filipino Veterans of World War II in recognition of the dedicated service of the veterans during World War II.
(b) DESIGN AND STRIKING.—For the purposes of the award referred to in subsection (a), the Secretary shall strike the Gold Medal with suitable emblems, devices, and inscriptions, to be determined by the Secretary.
(c) SMITHSONIAN INSTITUTION.—
(1) IN GENERAL.—Following the award of the gold medal in honor of the Filipino Veterans of World War II, the gold medal shall be given to the Smithsonian Institution, where it will be available for display as appropriate and made available for research.

(2) SENSE OF CONGRESS.—It is the sense of Congress that the Smithsonian Institution should make the gold medal received under paragraph (1) available for display elsewhere, particularly at other appropriate locations associated with the Filipino Veterans of World War II.
(d) DUPLICATE MEDALS.—
(1) IN GENERAL.—Under regulations that the Secretary may promulgate, the Secretary may strike and sell duplicates in bronze of the gold medal struck under this Act, at a price sufficient to cover the costs of the medals, including labor, materials, dies, use of machinery, and overhead expenses.
(2) SALE OF DUPLICATE MEDALS.—The amounts received from the sale of duplicate medals under paragraph (1) shall be deposited in the United States Mint Public Enterprise Fund.
SEC. 5. STATUS OF MEDALS.
(a) NATIONAL MEDALS.—Medals struck under this Act are national medals for purposes of chapter 51 of title 31, United States Code.
(b) NUMISMATIC ITEMS.—For purposes of section 5134 of title 31, United States Code, all medals struck under this Act shall be considered to be numismatic items.

The SPEAKER pro tempore. Pursuant to the rule, the gentleman from Michigan (Mr. HUIZENGA) and the gentleman from Illinois (Mr. FOSTER) each will control 20 minutes.

The Chair recognizes the gentleman from Michigan.

GENERAL LEAVE

Mr. HUIZENGA of Michigan. Mr. Speaker, I ask unanimous consent that all Members may have 5 legislative days in which to revise and extend their remarks and include extraneous material on the bill.

The SPEAKER pro tempore. Is there objection to the request of the gentleman from Michigan?

There was no objection.

Mr. HUIZENGA of Michigan. Mr. Speaker, I yield myself such time as I may consume.

Mr. Speaker, this is a special one for me, personally. I rise today in support of S. 1555, the Filipino Veterans of World War II Congressional Gold Medal Act of 2015, introduced by Senator HIRONO.

□ 1700

This bill, which was passed in the Senate on July 13, has companion legislation here in the House, H.R. 2737, introduced by our colleague, Representative GABBARD, which has 312 House cosponsors.

The reason why it is a special one to me is I have spent significant time in the Philippines and have many close Filipino friends, and know the dedication of the Philippines collectively, and those families who paid an ultimate sacrifice during World War II. I have actually visited our World War II cemetery in Manila, and have seen the headstones and gravestones of many Filipinos who were there fighting alongside of us as well. That is why it is a special opportunity for me, as chair of the subcommittee that has jurisdiction over this, to be involved.

So this bill authorizes the striking and awarding of a single Congressional Gold Medal of appropriate design to the Filipino Veterans of World War II in recognition of their heroic and dedicated service. Following the award, the medal will be given to the Smithsonian Institute, where it will be available for display as appropriate, or available for display elsewhere, particularly at other locations associated with the Filipino Veterans of World War II.

The Treasury Secretary is authorized to make and offer for sale bronze replicas of the medal at a price that will help defray the design and production costs of the actual medal.

Mr. Speaker, Japanese Imperial forces attacked the Philippines the day after bombing the U.S. base at Pearl Harbor almost exactly 75 years ago on December 7, 1941. At that point, the Philippines still were a United States colony, though the process that led to its independence in 1946 actually began in 1934.

Fortunately, the Philippines formed its own armed forces. Four months before the Pearl Harbor attack, President Roosevelt brought the 136,000 members of the force into a full state of readiness to defend the U.S. and its territories and colonies.

I will leave it to the House sponsor of the companion bill to describe the heroism of those soldiers and the sacrifices that they made in defense of the United States and their homeland; but suffice it to say that it was a difficult and costly defense that they waged.

I will note that our embassy sits right on the bay in Manila today and overlooks Corregidor and so many other places there in the Philippines that were witness to those battles, including my own uncle who, at the time, served in the Navy and helped deliver goods and services throughout the Pacific and into the Philippines as well.

Mr. Speaker, Congress has authorized Congressional Gold Medals in recognition of the heroic efforts of Japanese Americans, Native Americans, and Puerto Rican soldiers, among others, in defense of this country during World War II and in other conflicts. This recognition of Filipino veterans of World War II is long overdue, and I urge immediate passage of the bill.

I reserve the balance of my time.

HOUSE OF REPRESENTATIVES,
COMMITTEE ON HOUSE ADMINISTRATION,
Washington, DC, November 30, 2016.
Hon. JEB HENSARLING,
*Chairman, Committee on Financial Services,
Washington, DC.*

DEAR MR. CHAIRMAN: I write to you regarding S. 1555. As you know, the bill was received in the House of Representatives on July 17, 2016 and referred to the Committee on Financial Services and in addition to the Committee on House Administration. The bill seeks to award a Congressional Gold Medal, collectively, to the Filipino veterans of World War II, in recognition of the dedicated service of the veterans during World War II. S. 1555 passed the Senate without amendment by unanimous consent on July 13, 2016.

I realize that discharging the Committee on House Administration from further consideration of S. 1555 will serve in the best interest of the House of Representatives and agree to do so. It is the understanding of the Committee on House Administration that forgoing action on S. 1555 will not prejudice the Committee with respect to appointment of conferees or any future jurisdictional claim. I request that this letter and any response be included in in the Congressional Record.

Sincerely,
CANDICE S. MILLER,
Chairman.

———

HOUSE OF REPRESENTATIVES,
COMMITTEE ON FINANCIAL SERVICES,
Washington, DC, November 30, 2016.
Hon. CANDICE MILLER,
*Chairman, Committee on House Administration,
Washington, DC.*

DEAR CHAIRMAN MILLER: Thank you for your November 30th letter regarding S. 1555, the "Filipino Veterans of World War II Congressional Gold Medal Act of 2015."

I am most appreciative of your decision to forego action on S. 1555 so that it may move expeditiously to the House floor. I acknowledge that although you are waiving action on the bill, the Committee on House Administration is in no way waiving its jurisdictional interest in this or similar legislation. In addition, if a conference is necessary on this legislation, I will support any request that your committee be represented therein.

Finally, I shall be pleased to include your letter and this letter on S. 1555 in the Congressional Record during floor consideration of the same.

Sincerely,
JEB HENSARLING,
Chairman.

Mr. FOSTER. Mr. Speaker, I yield myself such time as I may consume.

I rise today in strong support of S. 1555, legislation to award a Congressional Gold Medal collectively to the Filipino Veterans of World War II in recognition of their service and sacrifice and their role in defeating the Imperial Japanese Army.

While we are taking up the Senate-passed version of the Filipino Veterans of World War II Congressional Medal Act today, I want to acknowledge the hard work and dedication of the gentlewoman from Hawaii, Representative TULSI GABBARD, who has led the effort to move this same legislation across the finish line here in the House. Since introducing the legislation, Representative GABBARD has garnered the support of more than 300 House cosponsors, and I am proud to be among them.

In 1934, the United States began a 10-year period of bringing its colonial rule to an end. During that time, the U.S. retained control over Philippine foreign policy and maintained the right to call Filipinos into the service of the United States Armed Forces.

As tensions with Japan began to rise in 1941, President Franklin Roosevelt invoked his authority to call all organized military forces of the Government of the Philippines into the service of the United States. Responding to his call to arms, more than 200,000 Filipinos fought on behalf of the U.S. as part of the United States Armed Forces in the Far East.

The force included the Philippine Scouts, the Philippine Commonwealth Army, the new Philippine Scouts, Filipino civilians who served on a voluntary basis, and the Guerrilla Services who fought behind enemy lines throughout the war.

Over the course of the war, an estimated 57,000 Filipinos in uniform perished, and many more Filipino civilian lives were lost. Despite this loyalty and tremendous sacrifice, and the U.S. commitment to provide Filipinos who served as part of the Allied struggle with full veterans benefits, this promise was shamefully withdrawn by the Rescission Act of 1946 at the close of the war.

While a number of benefits have since been made available to the Filipino veterans, we must continue to work to ensure that those who risked their lives to defend the United States and the free world are provided with the full benefits, honor, and respect that they deserve.

This legislation has the support of the Veterans of Foreign Wars, the Disabled American Veterans, the American Legion, the National Federation of Filipino American Associations, and many other distinguished organizations.

I urge Members to pass this legislation, which takes a modest but welcome step to recognize the contributions of Filipino veterans of World War II.

Mr. Speaker, I reserve the balance of my time.

Mr. HUIZENGA of Michigan. Mr. Speaker, I yield such time as he may consume to the gentleman from California (Mr. ROYCE), the chairman of the Foreign Affairs Committee.

Mr. ROYCE. Mr. Speaker, I rise in strong support here for the Filipino Veterans of World War II Congressional Gold Medal Act, and I am one of the proud cosponsors, along with my colleagues here, of this act.

I have had an opportunity over the last couple of years to travel twice to the Philippines. One of them was right after the cyclone hit Tacloban, and we took a delegation there.

As you travel across the islands of the Philippines, it is a constant reminder of the enormity of the sacrifice as you see those battle sites, the enormity of the sacrifice made by this unsung group of heroes who fought so courageously for the defense of our country, during what is really one of the most perilous moments of American history, and their valor and their patriotism is deserving of this recognition from Congress.

I don't think many Americans understand how quickly the reaction across the Philippines, in terms of Pearl Harbor, more than 250,000 Filipino soldiers responded to President Roosevelt's call to arms to fit under the American flag.

In addition to that, just in my State of California, we had 16,000 Filipino Americans that went forward and enlisted, where the U.S. Army then formed the 1st and 2nd Filipino American Infantry Regiments. That is where those regiments were organized.

On December 8, 1941—and this was not 24 hours after the bombing of Pearl Harbor—it was at that moment in time that the Japanese Imperial forces attacked the U.S. bases in the Philippines. Filipinos and Filipino Americans fought valiantly in the push to regain the Philippines from Imperial Japanese forces.

Mr. Speaker, 57,000 Filipinos in uniform died in the war effort. More than that, among the casualties of those who struggled against Japan, but 50,000 Filipinos in uniform, and they gave their lives in battles such as Bataan and Corregidor; and their sacrifice was absolutely instrumental in disrupting the enemy's advancement in the Pacific.

As President Harry Truman made clear: "They fought as American nationals under the American flag and under the direction of our military leaders. They fought with gallantry and courage under the most difficult conditions. . . ."

So I am honored to rise today in support of recognizing these great heroes. The contributions of the Filipino World War II veterans are a very important part of American military history, and their accomplishments deserve the recognition of the Congressional Gold Medal.

Mr. FOSTER. Mr. Speaker, I yield 5 minutes to the gentlewoman from Hawaii (Ms. GABBARD), the lead sponsor of the House version of this bill.

Ms. GABBARD. Mr. Speaker, I have the privilege of representing the Second Congressional District in Hawaii, a State that has deep cultural roots and ties to the contributions that Filipino Americans have made to our Nation throughout history, from driving Hawaii's plantation-based economy in the early 20th Century, serving in our Armed Forces, to becoming leaders in every industry and sector in our State and across the country.

It is an honor to stand here today as a voice for the more than 200,000 Filipino and Filipino American soldiers that served our country during World War II. These loyal and courageous soldiers suffered, sacrificed, fought, and gave their lives alongside their American counterparts throughout the war.

We have waited far too long to recognize these heroes, who deserve this honor, in standing alongside units like the Tuskegee Airmen and Hawaii's own 442nd/100th Infantry Battalion with being awarded the Congressional Gold Medal, our Nation's highest civilian honor.

With just 18,000 of these Filipino World War II veterans still alive and with us today, we cannot afford to wait any longer.

I would like to thank the 312 House Members, Republicans and Democrats, and 71 Senators that cosponsored this bipartisan legislation, representing nearly every State and territory in our country.

I also want to say a special mahalo nui loa to my colleagues, Congressman JOE HECK, who is the Republican lead on this legislation; Congresswoman JUDY CHU; and Congressman MIKE HONDA, for working with me to push this bill through the House; and my colleague, Senator MAZIE HIRONO, who is here today; as well as Senator DEAN HELLER, for championing this bill in the Senate; all of our staff; and both Democrat and Republican leadership for their efforts, commitment, and support to passing this legislation.

I would also like to recognize Major General Antonio Taguba, who joins us today in the gallery, and the Filipino Veterans Recognition and Education Project for their years of commitment to this historic effort and for continuing to fight to ensure we remember and recognize the legacy of our Filipino World War II veterans as a critical part of our American history.

Major General Taguba's father, Staff Sergeant Tomas Taguba, was a soldier in the 45th Infantry Regiment Philippine Division that served alongside the U.S. Army during the war, where he fought in the Battle of Bataan. He survived the Bataan Death March.

This legislation is a testament to Staff Sergeant Tomas Taguba, and the hundreds of thousands of Filipino World War II veterans who deserve a place of recognition amongst our greatest generation. Thank you very much to all of you: "Miraming salamat sa inyong lahat."

I urge my colleagues to join me in voting to pass this long overdue legislation today. Time is of the essence. We must honor these courageous men while they are still among us and recognize their dedicated service to our Nation and our history.

The SPEAKER pro tempore. Members are reminded not to reference guests in the gallery.

Mr. HUIZENGA of Michigan. Mr. Speaker, with that admonishment, I won't say Ma-Bu-Hi and welcome to our Filipino friends in the gallery; but I will yield such time as he may consume to the gentleman from Nevada (Mr. HECK), the lead sponsor on the Republican side.

Mr. HECK of Nevada. Mr. Speaker, during my time here in the House of Representatives, each Congressional Session I have introduced the World War II Filipino Veterans Recognition Act in an attempt to restore the benefits that were promised to these brave soldiers by Franklin Delano Roosevelt

when they were incorporated into the United States Armed Forces Far East during World War II, but then had those benefits denied by the Rescission Act of 1946.

These soldiers served side by side with American troops. They served under American officers. They bled, fought, and died to protect their homeland on behalf of the United States.

I have had the honor to get to know six of these gentlemen who lived in southern Nevada: Francisco Cedulla; Romeo Barreras; Silverio Cuaresma; Augusto Opus; Bataan Death March survivor, Jesse Baltazar; and Edilberto Briones. Unfortunately, over the last 6 years, five of them have passed on, never receiving the recognition that they justly deserve. That is why this bill is so important.

While it does not justly compensate these brave soldiers for the service that they gave to this country, this bill, S. 1555, and the companion introduced by my good friend, the gentlewoman from Hawaii (Ms. GABBARD), and of which I am the lead cosponsor, is in some small way a recognition of the service rendered by these brave patriots.

□ 1715

It is for that reason that I rise in strong support and urge all of my colleagues to vote in support of S. 1555, so that we can finally pay some level of recognition to those who served side by side with American soldiers under American command.

Mr. FOSTER. Mr. Speaker, I yield 2 minutes to the gentleman from Virginia (Mr. SCOTT), who is the ranking member of the Committee on Education and the Workforce.

Mr. SCOTT of Virginia. Mr. Speaker, I thank the gentleman for yielding.

Mr. Speaker, I rise today in support of S. 1555, the Filipino Veterans of World War II Congressional Gold Medal Act of 2015.

Filipino Americans have contributed to American life and culture in countless ways, and one of the most noble is through military service. Over 200,000 Filipino soldiers and guerrilla fighters served with the United States Armed Forces during World War II. Their invaluable service helped provide the necessary support to defeat the Japanese in the Pacific.

For over 60 years, Filipino veterans and community advocates have fought to obtain benefits and recognition that they were promised. In 2009, Congress created the Filipino Veterans Equity Compensation Fund, where eligible veterans who are U.S. citizens could receive a one-time payment of $15,000; eligible veterans who are not U.S. citizens could receive a one-time payment of $9,000. While this fund has allowed many of them to receive some compensation, in Congress we are still working to make sure these families get all of the benefits they earned, they deserved and were promised.

Another way that we can recognize these heroes is by awarding them the Congressional Gold Medal. The Senate unanimously passed the Filipino World War II Congressional Gold Medal Act in July. Mr. Speaker, as a cosponsor of the House version of the bill and co-chair of the U.S.-Philippines Friendship Caucus, I urge my colleagues to support the legislation so that approximately 18,000 surviving Filipino veterans of World War II may be recognized for their service to our Nation. We are forever indebted to these brave soldiers, and it is important that we appropriately express our gratitude for that service.

Mr. Speaker, I therefore urge my colleagues to support the bill.

Mr. FOSTER. Mr. Speaker, I yield 2 minutes to the gentlewoman from California (Ms. JUDY CHU), who is a member of the Judiciary Committee and the chair of the Congressional Asian Pacific American Caucus.

Ms. JUDY CHU of California. Mr. Speaker, over 70 years ago, more than 200,000 brave Filipino and Filipino American soldiers answered the call to fight alongside American servicemembers during World War II. These soldiers served on the front lines and played a critical role in ultimately helping the United States to achieve victory in the Pacific. It is because of their courage that we were able to protect Americans at home while defending democracy abroad. Many of these veterans are now in their twilight years, and it is long past time that we honor them for their sacrifice and service to our Nation.

While we can never fully repay the debt that we owe these veterans, today we have the opportunity to award them with our Nation's highest civilian honor by passing the Filipino Veterans of World War II Congressional Gold Medal Act. I urge my colleagues to join me in voting to pass this critical legislation to honor our Filipino World War II veterans with the recognition they have earned.

Mr. FOSTER. Mr. Speaker, I yield 4 minutes to the gentleman from California (Mr. HONDA), who is a member of the Appropriations Committee and chair emeritus of the Congressional Asian Pacific American Caucus.

Mr. HONDA. Mr. Speaker, I want to thank my colleague, Mr. FOSTER, and on the other side, Congressman HUIZENGA of Michigan, for bringing this up. It is an issue that has been a long time in coming forward. I thank Mr. HECK of Nevada, also, for the gentleman's comments regarding the Filipino veterans' history in World War II.

Prior to this, we talked about the merchant marines. I think that the merchant marines are a long time past in being recognized for their bravery and their willingness to forge through the oceans to bring materiel and artillery to fight fascism in Europe.

Today we stand here in 2016 to ask for support for the bravery, patriotism, and sacrifice of nearly 250,000 Filipinos and Filipino Americans to whom our Nation owes much. I ask this Chamber to show its commitment to those who have bled for our Nation's principles at a time of great adversity by honoring these brave souls with the Congressional Gold Medal.

The Congressional Gold Medal is a symbol of our recognition of their service, but it does very little to recognize the sacrifice and patience that they had to endure since World War II, when, as it was mentioned earlier, this Congress passed two rescission bills in the Appropriations in 1946 removing the Filipino veterans from veterans' benefits and the kinds of promises that President Roosevelt and MacArthur had given to the Filipino veterans.

The story of these proud veterans begins more than 70 years ago when President Roosevelt did ask Filipino and Filipino American soldiers to serve under U.S. authority during World War II. Under our flag, we drafted them and we asked for volunteers. We got both from them.

The people of the Philippines valiantly stepped up to the challenge and played a vital role in securing a victory for the U.S. and its Allies in the Pacific theater. Historians have long since concluded that these valiant efforts by the Filipino and Filipino American soldiers in Bataan helped keep Midway and the coral islands in America's hands at a crucial time during World War II.

Over 60,000 Filipino soldiers, alongside 15,000 American brothers in arms, were captured and forced to walk over 65 miles to the prison camps, which was called the infamous Bataan March—the infamous Bataan Death March—to the ships that would take them to Japan, where they became POWs.

Several thousand Filipinos and Americans died along the way making the ultimate sacrifice in our mutual struggle against fascism and for the promise of democracy and self-determination. A lot of these Filipinos had interceded during the march to the ships, endangering themselves of being beheaded or losing their arms or their lives because they were going to offer water as sustenance to our POWs who were being marched to the ships. We have forgotten that. Hopefully, today, this Congressional Medal of Honor will help us remember the kinds of things that they have sacrificed.

Congress shamefully passed the Rescission Act of 1946, as was mentioned earlier, betraying the promise of full eligibility of rights to Filipino soldiers turning their backs on these valiant souls. We did this consciously twice. In February of 2009, we were here in Congress and at long last passed legislation that included benefits for Filipino and World War II veterans.

The SPEAKER pro tempore. The time of the gentleman has expired.

Mr. FOSTER. Mr. Speaker, I yield the gentleman an additional 30 seconds.

Mr. HONDA. Mr. Speaker, this bittersweet victory comes at the end of a 50-year legislative battle which has seen thousands of veterans lose their lives due to the passage of time. This year we must send a clear message to the surviving 18,000 Filipino and Filipino American World War II veterans that we are honored by their spirit and moved by the heroism and their patience—the spirit that remained hopeful for many, many years that the American people, through their Representatives in this Congress, would do the right thing.

This is the right thing to do. Join me in honoring all of the Filipino World War II veterans with the Congressional Gold Medal.

Mr. FOSTER. Mr. Speaker, I yield 3 minutes to the gentlewoman from Hawaii (Ms. HANABUSA), who is a member of the Armed Services Committee.

Ms. HANABUSA. Mr. Speaker, I just returned to the 114th Congress, and I would like to have everyone remember that when I first came here in the 112th Congress is when we gave the Congressional Gold Medals to the Japanese Americans who fought in World War II. I remember how much pride they all had to receive that Gold Medal. That is why I introduced, in a subsequent Congress, the first attempt to get the Gold Medal for the Filipino war veterans.

In 7 days, Mr. Speaker, we will be commemorating, in Hawaii, the attack on Pearl Harbor—the 75th anniversary. Imagine, 75 years, and we have still not kept our promise to the Filipino war veterans. Many of them are in both Congresswoman GABBARD's and my district. I must tell you, all that they have asked for is a recognition by this country that we will keep our promises to them.

Mr. Speaker, I would like to say that it is with such pride that I stand here to see that, across the aisle, we have been able to have this piece of legislation hopefully pass and to also know the hard work of my colleagues, especially Senator HIRONO in the Senate and, of course, Congresswoman GABBARD.

There are two gentlemen that I also want us all to remember, and that is former Senator Daniel K. Inouye and Senator Daniel K. Akaka. The reason why is because they both said that the greatest regret they had was that we could not—they could not—change that act in 1946 and keep their word to the Filipino veterans that they would have full benefits, that they could not reunite them with their families as they had all promised.

But, Mr. Speaker, this act, the act of this Gold Medal, will make things somewhat right. It will at least say that this great country recognizes the promises that we have made and this great country will not forget the sacrifices that they have made for us.

Mr. Speaker, I ask that all my colleagues vote in favor of this bill.

Mr. FOSTER. Mr. Speaker, I have no further requests for time. I urge my colleagues to support this bill.

Mr. Speaker, I yield back the balance of my time.

Mr. HUIZENGA of Michigan. Mr. Speaker, I, too, urge passage of this bill by my colleagues and thank the Filipino people for their support and friendship for the many, many years.

Mr. Speaker, I yield back the balance of my time.

Ms. JACKSON LEE. Mr. Speaker, I rise in support of S. 1555, the "Filipino Veterans of World War II Congressional Gold Medal Act of 2015."

S. 1555 honors the brave Filipino soldiers who courageously fought for freedom in World War II by awarding the highest honor that this Congress can bestow.

More than 260,000 Filipino veterans, 18,000 of who are still alive today, who for decades had to fight for benefits and recognition, will now receive the recognition they have earned and deserve.

These Filipino soldiers were instrumental to the United States efforts in the Pacific.

After the invasion of the Philippines by Japanese forces they retired to the Bataan Peninsula and continued to fight valiantly.

Among these brave soldiers is Dominador Soriano, a resident of San Antonio, Texas, who fought as a member of both the Philippine and United States Armies.

He was drafted into the Philippine Army in 1938 and then inducted into the U.S. Army in the Far East on September 1, 1941.

Under the leadership of General Douglas MacArthur, Soriano commanded the Echo Company of the 83rd Infantry Regiment, keeping watch on Japanese ships moving through the Tanon Strait.

During the Japanese invasion he was shot and in July of 1944 was captured, beaten and then released, but could barely walk.

Soriano continued working with the resistance until the surrender of the Japanese on August 15, 1945.

Recently, the city of San Antonio honored Soriano and other Filipino veterans with a resolution that recognized their efforts during World War II and supported legislation to award these courageous men the Congressional Gold Medal.

The resolution is the first of its kind by any city in the United States, and I believe that it is time for Congress to follow suit.

These brave Filipino soldiers answered President Franklin D. Roosevelt's call to serve in World War II and they deserve the highest award that we can give, for there is no higher duty than putting one's life on the line for freedom and country.

For these reasons, Mr. Speaker, I rise in support of S. 1555 the "Filipino Veterans of World War II Congressional Gold Medal Act of 2015."

The SPEAKER pro tempore. The question is on the motion offered by the gentleman from Michigan (Mr. HUIZENGA) that the House suspend the rules and pass the bill, S. 1555.

The question was taken; and (two-thirds being in the affirmative) the rules were suspended and the bill was passed.

A motion to reconsider was laid on the table.

OFFICE OF STRATEGIC SERVICES CONGRESSIONAL GOLD MEDAL ACT

Mr. HUIZENGA of Michigan. Mr. Speaker, I move to suspend the rules and pass the bill (S. 2234) to award the Congressional Gold Medal, collectively, to the members of the Office of Strategic Services (OSS) in recognition of their superior service and major contributions during World War II.

The Clerk read the title of the bill.

The text of the bill is as follows:

S. 2234

Be it enacted by the Senate and House of Representatives of the United States of America in Congress assembled,

SECTION 1. SHORT TITLE.

This Act may be cited as the "Office of Strategic Services Congressional Gold Medal Act".

SEC. 2. FINDINGS.

The Congress finds the following:

(1) The Office of Strategic Services (OSS) was America's first effort to implement a system of strategic intelligence during World War II and provided the basis for the modern-day American intelligence and special operations communities. The U.S. Special Operations Command and the National Clandestine Service chose the OSS spearhead as their insignias.

(2) OSS founder General William J. Donovan is the only person in American history to receive our Nation's four highest decorations, including the Medal of Honor. Upon learning of his death in 1959, President Eisenhower called General Donovan the "last hero". In addition to founding and leading the OSS, General Donovan was also selected by President Roosevelt, who called him his "secret legs", as an emissary to Great Britain and continental Europe before the United States entered World War II.

(3) All the military branches during World War II contributed personnel to the OSS. The present-day Special Operations Forces trace their lineage to the OSS. Its Maritime Unit was a precursor to the U.S. Navy SEALs. The OSS Operational Groups and Jedburghs were forerunners to U.S. Army Special Forces. The 801st/492nd Bombardment Group ("Carpetbaggers") were progenitors to the Air Force Special Operations Command. The Marines who served in the OSS, including the actor Sterling Hayden (a Silver Star recipient), Col. William Eddy (a Distinguished Service Cross recipient who was described as the "nearest thing the United States has had to a Lawrence of Arabia"), and Col. Peter Ortiz (a two-time Navy Cross recipient), were predecessors to the Marine Special Operations Command. U.S. Coast Guard personnel were recruited for the Maritime Unit and its Operational Swimmer Group.

(4) The OSS organized, trained, supplied, and fought with resistance organizations throughout Europe and Asia that played an important role in America's victory during World War II. General Eisenhower credited the OSS's covert contribution in France to the equivalent to having an extra military division. General Eisenhower told General Donovan that if it did nothing else, the photographic reconnaissance conducted by the OSS prior to the D-Day Invasion justified its creation.

(5) Four future directors of central intelligence served as OSS officers: William Casey, William Colby, Allen Dulles, and Richard Helms.

(6) Women comprised more than one-third of OSS personnel and played a critical role in the organization. They included Virginia Hall, the only civilian female to receive a Distinguished Service Cross in World War II, and Julia Child.

(7) OSS recruited Fritz Kolbe, a German diplomat who became America's most important spy against the Nazis in World War II.

(8) America's leading scientists and scholars served in the OSS Research and Analysis Branch, including Ralph Bunche, the first African-American to receive the Nobel Peace Prize; Pulitzer Prize-winning historian Arthur Schlesinger, Jr.; Supreme Court Justice Arthur Goldberg; Sherman Kent; John King Fairbank; and Walt Rostow. Its ranks included seven future presidents of the American Historical Association, five of the American Economic Association, and two Nobel laureates.

(9) The U.S. Department of State's Bureau of Intelligence and Research traces its creation to the OSS Research and Analysis Branch.

(10) James Donovan, who was portrayed by Tom Hanks in the Steven Spielberg movie "Bridge of Spies" and negotiated the release of U-2 pilot Francis Gary Powers, served as General Counsel of the OSS.

(11) The OSS invented and employed new technology through its Research and Development Branch, inventing new weapons and revolutionary communications equipment. Dr. Christian Lambertsen invented the first underwater rebreathing apparatus that was first utilized by the OSS and is known today as SCUBA.

(12) OSS Detachment 101 operated in Burma and pioneered the art of unconventional warfare. It was the first United States unit to deploy a large guerrilla army deep in enemy territory. It has been credited with the highest kill/loss ratio for any infantry-type unit in American military history and was awarded a Presidential Unit Citation.

(13) Its X-2 branch pioneered counterintelligence with the British and established the modern counterintelligence community. The network of contacts built by the OSS with foreign intelligence services led to enduring Cold War alliances.

(14) Operation Torch, the Allied invasion of French North Africa in November 1942, was aided by the networks established and information acquired by the OSS to guide Allied landings.

(15) OSS Operation Halyard rescued more than 500 downed airmen trapped behind enemy lines in Yugoslavia, one of the most daring and successful rescue operations of World War II.

(16) OSS "Mercy Missions" at the end of World War II saved the lives of thousands of Allied prisoners of war whom it was feared would be murdered by the Japanese.

(17) The handful of surviving men and women of the OSS whom General Donovan said performed "some of the bravest acts of the war" are members of the "Greatest Generation". They have never been collectively

recognized for their heroic and pioneering service in World War II.

SEC. 3. CONGRESSIONAL GOLD MEDAL.

(a) PRESENTATION AUTHORIZED.—The Speaker of the House of Representatives and the President pro tempore of the Senate shall make appropriate arrangements for the presentation, on behalf of the Congress, of a gold medal of appropriate design in commemoration to the members of the Office of Strategic Services (OSS), in recognition of their superior service and major contributions during World War II.

(b) DESIGN AND STRIKING.—For purposes of the presentation referred to in subsection (a), the Secretary of the Treasury (referred to in this Act as the "Secretary") shall strike a gold medal with suitable emblems, devices, and inscriptions, to be determined by the Secretary.

(c) SMITHSONIAN INSTITUTION.—

(1) IN GENERAL.—Following the award of the gold medal in commemoration to the members of the Office of Strategic Services under subsection (a), the gold medal shall be given to the Smithsonian Institution, where it will be displayed as appropriate and made available for research.

(2) SENSE OF CONGRESS.—It is the sense of Congress that the Smithsonian Institution should make the gold medal received under paragraph (1) available for display elsewhere, particularly at other appropriate locations associated with the Office of Strategic Services.

SEC. 4. DUPLICATE MEDALS.

The Secretary may strike and sell duplicates in bronze of the gold medal struck pursuant to section 3 under such regulations as the Secretary may prescribe, at a price sufficient to cover the cost thereof, including labor, materials, dies, use of machinery, and overhead expenses, and the cost of the gold medal.

SEC. 5. STATUS OF MEDALS.

(a) NATIONAL MEDALS.—The medals struck pursuant to this Act are national medals for purposes of chapter 51 of title 31, United States Code.

(b) NUMISMATIC ITEMS.—For purposes of section 5134 of title 31, United States Code, all medals struck under this Act shall be considered to be numismatic items.

The SPEAKER pro tempore. Pursuant to the rule, the gentleman from Michigan (Mr. HUIZENGA) and the gentleman from Illinois (Mr. FOSTER) each will control 20 minutes.

The Chair recognizes the gentleman from Michigan.

GENERAL LEAVE

Mr. HUIZENGA of Michigan. Mr. Speaker, I ask unanimous consent that all Members may have 5 legislative days in which to revise and extend their remarks and include extraneous material on this bill.

The SPEAKER pro tempore. Is there objection to the request of the gentleman from Michigan?

There was no objection.

Mr. HUIZENGA of Michigan. Mr. Speaker, I yield myself such time as I may consume.

Mr. Speaker, every wartime President of the United States—and probably every wartime leader in history—has had some clandestine help from men and women who risked life and limb to report on and sometimes to dis-

rupt the actions of the enemy. No leader of such clandestine force was as uniformly successful, as visionary, or ultimately had as much impact on both his country's affairs and those of the entire world as Colonel William J. "Wild Bill" Donovan.

☐ 1730

President Franklin Roosevelt charged Colonel Donovan with the daunting task of unifying and streamlining the previously ad hoc U.S. efforts at intelligence gathering. The unit he founded, the Office of Strategic Services, was the foundation upon which the postwar government built the Central Intelligence Agency.

Each branch of the armed services contributed members of the OSS, which trained, equipped, and fought with resistance forces in the Atlantic and Pacific theaters. Its various operations were the forerunners of many of today's Special Operations Forces. Four future directors of central intelligence—Allen Dulles, William Casey, William Colby, and Richard Helms—were all OSS operatives, and at least a third of the operatives were women, including the world's first and favorite TV chef, Julia Child, of all people.

Mr. Speaker, I rise today in support of S. 2234, the Office of Strategic Services Congressional Gold Medal Act, introduced by Senator BLUNT of Missouri. The bill, which passed the Senate on February 23, has companion legislation to H.R. 3929, introduced by our Republican colleague, Representative LATTA, which has 320 House cosponsors.

The bill authorizes the striking and awarding of a single gold medal of appropriate design to commemorate the members of the Office of Strategic Services in recognition of their superior service and major contributions during World War II.

After awarding the medal, it will be given to the Smithsonian museum where it will be available for display there or elsewhere, as appropriate. The Treasury secretary is authorized to make and offer for sale bronze replicas of the medal at a price that will help defray the design and production costs of the actual medal.

Mr. Speaker, long after World War II ended, most of the efforts of the OSS remained classified, and we probably still do not know all of the hair-raising tales that might be told. One thing is not secret—we owe those men and women an enormous debt of gratitude, not only for their work during the war but for the groundwork that they laid towards what is clearly the best intelligence service in the world today. We should recognize those contributions by awarding the Congressional Gold Medal to these heroes.

I urge immediate passage of this bill.

I reserve the balance of my time.

HOUSE OF REPRESENTATIVES,
COMMITTEE ON HOUSE ADMINISTRATION,
Washington, DC, November 30, 2016.
Hon. JEB HENSARLING,
*Chairman, Committee on Financial Services,
Washington, DC.*

DEAR MR. CHAIRMAN: I write to you regarding S. 2234. As you know, the bill was received in the House of Representatives on February 23, 2016 and referred to the Committee on Financial Services and in addition to the Committee on the Committee on House Administration. The bill seeks to award the Congressional Gold Medal, collectively, to the members of the Office of Strategic Services (OSS) in recognition of their superior service and major contributions during World War II. S. 2234 passed the Senate without amendment by unanimous consent on February 22, 2016.

I realize that discharging the Committee on House Administration from further consideration of S. 2234 will serve in the best interest of the House of Representatives and agree to do so. It is the understanding of the Committee on House Administration that forgoing action on S. 2234 will not prejudice the Committee with respect to appointment of conferees or any future jurisdictional claim. I request that this letter and any response be included in the Congressional Record.

Sincerely,

CANDICE S. MILLER,
Chairman.

HOUSE OF REPRESENTATIVES,
COMMITTEE ON FINANCIAL SERVICES,
Washington, DC, November 30, 2016.
Hon. CANDICE MILLER,
*Chairman, Committee on House Administration,
Washington, DC.*

DEAR CHAIRMAN MILLER: Thank you for your November 30th letter regarding S. 2234, the "Office of Strategic Services Congressional Gold Medal Act."

I am most appreciative of your decision to forego action on S. 2234 so that it may move expeditiously to the House floor. I acknowledge that although you are waiving action on the bill, the Committee on House Administration is in no way waiving its jurisdictional interest in this or similar legislation. In addition, if a conference is necessary on this legislation, I will support any request that your committee be represented therein.

Finally, I shall be pleased to include your letter and this letter on S. 2234 in the Congressional Record during floor consideration of the same.

Sincerely,

JEB HENSARLING,
Chairman.

Mr. FOSTER. Mr. Speaker, I yield myself such time as I may consume.

I rise today in support of S. 2234, legislation to award a Congressional Gold Medal to members of the Office of Strategic Services in recognition of their significant service and contributions against the Axis Powers during World War II.

I am pleased to note that the legislation has already passed the Senate with unanimous consent, and that companion legislation, introduced here in the House, has already received the endorsement of 320 cosponsors. Upon passage here in the House, the legislation will be cleared for the President's signature.

Created at the start of World War II, the Office of Strategic Services was the

Nation's first effort to implement a coordinated intelligence system, laying the foundation for our modern-day intelligence and special operations capabilities.

In addition to honoring and recognizing the meaningful and personal sacrifice of the thousands of Americans who served as part of the Office of Strategic Services, the legacy of the OSS offers a number of lessons that continue to hold value to this day. Importantly, the legacy of the OSS serves as a reminder that effective coordination across our Nation's intelligence agencies continues to play a foundational role in promoting our national security interests.

The OSS also serves to remind us of the importance of working strategically and in concert with our longstanding allies to prevail against those who seek to do our Nation harm. Indeed, during World War II, the OSS played a critical role in organizing, training, supplying, and fighting alongside resistance organizations throughout Europe and Asia.

Moreover, throughout the war, the OSS demonstrated that our government is at its best when it brings together a wide range of individuals with diverse backgrounds. At its height in late 1944, the Office of Strategic Services employed nearly 13,000 individuals, nearly a third of whom were women. The service also drew its personnel not only from the military but also from civilians from all walks of life, including economists, psychologists, geographers, and a wide range of other fields.

Upon the dissolution of the Office of Strategic Services at the close of World War II, General William J. Donovan, who headed the OSS, stated that, "We have come to the end of an unusual experiment. That experiment was to determine whether a group of Americans constituting a cross section of racial origins, of abilities, of temperaments, and of talents could meet and risk an encounter with long-established and well-trained enemy organizations."

He went on to conclude that, "You can go with the assurance that you have made a beginning in showing the people of America that only by decisions of national policy based upon accurate information can we have the chance of a peace that will endure."

So I am pleased that we are honoring the thousands of men and women who made the sacrifice to serve as part of the Office of Strategic Services, whose contribution was so critical to America's ultimate triumph over the Axis Powers.

I am also pleased that the legislation will allow future generations to appreciate these contributions to our Nation and the world. By designating the Smithsonian Institution as the custodian of the medal, and by allowing for its display at other locations associated with the Office of Strategic Services, the legislation will ensure that the legacy and the lessons that can be drawn from the contributions made by members of the Office of Strategic Services will not be forgotten.

So as we enter into unchartered waters with the incoming administration, I hope that we will all take pause and heed the lessons of the OSS and remember that America is at its best when we work together with our longstanding allies and when we recruit diverse personnel to serve our government.

I also hope that it serves as a reminder of the importance of taking care of our veterans once their service has ended and they return to civilian life.

I urge adoption of the legislation.

I reserve the balance of my time.

Mr. HUIZENGA of Michigan. Mr. Speaker, I yield such time as he may consume to the gentleman from Ohio (Mr. LATTA), the author of the House bill.

Mr. LATTA. Mr. Speaker, I thank the gentleman for yielding.

Mr. Speaker, I rise today in support of S. 2234, the Office of Strategic Services Congressional Gold Medal Act, companion legislation I introduced earlier this Congress as H.R. 3929 to honor and recognize these brave veterans for their superior service and major contributions made during World War II.

The Office of Strategic Services, the OSS as it is often referred to, was America's first strategic intelligence service during World War II and provided the basis for the modern-day American intelligence and special operations communities.

Under the leadership of OSS founder, General Bill Donovan, the OSS conducted acts of great bravery during the war, and their efforts were another factor to the Allied victory in World War II. Let me name a few. These efforts included:

Organizing, training, supplying, and fighting with resistance organizations throughout Europe and Asia;

Engaging in successful guerrilla warfare deep in enemy territory;

Establishing intelligence networks before the successful Allied invasion of French North Africa, known as Operation Torch;

Rescuing more than 500 downed allied airmen behind enemy lines in Yugoslavia during Operation Halyard, one of the most daring and successful rescue missions of World War II;

Conducting mercy missions at the end of the war that saved thousands of Allied prisoners of war; and

Inventing and utilizing new technology, weapons, and revolutionary communications equipment never before seen.

General Eisenhower said that if it did nothing else, the photographic reconnaissance conducted by the OSS before the D-day invasion in June of 1944 justified its creation.

I am truly proud to be here today to honor these men and women who truly embody the greatest generation. Several members of the OSS came from northwest and west central Ohio, including Arthur Jibilian, who took part in Operation Helyard in Yugoslavia; Captain Stephanie Czech Rader; and another veteran who flew OSS missions in B–24s behind enemy lines into occupied France. They have earned and deserve this recognition. Congress and our Nation are proud of them, and we are grateful for their dedicated service. This Congressional Gold Medal is one way we can extend our gratitude.

Mr. Speaker, I want to thank Speaker RYAN, Leader MCCARTHY, and all of the leadership team, Senators BLUNT and WARNER, Chairman NUNES and Ranking Member SCHIFF, Chairman ED ROYCE, Representative MARCY KAPTUR, and all of my other colleagues, including the 320 Members that cosponsored this legislation, for their time, hard work, and support. I would also be remiss if I did not also thank the OSS Society and all those involved for their time and hard work in keeping the legacy of these OSS veterans forever alive.

Mr. Speaker, I urge my colleagues to join me in supporting passage of S. 2234 and bestow upon the OSS the Congressional Gold Medal.

I thank the gentleman for yielding.

Mr. FOSTER. Mr. Speaker, I yield 4 minutes to the gentlewoman from Ohio (Ms. KAPTUR), a member of the Appropriations Committee.

Ms. KAPTUR. Mr. Speaker, I thank Congressman FOSTER for yielding the time.

I am deeply honored to rise today in an official capacity, but also personally, to pay tribute to the patriotic and fearless soldiers, heroes and heroines, of the OSS. Their worthiness to be awarded this Congressional Gold Medal by our Nation for heroism in battle is long overdue.

Over 13,000 exceptional Americans comprise the Office of Strategic Services formed clandestinely during World War II by President Franklin Roosevelt. Roosevelt aimed to create a corps of specially trained intelligence warriors to help win that harrowing conflict. For these many decades since the end of World War II, the secrecy of the OSS and its member soldiers have been maintained.

I can attest to this. Our family's beloved Uncle Tony, full name Anthony Rogowski, our mother's brother, was selected as one of its members. He was a corporal and his medals include: Army Good Conduct, American Theater Medal, Pacific Theater Medal, World War II Victory Medal, and Distinguished Unit badge; Army Serial Number: 35–33–943.

He is buried in a simple grave at Calvary Cemetery in Toledo, Ohio, with a gravestone marker provided by the U.S. Department of Veterans Affairs.

Yes, there is an Army crest on its facing. But there is nothing there, nor in any other location, that would tell his family, or those who will inherit our Nation in the years ahead, what a brilliant man and brave soldier he was.

After his death, it was my particular privilege to present his precious leather flight jacket to his daughter, RoseAnn Rogowski Koperski, and his son, John Rogowski of Toledo. Uncle Tony was part of the elite OSS, trained rigorously as warfighters. We still do not know where he was trained. We know he was dispatched to the Pacific front, flown over the hump in the China-Burma-India campaign. He parachuted at night behind enemy lines under fire as he hit the ground to gather intelligence. He drove Jeeps filled with dynamite to the front along the Burma Road, fighting to cut off the supply of oil to the Japanese military.

Our bill recognizes OSS Detachment 101 that operated in Burma and pioneered the art of unconventional warfare. It was the first United States unit to deploy a large guerrilla army deep in enemy territory. It has been credited with the highest kill/loss ratio for any infantry-type unit in American military history and was awarded a Presidential Unit Citation.

Our uncle was knifed in a foxhole in Burma by a soldier from the Imperial Japanese Army, wounded badly, and he suffered throughout his life with terrible malaria bouts and flashbacks contracted in theatre. He passed away in his mid 50s, far too young, of poor health, all due to war injuries.

He was never recognized or acknowledged for his heroism, like the other men and women who valiantly fought as members of the OSS. I loved Uncle Tony. He was a complicated man with a rare and devilish sense of humor and a hearty laugh and grin. You just knew on meeting him there was depth, as well as honor.

He was war wise, sharing gripping stories about the war when I was a child, peppered with his own conclusions about the merit of the conflicts in which he participated.

His letters sent home during the war to our mother, which she kept banded in a special corner of our parents' cedar chest, were unusual. Parts of the letters had been cut out by his superiors; others had lines that were blackened out so as not to reveal his location or any aspect of what he was doing. As a child, that fascinated me, though I did not completely understand what it meant. His family never really knew where he was deployed nor how he arrived where he was sent. He never revealed the specific details of what he actually did.

And now through this legislation, sponsored by my dear friend and colleague, Ohio Congressman BOB LATTA, and 320 other Members, on a bipartisan basis, we now make America's military history more whole and complete. Frankly, it is the highest honor to pay just tribute to the OSS members, though long overdue.

□ 1745

As I participate in the passage of this legislation, I am reminded of how America's greatest strength is the weaving together of intergenerational experience from one era to another within our families and communities and then extended to the American family.

The SPEAKER pro tempore. The time of the gentlewoman has expired.

Mr. FOSTER. I yield the gentlewoman an additional 1 minute.

Ms. KAPTUR. I thank the gentleman.

Today, in the gallery, we have noble veterans of the OSS.

We know our Nation stands on your broad shoulders.

Through their patriotism and sacrifice, America still is a young nation but is growing and is keeping what we have learned close to our hearts. In paying Gold Medal tribute to the members of the OSS, America honors those who bequeathed precious liberty to us, and we must carry that torch forward as it was carried at such a great price by our forebears.

I would like to acknowledge Charles Pinck, whose father served as a member of the OSS, for his commitment to educate the public about this valiant group.

May God bless the members of the OSS, their families and friends. May our efforts here award them the Gold they so nobly, royally, and selflessly earned, and may God continue to bless America.

Mr. HUIZENGA of Michigan. Mr. Speaker, I yield such time as he may consume to the gentleman from Pennsylvania (Mr. ROTHFUS).

Mr. ROTHFUS. Mr. Speaker, I rise in strong support of S. 2234, to award the Congressional Gold Medal to the members of the Office of Strategic Services in recognition of their superior service and major contributions during World War II.

The accomplishments of the OSS are too numerous to mention here. We cannot imagine what the world would look like today had evil forces prevailed over good in World War II, but thanks to the invaluable contribution of the brave servicemembers of the OSS, we do not have to. The OSS organized, trained, supplied, and fought resistance organizations throughout Europe and Asia that played an important role in America's victory during World War II. The men and women of the OSS were pioneers in counterintelligence, technology, and unconventional warfare.

The OSS was the prototype for modern-day American intelligence and special operations communities. The outstanding Americans who serve today as Navy SEALs, U.S. Army Special Forces, Air Force Special Operations Command, Marine Special Operations Command, and more can trace their roots to the OSS.

For these and many other reasons, it is right that we honor the servicemembers of the OSS for their extraordinary contributions to American history and that future generations of Americans learn about the crucial role they played in keeping America safe.

While so many of the OSS servicemembers have already gone to their eternal rest, including my own father-in-law, Edgar Lewis, it is fitting and good that we pass this legislation while we continue to have OSS members among us today.

Mr. FOSTER. Mr. Speaker, I urge my colleagues to support this bill.

I yield back the balance of my time.

Mr. HUIZENGA of Michigan. Mr. Speaker, I appreciated the personal touches and discussions from Representative LATTA and Representative KAPTUR as they talked about their family members in this very important organization. With that, I urge the bill's passage.

I yield back the balance of my time.

The SPEAKER pro tempore. The question is on the motion offered by the gentleman from Michigan (Mr. HUIZENGA) that the House suspend the rules and pass the bill, S. 2234.

The question was taken; and (two-thirds being in the affirmative) the rules were suspended and the bill was passed.

A motion to reconsider was laid on the table.

────────

ANNOUNCEMENT BY THE SPEAKER PRO TEMPORE

The SPEAKER pro tempore. The Chair would remind persons in the gallery that it is a violation of the rules of the House to show approval or disapproval of the proceedings of the House.

────────

INTELLIGENCE AUTHORIZATION ACT FOR FISCAL YEAR 2017

Mr. NUNES. Mr. Speaker, I move to suspend the rules and pass the bill (H.R. 6393) to authorize appropriations for fiscal year 2017 for intelligence and intelligence-related activities of the United States Government, the Community Management Account, and the Central Intelligence Agency Retirement and Disability System, and for other purposes.

The Clerk read the title of the bill.

The text of the bill is as follows:

H.R. 6393

Be it enacted by the Senate and House of Representatives of the United States of America in Congress assembled,

SECTION 1. SHORT TITLE; TABLE OF CONTENTS.

(a) SHORT TITLE.—This Act may be cited as the "Intelligence Authorization Act for Fiscal Year 2017".

(b) TABLE OF CONTENTS.—The table of contents for this Act is as follows:

Sec. 1. Short title; table of contents.
Sec. 2. Definitions.

TITLE I—INTELLIGENCE ACTIVITIES

Sec. 101. Authorization of appropriations.
Sec. 102. Classified Schedule of Authorizations.
Sec. 103. Personnel ceiling adjustments.
Sec. 104. Intelligence Community Management Account.

TITLE II—CENTRAL INTELLIGENCE AGENCY RETIREMENT AND DISABILITY SYSTEM

Sec. 201. Authorization of appropriations.

TITLE III—GENERAL INTELLIGENCE COMMUNITY MATTERS

Sec. 301. Restriction on conduct of intelligence activities.
Sec. 302. Increase in employee compensation and benefits authorized by law.
Sec. 303. Support to nonprofit organizations assisting intelligence community employees.
Sec. 304. Promotion of science, technology, engineering, and math education in the intelligence community.
Sec. 305. Retention of employees of the intelligence community who have science, technology, engineering, or math expertise.
Sec. 306. Modifications to certain requirements for construction of facilities.
Sec. 307. Protections for independent inspectors general of certain elements of the intelligence community.
Sec. 308. Modification of certain whistleblowing procedures.
Sec. 309. Congressional oversight of policy directives and guidance.
Sec. 310. Notification of memoranda of understanding.
Sec. 311. Technical correction to Executive Schedule.
Sec. 312. Maximum amount charged for declassification reviews.

TITLE IV—MATTERS RELATING TO ELEMENTS OF THE INTELLIGENCE COMMUNITY

Subtitle A—Office of the Director of National Intelligence

Sec. 401. Designation of the Director of the National Counterintelligence and Security Center.
Sec. 402. Analyses and impact statements by Director of National Intelligence regarding investment into the United States.
Sec. 403. Assistance for governmental entities and private entities in recognizing online violent extremist content.

Subtitle B—Central Intelligence Agency

Sec. 411. Enhanced death benefits for personnel of the Central Intelligence Agency.
Sec. 412. Pay and retirement authorities of the Inspector General of the Central Intelligence Agency.

Subtitle C—Other Elements

Sec. 421. Clarification of authority, direction, and control over the information assurance directorate of the National Security Agency.
Sec. 422. Enhancing the technical workforce for the Federal Bureau of Investigation.

Sec. 423. Plan on assumption of certain weather missions by the National Reconnaissance Office.

TITLE V—MATTERS RELATING TO FOREIGN COUNTRIES

Sec. 501. Committee to counter active measures by the Russian Federation to exert covert influence over peoples and governments.
Sec. 502. Limitation on travel of accredited diplomats and consulars of the Russian Federation in the United States from their diplomatic post.
Sec. 503. Study and report on enhanced intelligence and information sharing with Open Skies Treaty member states.

TITLE VI—PRIVACY AND CIVIL LIBERTIES OVERSIGHT BOARD

Sec. 601. Information on activities of the Privacy and Civil Liberties Oversight Board.
Sec. 602. Authorization of appropriations for Privacy and Civil Liberties Oversight Board.

TITLE VII—REPORTS AND OTHER MATTERS

Sec. 701. Declassification review with respect to detainees transferred from United States Naval Station, Guantanamo Bay, Cuba.
Sec. 702. Cyber Center for Education and Innovation Home of the National Cryptologic Museum.
Sec. 703. Oversight of national security systems.
Sec. 704. Joint facilities certification.
Sec. 705. Leadership and management of space activities.
Sec. 706. Advances in life sciences and biotechnology.
Sec. 707. Reports on declassification proposals.
Sec. 708. Improvement in Government classification and declassification.
Sec. 709. Report on implementation of research and development recommendations.
Sec. 710. Report on Intelligence Community Research and Development Corps.
Sec. 711. Report on information relating to academic programs, scholarships, fellowships, and internships sponsored, administered, or used by the intelligence community.
Sec. 712. Report on intelligence community employees detailed to National Security Council.
Sec. 713. Intelligence community reporting to Congress on foreign fighter flows.
Sec. 714. Report on cybersecurity threats to seaports of the United States and maritime shipping.
Sec. 715. Report on counter-messaging activities.
Sec. 716. Report on reprisals against contractors of the intelligence community.

SEC. 2. DEFINITIONS.

In this Act:

(1) CONGRESSIONAL INTELLIGENCE COMMITTEES.—The term "congressional intelligence committees" means—

(A) the Select Committee on Intelligence of the Senate; and

(B) the Permanent Select Committee on Intelligence of the House of Representatives.

(2) INTELLIGENCE COMMUNITY.—The term "intelligence community" has the meaning given that term in section 3(4) of the National Security Act of 1947 (50 U.S.C. 3003(4)).

TITLE I—INTELLIGENCE ACTIVITIES

SEC. 101. AUTHORIZATION OF APPROPRIATIONS.

Funds are hereby authorized to be appropriated for fiscal year 2017 for the conduct of the intelligence and intelligence-related activities of the following elements of the United States Government:

(1) The Office of the Director of National Intelligence.

(2) The Central Intelligence Agency.

(3) The Department of Defense.

(4) The Defense Intelligence Agency.

(5) The National Security Agency.

(6) The Department of the Army, the Department of the Navy, and the Department of the Air Force.

(7) The Coast Guard.

(8) The Department of State.

(9) The Department of the Treasury.

(10) The Department of Energy.

(11) The Department of Justice.

(12) The Federal Bureau of Investigation.

(13) The Drug Enforcement Administration.

(14) The National Reconnaissance Office.

(15) The National Geospatial-Intelligence Agency.

(16) The Department of Homeland Security.

SEC. 102. CLASSIFIED SCHEDULE OF AUTHORIZATIONS.

(a) SPECIFICATIONS OF AMOUNTS.—The amounts authorized to be appropriated under section 101 and, subject to section 103, the authorized personnel ceilings as of September 30, 2017, for the conduct of the intelligence activities of the elements listed in paragraphs (1) through (16) of section 101, are those specified in the classified Schedule of Authorizations prepared to accompany this Act.

(b) AVAILABILITY OF CLASSIFIED SCHEDULE OF AUTHORIZATIONS.—

(1) AVAILABILITY.—The classified Schedule of Authorizations referred to in subsection (a) shall be made available to the Committee on Appropriations of the Senate, the Committee on Appropriations of the House of Representatives, and to the President.

(2) DISTRIBUTION BY THE PRESIDENT.—Subject to paragraph (3), the President shall provide for suitable distribution of the classified Schedule of Authorizations referred to in subsection (a), or of appropriate portions of such Schedule, within the executive branch.

(3) LIMITS ON DISCLOSURE.—The President shall not publicly disclose the classified Schedule of Authorizations or any portion of such Schedule except—

(A) as provided in section 601(a) of the Implementing Recommendations of the 9/11 Commission Act of 2007 (50 U.S.C. 3306(a));

(B) to the extent necessary to implement the budget; or

(C) as otherwise required by law.

SEC. 103. PERSONNEL CEILING ADJUSTMENTS.

(a) AUTHORITY FOR INCREASES.—The Director of National Intelligence may authorize employment of civilian personnel in excess of the number authorized for fiscal year 2017 by the classified Schedule of Authorizations referred to in section 102(a) if the Director of National Intelligence determines that such action is necessary to the performance of important intelligence functions, except that the number of personnel employed in excess of the number authorized under such section may not, for any element of the intelligence community, exceed 3 percent of the number of civilian personnel authorized under such schedule for such element.

(b) TREATMENT OF CERTAIN PERSONNEL.—The Director of National Intelligence shall establish guidelines that govern, for each element of the intelligence community, the treatment under the personnel levels authorized under section 102(a), including any exemption from such personnel levels, of employment or assignment in—

(1) a student program, trainee program, or similar program;

(2) a reserve corps or as a reemployed annuitant; or

(3) details, joint duty, or long-term, full-time training.

(c) NOTICE TO CONGRESSIONAL INTELLIGENCE COMMITTEES.—The Director of National Intelligence shall notify the congressional intelligence committees in writing at least 15 days prior to each exercise of an authority described in subsection (a).

(d) CONTRACTOR CONVERSIONS.—

(1) AUTHORITY FOR INCREASES.—In addition to the authority under subsection (a), the Director of National Intelligence may authorize employment of civilian personnel in an element of the intelligence community in excess of the number authorized for fiscal year 2017 by the classified Schedule of Authorizations referred to in section 102(a), as such number may be increased pursuant to subsection (a), if—

(A) the Director determines that the increase under this paragraph is necessary to convert the performance of any function of the element by contractors to performance by civilian personnel; and

(B) the number of civilian personnel of the element employed in excess of the number authorized under such section 102(a), as such number may be increased pursuant to both subsection (a) and this paragraph, does not exceed 10 percent of the number of civilian personnel authorized under such schedule for the element.

(2) NOTICE TO CONGRESSIONAL INTELLIGENCE COMMITTEES.—Not less than 30 days prior to exercising the authority described in paragraph (1), the Director of National Intelligence shall submit to the congressional intelligence committees, in writing—

(A) notification of exercising such authority;

(B) justification for making the conversion described in subparagraph (A) of such paragraph; and

(C) certification that such conversion is cost effective.

SEC. 104. INTELLIGENCE COMMUNITY MANAGEMENT ACCOUNT.

(a) AUTHORIZATION OF APPROPRIATIONS.—There is authorized to be appropriated for the Intelligence Community Management Account of the Director of National Intelligence for fiscal year 2017 the sum of $559,796,000. Within such amount, funds identified in the classified Schedule of Authorizations referred to in section 102(a) for advanced research and development shall remain available until September 30, 2018.

(b) AUTHORIZED PERSONNEL LEVELS.—The elements within the Intelligence Community Management Account of the Director of National Intelligence are authorized 787 positions as of September 30, 2017. Personnel serving in such elements may be permanent employees of the Office of the Director of National Intelligence or personnel detailed from other elements of the United States Government.

(c) CLASSIFIED AUTHORIZATIONS.—

(1) AUTHORIZATION OF APPROPRIATIONS.—In addition to amounts authorized to be appropriated for the Intelligence Community Management Account by subsection (a), there are

authorized to be appropriated for the Community Management Account for fiscal year 2017 such additional amounts as are specified in the classified Schedule of Authorizations referred to in section 102(a). Such additional amounts for advanced research and development shall remain available until September 30, 2018.

(2) AUTHORIZATION OF PERSONNEL.—In addition to the personnel authorized by subsection (b) for elements of the Intelligence Community Management Account as of September 30, 2017, there are authorized such additional personnel for the Community Management Account as of that date as are specified in the classified Schedule of Authorizations referred to in section 102(a).

TITLE II—CENTRAL INTELLIGENCE AGENCY RETIREMENT AND DISABILITY SYSTEM

SEC. 201. AUTHORIZATION OF APPROPRIATIONS.

There is authorized to be appropriated for the Central Intelligence Agency Retirement and Disability Fund for fiscal year 2017 the sum of $514,000,000.

TITLE III—GENERAL INTELLIGENCE COMMUNITY MATTERS

SEC. 301. RESTRICTION ON CONDUCT OF INTELLIGENCE ACTIVITIES.

The authorization of appropriations by this Act shall not be deemed to constitute authority for the conduct of any intelligence activity which is not otherwise authorized by the Constitution or the laws of the United States.

SEC. 302. INCREASE IN EMPLOYEE COMPENSATION AND BENEFITS AUTHORIZED BY LAW.

Appropriations authorized by this Act for salary, pay, retirement, and other benefits for Federal employees may be increased by such additional or supplemental amounts as may be necessary for increases in such compensation or benefits authorized by law.

SEC. 303. SUPPORT TO NONPROFIT ORGANIZATIONS ASSISTING INTELLIGENCE COMMUNITY EMPLOYEES.

(a) DIRECTOR OF NATIONAL INTELLIGENCE.—Section 102A of the National Security Act of 1947 (50 U.S.C. 3024) is amended by adding at the end the following:

"(y) FUNDRAISING.—(1) The Director of National Intelligence may engage in fundraising in an official capacity for the benefit of nonprofit organizations that—

"(A) provide support to surviving family members of a deceased employee of an element of the intelligence community; or

"(B) otherwise provide support for the welfare, education, or recreation of employees of an element of the intelligence community, former employees of an element of the intelligence community, or family members of such employees.

"(2) In this subsection, the term 'fundraising' means the raising of funds through the active participation in the promotion, production, or presentation of an event designed to raise funds and does not include the direct solicitation of money by any other means.

"(3) Not later than 7 days after the date the Director engages in fundraising authorized by this subsection or at the time the decision is made to participate in such fundraising, the Director shall notify the congressional intelligence committees of such fundraising.

"(4) The Director, in consultation with the Director of the Office of Government Ethics, shall issue regulations to carry out the authority provided in this subsection. Such regulations shall ensure that such authority

is exercised in a manner that is consistent with all relevant ethical constraints and principles, including the avoidance of any prohibited conflict of interest or appearance of impropriety.".

(b) DIRECTOR OF THE CENTRAL INTELLIGENCE AGENCY.—Section 12(f) of the Central Intelligence Agency Act of 1949 (50 U.S.C. 3512(f)) is amended by adding at the end the following:

"(3) Not later than the date that is 7 days after the date the Director engages in fundraising authorized by this subsection or at the time the decision is made to participate in such fundraising, the Director shall notify the Select Committee on Intelligence of the Senate and the Permanent Select Committee on Intelligence of the House of Representatives of the fundraising.".

SEC. 304. PROMOTION OF SCIENCE, TECHNOLOGY, ENGINEERING, AND MATH EDUCATION IN THE INTELLIGENCE COMMUNITY.

(a) REQUIREMENT FOR INVESTMENT STRATEGY FOR STEM RECRUITING AND OUTREACH ACTIVITIES.—Along with the budget for fiscal year 2018 submitted by the President pursuant to section 1105(a) of title 31, United States Code, the Director of National Intelligence shall submit a five-year investment strategy for outreach and recruiting efforts in the fields of science, technology, engineering, and mathematics (STEM), to include cybersecurity and computer literacy.

(b) REQUIREMENT FOR INTELLIGENCE COMMUNITY PLANS FOR STEM RECRUITING AND OUTREACH ACTIVITIES.—For each of the fiscal years 2018 through 2022, the head of each element of the intelligence community shall submit an investment plan along with the materials submitted as justification of the budget request of such element that supports the strategy required by subsection (a).

SEC. 305. RETENTION OF EMPLOYEES OF THE INTELLIGENCE COMMUNITY WHO HAVE SCIENCE, TECHNOLOGY, ENGINEERING, OR MATH EXPERTISE.

(a) SPECIAL RATES OF PAY FOR CERTAIN OCCUPATIONS IN THE INTELLIGENCE COMMUNITY.—The National Security Act of 1947 (50 U.S.C. 3001 et seq.) is amended by inserting after section 113A the following:

"SEC. 113B. SPECIAL PAY AUTHORITY FOR SCIENCE, TECHNOLOGY, ENGINEERING, OR MATH POSITIONS.

"(a) AUTHORITY TO SET SPECIAL RATES OF PAY.—Notwithstanding part III of title 5, United States Code, the head of each element of the intelligence community may establish higher minimum rates of pay for one or more categories of positions in such element that require expertise in science, technology, engineering, or math (STEM).

"(b) MAXIMUM SPECIAL RATE OF PAY.—A minimum rate of pay established for a category of positions under subsection (a) may not exceed the maximum rate of basic pay (excluding any locality-based comparability payment under section 5304 of title 5, United States Code, or similar provision of law) for the position in that category of positions without the authority of subsection (a) by more than 30 percent, and no rate may be established under this section in excess of the rate of basic pay payable for level IV of the Executive Schedule under section 5315 of title 5, United States Code.

"(c) NOTIFICATION OF REMOVAL FROM SPECIAL RATE OF PAY.—If the head of an element of the intelligence community removes a category of positions from coverage under a rate of pay authorized by subsection (a) after that rate of pay takes effect—

"(1) the head of such element shall provide notice of the loss of coverage of the special rate of pay to each individual in such category; and

"(2) the loss of coverage will take effect on the first day of the first pay period after the date of the notice.

"(d) REVISION OF SPECIAL RATES OF PAY.— Subject to the limitations in this section, rates of pay established under this section by the head of the element of the intelligence community may be revised from time to time by the head of such element and the revisions have the force and effect of statute.

"(e) REGULATIONS.—The head of each element of the intelligence community shall promulgate regulations to carry out this section with respect to such element, which shall, to the extent practicable, be comparable to the regulations promulgated to carry out section 5305 of title 5, United States Code.

"(f) REPORTS.—

"(1) REQUIREMENT FOR REPORTS.—Not later than 90 days after the date of the enactment of the Intelligence Authorization Act for Fiscal Year 2017, the head of each element of the intelligence community shall submit to the congressional intelligence committees a report on any rates of pay established for such element under this section.

"(2) CONTENTS.—Each report required by paragraph (1) shall contain for each element of the intelligence community—

"(A) a description of any rates of pay established under subsection (a); and

"(B) the number of positions in such element that will be subject to such rates of pay.".

(b) TABLE OF CONTENTS AMENDMENT.—The table of contents in the first section of the National Security Act of 1947 is amended by inserting after the item relating to section 113A the following:

"Sec. 113B. Special pay authority for science, technology, engineering, or math positions.".

SEC. 306. MODIFICATIONS TO CERTAIN REQUIREMENTS FOR CONSTRUCTION OF FACILITIES.

(a) INCLUSION IN BUDGET REQUESTS OF CERTAIN PROJECTS.—Section 8131 of the Department of Defense Appropriations Act, 1995 (50 U.S.C. 3303) is repealed.

(b) NOTIFICATION.—Section 602(a)(2) of the Intelligence Authorization Act for Fiscal Year 1995 (50 U.S.C. 3304(a)(2)) is amended by striking "improvement project to" and inserting "project for the improvement, repair, or modification of".

SEC. 307. PROTECTIONS FOR INDEPENDENT INSPECTORS GENERAL OF CERTAIN ELEMENTS OF THE INTELLIGENCE COMMUNITY.

(a) LIMITATION ON ACTIVITIES OF EMPLOYEES OF AN OFFICE OF INSPECTOR GENERAL.—

(1) LIMITATIONS.—Not later than 180 days after the date of the enactment of this Act, the Director of National Intelligence shall develop and implement a uniform policy for each covered office of an inspector general to better ensure the independence of each such office. Such policy shall include—

(A) provisions to prevent any conflict of interest related to a matter any employee of a covered office of an inspector general personally and substantially participated in during previous employment;

(B) standards to ensure personnel of a covered office of an inspector general are free both in fact and in appearance from personal, external, and organizational impairments to independence;

(C) provisions to permit the head of each covered office of an inspector general to waive the application of the policy with respect to an individual if such head—

(i) prepares a written and signed justification for such waiver that sets out, in detail, the need for such waiver, provided that such a waiver shall not be issued for in fact impairments to independence; and

(ii) submits to the congressional intelligence committees each such justification; and

(D) any other protections the Director determines appropriate.

(2) COVERED OFFICE OF AN INSPECTOR GENERAL DEFINED.—The term "covered office of an inspector general" means—

(A) the Office of the Inspector General of the Intelligence Community; and

(B) the office of an inspector general for—

(i) the Office of the Director of National Intelligence;

(ii) the Central Intelligence Agency;

(iii) the National Security Agency;

(iv) the Defense Intelligence Agency;

(v) the National Geospatial-Intelligence Agency; or

(vi) the National Reconnaissance Office.

(3) BRIEFING TO THE CONGRESSIONAL INTELLIGENCE COMMITTEES.—Prior to the date that the policy required by paragraph (1) takes effect, the Director of National Intelligence shall provide the congressional intelligence committees a briefing on such policy.

(b) LIMITATION ON ROTATION OF EMPLOYEES OF AN OFFICE OF INSPECTOR GENERAL.—Section 102A(l)(3) of the National Security Act of 1947 (50 U.S.C. 3024(l)(3)) is amended by adding at the end the following:

"(D) The mechanisms prescribed under subparagraph (A) and any other policies of the Director—

"(i) may not require an employee of an office of inspector general for an element of the intelligence community, including the Office of the Inspector General of the Intelligence Community, to rotate to a position in an office or organization of such an element over which such office of inspector general exercises jurisdiction; and

"(ii) shall be implemented in a manner that exempts employees of an office of inspector general from a rotation that may impact the independence of such office.".

SEC. 308. MODIFICATION OF CERTAIN WHISTLEBLOWING PROCEDURES.

(a) CLARIFICATION OF WHISTLEBLOWING PROCEDURES AVAILABLE TO CERTAIN PERSONNEL.—Subsection (a)(1)(A) of section 8H of the Inspector General Act of 1978 (5 U.S.C. App.) is amended by inserting after "Security Agency," the following: "including any such employee who is assigned or detailed to a combatant command or other element of the Federal Government,".

(b) CENTRAL INTELLIGENCE AGENCY.—

(1) ROLE OF DIRECTOR.—Section 17(d)(5) of the Central Intelligence Agency Act of 1949 (50 U.S.C. 3517(d)(5)) is amended—

(A) in subparagraph (B)—

(i) by striking clause (ii);

(ii) by striking "(i) Not" and inserting "Not"; and

(iii) by striking "to the Director" and inserting "to the intelligence committees"; and

(B) in subparagraph (D)—

(i) in clause (i), by striking "the Director" and inserting "the intelligence committees"; and

(ii) in clause (ii)—

(I) in subclause (I), by striking "the Director, through the Inspector General," and inserting "the Inspector General"; and

(II) in subclause (II), by striking "the Director, through the Inspector General," and inserting "the Inspector General, in consultation with the Director,".

(2) CONFORMING AMENDMENTS.—

(A) IN GENERAL.—Section 17(d)(5) of such Act is further amended—

(i) by striking subparagraph (C); and

(ii) by redesignating subparagraphs (D) through (H) as subparagraphs (C) through (G), respectively.

(B) INTELLIGENCE REFORM AND TERRORISM PREVENTION ACT OF 2004.—Section 3001(j)(1)(C)(ii) of the Intelligence Reform and Terrorism Prevention Act of 2004 (50 U.S.C. 3341(j)(1)(C)(ii)) is amended by striking "subparagraphs (A), (D), and (H)" and inserting "subparagraphs (A), (C), and (G)".

(c) OTHER ELEMENTS OF INTELLIGENCE COMMUNITY.—

(1) ROLE OF HEADS.—Section 8H of the Inspector General Act of 1978 (5 U.S.C. App.) is amended—

(A) in subsection (b)—

(i) by striking paragraph (2);

(ii) by striking "(1) Not" and inserting "Not"; and

(iii) by striking "to the head of the establishment" and inserting "to the intelligence committees"; and

(B) in subsection (d)—

(i) in paragraph (1), by striking "the head of the establishment" and inserting "the intelligence committees"; and

(ii) in paragraph (2)—

(I) in subparagraph (A), by striking "the head of the establishment, through the Inspector General," and inserting "the Inspector General"; and

(II) in subparagraph (B), by striking "the head of the establishment, through the Inspector General," and inserting "the Inspector General, in consultation with the head of the establishment,".

(2) CONFORMING AMENDMENTS.—Section 8H of such Act is further amended—

(A) by striking subsection (c);

(B) by redesignating subsections (d) through (i) as subsections (c) through (h), respectively; and

(C) in subsection (e), as so redesignated, by striking "subsections (a) through (e)" and inserting "subsections (a) through (d)".

(d) OFFICE OF THE DIRECTOR OF NATIONAL INTELLIGENCE.—

(1) IN GENERAL.—Section 103H(k)(5) of the National Security Act of 1947 (50 U.S.C. 3033(k)(5)) is amended—

(A) in subparagraph (B), by striking "to the Director" and inserting "to the congressional intelligence committees"; and

(B) in subparagraph (D)—

(i) in clause (i), by striking "the Director" and inserting "the congressional intelligence committees"; and

(ii) in clause (ii)—

(I) in subclause (I), by striking "the Director, through the Inspector General," and inserting "the Inspector General"; and

(II) in subclause (II), by striking "the Director, through the Inspector General," and inserting "the Inspector General, in consultation with the Director,".

(2) CONFORMING AMENDMENTS.—Section 103H(k)(5) of such Act is further amended—

(A) by striking subparagraph (C); and

(B) by redesignating subparagraphs (D) through (I) as subparagraphs (C) through (H), respectively.

(e) RULE OF CONSTRUCTION.—None of the amendments made by this section may be construed to prohibit or otherwise affect the authority of an Inspector General of an element of the intelligence community, the Inspector General of the Central Intelligence Agency, or the Inspector General of the Intelligence Community to notify the head of the element of the intelligence community, the Director of the Central Intelligence Agency, or the Director of National Intelligence, as the case may be, of a complaint or information otherwise authorized by law.

SEC. 309. CONGRESSIONAL OVERSIGHT OF POLICY DIRECTIVES AND GUIDANCE.

(a) COVERED POLICY DOCUMENT DEFINED.— In this section, the term "covered policy document" means any classified or unclassified Presidential Policy Directive, Presidential Policy Guidance, or other similar policy document issued by the President, including any annex to such a Directive, Guidance, or other document, that assigns takes, roles, or responsibilities the intelligence community.

(b) SUBMISSIONS TO CONGRESS.—The Director of National Intelligence shall submit to the congressional intelligence committees the following:

(1) Not later than 15 days after the date that a covered policy document is issued, a notice of the issuance and a summary of the subject matter addressed by such covered policy document.

(2) Not later than 15 days after the date that the Director issues any guidance or direction on implementation of a covered policy document or implements a covered policy document, a copy of such guidance or direction or a description of such implementation.

(3) Not later than 15 days after the date of the enactment of this Act, for any covered policy document issued prior to such date that is being implemented by any element of the intelligence community or that is in effect on such date—

(A) a notice that includes the date such covered policy document was issued and a summary of the subject matter addressed by such covered policy document; and

(B) if the Director has issued any guidance or direction on implementation of such covered policy document or is implementing such covered policy document, a copy of the guidance or direction or a description of such implementation.

SEC. 310. NOTIFICATION OF MEMORANDA OF UNDERSTANDING.

(a) IN GENERAL.—The head of each element of the intelligence community shall submit to the congressional intelligence committees a copy of each memorandum of understanding or other agreement regarding significant operational activities or policy between or among such element and any other entity or entities of the United States Government—

(1) for such a memorandum or agreement that is in effect on the date of the enactment of this Act, not later than 60 days after such date; and

(2) for such a memorandum or agreement entered into after such date, in a timely manner and not more than 60 days after the date such memorandum or other agreement is entered into.

(b) ADMINISTRATIVE MEMORANDUM OR AGREEMENT.—Nothing in this section may be construed to require an element of the intelligence community to submit to the congressional intelligence committees any memorandum or agreement that is solely administrative in nature, including a memorandum or agreement regarding joint duty or other routine personnel assignments.

SEC. 311. TECHNICAL CORRECTION TO EXECUTIVE SCHEDULE.

Section 5313 of title 5, United States Code, is amended by striking the item relating to "Director of the National Counter Proliferation Center.".

SEC. 312. MAXIMUM AMOUNT CHARGED FOR DECLASSIFICATION REVIEWS.

In reviewing and processing a request by a person for the mandatory declassification of information pursuant to Executive Order No. 13526, a successor executive order, or any other provision of law, the head of an element of the intelligence community—

(1) may not charge the person reproduction fees in excess of the amount of fees that the head would charge the person for reproduction required in the course of processing a request for information under section 552 of title 5, United States Code (commonly referred to as the "Freedom of Information Act"); and

(2) may waive or reduce any processing fees in the same manner as the head waives or reduces fees under such section 552.

TITLE IV—MATTERS RELATING TO ELEMENTS OF THE INTELLIGENCE COMMUNITY

Subtitle A—Office of the Director of National Intelligence

SEC. 401. DESIGNATION OF THE DIRECTOR OF THE NATIONAL COUNTERINTELLIGENCE AND SECURITY CENTER.

(a) IN GENERAL.—

(1) IN GENERAL.—Section 902 of the Counterintelligence Enhancement Act of 2002 (50 U.S.C. 3382) is amended to read as follows:

"**SEC. 902. DIRECTOR OF THE NATIONAL COUNTERINTELLIGENCE AND SECURITY CENTER.**

"(a) ESTABLISHMENT.—There shall be a Director of the National Counterintelligence and Security Center (referred to in this section as the 'Director'), who shall be appointed by the President, by and with the advice and consent of the Senate.

"(b) MISSION.—The mission of the Director shall be to serve as the head of national counterintelligence for the United States Government.

"(c) DUTIES.—Subject to the direction and control of the Director of National Intelligence, the duties of the Director are as follows:

"(1) To carry out the mission referred to in subsection (b).

"(2) To act as chairperson of the National Counterintelligence Policy Board established under section 811 of the Counterintelligence and Security Enhancements Act of 1994 (50 U.S.C. 3381).

"(3) To act as head of the National Counterintelligence and Security Center established under section 904.

"(4) To participate as an observer on such boards, committees, and entities of the executive branch as the Director of National Intelligence considers appropriate for the discharge of the mission and functions of the Director and the National Counterintelligence and Security Center under section 904.".

(2) TABLE OF CONTENTS AMENDMENT.—The table of contents in section 1(b) of the Intelligence Authorization Act for Fiscal Year 2003 (Public Law 107–306; 116 Stat. 2383) is amended by striking the item relating to section 902 and inserting the following:

"Sec. 902. Director of the National Counterintelligence and Security Center.".

(3) TECHNICAL EFFECTIVE DATE.—The amendment made by subsection (a) of section 401 of the Intelligence Authorization Act for Fiscal Year 2016 (division M of Public Law 114–113) shall not take effect, or, if the date of the enactment of this Act is on or after the effective date specified in subsection (b) of such section, such amendment shall be deemed to not have taken effect.

(b) NATIONAL COUNTERINTELLIGENCE AND SECURITY CENTER.—

(1) IN GENERAL.—Section 904 of the Counterintelligence Enhancement Act of 2002 (50 U.S.C. 3383) is amended—

(A) by striking the section heading and inserting "**NATIONAL COUNTERINTELLIGENCE AND SECURITY CENTER.**"; and

(B) by striking subsections (a), (b), and (c) and inserting the following:

"(a) ESTABLISHMENT.—There shall be a National Counterintelligence and Security Center.

"(b) HEAD OF CENTER.—The Director of the National Counterintelligence and Security Center shall be the head of the National Counterintelligence and Security Center.

"(c) LOCATION OF CENTER.—The National Counterintelligence and Security Center shall be located in the Office of the Director of National Intelligence.".

(2) FUNCTIONS.—Section 904(d) of the Counterintelligence Enhancement Act of 2002 (50 U.S.C. 3383(d)) is amended—

(A) in the matter preceding paragraph (1), by striking "National Counterintelligence Executive, the functions of the Office of the National Counterintelligence Executive" and inserting "Director of the National Counterintelligence and Security Center, the functions of the National Counterintelligence and Security Center";

(B) in paragraph (5), in the matter preceding subparagraph (A), by striking "In consultation with" and inserting "At the direction of"; and

(C) in paragraph (6), in the matter preceding subparagraph (A), by striking "Office" and inserting "National Counterintelligence and Security Center".

(3) PERSONNEL.—Section 904(f) of the Counterintelligence Enhancement Act of 2002 (50 U.S.C. 3383(f)) is amended—

(A) in paragraph (1), by striking "Office of the National Counterintelligence Executive may consist of personnel employed by the Office" and inserting "National Counterintelligence and Security Center may consist of personnel employed by the Center"; and

(B) in paragraph (2), by striking "National Counterintelligence Executive" and inserting "Director of the National Counterintelligence and Security Center".

(4) TREATMENT OF ACTIVITIES UNDER CERTAIN ADMINISTRATIVE LAWS.—Section 904(g) of the Counterintelligence Enhancement Act of 2002 (50 U.S.C. 3383(g)) is amended by striking "Office shall be treated as operational files of the Central Intelligence Agency for purposes of section 701 of the National Security Act of 1947 (50 U.S.C. 431)" and inserting "National Counterintelligence and Security Center shall be treated as operational files of the Central Intelligence Agency for purposes of section 701 of the National Security Act of 1947 (50 U.S.C. 3141)".

(5) OVERSIGHT BY CONGRESS.—Section 904(h) of the Counterintelligence Enhancement Act of 2002 (50 U.S.C. 3383(h)) is amended—

(A) in the matter preceding paragraph (1), by striking "Office of the National Counterintelligence Executive" and inserting "National Counterintelligence and Security Center"; and

(B) in paragraphs (1) and (2), by striking "Office" and inserting "Center" both places that term appears.

(6) TABLE OF CONTENTS AMENDMENT.—The table of contents in section 1(b) of the Intelligence Authorization Act for Fiscal Year 2003 (Public Law 107–306; 116 Stat. 2383), as amended by subsection (a)(2), is further amended by striking the item relating to section 904 and inserting the following:

"Sec. 904. National Counterintelligence and Security Center.".

(c) OVERSIGHT OF NATIONAL INTELLIGENCE CENTERS.—Section 102A(f)(2) of the National Security Act of 1947 (50 U.S.C. 3024(f)(2)) is amended by inserting ", the National Counterproliferation Center, and the National Counterintelligence and Security Center" after "National Counterterrorism Center".

(d) DIRECTOR OF THE NATIONAL COUNTERINTELLIGENCE AND SECURITY CENTER WITHIN THE OFFICE OF THE DIRECTOR OF NATIONAL INTELLIGENCE.—Paragraph (8) of section 103(c) of the National Security Act of 1947 (50 U.S.C. 3025(c)) is amended to read as follows:

"(8) The Director of the National Counterintelligence and Security Center.".

(e) DUTIES OF THE DIRECTOR OF THE NATIONAL COUNTERINTELLIGENCE AND SECURITY CENTER.—

(1) IN GENERAL.—Section 103F of the National Security Act of 1947 (50 U.S.C. 3031) is amended—

(A) by striking the section heading and inserting "DIRECTOR OF THE NATIONAL COUNTERINTELLIGENCE AND SECURITY CENTER";

(B) in subsection (a)—

(i) by striking the subsection heading and inserting "DIRECTOR OF THE NATIONAL COUNTERINTELLIGENCE AND SECURITY CENTER.—"; and

(ii) by striking "National Counterintelligence Executive under section 902 of the Counterintelligence Enhancement Act of 2002 (title IX of Public Law 107–306; 50 U.S.C. 402b et seq.)" and inserting "Director of the National Counterintelligence and Security Center appointed under section 902 of the Counterintelligence Enhancement Act of 2002 (50 U.S.C. 3382)"; and

(C) in subsection (b), by striking "National Counterintelligence Executive" and inserting "Director of the National Counterintelligence and Security Center".

(2) TABLE OF CONTENTS AMENDMENT.—The table of contents in the first section of the National Security Act of 1947 is amended by striking the item relating to section 103F and inserting the following:

"Sec. 103F. Director of the National Counterintelligence and Security Center.".

(f) COORDINATION OF COUNTERINTELLIGENCE ACTIVITIES.—Section 811 of the Counterintelligence and Security Enhancements Act of 1994 (50 U.S.C. 3381) is amended—

(1) in subsection (b), by striking "National Counterintelligence Executive under section 902 of the Counterintelligence Enhancement Act of 2002" and inserting "Director of the National Counterintelligence and Security Center appointed under section 902 of the Counterintelligence Enhancement Act of 2002 (50 U.S.C. 3382)";

(2) in subsection (c)(1), by striking "National Counterintelligence Executive." and inserting "Director of the National Counterintelligence and Security Center."; and

(3) in subsection (d)(1)(B)(ii)—

(A) by striking "National Counterintelligence Executive" and inserting "Director of the National Counterintelligence and Security Center"; and

(B) by striking "by the Office of the National Counterintelligence Executive under section 904(e)(2) of that Act" and inserting "pursuant to section 904(d)(2) of that Act (50 U.S.C. 3383(d)(2))".

(g) INTELLIGENCE AND NATIONAL SECURITY ASPECTS OF ESPIONAGE PROSECUTIONS.—Section 341(b) of the Intelligence Authorization Act for Fiscal Year 2004 (Public Law 108–177, 28 U.S.C. 519 note) is amended by striking

"Office of the National Counterintelligence Executive," and inserting "National Counterintelligence and Security Center,".

SEC. 402. ANALYSES AND IMPACT STATEMENTS BY DIRECTOR OF NATIONAL INTELLIGENCE REGARDING INVESTMENT INTO THE UNITED STATES.

Section 102A of the National Security Act of 1947 (50 U.S.C. 3024) is amended by adding at the end the following new subsection:

"(y) ANALYSES AND IMPACT STATEMENTS REGARDING PROPOSED INVESTMENT INTO THE UNITED STATES.—

"(1) IN GENERAL.—Not later than 20 days after the completion of a review or an investigation of any proposed investment into the United States for which the Director has prepared analytic materials, the Director shall submit to the Select Committee on Intelligence of the Senate and the Permanent Select Committee on Intelligence of the House of Representative copies of such analytic materials, including any supplements or amendments to such analysis made by the Director.

"(2) IMPACT STATEMENTS.—Not later than 60 days after the completion of consideration by the United States Government of any investment described in paragraph (1), the Director shall determine whether such investment will have an operational impact on the intelligence community, and, if so, shall submit a report on such impact to the Select Committee on Intelligence of the Senate and the Permanent Select Committee on Intelligence of the House of Representatives. Each such report shall—

"(A) describe the operational impact of the investment on the intelligence community; and

"(B) describe any actions that have been or will be taken to mitigate such impact.".

SEC. 403. ASSISTANCE FOR GOVERNMENTAL ENTITIES AND PRIVATE ENTITIES IN RECOGNIZING ONLINE VIOLENT EXTREMIST CONTENT.

(a) ASSISTANCE TO RECOGNIZE ONLINE VIOLENT EXTREMIST CONTENT.—Not later than 180 days after the date of the enactment of this Act, and consistent with the protection of intelligence sources and methods, the Director of National Intelligence shall publish on a publicly available Internet website a list of all logos, symbols, insignia, and other markings commonly associated with, or adopted by, an organization designated by the Secretary of State as a foreign terrorist organization under section 219(a) of the Immigration and Nationality Act (8 U.S.C. 1189(a)).

(b) UPDATES.—The Director shall update the list published under subsection (a) every 180 days or more frequently as needed.

Subtitle B—Central Intelligence Agency

SEC. 411. ENHANCED DEATH BENEFITS FOR PERSONNEL OF THE CENTRAL INTELLIGENCE AGENCY.

Section 11 of the Central Intelligence Agency Act of 1949 (50 U.S.C. 3511) is amended to read as follows:

"BENEFITS AVAILABLE IN EVENT OF THE DEATH OF PERSONNEL

"SEC. 11. (a) AUTHORITY.—The Director may pay death benefits substantially similar to those authorized for members of the Foreign Service pursuant to the Foreign Service Act of 1980 (22 U.S.C. 3901 et seq.) or any other provision of law. The Director may adjust the eligibility for death benefits as necessary to meet the unique requirements of the mission of the Agency.

"(b) REGULATIONS.—Regulations issued pursuant to this section shall be submitted to the Select Committee on Intelligence of

the Senate and the Permanent Select Committee on Intelligence of the House of Representatives before such regulations take effect.".

SEC. 412. PAY AND RETIREMENT AUTHORITIES OF THE INSPECTOR GENERAL OF THE CENTRAL INTELLIGENCE AGENCY.

(a) IN GENERAL.—Section 17(e)(7) of the Central Intelligence Agency Act of 1949 (50 U.S.C. 3517(e)(7)) is amended by adding at the end the following new subparagraph:

"(C)(i) The Inspector General may designate an officer or employee appointed in accordance with subparagraph (A) as a law enforcement officer solely for purposes of subchapter III of chapter 83 or chapter 84 of title 5, United States Code, if such officer or employee is appointed to a position with responsibility for investigating suspected offenses against the criminal laws of the United States.

"(ii) In carrying out clause (i), the Inspector General shall ensure that any authority under such clause is exercised in a manner consistent with section 3307 of title 5, United States Code, as it relates to law enforcement officers.

"(iii) For purposes of applying sections 3307(d), 8335(b), and 8425(b) of title 5, United States Code, the Inspector General may exercise the functions, powers, and duties of an agency head or appointing authority with respect to the Office.".

(b) RULE OF CONSTRUCTION.—Subparagraph (C) of section 17(e)(7) of the Central Intelligence Agency Act of 1949 (50 U.S.C. 3517(e)(7)), as added by subsection (a), may not be construed to confer on the Inspector General of the Central Intelligence Agency, or any other officer or employee of the Agency, any police or law enforcement or internal security functions or authorities.

Subtitle C—Other Elements

SEC. 421. CLARIFICATION OF AUTHORITY, DIRECTION, AND CONTROL OVER THE INFORMATION ASSURANCE DIRECTORATE OF THE NATIONAL SECURITY AGENCY.

Section 142(b)(1) of title 10, United States Code, is amended—

(1) in subparagraph (B), by striking the semicolon and inserting "; and";

(2) in subparagraph (C), by striking "; and" and inserting a period; and

(3) by striking subparagraph (D).

SEC. 422. ENHANCING THE TECHNICAL WORKFORCE FOR THE FEDERAL BUREAU OF INVESTIGATION.

(a) REPORT REQUIRED.—Building on the basic cyber human capital strategic plan provided to the congressional intelligence committees in 2015, not later than 180 days after the date of the enactment of this Act and updated two years thereafter, the Director of the Federal Bureau of Investigation shall submit to the congressional intelligence committees a comprehensive strategic workforce report regarding initiatives to effectively integrate information technology expertise in the investigative process.

(b) ELEMENTS.—The report required by subsection (a) shall include the following:

(1) An assessment, including measurable benchmarks, of progress on initiatives to recruit, train, and retain personnel with the necessary skills and experiences in vital areas, including encryption, cryptography, and big data analytics.

(2) An assessment of whether officers of the Federal Bureau of Investigation who possess such skills are fully integrated into the Bureau's work, including Agent-led investigations.

(3) A description of the quality and quantity of the collaborations between the Bureau and private sector entities on cyber issues, including the status of efforts to benefit from employees with experience transitioning between the public and private sectors.

(4) An assessment of the utility of reinstituting, if applicable, and leveraging the Director's Advisory Board, which was originally constituted in 2005, to provide outside advice on how to better integrate technical expertise with the investigative process and on emerging concerns in cyber-related issues.

SEC. 423. PLAN ON ASSUMPTION OF CERTAIN WEATHER MISSIONS BY THE NATIONAL RECONNAISSANCE OFFICE.

(a) PLAN.—

(1) IN GENERAL.—Except as provided in subsection (c), the Director of the National Reconnaissance Office shall develop a plan for the National Reconnaissance Office to address how to carry out covered space-based environmental monitoring missions. Such plan shall include—

(A) a description of the related national security requirements for such missions;

(B) a description of the appropriate manner to meet such requirements; and

(C) the amount of funds that would be necessary to be transferred from the Air Force to the National Reconnaissance Office during fiscal years 2018 through 2022 to carry out such plan.

(2) ACTIVITIES.—In developing the plan under paragraph (1), the Director may conduct pre-acquisition activities, including with respect to requests for information, analyses of alternatives, study contracts, modeling and simulation, and other activities the Director determines necessary to develop such plan.

(3) SUBMISSION.—Not later than July 1, 2017, and except as provided in subsection (c), the Director shall submit to the appropriate congressional committees the plan under paragraph (1).

(b) INDEPENDENT COST ESTIMATE.—The Director of the Cost Assessment Improvement Group of the Office of the Director of National Intelligence, in coordination with the Director of Cost Assessment and Program Evaluation, shall certify to the appropriate congressional committees that the amounts of funds identified under subsection (a)(1)(C) as being necessary to transfer are appropriate and include funding for positions and personnel to support program office costs.

(c) WAIVER BASED ON REPORT AND CERTIFICATION OF AIR FORCE ACQUISITION PROGRAM.—The Director of the National Reconnaissance Office may waive the requirement to develop a plan under subsection (a), if the Under Secretary of Defense for Acquisition Technology, and Logistics and the Chairman of the Joint Chiefs of Staff jointly submit to the appropriate congressional committees a report by not later than July 1, 2017, that contains—

(1) a certification that the Secretary of the Air Force is carrying out a formal acquisition program that has received milestone A approval to address the cloud characterization and theater weather imagery requirements of the Department of Defense; and

(2) an identification of the cost, schedule, requirements, and acquisition strategy of such acquisition program.

(d) DEFINITIONS.—In this section:

(1) The term "appropriate congressional committees" means—

(A) the congressional intelligence committees; and

(B) the congressional defense committees (as defined in section 101(a)(16) of title 10, United States Code).

(2) The term "covered space-based environmental monitoring missions" means the acquisition programs necessary to meet the national security requirements for cloud characterization and theater weather imagery.

TITLE V—MATTERS RELATING TO FOREIGN COUNTRIES

SEC. 501. COMMITTEE TO COUNTER ACTIVE MEASURES BY THE RUSSIAN FEDERATION TO EXERT COVERT INFLUENCE OVER PEOPLES AND GOVERNMENTS.

(a) DEFINITIONS.—In this section:

(1) ACTIVE MEASURES BY RUSSIA TO EXERT COVERT INFLUENCE.—The term "active measures by Russia to exert covert influence" means activities intended to influence a person or government that are carried out in coordination with, or at the behest of, political leaders or the security services of the Russian Federation and the role of the Russian Federation has been hidden or not acknowledged publicly, including the following:

(A) Establishment or funding of a front group.

(B) Covert broadcasting.

(C) Media manipulation.

(D) Disinformation and forgeries.

(E) Funding agents of influence.

(F) Incitement and offensive counterintelligence.

(G) Assassinations.

(H) Terrorist acts.

(2) APPROPRIATE COMMITTEES OF CONGRESS.—The term "appropriate committees of Congress" means—

(A) the congressional intelligence committees;

(B) the Committee on Armed Services and the Committee on Foreign Relations of the Senate; and

(C) the Committee on Armed Services and the Committee on Foreign Affairs of the House of Representatives.

(b) ESTABLISHMENT.—There is established within the executive branch an interagency committee to counter active measures by the Russian Federation to exert covert influence.

(c) MEMBERSHIP.—

(1) IN GENERAL.—

(A) APPOINTMENT.—Each head of an agency or department of the United States Government set out under subparagraph (B) shall appoint one member of the committee established by subsection (b) from among officials of such agency or department who occupy a position that is required to be appointed by the President, with the advice and consent of the Senate.

(B) HEAD OF AN AGENCY OR DEPARTMENT.—The head of an agency or department of the United States Government set out under this subparagraph are the following:

(i) The Director of National Intelligence.

(ii) The Secretary of State.

(iii) The Secretary of Defense.

(iv) The Secretary of the Treasury.

(v) The Attorney General.

(vi) The Secretary of Energy.

(vii) The Director of the Federal Bureau of Investigation.

(viii) The head of any other agency or department of the United States Government designated by the President for purposes of this section.

(d) MEETINGS.—The committee shall meet on a regular basis.

(e) DUTIES.—The duties of the committee established by subsection (b) shall be as follows:

(1) To counter active measures by Russia to exert covert influence, including by exposing falsehoods, agents of influence, corruption, human rights abuses, terrorism, and assassinations carried out by the security services or political elites of the Russian Federation or their proxies.

(2) Such other duties as the President may designate for purposes of this section.

(f) STAFF.—The committee established by subsection (b) may employ such staff as the members of such committee consider appropriate.

(g) BUDGET REQUEST.—A request for funds required for the functioning of the committee established by subsection (b) may be included in each budget for a fiscal year submitted by the President pursuant to section 1105(a) of title 31, United States Code.

(h) ANNUAL REPORT.—

(1) REQUIREMENT.—Not later than 180 days after the date of the enactment of this Act, and annually thereafter, and consistent with the protection of intelligence sources and methods, the committee established by subsection (b) shall submit to the appropriate committees of Congress a report describing steps being taken by the committee to counter active measures by Russia to exert covert influence.

(2) MATTERS INCLUDED.—Each report under paragraph (1) shall include a summary of the following:

(A) Active measures by Russia to exert covert influence during the previous year, including significant incidents and notable trends.

(B) Key initiatives of the committee.

(C) Implementation of the committee's initiatives by the heads of the agencies and departments of the United States Government specified in subsection (c)(1)(B).

(D) Analysis of the success of such initiatives.

(E) Changes to such initiatives from the previous year.

(3) SEPARATE REPORTING REQUIREMENT.—The requirement to submit an annual report under paragraph (1) is in addition to any other reporting requirements with respect to Russia.

SEC. 502. LIMITATION ON TRAVEL OF ACCREDITED DIPLOMATS AND CONSULARS OF THE RUSSIAN FEDERATION IN THE UNITED STATES FROM THEIR DIPLOMATIC POST.

(a) APPROPRIATE COMMITTEES OF CONGRESS DEFINED.—In this section, the term "appropriate committees of Congress" means—

(1) the congressional intelligence committees;

(2) the Committee on Foreign Relations and the Committee on the Judiciary of the Senate; and

(3) the Committee on Foreign Affairs and the Committee on the Judiciary of the House of Representatives.

(b) QUARTERLY LIMITATION ON TRAVEL DISTANCE.—Accredited diplomatic personnel and consulars of the Russian Federation in the United States may not be permitted to travel a distance in excess of 25 miles from their diplomatic post in the United States in a calendar quarter unless, on or before the last day of the preceding calendar quarter, the Director of the Federal Bureau of Investigation has certified in writing to the appropriate committees of Congress that during the preceding calendar quarter the Bureau did not identify any violations by accredited diplomatic personnel and consulars of the

Russian Federation of applicable requirements to notify the United States Government in connection with travel by such diplomatic personnel and consulars of a distance in excess of 25 miles from their diplomatic post in the United States.

(c) APPLICABILITY.—Subsection (b) shall apply to each calendar quarter that begins more than 90 days after the date of the enactment of this Act.

(d) WAIVER AUTHORITY.—

(1) IN GENERAL.—The Director of the Federal Bureau of Investigation may waive any travel distance limitation imposed by subsection (b) if the Director determines that such a waiver will further the law enforcement or national security interests of the United States.

(2) NOTIFICATION.—Not later than 15 days after issuing a waiver under paragraph (1), the Director of the Federal Bureau of Investigation shall submit to the appropriate committees of Congress a notification that such waiver has been issued and the justification for the issuance of such waiver.

SEC. 503. STUDY AND REPORT ON ENHANCED INTELLIGENCE AND INFORMATION SHARING WITH OPEN SKIES TREATY MEMBER STATES.

(a) DEFINITIONS.—In this section:

(1) APPROPRIATE COMMITTEES OF CONGRESS.—The term "appropriate committees of Congress" means—

(A) congressional intelligence committees;

(B) the Committee on Armed Services and the Committee on Foreign Relations of the Senate; and

(C) the Committee on Armed Services and the Committee on Foreign Affairs of the House of Representatives.

(2) COVERED STATE PARTY.—The term "covered state party" means a foreign country, that—

(A) was a state party to the Open Skies Treaty on February 22, 2016; and

(B) is not the Russian Federation or the Republic of Belarus.

(3) OPEN SKIES TREATY.—The term "Open Skies Treaty" means the Treaty on Open Skies, done at Helsinki March 24, 1992, and entered into force January 1, 2002.

(b) FEASIBILITY STUDY.—

(1) REQUIREMENT FOR STUDY.—Not later than 180 days after the date of the enactment of this Act, the Director of National Intelligence shall conduct and submit to the appropriate committees of Congress a study to determine the feasibility of creating an intelligence sharing arrangement and database to provide covered state parties with imagery that is comparable, delivered more frequently, and in equal or higher resolution than imagery available through the database established under the Open Skies Treaty.

(2) ELEMENTS.—The study required by paragraph (1) shall include an evaluation of the following:

(A) The methods by which the United States could collect and provide imagery, including commercial satellite imagery, national technical means, and through other intelligence, surveillance, and reconnaissance platforms, under an information sharing arrangement and database referred to in paragraph (1).

(B) The ability of other covered state parties to contribute imagery to the arrangement and database.

(C) Any impediments to the United States and other covered states parties providing such imagery, including any statutory barriers, insufficiencies in the ability to collect the imagery or funding, under such an arrangement.

(D) Whether imagery of Moscow, Chechnya, the international border between Russia and Georgia, Kaliningrad, or the Republic of Belarus could be provided under such an arrangement.

(E) The annual and projected costs associated with the establishment of such an arrangement and database, as compared with costs to the United States and other covered state parties of being parties to the Open Skies Treaty, including Open Skies Treaty plane maintenance, aircraft fuel, crew expenses, mitigation measures necessary associated with Russian Federation overflights over the United States or covered state parties, and new sensor development and acquisition.

(3) SUPPORT FROM OTHER FEDERAL AGENCIES.—Each head of a Federal agency shall provide such support to the Director as may be necessary for the Director to conduct the study required by paragraph (1).

(c) REPORT.—

(1) REQUIREMENT FOR REPORT.—Not later than 180 days after the date of the enactment of this Act, the Director of National Intelligence shall submit to the appropriate committees of Congress the report described in this subsection.

(2) CONTENT OF REPORT.—The report required by paragraph (1) shall include the following:

(A) An intelligence assessment on Russian Federation warfighting doctrine and the extent to which Russian Federation flights under the Open Skies Treaty contribute to such doctrine.

(B) A counterintelligence analysis as to whether the Russian Federation has, could have, or intends to have the capability to exceed the imagery limits set forth in the Open Skies Treaty.

(C) A list of intelligence exchanges with covered state parties that have been updated on the information described in subparagraphs (A) and (B) and the date and form such information was provided.

(d) FORM OF SUBMISSION.—The study required by subsection (b) and the report required by subsection (c) shall be submitted in an unclassified form but may include a classified annex.

TITLE VI—PRIVACY AND CIVIL LIBERTIES OVERSIGHT BOARD

SEC. 601. INFORMATION ON ACTIVITIES OF THE PRIVACY AND CIVIL LIBERTIES OVERSIGHT BOARD.

Subsection (e) of section 1061 of the Intelligence Reform and Terrorism Prevention Act of 2004 (42 U.S.C. 2000ee(e)) is amended—

(1) by striking the subsection heading and inserting "REPORTS AND OVERSIGHT ACTIVITIES.—"; and

(2) by adding at the end the following:

"(3) INFORMATION.—

"(A) OVERSIGHT ACTIVITIES.—In addition to the reports submitted under paragraph (1)(B), the Board shall ensure that each official and congressional committee specified in subparagraph (B) is kept fully and currently informed of the oversight activities of the Board, including any significant anticipated oversight activities.

"(B) OFFICIALS AND CONGRESSIONAL COMMITTEES SPECIFIED.—The officials and congressional committees specified in this subparagraph are the following:

"(i) The Director of National Intelligence.

"(ii) The head of any element of the intelligence community (as defined in section 3(4) of the National Security Act of 1947 (50 U.S.C. 3003(4)) the activities of which are, or are anticipated to be, the subject of the Board's oversight activities.

"(iii) The Select Committee on Intelligence of the Senate and the Permanent Select Committee on Intelligence of the House of Representatives.

"(C) EXEMPTION FOR STATUTORY ADVICE FUNCTION.—This paragraph shall not apply to exercises of the Board's advice function as set out in subsection (d)(1).

"(D) PRESERVATION OF PRIVILEGE.—Nothing in this paragraph may be construed to abridge or require waiver of any applicable privilege.

"(4) REPORTS ON ADVICE TO ELEMENTS OF THE INTELLIGENCE COMMUNITY.—Whenever an element of the intelligence community acts in contravention of the advice provided by the Board under subsection (d)(1), the Board shall, no less than 30 days after the action in contravention of the Board's advice, notify the Select Committee on Intelligence of the Senate and the Permanent Select Committee on Intelligence of the House of Representatives of the provision of advice and of the action by the element of the intelligence community.".

SEC. 602. AUTHORIZATION OF APPROPRIATIONS FOR PRIVACY AND CIVIL LIBERTIES OVERSIGHT BOARD.

(a) REQUIREMENT FOR AUTHORIZATIONS.—Subsection (m) of section 1061 of the Intelligence Reform and Terrorism Prevention Act of 2004 (42 U.S.C. 2000ee(m)) is amended to read as follows:

"(m) FUNDING.—

"(1) SPECIFIC AUTHORIZATION REQUIRED.—Appropriated funds available to the Board may be obligated or expended to carry out activities under this section only if such funds were specifically authorized by Congress for use for such activities for such fiscal year.

"(2) DEFINITION.—In this subsection, the term 'specifically authorized by Congress' has the meaning given that term in section 504(e) of the National Security Act of 1947 (50 U.S.C. 3094(e)).".

(b) AUTHORIZATION OF APPROPRIATIONS.—There is authorized to be appropriated to the Privacy and Civil Liberties Oversight Board for fiscal year 2017 the sum of $10,081,000 to carry out the activities of the Board under section 1061 of the Intelligence Reform and Terrorism Prevention Act of 2004 (42 U.S.C. 2000ee).

TITLE VII—REPORTS AND OTHER MATTERS

SEC. 701. DECLASSIFICATION REVIEW WITH RESPECT TO DETAINEES TRANSFERRED FROM UNITED STATES NAVAL STATION, GUANTANAMO BAY, CUBA.

(a) IN GENERAL.—For each individual detained at United States Naval Station, Guantanamo Bay, Cuba, after September 11, 2001, who was transferred or released from United States Naval Station, Guantanamo Bay, Cuba, the Director of National Intelligence shall—

(1)(A) complete a declassification review of intelligence reports regarding past terrorist activities of that individual prepared by the National Counterterrorism Center for the individual's Periodic Review Board sessions, transfer, or release; or

(B) if the individual's transfer or release occurred prior to the date on which the National Counterterrorism Center first began to prepare such reports regarding detainees, such other intelligence report or reports that contain the same or similar information regarding the individual's past terrorist activities;

(2) make available to the public—

(A) any intelligence reports declassified as a result of the declassification review; and

(B) with respect to each individual transferred or released, for whom intelligence reports are declassified as a result of the declassification review, an unclassified summary which shall be prepared by the President of measures being taken by the country to which the individual was transferred or released to monitor the individual and to prevent the individual from carrying out future terrorist activities; and

(3) submit to the congressional intelligence committees a report setting out the results of the declassification review, including a description of intelligence reports covered by the review that were not declassified.

(b) SCHEDULE.—

(1) TRANSFER OR RELEASE PRIOR TO ENACTMENT.—Not later than 210 days after the date of the enactment of this Act, the Director of National Intelligence shall submit the report required by subsection (a)(3), which shall include the results of the declassification review completed for each individual detained at United States Naval Station, Guantanamo Bay, Cuba, who was transferred or released from United States Naval Station, Guantanamo Bay, prior to the date of the enactment of this Act.

(2) TRANSFER OR RELEASE AFTER ENACTMENT.—Not later than 120 days after the date an individual detained at United States Naval Station, Guantanamo Bay, on or after the date of the enactment of this Act is transferred or released from United States Naval Station, Guantanamo Bay, the Director shall submit the report required by subsection (a)(3) for such individual.

(c) PAST TERRORIST ACTIVITIES.—For purposes of this section, the past terrorist activities of an individual shall include all terrorist activities conducted by the individual before the individual's transfer to the detention facility at United States Naval Station, Guantanamo Bay, including, at a minimum, the following:

(1) The terrorist organization, if any, with which affiliated.

(2) The terrorist training, if any, received.

(3) The role in past terrorist attacks against United States interests or allies.

(4) The direct responsibility, if any, for the death of United States citizens or members of the Armed Forces.

(5) Any admission of any matter specified in paragraphs (1) through (4).

SEC. 702. CYBER CENTER FOR EDUCATION AND INNOVATION HOME OF THE NATIONAL CRYPTOLOGIC MUSEUM.

(a) AUTHORITY TO ESTABLISH AND OPERATE CENTER.—Chapter 449 of title 10, United States Code, is amended by adding at the end the following new section:

"§ 4781. Cyber Center for Education and Innovation Home of the National Cryptologic Museum

"(a) ESTABLISHMENT.—(1) The Secretary of Defense may establish at a publicly accessible location at Fort George G. Meade the 'Cyber Center for Education and Innovation Home of the National Cryptologic Museum' (in this section referred to as the 'Center').

"(2) The Center may be used for the identification, curation, storage, and public viewing of materials relating to the activities of the National Security Agency, any predecessor or successor organizations of such Agency, and the history of cryptology.

"(3) The Center may contain meeting, conference, and classroom facilities that will be used to support such education, training, public outreach, and other purposes as the Secretary considers appropriate.

"(b) DESIGN, CONSTRUCTION, AND OPERATION.—The Secretary may enter into an agreement with the National Cryptologic Museum Foundation (in this section referred to as the 'Foundation'), a nonprofit organization, for the design, construction, and operation of the Center.

"(c) ACCEPTANCE AUTHORITY.—(1) If the Foundation constructs the Center pursuant to an agreement with the Foundation under subsection (b), upon satisfactory completion of the Center's construction or any phase thereof, as determined by the Secretary, and upon full satisfaction by the Foundation of any other obligations pursuant to such agreement, the Secretary may accept the Center (or any phase thereof) from the Foundation, and all right, title, and interest in the Center or such phase shall vest in the United States.

"(2) Notwithstanding section 1342 of title 31, the Secretary may accept services from the Foundation in connection with the design construction, and operation of the Center. For purposes of this section and any other provision of law, employees or personnel of the Foundation shall not be considered to be employees of the United States.

"(d) FEES AND USER CHARGES.—(1) The Secretary may assess fees and user charges to cover the cost of the use of Center facilities and property, including rental, user, conference, and concession fees.

"(2) Amounts received under paragraph (1) shall be deposited into the fund established under subsection (e).

"(e) FUND.—(1) Upon the Secretary's acceptance of the Center under subsection (c)(1)) there is established in the Treasury a fund to be known as the 'Cyber Center for Education and Innovation-Home of the National Cryptologic Museum Fund' (in this subsection referred to as the 'Fund').

"(2) The Fund shall consist of the following amounts:

"(A) Fees and user charges deposited by the Secretary under subsection (d).

"(B) Any other amounts received by the Secretary which are attributable to the operation of the Center.

"(3) Amounts in the Fund shall be available to the Secretary for the benefit and operation of the Center, including the costs of operation and the acquisition of books, manuscripts, works of art, historical artifacts, drawings, plans, models, and condemned or obsolete combat materiel.".

(b) CLERICAL AMENDMENT.—The table of sections at the beginning of chapter 449 of title 10, United State Code, is amended by adding at the end the following new item:

"4781. Cyber Center for Education and Innovation Home of the National Cryptologic Museum.".

SEC. 703. OVERSIGHT OF NATIONAL SECURITY SYSTEMS.

(a) IN GENERAL.—Section 3557 of title 44, United States Code, is amended—

(1) by striking "The head" and inserting the following:

"(c) RESPONSIBILITIES OF AGENCIES.—The head"; and

(2) by inserting before subsection (c), as designated by paragraph (1), the following:

"(a) DEFINITIONS.—In this section:

"(1) BINDING OPERATIONAL DIRECTIVE.—Notwithstanding section 3552(b), the term 'binding operational directive' means a compulsory direction to an agency that—

"(A) is for purposes of safeguarding national security information and information systems from a known or reasonably suspected information security threat, vulnerability, or risk; and

"(B) shall be in accordance with policies, principles, standards, and guidelines issued by the Committee.

"(2) COMMITTEE.—The term 'Committee' means the committee established pursuant to National Security Directive 42, signed by the President on July 5, 1990.

"(3) NATIONAL MANAGER.—The term 'National Manager' means the national manager referred to in National Security Directive 42, signed by the President on July 5, 1990.

"(b) OVERSIGHT BY NATIONAL MANAGER.—

"(1) DESIGNATION.—The Director of the National Security Agency shall serve as the National Manager.

"(2) REGISTRATION OF NATIONAL SECURITY SYSTEMS.—

"(A) IN GENERAL.—Each head of an agency that operates or exercises control of a national security system shall register such system and its configuration with the National Manager.

"(B) LIMITATION.—The head of an agency operating or exercising control of a national security system may not operate or exercise control of such national security system until such head receives a letter from the National Manager that acknowledges registration of such national security system.

"(3) AUTHORITY TO INSPECT.—The National Manager, in consultation with the head of an agency that operates or exercises control of a national security system, may, as the National Manager considers appropriate, inspect such system—

"(A) for adherence to such standards as the Committee may establish for national security systems; and

"(B) to confirm whether the national security system coheres with its configuration registered under paragraph (2).

"(4) BINDING OPERATIONAL DIRECTIVES.—

"(A) IN GENERAL.—Except as provided in subparagraph (B), the National Manager, in consultation with the Committee, may issue such binding operational directives as the National Manager considers appropriate to ensure the security of a national security system.

"(B) LIMITATION.—In any case in which the National Manager issues an operational directive under subparagraph (A) with respect to a national security system operated or controlled by an agency, such operational directive shall not be considered binding if the head of such agency submits to the National Manager a certification that the operational directive would degrade national security.

"(C) ANNUAL REPORT.—Not less frequently than once each year, the National Manager shall submit to the Select Committee on Intelligence of the Senate and the Permanent Select Committee on Intelligence of the House of Representatives a report on the certifications submitted to the National Manager under subparagraph (B) in the most recent year preceding the report.".

(b) CONSIDERATION OF CERTAIN ROUTINE ADMINISTRATIVE AND BUSINESS APPLICATIONS AS NATIONAL SECURITY SYSTEMS.—

(1) TITLE 40.—Section 11103(a) of title 40, United States Code, is amended—

(A) by striking paragraph (2);

(B) in paragraph (1)(E), by striking "subject to paragraph (2),";

(C) by striking "DEFINITION.—" and all that follows through "In this section" and inserting "NATIONAL SECURITY SYSTEM DEFINED.—In this section"; and

(D) by redesignating subparagraphs (A) through (E) as paragraphs (1) through (5), respectively, and moving such paragraphs 2 ems to the left.

(2) TITLE 44.—Section 3552(b)(6) of title 44, United States Code, is amended—

(A) by striking subparagraph (B);

(B) in subparagraph (A), by striking "(A)";

(C) by redesignating clauses (i) and (ii) as subparagraphs (A) and (B), respectively;

(D) by redesignating subclauses (I) through (V) as clauses (i) through (v), respectively; and

(E) in subparagraph (A)(v), as redesignated, by striking "subject to subparagraph (B),".

SEC. 704. JOINT FACILITIES CERTIFICATION.

(a) FINDINGS.—Congress finds the following:

(1) The Director of National Intelligence set a strategic goal to use joint facilities as a means to save costs by consolidating administrative and support functions across multiple elements of the intelligence community.

(2) The use of joint facilities provides more opportunities for operational collaboration and information sharing among elements of the intelligence community.

(b) CERTIFICATION.—Before an element of the intelligence community purchases, leases, or constructs a new facility that is 20,000 square feet or larger, the head of that element of the intelligence community shall submit to the Director of National Intelligence—

(1) a certification that, to the best of the knowledge of the head of such element, all prospective joint facilities in the vicinity have been considered and the element is unable to identify a joint facility that meets the operational requirements of such element; and

(2) a statement listing the reasons for not participating in the prospective joint facilities considered by the element.

SEC. 705. LEADERSHIP AND MANAGEMENT OF SPACE ACTIVITIES.

(a) APPROPRIATE COMMITTEES OF CONGRESS DEFINED.—In this section, the term "appropriate committees of Congress" means the congressional intelligence committees, the Committee on Armed Services of the Senate, and the Committee on Armed Services of the House of Representatives.

(b) UPDATE TO STRATEGY FOR COMPREHENSIVE INTERAGENCY REVIEW OF THE UNITED STATES NATIONAL SECURITY OVERHEAD SATELLITE ARCHITECTURE.—Not later than 180 days after the date of the enactment of this Act, the Director of National Intelligence, in consultation with the Secretary of Defense and the Chairman of the Joint Chiefs of Staff, shall issue an update to the strategy required by section 312 of the Intelligence Authorization Act for Fiscal Year 2016 (division M of Public Law 114–113; 129 Stat. 2919).

(c) UNITY OF EFFORT IN SPACE OPERATIONS BETWEEN THE INTELLIGENCE COMMUNITY AND DEPARTMENT OF DEFENSE.—

(1) REQUIREMENT FOR PLAN.—Not later than 90 days after the date of the enactment of this Act, the Director of National Intelligence, in consultation with the Secretary of Defense, shall submit to the appropriate committees of Congress a plan to functionally integrate the governance, operations, analysis, collection, policy, and acquisition activities related to space and counterspace carried out by the intelligence community. The plan shall include analysis of no fewer than 2 alternative constructs to implement this plan, and an assessment of statutory, policy, organizational, programmatic, and resources changes that may be required to implement each alternative construct.

(2) APPOINTMENT BY THE DIRECTOR OF NATIONAL INTELLIGENCE.—Not later than 30 days after the date of the enactment of this Act, the Director of National Intelligence, in consultation with the Secretary of Defense, shall appoint a single official to oversee development of the plan required by paragraph (1).

(3) SCOPE OF PLAN.—The plan required by paragraph (1) shall include methods to functionally integrate activities carried out by—

(A) the National Reconnaissance Office;

(B) the functional managers for signals intelligence and geospatial intelligence;

(C) the Office of the Director of National Intelligence;

(D) other Intelligence Community elements with space-related programs;

(E) joint interagency efforts; and

(F) other entities as identified by the Director of National Intelligence in coordination with the Secretary of Defense.

(d) INTELLIGENCE COMMUNITY SPACE WORKFORCE.—Not later than 90 days after the date of the enactment of this Act, the Director of National Intelligence shall submit to the congressional intelligence committees a workforce plan to recruit, develop, and retain personnel in the intelligence community with skills and experience in space and counterspace operations, analysis, collection, policy, and acquisition.

(e) JOINT INTERAGENCY COMBINED SPACE OPERATIONS CENTER.—

(1) SUBMISSION TO CONGRESS.—The Director of the National Reconnaissance Office and the Commander of the United States Strategic Command, in consultation with the Director of National Intelligence and Under Secretary of Defense for Intelligence, shall submit to the appropriate committees of Congress concept of operations and requirements documents for the Joint Interagency Combined Space Operations Center by the date that is the earlier of—

(A) the completion of the experimental phase of such Center; or

(B) 30 days after the date of the enactment of this Act.

(2) QUARTERLY BRIEFINGS.—The Director of the National Reconnaissance Office and the Commander of the United States Strategic Command, in coordination with the Director of National Intelligence and Under Secretary of Defense for Intelligence, shall provide to the appropriate committees of Congress briefings providing updates on activities and progress of the Joint Interagency Combined Space Operations Center to begin 30 days after the date of the enactment of this Act. Such briefings shall be quarterly for the first year following enactment, and annually thereafter.

SEC. 706. ADVANCES IN LIFE SCIENCES AND BIOTECHNOLOGY.

(a) REQUIREMENT FOR PLAN.—Not later than 180 days after the date of the enactment of this Act, the Director of National Intelligence shall brief the congressional intelligence committees on a proposed plan to monitor advances in life sciences and biotechnology to be carried out by the Director.

(b) CONTENTS OF PLAN.—The plan required by subsection (a) shall include—

(1) a description of the approach the elements of the intelligence community will take to make use of organic life science and biotechnology expertise within and outside the intelligence community on a routine and contingency basis;

(2) an assessment of the current collection and analytical posture of the life sciences and biotechnology portfolio as it relates to United States competitiveness and the global bio-economy, the risks and threats evolving with advances in genetic editing technologies, and the implications of such advances on future biodefense requirements; and

(3) an analysis of organizational requirements and responsibilities, including potentially creating new positions.

(c) REPORT TO CONGRESS.—Not later than 180 days after the date of the enactment of this Act, the Director of National Intelligence shall submit to the congressional intelligence committees, the Committee on Armed Services of the Senate, and the Committee on Armed Services of the House of Representatives a report and provide a briefing on the role of the intelligence community in the event of a biological attack on the United States, including an assessment of the capabilities and gaps in technical capabilities that exist to address the potential circumstance of a novel unknown pathogen.

SEC. 707. REPORTS ON DECLASSIFICATION PROPOSALS.

(a) COVERED STUDIES DEFINED.—In this section, the term "covered studies" means the studies that the Director of National Intelligence requested that the elements of the intelligence community produce in the course of producing the fundamental classification guidance review for fiscal year 2017 required by Executive Order No. 13526 (50 U.S.C. 3161 note), as follows:

(1) A study of the feasibility of reducing the number of original classification authorities in each element of the intelligence community to the minimum number required and any negative impacts that reduction could have on mission capabilities.

(2) A study of the actions required to implement a proactive discretionary declassification program distinct from the systematic, automatic, and mandatory declassification review programs outlined in part 2001 of title 32, Code of Federal Regulations, including section 2001.35 of such part.

(3) A study of the benefits and drawbacks of implementing a single classification guide that could be used by all elements of the intelligence community in the nonoperational and more common areas of such elements.

(4) A study of whether the classification level of "confidential" could be eliminated within agency-generated classification guides from use by elements of the intelligence community and any negative impacts that elimination could have on mission success.

(b) REPORTS AND BRIEFINGS TO CONGRESS.—

(1) PROGRESS REPORT.—Not later than 30 days after the date of the enactment of this Act, the Director of National Intelligence shall submit a report to the congressional intelligence committees and provide the congressional intelligence committees a briefing on the progress of the elements of the intelligence community in producing the covered studies.

(2) FINAL REPORT.—Not later than the earlier of 120 days after the date of the enactment of this Act or June 30, 2017, the Director of National Intelligence shall submit a report and provide a briefing to the congressional intelligence committees on—

(A) the final versions of the covered studies that have been provided to the Director by the elements of the intelligence community; and

(B) a plan for implementation of each initiative included in each such covered study.

SEC. 708. IMPROVEMENT IN GOVERNMENT CLASSIFICATION AND DECLASSIFICATION.

(a) REVIEW OF GOVERNMENT CLASSIFICATION AND DECLASSIFICATION.—Not later than 180 days after the date of the enactment of this Act, the Director of National Intelligence shall—

(1) review the system by which the Government classifies and declassifies information;

(2) develop recommendations—

(A) to make such system a more effective tool for the protection of information relating to national security;

(B) to improve the sharing of information with partners and allies of the Government; and

(C) to support the appropriate declassification of information; and

(3) submit to the congressional intelligence committees a report with—

(A) the findings of the Director with respect to the review conducted under paragraph (1); and

(B) the recommendations developed under paragraph (2).

(b) ANNUAL CERTIFICATION OF CONTROLLED ACCESS PROGRAMS.—

(1) IN GENERAL.—Not less frequently than once each year, the Director of National Intelligence shall certify to the congressional intelligence committees whether the creation, validation, or substantial modification, including termination, for all existing and proposed controlled access programs, and the compartments and subcompartments within each, are substantiated and justified based on the information required by paragraph (2).

(2) INFORMATION REQUIRED.—Each certification pursuant to paragraph (1) shall include—

(A) the rationale for the revalidation, validation, or substantial modification, including termination, of each controlled access program, compartment and subcompartment;

(B) the identification of a control officer for each controlled access program; and

(C) a statement of protection requirements for each controlled access program.

SEC. 709. REPORT ON IMPLEMENTATION OF RESEARCH AND DEVELOPMENT RECOMMENDATIONS.

Not later than 120 days after the date of the enactment of this Act, the Director of National Intelligence shall submit to the congressional intelligence committees a report that includes the following:

(1) An assessment of the actions each element of the intelligence community has completed to implement the recommendations made by the National Commission for the Review of the Research and Development Programs of the United States Intelligence Community established under section 1002 of the Intelligence Authorization Act for Fiscal Year 2003 (Public Law 107–306; 50 U.S.C. 3001 note).

(2) An analysis of the balance between short-, medium-, and long-term research efforts carried out by each element of the intelligence community.

SEC. 710. REPORT ON INTELLIGENCE COMMUNITY RESEARCH AND DEVELOPMENT CORPS.

Not later than 120 days after the date of the enactment of this Act, the Director of National Intelligence shall submit to the congressional intelligence committees a report and a briefing on a plan, with milestones and benchmarks, to implement an Intelligence Community Research and Development Corps, as recommended in the Report of the National Commission for the Review of the Research and Development Programs of the United States Intelligence Community, including an assessment—

(1) of the funding and modification to existing authorities needed to allow for the implementation of such Corps; and

(2) of additional legislative authorities, if any, necessary to undertake such implementation.

SEC. 711. REPORT ON INFORMATION RELATING TO ACADEMIC PROGRAMS, SCHOLARSHIPS, FELLOWSHIPS, AND INTERNSHIPS SPONSORED, ADMINISTERED, OR USED BY THE INTELLIGENCE COMMUNITY.

(a) REPORT.—Not later than 120 days after the date of the enactment of this Act, the Director of National Intelligence shall submit to the congressional intelligence committees a report by the intelligence community regarding covered academic programs. Such report shall include—

(1) a description of the extent to which the Director and the heads of the elements of the intelligence community independently collect information on covered academic programs, including with respect to—

(A) the number of applicants for such programs;

(B) the number of individuals who have participated in such programs; and

(C) the number of individuals who have participated in such programs and were hired by an element of the intelligence community after completing such program;

(2) to the extent that the Director and the heads independently collect the information described in paragraph (1), a chart, table, or other compilation illustrating such information for each covered academic program and element of the intelligence community, as appropriate, during the three-year period preceding the date of the report; and

(3) to the extent that the Director and the heads do not independently collect the information described in paragraph (1) as of the date of the report—

(A) whether the Director and the heads can begin collecting such information during fiscal year 2017; and

(B) the personnel, tools, and other resources required by the Director and the heads to independently collect such information.

(b) COVERED ACADEMIC PROGRAMS DEFINED.—In this section, the term "covered academic programs" means—

(1) the Federal Cyber Scholarship-for-Service Program under section 302 of the Cybersecurity Enhancement Act of 2014 (15 U.S.C. 7442);

(2) the National Security Education Program under the David L. Boren National Security Education Act of 1991 (50 U.S.C. 1901 et seq.);

(3) the Science, Mathematics, and Research for Transformation Defense Education Program under section 2192a of title 10, United States Code;

(4) the National Centers of Academic Excellence in Information Assurance and Cyber Defense of the National Security Agency and the Department of Homeland Security; and

(5) any other academic program, scholarship program, fellowship program, or internship program sponsored, administered, or used by an element of the intelligence community.

SEC. 712. REPORT ON INTELLIGENCE COMMUNITY EMPLOYEES DETAILED TO NATIONAL SECURITY COUNCIL.

Not later than 60 days after the date of the enactment of this Act, the Director of National Intelligence shall submit to the congressional intelligence committees a report listing, by year, the number of employees of an element of the intelligence community who have been detailed to the National Security Council during the 10-year period preceding the date of the report.

SEC. 713. INTELLIGENCE COMMUNITY REPORTING TO CONGRESS ON FOREIGN FIGHTER FLOWS.

(a) REPORTS REQUIRED.—Not later than 60 days after the date of the enactment of this

Act, and every 180 days thereafter, the Director of National Intelligence, consistent with the protection of intelligence sources and methods, shall submit to the appropriate congressional committees a report on foreign fighter flows to and from terrorist safe havens abroad.

(b) CONTENTS.—Each report submitted under subsection (a) shall include, with respect to each terrorist safe haven, the following:

(1) The total number of foreign fighters who have traveled or are suspected of having traveled to the terrorist safe haven since 2011, including the countries of origin of such foreign fighters.

(2) The total number of United States citizens present in the terrorist safe haven.

(3) The total number of foreign fighters who have left the terrorist safe haven or whose whereabouts are unknown.

(c) FORM.—The reports submitted under subsection (a) may be submitted in classified form. If such a report is submitted in classified form, such report shall also include an unclassified summary.

(d) SUNSET.—The requirement to submit reports under subsection (a) shall terminate on the date that is two years after the date of the enactment of this Act.

(e) APPROPRIATE CONGRESSIONAL COMMITTEES DEFINED.—In this section, the term "appropriate congressional committees" means—

(1) in the Senate—

(A) the Committee on Armed Services;

(B) the Select Committee on Intelligence;

(C) the Committee on the Judiciary;

(D) the Committee on Homeland Security and Governmental Affairs;

(E) the Committee on Banking, Housing, and Urban Affairs;

(F) the Committee on Foreign Relations; and

(G) the Committee on Appropriations; and

(2) in the House of Representatives—

(A) the Committee on Armed Services;

(B) the Permanent Select Committee on Intelligence;

(C) the Committee on the Judiciary;

(D) the Committee on Homeland Security;

(E) the Committee on Financial Services;

(F) the Committee on Foreign Affairs; and

(G) the Committee on Appropriations.

SEC. 714. REPORT ON CYBERSECURITY THREATS TO SEAPORTS OF THE UNITED STATES AND MARITIME SHIPPING.

(a) REPORT.—Not later than 180 days after the date of the enactment of this Act, the Under Secretary of Homeland Security for Intelligence and Analysis, in consultation with the Director of National Intelligence, and consistent with the protection of sources and methods, shall submit to the appropriate congressional committees a report on the cybersecurity threats to, and the cyber vulnerabilities within, the software, communications networks, computer networks, or other systems employed by—

(1) entities conducting significant operations at seaports in the United States;

(2) the maritime shipping concerns of the United States; and

(3) entities conducting significant operations at transshipment points in the United States.

(b) MATTERS INCLUDED.—The report under subsection (a) shall include the following:

(1) A description of any recent and significant cyberattacks or cybersecurity threats directed against software, communications networks, computer networks, or other systems employed by the entities and concerns described in paragraphs (1) through (3) of subsection (a).

(2) An assessment of—

(A) any planned cyberattacks directed against such software, networks, and systems;

(B) any significant vulnerabilities to such software, networks, and systems; and

(C) how such entities and concerns are mitigating such vulnerabilities.

(3) An update on the status of the efforts of the Coast Guard to include cybersecurity concerns in the National Response Framework, Emergency Support Functions, or both, relating to the shipping or ports of the United States.

(c) APPROPRIATE CONGRESSIONAL COMMITTEES DEFINED.—In this section, the term "appropriate congressional committees" means—

(1) the congressional intelligence committees; and

(2) the Committee on Homeland Security and Governmental Affairs of the Senate and the Committee on Homeland Security of the House of Representatives.

SEC. 715. REPORT ON COUNTER-MESSAGING ACTIVITIES.

(a) REPORT.—Not later than 60 days after the date of the enactment of this Act, the Under Secretary of Homeland Security for Intelligence and Analysis, consistent with the protection of sources and methods, shall submit to the appropriate congressional committees a report on the counter-messaging activities of the Department of Homeland Security with respect to the Islamic State and other extremist groups.

(b) ELEMENTS.—The report under subsection (a) shall include the following:

(1) A description of whether, and to what extent, the Secretary of Homeland Security, in conducting counter-messaging activities with respect to the Islamic State and other extremist groups, consults or coordinates with the Secretary of State, regarding the counter-messaging activities undertaken by the Department of State with respect to the Islamic State and other extremist groups, including counter-messaging activities conducted by the Global Engagement Center of the Department of State.

(2) Any criteria employed by the Secretary of Homeland Security for selecting, developing, promulgating, or changing the counter-messaging approach of the Department of Homeland Security, including any counter-messaging narratives, with respect to the Islamic State and other extremist groups.

(c) APPROPRIATE CONGRESSIONAL COMMITTEES DEFINED.—In this section, the term "appropriate congressional committees" means—

(1) the congressional intelligence committees; and

(2) the Committee on Homeland Security and Governmental Affairs of the Senate and the Committee on Homeland Security of the House of Representatives.

SEC. 716. REPORT ON REPRISALS AGAINST CONTRACTORS OF THE INTELLIGENCE COMMUNITY.

(a) REPORT.—Not later than 180 days after the date of the enactment of this Act, the Inspector General of the Intelligence Community, consistent with the protection of sources and methods, shall submit to the congressional intelligence committees a report on reprisals made against covered contractor employees.

(b) ELEMENTS.—The report under subsection (a) shall include the following:

(1) Identification of the number of known or claimed reprisals made against covered contractor employees during the 3-year pe-

riod preceding the date of the report and any evaluation of such reprisals.

(2) An evaluation of the usefulness of establishing a prohibition on reprisals against covered contractor employees as a means of encouraging such contractors to make protected disclosures.

(3) A description of any challenges associated with establishing such a prohibition, including with respect to the nature of the relationship between the Federal Government, the contractor, and the covered contractor employee.

(4) A description of any approaches taken by the Federal Government to account for reprisals against non-intelligence community contractors who make protected disclosures, including pursuant to section 2409 of title 10, United States Code, and sections 4705 and 4712 of title 41, United States Code.

(5) Any recommendations the Inspector General determines appropriate.

(c) DEFINITIONS.—In this section:

(1) COVERED CONTRACTOR EMPLOYEE.—The term "covered contractor employee" means an employee of a contractor of an element of the intelligence community.

(2) REPRISAL.—The term "reprisal" means the discharge or other adverse personnel action made against a covered contractor employee for making a disclosure of information that would be a disclosure protected by law if the contractor were an employee of the Federal Government.

The SPEAKER pro tempore. Pursuant to the rule, the gentleman from California (Mr. NUNES) and the gentleman from California (Mr. SCHIFF) each will control 20 minutes.

The Chair recognizes the gentleman from California (Mr. NUNES).

GENERAL LEAVE

Mr. NUNES. Mr. Speaker, I ask unanimous consent that all Members have 5 legislative days to revise and extend their remarks and to include extraneous material on H.R. 6393.

The SPEAKER pro tempore. Is there objection to the request of the gentleman from California?

There was no objection.

Mr. NUNES. Mr. Speaker, I yield myself such time as I may consume.

Passing an annual intelligence authorization bill is the most important tool Congress has to conduct effective oversight of the activities of the United States Government. Today, Ranking Member SCHIFF and I are bringing a fiscal year 2017 intelligence authorization bill to the floor for the second time this year. When enacted, it will mark the seventh consecutive Intelligence Authorization Act.

In May, H.R. 5077 passed the House with a strong bipartisan vote. I am pleased to say that this bill, H.R. 6393, is likewise a bipartisan product that reflects the contributions of all of the committee's members.

The bill contains provisions from H.R. 5077 that won wide bipartisan support in May and, after extensive negotiations with the Senate, incorporates numerous provisions from S. 3017, which was reported by the Senate Select Committee on Intelligence in June.

Because most of the intelligence budget involves highly classified programs, the committee's schedule of authorizations and the bulk of the committee's direction is found in the classified annex to the bill. This classified annex has been available in HVC–304 for all Members to review since yesterday.

At the unclassified level, I can report that the total funding authorized by H.R. 6393 balances fiscal discipline and national security. This bill will keep the intelligence base funding at the same share of the Bipartisan Budget Act discretionary cap as in fiscal year 2016 and is consistent with the administration's amended budget request for overseas contingency operations. Furthermore, the bill funds the Military Intelligence Program in line with the levels of the conference version of the National Defense Authorization Act for Fiscal Year 2017.

The agreed text preserves key committee, House, and Senate funding initiatives that are vital to national security. The bill funds high-priority initiatives not included in the President's request and trims requested increases that lack clear justifications. It reflects careful judgments as to which programs represent the best value for intelligence dollars in a challenging budget environment.

The bill will ensure that the men and women of our intelligence community have the funding, authorities, and support they need to carry out their mission and to keep us safe.

Before closing, I want to take a moment to thank the men and women of this country who serve in our intelligence community and thank the families of those who have lost their lives while serving in silence. I am honored to have gotten to know so many dedicated intelligence personnel in the course of the committee's oversight work.

I would also like to thank all of the committee's members—majority and minority—for their contributions to this bill. The many hearings, briefings, and oversight visits by our members carried out during the year provide the inputs for the authorization and direction in this annual bill and ensure the intelligence community remains accountable to the robust oversight of the people's elected Representatives.

I would like to thank my staff, including our staff director—Damon Nelson—George Pappas, Derek Harvey, Geof Kahn, Shannon Stuart, Michael Ellis, Scott Glabe, Jack Langer, Nick Ciarlante, Marissa Skaggs, Bill Flanigan, Lisa Major, Chelsey Campbell, Doug Presley, Andrew House, Steve Keith, and Angel Smith. I would also like to thank our two fellows from Los Alamos National Laboratory—Scott Miller and Phil Tubesing. I would also like to thank the committee's shared staff—Brandon Smith, Kristin Jepson, and Kimberlee Kerr.

In closing, I would like to thank Mr. SCHIFF, my ranking member, who has been just a pleasure to work with over the last couple of years. Without his work and his staff's hard work, we would not be in a position today in which we could stand up here with a strong bipartisan product.

Mr. Speaker, I would like to outline the joint explanatory statement to accompany the Intelligence Authorization Act of Fiscal Year 2017:

JOINT EXPLANATORY STATEMENT TO ACCOMPANY THE INTELLIGENCE AUTHORIZATION ACT FOR FISCAL YEAR 2017

This joint explanatory statement reflects negotiations between the House Permanent Select Committee on Intelligence and the Senate Select Committee on Intelligence (hereinafter, "the Agreement"). The joint explanatory statement shall have the same effect with respect to the implementation of this Act as if it were a joint explanatory statement of a conference committee.

The joint explanatory statement comprises three parts: an overview of the application of the annex to accompany this statement; unclassified congressional direction; and a section-by-section analysis of the legislative text.

PART I: APPLICATION OF THE CLASSIFIED ANNEX

The classified nature of U.S. intelligence activities prevents the congressional intelligence committees from publicly disclosing many details concerning the conclusions and recommendations of the Agreement. Therefore, a classified Schedule of Authorizations and a classified annex have been prepared to describe in detail the scope and intent of the congressional intelligence committees' actions. The Agreement authorizes the Intelligence Community (IC) to obligate and expend funds not altered or modified by the classified Schedule of Authorizations as requested in the President's budget, subject to modification under applicable reprogramming procedures.

The classified annex is the result of negotiations between the House Permanent Select Committee on Intelligence and the Senate Select Committee on Intelligence. It reconciles the differences between the committees' respective versions of the bill for the National Intelligence Program (NIP) and the Homeland Security Intelligence Program (HSIP) for Fiscal Year 2017. The Agreement also makes recommendations for the Military Intelligence Program (MIP), and the Information Systems Security Program (ISSP), consistent with the National Defense Authorization Act for Fiscal Year 2017, and provides certain direction for these two programs.

The Agreement supersedes the classified annexes to the reports accompanying H.R. 5077—passed by the House on May 24, 2016— and S. 3017—reported by the Senate Select Committee on Intelligence on June 15, 2016. All references to the House-passed and Senate-reported annexes are made solely to provide the heritage of, and context for, specific provisions.

The classified Schedule of Authorizations is incorporated into the bill pursuant to Section 102. It has the status of law. The classified annex supplements and adds detail to clarify the authorization levels found in the bill and the classified Schedule of Authorizations. The classified annex shall have the same legal force as the report to accompany the bill.

PART II: SELECT UNCLASSIFIED CONGRESSIONAL DIRECTION

The Agreement supersedes H. Rept. 114–573 accompanying H.R. 5077—passed by the House on May 24, 2016—and S. Rept. 114–277 accompanying S. 3017—reported by the Senate Select Committee on Intelligence on June 15, 2016. The phrase "consistent with" is used solely to provide the heritage of, and context for, specific provisions by denoting the report(s) from which the Agreement's unclassified direction derives.

Commercial Geospatial Intelligence Strategy

Consistent with S. Rept. 114–277 accompanying S. 3017, the Agreement encourages the Department of Defense (DoD), in building future-year budgets, to ensure continued funding is provided for implementation, through at least Fiscal Year 2021, of the Commercial Geospatial Intelligence Strategy issued by the National Geospatial-Intelligence Agency (NGA) in October 2015.

Space Launch Facilities

Consistent with S. Rept. 114–277 accompanying S. 3017, the Agreement directs the IC, in partnership with the U.S. Air Force, to consider the role and contribution of spaceports or launch and range complexes to our national security space launch capacity, and directs the Office of the Director of National Intelligence (ODNI), in consultation with DoD and the U.S. Air Force, no later than 90 days after the enactment of this Act, to brief the congressional intelligence committees on their plans to utilize such facilities.

National Reconnaissance Office Workforce Optimization Strategy

Consistent with S. Rept. 114–277 accompanying S. 3017, the Agreement directs the National Reconnaissance Office (NRO), no later than 90 days after the enactment of this Act, to conduct a workforce review to optimize the mix between government civilians and contractors and submit to the congressional intelligence committees a report containing a workforce optimization strategy.

Review of the National Intelligence University

The National Intelligence University (NIU) has made significant progress in recent years in its transition from a defense intelligence college to a national intelligence university that provides advanced education in a classified format. Such advanced education is integral to making intelligence a profession with recognized standards for performance and ethics and fostering an integrated IC workforce. While progress has been significant since the Director of National Intelligence (DNI) and Secretary of Defense agreed to redesignate Defense Intelligence Agency's (DIA) National Defense Intelligence College as NIU in 2011, the institution must continue to adapt to functioning as a university with a robust research agenda, and to serving the entire IC, not just elements of DoD.

Fiscal years 2017 and 2018 are of great significance for NIU, as it moves its principal facility to the IC Campus at Bethesda, completes activities associated with its 2018 decennial regional accreditation reaffirmation, and receives a new president. The congressional intelligence committees believe that these developments position NIU to make further progress in its vision to become the center of academic life for the IC.

To guide these next steps, the Agreement directs DIA, in coordination with ODNI and the Office of the Under Secretary of Defense for Intelligence, to, no later than 30 days after enactment of this Act, select a five-

member, external, and independent panel to conduct a review of NIU. The panel shall submit a report detailing the results of such review to the congressional intelligence and defense committees within 180 days of enactment of this Act. The panel should be composed of recognized academics, personnel from other DoD joint professional military education institutions, national security experts, and, at least one member of NIU's Board of Visitors.

This review and the resulting report shall, among other things, assess:

(1) Methods for ensuring a student body that is more representative of all IC elements;

(2) Incentives for IC elements to send personnel to NIU to earn a degree or certificate, to include designating attendance at NIU as positions reimbursable by ODNI and requiring IC elements to employ the workforce concept of "float" for personnel enrolled in higher-education programs;

(3) How certificate programs align with NIU's unique value as an institution of advanced intelligence education;

(4) Methods to enhance NIU's research program, to include publication of a journal, hosting of conferences and other collaborative fora, and more formalized relationships with intelligence studies scholars;

(5) Whether and how educational components of other IC elements could provide educational offerings as part of the NIU curriculum;

(6) Potential advantages and risks associated with alternative governance models for NIU, to include moving it under the auspices of ODNI; and

(7) The feasibility and resource constraints of NIU tailoring degree offerings to meet the needs of IC personnel at different stages in their careers, similar to DoD's joint professional military education model.

Privacy and Civil Liberties Oversight Board priorities

Consistent with H. Rept. 114–573 accompanying H.R. 5077 and S. Rept. 114–277 accompanying S. 3017, the Agreement strongly encourages the Privacy and Civil Liberties Oversight Board (PCLOB) to prioritize the privacy rights and civil liberties of U.S. persons in any findings, recommendations, or other reports stemming from its in-depth examinations of counterterrorism activities governed by Executive Order 12333. The Agreement further encourages PCLOB to refrain from publishing any such materials in unclassified form until PCLOB has completed a thorough fact-finding process, and the congressional intelligence committees expect the IC will provide timely cooperation with that process.

Cost of living consideration

Consistent with H. Rept. 114–573 accompanying H.R. 5077, the Agreement recommends that DIA evaluate alternate mechanisms for staffing overseas Combatant Command intelligence centers, particularly those that are not co-located with Combatant Command headquarters, and identify cost-savings opportunities by reducing the number of personnel receiving living quarters allowance payments and shifting personnel to lower cost locations, including in the continental United States.

Defense Intelligence Agency education opportunities

Consistent with H. Rept. 114–573 accompanying H.R. 5077, the Agreement directs DIA, no later than 180 days after the enactment of this Act, to:

(1) Provide for and fund a program that allows for DIA employees to attend civilian

graduate degree programs for up to two years each, based on the standard length of the relevant program, provided that:

(a) Where DIA deems appropriate, employees may pursue academic programs extending beyond two years. Consistent with current practices, the program should be made available to at least five employees each year, with each employee receiving a full-time salary while participating in the program; and

(b) Each DIA participant shall be subject to any program approvals, service obligations, repayment obligations, and other requirements pertaining to academic programs, as prescribed by applicable laws and policies.

(2) Brief the congressional intelligence committees on the status of the program's implementation.

Mental health prevalence

Consistent with H. Rept. 114–573 accompanying H.R. 5077, the Agreement directs the National Security Agency (NSA), NGA, the Central Intelligence Agency (CIA), and DIA, no later than 180 days after the enactment of this Act, to provide a joint briefing to the congressional intelligence committees on the mental health screenings and related services that these agencies offer employees, both before and after they deploy to combat zones. Such briefing shall include a description of:

(1) Existing services available;

(2) Agency resources for and analysis of these services, including the frequency of use by employees compared to the total number returning from deployment; and

(3) How agencies with deployed civilian employees are sharing best practices and leveraging services or resources outside their agencies.

Review of the Office of the Director of National Intelligence

Consistent with H. Rept. 114–573 accompanying H.R. 5077, the Agreement directs the President to form an independent, external panel of at least five individuals with significant intelligence and national security expertise to review ODNI's roles, missions and functions and make recommendations, as needed, regarding its authorities, organization and resources. The panel shall:

(1) Evaluate ODNI's ability to fulfill the responsibilities assigned to it in law given its current scope and structure;

(2) Assess whether any roles and responsibilities currently assigned to the DNI could be more effectively or efficiently executed by other IC components or government agencies outside the IC;

(3) Analyze the personnel, funding, and authorities required for each component of ODNI to perform each of its assigned responsibilities;

(4) Evaluate the organizational structure of ODNI;

(5) Review the size, role, purpose and function of ODNI's mission centers;

(6) Assess the value of the national intelligence manager construct;

(7) Review the size and mix of the ODNI workforce—to include the ratio between cadre and detailees, the balance between government and contractors, and grade structure—to perform its roles, missions and functions; and

(8) Make recommendations regarding the above.

The Agreement directs the President, no later than 30 days after the enactment of this Act, to select the individuals who will serve on the external panel and notify the congressional intelligence committees of such selection.

In addition, the Agreement directs the panel, no later than 180 days after the enactment of this Act, to provide a report on this review to the congressional intelligence committees. This report shall be unclassified, but may contain a classified annex. The Agreement further directs ODNI to reimburse the Executive Office of the President for any costs associated with the review.

Improving pre-publication review

Consistent with H. Rept. 114–573 accompanying H.R. 5077, the Agreement directs that, no later than 180 days after the enactment of this Act, the DNI shall issue an IC-wide policy regarding pre-publication review. The DNI shall transmit this policy to the congressional intelligence committees concurrently with its issuance. The policy should require each IC agency to develop and maintain a pre-publication policy that contains, at a minimum, the following elements:

(1) Identification of the individuals subject to pre-publication review requirements ("covered individuals");

(2) Guidance on the types of information that must be submitted for pre-publication review, including works (a) unrelated to an individual's IC employment; or (b) published in cooperation with a third party, e.g.—

(a) Authored jointly by covered individuals and third parties;

(b) Authored by covered individuals but published under the name of a third party; or

(c) Authored by a third party but with substantial input from covered individuals.

(3) Guidance on a process by which covered individuals can participate in pre-publication reviews, and communicate openly and frequently with reviewers;

(4) Requirements for timely responses, as well as reasoned edits and decisions by reviewers;

(5) Requirements for a prompt and transparent appeal process;

(6) Guidelines for the assertion of interagency equities in pre-publication review;

(7) A summary of the lawful measures each agency may take to enforce its policy, to include civil and criminal referrals; and

(8) A description of procedures for post-publication review of documents that are alleged or determined to reveal classified information but were not submitted for pre-publication review.

Additionally, the Agreement directs ODNI, no later than 180 days after the enactment of this Act, to provide to the congressional intelligence committees a report on the adequacy of IC information technology efforts to improve and expedite pre-publication review processes, and the resources needed to ensure that IC elements can meet this direction.

The Agreement further directs the DNI, no later than 270 days after the enactment of this Act, to certify to the congressional intelligence committees that IC elements' pre-publication review policies, non-disclosure agreements, and any other agreements imposing pre-publication review obligations reflect the policy described above.

Student loan debt report

Consistent with H. Rept. 114–573 accompanying H.R. 5077, the Agreement directs ODNI, no later than 180 days after the enactment of this Act, to provide a report to the congressional intelligence committees on programs that seek to help IC personnel manage student loan debt. The report shall include details about each IC element's program, including loan forgiveness, loan repay-

ment, and financial counseling programs; efforts to inform prospective and current employees about such programs; and the number of employees who use such programs. The report shall also include an analysis of the benefits and drawbacks of creating new programs and expanding existing programs, and shall identify any barriers to the establishment of IC-wide programs.

Workforce development partnership

Consistent with H. Rept. 114–573 accompanying H.R. 5077, the Agreement directs the DNI Chief Human Capital Officer, no later than 180 days after the enactment of this Act, to provide to the congressional intelligence committees an interagency briefing on new approaches, including outreach and advertising, the IC is considering or conducting to attract a diverse, robust information technology and Science, Technology, Engineering, and Math workforce to meet the increasing demands in the IC.

Distributed Common Ground/Surface System-Army

Consistent with H. Rept. 114–573 accompanying H.R. 5077, the Agreement requests that the Army, no later than 90 days after the enactment of this Act, submit a plan to the congressional intelligence and defense committees on how the Army will fully incorporate Distributed Common Ground/Surface System-Army (DCGS–A) training into the readiness cycle for Army personnel. The plan should specifically address any lessons learned from the fielding of DCGS–A Increment 1 and any ongoing corrective actions to improve the roll-out of Increment 1, Release 2.

Common controller for unmanned aircraft systems

Consistent with H. Rept. 114–573 accompanying H.R. 5077, the Agreement requests that the Army and the Marine Corps Intelligence Activity (MCIA), no later than 90 days after the enactment of this Act, jointly submit a report to the congressional intelligence and defense committees on the feasibility of developing a common controller for all Brigade and Below unmanned aircraft systems (UAS) airframes, as well as U.S. Marine Corps small unit UAS. The report should address the potential performance and operational benefits of a common controller, anticipated development costs, and anticipated life-cycle cost savings of a common controller.

Review of dual-hatting relationship

The congressional intelligence committees support further evaluation of the dual-hatting of a single individual as both Commander of U.S. Cyber Command (USCYBERCOM) and Director of the National Security Agency (DIRNSA).

Therefore, the Agreement directs the Secretary of Defense, no later than 180 days after the enactment of this Act, to provide to the congressional intelligence and defense committees a briefing that reviews and provides an assessment of the dual-hatting of DIRNSA and Commander, USCYBERCOM, This briefing should address:

(1) Roles and responsibilities, including intelligence authorities, of USCYBERCOM and NSA;

(2) Assessment of the current impact of the dual-hatting relationship, including advantages and disadvantages;

(3) Plans and recommendations on courses of action that would be necessary to end the dual-hatting of DIRNSA and Commander, USCYBERCOM;

(4) Suggested timelines for carrying out such courses of action;

(5) Recommendations for any changes in law that would be required by the end of dual-hatting; and

(6) Any additional topics as identified by the intelligence and defense committees.

The congressional intelligence committees further believe that a larger organizational review of NSA should be conducted with respect to the eventual termination of the dual-hatting relationship. The congressional intelligence committees seek to promote the efficient and effective execution of NSA's national intelligence mission, Specifically, the congressional intelligence committees believe that the organization of NSA should be examined to account for the evolution of its mission since its establishment, the current structure of the intelligence community, and the fact that the NSA is predominantly funded through the NIP.

Therefore, the Agreement further directs the DNI, no later than 180 days after the enactment of this Act, to conduct an assessment and provide a briefing to the congressional intelligence committees on options to better align the structure, budgetary procedures, and oversight of NSA with its national intelligence mission in the event of a termination of the dual-hafting relationship. This briefing should include:

(1) An assessment of the feasibility of transitioning NSA to civilian leadership appointed by the DNI in lieu of military leadership appointed by the Secretary of Defense;

(2) How NSA could be organizationally separated from DoD if USCYBERCOM were elevated to become a unified combatant command; and

(3) Any challenges, such as those requiring changes in law, associated with such a separation.

Acquisition security improvement

Consistent with H. Rept. 114–573 accompanying H.R. 5077, the Agreement directs ODNI, no later than 180 days after the enactment of this Act, to review and consider amendments to Intelligence Community Directive (ICD) 801 to better reflect and anticipate supply chain and cybersecurity risks and threats, as well as to outline policies to mitigate both risks and threats. In particular, the review should examine whether to:

(1) Expand risk management criteria in the acquisition process to include cyber and supply chain threats;

(2) Require counterintelligence and security assessments as part of the acquisition and procurement process;

(3) Propose and adopt new education requirements for acquisition professionals on cyber and supply chain threats; and

(4) Factor in the cost of cyber and supply chain security.

The Agreement further directs ODNI, no later than 210 days after the enactment of this Act, to provide to the congressional intelligence committees a report describing the review, including ODNI's process for considering amendments to ICD 801, and specifically addressing ODNI's analysis and conclusions with respect to paragraphs (1) through (4) above.

Cyber information sharing and customer feedback

Consistent with H. Rept. 114–573 accompanying H.R. 5077, the Agreement directs ODNI, no later than 120 days after the enactment of this Act, to brief the congressional intelligence committees on IC-wide efforts to share more information with the Department of Homeland Security (DHS) for further dissemination to the private sector.

This briefing shall specifically address types of information shared, metrics on output, tabulation of low output producing agencies, recommendations on how low output agencies can increase sharing, timeliness of information shared, and average total time it takes for information to transit the system.

The Agreement also directs ODNI, in coordination with the DHS Office of Intelligence and Analysis (I&A), to conduct a survey of government and private sector participants of the National Cybersecurity and Communications Integration Center (NCCIC). The survey shall be anonymous, provide an accurate assessment of the usefulness and timeliness of the data received, and determine if customers are satisfied with intelligence briefings on threat actors impacting their specific industry. The Agreement further directs ODNI, no later than one year after the enactment of this Act, to provide to the congressional intelligence and homeland security committees an unclassified report detailing the results of this survey.

Department of Homeland Security utilization of National Labs expertise

Consistent with H. Rept. 114–573 accompanying H.R. 5077, the Agreement directs, no later than 180 days after the enactment of this Act, DHS I&A, in coordination with DOE Office of Intelligence and Counterintelligence (DOE-IN), to provide to the congressional intelligence committees a report on the current utilization of Department of Energy (DOE) National Labs expertise by DHS I&A. This report should address opportunities to increase DHS I&A's utilization of cybersecurity expertise of the National Labs as well as the budgetary implications of taking advantage of these potential opportunities.

Cybersecurity courses for Centers of Academic Excellence

Consistent with H. Rept. 114–573 accompanying H.R. 5077, the Agreement directs ODNI, no later than 180 days after the enactment of this Act, to submit to the congressional intelligence committees a report on improving cybersecurity training within NIP-funded undergraduate and graduate computer science programs. The report should specifically address:

(1) The potential advantages and disadvantages of conditioning an institution's receipt of such funds on its computer science program's requiring cybersecurity as a precondition to graduation;

(2) How Centers of Academic Excellence programs might bolster cybersecurity educational requirements; and

(3) Recommendations to support the goal of ensuring that federally-funded computer science programs properly equip students to confront future cybersecurity challenges.

PART III: SECTION-BY-SECTION ANALYSIS AND EXPLANATION OF LEGISLATIVE TEXT

The following is a section-by-section analysis and explanation of the Intelligence Authorization Act for Fiscal Year 2017.

TITLE I—INTELLIGENCE ACTIVITIES

Section 101. Authorization of appropriations

Section 101 lists the United States Government departments, agencies, and other elements for which the Act authorizes appropriations for intelligence and intelligence-related activities for Fiscal Year 2017.

Section 102. Classified Schedule of Authorizations

Section 102 provides that the details of the amounts authorized to be appropriated for intelligence and intelligence-related activities and the applicable personnel levels by program for Fiscal Year 2017 are contained in the classified Schedule of Authorizations and that the classified Schedule of Authorizations shall be made available to the Committees on Appropriations of the Senate and House of Representatives and to the President.

Section 103. Personnel ceiling adjustments

Section 103 provides that the DNI may authorize employment of civilian personnel in Fiscal Year 2017 in excess of the number of authorized positions by an amount not exceeding three percent of the total limit applicable to each intelligence community (IC) element under Section 102, if necessary to the performance of important intelligence functions, and an amount not exceeding 10 percent of such limit, if necessary to convert the performance of any function of the element by contractors to performance by civilian personnel. The congressional intelligence committees intend that, for the purpose of Section 103, "contractor conversion" means that the number of contractor full-time equivalents shall decrease commensurate—on a one-for-one basis—with the number of contractors converted to government civilians.

Section 103 also requires that, not less than 30 days prior to authorizing a contractor conversion under this section, the DNI shall submit to the congressional intelligence committees a notification that includes a justification for making the conversion and a certification that such conversion is cost effective. The congressional intelligence committees intend that, in certifying that such conversion is cost effective, the DNI shall include a comparison of costs using a mature model that has been reviewed and accepted by the congressional intelligence committees.

Section 104. Intelligence Community Management Account

Section 104 authorizes appropriations for the Intelligence Community Management Account (ICMA) of the DNI and sets the authorized personnel levels for the elements within the ICMA for Fiscal Year 2017.

TITLE II—CENTRAL INTELLIGENCE AGENCY RETIREMENT AND DISABILITY SYSTEM

Section 201. Authorization of appropriations

Section 201 authorizes appropriations in the amount of $514,000,000 for Fiscal Year 2017 for the Central Intelligence Agency Retirement and Disability Fund.

TITLE III—GENERAL INTELLIGENCE COMMUNITY MATTERS

Section 301. Restriction on conduct of intelligence activities

Section 301 provides that the authorization of appropriations by the Act shall not be deemed to constitute authority for the conduct of any intelligence activity that is not otherwise authorized by the Constitution or laws of the United States.

Section 302. Increase in employee compensation and benefits authorized by law

Section 302 provides that funds authorized to be appropriated by the Act for salary, pay, retirement, and other benefits for federal employees may be increased by such additional or supplemental amounts as may be necessary for increases in compensation or benefits authorized by law.

Section 303. Support to nonprofit organizations assisting intelligence community employees

Section 303 permits the DNI to engage in fundraising in an official capacity for the benefit of nonprofit organizations that provide support to surviving family members of a deceased employee of an element of the IC or otherwise provide support for the welfare, education, or recreation of IC employees, former employees, or their family members. Section 303 requires the DNI to issue regulations ensuring that the fundraising authority is exercised consistent with all relevant ethical limitations and principles. Section 303 further requires that the DNI and the Director of the CIA notify the congressional intelligence committees within seven days after they engage in such fundraising.

Section 304. Promotion of science, technology, engineering, and math education in the intelligence community

Section 304 requires the DNI to submit a five-year investment strategy for outreach and recruiting efforts in the fields of science, technology, engineering, and mathematics (STEM), to include cybersecurity and computer literacy. Section 304 further requires elements of the IC to submit STEM investment plans supporting this strategy for each of the fiscal years 2018 through 2022, along with the materials justifying the budget request of each element for these STEM recruiting and outreach activities.

Section 305. Retention of employees of the intelligence community who have science, technology, engineering, or math expertise

Section 305 authorizes a new payscale to permit salary increases for employees in the IC with STEM backgrounds. Section 305 also requires notifications to individual employees if a position is removed from this new payscale. Section 305 further requires the head of each IC element to submit to the congressional intelligence committees a report on the new rates of pay and number of positions authorized under this payscale.

Section 306. Modifications to certain requirements for construction of facilities

Section 306 amends existing law regarding the requirements for inclusion in the Administration's annual budget request and clarifies that the requirement to notify the congressional intelligence committees of improvement projects with an estimated cost greater than $1,000,000 for facilities used primarily by IC personnel includes repairs and modifications.

Section 307. Protections for independent inspectors general of certain elements of the intelligence community

Section 307 requires the ODNI to develop and implement a uniform policy for each identified Inspector General (IG) office in the IC to better ensure their independence. The provision specifies elements to be incorporated in such a policy including (a) guidance regarding conflicts of interest, (b) standards to ensure independence, and (c) a waiver provision. Section 307 further prohibits the DNI from requiring an employee of an OIG to rotate to a position in the element for which such office conducts oversight.

Section 308. Modification of certain whistleblowing procedures

Section 308 amends current law, including the Intelligence Community Whistleblower Protection Act (ICWPA), to provide for the direct transmission to Congress by IC inspectors general of whistleblower complaints containing classified information. Section 308 also makes clear that the provision does not prohibit IC inspectors general from notifying, or otherwise affect the authority of IC inspectors general to notify, heads of IC elements or the DNI, as the case may be, of a complaint or information.

Section 309. Congressional oversight of policy directives and guidance

Section 309 requires the DNI to submit to the congressional intelligence committees

notifications of the issuance and a summary of the subject matter of any classified or unclassified Presidential Policy Directive, Presidential Policy Guidance, or other similar policy document issued by the President that assigns tasks, roles, or responsibilities to the IC, within the specified timeframes. Section 309 further requires the DNI to notify the congressional intelligence committees when the DNI has issued guidance or direction to implement such policies, and to submit a copy of such guidance or direction to the committees.

Section 310. Notification of memoranda of understanding

Section 310 requires the head of each element of the IC to submit to the congressional intelligence committees copies of each memorandum of understanding or other agreement regarding significant operational activities or policy entered into between, or among, such element and any other entity or entities of the federal government within specified timeframes.

Section 310 does not require an IC element to submit to the congressional intelligence committees any memorandum or agreement that is solely administrative in nature, including a memorandum or agreement regarding joint duty or other routine personnel assignments. An IC element also may redact any personally identifiable information from a memorandum or agreement that must be submitted to the intelligence committees.

Section 311. Technical correction to Executive Schedule

Section 311 contains a technical correction regarding the annual rate of basic pay for the Director of the National Counter Proliferation Center.

Section 312. Maximum amount charged for declassification reviews

Section 312 prohibits the head of an element of the IC from charging reproduction fees for a mandatory declassification review in excess of reproduction fees that the head would charge for a request for information under the Freedom of Information Act (FOIA). It also permits agency heads to waive processing fees for declassification reviews in the same manner as for FOIA.

TITLE IV—MATTERS RELATING TO ELEMENTS OF THE INTELLIGENCE COMMUNITY

SUBTITLE A—OFFICE OF THE DIRECTOR OF NATIONAL INTELLIGENCE

Section 401. Designation of the Director of the National Counterintelligence and Security Center

Section 401 renames the National Counterintelligence Executive as the "National Counterintelligence and Security Center," with conforming amendments.

Section 402. Analyses and impact statements by Director of National Intelligence regarding proposed investment into the United States

Section 402 directs the DNI to submit to the congressional intelligence committees, after the completion of a review or an investigation of any proposed investment into the United States, any analytic materials prepared by the DNI. This requirement includes, but is not limited to, national security threat assessments provided to the Committee on Foreign Investment in the United States (CFIUS) in connection with national security reviews and investigations conducted by CFIUS pursuant to Section 721(b) of the Defense Production Act of 1950 (50 U.S.C. 4565). This section is not intended to limit the ability of the DNI to transmit supplementary materials to the congressional

intelligence committees along with the threat assessments.

Section 402 also directs the DNI to provide the congressional intelligence committees with impact statements when the DNI determines a proposed investment into the United States will have an operational impact on the IC.

Section 403. Assistance for governmental entities and private entities in recognizing online violent extremist content

Section 403 requires the DNI to publish on a publicly available Internet website a list of all logos, symbols, insignia, and other markings commonly associated with, or adopted by, State Department-designated foreign terrorist organizations.

Subtitle B—Central Intelligence Agency

Section 411. Enhanced death benefits for personnel of the Central Intelligence Agency

Section 411 authorizes the Director of the CIA to pay death benefits substantially similar to those authorized for members of the Foreign Service, and requires the Director to submit implementing regulations to the congressional intelligence committees.

Section 412. Pay and retirement authorities of the Inspector General of the Central Intelligence Agency

Section 412 amends the Central Intelligence Agency Act of 1949 to authorize the IG of the CIA to consider certain positions as law enforcement officers for purposes of calculating retirement eligibility and entitlements under chapters 83 and 84 of title 5, United States Code, if such officer or employee is appointed to a position with responsibility for investigating suspected offenses against the criminal laws of the United States. Section 412 may not be construed to confer on the IG of the CIA, or any other officer or employee of the CIA, any police or law enforcement or internal security functions or authorities.

Subtitle C—Other Elements

Section 421. Clarification of authority, direction, and control over the Information Assurance Directorate of the National Security Agency

Section 421 restores authority, direction, and control over the Information Assurance Directorate of the NSA to the Under Secretary of Defense for Intelligence.

Section 422. Enhancing the technical workforce for the Federal Bureau of Investigation

Section 422 requires the Federal Bureau of Investigation (FBI) to produce a comprehensive strategic workforce report to demonstrate progress in expanding initiatives to effectively integrate information technology expertise in the investigative process. Section 422 further requires the report to include assessments of: (1) progress on training, recruitment, and retention of cyber-related personnel; (2) whether FBI officers with these skill sets are fully integrated in the FBI's workforce; (3) the FBI's collaboration with the private sector on cyber issues; and (4) the utility of reinstituting and leveraging the FBI Director's Advisory Board.

Section 423. Plan on assumption of certain weather missions by the National Reconnaissance Office

Section 423 requires the Director of the NRO to develop a plan to carry out certain space-based environmental monitoring missions currently performed by the Air Force. It also authorizes certain pre-acquisition activities and directs that an independent cost estimate be submitted to the congressional intelligence and defense committees. The Director of NRO may waive the requirement of

Section 423 if the Under Secretary of Defense for Acquisition, Technology, and Logistics, and the Chairman of the Joint Chiefs of Staff, jointly submit a certification to the congressional intelligence and defense committees.

TITLE V—MATTERS RELATING TO FOREIGN COUNTRIES

Section 501. Committee to counter active measures by the Russian Federation to exert covert influence over peoples and governments

Section 501 requires the President to establish an interagency committee to counter active measures by the Russian Federation to exert covert influence over peoples and governments, and requires the Committee to report to appropriate committees of Congress annually on trends in active measures by the Russian Federation and on the Committee's key initiatives.

Section 502. Limitation on travel of accredited diplomats and consulars of the Russian Federation in the United States from their diplomatic post

Section 502 requires the Director of the FBI to certify that the FBI did not identify any violations by Russian diplomats and consulars of the applicable requirements to notify the United States Government in connection with the Russian diplomats' or consulars' travel, before the Secretary of State can permit Russian diplomats or consulars to travel in excess of 25 miles outside their diplomatic post. Section 502 also permits the Director to waive the aforementioned travel distance restrictions if the Director determines that such a waiver will further the law enforcement or national security interests of the United States.

Section 503. Study and report on enhanced intelligence and information sharing with Open Skies Treaty member states

Section 503 requires the DNI, with support of other federal agencies, to conduct a study to determine the feasibility of creating an intelligence sharing arrangement and database among parties to the Open Skies Treaty (OST) with higher frequency, quality, and efficiency than that currently provided by the parameters of the OST. Section 503 also requires the Director to issue a report that includes an intelligence assessment on Russian Federation warfighting doctrine, the extent to which Russian Federation flights under the Open Skies Treaty contribute to the warfighting doctrine, a counterintelligence analysis as to the Russian Federation's capabilities, and a list of the covered parties that have been updated with this information.

TITLE VI—PRIVACY AND CIVIL LIBERTIES OVERSIGHT BOARD

Section 601. Information on activities of the Privacy and Civil Liberties Oversight Board

Section 601 requires the PCLOB to keep Congress and relevant IC elements fully and currently informed of its oversight activities.

Section 602. Authorization of appropriations for Privacy and Civil Liberties Oversight Board

Section 602 requires funds available to the PCLOB to be obligated or expended during a fiscal year only if such funds were specifically authorized by Congress for that fiscal year, and authorizes the full amount of the Administration's budget request for PCLOB for Fiscal Year 2017.

TITLE VII—REPORTS AND OTHER MATTERS

Section 701. Declassification review with respect to detainees transferred from United States Naval Station, Guantanamo Bay, Cuba.

Section 701 requires the DNI to complete a declassification review of intelligence reports prepared by the National Counterterrorism Center (NCTC) on past terrorist activities of each Guantanamo detainee held at Guantanamo after September 11, 2001, for the detainee's Periodic Review Board (PRB) sessions, transfer, or release from Guantanamo. The requirement applies both to detainees who have been transferred or released previously and to detainees transferred or released in the future. The provision also accounts for detainees whose transfer or release predated the establishment of the PRB or NCTC, or the latter's production of intelligence reports for PRB sessions, transfers, or releases.

Section 701 further requires the President to make any declassified intelligence reports publicly available and, with respect to each detainee for whom intelligence reports are declassified, also make public unclassified summaries of measures being taken by receiving countries to monitor the detainee and prevent future terrorist activities. Section 701 requires the DNI to submit to the congressional intelligence committees a report setting forth the results of the declassification review, including a description of covered reports that were not declassified.

Section 702. Cyber Center for Education and Innovation Home of the National Cryptologic Museum

Section 702 amends 10 U.S.C. §449 to enable the establishment of a Cyber Center for Education and Innovation Home of the National Cryptologic Museum (the "Center"). Section 702 also establishes in the Treasury a fund for the benefit and operation of the Center.

Section 703. Oversight of national security systems

Section 703 amends 44 U.S.C. §3557 to codify and strengthen existing roles and responsibilities with regard to the oversight of national security systems.

Section 704. Joint facilities certification

Section 704 requires that before an element of the IC purchases, leases, or constructs a new facility that is 20,000 square feet or larger, the head of that element must first certify that all prospective joint facilities have been considered and that it is unable to identify a joint facility that meets its operational requirements, and it must list the reasons for not participating in joint facilities in that instance.

Section 705. Leadership and management of space activities

Section 705 requires the DNI, in consultation with the Secretary of Defense and the Chairman of the Joint Chiefs of Staff, to issue an update to the strategy for a comprehensive review of the United States national security overhead satellite architecture required in the Intelligence Authorization Act for Fiscal Year 2016. Section 705 further requires the DNI, in consultation with the Secretary of Defense, to submit a plan to functionally integrate the IC's governance, operations, analysis, collection, policy, and acquisition activities related to space and counterspace under the oversight of a single official, to be appointed by the DNI, in consultation with the Secretary of Defense. Section 705 also requires the DNI to submit a workforce plan for space and counterspace operations, policy, and acquisition. Section 705 further requires the Director of the NRO and the Commander of U.S. Strategic Command to submit a concept of operations and requirements documents for the Joint Interagency Combined Space Operations Center.

Section 706. Advances in life sciences and biotechnology

Section 706 requires the DNI to brief the congressional intelligence committees and the congressional defense committees on a proposed plan and actions to monitor advances in life sciences and biotechnology to be carried out by the DNI. Section 706 further requires the DNI to submit a written report and provide a briefing to the congressional intelligence committees and the congressional defense committees on the role of the IC in the event of a biological attack, including a technical capabilities assessment to address potential unknown pathogens.

Section 707. Reports on declassification proposals

Section 707 requires the DNI to provide the congressional intelligence committees with a report and briefing on the IC's progress in producing four feasibility studies undertaken in the course of the IC's fundamental classification guidance review, as required under Executive Order 13526. Section 707 further requires the Director to provide the congressional intelligence committees with a briefing, interim report, and final report on the final feasibility studies produced by elements of the IC and an implementation plan for each initiative.

Section 708. Improvement in government classification and declassification

Section 708 assesses government classification and declassification in the digital era by requiring the DNI to review the system by which the Government classifies and declassifies national security information to improve the protection of such information, enable information sharing with allies and partners, and support appropriate declassification. Section 708 requires the DNI to submit a report with its findings and recommendations to the congressional intelligence committees. Section 708 further requires the DNI to provide an annual written notification to the congressional intelligence committees on the creation, validation, or substantial modification (to include termination) of existing and proposed controlled access programs, and the compartments and subcompartments within each. This certification shall include the rationale for each controlled access program, compartment, or subcompartment and how each controlled access program is being protected.

Section 709. Report on implementation of research and development recommendations

Section 709 requires the DNI to conduct and provide to the congressional intelligence committees a current assessment of the IC's implementation of the recommendations issued in 2013 by the National Commission for the Review of the Research and Development (R&D) Programs of the IC.

Section 710. Report on Intelligence Community Research and Development Corps

Section 710 requires the DNI to develop and brief the congressional intelligence committees on a plan, with milestones and benchmarks, to implement a R&D Reserve Corps, as recommended in 2013 by the bipartisan National Commission for the Review of the R&D Programs of the IC, including any funding and potential changes to existing authorities that may be needed to allow for the Corps' implementation.

Section 711. Report on information relating to academic programs, scholarships, fellowships, and internships sponsored, administered, or used by the intelligence community

Section 711 requires the DNI to submit to congressional intelligence committees a report on information that the IC collects on certain academic programs, scholarships, and internships sponsored, administered, or used by the IC.

Section 712. Report on intelligence community employees detailed to National Security Council

Section 712 requires the DNI to submit to the congressional intelligence committees a report listing, by year, the number of employees of an element of the IC who have been detailed to the National Security Council during each of the previous ten years.

Section 713. Intelligence community reporting to Congress on foreign fighter flows

Section 713 directs DNI to submit to the congressional intelligence committees a report on foreign fighter flows to and from terrorist safe havens abroad.

Section 714. Report on cybersecurity threats to seaports of the United States and maritime shipping

Section 714 directs the Under Secretary of Homeland Security for Intelligence and Analysis (I&A) to submit to the congressional intelligence committees a report on the cybersecurity threats to seaports of the United States and maritime shipping.

Section 715. Report on counter-messaging activities

Section 715 directs the Under Secretary of Homeland Security for I&A to submit to the congressional intelligence committees a report on the counter-messaging activities of DHS with respect to the Islamic State and other extremist groups.

Section 716. Report on reprisals against contractors of the intelligence community

Section 716 directs the IC IG to submit to the congressional intelligence committees a report on known or claimed reprisals made against employees of contractors of elements of the IC during the preceding three-year period. Section 716 further requires the report to include an evaluation of the usefulness of establishing a prohibition on reprisals as a means of encouraging IC contractors to make protected disclosures, and any recommendations the IC IG deems appropriate.

Mr. Speaker, I reserve the balance of my time.

Mr. SCHIFF. Mr. Speaker, I yield myself such time as I may consume.

Today, we are voting on the fiscal year 2017 Intelligence Authorization Act, which is the fourth major piece of legislation I have had the privilege of working on with Chairman NUNES and the membership of our committee.

I want to just return the compliment from the chairman. It is a great pleasure to work with him. One of the things I love about our committee is it is truly a refuge from a lot of the partisanship of this institution. To be able to grapple with some of the enormous challenges facing the country and to do so in a nonpartisan way is, I think, a real honor and privilege for all of us on the committee, and I thank the chairman for his leadership in making it so. He continues to be just an invaluable partner on the committee. Each bill we work on together proves anew what can be done when people work together constructively and in a nonpartisan manner to solve real problems.

Mr. Speaker, in this iteration of the bill, which the House first passed in the spring by an overwhelming 371–35 votes, we also had the privilege of working closely with our colleagues in

the Senate, particularly Chairman BURR and Vice Chairman FEINSTEIN. As always, they have proven to be invaluable partners. Although we still have one or two issues unresolved, 98 percent of this bill represents agreements forged by bipartisan and bicameral behind-the-scenes efforts over the past few months.

We should be very proud of this bill, and I believe it is an even better bill than the one we passed in the spring. It preserves—and, in some cases, furthers—all of the priorities of our Members, including the initiatives of our Democratic Members. In particular, I want to highlight some of their contributions:

The bill includes Representative HIMES' provision to improve the timeliness and fairness of prepublication review process throughout the IC.

It includes Representative SEWELL's language on investment in Centers of Academic Excellence programs, helping to guarantee that a diverse array of students can take part in IC internships. It also includes her requirement to collect data to evaluate the IC's federally funded academic programs.

The bill includes Representative CARSON's provision to assist public and private entities in their swiftly removing terrorist content online; his provision on the cooperation and deconfliction between the Departments of Homeland Security and State regarding countering violent extremism programs; and his requirement to have the committee receive information on the operational impacts of foreign investment in the United States.

Representative SPEIER's four provisions are included, which would standardize declassification photocopying fees across the IC to promote the increased availability of information and enhance transparency; her provision to expand access to graduate education programs at the Defense Intelligence Agency; her language on obtaining information on the mental health resilience programs that are available to IC civilians returning from tours in combat zones; and her provision to study reprisals taken against IC contractors who make disclosures that would be legally protected if made by IC employees.

The bill includes Representative QUIGLEY's language to continue support to security services in Ukraine.

It includes Representative SWALWELL's three provisions, including one to track foreign fighters, another to analyze the status of loan forgiveness and debt counseling programs within the IC, and a provision to better understand how the Departments of Homeland Security and Energy take advantage of the expertise resident at our national labs.

It includes Representative MURPHY's three provisions to provide a report detailing cybersecurity threats to—or

vulnerabilities in—systems employed by seaports and transshipment hubs, including efforts to improve our preparedness and response to a cyber attack; it has language to improve intelligence reporting with respect to Iran's compliance with the Joint Comprehensive Plan of Action; and it requires a report on security threats emanating from maritime smuggling routes and ways to better cooperate with other nations to mitigate these threats.

Let me also say that Patrick will be dearly missed when he leaves our committee at the end of this session. He has been a tremendously valuable member of the committee.

The IAA also furthers important privacy and transparency goals, including by fully authorizing the Privacy and Civil Liberties Oversight Board. The bill does not contain any legislative restrictions on the scope of the PCLOB's authority to review the impact of IC programs on the privacy and civil liberties of Americans and non-U.S. persons. Thanks to Senate provisions that we have incorporated, it also advances declassification efforts, potentially getting much more information to the public.

There are no GTMO transfer restrictions from the bill, and the legislative text adds important provisions that are aimed at countering Russia's destabilizing efforts, including those targeting elections.

The legislation accommodates and resolves the vast majority of the administration's objections, which were laid out earlier this year.

Critically, this IAA also continues to address the key strategic questions we must continue to ask now and in the next administration in Congress:

First, are we focusing too much on the threats of the day at the expense of the threats of tomorrow?

It is easy to get distracted by nonstop crises, and it is harder to remain focused on the long term, even when the future can be far more dangerous than the present.

☐ 1800

We have spent significant resources on counterterrorism priorities in the Middle East and South Asia. We have to continue to focus on CT and the threat posed by ISIS and its followers, but we must not disregard the growing threat posed by Russia, whose global efforts at disruption must be checked, particularly against our allies and our alliances.

We must not turn away from threats posed by China, whose Naval adventurism, infiltration of the supply chain, and efforts to get around the CFIUS process in the United States—and to undermine data security more generally—challenge our security and business interests abroad and threaten our Asian partners.

Second, are we sufficiently protecting what we currently have, whether in space, at sea, or in the cyber realm?

Third, are we leveraging commercial products and services while at the same time making investments in revolutionary technologies that do not yet have commercial application?

Fourth, are we recruiting, training, and developing the most effective and diverse workforce as well as leveraging foreign intelligence relationships and building foreign partner capacity?

The U.S. has unquestionably the most advanced, capable, and reliable intelligence community in the world. This bill supports that workforce by identifying ways to promote travel, support language training, and increase diversity. It does this, in part, by expanding internship opportunities in the IC to students from diverse regions and backgrounds and allocates resources to building the capacity of our foreign partners. These are values we expect and demand from those partners, and they are central tenets of who we are as a country.

There are many unknowns about the incoming administration, particularly how it will utilize and interact with the IC. It is now more important than ever that we give the IC the tools it needs to keep us safe and provide the necessary oversight required to ensure that they act in a manner consistent with our values and at all times. That is why I am pleased that this year's IAA provides such critical oversight of the IC, ensuring our Nation is secure, privacy and civil liberties are safeguarded, and transparency and accountability are paramount.

I am proud to support the Intelligence Authorization Act, and I urge my colleagues to do the same. I urge the Senate to pass this bill and send the fiscal year '17 IAA to the President's desk or to continue to work with us to resolve any last differences before the end of the Congress.

I reserve the balance of my time.

Mr. NUNES. Mr. Speaker, I yield 2 minutes to the gentleman from Utah (Mr. STEWART).

Mr. STEWART. Mr. Speaker, I thank Chairman NUNES for allowing me to speak in support of the Intelligence Authorization Act.

Mr. Speaker, sometimes it is easiest for us to forget that the primary responsibility of the Federal Government is to help to keep us safe. I felt the weight of that responsibility while I was serving as an Air Force pilot for 14 years, and now I am reminded almost every day of that same responsibility in my role on the House Permanent Select Committee on Intelligence.

The truth is that we live in a dangerous world. The news is filled daily with troubling reports of terrorist attacks and dangerous activities. All of us are aware that just this week a young man, almost certainly inspired by terrorist ideology, attacked students and faculty at The Ohio State University.

It doesn't stop with terrorism. We also face tremendous threats from China, Russia, North Korea, the Ya'alons in Iran, and the list goes on and on.

I am grateful for the brave men and women around the world serving our military and in our intelligence communities who operate critical national security programs which protect Americans and keep us safe. That is why we must pass the Intelligence Authorization Act. Not only does this bill continue to authorize critical national security programs at a time when we face the most significant threat level since 9/11, it also contains good government provisions that have gained bipartisan support.

This bill shines light on Guantanamo Bay detainees, requiring a review of their past terrorist activities. It strengthens congressional oversight of privacy and civil liberties, and it also updates intelligence community whistle-blowing procedures.

Importantly, this bill does not contain any provisions related to surveillance authorities.

Mr. Speaker, this bill is critical to providing the intelligence community with the tools and the authorizations they need to protect Americans and our national security. I urge my colleagues to vote "yes" on this important bill.

Mr. SCHIFF. Mr. Speaker, I yield 3 minutes to the gentleman from California (Mr. SWALWELL), a very valuable member of our committee.

Mr. SWALWELL of California. Mr. Speaker, I stand here today in support of this bipartisan IAA and the many provisions that it has that will continue to strengthen and empower our intelligence community and those who serve and toil away for our national security.

This bill also contains a few provisions I have personally championed during my time on the House Permanent Select Committee on Intelligence. First, it includes the provision I added requiring a report from the Office of the Director of National Intelligence on programs across the IC, the intelligence community, to help students manage student loan debt and the viability of an IC-wide program, knowing that this is critical for our recruitment and retention of quality intelligence community members.

Second, the bill includes a provision that was originally a bipartisan, standalone bill with Representative LoBiondo of New Jersey to track foreign fighters as they attempt to move to and from terrorist safe havens abroad. This bill passed the House at the end of last year by a vote of 423–0.

Finally, it includes a requirement for a report on the current utilization of our national laboratories by the intelligence divisions within the Department of Homeland Security and the Department of Energy, as well as ways these divisions can expand utilization of lab expertise on cybersecurity. I am honored to represent two of these laboratories, Lawrence Livermore and Sandia, and I have seen firsthand how important their work is to our national security.

This bill is the result of both parties and both Chambers coming together to prioritize our intelligence community and national security needs.

I also just want to echo what I have heard from our chairman and ranking member, which is that there is really nothing more fulfilling, especially during such national discord, to come to work every day and work with the members on this committee. I think maybe the secret sauce here is that the chairman and the ranking member are both Oakland Raiders fans. I don't know if there are other reasons they work well together, but it really is fulfilling to see that when you go into our committee hearing, Republicans and Democrats put party aside and put national security first.

I also want to say that I am going to miss two members as they depart the committee. That is, Congressman PATRICK MURPHY of Florida. He and I sat next to each other. Although he was in a 2-year-long Senate race, he showed up every day, worked hard, asked tough questions on behalf of his constituents and national security. I am also going to miss Congressman MIKE POMPEO of Kansas, and I congratulate him on being nominated as the next director of the Central Intelligence Agency. I find him to be a person of deep integrity and character. I enjoyed traveling with him to Iraq last Easter, and I look forward to serving with him in his new role.

Mr. NUNES. Mr. Speaker, I have no other speakers. I reserve the balance of my time.

Mr. SCHIFF. Mr. Speaker, let me just say on behalf of the chairman and myself, we were Raiders fans even when they were a losing team. This is not a newfound preoccupation with the team.

Mr. Speaker, I yield 3 minutes to the gentlewoman from Alabama (Ms. SEWELL), another fabulous member of our committee.

Ms. SEWELL of Alabama. Mr. Speaker, today I rise in support of this year's Intelligence Authorization Act. Our national security is truly a bipartisan issue, and this legislation is a reflection of both parties' shared commitment to the safety and security of all Americans.

This bill helps provide our intelligence community with the necessary resources and capabilities to defend our Nation against ongoing and emerging threats around the world.

As the ranking member on the DOD Intelligence and Overhead Architecture Subcommittee, I was pleased that the language and direction in this bill continues to advance our capabilities on the ground and in space and provides necessary oversight of many critical DOD, NRO, and NGA programs. Additionally, this legislation takes important steps toward enhancing thorough oversight of our surveillance capabilities while continuing to make calculated investments in critically important strategic efforts.

In the IAA, we also invested in our greatest national resource, our people. I want to thank the chairman and ranking member for accepting provisions that I drafted to promote diversity in the IC workforce. We are now able to provide a summer internship program to students from the existing Centers of Academic Excellence and Intelligence. We also now hold the IC more accountable for doing a better job of developing a matrix to assess minority fellowship and internship programs and how they actually achieve their desired results, which is to increase the number of minorities hired by the IC.

Recently, I had the privilege of hosting a diversity in Intel summit. This event served as a rare opportunity for minority groups interested in the IC to gain insightful and helpful advice from top national security officials. It was truly a great occasion and it further reaffirms our committee's shared commitment to helping to ensure robust diversity throughout the entire IC.

I was also pleased to successfully include bipartisan language that promotes accountability and transparency in the IC federally funded academic programs by requiring agencies to report on their recruitment and retention efforts. Increasing diversity and accountability in the IC is an issue of good governance and makes all of us better because it encourages unique and creative ways of problem-solving, which is increasingly necessary as we develop and we face more complex intelligence challenges.

As a committee, I am extremely proud of the work we have done. We took great pains to cut unnecessary funding while prioritizing the need to improve upon processes and be more efficient in the IC generally. The reality is that we live in a world where potential threats to our Nation are constantly developing and changing. As our military missions and intelligence objectives continue to evolve, we need an IC that is both diverse, agile, and adequately funded.

I am proud to support this year's Intelligence Authorization Act. I want to, again, thank the chairman and ranking member for all of their hard work. I urge my colleagues to support this important legislation.

Mr. NUNES. Mr. Speaker, I reserve the balance of my time.

Mr. SCHIFF. Mr. Speaker, I yield myself such time as I may consume.

Earlier this afternoon, we debated H.R. 3929, honoring the heroes of the Office of Strategic Services, the forerunner to our modern-day intelligence and special operations communities.

We honor them today to express our deepest gratitude for the contributions they made during World War II and its aftermath and our appreciation for the example they set for the present intelligence community and special operations heroes. They were part of America's Greatest Generation, one we will continue to honor, remember, and emulate. They faced a complex and dangerous world. They met those grave challenges on the desolate fields of Europe, the torrid seas of the Pacific, and in the shadows. Espionage and intelligence were critical to winning the war and to preserving the peace.

As we look forward to the future and to the dangerous world we inhabit today, we would do well to keep the examples set by that Greatest Generation in our minds. As they did, we should lead by example as much as by strength.

Thankfully, our intelligence community is the most capable and committed in the world to our ideals and to the rule of law. Every day, they seek to ensure that we are given the information necessary to guard and defend ourselves, our allies, and our partners. We remain grateful always for their hard work and dedication.

Again, my thanks to Chairman NUNES, to the members of HPSCI, particularly those who are leaving the committee, to the Senate for a remarkable bipartisan and bicameral effort, and to our excellent committee staff.

I want to thank the many public servants who have led the IC with whom we have had the chance to work over the past several years. In particular, I want to extend my thanks to those retiring or leaving their roles at the IC at the end of this administration, including Director of National Intelligence James Clapper and his deputy, Stephanie O'Sullivan; CIA Director John Brennan and his deputy, David Cohen; Assistant Secretary of the Treasury for Intelligence and Analysis Leslie Ireland, who today is retiring after 31 years of Federal service; and Under Secretary of Defense for Intelligence, Marcel Lettre.

Thank you as well to the incredibly capable leaders of the other elements of the IC who may remain beyond January 20th. Of course, most importantly, thank you to all the men and women of the intelligence community who silently and courageously protect our country day and night through their crucial work. We appreciate everything they do, and they have our continued support.

I also want to thank not only the HPSCI members, but the entire staff, including Michael Bahar, Tim Bergreen, Carly Blake, Robert Minehart, Linda Cohen, Amanda Rogers Thorpe, Wells Bennett, Rheanne Wirkkala, Thomas Eager, Patrick Boland, Kristin Jepson, Brandon Smith, and Kimberlee Kerr for all their valuable service.

I yield back the balance of my time.

Mr. NUNES. Mr. Speaker, I yield myself the balance of my time.

We have four retiring members from our committee this year: Representative MURPHY, who was already spoken about earlier, did a great job attending a lot of the committee hearings or almost all of the committee hearings. We also have Representative JEFF MILLER, who served on this committee for a very long time and who is chairman of the Veterans' Affairs Committee; he is retiring. Also, Representative LYNN WESTMORELAND did a great job chairing our National Security Agency and Cybersecurity Subcommittee. Dr. JOE HECK, who chaired the Department of Defense Intelligence and Overhead Architecture Subcommittee, he is here on the floor with us this evening.

Finally, it is possibly premature, but we may not be able to congratulate Representative POMPEO on the House floor. He will have to have Senate confirmation next year, so I imagine he will be with the committee for a few months. But if we don't get a chance to come down to the House floor before he is approved by the Senate, I want to congratulate Mr. POMPEO. We are quite excited to have somebody from our committee to be chosen in the next administration to run the CIA.

I would urge my colleagues to support this bipartisan, bicameral bill, H.R. 6393.

I yield back the balance of my time.

The SPEAKER pro tempore. The question is on the motion offered by the gentleman from California (Mr. NUNES) that the House suspend the rules and pass the bill, H.R. 6393.

The question was taken.

The SPEAKER pro tempore. In the opinion of the Chair, two-thirds being in the affirmative, the ayes have it.

Mr. NUNES. Mr. Speaker, on that I demand the yeas and nays.

The yeas and nays were ordered.

The SPEAKER pro tempore. Pursuant to clause 8 of rule XX, further proceedings on this question will be postponed.

□ 1815

REPORT ON RESOLUTION PROVIDING FOR CONSIDERATION OF CONFERENCE REPORT ON S. 2943, NATIONAL DEFENSE AUTHORIZATION ACT FOR FISCAL YEAR 2017

Mr. BYRNE, from the Committee on Rules, submitted a privileged report (Rept. No. 114–844) on the resolution (H. Res. 937) providing for consideration of the conference report to accompany the bill (S. 2943) to authorize appropriations for fiscal year 2017 for military activities of the Department of Defense, for military construction, and for defense activities of the Department of Energy, to prescribe military personnel strengths for such fiscal year, and for other purposes, which was referred to the House Calendar and ordered to be printed.

ANNOUNCEMENT BY THE SPEAKER PRO TEMPORE

The SPEAKER pro tempore. Pursuant to clause 8 of rule XX, and the order of the House of today, proceedings will resume on questions previously postponed.

Votes will be taken in the following order:

The question on the motion to concur in the Senate amendment to H.R. 34 with an amendment;

The motion to suspend the rules and pass H.R. 6393; and

The motion to suspend the rules and pass H.R. 6304, if ordered.

The first electronic vote will be conducted as a 15-minute vote. Remaining electronic votes will be conducted as 5-minute votes.

TSUNAMI WARNING, EDUCATION, AND RESEARCH ACT OF 2015

The SPEAKER pro tempore. The unfinished business is the question on agreeing to the motion to concur in the Senate amendment to the bill (H.R. 34) to authorize and strengthen the tsunami detection, forecast, warning, research, and mitigation program of the National Oceanic and Atmospheric Administration, and for other purposes, with an amendment offered by the gentleman from Michigan (Mr. UPTON), on which a recorded vote was ordered.

The Clerk read the title of the bill.

The SPEAKER pro tempore. The question is on agreeing to the motion.

The vote was taken by electronic device, and there were—ayes 392, noes 26, not voting 16, as follows:

[Roll No. 592]

AYES—392

Abraham	Blackburn	Capuano
Adams	Blum	Cárdenas
Aderholt	Blumenauer	Carson (IN)
Aguilar	Bonamici	Carter (GA)
Allen	Bost	Carter (TX)
Amodei	Boustany	Cartwright
Ashford	Boyle, Brendan	Castor (FL)
Barletta	F.	Castro (TX)
Barr	Brady (PA)	Chabot
Barton	Brady (TX)	Chaffetz
Bass	Brat	Chu, Judy
Beatty	Brooks (IN)	Cicilline
Becerra	Brownley (CA)	Clark (MA)
Benishek	Buchanan	Clarke (NY)
Bera	Bucshon	Clawson (FL)
Beyer	Burgess	Clay
Bilirakis	Bustos	Cleaver
Bishop (GA)	Butterfield	Clyburn
Bishop (MI)	Byrne	Coffman
Bishop (UT)	Calvert	Cohen
Black	Capps	Cole

Collins (GA)	Hill	Mullin
Collins (NY)	Himes	Murphy (FL)
Comer	Hinojosa	Murphy (PA)
Comstock	Holding	Nadler
Conaway	Honda	Napolitano
Connolly	Hoyer	Neal
Conyers	Hudson	Neugebauer
Cook	Huffman	Newhouse
Cooper	Huizenga (MI)	Noem
Costa	Hultgren	Nolan
Costello (PA)	Hunter	Norcross
Courtney	Hurd (TX)	Nunes
Cramer	Hurt (VA)	O'Rourke
Crawford	Israel	Olson
Crenshaw	Issa	Palazzo
Crowley	Jackson Lee	Pallone
Cuellar	Jeffries	Palmer
Culberson	Jenkins (KS)	Pascrell
Cummings	Jenkins (WV)	Paulsen
Curbelo (FL)	Johnson (GA)	Payne
Davidson	Johnson (OH)	Pearce
Davis (CA)	Johnson, E. B.	Pelosi
Davis, Danny	Johnson, Sam	Perlmutter
Davis, Rodney	Joyce	Perry
DeFazio	Kaptur	Peters
DeGette	Katko	Peterson
Delaney	Keating	Pingree
DelBene	Kelly (IL)	Pittenger
Denham	Kelly (MS)	Pitts
Dent	Kelly (PA)	Pocan
DeSantis	Kennedy	Poliquin
DeSaulnier	Kildee	Polis
Deutch	Kilmer	Pompeo
Diaz-Balart	Kind	Posey
Dingell	King (IA)	Price (NC)
Dold	King (NY)	Price, Tom
Donovan	Kinzinger (IL)	Quigley
Doyle, Michael	Kline	Reed
F.	Knight	Reichert
Duckworth	Kuster	Renacci
Duffy	LaHood	Ribble
Duncan (SC)	LaMalfa	Rice (NY)
Duncan (TN)	Lamborn	Rice (SC)
Edwards	Lance	Richmond
Ellison	Langevin	Roby
Ellmers (NC)	Larsen (WA)	Roe (TN)
Emmer (MN)	Larson (CT)	Rogers (AL)
Engel	Latta	Rogers (KY)
Eshoo	Lawrence	Rohrabacher
Esty	Levin	Rokita
Evans	Lieu, Ted	Rooney (FL)
Farr	Lipinski	Ros-Lehtinen
Fincher	LoBiondo	Roskam
Fleischmann	Loebsack	Ross
Fleming	Lofgren	Rothfus
Flores	Long	Rouzer
Fortenberry	Loudermilk	Roybal-Allard
Foster	Love	Royce
Foxx	Lowenthal	Ruiz
Frankel (FL)	Lowey	Ruppersberger
Franks (AZ)	Lucas	Rush
Frelinghuysen	Luetkemeyer	Russell
Fudge	Lujan Grisham	Ryan (OH)
Gallego	(NM)	Salmon
Garamendi	Luján, Ben Ray	Sánchez, Linda
Garrett	(NM)	T.
Gibbs	Lynch	Sanchez, Loretta
Gibson	MacArthur	Sarbanes
Goodlatte	Maloney,	Scalise
Gowdy	Carolyn	Schiff
Graham	Maloney, Sean	Schrader
Granger	Marchant	Schweikert
Graves (GA)	Marino	Scott (VA)
Graves (LA)	Matsui	Scott, Austin
Graves (MO)	McCarthy	Scott, David
Grayson	McCaul	Sensenbrenner
Green, Al	McClintock	Serrano
Green, Gene	McCollum	Sessions
Griffith	McGovern	Sewell (AL)
Grothman	McHenry	Sherman
Guinta	McKinley	Shimkus
Guthrie	McMorris	Shuster
Gutiérrez	Rodgers	Simpson
Hanabusa	McNerney	Sinema
Hanna	McSally	Sires
Hardy	Meehan	Slaughter
Harper	Meeks	Smith (MO)
Harris	Meng	Smith (NE)
Hartzler	Messer	Smith (NJ)
Hastings	Mica	Smith (TX)
Heck (NV)	Miller (FL)	Smith (WA)
Heck (WA)	Miller (MI)	Speier
Hensarling	Moolenaar	Stefanik
Herrera Beutler	Mooney (WV)	Stewart
Hice, Jody B.	Moore	Stivers
Higgins	Moulton	Stutzman

Swalwell (CA)	Vargas	Welch
Takano	Veasey	Wenstrup
Thompson (CA)	Vela	Westerman
Thompson (MS)	Velázquez	Wilson (SC)
Thompson (PA)	Visclosky	Wittman
Thornberry	Wagner	Womack
Tiberi	Walberg	Woodall
Tipton	Walden	Yarmuth
Titus	Walker	Yoder
Tonko	Walorski	Yoho
Torres	Walters, Mimi	Young (AK)
Trott	Walz	Young (IA)
Tsongas	Wasserman	Young (IN)
Turner	Schultz	Zeldin
Upton	Waters, Maxine	Zinke
Valadao	Watson Coleman	
Van Hollen	Webster (FL)	

NOES—26

Amash	Fitzpatrick	Massie
Babin	Gohmert	McDermott
Bridenstine	Gosar	Meadows
Brooks (AL)	Grijalva	Mulvaney
Buck	Huelskamp	Ratcliffe
DeLauro	Jordan	Sanford
DesJarlais	Labrador	Schakowsky
Doggett	Lee	Weber (TX)
Farenthold	Lummis	

NOT VOTING—16

Brown (FL)	Jones	Rigell
Carney	Kirkpatrick	Westmoreland
Forbes	Lewis	Williams
Gabbard	Nugent	Wilson (FL)
Hahn	Poe (TX)	
Jolly	Rangel	

□ 1838

Messrs. DIAZ-BALART, ELLISON, and Ms. LOVE changed their vote from "no" to "aye."

So the motion to concur was agreed to.

The result of the vote was announced as above recorded.

A motion to reconsider was laid on the table.

Stated for:

Ms. WILSON of Florida. Mr. Speaker, I was unavoidably detained. Had I been present, I would have voted "yea" on rollcall No. 592.

INTELLIGENCE AUTHORIZATION ACT FOR FISCAL YEAR 2017

The SPEAKER pro tempore (Mr. BYRNE). The unfinished business is the vote on the motion to suspend the rules and pass the bill (H.R. 6393) to authorize appropriations for fiscal year 2017 for intelligence and intelligence-related activities of the United States Government, the Community Management Account, and the Central Intelligence Agency Retirement and Disability System, and for other purposes, on which the yeas and nays were ordered.

The Clerk read the title of the bill.

The SPEAKER pro tempore. The question is on the motion offered by the gentleman from California (Mr. NUNES) that the House suspend the rules and pass the bill.

This is a 5-minute vote.

The vote was taken by electronic device, and there were—yeas 390, nays 30, not voting 14, as follows:

[Roll No. 593]

YEAS—390

Abraham	Aderholt	Allen
Adams	Aguilar	Amodei

Ashford
Babin
Barletta
Barr
Barton
Beatty
Becerra
Benishek
Bera
Beyer
Bilirakis
Bishop (GA)
Bishop (MI)
Bishop (UT)
Black
Blackburn
Blum
Bonamici
Bost
Boustany
Boyle, Brendan
  F.
Brady (PA)
Brady (TX)
Brat
Bridenstine
Brooks (AL)
Brooks (IN)
Brownley (CA)
Buchanan
Buck
Bucshon
Burgess
Bustos
Butterfield
Byrne
Calvert
Capps
Cárdenas
Carson (IN)
Carter (GA)
Carter (TX)
Cartwright
Castor (FL)
Castro (TX)
Chabot
Chaffetz
Cicilline
Clark (MA)
Clawson (FL)
Clay
Cleaver
Clyburn
Coffman
Cohen
Cole
Collins (GA)
Collins (NY)
Comer
Comstock
Conaway
Connolly
Cook
Cooper
Costa
Costello (PA)
Courtney
Cramer
Crawford
Crenshaw
Crowley
Cuellar
Culberson
Cummings
Curbelo (FL)
Davidson
Davis (CA)
Davis, Danny
Davis, Rodney
DeFazio
DeGette
Delaney
DeLauro
Denham
Dent
DeSantis
DeSaulnier
DesJarlais
Deutch
Diaz-Balart
Dingell
Doggett
Dold
Donovan
Doyle, Michael
  F.

Duckworth
Duffy
Duncan (SC)
Edwards
Ellmers (NC)
Emmer (MN)
Engel
Eshoo
Esty
Evans
Farenthold
Farr
Fincher
Fitzpatrick
Fleischmann
Fleming
Flores
Fortenberry
Foster
Foxx
Frankel (FL)
Franks (AZ)
Frelinghuysen
Fudge
Gallego
Garamendi
Garrett
Gibbs
Gibson
Gohmert
Goodlatte
Gosar
Gowdy
Graham
Granger
Graves (GA)
Graves (LA)
Graves (MO)
Grayson
Green, Al
Green, Gene
Griffith
Grothman
Guinta
Guthrie
Hanabusa
Hanna
Hardy
Harper
Harris
Hartzler
Hastings
Heck (NV)
Heck (WA)
Hensarling
Herrera Beutler
Hice, Jody B.
Higgins
Hill
Himes
Hinojosa
Holding
Hoyer
Hudson
Huelskamp
Huffman
Huizenga (MI)
Hultgren
Hunter
Hurd (TX)
Hurt (VA)
Israel
Issa
Jackson Lee
Jeffries
Jenkins (KS)
Jenkins (WV)
Johnson (GA)
Johnson (OH)
Johnson, E. B.
Johnson, Sam
Jordan
Joyce
Kaptur
Katko
Keating
Kelly (IL)
Kelly (MS)
Kelly (PA)
Kennedy
Kildee
Kilmer
Kind
King (IA)
King (NY)
Kinzinger (IL)

Kline
Knight
Kuster
LaHood
LaMalfa
Lamborn
Lance
Langevin
Larsen (WA)
Larson (CT)
Latta
Lawrence
Levin
Lewis
Lipinski
LoBiondo
Loebsack
Long
Loudermilk
Love
Lowenthal
Lowey
Lucas
Luetkemeyer
Lujan Grisham
  (NM)
Luján, Ben Ray
  (NM)
Lynch
MacArthur
Maloney,
  Carolyn
Maloney, Sean
Marchant
Marino
Matsui
McCarthy
McCaul
McClintock
McCollum
McHenry
McKinley
McMorris
  Rodgers
McSally
Meadows
Meehan
Meeks
Meng
Messer
Mica
Miller (FL)
Miller (MI)
Moolenaar
Mooney (WV)
Moore
Moulton
Mullin
Murphy (FL)
Murphy (PA)
Nadler
Napolitano
Neal
Neugebauer
Newhouse
Noem
Nolan
Norcross
Nunes
Olson
Palazzo
Pallone
Palmer
Pascrell
Paulsen
Payne
Pearce
Pelosi
Perlmutter
Perry
Peters
Peterson
Pingree
Pittenger
Pitts
Poliquin
Pompeo
Posey
Price (NC)
Price, Tom
Quigley
Ratcliffe
Reed
Reichert
Renacci
Ribble

Rice (NY)
Rice (SC)
Richmond
Roby
Roe (TN)
Rogers (AL)
Rogers (KY)
Rohrabacher
Rokita
Rooney (FL)
Ros-Lehtinen
Roskam
Ross
Rothfus
Rouzer
Royball-Allard
Royce
Ruiz
Ruppersberger
Rush
Russell
Ryan (OH)
Salmon
Sánchez, Linda
  T.
Sanchez, Loretta
Sanford
Sarbanes
Scalise
Schiff
Schrader
Schweikert
Scott (VA)
Scott, Austin
Scott, David

Sensenbrenner
Serrano
Sessions
Sewell (AL)
Sherman
Shimkus
Shuster
Simpson
Sinema
Sires
Slaughter
Smith (MO)
Smith (NE)
Smith (NJ)
Smith (TX)
Smith (WA)
Speier
Stefanik
Stewart
Stivers
Stutzman
Swalwell (CA)
Thompson (CA)
Thompson (MS)
Thompson (PA)
Thornberry
Tiberi
Tipton
Titus
Tonko
Torres
Trott
Tsongas
Turner
Upton

Valadao
Van Hollen
Vargas
Veasey
Vela
Velázquez
Visclosky
Wagner
Walberg
Walden
Walker
Walorski
Walters, Mimi
Walz
Wasserman
  Schultz
Waters, Maxine
Weber (TX)
Webster (FL)
Wenstrup
Westerman
Wilson (FL)
Wilson (SC)
Wittman
Womack
Woodall
Yarmuth
Yoder
Yoho
Young (AK)
Young (IA)
Young (IN)
Zeldin
Zinke

NAYS—30

Amash
Bass
Blumenauer
Capuano
Chu, Judy
Clarke (NY)
Conyers
DelBene
Duncan (TN)
Ellison

Gabbard
Grijalva
Gutiérrez
Honda
Labrador
Lee
Lieu, Ted
Lofgren
Lummis
Massie

McDermott
McGovern
Mulvaney
O'Rourke
Pocan
Polis
Schakowsky
Takano
Watson Coleman
Welch

NOT VOTING—14

Brown (FL)
Carney
Forbes
Hahn
Jolly

Jones
Kirkpatrick
McNerney
Nugent
Poe (TX)

Rangel
Rigell
Westmoreland
Williams

ANNOUNCEMENT BY THE SPEAKER PRO TEMPORE

The SPEAKER pro tempore (during the vote). There are 2 minutes remaining.

□ 1847

Mr. ELLISON and Ms. CLARKE of New York changed their vote from "yea" to "nay."

So (two-thirds being in the affirmative) the rules were suspended and the bill was passed.

The result of the vote was announced as above recorded.

A motion to reconsider was laid on the table.

PERSONAL EXPLANATION

Mr. RIGELL. Mr. Speaker, personal circumstances kept me from voting on the following votes. Had I been present, I would have voted "yea" on rollcall No. 592—21st Century Cures. "Yea" on rollcall No. 593—Intel Reauthorization.

ANNOUNCEMENT BY COMMITTEE ON RULES REGARDING AMENDMENT PROCESS FOR H.R. 5143, TRANSPARENT INSURANCE STANDARDS ACT OF 2016

Mr. SESSIONS. Mr. Speaker, this morning, the Rules Committee issued an announcement outlining the amendment process for H.R. 5143, the Transparent Insurance Standards Act of 2016.

The amendment deadline is set for Monday, December 5, at 10 a.m. Amendments should be drafted to the text of the Rules Committee Print 114–68, which contains the text of the bill, as reported by the Committee on Financial Services, with a modification, and can be found on the Rules Committee Web site.

Feel free to contact me or the staff if you have any questions.

ADOLFO "HARPO" CELAYA POST OFFICE

The SPEAKER pro tempore. The unfinished business is the question on suspending the rules and passing the bill (H.R. 6304) to designate the facility of the United States Postal Service located at 501 North Main Street in Florence, Arizona, as the "Adolfo 'Harpo' Celaya Post Office".

The Clerk read the title of the bill.

The SPEAKER pro tempore. The question is on the motion offered by the gentleman from Arizona (Mr. GOSAR) that the House suspend the rules and pass the bill.

The question was taken; and (two-thirds being in the affirmative) the rules were suspended and the bill was passed.

A motion to reconsider was laid on the table.

DIRECTING THE CLERK OF THE HOUSE OF REPRESENTATIVES TO MAKE A CORRECTION IN THE ENROLLMENT OF H.R. 34

Mr. LANCE. Mr. Speaker, I send to the desk a concurrent resolution and ask unanimous consent for its immediate consideration in the House.

The Clerk read the title of the concurrent resolution.

The SPEAKER pro tempore. Is there objection to the request of the gentleman from New Jersey?

There was no objection.

The text of the concurrent resolution is as follows:

H. CON. RES. 174

Resolved by the House of Representatives (the Senate concurring), That in the enrollment of the bill (H.R. 34) to authorize and strengthen the tsunami detection, forecast, warning, research, and mitigation program of the National Oceanic and Atmospheric Administration, and for other purposes, the Clerk of the House of Representatives shall make the following correction: Amend the long title so as to read: "An Act to accelerate the discovery, development, and delivery of 21st century cures, and for other purposes.".

The concurrent resolution was agreed to.

A motion to reconsider was laid on the table.

END OF CUBA'S BRUTAL REGIME OF REPRESSION

(Mr. LaMALFA asked and was given permission to address the House for 1 minute.)

Mr. LaMALFA. Mr. Speaker, Fidel Castro led a brutal regime of oppression that imprisoned an island nation. While he and his family live like kings, the people of Cuba are repressed, starved, and forbidden any outside information.

According to credible sources and The Wall Street Journal, his regime may have killed up to 100,000 people. Thousands of political prisoners and human rights activists were brutally tortured and killed over the years.

Castro was eager to see the Soviet Union and the United States engage in a nuclear war, and even Soviet leader Nikita Khrushchev had to remind Castro that the point of putting the missiles in Cuba was to further Communist interests, not start Armageddon. "This is insane." Khrushchev said. "Fidel wants to drag us into the grave with him."

Under Castro, the Cuban Government refused to recognize the legitimacy of Cuban human rights organizations, alternative political parties, independent labor unions, or even a free press. He also denied international monitors, such as the International Committee of the Red Cross, to access the island to investigate human rights conditions.

With this vicious dictator finally dead, perhaps our close neighbor can finally be free. The people of Cuba can choose for themselves what they would like for their lives, rather than death squads and secret police imposing the will of a madman. I hope we can be supportive of a free Cuba and not further a bad regime.

PRESIDENT-ELECT TRUMP'S TREASURY NOMINATION

(Ms. KAPTUR asked and was given permission to address the House for 1 minute.)

Ms. KAPTUR. Mr. Speaker, I rise tonight in alarm over the stacking of Wall Street insiders in top positions for the incoming administration.

During his campaign, President-elect Donald Trump said the system is rigged. He said hedge fund managers are "getting away with murder" and that he would "tax Wall Street" and called Washington, D.C., corrupt and promised to "drain the swamp." President-elect Trump even closed his campaign with a political ad bashing Goldman Sachs.

Yet now, according to media reports, he has chosen a second-generation Goldman Sachs partner, Steven Mnuchin, to serve as Treasury Secretary. He will take the post most responsible for watching and regulating the dangerous, high-risk, high-stakes gambling behavior of Wall Street,

which he has himself engaged in for decades. He worked at Goldman Sachs for 17 years. His father worked there. His brother still works there, and he frequently returns for alumni and social gatherings. He was named the "Foreclosure King" after buying up the remains of IndyMac, a California-based mortgage lender, and evicted approximately 36,000 people who could not keep up their mortgage payments.

The last three administrations have had Goldman executives at the helm inside the White House and Treasury. While President-elect Trump promises to drain the swamp, he is not doing it. He is enlarging it.

GUARDING AGAINST FOREIGN INTERFERENCE IN FUTURE ELECTIONS

(Mr. CONNOLLY asked and was given permission to address the House for 1 minute and to revise and extend his remarks.)

Mr. CONNOLLY. Mr. Speaker, on October 7, 2016, the Department of Homeland Security and the Office of the Director of National Intelligence on Election Security released a joint statement saying: "The U.S. Intelligence Community is confident that the Russian Government directed the recent compromises of emails from U.S. persons and institutions, including from U.S. political organizations."

The U.S. Intelligence Community went on to explicitly state that "these thefts and disclosures are intended to interfere with the U.S. election process . . . only Russia's senior-most officials could have authorized these activities."

Despite this certification, the majority in this body has demonstrated zero interest in examining the unprecedented attack on one of our most cherished institutions, democratic free elections.

I am here today to plead with the majority to take an interest, not because I seek to undermine the results of the recent Presidential election. That is not my intention. Rather, it is my sincere hope that we understand the nature of the foreign interference and how to guard against it in all future elections.

PRECISION MEDICINE INITIATIVE

(Ms. JACKSON LEE asked and was given permission to address the House for 1 minute and to revise and extend her remarks.)

Ms. JACKSON LEE. Mr. Speaker, I rise in celebratory support of H.R. 34, the House amendment to the Senate amendment to the 21st Century Cures Act. As a breast cancer survivor, I am celebrating. As a Representative from the City of Houston, I am celebrating.

Because of the Texas Medical Center, this plan will provide an ambitious ac-

tion that called for $6.3 billion in mandatory funding to be delivered over the next 10 years to the National Institutes of Health. It also provides and estimated that every $1 of NIH funding generates about $2.21 in local economic growth and 402,000 jobs. But most of all, it will deal with the curing of diseases and developing research that will help save lives.

In furtherance of this initiative, this legislation before us allows for the creation of an innovation fund through the National Institutes of Health so that we can design the most innovative ways of curing disease, of helping children, of helping seniors, of helping people who are dealing with incurable disease.

The Cures Act is an act of the 21st century. It moves forward on the President's Precision Medicine Initiative.

I thank Mr. UPTON, Ms. DeGETTE, and all the Members. I serve as an original cosponsor. I am excited about the legislation, for it will save lives.

□ 1900

COMMEMORATING AND CELEBRATING THE LIFE OF MS. JACQUELINE ELLIS

The SPEAKER pro tempore (Mr. CARTER of Georgia). Under the Speaker's announced policy of January 6, 2015, the gentleman from Texas (Mr. AL GREEN) is recognized for 60 minutes as the designee of the minority leader.

Mr. AL GREEN of Texas. Mr. Speaker, I am honored to stand before the House tonight to commemorate and celebrate the life of my former Chief of Staff, Ms. Jacqueline Ellis.

Mr. Speaker, Ms. Ellis served well. In the sense of many, she was the 436th Member of Congress. She helped to educate not only new persons who were here in administrative capacities, but also Congresspersons. She helped us to understand what Congress was all about.

I am honored tonight to say some kind words about her and to acknowledge a colleague who is here and will be saying a word as well.

To my right is a photograph of my very dear friend and former coworker, Jacqueline Ellis. She was born in Mobile, Alabama. She was born at a time when persons of African ancestry could buy a hat, but they couldn't try it on; at a time when persons of African ancestry would have to step aside so that others could step forward; and at a time when persons of African ancestry were relegated to certain places in life, certain schools, and certain places of business. They had to go to the back door for their food. They would drink from colored water fountains. She was born at a time when this country did not respect all of her rights.

Who could have known that when she was born in Mobile, Alabama, that she would make her way from Mobile to Capitol Hill?

There was no way to predict at the time of her birth that she would come to this Nation's Capitol and that she would serve three Members of Congress—one United States Senator and two U.S. Representatives: the Honorable Major Owens from New York's 11th Congressional District, the Honorable Senator Heflin. And, of course, she served in my office. No one could have known.

I think, quite frankly, that this speaks to the greatness of the country, that we have moved light years away from some of the circumstances that we had to endure earlier in the history of this country.

Notwithstanding all that has been done, there is still great work to be done. Tonight I want to say to you that this person born in Mobile during very difficult times has received an indication from the President of the United States of America that he was saddened to learn of her demise. I include in the RECORD a letter from the President.

THE WHITE HOUSE,
Washington, September 28, 2016.
Mr. CHRIS ELLIS,
Bowie, Maryland.

DEAR CHRIS: I was deeply saddened to learn of the loss of your sister, Jacqueline. My heartfelt condolences are with you as you reflect upon her life.

May cherished memories help temper your grief, and may you find comfort in the support of loved ones. Please know you will remain in my thoughts.

Sincerely,
BARACK OBAMA.

Mr. AL GREEN of Texas. She has also been honored by a good many of my colleagues here on the Hill, including the Honorable NANCY PELOSI, who sent a letter to my office and expressed verbally her condolences and her sympathies. She has also been honored by the Honorable STENY HOYER, by the Honorable JIM CLYBURN, and by the Honorable XAVIER BECERRA. She has been honored by Members of Congress in many capacities. We have a resolution that has been filed. This resolution is one that pays tribute to her. It has been signed on to by a good many Members of Congress as well.

So tonight I am pleased to say that Jacqueline Ellis, born in Mobile, Alabama, and matriculated her way to and through the Halls of Congress is now resting in peace.

She was a person that lived every day of her life in the sense that she was busy doing something for someone every day of her adult life. She worked up until the moment she was hospitalized. Literally, I was the last person to speak to her. She and I were going to an event, the ALC dinner, the Congressional Black Caucus dinner as it is called, and she was there to pick me up and take me to the dinner. She called me and said to me: I will be waiting for you. I am downstairs.

I said that I will be down in about 10 minutes.

Within that period of time, she called me back and informed me that she needed to go to the hospital. I rushed down to her, and when I got there, the emergency assistance was already there. She called them prior to calling me apparently. I immediately assisted them, and we went to the hospital together. She stayed in the hospital for some days and made her transition.

The important point to make is that she was working. Her work was her life. She lived to perform her duties. She was on her job in the sense that she was assisting that evening, and she was there all day long. She was ill, but she would not stop working. There were times when we would ask that she take some time off, but she always wanted to come to work.

Her work was her inspiration in a sense. Her work was the thing that gave her a reason to continue to go on, and she never, ever complained. There is a song that speaks to the kind of person that she was because there are many of us right here in Congress who can relate to this. When you see the great eagle flying, you assume that it is the wings. But there is a song that addresses how it is that the eagle can soar to these high heights. That song says that it is not the wings, but rather it is the wind beneath the wings. She was the wind beneath the wings of a lot of people who were able to soar to high heights, a lot of people who did not understand all of what was before them when they accepted the responsibility to become a part of a congressional staff or a Member of Congress. She became the wind beneath their wings and helped to guide them through Congress.

I am pleased to tell you that we have had several celebrations of her life. We had one in this area immediately after her untimely demise—untimely to me because I had hoped that she would be with us a lot longer than she was. We also had a celebration of her life in her hometown of Mobile, Alabama, attended by a good many dignitaries and staffers from the Hill; a celebration of her life in Houston, Texas, similarly attended. She has been recognized and honored by people that she came in contact with.

She made a difference. I will relate one brief vignette before I ask my colleague to come to the podium. When I was looking for my first chief of staff—and she was my first and only chief of staff, I might add. When I was looking for my chief of staff, I was a neophyte in Congress, and I brought her on board. You are always unsure about a new hire, especially a person who is going to be key to the office, a person that everything sort of evolves around. So I was unsure as to whether or not I had made the right decision.

She and I were together, and I saw her pull over rather abruptly. She was driving. My recollection is that this happened more than once, but on this occasion, she was driving. When she pulled over, she ran over to a person, and I saw her hand the person something, and then she came back to the car. I immediately wanted to know who this was. Was it somebody that she knew? Because she did it so abruptly.

She said: No, I didn't know that person.

The person was not dressed in a suit and tie. The person did not have the appearance of what we would call status, although I think everybody has status. The person did not appear to be a captain of industry, if you will. She went over and she gave that person money. I found out later on that she would go to the credit union, and she would extract dollar bills—some stack; I don't know how many in the stack—and she would use that money to just give to people that she would encounter that she was of the opinion needed some help.

When she did it on that day, I knew that I had made the right decision because I then knew that I saw the sermon that many people preach. It is truly better to see a sermon than to say one, or to be one than to say one. I saw that day "love your neighbor as you love yourself." I saw on that occasion "help somebody."

I saw her live up to the true meaning of the spirit of the story of the Good Samaritan who saw the person in the streets of life and went over and took that person to the inn and said: Here is money. Use this to help this person. And if this is not enough, when I come back, I will give you more.

I saw the good neighbor in Jacqui Ellis. I knew then that I made a good hire because I had a person who would not only speak a sermon, but would be a sermon.

Mr. Speaker, I yield to the gentlewoman from Texas (Ms. JACKSON LEE), who is my colleague from Houston, Texas. The Honorable SHEILA JACKSON LEE hails from the 18th Congressional District. She serves on the Judiciary Committee, she serves on the Committee on Homeland Security, and she has served us in Congress for a good many years.

Ms. JACKSON LEE. Mr. Speaker, I thank my colleague, the Honorable AL GREEN of Texas.

Mr. Speaker, we are like family in this House, Republicans and Democrats, as we work together and work with our staff. I am very clear in the fact that Ms. Ellis was the only chief of staff that Congressman AL GREEN of Texas had, and that he made an A-plus choice, and she, likewise, in accepting his offer to be his chief of staff.

She was a 30-year veteran, and she brought to his office and brought to this House a sense of affection and love for the institution, for democracy, and for America. Not only did she have the privilege of working for Congressman AL GREEN of Texas and he the privilege of having her as his chief of staff, she worked previously for Congressman Major Owens of New York, and the late former Alabama Senator Howard Heflin.

□ 1915

It means that she understood the institutions that helped to lay down the pillars of democracy.

She was a spiritual mother to the tens upon thousands of young people who came to this place with starry eyes to make a difference—spiritual mother, sister, mentor, and friend to many people, including elected and people of high ranking status.

She was a graduate of a historically Black college, and, as well, she had a background in government affairs.

But, more importantly, she had a big heart. And she was eager, as I am told by the staff, to be able to help all the new and young staff. They knew they could go to Jacqui Ellis.

She was a Christian woman as well, and she served on many important organizations. In particular, I worked for the Southern Christian Leadership Conference. She was a national board member, the organization founded by Dr. Martin Luther King, and Ralph David Abernathy, and where Andrew Young worked, and Josea Williams, and so many others. James Orange, and those of us young people who believed that we could overcome.

She was a recipient of the Ella Baker Award from the SCLC and Martin Luther King, III.

But where I got to see Jacqui really making it and doing it was in her leadership with C. Delores Tucker, and her work with the National Congress of Black Women. As a board member, I remember coming as a young Member of Congress, and we would go to that very famous breakfast, Congressman GREEN, the Sunday after the Congressional Black Caucus, and there was Jacqui. She was the orchestrator, the guider. She respected C. Delores Tucker. She honored the women who came. She was at their beck and call—we need this.

She was the person that the likes of Malcolm X's wife, Rosa Parks, and Coretta Scott King, because they used to come during their lifetime every year, and those of us who were young Members of Congress, she welcomed us with open arms and allowed us to sit in the royal place at the feet of these great women who she had come to know, and they had come to know and love her, as we held this wonderful program about the empowerment of women and, in particular, African American women.

She was, as well, the co-chair of the Bethune DuBois Institute, Inc. Leadership Forum and, as well, she has received awards from the Congressional Black Caucus.

So I close by simply saying, yes, she has a litany of accolades and honors. We wish that she could have lived on and on and on. Some say that the young die young. We certainly believe that Jacqui Ellis, our friend, our lover of this institution, this great staff person, was taken way too young.

As I told my friend and colleague, earlier this year, I experienced an enormous tragedy in losing a dear staff person, who, though a short time, had become so much a part of our extended family. And so, Congressman GREEN, I know it hurts. It hurts many of her fellow staffers and friends. Certainly we know her family suffered great pain.

But I can say, as we salute great Americans, and each have done something in their way to move this country forward, I want to say that Jacqui Ellis lived in the greatest country in the world. It was already a great country. But she was so much a part of making this country a country that welcomed all of the young talent and those new faces that desired to be part of the greatness of this country. She did it with open arms and a big heart. We will miss her greatly, but she has left a legacy of service. As you have noted, she stopped along the highway of life and gave what she had to someone who looked like they needed it more.

So to Jacqui I say: farewell our dear friend, farewell, for you are certainly one who is a good and faithful servant. May you rest in peace.

Mr. AL GREEN of Texas. Mr. Speaker, I thank Ms. JACKSON LEE for her very, very kind words. She did know Jacqui well. She had a lot of respect for her. I appreciate her taking the time to come by this evening.

I want to also acknowledge that the Honorable EDDIE BERNICE JOHNSON was here but had to step away.

I want to also acknowledge that some 150 individuals have given us expressions concerning Jacqui, a number of organizations, at least 20, and we have 41 cosponsors of the resolution that I spoke of earlier, H. Res. 905, which expresses condolences to her family, and it commemorates her life.

Finally, we have elected officials, at least 64, including the President and former Secretary of State Hillary Clinton, who have expressed their sympathies and condolences. She was truly a person who touched a lot of people in a very positive way. I am honored to say that I was associated with her and that she truly made a difference in my life.

Mr. Speaker, as we travel the road of life, we meet many people. We remember some and a good many we do not. Jacqueline Ellis is someone that I will remember, and my belief is that a good many other persons who came into contact with her, whether it was for a very short period of time or for some duration, will remember her as well.

These would include the members of the sorority that she was affiliated with, Delta Sigma Theta. She was very active in this sorority. She was loved, and is still loved, by the members of Delta Sigma Theta. They would come to the Hill on an annual basis and they always took time to come by and visit her. She would always welcome them and provide services.

This is but one of the many organizations that will continue to honor her, I am sure. The others that will remember her that she came in contact with would be SCLC, as was mentioned by my colleague, the Southern Christian Leadership Conference. This was the organization that Dr. King led. This was the organization that fought for human rights, civil rights, and human dignity across the length and breadth of this country. She was part of that organization. In fact, she was on the board.

She and Martin King, not Martin King the father but Martin King, III, the son of Dr. King, were the very best of friends—the very best of friends. He has traveled great distances to pay tribute to her. He was there in Mobile, Alabama. He came here for the services that we had. And he always, when he was in Washington, DC, would take the time to come by our office to say hello to Jacqui.

People who met her along life's way would also include the Links. The Links was an organization that she was affiliated with and that she took great pride in assisting as they were having their various events. She was always helpful to other people to make sure that they were able to be successful in their endeavors. When you travel the road of life, the highway of life, you meet many people. You don't remember them all, but there are some who are special, and these are the persons who will stand out in your mind and will be remembered in the very years to come of your life.

So tonight, I am grateful that the leadership has allowed us this time to pay tribute to Jacqueline Ellis, who was born in Mobile, Alabama, on October 22, 1957, a very difficult time in the life of the country, and who made a transition on September 21 of 2016. She is gone, but she is not forgotten. She will be remembered. We are grateful that we have had an opportunity to commemorate her life and celebrate the wonderful person that she was.

GENERAL LEAVE

Mr. AL GREEN of Texas. Mr. Speaker, I ask unanimous consent that all Members may have 5 legislative days in which to revise and extend their remarks and include extraneous material on the subject of my Special Order.

The SPEAKER pro tempore. Is there objection to the request of the gentleman from Texas?

There was no objection.

Mr. AL GREEN of Texas. Mr. Speaker, I yield back the balance of my time.

Ms. EDDIE BERNICE JOHNSON of Texas. Mr. Speaker, today, I join my colleagues to recognize a true pillar in the congressional community, Ms. Jacqueline Ellis. Jacqui began working on Capitol Hill when it was not common for a woman, let alone a woman of color to work here, but she never let that stop her. Her path in life is admirable and truly shows her resilience and dedication to public service.

During her tenure, she changed the lives of countless men and women, particularly those of color that she came in contact with. It was not uncommon for her to give her all to anyone that came through her door without asking for recognition. She stayed humbled and committed to her purpose to fulfill her life's mission of service.

Her love and dedication to Delta Sigma Theta Sorority, Inc. was felt with all her sorors, especially those who work on Capitol Hill. She assisted with hosting Delta Days at the Nation's Capitol and ensured that all who attended felt welcomed and loved. She also was the matriarchic for Deltas on the Hill, which gave members of her sorority at space to laugh, love and support each other on Capitol Hill. To my colleagues who are members of Delta Sigma Theta Sorority, Inc., I mourn with you all today for the loss of your sister.

She was a true humanitarian and her presence is missed throughout the halls of the Capitol. My thoughts and prayers go out to her family, Congressman AL GREEN's staff, her sorors, and all those who she impacted in her lifetime.

Mrs. BEATTY. Mr. Speaker, I thank my good friend and Congressional Black Caucus colleague, Congressman AL GREEN of Texas, for leading tonight's Special Order Hour to honor and in memorial to beloved Congressional staffer, Jacqueline A. Ellis, known to most of us as Jacqui.

On September 21, 2016, the world lost Jacqueline Ellis, a beloved mentor, friend, colleague, and sister, and we, here in the halls of Congress, lost a legend.

Through her nearly 30 years of service in the people's House, Jacqui helped to expand diversity on the Hill and inspired countless young people to dedicate their lives to public service.

She served as a mentor for many young African-American staffers who came to Capitol Hill looking to make a difference in our nation.

When Jacqui became a House staffer in 1988, there were few people of color in the corridors of the Congress, but that did not dissuade Jacqui. Instead, it inspired her to assist and help numerous Black staffers thrive.

Upon her passing, hundreds of former and current Congressional staffers took to social media to share their stories and memories of Jacqui. Words like "good listener"—"wonderful woman"—"especially there to help young people"—and "enormously respected" were used.

As one of the first Black women to serve as a Chief of Staff on Capitol Hill, she was a trailblazer who opened the door so other that women of color could follow in her footsteps.

She founded the Organization of African-American Administrative Assistants for Chiefs of Staff in the House. And, she worked quietly behind the scenes to expand equality of opportunity and to strengthen our democracy.

Jacqui was also a proud member of Delta Sigma Theta Sorority, Inc., and one of my sorors. She was instrumental in planning and executing the annual "Delta Days" on the Hill.

She was also a proud member of The LINKS Incorporated and coordinated its Congressional Black Caucus Foundation Issues Forum.

Her charitable nature, her unbridled spirit, her selfless dedication to public service, and her strong faith will certainly be missed.

RECOGNIZING THE VIRGINIA DELEGATION

The SPEAKER pro tempore. Under the Speaker's announced policy of January 6, 2015, the gentleman from Virginia (Mr. GOODLATTE) is recognized for 60 minutes as the designee of the majority leader.

GENERAL LEAVE

Mr. GOODLATTE. Mr. Speaker, I ask unanimous consent that all Members may have 5 legislative days in which to revise and extend their remarks and include extraneous material on the subject of my Special Order.

The SPEAKER pro tempore. Is there objection to the request of the gentleman from Virginia?

There was no objection.

Mr. GOODLATTE. Mr. Speaker, today I and other Members of the House, most especially members of the Virginia delegation, but other House Members who served with three of our Virginia colleagues, are here to express our thanks and pay tribute to their service, to the people of Virginia, and the people of the United States of America. We are saddened to lose three members of our great Virginia delegation, but we have the utmost regard for all of them, and we wish them well in their future endeavors.

I am going to start by recognizing my dear friend and colleague on the House Judiciary Committee, Congressman RANDY FORBES. I remember when RANDY arrived here. I had known him many years before he was elected to the House. I was, frankly, thrilled when he decided to run for the House of Representatives and got elected. Of course, his first priority, representing the Fourth Congressional District, was to get on the House Armed Services Committee.

Once he secured that, he was looking for a second committee. I encouraged him to seek a position on the House Judiciary Committee and helped him in his effort to do that. He is a fine attorney and someone who was a great value to me and my predecessors who have had the honor of chairing the House Judiciary Committee.

Born and raised in Chesapeake, Virginia, RANDY FORBES has never forgotten who he is or where he came from. Growing up as the son of a World War II Normandy veteran, RANDY was raised on the values of duty, hard work, family, and faith. He carried those principles with him to Randolph-Macon College, where he graduated as valedictorian of his 1974 class, and throughout his years at the University of Virginia School of Law.

Since first elected to Congress in 2001, RANDY's highest priority has been to protect and defend our Nation, the fundamental freedoms it was founded upon, and the men and women who fight for those freedoms. As chairman of the House Armed Services Seapower and Projection Forces Subcommittee, RANDY is one of the Nation's forceful advocates for a strong national defense.

As a result of his dedicated efforts, Chairman FORBES is one of the few individuals to be honored with the highest civilian awards offered by both the United States Army and the United States Navy. He is also a senior member, as I mentioned, of the House Judiciary Committee where he serves as a member of the Subcommittee on Courts, Intellectual Property, and the Internet, as well as the Subcommittee on Crime, Terrorism, Homeland Security, and Investigations. And he is the founder and co-chairman of the Congressional Prayer Caucus and the Congressional China Caucus.

RANDY began his career in private law practice, ultimately becoming a partner in the largest law firm in southeastern Virginia. From 1989 to 2001, he served the Commonwealth of Virginia in the General Assembly.

He and his wife, Shirley, have four children and three grandchildren, which RANDY personally regards as his greatest achievement. And, no doubt, as a grandfather myself, I understand well that sentiment, and I wish him very well with his family and hope that he has much time to enjoy with them, but not too much time because he is too valuable to our country not to be afforded another opportunity to serve our country in some great capacity.

Congressman ROBERT HURT also served with distinction in the Virginia General Assembly, and then a little over 6 years ago came to visit me and my wife, Maryellen, in our home to talk about his possibility of seeking election to the Congress. We encouraged him to do just that, he did, and was successful.

ROBERT HURT is a member of the Financial Services Committee, which has jurisdiction over all aspects of the Nation's financial and housing sectors. Within the committee, he serves as the vice chairman of the Capital Markets and Government Sponsored Enterprises Subcommittee, and serves on the Housing and Insurance Subcommittee, as well as the Oversight and Investigations Subcommittee.

A native of Pittsylvania County, ROBERT began his time in public service in 2001, as a member of the Chatham Town Council. From 2002 to 2007, ROBERT served in the Virginia House of Delegates, representing parts of Pittsylvania County, Henry County, and the city of Martinsville.

□ 1930

Starting in 2008, ROBERT represented the 19th district in the Senate of Virginia for 2 years, which includes the city of Danville, Pittsylvania County, Franklin County, and part of Campbell County. He received his college education at Hampden-Sydney College in the district that he now represents in 1991. He obtained his law degree from the Mississippi College School of Law in 1995. From 1999 to 2010, ROBERT was engaged in a general law practice in the courthouse town of Chatham, where he lives with his wife, Kathy, and their three sons—Charles, Clement, and John.

SCOTT RIGELL also was elected to Congress in the same year that Congressman HURT was, and we were delighted to have him come and join us as well, being another strong advocate for our Nation's defense. He serves on the House Committee on Appropriations. Since taking office in January 2011, Congressman RIGELL has made creating jobs, strengthening our military, controlling Federal spending, and changing Congress his most urgent priorities. In representing the Nation's largest military district, Congressman RIGELL is working to preserve our region's unique military assets and to support our men and women in uniform.

He was instrumental in the successful effort to keep all East Coast aircraft carriers based in Norfolk, and he introduced language that improved the maintenance of military housing, including in the fiscal year 2013 National Defense Authorization Act. With strong bipartisan support, the House and Senate passed Congressman RIGELL's Drywall Safety Act of 2012, which was signed into law by the President in early 2013. This legislation sets chemical standards for domestic and imported drywalls, establishes remediation guidelines for the disposal of all drywall, and expresses a sense of Congress that China must be held accountable for the damage this product has already caused in our community and across America.

Prior to his election to Congress, he was a successful entrepreneur, businessowner, and community leader—the founder of Freedom Automotive. Congressman RIGELL and his wife, Teri, previously owned automobile dealerships in Chesapeake, Hampton, Norfolk, and Virginia Beach. He served 6 years in the United States Marine Corps Reserve and rose to the rank of sergeant before receiving an honorable discharge. He earned his BBA from Mercer University and an MBA from Regent University.

He and his wife are the proud parents of four children and four grandchildren. They are competing well with the Forbes family in the grandchildren department, and I know they also will enjoy more time with those grand-children; but I hope we see Congressman RIGELL serving his country in another capacity in the future as well.

At this time, I am delighted that we have Members whose districts adjoin Congressman RIGELL's, Congressman HURT's, and Congressman FORBES'. I know that Congressman ROB WITTMAN, who served on the Armed Services Committee with Congressman FORBES, has to be somewhere else; so I am going to turn to him first, and then I will turn to Congressman SCOTT. I am happy to yield to the gentleman.

Mr. WITTMAN. I thank the chairman.

Mr. Speaker, it truly is an honor and a privilege to reflect on the careers of three dear friends as the gentleman spoke so eloquently about Congressman RANDY FORBES, Congressman SCOTT RIGELL, and Congressman ROBERT HURT. They have been true Virginia leaders. They are all statesmen in the truest sense of the word. They are all servant leaders in their putting others before themselves, and they have done that throughout their tremendous careers in public service.

RANDY FORBES is a dear friend. RANDY is one of those unique individuals who truly, truly puts others first in everything that he has done. I have known RANDY through the years, back to his days in the Virginia General Assembly, where he created great opportunities for folks, not only in the district that he represented, but he also made an impact on the State of Virginia. He was a very thoughtful and eloquent legislator. He understood what government's role was. He wanted to make sure that that was done properly. He also played a critical role in his party. The Grand Old Party was better off in Virginia because of RANDY FORBES' leadership. We were blessed to have him in that capacity there for a number of years. I have known RANDY as a dear friend but also, truly, as one of the most effective legislators whom we have seen up here on Capitol Hill.

His time, Mr. Chairman, on your Committee on the Judiciary is marked by many great accomplishments there as well as by some very sound and thoughtful judgments and, most importantly, by some very probing questions when it came time to interview panelists or witnesses who came before the Judiciary Committee.

He was extraordinarily adept at that as he was—and still is—on the House Armed Services Committee. It was tremendous to watch RANDY as he would pick apart an issue and get critical information from witnesses or panelists who came before our committee. Whether it was in a briefing or whether it was to really ascertain the facts of a situation, he was extraordinary in his opportunities there.

He really cares passionately about our Nation's military, about the men and women who serve and what we provide for them to serve. He has done a spectacular job in efforts to rebuild our Nation's Navy. In fact, this year, for the first time in 8 years, our Navy is actually back to growing again. We are building more ships than we are retiring, and that is due in no small part to RANDY FORBES' leadership and the things that he has done to make sure that things like our new carrier program with the *Ford*-class carriers and with our new *Ohio*-class replacement submarines, termed the *Columbia*-class, are on track, as well as the *Virginia*-class with our new destroyers. He has been extraordinary in making sure that he has been an advocate to ensure that our sailors have what they need as well as our marines have what they need, and he has done that every minute that he has served there on the Armed Services Committee.

I have learned a lot from RANDY. I have valued his counsel, but I have also watched his leadership as he has done things for our Nation that I think are extraordinarily important. I believe those accomplishments are things that will be valued and will have an effect on this Nation, not just in years to come but for decades to come. He has truly had that type of influence.

Mr. Chairman, I agree with you. I hope that Chairman RANDY FORBES of the Seapower and Projection Forces Subcommittee has an opportunity to continue to serve this Nation in another capacity in which he can use that expertise, that extraordinary history of leadership and legacy of leadership there on the House Armed Services Committee. I think our Nation will be better off for having RANDY there in a future capacity in leadership. I am hopeful that that will happen, and I truly value the things that he has done.

RANDY isn't somebody who just focuses on the Nation's military. He is also a fighter for our individual liberties and freedoms, specifically our religious liberties and freedoms. He has been the cofounder and co-chairman of the Congressional Prayer Caucus, where he has been a staunch advocate to make sure that we push back against those intrusions on our religious liberties and freedoms. He has done an extraordinary job there.

I value that relationship that I have with RANDY as a member of the Prayer Caucus and for the things that he has done. He has been unafraid to be out there in the forefront to make sure that he points out those efforts that are antifaith efforts and to make sure that he stands strong on the side of those folks who want to make sure that their religious beliefs are protected. He has done an extraordinary job there, not just here in Virginia, but also across the Nation. He has been seen as a true leader there. Again, it goes to the heart of that servant leader that RANDY truly is. We will miss him in those capacities. I know that he will continue to make sure that he is a beacon defending religious freedoms and liberties in whatever capacity he continues after his term here in Congress. We look forward to his efforts there also.

As well, the gentleman spoke of Congressman ROBERT HURT. ROBERT and I have a lot in common. ROBERT comes from the small town of Chatham in Pittsylvania County. He began there on the town council—the same place as I began in the little town of Montross. Both are very, very similar towns. ROBERT also has that heart of a servant leader by which he looked at where he could best serve his citizens there in the town of Chatham as well as going on to the general assembly there in Richmond, which is where he and I served in the house for a number of years. He went on to the State senate and then, later, here to the House of Representatives.

Mr. Chairman, just as you spoke of them, ROBERT and his wife, Kathy, graciously sat down with Kathryn and me to ask questions about what service would be like if he were to decide to run for the U.S. House of Representatives. Of course, we told him what the challenges were but also what he could accomplish in that role. I believe that he, again, put the Virginia way first in making sure that he was there to serve when he made that decision. It certainly was one that I know was a difficult one for him but was one that he came here with a lot of passion about as to what he could do to make a difference in the direction of this country, and ROBERT has continued that.

I have known ROBERT through the years. He has always been a man of deep personal conviction but also a man of deep passion. ROBERT is a lover of life, but he is also one who never backs away from an issue that he feels passionately about. As you know, I have watched ROBERT get up and give speeches. Boy, I will tell you, if it doesn't make the hair stand up on the back of your neck, nothing will. He is an effective standard-bearer for issues that are important to the Nation and to Virginia. He has been a real leader there on the Financial Services Committee, whereby he knows those issues backwards and forwards. Again, it is that background that he brings from his time in local and State government that, I think, makes him an extraordinarily effective legislator here.

We will certainly miss him, but I know that the next step in his career—with his wife, Kathy, and his three sons—will be one in which he will enjoy the time there in the small town of Chatham. I know he intends to go back and practice law there and get back to the important elements of what makes Chatham special and what makes Virginia special. We will miss him, but I know that he will be extraordinarily successful there.

I have known Representative SCOTT RIGELL for a number of years even prior to his coming to Congress. I will never forget the conversation that I had with him as he was—again, like ROBERT—thinking about running for Congress and how passionate he was about the direction this Nation was taking both in its deficit and its debt and as to what was happening to small businesses out there. As a small-business owner, he later went on to own some significant businesses there in the Tidewater area. He really saw what was unfolding in our Nation, and it caused him deep, deep concerns not only for himself and Teri, but also for his children and now for his grandchildren.

What a person of passion—and very eloquent. He was also a person who wanted to make sure that we reformed the way government conducted business. He and I had many, many deep conversations about what that would look like and how process is important and how doing the work of the Nation was absolutely critical. Whether what we were doing was to help small businesses or what we were doing was to ensure that our Nation's military had what it needed or what we were doing was to address the Nation's finances, he was equally adept and well schooled in those subject areas. He was a quick study on issues but a thorough study. He was exhaustive in how he would look at information concerning legislation or what he could do on a particular issue, and I admired him for that because you knew, when SCOTT RIGELL came to the floor to vote, that he knew that bill and that issue backwards and forwards. In fact, many times, I would go to talk to him about a bill that was coming up, and I could guarantee that SCOTT knew it without limitations. He was very, very passionate about that.

That is the reason he came to Congress and what he came here to accomplish, and he did an extraordinary job in his years here. I deeply appreciate his service and the sacrifice that his family has put into this. As I know Teri will attest, there were long hours that were spent here. Teri came up here on the Hill many times and was by SCOTT's side; so, for the Rigell family, it really was a family affair in service. I know that he also has exciting things facing him in his next chapter of life and that his efforts will, indeed, continue to include public service; so we wish SCOTT and Teri and his entire family the best.

We all are changed for the better because of the service of these three Virginia gentlemen—three Virginia statesmen—and what they have done here to affect not only their communities, whether it is in Chesapeake or in Virginia Beach or in Chatham, Virginia, but what they all have done to affect our great Commonwealth of Virginia and the lasting mark that they have left here for our Nation. We are all indebted to their service, indebted to the legacies that they have left behind, and indebted in our making sure that we continue the legacies of passion for the issues that are important to our Nation, whether it is for our military, whether it is for our small businesses, whether it is for our Nation's financial predicament it finds itself in.

□ 1945

All of them have brought lasting change to this body and will continue, I know, in further capacities in their life after. We thank them immensely. We are all better off for their service, and I know that we will continue to confer with them now as repositories of wisdom in the issues that we have to deal with going forward.

Mr. Speaker, I thank Chairman GOODLATTE, too, for taking the time tonight for all of us to be able to recognize their true servant leadership for the State of Virginia, their sacrifice, and truly the sacrifice of their families. As we all know, there is a sacrifice of families, too, for Members that serve here in Congress.

Again, we wish SCOTT, RANDY, and ROBERT all the best. We wish them God's blessings in the years ahead. I know that they will continue to lead and to serve in different capacities, but in equally as effective capacities.

Mr. GOODLATTE. Mr. Speaker, I thank the gentleman for sharing his personal experiences, his friendships with these three outstanding Members of Congress.

I turn to the other neighboring Congressman, the Congressman from the Third Congressional District who has served with me for many years on the House Judiciary Committee until he went to become the ranking member on the House Education and the Workforce Committee and has served here as long as I have. He has much knowledge about that part of the world and about these three gentleman. I thank him for taking time this evening.

I yield to Congressman SCOTT.

Mr. SCOTT of Virginia. Mr. Speaker, I thank the gentleman from Virginia for yielding and for organizing tonight's Special Order.

Tonight, we honor three retiring members from the Virginia delegation to Congress: Congressmen RANDY FORBES, ROBERT HURT, and SCOTT RIGELL.

Despite our differences from time to time on national policy, the Virginia delegation has a long history of being able to constructively work together on issues of importance to the citizens of the Commonwealth of Virginia. Former-Senator John Warner, the longtime dean of our delegation, embodied this bipartisan work ethic, and we have already heard it referred to as the Virginia way of doing things.

During their service in Congress, RANDY, ROBERT, and SCOTT have each put their mark on this institution and on national policy.

ROBERT HURT has been a leader on the Financial Services Committee and focused on policies to expand economic opportunity in south side Virginia and communities around the Nation. A strong advocate for community banks and credit unions over his three terms in Congress, ROBERT has also worked to ensure that consumers are financially literate with the necessary information to make the best financial choices for their families. ROBERT has always fought for what he believed to be the best interest of his constituents, and so I wish him and his family well as he returns to his home in Chatham.

I have come to know SCOTT and RANDY very well as our congressional districts are adjacent to one another in the Hampton Roads area of Virginia. Along with our colleague, ROB WITTMAN, we have participated in countless joint appearances and events across Hampton Roads.

In both the private and public sector, SCOTT RIGELL has dedicated his life to serving the Hampton Roads community. In his three terms in Congress, he has developed a well-deserved reputation as a pragmatic, bipartisan leader as he addresses the Nation's fiscal issues and reforming how Congress operates. We have been working together on many issues, but I especially appreciate his strong support and advocacy of the SAFE Justice Act, a comprehensive criminal justice reform bill that the gentleman from Wisconsin (Mr. SENSENBRENNER) and I introduced last year. I wish SCOTT, his wife Terry, and his children and grandchildren all the best as he transitions back to private life.

RANDY and I have become good friends during his time in Congress as we served together for many years on the House Judiciary Committee. Hampton Roads is the home to many military facilities, both private-sector defense contractors and military facilities, particularly those associated with the Navy. There is no Member of Congress who knows more about our Navy than RANDY FORBES. As chairman of the Seapower and Projection Forces Subcommittee of the Armed Services Committee, he has been an important voice on defense and shipbuilding policy. Hampton Roads has been fortunate to have RANDY fighting for our region's military and shipbuilding interests over the last 50 years. I will also miss working with him on modeling and simulation. He was the founder of the Modeling and Simulation Caucus. He promoted the modeling and simulation technology as a way to increase efficiency and to save the taxpayers money.

I wouldn't count RANDY out just yet. I know he will find ways to continue to serve our men and women in uniform in the months and years ahead, and so I wish him, his wife Shirley, and children and grandchildren well as they start the next chapter of their lives.

Mr. Speaker, I, again, want to thank the gentleman from Virginia (Mr. GOODLATTE) for organizing tonight's Special Order. The departure of Congressmen ROBERT HURT, SCOTT RIGELL, and RANDY FORBES is a loss for the House of Representatives and the Commonwealth of Virginia. Each of these men deserve our sincere gratitude for their service to our Nation and the civility that they have exemplified during their service.

Mr. GOODLATTE. Mr. Speaker, I thank the gentleman for his kind remarks about all three of these fine Representatives.

I yield to the gentlewoman from Indiana (Mrs. WALORSKI), who knows them as well.

Mrs. WALORSKI. Mr. Speaker, I rise today as we honor the exemplary service of three departing Members of this distinguished body. Congressmen RANDY FORBES, ROBERT HURT, and SCOTT RIGELL have served their districts and our Nation with honor and distinction, and they will be sorely missed.

I must take a moment and talk about the privilege I have had of serving alongside my friend, RANDY FORBES, on the Armed Services Committee and on the Seapower and Projection Forces Subcommittee he chairs.

Over the past few years, as the Obama administration has sought to shrink the size of our Armed Forces and reduce the number of ships in our Navy, it has been RANDY that has led with a strong, passionate advocacy for our servicemembers and a strong, informed defender of our Navy.

Article I of the Constitution states that Congress shall have the power to provide and maintain a Navy. No one has fulfilled that task more honorably or diligently than Congressman RANDY FORBES.

RANDY, your experience and your insights will be missed in Congress and on the Armed Services Committee, but I look forward to see where your commitment to service leads you. Until then, my friend, I wish you fair winds and following seas.

Mr. GOODLATTE. Mr. Speaker, I yield to the gentleman from Iowa (Mr. KING), another valued member of the House Judiciary Committee who has served literally alongside Congressman FORBES.

I think you have sat next to him, if not close to each other, for many years on the committee.

Mr. KING of Iowa. Mr. Speaker, I am very pleased to have the privilege to have been yielded to from Chairman GOODLATTE of Virginia, who I know laments the departure of three very esteemed members of the Virginia delegation and people I have had a privilege to serve with. I certainly tip my hat to, bow to, and salute all three of them: Congressmen RANDY FORBES, SCOTT RIGELL, and ROBERT HURT.

I came here this evening to focus a majority of my remarks on that of Representative RANDY FORBES because, as Chairman GOODLATTE said, I have had the privilege to sit next to RANDY FORBES on the Judiciary Committee—and our memories are never always exactly right—but it could be for the full 14 years that I have been here. We have been either next to each other or within one seat of each other all that period of time.

I have long viewed RANDY FORBES as my wingman on the House Judiciary Committee. He is the anchor. He is a man who we know is a man of faith. He led the Prayer Caucus here for a good number of years. We know that he is a constitutionalist. He served on the Constitution and Civil Justice Subcommittee also with me for many, if not, all of those years. When a man puts that kind of commitment and effort into defending the Constitution and defending innocent unborn human life and defending the values and the anchors of our faith, of our families, of our Constitution and—by the way, on the Crime, Terrorism, Homeland Security, and Investigations Subcommittee—defending the rule of law and bringing about appropriate punishment for people who violate that law, that is the life of RANDY FORBES.

I may be wired a little tighter than RANDY. I would come and sit down on the Judiciary Committee, and I might be all wound up. RANDY was always the calming influence on me. I am sure Chairman GOODLATTE appreciates that; that RANDY would reach over and put his hand on my arm and he said: Now, STEVE, here is where we are, here is where we are going.

There would also be times, though, he would turn his ear and he would listen to the arguments that I would make. We had hundreds and hundreds of conversations that helped shaped me as a Member of Congress, and they always were anchored in the right values. These are values you know come from a man who has demonstrated that here in the House of Representatives.

I thought, too, that RANDY was one of the best cross-examiners of a witness that I have seen in this United States Congress, and those among the best do serve on the Judiciary Committee. Those issues seem to come to us, and they refine your skill sets. RANDY would be sitting there. And as the line was coming down toward us on where we sat on seniority, I might want to talk about what is on my mind and chat with him a little bit on the other side.

I always knew that when RANDY had his pen up and he would have his research paper there and he would be taking notes in between that, what he was really doing, Mr. Speaker, was preparing himself to take—most of the times we only had 5 minutes—to take that witness down to the base facts that were necessary. RANDY did that as well as anybody that I have seen. It always was anchored in the rule of law, the Constitution, the faith, freedom, values and, of course, his strong support for the military and strengthening our military.

I wanted to put into the CONGRESSIONAL RECORD tonight, Mr. Speaker, something that impressed me about RANDY. It was after Hurricane Katrina hit New Orleans and RANDY FORBES went down in that area 6 months or a year afterwards. He came back with this data, which I wrote down and typed into my notes because it was something that just really gripped me.

The murder rate in New Orleans post-Katrina had risen to the point that it was 90 out of each 100,000 people who were victims of murder in New Orleans at that time. Only 1 out of 83.33 murders resulted in prison time, and only 1 in 10 murders resulted in an arrest. And of those total murders, only 1 in 8.33 resulted in convictions. So roughly 1 in 8 murders were solved. And that was a rate that is astonishingly high when you compare those numbers—90 of 100,000 murders, the violent death rate or the murder rate for New Orleans—where in the United States broadly it is around 6 per 100,000 as opposed to the 90 per hundred thousand. RANDY brought that kind of information back to me.

He was also a leader in the fight against gang violence and gang crime, and he brought that case before the Judiciary Committee a number of times for us. Each time RANDY spoke, we did listen and it moved policy in the right directions.

One of the other things, Mr. Speaker, that I cherish is my perspective of this: Jo Ann Davis represented Virginia's First Congressional District at the time and passed away untimely in the year 2007. I went down to her funeral. I had, of course, served with Jo Ann and traveled overseas with her into the war zones. She was also on the Armed Services Committee.

RANDY FORBES gave the eulogy for former Congresswoman Jo Ann Davis. I remember sitting in that church in Virginia, and RANDY stepped up to speak about the life of Jo Ann Davis and, without notes, gave one of the most moving and deepest eulogies I have heard in my life. It would have been impossible for RANDY FORBES to give such a presentation had he not respected, revered, and loved Jo Ann Davis the way that he did and watched her moves. The things that she did in her life reflected upon him in a way that he could honor her life at a time like that that had to give comfort to the family and friends that were in that church that day.

I would express this about RANDY—and I hope he has a long time to serve America—but he has affected my life in a similar way. He has made me a better Congressman, and he has done so with dignity and with class.

The time that RANDY spent in public life, Mr. Speaker, from the time he was elected to the Virginia House of Delegates in 1990 until 1998, and then to the State Senate of Virginia in 1998 until 2001, when he came here midterm in June of 2001 and served in this Congress, and he will serve in this Congress until January 3 of 2017. That is going to add up to somewhere really close to 27 years—26½ years, at least—of service to the Commonwealth of Virginia and the United States of America.

His wife, Shirley, is a class act and anyone that knows her knows that. Their four children—Neil, Jamie, Jordan, and Justin—I hope they know tonight that they hit the jackpot when they were born into the family of RANDY and Shirley Forbes.

I hit the jackpot when I had the privilege to be seated next to RANDY FORBES, and I hope that I can do my best to carry on that kind of legacy that he is leaving with us. He has made us all better. The United States of America is better, the Commonwealth of Virginia is better, and I appreciate the service that Congressman RANDY FORBES has given to our country.

Mr. GOODLATTE. Mr. Speaker, I thank the gentleman from Iowa for that heartfelt appreciation of these three Members.

I yield to the gentleman from the great State of Maine (Mr. POLIQUIN). He represents my alma mater, Bates College. He is just about to start his second term in Congress, but he makes friends fast. So I am delighted that he is here to say a few words about these three outstanding individuals as well.

□ 2000

Mr. POLIQUIN. Mr. Speaker, I thank Chairman GOODLATTE for yielding. We are very proud in our Second District of Maine to house Bates College, which I understand is the chairman's alma mater.

I would like to speak a little bit today, Mr. Speaker, about these three gentlemen from Virginia, from a slightly different perspective, as a freshman Member of Congress and someone who has a business background but not a legislative background.

RANDY FORBES has been a tremendous help to my district by giving me counsel when it comes to Bath Iron Works and the tremendous shipbuilding skills that BIW has, making the best destroyers that keep our country safe and the best shipbuilders in the world. RANDY FORBES' guidance on the Committee on Armed Services to help secure additional funding for BIW

is something that I will never forget and something that the 6,000 workers at Bath Iron Works in Bath, Maine, have a debt of gratitude to Mr. FORBES for his help in that regard.

SCOTT RIGELL, as a businessowner here in Virginia in the auto dealership area, has also been incredibly helpful to me in sitting on the Committee on Financial Services, Mr. Speaker, that deals with credit when it comes to the auto dealerships extending that credit to consumers, and SCOTT's guidance in that regard has been very, very helpful.

I do serve on the House Committee on Financial Services with Representative ROBERT HURT, who has become a very good friend and someone whom I have turned to on many occasions to make sure I understand what the legislative process is, Mr. Speaker.

As a business professional, I understand what needs to be done to move our country forward, move our economy forward, and to create more jobs in Maine and throughout the country; but the gears of how Congress works is something that has been new to me, and I want to thank ROBERT HURT very much for the patience he has extended to me to answer questions I have had. He is a very thoughtful man. He is someone who knows this process inside and out, and he has been very helpful to me, along with Mr. FORBES and Mr. RIGELL.

I thank Chairman GOODLATTE for giving me an opportunity to salute these tremendous gentlemen from the Commonwealth of Virginia, for extending their help to me as a freshman, to our State, and to our country. Congratulations to all these wonderful Congressmen.

Mr. GOODLATTE. I thank the gentleman for his kind words and for taking the time to share them with us this evening.

I yield now to the gentleman from the Ninth Congressional District of Virginia (Mr. GRIFFITH), my friend and neighboring Congressman. He served in the Virginia General Assembly with both RANDY FORBES and ROBERT HURT and was elected to Congress the same year that ROBERT HURT was. He knows all three of these individuals well, and I appreciate him taking the time this evening to participate as well.

Mr. GRIFFITH. Mr. Speaker, I thank Congressman GOODLATTE for yielding. It is my honor and privilege to be here to recognize these three Virginians who have served their Commonwealth so well.

SCOTT RIGELL and I were elected along with ROBERT HURT back in the same year, back in 2010. I got to know SCOTT when I got here. He is the one of the three who are retiring whom I did not know prior to coming to service in Congress. I learned that he was a hard worker, a dedicated public servant, someone who truly believed in trying to do everything the right way. Like myself every now and then, he was a little bit of a maverick and would cut his own way, but that is important in Congress, that we don't all walk in lockstep, that we work together but that we respect each other's opinions. SCOTT RIGELL is a gentleman who certainly does that, and as a Representative, he has done that very well.

I go next to RANDY. With the exception of, I think, probably Congressman SCOTT has known RANDY longer, having served a couple years in the State legislature before he came to Congress with RANDY, I think I have served longer with RANDY because I served with him first in the house of delegates, where he was a role model, one of the leaders on the floor in the Virginia House.

He then moved on to the Senate just before Republicans took control of the House for the first time in 120-some years. He was a feisty floor debater, one who was always prepared, and somebody that I looked up to and used as a role model in trying to figure out how I was going to behave on the floor and act as a gentleman and yet be determined and fierce in defending my positions. RANDY FORBES always did that in the Virginia House. He then went on to the Virginia Senate, where he, likewise, defended his positions and was known as a leader.

Then he came to Congress, where he kept saying to me: You would love it. There are so many policy issues that you would get into.

He enjoyed his time here very much, and not because he felt that it was just something that he enjoyed doing, but because he could take his talents and serve the people of the Commonwealth of Virginia with those talents and serve his Nation, the United States of America, with those talents as well.

I suspect that we will see RANDY doing other public service in the not-too-distant future, but I am so very glad that I had the opportunity tonight to talk about his service to the Commonwealth of Virginia and to the United States.

Last but certainly not least, my friend ROBERT HURT. ROBERT came after me into the Virginia House of Delegates. He, too, made the error of moving over to the senate. I think Congressman SCOTT made that error, too. But ROBERT HURT and I got to be friends in the house of delegates. He was a newer member. He had to make some tough decisions early on. We didn't always agree, but I told him to stick to his viewpoint and that he would be fine.

He is just a fantastic individual, a good friend. I am sorry that he decided to retire. I welcome his successor, but I am sorry that he decided to retire because I really enjoyed bouncing ideas off of him and sitting in the back row and talking about everything from birds that we might have seen alive or

dead somewhere along the highway or keeping notes on some of the flora and fauna of our part of Virginia. Our districts abutted. Where Congressman GOODLATTE and I share the Roanoke Valley, Congressman HURT and I shared Henry County and that area as well, and it was truly an honor to serve with him.

I didn't get to serve with any of the gentlemen on a committee. We have heard a lot of great testimony about what great committee members they were. I did not have that opportunity, but I did get to serve with them in the House for two of them and here on this floor for 6 years. It was an honor and a privilege to work with them and to learn from them and to watch as they behaved as gentlemen ought to do in a society and in a place where we may disagree, but we can be agreeable while we disagree on issues.

Mr. GOODLATTE. I thank the gentleman for his kind remarks as well. Does the gentleman have any further remarks? I want to thank all of the Members who took time this evening to honor these three colleagues. I know that there are many more who wish them well.

The RECORD is open, and I know some additional Members will put remarks into the RECORD, but I just want to close by saying that I was proud to serve with all three of them. They are strong advocates for their constituents. They have a strong love for their country, and they are fighters for limited government and individual responsibility and the free enterprise system. They believe very strongly in lower taxes and less government regulation.

They work hard for their families in passing legislation that strengthens American families and, most especially, they are all strong believers in a strong national defense and have worked hard for their Nation in this body. They deserve all of the accolades they have received this evening and many, many more. I wish them Godspeed and great futures with their families and their future endeavors.

Mr. Speaker, I yield back the balance of my time.

Mr. HULTGREN. Mr. Speaker, I rise today to recognize three friends and colleagues from Virginia who have served the House of Representatives and the American people faithfully and with whom I have enjoyed working during our time together in the House.

Congressmen SCOTT RIGELL, RANDY FORBES and ROBERT HURT will be greatly missed, and I personally will miss them as they leave office at the end of this 114th Congress.

I have valued SCOTT RIGELL's strong faith and commitment to regular Bible study ever since we entered Congress together in 2011.

He regularly seeks God's wisdom as he serves his constituents. I have appreciated the way in which he models his faith and convictions as a servant of the people.

RANDY FORBES has also demonstrated that true wisdom comes from the Source of all wisdom.

His founding of the Congressional Prayer Caucus as a body to encourage Members of Congress as they seek the Lord in all things has been meaningful to me personally and an inspiration to many of our like-minded colleagues.

ROBERT HURT and I have worked together on the Financial Services Committee, and I have appreciated his role defending our community banks as Vice-Chair of the Capital Markets Subcommittee.

I've had the great opportunity to work with him on the Investment Advisers Modernization Act and his contribution has made it easier for private equity to invest in our economy and grow jobs.

As they return to private life, each one of these men should be proud of the service they have rendered to their constituents and their country and the mark they have left on this institution and on those, like myself, who have had the privilege to serve alongside them.

SENATE BILLS REFERRED

Bills of the Senate of the following titles were taken from the Speaker's table and, under the rule, referred as follows:

S. 2944. An act to require adequate reporting on the Public Safety Officers' Benefits program, and for other purposes; to the Committee on the Judiciary.

S. 3438. An act to authorize the Secretary of Veterans Affairs to carry out a major medical facility project in Reno, Nevada; to the Committee on Veterans' Affairs.

ENROLLED BILL SIGNED

Karen L. Haas, Clerk of the House, reported and found truly enrolled a bill of the House of the following title, which was thereupon signed by the Speaker:

H.R. 4665. An act to require the Secretary of Commerce to conduct an assessment and analysis of the outdoor recreation economy of the United States, and for other purposes.

ADJOURNMENT

Mr. GOODLATTE. Mr. Speaker, I move that the House do now adjourn.

The motion was agreed to; accordingly (at 8 o'clock and 10 minutes p.m.), under its previous order, the House adjourned until tomorrow, Thursday, December 1, 2016, at 10 a.m. for morning-hour debate.

EXECUTIVE COMMUNICATIONS, ETC.

Under clause 2 of rule XIV, executive communications were taken from the Speaker's table and referred as follows:

7660. A letter from the Chief Counsel, Federal Emergency Management Agency, Department of Homeland Security, transmitting the Department's final rule — Suspension of Community Eligibility, Ulster County, NY, et al. [Docket ID: FEMA-2016-0002; Internal Agency Docket No.: FEMA-8453] received November 21, 2016, pursuant to 5 U.S.C. 801(a)(1)(A); Public Law 104-121, Sec.

251; (110 Stat. 868); to the Committee on Financial Services.

7661. A letter from the Regulations Coordinator, Centers for Medicare and Medicaid Services, Department of Health and Human Services, transmitting the Department's Major final rule — Medicaid and Children's Health Insurance Programs: Eligibility Notices, Fair Hearing and Appeal Processes for Medicaid and Other Provisions Related to Eligibility and Enrollment for Medicaid and CHIP [CMS-2334-F2] (RIN: 0938-AS27) received November 28, 2016, pursuant to 5 U.S.C. 801(a)(1)(A); Public Law 104-121, Sec. 251; (110 Stat. 868); to the Committee on Energy and Commerce.

7662. A letter from the Director, Regulatory Management Division, Environmental Protection Agency, transmitting the Agency's final rule — Spodoptera frugiperda Multiple Nucleopolyhedrovirus strain 3AP2; Exemption from the Requirement of a Tolerance [EPA-HQ-OPP-2015-0488; FRL-9953-40] received November 18, 2016, pursuant to 5 U.S.C. 801(a)(1)(A); Public Law 104-121, Sec. 251; (110 Stat. 868); to the Committee on Energy and Commerce.

7663. A letter from the Director, Regulatory Management Division, Environmental Protection Agency, transmitting the Agency's final rule — Greenhouse Gas Reporting Rule: Leak Detection Methodology Revisions and Confidentiality Determinations for Petroleum and Natural Gas Systems [EPA-HQ-OAR-2015-0764; FRL-9955-12-OAR] (RIN: 2060-AS73) received November 18, 2016, pursuant to 5 U.S.C. 801(a)(1)(A); Public Law 104-121, Sec. 251; (110 Stat. 868); to the Committee on Energy and Commerce.

7664. A letter from the Director, Regulatory Management Division, Environmental Protection Agency, transmitting the Agency's Major final rule — Formaldehyde Emission Standards for Composite Wood Products [EPA-HQ-OPPT-2016-0461; FRL-9949-90] (RIN: 2070-AJ44) received November 18, 2016, pursuant to 5 U.S.C. 801(a)(1)(A); Public Law 104-121, Sec. 251; (110 Stat. 868); to the Committee on Energy and Commerce.

7665. A letter from the Director, Regulatory Management Division, Environmental Protection Agency, transmitting the Agency's final rule — Findings of Failure to Attain the 1997 PM2.5 Standards; California; San Joaquin Valley [EPA-R09-OAR-2016-0494; FRL-9955-53-Region 9] received November 18, 2016, pursuant to 5 U.S.C. 801(a)(1)(A); Public Law 104-121, Sec. 251; (110 Stat. 868); to the Committee on Energy and Commerce.

7666. A letter from the Director, Regulatory Management Division, Environmental Protection Agency, transmitting the Agency's final rule — Endothall; Pesticide Tolerances [EPA-HQ-OPP-2014-0613; FRL-9953-97] received November 18, 2016, pursuant to 5 U.S.C. 801(a)(1)(A); Public Law 104-121, Sec. 251; (110 Stat. 868); to the Committee on Energy and Commerce.

7667. A letter from the Director, Regulatory Management Division, Environmental Protection Agency, transmitting the Agency's final rule — Designation of Areas for Air Quality Planning Purposes; Ohio; Redesignation of the Ohio Portion of the Campbell-Clermont KY-OH Sulfur Dioxide Nonattainment Area [EPA-R05-OAR-2015-0599; FRL-9955-37-Region 5] received November 18, 2016, pursuant to 5 U.S.C. 801(a)(1)(A); Public Law 104-121, Sec. 251; (110 Stat. 868); to the Committee on Energy and Commerce.

7668. A letter from the Director, Regulatory Management Division, Environmental Protection Agency, transmitting the Agency's final rule — Clarification of Require-

ments for Method 303 Certification Training [EPA-HQ-OAR-2014-0492; FRL-9955-50-OAR] (RIN: 2060-AR97) received November 18, 2016, pursuant to 5 U.S.C. 801(a)(1)(A); Public Law 104-121, Sec. 251; (110 Stat. 868); to the Committee on Energy and Commerce.

7669. A letter from the Director, Regulatory Management Division, Environmental Protection Agency, transmitting the Agency's final rule — Air Plan Approval; FL Infrastructure Requirements for the 2010 1-hour NO2 NAAQS [EPA-R04-OAR-2014-0507; FRL-9955-49-Region 4] received November 18, 2016, pursuant to 5 U.S.C. 801(a)(1)(A); Public Law 104-121, Sec. 251; (110 Stat. 868); to the Committee on Energy and Commerce.

7670. A letter from the Director, Regulatory Management Division, Environmental Protection Agency, transmitting the Agency's final rule — Air Plan Approval/Disapproval; AL Infrastructure Requirements for the 2010 1-hour NO2 NAAQS [EPA-R04-OAR-2014-0756; FRL-9955-29-Region 4] received November 18, 2016, pursuant to 5 U.S.C. 801(a)(1)(A); Public Law 104-121, Sec. 251; (110 Stat. 868); to the Committee on Energy and Commerce.

7671. A letter from the Director, Regulatory Management Division, Environmental Protection Agency, transmitting the Agency's final rule — Addition of Hexabromocyclododecane (HBCD) Category; Community Right-to-Know Toxic Chemical Release Reporting [EPA-HQ-TRI-2015-0607; FRL-9953-28] (RIN: 2025-AA42) received November 18, 2016, pursuant to 5 U.S.C. 801(a)(1)(A); Public Law 104-121, Sec. 251; (110 Stat. 868); to the Committee on Energy and Commerce.

7672. A letter from the Deputy Director, Regulations Policy and Management Staff, FDA, Department of Health and Human Services, transmitting the Department's final rule — Amendments to Regulations on Citizen Petitions, Petitions for Stay of Action, and Submission of Documents to Dockets [Docket No.: FDA-2011-N-0697] (RIN: 0910-AG26) received November 23, 2016, pursuant to 5 U.S.C. 801(a)(1)(A); Public Law 104-121, Sec. 251; (110 Stat. 868); to the Committee on Energy and Commerce.

7673. A letter from the Secretary, Department of the Treasury, transmitting a six-month periodic report on the national emergency with respect to the stabilization of Iraq that was declared in Executive Order 13303 of May 22, 2003, pursuant to 50 U.S.C. 1641(c); Public Law 94-412, Sec. 401(c); (90 Stat. 1257) and 50 U.S.C. 1703(c); Public Law 95-223, Sec 204(c); (91 Stat. 1627); to the Committee on Foreign Affairs.

7674. A letter from the Secretary, Department of the Treasury, transmitting a final report on the national emergency with respect to Burma that was declared in Executive Order 13047 of May 20, 1997, pursuant to 50 U.S.C. 1641(c); Public Law 94-412, Sec. 401(c); (90 Stat. 1257) and 50 U.S.C. 1703(c); Public Law 95-223, Sec 204(c); (91 Stat. 1627); to the Committee on Foreign Affairs.

7675. A letter from the Secretary, Department of the Treasury, transmitting a six-month periodic report on the national emergency with respect to Yemen that was declared in Executive Order 13611 of May 16, 2012, pursuant to 50 U.S.C. 1641(c); Public Law 94-412, Sec. 401(c); (90 Stat. 1257) and 50 U.S.C. 1703(c); Public Law 95-223, Sec 204(c); (91 Stat. 1627); to the Committee on Foreign Affairs.

7676. A letter from the Assistant Legal Adviser, Office of Treaty Affairs, Department of State, transmitting a report concerning international agreements other than treaties entered into by the United States to be

transmitted to the Congress within the sixty-day period specified in the Case-Zablocki Act, pursuant to 1 U.S.C. 112b(a); Public Law 92-403, Sec. 1(a) (as amended by Public Law 108-458, Sec. 7121(b)); (118 Stat. 3807); to the Committee on Foreign Affairs.

7677. A letter from the Assistant Secretary for Export Administration, Bureau of Industry and Security, Department of Commerce, transmitting the Department's final rule — Clarifications and Revisions to Military Aircraft, Gas Turbine Engines and Related Items License Requirements [Docket No.: 151030999-6552-02] (RIN: 0694-AG76) received November 28, 2016, pursuant to 5 U.S.C. 801(a)(1)(A); Public Law 104-121, Sec. 251; (110 Stat. 868); to the Committee on Foreign Affairs.

7678. A letter from the Assistant Secretary, Legislative Affairs, Department of State, transmitting the Department's final rule — Amendment to the International Traffic in Arms Regulations: Corrections and Clarifications [Public Notice: 9757] (RIN: 1400-AE05) received November 22, 2016, pursuant to 5 U.S.C. 801(a)(1)(A); Public Law 104-121, Sec. 251; (110 Stat. 868); to the Committee on Foreign Affairs.

7679. A letter from the Supervisory Management and Program Analyst, M/MPBP/POL, Office of Acquisition and Assistance, U.S. Agency for International Development, transmitting the Agency's final rule — Requirement for Nondiscrimination against End-Users of Supplies or Services ("Beneficiaries") under USAID-Funded Contracts (RIN: 0412-AA81) received November 28, 2016, pursuant to 5 U.S.C. 801(a)(1)(A); Public Law 104-121, Sec. 251; (110 Stat. 868); to the Committee on Foreign Affairs.

7680. A letter from the Senior Procurement Executive, Office of Acquisition Policy, General Services Administration, transmitting the Administration's summary presentation of final rules — Federal Acquisition Regulation; Federal Acquisition Circular 2005-92; Introduction [Docket No.: FAR 2016-0051, Sequence No.: 6] received November 21, 2016, pursuant to 5 U.S.C. 801(a)(1)(A); Public Law 104-121, Sec. 251; (110 Stat. 868); to the Committee on Oversight and Government Reform.

7681. A letter from the Senior Procurement Executive, Office of Acquisition Policy, General Services Administration, transmitting the Administration's final rule — Federal Acquisition Regulation: Removal of Regulations Relating to Telegraphic Communication [FAC 2005-92; FAR Case 2015-035; Item II; Docket No.: 2015-0035, Sequence No.: 1] (RIN: 9000-AN23) received November 21, 2016, pursuant to 5 U.S.C. 801(a)(1)(A); Public Law 104-121, Sec. 251; (110 Stat. 868); to the Committee on Oversight and Government Reform.

7682. A letter from the Senior Procurement Executive, Office of Acquisition Policy, General Services Administration, transmitting the Administration's final rule — Federal Acquisition Regulation; Federal Acquisition Circular 2005-92, Technical Amendments [FAC 2005-92; Item III; Docket No.: 2016-0052; Sequence No.: 5] received November 21, 2016, pursuant to 5 U.S.C. 801(a)(1)(A); Public Law 104-121, Sec. 251; (110 Stat. 868); to the Committee on Oversight and Government Reform.

7683. A letter from the Senior Procurement Executive, Office of Acquisition Policy, General Services Administration, transmitting the Administration's final rule — Federal Acquisition Regulation; Public Disclosure of Greenhouse Gas Emissions and Reduction Goals-Representation [FAC 2005-92; FAR Case 2015-024; Item I; Docket No.: 2015-0024,

Sequence No.: 1] (RIN: 9000-AM90) received November 21, 2016, pursuant to 5 U.S.C. 801(a)(1)(A); Public Law 104-121, Sec. 251; (110 Stat. 868); to the Committee on Oversight and Government Reform.

7684. A letter from the Administrator, U.S. Agency for International Development, transmitting the Agency's Semiannual Report of the Office of the Inspector General for the period ending September 30, 2016, pursuant to Sec. 5 of the Inspector General Act of 1978, as amended; to the Committee on Oversight and Government Reform.

7685. A letter from the Director, Office of Sustainable Fisheries, NMFS, National Oceanic and Atmospheric Administration, transmitting the Administration's temporary rule — Fisheries of the Northeastern United States; Atlantic Bluefish Fishery; Quota Transfer [Docket No.: 151130999-6225-01] (RIN: 0648-XE868) received November 18, 2016, pursuant to 5 U.S.C. 801(a)(1)(A); Public Law 104-121, Sec. 251; (110 Stat. 868); to the Committee on Natural Resources.

7686. A letter from the Acting Director, Office of Sustainable Fisheries, NMFS, National Oceanic and Atmospheric Administration, transmitting the Administration's temporary rule — Snapper-Grouper Fishery of the South Atlantic; 2016 Recreational Accountability Measure and Closure for the South Atlantic Other Jacks Complex [Docket No.: 120815345-3525-02] (RIN: 0648-XE774) received November 18, 2016, pursuant to 5 U.S.C. 801(a)(1)(A); Public Law 104-121, Sec. 251; (110 Stat. 868); to the Committee on Natural Resources.

7687. A letter from the Secretary, Department of Transportation, transmitting the Department's report titled "Transportation Infrastructure Finance and Innovation Act 2016 Report to Congress", pursuant to 23 U.S.C. 609(a); Public Law 105-178, Sec. 1503(a) (amended by Public Law 114-94, Sec. 2001(h)); (129 Stat. 1444); to the Committee on Transportation and Infrastructure.

7688. A letter from the Assistant Secretary for Legislation, Department of Health and Human Services, transmitting the Department's report entitled "Recovery Auditing in Medicare Fee-For-Service for Fiscal Year 2015", pursuant to 42 U.S.C. 1395ddd(h)(8); Aug. 14, 1935, ch. 531, title XVIII, Sec. 1893(h)(8) (as amended by Public Law 109-432, Sec. 302(a)); (120 Stat. 2992); ; jointly to the Committees on Energy and Commerce and Ways and Means.

REPORTS OF COMMITTEES ON PUBLIC BILLS AND RESOLUTIONS

Under clause 2 of rule XIII, reports of committees were delivered to the Clerk for printing and reference to the proper calendar, as follows:

Mr. THORNBERRY: Committee on Conference. Conference report of S. 2943. An act to authorize appropriations for fiscal year 2017 for military activities of the Department of Defense, for military construction, and for defense activities of the Department of Energy, to prescribe military personnel strengths for such fiscal year, and for other purposes (Rept. 114-840). Ordered to be printed.

Mr. CHAFFETZ: Committee on Oversight and Government Reform. H.R. 5384. A bill to amend title 44, United States Code, to restrict the distribution of free printed copies of the Federal Register to Members of Congress and other officers and employees of the United States, and for other purposes (Rept. 114-841, Pt. 1). Referred to the Committee of the Whole House on the state of the Union.

Mr. CHAFFETZ: Committee on Oversight and Government Reform. H.R. 6186. A bill to amend title 5, United States Code, to extend certain protections against prohibited personnel practices, and for other purposes (Rept. 114-842). Referred to the Committee of the Whole House on the State of the Union.

Mr. CHAFFETZ: Committee on Oversight and Government Reform. H.R. 6303. A bill to designate facilities of the United States Postal Service, to establish new ZIP Codes, and for other purposes (Rept. 114-843). Referred to the House Calendar.

Mr. BYRNE: Committee on Rules. House Resolution 937. Resolution providing for consideration of the conference report to accompany the bill (S. 2943) to authorize appropriations for fiscal year 2017 for military activities of the Department of Defense, for military construction, and for defense activities of the Department of Energy, to prescribe military personnel strengths for such fiscal year, and for other purposes (Rept. 114-844). Referred to the House Calendar.

DISCHARGE OF COMMITTEE

Pursuant to clause 2 of rule XIII, the Committee on House Administration discharged from further consideration. H.R. 5384 referred to the Committee of the Whole House on the state of the Union, and ordered to be printed.

PUBLIC BILLS AND RESOLUTIONS

Under clause 2 of rule XII, public bills and resolutions of the following titles were introduced and severally referred, as follows:

By Mr. JENKINS of West Virginia:
H.R. 6403. A bill to amend the Internal Revenue Code of 1986 to provide additional new markets tax credits for distressed coal communities; to the Committee on Ways and Means.

By Mr. BOUSTANY (for himself and Mr. DOGGETT):
H.R. 6404. A bill to permit occupational therapists to conduct the initial assessment visit under a Medicare home health plan of care for certain rehabilitation cases; to the Committee on Ways and Means, and in addition to the Committee on Energy and Commerce, for a period to be subsequently determined by the Speaker, in each case for consideration of such provisions as fall within the jurisdiction of the committee concerned.

By Mr. GRAYSON:
H.R. 6405. A bill to amend the Internal Revenue Code of 1986 to extend for one year the exclusion from gross income of discharge of qualified principal residence indebtedness; to the Committee on Ways and Means.

By Mr. GRAYSON:
H.R. 6406. A bill to amend the Internal Revenue Code of 1986 to extend for two years the exclusion from gross income of discharge of qualified principal residence indebtedness; to the Committee on Ways and Means.

By Mr. KILMER (for himself and Mr. NEWHOUSE):
H.R. 6407. A bill to direct the Secretary of Veterans Affairs to submit to the Committees on Veterans' Affairs of the Senate and the House of Representatives a report regarding the organizational structure of the Department of Veterans Affairs, and for other purposes; to the Committee on Veterans' Affairs.

By Mr. LANGEVIN:
H.R. 6408. A bill to amend the Internal Revenue Code of 1986 to expand the new energy efficient home credit, and for other purposes; to the Committee on Ways and Means.

By Mr. MEADOWS:
H.R. 6409. A bill to protect freedom of speech in America's electoral process and ensure transparency in campaign finance; to the Committee on House Administration.

By Mr. PALLONE:
H.R. 6410. A bill to prohibit the commercial harvesting of Atlantic striped bass in the coastal waters and the exclusive economic zone; to the Committee on Natural Resources.

By Mr. PALLONE:
H.R. 6411. A bill to amend the Federal Water Pollution Control Act to clarify that fill material cannot be comprised of waste; to the Committee on Transportation and Infrastructure.

By Mr. PALLONE:
H.R. 6412. A bill to amend the Oil Pollution Act of 1990 to require oil polluters to pay the full cost of oil spills, and for other purposes; to the Committee on Transportation and Infrastructure.

By Mr. PALLONE:
H.R. 6413. A bill to amend the Internal Revenue Code of 1986 to require oil polluters to pay the full cost of oil spills, and for other purposes; to the Committee on Transportation and Infrastructure, and in addition to the Committees on the Budget, and Ways and Means, for a period to be subsequently determined by the Speaker, in each case for consideration of such provisions as fall within the jurisdiction of the committee concerned.

By Mr. TONKO (for himself, Mr. McKINLEY, and Mr. KILMER):
H.R. 6414. A bill to encourage and increase the use of crowdsourcing and citizen science methods within the Federal Government to advance and accelerate scientific research, literacy, and diplomacy, and for other purposes; to the Committee on Oversight and Government Reform.

By Mr. LANCE:
H. Con. Res. 174. Concurrent resolution directing the Clerk of the House of Representatives to make a correction in the enrollment of H.R. 34; considered and agreed to.

By Mr. LIPINSKI (for himself and Mr. BROOKS of Alabama):
H. Con. Res. 175. Concurrent resolution expressing the sense of Congress that Congress and the President should prioritize the reduction and elimination, over a reasonable period of time, of the overall trade deficit of the United States; to the Committee on Ways and Means.

By Mr. SALMON (for himself, Mr. HECK of Nevada, Ms. DUCKWORTH, Ms. JUDY CHU of California, Mr. ROHRABACHER, Mr. CLEAVER, Ms. GABBARD, Mr. CARTER of Georgia, Mr. BARTON, Mr. MARINO, Ms. BORDALLO, Mr. HONDA, Mr. BISHOP of Michigan, and Mr. PETERS):
H. Con. Res. 176. Concurrent resolution honoring in praise and remembrance the extraordinary life, steady leadership, and remarkable, 70-year reign of King Bhumibol Adulyadej of Thailand; to the Committee on Foreign Affairs.

By Mr. TONKO (for himself and Mr. McKINLEY):
H. Res. 938. A resolution recognizing the Weatherization Assistance Program during its 40th anniversary year for its history of reducing the energy costs of families with low incomes, making low-income households healthier and safer, positively impacting the environment, and supporting jobs and new technology; to the Committee on Energy and Commerce.

By Mr. WELCH:
H. Res. 939. A resolution expressing the sense of the House of Representatives that

access to digital communications tools and connectivity is necessary to prepare youth in the United States to compete in the 21st century economy; to the Committee on Energy and Commerce.

CONSTITUTIONAL AUTHORITY STATEMENT

Pursuant to clause 7 of rule XII of the Rules of the House of Representatives, the following statements are submitted regarding the specific powers granted to Congress in the Constitution to enact the accompanying bill or joint resolution.

By Mr. JENKINS of West Virginia:
H.R. 6403.
Congress has the power to enact this legislation pursuant to the following:
Article 1 Section 8 of the United States Constitution.
By Mr. BOUSTANY:
H.R. 6404.
Congress has the power to enact this legislation pursuant to the following:
Clause 1 of Section 8 of Article I of the United States Constitution.
By Mr. GRAYSON:
H.R. 6405.
Congress has the power to enact this legislation pursuant to the following:
Article 1, Section 8, of the United States Constitution.
By Mr. GRAYSON:
H.R. 6406.
Congress has the power to enact this legislation pursuant to the following:
Article 1, Section 8, of the United States Constitution.
By Mr. KILMER:
H.R. 6407.
Congress has the power to enact this legislation pursuant to the following:
Article 1, Section 8 of the United States Constitution.
By Mr. LANGEVIN:
H.R. 6408.
Congress has the power to enact this legislation pursuant to the following:
Article I, Section 8, Clause 1
By Mr. MEADOWS:
H.R. 6409.
Congress has the power to enact this legislation pursuant to the following:
According to Article 1, Section 4, Clause I "The Times and Manner of holding Elections for Senators and Representatives, shall be prescribed in each State by the Legislature thereof; but the Congress may at any time by Law make or alter such Regulations, except as to the Places of chusing Senators."
By Mr. PALLONE:
H.R. 6410.
Congress has the power to enact this legislation pursuant to the following:
Clause 7 of Section 9 of Article I of the Constitution
By Mr. PALLONE:
H.R. 6411.
Congress has the power to enact this legislation pursuant to the following:
Clause 7 of Section 9 of Article I of the Constitution
By Mr. PALLONE:
H.R. 6412.
Congress has the power to enact this legislation pursuant to the following:
Clause 3 of Section 8 of Article I of the Constitution
By Mr. PALLONE:
H.R. 6413.
Congress has the power to enact this legislation pursuant to the following:
Clause 1 of Section 8 of Article I of the Constitution
By Mr. TONKO:
H.R. 6414.
Congress has the power to enact this legislation pursuant to the following:
Article I, Section 8, Clause 1
The Congress shall have Power to lay and collect Taxes, Duties, Imposts and Excises, to pay the Debts and provide for the common Defence and general Welfare of the United States; but all Duties, Imposts, and Excises shall be uniform throughout the United States.

ADDITIONAL SPONSORS

Under clause 7 of rule XII, sponsors were added to public bills and resolutions, as follows:

H.R. 188: Ms. KELLY of Illinois, Mr. RANGEL, and Ms. LOFGREN.
H.R. 213: Mr. QUIGLEY, Mr. FOSTER, Mr. WELCH, and Mr. SESSIONS.
H.R. 2274: Mr. LOEBSACK.
H.R. 2573: Mr. LOBIONDO.
H.R. 2920: Mrs. DAVIS of California, Ms. LEE and Mr. GUTIÉRREZ.
H.R. 3119: Ms. NORTON, Ms. WILSON of Florida, Mr. QUIGLEY, Mr. SEAN PATRICK MALONEY of New York, Ms. LEE, Mr. McDERMOTT, Mr. HIMES, Mr. SMITH of Washington, and Mr. HECK of Washington.
H.R. 3166: Mr. POLIS.
H.R. 3314: Mr. JORDAN.
H.R. 3535: Ms. ROS-LEHTINEN.
H.R. 3770: Ms. NORTON.
H.R. 3799: Mr. JENKINS of West Virginia.
H.R. 4298: Mr. ROGERS of Alabama, Ms. KUSTER, Ms. MOORE, Mr. PASCRELL, and Mr. BROOKS of Alabama.
H.R. 4380: Ms. LOFGREN.
H.R. 4621: Mr. COHEN.
H.R. 4818: Mr. MOONEY of West Virginia.
H.R. 4907: Ms. SCHAKOWSKY and Mr. GOHMERT.
H.R. 4919: Mrs. HARTZLER.
H.R. 4938: Ms. FUDGE and Ms. ADAMS.
H.R. 5167: Mr. MULLIN.
H.R. 5373: Ms. DELAURO.
H.R. 5488: Mr. QUIGLEY, Mr. LOWENTHAL, and Mr. GUTIÉRREZ.
H.R. 5500: Ms. DELBENE.
H.R. 5650: Mr. CUMMINGS.
H.R. 5899: Mr. DESAULNIER.
H.R. 5902: Mr. CICILLINE.
H.R. 5951: Mr. BYRNE.
H.R. 5965: Mr. GUTIÉRREZ.
H.R. 5980: Mr. QUIGLEY.
H.R. 5999: Mr. LOUDERMILK, Mr. BABIN, and Mr. WITTMAN,
H.R. 6037: Mr. WALZ, Mr. YOUNG of Alaska, Ms. MICHELLE LUJAN GRISHAM of New Mexico, Mrs. BEATTY, Mr. BLUMENAUER, and Mr. CICILLINE.
H.R. 6166: Mr. BUCSHON and Mr. CARSON of Indiana.
H.R. 6176: Mr. RATCLIFFE.
H.R. 6226: Mr. CONAWAY and Mr. KEATING.
H.R. 6234: Mr. THOMPSON of California.
H.R. 6287: Mr. BROOKS of Alabama.
H.R. 6292: Mr. SENSENBRENNER.
H.R. 6329: Mr. VARGAS, Mr. CONYERS, and Ms. LOFGREN.
H.R. 6339: Mr. STEWART.
H.R. 6340: Mr. ENGEL, Mr. KENNEDY, Ms. TSONGAS, Mr. RUIZ, Mr. POCAN, Ms. HANABUSA, Ms. ROYBAL-ALLARD, Mr. CARSON of Indiana, Ms. DELAURO, Mr. RIBBLE, and Ms. TITUS.
H.R. 6346: Ms. MENG.
H.R. 6382: Mr. SCHIFF, Mr. CAPUANO, Mr. MEEKS, Mr. RUIZ, Mr. POCAN, Mr. CONNOLLY, and Mr. McDERMOTT.
H.J. Res. 9: Mr. ROGERS of Alabama.
H.J. Res. 103: Mr. COHEN.
H. Con. Res. 33: Mr. GOHMERT.
H. Con. Res. 159: Mr. TIPTON, Ms. JACKSON LEE, and Mr. COHEN.
H. Res. 540: Mr. HIGGINS, Mr. GARAMENDI, and Ms. PINGREE.
H. Res. 750: Mr. GENE GREEN of Texas.
H. Res. 861: Mr. QUIGLEY and Ms. KUSTER.
H. Res. 931: Ms. LEE.

EXTENSIONS OF REMARKS

HONORING TOM WILSON

HON. JARED HUFFMAN

OF CALIFORNIA

IN THE HOUSE OF REPRESENTATIVES

Wednesday, November 30, 2016

Mr. HUFFMAN. Mr. Speaker, I rise today in recognition of Tom Wilson as he retires as executive director of the Canal Alliance after 24 years of service. Under Mr. Wilson's leadership, the Canal Alliance has added numerous programs and services, added more than 30 employees, and has maintained four county contracts and 400 active volunteers a year. He has expanded the organization's budget from $350,000 to $3.8 million today, helping to reach more residents in need.

Mr. Wilson has been instrumental in developing an organization that touches the lives of more than 3,500 people per year with educational, vocational, and legal services, as well as family support. The Canal Alliance helps to provide supplemental food distribution to 400 families every week and English as a second language instruction to 1,200 adults per year. After Immigration and Custom Enforcement officers conducted raids in the community, the Canal Alliance began talks with the Marin County Human Rights Commission, city and county officials, and ICE—conversations that ultimately helped stop the immigration raids.

As a result of the cutting-edge work done by Canal Alliance, the organization has been honored with the 2013 North Bay Leadership Council Award for empowering the Latino Community, the Heart of Marin Award for Achievement in Nonprofit Excellence, the Marin Community Foundation's Beryl Buck Achievement Award for Promoting Diversity and Inclusiveness, the Tipping Point Community Award, the U.S. Mayors' End Hunger Award, among others.

In addition to these recognitions, Tom Wilson has been awarded both the Benjamin Dreyfus Civil Liberties Award by the ACLU, and the Martin Luther King Jr. Humanitarian Award by the Marin County Human Rights Commission.

Tom Wilson's legacy is one of dedicated service to the children and families of San Rafael. Please join me in congratulating him on his retirement and expressing our deep appreciation for his long and exceptional career and outstanding contributions to the Canal Alliance.

HONORING ZANE GREEN

HON. SAM GRAVES

OF MISSOURI

IN THE HOUSE OF REPRESENTATIVES

Wednesday, November 30, 2016

Mr. GRAVES of Missouri. Mr. Speaker, I proudly pause to recognize Zane Green. Zane is a very special young man who has exemplified the finest qualities of citizenship and leadership by taking an active part in the Boy Scouts of America, Troop 412, and earning the most prestigious award of Eagle Scout.

Zane has been very active with his troop, participating in many scout activities. Over the many years Zane has been involved with scouting, he has not only earned numerous merit badges, but also the respect of his family, peers, and community. Most notably, Zane contributed to his community through his Eagle Scout project.

Mr. Speaker, I proudly ask you to join me in commending Zane Green for his accomplishments with the Boy Scouts of America and for his efforts put forth in achieving the highest distinction of Eagle Scout.

HONORING BRENDA FREEMAN

HON. ELIOT L. ENGEL

OF NEW YORK

IN THE HOUSE OF REPRESENTATIVES

Wednesday, November 30, 2016

Mr. ENGEL. Mr. Speaker, I rise today to honor Brenda Freeman, an individual who has been instrumental in shaping young hearts and minds as a member of the Yonkers public school system for nearly three decades.

A graduate of Yonkers Public Schools, Brenda earned her degree from Westchester Community College and has held the position of School Aide and School Number 16 since 1988. In addition to helping students in the Copy Room, Brenda has been instrumental in organizing many school fundraisers, including the Pasta for Pennies event which benefited the Leukemia Foundation and the American heart association Relay for Life. She also spearheaded the P.T.A. membership drive for her local CSEA union, for which she also served as Building Rep. Brenda also created and organized a Multicultural Food Week event for the entire School Number 16 staff, and has served as School social Committee Coordinator.

School Principal Cynthia Eisner has said of Brenda, "She is the Miss Congeniality of School 16 welcoming new staff. She facilitates our SMART Program, picking up the students for the senior citizens that volunteer in our building each week. Ms. Freeman is a well-respected member of the CSEA union and counsels her members wisely. She approaches problems with confidentiality and has a wonderful way of arranging consensus between parties. Ms. Freeman is a dependable reliable, humble person. She finds gratitude in a job done well and does everything with a pleasant attitude."

This year, the Exchange Club of Club of Yonkers is honoring Brenda as their 2016 Civil Service Employee of the Year. She is most deserving of this wonderful recognition. Congratulations to Brenda on receiving this great honor.

IN CELEBRATION OF THE AMERICAN RED CROSS CENTENNIAL ANNIVERSARY IN INDIANA

HON. SUSAN W. BROOKS

OF INDIANA

IN THE HOUSE OF REPRESENTATIVES

Wednesday, November 30, 2016

Mrs. BROOKS of Indiana. Mr. Speaker, I rise today to pay tribute to the Indiana Chapter of the American Red Cross in celebration of its 100th anniversary. This dynamic humanitarian organization has made significant contributions to the state of Indiana, to the nation, and around the world. It is my privilege to honor the American Red Cross as it celebrates 100 years of excellence in Indiana. The people of Indiana's Fifth Congressional District are forever grateful for their exceptional service and dedication to our Hoosier community.

Inspired by the Swiss Red Cross Network, Clara Barton founded the American Red Cross on May 21, 1881, in Washington, DC. The Red Cross received its first congressional charter in 1900 and the second in 1905. Shortly thereafter, the American Red Cross opened their Indiana Chapter in 1916. They have delivered aid in disaster relief, helped feed hungry children, and provided care for the sick. They provide care, shelter, service to veterans, and access to lifesaving blood. Through its strong network of volunteers, donors and partners, the American Red Cross has made a lasting impact in the lives of Hoosiers in their time of greatest need. Over 500,000 volunteers work across America, and more than 3,500 volunteers work to help their fellow Hoosiers in the face of disaster here at home. In 2015 alone the Indiana Red Cross helped 1,300 families through the aftermath of home fires. The Red Cross currently serves 6.3 million Hoosiers across 87 counties in Indiana.

The American Red Cross prevents and alleviates human suffering in the face of emergencies by mobilizing the power of volunteers and the generosity of donors. Born out of the desire to help without discrimination those wounded on the battlefield, the American Red Cross carries on its legacy by working to prevent and alleviate human suffering wherever it is found, both nationally and internationally. All people receive the care, shelter, and hope they need in the face of a disaster. Since 2006, the Red Cross and FEMA have worked together to help government agencies and community organizations plan, coordinate and provide feeding, sheltering and family reunification services for people affected by disasters.

Volunteers carry out 90 percent of the humanitarian work done by the Red Cross. Hoosiers and Americans across the country have the opportunity to translate their care and concern for people down the street, across the country and around the world through the American Red Cross. They not only give back to the community, but it also gives the community the ability to give back to the world.

On behalf of the citizens of Indiana's Fifth Congressional District, I would like to congratulate the Indiana Chapter of the American Red Cross on the celebration of its centennial anniversary. I am proud that our Hoosier state is home to an exemplary organization such as this one. I wish the Indiana Chapter of the American Red Cross all the best as it embarks on its next 100 years of excellence in Indiana.

HONORING THE CAREER OF PROFESSOR ANITA HILL

HON. JIM COSTA
OF CALIFORNIA
IN THE HOUSE OF REPRESENTATIVES
Wednesday, November 30, 2016

Mr. COSTA. Mr. Speaker, I rise today to give homage to the career and undertakings of Professor Anita Hill; a woman who has been at the center of American political discourse for over 25 years. Professor Hill's Senate testimony against Justice Clarence Thomas in 1991 shed light on important issues and generated significant legal change for sexual harassment protections for women and men in the workplace. For these reasons, it is both fitting and appropriate that Professor Hill is the 10th recipient of the Alice and Clifford Spendlove Prize in Social Justice, Diplomacy, and Tolerance; one of U.C. Merced's highest honors.

Professor Hill's early career was one marked by excellence. After obtaining her Bachelor's degree with honors in Psychology from Oklahoma State University, she moved on to receive her Juris Doctor degree from Yale in 1980. By 1983, Professor Hill had already served in major roles under the Department of Education's Office for Civil Rights and the U.S. Equal Employment Opportunity Commission (EEOC). By 1986, she had executed faculty positions at Oral Roberts University and became the first tenured African American Professor at the University of Oklahoma.

Professor Hill rose to national prominence after her Senate hearing regarding the misconduct of Justice Clarence Thomas during their time working together at the Department of Education and the EEOC. Professor Hill's statements facilitated a nationwide discussion about the common experiences of women in the workplace, which has empowered countless women to speak out against the injustices they have faced throughout the course of their careers. The subsequent tripling of the amount of women in the Senate, and the 60 percent increase in the number of female Representatives in the House that followed in the next election cycle are often attributed to the Senate hearings.

Professor Hill has become one of the most recognizable national voices on issues of race and gender equality. Professor Hill has been featured on numerous high profile television shows such as 60 Minutes, Meet the Press, and more recently was depicted by Kerry Washington in an HBO movie about her life and the hardships she endured during the Senate hearings. She has published a number of academic articles with profound content, and has written two books which have won national acclaim. In 2015, Professor Hill was appointed to serve as a Private University Professor of Social Policy, Law, and Women's Studies at Brandeis University.

Mr. Speaker, I urge my colleagues to join me in honoring Professor Anita Hill and the legacy she established in our country. The United States has seen a great deal of strife and conflict, but figures like Professor Hill ingrain an unshakable feeling of strength and hope for the people of this nation. As Professor Hill continues to advocate for noble causes, we hope that she can remain a stalwart figure in discourse on social justice and equality.

HONORING KRISTOPHER EVANS

HON. SAM GRAVES
OF MISSOURI
IN THE HOUSE OF REPRESENTATIVES
Wednesday, November 30, 2016

Mr. GRAVES of Missouri. Mr. Speaker, I proudly pause to recognize Kristopher Evans. Kristopher is a very special young man who has exemplified the finest qualities of citizenship and leadership by taking an active part in the Boy Scouts of America, Troop 1376, and earning the most prestigious award of Eagle Scout.

Kristopher has been very active with his troop, participating in many scout activities. Over the many years Kristopher has been involved with scouting, he has not only earned numerous merit badges, but also the respect of his family, peers, and community. Most notably, Kristopher has become an Ordeal Member of the Order of the Arrow and earned the rank of Warrior in the Tribe of Mic-O-Say. Kristopher has also contributed to his community through his Eagle Scout project. Kristopher built six large bat houses for Immacolata Manor in Liberty, Missouri, to control mosquitoes and other pests.

Mr. Speaker, I proudly ask you to join me in commending Kristopher Evans for his accomplishments with the Boy Scouts of America and for his efforts put forth in achieving the highest distinction of Eagle Scout.

HONORING REVEREND FATHER JON E. MAGOULIAS

HON. JEFF DENHAM
OF CALIFORNIA
IN THE HOUSE OF REPRESENTATIVES
Wednesday, November 30, 2016

Mr. DENHAM. Mr. Speaker, I rise today to recognize and honor Reverend Father Jon E. Magoulias from Modesto, California, for his thirty years of service to the Greek Orthodox Church of the Annunciation.

Father Jon has followed in his father's and grandfather's footsteps by obtaining his Bachelor of Arts in Philosophy of Religion and Masters of Divinity from the Holy Cross Greek Orthodox School of Theology.

In addition to being recognized as a Scholar for his depth of knowledge of the Orthodox Christian Faith, Father Jon has also written extensively on his faith. "The Divine Liturgy of St. John Chrysostom" (2004) translated a compilation of the most celebrated liturgy of the Orthodox from Greek to English. His work is used by at least seventy-nine Greek Orthodox Parishes.

In 2010, Father Jon published his second book, "The Priest as a Liturgist: A Handbook of Rubrics," which serves as a manual for priests in fulfilling their duties in celebrating the liturgies of the church. This book was written for and at the request of the ordained clergy of the Metropolitan Gerasimos of San Francisco. In addition, the book has been requested by over 350 priests across the world.

In his thirty years of ministry as Parish Priest, Father Jon has impacted the community by conducting over 500 baptisms, 200 weddings, and 300 funerals. He has encouraged philanthropic giving not just for the ministries of the Church, but also for local charities such as Modesto Gospel Mission, Sierra Vista Home, and Habitat for Humanity.

Father Jon is married to his beloved wife, Presvytera Georgia Magoulias, and together they have three daughters, Stamatia, Maria and Anastasia, and a son named Efstratios Jon.

Mr. Speaker, please join me in honoring Father Jon E. Magoulias for his 30 years of service and outstanding contributions to the Greek Orthodox Church of the Annunciation and the community.

EXCHANGE OF LETTERS REGARDING H.R. 5160

HON. CANDICE S. MILLER
OF MICHIGAN
IN THE HOUSE OF REPRESENTATIVES
Wednesday, November 30, 2016

Mrs. MILLER of Michigan. Mr. Speaker, I include in the RECORD two letters concerning Committee jurisdiction regarding H.R. 5160.

COMMITTEE ON TRANSPORTATION AND
INFRASTRUCTURE, HOUSE OF REP-
RESENTATIVES,
Washington, DC, May 27, 2016.
Hon. CANDICE S. MILLER,
*Chairman, Committee on House Administration,
Washington, DC.*

DEAR CHAIRMAN MILLER: I write concerning H.R. 5160, a bill to amend title 40, United States Code, to include as part of the buildings and grounds of the National Gallery of Art any buildings and other areas within the boundaries of any real estate or other property interests acquired by the National Gallery of Art. This legislation includes matters that fall within the Rule X jurisdiction of the Committee on Transportation and Infrastructure.

In order to expedite Floor consideration of H.R. 5160, the Committee on Transportation and Infrastructure will forgo action on this bill. However, this is conditional on our mutual understanding that forgoing consideration of the bill does not prejudice the Committee with respect to the appointment of conferees or to any future jurisdictional claim over the subject matters contained in the bill or similar legislation that fall within the Committee's Rule X jurisdiction. I request you urge the Speaker to name members of the Committee to any conference committee named to consider such provisions.

Please place a copy of this letter and your response acknowledging our jurisdictional interest into the committee report on H.R. 5160 and into the Congressional Record during consideration of the measure on the House floor. I appreciate the Committee on House Administration working with me to address my concerns.

Sincerely,

BILL SHUSTER,
Chairman.

CONGRESS OF THE UNITED STATES,
HOUSE OF REPRESENTATIVES,
Washington, DC, June 13, 2016.
Hon. BILL SHUSTER,
Chairman, Committee on Transportation and Infrastructure, Washington, DC.

DEAR CHAIRMAN SHUSTER: Thank you for your letter regarding H.R. 5160. As you know, the bill was introduced on April 29, 2016, and referred solely to the Committee on House Administration. The bill would amend section 6301(2) of title 40 of the United States Code, to include as part of the buildings and grounds of the National Gallery of Art any buildings and other areas within the boundaries of any real estate or other property interests acquired by the National Gallery of Art. On May 17, 2016 the Committee on House Administration reported H.R. 5160 favorably out of Committee by voice vote.

The Committee on House Administration recognizes that the Committee on Transportation and Infrastructure has a jurisdictional interest in H.R. 5160 under Rule X of the House Rules. The Committee appreciates the Committee on Transportation and Infrastructure forgoing action on H.R. 5160 in order to expedite the bill. It is the understanding of the Committee on House Administration that forgoing action on H.R. 5160 will not prejudice the Committee on Transportation and Infrastructure with respect to appointment of conferees or any future jurisdictional claim over the subject matters contained in the bill that fall under your Committee's Rule X jurisdiction.

A copy of this letter and your initial letter will be included in the Congressional Record during consideration on the House floor.

Sincerely,

CANDICE S. MILLER,
Chairman.

HONORING GINA ELIZABETH LAWSON, DO

HON. SAM GRAVES

OF MISSOURI

IN THE HOUSE OF REPRESENTATIVES

Wednesday, November 30, 2016

Mr. GRAVES of Missouri. Mr. Speaker, I proudly pause to congratulate Gina Elizabeth Lawson, DO, for being named the 2016 Catholic Doctor of the Year by the Mission Doctors Association.

The Mission Doctors Association chose Dr. Lawson out of more than 1,000 nominations in recognition of her efforts in responding to Christ's call to "Heal the Sick." Dr. Lawson serves as the Medical Director of the St. Luke's Transfer Team and the Medical Director of the Women's Center of St. Luke's Northland Hospital, where she serves as a Eucharistic Minister and brings Communion to the hospital. Dr. Lawson also participated in a

short-term mission to the mountain villages in Jamaica to care for the poor and overlooked.

Mr. Speaker, I proudly ask you to join me in congratulating Gina Elizabeth Lawson, DO, for her accomplishments and her service to her community.

PERSONAL EXPLANATION

HON. DINA TITUS

OF NEVADA

IN THE HOUSE OF REPRESENTATIVES

Wednesday, November 30, 2016

Ms. TITUS. Mr. Speaker, I was unavoidably absent in the House Chamber for votes on Tuesday, November 29, 2016. Had I been present, I would have voted "yea" on roll call votes 588 and 589.

HONORING LUISA DeCICCO, PhD

HON. ELIOT L. ENGEL

OF NEW YORK

IN THE HOUSE OF REPRESENTATIVES

Wednesday, November 30, 2016

Mr. ENGEL. Mr. Speaker, I rise today to recognize a leader in our community, Luisa DeCicco, PhD, whose humanitarian work is being recognized by The Pelham Civic Association at their Annual Dinner Dance Gala. Luisa is one of three honorees for "Persons of the Year" on November 4, 2016 in my district.

Luisa is the Director of Human Resources at DeCicco & Sons Food Markets and is the founder of the Pelham Business Club. She is also the founder and manager of the unique, free Pelham Business Club Facebook community. With over 850 current members, the community provides residents, businesses and not-for-profit organizations in Pelham free access to information and free opportunities to advertise their businesses' and organizations' events.

As head of the Business Club, Luisa works in coordination with the Town of Pelham and Villages of Pelham and Pelham Manor engendering a strong working relationship with all entities. She created and spearheads the town-wide free Easter Bunny Boulevard, Pelham Block Party, Candy Cane Lane events, and three Town Meetings with Town Supervisor and Mayors to inspire a strong community spirit and commitment for businesses and residents, with the theme: "Neighbors Helping Neighbors."

DeCiccos is also an active corporate sponsor of the "Hungry Kidzz" programs and events throughout the year, providing food to children in need throughout tristate area. In addition, they are an active corporate partner with "County Harvest," replenishing food pantries and soup kitchens throughout Westchester County. In Pelham, Luisa is also an active supporter of school PTAs and fundraising events. She married John DeCicco Jr. and together they have two wonderful children.

It is an honor to present Luisa DeCicco with a CONGRESSIONAL RECORD. Congratulations to all honorees of the evening.

HONORING GERALD S. CLARK, SR. ON THE OCCASION OF HIS RETIREMENT

HON. ROSA L. DeLAURO

OF CONNECTICUT

IN THE HOUSE OF REPRESENTATIVES

Wednesday, November 30, 2016

Ms. DeLAURO. Mr. Speaker, it gives me great pleasure to rise today to join friends, family, and colleagues in celebration of my good friend, Gerald S. Clark, Sr., as he marks his retirement as Executive Director of the Greater New Haven Business and Professional Association—an organization that he founded and has led for the last fifty years.

A visionary business leader for as long as most of us can remember, Gerry has left an indelible mark on Greater New Haven and particularly the minority business community. Born in Tuskegee, Alabama on New Year's Day of 1929, Gerry joined the U.S. Army in 1950 following his graduation from Hampton University. He served our nation with distinction during his two years of active service and twenty-eight years of service in the U.S. Army Reserves, retiring as a Lieutenant Colonel.

His graduate studies brought him to New York University and he soon settled in New Haven, Connecticut with his late wife, Yvonne. He opened the Gerald S. Clark Insurance Agency in 1965 and spearheaded the development of Dixwell Plaza as well as serving as a founding member of the Dixwell Merchants Association. Gerry quickly became a driving force in Greater New Haven's business community. He has served as a member of the Chamber of Commerce Board of Directors, the Tennis Foundation of Connecticut Board of Directors, Science Park Development Corporation, Chapel Square of New Haven, the Minority Enterprise Small Business Investment Corporation, the Airport Commission, the City-Wide School Building Committee, the New Haven Scholarship Fund, the Greater New Haven NAACP, and the Technology Investment Fund. Indeed there is no part of our City that has not been impacted by his dedicated efforts.

Perhaps his greatest contribution to the Greater New Haven community has been the establishment of the Greater New Haven Business and Professional Association. An organization dedicated to helping improve small and minority businesses and professions within Connecticut, to assisting in the development of new enterprises among minority businesses inside and around the community, enhancing the cultural and spiritual values of the community through communications and economic cooperation, and to promoting the development of business and economic resources in the minority community. For more than fifty years, Gerry has led this organization and helped to ensure that its members have had access to services that have enabled their businesses to flourish. Small businesses are the backbone of our nation's economy and one of the keys to creating new jobs. In today's challenging economic climate, organizations like the Greater New Haven Business & Professional Association are more important than ever—fostering the entrepreneurial spirit of small business owners in our community.

I would be remiss if I did not extend a special note of thanks to Gerry for his many years of friendship. There are few who have dedicated more of themselves to the New Haven community and its residents than Gerry Clark. His unique vision and leadership have made this organization the success it is today and his good work has helped to shape the very character of our City. I am honored to stand today to join his children, Gerald, Tanya, and William, his seven grandchildren and ten great-grandchildren as well as the many friends, colleagues, and community leaders who have gathered today in extending my deepest thanks and appreciation to Gerald Clark, Sr. for his invaluable contributions to our community as well as my very best wishes for many more years of health and happiness as he enjoys his retirement.

HONORING MORGAN ATKINSON

HON. SAM GRAVES
OF MISSOURI
IN THE HOUSE OF REPRESENTATIVES
Wednesday, November 30, 2016

Mr. GRAVES of Missouri. Mr. Speaker, I proudly pause to recognize Morgan Atkinson. Morgan is a very special young man who has exemplified the finest qualities of citizenship and leadership by taking an active part in the Boy Scouts of America, Troop 412, and earning the most prestigious award of Eagle Scout.

Morgan has been very active with his troop, participating in many scout activities. Over the many years Morgan has been involved with scouting, he has not only earned numerous merit badges, but also the respect of his family, peers, and community. Most notably, Morgan contributed to his community through his Eagle Scout project.

Mr. Speaker, I proudly ask you to join me in commending Morgan Atkinson for his accomplishments with the Boy Scouts of America and for his efforts put forth in achieving the highest distinction of Eagle Scout.

HONORING THE LIFE OF DAVID LUIS

HON. JEFF DENHAM
OF CALIFORNIA
IN THE HOUSE OF REPRESENTATIVES
Wednesday, November 30, 2016

Mr. DENHAM. Mr. Speaker, I rise today to acknowledge and honor the life of David Luis, former battalion chief for the Ripon Consolidated Fire Department. He passed away on November 24, 2016, surrounded by loved ones.

Over 26 years, David dedicated himself to the Ripon Consolidated Fire Department. He advanced from firefighter to captain to battalion chief. He had a passion for helping people, which was reflected not only in his professional career, but also in his personal life.

When David was not working, you could find him coaching youth football or helping FFA members with their projects. He also served as a member of the Ripon High School Ag Advisory Board. His selfless service has left an impact on multiple generations.

An inspiration to his family, friends and community, David brought out the best in people. His life embodied simple principles of authenticity, kindness, loyalty, humility, hard work, integrity, and above all else, service. Our community will greatly miss David's presence, but his legacy will live on.

David leaves behind his wife Clarice, three children, Josh, Kaleigh, and Courtney, as well as his father, brother, sister, nieces and nephews.

Mr. Speaker, please join me in honoring and recognizing Dave Luis and thanking him for his many years of outstanding and heroic service to the Ripon community. God bless him always.

TRIBUTE TO THE 2016 ELLIS ISLAND MEDAL OF HONOR RECIPIENTS

HON. CHARLES B. RANGEL
OF NEW YORK
IN THE HOUSE OF REPRESENTATIVES
Wednesday, November 30, 2016

Mr. RANGEL. Mr. Speaker, I rise today to congratulate the 2016 recipients of the prestigious Ellis Island Medal of Honor.

Presented annually by the National Ethnic Coalition of Organizations—NECO, the Ellis Island Medals of Honor pay tribute to our Nation's immigrant heritage, as well as individual achievement. The Medals are awarded to U.S. citizens from diverse ethnic backgrounds who exemplify outstanding qualities in both their personal and professional lives, while continuing to preserve the richness of their particular heritage and culture. We honor these outstanding individuals because the important work they do today, creates a better world for all of us tomorrow. 2016 marks NECO's 30th anniversary. This momentous occasion was celebrated with a patriotic ceremony on Ellis Island and a re-commitment by the leaders of the organization to their mission of honoring diversity, fostering tolerance and promoting religious and racial unity across America.

Since the Medals' founding, more than 2,500 American citizens have received the Ellis Island Medal of Honor, including six American Presidents, United States Senators, Congressmen, Nobel Laureates, athletes, artists, clergy, and military leaders. This Medal is not about material success, nor is it about the politics of immigration; it is about the people who have committed themselves to this nation, embraced the opportunities America has to offer, and most importantly, who have used those opportunities to not only better their own lives but make a difference in our country and in the lives of its people.

Citizens of the United States hail from every nation known to man. The iconic metaphor of this nation as a veritable melting pot of cultures continues to ring true, and it is this diversity that adds to the unique richness of American life. It is the key to why America is the most innovative, progressive and forward thinking country in the world. The Ellis Island Medals of Honor not only celebrate select individuals but also the pluralism and democracy that enabled our forebearers to celebrate their

cultural identities while still embracing the American way of life. This award serves to remind us all that with hard work and perseverance anyone can still achieve the American dream. In addition, by honoring these remarkable Americans, we honor all who share their origins and we acknowledge the contributions they have made to America. I commend NECO and its Board of Directors headed by my good friend, Nasser J. Kazeminy, for honoring these truly outstanding individuals for their tireless efforts to foster dialogue and build bridges between different ethnic groups, as well as to promote unity and a sense of common purpose in our nation.

Mr. Speaker, I ask all of my colleagues to join me in recognizing the good works of NECO and in congratulating all of the 2016 recipients of the Ellis Island Medal of Honor. I also include in the RECORD the names of this year's recipients.

2016 ELLIS ISLAND MEDAL OF HONOR RECIPIENTS

Mustafa K. Abadan FAIA, Bahram Akradi, Dr. Fariba Etemadi-Nejad Alamdari, George C. Albano, Mark O. Asperilla, MD, Edward Avedisian, George A. Bannayan, MD, Dr. Rekha Bhandari, David C. Bohnett, VADM Raquel Cruz Bono, MD, Stephen Briganti, Rinaldo S. Brutoco, Barbara Peterson Burwell, John Campion, Ms. Teresa Carlson, Commissioner Patrick Carroll, Stephen J. Cassidy, Gen. Martin E. Dempsey (Ret.), Wendy Diamond, General Ann Dunwoody, Kamran Elahian, Reverend Kail C. Ellis, SA, PhD, Bill Evans, Tamsen Fadal, Hamed Faridi, PhD.

Omid Farokhzad, M.D., VADM James Gordon Foggo, Paul G. Gaffney II VADM (Ret.), Garo S. Garibian, MD, Augie Garrido, FBI Special Agent Stephen Gaudin, Colonel Peter T. Green III, Timothy Haahs, PE, AIA, Leroy Hood, M.D., Ph.D., Appo K. Jabarian, Hon. Richard A. Jones, Brigadier General Paul J. Kennedy, Mehmood Khan, MD, Prerna Mona Khanna, MD, MPH, FACP, FACPM, FACOEM, Gissou R. Kian, George Spiros Kleris, MD, PhD, Vreij Kolandjian, Jerry Kyser, Joshua Laird, Padma Lakshmi, Risa J. Lavizzo-Mourey, MD, Mr. Hyung Ro Lee, Dr. Devorah Lieberman, Dr. Ajay Lodha, Asad M. Madni, PhD, DSc(H), ScD(H), DEng(H).

The Hon. Rosario Marin-Former US Treasurer, Eileen C. McDonnell, Captain Thomas S. Morkan, Robert Muzikowski, Alexander Navab, Dr. Chrysostomos L. Nikias, Ronald K. Noble, Thomas J. O'Donnell, Dr. Tony Orlando, Andrew F. Ortiz, JD, MPA, Carl Peterson, Charles Pinajian, Shervin Pishevar, Vincent F. Pitta, Esq., Lori Pollock, Jean Lenti Ponsetto, Issam Raad, MD, FACP, FIDSA, FSHEA, Daniel Ritchie, Kaitlin Roig-DeBellis, M.A. Ed, DHL, Peter Salovey, Ph.D., Akkaraju V.N. Sarma, MD, PhD, FAAFP, Michael H. Saudino, Sr, Edward H. Schauder, Esq., Major General Errol Schwartz.

Andrew Sieja, Major General John K. Singlaub (Ret.), Dr. Massih Tayebi, I. Lorraine Thomas, Edward Tom, Alice (Ali) Torre, Commissioner Benjamin Tucker, Mike Utley, Emmanuel E. Velivasakis, PE, FASCE, Jeanette Sarkisian Wagner, John C. Wobensmith, Doreen Wohl, Ambassador R. James Woolsey, Arthur William Zeckendorf.

INTERNATIONAL ELLIS ISLAND MEDAL OF HONOR RECIPIENTS

Anthony von Mandl, Bedriska v. Mandl, Bill S. Hansson, PhD.

HONORING THOMAS BEALE

HON. SAM GRAVES

OF MISSOURI

IN THE HOUSE OF REPRESENTATIVES

Wednesday, November 30, 2016

Mr. GRAVES of Missouri. Mr. Speaker, I proudly pause to recognize Thomas Beale. Thomas is a very special young man who has exemplified the finest qualities of citizenship and leadership by taking an active part in the Boy Scouts of America, Troop 714, and earning the most prestigious award of Eagle Scout.

Thomas has been very active with his troop, participating in many scout activities. Over the many years Thomas has been involved with scouting, he has not only earned numerous merit badges, but also the respect of his family, peers, and community. Most notably, Thomas earned the rank of Warrior of the Tribe of Mic-O-Say. Thomas has also contributed to his community through his Eagle Scout project. Thomas built a patio and fire pit for an outdoor worship and recreation area at Dearborn Christian Church in Dearborn, Missouri.

Mr. Speaker, I proudly ask you to join me in commending Thomas Beale for his accomplishments with the Boy Scouts of America and for his efforts put forth in achieving the highest distinction of Eagle Scout.

PERSONAL EXPLANATION

HON. ROBERT HURT

OF VIRGINIA

IN THE HOUSE OF REPRESENTATIVES

Wednesday, November 30, 2016

Mr. HURT of Virginia. Mr. Speaker, I was not present for Roll Call vote Number 589 on H.R. 4757, to expand the eligibility for headstones, markers, and medallions furnished by the Secretary of Veterans Affairs for deceased individuals who were awarded the Medal of Honor and are buried in private cemeteries, and for other purposes. Had I been present, I would have voted "yes.'

HONORING THE LIFE OF ELIZABETH WALLACE

HON. JIM COSTA

OF CALIFORNIA

IN THE HOUSE OF REPRESENTATIVES

Wednesday, November 30, 2016

Mr. COSTA. Mr. Speaker, I rise today in memory of Elizabeth Wallace. She was a loving mother, grandmother, and wife. Elizabeth passed away peacefully on October 19th, 2016.

Elizabeth was born in Harbin, China, on March 16th, 1944. At age 11 she emigrated with her mother, Edith, from China to Brazil, where she remained through high school. Elizabeth then traveled to California, where she met her future husband Joel "Bud" Wallace in San Francisco. They married in 1966 and moved to Merced, their home for the next 50 years. Although the Wallaces resided in Merced, Elizabeth identified herself as a "Citizen of the World", continuing to travel to many countries and fostering a lifetime passion for travel.

Between her travels Elizabeth was active in the Merced community. She played an important role in establishing the University of California, Merced. UC Merced's Yablokoff-Wallace Dining Hall and Elizabeth's Garden, named in recognition of her, are used and appreciated by students each and every day. She volunteered regularly at the historic Courthouse Merced and was active in bringing St. Mary Magdalene Orthodox church to Merced. She and Bud built Red Rock Winery, where she spent time in the tasting room.

Elizabeth is survived by her loving husband of 50 years, Joel "Bud" Wallace; her daughter and son-in-law, Lillian and Mark Dutra; and her son and daughter-in-law, Nicholas and Lisa Wallace. She has three grandchildren, Alison Dutra, Michael Dutra, and Vladimir Wallace; and her dog, Tippy.

Mr. Speaker, I urge my colleagues to join me in honoring Elizabeth Wallace's memory. Her love of family and commitment to her community serve as an example to all citizens, not just of our nation but also of our world.

HONORING WILL CAVANAGH

HON. ELIOT L. ENGEL

OF NEW YORK

IN THE HOUSE OF REPRESENTATIVES

Wednesday, November 30, 2016

Mr. ENGEL. Mr. Speaker, I rise today to recognize a leader in our community, Will Cavanagh, whose humanitarian work is being recognized by The Pelham Civic Association at their Annual Dinner Dance Gala. Will is one of three honorees for "Persons of the Year" on November 4, 2016 in my district.

Will is a student advocate and visionary with over two decades of volunteer service to the Pelham School District, including four consecutive terms—12 years—on the Pelham Board of Education, where he served as Vice-President of the Board. Will actively participated in the implementation and improvement of educational programming in the district, which included giving students more access to Advanced Placement/Honors classes; expanding course offerings and building the Science Research program; and developing the Bridge Academy Program.

Will also supported the Pelham School District's work on scope and sequence of subject matter for all grades, which has been instrumental to programmatic improvements, particularly in light of Common Core standards.

Will chaired the District Committee that oversaw development of the School District's Five-Year Strategic Plan (2006–2011) and headed up the District's Turf Field Committee leading to the installation of the Pelham's turf field. Will also served as the Pelham Rec Soccer Commissioner for eight years during a period of great expansion. In addition, he is a member of the Pelham Civic Association and long-time volunteer in the community.

It is an honor to present Will Cavanagh with a CONGRESSIONAL RECORD. Congratulations to all honorees of the evening.

HONORING DAVID GARCIA

HON. SAM GRAVES

OF MISSOURI

IN THE HOUSE OF REPRESENTATIVES

Wednesday, November 30, 2016

Mr. GRAVES of Missouri. Mr. Speaker, I proudly pause to recognize David Garcia. David is a very special young man who has exemplified the finest qualities of citizenship and leadership by taking an active part in the Boy Scouts of America, Troop 1376, and earning the most prestigious award of Eagle Scout.

David has been very active with his troop, participating in many scout activities. Over the many years David has been involved with scouting, he has not only earned numerous merit badges, but also the respect of his family, peers, and community. Most notably, David has become an Ordeal Member of the Order of the Arrow and earned the rank of Warrior in the Tribe of Mic-O-Say. David has also contributed to his community through his Eagle Scout project. David coordinated with the Liberty Parks and Recreation department and planted 83 native Missouri plants at the Rush Creek Parkway roundabout near Liberty Hospital in Liberty, Missouri.

Mr. Speaker, I proudly ask you to join me in commending David Garcia for his accomplishments with the Boy Scouts of America and for his efforts put forth in achieving the highest distinction of Eagle Scout.

RECOGNIZING GALE McCOY FOR 33 YEARS OF PUBLIC SERVICE

HON. TOM PRICE

OF GEORGIA

IN THE HOUSE OF REPRESENTATIVES

Wednesday, November 30, 2016

Mr. TOM PRICE of Georgia. Mr. Speaker, today I rise to recognize a remarkable civil servant, Gale McCoy. This year Gale is retiring from the U.S. Department of State after 33 years of service. I want to take this moment to highlight the career of this lifelong public servant.

Over the years, Ms. McCoy has served in several capacities. In 2007, she became the director of the Special Issuance Agency, which is charged with the task of processing diplomatic and official passport applications for the Department of Defense, the White House, and Congress. In 2011, Gale McCoy opened the Atlanta Passport Agency, which serves as the central hub for citizens across southeast. In 2016, the Agency issued over 38,000 passports. Under the leadership of Director McCoy the Atlanta Passport Agency has streamlined operations and put customer service at the forefront of their mission. Mr. Speaker, as a result of the hard work of Director McCoy and her staff, families are able to visit loved ones overseas, local business are able to grow internationally, and diplomatic work can continue without any impediments to travel.

On behalf of the citizens of the Sixth District of Georgia, I would like to thank Gale McCoy for the foundation she created that will ensure the Atlanta Passport Agency will continue serving the people of the Southeast. I would like to wish Gale and her family many more years of health and happiness.

PERSONAL EXPLANATION

HON. JAMES B. RENACCI
OF OHIO
IN THE HOUSE OF REPRESENTATIVES
Wednesday, November 30, 2016

Mr. RENACCI. Mr. Speaker, had I been present, I would have voted:
YEA on Roll Call No. 588
YEA on Roll Call No. 589

CONGRATULATIONS DR. JOHN JUNGMANN ON BEING NAMED AS MISSOURI'S TOP SUPERINTENDENT DEVELOPER OF THE YEAR

HON. BILLY LONG
OF MISSOURI
IN THE HOUSE OF REPRESENTATIVES
Wednesday, November 30, 2016

Mr. LONG. Mr. Speaker, I rise today to recognize Dr. John Jungmann, superintendent of Springfield Public Schools, who has been named as Missouri's top superintendent and later this year will be a candidate for the nation's top superintendent.

Dr. Jungmann was recognized by the Missouri Association of School Administrators for his efforts in moving Springfield Public Schools forward and understanding and addressing opportunity gaps for all students. In addition to these accomplishments, Dr. Jungmann challenged the community to think of ways to improve teaching and learning. He created innovative programs which included flexible schedules and the growth of summer learning, and initiated a three year plan that would grant laptops and tablets to every student, grades 3–12.

Dr. Jungmann is truly dedicated to improving the lives of our youth and has shown a passion for education that is worthy of deep admiration. I urge my colleagues to join me in congratulating him for this achievement. On behalf of Missouri's Seventh Congressional District, I wish Dr. Jungmann the best of luck in all his future endeavors.

HONORING LPL FINANCIAL ON THEIR NEW CAMPUS IN FORT MILL, SC

HON. MICK MULVANEY
OF SOUTH CAROLINA
IN THE HOUSE OF REPRESENTATIVES
Wednesday, November 30, 2016

Mr. MULVANEY. Mr. Speaker, I rise today to recognize LPL Financial and celebrate the grand opening of their new campus in my district in Fort Mill, South Carolina.

I have had the privilege to work with employees of LPL Financial through my service on the House Financial Services Committee.

LPL Financial is the largest independent broker-dealer in the United States, with more than 14,000 financial advisors and approximately $500 billion in assets. Through their advisors, LPL Financial helps my constituents and those across the country save to meet their financial goals, such as retirement or college, through investments in stocks, bonds, mutual funds and insurance.

Today, LPL Financial is celebrating the grand opening of their new campus in my district. I am sorry that I am not able to be at the ceremony in Fort Mill, but I have visited the new location and it is indeed impressive. It is a state of the art facility and incorporates sustainable design strategies to have minimal environmental impact. The campus will provide its employees with access to nature trails and proximity to retail shopping and restaurants. Onsite they included a health clinic and gym. I know that with this campus, LPL Financial has made a significant commitment to work-life balance and quality for its employees.

The new campus hosts more than 1,400 current LPL Financial employees, and the company has shared that this Fort Mill location will be the center for its continued growth and long-term expansion.

I am honored that LPL Financial selected my district and our state, and I am excited about the numerous opportunities this relocation will bring to South Carolina in the form of jobs and economic growth. I warmly welcome LPL Financial and all of its employees to South Carolina and wish them every success at this new location.

IN MEMORY OF LIEUTENANT COLONEL CECIL GLENN FOSTER

HON. BILL HUIZENGA
OF MICHIGAN
IN THE HOUSE OF REPRESENTATIVES
Wednesday, November 30, 2016

Mr. HUIZENGA of Michigan. Mr. Speaker, I rise today to honor Lt. Col. Cecil G. Foster, the 23rd Jet Ace pilot of the Korean War and a veteran of the Vietnam War. Lt. Col. Foster, a Midland, Michigan native, passed away at the age of 90 in July of 2016.

Lt. Col Foster was born on August 30, 1925. Upon completing high school he immediately enlisted in the United States Army Air Corps Aviation Cadet Program. In 1945, he achieved the rank of Second Lieutenant and became the Air Corps' 23rd Ace pilot when he shot down nine enemy aircraft during the Korean War.

In May of 2015, Lt. Col. Foster received the Congressional Gold Medal for his service to our nation. He also earned more than 65 military decorations during his 32 years of service with the United States Air Force. Lt. Col. Foster will be buried today at Arlington National Cemetery with full military honors.

Mr. Speaker, on behalf of the Second District of Michigan, we remember, honor, and thank Lt. Col. Foster for his service to Michigan and to our nation.

RECOGNIZING THE 40TH ANNIVERSARY OF LIGHTHOUSE CENTRAL FLORIDA

HON. DANIEL WEBSTER
OF FLORIDA
IN THE HOUSE OF REPRESENTATIVES
Wednesday, November 30, 2016

Mr. WEBSTER of Florida. Mr. Speaker, it is my pleasure to recognize the 40th anniversary of Lighthouse Central Florida. Lighthouse Central Florida has been serving individuals with visual impairment since 1976. Lighthouse Central Florida is dedicated to their mission to chart a course for living, learning and earning with vision loss.

Envisioning a community that engages and embraces environments accessible to all persons, Lighthouse is the only private non-profit offering services to people with visual impairment in the tri-county area. Lighthouse Central Florida has provided education, independent life skills and job training and placement to more than 100,000 people with visual impairment. The training programs are designed to help individuals who have recently lost part or all of their vision gain the skills needed to perform daily tasks and maintain employment.

Over the past 40 years, Lighthouse Central Florida has enriched the lives of individuals by providing them with the opportunity to gain greater independence and quality of life, and enjoy and benefit from participation in their communities. On behalf of the citizens of Central Florida, I applaud the efforts of those involved and the investments they are making in the lives of individuals with vision loss to provide them with job training, work experience and other tools necessary to lead independent, successful lives. I wish Lighthouse Central Florida many more years of quality service to our community.

CELEBRATING THE 100TH ANNIVERSARY OF THE ROTARY CLUB OF MICHIGAN CITY

HON. PETER J. VISCLOSKY
OF INDIANA
IN THE HOUSE OF REPRESENTATIVES
Wednesday, November 30, 2016

Mr. VISCLOSKY. Mr. Speaker, it is my distinct pleasure to congratulate the members of the Rotary Club of Michigan City, Indiana, as they celebrate the organization's 100th anniversary. In honor of this momentous occasion, the Rotary Club of Michigan City will be hosting an anniversary banquet on December 1, 2016, at the Barker Mansion in Michigan City.

On October 19, 1916, the Rotary Club was founded with goal of promoting civic development and public welfare. The original sixty-five members helped to develop a successful community in Michigan City. The club was officially chartered by Rotary International on December 1, 1916. Throughout the years, the Rotary Club motto of "service above self" has been the cornerstone of the organization's successes. Among its many extraordinary accomplishments, the Rotary Club has been a leader in the movement to establish the Indiana

Dunes State Park, and it assisted with the formation of a local Chamber of Commerce, the City Planning and Zoning Commission, and the Michigan City Historical Society. The organization's charitable endeavors include extensive fund-raising and support for the Boy Scouts of America, the Salvation Army, local law enforcement, the Rotary Polio Plus, a program that aids in bringing vaccinations to third world countries, and ShelterBox, which supplies immediate relief to disaster survivors. In 1990, the Michigan City Club Foundation was established. This outstanding foundation was created to support charitable programs involved in enhancing educational efforts. It has helped provide financial assistance for high school student scholarships, the Rotary Youth Leadership Awards, high school robotics programs, and various after-school programs.

The Rotary Club of Michigan City has been successful due to the unwavering dedication of its leadership and members. Northwest Indiana is not only grateful, but proud to have the organization's support for the past 100 years. For their significant contributions to their community and beyond, the members and leaders of the Michigan City Rotary Club are truly an inspiration to us all.

Mr. Speaker, I ask that you and my other distinguished colleagues join me in congratulating the Rotary Club of Michigan City on its 100th anniversary. For their remarkable dedication, commitment, and compassion shown through their service to the community of Northwest Indiana, the membership, past and present, is worthy of the highest praise.

HONORING ADAM CWERNER

HON. ELIOT L. ENGEL

OF NEW YORK

IN THE HOUSE OF REPRESENTATIVES

Wednesday, November 30, 2016

Mr. ENGEL. Mr. Speaker, I rise today to recognize the valuable civic engagement of one of our community members, Adam Cwerner, who is also being recognized by the Northeast Jewish Center at their Annual Gala Dinner Dance. Adam is one of two honorees on November 4, 2016.

Adam was born in Brooklyn to Betty and Jacob Cwerner. Along with his sister Gil, he spent many of his formative years in Brooklyn. Adam was a member of East New York Jewish Center which was located across the street from where his family lived.

After moving to Massapequa, Long Island, the family joined the Farmingdale Jewish Center. Adam went on to attend Stony Brook University, where he earned a Bachelor of Science in Economics. He continued his education at the State University of New York at Albany where he attained a Masters in Business Administration.

A position at an architectural firm in Westchester led to a move northward, and Adam settled in at Richard Meier & Partners Architects, where he has worked for almost thirty years as the firm's Controller.

After trying out five different synagogues when he moved to Yonkers, Adam decided to attend and eventually join the Northeast Jew-

ish Center, and he hasn't looked back. Adam was soon recruited by Marge Wise, then President of NEJC, for a seat on the Board of Trustees. He continued to serve on the Board for almost a decade, when the then Chairman of the Board suggested he take over the position. To this day, Adam still serves his congregants in that capacity.

Adam has meant so much to the Northeast Jewish Center community, and has been instrumental in the Center's growth and success. He is most deserving of this great recognition, and it is an honor to present him with a CONGRESSIONAL RECORD. Thank you again for all of your service to Yonkers.

IN HONOR OF J. TYLER WHITE

HON. ANDY BARR

OF KENTUCKY

IN THE HOUSE OF REPRESENTATIVES

Wednesday, November 30, 2016

Mr. BARR. Mr. Speaker, I rise to honor Justin Tyler White of Lexington, Kentucky who is stepping down as my District Director to take on a new role as the President of the Kentucky Coal Association. Tyler served our nation proudly as a member of the United States Marine Corps. He was deployed in both Iraq and Afghanistan. On behalf of a grateful nation, I thank him for his service and patriotism.

After eight years of service, Mr. White returned to Kentucky. He had great passion for his fellow veterans and was determined to improve the services provided by the Veterans Administration. He came to work in the Sixth Congressional District office, serving as a field representative and then as District Director. In his work in the district office, Mr. White continued to advocate for veterans. He organized a Veterans Coalition that meets regularly and has grown tremendously. He led the way on many successful programs and projects directed at improving the lives of America's veterans.

The leadership skills that Tyler learned in the Marine Corps carried over into private life. He built a strong team in the district office and served as a motivating and inspiring leader. He tirelessly served the people of the Sixth Congressional District. He leaves a lasting legacy as a servant leader.

I am honored to call Tyler White a loyal and trusted friend. I wish him all the best as he leaves to take on a new opportunity. Thank you to Tyler White for his friendship, his tireless work on behalf of the people of the Sixth District, and his outstanding service to our country.

HONORING THE REVEREND DR. BOISE KIMBER ON THE CELEBRATION OF HIS 30TH PASTORAL ANNIVERSARY

HON. ROSA L. DeLAURO

OF CONNECTICUT

IN THE HOUSE OF REPRESENTATIVES

Wednesday, November 30, 2016

Ms. DeLAURO. Mr. Speaker, it is with great pleasure that I rise today to join the congrega-

tion of the First Calvary Baptist Church and the many family, friends, and colleagues who have gathered this evening in extending my heartfelt congratulations to the Reverend Dr. Boise Kimber as he marks his 30th Pastoral Anniversary—a remarkable milestone for this outstanding member of our community.

Over the course of the last thirty years, Reverend Kimber's commitment to service through religious leadership has been unwavering. Under his direction, the First Calvary Baptist Church and its congregation have flourished, and as the former President of the Greater New Haven Clergy Association he brought spiritual growth to the entire community. In addition to his work in New Haven, Dr. Kimber is past immediate president of the Connecticut State Missionary Baptist Convention, an alliance of approximately eighty churches across the state, where he launched the Christian Leadership School, an accredited four-year Christian Education degree program. He has long been an active member of the National Baptist Convention, USA, Inc. serving as an Administrative Assistant for ten years and as the Executive Secretary of the Board of Directors for the past five years. Reverend Kimber also serves as a staff member for the Institute of Church Administration and Management at the Interdenominational Theological Center in Atlanta, Georgia.

Reverend Kimber has not only been a dedicated religious leader, but a strong voice for social justice, here in Connecticut and across the country. From housing development, police brutality and profiling, to workers' rights and other social issues, Reverend Kimber has stood against discrimination and injustice in its many forms. He is consultant to the office of Multicultural Affairs and the Multicultural Center at Southern Connecticut State University, a Fire Commissioner for the City of New Haven, a Director for Aids Interfaith Network, Inc., an advisor to local labor unions, and a member of Omega Psi Phi Fraternity, Inc. He is also the Director of the National Action Network, Inc., the Conference of National Black Churches, and Executive Director of the Social Justice Initiative.

Above and beyond his work in the church and on behalf of social justice issues, community leadership has always been a driving force for Reverend Kimber. His work to improve the quality of life for New Haven residents led him to political involvement. By encouraging citizens to participate and ensuring local concerns are heard by political leaders, Reverend Kimber has given voice to many who may not have otherwise been heard.

Tonight, as he marks his 30th pastoral anniversary, Reverend Kimber can be sure that his good work has touched the lives of many. As a spiritual guide, he has nourished the souls of many—often providing much needed comfort in the hardest of personal trials. Religious leader, community activist, mentor, and friend, the Reverend Dr. Boise Kimber has and continues to be an invaluable member of our community—striving to enrich the lives of others and inspiring a new generation to service. I am so pleased to join him his wife, Shevalle, his children LaShawn, Sherine, Shevalle and Savion, and his congregation in celebrating this remarkable milestone.

CELEBRATING THE 12TH ANNUAL NORTHWEST INDIANA INNOVATION INDUCTION CEREMONY

HON. PETER J. VISCLOSKY

OF INDIANA

IN THE HOUSE OF REPRESENTATIVES

Wednesday, November 30, 2016

Mr. VISCLOSKY. Mr. Speaker, it is with great respect and admiration that I congratulate Ivy Tech Community College and its regional partners who recently celebrated their 12th Annual Northwest Indiana Innovation Induction Ceremony. At the ceremony, which reflects the "Spirit of Innovation" in Indiana, eighteen individuals and twenty-one teams were inducted as members of the 2016–2017 Class of the Society of Innovators of Northwest Indiana. Of these individuals, several members were inducted as Society Fellows for their exceptional efforts in innovation. These individuals are Jon Groth, Chancellor Thomas Keon, Ph.D., Elizabeth Lynn, Ph.D., Sandra Chimon-Peszek Rogers, Ph.D., Mayor Joseph Stahura, and Barbara Eason-Watkins. Also honored were the recipients of the Society's team awards, Urschel Laboratories, Inc., which received the Accelerating Greatness Award, and the Grand Calumet River Partners in Restoration, which was honored with the Chanute Prize for Team Innovation. For their truly remarkable contributions to the community of Northwest Indiana and their unwavering commitment to cultivate a culture of innovation, these honorees were inducted at Horseshoe Casino, Hammond, on October 20, 2016.

The Society of Innovators of Northwest Indiana was created by Ivy Tech Northwest with the goal of highlighting and encouraging innovative individuals and groups within the not-for-profit, public, and private sectors, as well as building a culture of innovation in Northwest Indiana. The Northwest Region is led by Dr. Thomas G. Coley, Chancellor, Ivy Tech Community College, Northwest and North Central Regions. The importance of innovation in Northwest Indiana, as well as globally, is crucial in today's ever-changing economy.

The fellows selected by the Society of Innovators were chosen for their innovative leadership throughout Northwest Indiana and beyond. Jon Groth is the area director/principal of Porter County Career and Technical Education. Among his many accomplishments, Jon led the repurposing of a historic 1912 Grand Trunk Rail Depot, turning it into a 21st century classroom. He also initiated the first student-built energy alternative project in Indiana on a school roof. Chancellor Thomas Keon, Ph.D., led the unification of two college campuses into a single university, Purdue University Northwest, which is one of the first innovative educational mergers in Indiana. The merger creates more choices for students, promotes regional identity, and contributes to economic development in Northwest Indiana. Elizabeth Lynn, Ph.D., is the director and founder of Valparaiso University's Center for Civic Reflection (CCR). A truly innovative learning center, the CCR is nationally recognized and applies the use of humanities and civic conversations within communities in America. The center has trained more than 7,000 facilitators and led more than 20,000

people in public, community, and workplace dialogues. Sandra Chimon-Peszek Rogers, Ph.D., is the director of Calumet College of Saint Joseph's Biophysical Chemistry Department and a researcher of Alzheimer's disease. She developed an innovative curriculum combining lecture and hands-on learning that is especially helpful for struggling students. This award winning program has thrived and is a source of pride for the college. Mayor Joseph Stahura, of Whiting, Indiana, led the city's transformation into a flourishing 21st century destination. He has put life back into the community by re-establishing and beautifying the Whiting lakefront, revitalizing the downtown area, and bringing the National Mascot Hall of Fame to Whiting, to name just a few of his major accomplishments. Dr. Barbara Eason-Watkins is the Superintendent of Michigan City Area Schools. Under her leadership, the school system has flourished due to the collaboration of the community and county. Among her achievements, she launched the first NIPSCO Energy Academy in Indiana, the first STEM public elementary school, and the first construction technology program in Indiana.

Urschel Laboratories received the Greatness Award for Team Innovation, presented to Rick Urschel, President, for the company's inspiration to create future innovation. Urschel is now owned by its employees and recently completed a new $100 million, 350,000 square foot manufacturing facility and headquarters.

The Chanute Prize for Team Innovation was presented to the Grand Calumet River Partners in Restoration. Collaborating with eight companies and working with regulatory agencies, the clean-up and transformation of the Grand Calumet River has been astounding, with more than 80 percent of the river being revitalized over the past decade.

Mr. Speaker, I ask you and my other distinguished colleagues to join me in commending these noteworthy, inspiring innovators. The contributions each has made to society here in Northwest Indiana and worldwide are immeasurable and lifelong. For their truly brilliant innovative ideas, projects, and leadership, these recipients are worthy of the highest commendation.

CONGRATULATING THE CENTERS FOR CHILDREN AND FAMILIES ON THEIR NEW FACILITY

HON. K. MICHAEL CONAWAY

OF TEXAS

IN THE HOUSE OF REPRESENTATIVES

Wednesday, November 30, 2016

Mr. CONAWAY. Mr. Speaker, I rise today to congratulate an organization in my district, Centers for Children and Families, on the opening of their new facility.

Since 1957, Centers has helped strengthen individuals and families throughout West Texas by providing counseling for those who would otherwise be unable to afford these services. In addition to counseling services, Centers also provides assistance with life management skills, parenting classes, post-adoption support, and programs that help children have safe and positive supervised parental visits.

As a prior Chairman of the Board for Centers, I have been fortunate enough to see first-hand the great work that this organization does for the Permian Basin community. With the opening of their new facility, Centers will have quality space to carry on their long-standing legacy of helping people get through the difficult times they may be facing. I wish them best of luck in their future endeavors.

UNITED STATES GREEN BERET JAMES "JIMMY" MORIARTY

HON. TED POE

OF TEXAS

IN THE HOUSE OF REPRESENTATIVES

Wednesday, November 30, 2016

Mr. POE of Texas. Mr. Speaker, on Friday, November 4, 2016, a military base in Jafr, Jordan was attacked. A hail of gunfire suddenly rang out while three American soldiers were returning to base. The reason for the shots fired is still publicly unknown. Three Green Berets from the 5th Special Forces Group were killed in support of Operation Inherent Resolve.

One of these heroic men was Staff Sergeant James "Jimmy" Moriarty (27). SSgt. Moriarty was a Texas native, one of Houston's own. He was scheduled to come home to spend the holiday season with his family. His chair was empty at the Thanksgiving table this year. His voice was missing from the conversation. But he will not be forgotten.

Jimmy was unquestionably one of the best. Growing up in Houston, he earned his bachelor's degree in economics from the University of Texas and spoke fluent Arabic. As part of the 5th Special Forces Group, based out of Fort Campbell, Ky., he was more than three months into his third tour in Jordan.

Upon graduation from the University of Texas, Jimmy made the choice to serve his nation in the United States Army. Jimmy was a proud member of the United States Army Special Forces. He was a special breed, one of the few who met the requirements to be among the highest ranked military professionals in the United States, the Green Berets.

During his service, he earned the Good Conduct Medal, National Defense Service Medal, Global War on Terrorism Expeditionary Medal, Global War on Terrorism Service Medal, NCO Professional Development Ribbon and an Army Service Ribbon.

The brave men of the Green Beret are our nation's warriors. They take on the toughest missions that our nation faces. They are the absolute best that America has. These men are the forces who deter enemies who seek to harm the United States. They respond to terrorist activities to keep the United States safe. Proudly wearing silver wings on their chests they are without question America's finest.

Mr. Speaker, in the words of Marcus Luttrell, "In times of uncertainty there is a special breed of warrior ready to answer our Nation's call; a common man with uncommon desire to succeed. Forged by adversity, he stands alongside America's finest special operations forces to serve his country and the American people, and to protect their way of life." Jimmy Moriarty was one of these men.

Jimmy's father, U.S. Marine Corps Vietnam Veteran, James R. Moriarty wrote, "This is a young man who loved serving in the Army, was where he wanted to be, doing what he wanted to do." Moriarty was loved by his two sisters who incessantly saw to it that their younger brother would be a well rounded young man. It is without a doubt that this distinguished soldier will be missed by his family, friends, and community.

We grieve the loss of this American warrior, but we celebrate and honor his life and his service. We are fortunate to have a Green Beret like Moriarty standing in support of our country. We are fortunate that a man like Jimmy served our great nation. He stood for the best of those American ideals and values exemplified in Special Forces. He is a son of liberty. He epitomizes everything that America stands for. Our thoughts and prayers are with his family and friends.

At noon on December 5, 2016 taps will be played for the last time as Staff Sergeant James Moriarty is surrounded by his family and friends and will be buried in Arlington National cemetery next to thousands of other warriors who died for America.

And that's just the way it is.

PERSONAL EXPLANATION

HON. ROBERT HURT
OF VIRGINIA
IN THE HOUSE OF REPRESENTATIVES
Wednesday, November 30, 2016

Mr. HURT of Virginia. Mr. Speaker, I was not present for Roll Call vote #588 on H.R. 5422, To ensure funding for the National Human Trafficking Hotline, and for other purposes. Had I been present, I would have voted "yes."

COMMEMORATING THE CONTRIBUTIONS MADE BY CHARLES OGLETREE JR.

HON. JIM COSTA
OF CALIFORNIA
IN THE HOUSE OF REPRESENTATIVES
Wednesday, November 30, 2016

Mr. COSTA. Mr. Speaker, I rise today to recognize the achievements and contributions that Professor Charles Ogletree Jr. has made to the County of Merced. Professor Ogletree has positively impacted the lives of many people in Merced and throughout the nation. His efforts to transform the educational experience of underprivileged youth in Merced have created new pathways of opportunity for students.

Professor Ogletree has used his career experience as a Professor of Law at Harvard to give back to his hometown. Born in Merced, California, Professor Ogletree attended public schools and earned admission to Stanford University. He earned his Bachelor's degree and a Master's degree in Political Science. Upon receiving his Master's degree, Professor Ogletree earned his Juris Doctor from Harvard Law School. To list the publications authored, awards received, and lives changed by Professor Ogletree would present a task com-

parable to the writing of a small novel. Professor Ogletree's passion to promote equality of law under the constitution is a theme that has persisted throughout his entire career.

From 2002 to 2007, Professor Ogletree established a scholarship program with $50,000 in Merced. The scholarship offered low income youth a chance to work in recreation programs over the summer for up to 100 hours, making $7.00 an hour. Professor Ogletree has extended numerous scholarships to high schools in Merced County, including Golden Valley High School, Merced High School, and El Capitan High School. The tens of thousands of dollars he has offered to students in memory of fellow educators, family members, and friends, have substantially altered future education for Merced students around the country. To this day, the Charles Ogletree Family Scholarships are still offered to high school students in Merced.

As a Professor of Law and Founder and Executive Director of the Houston Institute for Race and Justice, Professor Ogletree will continue to promote the cause of equality. His unfailing willingness to give back to the people of Merced reminds us that his career is not one that has forgotten its humble roots.

Mr. Speaker, I respectfully ask my colleagues in the U.S. House of Representatives to join me in wishing Professor Ogletree continued success in his remarkable career as an academic and advocate for equality and justice. His life is a reminder of the success that follows an insatiable thirst for knowledge, and the charity that can come in its wake.

HONORING BERNICE SPRECKMAN

HON. ELIOT L. EMGEL
OF NEW YORK
IN THE HOUSE OF REPRESENTATIVES
Wednesday, November 30, 2016

Mr. ENGEL. Mr. Speaker, I rise today to honor an amazing public servant and an even better friend, former Westchester County Legislator Bernice Spreckman, who recently resigned after serving for 20 years as the Representative for the county's 14th District.

A longtime resident of Yonkers, Bernice was first elected in 1995 to the 14th district's legislative seat where she proudly represented and passionately advocated for the hard-working taxpayers of Yonkers and parts of Mount Vernon. Prior to becoming a county legislator, she served in several posts in Yonkers City government, including three terms as 2nd ward Council Member, Council Member-at-large, Vice Mayor and Chair of the City Council's Committees on Rules and Real Estate; she was also elected the first female President of the New York State Councilman's Association.

As County Legislator, Bernice was a tireless advocate for senior citizens, working to expand the epic program; organized an annual lobby day in Albany; worked in a bi-partisan manor to pass universal design legislation to benefit senior citizens and the disabled community; co-hosted an annual legislative speakout; and worked with State representatives to enact new "independent living" legislation to help protect seniors from being wrongfully displaced.

But for all of her great accomplishments, Bernice's greatest joy in life was always family. She has enjoyed the love and support of her wonderful family; her late husband Harry, who was her constant companion and champion supporter; her devoted sons Alan, and his wife Jill, Rory, Howie, and his wife Dana; she is the loving grandmother to Andrew, Evan, Jake, Jaclyn, Brian, Craig, Mason, Jackson and Julianna.

Though we never sat on the same side of the aisle, I always knew I could count on Bernice when it came to working together on behalf of our shared constituents. She was a tremendous force for good in the community, and I want to congratulate her on a remarkable career.

HONORING JOHN MONTY "JACK" ALLEN

HON. ZOE LOFGREN
OF CALIFORNIA
IN THE HOUSE OF REPRESENTATIVES
Wednesday, November 30, 2016

Ms. LOFGREN. Mr. Speaker, I rise today to recognize and honor the life of John Monty "Jack" Allen, who passed away on September 11, 2016. Jack was a wonderful friend and beloved member of our community whose passing is deeply felt. I have known Jack for all his life, and he will be greatly missed.

John Monty "Jack" Allen was born in 1946, the eldest of two children. Although an avid traveler, Jack lived his entire life in San Jose, California. Jack's family, the Aiellos, settled in Santa Clara Valley in Delight, Contadina Canning Company. Jack's father, Pete, owned a furniture store in Downtown San Jose for more than 50 years, was one of the founders of the Century Club, and was a mentor to me. His uncle, Jack, owned Paolo's Restaurant, a popular destination for local celebrities, including Joe DiMaggio and many elected officials. In fact, my husband, John, proposed to me at Paolo's.

Jack attended Trace Elementary, Hoover Junior High, and Lincoln High Schools, all within walking distance of his family home. He was indoctrinated into local politics from a very young age through his parents' involvement with the Democratic Party, and he volunteered for Democratic candidates and causes throughout his life.

Jack graduated from San Jose State University and became a Certified Public Accountant, a role that he held for the last forty years of his life. At any time, he served more than 400 clients, from small businesses to family members to corporations and trusts. He was known by all as a generous, efficient, and dedicated accountant, as evidenced by the loyalty of his clients.

Jack married Janice Paul in 1974, and they settled in the Willow Glen neighborhood of San Jose in 1976, raising three boys—all of whom attended local schools and shared Jack's passion for politics and history.

Jack was a curious and well-traveled soul, having crisscrossed Europe on a number of occasions, not to mention extensive domestic travels that took him to nearly all 50 states. His wife, Janice, was his favorite travel companion, even after their divorce. (Indeed, they had trips in the works at the time of his sudden passing.)

Jack was also dedicated to serving others and volunteered his time as treasurer and board member for local clubs and charities, from the San Jose Library Foundation to the Democratic Century Club and many more. He could always be counted on to be there for a friend—or a total stranger—in need and would never hesitate to help those who could not help themselves.

For all of this, Jack never sought fanfare, nor acclaim. His reward was the action itself and the knowledge that he made his corner of the world a little brighter for having been there.

He is survived by sons Peter, Chris, and Danny; their mother, Janice; sister, Judy; nieces Corinne and Tina; cousins Carolyn, Jenny, and John; dog, Cooper; and countless friends.

Mr. Speaker, our San Jose community mourns the passing of Jack Allen, but we are grateful for his life, his generosity, and his contributions.

IN RECOGNITION OF KEITH ORR AND MARTIN CONTRERAS FOR THEIR COMMUNITY ACTIVISM

HON. DEBBIE DINGELL

OF MICHIGAN

IN THE HOUSE OF REPRESENTATIVES

Wednesday, November 30, 2016

Mrs. DINGELL. Mr. Speaker, I rise today to recognize Keith Orr and Martin Contreras, two Ann Arbor LGBTQ businessmen and activists, on the date of UNIFIED—HIV Health and Beyond's 13th Annual Wine Cellar fundraiser. Mr. Orr and Mr. Contreras are successful business owners who have worked tirelessly to raise awareness and provide resources to the LGBTQ community in southeast Michigan.

Mr. Contreras and Mr. Orr have played a crucial role in building the LGBTQ community through their business and philanthropic initiatives. In 1995, they founded /aut/Bar, a gay bar and restaurant that today serves as a key pillar of the LGBTQ community in the Ann Arbor area. The couple also runs Common Language Books, an LGBTQ bookstore that also hosts authors, forums and serves as a social center for the gay community. Additionally, Mr. Contreras and Mr. Orr have been involved in many charitable causes, including UNIFIED—HIV Health and Beyond, which provides care, prevention and outreach services to individuals affected by HIV in southeast Michigan. Their sponsorship and support has been critical to the growth and development of UNIFIED and has allowed the organization to provide better care throughout the region.

Mr. Contreras and Mr. Orr's involvement in the LGBTQ and greater Ann Arbor area has helped make the city a great place to live and work. Their businesses not only effectively serve the gay community, but they also contribute to the multicultural and welcoming environment that has been critical to the growth and development of Ann Arbor. It is my hope that Mr. Contreras and Mr. Orr will remain active in promoting the values of tolerance and respect. Their leadership has effectively served the city's residents.

Mr. Speaker, I ask my colleagues to join me today in recognizing the Keith Orr and Martin Contreras for their success in business and impactful leadership in the community. Their success and activism are worthy of commendation, and it is my hope that they continue to play a leading role in the Ann Arbor community in the years ahead.

CONGRATULATING SOKA GAKKAI INTERNATIONAL

HON. MARC A. VEASEY

OF TEXAS

IN THE HOUSE OF REPRESENTATIVES

Wednesday, November 30, 2016

Mr. VEASEY. Mr. Speaker, I rise today to congratulate Soka Gakkai International (SGI), the Buddhist association of more than 12 million people, on celebrating 86 years since its founding.

On November 18, 1930, Tsunesaburo Makiguchi and Josei Toda founded the Soka Gakkai in Tokyo, Japan to spread the Buddhist ideals of equality, respect for all life and the connection of self and the environment. Makiguchi served as the first president of The Soka Gakkai and was succeeded by Toda as the second Soka Gakkai president. With the desire to further spread Buddhist philosophy across the world, Daisaku Ikeda founded Soka Gakkai International while he served as the third president of Soka Gakkai.

Today, Ikeda and the other founding presidents' work is evident in the 12 million individuals in 192 countries and territories who share the same beliefs and mission the founders established years ago. Most notably, the American branch of Soka Gakkai International is the largest and most diverse Buddhist community in the United States with 350,000 members organized in more than 500 chapters nationwide. In combination with its 100 centers, the members all actively engage in the promotion of sustainable living, human rights, and peace.

November the 18th has come to symbolize a day when each SGI member strengthens their own determination and sense of responsibility to be ambassadors of goodwill in the communities they serve. In the DFW Metroplex, members of Soka Gakkai International provide enormous contributions to the community they serve where their members are making individual contributions for peace and freedom.

I honor Soka Gakkai International's 86th anniversary celebration and for their lifetime commitment to peace.

CONGRATULATIONS TO SWI INDUSTRIAL SOLUTIONS FOR BEING AWARDED THE FOUNDER AWARD DEVELOPER OF THE YEAR

HON. BILLY LONG

OF MISSOURI

IN THE HOUSE OF REPRESENTATIVES

Wednesday, November 30, 2016

Mr. LONG. Mr. Speaker, I rise today to recognize and congratulate SWI Industrial Solu-

tions, an outstanding non-profit that provides more than 200 individuals with disabilities meaningful and dignified work, while expanding the work forces of other manufacturers. SWI Industrial Solutions was recognized by the Missouri Association of Manufacturers (MAM) and given the Founders Award for their 50 years of business in the Springfield community.

The Founder's award honors MAM founder, the late Jack T. Gentry, and is presented to select MAM member companies that preserve the manufacturing tradition and promote and advance manufacturing in Missouri.

In these 50 years, SWI Industrial Solutions has directly impacted the local economy in a positive way and has given countless individuals the confidence and training on how to be a good employee, and how to succeed at their jobs.

It is my honor to recognize SWI Industrial Solutions for this great achievement and wish its workers a joyous and well-earned celebration of their success. By creating jobs, delivering top-class products, and exhibiting exemplary work ethic for 50 years, SWI Industrial Solutions have made southwest Missouri a better place to live. It makes me proud to serve them, and all of Missouri's Seventh Congressional District.

HONORING CAREGIVERS OUTREACH MINISTRY EMPOWERMENT INC. 10TH ANNIVERSARY

HON. ELIOT L. ENGEL

OF NEW YORK

IN THE HOUSE OF REPRESENTATIVES

Wednesday, November 30, 2016

Mr. ENGEL. Mr. Speaker, I rise today to honor Caregivers Outreach Ministry Empowerment Inc. (C.O.M.E.) a remarkable organization in New York City that for 10 years has empowered family caregivers with accessible resources and knowledge to make comfortable choices and decisions that will have a positive impact upon the quality of life for themselves and their loved ones.

A family caregiver, sometimes called an informal caregiver is an unpaid individual—a spouse, partner, family member, friend coworker or neighbor—assisting others with activities of daily living and/or medical tasks. In New York City, 1.25 million family caregivers provide over one billion hours of unpaid care to elderly loved ones. Nationally, there are approximately 1.3 to 1.4 million-child caregivers who are between the ages of 8 and 18 providing care to a family member. Youth caregivers are often called a "hidden population," because they suffer from a systemic lack of support from their schools and communities.

Since its founding in 2006 by Diane Leona Cooper, C.O.M.E. has worked to educate, equip and empower community leaders with the tools to develop and implement the C.O.M.E. Outreach Support Model. The group has collaborated with a wide array of elected officials and organizations to advocate for family caregivers, and the work they have done in the community has been nothing short of remarkable.

As C.O.M.E. celebrates its 10th anniversary, I want to take the opportunity to thank their leadership team and staff for all of the good works they have done. It is wonderful to know I have such an amazing partner fighting for families in the community.

HONORING CHRIS GEORGE, RECIPIENT OF THE 2016 WILLARD M. McCRAE COMMUNITY DIVERSITY AWARD

HON. ROSA L. DeLAURO
OF CONNECTICUT

IN THE HOUSE OF REPRESENTATIVES

Wednesday, November 30, 2016

Ms. DeLAURO. Mr. Speaker, I am honored to rise today to join family, friends, and colleagues in extending my heartfelt congratulations to Chris George, Executive Director of Integrated Refugee and Immigrant Services (IRIS), as he is honored by Liberty Bank with their 2016 Willard M. McCrae Community Diversity Award.

Named in honor of Willard McCrae, past chairman of the Liberty Bank Board of Directors and founding member of the Liberty Bank Foundation Board of Directors, this annual award honors an individual who has made an "outstanding and ongoing contribution to the cause of promoting and celebrating diversity in the communities served by Liberty Bank." I can think of no one more deserving of such a recognition than Chris George.

Chris has dedicated a lifetime to promoting human rights, social justice and equal access to all. He began his career as a Peace Corps volunteer in the Sultanate of Oman and later worked with Quakers in Lebanese villages and refugee camps. He worked with Save the Children, primarily in the West Bank/Gaza Strip, was the director of the Middle East division of Human Rights Watch, and he directed the legislative strengthening project for the Palestinian Parliament during his tenure with the United States Agency for International Development (USAID).

He continued that unique dedication here in Connecticut through his work at IRIS and it is that good work that has earned him this very special honor. As the Executive Director, it has been through Chris' leadership that IRIS has grown into one of the most respected, vibrant refugee resettlement programs in Connecticut. Welcoming refuges from Somali, Iraq, Congo, Sudan, Cuba, and Columbia, IRIS has helped many families navigate the many difficulties associated with resettling in a new community, country, and culture.

From the time of its founding, our nation has welcomed those from other shores, particularly those whose own home countries have become too dangerous for them to stay. Whether boarding the Mayflower to escape religious persecution or fleeing from the many countries that are today caught in the midst of civil war, America has long been a safe haven for many. Chris has long championed the contributions refugees make to our communities and our country. Encouraging faith communities and other groups to co-sponsor refugee families, he has worked to bring together Connecticut's diverse residents to support refugee resettlement and has advocated vigorously for the U.S. government to allow more refugees

into the country. Most recently, when that increase was approved, IRIS and its community partners stepped up to welcome four hundred and sixty to our state. Under Chris' leadership, IRIS has not only built relationships and better understanding between Americans and the refugees, but between the different local organizations.

Throughout his professional life, Chris George has demonstrated a compassion and commitment that is second to none. He embodies the spirit in which the Willard McCrae Community Diversity Award was created and I am honored to join all of those gathered this evening in extending my sincere congratulations to him as he is bestowed with this very special recognition. Chris—many thanks for your service and best wishes for continued success.

TRIBUTE TO THE CAREER OF JOHN PEDROZO

HON. JIM COSTA
OF CALIFORNIA

IN THE HOUSE OF REPRESENTATIVES

Wednesday, November 30, 2016

Mr. COSTA. Mr. Speaker, I rise today to honor the career and achievements of Mr. John Pedrozo. John has been a life-long advocate and community leader for the people of the San Joaquin Valley and has passed on his committed spirit of service to others. His awareness of the unique issues that face Merced County, and the solutions he has offered in response, have proven to be valuable assets in the development of our Valley.

John's community ties to Merced are diverse and long-standing. After graduating from Our Lady of Mercy Catholic School in Merced, John moved on to graduate from Merced High School and Merced College soon after. John married his wife Kelly in 1979, and in her found someone who shared his commitment to improving the lives of others. Together John and Kelly raised three wonderful children: Kacie, Josh, and Anthony. They have followed John's example through both professional, and faith based engagements by assisting countless residents of the San Joaquin Valley throughout their careers.

John has served Merced County in multiple capacities, ranging from leadership roles in the Future Farmers of America during his youth, to his service on the Merced County Board of Supervisors. John was a member of the Merced Union High School District Board of Trustees before assuming his 12 year tenure on the Board of Supervisors. He has also served on the San Joaquin Joint Powers Authority for a number of years, some as chairman, which has enabled him to be a guiding voice on the direction of transportation projects in the San Joaquin Valley.

During his time on the Board of Supervisors, John was a tireless proponent for enhancing educational opportunities for the youth in his district. His commitment to expanding access to youth programs for the children of Merced has been instrumental in improving the state of education countywide. John's steadfast support of law enforcement has also helped make Merced County a safer place, and will not be forgotten.

As John moves forward in his life, there is no doubt that he will continue to find ways to help make Merced County a better area for all of its residents. His dedication to his family, friends, and constituents have provided a better future for the people of Merced County, and I am confident that his service will gain him further recognition as a man of honor and selflessness in the years to come.

Mr. Speaker, I urge my colleagues to join me in recognizing Mr. John Pedrozo for his contributions to Merced County. John's service and commitment to improving Merced County has laid the foundation for others to contribute as he has.

TRIBUTE IN HONOR OF THE LIFE OF KENNETH L. SCHROEDER

HON. ANNA G. ESHOO
OF CALIFORNIA

IN THE HOUSE OF REPRESENTATIVES

Wednesday, November 30, 2016

Ms. ESHOO. Mr. Speaker, I rise today to honor the life and work of a pioneer in Silicon Valley, Kenneth L. Schroeder, who died on October 26, 2016 at his home in Los Altos Hills, California, at the age of 70, due to complications of ALS.

Ken Schroeder was born in Illinois, earned a BSEE from the University of Wisconsin and an MBA from University of Pennsylvania's Wharton School of Business. He received numerous academic honors, including membership in Tau Beta Pi and was selected as one of the "125 People of Impact" at UW. His first job after Wharton was at Hewlett-Packard. He then joined Spectra Physics where he became General Manager of the Construction Laser Division. In 1979, Ken joined KLA Instruments as Vice President of Manufacturing, and became President and COO in 1991.

Under Ken's leadership, the company made great strides. Semiconductor test equipment became a multibillion dollar market, and KLA-Tencor was named one of the "Best Managed Companies" by Forbes Magazine. Electronic Business Magazine rated KLA-Tencor one of the best run semiconductor equipment companies in the world, and the company received accolades for its employee training programs. San Jose Magazine ranked KLA-Tencor as "one of the best places to work" in Silicon Valley. VLSI Research named Ken Schroeder "Most Valuable Executive" and elected him to its Hall of Fame. During his time as CEO of KLA-Tencor, sales doubled and retained earnings tripled.

Ken leaves his beloved wife, Fran Codispoti, his son Christian, his daughter-in-law Sarah and grandson Erik; his daughter Margaux and his son-in-law Brian. He also leaves his sister Nancy, his brother Robert, many loving family members and countless friends.

Ken Schroeder was a national treasure. He was a giant of a man, tremendously effective in business, big of heart, huge in his generosity and tall in stature. I consider it a great privilege to have known him and called him my friend, and he will be missed by all who had the privilege of knowing him.

Mr. Speaker, I ask the entire House of Representatives to join me in extending our most sincere condolences to the love of Ken's life, Fran, and to the entire Schroeder family.

HONORING JERRY CLUPPER AS HE IS AWARDED THE 2016 AMERICAN MANUFACTURING HALL OF FAME LEADERSHIP AWARD

HON. ROSA L. DeLAURO
OF CONNECTICUT
IN THE HOUSE OF REPRESENTATIVES
Wednesday, November 30, 2016

Ms. DeLAURO. Mr. Speaker, it is with great pleasure that I rise today to join the New Haven Manufacturers Association and the many family, friends, and colleagues who have gathered as Jerry Clupper, Executive Director of the Association, is honored with the 2016 American Manufacturing Hall of Fame Leadership Award. For more than two decades, Jerry has played an integral role in advancing manufacturing, as an industry and a career path and this award is a reflection of all of his good work.

Owner of Process Services, LLC and Executive Director of the New Haven Manufacturing Association for the last fifteen years, there are few who devoted as much time and energy to advocating for manufacturing in our state. Manufacturing has grown in so many ways yet too many hold tight to the stereotypical images of grimy factory floors and workers faces stained with grease and dirt. No one has worked harder to change that image than Jerry. He has spent countless hours meeting with his fellow manufacturers, collaborating with high school and college educators, and advocating for changes in the halls of Connecticut's General Assembly. From workforce development to investment in manufacturing, Jerry has and continues to be a catalyst for change—strengthening relationships between the community and the industry and inspiring a new generation of manufacturers.

I would be remiss if I did not take a moment to extend a personal note of thanks to Jerry. Over the years, he has helped myself and my staff on a variety of projects. He has joined me at local technical high schools to look at ways Congress can support skills training that better prepares students for local manufacturing jobs. We have visited community colleges where he has helped to develop curriculums for advanced manufacturing degrees that help those graduates meet the changing needs of our manufacturing industry. And it was under his leadership that the New Haven Manufacturing Association and I developed the concept and legislation for the Manufacturing Reinvestment Act. He has been an invaluable resource and what began as a working collaborative has grown into a cherished friendship.

Jerry Clupper has been a leader in Connecticut's manufacturing industry in every sense of the. word. His vision, dedication, and advocacy have renewed the spirit of an industry that has a long and proud Connecticut history. There is no one more deserving of being honored with the 2016 American Manufacturing Hall of Fame Leadership Award. I am honored to rise today to extend my heartfelt

congratulations to Jerry on this very special and prestigious recognition.

HONORING EMPRESS AMBULANCE SERVICES

HON. ELIOT L. ENGEL
OF NEW YORK
IN THE HOUSE OF REPRESENTATIVES
Wednesday, November 30, 2016

Mr. ENGEL. Mr. Speaker, I rise today to honor one of the great companies in my district, Empress Ambulance, which has provided outstanding emergency medical service to the City of Yonkers for over three decades.

In 1985, when Dan and Lenore Minerva acquired Empress Ambulance it was their mission, that since has been handed down to their sons Michael, Daniel and Matthew, that patient care and compassion would be the cornerstone on which the company would be built.

As the landscape in the healthcare industry changed for hospitals over the years, so too has it changed dramatically in the pre-hospital seam: These days an EMS company needs to have trained professionals and state of the art equipment to manage a medical emergency on the street or in someone's home. Empress has accepted this challenge and today they are the preeminent provider of pre-hospital care and ambulance transportation services in our region. With over 90 vehicles and more than 400 highly trained and compassionate employees, Empress is answering the call 24 hours a day, seven days a week.

In recent years, Empress has seen unprecedented growth in the region. In addition to Yonkers, Empress Ambulance is currently the emergency medical services provider for the cities of New Rochelle, White Plains, Mount Vernon and Pelham. Additionally, the company provides advanced life support services in Yorktown and basic life support supplemental staff in Hawthorne, Mohegan Lake and Peekskill. They have also recently been named the provider of choice to operate four 9-1-1 advanced life support ambulances by Montefiore Medical Center for the Fire Department of New York 9-1-1 System.

This year, St. Joseph's Medical Center is honoring Empress Ambulance Service for the remarkable contributions the company has made to both the Center and the community as a whole. I want to take the opportunity to congratulate the entire Empress team, and thank them for all their incredible work in our area.

CONGRATULATIONS TO HARRY S. TRUMAN FOR RECEIVING THE PRESTIGIOUS HONOR OF BEING NAMED A NATIONAL BLUE RIBBON SCHOOL

HON. BILLY LONG
OF MISSOURI
IN THE HOUSE OF REPRESENTATIVES
Wednesday, November 30, 2016

Mr. LONG. Mr. Speaker, I rise today to recognize Harry S. Truman Elementary School

for receiving the prestigious honor of being named a National Blue Ribbon School.

Harry S. Truman was one of 329 schools nationwide to be recognized as a Blue Ribbon School.

This national award recognizes schools that practice exemplary teaching and learning. For 34 years, the National Blue Ribbon Schools Program has been rewarding excellence in students and faculty and to date fewer than 8,500 schools have been granted this honor.

Harry S. Truman Elementary was granted this award in large part due to their high academic performance on standardized tests. This is a distinguished award that recognizes the academic success of a school.

I am honored to recognize Harry S. Truman Elementary School for their hard work and dedication in educating our future leaders of Missouri. On behalf of Missouri's Seventh Congressional District I ask all of my colleagues to join me to congratulate Harry S. Truman Elementary School.

HONORING MOUNT SINAI MISSIONARY BAPTIST CHURCH

HON. MARC A. VEASEY
OF TEXAS
IN THE HOUSE OF REPRESENTATIVES
Wednesday, November 30, 2016

Mr. VEASEY. Mr. Speaker, I rise today to honor Mount Sinai Missionary Baptist Church in celebration of its 60th Anniversary and its six-decade history of service to the community of Fort Worth, Texas.

Founded in 1956, Mount Sinai Missionary Baptist Church began through its commitment to fellowship. Since its founding, Mount Sinai Missionary Baptist Church has committed its efforts to establishing a safe environment for all those seeking spiritual guidance and the desire to share the Gospel of Jesus Christ through preaching, teaching, and ministry. For six decades, Mount Sinai Missionary Baptist Church's ministry team has inspired and positively changed the lives of people throughout Fort Worth.

For the past twenty years, Bishop B.C. McPherson II has led Mount Sinai Missionary Baptist Church's membership and its affiliate company Sininian Development Inc. (SDI), a community development organization. Together, they have invigorated the Southside communities of Fort Worth through crime reduction and affordable housing. Bishop McPherson has ensured throughout his tenure that every member can still receive a personal word with him even as the Church has grown its congregation.

Mount Sinai not only offers fellowship for those seeking spiritual guidance at the church in Fort Worth, but also extends its services through its Real Alive Word, R.A.W., online classes. These classes offer spiritual seekers with biblical foundations, syntax, culture and much more. Both traditional and non-traditional religious avenues have contributed to an increase in the number of new hopeful leaders in the DFW Metroplex.

I honor Mount Sinai Missionary Baptist Church's 60th Anniversary celebration and its dedication to the spiritual development of the Fort Worth community.

CONGRATULATING ROBYN STUART ON HER RETIREMENT FROM THE GRAPEVINE POLICE DEPARTMENT

HON. KENNY MARCHANT

OF TEXAS

IN THE HOUSE OF REPRESENTATIVES

Wednesday, November 30, 2016

Mr. MARCHANT. Mr. Speaker, I rise today to congratulate Senior Officer Robyn Stuart on her well-earned retirement from the Grapevine Police Department, in the city of Grapevine, Texas, after twenty-two years of dedicated service.

Stuart's esteemed career began with the Brownfield Police Department in 1993 where she served with distinction until joining the Fort Worth Marshal's Office in 1995 as a Deputy Marshal.

In 1996 she began her service in Grapevine, where she honorably served her community with the highest degree of professionalism for more than two decades. Throughout her tenure with the department, Stuart received seven commendation letters recognizing her outstanding service and dedication to the City of Grapevine.

Over her twenty-two year career, Stuart has completed more than 1,580 hours of training and has achieved the certification of Master Peace Officer. Additionally, she has served as a member of the Grapevine Police Department SWAT team, specializing as a hostage negotiator; a National Academy of Professional Driving (NAPD) instructor; and as a member of the Grapevine Police Department Critical Incident Stress Management/Peer Support Team.

Mr. Speaker, it is a pleasure to recognize the tireless efforts Senior Officer Robyn Stuart has contributed to the safety and security of the City of Grapevine. I ask all of my distinguished colleagues to join me in congratulating Robyn Stuart and her many years of service.

HONORING MICHAEL MINERVA

HON. ELIOT L. ENGEL

OF NEW YORK

IN THE HOUSE OF REPRESENTATIVES

Wednesday, November 30, 2016

Mr. ENGEL. Mr. Speaker, those who dedicate their lives to serving others professionally are a true asset to the community. For 28 years, Michael Minerva has been an asset to Westchester, through his amazing work with Empress Ambulance Service and our friends at St. Joseph's Medical Center.

Mike got his start in Yonkers working for American Ambulette, the company his parents, Dan and Lenore started in 1976. It was during this time that Mike was first introduced to the leadership and mission at St. Joseph's Medical Center.

In 1985, his family bought Empress Ambulance Service. For the next twenty years, Mike was fortunate to work side by side with the biggest driving force of his professional career, his mentor, business partner and "Mom" Lenore Minerva.

In 2008 Mike was promoted to President of Empress and has worked tirelessly to continue to grow the business and provide the highest level of pre-hospital care in the State. Under his guidance, Empress has been recognized as the leader in the ambulance industry with over 400 EMS professionals on staff and a fleet of over 90 vehicles. Mike was asked to serve on the Saint Joseph's Medical Center's Board of Directors in 2005, and his extensive knowledge of the healthcare industry, especially in the field of emergency services has been a tremendous asset to Saint Joseph's Medical Center for the many years he has served as a member of its Board of Trustees.

Mike also finds many ways to give back to the community that has afforded him so much. In addition to volunteering his time to Saint Joseph's Medical Center's Board of Trustees, where he is part of the Executive Committee, he is also on the Board of the Yonkers Police Athletic League and the Yonkers Chamber of Commerce.

But Mike's great love is always family. He has been married to his high school sweetheart, Bobbi, for over 27 years. Together they have raised five wonderful and accomplished children. Danielle, the head athletic trainer for Mercy College, Hayle, a full-time performer for Disney World FL, Michael, a recent college graduate who now works at Empress, and Jack and Lyndsey, a junior and sophomore respectively at Pleasantville High School.

This year, St. Joseph's Medical Center is honoring Mike at their annual Autumn in New York Ball. He is incredible deserving of this great honor. Congratulations to Mike and his family.

21ST CENTURY CURES ACT

HON. MICHAEL G. FITZPATRICK

OF PENNSYLVANIA

IN THE HOUSE OF REPRESENTATIVES

Wednesday, November 30, 2016

Mr. FITZPATRICK. Mr. Speaker, I do support many of the measures in the 21st Century Cures Act. It will increase choice, access, and quality in health care for all Americans by accelerating the discovery and development of new treatments for patients. The bill ensures our nation's standing as the biomedical innovation capital of the world. It provides funding at the National Institutes for Health to support cancer research and make progress in prevention, screening, treatment, and care.

The 21st Century Cures act will establish a data collection system to track the incidence and prevalence of neurological conditions, which includes MS. This new data system could one day lead to a cure for debilitating diseases, which have aspects we currently do not understand.

I wish this bill contained the "Right-to-Try," which would give my constituents Matt Bellina and Frank Mongiello, both diagnosed with ALS, access to experimental and clinical stage treatments to improve their quality of life.

But this bill does emphasize rare disease research and provides funding which will have a meaningful impact on those afflicted with rare diseases like ALS, Alzheimer's, Parkinson's, Duchenne muscular dystrophy, and mitochondrial disease. As a member of the Mitochondrial Disease Caucus and Rare Disease Caucus, I know this bill will have a big impact for those like Liz Kennerley, who has been a passionate advocate for all those suffering from mitochondrial disease and other rare diseases.

By establishing new review pathways at the FDA, 21st Century Cures will advance new drug therapies for patients with rare, serious, or life-threatening disease. It gives my young constituents living with Duchenne's, like Jake Wesley, a chance to live a longer, better life.

The 21st Century Cures helps individuals and families in mental health crisis. It will serve to increase access to trained professionals, improves communications between doctors and families while ensuring that federal funds are applied to programs that work, supporting organizations in Bucks County like the Lenape Valley Foundation and the National Alliance on Mental Illness. Enhancing crisis response, promoting early intervention, and integrating mental health, substance use and primary care will go a long way in helping the one in five individuals who have a mental health condition so they can live well and thrive.

The bill will grant funds to states to supplement opioid abuse prevention and treatment activities, such as improving prescription drug monitoring programs.

Mr. Speaker, while this bill accelerates the development of life-saving devices and therapies, the 21st Century Cures Act fails to protect patients against dangerous medical devices. For the past two years, I've sought medical device reform in Congress. I sought to raise awareness and advance legislation that protected patients and altered FDA processes and procedures to allow for maximum innovation and maximum safety. Congress ignored the victims affected by faulty, dangerous medical devices and what is more disappointing we were denied a hearing.

I support the measures in the 21st Century Cures Act, but I am concerned that it fails to provide adequate medical device protections for patients. There are two amendments missing to the 21st Century Cures Act: the Medical Device Guardians Act and Ariel Grace's Law.

CONGRATULATIONS RICK ZIEGENFUSS FOR RECEIVING THE 2016 MISSOURIAN AWARD DEVELOPER OF THE YEAR

HON. BILLY LONG

OF MISSOURI

IN THE HOUSE OF REPRESENTATIVES

Wednesday, November 30, 2016

Mr. LONG. Mr. Speaker, I rise today to recognize and congratulate Rick Ziegenfuss, for receiving the 2016 Missourian Award. Rick is the city administrator for Hollister, Missouri. The Missourian Award recognizes native Missourians for their outstanding accomplishments in business, civic, arts or politics.

It is important that we strive to better the community we live in and it is apparent that Mr. Ziegenfuss from Missouri's 7th Congressional District has continually done that.

The Missourian Award, created by local Springfield business and community leader

Ralph Slavens and his late wife Corrine, is a prestigious award that acknowledges the most accomplished citizens of Missouri and to receive the award one must have been born in the state of Missouri.

I am proud of the initiative that Mr. Ziegenfuss has taken to make the great state of Missouri the best it can be. I urge my colleagues to join me in congratulating him on this tremendous honor.

HONORING RICHARD H. GREIF, MD

HON. ELIOT L. ENGEL
OF NEW YORK
IN THE HOUSE OF REPRESENTATIVES
Wednesday, November 30, 2016

Mr. ENGEL. Mr. Speaker, I rise today to honor a distinguished member of the community whose work at St. Joseph's Medical Center has been of great service to countless Westchester residents, Dr. Richard H. Greif.

Dr. Greif was born in New York City and grew up in Morristown, New Jersey. After high school, he attended Cornell University, majoring in biology. He then went on to medical school at New York Medical College where he was inducted into Alpha Omega Alpha—the Medical Honor Society—and graduated in 1975. After medical school he completed an Internal Medical Residency at Metropolitan Hospital and a Cardiovascular Disease Fellowship at St. Vincent's Medical Center in New York City.

Dr. Greif joined the Saint Joseph's Medical Staff in 1981. He is currently President of the Medical Board and has been serving as the Co-Director of Cardiology since 2013. He has been a member of the Saint Joseph's Medical Board and Chairman of the Quality and Performance Improvement Committee for over 30 years. He has been an Assistant Professor at New York Medical College since 1981; Adjunct Professor at Manhattan College since the late 1980's and is a Fellow of the American College of Cardiology.

Dr. Greif has supervised the Medical Center's Family Medicine Resident ICU and Cardiology rotations since 1981 and precepted New York Medical College students from 1983 to 2015. In the field of research he was the co-investigator in the landmark multi-center TIMI 2B trial testing thrombolytic therapy for acute myocardial infarction. He has been listed many times among "Best Doctors in Westchester" by Westchester Magazine and recognized by Castle Connolly as a "Top Doctor" in the New York Metro Area from 2006 to 2016.

Of course, Dr. Greif's true passion is his family. He resides in Westchester with his wife Victoria. They have three children; Arel, Dylan and Shana. Arel works in New York City in the media industry, Dylan is a graphic designer working and living in Brooklyn and Shana is a second year Internal Medicine Resident in Los Angeles. All three children did volunteer work at Saint Joseph's.

This year, St. Joseph's Medical Center is honoring Dr. Richard Greif at their annual Autumn in New York Ball. I want to take the opportunity to congratulate him on this wonderful honor, and thank him for all of his amazing work in the community. He is most deserving of this incredible recognition.

HONORING THE LIFE OF JOHN J. AREIAS

HON. JIM COSTA
OF CALIFORNIA
IN THE HOUSE OF REPRESENTATIVES
Wednesday, November 30, 2016

Mr. COSTA. Mr. Speaker, I rise today to honor the life and achievements of John J. Areias, who recently passed away this week at age 96. Mr. Areias was an exceptional father, grandfather, husband, dairyman, and friend, whose depth of commitment to improving the San Joaquin Valley can be matched only by his depth of commitment to those he loved.

Born on April 21st, 1921 to Jesse Areias and Genevieve Silva Areias, John J. Areias was a first generation Portuguese-American from Volta, California. His family moved from Portugal's Azore Islands to California to begin a dairy, and to support a family. John's father put $10 down on 640 acres of land in western Merced County, where John spent much of his youth learning how to be a dairyman alongside his eight siblings. He was the valedictorian of Volta elementary, and moved on to graduate from Los Banos high school in 1940.

John had an insatiable hunger for community involvement, which began with his high school's student government, and the Future Farmers of America. His leadership position in the FFA granted him many opportunities early on, one of which called on him to present cattle at the California State Fair. This is also where he would meet the love of his life, Mary, whom he married shortly thereafter. John and his brother Jesse then moved on to begin their own dairy, which quickly became the first grade A dairy in the Los Banos Dairymen's Association. Eventually their dairy became one of the biggest and most successful in California, but they never lost sight of the role family should play in their business. John's children played the same part that he did when he was younger, lending a hand in day to day dairy operations to support the family business.

John was also very politically connected with Central California Democratic circles. He served as Chairman of the Merced County Democratic Central Committee and had been a delegate to the Democratic National Convention in 1960, where John F. Kennedy earned the nomination of his party as candidate for President of the United States. John was also a devout Catholic, serving as the Grand Knight for the Knights of Columbus.

John is survived by his four children, Marcia, Lucia, Kathleen, and Rusty, all of whom left John immensely proud of their success. He is also succeeded by his five grandchildren, Eva, Nina, Bianca, Alexis, and Austin.

Mr. Speaker, I rise to commemorate John Areias Sr.'s life for his outstanding character as an entrepreneur, public servant, family man, and friend. His life is a testament to the power of the American dream, and the joy that can accompany it. He was a powerful role model for the people of the Central Valley, and will be deeply missed by everyone that had the pleasure of knowing him. I join John's family in honoring his life, and love for our community.

HONORING THE CONNECTICUT MENTAL HEALTH CENTER ON THE OCCASION OF THEIR 50TH ANNIVERSARY

HON. ROSA L. DeLAURO
OF CALIFORNIA
IN THE HOUSE OF REPRESENTATIVES
Wednesday, November 30, 2016

Ms. DeLAURO. Mr. Speaker, it is with my sincere thanks and appreciation that I rise today to join the many who have gathered to mark the 50th Anniversary of the Connecticut Mental Health Center—a remarkable milestone for this exceptional institution.

In 1963, President John F. Kennedy signed into law the Community Mental Health Act, a pioneering piece of legislation that sought to transform the way in which we, as a society, approached mental health treatment. It was from this legislation that the Connecticut Mental Health Center, a unique partnership between the State of Connecticut and Yale University, was inspired and conceived. Opening its doors in 1966, CMHC has been an invaluable resource to our community for half a century, not only as a service provider but as a leader in research, education, and community.

Each year, more than five thousand of our most vulnerable citizens count on the Center for comprehensive clinical, addiction, and rehabilitative services. For fifty years, the Connecticut Mental Health Center has been transforming the lives of those with mental illness and addiction issues by providing a safe space where they can find the services they need to live, work, learn, and participate fully in their community.

Their outreach programs for the homeless, those who are at serious risk for mental illness, or involved with the criminal justice system have helped to ensure that those most at risk are able to find the care they need. CMHC's community education programs have helped community leaders better understand mental illness and addiction and their professional education programs have trained hundreds in Psychiatry, Neuropharmacology, Psychology, Psychiatric Nursing, as well as Pastoral and Social Work. In addition, CMHC is a national leader in cutting-edge research and innovation.

CMHC's mission statement concludes with a message to which they have strived for fifty years: "Continued success means transforming our systems of care to be suitable to the new environment, while preserving our fundamental commitment to excellent culturally sensitive, clinical, rehabilitative, and preventative services, linked to nationally recognized research and educational programs." It is their dedication to continually ensuring that the care they are providing is meeting the changing needs of their clients and community that has been their greatest gift.

I have had the privilege to work with the Connecticut Mental Health Center on a variety of issues over my tenure in Congress and have always been in awe of the outstanding work that they do. Today, as administrators, staff, supporters, and community leaders gather to mark this golden milestone, I am honored to extend my heartfelt congratulations to the Connecticut Mental Health Center on their

50th Anniversary. I have no doubt that they will continue their invaluable work for many more years to come.

TRIBUTE TO PAUL E. SCHICKLER

HON. DAVID YOUNG
OF IOWA

IN THE HOUSE OF REPRESENTATIVES

Wednesday, November 30, 2016

Mr. YOUNG of Iowa. Mr. Speaker, I rise today to recognize Paul E. Schickler, President of DuPont Pioneer, ahead of his retirement on January 1, 2017. Paul began his tenure with Pioneer as an accountant back in 1974. His 42 years of dedicated service has produced enduring success, and with his leadership, the company has experienced some of its most prosperous and successful years of operation.

Paul joined Pioneer after receiving an undergraduate degree from Drake University. He displayed a tireless work ethic as he pursued his MBA while working full-time at Pioneer. It was apparent from the start that he was destined for excellence within the company. Throughout his years at Pioneer, Paul has served in a number of roles, including: Controller; Vice President of Human Resources, Learning and Development, Communications and Real Estate Management; Vice President, Director, Latin America Operations, later expanding to include Mexico and Africa; Vice President, International Operations; Agriculture and Nutrition Business Development Director; and finally, in 2007, DuPont Vice President and the 11th President of Pioneer.

Paul's commitment to global agriculture and the fight against world hunger goes even beyond his work at Pioneer. He and his wife Claudia have used their own personal success to benefit the World Food Prize, donating resources to expand the foundation's Global Youth Institute to every Iowa high school. For the last several years Paul has shared his vision for global agriculture with the delegation of youth in attendance of the World Food Prize Week.

Mr. Speaker, I applaud and congratulate Paul on his upcoming retirement. He will now be able to spend his well-deserved time off sharing his love of golfing and skiing with his daughters, their husbands, and six grandchildren. It is with great honor that I recognize him today. I ask that my colleagues in the United States House of Representatives join me in recognizing Paul's accomplishments and service and in wishing him and his family nothing but the best.

CHARITY DOES NOT COME FROM GOVERNMENT AGENCIES

HON. JOHN J. DUNCAN, JR.
OF TENNESSEE

IN THE HOUSE OF REPRESENTATIVES

Wednesday, November 30, 2016

Mr. DUNCAN of Tennessee. Mr. Speaker, the best, most effective charity does not come from government agencies, which mainly help those who work for the agencies. The best,

kindest charity comes from one individual helping another. I often tell young people to try to pull themselves away from their very addictive screens (computer, iPads, television) and go out and help a live human being. Their lives will mean more if they do. That is why I was so impressed by Bob Hunt's column in the November 25 Knoxville News-Sentinel by the work started by Christine Maentz, and carried on now by her, her husband Scott, and others helping feed Knoxville's homeless. I would like to call this column to the attention of my colleagues and other readers.

DROPS OF CHARITY BETTER THAN DROUGHT

(By Bob Hunt)

"In the first centuries of Christianity, the hungry were fed at a personal sacrifice, the naked were clothed at a personal sacrifice, the homeless were sheltered at a personal sacrifice. And because the poor were fed, clothed and sheltered at a personal sacrifice, the pagans used to say about the Christians 'See how they love each other.'

"In our own day the poor are no longer fed, clothed and sheltered at a personal sacrifice, but at the expense of the taxpayers. And because the poor are no longer fed, clothed and sheltered, the pagans say about the Christians 'See how they pass the buck.'"—Feeding the Poor at a Sacrifice, by Peter Maurin (1877–1949)

Peter Maurin was a Catholic philosopher in the tradition of Christian personalism. He, along with Dorothy Day, founded the Catholic Worker movement, which today is represented by over 200 houses of hospitality that offer food, clothing and shelter to the poor. Not willing to wait for the government or church to organize official relief efforts, Maurin believed that it was the personal responsibility of Christians to commit themselves to serving those in need by way of personal sacrifice through the corporal and spiritual works of mercy. Maurin pointed to St. Francis of Assisi as the inspiration for Christian personalism. Today, another Francis is inspiring many with his message that the Church is a field hospital for the wounded, and that Christians must leave the confines of the church building and, "go outside and look for people where they live, where they suffer, and where they hope."

Christine Maentz saw a need last December. She was concerned that the poor who often gather under the bridge at Broadway and Magnolia would have nothing to eat on Christmas. She convinced her husband, Scott, to make dozens of peanut butter and jelly sandwiches with her and take them downtown. They passed them out to the homeless under the bridge while a rainstorm poured down around them. Christine and Scott have been back every month since, now bringing bunches of friends with them along with items of clothing and hygiene packs, in what they call their Bridge Ministry. It's an example of Christian personalism. The Maentz' didn't ask permission from their pastor or the City Council. The money spent in the effort was their own. They saw the need, took personal responsibility and made a personal sacrifice to meet it. Will it solve all the problems of the homeless? No. Will it feed every hungry person in the city? No. But, it's a drop.

A journalist once asked Mother Teresa, "Mother, all that you do here amounts to nothing more than a drop in the bucket. Why do

you bother?" Mother replied, "It's a drop." The question to ask, I think, isn't, "Why bother?" The question to ask is, "Where are all the other drops? Why isn't that bucket full yet? Where's your drop? Where's mine?"

Christine and Scott Maentz, and the others who now join them, offer their drops. They would like to eventually expand the Bridge Ministry to every Saturday. But, that will require more people willing to offer their drops. There are other needs in the city waiting to be filled, waiting for others to offer their drops. The bucket is very large. But, each drop is one more drop toward filling that bucket. Perhaps another rainstorm can be started. It all begins with one person taking personal responsibility and making a personal sacrifice. So, what's your Saturday look like?

HONORING CRAIG RAPPOPORT

HON. ELIOT L. ENGEL
OF NEW YORK

IN THE HOUSE OF REPRESENTATIVES

Wednesday, November 30, 2016

Mr. ENGEL. Mr. Speaker, I rise today to recognize a member of our community, Craig Rappoport, who is also being recognized by the Northeast Jewish Center at their Annual Gala Dinner Dance.

Craig was born in the Bronx in 1966 to Herman and Shirley Rappoport. The family quickly moved to Yonkers and he has lived at his house on Minerva Drive since he was a year old. Craig attended Westchester Day School and attended high school at Mesivta Ohr Torah. He majored in both accounting and economics at Queens College and graduated Magna Cum laude with an award for highest grade point average in economics. He worked for the CPA firm Miller Ellin & Co. located in Manhattan until 1995.

Craig and his family joined Midchester Jewish Center when Craig was a youngster, and they quickly became active members. Craig later joined and was very active in the newly formed Yonkers Orthodox Minyan in 1989.

In 2005, Craig came to Northeast Jewish Center and continued his active involvement. He first served as finance committee chair and then Vice President, in addition to a 2 year stint as housing committee chair. Craig then became Treasurer of the Men's Club and then Treasurer of the Synagogue. He is still instrumental in the synagogue's finances today and helps run the office. He maintains the synagogue's mailing list of members and nonmembers and updates the yahrtzeit lists, and he helps chair the Book of Remembrance and New Years' Greetings fundraisers.

Craig is also very active in other aspects of the synagogue's operations. He helps prepare for the high holidays by selling seats, helping to set up for the services, ushering at the services, and he even buys the wine and grape juice for the weekly kiddush and davens pesukei d'zimrah on Shabbat mornings.

It is no surprise why Craig has been selected as one of two honorees this year by the Center, as he has made so many tremendous contributions to its community. It is an honor to present Craig Rappoport with a CONGRESSIONAL RECORD and I wish to congratulate him on receiving this wonderful recognition. He is certainly most deserving of this great honor.

HONORING THE CAREER OF SERGEANT JIM PACHECO

HON. JIM COSTA
OF CALIFORNIA

IN THE HOUSE OF REPRESENTATIVES

Wednesday, November 30, 2016

Mr. COSTA. Mr. Speaker, I rise today to recognize the career and achievements of Sergeant Jim Pacheco in honor of his retirement from the Merced County Sheriff's Department. Jim Pacheco's wide ranging engagements in law enforcement have provided the Merced Sheriff's Department with a well-rounded law enforcement officer that will be deeply missed by those who had the pleasure to serve by his side.

Sergeant Pacheco has served for the Merced Sheriff's Department for nearly 30 years. He was first hired as a reserve deputy sheriff in 1987, and was sworn in as a deputy sheriff only two years later in 1989. He then served for 14 years until he was promoted to the rank of Sergeant in 2003. During the progression of his career, Sergeant Pacheco had a wide sampling of the many duties performed by the Merced Sheriff's Department. From the Sheriff's Dive Team, to numerous narcotics task forces, and as a SWAT negotiator, Jim Pacheco has served in many capacities to ensure public safety.

In 1999, Sergeant Pacheco was recognized with the Officer of the Year award. His colleagues overwhelmingly recall his willingness to rise above the call of duty to serve his community well beyond the normal scope of expectations. Jim Pacheco's heroism has been resoundingly felt and heard by the people of Merced County, and we hope that his retirement can bring him the solace and relaxation that he has so rightly earned.

Mr. Speaker, I urge my colleagues to join me in recognizing Sergeant Jim Pacheco's career in the Merced Sheriff's Department over the course of the last 30 years. The retirement of distinguished officers like Sergeant Pacheco leave a tangibly positive mark on law enforcement agencies that can be seen and felt by communities in both the immediate, and future. We honor Jim Pacheco's commitment to the County of Merced, and hope that future law enforcement agents can take reference from such a fine officer's career.

H. CON. RES. 165

HON. EARL BLUMENAUER
OF OREGON

IN THE HOUSE OF REPRESENTATIVES

Wednesday, November 30, 2016

Mr. BLUMENAUER. Mr. Speaker, yesterday, the House of Representatives passed unanimously H. Con. Res. 165, a resolution reaffirming the longstanding United States policy in support of a bilaterally-negotiated settlement of the Israeli-Palestinian conflict and our continued opposition to United Nations Security Council resolutions imposing a solution to the conflict.

To be clear, though only the parties themselves can agree to end the conflict, the United States has engaged in efforts to create better conditions for peace, beyond bilateral negotiations. The United Nations Security Council has also played a useful role in acknowledging harmful actions, rhetoric or policies of both parties to the conflict. The December 2000 parameters under President Bill Clinton, the 2002 Road Map under President George W. Bush and the United Nations Security Council non-binding resolutions 242 and 338 all provided suggestions for bridging differences between the parties, without imposing a solution to the conflict.

There is a nuanced role for the international community to play in fostering the context for peace and enabling the parties to directly negotiate a two-state solution. We should not lose sight of this critical objective.

SENATE COMMITTEE MEETINGS

Title IV of Senate Resolution 4, agreed to by the Senate of February 4, 1977, calls for establishment of a system for a computerized schedule of all meetings and hearings of Senate committees, subcommittees, joint committees, and committees of conference. This title requires all such committees to notify the Office of the Senate Daily Digest—designated by the Rules Committee—of the time, place and purpose of the meetings, when scheduled and any cancellations or changes in the meetings as they occur.

As an additional procedure along with the computerization of this information, the Office of the Senate Daily Digest will prepare this information for printing in the Extensions of Remarks section of the CONGRESSIONAL RECORD

on Monday and Wednesday of each week.

Meetings scheduled for Thursday, December 1, 2016 may be found in the Daily Digest of today's RECORD.

MEETINGS SCHEDULED
DECEMBER 6

2:30 p.m.
Committee on Foreign Relations
To hold hearings to examine defeating the Iranian threat network, focusing on options for countering Iranian proxies.
SD–419
Committee on the Judiciary
Subcommittee on Crime and Terrorism
To hold hearings to examine whether additional firewalls are needed to protect Congressional oversight staff from retaliatory criminal referrals.
SD–226

DECEMBER 7

10 a.m.
Committee on the Judiciary
Subcommittee on Antitrust, Competition Policy and Consumer Rights
To hold hearings to examine the competitive impact of the AT&T–Time Warner transaction.
SD–226
2:15 p.m.
Committee on Indian Affairs
To hold an oversight hearing to examine the Department of the Interior's Land Buy-Back Program for Tribal Nations, four years later.
SD–628
2:30 p.m.
Committee on Commerce, Science, and Transportation
Subcommittee on Surface Transportation and Merchant Marine Infrastructure, Safety and Security
To hold hearings to examine assessing the security of our critical surface transportation infrastructure.
SR–253

DECEMBER 8

10 a.m.
Committee on Foreign Relations
Subcommittee on State Department and USAID Management, International Operations, and Bilateral International Development
To hold hearings to examine State Department and United States Agency for International Development management challenges and opportunities for the next administration.
SD–419

SENATE—*Thursday, December 1, 2016*

The Senate met at 9:30 a.m. and was called to order by the President pro tempore (Mr. HATCH).

PRAYER

The Chaplain, Dr. Barry C. Black, offered the following prayer:

Let us pray.

Eternal God, thank You for the joy of Your surprises. You do more for us than we can ask or imagine.

Keep the hearts of our Senators steadfast toward You. Lord, lead them safely to the refuge of Your choosing, for we know You desire to give them a future and a hope. Today, provide them with the power to do Your will as they more fully realize that they are Your servants. Give them the wisdom to make Your Holy Word the litmus test by which they evaluate each action as they refuse to deviate from the path of integrity. May they maintain a conscious void of offense toward You or humanity.

We pray in Your great Name. Amen.

PLEDGE OF ALLEGIANCE

The President pro tempore led the Pledge of Allegiance, as follows:

I pledge allegiance to the Flag of the United States of America, and to the Republic for which it stands, one nation under God, indivisible, with liberty and justice for all.

RECOGNITION OF THE MAJORITY LEADER

The PRESIDING OFFICER (Mr. HELLER). The majority leader is recognized.

TRIBUTE TO HAL ROGERS

Mr. McCONNELL. Mr. President, this morning I would like to pay tribute to a fellow Kentuckian who has devoted much of his life to public service, my good friend Congressman HAL ROGERS of Kentucky's Fifth District. HAL, of course, just won reelection in his district with a modest 100 percent of the vote. I imagine he will serve here in Congress for many years to come, but his term as chairman of the House Appropriations Committee is drawing to a close at the end of this 114th Congress. So I thought it fitting to say a few words about the extraordinary tenure of this remarkable man.

HAL has served on the Appropriations Committee for more than 30 years and was selected as the 31st chairman 6 years ago. To mark the end of his chairmanship, family and friends and several special guests assembled a few months back in the House Appropriations Committee hearing room to unveil his official portrait as chairman of the committee.

HAL's portrait hangs alongside those of former chairmen, including some who went on to become Speakers of the House and, in the case of James Garfield, President of the United States. Adding his portrait to this distinguished group is the continuation of a century-old tradition. Many of HAL's colleagues, including Speaker RYAN, were on hand to mark the occasion of a well-deserved tribute to a man I have been honored to serve alongside for many years and to have known for even longer.

I first met HAL ROGERS several decades ago and later worked with him during the 1971 Kentucky gubernatorial campaign. While the Republican candidate that year, Tom Emberton, did not win the race, it was clear to me after getting to know HAL that he was destined for great things. Born in the small town of Barrier, KY, HAL became first a country lawyer in the town of Somerset and then the Commonwealth attorney for the region. He was first elected to the Congress with the Reagan revolution back in 1980 and is now the dean of Kentucky's congressional delegation.

Chairman ROGERS is legendary in Congress and back home for his relentless focus on the concerns and priorities of the people of the Fifth District. Long before the issue of opioid abuse dominated national headlines, HAL played an instrumental role in highlighting and preventing the scourge of drug abuse that has impacted many in Eastern Kentucky.

He has helped bring jobs and hope to the people of Southeastern Kentucky, thanks to projects like PRIDE, which promotes environmental responsibility, Operation UNITE, which helps fight substance abuse, and the Southeast Kentucky Economic Development Corporation, which encourages economic development and growth.

Through the years, HAL spearheaded numerous educational initiatives for all ages: Forward in the Fifth, Rogers Scholars, Rogers Explorers, and the Rogers Entrepreneurial Leadership Institute, just to name a few.

HAL helped launched TOUR Southern and Eastern Kentucky in order to boost tourism in the region and the Center for Rural Development as a way to help transform the area's economy. He has helped secure millions for the Kentucky National Guard, in which he proudly served, and the U.S. Forest Service for marijuana eradication efforts, and he recently spearheaded the Shaping Our Appalachian Region, or SOAR, initiative as a way to unite Kentucky's Appalachian counties around a common vision for attracting jobs and economic development to the region. He has also supported the Appalachian Regional Commission, pushed back against the Obama administration's War on Coal, and has earned a reputation as a tireless advocate for a strong national defense. I am proud to have worked closely with HAL on these and many other projects on behalf of the Bluegrass State.

His constituents can also be proud of the work that he has done for his Nation in his role as Appropriations chair. Under his leadership, the Appropriations Committee responsibly refocused efforts on regular order, reviewing and approving all—I repeat all—12 annual government spending bills through the committee during his tenure. As chairman, HAL has made oversight of Federal spending a top priority, and his Appropriations Committee has held more than 600 hearings to ensure that Federal tax dollars were being spent properly. Under his leadership, the Appropriations Committee has gotten results, such as reducing wasteful spending by $126 billion in total annual spending cuts since fiscal year 2010.

HAL is only the third Kentuckian to chair the House Appropriations Committee. The last was Congressman William Natcher, who held that position until 1994. He is, of course, the only Republican chairman from the Commonwealth. I know that becoming Appropriations Committee chairman was a great achievement for HAL and something he worked hard to earn.

Just on a personal note, I would like to add that HAL ROGERS is a great friend of mine. Elaine and I have always enjoyed spending time with him and his wife Cynthia. As the senior Republican in Kentucky politics, he has been a leader in getting things done for the benefit of the people of his district and of the Commonwealth for nearly four decades.

You can see his impact in many places. One can drive across the Hal Rogers Parkway in Southeastern Kentucky or visit one of the many institutions in service to Kentuckians. HAL is literally beloved in Southeastern Kentucky where he regularly wins reelection, as I indicated earlier, with an overwhelming majority of the votes.

HAL loves the people he serves. He is one of them. He is proud to champion their causes here in the Nation's Capital.

I thank Chairman ROGERS for his steady hand at the helm of the House Appropriations Committee for the last 6 years and for all he has done for Kentucky. Both Kentucky and the Nation are thankful for his service. As he turns his considerable energies to other important roles in Congress, I wish him the very best and look forward to partnering with him many more times in the future on behalf of the Commonwealth we both love.

Mr. REID. Mr. President, will my friend yield for a brief comment?

Mr. McCONNELL. Yes.

Mr. REID. Mr. President, I am going to give a speech here in a minute regarding Senator MIKULSKI. But the reason I mention that is I want the record to reflect that Chairman ROGERS has been so nice to me whenever we have gone to public events and events dealing with the work of the Hill. He has been always a gentleman—I mean first class.

In meetings with just Democrats, I have heard Senator MIKULSKI talk about her great relationship with this good man, so it has been pleasant for me to listen to the description of the relationship of the Republican leader and the chairman of the Appropriations Committee. I just wanted to take a minute and let everyone know that I have also been honored by his presence wherever it has been.

TRIBUTE TO DAVID VITTER

Mr. McCONNELL. Mr. President, after two terms in the Senate and more than two decades of public service, our friend and colleague Senator DAVID VITTER will be leaving us at the end of his term. I would like to say a few words before he does.

Our friend from Louisiana is the first Republican Senator popularly elected from his home State. It is an impressive achievement that history will long record. But Senator VITTER had little opportunity to celebrate at the time. Hurricane Katrina hit just a few months after he took office. It was a catastrophic natural disaster that presented massive and immediate challenges for Louisiana.

Our colleague did not miss a beat. Back home, he and his team worked tirelessly to set up mobile offices. Here in the Senate he fought hard to bring aid to those in need. It underlined something we have all come to know about Senator VITTER: He is passionate about his home State. That has been a constant throughout his career. He simply loves Louisiana. He loves the richness of its history, loves the richness of its culture, loves the richness of its food, too—crawfish pie etouffee and several other things I can't pronounce. Senator VITTER loves it all.

He flies home just about every chance he gets. When he was younger, he turned down offers from Harvard and Yale to study law in the Pelican State. This is after he spent some time in Cambridge, MA, and Oxford, as a Rhodes Scholar, by the way—pretty impressive—so perhaps it was born of a simple lesson: You're just not going to find alligator sauce piquante anywhere else.

Nor are you likely to find many Saints fans, certainly none as enthusiastic as our colleague. You will find Senator VITTER glued to a TV every football Sunday. If the Senate is in session, he will watch between votes in the cloakroom behind me. He has been a diehard fan of the Black and Gold for as long as he can remember. It was not as though he had much choice, of course, growing up in the Big Easy, but he has stuck by his team through thick and thin—often thin. It is what made the Saints eventual Super Bowl win in 2010 that much sweeter. He called it a dream come true.

This tenacity and determination carries over to his political career as well. Whatever the issue, Senator VITTER's staff says he is always looking for solutions that can improve the lives of Louisianans. They say he is always ready to roll up his sleeves and stay the course on legislation that will do just that.

Senator VITTER has worked hard to protect his constituents from the effects of hurricanes and floods before they occur and to rebuild when they do. He has taken the lead on important initiatives to reform the Army Corps of Engineers and improve our Nation's waterways.

Most recently, he helped to pass the first significant reform of the Toxic Substances Control Act in nearly four decades. Senator VITTER was a critical player throughout, working across the aisle with our late colleague Senator Lautenberg and then Senator Udall to steer this much needed legislation to passage and eventually law.

Senator VITTER says he believes his most important job is to keep an open-door policy for constituents who need help. I know he would tell you that, although it may not be the most publicized part of the job, he considers it the most fulfilling.

He still remembers the woman in desperate need of a liver transplant. With the help of his office, she got it. He still remembers the veteran who needed an operation to save his leg and his life. With the help of Team Vitter, he received that too.

Senator VITTER will never forget the countless families in need of assistance following Hurricanes Katrina and Rita, the oil spill, and recent flooding. He has seen firsthand the life-changing, even lifesaving impacts constituent casework can have. It is what inspired him to compile these powerful stories and best practices into a constituent service guidebook that will help guide his successor from day one.

Of course, none of this would have been possible without a great staff, and Senator VITTER has built a strong team that is as committed to the people of Louisiana as he is. It is tight-knit. It is loyal. It is a group of men and women who know they have a boss who takes genuine interest in their success, who trusts their judgment, and who is always eager for their input.

Senator VITTER awards a Reform Trophy each week to the staffer with the best new policy idea. He truly believes in a heavy dose of competition. That includes when his son Jack is in town. Staffers can expect to be enlisted in an entirely different competition then; it is called Office Olympics. Team Vitter knows to bring their A game when Jack is around. They also know to bring their sense of humor. It turns out Jack is a bit of a prankster. I hear you don't want Jack laying hands on a Post-it note or a roll of aluminum foil when he is in the office, but lifelong memories are often made when he does just that.

It is these relationships and it is this capacity to make a difference for the people of Louisiana through constituent service and the legislative process that I am sure our colleague will miss most when he leaves the Senate.

Senator VITTER may be retiring from his post in this Chamber, but we know he will continue to look for ways to serve the State he loves so much. Today we join with his team and his family in recognizing his many years of service. I know each of us is looking forward to seeing what else our colleague is able to achieve on behalf of Louisiana in the years to come.

Mr. VITTER. Mr. President, if the majority leader will yield for one moment, I want to thank the majority leader for his very kind words. Serving in the Senate for two terms has been the highest honor of my professional career. I have enjoyed it so much and have been honored by the relationship with all of my colleagues, certainly including the majority leader. I will have a few more reflections next Monday, but I sincerely thank him and also congratulate him for getting the Senate, particularly in the past 2 years, back to working order and some of its best practices. Not as a Member but as a cheerleader on the outside, I will be very much looking forward to even greater successes this coming Congress.

Mr. McCONNELL. I thank my colleague.

I have one more statement, and then I will be through.

21ST CENTURY CURES BILL

Mr. McCONNELL. Mr. President, yesterday the House passed the 21st Century Cures bill with overwhelming bipartisan support, and I hope to see the same in the Senate. The medical innovation bill is one that can have a substantial impact for families across our country. It supports medical research, including promoting regenerative medicine. It provides real funding to help combat the prescription opioid epidemic that swept our Nation, particularly in places such as my home State of Kentucky. It improves mental health programs, among other bipartisan priorities.

I thank Senator ALEXANDER, chairman of the HELP Committee, for his tireless work in driving this critical legislation forward. We should also thank Senator HATCH, who worked with our Finance colleagues on a significant number of Medicare provisions in the package to protect care for America's seniors. I would like to note the great work by Senator CORNYN and Senator CASSIDY to incorporate key mental health reforms into the Cures legislation.

Let's work together to send it to the President's desk as soon as possible.

IRAN SANCTIONS EXTENSION BILL

Mr. McCONNELL. Mr. President, later today we will have a chance to pass the Iran sanctions extension legislation that passed the House by a large margin.

Given Iran's continued pattern of aggression and the country's persistent efforts to expand its sphere of influence across the region, preserving these sanctions is critical. This is even more important given how the current administration has been held hostage by Iran's threats to withdraw from the nuclear agreement and how it has ignored Iran's overall efforts to upset the balance of power in the greater Middle East.

The authorities extended by this legislation give us some of the tools needed to, if necessary, impose sanctions to hold the regime to account and to keep the American people safer. Next year I expect the new administration and new Congress will undertake a total review of our overall Iran policy. These authorities should remain in place as we address how best to deal with the Iranian missile test, their support for Hezbollah, and their support for the Syrian regime.

I urge all Senators to support this legislation later today.

RECOGNITION OF THE MINORITY LEADER

The PRESIDING OFFICER (Mr. ROUNDS). The Democratic leader is recognized.

TRIBUTE TO BARBARA MIKULSKI

Mr. REID. Mr. President, at times it seems that Democrats and Republicans in the Senate don't agree on very much, but the one thing we all agree on without any exception is this: Our colleague BARBARA MIKULSKI of Maryland can turn a phrase better than anyone else. It is one of her many gifts. Just listen to some of the memorable lines we have heard her utter.

Running for her first term in the Senate, BARBARA said:

I might be short, but I won't be overlooked.

Just prior to the 2013 government shutdown, she told Senate Republicans:

You can huff and puff for 21 hours, but you can't be the magic dragon that blows the Affordable Care Act away.

Earlier this year, she spoke of the Zika virus as follows:

The mosquitoes are coming. The mosquitoes are already here. You can't build a fence to keep them out, and the mosquitoes won't pay for it. The mosquitoes are here—this is not an Obama fantasy.

My personal favorite was something she said at a welcome reception for the 1986 class. We gathered in the Russell Building, and it was a festive occasion for Democrats. We had many new Democrats. It was a huge class—Daschle, SHELBY, Breaux, GRAHAM, Conrad, and Fowler. There were many Democratic Senators, but the day was stolen by BARBARA MIKULSKI. We were all asked to say a word. About her opponent, she stood up and said: "I may be short, but it sure wasn't hard for me to slam dunk Linda Chavez," her opponent.

It is safe to say that with that quip, BARBARA immediately hit it off with all the Members of the Senate class.

From the moment she first set foot in the Senate, Senator MIKULSKI was determined to be herself—honest, disciplined, principled, undaunted, with an incredible wit and a fierce love of Maryland.

You will not find a Member of this body more devoted to her circumstances—and we will talk about those in a little bit—devoted to her constituents and her State than Senator BARBARA MIKULSKI. She served the State of Maryland for more than 50 years. A graduate of Mount Saint Agnes College and the University of Maryland, she made her name as a social worker and a political activist.

Her grandparents are well known, especially her grandmother. They ran a bakery. I have heard her talk about that bakery so many times, how the people in the neighborhood would come and wait for that bakery to open. Her grandparents went there very early, as bakers do. She speaks with nostalgia, warmth, and love of her grandparents.

Her own parents ran a little grocery store next to a steel mill. They would get there early in the morning, and the steelworkers would come and get their lunches and sometimes their breakfasts in that grocery store. Her parents were part of her life, as were her grandparents. She is so proud of them.

In 1966 the Baltimore City Council proposed building a large highway through the center of the city of Baltimore. There was a downside to the plan: It would have razed entire neighborhoods, African-American neighborhoods and especially immigrant neighborhoods. They would have to leave their homes.

The city's leaders, political bosses, and, of course, the wealthy real estate interests and many others—the power brokers of the State of Maryland, the city of Baltimore—knew this was a done deal, but the power brokers didn't count on a young social worker named MIKULSKI to fight for these families. It was her first political activism, and activism it was. It was hers alone. Because of her magnetism, her warmth, and her ability to organize, she organized an effort to stop the highway. Everyone said it couldn't be done, but no one bothered to tell BARBARA. She rallied the citizens of Baltimore in opposing the highway, and what a rally it was—not one rally, not two, but many of them until it was determined that she had won and the power brokers had lost. These people got to keep their homes, and today there is no superhighway towering over the center of Baltimore. People remember BARBARA MIKULSKI for that.

BARBARA's fight against the highway made her a hero in Baltimore and propelled her to the city council in 1971. In 1976 BARBARA MIKULSKI fought her way to the Congress of the United States as a Member of the House of Representatives. After five terms in the House, BARBARA MIKULSKI ran for a seat in the Senate, in the one I just told you about. She slam-dunked her opponent, making her the first Democratic woman in history to win seats in both the House of Representatives and the Senate of the United States. Today Senator MIKULSKI is the longest serving woman to serve in the U.S. Congress. For more than 40 years she has served the people of Maryland.

She is the first woman and first Marylander to chair the prestigious Senate Appropriations Committee. Her legislative record reflects her hard work for women and for equality. She worked with then-Senator JOE BIDEN to pass the first Violence Against Women Act in 1994. She was the architect of the Lilly Ledbetter Fair Pay Act. She was repeatedly in the forefront to fight for paycheck fairness, which determined that men and women who do the same work should be paid the same money.

When so many of us were duped by misinformation about the Iraq war, BARBARA MIKULSKI was not duped. She voted against the war.

BARBARA's career in the Senate has been historic, but I would be remiss if I failed to note her impact on my life and my career. As I said, we came to the Senate together. We served together. We got the same committees.

We, of course, served together in the House, but that is a huge body—435 Members. Frankly, I served there two terms. I know the Presiding Officer served in the House. It is a huge body. When I left there after 4 years, I can remember a vote taking place. Where did these people come from? It is hard to get to know 435 people, but I knew BARBARA. Everybody knew BARBARA. But in the Senate we came together, served on the same committees, and we got to know each other very well early on. BARBARA MIKULSKI has always protected me, looked out for me.

One of my first memories took place right here in the well. I was new, she was new, and it was a very close vote. It was an issue that was her issue, and I couldn't vote her way. That happens here. It was a close vote. People were nudging me: You have to change. You are going to upset everybody. You are a Democrat; you can't do that.

In walked BARBARA MIKULSKI into this crowd. I was there. I was really kind of afraid, but she wasn't. She walked in. People moved away. She said: "Leave him alone. It is a matter of principle." People left me alone. That is who she is. Was she disappointed? I know she would have been disappointed had I not done what I believed in.

I served for 10 years with John Ensign, the Senator from Nevada. John and I had a unique relationship. In 1998 I won an election for the Senate between Ensign and REID by 428 votes. That was a close election. But as fate would have it, 2 years later he came to the Senate. Senator Bryan retired, and he came to the Senate.

Well, John had some personal issues. He hadn't been here very long at all and had some personal issues. I called him at home, and he said: Yes, I have some problems here. I thought how I could help him. Here in the Senate we have the right to do what is called pair. Senator Ensign and I rarely voted alike anyway. So I said: Well, John, what I will do, so it won't affect your voting record, is that I will just pair with you and that way it won't show you have missed votes. So I agreed to do that, and for 2 weeks I told him I would do that.

Well, it worked out fine because we voted differently on everything, except there came an issue that affected Senator MIKULSKI. She came to me and said: Why are you voting that way? I told her: Senator Ensign has a personal issue, and I told him I would pair with him. She said: If you had done anything else—and I won't use her exact language—you would have been a fool. I wasn't a fool in her mind. Even though it was not good for her, she was supportive of me. She would not have been satisfied that I had done something that was wrong in her mind, and she accepted my explanation and that I had to do what I did. We have always had a lot of respect for each other.

Senator David Pryor of Arkansas had a heart attack and became very, very ill. He was a wonderful Senator. Everyone liked him. But he announced he couldn't serve as secretary of the Democratic caucus, and that was something that I was interested in. But I also heard BARBARA MIKULSKI was interested in it. She had been so good to me so often that I immediately went to BARBARA, and with the two of us together, I said: BARBARA, do you want this secretary's job? She said: Yes. I said: You have it. That was the end of that. Nobody opposed her.

Well, surprisingly, a few years later, out of nowhere, Wendell Ford, who was the whip, decided he wasn't going to run for reelection. It was a surprise to everyone. He was assistant Democratic leader, and that was something I was interested in, but again there was MIKULSKI. I didn't say a word. The word was out there that I was interested in it. So as fate would have it, I was walking from my office in the Hart Building over toward the Russell Building, and she was coming in the other direction. Those of us who know BARBARA know that a lot of times she is a person of few words. She is not a gadfly. Sometimes she talks a lot, but sometimes she doesn't want to talk. We were passing each other in the hall, and she said: I want to talk to you for a minute. She said: You took care of me in the Senate; the whip's job is yours. That ended it. It was all over. When that was done, I had a clear route to be the whip of the Senate—the Democratic Senate.

That is the relationship I have with BARBARA MIKULSKI. So she is as responsible as anyone for my years in Democratic leadership. Without her friendship and her loyalty my last 20 years in the Senate would have been much, much different. Working with BARBARA MIKULSKI is one of the highlights of my congressional career. Just hearing her speak is a privilege.

I have seen and listened to good orators. When I was in the House—and my friend, the Democratic whip is here— we heard Jim Wright. Jim Wright was a great orator. He was the majority leader and the Speaker of the House. He was really good. Tom Lantos, an immigrant from Hungary, could speak. He was so dynamic, so good. Claude Pepper had a different style but was someone you listened to. Here in the Senate I have listened to some great orators. Back there was Dale Bumpers. I can still see him. He had a long cord here. He had an extra-long one, and he would walk up and down these aisles speaking. He was a great orator. I listened to him. George Mitchell, one of my predecessors, was so good, so articulate—and DICK DURBIN, from Illinois. They are all terrific orators.

But in my estimation, there is no better orator who I have come across in my congressional service than BARBARA MIKULSKI. We have talked about her one-liners, but I would like, just for a minute, to talk about a trip I took with a congressional delegation led by the very famous John Glenn—war hero, astronaut, and gentleman. We went to places in Europe. The Iron Curtain was down. We went to Poland. BARBARA MIKULSKI's heritage is Polish. They called in John Glenn to give a speech. Ted Stevens from Alaska was also on that trip. I said: We have someone here who is of Polish heritage. Let's listen to her. Oh, what a speech—I mean it was spellbinding. She talked about how she felt about who she was and about her grandparents and her parents.

So I know there is no better orator than BARBARA MIKULSKI. That is because she speaks from the heart. She is honest and so genuine. As the Baltimore Sun wrote: "People know authenticity when they see it, and there's nothing fake about BARBARA MIKULSKI, most especially her love of her job." That is pretty good, coming from the biggest newspaper in the State.

BARBARA has loved her job in the Senate, and the people of Maryland and the United States have loved having her as their advocate and defender. She leaves the Senate as she entered it, as a political activist and a fighter.

So, BARBARA, thank you very much for your guidance, your mentoring, your friendship. It has been an honor to work by your side. We are forever friends. Godspeed, BARBARA MIKULSKI.

I yield the floor.

RESERVATION OF LEADER TIME

The PRESIDING OFFICER. Under the previous order, the leadership time is reserved

---

MORNING BUSINESS

The PRESIDING OFFICER. Under the previous order, the Senate will be in a period of morning business, with Senators permitted to speak therein for up to 10 minutes each.

The Democratic whip.

SENIOR SENATOR FROM MARYLAND

Mr. DURBIN. Mr. President, let me just echo the comments of our Democratic leader, Senator REID, in relation to Senator MIKULSKI. I will save a few moments perhaps next week to speak my own tribute to her and give my own reminiscences. But I didn't want to abruptly change the subject without saying I am in total agreement with Senator REID in terms of the quality of service and friendship that we have had with the senior Senator from the State of Maryland.

DACA

Mr. DURBIN. Mr. President, I come to the floor this morning to talk about an issue that I have raised many times from this very spot, and it is an issue relative to the undocumented young people living in America—undocumented because they are not legally in this country. They were brought here—many of them as infants, toddlers, or children—by their families. They were not aware of the family decision, other than the fact that they were in a car and moving into the United States. They didn't really appreciate where they came from. Many of them never knew where they came from. Some of them don't even speak the language of the country of their birth. They were brought here as children. They believed from the beginning they were part of America. In most, except in extraordinary circumstances, they were not even told of their immigration status at an early age.

So they grew up going to school in America. They learned English. They pledged allegiance to the only flag they had ever known. They sang the national anthem of this country believing they were part of this country. At some point, though, there was this realization and disclosure that they were not. Legally, they weren't. They were undocumented.

So these children were raised in the shadow of uncertainty—uncertain as to whether a knock on the door at any time of day or night might change their world forever; whether or not their parents might be deported from this country and they would have to go with them; or, God forbid, that something would happen to them and they would be deported. They lived with that fear for a long time.

I came to understand it when a Korean girl in Chicago who was looking for an opportunity to go to college because of her musical skills, realized she was undocumented and might not be able to do it. So she came to our office, told us of her situation, and we tried to help.

So 15 years ago I introduced a bill called the DREAM Act. The DREAM Act said that for young people brought to this country under the age of 16 and who have lived here successfully, completed school, and have no criminal record to disqualify them, we should give them a chance—give them a chance to become legal in America and give them a chance, from my point of view, to become citizens. I introduced the bill 15 years ago. It has been debated. The word DREAMer came out of it and has now become pretty well-known across America to describe this group of young people.

A few years ago, I prevailed on the President of the United States, Barack Obama, to give them a fighting chance to stay here. So by Executive action, he created something called DACA. DACA is the Deferred Action for Childhood Arrivals Program. This would allow these young people, undocu-

mented, to step forward and disclose their status, come up with a filing fee of almost $500, and go through a process where they were submitted to a criminal background check. If they cleared all the hurdles, they would be given a temporary—underline the word temporary—right to live in the United States without fear of deportation and to work in this country.

So over the years, since the President's Executive action, 744,000 young people have come forward. Their lives are amazing. I have told their stories over and over. Imagine, if you will, that you lived in fear of being deported tomorrow or fear that your family would be broken up and how that would weigh on you as a young person. So they did something that was maybe rash in the eyes of their parents but heroic in my eyes. They stepped forward, out of the shadows, and said: If the United States of America has set legal standards for us to follow to stay here, we will comply with them. Their parents warned them and their friends warned them: You are turning yourself in. You are telling this government who you are, where you are, and where they can find you. But they did it anyway, and I encouraged them to do it, and many others did as well, saying: If you show good faith in this country, good faith in this government, I will do everything in my power to make sure it isn't used against you.

Now we have reached a new stage in our history with a new President coming who has different views on immigration than the outgoing President. My concern, and a concern shared by millions across America, is this: What is going to happen to these young kids—744,000 of them—who are currently in college, in high school, in professional schools, such as medical schools and law schools? They are doing amazing things with their lives, and yet things could happen immediately to change their status.

I have talked to a number of my colleagues on the floor on both sides of the aisle about this, and there are pretty strong emotions about helping these young people. One of the leaders on this has been my friend and ally on immigration issues—on some immigration issues—and that is Lindsey Graham of South Carolina. He and I talked about introducing legislation that would give a temporary stay so these young people could be protected until Congress does its work and comes up with an immigration bill that addresses this issue and many more.

Senator Graham and I discussed it again this morning, and we even hope to have this bill ready before we leave next week—a bipartisan effort to say to the new President: Give these young people a fighting chance. At least protect them until we have had a chance to act on the larger immigration issues before us. I hope that colleagues on both sides will join us.

There has been a lot of talk about what the next Congress will look like and what we will do, how we will tackle the biggest issues of our time. The Affordable Care Act, for example, which I was proud to support, is clearly controversial. There wasn't a single Republican Senator who voted for it. Some want to repeal it and replace it. Some are suggesting we will repeal it, but do it with 2 years in advance.

So 2 years from now there might be a new Affordable Care Act. That puts us in a responsible position of coming up with an alternative in that period of time. I don't know if that is how this conversation will end, but I would suggest the same logic could apply when it comes to immigration: At least give us the time to come up with an alternative on immigration, and during that period of time, let us protect these youngest people.

The stories I have told on the floor say more about this issue than any words I can express, and I want to tell another one of those stories this morning. This is about a young man from Illinois. His name is Asael Reyes. Here is his picture. He has his University of Illinois at Chicago T-shirt on. He is an interesting young man.

He came to the United States at the age of 5, brought here from Mexico. He grew up on the North Side of Chicago. He is a bright young man, but he learned he was undocumented early in life. He really got despondent over the thought that he could lose everything and have to be forced to leave America. His classes were a challenge to him, and with this fear in his mind he started doing very poorly. In fact, he dropped out of high school. He said it weighed heavily on his mind that he might have to leave.

He said:

I felt that because of my status, I had no future. As a result, my grades and attendance plummeted and I struggled to do anything productive.

Then, in 2012, President Obama announced DACA, and everything changed for Asael Reyes. Here is how he explains it:

DACA meant that I had a future worth fighting for, and because of that I returned to school and reignited my passion for study. Because of DACA, I want to do whatever I can to contribute to my country.

When Asael says "my country," he means the United States of America—the only country he has ever known.

In his senior year in high school, this young man turned his life around because of DACA. He improved his grades, he was active in his community, he was head of his school's fund raising committee, he volunteered in a mentoring program, and he worked full time to support himself and his family. You see, young people like him—undocumented—don't qualify for any Federal assistance to go to college. If you want to go to college, you have to pay for it. For most of them, it means working pretty hard to come up with the money to do it.

Today Asael is in his sophomore year in the Honors College—the Honors College—at the University of Illinois at Chicago. He is a double major in psychology and political science, and he has a perfect 4.0 grade point average. Talk about a turnaround. He is involved with student government, leads a recreational bike club called College of Cycling. Every week he delivers food from the college dining halls on bike to a local homeless shelter. This effort has inspired other student groups to start similar initiatives. He mentors middle school students, and he is the youngest board member of the Erie Neighborhood House—a place I have visited many times—a social service agency that provides assistance to low-income families in the city of Chicago. In addition to all this, he works part time as a security guard at local events like Cubs baseball games and Bears football games.

Asael dreams of working in Chicago's city government someday. He says: "I have a passion for my city, and I feel an obligation to do whatever I can to make it great by serving its communities." This is one story—one story out of 744,000.

Will America be better if Asael Reyes is given his chance to stay here to make this a better nation? Of course, it will. At an early age, this young man was able to do a turnaround just on the hope that someday he might be able to live in this country legally.

There are so many stories just like his. In that same city of Chicago, at Loyola University School of Medicine, there are 28 students who are undocumented. The school opened up competition, and some of the brightest kids around America for the first time saw a chance for an undocumented student to be a doctor.

They have to sign up, incidentally—borrowing the money from the State of Illinois for their education—to serve a year of their lives as doctors in underserved areas of Illinois, in rural areas, and in the inner city, for each year they go to medical school. They willingly do it. They are prepared to give back. Asael is prepared to give back. The question is, Will we give them a chance?

I am not an expert in the area of social media, but yesterday we tweeted a short message about this DACA challenge and what is going to happen to these 744,000 young people across America. The hashtag "save DACA" went out. My staff reports to me—and they are expert on this, I am not—in the span of 2 hours, we were trending across the United States of America. Six million people saw this hashtag over 10 million times. Think of that, 6 million people in 2 hours. It touched them what can happen to this young man and so many others.

So will Congress rise to this challenge? Will Democrats and Republicans come to the rescue of these young people who are asking for just a chance—brought to this country not by their decision but the decision of their parents—asking for a chance now to have a life? I hope we will. It will be good for them. It will sure be good for America.

TRIBUTE TO MARK KIRK

Mr. DURBIN. Mr. President, on January 3, there will be a new Senate sworn in. Members come down this aisle, to be sworn in over here by the Vice President of the United States, to become Members of the U.S. Senate. It will be the passing of the Senate seat in our State from Senator MARK KIRK to Senator-elect TAMMY DUCKWORTH. I would like to say a few words about my colleague MARK KIRK.

For the last 6 years, MARK and I have had a very positive professional relationship. The night he won the election, I was standing with his opponent Alexi Giannoulias when Alexi made the call to MARK KIRK to congratulate him. MARK asked that I take the phone, and I did.

He said: I want to work with you. I know we just competed against one another in the election, but we now have a responsibility together to represent the State of Illinois, and we started a positive working relationship—a relationship based on mutual respect. One of the things we did was to continue a tradition.

Since 1985, my mentor and colleague in the House, and my predecessor in the Senate, Paul Simon of Illinois, started a Thursday morning breakfast, inviting people from Illinois who were in Washington and those who wish they were from Illinois, to come in for free coffee and donuts at no taxpayer expense. It was an hour-long public meeting so we could talk about what was happening in the Senate and then answer any questions and pose for pictures if they wanted them. I asked MARK KIRK to continue this, even though we were of opposite political faith, and we did, for a long time. We worked together to make sure the people of Illinois felt welcomed. We often took differing views on issues—that is understandable—but we did it in a civil way. People said they thought it was one of the highlights of their trip to see two Senators from two different parties working together. We did—and not just on those Thursday mornings. We found reasons to do it on the floor.

In the vast majority of cases, when it came to filling Federal judicial vacancies, MARK KIRK and I worked together to agree. Rarely did we disagree on those who needed to be chosen. As a result, we have had a pretty good record of filling vacancies in the State of Illinois.

Then, of course, it was in 2012 that a disaster struck and MARK KIRK suffered

a stroke. It was almost a life-ending experience. He is lucky—lucky—to be alive today. He knows it, and we all know it too. I primarily kept in touch with his staff, and with him, during the course of his rehabilitation after that stroke. It was a calendar year he had to give to rehabilitation, to learn how to walk again and speak again and do the basic things we take for granted. It was an extraordinary show of courage and determination on his part.

Finally, before he could return to the Senate, I visited with him and saw him some 10 months after the stroke and realized the devastation he weathered and how much he had managed to recover because of his sheer determination. The one thing he told me, though, was that he was determined to come back to the United States Senate and walk up those steps right into the Senate Chamber. He was working every single day on treadmills and with rehab experts to reach that day when he could get out of a car and walk up those steps. He asked me if I would ask other Senators to join him—especially his close friend JOE MANCHIN, a Democratic Senator from West Virginia, and we did. That day came and it was an amazing day. He started at the bottom of those steps and worked his way up, all the way into the Senate Chamber, to the applause of his colleagues—Democrats and Republicans—all the way up those steps. We realized what an amazing recovery he had made.

Our colleague Tim Johnson of the State of South Dakota had gone through a similar devastating experience. MARK KIRK said many times, when he was about to give up, he thought, Tim Johnson got back to the Senate. I can get back there if I work hard enough. He did just that.

He was an exceptional colleague of mine in the Senate. There were a lot of things we agreed on. One of them was Lake Michigan. As a Congressman from the 10th Congressional District, which is on the shores of Lake Michigan, he was always committed to that lake.

After the election, when the results didn't come out as he wished, I sat down with him and said: MARK, what do you want me to do in memory of your commitment to public service?

He said: Do everything you can to protect Lake Michigan. And I am going to. I asked his successor TAMMY DUCKWORTH to join me in that effort, and we will in his name and in his memory.

I thank him for the service he has given to our State, the service he has given our Nation as an officer in the Navy Reserve, and for the years he put in as a staff member to Congressman John Porter, for the work he did in the House of Representatives representing the 10th Congressional District, and for his term in the United States Senate. It has been a pleasure and an honor to serve with him. Despite our political differences, I count him as a friend, as an ally, and as a true champion for the State of Illinois.

I wish my colleague MARK KIRK the very best in his future endeavors.

Mr. President, I yield the floor.

I suggest the absence of a quorum.

The PRESIDING OFFICER. The clerk will call the roll.

The senior assistant legislative clerk proceeded to call the roll.

Mr. MENENDEZ. Mr. President, I ask unanimous consent that the order for the quorum call be rescinded.

The PRESIDING OFFICER. Without objection, it is so ordered.

IRAN SANCTIONS EXTENSION BILL

Mr. MENENDEZ. Mr. President, I rise to voice my support of the extension of the Iran Sanctions Act, which I believe we must treat as just one step in our continued efforts to counter Iran's destabilizing and nefarious actions throughout the world. This bill merely extends the basis of our extensive sanctions network against Iran aimed at crippling the Ayatollah's deadly pursuit of a nuclear weapon for 10 years.

The Iran Sanctions Act, which is part of the extensive network of sanctions that I helped author for the United States and our allies to levy against the Iranian regime, serves as the basis of the economic leverage that brought Iran to the negotiating table in the first place. Throughout my tenure in Congress, I have authored and championed the foundation of our network of sanctions that crippled Iran's economy and kept its nuclear pursuits at bay. It has been my consistent position that the United States must address these nefarious activities apart from the nuclear portfolio. We need to send a signal to Iran that the United States, while meeting its obligations under the JCPOA, will continue to respond to other threatening and dangerous activities the Iranian regime has taken.

Throughout debate over the Joint Comprehensive Plan of Action, its proponents made a number of repeated claims. Among these were that it was crippling sanctions that brought Iran to the negotiating table and that in the event of a breach of the agreement, the United States and our implementing partners would have every authority to "snap back"—the term that was coined—the sanctions that have been lifted. If the sanctions architecture has expired, then we have no sanctions which we can snap back. These sanctions were in place when the JCPOA was authored and signed, and it follows that they should remain in place.

Many of the agreement's proponents argued that putting the JCPOA in place would give the United States and our allies the opportunity to focus on countering Iran's more conventional threats to American security and regional stability. Since the nuclear agreement came into force, Iran has continued its efforts to destabilize the region and increase its power through proxy and terrorist networks.

Since we signed the nuclear agreement with Iran, Iran has been testing the agreement, testing our resolve, and quite literally testing long-range ballistic missiles. We have seen multiple ballistic missile tests in the past year and a half—in October and November of last year and in March and May of this year and one launch not far from U.S. naval vessels. We have seen American sailors humiliated and detained at gunpoint. Just this weekend, a vessel controlled by the IRGC—the Iranian Revolutionary Guard—pointed a weapon at a U.S. military helicopter in the Strait of Hormuz.

Iran continues to support a Houthi insurgency that toppled the legitimate Government of Yemen. It supports Shia militias in Iraq who seek to control the democratically elected Iraqi Government and bring it closer in line with Iran, threatening to return Iraq to civil war or worse. It supports Assad in Syria and continues to send millions of dollars and sophisticated weapons to Hezbollah and Hamas, threatening innocent civilians in Syria and Israel's security. It continues human rights violations and sustains an aging clergy who is losing touch with the hopes and dreams of young Iranians and moderates, an out-of-touch clergy who dominates the power structures and the security apparatus that restricts civil liberties and promotes its hegemonic regional destabilization. It has the largest inventory of ballistic missiles in the Middle East, capable of delivering weapons of mass destruction, chemical weapons, biological weapons, and continues to develop cyber war capabilities.

Iran continues its development of space-launch vehicles that can lead to a longer range missile capability. It has cooperated with North Korea on the transfer of ballistic missile technology. This is in addition to the fact that Iran has, by its own admission, violated the JCPOA itself. The International Atomic Agency reported that Iran has twice violated the terms of the agreement by producing more heavy water than the deal allows for. An excess stockpile of heavy water—a critical component of operating nuclear reactors—reduces Iran's nuclear breakout time. Yet, even with this violation, the United States and our implementing partners have upheld our end of the bargain.

As I have repeatedly said and which I outlined in the bill I authored earlier this year, we must take decisive action in response to Iran's behavior which is in violation, among other things, of the United Nations Security Council resolutions and threatens America's interests and regional stability. The United States must reserve the right to hold Iran accountable for all of its actions, and that is exactly what my legislation would do by imposing stricter sanctions tied to specific nefarious actions outside the nuclear portfolio.

After months of consultations with my colleagues in the Senate, outside experts, and constituents, I introduced a bipartisan bill, S. 3267, the Countering Iranian Threats Act, on July 14, just before Congress broke for recess. Its acronym, CITA, not only extends the Iran Sanctions Act, which we will do independently today, it also expands sanctions for ballistic missile development, support for terrorism, and other illicit Iranian actions, and it sanctions transfers of conventional weapons to or from Iran—the totality of Iran's dangerous behavior outside of the nuclear portfolio. Specifically, it requires the administration to identify the specific Iranians, persons, or entities that are engaged in these activities and then apply sanctions that freeze their assets and block their international travel and business interests. In this way, the sanctions are surgical and designed to avoid interference with the terms of the Iran nuclear deal.

We must provide leverage to seek necessary change in the conduct of the Iranian regime and hold Iran accountable for meeting its international obligations, including the terms of the JCPOA. We will improve the deplorable human rights situation in Iran and double down on our reassurances to Israel and American allies in the region of our full commitment to regional security.

The fact is, there is much we can do to ensure a bright future undimmed by a nuclear cloud. We must authorize the Iran Sanctions Act that I have authored so that, as flawed as the JCPOA was, in my view, the Iranians will know the consequences of any breach and we will deal with missile proliferation, terrorism, and regional destabilization that is just as dangerous and just as threatening to American security and to our ally, the State of Israel, and our other allies in the region. I hope we will get to that new phase in the next Congress.

With that, I yield the floor.

I suggest the absence of a quorum.

The PRESIDING OFFICER. The clerk will call the roll.

The senior assistant legislative clerk proceeded to call the roll.

Mr. PORTMAN. Mr. President, I ask unanimous consent that the order for the quorum call be rescinded.

The PRESIDING OFFICER (Mr. RUBIO). Without objection, it is so ordered.

OPIOID EPIDEMIC

Mr. PORTMAN. Mr. President, I rise today on another topic that is affecting every single State represented here in this Chamber, and that is the opioid epidemic. This is heroin, prescription drugs, and increasingly the synthetic heroin coming into our State and poisoning the people we represent, leading to a situation where we have about 120 people dying every day of overdoses—about 5 a day in my State of Ohio. Unfortunately, I have to report today that it is getting worse, not better.

I also believe that Congress is beginning to take the right steps to address that, and that is what I want to talk about today. This is the 28th time I have come to the floor to talk about this issue this year because it is one that affects every State, but particularly mine.

I come from Ohio. It is a State that recently, based on a new report, was named as one of the top States in the country for overdoses and, unfortunately, the tragedy of overdose deaths.

For those who die from overdoses, it is a tragedy, of course. But, frankly, it is the tip of the iceberg because there are so many people whose lives are shattered, whose lives are torn apart, who are not going to work and whose communities are facing more and more crime because of this issue.

It was addressed here in this Chamber recently by the legislation I want to talk about today, but it is something we must find a way to deal with immediately because of the urgency of the problem. To this Senator, it is much like other public health crises that we face as a country, whether it is a Zika virus or other issues that come up where Congress has said that we need to have immediate funding and immediate changes in policies to address it. What Congress has done already and the President has signed into law as of a couple of months ago is broad legislation called CARA, or the Comprehensive Addiction and Recovery Act, and that legislation is historic in the sense that it is the first time in over 20 years that Congress has taken a look at this issue and come up with a comprehensive approach. It focuses on education and prevention to help people make the right decision and not get into the funnel of addiction, particularly focusing on young people. But it also focuses on better treatment services and recovery.

Right now there are people who cannot access treatment, and part of the problem is that there is not adequate funding for that treatment. Part of the problem is that there is a stigma attached to addiction and people aren't willing to come forward. Our legislation, broadly speaking, addresses that as well because it says that addiction is a disease and ought to be treated as such, which should help to get people into treatment.

For the first time Congress is supporting not just treatment and detox but actually getting people into longer term recovery programs. Think of housing arrangements or other supportive recovery services that we found from our experience in doing the research around the country, which are much more successful in terms of helping people to turn their lives around and to lead a productive life. What we have found in the last 3 years with five conferences here in Washington, DC, bringing experts in from all around the country, is that this is something that can actually help to turn the tide. It is the first time Congress has focused on that. We also focused on the issue of ensuring that the law enforcement community and first responders—our firefighters and others—have access to this miracle drug called Narcan or naloxone, which is able to reverse the effects of an overdose. There is a program to allow them to apply to get the Narcan they need to help save lives, and it is amazing. It was administered 16,000 times in Ohio last year. This year it will be a lot more than that. Those are lives that are saved. It is not the ultimate solution. The solution is getting people into treatment and the recovery they need, but it is necessary right now given the epidemic that we face.

There are other aspects of the legislation, as well, that help ensure that we get the prescription drugs off the shelves, which unfortunately are being abused by having more drug take-back programs. We provide more resources to ensure that people can get the help they need in terms of treatment and recovery.

I am happy to say that the legislation is beginning to be implemented. I would ask the administration again today to expedite that implementation. Of the seven larger programs that are part of this legislation, I think it is fair to say that two are being implemented at this point already, and we need to move forward with others as well. I know it takes a while. We need to be sure that the programs are properly implemented. But again, there needs to be an urgency about this issue.

Section 303 of the legislation is being implemented now by the Department of Health and Human Services, as one example. It expands access to medication-assisted treatment by allowing nurse practitioners and physician assistants to prescribe medication-assisted treatment to help treat an opioid use disorder. This is important. Back in my home State, I am hearing a lot from people who are already training people to be able to provide this assistance to those who are addicted and need to have this medication-assisted treatment using methadone, Suboxone or Vivitrol. To allow nurse practitioners and physician assistants to participate in this is incredibly important. This is progress, but we are pushing the administration to implement the law even more quickly.

CARA also deals with the growing demand for drugs, as I said, by improving access to longer term recovery. Recently, I was able to go to a recovery house in Canton, OH, called the Phoenix Recovery Home. I was able to talk to some of the recovering addicts there, in one case several times where it had not been successful, but this longer term recovery was working for them. Again, this legislation is so important to implement the recovery aspect of it.

The funding for this has also been a work in progress. We have made some progress toward increasing the funding. This year there is a 47-percent increase in funding for the opioid crisis. In the CARA legislation there is an authorization for additional funding in the amount of $181 million every single year. That is important. That $181 million every year going forward is something that will be important in this comprehensive approach.

In the short term, we are working under a short-term spending bill right now called the continuing resolution. We were able to get funding of $37 million that expires next week. We have to be sure that funding continues. That is adequate funding to implement the program now, but we need to ensure that we have short-term funding over the next period of time, whenever that is—some say it will be from now until March—to ensure we keep CARA implemented.

What I am pleased to report today is that the 21st Century Cures legislation, which the House has sent over to the Senate, includes a dramatic increase in funding for this issue. It is about $500 million per year over the next 2 years of additional funding that will be block-granted to the States for prevention and treatment. This is incredibly important to my State of Ohio and other States. My understanding is that States that have a higher prevalence of overdoses will be given priority in terms of these funding dollars. I think that is appropriate. It will be helpful to those States hardest hit.

I wish that some of the parameters of the funding instructions had been a little broader to include this issue we talked about earlier having to deal with the recovery aspect. But we are working to ensure that, as this legislation is implemented, the States have maximum flexibility to address this problem.

This legislation will be bipartisan. I think you will see the vote to be very bipartisan next week when we take it up, and in part it is because of this legislation. So between CARA and this new legislation in the Cures Act, we are going to see additional funding and it is urgent that we see it.

The Kaiser Family Foundation recently released a report based on information from the Centers for Disease Control and Prevention that found that one in nine heroin deaths in the United States happened in our home State of Ohio. We have the most deaths from synthetic opioids, such as fentanyl and Carfentanil, that is coming into our communities. We are seeing unfortunately an increase not just in Ohio, but in other States around the country.

Every day I hear about this issue from Ohioans. Sometimes when I am back home at events that have nothing to do with this substance abuse issue, people will come up to me, as they will this weekend, and talk about their personal stories.

Recently, I received a couple of letters. Just before Thanksgiving I got a letter from Elaine. She is from Cincinnati, my hometown. She wrote that her daughter was lost to a drug overdose in 2013 and her grandson from a drug overdose on August 1 of this year. She writes that her other son is now an active heroin addict. She went through a story about trying to get him into a detox center for treatment but she faced barriers. One of the barriers in her case was being able to afford it. The insurance initially wouldn't cover it. We tried to help her with that, but in the meantime, she is at her wit's end to do something now to save her son's life, having lost two other members of her family. Again, this legislation we are going to vote on early next week, the Cures Act will help with regard to Elaine's inability to find detox and treatment for her son.

Barbara in Columbus has been in touch with my office a lot. She lost her son Eric to an overdose in 2012. He was just a week shy of his 24th birthday. She writes that Eric wanted to go to rehab. His sister took him to every place in Columbus, and no one had room. There was no room at the inn. This is another issue we are finding across the country. Sometimes these resources are available in larger urban areas, but they are frankly oversubscribed given the issue of heroin and prescription drug addiction and the growing problem that we have. She writes:

We need to stop jailing people for drug use. We need to stop people from dying in the streets, and get them into treatment clinics. We need to recognize the difference between drug use and drug abuse. We need focus on creating a society where people do not feel the need to numb the pain of their existence through drug abuse.

I agree with her, and that is the focus of the legislation, the Comprehensive Addiction and Recovery Act.

The PRESIDING OFFICER. The Senator's time has expired.

Mr. PORTMAN. Mr. President, I ask for an additional 30 seconds.

The PRESIDING OFFICER. Without objection, it is so ordered.

Mr. PORTMAN. Mr. President, again, I am pleased that Congress has made so much progress in this area. I see my colleague from the Judiciary Committee is here, Senator LEAHY, who

helped get this legislation through his committee, along with Senator GRASSLEY. It is called the Comprehensive Addiction and Recovery Act.

Now we have a chance with the Cures Act to put even more funding immediately against this problem. I encourage my colleagues to support that legislation. It is good legislation for other reasons, as well, but also because of the fact that this epidemic of opioid abuse must be addressed.

I yield the floor.

The PRESIDING OFFICER. The Senator from Vermont.

Mr. LEAHY. Mr. President, I appreciate the work of my colleague, and I am glad to work with him on this.

JUSTICE FOR ALL REAUTHORIZATION BILL

Mr. LEAHY. Mr. President, on another subject, each morning in this Chamber, we pledge allegiance to our flag. We end by declaring that we are "one Nation under God with liberty and justice for all." I believe in those words, but it is not enough just to say the words. It is our obligation to bring meaning to this promise.

Today I hope that Congress will finally take an important step forward by passing the bipartisan Justice for All Reauthorization Act. I have long championed the Justice for All Act to make our justice system more fair. Our bill will strengthen indigent defense and expand the rights of crime victims. It will improve the use of forensic evidence, including rape kits, to provide justice swiftly. It will help protect the innocent by increasing access to postconviction DNA testing. The Senate passed this bipartisan legislation in June, and the House approved a slightly modified version earlier this week. I am disappointed the House decreased authorizations for many programs I support. Still, the bill makes important changes and will improve the lives of many of our most vulnerable citizens. I urge my fellow Senators to consent to its immediate passage.

As a former prosecutor, I am dedicated to ensuring that our criminal justice system has integrity and the confidence of the public it serves. I started out on the front lines as State's attorney in Chittenden County, VT. And for the past 20 years, I have served as chairman or ranking member of the Senate Judiciary Committee. During that time, it has become clear to me that our system is deeply flawed—there is not always justice for all.

I have met many people who were wrongly convicted of crimes they did not commit. Kirk Bloodsworth—let me tell you a story about Kirk Bloodsworth, who is one such young man. He was just out of the Marines in 1984 when he was falsely convicted and sentenced to death for the rape and murder of a 9-year-old girl.

He always declared his innocence, but he was nearly executed, until DNA evidence proved he was innocent in 1993 and helped law enforcement find the person who actually committed the crime. He became the first death row inmate in the United States exonerated by DNA evidence.

I have always been impressed with his courage, but he was not the last. There were 149 innocent people exonerated just last year—in 1 year, 149—the highest number on record. Our justice system failed not only these innocent people, but also the victims of crime. Those of us who have been prosecutors know what it means if you convict the wrong person, aside from the injustice to the person who was convicted. It means that somebody who committed the crime is still out there free and has not been arrested and has not been convicted. Our justice system failed not only these innocent people but also the victims of crime. We can and we must do more to fix this injustice.

I believe we should eliminate the death penalty entirely because I know the system gets it wrong. But until we do away with the death penalty, we must improve the integrity of our criminal justice system. That is why I joined with Kirk years ago to enact the Post-Conviction DNA Testing Grant Program. This was originally part of the Innocence Protection Act enacted in 2000, and it gives defendants like Kirk a chance to prove their innocence. That should not be too much to ask.

We can and we must do more to fix this injustice. We must do more to ensure that our justice system gets it right from the beginning. That means improving the quality of indigent defense. Our system too often fails to provide a lawyer for every person accused of a crime, even if they cannot afford one. Our Founding Fathers recognized that no system could be fair if accusations by a king or a government went unchallenged. Without a vigorous defense, it is impossible to determine who is actually guilty and who has been wrongly accused. This legislation requires the Department of Justice to provide technical assistance to States to improve their indigent defense systems, and it ensures that public defenders will have a seat at the table when States determine how to use their Byrne JAG criminal justice funding.

Improving systems of indigent defense will mean fewer innocent people behind bars. It is an outrage when an innocent person is wrongly punished. Of course, this injustice is compounded when the true perpetrator remains on the streets, able to commit more crimes. We lock up the wrong person, and the person who committed the crime is still out there to commit more crimes.

My brave friend Debbie Smith, a champion for victims of sexual assault, waited 6 years after being attacked before her rape kit was tested and the perpetrator, the criminal, was caught. Survivors like Debbie should not have to live in anguish, knowing their attacker remains free. Our bill provides resources for forensic testing. Specifically, it creates a new tracking system so testing can be done more efficiently. It will also expand access to forensic exams in rural areas and for underserved populations. Coming from a State like Vermont, I know how important that will be in rural areas.

Sexual assaults must be prevented wherever they occur, including in our Nation's prisons. That is why I strongly supported the Prison Rape Elimination Act when it was enacted in 2003. This bill imposes true accountability by withholding Federal funds from States who do not implement protections to prevent sexual assaults in our prisons. It also protects grants designed to provide services for survivors of domestic and sexual violence.

Our legislation also builds on the landmark protections provided for victims of domestic violence in the 2013 Leahy-Crapo Violence Against Women Act. Imagine a woman living with an abusive partner in public housing, but her name is not on the lease. One night he beats her. She calls the police. The man is arrested. The women believes she is finally safe. But then the landlord says she has to leave immediately because the man is being evicted and she has no right to stay. The Justice for All Act will allow this woman time to remain there while she either finds another place to live or she can demonstrate she is eligible to remain under her own name. No person should be forced to choose between abuse and a place to live.

And finally, our bill expands rights for victims of all crime. It builds upon the success of the Crime Victims' Rights Act by making it easier for crime victims to have an interpreter present during court proceedings and to obtain court-ordered restitution.

It has been my great honor to serve as the most senior Democrat on the Senate Judiciary Committee since 1997. During that time, I have worked with Senators from both sides of the aisle to craft solutions to some of the most important problems of our time. I am proud to join with my good friend the Senator from Texas, Mr. CORNYN, on this legislation and the many advocates who have helped guide our work. I especially appreciate the work of the Innocence Project, the Rape, Abuse & Incest National Network, the National Domestic Violence Hotline, the Consortium of Forensic Science Organizations, Just Detention International, the National Criminal Justice Association, the National District Attorneys Association, Legal Aid DC, the National Network to End Domestic Violence, the Joyful Heart Foundation, the ACLU, the National Juvenile Justice Network, and the National Center for Victims of Crime.

Senator CORNYN and I have proved this is not a Republican or Democratic issue; this is a justice for all issue. That is why so many in both parties have joined, along with so many people around the country.

As we consider legislation next Congress, we must remember that we have an obligation to look out for all victims and to create fairness in our criminal justice system. While we made some improvements this year, including passing the bipartisan Comprehensive Addiction and Recovery Act and the Sexual Assault Survivors' Rights Act, I am disappointed the Republican-led Congress failed to even allow a vote on bipartisan criminal justice reform legislation despite its strong support. As we look to the new Congress, I hope those who worked with me on this important issue will continue to support efforts to correct the costly mistakes of mandatory minimum sentences. I hope we can again build the same kind of broad bipartisan consensus in support of all victims of sexual assault and domestic violence as we did last Congress when we passed the Leahy-Crapo Violence Against Women Reauthorization Act through the Senate.

I yield the floor.

I suggest the absence of a quorum.

The PRESIDING OFFICER. The clerk will call the roll.

The legislative clerk proceeded to call the roll.

Mr. MERKLEY. Mr. President, I ask unanimous consent that the order for the quorum call be rescinded.

The PRESIDING OFFICER. Without objection, it is so ordered.

APPOINTMENTS AND VOTER RIGHTS

Mr. MERKLEY. Mr. President, it has now been 23 days since the election—3 weeks and 2 days. Certainly it has been a time of great frustration and anxiety for Americans across the board, anticipating what our government will look like, what our executive branch will look like under the leadership of President-Elect Donald Trump.

The early signs have been ones that have indeed given a great deal of concern to many groups across America, beginning with the appointment by Mr. Trump of a White nationalist as his Chief Strategist, an individual, Steve Bannon, who has run a Web site, Breitbart, that specialized in hate, specialized in division.

It certainly reverberated in the campaign, but to bring that into the White House was something very few people anticipated would occur. It has been followed up by other appointments that were certainly a cause of deep concern. Just yesterday, there was the nomination of Steve Mnuchin, a Wall Street banker being assigned to the key post in our economy, the Treasury

Secretary post—a post that will come before this Chamber for confirmation.

This is not just someone from Wall Street but someone who specialized in acquiring a bank that had been deeply involved in predatory lending, proceeded to foreclosure on thousands and thousands of families, was using robosigning to accelerate that in violation of the law, was a specialist in turning people out of their homes, profited enormously in the strategy at the expense of working Americans seeking to have the fundamental comfort of owning their own home.

There is a list of other appointments, nominees who have certainly more than raised eyebrows, raised anxiety, other individuals who have specialized in hate and division, and other incidents such as the attack on the cast of "Hamilton" for proposing that individuals with a background of hate and division not be put into the Cabinet

Then we have this from our President-elect. I quote his tweet: "In addition to winning the Electoral College in a landslide, I won the popular vote if you deduct the millions of people who voted illegally."

It is a straight falsehood. It has been debunked by every major analytical group, news organization in America. It is a complete fiction created in the middle of the night by our President-elect, but why? I think most people conclude that the fact he lost the popular vote is so disturbing to the President-elect because he wants to claim a mandate, but he cannot claim a mandate because the majority of Americans voted against him. They have voted against his strategy of division. They have voted against his strategy of incurring hate against Muslims, against immigrants, against women, against Hispanics, against African Americans.

No, Donald Trump, you did not get the popular vote, you lost it. You lost it straight out by more than 2 million votes and perhaps a great deal more.

No fiction you can stir up in the middle of the night can change that fundamental fact that you have no mandate in America for these politics of hate and division.

The fact is, the citizens' vote against Donald Trump would have been far larger except for a strategy of voter suppression. Voter suppression is a crime against the Constitution. Our Nation was founded on the vision of citizens being empowered to have a direct voice.

President Jefferson wrote a letter in which he referred to the mother principle of our democracy. He described the mother principle as we can only claim to be a democratic republic to the degree that our decisions reflect the will of the people. Then he went on and said and that will only happen if the people, each person, has an equal voice. Then he went on to say that the biggest factor in equal voice is the power to vote.

We know the original Constitution was incomplete in this vision, that it did not provide that full empowerment to women or to minorities—flaws that we have addressed over time in this vision and understanding that the power to vote is fundamental to a democracy.

Indeed, President after President over the course of our Nation has recognized the power of the individual to vote as fundamental to our democratic Republic.

LBJ said: "The vote is the most powerful instrument ever devised by man for breaking down injustice and destroying the terrible walls which imprison men because they are different from other men."

Of course, he was referring to race and the battle over the Voting Rights Act in 1965.

FDR said: "The ultimate rulers of our democracy are not a President and Senators and Congressmen and Government officials but the voters of this country."

Robert Kennedy put it this way: "Each citizen's right to vote is fundamental to all the other rights of citizenship."

These are not simply ideas that Democrats put forward, these are not simply ideas that our Founders put forward, these are ideas that Republican Presidents have put forward.

Let's turn to Ronald Reagan, who said: "For this Nation to remain true to its principles, we cannot allow any American's vote to be denied, diluted, or defiled."

Ronald Reagan was right and that is why voter suppression is wrong. It is an attack on the vision of our Nation in which citizens are in charge, not powerful elites, powerful special interests. Citizens are in charge. When you deliberately set out to take away the vote from citizens, you really are trying to shred the Constitution.

So those in this Chamber who have been so engaged in promoting voter suppression and your attack on our Constitution—because it is simply wrong. As Ronald Reagan put it, it takes away the power of the individual, it denies, it dilutes, and it defiles. Quit denying, quit diluting, and quit defiling. Honor the vision of this Nation in which citizens are in charge.

Unfortunately, we have seen quite the opposite. We have seen a systematic Republican strategy to tear down the power to vote in our Nation, and this must end.

The Supreme Court set the stage for this by saying enough years have passed that the Voting Rights Act, which required areas and counties that had been active in voter suppression in the past, to get preapproval for changes in their law so they wouldn't go back to defiling and denying the right to vote, said: Enough time has passed. We can now trust them.

That Supreme Court decision was clearly a mistake because, immediately, jurisdiction after jurisdiction proceeded to enact voter suppression laws, often carrying out a debate deliberately about how to keep minorities from voting. This wasn't something hidden. This wasn't sneaky. This was straight out: We don't want those people to vote who might vote against us.

I tell you what I believe in. I believe in our Constitution. I believe in the power of citizens to vote, to be the rulemakers in our country, to have Jefferson's vision, his mother principle of a democratic republic to make decisions in accordance with the will of the people, not the will of the powerful, special interests who are driving this voter suppression attack on Americans' right to vote.

A study of nearly 400 counties in Alabama, Arizona, Texas, Louisiana, North Carolina, South Carolina, and Mississippi found more than 860 polling places were eliminated in those counties. In Arizona, almost every single county shut down voting locations. More than half the counties in Louisiana, Texas, and Alabama did so. They provided data to the researchers.

Let's take a look at North Carolina, a State that passed a voter suppression law which included restrictive voter ID, ending same-day registration, requiring votes cast at the wrong polling location to be thrown out, and shrinking the time for early voting a week—and which did these things after debating directly how to suppress the right of minorities to vote. That is an evil crime against our Constitution and against citizens of the United States of America. The law targeted African-American voters with what the Fourth Circuit of Appeals described as almost surgical precision.

The law was overturned by the court, but that didn't stop the North Carolina Republican Party's very direct efforts to suppress the vote, to eliminate early voting days—especially on Sunday, to severely curtail the number and hours of voting places, of closing all but one early voting location in largely African-American counties, and leaving 27 fewer polling locations than in 2012.

This strategy, successful in Mecklenburg County, which includes Charlotte and has more than 15 percent of the State's Black voters. The State reduced early voting sites from 22 to 4. In three North Carolina counties with large African-American populations, the Republican Party put out a piece of mail and challenged thousands of voter registrations and tried to get them stripped from the rolls until the Federal court ordered them to stop.

Long lines were the result at polling places that "put early voting totally out of reach for people without the time or resources to travel long distances to vote."

It is a crime against the Constitution, it is a crime against the citizens, and it significantly reduced turnout. It was successful.

In 2008, 70 percent of African-American voters in North Carolina voted early. The rough estimates are that about 10 percent fewer ballots were cast in North Carolina in 2016, and at least a substantial share of that change has to be attributed to these voter suppression efforts that produced those long lines and made it so hard for individuals to vote.

We saw glaring examples of voter suppression in Wisconsin, which has one of the strictest voter photo ID laws in the country. It is a law that by lower courts was ruled to serve no legitimate purpose, to make it unnecessarily harder to vote, and designed to disenfranchise African Americans, Latino students, the elderly people with disabilities, and low-income residents. It is a pure, partisan crime against the Constitution, a partisan crime against the citizens of Wisconsin.

As a result of this law, Wisconsin saw its lowest voter turnout in two decades for an election decided by fewer than 30,000 votes in the Presidential election.

Neil Albrecht, executive director of the Milwaukee Election Commission, said: "Some of the greatest declines were in districts we projected would have the most trouble with voter ID requirements."

That is not all. There were online voter suppression strategies. In the final days before the election, there were a series of ads put out that were claiming to be from Secretary Clinton's campaign and basically said to folks "vote from home" by text message or online.

Well, of course, the law doesn't allow people to vote by text message. It doesn't allow people to vote online, although there may be a few exceptions around the country, the vast majority of places you cannot vote online.

We have come a long way technologically in this country, but by and large you still have to show up in person. You still have to vote your ballot. In Oregon, you have to fill out your ballot, drop it off or mail it in. In other places around the country, you have to show up in that voting booth, whether it be early voting or day-of voting.

An effort to mislead people is akin to the other voting suppression tactics where we have seen people put out messages that tell people the voting location has changed. People put out messages that the voting hours have changed. This—a new clever strategy—is saying: Don't bother to go to the voting place, you can vote by text or you can vote online, encouraging people not to go to the polls.

When somebody does something like that, it should be a crime that puts them in jail for years, misleading voters about where to vote, the times to vote, or how you can legally vote. It should be a crime that puts people in jail for years. Why is that? Because it is an attack on the foundation of our democratic Republic, the right to vote.

It is this voter suppression strategy, a tactic which is completely at odds with the vision of a nation in which citizens are in charge—not powerful special interests, not powerful special interests like the Koch brothers who promised, in January of 2015, to put nearly a billion dollars into the 2016 election. The Koch brothers take credit for essentially controlling this Chamber. Indeed, their money played a key role in race after race after race. We saw it in 2014. We saw it this year in 2016.

What kind of Nation do we want? A nation where oil-and-coal billionaires control this Chamber, the Senate, or a nation in which the citizens control this Chamber, a nation in which we honor Jefferson's mother principle or a nation in which we have handed over the keys to a few powerful special interests and billionaires.

Do we want a nation of, by, and for the people or a nation of, by, and for the powerful and the privileged? That is what is at stake here. A senior member of the Trump campaign publicly said: "We have three major voter suppression operations under way."

One of those was Operation Project Alamo, the campaign's custom online database that contained detailed identity profiles on 220-million Americans. The point is, they used this information on more than 200 million Americans to target Secretary Clinton supporters with negative and misleading Facebook ads, the goal being voter suppression, as clearly stated by a senior member of the Trump campaign.

Well, let's go back to the principle laid out by President Ronald Reagan, and again I quote him: "For this Nation to be true to its principles, we cannot allow any American's vote to be denied, diluted or defiled."

So I call on my colleagues who have been the proponents of voter suppression, who have been the proponents of attacking the Constitution, who have been the proponents of government of, by, and for the most powerful and the most privileged rather than the people, to listen.

The PRESIDING OFFICER (Mrs. FISCHER). The Senator's time has expired.

Mr. MERKLEY. I ask unanimous consent for 2 more minutes.

The PRESIDING OFFICER. Is there objection?

Mr. CORNYN. Madam President, I didn't hear how long.

The PRESIDING OFFICER. Two minutes.

Mr. CORNYN. No objection here.

The PRESIDING OFFICER. Without objection, it is so ordered.

Mr. MERKLEY. I thank the Chair.

Those words should continue to reverberate in this Chamber. Colleagues, set your sights on the vision of ending your denying, diluting, and defiling of the most fundamental right close to the hearts of Americans and the foundation of a government of, by, and for the people. Only then will we have a government that responds to the real issues Americans face rather than the special goals of the most powerful and the most privileged.

I thank the Chair.

The PRESIDING OFFICER. The majority whip.

21ST CENTURY CURES BILL

Mr. CORNYN. Madam President, yesterday I spoke about the 21st Century Cures bill the House passed by a very large margin last night, and I am looking forward to taking up that legislation here in the Senate. I am particularly grateful that it includes some mental health reform legislation that I introduced here in the Senate. This represents the very first mental health reform in more than a decade, and it is high time we got it done. There are a lot of people who contributed to this effort, and I think it is something we can all be proud of.

With the mental health portion of the bill, we have two chief goals in mind—first, to help those who are mentally ill get the treatment they need, and secondly, to help law enforcement and first responders know how to respond to a potential mental health crisis in order to keep the person they are responding to safe, as well as the first responders themselves.

It opens up existing funds so that they can be used for more outpatient treatment options. That way, local and State governments can help identify mentally ill offenders, assess their mental health needs, and get them in the right treatment to improve their condition, rather than sending them to jail, where they will be warehoused and their condition will likely just get worse and worse.

This legislation will also provide flexibility to State and local authorities so they can use what works in their communities to help mentally ill individuals in the criminal justice system get healthy. This could include things such as assisted outpatient treatments, where families can help their loved ones, with a backstop of court supervision so they will remain compliant with their doctors' orders and take their medication, which will allow them to lead productive lives.

This legislation will make available Federal grants so that our law enforcement officials have the resources to get the kind of training they need. When law enforcement officials are called to the scene of an incident with somebody suffering from a mental health crisis, it is very important that they know

how to deescalate that crisis, both for the well-being of the individual suffering that crisis as well as the law enforcement officials responding.

It will allow the creation of more crisis-intervention teams comprised of law enforcement and first responders and even school officials, where appropriate, so they can rapidly respond to and counter a threat of violence in the community.

Yesterday I received messages from some of the people who have worked with us on this legislation and know all too well how mental illness can affect our families. One individual wrote:

After losing both [a] son and a husband to suicide, and having an adult son with bipolar disorder, I know only too well the frustrations of the mental health system. Thank you, Senator, for your determination and hard work to bring change to this broken system.

This is why these mental health reforms are so important. People need help and the mental health system needs reform, and that is why we need to pass the 21st Century Cures bill—for all the good it will do in addition to these important reforms in dealing with mental health challenges around the country. So I look forward to finishing the job next week and sending it to the President's desk.

MILITARY READINESS

Mr. CORNYN. Separately, Madam President, I come to the floor today to highlight a pressing national security concern that just doesn't get enough attention. Members often come to the floor to talk about specific military threats that other nations pose to the United States, and that is good and right. For example, we have heard a lot about Iran this week as the Senate considers the Iran Sanctions Extension Act—a bill that will help ensure that President-Elect Trump and future Presidents will have the authority they need to reimpose sanctions on Iran, even in spite of President Obama's flawed nuclear deal which provided relief from these same types of sanctions and others without getting a whole lot of meaningful concessions from Tehran in return. This bill passed the House a few weeks ago with more than 400 votes, and I am glad there has been significant bipartisan support to move it forward here.

But today I want to talk about a problem that is partly of our own making, and that is threats to our long-term military readiness. It is no secret that our military leaders continually call on Congress to adequately fund the weapons programs that enable our troops to defend our Nation.

The major concern I have and one that is shared by leadership at the Pentagon is that our military's technological edge on the battlefield is being whittled away by other countries, such as China and Russia, that are working at breakneck speed, investing millions of dollars to erase our advantage in many areas of military capability. That means we have to wake up to the risks that are inherent in this situation and do more to invest in the next generation of weapons to meet the challenges on the battlefields of tomorrow. The nations that are most belligerent and hostile to America and our interests are not cutting back on their investment in military technology, so we simply do not have the luxury of being complacent.

Recently, I had a chance to meet with Under Secretary of Defense Frank Kendall, the Defense Department's top acquisitions person or top weapons buyer. He is charged with equipping our men and women in uniform, and he has been thinking long and hard about the need to get the next generation of our military the very best capabilities possible. As he has said publicly in speeches and in congressional testimony, he is concerned that our enemies are rapidly expanding and building out their technological innovations for military applications.

But it is important to understand that these countries aren't just building up their own militaries to simply defend themselves; countries such as China and Russia are doing all they can to invest in specific technologies to defeat our forces and to be used for purposes of aggressive activity, whether it is in the South China Sea or in Europe, where Russia continues to threaten the NATO alliance. Countries such as China and Russia are preparing not for next week but for the coming decades to effectively counter and defeat the U.S. militarily. That is a big concern of Secretary Kendall, and it should be a major concern for all of us here in light of the responsibility of Congress to provide for our military.

I have a chart that helps explain where we are headed. Here we can see the research and development projections for the United States, China, and the European Union. It is not hard to see that China will soon outpace the United States.

This represents total research and development spending for the countries involved—not just in military R&D, but given the fact that a large percentage of research and development is spent on defense-related efforts, on military weaponry, it is a useful bellwether for understanding what the future holds in terms of Chinese and Russian military investment relative to our own. Clearly, we can see that China is on track to overtake the United States in this critical area in the next decade.

I should also point out that, according to one report, this isn't just because China is so committed to research and development; it is also because in recent years, due to austerity

measures in our own country, U.S. investment in research and development is increasing at a historically low rate.

Why is this important? Well, it is important because China is using some of this R&D to make weapons that are designed to undermine interests of the United States in the Asia-Pacific region. One recent study made headlines just this week, highlighting that both China and Russia are developing high-speed, high-altitude weapons designed to penetrate traditional U.S. defensive systems, such as our ballistic missile defenses, to attack not only our allies but to potentially attack the mainland of the United States as well.

Reports continue to surface about Chinese cyber theft of top U.S. military and industry secrets. Once they have stolen our trade secrets, the Chinese military can create copycat or cloned weapons for their own use without having to invest the years and billions of dollars that we have to in this country for research and testing and development of those weapons. They can simply steal the blueprints and copy them, saving themselves a lot of money and a lot of time in producing those weapons.

So while nations like China are doing all they can to build their capabilities and research the next cutting-edge weapons, the U.S. military is extremely limited in the amount of money we are investing in our own future, instead having to spend that money to maintain the readiness of current forces. That is where the money has gone—to try to maintain the readiness of our current forces, not looking out to the next 5 and 10 years, to the growing threat of our adversaries having weapon systems that will have the capability not only to be used offensively but potentially to defeat American forces around the world.

We know we need a robust military budget in order to allow us to walk and chew gum at the same time—to both maintain these world-class forces at high levels of readiness and ensure our troops have the cutting-edge weapons of tomorrow. Back in March, the Committee on Armed Services heard testimony by current Secretary of Defense Ash Carter. At the end of his prepared remarks, Secretary Carter made a point we all need to better understand. He said:

We don't have the luxury of just one opponent, or the choice between the current fight and future fights—we have to do both, and we have to have a budget that supports both.

He went on to explain that means being ready to fight the battles of today and train our current troops but also to develop the technologies and perfect the strategies to fight the wars of the future. And we know from Ronald Reagan's doctrine of peace through strength that military readiness is much more likely to make sure that we don't have to fight those battles be-

cause it deters the aggressive actions of our adversaries when America leads and when America is the strongest military in the world. But when our opponents see us pulling back, both in terms of our investment and in terms of American leadership, they are all too happy to fill the void left by that withdrawal.

Unfortunately, the Obama administration has apparently failed to see that national defense is the most critical function the Federal Government performs, and so every time we get into this discussion about how do we spend more money to keep the American people safe and secure, they want to enter into a discussion about how we can raise spending caps so we can spend more money on nondefense discretionary spending, and so it goes.

I believe that defense spending—making sure our men and women in uniform have the training and equipment they need for the current fight but also that we are preparing for the mid- and long-term so they will have the weapons and resources they need to fight the fights of the future—is job No. 1 for us here in the Congress.

It is not too late to eliminate some of these spending caps and to adequately fund the Department of Defense. I look forward to working with all of our colleagues to make sure we take care of job No. 1 before we then look to other priorities in our Federal budget.

We can't take for granted the fact that the U.S. military is the best in the world. We are the best in the world, but there is no certainty or guarantee that will always be the case, especially when our adversaries are making investments for the future and as America's leadership pulls back out of the world and allows others to fill that void. There are other nations at our heels spending a lot of money specifically to neutralize our military advantages and defeat us. The threat extends far beyond China. North Korea, for example, continues to threaten us and our allies with their nuclear weapons and their missile tests. As I indicated earlier, Russia continues to make tremendous advancements in areas such as cyber and electronic warfare, working to render our most effective and advanced capabilities ineffective.

We don't have any time to waste, and we have to spend more time and more energy looking not just at the threats of today but those of tomorrow and beyond. Frankly, once the threat is upon us, it may be too late to do the sort of research and development and investment we need in order to be prepared.

So I am hopeful that the next Congress, working with the new administration, will be able to move the needle in the right direction. We certainly can't just cross our fingers and hope for the best. That is not fulfilling our responsibilities and doing our duty as Members of the Congress. If we want to maintain our position as the most capable military in the world, we have to continue to act, and act without delay.

Madam President, I yield the floor.

The PRESIDING OFFICER. The Senator from Connecticut.

IRAN SANCTIONS EXTENSION BILL

Mr. BLUMENTHAL. Madam President, the Senate will soon act on a measure, the Iran Sanctions Extension Act, that I have long advocated, and I am proud to be a main cosponsor of this measure. It is a critical step toward deterring and impeding support of Iran's development of conventional weapons and weapons of mass destruction.

I am here to encourage my colleagues to support this 10-year reauthorization of the ISA, as it is known. We must act before it expires, before the end of the year. We really have no practical choice. The practical effect of the Iran nuclear agreement depends on our resolve and on our commitment to reliably and durably stop a nuclear-armed Iran by using sanctions and other means, if necessary. This measure should remove all doubt and dispel all question that we have that resolve and commitment to make sure the Iran nuclear commitment is enforced effectively. It must be enforced effectively not only for our own security but really the entire world's security. That is the reason I have championed efforts to stop a nuclear-armed Iran and make sure this agreement is both verifiable and enforceable.

I have long advocated for this renewal and most recently urged Leader McCONNELL to prioritize passage of this measure in the waning days of this Congress. I was joined in this effort by Senators STABENOW, MERKLEY, WYDEN, KLOBUCHAR, HEINRICH, and SCHATZ. I thank Senator McCONNELL for following through on this request and bringing this bill to the floor for a vote today.

This important bipartisan bill has already been approved by the House—in fact, overwhelmingly passed in November—and now the Senate must do the same. It must leave no question or doubt that we have the resolve and commitment to continue bipartisan support for efforts to block a nuclear-armed Iran.

The ISA is essential to ensuring that the Joint Comprehensive Plan of Action continues to prevent Iran from realizing its nuclear ambitions. For the United States to maintain its unambiguous ability to immediately snap back sanctions in coming years, the ISA must be renewed—and I hope it will be by a strong and overwhelming bipartisan majority—or we will surrender this critical capability.

Reauthorization is a significant step that will send a strong signal to Iran that our Nation is fully and irrev-

ocably committed to vigorously enforcing the nuclear agreement regardless of the administration and irrespective of the Congress. Future administrations need this ability to snap back existing sanctions—a step necessary for its enforcement, consistent with the agreement and anticipated by it. There is nothing inconsistent in what we do today with the agreement.

This strong message to Iran is that we are ready, willing, and able to hold Iran accountable. We can ill-afford to allow sanctions that deter and impede Iran's development of conventional weapons of mass destruction to expire, as they would expire at the end of the year. My hope is that as many as possible of my Senate colleagues will join in this effort today.

But holding Iran accountable will scarcely end here. We must confront Iran's maligned activities beyond its nuclear program, its continued pursuit of intercontinental missile development, its suppression of free speech and other vital civil liberties in its own country, and, of course, its sponsorship of terrorism around the world. We must fortify the security of our allies in the Middle East, most especially Israel, and our Nation. Our major strategic partner in that region is Israel. I look forward to working with my colleagues on the NDAA, which will provide additional missile defense capabilities to that great ally. And we must see what we do today in renewing the Iran sanctions agreement as part of an overall effort to secure the freedom and democracies that exist in that region insofar as they are always threatened and make sure we protect our Nation from a nuclear-armed Iran.

The Iran sanctions renewal sends a signal and a message, unmistakable to Iran and the world, that we are committed not just to the words of this agreement on paper but to the real enforcement of them and to making sure Iran is held accountable if it violates this agreement in the slightest way.

Madam President, I yield the floor.

I suggest the absence of a quorum.

The PRESIDING OFFICER. The clerk will call the roll.

The bill clerk proceeded to call the roll.

Mr. KIRK. Madam President, I ask unanimous consent that the order for the quorum call be rescinded.

The PRESIDING OFFICER. Without objection, it is so ordered.

Mr. KIRK. Madam President, on December 1, 2011, the Senate voted 100 to 0 to pass the Menendez-Kirk amendment to impose crippling sanctions on the Central Bank of Iran. As this chart shows, the Menendez-Kirk amendment decreased the value of Iran's currency by 73 percent the following year.

On November 30, 2012, the Senate passed the second Menendez-Kirk amendment by a 94 to 0 vote. This amendment cut off Iran's energy and

shipping sectors from international markets. It also restricted Iran's ability to barter in gold and other precious metals. These Iran sanctions played an indispensable role in forcing Iran to the negotiating table, but the administration wasted our powerful economic leverage when it agreed to a bad deal with Iran.

Since this disastrous deal, Iran's behavior has worsened. Iran has taken more American hostages, including Baquer Namazi and Reza Shahini. Iran received over $100 billion in sanctions relief and has increased support to terrorists groups, such as Hezbollah and Hamas. In fact, Iran announced the creation of its own foreign service to cause problems in Yemen, Iraq, and Iran and those places. Iran has conducted multiple missile tests on October 15, 2015; October 21, 2015; March 8 and 9, 2016; April 19, 2016; and July 11, 2016.

In June of 2015, Senator MENENDEZ and I introduced S. 1682, a bill to renew the Iran Sanctions Act of 1996 for 10 more years. I am glad to see the Senate is again taking up a similar bill based on legislation by Congressman ED ROYCE that passed the House by 419 to 1.

I urge my colleagues to support the Iran sanctions bill with overwhelming numbers. President Obama should immediately sign the Iran Sanctions Extension Act into law.

I urge the next President to join with the Congress to do much more. Our children should never be asked to clean up a nuclear war in the Persian Gulf. Iran, which is the biggest sponsor of world terrorism, should not have nuclear weapons.

I thank the Presiding Officer and yield back my time.

The PRESIDING OFFICER. The Senator from Michigan.

Mr. PETERS. Madam President, I rise to express my support for legislation that the Senate is considering today that will extend the Iran Sanctions Act for 10 years before it expires in just 30 days.

I will be voting for this bill later today, and I am proud to have cosponsored similar legislation earlier this year. The Iran Sanctions Act, or ISA, is an important aspect of U.S. sanctions on Iran.

The ISA was enacted in 1996 to tighten sanctions on Iran in response to its growing nuclear program and support for terrorist organizations, such as Hamas and Hezbollah. The ISA provides the legislative authority for many of the sanctions on Iran that were lifted but may be reimplemented if Iran violates the Joint Comprehensive Plan of Action, or JCPOA. These include sanctions on foreign investment in Iran's oil and gas fields, sales of gasoline to Iran, and transportation of Iranian crude oil. Even though these sanctions were suspended by the

JCPOA, we need this legal framework to address any Iranian violations of the deal so that sanctions can be rapidly put back in place if necessary.

Additionally, this framework maintains some sanctions that were not lifted under the JCPOA. The ISA still requires the United States to sanction entities that assist Iran with acquiring or developing weapons of mass destruction—that provide "destabilizing numbers and types" of advanced conventional weapons or participate in uranium mining ventures with Iran.

These provisions remain in place, and it is absolutely critical that Congress not allow them to expire at the end of the year.

I believe the Iran Sanctions Act has been effective and must be renewed. Tough sanctions were absolutely critical to bringing Iran to the negotiating table—sanctions such as those in the ISA and the Comprehensive Iran Sanctions, Accountability, and Divestment Act of 2010, which I voted for as a Member of the U.S. House of Representatives.

The JCPOA is the result of these and other tough multilateral sanctions put in place through cooperation with international partners, but it is essential that the deal is strictly enforced.

Earlier this year, I led a letter to President Obama, along with 14 of my colleagues, to express our concern about the lack of technical details published by the International Atomic Energy Agency, or IAEA, in reports on Iran's compliance with the JCPOA.

While the IAEA is the watchdog responsible for monitoring Iran's compliance with the JCPOA, it is up to the United States and other parties of the JCPOA to respond to any violations.

To ensure strict compliance, the IAEA should also publish technical details, including the total quantity of low-enriched uranium in Iran and the amount produced in Natanz, specifics on Iran's centrifuge research and development, and progress made on converting Iran's nuclear facilities. These details will provide independent experts and Members of Congress conducting oversight of the JCPOA the opportunity to renew the data behind the IAEA's analysis.

Iran opposes what we are doing here today, and they will say that renewing the Iran Sanctions Act is a violation of the JCPOA. Well, let me say, that is simply not true. Reauthorization of the Iran Sanctions Act in no way violates the JCPOA. The Iran Sanctions Act has been the law of the land since 1996. It was in place when the JCPOA was adopted, and it remains in effect today.

With our vote today, Congress will make clear that the United States will not hesitate to maintain sanctions on Iran and those that seek to provide the world's largest State sponsor of terrorism with weapons of mass destruction. We stand ready to impose rapid and strict punishments for any violation of the JCPOA. This sanctions regime is how we hold Iran accountable, strengthen our security, and deter Iranian hostility towards our allies, especially the State of Israel, which Iran has singled out as a target for destruction.

Diplomacy is always our preferred course of action, but it does not work in a vacuum. It only works if it is backed up with credible deterrence.

Today we show that the United States will continue our leadership against Iranian aggression—work that must continue in the years ahead.

Madam President, I yield the floor.

Mr. BROWN. Madam President, continued implementation of the Iran nuclear agreement, known as the Joint Comprehensive Plan of Action, JCPOA, is our best shot at stopping Iran from developing a nuclear weapon. And so far at least, that agreement has been working.

The Iranians are fulfilling their JCPOA commitments. And so we must also maintain our commitment both to the letter and to the spirit of this historic agreement. Assuming Iran continues to comply, the agreement can and should last for many years. I know many have noted President-Elect Trump's negative comments about renegotiating its terms or even scrapping it outright. I suspect—at least I hope—that once he learns more about the actual national security consequences of scrapping the agreement—of which we were all reminded yesterday by CIA Director John Brennan—he may reconsider.

We know Iran is a state sponsor of terrorism, that it destabilizes the region and violates the human rights of its people. That is why Western policymakers agreed to separate out and try to secure agreement on this one discrete issue. They knew an Iran with a nuclear weapon would be especially dangerous—to us, to Israel, and to the region.

In fact, it is important to keep in mind that this whole process began in the Bush administration, with a Republican President who was—in the wake of the Iraq War—willing to engage Iran diplomatically. The Bush administration laid the foundation for what eventually became the Iran Nuclear Agreement—sanctions relief in return for strict limits on Iran's nuclear program.

In June 2008, President Bush's National Security Adviser Condoleezza Rice signed a memorandum with the P5+1, which said that, in return for Iran doing key things to limit its nuclear program, the U.S. was ready to recognize Iran's right to nuclear energy for peaceful purposes; treat Iran's nuclear program like any nonnuclear weapons state party to the nonproliferation treaty, if international confidence in the peaceful nature of its program could be restored; provide technical and financial aid for peaceful nuclear energy; and work with Iran on confidence-building measures, begin to normalize trade and economic relations, and allow for civil aviation cooperation.

All of this should sound familiar because it was effectively the early outline of the Iran Nuclear Agreement.

As you know, the scope of the sanctions relief provided to Iran under the JCPOA is explicitly limited to nuclear-related sanctions. The United States continues to enforce vigorously a variety of nonnuclear sanctions against Iran, including for ballistic missile violations, human rights abuses, and acts of state-supported terrorism. Our primary trade embargo against Iran remains largely intact. Thus, our ability to maintain sanctions pressure on Iran has been preserved, even as we secured an agreement to prevent a state sponsor of terrorism from acquiring a nuclear weapon.

Today we are debating a simple 10-year extension of the Iran Sanctions Act. Strictly speaking, extension of the act is not legally necessary to continue to enforce our existing sanctions against Iran. As administration officials have testified before the Banking Committee and elsewhere, the International Emergency Economic Powers Act and other authorities provide all of the tools that we would need in order to keep the pressure on Iran—or even to ratchet up the pressure incrementally, if warranted.

But I believe that extending it today is important for two reasons. First, it is a signal of our resolve to keep the heat on Iran and its leaders and to ensure that, if they stray from the agreement through any significant violations, together with our partners in Europe, we would respond forcefully—including if necessary by immediately snapback sanctions on Iran. And second, today's action will make even clearer that we will continue to enforce the nonnuclear sanctions on Iran related to terrorism and ballistic missiles and human rights violations.

As we consider extension of the Iran Sanctions Act today, I hope that we will keep in mind what is truly necessary in order to maintain our current sanctions architecture. The JCPOA was a groundbreaking agreement designed to prevent Iran from obtaining a weapon of mass destruction—but it is also a relatively new and somewhat fragile agreement. We should be very careful, going forward, not to violate the terms of the JCPOA by simply imposing under another guise the old sanctions that were waived or suspended under the nuclear agreement. If that were to happen, our success in preventing Iran from obtaining a nuclear weapon could be unwound in a matter of weeks—or even days. And then we would be isolated internationally, instead of Iran being isolated as the outlier by the international community, as it was under the JCPOA.

Our debate today sends an important signal to Iran: We resolve to continue our fight against terrorism worldwide, to counter Iran's moves to further destabilize the Middle East region, and to impose consequences for the grave human rights abuses that, sadly, continue in Iran to this day. Of course, in addition to renewing these sanctions and maintaining tough JCPOA oversight, Congress must also continue to support robust military and other aid to regional partners like Israel. We should focus both on ensuring strict implementation of the agreement and on the most effective ways to pressure Iran's leaders to change their destabilizing behaviors in the region.

There is no question of our willingness to maintain our current Iran sanctions architecture. We can and we will continue to vigorously enforce non-nuclear sanctions against Iran. And I believe we presently have all of the tools we need to do so. I urge my colleagues to support this measure.

Mr. PETERS. I suggest the absence of a quorum.

The PRESIDING OFFICER (Mrs. ERNST). The clerk will call the roll.

The senior assistant legislative clerk proceeded to call the roll.

Mr. ALEXANDER. Madam President, I ask unanimous consent that the order for the quorum call be rescinded.

The PRESIDING OFFICER. Without objection, it is so ordered.

21ST CENTURY CURES BILL

Mr. ALEXANDER. Madam President, I come today to the Senate floor to offer congratulations to the U.S. House of Representatives because last night, in an overwhelming vote, they passed what Senate Majority Leader MITCH MCCONNELL has described as the single most important piece of legislation the Congress is likely to enact this year.

I am referring to the 21st Century Cures Act, combined with the mental health bill, which is the most significant set of reforms of major mental health programs in 10 years. The Cures package is the result of bipartisan work over the last 2 years. Its purpose is to move cures and treatments through the expensive development process and the extensive regulatory process and into the medicine cabinets and doctors' offices of America more rapidly and safely at the same time. That also helps to lower costs, and we hear a great deal of talk about the affordability of prescription medicines. If it takes more than 10 or 15 years and more than $1 billion to develop a drug, such as a treatment for Alzheimer's, that all adds to the final cost. We would like to lower that cost and speed that time up as long as we continue to do it safely.

I wish to especially compliment the chairman of the House committee that

worked on this, Chairman FRED UPTON, as well as Congressman PALLONE and Congresswoman DEGETTE, Democratic Members of the House of Representatives. They have worked with Senator MURRAY, the ranking Democrat on the Senate's HELP Committee, and with me for the last 2 years on a very complex but very important bill.

Part of the bill has to do with money, and one part of that is $1 billion of funding for State grants for opioids. Now, I suspect one reason there was such a large vote in the House of Representatives yesterday—only 26 Members voted no and 392 voted yes—was because of this $1 billion for opioids. At least in Tennessee—and I am sure it is true in most States of the country—there is no more urgent epidemic than opioid misuse. It is filling up the courts. It is filling up the jails. It is filling up the hospitals. It is causing tragedies in families all across America.

The Senate passed important legislation earlier this year on programs authorizing new money, but this is the money for State grants to Iowa, to Tennessee, to California, and to every State to help deal with the opioid epidemic abuse. So I suspect that one reason so many Members of the House voted yes yesterday and so few voted no would be that it would be pretty hard to explain a "no" vote against $1 billion of State grants for opioid abuse.

There is also $4.8 billion of funding for the National Institutes of Health, which Francis Collins, the distinguished Director, calls the "national institutes of hope," and there is $1.8 billion for the Cancer Moonshot led by Vice President BIDEN. There is $1.4 for the Precision Medicine Initiative, or personalized medicine initiative, a special project of President Obama, and $1.6 billion is for the BRAIN Initiative. There are remarkable advances being made in the ability to identify Alzheimer's before symptoms are evident and then to slow its progression. It is hard to imagine how much grief that would end and the billions it would save if we could do that. So those are other reasons why there are only 26 Members of the House of Representatives who voted no yesterday and 392 who voted yes.

The Mayo Clinic has sent a letter to me:

On behalf of the Mayo Clinic, I write in enthusiastic support of the 21st Century Cures Act and salute your strong, bipartisan leadership on this essential legislation.

We are pleased to see the inclusion of dedicated streaming funds for the Food and Drug Administration and National Institutes of Health. . . .

I ask unanimous consent that this letter be printed in the RECORD following my remarks.

So next Monday the Senate will have a chance to see whether we can do as well as the House of Representatives. I ask my colleagues to think long and

hard about a big vote. We need a big vote. Let me give my colleagues one reason especially why. This $6.3 billion that is in the 21st Century Cures bill is designated for opioids, for precision medicine, for cancer, for brain, and for FDA, and it has to be approved every year by a vote. That is the way our appropriations process works. I would say to my Democratic friends as well as to my Republican friends that if you are concerned about whether the $6.3 billion will be available next year and the next year, the best way to ensure that it is will be to cast a big vote on Monday for it this year, because it will be very hard to explain, if you vote for $6.3 billion this year spread over the next few years, why you did not vote to support it next year and the following year.

The big vote in the House should give assurance to Democrats as well as Republicans in the Senate that these are real dollars, that they are provided in a fundamentally responsible way. To Republicans who look at the $6.3 billion and say: I like the idea of funding opioids; I like the idea of improving funding for the National Institutes of Health, let me say that this is done in a responsible way.

Speaker RYAN, who everybody knows is a conservative budget hawk, created the mechanism for this funding. It was approved by TOM PRICE, the House Budget Committee chairman. It goes like this: $6.3 billion over the next several years for these dedicated purposes. It can only be spent for those purposes. It has to be approved every year. It does not increase the overall spending of the budget by one penny because it is offset by reductions in mandatory spending on the other side. So $6.3 billion up here and $6.3 billion down there over the next 10 years.

So this is a compromise, but it is a magnificent compromise. It is, as Senator MCCONNELL has said, the most important piece of legislation we will deal with this year. The House passed it with a huge bipartisan vote: 392 to 26. I hope that we in the Senate do just as well next Monday because the real winners will be the American people as they look forward to treatments for Alzheimer's, for cancer, a vaccine for Zika, a non-addictive pain medicine that will help deal with the opioid misuse epidemic, and regenerative medicine, which may help restore hearts and perhaps even eyesight in miraculous ways.

This is truly an exciting time, and this is truly an effective piece of legislation that deserves our support by coming to the floor on Monday and then by passing it on Tuesday or Wednesday.

There being no objection, the material was ordered to be printed in the RECORD, as follows:

MAYO CLINIC,
Rochester, MN, November 30, 2016.
Sen. LAMAR ALEXANDER,
Washington, DC.

DEAR SENATOR ALEXANDER: On behalf of Mayo Clinic, I write in enthusiastic support of the 21st Century Cures Act and salute your strong, bipartisan leadership on this essential legislation.

Efforts to advance biomedical innovation and accelerate the development and delivery of cures are of great importance to Mayo Clinic and our patients. We are pleased to see the inclusion of dedicated funding streams for the Food and Drug Administration and National Institutes of Health—including funds for research efforts such as the President's Precision Medicine initiative, the Vice President's Cancer Moonshot, and the BRAIN initiative to speed diagnosis and treatment of conditions such as Alzheimer's disease.

In addition, provisions to promote administrative streamlining, telehealth efforts and mental health reform are also of critical importance in allowing Mayo Clinic physicians and researchers to provide the best possible care to patients.

Mayo Clinic is grateful for your leadership, wholeheartedly supports this comprehensive legislation and looks forward to this innovative effort being signed into law, and we pledge to be a committed partner in its implementation. Thank you.

With best regards,
JOHN H. NOSEWORTHY, M.D.,
President & CEO.

Mr. ALEXANDER. Madam President, I thank the Presiding Officer, and I yield the floor.

I suggest the absence of a quorum.

The PRESIDING OFFICER. The clerk will call the roll.

The legislative clerk proceeded to call the roll.

Mr. COATS. Madam President, I ask unanimous consent that the order for the quorum call be rescinded.

The PRESIDING OFFICER. Without objection, it is so ordered.

WASTEFUL SPENDING

Mr. COATS. Madam President, today marks the 54th version of "Waste of the Week"—54 times I have been down here in the Senate to highlight documented examples of waste, fraud, and abuse. When I first started this endeavor, I told my staff: I hope we can reach $100 billion or so—some target. Do you think there is that much waste, fraud, and abuse floating around through the Federal Government?

Well, we hit that $100 billion a long time ago—I think about the 20th week—and we now have moved to a pretty staggering number, which is more than one-third of a trillion dollars of waste that has been documented by independent agencies of the government that are supporting us with information as to why this money should not have been spent or how it was wasted or lost through fraud or abuse.

I have had a number of serious issues here that run into the billions of dollars that could easily be fixed. Some of them we started by pointing this out

with legislation to try to fix these things, but it just keeps piling on here. So every once in a while, I throw in something so ridiculous, people will understand the fact that there may have been some benefit to that program—we don't understand what the benefit was—but surely these ridiculous examples of money spent, hard-earned tax money spent, are not used for this purpose. Tell me it is not true. Unfortunately, it is true. So today I am adding two more examples of something where people say: How can this be possible? The total ends up at about another $1.5 million.

One of the studies funded by grants from the National Science Foundation totaled $1.3 million. The researcher's application stated they would use the grant funds to examine a variety of factors, one of which was, how does humidity affect the heat that we feel? So, you know, if you go to Florida and it is 90 degrees, you have to shower three times a day. You are sweating, and it feels like it is 110, but the temperature says 90. If you go to Arizona and it is 90 degrees, you don't have to take a shower at all because you can go out and take a run, and it is so dry, you don't feel that heat you would feel in Florida.

I have the same situation in Indiana. Northern Indiana is up near the Great Lakes. It is much cooler and has lower humidity than Southern Indiana, which lies down along the Ohio River. So it can be the same temperature down in southern Indiana as northern Indiana, but people really feel that it is different.

I think we all know this. We have all experienced this through summers, through dry days and through humid days. But, no, the National Science Foundation said: We need a study. Let's give a grant for someone who has made an application—$1.3 million—to see if we can prove that humidity makes it feel as though it is a lot hotter.

So that is what they did. Folks, I can't make this up. This is true. In their initial study, they took beer cans and koozies. Do you know what koozies are? Koozies are those things that you wrap around a cold bottle of Coca Cola or a cold bottle of beer or a can of this or that in order to keep it cold. They put these beer cans in koozies to see if that would be successful in moderating the humidity or what it would do to it.

The researcher's initial round of testing was done in a basement bathroom, where researchers adjusted the temperature and humidity by turning on a hot-water shower and a space heater.

Now, you think, OK, NSF gave us $1.3 million to try to put a study together. You would think they would go to some kind of lab and get sophisticated equipment and so forth. Instead, they went down into the basement bathroom, shut the door, and turned on the

shower, hot water. That wasn't enough, so they put a space heater in there to heat it up. Guess what. The koozies worked.

Well, when you go buy a product this winter at Christmastime, everybody is going to go out and buy stuff. Companies will test something that they want to sell, that they think is going to be bought by the American people. They are successful. Do we have to provide a government grant to help determine whether this works? Can't we just go to the company and say: Hey, you developed this. What were your studies? What did you learn?

Anyway, that was $1.3 million. I think we have a photo. Here it is. Here, essentially, is what $1.3 million bought. They got a little something to measure with, and they put a can over this—looks like Gatorade or some kind of Powerade or whatever. I suppose the money went to buy some of this equipment here to test that. But does the taxpayer have to do this? Is $1.38 million of money taken from taxpayers' paychecks—is that what it is used for? Well, I guess this is great news for beverage drinkers, but it is mind-boggling that we spend that kind of money.

The second thing I would highlight here is another study, this one by DARPA. DARPA is the Federal Defense Advanced Research Projects Agency. For over 50 years—and I admire this Agency—it has done a lot of good things. This little-known Agency states that it is held to a singular and enduring mission that is on their literature: to make pivotal investments in breakthrough technologies for national security purposes. That is a needed, essential use of Federal dollars, to make sure that our warfighters have the kind of equipment and have the kind of research backing up what they are doing. So that is a legitimate expenditure. But why did DARPA decide that understanding why coffee sometimes spills when you are walking is a matter of national security? Now, maybe if the coffee is hot and it gets on the soldier's hands or whatever—the Presiding Officer has had military experience. I am not sure that, as someone in command, you would authorize a study to see that if you were moving when you had a cup of coffee in your hand, you were more likely to spill the coffee than if you were standing still. Trust me, folks—that is what this study was all about. Here was the conclusion of the study: To prevent a spill, you need to pay attention to your coffee while you are walking because the movement might result in a spill.

Now, a confession here. On my way to work—I drive in from Virginia. I have to go by a bakery shop on Lee Highway. I slip in there every morning—it has now become a habit; I have gotten to know the people—for a donut and a cup of coffee. But I don't want to waste time trying to get to work, so I jump into the car and eat the donut and drink the coffee while I am trying to deal with traffic in Washington and get over the bridges and get to work. I have noticed over time that if I have to put the brakes on a little hard or start a little fast or make a quick turn, my coffee spills out of the cup. So all they would have had to do was to buy my coffee, and I could have proved to them that movement would require liquid to move also, and if they are worried about coffee spilling out of the cup, I could have proved that, and all they had to do was buy me a donut and a cup of coffee.

Where does all of this come down? Where this all comes down is the fact that we are nearly $20 trillion in debt. We cannot balance our budget. We spend more every year than we take in. We have to go out and borrow that money, on which we then have to pay interest. By the way, interest rates are going up. When we are in this kind of a fiscal situation, can we not at least, as a body, stop this waste, fraud, and abuse and these stupid expenditures and ridiculous expenditures of taxpayer money?

This here is just a drop in the bucket. We have much bigger things to do to save taxpayers' dollars. But at the very least, could we not address the waste, abuse, and fraud that is taking place? I have offered legislation on a number of ways to do that.

I know the majority leader is moving to the floor here and I need to wrap up, so I will. At the end of 54 times down here on the Senate floor, we have a total of $351,587,239,536 of documented, certified waste, fraud, and abuse. We wonder why the American people are fed up with the status quo of what is happening here in Washington.

I yield the floor.

The PRESIDING OFFICER. The majority leader.

TSUNAMI WARNING, EDUCATION, AND RESEARCH ACT OF 2015

Mr. McCONNELL. Madam President, I ask the Chair to lay before the body the message to accompany H.R. 34.

The Presiding Officer laid before the Senate the following message from the House of Representatives:

Resolved, That the House agree to the amendment of the Senate to the bill (H.R. 34) entitled "An Act to authorize and strengthen the tsunami detection, forecast, warning, research, and mitigation program of the National Oceanic and Atmospheric Administration, and for other purposes", with an amendment.

MOTION TO CONCUR

Mr. McCONNELL. Madam President, I move to concur in the House amendment to the Senate amendment to H.R. 34.

CLOTURE MOTION

Mr. McCONNELL. Madam President, I send a cloture motion to the desk on the motion to concur.

The PRESIDING OFFICER. The cloture motion having been presented under rule XXII, the Chair directs the clerk to read the motion.

The legislative clerk read as follows:

CLOTURE MOTION

We, the undersigned Senators, in accordance with the provisions of rule XXII of the Standing Rules of the Senate, do hereby move to bring to a close debate on the motion to concur in the House amendment to the Senate amendment to H.R. 34, an act to authorize and strengthen the tsunami detection, forecast, warning, research, and mitigation program of the National Oceanic and Atmospheric Administration, and for other purposes.

> Mitch McConnell, Johnny Isakson, Bob Corker, Richard Burr, Pat Roberts, Roy Blunt, Thom Tillis, Lindsey Graham, Lamar Alexander, John Cornyn, Chuck Grassley, Michael B. Enzi, John Barrasso, Shelley Moore Capito, John McCain, Bill Cassidy.

MOTION TO CONCUR WITH AMENDMENT NO. 5117

Mr. McCONNELL. Madam President, I move to concur in the House amendment to the Senate amendment to H.R. 34, with a further amendment.

The PRESIDING OFFICER. The clerk will report.

The legislative clerk read as follows:

The Senator from Kentucky [Mr. McCONNELL] moves to concur in the House amendment to the Senate amendment to H.R. 34 with an amendment numbered 5117.

Mr. McCONNELL. Madam President, I ask unanimous consent that the reading of the amendment be dispensed with.

The PRESIDING OFFICER. Without objection, it is so ordered.

The amendment is as follows:

At the end add the following:
"This Act shall take effect 1 day after the date of enactment."

Mr. McCONNELL. Madam President, I ask for the yeas and nays on the motion to concur with the amendment.

The PRESIDING OFFICER. Is there a sufficient second?

There appears to be a sufficient second.

The yeas and nays were ordered.

AMENDMENT NO. 5118 TO AMENDMENT NO. 5117

Mr. McCONNELL. Madam President, I have a second-degree amendment at the desk.

The PRESIDING OFFICER. The clerk will report.

The legislative clerk read as follows:

The Senator from Kentucky [Mr. McCONNELL] proposes an amendment numbered 5118 to amendment No. 5117.

Mr. McCONNELL. I ask unanimous consent that the reading of the amendment be dispensed with.

The PRESIDING OFFICER. Without objection, it is so ordered.

The amendment is as follows:

Strike "1 day" and insert "2 days".

MOTION TO REFER WITH AMENDMENT NO. 5119

Mr. McCONNELL. Madam President, I move to refer the House message on H.R. 34 to the Committee on Health, Education, Labor, and Pensions with

instructions to report back forthwith an amendment numbered 5119.

The PRESIDING OFFICER. The clerk will report.

The legislative clerk read as follows:

The Senator from Kentucky [Mr. McCONNELL] moves to refer the House message on H.R. 34 to the Committee on Health, Education, Labor, and Pensions with instructions to report back forthwith with an amendment numbered 5119.

The amendment is as follows:

At the end add the following:
"This Act shall take effect 3 days after the date of enactment."

Mr. McCONNELL. Madam President, I ask for the yeas and nays on my motion.

The PRESIDING OFFICER. Is there a sufficient second?

There appears to be a sufficient second.

The yeas and nays were ordered.

AMENDMENT NO. 5120

Mr. McCONNELL. Madam President, I have an amendment to the instructions at the desk.

The PRESIDING OFFICER. The clerk will report.

The legislative clerk read as follows:

The Senator from Kentucky [Mr. McCONNELL] proposes an amendment numbered 5120 to the instructions of the motion to refer H.R. 34.

Mr. McCONNELL. I ask unanimous consent that the reading of the amendment be dispensed with.

The PRESIDING OFFICER. Without objection, it is so ordered.

The amendment is as follows:

Strike "3 days" and insert "4 days".

Mr. McCONNELL. Madam President, I ask for the yeas and nays on my amendment.

The PRESIDING OFFICER. Is there a sufficient second?

There appears to be a sufficient second.

The yeas and nays were ordered.

AMENDMENT NO. 5121 TO AMENDMENT NO. 5120

Mr. McCONNELL. Madam President, I have a second-degree amendment at the desk.

The PRESIDING OFFICER. The clerk will report.

The legislative clerk read as follows:

The Senator from Kentucky [Mr. McCONNELL] proposes an amendment numbered 5121 to amendment No. 5120.

The amendment is as follows:

Strike "4" and insert "5".

Mr. McCONNELL. Madam President, I ask unanimous consent that notwithstanding rule XXII, the cloture vote on the motion to concur occur at 5:30 p.m. on Monday, December 5.

The PRESIDING OFFICER. Without objection, it is so ordered.

CONCLUSION OF MORNING BUSINESS

The PRESIDING OFFICER. Morning business is closed.

IRAN SANCTIONS EXTENSION ACT

The PRESIDING OFFICER. Under the previous order, the Senate will proceed to the consideration of H.R. 6297, which the clerk will report.

The legislative clerk read as follows:

A bill (H.R. 6297) to reauthorize the Iran Sanctions Act of 1996.

The bill was ordered to a third reading and was read the third time.

The PRESIDING OFFICER. The bill having been read the third time, the question is, Shall the bill pass?

Mr. ISAKSON. Madam President, I ask for the yeas and nays.

The PRESIDING OFFICER. Is there a sufficient second?

There appears to be a sufficient second.

The clerk will call the roll.

The bill clerk called the roll.

Mr. DURBIN. I announce that the Senator from Vermont (Mr. SANDERS) is necessarily absent.

The PRESIDING OFFICER (Mr. HOEVEN). Are there any other Senators in the Chamber desiring to vote?

The result was announced—yeas 99, nays 0, as follows:

[Rollcall Vote No. 155 Leg.]

YEAS—99

Alexander	Fischer	Murphy
Ayotte	Flake	Murray
Baldwin	Franken	Nelson
Barrasso	Gardner	Paul
Bennet	Gillibrand	Perdue
Blumenthal	Graham	Peters
Blunt	Grassley	Portman
Booker	Hatch	Reed
Boozman	Heinrich	Reid
Boxer	Heitkamp	Risch
Brown	Heller	Roberts
Burr	Hirono	Rounds
Cantwell	Hoeven	Rubio
Capito	Inhofe	Sasse
Cardin	Isakson	Schatz
Carper	Johnson	Schumer
Casey	Kaine	Scott
Cassidy	King	Sessions
Coats	Kirk	Shaheen
Cochran	Klobuchar	Shelby
Collins	Lankford	Stabenow
Coons	Leahy	Sullivan
Corker	Lee	Tester
Cornyn	Manchin	Thune
Cotton	Markey	Tillis
Crapo	McCain	Toomey
Cruz	McCaskill	Udall
Daines	McConnell	Vitter
Donnelly	Menendez	Warner
Durbin	Merkley	Warren
Enzi	Mikulski	Whitehouse
Ernst	Moran	Wicker
Feinstein	Murkowski	Wyden

NOT VOTING—1

Sanders

The bill (H.R. 6297) was passed.

TSUNAMI WARNING, EDUCATION, AND RESEARCH ACT OF 2015—Continued

The PRESIDING OFFICER. The Senator from Georgia.

FILLING THE SUPREME COURT VACANCY

Mr. PERDUE. Mr. President, I rise to discuss the vacancy of the U.S. Supreme Court.

We have been on this issue and what needs to happen next year when our next President is sworn in. For months this year, I and other Members of this body held our ground in saying that the American people deserve a voice in this process. We talked about how the integrity of the advice and consent process, clearly outlined in article II, section 2 of the U.S. Constitution, was at stake. We outlined years of precedent against nominating and confirming a Supreme Court Justice during a Presidential election cycle.

The last time a vacancy arose and a nominee was confirmed in a Presidential election year was 1932, and 1888 was the last Presidential election year in which a Justice was nominated and confirmed by a divided government. Confirming a nominee to the U.S. Supreme Court should never be distorted by political theater of a Presidential election cycle. This is a bipartisan position. Both parties have said at different times in the past decade or so what I and many colleagues on this floor have said just this year.

Since day one, I have consistently said that no Supreme Court nominee should be considered for the Supreme Court or considered by the Senate before the next President is sworn in. That also meant no consideration during the lameduck, either, no matter the outcome of the election. You can't have it both ways. This was my position before the election. This is still my position today. It was and is about the principle, not the individual. As an outsider to the political process, this was a logical and an easy position to take from the very beginning. The process for nominating and confirming a Justice to the U.S. Supreme Court is enshrined in our Constitution.

The hyperpartisanship and politics of a Presidential election cycle should have absolutely no place in this process. Confirming any individual to a lifetime appointment to the U.S. Supreme Court must rise from that kind of political posturing. It must be above any political theater.

Furthermore, as I said previously, the American people deserved a voice in this process. Election day was not only about changing the direction of our country, but it was also a referendum on the ballots of the Supreme Court for generations to come.

Our decision to withhold consent on any Supreme Court nominee, until after a new President is sworn in, protected the integrity of the advice-and-consent process from political games in a heated Presidential campaign cycle. That decision was entirely within the rights and responsibilities of the Senate, as outlined in the Constitution.

We did our job, and next year we are going to continue to do that job of advice and consent as we consider the next nomination for the Supreme Court. With a new President sworn in, it will be time for the Senate to confirm a nominee to the U.S. Supreme Court. The election is over. The people have spoken. Americans have elected a new President. They chose a new direction.

I urge Members of this body to listen to them, and I urge this body to remember the integrity of the process. I also look forward to learning from whomever President-Elect Trump nominates to serve on the Supreme Court and having the opportunity to vote on his or her confirmation.

I yield my time.

I suggest the absence of a quorum.

The PRESIDING OFFICER. The clerk will call the roll.

The senior assistant legislative clerk proceeded to call the roll.

Mr. MORAN. Mr. President, I ask unanimous consent that the order for the quorum call be rescinded.

The PRESIDING OFFICER. Without objection, it is so ordered.

Mr. MORAN. Mr. President, since my arrival in the U.S. Senate a few years ago, I have been a proponent and advocate and have attempted to champion an issue many in the Senate care about; that is, the desire to increase America's investment in medical research, increase the likelihood of outcomes that are desirable in improving every American's well-being, and end the pain and heartache that comes with diagnoses that often end in difficult lives and ultimately death. We have worked hard as a Senate on this issue.

I serve on the Appropriations Committee with the Presiding Officer. I serve on the appropriations subcommittee that funds the National Institutes of Health, and from my vantage point, it is clear to me that we have made a significant investment in increasing the amount of dollars that taxpayers pay to try to find those cures for cancer, eliminate the onset of Alzheimer's, help with diabetes and mental health issues.

Leadership has been busy for a number of months, and that hard work will culminate with a vote next week on the 21st Century Cures Act. It is an important component of this medical innovation I find so necessary for the benefit of Kansans, Americans, and for people who live around the globe.

This Cures Act invests in the future of our country by providing a significant increase in Federal support for lifesaving biomedical research that will simply impact the life of every American—certainly every American family. These important investments range from increasing the funding at the National Institutes of Health, advancing the precision medicine initiative, funding important cancer research through the cancer Moonshot, and supporting the BRAIN Initiative to improve our understanding of diseases like Alzheimer's.

There are also provisions that will accelerate the FDA approval and drug development process as well as fight opioid abuse and suicides.

The subcommittee the Presiding Officer and I serve on in the Appropriations Committee, or the subcommittee that deals with agriculture and the Food and Drug Administration, wants to give the FDA the tools necessary to accelerate the process by which lifesaving drugs and devices are available for Americans and citizens around the globe.

Under the 21st Century Cures Act, the National Institutes of Health will receive a significant dollar investment increase over the next 10 years. We know that will drive research forward to develop a greater understanding of rare diseases. We often think about NIH as dealing with those major afflictions—cancer and Alzheimer's and diabetes—but many Americans unfortunately suffer from rare diseases, and we want to help find the treatments that are patient-centric that treat rare diseases as well.

This funding will send a message that we acknowledge the benefits of NIH research in a strong bipartisan way. This funding will also work in tandem with those increases that we have provided at NIH through the normal annual appropriations process.

We have always given NIH the ability to prioritize their research that could result in the biggest bang for the buck, the most lifesaving opportunities, but obviously the more resources NIH has, the more opportunities they have to find those cures and advancements in treatments.

This effort also supports the best and brightest among us—those researchers and scientists. I want young Kansans to have a future, if they are interested in science and mathematics and engineering and research, and an opportunity to pursue those careers, hopefully in our State, but certainly in this country. We want the United States to continue to be at the forefront of medical research and within the realm of science and engineering as well. This is an economic engine for our Nation. It can be and is an economic engine for my State. The Cures Act accelerates those opportunities for young people and others across the country who want to devote their lives toward a noble cause of making life longer, greater longevity, but also with fewer challenges and afflictions that come to many people who encounter disease.

The burdens of diseases like Alzheimer's, cancer, stroke, and mental illness can be lessened through research. A long time ago, well before the Affordable Care Act and ObamaCare, I sat down and put my thoughts on paper as to what we should do to try to reduce the cost of health care in this country. What can we do to reduce the price people have to pay to be insured? That list is long. In my view, the way to do this is incremental, but one of

those increments is to invest in medical research. The amount of money that we can save if we can find the cure for cancer, if we can find the delay for the onset of Alzheimer's, is certainly in the billions of dollars, and the investment in medical research helps us to save health care dollars, therefore helping us to make health insurance more affordable for all Americans. It certainly is an investment in economics, it is an investment in the ability to save money, as well as what we know about saving lives and making treatments available to people who otherwise would have less life enjoyment as a result of disease.

New scientific findings are what yields breakthroughs that enable us to confront the staggering challenges of disease and illness, and we can do that through the Cures Act and the efforts we have made over the last several years to make certain that NIH has additional resources.

When it comes to cancer, half of all men and a third of all women in the United States will develop cancer in their lifetime. This bill includes the Cancer Moonshot provision for $1.8 billion of funding. It seeks to combat those statistics to reduce the chances that somebody encounters cancer in their lives and to reduce the costs associated with it. This research will focus on accelerating cancer research and make more therapies more available to more people, to a wider range of patients, and improve our ability to detect cancers at earlier stages of its development and, hopefully, prevent that disease altogether.

So cancer is front and center with the Moonshot and the Cures Act.

For the Food and Drug Administration, an agency that I have learned more about in the last couple of years and have taken a greater interest in, we need to have reforms that are included in the Cures Act that target speeding up the FDA's approval of new medicines and medical equipment.

Pharmaceuticals have become a significant portion of how we treat disease. It used to be in the early days of my life, and certainly in my parents' lives, that you went to the doctor and you were examined and you may be admitted to the hospital. So often today you are examined, and you are given a prescription. It is a way now that we treat patients. We have today a wider variety of opportunities that pharmaceuticals provide, and we need to make certain that the FDA has the resources, has the right mentality, the mindset—is not a bureaucratic organization—that can advance the production of new drugs available to treat Americans with a wide array of options. This legislation brings a patient-focused view to drug development that will be so relevant in the process of bringing forward the things we need to cure and treat Americans.

Opioids have been a topic of conversation of this Senate for a number of months—for the last several years, in fact—and, unfortunately, millions across the country struggle with an addiction to opioids. It is a heartbreaking reality. The Presiding Officer and I come from rural States. We wish we could say that our States are immune, that it is a problem for folks in the cities or suburbs or someplace else. But, unfortunately, opioids and other drug addictions are a significant component of the challenges we face at home. We include in the Cures bill additional dollars to address the addiction issue, including prevention and treatment, prescription drug monitoring programs, and efforts to reform our current system.

It is important that this legislation pass as a followup to the Comprehensive Addiction and Recovery Act, which I voted for earlier this year, to try to stop the spread of opioid abuse in communities across the country.

I have started paying more attention to mental health issues at home as well, visiting our community mental health centers, visiting our State and mental health hospitals. We need to make certain that in our efforts to focus on health care, we have an appropriate prioritization of mental health as well. The 21st Century Cures Act takes steps forward in that regard in providing solutions for more than 11.5 million American adults who live with mental illness that is considered disabling. Important sections of the Helping Families in Mental Health Crisis Act, which represents some of the most significant reforms to the mental health system in more than a decade, are included in the Cures Act. These efforts are aided by establishing a new Assistant Secretary for Mental Health and Substance Abuse at the Department of Health and Human Services, and we are hopeful that this person will help us coordinate direct funding and remove the regulatory barriers that hold back our abilities to find treatment and cures and care for people who suffer from mental illness.

Suicides are a significant problem. The Presiding Officer and I serve on the Veterans' Committee together, where suicides by veterans are an ever-present problem. Twenty-two veterans a day commit suicide. Our efforts at focusing research and treatment in regard to mental health can help save the lives of those who sacrificed so much for us and comfort their families and avoid disasters and tragedies that occur way too often.

There are a couple of provisions that were included in this legislation as it works its way through the Senate. I am supportive of many of those related to rural health care. For my time in Congress, I have been an active member of the rural health care caucus. I represent a State that has 127 hospitals in communities across our State. Those hospitals provide health care and jobs for people in rural America. Rural Kansans have paid into FICA and Social Security taxes and deserve to have the attention they need for treating individuals who choose to live in rural America, in keeping those hospital doors open, keeping physicians in our communities, and keeping the pharmacy open on Main Street. Those are things that matter greatly to me.

Unfortunately, the Centers for Medicare & Medicaid Services, a component of the Department of Health and Human Services, often creates rules and regulations that make no sense in the places that the Presiding Officer and I come from. So I am supporting a couple of things in particular that are included in this bill. We had a regulation that came from CMS—the Centers for Medicare & Medicaid Services—generally called physician supervision. Its enforcement is delayed 1 year in the Cures Act. I am the sponsor of legislation to rid us of that regulation permanently, but it is a benefit for us to have it out of the system for another year as we work to find that permanent solution. But the idea that there must be a physician present in certain circumstances—it is difficult for us to have a physician on site in a room with a patient in every circumstance, and our mid-levels and others are important to us in rural communities in particular. That delay is something we have worked hard on, and I am pleased to see that we were successful in getting it included in this legislation.

Many of those hospitals that I mentioned in Kansas—127 hospitals in our State, 80-plus—90 or so—are what are called critical access hospitals, which is a special designation that allows them a so-called cost-based reimbursement. When I was in the House of Representatives, I authored legislation that created an opportunity to expand the critical access hospital designation to hospitals that are slightly larger and that wouldn't otherwise meet the criteria, which is 25 beds or less. There is a demonstration project, a pilot program that has been operating in the country for the last 5 years, trying to determine what cost-based reimbursement would mean for hospitals that are slightly larger than 25 beds. That demonstration project is expiring. Fortunately, language in the Cures Act extends that community health demonstration project—something, again, we have worked hard to make certain happens. I am pleased that the lead sponsors of this legislation were amenable to our request to include these provisions.

I would conclude by saying the United States has a responsibility to continue our leadership in providing medical breakthroughs that will help change the world, and certainly change people's lives, to develop those cures

and treat diseases, and we must commit ourselves to significant support for research that is supported in legislation just like the 21st Century Cures Act. This legislation has the capacity to benefit millions of Americans suffering from chronic diseases. It can help our grandparents, our children, our lifelong best friends, and we can avoid the tragedy that comes with a diagnosis that often ends in death. People's lives depend upon the decisions we make, and this is a decision we can make that will benefit many Americans and their families.

Our researchers must be able to rely on consistent, sustainable funding support from Congress; otherwise we will lose the best and brightest, and we will lose men and women who think maybe they want to be a researcher and find a cure for a disease, but because of their uncertainty as to whether or not their research might get funded or whether the funding is going to be there next year—they get it, but they are uncertain as to whether it will continue. We don't want to lose those bright minds and noble colleagues, people across our country who might enter into the profession of medical research to help find ways to meet the needs of Americans and their health care.

NIH-supported research has raised life expectancy, improved the quality of life, and lowered overall health care costs. This legislation strengthens that circumstance and allows us to better remain globally competitive in the arena of medical research. The 21st Century Cures Act is a powerful statement by Congress, but, more important than being a statement, it is something that will actually make a difference in the future of the people that we care about.

I commend the efforts by many Senators and Members of the House to make certain that this legislation arrives here in the Senate before there is a recess for the holidays. It will be a strong statement, but, more importantly, we expect significant results and the improvement of people's lives across the Nation and around the globe.

Mr. President, I yield the floor.

I suggest the absence of a quorum.

The PRESIDING OFFICER. The clerk will call the roll.

The senior assistant legislative clerk proceeded to call the roll.

Mr. SCOTT. Mr. President, I ask unanimous consent that the order for the quorum call be rescinded.

The PRESIDING OFFICER (Mr. CASSIDY). Without objection, it is so ordered.

ANTI-SEMITISM AWARENESS ACT OF 2016

Mr. SCOTT. Mr. President, I ask unanimous consent that the Senate proceed to the immediate consideration of S. 10, introduced earlier today.

The PRESIDING OFFICER. The clerk will report the bill by title.

The legislative clerk read as follows:

A bill (S. 10) to provide for the consideration of a definition of anti-Semitism for the enforcement of Federal antidiscrimination laws concerning education programs or activities.

There being no objection, the Senate proceeded to consider the bill.

Mr. CASEY. Mr. President, I rise today, along with my colleague from South Carolina, to talk about a bill we have introduced entitled the "Anti-Semitism Awareness Act of 2016."

Let me say first that I wish we were living in a time where we would not have to introduce legislation like this, but unfortunately what we have seen over a long period of time—and I think a problem that is getting worse—is the rising tide of anti-Semitism in substantial sectors of our society. We have, in fact, a rise in the incidence of religious discrimination and religiously motivated hate crimes. To say that is unacceptable, even un-American, is an understatement.

We have to take action at long last to do what we can in the U.S. Senate, and I hope in the House as well, to not just speak out against anti-Semitism but to take action which will lead to a better strategy to deal with it. What do I mean by that? Well, it is simple. It is about definitions, and it is about making sure that Federal agencies, such as the Department of Education, do their job when it comes to combating anti-Semitism. We know that one piece of legislation is not somehow going to magically eradicate anti-Semitism. We don't have that naive hope. But what we do believe is that if we don't take action, this problem is only going to get worse.

Some of the problem, frankly, is on our college campuses, and I know that is true, unfortunately and regrettably, in my home State of Pennsylvania. We don't have time to list every incident, every action, every terrible example of this, but I will just provide one for the record.

In September, students at Swarthmore College in Pennsylvania—one of our great institutions of higher education not only in Pennsylvania but across the country—Swarthmore is a great school, but here is what they found. They found swastikas spray-painted in a bathroom in the library. The college leadership did the right thing in swiftly condemning these actions and removing the graffiti, and I am glad they did that.

I can only try to imagine—and I can literally only try to understand because I have never been the victim of this kind of hate—the horror that was experienced by those students and their families. A person comes to a college or a university as a place where they are going to learn and grow and live in a community, and then there are people—for whatever reason, and I will never understand the reason anyone would do that—painting those images and using language and taking other actions that discriminate against people because of who they are. We have to be not just concerned about this, as I said, but we have to figure out a way to take action.

This particular piece of legislation is aimed at a terrible manifestation of this problem. When anti-Semitic views lead to discrimination against students of Jewish faith or Jewish ancestry, that is the result, and they are the victims of this. The intent here is simple and narrowly circumscribed to make sure we are getting at the problem as best we can to define anti-Semitism at long last—this hasn't been done before—to define anti-Semitism so that the Department of Education can effectively investigate allegations of discrimination motivated by anti-Semitism under the Civil Rights Act. The bill does not infringe on the First Amendment. It does not infringe on those rights of free speech. It is intended to help protect students from discrimination on the basis of their faith.

We all agree that religious discrimination has no place on campuses, has no place in our society, and we have to do more than just speak out against it. That is fundamental, but we can do more than just speak out; we can define it and thereby give in this case one Federal Government agency one tool it needs to deal with this issue. This is a bill which is timely not only because of what is happening on college campuses but unfortunately what has happened in too many parts of our society. We want to make sure the Department of Education has at least one of those tools to deal with this problem.

Because of the nature of this problem, we have people on both sides of the aisle here who are very concerned about it. I am particularly grateful that I am joined by my colleague from South Carolina, Senator SCOTT, who is joining with me. We are a Democrat and a Republican from different parts of the country and a different point of view on a lot of issues. On this issue we are unified, and we have a solidarity about not just the problem, but there is a solidarity and a consensus about one of the things we can do to take action on this issue.

I am grateful to be joined by my colleague from South Carolina.

I yield the floor to him.

The PRESIDING OFFICER. The Senator from South Carolina.

Mr. SCOTT. Mr. President, I thank Senator CASEY for joining me on the floor.

There is no question that much of our country yearns for a day when Republicans and Democrats come together on issues that impact who we are as a nation. I am thankful that Senator CASEY has joined me in this objective of making sure hate is pushed out of this Nation every single day.

Today I come to speak about an alarming issue—the issue of hate. It truly tears at the very fabric of our great Nation and should inspire all of us to stand up and be counted on the side of justice, on the side of common sense, and on the side of making sure this great American family remains one Nation.

Over the past several years, there has been a sharp rise in religiously motivated hate crimes, particularly on our college and university campuses all over America. According to the FBI, close to 60 percent of these crimes were due to anti-Jewish sentiments. From 2014 to 2015, we saw the number of reported incidents double. Let me say that one more time. In a year, we saw a doubling of the incidence of religious discrimination on college campuses, and the vast majority of those issues and situations focused on the Jewish community. There were 90 anti-Jewish incidents reported at 60 schools last year, compared with 47 incidents on 43 campuses just the year before. These numbers are staggering.

Senator CASEY noted that there have been college campuses and buildings on college campuses where we have seen swastikas. We have heard protests that call for Zionists to leave the school, and we have heard references being made to burning in Auschwitz. I am stunned and saddened by the careless and hateful reminders of such an incredibly dark and daunting time in our world's history, but I also feel empowered and committed to taking a stand against hate. No one, not a single person should ever have to experience being singled out because of who they are or attacked based on the religion they choose to follow. There is simply no place in our country for this kind of intolerance, especially not in our country, the greatest country on Earth.

As citizens of this great Nation, it falls on us to stand up and do more to protect our students from being targeted by any form of hate and bigotry. It is important that we work together to stamp out anti-Semitism and other forms of religious discrimination. Our students should be able to go to school, to grow, to learn, and to develop without having to worry about being discriminated against. Although the Department of Education's Office of Civil Rights has stated that they will not tolerate incidents such as these, there exists a lack of firm guidance on what constitutes anti-Semitic acts. That is why Senator CASEY and I stand before you today to introduce the bipartisan Anti-Semitism Awareness Act. We have come together to ensure that the U.S. Department of Education has the necessary tools at their disposal to investigate anti-Jewish discrimination.

Our proposed legislation uses the very definition of anti-Semitism adopted by the U.S. State Department's Special Envoy to monitor and combat anti-Semitism. This important clarification will provide necessary direction to assist officials and administrators to understand when anti-Semitic activities are occurring. By clarifying exactly what anti-Semitism is, we will leave no question as to what constitutes an illegal anti-Semitic incident.

As we seek to tackle this concerning issue, it is important to note that this act will in no way infringe on any individual right protected under the First Amendment of the Constitution. I think we have to emphasize that. Our legislation in no way, shape, or form infringes upon any individual rights protected under the First Amendment of the Constitution. It simply and specifically provides clarity on the definition that the Department of Education can and will use for defining anti-Semitic acts.

We must act now. This increase in religiously motivated hate crimes must be addressed. It must be addressed by the entire American family, and it ought to start here. We will come together because we will not allow others to tear us apart. We must hold to the ideals that our Nation was founded on and promote freedom of religion. We must protect that freedom and encourage it. We must—as a Nation, as an American family—call out hate wherever and whenever we see it.

I thank Senator CASEY for his involvement and leadership on such an important issue.

I yield the floor.

Mr. PORTMAN. Mr. President, I would like to thank Senators SCOTT and CASEY for their work on the anti-discrimination legislation, particularly as it relates to anti-Semitism. I support them in that effort and look forward to getting something done in Congress to help address the definition of anti-Semitism for the Department of Education.

Mr. SCOTT. Mr. President, I ask unanimous consent that the bill be read a third time and passed and the motion to reconsider be considered made and laid upon the table.

The PRESIDING OFFICER. Without objection, it is so ordered.

The bill (S. 10) was ordered to be engrossed for a third reading, was read the third time, and passed, as follows:

S. 10

Be it enacted by the Senate and House of Representatives of the United States of America in Congress assembled,

SECTION 1. SHORT TITLE.

This Act may be cited as the "Anti-Semitism Awareness Act of 2016".

SEC. 2. FINDINGS.

Congress makes the following findings:

(1) Title VI of the Civil Rights Act of 1964 (referred to in the section as "title VI") is one of the principal antidiscrimination statutes enforced by the Department of Education's Office for Civil Rights.

(2) Title VI prohibits discrimination on the basis of race, color, or national origin.

(3) Both the Department of Justice and the Department of Education have properly concluded that title VI prohibits discrimination against Jews, Muslims, Sikhs, and members of other religious groups when the discrimination is based on the group's actual or perceived shared ancestry or ethnic characteristics or when the discrimination is based on actual or perceived citizenship or residence in a country whose residents share a dominant religion or a distinct religious identity.

(4) A September 8, 2010 letter from Assistant Attorney General Thomas E. Perez to Assistant Secretary for Civil Rights Russlynn H. Ali stated that "[a]lthough Title VI does not prohibit discrimination on the basis of religion, discrimination against Jews, Muslims, Sikhs, and members of other groups violates Title VI when that discrimination is based on the group's actual or perceived shared ancestry or ethnic characteristics".

(5) To assist State and local educational agencies and schools in their efforts to comply with Federal law, the Department of Education periodically issues Dear Colleague letters. On a number of occasions, these letters set forth the Department of Education's interpretation of the statutory and regulatory obligations of schools under title VI.

(6) On September 13, 2004, the Department of Education issued a Dear Colleague letter regarding the obligations of schools (including colleges) under title VI to address incidents involving religious discrimination. The 2004 letter specifically notes that "since the attacks of September 11, 2001, OCR has received complaints of race or national origin harassment commingled with aspects of religious discrimination against Arab Muslim, Sikh, and Jewish students.".

(7) An October 26, 2010 Dear Colleague letter issued by the Department of Education stated, "While Title VI does not cover discrimination based solely on religion, groups that face discrimination on the basis of actual or perceived shared ancestry or ethnic characteristics may not be denied protection under Title VI on the ground that they also share a common faith. These principles apply not just to Jewish students, but also to students from any discrete religious group that shares, or is perceived to share, ancestry or ethnic characteristics (e.g., Muslims or Sikhs).".

(8) Anti-Semitism remains a persistent, disturbing problem in elementary and secondary schools and on college campuses.

(9) Jewish students are being threatened, harassed, or intimidated in their schools (including on their campuses) on the basis of their shared ancestry or ethnic characteristics including through harassing conduct that creates a hostile environment so severe, pervasive, or persistent so as to interfere with or limit some students' ability to participate in or benefit from the services, activities, or opportunities offered by schools.

(10) The 2010 Dear Colleague letter cautioned schools that they "must take prompt and effective steps reasonably calculated to end the harassment, eliminate any hostile environment, and its effects, and prevent the harassment from recurring," but did not provide guidance on current manifestation of anti-Semitism, including discriminatory anti-Semitic conduct that is couched as anti-Israel or anti-Zionist.

(11) The definition and examples referred to in paragraphs (1) and (2) of section 3 have been valuable tools to help identify contemporary manifestations of anti-Semitism, and

include useful examples of discriminatory anti-Israel conduct that crosses the line into anti-Semitism.

(12) Awareness of this definition of anti-Semitism will increase understanding of the parameters of contemporary anti-Jewish conduct and will assist the Department of Education in determining whether an investigation of anti-Semitism under title VI is warranted.

SEC. 3. DEFINITIONS.

For purposes of this Act, the term "definition of anti-Semitism"—

(1) includes the definition of anti-Semitism set forth by the Special Envoy to Monitor and Combat Anti-Semitism of the Department of State in the Fact Sheet issued on June 8, 2010, as adapted from the Working Definition of Anti-Semitism of the European Monitoring Center on Racism and Xenophobia (now known as the European Union Agency for Fundamental Rights); and

(2) includes the examples set forth under the headings "Contemporary Examples of Anti-Semitism" and "What is Anti-Semitism Relative to Israel?" of the Fact Sheet.

SEC. 4. RULE OF CONSTRUCTION FOR TITLE VI OF THE CIVIL RIGHTS ACT OF 1964.

In reviewing, investigating, or deciding whether there has been a violation of title VI of the Civil Rights Act of 1964 (42 U.S.C. 2000d et seq.) on the basis of race, color, or national origin, based on an individual's actual or perceived shared Jewish ancestry or Jewish ethnic characteristics, the Department of Education shall take into consideration the definition of anti-Semitism as part of the Department's assessment of whether the alleged practice was motivated by anti-Semitic intent.

SEC. 5. CONSTITUTIONAL PROTECTIONS.

Nothing in this Act, or an amendment made by this Act, shall be construed to diminish or infringe upon any right protected under the First Amendment to the Constitution of the United States.

Mr. SCOTT. Mr. President, I suggest the absence of a quorum.

The PRESIDING OFFICER. The clerk will call the roll.

The legislative clerk proceeded to call the roll.

Mr. TESTER. Mr. President, I ask unanimous consent that the order for the quorum call be rescinded.

The PRESIDING OFFICER. Without objection, it is so ordered.

TSUNAMI WARNING, EDUCATION, AND RESEARCH ACT OF 2015—Continued

TRIBUTE TO TRECIA BICKFORD MC EVOY

Mr. TESTER. Mr. President, I rise today, not a minute too late, not a minute too early but at the exact time I am scheduled to speak. That is because of a remarkable woman, my scheduler Trecia Bickford McEvoy. Trecia has dedicated 25 years of her life to serving her country and the United States Senate. She has worked for a Republican, she has worked for an Independent, and she has worked for a Democrat, a true bipartisan public servant we can all learn a thing or two from.

As a farmer, the schedule is rigorous but simple: You plant, you harvest, and

then everything else in between, but when I got to the Senate, I found Washington, DC, is not as cut and dry as the farm. Luckily for me, after Trecia served Vermont Senator Jim Jefford's office for over 15 years, she came to my office to help me and my staff find the bathrooms.

Since 2008, I have been lucky enough to have her in my office, and the State of Montana is better off for it. Thanks to her remarkable work, I have been able to see thousands of Montanans, in between thousands of committee hearings and briefings and runs to the airport, all because of an airtight schedule curated by Trecia.

At an all-staff meeting, one of my staffers was asked to draw a picture of what she believes Trecia does every day. With her trademark humility, Trecia said: "Well, that would be kind of boring," but what landed on that paper was a set of hands, a generous set of hands, that ensures that all Montanans can engage with the important policy decisions that shape our lives every day.

Trecia acts as the hands that carry Montanans from all across the State to see their Senator. It is not boring at all. In fact, it is really important. If scheduling was an art, my schedules would be enshrined not just on my Web site but also down the street at the National Gallery. Trecia would know exactly how many minutes it takes every day to drive from the Hill to the museum.

As my colleagues know, a good scheduler is hard to find and even harder to keep. Trecia has shown a staying quality that puts her in the Scheduler Hall of Fame, a hall that would be erected along the road from the Capitol to National Airport. Whether it is a call from my farm at 3 a.m. to tell her I am going to miss my flight because my truck can't make it through the snow or a text from the plane in Minneapolis asking which gate I need to get to for a tight connection, Trecia has always been ready and willing to answer the call.

After 25 years on the Hill, I know I am not the only one who can attest to Trecia's talents as a scheduler, as a friend, and as a person. She is a critical part of my office, not only because she keeps me on schedule, but she is also a relentless mentor to my younger staffers, always sharing in their joys and consoling them in their tougher times.

I will never forget that the first time I met Trecia is when I interviewed her for the job as my scheduler. A few months earlier, my wife and I had just been on an airplane from Seattle to Washington National Airport. My wife sat in the middle seat in row 12, and I sat in the middle seat in row 27.

I said to Trecia: What is going to happen when you schedule me on a cross-country flight in a middle seat in the back of the plane and my wife in a middle seat in the front of the plane?

She looked at me and said: That ain't ever going to happen.

And it never has.

Her smarts, her generosity, and her quick wit not only make my life easier but also make the lives of other Senators' staffs and, most importantly, Montanans' easier. As one of my former chiefs of staff pointed out, whether it is a veteran from Columbia Falls, a high school student from Billings, or a mom from Havre, Trecia has played a vital role in improving the lives of everyday Montanans. They may not know who made that moment happen, but I do.

To me and to many others on the Hill and in the office, Trecia is more than just a scheduler. When I asked for the quintessential Trecia McEvoy story, one of her former bosses told a story—not about Trecia getting a meeting scheduled or pulling off an air traffic miracle, but they told a story about Trecia the coworker and friend. According to one of her former chiefs of staff, Trecia would give a secret heads-up to young, junior staff members any time their boss was coming by so that their pencils were sharpened and everything was on the up and up, even late on a Friday afternoon long after the Senator had flown home. This type of kindness, humor, and leadership shines through with Trecia's work every day.

Whether it is a bright-eyed intern from Helena looking for a place to live for the summer, the ambitious staff assistant looking for professional guidance, or the know-it-all executive assistant who thinks he knows best, Trecia has been there to give advice, to listen, and to keep all of us grounded in a town where often the only thing bigger than the monuments are the egos.

Despite a reputation as a miracle worker, her greatest accomplishment has been balancing the hectic profession of a scheduler with her critically important duties as a parent. When I call on Thursday night because a flight is delayed, it is not uncommon for me to hear in the background the cheer of a crowd from Ian's hockey game or a hushed whisper from an audience at one of Zachary's plays. Despite the long hours, frantic phone calls, and countless emails, Trecia's No. 1 priority has always been crystal clear: her family. Over the past 25 years, Trecia and her husband Jeff have made sure that their kids—Alexis, Zachary, and Ian—have everything they need to be able to succeed.

In the office and in life, Trecia is more than a scheduler. What has made Trecia a great scheduler over the years are the same qualities that have made her a great friend, counselor, and mother. Trecia's generosity, sympathetic ear, sharp wit, and understanding nature have made her a phenomenal scheduler, a great friend, and, most importantly, an ideal mother.

On behalf of Montana, Vermont, countless staff members, and from this dirt farmer from Big Sandy, I thank Trecia for 25 years of service.

Mr. President, I yield the floor.

I suggest the absence of a quorum.

The PRESIDING OFFICER. The clerk will call the roll.

The legislative clerk proceeded to call the roll.

Mr. FRANKEN. Mr. President, I ask unanimous consent that the order for the quorum call be rescinded.

The PRESIDING OFFICER. Without objection, it is so ordered.

OVERTIME RULE

Mr. FRANKEN. Mr. President, as we enter the holiday season, today should be a special day for 4.2 million working Americans, including 75,000 Minnesotans. That is because today was supposed to be the day that the overtime rule would go into effect to ensure that workers are paid overtime wages when they work more than 40 hours in a week. Instead, the rule has been blocked, meaning that many of these working people will not be able to benefit from this rule, which is especially unfortunate given that the holidays are coming upon us. Right now, these 4.2 million employees don't have to be paid at all for overtime work they perform. That is what we are trying to change.

As you know, we had a big election in which working people sent the clear message they are hurting. Yet less than a month later, Republicans have decided to attack a rule that would ensure that American workers are paid for every hour they work. This is exactly the type of policy we should all be able to agree on to help working people across the country.

During the campaign, President-Elect Trump repeatedly said he was for working people. One important action he could take immediately would be to go on his twitter account and express support for the overtime rule.

Here is why this rule matters so much. As our economy has changed in the past couple of decades, the rule on overtime pay has not kept pace at all. The last meaningful improvement for workers covered by this rule came in 1975, when the rule made 62 percent of so-called administrative and professional employees eligible for overtime pay. As a result of failing to keep the rule up-to-date and current with the rate of inflation, right now only 7 percent of employees in that category must be paid overtime.

The Obama administration's update to the overtime rule was intended to change the fact that under the standard right now, employers aren't required to pay overtime to these employees unless the employees earn less than $23,000 a year. If you are paid on a salary basis and earn more than $23,000 a year, your employer can make you work more than 40 hours a week and not pay you anything at all for your extra hours. Twenty-three thousand dollars is simply too low of a threshold. A salary of $23,000 a year is below the poverty line for a family of four. I believe workers and their families deserve better.

That is why the Obama administration instituted an update to the overtime rule, to lift the salary threshold to $47,000 a year, bringing it closer to the original standard in place in 1975. It still wouldn't be as high as the comparable level in 1975, but it would be a vast improvement, and it would mean that 4.2 million more workers across the United States would qualify for overtime pay.

Consider a retail manager making a salary of $40,000 a year at a big box store or fast-food chain. Right now, many employers are legally allowed to require such an employee to work 50, 60 or more hours in a week without paying him or her anything extra. This new rule would mean the employee would be paid extra when they work more than 40 hours a week.

Similarly, the rule would make sure a trucking dispatcher earning $45,000 a year would not be forced to work late at night without compensation. The rule encourages his or her employer to send employees home to his or her family on time or else the employer will pay them for the overtime he or she works.

This is very important for working men and women in America. That is why many of my colleagues and I have been strong supporters of this rule. That is why it has been very disappointing to see so many of my Republican colleagues attack and ultimately try to dismantle this rule.

They have been attacking the rule ever since it was proposed. They have set out on a campaign to delay, to water down, or to block the rule entirely. In the Senate, 45 Republicans have signed on to a bill to block it. In the House, 202 Members have signed on to a companion measure to that bill. House Speaker PAUL RYAN claims the rule is an "absolute disaster," and Senator VITTER claims the rule will "reduce worker's opportunity for long-term advancement and increased pay."

Despite their attacks on this updated rule in the House and in the Senate, Republicans weren't able to block it through the legislative process. So they took their fight to the courts, where they used their old tactic of forum shopping, where they file a suit in the court they think is most likely to be favorable for their arguments. As a result, 9 days ago, they convinced a Texas judge to put the updated overtime rule on hold. The 4.2 million workers who today were scheduled to be paid for every hour they work above the 40 could continue to be forced to work overtime without the additional compensation they deserve.

As our economy has continued to recover from the Great Recession, too much of the wealth in the last few years has accrued to the top 1 percent in this country and often the top one-tenth of 1 percent. While new data suggests the economy has improved a bit for middle-class workers since last year, the median household income in the United States remains lower than it was in the year 2000 in real dollars. Updating our overtime pay rule is one of the most effective steps we can take to put working people back on a more level economic playing field.

I hope my colleagues will join me today in pledging to fight in Congress, the executive branch, and the courts for a fairer system for all workers and for updating this incredibly outdated overtime rule. Let's hope that the postponement of the new rule today will be temporary. Let's join forces on behalf of American workers to stand strong in support of a fair overtime rule and to work together to build a stronger American middle class.

I thank the Presiding Officer.

The PRESIDING OFFICER. The Senator from Oregon.

Mr. MERKLEY. Mr. President, I appreciate the comments made by my colleague from Minnesota. He has been a strong champion for America's workers and believes we should make this Nation and our economy work for working Americans. His leadership on this overtime rule is certainly much appreciated.

Today should be a day of celebration. It should be a day in which 4 million American workers who work overtime without getting paid but earn very modest salaries were going to get rewarded for their overtime work—get paid for their overtime work—but instead those 4 million Americans are getting scrooged.

You all remember the story of Ebenezer Scrooge. He made a lot of money as a very successful businessman. He enjoyed counting his coins while treating his workers in a terrible fashion and paying them as little as he could get away with. That is exactly what is at stake with this overtime rule. The vision of the overtime rule was that when you had a very well-paid manager who was clearly earning far more than they would if they were earning a more modest amount plus overtime, you could reduce the complexity of tracking their overtime hours and instead simply pay them a salary without compensation for overtime. The key to that was that it was a very well-paid worker or manager and not someone earning near the bottom of the scale and barely making more than minimum wage.

As I said, today should be a day of celebration with the overtime rule being modified so that it would catch up with inflation. Many decades have passed since it was put forward. It was supposed to be adjusted for inflation from here forward, but it was not adjusted.

This is not a day of celebration; it is a day in which approximately 4 million Americans are getting scrooged, and that also means 40,000 Oregonians who were looking forward to finally getting compensated for the overtime they will be working during this coming holiday season will also be told: No go. No paycheck. No compensation for your overtime.

These folks earn as little as $23,000 a year. Going into the holidays, a lot of retail workers are asked to work far more than 40 hours a week. They are asked to work 50, 60, 70, 80 hours a week without a dime of overtime, and that is wrong.

A whole lot of these workers are parents raising children. It is pretty hard to raise a child on $23,000 a year. I don't think anyone in this Chamber—any one of the Senators here in this Chamber—has raised a child on $23,000 a year. If they had attempted to do so, they would have an understanding of why they should be up here right now joining this fight for the overtime rule—which is hopelessly outdated and hopelessly unfair to America's workers—to be implemented in a timely fashion with legislation that we could pass today. Instead, Senators with their far larger salaries are very happily preparing for their holiday without considering that today is a day in which 4 million American workers are getting treated unfairly.

Since 1975, the salary of full-time workers who qualify for overtime has plummeted from 62 percent to 7 percent. That is a pretty dramatic reduction. For over a year now, millions of American workers have been looking forward to today when their long hours of overtime were finally going to be compensated, and it is only fair that they have that compensation. But just like Ebenezer Scrooge, the Republican Party, in coordination with 21 States, has said to those 4 million American workers: Bah humbug. You don't get compensated for your overtime. We are putting a lump of coal in your stocking, and it is too bad that you are trying to raise kids. This happened because States filed a lawsuit and got a preliminary injunction granted by a judge to take away the power of today's overtime rule, the modified overtime rule, to assist American workers.

I grew up in a blue-collar family. My dad was a mechanic, and my mother was a stay-at-home mom. My father, who had a basic blue-collar wage, was able to put food on the table, buy a three-bedroom ranch house with a garage, acquire a car, and have modest family camping vacations. It was a pretty square deal to provide a foundation for his children to thrive and have opportunities by working with his hands. Our blue-collar community was in much the same situation. When he worked overtime and stayed on the job because a machine needed to be re-paired and finished in time for a client of the company to be able to put that heavy equipment to work to build highways, work in the forest, or work to build dams, he got paid for that overtime, and it was right and fair that he did.

It is not right and fair that today America's workers are not getting paid for their overtime. They are working longer and harder only to see that extra wealth go to the CEO of the company. American workers are working longer hours, but their wages and paychecks are getting spread thinner and thinner. The overtime rule is a long overdue adjustment for those who are working those long hours. You don't get any help from this rule if you are not working more than 40 hours a week.

When President Franklin Roosevelt was talking about the importance of living wages to support families, he said: "By living wages I mean more than a bare subsistence level—I mean the wages of decent living." Isn't that what we are talking about, the wages of decent living?

Is there anyone who would contend that a parent raising a child on $23,000 a year is making a wage that would allow them to have a decent living? I don't think so, at least not at the cost of what it is to exist in today's society, not when rent on a two-bedroom apartment is $800 to $900 in Portland, not when the cost of groceries is where it is, and not when the cost of health care is where it is. Franklin Roosevelt said that no one who works full time should live in poverty. He said that working Americans should make enough to raise and support a family and provide a foundation for their children to thrive. He meant that you should be able to earn enough to save up over time and retire with dignity. He meant that a working American should be able earn enough to cover the basic necessities of life, such as food, clothes, and shelter, but for many Americans, those goals are out of reach even though they are working a lot of overtime, overtime in which they are not getting paid. We just haven't kept pace with the vision of families being able to earn, as Roosevelt put it, the wages of a decent living—the wages that enable you to live decently. This rule is critical to changing and fixing that.

While the courts tie up the process at the request of my Republican colleagues and State governments, we should instead have a bill here on the floor and simply pass this adjustment ourselves.

Has anyone noticed that we just had a Presidential campaign in which both candidates talked about making America work for working Americans? The candidate who won the vote in the electoral college but lost the popular vote, by the way, has claimed he is going to watch out for working Americans.

Well, where is he today on the day 4 million Americans are getting scrooged? Where is Donald Trump today on the day that those who worked overtime are now told they will not get paid for that overtime? How about a tweet in the middle of the night saying: I get it.

If we return to the story of Ebenezer Scrooge, we remember the fact that he was resisting any effort to enable his employee, Bob Cratchit, to have Christmas Day off with his family or to be able to have a decent amount of food on the table on that day. His heart was a few sizes too small. The night before Christmas he had a dream, and in that dream ghosts of Christmas past, Christmas present, and Christmas future came to him and showed the poverty—the spiritual poverty of his life. They showed him the emptiness of his life. That life is not about building up treasures you can count coin by coin, but helping other families to thrive and succeed and share in their joy. When he woke up, he was a changed man. He woke up and said: Yes, my team—my workers—shouldn't be working on Christmas Day. Yes, I should pay them more. Yes, I should make sure they have bountiful food so they can care for their family. Yes, their son, Tiny Tim, should have the health care he needs so he can live a full and productive life. He took care of these things and personally went out and acquired the largest turkey he could for the Cratchit family.

Isn't today the day when my colleagues who have been playing the role of Ebenezer Scrooge and fighting fair compensation for overtime—isn't today the day when they should take a nap and go to sleep tonight and have a little bit of a dream about the circumstances of working Americans? Here we are, just coming off a campaign where everyone talked about the plight of working Americans. Maybe a little of that should reverberate in their dreams tonight so that they might think about how families are struggling across America and how hard it is to put food on the table, not just during the holiday season but throughout the year. They should think about how unfair it is for someone to work 80 hours a week and not get paid overtime because they are being paid only $23,000 a year.

Do I hear a single colleague volunteer to work for 80 hours a week for a year and get paid $23,000? I would love to hear that speech on this floor when someone says: I get it. I am all for the overtime rule of the past because I am willing to live on $23,000 a year.

I don't think I have heard that from a single colleague. Colleagues here are paid many times that increment. Maybe it is a little hard to understand the plight of American workers when you are living in a bubble. Think about what it would be like to raise a family on $23,000 a year, given the expenses you experience in today's society.

So tonight, let's have a few of our colleagues who have been such advocates of the Ebenezer Scrooge strategy of denying overtime to workers who are paid very little go to sleep and maybe get visited by the ghosts of the past and the present and the future. Maybe they will be able to put themselves in the same pair of shoes that working Americans work in and place themselves in the same set of circumstances and financial challenges that American workers have. Maybe they can wake up tomorrow with a different vision—a vision of being a partner with working America—to make this Nation work for working America, make our economy work for working America. Maybe they can come to this floor and insist that we immediately pass a bill to take care of these workers so they are compensated for their overtime. That would be a Christmas story to celebrate.

Maybe, while we are at it, our President-elect can tweet tonight in the middle of the night that he had a dream and he was visited by the ghosts of the past and the present and the future and he saw a vision of treating workers fairly, and he wants the Senate to act tomorrow morning. Wouldn't that be a fabulous Christmas story—one that is completely consistent with the rhetoric we heard in the campaign about an economy that works for working Americans. I hope tomorrow morning that is exactly what we hear.

Thank you, Mr. President.

The PRESIDING OFFICER. The Senator from Alaska.

THE ECONOMY

Mr. SULLIVAN. Mr. President, one of the things I have been focused on—and I know many of my colleagues have been as well, such as the Presiding Officer—in the last couple of years in the Senate is coming to the Senate floor and speaking about this issue, certainly one of the most important issues we can be focused on in the Congress, and that is the economy and the economic growth for the United States.

What we have here, shown by this chart, is really a lost decade of economic growth that we have had in America over the last 10 years—a lost decade. This chart reflects the gross domestic product, or GDP growth, in the United States over the last several decades. GDP is essentially really a measure of the health of the economy, the health of the opportunity that we have in this country. By any measure, over the last 10 years we have had a sick economy.

So if we look here at the 3-percent GDP growth, this is OK growth. It is not considered that great. The average rate of growth for the United States over the last 200 years—what really has made our country great—has been

about 3.9 percent, almost 4 percent. Three percent is not great. It is certainly below average. But we have a President—President Obama—and an administration that is going to be the first President ever to never in 1 year, even once, hit 3 percent GDP growth ever.

Let me cite a couple of recent numbers. In the fourth quarter of 2015, we grew at 0.9 percent of GDP and did not even hit 1 percent. In the first quarter of 2016, it was 0.8 percent of GDP. In the second quarter of 2016, it was 1.1 percent GDP growth. It is true that the third quarter numbers came out estimated just a little above 3 percent for the quarter, but the year will be way off of even 3 percent.

Again, traditional levels of American growth are close to 4 percent.

So each quarter, when these numbers have come out—these dismal, anemic economic growth numbers—what I have tried to do is come to the Senate floor, talk about the issue, and then ask the question: Where is the Secretary of the Treasury? Where is the President of the United States? What is the plan? Is this really what we expect for Americans? We can't even hit 3 percent GDP growth.

Look at every other administration, including Kennedy, Johnson, Eisenhower, Nixon, Ford, Carter, Reagan—holy cow—6 percent, 5.5 percent; Bill Clinton, 4.5, 5 percent; even George Bush, well above 3 percent. Not once in 8 years—the lost decade of economic growth under President Obama. That is with low energy prices, and that is with super-low interest rates.

So when we ask what the plan is, what the administration is doing to grow the economy, they come back and say: Well, listen, the new normal is about 2 percent, 1.5 percent GDP growth. They don't say we are going to grow the economy. They just dumb down American expectations. Go google the term "new normal." Everybody uses it now in Washington. Essentially, they are saying that 1.5, 2 percent GDP growth is the best we can do.

I have a lot of respect for my colleague from Oregon, but if you want to talk about an Ebenezer Scrooge strategy—growing the U.S. economy at 1.5 percent and not even trying to grow at traditional levels of American growth—that is the ultimate Ebenezer Scrooge strategy because the entire country, especially middle class families, are hurt by it.

So this answer that, no, we can't even hit 3 percent, that the new normal is 1.5, 2 percent, that is an answer that we get from the Obama administration. The Secretary of the Treasury never comes out and tells us how we are going to get back to traditional levels of growth. That is an answer that consigns millions of Americans to lives where they no longer believe in economic opportunity, no longer believe in strong wages and in terms of growth for our wages, and no longer believe in a future in which their kids are going to do better than they did.

We talk a lot about stats, which are important to understand. So let me give my colleagues some of the numbers behind them. In the last 8 years, we have now had, in terms of people working in the workforce, the lowest labor-force participation rate since 1978. What does that mean? Again, that is a health issue of our economy. It means that millions of Americans have just quit looking for work. Can we imagine being that discouraged because the economy is not growing and so you just quit looking?

The percentage of Americans below the poverty line has grown by almost 4 percent over this period, where we see no growth. Real medium household income during this period sank by almost $2,000. Food stamp participation in this period—again, 8 years—has soared by almost 40 percent. The percentage of Americans who own homes, which is one of the ultimate markers of the American dream, is the lowest it has been since 1965. So we were talking about Ebenezer Scrooge. My colleague was just talking about him. Those are Ebenezer Scrooge numbers, and those are Americans who are hurting because we can't grow the economy.

We need to change that. The Obama administration has not been focused on this issue. We never hear the Secretary of the Treasury come out—or even the President—and talk about how we get back to traditional levels of American growth, like every Republican and Democratic President has done for decades. They don't talk about it. They haven't been focused on it. But I think on November 8, we saw that the American people are very focused on this issue. Millions and millions of Americans rejected the idea that, because of these growth rates, they had to give up on the American dream and a strong U.S. economy and good jobs. They did not want to give up on it. We do not want to give up on that.

In essence, Americans saw that the idea of the new normal—which is this, peddled by the Obama administration—is a surrender, and they didn't want to surrender. We shouldn't surrender. We need to grow this economy.

So what now? Well, I find it very encouraging that the President-elect and his team, including his nominee for the Secretary of the Treasury, have been talking very regularly about this issue. We need to grow the economy—not at new normal rates of 1.5 percent or 2 percent but at 3, 3.5, or 4 percent GDP growth. That is what we need to do. We in this body need to help them do that because that is what the American people want. In fact, with the exception of having a strong military and keeping this country safe in terms of national defense, growing our economy, creating

economic opportunity for all Americans is certainly one of the most important things we can do in the Senate. But we need a partner in the executive branch. We need a partner in the executive branch that is actually focused on the issue, that actually cares about these numbers, and we haven't had it in 8 years. So where do we start?

I think we need to start on this issue of the overregulation of our economy. Again, the incoming administration has talked a lot about this issue. When we ask people outside of Washington what is keeping our economy down, they refer to this. This chart is a chart of the cumulative number of Federal rules that have come out of this town onto American businesses, small businesses, and working-class families. That is what we see—pure growth, pure growth.

President Obama has enacted more than 600 new major regulations, totaling close to $800 billion or $2,300 per American. What is really interesting is that, despite the fact that the American people on November 8 said they want to grow the economy and they don't want to see this continue, this administration is putting its pedal to the metal on trying to see how many more regulations they can issue and promulgate to crush our economy and opportunity.

My State has been ground zero for a lot of these regulations. We are a resource development State in Alaska. The President just last week came out with a new regulation that said: I know that the vast majority of Alaskans want to responsibly develop their resources, but I am going to take the entire Outer Continental Shelf off the table for Alaska. Sorry, Alaska. Sorry, workers. Sorry, American energy independence. I am taking it all off the table. That was a regulation the President put on the table and issued last week that is going to hurt our economy, that is going to hurt American energy independence, that is going to hurt jobs, that is going to hurt our national security, and he did it anyway. There are no leases in my State because the President, in Executive order, issued that. That is not what the American people voted for on November 8.

So several Senators, led by Senator GARDNER, are going to be sending the President a letter very soon saying: Mr. President, the American people have spoken. The American people are tired of this. You are on your way out. Please, respect the results of the election and quit issuing these regulations that are stifling economic growth and crushing middle-class families. I hope he will abide by that. I hope he listens to us. I hope he listens to the American people. But, somehow, I think we are going to see even more of these in the next month or so.

I wish to conclude by noting something that I think most Americans understand intuitively. When it comes to our Nation and the comparative advantages that we have over other countries—and I am talking about the major countries in the world, whether it is China or Russia or the EU or Brazil or Japan—we have so many incredible comparative advantages relative to anyone. We have energy. We have great entrepreneurs. We have world class universities. We have agriculture and fisheries that literally feed the world. We have some of the brightest young people, like our pages here. We have a military that is the most professional and lethal in the world, by far. We have alliances all over the world where countries want to be close to the United States. Our adversaries and potential adversaries, such as China, Russia, North Korea, and Iran, have very few, if any, allies.

We have so many advantages, and yet the majority of Americans think we are heading in the wrong direction. I believe they think that because we can't grow the economy. So what we need to do is for all of us to work closely with the new administration, and I would encourage all of my colleagues here in the Senate to focus back on this issue. We need to return to traditional levels of American economic growth, and we can do it with the right policies.

I yield the floor.

Mr. President, I suggest the absence of a quorum.

The PRESIDING OFFICER. The clerk will call the roll.

The senior assistant legislative clerk proceeded to call the roll.

Mr. GRASSLEY. Mr. President, I ask unanimous consent that the order for the quorum call be rescinded.

The PRESIDING OFFICER. Without objection, it is so ordered.

UNANIMOUS CONSENT REQUEST—S. 579

Mr. GRASSLEY. Mr. President, Members of the Senate, I come to the floor to speak about and to propound a unanimous consent request in regard to the Inspector General's Empowerment Act. I would like to defer. I ask unanimous consent to not lose the floor but yield to Senator JOHNSON.

The PRESIDING OFFICER. Without objection, it is so ordered.

Mr. JOHNSON. Mr. President, I thank the Senator from Iowa for letting me speak to a very important issue. I also thank him for his leadership. Long before I came to the Senate, I know the Senator from Iowa was working tirelessly to make sure government was more efficient, more effective, and more accountable. He has done an awful lot of work to ensure that. Certainly he has relied on inspectors general to bolster his efforts.

So I am completely in support of S. 579, the Inspector General Empowerment Act of 2015. When I took over the chairmanship of the Senate Committee on Homeland Security and Governmental Affairs, the Senator from Iowa had been working long and hard on this act. I was happy—I was pleased to utilize our committee to move this bill through our committee unanimously.

The bill has 18 bipartisan cosponsors. It is just incredibly important. The Senator from Iowa will certainly fill us in on the details of what has happened and what has made this bill so important. I just want to spend a little bit of time on how important inspector generals are.

We, working together with the Senator from Iowa, asked the inspectors general, for example, to report back to us how many of their recommendations—off of their tireless work—have gone unimplemented. We just received that report. Over 15,000 recommendations from inspectors general have not been implemented. The total aggregate savings could be as high as $87 billion. Even in this massive Federal Government, $87 billion is real money. Of course, inspectors general need access to the records from their agencies, from their departments, so they can determine what is happening so they can make these kind of recommendations.

We also have had and witnessed a real tragedy, for example, at the Tomah VA Medical Center. We had an inspector general who had inspected and investigated over 140 different instances, then issued reports on those inspections, investigations, and then buried those reports—did not make those reports public.

One of those had to do with the Tomah VA Center in terms of the overprescription of opioids. Because that report was not made public, we were unaware of the problems there, and the problems persisted. For over a decade, opioids were being overprescribed. The result was that veterans—the finest among us—some of them died because of overprescription.

It is not an overstatement to say that the work of the inspector general is crucial and that work—those reports, those inspections, those investigations—literally is the difference between life and death. Again, I am here supporting the Senator from Iowa in his tireless efforts to get this bill passed, the Inspector General Empowerment Act of 2015. I urge all of my colleagues to allow this to pass by unanimous consent so we can get this put on the President's desk and it can be signed into law as quickly as possible.

With that, I yield the floor.

Mr. GRASSLEY. Mr. President, while I am waiting for Senator MCCAIN to come to the floor before I speak about the specific unanimous consent request I am going to make, I would like to point out, in a very general way, that the pursuit of what we are doing, in so many other ways, is part of Congress's constitutional responsibility and constitutional authority under the checks and balances of government to make sure the laws are faithfully executed.

There are several different tools that are used in that direction. They can be individual Senators. Any time an individual Senator wants to ask questions of whether the laws are being faithfully executed, that Senator can do it, that Member of the House of Representatives can do it, through the particular committees of the Senate and the House of Representatives, through both letter as well as open hearings about certain subjects of whether money being spent by the executive branch is according to Congressional intent or whether laws are being carried out the way Congress intended.

That is all part of congressional oversight, but there has also been seen a need, over a course of many years, for other ways to make sure it is done. One of those was the setting up of the Government Accountability Office that has authority, at the request of committees and request of individual Members of Congress, to investigate and do research on certain problems we have in the executive branch of government.

That predates, by a long time, the passage of the inspectors general law that we are dealing with, with this subject I have before the Senate now. The inspector general was set up for the purpose of being within the executive branch to see that the laws are faithfully executed and the money spent according to Congress. I see that Senator MCCAIN has come to the floor. I would like to make my opening statement on the legislation. I thank Senator MCCAIN for the courtesy he gives me to come and listen to my request. Whatever he decides to do with it will be his choice, but I want to tell him I appreciate the cooperation he has given me on so many different things

To justify my unanimous consent request, I start out with some of the issues that are involved with the legislation, the Inspector General Empowerment Act. In 1978, Congress created inspectors general or IGs as they are often known, to be the eyes and ears within the executive branch.

These independent watchdogs are designed to keep Congress and the public informed about waste, fraud, and abuse in government. They also help agency leaders identify problems and inefficiencies they may not be aware of. IGs are a very critical part to good governance and to the rule of law.

In order for IGs to do their job, they need independent access to information. That is why, when Congress passed the Inspector General Act of 1978, we explicitly said IGs should have access to all records of the agency they are charged with overseeing.

However, since 2010, more and more agencies have refused to comply with this legal obligation. This obstruction has slowed down far too many important investigations, ranging from sexual assault in the Peace Corps to the FBI's exercise of anti-terrorism authority under the PATRIOT Act.

Those are just two of the things I have been involved in. Every one of the other 99 Senators would probably have to say that in their oversight work, somehow the executive branch agencies have not carried out the spirit of the 1978 legislation.

It got worse in July of 2016. The Justice Department's Office of Legal Counsel released a memo supporting this obstruction of congressional intent. Now, let me put this in a commonsense form that surely everybody ought to understand. In 1978, Congress passes the inspectors general law. It is voted on by a majority of the Congress. It is sent to the President. The President signs it. It has been law since that period of time, but we have a situation where 1 bureaucrat out of 2 million Federal employees sits and reads something into a piece of legislation that was never intended because the legislation says the inspector general should be entitled to all records, but the Office of Legal Counsel opinion says: Well, maybe not all. It kind of depends on the head of the department. There are some exceptions in the inspectors general law that ought to be there—those are spelled out—some of them dealing with national security, some of them dealing with the Department of Defense, as just one example.

So we have this opinion in July of 2016. The memo argued that Congress did not mean what it very clearly said; that the IG gets access to all records. This is unacceptable. It undermines Congress's intent. It undermines the rule of law. It makes a mockery of government transparency. The public deserves a robust scrutiny of the Federal Government. Every eighth grade civics student understands what checks and balances is all about.

Congressional oversight is one of those checks. Since September 2015, a bipartisan group of Senators and I have been working to overturn the Justice Department's opinion through S. 579, the Inspector General Empowerment Act. Among other things, this bill further clarifies that Congress intended IGs to access all agency records, notwithstanding any other provision of law, unless—and this is a big unless—other laws specifically state that the IGs are not entitled to receive such access.

A lot of those fall into the area of national security and defense. The bill has a total of 20 cosponsors, including seven of my Democratic colleagues: MCCASKILL, CARPER, MIKULSKI, WYDEN, BALDWIN, MANCHIN and PETERS. At the Judiciary Committee hearing in August of last year, Senator LEAHY also agreed that this access problem needs to be fixed by legislation because it is "blocking what was once a free flow of information." Even the Justice Department witness at that hearing disagreed with the results of the Office of Legal Counsel opinion and supported legislative action to solve the problem.

As of today, a large majority of Senators, the Las Vegas Review Journal—and I say that for the benefit of Senator REID who at one time objected—the New York Times, the Washington Post, good governance groups like Project on Government Oversight and Citizens Against Government Waste, all support restoring the intent of that act through S. 579.

I want to emphasize that the intent of the act was destroyed by one bureaucrat writing a legal opinion that has been a crutch for a lot of people who don't want to cooperate with the inspector general.

Despite strong bipartisan and public support for the bill, we have not been able to pass the bill by unanimous consent. We attempted to pass the bill by unanimous consent September 2015 and again December 2015.

In December, the Armed Services Committee and the Intelligence Committee raised concerns about the bill. It is perfectly legitimate for them to do that. My cosponsors and I worked with our colleagues on those committees to address and resolve their concerns. Ultimately, Chairman McCAIN and Chairman BURR lifted their holds, and in December 2015 the bill cleared the Republican side with no objections. But when we tried to pass the bill on the floor by unanimous consent, Senator REID, as I previously said, objected on the Democratic side.

In the meantime, the House passed its own version of the bill. Since then, we have worked closely with the House to resolve minor differences between the House and Senate bills. Now it is time to press forward and finally pass this critical bill to ensure the effective oversight of waste, fraud, and abuse in government—in other words, to make very clear that when the act says they are entitled to all records, "all" means all.

There is one provision of the bill we had to remove from this version at the insistence of Senator LEAHY. It relates to testimonial subpoena authority for inspectors general.

First, let me be clear about why the testimonial subpoena authority is important to the ability of IGs to conduct effective investigations. When employees of the U.S. Government are accused of wrongdoing or misconduct, IGs should be able to conduct a full and thorough investigation. Unfortunately, employees who may have violated that trust are often able to evade the IG's inquiry simply by retiring from the government. Testimonial subpoena authority empowers IGs to obtain testimony about waste, fraud, and abuse from employees after they leave the agency.

Similarly, the subpoena authority helps IGs investigate entities that re-

ceive Federal funds. In other words, if you want to know what is wrong, follow the money. The subpoena authority enables IGs to require testimony from government contractors, subcontractors, grantees, and subgrantees. Currently, most IGs can subpoena documents from entities outside of their agency, but most cannot subpoena testimony. The ability to require witnesses outside the agency to talk to the IG can be critical in carrying out an inspector general's statutory duties or recovering wasted Federal funds.

Let me also be clear that when we learned of Senator LEAHY's concerns with this provision in November 2015, my bipartisan cosponsors and I worked in good faith for 12 months to address them. We offered at least half a dozen accommodations that would provide meaningful and appropriate limitations on the subpoena in question, but Senator LEAHY continued to demand the removal of that from the bill.

Despite a year of negotiation, we were unable to reach a resolution, so I proposed bringing the provision to the floor for debate. I offered Senator LEAHY the option of debating on the floor the merits of the testimonial subpoena authority so that the Senate could vote on whether to keep or remove the provision from the bill, but my colleague declined to agree to floor time so that we could have an open debate on the issue.

His continued refusal to debate and vote on the much needed testimonial subpoena authority threatens to derail the entire bill, which has such substantial bipartisan public support.

Despite my strong belief that IGs need that subpoena authority, I also recognize that the IG bill contains many other critical provisions the IG needs to move forward with it, and now is the time to do that. We cannot afford to wait any longer for those provisions that empower the IG. This bill is still necessary to help IGs and to ensure to the American people that there is transparency and accountability within the government.

Before I ask unanimous consent, I wish to say for the benefit of the position that I think Senator McCAIN is going to take that the Secretary, under existing law, may block an IG investigation if it is necessary to preserve the national security and interests of the United States and if the information the IG has requested concerns any one of five categories: sensitive operation plans, intelligence matters, counterintelligence matters, ongoing criminal investigations, or other matters that would constitute a serious threat to national security if they were to be disclosed.

Mr. President, I ask unanimous consent that the Senate proceed to the immediate consideration of Calendar No. 68, S. 579. I further ask that the Johnson substitute amendment be agreed

to; the bill, as amended, be read a third time and passed; and that the motion to reconsider be considered made and laid upon the table.

The PRESIDING OFFICER. Is there objection?

Mr. McCAIN. Reserving the right to object.

The PRESIDING OFFICER. The Senator from Arizona.

Mr. McCAIN. Mr. President, I appreciate the hard work the Senator from Iowa and his staff have done. The Senator and I are old friends, and I know he is one of the most zealous advocates for government oversight and reform in the Senate. I am aware of the many years of hard work he has put into this legislation.

I believe we share the same goal of ensuring that inspectors general across the Federal Government have the authorities and support they need to do their vital work on behalf of the American people. At the same time, I have serious concerns about a few aspects of this regulation as written.

I have been working with the Senator from Iowa. I wish to continue working with him.

To tell you the truth, I say to my friend from Iowa, I don't know why we cannot reach agreement. What we are really talking about are a few words. For example, this legislation would substitute the words "under the nominal supervision of the head of the establishment involved"—that takes the place of the wording "under the general supervision of the establishment involved." I say to my friend from Iowa, what springs to mind is, why would we want to change that wording unless there was some intent to do so? Isn't the "general supervision of the establishment involved"—we have to have "under the nominal supervision"? What is this wordsmithing stuff that, frankly, I can only assume has some underlying purpose? Why would you want to substitute "under the nominal supervision" for "under the general supervision" without some reason? I don't get it. There is no explanation for why this change is necessary. It is unclear what "nominal supervision" means. If "nominal" means literally "in name only"—that is what "nominal" means—then it would remove the IG from the supervisory authority of the agency or department head.

The legislation would impose further restrictions on the ability of the Secretary of Defense—which is the area of my responsibility—to supervise and support the inspector general of the Department of Defense, so it is a reach too far.

The legislation would also restrict the President from placing an inspector general in an involuntary nonduty status, either paid or not paid, except as narrowly defined, for cause. This is likely an unconstitutional restriction on the authority of the President, who has the authority to appoint and to remove his or her own appointees. Constitutionally appointed officers serve at the pleasure of the President. Constitutionally appointed officers serve at the pleasure of the President, some subject to advice and consent of the Senate, some not. In other words, us saying what a Member of Congress can do to put someone on nonduty status is not the responsibility or the authority of the Congress of the United States.

It would limit the President's authority to place an inspector general in an involuntary, paid or unpaid, nonduty status for more than 14 days, unless the Integrity Committee of the Council of the Inspectors General on Integrity and Efficiency, a well-known organization, submits to the President a written recommendation for additional time, which is acted upon by the President, and the decision is communicated immediately to both Houses of Congress. That is a further restriction on Presidential power by a committee of the Council of the Inspectors General on Integrity and Efficiency—by the way, an organization whose existence I was unaware of.

The people expect the President to have both control and responsibility over employees and officers in the executive branch, subject to advice and consent—the constitutional authorities of the Senate of the United States. It is clearly outlined in the Constitution.

The people expect the President to have both control and responsibility over employees and officers in the executive branch. The Founders believed that this design ensured effective government but, most importantly, protected our liberty from rogue government agents who might accrue vast power but be responsive and responsible to no elected, accountable authority. We just saw a dramatic example of that, as I know my colleague from Iowa understands, in the Dodd-Frank legislation, which created agencies of government that have no accountability whatsoever, even to the appropriations process.

The legislation would also undermine congressional oversight of the IGs. For example, with this language, a congressional investigation conducted by committees into complaints that the IG has violated whistleblower protections could be labeled as "interfering with the independence of the IG" if the committee is communicating with an agency or department as part of that investigation.

While I appreciate the effort to provide exemptions to the Department of Defense from this legislation, that exemption only relates to certain subsections and sentences of the overall Inspector General Act. Thus, many of these new rules and requirements would apply to the Department of Defense. For example, the new "timely access to information" requirement is

included in the legislation, but there is no exemption for DOD from that requirement. It is unclear that existing exemptions would apply.

The Senate Armed Services Committee conducts a regular, stringent oversight of the Department of Defense, including its inspector general. The committee and the Congress pass defense legislation on an annual basis, and this will be the 55th year we will do so. I do not believe there is any problem at present in the DOD IG that requires the solution this legislation would require, and in the event the Senate Armed Services Committee uncovers problems in the course of our oversight work, we will address those issues in our annual authorization legislation.

Look, I have great affection for my friend from Iowa. It is obvious that this issue is important to him. It is obvious he has been working on it for years. If I could make a suggestion to my friend from Iowa, let's set a time tomorrow to sit down with our staffs, find out what the problem is, see if we can get it resolved, and then that will give us 24 hours to try to resolve these issues.

I understand what the Senator from Iowa is seeking and trying to do. I support the intent of that legislation. My responsibilities are oversight of the Department of Defense, the largest part of our government, and I have these concerns about it. I believe we can resolve these problems maybe with a face-to-face with our staffs's engagement.

For all those reasons, I regret to tell my friend from Iowa that I object.

The PRESIDING OFFICER. Objection is heard.

The Senator from Iowa.

Mr. GRASSLEY. Mr. President, I knew ahead of time that we would have this objection. The only difference between this objection this time and a year ago is the fact that a year ago we worked out differences with other committees of the Congress and had, evidently, 99 Senators ready to pass this bill, except for Senator REID. So it is disappointing that when we work out one problem we had a year ago, that now we have serious objections, very numerous, as it worked out, considering the fact that the committee of jurisdiction—Senator JOHNSON is chair of the Homeland Security and Governmental Affairs Committee, passing this bill out unanimously, getting it cleared on both sides a year ago, except for Senator REID, and now all these other problems come up.

It is impossible for me to respond to all the problems that have been presented by the Senator from Arizona. Obviously, the legislative process does emphasize cooperation between Members when there are differences, but I believe that it is probably going to be impossible this year for us to work out

those differences. So I will be prepared to come back next year and pursue this legislation again and see what we can do.

Mr. McCAIN. Mr. President, could I just say to my friend from Iowa that I am willing to maybe have a sit-down sometime in the next 24 hours to see if we can get this done.

Mr. GRASSLEY. OK. I will take that under advisement.

I would simply close with further evidence of the importance of this legislation and try to respond to what the Senator from Arizona said about its impact on the Defense Department.

Section 8 of the IG Act already contains an exception that allows the Secretary of Defense to prohibit the inspector general from conducting an investigation and gathering documents to protect national security. The exception is broad. The Secretary may block an IG investigation if it is necessary to preserve the national security interests of the United States and if the information the IG has requested concerns sensitive operation plans, intelligence matters, counterintelligence matters, ongoing criminal investigations, and other matters that would constitute a serious threat to national security if disclosed.

In addition, cosponsors and I worked with the Committee on Armed Services last year to ensure that the bill makes the Secretary of Defense's authority to restrict certain types of sensitive information even more clear than it was in the 1978 legislation. After we made those changes, Senator McCAIN, as I have already said, cleared this version of the access language last year.

I guess at this point I am going to yield the floor.

I suggest the absence of a quorum.

The PRESIDING OFFICER. The clerk will call the roll.

The legislative clerk proceeded to call the roll.

Mr. CORKER. Mr. President, I ask unanimous consent that the order for the quorum call be rescinded.

The PRESIDING OFFICER. Without objection, it is so ordered.

TENNESSEE TRAGEDIES

Mr. CORKER. Mr. President, I rise today to express my deepest sympathies and offer steadfast support to the countless Tennesseans who have experienced tragedy in the recent days.

It has been a rough few weeks in our great State. Last week, my hometown of Chattanooga lost six young children in a tragic schoolbus crash. Today, countless East Tennesseans face a long road ahead after severe storms and tornadoes ripped through southeast Tennessee, leaving tremendous damage and taking the lives of two individuals in Polk County.

Tomorrow morning, I will be in another area of our State that is dealing with unimaginable tragedy. As you have likely seen by now, the damage caused by wildfires in Sevier County, the place where my wife was raised, is heartbreaking. While officials continue to assess the full extent of the damage, we know that many have suffered tremendous loss. As of this morning, officials confirmed that they are still addressing the remnants of smoldering wildfires. More than 400 firefighters are supporting the effort. The exact number of structures affected remains unknown, but local officials are estimating 700 impacted structures and more than 17,000 acres burned. More than 200 individuals remain in shelters, and just moments ago, we learned that 10 fatalities have been confirmed.

Sevier County is a special place, surrounded by some of the country's most beautiful God-given amenities. Millions of people from around the world visit each year and have built memories in this treasured community. But as the mayor of Gatlinburg noted earlier today, "it's not the attractions or the restaurants that make this place special, it's the people" who live there.

So many wonderful families call Sevier County home—tough, proud people whose roots in the area span generations.

Those who know the area and these people are not at all surprised by the community response. The Nation has watched and read countless stories of selfless individuals—many who lost everything themselves—helping others. We have watched the mayor and city manager of Gatlinburg, both of whom lost their own homes, provide steadfast strength and grace. We have watched the Sevier County mayor close each press conference with a simple request: "Pray for us."

The coming days, weeks, and months will not be easy. The recovery will take time. We are committed to doing everything that we all can do to help you rebuild. The support does not end when the cameras leave. Governor Haslam, Senator ALEXANDER, Congressman ROE, and I are ready to support requests for assistance for the recovery efforts. People throughout Tennessee and across the Nation will be back to visit very soon. Of course, as has been requested, we will continue to pray.

I yield the floor.

I suggest the absence of a quorum.

The PRESIDING OFFICER. The clerk will call the roll.

The legislative clerk proceeded to call the roll.

Mr. SULLIVAN. Mr. President, I ask unanimous consent that the order for the quorum call be rescinded.

The PRESIDING OFFICER. Without objection, it is so ordered.

MORNING BUSINESS

Mr. SULLIVAN. Mr. President, I ask unanimous consent that the Senate be in a period of morning business, with Senators permitted to speak therein for up to 10 minutes each.

The PRESIDING OFFICER. Without objection, it is so ordered.

WORLD AIDS DAY

Mr. CARDIN. Mr. President, today I wish to discuss World AIDS Day. Thirty years ago, the National Academy of Sciences's Institute of Medicine issued a report calling for a "massive media, educational and public health campaign to curb the spread of the HIV infection." The global community heeded that call and today, on World AIDS Day, we celebrate progress that we have made in treating and preventing HIV/AIDS both at home and abroad and recommit ourselves to creating an AIDS-free generation.

Earlier this year, I had the opportunity to visit an HIV/AIDS clinic in Namibia supported by the President's Emergency Plan for AIDS Relief, PEPFAR, and the Global Fund. While there, I met a 30-year-old man named Simon who said he would not be alive without the international community's HIV/AIDS assistance. While the individual stories of people like Simon are a testament to the hard-fought progress this global response has achieved, the aggregate impact of our efforts cannot be understated. PEPFAR has been a bipartisan success story that began with a strong commitment by President George W. Bush and grew under President Obama. It must continue to have broad-based support in a Trump administration and in the 115th Congress, so we can keep making inroads against this pernicious disease.

Since 2005, AIDS-related deaths have fallen by 45 percent globally. In Africa, new HIV infections have declined 14 percent since 2010, including a 66 percent reduction in new infections in children in the region. And today, 18.2 million men, women, and children worldwide are on antiretroviral therapy, double the number of people who had access just 5 years ago.

Nevertheless, there remains more work to be done. In my home State of Maryland, there were 1,334 new HIV diagnoses in 2015, ranking it the third highest adult HIV diagnosis rate per capita in the country. And globally, we are seeing data that indicates that AIDS-related deaths are actually increasing among adolescents. At home and abroad, such trends are troubling.

We therefore cannot rest on our laurels. The United States must continue to lead this global fight. Through strong funding for PEPFAR and multilateral organizations like the Global Fund, we will ensure the continued commitment and leadership of partner countries reinforced with support from donor nations, civil society, and people living with HIV, faith-based organizations, the private sector, and foundations. And at here at home, we must ensure that the Centers for Disease Control and Prevention, CDC, the National Institutes of Health, NIH, the Ryan White HIV/AIDS Program, and our State, local, and community partners have the resources they need to continue making significant progress to prevent, treat, and eventually cure this disease.

With our work cut out for us and the memories of far too many loved ones in our hearts, we strive on this World AIDS Day as an international community toward a world free of HIV/AIDS and recommit to mobilize the resources needed for treatment, to summon the compassion and understanding to prevent stigma, and to unleash our collective ingenuity and persistence in search of a cure.

REMEMBERING BISHOP EMERSON COLAW

Mr. PORTMAN. Mr. President, today I wish to remember a dear friend, Bishop Emerson Colaw, a devoted and widely respected leader of the United Methodist Church. Bishop Colaw passed away on October 11, 2016, at the age of 94 in Ohio, where he lived during the final years of his life.

Emerson Stephen Colaw was born November 13, 1921, in Chanute, KS, and moved to Cincinnati at the age of 16 to attend God's Bible School and College. A committed student, Colaw went on to earn a B.S. degree in 1944 from the University of Cincinnati, a bachelor of divinity, magna cum laude, in 1947 from Drew Theological Seminary, and a master of arts in 1953 from Northwestern University in Evanston, IL. He also received honorary doctorates from five different institutions.

Remembered as a strong preacher and compassionate leader who loved the church and had a heart for the clergy, Colaw served as a mentor and role model of Christian discipleship for colleagues, congregants, friends, and family. He began his ministry as a clergyperson for the United Methodist Church serving the New York Annual Conference and the Northern Illinois Annual Conference, where he served three pastorates over 14 years.

In 1961, Colaw was appointed to Hyde Park Community United Methodist Church in Cincinnati, OH, part of the West Ohio Annual Conference. During his time in Cincinnati, Colaw spent many years as the moderator of a weekly television program titled "Dialogue" which featured area clergy from a variety of faiths.

After 19 years of service to Hyde Park Community Methodist Church, in 1980, Colaw was elected Bishop of the Minnesota Conference, where he served until retiring from the episcopacy in 1988. He went on to serve as professor of Homiletics and Christian Ministry at the United Theological Seminary in Dayton, OH, from 1988 to 1999 and was its acting president in 1995–96. He later spent winters in Florida and served as bishop-in-residence at North Naples United Methodist Church.

Emmerson and his late wife, Jane, were married more than 70 years and raised 4 children, 8 grandchildren, 12 great-grandchildren, and a great-great-granddaughter.

I would like to honor Emmerson Colaw for his contributions to the United Methodist Church, his community, and our State.

REMEMBERING JAMES "JIM" F. DICKE

Mr. PORTMAN. Mr. President, today I wish to remember James "Jim" F. Dicke, a WWII veteran, an Ohio business leader, and a philanthropist. Mr. Dicke passed away on Friday, November 11, 2016, at the age of 94.

Jim Dicke was born in New York in 1922 and raised in Dayton, OH, graduating from Stivers High School in 1939. He was an honorary graduate of Culver Military Academy and was awarded an honorary DBA by Ohio Northern University. A WWII veteran, Jim served as a lieutenant instructor in the Army Air Corps.

Following his military service, Jim returned to the Dayton region and worked with his father, Carl, and other family members to found a company called Crown Controls Company, now known as Crown Equipment Corporation, which is a leading global manufacturer of material handling equipment, currently in its fourth generation of family leadership. With over 4,400 Ohio employees, the New Bremen, OH, based company has three manufacturing facilities along I–75 in west Ohio, as well as a branch in Vandalia. We are proud to have this innovative, successful, and competitive manufacturer in the Buckeye State.

In addition to being a job creator and business leader, Jim Dicke was involved in many important community activities. He was a major benefactor to Ohio Northern University, where he was given an honorary doctorate in 2000 and where there are a number of namesakes there in his honor, including James F. Dicke Hall, home to the James F. Dicke College of Business Administration, as well as the Dicke House, home of the university's president.

Jim and his late wife, Eilleen, were married for almost 73 years and raised two sons, six grandchildren, and seven great-grandchildren.

I would like to honor James Frank Dicke for his many contributions to his community and our State.

150TH ANNIVERSARY OF THE COLLEGE OF WOOSTER

Mr. PORTMAN. Mr. President, today I wish to honor the College of Wooster in recognition of its 150th anniversary of providing quality higher education to the citizens of Ohio. In 1865, Reverend James Reed, the minister of the First Presbyterian Church in Wooster, rallied the community to create a Presbyterian college in Wooster. On December 18, 1866, the then University of Wooster was incorporated by the Presbyterian Synod. In order to better reflect the institution's offerings, the University of Wooster became the College of Wooster. Wooster's first class consisted of 30 men and 4 women instructed by five faculty members; the college now enrolls over 2,000 students, representing 45 States and 44 countries, and instructed by 171 faculty members. Wooster now has more than 50 academic programs in business, the arts, humanities, and the sciences.

The mission of the College of Wooster is to create "a community of independent minds, working together to become leaders of character and influence in an interdependent global community." Wooster accomplishes this by offering a rigorous and dynamic liberal education that focuses on mentoring, applied learning, and project based learning where students develop attributes that are valued by employers and important for developing the leaders of tomorrow. It is helping to ensure that students are prepared with the skills they need for the jobs of the 21st century. Because of this, 92 percent of Wooster graduates are either employed or in graduate school within 1 year after receiving their diplomas. We are proud to have this extraordinary independent college in Ohio.

I am here to honor the College of Wooster and to congratulate all of those who contributed to making its first 150 years such a success.

HONORING ERIC DALE ELLSWORTH

Mr. LEE. Mr. President, on Friday, November 18, 2016, Eric Ellsworth of Brigham City, UT, began his day like virtually every other day of his adult life. He put on his uniform and drove to work fully aware that it could be his last day on Earth. Eric was a State trooper with the Utah Highway Patrol, and for 7 years this is how he began each day: by summoning enough courage to last most men a lifetime.

Why did he do it?

I never had the privilege of meeting Eric. But over the past several days I have read a great deal about him, and based on the comments of his family, friends, and colleagues, I suspect the answer is that Eric wouldn't have wanted it any other way.

Like all law enforcement officers, the life of a trooper is a life of service to one's community and one's fellow man—the vulnerable, the needy, and the insecure. It is also a life of sacrifice. And on November 18, 2016—that Friday that began like all the others—Trooper Ellsworth made the ultimate sacrifice.

While directing traffic to avoid a roadway hazard along a rural stretch of State Route 13 near Garland in Box Elder County, Trooper Ellsworth was accidentally struck by a passing vehicle. For 4 days, he remained in critical condition at Intermountain Medical Center, defying the odds and fighting to live another day in that uniform. But on November 22, 2016, Eric succumbed to the injuries sustained in the crash and passed from this life into the next. He died honorably, doing what he loved—and lived—to do: helping others and serving his community.

Indeed, if you look at the trajectory of Eric's life, you are left with the distinct impression that the man was destined, from the very start, to be a highway patrol trooper.

He was the seventh of nine children—and the eldest brother—which must have taught him at an early age what it means to live with duties and obligations toward others. And his hero—his father, Ronald Ellsworth, who was also a highway trooper—showed him what courage as a daily discipline looks like.

Like most sons who revere their dads, Eric grew up wanting to follow in his father's footsteps. And so he served.

He served his community, as an Eagle Scout and an active member of his church, the Church of Jesus Christ of Latter-day Saints. He served his family, as a loving husband to his wife and high-school sweetheart, Janica, and a nurturing father to their three sons, Bennett, Ian, and Oliver. He served his fellow citizens and countrymen as a highway trooper who kept watch over the roads in northern Utah. And most importantly to Eric, he served his Heavenly Father, as a missionary in Winnipeg, Canada, and as a faithful witness of Jesus Christ.

At 31 years of age, Trooper Ellsworth's life was cut tragically short. But in those 31 years, he did more to help his fellow man than most of us can hope to accomplish in a lifetime. He lived a full and bighearted life, always ready to answer the call of service and dedicated to making the world not just safer but better for everyone.

This is Eric Ellsworth's legacy, his gift to the world, and his sons' greatest inheritance: the enduring example of a life well lived.

May he rest in peace, and may God bless his family and the community he served—it will never be the same without him.

Thank you.

ADDITIONAL STATEMENTS

IDAHO HOMETOWN HERO MEDAL

● Mr. CRAPO. Mr. President, today I wish to honor the 2016 Idaho Hometown Hero medalists.

Drs. Fahim and Naeem Rahim established the Idaho Hometown Hero medal in 2011 to recognize outstanding Idahoans working for the betterment of our communities. Medalists are selected from nominations sought from the public throughout the State and must meet criteria that include being dedicated to hard work, self-improvement, and community service.

In this 6th year of the presentation of this honor, 10 Idahoans from communities across Idaho are 2016 Hometown Hero medal recipients. Executive Director of Suicide Prevention Action Network of Idaho Jeni Griffin of Idaho Falls is recognized for her dedication of more than 10 years to promoting suicide prevention in Idaho. Nationally recognized teacher, coach, and mentor Holly Kartchner of Blackfoot received the award for her commitment to education in southeastern Idaho, leading her students to reach national championships. Former Coeur d'Alene police officer and Air Force veteran Mike Kralicek is honored for the inspiration he provides to other public servants to be better prepared for overcoming adversity and his leadership in helping law enforcement families in times of crisis.

Idaho Falls attorney Doug Nelson is recognized for dedicating more than three decades to leading, supporting, and advocating for children's activity programs and multiple charitable organizations and mentoring disadvantaged single mothers. Wiley Petersen, a professional bullrider, coach, motivational speaker, and mentor who grew up in Fort Hall received the medal for his efforts to give back to his Native American community and help further the progress of the Native American people. Sonya Rosario, a filmmaker from Meridian and the founder and executive director of Women of Color Alliance, is honored for her work and films to help heal Native communities. Zeze Rwasama of Twin Falls, who is originally from Congo, is the director of the College of Southern Idaho's refugee program, and is recognized for his work to educate, integrate and build bridges between refugees and their new communities.

Tyvan Schmitt, of Pocatello, who served in the U.S. Navy, is a posthumous awardee for his bravery and courage as he attempted to prevent a large catastrophe and for his devotion to helping the homeless, the schools, and neighbors. Linda Scott, a Pocatello native who served in the U.S. Army, is recognized for her volunteer efforts and commitment of her time, energy, resources, and compassion to helping others in need. Pocatello resident and Spanish professor Dr. Helen Cathleen Tarp is recognized for her work as founding program director of the Spanish for Health Professions major at Idaho State University, which is the only major of its kind in the country.

These remarkable Idahoans are among the 56 Idahoans of diverse backgrounds and a wide range of ages who have been honored as Hometown Hero Award recipients since the award's establishment. I commend the Rahims, the award's committee members, the cosponsors, volunteers, and other organizations supporting this honor for their work to shed light on extraordinary service in our communities.

These Hometown Hero award recipients and countless other Idahoans lead by example, inspiring others to go above and beyond in assisting others and improving our communities. Congratulations to the 2016 Hometown Hero award recipients on your achievements, and thank you for your efforts to better our communities.●

TRIBUTE TO ROYCE PERRETT

● Mr. DAINES. Mr. President, this week, I have the distinct honor of recognizing Royce Perrett of Wibaux County, a true American cowboy, who will celebrate his 93rd birthday this weekend. While ranching has been his profession for most of his life, he is also a Navy veteran, a devoted husband of over 70 years, a father of three children, and a valued member of the ranching community between Sidney and Wibaux.

Growing up in rural Nebraska, Mr. Perrett made do without many of the modern comforts we enjoy today: electricity, refrigeration, and modern transportation. When courting Nell Anderson, who would later become his wife, he traveled 10 miles by horse on the weekend to spend time with her, and on his way home Sunday night, he would sleep on his horse, waking up when the horse would stop to open gates.

After WWII and his service in the Navy was completed, Mr. Perrett returned to doing what he loves: ranching. His pursuits took him and his family from the Sandhills of Nebraska, to Isabel, SD, and then in his early 60s, when most would be considering retirement, Mr. Perrett came to Montana to manage the Blue Mountain Ranch, a 13,000-acre ranch north of Wibaux. While Mr. Perrett has had to trade in his saddle for a seat in a side-by-side ATV in recent years, he still manages the Blue Mountain Ranch full time for Gartner-Denowh Angus Ranch and puts in long hours fixing fences, checking water, and watching over 500 cows that graze there in the summer and fall.

When he isn't busy working, he enjoys collecting Western memorabilia and sharing his many stories about ranching, his life adventures, and his self-described greatest achievement: his marriage of over 70 years. As I found out recently when I stopped to visit Mr. Perrett, his door is always open to visitors and you had better be ready for a good conversation and history lesson if you stop by.●

MESSAGES FROM THE HOUSE

At 11:32 a.m., a message from the House of Representatives, delivered by Mrs. Cole, one of its reading clerks, announced that the House agrees to the amendment of the Senate to the bill (H.R. 34) to authorize and strengthen the tsunami detection, forecast, warning, research, and mitigation program of the National Oceanic and Atmospheric Administration, and for other purposes, with an amendment, in which it requests the concurrence of the Senate.

At 12:30 p.m., a message from the House of Representatives, delivered by Mrs. Cole, one of its reading clerks, announced that the Speaker has signed the following enrolled bills:

H.R. 4419. An act to update the financial disclosure requirements for judges of the District of Columbia courts and to make other improvements to the District of Columbia courts.

H.R. 5785. An act to amend title 5, United States Code, to provide for an annuity supplement for certain air traffic controllers.

The enrolled bills were subsequently signed by the President pro tempore (Mr. HATCH).

At 1:37 p.m., a message from the House of Representatives, delivered by Mrs. Cole, one of its reading clerks, announced that the House has passed the following bills, without amendment:

S. 1555. An act to award a Congressional Gold Medal, collectively, to the Filipino veterans of World War II, in recognition of the dedicated service of the veterans during World War II.

S. 2234. An act to award the Congressional Gold Medal, collectively, to the members of the Office of Strategic Services (OSS) in recognition of their superior service and major contributions during World War II.

The message also announced that the House has passed the following bills, in which it requests the concurrence of the Senate:

H.R. 2992. An act to award a Congressional Gold Medal, collectively, to the U.S. Merchant Marine of World War II, in recognition of their dedicated and vital service during World War II.

H.R. 5047. An act to direct the Secretary of Veterans Affairs and the Secretary of Labor to provide information to veterans and members of the Armed Forces about articulation agreements between institutions of higher learning, and for other purposes.

H.R. 5384. An act to amend title 44, United States Code, to restrict the distribution of free printed copies of the Federal Register to Members of Congress and other officers and employees of the United States, and for other purposes.

H.R. 5948. An act to designate the facility of the United States Postal Service located at 830 Kuhn Drive in Chula Vista, California, as the "Jonathan 'J.D.' De Guzman Post Office Building".

H.R. 6009. An act to ensure the effective processing of mail by Federal agencies, and for other purposes.

H.R. 6138. An act to designate the facility of the United States Postal Service located at 560 East Pleasant Valley Road, Port Hueneme, California, as the U.S. Naval Construction Battalion "Seabees" Fallen Heroes Post Office Building.

H.R. 6186. An act to amend title 5, United States Code, to extend certain protections against prohibited personnel practices, and for other purposes.

H.R. 6282. An act to designate the facility of the United States Postal Service located at 2024 Jerome Avenue, in Bronx, New York, as the "Dr. Roscoe C. Brown, Jr. Post Office Building".

H.R. 6302. An act to provide an increase in premium pay for United States Secret Service agents performing protective services during 2016, and for other purposes.

H.R. 6303. An act to designate facilities of the United States Postal Service, to establish new ZIP Codes, and for other purposes.

H.R. 6304. An act to designate the facility of the United States Postal Service located at 501 North Main Street in Florence, Arizona, as the "Adolfo 'Harpo' Celaya Post Office".

H.R. 6393. An act to authorize appropriations for fiscal year 2017 for intelligence and intelligence-related activities of the United States Government, the Community Management Account, and the Central Intelligence Agency Retirement and Disability System, and for other purposes.

The message further announced that the House agreed to the following concurrent resolution, in which it requests the concurrence of the Senate:

H. Con. Res. 174. Concurrent resolution directing the Clerk of the House of Representatives to make a correction in the enrollment of H.R. 34.

EXECUTIVE AND OTHER COMMUNICATIONS

The following communications were laid before the Senate, together with accompanying papers, reports, and documents, and were referred as indicated:

EC–7767. A communication from the Associate General Counsel, Office of the General Counsel, Department of Agriculture, transmitting, pursuant to law, a report relative to a vacancy in the position of Deputy Secretary of Agriculture, received in the Office of the President of the Senate on November 29, 2016; to the Committee on Agriculture, Nutrition, and Forestry.

EC–7768. A communication from the Associate General Counsel, Office of the General Counsel, Department of Agriculture, transmitting, pursuant to law, a report relative to a vacancy in the position of Under Secretary for Marketing and Regulatory Programs, received in the Office of the President of the Senate on November 29, 2016; to the Committee on Agriculture, Nutrition, and Forestry.

EC–7769. A communication from the Assistant Secretary for Export Administration, Bureau of Industry and Security, Department of Commerce, transmitting, pursuant to law, the report of a rule entitled "Clarifications and Revisions to Military Aircraft, Gas Turbine Engines and Related Items License Requirements" (RIN0694–AG76) received in the Office of the President of the Senate on November 28, 2016; to the Committee on Banking, Housing, and Urban Affairs.

EC–7770. A communication from the Chief Counsel, Federal Emergency Management Agency, Department of Homeland Security,

transmitting, pursuant to law, the report of a rule entitled "Suspension of Community Eligibility; Massachusetts: Marshfield, Town of, Plymouth County" ((44 CFR Part 64) (Docket No. FEMA–2016–0002)) received in the Office of the President of the Senate on November 28, 2016; to the Committee on Banking, Housing, and Urban Affairs.

EC–7771. A communication from the Secretary of the Treasury, transmitting, pursuant to law, a six-month periodic report on the national emergency with respect to the stabilization of Iraq that was declared in Executive Order 13303 of May 22, 2003; to the Committee on Banking, Housing, and Urban Affairs.

EC–7772. A communication from the Secretary of the Treasury, transmitting, pursuant to law, a final report on the national emergency with respect to Burma that was declared in Executive Order 13047 of May 20, 1997; to the Committee on Banking, Housing, and Urban Affairs.

EC–7773. A communication from the Secretary of the Treasury, transmitting, pursuant to law, a six-month periodic report on the national emergency with respect to Yemen that was originally declared in Executive Order 13611 on May 16, 2012; to the Committee on Banking, Housing, and Urban Affairs.

EC–7774. A communication from the Director of Legislative Affairs, Federal Deposit Insurance Corporation, transmitting, pursuant to law, the report of a rule entitled "Revision of the FDIC's Freedom of Information Act Regulations" (RIN3064–AE53) received in the Office of the President of the Senate on November 29, 2016; to the Committee on Banking, Housing, and Urban Affairs.

EC–7775. A communication from the General Counsel of the National Credit Union Administration, transmitting, pursuant to law, the report of a rule entitled "Civil Monetary Penalty Inflation Adjustment" (RIN3133–AE59) received in the Office of the President of the Senate on November 30, 2016; to the Committee on Banking, Housing, and Urban Affairs.

EC–7776. A communication from the Senior Counsel, Legal Division, Bureau of Consumer Financial Protection, transmitting, pursuant to law, the report of a rule entitled "Prepaid Accounts Under the electronic Fund Transfer Act (Regulation E) and the Truth in Lending Act (Regulation Z)" (RIN3170–AA22) received in the Office of the President of the Senate on November 30, 2016; to the Committee on Banking, Housing, and Urban Affairs.

EC–7777. A communication from the Assistant Secretary, Legislative Affairs, Department of State, transmitting, pursuant to law, a six-month periodic report relative to the continuation of the national emergency with respect to the proliferation of weapons of mass destruction that was originally declared in Executive Order 12938 of November 14, 1994; to the Committee on Banking, Housing, and Urban Affairs.

EC–7778. A communication from the Chief of the Forest Service, Department of Agriculture, transmitting, pursuant to law, a report relative to the Department's proposal to accept a 3,323-acre donation from the American River Conservancy; to the Committee on Energy and Natural Resources.

EC–7779. A communication from the Counsel to the Director, Office of Hearings and Appeals, Department of the Interior, transmitting, pursuant to law, the report of a rule entitled "Resource Agency Hearings and Alternatives Development Procedures in Hydropower Licenses" (RIN0596–AC42; RIN1090–

AA91; RIN0648–AU01) received in the Office of the President of the Senate on November 29, 2016; to the Committee on Energy and Natural Resources.

EC–7780. A communication from the Director of the Regulatory Management Division, Environmental Protection Agency, transmitting, pursuant to law, the report of a rule entitled "Revision of Certain Federal Water Quality Criteria Applicable to Washington" ((RIN2040–AF56) (FRL No. 9955–40–OW)) received in the Office of the President of the Senate on November 28, 2016; to the Committee on Environment and Public Works.

EC–7781. A communication from the Director of the Regulatory Management Division, Environmental Protection Agency, transmitting, pursuant to law, the report of a rule entitled "National Pollutant Discharge Elimination System (NPDES) Municipal Separate Storm Sewer System General Permit Remand Rule" ((RIN2040–AF57) (FRL No. 9955–11–OW)) received in the Office of the President of the Senate on November 28, 2016; to the Committee on Environment and Public Works.

EC–7782. A communication from the Director of the Regulatory Management Division, Environmental Protection Agency, transmitting, pursuant to law, the report of a rule entitled "Air Quality Plans; Tennessee; Infrastructure Requirements for the 2010 Sulfur Dioxide National Ambient Air Quality Standard" (FRL No. 9955–58–Region 4) received in the Office of the President of the Senate on November 28, 2016; to the Committee on Environment and Public Works.

EC–7783. A communication from the Director of the Regulatory Management Division, Environmental Protection Agency, transmitting, pursuant to law, the report of a rule entitled "Air Plan Approval: AK; Permitting Fees Revision" (FRL No. 9955–48–Region 10) received in the Office of the President of the Senate on November 28, 2016; to the Committee on Environment and Public Works.

EC–7784. A communication from the Director of the Regulatory Management Division, Environmental Protection Agency, transmitting, pursuant to law, the report of a rule entitled "Air Plan Approval; MA; Decommissioning of Stage II Vapor Recovery Systems" (FRL No. 9950–92–Region 1) received in the Office of the President of the Senate on November 28, 2016; to the Committee on Environment and Public Works.

EC–7785. A communication from the Director of the Regulatory Management Division, Environmental Protection Agency, transmitting, pursuant to law, the report of a rule entitled "2015 Revision and Confidentiality Determinations for Data Elements Under the Greenhouse Gas Reporting Rule" ((RIN2060–AS60) (FRL No. 9954–42–OAR)) received in the Office of the President of the Senate on November 28, 2016; to the Committee on Environment and Public Works.

EC–7786. A communication from the Director of the Regulatory Management Division, Environmental Protection Agency, transmitting, pursuant to law, the report of a rule entitled "Effluent Limitations Guidelines and Standards for the Oil and Gas Extraction Point Source Category—Implementation Date Extension" ((RIN2040–AF68) (FRL No. 9955–65–OW)) received in the Office of the President of the Senate on November 28, 2016; to the Committee on Environment and Public Works.

EC–7787. A communication from the Assistant Secretary for Legislation, Department of Health and Human Services, transmitting, pursuant to law, a report entitled "Recovery Auditing in Medicare Fee-for-Service for Fiscal Year 2015"; to the Committee on Finance.

EC–7788. A communication from the Director, Office of Regulations and Reports Clearance, Social Security Administration, transmitting, pursuant to law, the report of a rule entitled "Revised Medical Criteria for Evaluating Human Immunodeficiency Virus (HIV) Infection and for Evaluating Functional Limitations in Immune system Disorders" (RIN0960–AG71) received in the Office of the President of the Senate on November 28, 2016; to the Committee on Finance.

EC–7789. A communication from the Assistant Secretary, Legislative Affairs, Department of State, transmitting, pursuant to law, the report of a rule entitled "Amendment to the International Traffic in Arms Regulations: Corrections and Clarifications" (RIN1400–AE05) received in the Office of the President of the Senate on November 28, 2016; to the Committee on Foreign Relations.

EC–7790. A communication from the Supervisory Management and Program Analyst, Office of Acquisition and Assistance, U.S. Agency for International Development, transmitting, pursuant to law, the report of a rule entitled "Requirement for Nondiscrimination against End-Users of Supplies or Services ('Beneficiaries') under USAID-Funded Contracts" (RIN0412–AA81) received in the Office of the President of the Senate on November 28, 2016; to the Committee on Foreign Relations.

EC–7791. A communication from the Director of Regulations and Policy Management Staff, Food and Drug Administration, Department of Health and Human Services, transmitting, pursuant to law, the report of a rule entitled "Indirect Food Additives: Paper and Paperboard Components" (Docket No. FDA–2016–F–1153) received in the Office of the President of the Senate on November 28, 2016; to the Committee on Health, Education, Labor, and Pensions.

EC–7792. A communication from the Director of Regulations and Policy Management Staff, Food and Drug Administration, Department of Health and Human Services, transmitting, pursuant to law, the report of a rule entitled "Medical Gas Containers and Closures; Current Good Manufacturing Practice Requirements" ((RIN0910–AC53) (Docket No. FDA–2005–N–0343)) received in the Office of the President of the Senate on November 28, 2016; to the Committee on Health, Education, Labor, and Pensions.

EC–7793. A communication from the Director of Regulations and Policy Management Staff, Food and Drug Administration, Department of Health and Human Services, transmitting, pursuant to law, the report of a rule entitled "Uniform Compliance Date for Food Labeling Regulations" (Docket No. FDA–2000–N–0011) received in the Office of the President of the Senate on November 28, 2016; to the Committee on Health, Education, Labor, and Pensions.

EC–7794. A communication from the Director of Regulations and Policy Management Staff, Food and Drug Administration, Department of Health and Human Services, transmitting, pursuant to law, the report of a rule entitled "Food and Drug Administration Review and Action on Over-the-Counter Time and Extent Applications" ((RIN0910–AH30) (Docket No. FDA–2016–N–0543)) received in the Office of the President of the Senate on November 28, 2016; to the Committee on Health, Education, Labor, and Pensions.

EC–7795. A communication from the Assistant General Counsel for Regulatory Affairs, Pension Benefit Guaranty Corporation, transmitting, pursuant to law, the report of a rule entitled "Allocation of assets in Single-Employer Plans; Valuation of Benefits and Assets; Expected Retirement Age" (29 CFR Part 4044) received in the Office of the President of the Senate on November 28, 2016; to the Committee on Health, Education, Labor, and Pensions.

EC–7796. A communication from the Administrator, Environmental Protection Agency, transmitting, pursuant to law, the Department's Semiannual Report from the Office of the Inspector General for the period from April 1, 2016 through September 30, 2016; to the Committee on Homeland Security and Governmental Affairs.

EC–7797. A communication from the Chairman, National Endowment for the Arts, transmitting, pursuant to law, the Endowment's Agency Financial Report for fiscal year 2016; to the Committee on Homeland Security and Governmental Affairs.

EC–7798. A communication from the Chairman of the National Endowment for the Arts, transmitting, pursuant to law, the Semiannual Report of the Inspector General and the Chairman's Semiannual Report on Final Action Resulting from Audit Reports, Inspection Reports, and Evaluation Reports for the period from April 1, 2016 through September 30, 2016; to the Committee on Homeland Security and Governmental Affairs.

EC–7799. A communication from the Acting Director, Office of Personnel Management, transmitting, pursuant to law, the report of a rule entitled "Career and Career-Conditional Employment" (RIN3206–AM64) received in the Office of the President of the Senate on November 28, 2016; to the Committee on Homeland Security and Governmental Affairs.

EC–7800. A communication from the Acting Director, Office of Personnel Management, transmitting, pursuant to law, the report of a rule entitled "Veterans' Preference" (RIN3206–AM79) received in the Office of the President of the Senate on November 28, 2016; to the Committee on Homeland Security and Governmental Affairs.

EC–7801. A communication from the Acting Director, Planning and Policy Analysis, Office of Personnel Management, transmitting, pursuant to law, the report of a rule entitled "Federal Employees' Health Benefits Program Coverage for Certain Firefighters and Intermittent Emergency Response Personnel" (RIN3206–AM66) received in the Office of the President of the Senate on November 28, 2016; to the Committee on Homeland Security and Governmental Affairs.

EC–7802. A communication from the Secretary of Energy, transmitting, pursuant to law, the Department of Energy's Agency Financial Report for fiscal year 2016; to the Committee on Homeland Security and Governmental Affairs.

EC–7803. communication from the Under Secretary of Defense (Comptroller), transmitting, pursuant to law, a report relative to the Department of Defense Agency Financial Report (AFR) for fiscal year 2016; to the Committee on Homeland Security and Governmental Affairs.

EC–7804. A communication from the Secretary of Veterans Affairs, transmitting, pursuant to law, the Department of Veterans Affairs' Semiannual Report of the Inspector General for the period from April 1, 2016 through September 30, 2016; to the Committee on Homeland Security and Governmental Affairs.

EC–7805. A communication from the Chairman, National Endowment for the Arts, transmitting, pursuant to law, the Endowment's Agency Financial Report for fiscal year 2016; to the Committee on Homeland Security and Governmental Affairs.

EC–7806. A communication from the Chairman, Consumer Product Safety Commission, transmitting, pursuant to law, the Agency Financial Report for fiscal year 2016; to the Committee on Homeland Security and Governmental Affairs.

EC–7807. A communication from the Chairman, Merit Systems Protection Board, transmitting, pursuant to law, the Board's Agency Financial Report for fiscal year 2016; to the Committee on Homeland Security and Governmental Affairs.

EC–7808. A communication from the Chairman, Federal Maritime Commission, transmitting, pursuant to law, the Commission's Performance and Accountability Report for fiscal year 2016; to the Committee on Homeland Security and Governmental Affairs.

EC–7809. A communication from the Administrator, Saint Lawrence Seaway Development Corporation, Department of Transportation, transmitting, pursuant to law, the Corporation's annual financial audit and management report for the fiscal year ending September 30, 2016; to the Committee on Homeland Security and Governmental Affairs.

EC–7810. A communication from the Chairwoman of the Federal Trade Commission, transmitting, pursuant to law, the Commission's fiscal year 2016 Agency Financial Report and the Uniform Resource Locator (URL) for the report; to the Committee on Homeland Security and Governmental Affairs.

EC–7811. A communication from the Secretary of Energy, transmitting, pursuant to law, the Department of Energy's Agency Financial Report for fiscal year 2016; to the Committee on Homeland Security and Governmental Affairs.

EC–7812. A communication from the Chief Executive Officer, Millennium Challenge Corporation, transmitting, pursuant to law, the Office of Inspector General's Semiannual Report for the period of April 1, 2016 through September 30, 2016, and the Millennium Challenge Corporation's response; to the Committee on Homeland Security and Governmental Affairs.

EC–7813. A communication from the Associate Administrator, Office of Congressional and Legislative Affairs, Small Business Administration, transmitting, pursuant to law, the Uniform Resource Locator (URL) for the Administration's fiscal year 2016 Agency Financial Report; to the Committee on Homeland Security and Governmental Affairs.

EC–7814. A communication from the Chief Executive Officer, Corporation for National and Community Service, transmitting, pursuant to law, the Semiannual Report of the Inspector General and the Corporation for National and Community Service's Response and Report on Final Action for the period from April 1, 2016 through September 30, 2016; to the Committee on Homeland Security and Governmental Affairs.

EC–7815. A communication from the Secretary of Health and Human Services, transmitting, pursuant to law, the Department's Semiannual Report of the Inspector General for the period from April 1, 2016 through September 30, 2016; to the Committee on Homeland Security and Governmental Affairs.

EC–7816. A communication from the Secretary of Transportation, transmitting, pursuant to law, the Department of Transportation's Semiannual Report of the Inspector General for the period from April 1, 2016 through September 30, 2016; to the Committee on Homeland Security and Governmental Affairs.

EC–7817. A communication from the Federal Co-Chair, Appalachian Regional Commission, transmitting, pursuant to law, the

Commission's Semiannual Report of the Inspector General for the period from April 1, 2016 through September 30, 2016; to the Committee on Homeland Security and Governmental Affairs.

EC–7818. A communication from the Chairman, Consumer Product Safety Commission, transmitting, pursuant to law, the Agency Financial Report for fiscal year 2016; to the Committee on Homeland Security and Governmental Affairs.

EC–7819. A communication from the Board Members of the Railroad Retirement Board, transmitting, pursuant to law, the Semiannual Report of the Inspector General for the period from April 1, 2016 through September 30, 2016; to the Committee on Homeland Security and Governmental Affairs.

EC–7820. A communication from the Assistant Secretary for Legislation, Department of Health and Human Services, transmitting, pursuant to law, a report entitled "2015 Outcome Evaluations of Administration for Native Americans (ANA) Projects Report to Congress"; to the Committee on Indian Affairs.

EC–7821. A communication from the Assistant Secretary for Legislation, Department of Health and Human Services, transmitting, pursuant to law, a report entitled "Fiscal Year (FY) 2015 Report to Congress on Contract Funding of Indian Self-Determination and Education Assistance Act Awards"; to the Committee on Indian Affairs.

EC–7822. A communication from the Assistant Secretary for Legislation, Department of Health and Human Services, transmitting, pursuant to law, a report entitled "Fiscal Year 2012 Report to Congress on Administration of the Tribal Self-Governance Program"; to the Committee on Indian Affairs.

EC–7823. A communication from the Assistant Secretary for Legislation, Department of Health and Human Services, transmitting, pursuant to law, a report entitled "Fiscal Year 2013 Report to Congress on Administration of the Tribal Self-Governance Program"; to the Committee on Indian Affairs.

EC–7824. A communication from the Assistant Secretary for Legislation, Department of Health and Human Services, transmitting, pursuant to law, a report entitled "Fiscal Year 2014 Report to Congress on Administration of the Tribal Self-Governance Program"; to the Committee on Indian Affairs.

EC–7825. A communication from the Executive Analyst (Political), Department of Health and Human Services, transmitting, pursuant to law, a report relative to a vacancy in the position of Commissioner, Administration on Native Americans, Department of Health and Human Services, received in the Office of the President of the Senate on November 30, 2016; to the Committee on Indian Affairs.

EC–7826. A communication from the Executive Director, Consumer Product Safety Commission, transmitting, pursuant to law, the Commission's 2016–2020 Strategic Plan; to the Committee on Commerce, Science, and Transportation.

EC–7827. A communication from the Executive Director, Consumer Product Safety Commission, transmitting, pursuant to law, the Commission's 2016–2020 Strategic Plan; to the Committee on Commerce, Science, and Transportation.

EC–7828. A communication from the Attorney-Advisor, Office of the Secretary, Department of Transportation, transmitting, pursuant to law, a report relative to a vacancy for the position of Assistant Secretary for Research and Technology, Department of Transportation, received in the office of the President of the Senate on November 30, 2016; to the Committee on Commerce, Science, and Transportation.

EC–7829. A communication from the Deputy Chief, Wireline Competition Bureau, Federal Communications Commission, transmitting, pursuant to law, the report of a rule entitled "Protecting the Privacy of Customers of Broadband and Other Telecommunications Services" ((FCC 16–148) (WC Docket No. 16–106)) received in the Office of the President of the Senate on November 30, 2016; to the Committee on Commerce, Science, and Transportation.

EC–7830. A communication from the Deputy Bureau Chief, Wireline Competition Bureau, Federal Communications Commission, transmitting, pursuant to law, the report of a rule entitled "Connect America Fund" ((FCC 16–143) (WC Docket No. 10–90)) received in the Office of the President of the Senate on November 30, 2016; to the Committee on Commerce, Science, and Transportation.

PETITIONS AND MEMORIALS

The following petitions and memorials were laid before the Senate and were referred or ordered to lie on the table as indicated:

POM–256. A joint resolution adopted by the General Assembly of the State of Indiana requesting the United States Congress to call a constitutional convention for the purpose of proposing an amendment to the United States Constitution concerning imposition of fiscal restraints on the federal government, limitations of the powers and jurisdiction of federal powers, and the limitation of the terms of office for its officials and for members of Congress; to the Committee on the Judiciary.

SENATE ENROLLED JOINT RESOLUTION NO. 14

Section 1. The legislature of the State of Indiana hereby applies to Congress, under the provisions of Article V of the Constitution of the United States, for the calling of a convention of the states limited to proposing amendments to the Constitution of the United States that impose fiscal restraints of the federal government, limit the power and jurisdiction of the federal government, and limit the terms of office for its officials and for members of Congress.

Section 2. The secretary of state is hereby directed to transmit copies of this application to the President and Secretary of the United States Senate and to the Speaker and Clerk of the United States House of Representatives, and copies to the members of the said Senate and House of Representatives from this State; also to transmit copies hereof to the presiding officers of each of the legislative houses in the several States, requesting their cooperation.

Section 3. This application constitutes a continuing application in accordance with Article V of the Constitution of the United States until the legislatures of at least two-thirds of the several States have made applications on the same subject.

POM–257. A petition from a citizen of the State of Texas relative to a proposed amendment to the United States Constitution; to the Committee on the Judiciary.

REPORTS OF COMMITTEES

The following reports of committees were submitted:

By Mr. THUNE, from the Committee on Commerce, Science, and Transportation, with an amendment in the nature of a substitute:

S. 3084. A bill to invest in innovation through research and development, and to improve the competitiveness of the United States (Rept. No. 114–389).

By Mr. CORKER, from the Committee on Foreign Relations, with an amendment in the nature of a substitute:

S. 2201. A bill to promote international trade, and for other purposes.

EXECUTIVE REPORTS OF COMMITTEES

The following executive reports of nominations were submitted:

By Mr. McCAIN for the Committee on Armed Services.

Air Force nomination of Brig. Gen. Robert N. Polumbo, to be Major General.

Air Force nomination of Maj. Gen. Jerry D. Harris, Jr., to be Lieutenant General.

Air Force nomination of Lt. Gen. James M. Holmes, to be General.

Navy nomination of Rear Adm. William K. Lescher, to be Vice Admiral.

Navy nomination of Capt. Kelly A. Aeschbach, to be Rear Admiral (lower half).

Navy nomination of Vice Adm. Dixon R. Smith, to be Vice Admiral.

Air Force nominations beginning with Col. Joel E. DeGroot and ending with Col. David D. Zwart, which nominations were received by the Senate and appeared in the Congressional Record on November 15, 2016.

Air Force nominations beginning with Brig. Gen. David P. Baczewski and ending with Brig. Gen. Roger E. Williams, Jr., which nominations were received by the Senate and appeared in the Congressional Record on November 15, 2016.

Air Force nomination of Brig. Gen. Jesse T. Simmons, Jr., to be Major General.

Air Force nominations beginning with Brig. Gen. David M. McMinn and ending with Brig. Gen. Ronald E. Paul, which nominations were received by the Senate and appeared in the Congressional Record on November 15, 2016.

Air Force nomination of Col. William E. Dickens, Jr., to be Brigadier General.

Air Force nominations beginning with Col. Brian K. Borgen and ending with Col. Constance M. Von Hoffman, which nominations were received by the Senate and appeared in the Congressional Record on November 15, 2016.

Air Force nomination of Brig. Gen. Randolph J. Staudenraus, to be Major General.

Air Force nominations beginning with Brig. Gen. Craig L. LaFave and ending with Brig. Gen. Patrick M. Wade, which nominations were received by the Senate and appeared in the Congressional Record on November 15, 2016.

Air Force nomination of Col. Stephen C. Melton, to be Brigadier General.

Army nomination of Maj. Gen. Paul E. Funk II, to be Lieutenant General.

Army nomination of Maj. Gen. Gary J. Volesky, to be Lieutenant General.

Army nomination of Maj. Gen. James H. Dickinson, to be Lieutenant General.

Army nomination of Brig. Gen. Patrick M. Hamilton, to be Major General.

Army nominations beginning with Brig. Gen. Benjamin F. Adams III and ending with Brig. Gen. Michael R. Zerbonia, which nominations were received by the Senate and appeared in the Congressional Record on November 15, 2016.

Army nomination of Col. Mark A. Piterski, to be Brigadier General.

Army nomination of Col. Ellis F. Hopkins III, to be Brigadier General.

Army nominations beginning with Col. Michael A. Abell and ending with Col. Louis W. Wilham, which nominations were received by the Senate and appeared in the Congressional Record on November 15, 2016.

Navy nomination of Rear Adm. (lh) Mary M. Jackson, to be Vice Admiral.

Mr. McCAIN. Mr. President, for the Committee on Armed Services I report favorably the following nomination lists which were printed in the RECORD on the dates indicated, and ask unanimous consent, to save the expense of reprinting on the Executive Calendar that these nominations lie at the Secretary's desk for the information of Senators.

The PRESIDING OFFICER. Without objection, it is so ordered.

Air Force nominations beginning with Daniel J. Bessmer and ending with Christie Barton Walton, which nominations were received by the Senate and appeared in the Congressional Record on June 16, 2016.

Air Force nominations beginning with Kip T. Averett and ending with Daniel S. Walker, which nominations were received by the Senate and appeared in the Congressional Record on November 15, 2016.

Air Force nominations beginning with Shawn M. Garcia and ending with Morgan H. Laird, which nominations were received by the Senate and appeared in the Congressional Record on November 15, 2016.

Air Force nominations beginning with Daniel C. Abell and ending with Peter Zwart, which nominations were received by the Senate and appeared in the Congressional Record on November 15, 2016.

Air Force nomination of Gary A. Fairchild, to be Colonel.

Air Force nomination of Megan M. Luka, to be Major.

Air Force nominations beginning with Brandon D. Clint and ending with Edmund J. Rutherford, which nominations were received by the Senate and appeared in the Congressional Record on November 15, 2016.

Air Force nominations beginning with Isamettin A. Aral and ending with Leslie Ann Zyzda-Martin, which nominations were received by the Senate and appeared in the Congressional Record on November 15, 2016.

Army nomination of Brian C. Garver, to be Major.

Army nomination of Clifford D. Johnston, to be Major.

Army nomination of Reinaldo Gonzalez II, to be Major.

Army nomination of Graham F. Inman, to be Major.

Army nomination of Eileen K. Jenkins, to be Lieutenant Colonel.

Army nomination of Jeffrey M. Farris, to be Colonel.

Army nomination of Matthew T. Bell, to be Lieutenant Colonel.

Army nomination of Melissa B. Reister, to be Major.

Army nomination of Charles M. Causey, to be Colonel.

Army nominations beginning with Stephen A. Labate and ending with Raymond J. Orr, which nominations were received by the Senate and appeared in the Congressional Record on November 15, 2016.

Army nomination of Roxanne E. Wallace, to be Lieutenant Colonel.

Army nomination of Eric A. Mitchell, to be Major.

Army nomination of Jonathan J. Vannatta, to be Colonel.

Army nomination of Dennis D. Calloway, to be Lieutenant Colonel.

Army nominations beginning with Kenneth L. Alford and ending with Bruce T. Sidebotham, which nominations were received by the Senate and appeared in the Congressional Record on November 15, 2016.

Army nomination of Henry Spring, Jr., to be Colonel.

Army nomination of Craig A. Yunker, to be Colonel.

Army nomination of Cornelius J. Pope, to be Lieutenant Colonel.

Army nomination of Anthony K. McConnell, to be Colonel.

Army nomination of Jennifer L. Cummings, to be Lieutenant Colonel.

Army nominations beginning with Donald J. Erpenbach and ending with Timothy A. Fanter, which nominations were received by the Senate and appeared in the Congressional Record on November 15, 2016.

Army nomination of Carl I. Shaia, to be Colonel.

Army nomination of Lisa M. Barden, to be Lieutenant Colonel.

Army nomination of Roger D. Lyles, to be Colonel.

Army nomination of Clara A. Bieganek, to be Lieutenant Colonel.

Army nomination of Isaiah M. Garfias, to be Major.

Army nomination of Louis E. Herrera, to be Colonel.

Army nomination of Schnicka L. Singleton, to be Major.

Army nomination of John R. Burchfield, to be Colonel.

Army nomination of Elizabeth S. Eatonferenzi, to be Major.

Army nomination of Richard D. Mina, to be Major.

Army nominations beginning with Temidayo L. Anderson and ending with D0127914, which nominations were received by the Senate and appeared in the Congressional Record on November 15, 2016.

Army nomination of Richard A. Gautier, Jr., to be Major.

Army nomination of Joseph A. Papenfus, to be Colonel.

Army nominations beginning with Stuart G. Baker and ending with Walter D. Venneman, which nominations were received by the Senate and appeared in the Congressional Record on November 15, 2016.

Army nomination of David S. Yuen, to be Colonel.

Army nomination of Donta A. White, to be Major.

Army nomination of Tony A. Hampton, to be Major.

Army nominations beginning with Charles C. Anderson and ending with James D. Willson, which nominations were received by the Senate and appeared in the Congressional Record on November 15, 2016.

Army nomination of David A. Yasenchock, to be Colonel.

Army nomination of Aaron C. Ramiro, to be Major.

Army nomination of Richard M. Strong, to be Lieutenant Colonel.

Army nomination of Brendon S. Baker, to be Major.

Army nominations beginning with Lanny J. Acosta, Jr. and ending with Lance B. Turlington, which nominations were received by the Senate and appeared in the Congressional Record on November 15, 2016.

Army nomination of Andrew J. Wade, to be Colonel.

Army nomination of Christopher S. Besser, to be Lieutenant Colonel.

Army nomination of Chad C. Black, to be Major.

Army nomination of Thomas D. Starkey, to be Colonel.

Marine Corps nomination of Joshua D. Fitzgarrald, to be Major.

Marine Corps nomination of Anthony C. Lyons, to be Lieutenant Colonel.

Navy nomination of Suzanne L. Hopkins, to be Lieutenant Commander.

Navy nominations beginning with Jafar A. Ali and ending with Anthony K. Wolverton, which nominations were received by the Senate and appeared in the Congressional Record on November 15, 2016.

Navy nomination of Meryl A. Severson III, to be Captain.

Navy nomination of Ashley R. Bjorklund, to be Lieutenant Commander.

Navy nomination of Adeleke O. Mowobi, to be Lieutenant Commander.

Navy nominations beginning with Mary K. Arbuthnot and ending with John K. Werner, Jr., which nominations were received by the Senate and appeared in the Congressional Record on November 15, 2016.

Navy nomination of Stephen W. Hedrick, to be Lieutenant Commander.

Navy nomination of Vincent M.J. Ambrosino, to be Lieutenant Commander.

Navy nomination of Neal P. Ridge, to be Captain.

Navy nomination of Abdeslam Bousalham, to be Lieutenant Commander.

Navy nomination of Scott M. Morey, to be Lieutenant Commander.

Navy nomination of Christian R. Foschi, to be Lieutenant Commander.

By Mr. HATCH for the Committee on Finance.

*Charles P. Blahous, III, of Maryland, to be a Member of the Board of Trustees of the Federal Supplementary Medical Insurance Trust Fund for a term of four years.

*Charles P. Blahous, III, of Maryland, to be a Member of the Board of Trustees of the Federal Old-Age and Survivors Insurance Trust Fund and the Federal Disability Insurance Trust Fund for a term of four years.

*Charles P. Blahous, III, of Maryland, to be a Member of the Board of Trustees of the Federal Hospital Insurance Trust Fund for a term of four years.

*Robert D. Reischauer, of Maryland, to be a Member of the Board of Trustees of the Federal Supplementary Medical Insurance Trust Fund for a term of four years.

*Robert D. Reischauer, of Maryland, to be a Member of the Board of Trustees of the Federal Old-Age and Survivors Insurance Trust Fund and the Federal Disability Insurance Trust Fund for a term of four years.

*Robert D. Reischauer, of Maryland, to be a Member of the Board of Trustees of the Federal Hospital Insurance Trust Fund for a term of four years.

*Nomination was reported with recommendation that it be confirmed subject to the nominee's commitment to respond to requests to appear and testify before any duly constituted committee of the Senate.

(Nominations without an asterisk were reported with the recommendation that they be confirmed.)

INTRODUCTION OF BILLS AND JOINT RESOLUTIONS

The following bills and joint resolutions were introduced, read the first and second times by unanimous consent, and referred as indicated:

By Mr. VITTER (for himself and Ms. KLOBUCHAR):

S. 7. A bill to amend title XVIII of the Social Security Act to make permanent the removal of the rental cap for durable medical equipment under the Medicare program with respect to speech generating devices; to the Committee on Finance.

By Mr. CORKER (for himself and Mr. CARDIN):

S. 8. A bill to provide for the approval of the Agreement for Cooperation Between the Government of the United States of America and the Government of the Kingdom of Norway Concerning Peaceful Uses of Nuclear Energy; to the Committee on Foreign Relations.

By Ms. WARREN (for herself and Mr. GRASSLEY):

S. 9. A bill to provide for the regulation of over-the-counter hearing aids; to the Committee on Health, Education, Labor, and Pensions.

By Mr. SCOTT (for himself, Mr. CASEY, Mr. WYDEN, Mr. GRAHAM, and Mr. BENNET):

S. 10. A bill to provide for the consideration of a definition of anti-Semitism for the enforcement of Federal antidiscrimination laws concerning education programs or activities; considered and passed.

By Mr. BOOKER (for himself and Mrs. GILLIBRAND):

S. 3489. A bill to prohibit a court from awarding damages based on race, ethnicity, gender, religion, or actual or perceived sexual orientation, and for other purposes; to the Committee on the Judiciary.

By Mr. MENENDEZ (for himself, Mr. PERDUE, and Mrs. GILLIBRAND):

S. 3490. A bill to direct the Secretary of Homeland Security to provide for an option under the Secure Mail Initiative under which a person to whom a document is sent under that initiative may require that the United States Postal Service obtain a signature from that person in order to deliver the document, and for other purposes; to the Committee on Homeland Security and Governmental Affairs.

By Mr. BROWN (for himself, Mr. LEAHY, Mr. FRANKEN, Mr. DURBIN, Mr. TESTER, Mrs. MURRAY, Mr. MERKLEY, Ms. WARREN, Ms. HIRONO, Mr. CASEY, Mr. WARNER, Mr. MENENDEZ, Mr. BLUMENTHAL, Ms. HEITKAMP, and Mr. REED):

S. 3491. A bill to amend the Truth in Lending Act and the Electronic Fund Transfer Act to provide justice to victims of fraud; to the Committee on Banking, Housing, and Urban Affairs.

By Mr. PETERS (for himself and Ms. STABENOW):

S. 3492. A bill to designate the Traverse City VA Community-Based Outpatient Clinic of the Department of Veterans Affairs in Traverse City, Michigan, as the "Colonel Demas T. Craw VA Clinic"; considered and passed.

By Mr. BOOKER (for himself and Mr. MENENDEZ):

S. 3493. A bill to revise the boundaries of certain John H. Chafee Coastal Barrier Resources System units in New Jersey; to the Committee on Environment and Public Works.

SUBMISSION OF CONCURRENT AND SENATE RESOLUTIONS

The following concurrent resolutions and Senate resolutions were read, and referred (or acted upon), as indicated:

By Mr. ISAKSON (for himself and Ms. BALDWIN):

S. Res. 627. A resolution designating December 3, 2016, as "National Phenylketonuria Awareness Day"; considered and agreed to.

By Mr. BLUNT:

S. Res. 628. A resolution authorizing the printing of a revised edition of the Senate Rules and Manual; considered and agreed to.

ADDITIONAL COSPONSORS

S. 290

At the request of Mr. MORAN, the name of the Senator from Montana (Mr. DAINES) was added as a cosponsor of S. 290, a bill to amend title 38, United States Code, to improve the accountability of employees of the Department of Veterans Affairs, and for other purposes.

S. 497

At the request of Mrs. MURRAY, the name of the Senator from Maryland (Mr. CARDIN) was added as a cosponsor of S. 497, a bill to allow Americans to earn paid sick time so that they can address their own health needs and the health needs of their families.

S. 1490

At the request of Ms. KLOBUCHAR, the name of the Senator from Montana (Mr. DAINES) was added as a cosponsor of S. 1490, a bill to establish an advisory office within the Bureau of Consumer Protection of the Federal Trade Commission to prevent fraud targeting seniors, and for other purposes.

S. 1794

At the request of Mr. MERKLEY, the name of the Senator from New Jersey (Mr. MENENDEZ) was added as a cosponsor of S. 1794, a bill to prohibit drilling in the Arctic Ocean.

S. 2208

At the request of Mrs. MURRAY, the name of the Senator from Maryland (Mr. CARDIN) was added as a cosponsor of S. 2208, a bill to promote the economic security and safety of survivors of domestic violence, dating violence, sexual assault, or stalking, and for other purposes.

S. 2577

At the request of Mr. LEAHY, the name of the Senator from Washington (Mrs. MURRAY) was added as a cosponsor of S. 2577, a bill to protect crime victims' rights, to eliminate the substantial backlog of DNA and other forensic evidence samples to improve and expand the forensic science testing capacity of Federal, State, and local crime laboratories, to increase research and development of new testing technologies, to develop new training programs regarding the collection and use of forensic evidence, to provide post-conviction testing of DNA evidence to exonerate the innocent, to support accreditation efforts of forensic science laboratories and medical examiner offices, to address training and equipment needs, to improve the performance of counsel in State capital cases, and for other purposes.

S. 2645

At the request of Mrs. SHAHEEN, the name of the Senator from Maryland (Mr. CARDIN) was added as a cosponsor of S. 2645, a bill to impose sanctions with respect to foreign persons responsible for gross violations of internationally recognized human rights against lesbian, gay, bisexual, and transgender individuals, and for other purposes.

S. 2671

At the request of Mr. NELSON, the name of the Senator from Montana (Mr. TESTER) was added as a cosponsor of S. 2671, a bill to amend title XVIII of the Social Security Act to establish rules for payment for graduate medical education (GME) costs for hospitals that establish a new medical residency training program after hosting resident rotators for short durations.

S. 2868

At the request of Mr. SCOTT, the name of the Senator from New York (Mrs. GILLIBRAND) was added as a cosponsor of S. 2868, a bill to amend the Internal Revenue Code of 1986 to provide for the deferral of inclusion in gross income for capital gains reinvested in economically distressed zones.

S. 2878

At the request of Mr. RUBIO, the name of the Senator from Nebraska (Mr. SASSE) was added as a cosponsor of S. 2878, a bill to amend the International Religious Freedom Act of 1998 to improve the ability of the United States to advance religious freedom globally through enhanced diplomacy, training, counterterrorism, and foreign assistance efforts, and through stronger and more flexible political responses to religious freedom violations and violent extremism worldwide, and for other purposes.

S. 2989

At the request of Ms. MURKOWSKI, the name of the Senator from Indiana (Mr. COATS) was added as a cosponsor of S. 2989, a bill to award a Congressional Gold Medal, collectively, to the United States merchant mariners of World War II, in recognition of their dedicated and vital service during World War II.

S. 3111

At the request of Mr. PORTMAN, the name of the Senator from Maine (Ms. COLLINS) was added as a cosponsor of S. 3111, a bill to amend the Internal Revenue Code of 1986 to extend the 7.5 percent threshold for the medical expense deduction for individuals age 65 or older.

S. 3164

At the request of Mrs. SHAHEEN, the name of the Senator from Michigan (Ms. STABENOW) was added as a cosponsor of S. 3164, a bill to provide protection for survivors of domestic violence or sexual assault under the Fair Housing Act.

S. 3299

At the request of Mr. DAINES, his name was added as a cosponsor of S. 3299, a bill to direct the Secretary of Homeland Security to notify air carriers and security screening personnel of the Transportation Security Administration of the guidelines of the Administration regarding permitting baby formula, breast milk, and juice on aircraft, and for other purposes.

S. 3373

At the request of Mr. WARNER, the name of the Senator from Idaho (Mr. CRAPO) was added as a cosponsor of S. 3373, a bill to amend the Federal Deposit Insurance Act to ensure that the reciprocal deposits of an insured depository institution are not considered to be funds obtained by or through a deposit broker, and for other purposes.

S. 3391

At the request of Mr. REED, the name of the Senator from Rhode Island (Mr. WHITEHOUSE) was added as a cosponsor of S. 3391, a bill to reauthorize the Museum and Library Services Act.

S. 3447

At the request of Mr. SULLIVAN, the names of the Senator from South Dakota (Mr. ROUNDS) and the Senator from Maine (Mr. KING) were added as cosponsors of S. 3447, a bill to direct the Secretary of the Army to place in Arlington National Cemetery a memorial honoring the helicopter pilots and crew members of the Vietnam era, and for other purposes.

S. 3472

At the request of Mr. LEE, the names of the Senator from Kentucky (Mr. PAUL), the Senator from Florida (Mr. RUBIO) and the Senator from Texas (Mr. CRUZ) were added as cosponsors of S. 3472, a bill to require the Bureau of the Census to conduct a survey to determine income and poverty levels in the United States in a manner that accounts for the receipt of Federal means-tested benefits, and for other purposes.

S. 3476

At the request of Mrs. FEINSTEIN, the name of the Senator from Michigan (Ms. STABENOW) was added as a cosponsor of S. 3476, a bill to waive recoupment by the United States of certain bonuses and similar benefits erroneously received by members of the Army National Guard, and for other purposes.

S. 3478

At the request of Mr. RUBIO, the name of the Senator from Georgia (Mr. PERDUE) was added as a cosponsor of S. 3478, a bill to require continued and enhanced annual reporting to Congress in the Annual Report on International Religious Freedom on anti-Semitic incidents in Europe, the safety and security of European Jewish communities, and the efforts of the United States to partner with European governments, the European Union, and civil society groups, to combat anti-Semitism, and for other purposes.

S. CON. RES. 51

At the request of Mr. GRASSLEY, the name of the Senator from South Dakota (Mr. ROUNDS) was added as a cosponsor of S. Con. Res. 51, a concurrent resolution expressing the sense of Congress that those who served in the bays, harbors, and territorial seas of the Republic of Vietnam during the period beginning on January 9, 1962, and ending on May 7, 1975, should be presumed to have been exposed to the toxin Agent Orange and should be eligible for all related Federal benefits that come with such presumption under the Agent Orange Act of 1991.

S. CON. RES. 56

At the request of Mr. CARDIN, the name of the Senator from Minnesota (Ms. KLOBUCHAR) was added as a cosponsor of S. Con. Res. 56, a concurrent resolution clarifying any potential misunderstanding as to whether actions taken by President-elect Donald Trump constitute a violation of the Emoluments Clause, and calling on President-elect Trump to divest his interest in, and sever his relationship to, the Trump Organization.

S. RES. 580

At the request of Mr. BOOKER, the name of the Senator from Oregon (Mr. WYDEN) was added as a cosponsor of S. Res. 580, a resolution supporting the establishment of a President's Youth Council.

S. RES. 616

At the request of Mrs. SHAHEEN, the name of the Senator from Montana (Mr. TESTER) was added as a cosponsor of S. Res. 616, a resolution supporting the goals and ideals of American Diabetes Month.

STATEMENTS ON INTRODUCED BILLS AND JOINT RESOLUTIONS

By Mr. BROWN (for himself, Mr. LEAHY, Mr. FRANKEN, Mr. DURBIN, Mr. TESTER, Mrs. MURRAY, Mr. MERKLEY, Ms. WARREN, Ms. HIRONO, Mr. CASEY, Mr. WARNER, Mr. MENENDEZ, Mr. BLUMENTHAL, Ms. HEITKAMP, and Mr. REED):

S. 3491. A bill to amend the Truth in Lending Act and the Electronic Fund Transfer Act to provide justice to victims of fraud; to the Committee on Banking, Housing, and Urban Affairs.

Mr. BOOKER. Mr. President, I rise to introduce the Fair Calculations in Civil Damages Act of 2016, also known as the Fair Calculations Act. This critical civil rights legislation would ensure that Federal judicial awards of civil damages do not value women and minorities less than other Americans. By combating discrimination in the award of civil damages, the Fair Calculations Act would help bring our nation one step closer to fulfilling the promise of equal justice under law. I thank Senator GILLIBRAND for her support, and I am proud she is an original cosponsor of this bill. I also thank Rep. KENNEDY, who is introducing the House companion to this bill, for his leadership.

A basic tenet of the American legal system is our shared belief that "all men are created equal," an idea so critical to who we are and what we believe that it is explicitly reflected in our Declaration of Independence. Even our national charter reflects the idea that everyone must be given equal protection under the laws. Out of this constitutional foundation lays a simple truth: to be equal under the law means, at a minimum, that neither our government nor the rule of the law should discriminate against anyone by virtue of his or her membership in a group.

Sadly, our Nation fails to live up to those promises when courts award damages in civil cases. Far too often, Federal and State judges use race or gender as factors to weigh when deciding how much money to award a plaintiff in a civil case. As a result, individuals of a certain race or gender often receive larger awards than people of a different race or gender, even in similar cases. This damages awards gap derives from estimates of how much money an individual would have earned over their lifetimes had they not been injured and, far too often, that estimate considers earnings and job levels by race and gender.

Consider the case of James McMillan, an African-American man who was injured during the 2003 Staten Island ferry crash. As a result of the crash, Mr. McMillan suffered a severe spinal cord injury that caused him to need medical care for the remainder of his life. He sued the City of New York. In response to his suit, the City of New York argued that he should receive less money for his injury because data demonstrated that African-American victims of spinal cord injuries lived fewer years than white victims and, therefore, he would incur fewer medical costs. Fortunately, the judge in that case rejected the city's argument. But no American should have to endure the indignity of having the value of their life determined by their race or gender.

The use of race and gender to project future earnings in courts is a widespread problem. According to a 2009 survey by the National Association of Forensic Economics, 44 percent of forensic economists reported considering race and 92 percent reported considering gender when estimating future earning rates for injured children.

Even leading scholars have been critical of this practice. Martha Chamallas, a law professor at the Ohio State University Law School, called the practice reminiscent of something "civil rights advocates [fought] in the 1960s." Jennifer Wiggins, a law professor at the University of Maine Law School, has emphasized that the practice "reinforces past discrimination and pushes it out into the future and endorses." I could not agree more.

The Fair Calculations Act, which I introduce today, would bar Federal courts from awarding damages based on race, ethnicity, gender, religion, or actual or perceived sexual orientation. Justice in an American court should not turn on race or gender, and the time has come to put an end to this discriminatory practice in Federal courts. I also believe this bill would serve as a road map for States who I hope will end this discriminatory practice in their courts.

The legislation would require the Department of Justice and the Department of Labor to develop guidance to the States on how calculations of future earnings for a violation of State tort law could violate Federal equal protection laws. That is yet another example of how this bill aims to persuade states to follow our lead. By issuing guidance to the states on this issue, the impact of this bill has the potential to be even more far-reaching.

The bill would require the Department of Labor to issue guidance to forensic economists on how to create inclusive future earnings tables that do not rely on race, ethnicity, gender, religion, or actual or perceived sexual orientation. Forensic economists are often used as experts in both Federal and State courts to advise lawyers and judges on the proper amounts to award for damages. Instructing these experts on the benefits of more representative future earnings tables and the legal hurdles of using less inclusive earning tables is yet another way to ensure that future earnings in State courts do not harm women or minorities.

Finally, the Fair Calculations Act would direct the Judicial Conference of the United States to conduct a study and report to Congress on the use of race, ethnicity, gender, age, disability, or actual or perceived sexual orientation in the calculation of future earnings in civil court cases. This provision provides for more transparency and record keeping. The first step to fixing a problem is understanding the extent of the problem you have, and this provision allows for Congress to track the extent of Federal judicial awards based on demographics. It also allows for more open government, which is important because transparency allows the American people to hold its government accountable.

Our Nation was founded on the idea that all people are created equal. Valuing one person's life more than another merely because of the color of their skin or sex belies this core value that makes our Nation great. The Fair Calculations Act would remedy this wrong and continue our country down the path towards fulfilling our Nation's promise of liberty and justice for all. I am proud to stand here today and introduce this critical bill and I urge its speedy passage.

SUBMITTED RESOLUTIONS

SENATE RESOLUTION 627—DESIGNATING DECEMBER 3, 2016, AS "NATIONAL PHENYLKETONURIA AWARENESS DAY"

Mr. ISAKSON (for himself and Ms. BALDWIN) submitted the following resolution; which was considered and agreed to:

S. RES. 627

Whereas phenylketonuria (in this preamble referred to as "PKU") is a rare, inherited metabolic disorder that is characterized by the inability of the body to process the essential amino acid phenylalanine and which causes intellectual disability and other neurological problems, such as memory loss and mood disorders, when treatment is not started within the first few weeks of life;

Whereas PKU is also referred to as Phenylalanine Hydroxylase Deficiency;

Whereas newborn screening for PKU was initiated in the United States in 1963 and was recommended for inclusion in State newborn screening programs under the Newborn Screening Saves Lives Act of 2007 (Public Law 110–204);

Whereas approximately 1 out of every 15,000 infants in the United States is born with PKU;

Whereas PKU is treated with medical food;

Whereas the 2012 Phenylketonuria Scientific Review Conference affirmed the recommendation of lifelong dietary treatment for PKU made by the National Institutes of Health Consensus Development Conference Statement 2000;

Whereas, in 2014, the American College of Medical Genetics and Genomics and Genetic Metabolic Dieticians International published medical and dietary guidelines on the optimal treatment of PKU;

Whereas medical foods are medically necessary for children and adults living with PKU;

Whereas adults with PKU who discontinue treatment are at risk for serious medical issues, such as depression, impulse control disorder, phobias, tremors, and pareses;

Whereas women with PKU must maintain strict metabolic control before and during pregnancy to prevent fetal damage;

Whereas children born from untreated mothers with PKU may have a condition known as "maternal phenylketonuria syndrome", which can cause small brains, intellectual disabilities, birth defects of the heart, and low birth weights;

Whereas, although there is no cure for PKU, treatment involving medical foods, medications, and restriction of phenylalanine intake can prevent progressive, irreversible brain damage;

Whereas access to health insurance coverage for medical food varies across the United States and the long-term costs associated with caring for untreated children and adults with PKU far exceed the cost of providing medical food treatment;

Whereas gaps in medical foods coverage has a detrimental impact on individuals with PKU, their families, and society;

Whereas scientists and researchers are hopeful that breakthroughs in PKU research will be forthcoming;

Whereas researchers across the United States are conducting important research projects involving PKU; and

Whereas the Senate is an institution that can raise awareness of PKU among the general public and the medical community: Now, therefore, be it

Resolved, That the Senate—

(1) designates December 3, 2016, as "National Phenylketonuria Awareness Day";

(2) encourages all people in the United States to become more informed about phenylketonuria and the role of medical foods in treating phenylketonuria; and

(3) respectfully requests that the Secretary of the Senate transmit an enrolled copy of this resolution to the National PKU Alliance, a nonprofit organization dedicated to improving the lives of individuals with phenylketonuria.

SENATE RESOLUTION 628—AUTHORIZING THE PRINTING OF A REVISED EDITION OF THE SENATE RULES AND MANUAL

Mr. BLUNT submitted the following resolution; which was considered and agreed to:

S. RES. 628

Resolved, That—

(1) the Committee on Rules and Administration shall prepare a revised edition of the Senate Rules and Manual for the use of the 114th Congress;

(2) the manual shall be printed as a Senate document; and

(3) in addition to the usual number of copies, 1,500 copies of the manual shall be bound, of which—

(A) 500 paperbound copies shall be for the use of the Senate; and

(B) 1,000 copies shall be bound (550 paperbound, 250 nontabbed black skiver, 200 tabbed black skiver) and delivered as may be directed by the Committee on Rules and Administration.

AMENDMENTS SUBMITTED AND PROPOSED

SA 5117. Mr. McCONNELL proposed an amendment to the bill H.R. 34, to authorize and strengthen the tsunami detection, forecast, warning, research, and mitigation program of the National Oceanic and Atmospheric Administration, and for other purposes.

SA 5118. Mr. McCONNELL proposed an amendment to amendment SA 5117 proposed by Mr. McCONNELL to the bill H.R. 34, supra.

SA 5119. Mr. McCONNELL proposed an amendment to the bill H.R. 34, supra.

SA 5120. Mr. McCONNELL proposed an amendment to amendment SA 5119 proposed by Mr. McCONNELL to the bill H.R. 34, supra.

SA 5121. Mr. McCONNELL proposed an amendment to amendment SA 5120 proposed by Mr. McCONNELL to the amendment SA 5119 proposed by Mr. McCONNELL to the bill H.R. 34, supra.

SA 5122. Mr. JOHNSON submitted an amendment intended to be proposed by him to the bill H.R. 34, supra; which was ordered to lie on the table.

SA 5123. Mr. SULLIVAN (for Mr. BURR (for himself and Ms. CANTWELL)) proposed an amendment to the bill S. 2058, to require the Secretary of Commerce to study the coverage gaps of the Next Generation Weather Radar of the National Weather Service and to develop a plan for improving radar coverage and hazardous weather detection and forecasting.

SA 5124. Mr. SULLIVAN (for Mr. BURR) proposed an amendment to the bill S. 2058, supra.

SA 5125. Mr. SULLIVAN (for Mr. THUNE (for himself and Mr. NELSON)) proposed an amendment to the bill H.R. 1561, to improve the National Oceanic and Atmospheric Administration's weather research through a focused program of investment on affordable and attainable advances in observational, computing, and modeling capabilities to support substantial improvement in weather forecasting and prediction of high impact weather events, to expand commercial opportunities for the provision of weather data, and for other purposes.

SA 5126. Mr. SULLIVAN (for Ms. CANTWELL) proposed an amendment to amendment SA 5125 proposed by Mr. SULLIVAN (for Mr. THUNE (for himself and Mr. NELSON)) to the bill H.R. 1561, supra.

TEXT OF AMENDMENTS

SA 5117. Mr. McCONNELL proposed an amendment to the bill H.R. 34, to authorize and strengthen the tsunami detection, forecast, warning, research, and mitigation program of the National Oceanic and Atmospheric Administration, and for other purposes; as follows:

At the end add the following:

"This Act shall take effect 1 day after the date of enactment."

SA 5118. Mr. McCONNELL proposed an amendment to amendment SA 5117 proposed by Mr. McCONNELL to the bill H.R. 34, to authorize and strengthen the tsunami detection, forecast, warning, research, and mitigation program of the National Oceanic and Atmospheric Administration, and for other purposes; as follows:

Strike "1 day" and insert "2 days".

SA 5119. Mr. McCONNELL proposed an amendment to the bill H.R. 34, to authorize and strengthen the tsunami detection, forecast, warning, research, and mitigation program of the National Oceanic and Atmospheric Administration, and for other purposes; as follows:

At the end add the following:

"This Act shall take effect 3 days after the date of enactment."

SA 5120. Mr. McCONNELL proposed an amendment to amendment SA 5119 proposed by Mr. McCONNELL to the bill H.R. 34, to authorize and strengthen the tsunami detection, forecast, warning, research, and mitigation program of the National Oceanic and Atmospheric Administration, and for other purposes; as follows:

Strike "3 days" and insert "4 days".

SA 5121. Mr. McCONNELL proposed an amendment to amendment SA 5120 proposed by Mr. McCONNELL to the amendment SA 5119 proposed by Mr. McCONNELL to the bill H.R. 34, to authorize and strengthen the tsunami detection, forecast, warning, research, and mitigation program of the National Oceanic and Atmospheric Administration, and for other purposes; as follows:

Strike "4" and insert "5".

SA 5122. Mr. JOHNSON submitted an amendment intended to be proposed by him to the bill H.R. 34, to authorize and strengthen the tsunami detection, forecast, warning, research, and mitigation program of the National Oceanic and Atmospheric Administration, and for other purposes; which was ordered to lie on the table; as follows:

At the appropriate place in division A, insert the following:

SEC. ___. USE OF UNAPPROVED MEDICAL PRODUCTS BY PATIENTS DIAGNOSED WITH A TERMINAL ILLNESS.

(a) SHORT TITLE.—This section may be cited as the "Trickett Wendler Right to Try Act of 2016".

(b) USE OF UNAPPROVED MEDICAL PRODUCTS BY PATIENTS DIAGNOSED WITH A TERMINAL ILLNESS.—

(1) IN GENERAL.—Notwithstanding the Federal Food, Drug, and Cosmetic Act (21 U.S.C. 301 et seq.), the Controlled Substances Act (21 U.S.C. 801 et seq.), and any other provision of Federal law, the Federal Government shall not take any action to prohibit or restrict—

(A) the production, manufacture, distribution, prescribing, or dispensing of an experimental drug, biological product, or device that—

(i) is intended to treat a patient who has been diagnosed with a terminal illness; and

(ii) is authorized by, and in accordance with, State law; and

(B) the possession or use of an experimental drug, biological product, or device—

(i) that is described in clauses (i) and (ii) of subparagraph (A); and

(ii) for which the patient has received a certification from a physician, who is in good standing with the physician's certifying organization or board, that the patient has exhausted, or otherwise does not meet qualifying criteria to receive, any other available treatment options.

(2) NO LIABILITY OR USE OF OUTCOMES.—

(A) NO LIABILITY.—Notwithstanding any other provision of law, no liability shall lie against a producer, manufacturer, distributor, prescriber, dispenser, possessor, or user of an experimental drug, biological product, or device for the production, manufacture, distribution, prescribing, dispensing, possession, or use of an experimental drug, biological product, or device that is in compliance with paragraph (1).

(B) NO USE OF OUTCOMES.—Notwithstanding any other provision of law, the outcome of any production, manufacture, distribution, prescribing, dispensing, possession, or use of an experimental drug, biological product, or device that was done in compliance with paragraph (1) shall not be used by a Federal agency reviewing the experimental drug, biological product, or device to delay or otherwise adversely impact review or approval of such experimental drug, biological product, or device.

(3) DEFINITIONS.—In this section:

(A) BIOLOGICAL PRODUCT.—The term "biological product" has the meaning given to such term in section 351 of the Public Health Service Act (42 U.S.C. 262).

(B) DEVICE; DRUG.—The terms "device" and "drug" have the meanings given to such terms in section 201 of the Federal Food, Drug, and Cosmetic Act (21 U.S.C. 321).

(C) EXPERIMENTAL DRUG, BIOLOGICAL PRODUCT, OR DEVICE.—The term "experimental drug, biological product, or device" means a drug, biological product, or device that—

(i) has successfully completed a phase 1 clinical investigation;

(ii) remains under investigation in a clinical trial approved by the Food and Drug Administration; and

(iii) is not approved, licensed, or cleared for commercial distribution under section 505, 510(k), or 515 of the Federal Food, Drug, or Cosmetic Act (21 U.S.C. 355, 360(k), 360(e)) or section 351 of the Public Health Service Act (42 U.S.C. 262).

(D) PHASE 1 CLINICAL INVESTIGATION.—The term "phase 1 clinical investigation" means a phase 1 clinical investigation, as described in section 312.21 of title 21, Code of Federal Regulations (or any successor regulations).

(E) TERMINAL ILLNESS.—The term "terminal illness" has the meaning given to such term in the State law specified in paragraph (1)(A)(ii).

SA 5123. Mr. SULLIVAN (for Mr. BURR (for himself and Ms. CANTWELL)) proposed an amendment to the bill S. 2058, to require the Secretary of Commerce to study the coverage gaps of the Next Generation Weather Radar of the National Weather Service and to develop a plan for improving radar coverage and hazardous weather detection and forecasting; as follows:

Strike all after the enacting clause and insert the following:

SEC. ___. STUDY ON GAPS IN NEXRAD COVERAGE AND REQUIREMENT FOR PLAN TO ADDRESS SUCH GAPS.

(a) STUDY ON GAPS IN NEXRAD COVERAGE.—

(1) IN GENERAL.—Not later than 90 days after the date of the enactment of this Act, the Secretary of Commerce shall complete a study on gaps in the coverage of the Next Generation Weather Radar of the National Weather Service (referred to in this section as "NEXRAD").

(2) ELEMENTS.—In conducting the study required under paragraph (1), the Secretary shall—

(A) identify areas in the United States with limited or no NEXRAD coverage below 6,000 feet above ground level of the surrounding terrain;

(B) for the areas identified under subparagraph (A)—

(i) identify the key weather effects for which prediction would improve with improved radar detection;

(ii) identify additional sources of observations for high impact weather that were available and operational for such areas on the day before the date of the enactment of this Act, including Terminal Doppler Weather Radar (commonly known as "TDWR"), air surveillance radars of the Federal Aviation Administration, and cooperative network observers; and

(iii) assess the feasibility and advisability of efforts to integrate and upgrade Federal radar capabilities that are not owned or controlled by the National Oceanic and Atmospheric Administration, including radar capabilities of the Federal Aviation Administration and the Department of Defense;

(C) assess the feasibility and advisability of incorporating State-operated and other non-Federal radars into the operations of the National Weather Service;

(D) identify options to improve radar coverage in the areas identified under subparagraph (A); and

(E) estimate the cost of, and develop a timeline for, carrying out each of the options identified under subparagraph (D).

(3) REPORT.—Upon the completion of the study required under paragraph (1), the Secretary shall submit a report to the Committee on Commerce, Science, and Transportation of the Senate, the Committee on Appropriations of the Senate, the Committee on Science, Space, and Technology of the House of Representatives, and the Committee on Appropriations of the House of Representatives that includes the findings of the Secretary with respect to the study.

(b) PLAN TO IMPROVE RADAR COVERAGE.— Not later than 30 days after the completion of the study under subsection (a)(1), the Secretary of Commerce shall submit a plan to the congressional committees referred to in subsection (a)(3) for improving radar coverage in the areas identified under subsection (a)(2)(A) by integrating and upgrading, to the extent practicable, additional observation solutions to improve hazardous weather detection and forecasting.

(c) REQUIREMENT FOR THIRD-PARTY REVIEWS REGARDING PLAN TO IMPROVE RADAR COVERAGE.—The Secretary of Commerce shall seek third-party reviews on scientific methodology relating to, and the feasibility and advisability of, implementing the plan submitted under subsection (b), including the extent to which warning and forecast services of the National Weather Service would be improved by additional NEXRAD coverage.

SA 5124. Mr. SULLIVAN (for Mr. BURR) proposed an amendment to the bill S. 2058, to require the Secretary of Commerce to study the coverage gaps of the Next Generation Weather Radar of the National Weather Service and to develop a plan for improving radar coverage and hazardous weather detection and forecasting; as follows:

Amend the title so as to read: "A bill to require the Secretary of Commerce to study the coverage gaps of the Next Generation Weather Radar of the National Weather Service and to develop a plan for improving radar coverage and hazardous weather detection and forecasting.".

SA 5125. Mr. SULLIVAN (for Mr. THUNE (for himself and Mr. NELSON)) proposed an amendment to the bill H.R. 1561, to improve the National Oceanic and Atmospheric Administration's weather research through a focused program of investment on affordable and attainable advances in observational, computing, and modeling capabilities to support substantial improvement in weather forecasting and prediction of high impact weather events, to expand commercial opportunities for the provision of weather data, and for other purposes; as follows:

Strike all after the enacting clause and insert the following:

SECTION 1. SHORT TITLE; TABLE OF CONTENTS.

(a) SHORT TITLE.—This Act may be cited as the "Weather Research and Forecasting Innovation Act of 2016".

(b) TABLE OF CONTENTS.—The table of contents for this Act is as follows:

Sec. 1. Short title; table of contents.
Sec. 2. Definitions.

TITLE I—UNITED STATES WEATHER RESEARCH AND FORECASTING IMPROVEMENT

Sec. 101. Public safety priority.
Sec. 102. Weather research and forecasting innovation.
Sec. 103. Tornado warning improvement and extension program.
Sec. 104. Hurricane forecast improvement program.
Sec. 105. Weather research and development planning.
Sec. 106. Observing system planning.
Sec. 107. Observing system simulation experiments.
Sec. 108. Annual report on computing resources prioritization.
Sec. 109. United States Weather Research program.
Sec. 110. Authorization of appropriations.

TITLE II—SUBSEASONAL AND SEASONAL FORECASTING INNOVATION

Sec. 201. Improving subseasonal and seasonal forecasts.

TITLE III—WEATHER SATELLITE AND DATA INNOVATION

Sec. 301. National Oceanic and Atmospheric Administration satellite and data management.
Sec. 302. Commercial weather data.
Sec. 303. Unnecessary duplication.

TITLE IV—FEDERAL WEATHER COORDINATION

Sec. 401. Environmental Information Services Working Group.
Sec. 402. Interagency weather research and forecast innovation coordination.
Sec. 403. Office of Oceanic and Atmospheric Research and National Weather Service exchange program.
Sec. 404. Visiting fellows at National Weather Service.
Sec. 405. Warning coordination meteorologists at weather forecast offices of National Weather Service.
Sec. 406. Improving National Oceanic and Atmospheric Administration communication of hazardous weather and water events.
Sec. 407. National Oceanic and Atmospheric Administration Weather Ready All Hazards Award Program.
Sec. 408. Department of Defense weather forecasting activities.
Sec. 409. National Weather Service; operations and workforce analysis.
Sec. 410. Water resources.
Sec. 411. Report on contract positions at National Weather Service.
Sec. 412. Weather impacts to communities and infrastructure.
Sec. 413. Weather enterprise outreach.

SEC. 2. DEFINITIONS.

In this Act:

(1) SEASONAL.—The term "seasonal" means the time range between 3 months and 2 years.

(2) STATE.—The term "State" means a State, a territory, or possession of the United States, including a Commonwealth, or the District of Columbia.

(3) SUBSEASONAL.—The term "subseasonal" means the time range between 2 weeks and 3 months.

(4) UNDER SECRETARY.—The term "Under Secretary" means the Under Secretary of Commerce for Oceans and Atmosphere.

(5) WEATHER INDUSTRY AND WEATHER ENTERPRISE.—The terms "weather industry" and "weather enterprise" are interchangeable in this Act, and include individuals and organizations from public, private, and academic sectors that contribute to the research, development, and production of weather forecast products, and primary consumers of these weather forecast products.

TITLE I—UNITED STATES WEATHER RESEARCH AND FORECASTING IMPROVEMENT

SEC. 101. PUBLIC SAFETY PRIORITY.

In conducting research, the Under Secretary shall prioritize improving weather data, modeling, computing, forecasting, and warnings for the protection of life and property and for the enhancement of the national economy.

SEC. 102. WEATHER RESEARCH AND FORECASTING INNOVATION.

(a) PROGRAM.—The Assistant Administrator for the Office of Oceanic and Atmospheric Research shall conduct a program to develop improved understanding of and forecast capabilities for atmospheric events and their impacts, placing priority on developing more accurate, timely, and effective warnings and forecasts of high impact weather events that endanger life and property.

(b) PROGRAM ELEMENTS.—The program described in subsection (a) shall focus on the following activities:

(1) Improving the fundamental understanding of weather consistent with section 101, including the boundary layer and other processes affecting high impact weather events.

(2) Improving the understanding of how the public receives, interprets, and responds to warnings and forecasts of high impact weather events that endanger life and property.

(3) Research and development, and transfer of knowledge, technologies, and applications to the National Weather Service and other appropriate agencies and entities, including the United States weather industry and academic partners, related to—

(A) advanced radar, radar networking technologies, and other ground-based technologies, including those emphasizing rapid, fine-scale sensing of the boundary layer and lower troposphere, and the use of innovative, dual-polarization, phased-array technologies;

(B) aerial weather observing systems;

(C) high performance computing and information technology and wireless communication networks;

(D) advanced numerical weather prediction systems and forecasting tools and techniques that improve the forecasting of timing, track, intensity, and severity of high impact weather, including through—

(i) the development of more effective mesoscale models;

(ii) more effective use of existing, and the development of new, regional and national cloud-resolving models;

(iii) enhanced global weather models; and

(iv) integrated assessment models;

(E) quantitative assessment tools for measuring the impact and value of data and observing systems, including Observing System Simulation Experiments (as described in section 107), Observing System Experiments, and Analyses of Alternatives;

(F) atmospheric chemistry and interactions essential to accurately characterizing atmospheric composition and predicting meteorological processes, including cloud microphysical, precipitation, and atmospheric electrification processes, to more effectively understand their role in severe weather; and

(G) additional sources of weather data and information, including commercial observing systems.

(4) A technology transfer initiative, carried out jointly and in coordination with the Director of the National Weather Service, and in cooperation with the United States weather industry and academic partners, to ensure continuous development and transition of the latest scientific and technological advances into operations of the National Weather Service and to establish a process to sunset outdated and expensive operational methods and tools to enable cost-effective transfer of new methods and tools into operations.

(c) EXTRAMURAL RESEARCH.—

(1) IN GENERAL.—In carrying out the program under this section, the Assistant Administrator for Oceanic and Atmospheric Research shall collaborate with and support the non-Federal weather research community, which includes institutions of higher education, private entities, and nongovernmental organizations, by making funds available through competitive grants, contracts, and cooperative agreements.

(2) SENSE OF CONGRESS.—It is the sense of Congress that not less than 30 percent of the funds for weather research and development at the Office of Oceanic and Atmospheric Research should be made available for the purpose described in paragraph (1).

(d) ANNUAL REPORT.—Each year, concurrent with the annual budget request submitted by the President to Congress under section 1105 of title 31, United States Code, for the National Oceanic and Atmospheric Administration, the Under Secretary shall submit to Congress a description of current and planned activities under this section.

SEC. 103. TORNADO WARNING IMPROVEMENT AND EXTENSION PROGRAM.

(a) IN GENERAL.—The Under Secretary, in collaboration with the United States weather industry and academic partners, shall establish a tornado warning improvement and extension program.

(b) GOAL.—The goal of such program shall be to reduce the loss of life and economic losses from tornadoes through the development and extension of accurate, effective, and timely tornado forecasts, predictions, and warnings, including the prediction of tornadoes beyond one hour in advance.

(c) PROGRAM PLAN.—Not later than 180 days after the date of the enactment of this Act, the Assistant Administrator for Oceanic and Atmospheric Research, in coordination with the Director of the National Weather Service, shall develop a program plan that details the specific research, development, and technology transfer activities, as well as corresponding resources and timelines, necessary to achieve the program goal.

(d) ANNUAL BUDGET FOR PLAN SUBMITTAL.—Following completion of the plan, the Under Secretary, acting through the Assistant Administrator for Oceanic and Atmospheric Research and in coordination with the Director of the National Weather Service, shall, not less frequently than once each year, submit to Congress a proposed budget corresponding with the activities identified in the plan.

SEC. 104. HURRICANE FORECAST IMPROVEMENT PROGRAM.

(a) IN GENERAL.—The Under Secretary, in collaboration with the United States weather industry and such academic entities as the Administrator considers appropriate, shall maintain a project to improve hurricane forecasting.

(b) GOAL.—The goal of the project maintained under subsection (a) shall be to develop and extend accurate hurricane forecasts and warnings in order to reduce loss of life, injury, and damage to the economy, with a focus on—

(1) improving the prediction of rapid intensification and track of hurricanes;

(2) improving the forecast and communication of storm surges from hurricanes; and

(3) incorporating risk communication research to create more effective watch and warning products.

(c) PROJECT PLAN.—Not later than 1 year after the date of the enactment of this Act, the Under Secretary, acting through the Assistant Administrator for Oceanic and Atmospheric Research and in consultation with the Director of the National Weather Service, shall develop a plan for the project maintained under subsection (a) that details the specific research, development, and technology transfer activities, as well as corresponding resources and timelines, necessary to achieve the goal set forth in subsection (b).

SEC. 105. WEATHER RESEARCH AND DEVELOPMENT PLANNING.

Not later than 1 year after the date of the enactment of this Act, and not less frequently than once each year thereafter, the Under Secretary, acting through the Assistant Administrator for Oceanic and Atmospheric Research and in coordination with the Director of the National Weather Service and the Assistant Administrator for Satellite and Information Services, shall issue a research and development and research to operations plan to restore and maintain United States leadership in numerical weather prediction and forecasting that—

(1) describes the forecasting skill and technology goals, objectives, and progress of the National Oceanic and Atmospheric Administration in carrying out the program conducted under section 102;

(2) identifies and prioritizes specific research and development activities, and performance metrics, weighted to meet the operational weather mission of the National Weather Service to achieve a weather-ready Nation;

(3) describes how the program will collaborate with stakeholders, including the United States weather industry and academic partners; and

(4) identifies, through consultation with the National Science Foundation, the United States weather industry, and academic partners, research necessary to enhance the integration of social science knowledge into weather forecast and warning processes, including to improve the communication of threat information necessary to enable improved severe weather planning and decision-making on the part of individuals and communities.

SEC. 106. OBSERVING SYSTEM PLANNING.

The Under Secretary shall—

(1) develop and maintain a prioritized list of observation data requirements necessary to ensure weather forecasting capabilities to protect life and property to the maximum extent practicable;

(2) consistent with section 107, utilize Observing System Simulation Experiments, Observing System Experiments, Analyses of Alternatives, and other appropriate assessment tools to ensure continuous systemic evaluations of the observing systems, data, and information needed to meet the requirements of paragraph (1), including options to maximize observational capabilities and their cost-effectiveness;

(3) identify current and potential future data gaps in observing capabilities related to the requirements listed under paragraph (1); and

(4) determine a range of options to address gaps identified under paragraph (3).

SEC. 107. OBSERVING SYSTEM SIMULATION EXPERIMENTS.

(a) IN GENERAL.—In support of the requirements of section 106, the Assistant Administrator for Oceanic and Atmospheric Research shall undertake Observing System Simulation Experiments, or such other quantitative assessments as the Assistant Administrator considers appropriate, to quantitatively assess the relative value and benefits of observing capabilities and systems. Technical and scientific Observing System Simulation Experiment evaluations—

(1) may include assessments of the impact of observing capabilities on—

(A) global weather prediction;

(B) hurricane track and intensity forecasting;

(C) tornado warning lead times and accuracy;

(D) prediction of mid-latitude severe local storm outbreaks; and

(E) prediction of storms that have the potential to cause extreme precipitation and flooding lasting from 6 hours to 1 week; and

(2) shall be conducted in cooperation with other appropriate entities within the National Oceanic and Atmospheric Administration, other Federal agencies, the United States weather industry, and academic partners to ensure the technical and scientific merit of results from Observing System Simulation Experiments or other appropriate quantitative assessment methodologies.

(b) REQUIREMENTS.—Observing System Simulation Experiments shall quantitatively—

(1) determine the potential impact of proposed space-based, suborbital, and in situ observing systems on analyses and forecasts, including potential impacts on extreme weather events across all parts of the Nation;

(2) evaluate and compare observing system design options; and

(3) assess the relative capabilities and costs of various observing systems and combinations of observing systems in providing data necessary to protect life and property.

(c) IMPLEMENTATION.—Observing System Simulation Experiments—

(1) shall be conducted prior to the acquisition of major Government-owned or Government-leased operational observing systems, including polar-orbiting and geostationary satellite systems, with a lifecycle cost of more than $500,000,000; and

(2) shall be conducted prior to the purchase of any major new commercially provided data with a lifecycle cost of more than $500,000,000.

(d) PRIORITY OBSERVING SYSTEM SIMULATION EXPERIMENTS.—

(1) GLOBAL NAVIGATION SATELLITE SYSTEM RADIO OCCULTATION.—Not later than 30 days after the date of the enactment of this Act, the Assistant Administrator for Oceanic and Atmospheric Research shall complete an Observing System Simulation Experiment to assess the value of data from Global Navigation Satellite System Radio Occultation.

(2) GEOSTATIONARY HYPERSPECTRAL SOUNDER GLOBAL CONSTELLATION.—Not later than 120 days after the date of the enactment of

this Act, the Assistant Administrator for Oceanic and Atmospheric Research shall complete an Observing System Simulation Experiment to assess the value of data from a geostationary hyperspectral sounder global constellation.

(e) RESULTS.—Upon completion of all Observing System Simulation Experiments, the Assistant Administrator shall make available to the public the results an assessment of related private and public sector weather data sourcing options, including their availability, affordability, and cost-effectiveness. Such assessments shall be developed in accordance with section 50503 of title 51, United States Code.

SEC. 108. ANNUAL REPORT ON COMPUTING RESOURCES PRIORITIZATION.

Not later than 1 year after the date of the enactment of this Act and not less frequently than once each year thereafter, the Under Secretary, acting through the Chief Information Officer of the National Oceanic and Atmospheric Administration and in coordination with the Assistant Administrator for Oceanic and Atmospheric Research and the Director of the National Weather Service, shall produce and make publicly available a report that explains how the Under Secretary intends—

(1) to continually support upgrades to pursue the fastest, most powerful, and cost-effective high performance computing technologies in support of its weather prediction mission;

(2) to ensure a balance between the research to operations requirements to develop the next generation of regional and global models as well as highly reliable operational models;

(3) to take advantage of advanced development concepts to, as appropriate, make next generation weather prediction models available in beta-test mode to operational forecasters, the United States weather industry, and partners in academic and Government research; and

(4) to use existing computing resources to improve advanced research and operational weather prediction.

SEC. 109. UNITED STATES WEATHER RESEARCH PROGRAM.

Section 108 of the Oceanic and Atmospheric Administration Authorization Act of 1992 (Public Law 102–567; 15 U.S.C. 313 note) is amended—

(1) in subsection (a)—

(A) in paragraph (3), by striking "; and" and inserting a semicolon;

(B) in paragraph (4), by striking the period at the end and inserting a semicolon; and

(C) by inserting after paragraph (4) the following:

"(5) submit to the Committee on Commerce, Science, and Transportation of the Senate and the Committee on Science, Space, and Technology of the House of Representatives, not less frequently than once each year, a report, including—

"(A) a list of ongoing research projects;

"(B) project goals and a point of contact for each project;

"(C) the 5 projects related to weather observations, short-term weather, or subseasonal forecasts within Office of Oceanic and Atmospheric Research that are closest to operationalization,

"(D) for each project referred to in subparagraph (C)—

"(i) the potential benefit;

"(ii) any barrier to operationalization; and

"(iii) the plan for operationalization, including which line office will financially support the project and how much the line office intends to spend;

"(6) establish teams with staff from the Office of Oceanic and Atmospheric Research and the National Weather Service to oversee the operationalization of research products developed by the Office of Oceanic and Atmospheric Research;

"(7) develop mechanisms for research priorities of the Office of Oceanic and Atmospheric Research to be informed by the relevant line offices within the National Oceanic and Atmospheric Administration, the relevant user community, and the weather enterprise;

"(8) develop an internal mechanism to track the progress of each research project within the Office of Oceanic and Atmospheric Research and mechanisms to terminate a project that is not adequately progressing;

"(9) develop and implement a system to track whether extramural research grant goals were accomplished;

"(10) provide facilities for products developed by the Office of Oceanic and Atmospheric Research to be tested in operational simulations, such as test beds; and

"(11) encourage academic collaboration with the Office of Oceanic and Atmospheric Research and the National Weather Service by facilitating visiting scholars.";

(2) in subsection (b), in the matter preceding paragraph (1), by striking "Not later than 90 days after the date of enactment of this Act, the" and inserting "The"; and

(3) by adding at the end the following new subsection:

"(c) SUBSEASONAL DEFINED.—In this section, the term 'subseasonal' means the time range between 2 weeks and 3 months.".

SEC. 110. AUTHORIZATION OF APPROPRIATIONS.

(a) FISCAL YEARS 2016 THROUGH 2018.—For each of fiscal years 2016 through 2018, there are authorized to be appropriated to Office of Oceanic and Atmospheric Research—

(1) $111,516,000 to carry out this title, of which—

(A) $85,758,000 is authorized for weather laboratories and cooperative institutes; and

(B) $25,758,000 is authorized for weather and air chemistry research programs; and

(2) an additional amount of $20,000,000 for the joint technology transfer initiative described in section 102(b)(4).

(b) LIMITATION.—No additional funds are authorized to carry out this title and the amendments made by this title.

TITLE II—SUBSEASONAL AND SEASONAL FORECASTING INNOVATION

SEC. 201. IMPROVING SUBSEASONAL AND SEASONAL FORECASTS.

Section 1762 of the Food Security Act of 1985 (Public Law 99–198; 15 U.S.C. 313 note) is amended—

(1) in subsection (a), by striking "(a)" and inserting "(a) FINDINGS.—";

(2) in subsection (b), by striking "(b)" and inserting "(b) POLICY.—"; and

(3) by adding at the end the following:

"(c) FUNCTIONS.—The Under Secretary, acting through the Director of the National Weather Service and the heads of such other programs of the National Oceanic and Atmospheric Administration as the Under Secretary considers appropriate, shall—

"(1) collect and utilize information in order to make usable, reliable, and timely foundational forecasts of subseasonal and seasonal temperature and precipitation;

"(2) leverage existing research and models from the weather enterprise to improve the forecasts under paragraph (1);

"(3) determine and provide information on how the forecasted conditions under paragraph (1) may impact—

"(A) the number and severity of droughts, fires, tornadoes, hurricanes, floods, heat waves, coastal inundation, winter storms, high impact weather, or other relevant natural disasters;

"(B) snowpack; and

"(C) sea ice conditions; and

"(4) develop an Internet clearinghouse to provide the forecasts under paragraph (1) and the information under paragraphs (1) and (3) on both national and regional levels.

"(d) COMMUNICATION.—The Director of the National Weather Service shall provide the forecasts under paragraph (1) of subsection (c) and the information on their impacts under paragraph (3) of such subsection to the public, including public and private entities engaged in planning and preparedness, such as National Weather Service Core partners at the Federal, regional, State, tribal, and local levels of government.

"(e) COOPERATION.—The Under Secretary shall build upon existing forecasting and assessment programs and partnerships, including—

"(1) by designating research and monitoring activities related to subseasonal and seasonal forecasts as a priority in 1 or more solicitations of the Cooperative Institutes of the Office of Oceanic and Atmospheric Research;

"(2) by contributing to the interagency Earth System Prediction Capability; and

"(3) by consulting with the Secretary of Defense and the Secretary of Homeland Security to determine the highest priority subseasonal and seasonal forecast needs to enhance national security.

"(f) FORECAST COMMUNICATION COORDINATORS.—

"(1) IN GENERAL.—The Under Secretary shall foster effective communication, understanding, and use of the forecasts by the intended users of the information described in subsection (d). This may include assistance to States for forecast communication coordinators to enable local interpretation and planning based on the information.

"(2) REQUIREMENTS.—For each State that requests assistance under this subsection, the Under Secretary may—

"(A) provide funds to support an individual in that State—

"(i) to serve as a liaison among the National Oceanic and Atmospheric Administration, other Federal departments and agencies, the weather enterprise, the State, and relevant interests within that State; and

"(ii) to receive the forecasts and information under subsection (c) and disseminate the forecasts and information throughout the State, including to county and tribal governments; and

"(B) require matching funds of at least 50 percent, from the State, a university, a nongovernmental organization, a trade association, or the private sector.

"(3) LIMITATION.—Assistance to an individual State under this subsection shall not exceed $100,000 in a fiscal year.

"(g) COOPERATION FROM OTHER FEDERAL AGENCIES.—Each Federal department and agency shall cooperate as appropriate with the Under Secretary in carrying out this section.

"(h) REPORTS.—

"(1) IN GENERAL.—Not later than 18 months after the date of the enactment of the Weather Research and Forecasting Innovation Act of 2016, the Under Secretary shall submit to the Committee on Commerce, Science, and Transportation of the Senate and the Committee on Science, Space, and Technology of the House of Representatives a report, including—

"(A) an analysis of the how information from the National Oceanic and Atmospheric Administration on subseasonal and seasonal forecasts, as provided under subsection (c), is utilized in public planning and preparedness;

"(B) specific plans and goals for the continued development of the subseasonal and seasonal forecasts and related products described in subsection (c); and

"(C) an identification of research, monitoring, observing, and forecasting requirements to meet the goals described in subparagraph (B).

"(2) CONSULTATION.—In developing the report under paragraph (1), the Under Secretary shall consult with relevant Federal, regional, State, tribal, and local government agencies, research institutions, and the private sector.

"(i) DEFINITIONS.—In this section:

"(1) FOUNDATIONAL FORECAST.—The term 'foundational forecast' means basic weather observation and forecast data, largely in raw form, before further processing is applied.

"(2) NATIONAL WEATHER SERVICE CORE PARTNERS.—The term 'National Weather Service core partners' means government and non-government entities which are directly involved in the preparation or dissemination of, or discussions involving, hazardous weather or other emergency information put out by the National Weather Service.

"(3) SEASONAL.—The term 'seasonal' means the time range between 3 months and 2 years.

"(4) STATE.—The term 'State' means a State, a territory, or possession of the United States, including a Commonwealth, or the District of Columbia.

"(5) SUBSEASONAL.—The term 'subseasonal' means the time range between 2 weeks and 3 months.

"(6) UNDER SECRETARY.—The term 'Under Secretary' means the Under Secretary of Commerce for Oceans and Atmosphere.

"(7) WEATHER INDUSTRY AND WEATHER ENTERPRISE.—The terms 'weather industry' and 'weather enterprise' are interchangeable in this section and include individuals and organizations from public, private, and academic sectors that contribute to the research, development, and production of weather forecast products, and primary consumers of these weather forecast products.

"(j) AUTHORIZATION OF APPROPRIATIONS.— For each of fiscal years 2016 through 2018, there are authorized out of funds appropriated to the National Weather Service, $26,500,000 to carry out the activities of this section.".

TITLE III—WEATHER SATELLITE AND DATA INNOVATION

SEC. 301. NATIONAL OCEANIC AND ATMOSPHERIC ADMINISTRATION SATELLITE AND DATA MANAGEMENT.

(a) SHORT-TERM MANAGEMENT OF ENVIRONMENTAL OBSERVATIONS.—

(1) MICROSATELLITE CONSTELLATIONS.—

(A) IN GENERAL.—The Under Secretary shall complete and operationalize the Constellation Observing System for Meteorology, Ionosphere, and Climate-1 and Climate-2 (COSMIC) in effect on the day before the date of the enactment of this Act—

(i) by deploying constellations of microsatellites in both the equatorial and polar orbits;

(ii) by integrating the resulting data and research into all national operational and research weather forecast models; and

(iii) by ensuring that the resulting data of National Oceanic and Atmospheric Administration's COSMIC-1 and COSMIC-2 programs are free and open to all communities.

(B) ANNUAL REPORTS.—Not less frequently than once each year until the Under Secretary has completed and operationalized the program described in subparagraph (A) pursuant to such subparagraph, the Under Secretary shall submit to Congress a report on the status of the efforts of the Under Secretary to carry out such subparagraph.

(2) INTEGRATION OF OCEAN AND COASTAL DATA FROM THE INTEGRATED OCEAN OBSERVING SYSTEM.—In National Weather Service Regions where the Director of the National Weather Service determines that ocean and coastal data would improve forecasts, the Director, in consultation with the Assistant Administrator for Oceanic and Atmospheric Research and the Assistant Administrator of the National Ocean Service, shall—

(A) integrate additional coastal and ocean observations, and other data and research, from the Integrated Ocean Observing System (IOOS) into regional weather forecasts to improve weather forecasts and forecasting decision support systems; and

(B) support the development of real-time data sharing products and forecast products in collaboration with the regional associations of such system, including contributions from the private sector, academia, and research institutions to ensure timely and accurate use of ocean and coastal data in regional forecasts.

(3) EXISTING MONITORING AND OBSERVATION-CAPABILITY.—The Under Secretary shall identify degradation of existing monitoring and observation capabilities that could lead to a reduction in forecast quality.

(4) SPECIFICATIONS FOR NEW SATELLITE SYSTEMS OR DATA DETERMINED BY OPERATIONAL NEEDS.—In developing specifications for any satellite systems or data to follow the Joint Polar Satellite System, Geostationary Operational Environmental Satellites, and any other satellites, in effect on the day before the date of enactment of this Act, the Under Secretary shall ensure the specifications are determined to the extent practicable by the recommendations of the reports under subsection (b) of this section.

(b) INDEPENDENT STUDY ON FUTURE OF NATIONAL OCEANIC AND ATMOSPHERIC ADMINISTRATION SATELLITE SYSTEMS AND DATA.—

(1) AGREEMENT.—

(A) IN GENERAL.—The Under Secretary shall seek to enter into an agreement with the National Academy of Sciences to perform the services covered by this subsection.

(B) TIMING.—The Under Secretary shall seek to enter into the agreement described in subparagraph (A) before September 30, 2018.

(2) STUDY.—

(A) IN GENERAL.—Under an agreement between the Under Secretary and the National Academy of Sciences under this subsection, the National Academy of Sciences shall conduct a study on matters concerning future satellite data needs.

(B) ELEMENTS.—In conducting the study under subparagraph (A), the National Academy of Sciences shall—

(i) develop recommendations on how to make the data portfolio of the Administration more robust and cost-effective;

(ii) assess the costs and benefits of moving toward a constellation of many small satellites, standardizing satellite bus design, relying more on the purchasing of data, or acquiring data from other sources or methods;

(iii) identify the environmental observations that are essential to the performance of weather models, based on an assessment of Federal, academic, and private sector weather research, and the cost of obtaining the environmental data;

(iv) identify environmental observations that improve the quality of operational and research weather models in effect on the day before the date of enactment of this Act;

(v) identify and prioritize new environmental observations that could contribute to existing and future weather models; and

(vi) develop recommendations on a portfolio of environmental observations that balances essential, quality-improving, and new data, private and nonprivate sources, and space-based and Earth-based sources.

(C) DEADLINE AND REPORT.—In carrying out the study under subparagraph (A), the National Academy of Sciences shall complete and transmit to the Under Secretary a report containing the findings of the National Academy of Sciences with respect to the study not later than 2 years after the date on which the Administrator enters into an agreement with the National Academy of Sciences under paragraph (1)(A).

(3) ALTERNATE ORGANIZATION.—

(A) IN GENERAL.—If the Under Secretary is unable within the period prescribed in subparagraph (B) of paragraph (1) to enter into an agreement described in subparagraph (A) of such paragraph with the National Academy of Sciences on terms acceptable to the Under Secretary, the Under Secretary shall seek to enter into such an agreement with another appropriate organization that—

(i) is not part of the Federal Government;

(ii) operates as a not-for-profit entity; and

(iii) has expertise and objectivity comparable to that of the National Academy of Sciences.

(B) TREATMENT.—If the Under Secretary enters into an agreement with another organization as described in subparagraph (A), any reference in this subsection to the National Academy of Sciences shall be treated as a reference to the other organization.

(4) AUTHORIZATION OF APPROPRIATIONS.— There are authorized to be appropriated, out of funds appropriated to National Environmental Satellite, Data, and Information Service, to carry out this subsection $1,000,000 for the period encompassing fiscal years 2018 through 2019.

SEC. 302. COMMERCIAL WEATHER DATA.

(a) DATA AND HOSTED SATELLITE PAYLOADS.—Notwithstanding any other provision of law, the Secretary of Commerce may enter into agreements for—

(1) the purchase of weather data through contracts with commercial providers; and

(2) the placement of weather satellite instruments on cohosted government or private payloads.

(b) STRATEGY.—

(1) IN GENERAL.—Not later than 180 days after the date of the enactment of this Act, the Secretary of Commerce, in consultation with the Under Secretary, shall submit to the Committee on Commerce, Science, and Transportation of the Senate and the Committee on Science, Space, and Technology of the House of Representatives a strategy to enable the procurement of quality commercial weather data. The strategy shall assess the range of commercial opportunities, including public-private partnerships, for obtaining surface-based, aviation-based, and space-based weather observations. The strategy shall include the expected cost-effectiveness of these opportunities as well as provide a plan for procuring data, including an expected implementation timeline, from these nongovernmental sources, as appropriate.

(2) REQUIREMENTS.—The strategy shall include—

(A) an analysis of financial or other benefits to, and risks associated with, acquiring commercial weather data or services, including through multiyear acquisition approaches;

(B) an identification of methods to address planning, programming, budgeting, and execution challenges to such approaches, including—

(i) how standards will be set to ensure that data is reliable and effective;

(ii) how data may be acquired through commercial experimental or innovative techniques and then evaluated for integration into operational use;

(iii) how to guarantee public access to all forecast-critical data to ensure that the United States weather industry and the public continue to have access to information critical to their work; and

(iv) in accordance with section 50503 of title 51, United States Code, methods to address potential termination liability or cancellation costs associated with weather data or service contracts; and

(C) an identification of any changes needed in the requirements development and approval processes of the Department of Commerce to facilitate effective and efficient implementation of such strategy.

(3) AUTHORITY FOR AGREEMENTS.—The Assistant Administrator for National Environmental Satellite, Data, and Information Service may enter into multiyear agreements necessary to carry out the strategy developed under this subsection.

(c) PILOT PROGRAM.—

(1) CRITERIA.—Not later than 30 days after the date of the enactment of this Act, the Under Secretary shall publish data and metadata standards and specifications for space-based commercial weather data, including radio occultation data, and, as soon as possible, geostationary hyperspectral sounder data.

(2) PILOT CONTRACTS.—

(A) CONTRACTS.—Not later than 90 days after the date of enactment of this Act, the Under Secretary shall, through an open competition, enter into at least one pilot contract with one or more private sector entities capable of providing data that meet the standards and specifications set by the Under Secretary for providing commercial weather data in a manner that allows the Under Secretary to calibrate and evaluate the data for its use in National Oceanic and Atmospheric Administration meteorological models.

(B) ASSESSMENT OF DATA VIABILITY.—Not later than the date that is 3 years after the date on which the Under Secretary enters into a contract under subparagraph (A), the Under Secretary shall assess and submit to the Committee on Commerce, Science, and Transportation of the Senate and the Committee on Science, Space, and Technology of the House of Representatives the results of a determination of the extent to which data provided under the contract entered into under subparagraph (A) meet the criteria published under paragraph (1) and the extent to which the pilot program has demonstrated—

(i) the viability of assimilating the commercially provided data into National Oceanic and Atmospheric Administration meteorological models;

(ii) whether, and by how much, the data add value to weather forecasts; and

(iii) the accuracy, quality, timeliness, validity, reliability, usability, information technology security, and cost-effectiveness of obtaining commercial weather data from private sector providers.

(3) AUTHORIZATION OF APPROPRIATIONS.—For each of fiscal years 2017 through 2020,

there are authorized to be appropriated for procurement, acquisition, and construction at National Environmental Satellite, Data, and Information Service, $6,000,000 to carry out this subsection.

(d) OBTAINING FUTURE DATA.—If an assessment under subsection (c)(2)(B) demonstrates the ability of commercial weather data to meet data and metadata standards and specifications published under subsection (c)(1), the Under Secretary shall—

(1) where appropriate, cost-effective, and feasible, obtain commercial weather data from private sector providers;

(2) as early as possible in the acquisition process for any future National Oceanic and Atmospheric Administration meteorological space system, consider whether there is a suitable, cost-effective, commercial capability available or that will be available to meet any or all of the observational requirements by the planned operational date of the system;

(3) if a suitable, cost-effective, commercial capability is or will be available as described in paragraph (2), determine whether it is in the national interest to develop a governmental meteorological space system; and

(4) submit to the Committee on Commerce, Science, and Transportation of the Senate and the Committee on Science, Space, and Technology of the House of Representatives a report detailing any determination made under paragraphs (2) and (3).

(e) DATA SHARING PRACTICES.—The Under Secretary shall continue to meet the international meteorological agreements into which the Under Secretary has entered, including practices set forth through World Meteorological Organization Resolution 40.

SEC. 303. UNNECESSARY DUPLICATION.

In meeting the requirements under this title, the Under Secretary shall avoid unnecessary duplication between public and private sources of data and the corresponding expenditure of funds and employment of personnel.

TITLE IV—FEDERAL WEATHER COORDINATION

SEC. 401. ENVIRONMENTAL INFORMATION SERVICES WORKING GROUP.

(a) ESTABLISHMENT.—The National Oceanic and Atmospheric Administration Science Advisory Board shall continue to maintain a standing working group named the Environmental Information Services Working Group (in this section referred to as the "Working Group")—

(1) to provide advice for prioritizing weather research initiatives at the National Oceanic and Atmospheric Administration to produce real improvement in weather forecasting;

(2) to provide advice on existing or emerging technologies or techniques that can be found in private industry or the research community that could be incorporated into forecasting at the National Weather Service to improve forecasting skill;

(3) to identify opportunities to improve—

(A) communications between weather forecasters, Federal, State, local, tribal, and other emergency management personnel, and the public; and

(B) communications and partnerships among the National Oceanic and Atmospheric Administration and the private and academic sectors; and

(4) to address such other matters as the Science Advisory Board requests of the Working Group.

(b) COMPOSITION.—

(1) IN GENERAL.—The Working Group shall be composed of leading experts and

innovators from all relevant fields of science and engineering including atmospheric chemistry, atmospheric physics, meteorology, hydrology, social science, risk communications, electrical engineering, and computer sciences. In carrying out this section, the Working Group may organize into subpanels.

(2) NUMBER.—The Working Group shall be composed of no fewer than 15 members. Nominees for the Working Group may be forwarded by the Working Group for approval by the Science Advisory Board. Members of the Working Group may choose a chair (or co-chairs) from among their number with approval by the Science Advisory Board.

(c) ANNUAL REPORT.—Not less frequently than once each year, the Working Group shall transmit to the Science Advisory Board for submission to the Under Secretary a report on progress made by National Oceanic and Atmospheric Administration in adopting the Working Group's recommendations. The Science Advisory Board shall transmit this report to the Under Secretary. Within 30 days of receipt of such report, the Under Secretary shall submit to the Committee on Commerce, Science, and Transportation of the Senate and the Committee on Science, Space, and Technology of the House of Representatives a copy of such report.

SEC. 402. INTERAGENCY WEATHER RESEARCH AND FORECAST INNOVATION COORDINATION.

(a) ESTABLISHMENT.—The Director of the Office of Science and Technology Policy shall establish an Interagency Committee for Advancing Weather Services to improve coordination of relevant weather research and forecast innovation activities across the Federal Government. The Interagency Committee shall—

(1) include participation by the National Aeronautics and Space Administration, the Federal Aviation Administration, National Oceanic and Atmospheric Administration and its constituent elements, the National Science Foundation, and such other agencies involved in weather forecasting research as the President determines are appropriate;

(2) identify and prioritize top forecast needs and coordinate those needs against budget requests and program initiatives across participating offices and agencies; and

(3) share information regarding operational needs and forecasting improvements across relevant agencies.

(b) CO-CHAIR.—The Federal Coordinator for Meteorology shall serve as a co-chair of this panel.

(c) FURTHER COORDINATION.—The Director of the Office of Science and Technology Policy shall take such other steps as are necessary to coordinate the activities of the Federal Government with those of the United States weather industry, State governments, emergency managers, and academic researchers.

SEC. 403. OFFICE OF OCEANIC AND ATMOSPHERIC RESEARCH AND NATIONAL WEATHER SERVICE EXCHANGE PROGRAM.

(a) IN GENERAL.—The Assistant Administrator for Oceanic and Atmospheric Research and the Director of National Weather Service may establish a program to detail Office of Oceanic and Atmospheric Research personnel to the National Weather Service and National Weather Service personnel to the Office of Oceanic and Atmospheric Research.

(b) GOAL.—The goal of this program is to enhance forecasting innovation through regular, direct interaction between the Office of Oceanic and Atmospheric Research's world-class scientists and the National Weather Service's operational staff.

(c) ELEMENTS.—The program shall allow up to 10 Office of Oceanic and Atmospheric Research staff and National Weather Service staff to spend up to 1 year on detail. Candidates shall be jointly selected by the Assistant Administrator for Oceanic and Atmospheric Research and the Director of the National Weather Service.

(d) ANNUAL REPORT.—Not less frequently than once each year, the Under Secretary shall submit to the Committee on Commerce, Science, and Transportation of the Senate and the Committee on Science, Space, and Technology of the House of Representatives a report on participation in such program and shall highlight any innovations that come from this interaction.

SEC. 404. VISITING FELLOWS AT NATIONAL WEATHER SERVICE.

(a) IN GENERAL.—The Director of the National Weather Service may establish a program to host postdoctoral fellows and academic researchers at any of the National Centers for Environmental Prediction.

(b) GOAL.—This program shall be designed to provide direct interaction between forecasters and talented academic and private sector researchers in an effort to bring innovation to forecasting tools and techniques to the National Weather Service.

(c) SELECTION AND APPOINTMENT.—Such fellows shall be competitively selected and appointed for a term not to exceed 1 year.

SEC. 405. WARNING COORDINATION METEOROLOGISTS AT WEATHER FORECAST OFFICES OF NATIONAL WEATHER SERVICE.

(a) DESIGNATION OF WARNING COORDINATION METEOROLOGISTS.—

(1) IN GENERAL.—The Director of the National Weather Service shall designate at least 1 warning coordination meteorologist at each weather forecast office of the National Weather Service.

(2) NO ADDITIONAL EMPLOYEES AUTHORIZED.—Nothing in this section shall be construed to authorize or require a change in the authorized number of full time equivalent employees in the National Weather Service or otherwise result in the employment of any additional employees.

(3) PERFORMANCE BY OTHER EMPLOYEES.—Performance of the responsibilities outlined in this section is not limited to the warning coordination meteorologist position.

(b) PRIMARY ROLE OF WARNING COORDINATION METEOROLOGISTS.—The primary role of the warning coordination meteorologist shall be to carry out the responsibilities required by this section.

(c) RESPONSIBILITIES.—

(1) IN GENERAL.—Subject to paragraph (2), consistent with the analysis described in section 409, and in order to increase impact-based decision support services, each warning coordination meteorologist designated under subsection (a) shall—

(A) be responsible for providing service to the geographic area of responsibility covered by the weather forecast office at which the warning coordination meteorologist is employed to help ensure that users of products of the National Weather Service can respond effectively to improve outcomes from weather events;

(B) liaise with users of products and services of the National Weather Service, such as the public, media outlets, users in the aviation, marine, and agricultural communities, and forestry, land, and water management interests, to evaluate the adequacy and usefulness of the products and services of the National Weather Service;

(C) collaborate with such weather forecast offices and State, local, and tribal government agencies as the Director considers appropriate in developing, proposing, and implementing plans to develop, modify, or tailor products and services of the National Weather Service to improve the usefulness of such products and services;

(D) ensure the maintenance and accuracy of severe weather call lists, appropriate office severe weather policy or procedures, and other severe weather or dissemination methodologies or strategies; and

(E) work closely with State, local, and tribal emergency management agencies, and other agencies related to disaster management, to ensure a planned, coordinated, and effective preparedness and response effort.

(2) OTHER STAFF.—The Director may assign a responsibility set forth in paragraph (1) to such other staff as the Director considers appropriate to carry out such responsibility.

(d) ADDITIONAL RESPONSIBILITIES.—

(1) IN GENERAL.—Subject to paragraph (2), a warning coordination meteorologist designated under subsection (a) may—

(A) work with a State agency to develop plans for promoting more effective use of products and services of the National Weather Service throughout the State;

(B) identify priority community preparedness objectives;

(C) develop plans to meet the objectives identified under paragraph (2); and

(D) conduct severe weather event preparedness planning and citizen education efforts with and through various State, local, and tribal government agencies and other disaster management-related organizations.

(2) OTHER STAFF.—The Director may assign a responsibility set forth in paragraph (1) to such other staff as the Director considers appropriate to carry out such responsibility.

(e) PLACEMENT WITH STATE AND LOCAL EMERGENCY MANAGERS.—

(1) IN GENERAL.—In carrying out this section, the Director of the National Weather Service may place a warning coordination meteorologist designated under subsection (a) with a State or local emergency manager if the Director considers doing so is necessary or convenient to carry out this section.

(2) TREATMENT.—If the Director determines that the placement of a warning coordination meteorologist placed with a State or local emergency manager under paragraph (1) is near a weather forecast office of the National Weather Service, such placement shall be treated as designation of the warning coordination meteorologist at such weather forecast office for purposes of subsection (a).

SEC. 406. IMPROVING NATIONAL OCEANIC AND ATMOSPHERIC ADMINISTRATION COMMUNICATION OF HAZARDOUS WEATHER AND WATER EVENTS.

(a) PURPOSE OF SYSTEM.—For purposes of the assessment required by subsection (b)(1)(A), the purpose of National Oceanic and Atmospheric Administration system for issuing watches and warnings regarding hazardous weather and water events shall be risk communication to the general public that informs action to prevent loss of life and property.

(b) ASSESSMENT OF SYSTEM.—

(1) IN GENERAL.—Not later than 2 years after the date of the enactment of this Act, the Under Secretary shall—

(A) assess the National Oceanic and Atmospheric Administration system for issuing watches and warnings regarding hazardous weather and water events; and

(B) submit to Congress a report on the findings of the Under Secretary with respect to the assessment conducted under subparagraph (A).

(2) ELEMENTS.—The assessment required by paragraph (1)(A) shall include the following:

(A) An evaluation of whether the National Oceanic and Atmospheric Administration system for issuing watches and warnings regarding hazardous weather and water events meets the purpose described in subsection (a).

(B) Development of recommendations for—

(i) legislative and administrative action to improve the system described in paragraph (1)(A); and

(ii) such research as the Under Secretary considers necessary to address the focus areas described in paragraph (3).

(3) FOCUS AREAS.—The assessment required by paragraph (1)(A) shall focus on the following:

(A) Ways to communicate the risks posed by hazardous weather or water events to the public that are most likely to result in action to mitigate the risk.

(B) Ways to communicate the risks posed by hazardous weather or water events to the public as broadly and rapidly as practicable.

(C) Ways to preserve the benefits of the existing watches and warnings system.

(D) Ways to maintain the utility of the watches and warnings system for Government and commercial users of the system.

(4) CONSULTATION.—In conducting the assessment required by paragraph (1)(A), the Under Secretary shall—

(A) consult with such line offices within the National Oceanic and Atmospheric Administration as the Under Secretary considers relevant, including the the the National Ocean Service, the National Weather Service, and the Office of Oceanic and Atmospheric Research;

(B) consult with individuals in the academic sector, including individuals in the field of social and behavioral sciences, and other weather services;

(C) consult with media outlets that will be distributing the watches and warnings;

(D) consult with non-Federal forecasters that produce alternate severe weather risk communication products;

(E) consult with emergency planners and responders, including State and local emergency management agencies, and other government users of the watches and warnings system, including the Federal Emergency Management Agency, the Office of Personnel Management, the Coast Guard, and such other Federal agencies as the Under Secretary determines rely on watches and warnings for operational decisions; and

(F) make use of the services of the National Academy of Sciences, as the Under Secretary considers necessary and practicable, including contracting with the National Research Council to review the scientific and technical soundness of the assessment required by paragraph (1)(A), including the recommendations developed under paragraph (2)(B).

(5) METHODOLOGIES.—In conducting the assessment required by paragraph (1)(A), the Under Secretary shall use such methodologies as the Under Secretary considers are generally accepted by the weather enterprise, including social and behavioral sciences.

(c) IMPROVEMENTS TO SYSTEM.—

(1) IN GENERAL.—The Under Secretary shall, based on the assessment required by subsection (b)(1)(A), make such recommendations to Congress to improve the system as the Under Secretary considers necessary—

(A) to improve the system for issuing watches and warnings regarding hazardous weather and water events; and

(B) to support efforts to satisfy research needs to enable future improvements to such system.

(2) REQUIREMENTS REGARDING RECOMMENDATIONS.—In carrying out paragraph (1)(A), the Under Secretary shall ensure that any recommendation that the Under Secretary considers a major change—

(A) is validated by social and behavioral science using a generalizable sample;

(B) accounts for the needs of various demographics, vulnerable populations, and geographic regions;

(C) accounts for the differences between types of weather and water hazards;

(D) responds to the needs of Federal, State, and local government partners and media partners; and

(E) accounts for necessary changes to Federally-operated watch and warning propagation and dissemination infrastructure and protocols.

(d) WATCHES AND WARNINGS DEFINED.—

(1) IN GENERAL.—Except as provided in paragraph (2), in this section, the terms "watch" and "warning", with respect to a hazardous weather and water event, mean products issued by the Administration, intended for consumption by the general public, to alert the general public to the potential for or presence of the event and to inform action to prevent loss of life and property.

(2) EXCEPTION.—In this section, the terms "watch" and "warning" do not include technical or specialized meteorological and hydrological forecasts, outlooks, or model guidance products.

SEC. 407. NATIONAL OCEANIC AND ATMOSPHERIC ADMINISTRATION WEATHER READY ALL HAZARDS AWARD PROGRAM.

(a) PROGRAM.—The Director of the National Weather Service is authorized to establish the National Oceanic and Atmospheric Administration Weather Ready All Hazards Award Program. This award program shall provide annual awards to honor individuals or organizations that use or provide National Oceanic and Atmospheric Administration Weather Radio All Hazards receivers or transmitters to save lives and protect property. Individuals or organizations that utilize other early warning tools or applications also qualify for this award.

(b) GOAL.—This award program draws attention to the life-saving work of the National Oceanic and Atmospheric Administration Weather Ready All Hazards Program, as well as emerging tools and applications, that provide real-time warning to individuals and communities of severe weather or other hazardous conditions.

(c) PROGRAM ELEMENTS.—

(1) NOMINATIONS.—Nominations for this award shall be made annually by the Weather Field Offices to the Director of the National Weather Service. Broadcast meteorologists, weather radio manufacturers and weather warning tool and application developers, emergency managers, and public safety officials may nominate individuals or organizations to their local Weather Field Offices, but the final list of award nominees must come from the Weather Field Offices.

(2) SELECTION OF AWARDEES.—Annually, the Director of the National Weather Service shall choose winners of this award whose timely actions, based on National Oceanic and Atmospheric Administration Weather Radio All Hazards receivers or transmitters or other early warning tools and applica-

tions, saved lives or property, or demonstrated public service in support of weather or all hazard warnings.

(3) AWARD CEREMONY.—The Director of the National Weather Service shall establish a means of making these awards to provide maximum public awareness of the importance of National Oceanic and Atmospheric Administration Weather Radio, and such other warning tools and applications as are represented in the awards.

SEC. 408. DEPARTMENT OF DEFENSE WEATHER FORECASTING ACTIVITIES.

Not later than 60 days after the date of the enactment of this Act, the Under Secretary shall submit to the Committee on Commerce, Science, and Transportation of the Senate and the Committee on Science, Space, and Technology of the House of Representatives a report analyzing the impacts of the proposed Air Force divestiture in the United States Weather Research and Forecasting Model, including—

(1) the impact on—

(A) the United States weather forecasting capabilities;

(B) the accuracy of civilian regional forecasts;

(C) the civilian readiness for traditional weather and extreme weather events in the United States; and

(D) the research necessary to develop the United States Weather Research and Forecasting Model; and

(2) such other analysis relating to the divestiture as the Under Secretary considers appropriate.

SEC. 409. NATIONAL WEATHER SERVICE; OPERATIONS AND WORKFORCE ANALYSIS.

The Under Secretary shall contract or continue to partner with an external organization to conduct a baseline analysis of National Weather Service operations and workforce.

SEC. 410. WATER RESOURCES.

(a) NATIONAL WATER CENTER.—

(1) ESTABLISHMENT.—The Under Secretary shall maintain a National Water Center.

(2) FUNCTIONS.—The National Water Center may—

(A) facilitate collaboration across Federal and State departments and agencies, academia, and the private sector to improve understanding of water resources;

(B) make recommendations to water resource managers;

(C) make recommendations to improve water resource forecasts; and

(D) facilitate the transition of water research into applications.

(b) TOTAL WATER PREDICTION.—The Under Secretary, through the National Water Center, shall—

(1) initiate research and development activities to develop operational water resource prediction products;

(2) collaborate with, and provide decision support regarding total water prediction to, other relevant Federal and State agencies, including—

(A) the Army Corps of Engineers;

(B) the United States Geological Survey;

(C) the Federal Emergency Management Agency;

(D) the National Science Foundation;

(E) the Environmental Protection Agency;

(F) State water resource agencies; and

(G) State emergency management agencies; and

(3) in carrying out the responsibilities described in paragraphs (1) and (2), develop capabilities necessary for total water predictive capacity, including observations, modeling, data management, supercomputing, social science, and communications.

(c) REPORT.—

(1) IN GENERAL.—Not later than 3 years after the date of the enactment of this Act, the National Water Center shall submit to the Assistant Secretary of the Army for Civil Works a report on total water predictive capabilities and products.

(2) CONTENTS.—The report may include recommendations to improve engineering, design, operations, and management of civil works projects, including the Central and Southern Florida Project and any project in the Apalachicola-Chattahoochee-Flint River System, to optimize water management, including the implications of total water predictive products for—

(A) environmental protection and restoration, including restoration of water quality, water flows, fish, and other aquatic species;

(B) reduced flood risk; and

(C) improved recreation.

SEC. 411. REPORT ON CONTRACT POSITIONS AT NATIONAL WEATHER SERVICE.

(a) REPORT REQUIRED.—Not later than 180 days after the date of the enactment of this Act, the Under Secretary shall submit to Congress a report on the use of contractors at the National Weather Service for the most recently completed fiscal year.

(b) CONTENTS.—The report required by subsection (a) shall include, with respect to the most recently completed fiscal year, the following:

(1) The total number of full-time equivalent employees at the National Weather Service, disaggregated by each equivalent level of the General Schedule.

(2) The total number of full-time equivalent contractors at the National Weather Service, disaggregated by each equivalent level of the General Schedule that most closely approximates their duties.

(3) The total number of vacant positions at the National Weather Service on the day before the date of enactment of this Act, disaggregated by each equivalent level of the General Schedule.

(4) The 5 most common positions filled by full-time equivalent contractors at the National Weather Service and the equivalent level of the General Schedule that most closely approximates the duties of such positions.

(5) Of the positions identified under paragraph (4), the percentage of full-time equivalent contractors in those positions that have held a prior position at the National Weather Service or another entity in National Oceanic and Atmospheric Administration.

(6) The average full-time equivalent salary for Federal employees at the National Weather Service for each equivalent level of the General Schedule.

(7) The average salary for full-time equivalent contractors performing at each equivalent level of the General Schedule at the National Weather Service.

(8) A description of any actions taken by the Under Secretary to respond to the issues raised by the Inspector General of the Department of Commerce regarding the hiring of former National Oceanic and Atmospheric Administration employees as contractors at the National Weather Service such as the issues raised in the Investigative Report dated June 2, 2015 (OIG–12–0447).

(c) ANNUAL PUBLICATION.—For each fiscal year after the fiscal year covered by the report required by subsection (a), the Under Secretary shall, not later than 180 days after the completion of the fiscal year, publish on a publicly accessible Internet website the information described in paragraphs (1) through (8) of subsection (b) for such fiscal year.

SEC. 412. WEATHER IMPACTS TO COMMUNITIES AND INFRASTRUCTURE.

(a) REVIEW.—

(1) IN GENERAL.—The Director of the National Weather Service shall review existing research, products, and services that meet the specific needs of the urban environment, given its unique physical characteristics and forecasting challenges.

(2) ELEMENTS.—The review required by paragraph (1) shall include research, products, and services with the potential to improve modeling and forecasting capabilities, taking into account factors including varying building heights, impermeable surfaces, lack of tree canopy, traffic, pollution, and inter-building wind effects.

(b) REPORT AND ASSESSMENT.—Upon completion of the review required by subsection (a), the Under Secretary shall submit to Congress a report on the research, products, and services of the National Weather Service, including an assessment of such research, products, and services that is based on the review, public comment, and recent publications by the National Academy of Sciences.

SEC. 413. WEATHER ENTERPRISE OUTREACH.

(a) IN GENERAL.—The Under Secretary may establish mechanisms for outreach to the weather enterprise—

(1) to assess the weather forecasts and forecast products provided by the National Oceanic and Atmospheric Administration; and

(2) to determine the highest priority weather forecast needs of the community described in subsection (b).

(b) OUTREACH COMMUNITY.—In conducting outreach under subsection (a), the Under Secretary shall contact leading experts and innovators from relevant stakeholders, including the representatives from the following:

(1) State or local emergency management agencies.

(2) State agriculture agencies.

(3) Indian tribes (as defined in section 4 of the Indian Self-Determination and Education Assistance Act (25 U.S.C. 5304)) and Native Hawaiians (as defined in section 6207 of the Elementary and Secondary Education Act of 1965 (20 U.S.C. 7517)).

(4) The private aerospace industry.

(5) The private earth observing industry.

(6) The operational forecasting community.

(7) The academic community.

(8) Professional societies that focus on meteorology.

(9) Such other stakeholder groups as the Under Secretary considers appropriate.

SA 5126. Mr. SULLIVAN (for Ms. CANTWELL) proposed an amendment to amendment SA 5125 proposed by Mr. SULLIVAN (for Mr. THUNE (for himself and Mr. NELSON)) to the bill H.R. 1561, to improve the National Oceanic and Atmospheric Administration's weather research through a focused program of investment on affordable and attainable advances in observational, computing, and modeling capabilities to support substantial improvement in weather forecasting and prediction of high impact weather events, to expand commercial opportunities for the provision of weather data, and for other purposes; as follows:

At the appropriate place, insert the following:

TITLE __—TSUNAMI WARNING, EDUCATION, AND RESEARCH ACT OF 2016

SEC. __01. SHORT TITLE.

This title may be cited as the "Tsunami Warning, Education, and Research Act of 2016".

SEC. __02. REFERENCES TO THE TSUNAMI WARNING AND EDUCATION ACT.

Except as otherwise expressly provided, whenever in this title an amendment or repeal is expressed in terms of an amendment to, or repeal of, a section or other provision, the reference shall be considered to be made to a section or other provision of the Tsunami Warning and Education Act (Public Law 109–424; 33 U.S.C. 3201 et seq.).

SEC. __03. EXPANSION OF PURPOSES OF TSUNAMI WARNING AND EDUCATION ACT.

Section 3 (33 U.S.C. 3202) is amended—

(1) in paragraph (1), by inserting "research," after "warnings,";

(2) by amending paragraph (2) to read as follows:

"(2) to enhance and modernize the existing United States Tsunami Warning System to increase the accuracy of forecasts and warnings, to ensure full coverage of tsunami threats to the United States with a network of detection assets, and to reduce false alarms;";

(3) by amending paragraph (3) to read as follows:

"(3) to improve and develop standards and guidelines for mapping, modeling, and assessment efforts to improve tsunami detection, forecasting, warnings, notification, mitigation, resiliency, response, outreach, and recovery;";

(4) by redesignating paragraphs (4), (5), and (6) as paragraphs (5), (6), and (8), respectively;

(5) by inserting after paragraph (3) the following:

"(4) to improve research efforts related to improving tsunami detection, forecasting, warnings, notification, mitigation, resiliency, response, outreach, and recovery;";

(6) in paragraph (5), as redesignated—

(A) by striking "and increase" and inserting ", increase, and develop uniform standards and guidelines for"; and

(B) by inserting ", including the warning signs of locally generated tsunami" after "approaching";

(7) in paragraph (6), as redesignated, by striking ", including the Indian Ocean; and" and inserting a semicolon; and

(8) by inserting after paragraph (6), as redesignated, the following:

"(7) to foster resilient communities in the face of tsunami and other similar coastal hazards; and".

SEC. __04. MODIFICATION OF TSUNAMI FORECASTING AND WARNING PROGRAM.

(a) IN GENERAL.—Subsection (a) of section 4 (33 U.S.C. 3203(a)) is amended by striking "Atlantic Ocean, Caribbean Sea, and Gulf of Mexico region" and inserting "Atlantic Ocean region, including the Caribbean Sea and the Gulf of Mexico".

(b) COMPONENTS.—Subsection (b) of section 4 (33 U.S.C. 3203(b)) is amended—

(1) in paragraph (1), by striking "established" and inserting "supported or maintained";

(2) by redesignating paragraphs (7) through (9) as paragraphs (8) through (10), respectively;

(3) by redesignating paragraphs (2) through (6) as paragraphs (3) through (7), respectively;

(4) by inserting after paragraph (1) the following:

"(2) to the degree practicable, maintain not less than 80 percent of the Deep-ocean Assessment and Reporting of Tsunamis buoy array at operational capacity to optimize data reliability;";

(5) by amending paragraph (5), as redesignated by paragraph (3), to read as follows:

"(5) provide tsunami forecasting capability based on models and measurements, including tsunami inundation models and maps for use in increasing the preparedness of communities and safeguarding port and harbor operations, that incorporate inputs, including—

"(A) the United States and global ocean and coastal observing system;

"(B) the global Earth observing system;

"(C) the global seismic network;

"(D) the Advanced National Seismic system;

"(E) tsunami model validation using historical and paleotsunami data;

"(F) digital elevation models and bathymetry; and

"(G) newly developing tsunami detection methodologies using satellites and airborne remote sensing;";

(6) by amending paragraph (7), as redesignated by paragraph (3), to read as follows:

"(7) include a cooperative effort among the Administration, the United States Geological Survey, and the National Science Foundation under which the Director of the United States Geological Survey and the Director of the National Science Foundation shall—

"(A) provide rapid and reliable seismic information to the Administrator from international and domestic seismic networks; and

"(B) support seismic stations installed before the date of the enactment of the Tsunami Warning, Education, and Research Act of 2016 to supplement coverage in areas of sparse instrumentation;";

(7) in paragraph (8), as redesignated by paragraph (2)—

(A) by inserting ", including graphical warning products," after "warnings";

(B) by inserting ", territories," after "States"; and

(C) by inserting "and Wireless Emergency Alerts" after "Hazards Program"; and

(8) in paragraph (9), as redesignated by paragraph (2)—

(A) by inserting "provide and" before "allow"; and

(B) by inserting "and commercial and Federal undersea communications cables" after "observing technologies".

(c) TSUNAMI WARNING SYSTEM.—Subsection (c) of section 4 (33 U.S.C. 3203(c)) is amended to read as follows:

"(c) TSUNAMI WARNING SYSTEM.—The program under this section shall operate a tsunami warning system that—

"(1) is capable of forecasting tsunami, including forecasting tsunami arrival time and inundation estimates, anywhere in the Pacific and Arctic Ocean regions and providing adequate warnings;

"(2) is capable of forecasting and providing adequate warnings, including tsunami arrival time and inundation models where applicable, in areas of the Atlantic Ocean, including the Caribbean Sea and Gulf of Mexico, that are determined—

"(A) to be geologically active, or to have significant potential for geological activity; and

"(B) to pose significant risks of tsunami for States along the coastal areas of the Atlantic Ocean, Caribbean Sea, or Gulf of Mexico; and

"(3) supports other international tsunami forecasting and warning efforts.".

(d) TSUNAMI WARNING CENTERS.—Subsection (d) of section 4 (33 U.S.C. 3203(d)) is amended to read as follows:

"(d) TSUNAMI WARNING CENTERS.—

"(1) IN GENERAL.—The Administrator shall support or maintain centers to support the tsunami warning system required by subsection (c). The Centers shall include—

"(A) the National Tsunami Warning Center, located in Alaska, which is primarily responsible for Alaska and the continental United States;

"(B) the Pacific Tsunami Warning Center, located in Hawaii, which is primarily responsible for Hawaii, the Caribbean, and other areas of the Pacific not covered by the National Center; and

"(C) any additional forecast and warning centers determined by the National Weather Service to be necessary.

"(2) RESPONSIBILITIES.—The responsibilities of the centers supported or maintained under paragraph (1) shall include the following:

"(A) Continuously monitoring data from seismological, deep ocean, coastal sea level, and tidal monitoring stations and other data sources as may be developed and deployed.

"(B) Evaluating earthquakes, landslides, and volcanic eruptions that have the potential to generate tsunami.

"(C) Evaluating deep ocean buoy data and tidal monitoring stations for indications of tsunami resulting from earthquakes and other sources.

"(D) To the extent practicable, utilizing a range of models, including ensemble models, to predict tsunami, including arrival times, flooding estimates, coastal and harbor currents, and duration.

"(E) Using data from the Integrated Ocean Observing System of the Administration in coordination with regional associations to calculate new inundation estimates and periodically update existing inundation estimates.

"(F) Disseminating forecasts and tsunami warning bulletins to Federal, State, tribal, and local government officials and the public.

"(G) Coordinating with the tsunami hazard mitigation program conducted under section 5 to ensure ongoing sharing of information between forecasters and emergency management officials.

"(H) In coordination with the Coast Guard, evaluating and recommending procedures for ports and harbors at risk of tsunami inundation, including review of readiness, response, and communication strategies, and data sharing policies, to the maximum extent practicable.

"(I) Making data gathered under this Act and post-warning analyses conducted by the National Weather Service or other relevant Administration offices available to the public.

"(J) Integrating and modernizing the program operated under this section with advances in tsunami science to improve performance without compromising service.

"(3) FAIL-SAFE WARNING CAPABILITY.—The tsunami warning centers supported or maintained under paragraph (1) shall maintain a fail-safe warning capability and perform back-up duties for each other.

"(4) COORDINATION WITH NATIONAL WEATHER SERVICE.—The Administrator shall coordinate with the forecast offices of the National Weather Service, the centers supported or maintained under paragraph (1), and such program offices of the Administration as the Administrator or the coordinating committee, as established in section 5(d), consider appropriate to ensure that regional and local forecast offices—

"(A) have the technical knowledge and capability to disseminate tsunami warnings for the communities they serve;

"(B) leverage connections with local emergency management officials for optimally disseminating tsunami warnings and forecasts; and

"(C) implement mass communication tools in effect on the day before the date of the enactment of the Tsunami Warning, Education, and Research Act of 2016 used by the National Weather Service on such date and newer mass communication technologies as they are developed as a part of the Weather-Ready Nation program of the Administration, or otherwise, for the purpose of timely and effective delivery of tsunami warnings.

"(5) UNIFORM OPERATING PROCEDURES.—The Administrator shall—

"(A) develop uniform operational procedures for the centers supported or maintained under paragraph (1), including the use of software applications, checklists, decision support tools, and tsunami warning products that have been standardized across the program supported under this section;

"(B) ensure that processes and products of the warning system operated under subsection (c)—

"(i) reflect industry best practices when practicable;

"(ii) conform to the maximum extent practicable with internationally recognized standards for information technology; and

"(iii) conform to the maximum extent practicable with other warning products and practices of the National Weather Service;

"(C) ensure that future adjustments to operational protocols, processes, and warning products—

"(i) are made consistently across the warning system operated under subsection (c); and

"(ii) are applied in a uniform manner across such warning system;

"(D) establish a systematic method for information technology product development to improve long-term technology planning efforts; and

"(E) disseminate guidelines and metrics for evaluating and improving tsunami forecast models.

"(6) AVAILABLE RESOURCES.—The Administrator, through the National Weather Service, shall ensure that resources are available to fulfill the obligations of this Act. This includes ensuring supercomputing resources are available to run, as rapidly as possible, such computer models as are needed for purposes of the tsunami warning system operated under subsection (c).".

(e) TRANSFER OF TECHNOLOGY; MAINTENANCE AND UPGRADES.—Subsection (e) of section 4 (33 U.S.C. 3203(e)) is amended to read as follows:

"(e) TRANSFER OF TECHNOLOGY; MAINTENANCE AND UPGRADES.—In carrying out this section, the Administrator shall—

"(1) develop requirements for the equipment used to forecast tsunami, including—

"(A) provisions for multipurpose detection platforms;

"(B) reliability and performance metrics; and

"(C) to the maximum extent practicable, requirements for the integration of equipment with other United States and global ocean and coastal observation systems, the global Earth observing system of systems, the global seismic networks, and the Advanced National Seismic System;

"(2) develop and execute a plan for the transfer of technology from ongoing research conducted as part of the program supported or maintained under section 6 into the program under this section; and

"(3) ensure that the Administration's operational tsunami detection equipment is properly maintained.".

(f) FEDERAL COOPERATION.—Subsection (f) of section 4 (33 U.S.C. 3203(f)) is amended to read as follows:

"(f) FEDERAL COOPERATION.—When deploying and maintaining tsunami detection technologies under the program under this section, the Administrator shall—

"(1) identify which assets of other Federal agencies are necessary to support such program; and

"(2) work with each agency identified under paragraph (1)—

"(A) to acquire the agency's assistance; and

"(B) to prioritize the necessary assets in support of the tsunami forecast and warning program.".

(g) UNNECESSARY PROVISIONS.—Section 4 (33 U.S.C. 3203) is further amended—

(1) by striking subsection (g);

(2) by striking subsections (i) through (k); and

(3) by redesignating subsection (h) as subsection (g).

(h) CONGRESSIONAL NOTIFICATIONS.—Subsection (g) of section 4 (33 U.S.C. 3203(g)), as redesignated by subsection (g)(3), is amended—

(1) by redesignating paragraphs (1) and (2) as subparagraphs (A) and (B), respectively, and moving such subparagraphs 2 ems to the right;

(2) in the matter before subparagraph (A), as redesignated by paragraph (2), by striking "The Administrator" and inserting the following:

"(1) IN GENERAL.—The Administrator";

(3) in paragraph (1), as redesignated by paragraph (3)—

(A) in subparagraph (A), as redesignated by paragraph (2), by striking "and" at the end;

(B) in subparagraph (B), as redesignated by paragraph (2), by striking the period at the end and inserting "; and"; and

(C) by adding at the end the following:

"(C) the occurrence of a significant tsunami warning."; and

(4) by adding at the end the following:

"(2) CONTENTS.—In a case in which notice is submitted under paragraph (1) within 30 days of a significant tsunami warning described in subparagraph (C) of such paragraph, such notice shall include, as appropriate, brief information and analysis of—

"(A) the accuracy of the tsunami model used;

"(B) the specific deep ocean or other monitoring equipment that detected the incident, as well as the deep ocean or other monitoring equipment that did not detect the incident due to malfunction or other reasons;

"(C) the effectiveness of the warning communication, including the dissemination of warnings with State, territory, local, and tribal partners in the affected area under the jurisdiction of the National Weather Service; and

"(D) such other findings as the Administrator considers appropriate.".

SEC. _05. MODIFICATION OF NATIONAL TSUNAMI HAZARD MITIGATION PROGRAM.

(a) IN GENERAL.—Section 5(a) (33 U.S.C. 3204(a)) is amended to read as follows:

"(a) PROGRAM REQUIRED.—The Administrator, in coordination with the Administrator of the Federal Emergency Management Agency and the heads of such other agencies as the Administrator considers relevant, shall conduct a community-based tsunami hazard mitigation program to improve tsunami preparedness and resiliency of at-risk areas in the United States and the territories of the United States.''.

(b) NATIONAL TSUNAMI HAZARD MITIGATION PROGRAM.—Section 5 (33 U.S.C. 3204) is amended by striking subsections (c) and (d) and inserting the following:

''(c) PROGRAM COMPONENTS.—The Program conducted under subsection (a) shall include the following:

''(1) Technical and financial assistance to coastal States, territories, tribes, and local governments to develop and implement activities under this section.

''(2) Integration of tsunami preparedness and mitigation programs into ongoing State-based hazard warning, resilience planning, and risk management activities, including predisaster planning, emergency response, evacuation planning, disaster recovery, hazard mitigation, and community development and redevelopment planning programs in affected areas.

''(3) Activities to promote the adoption of tsunami resilience, preparedness, warning, and mitigation measures by Federal, State, territorial, tribal, and local governments and nongovernmental entities, including educational and risk communication programs to discourage development in high-risk areas.

''(4) Activities to support the development of regional tsunami hazard and risk assessments. Such regional risk assessments may include the following:

''(A) The sources, sizes, and other relevant historical data of tsunami in the region, including paleotsunami data.

''(B) Inundation models and maps of critical infrastructure and socioeconomic vulnerability in areas subject to tsunami inundation.

''(C) Maps of evacuation areas and evacuation routes, including, when appropriate, traffic studies that evaluate the viability of evacuation routes.

''(D) Evaluations of the size of populations that will require evacuation, including populations with special evacuation needs.

''(E) Evaluations and technical assistance for vertical evacuation structure planning for communities where models indicate limited or no ability for timely evacuation, especially in areas at risk of near shore generated tsunami.

''(F) Evaluation of at-risk ports and harbors.

''(G) Evaluation of the effect of tsunami currents on the foundations of closely-spaced, coastal high-rise structures.

''(5) Activities to promote preparedness in at-risk ports and harbors, including the following:

''(A) Evaluation and recommendation of procedures for ports and harbors in the event of a distant or near-field tsunami.

''(B) A review of readiness, response, and communication strategies to ensure coordination and data sharing with the Coast Guard.

''(6) Activities to support the development of community-based outreach and education programs to ensure community readiness and resilience, including the following:

''(A) The development, implementation, and assessment of technical training and public education programs, including education programs that address unique characteristics of distant and near-field tsunami.

''(B) The development of decision support tools.

''(C) The incorporation of social science research into community readiness and resilience efforts.

''(D) The development of evidence-based education guidelines.

''(7) Dissemination of guidelines and standards for community planning, education, and training products, programs, and tools, including—

''(A) standards for—

''(i) mapping products;

''(ii) inundation models; and

''(iii) effective emergency exercises; and

''(B) recommended guidance for at-risk port and harbor tsunami warning, evacuation, and response procedures in coordination with the Coast Guard.

''(d) AUTHORIZED ACTIVITIES.—In addition to activities conducted under subsection (c), the program conducted under subsection (a) may include the following:

''(1) Multidisciplinary vulnerability assessment research, education, and training to help integrate risk management and resilience objectives with community development planning and policies.

''(2) Risk management training for local officials and community organizations to enhance understanding and preparedness.

''(3) Interagency, Federal, State, tribal, and territorial intergovernmental tsunami response exercise planning and implementation in high risk areas.

''(4) Development of practical applications for existing or emerging technologies, such as modeling, remote sensing, geospatial technology, engineering, and observing systems, including the integration of tsunami sensors into Federal and commercial submarine telecommunication cables if practicable.

''(5) Risk management, risk assessment, and resilience data and information services, including—

''(A) access to data and products derived from observing and detection systems; and

''(B) development and maintenance of new integrated data products to support risk management, risk assessment, and resilience programs.

''(6) Risk notification systems that coordinate with and build upon existing systems and actively engage decisionmakers, State, local, tribal, and territorial governments and agencies, business communities, nongovernmental organizations, and the media.

''(e) NO PREEMPTION WITH RESPECT TO DESIGNATION OF AT-RISK AREAS.—The establishment of national standards for inundation models under this section shall not prevent States, territories, tribes, and local governments from designating additional areas as being at risk based on knowledge of local conditions.

''(f) NO NEW REGULATORY AUTHORITY.—Nothing in this Act may be construed as establishing new regulatory authority for any Federal agency.''.

(c) REPORT ON ACCREDITATION OF TSUNAMIREADY PROGRAM.—Not later than 180 days after the date of enactment of this Act, the Administrator of the National Oceanic and Atmospheric Administration shall submit to the Committee on Commerce, Science, and Transportation of the Senate and the Committee on Science, Space, and Technology of the House of Representatives a report on which authorities and activities would be needed to have the TsunamiReady program of the National Weather Service accredited by the Emergency Management Accreditation Program.

SEC. 06. MODIFICATION OF TSUNAMI RESEARCH PROGRAM.

Section 6 (33 U.S.C. 3205) is amended—

(1) in the matter before paragraph (1), by striking ''The Administrator shall'' and all that follows through ''establish or maintain'' and inserting the following:

''(a) IN GENERAL.—The Administrator shall, in consultation with such other Federal agencies, State, tribal, and territorial governments, and academic institutions as the Administrator considers appropriate, the coordinating committee under section 5(d), and the panel under section 8(a), support or maintain'';

(2) in subsection (a), as designated by paragraph (1), by striking ''and assessment for tsunami tracking and numerical forecast modeling. Such research program shall—'' and inserting the following: ''assessment for tsunami tracking and numerical forecast modeling, and standards development.

''(b) RESPONSIBILITIES.—The research program supported or maintained under subsection (a) shall—''; and

(3) in subsection (b), as designated by paragraph (2)—

(A) by amending paragraph (1) to read as follows:

''(1) consider other appropriate and cost effective solutions to mitigate the impact of tsunami, including the improvement of near-field and distant tsunami detection and forecasting capabilities, which may include use of a new generation of the Deep-ocean Assessment and Reporting of Tsunamis array, integration of tsunami sensors into commercial and Federal telecommunications cables, and other real-time tsunami monitoring systems and supercomputer capacity of the Administration to develop a rapid tsunami forecast for all United States coastlines;'';

(B) in paragraph (3)—

(i) by striking ''include'' and inserting ''conduct''; and

(ii) by striking ''and'' at the end;

(C) by redesignating paragraph (4) as paragraph (5);

(D) by inserting after paragraph (3) the following:

''(4) develop the technical basis for validation of tsunami maps, numerical tsunami models, digital elevation models, and forecasts; and'' and

(E) in paragraph (5), as redesignated by subparagraph (C), by striking ''to the scientific community'' and inserting ''to the public and the scientific community''.

SEC. 07. GLOBAL TSUNAMI WARNING AND MITIGATION NETWORK.

Section 7 (33 U.S.C. 3206) is amended—

(1) by amending subsection (a) to read as follows:

''(a) SUPPORT FOR DEVELOPMENT OF AN INTERNATIONAL TSUNAMI WARNING SYSTEM.—The Administrator shall, in coordination with the Secretary of State and in consultation with such other agencies as the Administrator considers relevant, provide technical assistance, operational support, and training to the Intergovernmental Oceanographic Commission of the United Nations Educational, Scientific, and Cultural Organization, the World Meteorological Organization of the United Nations, and such other international entities as the Administrator considers appropriate, as part of the international efforts to develop a fully functional global tsunami forecast and warning system comprised of regional tsunami warning networks.'';

(2) in subsection (b), by striking ''shall'' each place it appears and inserting ''may''; and

(3) in subsection (c)—

(A) in paragraph (1), by striking ''establishing'' and inserting ''supporting''; and

(B) in paragraph (2)—

(i) by striking "establish" and inserting "support"; and

(ii) by striking "establishing" and inserting "supporting".

SEC. __08. TSUNAMI SCIENCE AND TECHNOLOGY ADVISORY PANEL.

(a) IN GENERAL.—The Act is further amended—

(1) by redesignating section 8 (33 U.S.C. 3207) as section 9; and

(2) by inserting after section 7 (33 U.S.C. 3206) the following:

"SEC. 8. TSUNAMI SCIENCE AND TECHNOLOGY ADVISORY PANEL.

"(a) DESIGNATION.—The Administrator shall designate an existing working group within the Science Advisory Board of the Administration to serve as the Tsunami Science and Technology Advisory Panel to provide advice to the Administrator on matters regarding tsunami science, technology, and regional preparedness.

"(b) MEMBERSHIP.—

"(1) COMPOSITION.—The Panel shall be composed of no fewer than 7 members selected by the Administrator from among individuals from academia or State agencies who have academic or practical expertise in physical sciences, social sciences, information technology, coastal resilience, emergency management, or such other disciplines as the Administrator considers appropriate.

"(2) FEDERAL EMPLOYMENT.—No member of the Panel may be a Federal employee.

"(c) RESPONSIBILITIES.—Not less frequently than once every 4 years, the Panel shall—

"(1) review the activities of the Administration, and other Federal activities as appropriate, relating to tsunami research, detection, forecasting, warning, mitigation, resiliency, and preparation; and

"(2) submit to the Administrator and such others as the Administrator considers appropriate—

"(A) the findings of the working group with respect to the most recent review conducted under paragraph (1); and

"(B) such recommendations for legislative or administrative action as the working group considers appropriate to improve Federal tsunami research, detection, forecasting, warning, mitigation, resiliency, and preparation.

"(d) REPORTS TO CONGRESS.—Not less frequently than once every 4 years, the Administrator shall submit to the Committee on Commerce, Science, and Transportation of the Senate, and the Committee on Science, Space, and Technology of the House of Representatives a report on the findings and recommendations received by the Administrator under subsection (c)(2).".

SEC. __09. REPORTS.

(a) REPORT ON IMPLEMENTATION OF TSUNAMI WARNING AND EDUCATION ACT.—

(1) IN GENERAL.—Not later than 1 year after the date of the enactment of this Act, the Administrator of the National Oceanic and Atmospheric Administration shall submit to Congress a report on the implementation of the Tsunami Warning and Education Act (33 U.S.C. 3201 et seq.).

(2) ELEMENTS.—The report required by paragraph (1) shall include the following:

(A) A detailed description of the progress made in implementing sections 4(d)(6), 5(b)(6), and 6(b)(4) of the Tsunami Warning and Education Act.

(B) A description of the ways that tsunami warnings and warning products issued by the Tsunami Forecasting and Warning Program established under section 4 of the Tsunami Warning and Education Act (33 U.S.C. 3203)

can be standardized and streamlined with warnings and warning products for hurricanes, coastal storms, and other coastal flooding events.

(b) REPORT ON NATIONAL EFFORTS THAT SUPPORT RAPID RESPONSE FOLLOWING NEARSHORE TSUNAMI EVENTS.—

(1) IN GENERAL.—Not later than 1 year after the date of the enactment of this Act, the Administrator and the Secretary of Homeland Security shall jointly, in coordination with the Director of the United States Geological Survey, Administrator of the Federal Emergency Management Agency, the Chief of the National Guard Bureau, and the heads of such other Federal agencies as the Administrator considers appropriate, submit to the appropriate committees of Congress a report on the national efforts in effect on the day before the date of the enactment of this Act that support and facilitate rapid emergency response following a domestic near-shore tsunami event to better understand domestic effects of earthquake derived tsunami on people, infrastructure, and communities in the United States.

(2) ELEMENTS.—The report required by paragraph (1) shall include the following:

(A) A description of scientific or other measurements collected on the day before the date of the enactment of this Act to quickly identify and quantify lost or degraded infrastructure or terrestrial formations.

(B) A description of scientific or other measurements that would be necessary to collect to quickly identify and quantify lost or degraded infrastructure or terrestrial formations.

(C) Identification and evaluation of Federal, State, local, tribal, territorial, and military first responder and search and rescue operation centers, bases, and other facilities as well as other critical response assets and infrastructure, including search and rescue aircraft, located within near-shore and distant tsunami inundation areas on the day before the date of the enactment of this Act.

(D) An evaluation of near-shore tsunami response plans in areas described in subparagraph (C) in effect on the day before the date of the enactment of this Act, and how those response plans would be affected by the loss of search and rescue and first responder infrastructure described in such subparagraph.

(E) A description of redevelopment plans and reports in effect on the day before the date of the enactment of this Act for communities in areas that are at high-risk for near-shore tsunami, as well identification of States or communities that do not have redevelopment plans.

(F) Recommendations to enhance near-shore tsunami preparedness and response plans, including recommended responder exercises, predisaster planning, and mitigation needs.

(G) Such other data and analysis information as the Administrator and the Secretary of Homeland Security consider appropriate.

(3) APPROPRIATE COMMITTEES OF CONGRESS.—In this subsection, the term "appropriate committees of Congress" means—

(A) the Committee on Commerce, Science, and Transportation and the Committee on Homeland Security and Governmental Affairs of the Senate; and

(B) the Committee on Science, Space, and Technology and the Committee on Homeland Security of the House of Representatives.

SEC. __10. AUTHORIZATION OF APPROPRIATIONS.

Section 9 of the Act, as redesignated by section 8(a)(1) of this Act, is amended—

(1) in paragraph (4)(B), by striking "and" at the end;

(2) in paragraph (5)(B), by striking the period at the end and inserting "; and"; and

(3) by adding at the end the following:

"(6) $25,800,000 for each of fiscal years 2016 through 2021, of which—

"(A) not less than 27 percent of the amount appropriated for each fiscal year shall be for activities conducted at the State level under the tsunami hazard mitigation program under section 5; and

"(B) not less than 8 percent of the amount appropriated shall be for the tsunami research program under section 6.".

SEC. __11. OUTREACH RESPONSIBILITIES.

The Administrator of the National Oceanic and Atmospheric Administration, in coordination with State and local emergency managers, shall develop and carry out formal outreach activities to improve tsunami education and awareness and foster the development of resilient communities. Outreach activities may include—

(1) the development of outreach plans to ensure the close integration of tsunami warning centers supported or maintained under section 4(d) of the Tsunami Warning and Education Act (33 U.S.C. 3203(d)) with local Weather Forecast Offices of the National Weather Service and emergency managers;

(2) working with appropriate local Weather Forecast Offices to ensure they have the technical knowledge and capability to disseminate tsunami warnings to the communities they serve; and

(3) evaluating the effectiveness of warnings and of coordination with local Weather Forecast Offices after significant tsunami events.

SEC. __12. REPEAL OF DUPLICATE PROVISIONS OF LAW.

(a) REPEAL.—The Magnuson-Stevens Fishery Conservation and Management Reauthorization Act of 2006 (Public Law 109–479) is amended by striking title VIII (relating to tsunami warning and education).

(b) CONSTRUCTION.—Nothing in this section shall be construed to repeal, or affect in any way, Public Law 109–424.

AUTHORITY FOR COMMITTEES TO MEET

Mr. CORNYN. Mr. President, I have five requests for committees to meet during today's session of the Senate. They have the approval of the Majority and Minority leaders.

Pursuant to rule XXVI, paragraph 5(a), of the Standing Rules of the Senate, the following committees are authorized to meet during today's session of the Senate:

COMMITTEE ON ARMED SERVICES

The Committee on Armed Services is authorized to meet during the session of the Senate on December 1, 2016, at 9:30 a.m.

COMMITTEE ON FINANCE

The Committee on Finance is authorized to meet during the session of the Senate on December 1, 2016, at 1:45 p.m., in room S–216.

COMMITTEE ON FOREIGN RELATIONS

The Committee on Foreign Relations is authorized to meet during the session of the Senate on December 1, 2016, at 10:30 a.m., to conduct a hearing entitled "The Future of Counter-Terrorism Strategy."

SELECT COMMITTEE ON INTELLIGENCE

The Select Committee on Intelligence is authorized to meet during the session of the

Senate on December 1, 2016, at 2 p.m., in room SH–219 of the Hart Senate Office Building.

SUBCOMMITTEE ON REGULATORY AFFAIRS AND
FEDERAL MANAGEMENT

The Subcommittee on Regulatory Affairs and Federal Management of the Committee on Homeland Security and Governmental Affairs is authorized to meet during the session of the Senate on December 1, 2016, at 2:30 p.m., to conduct a hearing entitled, "Examining Two GAO Reports regarding the Renewable Fuel Standard."

PRIVILEGES OF THE FLOOR

Mr. MERKLEY. Mr. President, I ask unanimous consent my intern, Jill Goatcher, be given the privileges of the floor for the balance of the day.

The PRESIDING OFFICER. Without objection, it is so ordered.

JUSTICE FOR ALL REAUTHORIZATION ACT OF 2016

Mr. SULLIVAN. Mr. President, I ask that the Chair lay before the Senate the message from the House to accompany S. 2577.

The Presiding Officer laid before the Senate the following message from the House of Representatives:

Resolved, That the bill from the Senate (S. 2577) entitled "An Act to protect crime victims' rights, to eliminate the substantial backlog of DNA and other forensic evidence samples to improve and expand the forensic science testing capacity of Federal, State, and local crime laboratories, to increase research and development of new testing technologies, to develop new training programs regarding the collection and use of forensic evidence, to provide post-conviction testing of DNA evidence to exonerate the innocent, to support accreditation efforts of forensic science laboratories and medical examiner offices, to address training and equipment needs, to improve the performance of counsel in State capital cases, and for other purposes.", do pass with an amendment.

Mr. SULLIVAN. Mr. President, I move to concur in the House amendment; and I ask unanimous consent that the motion be agreed to and the motion to reconsider be considered made and laid upon the table without intervening action or debate.

The PRESIDING OFFICER. Without objection, it is so ordered.

METROPOLITAN WEATHER HAZARDS PROTECTION ACT OF 2015

Mr. SULLIVAN. Mr. President, I ask unanimous consent that the Senate proceed to the immediate consideration of Calendar No. 629, S. 2058.

The PRESIDING OFFICER. The clerk will report the bill by title.

The legislative clerk read as follows:

A bill (S. 2058) to require the Secretary of Commerce to maintain and operate at least one Doppler weather radar site within 55 miles of each city in the United States that has a population of more than 700,000 individuals, and for other purposes.

There being no objection, the Senate proceeded to consider the bill, which had been reported from the Committee on Commerce, Science, and Transportation, with an amendment to strike all after the enacting clause and insert in lieu thereof the following:

SECTION 1. SHORT TITLE.

This Act may be cited as the "Metropolitan Weather Hazards Protection Act of 2015".

SEC. 2. STUDY ON GAPS IN NEXRAD COVERAGE AND REQUIREMENT FOR PLAN TO ADDRESS SUCH GAPS.

(a) STUDY ON GAPS IN NEXRAD COVERAGE.—

(1) IN GENERAL.—Not later than 90 days after the date of the enactment of this Act, the Secretary of Commerce shall complete a study on gaps in the coverage of the Next Generation Weather Radar of the National Weather Service (known as "NEXRAD").

(2) ELEMENTS.—Under the study required by paragraph (1), the Secretary shall—

(A) identify areas in the United States with limited or no Next Generation Weather Radar coverage below 6,000 feet above ground level of the surrounding terrain;

(B) for the areas identified under subparagraph (A), Charlotte, North Carolina, and surrounding counties, central Washington State, northwest New Mexico, and Columbus, Ohio, and surrounding counties—

(i) identify the key weather effects for which prediction would improve with improved radar detection;

(ii) identify additional sources of observations for high impact weather that were available and operational for such areas on the day before the date of the enactment of this Act, including Terminal Doppler Weather Radar (known as "TDWR"), air surveillance radars of the Federal Aviation Administration, and cooperative network observers; and

(iii) assess the feasibility and advisability of efforts to integrate and upgrade Federal radar capabilities in such areas that are not owned or controlled by of the National Oceanic and Atmospheric Administration, including radar capabilities of the Federal Aviation Administration and the Department of Defense;

(C) assess the feasibility and advisability of incorporating State-operated and other non-Federal radars into the operations of the National Weather Service;

(D) identify options to improve radar coverage in the areas identified under subparagraph (A); and

(E) estimate the cost of, and develop a timeline for, carrying out each of the options identified under subparagraph (D).

(3) REPORT.—Upon the completion of the study required by paragraph (1), the Secretary shall submit to the Committee on Commerce, Science, and Transportation of the Senate and the Committee on Science, Space, and Technology of the House of Representatives a report on the findings of the Secretary with respect to the study.

(b) PLAN TO IMPROVE RADAR COVERAGE.—Not later than 30 days after the completion of the study required by subsection (a)(1), the Secretary shall develop and submit to the Committee on Commerce, Science, and Transportation of the Senate and the Committee on Science, Space, and Technology of the House of Representatives a plan to improve radar coverage in the areas identified under subsection (a)(2)(A) by integrating, and upgrading where practicable, additional observation solutions to improve hazardous weather detection and forecasting.

(c) REQUIREMENT FOR THIRD-PARTY REVIEWS REGARDING PLAN TO IMPROVE RADAR COVERAGE.—The Secretary shall seek third-party re- *views on scientific methodology relating to, and the feasibility and advisability of, implementing the plan developed and submitted under subsection (b), including the extent to which warning and forecast services of the National Weather Service would be improved by additional Next Generation Weather Radar coverage.*

Mr. SULLIVAN. Mr. President, I ask unanimous consent that the committee-reported substitute amendment be withdrawn, the Burr substitute amendment be agreed to, the bill, as amended, be considered read a third time and passed, the title amendment be agreed to, and the motions to reconsider be considered made and laid upon the table.

The PRESIDING OFFICER. Without objection, it is so ordered.

The committee-reported amendment in the nature of a substitute was withdrawn.

The amendment (No. 5123) in the nature of a substitute was agreed to, as follows:

(Purpose: In the nature of a substitute)

Strike all after the enacting clause and insert the following:

SEC. ___ . STUDY ON GAPS IN NEXRAD COVERAGE AND REQUIREMENT FOR PLAN TO ADDRESS SUCH GAPS.

(a) STUDY ON GAPS IN NEXRAD COVERAGE.—

(1) IN GENERAL.—Not later than 90 days after the date of the enactment of this Act, the Secretary of Commerce shall complete a study on gaps in the coverage of the Next Generation Weather Radar of the National Weather Service (referred to in this section as "NEXRAD").

(2) ELEMENTS.—In conducting the study required under paragraph (1), the Secretary shall—

(A) identify areas in the United States with limited or no NEXRAD coverage below 6,000 feet above ground level of the surrounding terrain;

(B) for the areas identified under subparagraph (A)—

(i) identify the key weather effects for which prediction would improve with improved radar detection;

(ii) identify additional sources of observations for high impact weather that were available and operational for such areas on the day before the date of the enactment of this Act, including Terminal Doppler Weather Radar (commonly known as "TDWR"), air surveillance radars of the Federal Aviation Administration, and cooperative network observers; and

(iii) assess the feasibility and advisability of efforts to integrate and upgrade Federal radar capabilities that are not owned or controlled by the National Oceanic and Atmospheric Administration, including radar capabilities of the Federal Aviation Administration and the Department of Defense;

(C) assess the feasibility and advisability of incorporating State-operated and other non-Federal radars into the operations of the National Weather Service;

(D) identify options to improve radar coverage in the areas identified under subparagraph (A); and

(E) estimate the cost of, and develop a timeline for, carrying out each of the options identified under subparagraph (D).

(3) REPORT.—Upon the completion of the study required under paragraph (1), the Secretary shall submit a report to the Committee on Commerce, Science, and Transportation of the Senate, the Committee on Appropriations of the Senate, the Committee on Science, Space, and Technology of the House of Representatives, and the Committee on Appropriations of the House of Representatives that includes the findings of the Secretary with respect to the study.

(b) PLAN TO IMPROVE RADAR COVERAGE.—Not later than 30 days after the completion of the study under subsection (a)(1), the Secretary of Commerce shall submit a plan to the congressional committees referred to in subsection (a)(3) for improving radar coverage in the areas identified under subsection (a)(2)(A) by integrating and upgrading, to the extent practicable, additional observation solutions to improve hazardous weather detection and forecasting.

(c) REQUIREMENT FOR THIRD-PARTY REVIEWS REGARDING PLAN TO IMPROVE RADAR COVERAGE.—The Secretary of Commerce shall seek third-party reviews on scientific methodology relating to, and the feasibility and advisability of, implementing the plan submitted under subsection (b), including the extent to which warning and forecast services of the National Weather Service would be improved by additional NEXRAD coverage.

The bill (S. 2058), as amended, was ordered to be engrossed for a third reading, was read the third time, and passed.

The amendment (No. 5124) was agreed to, as follows:

(Purpose: To amend the title)

Amend the title so as to read: "A bill to require the Secretary of Commerce to study the coverage gaps of the Next Generation Weather Radar of the National Weather Service and to develop a plan for improving radar coverage and hazardous weather detection and forecasting.".

ALLOWING THE ADMINISTRATOR OF THE FAA TO ENTER INTO REIMBURSABLE AGREEMENTS FOR CERTAIN AIRPORT PROJECTS

Mr. SULLIVAN. Mr. President, I ask unanimous consent that the Committee on Commerce, Science, and Transportation be discharged from further consideration of H.R. 6014 and the Senate proceed to its immediate consideration.

The PRESIDING OFFICER. Without objection, it is so ordered.

The clerk will report the bill by title.

The legislative clerk read as follows:

A bill (H.R. 6014) to allow the Administrator of the Federal Aviation Administration to enter into reimbursable agreements for certain airport projects.

There being no objection, the Senate proceeded to consider the bill.

Mr. SULLIVAN. Mr. President, I ask unanimous consent that the bill be considered read a third time and passed and the motion to reconsider be considered made and laid upon the table.

The PRESIDING OFFICER. Without objection, it is so ordered.

The bill (H.R. 6014) was ordered to a third reading, was read the third time, and passed.

WEATHER RESEARCH AND FORECASTING INNOVATION ACT OF 2015

Mr. SULLIVAN. Mr. President, I ask unanimous consent that the Committee on Commerce, Science, and Transportation be discharged from further consideration of H.R. 1561 and the Senate proceed to its immediate consideration.

The PRESIDING OFFICER. Without objection, it is so ordered.

The clerk will report the bill by title.

The legislative clerk read as follows:

A bill (H.R. 1561) to improve the National Oceanic and Atmospheric Administration's weather research through a focused program of investment on affordable and attainable advances in observational, computing, and modeling capabilities to support substantial improvement in weather forecasting and prediction of high impact weather events, to expand commercial opportunities for the provision of weather data, and for other purposes.

There being no objection, the Senate proceeded to consider the bill.

Mr. SULLIVAN. Mr. President, I ask unanimous consent that the Thune substitute amendment at the desk be considered, the Cantwell amendment at the desk be considered and agreed to, the Thune substitute amendment, as amended, be agreed to, the bill, as amended, be considered read a third time and passed, and the motion to reconsider be considered made and laid upon the table.

The PRESIDING OFFICER. Without objection, it is so ordered.

The amendment (No. 5126) was agreed to.

(The amendment is printed in today's RECORD under "Text of Amendments.")

The amendment (No. 5125) in the nature of a substitute, as amended, was agreed to.

(The amendment is printed in today's RECORD under "Text of Amendments.")

The amendment was ordered to be engrossed and the bill to be read a third time.

The bill was read the third time.

The bill (H.R. 1561), as amended, was passed.

HONORING THE MEMORIES AND LEGACIES OF THE 3 LAW ENFORCEMENT OFFICERS WHO LOST THEIR LIVES IN THE ATTACK ON JULY 17, 2016, IN BATON ROUGE, LOUISIANA

Mr. SULLIVAN. Mr. President, I ask unanimous consent that the Judiciary Committee be discharged from further consideration of and the Senate now proceed to the consideration of S. Res. 606.

The PRESIDING OFFICER. Without objection, it is so ordered.

The clerk will report the resolution by title.

The legislative clerk read as follows:

A resolution (S. Res. 606) honoring the memories and legacies of the 3 law enforcement officers who lost their lives in the attack on July 17, 2016, in Baton Rouge, Louisiana, condemning that attack, and recognizing the heroism of law enforcement personnel and first responders.

There being no objection, the Senate proceeded to consider the resolution.

Mr. SULLIVAN. Mr. President, I ask unanimous consent that the resolution be agreed to, the preamble be agreed to, and the motions to reconsider be considered made and laid upon the table.

The PRESIDING OFFICER. Without objection, it is so ordered.

The resolution (S. Res. 606) was agreed to.

The preamble was agreed to.

(The resolution, with its preamble, is printed in the RECORD of September 29, 2016, under "Submitted Resolutions.")

COLONEL DEMAS T. CRAW VA CLINIC

Mr. SULLIVAN. Mr. President, I ask unanimous consent that the Senate proceed to the immediate consideration of S. 3492, introduced earlier today.

The PRESIDING OFFICER. The clerk will report the bill by title.

The legislative clerk read as follows:

A bill (S. 3492) to designate the Traverse City VA Community-Based Outpatient Clinic of the Department of Veterans Affairs in Traverse City, Michigan, as the "Colonel Demas T. Craw VA Clinic."

There being no objection, the Senate proceeded to consider the bill.

Mr. SULLIVAN. I ask unanimous consent that the bill be read a third time and passed and the motion to reconsider be considered made and laid upon the table with no intervening action or debate.

The PRESIDING OFFICER. Without objection, it is so ordered.

The bill (S. 3492) was ordered to be engrossed for a third reading, was read the third time, and passed, as follows:

S. 3492

Be it enacted by the Senate and House of Representatives of the United States of America in Congress assembled,

SECTION 1. DESIGNATION OF COLONEL DEMAS T. CRAW VA CLINIC IN TRAVERSE CITY, MICHIGAN.

(a) FINDINGS.—Congress finds the following:

(1) Demas T. Craw was born on April 9, 1900, in Long Lake Township, Michigan.

(2) While residing in Traverse City, Michigan, Demas T. Craw enlisted in the United States Army at Columbus Barracks, Ohio, on April 18, 1918, and trained with the 12th Cavalry at Camp Stanley, Texas.

(3) Colonel Craw achieved the position of senior pilot and was awarded—

(A) the Medal of Honor for action in North Africa;

(B) the World War I Victory Medal;

(C) the World War II Victory Medal;

(D) the European-African-Middle Eastern Campaign Medal;

(E) the Mexican Service Medal;

(F) the American Defense Service Medal;

(G) the Purple Heart;

(H) the Royal Order of George I; and

(I) the Observer Badge.

(4) Colonel Craw's citation for the Medal of Honor said, "For conspicuous gallantry and intrepidity in action above and beyond the call of duty. On November 8, 1942, near Port Lyautey, French Morocco, Col. Craw volunteered to accompany the leading wave of assault boats to the shore and pass through the enemy lines to locate the French commander with a view to suspending hostilities. This request was first refused as being too dangerous but upon the officer's insistence that he was qualified to undertake and accomplish the mission he was allowed to go. Encountering heavy fire while in the landing boat and unable to dock in the river because of shell fire from shore batteries, Col. Craw, accompanied by 1 officer and 1 soldier, succeeded in landing on the beach at Mehdia Plage under constant low-level strafing from 3 enemy planes. Riding in a bantam truck toward French headquarters, progress of the party was hindered by fire from our own naval guns. Nearing Port Lyautey, Col. Craw was instantly killed by a sustained burst of machinegun fire at pointblank range from a concealed position near the road.".

(5) Colonel Craw was killed in action on November 8, 1942, while attempting to deliver a message to broker a cease fire with France.

(b) DESIGNATION.—The Traverse City VA Community-Based Outpatient Clinic of the Department of Veterans Affairs in Traverse City, Michigan, shall after the date of the enactment of this Act be known and designated as the "Colonel Demas T. Craw VA Clinic".

(c) REFERENCE.—Any reference in any law, regulation, map, document, paper, or other record of the United States to the community-based outpatient clinic referred to in subsection (b) shall be considered to be a reference to the Colonel Demas T. Craw VA Clinic.

NATIONAL PHENYLKETONURIA AWARENESS DAY

Mr. SULLIVAN. Mr. President, I ask unanimous consent that the Senate proceed to the consideration of S. Res. 627, submitted earlier today.

The PRESIDING OFFICER. The clerk will report the resolution by title.

The legislative clerk read as follows:

A resolution (S. Res. 627) designating December 3, 2016, as "National Phenylketonuria Awareness Day."

There being no objection, the Senate proceeded to consider the resolution.

Mr. SULLIVAN. I ask unanimous consent that the resolution be agreed to, the preamble be agreed to, and the motions to reconsider be considered made and laid upon the table with no intervening action or debate.

The PRESIDING OFFICER. Without objection, it is so ordered.

The resolution (S. Res. 627) was agreed to.

The preamble was agreed to.

(The resolution, with its preamble, is printed in today's RECORD under "Submitted Resolutions.")

AUTHORIZING THE PRINTING OF A REVISED EDITION OF THE SENATE RULES AND MANUAL

Mr. SULLIVAN. Mr. President, I ask unanimous consent that the Senate proceed to the consideration of S. Res. 628, submitted earlier today.

The PRESIDING OFFICER. The clerk will report the resolution by title.

The legislative clerk read as follows:

A resolution (S. Res. 628) authorizing the printing of a revised edition of the Senate Rules and Manual.

There being no objection, the Senate proceeded to consider the resolution.

Mr. SULLIVAN. I ask unanimous consent that the resolution be agreed to and the motion to reconsider be considered made and laid upon the table with no intervening action or debate.

The PRESIDING OFFICER. Without objection, it is so ordered.

The resolution (S. Res. 628) was agreed to.

(The resolution is printed in today's RECORD under "Submitted Resolutions.")

ORDERS FOR MONDAY, DECEMBER 5, 2016

Mr. SULLIVAN. Mr. President, I ask unanimous consent that when the Senate completes its business today, it adjourn until 3 p.m. on Monday, December 5; that following the prayer and pledge, the morning hour be deemed expired, the Journal of proceedings be approved to date, and the time for the two leaders be reserved for their use later in the day; further, that following leader remarks, the Senate resume consideration of the House message to accompany H.R. 34; further, that the filing deadline for first-degree amendments under rule XXII for the cloture motion filed during today's session be 4 p.m., Monday, December 5; finally, that the mandatory quorum call under rule XXII with respect to the cloture motion be waived.

The PRESIDING OFFICER. Without objection, it is so ordered.

ADJOURNMENT UNTIL MONDAY, DECEMBER 5, 2016, AT 3 P.M.

Mr. SULLIVAN. Mr. President, if there is no further business to come before the Senate, I ask unanimous consent that it stand adjourned under the previous order.

There being no objection, the Senate, at 6:07 p.m., adjourned until Monday, December 5, 2016, at 3 p.m.

HOUSE OF REPRESENTATIVES—*Thursday, December 1, 2016*

The House met at 10 a.m. and was called to order by the Speaker pro tempore (Mr. BOST).

DESIGNATION OF SPEAKER PRO TEMPORE

The SPEAKER pro tempore laid before the House the following communication from the Speaker:

WASHINGTON, DC,
December 1, 2016.

I hereby appoint the Honorable MIKE BOST to act as Speaker pro tempore on this day.

PAUL D. RYAN,
Speaker of the House of Representatives.

MORNING-HOUR DEBATE

The SPEAKER pro tempore. Pursuant to the order of the House of January 5, 2016, the Chair will now recognize Members from lists submitted by the majority and minority leaders for morning-hour debate.

The Chair will alternate recognition between the parties, with each party limited to 1 hour and each Member other than the majority and minority leaders and the minority whip limited to 5 minutes, but in no event shall debate continue beyond 11:50 a.m.

DISCOVERY, DEVELOPMENT, AND DELIVERY OF NEW CURES

The SPEAKER pro tempore. The Chair recognizes the gentleman from Pennsylvania (Mr. THOMPSON) for 5 minutes.

Mr. THOMPSON of Pennsylvania. Mr. Speaker, yesterday, the House passed the 21st Century Cures Act with a vote of 392–26. I was proud to support the Cures Act that expedites the discovery, the development, and the delivery of new cures for illnesses and disabling conditions where none exist today. This legislation also included long overdue reforms to our Nation's mental health system.

Mr. Speaker, the text of the Cures Act additionally contains my Special Needs Trust Fairness Act language. This corrects a civil rights oversight or issue for persons living with any disability to be allowed to establish their own special needs trust. Without this legislation, the way the law exists today, a person, any person living with a label of a disability, is deemed incompetent to be able to set up and manage their own special needs trust. Their parents can do it, their grandparents, a court-appointed guardian, but they are deemed incompetent.

I want to thank my colleagues for their support, and encourage the Senate to take swift action on the Cures Act that contains all this language.

RECOGNIZING THE LIFE OF DR. DAVID WRIGHT

Mr. THOMPSON of Pennsylvania. Mr. Speaker, I rise today to recognize the life of Dr. David Wright, a dedicated public servant and community leader from Clarion County, Pennsylvania, in Pennsylvania's Fifth Congressional District. He was a beloved professor and department head at Clarion University, where he passionately taught for nearly 30 years.

Dr. Wright also served in the Pennsylvania House of Representatives from 1976 to 1996. His 20-year tenure is the longest served in the State house by any Representative from Clarion County.

As a house member, Dr. Wright served as chairman on several committees and took on various leadership roles. He continually advocated for rural Pennsylvanians and authored language that created the Center for Rural Pennsylvania. He also played a major role in establishing the State System for Higher Education, which unified Pennsylvania's 14 State colleges into a comprehensive system.

Dr. Wright passed away on November 18, at the age of 80, leaving behind a legacy that will continue to benefit Pennsylvanians for generations to come. My thoughts and prayers are with the Wright family.

RECOGNIZING 75TH ANNIVERSARY OF AMERICAN TREE FARM SYSTEM

Mr. THOMPSON of Pennsylvania. Mr. Speaker, I rise today in recognition of the 75th anniversary of the American Tree Farm System, the largest and oldest woodland certification system in the Nation.

The American Tree Farm System was founded in 1941 to protect landowners across the country and help meet the growing demand for forest products. In 1954, the Principles of the American Tree Farm System created a system for tree farm certification, establishing a clear outline for proper forest management and conservation.

Today, the American Tree Farm System is comprised of more than 70,000 individuals and families that manage more than 20.5 million acres of forest. These tree farmers benefit our Nation's forests and our economy, while providing timber, homes for wildlife, recreational space, and clean water.

In honor of its legacy, last June I introduced H. Con. Res. 144, bipartisan legislation celebrating the American Tree Farm System and recognizing the 75th anniversary.

I congratulate the members of the American Tree Farm System on this remarkable milestone and applaud their work with landowners and foresters across the United States.

TRUMP ADMINISTRATION AND U.S. FOREIGN POLICY TOWARD ISRAEL

The SPEAKER pro tempore. The Chair recognizes the gentleman from Oregon (Mr. BLUMENAUER) for 5 minutes.

Mr. BLUMENAUER. Mr. Speaker, day by day we are learning more about the future Trump administration, and as the picture becomes clearer, usually the news is troubling.

One of the most unsettling indications about the Trump administration and the Republican Party is the abandonment of a half century of bipartisan foreign policy regarding Israel and our commitment to a two-state solution.

Israel has no greater friend in the world than the United States, but one of the ways to demonstrate friendship is to be clear when your friends are making mistakes. Settlement activity by Israel on the West Bank and the renewed destruction of Palestinian homes and confiscation of property are mistakes. The overwhelming majority of Israelis still favor a two-state solution, they just despair of it being possible. The steps the Netanyahu government is taking on that path make it more remote.

Donald Trump and the Republican Party he dominated at the Republican Convention abandoned the two-state solution. For the first time in a half century, the bipartisan commitment to a two-state solution has been stripped from the Republican Party platform.

This matters.

Donald Trump has empowered two of the most extreme voices, who have emboldened and defended settlement activity and undercut the necessary two-state solution, to manage his policy advice on Israel. This should be disturbing for everyone concerned about Middle East peace.

The world is a complicated and dangerous place. There are hints that Donald Trump is starting to learn about this complexity in fits and starts. Witness his statements after visiting with President Obama and his walking back some of his most extreme and definitive campaign promises.

It is important that the reality in the Middle East catches up sooner

---

☐ This symbol represents the time of day during the House proceedings, e.g., ☐ 1407 is 2:07 p.m.

Matter set in this typeface indicates words inserted or appended, rather than spoken, by a Member of the House on the floor.

rather than later. A prime example is the Iranian nuclear agreement, one of the few things that China, Russia, Great Britain, France, Germany, and the United States all agreed upon. It is not perfect, and there are certainly Iranian leaders who are dangerous people, but this agreement was the best alternative and the only thing that all these parties could agree upon.

Now, it is easy to talk on the campaign trail about blowing it up; it is harder to do in reality when it is actually working as it was supposed to and, in fact, is supported even by an overwhelming majority of American Jewish voters.

We all have responsibility for a thoughtful foreign policy, and Democrats must stand firm to reject some of the reckless proposals from the Trump administration; but our Republican friends in Congress should not allow a half century of bipartisan foreign policy to become a casualty of some of the most extreme voices of American and Israeli politics.

The time to speak out is now. Everyone must find their voice. Failure to support a two-state solution and reject the misguided settlement efforts which would make that solution impossible is a prescription for more pain, unrest, and violence between Israelis and Palestinians. Middle East peace should not be a casualty of the American election.

HONORING THE LIFE AND SERVICE OF FORMER CONGRESSMAN TOM LANTOS

The SPEAKER pro tempore. The Chair recognizes the gentlewoman from Florida (Ms. ROS-LEHTINEN) for 5 minutes.

Ms. ROS-LEHTINEN. Mr. Speaker, Congressman Tom Lantos was a giant of a man, an inspiration to all of us who knew him, and greatly admired by his peers. Tom was a patriot, a recipient of the Presidential Medal of Freedom who championed justice, human rights, and human dignity across the globe.

Tom Lantos was a Holocaust survivor, the only Holocaust survivor ever elected to serve in this esteemed institution. Coming to America as a penniless immigrant, Tom's life story is one of perseverance and fortitude, yet, a kinder, more loving man you would not ever find.

Tom was the embodiment of the American Dream, building a wonderful life for himself, for his wife, Annette, and their two daughters. He made it his life's work to see to it that the horrors that he had seen, the horrors that he had lived through, would never be brought upon others ever again.

His background as a survivor and a Member of Congress gave him a unique opportunity to forge an ever stronger relationship between the United States and our ally, the democratic Jewish

State of Israel and to guarantee that the Jewish people will always have a homeland.

Now Tom's legacy and his memory are being honored on December 19 in Netanya, Israel, where a statue will be dedicated in his honor. I extend my most sincere and heartfelt words of admiration to Tom's family. I congratulate them all on this auspicious occasion.

Tom Lantos was an honorable gentleman, Mr. Speaker, and few are more deserving of such a great honor.

HONORING BROTHER KEVIN HANDIBODE, PRESIDENT OF CHRISTOPHER COLUMBUS HIGH SCHOOL

Ms. ROS-LEHTINEN. Mr. Speaker, I rise today to recognize Brother Kevin, president of Christopher Columbus High School, for his 45 years of service to this wonderful institution and for his 60th anniversary as a Marist Brother this upcoming year.

Since arriving at Christopher Columbus High School in 1966, Brother Kevin has been an all-around champion for CCHS and its students while serving in many capacities, including teacher, dean of discipline, athletic director, varsity coach for over 18 years, developmental director, and principal.

His legendary reputation has carried him through many recognitions and accolades, including the respect and admiration of his peers, his coworkers, and our loving community. In 2008, for his distinguished service to the church and devotion to the Catholic education system, Brother Kevin was bestowed the Cross, the highest medal that can be awarded by the Pope.

So, again, Brother Kevin, congratulations on this magnificent milestone. As the heart and soul of Columbus High School, you have been a leader, you have been a role model, but, more importantly, you have given countless students the ability to pursue their dreams and reach their full potential.

Go Explorers. Go Brother Kevin.

CELEBRATING THE 40TH ANNIVERSARY OF HIGHPOINT ACADEMY

Ms. ROS-LEHTINEN. Mr. Speaker, it gives me great joy to recognize Highpoint Academy, a well-respected bilingual private school located in my community, on its 40th anniversary.

Since its founding in 1976, Highpoint Academy has provided generations of students with an excellent education in a positive and nurturing academic environment. This prestigious institution is a model of academic excellence, imagination, innovation, and creative thinking. I am proud that, over the last 40 years, the gifted educators at Highpoint Academy have helped develop successful students who have gone on to become leaders in our south Florida community and, indeed, throughout our Nation.

To Principal Alicia Casanova and the whole Highpoint Academy family, congratulations on this very special anni-

versary, and thank you for decades of outstanding educational contributions to our south Florida community.

WORLD AIDS DAY

Ms. ROS-LEHTINEN. Mr. Speaker, today is a milestone in the history of the fight against AIDS because we are celebrating the 28th World AIDS Day. For sure, we must continue to build upon a bipartisan commitment to ending AIDS by the year 2030, both here in the U.S. and around the world.

I will remain deeply involved as the Republican co-chair of the Congressional HIV/AIDS Caucus because south Florida, my community, is ground zero for the next phase of the battle against HIV/AIDS.

Sadly, Florida is number one in the Nation for new HIV cases, and south Florida accounts for more than half of all new HIV cases in our State. Florida's growing struggle with HIV/AIDS mirrors a larger dynamic taking place across the South for which the region, as a whole, is not well-prepared. South Florida's issues, in particular, are exacerbated by the demographics of HIV, our magnetism as a tourist destination, and the international character of both our community and the AIDS epidemic.

Next year is a big year for the fight against HIV/AIDS. The AIDS community and the Congressional HIV/AIDS Caucus will remain committed to putting an end to AIDS by the year 2030.

□ 1015

PRESIDENT OBAMA'S LEGACY

The SPEAKER pro tempore. The Chair recognizes the gentleman from Illinois (Mr. QUIGLEY) for 5 minutes.

Mr. QUIGLEY. Mr. Speaker, 8 years ago, our Nation was in the midst of the Great Recession. It was the worst economic downturn since the Great Depression, unprecedented in both severity and duration. It was an economic tailspin that blindsided many, devastated millions, and robbed good people of their savings, their security, and their way of life. It was a disastrous combination of irresponsible lending, overly complex derivatives, and inadequate regulatory oversight that led to a near collapse of our financial system.

Over the course of this economic catastrophe, more than 5 million Americans lost the roof over their head, and another 9 million lost the paycheck they relied on to support themselves and their families. People were terrified for their futures, and for the first time in generations, it looked as if moms and dads might have it better off than their sons and daughters.

This chaos and despair extended far beyond economics. At the end of 2008, almost 16 percent of the population was uninsured. This meant that over 50 million Americans were crossing their fingers, holding their breath, and hoping to avoid any unpredictable, unanticipated, and uncontrollable health concerns that would turn their lives upside down. Simply being a woman or having asthma was enough for insurance companies to deny you quality care, and basic preventive and primary care services were hard to come by.

Thousands of brave men and women in uniform had been killed, and scores more were wounded in a long and polarizing war in Iraq. LGBT Americans had to keep their true identities hidden. Gay men and women who served their Nation in uniform and risked their lives in defense of our freedom had to stay quiet about whom they loved, and those who were open about their sexual orientation were not allowed to join their partner in marriage if they lived in one of the 48 States that prohibited same-sex marriage.

This was the state of our Nation. This is the America that President Obama inherited on January 20, 2009.

Things look a little different today, and I know that I speak for millions of Americans who are grateful for the past 8 years fueled by real change that made our economy stronger and our society much more just.

When President Obama took his oath of office, the economy was bleeding 800,000 jobs a month. Today, we have seen record private sector job growth marked by over 15 million new jobs over the past 80 months.

At the height of the recession in 2009, unemployment hit an alarming 10 percent; but, today, the unemployment rate is below 5 percent. Today, thanks to the Dodd-Frank Act, systemic risk in our financial system has been significantly reduced, and our largest banking institutions are more transparent and accountable than they have been in decades.

Today, marriage equality is now the law of the land in all 50 States. Today, nearly 18 million previously uninsured Americans have gained coverage under the Affordable Care Act, resulting in the lowest uninsured rate in history. Today, men and women are charged the same price for health care. Americans can access preventive care services at no cost. Preexisting conditions don't bar individuals from treatment, and young people can stay on their parents' plan until they are 26.

Today, because of the Lilly Ledbetter Fair Pay Act, which was the first piece of legislation signed by President Obama, women can more effectively challenge unequal pay practices.

Today, previously fraught relationships with many allied countries have been restored. Today, the combat mission in Iraq is over and tens of thousands of troops are back home with their families after years of war. Today, justice has been served, and Osama bin Laden is dead.

Today, our Nation has championed some of the most profound climate change initiatives in the world, like the Clean Power Plan and the Paris Ac-

cords, which will help protect our precious natural resources and defend our environment for generations to come.

It is up to us to decide if we want to move forward or back. Nearly a decade of progress is on the chopping block.

There is no doubt that everyone is still reeling from the long and divisive campaign season that culminated in an election that left millions of Americans scared once again.

The economic recovery and social victories we have seen during the Obama presidency have been substantial, but much more work remains to ensure that Americans have an equal opportunity to succeed; because even though today looks better than it did 8 years ago, what will tomorrow look like?

As for now, and as for me, I am proud to have served in the people's House under this President.

PAYING FOR INFRASTRUCTURE WITHOUT SOAKING THE TAXPAYER

The SPEAKER pro tempore. The Chair recognizes the gentleman from California (Mr. McCLINTOCK) for 5 minutes.

Mr. McCLINTOCK. Mr. Speaker, President-elect Trump has many difficult tasks ahead—one of which is to promote long overdue infrastructure construction at a time when the national debt exceeds our entire economy and interest costs alone are eating us alive. Now, some have said that a rebounding economy resulting from tax reform can pay for it. Well, that may be, but it is not guaranteed, it cannot be accurately forecasted, and we will need any new revenues to beef up our defenses and reduce our deficit—two other critical objectives of the new administration.

Others have proposed tax credits to leverage private capital for infrastructure improvements. But tax credits reduce revenue and widen the deficit. Worse, such public-private partnerships have proven a fertile breeding ground for corruption, crony capitalism, waste, and fraud; and as we learned during the Obama stimulus fiasco, massive government spending might stimulate government, but it does little to stimulate the economy when it is squandered for boondoggles like subsidizing Solyndra and paying cash for clunkers.

So how do we avoid mistakes of the past, control the deficit, protect taxpayers, and yet add $1 trillion of new infrastructure in a way that helps the economy and not just lines the pockets of politically well-connected interests?

First, get government out of the way. Stop obstructing major infrastructure projects like the Keystone Pipeline. Keystone and many other projects like it across the country already have private capital ready to finance them.

Keystone by itself would unleash an estimated $8 billion of privately financed infrastructure construction, and when complete, would mean a half million barrels a day of Canadian crude oil entering U.S. markets.

In my district alone, one abusive official at the Sacramento office of the Army Corps of Engineers single-handedly blocked tens of millions of dollars of critical infrastructure construction desperately sought by local governments in the region. Multiply that across the country, and you can see how many infrastructure projects already are financed but cannot move forward because of Federal obstructionism.

Second, streamline radical regulations that have made many infrastructure projects cost-prohibitive. In my district, the little town of Foresthill gets its water from the Sugar Pine Reservoir, formed by a dam that has an 18-foot spillway, but no spillway gate. The town is trying to increase the reservoir's capacity by adding the missing gate. The gate will cost $2 million, but environmental studies, environmental litigation, and U.S. Forest Service fees have inflated that cost to $11 million. So this project has stalled. Multibillion dollar expansion of Shasta Dam is stalled for similar reasons. Once again, multiply this across the rest of the country.

Third, use revenue bonds to finance capital-intensive projects like dams and bridges. California built its iconic Golden Gate and Bay Bridges with loans from private investors—repaid by tolls that were charged only to the users of the bridges. The taxpayers were never on the hook for a dime, and the loans were paid back ahead of schedule.

The famous California State Water Project constructed 21 dams and more than 700 miles of canals. The revenue bonds and self-liquidating general obligation bonds that financed it were paid back not by general taxpayers, but by the users of the water and power.

Fourth, restore the integrity of our highway trust fund. We built the modern interstate system with the Federal excise tax paid by highway users at the gas pump. The more you drove, the more you paid for the roads you were using. But over the decades, more and more of these funds were bled away to subsidize mass transit and other purposes unrelated to highway construction. Restoring highway taxes for highways would go a long way toward addressing the maintenance and construction backlog.

Fifth, repeal the outdated Davis-Bacon Act that requires Federal projects to pay grossly inflated wages. Think tanks like The Heritage Foundation and the Competitive Enterprise Institute estimate that Davis-Bacon alone inflates total construction costs by roughly 10 percent. That means that just repealing this single act would add one new project for every 10 existing ones at no additional cost.

These are just a few of the ways that massive infrastructure projects can be financed at zero cost to general taxpayers; and because these reforms are actually directed at projects for which there is a demonstrated economic need, political favoritism and corruption inherent in government-directed programs can be greatly reduced.

Mr. Speaker, freedom works; and it is time that we put it and America back to work.

RECOGNIZING LESLIE McGOWAN, HEROINE OF THE MONTH

The SPEAKER pro tempore. The Chair recognizes the gentleman from California (Mr. COSTA) for 5 minutes.

Mr. COSTA. Mr. Speaker, I rise today to recognize Leslie McGowan as November's Heroine of the Month.

The Hero or the Heroine of the Month is an individual in the community in the San Joaquin Valley in California who goes the extra mile to make a positive difference for the people whom I serve.

Leslie is the CEO of Livingston Community Health, a medical and dental provider with community health center locations throughout Merced County.

Leslie has been a part of the team at the Livingston health center for over 10 years, and she has been instrumental in the development of the success of the health center, which enables residents in Merced County to receive health services that would not be otherwise available.

One hundred percent of Merced County is a Health Professional Shortage Area—not enough health care. In other words, the county has a major shortage of primary care physicians.

The Livingston health center has an important role in working to fill that gap so that no one goes untreated. Most recently, Leslie led the efforts for the opening of the Wolves Wellness Center at Livingston High School. It is the only school-based health center in Merced County. It provides medical care, counseling, and dental services to students, their families, and local residents at no or very low cost.

Additionally, Leslie has implemented programs like the Back to School Fair, Homeless Health Day, and an annual scholarship fundraiser to help ensure that people know that they have access to quality and affordable health services. This was all made available as a result of the Affordable Care Act.

Livingston Community Health and its doctors, nurses, and staff work to ensure that individuals who live in rural communities—many rural communities throughout this country, many that I represent—and throughout Merced County have access to quality, affordable health services.

As a strong supporter of community health centers, it is a pleasure to recognize and give a big thank-you to Leslie McGowan and her staff of doctors and nurses at Livingston Community Health.

WATER AND CALIFORNIA'S DROUGHT

Mr. COSTA. Mr. Speaker, I rise today to speak about water and California's ongoing drought. This week, the California Department of Water Resources announced that the 2017 initial allocation for the State Water Project is 20 percent—not good.

I join with drought-stricken communities like those in the San Joaquin Valley and California farmers, farm workers, and farm communities who are all praying that the initial water allocation of 20 percent improves when the Department of Water Resources issues a final allocation not just for the State water projects, but for the Federal water projects as well.

However, with the current operations of California's water system, it would take storms of Biblical proportions for these agencies that are served by the State and Federal Water Project to be able to increase those allocations to 100 percent.

That is why Congress must act now to pass a California water bill that will improve operations to fix our broken water system. We need legislation to provide funding to improve our water infrastructure and to move more water when larger storms make it available, as in last weekend.

California may soon face a sixth consecutive dry year. Therefore, as a result of the drought and the inadequate and broken water system, hundreds of thousands of acre-feet of water have been lost, and 600,000 acres of productive farmland has, unfortunately, been left unplanted.

Some families in my district do not have reliable water to drink, to cook, or to bathe in. The drought, together with the current water policies, are devastating to the San Joaquin Valley.

So, Mr. Speaker, I urge my colleagues to work together in these last few days as we try to assist the people in Flint, Michigan, and to bring together a package of legislation that will end the impasse that we have had and provide water if, in fact, the good Lord sees to bringing rain and snow to the mountains this winter in California.

□ 1030

5A STATE CHAMPIONS: ELK RIVER ELKS

The SPEAKER pro tempore. The Chair recognizes the gentleman from Minnesota (Mr. EMMER) for 5 minutes.

Mr. EMMER of Minnesota. Mr. Speaker, I rise today to congratulate the Elk River High School football team on their Class 5A State Championship victory. Entering the State title game undefeated, the Elks scored an impressive 42 points and rushed for a total of 446 yards over Spring Lake Park at U.S. Bank Stadium last Saturday.

The Elks had an incredible season, averaging 45 points and 449 rushing yards per game. Every Elk deserves mention, but two in particular played a special role in their success—Nick Rice and Sam Gibas.

Rice finished the season with 2,154 rushing yards and a total of 25 touchdowns, and Gibas finished with 1,330 rushing yards and 23 touchdowns.

The Elk River football team worked hard this season under the guidance of Coach Steve Hamilton, and their efforts paid off.

Congratulations for being the 2016 Minnesota State high school football champions.

REMEMBERING A TRUE PUBLIC SERVANT

Mr. EMMER of Minnesota. Mr. Speaker, I rise today to remember the life of St. Francis Police Chief Jake Rehling, who lost his battle with a rare form of cancer last month. What a life he lived. Jake Rehling spent his life working tirelessly to better the St. Francis community and the lives of those around him.

A native Minnesotan, Jake grew up in Onamia and attended Bethel University, where he studied criminal justice. Upon graduation, Jake joined the St. Francis Police Department where he served for 17 years. His passion for his work and the compassion he displayed to others ultimately led to his promotion to St. Francis police chief earlier this year.

Jake was committed to his family and his community. His life is the definition of public service. He will be missed.

I would like to express my sincere condolences to Jake's wife, Brooke, and son, Aiden. Please know the impact Jake had on this world will always be remembered.

REMEMBERING DR. WARREN WARWICK

Mr. EMMER of Minnesota. Mr. Speaker, I rise today to pay tribute to the life and work of Dr. Warren Warwick.

As a professor of pediatrics at the University of Minnesota, Dr. Warwick was a pioneer in the advancement of care for cystic fibrosis patients.

Early in his career, Dr. Warwick founded the University of Minnesota Cystic Fibrosis Clinic, where he served as director for nearly 40 years. Dr. Warwick was known for his compassion, kindness, ingenuity, and tireless commitment to the improvement of patient care.

Because of his work, the Cystic Fibrosis Foundation patient registry was created. Before the creation of the cystic fibrosis registry, cystic fibrosis patients typically lived into their early childhood. Today, many live well beyond their 50s, thanks largely to the advancements and treatment only possible through the patient registry and Dr. Warwick's unwavering commitment to research and excellence in patient care.

In addition to serving his patients, Dr. Warwick honorably served his country for over 30 years in the United States Army Reserve Medical Corps, retiring as a colonel.

His legacy—one of a passionate pursuit of excellence and dedicating his life to helping others—will live on.

DAKOTA ACCESS PIPELINE

The SPEAKER pro tempore. The Chair recognizes the gentlewoman from Hawaii (Ms. GABBARD) for 5 minutes.

Ms. GABBARD. Mr. Speaker, growing up in Hawaii, I learned the value of caring for our home, caring for our planet, and the basic principle that we are all connected in this great chain of cause and effect.

The Dakota Access Pipeline is a threat to this great balance of life. Despite strong opposition from the Standing Rock Sioux and serious concerns raised by the EPA, the Department of the Interior, the Advisory Council on Historic Preservation, and other Federal agencies, the Army Corps of Engineers approved permits to construct the Dakota Access Pipeline without adequately consulting the tribes and without fully evaluating the potential impacts to the neighboring tribal lands, sacred sites, and their water supply. Just one spill near the tribe's reservation could release thousands of barrels of crude oil, contaminating the tribe's drinking water.

The impact of the Dakota Access Pipeline is clear. Energy Transfer Partners, the company that is constructing the Dakota pipeline, has a history of serious pipeline explosions, which have caused injury, death, and significant property damage in the past decade. The future operator of the planned pipeline, Sunoco Logistics Partners, has had over 200 environmentally damaging oil spills in the last 6 years alone, more than in any of its competitors.

Protecting our water is not a partisan political issue; it is an issue that is important to all people and all living beings everywhere. Water is life. We cannot survive without it. Once we allow an aquifer to be polluted, there is very little that can be done about it. This is why it is essential that we prevent our water resources from being polluted in the first place.

Our Founding Fathers took great inspiration from Native American forms of governance and the democratic principles that they were founded on. Their unique form of governance was built on an agreement called the Great Law of Peace, which states that before beginning their deliberations, the council shall be obliged "to express their grati-

tude to their cousins and greet them, and they shall make an address and offer thanks to the Earth where men dwell, to the streams of water, the pools, the springs and the lakes, to the maize and the fruits, to the medicinal herbs and trees, to the forest trees for their usefulness . . . and to the Great Creator who dwells in the heavens above, who gives all the things useful to men, and who is the source and the ruler of health and life."

This recognition of our debt to the Creator and our responsibility to be responsible members of this great web of life was there from the beginning of western democracy.

Freedom is not a buzzword. The freedom of our Founding Fathers was not the freedom to bulldoze wherever you like.

Our freedom is a freedom of mind, a freedom of heart, a freedom to worship as we see fit, freedom from tyranny, and freedom from terror. That is the freedom this country was founded on—the freedom cultivated by America's native people and the freedom that the Standing Rock Sioux are now exercising.

This weekend, I am joining thousands of veterans from all across the country at Standing Rock to stand in solidarity with our Native American brothers and sisters. Together, we call on President Obama to immediately halt the construction of this pipeline, respect the sacred lands of the Standing Rock Sioux, and respect their right to clean water. The truth is whether it is the threat to essential water sources in this region, the lead contaminated water in Flint, Michigan, or the threat posed to a major Hawaii aquifer by the Red Hill fuel leak, each example underscores the vital importance of protecting our water resources.

We cannot undo history, but we must learn lessons from the past and carry them forward, to encourage cooperation among free people, to protect the sacred, and to care for the Earth, for our children and our children's children. What is at stake is our shared heritage of freedom and democracy and our shared future on this great Turtle Island, our United States of America.

RECOGNIZING CAPTAIN WILLIAM B.J. FORE

The SPEAKER pro tempore. The Chair recognizes the gentleman from North Carolina (Mr. MEADOWS) for 5 minutes.

Mr. MEADOWS. Mr. Speaker, I rise today to recognize the service of a great public servant on his retirement—Captain William B.J. Fore.

B.J., as I call him, a great friend from Caldwell County, North Carolina, has served in the Caldwell County Sheriff's Office for a number of years. Today, Mr. Speaker, I could rise and go through a litany of different positions

on how he has served that great county, but it would miss the point, it would miss the point of who B.J. Fore really is.

He is a gentleman that not only do I call a friend, but he is someone who has served Caldwell County over and over again, consistently answering the call with the word "yes."

B.J. Fore has not only served the Caldwell County area in public service as a law enforcement officer, but he has consistently been someone who is always there to serve those that are in need. I remember specifically just a few years back where he and I were working together on trying to serve some of those that were in most need during an event at Halloween time. Some would come in, and there he was making sure that not only children and families were recognized for what they had or didn't have, but some of them, perhaps even that day, showed up to get the meal that only they could have provided at that particular event.

It is a heart of a big man, a big man of courage, that I recognize today on his retirement. I wish him the very heartfelt congratulations on a life that has served Caldwell County so well, and I wish him the very best in his future endeavors.

COMMERCE LEXINGTON

The SPEAKER pro tempore. The Chair recognizes the gentleman from Kentucky (Mr. BARR) for 5 minutes.

Mr. BARR. Mr. Speaker, I rise today to honor Commerce Lexington, the chamber of commerce for my hometown of Lexington, Kentucky, which has been named the 2016 Chamber of the Year by the Association of Chamber of Commerce Executives.

Commerce Lexington won the large chamber category over the great cities of Brooklyn, New York; Jacksonville, Florida; and Tacoma, Washington. This award is recognition of Commerce Lexington's work to promote economic development, job creation, and overall business growth in Lexington and neighboring communities through its many programs and services.

As a member-driven organization, the award is also a reflection of Commerce Lexington's 1,700 members, as well as their volunteers and staff, ably led by CEO and President Bob Quick.

In addition to the Chamber of the Year award, Commerce Lexington also received a Grand Award in Communications for their "Here's Our Proof" marketing campaign during the 2015 Breeders' Cup World Thoroughbred Championships, which showcased central Kentucky and the Bluegrass region as a great place to do business, as well as an ideal location for conventions and tourism. It helped, of course, that American Pharoah did what no other thoroughbred had done in history—win not only the Triple Crown, but also the

Grand Slam of thoroughbred racing going wire to wire in the Breeders' Cup Classic at Keeneland Racecourse—Keeneland, of course, a key member of Commerce Lexington.

Mr. Speaker, I hope that all of my colleagues will join me in congratulating Commerce Lexington on achieving this national honor, and for their hard work to encourage jobs and economic growth in central Kentucky and to share how special our city and our region are with the world—of course, Lexington, the world's horse capital of the world.

RECOGNIZING MASTER FIREFIGHTER MICHAEL CURRY

The SPEAKER pro tempore. The Chair recognizes the gentleman from Georgia (Mr. CARTER) for 5 minutes.

Mr. CARTER of Georgia. Mr. Speaker, I rise today in recognition of Master Firefighter Michael Curry, who passed away in the line of duty on Saturday, November 19, in Savannah, Georgia.

Mr. Curry's work as a firefighter allowed him to do what he loved most—help people. On his last alarm as a firefighter, he rescued seven people from the Savannah River after a ferry boarding platform collapsed. His 13 years of dedication to the Savannah community and the fire department shows in his numerous volunteer activities.

He worked as an emergency medical responder, disaster search and rescue technician, swift water rescue technician, advanced rescue diver, and was involved in groups, including the Alee Temple, the Georgia Critical Incident Stress Foundation, and was the cub master for pack number 4102.

Mr. Michael Curry is a true hero, who died in service to our community running toward an emergency while others sought out safety.

I am heartbroken by this loss. Our community is heartbroken by this loss. I encourage everyone to keep the Curry family and first responders everywhere in your thoughts and prayers.

RECOGNIZING DON LOGANA

Mr. CARTER of Georgia. Mr. Speaker, I rise today in recognition of Don Logana, a longtime reporter in the Savannah community, who passed away on Sunday, November 20.

Mr. Logana joined the local Savannah news station, WTOC, in 2004, and quickly became an integral part of the Savannah news scene and a familiar face in our homes.

□ 1045

His career began in Syracuse, New York, as an intern, but his talent for finding a story and bringing a unique point of view allowed him to quickly rise up the ranks.

When he moved to Savannah, he became the weekday morning anchor for WTOC's "The News at Daybreak" and an investigative reporter who exposed consumer issues. A testament to his talent, Mr. Logana received multiple awards and was honored throughout his career, with the most recent being for the Best Local TV News Anchor 2016 by Connect Savannah.

In addition to his news accomplishments, Mr. Logana had a heart of gold and was constantly involved in the community. In 2011, he competed in "Dancing with Savannah Stars," raising the most money for abused and neglected children.

Mr. Logana's colleagues describe him as a trusted friend to all and someone whose bright, loving personality will be deeply missed.

Mr. Logana's loss is felt by the whole Savannah community. I encourage everyone to keep the Logana family and WTOC Savannah in their thoughts and prayers.

3RD INFANTRY DIVISION'S 99 YEARS OF SERVICE

Mr. CARTER of Georgia. Mr. Speaker, I rise to recognize the U.S. Army's 3rd Infantry Division and its 99 years of service to the United States Armed Forces. The 3rd ID has been located in coastal Georgia for the past 20 years; yet its amazing history dates back to 1917.

During World War I, the 3rd Infantry Division earned the name "Rock of the Marne" by pushing the Germans back across the Marne River and stopping their march to occupy the important allied city of Paris. The 3rd ID continued to fight the Germans at the Marne even as other units retreated.

In 1943, during World War II, the 3rd ID was one of the few divisions to fight the Axis Powers on all European fronts. They fought in north Africa, Italy, France, Germany, and Austria. The 3rd ID even liberated half of French Morocco from the Nazi influence.

Since the World Wars, the 3rd ID has continued to support America's safety and freedom by fighting bravely in the Vietnam war, the Korean war, Operation Desert Storm, and the global war on terrorism.

Thank you to the 3rd ID for your courage, your sacrifice, and your commitment to our national security.

THE DEATH OF FIDEL CASTRO BRINGS AN OPPORTUNITY OF HOPE FOR CUBA

The SPEAKER pro tempore. The Chair recognizes the gentleman from South Carolina (Mr. WILSON) for 5 minutes.

Mr. WILSON of South Carolina. Mr. Speaker, last Friday began a new era for the people of Cuba. For too long, the murderous dictatorship of Fidel Castro has reduced one of Latin America's wealthiest countries to mass poverty in order to benefit the Communist elite and the military.

A recent editorial in The Charleston Post and Courier stated: "Fidel, though he thrived on opposing the U.S., he was long subservient to another superpower, the Soviet Union, until its welcome demise in 1991. He also was an enthusiastic proponent of the Soviets' reckless decision to put weapons of mass destruction aimed at the U.S. in his country."

President-elect Trump has correctly reviewed: "It is my hope that today marks a move away from the horrors endured for too long, and toward a future in which the wonderful Cuban people finally live in the freedom they so richly deserve."

I have been inspired by the late Louis and Nena Gonda, who fled Cuba with their three daughters as all of their property was stolen. They told me about their daughters. They were told to pack for a 2-week visit to visit a sick aunt in New York. They went to a department store there in Cuba, and they bought suitcases. When they arrived home, the secret police were already at the house. They asked them: What are you buying suitcases for? It was explained that they were buying suitcases to go visit a sick aunt in New York and that they would be returning in 2 weeks.

They just didn't have the heart to tell their children—their three young girls—that they would never return to their home, that they would never see their personal property. Their cars, the ones that now appear to be unique, are all stolen cars when you see the classic cars in Cuba. Everything that the family owned was stolen by the Communist government.

They fled to West Columbia, South Carolina, where they worked hard to achieve the American Dream of extraordinary economic success as neighbors in my home County of Lexington, South Carolina.

In conclusion, God bless our troops; and may the President, by his actions, never forget September the 11th in the global war on terrorism.

RECESS

The SPEAKER pro tempore. Pursuant to clause 12(a) of rule I, the Chair declares the House in recess until noon today.

Accordingly (at 10 o'clock and 49 minutes a.m.), the House stood in recess.

□ 1200

AFTER RECESS

The recess having expired, the House was called to order by the Speaker at noon.

PRAYER

The Chaplain, the Reverend Patrick J. Conroy, offered the following prayer:

Loving and gracious God, we give You thanks for giving us another day.

Help us this day to draw closer to You so that, with Your Spirit and aware of Your presence among us, we may all face the tasks of this day.

Bless the Members of the people's House. Help them to think clearly, speak confidently, and act courageously in the belief that all noble service is based upon patience, truth, and love.

You know well the pressing issues facing our Nation. Grant our leaders, especially, the wisdom and magnanimity to do what is best; and may we all join in a common will for the benefit of all constituencies, even though this will take some sacrifice.

May all that is done this day be for Your greater honor and glory.

Amen.

THE JOURNAL

The SPEAKER. The Chair has examined the Journal of the last day's proceedings and announces to the House his approval thereof.

Pursuant to clause 1, rule I, the Journal stands approved.

PLEDGE OF ALLEGIANCE

The SPEAKER. Will the gentleman from Florida (Mr. BILIRAKIS) come forward and lead the House in the Pledge of Allegiance.

Mr. BILIRAKIS led the Pledge of Allegiance as follows:

I pledge allegiance to the Flag of the United States of America, and to the Republic for which it stands, one nation under God, indivisible, with liberty and justice for all.

ANNOUNCEMENT BY THE SPEAKER

The SPEAKER. The Chair will entertain up to 15 requests for 1-minute speeches on each side of the aisle.

RECOGNIZING THE SERVICE OF KIM HOLMES OF DAYTON, OHIO

(Mr. TURNER asked and was given permission to address the House for 1 minute.)

Mr. TURNER. Mr. Speaker, I am here today to recognize the service of Kim Holmes as she retires from over 32 years of combined constituent services to the citizens of Ohio.

Kim Holmes joined my Dayton office in July of 2007 as a caseworker. She began working for me after the retirement of her former boss, Congressman Mike Oxley. Since 2007, Kim has helped thousands of people on my constituent services team. Those numbers increase exponentially when you factor in 23 years of service in Congressman Oxley's office.

Kim's direct, persistent, and dedicated work has helped make a difference in the lives of Ohioans in several of the counties in Ohio: Montgomery, Greene, Fayette, Allen, Auglaize, Champaign, Hancock, Hardin, Logan, Marion, Morrow, Richland, Shelby, and part of Wyandot.

Kim expeditiously resolved problems across multiple issues from veterans, Social Security, Medicare, and immigration by developing a strong and long-lasting relationship with fellow agencies.

I made the point to stop by her office every day I saw her and thanked her for being there. In the words of her constituents, it is probably best reported as to her impact. They have said:

"I don't know what I would have done without you."

"I will never forget your kindness."

"We deeply appreciate your attention to our claim."

"We cannot express our gratitude to you enough."

"I appreciate your help more than words can express."

"There are still good people in this world who still care and want to help. You are one of those."

On behalf of your coworkers and the countless constituents you have assisted, your knowledge, compassion, and efficiency will be sorely missed. Thank you for representing my office in the highest standards. I hope that you enjoy your retirement with your grown children, Jason and Tori, as well as your grandson, Luke.

I wish you all the best.

OHIO STATE UNIVERSITY ATTACK

(Mrs. BEATTY asked and was given permission to address the House for 1 minute.)

Mrs. BEATTY. Mr. Speaker, I rise today to salute the Ohio State University Buckeye community for its strength and resilience in response to the tragic incident when an Ohio State University student rammed his car into a crowd of students on the campus and then stabbed several of them in an attack that ended when a police officer shot and killed him.

I applaud the university president, Michael Drake, university leadership, and its incredible student alert system, along with multiagency police officials for working together to enhance the safety and security of the university. These first responders acted quickly and selflessly, including an Ohio State University police officer who, within seconds, responded to the violence, containing injuries and diffusing the situation.

I thank the medical team and staff at the Wexner Medical Center and surrounding hospitals for treating 11 patients to ensure full recovery.

As the former senior vice president of outreach and engagement at the university, I was never prouder of how we came together quickly in the face of terror. I thank all at the university for continuing to exemplify the Buckeye spirit and remaining united, even in the face of adversity.

Go Bucks.

CONGRATULATING COACH BROOKE GOOD AND THE MESSIAH COLLEGE FIELD HOCKEY TEAM

(Mr. PERRY asked and was given permission to address the House for 1 minute and to revise and extend his remarks.)

Mr. PERRY. Mr. Speaker, I rise today to congratulate Coach Brooke Good and the Messiah College field hockey team of Pennsylvania's Fourth District on their NCAA Division III national championship.

Messiah College played through freezing temperatures, wind, and snow against Tufts University in the NCAA Division III national championship on November 20, and they came away with a 1–0 decision in penalty strokes that will go down as one of the best games in Division III field hockey history.

The Falcons are a great team with a great leader who inspired them to be their best—not only as athletes, but as women of character, determination, pride, and loyalty to each other and to their school.

We are all incredibly proud of you.

THE PUBLIC GOOD

(Ms. JACKSON LEE asked and was given permission to address the House for 1 minute.)

Ms. JACKSON LEE. Mr. Speaker, first, I want to acknowledge that this is World AIDS Day, and much of the success has come because of public funding. That is why I rise today, to talk about the public good and the responsibility of the President and his Cabinet members to do the public good.

I remember when President Clinton was in and generated a major surplus in our budget, 22 million jobs, pursuant to the 1997 budget. We also recognized that the next administration generated enormous tax cuts, low job creation, and a seismic debt that was created because of those tax cuts to the 1 percent.

Now, today, we have the toxicity of two billionaires who head the Treasury Department: the "King of Foreclosures," forced foreclosures, and the other who will head the no-job-creating Commerce Department by this individual.

Rather than supporting full employment or creating jobs, everything will be for the big pockets of the big corporations, not the pockets of the working families, like my constituents.

So I raise the question to Mr. Trump: Where are the appointees that are going to work for the public good? Where are the individuals that are going to have the sufficient wisdom to provide the funding that will support continued work on stifling out and snuffing out HIV/AIDS? Where are those that are going to listen to the people?

This toxic brand has to stop.

HONORING NAVAL SUPPORT ACTIVITY CRANE

(Mr. BUCSHON asked and was given permission to address the House for 1 minute and to revise and extend his remarks.)

Mr. BUCSHON. Mr. Speaker, I rise in honor of a premier U.S. military base in my district, Naval Support Activity Crane.

Seventy-five years ago today, December 1, 1941, Crane Naval Installation officially opened. One week later, Pearl Harbor was bombed, and the need for an ordnance facility safe from attack on the coasts became obvious.

Today, at 100 square miles, Naval Support Activity Crane is the U.S. Navy's third largest installation in the world. The base is home to two vital tenant commands: Naval Surface Warfare Center, a center of excellence in strategic systems, electronic warfare, and expeditionary systems; and Crane Army Ammunition Activity, through which 25 percent of the Department of Defense conventional munitions passes every year.

Crane is also a regional economic powerhouse, supporting 5,000 civilian employees and contributing $2 million a day to Indiana's economy. This critical military asset is a national treasure for research and development and an outstanding Hoosier neighbor. I proudly salute the men and women who call it home.

BUFFALO'S CENTRAL TERMINAL

(Mr. HIGGINS asked and was given permission to address the House for 1 minute.)

Mr. HIGGINS. Mr. Speaker, Buffalo will select a new site for a train station in the next several months and will build a new passenger train terminal in the next 2 years. This offers an opportunity to remake Buffalo's storied Central Terminal.

Selection of the Central Terminal will be a catalyst for the redevelopment of the city's Broadway-Fillmore neighborhood, improve destination choice, and will represent the next exciting iteration of what is possible in the new Buffalo.

This is not simply about building a new train station. Selection of the Central Terminal is a bold statement of confidence and commitment by a city of limitless potential and possibility.

SARAH HUGHES' MIRACLE CURE

(Mr. OLSON asked and was given permission to address the House for 1 minute and to revise and extend his remarks.)

Mr. OLSON. Mr. Speaker, I want the American people to know why I proudly voted for the 21st Century Cures Act last night—six words: Sarah Hughes and systemic juvenile idiopathic arthritis.

Sarah found out she had this autoimmune disorder when she was 11 months old. For over 20 years, she fought intense pain, fevers of 107 degrees, and getting fed through a tube for over a decade.

Her mom, Fiona, was told by her doctors that she would watch her daughter die before she turned 20 years old. Sarah proved those doctors wrong by getting stem cell therapy from Celltex Therapeutics from my own town of Sugar Land, Texas.

Within 2 hours of her first infusion, Sarah felt a change. Here she is today. Her mom, Fiona, summed up Sarah's amazing miracle. She said: "She's her, and I'm me. We're enjoying life together, the way it should be."

REMEMBERING THE SERVICE AND SACRIFICE OF OFFICER COLLIN ROSE

(Mr. KILDEE asked and was given permission to address the House for 1 minute.)

Mr. KILDEE. Mr. Speaker, I rise to pay respects and remember Officer Collin Rose, who was killed in the line of duty last week in Detroit while on patrol near Wayne State University.

To the Rose family, including Collin's fiancee, Nikki, I am terribly sorry for your loss. At just 29 years old, Collin was taken from your family and this world far too soon. Our community, our State, and our country are all standing with you during this difficult time.

His fellow officers described Collin as always being kindhearted and hardworking. One officer said that Collin always had an engaging smile and generous spirit. Another officer said that he was the hardest working person he had ever met.

His grandfather, Clifford Rose, told a local news outlet that at the age of 8, Collin knew he wanted to be a police officer. As an officer at Wayne State, Collin was most passionate, though, about canines and training Clyde, his rottweiler, and Wolverine, a German shorthaired pointer. "His passion was training those dogs," said one of his fellow officers.

This is a terrible loss, and I ask all of my fellow Members of the House of Representatives present to join me in observing and honoring the memory of Collin Rose, his service, and his sacrifice.

HONORING THE LIFE AND SERVICE OF TUSKEGEE AIRMAN WILLIE ROGERS

(Mr. BILIRAKIS asked and was given permission to address the House for 1 minute and to revise and extend his remarks.)

Mr. BILIRAKIS. Mr. Speaker, I rise today to honor the life and service of an American hero from St. Petersburg, Florida, Tuskegee Airman Willie Rogers.

Willie was the oldest remaining Tuskegee Airman from the original legendary 100th Fighter Squadron, the first African American military aviators in the history of the U.S. Armed Forces. He was a part of history, and I am saddened to hear he passed away recently at the incredible age of 101.

Willie truly represented the Greatest Generation: humble, hardworking, and dedicated to his country and his family. He fought the Axis powers and protected our freedom and our way of life, despite the disgraceful way the Tuskegee Airmen were treated.

We would not be the Nation we are today without those who served, Mr. Speaker, and I would like to sincerely thank Willie and his family again for Willie's honorable service and his unwavering love of country.

□ 1215

STOP GUN VIOLENCE

(Ms. KELLY of Illinois asked and was given permission to address the House for 1 minute.)

Ms. KELLY of Illinois. Mr. Speaker, I have spoken on this floor many times about gun violence. This summer, many of us took to the House floor and shut this Chamber down for 26 hours, demanding that Congress do something to stop gun deaths. We almost lost a colleague, Gabby Giffords, to this violence. We stand not too far from the Gabe Zimmerman Room memorializing the brave staffer who lost his life in that Tucson shooting.

I often question if the loss of one of our own family members would be enough for us to act. Just 2 weeks ago, we learned that our esteemed colleague DANNY DAVIS' grandson, Javon Wilson, was shot and killed in Chicago. He was only 15. Javon joins the list of over 700 Chicagoans killed by guns this year.

To those Members that have offered their condolences to Congressman DAVIS, I say this: True concern and compassion requires some action. We can start with the bipartisan background check legislation. We have to start somewhere. Do something so no parent or grandparent has to feel this pain—Congressman DAVIS' pain—ever again.

POLL: MEDIA BIAS THREATENS DEMOCRACY

(Mr. SMITH of Texas asked and was given permission to address the House for 1 minute and to revise and extend his remarks.)

Mr. SMITH of Texas. Mr. Speaker, media bias is a direct threat to our democracy.

When the media doesn't report the facts or reports them in a biased manner, Americans can't make good decisions. If Americans can't make good decisions, our democracy is at risk.

Americans understand this. A recent USA Today/Suffolk University poll found that a majority of Americans believe the media poses a threat to our democracy. Due to its bias, particularly over the last few months, the national media has lost much of its credibility. In fact, the same poll found that less than 8 percent of voters trust the Big Three networks to provide fair and balanced coverage of the news.

Americans agree, the liberal national media is neither objective nor trustworthy.

HONORING DR. DEBRA SAUNDERS-WHITE

(Ms. ADAMS asked and was given permission to address the House for 1 minute.)

Ms. ADAMS. Mr. Speaker, I rise today to honor the life of the late Dr. Debra Saunders-White, a dedicated public servant and chancellor of North Carolina Central University. A cherished friend and confidant, I have never met anyone who worked harder and who gave more.

We often worked together on legislation related to HBCUs. I could always count on her to bring pertinent issues to my attention. She remained involved, even during her illness with cancer.

Prior to joining the Eagle family, Dr. Saunders-White served as acting Assistant Secretary for the Office of Postsecondary Education in the U.S. Department of Education and in university administrations of UNC Wilmington and Hampton University.

As chancellor of North Carolina Central University, Dr. Saunders-White expanded NCCU's course curriculum, helped secure critical investments for the university, and increased graduation rates. During her first week on campus, a campus food bank was opened to serve the needs of students, faculty, and staff.

Dr. Debra Saunders-White, educator-chancellor par excellence, will be sorely missed, but her legacy will live forever.

My thoughts and prayers continue to be with the Saunders-White family, friends, and the NCC University campus.

ADVANCES IN HEALTH

(Mr. LAMALFA asked and was given permission to address the House for 1 minute and to revise and extend his remarks.)

Mr. LAMALFA. Mr. Speaker, yesterday, the House overwhelmingly passed H.R. 34, the 21st Century Cures Act, a bill that offers help to millions of Americans whose needs have been pushed aside for far too long and marks the first step in helping improve our healthcare system, notably in mental health.

I commend my Pennsylvania colleague, Congressman TIM MURPHY, for his dedication and years of hard work on this issue. Back in my district in northern California, these failures have reached crisis levels of this system. In some areas, there are no psychiatric inpatient beds, leaving patients who are suffering to wait days, even weeks, to be seen. That could mean having to travel hundreds of miles for people who need care immediately. In other areas, there is virtually no access to psychiatric care, due to severe physician shortages.

Law enforcement struggle while responding to crisis calls due to lack of training, which has, unfortunately, resulted in tragic outcomes that we see way too many times; as well as the opioid struggles, which is a big challenge for law enforcement and our prosecutors. Heroin really has had a great grip in rural areas like mine in northern California. Indeed, 1,100 overdoses in 8 years.

This bill marks a significant historic, bipartisan effort to right what is wrong with our mental health system. It not only offers solutions, but it offers hope.

I ask my colleagues in the Senate to please take quick action.

WORLD AIDS DAY

(Ms. LEE asked and was given permission to address the House for 1 minute.)

Ms. LEE. Mr. Speaker, I rise today to commemorate World AIDS Day. The theme this year is "Leadership, Commitment, Impact."

First, I would like to thank Leader PELOSI for her steadfast commitment to fighting HIV and AIDS, and for guaranteeing strong United States leadership in this area. Also, to the Congressional Black Caucus for its leadership in the establishment of PEPFAR, which was a bipartisan effort that President Bush signed into law.

As the cofounder and co-chair of the bipartisan Congressional HIV/AIDS Caucus, with Congresswoman ILEANA ROS-LEHTINEN and Congressman MCDERMOTT, we have seen significant progress that we have made in the global fight against AIDS. From PEPFAR and the Global Fund to fight AIDS, TB, and malaria, to the Ryan White Care Act and the Minority AIDS Initiative led by Congresswoman MAXINE WATERS, year after year we have committed critical resources to end this disease.

Partly due to our efforts, 18.2 million people around the world are now living on antiretroviral drugs, and 37 million lives have been saved. But much work remains, which must continue to be bipartisan.

Still, stigma and discrimination prevents too many people from seeking testing and treatment. Around the world, countries criminalize LGBT people and prevent them from accessing critical HIV care. Here in the United States, we preserve stigma through outdated, unscientific laws that criminalize HIV in over 30 States.

We must end these laws and repeal the discrimination laws against people.

COMMUNICATION FROM THE CLERK OF THE HOUSE

The SPEAKER pro tempore (Mr. FORTENBERRY) laid before the House the following communication from the Clerk of the House of Representatives:

OFFICE OF THE CLERK,
HOUSE OF REPRESENTATIVES,
Washington, DC, December 1, 2016.
Hon. PAUL D. RYAN,
The Speaker, House of Representatives,
Washington, DC.

DEAR MR. SPEAKER: Pursuant to the permission granted in Clause 2(h) of Rule II of the Rules of the U.S. House of Representatives, the Clerk received the following message from the Secretary of the Senate on December 1, 2016, at 11:49 a.m.:

That the Senate has made a technical correction to the engrossment of the Senate amendments to the House Concurrent Resolution of September 29, 2016 and hereby returns to the House the papers to accompany the resolution H. Con. Res. 122.

That the Senate concur in House Amendment S. 1550.

With best wishes, I am,

Sincerely,

KAREN L. HAAS.

COMMUNICATION FROM THE CLERK OF THE HOUSE

The SPEAKER pro tempore laid before the House the following communication from the Clerk of the House of Representatives:

OFFICE OF THE CLERK,
HOUSE OF REPRESENTATIVES,
Washington, DC, December 1, 2016.
Hon. PAUL D. RYAN,
The Speaker, House of Representatives,
Washington, DC.

DEAR MR. SPEAKER: Pursuant to the permission granted in Clause 2(h) of Rule II of the Rules of the U.S. House of Representatives, the Clerk received the following message from the Secretary of the Senate on December 1, 2016, at 9:12 a.m.:

That the Senate passed S. 2971.

That the Senate passed S. 3183.

That the Senate passed S. 3386.

That the Senate passed without amendment H.R. 5509.

That the Senate passed without amendment H.R. 5995.

With best wishes, I am,

Sincerely,

KAREN L. HAAS.

PROVIDING FOR CONSIDERATION OF CONFERENCE REPORT ON S. 2943, NATIONAL DEFENSE AUTHORIZATION ACT FOR FISCAL YEAR 2017

Mr. BYRNE. Mr. Speaker, by direction of the Committee on Rules, I call up House Resolution 937 and ask for its immediate consideration.

The Clerk read the resolution, as follows:

H. RES. 937

Resolved, That upon adoption of this resolution it shall be in order to consider the conference report to accompany the bill (S. 2943) to authorize appropriations for fiscal year 2017 for military activities of the Department of Defense, for military construction, and for defense activities of the Department of Energy, to prescribe military personnel strengths for such fiscal year, and for other purposes. All points of order against the conference report and against its consideration are waived. The conference report shall be considered as read. The previous question shall be considered as ordered on the conference report to its adoption without intervening motion except: (1) one hour of debate; and (2) one motion to recommit if applicable.

The SPEAKER pro tempore. The gentleman from Alabama is recognized for 1 hour.

Mr. BYRNE. Mr. Speaker, for the purpose of debate only, I yield the customary 30 minutes to the gentleman from Massachusetts (Mr. McGOVERN), pending which I yield myself such time as I may consume. During consideration of this resolution, all time yielded is for the purpose of debate only.

GENERAL LEAVE

Mr. BYRNE. Mr. Speaker, I ask unanimous consent that all Members may have 5 legislative days to revise and extend their remarks.

The SPEAKER pro tempore. Is there objection to the request of the gentleman from Alabama?

There was no objection.

Mr. BYRNE. Mr. Speaker, House Resolution 937 provides for consideration of the conference report for the National Defense Authorization Act for fiscal year 2017. This marks the 55th consecutive year that the House and Senate are coming together to pass a bill to authorize spending and set policy for our Nation's military.

Just as important, as is the case with most of our work on the Armed Services Committee that I have the privilege to serve on, this was a bipartisan process that allowed for numerous members to have input into the final bill. That is a testament to the great work and leadership of Chairman MAC THORNBERRY, Ranking Member ADAM SMITH, our subcommittee chairmen and the entire committee staff. This is truly a professional team that puts in long hours to make this bill possible, and they deserve a lot of credit for their efforts.

Mr. Speaker, I have said on this floor many times before that our military faces a serious readiness crisis. Budget cuts have really thinned out our military and hurt our ability to train and prepare for conflict.

One of the most startling examples of this readiness crisis is the fact that some of our marines have been forced to get parts for their F–18s off of planes in a museum. That is simply absurd and it is deeply troubling.

Just as bad, less than one-third of Army forces are at acceptable readiness levels for ground combat and our pilots are getting less training than many of our adversaries.

Thankfully, this NDAA stops the drawdown of the military and authorizes critical funding for the operation and maintenance of our military. The bill authorizes important funding for training, helps rebuild outdated infrastructure, and ensures our military men and women have the munitions they need for ongoing operations.

The bill also provides for a 2.1 percent pay increase for our military. This is the largest pay raise for our troops in 6 years, and it is especially important for our military families.

Additionally, the bill supports our Nation's military operations around the globe. As we fight the Islamic State in Iraq and Syria and continue to have a presence in Afghanistan, it is vital that our military has the tools they need to carry out their mission and defeat radical Islamic terrorism.

Just as important, this NDAA provides for a continued military presence in Europe to support our allies and deter Russian aggression, as well as resources to support U.S. operations in the ever-important Pacific.

Finally, the NDAA includes some important reforms to make our military and the Pentagon more effective and more efficient. This includes updates to the Goldwater-Nichols Act to improve the overall organizational structure at the Pentagon and throughout our military.

The bill builds upon recent reforms to the Pentagon's acquisition programs to cut down on red tape and spur innovation and research.

It also updates the Uniform Code of Military Justice to promote accountability within our military.

□ 1230

Mr. Speaker, this is a good bill, but it alone will not be enough to fully turn the tide back in favor of the fully trained, fully capable, and fully equipped military that we need.

Congress and the incoming President must act early next year on a funding bill to fully fund our military, and we need to go above even what is included in this bill. As Chairman THORNBERRY has indicated, we need to push for a defense supplemental that includes important military programs that were, unfortunately, left out of this final bill.

I look forward to working with Chairman THORNBERRY, Ranking Member SMITH, the Appropriations Committee, and the incoming administration to get this funding bill taken care of as soon as possible next year because, without supplemental funding, we will leave the job half done.

While this is just one step in ensuring our military is ready for the fight, it is an important one nonetheless; so I urge my colleagues to join me in supporting this truly bipartisan legislation. For the 55th consecutive year, let's send a message to our servicemembers that supporting the United States military isn't a Republican goal or a Democrat goal—it is an American goal. I urge my colleagues to support House Resolution 937 and the underlying bill.

Mr. Speaker, I reserve the balance of my time.

Mr. McGOVERN. Mr. Speaker, I yield myself such time as I may consume.

Mr. McGOVERN. Mr. Speaker, I thank the gentleman from Alabama (Mr. BYRNE) for yielding me the customary 30 minutes.

Mr. Speaker, I thank the chairman of the House Armed Services Committee, the gentleman from Texas (Mr. THORNBERRY), and the honorable ranking member, the gentleman from Washington (Mr. SMITH), for their service and for concluding work on this conference report, which authorizes resources for our uniformed men and women, civilian defense workforce, our veterans and their families.

The defense bill is one of the most complex bills that comes each year before Congress for consideration and action, and I know the hours'—and the weeks'—and the months'—worth of work that goes into these negotiations by staff and Members. It is also, in general, a bill that receives broad bipartisan support, which is a reflection of the leadership, character, and abilities of the chairman, of the ranking member, and of their staffs.

Mr. Speaker, there is a great deal to support in this conference report and some provisions that continue to raise concern. Some items that were of grave concern have been dropped from the final conference report, like the fiscal cliff, language that would have authorized discrimination by Federal contractors, and some anti-environment riders.

I am very upset, however, that, for the second year in a row, the House caved to unreasonable Senate demands to drop the House-passed provision to honor our Atomic Veterans with a simple service medal. These uniformed men and women literally gave their lives in service to our country. In many cases, totally unprotected, they were exposed to extreme levels of radiation during the post-World War II era and the subsequent cold war period. Because they signed secrecy oaths, they could not even inform their doctors that their many illnesses might be related to radiation exposure.

They never complained, and they did their duty. Their heroism and their service have been publicly recognized by Presidents George H. W. Bush and Bill Clinton. All we are seeking is for them to receive a simple service medal. More than three out of every four of these veterans have already passed away unrecognized for their service; yet the Senate—and Senate Armed Services Committee Chairman JOHN MCCAIN and a handful of Pentagon bureaucrats in particular—seems to think it is a major scandal to provide them with a service medal. My meetings with some at the Pentagon have been particularly troubling because of what I have perceived to be their total lack of sensitivity and their total lack of appreciation for the service that these veterans have provided to our country.

These men and women deserve better from their government. I hope, next year, when the House, once again, includes this bipartisan measure in the defense bill, that it won't be so weak-kneed as to cave for a third time before such unreasonable intransigence.

This conference report, like its most recent predecessors, continues to authorize billions of dollars for our wars against the Islamic State in Syria, Iraq, and elsewhere without any debate on an Authorization for Use of Military Force in those countries and elsewhere.

I hope that one of Speaker RYAN's priorities during the first week of January will be to meet with President-elect Trump and work out a timeline for when Mr. Trump will send an AUMF to Congress on these wars and when the House will finally fulfill its constitutional duty to debate and vote on this matter. For over 2½ years, this House has failed, time and time again, to take up this serious debate even after President Obama sent an AUMF to Capitol Hill for action.

Enough is enough. With a Republican in the White House, I hope the Republican-controlled Congress will finally do its duty. The cowardice of the 113th and 114th Congresses must not be allowed to extend into and infect the 115th Congress.

Mr. Speaker, I want to say one more thing about the NDAA conference report.

This conference report includes a very important title that incorporates the Global Magnitsky Human Rights Accountability Act. As many of my colleagues know, this is a bipartisan measure, championed and introduced in the House by my friend and colleague, Congressman CHRIS SMITH; me; and by BEN CARDIN in the United States Senate.

The Global Magnitsky Act builds on the seminal Sergei Magnitsky Rule of Law Accountability Act, which is legislation that I authored that focused on

Russia, which was approved by Congress and signed into law in 2012. That law targets individual Russian officials who are accountable for the death of Russian lawyer Sergei Magnitsky, as well as other Russian officials engaged in corruption, human rights abuses, or who seek to undermine the rule of law. It denies them visas to the United States and freezes their assets in the United States.

The Global Magnitsky Act will extend the use of those same targeted sanctions to all countries, not just to Russia. It will ensure that visiting the United States and having access to our financial system, including to U.S. dollars, are privileges that should not be granted to those officials who violate basic human rights and the rule of law.

Mr. Speaker, as we enter the uncharted territory of a Trump administration, it is critical that Congress maintain its bipartisan leadership and support for human rights. It is critical that Congress continue to hold accountable the Russian Government and government officials around the world who engage in corruption, human rights abuses, and who flout the rule of law.

During the long campaign, two words I never heard Mr. Trump utter were "human rights." Quite frankly, I was disturbed by his public admiration of Russian strongman Vladimir Putin, whose government has jailed and even killed human rights defenders and political opponents.

Mr. Speaker, in past years, I have often voted against the final passage of the NDAA conference report. In general, I can't vote for a bill that provides tens of billions of dollars for wars that Congress refuses to debate and authorize. I can't vote for a bill that ties the hands of a President—any President—to shut down the prison at the U.S. Naval Base at Guantanamo Bay. I can't support a bloated budget that fails to make hard choices, that provides the Pentagon with even more money than it asks for, and that continues to increase in size—without end—for the foreseeable future.

However, because of the inclusion of the Global Magnitsky Human Rights Accountability Act, this year, I will vote in support of the FY 2017 NDAA conference report. The Global Magnitsky Act will give Congress a tool with which to hold accountable human rights abusers even if our new President ends up turning a blind eye. This language in this authorization bill is important because it sends a signal—no matter what our next President believes on the issue of human rights—that, in this Congress, in a bipartisan way, we believe that, if the United States of America stands for anything, it needs to stand out loud and foursquare for human rights.

I urge all of my colleagues to support the conference report notwithstanding the many reservations we may have.

Mr. Speaker, I reserve the balance of my time.

Mr. BYRNE. Mr. Speaker, I yield 3 minutes to the gentleman from Oklahoma (Mr. COLE), a distinguished member of the Rules Committee and a distinguished member of the Appropriations Committee.

Mr. COLE. I thank the gentleman from Alabama for yielding. Frankly, I thank him for the wonderful work he provided as a member of the Armed Services Committee to bring this legislation to the floor today.

Mr. Speaker, I also want to quickly associate myself with my friend from Massachusetts' remarks about the authorization. I think he is absolutely right on that issue—we have worked together on that—and it is something that ought to happen. It is an institutional question of whether or not we retain our war-making authority, and he has done admirable work in that area.

The bill, itself, which I support—and, of course, the rule and the underlying legislation—is a very important piece of legislation.

I commend our friends on the Armed Services Committee for working in a bipartisan fashion, first, to make sure they stop the erosion of the end strength of the military. It is an absolutely critical thing to do. It could not have happened had they not worked together and made some tough decisions.

Second, I want to point out all of the reforms in this legislation—procurement reforms, in particular. They have gone well beyond simply appropriating money for the military as they have done some important work to put important tools in our hands that, I think in going forward, will save billions of dollars.

I also commend them for fully funding a pay raise for the men and women in uniform. That is an important thing. The amount of money—a 2.1 percent increase—is relatively modest but appropriate. The more important thing is the signal it sends to the men and women who put themselves between us and harm's way, and I thank the gentleman for his role in that.

Finally, I want to pick up on one of the points that my friend from Alabama made that I couldn't agree with more. As important and as good as this legislation is, if we do not marry it with the money that it takes to actually implement it, we are making the mistake of a lifetime. In my opinion, we could do that, literally, this year if we were to do an omnibus; but if we fail to do that and if we do a CR, my friend is exactly right in that we should act as rapidly as possible in January to make sure that we actually put the money together with the excellent authorization work that is done here. Otherwise, we simply undercut all of the good work of the Armed Services Committee.

This is something that we need to focus on. The authorization is important, but if we don't appropriate the money, a lot of the hard work that was done on the Armed Services Committee will be for naught, and it will be for naught until we actually make that decision. We shouldn't wait until the end of April or the end of May. We ought to get it done as quickly as we can. I would like to get it done before we go home, but if we can't do that, we certainly ought to get it done as quickly as we can when we get back.

With all of that aside, again, I congratulate both sides of the aisle. This is a model of bipartisanship. My friend from Massachusetts mentioned some other measures in here with regard to Russia that, I think, are absolutely also appropriate, and I applaud their inclusion.

I urge every Member to support the rule and, certainly, to vote for the underlying legislation.

Mr. MCGOVERN. Mr. Speaker, I yield 3 minutes to the gentleman from New York (Mr. ENGEL), the distinguished ranking member of the Committee on Foreign Affairs.

Mr. ENGEL. I thank the gentleman for yielding to me.

Mr. Speaker, I support the defense authorization bill. Our men and women in uniform are the greatest fighting force in the world, and they deserve our unwavering support. I thank Chairman THORNBERRY and Ranking Member SMITH for their hard work on this year's effort, but I oppose the rule because this bill could be made better not by expanding it, but by taking out parts that don't belong there in the first place.

Year after year, Congress has placed more and more diplomatic prerogatives under the military's purview. There are 80 provisions from the House and Senate bills in the conference report that cross into the jurisdiction of the Foreign Affairs Committee. As that committee's ranking member, I am grateful to my friend, Mr. SMITH of Washington, as we have worked together to improve these parts of the bill; but different agencies have different responsibilities and capabilities. That is why different committees oversee these issues.

We would never ask a group of Foreign Service Officers to carry out a targeted strike on an enemy. That is not their job. So why would we assign diplomatic functions to those who are already handling the tall order of protecting and defending us?

Take the Asia Maritime Security Initiative—a program seeking greater collaboration among our Asian partners to solve maritime disputes peacefully. This is the sort of effort that our diplomats are trained to deal with. It takes time and precision and patience to develop interest among governments and to ramp up capacity; but the Pentagon moved ahead without the State Department, and the DOD's approach was like performing surgery with a hacksaw.

The Philippines and Vietnam were slow to come on board. That is where, I believe, careful diplomacy would have paid off. Instead, the DOD threw money at the problem. The Philippines didn't want the money, and they weren't ready to absorb it; so the effort fell apart. Now, in a difficult time in American-Philippines relations, we have a gaping hole in our maritime security strategy. This should be a lesson learned, but, instead, this bill will put even more diplomatic responsibility in military hands.

For instance, the bill diverts Defense Department dollars to the Global Engagement Center, the GEC. It is a State Department program that is focused on countering violent extremist propaganda overseas. The goal of this provision is worthwhile, but the way it is written ignores overwhelming advice from experts in the field and from our public diplomacy officials who are already hard at work in Foggy Bottom. Instead of building on what we already know from years of countering propaganda, it says that the DOD should decide how much money to give a State Department program. Mr. Speaker, that is just bad policy, and that example just scratches the surface.

□ 1245

So I support the underlying bill because it is good for our military, but I don't support this rule. I did not sign the conference report because I have deep concerns that the line between our military and diplomatic efforts is blurring. We will be back here in a year, and I hope at that time we will pass a defense authorization that deals just with defense.

Mr. BYRNE. Mr. Speaker, I am prepared to close.

I reserve the balance of my time.

Mr. MCGOVERN. Mr. Speaker, I yield myself such time as I may consume.

I am going to urge my colleagues to defeat the previous question. And if we defeat the previous question, I will offer an amendment to the rule to bring up legislation authored by the gentlewoman from California (Ms. ESHOO), who has been a leader on this issue, that would require Presidential nominees to disclose 3 years of their tax returns.

Mr. Speaker, tax returns provide the public with vital information about our Presidential candidates. Have they paid taxes at all? Do they keep money offshore? Or have they taken advantage of tax loopholes? This is important information that voters have a right to know. The American people should expect candidates running for President to be open and transparent about their tax returns, and this legislation would ensure that transparency. It is hard for me to believe that giving the people the right to know about a Presidential candidate's financial dealings is controversial. I hope that this isn't.

Mr. Speaker, I ask unanimous consent to insert the text of the amendment in the RECORD, along with extraneous material immediately prior to the vote on the previous question.

The SPEAKER pro tempore. Is there objection to the request of the gentleman from Massachusetts?

There was no objection.

Mr. MCGOVERN. Mr. Speaker, to discuss our proposal, I yield 3 minutes to the distinguished gentlewoman from California (Ms. ESHOO).

Ms. ESHOO. Mr. Speaker, I rise today to urge all House Members to defeat the previous question so that this bipartisan, bicameral legislation, the Presidential Tax Transparency Act, can be made in order for immediate floor debate and a vote.

Now, the legislation is really very simple. It requires Presidential nominees of major political parties to file 3 previous years of their Federal tax returns with the Federal Election Commission. Now, tax returns contain vital information. We all know that. But it is also vital for the public, for voters, to consider. They should be able to know whether a candidate has paid taxes, if they have paid any taxes, how much they have paid, whether they have made charitable contributions and to whom, and whether they took advantage of tax loopholes or offshore tax shelters.

This election year, we experienced a bipartisan problem in this area. For the first time since 1976, Mr. Trump, who is now the President-elect, would not release any tax returns to the public whatsoever. And on the Democratic side, Senator SANDERS only disclosed a summary of 1 year of his tax returns. I think that these are areas that demonstrate themselves to fall far short of what the American people deserve in terms of transparency. So this legislation ensures that the custom of disclosing—and it has been a custom since 1976—that they disclose multiple years of tax returns and that it be required by Federal law for future Presidential candidates to do so.

Former Presidential candidate Mitt Romney stated earlier this year that: "Tax returns provide the public with its sole confirmation of the veracity of a candidate's representations regarding charities, priorities, wealth, tax conformance, and conflicts of interest."

One of the Republican cosponsors of my bill, Congressman MARK SANFORD, wrote in The New York Times in August: "The Presidency is the most powerful political position on Earth, and the idea of enabling the voter the chance to see how a candidate has handled his or her finances is a central part of making sure the right person gets the job."

So I rise today because I believe Congress should write this important disclosure tradition into law. I urge my colleagues to reject the previous question so we can hold an immediate vote on the Presidential Tax Transparency Act.

Mr. BYRNE. Mr. Speaker, I yield myself such time as I may consume.

It is not unusual for me to come down here to handle pieces of legislation for the Rules Committee that pertain to our national defense and find myself in a debate about issues that have nothing to do with national defense. Whatever else you can say about the issue about the President or the President-elect providing tax returns, it has nothing to do with the defense of the United States of America. It has nothing to do with authorizing what the Army, the Marine Corps, the Air Force, and the Navy need to defend this country.

So whatever may be the merits of the proposal we just heard from the gentlewoman from California, it is totally irrelevant to the piece of legislation and the resolution on the rules before this body. So I think that it is an interesting argument. Maybe there is another time to have it, but this is not that time.

We need to stay focused on what needs to be authorized to defend the United States of America, and I would urge my colleagues to reject the notion that we just heard.

I reserve the balance of my time.

Mr. McGOVERN. Mr. Speaker, I yield myself the balance of my time.

Mr. Speaker, let me disagree with my distinguished colleague that somehow this has nothing to do with national defense. I strongly disagree with him on that. I think where a Presidential candidate or a soon-to-be President has financial dealings is related directly to our national defense. Does he have investments in Russia? Does he have investments in countries that have been hostile to human rights or to U.S. interests in various parts of the world? That is very relevant.

One of the reasons why we are utilizing this mechanism of defeating the previous question—by the way, if we defeat the previous question, we still get to bring up the defense authorization conference report. But one of the reasons that we do it is because—the way this House operates is that, if you are in the minority, you don't get an opportunity to get any of your amendments made in order or your bills made in order, especially bills of any consequence. So that is why we are utilizing this. This is very relevant to our national defense.

As I said, I normally vote against these authorization bills because I think they are overbloated. I think there are issues concerning the fact that we spend billions of dollars on wars that we never debate or we don't

properly authorize here in the Congress.

But I am voting for this one because of the Global Magnitsky legislation because of the human rights provisions. Because I don't know where the head of our next President is going to be when it comes to standing up to abuses by people like Vladimir Putin, against opposition leaders and journalists and anybody he disagrees with.

This bill is named after a guy named Sergei Magnitsky who, by the way, was an accountant in Russia who uncovered the largest corruption scandal in Russia's history. What was his reward for doing that? Putin had him put in jail. He was tortured, and he was beaten to death. You know, that is what happens in places that are run by strongmen like Vladimir Putin.

So, yeah, I would like to know whether or not our next President has investments in Russia. I think that would be very relevant to know. Quite frankly, the reason why this Magnitsky legislation is so important is it gives us a tool to pressure the next administration on the issue of human rights, and it is a signal to people like Putin and other dictators and strongmen around the world that Congress is not going to be silent in the face of human rights abuses. So I think this is all very relevant.

I would urge my colleagues to vote "no" on the previous question so we can do what I would think most people in this country think is noncontroversial, which is to have people running for President release their tax returns so we know. This shouldn't be a big deal. We should do it now, and we have an opportunity to do it now and still vote on this NDAA bill. I hope that we will do that.

Mr. Speaker, I include in the RECORD a letter from 20 national organizations voicing concern about the $3.2 billion added to the overseas contingency operations account in funds not requested by the Pentagon.

DEAR SENATOR/REPRESENTATIVE: The recently released conference report for the Fiscal Year 2017 National Defense Authorization Act (NDAA) would authorize an additional $3.2 billion unrequested by the Pentagon, effectively exceeding the spending limits set in place previously by Congress as part of the Budget Control Act of 2011 and Bipartisan Budget Act of 2015. As organizations representing Americans across the political spectrum, we are writing to voice our disagreement with this tactic.

The very real challenges facing our military are not the result of a lack of funds. They are the result of years of failing to make necessary, tough choices our nation's security requires. If Congress votes to simply throw additional billions of dollars at this problem by using a budgetary gimmick involving the Overseas Contingency Operations (OCO) account, you will do nothing to solve these problems. Rather, you will simply be guaranteeing another year of massive spending at the Pentagon. Refusing to make hard choices and trade-offs does not strengthen our security, it undermines it.

Earlier this year, many of our organizations expressed our opposition to the House Armed Services Committee's draft NDAA which included an $18 billion gimmick to fund the OCO account above previously agreed upon levels. What was a bad idea at $18 billion is still a bad idea at $3.2 billion. We strongly urge you to scrap any plans to fund the OCO account above the levels set in existing law and finally pursue a path of fiscal responsibility at the Pentagon.

Sincerely,

Campaign for Liberty, Center for International Policy, Council for a Livable World, Council for Citizens Against Government Waste, FreedomWorks, Friends Committee on National Legislation, Just Foreign Policy, National Priorities Project, National Taxpayers Union, Peace Action, Project on Government Oversight, Taxpayers for Common Sense, Taxpayers Protection Alliance, Taxpayers United of America, The Libertarian Institute, The London Center, United for Peace and Justice, Win Without War, Women's Action for New Directions.

Mr. McGOVERN. Mr. Speaker, one of my many concerns about this bill—and if it wasn't for the Global Magnitsky Human Rights Accountability Act, I would be voting against this bill because of things like that.

Vote "no" on the previous question. Let the American people know what the financial dealings of their Presidential candidates and soon-to-be Presidents are, and then we get on to dealing with passing the National Defense Authorization Act.

I yield back the balance of my time.

Mr. BYRNE. Mr. Speaker, I yield myself the balance of my time to close.

The Presidential election is over. Maybe some people would like to relitigate the results, but certainly the National Defense Authorization Act is not the place to do that. So we need to get back to the focus of what we are here about today, and that is authorizing the defense of the United States of America.

I appreciate the gentleman's support for the rule. I appreciate his support, which he says is unusual for the underlying bill. I also agree with him, as I heard the gentleman from Oklahoma agree with him, about the need for us in the future to address an authorization for the use of military force in the Middle East.

I don't know what the authorization is under law for what we are undertaking today in Yemen, what we are undertaking today in Libya, or what we are undertaking today in other countries like Somalia. I hope the new administration will take a complete new look at that and come to us and tell us what they think a real strategy for success and victory is. Now, that is something we could all get together and authorize. This is not the piece of legislation to address it, and I appreciate the fact that my friend is willing to drop his concerns about that to support it.

We are here to do one very important thing—and it is the most important thing that the Congress does—and that is to provide for the defense of the American people, pure and simple. This rule, the underlying legislation, does that.

There is more work to be done at the beginning of next year, and I hope and am confident that there will be a real effort to come back and do that. At this point in time, it is important that we move forward with this National Defense Authorization Act for the 55th straight year.

Mr. Speaker, I again urge my colleagues to support House Resolution 937 and the underlying bill.

The material previously referred to by Mr. McGovern is as follows:

AN AMENDMENT TO H. RES. 937 OFFERED BY MR. McGOVERN

At the end of the resolution, add the following new sections:

SEC. 2. Immediately upon adoption of this resolution the Speaker shall, pursuant to clause 2(b) of rule XVIII, declare the House resolved into the Committee of the Whole House on the state of the Union for consideration of the bill (H.R. 5386) to amend the Federal Election Campaign Act of 1971 to require candidates of major parties for the office of President to disclose recent tax return information. The first reading of the bill shall be dispensed with. All points of order against consideration of the bill are waived. General debate shall be confined to the bill and shall not exceed one hour equally divided among and controlled by the chair and ranking minority member of the Committee on Ways and Means and the chair and ranking minority member of the Committee on House Administration. After general debate the bill shall be considered for amendment under the five-minute rule. All points of order against provisions in the bill are waived. At the conclusion of consideration of the bill for amendment the Committee shall rise and report the bill to the House with such amendments as may have been adopted. The previous question shall be considered as ordered on the bill and amendments thereto to final passage without intervening motion except one motion to recommit with or without instructions. If the Committee of the Whole rises and reports that it has come to no resolution on the bill, then on the next legislative day the House shall, immediately after the third daily order of business under clause 1 of rule XIV, resolve into the Committee of the Whole for further consideration of the bill.

SEC. 3. Clause 1(c) of rule XIX shall not apply to the consideration of H.R. 5386.

THE VOTE ON THE PREVIOUS QUESTION: WHAT IT REALLY MEANS

This vote, the vote on whether to order the previous question on a special rule, is not merely a procedural vote. A vote against ordering the previous question is a vote against the Republican majority agenda and a vote to allow the Democratic minority to offer an alternative plan. It is a vote about what the House should be debating.

Mr. Clarence Cannon's Precedents of the House of Representatives (VI, 308–311), describes the vote on the previous question on the rule as "a motion to direct or control the consideration of the subject before the House being made by the Member in charge." To defeat the previous question is to give the opposition a chance to decide the subject before the House. Cannon cites the Speaker's ruling of January 13, 1920, to the effect that

"the refusal of the House to sustain the demand for the previous question passes the control of the resolution to the opposition" in order to offer an amendment. On March 15, 1909, a member of the majority party offered a rule resolution. The House defeated the previous question and a member of the opposition rose to a parliamentary inquiry, asking who was entitled to recognition. Speaker Joseph G. Cannon (R–Illinois) said: "The previous question having been refused, the gentleman from New York, Mr. Fitzgerald, who had asked the gentleman to yield to him for an amendment, is entitled to the first recognition."

The Republican majority may say "the vote on the previous question is simply a vote on whether to proceed to an immediate vote on adopting the resolution . . . [and] has no substantive legislative or policy implications whatsoever." But that is not what they have always said. Listen to the Republican Leadership Manual on the Legislative Process in the United States House of Representatives, (6th edition, page 135). Here's how the Republicans describe the previous question vote in their own manual: "Although it is generally not possible to amend the rule because the majority Member controlling the time will not yield for the purpose of offering an amendment, the same result may be achieved by voting down the previous question on the rule. . . . When the motion for the previous question is defeated, control of the time passes to the Member who led the opposition to ordering the previous question. That Member, because he then controls the time, may offer an amendment to the rule, or yield for the purpose of amendment."

In Deschler's Procedure in the U.S. House of Representatives, the subchapter titled "Amending Special Rules" states: "a refusal to order the previous question on such a rule [a special rule reported from the Committee on Rules] opens the resolution to amendment and further debate." (Chapter 21, section 21.2) Section 21.3 continues: "Upon rejection of the motion for the previous question on a resolution reported from the Committee on Rules, control shifts to the Member leading the opposition to the previous question, who may offer a proper amendment or motion and who controls the time for debate thereon."

Clearly, the vote on the previous question on a rule does have substantive policy implications. It is one of the only available tools for those who oppose the Republican majority's agenda and allows those with alternative views the opportunity to offer an alternative plan.

Mr. BYRNE. Mr. Speaker, I yield back the balance of my time, and I move the previous question on the resolution.

The SPEAKER pro tempore. The question is on ordering the previous question.

The question was taken; and the Speaker pro tempore announced that the ayes appeared to have it.

Mr. McGOVERN. Mr. Speaker, on that I demand the yeas and nays.

The yeas and nays were ordered.

The SPEAKER pro tempore. Pursuant to clause 8 of rule XX, further proceedings on this question will be postponed.

□ 1300

PERMISSION TO POSTPONE PROCEEDINGS ON MOTION TO RECOMMIT ON H.R. 6392, SYSTEMIC RISK DESIGNATION IMPROVEMENT ACT OF 2016

Mr. HENSARLING. Mr. Speaker, I ask unanimous consent that the question of adopting a motion to recommit on H.R. 6392 may be subject to postponement as though under clause 8 of rule XX.

The SPEAKER pro tempore. Is there objection to the request of the gentleman from Texas?

There was no objection.

SYSTEMIC RISK DESIGNATION IMPROVEMENT ACT OF 2016

Mr. HENSARLING. Mr. Speaker, pursuant to House Resolution 934, I call up the bill (H.R. 6392) to amend the Dodd-Frank Wall Street Reform and Consumer Protection Act to specify when bank holding companies may be subject to certain enhanced supervision, and for other purposes, and ask for its immediate consideration.

The Clerk read the title of the bill.

The SPEAKER pro tempore. Pursuant to House Resolution 934, the bill is considered read.

The text of the bill is as follows:

H.R. 6392

Be it enacted by the Senate and House of Representatives of the United States of America in Congress assembled,

SECTION 1. SHORT TITLE.

This Act may be cited as the "Systemic Risk Designation Improvement Act of 2016".

SEC. 2. TABLE OF CONTENTS.

The table of contents for the Dodd-Frank Wall Street Reform and Consumer Protection Act (12 U.S.C. 5301 et seq.) is amended by striking the item relating to section 113 and inserting the following:

"Sec. 113. Authority to require enhanced supervision and regulation of certain nonbank financial companies and certain bank holding companies.".

SEC. 3. REVISIONS TO COUNCIL AUTHORITY.

(a) PURPOSES AND DUTIES.—Section 112 of the Dodd-Frank Wall Street Reform and Consumer Protection Act (12 U.S.C. 5322) is amended in subsection (a)(2)(I) by inserting before the semicolon ", which have been the subject of a final determination under section 113".

(b) BANK HOLDING COMPANY DESIGNATION.— Section 113 of the Dodd-Frank Wall Street Reform and Consumer Protection Act (12 U.S.C. 5323) is amended—

(1) by amending the heading for such section to read as follows: "**AUTHORITY TO REQUIRE ENHANCED SUPERVISION AND REGULATION OF CERTAIN NONBANK FINANCIAL COMPANIES AND CERTAIN BANK HOLDING COMPANIES**";

(2) by redesignating subsections (c), (d), (e), (f), (g), (h), and (i) as subsections (d), (e), (f), (g), (h), (i), and (j), respectively;

(3) by inserting after subsection (b) the following:

"(c) BANK HOLDING COMPANIES SUBJECT TO ENHANCED SUPERVISION AND PRUDENTIAL STANDARDS UNDER SECTION 165.—

"(1) DETERMINATION.—The Council, on a nondelegable basis and by a vote of not fewer than ⅔ of the voting members then serving, including an affirmative vote by the Chairperson, may determine that a bank holding company shall be subject to enhanced supervision and prudential standards by the Board of Governors, in accordance with section 165, if the Council determines, based on the considerations in paragraph (2), that material financial distress at the bank holding company, or the nature, scope, size, scale, concentration, interconnectedness, or mix of the activities of the bank holding company, could pose a threat to the financial stability of the United States.

"(2) CONSIDERATIONS.—In making a determination under paragraph (1), the Council shall use the indicator-based measurement approach established by the Basel Committee on Banking Supervision to determine systemic importance, which considers—

"(A) the size of the bank holding company;

"(B) the interconnectedness of the bank holding company;

"(C) the extent of readily available substitutes or financial institution infrastructure for the services of the bank holding company;

"(D) the global cross-jurisdictional activity of the bank holding company; and

"(E) the complexity of the bank holding company.

"(3) GSIBs DESIGNATED BY OPERATION OF LAW.—Notwithstanding any other provision of this subsection, a bank holding company that is designated, as of the date of enactment of this subsection, as a Global Systemically Important Bank by the Financial Stability Board shall be deemed to have been the subject of a final determination under paragraph (1).";

(4) in subsection (d), as so redesignated—

(A) in paragraph (1)(A), by striking "subsection (a)(2) or (b)(2)" and inserting "subsection (a)(2), (b)(2), or (c)(2)"; and

(B) in paragraph (4), by striking "Subsections (d) through (h)" and inserting "Subsections (e) through (i)";

(5) in subsections (e), (f), (g), (h), (i), and (j)—

(A) by striking "subsections (a) and (b)" each place such term appears and inserting "subsections (a), (b), and (c)"; and

(B) by striking "nonbank financial company" each place such term appears and inserting "bank holding company for which there has been a determination under subsection (c) or nonbank financial company";

(6) in subsection (g), as so redesignated, by striking "subsection (e)" and inserting "subsection (f)";

(7) in subsection (h), as so redesignated, by striking "subsection (a), (b), or (c)" and inserting "subsection (a), (b), (c), or (d)"; and

(8) in subsection (i), as so redesignated, by striking "subsection (d)(2), (e)(3), or (f)(5)" and inserting "subsection (e)(2), (f)(3), or (g)(5)".

(c) ENHANCED SUPERVISION.—Section 115 of the Dodd-Frank Wall Street Reform and Consumer Protection Act (12 U.S.C. 5325) is amended—

(1) in subsection (a)(1), by striking "large, interconnected bank holding companies" and inserting "bank holding companies which have been the subject of a final determination under section 113";

(2) in subsection (a)(2)—

(A) in subparagraph (A), by striking "; or" at the end and inserting a period;

(B) by striking "the Council may" and all that follows through "differentiate" and inserting "the Council may differentiate"; and

(C) by striking subparagraph (B); and

(3) in subsection (b)(3), by striking "subsections (a) and (b) of section 113" each place such term appears and inserting "subsections (a), (b), and (c) of section 113".

(d) REPORTS.—Section 116(a) of the Dodd-Frank Wall Street Reform and Consumer Protection Act (12 U.S.C. 5326(a)) is amended by striking "with total consolidated assets of $50,000,000,000 or greater" and inserting "which has been the subject of a final determination under section 113".

(e) MITIGATION.—Section 121 of the Dodd-Frank Wall Street Reform and Consumer Protection Act (12 U.S.C. 5331) is amended—

(1) in subsection (a), by striking "with total consolidated assets of $50,000,000,000 or more" and inserting "which has been the subject of a final determination under section 113"; and

(2) in subsection (c), by striking "subsection (a) or (b) of section 113" and inserting "subsection (a), (b), or (c) of section 113".

(f) OFFICE OF FINANCIAL RESEARCH.—Section 155 of the Dodd-Frank Wall Street Reform and Consumer Protection Act (12 U.S.C. 5345) is amended in subsection (d) by striking "with total consolidated assets of 50,000,000,000 or greater" and inserting "which have been the subject of a final determination under section 113".

SEC. 4. REVISIONS TO BOARD AUTHORITY.

(a) ACQUISITIONS.—Section 163 of the Dodd-Frank Wall Street Reform and Consumer Protection Act (12 U.S.C. 5363) is amended by striking "with total consolidated assets equal to or greater than $50,000,000,000" each place such term appears and inserting "which has been the subject of a final determination under section 113".

(b) MANAGEMENT INTERLOCKS.—Section 164 of the Dodd-Frank Wall Street Reform and Consumer Protection Act (12 U.S.C. 5364) is amended by striking "with total consolidated assets equal to or greater than $50,000,000,000" and inserting "which has been the subject of a final determination under section 113".

(c) ENHANCED SUPERVISION AND PRUDENTIAL STANDARDS.—Section 165 of the Dodd-Frank Wall Street Reform and Consumer Protection Act (12 U.S.C. 5365) is amended—

(1) in subsection (a), by striking "with total consolidated assets equal to or greater than $50,000,000,000" and inserting "which have been the subject of a final determination under section 113";

(2) in subsection (a)(2)—

(A) by striking "(A) IN GENERAL.—"; and

(B) by striking subparagraph (B);

(3) by striking "subsections (a) and (b) of section 113" each place such term appears and inserting "subsections (a), (b), and (c) of section 113"; and

(4) in subsection (j), by striking "with total consolidated assets equal to or greater than $50,000,000,000" and inserting "which has been the subject of a final determination under section 113".

(d) CONFORMING AMENDMENT.—The second subsection (s) (relating to "Assessments, Fees, and Other Charges for Certain Companies") of section 11 of the Federal Reserve Act (12 U.S.C. 248) is amended—

(1) by redesignating such subsection as subsection (t); and

(2) in paragraph (2)—

(A) in subparagraph (A), by striking "having total consolidated assets of $50,000,000,000 or more;" and inserting "which have been the subject of a final determination under section 113 of the Dodd-Frank Wall Street Reform and Consumer Protection Act; and";

(B) by striking subparagraph (B); and

(C) by redesignating subparagraph (C) as subparagraph (B).

SEC. 5. EFFECTIVE DATE; RULE OF APPLICATION.

(a) EFFECTIVE DATE.—The Financial Stability Oversight Council may begin proceedings with respect to a bank holding company under section 113(c)(1) of the Dodd-Frank Wall Street Reform and Consumer Protection Act, as added by this Act, on the date of the enactment of this Act, but may not make a final determination under such section 113(c)(1) with respect to a bank holding company before the end of the 1-year period beginning on the date of the enactment of this Act.

(b) IMMEDIATE APPLICATION TO LARGE BANK HOLDING COMPANIES.—During the 1-year period described under subsection (a), a bank holding company with total consolidated assets equal to or greater than $50,000,000,000 shall be deemed to have been the subject of a final determination under section 113(c)(1) of the Dodd-Frank Wall Street Reform and Consumer Protection Act.

SEC. 6. EXISTING ASSESSMENT TERMINATION SCHEDULE.

(a) TEMPORARY EXTENSION OF EXISTING ASSESSMENT.—

(1) IN GENERAL.—Each bank holding company with total consolidated assets equal to or greater than $50,000,000,000 and which has not been the subject of a final determination under section 113 of the Dodd-Frank Wall Street Reform and Consumer Protection Act (12 U.S.C. 5323) shall be subject to assessments by the Secretary of the Treasury to the same extent as a bank holding company that has been subject to such a final determination.

(2) LIMITATION ON AMOUNT OF ASSESSMENTS.—The aggregate amount collected pursuant to paragraph (1) from all bank holding companies assessed under such paragraph shall be $115,000,000.

(3) EXPEDITED ASSESSMENTS.—If necessary, the Secretary of the Treasury shall expedite assessments made pursuant to paragraph (1) to ensure that all $115,000,000 of assessments permitted by paragraph (2) is collected before fiscal year 2018.

(4) PAYMENT PERIOD OPTIONS.—The Secretary of the Treasury shall offer the option of payments spread out before the end of fiscal year 2018, or shorter periods including the option of a one-time payment, at the discretion of each bank holding company paying assessments pursuant to paragraph (1).

(5) ASSESSMENTS TO BE MADE IN ADDITION TO ANY OTHER ASSESSMENTS.—The assessments collected pursuant to paragraph (1) shall be in addition to, and not as a replacement of, any assessments required under any other law.

(b) USE OF ASSESSMENTS.—Of the total amount collected pursuant to subsection (a)—

(1) $60,000,000 shall be transferred to the Financial Stability Oversight Council to pay for any administrative costs resulting from this Act and the amendments made by this Act, of which the Financial Stability Oversight Council shall distribute $20,000,000 to the Board of Governors of the Federal Reserve System, $20,000,000 to the Federal Deposit Insurance Corporation, and $20,000,000 to the general fund of the Treasury; and

(2) $55,000,000 shall be transferred to the Federal Deposit Insurance Corporation to pay for any resolution costs resulting from this Act and the amendments made by this Act.

(c) TREATMENT UPON DETERMINATION.—A bank holding company assessed under this section shall no longer be subject to such assessments in the event it is subject to a final determination under section 113 of the Dodd-Frank Wall Street Reform and Consumer Protection Act (12 U.S.C. 5323). Any prior payments made by such a banking holding company pursuant to an assessment under this section shall be nonrefundable.

(d) RULE OF CONSTRUCTION.—A bank holding company deemed to have been the subject of a final determination under section 113 of the Dodd-Frank Wall Street Reform and Consumer Protection Act (12 U.S.C. 5323) under section 5(b) shall not be subject to assessments under subsection (a) solely by operation of section 5(b).

The SPEAKER pro tempore. The bill shall be debatable for 1 hour, equally divided and controlled by the chair and ranking minority member of the Committee on Financial Services.

After 1 hour of debate, it shall be in order to consider the amendment printed in part B of House Report 114–839, if offered by the Member designated in the report, which shall be considered read, shall be separately debatable for the time specified in the report equally divided and controlled by the proponent and an opponent, and shall not be subject to a demand for a division of the question.

The gentleman from Texas (Mr. HENSARLING) and the gentlewoman from California (Ms. MAXINE WATERS) each will control 30 minutes.

The Chair recognizes the gentleman from Texas.

GENERAL LEAVE

Mr. HENSARLING. Mr. Speaker, I ask unanimous consent that all Members may have 5 legislative days in which to revise and extend their remarks and submit extraneous materials on the bill under consideration.

The SPEAKER pro tempore. Is there objection to the request of the gentleman from Texas?

There was no objection.

Mr. HENSARLING. Mr. Speaker, I yield myself such time as I may consume.

Mr. Speaker, I rise in support of H.R. 6392, the Systemic Risk Designation Improvement Act, which is a very important bill cosponsored by a bipartisan group of Members of the House, the text of which was approved by our committee with a strong bipartisan support of 39–16.

I thank Chairman LUETKEMEYER, chairman of our Subcommittee on Housing and Insurance, one of the key leaders on our Committee on Financial Services, for his leadership and for introducing this legislation. He has led these efforts valiantly to reform a flawed and arbitrary framework used by regulators to designate so-called systemically important financial institutions, also known as SIFIs. Designation, Mr. Speaker, anoints these institutions as too big to fail, meaning that today's SIFI designations are tomorrow's tax-funded bailouts.

It is clear that this issue has found, again, a fair amount of consensus on both sides of the aisle, and this legisla-

tion represents a very good-faith effort by the gentleman from Missouri to forge a bipartisan piece of legislation that, at the very least, at the minimum, would get rid of a totally arbitrary and static threshold currently used to designate institutions as systemically important.

Mr. Speaker, I speak for many on this floor when I say I do not believe in the SIFI architecture at all. I think it is harmful. I think it is dangerous, and clearly it should be replaced by high levels of loss-absorbing private capital. But that is not what we are debating today.

Today in the 114th Congress, we continue to try to find a bipartisan consensus to support needed reforms; and, again, that is what this bill is: bipartisan. It recognizes that regulations should consider different components of risk and not simply a Washington one-size-fits-all definition.

The current approach—and this is very important, Mr. Speaker, as the coauthor of the Dodd-Frank Act, himself, admits—is a mistake. It is a mistake because it fails to take into account differences in the various business models or systemic risk institutions pose to our financial system. In fact, it is indisputable that the asset threshold used in Dodd-Frank is not based on a logical formula, on research, or on any evidence at all. Instead, it is simply a random number picked out of thin air.

Concerns with this arbitrary number have been recognized, as I just mentioned, by none other than former Committee on Financial Services Chairman Barney Frank, himself. As I recall, he is the Frank of Dodd-Frank. In testimony before our committee, Mr. Speaker, former Chairman Frank agreed that the threshold he wrote into law was "arbitrary." He expressed support for adjusting it. Then just last week, he stated the asset threshold was a "mistake." I hope all Members on the other side of the aisle take careful note.

Federal Reserve Board member Dan Tarullo has also expressed skepticism, as has the Comptroller of the Currency Thomas Curry. Even the ranking member, the Democrat ranking member of the Senate Banking Committee, Senator SHERROD BROWN, has stated: "I do agree that some banks above $50 billion should not"—not—"be regulated like Wall Street megabanks."

So what we are trying to do here today with this bipartisan bill is trying to provide a solution to try to fix a generally recognized mistake in Dodd-Frank, and what those who oppose the bill are trying to do is to preserve that mistake in the law. Perhaps again, Mr. Speaker, some of my colleagues need to be reminded that small banks on Main Street and even our regional banks did not cause the financial crisis, and arbitrarily painting big banks and small and midsized banks with ex-

actly the same broad brush is wrong. It is bad policy, and it is bad for our economy.

So the discussion today, Mr. Speaker, should instead focus on the appropriate measure of systemic importance and the regulatory burden imposed by the so-called enhanced prudential standards once an institution has been designated. By focusing exclusively on asset size, you ignore other factors that may be more relevant in determining whether a financial institution should be subject to, again, so-called enhanced prudential standards. Furthermore, an asset-based approach does not capture the types of risk that enhanced prudential standards are designed to mitigate in the first place.

By determining risk using activity-based standards, no matter how flawed these standards may be, our regulators would be better equipped to differentiate between stable activities and those that may pose a threat to financial stability. It would allow more precision in identifying systemic importance, while also providing flexibility for institutions engaging in more prudent lending activities.

Mr. Speaker, it is just so important that we note the effect these regulations are having today on the U.S. economy. They are harming our economy. Instead of helping to capitalize small businesses, leading to more jobs and opportunity for people who still lack both, financial institutions are, instead, having to expend capital on compliance, compliance that even the coauthor of Dodd-Frank admits is a mistake.

Mr. Speaker, regrettably, I need not remind us that we remain stuck in the slowest and weakest economic recovery since the end of World War II. The economy simply is not working for working Americans. They can't get ahead, and they fear for the future of their families. Their paychecks have remained stagnant. Their savings have declined. The American people deserve better.

I urge adoption of this measure. I thank Chairman LUETKEMEYER for his leadership in forging this bipartisan consensus solution. I urge us to correct this Dodd-Frank mistake.

Mr. Speaker, I reserve the balance of my time.

COMMITTEE ON WAYS AND MEANS,
HOUSE OF REPRESENTATIVES,
Washington, DC, November 29, 2016.
Hon. JEB HENSARLING,
Chairman, Committee on Financial Services.

DEAR CHAIRMAN HENSARLING: I am writing concerning H.R. 6392, the "Systemic Risk Designation Improvement Act of 2016." This legislation contains provisions that fall within the Ways and Means Committee's Rule X jurisdiction over revenue.

I appreciate your willingness to work with me on the provisions in my Committee's jurisdiction. In order to allow H.R. 6392 to move expeditiously to the House floor, I agree not to seek a sequential referral on this bill. The Committee on Ways and Means takes this action with our mutual understanding that by foregoing formal action on H.R. 6392, we do not waive any jurisdiction over subject matter contained in this or similar legislation, and that our Committee will be appropriately consulted and involved as this bill or similar legislation moves forward. Our Committee also reserves the right to seek appointment of an appropriate number of conferees to any House-Senate conference involving this or similar legislation, and asks that you support any such request.

I would appreciate your response to this letter confirming this understanding, and would request that you include a copy of this letter and your response in the Congressional Record during the floor consideration of this bill. Thank you in advance for your cooperation.

Sincerely,

KEVIN BRADY,
Chairman.

COMMITTEE ON FINANCIAL SERVICES,
HOUSE OF REPRESENTATIVES,
Washington, DC, November 29, 2016.
Hon. KEVIN BRADY,
Chairman, Ways and Means Committee.

DEAR CHAIRMAN BRADY: Thank you for your November 29th letter regarding H.R. 6392, the "Systemic Risk Designation Improvement Act of 2016."

I am most appreciative of your decision to forego action on H.R. 6392 so that it may move expeditiously to the House floor. I acknowledge that although you are waiving action on the bill, the Ways and Means Committee is in no way waiving its jurisdictional interest in this or similar legislation. In addition, if a conference is necessary on this legislation, I will support any request that your committee be represented therein.

Finally, I shall be pleased to include your letter and this letter on H.R. 6392 in the Congressional Record during floor consideration of the same.

Sincerely,

JEB HENSARLING,
Chairman.

Ms. MAXINE WATERS of California. Mr. Speaker, I yield myself such time as I may consume.

Mr. Speaker, I rise today in strong opposition to H.R. 6392. This is the first step in the Trump agenda to deregulate Wall Street, despite candidate Trump's pledges to hold elite bankers accountable. In fact, as we debate this bill today, Trump Tower's revolving door is spinning with Wall Street insiders.

Yes, in a skyscraper in midtown Manhattan, Trump and his transition team are plotting their agenda to weaken financial reform and bring us back to the precrisis Wild West days when banks could gamble with taxpayer money. Bank stocks are up on news of gifts to come, and newspaper headlines are already documenting Republicans' aggressive plans.

In fact, President-elect Trump just announced that he will nominate Steven Mnuchin, a former Goldman Sachs executive who now sits on the board of the megabank CIT, to be his Treasury Secretary. Mr. Mnuchin's bank is just one of 27 banks that stands to benefit directly from this legislation. Though CIT crashed—that is the bank—and went bankrupt during the crisis be-

cause of high-risk commercial lending and subprime loans, somehow Mr. Mnuchin still managed to sign an employment deal, handing him $4.5 million a year in 2016. I suppose passing this legislation is just the Republican Congress' way of giving him a signing bonus for coming into government.

We enacted the Dodd-Frank Wall Street Reform and Consumer Protection Act in response to the stunning greed and regulatory failures in our financial system; and yet, with this bill, the Republicans are displaying a staggering degree of historical amnesia.

☐ 1315

This bill is the epitome of that dangerous agenda, with H.R. 6392 gutting our banking regulators' oversight of $4.5 trillion in banking assets, or approximately 30 percent of the industry currently subject to enhanced rules.

Make no mistake. This bill is not about helping the community banks because 99 percent of our country's community banks and credit unions are already exempt from most rules in Dodd-Frank. So I don't want anybody to come out here saying: we are helping the community banks. This has nothing to do with the community banks. This is about deregulating the big banks over $50 billion.

It is also not about tailoring regulations for regional banks. Wall Street reform already required that, and the Federal Reserve is already taking steps to do so. No, this bill is about a wholesale regulatory exemption for just 27 of the biggest banks in America—banks with $100 billion, $200 billion, and even $400 billion in assets.

Many of the types of banks that would benefit from this bill failed spectacularly during the financial crisis. In fact, large bank holding companies with more than $50 billion in assets received twice as much bailout money per dollar than banks with less than $50 billion in assets.

Contrary to the talking points from the other side of the aisle, these megaregional banks are not just big community banks. No, these regional banks are some of the worst players in predatory, subprime lending leading up to the financial crisis. They have preyed on minority and rural communities and have passed the buck onto taxpayers when their bets failed.

Remember Countrywide, a $200 billion thrift? They were the number three subprime mortgage originator and number one issuer of mortgage bonds in 2006. They are a poster child of the crisis.

Remember Washington Mutual, with $300 billion in assets, whose hometown paper, The Seattle Times, described as "predatory"?

Remember Wachovia, with their exotic "pick-a-payment" mortgage loans? Remember in October of 2008, when they posted a $24 billion quar-

terly loss and the FDIC had to facilitate a midnight acquisition by Wells Fargo?

Remember New Century, AmeriQuest, or Option One? This bill would enable more blowups like these.

H.R. 6392 would repeal Dodd-Frank's $50 billion threshold above which banks are subject to closer regulatory scrutiny and prevent the Federal Reserve Board from regulating these banks. Instead, it would hand over that responsibility to what is known as FSOC, the Financial Stability Oversight Council.

In order to regulate the banks, the FSOC would have to go through a Byzantine and litigious process of designation, which takes 2 to 4 years to complete. This would give them plenty of time to go back to the old ways that Dodd-Frank is trying to prevent. Even if a potential Treasury Secretary Mnuchin decided to regulate his former employer, by the time he got around to it, the damage would likely already be done.

It is also significant to note that Republicans have repeatedly tried to dismantle the FSOC and its existing designation authority for large nonbanks. They have called the Council "unconstitutional," introduced bills to make it harder for the FSOC to do its job, and helped companies like MetLife fight its designation in court.

What is more, Chairman HENSARLING's sweeping Wall Street deregulation bill, the "Wrong Choice Act," would repeal this exact same designation authority altogether.

Why is the majority even considering this bill today when the chairman's Wall Street reform repeal package would render this bill moot? It is clear that this is just the first act in a long, dangerous play that will continue well into next year. I, therefore, urge my colleagues to join me in opposing this harmful bill.

Mr. Speaker, as I said when I took the floor to debate this bill, this is the first act in Trump's promise that he is going to deregulate, his promise that he is going to get rid of Dodd-Frank, his promise that he is going to get rid of the Consumer Financial Protection Bureau, and his promise that he is going to, in essence, turn all of this back over to Wall Street.

Mr. Speaker, I reserve the balance of my time.

Mr. HENSARLING. Mr. Speaker, I yield myself 5 seconds just to say, if the ranking member believes this is the first act in getting rid of Dodd-Frank, she ain't seen nothing yet.

Mr. Speaker, I yield 2 minutes to the gentleman from Texas (Mr. SESSIONS), the distinguished chairman of the House Rules Committee, and I thank him for his leadership in helping bring this bill to the floor.

Mr. SESSIONS. Mr. Speaker, I thank my dear colleague from Dallas for not only yielding, but I want to commend him in working with his committee, including the gentleman from Missouri (Mr. LUETKEMEYER), on this awesome legislation.

Mr. Speaker, the point is simple: Washington has once again gotten in the way of legitimate business and is harming the American people, the American economy, and job growth in this country by imposing unnecessary and burdensome compliance costs on medium-sized banks all across America.

Asset thresholds, regardless of how high or low, are disincentives to growth. There will always be an institution that lies somewhere that is slightly above or below some threshold, but the bottom line is that arbitrary numbers tell us very little about the risk that is actually involved. It is the risk to institutions in America that we should be talking about.

So, simply put, the SIFI designation is arbitrary. It simply subjects smaller banks to the same standards as trillion-dollar, globally systematic organizations, which is something that would only make sense here in Washington.

The bottom line is, it is an impediment to free economic growth, and it is an impediment that is burdening not only our banks but consumers also.

I commend Congressman LUETKEMEYER for advancing this important, commonsense regulation. By the way, it has taken several years to get here.

We now understand that the American economy can move in the right direction. The American economy, with good and proper leadership, not only in Washington but by the rules and regulations that are balanced, will help United States families, small businesses, and specifically smaller banks be more competitive to offer the services that are necessary.

I commend the young chairman of the Financial Services Committee, Mr. HENSARLING, for allowing this bill to come here today.

Ms. MAXINE WATERS of California. Mr. Speaker, Democrats, small town America, Rust Belt America, you just heard what he said. Mr. HENSARLING just said: You ain't seen nothing yet. You heard it coming out of his mouth as they stand here and defend deregulation of these big banks.

Mr. Speaker, I yield 3 minutes to the gentleman from Texas (Mr. AL GREEN) a member of the Financial Services Committee.

Mr. AL GREEN of Texas. Mr. Speaker, I think it appropriate to reflect for just a moment on what the crisis was like in 2008.

In 2008, when this crisis hit and it started to blossom, started to blow up, banks would not lend to each other. The crisis was so serious that banks would not bail each other out.

We had a circumstance such that people were losing their homes. They were losing their homes because of

these so-called exotic products that allowed them to buy homes that they could not afford, homes that would allow them to have a teaser rate that would coincide with a prepayment penalty such that they couldn't get out of the rate that was to follow, which was going to be higher than they can afford.

Mr. Speaker, this bill, H.R. 6392, should be appropriately named the "Systemic Risk Creation Act," because that is what it does. It creates the opportunity for systemic risk to exist, and it puts us back where we were before Dodd-Frank such that these various banks and lending institutions and other institutions of great amount of finance would be in a position to fail without our having the opportunity to immediately act upon them, as was the case with AIG. There was no system in place to deal with the AIGs of the world.

Dodd-Frank allows us to do this in a systemic way, a systematic way, an orderly way. It allows us to, if we need to, wind down these huge institutions—wind them down such that they don't create harm to the broader economy.

I want you to know, Mr. Speaker, for those who think that these are all small banks, let me just give you some indication as to how small they are. I am looking now at the top five of the 27 in question. The top five:

Number five is $217 billion.

Number four, $255 billion.

Number three, $278 billion.

Number two, $350 billion.

Number one, $433 billion.

Only in the Congress of the United States of America would this be considered small change.

We must not allow this deregulation to take place such that we put the economic order at risk again. This bill, Dodd-Frank, when it passed, allowed us to look at the entire economic order and to determine whether or not there were institutions that were a systemic risk to the economic order. Prior to Dodd-Frank, they were all siloed. Prior to Dodd-Frank, we had long-term capital. Long-term capital was the first canary in the coal mine.

The SPEAKER pro tempore. The time of the gentleman has expired.

Ms. MAXINE WATERS of California. Mr. Speaker, I yield the gentleman an additional 30 seconds.

Mr. AL GREEN of Texas. Long-term capital had its demise in 1998. It was a canary in the coal mine. Bear Stearns followed, as well as IndyMac, Countrywide, and WaMu. They followed in 2008.

We didn't have a system that allowed us to recognize these canaries in the coal mine and take affirmative action. This is what Dodd-Frank does. This is what FSOC does. And it would be a severe mistake to vote for legislation to repeal these bills. We are going to live to regret this vote. Those who vote to repeal will live to regret it.

Mr. HENSARLING. Mr. Speaker, I yield myself 10 seconds to say I appreciate the passion of my colleagues on the other side of the aisle and their concern for taxpayers and systemic risk. So I certainly look forward to their cosponsorship of our legislation to get rid of Dodd-Frank's taxpayer-funded bailout fund.

Mr. Speaker, I yield 3½ minutes to the gentleman from Missouri (Mr. LUETKEMEYER), a real leader on our committee and the author of H.R. 6392, the Systemic Risk Designation Improvement Act.

Mr. LUETKEMEYER. Mr. Speaker, today, the House will consider H.R. 6392, the Systemic Risk Designation Improvement Act of 2016, legislation to address an inefficient regulatory structure by accounting for actual risk, rather than asset size alone, in the designation of systemically important financial institutions, or SIFIs.

Under the current regulatory framework for the designation of SIFIs, any bank holding company with more than $50 billion in assets is subject to enhanced regulatory supervision and special assessments. This approach fails to take into account differences in business models or risk imposed to the financial system. It has real-world implications, too, stunting economic growth and limiting access to credit.

The risk of a traditional bank is not the same as an internationally active, complex firm. H.R. 6392 would remove the completely arbitrary approach and replace it with analysis of actual risk imposed to the financial system.

□ 1330

More specifically, my legislation would require regulators to examine not just size, but also interconnectedness, the extent of readily available substitutes, global cross-jurisdictional activity, and complexity of each bank holding company. These are metrics that are presently being used by the Financial Stability Board and the Office of Financial Research to determine what a G-SIFI is, a Global Systemically Important Financial Institution.

This bill number may be new, but the concept is not. With the exception of the offset language contained in section 6 of this bill, H.R. 6392 is identical to H.R. 1309, which was the legislation I introduced last year that attracted broad bipartisan support and garnered 135 cosponsors.

Even Dodd-Frank's author, the former chairman of the Financial Services Committee, Barney Frank, said this issue needs to be addressed. During a November 20 radio interview, Chairman Frank said: "We put in there that banks got the extra supervision if they were $50 billion in assets. That was a mistake."

Chairman Frank further went on to say: "When it comes to lending and job creation, the regional banks are obviously very, very important. I hope that if we get some regulatory changes, we give some regulatory relaxation to those banks.''

Chairman Frank testified to that effect—and this is a picture of him in front of our committee—and expressed support for our bill back in 2014. This week we have the opportunity to remedy this oversight.

This legislation will not impact the authority of the regulatory agencies to oversee institutions. It will, however, encourage enhanced and more appropriate oversight of institutions that could actually have a greater impact on the overall economy, financial system, and, most importantly, consumers.

Mr. Speaker, this is a bill to take a more pragmatic approach to financial regulation. Mr. Speaker, it is time to actually manage risk and limit threats to our financial system.

I want to thank my colleagues for their work on this legislation, namely, Mr. MURPHY, Mr. STIVERS, Mr. SCOTT, Mr. WILLIAMS, Ms. SEWELL, Mr. HILL, and Ms. SINEMA, and ask my colleagues for their support today. And a special thanks to Chairman HENSARLING for his tireless support for efforts on this bill.

Just one moment, if I could, to address a couple of comments that were made earlier. We are talking about systemically important financial institutions, and the definition of a SIFI is it has got to be something that is going to cause the economy to go down. A $50 billion bank is going to be something that may be important to a local economy, but it is not going to be something important to the entire economy. This is what we are talking about.

Big banks have big problems. Medium-sized banks do not affect the systemic concern that we should have about the economy, and this is where this bill is directed. Somebody who doesn't understand that, I think they are missing the point.

The SPEAKER pro tempore. The time of the gentleman has expired.

Mr. HENSARLING. I yield the gentleman an additional 30 seconds.

Mr. LUETKEMEYER. So I think even the ranking member made my point a while ago when she said 27 banks, a total of $4.6 trillion. We have got a half dozen banks over $1 trillion, so we are talking about some small banks that are really going to have a small impact with regard to if they went down or not.

That is what the purpose of this legislation, Dodd-Frank, was about: to stop the big guys from bringing the whole economy down. The ranking member, with all due respect, misses the entire point of what Dodd-Frank is supposed to be and what the intent of this bill is.

Ms. MAXINE WATERS of California. Mr. Speaker, while the other side fights for the big banks and we over here are fighting for the consumers, let me just say that Mr. Frank has not supported H.R. 6392, and you need to stop saying that.

I yield 3 minutes to the gentleman from Washington (Mr. HECK), a member of the Financial Services Committee.

Mr. HECK of Washington. Mr. Speaker, I have a little different take on this. I oppose this bill. In fact, I strongly oppose it, but I don't exactly oppose the idea at all. Let me explain that.

The Dodd-Frank legislation was written, as we all know, during a period of financial crisis, and legislators and regulators had to act quickly. Sometimes, when you have to act quickly, you take shortcuts to get the financial system stabilized. But today, the difference is we have the luxury of time to go back and replace those shortcuts with some more deliberative decision-making.

Now, Dodd-Frank said that every bank holding company over $50 billion gets heightened supervision. Well, frankly, back then, for stabilizing a financial crisis, that was a great way to move quickly and to get it done and to bring about the intended result. But again, for making policy over the long term, that doesn't make sense because, in fact, it is an arbitrary-size threshold. So it was a shortcut that made sense at the time, and I join with you in supporting a reevaluation of that particular threshold level. That is the idea of this bill, and I support the bill—or support the idea. But, again, I don't support this bill at all because, instead of taking the luxury of time to make good policy, frankly, it acts like we are still back in that crisis, and we are taking another shortcut.

The bill says FSOC should determine which banks need heightened supervision, and that is a great idea. That is what they are there for. And then it says FSOC has to complete all of its work on all of the banks within 12 months. That is a terrible idea. That is a terrible idea.

The last determination that FSOC took lasted 16 months, and they were working on one company at the time—and it took 16 months. And even then, the judge said: You took 16 months, and you acted too rashly and should have deliberated more. But this bill says only 12 months are allowed. And it is not just one company they would be looking at. It could be up to 40 companies with over $50 billion in assets.

So I would say to my friend from Missouri, I think you have a good idea. I wish you would have brought a bill reflecting that idea out here.

Let's remember that Bear Stearns was $400 billion; it contributed. Washington Mutual, $300 billion; it contributed. All of those banks are going to be in one pot that have 12 months to be looked at. We are, in fact, gutting Dodd-Frank; and, no, I do not agree with my friend from Texas, the chairman, that that is a good idea at all.

The authors kind of recognized this, which is why they said banks get heightened supervision if FSOC says so or if the Financial Stability Board in Basel, Switzerland, says so. I don't know why we would cede sovereignty. I have been working with the gentleman from Missouri on exactly that issue as it relates to insurance companies. Why are we ceding our sovereignty to some regulatory entity in another country?

So I do take a different view of this bill.

The SPEAKER pro tempore. The time of the gentleman has expired.

Ms. MAXINE WATERS of California. I yield an additional 30 seconds to the gentleman.

Mr. HECK of Washington. I urge my colleagues to support the idea by rejecting this bill which will not achieve the intended result because it can't work. But the idea can. Go back. Put in a reasonable timeframe. Drop that crazy FSB provision, and let the regulators get to work looking for the risks that devastated the economy a decade ago so we don't have to relive that. If we pass this bill, we very well may.

The SPEAKER pro tempore (Mr. JODY B. HICE of Georgia). Without objection, the gentleman from Missouri (Mr. LUETKEMEYER) will control the remainder of the time of the gentleman from Texas (Mr. HENSARLING).

There was no objection.

Mr. LUETKEMEYER. Mr. Speaker, I yield 2 minutes to the gentleman from Texas (Mr. NEUGEBAUER), the chair of the Financial Institutions and Consumer Credit Subcommittee, who is set to retire shortly, and whose expertise and hard work we are going to miss; but his guidance over these years has certainly given us a lesson on how to get things done. And we certainly hope that he will have a great retirement.

Mr. NEUGEBAUER. I thank the gentleman for those kind words.

Mr. Speaker, I rise today in support of H.R. 6392, offered by my good friend from Missouri (Mr. LUETKEMEYER).

H.R. 6392, known as the Systemic Risk Designation Improvement Act, is bipartisan legislation that ensures that the Federal Government takes a thoughtful and comprehensive approach when evaluating the financial stability concerns posed by U.S. bank holding companies.

Under H.R. 6392, the bank holding companies will no longer be measured by their size alone when evaluated for the application of heightened prudential standards. Instead, the Financial Stability Oversight Council will use a metrics-based approach that takes into consideration the totality of the bank holding company's operations. Using this framework, bank holding companies will be measured on size, complexity, their interconnectedness, cross-jurisdictional activity, and available substitutes.

This approach is similar to the framework used by the international body known as the Financial Stability Board, which designates global systemically important banks. Further, it is the framework already being used by the Federal Reserve when it evaluates financial stability concerns stemming from bank mergers.

Mounting evidence coming from regulators and academics have highlighted the flaws in using a size-only approach to measuring systemic risk. Further, several democratically appointed regulators have noted the flaws with Dodd-Frank's threshold of $50 billion in assets.

Put simply, many bank holding companies are being subjected to enhanced regulatory requirements for no sound policy reasons. That results in restricted lending, decreased services to customers, and inefficiencies in the marketplace.

We must strive to ensure that the government policy is thoughtful and properly calibrated. H.R. 6392 is absolutely necessary to ensure that we meet those principles.

I urge my colleagues to vote "yes" for H.R. 6392.

Ms. MAXINE WATERS of California. Mr. Speaker, I yield 3 minutes to the gentleman from Illinois (Mr. FOSTER), a member of the Financial Services Committee.

Mr. FOSTER. I thank Ranking Member WATERS for yielding.

Mr. Speaker, I rise in opposition to H.R. 6392, the Systemic Risk Designation Improvement Act of 2016. Although many aspects of this bill have sound arguments behind them, it contains fatal flaws which should preclude our support.

The financial crisis taught us many things about our markets and overturned some fairly fundamental assumptions that were widely held prior to it. One of the things we learned was the extent to which systemic risk could build up in a regulatory paradigm that was focused entirely on entity risk. It was quickly evident that the failure of a large institution posed a greater threat than previously believed.

At the same time the phrase "too big to fail" became public shorthand for some of these firms, economists and other experts talked about another important aspect, too interconnected to fail.

Asset size is a quick and useful metric for determining whether a firm is potentially so large that a failure could have a massive impact on systemwide stability, and evaluating the risks that single institutions can pose to the system often require a more nuanced approach.

The exposure of counterparties to a failing firm or exposures of other institutions to the same risks are systemic risk factors that should rightly be considered. Also, as the economy grows, many fixed thresholds, such as $50 bil-

lion, will shrink in importance. At the very least, the importance given to any asset size threshold needs to be periodically reconsidered in the scope of an economic indicator like GDP. Wherever the line is drawn, it should reflect the macroeconomic factors that the bank is nested in.

Moreover, there is anecdotal evidence that firms will avoid growth—meaning, cutting back in lending—as they approach any fixed threshold. I see this as a market distortion that reflects risks of increasing concentration rather than prudent risk management. I see this concern with nearly any fixed threshold for being deemed a SIFI.

However, I think that a nuanced, weighted process that gives deference to the expertise of regulatory agencies is appropriate. Drawing lines to determine which firms warrant additional scrutiny will always be a difficult process. To the extent that the bill we consider today looks to other factors that a strong Financial Stability Oversight Council with adequate resources and leadership should consider, I believe that this is a good start.

I do think that there are improvements to be made in the designation threshold, but I think this bill has two core problems that prevent my support.

First, legislation to change the threshold should give sufficient specific direction that it would not move with changes to the political leadership of the FSOC. The concentration of an effective veto power in the hands of a single political appointee basically aggravates that concern tremendously.

The SPEAKER pro tempore. The time of the gentleman has expired.

Ms. MAXINE WATERS of California. I yield the gentleman an additional 30 seconds.

Mr. FOSTER. Second, thorough analysis of the institutions presently categorized as SIFIs but not G-SIBs requires more than a year. The bill today rightly looks to characteristics that are important in assessing systemic risk, but it does not provide predictability or an adequate transition period.

The most recent financial crisis saw the failure of institutions of a variety of sizes, but, for example, the savings and loan crisis was the simultaneous failure of many smaller firms.

I support an approach that looks at many different factors and gives discretion to a strong, well-resourced FSOC to designate forms based on objective characteristics of the firm so we can prevent another crisis. However, I urge my colleagues to vote "no" on H.R. 6392 because it does not set up the thoughtful framework we need.

□ 1345

Mr. LUETKEMEYER. Mr. Speaker, may I inquire as to the amount of time remaining on both sides, please?

The SPEAKER pro tempore. The gentleman from Missouri has 15 minutes remaining. The gentlewoman from California has 10¾ minutes remaining.

Mr. LUETKEMEYER. Mr. Speaker, I yield 2 minutes to the gentleman from Michigan (Mr. HUIZENGA), chairman of the Monetary Policy and Trade Subcommittee. He is obviously one of the greater, deeper thinkers on our committee from the standpoint of being able to handle that sort of subcommittee. It is certainly an honor to have him with us today.

Mr. HUIZENGA of Michigan. Mr. Speaker, I appreciate my fellow subcommittee chairman who has written a great piece of legislation here.

We all have been talking about Dodd-Frank creating this Financial Stability Oversight Council, or FSOC, which was charged with monitoring systemic risk in the U.S. financial sector and coordinating regulatory responses by its member agencies—a good goal, but an idea gone bad, unfortunately.

FSOC designates these banking companies with over $50 billion in assets, they are automatically considered systemically important financial institutions, and the act subjects those institutions to enhanced regulatory standards.

Here is the issue, Mr. Speaker: this is not about Wall Street banks. This is really affecting and hitting Main Street banks. The SIFI designation really is arbitrary, and it subjects these companies with those assets. Which, don't get me wrong, $50 billion is a lot of money. However, if you look at the totality of our financial institutions, it is actually quite small. It suddenly says that they are globally now systemically important that, if this particular bank or company went out of business, we could take down the whole economy. It is just ludicrous.

The process that FSOC uses to designate these institutions is flawed in its current design and lacks the transparency and accountability that the American taxpayers deserve and, frankly, expect.

In fact, the former Financial Services chairman, Barney Frank, under which Dodd-Frank is named, even agreed that the $50 billion SIFI threshold that he wrote into law and that the Senate wrote into law was "arbitrary." Maybe 75 was too big and 25 was too small, so they settled on 50. There is no basis as to why that number was picked. I couldn't agree more with that former chairman.

This bill, H.R. 6392, the Systemic Risk Designation Improvement Act, is a bipartisan bill that passed out of our committee 39–16 with eight Democrats joining the majority, and it would require instead that FSOC use an indicator-based measurement that has five different operational indicators.

The SPEAKER pro tempore. The time of the gentleman has expired.

Mr. LUETKEMEYER. Mr. Speaker, I yield the gentleman an additional 30 seconds.

Mr. HUIZENGA of Michigan. Those five operational indicators are size, interconnectedness, complexity, cross-jurisdictional activity, and available substitutes. Therefore, what is happening is we are seeing fewer products and services available to bank customers because these banks are having to pour more additional resources that could go towards servicing those customers into a regulation that isn't doing anything to protect our economy.

That ultimately needs to be our goal. Our goal here needs to make sure that we restore transparency by allowing regulators to review all of the circumstances surrounding that and not have a Washington, D.C.-driven one-size-fits-all approach.

Mr. Speaker, I urge my colleagues to support this important bill.

Ms. MAXINE WATERS of California. Mr. Speaker, it was just said that this is affecting Main Street. It is not. All that passion you see on the other side is about the big banks, not about community banks.

Mr. Speaker, I yield 3 minutes to the gentleman from Maryland (Mr. SARBANES), who is a member of the Energy and Commerce Committee and a strong advocate for the protection of Wall Street reform.

Mr. SARBANES. Mr. Speaker, I thank the gentlewoman for yielding.

Mr. Speaker, I rise today to oppose this legislation, but I also want to speak to the millions of Americans of all political stripes who want Washington to change, who want to reclaim their voice in their democracy, and who long, actually, for the interests of Main Street to be put ahead of the interests of Wall Street.

Unfortunately, Washington hasn't heard you, America. The system is still rigged and the swamp is only getting deeper. Special interest lobbyists are sharpening their knives in advance of the new Congress, and President-elect Trump's administration is ready to carve up the Tax Code for their benefit and eliminate oversight of Wall Street.

In fact, bank stocks are surging now with Wall Street giddy at the prospect of tossing out critical rules and regulations designed to prevent another financial collapse and taxpayer bailout.

As one Wall Street analyst put it immediately after the election: "Everything is in play."

Or maybe we should just use Mr. HENSARLING's words: "You ain't seen nothing yet."

If you need further proof that special interests and the Wall Street elite will be empowered in the new Congress and administration, look no further than President-elect Trump's nomination for the Treasury Department: Steve Mnuchin—a billionaire hedge fund manager, former Goldman Sachs executive and bank CEO. President-elect Trump, a supposed champion of the working class, now seeks to appoint a financier who, like Trump, personally profited on the financial ruin of hard-working Americans.

What does this have to do with the bill we have before us, you may ask?

Well, a lot. Today, before the new President is even seated and Steven Mnuchin is even confirmed, H.R. 6392 will dramatically upend sensible oversight of some of the Nation's largest banks, many of which were directly implicated in the financial collapse of 2008.

Taxpayers lose under this legislation, but guess who stands to benefit from it?

Steve Mnuchin. He serves on the board of the bank CIT, receiving a salary of $4.5 million. CIT is one of only 27 banks in the country that will benefit from this terrible legislation. What is more, under this legislation, Mnuchin, if confirmed, will be in charge of overseeing the replacement designation process for CIT and the other 26 large regional banks rewarded by this legislation.

Mr. Speaker, this legislation and the nomination of Steve Mnuchin is a direct rebuke of President-elect Trump's promise to "drain the swamp." The only thing cleaner about the swamp is that the alligators will be wearing suits and ties.

Millions of Americans of all political stripes are hurting. They want a more representative democracy. They want public policy designed for the public interest, not the special interests. They want a fair shake. Let's show them we are still fighting for them. Let's defeat this Wall Street giveaway.

Mr. LUETKEMEYER. Mr. Speaker, I yield 2½ minutes to the gentleman from Wisconsin (Mr. DUFFY), who is the chairman of the Oversight and Investigations Subcommittee. He is one of our toughest guys on the committee. He has got one of the toughest committees to be able to go after some of the issues that we are working on.

Mr. DUFFY. Mr. Speaker, I thank Chairman LUETKEMEYER for all his hard work on what I think is an excellent bill. It is fascinating to sit in this Chamber and listen to the debate and the fear-mongering that takes place.

Before I get into that, let's just take a trip down memory lane. We have to look at the financial crisis and what the Democrats chose to do, the idea that you can't let any good crisis go to waste. There is a financial crisis, so we go to our file cabinets, we open them up, and every progressive, liberal idea we take out and put them into Dodd-Frank—a 2,300-page bill, a bill that was written before the Financial Crisis Inquiry Commission even came out with their report on the cause of the crisis.

This is a very, very simple tweak. Right now we have designations for systemically risky banks at a set assets threshold of $50 billion. Let me tell you what, I have banks in Wisconsin. They are small, regional banks—not Wall Street banks—that are getting crushed by these new rules and regulations.

So all we are saying to my friends across the aisle is: You love the regulators. You think that the regulators are awesome.

We are trying to empower the regulators to look at the facts on the ground and to look at the interconnectedness and complexity to determine risk, not just have a one-size-fits-all mentality. It is not one size fits all. We are more complex. Banks are as different as people.

Let's look at the complexity at every bank and make sure they can operate within their communities in a way that fits the risk to the financial system.

This gets back to the American people. Why does this matter? Why is this not just about finance and complex rules?

Because if banks can't lend, or if they lend and you are driving up the cost of their lending, then that has a real impact on the small businesses in my community and the families in my community that can't get a loan, or the loans they do get, the costs are going through the roof because of all the new compliance costs.

The bottom line is why do we want to have increased regulatory burdens on banks that aren't risky?

Let's have the regulators focus like a laser on the banks on Wall Street who do need the increased regulation, but not the ones that don't.

One size doesn't fit all. Let's work together. Let's modify Dodd-Frank. This isn't Holy Scripture. It didn't come down from Heaven on high. It can be fixed. It is not perfect. Again—we are going to say this all day—Barney Frank even thinks the threshold is too low. It can be fixed.

The SPEAKER pro tempore. The time of the gentleman has expired.

Mr. LUETKEMEYER. I yield the gentleman an additional 30 seconds.

Mr. DUFFY. Mr. Speaker, I look forward to working with my good friend, the ranking member. Commonsense reform that looks to your good friends, the regulators, to take a sound look at risk profiles, and then decide what kind of regulatory regime is necessary for the risk that is presented by each of these banks.

I thank the chairman for his work. I encourage everyone on both sides of the aisle to support this commonsense bill that supports small businesses and American families to make America great again.

Ms. MAXINE WATERS of California. Mr. Speaker, the gentleman from Wisconsin has the audacity to come to this floor and say that we are crushing these pitiful little banks with $50 billion or more. No. You are crushing the average person who gets up every morning, who goes to work, and who is trying to take care of their families and is getting ripped off by these financial institutions.

Mr. Speaker, I yield 3 minutes to the gentlewoman from Hawaii (Ms. GABBARD), who is a member of the Foreign Affairs Committee.

Ms. GABBARD. Mr. Speaker, I am rising today in strong opposition to H.R. 6392. It is a dangerous bill that puts the economic security of millions of Americans at risk.

Let's not forget that just 8 short years ago, the lives of Americans all across the country were shaken and devastated by the worst economic crisis since the Great Depression. The livelihoods of hardworking families were put at risk and millions of Americans lost their homes and saw their lifesavings wiped out all because of risky banking practices and the overgrown "too big to fail" banks. At that time, Republicans and Democrats railed against the travesty that these banks exacted on the American people.

This bill threatens to unravel the very protections that were put in place to prevent a repeat of this economic crisis. It would gut the higher capital requirements on 27 banks that together hold over $4 trillion in assets—nearly one-quarter of all banking system assets in the United States—and water down the independent authority of the Federal Reserve to regulate large bank risk.

Eight years ago, the failure of large regional banks like Countrywide, Washington Mutual, and Wachovia—major subprime mortgage lenders leading up to the crisis—created shock waves throughout our financial system and hurt the American people. This bill would scale back the Federal Reserve's ability to regulate these banks, placing greater risk and burden on the backs of the American people.

I urge my colleagues to stand with the people and vote against this dangerous legislation.

Mr. LUETKEMEYER. Mr. Speaker, I yield 3 minutes to the gentleman from Kentucky (Mr. BARR), who is one of our bright and shining stars on the Financial Services Committee.

Mr. BARR. Mr. Speaker, I rise in strong support of H.R. 6392, the Systemic Risk Designation Improvement Act, and I applaud the gentleman's excellent work on this bill.

The ranking member, my friend, says that this is not about Main Street. Let me talk about what this bill is trying to fix, the problem we are trying to solve here.

Dodd-Frank, the legislation that my friends on the other side of the aisle are defending, has produced this: small-business lending from banks is at the lowest level it has been in 20 years, and

more than 75 percent of corporate treasurers in this country say that Federal regulations are stifling access to financial services. As a result, new business formation in this country is at a 35-year low.

This bill is about Main Street because Main Street cannot access financial services because of Dodd-Frank. This bill is about fixing an arbitrary provision in the Dodd-Frank law that harms consumers and does absolutely nothing to stabilize markets.

Dodd-Frank directs the Financial Stability Oversight Council to designate banks as systemically important financial institutions, or SIFIs. These designated institutions are subject to surcharges, additional regulation, and an implicit taxpayer bailout. That's right, their bill is what gives Wall Street a bailout.

□ 1400

What we are saying is: let's focus our attention on Wall Street, but let's get regional banks some regulatory relief so that they can serve their customers on Main Street.

The primary test for systemic importance is an arbitrary threshold of $50 billion. Above that line, an institution is designated systemically important or too big to fail. Above that line, regardless of the institution's risky activities, it is exempt.

This bill that we are supporting does away with this blunt threshold and directs FSOC and its constituent agencies to consider the institution's actual activities to determine if it actually is risky. If it is not, it deserves relief so that it can serve its customers better.

Size is not the only issue. It is interconnectedness. It is risky activities. Many of these regional banks that serve my constituents in central and eastern Kentucky, not Wall Street—central and eastern Kentucky. Farmers, small business owners, and homeowners in Kentucky are being crushed and denied access to capital because of a one-size-fits-all regulation from Washington.

Unlike Dodd-Frank's arbitrary approach, this will better promote financial stability because it actually targets the enhanced regulation to where it belongs and not on Wall Street.

The bottom line is, we are hearing from regional banks around this country, in central Kentucky and other places, that the expense of complying with these enhanced regulations and the SIFI surcharge means less capital for deployment in mortgages, in automobile loans, and in small business loans, it means higher credit card rates, and it means fewer customer rewards. It impacts these institutions' ability to engage in philanthropy and community development activities.

Treating these regional banks as complex Wall Street firms is simply illogical. These are not multinational

Wall Street firms. These are traditional banks that serve Americans on Main Street.

Ms. MAXINE WATERS of California. Mr. Speaker, I reserve the balance of my time.

Mr. LUETKEMEYER. Mr. Speaker, I yield 2 minutes to the gentleman from Pennsylvania (Mr. ROTHFUS), one of our most thoughtful members on the Financial Services Committee.

Mr. ROTHFUS. Mr. Speaker, I rise today in strong support of H.R. 6392.

This bill, the Systemic Risk Designation Improvement Act, offers a commonsense approach to the process of designating systemically important financial institutions. In doing so, it addresses a problem that Republicans and Democrats have complained about for some time.

Dodd-Frank's $50 billion threshold for identifying SIFIs is a crude and arbitrary way to decide which firms pose a risk to the stability of the financial system. It is important to remember that SIFI designation isn't trivial. When a financial institution is labeled as a SIFI, it faces enhanced regulation, supervision, and costs without regard to the nature of the bank or the bank's business.

Accordingly, SIFI designation impacts a firm's lending ability, and, therefore, the firm's customers, and their customer's ability to thrive.

If we really care about protecting financial stability and having a healthy financial system, we have a responsibility to pursue a fairer, more transparent, and more accurate process. The approach set forth under H.R. 6392 represents a more rational process for evaluating financial institutions, as opposed to the Washington tradition of one-size-fits-all.

Under this bill, the Financial Stability Oversight Council will be required to look at not only the size of a financial institution but also its interconnectedness, complexity, cross-jurisdictional activity, and availability of substitutes. Keep in mind that banks designated as SIFIs today may still be designated as SIFIs under this new approach.

This bill's reforms will inject the FSOC's SIFI designation process with greater clarity and fairness, and it will result in more appropriately targeted regulatory efforts.

I commend Chairman LUETKEMEYER for his work on this important issue, and I am proud to be a cosponsor of this bill in its original form.

I urge my colleagues to support this bill.

Ms. MAXINE WATERS of California. Madam Speaker, I yield 1 minute to the gentleman from Texas (Mr. AL GREEN).

Mr. AL GREEN of Texas. Madam Speaker, let's take a look at this size question because $50 billion was selected for a reason, and the reason is this: If you don't have a threshold, we knew at the time, as we know now, that you won't get any banks designated because the banks are going to sue, and they are going to tie you up in court. Well, maybe some will not, but you are going to have a real fight on your hands getting them to be designated, and it can take 2 to 4 years to get it done.

Looking at the banks that are covered, only three of the banks covered are in the $50-billion range. The top 15 are over $100 billion, and the top bank is about a half trillion dollars. Again, only in Washington, D.C., would this kind of money—a half trillion dollars for one bank—be considered small change.

We cannot allow the banks to dominate the process. We put the process in the hands of the banks when the regulators have to take them on one at a time.

Finally, what is wrong with telling a bank, "You have to tell us how to eliminate you if you become a systemic risk"? That is what Dodd-Frank does. This bill eliminates the ability of FSOC to determine and tell banks that they must give up.

Mr. LUETKEMEYER. Madam Speaker, I yield 2 minutes to the gentleman from Colorado (Mr. TIPTON), one of our hardest working members on the committee.

Mr. TIPTON. Madam Speaker, I thank my colleague from Missouri (Mr. LUETKEMEYER) for offering this important piece of legislation under consideration today.

The bipartisan Systemic Risk Designation Improvement Act replaces an arbitrary asset threshold with an indicator-based approach, which will better assist the Financial Stability Oversight Council in determining the true systemic risk of a financial institution.

It is a mistake for regulators to continue regulating a $50-billion bank in the same way they regulate trillion-dollar global systemically important institutions. In fact, this view is shared among regulators and legislators. Comptroller Curry, Federal Reserve Board member Tarullo, Senator SHERROD BROWN, and even former Chairman Barney Frank have all made public comments agreeing that the $50-billion SIFI threshold is not the best determination for imposing heightened prudential standards.

This bill introduces a better, analysis-driven approach, requiring the council to require metrics already established by the Basel Committee on Banking Supervision when it identifies Global Systemically Important Banks.

The Systemic Risk Designation Improvement Act will stop the current regulatory model of needlessly increasing compliance costs and forcing institutions to decrease financial services. By ensuring that the SIFI designation process takes into account indicator factors, financial institutions that were not the cause of the financial crisis will once again be able to fully serve their communities. Not only will this legislation provide relief for stable financial institutions, but it will also allow regulators to focus their resources, working with institutions that pose an actual systemic risk to the financial system.

It is important to note that this legislation does not strip the FSOC of designation powers. It is concerning that some groups oppose a bill that encourages the council to use accepted measuring standards to justify a SIFI designation.

Systemic importance should be determined by appropriate criteria rather than by an arbitrary line that has no justifiable purpose. To advocate for the status quo, and against this legislation, shows a fundamental misunderstanding of the financial system and systemic risk.

I am happy to lend my support to this bill and encourage my colleagues to support this commonsense measure. I, again, thank the gentleman from Missouri (Mr. LUETKEMEYER) for his leadership on this measure.

Ms. MAXINE WATERS of California. Madam Speaker, I continue to reserve the balance of my time.

Mr. LUETKEMEYER. Madam Speaker, may I inquire as to how much time is remaining on both sides?

The SPEAKER pro tempore (Mrs. BLACK). The gentleman from Missouri has 2½ minutes remaining. The gentlewoman from California has 5 minutes remaining.

Mr. LUETKEMEYER. Madam Speaker, I yield 1 minute to the gentlewoman from Utah (Mrs. LOVE). Again, we have a good crop of young folks on our committee, and she is one of those bright stars for us.

Mrs. LOVE. Madam Speaker, we have before us a solution to regulation that causes real harm to an important financial institution, especially in my State, Zions Bancorporation, which supports the financial needs of many families and businesses throughout Utah and the Western States.

Last year, Zions Bancorporation chairman and CEO, Harris Simmons, spoke about increased compliance costs his institution has to face as a result of the enhanced prudential standards requirements of the Dodd-Frank Act. Specifically, Zions has had to divert resources to add nearly 500 additional full-time staff to areas such as compliance, internal audits, credit administration, and enterprise risk management.

Mr. Simmons also testified at the House Financial Services' Financial Institutions and Consumer Credit Subcommittee that these increased compliance costs are offset by reductions in other areas of the organization. Many of them are consumer-facing functions. In other words, Zions Bank had to move resources away from lending to customers and consumer service because of these extra regulations. Yet, Zions is one of the smallest SIFIs, with a business model centered on very traditional banking activities, primarily commercial lending with a particular focus on lending to smaller businesses.

I support H.R. 6392. It allows banks like Zions Bank to get back to what they do best.

Ms. MAXINE WATERS of California. Madam Speaker, I continue to reserve the balance of my time.

Mr. LUETKEMEYER. Madam Speaker, I yield 1 minute to the gentleman from Arkansas (Mr. HILL), who brings a wealth of financial services background to the committee.

Mr. HILL. Madam Speaker, I thank the chairman and congratulate him on this constructive bill.

This bill today is not about dangerous agendas, greed, signing bonuses, or wholesale exemptions of regulation for 27 big banks—not at all. This bill is about using common sense and taking off the autopilot that is in Dodd-Frank, which designates our SIFIs on size alone. In fact, it includes all the factors that should be considered for institutions that might present a systemic risk.

This is a bipartisan bill that has support on both sides of the aisle. Former Chairman Frank's comments have been read into the RECORD, but how about Governor Dan Tarullo: "Resolution planning and the quite elaborate requirements of our supervisory stress testing process do not seem to me to be necessary for banks between $50 billion and $100 billion in assets."

Tom Curry, our comptroller of the currency: "The better approach is to use an asset figure as a first screen and give discretion to the supervisors based on the risks in the business plan and operations."

And Senator SHERROD BROWN, certainly a supporter of Dodd-Frank: "I do agree that some banks above $50 billion should not be regulated like Wall Street megabanks."

I support this bill.

Ms. MAXINE WATERS of California. Madam Speaker, I yield myself such time as I may consume.

Here we are in the lameduck session of Congress, and we are signaling to special interests all the giveaways that are about to come with Republicans in control of Washington. And we do this just after the President-elect selected a man to head the Treasury Department whose bank has been accused of redlining and violating the Fair Housing Act, whose bank was responsible for about 40 percent of reverse mortgage foreclosures in 2009 to 2014, and whose bank was characterized by a New York judge as engaging in harsh, repugnant, shocking, and repulsive acts against debtors.

Donald Trump ran a campaign on anti-Wall Street rhetoric, but appointing a former hedge fund manager, Goldman Sachs, executive and bank CEO, as Treasury Secretary shows his true colors. Mr. Mnuchin is a Wall Street insider with ties to big banks that have a troubling past of putting profits ahead of consumers and taxpayers. Mnuchin, during his time at OneWest, during his time, foreclosed on homes of 36,000 families.

Mr. Mnuchin now sits on the board of CIT, which bought his former bank. Mnuchin took a reported $10.9-million payout when the merger was completed. CIT's regulatory filings indicate that the bank provides Mr. Mnuchin with annual compensation of $4.5 million for each of 2015, 2016, and 2017, which gives a base salary of $800,000, short-term incentives of $1.4 million, and long-term incentives of $2.3 million. That is 88 times the household income of the average American family.

What is worse, CIT is a megabank, and, instead of paying back taxpayers, it went bankrupt, like many of Mr. Trump's failed businesses.

□ 1415

Mnuchin is a man who got rich off of the foreclosure crisis and taxpayer bailouts again—not unlike Mr. Trump himself—and he will now have oversight over significant swaps of our financial regulatory system.

H.R. 6392, in particular, is President-elect Trump's and the congressional GOP's first effort to deregulate Wall Street since the election.

This bill stands to benefit just 27 banks in the United States, and one of those banks is Mr. Mnuchin's bank, CIT. In fact, CIT just recently completed a merger with OneWest, which made Mr. Mnuchin rich. That merger also pushed CIT over the $50-billion threshold that would make the bank subject to Dodd-Frank rules. Rather than submit to more stringent regulation, CIT is trying to grease the skids to get favorable treatment in Congress so that its megamerger won't come with any strings attached. Specifically, this legislation would eliminate CIT from being subjected to more stringent Dodd-Frank rules related to capital, liquidity, risk management, living wills, stress testing, and other crucial requirements that prevent bailouts.

What is more, the legislation would take authority to regulate banks away from our independent regulators and hand that power over to this man, who I am telling you all about, who has a history of proving to have not only foreclosed on a lot of innocent homeowners, but who is, maybe, I think, under investigation now by HUD.

Again, this legislation would take the authority to regulate banks away from our independent regulators and would hand that power over to him.

Mr. Mnuchin would now, per H.R. 6392, be in the driver's seat to determine which banks get regulated and how. That means he could give special favors to his bank while ignoring similarly situated banks, not to mention our financial stability.

My friends on the opposite side of the aisle will tell us: Oh, that is a bailout we had to do in order to keep this country from going into a depression.

You force taxpayers to make that bailout—to pay for it. Now here we are today with a President-elect who pays no taxes. So why would he be worried about whether or not we have a bailout?

I would say this is one of the worst bills that is going to come before us; but just like Mr. HENSARLING said: We ain't seen nothing yet.

Madam Speaker, I yield back the balance of my time.

Mr. LUETKEMEYER. Madam Speaker, I yield myself such time as I may consume.

Just to recap, the Dodd-Frank came into being as a result of the crisis. One of the solutions was to be able to fine systemically important financial institutions before they brought the economy down. Coming up with the SIFI definition was one way to do that. The problem was that the SIFI designation was too large and was being impacted in too many different and wrongful ways. Even Dodd-Frank's original author, Barney Frank, recognized that with his testimony this past week as well as in our committee.

The metrics that we have in the bill are very simple. They are things that are used by the Financial Stability Board and by the Office of Financial Research when they look at global SIFIs. The CIT and OneWest merger that the ranking member keeps talking about are metrics that were used by the regulators to determine whether that was something they should be doing.

We are not reinventing the wheel here. What we are doing is taking the burden off of the midsized regional banks, which is causing fewer products and services to be able to be provided to the customers at an increased cost; so I ask for the passage of the bill.

Madam Speaker, I yield back the balance of my time.

The SPEAKER pro tempore. All time for debate on the bill has expired.

AMENDMENT NO. 1 PRINTED IN PART B OF HOUSE REPORT 114–839 OFFERED BY MR. DAVIDSON

Mr. DAVIDSON. Madam Speaker, I have an amendment at the desk that would ensure the integrity of H.R. 6392, the Systemic Risk Designation Improvement Act of 2016.

The SPEAKER pro tempore. The Clerk will designate the amendment.

The text of the amendment is as follows:

Add at the end the following:
SEC. 7. RULE OF CONSTRUCTION.

Nothing in this Act or the amendments made by this Act may be construed as broad-ly applying international standards except as specifically provided under paragraphs (2) and (3) of section 113(c) of the Dodd-Frank Wall Street Reform and Consumer Protection Act, as added by section 3.

The SPEAKER pro tempore. Pursuant to House Resolution 934, the gentleman from Ohio (Mr. DAVIDSON) and a Member opposed each will control 5 minutes.

The Chair recognizes the gentleman from Ohio.

Mr. DAVIDSON. Madam Speaker, I yield myself 2½ minutes.

Today's bill spells out the criteria the Financial Stability Oversight Council, FSOC, must use in determining institutions of systemic risk.

My amendment will prevent the Federal Reserve and the Treasury from blindly implementing new regulations proposed by an international entity, whether coming from the Basel Commission or from the unelected bureaucrats on the Financial Stability Board. When Congress begins to apply international standards, we need to make certain that executive agencies don't overreach by simply ratifying every decision that is made internationally.

Recently, the Treasury and the Fed have been found to have made determinations that mirror the standards issued by the Financial Stability Board but without sufficient review—simply rubberstamping them. They have gone along with the decisions that have been made by international unelected bureaucrats and, in the process, have harmed our regional and community banks and Americans' access to credit. Similar concerns have been raised by U.S. insurance companies. That is why Mr. LUETKEMEYER is also sponsoring legislation to make sure that these one-size-fits-all regulations are not used to supersede our State-based insurance regulations here in the United States.

H.R. 6392 will provide the necessary relief and transparency that is needed in these systemic risk designations. I am proud to offer this amendment to clarify that our Federal agencies cannot use the loophole of international recommendations to expand their powers and subject our community and local banks to even more burdensome regulations.

Madam Speaker, I reserve the balance of my time.

Ms. MAXINE WATERS of California. Madam Speaker, I rise in opposition to the gentleman's amendment.

The SPEAKER pro tempore. The gentlewoman is recognized for 5 minutes.

Ms. MAXINE WATERS of California. Madam Speaker, this bill outsources our domestic regulation by the Federal Reserve and hands it over to an international group of regulators known as the Financial Stability Board, or the FSB, to determine which banks should be regulated by our regulators. It says this international body should decide which banks are regulated, not the United States Congress.

The U.S. is just one member nation among many represented on the FSB, and the Republicans have often criticized this board of regulators for being "shadowy" and not sufficiently deferential to American interests.

Currently, the FSB makes determinations on which global banks are systemically significant—not significant to the U.S., but to the entire global economy. This legislation imports those determinations and sets our domestic regulation on autopilot. If the international regulators say you are important, then this bill would grandfather you into Dodd-Frank. If not, then you get the big giveaway of deregulation.

This amendment rightfully says that the U.S. shouldn't be giving away our sovereignty over our economy to international regulators, but the amendment fails to have the courage of its convictions. Curiously, it says that nothing in this bill shall broadly apply international regulatory standards to the U.S., with an exception for the part of the bill that applies international regulatory standards to the U.S.

In summary, Democrats who oppose the deregulation of big banks should oppose H.R. 6392, and Republicans who oppose outsourcing our regulation to foreign bureaucrats should oppose H.R. 6392. This amendment does nothing to solve this fundamental issue in the bill, and this legislation is still deeply problematic even if the amendment is accepted.

Madam Speaker, I reserve the balance of my time.

Mr. DAVIDSON. Madam Speaker, I yield the balance of my time to the gentleman from Missouri (Mr. LUETKEMEYER).

Mr. LUETKEMEYER. I thank the gentleman from Ohio (Mr. DAVIDSON) for his interest and for his authoring this amendment.

Madam Speaker, the amendment makes clear that H.R. 6392 should not be construed to allow international standards to be imposed on U.S. institutions. The underlying bill, in two separate places, does rely on a similar framework that is utilized by the Basel Commission and that is used by the Federal Reserve and the Treasury in an effort to ensure that the largest U.S. banks maintain their SIFI designations.

Beyond these provisions, however, it would be highly inappropriate for any international body to use H.R. 6392 to impose any standard on a U.S. entity. It is important to make the point, as we advocate today for risk-based supervision, that we avoid any sort of blanket approach that is so commonly seen out of international regulatory bodies.

In the case of foreign banks in their doing business in the United States, for example, the $50-billion threshold and its interpretation by the Federal Reserve results in a huge number of banks being treated as SIFIs despite the fact that many of them have under $10 billion in assets. As we consider these designations, we need to avoid one-size-fits-all models and look at factors like comparable home-country standards before we move forward on enhanced prudential regulation.

I hope we can address some of these issues in the next Congress and that we can work with international regulators, particularly those in the European Union, to avoid the escalation of the ongoing standoff on bank capital rules. We should work collaboratively to inject commonsense into financial regulation that will protect U.S. taxpayers and the financial system without constricting economic growth.

Mr. DAVIDSON. Madam Speaker, I yield back the balance of my time.

Ms. MAXINE WATERS of California. Madam Speaker, I yield back the balance of my time.

The SPEAKER pro tempore. Pursuant to the rule, the previous question is ordered on the bill and on the amendment offered by the gentleman from Ohio (Mr. DAVIDSON).

The question is on the amendment by the gentleman from Ohio (Mr. DAVIDSON).

The amendment was agreed to.

The SPEAKER pro tempore. The question is on the engrossment and third reading of the bill.

The bill was ordered to be engrossed and read a third time, and was read the third time.

MOTION TO RECOMMIT

Ms. MAXINE WATERS of California. Madam Speaker, I have a motion to recommit at the desk.

The SPEAKER pro tempore. Is the gentlewoman opposed to the bill?

Ms. MAXINE WATERS of California. I am opposed in its current form.

The SPEAKER pro tempore. The Clerk will report the motion to recommit.

Ms. MAXINE WATERS of California. Madam Speaker, I ask unanimous consent to dispense with the reading.

The SPEAKER pro tempore. Is there objection to the request of the gentlewoman from California?

Mr. LUETKEMEYER. Madam Speaker, I object to the dispensing of the reading.

The SPEAKER pro tempore. Objection is heard.

The Clerk will report the motion to recommit.

The Clerk read as follows:

Ms. Maxine Waters of California moves to recommit the bill H.R. 6392 to the Committee on Financial Services with instructions to report the same back to the House forthwith with the following amendment:

Page 4, line 17, strike the quotation mark and following semicolon and insert the following:

"(4) CERTAIN COMPANIES WITH PENDING LAWSUITS OR ENFORCEMENT ACTIONS DESIGNATED BY OPERATION OF LAW.—Notwithstanding any other provision of this subsection, a bank holding company shall be deemed to have been the subject of a final determination under paragraph (1) if the bank holding company, as of the date of enactment of this subsection—

"(A) has total consolidated assets equal to or greater than $50,000,000,000; and

"(B) has disclosed in a filing with the Commission that a department or agency of the United States Government has a pending lawsuit or enforcement action against the bank holding company related to the origination, securitization, or sale of residential mortgage-backed securities.".

Mr. LUETKEMEYER. Madam Speaker, I reserve a point of order.

The SPEAKER pro tempore. A point of order is reserved.

Pursuant to the rule, the gentlewoman from California is recognized for 5 minutes.

Ms. MAXINE WATERS of California. Madam Speaker, this is the final amendment to the bill, which will not kill the bill or send it back to committee. If adopted, the bill will immediately proceed to final passage, as amended.

Madam Speaker, make no mistake. This bill is the opening salvo in the Trump plan to dismantle Dodd-Frank. The House Republicans have been trying for 6 years, ever since we passed Wall Street reform; and on the eve of the President-elect's taking office, this is their big chance to deregulate 27 of the Nation's largest banks.

This bill would strip rules around capital, liquidity, stress testing, and living wills—key components to guard against catastrophic bank failures. These are not community banks. No. These are $50-, $100-, $200-, and $400-billion banks that engage in exotic products like "pick-a-payment," which is when you choose how much you want to pay; and "negative amortization" loans, which is when, incredibly, the loan principal goes up, not down, leading up to the financial crisis.

□ 1430

This bill would strip Fed Chair Janet Yellen of the Fed's independent authority and hand it over to Trump's Wall Street Treasury Secretary, a man who foreclosed on 36,000 families when he ran this bank, a man who has been accused of redlining and fair lending discrimination by civil rights and advocacy groups, a man who would be handed the authority to deregulate the bank on whose board he now serves, if this bill became law. But those conflicts of interest are par for the course in this incoming administration.

President-elect Donald Trump has more conflicts of interest than any incoming President in the history of this country. Trump's son-in-law and close adviser, Jared Kushner, has hundreds of millions of dollars in loans outstanding from domestic and foreign banks and has obtained development financing through a controversial U.S. program that sells green cards.

Legal scholars believe Trump's lease with the government over the Old Post Office Building where his hotel in Washington, D.C., stands will trigger a breach of contract and a conflict of interest the moment he is sworn in. And Trump may even violate the Constitution on the day he takes office, with former-President Bush's ethics lawyer saying that foreign diplomats staying in his hotels would be an unlawful foreign gift.

Madam Speaker, this amendment highlights yet another conflict of interest we are facing. President-elect Trump is deeply indebted to Deutsche Bank. Over the past two decades, Deutsche Bank has been a lender or a co-lender in at least $2.5 billion in loans to Donald Trump or his companies.

Here is a sampling of Trump's indebtedness to Deutsche: The businesses within Trump's network currently owe Deutsche Bank nearly $360 million in outstanding principal, including $125 million for his Florida golf course, up to $69 million for his Chicago high-rise, and a $170 million line of credit used to fund the development of his new hotel in Washington, DC.

This legislation, H.R. 6392, deregulates huge megabanks representing almost 30 percent of the assets currently subject to stricter rules under Dodd-Frank. In the bill, it is possible that the U.S. operations of global megabanks—megabanks like Deutsche Bank—would also be deregulated. And with Donald Trump's appointments interpreting the law, I suspect they will indeed deregulate these global megabanks.

Why is this important? Well, it is important because Deutsche Bank has a potential $14 billion settlement with the Department of Justice pending related to toxic mortgages they packaged and sold leading up to the financial crisis. They sliced and diced subprime loans and duped not only homeowners, but unsuspecting investors. Just like President-elect Trump, they saw the specter of a foreclosure crisis and financial collapse as a business opportunity, not a human tragedy. After Trump's election, news headlines said that Deutsche Bank stood to get a windfall because the new sheriffs in town would go easy on them.

This amendment says enough is enough. While the Trump Justice Department may give Deutsche Bank a break, the United States Congress will not stand idly by and let Trump's conflicts of interest grease the skids for powerful interests in Washington.

I yield back the balance of my time.

Mr. LUETKEMEYER. Madam Speaker, I withdraw my reservation of a point of order.

The SPEAKER pro tempore. The reservation of a point of order is withdrawn.

Mr. LUETKEMEYER. Madam Speaker, I claim time in opposition.

The SPEAKER pro tempore. The gentleman from Missouri is recognized for 5 minutes.

Mr. LUETKEMEYER. Madam Speaker, just to highlight some comments here with regard to the ranking member's last discussion on this point of order, we believe the motion to recommit has absolutely nothing to do with financial stability.

Title 1 of the bill deals with operational standards of bank holding companies. This bill we are working with deals directly with how regulators deal with banks. A pending lawsuit has nothing to do with the financial stability of this bank. This may belong somewhere else in the Dodd-Frank bill, but it doesn't belong in here.

With regards to the underlying bill as well, Madam Speaker, to reiterate some of the points that have been discussed already, we have a situation where the fix for the crisis of 2008 was Dodd-Frank, as was spoken to eloquently by some of my colleagues. Some of the fixes—no bill we put together around here is ever perfect. There are always problems with it. It always needs to be tweaked down the road.

This particular issue we are talking about today, systemically important designation of institutions, was part of a solution to try and be able to identify banks, by definition, that would bring down the entire economy so this couldn't ever happen again. If we have a big bank go down, it could be of such a size and magnitude and connectedness that it would bring down the entire economy. One of the unintended consequences of this is that these regulations have rolled downhill to small, midsized banks. It was unintended, but they are a consequence.

Barney Frank, the author of the bill, has said on numerous occasions—in fact, in our committee, he testified to the fact that this is an unintended consequence—it should be fixed. That is what this bill does. It fixes that problem.

These unintended consequences of all these rules and regulations, which carry costs with them, are rolling downhill to these midsized regional banks; and even at that, they are rolling below that, below 50. If you are talking $10 billion to $50 billion banks, they will tell you that all of the things that the midsized banks above are dealing with, they are dealing with that as well. So these regulations that are supposed to be for the big banks—a trillion dollars and over or whatever—are rolling all the way downhill to the small banks, the small community banks.

Now, they will argue about the fact that $50 billion is an arbitrary figure. It is something we need to keep. That is a big bank.

I am sorry. Madam Speaker, I was a regulator in my former life, and I was a banker in a former life. I can tell you that is a big bank, but that is not something that is going to bring down the economy unless they are interconnected. The metrics in my bill say that if they are interconnected—they have got all sorts of other risky actions they are engaged in—$50 billion is not going to do it.

Things that you have to look at are size and all these other criteria that we have in here. And these are not criteria pulled out of the air. These are criteria that the Federal Stability Board uses, that the Office of Financial Research uses when they look at G-SIBs, which are global SIBs. So these are analysis tools that are there and have been there for a long time.

Why not give the examiners, the regulators, these tools? I can tell you, as a regulator, they already do this.

A while ago, the point was made it takes the regulator about 12 months, in my bill, to come up with these designations. The regulators already do this. They have got the information in hand. There is no reason that they can't do this in a 12-month period. I have been there. I have done that. It is easy to do. They have the information.

So what we are doing is taking existing criteria and asking them to look at the risk and the business model of this particular entity to see if it is something that is big enough and connected enough to go down. $50 billion is not someplace where a bank should be that it is going to cause the entire economy to collapse, no way. Common sense will tell you that.

So, to close out here very quickly, I think that we have a situation where these regulations are costing money to the consumers, to the businesses that the banks lend to. One quick factoid is 75 percent of the banks before Dodd-Frank had free checking, now only 37 percent.

Those are just some of the facts, as they roll downhill, that show that these regulations are having a negative effect on our economy and our local communities. The banks we are talking about are not the gigantic interconnected globals, folks. These are large community banks, which is basically what they all are, that serve communities and mom-and-pop shops. We want to keep them in business. We want to keep our communities growing.

I yield back the balance of my time.

The SPEAKER pro tempore. Without objection, the previous question is ordered on the motion to recommit.

There was no objection.

The SPEAKER pro tempore. The question is on the motion to recommit.

The question was taken; and the Speaker pro tempore announced that the ayes appeared to have it.

Ms. MAXINE WATERS of California. Madam Speaker, on that I demand the yeas and nays.

The yeas and nays were ordered.

The SPEAKER pro tempore. Pursuant to clause 8 of rule XX and the order of the House of today, further proceedings on this question will be postponed.

PERMISSION TO POSTPONE PROCEEDINGS ON MOTION TO RECOMMIT ON H. RES. 933, PROVIDING AMOUNTS FOR FURTHER EXPENSES OF THE COMMITTEE ON ENERGY AND COMMERCE IN THE ONE HUNDRED FOURTEENTH CONGRESS

Mr. HARPER. Madam Speaker, I ask unanimous consent that the question of adopting a motion to recommit on H. Res. 933 may be subject to postponement as though under clause 8 of rule XX.

The SPEAKER pro tempore (Mrs. WAGNER). Is there objection to the request of the gentleman from Mississippi?

There was no objection.

PROVIDING AMOUNTS FOR FURTHER EXPENSES OF THE COMMITTEE ON ENERGY AND COMMERCE IN THE ONE HUNDRED FOURTEENTH CONGRESS

Mr. HARPER. Madam Speaker, by direction of the Committee on House Administration, I call up the resolution (H. Res. 933) providing amounts for further expenses of the Committee on Energy and Commerce in the One Hundred Fourteenth Congress, and ask for its immediate consideration.

The Clerk read the title of the resolution.

The text of the resolution is as follows:

H. RES. 933

Resolved,

SECTION 1. AMOUNTS FOR COMMITTEE EXPENSES.

For further expenses of the Committee on Energy and Commerce (hereafter in this resolution referred to as the "Committee") for the One Hundred Fourteenth Congress, there shall be paid out of the applicable accounts of the House of Representatives not more than $800,000.

SEC. 2. VOUCHERS.

Payments under this resolution shall be made on vouchers authorized by the Committee, signed by the Chairman of the Committee, and approved in the manner directed by the Committee on House Administration.

SEC. 3. REGULATIONS.

Amounts made available under this resolution shall be expended in accordance with regulations prescribed by the Committee on House Administration.

The SPEAKER pro tempore. The gentleman from Mississippi (Mr. HARPER) is recognized for 1 hour.

Mr. HARPER. Madam Speaker, for the purpose of debate only, I yield the customary 30 minutes to the gentleman from Pennsylvania (Mr. BRADY), pending which I yield myself such time as I may consume. During consideration of this resolution, all time yielded is for the purpose of debate only.

GENERAL LEAVE

Mr. HARPER. Madam Speaker, I ask unanimous consent that all Members have 5 legislative days to revise and extend their remarks and to include extraneous matter in the RECORD on the consideration of H. Res. 933, currently under consideration.

The SPEAKER pro tempore. Is there objection to the request of the gentleman from Mississippi?

There was no objection.

Mr. HARPER. Madam Speaker, I rise in support of H. Res. 933, a resolution that authorizes additional funds for the Committee on Energy and Commerce's budget for the remainder of the 114th Congress.

Last year, on October 7, the House passed, by a majority vote, a measure creating a Select Investigative Panel on Infant Lives within the Committee on Energy and Commerce. Our committee has the responsibility to ensure that each committee of the House has sufficient resources to fulfill their assigned oversight duties.

Last year, our committee transferred funds from the committee reserve account to the Energy and Commerce Committee so that the panel could begin its work. An additional transfer was made earlier this year. These funds were allocated based on the full committee's need to fulfill its mission. These initial transfers were insufficient to cover the costs associated with the select panel.

The measure before us on the House floor today will rectify this situation and allow the Committee on Energy and Commerce and the Select Investigative Panel on Infant Lives to continue to operate until the end of this Congress.

□ 1445

Passing this measure to provide additional funds is an institutional responsibility. If we do not allocate these additional funds, the work of the entire Committee on Energy and Commerce, both for the majority and minority, would grind to a halt. The committee would be unable to complete its vital work. This work covers important areas, such as electronic communications, environmental protection, and health care. We saw this week the important work of the committee in the 21st Century Cures Act.

There are differences of opinion on the creation of the select investigative panel. However, we are not here to relitigate a decision that the House made more than a year ago but to fulfill our institutional responsibilities. It is my hope that we will swiftly pass this measure today.

I reserve the balance of my time.

Mr. BRADY of Pennsylvania. Madam Speaker, I yield myself such time as I may consume.

I rise in opposition to this resolution and in opposition to the existence of the panel generally. It has been nothing more than a partisan witch hunt that will ultimately cost taxpayers over a million dollars and has found no wrongdoing by the people it was created to investigate. Three House committees and 13 States have launched their own similar investigations and came to the same conclusion.

The panel has been a one-sided operation from the start, with the majority failing to consult and inform the minority on official actions and withholding panel records and documents.

The dangers of this panel go far beyond simply wasting taxpayer money. It is a direct assault on women's health care and the right to choose. The panel's actions also put at risk the lives of researchers working to find cures to our most debilitating and deadly diseases. It is my hope that this is the last we hear of it.

Madam Speaker, I yield 26 minutes to the gentlewoman from Illinois (Ms. SCHAKOWSKY), and ask unanimous consent that she be permitted to control that time.

The SPEAKER pro tempore. Is there objection to the request of the gentleman from Pennsylvania?

There was no objection.

Mr. HARPER. Madam Speaker, I yield 3 minutes to the gentlewoman from Tennessee (Mrs. BLACKBURN), the chairman of the select investigative panel.

Mrs. BLACKBURN. Madam Speaker, the select investigative panel was formed to investigate areas that, prior to the revelations of undercover journalists, received too little attention. For most of us, it is nothing short of an outrage that Planned Parenthood and other abortion clinics supplement their budgets by selling the leftover parts of babies they have aborted.

This Chamber charged the panel with investigating fetal tissue trafficking, second and third trimester abortion practices, the standard of care for infants who survive abortions, and the role our taxpayer dollars play in this sector of society. Over the last year, we have held hearings that explored the bioethics surrounding fetal tissue use, and that revealed the sobering reality of how fetal tissue is priced.

Our investigation revealed four models by which the subjects of our investigation implicate serious public policy concerns. The first, the middleman model, comprises a middleman and tissue procurer that obtains tissue directly from a source such as an abortion clinic or hospital and then transfers the tissue to a customer, usually a university researcher.

As the example of StemExpress illustrates, the procurement company would embed a lab technician inside an abortion clinic, where the technician would receive the day's orders for body parts at specified gestation periods, access patient files in violation of women's HIPAA privacy rights, and collect the tissue. Then the technician would receive pay and even bonuses based on the tissue she secured.

A second model, the university clinic model, reveals the cozy relationship between abortion clinics and research institutions, most of them State universities funded by the taxpayers. The clinic provides the university the tissue used for research. The university adopts the clinic doctors as faculty members, giving them benefits regardless of whether they actually teach. And, in many cases, thanks to programs like the Ryan Fellowship, medical students are deployed to abortion clinics to be trained as the next generation of abortion providers.

The panel's investigation into a third model, the late-term abortion clinic, revealed the appalling absence of mechanisms or procedures to safeguard those infants who survive the abortion procedure. Put bluntly, even though we have the Born-Alive Infants Protection Act and the prohibition of partial birth abortion on the books, they are not enforced.

Fourth, the panel investigated the model by which Federal tax dollars make their way to abortion clinics, typically by Medicaid payments under title XIX, and fetal tissue researchers.

The SPEAKER pro tempore. The time of the gentlewoman has expired.

Mr. HARPER. Madam Speaker, I yield an additional 1 minute to the gentlewoman from Tennessee.

Mrs. BLACKBURN. Madam Speaker, to provide just a snapshot of the 51 known external audits of Planned Parenthood clinics, nearly all found title XIX overpayments for family planning and reproductive health service claims. The overbilling totalled more than $8.5 million, and that is without counting several False Claims Act lawsuits that allege millions more in overbilling.

Consider all that our panel has identified, despite having just barely a year—even less by the time we were fully staffed—to conduct the investigation. It is now up to us to build on the work, to hold the government accountable, and to stop these affronts to human dignity.

Ms. SCHAKOWSKY. I thank the gentleman from Pennsylvania for yielding the time to me, and I yield myself such time as I may consume.

Madam Speaker, I rise in opposition to this legislation to fund the select investigative panel, the panel that we call the select panel to attack women's health.

It really shouldn't come as any surprise that one of the very first things that the Republicans have done coming back now to Washington is to approve additional funding for this select so-called investigative panel, doubling its budget and putting it on track to spend nearly $1.6-million taxpayer funds by the end of this year.

This investigation is essentially built on a pack of lies that are perpetrated by anti-abortion extremists and has never been and has no chance of becoming a fact-based investigation. The panel Republicans have continually relied on, even today, doctored videotapes, so-called evidence, even though that evidence and those videotapes have been discredited already by three House committees, 13 States, and a Texas grand jury.

Throughout this investigation, Republicans have abused congressional authority, issuing 42 unilateral subpoenas in violation of House rules, demanding that clinics and universities name names of their doctors, students, and staff, and releasing some of these names knowing that doing so puts lives in danger, a truly McCarthyesque attack on individuals. They have compared researchers to Nazi war criminals and echoed the words of anti-abortion activists that were also used by a gunman who shot 12 people, killing 3 at a Planned Parenthood clinic in Colorado Springs.

Despite Republicans' failure to find any evidence of wrongdoing, they continue to make inflammatory, grotesque allegations to justify the panel's existence, and, by their words and actions, have put lifesaving research and women's health care at risk.

The panel has already had a chilling effect on research, drying up the supply of needed tissue for research on multiple sclerosis and threatening research on other diseases from A to Z, Alzheimer's to Zika.

Fetal tissue research has historically had broad, bipartisan support. It is the basis for key vaccines that have saved, literally, millions and millions of lives, including the polio vaccine. That is why over 60 of our Nation's leading medical institutions released an open letter in support of scientific research using fetal tissue.

We cannot afford to let a set of reckless and irresponsible claims stop this vital medical research. This panel and its investigation are a disgrace to this House of Representatives. We need to end this dangerous and unjustified witch hunt, and, instead of providing more funding for this divisive and dangerous inquisition, Congress should shut down this panel and put an end to its shameful proceedings.

Madam Speaker, I reserve the balance of my time.

Mr. HARPER. Madam Speaker, I yield 3 minutes to the gentleman from Pennsylvania (Mr. PITTS).

Mr. PITTS. I thank the gentleman. As a member of the select investigative panel, I rise in support of H. Res. 933.

Madam Speaker, after the release of the undercover videos of Planned Parenthood, one little known tissue procurement company became a household name: StemExpress. They are one of the biggest players in the sale of aborted-baby body parts in the United States. In clear violation of the intent of Federal law, they promise profits to abortion clinics in return for otherwise discarded—and I will use their quote—products of conception.

The select panel learned that in order to make as much tissue available for sale as possible, and thus rake in huge profits, StemExpress sought to contract with the National Abortion Federation. Contracting with this network of abortion clinics would mean access to thousands of baby body parts, which StemExpress could procure, then turn around and sell at huge markups.

Our investigation found that they had created a drop-down menu—here is a copy of part of it—on their Web site, such as one might find on Amazon.com, to facilitate their sales. Their buyers could select the gestational age, the type of tissue, and the number of specimens. For example, you could select three 12-week-old baby scalps, twelve 14-week-old baby brains, one 15-week pair of baby eyes, or seven 16-week baby livers, to name just a few of the combinations. For crying out loud, this is the Amazon.com of baby body parts. It is outrageous. It is disgusting. It is a very disturbing practice that has been tucked away and out of sight for too long.

The CEO of StemExpress told one undercover journalist over lunch and a glass of wine that some of the buyers' lab techs "freak out and have meltdowns" when they see little baby hands and little baby feet attached to an order of limbs. So she makes sure her techs cut off the hands and the feet before shipping off boxes of these body parts. It is this callous, dark talk that has so many Americans concerned with the state of research in our country.

The select panel is proud to support lifesaving ethical research, but, like the rest of America, my colleagues and I know that ethical boundaries do exist, and I hope StemExpress' research will cease to come at the expense of unborn children who have had no say in the so-called donation of their body parts. Many years from now, we will look back on this practice as a dark and horrible time where humanity and human dignity lost to financial profits. We must end this horrific practice. I urge support for this resolution.

Ms. SCHAKOWSKY. Madam Speaker, I yield 2 minutes to the gentleman from New York (Mr. NADLER), the distinguished member on our team of the select panel.

Mr. NADLER. I thank the gentlewoman for yielding.

Madam Speaker, from start to finish, this select panel has abused congressional power in order to intimidate and threaten private people and entities engaged in legal businesses in constitutionally protected health care.

Republicans on the select panel have now spent $1.5 million on this so-called investigation. What do they have to show the American people for spending their hard-earned tax dollars? They have not presented any evidence that any entity broke the law surrounding fetal tissue donation or research. They have not presented any evidence that any entity or physician engaged in the horrifying behavior of which Republicans accuse them. We have heard today on this floor, as we have repeatedly from the select panel, the oft-proven lies that Planned Parenthood sold fetal tissue for profit. We have heard the lie that the clearly doctored and disproven videotapes bore some relationship to reality.

□ 1500

We have heard today on this floor, as we have repeatedly from the select panel, the oft disproved lies that Planned Parenthood sold fetal tissue for profit. We have heard the lie that the clearly doctored and disproved videotapes bore some relationship to reality. We have heard the disproved lie that StemExpress procured fetal tissue not for lifesaving medical research, but for profit.

The Republicans have wasted countless hours and millions of dollars running in circles after evidence that doesn't exist. They have insisted over and over again that entities name names, with no promise or plan to protect those individuals; and when asked to explain why they needed names, they simply refused to answer. When Republicans on the panel did get names, they released some of them publicly, even though they knew that doing so would expose the doctors, researchers, and other private individuals to harassment, threats, and even murder.

The Republicans on the panel have repeatedly made baseless accusations of wrongdoing, with no concern for the consequences. They have had a chilling effect on lifesaving medical research through their intimidation tactics. They have flown in the face of congressional rules and abused congressional power to meet their own blatantly partisan ends. And now the Republicans on the select panel have the audacity to ask for more taxpayer money to fund this witch hunt.

In words once addressed to the last Member of Congress to so clearly violate congressional authority, Senator Joseph McCarthy, I ask my Republican colleagues: "At long last, have you no sense of decency?"

I call on all of my colleagues today to remember their decency. This grotesque and murderous panel should have been shut down long ago. Vote against the previous question, vote against this absurd funding bill, and stand up for the American taxpayer and for the dignity of this institution.

Mr. HARPER. Madam Speaker, I yield 3 minutes to the gentlewoman from Tennessee (Mrs. BLACK).

Mrs. BLACK. Madam Speaker, one of the striking discoveries we have made in this investigation has been the sheer number of laws implicated by the troubling actions of abortion providers, tissue procurement businesses, and researchers. One such law is the HIPAA privacy rule.

The panel's investigation uncovered a series of business contracts between StemExpress, which is a tissue procurement business that is not covered by HIPAA, and several abortion clinics that are. StemExpress paid fees to the abortion clinics for fetal tissue and maternal blood and then resold the fetal tissue and the blood to researchers.

Here is a quick HIPAA privacy tutorial:

The HIPAA privacy rule protects all individually identifiable health information, known as protected health information, or PHI, that is held or transmitted by a covered entity. This information identifies an individual or can reasonably be believed to be useful in identifying an individual, such as a name or an address, and includes demographic data related to her physical or mental health, condition, treatment, and payments.

The panel's investigation indicates that StemExpress and four abortion clinics, including three Planned Parenthood locations, committed systemic violations of a HIPAA privacy rule over a course of about 5 years. The abortion clinics provided patients' private, protected health information to StemExpress to help them obtain human fetal tissue for resale.

How did they do this? Well, the abortion clinics permitted the employees of StemExpress to enter their clinics to obtain human fetal tissue from the aborted infants, obtain protected health information about their patients, interact with the patients, and, yes, even seek and obtain patient consent for the tissue donation.

StemExpress did not have a medically valid reason to see, and the abortion clinics did not have a reason to disclose, the patients' private information. Instead, the abortion clinics intentionally shared patients' most intimate private information with StemExpress to financially benefit StemExpress and the clinics.

The panel has made a referral of each of these entities to the Department of Health and Human Services and has requested a swift and full investigation by the HHS Office for Civil Rights. But more importantly, we have discovered a deeply concerning violation of a law that protects the most cherished privacy rights.

Ms. SCHAKOWSKY. Madam Speaker, I just find it so hypocritical that the majority is talking about putting peoples' private names out into the public when we have had people who have been attacked and lives threatened as a result of them putting names out there.

Madam Speaker, I yield 2 minutes to the gentlewoman from Washington (Ms. DELBENE), another distinguished member of our select panel.

Ms. DELBENE. Madam Speaker, I rise in strong opposition.

This resolution provides an additional $800,000 of taxpayer money to a select investigative panel that should never have been created in the first place. As a member of that panel, I can tell you it has been nothing more than a bully pulpit for the majority to spread extreme anti-choice falsehoods and fabrications, with no basis in reality. This so-called investigation has repeatedly shown contempt for the facts and disdain for the truth.

Instead of carrying out a fair and evidence-based process, the panel has spent the last year publicly targeting women's healthcare providers, bullying scientists and medical students, delaying medical research, and trying to cut off lines of scientific inquiry, all because the majority opposes a woman's constitutional right to choose.

Now we are voting to double the panel's budget. It is ridiculous. No one in this Chamber should be condoning this kind of harassment and intimidation, let alone approving hundreds of thousands of additional taxpayer dollar to do so. This has been a brazenly partisan and ideological witch hunt, and it should have been shut down months ago.

Rather than wasting another $800,000 on this dangerous panel, Congress could use that money to provide more than 270,000 school lunches to low-income students, purchase nearly 12,000 textbooks to make higher education more affordable for college students, or purchase more than 3 million diapers to help new mothers care for their babies. But instead, that money will go toward intimidating doctors, harassing researchers, and delaying the progress of science. It is shameful.

We shouldn't throw good many after bad by passing this legislation. I urge my colleagues to vote "no."

Mr. HARPER. Madam Speaker, I yield 3 minutes to the gentleman from Indiana (Mr. BUCSHON), who is a medical doctor.

Mr. BUCSHON. Madam Speaker, this is about infant lives, but I would like address what else it is about. It is about science and research. The other side seems to only want to focus on politics and scare tactics.

From the beginning, we recognized the other side would try to avert attention from our investigation by falsely claiming we are opposed to science. As a doctor, I find that offensive, and I think it is a dangerous practice to introduce fear into important scientific debates.

Every member of the panel is committed to medical research that finds cures. The rhetoric that we are opposed to cures for Zika, HIV, Alzheimer's, or Parkinson's is just ridiculous and wrong.

The United States of America is a global leader in scientific research. We should all be proud of the research enterprise in our country and support it with tax dollars. The House Select Panel on Infant Lives shares this support. We are strongly committed to promoting both basic and clinical research.

The goal of the House select panel is not to oppose science but, rather, to determine how best to support science so that this important work can advance as rapidly as possible without ethical compromise. As the history of biomedical research in the 20th century clearly demonstrates, when scientific research is separated from ethics or the law, grave injustice can occur.

We here in Congress, like the rest of Americans, care deeply about protecting the rights of patients and ensuring ethical oversight of research procedures. These are not meant to "hinder" advances in science but, rather, to ensure that the scientific enterprise more perfectly fulfills its promise to society by advancing in a manner that is both just and ethical.

Through the panel's investigation, we have discovered inaccuracies about the role of human fetal tissue and have sought to correct them to realistically address the obstacles facing research.

Any argument from the 1950s—or even the 1990s, for that matter—about biomedical research is outdated, and the actual record is clear: human fetal tissue did not directly result in a vaccine for diseases like measles. Similarly, the Nobel Prize was not awarded for curing polio using human fetal tissue. In fact, of the 75 vaccines in use today, not one was produced using fetal tissue.

Furthermore, the NIH has not funded fetal tissue transplant grants for nearly 10 years. That should tell us something. We examined 30 major grants that were funded by the NIH over the last 5 years and found that human fetal tissue research represents only a tiny fraction of the overall scientific enterprise. In fact, only 0.2 percent used human fetal tissue.

Hysterical calls for enhanced fetal tissue research through expanded abortion licenses are a matter of politics, not medicine or science. A small subset of NIH-funded grants use fetal tissue to study things like birth defects. These types of grants represent only 1 in 100,000.

The SPEAKER pro tempore. The time of the gentleman has expired.

Mr. HARPER. Madam Speaker, I yield the gentleman an additional 1 minute.

Mr. BUCSHON. Tissue or cells for these studies could be derived from an-

other source than aborted babies, like premature natural demise infants whose parents are willing to donate. The other grants use fetal tissue when alternatives are easily available, like placenta, cord blood, or modified adult stem cells.

Some grants even study adult macular degeneration. Research on adult macular degeneration should be conducted on adult donor eyes, but these grants are instead using fetal eyes from aborted infants—not because of science, but because of convenience.

Madam Speaker, I know these things can be uncomfortable to discuss, but that is why the other side wants to avoid the facts and that is why this debate is so important. It is about conducting medical research in an ethical and just manner. So let's sit down and talk science with the NIH and others so that research works for everyone in an ethical and moral way.

Mr. HARPER. Madam Speaker, may I inquire as to how much time is remaining?

The SPEAKER pro tempore. The gentleman from Mississippi has 14 minutes remaining, and the gentlewoman from Illinois has 21½ minutes remaining.

Ms. SCHAKOWSKY. Madam Speaker, I yield 2 minutes to the gentlewoman from New Jersey (Mrs. WATSON COLEMAN).

Mrs. WATSON COLEMAN. Madam Speaker, I am disappointed that we are here today asking the American taxpayers to waste another $800,000 on an unnecessary, dangerous investigation.

This select panel was formed based on fraudulent videos created by anti-abortion extremists to attack Planned Parenthood, an organization that has always fought for women's rights and provides healthcare services to 3 million women and men each year.

I was proud to be the first Member of Congress to speak out against these videos immediately after their release. And here we are, a year and a half later, with no evidence of wrongdoing after 17 separate investigations in three House committees, 13 States, and one grand jury. Yet Republicans continue to chase false, inflammatory allegations, at a severe cost to advances in medicine and to the safety of those involved in this lifesaving research.

Panel Republicans have conducted themselves in ways reminiscent of Joe McCarthy's abusive tactics: witnesses have been harassed and intimated during testimony; names of researchers, students, clinical personnel, and doctors have been released publicly, placing their lives in great danger; misleading "exhibits" have been manufactured; critical documents have been withheld from Democrats; and Republicans have continued to fan the flames of anti-abortion extremism with their inflammatory rhetoric.

Let us not forget the horrible tragedy that occurred in a Colorado

Planned Parenthood clinic where a gunman shot 12 people and killed 3, echoing the same anti-abortion rhetoric used by Republicans to this day.

What this investigation truly is is an attack on women's rights and women's access to legal health services. The select panel comes at a time when Republicans have repeatedly voted to defund Planned Parenthood, eliminate family planning services, and restrict access to abortions.

This investigation dishonors this institution and hurts the American people that Congress is elected to serve. Let's put an end to the witch hunt, stop wasting taxpayer dollars, and reject this resolution.

☐ 1515

Mr. HARPER. Madam Speaker, I yield 3 minutes to the gentlewoman from Missouri (Mrs. HARTZLER).

Mrs. HARTZLER. Madam Speaker, the Select Investigative Panel on Infant Lives investigation has uncovered many valid concerns and potential law violations that are disturbing, horrific, and unacceptable.

In the course of our investigation, we discovered a hardness, a callousness, and a track record of deceptive tactics that some abortion clinics and fetal tissue procurers exercised toward vulnerable women. It is difficult to imagine a more vulnerable time in a woman's life than when she is considering an abortion.

What if, during that time, the woman is lied to and told that, by having an abortion, she will facilitate research that will cure tragic diseases?

This is exactly the type of concern that our panel addressed during our hearing on bioethics and fetal tissue. During that hearing, I shared a consent form widely used by abortion clinics to obtain a mother's consent to donate fetal tissue. And the form stated that research using the blood from pregnant women and tissue that has been aborted has been used to treat and find a cure for such diseases as diabetes, Parkinson's Disease, Alzheimer's disease, cancer, and AIDS. This is clearly false.

The witness, who is an ethics expert, agreed and he said that the idea of promise of cures found in the form was a "very powerful motivator." He also expressed concern that the scientific community's standards for fetal tissue donation are absent in that consent form, saying, "the thoroughness of the consent seems to be missing in this form."

A researcher for the minority testified during the hearing. He also agreed, stating the form would not have made it past his institutional review board. Yet, this is what is being used in abortion clinics with vulnerable women.

In other words, the testimony provided by both of the witnesses from the majority and the minority raised concerns that the principles embodied in ethics reports, and later incorporating the Federal regulations, are not being followed by abortion providers seeking consent for the donation of human fetal tissue.

We must raise this awareness, make sure people know, and make sure that women are protected.

Ms. SCHAKOWSKY. Madam Speaker, I yield 2 minutes to the gentlewoman from Colorado (Ms. DEGETTE), not only someone who has been such a stalwart for women's rights and reproductive rights, but the co-chair of the Pro-Choice Caucus in the House of Representatives.

Ms. DEGETTE. Madam Speaker, so this panel was supposed to be set up to investigate the alleged sale of fetal tissue, which is illegal under current law. That didn't turn out so well.

So now, as you can hear from the other side of the aisle, they are going after fetal tissue research itself, something that has been legal and used in an ethical way since the 1930s, something which has been used to find most vaccines and other cures for diseases in this country, something which a panel appointed by President Ronald Reagan, found unanimously in 1980 to be ethical.

So I want to ask, Madam Speaker, what the heck are we being asked to spend another $800,000 on?

The total funding for this witch hunt and this reckless endeavor is now more than $1.5 million. We have gone after women and punished them. We have gone after medical professionals and put their lives at risk, like what happened in my neighborhood of Colorado Springs, Colorado. We have put doctors and researchers on the line, and we have had a chilling effect on important biomedical research.

I say enough is enough. We need to disband this select committee. We need to continue to make sure that we have ethical medical research in this country because, frankly, that will lead to the cures that affect diseases that affect millions of Americans.

Mr. Speaker, from its start, the Select Panel has been nothing but a partisan witch hunt. The apparent goal of the Select Panel is to punish and intimidate women medical professionals and researchers who are following the law. Through wanton use of subpoenas, inflammatory language and release of private information—including addresses and phone numbers where those wishing to harass health care providers can find them—the Select Panel as put many, many people at risk. It has also threatened life-saving research and health care that these people provide.

Make no mistake: this threat is very real. Clinics are picketed and fire-bombed, doctors and their families are targeted at their homes, and some have even been murdered.

Furthermore, the Select Panel is trying to force universities and clinics to turn over the names of their researchers, graduate students, lab and clinic staff and doctors—for no legitimate congressional reason. Not since Joe

McCarthy have we seen such abusive pressure tactics to "name names."

The Select Panel is acting as judge, jury, and executioner and endangering lives. It is time for Speaker RYAN to disband this panel—rather than let it gorge even more on taxpayer funds.

Like the seventeen investigations that preceded it, the Select Panel has found no evidence of wrongdoing by Planned Parenthood, other providers, researchers or the companies that facilitate life-saving research and health care for women.

The Washington Post editorial board called on Speaker RYAN to disband the Select Committee months ago, noting that it "has issued indiscriminate subpoenas, intimidated witnesses and relied on misleading information. It is abusing power at taxpayer expense, and Democrats are right to demand its shutdown." The paper added, "There is no legitimate reason for this inquiry."

The Select Panel is a waste of funds, an attack on women's rights, a danger to life-saving medical research and an abusive use of Congressional power for mere partisan gain.

So Mr. Speaker, I say enough with the smear campaigns, fishing expeditions and endless stream of subpoenas. Congressional bullying to frighten women out of exercising their rights, and to drive researchers and healthcare providers out of business, has to stop.

We in the minority have long called for the Select Committee to be disbanded before it does any more damage. I look forward to closing this shameful chapter in Congressional history at the end of this year.

Mr. HARPER. Madam Speaker, I yield 3 minutes to the gentleman from Maryland (Mr. HARRIS), who is also a medical doctor.

Mr. HARRIS. Madam Speaker, I am glad the gentlewoman talked about the need for ethical medical research because one of our panel's accomplishments is to show how StemExpress undermined the very foundations of ethical American scientific research.

First, Federal regulations require researchers to obtain informed consent from each person used as a subject. The basic element of informed consent includes a detailed explanation of the purposes of the research for which tissue is being obtained. StemExpress, as we found, simply did not follow that requirement.

HHS regulations also require that in obtaining consent, researchers "minimize the possibility of coercion or undue influence." Well, StemExpress documents that we uncovered shows that its employees were already promising to deliver baby body parts even before the abortions were performed. That raises serious concerns that there may have been coercion or undue influence on women to donate parts of their aborted babies.

Now, second, Federal regulations require that all research that involves human subjects needs approval from an institutional review board, or IRB. As a medical researcher, I had to file IRB

applications and receive IRB approval from my university's IRB.

Now, it turns out that StemExpress received their IRB approval from a company called BioMed IRB, a California firm that is basically an online, mail order IRB that the Federal Government actually barred for 2 years because they violated FDA rules in granting their IRB approval.

The FDA gave the panel its file on BioMed IRB. Madam Speaker, that file literally was more than a foot high.

HHS regulations require IRBs to "prepare and maintain adequate documentation" of their activities, including: copies of all research proposals reviewed, records of continuing review activities, and copies of all correspondence between the IRB and the investigators, in this case, StemExpress' founder and CEO, Cate Dyer.

Now, the panel subpoenaed BioMed IRB for all documents related to its approval of StemExpress' research protocol. BioMed IRB's executive director informed the panel that, in regards to those records, "there are none." In other words, BioMed clearly violated Federal regulations on IRBs.

The head of BioMed went further. He told the panel to just bring on a contempt proceeding. That is the IRB StemExpress used. That says a lot about StemExpress' motives and it says a lot about the accomplishments of the select panel. None of these shameful practices would have been discovered if not for the panel's investigative work this year.

As a physician and researcher, I know that if I had used the same shady tactics as StemExpress and BioMed IRB, at best, my research reputation would be at risk and, at worst, I would be facing prison.

Ms. SCHAKOWSKY. Madam Speaker, I yield 1 minute to the gentlewoman from Connecticut (Ms. ESTY).

Ms. ESTY. Madam Speaker, I rise today in opposition to H. Res. 933, legislation that would waste an additional 800,000 taxpayer dollars on the partisan witch hunt against Planned Parenthood.

I learned from a young age the value of making quality reproductive health care available to everyone. In the rural town I grew up in, too many young women didn't have access to family planning services. Too many got pregnant, dropped out of school, and never pursued their dreams. That is why, in college, I volunteered with Planned Parenthood to ensure legal access to the full range of safe family planning services for all women.

So instead of funding a sham investigation, $800,000 could fund lifesaving breast exams, pregnancy tests, Pap smears, and ovarian cancer screenings.

Today I stand with women and men across this country to speak out against a baseless investigation, which has shamefully wasted tax dollars to attack the very people who most need our help.

Mr. HARPER. Madam Speaker, I yield 3 minutes to the gentlewoman from Utah (Mrs. LOVE).

Mrs. LOVE. Madam Speaker, my colleagues on the other side have said that the three House Committee investigations related to the sale of fetal tissue have produced nothing. Others have said that the State Attorney General investigations have also looked into the matter and have found nothing. They complain that this is a waste of time and they complain that it is a waste of money.

First of all, there is so much that we don't know and the American people don't know and still don't understand about this industry. However, since the panel's investigation, we have uncovered alarming revelations about the fetal tissue industry and, because of this, there have been criminal and regulatory referrals. They have resulted in numerous investigations around the Nation, and I will highlight eight of these.

First, the panel discovered that the University of New Mexico was violating their State's Anatomical Gift Act by receiving tissue from late-term abortion clinics. This is currently being investigated.

Second, the panel made a forensic accounting analysis of StemExpress' limited production and determined that they were profiting from the sale of baby body parts. Now the El Dorado District Attorney and the United States Department of Justice are investigating this.

Third, the panel learned that StemExpress and certain abortion clinics were violating HIPAA privacy rights of vulnerable women for the sole purpose of increasing and harvesting fetal tissue to make money.

Fourth, the panel discovered that an abortion clinic in Arkansas violated State law when it sent tissue to StemExpress. This, too, is under investigation.

Fifth, the panel discovered that a university in Ohio was trafficking in baby body parts, an illegal act under Ohio State law.

Sixth, it was discovered that DV Biologics, another tissue procurement company, was profiting from the sale of fetal tissue and violated California State law. This case has been filed.

Seventh, recently the panel learned that Planned Parenthood of Gulf Coast violated both Texas and U.S. law when it sold baby body parts to the University of Texas.

Eighth, the panel also learned that Advanced Bioscience Resources made a profit when it sold tissue to various universities.

As elected Representatives, we are tasked with oversight of our government that enforces our laws. These eight referrals are proof of potential criminal activity in the fetal tissue industry. They justify the existence of the panel and their investigations.

The work of the select panel is not over. More referrals will come, and we need to complete this process. Continued funding for the panel's unfinished work is needed.

I urge my colleagues to support this resolution to fund the investigative work and fulfill the obligations that we have to the American people and the rule of law.

Ms. SCHAKOWSKY. Madam Speaker, let me just say that bogus referrals do not a conviction make, and that StemExpress had offered many times to come in with its procurement officers and answer all the questions. They were denied that.

Madam Speaker, I yield 1 minute to the gentlewoman from Massachusetts (Ms. CLARK).

Ms. CLARK of Massachusetts. Madam Speaker, I thank the gentlewoman for yielding.

Republicans today are asking us to spend more than $1.5 million to conduct a radical, dangerous inquisition that targets and intimidates private citizens.

To satisfy their seemingly unquenchable obsession with rolling back women's reproductive rights and access to basic health care, this overreaching panel recklessly has demanded names, and interferes in the lives of law-abiding students, scientists, and researchers whose private lives and jobs have been turned upside down by their own government.

What do we have to show for this display of government abuse?

Absolutely nothing. In fact, it is worse than nothing.

Today, they are invoking institutional responsibility to ask the taxpayers to foot a bill for $800,000 of their own cost overruns. This is money that could have been used to help families, feed the hungry, help our veterans and military families, and go toward education.

I urge my colleagues to reject this dangerous abuse of power and taxpayer funding.

Mr. HARPER. Madam Speaker, I yield 3 minutes to the gentleman from Wisconsin (Mr. DUFFY).

Mr. DUFFY. Madam Speaker, I thank the gentleman from Mississippi for yielding.

Let's be really clear about what this is about. This is about following the law. We negotiate, we vote, we pass laws, the President signs them, and they should be enforced. That is what this conversation is about, Madam Speaker.

StemExpress has thumbed its nose against the select investigative panel and obstructed our efforts to bring light to the fetal tissue procurement industry.

□ 1530

Nearly a year ago, the panel requested information from StemExpress regarding where they procured their fetal tissue, whom they distributed the fetal tissue to, any communications instructing the company's employees to procure fetal tissue, and all accounting records and banking records related to fetal tissue.

StemExpress, in response to that request, has given us none—zero—no document. So to compel StemExpress to provide the panel with this information, the panel issued the company a subpoena. Instead of complying with the subpoena, StemExpress only turned over limited information to the panel, and the information that they turned over to us was so heavily redacted that it was completely useless for investigative purposes.

To date, the select panel has not received a single accounting or bank record from StemExpress. So they have failed to comply with our requests and our subpoenas in violation of the law.

If StemExpress is within the limits of the law, if nothing is illegal or immoral, then why does StemExpress refuse to turn over all the documents that our panel has requested? Opening your accounting records to a congressional panel shouldn't be that difficult.

StemExpress has had plenty of time to get their act together and provide us with the requested documents that we have asked for. Other organizations that we have reached out to and made the same requests to have turned over the documents in a pretty timely fashion.

For failure to comply with our subpoenas, this panel has recommended the House hold Cate Dyer, the CEO of StemExpress, in contempt of Congress.

Despite StemExpress' best efforts to stonewall this investigation, the panel did find out the name of StemExpress' bank which we subpoenaed. The bank provided us with StemExpress' banking records. So, again, StemExpress won't give us the records, but we got them from the bank.

We now know why StemExpress was hiding these documents. The banking records reveal that StemExpress may have been shredding documents that were directly related to this panel's investigation. The bank records show that payments were made to a shredding company—a shredding company. We looked back at all the records we sought from StemExpress back to 2012, and there is no payments to a shredding company. But when this panel started its investigation and when we started asking for documentation, guess what? You have bank records that show they hired a shredding company. Why hire a shredding company when we were starting our investigation?

The SPEAKER pro tempore. The time of the gentleman has expired.

Mr. HARPER. Madam Speaker, may I inquire as to how much time is remaining.

The SPEAKER pro tempore. The gentleman from Mississippi has 3 minutes remaining. The gentlewoman from Illinois has 16 minutes remaining.

Mr. HARPER. Madam Speaker, I yield the gentleman an additional 1 minute.

Mr. DUFFY. Madam Speaker, there is no cause and no reason why StemExpress would allegedly shred these documents. We both know on both sides of the aisle—though we may have a disagreement on this issue—that when this Congress sends a lawful request to an institution, they are required to provide the documents that are requested. Both sides of the aisle know that when we send a subpoena, those who are subpoenaed are required to provide those documents to us.

So if StemExpress has failed to comply with these requests and these subpoenas, and if they are willing to violate the law in regard to subpoenas to hide information, the question becomes: What laws are they willing to violate in regard to the sale of baby body parts? I think that question deserves to be answered by StemExpress, by this institution, and for the American people.

So I would ask support for this additional funding to complete this investigation and provide documentation to this country and to this House about what has been taking place in regard to the procurement and sale of fetal tissue.

1. Date of Congressional Action: August 7, 2015.

a. Event: Energy & Commerce Committee letter to StemExpress requesting a briefing.

b. Date of StemExpress Payment to Shred-It Us: August 13, 2015.

2. Date of Congressional Action: August 21, 2015.

a. Event: StemExpress briefing to Energy & Commerce Committee.

b. Date of StemExpress Payment to Shred-It Us: August 13, 2015.

3. Date of Congressional Action: September 17, 2015.

a. Event: Senate Judiciary Committee document request letter to StemExpress.

b. Date of StemExpress Payment to Shred-It Us: September 29, 2015; November 10, 2015; December 10, 2015.

4. Date of Congressional Action: December 17, 2015.

a. Event: Select Investigative Panel document request letter to StemExpress.

b. Date of StemExpress Payment to Shred-It Us: January 12, 2016.

5. Date of Congressional Action: January 15, 2016.

a. Event: StemExpress first production in response to Select Panel document request letter.

b. Date of StemExpress Payment to Shred-It Us: January 12, 2016.

6. Date of Congressional Action: February 9, 2016.

a. Event: StemExpress production in response to Select Panel document request letter.

b. Date of StemExpress Payment to Shred-It Us: January 27, 2016.

7. Date of Congressional Action: February 12, 2016.

a. Event: Select Panel Subpoena to StemExpres.

b. Date of StemExpress Payment to Shred-It Us.

8. Date of Congressional Action: March 28, 2016.

a. Event: StemExpress production in response to Panel subpoena.

b. Date of StemExpress Payment to Shred-It Us: March 21, 2016.

9. Date of Congressional Action: May 10, 2016.

a. Event: StemExpress production in response to Panel subpoena.

b. Date of StemExpress Payment to Shred-It Us: April 26, 2016.

Ms. SCHAKOWSKY. Madam Speaker, I yield 1 minute to the gentleman from Pennsylvania (Mr. EVANS) who is a new Member. He has served over three decades in the Pennsylvania legislature and now has joined us.

Mr. EVANS. Madam Speaker, I would like to thank the gentlewoman from Illinois.

In the short 2 weeks that I have been here, Madam Speaker, I have observed a lot of interesting things take place. But what I especially have observed at this particular point, Madam Speaker, is that the American taxpayers shouldn't be asked to spend another $800,000 on an unnecessary and dangerous selective investigation.

Don't take my word, Madam Speaker, look at the aspect of quotes from around the United States.

The Tennessean: "Right now, the panel is creating the perception that it is embroiled in a wild goose chase."

The New York Times: "Neither the videos nor the many investigations that followed have found any evidence that Planned Parenthood offered to sell fetal tissue for a profit."

"Elected officials should not use the power of the office to intimidate citizens who hold different points of view."

The New York Times: "Nor is there any reason to conduct this investigation . . . Republicans are pointlessly attacking a practice that could save lives and, in the process, potentially putting researchers' lives at risk."

The Hill: "The committee is abusing its power and the effect is very troubling for researchers and patients alike."

The SPEAKER pro tempore. The time of the gentleman has expired.

Ms. SCHAKOWSKY. Madam Speaker, I yield the gentleman an additional 1 minute.

Mr. EVANS. The fact is Planned Parenthood does not sell fetal tissue for profit and never has. A Republican-led House panel is undeterred and conducting its own investigation and, more accurately, witch hunt. Even more troubling is the considerable time and money that will be wasted on this political damage to health care and medical research.

Madam Speaker, this is not needed. We should be against it.

Ms. SCHAKOWSKY. Madam Speaker, I yield 1 minute to the gentlewoman from California (Ms. JUDY CHU).

Ms. JUDY CHU of California. Today, Republicans are asking taxpayers to spend $800,000 to cover for their mistakes. The select panel to investigate Planned Parenthood, which was created based on lies spread by anti-abortion extremists, has already overspent the $1 million this Republican Congress has allocated them with no real findings. Now they want to continue their attack on women and Planned Parenthood. This is outrageous.

This select panel—along with 13 States, three House committees, and a Texas grand jury investigation—has found no wrongdoing on the part of Planned Parenthood. It is clear that, after over a year of investigations, Republicans are not seeking truth or better policy.

Instead, this panel has released confidential documents to the public, compared researchers to Nazi war criminals, and exposed doctors and researchers to harassment and violence. We cannot continue to fund this fruitless witch hunt that endangers our researchers and slows important medical discoveries.

I strongly oppose this committee and urge my colleagues to vote "no."

Mr. HARPER. Madam Speaker, may I inquire as to how many additional speakers the minority may have?

Ms. SCHAKOWSKY. Madam Speaker, I have six additional speakers and still, I think, some additional time beyond that.

Mr. HARPER. Madam Speaker, I yield 1 minute to the gentleman from Pennsylvania (Mr. ROTHFUS).

Mr. ROTHFUS. Madam Speaker, I rise today in support of this resolution. The Select Investigative Panel on Infant Lives has been investigating potential violations of the Federal law that makes it illegal to sell fetal tissue—that is body parts—for profit. The evidence reveals appalling practices. For example, on video, we saw a Planned Parenthood doctor talking about doing "less crunchy" types of abortion. That was to make sure they had intact body parts to sell.

The gruesome practices the panel discovered shocked the conscience. Where does this end?

Consider this: It was startling to learn that the University of New Mexico had a summer camp program in which students dissected the brains of unborn children. According to documents obtained by the panel, the university ordered from a late-term abortion doctor "whole, fixed brains to dissect with summer camp students."

Think about that. We are talking about students—teenagers—dissecting the brains of someone within the age group of their own siblings. What barbarity are we teaching our children? How seared have our consciences become?

The select panel must move forward with its investigation into these alarming violations of law and assaults on human dignity and conscience.

Ms. SCHAKOWSKY. Madam Speaker, I yield 1 minute to the gentleman from California (Mr. RUIZ) who is a doctor.

Mr. RUIZ. Madam Speaker, I rise in strong opposition to H. Res. 933. I oppose funding for the select panel to attack and intimidate women's health care.

The select panel is a baseless committee formed with no regard to the facts or evidence of this case. In fact, the creators of the purposefully doctored and highly manipulated videos that they consistently bring up that this investigation is based on have been indicted on criminal felony charges, and we should be investigating their legal practices instead. Continuing to fund this panel is a disgrace, and this investigation must cease immediately.

Instead of taking action that would improve the lives of women and families across the country, this panel continues to chase baseless allegations.

As an emergency physician, I am exceptionally disappointed. The reckless work of the panel puts women's reproductive rights in jeopardy and threatens to undo the progress we have made over the last 40 years. It is also a complete waste of taxpayer money.

I stand in strong opposition to this resolution and call on this panel to be disbanded. Let's take real action to improve the health and well-being of this country.

Ms. SCHAKOWSKY. Madam Speaker, I yield 1 minute to the gentlewoman from Wisconsin (Ms. MOORE) who is my friend.

Ms. MOORE. Madam Speaker, I thank the gentlewoman from Illinois.

Madam Speaker, I rise today in strident opposition to H. Res. 933.

Madam Speaker, we have heard so much about fake news lately, and now we are being asked for taxpayer funding for fake congressional committees. This resolution provides another 800,000 taxpayer dollars to the Republicans' ongoing hatchet job against Planned Parenthood. We already know the facts on the faked Planned Parenthood videos and the unethical videographer. The fake committee's only goal is to create Orwellian unfacts.

So far, this fake committee has found no wrongdoing by Planned Parenthood or their doctors. Of course, this panel knows that they wouldn't find anything because Planned Parenthood has been cleared of wrongdoing 17 times by three different House committees, 17 State investigations, and a grand jury.

Now, despite all this, Republicans want to waste more taxpayer dollars.

The SPEAKER pro tempore. The time of the gentlewoman has expired.

Ms. SCHAKOWSKY. Madam Speaker, I yield the gentlewoman an additional 30 seconds.

Ms. MOORE. Madam Speaker, despite all this, Republicans want to waste more taxpayer dollars for their smear campaign, money that could be used on meaningful measures to reduce infant mortality, feed hungry children, or improve early childhood education. What we really need to get to the bottom of is: What will it take to get Republicans to get the target off women's backs?

Do that, and we might actually make some progress.

Ms. SCHAKOWSKY. Madam Speaker, I yield 1 minute to the gentleman from Michigan (Mr. KILDEE).

Mr. KILDEE. Madam Speaker, I thank my friend and colleague for her leadership and for yielding.

Let's just be clear. We know what this is. This is yet another attempt to fund with Federal taxpayer dollars a Republican messaging effort to attack Planned Parenthood.

More than 2.5 million people—2.5 million women—every year rely on Planned Parenthood for lifesaving cancer screenings and for other health services. We have important legislative work to do, and we ought not be using taxpayer dollars to fund this effort which has clearly been described in all sorts of lofty tones but is essentially a political witch hunt after an organization that provides essential services to women.

The majority cannot deny the chilling effect that this effort has had on medical research. It has already been revealed that this is also an attack on stem cell research. You just have to listen to the debate.

The SPEAKER pro tempore. The time of the gentleman has expired.

Ms. SCHAKOWSKY. Madam Speaker, I yield the gentleman an additional 30 seconds.

Mr. KILDEE. We need to make sure that we are pursuing scientific research to fight diseases like diabetes, like Alzheimer's, and like multiple sclerosis, a disease my wife, Jennifer, has been fighting for 18 years.

□ 1545

We are one of those families that, when we hear about medical research and we hear about stem cell research, in particular, our ears perk up because we know there is hope in that research.

This effort—no matter what anybody wants to say, it is well documented—has had a chilling effect on that medical research, and we ought to shut this down.

Mr. HARPER. Madam Speaker, I continue to reserve the balance of my time.

Ms. SCHAKOWSKY. Madam Speaker, I yield 1 minute to the gentleman from Florida (Mr. DEUTCH).

Mr. DEUTCH. Madam Speaker, I thank my friend, the gentlewoman from Illinois (Ms. SCHAKOWSKY) for yielding.

Madam Speaker, it is time to move on from this dangerous, partisan, and wasteful investigation into Planned Parenthood. This case is closed—after investigations with 13 States, three House committees, and a Texas Grand Jury that found no wrongdoing by Planned Parenthood.

The majority wants $1.5 million from the American taxpayers to fund this dangerous sham when they know that they will never find evidence of wrongdoing by Planned Parenthood.

But the evidence doesn't matter, Madam Speaker. The majority knows that, if they keep this farce in the headlines, it will do real damage to women seeking health care. They know that it will feed fake news sites on the Internet. They know that it will block women from exercising their constitutional rights. And they know that it will unfairly harass women's health clinics. Madam Speaker, they know that this will put abortion providers and their staff in danger.

This panel serves no true investigatory purpose. It is a political tool. It is a disgrace.

I urge my colleagues to vote "no."

Mr. HARPER. Madam Speaker, I continue to reserve the balance of my time.

Ms. SCHAKOWSKY. Madam Speaker, if I could inquire how much time I have left.

The SPEAKER pro tempore. The gentlewoman from Illinois has 8½ minutes remaining.

Ms. SCHAKOWSKY. Madam Speaker, I yield 1 minute to the gentlewoman from California (Ms. LEE).

Ms. LEE. Madam Speaker, I thank Congresswoman SCHAKOWSKY for yielding and for her tremendous leadership on this issue and so many issues that affect women.

I rise in strong opposition to H. Res. 933, which is nothing more than a politically motivated resolution. It would shamefully—shamefully—provide an additional $800,000 to the select investigative panel to so-called investigate Planned Parenthood and attack women's health.

Republicans are asking for more money to continue their baseless attacks to undermine medical and scientific research and intimidate and harass providers. How outrageous. Let's be clear. This is yet another attempt to deny women, especially low-income women, access to health care.

There have been multiple hearings and there have been committee investigations, none of which have resulted in any evidence of wrongdoing by Planned Parenthood, doctors, or researchers.

Madam Speaker, this resolution and the absurd select panel investigation amounts to nothing more than a witch hunt. Instead of wasting millions of taxpayer dollars on this smear campaign, we should be fully investing in women's health and childcare.

I urge my colleagues to vote "no" on this dangerous resolution and, instead, call for an end of the select panel to attack women's health.

Mr. HARPER. Madam Speaker, I continue to reserve the balance of my time.

Ms. SCHAKOWSKY. Madam Speaker, I yield 1 minute to the gentlewoman from Florida (Ms. FRANKEL).

Ms. FRANKEL of Florida. Madam Speaker, I join my Democratic colleagues in opposing funding for a legislative panel that, instead of protecting, is jeopardizing life. Just ask the wife and 4 children and 10 grandchildren of George Tiller, a good doctor, who, while attending church, was shot dead by an anti-abortion extremist. His loved ones know the tragic consequences of having a target on one's back. And what this panel is doing is funding and creating new targets.

Reports naming names with bogus accusations; every day, clinics dealing with social media threats, bomb scares, harassment. We are playing deadly politics here, endangering lives and halting lifesaving medical breakthroughs. Enough is enough.

I urge my colleagues to oppose this resolution.

Mr. HARPER. Madam Speaker, I continue to reserve the balance of my time.

Ms. SCHAKOWSKY. Madam Speaker, I yield myself such time as I may consume.

I just want to say a few things before yielding to the gentleman from Pennsylvania (Mr. BRADY).

We have heard a lot of accusations against certain businesses, et cetera, and institutions, and the Republicans have selectively and repeatedly released documents and letters, including a so-called criminal referral to the New Mexico attorney general, to the press before sending them or sharing them with Democrats. This is clearly a political move.

They have also manufactured their own misleading so-called exhibits and withheld documents and information from Democrats in violation of the House rules. They have abused their power throughout the whole time and should now not be allowed to continue to get any more money for this panel.

Madam Speaker, I urge my colleagues to defeat the previous question. If we defeat the previous question, I would offer an amendment to the resolution that would abolish the select panel instead of funding it. Let's be done with this once and for all.

Madam Speaker, I yield the remainder of my time to the gentleman from Pennsylvania (Mr. BRADY).

Mr. BRADY of Pennsylvania. Madam Speaker, I also urge my colleagues to vote "no" on H. Res. 933.

I reserved a little bit of my time because I thought that this would be the last time that our chairman, CANDICE MILLER, would be here orchestrating the resolution. Instead we got my dear friend, Mr. HARPER. That is okay. We will take the second.

CANDICE MILLER is going on to other things, and we wish her well. She is on other endeavors, and it is bittersweet. The sweetness is that she is leaving here and going home. The bitterness is that she is leaving here and going home. She has been a great chairman. We have had the pleasure of working together. We agreed 99.9 percent of the time. Without question, she was the classiest lady—without question, the classiest person, not only the classiest lady—in this institution.

Again, I wish her well. And whatever I can do—if I am ever in Michigan, I am going to stop to see her; if she is ever in Philadelphia, she can come to see me; and if she comes back here, I would love to see her again.

Ms. SCHAKOWSKY. Madam Speaker, I reserve the balance of my time.

Mr. HARPER. Madam Speaker, I yield myself such time as I may consume.

I share that admiration for CANDICE MILLER, who will be leaving at the end of this term. It has been great to see the working relationship that Mr. BRADY and Mrs. MILLER have had together on the Committee on House Administration. It has been an excellent example of how this place can operate.

Let us come together, though, here to fulfill our responsibility to one of the House's standing committees and provide the Committee on Energy and Commerce, both the majority and the minority, the funding that they need to finish their work this year.

I reserve the balance of my time.

Ms. SCHAKOWSKY. Madam Speaker, I ask unanimous consent to insert the text of the amendment in the RECORD along with extraneous material immediately prior to the vote on the previous question.

The SPEAKER pro tempore. Is there objection to the request of the gentlewoman from Illinois?

There was no objection.

Ms. SCHAKOWSKY. I yield back the balance of my time.

Ms. SLAUGHTER. Madam Speaker, the Select Investigative Panel was created solely to attack Planned Parenthood and intimidate women, health care providers, and scientific researchers. Its investigation has never been fair or fact-based.

It is shameful that the Majority is continuing to use the taxpayer's money to advance its own political purposes. This privileged resolution would waste another $800,000 of the American people's tax dollars on this partisan witch hunt. The Majority is now on track to spend more than $1.5 million on this dangerous smear campaign.

Madam Speaker, I call on every Member of the House who does not want to fund witch hunts to support Ms. SCHAKOWSKY's amendment.

Ms. JACKSON LEE. Madam Speaker, as a senior member of the Judiciary, and Ranking Member of the Subcommittee on Crime, Terrorism, Homeland Security, and Investigations, I rise in strong opposition to H. Res. 933, which would increase funding by $800,000 for the Select Investigative Panel of the Energy and Commerce Committee, which more accurately should be called the "Planned Parenthood Witchunt."

The ostensible purpose of this Select Investigative Panel is to investigate and report on all issues related to medical procedures and practices involving fetal tissue donation and procurement; federal funding and support for abortion providers; and late-term abortions.

But make no mistake, the Republican majority's real purpose in establishing this panel is (1) to open another front in their ongoing War Against Women, (2) impede women in the exercise of their right to make their own choices when it comes to their reproductive health, and (3) to persecute, smear, and demonize Planned Parenthood.

We know this from our experience with the so-called "Benghazi Committee," which the Republican leadership claimed was a non-partisan inquiry into the facts and circumstances surrounding the 2012 tragedy in Libya which claimed the lives of four brave and heroic Americans.

We know now, as confirmed by the Majority Leader and the Speaker-apparent, that the Benghazi Committee was in reality part of politically-motivated strategy to disparage and damage the former Secretary of State and leading candidate for the Democratic presidential nomination that wasted $4.5 million of the taxpayers' money.

Madam Speaker, with so many pressing challenges facing our nation, wasting time and taxpayer money on another partisan witch hunt is a luxury we simply cannot afford.

The structure and powers to be given the Select Investigative Panel does not inspire any confidence that it will operate in a fair and impartial manner.

For example, the composition of the committee is lopsided in favor of the majority (8 Republican; 5 Democrat), instead of more equally divided as select committees are comprised.

Second, the chairman of the select panel is given subpoena power and deposition authority, including the authority to order the taking of depositions by a member of the select panel or the panel's counsel.

Third, the the chairman of the select committee is authorized to recognize members to question witness for periods longer than the traditional five minutes and to recognize staff to question witnesses.

Taken together, these unusual powers are susceptible to abuse and are valued tools to any party wishing to conduct a fishing expedition as opposed to a dispassionate search for facts.

Madam Speaker, let me save our Republican colleagues some time by pointing out the facts that an objective, fair-minded inquiry would reveal.

In 2011, approximately 1.06 million abortions took place in the U.S., down from an estimated 1.21 million abortions in 2008, 1.29 million in 2002, 1.31 million in 2000 and 1.36 million in 1996.

Based on available state-level data, an estimated 984,000 abortions took place in 2013—

down from an estimated 1.02 million abortions in 2012.

Fetal tissue research has been scientifically accepted since the Reagan Administration.

In 1988 the Human Fetal Tissue Transplantation Research Panel (or the Blue Ribbon Commission) sought to separate the question of ethics of abortion from the question ethics of using fetal tissue from legal elective abortions for medical research.

The report of this commission laid the foundation for the NIH Health Revitalization Act of 1993 (which passed overwhelmingly with bipartisan support), prohibits the payment or receipt of money or any other form of valuable consideration for fetal tissue, regardless of whether the program to which the tissue is being provided is funded or not.

The law contains a limited exception that permits reimbursement for actual expenses (e.g. storage, processing, transportation, etc.) of the tissue.

These fees generally amount to less than $100.

Less than 1 percent of Planned Parenthood chapters participate in this area of research.

Planned Parenthood reports revenue by source (either government or non-government) rather than the manner of disbursement (income versus grants and contracts).

Payments from Medicaid managed care plans are listed as "Government Health Services Grants and Reimbursements" to reflect the ultimate source of the funds.

Planned Parenthood spends about $1.1 billion annually on 11.4 million services, 83 percent of which is spent on research, client services and education.

Client services are divided into six categories: Cancer Prevention and Screenings, STI Testing, Contraception, Abortion Services, Other Women's Health Services & Other Services.

According to Planned Parenthood financial statements from 2009 through 2014, 86 percent of Planned Parenthood's Services fall under the categories of Cancer Prevention and Screenings (12–16 percent), STI Testing for men and women (35–41 percent), and Contraception (32–35 percent).

Only about about 3 percent of its services fall under the Abortion category nationally.

Additionally, Planned Parenthood is already prohibited from spending federal funds on abortion services anyway.

Finally, Madam Speaker, H. Res. 933 is an irresponsible diversion from tackling and addressing the following critical challenges facing this Congress and the American people.

Funding to keep the government open expires on December 9 and Congress must find a way to keep the government open in the face of irresponsible opposition from 151 Republicans who previously voted to shut down the government rather than allow women access to affordable family planning and life-saving preventive health care.

Madam Speaker, we have far more important things to do than waste more time and taxpayer money on another partisan attempt to deprive women of their right to make their own decisions regarding their reproductive health that has been recognized as constitutionally guaranteed since 1973 by the Supreme Court decision in Roe v. Wade.

I oppose H. Res. 933 and urge all Members to join me in voting against this wasteful and irresponsible measure.

HEALTH IMPACT OF PLANNED PARENTHOOD AFFILIATES

BY THE NUMBERS

378,692—Pap tests performed.

487,029—breast exams performed.

87,988—women whose cancer was detected early or whose abnormalities were identified.

865,721—Total Pap tests and breast exams performed.

1,440,495—emergency contraception kits provided.

516,000—unintended pregnancies averted by contraceptive services.

3,577,348—Birth control information and services provided.

704,079—HIV tests conducted.

169,008—STIs diagnosed, enabling people to get treatment and to learn how to prevent the further spread of STIs.

4,470,597—Tests and treatment for sexually transmitted infections provided.

Planned Parenthood health centers saw 2.7 million patients, who collectively received 10.6 million services during 4.6 million clinical visits.

PARENTHOOD CLIENTS RECEIVING CONTRACEPTIVE SERVICES IN 2013

42 percent—STI/STD Testing & Treatment.

11 percent—Other Women's Health Services.

3 percent—Abortion Services.

1 percent—Other Services.

9 percent—Cancer Screening and Prevention.

34 percent—Contraception.

MEDICAL SERVICES PROVIDED BY AFFILIATES (2013)

STI/STD Testing & Treatment Total: 4,470,597.

STI Tests, Women and Men: 3,727,359.

Genital Warts (HPV) Treatments: 38,612.

HIV Tests, Women and Men: 704,079.

Other Treatments: 547.

Contraception Total: 3,577,348.

Reversible Contraception Clients, Women 2,131,865.

Emergency Contraception Kits 1,440,495.

Female Sterilization Procedures 822.

Vasectomy Clients 4,166.

Cancer Screening and Prevention Total: 935,573.

Pap Tests 378,692.

HPV Vaccinations 34,739.

Breast Exams/Breast Care 487,029.

Colposcopy Procedures 32,334.

LEEP Procedures 2,095.

Cryotherapy Procedures 684.

Other Women's Health Services Total: 1,147,467.

Pregnancy Tests 1,128,783.

Prenatal Services 18,684.

Abortion Services Total: Abortion Procedures 327,653.

Other Services Total: 131,795.

Family Practice Services, Women and Men 65,464.

Adoption Referrals to Other Agencies 1,880.

Urinary Tract Infections Treatments 47,264.

Other Procedures, Women and Men 517,187.

Total of All Services Provided: 10,590,433.

GOVERNMENT FUNDING FOR PLANNED PARENTHOOD

National and Affiliate Chapters (FY2004–FY2014)

$4,529,900,000: Amount that Planned Parenthood and its affiliates have received in government funding over the last ten years, according to the organization's annual reports.

This represents less than half, approximately 45 percent, of the organization total revenues.

There are 38 Planned Parenthood locations in Texas.

Planned Parenthood reports revenue by source (either government or non-government) rather than the manner of disbursement (income versus grants and contracts).

Payments from Medicaid managed care plans are listed as "Government Health Services Grants and Reimbursements" to reflect the ultimate source of the funds.

The government funding comes from both federal and state governments.

Government Health Service Grants and Reimbursements:

FY 2014: $528.5 million.

FY 2013: $540.6 million.

FY 2012: $542.4 million.

FY 2011: $538.5 million.

FY 2010: $487.4 million.

FY 2009: $363 million.

FY 2008: $349.6 million.

FY 2007: $305.3 million.

FY 2006: $305.3 million.

FY 2005: $272.7 million.

FY 2004: $265.2 million.

The material previously referred to by Ms. SCHAKOWSKY is as follows:

AN AMENDMENT TO H. RES. 933 OFFERED BY MS. SCHAKOWSKY

Strike all after the resolved clause and insert:

That the Select Investigative Panel of the Committee on Energy and Commerce established pursuant to House Resolution 461, agreed to October 7, 2015, is hereby terminated.

THE VOTE ON THE PREVIOUS QUESTION: WHAT IT REALLY MEANS

This vote, the vote on whether to order the previous question on a special rule, is not merely a procedural vote. A vote against ordering the previous question is a vote against the Republican majority agenda and a vote to allow the Democratic minority to offer an alternative plan. It is a vote about what the House should be debating.

Mr. Clarence Cannon's Precedents of the House of Representatives (VI, 308–311), describes the vote on the previous question on the rule as "a motion to direct or control the consideration of the subject before the House being made by the Member in charge." To defeat the previous question is to give the opposition a chance to decide the subject before the House. Cannon cites the Speaker's ruling of January 13, 1920, to the effect that "the refusal of the House to sustain the demand for the previous question passes the control of the resolution to the opposition" in order to offer an amendment. On March 15, 1909, a member of the majority party offered a rule resolution. The House defeated the previous question and a member of the opposition rose to a parliamentary inquiry, asking who was entitled to recognition. Speaker Joseph G. Cannon (R–Illinois) said: "The previous question having been refused, the gentleman from New York, Mr. Fitzgerald, who had asked the gentleman to yield to him for an amendment, is entitled to the first recognition."

The Republican majority may say "the vote on the previous question is simply a vote on whether to proceed to an immediate vote on adopting the resolution . . . [and] has no substantive legislative or policy implications whatsoever." But that is not what they have always said. Listen to the Republican Leadership Manual on the Legislative

Process in the United States House of Representatives, (6th edition, page 135). Here's how the Republicans describe the previous question vote in their own manual: "Although it is generally not possible to amend the rule because the majority Member controlling the time will not yield for the purpose of offering an amendment, the same result may be achieved by voting down the previous question on the rule. . . . When the motion for the previous question is defeated, control of the time passes to the Member who led the opposition to ordering the previous question. That Member, because he then controls the time, may offer an amendment to the rule, or yield for the purpose of amendment."

In Deschler's Procedure in the U.S. House of Representatives, the subchapter titled "Amending Special Rules" states: "a refusal to order the previous question on such a rule [a special rule reported from the Committee on Rules] opens the resolution to amendment and further debate." (Chapter 21, section 21.2) Section 21.3 continues: "Upon rejection of the motion for the previous question on a resolution reported from the Committee on Rules, control shifts to the Member leading the opposition to the previous question, who may offer a proper amendment or motion and who controls the time for debate thereon."

Clearly, the vote on the previous question on a rule does have substantive policy implications. It is one of the only available tools for those who oppose the Republican majority's agenda and allows those with alternative views the opportunity to offer an alternative plan.

Mr. HARPER. Madam Speaker, I yield back the balance of my time, and I move the previous question on the resolution.

The SPEAKER pro tempore. The question is on ordering the previous question.

The question was taken; and the Speaker pro tempore announced that the ayes appeared to have it.

Mr. BRADY of Pennsylvania. Madam Speaker, on that I demand the yeas and nays.

The yeas and nays were ordered.

The SPEAKER pro tempore. Pursuant to clause 8 of rule XX, further proceedings on this question will be postponed.

RECESS

The SPEAKER pro tempore. Pursuant to clause 12(a) of rule I, the Chair declares the House in recess subject to the call of the Chair.

Accordingly (at 3 o'clock and 54 minutes p.m.), the House stood in recess.

□ 1710

AFTER RECESS

The recess having expired, the House was called to order by the Speaker pro tempore (Mr. BYRNE) at 5 o'clock and 10 minutes p.m.

COMMUNICATION FROM THE CLERK OF THE HOUSE

The SPEAKER pro tempore laid before the House the following communication from the Clerk of the House of Representatives:

OFFICE OF THE CLERK,
HOUSE OF REPRESENTATIVES,
Washington, DC, December 1, 2016.
Hon. PAUL D. RYAN,
The Speaker, House of Representatives,
Washington, DC.
DEAR MR. SPEAKER: Pursuant to the permission granted in Clause 2(h) of Rule II of the Rules of the U.S. House of Representatives, the Clerk received the following message from the Secretary of the Senate on December 1, 2016, at 4:18 p.m.:
That the Senate passed without amendment H.R. 6297.
With best wishes, I am,
Sincerely,

KAREN L. HAAS.

ANNOUNCEMENT BY THE SPEAKER PRO TEMPORE

The SPEAKER pro tempore. Pursuant to clause 8 of rule XX and the order of the House of today, proceedings will resume on questions previously postponed.

Votes will be taken in the following order:

Ordering the previous question on House Resolution 933;

Adoption of House Resolution 933, if ordered;

Ordering the previous question on House Resolution 937;

Adoption of House Resolution 937, if ordered;

Adoption of the motion to recommit on H.R. 6392; and

Passage of H.R. 6392, if ordered.

The first electronic vote will be conducted as a 15-minute vote. Remaining electronic votes will be conducted as 5-minute votes.

PROVIDING AMOUNTS FOR FURTHER EXPENSES OF THE COMMITTEE ON ENERGY AND COMMERCE IN THE ONE HUNDRED FOURTEENTH CONGRESS

The SPEAKER pro tempore. The unfinished business is the vote on ordering the previous question on the resolution (H. Res. 933) providing amounts for further expenses of the Committee on Energy and Commerce in the One Hundred Fourteenth Congress, on which the yeas and nays were ordered.

The Clerk read the title of the resolution.

The SPEAKER pro tempore. The question is on ordering the previous question.

The vote was taken by electronic device, and there were—yeas 235, nays 177, not voting 22, as follows:

[Roll No. 594]

YEAS—235

Abraham	Barletta	Bishop (UT)
Aderholt	Barr	Black
Allen	Barton	Blackburn
Amash	Benishek	Blum
Amodei	Bilirakis	Bost
Babin	Bishop (MI)	Boustany

Brady (TX)	Hice, Jody B.	Pittenger
Brat	Hill	Pitts
Bridenstine	Holding	Poliquin
Brooks (AL)	Hudson	Pompeo
Brooks (IN)	Huelskamp	Posey
Buchanan	Huizenga (MI)	Price, Tom
Buck	Hultgren	Ratcliffe
Bucshon	Hunter	Reed
Burgess	Hurd (TX)	Reichert
Byrne	Hurt (VA)	Ribble
Calvert	Issa	Rice (SC)
Carter (GA)	Jenkins (KS)	Rigell
Carter (TX)	Jenkins (WV)	Roby
Chabot	Johnson (OH)	Roe (TN)
Chaffetz	Johnson, Sam	Rogers (AL)
Clawson (FL)	Jordan	Rogers (KY)
Coffman	Joyce	Rohrabacher
Cole	Katko	Rokita
Collins (GA)	Kelly (MS)	Rooney (FL)
Collins (NY)	Kelly (PA)	Ros-Lehtinen
Comer	King (IA)	Roskam
Comstock	King (NY)	Ross
Conaway	Kinzinger (IL)	Rothfus
Cook	Kline	Rouzer
Costello (PA)	Knight	Royce
Cramer	Labrador	Russell
Crawford	LaHood	Salmon
Crenshaw	LaMalfa	Sanford
Culberson	Lamborn	Scalise
Davidson	Lance	Schweikert
Davis, Rodney	Latta	Scott, Austin
Denham	Lipinski	Sensenbrenner
Dent	LoBiondo	Sessions
DeSantis	Long	Shimkus
DesJarlais	Loudermilk	Shuster
Diaz-Balart	Love	Smith (MO)
Dold	Lucas	Smith (NE)
Donovan	Luetkemeyer	Smith (NJ)
Duffy	Lummis	Smith (TX)
Duncan (SC)	MacArthur	Stefanik
Duncan (TN)	Marchant	Stewart
Ellmers (NC)	Marino	Stivers
Emmer (MN)	Massie	Stutzman
Farenthold	McCarthy	Thompson (PA)
Fitzpatrick	McCaul	Thornberry
Fleischmann	McClintock	Tiberi
Fleming	McHenry	Tipton
Fortenberry	McKinley	Trott
Foxx	McMorris	Turner
Franks (AZ)	Rodgers	Upton
Frelinghuysen	McSally	Valadao
Gibbs	Meadows	Wagner
Gibson	Meehan	Walberg
Gohmert	Messer	Walden
Goodlatte	Mica	Walker
Gosar	Miller (FL)	Walorski
Gowdy	Miller (MI)	Walters, Mimi
Granger	Moolenaar	Weber (TX)
Graves (GA)	Mooney (WV)	Webster (FL)
Graves (LA)	Mullin	Wenstrup
Graves (MO)	Mulvaney	Westerman
Griffith	Murphy (PA)	Wilson (SC)
Grothman	Neugebauer	Wittman
Guinta	Newhouse	Womack
Guthrie	Noem	Woodall
Hanna	Nunes	Yoder
Hardy	Olson	Yoho
Harper	Palazzo	Young (AK)
Harris	Palmer	Young (IA)
Hartzler	Paulsen	Young (IN)
Heck (NV)	Pearce	Zeldin
Hensarling	Perry	Zinke
Herrera Beutler	Peterson	

NAYS—177

Adams	Carson (IN)	Davis (CA)
Aguilar	Cartwright	Davis, Danny
Ashford	Castor (FL)	DeGette
Bass	Castro (TX)	Delaney
Beatty	Chu, Judy	DeLauro
Becerra	Cicilline	DelBene
Bera	Clark (MA)	DeSaulnier
Beyer	Clarke (NY)	Deutch
Bishop (GA)	Clay	Dingell
Blumenauer	Cleaver	Doggett
Bonamici	Clyburn	Doyle, Michael
Boyle, Brendan	Cohen	F.
F.	Connolly	Duckworth
Brady (PA)	Conyers	Edwards
Brownley (CA)	Cooper	Ellison
Bustos	Costa	Engel
Butterfield	Courtney	Eshoo
Capps	Crowley	Esty
Capuano	Cuellar	Evans
Cárdenas	Cummings	Farr

Foster
Frankel (FL)
Fudge
Gabbard
Gallego
Garamendi
Graham
Grayson
Green, Al
Green, Gene
Grijalva
Gutiérrez
Hanabusa
Hastings
Heck (WA)
Higgins
Himes
Hinojosa
Honda
Hoyer
Huffman
Israel
Jackson Lee
Jeffries
Johnson (GA)
Johnson, E. B.
Kaptur
Keating
Kelly (IL)
Kennedy
Kildee
Kilmer
Kind
Kuster
Langevin
Larsen (WA)
Larson (CT)
Lawrence
Lee
Levin
Lewis
Lieu, Ted

Loebsack
Lowenthal
Lowey
Lujan Grisham (NM)
Luján, Ben Ray (NM)
Lynch
Maloney, Carolyn
Maloney, Sean
Matsui
McCollum
McDermott
McGovern
McNerney
Meeks
Meng
Moore
Moulton
Murphy (FL)
Nadler
Napolitano
Nolan
Norcross
O'Rourke
Pallone
Pascrell
Pelosi
Perlmutter
Peters
Pingree
Pocan
Polis
Price (NC)
Quigley
Rangel
Rice (NY)
Richmond
Roybal-Allard
Ruiz
Ruppersberger

Rush
Ryan (OH)
Sánchez, Linda T.
Sanchez, Loretta
Sarbanes
Schakowsky
Schiff
Schrader
Scott (VA)
Scott, David
Serrano
Sewell (AL)
Sherman
Sinema
Sires
Slaughter
Smith (WA)
Speier
Swalwell (CA)
Takano
Thompson (CA)
Thompson (MS)
Titus
Tonko
Torres
Tsongas
Van Hollen
Vargas
Veasey
Velázquez
Visclosky
Walz
Wasserman Schultz
Waters, Maxine
Watson Coleman
Welch
Wilson (FL)
Yarmuth

NOT VOTING—22

Brown (FL)
Carney
Curbelo (FL)
DeFazio
Fincher
Flores
Forbes
Garrett

Hahn
Jolly
Jones
Kirkpatrick
Lofgren
Neal
Nugent
Payne

Poe (TX)
Renacci
Simpson
Vela
Westmoreland
Williams

☐ 1735

Mr. ASHFORD changed his vote from "yea" to "nay."

Mr. MULLIN and Ms. GRANGER changed their vote from "nay" to "yea."

So the previous question was ordered.

The result of the vote was announced as above recorded.

The SPEAKER pro tempore. The question is on the resolution.

The question was taken; and the Speaker pro tempore announced that the ayes appeared to have it.

RECORDED VOTE

Mr. BRADY of Pennsylvania. Mr. Speaker, I demand a recorded vote.

A recorded vote was ordered.

The SPEAKER pro tempore. This is a 5-minute vote.

The vote was taken by electronic device, and there were—ayes 234, noes 181, not voting 19, as follows:

[Roll No. 595]

AYES—234

Abraham
Aderholt
Allen
Amash
Amodei
Babin
Barletta
Barr
Barton

Benishek
Bilirakis
Bishop (MI)
Bishop (UT)
Black
Blackburn
Blum
Bost
Boustany

Brady (TX)
Brat
Bridenstine
Brooks (AL)
Brooks (IN)
Buchanan
Buck
Bucshon
Burgess

Byrne
Calvert
Carter (GA)
Carter (TX)
Chabot
Chaffetz
Clawson (FL)
Coffman
Cole
Collins (GA)
Collins (NY)
Comer
Comstock
Conaway
Cook
Costello (PA)
Cramer
Crawford
Crenshaw
Culberson
Curbelo (FL)
Davidson
Davis, Rodney
Denham
Dent
DeSantis
DesJarlais
Diaz-Balart
Dold
Donovan
Duffy
Duncan (SC)
Duncan (TN)
Ellmers (NC)
Emmer (MN)
Farenthold
Fitzpatrick
Fleischmann
Fleming
Fortenberry
Foxx
Franks (AZ)
Frelinghuysen
Gibbs
Gibson
Gohmert
Goodlatte
Gosar
Gowdy
Granger
Graves (GA)
Graves (LA)
Graves (MO)
Griffith
Grothman
Guinta
Guthrie
Hardy
Harper
Harris
Hartzler
Heck (NV)
Hensarling
Herrera Beutler
Hice, Jody B.
Hill
Holding
Hudson
Huelskamp
Huizenga (MI)

Hultgren
Hunter
Hurd (TX)
Hurt (VA)
Issa
Jenkins (KS)
Jenkins (WV)
Johnson (OH)
Johnson, Sam
Jordan
Joyce
Katko
Kelly (MS)
Kelly (PA)
King (IA)
King (NY)
Kinzinger (IL)
Kline
Knight
Labrador
LaHood
LaMalfa
Lamborn
Lance
Latta
Lipinski
LoBiondo
Long
Loudermilk
Love
Lucas
Luetkemeyer
Lummis
MacArthur
Marchant
Marino
Massie
McCarthy
McCaul
McClintock
McHenry
McKinley
McMorris Rodgers
McSally
Meadows
Meehan
Messer
Mica
Miller (FL)
Miller (MI)
Moolenaar
Mooney (WV)
Mullin
Mulvaney
Murphy (PA)
Neugebauer
Newhouse
Noem
Nunes
Olson
Palazzo
Palmer
Paulsen
Pearce
Perry
Peterson
Pittenger
Pitts
Poliquin

Pompeo
Posey
Price, Tom
Ratcliffe
Reed
Reichert
Ribble
Rice (SC)
Rigell
Roby
Roe (TN)
Rogers (AL)
Rogers (KY)
Rohrabacher
Rokita
Rooney (FL)
Ros-Lehtinen
Roskam
Ross
Rothfus
Rouzer
Royce
Russell
Salmon
Sanford
Scalise
Schweikert
Scott, Austin
Sessions
Shimkus
Shuster
Simpson
Smith (MO)
Smith (NE)
Smith (NJ)
Smith (TX)
Stefanik
Stewart
Stutzman
Thompson (PA)
Thornberry
Tiberi
Tipton
Trott
Turner
Upton
Valadao
Wagner
Walberg
Walden
Walker
Walorski
Walters, Mimi
Weber (TX)
Webster (FL)
Wenstrup
Westerman
Wilson (SC)
Wittman
Womack
Woodall
Yoder
Yoho
Young (AK)
Young (IA)
Young (IN)
Zeldin
Zinke

NOES—181

Adams
Aguilar
Ashford
Bass
Beatty
Becerra
Bera
Beyer
Bishop (GA)
Blumenauer
Bonamici
Boyle, Brendan F.
Brady (PA)
Brownley (CA)
Bustos
Butterfield
Capps
Capuano
Cárdenas
Carson (IN)
Cartwright
Castor (FL)

Castro (TX)
Chu, Judy
Cicilline
Clark (MA)
Clarke (NY)
Clay
Cleaver
Clyburn
Cohen
Connolly
Conyers
Cooper
Costa
Courtney
Crowley
Cuellar
Cummings
Davis (CA)
Davis, Danny
DeGette
Delaney
DeLauro
DelBene

DeSaulnier
Deutch
Dingell
Doggett
Doyle, Michael F.
Duckworth
Edwards
Ellison
Engel
Eshoo
Esty
Evans
Farr
Foster
Frankel (FL)
Fudge
Gabbard
Gallego
Garamendi
Graham
Grayson
Green, Al

Green, Gene
Grijalva
Gutiérrez
Hanabusa
Hanna
Hastings
Heck (WA)
Higgins
Himes
Hinojosa
Honda
Hoyer
Huffman
Israel
Jackson Lee
Jeffries
Johnson (GA)
Johnson, E. B.
Kaptur
Keating
Kelly (IL)
Kennedy
Kildee
Kilmer
Kind
Kuster
Langevin
Larsen (WA)
Larson (CT)
Lawrence
Lee
Levin
Lewis
Lieu, Ted
Loebsack
Lowenthal
Lowey
Lujan Grisham (NM)

Luján, Ben Ray (NM)
Lynch
Maloney, Carolyn
Maloney, Sean
Matsui
McCollum
McDermott
McGovern
McNerney
Meeks
Meng
Moore
Moulton
Murphy (FL)
Nadler
Napolitano
Neal
Nolan
Norcross
O'Rourke
Pallone
Pascrell
Payne
Pelosi
Perlmutter
Peters
Pingree
Pocan
Polis
Price (NC)
Quigley
Rangel
Rice (NY)
Richmond
Roybal-Allard
Ruiz
Ruppersberger
Rush

Ryan (OH)
Sánchez, Linda T.
Sanchez, Loretta
Sarbanes
Schakowsky
Schiff
Schrader
Scott (VA)
Scott, David
Sensenbrenner
Serrano
Sewell (AL)
Sherman
Sinema
Sires
Slaughter
Smith (WA)
Speier
Swalwell (CA)
Takano
Thompson (CA)
Thompson (MS)
Titus
Tonko
Torres
Tsongas
Van Hollen
Vargas
Veasey
Velázquez
Visclosky
Walz
Wasserman Schultz
Waters, Maxine
Watson Coleman
Welch
Wilson (FL)
Yarmuth

NOT VOTING—19

Brown (FL)
Carney
DeFazio
Fincher
Flores
Forbes
Garrett

Hahn
Jolly
Jones
Kirkpatrick
Lofgren
Nugent
Poe (TX)

Renacci
Stivers
Vela
Westmoreland
Williams

☐ 1743

So the resolution was agreed to.

The result of the vote was announced as above recorded.

A motion to reconsider was laid on the table.

PROVIDING FOR CONSIDERATION OF CONFERENCE REPORT ON S. 2943, NATIONAL DEFENSE AUTHORIZATION ACT FOR FISCAL YEAR 2017

The SPEAKER pro tempore (Ms. ROS-LEHTINEN). The unfinished business is the vote on ordering the previous question on the resolution (H. Res. 937) providing for consideration of the conference report to accompany the bill (S. 2943) to authorize appropriations for fiscal year 2017 for military activities of the Department of Defense, for military construction, and for defense activities of the Department of Energy, to prescribe military personnel strengths for such fiscal year, and for other purposes, on which the yeas and nays were ordered.

The Clerk read the title of the resolution.

The SPEAKER pro tempore. The question is on ordering the previous question.

This will be a 5-minute vote.

The vote was taken by electronic device, and there were—yeas 235, nays 180, not voting 19, as follows:

[Roll No. 596]

YEAS—235

Abraham	Graves (MO)	Palazzo
Aderholt	Griffith	Palmer
Allen	Grothman	Paulsen
Amash	Guinta	Pearce
Amodei	Guthrie	Perry
Babin	Hanna	Pittenger
Barletta	Hardy	Pitts
Barr	Harper	Poliquin
Barton	Harris	Pompeo
Benishek	Hartzler	Posey
Bilirakis	Heck (NV)	Price, Tom
Bishop (MI)	Hensarling	Ratcliffe
Bishop (UT)	Herrera Beutler	Reed
Black	Hice, Jody B.	Reichert
Blackburn	Hill	Ribble
Blum	Holding	Rice (SC)
Bost	Hudson	Rigell
Boustany	Huelskamp	Roby
Brady (TX)	Huizenga (MI)	Roe (TN)
Brat	Hultgren	Rogers (AL)
Bridenstine	Hunter	Rogers (KY)
Brooks (AL)	Hurd (TX)	Rohrabacher
Brooks (IN)	Hurt (VA)	Rokita
Buchanan	Issa	Rooney (FL)
Buck	Jenkins (KS)	Ros-Lehtinen
Bucshon	Jenkins (WV)	Roskam
Burgess	Johnson (OH)	Ross
Byrne	Johnson, Sam	Rothfus
Calvert	Jordan	Rouzer
Carter (GA)	Joyce	Royce
Carter (TX)	Katko	Russell
Chabot	Kelly (MS)	Salmon
Chaffetz	Kelly (PA)	Sanford
Clawson (FL)	King (IA)	Scalise
Coffman	King (NY)	Schweikert
Cole	Kinzinger (IL)	Scott, Austin
Collins (GA)	Kline	Sensenbrenner
Collins (NY)	Knight	Sessions
Comer	Labrador	Shimkus
Comstock	LaHood	Shuster
Conaway	LaMalfa	Simpson
Cook	Lamborn	Smith (MO)
Costello (PA)	Lance	Smith (NE)
Cramer	Latta	Smith (NJ)
Crawford	LoBiondo	Smith (TX)
Crenshaw	Long	Stefanik
Culberson	Loudermilk	Stewart
Curbelo (FL)	Love	Stivers
Davidson	Lucas	Stutzman
Davis, Rodney	Luetkemeyer	Thompson (PA)
Denham	Lummis	Thornberry
Dent	MacArthur	Tiberi
DeSantis	Marchant	Tipton
DesJarlais	Marino	Trott
Diaz-Balart	Massie	Turner
Dold	McCarthy	Upton
Donovan	McCaul	Valadao
Duffy	McClintock	Wagner
Duncan (SC)	McHenry	Walberg
Duncan (TN)	McKinley	Walden
Ellmers (NC)	McMorris	Walker
Emmer (MN)	Rodgers	Walorski
Farenthold	McSally	Walters, Mimi
Fitzpatrick	Meadows	Weber (TX)
Fleischmann	Meehan	Webster (FL)
Fleming	Messer	Wenstrup
Fortenberry	Mica	Westerman
Foxx	Miller (FL)	Wilson (SC)
Franks (AZ)	Miller (MI)	Wittman
Frelinghuysen	Moolenaar	Womack
Gibbs	Mooney (WV)	Woodall
Gibson	Mullin	Yoder
Gohmert	Mulvaney	Yoho
Goodlatte	Murphy (PA)	Young (AK)
Gosar	Neugebauer	Young (IA)
Gowdy	Newhouse	Young (IN)
Granger	Noem	Zeldin
Graves (GA)	Nunes	Zinke
Graves (LA)	Olson	

NAYS—180

Adams	Boyle, Brendan	Castor (FL)
Aguilar	F.	Castro (TX)
Ashford	Brady (PA)	Chu, Judy
Bass	Brownley (CA)	Cicilline
Beatty	Bustos	Clark (MA)
Becerra	Butterfield	Clarke (NY)
Bera	Capps	Clay
Beyer	Capuano	Cleaver
Bishop (GA)	Cárdenas	Clyburn
Blumenauer	Carson (IN)	Cohen
Bonamici	Cartwright	Connolly

Conyers	Kaptur
Cooper	Keating
Costa	Kelly (IL)
Courtney	Kennedy
Crowley	Kildee
Cuellar	Kilmer
Cummings	Kind
Davis (CA)	Kuster
Davis, Danny	Langevin
DeGette	Larsen (WA)
Delaney	Larson (CT)
DeLauro	Lawrence
DelBene	Lee
Deutch	Levin
Dingell	Lewis
Doggett	Lieu, Ted
Doyle, Michael	Lipinski
F.	Loebsack
Duckworth	Lowenthal
Edwards	Lowey
Ellison	Lujan Grisham
Engel	(NM)
Eshoo	Luján, Ben Ray
Esty	(NM)
Evans	Lynch
Farr	Maloney,
Foster	Carolyn
Frankel (FL)	Maloney, Sean
Fudge	Matsui
Gabbard	McCollum
Gallego	McDermott
Garamendi	McGovern
Graham	McNerney
Grayson	Meeks
Green, Al	Meng
Green, Gene	Moore
Grijalva	Moulton
Gutiérrez	Murphy (FL)
Hanabusa	Nadler
Hastings	Napolitano
Heck (WA)	Neal
Higgins	Nolan
Himes	Norcross
Hinojosa	O'Rourke
Honda	Pallone
Hoyer	Pascrell
Huffman	Payne
Israel	Pelosi
Jackson Lee	Perlmutter
Jeffries	Peters
Johnson (GA)	Peterson
Johnson, E. B.	Pingree

Pocan	
Polis	
Price (NC)	
Quigley	
Rangel	
Rice (NY)	
Richmond	
Roybal-Allard	
Ruiz	
Ruppersberger	
Rush	
Ryan (OH)	
Sánchez, Linda	
T.	
Sanchez, Loretta	
Sarbanes	
Schakowsky	
Schiff	
Schrader	
Scott (VA)	
Scott, David	
Serrano	
Sewell (AL)	
Sherman	
Sinema	
Sires	
Slaughter	
Smith (WA)	
Speier	
Swalwell (CA)	
Takano	
Thompson (CA)	
Thompson (MS)	
Titus	
Tonko	
Torres	
Tsongas	
Van Hollen	
Vargas	
Veasey	
Velázquez	
Visclosky	
Walz	
Wasserman	
Schultz	
Waters, Maxine	
Watson Coleman	
Welch	
Wilson (FL)	
Yarmuth	

NOT VOTING—19

Brown (FL)	Garrett	Poe (TX)
Carney	Hahn	Renacci
DeFazio	Jolly	Vela
DeSaulnier	Jones	Westmoreland
Fincher	Kirkpatrick	Williams
Flores	Lofgren	
Forbes	Nugent	

□ 1750

So the previous question was ordered.

The result of the vote was announced as above recorded.

The SPEAKER pro tempore. The question is on the resolution.

The question was taken; and the Speaker pro tempore announced that the ayes appeared to have it.

RECORDED VOTE

Mr. BYRNE. Madam Speaker, I demand a recorded vote.

A recorded vote was ordered.

The SPEAKER pro tempore. This is a 5-minute vote.

The vote was taken by electronic device, and there were—ayes 277, noes 139, not voting 18, as follows:

[Roll No. 597]

AYES—277

Abraham	Babin	Bishop (GA)
Aderholt	Barletta	Bishop (MI)
Aguilar	Barr	Bishop (UT)
Allen	Barton	Black
Amash	Benishek	Blackburn
Amodei	Beyer	Blum
Ashford	Bilirakis	Bost

Boustany	Higgins	Pittenger
Brady (TX)	Hill	Pitts
Brat	Holding	Poliquin
Bridenstine	Hoyer	Pompeo
Brooks (AL)	Hudson	Posey
Brooks (IN)	Huelskamp	Price (NC)
Brownley (CA)	Huizenga (MI)	Price, Tom
Buchanan	Hultgren	Quigley
Buck	Hunter	Rangel
Bucshon	Hurd (TX)	Ratcliffe
Burgess	Hurt (VA)	Reed
Byrne	Issa	Reichert
Calvert	Jenkins (KS)	Ribble
Carter (GA)	Jenkins (WV)	Rice (NY)
Carter (TX)	Johnson (GA)	Rice (SC)
Chabot	Johnson (OH)	Rigell
Chaffetz	Johnson, Sam	Roby
Clawson (FL)	Jordan	Roe (TN)
Coffman	Joyce	Rogers (AL)
Cole	Katko	Rogers (KY)
Collins (GA)	Kelly (MS)	Rohrabacher
Collins (NY)	Kelly (PA)	Rokita
Comer	Kilmer	Rooney (FL)
Comstock	King (IA)	Ros-Lehtinen
Conaway	King (NY)	Roskam
Cook	Kinzinger (IL)	Ross
Cooper	Kline	Rothfus
Costa	Knight	Rouzer
Costello (PA)	Labrador	Royce
Courtney	LaHood	Ruppersberger
Cramer	LaMalfa	Russell
Crawford	Lamborn	Salmon
Crenshaw	Lance	Sanford
Cuellar	Langevin	Scalise
Culberson	Larsen (WA)	Schweikert
Curbelo (FL)	Larson (CT)	Scott (VA)
Davidson	Latta	Scott, Austin
Davis (CA)	Lieu, Ted	Scott, David
Davis, Rodney	Lipinski	Sensenbrenner
Denham	LoBiondo	Sessions
Dent	Long	Shimkus
DeSantis	Loudermilk	Shuster
DesJarlais	Love	Simpson
Diaz-Balart	Lucas	Sinema
Dold	Luetkemeyer	Slaughter
Donovan	Lummis	Smith (MO)
Duffy	MacArthur	Smith (NE)
Duncan (SC)	Marchant	Smith (NJ)
Duncan (TN)	Marino	Smith (TX)
Ellmers (NC)	Massie	Smith (WA)
Emmer (MN)	McCarthy	Stefanik
Eshoo	McCaul	Stewart
Esty	McClintock	Stivers
Evans	McGovern	Stutzman
Farenthold	McHenry	Thompson (PA)
Fitzpatrick	McKinley	Thornberry
Fleischmann	McMorris	Tiberi
Fleming	Rodgers	Tipton
Fortenberry	McSally	Trott
Foxx	Meadows	Tsongas
Franks (AZ)	Meehan	Turner
Frelinghuysen	Messer	Upton
Garamendi	Mica	Valadao
Gibbs	Miller (FL)	Veasey
Gibson	Miller (MI)	Wagner
Gohmert	Moolenaar	Walberg
Goodlatte	Mooney (WV)	Walden
Gosar	Moulton	Walker
Gowdy	Mullin	Walorski
Granger	Mulvaney	Walters, Mimi
Graves (GA)	Murphy (PA)	Weber (TX)
Graves (LA)	Neugebauer	Webster (FL)
Graves (MO)	Newhouse	Wenstrup
Griffith	Noem	Westerman
Grothman	Norcross	Wilson (SC)
Guinta	Nunes	Wittman
Guthrie	Olson	Womack
Hanna	Palazzo	Woodall
Hardy	Palmer	Yoder
Harper	Paulsen	Yoho
Harris	Pearce	Young (AK)
Hartzler	Perlmutter	Young (IA)
Heck (NV)	Perry	Young (IN)
Hensarling	Peters	Zeldin
Herrera Beutler	Peterson	Zinke
Hice, Jody B.	Pingree	

NOES—139

Adams	Boyle, Brendan	Cárdenas
Bass	F.	Carson (IN)
Beatty	Brady (PA)	Cartwright
Becerra	Bustos	Castor (FL)
Bera	Butterfield	Castro (TX)
Blumenauer	Capps	Chu, Judy
Bonamici	Capuano	Cicilline

Clark (MA)
Clarke (NY)
Clay
Cleaver
Clyburn
Cohen
Connolly
Conyers
Crowley
Cummings
Davis, Danny
DeGette
Delaney
DeLauro
DelBene
DeSaulnier
Deutch
Dingell
Doggett
Doyle, Michael F.
Duckworth
Edwards
Ellison
Engel
Farr
Foster
Frankel (FL)
Fudge
Gabbard
Gallego
Graham
Grayson
Green, Al
Green, Gene
Grijalva
Gutiérrez
Hanabusa
Hastings
Heck (WA)
Himes
Hinojosa

Honda
Huffman
Israel
Jackson Lee
Jeffries
Johnson, E. B.
Kaptur
Keating
Kelly (IL)
Kennedy
Kildee
Kind
Kuster
Lawrence
Lee
Levin
Lewis
Loebsack
Lowenthal
Lowey
Lujan Grisham (NM)
Luján, Ben Ray (NM)
Lynch
Maloney, Carolyn
Maloney, Sean
Matsui
McCollum
McDermott
McNerney
Meeks
Meng
Moore
Murphy (FL)
Nadler
Napolitano
Neal
Nolan
O'Rourke
Pallone

Pascrell
Payne
Pelosi
Pocan
Polis
Richmond
Roybal-Allard
Ruiz
Rush
Ryan (OH)
Sánchez, Linda T.
Sanchez, Loretta
Sarbanes
Schakowsky
Schiff
Schrader
Serrano
Sewell (AL)
Sherman
Sires
Speier
Swalwell (CA)
Takano
Thompson (CA)
Thompson (MS)
Titus
Tonko
Torres
Van Hollen
Vargas
Velázquez
Visclosky
Walz
Wasserman Schultz
Waters, Maxine
Watson Coleman
Welch
Wilson (FL)
Yarmuth

NOT VOTING—18

Brown (FL)
Carney
DeFazio
Fincher
Flores
Forbes

Garrett
Hahn
Jolly
Jones
Kirkpatrick
Lofgren

Nugent
Poe (TX)
Renacci
Vela
Westmoreland
Williams

☐ 1757

So the resolution was agreed to.

The result of the vote was announced as above recorded.

A motion to reconsider was laid on the table.

SYSTEMIC RISK DESIGNATION IMPROVEMENT ACT OF 2016

The SPEAKER pro tempore. Pursuant to clause 8 of rule XX and the order of the House of today, the unfinished business is the question on the motion to recommit on the bill (H.R. 6392) to amend the Dodd-Frank Wall Street Reform and Consumer Protection Act to specify when bank holding companies may be subject to certain enhanced supervision, and for other purposes, offered by the gentlewoman from California (Ms. MAXINE WATERS), on which the yeas and nays were ordered.

The Clerk will redesignate the motion.

The Clerk redesignated the motion.

The SPEAKER pro tempore. The question is on the motion to recommit.

This is a 5-minute vote.

The vote was taken by electronic device, and there were—yeas 178, nays 236, not voting 20, as follows:

[Roll No. 598]

YEAS—178

Adams
Aguilar
Bass
Beatty
Becerra
Bera
Beyer
Bishop (GA)
Blumenauer
Bonamici
Boyle, Brendan F.
Brady (PA)
Brownley (CA)
Bustos
Butterfield
Capps
Capuano
Cárdenas
Carson (IN)
Cartwright
Castor (FL)
Castro (TX)
Chu, Judy
Cicilline
Clark (MA)
Clarke (NY)
Clay
Cleaver
Clyburn
Cohen
Connolly
Conyers
Cooper
Costa
Courtney
Crowley
Cuellar
Cummings
Davis (CA)
Davis, Danny
DeGette
Delaney
DeLauro
DelBene
DeSaulnier
Deutch
Dingell
Doggett
Doyle, Michael F.
Duckworth
Edwards
Ellison
Engel
Eshoo
Esty
Evans
Farr
Foster
Frankel (FL)
Fudge

Gabbard
Gallego
Garamendi
Graham
Grayson
Green, Al
Green, Gene
Grijalva
Gutiérrez
Hanabusa
Hastings
Heck (WA)
Higgins
Himes
Hinojosa
Honda
Hoyer
Huffman
Israel
Jackson Lee
Jeffries
Johnson (GA)
Johnson, E. B.
Kaptur
Keating
Kelly (IL)
Kennedy
Kildee
Kilmer
Kind
Kuster
Langevin
Larsen (WA)
Larson (CT)
Lawrence
Lee
Levin
Lewis
Lieu, Ted
Lipinski
Loebsack
Lowenthal
Lowey
Lujan Grisham (NM)
Luján, Ben Ray (NM)
Lynch
Maloney, Carolyn
Maloney, Sean
Matsui
McCollum
McDermott
McGovern
McNerney
Meeks
Meng
Moore
Moulton
Murphy (FL)
Nadler

Napolitano
Neal
Nolan
Norcross
O'Rourke
Pallone
Pascrell
Payne
Pelosi
Perlmutter
Peters
Peterson
Pingree
Pocan
Polis
Price (NC)
Quigley
Rangel
Rice (NY)
Richmond
Roybal-Allard
Ruiz
Ruppersberger
Rush
Ryan (OH)
Sánchez, Linda T.
Sanchez, Loretta
Sarbanes
Schakowsky
Schiff
Schrader
Scott (VA)
Scott, David
Serrano
Sewell (AL)
Sherman
Sires
Slaughter
Smith (WA)
Speier
Swalwell (CA)
Takano
Thompson (CA)
Thompson (MS)
Titus
Tonko
Torres
Tsongas
Van Hollen
Vargas
Veasey
Velázquez
Visclosky
Walz
Wasserman Schultz
Waters, Maxine
Watson Coleman
Welch
Yarmuth

NAYS—236

Abraham
Aderholt
Allen
Amash
Amodei
Ashford
Babin
Barr
Barton
Benishek
Bilirakis
Bishop (MI)
Bishop (UT)
Black
Blackburn
Blum
Bost
Boustany
Brady (TX)
Brat
Bridenstine
Brooks (AL)
Brooks (IN)
Buchanan
Buck
Bucshon
Burgess
Byrne

Calvert
Carter (GA)
Carter (TX)
Chabot
Chaffetz
Clawson (FL)
Coffman
Cole
Collins (GA)
Collins (NY)
Comer
Comstock
Conaway
Cook
Costello (PA)
Cramer
Crawford
Crenshaw
Culberson
Curbelo (FL)
Davidson
Davis, Rodney
Denham
Dent
DeSantis
DesJarlais
Diaz-Balart
Dold

Donovan
Duffy
Duncan (SC)
Duncan (TN)
Ellmers (NC)
Emmer (MN)
Farenthold
Fitzpatrick
Fleischmann
Fleming
Fortenberry
Foxx
Franks (AZ)
Frelinghuysen
Gibbs
Gibson
Gohmert
Goodlatte
Gosar
Gowdy
Granger
Graves (GA)
Graves (LA)
Graves (MO)
Griffith
Grothman
Guinta
Guthrie

Hanna
Hardy
Harper
Harris
Hartzler
Heck (NV)
Hensarling
Herrera Beutler
Hice, Jody B.
Hill
Holding
Hudson
Huelskamp
Huizenga (MI)
Hultgren
Hunter
Hurd (TX)
Hurt (VA)
Issa
Jenkins (KS)
Jenkins (WV)
Johnson (OH)
Johnson, Sam
Jordan
Joyce
Katko
Kelly (MS)
Kelly (PA)
King (IA)
King (NY)
Kinzinger (IL)
Kline
Knight
Labrador
LaHood
LaMalfa
Lamborn
Lance
Latta
LoBiondo
Long
Loudermilk
Love
Lucas
Luetkemeyer
Lummis
MacArthur
Marchant
Marino
Massie
McCarthy

McCaul
McClintock
McKinley
McMorris Rodgers
McSally
Meadows
Meehan
Messer
Mica
Miller (FL)
Miller (MI)
Moolenaar
Mooney (WV)
Mullin
Mulvaney
Murphy (PA)
Neugebauer
Newhouse
Noem
Nunes
Olson
Palazzo
Palmer
Paulsen
Pearce
Perry
Pittenger
Pitts
Poliquin
Pompeo
Posey
Price, Tom
Ratcliffe
Reed
Reichert
Ribble
Rice (SC)
Rigell
Roby
Roe (TN)
Rogers (AL)
Rogers (KY)
Rohrabacher
Rokita
Rooney (FL)
Ros-Lehtinen
Roskam
Ross
Rothfus
Rouzer

Royce
Russell
Salmon
Sanford
Scalise
Schweikert
Scott, Austin
Sensenbrenner
Sessions
Shimkus
Shuster
Simpson
Sinema
Smith (MO)
Smith (NE)
Smith (NJ)
Smith (TX)
Stefanik
Stewart
Stivers
Stutzman
Thompson (PA)
Thornberry
Tiberi
Tipton
Trott
Turner
Upton
Valadao
Wagner
Walberg
Walden
Walker
Walorski
Walters, Mimi
Weber (TX)
Webster (FL)
Wenstrup
Westerman
Wilson (FL)
Wilson (SC)
Wittman
Womack
Woodall
Yoder
Yoho
Young (AK)
Young (IA)
Young (IN)
Zeldin
Zinke

NOT VOTING—20

Barletta
Brown (FL)
Carney
DeFazio
Fincher
Flores
Forbes

Garrett
Hahn
Jolly
Jones
Kirkpatrick
Lofgren
McHenry

Nugent
Poe (TX)
Renacci
Vela
Westmoreland
Williams

☐ 1805

Ms. WILSON of Florida changed her vote from "yea" to "nay."

So the motion to recommit was rejected.

The result of the vote was announced as above recorded.

The SPEAKER pro tempore. The question is on the passage of the bill.

The question was taken; and the Speaker pro tempore announced that the ayes appeared to have it.

Ms. MAXINE WATERS of California. Madam Speaker, on that I demand the yeas and nays.

The yeas and nays were ordered.

The SPEAKER pro tempore. This will be a 5-minute vote.

The vote was taken by electronic device, and there were—yeas 254, nays 161, not voting 19, as follows:

[Roll No. 599]

YEAS—254

Abraham
Aderholt
Allen
Amash

Amodei
Ashford
Babin
Barletta

Barr
Barton
Beatty
Benishek

Bilirakis
Bishop (GA)
Bishop (MI)
Bishop (UT)
Black
Blackburn
Blum
Bost
Boustany
Brady (TX)
Brat
Bridenstine
Brooks (AL)
Brooks (IN)
Buchanan
Buck
Bucshon
Burgess
Byrne
Calvert
Carter (GA)
Carter (TX)
Chabot
Chaffetz
Clawson (FL)
Coffman
Cole
Collins (GA)
Collins (NY)
Comer
Comstock
Conaway
Cook
Cooper
Costa
Costello (PA)
Cramer
Crawford
Crenshaw
Cuellar
Culberson
Curbelo (FL)
Davidson
Davis, Rodney
Delaney
Denham
Dent
DeSantis
DesJarlais
Diaz-Balart
Dold
Donovan
Duffy
Duncan (SC)
Duncan (TN)
Ellmers (NC)
Emmer (MN)
Farenthold
Fitzpatrick
Fleischmann
Fleming
Fortenberry
Foxx
Franks (AZ)
Frelinghuysen
Gibbs
Gibson
Gohmert
Goodlatte
Gosar
Gowdy
Granger
Graves (GA)
Graves (LA)
Graves (MO)
Green, Gene
Griffith
Grothman
Guinta
Guthrie
Hanna

Hardy
Harper
Harris
Hartzler
Heck (NV)
Hensarling
Herrera Beutler
Hice, Jody B.
Higgins
Hill
Holding
Hudson
Huelskamp
Huizenga (MI)
Hultgren
Hunter
Hurd (TX)
Hurt (VA)
Issa
Jackson Lee
Jenkins (KS)
Jenkins (WV)
Johnson (OH)
Johnson, Sam
Jordan
Joyce
Katko
Kelly (MS)
Kelly (PA)
King (IA)
King (NY)
Kinzinger (IL)
Kline
Knight
Labrador
LaHood
LaMalfa
Lamborn
Lance
Latta
Lipinski
LoBiondo
Long
Loudermilk
Love
Lucas
Luetkemeyer
Lummis
MacArthur
Marchant
Marino
Massie
McCarthy
McCaul
McClintock
McHenry
McKinley
McMorris
　Rodgers
McSally
Meadows
Meehan
Meeks
Messer
Mica
Miller (FL)
Miller (MI)
Moolenaar
Mooney (WV)
Mullin
Mulvaney
Murphy (FL)
Murphy (PA)
Neugebauer
Newhouse
Noem
Nunes
Olson
Palazzo
Palmer
Paulsen

Payne
Pearce
Perry
Peters
Peterson
Pittenger
Pitts
Poliquin
Pompeo
Posey
Price, Tom
Ratcliffe
Reed
Reichert
Ribble
Rice (SC)
Rigell
Roby
Roe (TN)
Rogers (AL)
Rogers (KY)
Rohrabacher
Rokita
Rooney (FL)
Ros-Lehtinen
Roskam
Ross
Rothfus
Rouzer
Royce
Russell
Sanford
Scalise
Schweikert
Scott, Austin
Scott, David
Sensenbrenner
Sessions
Sewell (AL)
Shimkus
Shuster
Simpson
Sinema
Sires
Smith (MO)
Smith (NE)
Smith (NJ)
Smith (TX)
Stefanik
Stewart
Stivers
Stutzman
Thompson (PA)
Thornberry
Tiberi
Tipton
Trott
Turner
Upton
Valadao
Wagner
Walberg
Walden
Walker
Walorski
Walters, Mimi
Weber (TX)
Webster (FL)
Wenstrup
Westerman
Wilson (SC)
Wittman
Womack
Woodall
Yoder
Yoho
Young (AK)
Young (IA)
Young (IN)
Zeldin
Zinke

NAYS—161

Adams
Aguilar
Bass
Becerra
Bera
Beyer
Blumenauer
Bonamici
Boyle, Brendan
　F.
Brady (PA)
Brownley (CA)

Bustos
Butterfield
Capps
Capuano
Cárdenas
Carson (IN)
Cartwright
Castor (FL)
Castro (TX)
Chu, Judy
Cicilline
Clark (MA)

Clarke (NY)
Clay
Cleaver
Clyburn
Cohen
Connolly
Conyers
Courtney
Crowley
Cummings
Davis (CA)
Davis, Danny

DeGette
DeLauro
DelBene
DeSaulnier
Deutch
Dingell
Doggett
Doyle, Michael
　F.
Duckworth
Edwards
Ellison
Engel
Eshoo
Esty
Evans
Farr
Foster
Frankel (FL)
Fudge
Gabbard
Gallego
Garamendi
Graham
Grayson
Green, Al
Grijalva
Gutiérrez
Hanabusa
Hastings
Heck (WA)
Himes
Hinojosa
Honda
Hoyer
Huffman
Israel
Jeffries
Johnson (GA)
Johnson, E. B.
Kaptur
Keating
Kelly (IL)
Kennedy

Kildee
Kilmer
Kind
Kuster
Langevin
Larsen (WA)
Larson (CT)
Lawrence
Lee
Levin
Lewis
Lieu, Ted
Loebsack
Lowenthal
Lowey
Lujan Grisham
　(NM)
Luján, Ben Ray
　(NM)
Lynch
Maloney,
　Carolyn
Maloney, Sean
Matsui
McCollum
McDermott
McGovern
McNerney
Meng
Moore
Moulton
Nadler
Napolitano
Neal
Nolan
Norcross
O'Rourke
Pallone
Pascrell
Pelosi
Perlmutter
Pingree
Pocan
Polis

Price (NC)
Quigley
Rangel
Rice (NY)
Richmond
Roybal-Allard
Ruiz
Ruppersberger
Rush
Ryan (OH)
Sánchez, Linda
　T.
Sanchez, Loretta
Sarbanes
Schakowsky
Schiff
Schrader
Scott (VA)
Serrano
Sherman
Slaughter
Smith (WA)
Speier
Swalwell (CA)
Takano
Thompson (CA)
Thompson (MS)
Titus
Tonko
Torres
Tsongas
Van Hollen
Vargas
Veasey
Velázquez
Visclosky
Walz
Wasserman
　Schultz
Waters, Maxine
Watson Coleman
Welch
Wilson (FL)
Yarmuth

NOT VOTING—19

Brown (FL)
Carney
DeFazio
Fincher
Flores
Forbes
Garrett

Hahn
Jolly
Jones
Kirkpatrick
Lofgren
Nugent
Poe (TX)

Renacci
Salmon
Vela
Westmoreland
Williams

☐ 1815

Ms. GRAHAM changed her vote from "yea" to "nay."

So the bill was passed.

The result of the vote was announced as above recorded.

A motion to reconsider was laid on the table.

PROTECTION OF THE RIGHT OF TRIBES TO STOP THE EXPORT OF CULTURAL AND TRADITIONAL PATRIMONY RESOLUTION

Mr. GOODLATTE. Mr. Speaker, I ask unanimous consent to take from the Speaker's table the concurrent resolution (H. Con. Res. 122) supporting efforts to stop the theft, illegal possession or sale, transfer, and export of tribal cultural items of American Indians, Alaska Natives, and Native Hawaiians in the United States and internationally, with the Senate amendments thereto, and concur in the Senate amendments.

The Clerk read the title of the concurrent resolution.

The Clerk read the Senate amendments, as follows:

Senate amendments:
(1)Strike all after the resolving clause and insert the following:

SECTION 1. SHORT TITLE.

This concurrent resolution may be cited as the "Protection of the Right of Tribes to stop the Export of Cultural and Traditional Patrimony Resolution" or the "PROTECT Patrimony Resolution".

SEC. 2. DEFINITIONS.

In this resolution:

(1) NATIVE AMERICAN.—The term "Native American" means—

(A) with respect to an individual, an individual who is a member of an Indian tribe (as defined in section 2 of the Native American Graves Protection and Repatriation Act (25 U.S.C. 3001)); and

(B) with respect to the cultural nature or significance of an item, right, or other object or concept, being of or significant to—

(i) an Indian tribe (as defined in section 2 of the Native American Graves Protection and Repatriation Act (25 U.S.C. 3001)); or

(ii) a Native Hawaiian organization (as defined in that section (25 U.S.C. 3001)).

(2) TRIBAL CULTURAL ITEM.—The term "tribal cultural item" has the meaning given the term "cultural item" in section 2 of the Native American Graves Protection and Repatriation Act (25 U.S.C. 3001).

SEC. 3. FINDINGS.

Congress finds the following:

(1) Tribal cultural items—

(A) have ongoing historical, traditional, or cultural importance central to a Native American group or culture;

(B) cannot be alienated, appropriated, or conveyed by any individual; and

(C) are vital to Native American cultural survival and the maintenance of Native American ways of life.

(2) The nature and description of tribal cultural items are sensitive and to be treated with respect and confidentiality, as appropriate.

(3) Violators often export tribal cultural items internationally with the intent of evading Federal and tribal laws.

(4) Tribal cultural items continue to be removed from the possession of Native Americans and sold in black or public markets in violation of Federal and tribal laws, including laws designed to protect Native American cultural property rights.

(5) The illegal trade of tribal cultural items involves a sophisticated and lucrative black market, where the items are traded through domestic markets and then are often exported internationally.

(6) Auction houses in foreign countries have held sales of tribal cultural items from the Pueblo of Acoma, the Pueblo of Laguna, the Pueblo of San Felipe, the Hopi Tribe, and other Indian tribes.

(7) After tribal cultural items are exported internationally, Native Americans have difficulty stopping the sale of the items and securing their repatriation to their home communities, where the items belong.

(8) Federal agencies have a responsibility to consult with Native Americans to stop the theft, illegal possession or sale, transfer, and export of tribal cultural items.

(9) An increase in the investigation and successful prosecution of violations of the Native American Graves Protection and Repatriation Act (25 U.S.C. 3001 et seq.) and the Archaeological Resources Protection Act of 1979 (16 U.S.C. 470aa et seq.) is necessary to deter illegal trading in tribal cultural items.

(10) Many Indian tribes and tribal organizations have passed resolutions condemning the theft and sale of tribal cultural items, including the following:

(A) The National Congress of American Indians passed Resolutions SAC–12–008 and SD–15–075 to call on the United States, in consultation with Native Americans—

(i) to address international repatriation; and

(ii) to take affirmative actions to stop the theft and illegal sale of tribal cultural items both domestically and internationally.

(B) The All Pueblo Council of Governors, representative of 20 Pueblo Indian tribes—

(i) noted that the Pueblo Indian tribes of the Southwestern United States have been disproportionately affected by the sale of tribal cultural items both domestically and internationally in violation of Federal and tribal laws; and

(ii) passed Resolutions 2015–12 and 2015–13 to call on the United States, in consultation with Native Americans—

(I) to address international repatriation; and

(II) to take affirmative actions to stop the theft and illegal sale of tribal cultural items both domestically and internationally.

(C) The United South and Eastern Tribes, an intertribal organization comprised of 26 federally recognized Indian tribes, passed Resolution 2015:007, which calls on the United States to address all means to support the repatriation of tribal cultural items from beyond United States borders.

(D) The Inter-Tribal Council of the Five Civilized Tribes, uniting the Chickasaw, Choctaw, Cherokee, Muscogee (Creek), and Seminole Nations, passed Resolution 12–07, which requests that the United States, after consultation with Native Americans, assist in international repatriation and take immediate action to address repatriation.

SEC. 4. DECLARATION OF CONGRESS.

Congress—

(1) condemns the theft, illegal possession or sale, transfer, and export of tribal cultural items;

(2) calls on the Secretary of the Interior, the Secretary of State, the Secretary of Commerce, the Secretary of Homeland Security, and the Attorney General to consult with Native Americans, including traditional Native American religious leaders, in addressing the practices described in paragraph (1)—

(A) to take affirmative action to stop the practices; and

(B) to secure repatriation of tribal cultural items to Native Americans;

(3) supports the efforts of the Comptroller General of the United States—

(A) to determine the scope of illegal trafficking in tribal cultural items domestically and internationally; and

(B) to discuss with Native Americans, including traditional Native American religious leaders, relevant Federal officials, and other individuals and entities, as appropriate, the steps required—

(i) to end illegal trafficking in, and the export of, tribal cultural items; and

(ii) to secure repatriation of tribal cultural items to the appropriate Native Americans;

(4) supports the development of explicit restrictions on the export of tribal cultural items; and

(5) encourages State and local governments and interested groups and organizations to work cooperatively in—

(A) deterring the theft, illegal possession or sale, transfer, and export of tribal cultural items; and

(B) securing the repatriation of tribal cultural items to the appropriate Native Americans.

(2)Strike the preamble.

Mr. GOODLATTE (during the reading). Mr. Speaker, I ask unanimous consent to dispense with the reading of the Senate amendments.

The SPEAKER pro tempore (Mr. GROTHMAN). Is there objection to the request of the gentleman from Virginia?

There was no objection.

The SPEAKER pro tempore. Is there objection to the original request of the gentleman from Virginia?

There was no objection.

A motion to reconsider was laid on the table.

SMALL BUSINESS SATURDAY

(Mr. THOMPSON of Pennsylvania asked and was given permission to address the House for 1 minute and to revise and extend his remarks.)

Mr. THOMPSON of Pennsylvania. Mr. Speaker, I rise in recognition of Small Business Saturday this past weekend, a day to support small businesses and celebrate the role that they play in our communities. This year, Small Business Saturday saw a record 112 million shoppers, a number which highlights the effectiveness of this movement across the United States.

Small businesses have proven time and time again that they are the backbone of a strong economy. In Pennsylvania's Fifth Congressional District, which I am proud to represent, small businesses provide valuable services, ranging from construction and manufacturing to health care and social assistance, bettering the lives of residents and consumers.

Academic institutions also play an important role in growing small businesses. For example, Penn State University introduced a business pre-accelerator this year, known as the Happy Valley Launchbox. This unique venture is a signature program of the Invent Penn State initiative, and I am confident it will serve as a platform for entrepreneurship and innovation.

I look forward to the continued success of small businesses both in Pennsylvania and across the United States, and I remain grateful for their contribution to our Nation's economy.

IMPROVING THE HEALTH OF AMERICANS

The SPEAKER pro tempore. Under the Speaker's announced policy of January 6, 2015, the gentleman from Oklahoma (Mr. MULLIN) is recognized for 60 minutes as the designee of the majority leader.

GENERAL LEAVE

Mr. MULLIN. Mr. Speaker, I ask that all Members may have 5 legislative days to revise and extend their remarks and include any extraneous materials in the RECORD.

The SPEAKER pro tempore. Is there objection to the request of the gentleman from Oklahoma?

There was no objection.

Mr. MULLIN. Mr. Speaker, I rise in support of the 21st Century Cures Act that passed yesterday. It is not too often that we get to be proactive in such important legislative business in this House. However, yesterday we saw a great victory for the families that so many of us have heard from. We have heard from mothers and fathers, brothers and sisters, and aunts and uncles about loved ones who are dealing with mental illness or dealing with drug addiction or dealing with a disease that we haven't been able to accurately address because we have had roadblocks because of legislation and rules that have been put in place by the FDA. But yesterday we got to pass a piece of legislation by overwhelming bipartisan support to say: Yes, we are listening; yes, we hear you; and yes, we are going to make changes.

I am going to let my other colleagues speak. At this time I yield to the gentleman from Pennsylvania (Mr. MURPHY), my chairman.

Mr. MURPHY of Pennsylvania. Mr. Speaker, I thank the gentleman for yielding and heading up this very important Special Order on a topic that affects every single family in America, and that is their health.

As the gentleman said, yesterday we passed a very important bill, the 21st Century Cures Act, with the charge led by the chairman of the Committee on Energy and Commerce, FRED UPTON. I was pleased that they included in that package our mental health reform bill, which we moved out of the Committee on Energy and Commerce unanimously in July.

We have spoken about this issue at great length for the last few years because it is worthy of that time. We have spoken because of the 60 million Americans who suffer from some level of mental illness and the 10 million Americans who suffer from severe mental illness and the fact that 40 percent of them cannot get care; that half the counties in America have no psychiatrists, psychologists or social workers; that we do not have enough hospital beds for people in crisis, a shortage of 100,000; that there are only 9,000 child and adolescent psychiatrists when we need 30,000, particularly important because severe mental illness in half the cases emerges by age 14 and 75 percent by age 24; that we have seen too many lives lost, that the body count in this Nation last year related primarily and secondarily to mental illness exceeds the total combat body counts of United States soldiers in World War I, Korea, Vietnam, Desert Storm, Bosnia, Afghanistan, and Iraq combined; because millions of families continue to suffer, because our prisons are filled with the mentally ill, our emergency rooms are backed up with people with mental illness-related disorders, and because our morgues are also filled.

Yesterday, the House took a definitive bipartisan approach in changing that trajectory. The issues we have covered on mental health, along with the advances in the 21st Century Cures bill, sets a new direction for where we need to be going in this Nation to approaching health care overall. When we look at the research changes that we have made in advancing cures not only in small population orphan diseases, but also with regard to the total 10,000 diseases out there, we will be able to sufficiently and more effectively identify medical disorders and psychiatric disorders early on and get them treatment sooner.

One of the aspects that was taken care of in the Helping Families With Mental Health Crisis Act is a program called RAISE, Response After Initial Schizophrenic Episode. As we know, research tells us that when you provide medication and effective targeted counseling early on, you can reduce the trajectory of severe mental illness and improve the prognosis greatly. But when that is not provided, every crisis moment of severe mental illness leads to other neurological damage, worsens the prognosis and, sadly, increases the chances that a person will have time in prison 10 times more likely than to be in a hospital when they are in crisis.

We are changing that trajectory. New research will get us in that direction. Let me lay out for a few minutes today where this takes us as Congress is looking to change the Affordable Care Act. People have spoken ad nauseam about the problems with that act, how it has cost families a great deal, how it is supposed to be affordable but it is not, how premiums have gone up dramatically in double digits and triple digits over the last few years, how the deductibles and copays put it out of families' reach, and how it is not really a comprehensive approach because it does not stem the tide of increasing healthcare costs.

There are some specific reasons for that. As long as we have a system that is based on a fee-for-service model and as long as we have a system that does not put the patient at the center of this focus, we are going to continue to have problems with cost overruns and, quite frankly, care problems.

We have seen changes in the trajectory of improvements in reduction in mortality and morbidity. For example, over the last couple decades, we have seen a reduction in mortality rates for cancer, for heart disease, for stroke, for accidental deaths, for HIV/AIDS; but we have seen increases in mortality rates for suicide and also for drug overdose deaths.

This really means we need to be looking at a different kind of model, and that model is the integrated care model, the model where behavioral medicine and physical medicine work together.

Why is that important?

We know that 75 percent of the people with a severe mental illness will have some other chronic illness like heart disease, lung disease, diabetes, infectious disease; and 50 percent of them have at least two chronic diseases; a third will have at least three. We know that a person with severe mental illness has triple the chance of moving into poverty, and we know that people in poverty have three times the rate of mental illness.

Beyond that, if we look at people who enter into using the medical field from the area of chronic illness, that perhaps the first diagnosis might be anything from cancer, inflammatory bowel disease, diabetes, et cetera, the chances of them developing a psychological problem such as depression, panic disorder, anxiety, is massive, twice the rate of the rest of the population.

This is where the costs begin to soar, because when a person recognizes they have this long-term problem with pain, with doctors' appointments, with disruption of their lifestyle, with immobility, with disability, et cetera, it is expected and it is common for them to develop other psychiatric disorders. But we have had a system that has ignored that.

What happens when we ignore that?

If a person has a chronic illness and depression, for example, untreated depression, it doubles. It doubles their healthcare costs. When there are models out there, however, that say let's integrate behavioral medicine and physical medicine so that a physician, being a coordinated care model, when they have a patient with one of those illnesses, a chronic illness, they begin to treat the whole patient, the patient-centered model, the team approach between the doctor and patient there.

□ 1830

What can it do? Well, I want to cite a study done by a young doctor by the name of Jeffrey Brenner, who was out in New Jersey.

You recognize that people with complex health and social issues have these high rates of going to emergency rooms. They are called super-utilizers. Medicaid points out that 5 percent of the people on Medicaid account for 50 percent of Medicaid spending and, I might add, virtually all of those are people who have a concurrent psychiatric disorder, such as depression.

But what Brenner did in his particular study is recognize that there were a number of people who had a huge number of visits to emergency rooms in a very costly way. He said, for example, nearly half of the city of Camden's 77,000 residents were visiting an emergency department annually, most often for head colds, viral infections, ear infections, and sore throats. Thirteen percent of the patients accounted for 80 percent of hospital costs, and 20 percent of the patients accounted for 90 percent of the costs.

What he looked at were models that police use called hot spotting—where are the areas of a city where you have a great deal of crime, and, instead of avoiding those areas, the police would go in and work to prevent crime. Well, similarly, in Brenner's model, he looked at managing these patients' care instead of ignoring them. If you ignore them, they go to emergency rooms repeatedly.

Studies done, for example, at the University of Pittsburgh Medical Center with inflammatory bowel disease found when you ignore folks, they continue to go to emergency rooms. Overutilizers of the system. And on a fee-for-service model, it is worth it for the doctor. They made a lot of money. Hospitals made money, as long as the people continued to come back.

But what was it that was driving people repeatedly to get this care at an emergency room, or expensive care, instead of doing something else? What Brenner did and other studies have found is that people could not access their primary care physician or their specialist, so that is where they would go for care. They would panic. Worry, anxiety, depression. They weren't managing their medication well. There are neurobiological things that take place in the system of someone with depression which makes them more prone toward other infections and viruses, et cetera.

What Brenner did was identified folks with a fairly complicated model here and developed a care management team where the goal is leaving patients with the ability to manage health care on their own. And how do they do that? By helping them see doctors more frequently.

The studies done with the inflammatory bowel disease clinic at the University of Pittsburgh did the same thing. They developed an integrative care team, including psychiatric and psychological consulting, to help the person deal with their pain, help them change their behavior patterns, and make sure they had easy access to the doctors, so even getting the doctor's cell phone number, email address, and respond within 72 hours for doctor visits.

What Brenner found, the first 36 patients had a total of 62 hospital emergency room visits per month before they began intervention. It dropped to 37 visits per month afterwards. Then they also found the hospital bill fell from a monthly average of $1.2 million to just over $500,000, savings that benefited State and Federal healthcare plans. Similar results have been found in other areas when this is targeted.

Now, we know the Affordable Care Act had some models of this, but the results have been somewhat equivocal because they haven't looked at these as closely and really worked with the patients as closely. But the point is this: Recognizing if we are going to get hold of the cost overruns with health care, it needs to be that integrated care model—behavioral and physical medicine working together—a coordinated care model, where a primary care physician and/or the specialists are working to coordinate the patient's care instead of leaving them on their own, and, quite frankly, a capitated care model, where it is worth it financially for the physician and patient to work together, not to just say: Go to the hospital whenever you want; go to the emergency room whenever you want; but get the care you need, the time you need it, with the quality you need.

The Affordable Care Act started down this road, but it wasn't fully followed. But this bill we passed yesterday, and our hope is that the Senate passes next week, by moving forward on research; by making sure physicians get timely, quality information for what they should do; by making sure that it is disseminated to physicians, whether they are in urban downtown Manhattan or they are out in rural South Dakota, that through telemedicine they have access to the best decisionmaking; and by making sure that, through telehealth, which we funded in the Helping Families with Mental Health Crisis Act, no matter where physicians are in America, to have access to psychologists and psychiatrists and social workers and to integrate that care together, this is what makes a huge difference.

Children's Hospital of Pittsburgh did a study of when that behavioral health consultation is done during the pediatrician visit, when there is a warm handoff, right away the family meets the mental health professional, there is over a 90-percent followup for that patient with the doctor. When they are given a card and said to call another day, it plummets to less than half.

Similarly, look at the problems we face with opioid abuse in America. Last year, we had a death total of 47,000. We are reaching the point of the number of people who die from opioid substance abuse is reaching that of the level of our combat deaths during the entire Vietnam war. It is an embarrassing, shameful, and painful thing for our Nation to have, and that doesn't even include the many, many folks who still remain addicted.

But here is what happens with care for the addicted. Out of every 1,000 persons who has an addiction disorder, 900 will not seek care. Of the 100 who do seek care, 37 can't find it. It is not available in their community. Of the 63 who do seek care and find it, only 6 of them will find evidence-based care.

But what if we change that trajectory? What if we say as part of moving forward in our revision of the Affordable Care Act and making it really effective health care we made sure we integrated behavioral and physical medicine together?

A study done at the University of Michigan, I believe, or Michigan State—I have to make sure I get those right because I know Chairman UPTON would not forgive me, but let's say it was done in Michigan—they did a fascinating study where they made sure when someone came to the emergency room with a drug overdose, they didn't do the typical thing and hand someone a card and say: you know, you have a drug problem; you need to go get help. In those cases, many times the vast majority of people don't follow up.

Instead, what they did is they provided qualified drug counseling in the emergency room. From the same model, if a person had a broken arm, the hospital would set it before they went home. They wouldn't say: here is a card; call an orthopedic surgeon on Monday and get that arm set. If a person came in with chest pains, they wouldn't say: why don't you make an appointment in a week or two with a cardiologist. They would treat it right away. Well, the same thing goes with psychiatric disorders and drug abuse.

What Michigan found in their study and replicated in other communities is there was a 50-percent increase of people following through on drug treatment.

So look at the things that are done. The bill we passed yesterday also invests hundreds of millions of dollars into more effective treatment for people with a substance abuse problem. It isn't enough just to have them in methadone maintenance or buprenorphine programs. Those will not be as effective. You have got to get them into effective counseling programs.

So what we see is this: The bipartisan efforts that have worked through here and have made some big differences in where we are going with research and care will set us on a strong trajectory to making a big difference as this Congress and the new President work to change the Affordable Care Act to really being affordable and really being care-focused.

That being said, we will still have, tragically, too many stories while we are waiting to get that care out there. We will still have too many episodes: a homicide, or a suicide, or a drug overdose death, or someone has lost their job, or a marriage is broken up, or families who have been abandoned by someone else, or children who are lost, or those who are homeless. It continues on as long as we are not properly addressing the issues of mental illness in America.

I tell you, even though we have those long, somber moments of sadness, there is some joy in what this House did yesterday in this strong, bipartisan, coordinated effort to say we are changing the direction of how we recognize mental health care, what we are going to do about that, and how that has to be an integral component as we move forward to change health overall. We can do this. We can reduce costs dramatically by providing better and more effective care.

So for all those families who have been contacting us Members of Congress, literally the millions of Americans who are suffering from these diseases of mental illness and the tens of millions of families who recognize the suffering there, help is on its way. The actions that Congress took yesterday, the actions that we anticipate the Senate will take next week, the signature of the President will move these things forward. We will create a new dawn, a brighter horizon for people who, up to this point, had very little hope of where things are.

We know we have a long way to go, and we know this next Congress, as we move into the next session next year, is going to have their hands full, but we can do this. And I know there are dedicated people here on both sides of the aisle just waiting and eager to make a big difference for America's families. And where there is help, there is hope.

Mr. MULLIN. Mr. Speaker, as you can see, the gentleman from Pennsylvania is extremely passionate about this. He has been the leader and a voice for mental illness for my entire time that I have been up here, which hasn't been that long—only 4 years—but we appreciate his passion and his dedication to this.

Unfortunately, mental illness isn't going away. It is becoming more of a problem. And we, as Members of Congress, are going to have to address this. I look forward to continuing to work with the chairman on this.

Yesterday was a step in the right direction, but we have a long way to go. We are in this fight, and we are in this fight together. I couldn't imagine being with anyone better than the gentleman from Pennsylvania. So I thank him for his dedication.

Mr. Speaker, I yield to the gentlewoman from Indiana (Mrs. BROOKS).

Mrs. BROOKS of Indiana. Before the chairman of our committee steps away, I just want to acknowledge the leadership that Congressman MURPHY of Pennsylvania has given to this issue—an issue that so many Members of Congress haven't talked about enough until he began talking about it.

I want to thank the gentleman from Oklahoma (Mr. MULLIN) for leading this Special Order. We have heard from our constituents, and we know families where 1 in 4 adults—a total of 61.5 million Americans—will struggle with mental illness in any given year. While the numbers are staggering—and certainly, my colleague from Pennsylvania knows the numbers and statistics better than maybe this Chamber combined—they don't actually tell the deeply personal and typically painful stories that this disease inflicts on those it touches, their friends, neighbors, and families.

Whether it was Columbine, Aurora, or Sandy Hook, time and time again, tragedies have left our communities devastated and reeling, wondering if our fellow citizens could have been spared the violence and bloodshed had we simply been able to see the signs of mental illness.

Many lessons followed in the wake of all of these tragedies, but chief among them always came out the fact that our mental health system is broken: we are unable to fully recognize the signs and symptoms of an individual suffering from mental illness; we often don't have the resources to help these individuals and their families; and we have very limited mental health workforce, which is overwhelmed and often underprepared for the vast challenges they face day in and day out.

Mental illness is sometimes referred to as an invisible illness. However, just because you can't see the illness, it doesn't mean it isn't there. It is a serious disease, and in order to make any progress in more effectively identifying it, we must begin to recognize it as such.

Before the end of this year, we have a chance to make the first major mental health reforms this country has seen in over 50 years. And I am very proud to stand with the gentleman from Pennsylvania in support of his years of tireless work to bring to the forefront this health crisis we are facing in America—a crisis often pushed to the side because it may be too difficult or too uncomfortable to talk about. I applaud his efforts and the efforts of so many from our committee, particularly the staff, who have made it possible to work to include these important reforms to our mental health system in the critical 21st Century Cures bill that passed the House last night overwhelmingly.

Right now, our medical system does not allow families of those suffering from mental illness to become true partners in their care. The language in our bill takes significant steps toward easing these barriers and making sure that people struggling with mental illness will have more access to the care and treatment that they need.

Our prisons and emergency rooms have become de facto psychiatric treatment centers and are overcrowded with individuals suffering from mental illness; however, we have learned over the years we cannot simply arrest away this problem. I am pleased that there are reforms to the way our criminal justice system handles individuals with mental illness. As someone who has worked in the criminal justice system most of my career, I can assess that such support is long overdue and so very necessary.

One of the greatest issues with our mental health system is there is a critical shortage, as Dr. Murphy just mentioned, in our mental health workforce. This effort contains significant measures to train and expand this critically important workforce.

□ 1845

These are simply a few of the important reforms included in 21st Century Cures which, above all else, sets a new and higher standard for mental health care and treatment in America.

Once again, I applaud Congressman MURPHY's incredible work to fix our broken mental health care system. I am proud to have supported this effort throughout the legislative process and look to the Senate to now take up the 21st Century Cures and bring relief to the individuals and families across America who need it the most.

Mr. MULLIN. Mr. Speaker, it is always an honor to have people that are willing to come down and share their time and their passion with us, so I would like to thank my colleague from Indiana for laying it out in such an eloquent form like she always does.

Also, congratulations on the committee assignment. I don't know if I wish the gentlewoman good luck or not.

Mr. Speaker, at this time I yield to the gentleman from Illinois (Mr. DOLD).

Mr. DOLD. Mr. Speaker, I want to thank my friend from Oklahoma for yielding on what is an incredibly important topic.

I also want to weigh in and thank my good friend, Dr. TIM MURPHY, for his incredible work on a really comprehensive piece of mental health legislation. I want to not only congratulate him, I want to thank him for successfully shepherding this first real piece of mental health legislation, honestly, since 1962. It is now up to the Senate to move this forward.

I am pleased to be here as not only an original cosponsor, but helped introduce the Helping Families in Mental Health Crisis Act, which was now attached to this recent 21st Century Cures bill, another bill that I am proud to not only stand up and support.

As we look at cures, as we look at what we are doing, we see so much tension across our country today. We just got done with a national election, and, frankly, it seems as people are at each others' throats. And the one thing that we can agree on, I hope, regardless of whom you voted for, we should all be on the same page that we want 21st Century Cures to move forward; because, frankly, as we look at the number of people that are suffering from diabetes, Alzheimer's, Parkinson's, and the like, they don't care what political persuasion you are. They are just impacting families all across our country.

Another huge piece of that is mental health; and as we look at mental health, there is no question, family after family, an enormous number of people, nearly 10 million Americans, suffer from a serious mental health issue, including schizophrenia, bipolar disorder, major depression, amongst others. Yet millions of these people are

going without treatment, and their families are struggling to care for them each and every day.

We need to talk about treatment. Treatment before tragedy is something that I know has been talked about time and again.

The Federal Government currently dedicates about $130 billion towards 112 programs intended to address mental health, but there is still a nationwide shortage of nearly 100,000 beds needed for psychiatric care and only one child and adolescent psychiatrist for every 2,000 children with a mental health disorder. Frankly, that is just unacceptable.

My constituents have come to me time and again demanding that we do better. The Filler Foundation comes to mind as something that we have to do because, again, as we look at mental health, one of the things that we know is tied to that is this incredible epidemic of prescription drugs and opiates that are really just impacting every single community across our country. Ultimately, we know that this mental health disorder is a huge part of that, as people are trying to self-medicate, and so people are overdosing and dying on a regular basis.

Ultimately, this bill that we are talking about today helps and now allows those families to give better care, be better informed, so that parents or caregivers can actually play a more vital role.

In July, we passed the Helping Families in Mental Health Crisis Act, 422–2. And just recently, this other bill that we just passed, the 21st Century Cures, that included this mental health legislation, passed with enormous bipartisan support right here in this body. It is time that the Senate take up this legislation and pass it.

I am confident that the incredible providers that are in my district, the families who are in need that have been asking for help, will benefit from the many grants that we reauthorized, the updates that we have made to improve communication between the patients, the families, and the providers, and the steps that we took to ensure that insurance providers are complying with existing mental health parity laws.

Over the past 2 years, Dr. Murphy's efforts have engaged Democrats and Republicans from every region of the country. Just a few short months ago, and I am sure—I don't know if he was in Oklahoma with my good friend, but I know he came out to my district. We had a roundtable talking about mental health issues. We went and visited some of the facilities together to talk about the real needs that are out there. Ultimately, we know that mental health impacts so many families across our country.

I would venture to say, Mr. Speaker, that not a single Member in this body has not been impacted in some way, shape, or form, by a loved one, a friend, a family member that is suffering from some sort of mental illness. So I believe that we have an incredible opportunity here.

Ultimately, when I go out and I talk to people—and I know my good friend, I am sure, has done the same—they say: Is Congress working? And the answer oftentimes is no. But I do think that we have to step back and take a look at what we can accomplish when we actually do come together.

Something that we all should be proud of is the fact that we were able to move forward in this body to talk about not only 21st Century Cures, talking about funding for the National Institutes of Health, talking about trying to deal with some of the prescription drug and opiate epidemics, but really trying to tackle head-on the issue of mental health and the impacts that this has for our Nation.

So I want to thank my good friend from Oklahoma for organizing this Special Order. I want to thank, obviously, my good friend, Dr. MURPHY, for the great work that he has been doing for years on this.

And I do want to make sure that the American people know that today we took a big step forward and, honestly, we are not going to rest until this is signed into law by the President and really enabling so many families to get a tremendous amount of relief.

Mr. MULLIN. I thank the gentleman for his service. My good friend from Illinois is going to be missed. His service has been something we can all hold in great respect. I am going to miss seeing him in the morning at our workout, but he has influenced us in a better way. If we can always leave where we have been better than we found it, that is a legacy we can all walk with. I thank the gentleman for his service, and I hope our friendship will continue.

Mr. Speaker, as my friend from Illinois was saying about the opioid addiction, I want to point out a sad statistic. Oklahoma is ranked 28th in population throughout the country, and yet we had the 10th highest—10th highest—accidental opioid overdose deaths. We have more accidental drug overdose deaths caused by painkiller addictions than vehicle accidents in the State of Oklahoma.

And these aren't from the young who may be going through a time of experimenting. This isn't from the elderly who may not understand the prescription which they are taking. This is coming from our mothers. Our number one—number one—individual that is losing their life to opioid overdose is our middle-aged mothers. There is a problem.

The 21st Century Cures does address this, but just the same as mental health, it is a first step in the right direction.

Mr. Speaker, at this time I yield to the gentleman from Pennsylvania (Mr.

PERRY), another good friend of mine, a true patriot to this country, one who has years and years of service. I have a tremendous amount of respect for him.

Mr. PERRY. Mr. Speaker, I thank the gentleman, my friend from the great State of Oklahoma. I am privileged to have visited not only his State, but his district, and met the fabulous and wonderful people there, and they are lucky to have him representing them here.

You talk about that statistic, and I am here to talk specifically about mental illness, but this opioid epidemic has touched every single community. You don't have to live in the city. You don't have to live in underprivileged areas. I know very good friends that it has wracked their families, and it has wracked our communities.

Certainly, one of the great things about the 21st Century Cures Act is the help that is on the way. It is probably not going to be enough, but we need to do everything we can, at least in making these first steps in wrapping our minds and our hands around this problem and getting to a solution.

So I am thankful that the gentleman has taken the time to hold this Special Order, to bring that, as well as the other issues, up, and I appreciate that.

Mr. Speaker, I want to talk a little bit about the mental health situation in our country, and I think the gentleman has alluded to much of it in his conversation.

Mr. Speaker, more than 11 million Americans suffer from severe schizophrenia, bipolar disorder, and major depression, yet millions—literally millions—are going without any treatment whatsoever. And families, these families are struggling to care for these people.

You have a broken arm or some physical malady, you can see that and you can get to a cure in many, many cases. But these mental illnesses vex us, where your loved one is fine one moment and the next moment is not, and you don't know when that is going to happen or the gravity of the situation, how bad it might be at any given moment. These are our loved ones. These are our family members and our neighbors.

The Federal Government's approach to mental health has been a chaotic patchwork of antiquated programs and ineffective policies spread across numerous bureaucratic agencies that simply don't get to the issue at hand, and I think we can all see that.

Sadly, many patients end up in the criminal justice system or are on the street because services are unavailable. I know that in the State that I reside in, the great State of Pennsylvania, years back, we closed our State hospitals where much of the care was given to these people, and they just ended up out on the street or back with their families, which often are cases

that their families just don't know what to do. They don't know how to handle it. They can't handle it.

Then these folks end up in the penal system, which is no place for people that justifiably are sick. They have an issue. They are sick. They are not criminals, but they are sick.

In the worst case scenarios, some individuals commit acts of violence. And every one of us has heard the stories and seen the film footage on the news of these acts of violence that can be directly attributable to mental illness.

Now, we should be able to feel safe in our homes, all of us, in our communities, and our hearts just break every single time a senseless act of violence occurs and we see that. And certainly, for parents, these tragedies, they hit especially close to home.

We need to remember that the beneficiaries of mental health treatment aren't only those directly treated for mental illness, but also our broader community when we see those things, those images on TV, because mental health treatment is a preventive measure to reducing acts of violence. It is a preventive measure. It actually stops those things from ever occurring if we get to it.

Now, I was an enthusiastic supporter and cosponsor of my colleague Congressman TIM MURPHY's Helping Families in Mental Health Crisis Act. He literally worked on it for years, and I watched him struggle through that. And that bill was actually included in the 21st Century Cures Act, which passed this very House last night.

This legislation coordinates programs across different agencies, those disparate agencies that don't seem to work with one another, where information is siloed. It coordinates that, those programs, and promotes effective evidence-based programs, evidence-based so we can get to solutions.

Just like most other things with the Federal Government, by removing Federal barriers to care, advancing early intervention programs, adding alternatives to institutionalization, and improving the transition from one level of care to another, we directly address our Nation's broken mental health care system, finally. Finally, a step in the right direction.

So, once again, I applaud and thank the gentleman from Oklahoma for allowing me this time and bringing this issue to the floor; and I urge my colleagues in the Senate to send this bill directly to the President's desk, absolutely, as soon as possible. We can't wait for another tragedy to occur where we are all watching on television the footage of something that could have been prevented and avoided.

Mr. MULLIN. Mr. Speaker, I thank my colleague from Pennsylvania for also being extremely passionate about moving in the right direction with mental health. It is something that we continue to look over.

As I stated when we first started tonight, we had an overwhelming amount of bipartisan support on passing the 21st Century Cures Act. We could see that the hard work that the staff over in the Energy and Commerce Committee, on both sides, the Republican staff and the Democratic staff, worked together to come up with a bipartisan bill to make sure that we are putting our families first, that we are putting our constituents first.

☐ 1900

We are setting aside the partisanship that often finds its way inside our conversations. We set it aside and actually were very proactive on a very important piece of legislation.

I would like to thank Chairman MURPHY, with his passion on mental health, and our outgoing chairman, Mr. FRED UPTON, who has dedicated his years of service to the betterment of our constituents and his passion for fighting this and seeing this through. I would like to thank him for his dedication. The gentleman will be missed as our chairman.

Mr. Speaker, I see no other speakers at this time. I yield back the balance of my time.

CELEBRATING THE DREAMERS

The SPEAKER pro tempore. Under the Speaker's announced policy of January 6, 2015, the gentleman from Texas (Mr. O'ROURKE) is recognized for 60 minutes as the designee of the minority leader.

GENERAL LEAVE

Mr. O'ROURKE. Mr. Speaker, I ask unanimous consent that all Members may have 5 legislative days to revise and extend their remarks and include extraneous material on the subject of this Special Order.

The SPEAKER pro tempore. Is there objection to the request of the gentleman from Texas?

There was no objection.

Mr. O'ROURKE. Mr. Speaker, I rise today to share the stories of and celebrate the DREAMers who live in our communities, mine in El Paso, Texas, and nearly every single community across the great United States.

All together, we estimate there are close to 750,000 DREAMers in the United States. These are beneficiaries of an executive action under this President, known as the Deferred Action for Childhood Arrivals, that ensured that young people in our communities who arrived in this country at a very early age, brought here by their parents from another country of origin, who are going to school, living by our laws, being productive and net contributors to their communities and who, in some cases, strive to serve in the military or perform some other community or civic service, are able to reside in this country after they come forward

voluntarily out of the shadows to give their personal information, their fingerprints, their contact information, their names, their addresses, and their telephone numbers, in other words, to register with the government so that we know who is in this country and satisfy some legitimate security concerns that we have when it comes to undocumented immigration. So these young DREAMers have satisfied those concerns by coming forward.

This temporary reprieve from deportation allows them to continue to live in our communities, to continue to be our neighbors, to continue to make this country great, and to make cities like El Paso the safe and wonderful communities that they are. It is no accident that El Paso has more than its fair share of DREAMers and also is the safest city not just along the U.S.-Mexico border, it is the safest city not just in the State of Texas, but it is the safest city in the United States today.

The urgency behind our actions today lies with the commitment from the President-elect to immediately terminate the current President's executive actions when it comes to these DREAMers. This commitment to terminate this action will also terminate any certainty these young people have. It will reduce the security of our communities when young people no longer feel comfortable approaching or working with law enforcement for fear of deportation; and it produces extreme anxiety and fear that I can only begin to imagine for myself or for my kids if I knew that I had given all of my personal identifiable information, including the address at which I reside, my telephone number, and the names of my parents, to the Federal Government which now may have a policy to immediately deport me back to the country of origin and, if I were, as a typical DREAMer might be, 20 years old and attending the University of Texas in El Paso, may have lived in El Paso for the majority of my life. I may have come over at the age of 3, and for the last 17 years, the only life I knew was in the United States; the only city I knew was in El Paso, Texas; the only language I spoke was English. I had no family, no connections, no place in my country of original origin, and I didn't speak the language. Then I would be unable to thrive.

I think for some of these young people, they question whether they will have the ability to survive. I think it is really that critical, and it is very important that we remind ourselves, the rest of the country, and certainly our colleagues here in the House of the gravity of the situation.

Beyond the moral imperative, which I think is the most important, there is also an economic dynamic to this. The Department of Commerce estimates that the DREAMers, these 750,000-strong DREAMers who are contrib-

uting every single day in our communities, going to our high schools and making our country better, that over their lifetimes in the United States they will earn up to $4 trillion of taxable income—taxable income that will allow the community they live in to flourish, to thrive, to enrich those that they hire and work with, and to add significantly to the Federal Treasury.

That is just one point in terms of the economic advantage of creating additional certainty and, at a minimum, not forcibly removing these DREAMers or terminating the protection under which they currently reside.

Before I yield to my colleagues to share their stories about the DREAMers in their communities—and, again, they are in every single State of the Union and almost every community in every one of those States—I thought I would share the story of one of the DREAMers that I met this Monday in El Paso, Texas, when I held a townhall on short notice, a few days' notice to my constituents over Facebook and Twitter and published in the newspaper.

More than 300 El Pasoans showed up to share their stories of how they came to this country and what they are now doing in our communities. What was even more impressive and poignant for me and many in the audience that night were the U.S. citizens in El Paso who showed up to stand in solidarity and in strength with these DREAMers and to let them know that, come what may, whatever executive actions are terminated, whatever necessary immigration reform laws are not enacted, that we as a community in El Paso, Texas, are going to stand with these DREAMers, make sure that they are successful, and make sure that they have nothing to fear going forward.

One of these DREAMers that had the courage to stand up and be counted on Monday night was Estefania Garcia Ruvalcaba. She is 17 years old. She arrived in the United States in El Paso, Texas, which has served as the Ellis Island for much of the Western Hemisphere, at the age of 3 years old. I ask you to tell me what 3-year-old understands concepts like citizenship or nationality.

She doesn't speak the Spanish language anymore that she barely knew at the age of 3. She only speaks English. She is a junior at Del Valle High School in El Paso. She is captain of the soccer team. She is on the student council. She is the press box manager, and so she is earning a little bit of money to be able to take home at the end of the day and help out; and she goes to every single football game to be able to support the hometown and home high school team. On top of that, she runs on the cross-country team.

My 8-year-old daughter, Molly O'Rourke, has an example in Estefania. I want Molly to be able to do all those things. I am proud of Estefania. She is part of what makes El Paso such a wonderful place to live and what makes me so proud to represent the community and helps us, again, stay the safest city in America, bar none.

There are 750,000-plus Estefanias who have come forward to register with their government to make sure that we know that they are in our communities to defer the action that otherwise would deport them back to their countries of origin and to make this country successful.

At this time, I yield to a good friend and colleague from the great State of Texas, who understands these issues just as well as anyone, who has thousands of DREAMers in his community, and whom I am so grateful to for being here tonight.

Mr. Speaker, I yield to the gentleman from Texas (Mr. CASTRO).

Mr. CASTRO of Texas. I thank Congressman O'ROURKE. I thank the gentleman for all of his work on behalf of these DREAMers, these young students who were brought to the United States through no fault of their own. They have grown up here, many of them knowing no other life except an American life.

President Obama, during his term, was so good to issue an executive action known as DACA to give these folks who were in a legal limbo a chance to participate in American society. So many of them have gone on and are doing great things. DACA allows them to work, to go to school, and, most of all, to not have to live in fear, not have to live in fear of deportation.

As you mentioned, many of these folks are people who were brought here at the age of 3 or 5 or 9 and had no choice about coming. Some of them didn't even realize that they were not American citizens until they had to apply to college or try to get a driver's license or in some other way interact with the government.

There has been a lot of rhetoric over the past few years about immigrants. They have been called rapists, murderers, and criminals. There is so much of that kind of rhetoric that is used when people talk about the border, for example, and even the people that live in our border cities, whether it is El Paso or San Diego or McAllen, Texas. My wife is from the Rio Grande Valley, where you have a high concentration of DREAMers, for example. Sometimes, in all of that rhetoric and ugliness, there is a profound misunderstanding about who these people are. So I thank the gentleman for helping to highlight their stories and, really, for the country, to put a human face to these folks who are good people.

I will tell you, because I know other Members have stories of DREAMers in their districts, just a quick story about somebody from San Antonio, a young man named Eric Balderas. His story was in the news in the last few years.

Eric was the valedictorian in 2009 of Highlands High School. He was number one in his class at Highlands High School, and he was on the academic decathlon team, student council, and even played varsity soccer. He also received a full scholarship to Harvard University.

While returning to Harvard in 2010 to complete summer research in molecular biology, Eric was detained at the San Antonio International Airport for traveling without acceptable identification. After efforts from Senator DURBIN and the Harvard University president, U.S. Citizenship and Immigration Services was able to grant him deferred action status. Eric's story, so far, has had a happy ending. He graduated from Harvard in 2013.

There have been other folks who have achieved just as much, who are productive members of our country and our society, but oftentimes they are maligned, and they are often misunderstood.

Right now, we are at a critical moment in our country's history. There is a question hanging over the Nation about how we will treat these DREAMers, these young students, these young people, again, who find themselves in legal limbo, who are as American as we are, and who have only known America as their homeland. There is a big question about what will happen with them.

The President-elect has talked about getting rid of DACA early on, perhaps on the first day in office. So, as I am sure you found, there is a lot of anxiety from these young people and also their families about what is going to happen to them. They have played by the rules; they are being productive; they are working hard; they are going to school; they are paying their taxes; and they are living as Americans.

This will be a real test for the Congress, for the President-elect, who, on January 20, will be the new President, and, really, for the Nation about what kind of nation we are. This really tugs at our conscience.

When we think about some of the rhetoric that has been used—some people call them criminals. They say that they broke the law. I think when I hear that, as an attorney, I think about the different legal standards that we apply in criminal cases. For example, there is something known as mens rea, state of mind. Often when you are charged with a crime, a jury or a judge asks: Did you intend to do what you did? Did you know what you were doing?

Even in our civil cases when we think about the negligence standard, there is still a question about whether somebody was indifferent to what they were doing. Well, in this case, these young people had no idea what was going on. They had no participation in even coming to the United States, but they find themselves here as Americans.

□ 1915

I hope that our Nation and this Congress and the next President will be big enough, will be gracious enough, will respect their humanity, do the right thing, and make sure that they are protected under the law.

First of all, thank you for holding your town hall, which may have been the first one in this season after the election. We are going to have one in San Antonio on December 11, which is a Sunday, with State Representative Diego Bernal, who really helped organize it and spearhead it; Congressman LLOYD DOGGETT, who also represents part of San Antonio; State Senator Jose Menendez.

There are also other Members who I know are going to hold similar town halls in their cities. I will read off just a few of them because I think it is important to acknowledge that work:

PETE AGUILAR in San Bernardino, California; TONY CÁRDENAS in Los Angeles, California; RUBEN GALLEGO in Phoenix, Arizona; RAÚL GRIJALVA in Tucson, Arizona; MICHELLE LUJAN GRISHAM in New Mexico; and RAUL RUIZ, who has a district in southern California. I know that there are others that are being scheduled.

I think all of this work is so important because when we talk about DACA, we are not talking about a piece of legislation that is going to take months to come through the House of Representatives and the Senate. This is something, a decision, that the new President on January 20 can make a decision to do away with it completely and to subject these kids to deportation, often to a country that they have never known, that they have no recollection of being a part of or growing up in. This really is a moral question, as you mentioned, for the country that pulls at our conscience.

Thank you for all your work.

Mr. O'ROURKE. Mr. Speaker, I can't thank the gentleman from Texas (Mr. CASTRO) enough for taking the time to be here for his leadership on this issue. Not just after this election, and not just since he has been in the House of Representatives, but really his whole life has been exemplary in his advocacy for the most vulnerable amongst us in ensuring the truth about the story of these young people who come to our country.

It is not simply a matter of sympathy—although, I sympathize with their situation—it is also a matter of our self-interest as a country. As we continue to look for ways to become a stronger and better country, so much of that lies with those who have made the very difficult choice to come here and contribute to our success and contribute to the American Dream. I am grateful to you for continuing to advocate for them and to share those stories with the rest of the country.

Mr. Speaker, I yield to the gentleman from the State of Massachusetts (Mr.

KENNEDY), another very good friend from a State that has known its share of amazing stories of immigration and seeing those immigrants flourish and become the best of us in this country.

Mr. KENNEDY. Mr. Speaker, I thank Congressman O'ROURKE for yielding and for organizing this critical Special Order.

Most importantly, thank you for your fierce advocacy for people of your district, for people of our country, for immigrants, and for DREAMers.

Let me begin by echoing your comments and that of our colleague, Mr. CASTRO's, as well. The stories that you both have shared underscore the urgency that we face in protecting these children and young adults from deportation under the next administration.

Tonight, right now, there are high school seniors across our country writing college essays, compiling recommendations, and filling out applications who are not sure if they will be allowed to stay in this country when it comes time to enroll in classes.

There are elementary and middle school students that are working diligently on their homework because, one day, they want to pursue a college education or work in their communities, but now they are not sure if that day will come.

There are young professionals working in our factories, teaching in our schools, volunteering in our neighborhoods, or even preparing to join the military that are going to sleep tonight worried that, when the calendar strikes 2017, the only life that they have ever known might be shattered.

All of these children, these young people, all 740,000 of them, they are our future. They put their trust in us, their government, in our promise to protect them if they stepped out of the shadows.

Today, that faith is frayed. It is our responsibility, all of ours, as this body, to commit to them that the only country that they know will not wash away their contributions, those that they have made, and send them to an unfamiliar land; because they believe in the American Dream just as our ancestors did and as we do today; because they are DREAMers; because they are our neighbors, our friends, our classmates, our community, and so much more; because they are countrymen.

Down this hallway in the Senate, a few of our Republican colleagues have already started on legislation to protect DACA beneficiaries. In order to lift the cloud of doubt for thousands in our country, fighting for their rights must be our priority today and every day until we succeed.

Congressman O'ROURKE, Congressman CASTRO, and my colleagues gathered here with us this evening, thank you for your work, thank you for your passion, thank you for your commitment. I know that we are on the right side of this fight when I see all of you standing here.

Mr. O'ROURKE. Mr. Speaker, I thank the gentleman from Massachusetts (Mr. KENNEDY) for his eloquence on this and for his empathy in allowing us to try to think about what it must feel like to be working on that finals paper or that homework assignment in high school or at community college or at one of our great universities and not know if at the start of next semester you will find yourself in another country, in a place that is now strange to you, with a language that you don't speak.

When we think about this, when we think about these mass deportations, literally using the information that these young people and their families came forward with to register under the DACA program, and then using that against them after they voluntarily came forward, to find out where they live, pick them up, process them, deport them back to their country of origin, beyond the incalculable emotional human psychological toll, beyond what that would do to the conscience of this country, look at what it would cost us in financial terms. We would lose 2 to 2.6 percent of our GDP. We would lose nearly $5 trillion over the next 10 years, and government receipts on the trillions of dollars that these DREAMers would otherwise earn would also be gone with those DREAMers—nearly $900 billion that we would lose from the United States Treasury.

We would lose young Americans like the one who is pictured next to me, David Gamez, who is now 20 years old and who joined us Monday at our town hall in El Paso, Texas, one of these brave young El Pasoans, young Americans, who had the courage to come forward, and shared with us at that town hall that he came to this country at the age of 10. He came from Mexico City. He immediately applied himself, learned English, rose to the top of the ranks in his high school classes, took AP courses, is now a member of the STEM club at the El Paso Community College, and is pursuing a career in electrical engineering. He is an artist, he loves to draw, he loves to paint, and he wants to be an innovator. His heroes are all American heroes. His heroes are Elon Musk, Bill Gates, and Larry Ellison, those people who are contributing to our country, creating jobs, innovating, creating, growing this economy. That is what David wants to do. That is what he will do if he is able to stay in this country.

I think it is so important for us to give David the certainty and, also at the same time, not to provoke anxiety and fear that will cause him to lose this opportunity, to lose his way, and for us to lose out on all the amazing things that he can create.

Mr. Speaker, I yield to the gentlewoman from Nevada (Ms. TITUS), who I have the pleasure of sitting with on the Veterans' Affairs Committee and who, over the last 4 years, I have learned from because she is the most tireless champion for veterans. She is the most tireless champion for the LGBT community. She is often the most tireless champion for those who do not have a voice in our system or whose voice is not loud enough. So it is up to Ms. TITUS to amplify that voice and become their advocate.

Ms. TITUS. Mr. Speaker, I thank Congressman O'ROURKE for yielding. You are too kind in your compliments. I give them right back to you. We have worked together on many things, including veterans and public lands, and now this very pressing issue of what we can do to protect our DREAMers.

Since the election, my office has just been deluged by phone calls from the DACA recipients, those we call DREAMers, from their friends, and from their family. They are afraid. You can just hear the fear in their voice. They are just calling to ask questions: Will I be deported? Will my friends be deported? Will my family be separated? Will I lose my house? Will I lose my job? Will I lose my scholarship? Should I apply for DACA? Should I apply to renew DACA? Or should I just keep my head down and hope that they don't notice that I am here?

It just tears your heart out. That is one of the reasons that in my district, in Las Vegas, we held a round table, not a town hall. We started with those organizations who help DREAMers. We had Catholic charities; we had the university, UNLV; we had other institutions of higher education; we had the Latin Chamber; and we had the Mexican and the Salvadoran Consulate all gathered around the table because we don't know how to answer those questions. We wanted to be sure we were all on the same page, giving people the same advice, and reassuring them that whatever happens, we will be there for them. That helps a little, but still you want to be able to say: This is what you are facing.

I know I am not the only one getting these calls. They are coming from kitchens and living rooms and restaurants and stores and families all across this country, as you have heard from some of the other speakers here tonight. For our DREAMers and their families, this fear and anxiety will continue to grow. I am afraid they are just going to return to the shadows if we don't act soon to responsibly reform our immigration system.

Now, as yet, we have heard very little from the Trump transition team about what is actually going to happen to the DREAMers once President Obama leaves office.

Will they round up people and send them back? Will they build that wall?

We don't know. But what we do know is that Mr. SESSIONS has been appointed as Attorney General, who has a very long record of opposing comprehensive immigration reform, actually railing against it; and that is not a very good sign.

After months of just disgraceful campaign rhetoric speeches that denigrate immigrants, Trump and his team now have to really deal with the gravity of the situation. I would suggest, to begin with, they should acquaint themselves with some of the young men and women who have been able to go to work, go to school, contribute to the tax base, contribute to society and our culture, like those that Mr. O'ROURKE mentioned, because they had that protection of DACA.

Instead of demoralizing and degrading them, they should take the time to learn about people like Brenda Romero. Brenda is a young DREAMer who interned in my office this past summer. She is one of 12,000 DREAMers in Nevada. She is not a rapist and she is not a drug dealer. She is a high school graduate and the first immigrant to be the student body president of a small college in my home State. She is now pursuing a law degree.

Brenda was brought to the United States from Mexico when she was just 2 years old. Like so many of the over 700,000 DREAMers, she didn't really have any choice in that decision. She has had a choice about her life, and she has made the most of it, like so, so many DREAMers, including another dreamer from Las Vegas who many of you have seen on television, an amazing national spokeswoman for this campaign for DREAMers, Astrid Silva.

□ 1930

They have contributed, and they inspire me. That is the reason I am joining the gentleman here tonight to talk about their stories, and they are the reason that I will continue to be on the front line—to fight to make this country a better place for them so they, in turn, can make it a better place for all of us.

I want you to go out and meet these people. I want you to sit down with them eye to eye. I call on all of my colleagues to do that. Hear their stories, and you will understand just how remarkable they are. They will make you feel very proud, and you will find that you have more in common with them and their families than you have apart.

We are not a country that should alienate immigrants. We are a country that is characterized by the Statue of Liberty: give me your tired, your poor, your hungry, those yearning to be free. Surely, we can't forget that kind of history and heritage that we have of welcoming immigrants with open arms. We are not a country that should be tearing families apart. As we stand here tonight on the floor of the House, I would just ask you to make that effort to get to know the DREAMers in your community. Hear their stories,

and I think you will agree with me just how remarkable they are.

So I thank the gentleman for letting me speak. Count on me to continue this fight. I think, if we can't get comprehensive immigration reform done in the short term, let's at least protect those DREAMers who already have that status so that they don't have to live in fear.

Mr. O'ROURKE. I thank the gentlewoman from Nevada for sharing these personal stories of the people in her community who inspire her. It is these stories of courage that the gentlewoman just recounted and that I have been trying to share about the young DREAMers in my community of El Paso that were the impetus for our coming together this evening and sharing with our colleagues and the people of this country the truth about a group of very special young people who are too often misunderstood, if not outright maligned; so I am grateful to the gentlewoman for her efforts to improve our understanding of this very special group of people.

When I am thinking about these courageous, young people whom I have been introducing you to tonight from the city of El Paso who happen to have come to this country, to my city, from another country at a very tender age— be it 3, be it 5, be it 7 years old—now, as they are in their teens and in their early twenties, we find them to be flourishing and inspiring us.

I want to share a story that goes back a few generations as I introduce the next Member who will speak. That is the story of Mildred Parish Tutt, who in El Paso, Texas, in 1955, after having graduated from Douglass High School—a segregated, all-Black institution in my community of El Paso, Texas—had the audacity to apply for enrollment at Texas Western College, now known as the University of Texas at El Paso, and her application was rejected solely based on her race.

Mildred and her friend Thelma White and a few other students who were denied enrollment teamed up and, with the help of the NAACP and an attorney named Thurgood Marshall, they took this issue and their aspiration and this case to a Federal court. Thanks to the wisdom and the judgment of our Federal judge at the time, R.E. Thomason, not only was it found that Texas Western's ban on African American students was unconstitutional, but his ruling and their effort and Mildred's courage effectively desegregated the institutions of higher learning in the State of Texas for every single Texan.

As I was sharing with some of our colleagues yesterday, as I was introducing my very good friend BARBARA LEE, this took incredible personal sacrifice. I can only imagine the difficulty that Mildred faced on that day; yet it was so incredibly important for this country. That is the kind of story that

we are telling today about these, again, courageous, special young people in our midst whom we want to continue to allow to flourish.

I want to, at this time, yield to the gentlewoman from California, BARBARA LEE, who has her roots deeply in the State of Texas at El Paso.

Ms. LEE. I thank the gentleman very much.

First of all, I thank Congressman O'ROURKE for lifting up my mother, who was a phenomenal woman, who passed away last year, and who broke many glass ceilings. I want to thank the gentleman for recognizing what a true shero she was; so I just had to tell you. I want to thank the gentleman also for his tireless advocacy on behalf of my hometown and the place of my birth, El Paso, Texas, on so many fronts but especially on behalf of immigrants.

I grew up in an immigrant community. I can tell you my mother, my grandfather, my sisters, and my brothers-in-law—everybody from El Paso—consider the gentleman our Representative, so I thank him very much. We are very proud of him.

Mr. Speaker, I attended St. Joseph's Elementary School on Waco Avenue, and we were taught that we must value the dignity of all human beings. I was taught by the Sisters of Loretto in El Paso. So now, in representing the beautiful East Bay of northern California, my values and what I learned from my mother and my grandfather and my parents in El Paso really drive me to continue our fight on behalf of our young people, on behalf of our DREAMers.

Four years ago, President Obama made history by announcing the Deferred Action for Childhood Arrivals program, DACA. This critical program provides—and this is just commonsense—humane protections for undocumented Americans, mind you, who were brought to our Nation as young children. Since the executive action, about 744,000 young people have benefited from this important program.

I am proud to say, though, that now one in three DREAMers in the United States is from my State of California. These are brilliant young people who deserve the chance to live the American Dream. DACA empowers young people and keeps families together even in the face of Republican inaction on comprehensive immigration reform.

This is an issue that is dear to my heart. As I said, I grew up in El Paso in an immigrant community; so I know no option. I mean, we have to protect our young people and keep families together. More than a quarter of the residents now in my congressional district were born outside of the United States. Tens of thousands of young people have benefited from the DACA program.

We sponsored a town meeting several weeks ago. Actually, it was sponsored by Oakland Community Organizations, which is an affiliate of PICO. It was an amazing town meeting. Everyone participated. It was multiracial. It was held in the Catholic cathedral. There are several stories I would like to share, just very quickly, that we heard that night.

One DREAMer and DACA recipient—let's call her Amy—was born in Venezuela and immigrated to the United States as a child. DACA opened doors for Amy. She received her bachelor's degree at UCLA and then went on to obtain her law degree. This is really impressive. Through her hard work, Amy became the first DACA recipient to be admitted to the California bar. I am so proud of Amy. She has taken her skills and experiences to give back to our community. Today, she works at a nonprofit in the East Bay where she is an advocate for immigration reform and helps other young people benefit from the DACA program; but while she spends her days helping her community, she still lives in fear—in fear for her family, in fear for her friends, in fear of being deported at any moment.

I have another constituent—let's call him Gabriel—whom I met recently at the same event. Gabriel was born in Mexico and immigrated to the United States 10 years ago. Since then, he has used his voice to empower his community and advocate for immigrants. In high school, he started a local DREAMers club that advocates for the inclusion and advancement of undocumented students. He went on to attend UC Berkeley and was able to receive funds to cover most of his studies. Through DACA and State policies, he was able to afford the high cost of living in the Bay Area and receive a world-class education.

He and Amy show the incredible potential of our Nation's young people. Their determination to live the American Dream, to receive a quality education, and to help their communities was really unlocked through DACA. It is terrible to think of the dreams that would be destroyed by rolling back DACA now.

Time and time again, I hear stories like Gabriel's and Amy's—stories of families who are kept together because of DACA and of young people who are able to attend college and pursue these dreams. Now these young people are afraid. They fear that their families will be torn apart, that their parents may be deported, and that their American Dreams are truly in jeopardy.

We have always been a nation of immigrants. This is a history that we should be proud of; but, right now, we know that immigrants in my district, in El Paso, and all across our Nation are scared to death about what this next administration will bring. There are families who wake up in fear that, come January 21, their work or their school will be raided. There are

DREAMers who dread being forced to leave the country—the only country that they have ever known. This is morally wrong. The nuns who taught me at St. Joseph's would be shocked if they knew what was taking place now. We are better than this. These young people deserve better from our country, and they deserve better from this Congress.

Again, I am calling on my Republican colleagues to let us vote on bipartisan comprehensive immigration reform—legislation that will reunify families, that will grow our economy, and that will provide a clear pathway to citizenship. I know the gentleman and all of our colleagues are going to continue to fight for and to pass immigration reform and the DREAM Act; but, minimally, we have to protect our Nation's DREAMers, our immigrants, and all families.

I thank the gentleman again for his leadership. I thank him for inviting me to be with him tonight. Again, my family is very proud of him, our Congressman.

Mr. O'ROURKE. I thank the gentlewoman from California, and I thank her for continuing to cut the profile in courage in Congress and for her fierce advocacy on the issues that matter most. She continues to stand out as an example to me, and tonight is testimony to that; so I am grateful to her for being here.

I now want to yield to yet another good friend. It is an embarrassment of riches, in the Chamber this evening, to have so many talented Members who have decided to stand up with some of the best among us. In my opinion, the gentleman from Oregon, who in the 4 years that I have been here has taught me so much and much of that by example, is perfectly suited to share his experiences, those of the community he represents, and what he wants to see going forward for this great country.

I yield to the gentleman from Oregon (Mr. BLUMENAUER).

Mr. BLUMENAUER. I appreciate the gentleman's courtesy in permitting me to speak this evening and for his thoughtfulness in organizing this conversation and inviting others of our colleagues to come forward.

Mr. Speaker, I think it is so important to be able to put a human face on an issue that sometimes gets lost in the rhetoric. We have had a lot of rhetoric this last year. The fears that were stoked by the campaign with harsh words about immigrants, people of different religions, people who would be at risk of deportation, to maybe having a registry, having denial based on people's religions or what their perceived religions might be has sent shock waves, but it is nothing compared to what I have experienced in the days immediately after the election.

People who were apprehensive and concerned are terrified—children un-

sure about whether parents will be there when they come home from school, people who are concerned about whether they will be able to have employment. It is not just people who may not have their documents in order. This touches millions of Americans who are part of extended families, who are part of families in the workplace.

I was honored to be part of a fundraising event 2 weeks ago that was hosted by Oregon's wine industry. We came together in a lavish fundraising dinner and raised hundreds of thousands of dollars for the health care for the employees in their vineyards. Now, they are not asking about their documentation. They understand that there may be some who are questionable, but they are not seeking in terms of what people's histories are.

□ 1945

They have people here who have worked with them for years who are like family and who are connected to the community. The notion of sending these young people back, who, as you and our other colleagues have pointed out, came here as children—they didn't have any choice. What 4-year-old, 3-year-old, 2-year-old infant is making this perilous journey on their own? They were brought here. They were raised here.

Many of these young people, as you have already had testimony this evening, have had amazing records of success. They took the United States Government and its President at his word and came forward and took a little bit of a risk because they wanted to be part of the fabric of this country. They are in this situation, sadly, because of a failure of will by my Republican friends in the House.

As the gentleman knows, he was here when we had an opportunity to vote on comprehensive immigration reform that passed the Senate on a bipartisan basis. It wasn't a great bill, but it was an important step forward, on a bipartisan basis, that would have prevented some of this confusion, some of this pain, and some of this uncertainty.

If the Republican leadership had allowed it to come to the floor for a vote, they wouldn't have had to twist any arms. There would have been more than enough votes on both sides of the aisle to enact it. That failure of courage stoked part of this hateful campaign that we have all experienced and has kept these unfortunate people and their families and friends—whether they are citizens, employees, they're part of the community—under a cloud.

This is a failure of the House of Representatives that has created this situation. We should not, as a country, compound it by raising the specter of decent, hardworking, young people who are here through no act of their own, who have taken a step forward, a little risk to try and integrate into our society, who are high performing.

I could give examples tonight of a young man who is completing his dental studies at the Oregon Health & Science University, a DREAMer who dreams big about serving his community as a professional dealing with dental health. There is a young woman who is a human resource professional at the largest school district in our State, who isn't just adding her competence, but is being able to provide opportunities to deal with some of the real serious human resource questions from first-line experience. We could all do this if we tried.

Representative O'ROURKE, I deeply appreciate your bringing this forward. I think it would be a tragedy if we were to punish people who took the President at his word, who put confidence in this Congress, to unwind this unfortunate situation. But I think it is important that all of us add our voices, that we connect with the people at home who are desperate, apprehensive, and vulnerable, to be able to make sure the American public knows what is at stake; because if we add our voices, our examples, and engage them, there is no doubt in my mind that there will be enough public pressure to prevent a tragedy of immense proportions.

Mr. O'ROURKE. Mr. Speaker, I am so grateful to the gentleman from Oregon (Mr. BLUMENAUER) and could not agree more forcefully with his words. In addition to these, again, inspiring examples of what the DREAMers mean to us as a country and what they mean to the gentleman personally, I also enjoyed hearing about how the community he represents is rallying around them and supporting them and ensuring that they know that they are not alone, despite the rhetoric, despite the changes that we might see in executive actions going forward.

I am also deeply appreciative of the gentleman's reminder that it is this institution that really has the opportunity, the responsibility, and the power to correct this. In these 4 years that I have had the pleasure of joining you here in the House, I know that both of us and dozens of our colleagues have tried mightily to do that, but, unfortunately, to no avail. That does not in any way damper my enthusiasm to do this. In fact, these stories that we are sharing tonight only cause me to want to redouble my efforts and work with you and our colleagues to make sure that we do everything we can and, beyond that, that we are ultimately effective and successful in setting this country, when it comes to our immigration laws and it comes to the lives of these 750,000 DREAMers, in the right direction. So I thank the gentleman for being here this evening.

One thing that the gentleman from Oregon said that really struck home and helps me to introduce a very good friend of mine from El Paso, Claudia Yoli—were his comments about family and the importance of family and how fundamental family is to our success.

So I ask those in the Chamber this evening to think about Claudia Yoli, who is pictured here, to my right, in front of the White House, perhaps in 2013 when she served as an intern in my congressional office here. She came to this country for the first time at the age of 8, from Venezuela, and has been nothing but exceptional to the community that she lives in, to the country that is now her home, and to those that she has worked with, including me and my office, and our State Senator Jose Rodriguez, for whom she works today. She showed courage in coming to our townhall on Monday evening, where she told us about all of this and then shared something that was so personally painful and tragic that it could only help me to understand truly what is at stake here.

In 2010, Claudia's mother traveled back to Venezuela. Because of Claudia's status, because she was a DREAMer and because of provisions within the Deferred Action for Childhood Arrivals, she was not able to go back to Venezuela with her mother. Unfortunately, last year, Claudia's mother passed away in Venezuela, and Claudia could not be there to comfort her mother in her dying days, nor could she be there for the funeral, nor could she be there with those family members who came together to grieve her mother's passing. Our inaction causes tremendous pain and suffering for those whom we have the power to help right now.

I yield at this point to the gentleman from Illinois (Mr. FOSTER), another colleague with whom I was elected in 2012.

Mr. FOSTER. Mr. Speaker, I am Congressman BILL FOSTER, and I am proud to represent the 11th District of Illinois.

In our district, we have vibrant immigrant communities from all over the world. I have met many DREAMers, both at home in Illinois and right here in the Halls of Congress. For many of them, the United States is the only country that they have ever called home.

Our district includes the diverse cities of Aurora, Bolingbrook, Joliet, and others. In Aurora, the East Aurora High School District 131 has one of the largest Naval Junior ROTCs in the world. Many of these young ROTC students come from immigrant families, and they dream one day of serving our country in the Armed Forces. You can see it in their faces during flag ceremonies, parades, and you can see the admiration of the younger children looking up to these ROTC DREAMers. Many of them are here because their parents dreamed of a better life for their children.

The DACA program has been incredibly successful. Over half a million young people are currently enrolled in it. They are living examples of the American Dream, the idea that anyone could come here and have a fulfilling and prosperous life regardless of where you come from and where you live.

Instead of creating new opportunities for these great young people, Republicans in Congress have repeatedly voted to end the DACA program. We need to reform our outdated immigration laws and not double down on a broken system. As their Representatives, we should honor their patriotism and dedication to our country with support, not fear and degradation. It is a pretty simple proposition.

Mr. O'ROURKE. Mr. Speaker, I thank the gentleman from Illinois (Mr. FOSTER) for being here this evening, for standing up for some who, especially right now, feel that perhaps their government is not with them and perhaps these commitments that were made to them that engendered their trust, their willingness to come forward to share their personal information, their addresses, their identities, perhaps have been abandoned. Your presence here tonight, your words, I think, do much to show them that that is not the case and that there is still a chance in this country that we will do the right thing. I appreciate the gentleman from Illinois (Mr. FOSTER) for being here tonight.

Mr. Speaker, in closing, let me say that, whether it is these 750,000-plus DREAMers, these young Americans who, at a very tender age, were brought to this country by their parents or relatives and in every single way, except for citizenship, are no different than my three children or anyone else that I represent in the great City of El Paso, Texas—these DREAMers are going to high school, are serving in our Armed Forces, are attending our universities, are, in many respects, the future of our communities, of our country, who have so much to gain personally and so much to give back to this country. These DREAMers must be spared from any decisions that would break the trust that was created with them, that would force them back to their countries of origin, which they no longer know as home, whose language they no longer speak, where they no longer have family with whom they can reside.

Mr. Speaker, I think it is also important, on the larger subject of how we talk about those who are in our country from another country, that we remember a few facts. For example, the border that connects us with our country and neighbor to the south, Mexico, is as safe today as it has ever been. The community that I have the honor to represent and to serve, El Paso, Texas, which is conjoined with Ciudad Juarez to form the largest binational community anywhere in the world, is the safest city in the United States. It is safe not in spite of, but precisely because of, our connection to Mexico, the Mexican immigrants, the Mexican Americans, and those who are in our community, documented or otherwise, that make El Paso such a tremendously safe, wonderful, thriving community.

We know that U.S. cities on the border with Mexico and U.S. cities with large immigrant populations are, in fact, far safer than the average U.S. city in the interior, be that in Kentucky, be that in Iowa. That is what we have to be proud of. That is what we need to share with the American public.

We also need them to know that immigrants, documented or otherwise—and including, especially, those who are undocumented—commit crimes, including violent crimes, at a far lower rate than do native-born U.S. citizens.

We need to remember that we have so much to be proud of, so much to be grateful for, so much to celebrate in the immigrants' story, especially these DREAMers who, right now, live in a period of uncertainty, fear, and anxiety. It is incumbent upon us in this Chamber to do what we must to change our laws to reflect our values and the reality in our communities and in our country. Mr. Speaker, I stand ready to work with any Member on either side of the aisle to do just that.

I want to thank my colleagues who joined me tonight to help drive home the very important point that everyone who is in our country that has registered with the government, that has come forward, that has applied successfully under the DACA program deserves to stay here and deserves our help to ensure our laws allow them to do that going forward.

I yield back the balance of my time.

Mr. VEASEY. Mr. Speaker, thank you to my colleague Mr. O'ROURKE for his work to highlight such an important issue.

Since November 9th, many of the immigrants in my district of Dallas-Fort Worth have been rightfully nervous about their future in the United States.

It is no secret where the President-Elect stands on immigration.

He has vowed to repeal the highly successful Deferred Action for Childhood Arrivals program, commonly known as DACA.

This move is wrong for America and for the immigrants whose lives have been forever changed by the program.

Since 2012, over 135,000 bright young Texans have successfully applied for the program.

It has been life changing for all those who qualified.

This has been especially true for one of my constituents, Erik.

Erik is a 27-year-old DACA recipient who immigrated to the United States from Mexico with his mother when he was just two years old.

Erik was unaware of his immigration status for the majority of his life until he reached a critical milestone at the age of 16.

When he asked his mother if he could apply for his driver's license, what normally would be an exciting event turned into a difficult conversation with his mother about his immigration status.

Erik was devastated because although he called the United States home, he would be unable to move forward with his life as he planned.

Once he graduated from high school, Erik knew that attending college would be a significant challenge—one he almost didn't take on.

He shared that he wasn't even sure college was the right decision because he was unsure that he could get a job after he graduated.

Yet, he persevered and graduated in 2011—but once again was confronted with the reality that his undocumented status created additional challenges.

Although he was college educated, Erik couldn't legally work in the United States.

But with the announcement of DACA in 2012, Erik had a ray of hope.

Finally, Erik could legally work and better participate in the country he's called home since the age of two.

Since successfully receiving DACA status, Erik has worked as a Store Systems Engineer at Rent-A-Car and has advocated for other undocumented immigrants.

Unfortunately, the newly found freedom Erik enjoyed under DACA is now in jeopardy.

Now, with just weeks away until the President-Elect is sworn into office, millions of DREAMERs are frightened they will be forced to return to the shadows or be targeted for deportation.

These young aspiring immigrants are already part of our communities.

They attend our schools, work alongside us, and live in our neighborhoods.

For Erik and the thousands of other DREAMERs across Texas, the revocation of DACA could mean returning to countries they haven't called home since they were children.

While we work to reform our broken immigration system, we must remember that the immigrants we speak of are just like us—they have hopes, dreams, and want to live a good life.

Like Erik, I believe that we need to move forward with immigration reform.

I believe we can do so in a way that keeps families together and benefits our country as a whole at the same time.

I stand here alongside my colleagues to remind our country's DREAMers that the fight isn't over.

Our fight here in Congress has just begun.

Ms. TITUS. Mr. Speaker, my office was overwhelmed with phone calls in the days following the election.

DACA recipients, their friends, and their family were afraid: Will I be deported, they asked. Will my cousin be deported? Will my friends be deported?

I know these questions were not just being uttered in Southern Nevada. People were asking them in living rooms, kitchens, restaurants, schools, and countless other places across the country.

For our DREAMers and their loved ones, the fear and anxiety will continue if we don't responsibly act to reform our broken immigration system.

Since the election we've heard very little from the incoming administration about what's actually going to happen once President Obama leaves office.

That is why I recently held an immigration advocacy roundtable with local community leaders like The Legal Aid Center of Southern Nevada, UNLV, the Latin Chamber of Commerce, and other local officials.

We wanted to let families know that despite the uncertainty, we are here to help them.

Together, we want to change the tone that we heard from Donald Trump during the election.

After months of disgraceful speeches about walls and deportations, Trump and his administration must now deal with the gravity of the situation.

It's time they acquaint themselves with the young men and women who have been able to work, go to school, contribute to the tax base, and live life without fear of being thrown out of the country they call home.

PROTESTS OF THE DAKOTA ACCESS PIPELINE

The SPEAKER pro tempore (Mr. DONOVAN). Under the Speaker's announced policy of January 6, 2015, the Chair recognizes the gentleman from North Dakota (Mr. CRAMER) for 30 minutes.

Mr. CRAMER. Mr. Speaker, I rise this evening to talk about the rule of law, the importance of enforcement of the rule of law, the importance of a government that stands for law and order.

I ask your indulgence, Mr. Speaker, as I begin my comments tonight by reading a resolution of support, a resolution that illustrates the position of a very important organization in my State of North Dakota, the North Dakota Veterans Coordinating Council.

□ 2000

It reads like this:

Whereas: The protests against the Dakota Access Pipeline have been going on for over 100 days in North Dakota.

Whereas: The protests have been conducted on public and private land without proper permission.

Whereas: The protests have not remained peaceful. In fact, the protesters have caused millions of dollars in damage. They have destroyed public and privately owned property, vehicles, and equipment to include heavy equipment and trucks owned by private contractors, at least two government trucks, cut privately owned fences, and slaughtered farm animals owned by private farms. Protesters have assaulted and thrown Molotov cocktails and hard objects at North Dakota law enforcement officers and military personnel who are sworn to keep the peace and protect North Dakota's citizens.

Whereas: Protesters have desecrated North Dakota State and Federal property, to include the North Dakota State Capitol and, yes, the North Dakota pillar of the World War II Monument right here in Washington, D.C., located at The National Mall.

Whereas: The protesters of the Dakota Access Pipeline in and around Standing Rock have desecrated the American flag by flying it upside down, sewing emblems over the flag, and displaying emblems and non-U.S. flags in a dominant manner to the U.S. flag in violation of North Dakota Century Code.

Whereas: 95 percent of the protesters are not North Dakota citizens or Native Americans. Many are professional paid protesters unaware of the true understanding of the issues at hand.

Whereas: As former military members, we have all taken an oath to defend the Constitution of the United States against foreign and domestic enemies, the American flag, and our freedom. As veterans, we continue to support our military, law enforcement, and all of our constitutional rights we have fought for.

Whereas: As veterans of the U.S. military, we have fought for and maintained the rights of our citizens to peacefully protest. The protests in Standing Rock have not been peaceful and, therefore, violate the rights of those living peacefully around the protest site and threaten the sanctity and sustainability of our basic freedom of peaceful protests by crossing the line into unlawful activities.

Whereas: Individual veterans and veteran groups from outside of the State of North Dakota have reached out to North Dakota veterans and veterans service organizations for support in their plan to recruit veterans to assemble in North Dakota in support of the Standing Rock protest against the Dakota Access Pipeline.

Whereas: Veterans standing in a nonpeaceful protest against the Dakota Access Pipeline, will also be standing against North Dakota law enforcement, military, private and government entities, reflects poorly upon themselves, our veterans organizations, veterans as a whole, the State of North Dakota, and our country.

Therefore: Let it be the position of the North Dakota Veterans Coordinating Council made up of the North Dakota AMVETS, American Legion, Disabled American Veterans, Veterans of Foreign Wars, and the Vietnam Veterans of America adamantly oppose and condemn any veteran organization or persons representing themselves as U.S. military veterans who associate or involve themselves with the illegal activities which have occurred or take part in any unlawful or unbecoming conduct or assembly in protest to the Dakota Access Pipeline in North Dakota.

Mr. Speaker, I could never say it better than the men and women who have fought and who have been willing to die for our liberties. They have said it perfectly in this position in support of a legally permitted pipeline and in support of our law enforcement officers who have exercised tremendous restraint against violence thrown at them. I, for one, am tired, as are the vast majority of North Dakotans, of people from outside of our State with a political agenda who have co-opted the reasonable, peaceful protests that once began what has become a full-fledged riot.

Mr. Speaker, for more than 3 months, thousands of rioters disguising themselves as prayerful people, peaceful protesters, have illegally camped on Federal land owned or at least managed by the U.S. Army Corps of Engineers, owned by the taxpayers of this country. They have illegally camped on the shores of the Missouri River.

By the way, Mr. Speaker, if you and I decided to go for a walk on that same land and picked up a rock and threw it in the river, we would be fined by this government. But, oh, no, not antifossil fuel rioters. No, they are enabled; no, they are encouraged by our Federal Government, at least this current Administration.

Celebrities, bad actors; celebrities, political activists; and anti-oil extremists are blocking this pipeline's progress, and they are doing so based not on good information, not on the law, but rather on a leftwing political agenda. Oh, by the way, these celebrities and these rioters fly in on jet airplanes that are fueled by jet fuel that is refined from oil, in many cases Bakken oil; but let's ignore the irony and the hypocrisy for the moment.

North Dakotans like these veterans that I just read about have respected the rights of peaceful protesters, but this has gone way beyond that. It has become rioting, plain and simple. In fact, I think it is important to note, Mr. Speaker, that two Federal courts right here in the District of Columbia have upheld the legality of this pipeline. First, a D.C. Circuit district judge appointed by President Obama, I might add, denied a request for an injunction to stop this pipeline based on the fact that not only has the company and the Corps of Engineers and the North Dakota Public Service Commission met every letter of the law, but exceeded it, including, according to this judge's own opinion, exceeding the requirements for consultation with the sovereign tribes. The project developer and the Army Corps tried desperately to engage the Standing Rock Sioux tribe dozens of times, only to be rejected for more than 2 years.

Mr. Speaker, all that remains for the pipeline to be finished is an easement to begin the process and to finish the process of connecting this pipeline under the Missouri River in North Dakota, an easement that has been prepared and finished for months. Of course, the Obama administration rescinded a permit that had already been issued, a 408 permit to allow the pipeline to be built under this river. The same administration, by the way, who has gone to court to defend it. It is ironic, to say the least. It is chaos, to say the best.

At the center of this issue is an administration that refuses—not just refuses to follow the rule of law, but enables and encourages the breaking of the law, beginning with the fact that thousands of illegal protesters are allowed to camp, to trespass on federally owned land.

Now, if you allow somebody to illegally assemble, why would they not think that they should be allowed to burn property? Why would they not think they should be allowed to trespass on private land? Why would they

think they shouldn't be allowed to throw Molotov cocktails at police officers trying to protect innocent citizens? Why would they not think they could follow a police officer home and harass his family until they had to move out of their home, or follow a National Guard member to their apartment and then harass them at their apartment and force their family to leave, to spit on them? Why would they think they shouldn't be allowed to do that if the President of the United States says go ahead and trespass?

Never mind that this is a legally permitted pipeline. Let's just ignore that. Let's withdraw the permit that we have already issued, that we are defending in court. Why wouldn't they think that?

What has happened, Mr. Speaker, to virtue in this country?

When I see these protesters, rioters, criminals, thugs—yes, thugs; it is not a racial comment; it is just what you call people who are thugs—I look at them and I think, who is their mother? Where were they raised? How were they raised?

What has happened in this country when we stand here in this Chamber, in this assembly, in this town, and we hear some people, politicians, supposed leaders, talk about law enforcement as though they are the problem? What has happened that people have become confused about the difference between breaking the law and enforcing the law?

It is hard for North Dakotans to see that because we are not confused by that. We were raised by parents who told us what was right and what was wrong, who taught us to respect the legal system, to respect law enforcement officers. We have really respectable police officers in North Dakota, and we do throughout this country, because we have seen them come from multiple States. The National Sheriffs' Association has sent many officers. Other States and city police departments and counties have sent law enforcement officers to give some assistance to our overworked, overtaxed law enforcement officers right in North Dakota. We are tired of it.

Stay home, Jane Fonda; don't come back and deliver food, pretend that somehow you care and take off again in your private jet; unless you want to try to fly that jet on solar panels, then come on, we will take you.

You can't encourage illegal behavior and then wonder why there is violence, Mr. Speaker; and that is what our President has done.

Let's give a little background on this. I know a little bit about siting pipelines. I was a regulator for nearly 10 years. I have sited several of them. This 1,172-mile Dakota Access Pipeline will deliver as many as 570,000 barrels of Bakken crude oil every day to Patoka, Illinois, and then to other markets beyond. This is 570,000 barrels of oil that is currently being produced every single day. It is being transported now. It will always find its way to market. It is just that it is being transported by trains and trucks. Oh, those aren't as safe or as efficient or even as environmentally friendly ways to move oil as a safe pipeline is, especially one that is going to be buried 100 feet below the bottom of the river, to make sure that the water is safe.

From the outset of this process, the Standing Rock Sioux leaders have refused to sit down and meet with either the Corps of Engineers or the pipeline developer. However, 55 other tribes have. The Corps consulted with 55 Native American tribes at least 389 times, after which they proposed 140 variations of the current route to avoid culturally sensitive areas in North Dakota alone.

That is right, Mr. Speaker, you are not going to read about that in the New York Times or the Washington Post. You are never going to hear about it on NBC or ABC or CBS. You may not even hear about it in North Dakota because, frankly, even our media are afraid of the ramifications of violent rioters who are willing to commit violent acts if you cross them. Yes, even my home address has been posted on their Web sites and on their Facebook pages so that they know where my family and I live. These are the prayerful, peaceful protesters you hear so much about on the NBC News.

This project route was examined, reviewed, studied, and ultimately supported by the North Dakota Public Service Commission, the State Historic Preservation Office, assorted tribal consultants from around the country, and multiple professional independent archaeologists. This is a thoroughly vetted pipeline, which is why it has over 200 Federal permits, all of which have been delivered and have been built, except for this one, which was rescinded to make a political statement.

They say that they object to the pipeline being close to the water intake of the Standing Rock Sioux Reservation. However, it shouldn't be of any concern. As I said, this is going to go between 90 and 115 feet below the floor of the river. It is double-lined pipe. It has got control valves at both ends and sensors at both ends. It is the safest pipeline in the world.

By the way, the intake for Standing Rock's drinking water, the new one, which will be in service before the end of this year, is 70 miles away. There is a railroad track that carries hundreds of thousands of barrels every day over the top of the Missouri, as close as that.

By the way, the other thing you often hear is that this was not the original route, that there were other preferred routes, but because they crossed at places that affected a different kind of people than the Standing Rock Sioux tribe, that this was somehow discriminatory.

Let me set that record straight as well. I know, as I said, a fair bit about pipelines. I have read the permit. I have read the application. I have read the judge's opinions. It was always planned for this location for a very good reason, Mr. Speaker. By the way, there are at least 10 to 12 other petroleum pipelines north of this same location. This is just going to be the latest and greatest of them. The main reason this route was chosen was because it was the least intrusive on the environment, on waterways, on private property, and on cultural resources.

□ 2015

The other locations that were under consideration that were not chosen crossed many more bodies of water and were much closer to many wells and cultural resources and very important historical resources. It was 48 extra miles of previously undisturbed field areas. This is and was the best route because it is an existing corridor. In this same corridor, there is already a natural gas pipeline. There is already a large electric transmission line. That is why it was chosen.

Let me talk a little bit about the impact this is having on my State. We had the recent vandalism of the graves in Bismarck. That is right. They vandalized graves in a Bismarck cemetery. Of course, the unconscionable graffiti markings on the North Dakota World War II pillar that the veterans wrote about earlier are examples of how these peaceful protestors' actions don't match their claims.

The responsibility of protecting property and residents has fallen on the shoulders of the State of North Dakota because, guess what, when we asked the Obama administration for law enforcement help, for reimbursement, at least, for our State and for our counties for a situation that they created by their refusal to obey the law themselves, they sent some PR people from the Department of Justice. They sent people to watch our cops to make sure they don't do something wrong. See, again, they are confused about the difference between breaking the law and enforcing the law. We are not confused about that in North Dakota.

Attempts to get reimbursement or to get U.S. Federal help have fallen on deaf ears. So far, North Dakota has had to borrow $17 million to cover law enforcement costs. I will tell you this—and we have heard in the Chamber a lot of bad-mouthing of the incoming administration—I can't wait. I can't wait to go to Attorney General JEFF SESSIONS and explain the situation to him and ask him for assistance. I am very encouraged by President-elect Trump's favorable comments about the Dakota Access Pipeline earlier today.

These protesters, these demonstrators, these rioters have brought protests into the communities of Bismarck and Mandan. They blocked roads and traffic, forcing lock-downs at the State capital and Federal buildings. They have forced people to leave their homes. They forced daycare centers to close. This daycare was forced into lockdown twice. Can you imagine explaining to children, who don't know anything about a pipeline and they don't care—and they shouldn't have to—why they are in a lockdown, why they have to be careful. Some out-of-State thugs are circling the block, harassing the owners.

Many of our residents are fearful for the safety of their neighborhoods and volunteers are hesitant even to deliver Meals on Wheels. We have had people call us and say they can't deliver Meals on Wheels because people won't even answer their doors because they have seen these rioters walking around their property.

Law enforcement and their families have been stopped and rioters have repeatedly tried to intimidate them. On Thanksgiving Day, 300 protesters blocked traffic in Mandan, North Dakota, carrying a large dead pig on a stick while at least as many protesters, again, trespassed and built a bridge to reach a hilltop on private property.

Law enforcement has shown tremendous constraint, giving verbal warnings that if they stop making the bridge, there would not be any arrests. It was ignored. The bridge was built. Rioters crossed, dismantled the bridge, and law enforcement held the line for hours against tremendous numbers—they were well outnumbered—without a single arrest.

The protesters are the clear agitators and the criminals here, not the police officers. There would be no law enforcement presence if these protests were truly peaceful.

For example, most media have demonized their law enforcement for use of water as a less than lethal tool during a protest in cold temperatures. They used it to hold back protestors only after they used the water to put out prairie fires that were started by the protesters. And the protestors got wet from a water cannon. By the way, that is a made-up term by the national media to make it sound like some sort of violent act by our police department. It was a water hose brought there to put out fires. And when they used that to push back hundreds of protesters when there were only dozens of police officers, now they are blamed for being the agitators.

As you can tell, I am frustrated, Mr. Speaker. I am frustrated not just by the actions of these thugs, because we have come to expect that from certain people in this country, unfortunately. I am frustrated by this administration's refusal to obey the law, to enforce the law, to support the law, but instead enable and actually encourage the breaking of the law. That is not what we elect the President for. I am so grateful we have a law-and-order President coming into office shortly.

They have been forced to arrest more than 400 people, most of them from out of State. They get bailed out rather quickly. Somehow they have a source of lots of money readily available to bail people out and cover their expenses. They have chained themselves to equipment to prevent work from being done.

Here is an interesting fact. When it was much warmer in North Dakota than it is today, they would chain themselves to the equipment. And then, after hours of being there, they would get thirsty. And police officers, rather than just letting them stay there, actually helped provide them water and held the water so that the protesters, the illegal rioters, could get a drink of water. That is the quality of our law enforcement officers.

They burned tires and fields, as I said earlier. They damaged cars and bridges. They harassed residents and have torn down fences. They killed and slaughtered neighbors' cattle and bison and horses. There was at least one report where gunshots were fired at the police.

By the way, this protest is not about climate. We hear about that. By the way, it shouldn't have anything to do with climate. The oil is being produced. Now the issue is: How do you transport it? Do you transport it in the most environmentally and economical and efficient way in a pipeline? Or, do you transport it in some less safe, less efficient, less environmentally friendly way?

The simple fact is, our Nation will continue to produce and consume oil, and pipelines are the best way to move that oil. Legally permitting infrastructure projects have to be allowed to proceed without the threat of improper governmental meddling and activity.

By the way, what of shovel-ready jobs, Mr. Speaker? What of that? What of building the infrastructure of this country with private sector money? What a great thing. But for the Bakken and other shale oil plays in this country in the last 8 years, we still would be in a recession. Most of the jobs that have been created in the last 8 years in this country have been created in the energy sector.

It is not about water protection, as I said. There is a brand new intake system being built. It will be operational 73 miles from this pipeline. That is not the issue. That is just an excuse. By the way, that new intake is about 1.6 miles downstream of a railroad track, a railroad bridge that will carry crude oil, as well.

The pipeline is not going to come in contact with the water. It employs the latest and greatest in advanced technology. As I said, a dozen or more oil and gas and refined product pipelines already cross the Missouri River upstream from the tribe's drinking water intake, and this pipeline is crossing at a point where there is existing infrastructure. It is an infrastructure corridor.

Mr. Speaker, the rule of law matters. I am so grateful for our law enforcement officers, as I said, not just in Morton County, not just around Bismarck, Mandan, and not just in North Dakota, but from around the country who have come to the assistance of our State. But, Mr. Speaker, if we think we are going to rebuild the infrastructure of this country, and every time we build a railroad track or a highway or a bridge or a pipeline or a transmission line or wind farm or factory, we are going to have to put up with this, what kind of investment is going to take place in this country?

As I said, we are not confused in North Dakota about the difference between breaking the law and enforcing the law. The vast majority of North Dakotans—and when I say vast, well into 90 percent—support law enforcement. We are grateful for what they do. We are sorry that you are going through this.

I will fight with everything I have and use every ounce of influence I have over the next administration and with my colleagues in this Chamber to provide the resources to make sure that you get a day off, to make sure that our State gets reimbursed, and that your families are compensated for what you have gone through.

I thank law enforcement officers for taking and making the tremendous sacrifice they make to protect legal commerce, peaceful citizens, and yes, ironically, Mr. Speaker, I thank the law enforcement officers for protecting the right to express ourselves in a peaceful manner.

Mr. Speaker, I yield back the balance of my time.

EVENTS IN CUBA

The SPEAKER pro tempore. Under the Speaker's announced policy of January 6, 2015, the Chair recognizes the gentleman from Iowa (Mr. KING) for 30 minutes.

Mr. KING of Iowa. Mr. Speaker, it is my honor and privilege to be recognized to address the floor of the United States House of Representatives. It was quite interesting to listen to the gentleman from North Dakota and the stress that they have up there; in particular, with regard to the pipeline being built through there.

I would just want to reinforce the statements made by the gentleman from North Dakota and point out that the permits are there, the process is there. We have tens of thousands of miles of pipelines in the United States of America, and we have very, very few problems with leaks or other circumstances that would cause one to think that there is a safer way to transport oil. There is not. The safest way is with the pipeline.

I am one who has actually started out in the construction business building pipelines. We have been in the construction business for 42 years. We dig in the ground, and we are doing underground utility work every day, except for Sundays, and we go deep sometimes. We go into hydraulic soil from time to time. Water tables are above where we are working. We do well points. We are working with the flow of water in the soil and underground, and we have got as good a look at this as anybody I know.

I would point out to those that are detractors that say: well, we can pollute the underground aquifer if we have a pipeline that we build and if that pipeline should leak. And I would point out something that they ought to know if they ever saw a movie of a shipwreck: oil floats on water. Therefore, it cannot penetrate down into the aquifer. You are not pumping off of the top-skimmed surface of the aquifer. You are pumping down below. And if you should get a leak, which is extraordinarily rare, the oil pools and floats on the top and can be pumped off.

There is no safer way to transfer petroleum products and no more efficient way. It is by far the best way, which is why we have tens of thousands of pipelines all over this country moving all kinds of product, including crude oil, but also anhydrous ammonia and a number of other products across the country.

I have built the pipelines. I have been down in the trench. I have been tossed into the air and slammed to the ground and climbed down the machine. The wind, the dust, the noise, the heat, the cold, has all been around me. What I don't understand is why anybody would take people seriously that think that oil doesn't float on water, or that there is a better way to transport oil, or that somehow if they just get organized and people fund them, we are going to pay attention to them as if they were logical. They are not.

So that concludes my statement on the oil pipeline. I am hopeful, though, that in the upcoming Trump administration the future Secretary of State signs that permit that opens up that they need one section of pipe to go across the 49th parallel, Mr. Speaker, in order to facilitate the Keystone XL pipeline. We can build that pipeline down to the Canadian border from the north, and we can build the pipeline up to the Canadian border from the south. But what has always been short on the Obama administration is a Hillary Clinton or a John Kerry signature on the document that says: we have an agreement with Canada to connect these pipelines together at our border. That is one section of pipe that would need to go in there.

I believe that happens under the Trump administration. And we should set aside these ridiculous arguments earlier rather than later. But America looks ridiculous in the world if we are going to argue against that very logic that, if petroleum needs to move and we are going to use it to move product around America and heat our homes and generate electricity and all the things that we do, then we need to do it as effectively and efficiently as possibly or we will become noncompetitive for the rest of the country.

□ 2030

So, Mr. Speaker, I emphasize the points made by the gentleman from North Dakota, and I urge that the Corps of Engineers accelerate the operation up there, and they can commence to finish their work that goes across what is the reservoir and river, the Missouri River, get that connected and get it done. This demonstration isn't going to be over till you get done, so bore on through would be my advice.

THE DEATH OF FIDEL CASTRO

Mr. KING of Iowa. I made myself a promise yesterday, Mr. Speaker, when I stopped in to ILEANA ROS-LEHTINEN's office to congratulate her; and I would do that with many of the people who are related to, from, or descended from folks who had to leave Cuba, especially those who are there today who weren't able to leave Cuba.

We have been looking for the biological solution, which would be Castro being transferred into the next life. The very definition of the biological solution in the vernacular around this town was the eventual death of Fidel Castro.

Well, it happened, finally happened, Mr. Speaker, and so I had a celebratory cup of Cuban coffee in the office of ILEANA ROS-LEHTINEN. And now I would make this call, that it is time for the Cuban people and it is time for the incoming Trump administration to put together what amounts to the need for a regime change on the island of Cuba for the 11 million people that are free-spirited, hardworking, happy people, given all the circumstances that they have to fight against in the poorest country in all of the Western Hemisphere as far as their spirit is concerned.

I would pass the message along. There is a wonderful, wonderful nun in my district named Sister Marie. She served under Mother Teresa for 27 years. She served in Cuba for a long, long time, but she has been to all the—well, maybe not all, but many of the worst places in the world to serve the Lord and to help people.

She used to sneak into Cuba with seeds sewn in her clothing, into the

seams of her clothing, so that she could plant a garden, and that garden then could grow and prosper and help feed the Cuban people that were living off of their monthly supply of the ration of rice, beans, and sugar.

She told me that, of all the places she has been, Cuba is the poorest place—$20 a month for income, but the poorest place because of their spirit. The spirit of their Christian faith has been so suppressed by Castro, who has closed so many of the churches, the cathedrals. I walked into a cathedral down in Cuba, and you could see that where the pews were, that there was dust there and there weren't tracks by the pews.

But the line down through the center aisle was all polished from people walking down through the center aisle. And when you look at that, you realize the reason that there is dust out in the pews and there is not a path of people's feet moving back and forth down through the seats and the pews of this cathedral in Cuba is because that church does not function any longer as a church; it is functioning as a museum.

Castro shut down many, many of the religious institutions throughout Cuba and did his best to suppress Christian faith on that island. Occasionally, a little chapel pops up here and there, and you can see, if you are looking closely, you will see a little bit of it. But he has been an aggressive opponent to our Christian faith, which is the foundation of the faith in Cuba.

So I am not sorry to see the end of the life of Fidel Castro. And I have made a pact with some of my Cuban friends that one day we will return to Cuba and we will swim ashore at the Bay of Pigs. And that would be the ultimate symbolic act that, when the day comes, that it is possible for, let's say, Cuban exiles to come towards the shore.

I will say, I would want to dive out of that boat and swim ashore and wade out onto a free Cuba. That is our pact. That is our mission. I am going to do my best to stay in shape to be able to accomplish that mission.

Here are some things that I saw in my trip down to Cuba, Mr. Speaker, and I think it is important that the body here pay attention to some of this.

I hear a lot of stories about how good the health care system is, about how good the educational system is. Well, we went to visit some of the educational system, Mr. Speaker, and one of them was a country school. They had, oh, I don't know, 15 or 18 kids sitting at desks in this little shack out in the country with the teacher up front looking like this was a country school from 150 years ago in my home State of Iowa.

There, when we walked in, of course, everything stopped and the kids all

paid attention. They didn't get to see Americans very often. I suppose we look a little bit different, on balance, than they do and their parents do.

But we had a pretty good handful of pencils there, and that handful of pencils was swept up immediately. They couldn't wait to get their hands on pencils so that they could write. That is one of the examples of the shortage of supplies that are there.

The educational system, also, we took a ride up to the top of the mountains about 70 kilometers from Santa Clara in Cuba. There is an extension college up there that teaches agriculture. This was a ride up there that took, oh, at least 90 minutes to get up the mountain. We were sitting in the back of a Russian deuce and a half that gave us a ride up the mountain.

When we got there to this little campus built into the mountains, we had the equivalent of—we had about 40 people on this tour altogether. And as we were standing there, they brought out—the Cuban minders brought out the spokesmen for the university, and they stood there in their gray smocks, and the Cuban minders began transferring our questions to them.

So I was asking questions of the faculty at the extension college in the mountains there, and as I would ask the question, then the Cuban minder would translate the question from English into Spanish and ask in Spanish a question of the representatives of the university. They would hear the question. They would answer in Spanish. The Cuban minder would interpret it back into English, and he would tell us what he supposedly said.

Well, I am trying to learn the things I came there to learn, and the interpreter standing next to me, he was on the tour and he was not designed to be the interpreter, but he was the best interpreter I have ever had. His name was Ed Sabatini, and his parents owned real estate in Cuba that had been nationalized by Castro, taken away from them, and they had escaped from the island and lived in Miami.

But Ed Sabatini, the son of the refugees that had gotten out of Cuba, he said to me, as I am listening to the responses to the questions that I think are being asked, he said: You realize, don't you, that these Castro minders are not asking the questions that you are asking, and when they get the answers back, they are not giving back to you the answers that were given to them by the faculty here at this university. And I said: No, I didn't realize that. Of course, I didn't understand enough Spanish to realize that.

So he began to interpret this for me, and he was interpreting not only what was said, but he was interpreting what wasn't said, what body language was there, and filling me in on the things that he was soaking up in that encounter.

So after a little while, we realized it doesn't pay for us to stand here and talk to these people because we are not going to get the truth out of them anyway. They are just putting us through this exercise. And so we stepped away from the group and went down and spoke to some students who were sitting on the curb.

I had already asked the faculty: Do you have Internet services up here on the mountain? And the faculty had answered back, or at least through the minder: Yes, we have Internet services. So we began to talk to the students, and we got straighter answers.

Well, they did have Internet service. They had a computer class going on right then up in a building adjacent to where we were. And so I asked them: So, if you want to access the Internet, how do you get to that Internet? Tell me how that works.

Their answer was: Well, if we have research or a question that we want to get resolved, we write that question down on a piece of paper, and then we hand that to our instructor. Our instructor decides whether to approve our request or not.

If he approves it, then that goes into a packet that goes down the mountain, in a Russian deuce and a half, 70 kilometers to Santa Clara, where the Internet connection is. It is run by Castro's people. Then they look at the request. They type that request out onto the Internet if they are approved that the question can be allowed to be asked and answered, and then the question goes out on the Internet. They download the response that they are looking for. If they approve it, they will take that response down and then redact the things they don't want the student to know, but print the document, put that document back on a Russian deuce and a half, and it goes 70 kilometers back up the mountain. It takes days or even weeks to get an answer from the Internet.

I asked them: Tell me about your Internet service. Their answer was: Oh, yes, we have Internet service here, good access to Internet service. That is what it is. Give a piece of paper a ride down a mountain on a Russian deuce and a half 70 kilometers, going through the minders and through the censors and out to the Internet, back again, redacted, back on the deuce and a half, back up the mountain.

Now, how long would it take you to research anything on the Internet if you have to process things through that means?

It was amazing to me that anyone could even seriously suggest such a thing, that it was Internet access, when it had to take two rides in a Russian deuce and a half and go through a censor and a couple of minders. That is what we saw down there at that university.

So I said: I want to go look at this computer class that is going on. As I

headed up that way, the leader of our tour group was gathering people together, and I said: I am going to go look at this computer class up here.

He said: We are going to leave. That meant we were supposed to jump in these deuce and a halfs and take our ride back down the mountain.

I said: I am going to go up and see the computers.

He said: Well, we are going to leave you here.

I said: Then I will see you in Havana.

So I thought they were bluffing, and they were, but Ed Sabatini and I went into that classroom, kind of down in the basement of a school building there, and there sat about 12 computers, all old 386s or maybe even earlier, and they had two or three male students all sitting in front of each computer. And there on the screen was the five points of why capitalism is bad and Marxism is good. They were teaching the lesson of Marxist ideology right there on the screens of those old computers while these students sat there sharing a screen to look at.

When we walked in, it kind of took over the room. And once they found out that we were from America, the students had questions they wanted to ask, and they began to ask the questions. They were interpreted through Ed Sabatini, and then to me, and I answered them. After awhile, it became so rapid-fire that Ed just answered the questions and he told me what happened as we walked out of there.

But they were asking questions like—and this was agriculture. I said extension. So they were asking questions like, let's see: Who sets the price on the markets for, say, grain? And they are probably thinking rice and sugar, maybe beans, and I am thinking corn and soybeans. Who sets the price?

And we say: The market sets the price.

Well, what is the market?

Well, it is supply and demand. Buyers come in and they make an offer, and if they can buy what they want at that price, then that is the price. If they are getting more than they want, they lower the price. If they are getting less than they want, they raise the price.

Pretty big idea. You could see them try to figure out what that meant.

Then they said: How many times does the price—when does the price change? They were thinking that there still was some government that set our commodity prices, our grain prices, maybe once a month or twice a year or whatever they might do.

I said to them: That price can change, actually, several times a minute. It is kind of a living, moving market because it reacts to the bids that are out there.

Hard to think of what that means.

Who sets—they wanted to know what are our land values, and I told them.

Who set the values on land?

Well, the buyers and the sellers set the value on land. They just didn't have a concept of that.

And then it would be: Why would anyone sell land if they owned land?

Well, there is a concept of real estate ownership that doesn't exist in any significant way in a Marxist economy that controls and owns everything.

So we went through that. It was a fascinating time for them, and it was fascinating for me to see how they reacted, the inquisitiveness of those young students that had an opportunity to hear what it is like in America.

And you heard from them: I want to go to America. I would say everyone in that room wanted to go to America. That is the sense of not only the deprivation that is there because they are on rations of rice and beans and sugar, but deprived, also, of ideas, the opportunity to have access to information, to exchange ideas. That has been crushed by Castro.

So the potential of the people in Cuba, which I think is terrific, has been so badly damaged by the oppressing oppression of Castro, who threw thousands of his political enemies into prison.

□ 2045

He tortured them, he beat them, and he executed many, many of them.

I remember, Mr. Speaker, the vision, the images that I saw on television back in 1959, 1960, and beyond when Castro and Che Guevara took over Cuba and they executed the political enemies. They took them up against a wall. Many of them were wearing white slacks and white Cuban shirts that hang outside their belt, and they were put up to the wall, blindfolded. They stood there with their hands tied, and they were shot. That was back when television showed the reality of what was taking place. We hadn't gotten so sensitive that when there was murder that was picked up on cameras, it went on television without being blurred out as if somehow we are too sensitive to see things like that. It was an awful sight.

I recall a man who was about to be executed, one of Castro's enemies, and he insisted that he not be blindfolded, he insisted that he not be tied, and he insisted that he give the order for them to fire. So, Mr. Speaker, he stood in front of that execution wall in his white Cuban shirt, his white slacks, and his sandals. He raised his hand with no blindfold on him. He looked at that firing squad, he raised his hand, and in a moment of, I will say, just an amazing display of courage and nerve dropped his hand, and that firing squad fired and executed that probably very innocent Cuban there in front of that wall. He became one of thousands who were put into their graves because they were political opponents of the Marxist, the Communist, the dictator, the tyrant that had turned Cuba into a prison island; and it has been a prison island ever since 1959.

Finally, the biological solution has kicked in, and Fidel Castro is no more. There is one more to go, and that is Raul. The Cuban people need to know that when they go to their grave, their grip on the island of Cuba is letting go. It has got to let go, and the free spirit that exists within the hearts of the Cuban people needs to be released. They need to be freed up on that island so they can control their own destiny, they can live their own lives, they can become prosperous by their brains and the sweat of their own brow and have the opportunities that we have here in this country.

This new administration needs to be about regime change in Cuba. The Western Hemisphere has been terrorized by the policies of Fidel Castro and by his support for the Marxists throughout a number of countries in Central and South America. That includes Nicaragua, and it includes Venezuela with Hugo Chavez and now his successor. It includes a number of other countries. Castro has engaged in trouble in Grenada and also over into Africa. He has fomented that kind of terror and sent his army out there for hire to take freedom away from other people. If we had been absent his influence in this hemisphere, chances are South America itself would be much more free than it is today. That is Castro.

I recall visiting the Hotel Nacional. In there, when you walk inside, that was a place where the rich and famous from America used to play down in Cuba at the Hotel Nacional in Havana. It looks out across the sea, and there is a gun emplacement there, a cannon that sits down in a bunker that was used to defend the shores of Cuba back during the Spanish-American War— they say the Spanish-Cuban-American War—in 1898. There in that hotel, you will see pictures of the celebrities of the time: Marilyn Monroe, Stan Musial, Rocky Marciano. When you walk through, you see the people that I will say lived in black-and-white fame in America. Their pictures are on the wall in the Hotel Nacional. Also, there in the parking lot was the 1959 Jaguar station wagon that was the vehicle of the previous dictator, Batista's, wife, who had that green 1959 Jaguar station wagon.

But things have stopped. They are frozen in time. The most typical taxicab in Havana was a 1954 Chevy, and it had a 3-cylinder Russian diesel engine under the hood. If you look around the island, you would see Russian tractors that were parked, and they had been stripped for parts. I didn't see any of them out there running. It is the only place in civilization that I know that once went from animal husbandry agriculture where they used beasts of bur-

den to till the fields to Russian tractors when the Russians were subsidizing the Cubans, and then when the Soviet Union imploded, Mr. Speaker; and that ended Christmas Day 1991, when the Soviet Union went under and was no more. Over a period of time their subsidy for the island of Cuba dried up.

They were subsidizing Cubans this way. Cubans then were producing sugar. The open market on sugar was 6 cents a pound. The Russians were sending them oil for sugar, making a trade. The sugar that was going to Russia was costing the Russians 51 cents worth of oil. So you have a more than eight times multiplier effect sugar for oil, and that profit that was in there was what was propping up the failed, failed, failed economy of Cuba.

The Soviet Union imploded. That subsidy ended, and those Russian tractors broke down and finally died. So you end up with brahma oxen that are out there doing the tillage in the field. They would tie them on a piece of rope, and they would have what I called a pivot grazing system rather than a pivot irrigation system. I happened to plow behind a team of brahma oxen out there just kind of for sport. He was out in the field working. I asked him: Can I take a round? So I got to do that and got a picture of that, Mr. Speaker. That island had regressed so much that the tractors were parked and the animals had been put back to work.

Hugo Chavez decided he would prop up the Cuban island with the wealth of his oil. Of course, when Chavez himself went to his Maker, thankfully, and the prosperity that Venezuela enjoyed collapsed around the failed ideology of a Marxist-controlled economy, that then shut down the subsidy for Cuba.

Who should come along to save the day?

Barack Obama, who decided he is going to open up trade with Cuba, establish an embassy there, and let American dollars come down into Cuba so the island could become prosperous again.

We needed to let the Marxist regime finally be starved out. That was the purpose of the sanctions against Cuba, and that is why it has never been wise to open up free trade with Cuba. Now it is wise for this incoming Trump administration to promote regime change in Cuba. Raul can't last much longer. Freedom must come to the Cuban people, and I want to swim ashore at the Bay of Pigs and walk out on a free Cuba. I have done that at GTMO, but I want to do that at the Bay of Pigs, Mr. Speaker.

Another way that Cuba was propped up would be any foreign currency that came in—tourists could come into Cuba, and they would come into Cuba especially from Europe. They would go to the beaches at Varadero and other places, and so they spent their euros

there. Americans would sneak into Cuba by going through the Bahamas and get their passport punched out there and take a separate flight and fly into Cuba. They might also come in through the south or come in through Mexico, but American dollars came down.

Now, here is the rule: we think we are helping Cubans by doing business with Cuba with American dollars. Here is how it was when I was there—and I don't think it is any different today— the exchange rate of the Cuban peso to the dollar was 21 pesos to the dollar. Cubans could earn American dollars, they could hold American dollars, but they can't spend American dollars unless they go to a Cuban bank where they have to take their American dollar, lay that down on the counter and get an exchange for Cuban currency. But the Cuban currency doesn't give them 21 pesos, which is the exchange rate for their American dollar. It gives them one peso for the American dollar, and 20 pesos go into Castro's bank account to prop up Cuba.

That is how he is raking the vigorish out of those transactions that are there. Or they could go into a Dollar Store where their dollar would only get them a peso. That is how that money went back into the hands of Castro. He is raking up the foreign currency and using that to prop up the military, keep his prisons open, and suppress and repress the Cuban people.

Mr. Speaker, we are in a place in history here where I am glad to see that the Trump administration understands what needs to happen in Cuba. I am hopeful the Cuban people have enough of that spirit left in them to understand what they need to do. Mourn for Fidel is not what they need to do, but replace him with a leader of, by, and for the Cuban people, and a constitution that protects the individual interest and rights of the Cuban people is what needs to happen.

I fully support the effort of the free-minded and free-spirited Cuban people to one day also be free, all 11 million of them. Mr. Speaker, I will do my best to stay in shape so I can swim ashore and wade out onto a free Cuba.

Mr. Speaker, I yield back the balance of my time.

LEAVE OF ABSENCE

By unanimous consent, leave of absence was granted to:

Mr. DeFazio (at the request of Ms. Pelosi) for today after 5 p.m. and December 2 on account of medical appointment.

SENATE BILL REFERRED

A bill of the Senate of the following title was taken from the Speaker's table and, under the rule, referred as follows:

S. 2971. An act to authorize the National Urban Search and Rescue Response System; to the Committee on Transportation and Infrastructure.

ENROLLED BILLS SIGNED

Karen L. Haas, Clerk of the House, reported and found truly enrolled bills of the House of the following titles, which were thereupon signed by the Speaker:

H.R. 4419. An act to update the financial disclosure requirements for judges of the District of Columbia courts and to make other improvements to the District of Columbia courts.

H.R. 5785. An act to amend title 5, United States Code, to provide for an annuity supplement for certain air traffic controllers.

BILL PRESENTED TO THE PRESIDENT

Karen L. Haas, Clerk of the House, reported that on December 1, 2016, she presented to the President of the United States, for his approval, the following bill:

H.R. 4665. To require the Secretary of Commerce to conduct an assessment and analysis of the outdoor recreation economy of the United States, and for other purposes.

ADJOURNMENT

Mr. KING of Iowa. Mr. Speaker, I move that the House do now adjourn.

The motion was agreed to; accordingly (at 8 o'clock and 55 minutes p.m.), the House adjourned until tomorrow, Friday, December 2, 2016, at 9 a.m.

EXECUTIVE COMMUNICATIONS, ETC.

Under clause 2 of rule XIV, executive communications were taken from the Speaker's table and referred as follows:

7689. A letter from the Alternate OSD FRLO, Office of the Secretary, Department of Defense, transmitting the Department's final rule — DoD Environmental Laboratory Accreditation Program (ELAP) [Docket ID: DOD-2013-OS-0230] (RIN: 0790-AJ16) received November 28, 2016, pursuant to 5 U.S.C. 801(a)(1)(A); Public Law 104-121, Sec. 251; (110 Stat. 868); to the Committee on Armed Services.

7690. A letter from the Associate General Counsel for Legislation and Regulations, Office of the Secretary, Department of Housing and Urban Development, transmitting the Department's final rule — Equal Access to Housing in HUD's Native American and Native Hawaiian Programs — Regardless of Sexual Orientation or Gender Identity [Docket No.: FR-5861-F-03] (RIN: 2506-AC40) received November 28, 2016, pursuant to 5 U.S.C. 801(a)(1)(A); Public Law 104-121, Sec. 251; (110 Stat. 868); to the Committee on Financial Services.

7691. A letter from the Assistant Secretary for Legislation, Office of the Secretary, Department of Health and Human Services, transmitting the 2015 Outcome Evaluations of Administration for Native Americans (ANA) Projects Report to Congress, pursuant to Sec. 811(e) of the Native American Programs Act of 1974, as amended; to the Committee on Education and the Workforce.

7692. A letter from the Assistant General Counsel for Regulatory Affairs, Pension Benefit Guaranty Corporation, transmitting the Corporation's final rule — Benefits Payable in Terminated Single-Employer Plans; Interest Assumptions for Paying Benefits received November 28, 2016, pursuant to 5 U.S.C. 801(a)(1)(A); Public Law 104-121, Sec. 251; (110 Stat. 868); to the Committee on Education and the Workforce.

7693. A letter from the Director, Regulatory Management Division, Environmental Protection Agency, transmitting the Agency's final rule — Air Plan Approval; MA; Decommissioning of Stage II Vapor Recovery Systems [EPA-R01-OAR-2015-0351; A-1-FRL-9950-92-Region 1] received November 28, 2016, pursuant to 5 U.S.C. 801(a)(1)(A); Public Law 104-121, Sec. 251; (110 Stat. 868); to the Committee on Energy and Commerce.

7694. A letter from the Director, Regulatory Management Division, Environmental Protection Agency, transmitting the Agency's final rule — 2015 Revisions and Confidentiality Determinations for Data Elements Under the Greenhouse Gas Reporting Rule [EPA-HQ-OAR-2015-0526; FRL-9954-42-OAR] (RIN: 2060-AS60) received November 28, 2016, pursuant to 5 U.S.C. 801(a)(1)(A); Public Law 104-121, Sec. 251; (110 Stat. 868); to the Committee on Energy and Commerce.

7695. A letter from the Assistant Secretary, Legislative Affairs, Department of State, transmitting a six-month periodic report, covering May 15, 2016 to November 15, 2016, on the national emergency with respect to the proliferation of weapons of mass destruction that was declared in Executive Order 12938 of November 14, 1994, and has been continued by the President each year, most recently on November 8, 2016, pursuant to 50 U.S.C. 1641(c); Public Law 94-412, Sec. 401(c); (90 Stat. 1257) and 50 U.S.C. 1703(c); Public Law 95-223, Sec 204(c); (91 Stat. 1627); to the Committee on Foreign Affairs.

7696. A letter from the Assistant Secretary for Export Administration, Bureau of Industry and Security, Department of Commerce, transmitting the Department's final rule — Commerce Control List: Removal of Certain Nuclear Nonproliferation (NP) Column 2 Controls [Docket No.: 160718621-6621-01] (RIN: 0694-AH04) received November 28, 2016, pursuant to 5 U.S.C. 801(a)(1)(A); Public Law 104-121, Sec. 251; (110 Stat. 868); to the Committee on Foreign Affairs.

7697. A letter from the Assistant Secretary for Export Administration, Bureau of Industry and Security, Department of Commerce, transmitting the Department's final rule — Temporary General License: Extension of Validity [Docket No.: 160106014-6728-04] (RIN: 0694-AG82) received November 28, 2016, pursuant to 5 U.S.C. 801(a)(1)(A); Public Law 104-121, Sec. 251; (110 Stat. 868); to the Committee on Foreign Affairs.

7698. A letter from the Associate General Counsel, Department of Agriculture, transmitting a notification of a federal vacancy and a notification of a discontinuation of service in acting role, pursuant to 5 U.S.C. 3349(a); Public Law 105-277, 151(b); (112 Stat. 2681-614); to the Committee on Oversight and Government Reform.

7699. A letter from the Acting Director, Employee Services, Office of Personnel Management, transmitting the Office's final rule — Veterans' Preference (RIN: 3206-AM79) received November 28, 2016, pursuant to 5 U.S.C. 801(a)(1)(A); Public Law 104-121, Sec.

251; (110 Stat. 868); to the Committee on Oversight and Government Reform.

7700. A letter from the Acting Director, Employee Services, Office of Personnel Management, transmitting the Office's final rule — Career and Career-Conditional Employment (RIN: 3206-AM64) received November 28, 2016, pursuant to 5 U.S.C. 801(a)(1)(A); Public Law 104-121, Sec. 251; (110 Stat. 868); to the Committee on Oversight and Government Reform.

7701. A letter from the Deputy Assistant to the President and Director, Office of Administration, Executive Office of the President, transmitting the personnel report as required by 3 U.S.C. 113 (2016), for personnel employed in the White House Office, the Executive Residence at the White House, the Office of the Vice President, the Office of Policy Development (Domestic Policy Staff), and the Office of Administration for FY 2016; to the Committee on Oversight and Government Reform.

7702. A letter from the Acting Director, Planning and Policy Analysis, Office of Personnel Management, transmitting the Office's final rule — Federal Employees Health Benefits Program Coverage for Certain Firefighters and Intermittent Emergency Response Personnel (RIN: 3206-AM66) received November 28, 2016, pursuant to 5 U.S.C. 801(a)(1)(A); Public Law 104-121, Sec. 251; (110 Stat. 868); to the Committee on Oversight and Government Reform.

7703. A letter from the Assistant Secretary for Legislation, Office of the Secretary, Department of Health and Human Services, transmitting a report titled "Fiscal Year 2015 Report to Congress on Contract Funding of Indian Self-Determination and Education Assistance Act Awards (Includes Fiscal Year 2012-2015 Data)", pursuant to 25 U.S.C. 450j-1(c); Public Law 93-638, Sec. 106(c) (as added by Public Law 106-260, Sec. 9(2)); (114 Stat. 733); to the Committee on Natural Resources.

7704. A letter from the Division Chief, Regulatory Affairs, Bureau of Land Management, Department of the Interior, transmitting the Department's Major final rule — Waste Prevention, Production Subject to Royalties, and Resource Conservation [17X.LLWO310000.L13100000.PP0000] (RIN: 1004-AE14) received November 18, 2016, pursuant to 5 U.S.C. 801(a)(1)(A); Public Law 104-121, Sec. 251; (110 Stat. 868); to the Committee on Natural Resources.

7705. A letter from the Director, Regulatory Management Division, Environmental Protection Agency, transmitting the Agency's withdrawal of direct final rule — Effluent Limitations Guidelines and Standards for the Oil and Gas Extraction Point Source Category — Implementation Date Extension [EPA-HQ-OW-2014-0598; FRL-9955-65-OW] (RIN: 2040-AF68) received November 28, 2016, pursuant to 5 U.S.C. 801(a)(1)(A); Public Law 104-121, Sec. 251; (110 Stat. 868); to the Committee on Transportation and Infrastructure.

7706. A letter from the Deputy General Counsel, Office of the General Counsel, Small Business Administration, transmitting the Administration's interim final rule — Debt Refinancing in 504 Loan Program (RIN: 3245-AG79) received November 28, 2016, pursuant to 5 U.S.C. 801(a)(1)(A); Public Law 104-121, Sec. 251; (110 Stat. 868); to the Committee on Small Business.

7707. A letter from the Director, Office of Regulations and Reports Clearance, Social Security Administration, transmitting the Administration's final rule — Revised Medical Criteria for Evaluating Human Immunodeficiency Virus (HIV) Infection and for

Evaluating Functional Limitations in Immune System Disorders [Docket No.: SSA-2007-0082] (RIN: 0960-AG71) November 28, 2016, pursuant to 5 U.S.C. 801(a)(1)(A); Public Law 104-121, Sec. 251; (110 Stat. 868); to the Committee on Ways and Means.

7708. A letter from the Chief, Border Security Regulations Branch, U.S. Customs and Border Protection, Department of Homeland Security, transmitting the Department's final rule — The U.S. Asia-Pacific Economic Cooperation Business Travel Card Program [Docket No.: USCBP-2013-0029] (RIN: 1651-AB01) received November 21, 2016, pursuant to 5 U.S.C. 801(a)(1)(A); Public Law 104-121, Sec. 251; (110 Stat. 868); to the Committee on Homeland Security.

PUBLIC BILLS AND RESOLUTIONS

Under clause 2 of rule XII, public bills and resolutions of the following titles were introduced and severally referred, as follows:

By Mrs. MILLER of Michigan (for herself and Mr. BRADY of Pennsylvania):

H.R. 6415. A bill to provide for the appointment of members of the Board of Directors of the Office of Compliance to replace members whose terms expire during 2017, and for other purposes; to the Committee on House Administration.

By Mr. ROE of Tennessee (for himself, Mr. MILLER of Florida, Mr. BILIRAKIS, Mr. BOST, Mrs. RADEWAGEN, and Mr. ABRAHAM):

H.R. 6416. A bill to amend title 38, United States Code, to make certain improvements in the laws administered by the Secretary of Veterans Affairs, and for other purposes; to the Committee on Veterans' Affairs, and in addition to the Committees on the Budget, and Armed Services, for a period to be subsequently determined by the Speaker, in each case for consideration of such provisions as fall within the jurisdiction of the committee concerned.

By Mr. KENNEDY (for himself and Mrs. LOVE):

H.R. 6417. A bill to prohibit a court from awarding damages based on race, ethnicity, gender, religion, or actual or perceived sexual orientation, and for other purposes; to the Committee on the Judiciary.

By Mr. LATTA:

H.R. 6418. A bill to amend certain provisions of the Safe Drinking Water Act, and for other purposes; to the Committee on Energy and Commerce.

By Mr. LEWIS:

H.R. 6419. A bill to amend the Omnibus Crime Control and Safe Streets Act of 1968 to provide that COPS grant funds may be used to hire and train new, additional career law enforcement officers who are residents of the communities they serve, and for other purposes; to the Committee on the Judiciary.

By Miss RICE OF NEW YORK:

H.R. 6420. A bill to improve the screening of transgender persons at airport security checkpoints, and for other purposes; to the Committee on Homeland Security.

By Mr. ROSKAM (for himself, Mr. DEUTCH, Mrs. LOWEY, Ms. ROS-LEHTINEN, Mr. ENGEL, and Mr. ISRAEL):

H.R. 6421. A bill to provide for the consideration of a definition of anti-Semitism for the enforcement of Federal antidiscrimination laws concerning education programs or activities; to the Committee on the Judiciary.

By Mr. ROSKAM (for himself and Mr. BLUMENAUER):

H.R. 6422. A bill to amend the Internal Revenue Code of 1986 to treat qualified alternative commuter programs as an excludable qualified transportation fringe benefit; to the Committee on Ways and Means.

By Mr. SHERMAN (for himself, Mr. CONYERS, Mr. CAPUANO, Ms. JUDY CHU of California, Mrs. NAPOLITANO, Ms. EDWARDS, Ms. NORTON, Mr. DANNY K. DAVIS of Illinois, Mrs. LAWRENCE, Mr. CARTWRIGHT, and Mr. GRIJALVA):

H.R. 6423. A bill to amend the Truth in Lending Act and the Electronic Fund Transfer Act to provide justice to victims of fraud; to the Committee on Financial Services.

By Mr. COHEN:

H.J. Res. 104. A joint resolution proposing an amendment to the Constitution of the United States to abolish the electoral college and to provide for the direct election of the President and Vice President of the United States; to the Committee on the Judiciary.

By Ms. LEE (for herself, Ms. KELLY of Illinois, Ms. WASSERMAN SCHULTZ, Ms. ROYBAL-ALLARD, Mr. PASCRELL, Ms. WILSON of Florida, Mr. SIRES, Mr. PRICE of North Carolina, Ms. CLARKE of New York, Ms. ADAMS, Mr. TAKANO, Ms. SPEIER, Mr. ELLISON, Mr. CICILLINE, Ms. BASS, Mr. DEUTCH, and Ms. JACKSON LEE):

H. Con. Res. 177. Concurrent resolution supporting the goals and ideals of World AIDS Day; to the Committee on Energy and Commerce, and in addition to the Committee on Foreign Affairs, for a period to be subsequently determined by the Speaker, in each case for consideration of such provisions as fall within the jurisdiction of the committee concerned.

By Mr. WELCH:

H. Con. Res. 178. Concurrent resolution clarifying any potential misunderstanding as to whether actions taken by President-elect Donald Trump constitute a violation of the Emoluments Clause, and calling on President-elect Trump to divest his interest in, and sever his relationship to, the Trump Organization; to the Committee on Oversight and Government Reform.

CONSTITUTIONAL AUTHORITY STATEMENT

Pursuant to clause 7 of rule XII of the Rules of the House of Representatives, the following statements are submitted regarding the specific powers granted to Congress in the Constitution to enact the accompanying bill or joint resolution.

By Mrs. MILLER of Michigan:

H.R. 6415.

Congress has the power to enact this legislation pursuant to the following:

Article I, Section 8 of the U.S. Constitution, which grants Congress the authority to make laws governing the commerce among several states, including employment discrimination laws.

By Mr. ROE of Tennessee:

H.R. 6416.

Congress has the power to enact this legislation pursuant to the following:

Article 1, Section 8 of the United States Constitution.

By Mr. KENNEDY:

H.R. 6417.

Congress has the power to enact this legislation pursuant to the following:

Article I, Section 8 and the 14th Amendment

By Mr. LATTA:

H.R. 6418.

Congress has the power to enact this legislation pursuant to the following:

Article I, Section 8, Clause 18

To make all Laws which shall be necessary and proper for carrying into Execution the foregoing Powers, and all other Powers vested by this Constitution in the Government of the United States, or in any Department or Officer thereof.

By Mr. LEWIS:

H.R. 6419.

Congress has the power to enact this legislation pursuant to the following:

This bill is enacted pursuant to the power granted to Congress under Article I of the United States Constitution and its subsequent amendments, and further clarified and interpreted by the Supreme Court of the United States.

By Miss RICE of New York:

H.R. 6420.

Congress has the power to enact this legislation pursuant to the following:

Article I, Section 8, Clause 1 of the Constitution of the United States

By Mr. ROSKAM:

H.R. 6421.

Congress has the power to enact this legislation pursuant to the following:

Article I, Section 8 of the Constitution of the United States of America

By Mr. ROSKAM:

H.R. 6422.

Congress has the power to enact this legislation pursuant to the following:

Article I, Section 8, which states "The Congress shall have Power To lay and collect Taxes," and Article I, Section 7, which states "All Bills for raising Revenue shall originate in the House of Representatives."

By Mr. SHERMAN:

H.R. 6423.

Congress has the power to enact this legislation pursuant to the following:

Article 1, Section 8, Clause 3

By Mr. COHEN:

H.J. Res. 104.

Congress has the power to enact this legislation pursuant to the following:

Article V

ADDITIONAL SPONSORS

Under clause 7 of rule XII, sponsors were added to public bills and resolutions, as follows:

H.R. 169: Mr. COFFMAN.
H.R. 546: Mr. BEYER.
H.R. 590: Mr. HECK of Washington.
H.R. 1061: Mr. HECK of Washington.
H.R. 1147: Mr. DAVIDSON.
H.R. 1220: Mr. NEAL.
H.R. 1421: Mr. HECK of Washington.
H.R. 1707: Ms. LOFGREN.
H.R. 1787: Ms. LOFGREN.
H.R. 2197: Ms. CASTOR of Florida.
H.R. 2274: Ms. LOFGREN.
H.R. 2461: Mr. KING of New York.
H.R. 2493: Mr. BRENDAN F. BOYLE of Pennsylvania.
H.R. 2747: Mr. MOULTON.
H.R. 3244: Mr. MEEHAN.
H.R. 3559: Mr. PAYNE.
H.R. 4296: Mr. REICHERT.
H.R. 4298: Mr. KING of New York, Mr. LANGEVIN, Mr. WALZ, and Mr. COURTNEY.
H.R. 4376: Ms. LOFGREN.
H.R. 4456: Ms. LOFGREN and Mr. COSTELLO of Pennsylvania.

H.R. 4731: Mr. JORDAN.

H.R. 4907: Mr. KING of New York.

H.R. 5090: Mr. TAKANO, Mr. QUIGLEY, Mr. MEEKS, Mr. YODER, and Mr. GENE GREEN of Texas.

H.R. 5167: Ms. LOFGREN.

H.R. 5258: Ms. MENG.

H.R. 5296: Mr. FITZPATRICK.

H.R. 5334: Ms. KUSTER.

H.R. 5474: Mr. LOWENTHAL.

H.R. 5501: Ms. KUSTER.

H.R. 5932: Mr. WALZ.

H.R. 5956: Mr. LEWIS and Ms. STEFANIK.

H.R. 5961: Mr. CÁRDENAS and Mr. JODY B. HICE of Georgia.

H.R. 5999: Mr. MOOLENAAR, Mr. MCGOVERN, Mr. WILSON of South Carolina, and Mr. ROE of Tennessee

H.R. 6045: Mr. BUCHANAN.

H.R. 6100: Mr. AUSTIN SCOTT of Georgia.

H.R. 6117: Mr. SWALWELL of California.

H.R. 6132: Mr. HECK of Washington.

H.R. 6273: Ms. KUSTER.

H.R. 6306: Mr. CONYERS.

H.R. 6316: Mr. NUNES.

H.R. 6317: Ms. KUSTER.

H.R. 6336: Ms. KUSTER.

H.R. 6340: Ms. SLAUGHTER, Mr. WELCH, Ms. BROWNLEY of California, Mr. SWALWELL of California, Mr. DEFAZIO, Mr. PASCRELL, Mr. KIND, Mr. GRIJALVA, and Mr. O'ROURKE.

H.R. 6377: Mr. DESAULNIER, Mrs. DINGELL, Mr. HASTINGS, Mr. GRIJALVA, and Mr. BLUMENAUER.

H.R. 6382: Mr. MOULTON, Mrs. DINGELL, Mr. SWALWELL of California, Ms. MENG, Ms. LOFGREN, Mr. AL GREEN of Texas, Mr. GARAMENDI, Mr. KIND, Mr. LOWENTHAL, and Ms. BROWNLEY of California.

H. Con. Res. 159: Mr. COOK and Mr. MARINO.

H. Con. Res. 161: Ms. BROWNLEY of California.

H. Con. Res. 171: Mr. OLSON, Mr. HASTINGS, and Mr. VARGAS.

H. Res. 753: Mr. PERLMUTTER.

H. Res. 924: Mr. HECK of Washington.

EXTENSIONS OF REMARKS

TRIBUTE TO DAVID JOHNSON, CO-FOUNDER OF POLARIS INDUSTRIES

HON. COLLIN C. PETERSON
OF MINNESOTA

IN THE HOUSE OF REPRESENTATIVES

Thursday, December 1, 2016

Mr. PETERSON. Mr. Speaker, I rise today to pay tribute to a visionary business man from my district, David Johnson. He co-foundered Polaris Industries and designed its first snowmobile.

While Mr. Johnson was in the Navy he invested half of his paycheck . . . just $11 after he received a letter from his friend asking for help. When he returned home after his military service Mr. Johnson went to work for the company.

The company he helped found reached its first billion-dollar sales year in 1995. It now generates over $4 billion in sales yearly and has a major impact on the local economy.

Despite retiring in 1988, Mr Johnson was a regular fixture at the company's Roseau, Minnesota plant, which is in my district. He would check in on the newer models the company was producing and he would also give tours and share stories about company history.

Mr. Johnson was a lifelong snowmobile rider. For his 90th birthday, he took a three-day 150-mile ride aboard a Polaris snowmobile from Roseau to his old cabin in the Northwest angle.

Mr. Johnson was inducted into the snowmobile Hall of Fame in 1999. Mr. Johnson died in his Roseau MN home after a long illness. He was 93 years old.

David Johnson is survived by his wife of 68 years, Eleanor, and their children, Rodney, Mary, Mitchell, and Aaron. All Polaris employees were honorary pallbearers for his funeral service.

It was my sincere pleasure to know David Johnson and to work with him.

I ask my colleagues to join me in recognizing the life and achievements of David Johnson.

TRIBUTE TO STAFF SERGEANT CLAYTON E. MONEYMAKER

HON. MO BROOKS
OF ALABAMA

IN THE HOUSE OF REPRESENTATIVES

Thursday, December 1, 2016

Mr. BROOKS of Alabama. Mr. Speaker, I rise today to recognize the life and military service of Staff Sergeant Clayton E. Moneymaker, who, after service in the U.S. Army during World War II, dedicated 41 years of his life to the service of veterans in the Huntsville-Madison County community and the State of Alabama.

Clayton Eugene Moneymaker was born on January 1, 1918 in Heysworth, Illinois to Mr. and Mrs. Lee Moneymaker. On August 10, 1943, at 25 years old, Clayton joined the U.S. Army and officially entered active military service on August 31, 1943. Clayton served honorably, and on January 8, 1946, separated from the Army having attained the rank of Staff Sergeant.

In 1981, Clayton mortgaged his home to complete the purchase, construction, and completion of the new home for the Huntsville-Madison County American Legion Post 237.

Clayton served his fellow veterans from 1982 to 2011 in numerous positions including as the American Legion Department of Alabama Commander, the District 12 Commander, the Division 1 Commander, and twice he served as the American Legion Post 237 Commander, spanning 19 years.

In recognition of his dedication to veterans in our community, the American Legion Post 237 membership, living heirs of Clayton, the American Legion Department of Alabama, and the National Headquarters of the American Legion all agreed to rename the Huntsville-Madison County American Legion Post 237 as the Clayton E. Moneymaker American Legion Post 237.

Clayton Eugene Moneymaker dedicated 41 years of his life to serving veterans in the Huntsville-Madison County community and the State of Alabama.

Today I pay tribute to an extraordinary individual, Clayton E. Moneymaker, and express my sincere gratitude for his life of committed service to the veterans of Alabama.

HONORING THE 10TH ANNIVERSARY OF GRACE HEALTH CLINIC AND THE LEADERSHIP OF DR. RANDY HICKLE

HON. RANDY NEUGEBAUER
OF TEXAS

IN THE HOUSE OF REPRESENTATIVES

Thursday, December 1, 2016

Mr. NEUGEBAUER. Mr. Speaker, I rise today to recognize the 10th anniversary of Grace Health Clinic in Lubbock, Texas. I would also like to honor Grace Health Clinic's founder and CEO, Dr. Randy Hickle, and recognize his commitment to providing quality, service and value to the countless families throughout the South Plains.

To appreciate this accomplishment, one must understand the humble beginnings from which Grace Health Clinic came.

Dr. Hickle founded Grace Clinic in 2006 with just eight doctors on staff. Under his guidance, Grace Health Clinic has transformed into Grace Health System, growing to more than 50 doctors and specialists and expanding its operations to better serve their patients' needs.

The award-winning clinic is the only locally owned, doctor-operated health facility in the region. Thanks to the tireless efforts of Dr. Hickle, Grace Health Clinic has been able to grow without losing its focus on patients and their healthcare needs.

Mr. Speaker, it is my honor to recognize a clinic that has contributed so much to our community. It is my pleasure to take this opportunity and praise the vision that Dr. Hickle had when he founded this clinic 10 years ago and the leadership he has exhibited throughout this journey.

RECOGNIZING MR. WILLIAM "BILL" HALD

HON. DOUG LaMALFA
OF CALIFORNIA

IN THE HOUSE OF REPRESENTATIVES

Thursday, December 1, 2016

Mr. LAMALFA. Mr. Speaker, I would like to recognize Mr. William "Bill" Hald of Grass Valley, California, an artist and a veteran from the North State.

Bill served in the United States Navy from 1967 through 1973. After graduating 2nd in his class, he served as a computer fire control missile technician aboard the USS *Ramsey*, a *Brooke*-class destroyer escort for the USS *Hancock* aircraft carrier in the Western Pacific. Mr. Hald was one of the six crewmembers required to use the *Ramsey*'s Tartar Missile System—but during his first tour he was the sole technician able to use the system's analog computer, resulting in long days and nights. Throughout his tour in the Western Pacific, the USS *Ramsey* earned 5 Battle Stars in addition to a number of citations and campaign ribbons. After his service, Bill returned to the North State and began to sculpt, sometimes using patriotic symbols, such as the bald eagle.

Bill's wife Camille placed one of his sculptures, We The People, up for the 2016 National Veterans Administration Creative Arts Competition. This annual competition focuses on the use of the creative arts to assist in rehabilitative treatment for enrolled Veterans recovering from, and coping with physical and emotional disabilities. The competition has 51 categories, including sculptures. We The People quickly gained recognition, placing first in local and regional competitions. On October 16, 2016, at the National Veterans Creative Arts Festival in Jackson, Mississippi, We The People won first place in the sculpture category.

We The People portrays a bald eagle perched atop four books: the Holy Bible, on top, followed by three books labelled Legislative, Executive and Judicial to represent the first three Articles of the Constitution of the United States. The right talon of the eagle is placed on the Holy Bible, while it stands "on the wall," over the Constitution in a protective stance. In total, Bill spent over a year crafting the 100 pound pure bronze sculpture in his garage. There are 5,000 accurately handcrafted feathers on the piece. I am deeply grateful to Bill for his service in the United States Navy, but also for the incredible devotion and patriotism that he has shown to his country after his service ended.

HONORING THE LIFE OF THE HONORABLE GEORGE R. GROSSE OF JACKSONVILLE, FLORIDA

HON. ANDER CRENSHAW
OF FLORIDA
IN THE HOUSE OF REPRESENTATIVES
Thursday, December 1, 2016

Mr. CRENSHAW. Mr. Speaker, I rise today to honor the life of The Honorable George R. Grosse. We in Jacksonville, Florida, mourned Mr. Grosse's passing after 86 years of life on June 3, 2016.

Born in Jacksonville, Florida, in 1930, George dedicated his life to his faith, his family and his community. He graduated from Baldwin High School and was a lifelong resident of Jacksonville's Westside. George became an accomplished businessman, a successful law enforcement official, and a public servant who enjoyed a reputation for honesty, fair dealings, and a strong Christian faith. He was a member of Westside Baptist Church where he served as a Deacon for more than 25 years.

George always held an entrepreneurial spirit, a strong work ethic, and the American Dream in his heart. He started a chicken farm and later became a journeyman carpenter. Then in 1957, George joined the Duval County Road Patrol as a Deputy Sheriff. In 1968, he was elected President of the Duval County Fraternal Order of Police Lodge Number 30. Then, when the city and the county consolidated, he was elected as the first President of the consolidated FOP Lodge Number 5–30 and was selected as Officer of the Year for the Jacksonville Sheriff's Office. He continued to serve as FOP President until he left JSO in 1970 to devote his full attention to Gateway Concrete Contractors, Inc., a concrete business he founded and which ultimately grew to be the largest concrete contractor of its day in Northeast Florida.

In 1973, George was elected to the Florida House of Representatives for District 15. He represented West Duval County, as well as all of Baker, Nassau and Union counties for three terms. I had the privilege of serving with him in the State House for several years and considered him a valued friend and colleague. George resigned his seat in 1977, when President Jimmy Carter appointed him as the U.S. Marshall for the Middle District of Florida, a role he served in until 1982. Later he was appointed by Mayor Jake Godbold to the Jacksonville Electric Authority Board of Directors and was, subsequently, elected Board Chairman.

George was a role model to many and a well-respected leader of our community. He was recognized on several occasions for his active role in the leadership of the Boy Scouts of America's Great Northern District. In addition, he maintained an active role and presence in local politics his entire life. Each year, George and his wife Corene hosted a bar-beque at their farm in support of my candidacy for Congress. I was never sure if people came out to see me or George. He dedicated his life to the service of others and his generosity of spirit and warm affability endeared him to his family, his friends and his neighbors. I send my heartfelt condolences to his family and join with all of Jacksonville in mourning our loss.

Mr. Speaker, I ask you to join me in celebrating the outstanding life of one of Florida's and Jacksonville's most outstanding citizens, The Honorable George R. Grosse.

REMEMBRANCE AND HOPE ON WORLD AIDS DAY

HON. JAMES A. HIMES
OF CONNECTICUT
IN THE HOUSE OF REPRESENTATIVES
Thursday, December 1, 2016

Mr. HIMES. Mr. Speaker, today, December 1, 2016, marks the 28th World AIDS Day—a day to come together in support of people around the world who live with HIV/AIDS, to remember those we've lost, and to commit ourselves to eradicating this vile disease once and for all.

For me, this day conjures back a memory I have of visiting the Names Project AIDS Memorial Quilt on the National Mall on a sweltering day in Washington a few summers ago. Although I was sweating through my suit, it was impossible not to stand there without being profoundly moved. I was moved when I thought about the fathers, mothers, cousins, sisters, brothers, friends, and other loved ones whose lives were cut short by this wretched disease—many of whom had their stories memorialized on a panel of the AIDS quilt for the world to see. Stories like that of Ryan White, an Indiana teenager who was diagnosed with HIV in 1984 after receiving a contaminated blood treatment for Hemophilia. Just 13 years old, Ryan was barred from returning to school, cast asunder by a society that did not yet comprehend that the disease transmits independently of lifestyle. But he spent the rest of his young life advocating for understanding and against an unjust stigma, finally perishing far too young at 18. Countless stories like Ryan's are a reminder that we must never forget how far we've come, and how far we have left to go.

That said, we've made tremendous progress since the first World AIDS Day in 1988. So many people today are alive because of the investment, hard work, activism and commitment of those who fought for this progress, like Ryan—for housing, for prevention, for a fair shake for those who today live with this wretched disease.

In Congress, I have worked with my colleagues on the Congressional HIV/AIDS caucus to support policies that promote research, prevention, and, most importantly, a cure. Through my work with these magnificent colleagues—many of whom have been fighting this battle since long before I dreamed of running for Congress—I have resolved that we must fully fund programs that fight AIDS at home and abroad. Programs like the President's Emergency Plan for AIDS Relief (PEPFAR) and the Global Fund to Fight AIDS, Tuberculosis, and Malaria—both of which provide antiretroviral HIV treatments and screenings to millions of children and adults around the world. And the Housing Opportunities for Persons with AIDS—a program that allows Americans with AIDS to access subsidized, low-income housing.

Today, our government has made stopping the proliferation of HIV/AIDS a priority, and the impact is real. Last year, the U.S. government spent $26.42 billion on HIV/AIDS treatment, prevention, and accommodations domestically, and $6.57 billion for international programs. Between 2005 and 2014, the annual total of new cases has fallen 19 percent largely due to increased screenings and prevention measures. Even still, the lifetime cost of treating an HIV infection is $379,000—a staggering amount considering that 30 percent of those living with the disease lack health insurance.

I am especially pleased by news that the National Institutes of Health started a grant program in July of this year to fund research into a cure—$30 million per year over the next five years. amFAR, a non-profit research organization, has committed to investing $100 million to form the scientific basis for a cure by 2020.

The scientists tell us the moment is now. A cure is possible if we commit ourselves to it. As long as I am in Congress, I will fight to make the necessary resources available to eradicate HIV/AIDS and realize our shared dream of an AIDS-free generation.

IN HONOR OF DAVE POTTER

HON. SAM FARR
OF CALIFORNIA
IN THE HOUSE OF REPRESENTATIVES
Thursday, December 1, 2016

Mr. FARR. Mr. Speaker, I rise today to honor Dave Potter, a model public servant on this memorable occasion of his retirement from the Monterey County Board of Supervisors. I have had the tremendous pleasure in working with Dave over the years and the great honor to call him a dear friend.

Dave originally hails from Hingham, Massachusetts. In 1970, his van broke down on Highway 1 near Carmel and he just stayed and made the Monterey Peninsula his home. Starting in the early 70s, he built a general contracting business, Potter Construction. That work soon led him into the world of public policy as an appointee to the City of Monterey's Architectural Review Committee and then Planning Commission and ultimately to an elected seat on the Monterey City Council.

In 1996, Dave was elected to the Monterey County Board of Supervisors to represent the Fifth District, the same supervisorial district I represented from 1975 to 1980. He quickly gained a reputation on the Board as a doer, a leader who got stuff done. The Carmel Hill Highway 1 climbing lane is a good example, and one that many of us use on a daily basis. And then there were countless other tasks and efforts that made life in the Fifth District that much better: resolution to a parking problem, a new park, viable ambulance service, assistance with County Planning, etc. His service stood out particularly in response to disasters both small and large. During the 2008 Basin Complex Fire and this year's Sobranes Fire, Dave and his office were ever present in the thick of the action helping the community and incident command resolve countless issues that came up on an almost daily basis. This kind of service won Dave reelection in 2000, 2004, 2008, and 2012.

During his tenure on the Board, Dave served on many boards, committees and commissions including the California Coastal Commission for 12 years, Monterey Peninsula Water Management District, Fort Ord Reuse Authority, Legislative Committee, Fort Ord Committee, Capital Improvements Committee, Natividad Medical Center Board of Trustees, Chair of Transportation Agency for Monterey County, and Chair of the Rail Policy Committee. In addition, Dave received numerous awards of recognition from 1980 through 2015 from a multitude of local cities and organizations, Chambers of Commerce, including resolutions from California State Senate and Congress representatives.

Mr. Speaker, I know that I speak for the whole House in thanking Supervisor Potter for his many years of dedicated public service. I want to especially thank Dave's wife Janine and his three adult children Myles, Tyler, and Sarah, and grandchildren, Ciara and Bella for lending their husband, father, and grandfather to the people of this community. As a resident myself of the Fifth District, I know that my neighbors and I owe him a deep gratitude for doing so much to improve our quality of life. The world is a better place because of his efforts.

RECOGNIZING THE LIFE AND LEGACY OF NORTHWEST FLORIDA'S BELOVED WILLIAM LEE "BILL" SUTLER

HON. JEFF MILLER

OF FLORIDA

IN THE HOUSE OF REPRESENTATIVES

Thursday, December 1, 2016

Mr. MILLER of Florida. Mr. Speaker, I rise to recognize the life and legacy of Northwest Florida's beloved William Lee "Bill" Sutler, who passed away on November 24, 2016. His love for his family and community, as well as his dedicated service in the United States Navy, will be remembered by all those who knew him.

Bill was born August 31, 1932, in Stanton, Virginia where he grew up with his mother and two sisters. At the young age of 17, Bill made the choice to serve our Nation by joining the United States Navy, serving faithfully and honorably for the next 26 years. Bill utilized his talents as an aircraft mechanic aboard several ships including the USS *Franklin D. Roosevelt,* USS *Saratoga,* USS *Constellation,* and the USS *John F. Kennedy.* Chief Petty Officer Sutler also worked on aircrafts VF–11, VF–31,

VF–121, and the RVAH–11. In 1974, after 26 years of service, he retired as a Senior Chief Petty Officer. After retirement, Bill continued his career by working for the state agriculture department and remained active in both Pineview Methodist Church and his community.

Those who knew Bill, know that he was a kind, generous, and smart man. He will always be remembered fondly for the unwavering love that he held for his family and his country.

On behalf of the United States Congress, I am privileged to recognize the life of William Lee "Bill" Sutler. My wife Vicki and I extend our heartfelt prayers and condolences to his wife Shirley "Colleen" Sutler; sons, William Jr. "Billy" and Virginia Sutler, Michael and Cheryl Sutler, and Robert "Bobby" and Diane Sutler; six grandchildren, Penny, Jennifer, Emily, Emmett, and Caleb Sutler, and Amanda Bell; and two great-grandchildren.

HONORING DEPUTY COMMANDER PAT CAROTHERS

HON. BOB GOODLATTE

OF VIRGINIA

IN THE HOUSE OF REPRESENTATIVES

Thursday, December 1, 2016

Mr. GOODLATTE. Mr. Speaker, nearly two weeks ago, our nation lost another dedicated public servant committed to protecting our neighborhoods from criminals.

Deputy Commander Pat Carothers of the Southeast Regional Fugitive Task Force died in the line of duty while executing an arrest warrant for a fugitive wanted for attempted murder of police officers and domestic violence.

Deputy Commander Carothers served in the U.S. Marshals Service for 26 years. He was a native of Luray, Virginia, in the Sixth Congressional District which I represent, and spent his career serving the Northern District of Georgia. For over a quarter of a century, he risked his life every day to arrest fugitives of the law and see them brought to justice for their crimes.

In addition to wearing the badge, Deputy Commander Carothers was also a family man. He was married to his wife Terry for 30 years and was a loving father to five children. As the Carothers family mourns their devastating loss, we pray that God would comfort them and give them peace.

The murder of Deputy Commander Carothers reminds us once again that law enforcement officers face danger every day while on duty, whether simply knocking on a door or pulling someone over.

In 2016 alone, 132 law enforcement officers died in the line of duty. Attacks on those who protect our neighborhoods from criminals and keep the peace are not to be tolerated. I—and others in Congress—stand shoulder to shoulder with our nation's law enforcement officers and remain committed to finding solutions to reduce violence and aggression towards them.

In the Gospel of John, we are told that there is no greater love than to lay down one's life for one's friends. And this is true of Deputy Commander Carothers. Every day he risked

his life so that others would be safe from harm. He is a hero and deserves to be recognized and honored for his service to our country.

CELEBRATING THE TOWN OF WESTBOROUGH, MASSACHUSETTS

HON. JAMES P. McGOVERN

OF MASSACHUSETTS

IN THE HOUSE OF REPRESENTATIVES

Thursday, December 1, 2016

Mr. McGOVERN. Mr. Speaker, today I rise to celebrate the town of Westborough, Massachusetts as they enter the year of their 300th anniversary. Westborough was the 100th town to be incorporated in the Commonwealth of Massachusetts on November 18th, 1717. Westborough has had an impressive history.

Forty-six Minutemen left Westborough on April 19, 1775 under the command of Captain Edmund Brigham to fight in the opening battle of the Revolutionary War. In the early 1800s, Westborough became a key stop as travelers to and from Worcester and Boston stopped along their journey.

Today, Westborough is a vibrant, thriving, and diverse town with an excellent school system and a family-oriented community. Westborough has been named "one of the best places to live" and a "top ten best town for families."

Westborough's location at the center of Massachusetts has helped propel its thriving local economy. Westborough has many unique family-owned small businesses and is home to the headquarters of some of New England's most notable companies.

Congratulations, again, to the town of Westborough. As Westborough looks ahead to the next 300 years, I am proud to join so many in wishing them a bright and prosperous future.

TRIBUTE TO WAYNE STATE UNIVERSITY POLICE OFFICER COLLIN ROSE

HON. SANDER M. LEVIN

OF MICHIGAN

IN THE HOUSE OF REPRESENTATIVES

Thursday, December 1, 2016

Mr. LEVIN. Mr. Speaker, I rise today with a heavy heart to commemorate the life of Wayne State University police officer Collin Rose, who was killed in the line of duty on November 23, 2016. Officer Rose was my constituent, and lived in St. Clair Shores, Michigan.

A K9 officer with the Wayne State University Police Department in Detroit, Officer Rose not only protected the faculty, staff and student body at the University, but also the community surrounding Wayne State's campus. He was known to his friends and colleagues as a person of boundless energy, for his commitment to the safety of those he was sworn to serve, and for his kindness and generosity to others. A fellow member of the Wayne State University Police Department, Chris Powell, described Officer Rose as ". . . the light of the room. He was bears to honey. Everyone would befriend him."

As a memorial bicyclist with Chapter One of the Police Unity Tour, Officer Rose proudly honored police officers throughout the country who died in the line of duty. In addition to helping to broaden public awareness of the sacrifices made by fallen officers, Officer Rose and other Unity Tour participants throughout the nation have helped to raise millions of dollars for the National Law Enforcement Officers Memorial Fund and the National Law Enforcement Museum. An avid cyclist, Officer Rose proposed to his fiancée, Nikki Salgot, after completing the last leg of the Police Unity Tour on May 12th of this year.

A 13-year old boy, Kameren Greene, who lives near Wayne State and who came to know Officer Rose though his consistent outreach to young people in the neighborhood, told WXYZ-TV in Detroit, "It's sad that he lost his life, and we lost a good friend." So with profound sadness at his loss and deep gratitude for his service, I encourage my colleagues to join me in paying tribute to Officer Collin Rose, who was indeed a good friend to so many people, and in offering sincere condolences to Officer Rose's fiancée, Nikki Salgot; to his parents, Randy and Karen Rose and his brother Curtis Rose; to his colleagues with the Wayne State Police Department; and to the Wayne State community.

HONORING REVEREND FRANK E. COLEMAN JR.

HON. ELIOT L. ENGEL
OF NEW YORK
IN THE HOUSE OF REPRESENTATIVES
Thursday, December 1, 2016

Mr. ENGEL. Mr. Speaker, as Messiah Baptist Church in Yonkers celebrates the installation of a new Pastor, I wanted to take the opportunity to congratulate and welcome the congregation's new leader, Westchester's own Reverend Frank E. Coleman Jr.

A graduate of Tuckahoe High School, Rev. Coleman attended Virginia Union University where he graduated with a B.A. in Religion & Philosophy. Later he graduated from Almeda University where he received his Master's degree in Pastoral Studies.

Rev. Coleman began his Pastoral career at Zion Baptist Church in Westmoreland, Virginia, before moving back to Westchester as Pastor of Shiloh Baptist Church in Tuckahoe. In 2010, he once again returned to Virginia as Pastor of the First Baptist Church in South Boston and remained there until 2014, when he once again returned home to Westchester. Since September, 2015 Rev. Coleman has served as Pastor-Elect of the Mother Church, The Messiah Baptist Church in Yonkers, New York.

In addition to his Pastoral duties, Rev. Coleman has left a lasting legacy of helping others everywhere he goes. He was the Vice President of the Halifax County Substance Abuse Awareness Coalition, Commissioner of The Southside Planning District Commission, Board Member of The Department of Social Services in Halifax, member of the S.C.L.C.,

Danville Branch and he served as the President of the Halifax/South Boston NAACP. He has also served as V.P. of the Tuckahoe School District's school board, Member of the Tuckahoe Village's Ethics Board and Co-Founder/President of the Committee Worker for All Children (CWAC).

Of course, Rev. Coleman's true love has always been family. He is the husband of the Rev. Margaret Fountain Coleman of Mount Vernon New York and the father of one son and three daughters.

I am honored to help welcome Rev. Coleman to Messiah Baptist and I wish him nothing but the best in his tenure.

HONORING U.S. ARMY CORPS OF ENGINEERS SAINT PAUL DISTRICT ON 150 YEARS

HON. BETTY McCOLLUM
OF MINNESOTA
IN THE HOUSE OF REPRESENTATIVES
Thursday, December 1, 2016

Ms. McCOLLUM. Mr. Speaker, I rise to congratulate the U.S. Army Corps of Engineers Saint Paul District on 150 years of service to residents of Minnesota and the entire upper Mississippi region. The Saint Paul district has, over the past century-and-a-half, conserved our aquatic habitats, managed the effects of drought and flood damage, provided outdoor recreation areas for the public, and ensured that the products and services produced in our region have the ability to be transported safely via our waterways. This is only to name a few of the critical tasks performed by the U.S. Army Corps of Engineers Saint Paul District.

The Saint Paul District celebrates its birthday on August 17th every year because it was on that day in 1866 that Major General G.K. Warren, a West Point Graduate acclaimed for his leadership in the battle of Gettysburg, arrived in Saint Paul. His orders were seemingly modest: To establish an engineering office. He could not have known at the time, but the office that he established would go on to be entwined with the economy and history of the entire region. The first emergency that the St. Paul District responded to was the collapse of the Eastman Tunnel of Nicollet Island in Minneapolis. With expertise and precision, the Saint Paul district constructed structures to save both the island and nearby St. Anthony Falls. The structures that they built are still in use to this day.

Later on in its history, the Saint Paul District supported the nation's mobilization during World War II. The Saint Paul District dredged the Minnesota River to the Port of Cargill, where Minnesota-based Cargill was building ships for the war effort. In addition, they also built an ordnance plant in Arden Hills, Minnesota, and airports in Fargo and Devil's Lake, North Dakota.

Today, any visit to the Mississippi River in St. Paul, showcases the work that the Saint Paul District does. The 13 locks and dams, and 9 foot navigation channel that the Saint Paul District operates and maintains, goes to support economically crucial inland navigation that benefits the entire upper Mississippi re-

gion. One of the most important tasks that the Saint Paul District has is to help communities combat the effects of flooding through disaster support and by the construction of flood risk management projects. This includes 16 large reservoirs for flood risk reduction that also offer recreation and fish and wildlife habitat. Another little known operation of the Saint Paul District is the operation of 49 separate recreation areas open to the public.

The Saint Paul District has supported the citizens of the Fourth Congressional District, and thousands of people in the upper Mississippi River region for 150 years. Every task that they undertake goes to benefit the people they serve by strengthening the local economy, enabling the movement of goods and people, maintaining and restoring natural aquatic ecosystems, and reducing and preventing the effects of floods and droughts. Mr. Speaker, please join me in congratulating the Saint Paul District of the U.S. Army Corps of Engineers on 150 years of service.

USS "JOHN P. MURTHA" (LPD–26)

HON. MARCY KAPTUR
OF OHIO
IN THE HOUSE OF REPRESENTATIVES
Thursday, December 1, 2016

Ms. KAPTUR. Mr. Speaker, I rise today to recognize the commissioning of the USS *John P. Murtha,* the new naval vessel named in honor of the late Congressman Jack Murtha, who will fondly be remembered as a decorated combat Marine, statesman, and dear friend to colleagues on both sides of the aisle.

On Saturday, October 8, 2016 in Philadelphia, PA, the Navy's 10th *San Antonio*-class amphibious transport dock, named the USS *John P. Murtha* (LPD 26), was commissioned by his beloved widow Mrs. Joyce Murtha and daughter Ms. Donna Murtha.

During his 58 years of service to our nation, 38 in the U.S. Marine Corps and 35 as a Member of U.S. Congress from Johnstown, PA, Rep. Murtha was an indefatigable champion for the Armed Services, rising in 1989 to chair the House Defense Appropriations Subcommittee. His detailed knowledge of the U.S. military, deep friendships across the various services, respect from his Congressional colleagues on both sides of the aisle, and wry sense of humor drew people to him and made him a highly effective lawmaker. Jack was a father of three children, the first Vietnam War combat veteran elected to Congress, recipient of the John F. Kennedy Profile in Courage Award, and staunch representative of his people. His own wartime experience as a battalion staff officer in Vietnam, where he was awarded the Bronze Star, two Purple Hearts, and the Vietnamese Cross of Gallantry, gave him deep insight into the political and military complexities of modern warfare.

An author, From Vietnam to 9/11: On the Front Lines of National Security with a New Epilogue on the Iraq War, he wrote: The Congress—the people's branch of government—has an obligation to make an independent assessment of key foreign policy issues. The way we go about collecting, analyzing, and using intelligence information is one of the most important determinants of our success or failure in world events. Unfortunately, it is a lesson we have had to learn too often, at a heavy price in American blood and treasure. What is certain, is that intelligence must always be used as a tool of statecraft, not as a political tool.

As this ship performs its missions on behalf of the American people, I have full confidence Jack Murtha's patriotic and strong spirit—Semper Fidelis—will be guiding the vessel if it encounters troubled waters as it navigates toward fair winds and following seas.

I include in the RECORD the remarks of Democratic Leader NANCY PELOSI given at the commissioning of the USS *John P. Murtha.*

PELOSI REMARKS AT USS JOHN P. MURTHA
COMMISSIONING CEREMONY

PHILADELPHIA.—House Democratic Leader Nancy Pelosi delivered remarks today, October 8, 2016, at the commission ceremony of the USS John P. Murtha. Below are the Leader's remarks:

"Good morning. Thank you very much, Admiral William Moran for your kind introduction but more importantly, for your great leadership. As one that grew up in Baltimore, Maryland, I have a great loyalty to the Naval Academy, so I appreciate your comments about the Navy—but I had four brothers who served in the Army so . . .

[Laughter and applause]

"It is an honor to be with you today, with Secretary Valdez—please give our regards to Secretary Mabus—to Major General Christopher Owens—it is a proud day for all of us to come together for the Navy and the Marine Corps, for the Commissioning of the USS John P. Murtha.

"Chairman Murtha—as you have heard—was a legislator of unsurpassed talents, a soldier of extraordinary courage and a public servant to the end. Mr. Brady—my colleague, Congressman Brady is correct: we will never see his light again.

"I thank the Murtha family for the opportunity to make this address today. I appreciate this opportunity to bring the greetings and congratulations from Jack Murtha's many friends in the Congress of the United States, on both sides of the aisle, on both sides in the Capitol and all the way down Pennsylvania Avenue.

"I am glad to be with my colleagues—present and former—the Undersecretary of the Army Patrick Murphy—as he mentioned, the first Iraq veteran to serve in the Congress—Congressman Bob Brady, in whose district we are and great friend of Jack Murtha's, Congressman Keith Rothfus, he represents the district where Jack represented in Congress, and as well as Mark Critz, who followed in Jack's footsteps, and Marjorie Margolies-Mezvinsky, who is here as well—who represented Philadelphia in Congress. It is also an honor to be here with Lieutenant Governor Michael Stack—recognizing the important role that Pennsylvania and Philadelphia play in our national security.

"It is appropriate for us to be here in Pennsylvania to honor Jack Murtha—a state he loved and was proud to represent and to serve. In the House Chamber—Congressman Bob Brady mentioned the 'Pennsylvania Corner'—Jack took great pride that in the House of Representatives, the 'Pennsylvania Corner' was the most bipartisan corner in the Chamber. In the Chamber, everyone gravitated toward Jack Murtha—Democrats and Republicans alike.

"To Brian Cuccias—Brian and the Ingalls shipbuilders, thank you for the skill, hard work and patriotism of all the men and women of labor who built this fine ship that enters service today. And many of you were in Mississippi when Donna christened the ship. It is wonderful to see so many of you here today. Thank you. Thank you for making today possible.

[Applause]

"Commanding Officer, Captain Kevin J. Parker, it was a privilege to be with you last year in Mississippi at the Murtha's christening when you were the prospective commander, and now at this time-honored commissioning ceremony to become the Commanding Officer—that is when Donna gives the signal. When Donna gives the signal—we're all waiting for her.

"And to the sailors and the Marines—the men and women who will crew this ship over the oceans and perhaps ride it into battle, take it to humanitarian assistance—to you, and your families—thank you for honoring our country, all of us with your bravery and service.

[Applause]

"It is a joy to be with the family members, as my colleagues and others have said, Jack's daughter, our ship sponsor, Donna, his sons John and Pat, grandchildren, nephews and nieces and others.

"I send the congratulations and thanks of my colleagues in Congress to Joyce—Joyce, the love of Jack's life. She and Jack were both so proud of having this ship named in his honor but Admiral Joyce was very proud to comment that the ship that she christened, the USS Bonhomme Richard, was a bigger ship. Not a competition, though.

"Service runs deep in Jack Murtha's family from his brothers, Kit and Jim, to his nephews Brian and Bob—all proud Marines—and his grandson, Lieutenant Jack Murtha in the Air Force, and to Jack's wife, Captain Amanda Murtha.

"Today, as you commission, as we all commission, the USS John P. Murtha, I want to tell you a little bit about the man your ship is named for—his legacy of strength, effectiveness and fidelity. As was mentioned by my colleague, as a child, John's grandmother told him: 'You are put on this earth to make a difference.' And that's exactly what he did. John P. Murtha dedicated his entire life to the service of our nation.

"Jack Murtha was a fiercely proud Marine, who volunteered for combat in Vietnam—earning two Purple Hearts and a Bronze Star. In the end, Congressman Murtha would leave the Corps with 37 years of service to his name. How proud he was of that.

"In the Congress, Chairman Murtha was a formidable legislator and a towering leader. To watch Jack Murtha legislate was to observe a master at work. But more indicative of his character was to watch him communicate, with our troops in theater, at the Pentagon, and in their hospital rooms.

"His experiences in the battlefield of Vietnam was what fueled his boundless dedication to our men and women in uniform—with that connection to those warriors he frequently visited in Washington, across the country and around the world.

"A few of us had the privilege of traveling in bipartisan delegations with Jack—and this one in particular to Kuwait, a few weeks before the initiation of hostilities into Iraq—we observed the level of detail with which Jack conversed with the soldiers, whether it was the comfort of the seats in their Humvees—how much they could endure as they did their jobs—responding to their needs, providing body and vehicle armor and reliable radios—you name it. Again, not just the big picture, but down to the personal comfort and safety of our troops.

"In those moments, Jack bonded with them, sharing his own personal military experiences, and caring for them really as a father—as Secretary Murtha said, he treated them as family. And they returned his respect.

"We often saw this when he would take groups of us—as Bob mentioned—take groups of us on regular visits to our wounded warriors in the hospitals. One day as we were going into one of the rooms and the nurse came and said, 'Hold up. Hold up for a while.' We wanted to be very respectful and sensitive to the privacy of the soldiers. But when we walked in to the room, we saw a young, injured soldier standing at attention by his bed and saluting Jack Murtha wearing a Pittsburgh Steelers jersey right after they had won the Super Bowl.

[Applause]

"That was football but it was very personal with Jack.

"It is important to note that Jack defined our nation's strength, not only in our military might—as important as our military is and the priority that it is—but also our strength is measured by Jack in the health and well being of the American people.

"Chairman Murtha fought for the armed forces—whether it was for what they needed, for our troops, facilities—but he also fought to advance scientific research to seek treatments and cures for breast cancer, prostate cancer, diabetes, and HIV/AIDS—the list goes on and on. Today, at Walter Reed, the John P. Murtha Cancer Center carries forward his commitment to the health of our entire community.

"John Murtha made a difference—for our national defense, for our nation's health, for the men and women who wear our nation's uniform.

"Commander Parker, as this fine ship comes alive with her outstanding crew, the strength of the USS John P. Murtha will embody our nation's promise to stand with you and your crew—through the storm and the calm, both as you defend democracy abroad, and when you come home safely. And when our men and women in uniform come home, Jack wanted them to feel safe as well.

"In the military, he always told us: on the battlefield, we leave no soldier behind. And when they come home, we leave no veteran behind. So I join all of those saluting our veterans who are here today. That was a priority for Jack Murtha.

[Applause]

"'Semper Fi' was the watchword of Jack Murtha's life. And always faithful he was: to his principles, to his promises, to his family and to the nation he loved.

"As we place the Murtha into active service, we also renew our pledge to also always be faithful to you—the sailors and Marines who will board her today, and to every crew who follows.

"Like John P. Murtha, each of you has stepped forward and answered the call to 'make a difference'—for our country, and for the world. Be proud of the legacy that has been passed down to you, be proud of your ship's namesake and motto, and be proud of the values you share.

"May God bless the USS John P. Murtha.

"May God bless the brave men and women who will serve aboard it—and the privilege of serving as the first crew for one of these great ships, who will be transported within it—and the families who wait for their safe return. You are family to all of us. You will always be in our prayers.

"May God bless you and may God bless the United States of America."

HONORING BOB STAUF

HON. ELIOT L. ENGEL

OF NEW YORK

IN THE HOUSE OF REPRESENTATIVES

Thursday, December 1, 2016

Mr. ENGEL. Mr. Speaker, as a former school teacher, I know just how dedicated our educators are to their students as well as the community as a whole. In the Bronx and Westchester, no one has displayed that dedication more than Bob Stauf, one of the honorees at this year's American Irish Association of Westchester Annual Dinner.

Involved in the world of education for a half century, Bob Stauf has taught elementary and junior high students at St. Philip Neri School in the Bronx, in the Yonkers Public School system and Yonkers and Tarrytown Salvation Army citadels. His work with the Salvation Army has also extended to its Advisory Board, on which he currently serves as President for the Yonkers chapter. Bob is also the President of the 3rd Precinct Police Community Council, Vice President of the American Irish of Westchester, and facilitator of programming of Brahma Kumaris in Westchester. He has also taught adult education and home school instruction with the Yonkers School System and the Children's Village Yonkers Satellite program.

Bob has also made a difference at the local level through his work in City government. He has chaired the Yonkers Human Rights Commission under two administrations, chaired the Mayors Community Relations Committee and Mayor's Committee on Irish Affairs, chaired the Yonkers Community Action Program and was Vice Chair of New York State Community Agencies.

In addition, Bob is a good friend who was personally helpful to me just prior to my first trip as a Member of Congress to Ireland. He was a wonderful resource on Irish matters, and even traveled with me on that trip.

This year the American Irish Association of Westchester is honoring Bob Stauf at their Annual Dinner Dance. I want to congratulate Bob on this well-deserved honor and thank him for his many contributions to both the Bronx and Yonkers communities.

CELEBRATING KAZAKHSTAN'S 25 YEARS OF INDEPENDENCE

HON. DANA ROHRABACHER

OF CALIFORNIA

IN THE HOUSE OF REPRESENTATIVES

Thursday, December 1, 2016

Mr. ROHRABACHER. Mr. Speaker, on December 16th the people of Kazakhstan will celebrate 25 years of their independence. From the collapse of the Soviet Union to the present day, Kazakhstan has become a valued member in the international community and is a respected voice as a nonpermanent member of the United Nations Security Council. For the United States, the first country to recognize Kazakhstan's independence, this moment not only symbolizes Kazakhstan's remarkable development, but also marks 25 years of cooperation and friendship between our two nations.

Our strategic partnership was founded on a shared interest in nuclear nonproliferation and security. When the Soviet Union dissolved, Kazakhstan inherited the fourth largest nuclear stockpile in the world. Rather than using those resources in unproductive ways, through President Nursultan Nazarbayev's leadership this nuclear arsenal was decommissioned and Kazakhstan has continued to cooperate in these efforts.

Over the 25 years the economic relationship between Kazakhstan and the United States has greatly expanded as well. The Kazakh economy is dynamic and open to the world. From 1993 to 2013 American firms invested more than $42 billion in Kazakhstan, and trade between our nations is measured in the billions of dollars per year.

The government and the people of Kazakhstan have made great strides in building an economically diverse, multi-ethnic and prosperous country. Kazakhstan exemplifies a country of religious diversity and shows the world how people of various faiths can live together in peace. I congratulate them on that achievement. In the coming years, I hope to see the cooperation between the United States and Kazakhstan continue to grow as future leaders build on the successful foundation that has already been laid.

HONORING CHIEF KATHLEEN HARRELL ON HER RETIREMENT

HON. ALCEE L. HASTINGS

OF FLORIDA

IN THE HOUSE OF REPRESENTATIVES

Thursday, December 1, 2016

Mr. HASTINGS. Mr. Speaker, I rise today to honor Chief Kathleen Harrell, on the occasion of her retirement from the Florida Department of Corrections.

Chief Harrell has given 30 years of distinguished public service to the State of Florida through her knowledge, integrity and leadership. Her tenure at the Florida Department of Corrections began on August of 1986, where she worked as a Field Agent within the Correctional Probation sector. She then spent several years performing professional work investigating, assessing, supervising, counseling, administrating, and/or classifying offenders as a Correctional Probation Officer. It was in 1993 when she joined the Office of Inspector General and strived passionately to become the Assistant Chief of Investigations for the Florida Department in January of 2013. Chief Harrell deserves our admiration and respect for her dedication to public service.

Besides working tirelessly to ensure the wellbeing of Florida's citizens, Chief Harrell dedicates time to worship as a member of the New Mount Olive Baptist Church in Ft. Lauderdale, FL since 2011. She has also been an avid cyclist for ten years and frequently participates in fundraising rides for multiple sclerosis and HIV/AIDS charities. If there's something Chief Harrell loves as much as cycling, it is the Miami Dolphins, being a seasonal ticket holder for around fourteen years now.

Mr. Speaker, it is my distinct honor to congratulate Chief Kathleen Harrell on her retirement. I wish her the very best of luck in all her future endeavors.

REMEMBERING MR. TOM BAKER

HON. CATHY McMORRIS RODGERS

OF WASHINGTON

IN THE HOUSE OF REPRESENTATIVES

Thursday, December 1, 2016

Mrs. McMORRIS RODGERS. Mr. Speaker, I rise to honor the memory of Tom Baker of Waitsburg, Washington who passed away on November 14, 2016 at the age of 86.

Tom Baker was born on April 17, 1930 in Fort Morgan, Colorado. As a child, he was a member of the Boy Scouts of America, and active in various church, music, and social events. Following his high school graduation, Tom attended the Carnegie Institute of Technology, where he graduated with a Bachelor's of Science in Printing Management in 1953. It was during his college years that he met and fell in love with his wife Anita.

Tom's passion and dream from a young age was to work in newspapers. Following positions with various local newspapers in Colorado, Tom and Anita eventually moved to Waitsburg in 1963, where Tom bought stake in the Waitsburg Times, eventually becoming editor and publisher in 1964.

As publisher of the Waitsburg Times for 27 years, Tom was able to employ his dry wit and unique style while chronicling the life and times of the people of Waitsburg. Tom officially sold his stake in the Waitsburg Times in 1991, but happily contributed to the paper with his weekly column "TOMfoolery" until 2009. Tom understood the importance of providing the citizens of Waitsburg with a weekly print newspaper tailored to their interests and passions.

An active member of his community, Tom enjoyed spending his time working with the Waitsburg Commercial Club, Masonic Lodge No. 16, the Waitsburg Historical Society, the Waitsburg Presbyterian Church Choir and Board of Elders, the Walla Walla Community College Board of Trustees, and the Washington Newspaper Publishers Association among many others.

Tom was also an active and loyal community servant, who ably filled roles on the Waitsburg City Council and served as Mayor of Waitsburg on two separate occasions.

Tom is survived by his wife of 64 years, Anita, his sons Charles and Loyal, and daughter Peggy, as well as numerous grandchildren and great-grandchildren.

Mr. Speaker, Tom Baker was a dedicated public servant and important member of the greater Waitsburg community for many years who will be truly missed. His positive spirit, belief in the good of the community, and devotion to his passions was truly admirable. I will fondly remember Tom Baker and share my condolences with his family.

INTRODUCTION OF CONSTITUTIONAL AMENDMENT TO ELIMINATE THE ELECTORAL COLLEGE AND PROVIDE FOR THE DIRECT ELECTION OF THE PRESIDENT AND VICE PRESIDENT

HON. STEVE COHEN
OF TENNESSEE
IN THE HOUSE OF REPRESENTATIVES
Thursday, December 1, 2016

Mr. COHEN. Mr. Speaker, I rise today in support of a constitutional amendment I introduced today to eliminate the electoral college and provide for the direct election of our nation's President and Vice President.

For the second time in recent memory, and for the fifth time in our history, we have a President-elect, who lost the popular vote.

The reason is because of an antiquated system that was established to prevent citizens from directly electing our nation's President.

That notion—that citizens should be prevented from directly electing the President—is antithetical to our understanding of democracy.

In our country, "We the People," are supposed to determine who represents us in elective office.

Yet, we use an anachronistic process for choosing who will hold the highest offices in the land.

It is time for us to fix this, and that is why I have introduced this amendment today.

When the Founders established the electoral college it was in an era of limited nationwide communication. It was premised on a theory that citizens would have a better chance of knowing about electors from their home states than about presidential candidates from out-of-state.

The development of mass media and the internet, however, has made information about presidential candidates easily accessible to U.S. citizens across the country and around the world.

Today, citizens have a far better chance of knowing about out-of-state presidential candidates than knowing about presidential electors from their home states. Most people don't even know who their electors are.

As Thomas Jefferson said, "I am not an advocate for frequent changes in laws and constitutions, but laws and institutions must go hand in hand with the progress of the human mind. As that becomes more developed, more enlightened, as new discoveries are made, new truths discovered and manners and opinions change, with the change of circumstances, institutions must advance also to keep pace with the times. We might well as require a man to wear still the coat which fitted him when a boy as civilized society to remain ever under the regimen of their barbarous ancestors."

Since our nation first adopted our Constitution, "We the People," have amended it repeatedly to expand the opportunity for citizens to directly elect our leaders. What resulted was the following:

The 15th Amendment guarantees the right of all citizens to vote, regardless of race.

The 19th Amendment guarantees the right of all citizens to vote, regardless of gender.

The 26th Amendment guarantees the right of all citizens 18 years of age and older to vote, regardless of age.

And the 17th Amendment empowers citizens to directly elect U.S. Senators.

We need to empower citizens to directly elect the President and the Vice President of the United States.

I am privileged to serve as Ranking Member of the House Judiciary Committee's Subcommittee on the Constitution and Civil Justice. My colleagues and I at the Judiciary Committee will be holding a forum next week to examine our outdated presidential election process. I hope members will attend and share their views.

Working together, I know we can fix this historical anomaly, and make our Constitution better reflect the "more perfect Union" to which it aspires.

HONORING MARY KEEHAN

HON. ELIOT L. ENGEL
OF NEW YORK
IN THE HOUSE OF REPRESENTATIVES
Thursday, December 1, 2016

Mr. ENGEL. Mr. Speaker, I rise today to recognize a leader in our community, Mary Keehan, who is an honoree at the American Irish Association of Westchester Annual Dinner Dance.

Mary was born in White Plains, New York to Peter and Catherine Kevil, who emigrated from Ireland and married in Scarsdale. Mary attended White Plains High School and simultaneously worked part-time at Macy's department store. Eventually graduating with honors and becoming an office manager for a Chiropractor, Mary felt her passion in a different field and decided to return to school in the field of Electrolysis.

Mary combined passion for service and business, and she established her own practice in Electrolysis. Her business has served thousands of people for the past 34 years, while her service to her community through volunteerism made an equally lasting impact.

Mary became a member of the American Irish Association, where she held the office of President in 2008, and currently serves as the financial secretary. Mary is also a member of the Tarrytown LAOH, and is often seen leading the Rockland County Ancient Order of the Hibernian's Pipe Band in marches and parades as "Banner Mom".

With such an impressive record of civic engagement, it's no surprise Mary's list of accomplishments is extensive: President of the Ardsley American Legion Auxiliary for six years, President in 1981 of the Westchester County American Legion Auxiliary, National Board Member at the NYS Electrolysis Association, President of the Ardsley Garden Club, Board Member of the Ninth District of Federated Garden Club of NYS, Board Member of the Girls Scout of Westchester-Putnam, and committee member of Dobbs Ferry Woman's Club. She also serves on the Board of Elections for the Town of Greenburgh.

Married to George Keehan, Mary and her loving husband raised six wonderful children together. She is also the proud grandmother of six amazing grandchildren, her pride and joy.

Mary has shown incredible spirit through her service and love of family. It is an honor to recognize her as one of the American Irish Association of Westchester Annual Dinner Dance Honorees. Congratulations to Mary on this most deserved recognition.

RECOGNIZING THE PEORIA LIONS ON THEIR STATE TITLE

HON. CHERI BUSTOS
OF ILLINOIS
IN THE HOUSE OF REPRESENTATIVES
Thursday, December 1, 2016

Mrs. BUSTOS. Mr. Speaker, I rise today to honor The Peoria Lions for their Class 5A championship win against the Vernon Hills Cougars earlier this week.

Peoria struggled to stop the Cougars in the first half, but the Lions forced three second-half turnovers, allowing them to build a two-score lead. Junior quarterback Coran Taylor threw for 215 yards and two touchdowns, and added 134 yards and three scores on the ground. Fellow junior Geno Hess led all rushers with 215 yards and two touchdowns of his own. In the end the Lions racked up 621 yards in their 62–48 win.

I congratulate the Peoria Lions on their outstanding victory in their 5A championship win. The Lions are now first-time state champions, a testament to the impressive football program that coach Tim Thornton has built.

Mr. Speaker, as a former athlete, I understand how important this is to the young men, the coaches and the community. They never gave up. They kept playing their best, and their team spirit and belief in themselves helped them become state champions. Their efforts and resilience should inspire us all.

RECOGNIZING SYSCO NORTH TEXAS' OSHA "STAR SITE" HONOR

HON. KENNY MARCHANT
OF TEXAS
IN THE HOUSE OF REPRESENTATIVES
Thursday, December 1, 2016

Mr. MARCHANT. Mr. Speaker, I rise today to recognize Sysco North Texas and its nearly 600 employees for the achievement of being recognized as an OSHA Voluntary Protection Program "Star Site."

The Star Site designation is the highest honor within OSHA's Voluntary Protection Program. The Program rewards companies who lay out a comprehensive compliance and safety risk management plan for internal controls, which translates directly into fewer workplace injuries and illnesses. Sysco North Texas received this award by maintaining a workplace injury incident rating well below the industry average, and by meeting other strict metrics for workplace safety.

Sysco North Texas operates an 800,000 square foot facility in Lewisville, Texas, serving nearly 4,000 customers throughout the

Dallas-Fort Worth metro region and beyond. The facility has been in operation since 1973. As an upstanding business in the 24th District of Texas, I am proud to represent Sysco North Texas here in Congress. I commend them and all other businesses around my district as they continue to provide good jobs and safe work environments for Texas citizens.

Mr. Speaker, it is a pleasure to recognize the safe and beneficial work environment Sysco North Texas provides for its employees. I ask all of my distinguished colleagues to join me in recognizing this hard earned achievement.

IN RECOGNITION OF ROBERT W. LOHR, JR.'S 30 YEARS OF PUBLIC SERVICE

HON. BARBARA COMSTOCK

OF VIRGINIA

IN THE HOUSE OF REPRESENTATIVES

Thursday, December 1, 2016

Mrs. COMSTOCK. Mr. Speaker, I am honored to thank Mr. Robert W. Lohr, Jr. for his three decades of extraordinary leadership and service to the town of Purcellville, Virginia, located in my congressional district.

Mr. Lohr has served in local government for 30 years, and for the past 23 years he was the town manager of Purcellville. As town manager he has been instrumental in the growth and development of Purcellville. Mr. Lohr has overseen Purcellville's rapid growth to a community of around 9,000 residents.

In his role as town manager, Mr. Lohr, oversaw a number of important projects to improve the local infrastructure and quality of life for Purcellville's residents. Some of these projects include the development of the Basham Simms Wastewater Treatment Plant and the Purcellville Maintenance Facility, as well as the effort to preserve and improve historic downtown Purcellville. Mr. Lohr's dedication to bettering the town and the lives of its citizens has been evident during his years of tireless service.

Mr. Lohr's selfless desire to constantly improve Purcellville never went unnoticed, least of all to his colleagues in the town government. Working in close collaboration with the town council, Mr. Lohr was able to identify the needs of the town's citizens, and develop a strategy in order to complete their needed goals.

Mr. Speaker, I now ask that my colleagues join me in recognizing Mr. Robert Lohr, Jr.'s 30 years of public service, especially those 23 years as town manager of Purcellville, Virginia. Today, we honor and celebrate the contributions he has made to the town and all its citizens. I wish him all the best in his future endeavors.

RECOGNIZING JOHN NESGODA AS THE AMERICAN VETERANS (AMVETS) POST 1 OF PENNSYLVANIA'S VETERAN OF THE YEAR

HON. LOU BARLETTA

OF PENNSYLVANIA

IN THE HOUSE OF REPRESENTATIVES

Thursday, December 1, 2016

Mr. BARLETTA. Mr. Speaker, it is my privilege to honor Mr. John Nesgoda for receiving the American Veterans (AMVETS) Post 1 of Pennsylvania's Veteran of the Year Award. AMVETS' mission is to enhance and safeguard the entitlements for all American veterans that have served honorably. Through leadership, advocacy, and engagement, AMVETS work to improve the quality of life for our veterans, their families, and their communities, and John's years of dedication to these principles have earned him this important award.

During the height of the Vietnam War, John answered the call to serve his country and enlisted in the United States Air Force. From 1963 to 1967, John served overseas providing communications support to troops on the front lines. His service to others did not stop after leaving active duty. As 3rd Vice Commander, and a lifetime member of AMVETS Post 1, John leads by example and works every day to ensure that all Pennsylvania veterans are taken care of. He is a lifetime member in the McAdoo Veterans of Foreign Wars Post and a member of the Quakake American Legion. John has also spearheaded fundraising efforts that support veterans' programs like PTSD Working Dogs for PA Veterans, Hazleton Cold Weather Shelters for local veterans, coordinated numerous military funerals, and assists with cemetery maintenance.

Mr. Speaker, I wish to congratulate Mr. John Nesgoda for receiving the American Veterans (AMVETS) Post 1 of Pennsylvania's Veteran of the Year Award. His years of service, during both active duty and as a veteran, have exemplified his commitment to his country and the military veterans in the Commonwealth of Pennsylvania. On behalf of my constituents, I thank John for his dedication and wish him and his wife Carol all the best in their future endeavors.

HONORING MARY "SCOTTY" O'SULLIVAN

HON. ELIOT L. ENGEL

OF NEW YORK

IN THE HOUSE OF REPRESENTATIVES

Thursday, December 1, 2016

Mr. ENGEL. Mr. Speaker, I rise today to honor a beautiful spirit, Ms. Mary P. O'Sullivan, known commonly around the neighborhood as "Scotty." Mary went to her eternal home April 18th, 2016 surrounded by her loving family and friends. Though she is no longer with us, Scotty's contributions to the community will forever live on, as she has left a lasting impact on all of those she was able to touch in life.

Scotty, along with her husband, the late Jimmy "Sonny" O'Sullivan, were the propri-

etors of "Tara Irish Gift Shop" in Inwood for over 35 years. The store was a local mainstay for decades, selling everything from checkered Irish walking caps and Celtic crosses to green neckties bedecked with little Irish flags. She operated the shop at 609 West 207th Street with Thomas and Kathleen Traynor until 2001, a remarkable run for any business establishment in New York City.

Scotty was also incredibly active in an array of community groups, and was especially active in many Irish-American organizations. She was a long time, beloved active member of the American Irish Association of Westchester and always organized and ran the raffles at the annual Heritage Day. Of course, Scotty's great love was always family. She is survived by her loving in-laws and many nieces & nephews.

Scotty's life was an inspiration, and she will forever be a part of the amazing Irish-American community in New York. I want to thank the American Irish Association of Westchester for honoring her at this year's Annual Dinner Dance.

CELEBRATING SYLVIA ROSENBLATT'S 100TH BIRTHDAY

HON. LOIS FRANKEL

OF FLORIDA

IN THE HOUSE OF REPRESENTATIVES

Thursday, December 1, 2016

Ms. FRANKEL of Florida. Mr. Speaker, I rise today to celebrate Sylvia Rosenblatt, who turned 100 years young in November. Sylvia is a dedicated volunteer in our South Florida community and a beloved mother, grandmother, and great-grandmother.

Throughout her life Sylvia has been committed to helping others. She volunteers for numerous organizations including the Mandel Jewish Community Center and the Forgotten Soldiers Outreach, where she helps pack and ship care packages to soldiers overseas.

I join with Sylvia's friends, family, and the ACE Lifelong Learning Center in celebrating her birthday. I wish her good health and continued success in the coming year.

HONORING MARCUS JOHN BRADSHAW

HON. JANICE HAHN

OF CALIFORNIA

IN THE HOUSE OF REPRESENTATIVES

Thursday, December 1, 2016

Ms. HAHN. Mr. Speaker, I rise today to honor Marcus John Bradshaw, the grandson of Jimmie Bernstein, and a former neighbor of mine when I lived in Long Beach, California. Marcus John Bradshaw was born to John and Sheri (Bernstein) Bradshaw on July 26, 1988, in Hazel Crest, Illinois. Marcus was blessed to have three older brothers, Eric, John and Timothy. Known for his kindness, Marcus was steadfastly loyal and faithful to all who were blessed to know him.

Marcus attended Western Avenue Elementary School in Flossmoor, Illinois, where he played soccer and baseball. Marcus went to

Parker Junior High School in Flossmoor, where he played volleyball, golf, as well as participated in a national chorus. Outside of school, he was a member of a traveling baseball team, for which he played second base. Marcus graduated from Homewood-Flossmoor High School in 2006. He lettered in volleyball, participated in intramural sports, and became an official ball boy for the Chicago Bears. During the 2006 season, Marcus went to the Super Bowl when the Bears played the Indianapolis Colts. His school chronicled his experience as an NFL ball boy for the Chicago Bears in a feature article for its newspaper, the Homewood-Flossmoor High School Voyager. Marcus attended DePaul University, where he participated in the volleyball club and enjoyed playing flag football with friends. In 2010, he earned a Bachelor of Science degree in Business Management.

Marcus began his professional career as a Brand Ambassador for Powerade and Fuze. He was then promoted to Event Manager for Powerade. He also worked as a Construction Coordinator for Goodman Networks. Following his tenure there, he worked for Bradshaw Construction & Management, first as a Field Inspector at Chicago's Midway Airport and then as a Quality Assurance Inspector at O'Hare International Airport. Marcus proved to be a consummate professional, known for his strong work ethic and his consistent punctuality.

His travels included Mexico, the Caribbean islands, Australia, as well as two trips to China including the 2008 Olympics in Beijing. Marcus' sparkling personality, infectious smile, and winning ways reflected his humorous side. He was witty and fun to be around. His favorite pastimes included fantasy football and fantasy basketball. In addition, he skied, continued to play volleyball and golf, and as a testament to his athletic prowess, served as a wide receiver for the Chicago Thunder semi-professional football team.

Marcus truly enjoyed life to the fullest and experienced much in his 27 years. Marcus made his transition to everlasting peace and joy on July 5, 2016, from the rare incurable disease, autoimmune hemolytic anemia. Marcus will forever remain in the minds and hearts of those who love him as his spirit soars with the angels in the presence and love of God.

Marcus is survived by those that honor and cherish his memory including: his parents, John and Sheri Bradshaw; his brother Eric and his wife Ana; his brother John and his wife, Sylvia; his brother Timothy; his maternal grandmother Jimmie Bernstein; as well as a host of loving family members and a legion of friends throughout the nation.

IN RECOGNITION OF JOSHUA, JONLUKE, AND CALEB O'CAIN, AND ALEX MARJANOVICH

HON. BARBARA COMSTOCK
OF VIRGINIA
IN THE HOUSE OF REPRESENTATIVES
Thursday, December 1, 2016

Mrs. COMSTOCK. Mr. Speaker, I rise to acknowledge Joshua, Jonluke, and Caleb O'Cain, and their friend Alex Marjanovich from my district for their charitable service to our veterans through their book collection efforts. Eagle Scout candidate Joshua O'Cain decided on this endeavor for his final project, which consisted of making boxes where people can donate their used books for the children of our nation's veterans and active duty service members. Given the need at Walter Reed National Military Medical Center's pediatric department, these boys decided to focus their efforts at filling their high demand.

I am honored to have these young men living in Virginia's 10th Congressional District. I commend their hard work to help our veterans and their families who make so many sacrifices to preserve freedom and democracy for others. Their project is a reflection on the noble nature of the Boy Scouts of America's continuous work to better our great nation. These young men not only embody charity and selflessness, but are also helping inspire it in others.

The O'Cain family has also strived to help servicemen and women through their work with Military Operation Kindness, an organization which sends troops stationed overseas thank you letters and care packages. Astonishingly, the O'Cain family has sent over 600 of these thank you notes this year alone. I cannot express how grateful I am to the O'Cain family and others like them who do so much to aid the members of our armed forces.

Mr. Speaker, Joshua, Jonluke, and Caleb O'Cain and Alex Marjanovich exemplify a spirit of comradery and a dedication to serving others that makes America truly great. I would encourage my colleagues to join me in thanking these young men for their work to help the families of America's heroes. I wish them all the best in their future endeavors.

HONORING ST. BARNABAS PARISH

HON. ELIOT L. ENGEL
OF NEW YORK
IN THE HOUSE OF REPRESENTATIVES
Thursday, December 1, 2016

Mr. ENGEL. Mr. Speaker, as we in the Bronx and Westchester celebrate the installation of the seventh Pastor of the St. Barnabas Parish, I want to take a moment to celebrate both the Parish's rich history and the wonderful people who make up its congregation.

Established in 1910, the parish was placed under the patronage of St. Barnabas with the Reverend Michael Reilly as the first Pastor. The Parish included what is known as the Woodlawn section of the Bronx and McLean Heights/Yonkers entity, the Church and Rectory were erected on the actual line separating the two cities.

Monsignor George McWeeney was appointed the second Pastor and served until 1965. Under his leadership, a new High School building and Chapel were erected. The third Pastor was Monsignor John J. Considine who served until his retirement in 1986. His twenty-one years as Pastor saw a phenomenal growth in the Parish. The fourth Pastor was Monsignor Timothy S. Collins who served until 1994 when he was appointed Pastor of Our Lady of the Rosary (The Mother Seton Shrine). During his eight years tenure, Monsignor supervised the remodeling of the Rectory, Parish Center and High School Chapel.

The fifth Pastor Monsignor Francis X. Toner was appointed in 1994 until his death in 2003. Msgr. Toner re-organized the parish's services to accommodate the changing demographics of the parish. Monsignor Edward M. Barry, the sixth Pastor, was appointed in 2004. On the occasion of the parish's 100th anniversary Msgr. Barry conducted a fund raiser for the complete renovation of the church, as well as installing an elevator.

And just this year, the St. Barnabas community has warmly welcomed Father Brendan A. Fitzgerald, who served as Pastor of Regina Coeli Parish, Hyde Park, 2012–2016. A native of Ireland, Fr. Fitzgerald has already had a very distinguished career and will no doubt bring great wisdom to the parish. I want to congratulate him on his installation, and congratulate the entire St. Barnabas community.

REMARKS BY FORMER NATO SECRETARY GENERAL ANDERS FOGH RASMUSSEN

HON. STENY H. HOYER
OF MARYLAND
IN THE HOUSE OF REPRESENTATIVES
Thursday, December 1, 2016

Mr. HOYER. Mr. Speaker, I include in the RECORD the text of a speech delivered by former Secretary General of NATO Anders Fogh Rasmussen, who is a dear friend and former Prime Minister of our ally Denmark. He spoke at the "Celebration of Democracy" dinner hosted jointly by the National Democratic Institute and International Republican Institute, and his remarks testify to the strong bonds between our nation and its NATO allies. He also reaffirms a core component of our foreign policy: that the world needs strong American leadership in the years ahead, just as it benefitted from our leadership in the twentieth century.

I'm extremely pleased to see the International Republican Institute and the National Democratic Institute work so closely together in a bi-partisan manner to promote freedom and democracy.

During the last 70 years, we've got used to a world where protectionism was replaced by free trade, closed societies were replaced by open societies, and dictatorship was replaced by democracy. During these 70 years the world has experienced an unprecedented era of peace, prosperity and progress.

Now, we are living in an era where the fear of the consequences of globalization has led to stronger support for protectionism, fear over the influx of immigrants and refugees has led to stronger support for closed borders, the fear of chaos and weak leadership in democracies has led to stronger support for tough men and autocracy.

Under these circumstances, there is a strong need for good men and women who will stand up for the basic ideas upon which we so successfully have built and developed our free societies.

Secretary Albright and Senator McCain are such solid people.

As American ambassador to the United Nations and as Secretary of State you, Madeleine Albright, was a staunch proponent of

American engagement in the Balkans to stop the bloodshed. And it wasn't until the United States took leadership that a lasting peace was created.

As Secretary General of NATO, I asked you to lead the preparations for a new strategic concept. You and your group of experts did an outstanding job, and in 2010, we adopted a new strategic concept for NATO.

Madeleine, you have always been a steadfast fighter for freedom and democracy. And your mood can always be read in the pins you're wearing. In the book, "Read My Pins", you said: "I had this wonderful antique snake pin. So when we were dealing with Iraq, I wore the snake pin". You had balloons, butterflies and flowers to signify optimism and, when diplomatic talks were going slowly, crabs and turtles to indicate frustration.

John, I'm so happy to also be with you tonight. First of all, congratulations on your re-election as US senator. Recently you turned eighty, but if we didn't know, we wouldn't believe it. You are still going strong, and you are setting an example for all of us to continue working as long as we can.

We have met on several occasions in Europe. You have been a frequent guest at the Munich Security Conference, as leader of the US delegation and as a highly valued speaker. We have never doubted your position as one of the strongest American voices in favor of American global leadership and continued engagement in Europe.

You were disappointed that NATO did not engage more in Syria. You also criticized me. Tonight I can tell you, I agreed with you. But I couldn't get the allies to support even prudent planning for an operation.

John, you have always remembered America's friends and allies. I still recall how warmly you thanked me for my personal support for the United States and my country's contribution to international military operations all over the world.

John, we owe you great respect. And I would like to use this occasion to express my admiration and my gratitude for your service to the United States and to the world.

We all know that Secretary Albright and Senator McCain belong to different political parties. But they are united in their desire to see freedom and democracy flourish in the world. Madeleine and John, you represent the very best in the American democracy: the bi-partisan support for American global leadership.

Let me put it directly: the world needs a policeman. The only capable, reliable and desirable candidate for that position is the United States. We need determined American global leadership.

The world is on fire. The Middle East is being torn up by war, terrorism and humanitarian catastrophes that have forced millions of people to flee. Europe is almost sinking under the refugee burden and internal political division. In North Africa, Libya has collapsed and become a breeding ground for terrorists who are spreading instability throughout the region. In Eastern Europe, a resurgent Russia has brutally attacked and grabbed land by force from Ukraine. China is flexing its muscle against its neighbors around the South China Sea. North Korea is a rogue state that threatens its neighbors and the United States with a nuclear attack.

There is a link between the American reluctance to use hard power and this outbreak of fire. If the US retrenches and retreats or even if the world thinks that the US retreats, it leaves behind a vacuum that will be filled by the bad guys.

If the United States withdraws to concentrate on "nation building at home", the forces fighting against liberal democracy and our way of life will gain ground. The US will be faced with stronger foes, weaker friends and a more insecure world. That would definitely not make America great.

Appeasement doesn't lead to peace. It just incites tyrants. Any failure to counter oppression will only invite further oppression. That is the lesson of the twentieth century— a lesson we must never forget.

That's why President Truman established a new, rules-based world order, centered around a series of international institutions and economic programs. He created an American led world order that set the stage for the Cold War. Truman elevated engagement to moral choice directly affecting every single American citizen, because it was based on American values. He said: "I believe that we must assist free peoples to work out their own destinies in their own way."

In 1961, President Kennedy expressed what is probably the strongest commitment to American global leadership ever given by a president of the United States: "Let every nation know, whether it wishes us well or ill, that we shall pay any price, bear any burden, meet any hardship, support any friend, oppose any foe, to assure the survival and the success of liberty."

And President Reagan ended the Cold War peacefully due to his firm conviction that capitalism is superior to communism. He said: "America's economic success is freedom's success; it can be repeated a hundred times in a hundred nations". He was firmly convinced that peace does not come from weakness or retreat. It comes from economic and military superiority. Peace through strength.

President Truman showed strong leadership and effective conduct by establishing the world order that for seven decades secured an unprecedented peace, development and wealth. President Kennedy came to stand as a beacon for the free world with his energetic and eloquent communication. And President Reagan led the United States and the world to the victory over Communism and oppression by his firm conviction of American exceptionalism.

Hopefully, future US presidents will combine President Truman's effective conduct, President Kennedy's inspiring communication and President Reagan's firm conviction. This would prepare the ground for strong American global leadership and a better and safer world. And make America great again.

The United States is indispensable in its ability to protect and promote freedom and to prevent conflicts, to resolve conflicts and to help with post-conflict reconstruction. However, the United States should not be left to carry out that job alone: Smart American leadership should strive for alliance-building.

There is a need to create an overwhelming, credible, and strong democratic supremacy in order to counterbalance the rising and assertive autocracies.

To create a stronger global democratic community, the American president should use his convening power to assemble the world's true democracies in a strong "Alliance for Democracy". It would be a community of shared values, individual liberty, economic freedom, democracy, and the rule of law; a community that would bolster the identity and potency of democracy in a world where the forces of oppression are trying to regain ground.

The Alliance for Democracy could help confront common security challenges, in-

cluding terrorism. It could work to make the liberal capitalist democracies more prosperous, competitive, and attractive by promoting commerce, economic growth and job creation. It could help promote democracy directly through advice, support, and assistance. It could be a forum for the coordination of policies in other international organizations, including push for reforms to make the United Nations more effective. And the Alliance for Democracy could also be used for joint action, particularly humanitarian interventions.

Many of us are inclined to believe that the community of values with the best story will win, that the West won the Cold War because the better world view triumphed, and the progress is inevitable.

However, the rise of autocratic powers and Islamic radicalism reminds us that the victory of democratic powers over oppression is not inevitable and it needs not be lasting. History has taught us that we cannot be complacent.

Thomas Jefferson reminded us that "the price of liberty is eternal vigilance". I will continue dreaming of the predominance of capitalism and liberal democracy. I will not accept the argument that certain people are not well suited for democracy.

In a world that grows in freedom and democracy, people will have a chance to raise their families and live in peace and build a better future. The terrorists will lose their recruits and lose their sponsors and lose safe havens from which to launch new attacks, and there will be less room for tyranny and terror.

But to ensure the progress of freedom and democracy, we must ensure an invincible global balance in favor of the forces of freedom and democracy.

You have just had presidential elections. I don't think the American people have mandated retreat. On the contrary, I believe that the outcome of the elections was a reaction to the receding freedom and democracy and the growing terrorism and autocracy that you have witnessed during recent years.

I trust America and American leadership. Of course, also America makes mistakes. But who else should be the leader of the free world? I'm tempted to quote Winston Churchill who once said that the Americans will always do the right thing—after having tried everything else.

Ladies and gentlemen, the world's democracies must rise to the challenge. America must exercise determined global leadership.

HONORING ANDREA M. BROWN

HON. ELIOT L. ENGEL
OF NEW YORK
IN THE HOUSE OF REPRESENTATIVES
Thursday, December 1, 2016

Mr. ENGEL. Mr. Speaker, I rise today to recognize a community servant who has for years worked to improve the lives of her friends and neighbors in Yonkers, Ms. Andrea M. Brown.

Andrea was born and bred in Westchester, the eldest of eight children in Tarrytown, NY. She attended the Tarrytown public schools, Westchester Business School, and Westchester Community College. She began her community service when she was in her teens, in high school clubs and through her church. In 1970 she married and moved to Yonkers and began her community service in

1974 by volunteering at her oldest daughter's pre-kindergarten class at School 25 and joining the Parent's Group at the Nepperhan Community Center, which led to her becoming a Board Member and eventually Board President.

Andrea's volunteer work only grew from there. She has served her community as President of the Yonkers Branch of the NAACP; Trustee for the Yonkers Board of Education; 1st Vice President of the Empire State Federation of Women's Club, Westchester Region; Member of the Yonkers Mayor's African American Advisory Board; and Vice President of Aquehung Women's Democratic Club, just to name some of her work. She has also received numerous awards for her efforts, including the Martin Luther King Commission Profile Award; the Bethany Lutheran Church Woman of the Year Award; the Women's Civic Club of Nepperhan Woman of the Year Award; The Nepperhan Community Center Community Service Award; and the Dominican Cultural Association Community Service Award.

But for all of her accomplishments, Andrea's greatest treasure was always family. She was married to the late Bernard G. Brown, Sr. and is the mother of two adult children, three grandchildren and two great-grandchildren.

The Yonkers Democratic Committee is honoring Andrea this year at their Annual Road to Victory Dinner. Congratulations to her on this great honor.

SHIPPENSBURG UNIVERSITY FIELD HOCKEY WINS DIVISION II NATIONAL CHAMPIONSHIP

HON. LOU BARLETTA
OF PENNSYLVANIA
IN THE HOUSE OF REPRESENTATIVES

Thursday, December 1, 2016

Mr. BARLETTA. Mr. Speaker, it is my honor to recognize the Shippensburg University field hockey team as the 2016 NCAA Division II National Champions. Shippensburg, which is a university in my district, has always been about serving the educational, social and cultural needs of their students, both in the classroom and beyond. The Red Raiders defeated Long Island University Post by a score of 2 to 1 on Sunday, November 20, 2016, capping a 20 win season that was dedicated to former student-athlete and coach, Amanda Strous.

All season long, a number 22 jersey hung in the Robb Sports Complex in honor of Amanda Strous, a former student-athlete and coach at Shippensburg who tragically passed away before the start of the 2016 season. The mantra "Live, Laugh, Love" and hashtag "FlyHigh22" served as inspiration for the team as they sought to "Leave a Legacy" in honor of Amanda.

Shippensburg's emotional season concluded on a cold, fall day at the W.B. Mason Stadium at Stonehill College in Easton, MA. Winning three consecutive games as the lower seed, the No. 3 seeded Red Raiders were lifted to victory by goals from junior forward Emily Barnard and senior forward Katelyn Grazan. Finishing the year as the national leader in goals

against average (0.46), save percentage (.899) and shutouts (14), Shippensburg is only the second team in tournament history to emerge from their region as a No. 3 seed and win a national championship.

Mr. Speaker, it is with admiration and respect that I congratulate the Shippensburg University field hockey team for winning the 2016 NCAA Division II National Championship. Such an emotional season could not have a better ending, and I am confident that they will continue to achieve great things both on the field and in the classroom. On behalf of my constituents, I wish the Red Raiders all the best as they enjoy this accomplishment and look forward to next season.

H. CON. RES. 165

HON. DOUG COLLINS
OF GEORGIA
IN THE HOUSE OF REPRESENTATIVES

Thursday, December 1, 2016

Mr. COLLINS of Georgia. Mr. Speaker, today I rise to commend the House on passage of H. Con. Res. 165, which reaffirms Congress' approach to Israel and Palestine. This bipartisan resolution supports the long-standing approach of the United States as a facilitator of bilateral negotiations between Israel and Palestine. It properly recognizes that a lasting resolution to the Israeli-Palestinian conflict will only come about through direct, mutual negotiations between the two parties. Attempts by Congress or other outside bodies to interfere with bilateral negotiations by establishing parameters or imposing solutions on Israel and Palestine will inevitably complicate the situation and delay its peaceful resolution.

Since 1972, the United States has opposed and vetoed 42 United Nations Security Council resolutions dictating binding parameters on the peace process. The current Administration has time and again refused to aid Israel by tolerating Palestinian threats, harming the U.S.-Israeli relationship, and undermining Israel's peacemaking efforts. Israel is our strongest ally in the Middle East, and I believe the country deserves our full support. I have consistently demanded this Administration recognize the importance of Israel, and today's resolution provided another opportunity to affirm my commitment to our relationship with that nation. I strongly urge continued opposition to efforts by the UN Security Council to force agreements that are one-sided or anti-Israel.

Israel has continuously demonstrated its willingness to coexist with its neighbors, and the United States must promote direct talks between Israelis and Palestinians, not the international intervention of the United Nations or other bodies. Through passage of this resolution, the House of Representatives publicly reaffirmed our support for bilateral negotiations between Israel and Palestine, demonstrated the strength of our relationship with Israel, and rebuked faulty attempts to impose the terms of peace.

I was proud to join my colleagues in support of this important resolution.

ROBIN PERKINS NAMED WOMAN OF THE YEAR BY THE GREATER MANASSAS CHRISTMAS PARADE COMMITTEE

HON. BARBARA COMSTOCK
OF VIRGINIA
IN THE HOUSE OF REPRESENTATIVES

Thursday, December 1, 2016

Mrs. COMSTOCK. Mr. Speaker, I rise to congratulate Robin Perkins on being named Woman of the Year by the Greater Manassas Christmas Parade Committee. Mrs. Perkins has diligently served the Manassas community for many years and is more than deserving of this honor.

A lifelong resident of Manassas and devoted community leader, Mrs. Perkins has served her hometown for 33 years in the City of Manassas treasurer's office. After fifteen years of service in that office, she was elected to serve as Treasurer for the City of Manassas. Now, after over eighteen years of service as Treasurer, Mrs. Perkins is entering into a well-deserved retirement.

Though she is leaving her post as Treasurer, Mrs. Perkins will remain a fixture of the Manassas community. She serves as a scout leader, a youth bowling director, and has been a long-time volunteer with the city schools. Her lifelong dedication to her community is an inspiration and I'm proud to represent such a wonderful woman.

Mr. Speaker, I ask that my colleagues join me in congratulating Robin Perkins for being named Woman of the Year by the Greater Manassas Christmas Parade Committee. It is a privilege to represent her and I wish her all the best in her future endeavors.

HONORING THE LIFE OF DEBRA SAUNDERS-WHITE

HON. ROBERT C. "BOBBY" SCOTT
OF VIRGINIA
IN THE HOUSE OF REPRESENTATIVES

Thursday, December 1, 2016

Mr. SCOTT of Virginia. Mr. Speaker, I rise today to mourn the loss of one of our nation's finest public servants, Dr. Debra Saunders-White. She was a good friend and a tireless advocate for increasing access to higher education for all students. This past Saturday, Debra Saunders-White passed away, and I would like to take a brief moment to celebrate her life and legacy.

For many years, Debra Saunders-White was a leading voice in education as she fought to strengthen historical black colleges and universities and other minority serving institutions. As a first generation college graduate, Debra understood both the opportunities afforded by higher education and the many challenges that accompany students as they attempt to access and afford a higher education.

A native of Hampton, Virginia, she attended the University of Virginia before receiving her Masters of Business Administration from the College of William and Mary and her Doctorate in Higher Education Administration from George Washington University. After completing her education, Mrs. Saunders-White spent 15 years in the private sector, working for IBM as a systems engineer before transitioning to marketing.

From 1999 until 2006, Dr. Saunders-White served as the Assistant Provost of Technology at Hampton University. While at Hampton, she designed and implemented the university's first information technology organization. Her efforts made Hampton University the first HBCU in the nation to join the Internet2 community, where they earned the "most wired university" title by Forbes Magazine and the Princeton Review.

Ultimately, Dr. Saunders-White left Hampton University and spent some time at the University of North Carolina Wilmington (UNCW) as the Vice Chancellor and later served as the Deputy Assistant Secretary at the Department of Education in President Obama's administration. In 2011, Mrs. Saunders-White became the 11th chancellor of North Carolina Central University. During her tenure, Dr. Saunders-White was held in high regard by all of her colleagues and students. Known for her strong vision and leadership, Debra was extremely dedicated to ensuring the success of the students at NCCU while she carried out her vision for growth at the university.

Mr. Speaker, the education and NCCU communities have lost a tremendous advocate for our nation's students. I want to extend my deepest sympathies to her two children, Elizabeth Paige and Cecil III; her mother, Irene Saunders; her brothers, Roger, Ralph and Kyle Saunders, and the rest of her family, friends, and countless students she positively impacted during her life.

HONORING THE LIFE AND WORK OF NORTH CAROLINA CENTRAL UNIVERSITY CHANCELLOR DR. DEBRA SAUNDERS-WHITE

HON. G. K. BUTTERFIELD
OF NORTH CAROLINA
IN THE HOUSE OF REPRESENTATIVES
Thursday, December 1, 2016

Mr. BUTTERFIELD. Mr. Speaker, I rise today to honor the life and work of Dr. Debra Saunders-White, a dear friend, nationally recognized academic, and the eleventh Chancellor of North Carolina Central University in Durham, North Carolina. Dr. Saunders-White transitioned to her heavenly home on Saturday, November 26, 2016 after a courageous battle with cancer. She will be greatly missed by the entire NCCU family and all who knew her.

Dr. Saunders-White was born in Hampton, Virginia on January 8, 1957. As a first-generation college student, she received her undergraduate training at the University of Virginia in Charlottesville. Graduating in the Class of 1979 with a Bachelor's degree in history, Dr. Saunders-White went on to receive a Master's of Business Administration from the College of William and Mary (in 1993) and a Doctorate in Higher Education Administration from George Washington University (in 2004).

The massive outpouring of accolades that arose upon Dr. Saunders-White's passing speaks to her character and abilities. She was installed as the eleventh chancellor of my alma mater, North Carolina Central University, on June 1, 2013. And, I might add, she became the first permanent woman chancellor in the University's 106-year history.

Prior to assuming her duties at NCCU, she served as the acting Assistant Secretary for the Office of Postsecondary Education at the U.S. Department of Education in the Obama Administration under Secretary Arne Duncan. Dr. Saunders-White joined the Department of Education in May of 2011 as the Deputy Assistant Secretary for higher education programs.

Throughout her tenure as NCCU's Chancellor, Dr. Saunders-White made many important contributions to the University, including increasing the freshman-to-sophomore retention rate from 69 percent to 80 percent; growing faculty and staff annual giving from 19 percent to 76 percent; creating the Triangle area's first dual-enrollment, residential transfer program known as Eagle Connect, in conjunction with Durham Technical Community College; and opening a Fabrication Laboratory in 2015 that is part of a select number of such laboratories at HBCUs.

Always committed to uplifting Historically Black Colleges and Universities, Dr. Saunders-White was named a "cyber star" by Black Issues in Higher Education and has published articles and whitepapers on the role of technology in learning. At NCCU, she was instrumental in raising scholarship funds for students and prioritized innovative academic instruction to prepare students of color to be competitive in the global marketplace.

Beyond her academic contributions, what is more illuminating of Dr. Saunders-White's stellar character was the way she connected with students at the university. She took a personal interest in the scholarship and mentorship program by encouraging "Eagle Excellence" that went beyond success in the classroom. Her dedication to scholarship and preserving the legacy of our Historically Black Colleges and Universities earned her the respect and admiration of students and colleagues alike.

It is dedicated leaders like Dr. Debra Saunders-White whose passionate commitment to helping all students succeed will leave a lasting mark on the future of our students and our country. NCCU (and all of those connected with institutions of higher learning) have lost a great educator and friend. Mr. Speaker, the Nation has lost a great educator.

Dr. Saunders-White is survived by two children, Elizabeth Paige White and Cecil White, III; her mother, Mrs. Irene Saunders; and her brothers, Roger, Ralph, and Kyle. I hope the outpouring of love shared by the community has been a comfort to Dr. Saunders-White's family.

Today, we remember Dr. Debra Saunders-White and reflect on her motto 'Eagle Excellence.' That motto, which Dr. Saunders-White embodied in her work each day, will remain embedded in the fabric of the University for generations to come.

This is indeed a solemn occasion. But it's also an occasion to celebrate. Dr. Saunders-White fought the good fight, kept the faith, and was a friend to so many and we are all thankful that she was able to touch so many lives. I ask my colleagues to join me in celebrating the life, work, and legacy of Chancellor Debra Saunders-White.

HONORING WILLIAM STALLINGS

HON. ELIOT L. ENGEL
OF NEW YORK
IN THE HOUSE OF REPRESENTATIVES
Thursday, December 1, 2016

Mr. ENGEL. Mr. Speaker, I rise today to honor one of Yonkers' most active and dedicated community members, William Stallings, who is being honored at this year's Yonkers Democratic Committee Annual Road to Victory Dinner.

Originally a product of Charleston, South Carolina, Bill attended public school and became very active in the civil rights movement in his junior and senior years of high school. Upon completion of Burke High School he began working at the Citadel, the military college of South Carolina. After a year, he applied to Tuskegee Institute in Alabama and was accepted. At Tuskegee, he enrolled in the Air Force ROTC and was commissioned 2nd Lieutenant upon graduation. His bars were pinned on him by his grandmother and General Daniel "Chappy" James, and while in the Air Force, he reached the rank of Captain.

It was a recruitment by Pepsi Cola that ultimately brought Bill to Westchester County, where he has remained ever since. He became active in the local Democratic Party in 1974 by engaging in local voter registration drives, and later became a District Leader. He is a member of the NAACP and is very active in his church, Greater Centennial AME Zion Church. He has been an officer of the church for over 25 years, was President of the Greater Centennial Federal Credit Union for over 20 years, and is a founding member of the Greater Centennial Community Development Corporation. Bill has also served on the Board of Directors of the Human Development Services of Westchester (HDSW) for the past 20 years and on the Yonkers Democratic City Executive Committee for over 20 years.

Few have done more to help their local community thrive than Bill Stallings. He is most deserving of this wonderful recognition.

TRIBUTE TO DR. HIRAM SPAIN, JR.

HON. JAMES E. CLYBURN
OF SOUTH CAROLINA
IN THE HOUSE OF REPRESENTATIVES
Thursday, December 1, 2016

Mr. CLYBURN. Mr. Speaker, I rise to congratulate a great American, and outstanding South Carolinian, Reverend Dr. Hiram Spain, Jr. Dr. Spain, who was simply Hiram to me when we shared classes and hallways at South Carolina State College, is retiring from public service. Dr. Spain served as Executive Secretary of the Baptist Educational and Missionary Convention of South Carolina since his election in 2000 until his recent retirement.

Dr. Hiram Spain, Jr. is a native of Conway, South Carolina. In addition to graduating with honors from South Carolina State University, he received the degree of Juris Doctor from Howard University. He did additional studies at the University of South Carolina, Morris College Extension and the Columbia International

Seminary. He is presently pursuing the Master of Divinity degree at the Lutheran Theological Southern Seminary. Dr. Spain was ordained by the Gethsemane Baptist Association and retired as Pastor of the Saint Mark Baptist Church in Columbia, South Carolina.

During my tenure on the staff of Governor John West, I brought Dr. Spain on board where he headed the program that became the state's first Office of Rural Development to outstanding success. He has served as the Chief Executive Officer of the Columbia Urban League and as the first Black Bureau Chief of the South Carolina Department of Social Services.

Dr. Spain serves his community in several civic capacities, including the Board of The United Black Fund of the Midlands, The Executive Board of the Gethsemane Baptist Association, The Board of the South Carolina Christian Action Council, past Board Member of the Communities in Schools of South Carolina, member of the Interdenominational Ministerial Alliance of Greater Columbia, Board Member of the I.D. Quincy Newman Institute for social change at the University of South Carolina, Board Member of Partnership, South Carolina, and a life member of Kappa Alpha Psi Fraternity, Inc.

He has received numerous awards and honors for his civic and community service and was recently honored by the City of Columbia and the Midlands Authority for Conventions, Sports and Tourism for his outstanding service and leadership. He has never been reluctant to give of his time and energies to civic, professional and community service organizations. His favorite Bible verse is Psalm 121 verses 1 and 2, "I will lift up mine eyes to the Hills, from whence cometh my help. My help cometh from the Lord, which made heaven and earth."

Dr. Spain is married to the former Doris Bush, a Benedict College graduate and retired teacher at W.A. Perry Middle School. They are the parents of two adult children, both of whom are social work administrators.

Mr. Speaker, I ask that you and this Congress join me in wishing this outstanding South Carolinian, and longtime personal friend, the Reverend Dr. Hiram Spain, Jr., a long and productive retirement.

IN RECOGNITION OF THE 85TH ANNIVERSARY OF THE FAIRFAX ROTARY CLUB

HON. BARBARA COMSTOCK
OF VIRGINIA
IN THE HOUSE OF REPRESENTATIVES
Thursday, December 1, 2016

Mrs. COMSTOCK. Mr. Speaker, I rise to honor the Fairfax Rotary Club on their 85th Anniversary of community service this year. The Fairfax Rotary Club was chartered in 1931 and has grown from the original 16 members to 75 members today. This organization brings enormous benefit to the City of Fairfax and surrounding communities. I am very grateful for Fairfax Rotary Club's continued efforts to provide humanitarian service and assistance in the 10th Congressional District.

The Fairfax Rotary Club holds weekly meetings and organizes numerous charitable events in order to benefit the community. Their activities range from fundraising to acts of hands-on community service. Some examples of their generous deeds include creating college scholarships for local students, doing home repairs free of charge, providing free meals to families in need, and raising money for many other charitable causes, such as polio and access to clean water.

The members of the Fairfax Rotary Club are true pillars of their community, and I am proud to represent such service-minded citizens. This organization has a history of providing a setting that fosters fellowship between its members and that enables them to have a positive impact in the world. I applaud the Fairfax City Council's decision to honor this organization by declaring September 25th Fairfax Rotary Club Day in the city.

Mr. Speaker, I ask my colleagues to join in recognizing the 85th Anniversary of the Fairfax Rotary Club and thanking its members for all of the selfless community service work they undertake. I hope that the members of this service organization will continue to find success in their endeavors for many years to come.

HONORING JUDGE TODD J. CAMPBELL

HON. JIM COOPER
OF TENNESSEE
IN THE HOUSE OF REPRESENTATIVES
Thursday, December 1, 2016

Mr. COOPER. Mr. Speaker, I rise today to recognize Judge Todd J. Campbell on his retirement from the federal bench.

A graduate of Vanderbilt University and the University of Tennessee College of Law, Judge Campbell started his legal career in private practice. After the 1992 election, he joined President-elect Bill Clinton's transition team and later became counsel to Vice President Al Gore.

In 1995, President Clinton nominated Judge Campbell to fill a vacant seat on the U.S. District Court for the Middle District of Tennessee. Judge Campbell was confirmed the same year by the U.S. Senate, becoming one of America's youngest federal judges in modern times. He eventually was elevated to chief judge, serving many years in that role.

Judge Campbell has led a distinguished career on the federal bench, and he is a pillar of our community. For example, he has led more than 100 naturalization ceremonies, often relating his own family immigration history to Middle Tennessee's newest citizens.

Federal Public Defender Henry Martin best captured Judge Campbell in a recent letter to the editor published in The Tennessean newspaper:

Judge Todd Campbell's announced retirement as a United States District Judge last week was sad news to anyone interested in justice in this community.

I am confident that every lawyer and litigant experienced what I saw there for 20-plus years: an exceedingly well-prepared judge who favored neither side, but treated all who appeared before him with respect, courtesy

and usually a smile. I always warned lawyers about to appear in Judge Campbell's court for the first time to be prepared: "he will have read every case you cited, that your adversary cited and ask you about cases you missed that he had found. Then he would listen."

The challenge of determining what the law is in a particular situation and then applying it fairly to complex facts, where the outcome has a life-changing impact on the people in the case is not only intellectually demanding, but emotionally and physically exhausting. It can also be lonely and thankless work. And yet, Judge Campbell always took the time to thank the lawyers who took indigent defense appointments and was quick to proclaim how important their work was to the preservation of constitutional liberties.

The founders of this country knew that the viability of a society operating under the rule of law depended on the selection of judges who had the intellect to decipher the law, the common sense to shape it to fit human behavior and the courage and integrity to decide controversial issues regardless of popular sentiment.

For better than 20 years Judge Campbell gave exactly that to this community. We are the better for that service and owe him our utmost gratitude.

Henry A. Martin, Federal Public Defender, Nashville 37203.

Judge Campbell has dedicated himself to the federal bench every day he has served. I want to thank Judge Campbell, his wife, Margaret, and their children, Seth and Holt. Judge Campbell represents the very best of our judicial traditions, and I thank him for his long and patriotic service.

HONORING WILLIAM SCRIBNER

HON. ELIOT L. ENGEL
OF NEW YORK
IN THE HOUSE OF REPRESENTATIVES
Thursday, December 1, 2016

Mr. ENGEL. Mr. Speaker, I rise today to honor the life of an amazing artist and a true friend, William Scribner. Bill as he was better known brought so much light and beauty to the Bronx through his music, and his contributions to our borough will never be forgotten.

Renowned as one of New York's finest bassoonists, Bill always looked for ways to share his amazing gift with the world and spread his love of music to others. In 1972, he founded the Bronx Arts Ensemble, the premier professional music organization in the Bronx. With a mission to "nourish the arts in the Bronx, serving its diverse communities and developing audiences through arts education and musical performances of the highest professional standard," the organization has touched the lives of thousands of people over the years with their unique performances and beautiful shows. This is largely due in part to Bill's exceptional work, and the amazing assemblage of talent he nurtured and put together.

In addition to presenting over 100 concerts a year, the Bronx Arts Ensemble also specializes in an arts-in-education programming in over 40 schools in the Bronx and beyond with instruction in music, drama, dance, visual arts, capoeira, drumming and more.

Yet for all of Bill's incredible work bringing the arts to the Bronx, his first love was always his family. The beloved husband of Marsha Heller and loving father of Andrew Scribner, Bill is also survived by sister Janice Freeman, cousin Nancy Wirth, stepson Joshua Marantz, and first wife Louise Scribner.

Bill brought so much joy to our community, and enriched the lives of so many. Through the Bronx Arts Ensemble his legacy shall forever live on, and for that I am very thankful. It is an honor to celebrate his amazing life here today.

IN RECOGNITION OF FRAN PAVLEY OF AGOURA HILLS

HON. TED LIEU

OF CALIFORNIA

IN THE HOUSE OF REPRESENTATIVES

Thursday, December 1, 2016

Mr. TED LIEU of California. Mr. Speaker, I rise today to celebrate the retirement of my friend Senator Fran Pavley. I had the honor of serving with Fran in both the State Assembly and State Senate. Fran is an extraordinary individual who strove to ensure her community, state, and nation's best interests came first. Her legislative accomplishments are legendary.

Over the last 14 years, Fran became a titan when it came to developing innovative climate change solutions. Her laws elevated California's status as a global leader in fighting climate change and promoting sustainable clean energy. Her bill AB 32, of which I was a coauthor, became a model for climate change legislation in other states, nationally and internationally.

With California experiencing severe drought, Fran championed smart water policy by encouraging conservation, recycling, storm water capture, and ground water clean-up. Fran also passed legislation that increased fuel efficiency standards in California. Her law was then modeled at the federal level.

Fran also introduced legislation to encourage more college students to become teachers. In 2015, California had 43,000 teacher vacancies and one of the highest student-teacher ratios in the country. To reduce this burden, Fran presented legislation that would reinstate a loan forgiveness program to motivate more students to pursue a career in teaching.

In addition to Fran's exemplary record of protecting the environment and supporting teachers, she also passed a law that allowed women to receive up to a 12 month supply of birth control prescriptions at one time. Passage of this law was lauded by many health care providers because it reduced the stress of having women acquire birth control on a monthly or quarterly basis.

These tremendous accomplishments cut across various fields and demonstrate Fran's enormous impact. Fran's legacy in the community, state and country will be felt for generations to come.

Actually, this is Fran's second retirement. Prior to serving 14 years in the legislature, Fran was a beloved middle school teacher for 28 years.

After retiring, Fran will continue to spearhead the creation of the first urban and largest wildlife crossing at Liberty Canyon in Agoura Hills. I wish Fran, her husband, and children many years of happiness and good health.

LIBYA

HON. TED POE

OF TEXAS

IN THE HOUSE OF REPRESENTATIVES

Thursday, December 1, 2016

Mr. POE of Texas. Mr. Speaker, for six months, the U.S.-backed troops of the interim Libyan Government of National Accord has been fighting street by street to retake the ISIS stronghold of Sirte on the Libyan coast.

ISIS seized control of the city in early 2015 and extended its control along about 155 miles of Libya's coastline. That means that ISIS wields its influence over a territory roughly the distance from Houston to San Antonio.

How did the U.S. get here? How did Libya become an incubator for all stripes of terrorists?

In 2008, U.S. military leaders were calling Libya a top U.S. ally in combating international terrorism. Qaddafi realized that his regime was the target of terrorism, and he changed course from supporting terrorists in the 1980s to siding with the U.S. against the terrorist threat.

However, in 2011, in the midst of a rebellion against the Qaddafi regime, the U.S. decided to intervene and establish a no-fly zone to aid the Libyan rebels.

Under the safety of the no-fly zone the U.S. imposed, Islamist terrorist groups long subdued under Qaddafi's regime sprung up and amassed weapons, training, and military training.

Qaddafi was ultimately killed in October 2011. Within days, NATO and U.S. forces packed up and left Libya to its own devices. America's only Libya policy at the time was to remove Qaddafi—there was little planning regarding what to do the day after. The U.S. opened the Pandora's box and looked away.

Almost immediately after Qaddafi's ouster, Libya spiraled into chaos. Long simmering political, regional, and ethnic divisions suddenly emerged and set Libya on a path towards disaster. The country has never recovered.

Even the Administration has admitted its role in Libya's failure. Earlier this year, the President admitted that there was no plan for post-Qaddafi Libya, describing it as his biggest regret as President.

Libya has become a regional and international security threat due to this Administration's lack of planning. ISIS and al-Qaeda are the main beneficiaries.

Al-Qaeda's Libyan affiliate, Ansar al-Shariah, emerged shortly after Qaddafi's death and has since become deeply entrenched in the country.

They have successfully filled the void the U.S. helped create by providing social services—building schools and providing medical care.

But they did not stop there. They recruited, armed, and trained terrorist fighters intent on carrying out the group's ultimate goal: imposing Islamic law on the country.

Ansar al-Shariah fighters were among those who ultimately attacked the U.S. diplomatic compound in Benghazi in 2012, killing Ambassador Christopher Stevens and three of his colleagues.

Since then, things have gotten worse. ISIS announced the establishment of a Libyan affiliate at the end of 2014 and soon began consolidating its power around Sirte and expanding east, west, and south.

America should not fool itself into believing that once Sirte is liberated the ISIS threat is over. For close to a year now, ISIS has been redirecting recruits and even senior leaders to Libya. It has been laying the seeds for what many have called a "fallback Caliphate," where it could retreat to in case it is pushed out of Syria and Iraq.

Pentagon estimates from earlier this year suggested that the group's ranks in Libya have swelled to nearly 7,000 fighters.

Liberating Sirte will simply transform the ISIS threat in Libya from a concentrated one to a dispersed one. They have fanned out throughout the country and will continue to exploit the political mess in Libya.

Libya will unfortunately remain a terrorist foothold for years to come. This is the legacy of the current Administration in North Africa.

The mess the U.S. have left there has spread throughout the region. It endangers Egyptian allies to the east, and the weapons unleashed with Qaddafi's fall have fueled terrorism in places like Syria, Nigeria, and the Sinai Peninsula bordering Israel.

The United States' airstrike campaign in support of the Libyan forces retaking Sirte is only a small step. Until the U.S. can devise a truly comprehensive long-term strategy to stabilize Libya and defeat the terrorist groups hiding there, Libya will continue to threaten regional and international security. Treating the symptoms while ignoring the underlying disease will not solve the problem.

The U.S. forcibly overthrew a regime in Libya, creating chaos that led to a failed state where terrorists flourished and thousands of Libyans died. The U.S. now has a responsibility to work towards a stabilizing solution in Libya. Going forward, the U.S. should be much more cautious before it helps overthrow another regime.

IN RECOGNITION OF CONGRESS-MEN ROBERT HURT, RANDY FORBES, AND SCOTT RIGELL

HON. BARBARA COMSTOCK

OF VIRGINIA

IN THE HOUSE OF REPRESENTATIVES

Thursday, December 1, 2016

Mrs. COMSTOCK. Mr. Speaker, I rise today to honor three colleagues of mine who have served their Districts and the Commonwealth of Virginia with distinction. Congressman ROBERT HURT from Virginia's Fifth District, Congressman RANDY FORBES from Virginia's Fourth District, and Congressman SCOTT RIGELL from Virginia's Second District have dedicated years of their lives to public service.

Since coming to Congress in 2001, RANDY FORBES, as Chairman of the House Armed Services' Seapower and Projection Forces Subcommittee, has worked to build a stronger defense for America to help ensure the safety of our nation and has worked with all of us to help our veterans. He also made it a priority to foster partnerships with local officials and other community leaders, earning a reputation for stellar constituent service as a representative.

Congressman SCOTT RIGELL has more active duty and retired military personnel in his district than any other district and has made it a priority to assist them. He had a major role in keeping all East Coast aircraft carriers based in Norfolk.

I had the distinct pleasure of serving with Congressman HURT in the Virginia General Assembly, where he served beginning in 2001 before running for Congress, and he is a gentleman, statesman, constitutional scholar, and most important of all a true friend to the Commonwealth of Virginia. ROBERT has been a leader here in Washington with his great work on the Financial Services Committee and striving to help our small businesses as well as veterans, to name just some of the ways he has worked for a better life for those in his District.

While the Commonwealth of Virginia loses three committed public servants in this body, we all greatly appreciate the years they have put into advancing the priorities of their constituents and the lives of all those in Virginia and in our country.

I know they will continue to serve the public in a variety of ways.

Mr. Speaker, I ask my colleagues to join me in thanking and honoring these gentlemen for their service to their Districts and for representing their constituents and the Commonwealth in which we call home.

PERSONAL EXPLANATION

HON. ROBERT HURT

OF VIRGINIA

IN THE HOUSE OF REPRESENTATIVES

Thursday, December 1, 2016

Mr. HURT of Virginia. Mr. Speaker, I was unavoidably detained. Had I been present, I would have voted YEA on Roll Call No. 590, and YEA on Roll Call No. 591.

HONORING LOUIS A. PICANI

HON. ELIOT L. ENGEL

OF NEW YORK

IN THE HOUSE OF REPRESENTATIVES

Thursday, December 1, 2016

Mr. ENGEL. Mr. Speaker, as the son of an ironworker and former union member myself, I know firsthand just how critical our area's union members are to our country's shared prosperity and success. This year, the Yonkers Democratic Committee is honoring Louis Picani, a dedicated union member who has fought for working men and women in Westchester for over 30 years.

Louis has spent his entire career as a visionary, fighting for workers' rights, fair wages and benefits, workplace safety, and the right to organize. He has been a dedicated union member since he joined Teamsters Local 456 over 30 years ago, where his natural leadership ability quickly emerged and enabled him

to be appointed Shop Steward for the City of Yonkers Department of Public Works in 1992. In 1994, Louis became a Trustee of the Teamsters Health and Welfare Fund. In 2005, he was elected as a Teamsters Local 456 Trustee and appointed as a Teamsters Local 456 Business Agent. Louis has been a member of Joint Council 16's New York Teamsters Political Action Committee, and in 2016, was elected President and Principal Officer of Teamsters Local 456. He also serves as Vice President of the Westchester Putnam Central Labor Body.

But Louis' good works extend beyond his labor advocacy. Incredibly, he is also a licensed drug and alcohol counselor.

Louis continues to represent Teamsters members and all labor organizations who serve our work force so proudly. He is incredibly deserving of this honor and recognition, and on behalf of the 16th Congressional District I want to congratulate him on this special occasion.

CELEBRATING THE 75TH ANNIVERSARY OF THE CIVIL AIR PATROL

HON. JANICE D. SCHAKOWSKY

OF ILLINOIS

IN THE HOUSE OF REPRESENTATIVES

Thursday, December 1, 2016

Ms. SCHAKOWSKY. Mr. Speaker, I rise today to recognize the 75th anniversary of the Civil Air Patrol, celebrated on December 1st and to honor its all-volunteer members. Since 1941, volunteers have lent their talents in dedicated service to protect Americans and our nation. Their work is deeply appreciated.

The Civil Air Patrol came into existence just six days before the events of Pearl Harbor and was comprised of many civilian aviators, including women and African Americans who were not allowed to fly for the military at that time. Members flew in support of defense forces and provided the military with professional and cost-efficient assistance, which they have continued to provide ever since—chartered by Congress as non-combative, humanitarian force in 1946, becoming the official Auxiliary to the U.S. Air Force in 1948, and most recently becoming part of the U.S. Air Force's Total Force in 2015.

The Search and Rescue efforts of the Civil Air Patrol are credited with saving an average of 75 lives every year and their Disaster Relief efforts and ability to work closely with partner organizations have been vital to our nation's security and wellbeing. Their service was particularly notable following the terrible events of September 11th, 2001, Hurricane Katrina, and Hurricane Sandy.

I am proud to call myself a member of the Civil Air Patrol. Earlier this week, I was presented with the grade of Lieutenant Colonel and membership in the Patrol's Congressional Squadron. The distinction was presented to me by Lieutenant Colonel Harold Damron and two wonderful young members of the Civil Air Patrol from my district, Cadet Second Lieutenant Laivi Grossman and Cadet Airman Basic Nancy Kahdeman. I thank them and the entire Civil Air Patrol for this opportunity.

The organization's Cadet Program has been a tremendous resource to this nation, pro-

viding leadership training to youth, ages twelve through twenty-one. The Program promotes education in the fields of Science, Technology, Engineering, and Math, both for participants within the program and their local communities. This is done with a focus on Aerospace and Aviation, developing a passion for them in our younger citizens and ensuring our preeminence in these areas as well as Cyberspace. I believe this effort to be especially important now, as our nation's future and security depend upon the ability of the next generation to lead global progress in these areas.

Civil Air Patrol volunteer professionals serve in every state of the nation and as nonprofit resources within thousands of communities. I am proud to support the work that these men and women continue to do, and I am very pleased to be celebrating this milestone anniversary with them.

IN HONOR OF THE 155TH ANNIVERSARY OF THE BATTLE OF BALL'S BLUFF

HON. BARBARA COMSTOCK

OF VIRGINIA

IN THE HOUSE OF REPRESENTATIVES

Thursday, December 1, 2016

Mrs. COMSTOCK. Mr. Speaker, I would like to honor the 155th Anniversary of the Battle of Ball's Bluff fought in Loudoun County, Virginia, on October 21st, 1861. Being one of the earliest battles of the American Civil War, Ball's Bluff had an enormous impact on military affairs for the remaining four years of conflict.

On October 20th, 1861, Brigadier General Charles Pomeroy Stone and the Union forces under his command engaged the Confederate forces of Colonel Nathan Evans on the banks of the Potomac River near Leesburg, Virginia. Stone's forces had crossed the river and were subsequently repelled and defeated by their Confederate counterparts. This battle was unique in American history because, as Union forces were withdrawing across the Potomac, Colonel Edward Baker, a sitting U.S. Senator, was killed in action. The defeat, coupled with Colonel Baker's death, was the catalyst for the creation of the Congressional Joint Committee on the Conduct of the War. Colonel Baker remains the only United States Senator killed in battle, and Ball's Bluff proved to be indicative of the long war to come.

Mr. Speaker, I ask my colleagues to join in recognizing the 155th Anniversary of the Battle of Ball's Bluff. We must always remember and honor those who sacrificed their lives to preserve our nation in its darkest hour.

HONORING JOHN DeCICCO JR.

HON. ELIOT L. ENGEL

OF NEW YORK

IN THE HOUSE OF REPRESENTATIVES

Thursday, December 1, 2016

Mr. ENGEL. Mr. Speaker, I rise today to recognize a leader in our community, John DeCicco Jr. whose humanitarian work is being recognized by The Pelham Civic Association at their Annual Dinner Dance Gala. John is one of three honorees for "Persons of the Year" on November 4, 2016 in my district.

John is the President and CEO of DeCicco & Sons Food Markets. He is a longtime volunteer member of the Pelham Civics, a major contributor to Pelham Civics "Needy Cases Program," which provides food baskets for hundreds of needy families. He also spearheaded the Pelham Civics' 75th Anniversary Dinner Dance Journal in 2014, raising over $12,000.

John is known for his countless acts of altruism, philanthropy, and charity. He has worked with The Veterans of Foreign Wars, The Wounded Warriors, The Boy and Girl Scouts in an effort to support the community and those in need. He was the recipient of the 2015 Rotary Club of the Pelhams Award for his work supporting children and families.

John also works closely with career placement for special needs students, was a Past Advisory Board Member for the Fordham University Graduate School of Business Entrepreneurship, a former Junior Board Member for the Westchester Italian Cultural Center, Past President of the Pelham Chamber of Commerce, and has worked closely with Governor Cuomo, County Executive Rob Astorino, ConEdison, and NYSERDA in leading an effort to promote "GREEN Markets for the Future" the first of which was opened in Larchmont in December of 2015. The store, which is founded on the principle of being environmentally friendly, has received the EPA's Green Chill Platinum Certification.

John's business, DeCicco & Sons, is also a long-time contributor to Pelham School PTAs, and was the recipient of the 2015 New York State PTA Congress "Golden Oak Award" for exemplary support of the school districts, PTAs and students. DeCiccos also received the 2015 Westchester's Best Family-Owned Business Award, for continued commitment and active support to the communities in which they live and work, the 2016 Independent Green Business of the Year Award. John married Luisa DeCicco, Ph.D., another honoree, and have two children.

It is an honor to present John with a CONGRESSIONAL RECORD at The Pelham Civic Association Annual Dinner Gala. I want to thank him for all he has done in the community and all he continues to do on behalf of Pelham. Congratulations to all honorees of the evening.

HOUSE OF REPRESENTATIVES—*Friday, December 2, 2016*

The House met at 9 a.m. and was called to order by the Speaker.

PRAYER

The Chaplain, the Reverend Patrick J. Conroy, offered the following prayer:

Loving God, we give You thanks for giving us another day.

In the waning days of this 114th Congress, we ask Your blessing upon the Members of this people's House, and most especially upon the leadership. It is on their shoulders the most important negotiations of this Congress have been placed.

They have been entrusted by their fellow Americans with the awesome privilege and responsibility of sustaining the great experiment of democratic self-government. Give them wisdom, grace, insight, and courage to forge legislation that allows us all to move forward toward an encouraging future.

May all that is done this day be for Your greater honor and glory.

Amen.

THE JOURNAL

The SPEAKER. The Chair has examined the Journal of the last day's proceedings and announces to the House his approval thereof.

Pursuant to clause 1, rule I, the Journal stands approved.

Mr. WILSON of South Carolina. Mr. Speaker, pursuant to clause 1, rule I, I demand a vote on agreeing to the Speaker's approval of the Journal.

The SPEAKER. The question is on the Speaker's approval of the Journal.

The question was taken; and the Speaker announced that the ayes appeared to have it.

Mr. WILSON of South Carolina. Mr. Speaker, I object to the vote on the ground that a quorum is not present and make the point of order that a quorum is not present.

The SPEAKER. Pursuant to clause 8, rule XX, further proceedings on this question will be postponed.

The point of no quorum is considered withdrawn.

PLEDGE OF ALLEGIANCE

The SPEAKER. Will the gentleman from Washington (Mr. KILMER) come forward and lead the House in the Pledge of Allegiance.

Mr. KILMER led the Pledge of Allegiance as follows:

I pledge allegiance to the Flag of the United States of America, and to the Republic for which it stands, one nation under God, indivisible, with liberty and justice for all.

ANNOUNCEMENT BY THE SPEAKER

The SPEAKER. The Chair will entertain up to five requests for 1-minute speeches on each side of the aisle.

APPRECIATING MARINE LIEUTENANT COLONEL TRANE McCLOUD

(Mr. WILSON of South Carolina asked and was given permission to address the House for 1 minute and to revise and extend his remarks.)

Mr. WILSON of South Carolina. Mr. Speaker, sadly, this weekend marks the 10-year anniversary of the death of Marine Lieutenant Colonel Joseph Trane McCloud, a former Military Fellow in my office, an American hero.

Trane served in the office in 2003, promoting democracy and freedom. As an Active-Duty marine, Trane provided incredible insight into defense and national security issues. I am grateful that I had the opportunity to work with Trane, and it was a privilege to see his firsthand dedication to the Marine Corps, but equally to his wife, Maggie, and their three young children.

Trane was tragically killed in Iraq on December 3, 2006, when the helicopter he was riding in malfunctioned and was forced to make an emergency landing. In an interview in The Washington Post, Maggie described her husband as "a man of character and honor," words that I know accurately describe Trane.

To his wife, Maggie; their three children, Hayden, Grace, and Meghan; and the rest of the family: You are in my thoughts and prayers. His service will never be forgotten. Trane lived up to the highest ideals of the U.S. Marine Corps, semper fidelis.

In conclusion, God bless our troops, and may the President, by his actions, never forget September the 11th in the global war on terrorism.

For Trane, with General Jim Mattis, we will achieve victory to protect American families.

GRANT FOR COMPOSITE RECYCLING CENTER

(Mr. KILMER asked and was given permission to address the House for 1 minute.)

Mr. KILMER. Mr. Speaker, today I rise to talk about jobs and economic opportunity for the region I represent. In my hometown of Port Angeles, Washington, we recently opened up a new innovative center focused on composite manufacturing. This composite recycling center, one of the first in the Nation, is already showing that the peninsula can be a hub for groundbreaking innovation.

Just yesterday, they won a national investment, a grant from the U.S. Department of Commerce, that will give entrepreneurs the tools that they need to take yesterday's recycled parts and turn them into advanced products.

It will also encourage the growth of quality jobs in my region, investing in local citizens so that they can build careers working with composites. This is a terrific example, to use a Wayne Gretzky quote, of local economic developers skating to where the puck is going to be; and I want to congratulate the folks back home. I look forward to continuing to be a partner in the effort to bring good jobs to our neck of the woods.

CONGRATULATING THE LA SALLE LANCERS

(Mr. CHABOT asked and was given permission to address the House for 1 minute.)

Mr. CHABOT. Mr. Speaker, last night, my alma mater, the La Salle Lancers, did it again. They won their third straight Ohio high school football championship. By the way, my brother Dave and I both played for La Salle back in the day.

La Salle faced a tough Massillon Perry team in the championship game for the second straight season. The Lancers' back-to-back-to-back championships capped off a historic 2016 football season in which La Salle won its first outright GCL South championship, and became the first ever three-peat Division II champions in Ohio playoff history.

I also want to wish one of La Salle's rival teams, the St. X Bombers, the best in their quest to win the Division I championship this evening.

Again, congratulations to all of the La Salle players and their families, to Coach Jim Hilvert and his coaching staff, and to everyone involved with the Lancer football program. You have all made the entire Cincinnati area extremely proud.

Lancers roll deep.

WE WILL NOT END MEDICARE

(Mr. CICILLINE asked and was given permission to address the House for 1 minute.)

Mr. CICILLINE. Mr. Speaker, this is Trudy Willis. Trudy and her husband, William, are lifelong residents of Middletown in my district in Rhode Island. They have three children and four wonderful grandchildren.

Like millions of Americans, Trudy relies on Medicare to pay for her healthcare needs. For Trudy, Medicare isn't an entitlement; it is a benefit that she and millions of Americans have earned and is a promise our government made.

That is why I am disappointed that President-elect Donald Trump has announced he will appoint a Secretary of Health and Human Services who wants to end Medicare as we know it.

Let me be very clear. President-elect Trump does not have a mandate to end the guarantee of Medicare. He lost the popular vote by about 2.5 million votes. We are not going to let him kill one of the most effective tools that seniors have to live their retirement years with dignity.

If Republicans bring up legislation to end Medicare, we will stop this legislation dead in its tracks. We did it a decade ago when President George W. Bush tried to privatize Social Security, and we will do it again. And by doing so, we will maintain the promise we have made to Trudy and millions of seniors across our great country.

HONORING CONGRESSMAN JOHN KLINE

(Mr. THOMPSON of Pennsylvania asked and was given permission to address the House for 1 minute and to revise and extend his remarks.)

Mr. THOMPSON of Pennsylvania. Mr. Speaker, I rise today to recognize a great friend and leader, Congressman JOHN KLINE, who will be retiring at the end of this Congress. He has served the citizens of Minnesota's Second District in the U.S. House since 2002. A 25-year veteran of the Marine Corps, he also serves on the House Armed Services Committee.

I have had the honor of serving with JOHN KLINE on the Education and Workforce Committee for 8 years. He has chaired this committee as a great advocate for education and how this creates greater opportunity for all.

His steady leadership has navigated Congress to successfully developing and advancing legislation to improve job training, elementary and secondary education, career and technical education, and so much more. His service has truly made a difference throughout our Nation.

In addition to serving under Chairman KLINE's leadership, I have enjoyed the privilege to share a weekly Bible study with JOHN.

Thank you, and best wishes to Congressman JOHN KLINE and his wife, Vicky, for their service to the Nation.

ALLOW THE DREAMERS TO SUCCEED

(Mr. O'ROURKE asked and was given permission to address the House for 1 minute.)

Mr. O'ROURKE. Mr. Speaker, because of the inaction of this Congress, our President, in 2012, deferred action on childhood arrivals to this country, young boys and girls who were brought here at the tender age of 3 or 5 or 6 or 7, who are now flourishing in our communities and making this great country even better.

I call your attention to one of my constituents, Claudia Yoli, who arrived in this country at the age of 8 from Venezuela, interned in my office in 2013, and now works for our great State Senator Jose Rodriguez, and is making El Paso, Texas, and America an even greater place to live.

Unfortunately for Claudia, her mother had to return to Venezuela in 2010 and, because of her status, Claudia was not able to follow. Her mother died last year, and Claudia was unable to return to be with her mother in her dying days and to grieve with her family and be with them.

We owe Claudia and the 750,000 other DREAMers in this country certainty; and we certainly owe them something better than what the President-elect has promised, which is to terminate this deferred action.

So I ask this body, I ask the President-elect, and I ask every American to join together to make sure that we allow these DREAMers to succeed, because their success means America's success.

HONORING EXPLOSIVE ORDNANCE DISPOSAL TECHNICIANS WHO MADE ULTIMATE SACRIFICE

(Mr. CRAWFORD asked and was given permission to address the House for 1 minute.)

Mr. CRAWFORD. Mr. Speaker, this year marks the 75th anniversary of Explosive Ordnance Disposal in our Nation's Armed Forces, and their mission is even more important and dangerous today than it was 75 years ago. Today I rise to honor two EOD techs who gave their lives in just the past few weeks to keep others safe from harm.

U.S. Navy EOD Senior Chief Petty Officer Scotty C. Dayton, age 42, was killed in Syria on Thanksgiving Day, the 24th of November, 2016, in the ongoing conflict in Syria against ISIS. He died from wounds sustained from an improvised explosive device. Assigned to EOD Mobile Unit Two, Virginia Beach, Virginia, he was operating with Combined Joint Task Force-Operation Inherent Resolve near the ISIS stronghold of Raqqa. He is survived by his wife, Kristin; and two children, Hailey and Cole.

EOD Chief Jason Finan, age 34, was killed near Mosul, Iraq, 20 October, 2016. He also died from wounds sustained from an IED. Assigned to Mobile Unit Three, Coronado, California, he was operating while deployed with Navy SEALs, advising Iraqi forces in operations against ISIS and retaking the city of Mosul. He is survived by his wife, Chariss; son, Christopher; and mother, Gloria.

As a Nation, we will be forever grateful for the ultimate sacrifice both of these men made in service to their fellow sailors and their country. In this 75th year of Explosive Ordnance Disposal, please take the time to remember the important role that EOD techs play in our national security and the risks they take every day to keep us safe.

HONORING THE SERVICE OF GIBBIE BUCHHOLTZ

(Mr. DOLD asked and was given permission to address the House for 1 minute and to revise and extend his remarks.)

Mr. DOLD. Mr. Speaker, I rise today to honor Gibbie Buchholtz from Zion, Illinois. Gibbie has lived in Zion his entire life and works tirelessly to bring our community together. He works part time as a cameraman for the Zion Park District filming city council and township meetings.

Gibbie has become a staple in the community, documenting almost every single event in Zion, from local park openings to volunteer events at soup kitchens, to police and firefighter awards. He promotes events and special moments that often go unnoticed, and he recognizes individuals that go above and beyond.

It has been an honor and a privilege to work alongside him in the Zion community. Gibbie never asks for recognition behind the camera, and only asks that people cherish the special moments with others.

Today I am honored to be able to give Gibbie a little bit of recognition for his great service to our community.

Thank you, Gibbie, and keep up the great work.

RECESS

The SPEAKER pro tempore (Mr. THOMPSON of Pennsylvania). Pursuant to clause 12(a) of rule I, the Chair declares the House in recess subject to the call of the Chair.

Accordingly (at 9 o'clock and 13 minutes a.m.), the House stood in recess.

□ 1000

AFTER RECESS

The recess having expired, the House was called to order by the Speaker pro tempore (Mr. DOLD) at 10 o'clock and 1 minute a.m.

CONFERENCE REPORT ON S. 2943, NATIONAL DEFENSE AUTHORIZATION ACT FOR FISCAL YEAR 2017

Mr. THORNBERRY. Mr. Speaker, pursuant to House Resolution 937, I call up the conference report on the bill (S. 2943) to authorize appropriations for fiscal year 2017 for military activities of the Department of Defense, for military construction, and for defense activities of the Department of Energy, to prescribe military personnel strengths for such fiscal year, and for other purposes, and ask for its immediate consideration.

The Clerk read the title of the bill.

The SPEAKER pro tempore. Pursuant to House Resolution 937, the conference report is considered read.

(For conference report and statement, see proceedings of the House of November 30, 2016, at page 14795.)

The SPEAKER pro tempore. The gentleman from Texas (Mr. THORNBERRY) and the gentleman from Washington (Mr. SMITH) each will control 30 minutes.

The Chair recognizes the gentleman from Texas.

GENERAL LEAVE

Mr. THORNBERRY. Mr. Speaker, I ask unanimous consent that all Members may have 5 legislative days in which to revise and extend their remarks and insert extraneous material on the conference report to accompany S. 2943.

The SPEAKER pro tempore. Is there objection to the request of the gentleman from Texas?

There was no objection.

Mr. THORNBERRY. Mr. Speaker, I yield myself 5 minutes.

Mr. Speaker, I am pleased to bring to the House the conference report for the Fiscal Year 2017 National Defense Authorization Act. Once the President signs this measure into law, it will be the 55th consecutive year in which Congresses of both parties and Presidents of both parties have enacted a defense authorization bill.

I want to start by thanking the distinguished gentleman from Washington, Ranking Member SMITH. Not only has he focused on what is good for the troops and good for the country in this bill, that has been his focus throughout this Congress. It has certainly been my pleasure to work with him toward that end. We do not always agree on what is good for the troops and what is good for the country, but we always agree that that comes first. Our work together has certainly been productive, and I appreciate that opportunity.

Ranking Member SMITH and I have a terrific team on the Armed Services Committee; 63 outstanding members, all of whom have contributed to this product. I certainly appreciate the contributions they have made that have made such a large bill possible.

Mr. Speaker, this bill does good things for the men and women who serve our Nation in the military, and it supports our country's national security. I want to just touch on a few of the highlights, starting with the fact that this bill authorizes spending of $3.2 billion more than the President has requested. Now, that is not nearly enough, and my great hope is that the new incoming administration will submit to Congress a supplemental request that can really get about the job of rebuilding the military, which is so essential.

The $3.2 billion, in addition to what the President has requested, is focused on people; and that is exactly what the primary focus of this bill is. So, for example, it provides the full pay raise to which the troops are statutorily entitled for the first time in 6 years; that is in this bill. It stops the layoffs of military personnel, which have been going on, and, at least, prevents it from getting any worse.

It starts to stabilize the readiness problems that are making it more and more difficult for our troops to accomplish their mission and increasingly represents a danger to their lives.

It improves the military healthcare system for the benefit of our troops and their families so that they will have a more consistent experience, that they will get better care, more convenient hours, and a number of things that are in this bill.

In addition to the reforms related to military health care, there are a number of very significant reforms in other areas. For example, in acquisition, we try to make sure that not only we get more value for the taxpayer dollars but that we are more agile in being able to get new technology into the hands of the warfighters faster.

We have commissary reform, which maintains the benefit but reduces the burden on the taxpayers.

We have the first comprehensive rewrite of the Uniform Code of Military Justice in 30 years, and that is a big part of the reason that this bill is the size that it is.

We have organizational reform that streamlines the bureaucracy and helps reduce the overhead so more resources can go to the front lines.

There are many items in this bill, Mr. Speaker, from replenishing munitions of which we have shortages to dealing with the California National Guard repayment issue that has come up in recent weeks.

Other speakers will give more detail about many of those provisions. I just want to take this moment, first, to thank the staff on both sides of the aisle for their work in producing this product. We have a unified staff on the Armed Services Committee. We work together to solve problems. And through the ups and downs of the political calendar and all of the other issues that impact our bill, they have done a terrific job in getting us to this point

and have served the Nation by doing so. I want to express my appreciation to staff on both sides for that work.

Finally, I also want to pay tribute to the members of our committee who will not be with us in the next Congress for a variety of reasons. They include the gentleman from Virginia (Mr. FORBES), the gentleman from Florida (Mr. MILLER), the gentleman from Minnesota (Mr. KLINE), the gentleman from Louisiana (Mr. FLEMING), the gentleman from New York (Mr. GIBSON), the gentleman from Nevada (Mr. HECK), the gentleman from Florida (Mr. NUGENT), the gentlewoman from California (Ms. LORETTA SANCHEZ), the gentlewoman from Illinois (Ms. DUCKWORTH), the gentlewoman from Florida (Ms. GRAHAM), and the gentleman from Nebraska (Mr. ASHFORD).

I particularly want to thank Subcommittee Chairman RANDY FORBES, Subcommittee Chairman JOE HECK, and Ranking Member LORETTA SANCHEZ for their leadership and years of contributions to the military of our country. We will miss them.

I reserve the balance of my time.

Mr. SMITH of Washington. Mr. Speaker, I yield myself such time as I may consume.

First of all, I want to say that this is an excellent product. It was not easy to pull together. It is a very large bill with a lot of very important issues. As Chairman THORNBERRY indicated, a lot of people contributed to it. Certainly, everybody on our committee, but then many Members who aren't on the committee in the House and, of course, our friends in the Senate. We all worked together and found a way to get through the areas of disagreement and to get to a very good bill, with the central thought that it is our job in passing this bill to give the men and women who serve us in the Armed Services all of the tools they need to do the job we ask them to do.

So I really want to echo Chairman THORNBERRY's comments and thank our staff, first of all, for the outstanding work that they have done in putting together this product. I thank the Members for their contribution. Also, perhaps most importantly, I thank Mr. THORNBERRY for his leadership as the chairman of the committee.

I have been on this committee for 20 years, and we have had a tradition from the moment I showed up and before then that this is a bipartisan committee that is focused on getting its work done. Whatever the hurdles, whatever the difficulties, whatever the disagreements, we know how important it is to produce this bill and how important it is to our troops who are fighting to protect us and provide the national security that we need.

Mr. THORNBERRY has upheld that tradition. We have had many chairmen in those 20 years. They have all had that first and foremost in mind. This is not a partisan committee. This is a committee that works together to get its job done. Mr. THORNBERRY has done an outstanding job of that. He has certainly been an excellent partner for me, and we even found a way to work with the Senate and then made that work. So I thank all of those people who contributed to this.

Chairman THORNBERRY is also right. I think that the most striking thing about this bill is how much it does to help reform the way things are done at the Department of Defense. There is much on acquisition reform, all aimed at trying to get the taxpayers more for the money they spent. Because the chairman is right, as in many areas of government, there are more needs than there is money.

What we have to do is try to figure out how to make that money go as far as possible. Acquisition reform is a key part of that. We really struggled in the early part of the 21st century with a lot of programs that went overbudget. We are still dealing with the legacy of some of that, but very proud that, in the last few years, that has declined, as we have passed acquisition reform, and as we have figured out better ways to get things in the field, into service more quickly, commercial, off-the-shelf technology, more improvements in our acquisition. That is critical if we are going to be able to use the scarce resources we have to the best of our ability. So we put together an excellent product.

Also, as Chairman THORNBERRY mentioned, we do have the full pay raise for the troops that they need and desperately deserve. I will just close by saying, I think, that is the thing that you can really see from this bill. It prioritizes the men and women who serve in the military to try to make sure that we provide for them, give them all the training they need and all the support they need so that when we ask them to do something, they are trained and ready to do it. I really believe that is the most important thing that we do on this committee.

We can have many, many debates about what our national security strategy should be, where we should employ our forces, how we should use them, and what equipment we should provide for them. But the one thing that we have to agree on is, whatever we decide the mission should be, we have to make absolutely certain that we provide the men and women everything they need to be ready to carry out that mission so that we do not send them into a fight unprepared. I think we are doing a very good job of that.

There are many challenges ahead, as the chairman noted. We have a lot of demands. We do not have an infinite amount of money. So we are going to keep working hard to try to figure out how to make that money go as far as possible.

Again, I want to thank all the people who worked on this process. This, I think, is an example of how Congress should work, how legislation should work, people working together, having differences, working them out, and producing a product that improves our Nation and, in this case, improves the quality of national security.

Again, I thank Chairman THORNBERRY. I think this is an excellent bill. I urge passage.

I reserve the balance of my time.

Mr. THORNBERRY. Mr. Speaker, I yield 2 minutes to the distinguished gentleman from Virginia (Mr. FORBES), chairman of the Seapower and Projection Forces Subcommittee.

Mr. FORBES. Mr. Speaker, I rise in support of the National Defense Authorization Act for Fiscal Year 2017.

I want to thank Chairman THORNBERRY for his leadership in bringing to the floor this National Defense Authorization Act and for his incredible contribution to the national defense of this country. I also would like to recognize the efforts of Congressman SMITH, who is the ranking member, for his dedication and commitment to get this bill to the floor.

During the last 8 years, our military readiness has been impacted and our force structure has declined. For example, naval aviation has only 3 in 10 Navy jet aircraft that are fully mission capable. Aircraft carrier gaps in critical regions persist. Navy ship deployments have increased almost 40 percent, and submarine demand continues to outpace availability.

As to the Air Force, our B–1 fleet was pulled back from the Persian Gulf this year because of engine maintenance issues and replaced with B–52s that are over 50 years old. I think everyone would agree that these are disturbing trends.

It is obvious that we need to concurrently increase readiness and invest in critical capabilities to ensure that our Nation is capable of projecting force and deterring conflict in the future. A 350-ship Navy is a minimal investment in ensuring our Nation's strategic priorities.

I urge that our NDAA does a good job in arresting our national security's general decline. With the increases in force structure for the Army and the Marine Corps and a 2.1 percent pay raise for our servicemembers, these are good first steps, but we have a long way to go with getting our military ready to defend our Nation. With the election of President-elect Trump, I am optimistic as to our ability to make our military truly great again.

With this being my last NDAA, I want to thank all the members of the House Armed Services Committee and, most specifically, Ranking Member JOE COURTNEY. I have often said that our Seapower and Projection Forces Subcommittee is likely the most bipar-

tisan subcommittee in Congress, and I think that Ranking Member COURTNEY has been a resolute supporter of our national security. I will miss working with him on a daily basis to improve our Nation's military.

Once again, I thank Chairman THORNBERRY and urge my colleagues to support the National Defense Authorization Act.

☐ 1015

Mr. SMITH of Washington. Mr. Speaker, I yield 3 minutes to the gentleman from Connecticut (Mr. COURTNEY).

Mr. COURTNEY. Mr. Speaker, I rise to offer my strong support for the 2017 defense bill conference report.

This bill is the result of extraordinary work by Chairman THORNBERRY and Ranking Member SMITH, who, despite the extremely polarized environment of the 114th Congress, have managed to produce two bipartisan defense bills this year and last. The degree of difficulty accomplishing that feat cannot be overstated. I congratulate them both.

As ranking member of the Subcommittee on Seapower and Projection Forces, I am particularly pleased with the final bill. Working together, the members of our subcommittee produced a strong mark that makes important investments in new shipbuilding as well as introducing new acquisition reform that will strengthen our Navy. Nine new ships are authorized in the final bill, continuing to boost the numbers of our fleet that is on a path to 308 ships by 2021. As the Secretary of the Navy has publicly stated, the Department is on the verge of releasing a new naval force structure assessment that will call for raising that target even higher. Today's bill provides a sound footing to take on that task with enough work in the shipyards that produce amphibs, destroyers, and submarines to go to a higher level in short order.

To be clear, our subcommittee did not just rubberstamp the administration's budget. For example, the agreement pluses up critical advanced procurement funding for the Virginia class submarine program to ensure that the two-a-year build rate continues on its current pace. Given the important role that our submarines play in our Nation's defense, we cannot let that build rate slip by underfunding advanced procurement.

This agreement also authorizes a new national security multimission vessel that will replace the aging training ships at our Nation's maritime academies. This program is vital to ensuring that we retain a maritime workforce in the future, and this agreement puts us on that path.

I am particularly pleased that the measure also includes language that I helped to author with Chairman

FORBES in the House bill to enhance the National Sea-Based Deterrence Fund. Our language adds new authorities to the fund that will help reduce costs in the Ohio Replacement Submarine by procuring and building key components in an efficient level-loaded manner.

The Navy estimates that we could save as much as 25 percent of the total cost of the missile compartment alone with this new authority. At a time when we are looking to grow the fleet while also meeting the multigenerational commitment of Ohio replacement, this approach to reducing costs in shipbuilding is absolutely vital.

I want to conclude by saluting Chairman FORBES as he begins a new chapter in his life. I have seen firsthand the impact that he has made on our fleet, our shipbuilding industry, and, most importantly, the lives of sailors, marines, airmen, and mariners touched by his work, which has always been conducted in a bipartisan manner. I thank him for his service and express my hope that we will see him continue his work in these areas in whatever opportunity comes his way next.

I also want to salute the staff, and in particular Lieutenant Commander Jonathan Cebik, who is a Navy fellow in my office who is finishing up his duties in the next few days or so. He did great work in terms of advising not just my office, but also the subcommittee.

I thank all the Members of our panel for their hard work on this year's defense bill, and I urge my colleagues to vote "yes" on this agreement.

Mr. THORNBERRY. Mr. Speaker, I yield 2 minutes to the gentleman from South Carolina (Mr. WILSON), the distinguished chairman of the Subcommittee on Emerging Threats and Capabilities.

Mr. WILSON of South Carolina. Mr. Speaker, I thank Chairman MAC THORNBERRY for yielding. I am grateful for his success in promoting peace through strength.

I am in strong support of the National Defense Authorization Act of 2017. Generations of my family have served our Nation in uniform. My father was a Flying Tiger in India and China during World War II. I served for 31 years in the Army Reserve and South Carolina Army Guard. I am grateful to have four sons who have served in the military overseas in the global war on terrorism.

I know firsthand the positive impact this year's NDAA will have on our troops, veterans, and military families. After passing this bill, I look forward to telling my constituents at Fort Jackson, adjacent to McEntire Joint Air Base, neighboring Fort Gordon, and the thousands of veterans and countless families concerned about the safety of our citizens that Congress has done its job, just as it has for the past 54 years, by passing a defense authorization bill.

In this bill, readiness is first, protecting our servicemembers overseas and on training missions at home. Cybersecurity is enhanced, protecting American families and encouraging public-private partnerships. We are fully resourcing our Special Operations Forces and providing critical support to fight Islamic terrorists, including counter-propaganda measures. We have increased oversight by requiring a report from the President on Iran as it aggressively acts on ICBMs.

This bill is clear, if our enemies attack our soldiers and American families with new and unconventional attacks, we will ensure our military has the tools to respond. As chairman of the Subcommittee on Emerging Threats and Capabilities, I am very grateful as a military veteran and as a grateful dad that this is a very positive NDAA.

I would like to close again by thanking Chairman THORNBERRY for his remarkable persistence throughout this year's reforms. We also have been fortunate to have the visionary leadership of subcommittee chairman RANDY FORBES, who has successfully promoted a vibrant Navy. I additionally want to thank our ranking members ADAM SMITH and JIM LANGEVIN for their bipartisan manner. This bill will enable President-elect Donald Trump and the incoming Defense Secretary Jim Mattis to establish peace through strength.

Mr. SMITH of Washington. Mr. Speaker, I yield 2½ minutes to the gentlewoman from Guam (Ms. BORDALLO), the ranking member on the Subcommittee on Readiness.

Ms. BORDALLO. Mr. Speaker, I commend Chairman THORNBERRY and Ranking Member SMITH and the committee staff who have worked many, many long nights on this year's defense bill.

This conference report provides funding levels that work to address readiness shortfalls, a process that takes time and will continue to require stable, consistent funding. Unfortunately, that is something that we are not afforded under sequestration and reliance on continuing resolutions.

I also appreciated the efforts to fight in conference for the provisions that were important to the territory of Guam. In particular, I am pleased that the restrictions are lifted for remaining water and wastewater civilian infrastructure projects, as well as for the construction associated with the cultural artifact repository, and that military infrastructure projects were authorized at the President's budget request level.

I thank again Ranking Member SMITH for working with me to get a provision through conference mandating a review of distinguished Asian American and Pacific Islander veterans who may have been unjustly over-

looked in the Medal of Honor consideration. We must never overlook the past contributions of our brave men and women in uniform.

To that end, I am also heartened to see the inclusion of the Guam war claims. It is time that we bring resolution to the people of Guam after 70 years and all U.S. citizens who have suffered under enemy occupation during World War II. We have advanced this legislation this far in the past numerous times, but I hope that my colleagues in the Senate will also pass this critical legislation. Ultimately, finding an offset for this legislation has helped to bring resolution to the matter. The people of Guam deserve to close this chapter in our history.

I look forward to this bill passing the House as well as the Senate before being signed into law by the President later this month.

Mr. THORNBERRY. Mr. Speaker, I yield 2 minutes to the gentleman from Ohio (Mr. TURNER), the distinguished chair of the Subcommittee on Tactical Air and Land Forces.

Mr. TURNER. Mr. Speaker, I rise in support of the National Defense Authorization Act for Fiscal Year 2017.

Mr. Speaker, consideration of this important bill comes at a critical time for our Nation and for our military. Under the leadership of Chairman THORNBERRY, this bill, if funded, begins the process of rebuilding our military and restoring readiness back into the force. The bill stops the harmful end-strength reductions in our military service and it begins the process of reversing this damaging trend in reducing our military capacity. I thank CHRIS GIBSON, my colleague, for his efforts in ending those end-strength reductions.

The bill provides an additional $600 million to address shortfalls of critical munitions. I want to repeat that. We had to put in $600 million to address shortfalls in munitions. That is how much we are suffering in our military in spending.

The bill also continues to address the needs of the National Guard and Reserve components by authorizing an additional $250 million for equipment modernization for the Guard and the Reserve. Additionally, this bill calls for continued action to eradicate sexual assault in the military by providing greater transparency in the military criminal justice system. It also acknowledges the need for intensive treatment for male victims and continues to address the critical issues of retaliation.

This bill also includes important provisions on the protection of child custody rights of our members of the Armed Forces. However, it is important to note that the military services submitted over $22 billion of unfunded requirements for fiscal year 2017 alone. I had hoped we would be able to address these modernization shortfalls, as we did in the House-passed bill. This bill falls short of the House-passed bills. It is also essential that we begin to correct these funding shortfalls in the next Congress. Currently we have a lack of readiness and a heightened level of risk.

I look forward to working with the new Trump administration in regards to an early supplemental request to fully fund these requirements, and I would expect that the House-passed bill would be used as the minimum starting point in order to start the process for rebuilding our military and working with our allies to create conditions for credible U.S. deterrence. It saddens me that we might pass this bill fully funding the military and then pass a CR that underfunds our military.

Before I conclude, I thank our subcommittee's ranking member, Ms. LORETTA SANCHEZ, who has truly been my dear friend. She will be sorely missed. I will miss her guidance and her friendship.

Mr. SMITH of Washington. Mr. Speaker, I yield 3 minutes to the gentlewoman from California (Mrs. DAVIS), the ranking member of the Subcommittee on Military Personnel.

Mrs. DAVIS of California. Mr. Speaker, I thank Chairman THORNBERRY and Ranking Member SMITH for their leadership during this process.

The conference report includes many provisions that will provide the military services flexibility to recruit and retain members of our Armed Forces and to continue our commitment to taking care of military families. One provision I would like to highlight expands maternity leave for military members up to 12 weeks in conjunction with the birth of a child and authorizes 6 weeks of leave for the primary caregiver in the case of adoption. For the first time, it also grants 21 days to the secondary caregiver for both the birth of a child and adoption.

The conference report also begins to reform and modernize the military healthcare system by standardizing military treatment facilities across the services and increasing access for beneficiaries. The conference report reforms TRICARE into an HMO and a PPO system, but, unfortunately, it establishes a two-fee structure for the next 50 years, thus creating an inequity in a defined benefit for military retirees. I sincerely hope we can continue to work towards a better solution in the future.

Although it is not perfect, this bill is a necessary step toward ensuring our servicemembers, retirees, and their families continue to receive the best, the most efficient, and the most economical health care possible.

While I do agree with the increase in end strength for the military services in the conference report, I am still concerned about how it is paid for, espe-cially with a possible continuing resolution until April. If the fiscal year 2017 defense appropriations bill does not contain the $3.2 billion in OCO for this increase, the services, particularly the Army, may be forced to reprogram from other critical accounts or give pink slips to dedicated soldiers.

Lastly, I thank Chairman JOE HECK for his 2 years of leadership and bipartisanship on the subcommittee. His dedication to working with me and other members of the subcommittee on behalf of our servicemen and -women and their families is a credit to himself and his values as a public servant. I will miss working with him.

Mr. THORNBERRY. Mr. Speaker, I yield 2 minutes to the gentleman from Alabama (Mr. ROGERS), the distinguished chair of the Subcommittee on Strategic Forces.

Mr. ROGERS of Alabama. Mr. Speaker, I commend the chairman for his leadership in bringing the 55th consecutive NDAA across the finish line. This legislation includes vital provisions, such as a pay raise for our troops, a fix to the end strength, and it begins to address the readiness crisis that is literally claiming the lives of our men and women in uniform.

A special thank-you goes to my friend, the subcommittee ranking member, Mr. COOPER. He is a pleasure to work with—Roll Tide.

The conference report includes critical provisions resulting from oversight of the Subcommittee on Strategic Forces. For example, regarding the national security space, it enables a rational transition to the end of our reliance on the Russian RD–180 engine. The agreement prioritizes funding for U.S. replacement of the RD–180 engine. It rejects the Air Force strategy to pay for three new launch systems to commercial providers. In fact, the Air Force should only hold its industry day and take no further action until the new administration has a chance to conduct a full cost policy and legal analysis. It gives the Air Force one final opportunity to meet warfighter requirements and bring order to the Department's space-based weather collection program.

Concerning our nuclear forces and nuclear enterprise, the conference report prohibits funding for the administration's misguided proposal to accelerate dismantlement of retired nuclear weapons, authorizes an additional $100 million in funding to help pay for and address the massive infrastructure problems and deferred maintenance backlogs in the NSA, and gives the Air Force one final chance to appropriately prioritize the strategic missile warning system.

Concerning missile defense, the conference report restricts funding for the Army's Lower Tier Air and Missile Defense radar modernization program. The chief wanted more acquisition au-thority. The bill gives it to him, and I expect him to use it.

□ 1030

I am also proud to see the conference report includes language to repeal the cold war-minded National Missile Defense Act, which sought to limit U.S. missile defense deployments. It provides full funding of the request of our allies in Israel for $600 million for co-development and coproduction of Iron Dome, David's Sling, and Arrow 3.

Mr. SMITH of Washington. Mr. Speaker, I yield 3½ minutes to the gentleman from Rhode Island (Mr. LANGEVIN), the ranking member of the Subcommittee on Emerging Threats and Capabilities.

Mr. LANGEVIN. Mr. Speaker, I begin by thanking Ranking Member SMITH, Chairman THORNBERRY, and Chairman WILSON for their tireless work on this bill, as well as all the work on behalf of the staff of the full Armed Services Committee and my personal staff, Kathryn Mitchell and Amanda Donegan.

Mr. Speaker, there is a lot to be proud of in the conference report before us today. This legislation both provides for the needs of our warfighters and ultimately takes strong steps towards strengthening our national security.

The Emerging Threats and Capabilities portion of the NDAA, which I serve as ranking member of, first and foremost recognizes the importance of the cyber domain. After careful consideration, my colleagues and I came to the conclusion that the execution of cyberspace operations and the readiness of the Cyber Mission Forces warrants a new unified combatant command, now currently a sub-unified command under STRATCOM.

The bill reiterates the importance of transparency and regular updates to Congress on cyber operations, internal policies and authorities, and other relevant issues and activities. This sets the stage for creating a formalized framework for oversight of U.S. Cyber Command next year.

The legislation also formalizes the relationship between the principal cyber adviser to the Secretary of Defense and Cyber Command, aiding the successful execution of their respective roles and responsibilities. We have come to realize how important these distinctions are to both parties. Thus, the bill clarifies the roles and responsibilities of the Assistant Secretary of Defense for Special Operations and Low-Intensity Conflict.

Now, on research and development, my ETC colleagues and I strive to champion innovation wherever possible, so this bill authorizes a demonstration pilot program that allows select DOD laboratory directors more flexibility in the day-to-day operations of their labs. This will ensure they can use best management practices to advance science and technology break-throughs with greater levels of agility.

As directed energy technologies continue to mature and may be ready to be fielded in the near future, the bill designates a senior official within the DOD for coordination of directed energy efforts to reduce redundancy, leverage lessons learned, and advance key policy considerations for uses of such technology.

Earlier this year, the Global Engagement Center was created by executive order within the State Department and tasked with coordinating U.S. counterterrorism messaging with our allies around the world. This year, the ETC portion of the bill formally authorizes the Global Engagement Center and expands the scope of its mission to include countering propaganda of state actors by permitting the DOD to transfer funds to the organization. Mr. Speaker, it is time we counter the dangerous rhetoric both ISIL and Russia are using to influence populations across the world and here at home.

Finally, Mr. Speaker, this legislation continues to address the critical policies and programs within the scope of emerging threats and capabilities. Beyond that, I am also particularly pleased that this bill makes the necessary investments in our Navy's nuclear submarine force, the most survivable leg of the triad. The Virginia class submarine and the Ohio Replacement class submarine are critical to our Nation's defense, and I am very pleased that they are prioritized and properly resourced in this legislation.

I want to again thank the leadership of Chairman Thornberry, Ranking Member Smith, and Chairman Wilson, and I thank my colleagues for their work on this bill.

Mr. THORNBERRY. Mr. Speaker, I yield 2 minutes to the gentleman from Virginia (Mr. Wittman), the distinguished chair of the Subcommittee on Readiness.

Mr. WITTMAN. Mr. Speaker, I stand today in strong support of S. 2943, the National Defense Authorization Act for Fiscal Year 2017.

First, I would like to thank Chairman Thornberry and Ranking Member Smith for their leadership here, and also our Readiness Subcommittee ranking member, Ms. Madeleine Bordallo. I thank them so much for all of their help and constant and tireless efforts in this endeavor. The efforts behind the 2017 National Defense Authorization Act were truly bipartisan.

Mr. Speaker, throughout the year, we heard testimony from all of our service branches about the necessity to address our military's alarming readiness shortfalls. Their accounts were sobering, to say the least. We now confront the maintenance, sustainment, and readiness issues that we put off until tomorrow. Today, we have the responsibility of reducing the risk for our warfighters by making sure that they are well-trained and have combat-ready equipment.

There are a number of provisions in this conference report that aim to bolster our military readiness. In addition to the pay raise and increases in end strength, this report directs several assessments of the military departments' plans to rebuild readiness, enhance exercises, and modernize training requirements. It also provides for increased military construction above the President's budget request. It provides the Department of Defense with flexibility for hiring civilians to fill critical manpower capability gaps, in particular, at our defense industrial base facilities: our depots, arsenals, and shipyards. It increases funding to the military service operations and maintenance accounts, critical elements we need to do to restore readiness.

None of these readiness provisions were included arbitrarily. They were specifically targeted to begin to reverse the decline in the readiness of our Armed Forces and bring them closer to achieving full-spectrum readiness levels. That is an absolute must if we are to combat and deter the threats to our national security from around the world.

Mr. Speaker, in that vein, I strongly urge support for S. 2943, the National Defense Authorization Act for Fiscal Year 2017, and encourage my colleagues in the House to support it as well.

Mr. SMITH of Washington. Mr. Speaker, I yield 2½ minutes to the gentleman from Virginia (Mr. Scott), the ranking member on the Committee on Education and the Workforce, and who also was enormously helpful with a number of different aspects of this bill. I appreciate his help and support in that.

Mr. SCOTT of Virginia. Mr. Speaker, I rise in support of the National Defense Authorization Act for Fiscal Year 2017.

I have the honor of representing the Hampton Roads area of Virginia, the heart of our Nation's shipbuilding industrial base. I want to underscore my support for the shipbuilding and ship maintenance provisions in the bill, including the language urging the Secretary of the Navy to speed up the procurement schedule for aircraft carriers to ensure that our carrier fleet is not again reduced to just 10 carriers. These provisions will not only significantly benefit my region, but will be critical to our Nation's security.

I want to particularly commend my colleague from Virginia, the chair of the Seapower and Projection Forces Subcommittee, Mr. Forbes, and the ranking member of that subcommittee, Mr. Courtney, for their hard work on the shipbuilding aspects of the bill.

As ranking member of the Committee on Education and the Workforce, I am pleased to see that the final conference report eliminated three matters of grave concern that would have adversely affected working conditions for shipyard workers and employees of government contractors.

The first provision eliminated from the bill would have severely undermined the workers' compensation benefits that many shipyard workers now receive. A second problematic provision would have authorized taxpayer-funded employment discrimination. A third provision eliminated from the bill would have significantly diminished the application of the executive order on fair pay and safe workplaces. This order will now remain in effect and it will help level the playing field so that those contractors who willfully and repeatedly violate workplace safety, labor, and civil rights laws will not gain competitive advantages over those law-abiding contractors who faithfully comply with employment laws.

In closing, Mr. Speaker, I want to recognize the exceptional effort made by the ranking member of the committee, Mr. Smith, with the cooperation of the chair of the committee, Mr. Thornberry, to produce a bill that addresses the defense needs of our Nation, but also ensures that workers are treated fairly.

Before addressing matters of concern to the Education and the Workforce Committee, I want to underscore my strong support for the shipbuilding and ship maintenance provisions. I have the honor of representing Hampton Roads, Virginia, the heart of our nation's shipbuilding industrial base. I strongly support the conference report's shipbuilding and ship maintenance provisions, specifically language urging the Secretary of the Navy to speed up the procurement schedule for aircraft carriers to ensure that our carrier fleet is not again reduced to 10 carriers. These provisions in the conference report will not only significantly benefit my region, but will be critical for our nation's security. I'd like to commend Congressman Forbes and Congressman Courtney for their efforts on this area.

As a conferee and Ranking Member of the Education and the Workforce Committee, I was pleased to see that the final conference report eliminated matters of grave concern.

First, the Conference Report removed Section 3512 of the House bill which redefined "recreational vessels" across almost all statutes.

The aim of this provision was to exempt workers repairing vessels over 65 feet in length from coverage under the Longshore and Harbor Workers Act (LHWCA), such as very large yachts and luxury watercraft. By stripping injured workers of the protections under LWHCA, these workers would have been shifted into coverage under state workers' compensation laws. Many state workers' compensation benefit levels are substantially inferior to LHWCA coverage, especially in states such as Florida.

Earlier this year, the Florida Supreme Court found that the Florida workers' compensation law was unconstitutional because the duration of disability benefits was so truncated and the benefit levels so anemic that they did not constitute "a system of redress" that "functions as a reasonable alternative to tort litigation."

Both the U.S. Department of Labor (DOL) and the U.S. Coast Guard (USCG) opposed Section 3512.

The DOL noted that Section 3512 would "lead to uncertainty and foster litigation regarding Longshore Act coverage" because the new definition of "recreational" vessel introduced subjective criteria. For example, would vessels with paid crews or which are leased out for commercial purposes be deemed recreational or commercial? DOL also expressed concern that this "legislation will simply encourage employers to shift their employees out of the more protective federal longshore workers' compensation system," and into inferior state workers' comp coverage.

The Coast Guard noted changing the definition of "recreational vessel" under Section 4301 of Title 46 (the Federal Boat Safety Act of 1971) would have adverse impacts on Coast Guard regulatory and enforcement authorities.

Second, I was pleased to see that Impact Aid has been preserved for Local Educational Agencies consistent with past precedent.

Third, there were two provisions that adversely impacted employee protections in the workplace, which were deleted in the conference report.

One such provision was Section 1094 of the House bill, which was misleadingly labeled "Protections Relating to Civil Rights and Disabilities" authorized taxpayer-funded employment discrimination in every grant, cooperative agreement, contract, subcontract, and purchase order awarded by every Federal agency doing business with a religiously affiliated organization.

Section 1094 would effectively nullify the protections from workplace discrimination for LGBT workers that were provided in Executive Order 13672 (Prohibiting Discrimination Based on Sexual Orientation and Gender Identity by Contractors and Subcontractors) that was signed on July 21, 2014.

Further, the provision would incorporate an exemption from the Americans with Disabilities Act that could permit taxpayer-funded discrimination not only against employees and applicants who are not members of the same religion, but also against those who fail to adhere to the organization's religious tenets.

Accordingly, religious organizations in receipt of federal dollars could use their religious viewpoint to: discharge working women who use birth control or who is pregnant and unmarried; fire employees who engage in premarital sex; deny employment or health benefits to married same-sex couples that they already provide to married opposite-sex couples; or refuse to consider for employment anyone, however qualified, whose religion is inconsistent with the employer's religious tenets.

Ninety-one religious, education, civil rights, labor, and women's organizations wrote to express their opposition in a letter dated August 25, 2016. The groups noted that: "effective government collaboration with faith-based groups does not require the sanctioning of federally funded religious discrimination."

I am pleased that the conference report did not authorize religious employers to discriminate in hiring using federal funds. I want to applaud Senator BLUMENTHAL for his leadership in helping to remove this provision.

In addition, Sections 1095 of the House bill and Section 829–I of the Senate bill would have eliminated or diminished the application of the "Fair Pay and Safe Workplaces" Executive Order.

This executive order requires companies to disclose whether they have engaged in serious, repeated, willful or pervasive violations of any of 14 long-standing labor laws, including the Fair Labor Standards Act, the Occupational Safety and Health Act, the Vietnam Era Veterans Readjustment Assistance Act, and nondiscrimination laws.

Each year, thousands of federal contractor workers are deprived of overtime wages, denied basic workplace protections, forced to endure illegal discrimination, and made to tolerate unwarranted health and safety risks. Companies supported by and entrusted with federal government contracts should be expected to represent the gold standard in the American workplace.

The executive order aims to level the playing field so that those who repeatedly violate those laws do not gain competitive advantage over those law abiding contractors who expend the funds and make the effort to ensure full compliance.

Finally, I want to recognize the exceptional effort made by Ranking Member SMITH and his staff to work with the Education and Workforce Committee to produce a final bill that meets the defense needs of this nation and also ensures workers are treated fairly.

Mr. THORNBERRY. Mr. Speaker, I yield 2 minutes to the gentleman from New York (Mr. GIBSON), a member of the conference committee and a combat veteran who has played a key role in formulating this bill.

Mr. GIBSON. Mr. Speaker, I rise in strong support of this conference report. I thank the chairman and the ranking member for their leadership.

This may very well be the most significant piece of legislation to come out of the House Armed Services Committee since Goldwater-Nichols. I say that for five reasons:

One, it reforms the strategic planning process, reclaiming Article 1, section 8 responsibility for the Congress with regard to providing strategic guidance.

Two, it empowers the chairman of the Joint Chiefs of Staff. I think this is really important for unity of effort, efficient use of resources, and, quite frankly, also for civil military relations.

Three, bold acquisition reforms; it has been mentioned in terms of agility, transparency, and accountability. We bring forward major reforms here, and, quite frankly, we are empowering the services. This is some of the testimony we received, and, in the process, we have provided incentives and also consequences for noncompliance. I think this is all going to be good news for the

taxpayers who are counting on us to get this right.

Four, decisive steps to improve readiness. We are entering a new era, Mr. Speaker. The drawdown is over; in fact, we are increasing end strength. I think this is really important.

On a congressional delegation trip I led this summer listening to the commanders in the European Command, including the Supreme Allied Commander of Europe, this bill and all the resources that come with it are going to help strengthen deterrence. This is also a good bill for NATO.

I mentioned resources. This was so important to the Joint Chiefs and to their senior enlisted advisers. They said they welcomed the end strength, but it had to come with the resources. They did not want to hollow out the force. We have listened and we have done this.

Money for training; it is a very dangerous business, and it is important the training be realistic. We have reinforced the account for the CTCs, flying hours, and the spare parts to come with it.

Five, Mr. Speaker, the pay raise, which is so justifiably earned.

I am proud of this bill. I want to thank the staff. The staff on both sides of the aisle are second to none, and it has been a great privilege to serve on this committee.

God bless this Nation.

Mr. SMITH of Washington. Mr. Speaker, may I inquire how much time each side has remaining.

The SPEAKER pro tempore. The gentleman from Washington has 13 minutes remaining, and the gentleman from Texas also has 13 minutes remaining.

Mr. SMITH of Washington. Mr. Speaker, I yield 2 minutes to the gentleman from California (Mr. GARAMENDI), a member of the committee.

Mr. GARAMENDI. Mr. Speaker, I want to thank the chairman of the committee, Mr. THORNBERRY; the ranking member, Mr. SMITH; and the members, my colleagues, for an exceptional piece of work here. This is an extremely important bill. I do support it; however, I do have some reservations. I would like to speak to at least one of them at the moment.

I want to bring to the attention of the Members section 671 of the NDAA concerning the ongoing bonus clawback issue affecting thousands of California National Guardsmen. While I am pleased that a permanent legislative fix is one step closer to the President's desk, I think some of the language needs to be clarified further to ensure that guardsmen are treated fairly.

First and foremost, I have concerns with the standard use to determine if a guardsman's debt should be waived or not. The current language says the DOD needs to produce a preponderance of evidence to demonstrate fraud on the part of the guardsman and withhold their bonus.

What does that mean in practice? We are not sure. This is vague and subject to interpretation. I believe this standard must be better defined, and we will continue to work on that in the future.

I am also concerned about subsection (c)(1)(B), which gives the Department of Defense far too much leeway in determining which cases warrant review. Though Secretary Carter has pledged to review every case, this gives DOD the option of ignoring about 2,000 cases. That would be a problem.

Our job isn't yet done. There will be a hearing next week on this issue. We will attempt to get further clarification to protect those men and women who accepted a bonus, went to war, performed their duties, and are now subject to a clawback. That should not happen.

One more thing to bring to the attention of the committee is the strategic arms portion of this bill, which continues a trillion-dollar project of recapitalizing our entire nuclear arsenal. We should pay attention to that in the future. It is extraordinarily expensive and dangerous.

□ 1045

Mr. THORNBERRY. Mr. Speaker, I yield 2 minutes to the gentlewoman from Missouri (Mrs. HARTZLER), the distinguished chair of the Subcommittee on Oversight and Investigations, for the purpose of a colloquy.

Mrs. HARTZLER. Mr. Speaker, I thank the chairman for yielding and for his leadership on this bill, as well as Ranking Member SMITH, and the hardworking dedicated staff. This is a great bill. It is a win for our troops and it is a win for national defense, and I fully support it.

I do want to also convey, though, my concern about and the importance of the Russell amendment, which passed this House but was not in the final bill. The attacks on this commonsense language have been dishonest and grossly inaccurate. The truth is that this language uses existing Federal civil rights laws to clarify hiring practices of religious organizations when they partner with the government through grants and contracts.

Religious charities are selfless and crucial providers who often go where no one else will go to help the vulnerable. They resettle refugees, counsel victims of sex trafficking, pray for soldiers in war zones, and comfort veterans suffering from PTSD. The White House has lauded these partnerships with the government, and Senate Democrats included a nearly identical provision in ENDA in 2013, a bill which most of the Senators publicly opposing this provision voted for in the past.

We need to protect these basic rights and preserve these vital partnerships,

and I look forward to working with the chairman next Congress to address these most basic of interests.

Mr. THORNBERRY. Will the gentlewoman yield?

Mrs. HARTZLER. I yield to the gentleman from Texas.

Mr. THORNBERRY. Mr. Speaker, I want to reiterate the importance of this issue to House majority conferees. For many years, organizations of faith have been able to both contract with the Federal Government and hire according to their faith practices. That has been especially true with religious universities, chaplain services, and refugee service providers; yet executive action under the current administration has created a direct conflict between the White House policy and these longstanding legal protections for these organizations' religious tenets.

While the NDAA was always an imperfect vehicle for this discussion, majority conferees believe that these executive orders must be reviewed; and we look forward to working directly with the incoming administration to address the concerns, not just for DOD, but for the government nationwide.

I certainly appreciate the leadership of the gentlewoman from Missouri on these very issues.

Mr. SMITH of Washington. Mr. Speaker, I yield 1½ minutes to the gentlewoman from Guam (Ms. BORDALLO) for the purpose of a colloquy with the chairman, Mr. THORNBERRY.

Ms. BORDALLO. Mr. Speaker, I thank the ranking member for yielding and wish to engage the gentleman from Texas, the chairman of the Armed Services Committee, in a colloquy.

Mr. Speaker, let me first start by thanking the chairman and the committee staff again for working diligently with us to address a number of provisions important to our territory, our island, and U.S. posture in the Asia-Pacific region.

I especially appreciate your support for our efforts to address workforce issues through the inclusion in the House bill of a targeted remedy for the H–2B visa denial issue particularly affecting military health care and construction projects on Guam.

Though the House Judiciary majority and minority approved the language, it is my understanding that the provision was not included in the final conference agreement due to concerns raised by the Senate Judiciary majority. As we look toward next year, will the chairman commit to working with me to address this issue to ensure the realignment of U.S. Marines to Okinawa is not adversely impacted?

Mr. THORNBERRY. Will the gentlewoman yield?

Ms. BORDALLO. I yield to the gentleman from Texas.

Mr. THORNBERRY. First, I want to thank the distinguished ranking mem-

ber of the Readiness Subcommittee for her hospitality. I learned a lot about the issue that she raises during my recent visit to Guam. I understand the workforce issues there much better, as well as the unacceptable impacts it is already having on our military activity on Guam.

Our strategic presence there, Mr. Speaker, and the U.S. Marine realignment are critical national security interests, and this issue must be addressed soon. We need to ensure an adequate workforce is available to support the current military presence, as well as the activity associated with the increase to come; and I look forward to continuing to work with the gentlewoman from Guam and with the Members on the other side of the Capitol to find an acceptable solution in the coming year.

Ms. BORDALLO. I thank the chairman, and I appreciate that he took the time to stop on Guam in October to see and understand the strategic value of our island and also better understand, firsthand, some of the unique challenges. It was a real honor, his visit, for the people of Guam, and I thank both the chairman and our Ranking Member SMITH for their assistance.

Mr. THORNBERRY. Mr. Speaker, I yield 2 minutes to the gentleman from Nevada (Mr. HECK), the distinguished chair of the Military Personnel Subcommittee.

Mr. HECK of Nevada. Mr. Speaker, I rise in strong support of the conference report to S. 2943, the National Defense Authorization Act of 2017.

This conference report contains significant policy and funding priorities to continue our commitment to maintaining the readiness of our military personnel and their families.

Included in this conference report are many important initiatives:

Specifically, it provides a fully funded pay raise. This is the largest pay raise for our military in the last 5 years and the first full pay raise in 4 years. After 3 years of lower pay raises than allowed by law, it is time that we give our troops and their families the pay increase they deserve.

It stops the troop reductions in our Armed Forces, thereby increasing readiness, while reducing the stress and strain on our force and their families.

It reforms the military health system to ensure that we have a ready medical force and a medically ready force, while providing a quality healthcare benefit valued by its beneficiaries.

It modernizes the Uniform Code of Military Justice to improve the system's efficiency and transparency, while also enhancing victims' rights.

It reforms the commissary system in a way that preserves this valuable benefit, while also improving it so that the system remains an excellent value for the shoppers and a good value for taxpayer dollars.

In conclusion, I want to thank the ranking member, the gentlewoman from California (Mrs. DAVIS), for her contributions and support in this process. It has truly been an honor and a pleasure to work with her.

I also want to thank the subcommittee members and offer my sincere appreciation for the hard work and dedication of the subcommittee staff.

Lastly, I want to thank the chairman, the gentleman from Texas (Mr. THORNBERRY), for his support and for entrusting me with the great privilege and honor of chairing this subcommittee.

I strongly urge my colleagues to support the conference report to S. 2943.

Mr. SMITH of Washington. Mr. Speaker, I yield 2 minutes to the gentlewoman from Texas (Ms. JACKSON LEE).

Ms. JACKSON LEE. Mr. Speaker, I thank the ranking member, and I rise in support of the conference report to S. 2943, the National Defense Authorization Act for Fiscal Year 2017.

This act is designed to meet the threats we face today as well as in the future, and I thank the chairman of the committee from Texas, as well as the ranking member from Washington, both having worked together in this enormous task to be able to defend our Nation.

The results of our work here today will reflect our strong commitment to ensure the men and women of our armed services receive the benefits and support that they deserve for their faithful service. Building on these efforts, this bill contains initiatives designed to provide resources and support for these men and women.

This legislation recognizes the reality that we live in a dangerous world where threats are not always easily identifiable and our enemies are not bound by borders. Confronting this type of enemy deserves a well-prepared, ready military, which I strongly support.

Mr. Speaker, I am delighted and very pleased that the work that we did together with the chairman and the ranking member, amendments that I offered, are in this legislation:

The Jackson Lee amendment expressing the sense of Congress regarding the importance of increasing the effectiveness of NORTHCOM in fulfilling its critical mission of protecting the U.S. homeland in the event of war, and to provide support to local, State, and Federal authorities that we work with all the time in times of national emergency.

The Jackson Lee amendment calling for a report on American efforts to combat Boko Haram in Nigeria and the countries in the Lake Chad region by way of provision of technical training and evidence-gathering strategies, to name a few. Having gone to the region,

having been dealing with the missing Chibok girls for, now, some 4 years plus, we know devastation there.

The Jackson Lee amendment requiring the Department of Defense to conduct outreach programs to assist small-business concerns owned and controlled by women, veterans, and social and economic minorities.

And the Jackson Lee amendment requiring annual report to Congress listing the most common grounds for sustaining protests including and relating to bids.

This is important to pass this legislation, Mr. Speaker.

And let me just personally thank the gentleman from Washington for always welcoming Members and the ideas and needs that they have for their districts, but also for this Nation. We are better for it, and we are better that we are preparing the men and women of the United States military to keep them safe.

Mr. Speaker, I rise in support of the Conference Report to S. 2943, the "National Defense Authorization Act for Fiscal Year 2017."

The National Defense Authorization Act is designed to meet the threats we face today as well as into the future.

The results of our work here today will reflect our strong commitment to ensure that the men and women of our Armed Services receive the benefits and support that they deserve for their faithful service.

Building on our efforts from previous years, this bill contains a number of initiatives designed to provide the resources and support needed for the men and women who keep our nation safe.

This legislation recognizes the reality that we live in a dangerous world, where threats are not always easily identifiable, and our enemies are not bound by borders.

Confronting this unique type of enemy requires unique capabilities.

As we have seen time and time again, our military has the ability to track down violent extremists who wish to do our country harm, regardless of where they reside.

Mr. Speaker, I am pleased that four of my amendments adopted during House consideration of the NDAA are included in the final legislation or in language in the accompanying report:

1. Jackson Lee Amendment expressing the sense of Congress regarding the importance of increasing the effectiveness of the Northern Command ("NORTHCOM") in fulfilling its critical mission of protecting the U.S. homeland in the event of war and to provide support to local, state, and federal authorities in times of national emergency or in the event of an invasion.

2. Jackson Lee Amendment calling for a report on American efforts to combat Boko Haram in Nigeria and the countries in the Lake Chad Basin, by way of provision of technical training and evidence gathering strategies to name a few.

3. Jackson Lee Amendment requiring the Department of Defense to conduct outreach program to assist small business concerns owned and controlled by women, veterans, and socially and economically minorities.

4. Jackson Lee Amendment requiring annual report to Congress listing the most common grounds for sustaining protests relating to bids for contracts.

The passing of this bill today brings us one step closer to enacting the 54th consecutive National Defense Authorization Act.

This particular bill is seen as the gold standard for Congressional bipartisanship and transparency.

Despite disagreements on key issues, Members have not failed to reach consensus on behalf of our fighting men and women.

I am proud of the work we have done here today.

Mr. THORNBERRY. Mr. Speaker, I yield 1 minute to the gentleman from Ohio (Mr. WENSTRUP), a valued member of the committee.

Mr. WENSTRUP. Mr. Speaker, I rise in strong support of the conference report to accompany S. 2943, the National Defense Authorization Act for Fiscal Year 2017. Congress has upheld its constitutional duty to "provide for the common defense" by passing the NDAA 55 years in a row, and I am looking forward to making this the 56th.

This bipartisan bill contains a number of vitally important provisions to support our troops deployed overseas, stop the dangerous drawdown of the military, and begin rebuilding our force for the future. It increases the end strength of our Armed Forces, gives our troops a substantial pay raise, and maintains restrictions on the administration's ability to bring terrorist detainees from Guantanamo to U.S. soil.

One provision I am particularly proud of is the Joint Trauma Education and Training Directorate. Too often we take for granted the readiness of our military healthcare teams, doctors, and surgeons when, in reality, their skills and knowledge are earned through work in grueling, dangerous conditions and must be maintained through frequent practice.

The Joint Trauma Education and Training Directorate will support partnerships, allowing military trauma surgeons and physicians to embed within civilian trauma centers to treat critically injured patients, maintaining medical readiness and deployability for future armed conflicts. By connecting the Department of Defense with civilian hospitals, these partnerships will serve the needs of our military medical professionals and our local communities, to the benefit of the whole Nation.

I urge my colleagues to support this important bill.

Mr. SMITH of Washington. Mr. Speaker, I yield 1 minute to the gentlewoman from California (Ms. LEE).

Ms. LEE. Mr. Speaker, I want to thank our ranking member for yielding and for his tremendous leadership on so many of these very critical issues.

Mr. Speaker, I rise, though, in strong opposition to the National Defense Authorization Act, which would authorize another $618 billion in spending to our already out-of-control defense budget. It would also expand funding for wars that Congress has never debated. Once again, my Republican colleagues have used an off-the-books spending gimmick to further expand the already-bloated Pentagon budget.

Enough is enough. Instead of writing blank checks to the Pentagon, Congress needs to live up to its constitutional obligation to debate matters of war and peace. We need to rip up the 2001 blank check for endless war. We need to stop funding wars without end, with no debate on the costs and consequences to our troops or to the American people.

Mr. Speaker, I do have to say that I am pleased that my amendment, which I coauthored with my good friend Congressman BURGESS, to report on the audit-readiness of the Pentagon, that amendment passed, but much work remains.

So I call on our Speaker to act to bring some accountability to Pentagon spending and to bring forth an authorization to use force to support or oppose these new wars. We need to do our job.

I urge my colleagues to vote "no" on this bill and reject this wasteful spending.

Mr. THORNBERRY. Mr. Speaker, I yield 2 minutes to the gentlewoman from New York (Ms. STEFANIK), the distinguished vice chair of the Subcommittee on Readiness.

Ms. STEFANIK. Mr. Speaker, I rise today to express my strong support for the FY17 NDAA conference report.

I want to first thank Chairman THORNBERRY for his dedication and continuous support for our troops and for his leadership during the conference committee process.

I am proud to support this critical bill that truly hits home for my district and for our brave men and women in uniform across our great Nation. My district is the proud home of Fort Drum, and this bill provides for the ongoing combat operations where troops from the 10th Mountain Division continue to selflessly serve. It also fully supports our Navy's nuclear community, from operational capabilities, to nuclear training sites at Ballston Spa, New York.

□ 1100

One of the most important provisions is a full 2.1 percent pay raise for our troops—to our Nation's dedicated and brave servicemembers who risk it all to provide us with protection and security—and to their loved ones who are anxiously awaiting their return.

This bill also prevents a possible readiness crisis by investing in our military personnel and preserving their expertise.

In order for our military to continue its superiority in any battlefield and

through countless combat deployments, this bill ends the misguided drawdown of troops. It ensures we have the land forces end strength to face the world's challenges and protect our Nation.

Every day I am grateful and humbled to represent so many brave men and women in uniform and their resilient loved ones. I encourage all of my House colleagues to vote in support of this vital bill.

Mr. SMITH of Washington. Mr. Speaker, may I inquire how much time is remaining?

The SPEAKER pro tempore. The gentleman from Washington has 6½ minutes remaining. The gentleman from Texas has 6½ minutes.

Mr. SMITH of Washington. Mr. Speaker, I have no further speakers, and I reserve the balance of my time.

Mr. THORNBERRY. Mr. Speaker, I yield 1 minute to the gentlewoman from Arizona (Ms. MCSALLY) who is a very valued member of our Armed Services Committee.

Ms. MCSALLY. Mr. Speaker, I rise today in strong support of the NDAA. I thank Chairman THORNBERRY for his leadership on this issue and being a member of that committee.

As a retired Air Force colonel and A-10 pilot, I am deeply troubled by the dangerous atrophying of our military in recent years. For example, we once had 134 fighter squadrons. Today we have 55. We had 946,000 total force military and civilian airmen, and now we are down to 660,000. We are short 700 fighter pilots, 4,000 maintainers, and critical munitions. Yet the world isn't getting any safer.

This bill takes crucial steps to reverse the readiness crisis and helps ensure our military has the training, manpower, and resources they need to keep us safe. It increases end strength and funds the weapons systems we need to take on ISIS and other emerging threats, such as the Tomahawk missile.

It fully protects the mighty A-10 Warthog, our best close air support asset. It includes critical language I authored to require a fly-off between the A-10 and the F-35 before a single A-10 can be retired. It fully funds the EC-130H Compass Call, the Air Force's only dedicated electronic warfare asset. It fully funds the vital missions we need for the future, like cyber, intelligence, and electronic warfare—all of which are housed at Fort Huachuca in my district.

I am proud to have worked on the committee with Chairman THORNBERRY and Chairman MCCAIN on these important issues. I want to thank them for their leadership. I urge my colleagues on both sides of the aisle to support this critical bill and support our troops.

Mr. THORNBERRY. Mr. Speaker, I yield 1½ minutes to the gentleman

from Ohio (Mr. CHABOT) who is the distinguished chair of the House Committee on Small Business, which has made a number of contributions to this conference report.

Mr. CHABOT. Mr. Speaker, I also rise in strong support of this conference report because it provides for our national defense and also supports America's small businesses. As was mentioned, as chairman of the House Committee on Small Business, I have seen firsthand just how vital small businesses are in providing the Department of Defense with the goods and services it needs in a cost-effective and efficient manner.

Also included within this conference report are contracting reforms which will provide small businesses with greater access to defense contracting opportunities, as well as extend such important programs as the SBIR and the STTR research programs.

Finally, this conference report calls on agencies to provide cybersecurity resources to small businesses to protect themselves from cyber attacks which are becoming a greater and greater threat to businesses all across this country and really all across the world.

I want to thank Chairman THORNBERRY for his hard work and his leadership. He has done a tremendous job in getting this crucial legislation finally across the finish line. I also want to thank all the members of the Small Business Committee. Many of the small business provisions included within this report came out of our committee with strong—if not unanimous—bipartisan support. Working together through regular order, we have been able to strengthen the small business industrial base which is so fundamental to the health of our Nation as a whole.

Mr. Speaker, again, I want to thank all the members of Mr. THORNBERRY's committee for their hard work on this. It is really a job well done.

Mr. THORNBERRY. Mr. Speaker, I have no further speakers other than myself to close, and I reserve the balance of my time.

Mr. SMITH of Washington. Mr. Speaker, I yield myself the balance of my time.

I just want to make three issues, and some of them were raised during the course of the debate. First of all, I like a lot of what is in this bill. I think it is also important what is not in this bill. There were a number of issues that were extraneous to the actual business of national security that had been put in by one side or the other that, in conference, we were able to remove. One of the most prominent ones was one that was raised earlier, the so-called Russell amendment having to do with the ability of companies and businesses that are receiving government contracts to discriminate. I was very much opposed to the Russell amendment. I am happy that we agreed to take it out.

I just want to explain a little bit exactly what it is because it is really rather simple. All the President accomplished in this is that there already is an executive order saying: if you do business with the Federal Government, then you cannot discriminate against certain classes of people. I don't remember all the different classes, but certainly one of the big ones is you can't discriminate based on race. So in other words, if your religious tenets are racist—say, for instance, you don't like Black people and don't employ them and don't want to do business with them—we, as the Federal Government, have decided that that is not acceptable, and we will not allow you to do business with the Federal Government.

All this executive order did was add the LGBT community to those protected classes. So, basically, what we are saying is: not only is it not acceptable to be racist, but it is also not acceptable to be homophobic. I completely agree with that, and I would hope our country would get to the place where it would agree with that as well; that if you feel that you must discriminate against people simply based on their sexual preference, then we are not going to do business with you. That is a policy that, I think, we should have. That is what the executive order does.

To reverse that in the Defense bill, I think, would be an abomination, particularly since we have made such progress within the Department of Defense. We have finally gotten rid of Don't Ask, Don't Tell so that gay and lesbian people can serve openly in the military. They have served in the military for decades, and now they are allowed to serve openly. We have recently allowed transgender people to serve openly as well, which I think is a tremendous step forward. The Russell amendment would take us back.

So, again, I really want to emphasize that all the executive order does is say that it is not all right to be racist and it is also not all right to be homophobic. I think that is a principle that we should stand for as a country.

I want to further add that even within that executive order, there are many exceptions that already exist. Now, even though I am a lawyer, and even though lawyers have tried to explain this to me, I don't fully understand all those exceptions, but religious groups are allowed to discriminate based on the tenets of their belief within the existing executive order that was already passed. So even though the people who were pushing the Russell amendment already have what they want—even though, in my opinion, they shouldn't—there is no need to further emphasize the fact that we are going to

allow people who do contract with the Federal Government to discriminate against the LGBT community. I think that is basically wrong and should not be allowed.

The second point I want to make is on the money. We have heard over and over again about how underfunded everything is, and I get that. But we are spending $619 billion on the Department of Defense—far and away more money than any other country in the world, and we have been spending more money on defense for decades than any other country in the world. We ought to be able to build a military that can protect our national security interests for that amount of money, and not only should we be able to, we are going to have to because we are $19 trillion in debt. I forget exactly what the deficit is this year, but it is somewhere in the $500- to $600-billion range.

We have a President coming into office who is promising trillions of dollars in additional tax cuts. We also have a crumbling infrastructure in this country, and it is just as important that we maintain the strength of our country at home—that we have a transportation infrastructure, an education infrastructure, and a research infrastructure that continues to make us as strong as it is and that we have a national security apparatus that will protect our interests abroad. If we spend all of our money in tax cuts and defense, then we will wind up with a very hollow country.

We have got to make some tough choices going forward, and I believe that we can meet our national security needs, frankly, for less money than we spend. There are greater efficiencies; there are programs that we don't need to continue with.

Those are the choices that we are going to have to make in the years ahead because right now we are planning on more programs and more national security than we could possibly have money for in the next decade. We cannot continue to duck the tough choices that get us a national security apparatus and a Department of Defense that we can actually afford that also provides for our national security.

Lastly, I just want to close where I started and say that the product of this bill—I don't know how many pages it is this year, but it is a lot—requires a lot of work, and the people you see sitting behind us are the staff that do that work tirelessly night after night. It is a yearlong process to put it together and to negotiate with the Senate to get there. We have the most outstanding staff that I can imagine. I want to make sure that we thank them for that incredible work that they do, not just for us but for the men and women who serve in the military.

Again, I want to thank Chairman THORNBERRY. We work in a bipartisan manner on this committee, and, as

many of you are aware, that is not easy. I have been here 20 years, and the country and this place have suddenly become more partisan. It has become more and more difficult to do anything, to pass any kind of bill where Democrats and Republicans actually work together.

The National Defense Authorization Act is a shining example of the way the legislative process should work, and many people are to thank for that, but it all starts with the chairman. It all starts with Mr. THORNBERRY and also with Senator MCCAIN on the other side being dedicated to the principle, number one, of bipartisanship—of working together—and, number two, to the absolute commitment that we will get our job done. Sometimes it takes until December. I think we went all the way up to December 16 a couple of years ago, so we are way ahead of schedule this year by those standards. Sometimes it takes a long time, but we always get it done, and it is a credit to those chairmen that we do.

Mr. Speaker, again, I urge passage of this very important bill, and I thank the chairman again for his great work and all the staff for the work they did to make this possible.

Mr. Speaker, I yield back the balance of my time.

Mr. THORNBERRY. Mr. Speaker, I yield myself the balance of my time.

Mr. Speaker, I completely agree with the distinguished ranking member that to produce this bill requires a great deal of effort by a number of people, starting with him, other members of the committee, and other Members of the House. It is also essential that our staff, who support our work, be thanked, and he has done a great job of doing that.

I agree with him also about the leadership of Senator JOHN MCCAIN, a man who, I think, is unique in the country's military history at this point. His leadership, along with the ranking member, Senator JACK REED, has been obviously essential, not only in this bill but in Congress being able to fulfill its constitutional responsibilities.

I know there are disappointments with this bill, Mr. Speaker. There are things that people would like to see in here, a lot of them not really core defense issues, but those matters had to be dropped to get this bill to this point.

I am confident that the new administration will review the executive orders that the ranking member was talking about and that those unconstitutional restrictions on the First Amendment will be reviewed, modified, or repealed. All of that facilitated getting this bill before us today.

I am also hopeful that the new administration will send us a supplemental request, because there are desperately needed modernization items from ships, airplanes, munitions, and other things that are not authorized in this bill but are needed desperately by our troops. So I hope—and I expect—that we will do better in the coming year to, again, fulfill our responsibilities under the Constitution.

Mr. Speaker, I would just end with this: I believe the first job of the Federal Government is to defend the country. The Constitution puts specific responsibilities on our shoulders to raise, support, provide, and maintain the military forces of the United States. The most important part of that responsibility deals with the people, and this bill, if it is nothing else, supports the men and women who volunteer to risk their lives to defend us and protect our freedoms. For that reason alone, it deserves the support of every Member of the House. I hope it will receive that support.

Mr. Speaker, I yield back the balance of my time.

Mr. BLUMENAUER. Mr. Speaker, today I voted against the Conference Report to Accompany S. 2943, the National Defense Authorization Act (NDAA) for Fiscal Year 2017 (Roll No. 600). Though the legislation contains several provisions that I support, and I commend the House and Senate Armed Services Committee for tackling some difficult issues, I am concerned about many components of the bill, including the continued use of a budgetary gimmick to avoid making the tough decisions we need to make about our defense spending.

This NDAA includes $67.8 billion in Overseas Contingency Operations (OCO) funding, which isn't subject to budget caps, and $8.3 billion of this funding would go to base defense budget operations. Congress and the Administration should not be able to use the account, initially used to fund the wars in Iraq and Afghanistan, to pad their budgets in an era of fiscal uncertainty. The legislation also keeps intact funding for several unnecessary and outdated weapons programs and includes extraneous funding, unsolicited by the Navy, for an amphibious ship replacement program known as the LX (R).

The legislation also maintains prohibitions on closing the Guantanamo Bay detention facility and on transferring any detainees to the United States. It's past time that we closed this military prison.

Finally, it's concerning that the bill includes new language that marks a significant shift in U.S. missile defense policy which dates back to 1999. This adjustment could cement U.S. proliferation of nuclear weapons, while sending a counterproductive signal to other countries.

There are provisions of this legislation that I support. I've fought to defend and strengthen the Afghan Special Immigrant Visa (SIV) program since I helped establish the program with my colleagues in 2009. This legislation extends the program through 2020 and authorizes an additional 1,500 visas for our allies. Though the bill, unfortunately, restricts the eligibility of applicants—eligibility requirements that I sought to remove from the legislation when it was being considered by the House—I look forward to continue fighting for the viability of the program next year.

I'm also glad that we're taking a small step towards cost accountability with the bill's transparency requirements for the Air Force's new B–21 bomber. I offered an amendment to have the Department of Defense disclose the total cost of the bomber program in the House version of the bill.

Though I cannot support this legislation, I will continue to support our armed forces, while fighting for reductions in the bloated defense budget.

Mr. SANFORD. Mr. Speaker, I will ultimately vote today for the National Defense Authorization Act because it's a necessity, and I think it's important we authorize this spending so that procurement, research, and a host of other long-term projects stay on track.

That's the good news.

The bad is that there are many wrongs tucked into this bill. It continues to use wartime contingency funds for recurring operations. It has an earmark for New Balance shoes. I could go on, but I write to highlight what I think will be the most damaging part of the bill—exempting women from the draft.

In the spring, Secretary Carter made women eligible for combat roles, and this was supposedly about equality. This bill goes a step further and makes it law that woman will be preferentially treated. Doing so is not good for morale and readiness because troops know you can't have it both ways in life. Either we are all on the team together and treated equally—or we are not.

I said in February that the Secretary of Defense's new policy of opening front-line combat roles to women would unleash political forces that in the end would make our military weaker. All this could have been avoided if we had been allowed a national debate, but the administration rushed to stack up perceived political wins while it could—and so we are where we are.

What happened in this bill is the first of many inconsistencies that will come to weaken one of our military's real strengths: its leadership as an institution in treating people equally as it focuses on but one outcome—the defense of our nation. It needs to be remembered that 6 years before Brown vs. Board of Education, the armed forces had already been desegregated. Actions like this and its focus on equality of opportunity have something to do with Gallup polls showing our military as the most respected of American institutions.

The bill creates a daring double standard. Women are now eligible for combat roles but not the draft. It codifies the draft for men but not for women at the very time women are now eligible for combat roles. How is this equal?

To be clear, I'm not a fan of women in a draft or being a part of Seal Team 6. I just think we should offer equal roads to getting to the Seal unit, if billets are open to men and women. Our nation asks people in the elite units to do remarkably rugged things that pose serious physical challenge. The Marines have actually looked deeply at this and recently completed a 1,000-page study that concluded that male units overwhelmingly outperformed integrated units in physical tasks. Indeed, Navy Seals comprise but 1 percent of the Navy, Force Recon is about the same within the Marines—while Delta Force numbers are actually classified, and the problem in the elite forces is that physical prowess is not a part of what you do; it is part and parcel to what you do.

There is a reason we don't see a lot of women in the NFL, and if we really want to try a social experiment, let's make one-third of the Army football team female and see how it does next year against Navy. For that matter, my sister is a wonderful woman and a far better shot than I am, but she can't carry me very far. We begin to affect unit cohesion when members of a unit believe their counterparts can't carry them out of a bad spot in which they may have found themselves . . . but all this is a debate for another day.

The debate that needs to come in the wake of this bill is how we reconcile equality of opportunity in the military with people in this bill being treated quite differently. Our nation's defense is not a social experiment. Lives hang in the balance. For the sake of morale—so important to what makes our military strong—it's important we circle back on the draft issue this coming year.

Ms. BORDALLO. Mr. Speaker, I rise to speak on the Fiscal Year 2017 National Defense Authorization Act, which was passed by a 375–34 vote on Friday. I commend Chairman THORNBERRY, Ranking Member SMITH and the committee staff who worked many long nights on the FY17 NDAA. I worked with Mr. SMITH and members of the committee, particularly Readiness Chairman ROB WITTMAN, to include a number of provisions and funding levels that will address certain readiness shortfalls and continue to support the Asia-Pacific Rebalance.

This conference agreement, along with the House report passed in May, includes a number of provisions that are particularly important for the people of Guam. Over the past few months of negotiations, we were able to secure the provision that authorizes the payment of claims to the survivors of the occupation of Guam during World War II and the heirs of those who were killed during the occupation. During World War II, Guam was the only U.S. civilian population occupied by Japan, and during this time our people were subjected to rape, torture, assault, murder, and other inhumane atrocities. The provision does not add to federal spending and utilizes mandatory federal spending provided only to the Government of Guam for taxes paid by federal personnel stationed on Guam. This is an important step towards recognizing the men, women, and children who endured injustice yet remained and remain loyal and patriotic Americans, and its inclusion this year is a hard fought victory for the people of Guam. I look forward to working with the Foreign Claims Settlement Commission, the Trump Administration and stakeholders on Guam to ensure that the war claims program is implemented in a fair, transparent and equitable manner. I will work to ensure the process is as clear to the people of Guam as possible so that we can truly bring closure to this matter.

We also successfully repealed the remaining restrictions on civilian infrastructure projects related to water and wastewater, as well as the construction of a cultural artifact repository, and authorized $67.5 million for these investments. This bill also authorizes military infrastructure projects, including full funding for six military construction projects for housing, munitions, and power infrastructure development. These projects total nearly $250 million and demonstrate further the continued commitment of the U.S. government to the Guam build-up and the realignment of Marines.

At the same time, this build-up must continue to reflect the 2011 Four Pillars agreement that commits the Navy to being a responsible community partner. Because of local concerns raised about land returns and how that will be calculated and tracked, we hold the Navy accountable to its "Net Negative" commitment by including in this bill a reporting requirement on past, current, and future Navy land usage on Guam. It is important that we have a mutual understanding about what lands will be returned to ensure that the Navy's commitment to hold no more land than it already has is upheld.

There are other challenges associated with the Guam build-up that are addressed this year. The Senate Judiciary Committee majority objected to the House-passed provision that would address workforce challenges affecting the health care and construction industries by providing flexibility to U.S. Customs and Immigration Services as it evaluates H–2B visa renewal applications. These industries directly support the military mission on Guam and having an inadequate workforce on island could negatively impact our national security. However, in order to gather additional data and continue to build the argument in order to address the situation in the coming year, there is a reporting requirement that asks the Navy to document the mission specific impacts of a reduced workforce associated with increased denials of these applications. I am deeply disappointed that this tailored provision was not ultimately included in the Conference Report but I will work with the Department of Defense to address this matter in next year's defense bill or any other appropriate legislation next year. Immediately, I will work with USCIS to see if any additional emergency authorities exist to find a temporary solution to the matter so that we do not hold up military construction projects. We must find a more permanent solution to the repeated denials of H–2B labor on Guam so we can have a stable and consistent workforce to meet construction timelines and provide critical health care to the military and residents of Guam.

Additionally, ballooning cost estimates and associated scheduling delays because of Navy requirements for clearance of munitions and explosives of concern have disrupted numerous projects and need to be addressed. While the Navy has demonstrated a commitment to finding a balance that assures public safety while eliminating unnecessary, burdensome, and duplicative requirements, there is more that needs to be done. Early next spring. I expect the Navy to brief us on steps they are taking to mitigate redundancies and find acceptable efficiencies and we will continue to track this issue closely.

Additionally, this bill mandates a review of distinguished Asian American and Pacific Islander war heroes who may have been unjustly overlooked in consideration of the Medal of Honor. I especially want to thank Ranking Member SMITH for his leadership on issues important to Asian American Pacific Islanders

(AAPIs) and working to get that provision included in the Conference report. This review was first conducted for AAPIs who served during World War II, but did not include those who served during the Korean and Vietnam Wars. Similar reviews have been conducted for African, Jewish, and Hispanic Americans and I believe that it is prudent to also conduct a comprehensive review for AAPIs who may have faced similar discrimination. It's important we appropriately recognize those who have given so much in support of our freedoms.

There are numerous provisions in this year's NDAA which help develop or restate our national security priorities in the Asia-Pacific region. We included several provisions which aim to help continue to build our relationship with Taiwan, including requiring a feasibility report on replenishment stops for Taiwanese midshipmen during their annual exercise in the Pacific as well as encouraging the U.S. and Taiwan to work together to engage in senior military leader exchanges. These will help build our bilateral relationship and provide opportunities for mutual exchange of information and training. This relationship will continue to be a critical asset for U.S. engagement in the region. We also seek to clarify and document aerial and maritime freedom of navigation operations in the South China Sea. This requirement tasks the Navy and Air Force with reporting quarterly on important details pertaining to individual operations which are meant to challenge claims to disputed islands in the region and ensure freedom of navigation for all vessels and aircraft. Additionally, this report expresses a Sense of Congress in support of trilateral cooperation between the United States, Japan, and South Korea. Japan and South Korea are important American allies in the region and have taken steps to rebuild their bilateral relationship, which the U.S. must continue to encourage and foster. As we continue a unified approach to countering nuclear proliferation in North Korea, as well as deterring and destroying threats emanating from the unstable regime, there are opportunities to leverage the Guam National Guard in defense of the homeland. Building on discussions I have had with senior Army leaders, the bill report encourages the Department of the Army and the National Guard Bureau to ensure that there are resources made available in the Fiscal Year 2018 Budget to integrate the Guam Army National Guard into the security force mission for the THAAD deployed to Guam. Not only does this mission fit perfectly into the Total Force integration for which the Army has been an advocate, it contributes to Active and Reserve Component readiness, and enables the National Guard to utilize their capabilities for the homeland defense mission.

The bill also continues to promote invasive specific prevention and management and regional biosecurity issues and complements appropriations legislation for the Department of Agriculture and the National Oceanic and Atmospheric Administration which require briefing on the Regional Biosecurity Plan on recommendations that will minimize the harmful ecological, social, cultural, and economic impacts of invasive species. This will encourage the Department of Defense and other federal agencies to make progress on implementation of high priority proposals contained within the Plan.

Finally, this bill provides critical funding for a number of Department of Defense programs that are important to Guam, the Asia-Pacific rebalance, and our broader national security interests. We provide critical funding to the Long Range Strike Bomber program and additional funding to keep the fielding of the MQ–4 program on track. There is also $15 million in additional funding for the Readiness and Environmental Protection Integration Program. Though there needs to be greater allocation of resources for critical programs such as the National Guard State Partnership Program and the Naval Sea Cadet Corps, we were able to protect the President's Budget Request. However, these programs and their significant return on investment merit greater funding contributions.

The SPEAKER pro tempore. All time for debate has expired.

Pursuant to House Resolution 937, the previous question is ordered.

The question is on the conference report.

The question was taken; and the Speaker pro tempore announced that the ayes appeared to have it.

Mr. THORNBERRY. Mr. Speaker, on that I demand the yeas and nays.

The yeas and nays were ordered.

The SPEAKER pro tempore. Pursuant to clause 8 of rule XX, this 15-minute vote on adoption of the conference report will be followed by a 5-minute vote on agreeing to the Speaker's approval of the Journal, if ordered.

The vote was taken by electronic device, and there were—yeas 375, nays 34, not voting 25, as follows:

[Roll No. 600]

YEAS—375

Abraham	Carter (GA)	Dent
Adams	Carter (TX)	DeSantis
Aderholt	Cartwright	DesJarlais
Allen	Castor (FL)	Deutch
Amodei	Castro (TX)	Diaz-Balart
Ashford	Chabot	Dingell
Babin	Chaffetz	Doggett
Barletta	Cicilline	Dold
Barr	Clawson (FL)	Donovan
Barton	Clay	Doyle, Michael
Beatty	Cleaver	F.
Benishek	Clyburn	Duckworth
Bera	Coffman	Duffy
Beyer	Cole	Duncan (SC)
Bilirakis	Collins (GA)	Edwards
Bishop (GA)	Collins (NY)	Ellmers (NC)
Bishop (MI)	Comer	Emmer (MN)
Black	Comstock	Engel
Blackburn	Conaway	Eshoo
Blum	Connolly	Esty
Bonamici	Cook	Evans
Bost	Cooper	Farenthold
Boustany	Costa	Farr
Boyle, Brendan	Costello (PA)	Fitzpatrick
F.	Courtney	Fleischmann
Brady (PA)	Cramer	Fleming
Brady (TX)	Crawford	Forbes
Brat	Crenshaw	Fortenberry
Bridenstine	Crowley	Foster
Brooks (AL)	Cuellar	Foxx
Brooks (IN)	Culberson	Frankel (FL)
Brownley (CA)	Cummings	Franks (AZ)
Buchanan	Curbelo (FL)	Frelinghuysen
Buck	Davidson	Fudge
Bucshon	Davis (CA)	Gallego
Burgess	Davis, Danny	Garamendi
Bustos	Davis, Rodney	Gibbs
Byrne	DeGette	Gibson
Calvert	Delaney	Gohmert
Capps	DeLauro	Goodlatte
Cárdenas	DelBene	Gosar
Carson (IN)	Denham	Gowdy

Graham
Granger
Graves (GA)
Graves (LA)
Graves (MO)
Green, Al
Green, Gene
Grothman
Guinta
Guthrie
Hanabusa
Hanna
Hardy
Harper
Harris
Hartzler
Hastings
Heck (NV)
Heck (WA)
Hensarling
Herrera Beutler
Hice, Jody B.
Higgins
Hill
Himes
Hinojosa
Holding
Hoyer
Hudson
Huelskamp
Huizenga (MI)
Hultgren
Hunter
Hurd (TX)
Hurt (VA)
Israel
Issa
Jackson Lee
Jeffries
Jenkins (KS)
Jenkins (WV)
Johnson (GA)
Johnson (OH)
Johnson, E. B.
Johnson, Sam
Jolly
Jordan
Joyce
Kaptur
Katko
Keating
Kelly (IL)
Kelly (MS)
Kelly (PA)
Kildee
Kilmer
Kind
King (IA)
King (NY)
Kinzinger (IL)
Kline
Knight
Kuster
LaHood
LaMalfa
Lamborn
Lance
Langevin
Larsen (WA)
Larson (CT)
Latta
Lawrence
Levin
Lieu, Ted
Lipinski
LoBiondo
Loebsack
Long
Loudermilk
Lowenthal
Lowey
Lucas
Luetkemeyer
Lujan Grisham (NM)

Luján, Ben Ray (NM)
Lummis
Lynch
MacArthur
Maloney, Carolyn
Maloney, Sean
Marchant
Marino
Matsui
McCarthy
McCaul
McClintock
McCollum
McGovern
McHenry
McKinley
McMorris Rodgers
McNerney
McSally
Meadows
Meehan
Meeks
Meng
Messer
Mica
Miller (FL)
Miller (MI)
Moolenaar
Mooney (WV)
Moore
Moulton
Mullin
Mulvaney
Murphy (FL)
Murphy (PA)
Napolitano
Neal
Neugebauer
Newhouse
Noem
Nolan
Norcross
Nunes
O'Rourke
Olson
Palazzo
Palmer
Pascrell
Paulsen
Payne
Pearce
Pelosi
Perlmutter
Perry
Peters
Peterson
Pingree
Pittenger
Pitts
Poliquin
Posey
Price (NC)
Price, Tom
Quigley
Rangel
Ratcliffe
Reed
Reichert
Renacci
Ribble
Rice (NY)
Rice (SC)
Richmond
Rigell
Roby
Roe (TN)
Rogers (AL)
Rogers (KY)
Rohrabacher
Rokita
Rooney (FL)
Ros-Lehtinen
Roskam

Ross
Rothfus
Rouzer
Roybal-Allard
Royce
Ruiz
Ruppersberger
Rush
Russell
Ryan (OH)
Salmon
Sánchez, Linda T.
Sanford
Sarbanes
Scalise
Schiff
Schweikert
Scott (VA)
Scott, Austin
Scott, David
Sensenbrenner
Serrano
Sessions
Sherman
Shimkus
Shuster
Simpson
Sinema
Sires
Slaughter
Smith (MO)
Smith (NE)
Smith (NJ)
Smith (TX)
Smith (WA)
Speier
Stefanik
Stewart
Stivers
Stutzman
Swalwell (CA)
Thompson (CA)
Thompson (MS)
Thompson (PA)
Thornberry
Tiberi
Tipton
Titus
Tonko
Torres
Trott
Tsongas
Turner
Upton
Valadao
Van Hollen
Vargas
Veasey
Visclosky
Wagner
Walberg
Walden
Walker
Walorski
Walters, Mimi
Walz
Wasserman Schultz
Waters, Maxine
Weber (TX)
Webster (FL)
Wenstrup
Westerman
Wilson (FL)
Wilson (SC)
Wittman
Womack
Woodall
Yoder
Yoho
Young (AK)
Young (IA)
Young (IN)
Zeldin
Zinke

NAYS—34

Amash
Bass
Becerra
Blumenauer
Capuano
Chu, Judy
Clark (MA)

Clarke (NY)
Cohen
Conyers
DeSaulnier
Duncan (TN)
Gabbard
Grayson

Griffith
Grijalva
Gutiérrez
Honda
Huffman
Kennedy
Lee

Lewis
Massie
Nadler
Pallone
Pocan

Polis
Schakowsky
Schrader
Takano
Velázquez

Watson Coleman
Welch
Yarmuth

NOT VOTING—25

Aguilar
Bishop (UT)
Brown (FL)
Butterfield
Carney
DeFazio
Ellison
Fincher
Flores

Garrett
Hahn
Jones
Kirkpatrick
Labrador
Lofgren
Love
McDermott
Nugent

Poe (TX)
Pompeo
Sanchez, Loretta
Sewell (AL)
Vela
Westmoreland
Williams

ANNOUNCEMENT BY THE SPEAKER PRO TEMPORE

The SPEAKER pro tempore (during the vote). There are 2 minutes remaining.

□ 1137

Messrs. POLIS, COHEN, and NADLER changed their vote from "yea" to "nay."

Messrs. GALLEGO, CICILLINE, and RICHMOND changed their vote from "nay" to "yea."

So the conference report was agreed to.

The result of the vote was announced as above recorded.

A motion to reconsider was laid on the table.

Stated for:

Mr. AGUILAR. Mr. Speaker, I was not present for votes on Friday, December 2, 2016 because I was home in San Bernardino, CA to mark the one-year anniversary of the terrorist attack in our community. Had I been present, I would have voted "yea" on rollcall No. 600, the adoption of the Conference Report to accompany S. 2943, the National Defense Authorization Act for Fiscal Year 2017.

THE JOURNAL

The SPEAKER pro tempore. Pursuant to clause 8 of rule XX, the unfinished business is the question on agreeing to the Speaker's approval of the Journal, which the Chair will put de novo.

The question is on the Speaker's approval of the Journal.

Pursuant to clause 1, rule I, the Journal stands approved.

COMMUNICATION FROM THE CLERK OF THE HOUSE

The SPEAKER pro tempore (Mr. EMMER of Minnesota) laid before the House the following communication from the Clerk of the House of Representatives:

OFFICE OF THE CLERK,
HOUSE OF REPRESENTATIVES,
Washington, DC, December 2, 2016.
Hon. PAUL D. RYAN,
The Speaker, House of Representatives,
Washington, DC.
DEAR MR. SPEAKER: Pursuant to the permission granted in Clause 2(h) of Rule II of the Rules of the U.S. House of Representatives, the Clerk received the following message from the Secretary of the Senate on December 2, 2016, at 9:55 a.m.:

That the Senate passed without amendment H.R. 6014.

That the Senate passed S. 3492.
That the Senate passed S. 10.
That the Senate passed S. 2058.
With best wishes, I am,
Sincerely,
KAREN L. HAAS.

LEGISLATIVE PROGRAM

(Mr. HOYER asked and was given permission to address the House for 1 minute.)

Mr. HOYER. Mr. Speaker, I yield to the gentleman from California (Mr. MCCARTHY), the majority leader, for the purpose of inquiring of the schedule for the week to come.

Mr. MCCARTHY. I thank the gentleman for yielding.

Mr. Speaker, on Monday, the House will meet at noon for morning hour and 2 p.m. for legislative business. Votes will be postponed until 6:30 p.m.

On Tuesday and Wednesday, the House will meet at 10 a.m. for morning hour and noon for legislative business.

On Thursday, the House will meet at 9 a.m. for legislative business, and no votes are expected in the House on Friday.

Mr. Speaker, the House will consider a number of suspensions next week, a complete list of which will be announced by close of business today.

The House will also consider H.R. 5143, the Transparent Insurance Standards Act of 2016, sponsored by Representative BLAINE LUETKEMEYER, which specifies U.S. objectives regarding international insurance standards to ensure that our State-based system is preserved.

Additionally, the House is expected to consider the final Water Resources and Development bill as well as the continuing resolution to fund the government.

□ 1145

Mr. HOYER. Mr. Speaker, as the gentleman knows, the current CR expires on December 9. He has announced the CR will be on the floor next week, and it is my understanding that December 9 may be our last day in session, so I presume we need to act before December 8.

Does the gentleman have a perspective on the specific scheduling of the CR and when it will be on the floor?

I yield to the gentleman from California.

Mr. MCCARTHY. Mr. Speaker, the Appropriations Committee is continuing to work on the CR, including the length of time and when. As soon as it is done, it will be posted. It is our intention to have it done next week, and it would be our hope that we could finalize it on Thursday.

Mr. HOYER. Mr. Speaker, I want to make a comment that I know the CR will be the vehicle. I know Mr. TOM COLE made a comment—and I have talked to him about it—with which I agree. I am disappointed, our side is disappointed, and I think some on your side with whom I have talked are disappointed that we were unable to do an omnibus appropriations bill which would reflect the work of the committee on our side and, indeed, the work of the committees on the other side of the aisle.

A CR is not helpful to management, obviously, not knowing specifically what resources they will have available for the balance of the year. Very frankly, although there will be anomalies in the bill to reflect the changes from last year's funding levels, they will undoubtedly not take care of a funding stream which will be appropriate for good management in the Federal Government.

I would hope in the year ahead that we would certainly work toward having bipartisan appropriation bills done bill by bill. Both sides have had trouble doing that from time to time, but let's hope that we can work toward that end. Because a CR, in many ways, is simply a failure; and forgetting about who is at fault or who is not at fault, it is a failure to operate the government in a way that is rational, reasonable, and most effective.

So I want to make that comment. I know the gentleman agrees with me on trying to go through regular order, and it is unfortunate that we didn't get there.

I yield to the gentleman from California if he wants to say anything on that. I have another question.

Mr. McCARTHY. Mr. Speaker, I agree with the gentleman that we should go through regular order and get our appropriation bills done. It is our intention, as the gentleman knows from the new schedule coming out, especially loading more days in, to make sure, as we come back into the next Congress, that we start with appropriations and get that work done.

Mr. HOYER. Mr. Speaker, as a constructive suggestion, I notice that the gentleman has scheduled—and I want to thank him for his communication with our office so that we could work together on trying to get the schedule together—we have four working weeks in June. As you know, essentially, the Appropriations Committee tries to get its work done by the end of May in terms of its bills—they don't get all of them done by the end of May—so we can start moving them to the floor.

I congratulate the gentleman for putting sufficient time in so that we can do that in June and July, so that all the bills, hopefully—the objective, I would suggest, ought to be to have all of the 12 appropriation bills sent to the Senate prior to the August break. I thank him for his schedule on that.

Originally, March 31 was, as I understood, the CR date, but that is somewhat flexible now, I understand. Can the gentleman tell me what date he expects the CR to expire on?

I yield to the gentleman from California.

Mr. McCARTHY. Mr. Speaker, as I mentioned earlier, the Appropriations Committee is continuing to work on the CR, and that would be including the length of time. The gentleman is correct that March was the date we were looking at. I believe that date will change. But as soon as discussions have ended and we are able to post, it will include the date of the length of the CR.

Mr. HOYER. Mr. Speaker, one of the things that we are certainly very hopeful of—your office and my office were having a lot of discussions about that, as are Leader PELOSI and Speaker RYAN having a lot of discussions—is the WRRDA bill. This deals very critically with the Flint crisis that has been ongoing now for 2-plus years. I am very concerned, although we apparently have an agreement on the dollar figure, can the gentleman tell me whether that dollar figure will, in fact, be appropriated within the structure of the WRRDA bill?

I yield to the gentleman from California.

Mr. McCARTHY. Mr. Speaker, I do want to thank the gentleman from Maryland for his work with his staff on this issue of the Flint crisis when we were dealing with WRRDA and the continuing resolution just short months ago.

The Speaker and Minority Leader NANCY PELOSI are continuing to talk. It is our intention that it gets solved inside WRRDA, and we are hopeful that we can close out on that even today. As soon as it is finished, it will be posted as well.

Mr. HOYER. Mr. Speaker, when you say within WRRDA, in the event that that does not occur, would the gentleman believe that we would deal with the assurance of the funding in the CR itself?

I yield to the gentleman from California.

Mr. McCARTHY. Mr. Speaker, as soon as it is finished, we will be able to put it out. But it is our intention, on the work that we agreed to with Members on your side of the aisle—and I know Speaker RYAN has had discussions with him as well, and he feels very comfortable about where we are and with funding on that—as soon as we are able to finish that up, I think everybody will be quite happy with the outcome. I think this is a work-on-both-sides-of-the-aisle compromise to find common ground to actually solve a problem.

Mr. HOYER. Mr. Speaker, I want to say to the gentleman from California that I appreciate the fact that our offices work together, that the Speaker and the leaders' offices have been working together and that the committees have been working together.

I would urge, however this money is appropriated—whether it is appro-

priated within the CR, whether it is appropriated in the WRRDA bill itself—that the money needs to be made available before we leave this week because this is an issue that has dragged on for too long and the people of Flint are still in dire distress, which is terribly unfortunate given the length of this crisis and the causes of this crisis, in some respects.

Lastly, Mr. Leader, I asked this and you responded that December 9 was the date; but do you see any possibility of going beyond the 9th that we need to warn our Members about? We are hearing that both on the Senate side and on our side, that there is every expectation that next week will be the last week that we will be in session in the 114th Congress.

I yield to the gentleman from California.

Mr. McCARTHY. Mr. Speaker, the gentleman knows better than I—he has been here longer than I—that we can always set a date, but Congress sometimes has a problem making that date.

It is our hope that we can be finished by December 8, but no one can predict what happens on this floor, whether we have to be here longer. It is always my intention that Members understand, if the work is not done, we will not leave.

So we will not leave until we get a continuing resolution done and get WRRDA done. I believe that the prior work that we have done working together—and knowing where both of them are right now—that we can finish this up and be done on time.

Mr. HOYER. Mr. Speaker, the gentleman mirrors my words. When people would ask me when we are going to conclude, I would say we are going to conclude when we finish our work. Now, finishing, I guess, one's work is a subjective judgment; but certainly these two pieces of legislation need to get done, and hopefully we can get those done.

If we don't have a further week, this will be the last colloquy. I want to say to my friend that we have been able to work on a lot in the 114th Congress. We have had real substantive differences. We will continue to have those differences. But I look forward to working closely with the majority leader when, in fact, we agree, and when we disagree, to try to work constructively on trying to get to an agreement.

This election has caused us, I think, some real challenges. The election itself was a challenge, and I know we will have a lot more to say on that afterwards.

I want to thank the gentleman from California for the ability to work together and constructively on behalf of the American people where we have been able to do that.

I yield to the gentleman from California.

Mr. McCARTHY. Mr. Speaker, I want to take a moment and congratulate the gentleman from Maryland on his re-election to whip.

Hopefully, this is our last colloquy for the year, but you know as much as I know.

Mr. HOYER. Mr. Speaker, well, I know how much you look forward to these colloquies.

I yield to the gentleman from California.

Mr. McCARTHY. Mr. Speaker, it is the highlight of my week.

I look forward to the next Congress. I do enjoy working with the gentleman from Maryland, even when we disagree, because the gentleman is honest and forthright with his disagreements. The gentleman is willing to work where we do find common ground.

We are going to have philosophical differences, but we are going to have the same commitment that we are going to try to find a way to move forward. At times, we are going to disagree; but those times that we do agree, we work very well together. I admire the gentleman. The gentleman works very hard when he disagrees, and that is just part of what I think the American people expect. We have got a lot of work to go before us. The election is over. I think it is time that this country comes together. We are going to have a lot of work.

As the gentleman from Maryland knows, with the new schedule, Members are going to be here much more than they have been in the past, and we are probably going to be on this floor with legislation a little more than we were last year. I look forward to that and look forward to working with the gentleman on ways that we can work together.

I wish the gentleman from Maryland a very Merry Christmas.

Mr. HOYER. Mr. Speaker, I thank the gentleman from California and return that wish for a Merry Christmas. This is not our last week. We are going to be here next week, so maybe we will save that for then.

I do look forward and the people look forward. This election has been a deeply troubling one for all sides in many respects. I think it is our responsibility to try to bring some degree of confidence to all of our constituents, whatever they believe, whoever they voted for, that we are going to move forward in a constructive, positive way to make America an even greater country than it is now.

I yield back the balance of my time.

ADJOURNMENT FROM FRIDAY, DECEMBER 2, 2016, TO MONDAY, DECEMBER 5, 2016

Mr. McCARTHY. Mr. Speaker, I ask unanimous consent that when the House adjourns today, it adjourn to meet on Monday, December 5, 2016, when it shall convene at noon for morning-hour debate and 2 p.m. for legislative business.

The SPEAKER pro tempore (Mr. EMMER of Minnesota). Is there objection to the request of the gentleman from California?

There was no objection.

UNIVERSITY OF DETROIT JESUIT HIGH SCHOOL STUDENTS PAY TRIBUTE TO VETERANS

(Mr. BISHOP of Michigan asked and was given permission to address the House for 1 minute and to revise and extend his remarks.)

Mr. BISHOP of Michigan. Mr. Speaker, I rise today to recognize the students of University of Detroit Jesuit High School. They love this country, and they found a special way to pay tribute to our veterans.

Young men and women of University of Detroit Jesuit are volunteering their time to serve as pallbearers for homeless veterans at Great Lakes National Cemetery in my district, the final resting place for local military members who don't have families and are typically buried alone.

The students have never met these veterans, but they have a genuine sense of patriotism and gratitude for what they have done for our country. Their mission is simple: to give the proper burial that every veteran—every person—deserves.

Mr. Speaker, when no one else came forward, these young men and women stepped up to say thank you. Our district, our State, our country could not be more proud.

Our veterans are the backbone of what makes this Nation great, and we owe them the deepest respect and gratitude, even at the end of their journey. So thank you to our men and women of the military, and thank you to the young men and women of University of Detroit Jesuit for honoring their service to our Nation.

COOL SCIENCE TOPICS

(Mr. McNERNEY asked and was given permission to address the House for 1 minute and to revise and extend his remarks.)

Mr. McNERNEY. Mr. Speaker, I rise to continue a series of 1-minute speeches about cool science topics. Today I will be discussing applications of the National Science Foundation's funded research into arctic species.

In order to survive in the subzero temperatures of the Arctic, small organisms such as fish, insects, plants, fungi, and bacteria have evolved proteins that lower the freezing point of water solutions in order to protect themselves when temperatures drop.

Studies of the proteins of these arctic species will aid in the development of aircraft de-icing systems, cryopreservation of food, crop protection, frostbite prevention, and other innovations. These organisms and their ability to

survive in extreme temperatures will yield information of great value to society.

I applaud the NSF's funding of such important research.

□ 1200

HONORING OFFICER REGINALD GUTIERREZ

(Mr. REICHERT asked and was given permission to address the House for 1 minute and to revise and extend his remarks.)

Mr. REICHERT. Mr. Speaker, late in the afternoon on Wednesday, Officer Reginald "Jake" Gutierrez of Washington State's Tacoma Police Department responded to a domestic violence call. Despite the potential danger he knew lay ahead, he went forward with courage and a resolute focus on saving lives, sadly sacrificing his own life in the end.

Tragically, he was 1 of 133 law enforcement officers this year to die in the line of duty. That is a 20 percent increase, Mr. Speaker, over last year. Officer Gutierrez has served in law enforcement 17 years, and he is one of the few who accept the calling to serve.

The men and women who wear the badge like Officer Gutierrez have continued to show resilience during difficult times and have maintained an unshakeable commitment to perform their critical mission of keeping our families safe and protecting our freedoms, whether we are relaxing at home or protesting in the street. Wednesday was no exception.

During what became an 11-hour standoff with the suspect, the Tacoma Police Department was assisted by many of its neighboring partners to ensure the surrounding area was secure. What is exceptional about this demonstration, Mr. Speaker, of bravery is that it is not exceptional at all. Men and women every day in this country walk out of their home wearing the badge and the uniform to protect our children, protect our communities, protect our kids at school.

I ask all of us to keep our law enforcement officers in their prayers, Mr. Gutierrez's family, and the Tacoma Police Department.

PUERTO RICO AND THE PRESIDENTIAL VOTE

(Mr. GRAYSON asked and was given permission to address the House for 1 minute and to revise and extend his remarks.)

Mr. GRAYSON. Mr. Speaker, I rise today to call on Congress to give the people of Puerto Rico the most basic of rights, the right to vote for our national leader. In all of the world's democracies, Puerto Rico is the largest territory by population that cannot choose our national elected official.

Three-and-a-half million Americans in Puerto Rico have no say in who serves as President of the United States.

Women and African Americans were once denied this basic voting right. Now it is American citizens who reside in Puerto Rico who suffer this disenfranchisement. The contradictions are painfully clear. Puerto Ricans participate in the Presidential primary process, they send pledged delegates to each major party's convention, but they do not participate directly in the choice of President of the United States.

If these same American citizens move to the mainland, they can quickly and easily help to elect our national leader, but they are denied this very basic right to help choose the President and Vice President merely for living where they do.

The solution to this problem is a simple one, and we have accomplished it before. Fifty-five years ago, the District of Columbia was granted electors to the electoral college with the passage of the 23rd Amendment to the Constitution. Like Puerto Rico now, the District of Columbia was not and is not a State.

The SPEAKER pro tempore. The time of the gentleman has expired.

Mr. GRAYSON. Mr. Speaker, I ask unanimous consent for an additional 30 seconds.

The SPEAKER pro tempore. The Chair cannot entertain that request.

Mr. GRAYSON. I will simply say we must give Puerto Ricans the right to vote for President.

The SPEAKER pro tempore. The time of the gentleman has expired.

CONGRATULATIONS TO OWEN HOLMES ON HIS RETIREMENT

(Mr. ROYCE asked and was given permission to address the House for 1 minute and to revise and extend his remarks.)

Mr. ROYCE. Mr. Speaker, I rise today to recognize the service of Owen Holmes on the eve of his retirement from California State University, Fullerton.

Dedicating his life to education, Owen has received the Robert and Louise Lee Collaborative Teaching Award, served as an education policy fellow at the Institute for Educational Leadership, and Owen was the inaugural awardee of the Edwin Crawford Award for Innovation.

I have had the pleasure of working with Owen on many issues for CSUF over the years—gerontology, childhood obesity, the Strategic Language Initiative, water hazard mitigation, the advancement of teaching and learning in mathematics and science—all to help enhance the university's education experience, and on the Cal State DC Scholars program and bringing students from the university here to our

Nation's Capital, where he orchestrated that effort.

Throughout his over 30 years of service, he has touched the lives of thousands of students and improved government relations and advocacy at Cal State Fullerton. I am pleased to have had the opportunity to work with Owen over the years to help make CSUF one of the Nation's largest and most inclusive institutions of higher education.

Thank you, Owen, for dedicating your life to improving education. We wish you a happy retirement.

CELEBRATING 150 YEARS OF GENERAL MILLS

(Mr. PAULSEN asked and was given permission to address the House for 1 minute and to revise and extend his remarks.)

Mr. PAULSEN. Mr. Speaker, I rise to recognize the 150th anniversary of General Mills, an iconic Minnesota company. In 1866, on the banks of the Mississippi River, a bold and ambitious flour mill was founded, immediately becoming one of the largest in the country. Then in the 1920s, the company recognized that the milling industry needed to adapt, and so it expanded its scope and its vision and was renamed General Mills, turning its attention to food and consumer products, and brands such as Cheerios and Betty Crocker were born, becoming staples in homes across the United States and the world.

For 150 years, General Mills has made wonderful contributions to our great State. General Mills embodies the Minnesota spirit of hard work, innovation, perseverance, and generosity. They are an outstanding corporate citizen, representing the best of Minnesota and having an impact around the world.

Mr. Speaker, as Minnesotans, we take great pride in General Mills' success over the past 150 years, and we wish them continued success in the future with their leadership.

RECOGNIZING FILIPINO WORLD WAR II HEROES

(Mrs. RADEWAGEN asked and was given permission to address the House for 1 minute and to revise and extend her remarks.)

Mrs. RADEWAGEN. Mr. Speaker, I want to take this minute to applaud the passage, by unanimous consent, of the Filipino Veterans of World War II Congressional Gold Medal Act, which I was proud to cosponsor.

I want to thank both Senator HIRONO and Representative GABBARD for their efforts in seeing this measure get sent to the President's desk. They did a fantastic job, and I could not be more proud to work alongside other women in Congress who work so hard for those they serve.

This has been a long time coming, and I am happy to see that we are fi-

nally recognizing these heroes who helped the United States win the war in the Pacific. The countless sacrifices and efforts by those men and women of the Philippines who answered the call to arms in defense of the ideals and values we hold so dear can never be forgotten. With the passage of this important legislation, the people of the United States can finally say thank you to those brave men and women.

I look forward to seeing the President sign this legislation into law and want to once again thank the men and women of the Philippines who fought alongside the United States in defense of freedom.

HIGHLIGHTS OF THE NDAA

(Mr. LaMALFA asked and was given permission to address the House for 1 minute and to revise and extend his remarks.)

Mr. LaMALFA. Mr. Speaker, we are all very pleased to see the passage of the Defense Authorization Act today. This is how the process actually is supposed to work. The House and the Senate came together in conference to have a document that we can send to the White House. We urge the President, after previous veto threats, to pass this measure, to sign this measure so we can put these important priorities in place, such as stopping the decrease of our American troop levels—this has funding to do that; very importantly, finally, a 2.1 percent pay raise for our troops, largest in several years.

Other good highlights of this include the stoppage of any funding to close down Guantanamo Bay, which helps keep us safe on American soil. We are not going to do anything to reduce the housing allowance. Instead, we will keep that in place for our soldiers and their families on base.

There is much to be happy about with this. One of the things I am most happy about as a Californian is Cal Guard, the National Guard, will not be seeking to take back the bonuses. This has strong measures in it. My colleague, Representative DENHAM, and I sponsored a bill to do this. This has a lot of those pieces in that, in Mr. DENHAM's bill, to stop the required repayment of bonuses that were taken in good faith by our Guard members who served. A lot of good things about this. I urge the President to sign this.

WEEK IN REVIEW

The SPEAKER pro tempore. Under the Speaker's announced policy of January 6, 2015, the gentleman from Texas (Mr. GOHMERT) is recognized for 60 minutes as the designee of the majority leader.

Mr. GOHMERT. Mr. Speaker, it is an honor to be here, and, even after the voters have spoken, it is an honor to find when you and your positions actually don't make you special, they just make you completely in accord with over 70 percent of your constituents, not including newspapers.

The people have spoken, and, as President Obama referenced a number of times, elections do have consequences. What he failed to remember was, yes, but we had elections to Congress that also should have consequences. When we are accountable every 2 years, the President is only accountable every 4 years.

At this time, I yield to the gentleman from Louisiana (Mr. GRAVES), my friend.

LOUISIANA'S TRAGIC FLOODS

Mr. GRAVES of Louisiana. Mr. Speaker, I want to thank the gentleman from Texas (Mr. GOHMERT) for yielding to me.

Mr. Speaker, I have had the opportunity to come on the House floor a number of times and give an update to this body about the profound impacts of the flood we had in August of this year in south Louisiana. Just to remind you of a few statistics, this was believed to be a 1,000-year storm. There were trillions of gallons of water that fell in Louisiana. It was estimated to be about 31 inches of rain in about 36 hours in some areas of south Louisiana. That is more rain in 36 hours than the average American gets in a year's time. If that were a snowstorm, Mr. Speaker, that would have been 25 feet of snow.

We have been working now for months, working to try and make sure that we have an efficient recovery, make sure that these people can get back on their own two feet, that they can recover from this absolute tragedy that happened in south Louisiana, this once-in-a-lifetime event.

Starting out, Mr. Speaker, we saw unbelievable recovery, response, rescue activities, but it wasn't by government. That was the amazing thing. This was the community coming together, rescuing themselves, cooking for one another, sheltering one another, clothing one another. This wasn't government that came in and saved the day. While there were great first responders from our police departments and fire departments and others that came and helped out, the reality is, well over 90 percent of the response and rescue activities were done by other members of the community. They weren't trained. They weren't asked to do it. They just did it. So you saw a great spirit of recovery happening.

Then what happened is the Federal Government stepped in and began taking over some of the sheltering, began taking over the recovery activities, and we have seen a complete stop. Here we are, over 100 days after this flood event, and FEMA is telling people that they may get a trailer unit in January or February. Mr. Speaker, it is wintertime. People are living in tents. I heard about a veteran over the weekend who is living in a car wash. We have people who are living in their stripped and gutted uninsulated homes, and they can't get trailers.

Mr. Speaker, there is a guy by the name of Darrell Whitehead who lives in Denham Springs, Louisiana. Mr. Whitehead has had a trailer sitting in his front yard for 5 weeks, a trailer that FEMA brought, and they couldn't let him move in. He has stared at this thing for 5 weeks. I made phone calls, my chief of staff made phone calls, and we had other caseworkers in the office who made phone calls trying to get FEMA to simply get this guy in his trailer.

☐ 1215

Mr. Whitehead, already a victim of the flood, has been revictimized by FEMA by having a trailer sitting in his yard, not giving him a place to go for 5 weeks, and just having to sit there and be tortured because they needed a sink installed.

Mr. Speaker, this is ridiculous. And this isn't an isolated case. I can tell you case after case after case where this is the way FEMA has revictimized people flooded from this disaster.

Another example is Sheriff Jason Ard in Livingston Parish. Sheriff Ard was very concerned about the high percentage of sheriff's deputies that were flooded. He came in and he simply said: Look, we have got to get these deputies and their families in a safe, stable situation so they can focus not on having to figure out where their family is sleeping at night or what they are eating, but focus on law enforcement, focus on safety and security of the community that has been devastated by this flood.

So he came to FEMA and he said: Hey, look, I have got a plan. I have got a trailer dealer who is willing to give us trailers—and don't quote me on the numbers, but I am within the ball park—for $36,000. I will buy them back from you for $27,000 a year and you can find a piece of land. You can put all these trailers out. You can have a sheriff's deputy group housing area.

Instead, FEMA says: No. What we are going to do is get these deputies trailers not for a net of $10,000, roughly, as I explained, but for $100,000. That is how much FEMA is paying for these trailer units to buy them, store them, transport them—$100,000 versus the scenario that Sheriff Ard found for $10,000.

I have spoken to the Secretary of Homeland Security, the Deputy Secretary, Assistant Secretary, Regional Administrator of FEMA. Nobody can figure out how to do this and they are all telling him no.

So we have displaced deputies. We don't have the proper law enforcement focus in the community because the deputies, appropriately, are worried about their family and where they are going to sleep and eat. We have got FEMA spending 10 times the amount of money that Sheriff Ard has found a solution for. What is happening is absolutely ridiculous.

So, lastly, Mr. Speaker, in September of this year we did appropriate a down payment of money to help with the recovery efforts; and certainly it is a step in the right direction. As I have said several times, it is not anywhere near the level of funding that should be put forth for a cost-efficient recovery effort. We are going to end up spending more money by lowballing these numbers and having FEMA revictimize people for months here than if we had just appropriated the right amount to begin with.

Right now we are negotiating a second tranche, a second payment. Under HUD rules, they are requiring that the funds focus upon low- and moderate-income only. I want to be clear: low- and moderate-income folks need help in recovering.

What about the middle class? What about the upper class? What about the job creators? What about the businesses?

Focusing only on low- and moderate-income begins a partial restoration. Flood waters didn't recognize only one socioeconomic class, only one race. It flooded everybody. The recovery should treat everyone the same. We shouldn't be splitting this up and only recovering certain folks. It is inappropriate.

The State of Louisiana's plan, in complying with the National Environmental Policy Act and overhead and administrative costs, is saying it is going to cost 30 percent of the money just to deliver this program. Complying with all these crazy rules, 30 percent of the money gets eaten up. That is crazy. These people are rebuilding homes that were right there, in many cases, within the same four walls that are there now.

Why are we spending $100 million on environmental compliance? Who comes up with this stuff?

It is further delaying people getting back into their homes. This is crazy, Mr. Speaker. We have got to have a more commonsense, appropriate process to recovery.

Mr. Speaker, in closing, I just want to say that I have heard a lot of people in this country talk about how surprised they were with the outcome of the recent elections that we had. It is not a surprise to me that people are frustrated. What we are experiencing in south Louisiana today, being revictimized by FEMA, revictimized by the SBA in our recovery efforts, it is cause for extraordinary frustration. This is not what anybody in America wants—having to deal with a bureaucracy wasting money and taking months and spending 10 times to do what the local officials or our community could do for a fraction of the cost at a fraction of the time.

People want government to be responsive to them. People want government to be efficient. We can do better than this. The election results didn't surprise me. I ran because I was frustrated; and I understand the sentiment, unfortunately, more so than most right now, because watching the Federal Government absolutely screw up this recovery effort is revictimizing folks in south Louisiana.

Mr. GOHMERT. Mr. Speaker, I certainly appreciate my friend, Mr. GRAVES, bringing up a real problem. We have seen it in Louisiana—and not just in southern Louisiana, but other parts of Louisiana—with massive flooding. I am not even talking about Katrina, but there was a massive amount of waste in Hurricane Katrina that also affected my district in east Texas. I have a 120-mile border that I share with Louisiana, and we have seen the same problems.

We have had a massive flood of Caddo Lake, one time the largest freshwater natural lake besides the Great Lakes. A natural dam apparently was exploded years ago. It still is one of the great treasures of the State and our country. It had a massive flood.

I was visiting in Karnack, Texas, last week with some of the local emergency people that are trying to take care of the issue. The local folks there in Harrison County are acting very responsibly, the local government is acting responsibly, but you have outrageous things like my friend, Mr. GRAVES, was talking about.

One family got a loan to buy a new mobile home that wasn't destroyed like the last one. With the flood, it had too much water. So they got a new mobile home and got the loan. Well, as we have heard with FEMA, in this case there were requirements that the mobile home be lifted up much higher. The elevation had to be much higher where it was. In the process of lifting it up, the mobile home fell and was completely destroyed. They still have to make payments on their mobile home for the loan, and they have no home. They were doing everything within their power to comply with the governmental requirements.

There are other bureaucratic nightmares.

I was hearing stories about how some of the churches in east Texas banded together. The Baptist men came in and did amazing work. Yes, I understand women, too. I think they call themselves the Baptist men. Anyway, they came in and did extraordinary work. When people didn't have any plumbing, they had nothing, they brought in portable showers and restrooms and provided the help long before FEMA could get there and do what was needed.

You hear people who were so affected by massive floods say: If we ever have

another disaster like that, before we call FEMA, we are going to call the Baptist men. They come in and they get stuff done. They help people where it is, and they don't care who you are, all of your background information. They see who is hurting and they help them.

Well, that is the way it used to be, but then we became too reliant on letting the government fix everything. There were people in the Federal Government that realized that if we can make the Federal Government the ultimate insurer of everything—your school loans, your home, your flood insurance—we will start small, but we will work up until maybe one day we can even have the government behind everyone's health insurance.

If you really want to take away people's freedom and you really want to have Big Brother government dictating every aspect of your life, the way to do it is to have the government ensure all those aspects of your life. Once someone has the right to pay in the event that you are harmed, then they have the right to tell you how to avoid them having to pay, and there goes your freedom. So the power of more insurance has come to the Federal Government.

Many of us thought we could give up our liberty just for a little more security, but Benjamin Franklin, with all the wisdom that man had, understood back then that basically those who are willing to give up liberty for security deserve neither.

For too long in this country, people have been giving up their liberty in order to get security only to find that they are not even secure, just like Mr. GRAVES was talking about. We thought, Gee, if we set up a Federal Emergency Management Agency to help take care of emergencies, it will be fantastic. If we set up a Corps of Engineers to help with our water projects, it will be fantastic. If we set up an EPA, or Environmental Protection Agency, to protect the world, the environment, it will be a great thing. But the longer these agencies exist, the less sensitive they are to what they were supposed to do.

We found it right here in the Capitol. About 7 years ago, the Architect of the Capitol, who works for the House and Senate, had decided that we all work for him and he started making demands, one of which was that I could not cook ribs and share them with other Members of Congress, as I had been doing once a quarter. Most of the networks wanted to do stories on my cooking ribs and I said: No, we are not going to do a TV thing on this. This is just between the Members.

Well, I am grateful that STEVE SCALISE got involved and I got PAUL RYAN to help. The Speaker was able to persuade the bureaucracies here on Capitol Hill that we can make this work

and have it safe if we work with each other and are able to get people to work together.

Many of my colleagues tell me it is the best meat they have ever tasted. Some say they are the best ribs they have ever tasted. I have enough of my late mother in me that I enjoy cooking and enjoy people enjoying what I cook. It is probably the only time here on Capitol Hill when I actually leave a good taste in people's mouths instead of a bitter taste.

As we continue to see abuses by the Federal Government and we see abuses going on across the country, you think, Well, in the Federal Government, even though it has badly abused its authority, isn't it supposed to protect us from other abuses?

The answer is: yes, if they are federally related.

Well, when you have the electoral college and electors elected as part of that system, it is critical that that be a protected system of voting, just as the Constitution would require and as the law actually requires.

This story by Hans von Spakovsky and Jennifer Matthes says: "Before Donald Trump's stunning victory on November 8, liberals called for acceptance of election results. But since the election didn't go as they'd planned, some have taken to harassing and intimidating electors in an attempt to change the election results. Some of these threats may actually violate Federal law, yet the Justice Department acts strangely uninterested in investigating."

This takes us back to having people armed with billy clubs standing and trying to intimidate voters at their place of voting, and the "Department of Just Us," which was supposed to be "Justice," said: No, no, no, that is fine for them to do it. There are no problems with them doing that.

□ 1230

If anybody else were to do that, yeah, we would probably go after them; but these are the New Black Panther Party, or such as that, so, yeah, it is fine if they do it.

We have got to get back to being a nation where the laws are enforced evenly across the board. If the laws don't make sense, like our own rules here on Capitol Hill, if things do not accommodate people fairly and equally, they are just arbitrary decisions like we got from the Architect of the Capitol when the Visitor Center was being built, or when people are just wanting to have a life up here, we should be stopping the bureaucrats and getting rules that apply across the board, fairly across the board.

Yes, here we make the rules, and we should have rules that apply to everybody; but when you have an arbitrary dictator, they don't get applied quite so evenly.

Here we have the Justice Department, and this report of electors that are going to be voting very soon in the electoral college to elect the President, and their very lives are being threatened. Some of them have had to move their families.

This Justice Department is not interested in protecting the integrity of the election. That is the problem we have been suffering for quite some time around the country. They were not interested in enforcing the law fairly across the board, so we end up all the worse off for it.

This article goes on to say, in Georgia and Idaho, the threats have become so extreme that the secretaries of state both released statements calling for the harassment to end.

I absolutely know, without doubt, that if Hillary Clinton had won the election, as the rules set it up, with a republican form of government—little R. Not the Republican Party, but a republican form of government, just as Ben Franklin said when he was asked after the Constitution finally came together with what most of the members of the Constitutional Convention said was divine providence, or the finger of God. Without the finger of God being involved, they could never have come up with that Constitution. Franklin says: A republic, madam, if you can keep it.

So we had found, and our Founders had wisely, so many of them, sought truth in Scripture, a Bible that they used to argue positions; and they realized probably a complete, perfect democracy is not best for governing people because, if it is a true democracy, then the law gets changed on whims. If someone becomes the object of scorn and it is a true democracy, they are not governed by laws that we currently have in our Constitution which indicate you can't have ex post facto laws. You can't make a law criminalizing things after the act has already occurred. Our Constitution guarantees against that.

Well, in a perfect democracy, there is no such ex post facto law. A majority can make a decision to criminalize conduct that previously occurred so that, when the person committed the act, they were not violating the law. They were acting in accordance with the law, and it was later changed.

Of course we have had people violate the ex post facto law, like President Clinton shoved through, in 1993, taxes on Social Security, taxes on money that had already been earned under different rules of taxation. That was a violation of the Constitution that was not thrown out, but it was clearly a violation of the Constitution. So those things do happen, even in a republic.

But with a republic as the Founders gave us, this idea of liberty could take hold. It wasn't just might makes right, somebody powerful intimidate the rest

into voting to string you up or to throw you out of the community. No, you had to abide by existing laws; and your conduct, if appropriate under the law at the time, could not be changed to punish you for something that happened before it was a crime.

So much wisdom in the Constitution, and that wisdom is being cast aside. But that wisdom gave us the electoral college, without which you would never see the Presidential candidates going to all the different States. They would never go to all the different cities that they have because the elections would be decided by the big urban areas. And you can look on the map that shows, most of them have red for Republican, blue for Democrats. Years ago it was the other way around. Red depicted Democrats. But since so many of them were becoming socialists, they were offended that the red made it look like they are red Communists. So somewhere along the way—I can't find who decided to make the color change—but more started making red Republican and blue Democrat. Colors don't matter.

But if you look at the counties that voted for Hillary Clinton, you quickly see that she was a fringe candidate. She was fringe on the West Coast, the big cities on the West Coast; a fringe candidate on the East Coast, the big cities on the fringe of the Nation; fringe up in the very north, the big cities in the very north; fringe along the southern border, and basically just a fringe candidate, which I guess would make the Democratic Party, when you look at who voted for the Democratic candidate, you would have to say this is now a fringe party in the United States.

You have the Republican Party that, apparently, according to the votes of the majority, represents over 90 percent of the geographical United States, and you have this other party, this fringe party, that represents the fringes around the edge of the country, basically. There are a few larger in the middle, but they are a bit of an anomaly, because mostly what we see is a fringe candidate and a fringe party. So it will be interesting to see where we go from here.

Obviously, we have a Justice Department that is not interested in protecting our Constitution, protecting the election process as they are mandated to do; and, frankly, when you have a Department of Justice that selectively enforces the law and so totally disregards other parts of the law, then they are really not a Department of Justice. If this administration had continued on, then we would seriously need to look to provide a more appropriate name for the Department of Justice because this is not—it has not been—a Department of Justice.

When you look at what appear to have been crimes committed by IRS

personnel, like Lois Lerner, perjury committed before Congress, crimes across America, as my friend, John Fund, wrote in his book about illegal voting, one of the—as I have heard John Fund say, perhaps the biggest fraud in America about our elections is the fraud that has been telling people that there is no illegal voting going on. There is certainly illegal voting going on, and many have chosen to look the other way.

But a majority of the geographic and a majority of the electoral college, elected electors, indicate they want the law applied across the country fairly. Section 11(b) of the Voting Rights Act makes it a crime for anyone to "intimidate, threaten, or coerce, or attempt to intimidate, threaten, or coerce any person for voting or attempting to vote."

While this has been applied in the past to ordinary, everyday voters in Federal elections, the language does not limit it only to such voters. Electors who are casting their votes for President and Vice President are also protected by section 11(b), since the electoral college is an essential part of the Federal voting process.

This is supported by section 14(c) of the Voting Rights Act, which says that "voting includes all action necessary to make a vote effective in any primary, special, or general election."

Obviously, the votes cast by Americans on November 8 will not be effective if the electors they chose are intimidated from casting their votes in the electoral college.

Federal law, which is 3 U.S.C., section 7, requires electors to cast their votes on the first Monday after the second Wednesday of December, which this year is December 19. These are recorded as certificates of votes, signed, sealed, and delivered by December 28 to the President of the Senate and the Archivist of the United States. Congress is required to meet on January 6 in joint session to count the electoral college votes.

As we know from so much of the lame stream media, like CNN, MSNBC, there was outrage when Donald Trump said he wasn't sure. He couldn't say beforehand that he wouldn't have questions about the outcome of the election if there were indications of massive fraud in the election. But as we heard from the lame stream media, oh, that would threaten the very foundation of this country. It would destroy the basis for this country. It was just such a threat to our very existence.

Well, now those same people that said those things are, according to they, themselves, risking this country. They are putting the very foundation of our country at risk.

And we all know now—some raised this during the election, but it was not clear until a recount began to be demanded by a third-party candidate—we can now say, clearly, the evidence is in. I used to try felony cases as a judge, and before that, years before that, as a prosecutor. We can now rest our case.

Jill Stein was nothing more than a sham candidate to help Hillary Clinton, to try to pull votes away from others to help Hillary Clinton win the election. Clearly, that is what she was. Some suspected that. Some raised that issue. And now, obviously, she has no chance of winning anything in a recount—nothing. She has no chance of winning anything after a recount. So, clearly, the only reason she is doing it is to continue her effort to help Hillary Clinton become President, despite the will of the American people, through the electoral college, through the law as it was designed and set up.

Electors across the country should not be getting threatened. The Justice Department should be outraged, but they are not. They are not bothered in the least that the lives of the electors who will decide the Presidency are being threatened and that a constitutional crisis is at hand. And it shows, yet again, why over 90 percent of the—except for the fringes—Americans have said we want a change. We want an America that can actually move toward Dr. King's dream of people being judged not by the color of their skin, but by the content of their character. I hope and continue to pray that we will get there.

□ 1245

This quote in the article: "The U.S. Justice Department, which is charged with protecting all voters, should act to quash this outrage immediately."

Obviously, they are not interested in quashing an outrage. They have done more to stir up racial disharmony in this country. They have done more to supplant and subvert the intent of the Constitution and the clear meaning in the Constitution, and I cannot wait to have an administration that will at least make an overt effort to enforce the law as it exists.

The President, in his first term, told people over 20 times: I can't just do amnesty; that has to be done by Congress.

Somebody figured out—after his first term it appears to be when it really kicked up heavily—look, who will stop you? Sure, it is against the law. Sure, it is against the Constitution for you to do amnesty and to do executive orders that take away or rewrite laws that were passed by the House and Senate and signed by another President. You can just write them like any good monarch would. Who is going to stop you?

Somebody figured out to present that to the President. It had to be what happened because he had said so many times that he didn't have the power to do what he ultimately started doing.

You realize, gee, that is right. The soon-to-be-leaving HARRY REID will surely protect President Obama from the Senate allowing anything that follows the law coming out of the House to enforce the law, the Senate will be able to stop it. So if Congress wants to cut off funding for what the President is doing illegally, the Senate Democrats will protect the President and protect his illegal conduct. So you won't have to worry; you can do whatever you want.

Amnesty was often granted by not even an executive order. It was granted by a series of memos by the Secretary of Homeland Security, Jeh Johnson. He rewrote the law with memos. So it will be nice to get back to having enforcement of the law because this article yesterday from Paul Bedard says: "A United Nations mix of illegal immigrants are now flooding through the U.S.-Mexico border, especially from Haiti and Pakistan, raising concerns of terrorism costing Americans billions, according to a new report and Senate testimony."

They have a quote here from my friend, Representative HENRY CUELLAR from Texas, a Democrat, but a great man. He said: "It is because people from different parts of the world, Africa, Middle East, other parts of the world are now realizing that all you have to do is get to the southern border of the United States and there's a process there you can claim a legal defense and you just get to come in. I mean, people, the smuggling organizations know exactly what they're doing."

As the border patrolmen have told me during late hours and early mornings talking to them out on the border, the drug cartels control every inch of the Mexico-U.S. border. They do so from the Mexico side, but they control what happens on the U.S. side under this administration.

We saw routinely that there were groups that came across who were not threats criminally, but they either wanted jobs or they wanted U.S. welfare, and they knew that under this administration we would not turn them back and say: No, you cannot come in illegally.

They would not interdict and enforce the law. They would say: Come on in. We have some questions to ask you before we give you a slip of paper, send you on your way or house you or, as some of the border patrolmen said, We end up sending them wherever they want to go in the United States.

They call the Border Patrol logistics. They get them to our side of the border, and we ship them anywhere they want to go.

So it is no wonder that we would have a request for this administration asking for billions more money to process folks. Another $2.2 billion was mentioned. I saw another article where it lists the different components that the administration wanted to do. If you add up all the different requests and different ways that this administration wants to use the money from American taxpayers, and it is to take money away from Americans who are here legally who are working and who are struggling to provide for themselves and their family, take their money away and give that to people who are coming in illegally.

There was a law I found out about in England visiting with some of their social security-type folks in their government. They have a law that you are supposed to be there for 5 years contributing to that social security-type system for 5 years before you can ever make a claim for a dime of it. Now, I hear there are abuses of that system because they may not have the best control over it, but it is a system that we have in this country and some other countries. You are taking money from people that earned it and giving it to people who are breaking the law.

If you do that long enough, that place that at one time was a shining light on the hill goes broke. The light goes out. Once that happens in America, as friends from other parts of the world have said: If you lose your freedom in America, the rest of the world has no chance.

You will realize historically a United States of America where people will go fight for freedom, they will create strength, a strong economy in their own country, strong enough because they enforce the rule of law across the board and become strong enough economically that they will go shed their blood and spend their money to get freedom for people who are suffering under the forces of evil.

Every now and then you have a President like Jimmy Carter who will say: Let's get rid of the Shah. Then he welcomes the Ayatollah Khomeini who was, as he said, a man of peace which opened Pandora's box. Radical Islamists had been put in a box for many decades, but President Carter was complicit in helping because he is a well-intentioned man, a good man and well intentioned—yeah, maybe a little anti-Israel, but he wanted to help folks. Out of his ignorance on radical Islam, he, for the first time in many decades, placed radical Islamists in charge of a massive military and a whole country. Since then, the world has been paying a very heavy price for what happened.

So we have a job to do. We took an oath in this body to support and defend the Constitution of the United States. As Donald Trump was saying yesterday in Ohio: our devotion and our oath is to one country. We say a pledge to a flag. That used to be true. It used to be that people learned enough history.

I love history. People like coach Sam Parker inspired me to love history. We learned it, and we knew what it took to keep a republic, madam, if we could. Because of Federal intervention in education, we have not helped our kids in suffering schools. We have made them subjects to this master Federal Government: You do what we say or we don't send you any of the money you sent to us. We will fix up our offices, we will fix up a massive bureaucracy, and we will dictate to you from on high what we want done regardless of what Congress says.

They are not as bad as the Corps of Engineers, the EPA, and the FDA have been recently; but they have really not helped. As I said to President Bush's Secretary of Education—a very nice person. She had helped, I think, Texas schools when she was in Austin, but then she came here and disregarded the 10th Amendment and the Constitution that did not enumerate education as a Federal power. It was reserved to the States and the people. She began acting unconstitutionally.

As I explained to her, you ought to come to Gladewater, Texas. There is an amazing school there that helps between 120 and 130 special needs kids. One of them, if he touches something shiny, he has had a big day, and you mandate that they have to do a test for that child. They had a child at the Saint Louis School in Tyler. They told her she needed to come visit because they had a goal that by the end of the year this young man would be able to stick a fork in a piece of food and get it to his mouth. The goal they believed was reachable, but because the Federal Government was involved and they say, You don't get any of the money you sent us from Texas unless you do exactly what we say, that was not allowed. They allowed an alternative test that if he could point to a sticker that had a picture of food on it by the end of the year, then he would pass the test and that school would get back money from the Federal Government that those Texas taxpayers had sent to it to siphon off for whatever they wanted. So by the end of this year, that special needs young man—severe special needs—was able to point to a sticker that had a picture of food, but he could not feed himself.

That is the kind of insanity that has only gotten worse over the last 8 years. I thought a silver lining to President Obama being elected President was at least he is going to end the No Child Left Behind Act because that would mean returning the power to the States and the people that knew what they were doing.

A few years ago we were far higher in the studies of the capabilities of schoolchildren. We have dropped. We are not doing so well. There may be improvement in one year over another, but if you really want to leave no child behind, then you need to stop coddling the teachers' unions and coddle the teachers by letting them do what they know is best, subject to local control. If they are not doing their job, you don't have to go begging to Washington

or a teachers' union, you can go to the school board. If the school board won't do the right thing, you can run against them, get elected, and then fix it yourself.

☐ 1300

When Sonny Bono in California ran up against a city manager that was so bigoted he would not let Sonny have the license to open his restaurant, that is how he got involved in politics. He found out who hired and fired the city manager—it was the mayor—so he ran for mayor, and the first thing he did was fire the abusive city manager. That is how a Republic system is supposed to work. It is a form of democracy, not a pure democracy, so that we can have ex post facto laws, and we can keep people from having their conduct criminalized after they committed it.

But we have got to hit the ground running at the first of the year and start the process of trying to heal America. President Obama did not make the school system better; he made matters worst.

We had a voucher program here in D.C. that minority kids—actually, it is the minorities are a majority here; minority elsewhere. These poor kids were suffering from a broken school system that had more than enough money to properly educate the kids, but kids were the victims of the bureaucracy.

What else has this Justice Department done? Well, they have gone around and started up racial tensions where there shouldn't have been. They stirred up rumors that, for example, if you are a Black young man in America, you are 20 times more likely to be shot than if you are a White person in America of that same age, which is simply not true.

We saw in different parts of the country when we had a Black mayor or a Black police chief, he was not a racist, was not out to harm Blacks in America, but try to do justice by them. They ultimately found in most cases that had been brought, actually, the police were justified in what they were doing.

Since police are composed of human beings, there are going to be some rotten apples. When I was a judge, I saw one every now and then—very, very rarely. But every now and then you did. And I would contend, from my experience handling thousands of felony cases, that the law enforcement officers I dealt with have a much tinier percentage of problems than the general population of America. When we find a police officer who is abusive, who is problematic, he or she should be punished.

But after 9/11, America was jarred awake for the first time in decades and really began again to appreciate the job law enforcement officers have done for us to keep the peace, to allow us not to be beat up by a bigger bully on our block, but allow the law to be en-

forced more equally and fairly. It is never perfect. There is always room for improvement.

People began to appreciate our first responders without contempt because they were stopping traffic. And they began to appreciate our military more because it was willing to go lay down their lives for their friends, for the people in this country, which Jesus said was the greatest love. And he absolutely knew. He laid down his life for us.

But in the last 8 years, we have become so racially divided.

The regret I have from going back to Mount Pleasant is how choked up I got going back to my old high school that was so good to me, did such a great job—public-school educating me, my brothers, my sister. I loved Coach Willie Williams, and I saw him after so long and got a hug that just touched deeply. Somebody said: Did you take a picture?

I didn't even think about a picture. I wasn't thinking picture. Here was a man that coached me, who would not put up with anybody using race. It didn't matter to Coach Williams. He expected us to perform. I wish I had gotten a picture. I have got to do that. What a great man.

Well, unfortunately, we have other information. There was a damning Department of Homeland Security report that exposed the administration's claim that as many as 81 percent of people attempting to cross the border illegally were apprehended from the port. We found out that actually it is not anything like 81 percent. It may be more like 54 percent.

Shockingly, the report's authors find that the estimated apprehension rate between ports of entry in 2005 was only 36 percent—and that was 2005. It has not gotten better, even though tricks of adjusting the statistics have gotten more multiplied.

We have got to defend our Nation, we have got to enforce the law, we have got to get this country back to being a shining light on the hill, instead of one overwhelmed by people who want to violate our law. They don't want to do it, but failing to enforce our borders will eliminate our ability to be the most generous country when it comes to visas and legal entry.

No other countries are massively larger in size—geographically in size or populationwise. No one awards more visas than we do—over 1 million. Yet, that will end up coming to an end with the failure to enforce the law. Particularly, there were problems in the Bush administration, the Clinton administration, the Bush administration before that, but it has just gone exponentially crazy over this administration, and we have got to get it under control.

One other thing: I continue to hear some in America say the days of the

United States being a manufacturing powerhouse are over. Well, I know from history—and apparently Donald Trump knows from just his business instincts—that if a strong country cannot produce the things it needs to defend itself and defend freedom, it will cease being a free country after the next significant conflict. It is just a fact.

The Battle of the Bulge, so many don't realize, even as late as that occurred in World War II, it had a good shot of prevailing and driving the Allied forces from the bulge in the middle out to the water's edge. But one of the most fundamental problems was they ran out of fuel.

Well, east Texas was the largest known reserve when it was discovered, and it provided plenty of oil. Our tanks had fuel, but, as we became more dependent on other countries, that became a problem. American ingenuity has allowed us to find more natural gas and more oil. Now we find out in west Texas natural gas is far cleaner, and I hope and pray, under Donald Trump, we will move to use more of that.

If we don't get back the factories—and we didn't just lose them from the Rust Belt. I lost a lot of steel plants like Lufkin Industries. It got bought up by GE. They didn't care about Lufkin. They weren't going to sponsor any little-league teams. They didn't care. They just bought them up, took their patents. They told me their headquarters for that operation was in Italy, over in the Mediterranean. This is a company that doesn't pay us taxes, but the head of it is close friends with the President.

Well, it is time we got back to manufacturing steel in America, steel pipe in America, manufacturing what we need to make tanks, planes, cars, and buses. Do that here. It is time we got back jobs to make paper. We have renewable resources here we quit using. They are not sequoias. They are not redwoods. They are pine trees. They grow back every 20 years. You can find pictures of places in east Texas where there were no trees, and yet, after the timber industry came in, they became forested again.

We can become great again, but we have got to be more responsible. We have got to protect our borders from those who want to do us harm and violate our laws. If we would do that, a 10-year-old little girl in my county would be alive today.

Mr. Speaker, I yield back the balance of my time.

SENATE BILLS REFERRED

Bills of the Senate of the following titles were taken from the Speaker's table and, under the rule, referred as follows:

S. 10. An act to provide for the consideration of a definition of anti-Semitism for the enforcement of Federal antidiscrimination laws concerning education programs or activities; to the Committee on the Judiciary.

S. 2058. An act to require the Secretary of Commerce to study the coverage gaps of the Next Generation Weather Radar of the National Weather Service and to develop a plan for improving radar coverage and hazardous weather detection and forecasting; to the Committee on Science, Space and Technology.

S. 3492. An act to designate the Traverse City VA Community-Based Outpatient Clinic of the Department of Veterans Affairs in Traverse City, Michigan, as the "Colonel Demas T. Craw VA Clinic"; to the Committee on Veterans' Affairs.

ENROLLED BILLS SIGNED

Karen L. Haas, Clerk of the House, reported and found truly enrolled bills of the House of the following titles, which were thereupon signed by the Speaker:

H.R. 3471. An act to amend title 38, United States Code to make certain improvements in the provision of automobiles and adaptive equipment by the Department of Veterans Affairs.

H.R. 5111. An act to prohibit the use of certain clauses in form contracts that restrict the ability of a consumer to communicate regarding the goods or services offered in interstate commerce that were the subject of the contract, and for other purposes.

H.R. 6297. An act to reauthorize the Iran Sanctions Act of 1996.

SENATE ENROLLED BILLS SIGNED

The Speaker announced his signature to enrolled bills of the Senate of the following titles:

S. 1808. An act to require the Secretary of Homeland Security to conduct a Northern Border threat analysis, and for other purposes.

S. 1915. An act to direct the Secretary of Homeland Security to make anthrax vaccines available to emergency response providers, and for other purposes.

ADJOURNMENT

Mr. GOHMERT. Mr. Speaker, I move that the House do now adjourn.

The motion was agreed to; accordingly (at 1 o'clock and 10 minutes p.m.), under its previous order, the House adjourned until Monday, December 5, 2016, at noon for morning-hour debate.

EXECUTIVE COMMUNICATIONS, ETC.

Under clause 2 of rule XIV, executive communications were taken from the Speaker's table and referred as follows:

7709. A letter from the Chief Counsel, FEMA, Department of Homeland Security, transmitting the Department's final rule — Suspension of Community Eligibility; Massachusetts: Marshfield, Town of, Plymouth County [Docket ID: FEMA-2016-0002; Internal Agency Docket No.: FEMA-8453] received November 28, 2016, pursuant to 5 U.S.C. 801(a)(1)(A); Public Law 104-121, Sec. 251; (110 Stat. 868); to the Committee on Financial Services.

7710. A letter from the Associate General Counsel for Legislation and Regulations, Office of the Secretary, Department of Housing and Urban Development, transmitting the Department's final rule — Violence Against Women Reauthorization Act of 2013: Implementation in HUD Housing Programs [Docket No.: FR-5720-F-03] (RIN: 2501-AD71) received November 28, 2016, pursuant to 5 U.S.C. 801(a)(1)(A); Public Law 104-121, Sec. 251; (110 Stat. 868); to the Committee on Financial Services.

7711. A letter from the Associate General Counsel for Legislation and Regulations, Office of the Secretary, Department of Housing and Urban Development, transmitting the Department's Major final rule — Establishing a More Effective Fair Market Rent System; Using Small Area Fair Market Rents in the Housing Choice Voucher Program Instead of the Current 50th Percentile FMRs [Docket No.: FR-5855-F-03] (RIN: 2501-AD74) received November 28, 2016, pursuant to 5 U.S.C. 801(a)(1)(A); Public Law 104-121, Sec. 251; (110 Stat. 868); to the Committee on Financial Services.

7712. A letter from the Counsel to the Director, Office of Hearings and Appeals, Department of the Interior, transmitting the Department's final rules — Resource Agency Hearings and Alternatives Development Procedures in Hydropower Licenses [Docket No.: 080220223-6961-03] (RINs: 0596-AC42, 1090-AA91, and 0648-AU01) received November 28, 2016, pursuant to 5 U.S.C. 801(a)(1)(A); Public Law 104-121, Sec. 251; (110 Stat. 868); to the Committee on Energy and Commerce.

7713. A letter from the Director, Defense Security Cooperation Agency, Department of Defense, transmitting a proposed Letter of Offer and Acceptance to Poland, Transmittal No. 16-72, pursuant to Sec. 36(b)(1) of the Arms Export Control Act, as amended; to the Committee on Foreign Affairs.

7714. A letter from the Acting Assistant Secretary for Administration and Management, Department of Labor, transmitting notification of the link to the Department's FY 2014 and 2015 Inventory of Inherently Governmental Activities and of Commercial Activities, pursuant to 31 U.S.C. 501 note; Public Law 105-270, Sec. 2(c)(1)(A); (112 Stat. 2382); to the Committee on Oversight and Government Reform.

7715. A letter from the Administrator, Environmental Protection Agency, transmitting the Agency's Semiannual Report of the Office of the Inspector General for the period ending September 30, 2016, pursuant to Sec. 5 of the Inspector General Act of 1978, as amended; to the Committee on Oversight and Government Reform.

7716. A letter from the Director, Office of Legislative Affairs, Federal Deposit Insurance Corporation, transmitting the Corporation's interim final rule — Revision of the FDIC's Freedom of Information Act Regulations (RIN: 3064-AE53) received November 29, 2016, pursuant to 5 U.S.C. 801(a)(1)(A); Public Law 104-121, Sec. 251; (110 Stat. 868); to the Committee on Oversight and Government Reform.

7717. A letter from the Chairman, Federal Labor Relations Authority, transmitting the Authority's FY 2016 Performance and Accountability Report, pursuant to 31 U.S.C. 3515(a)(1); Public Law 101-576, Sec. 303(a)(1) (as amended by Public Law 107-289, Sec. 2(a)); (116 Stat. 2049); to the Committee on Oversight and Government Reform.

7718. A letter from the Chairman, Federal Maritime Commission, transmitting the

Commission's Fiscal Year 2016 Performance and Accountability Report, pursuant to 31 U.S.C. 3515(a)(1); Public Law 101-576, Sec. 303(a)(1) (as amended by Public Law 107-289, Sec. 2(a)); (116 Stat. 2049); to the Committee on Oversight and Government Reform.

7719. A letter from the Chairwoman, Federal Trade Commission, transmitting the Commission's Fiscal Year 2016 Agency Financial Report, pursuant to 31 U.S.C. 3515(a)(1); Public Law 101-576, Sec. 303(a)(1) (as amended by Public Law 107-289, Sec. 2(a)); (116 Stat. 2049); to the Committee on Oversight and Government Reform.

7720. A letter from the Chairman, National Endowment for the Arts, transmitting the Endowment's Fiscal Year 2016 Agency Financial Report, pursuant to 31 U.S.C. 3515(a)(1); Public Law 101-576, Sec. 303(a)(1) (as amended by Public Law 107-289, Sec. 2(a)); (116 Stat. 2049); to the Committee on Oversight and Government Reform.

7721. A letter from the Chairman, Occupational Safety and Health Review Commission, transmitting the Commission's Fiscal Year 2016 Performance and Accountability Report, pursuant to 31 U.S.C. 3515(a)(1); Public Law 101-576, Sec. 303(a)(1) (as amended by Public Law 107-289, Sec. 2(a)); (116 Stat. 2049); to the Committee on Oversight and Government Reform.

7722. A letter from the Chairman, U.S. Merit Systems Protection Board, transmitting the Board's FY 2016 Agency Financial Report, pursuant to 31 U.S.C. 3515(a)(1); Public Law 101-576, Sec. 303(a)(1) (as amended by Public Law 107-289, Sec. 2(a)); (116 Stat. 2049); to the Committee on Oversight and Government Reform.

7723. A letter from the Chief, Forest Service, Department of Agriculture, transmitting a proposal to accept a donation of approximately 3,323 acres of private land from the American River Conservancy, a California non-profit public benefit corporation, pursuant to 16 U.S.C. 1135(a); Public Law 88-577, Sec. 6(a); (78 Stat. 896); to the Committee on Natural Resources.

PUBLIC BILLS AND RESOLUTIONS

Under clause 2 of rule XII, public bills and resolutions of the following titles were introduced and severally referred, as follows:

By Mr. CARTWRIGHT (for himself and Mr. GRIJALVA):

H.R. 6424. A bill to require the National Institute of Standards and Technology to establish a premise plumbing research laboratory, and for other purposes; to the Committee on Science, Space, and Technology.

By Mr. CRAWFORD (for himself, Mr. THOMPSON of Mississippi, Ms. SEWELL of Alabama, Mr. HARPER, Mr. PALAZZO, Mr. WESTERMAN, Mr. HILL, Mr. WOMACK, and Mr. ADERHOLT):

H.R. 6425. A bill to provide the force and effect of law for certain regulations relating to the taking of double-crested cormorants to reduce depredation at aquaculture facilities and protect public resources; to the Committee on Natural Resources.

By Mr. BUCK:

H.R. 6426. A bill to amend title 5, United States Code, to provide for a 2 year prohibition on employment in a career civil service position for any former political appointee, and for other purposes; to the Committee on Oversight and Government Reform.

By Mr. GARRETT (for himself, Mr. NEUGEBAUER, Mr. DUFFY, Mr. CARNEY, Ms. VELÁZQUEZ, Mr. MCHENRY,

Mr. HUIZENGA of Michigan, Mr. POLIQUIN, Mr. SCHWEIKERT, Mr. HURT of Virginia, and Mr. LUETKEMEYER):

H.R. 6427. A bill to improve the operation of United States capital markets, and for other purposes; to the Committee on Financial Services.

By Ms. TITUS (for herself, Mr. BERA, Ms. HANABUSA, Ms. MATSUI, Mr. PETERSON, Mr. POCAN, Mr. CONYERS, Mr. COURTNEY, Mr. O'ROURKE, Mr. YARMUTH, Ms. SCHAKOWSKY, Mrs. LOWEY, Ms. KUSTER, Ms. DELBENE, Ms. MCCOLLUM, Ms. MICHELLE LUJAN GRISHAM of New Mexico, Mr. KEATING, Mr. BISHOP of Georgia, Mr. NOLAN, Mrs. DINGELL, Ms. EDWARDS, Ms. FRANKEL of Florida, Mr. GARAMENDI, Mr. DEUTCH, Mrs. BUSTOS, Mr. COHEN, Ms. SLAUGHTER, Ms. MOORE, Ms. CASTOR of Florida, Ms. PINGREE, Ms. WASSERMAN SCHULTZ, Mr. NADLER, Ms. KAPTUR, Mr. MCGOVERN, and Ms. BONAMICI):

H.R. 6428. A bill to amend title XVIII of the Social Security Act to limit Medicare part B premium increases for 2017; to the Committee on Energy and Commerce, and in addition to the Committee on Ways and Means, for a period to be subsequently determined by the Speaker, in each case for consideration of such provisions as fall within the jurisdiction of the committee concerned.

By Mr. BABIN (for himself, Mr. CONAWAY, Mr. FARENTHOLD, and Mr. WILLIAMS):

H.R. 6429. A bill to amend the Intermodal Surface Transportation Efficiency Act of 1991 to include certain areas in the Central Texas Corridor; to the Committee on Transportation and Infrastructure.

By Ms. KAPTUR (for herself, Mr. BENISHEK, and Mr. QUIGLEY):

H.R. 6430. A bill to require the Under Secretary of Commerce for Oceans and Atmosphere to conduct an assessment of cultural and historic resources in the waters of the Great Lakes, and for other purposes; to the Committee on Natural Resources.

By Ms. KUSTER (for herself and Ms. STEFANIK):

H.R. 6431. A bill to ensure United States jurisdiction over offenses committed by United States personnel stationed in Canada in furtherance of border security initiatives; to the Committee on the Judiciary.

By Ms. SLAUGHTER:

H.R. 6432. A bill to require the Secretary of Labor to monitor the trade deficits between the United States and other countries, and for other purposes; to the Committee on Ways and Means.

By Mr. TURNER (for himself, Mr. ZINKE, Mr. MILLER of Florida, Mr. LUETKEMEYER, Mr. DIAZ-BALART, Mr. COLLINS of Georgia, Mr. WITTMAN, Mr. BROOKS of Alabama, Mr. AUSTIN SCOTT of Georgia, Mr. ALLEN, Mr. KELLY of Mississippi, Mr. BRAT, Mr. YOHO, Mr. RIBBLE, Mr. DESJARLAIS, Mr. RICE of South Carolina, Mr. BOUSTANY, Mr. WALBERG, Mr. SCHWEIKERT, Mr. LAMBORN, Mr. SMITH of Missouri, Mrs. WAGNER, Mr. CHABOT, Mrs. HARTZLER, Mrs. BLACKBURN, Mr. WENSTRUP, Mr. MEADOWS, Mr. JOHNSON of Ohio, Mr. MCKINLEY, Mr. TIPTON, Mr. JENKINS of West Virginia, Mr. LANCE, Mr. DAVIDSON, Mr. ROE of Tennessee, Mr. ABRAHAM, Mrs. WALORSKI, Ms. GRANGER, Mr. NEUGEBAUER, Mr. PEARCE, Mr. WEBER of Texas, Mr. CARTER of Texas, Mr. ROGERS of Alabama, Mr. CONAWAY, Mr.

CULBERSON, Mr. OLSON, Mr. FARENTHOLD, Mr. REED, Mr. GUINTA, Mr. BISHOP of Utah, Mr. CHAFFETZ, Mr. STEWART, Mrs. LOVE, Mr. WALKER, and Mr. STIVERS):

H.R. 6433. A bill to render ineligible for Federal funds any institution of higher education that removes, censors, takes down, prohibits, or otherwise halts display of a flag of the United States; to the Committee on Education and the Workforce.

By Mr. GRAYSON:

H.J. Res. 105. A joint resolution proposing an amendment to the Constitution of the United States to treat Puerto Rico as if it were a State for purposes of the election of the President and Vice President; to the Committee on the Judiciary.

By Mr. FOSTER (for himself and Mr. TAKANO):

H. Res. 940. A resolution expressing support for designation of December 3, 2016, as the "National Day of 3D Printing"; to the Committee on Energy and Commerce.

CONSTITUTIONAL AUTHORITY STATEMENT

Pursuant to clause 7 of rule XII of the Rules of the House of Representatives, the following statements are submitted regarding the specific powers granted to Congress in the Constitution to enact the accompanying bill or joint resolution.

By Mr. CARTWRIGHT:
H.R. 6424.
Congress has the power to enact this legislation pursuant to the following:
Article I; Section 8; Clause 1 of the Constitution states The Congress shall have Power To lay and collect Taxes, Duties, Imposts and Excises, to pay the Debts and provide for the common Defence and general Welfare of the United States. . .
Article I; Section 8; Clause 18 of the Constitution states To make all laws which shall be necessary and proper for carrying into execution the foregoing powers, and all other powers vested by this Constitution in the government of the United States, or in any department or officer thereof.

By Mr. CRAWFORD:
H.R. 6425.
Congress has the power to enact this legislation pursuant to the following:
Article VI, Clause 2 of the United States Constitution as upheld by the Supreme Court in Missouri v. Holland, 252 U.S. 416 (1920)

By Mr. BUCK:
H.R. 6426.
Congress has the power to enact this legislation pursuant to the following:
Pursuant to clause 1, section 8 of Article I of the United States Constitution of the United States which states: "The Congress shall have Power to lay and collect Taxes, Duties, Imposts, and Excises, to pay the Debts, and provide for the common Defense and General Welfare of the United States; but all Duties and Imposts and Excises shall be uniform throughout the United States."

By Mr. GARRETT:
H.R. 6427.
Congress has the power to enact this legislation pursuant to the following:
Article I, Section 8, Clauses 1 ("The Congress shall have Power To lay and collect Taxes, Duties, Imposts and Excises, to pay the Debts and provide for the common Defense and general Welfare of the United States; but all Duties, Imposts and Excises

shall be uniform throughout the United States''), 3 (''To regulate Commerce with foreign Nations, and among the several States, and with the Indian Tribes''), and 18 (''To make all Laws which shall be necessary and proper for carrying into Execution the foregoing Powers, and all other Powers vested by this Constitution in the Government of the United States, or in any Department or Officer thereof'').

By Ms. TITUS:
H.R. 6428.
Congress has the power to enact this legislation pursuant to the following:
Article 1, Section 8, Clause 1

By Mr. BABIN:
H.R. 6429.
Congress has the power to enact this legislation pursuant to the following:
Article I, Section 8

By Ms. KAPTUR:
H.R. 6430.
Congress has the power to enact this legislation pursuant to the following:
Article I, Section 8, Clause 18:
To make all Laws which shall be necessary and proper for carrying into Execution the foregoing Powers, and all other Powers vested by this Constitution in the Government of the United States, or in any Department or Officer thereof.

By Ms. KUSTER:
H.R. 6431.
Congress has the power to enact this legislation pursuant to the following:
Article I, Section 8, Clause 3 of the United States Constitution, the Taxing and Spending Clause: ''To regulate Commerce with foreign Nations, and among the several States, and with the Indian Tribes. . .''

By Ms. SLAUGHTER:
H.R. 6432.
Congress has the power to enact this legislation pursuant to the following:
Article I, Section 8 of the Constitution of the United States.

By Mr. TURNER:
H.R. 6433.
Congress has the power to enact this legislation pursuant to the following:
Article I, Section 8, Clause 1 of the United States Constitution, to ''lay and collect Taxes, Duties, Imposts and Excises, to pay the Debts and provide for the common Defence and general Welfare of the United States. . . .''
Article I, Section 8, Clause 18 of the United States Constitution, ''To make all Laws which shall be necessary and proper for carrying into Execution the foregoing Powers, and all other Powers vested by this Constitution in the Government of the United States, or in any Department or Officer thereof.''

By Mr. GRAYSON:
H.J. Res. 105.
Congress has the power to enact this legislation pursuant to the following:
Article 5 of the United States Constitution.

ADDITIONAL SPONSORS

Under clause 7 of rule XII, sponsors were added to public bills and resolutions, as follows:
H.R. 704: Mr. LAMALFA.
H.R. 1151: Mr. DENHAM.
H.R. 1258: Mr. THOMPSON of California.
H.R. 1283: Mr. KNIGHT.

H.R. 1399: Mr. DAVID SCOTT of Georgia, Mr. BUTTERFIELD, and Ms. ADAMS.
H.R. 1733: Mr. KNIGHT.
H.R. 2903: Mr. DAVIDSON.
H.R. 3084: Ms. FRANKEL of Florida, Mr. JENKINS of West Virginia, and Ms. DELBENE.
H.R. 3683: Ms. PLASKETT.
H.R. 3713: Ms. PINGREE.
H.R. 3742: Mr. GARRETT and Ms. KUSTER.
H.R. 4298: Mr. BRADY of Pennsylvania, Mr. GRIFFITH, Mr. NORCROSS, and Mr. SHUSTER.
H.R. 4595: Mr. KILDEE.
H.R. 4770: Mr. JORDAN.
H.R. 5067: Mr. QUIGLEY.
H.R. 5082: Mr. REICHERT and Mr. NEAL.
H.R. 5310: Mr. COHEN.
H.R. 5947: Mr. COHEN.
H.R. 5999: Mr. FLORES, Mr. POLIQUIN, Mrs. BLACKBURN, Mr. PAULSEN, Mr. ISSA, Mr. WESTERMAN, Mr. MULLIN, Mr. BISHOP of Michigan, Mr. FLEISCHMANN, Mr. PITTENGER, Mr. GIBBS, Mr. WEBSTER of Florida, Mr. CHABOT, Mr. LAMBORN, and Mr. NEAL.
H.R. 6147: Mr. PERLMUTTER, Mr. POSEY, Ms. LOFGREN, Mr. LANGEVIN, Mr. BEYER, Ms. BONAMICI, Mr. GRAYSON, Mr. HONDA, and Mr. JOHNSON of Georgia.
H.R. 6149: Ms. STEFANIK.
H.R. 6208: Ms. MENG and Mr. LOWENTHAL.
H.R. 6340: Mr. GARAMENDI, Mr. HUFFMAN, Mr. YARMUTH, Mr. MOULTON, and Mr. DESAULNIER.
H.R. 6344: Mr. STEWART.
H.R. 6421: Mr. SMITH of New Jersey and Ms. GRANGER.
H.J. Res. 103: Ms. SPEIER.
H. Con. Res. 17: Mr. COMER.
H. Res. 831: Mr. PERRY.

EXTENSIONS OF REMARKS

RECOGNIZING THE HONORABLE JUDGE FAYE D'OPAL

HON. JARED HUFFMAN

OF CALIFORNIA

IN THE HOUSE OF REPRESENTATIVES

Friday, December 2, 2016

Mr. HUFFMAN. Mr. Speaker, I rise to recognize the Honorable Faye D'Opal as she retires from a long and distinguished career as Marin County Superior Court Judge on December 31, 2016.

First elected as Marin Superior Court Judge in 2004, Judge D'Opal served in the Felony and Civil Departments, Family Law, Probate, Conservatorships and the past two years as Presiding Judge of the Juvenile Department. She also served as the court's Assistant Presiding Judge (2012–2013) and Presiding Judge (2014–2015) with distinction.

Judge D'Opal's legacy of community service began in rural Arkansas where she participated in the historic efforts to desegregate Little Rock's public schools. She earned her bachelor's degree from Hendrix College in Arkansas and a law degree from the New College of California, San Francisco. She spent 12 years in Latin America working for the Peace Corps, and became a public-interest attorney.

Renowned for her 2013, now historic decision on the death penalty that virtually stopped it in the state of California, Judge D'Opal's career includes many additional legacies and positive impacts on others. From her work to establish a legal self-help center, to her advocacy for abused women for the Legal Aid of Marin, and her work as trustee of the Marin Community Foundation, Judge D'Opal has used her keen intellect to improve the quality of life for others less fortunate by supporting social justice and promoting fairness and equity for all.

In all aspects of her life, Judge D'Opal has acted with principles and courage. As a leader and role model for the LGBT community, and throughout her professional career and extensive public service, she has set a fabulous example for women and young girls everywhere. Even as she is approaching her retirement from the Superior Court, she has been encouraging more women and minorities to get involved in the legal system. Her positive impact on our community will continue as a pro tem judge in juvenile law, and in her pursuit to eliminate domestic violence.

Mr. Speaker, it is therefore fitting that we honor and thank the Honorable Faye D'Opal for her many good deeds, and wish her much enjoyment as she spends more time with her beloved partner, daughters and grandchildren, and hikes, bikes, and kayaks around the beautiful Northern Coast of California.

REMEMBERING CHANCELLOR DEBRA SAUNDERS-WHITE

HON. DAVID E. PRICE

OF NORTH CAROLINA

IN THE HOUSE OF REPRESENTATIVES

Friday, December 2, 2016

Mr. PRICE of North Carolina. Mr. Speaker, I rise today to honor the life and legacy of Dr. Debra Saunders-White, Chancellor of North Carolina Central University. Her death at 59, after a valiant battle with kidney cancer, is a tragic loss for the university and our state. My wife Lisa and I extend our condolences to the family of Dr. Saunders-White, the North Carolina Central community, and her extensive network of colleagues and friends.

Chancellor Debra Saunders-White was a first-generation college student, which gave her insight into the obstacles many students and families face and a passion to overcome them. She also understood the opportunities that come with higher education, especially for lower-income students. She was often found talking with students in the lunch hall or while walking around campus. Her warmth, the personal interest she took in students, and her courage in the face of adversity won the hearts of all who knew her.

Dr. Saunders-White began her career as Assistant Provost of Technology at Hampton University, where she later served as Chief Information Officer. In North Carolina, she first served at the University of North Carolina at Wilmington in the roles of Vice Chancellor of Information Technology, interim Associate Provost, and finally Chief Diversity Officer in the Office of Institutional Diversity. In May 2011, Dr. Saunders-White moved to Washington, D.C. to serve as Deputy Assistant Secretary for Higher Education Programs in the Department of Education.

On June 1st, 2013 Debra Saunders-White was appointed by UNC President Tom Ross and welcomed as the first female chancellor of North Carolina Central University, one of the top Historically Black Universities in this country.

During her time as chancellor, Dr. Saunders-White led an era of growth for North Carolina Central University, cultivating a theme of "Eagle Excellence". Her legacy includes the expansion of a dual degree program with North Carolina State University, as well as a collaboration with Durham Technical Community College to allow more students to transfer to NCCU. Construction of both a new business school and student center will begin next year thanks to Chancellor Saunders-White's efforts. It is a tribute to her legacy that this year North Carolina Central University was recognized as "HBCU of the Year" by HBCU Digest.

I join the North Carolina Central University and Durham communities in mourning the passing of Debra Saunders-White, who set the

university towards an even brighter future with her wise stewardship and strategic vision. We eagerly anticipate the new student center and will think of her every time we walk into it.

Chancellor Saunders-White combined professionalism and a collaborative style in a unique way, and I always enjoyed working with her. I especially admired her courage and determination in continuing to provide leadership throughout her battle with cancer. We join with her family, her many friends, and the students, faculty, and staff of NCCU, in mourning her passing and honoring her exemplary life.

HONORING SENIOR RESIDENT SUPERIOR COURT JUDGE PAUL L. JONES ON THE OCCASION OF HIS RETIREMENT

HON. G. K. BUTTERFIELD

OF NORTH CAROLINA

IN THE HOUSE OF REPRESENTATIVES

Friday, December 2, 2016

Mr. BUTTERFIELD. Mr. Speaker, it is with great pleasure that I rise today to honor Senior Resident Superior Court Judge Paul L. Jones. Judge Jones has been committed to the state of North Carolina and the people of Lenoir and Greene Counties through his work as a community based lawyer, jurist, Army Reservist and his commitment to nonprofit organizations.

Judge Jones is a proud graduate of historic Adkin High School in Kinston, North Carolina, Class of 1967. He received his undergraduate degree from North Carolina Agricultural and Technical State University and his law degree from my alma mater, North Carolina Central University. Judge Jones and I were law school classmates in the Class of 1974. We were the best of friends in law school and our friendship has endured.

Judge Jones work in the legal profession includes a variety of positions including his time serving as a staff attorney and Assistant Clerk of Court with the U.S. Supreme Court, a Judge Advocate Officer in the Army, supervising attorney for the North Carolina Central University Legal Clinic, managing attorney for Eastern Carolina Legal Services, and as a District Court Judge. When a vacancy was created for a Resident Superior Court judge position in 1999, Judge Jones was appointed to the Court and ran unopposed in 2000 and 2008, a position that he is now retiring.

While on the Superior Court bench, Judge Jones was an officer of the North Carolina Judicial Council and a founding member of the Equal Access to Justice Commission. He was a member of the North Carolina Judicial Standards Commission for a five-year term, which included the role of vice-chairman. In 2001, he was elected Vice-President of the North Carolina Bar Association.

Before retiring as a Colonel in the Army Reserves in 2000, Judge Jones served as a

---

Judge Advocate with the 108th Division IT in Charlotte, North Carolina. While serving, Judge Jones was awarded the Army Commendation Medal, Meritorious Service Medal, the National Defense Medal, and the Legion of Merit.

While his commitment to the legal field and the military is commendable, it is noteworthy that he is deeply rooted in his native community of Kinston, North Carolina. Judge Jones has volunteered and been active on more than 20 nonprofit boards within Kinston for over 30 years and received the Kinston-Lenoir County Chamber of Commerce award of Citizen of the Year for 2013.

Judge Jones is married to the former Edwina Link and has two children, Krystle and Erika.

Judge Jones is a man of integrity, valor, and service. I ask my colleagues to join me in applauding my dear friend, Judge Paul L. Jones, and recognize his lifelong devotion to the people of Lenoir County and the State of North Carolina.

HONORING MONSIGNOR EDWARD BARRY

HON. ELIOT L. ENGEL
OF NEW YORK
IN THE HOUSE OF REPRESENTATIVES
Friday, December 2, 2016

Mr. ENGEL. Mr. Speaker, I rise today to honor a man who has been an integral part of the Bronx and Westchester communities for more than four decades, Monsignor Edward Barry.

Born in Washington Heights, Msgr. Barry traces his roots from County Waterford. He graduated from St. Anthony's elementary school in Nanuet, NY in 1961 and then graduated Albertus Magnus High School in Bardonia, NY in 1965. In 1969, he graduated from Cathedral College in New York and then went on to St. Joseph's Seminary. After being ordained in 1973, he was appointed Parochial Vicar at St. Patrick's in Yorktown Heights, NY where he spent 7 years. As a young priest at St. Patrick's parish in Yorktown Heights, he was a member of the Yorktown Interfaith Alliance and a member of the Yorktown Substance Abuse Advisory Board. In 1980, Msgr. Barry was appointed Parochial Vicar of St. Frances de Chantal in the Bronx, NY. Following 6 years at St. Frances, he was appointed in 1986 as Executive Director of Youth Services and CYO for the Archdiocese of New York. From 1986–1991, he served as Chairman of the Board for the Kennedy Center in NYC and Chairman of the Board of Head Start at the Spellman Center in NYC.

In 1991 Msgr. Barry became pastor of St. Charles Borromeo in Dover Plains where he spent the next 13 years during which he was appointed Honorary Prelate. In 2004 he moved to become Dean of the Northeast Bronx Deanery and assigned as Pastor of St. Barnabas in the Bronx, before returning to Yorktown Heights.

Msgr. Barry's faith and devotion have served as a guiding light to countless men and women over the years. This year, the American Irish Association of Westchester is honoring Msgr. Barry at their annual dinner dance. They could not have picked a more deserving honoree. Congratulations to Msgr. Barry on receiving this wonderful recognition, and my thanks to him for all he has done to better his and our community.

GIRL SCOUT GUSTALINE SAMBA EARNS GIRL SCOUT GOLD AWARD

HON. PETE OLSON
OF TEXAS
IN THE HOUSE OF REPRESENTATIVES
Friday, December 2, 2016

Mr. OLSON. Mr. Speaker, I rise today to congratulate Gustaline Samba of Fort Bend County, TX, for earning her Girl Scout Gold Award.

The Gold Award is the highest achievement a Girl Scout can earn. To earn this distinguished award, Gustaline had to spend at least 80 hours developing and executing a project that would benefit the community and have a long-term impact on girls as well. To do this she created "Project Cycle Safety Shield," which addresses bike safety in her community where students often ride their bikes to school.

On behalf of the Twenty-Second Congressional District of Texas, congratulations again to Gustaline Samba for earning her Girl Scout Gold Award. We are confident she will have continued success in her future endeavors. We are very proud.

HONORING WILLIAM T. BROWN

HON. DAVID E. PRICE
OF NORTH CAROLINA
IN THE HOUSE OF REPRESENTATIVES
Friday, December 2, 2016

Mr. PRICE of North Carolina. Mr. Speaker, I rise today to honor the life and legacy of William T. Brown of Fayetteville, North Carolina, a committed advocate for civil rights and educational excellence. His place in history was secured by his leadership during the integration of Cumberland County schools, one of the largest and most diverse school districts in the state of North Carolina.

Mr. Brown passed away on November 14 at the age of 87. My wife Lisa and I wish to extend our deepest condolences to his family, friends, and colleagues.

A North Carolina native, William T. Brown graduated from North Carolina A&T State University in 1948 and North Carolina Central University in 1954. Mr. Brown also pursued graduate degrees at Columbia University and the University of North Carolina at Chapel Hill.

In 1955, Mr. Brown moved to Fayetteville and began teaching science at E.E. Smith High School. After leading Ferguson Elementary School, he served as principal of Washington Drive Junior High School from 1963 to 1971, where he oversaw the process of integration almost a decade after the landmark Supreme Court case, Brown v. Board of Education.

In 1971, Mr. Brown became principal of E.E. Smith High School. It was during this pivotal year that white students began attending the historically black high schools in Cumberland County. During this time, Mr. Brown emphasized to students and parents that their success in breaking down barriers would be remembered long after the racial backlash had subsided.

A career educator, Mr. Brown later became assistant superintendent and associate superintendent for Fayetteville City Schools. He retired in 1992 and served as special assistant to the chancellor at Fayetteville State University until 1995. He was then appointed to the University of North Carolina Board of Governors and served as trustee emeritus at Fayetteville State University.

In 1994, the Cumberland County Board of Education named William T. Brown Elementary in Spring Lake, North Carolina, the county's first year-round school, in his honor. In 2014, Fayetteville State University named a Distinguished Professorship in Economics in recognition of his many contributions.

The Fayetteville community and the State of North Carolina continue to benefit from William Brown's contributions to public education, desegregation, and expanded opportunity. He was a revered leader in the community, and his tireless efforts helped provide a better future for the people of Cumberland County, the Fourth District, and North Carolina.

HONORING SHAYA GUTLEIZER

HON. DANIEL M. DONOVAN, JR.
OF NEW YORK
IN THE HOUSE OF REPRESENTATIVES
Friday, December 2, 2016

Mr. DONOVAN. Mr. Speaker, I rise today to honor Brooklyn resident Shaya Gutleizer's ceaseless devotion to his community.

Born and raised in Brooklyn, Shaya knew as a child that he wanted to be a first responder like his father when he grew up. In fact, he signed up to be an Emergency Medical Technician (EMT) when he turned 18 and received his certification shortly after. When he wasn't saving lives on the clock, Shaya was giving his time working with multiple volunteer ambulance services. As an EMT, Shaya was responsible for numerous pre-hospital saves, which involves reviving individuals who are clinically dead. Due to his heroism, Shaya has been honored at various second-chance brunches, events where the honoree is thanked by the person he resuscitated.

Moreover, Shaya Gutleizer has not been afraid to put his life on the line in service to others. On September 11, 2001, Shaya rushed to the World Trade Center and remained there for several days to assist with the rescue efforts. Soon after, he decided to serve his country further by enlisting in the Army. However, due to the conditions he encountered at Ground Zero, Shaya developed breathing difficulties and received a medical discharge. After finding out how many fellow 9/11 first responders were developing health issues, Shaya became a tireless advocate for the passage and permanent extension of Zadroga health benefits for the courageous heroes, such as himself who risked their lives on that fateful day to save others.

Mr. Speaker, Shaya Gutleizer's devotion to serving his fellow man and saving lives reflects the good in each of us. This country is great due to individuals like him, and I am proud to take this moment to honor him.

RETIREMENT OF MARY ANNIE HARPER FROM THE U.S. HOUSE OF REPRESENTATIVES

HON. FRANK A. LoBIONDO
OF NEW JERSEY
IN THE HOUSE OF REPRESENTATIVES
Friday, December 2, 2016

Mr. LoBIONDO. Mr. Speaker, it is with a heavy heart and tremendous gratitude that I express my deepest appreciation to my Chief of Staff, Mary Annie Harper, for her more than 29 years of incredibly loyal service at my side on behalf of South Jersey residents.

In May 1987, Mary Annie joined in helping me as my Chief of Staff as I started my freshman term as a member of the New Jersey General Assembly. For almost three decades I have relied daily on her invaluable insights and sound judgment. She has helped me remain focused and motivated, reminding me daily to stay grounded and always remember my South Jersey roots.

Her clear passion for public policy and politics is evident to anyone who has worked with her. Without any hesitation I can say that there will never be another Mary Annie Harper in my office or my life. Her heart and humor will be two of her many character qualities I will miss going forward.

On behalf of all of the residents of South Jersey, the staff and myself, I wish Mary Annie a very rewarding and well-deserved retirement and thank her both for her steadfast friendship and loyal service to South Jersey.

PERSONAL EXPLANATION

HON. TERRI A. SEWELL
OF ALABAMA
IN THE HOUSE OF REPRESENTATIVES
Friday, December 2, 2016

Ms. SEWELL of Alabama. Mr. Speaker, during the votes held on December 2nd, 2016, I was inescapably detained and away handling important matters related to my District and the State of Alabama. If I had been present, I would have voted YES on Agreeing to the Conference Report to Accompany S. 2943, and YES on Approving the Journal.

HONORING MARTA I. BOOKBINDER

HON. JACKIE SPEIER
OF CALIFORNIA
IN THE HOUSE OF REPRESENTATIVES
Friday, December 2, 2016

Ms. SPEIER. Mr. Speaker, I rise to honor Marta I. Bookbinder, an outstanding educator, communicator and counselor, who is retiring after 17 years as the Collaborative Projects Coordinator of the adult and youth programs at the Community Learning Center in South San Francisco.

Marta is the last original founding member of the Community Learning Center which opened doors to countless preschool to adult learners. CLC is a program of the South San Francisco Public Library in the heart of the historic downtown area, easily accessible to the great number of immigrants from around the world. The center is an irreplaceable gem of the community and a perfect reflection of the values Marta has embraced her entire life and career.

In close partnership with the school district, CLC offers English and computer classes and Spanish language literacy tutoring for adults and homework help classes for elementary school students from the surrounding schools. Adults learn to maneuver education, health, transportation, employment, financial and voting systems, giving them the tools to help themselves and to make progress.

Having completed her own education in the U.S. and Latin America, Marta was perfectly positioned to become a global educator. She holds an M.A. in Counseling Psychology, a B.A. in International Relations, an A.A. in English and Psychology and a teaching credential for English as a Second Language, Citizenship and Conversational Spanish. She is fluent in English and Spanish and competent in Italian.

Marta began her career as a program assistant at the job placement and career center at Skyline College in 1989. She moved on to the College of Notre Dame as a staff assistant in 1993 and to the Family Council of Half Moon Bay as the director of parent services in 1997. While she held that position, she also became an adult education instructor at the Cabrillo Unified School District. From there she moved on to the San Mateo Union High School District in 1998, and to the South San Francisco Unified School District in 1999, teaching adult education. She will continue her work as an instructor and CBET coordinator of adult education at the South San Francisco Unified School District.

Marta never ceases to develop innovative ideas to improve the lives of others, a fact noted in the community. She has received numerous awards including the Employee of the Year and the Mayors Diversity awards from the city of South San Francisco, the San Mateo County Governing Board Association KENT Award for innovation in educational programs, the Julie Billiart Alumna Award for outstanding community service from Notre Dame de Namur University, and the KQED & Kaiser Permanente Bay Area Local Hero Award.

In her well-deserved retirement, Marta is looking forward to spending more time with her husband of 45 years, David N. Bookbinder, and their two daughters, Tamara and Tatiana.

Mr. Speaker, I ask the members of the House of Representatives to join me in honoring a friend and colleague, Marta Bookbinder, for creating empowering programs at the Community Learning Center that have turned hundreds of lives around. She is a role model for teachers in South San Francisco and beyond.

IN MEMORIAM: PATRICK J. MITCHELL

HON. KYRSTEN SINEMA
OF ARIZONA
IN THE HOUSE OF REPRESENTATIVES
Friday, December 2, 2016

Ms. SINEMA. Mr. Speaker, I rise today to honor the life and legacy of Patrick Mitchell.

Pat, a Yuma, Arizona native, dedicated his life to public service. He graduated from the University of Arizona and received a law degree from Arizona State University. He served the City of Phoenix as a member of the Public Employees Relations Board and was appointed special assistant attorney general for the State of Arizona, Department of Health.

Pat was a trusted advisor to many, working on presidential campaigns for Kansas Senator Gary Hart and Iowa Senator Paul Simon. He joined former Arizona Senator Dennis DeConcini's staff where he handled constituent and policy issues for 13 of Arizona's 15 counties. Pat also served as a political advisor to former Arizona Governor Janet Napolitano and Congressman Mo Udall and as chief of staff to New York Congresswoman Louise Slaughter.

I am thankful for Pat's dedication to service and appreciate his determination and willingness to make our state and country a better place for all Arizonans.

Please join me in honoring his memory.

HONORING HELEN ANN HENKEL

HON. ELIOT L. ENGEL
OF NEW YORK
IN THE HOUSE OF REPRESENTATIVES
Friday, December 2, 2016

Mr. ENGEL. Mr. Speaker, I rise today to honor a symbol of volunteerism for all of Yonkers: Helen Ann Henkel. For over forty years, Helen Henkel has affected hundreds of thousands of lives in Yonkers and beyond; through her selfless commitment to improving her community. It is an honor to recognize her service at her retirement honoring.

Born and raised in Yonkers, Helen is the daughter of Ann and Otto Rogewitz, and the proud granddaughter of Ukrainian and Polish immigrants who came to this country at the turn of the century and settled in Yonkers and Hastings-on-Hudson, New York. After earning her diploma from Yonkers High School of Commerce, Helen earned a degree in Business Administration from Westchester Community College.

Helen has been a motivating force for a great many Yonkers institutions, including the Exchange Club of Yonkers, the Enrico Fermi Educational Fund, and the Yonkers Board of Ethics, all of which she served in a leadership capacity. She has also been intimately involved in other organizations in the neighborhood, including the Yonkers Historical Society, Untermyer Performing Arts Council, Westchester Pulaski Association, Friends of Phillips Manor Hall, Sherwood House, Yonkers YWCA, Yonkers Beautification Conservancy, and Piper Theater Productions, just to name a few.

For her selfless service, Helen has received multiple awards and recognitions, including the

2013 Yonkers Woman of Distinction Award, the 2013 Yonkers Police Commissioner's Award, the 2009 Woman of Excellence Award, the Yonkers Chamber of Commerce Women in Business—Above and Beyond Award, and has also been bestowed the Key to the City of Yonkers.

Helen has done so much good for Yonkers community, and indeed the world, that it is hard to fathom the true scope of her impact. I want to wish Helen congratulations on her well-earned honor and thank her for all she has done on behalf of the people of Yonkers.

RICHMOND, TX EARNS COMMUNITY OF THE YEAR TITLE

HON. PETE OLSON
OF TEXAS
IN THE HOUSE OF REPRESENTATIVES
Friday, December 2, 2016

Mr. OLSON. Mr. Speaker, I rise today to congratulate the City of Richmond, TX, for receiving the Community of the Year award from the American Planning Association—Texas Chapter (Texas APA).

Richmond received this award due to its outstanding planning tools it adopted to prepare for the city's growth. Without submitting an application for the award this year, Richmond won anyway thanks to their impressive planning efforts that caught the attention of the Texas APA. Over the last year and a half, Richmond leaders have adopted three different planning tools without an existing internal Planning Department. The Texas APA's goal of rewarding cities with significantly notable contributions to planning projects, made Richmond a clear choice.

On behalf of the Twenty-Second Congressional District of Texas, congratulations again to the City of Richmond, TX for receiving the Community of the Year award from the Texas APA. We look forward to seeing your growth.

GREAT LAKES MARITIME HERITAGE ASSESSMENT ACT

HON. MARCY KAPTUR
OF OHIO
IN THE HOUSE OF REPRESENTATIVES
Friday, December 2, 2016

Ms. KAPTUR. Mr. Speaker, I rise today to introduce the Great Lakes Maritime Heritage Assessment Act, an important bill to promote and preserve the sunken treasures of the Great Lakes.

The Great Lakes have an amazing naval history which is unknown and unseen by too many Americans. Steamboats on the Great Lakes provided a route west for immigrants as they settled what was then called the Northwest Territory. As cities grew, Great Lakes ships and barges carried the timber, coal, and ore that fueled America's industrial might.

As commerce increased, so too did the number of ships which succumbed to the unpredictable and sometimes foreboding weather on the Lakes. Today, thousands of shipwrecks are scattered across the floor of the Great Lakes, including the remains of one of America's first great naval victories, the Battle of Lake Erie.

Despite this amazing heritage, only one marine sanctuary exists in the Great Lakes. The Thunder Bay Marine Sanctuary, located in Lake Huron off the coast of Alpena, Michigan, has been a major economic driver for the area, spurring tourism, research, and educational opportunities.

This bill builds on the success of Thunder Bay by setting the stage to establish additional sanctuaries across the Great Lakes. It directs the Administrator of NOAA to identify underwater areas throughout the Lakes that possess significant historical and archaeological resources and recommend whether they should be designated as National Marine Sanctuaries.

Preserving the cultural legacy of our region is an important component of caring for our Great Lakes. Marine sanctuaries will protect this history while providing the additional benefits of driving economic development and providing jobs to our region. I look forward to working with my colleagues to achieve these goals.

SUPPORT OF FEDERAL TRADE COMMISSION WE DON'T SERVE TEENS INITIATIVE

HON. DANNY K. DAVIS
OF ILLINOIS
IN THE HOUSE OF REPRESENTATIVES
Friday, December 2, 2016

Mr. DANNY K. DAVIS of Illinois. Mr. Speaker, I rise to address underage drinking, a public health and safety issue that is often lost in the pile of other stories in our 24-hour news cycle.

Back in 2005, the Federal Trade Commission initiated a consumer education program to reduce underage drinking called "We Don't Serve Teens." It is a valuable resource to raise awareness among parents, educators, and other adults that furnishing alcohol to minors is illegal and irresponsible. The program also encourages common-sense measures to further reduce illegal underage drinking and the dangers caused by teens who drink illegally and to the general public.

Over the last several years, I have checked with credible sources to see how we are doing as a nation on addressing underage drinking.

The Substance Abuse and Mental Health Services Administration (SAMHSA) indicates that progress has continued for more than a decade in reducing underage drinking, but it remains a serious public health problem for adolescents and young adults.

SAMSHA surveys find that significant numbers of younger persons between the ages of 12 and 14 drank alcohol in the month before they were surveyed, and that more than 90 percent obtain alcohol from their own home, the home of a friend, or an adult family member. Those findings clearly indicate the importance that family members can play in reducing young adolescents' access to alcohol and the associated risks of injury and the early onset of serious health problems.

Recent information on highway deaths from the National Highway Traffic Safety Adminis-

tration is very discouraging for adults and teens. Highway deaths increased in 2015 as did deaths from drunk driving. More than 10,000 Americans were killed in drunk-driving accidents, and younger drivers are a large portion of that terrible and preventable toll. Tens of thousands of people were also injured, including many young people who will be scarred or disabled for life.

Underage drinking is illegal and persons under the age of 21 are subject to arrest, fines, and license suspension for possession of alcohol beverages or driving after consumption of a single drink. This issue is often overlooked in stories about the criminal justice system. Thousands of young people get a criminal record and driver's license history that will prevent them from obtaining many jobs that involve driving or that require a clean record. In addition to the risk of injury and death, experimenting with alcohol can cause a young person permanent economic harm.

A substantial proportion of college students are under the age of 21. They face significantly higher risks than their non-college peers of injury or death from assault, car crashes, and other accidents after illegally consuming alcohol. This behavior must be challenged. Our best and brightest students, many of whom attend publicly supported schools and receive government grants and subsidies, have to do better.

For the last eleven years, members of the alcohol beverage industry have actively supported the We Don't Serve Teens initiative. Constellation Brands Beer Division and many retail stores in Chicago have made long-term commitments to underage drinking prevention in the district I represent and surrounding communities. Over the last couple of months, they sponsored electronic billboards, bus shelter signs, and media messages to promote the We Don't Serve Teens message. Other companies made similar efforts in their home cities. I commend those efforts. I also ask all adults and teens to work together to further reduce the tragic consequences of illegal underage drinking. All of these hazards are preventable.

As we approach the holiday season celebrations in our homes and elsewhere, I urge all adults to set an example of responsible behavior and compliance with laws designed to ensure the safety of our citizens. With a sincere commitment of parents, guardians, and concerned citizens to remain involved in the lives of our teens, we can all get home safely and to enjoy special holiday occasions together for years to come.

JANIECE LONGORIA NAMED 2017 MARITIME PERSON OF THE YEAR

HON. PETE OLSON
OF TEXAS
IN THE HOUSE OF REPRESENTATIVES
Friday, December 2, 2016

Mr. OLSON. Mr. Speaker, I rise today to congratulate Janiece Longoria of Houston, TX, for being named the 2017 Maritime Person of the Year by the Greater Houston Port Bureau.

Janiece was recognized for her leadership and accomplishments in the Port of Houston.

In 2013, she was unanimously appointed as Chairman of the Port Commission by the City of Houston and Harris County. Since her tenure began, the Port of Houston Authority has reached a historic high of handling more than 2 million loaded container units, increased revenue, made infrastructure investments, and worked on projects to keep the Houston Ship Channel deep and wide. Her enthusiasm and dedication to the Port of Houston have made the port competitive internationally and a continued boost to the Houston economy. Janiece's stellar accomplishments also previously earned her the Distinguished Alumnus Award for the University of Texas, the 2008 Sandra Day O'Connor Award for Board Excellence, Female Executive of the Year Award from the Houston Hispanic Chamber of Commerce, recognized as a "Breakthrough Woman," and inducted into the Hall of Fame by the Greater Houston Women's Chamber of Commerce.

On behalf of the Twenty-Second Congressional District of Texas, congratulations again to Janiece Longoria for being named the 2017 Maritime Person of the Year by the Greater Houston Port Bureau. She has done so much for the Port of Houston and the Houston area and makes us proud. We look forward to seeing her continued success.

IN MEMORIAM: PRIVATE FIRST CLASS DANIEL HUNT, FEBRUARY 10, 1933–SEPTEMBER 28, 1951

HON. KYRSTEN SINEMA

OF ARIZONA

IN THE HOUSE OF REPRESENTATIVES

Friday, December 2, 2016

Ms. SINEMA. Mr. Speaker, I rise today to honor the life and legacy of Private First Class (PFC) Daniel Hunt. PFC Daniel Hunt served our country as a member of A Company, 1st Battalion, 9th Infantry Regiment, 2nd Infantry Division with the United States Army.

Daniel was born February 10, 1933, to Ownie and Lillie (White) Hunt, the youngest of 17 children. Daniel and two of his brothers, John and Charles, served in the Korean War. Daniel never returned.

PFC Daniel Hunt was killed on September 28, 1951, while serving his country on Heartbreak Ridge in South Korea, where his remains were recovered earlier this year. Daniel was missing in action for over 65 years and is going home to Arizona to be buried with full military honors.

I am incredibly thankful for PFC Daniel Hunt and his family's sacrifice to our country.

Daniel is survived by his many nieces and nephews. Please join me in honoring his memory.

HONORING LAURA KORNFELD

HON. ELIOT L. ENGEL

OF NEW YORK

IN THE HOUSE OF REPRESENTATIVES

Friday, December 2, 2016

Mr. ENGEL. Mr. Speaker, I rise today to honor a constituent of mine and a pillar of the community, Ms. Laura Kornfeld, who on October 11, 2016 is celebrating her amazing 90th birthday.

A first generation American, Ms. Kornfeld graduated from Tilden High School in Brooklyn and was the first person in her family to attend college. She received her Bachelor's degree from Hunter College and later served as an officer on the Alumni Board of Columbia University Teachers College, the same institution where she received a Master's Degree in Adult Education. Ms. Kornfeld founded Academic Advisory Service, a company that assisted women new to the job market. She served on the New York State Advisory for Women and the League of Women Voters, Professional Womens' Caucus and the National Organization of Women.

In Rye, Ms. Kornfeld has been active in a wide array of organizations and a strong supporter of education and racial equality. She has been on the Board of Carver Center in Port Chester, supporting "grassroots organizers and advocates for the minority community in Port Chester". She served as President of the PTA for the City of Rye Schools, as well as on the board of Kids Space, a childcare and enrichment program for school children. She spearheaded Rye's campaign to pass the Equal Rights Amendment and attended the International Women's Year Conference in 1985 in Nairobi, Kenya.

Of course, Ms. Kornfeld's main love has always been family. Married to career Naval officer Leo Kornfeld since 1947, they have been residents of Rye, NY, since 1957. They have three grown children, Melanie, Hank and Nancy Danielle.

Ms. Kornfeld has led an amazingly full and active life. She has been a great member of the community, who has always given her time and effort to the issues that have made her neighborhood stronger. Congratulations to her on her 90th birthday.

MEMORIAL HERMANN SUGAR LAND HOSPITAL RECEIVES MALCOM BALDRIGE NATIONAL QUALITY AWARD

HON. PETE OLSON

OF TEXAS

IN THE HOUSE OF REPRESENTATIVES

Friday, December 2, 2016

Mr. OLSON. Mr. Speaker, I rise today to congratulate Memorial Hermann Sugar Land Hospital for receiving the Malcom Baldrige National Quality Award.

This prestigious award is given by the U.S. Department of Commerce through the National Institute of Standards and Technology (NIST). It is the nation's highest Presidential honor for sustainable excellence through visionary leadership, organizational alignment, systemic improvement and innovation. Memorial Hermann Sugar Land Hospital received this award thanks to ranking among the top 10 percent for its emergency center arrival-to-discharge time, compliance with regulations to reduce medication errors, bed turnaround times, radiology and laboratory result turnaround times, and the use of computerized physician order entry.

On behalf of the Twenty-Second Congressional District of Texas, congratulations again to Memorial Hermann Sugar Land Hospital for receiving the Malcom Baldrige National Quality Award. We all benefit from their commitment to quality healthcare and we thank them for their hard work to keep Houstonians healthy.

WAYZATA BOYS' CROSS COUNTRY WIN IT ALL

HON. ERIK PAULSEN

OF MINNESOTA

IN THE HOUSE OF REPRESENTATIVES

Friday, December 2, 2016

Mr. PAULSEN. Mr. Speaker, I rise today to congratulate the Wayzata Boys Cross Country team for winning the Minnesota High School State Championship.

The Trojans capped off their championship season with a strong team finish. Wayzata, led by junior Khalid Hussein, had five runners placing among the top 22 finishers in the state championship race. The diligence of each individual runner as well as the dedication of their coach, Mark Popp, is responsible for this team-wide success.

Everyone knows that cross country requires countless hours of practice and preparation. It's a sport that requires both mental and physical endurance and these outstanding student-athletes should be commended for their excellence.

Balancing school and athletics is not an easy task. It takes focus. It takes dedication. And, it takes hard work both in and out of the classroom as they continually make strides to improve their craft. The families, teachers, friends, and the entire community are very proud of the Wayzata Boys' Cross Country team. Congratulations on being state champs.

PERSONAL EXPLANATION

HON. CARLOS CURBELO

OF FLORIDA

IN THE HOUSE OF REPRESENTATIVES

Friday, December 2, 2016

Mr. CURBELO of Florida. Mr. Speaker, I unfortunately missed a vote during a vote series on 12/1/16. Had I been present, I would have voted yea on Roll Call No. 594.

HONORING WESTCHESTER HISPANIC LAW ENFORCEMENT ASSOCIATION 20TH ANNIVERSARY

HON. ELIOT L. ENGEL

OF NEW YORK

IN THE HOUSE OF REPRESENTATIVES

Friday, December 2, 2016

Mr. ENGEL. Mr. Speaker, the brave men and women who protect us every day as members of law enforcement are truly New York's Finest. For the last 20 years in Westchester County, The Westchester Hispanic Law Enforcement Association has dedicated itself to making a difference in the community, by paving the way for the future leaders in law enforcement who will someday serve and protect their communities with great honor.

The Mission of the Westchester Hispanic Law Enforcement Association (WHLEA) has been to "build an organization that will withstand the test of time." The pledge of their founding members to make a difference has been lived up to for two decades by members who work tirelessly to improve conditions for those less fortunate. The Association prides itself on representing those who for too long have remained disenfranchised, and left to do for themselves. Their commitment to keeping vigil over those in our communities whose voices and concerns have all too often fallen upon deaf ears has left a lasting impact on the lives of countless people.

Above all though, the Association's mission is to pave the way for future generations, sons and daughters who someday may choose the Honorable profession of law enforcement as a way of serving their communities. By working to inspire, instruct and create the future leaders of law enforcement throughout Westchester County, the WHLEA has provided a great service to the community. Congratulations to their members on 20 years.

SAN JACINTO COLLEGE TOP CONTESTANT FOR COMMUNITY COLLEGE AWARD

HON. PETE OLSON
OF TEXAS

IN THE HOUSE OF REPRESENTATIVES

Friday, December 2, 2016

Mr. OLSON. Mr. Speaker, I rise today to congratulate San Jacinto College of Houston, TX for being named a top-10 finalist for the 2017 Aspen Prize for Community College Excellence.

The Aspen Prize for Community College Excellence has nominated the top-notch community colleges in the country regarding student learning, certificate and degree completion, employment and earnings for graduates and accessibility and success of minority and lower income students. San Jacinto was recognized because of its extreme focus on supporting and working with students to ensure they are the most equipped to find a job and prepare for life after graduation. Between 2007 and 2015, the number of certificates and associate degrees San Jacinto College has awarded has increased by an impressive 140 percent. The winner of the $1 million prize will be announced in March.

On behalf of the Twenty-Second Congressional District of Texas, congratulations again to San Jacinto College for being named a top-10 finalist for the Aspen Prize for Community College Excellence. We are very proud of their strong commitment to prepare students for life after graduation. Keep up the good work.

RECOGNIZING BRUCE MULHEARN

HON. LORETTA SANCHEZ
OF CALIFORNIA

IN THE HOUSE OF REPRESENTATIVES

Friday, December 2, 2016

Ms. LORETTA SANCHEZ of California. Mr. Speaker, I rise today to recognize Mr. Bruce Mulhearn on his 50th Anniversary in the real estate industry and helping individuals, families, and businesses to achieve the American dream. Mr. Mulhearn immigrated to the United States via New Zealand in 1958. After working in leather tanneries and pipe manufacturing plants, he obtained his realty license and began work for the Apple Valley Land & Development Co., selling vacant home sites in the High Desert, California. Thereafter he served honorably in the United States Army for two years.

In 1967, Bruce and his wife Tomazina opened Bruce Mulhearn Inc., Realtors in a 600 square foot office and began their journey to build a company. The company grew to eight offices and several hundred agents, and by 1969, Mr. Mulhearn founded Castlehead Escrow Company as an insurance brokerage, a real estate school, new home development and a mortgage brokerage operation. Within twenty years the company was one of the leading firms in all of Southern California.

He went on to become a Senior lecturer for both the National Association of Realtors and the California Association of Realtors. Mr. Mulhearn was deeply involved in creating the Certified Residential Broker and Certified Residential Specialist designations for the industry. The company continued to grow and prosper adding various affiliates and branch offices.

In 2014, a merge resulted in the creation of Berkshire Hathaway HomeServices California Properties, with Bruce Mulhearn still the President and with his joint venture owners operating over twenty offices, doing business in five counties with thousands of transactions per year. After weathering five economic storms during that time frame, with interest rates soaring to as much as 24 percent including the Great Recession most recently, this is indeed a remarkable enterprise.

I applaud Mr. Bruce Mulhearn on his vision and on creating opportunities for many others within the real estate industry. I am delighted to join in celebration of this important 50th Anniversary milestone.

HONORING THE 80TH ANNIVERSARY OF CHI ST. JOSEPH HEALTH

HON. BILL FLORES
OF TEXAS

IN THE HOUSE OF REPRESENTATIVES

Friday, December 2, 2016

Mr. FLORES. Mr. Speaker, I rise today to honor the 80th anniversary of the founding of CHI St. Joseph Health of Bryan, Texas, and the 100th anniversary of the Sisters of St. Francis of Sylvania, Ohio. CHI St. Joseph Health is a healthcare leader in the Brazos Valley, drawing upon the rich legacy of the Sisters of St. Francis.

In 1936, the Sisters purchased Bryan Hospital and immediately began investing in improvements, making CHI St. Joseph part of its growing nation-wide healthcare ministry. The Sisters grew the small Bryan hospital into a major regional health system with five hospitals, two long-term care facilities, more than 30 clinics, and an exceptional physician network that is 250 physicians strong. The Sisters' investment has given CHI St. Joseph the privilege of caring for more patients, delivering more babies, and introducing more advancements in healthcare that any other provider in the region.

In 2014, through Supreme guidance and ministry, the Sisters pursued sponsorship with Catholic Health Initiatives, one of the largest healthcare systems in the nation. The Sisters believed this move would help CHI St. Joseph continue to thrive in a complex and ever-changing healthcare environment.

The 80th anniversary of CHI St. Joseph and the 100th anniversary of the Sisters of St. Francis are being celebrated by current and former CHI St. Joseph leaders, Sisters of St. Francis leadership, the Board of Directors, physicians, administration, team members with more than 25 years of tenure, the entire St. Joseph's team, and all of the Brazos Valley. Their hard work and dedication to improve their communities should be both appreciated and celebrated.

I, along with the residents of the 17th Congressional District, commend CHI St. Joseph's and the Sisters of Sylvania for their 80 years of unwavering commitment, dedication, and contributions to the Brazos Valley. All of us also wish them great success in the future.

As I close, I ask everyone to continue praying for our country, and for our military and first responders who selflessly serve and sacrifice to protect us. God bless important institutions like CHI St. Joseph's and God Bless America.

CONGRATS TO EDINA GIRLS' CROSS COUNTRY

HON. ERIK PAULSEN
OF MINNESOTA

IN THE HOUSE OF REPRESENTATIVES

Friday, December 2, 2016

Mr. PAULSEN. Mr. Speaker, I want to offer a big congratulations to the Edina Girls' Cross Country team for winning the Minnesota High School State Championship.

After winning it all last year, the Hornets were determined to defend their state title. In the final race, Edina put forward a great team effort with runners from all four grades placing for points, including three runners in the top 10 and five in the top 20. Led by senior captain Amanda Mosborg, the team was able to fend off its rivals and repeat as champs.

Cross country requires countless hours, and miles, of training and discipline. As the father of cross-country runners myself, I've seen firsthand the time and commitment it takes, from the challenging practices to the faraway travel to daylong meets, all while juggling academics and other obligations. These girls, along with Coach Matt Gabrielson, saw their dedication pay off with their victory.

Mr. Speaker, after winning the championship last year, the Edina Girls' Cross Country team didn't let up and came back to win it again. Congratulations to the runners, coaches, and parents on an excellent season. Our community is proud. Go Hornets.

ROBERT ROBBINS NAMED HOUSTON'S INTERNATONAL CITIZEN OF THE YEAR

HON. PETE OLSON
OF TEXAS

IN THE HOUSE OF REPRESENTATIVES

Friday, December 2, 2016

Mr. OLSON. Mr. Speaker, I rise today to congratulate Robert C. Robbins, M.D. for being named Houston's 2016 International Citizen of the Year.

The World Affairs Council of Greater Houston awarded Robert the International Citizen of the Year award for his partnership with the Texas Medical Center (TMC) and his vision and energetic efforts to engage with biotech leaders, investors and other stakeholders from around the world. Robert is an internationally recognized cardiac surgeon and joined the TMC as president and CEO in 2012. His expertise is in the surgical treatment of congestive heart failure and cardiothoracic transplantation and his research expands from cardiac transplant allograft to bioengineering blood vessels and automated vascular anastomotic devices.

On behalf of the Twenty-Second Congressional District of Texas, congratulations again to Robert C. Robbins, M.D. for being recognized as Houston's 2016 International Citizen of the Year. We benefit from his medical skills and commitment to quality care. We look forward to his future accomplishments.

U.S. ECONOMY

HON. EDDIE BERNICE JOHNSON
OF TEXAS

IN THE HOUSE OF REPRESENTATIVES

Friday, December 2, 2016

Ms. EDDIE BERNICE JOHNSON of Texas. Mr. Speaker, this morning, the U.S. Department of Labor released its November jobs report detailing the state of the U.S. workforce and employment throughout our nation. According to the report, the unemployment rate declined to its lowest point since August 2007, falling from 4.9 percent to 4.6 percent unemployment last month. U.S. employers also added 178,000 jobs to the economy—pointing to strength and stability throughout the country.

Our growing economy and burgeoning workforce is a testament to President Obama's policies and efforts to put Americans back to work by reversing years of damage caused by President Bush and the regressive policies of the right. President Obama has helped to steer us to the lowest period of unemployment in nine years, despite having to face the most serious economic downturn since the Great Depression and the most divided Congress this nation has seen in recent years. Businesses have been able to add 15.6 million jobs since early 2010 and this growth can endure as long as we continue to enact policies and embrace a culture that favors everyday men and women, and not just a select few.

As we inch closer to President-elect Trump's administration and a Congress dominated by Republicans in the House and Senate, I will continue to encourage the new Administration and my colleagues in Congress to stay on our current path of creating jobs and decreasing unemployment for all Americans. If we reverse course by handing out billions of dollars in tax breaks to only the largest corporations and the wealthiest Americans, gutting public programs and social safety nets, or slashing spending on research and development, then our economic growth will surely stall.

Mr. Speaker, our nation is at an important crossroad. The transition to this new administration and Republican-controlled Congress poses new opportunities and even greater challenges. Will we choose to continue on the path to prosperity? Or will President-elect Trump and the Republican majority work to reverse all of the progress that we have achieved for everyday Americans by instead favoring the super wealthy and the biggest corporations? Only time will tell, although it is imperative that we look to these gains throughout our economy over these eight years and work to continue that trend. Anything less would be an insult to the American people and a devastating step in the wrong direction after coming so far.

HONORING ANN MURO

HON. ELIOT L. ENGEL
OF NEW YORK

IN THE HOUSE OF REPRESENTATIVES

Friday, December 2, 2016

Mr. ENGEL. Mr. Speaker, those special individuals who dedicate their lives to improving the community have the power to transform lives for the better. In Yonkers, no one has had a more transformative effect than my friend, Ann Muro, an amazing public servant who has dedicated her life to helping others. Ann grew up in the Colonial Heights section of Yonkers and attended Annunciation School and Maria Regina High School. She then went on to Mercy College, where she received her degree in Behavioral Psychology. Always wanting to help people, Ann became a Social Worker for the County of Westchester and served on the steering committee for the implementation of the Medicaid Program into Westchester County. She also served as a Community Affairs Specialist for the Westchester County Human Rights Commission and as an Employment Specialist for the Yonkers Employment Center. In addition to her professional work helping others, Ann has also been extremely active in the community during her personal time. She serves as President of the Exchange Club of Yonkers; Board Member of PAL; President of the Crestwood Tenants Association; former Board Member of the Yonkers Chamber of Commerce; former Board Member of the American Cancer Society, and this is just a small fraction of her involvement. A published writer, Ann is also in the process of writing two books and is also an accomplished poet.

This year, the Yonkers Exchange Club is honoring Ann for all of her incredible work and contributions in the community. I want to congratulate her on this wonderful honor and thank her on behalf of the 16th Congressional District

RECOGNIZING ROBERT D. ESCALANTE

HON. LORETTA SANCHEZ
OF CALIFORNIA

IN THE HOUSE OF REPRESENTATIVES

Friday, December 2, 2016

Ms. LORETTA SANCHEZ of California. Mr. Speaker, I rise today to pay tribute to successful business owner Robert D. Escalante. Mr. Escalante is the owner of Custom Auto Service in my district. For decades the Packard Motor Car marketed some of America's most prestigious cars. Custom Auto Service specializes in rebuilding and selling Packard Automobiles. This year, Custom Auto Service and the Packard Automobile are celebrating their Golden Anniversary in Santa Ana, California; 50 years of dedication to the "American Dream" car—the PACKARD. Custom Auto Service also recently entered into a public-private partnership with other businesses to help establish a four-block development zone nationally known as Fiesta Marketplace. Its purpose is to help nurture the surrounding community in Santa Ana.

We give thanks to businesses like Custom Auto Service for doing their part to lift up our district. This small business is a reflection of what's in the heart of America and I thank Mr. Robert Escalante for his tremendous dedication.

PEARLAND 6U AMERICAN FORCE BASEBALL TEAM WINS WORLD TITLE

HON. PETE OLSON
OF TEXAS

IN THE HOUSE OF REPRESENTATIVES

Friday, December 2, 2016

Mr. OLSON. Mr. Speaker, I rise today to recognize the 6U American Force baseball team from Pearland, TX for winning the United States Specialty Sports Association Baseball World Series title in Dallas.

After going 3–0 in the pool play, the team was a Number 2 seed going into the first round of the tournament. From there American Force went undefeated in the tournament earning the championship title. The American Force coaches are Ruben Ramirez, James Turrubiartes, Tino Arredondo, Junior Vasques, Bryan White, and Cliff Santellana. Most Valuable Player (MVP) of the championship game was Alex Vasques and Offensive MVP was given to Thomas Turrubiartes.

On behalf of the Twenty-Second Congressional District of Texas, congratulations again to the 6U American Force team for their accomplishments. We wish them success in future baseball seasons and look forward to rooting for them next year. Pearland, Texas is proud of them.

SENATE—*Monday, December 5, 2016*

The Senate met at 3 p.m. and was called to order by the President pro tempore (Mr. HATCH).

PRAYER

The Chaplain, Dr. Barry C. Black, offered the following prayer:

Let us pray.

Heavenly Father, help us today to become people whose lives will be productive for Your glory. Forgive us when we come short of Your will for us and for our Nation.

Lord, show our lawmakers how to do things Your way, embracing Your precepts and walking in Your path. Remind them that the narrow and difficult road often leads to life and abundant joy. As You teach them to live abundantly, replace their anxiety with calm, their confusion with clarity, and their doubts with faith. May Your heavenly peace, which transcends human understanding, guard their hearts and minds today and always.

We pray in Your Holy Name. Amen.

PLEDGE OF ALLEGIANCE

The President pro tempore led the Pledge of Allegiance, as follows:

I pledge allegiance to the Flag of the United States of America, and to the Republic for which it stands, one nation under God, indivisible, with liberty and justice for all.

RECOGNITION OF THE MAJORITY LEADER

The PRESIDING OFFICER (Mr. LANKFORD). The majority leader is recognized.

WORK BEFORE THE SENATE

Mr. McCONNELL. Mr. President, last week the House overwhelmingly passed the bipartisan 21st Century Cures Act, the medical innovation bill. Now it is the Senate's turn to move this bill forward and send it to the President's desk for signature.

This legislation has earned wide support from both sides of the aisle, and it is one of the most important bills that will pass this year. It is not hard to see why. It will encourage investment in biomedical research to help deliver treatment and cures to patients. It will cut through redtape and burdensome regulations while also protecting safety, and it will build upon progress to support regenerative medicine and other innovative therapies.

Cures also includes provisions to strengthen mental health programs and to provide much needed resources to help combat the opioid epidemic. It is legislation that could have an impact on each of our States and on each of our constituents.

Later today, Senators will take the next step in advancing 21st Century Cures. With continued cooperation, we can pass this bipartisan bill very soon.

The Cures legislation is just one key area where the Senate has been working to complete its work before the holidays. Negotiations are ongoing on a continuing resolution, which we will consider this week.

This week we will also pass the Defense authorization conference report, and work continues to finalize other outstanding conference reports, including the Water Resources Development Act—the so-called WRDA bill—and the energy policy modernization bill.

As these efforts continue, I thank all of those who have been working around the clock to reach a conclusion on these important issues. We will have a busy week ahead. Let's keep working together to get it done.

COMMENDING THE SENATOR FROM TENNESSEE

Mr. McCONNELL. Mr. President, I see the Senator from Tennessee on the floor. I particularly commend him for his outstanding work on the Cures bill. The Senator has had two major accomplishments this Congress—the rewrite of No Child Left Behind last year and now this medical innovation bill. I may have more to say about that later, but I commend the Senator from Tennessee for his outstanding work on this important bill.

AUTHORIZING THE SECRETARY OF THE TREASURY TO INCLUDE ALL FUNDS WHEN ISSUING CERTAIN GEOGRAPHIC TARGETING ORDERS

Mr. McCONNELL. Mr. President, I ask unanimous consent that the Committee on Banking, Housing, and Urban Affairs be discharged from further consideration of H.R. 5602 and the Senate proceed to its immediate consideration.

The PRESIDING OFFICER. Without objection, it is so ordered.

The clerk will report the bill by title.

The senior assistant legislative clerk read as follows:

A bill (H.R. 5602) to amend title 31, United States Code, to authorize the Secretary of the Treasury to include all funds when issuing certain geographic targeting orders, and for other purposes.

There being no objection, the Senate proceeded to consider the bill.

Mr. McCONNELL. Mr. President, I ask unanimous consent that the Shelby-Brown substitute amendment be agreed to and the bill, as amended, be considered read a third time.

The PRESIDING OFFICER. Without objection, it is so ordered.

The amendment (No. 5127) in the nature of a substitute was agreed to.

(The amendment is printed in today's RECORD under "Text of Amendments.")

The amendment was ordered to be engrossed and the bill to be read a third time.

The bill was read the third time.

The PRESIDING OFFICER. The bill having been read the third time, the question is, Shall the bill pass?

The bill (H.R. 5602), as amended, was passed.

Mr. McCONNELL. Mr. President, I ask unanimous consent that the motion to reconsider be considered made and laid upon the table.

The PRESIDING OFFICER. Without objection, it is so ordered.

THE CALENDAR

Mr. McCONNELL. Mr. President, I ask unanimous consent that the Senate proceed to the immediate consideration of Calendar Nos. 675 through 683.

There being no objection, the Senate proceeded to consider the bills en bloc.

Mr. McCONNELL. Mr. President, I ask unanimous consent that the bills be read a third time and passed and the motions to reconsider be considered made and laid upon the table, all en bloc.

The PRESIDING OFFICER. Without objection, it is so ordered.

SPECIAL WARFARE OPERATOR MASTER CHIEF PETTY OFFICER (SEAL) LOUIS "LOU" J. LANGLAIS POST OFFICE BUILDING

The bill (H.R. 3218) to designate the facility of the United States Postal Service located at 1221 State Street, Suite 12, Santa Barbara, California, as the "Special Warfare Operator Master Chief Petty Officer (SEAL) Louis 'Lou' J. Langlais Post Office Building," was ordered to a third reading, was read the third time, and passed.

RICHARD ALLEN CABLE POST OFFICE

The bill (H.R. 4887) to designate the facility of the United States Postal Service located at 23323 Shelby Road in Shelby, Indiana, as the "Richard Allen Cable Post Office," was ordered to a

---

● This "bullet" symbol identifies statements or insertions which are not spoken by a Member of the Senate on the floor.

third reading, was read the third time, and passed.

LEONARD MONTALTO POST OFFICE BUILDING

The bill (H.R. 5150) to designate the facility of the United States Postal Service located at 3031 Veterans Road West in Staten Island, New York, as the "Leonard Montalto Post Office Building," was ordered to a third reading, was read the third time, and passed.

ARMY FIRST LIEUTENANT DONALD C. CARWILE POST OFFICE BUILDING

The bill (H.R. 5309) to designate the facility of the United States Postal Service located at 401 McElroy Drive in Oxford, Mississippi, as the "Army First Lieutenant Donald C. Carwile Post Office Building," was ordered to a third reading, was read the third time, and passed.

E. MARIE YOUNGBLOOD POST OFFICE

The bill (H.R. 5356) to designate the facility of the United States Postal Service located at 14231 TX–150 in Coldspring, Texas, as the "E. Marie Youngblood Post Office," was ordered to a third reading, was read the third time, and passed.

ZAPATA VETERANS POST OFFICE

The bill (H.R. 5591) to designate the facility of the United States Postal Service located at 810 N US Highway 83 in Zapata, Texas, as the "Zapata Veterans Post Office," was ordered to a third reading, was read the third time, and passed.

OFFICER JOSEPH P. CALI POST OFFICE BUILDING

The bill (H.R. 5676) to designate the facility of the United States Postal Service located at 6300 N. Northwest Highway in Chicago, Illinois, as the "Officer Joseph P. Cali Post Office Building," was ordered to a third reading, was read the third time, and passed.

ABNER J. MIKVA POST OFFICE BUILDING

The bill (H.R. 5798) to designate the facility of the United States Postal Service located at 1101 Davis Street in Evanston, Illinois, as the "Abner J. Mikva Post Office Building," was ordered to a third reading, was read the third time, and passed.

SEGUNDO T. SABLAN AND CNMI FALLEN MILITARY HEROES POST OFFICE BUILDING

The bill (H.R. 5889) to designate the facility of the United States Postal Service located at 1 Chalan Kanoa VLG in Saipan, Northern Mariana Islands, as the "Segundo T. Sablan and CNMI Fallen Military Heroes Post Office Building," was ordered to a third reading, was read the third time, and passed.

PROVIDING ARSENAL INSTALLATION REUTILIZATION AUTHORITY

Mr. McCONNELL. Mr. President, I ask unanimous consent that the Committee on Armed Services be discharged from further consideration of S. 3336 and the Senate proceed to its immediate consideration.

The PRESIDING OFFICER. Without objection, it is so ordered.

The clerk will report the bill by title.

The senior assistant legislative clerk read as follows:

A bill (S. 3336) to provide arsenal installation reutilization authority.

There being no objection, the Senate proceeded to consider the bill.

Mr. McCONNELL. Mr. President, I ask unanimous consent that the Ernst amendment be agreed to; that the bill, as amended, be considered read a third time and passed; that the title amendment be agreed to; and that the motions to reconsider be considered made and laid upon the table.

The PRESIDING OFFICER. Without objection, it is so ordered.

The amendment (No. 5128) was agreed to, as follows:

(Purpose: To improve the bill)

On page 1, strike lines 3 and 4 and insert the following:

SECTION 1. INSTALLATION REUTILIZATION AUTHORITY FOR ARSENALS, DEPOTS, AND PLANTS.

On page 1, line 6, strike "arsenal, the Secretary concerned" and insert "arsenal, depot, or plant, the Secretary of the Army".

On page 2, line 4, insert ", depot, or plant" after "arsenal".

On page 2, line 8, insert ", depot, or plant" after "arsenal".

On page 2, line 12, insert ", depot, or plant" after "arsenal".

On page 2, line 17, strike "Secretary concerned" and insert "Secretary of the Army".

On page 2, line 21, insert ", depot, or plant" after "arsenal".

On page 4, line 3, insert ", DEPOT, OR PLANT" after "ARSENAL".

On page 4, line 5, insert ", depot, or plant" after "arsenal".

On page 4, line 6, strike "Department of the Defense" and insert "Army".

The bill (S. 3336), as amended, was ordered to be engrossed for a third reading, was read the third time, and passed.

The amendment (No. 5129) was agreed to, as follows:

(Purpose: To amend the title)

Amend the title so as to read: "A bill to provide installation reutilization authority for arsenals, depots, and plants.".

NATIONAL DEFENSE AUTHORIZATION ACT FOR FISCAL YEAR 2017—CONFERENCE REPORT

Mr. McCONNELL. Mr. President, I ask that the Chair lay before the Senate the conference report accompanying S. 2943.

The PRESIDING OFFICER. The Chair lays before the Senate the conference report to accompany S. 2943, which will be stated by title.

The legislative clerk read as follows:

The committee of conference on the disagreeing votes of the two Houses on the amendment of the House to the bill (S. 2943), to authorize appropriations for fiscal year 2017 for military activities of the Department of Defense, for military construction, and for defense activities of the Department of Energy, to prescribe military personnel strengths for such fiscal year, and for other purposes, having met, have agreed that the Senate recede from its disagreement to the amendment of the House and agree to the same with an amendment and the House agree to the same. Signed by a majority of the conferees on the part of both Houses.

Thereupon, the Senate proceeded to consider the conference report.

The conference report is printed in the House proceedings of the RECORD of November 30, 2016.)

CLOTURE MOTION

Mr. McCONNELL. Mr. President, I send a cloture motion to the desk.

The PRESIDING OFFICER. The cloture motion having been presented under rule XXII, the Chair directs the clerk to read the motion.

The legislative clerk read as follows:

CLOTURE MOTION

We, the undersigned Senators, in accordance with the provisions of rule XXII of the Standing Rules of the Senate, do hereby move to bring to a close debate on the conference report to accompany S. 2943, National Defense Authorization Act for Fiscal Year 2017.

Mitch McConnell, Deb Fischer, Thom Tillis, Daniel Coats, James M. Inhofe, John Hoeven, Cory Gardner, Orrin G. Hatch, Mark Kirk, Tom Cotton, John Cornyn, Lindsey Graham, Mike Rounds, Lisa Murkowski, Dan Sullivan, John McCain.

Mr. McCONNELL. Mr. President, I ask unanimous consent that the mandatory quorum call be waived with respect to this cloture motion.

The PRESIDING OFFICER. Without objection, it is so ordered.

RECOGNITION OF THE MINORITY LEADER

The PRESIDING OFFICER. The Democratic leader is recognized.

COMMENDING THE SENIOR SENATOR FROM TENNESSEE

Mr. REID. Mr. President, before I give my remarks, as I planned, I wish to say a brief word about Senator ALEXANDER, the senior Senator from Tennessee.

During my time in Congress, he has always been one of the most pleasant people I have dealt with. He is always very thorough in whatever he wants to talk to you about, and I have found him to be a remarkably good Senator. He has a background that is stunningly important—a longtime Governor of the State of Tennessee and someone who has served in one of the Republican administrations as Secretary of Education.

This Cures bill is not everything I would wish it to be. I think it is too weak in some parts. I think we could have done better. But I have been around for a long time, and I understand what legislation is all about.

We have gotten money. We have been trying for a couple years to get money for opioids. There should be far more, and it should be given in a different way than we have it here, but it is money. We have people—as we are sitting here for a few minutes today—dying as a result of this scourge that is sweeping America. It is in Oklahoma, it is in Tennessee, and it is in places such as New Hampshire. It is all over. So that part of it is excellent.

As to the resources we give the National Institutes of Health, or NIH, there is not enough we can do. I would hope there would be much more. I am pleased to report that this is the beginning of the Moonshot that Senator BIDEN will lead in research to defeat cancer. It can be done. We have made tremendous progress, and we are making it on a monthly basis now.

There are a lot of good things in this legislation. One of the things that the senior Senator from Tennessee and I have spoken about is clinical trials. Sometimes you don't understand the importance of those until they could personally affect you.

With the injury that I suffered almost 2 years ago, I am hopeful that in my lifetime there will be something done to be able to take care of retinas that are damaged. We have a lot of those that are damaged—a lot of retinas that are damaged as a result of diabetes and other maladies—but not a lot has been done on injuries to retinas. But there is work being done on that now.

I had a very good meeting on Saturday with one of the foremost people in the world dealing with retinas, Dr. Bressler of Johns Hopkins, and they are doing some stuff. They are doing stem cell work. They are doing some transplants. They are doing some good things.

On a very personal basis, Senator ALEXANDER came and talked to me one evening. He asked if I had time. Of course, I always have time for any Senator who wants to see me.

He came with tears in his eyes to talk to me about some things he had learned about people who had damaged their eyes and how some work is being done with these people who once could not see and, as in the Biblical passages, can now see.

It was a very wonderful meeting, and I had the opportunity to meet one individual he introduced me to—a man named Doug Oliver, who was basically blind. Because of work done with stem cells, he can now see. He is off disability, he can drive a car, and he can read. He could not do that before.

I appreciate it. It perhaps could have passed without him, but I doubt it, and I admire his legislative skills. I hope, with the new Congress coming, he will pull even those skills he doesn't have now out of his back pocket so perhaps we can do even more. There is going to be a lot more that needs to be done in the new Republican Congress.

So I express my public admiration to the senior Senator from Tennessee for the good work he has done for his State and for the country for many decades.

CELEBRATION AT STANDING ROCK

Mr. REID. Mr. President, in the bitter cold of a North Dakota December yesterday—and it can be cold up there—there was a celebration at Standing Rock. Why?

Along the banks of the Missouri River, in this heavy snow, there were hugs and tears of joy and drumming and dancing as the people of the Standing Rock Tribe and others heard the good news. The Army Corps of Engineers did not—did not—approve the easement for the Dakota Access oil pipeline. Instead, the Corps of Engineers determined that the pipeline must be rerouted. I am so glad. It is so important.

This is a victory for the Standing Rock Sioux. We know the long history Native Americans have in the State of the Presiding Officer. We know that around the country—I have 26 Indian entities in Nevada—they have been treated so poorly. Nevada is no different from any other State. They were pushed off of the lands they dwelt on before we showed up, we White folks here in America. They have been pushed around. So when the Standing Rock people heard the good news that the Corps of Engineers had finally given them at least some small victory, it was very exciting for them. It is a victory for them. They have been objecting to this construction for more than 2 years.

The tribe was concerned about a number of issues, not the least of which were their ancestral grounds, some of which land has their ancestors buried there. They were afraid of water contamination and other problems.

In a statement to the press, the chairman of the Standing Rock Sioux Tribe said:

We wholeheartedly support the decision of the administration and commend with the utmost gratitude the courage it took on the part of President Obama, the Army Corps, the Department of Justice and the Department of Interior to take steps to correct the course of history and do the right thing.

The Standing Rock Sioux Tribe and all of Indian country will be forever grateful to the Obama administration for this historic decision.

Indians have taken one loss after another. Rare are there any victories for the Indians.

I agree with the chairman of the tribe. This is a historic decision, and it was a momentous step toward correcting the course of a disgraceful history.

As I said last week here on the floor, the treatment of the Standing Rock Sioux by our government has been shameful—not only recently but for more than a century. The Sioux were pushed to reservations first. I say "reservations"—plural. But even that land was taken—most of it—and then massive dams were built that put the tribe's best farmland underwater. The result of these actions was a crippling poverty that plagued the tribe for generations—even this generation.

This mistreatment was not unique, as I have indicated, to Standing Rock. Indeed, there are tribes all across the Nation with very similar histories. We have them in Nevada.

Yesterday's decision will not make up for the past, but the President's action was a huge step toward correcting a terrible wrong. Money, profits, and not human dignity, was the direction of the pipeline. The Obama administration changed that.

For far too long, the pleas for justice for Native Americans have gone unanswered. At least now, on this occasion, the Standing Rock Sioux and Native Americans throughout this country know that someone is listening and their concerns are being addressed by the U.S. Government.

I admire the support of those who locked arms with the Standing Rock Sioux. Appropriately enough, these people call themselves water protectors. Native Americans from all over America, politicians from all over America, entertainers from all over America, and other celebrities were some of the water protectors, and we must recognize the more than 2,000 veterans who traveled to Standing Rock from across America to protect the protestors from violence.

It is also important to note that speech after speech and demonstration after demonstration were peaceful. All the leaders of this demonstration said time after time after time that it would be peaceful, and it has been. The only aggression has not been from the Indians but from those people who are pushing the pipeline.

It is no surprise that many of these veterans are Native Americans because American Indians serve in our Nation's Armed Forces in greater numbers per capita than any other ethnic group.

Going back to World War II, of course, the great Ira Hayes, who was made famous by Johnny Cash—they have a long history of serving in all of our wars and stepping forward.

I am gratified at the strength of the Standing Rock Sioux. Their ancestral burial grounds will remain protected and their water clean.

I thank President Obama and his administration and the Army Corps of Engineers for their action. This victory was the culmination of months and months of analysis and deliberation. I appreciate the conclusion reached.

But everyone should know that this fight isn't over. We know from long experience that our decisionmakers keel over for fossil fuel interests. We must remain vigilant. My only hope is that the Trump administration will not undo the justice the Native Americans have finally received. All of us must support the Standing Rock Sioux and help them protect their history and their land and their water.

As one aside, many decades ago I was the Lieutenant Governor of the State of Nevada, and we had our Lieutenant Governors' conference in Oklahoma. It was a wonderful week that we spent in Oklahoma. One of the highlights of that trip was an education that I received one night of a—I assume it is still going on; I don't know—a wonderful pageant that took place in a place that I believe is called Tahlequah—I believe that was the name of the place—where in such detail and in such magnificence was described how Oklahoma has so many Native Americans who came from Florida. It was a wonderful story. I was very impressed with the Native Americans whom I met and have met since that time in Oklahoma. And a memento I was given there in Oklahoma—frankly, someone stole it from me, but each one of us, each Lieutenant Governor, was given a little painting by a famous Oklahoman—at the time, at least—whose time was Tiger. I don't know what his real name was, but he was a famous artist. It was a beautiful Indian scene he had painted. We all got one. It was an original. I am sorry someone took it out of my office. But I have fond memories of that convention in Oklahoma where I learned so much about the people of Oklahoma.

Some of us in the West had over the years kind of a negative impression of Oklahoma—the Okies coming into California, all of these uneducated people causing trouble—but that was a wonderful trip to Oklahoma. I was terribly impressed at the time and have always been impressed with the people of Oklahoma.

Just a little aside here: I have had some good fortune at being able to legislate things here in Washington. One of the things that can be looked at as good or bad—and maybe I won't get a lot of pats on the back for this with the

new administration—but a Senator from Oklahoma and I did some very good work. The Congressional Review Act was Reid-Nichols legislation. That was hard to do, but what it basically said is if there is a regulation promulgated by an administration, we as a Congress have an opportunity to look it over again to determine if, in fact, we have the ability, with enough folks, to overturn that regulation.

So, again, as the Presiding Officer is from Oklahoma, I want him to understand my affection for the State of Oklahoma and the people of Oklahoma. I have had some difficult tussles with people from Oklahoma over the years. There is no better example of that than Dr. Coburn. But having said that, I have never found more of a gentleman than Dr. Coburn. Even though we disagreed on some policy issues, he was always a gentleman and I have appreciated the things I learned from him.

I yield the floor.

———

RESERVATION OF LEADER TIME

The PRESIDING OFFICER. Under the previous order, the leadership time is reserved.

———

TSUNAMI WARNING, EDUCATION, AND RESEARCH ACT OF 2015

The PRESIDING OFFICER. Under the previous order, the Senate will resume consideration of the House message to accompany H.R. 34, which the clerk will report.

The legislative clerk read as follows:

House message to accompany H.R. 34, an act to authorize and strengthen the tsunami detection, forecast, warning, research, and mitigation program of the National Oceanic and Atmospheric Administration, and for other purposes.

Pending:

McConnell motion to concur in the amendment of the House to the amendment of the Senate to the bill.

McConnell motion to concur in the amendment of the House to the amendment of the Senate to the bill, with McConnell amendment No. 5117, to change the enactment date.

McConnell amendment No. 5118 (to amendment No. 5117), of a perfecting nature.

McConnell motion to refer the message of the House on the bill to the Committee on Health, Education, Labor, and Pensions, with instructions, McConnell amendment No. 5119, to change the enactment date.

McConnell amendment No. 5120 (to the instructions (amendment No. 5119) of the motion to refer), of a perfecting nature.

McConnell amendment No. 5121 (to amendment No. 5120), of a perfecting nature.

The PRESIDING OFFICER. The Senator from Utah.

REMEMBERING JAMES TANCILL LYONS

Mr. HATCH. Mr. President, I rise today to pay tribute to Jim Lyons, a longtime staffer on Capitol Hill—my staffer—and a fixture in tax policy here in DC, who passed away on September 29 of this year.

James Tancill Lyons was born on March 7, 1973, to Stephen and Ann Lyons, both natives of the DC-Virginia area with longstanding ties to the local community. Growing up in Springfield, VA, Jim was an accomplished athlete, excelling in both baseball and basketball. Oddly, for a sports fan in the DC area, his favorite football team was the Dallas Cowboys—a decision he made consciously because his older brother, Stephen, was a big Redskins fan.

Jim was also a great student, eventually graduating summa cum laude from James Madison University. He went to law school at the University of Texas, where he made the Editing Committee of the Texas Journal of Business Law and won a scholarship for being the best tax law student in his class after pulling the top grade in his business associations, income tax, international tax, corporate tax, and estate and gift tax classes.

After law school, he earned a clerkship at the Fifth Circuit Court of Appeals and then got a job working for Cleary Gottlieb, one of the finest law firms in the country. Of course, you would never guess any of this if you knew Jim. While he was always an incredibly valuable and often brilliant attorney and congressional staffer, he talked about his college and law school days as though he spent most of his time having fun and just barely skating by. That, of course, was vintage Jim Lyons—incredibly outgoing but unbelievably humble.

Jim could have a long conversation with anyone about pretty much anything, but he was never one to spend all that much time touting his own accomplishments. Make no mistake, Jim Lyons was very accomplished. After his time at the law firm in New York, Jim made his way to the House Ways and Means Committee, and, following a brief subsequent and successful stint at the Department of Justice, he was hired by Chairman CHUCK GRASSLEY to serve as tax counsel on the Senate Finance Committee.

In his 8 years on the Finance Committee, he made a mark on every major tax bill, not to mention a number of debt and budget deals that went through the Senate, including many tax-extenders bills, some of which he seemed to be able to cobble together singlehandedly.

Jim was smart as a whip. He was a tremendously valuable congressional staffer because he had both a remarkable understanding of tax policy and an uncanny ability to see all the traps and pitfalls that stood ahead for any particular proposal or piece of legislation. He had an encyclopedic knowledge of the technical aspects of the Tax Code, as well as a clear understanding of the real-world implications, immediately seeing where a particular tax policy or bill would fit in the larger policy and, when necessary, the political landscape. Jim was one of those people who could go into the weeds to discuss, debate, and negotiate tax policy literally with anyone on the planet but also break that same policy down to its essential elements and explain it to lesser mortals, including, I have to say, more than a few of us U.S. Senators.

Of course, like all of us, Jim had his own ideological views and opinions, and he made no secret about the way he saw the world and his beliefs about the best path forward for our country. When necessary, he was a fierce advocate for his own views, but more importantly, for someone in his position, he was able, when necessary, to dispassionately apply his accrued knowledge and expertise to any tax proposal, whether it came from a conservative or liberal or a Republican or Democrat, and then break it down to its essence and give a clear and concise assessment of the policy and its chances for being enacted.

All of this made him an essential and indispensable part of our efforts on the Senate Finance Committee for close to a decade. As I think all of my colleagues will attest, staffers with that kind of knowledge and ability to evaluate policy and lay out its chances for success really can be hard to come by.

However, in the weeks since Jim's passing, it hasn't been his accomplishments or his knowledge of the Tax Code that people have most remembered; instead, most of the focus has been on his friendly demeanor, his mischievous sense of humor, and most of all, his kind heart.

Dozens of Jimmy's friends and colleagues visited Jim and his family in the hospital during his final days, and during the October recess, hundreds attended a memorial service held here in the Capitol. Each one of these people had at least one personal story to share about Jim. Sure, some of the stories did touch on his successes as a staffer and his professional disposition, but far more often the stories were about Jim's kindness, even to strangers, or his ability to make people feel at ease—and sometimes laugh uncontrollably—even in tense situations.

Jim was always quick to offer assistance and comfort to those in need and to provide a much needed laugh when things got really tough. He is one of very few people I have come across on Capitol Hill—and keep in mind I have been here a while—who will be remembered more or less equally for the bills he successfully drafted and negotiated and for the way he cracked everyone up at the negotiating table.

I think my favorite story I have heard about Jim came from his mother Ann. In 2003, Jim was living in New York City when much of that part of the country suffered a massive blackout. It is difficult to be in a place like New York without power, and Jim noticed many people on his way home who were stranded and in need of as-

sistance. Rather than look down at the ground and head quickly for home, as many would probably want to do in that situation, Jim offered help to a dozen or so people, bringing them all home to his apartment, giving them both food and a comfortable space to ride out the power outage. Most of these people were strangers. Yet Jim, ever the kind soul, offered his time and his home to help them through a difficult evening.

Mr. President, I ask unanimous consent that a copy of pages 14 and 15 from the August 2003 edition of Cleargolaw News, a newsletter for the law firm where Jim worked at that time, be printed in the RECORD following my remarks.

The article tells the story of Jim's efforts during the power blackout.

These are the types of stories that have constantly been shared since Jim's passing, and I know these memories and stories from people who knew and worked with Jim have been helpful to his family during this difficult time.

When I hear these accounts of people's interactions with Jim, I am reminded of a popular hymn in my church, which reads:

Each life that touches ours for good
Reflects thine own great mercy, Lord;
Thou sendest blessings from above
Thru words and deeds of those who love.
What greater gift dost thou bestow,
What greater goodness can we know
Than Christ-like friends, whose gentle ways
Strengthen our faith, enrich our days.
When such a friend from us departs,
We hold forever in our hearts
A sweet and hallowed memory,
Bringing us nearer, Lord, to thee.

Jim Lyons led a life which touched many others for the better. His positive influence has been felt by countless people, pretty much anyone who had the opportunity to interact with him. I personally already miss Jim's stalwart presence on the Finance Committee. I miss his wise and plain-spoken advice and unequalled knowledge of tax policy. More than that, I miss the kind and humorous manner that endeared Jim to so many of us working in and around the Senate.

There is a simple quote—an anonymous proverb of sorts—that has often been attributed to Dr. Seuss, though its origin is ultimately in dispute: "Don't cry because it's over, smile because it happened."

Over the past couple of months, I think that has been the prevailing sentiment among those of us who were lucky enough to know Jim Lyons. While tears have been shed and great sadness has been felt, the remembrances we have had of Jim's life and our interactions with him have given all of us reason to smile and even laugh.

I want to once again express my condolences to Jim's family, his parents Stephen and Ann, his brother Steve, his two nephews, Tyler and Blake, and

of course his beloved dog Buddy. Recently, I have had the opportunity to spend time with and get to know Jim's wonderful family. They are truly extraordinary people, and my prayers continue to go out to them. I know I am not alone in that regard. I care for them. Everybody who knew Jim and has now known them cares for them. Our sympathy and our heartfelt thanks go out to them for allowing their son to become the great person he became, and, of course, allowing him to come and work with us on Capitol Hill.

There being no objection, the material was ordered to be printed in the RECORD, as follows:

THANK YOU FOR TAKING CARE OF US

(By Alice Steinert)

Here is a wonderfully refreshing story about a truly good, kind person.

The day of the blackout was scary for some, devastating for others, and just plain inconvenient for many. There are those of us who still have thighs and calves that ache from all those flights of stairs! Many people could not get home that night for a number of reasons—1) after walking down that many flights of stairs, some people were a bit lame and therefore could not walk the distance to their homes, or their homes were too far to walk to; 2) there were few, if any, buses, taxi cabs, cars, trains, ferries, no subways, and no hotel vacancies; 3) etc., etc., etc.

But, for those of us fortunate enough to know Jim Lyons, CGSH Associate extraordinaire, we certainly know the meaning of the true human spirit.

Jim invited many people to his home that day when we had to evacuate OLP. He provided an immediate "base" for people to relax, calm down, regroup, make contact with family/friends, eat, drink, whatever they needed. But, for nine of us (Ron Becton, Robert Franklin, Monica Gagnon, Glenville Hunter, Amy Menendez, Alice Steinert, Jason Steinert, Naj-Lah Toussaint and Carol Whatley), he provided much, much more. He provided a safe haven for the night.

At about 7:45 P.M. Jim walked from his home to OLP to see if there was anyone else in need of assistance. Well, he found nine of us who were seriously thinking about bunking down for the night in front of the lobby doors. Without hesitation Jim invited all of us to his home (he had never even met some of us before). Not only did he provide us with a roof over our heads, he also offered food and beverage, the use of his cell phone, pillows and blankets, and even gave up his bed to two of us ladies. Not only that, he bought toothbrushes for us; What ensued was a night we will all remember—good people, stimulating conversation, a lot of fun, and a great deal of bonding and comeraderie.

While we will individually, and as a group, thank Jim, I think everyone in the firm should recognize what an exceptional person Jim is. If there were more "Jim's" in the world, what a different place it would be. God Bless You Jim.

REMEMBERING KING BHUMIBOL ADULYADEJ OF THAILAND

Mr. HATCH. Mr. President, I rise today, December 5, 2016, in commemoration of the 89th birthday of the late King Bhumibol Adulyadej of Thailand and in recognition of the National Day of Thailand. In remembrance of the extraordinary life, steady leadership, and remarkable 70-year reign of the beloved King Bhumibol, I have introduced S. Con. Res. 57, along with Representative MATT SALMON in the House. This resolution honors the late King's lasting legacy, extends our collective condolences to the royal family and the people of Thailand, and celebrates the alliance and friendship between our two nations. I would like to thank the cosponsors of this resolution, Senators WHITEHOUSE, ROBERTS, MARKEY, FLAKE, COTTON, and GARDNER. Additionally, I express my appreciation to Chairman BOB CORKER for his assistance in receiving timely consideration of this bipartisan effort in the Senate Foreign Relations Committee.

His Majesty, King Bhumibol Adulyadej, enjoyed a special relationship with the United States, having been born in Cambridge, MA, in 1927, while his father was completing his medical studies at Harvard University. He was always a trusted friend of the United States in advancing a strong and enduring alliance and partnership between our two countries.

At the time of his death on October 13, 2016, King Bhumibol Adulyadej was the longest serving head of state in the world and the longest serving in the history of Thailand. He dedicated his life to the well-being of the Thai people and the sustainable development of his country. His Majesty was an anchor of peace and stability for Thailand and for the region, earning him the deep reverence of the Thai people and the respect of leaders around the world.

I hope my colleagues will join me tomorrow in passing S. Con. Res. 57 as a gesture of respect and appreciation for the life of this great leader and as a symbol of our continued commitment to and friendship with Thailand. Additionally, I am sure my colleagues in the Senate will join me in offering our warmest congratulations and best wishes to the new King of Thailand, His Majesty King Maha Vajiralongkorn.

Mr. President, I yield the floor.

I suggest the absence of a quorum.

The PRESIDING OFFICER. The clerk will call the roll.

The legislative clerk proceeded to call the roll.

Mr. HATCH. Mr. President, I ask unanimous consent that the order for the quorum call be rescinded.

The PRESIDING OFFICER. Without objection, it is so ordered.

PASSAGE VITIATED—H.R. 5602, S. 3336, AND CALENDAR NOS. 675 THROUGH 683

Mr. HATCH. Mr. President, I ask unanimous consent to vitiate passage of H.R. 5602, S. 3336, and Calendar Nos. 675 through 683.

The PRESIDING OFFICER. Is there objection?

Without objection, it is so ordered.

Mr. HATCH. Mr. President, I suggest the absence of a quorum.

The PRESIDING OFFICER. The clerk will call the roll.

The legislative clerk proceeded to call the roll.

Mr. VITTER. Mr. President, I ask unanimous consent that the order for the quorum call be rescinded.

The PRESIDING OFFICER. Without objection, it is so ordered.

FAREWELL TO THE SENATE

Mr. VITTER. Mr. President, I rise today to speak on the Senate floor for the last time. I am not generally big on nostalgic reminiscences, but I would like to briefly reflect on what is clearly the greatest honor of my professional life—my 12 years in the U.S. Senate and 5½ years in the U.S. House of Representatives and the enormous honor of serving the people of Louisiana to whom I will always be so deeply indebted.

In some ways it seems like just yesterday that I was on the floor of the U.S. House being sworn in, surrounded by our very young children, except for Jack, who wasn't born yet. I said then: "I am honored, humbled, awestruck to stand before you today." I stated my simple goal: to become at ease and comfortable as I learn the ways of Congress, as I hopefully become an effective representative and respected colleague and friend, but never to become so at ease and comfortable that I lose these feelings of honor, of humility, of awe, and, believe me, I haven't.

My very first year in the Senate was a very memorable one. That year Louisiana was struck by Hurricanes Rita and Katrina. After the initial shock of those cataclysmic events, I realized that for quite some time, my priorities as Louisiana Senator would be dominated by the desperate need to rebuild our State, including dramatically improving our hurricane and flood protection and restoring our coastline.

Katrina's devastation was hard to imagine, destroying much of Southeast Louisiana and Coastal Mississippi. Less than 1 month later, Hurricane Rita slammed into Southwest Louisiana as another one of the most intense hurricanes in history. I immediately went to work with Senator Landrieu and the rest of our Louisiana delegation as well as my good friends THAD COCHRAN, Trent Lott, and others to secure the necessary disaster recovery assistance and also to make reforms to the Army Corps of Engineers to better protect our families and communities from future natural disasters.

Louisiana has continued to face and survive other major disasters, including Hurricane Gustav in August and September 2008, Hurricane Ike in September of that same year, Hurricane Isaac in 2012, the Red River flooding in Northern and Central Louisiana, and the 1,000-year-flood event in greater Baton Rouge and Acadiana this past August.

As if all of that weren't enough, in April of 2010, the Deepwater Horizon oil rig exploded off the coast of Louisiana, killing 11 men and devastating our coastline. The disaster, followed by the horribly misguided offshore drilling moratorium President Obama put in place, caused economic and environmental chaos in Louisiana.

Once again, I immediately went to work with so many others to increase and improve safety measures and reopen the Gulf of Mexico to energy exploration and put people back to work. We introduced legislation to dedicate a majority of the BP penalties toward restoring coastal ecosystems and economies damaged by the spill. It was an uphill battle to ensure Louisiana was fairly compensated, but we did, and we achieved substantial wins, including passage of that critical RESTORE Act that I described.

During the recovery fight following each of these disasters, I found that the most effective leadership involved communicating clearly and employing solutions based on Louisiana common sense, and what always inspired me and kept me going was the unbelievable resilience, faith, and determination of my fellow Louisianans. Their strength and optimism have been oh so powerful reminders of how blessed I have been to serve them.

On a host of other important issues, I always sought to further two sets of political values, really modeled after my two favorite Presidents, Ronald Reagan and Teddy Roosevelt. I always strove to further the central American tradition of limited government and individual freedom, and I was never afraid to shake things up, to demand needed reforms to ensure that leaders in Washington served the American people and not the other way around.

I have had the honor of protecting Louisiana's traditions and proud heritage while here in the Senate. Louisianans love the outdoors and want strong environmental conservation and sportsmen's policies to maintain that culture, and that certainly includes securing the rights afforded to each American by the Second Amendment, which I have fought to do.

Louisianans respect the sanctity of life, which has been one of my top priorities while serving in Congress. I have introduced many bills that end taxpayer funding of abortion and abortion mills and have proudly stood in the defense of life.

When it comes to our Nation's immigration policies, I have been an advocate for targeted reforms that fix the immigration crisis, starting with border security and enforcing the immigration laws already on the books. I fought President Obama's unconstitutional attempts to implement Executive amnesty, which only encourages more immigrants to come here illegally and insults the millions of fine immigrants who do follow U.S. law.

I was also the first to introduce legislation in 2007 to end dangerous sanctuary city policies and have continued to do so each Congress since. I have also been critical of too big to fail in the banking sector and have found banking reform to be an area in which Republicans can absolutely find common ground with Democrats. That is where I found success in passing into law specific measures that restrict too-big-to-fail and tax-funded bailouts. Also during my time in Congress, I have introduced several important government reform bills so we can get back to the best traditions of our democracy, which includes electing citizen legislators, making sure they don't make themselves into a separate ruling class, and advocating for term limits so individuals don't remain in office for an eternity.

Americans of all backgrounds think Washington is on a different planet and Members of Congress just don't get it. That is why I fought to end Congress's automatic pay raises each year. I first introduced that language in 2009, and the raises have been successfully blocked each year since. Congress can be an effective representative body only when it lives under the same laws it imposes on the rest of the country, and one major way to support that is through term limits. When I was a member of the Louisiana State legislature, I was successful in establishing legislative term limits there, and I have offered the leading term limits measure for Congress here, as well as imposing it on myself.

I fought for commonsense legislation that helps all Americans have access to high-quality and affordable health care. That includes the work to dismantle ObamaCare and replace it with patient-centered health care reform, which I am very hopeful the incoming Trump administration will achieve. In the meantime, I have been fighting to end Washington's exemption from ObamaCare, an illegal Obama administration Executive order that allows Washington elites to avoid the most inconvenient, expensive aspects of the Affordable Care Act by giving themselves taxpayer subsidized health care through an exchange meant solely for small businesses. Also in the health care arena, I was able to pass into law the bipartisan Steve Gleason Act of 2015. It provided immediate relief for patients who have been denied access to lifesaving and life-altering medical equipment. It was about a 2014 Medicare policy change that we had to reverse. Our bill allowed these patients to have access to medical equipment that truly empowers them, that is a true lifeline, and it changes their lives absolutely for the better.

I have also fought against large drug manufacturing lobbies to allow for reimportation of safe and approved prescription medicine from other countries, which gives patients, especially our seniors, relief from rising health care costs.

I have been honored to serve in the Senate in additional ways as well, including as a top Republican on the Environment and Public Works Committee and most recently as chair of the Senate Committee on Small Business and Entrepreneurship. I am very proud to say that we have accomplished so many of our goals in those two roles.

We worked in a bipartisan fashion on EPW to pass several major pieces of legislation, including the Water Resources and Development Act of 2007 and the even more significant WRDA of 2014, several reauthorizations of the highway bill, the bipartisan and historic rewrite of the 40-year-old Toxic Substances Control Act, which began as conversations between Senator Frank Lautenberg and myself, a partnership which Senator TOM UDALL continued after Frank's unfortunate passing.

We were also able to hold the administration accountable by conducting investigations into some outright corruption within the Obama EPA, and we advanced key transparency initiatives that shed light on government's attempts to implement policies that were not based on sound science or strategic needs.

As chair of the Small Business Committee, I have been advocating to make sure the voices and concerns of small business owners across the country are heard in Washington. We have held 23 hearings here, 18 field hearings, numerous roundtable discussions. We have heard testimony from over 175 witnesses, usually about the disastrous negative effects of Obama policies like the new waters of the United States rule, key and disastrous effects on small businesses and job creators and their employees.

At the very same time, we found common ground with Ranking Member SHAHEEN and other Democrats on the committee. During my tenure as chair, we passed 32 bipartisan bills out of the committee, which is 22 more than my predecessors did over a much longer period, and 8 of our bills have passed through the entire legislative process and have been signed into law.

These accomplishments are but a fraction of the years of hard work my staff and I have dedicated to the people of Louisiana and, indeed, the American people. I have worked hard to be a champion for them because the government should serve the taxpayer and not the other way around, and that includes by working hard to stay in touch through 398 townhall meetings, at least 5 in each parish of Louisiana, through 231 telephone townhalls, and through active, energetic casework and constituent service.

Clearly what I will treasure most about my service here is the people with whom I have been honored to serve; my colleagues, including my fellow Louisianian Senator BILL CASSIDY, mentors like former Senator Rick Santorum and Senator JEFF SESSIONS, and most especially each of the dedicated people who have been part of Team Vitter. I have come to the Senate floor several times this year to thank key departing staff members.

That is for a very simple reason. My staff has been the key ingredient—the key—to every success we have enjoyed together in public service. Wendy and I consider them a part of the family. I truly thank my staff again for their tireless, dedicated service to Louisiana. I am so very grateful. Wendy joins me in that.

I want to specifically recognize some of our leaders: my chief of staff, Luke Bolar; my legislative director, Chris Stanley; my wonderful finance director, Courtney Guastela; our state director, Chip Layton; and committee staff director, Meredith West; our grants coordinator, Brenda Moore; my media head, John Brabender; and senior infrastructure policy advisor, Charles Brittingham; my senior economic adviser, David Stokes; campaign treasurer Bill Vanderbrook; and communications director, Cheyenne Klotz.

I know a few of our other former senior staff members are here or are watching, like Mac Abrams, Joel DiGrado, Bryan Zumwalt, Travis Johnson, and Michael Long. Last, and obviously not least, is my beloved family. My five wonderful brothers and sisters, our children, their children, the extended family, led by the ultimate leader of Team Vitter, my wife Wendy.

I can never thank them enough, and certainly I can never ever thank Wendy enough. Through it all, Wendy has been so enormously patient and supportive and understanding, not to mention being the life of every Team Vitter party, leading the rounds—rounds plural—of Fireball shots. She and our daughter Lise are in the Gallery today. I thank them and Sophie, Airey, and Jack for decades of love and support. Lise, up there, was in my arms as a 2-year-old when I was first sworn into the House of Representatives and made those previously quoted remarks: "I am honored, humbled, awestruck to stand before you." She has changed some, but as I said at the beginning of my reflections, those feelings certainly have not.

I would like to close as I did that day in the House over 17 years ago; that is, simply by recognizing the wonderful, loving forces that have brought me here today: God, family, led by my parents up above, and my wife Wendy, staff and friends, and of course the wonderful, wonderful people of Louisiana. They are here with me today. They are here with me always. I thank them from the depths of my heart.

For the last time, I yield the floor.

The PRESIDING OFFICER. The Senator from Louisiana.

TRIBUTE TO DAVID VITTER

Mr. CASSIDY. Mr. President, I have the honor to recognize and thank my colleague and friend, the Honorable Senator DAVID VITTER, for his 25 years of service to Louisiana. Our State has been fortunate to have him as its voice and advocate in this Chamber for the past 12 years.

On a personal note, when I arrived at the Senate, DAVID worked with me, sharing with me some of the privileges that normally he, as a senior Senator, could have kept all to himself. With great graciousness, he worked with me and said: Listen, this is how I think the process should be set up. I would like you to have some of this privilege as well. I will do the same with whoever replaces DAVID. He has set a pattern that, again, by his graciousness and magnanimity, deserves repetition.

As a new Senator, I was fortunate to have him as a resource for advice and knowledge that comes from time and experience in this body. There are some things that happen here that you have to kind of have experience to follow. DAVID had both the experience, the sharpness, and the insight to recognize.

I again look forward to sharing what he has taught me with whoever takes his place. I will note, as DAVID did, he helped lead our State through some of our worst times. From Hurricane Katrina in 2005 to the great flood of 2016, all of the way in between, DAVID has worked hard to make sure Louisiana and the people of Louisiana have what they need to recover.

The hallmark of Senator VITTER's tenure is that he has always cared deeply about our State, constantly looking for what he could do that would benefit our State, not just in the short term but doing that which is consistent with his principles to help Louisiana and the United States thrive in the long term.

He has been on the side of that family whose father goes for 2 weeks, works on an oil rig in the middle of the Gulf of Mexico, working hard so his family has a better future. DAVID has been on the side of that mom juggling two jobs to earn enough to make sure her children's needs are met.

A recent example—again for the short-term and long-term perspective DAVID handled so well—he stayed persistent for years working across the aisle, first with Senator Frank Lautenberg, then Senator UDALL, to pass the much needed reform of the Toxic Substances Control Act, the first reform of its kind in 40 years.

This reform protects both the workers—those people on that rig, perhaps, at least the people who would be processing the products of that rig—but also gives the manufacturers of Louisiana and across the country the certainty they need to expand their businesses and create more jobs.

On a lighter note, DAVID is a great Saints fan. We in Louisiana kind of liked the fact that when the slogan "Who Dat" came up spontaneously, and people started to put it on their shirts and the NFL was going to go to court to stop this from happening, DAVID wrote a letter to Roger Goddell. The letter started off by saying: "Who Dat." So speaking truth to power on behalf of the "Who Dat Nation" is one credit of his.

Similarly, DAVID was tweeting before our President-elect made it perhaps as high profile. I remember during the 2013 Super Bowl in New Orleans—and again the context of this is, the Saints had just been punished—of course Saints fans think unfairly—by Roger Goddell. So during the 2013 Super Bowl in New Orleans, when the power went out, DAVID's tweet, without missing a beat said: "Like most Saints fans, I am immediately assuming Roger Goddell is the chief suspect for the power outage." The quick-witted quip cut to the emotion of the "Who Dat Nation."

As the 114th Congress comes to a close, the Senate will be losing an important Member. DAVID brings a sound, strategic mind to this Chamber that will be missed. I wish him, Wendy, their children, Lise, Sophie, Airey, and Jack, the best of luck in their journey forward. On behalf of all Louisiana, I say thank you.

I yield the floor.

The PRESIDING OFFICER. The Senator from Louisiana.

Mr. VITTER. Mr. President, I thank the Senator from Louisiana for his very kind remarks. More importantly, I want to thank him for years of great partnership, great work on behalf of Louisiana. I know he will make an outstanding senior Senator. Thank you.

I yield the floor.

Mr. CASSIDY. Mr. President, I suggest the absence of a quorum.

The PRESIDING OFFICER. The clerk will call the roll.

The senior assistant legislative clerk proceeded to call the roll.

Ms. COLLINS. Mr. President, I ask unanimous consent that the order for the quorum call be rescinded.

The PRESIDING OFFICER. Without objection, it is so ordered.

Ms. COLLINS. Mr. President, I rise in strong support of the 21st Century Cures Act, and I commend the chairman and ranking member of the Senate Health, Education, Labor, and Pensions Committee, Senator LAMAR ALEXANDER and Senator PATTY MURRAY, for their unwavering commitment to this very significant bipartisan legislation.

The Senate HELP Committee, on which I am privileged to serve, has devoted considerable time and effort to this comprehensive legislation. It includes many reforms and priorities that will benefit so many families across our great country. The 21st Century Cures Act will support the research and development of safe treatments and cures for millions of Americans and their families who are coping with devastating diseases. It will improve the process of moving new discoveries from laboratory benches to patient bedsides.

I doubt that there is a family in America who will not be touched by this important legislation in some way. All of us have a family member, a co-worker, or a friend who has courageously faced the struggles of living with a debilitating chronic illness or a rare disease or who has received a devastating diagnosis and has passed away far too soon, leaving a hole in our hearts. Imagine how this could change with the passage of the 21st Century Cures Act and strong support of the research and development that will lead to new treatments and therapies that can help us achieve our dream of conquering so many devastating diseases.

Simply put, this legislation matters. It matters to the children who know firsthand the burden of living with type 1 diabetes and who beg their parents for just one day off—their birthday or Christmas—from having to deal with the consequences of their juvenile diabetes. It matters to the family members who know the agonizing experience of looking into the eyes of a loved one suffering from Alzheimer's disease, only to receive a confused look in return. It matters to the parents of young boys who have Duchenne muscular dystrophy, who know what it is like to give their all in an effort to help their sons achieve their dreams, whether it is finishing college or driving a car, even as every day their children battle the progression of this debilitating and ultimately terminal illness. The 21st Century Cures Act will drive progress in medical innovation so that we can prevail against these diseases and many more that cause so much pain and suffering, so much fear and uncertainty, and so much heartbreak.

There simply is no investment that we can make that provides greater return for Americans than our investment in biomedical research. It not only leads to new discoveries and the development of better treatments and even cures but also can have a dramatic effect on the budgets of families, States, and the Federal Government. The bill before us will help direct $4.8 billion to the National Institutes of Health, including $1.6 billion for the BRAIN Initiative to improve our understanding of diseases such as ALS, Parkinson's, and Alzheimer's, our Nation's most costly disease.

We spend $263 billion a year caring for people with Alzheimer's disease. Of that amount, approximately $160 billion comes from the Medicare and Medicaid Programs. If the current trajectory continues as our population grows older, this disease will bankrupt the Medicare and Medicaid Programs. That is why I am so pleased to see the BRAIN Initiative funded in this bill and also the work we are doing in the Appropriations Committee to boost funding for Alzheimer's disease and other dementias so that we can finally find effective treatments, a means of prevention, or perhaps even a cure for this disease that brings so much heartache not only to those suffering from it but to their families as well.

Our bill will also help provide $1.8 billion for the Vice President's Cancer Moonshot. We all know that Vice President BIDEN has taken on this cause—a very personal one for him—because he lost his beloved son Beau to cancer.

Another exciting field that will be funded by this bill is $30 million for regenerative medicine, using adult stem cells. How exciting it was to have an individual come before our policy lunch whose sight had been restored due to innovative stem cell surgery. This individual lives in Tennessee now but happens to be from Presque Isle, ME, just 13 miles from where I was born and grew up. How I wish so many older people in this country who are losing their vision to macular degeneration and glaucoma—in some cases, a combination of both—or injuries to their eyes could benefit from this exciting development with adult stem cells, which has restored the sight of someone who was legally blind. He now can drive. That is so exciting, and that is the promise of researching regenerative medicine.

In addition to support for NIH, the 21st Century Cures Act will help direct $1 billion in much needed funding to address the horrendous heroin and opioid abuse problem in this country. Maine has been particularly hard hit by this epidemic. In just the first 9 months of this year, Maine experienced a record 286 overdose deaths. That is more than one a day. Tragically, that number already exceeds the 272 overdose deaths in Maine during all of 2015.

I am distressed when I hear about the lack of treatment options for Mainers who are struggling with drug addiction, particularly in rural areas. As a result of the shortage of treatment alternatives, this epidemic is playing out in emergency rooms, county jails, and on the main streets of my State. I can't tell you how many sheriffs have come to me pleading for help, telling me that the intake area of their jail looks like a detox center or an emergency room of a hospital. They are overwhelmed by these cases.

We can and must do more to support access to treatment and to alert people of all ages to the risks of opioid abuse and heroin use. The 21st Century Cures Act will provide a vital infusion of $1 billion over 2 years to support grants to States to supplement treatment and prevention efforts.

I was talking with one of my colleagues earlier today. Both of us remember when we were in school hearing lectures from recovering heroin addicts who came into the schools, and I can state that it was highly effective. We would never have tried heroin. I can't even think of a proper analogy.

We know, unfortunately, that many of the people who are using heroin started with prescription opioids, and that is why I am encouraged by movements across our country and by actions taken, at my request and the request of other Senators, by the Centers for Medicare & Medicaid Services to make sure we are not putting pressure on providers to overprescribe opioids. Surely they are appropriate in certain cases, but the number of prescriptions has soared in this country and is twice the number prescribed on a per capita basis as in our neighboring country of Canada.

The 21st Century Cures Act also includes a bill that I introduced with several of my colleagues—Senators WARREN, KIRK, BALDWIN, ALEXANDER, and MURRAY—that is called the Advancing NIH Strategic Planning and Improving Representation in Medical Research Act. Despite its extremely cumbersome name, it is an important bill that has been incorporated into this legislation. It will require the NIH to release periodically a strategic plan outlining how the agency will meet its mission statement, and it will provide us with important guidance and metrics as we continue to work together to increase this vital funding.

It will also help to ensure that study populations in clinical research are more representative of the diverse population in our country. For example, women face many of the same health threats as men, such as heart disease and cancer, but they react differently to various treatments.

I remember years ago an infamous study that was called MRFIT. It had only men enrolled in it. I believe, if memory serves me correctly, it was to look at heart disease. Well, women often have different symptoms of heart disease than do men, and they respond differently to different medications, therapies, and treatments. We also know that women are at higher risk for certain chronic health conditions, such as Alzheimer's disease and osteoporosis. They suffer from those diseases in far greater numbers than do men. With Alzheimer's disease, I am wondering whether it is simply a matter that the biggest risk factor is age and women live longer than men, but perhaps there are other factors at play.

My point is that by helping to ensure that women, African Americans, Latinos, and other demographic groups are appropriately represented in clinical research, we can increase our scientific understanding of the causes, risk factors, prevention strategies, and effects of treatments for diseases that commonly or disproportionately affect these populations.

The bill before us also includes legislation that I introduced with my colleague from Wisconsin, Senator BALDWIN, to help address the educational debt burden that many young researchers face. This is so important to help ensure that America's finest, up-and-coming young researchers continue to help lead the world in biomedical discovery in this country. I don't want to lose these young talented people to other countries. I want them to stay right here. If they come to work for the NIH or the CDC or other federally funded institutions and agencies and we can get them help with their medical school, college, their advanced degrees, and their debt, that is a very good agreement for us to be making.

It is also of tremendous importance that we were able to add mental health legislation to the 21st Century Cures Act. The reforms in this bill will enhance coordination, address a lack of resources, and develop real solutions to improve outcomes for individuals with serious mental illness and to help their families, who are often desperate to get them the help they need.

I am pleased that the bill also includes the Mental Health on Campus Improvement Act, which I offered as an amendment when we considered the mental health legislation in committee. My colleague, Senator DICK DURBIN, and I introduced this legislation for the first time in 2009. I commend him for his leadership.

College students in Maine and across the country must have access to critical and often lifesaving mental health services. Despite growing demand for these critical services, far too many students still lack access. Without these services, students may experience detrimental effects that range from declining academic performance to drug dependence and to being at greater risk of suicide.

While millions of Americans suffer from mental illness, only a statistical few engage in unspeakable acts of violence against themselves or others. Suicide, however, is the leading cause of death among Americans between the ages of 15 and 34. In addition, recent tragedies on college campuses, such as the shooting at a community college in Roseburg, OR, or at Northern Illinois University, highlight the dire need for mental health outreach and counseling services on college campuses.

Perhaps some of the tragedies that we have witnessed might have been prevented had the resources been in place to support timely diagnosis, early intervention, and effective treatment for those struggling with severe mental illness.

One of the saddest meetings I have had in the last year was with a group of families from Maine who had adult children who were suffering from severe mental illness, yet these families felt powerless in getting them the help they needed. These adult children were not compliant with the medication they had been prescribed, and in many cases their families felt powerless to be able to get them the help they needed.

In one terrible case, a man's son was released from a hospital in the State of Maine—from a hospital for people with mental illness—and he killed his mother, thinking she was Al Qaeda. Only then could his father get his son the institutionalized help his son so desperately needed.

It was just such a painful, painful story to hear from this anguished father and husband. I believe the language in this bill will help to change that.

The 21st Century Cures Act passed the House last week by an overwhelming vote of 392 to 26. Think how few bills pass with that kind of strong, bipartisan support. It is supported by President Obama, who had an op-ed in Maine newspapers this weekend endorsing the bill. It is the product of years of bipartisan work on the Senate HELP Committee, and it has earned the support of more than 300 organizations.

Frankly, I am surprised that we are having a rollcall vote—a cloture vote on this bill. I am surprised because, while this bill may not be perfect—and no bill is—there is so much that is worthwhile, good, and significant in it that will make such a difference to so many American families.

I urge all of our colleagues to vote in support of this bill so that we can quickly send it to the President's desk, where he is eager to sign it into law. It may well be the most important, far-reaching legislation that we pass this year in terms of its benefits for families across this great Nation.

Mr. President, I suggest the absence of a quorum.

The PRESIDING OFFICER. The clerk will call the roll.

The senior assistant legislative clerk proceeded to call the roll.

Mr. TESTER. Mr. President, I ask unanimous consent that the order for the quorum call be rescinded.

The PRESIDING OFFICER. Without objection, it is so ordered.

SUPPORTING OUR VETERANS

Mr. TESTER. Mr. President, I rise today on behalf of nearly 100,000 veterans who live in Montana. These are folks who have earned our deep respect and gratitude.

I have traveled the State many times, listened to their ideas, and I have listened to their concerns. Montana's veterans have not been shy about expressing their views.

What I have heard is this. There is no doubt that we must hold the VA accountable and work to improve access to health care, jobs, education, transportation, and housing for veterans.

That is why it is critically important that we are taking marching orders from veterans and the advocacy organizations that are led by veterans, because we know that their top priority is to do right by the folks who they serve.

Veterans in Montana also tell me that when it comes to solving the problems facing veterans, they expect folks in Washington, DC, to check their politics at the door and go to work.

Unfortunately, there are groups out there that are funded by dark money. They hide their out-of-touch political agenda behind the veil of our Nation's veterans.

As the incoming ranking member of the Veterans' Affairs Committee, I have serious concerns about who President-Elect Trump is listening to when it comes to honoring our veterans and this Nation's commitment to those who have worn the uniform. That is why it is so troubling that recent news reports have indicated that the Trump administration is relying heavily on guidance from Concerned Veterans for America. Concerned Veterans for America is a political advocacy group funded by the Koch brothers, who want to dump unlimited amounts of dark money to push dangerous policies that would privatize the VA or to convert the Veterans Health Administration into an independent, nongovernment-chartered, for-profit corporation. CVA also wants to divert funds from the VA and cripple its ability to plan for the long term to recruit doctors and nurses and to invest in the information technology that can improve veterans' experiences at the VA. These cuts will undermine the quality of care at the VA.

There is nothing wrong with helping veterans get specialty care in the community in a timely fashion when the VA cannot do it. That often happens in rural communities, but CVA's push for wholesale dismantling of the VA is not what we want, and that is not what the veterans need.

We need to talk to the veterans—the veterans I have spoken to—and this is what we will see.

When folks volunteer to serve in the Armed Forces, this Nation is indebted to them. We must ensure that we deliver on those promises that are made. Privatizing the VA will fail our veterans and their families. It will reduce the quality of care that our veterans receive, and it will be more expensive for taxpayers. Privatizing the VA will ultimately mean that veterans will wait longer for doctors' appointments and the cost of care will go up.

All we have to do is take a look at the Veterans Choice Program, which allows veterans to access care at private facilities. It has resulted in longer wait times, and this is unacceptable.

Under this program, veterans are actually waiting longer to see doctors. Hospitals are increasingly frustrated and refusing to see veterans, and costs are going through the roof. Imagine this program on steroids. That is what the CVA wants to do—all while starving the VA's existing workforce and infrastructure. In fact, what CVA is pushing for is similar to what Speaker RYAN wants to do with Medicare, and we have seen the backlash to that proposal by seniors across this Nation.

The same is true with the veterans and proposals to privatize the VA. It is simply bad policy. Groups such as the VFW, the American Legion, Disabled American Veterans, Iraq and Afghanistan Veterans of America, and many others oppose privatization, and they oppose it for good reason.

The American Legion national commander, Dale Barnett, said it best:

> The private sector didn't send our heroes to war. Uncle Sam did.

Barnett is right. The Federal Government has an obligation to honor those incredible sacrifices. When we shirk that responsibility, it dishonors those brave men and women. We need to listen to the American Legion and countless other veterans groups, whose mission is to help the veterans, not unravel the VA. Veterans service organizations are very different and have a very different mission and tax structure than Concerned Veterans for America, the first being that VSOs take their cues from the veterans they represent, not from billionaire political activists who fund their operation. Groups such as the Legion, the VFW, and Iraq and Afghanistan Veterans of America are organized as nonprofit groups whose missions are simply to help veterans.

Concerned Veterans for America is an issue advocacy group with a political mission. VSOs disclose their donors. CVA doesn't have to. Yet CVA has incredible influence and the ear of the President-elect. This is deeply concerning to me and, more importantly, it is deeply concerning to the veterans across this Nation.

I talk to veterans every week when I am home in Montana. They universally tell me that they like the care they receive from the VA once they get in the door; the problem is getting in the door. They don't want to see a private doc; they want to be seen by a VA doc. They know that the VA understands their unique issues. They know that doctors and nurses at the VA are attentive to the wounds of war.

My hope is that President-elect Donald Trump starts talking with the folks who want to help veterans and not to organizations with a political agenda. My hope is that he will work with Chairman ISAKSON and me and countless other reputable veterans groups to hold the VA accountable while increasing access to care. My hope is that he will work with Democrats, Republicans, and Independents to reform our campaign finance laws so that we can increase transparency and know who is trying to influence this government.

My hope is that he will put veterans first as he chooses the next VA Secretary.

I remain hopeful that we can find common ground to work together to hold the VA accountable, to improve care, and to ensure that we are all delivering for veterans. When our brothers and sisters and sons and daughters are sent to war, we make promises to them—promises we must keep. When they come home, they are changed people, and we cannot expect the private sector to address these seen and unseen wounds of war.

In this upcoming Congress, there will be incredible opportunities to make progress, and I am fully committed to Montana's veterans and veterans across this country and their families, and I will push back against those who attempt to undermine the noble mission of the Veterans' Administration.

Mr. President, I yield the floor.

Mrs. FEINSTEIN. Mr. President, I wish to support the 21st Century Cures Act, which would make vital investments in research to develop new treatments for deadly diseases, including cancer. The bill would also dedicate desperately needed funding to address some of our country's most pressing public health problems—opioid addiction and mental illness.

First, I would like to speak about the bill's provisions for cancer and rare diseases. Cancer touches the lives of all Americans; it doesn't discriminate. We have all experienced the grief and pain that comes with losing a loved one, friend, or colleague to this terrible disease.

Cancer is the second leading cause of death in our country. Nearly 40 percent of Americans will be diagnosed with cancer at some point in their lives, according to the National Cancer Institute. We have made great strides in improving detection, treatment, and survival rates for many cancers, including early-stage breast cancer, prostate cancer, and melanoma.

Despite this progress, other cancers like pancreatic and certain brain cancers remain extremely deadly, with very low 5-year survival rates. These cancers are typically detected in late stages, and even the most cutting-edge treatments may result in just a few more months of life.

The Cures Act designates nearly $4.8 billion in additional funds for medical research through the National Institutes of Health, $1.8 billion of which will expand and accelerate cancer research, in line with Vice President BIDEN's Cancer Moonshot Initiative. This research funding also supports important initiatives focused on precision medicine and neurological research.

Next, I would like to talk about the bill's funding to combat opioid addiction, which is an epidemic in this country. Nearly 2 million Americans are addicted to opioids, and 19,000 Americans overdosed and died in 2014. This epidemic stems from a surge in the use of prescription drugs. It is not a coincidence that prescription overdose deaths quadrupled during the same period that opioid prescriptions quadrupled.

In 2012, 259 million prescriptions for opioids were written. That means 80 percent of Americans could have a bottle of pills. Prescription drug abuse frequently leads to heroin addiction because these drugs affect the brain in the same way. This problem is exacerbated because heroin is significantly cheaper that prescription opioids like OxyContin or fentanyl.

This crisis demands an immediate, comprehensive, national response. Congress took a first step earlier this year, passing the Comprehensive Addiction and Recovery Act in May. This bill authorizes grants to expand access to substance use disorder treatment, strengthen prescription drug monitoring programs, and supply first responders with naloxone, which can reverse the effects of an overdose. However, this bill didn't include any funding for the initiatives it authorized. The Cures Act takes that step, providing $1 billion for the Department of Health and Human Services to fund many of the prevention and treatment programs authorized by Congress earlier this year.

Lastly, I would like to highlight the bill's provisions to improve our country's mental health system. This is an area where we fall far short. We don't do nearly enough to ensure those with mental illness are able to access appropriate treatment and this has ripple effects throughout society.

In October, I was briefed on the homelessness crisis in Los Angeles and toured a shelter for homeless women. A significant percentage of the city's homeless population is battling mental illness. So, by improving our mental health system, we are also going to address connected issues like homelessness.

Under the bill, Health and Human Services will develop a strategic plan to address mental health priorities. There is increased funding to train our doctors and nurses to better integrate substance abuse and mental health treatment into primary care visits.

The bill also reauthorizes many important existing programs, including the National Suicide Prevention Lifeline and the National Child Traumatic Stress Network, and increases support for mental health and drug courts. These innovative approaches to criminal justice provide an alternative process for individuals to receive and comply with needed treatment and are supported by the law enforcement community.

The bill further provides for police training when police officers encounter individuals who exhibit mental illness.

I recently convened meetings in Los Angeles and San Francisco with law enforcement and community leaders, and they all stressed the importance of deescalating situations with mentally ill individuals to make sure that situations do not end with violent encounters.

In closing, I reiterate my support for the 21 Century Cures Act and urge its swift passage. This is a great opportunity to spur this century's medical innovation, improve access to needed treatments, and strengthen public health.

The PRESIDING OFFICER (Mr. COATS). The Senator from Tennessee.

Mr. ALEXANDER. Mr. President, I ask unanimous consent that Senator KIRK be recognized next and then Senator MURPHY following him and that after that, I be recognized. We will be voting at 5:30.

The PRESIDING OFFICER. Without objection, it is so ordered.

The Senator from Illinois.

Mr. KIRK. Mr. President, 4 years ago I climbed the Capitol steps for those who could not. I vowed to return to the Senate to create and establish a standard of care for rehabilitation in this legislation to make sure many people can have access to the best rehab, as I did. With the passage of the Cures Act tomorrow, we will achieve this lofty goal.

The Cures Act also contains bipartisan provisions to provide accelerated approval of regenerative medicines and therapies. The Regrow Act, which is also in this bill, is a major step forward so that Americans will not have to go to other countries for their own stem cells to be used in their own therapy. Making sure this faster approval process happens in this bill means that many more people will be able to receive advanced stem cell therapies that are also available overseas, right here at home.

I would like to thank everybody. We have made progress with the FDA. I championed with Senators COLLINS and MANCHIN on this. I thank my senior colleague from Tennessee for all of his action on the Regrow Act so we can make the fundamental point of using your own stem cells to accelerate healing. In the case of using your own stem cells, they already have your exact DNA match. I think it is wise that we go through a shorter process. I thank the Senator for putting the Kirk language in the Regrow Act.

I yield the floor.

Mr. ALEXANDER. Mr. President, while we are waiting for Senator MURPHY, let me salute Senator KIRK for his leadership from the very beginning. He has pointed out to the committee and the Senate that, as the Mayo Clinic has said, regenerative medicine is a game changer for stroke victims, for heart disease, and for people with retinal disease.

Thanks to Senator KIRK, Senator COLLINS, Senator MANCHIN, and Senator MCCONNELL, we have legislation that takes an important and responsible step forward to recognize the promise of regenerative medicine.

This bill includes $30 million to the National Institutes of Health for clinical trials to support regenerative medicine. Then there are two other provisions in the bill. One of them allows the Food and Drug Administration to make regenerative therapeutic products eligible for the FDA's existing accelerated drug approval pathway. We have had great success over the last 4 or 5 years with an accelerated pathway for drugs, similar to what Senators BURR and BENNET and others got enacted into law. We are doing the same thing with combination drugs and devices in this legislation. Now Senator KIRK has added regenerative medicine to the accelerated pathway, and I salute him for that leadership.

The PRESIDING OFFICER. The Senator from Illinois.

Mr. KIRK. Mr. President, I wish to remind my colleague, who is also the chairman of the Appropriations Energy Subcommittee that controls the exascale funding, one of the most complicated things we can face in our world is biological systems when we look at the new Aurora computer that is going to be built in the Argonne National Laboratories. I know that at Oak Ridge, we have exascale computers. My goal is to make sure we are always way ahead of the Chinese. In the case of Aurora, we now have $165 million to make sure that we have a computer that is far faster than the computer in China. With that, we will be able to model proteins themselves to make sure we make these advances much faster. My hope is that we will be stunned at how much biological work is being done at the Oak Ridge lab with their leading computer to make sure we accelerate progress on this.

Let me say one thing about the work of the Senator. Every piece of legislation that he touches goes through by a couple hundred votes. When we see LAMAR take over a bill, we know it is going to be going through on a big walloping. He got a huge vote in the Senate, and I hope he gets a big vote again. Everything he touches turns to gold, and we cannot have a better friend in medical care than we have in LAMAR ALEXANDER.

Mr. ALEXANDER. Mr. President, the Senator from Illinois is very generous, and I thank him, but I would remind him that he was the persistent agent for the change in support for regenerative medicine. That wasn't easy to do, and he has been the leader, along with others of us who cared about the same thing, in making sure the United States maintains its lead in supercomputing competition around the world.

Senator MURPHY, the Senator from Connecticut, is coming. I think what I will do is begin, and when he comes I will stop and let him make his 5 minutes of remarks and then resume so I don't delay the vote because I know everyone is looking forward to casting a great big "yes" vote in a few minutes.

The U.S. Senate majority leader, whose position in the Senate this is, has said more than once in private meetings I attended and on the floor of this body that the 21st Century Cures bill on which we will be voting in a few minutes is the most important legislation Congress will pass this year.

In his address to the Nation this past weekend, President Obama urged us to vote for the bill today and tomorrow. "It could help us find a cure for Alzheimer's," the President said. "It could end cancer as we know it and help those seeking treatment for opioid addiction." The President continued: "It's an opportunity to save lives and an opportunity we just can't miss."

Vice President BIDEN has been telephoning Senators urging support for 21st Century Cures because, in the Vice President's words, it is a big step for cancer research and the Cancer Moonshot that is so close to his heart.

Speaker PAUL RYAN in the House of Representatives has made 21st Century Cures explicitly a centerpiece of his vision for our country's future, describing it as "bipartisan legislation that would accelerate the discovery, development, and delivery of lifesaving treatments."

With such bipartisan support from the President of the United States, the Vice President of the United States, the Speaker of the House, the Senate majority leader—two Democrats, two Republicans—it is no wonder that on last Wednesday, the House of Representatives approved 21st Century Cures by the overwhelming vote of 392 to 26.

This legislation holds the promise of improving the life and health of virtually every family in the country.

It will provide $4.8 billion in a one-time surge of funding for biomedical research in a time of breathtaking opportunity.

It will advance Vice President BIDEN's Cancer Moonshot to find cures for cancer and President Obama's Precision Medicine Initiative, as well as the BRAIN Initiative.

It will help move safe and effective treatments and cures through the development and regulatory process more rapidly, and it will lower costs, making medicines available sooner and hopefully also at lower costs to patients.

It will provide $1 billion in grants to help deal with the raging opioid epidemic.

It includes legislation to help the one in five adults in this country suffering from a mental illness, help them receive treatment by updating many of our country's mental health programs for the first time in a decade.

It will improve health information technology for doctors who are eager to get rid of the overdocumentation of hospitals and their patients and help get the Nation's electronic health records system out of the ditch.

From a taxpayer's point of view, it does all of these things in a fiscally responsible way by reducing other spending to pay for every penny of the $6.3 billion cost.

I see the Senator from Connecticut on the floor, so I would like to suspend my remarks for 5 minutes so that he can make his, and then I would ask unanimous consent that the totality of my remarks follow his remarks.

Before he speaks, let me just say once again how much I appreciate his leadership and that of Senator CASSIDY and Senator CORNYN. One reason the majority leader calls this the most important piece of legislation Congress will act on this year is because it includes the mental health legislation that these Senators, including Senator MURPHY, Senator CORNYN, and Senator CASSIDY, have offered.

The PRESIDING OFFICER. The Senator from Connecticut.

Mr. MURPHY. Mr. President, I appreciate Senator ALEXANDER's kindness in allowing me to say a few words in support of this bill on behalf of myself and Senator MURRAY. I wish to congratulate Senator ALEXANDER for once again showing how the Senate can work properly, how we can bring together Republicans and Democrats for a priority that really has nothing to do with whether one is a Republican or a Democrat or whether one voted for Hillary Clinton or Donald Trump. If people are out there suffering from a life-altering or potentially terminal disease or suffering from mental illness or addiction, they need help, and we are coming together in maybe one of the most important pieces of health legislation that has passed this Congress in a very long time to deliver that help.

So I am not going to endeavor to recreate the remarks of Senator ALEXANDER when it comes to describing the important aspects of this bill except to say that after passage of this bill, it is going to be a whole heck of a lot more likely that a life-changing, lifesaving drug is going to be able to make it to market in time to save a life.

Every single one of the underlying reforms in this bill to the drug discovery process is bipartisan. I think about Senators BENNET and HATCH's bill, the promise for antibiotics and therapeutics for health, which establishes a new pathway for antibacterial and antifungal drugs that will treat serious, life-threatening infections for patients. I think about Senator CASEY and Senator ISAKSON working on the Advancing Hope Act, which will extend the pediatric priority review voucher program until 2020. It incentivizes drug companies to research treatment for life-altering diseases that impact pediatric patients.

Inside this bill are all sorts of good, important, bipartisan achievements. As Senator ALEXANDER noted, there is also help on the way for people suffering from addiction. In my tiny little State—only 1 percent of the Nation's population—we are going to have over 800 people die this year from drug overdoses. Yes, we need to get to the source of that epidemic and stop people from getting addicted to pain medications in the first place, but, boy, we have an awful lot of people showing up with overdoses in our emergency rooms who have no place to go, have no detox programs, no long-term residential programs. The $1 billion authorized in this legislation to fight the opioid epidemic is going to save lives in my little State.

Finally, when it comes to the issue of mental health—Senator ALEXANDER, Senator CASSIDY, and I were on the floor last week talking about this legislation; the focus on funding prevention, the focus on making sure parents are part of the care for their adult children, the focus on ensuring that insurance companies really do pay attention to the Parity Act we passed 10 years ago in this Congress to assure that you get covered for mental illness just like physical illness. A broken leg really isn't any different than a broken brain when we think about it. We can treat both. These are important advances in mental health as well.

I know this place has a bad reputation; that people pay attention to the fights here more often than they do to the moments where we get together and cooperate. The 21st Century Cures Act that Senator MURRAY and Senator ALEXANDER, with help from Senator CORNYN, me, Senator CASSIDY, and in the House Congressmen UPTON, PALLONE, TIM MURPHY, and EDDIE BERNICE JOHNSON—this is an example of how this place can work better.

As we head in to what may be a very charged atmosphere in January, I hope we remember this moment. I wanted to come down on behalf of Senator MURRAY, who has helped shepherd this process, to congratulate Senator ALEXANDER on it and recommend its passage to all of my colleagues.

I yield the floor.

The PRESIDING OFFICER. The Senator from Tennessee.

Mr. ALEXANDER. Mr. President, I thank the Senator for his words, support, and his leadership this year. I thank also Senator MURRAY from Washington. She would be here, except her plane is delayed. The vote will be held open to make sure she can be here, but Senator MURRAY is a Member of the Democratic leadership and well respected on that side of the aisle but also on this side of the aisle because, when she can, she creates an environment where we can do today exactly

what we are doing today. I think the American people appreciate that, and Senator MURPHY and I both benefit from that. I thank the Senator for those remarks and will now continue my remarks.

At a Senate hearing earlier this year, Dr. Francis Collins, the distinguished head of the National Institutes of Health—an agency he calls the "National Institutes of Hope"—offered "bold predictions" about major advances to expect in the next 10 years from sustained investments in biomedical research, such as we are doing with this bill.

One prediction is that scientists will find ways to identify individuals at risk for Alzheimer's even before symptoms appear, as well as how to slow or even prevent the disease. Today, Alzheimer's causes untold family grief and costs $236 billion a year. Left unchecked, the cost in 2050 would be more than our Nation spends on national defense.

Dr. Collins' other predictions are equally breathtaking. Using stem cells, doctors could use a patient's own cells to rebuild his or her heart. This personalized rebuilt heart, Dr. Collins says, would make transplant waiting lists and anti-rejection drugs obsolete. He expects development of an artificial pancreas to help diabetes patients by tracking blood glucose levels and creating precise doses of insulin. He says a Zika vaccine should be widely available by 2018, with universal flu vaccine and HIV/AIDS vaccine available within the decade. To relieve suffering and deal with the epidemic of opioid addiction that led to 28,000 overdose deaths in America in 2014, he predicts new nonaddictive medicines to manage pain, an even more effective antidote than the $1 billion we would be authorizing by our votes today. These truly would be miracles.

The bill has taken more than 2 years to assemble both in the Senate and the House. There have been major differences of opinion, but the resolution of those differences—thanks to Senator MURRAY and many other Senators—has been bipartisan every step of the way. We saw that on display in the work of the President, the Vice President, the Speaker of the House, and the Senate majority leader. We saw it in the House with its vote of 392 to 26 last week, thanks especially to the leadership of Chairman UPTON, Ranking Member PALLONE, and Representative DEGETTE. We saw it in our Senate Health Committee, where we approved 19 bills that include 50 proposals, and every one with both a Democratic and Republican sponsor, except for 1 bill offered solely by Senator MURRAY, who is the ranking Democratic member of our committee.

We have a diverse committee of 22 Members—that would be an understatement, actually—some of the most

liberal Members and some of the most conservative Members, but when our committee considered these 19 bills during our 3 markups held over several months, the largest number of votes against any one of these 19 bipartisan bills was 2. Let me say that again. The largest number of votes—recorded votes—against any one of these 19 bipartisan bills was 2 in our committee of 22.

Here is what some of those 19 bipartisan bills—again, approved unanimously or by a wide margin—would do to help move safe and effective treatments and cures more rapidly through the regulatory process and into patients' medicine cabinets and into doctors' offices.

For example, Senators BENNET, WARREN, BURR, and HATCH's act would allow researchers to use their own data from previously approved therapies when they submit for review a treatment or cure for serious rare genetic diseases, like Duchenne's, a rare kind of muscular dystrophy that could impact children as young as 3.

Senators BURR and FRANKEN's legislation will help to bring innovative medical devices—such as artificial knees, insulin pumps, and heart stents—to patients more quickly by getting rid of unnecessary burdens in medical device evaluations and streamlining the review process for clinical trials.

Senators BALDWIN and COLLINS have a bill to improve opportunities for our young researchers, essential to advancing biomedical research.

Senator KIRK just talked about his legislation with BENNET, HATCH, MURKOWSKI, ISAKSON, and COLLINS to improve rehabilitation research and help the approximately 800,000 Americans who suffer a stroke each year.

Senators ISAKSON, MURPHY, CASEY, WICKER, and VITTER will help advance our understanding of neurological diseases.

Senator MURRAY, as I mentioned earlier, will clarify that the FDA requires cleaning and validation data for reusable medical devices.

Senators MURRAY, HATCH, BENNET, CASSIDY and WHITEHOUSE's bill will improve health information technology for doctors and their patients. We had six hearings on medical information technology programs in a ditch. We think we are helping to get them out of the ditch. We have been working with the Obama administration to do that, and I look forward to working with the Trump administration to continue that.

Senators BURR, BENNET, HATCH, and DONNELLY would speed safe breakthrough devices, putting senior people in charge of the review process.

CASEY, ISAKSON, BROWN, and KIRK's legislation. If you are the parent of a child with a rare disease like brain cancer, their bill would increase the likelihood that your child will be able to take a drug that will help by giving a drug company that develops a drug for such a disease a voucher they could keep or sell that would speed up the review of another drug.

One may say this is getting boring. This is too long. It is not boring to the millions of Americans who stand to benefit from this, and it is exactly the kind of work we ought to be doing in the United States Senate and what the American people would like to see us do more of.

The Medical Electronic Data Technology Enhancement Act, with Senators BENNET and HATCH and many others interested in that.

Senators BURR and CASEY and ISAKSON and ROBERTS have important legislation for planning ahead for events like bioterror attacks, to help protect against anthrax, for example, or smallpox.

The Combination Products Innovation Act, with a number of Senators involved on the committee, will help prevent the growing field of combination products—like bandaids with Neosporin built in or a heart stent that can be implanted to deliver blood thinners to prevent clots—from being caught in redtape.

Then there is legislation that will give patients and their families a voice in drug development. There is one that is a top priority for the heads of FDA and NIH which will help those agencies attract and keep the kind of talent they need to approve all these exciting advances that are coming.

There is legislation to shorten the development of new treatments to help those affected with life-threatening superbugs.

The Advancing Precision Medicine Act, which Senator MURRAY and I cosponsored, is in direct support of President Obama's initiative to map 1 million genomes so researchers can develop treatments and cures tailored to a patient's genome.

There are five or six other major pieces of legislation that I will include in the RECORD but not read at this time because we are approaching the time for a vote, but let me conclude by saying that in addition to these bipartisan policies, the 21st Century Cures bill includes $6.3 billion in funding. We usually don't attach such funding to a bill authorizing programs. We usually work along two tracks; one track for authorizing programs and one deciding how much to spend on those programs.

During the last 2 years, while we have been working on our authorizing legislation, our appropriations committees have recommended major increases in support for biomedical research, and it is important that every Senator know this. In the current year, at the urging of Senators BLUNT and Senator MURRAY, Congress added $2 billion a year to the $32 billion budget of the National Institutes of Health,

which could total $20 billion over 10 years. Then, the Senate Appropriations Committee recommended another $2 billion increase for the next fiscal year, 2017, which could total another $20 billion over 10 years. This 21st Century Cures legislation adds $4.8 billion in a surge of one-time spending for the National Institutes of Health on top of the regular appropriated money toward key objectives: $1.8 billion for the Cancer Moonshot, $1.4 billion for precision medicine, $1.6 for the BRAIN Initiative, and it adds $1 billion for State grants to help States fight the opioid abuse epidemic. I believe that for every State represented by a Senator here tonight, the opioid epidemic is on the front pages of the newspapers. It adds $500 million for the Food and Drug Administration, and 21st Century Cures also gives the National Institutes of Health $30 million for clinical trials to support regenerative medicine, which the Mayo Clinic has described as a "game-changing area of medicine with the potential to fully heal damaged tissues and organs, offering solutions and hope for people who have conditions that are beyond repair." It gives the FDA authority to allow regenerative therapeutic products to be eligible for FDA's existing accelerated drug approval pathway.

I wish to acknowledge the work of Speaker RYAN and Leader MCCONNELL in designing a way to secure funding that both Democrats and Republicans can accept. That is not always easy. For those concerned about additional spending—often on our side of the aisle—Speaker RYAN and House Budget Chairman TOM PRICE made sure the funding is one time, not mandatory, paid for, and approved each year by Appropriations Committees. It doesn't add one penny to the overall budget because for every increase in the discretionary budget, we reduce the same amount in the mandatory ledger.

For those who worry that Congress might not approve the $6.3 billion in additional spending in later years—I have heard a little of that from the other side of the aisle—my answer is that the best way to ensure the money is spent in the following years is a big vote today and tomorrow when we finally pass the bill, just as the House did last week.

In conclusion, it will be hard to explain why you voted to spend $6.3 billion for cancer, the Precision Medicine Initiative, and opioids this year but then voted not to spend it next year, and the legislation provides that the money cannot be diverted for any other purpose than what we vote for today and tomorrow.

In addition, this year's portion of Cures funding—including one-half billion for opioid grants—is included in the continuing resolution that we will vote on later this week.

This is the kind of lasting legacy the President of the United States and our

Congress can be proud of. The next administration or the next Congress will not be repealing this law because we have taken the time to work out our differences and create a consensus of support. We did this at this time last year with an equally complicated bill to fix No Child Left Behind, which, despite its complexities, received 85 votes in this body. When he signed it, the President called it a "Christmas miracle."

The 21st Century Cures bill will present President Obama with another Christmas miracle, one that will help virtually every family. When we pass this legislation, the real winners will be the American families whose lives will be improved by this bipartisan legislation.

Mr. President, I yield the floor.

I suggest the absence of a quorum.

The PRESIDING OFFICER. The clerk will call the roll.

The senior assistant legislative clerk proceeded to call the roll.

Mr. WHITEHOUSE. Mr. President, I ask unanimous consent that the order for the quorum call be rescinded.

The PRESIDING OFFICER. Without objection, it is so ordered.

Mr. WHITEHOUSE. Mr. President, with the permission of my distinguished chairman, who has worked very hard on this bill and whose efforts I appreciate very much, I wanted to add, very briefly, that I hope very much and look forward to working with my colleagues to assure that the second tranche of the opioid funding is aligned with the CARA bill, or the Comprehensive Addiction and Recovery Act, which we just passed in such bipartisan fashion a few months ago.

We have not achieved that alignment yet, and I hope that we do very soon. I appreciate the terrific efforts of my chairman.

With that, I yield.

I suggest the absence of a quorum.

The PRESIDING OFFICER. The clerk will call the roll.

The senior assistant legislative clerk proceeded to call the roll.

Mr. MCCONNELL. Mr. President, I ask unanimous consent that the order for the quorum call be rescinded.

The VICE PRESIDENT. Without objection, it is so ordered.

DIRECTING THE CLERK OF THE HOUSE OF REPRESENTATIVES TO MAKE A CORRECTION IN THE ENROLLMENT OF H.R. 34

Mr. MCCONNELL. Mr. President, it is a rare day when we see the Vice President presiding. We welcome him here today. We look forward to welcoming him back later in the week. I know Members will have plenty to say about his life and his legacy later in the week, but today the Senate would like to specifically acknowledge his efforts to help Americans struggling with cancer.

He has known the cruel toll this disease can take, but he hasn't let it defeat him. He has chosen to fight back. He has taken a leading role, and the Senate will soon pass the 21st Century Cures Act as a testament to his tremendous effort.

I think it is fitting to dedicate this bill's critical cancer initiatives in honor of someone who would be proud of the Presiding Officer today, and that is his son Beau. In just a moment, that is exactly what the Senate will do—renaming the NIH's cancer initiatives in this bill after Beau Biden.

Mr. REID. Will the Senator yield for a brief statement?

Mr. McCONNELL. If I could say to my friend the Democratic leader, I have one more thing here.

Therefore, Mr. President, I ask unanimous consent that the Senate proceed to the consideration of H. Con. Res. 174, which is at the desk.

The VICE PRESIDENT. The clerk will report the concurrent resolution by title.

The senior assistant legislative clerk read as follows:

A concurrent resolution (H. Con. Res. 174) directing the Clerk of the House of Representatives to make a correction in the enrollment of H.R. 34.

There being no objection, the Senate proceeded to consider the concurrent resolution.

AMENDMENT NO. 5137

(Purpose: To make additional corrections in the enrollment of H.R. 34)

Mr. McCONNELL. I call up an amendment, which would rename a title of the bill.

I would say to the clerk that I would like for her to read it in its entirety.

The VICE PRESIDENT. The clerk will report.

The senior assistant legislative clerk read as follows:

The Senator from Kentucky [Mr. McCONNELL] proposes an amendment numbered 5137.

Beginning on page 1, line 7, strike "following correction:" and all that follows and insert the following:

"following corrections:

"(1) Amend the long title so as to read: 'An Act to accelerate the discovery, development, and delivery of 21st century cures, and for other purposes.'.

"(2) Amend the section heading for section 1001 so as to read: '**BEAU BIDEN CANCER MOONSHOT AND NIH INNOVATION PROJECTS**'.

"(3) Amend the table of contents in section 1 so that the item relating to section 1001 reads as follows:

"'1001. Beau Biden Cancer Moonshot and NIH innovation projects.'.".

Mr. McCONNELL. Mr. President, I ask unanimous consent that the amendment be agreed to, the concurrent resolution, as amended, be agreed to, and the motion to reconsider be laid upon the table with no intervening action or debate.

The VICE PRESIDENT. Without objection, it is so ordered.

The amendment (No. 5137) was agreed to.

The concurrent resolution, as amended, was agreed to.

(Applause, Senators rising.)

The VICE PRESIDENT. Thank you.

The Democratic leader.

Mr. REID. Mr. President, I say to all my colleagues, the Presiding Officer served in the Senate for 36 years. During that time he was here, he was about as much a man of the Senate as anyone could be. He was a Democrat, but he was also available to anybody anytime, and I so admire him. I know that he has worked very closely with the Republican leader on some very important issues the last 8 years.

I want the record to be spread with the fact that the Presiding Officer is as proud of his family as anyone could be, and doing this for Beau only furthers the effect that this man, the Presiding Officer, has had on this country. I am grateful to the Republican leader for allowing me to cosponsor this important amendment, changing the name of this bill to the Beau Biden Memorial Moonshot.

I am grateful to you, the Republican leader. All of the Senators understand that the man presiding is really a man of the Senate and always will be.

(Applause, Senators rising.)

―――――――

TSUNAMI WARNING, EDUCATION, AND RESEARCH ACT OF 2015—Continued

CLOTURE MOTION

The VICE PRESIDENT. Pursuant to rule XXII, the Chair lays before the Senate the pending cloture motion, which the clerk will state.

The senior assistant legislative clerk read as follows:

CLOTURE MOTION

We, the undersigned Senators, in accordance with the provisions of rule XXII of the Standing Rules of the Senate, do hereby move to bring to a close debate on the motion to concur in the House amendment to the Senate amendment to H.R. 34, an act to authorize and strengthen the tsunami detection, forecast, warning, research, and mitigation program of the National Oceanic and Atmospheric Administration, and for other purposes.

Mitch McConnell, Johnny Isakson, Bob Corker, Richard Burr, Pat Roberts, Roy Blunt, Thom Tillis, Lindsey Graham, Lamar Alexander, John Cornyn, Chuck Grassley, Michael B. Enzi, John Barrasso, Shelley Moore Capito, John McCain, Bill Cassidy.

The VICE PRESIDENT. By unanimous consent, the mandatory quorum call has been waived.

The question is, Is it the sense of the Senate that debate on the motion to concur in the House amendment to the Senate amendment to H.R. 34 shall be brought to a close?

The yeas and nays are mandatory under the rule.

The clerk will call the roll.

The bill clerk called the roll.

Mr. DURBIN. I announce that the Senator from Washington (Mrs. MURRAY) and the Senator from Oregon (Mr. WYDEN) are necessarily absent.

The VICE PRESIDENT. Are there any other Senators in the Chamber desiring to vote?

The yeas and nays resulted—yeas 85, nays 13, as follows:

[Rollcall Vote No. 156 Leg.]

YEAS—85

Alexander	Feinstein	Murphy
Ayotte	Fischer	Nelson
Baldwin	Flake	Paul
Barrasso	Franken	Perdue
Bennet	Gardner	Peters
Blumenthal	Graham	Reed
Blunt	Grassley	Reid
Booker	Hatch	Risch
Boozman	Heinrich	Roberts
Burr	Heitkamp	Rounds
Cantwell	Heller	Rubio
Cardin	Hirono	Sasse
Carper	Hoeven	Schatz
Casey	Inhofe	Scott
Cassidy	Isakson	Sessions
Coats	Johnson	Shaheen
Cochran	Kaine	Shelby
Collins	King	Stabenow
Coons	Kirk	Sullivan
Corker	Klobuchar	Tester
Cornyn	Lankford	Thune
Cotton	Leahy	Tillis
Crapo	Markey	Toomey
Cruz	McCain	Vitter
Daines	McCaskill	Warner
Donnelly	McConnell	Whitehouse
Durbin	Menendez	Wicker
Enzi	Mikulski	
Ernst	Moran	

NAYS—13

Boxer	Manchin	Schumer
Brown	Merkley	Udall
Capito	Murkowski	Warren
Gillibrand	Portman	
Lee	Sanders	

NOT VOTING—2

Murray	Wyden

The VICE PRESIDENT. On this vote, the yeas are 85, the nays are 13.

Three-fifths of the Senators duly chosen and sworn having voted in the affirmative, the motion is agreed to.

Cloture having been invoked, the motion to refer and the amendments thereto fall.

Mr. THUNE. I suggest the absence of a quorum.

The VICE PRESIDENT. The clerk will call the roll.

The bill clerk proceeded to call the roll.

Mr. DURBIN. Mr. President, I ask unanimous consent that the order for the quorum call be rescinded.

The PRESIDING OFFICER (Mr. LANKFORD). Without objection, it is so ordered.

DACA

Mr. DURBIN. Mr. President, last Friday I had a meeting in Chicago with about 50 in attendance. It was Friday morning, and we gathered groups of people from across the city of Chicago and the State of Illinois who were focusing on one make-or-break issue for many of us. It was an emotional issue, one that caused many to break down in tears as they told me their stories. It is the reason I have come back to the floor of the Senate today and every day since the election to talk about one specific issue that I believe is important for this Nation to reflect on.

Mr. President, 16 years ago a young lady contacted my office. Her name is Tereza Lee. She had been brought to the United States from Korea at the age of 2. She had grown up in Chicago with a family of modest means.

During the course of her childhood, she signed up for what is known as the Merit music program in Chicago. They offered free instruments and free musical instruction to kids from low-income families. It is a great program. Tereza Lee signed up, and it turned out she had an extraordinary talent at piano. When she came to contact my office, it was as she was leaving high school and applying to be accepted at the best music schools in the America—Juilliard in New York and the Conservatory of Music in Manhattan.

She went to fill out the application, and when it came to a question of her citizenship and nationality, she wasn't certain what to put. Her mother suggested that she call our office, and she did. We told her that under the law she was undocumented, brought here at the age of 2 on a visitor visa. Her mother had never filed any papers for her. She had grown up in America thinking she was an American citizen like her brother and sister who were born here, and she came to realize at the age of 17 or 18 that in the eyes of the law she had no legal standing in America.

The law is pretty harsh for people like Tereza. The law says she needs to leave the United States for 10 years and apply to return to the United States.

Where would she go—to Korea? She had never been there. She grew up in Brazil for a short period of time. She didn't speak the language. She doesn't speak Portuguese.

She was caught in the middle. That is why I introduced the DREAM Act. It said that young people brought to the United States by their parents before the age of 16, if they finish school and have no serious criminal issues, should be given a chance to go to school further and have a legal status in America and, ultimately, to earn their way to citizenship—going to the back of the line and waiting their turn but at least setting that as their goal. I introduced that bill 15 years ago. It has never become law, but there are 2.5 million people in that circumstance in America.

Six years ago, the President of the United States created something called DACA, the Deferred Action for Childhood Arrivals program, by an Executive action. As a result of that action, President Obama allowed these eligible DREAMers—as they have come to be known—to receive DACA status.

In order to do it, they have to apply, come out of the shadows, declare themselves, file a fee of about $500 with the government, go through a criminal background check, and then be given temporary—only temporary—legal status so they can't be deported and can legally work, which is renewable every 2 years. As of today, 744,000 young people have done that. Many of them were in the room—at least some of them were in the room in Chicago last Friday.

They are not certain what is going to happen next. The new President has promised to end DACA. If he ends it, what happens to these young people? For instance, there are 28 of these DACA young people who are in medical school at Loyola University in Chicago—28 students who are undocumented who are there without any Federal Government assistance, and most of them have promised to give a year of service to the State of Illinois in rural areas and poor neighborhoods when they become doctors. If they lose their DACA status, they lose their ability to work legally in the United States and they cannot go through the clinical experience, which is part of becoming a doctor. They would have to drop out of medical school. There is one thing we can say for certain: We don't have an oversupply of doctors serving inner cities and rural areas in my State and across the Nation. We need these doctors.

If DACA changes, if it is eliminated, what will happen to these young people? That is a challenge which I face, and other Members have as well. I salute Senator LINDSEY GRAHAM of South Carolina. He is working with me on legislation to address this, to at least give a temporary status to these DACA-eligible young people while we debate immigration reform in a larger context.

There are important issues at stake, but the most fundamental issue is one of fairness and justice. These young people did nothing wrong. They were brought to this country by their parents. They have grown up in this country, gone to our schools, and there are some amazing stories of what they have done with their lives. I wish to tell you one of those stories. I have done this over 100 times now on the floor of the Senate.

This is Barbara Olachea. In 2002, when Barbara was 5 years old, her family brought her to the United States from Mexico. She grew up in Phoenix, AZ, and she knew she would face challenges, being undocumented. Her older sister had been accepted to Arizona State University but couldn't afford to go to school there. As an undocumented immigrant, she is not eligible for Federal financial assistance. Arizona law specifically prohibits State financial assistance to DREAMers such as Barbara and her sister.

During her freshman year in high school, a mentor told her that as a DREAMer, "You're going to have to try harder than everybody else."

Barbara said:

Those words confirmed what I had known all along. Although I was only starting high school, I began to dread what most students anticipate with excitement: graduation day. What if I got into my dream school, but I still couldn't go because I couldn't afford it?

In high school, Barbara was a great student and was involved in many extracurricular and volunteer activities. She was a member of the Academic Decathlon team for 4 years and team captain when she was a senior. She was a member of student government, yearbook, and homecoming. She volunteered to tutor middle school students and worked part time to save money for her education. She participated in a number of programs at Arizona State University, including the Walter Cronkite School of Journalism. She recorded a story about her life that was aired on National Public Radio. This experience sparked her interest in journalism and led to an internship at KJZZ, the Phoenix affiliate for NPR.

Last year Barbara graduated as valedictorian of her high school class with a 4.5 grade point average. As a result of her accomplishments, Barbara was accepted at Dartmouth College, an Ivy League school, where she is now a sophomore.

Barbara wrote a letter to me and said this about DACA:

I am very grateful for DACA, as it allowed me to work and not be deported to a country I do not know and have not been to since I was five. Just like thousands of other undocumented students in the United States, I have grown up and become accustomed to the culture here. The U.S. is where I belong and I want to be a contributing member of society, as I have proved in my 13 years here.

Barbara and other DREAMers have so much to give. They are young, they are idealistic, they are energetic, and they are amazing. These young people have overcome odds that many young people never face in their lives. To think that in your freshman year of high school, you are reflecting on the fact that even if accepted to college, you may not be able to go—that was her future as she saw it then.

If DACA is eliminated, Barbara will lose her legal status and could be deported to Mexico—a country where she hasn't lived since she was 5. Will America be a better country if Barbara is deported or if she stays here and uses her talent, her determination, her energy, and her inspiration, for our future? I think the answer is clear.

Now is the time for America, this Nation of immigrants, to come together and heal the wounds that divided us in this election. I am just hoping that this President-elect, when he reflects on Barbara and 700,000-plus other DACA eligibles, will realize that they can bring important values and achievements to America's future. I am hoping that in the Senate, we can overcome our differences—and there are many deep differences, political differences—and give these young people a chance.

Senator GRAHAM and I are basically working on a bill that says at least suspend their status so they won't be deported, so they can continue to work. Do that while we do our business here on the issue of immigration. That is only fair. It is only right. It is the right American way to approach an issue that can affect so many innocent American people.

I yield the floor.

The PRESIDING OFFICER. The Senator from West Virginia.

MINERS PROTECTION ACT

Mrs. CAPITO. Mr. President, I rise today to talk about an issue of great urgency—the fate of tens of thousands of American workers.

In just a matter of weeks, 16,000 coal miners and their dependents will lose their health care coverage and roughly 6,000 others will join that group in the year 2017, and here we are just days away from Congress wrapping up its work for the year. This should be a time to motivate us to action.

I have served in Congress a long time, and I know nothing motivates Congress more than a deadline, being up against a deadline, as we are today. This time should be no different, and here is why: Without some resolution before Congress adjourns, the men and women who have powered our Nation and spurred economic growth for generations will have the carpet ripped out from under them. They will lose the health care benefits they so rely on and have been promised.

It is important to recognize the risks our coal miners take to better our lives every day. When you visit a coal mine, which I have done—I have been underground in a coal mine—you see the rigorous and often very dangerous working conditions where these men and women do their job every day to provide the energy we need to light this Chamber, to warm our homes, and to keep our classrooms lit. These miners are the pillars of our communities, and many of them are veterans of our Nation. For decades they have worked hard and played by the rules. Yet the realities facing these men and women are stark. They are up against the wall, and we are up against the wall with them. The challenges they face will only grow if we fail to accommodate and have immediate action.

We can talk about the realities of the War on Coal, but this is about more than that. This is about people—tens of thousands of people, mostly older, many suffering health issues—who rely on health care, and many are in need. This is about tens of thousands of coal jobs that have been lost, devastating my region of the country, forcing miners to rely on these modest benefits more than ever before. This is about employers who are bankrupt who can no longer fund these benefit plans.

We have a solution right here in front of us that is ready for a vote to prevent any lapse in benefits. It is a solution that has support from both sides of the aisle. We passed the Miners Protection Act out of the Finance Committee in a bipartisan way, and it is a solution that could make a difference in the livelihoods of tens of thousands of Americans.

I had really hoped that we could offer the Miners Protection Act as an amendment to the 21st Century Cures bill. The 21st Century Cures bill is all about health. The Miners Protection Act is a lot about the health and wellbeing of our miners.

That is why, despite the many good things and benefits in the 21st Century Cures Act, such as funding for the opioid epidemic that hit my State of West Virginia and many of our States very hard, advanced medicine, and Cancer Moonshot, I had to oppose us moving forward on the Cures Act tonight without an amendment process. That is how important this issue is to our miners.

Before Friday we will move forward on a bill to fund our government. We must take action in that bill—which I consider mostly our last chance, the continuing resolution—to protect these important benefits for our miners. If we don't, we will be failing to act for the benefit of thousands of American workers.

I yield the floor.

I suggest the absence of a quorum.

The PRESIDING OFFICER. The clerk will call the roll.

The senior assistant legislative clerk proceeded to call the roll.

Mr. MORAN. Mr. President, I ask unanimous consent that the order for the quorum call be rescinded.

The PRESIDING OFFICER. Without objection, it is so ordered.

MORNING BUSINESS

Mr. MORAN. Mr. President, I ask unanimous consent that the Senate be in a period of morning business, with Senators permitted to speak therein for up to 10 minutes each.

The PRESIDING OFFICER. Without objection, it is so ordered.

DACA

Mr. REID. Mr. President, 15 years ago Senator DICK DURBIN introduced the DREAM Act in the U.S. Senate. This legislation provided a path to citizenship for young people brought to the U.S. as children.

These young people call themselves DREAMers. And they are as American as you or me. They belong to this country culturally and linguistically and are American in all but paperwork. For many of them, this is the only country they have ever known.

In 2010, the DREAM Act passed the House and came to the Senate for a vote. Sadly, Republicans killed the bill—eliminating the hopes and dreams of hundreds of thousands of DREAMers. Because Republicans refused to act, it was up to President Obama.

In 2011, I joined 21 other Senators in asking President Obama to grant deferred action to immigrant youth who would have qualified under the DREAM Act and who are not an enforcement priority. And in 2012, President Obama's administration did just that. They announced that young people who were brought to the United States as children could apply for Deferred Action for Childhood Arrivals, also known as DACA.

This brought nearly 800,000 young people out of the shadows. These young men and women are our newest college students, teachers, engineers, and small business owners. They contribute to our communities and make America better.

In Nevada alone, DACA has helped over 12,000 DREAMers—DREAMers like Brenda Romero. Brenda was just 2 years old when she crossed the border in southern California with her mother to reunite with members of their family.

Growing up in Las Vegas, Brenda was like any other American kid. She excelled in school, participated in student government and played the cello in the orchestra. But soon enough, she realized what it truly meant to be undocumented. Her friends could get their driver's licenses; Brenda could not. Her peers could get legally paying jobs; Brenda could not. Her classmates could speak with recruiters from the Armed Services about career opportunities; Brenda could not. Brenda described the months after graduating high school as one of the lowest points in her life.

But that all changed with DACA. She was finally able to get a job and enrolled in the College of Southern Nevada as soon as she saved enough money. Brenda became student body president her second year at the College of Southern Nevada, working to help other students who faced struggles similar to hers. During her time as student body president, Brenda helped award $10,000 to her fellow classmates in scholarship funds.

Brenda graduated from CSN with an associate's degree in art and is currently pursuing a bachelor's degree in human services at the University of Nevada, Las Vegas. She wants to be a higher education counselor, and she is already well on her way. She is already making her mark on the UNLV campus. As part of the Undocu-network Club, Brenda is helping to bring counseling and services to students in need and promoting visibility for undocumented students to the school administration.

Brenda's story is impressive, but it is not unique. Every Senator has a story to tell like Brenda's. There are young men and women just like her in all 50 states.

In addition to the moral reasons for supporting DACA, there are strong economic reasons. DACA recipients will add $433 billion to the economy over 10 years. After DACA, more than two-thirds of recipients were able to secure a job and their wages rose by 42 percent. Six percent of recipients started their own businesses, a rate that is nearly double the rate among the entire U.S. population. Fifty-four percent of recipients bought cars, and 12 percent bought houses, all of which means significant new tax revenue for States and localities. DACA recipients will add $433 billion to the economy over 10 years. It is not surprising that the majority of Americans—almost 60 percent—oppose repeal of DACA.

As with Brenda, DACA has opened doors of opportunity for hundreds of thousands of young people.

We hoped that it would be a stop-gap measure until we passed immigration reform. The Senate overwhelmingly passed a bipartisan bill but the House refused to bring it to a vote. With the outcome of the election, it isn't likely that comprehensive immigration reform will happen over the next 4 years. That is why it is so important for the next administration to continue this vital program. For Brenda and hundreds of thousands like her, losing DACA status means being adrift in the only country she calls home.

I urge the next administration: Don't put almost 800,000 young people back in the shadows where they are afraid. Don't force hundreds of thousands of DREAMers to lose their jobs. And don't squander the huge economic benefits to this country.

If Republicans want to do something, then they should pass the DREAM Act.

ARMS SALES NOTIFICATION

Mr. CORKER. Mr. President, section 36(b) of the Arms Export Control Act requires that Congress receive prior notification of certain proposed arms sales as defined by that statute. Upon such notification, the Congress has 30 calendar days during which the sale may be reviewed. The provision stipulates that, in the Senate, the notification of proposed sales shall be sent to the chairman of the Senate Foreign Relations Committee.

In keeping with the committee's intention to see that relevant information is available to the full Senate, I ask unanimous consent to have printed in the RECORD the notifications which have been received. If the cover letter references a classified annex, then such annex is available to all Senators in the office of the Foreign Relations Committee, room SD–423.

There being no objection, the material was ordered to be printed in the RECORD, as follows:

DEFENSE SECURITY
COOPERATION AGENCY,
Arlington, VA.

Hon. BOB CORKER,
Chairman, Committee on Foreign Relations,
U.S. Senate, Washington, DC.

DEAR MR. CHAIRMAN: Pursuant to the reporting requirements of Section 36(b)(1) of the Arms Export Control Act, as amended, we are forwarding herewith Transmittal No. 16–76, concerning the Department of the Army's proposed Letter(s) of Offer and Acceptance for the Government of Peru for defense articles and services estimated to cost $668 million. After this letter is delivered to your office, we plan to issue a news release to notify the public of this proposed sale.

Sincerely,
J.W. RIXEY, *Vice Admiral, USN,*
Director.

Enclosures.

TRANSMITTAL NO. 16–76

Notice of Proposed Issuance of Letter of Offer Pursuant to Section 36(b)(1) of the Arms Export Control Act, as amended

(i) Prospective Purchaser: Government of Peru.

(ii) Total Estimated Value:

Major Defense Equipment* $434 million.

Other $234 million.

Total $668 million.

(iii) Description and Quantity or Quantities of Articles or Services under Consideration for Purchase:

Major Defense Equipment (MDE):

One hundred and seventy-eight (178) Reconditioned Stryker Infantry Carrier Vehicles.

One hundred and seventy-eight (178) M2 Flex .50 Cal Machine Guns.

One hundred and seventy-eight (178) Remote Weapon Stations (RWS).

Non-MDE includes: Driver's vision enhancers; Global Positioning System (GPS) navigational capability; sets of special tools testing equipment; associated M2 Flex spare parts and tripods; M6 Smoke Grenade launchers and associated spares; VIC–3 systems; Operators New Equipment Training (OPNET) and Field Level Maintenance Training (FLMNET); publications; training manuals; Contractor Field Service Representative support; contractor and concurrent spare parts; project office technical support; U.S. Government technical assistance; packaging, crating, and handling; de-processing services for shipment; and associated transportation.

(iv) Military Department: Army.

(v) Prior Related Cases, if any: None.

(vi) Sales Commission, Fee. etc., Paid, Offered, or Agreed to be Paid: None.

(vii) Sensitivity of Technology Contained in the Defense Article or Defense Services Proposed to be Sold: See Annex Attached.

(viii) Date Report Delivered to Congress: December 2, 2016.

*As defined in Section 47(6) of the Arms Export Control Act.

POLICY JUSTIFICATION

Government of Peru—Reconditioned Stryker Infantry Carrier Vehicles

The Government of Peru has requested a possible sale of one hundred and seventy-eight (178) Reconditioned Stryker Infantry Carrier Vehicles; one hundred and seventy-eight (178) M2 Flex .50 Cal Machine Guns; and one hundred and seventy-eight (178) Remote Weapon Stations (RWS). Also included are driver's vision enhancers; Global Positioning System (GPS) navigation capability; sets of special tools testing equipment; associated M2 Flex spare parts and tripods; M6 Smoke Grenade launchers and associated spares; VIC–3 systems; Operators New Equipment Training (OPNET) and Field Level Maintenance Training (FLMNET); publications; training manuals; Contractor Field Service Representative support; contractor and concurrent spare parts; project office technical support; U.S. Government technical assistance; packaging, crating, and handling; deprocessing services for shipment; and associated transportation. Total estimated program cost is $668 million.

This proposed sale will contribute to the foreign policy objectives of the United States by helping to improve the security of an important partner which has been and continues to be an important force for political stability, peace, and economic progress in South America. It is in the U.S. national security interest for Peru to field capable forces and multi-role equipment for border security, disaster response, and to confront de-stabilizing internal threats, such as the terrorist group Sendero Luminoso (Shining Path).

Peru intends to use these defense articles and services to modernize its armed forces. This will contribute to the Peruvian military's goal of updating its capabilities while further enhancing interoperability between Peru, the United States, and other allies and partners. This acquisition would support the first major step in Peru's acquisition strategy to build a multi-dimensional brigade by 2030. Peru will have no difficulty absorbing this equipment into its armed forces.

The proposed sale of this equipment and support will not alter the basic military balance in the region.

The prime contractor for this program is General Dynamics Land Systems. There are no known offset agreements in connect with this potential sale.

Implementation of this proposed sale will require the temporary assignment of U.S. Government or contractor representatives to Peru for up to three years.

There will be no adverse impact on U.S. defense readiness as a result of this proposed sale.

TRANSMITTAL NO. 16–76

Notice of Proposed Issuance of Letter of Offer Pursuant to Section 36(b)(1) of the Arms Export Control Act

Annex Item No. vii

(vii) Sensitivity of Technology:

1. The following Major Defense Equipment items do not contain any sensitive technologies or classified material: 178 M1126 Stryker Infantry Carrier Vehicles with M2 Flex .50 Cal machine guns and Remote Weapon Systems. The M1126 Stryker is an infantry carrier vehicle transporting nine soldiers, their mission equipment and a crew of two consisting of a driver and vehicle commander. It is equipped with armor protection, M2 machine guns and M6 smoke grenade launchers for self-protection. The Stryker is an eight-wheeled vehicle powered by a 350hp diesel engine. It incorporates a central tire inflation system, run-flat tires, and a vehicle height management system. The Stryker is capable of supporting a communications suite, a Global Positioning System (GPS), and a high frequency and near-term digital radio systems. The Stryker is deployable by C–130 aircraft and combat capable upon arrival. The Stryker is capable of self-deployment by highway and self-recovery. It has a low noise level that reduces crew fatigue and enhances survivability. It moves about the battlefield quickly and is optimized for close, complex, or urban terrain. The Stryker program leverages non-developmental items with common subsystems

and components to quickly acquire and filed these systems.

2. The AN/VAS–5 Driver's Vision Enhancer (DVE) is a compact thermal camera providing armored vehicle drivers with day or night time visual awareness in clear or reduced vision (fog, smoke, dust) situations. The system provides the driver a 180 degree viewing angle using a high resolution infrared sensor and image stabilization to reduce the effect of shock and vibration. The viewer and monitor are ruggedized for operation in tactical environments. The system is UNCLASSIFIED but considered sensitive technology. If a technically advanced adversary were to obtain knowledge of the AN/VAS–5, the information could be used to identify ways to countering the system or improve the adversary's ability to avoid detection by the system in low-visibility environments. This is a low-level concern because the thermal imaging technology used in the AN/VAS–5 is considered mature and available in other industrial nation's comparable performance thresholds.

3. A determination has been made that the recipient country can provide the same degree of protection for the sensitive technology being released as the U.S. Government. This sale is necessary in furtherance of the U.S. foreign policy and national security objectives outlined in the Policy Justification.

4. All defense articles and services listed in this transmittal have been authorized for release and export to Peru.

———

DEFENSE SECURITY
COOPERATION AGENCY,
Arlington, VA.
Hon. BOB CORKER,
Chairman, Committee on Foreign Relations,
U.S. Senate, Washington, DC.

DEAR MR. CHAIRMAN: Pursuant to the reporting requirements of Section 36(b)(1) of the Arms Export Control Act, as amended, we are forwarding herewith Transmittal No. 16–54, concerning the Department of the Navy's proposed Letter(s) of Offer and Acceptance to the Government of Australia for defense articles and services estimated to cost $115 million. After this letter is delivered to your office, we plan to issue a news release to notify the public of this proposed sale.

Sincerely,
J.W. RIXEY, *Vice Admiral, USN,*
Director.
Enclosures.

TRANSMITTAL NO. 16–54

Notice of Proposed Issuance of Letter of Offer Pursuant to Section 36(b)(1) of the Arms Export Control Act, as amended

(i) Prospective Purchaser: Government of Australia.

(ii) Total Estimated Value:
Major Defense Equipment (MDE)* $ 0.00 million.
Basic Case (GUW) $ 79.07 million.
Amendment Funding $ 35.93 million.
Total $115.00 million.

(iii) Description and Quantity or Quantities of Articles or Services under Consideration for Purchase:
Non-MDE: FMS case AT–P–GUW, originally offered below congressional notification threshold at $79.07 million, was for acquisition of two Range Systems to conduct Electronic Warfare (EW), Electronic Surveillance, and Airborne Electronic Attack for Royal Australian Air Force aircrew training on its twelve (12) Australian EA–18G aircraft. An amendment to AT–P–GUW is required to

add $35.93 million in funding, to provide for unfunded requirements to meet the scope of the basic case and provide for the sale of additional classified technical data and software, system integration and testing, tools and test equipment, support equipment, spare and repair parts, publications, operations manuals, and technical documents, personnel training, U.S. Government and contractor technical assistance, and other related elements of engineering, logistics, and program management. This amendment will push the original case value above notification threshold and thus requires notification of the entire case.

Military Department: Navy (AT–P–GUW–A1).

Prior Related Cases. if any:
FMS case AT–P–LEN: $992M September 13, 2012 (Airborne Electronic Attack Kits).
FMS case AT–P–SCI $1.3B July 4, 2013 (twelve EA–18G aircrafts).
FMS case AT–P–GUW $79M February 12, 2015 (Electronic Warfare Range System).

(vi) Sales Commission, Fee, etc., Paid, Offered, or Agreed to be Paid: None.

(vii) Sensitivity of Technology Contained in the Defense Article or Defense Services Proposed to be Sold: See Attached Annex.

(viii) Date Report Delivered to Congress: December 2, 2016.

*As defined in Section 47(6) of the Arms Export Control Act.

POLICY JUSTIFICATION

Government of Australia—AEA–18G
Electronic Warfare Range System

The Government of Australia has requested additional funding to a previously implemented case for two Electronic Warfare Range Systems to conduct Electronic Warfare and Electronic Surveillance training within the borders of Australia. The original FMS case, valued at $79.07 million, includes non-MDE costs for all support elements required to provide for system integration testing, tools and test equipment, support equipment, spare and repair parts, publications, operations manuals, technical documents, personnel training, U.S. Government and contractor technical assistance, and other related elements of logistics and program support. The addition of $35.93 million in non-MDE funding to the basic case will provide for unfunded requirements to meet the scope of the basic case and provide for the sale of additional classified technical data and software, system integration and testing, tools and test equipment, support equipment, spare and repair parts, publications, operations manuals, and technical documents, personnel training, U.S. Government and contractor technical assistance, and other related elements of engineering, logistics, and program management. This amendment will push the original case value above notification threshold and thus requires notification of the entire case. The total overall estimated value is $115 million.

This sale will contribute to the foreign policy and national security of the United States by helping to improve the security of a major contributor to political stability, security, and economic development in the Western Pacific. Australia is an important Major non-NATO Ally and partner that contributes significantly to peacekeeping and humanitarian operations around the world. It is vital to the U.S. national interest to assist our ally in developing and maintaining a strong and ready self-defense capability. By enabling Australian Defense Force (ADF) ranges, the U.S. Government will ensure consistency in training across platforms and

theaters, whether the exercises are conducted in the United States or in Australia, where U.S. aircrews will be able to participate in training exercises alongside their Australian counterparts. The proposed sale will allow continued efforts to improve Australia's capability in current and future coalition operations. Australia will use the range to enhance Electronic Warfare capabilities as a deterrent to regional threats and to strengthen its homeland defense. Australia will have no difficulty absorbing these items into its armed forces.

The proposed sale will not alter the basic military balance in the region.

The prime contractors will be Leidos (hardware) and General Dynamics Mission Systems (software). The U.S. Government is not aware of any known offsets associated with this sale.

Implementation of this sale will require ten (10) temporary U.S. Government or contractor representatives to Australia for assistance in integration and range operational and maintenance training.

There will be no adverse impact on U.S. defense readiness as a result of this proposed amendment.

TRANSMITTAL NO. 16–54

Notice of Proposed Issuance of Letter of Offer Pursuant to Section 36(b)(1) of the Arms Export Control Act

Annex Item No. vii

(vii) Sensitivity of Technology:

1. Provides two (2) in-country Electronic Warfare (EW) ranges for EA–18G aircrew training to detect, identify, locate, and suppress hostile emitters. Range technology transfers programmable equipment able to emulate generic Integrated Air Defense Systems, threat and other emitters, along with authentic threat emitters purchased from vendors in Former Soviet Block states. The range hardware is Unclassified either standalone or integrated. The range software is unclassified with the exception of one (1) Secret Digital Integrated Air Defense System (DIADS) software suite. The amendment facilitates transfer of classified information such as software, classified threat and flyout models, user event captured data, range operations manuals, and security classification guidance. The classified information enhances the usefulness of the range technology being transferred and provides guidance on safeguarding sensitive information.

2. When EW range hardware and software work together against a particular aircraft platform, the visual and recorded information becomes classified Secret. The range capability is unclassified until the networks touch a Secret network (e.g., Link 16) or perform against real world training missions. The customer may capture intelligence regarding the authentic threat emitters that is classified Confidential or Secret, as well as other training artifacts and debrief products capturing weapons capability and tactics.

3. If a technologically advanced adversary were to obtain knowledge of the specific hardware and software elements, the information could be used to develop countermeasures that might reduce EA–18G weapon system effectiveness or be used in the development of a system with similar or advanced capabilities.

4. All defense articles and services listed in this transmittal are authorized for release and export to the Government of Australia.

DEFENSE SECURITY
COOPERATION AGENCY,
Arlington, VA.

Hon. BOB CORKER,
Chairman, Committee on Foreign Relations,
U.S. Senate, Washington, DC.

DEAR MR. CHAIRMAN: Pursuant to the reporting requirements of Section 36(b)(1) of the Arms Export Control Act, as amended, we are forwarding herewith Transmittal No. 16–65, concerning the Department of the Navy's proposed Letter(s) of Offer and Acceptance for the Government of Finland for defense articles and services estimated to cost $156 million. After this letter is delivered to your office, we plan to issue a news release to notify the public of this proposed sale.

Sincerely,
JAMES WORM, *Acting Deputy Director,*
(for J.W. Rixey, Vice Admiral, USN,
Director).

Enclosures.

TRANSMITTAL NO. 16–65

Notice of Proposed Issuance of Letter of Offer Pursuant to Section 36(b)(1) of the Arms Export Control Act, as amended

(i) Prospective Purchaser: Government of Finland.

(ii) Total Estimated Value:
Major Defense Equipment* $ 57 million.
Other $ 99 million.
Total $156 million.

(iii) Description and Quantity or Quantities of Articles or Services under Consideration for Purchase:

Major Defense Equipment (MDE):

Ninety (90) Multifunctional Information Distribution System Joint Tactical Radio System (MIDS–JTRS) Variant(s).

Non-MDE includes: Follow-on equipment and support for Finland's F/A–18 Mid-Life Upgrade (MLU) program includes software test and integration center upgrades, flight testing, spare and repair parts, support and test equipment, transportation, publications and technical documentation, personnel training and training equipment, U.S. Government and contractor technical and logistics support services, and other related elements of logistics support.

(iv) Military Department: Navy.

(v) Prior Related Cases, if any:

FMS case FI–P–SAA $2.4 billion—9 Jun 1992.

FMS case FI–P–SAB $675 million—7 Feb 1994.

FMS case FI–P–GAD $25 million—13 Jul 2001.

FMS case FI–P–LBB $63 million—4 Aug 2001.

FMS case FI–P–LBC $127 million—1 Jan 2004.

FMS case FI–P–LBD $252 million—25 Jul 2007.

FMS case FI–P–LBH $307 million—3 Apr 2009.

FMS case FI–P–GAU $170 million—27 Jun 2013.

(vi) Sales Commission, Fee, etc., Paid, Offered, or Agreed to be Paid: None.

(vii) Sensitivity of Technology Contained in the Defense Article or Defense Services Proposed to be Sold: See Annex Attached.

(viii) Date Report Delivered to Congress: December 2, 2016.

*As defined in Section 47(6) of the Arms Export Control Act.

POLICY JUSTIFICATION

Government of Finland—F–18 Mid-Life Upgrade Program

The Government of Finland has requested a possible sale of follow-on equipment and support for Finland's F/A–18 Mid-Life Upgrade (MLU) program, consisting of: Ninety (90) Multifunctional Information Distribution System Joint Tactical Radio System (MIDS–JTRS) variant(s). The proposed program support also includes software test and integration center upgrades, flight testing, spare and repair parts, support and test equipment, transportation, publications and technical documentation, personnel training and training equipment, U.S. Government and contractor technical and logistics support services, and other related elements of logistics support. Total estimated program cost is $156 million.

This proposed sale will contribute to the foreign policy and national security objectives of the United State by helping to improve the security of a friendly country which has been and continues to be an important force for political stability and economic progress in Europe.

The Finnish Air Force (FAF) intend to purchase this MLU program equipment and services to extend the useful life of its F/A–18 fighter aircraft and enhance their survivability and communications connectivity. The FDF needs this upgrade to keep pace with technology advances in sensors, weaponry, and communications. Finland has extensive experience operating the F/A–18 aircraft and will have no difficulty incorporating the upgraded capabilities into its forces.

The proposed sale of this equipment and support will not alter the basic military balance in the region.

The principal contractors will be Raytheon in Waltham, Massachusetts; Lockheed Martin in Bethesda, Maryland; The Boeing Company in St. Louis, Missouri; BAE North America in Arlington, Virginia; General Electric in Fairfield, Connecticut; General Dynamics in West Falls Church, Virginia; Northrop Grumman in Falls Church, Virginia; Rockwell Collins in Cedar rapids, Iowa; ViaSat in Carlsbad, California; and Data Link Solutions in Cedar Rapids, Iowa. There are no known offset agreements proposed in connection with this potential sale.

Implementation of this proposed sale will require multiple trips to Finland involving U.S. Government and contractor representatives for technical reviews, support, and training.

There will be no adverse impact on U.S. defense readiness as a result of this proposed sale.

TRANSMITTAL NO. 16–65

Notice of Proposed Issuance of Letter of Offer Pursuant to Section 36(b)(1) of the Arms Export Control Act

Annex Item No. vii

(vii) Sensitivity of Technology:

1. The Multifunctional Information Distribution System Joint Tactical Radio System (MIDS–JTRS) is not classified but is considered a COMSEC Controlled Item (CCI). There are no training devices, associated documentation, or services to be provided with the sale of these MIDS–JTRS units. No sensitive information is provided or associated with this sale.

2. All defense articles and services listed in this transmittal have been authorized for release and export to the Government of Finland.

━━━━━

TRIBUTE TO GENERAL RAHEEL SHARIF

Mr. McCAIN. Mr. President, today I wish to recognize the accomplishments of General Raheel Sharif and to express my gratitude to him upon his retirement as Pakistan's Chief of Army Staff. General Sharif has been a vital partner for the United States in the battle against terrorism. Since taking office in November 2013, General Sharif has continued to target terrorists operating within the borders of Pakistan. He has carried the fight to the northwest frontier provinces of Pakistan, as well as promised to eliminate safe havens for terrorists from the country completely. In taking these actions, General Sharif has demonstrated that fighting against extremist groups is firmly in the national security interests of Pakistan.

General Sharif comes from a military family, with a long tradition of patriotism and service to country. Among his many brave military family members, his older brother Major Rana Shabbir Sharif, who was killed in action, is regarded as the most decorated officer of the Pakistan Army, having received the three most coveted awards of the Army, and is fondly addressed as the army's "Superman." This is a legacy difficult to live up to, but General Sharif has done so, honoring his brother and family's service, and continuing to serve and protect his country and its institutions.

Since taking on the role of Chief of Army Staff, General Sharif has been at the forefront of fighting the Taliban and other terrorist groups inside Pakistan. In 2014, he initiated the launch of Operation Zarb-e-Azb in North Waziristan, a tribal area along the Afghanistan-Pakistan border where militants had operated with impunity for decades. This operation didn't eliminate every terrorist, nor has it denied safe haven to many who continue to operate from Pakistan. But it has led to security improvements in the country, and this area is now safer than ever before. And importantly, the Pakistani Army is continuing to secure the gains it has achieved by building roads, border posts, schools, and healthcare facilities across North Waziristan to promote economic development and give citizens a more prosperous and peaceful future.

In the south, General Sharif also took on the task of clearing Karachi, one of Pakistan's largest cities, of an array of terrorist organizations, criminal groups, and even political corruption. The results were equally impressive, leading to a dramatic decline in militant attacks and ending the kind of targeted killings, kidnappings for ransom, and extortion that had become a feature of life in the city.

Much of the credit for the success of these operations is due to General Sharif and the service and sacrifice of tens of thousands of Pakistani soldiers who followed his lead. What was remarkable about General Sharif was not only the commitment he demonstrated to rooting out terrorism, but also his efforts to improve economic development, political life, and civic services for citizens throughout the country. He recognized that failure to focus on the root causes of radicalization, including economic and political corruption, had exacerbated the growth of extremism in Pakistan, and he showed foresight in seeking to remedy both cause and effect.

This is the kind of leadership that is imperative for the continued improvement of relations between the United States and Pakistan, which is important for the stability of the entire region, and for the national security of both Pakistan and the United States.

But despite the progress I witnessed firsthand when I visited Pakistan this past summer, the U.S.-Pakistan relationship has become strained. Among other things, limitations on U.S. assistance to Pakistan and congressional opposition to approve funding for the sale of defense articles have added to tensions between our two governments. But even with these difficulties, U.S. and Pakistani leaders cannot allow ambivalence and suspicion to fester in our relationship. Our common interests in counterterrorism, nuclear security, and regional stability are too important and too urgent. Both sides share responsibility to improve U.S.-Pakistan relations, and the United States must continue to make clear its enduring commitment to Pakistan's stability and economic growth.

As we look to the future, there remains much to be done. While Pakistan has made progress in its fight against terrorism, the Haqqani Network continues to operate within its border, increasing cross-border attacks are carried out by armed militants on neighboring countries, and political corruption has stilted economic growth. Pakistan must demonstrate that the commitment to fighting terrorism and improving conditions in the country is not dependent on a single individual. In that spirit, I look forward to working with General Qamar Javed Bajwa, Prime Minister Nawaz Sharif's selection to be the next Chief of Army Staff. By taking on all terrorist groups operating in its country, Pakistan will find that the United States remains willing and able to assist in this fight and develop an enduring strategic partnership.

I congratulate Pakistan on carrying out a second consecutive transition of power in the military, and I wish General Sharif well as he enters a well-earned retirement. He has vowed to serve Pakistan even after his retirement, and I would expect nothing less.

SECRETARY KERRY'S REMARKS AT COP22

Mr. MARKEY. Mr. President, last year the world came together in Paris to support a truly historic agreement on climate change. And 2015 was also historic for another reason: It was the hottest year in an observational record that stretches back to the 1880s. In fact, 15 of the 16 hottest years on the planet have occurred since 2000. Recently, July and August 2016 tied the global record for the hottest month, and 2016 is on track to be the warmest year yet. The evidence on climate change is overwhelming. Scientists have understood the fundamental physics for over a century. And the world agrees that we must take action to curb dangerous carbon pollution and reduce the effects of climate change. A majority of the United States agrees that we must take action.

The swiftness with which the Paris Climate Accord came into force demonstrates the global commitment to addressing the serious concerns of climate change. It is also a testament to the leadership of President Barack Obama and Secretary of State John Kerry. This year, the world again came together at the United Nations Climate Change Conference in Marrakesh, Morocco, to begin forging the path towards a lower-emissions world and clean energy future. And while there is much work to be done, we are heading in the right direction. We have seen the price of solar energy reach record lows and the rate of new solar installation reach record highs. We have seen States, regions, and countries reduce their carbon pollution while growing their economies. These positive steps will not only curb carbon pollution, but also create good, well-paying clean energy jobs.

Climate change is a challenge for the entire world. Through the Paris Climate Accord, the international community has decided to face this challenge head on, and the United States must continue to be the global leader. Under the leadership of Sectary of State John Kerry, the United States has carried this mantle. In the speech that Secretary Kerry delivered last month in Marrakesh, Morocco, at the 22nd meeting of the Conference of Parties to the United Nationals Framework Convention on Climate Change and first session of the Conference of Parties to the Paris Agreement, Secretary Kerry shared his vision for our future: a brighter, cleaner, healthier and more prosperous one.

He said:

Thank you so much, everybody. I apologize for being a few moments late. There was a fire and then there was some traffic backed up, and so here I am and here are you, and thank you for being here.

Let me begin by thanking our terrific U.S. Special Envoy for Climate Change Jonathan Pershing. I couldn't be luckier than to have him in this job. He was over at the Energy Department for a while. We stole him from Ernie Moniz, who is a great colleague and was gracious in my theft. And he has done a spectacular job working with all of our inter-national partners as we begin the hard work of implementing the Paris Agreement. And I also want to thank Ambassador Jennifer Haverkamp, who, along with Jonathan and a lot of the team that I see sitting here, has done an absolutely terrific job in leading the State Department's efforts to advance our climate goals this year. And I have to tell you—well, let me just divert for a minute. I also want to thank Brian Deese—I don't know if he's here—but I'm grateful for President Obama's senior advisor on climate issues and the entire intrepid U.S. delegation to the COP, whom I had a chance to meet with earlier this morning, but we've kind of traveled this road together.

I also thank our international partners, and particularly the executive secretary of the UNFCCC, Patricia Espinosa; the outgoing president of the COP, Minister Segolene Royal of France; and the incoming COP president, my friend and our host this week, Minister Salaheddine Mezouar, the foreign minister of Morocco. And I also want to thank our partners from Fiji, who will serve as president for the next COP, which I intend hopefully to attend as Citizen Kerry.

It's a great pleasure for me to be able to be here in Marrakech. I'm reminded of one of the 20th century's most outsized figures whose connection with this city is so famous—Sir Winston Churchill. He loved to paint the landscapes here and to absorb the beauty and the culture.

And in fact, at the very height of World War II, as he and President Franklin Roosevelt and Allied leaders gathered in Casablanca to plan the strategy for the European Theater, Churchill was absolutely stunned to learn that Roosevelt had never been to this part of Morocco.

So in a move that perhaps only Winston Churchill would get away with in the middle of a global war—world war—Churchill convinced Roosevelt to extend his visit and drive through what was still, at the time, a country engulfed in active combat.

So after several hours on the loose, and because we're talking about Winston Churchill, plenty of Scotch—(laughter)—the two leaders arrived in Marrakech in time to see the sun set on the Atlas Mountains.

And Churchill said it was the loveliest view on Earth.

So I think it's fitting, therefore, that almost three-quarters of a century later, friends and allies meet again in Marrakech in order to undertake a very important discussion—a discussion about the natural world that surrounds us and the importance of preserving it for generations to come.

As Jonathan mentioned, climate change is deeply personal to me, but it's personal to everyone in this room. I know that. And we obviously want it to be just as personal for everyone in every room: men, women, children, businesspeople, consumers, parents, teachers, students, grandparents. Wherever we live, whatever our calling, whatever our background must be, this is an imperative.

Now, I know the danger of preaching to the choir—and, obviously, all of us here are the proverbial choir. But I'm actually grateful for that, because here at the 22nd COP, no one can deny the remarkable progress that we have made—progress that actually was pretty hard to imagine even a few years ago. The global community is more united than ever not just in accepting the challenge, but in confronting it with real action, in making a difference. And no one should doubt the overwhelming majority of the citizens of the United States who know climate change is happening and who are determined to keep our commitments that were made in Paris. (Applause.)

None of us will forget the moment last December at Le Bourget, when the former foreign minister of France, with Segolene and a bunch of you there, led by our friend Laurent Fabius, who gaveled in the strongest, most ambitious global climate agreement ever negotiated. It was an accord that took literally decades to achieve—the proud work product of principled diplomacy, and ultimately, a deeply held, shared understanding that we're all in this together.

And when we left Paris, no one rested on their laurels. Instead, the world—unified—moved expeditiously to begin the—to pull the agreement permanently into force, crossing the thresholds of 55 countries representing 55 percent of global emissions, and doing so far faster than even the most optimistic among us might have predicted. In a powerful statement of the whole world's broad commitment to this agreement, in less than a year, 109 countries representing nearly 75 percent of the world's emissions have now formally committed to bold, decisive action—and we are determined to affirm that action and to stick with it out of Marrakech.

Now, we have in place—(applause)—so we have in place a foundation, based on national climate goals—109 nations, each of them have come up with their own plan, each of us setting goals that are based on our own abilities and our own circumstances. This agreement is, in fact, the essence of common but differentiated responsibilities. It provides support to countries that need help meeting the targets. It leaves no country to weather the storm of climate change alone. It marshals an array of tools in order to help developing nations to invest in infrastructure, technology, and the science to get the job done. It supports the most vulnerable countries, so they can better adapt to the climate impacts that many of those countries are already confronting.

And finally, it enables us to ratchet up ambition over time as technology develops and as the price of clean energy comes down. This is critical: the agreement calls on the parties to revisit their national pledges every five years, in order to ensure that we keep pace with the technology and that we accelerate the global transition to a clean energy economy.

This process—a cornerstone of our agreement—gives us a framework that is built to last, and a degree of global accountability that has never before existed. But I want to share with you that the progress that we've made this year goes well beyond Paris.

In early October, the International Civil Aviation Organization established a sector-wide agreement for carbon-neutral growth. Why is this so important? Because international aviation wasn't covered by what we did in Paris, and if that aviation was a country, it would rank among the top dozen greenhouse gas emitters in the world.

A few weeks later, I was pleased to be in Kigali, Rwanda, when representatives from again nearly 200 countries came together to phase down the global use and production of hydrofluorocarbons—which has been expected to increase very rapidly with a danger that is multiple of times more damaging than carbon dioxide. The Kigali agreement could singlehandedly help us to avoid an entire half a degree centigrade of warming by the end of the century—while at the same time opening up new opportunities for growth in a range of industries.

All of these steps combine to move the needle in the direction that we need to. And in

large part because global leaders have woken up to the enormity of this challenge, the world is now beginning to move forward together towards a clean energy future.

Over the past decade, the global renewable energy market has expanded more than sixfold. Last year, investment in renewable energy was at an all-time high—nearly $350 billion. But that only tells you part of the story. An average of—that 350 billion is the first time that we've been able to see that money outpacing what is being put into fossil fuels. An average of half a million new solar panels were installed every single day last year. And for the first time since the Pre-Industrial Era, despite the fact that you have global prices of oil and gas and coal that are lower than ever, still more of the world's money was invested in renewable energy technologies than in new fossil fuel plants.

And like many of you, I've seen this transformation take hold in my own country. That's why I'm confident about the future, regardless of what policy might be chosen, because of the marketplace. I've met with leaders and innovators in the energy industry all across our nation, and I am excited about the path that they are on. America's wind generation has tripled since 2008 and that will continue, and solar generation has increased 30 times over. And the reason both of those will continue is that the marketplace will dictate that, not the government. I can tell you with confidence that the United States is right now, today, on our way to meeting all of the international targets that we've set, and because of the market decisions that are being made, I do not believe that that can or will be reversed. (Applause.)

Now, much of this is due to President Obama's leadership, and our Congress also moving in a bipartisan fashion on things like tax credits for renewable energy. This leadership has helped to inspire targeted investment from the private sector. Today our emissions are being driven down because market-based forces are taking hold all over the world. And that's what we said we would do in Paris. None of us pretended that in Paris, the agreement itself was going to achieve two degrees. What we knew is we were sending that critical message to the marketplace, and businesses have responded, as I just described. Most businesspeople have come to understand: investing in clean energy simply makes good economic sense. You can make money. You can do good and do well at the same time.

Now, significantly, the renewable energy boom isn't limited to industrialized countries, and that's important to note. In fact, emerging economies like China, India, and Brazil invested even more in renewable technologies last year than the developed world.

China alone invested more than 100 billion dollars. Ultimately, clean energy is expected to be a multitrillion dollar market—the largest market the world has ever known. And no nation will do well if it sits on the sidelines, handicapping its new businesses from reaping the benefits of the clean-tech explosion.

My friends, we are in the midst of a global renewable energy surge, and as a result, in many places, clean energy has already reached cost parity with fossil fuels. Millions around the world are currently employed by the renewable energy industry. And if we make the right choices, millions more people will be put to work.

So good things are happening. The energy curve is bending towards sustainability. The

market is clearly headed towards clean energy, and that trend will only become more pronounced.

Now, for those of us who have been working on this challenge for decades, this really is a turning point. It is a cause for optimism, notwithstanding what you see in different countries with respect to politics and change. In no uncertain terms, the question now is not whether we will transition to energy economy—to a clean energy economy. That we've already begun to do. The question now is whether or not we are going to have the will to get this job done. That's the question now—whether we will make the transition in time to be able to do what we have to do to prevent catastrophic damage.

Ladies and gentlemen, I'm not a Cassandra. You can tell from what I've said. But I'm a realist. Time is not on our side. The world is already changing at an increasingly alarming rate with increasingly alarming consequences. The last time that Morocco hosted the COP was in 2001, and the intervening 15 years have been among the 16 hottest years in recorded history. 2016 is going to be the warmest year of all. Every month so far has broken a record. And this year will contribute its record-breaking heat to the hottest decade in recorded history, which was, by the way, preceded by the second-hottest decade, which was preceded by the third hottest decade. At some point, even the strongest skeptic has to acknowledge that something disturbing is happening.

We have seen record-breaking droughts everywhere—from India to Brazil to the west coast of the United States. Storms that used to happen once every 500 years are becoming relatively normal. In recent years, an average of 22.5 million people have been displaced by extreme weather events annually. We never saw that in the 20th Century.

Communities in island states like Fiji have already been forced to take steps to relocate permanently, because the places they have called home for generations are now uninhabitable. And there are many, many more who know it's only a matter of time before rising oceans begin to inundate their cities.

I know this is a lot for anyone to process—hard to process. That's why I have found that whenever possible, the best way to try to understand and to see whether people are pushing the envelope of thinking on this or not is to see for oneself what is happening. That's why this summer I went to Greenland to visit the incredible Jakobshavn glacier. Scientists pointed out to me the lines many meters above the water today that mark the glacier's retreat which it has done more in the past 15 years than it did in the entire previous century. And while I was there, I boarded a Danish naval vessel and I traveled through the ice fjord. I saw the massive ice chunks that had just broken off from the glacier to melt inexorably into the sea. And because they come off Greenland, which is on rock, every bit of that ice contributes to the rise of the ocean.

Since the 1990s, the painful pace of that melting has nearly tripled. Every day, 86 million metric tons of ice makes its way down that fjord into the ocean. And the total flow that comes off that glacier in a single year is enough water to meet the needs of New York City for two decades.

But experts in Greenland and elsewhere have always warned me, and they warned me on this trip this summer, if you really want to understand what's happening and what the threat is, go to Antarctica. Nowhere on the planet are the stakes as high as they are on the opposite end of the globe. For half a century, climate scientists have believed the West Antarctic Ice Sheet is a sword of Damocles hanging over our entire way of life. Should it break apart and melt into the sea, it alone could raise global sea levels by four to five meters. And the scientists down there described to me how the pressure of the ice and the weight of the ice pushes the entire continent down so that it's grounded on the base of Earth's crust and rock. But that allows warmer sea water to creep in under the glacier and speed up the process of the melting and destabilize the glacier.

Antarctica contains ice sheets that are, in some places, on the East Antarctic Ice Sheet three miles deep. And if all that ice were somehow able to melt away completely because we are irresponsible about climate change, in the coming centuries, sea level would rise somewhere over 100 to 200 feet.

That's why I flew last week to McMurdo Station in Antarctica to meet with our scientists and to understand better what is taking place. I flew by helicopter over the West Antarctic Ice Sheet. I walked out onto the Ross Sea ice shelf. And I talked with the scientists who are on the front lines, not people involved in day to day politics, but people who are making scientific judgment and doing extensive research. And they were crystal clear: The more they learn, the more alarmed they become about the speed with which these changes are happening. A scientist from New Zealand named Gavin Dunbar described what they're seeing there as the quote, "canary in the coal mine" and warned that some thresholds, if we cross them, cannot be reversed.

In other words, we can't wait too long to translate the science that we have today into the policies that are necessary to address this challenge. These scientists urged me to remind my own government and governments around the world and everyone here that what we do right now—today— matters, because if we don't go far enough and if we don't go fast enough, the damage we inflict could take centuries to undo—if it can be undone at all.

I underscore today: We don't get a second chance. The consequences of failure would in most cases be irreversible. And if we lose this moment for action, there's no speech decades from now that will put these massive ice sheets back together. There's no magic wand in any capital in the world that you can wave to refill all of the lakes and rivers that will dry up, or make farm—arid farm land fertile again. And we certainly won't have the power to hold back rising tides as they encroach on our shores. So we have to get this right, and we have to get it right now.

The scientists in Antarctica told me that they are still trying to figure out how quickly this is all happening. But they know for certain that it's happening, and it's happening faster than we previously thought possible. The alarm bells ought to be going off everywhere. As an American glacial geologist told me down there, a fellow by the name of John Stone, he said, "The catastrophic period could already be underway." That's why wise public policy demands that we take precautionary measures now.

Still, despite the real-life changes that are being done and the threat of more to come, it's important to remind ourselves that we are not on a pre-ordained path to disaster. This is not pre-ordained. It's not written in the stars. This is about choices—choices that we still have. This is a test of willpower, not capacity. It's within our power to put the planet back on a better track. But doing

that requires holding ourselves accountable to the hard truth. It requires holding ourselves accountable to facts, not opinion; to science, not theories that haven't been proven and can't be proven; and certainly not to political bromides and slogans.

For all the progress that we are making, at the current pace we will not meet our goal. I said that earlier. We knew in Paris that what we were doing was trying to start down a road. But we also knew it doesn't get us to the end of the journey. Yes, renewables make up more than half of all the new electricity installation last year. That's progress. But the reality is because of the existing energy infrastructure already in place, that new energy only generated a little more than 10 percent of the world's total energy. That is nowhere near what we need in order to achieve our goals.

If we're going to have the ability to stave off the worst impacts of climate change, we have to dramatically accelerate the transition that is already starting. We need to get to a point where clean sources are generating most of the world's energy, and we need to get there fast. Certainly experts tell us by the middle of this century we have to get there.

Now, I've said many times, and I'll say it again today: It is not going to be governments alone, or even principally, that solve the climate challenge. The private sector is the most important player. And already we are seeing real solutions coming from entrepreneurs and academia. It's going to be innovators, workers, and business leaders, many of whom have been hammering away at this challenge for years who are going to continue to create the technological advances that forever revolutionize the way that we power our world.

But make no mistake, government leadership is absolutely essential. And because today is the last opportunity I will have to address the COP as Secretary of State, I just want to take a moment to underscore the work that government leaders can do and should do, especially the 200—almost 200 nations represented here.

Now, we know that we have not come to Marrakech to bask in the glow of Paris. We've come here to move forward. In doing so, we cannot forget that the contributions we've each made thus far were never meant to be the ceiling. They're a foundation on which we expect to build. And unless our nations voluntarily ratchet up our ambition, and unless we continue to put sustained pressure on one another to act wisely, we will have difficulty meeting the current mitigation needs, let alone holding temperature increases at 2 degrees warming, which science tells us is a tipping point.

And if we fall short, it will be the single greatest instance in modern history of a generation in a time of crisis abdicating responsibility for the future. And it won't just be a policy failure; because of the nature of this challenge, it will be a moral failure, a betrayal of devastating consequence.

Now, I know not—that's not what any of us here signed up for. As Pope Francis said, "We receive this world as an inheritance from past generations, but also as a loan for future generations, to whom we will have to return it."

Now, I fully recognize the challenges that a number of countries face because they have a big population, they have a growing economy, they have a lot of people in poverty, they're determined to maintain stability and pull those people into the economy. And of course, they're concerned about stability—

we all are. Access to affordable energy is a key part of providing that stability. And the dirtiest sources of energy are, unfortunately, some of the cheapest. But I emphasize this: Only in the short term. In the long term, it's an entirely different story, folks. In the long term, carbon-intensive energy is actually today, right now, one of the costliest and most foolhardy investments any nation can possibly make. And that is because the final invoice for carbon-based energy includes a lot more than just the price of the oil or the coal, or the natural gas; it—or the price of building the power plant. The real cost accounting needs to fully consider all of the downstream consequences, which, in the case of dirty fuels, are enough to at least double or triple the initial expenses.

That's the kind of accounting that we need to do today. Just think about the price of environmental and agricultural degradation. Think about the loss of an ability of farmers in one area because of the lack of water or too much heat to be able to grow their crops today. Think of the hospital bills for asthma and emphysema patients, and the millions of deaths that are linked to air pollution caused by the use of fossil fuels.

In 2014, a study found that up to six million people in China have black lung because they lived and worked so close to coal-fired power plants. There are nearly 20 million new asthma cases a year in India linked to coal-related air pollution, and in the United States, asthma costs taxpayers more than $55 billion annually. The greatest cause of children being hospitalized in the summer in the United States is environmentally induced asthma. These are real costs, and they need to be added to the tally.

We also have to include the price tag of rebuilding after devastating storms and flooding. Just in the first three quarters of this year alone, extreme weather events have cost the United States—have cost American taxpayers $27 billion in damage. In August alone, Louisiana experienced flooding that resulted in roughly $10 billion worth of damage.

So none of us can afford to be oblivious to these expenses, and these initial costs are in reality just a glimpse of what the future could hold in store for us if we fail to respond. Just imagine: Sea barriers that have to be built. Go down to Miami—in south Miami, they're building—they're raising streets to deal with flooding that's already occurring, building new storm drains and assessing people additional tax in order to do it. Massive increases in cost of maintaining infrastructure to control flooding, withstand storms. Power outages. All of this and more has to be added to any honest assessment of high-carbon energy sources. And in an age of increasing transparency and public demand for accountability, citizens in the long run will not accept phony accounting or an obfuscation of the consequences of the decisions.

So everyone needs to make smarter choices—with the long game, not the short game, in mind.

Coal, unfortunately, is the single biggest contributor to global carbon pollution. It provides about 30 percent of the world's energy, but it produces nearly 50 percent of the world's greenhouse gases. The unprecedented investments that we are now seeing in clean energy will mean very, very little if, at the same time, new coal fire plants without carbon capture are coming online and at a rate dumping into the atmosphere more and more of the very pollution that we're all working so hard to reduce.

Some of these projections, I have to tell you, are deeply troubling. For example, between now and 2040, the demand for electricity in Southeast Asia is likely to triple—and the bulk of that demand is currently expected to be met by growth—where? In the coal-fired power sector, rather than clean energy. That threatens everything we're trying to achieve here.

We literally cannot use one hand to pat ourselves on the back for what we've done to take steps to address climate change, and then turn around and use the other hand to write a big fat check enabling the widespread development of the dirtiest source of fuel in an outdated way. It just doesn't make sense. That's suicide. And that's how we all lose this fight.

Make no mistake: People all over the world are working for victory in this. And this issue is increasingly capturing the attention of citizens everywhere, and certainly the private sector. The private sector welcomed the signals that we sent in Paris, but they are demanding even stronger signals now—the private sector—so that they can invest clean energy solutions with even greater confidence.

One of the strongest signals that government can send, one of the most powerful ways to reduce emissions at the lowest possible course—cost—is to move toward carbon pricing that puts basic, free-market economics to work in addressing this challenge.

Now obviously, this is not a new idea. Many have come to this conclusion already. The share of global emissions that are covered by a carbon price has tripled over the last decade. Last year, more than 1,000 businesses and investors—including sectors that might be surprising to some of you—all came together to voice their support for carbon pricing. The long list of supporters includes energy companies like BP, Royal Dutch Shell, utilities like PG&E, transportation companies like British Airways, construction firms like Cemex, financial institutions like Deutsche Bank, like Swiss Re, and consumer goods corporations like Unilever and Nokia. These companies all believe that carbon pricing will establish the necessary certainty in the marketplace that helps the private sector to move the capital that helps to solve the problem.

Carbon pricing allows citizens, innovators, and companies—it allows the market to make independent decisions free from the government to be able to best drive their emission reductions. And this is also, by the way, the chief reason that carbon pricing has received support from leaders and economists on both sides of the aisle in the United States of America. A price on carbon, coupled with government support for innovation in key sectors, is easily one of the most compelling tools for the world to accelerate the clean energy transformation that we are working to achieve. Now, while it may be some time before we see this ideal outcome, the effort to improve carbon markets ought to be a priority going forward.

The bottom line is that there are many tools at the world's disposal. The COP itself is an important tool, in a sense. It has become much more of a—much more than just a gathering of government officials. It's really a yearly summit, 25,000 people strong this year from all over the world, for all sectors to showcase their commitment to climate action and to discuss ways to expand shared efforts. It's a regular reminder of exactly how much this movement has grown—and how many people, in how many countries, are committed to action.

Walking around the conference here before I was coming in here and seeing this site in Marrakech, and seeing the delegations and the business leaders, the entrepreneurs and the activists who have traveled from near and far to be here, it's abundantly clear we have the ability to prevent the worst impacts of climate change.

But again, we're forced to ask: Do we have the collective will? Because our success is not going to happen by accident. It won't happen without sustained commitment, without cooperation and creative thinking. And it won't happen without confident investors and innovative entrepreneurs. And it certainly won't happen without leadership.

For those in power in all parts of the world, including my own, who may be confronted with decisions about which road to take at this critical juncture, I ask you, on behalf of billions of people around the world: Don't take my word for it. Don't take just the existence of this COP as the stamp of approval for it. I ask you to see for yourselves. Do your own due diligence before making irrevocable choices.

Examine closely what it is that has persuaded the Pope, presidents, and prime ministers all over the world, leaders around the world, to take on the responsibility of responding to this threat. Talk to the business leaders of Fortune 500 companies and smaller innovative companies, all of whom are eager to invest in the energy markets of the future. Get the best economists' judgment on the risk of inaction, of what the cost would be to global economies, versus the opportunities that are to be found in the clean energy market of the future. Speak with the military leaders who view climate change as a global security concern, as a threat multiplier. Ask farmers about—and fisherman about the impact of dramatic changes in weather patterns on their current ability to make a living and to support their families or on what they see for the future. Listen to faith leaders talk about the moral responsibility that human beings have to act as stewards of the planet that we have to share, the only planet we have. Bring in the activists and civil society, groups who have worked for years with communities all over the world to raise awareness and to respond to this threat. Ask young people about their legitimate concerns for the planet that their children will inherit in reducing emissions worldwide.

And above all, consult with the scientists who have dedicated their entire lives to expanding our understanding of this challenge, and whose work will be in vain unless we sound the alarm loud enough for everyone to hear. No one has a right to make decisions that affect billions of people based on solely ideology or without proper input.

Anyone who has these conversations, who takes the time to learn from these experts, who gets the full picture of what we're facing—I believe they can only come to one legitimate decision, and that is to act boldly on climate change and encourage others to do the same.

Now, I want to acknowledge that since this COP started, obviously, an election took place in my country. And I know it has left some here and elsewhere feeling uncertain about the future. I obviously understand that uncertainty. And while I can't stand here and speculate about what policies our president-elect will pursue, I will tell you this: In the time that I have spent in public life, one of the things I have learned is that some issues look a little bit different when you're actually in office compared to when you're on the campaign trail.

And the truth is that climate change shouldn't be a partisan issue in the first place. It isn't a partisan issue for our military leaders at the Pentagon who call climate change a threat multiplier. (Applause.) It isn't a partisan issue for those military leaders because of the way that climate change exacerbates conflicts all over the world and who view it as a threat to military readiness at their bases and could suffer the consequences of rising seas and stronger storms. It isn't a partisan issue for our intelligence community, who just this year released a report detailing the implications of climate change for U.S. national security: threats to the stability of fragile nations, heightened social and political tensions, rising food prices, increased risks to human health, and more.

It isn't a partisan issue for mayors from New Orleans to Miami, who are already working hard to manage sunny-day floods and stronger storm surges caused by climate change. It isn't partisan for liberal and conservative business leaders alike who are investing unprecedented amounts of money into renewables, voluntarily committing to reduce their own emissions, and even holding their supply chains accountable to their overall carbon footprint.

And there's nothing partisan about climate change for the world scientists who are near unanimous in their conclusion that climate change is real, it is happening, human beings for the most part are causing it, and we will have increasing catastrophic impacts on our way of life if we don't take the dramatic steps necessary to reduce the carbon footprint of our civilization.

Now, whether we are able to meet this moment is a big test—probably as big a test of courage and vision as you'll ever find. Every nation has a responsibility to do its part if we are going to pass that test—and only those nations who step up and respond to this threat can legitimately lay claim to a mantle of global leadership. That's a fact.

More than his love of Marrakech, Winston Churchill was known for his hard-nosed insight and the way that he expressed it. He once argued, tellingly: "It's not always enough that we do our best; sometimes we have to do what is required."

We know today what is required. And with all of the real-world evidence, with all of the peer-reviewed science, with all of the plain just old common sense, there isn't anyone who can credibly argue otherwise. So we have to continue this fight, my friends. We have to continue to defy expectations. We have to continue to accelerate the global transition to a clean energy economy. And we have to continue to hold one another accountable for the choices that our nations makes.

Earlier this year, on Earth Day, I had the great privilege of signing the Paris Agreement on behalf of President Obama and the United States. It was a special day. And because my daughter lives in New York, I invited her to join me at the UN. She surprised me by bringing my 2-year-old granddaughter, Isabelle, along as well.

And that morning, I had been thinking about the history that had brought us to that day. I thought about the first Earth Day in 1970 that I mentioned earlier, when I joined with millions of Americans in teach-ins to educate the public about the environmental challenges we faced. I thought about the first UN climate conference in Rio, which is actually where I met my wife Teresa, and I thought of the urgency that we all felt way back then in 1992. And of course,

I thought about that December night at Le Bourget, when it seemed—for the first time—that the world had finally found the path forward.

But as I sat and I played with my granddaughter, waiting for my turn to go out and sign the Agreement, I thought, not of the past, but I thought of the future. Her future. The world her children would one day inherit.

And when it was time for me to go up on that stage, I scooped her up and I brought her out with me. I wanted to share that moment with her. And I'll never forget it.

But to my surprise, people responded to her presence that day, and since then so many people have said to me, they've conveyed to me how that moment conveyed something special and moved them. They told me they thought of their own children, their own grandchildren. They thought of the future. They were reminded of the stakes.

Ladies and gentlemen, here in Marrakech, in the next hours, let us make clear to the world that we will always remember the stakes. Let us stand firm in support of the goals that we set in Paris and recommit ourselves to double our efforts to meet them. Let us say that when it comes to climate change, we will commit not just to doing our best, but as Winston Churchill admonished, we will do what is required.

I look forward to working with you in this important work for whatever number of years ahead I have a chance to. Thank you.

TRIBUTE TO CARDINAL JOSEPH WILLIAM TOBIN

Mr. DONNELLY. Mr. President, today I wish to recognize Archbishop Joseph William Tobin of Indianapolis on his recent elevation to cardinal by Pope Francis and for his extraordinary service to Indiana. As a leader in our State, Cardinal Tobin has demonstrated his lifelong, faith-filled commitment to serving others and giving a voice to the voiceless.

Born in Detroit, MI, Cardinal Tobin is the eldest of Joseph W. Tobin and Marie Terese Kerwin's 13 children. From an early age, it was apparent to his family that he was intellectually and spiritually gifted and wanted to use those talents by becoming a priest. Cardinal Tobin's family instilled in him the importance of faith and family, and he pursued the priesthood with purpose and determination. He received a bachelor of arts in philosophy from Holy Redeemer College in Waterford, WI, and a masters in religious education, as well as a masters in divinity from Mount Saint Alphonsus Seminary in Esopus, NY.

Cardinal Tobin professed first vows as a Redemptorist missionary on August 5, 1973, and he was ordained to the priesthood on June 1, 1978. Over the next 12 years, Cardinal Tobin served communities in the Midwest, including in his hometown of Detroit and in Chicago. He then was elected general consultor to the Superior General of the Redemptorists and moved to Rome, Italy. During his 21 years in Italy, he was recognized for his efforts to promote dialogue and resolve tensions between the Vatican and U.S. nuns. He was elected and reelected as superior general and later named archbishop by Pope Benedict XVI, as well as secretary of the Congregation for Institutes of Consecrated Life and Societies of Apostolic Life on August 2, 2010. Soon thereafter, he was ordained to the episcopacy on October 9, 2010, and approximately 2 years later, he was named Metropolitan Archbishop of Indianapolis.

For 4 years, the Indianapolis archdiocese benefited greatly from Cardinal Tobin's leadership. His commitment to serving those in the greatest need and his tireless dedication to sharing the teachings of the Catholic Church with the people of central and southern Indiana have benefited countless Hoosiers.

Pope Francis announced Archbishop Tobin's selection as cardinal on October 9, 2016, from the steps of St. Peter's Basilica in the Vatican. Less than a month later, the Pope selected him to lead the archdiocese of Newark, NJ, which serves 1.5 million Catholics and is among the 10 largest dioceses in the country.

Outside of the church, Cardinal Tobin has dedicated himself to various organizations including the Canon Law Society of America and the North American Orthodox-Catholic Theological Consultation. He also is a member of United States Conference of Catholic Bishops, USCCB, subcommittee on the Church in Africa and a consultant to the committee on ecumenical and interreligious affairs.

On behalf of Hoosiers, I congratulate Cardinal Tobin and thank him for blessing us with his leadership. Let us honor Cardinal Tobin for his selfless commitment to serving his fellow citizens of the world and steadfast efforts to make Indiana and the world a better place.

TRIBUTE TO LIEUTENANT COLONEL WADE E. WIEGEL

Mr. GRASSLEY. Mr. President, I would like to take a moment to recognize Lt. Col. Wade E. Wiegel for his 22 years of service in the U.S. Marine Corps. Wade is a native of Iowa, and I am proud to say that I nominated him for the U.S. Naval Academy in 1990. In May 1994, he earned a bachelor of science degree in mechanical engineering and reported to the Marine Corps' The Basic School. From there he completed flight training and was designated a naval aviator in March 1997. He deployed aboard the USS *Enterprise* in support of Operation Iraqi Freedom and Operation Enduring Freedom.

Wade later served as the commanding officer for the VMFA–122 "Crusaders" and forward deployed the squadron for 6 months into the Pacific Theater in support of theater security cooperation activities with Japan, South Korea, and the Philippines. After graduating from the National War College, he served as a military adviser in the Office of the Under Secretary of Defense for Policy. Most recently, Wade has served in the Office of Legislative Affairs as a congressional affairs officer. His personal decorations include the Defense Meritorious Service Medal, Meritorious Service Medal with Gold Star, the Navy and Marine Corps Commendation Medal, and the Navy and Marine Corps Achievement Medal with Gold Star.

As he prepares to retire from the Marine Corps, I would like to take this opportunity to thank him for his service to our country and to wish him well in his future endeavors.

REMEMBERING JIM LYONS

Mr. GRASSLEY. Mr. President, I would like to pay tribute to Jim Lyons.

Jim was a tax counsel for Chairman HATCH on the Finance Committee. Before that, he served as a tax counsel for the committee when I was ranking member.

Jim had a medical emergency during a basketball game for charity which, unfortunately for us all, he did not survive.

Those who knew Jim would not be surprised that he was spending an evening at an event to help others.

He was well known for his generosity, whether it was donating holiday gifts for children in foster care or sharing his extensive knowledge of the Tax Code with younger staff who were learning the ropes.

He was incredibly smart and had a zest for his work and for life that was joyous and inspiring to all of those around him.

He loved to laugh and had a gift for making others laugh. Jim's quick wit is legendary, and he drew others to his company to hear what funny story or observation he might share next.

Devising clever floor charts that made an insightful point about tax policy was a Jim Lyons specialty. He was extremely gifted in using humor to draw attention to a serious policy concern or to point out a political absurdity.

It is a rare skill and one that Jim used to great effect. People liked to hear what he had to say. The tragedy of his loss in the prime of his life is immeasurable. Those of us who knew him take comfort in learning from his example. We can do serious work without taking ourselves too seriously. In fact, we might be much more successful by finding room to share a laugh with others. I wish Jim eternal peace and send my best wishes to his loving family.

ADDITIONAL STATEMENTS

TRIBUTE TO VINCENT VESPIA, JR.

● Mr. WHITEHOUSE. Mr. President, South Kingstown Police Chief Vincent Vespia, Jr., has dedicated his career to protecting and serving the people of Rhode Island. He retired this month after nearly 60 years of exceptional service.

The State's longest serving police chief began his career in 1959 as a trooper with the Rhode Island State police. Chief Vespia would eventually go on to become a State police organized crime investigator. His work helped bring down New England's top organized crime family. There are many stories about Vin Vespia. One of the most famous was when he crashed through a second floor window of a Federal Hill crap game from a bucket of a cherry picker, brandishing a machine gun at the surprised dice players. As Pulitzer Prize winning author Mike Stanton wrote in his book "The Prince of Providence," "Vespia was a kick-ass cop who had grown up on the Hill, playing in the street with some of the wise guys he now pursued." As a young trooper, Vespia had busted a former playmate with a truckload of stolen furs. "How can you arrest me?" the man asked. "We played kick the can together." Replied Vespia: "You went one way, I went another."

After retiring from the State police, Vin was appointed chief of the South Kingstown Police Department in 1981. He would spend the next 35 years of his career building an effective, professional force with strong ties to the community. He created new leadership programs within the department's detective bureau and oversaw the construction of an innovative public safety facility with state-of-the-art information technology.

Chief Vespia will be remembered for his leadership and fairness. Those he led describe him as dedicated, rational, and respectable. He has been called "probably the most admired law enforcement officer in Rhode Island." I was honored to have worked with him when I was attorney general and am proud to call him my friend. Chief Vespia's 57 years of commitment and service to the people of Rhode Island represent the very best in law enforcement.

I commend him and his family for the sacrifices they have made. On behalf of those he has served throughout the years, I offer my thanks. I wish Vin and Judith-Ann, his wife of 40 years, a happy retirement and the best of luck in all future endeavors.●

MESSAGE FROM THE HOUSE RECEIVED DURING ADJOURNMENT

ENROLLED BILLS SIGNED

Under the authority of the order of the Senate of January 6, 2015, the Sec-retary of the Senate, on December 2, 2016, during the adjournment of the Senate, received a message from the House of Representatives announcing that the Speaker had signed the following enrolled bills:

S. 1808. An act to require the Secretary of Homeland Security to conduct a Northern Border threat analysis, and for other purposes.

S. 1915. An act to direct the Secretary of Homeland Security to make anthrax vaccines available to emergency response providers, and for other purposes.

H.R. 3471. An act to amend title 38, United States Code, to make certain improvements in the provision of automobiles and adaptive equipment by the Department of Veterans Affairs.

H.R. 5111. An act to prohibit the use of certain clauses in form contracts that restrict the ability of a consumer to communicate regarding the goods or services offered in interstate commerce that were the subject of the contract, and for other purposes.

H.R. 6297. An act to reauthorize the Iran Sanctions Act of 1996.

Under the authority of the order of the Senate of January 6, 2015, the enrolled bills were signed on December 2, 2016, during the adjournment of the Senate, by the President pro tempore (Mr. HATCH).

MESSAGES FROM THE HOUSE

ENROLLED BILLS SIGNED

At 3:06 p.m., a message from the House of Representatives, delivered by Mr. Novotny, one of its reading clerks, announced that the Speaker has signed the following enrolled bills:

S. 1550. An act to amend title 31, United States Code, to establish entities tasked with improving program and project management in certain Federal agencies, and for other purposes.

H.R. 5509. An act to name the Department of Veterans Affairs temporary lodging facility in Indianapolis, Indiana, as the "Dr. Otis Bowen Veteran House".

H.R. 5995. An act to strike the sunset on certain provisions relating to the authorized protest of a task or delivery order under section 4106 of title 41, United States Code.

The enrolled bills were subsequently signed by the President pro tempore (Mr. HATCH).

At 3:07 p.m., a message from the House of Representatives, delivered by Mrs. Cole, one of its reading clerks, announced that the House has passed the following bill, in which it requests the concurrence of the Senate:

H.R. 6392. An act to amend the Dodd-Frank Wall Street Reform and Consumer Protection Act to specify when bank holding companies may be subject to certain enhanced supervision, and for other purposes.

The message further announced that the House agrees to the report of the committee of conference on the disagreeing votes of the two Houses on the amendment of the House of Representatives to the bill (S. 2943) to authorize appropriations for fiscal year 2017 for military activities of the De-partment of Defense, for military construction, and for defense activities of the Department of Energy, to prescribe military personnel strengths for such fiscal year, and for other purposes.

The message also announced that the House agrees to the amendments of the Senate to the resolution (H.Con.Res. 122) supporting efforts to stop the theft, illegal possession or sale, transfer, and export of tribal cultural items of American Indians, Alaska Natives, and Native Hawaiians in the United States and internationally.

ENROLLED BILLS PRESENTED

The Secretary of the Senate reported that on December 2, 2016, she had presented to the President of the United States the following enrolled bills:

S. 1808. An act to require the Secretary of Homeland Security to conduct a Northern Border threat analysis, and for other purposes.

S. 1915. An act to direct the Secretary of Homeland Security to make anthrax vaccines available to emergency response providers, and for other purposes.

The Secretary of the Senate reported that on today, December 5, 2016, she had presented to the President of the United States the following enrolled bill:

S. 1550. An act to amend title 31, United States Code, to establish entities tasked with improving program and project management in certain Federal agencies, and for other purposes.

REPORTS OF COMMITTEES

The following reports of committees were submitted:

By Mr. THUNE, from the Committee on Commerce, Science, and Transportation, with an amendment in the nature of a substitute:

S. 3346. A bill to authorize the programs of the National Aeronautics and Space Administration, and for other purposes (Rept. No. 114–390).

By Mr. THUNE, from the Committee on Commerce, Science, and Transportation:

Report to accompany S. 3183, A bill to prohibit the circumvention of control measures used by Internet ticket sellers to ensure equitable consumer access to tickets for any given event, and for other purposes (Rept. No. 114–391).

By Mr. THUNE, from the Committee on Commerce, Science, and Transportation, with an amendment in the nature of a substitute:

S. 1403. A bill to amend the Magnuson-Stevens Fishery Conservation and Management Act to promote sustainable conservation and management for the Gulf of Mexico and South Atlantic fisheries and the communities that rely on them, and for other purposes.

INTRODUCTION OF BILLS AND JOINT RESOLUTIONS

The following bills and joint resolutions were introduced, read the first and second times by unanimous consent, and referred as indicated:

By Mr. FLAKE (for himself and Ms. HEITKAMP):

S. 3494. A bill to provide U.S. Customs and Border Protection with adequate flexibility in its employment authorities; to the Committee on Homeland Security and Governmental Affairs.

By Mr. DAINES (for himself and Mr. TESTER):

S. 3495. A bill to amend the Food, Agriculture, Conservation, and Trade Act of 1990 to designate certain research and extension grants to increase participation by women and underrepresented minorities in the fields of science, technology, engineering, and mathematics as "Jeannette Rankin Women and Minorities in STEM Fields Grants"; to the Committee on Agriculture, Nutrition, and Forestry.

By Mr. CORNYN (for himself and Mr. CASEY):

S. 3496. A bill to amend the Internal Revenue Code of 1986 to allow members of the Ready Reserve of a reserve component of the Armed Forces to make elective deferrals on the basis of their service to the Ready Reserve and on the basis of their other employment; to the Committee on Finance.

By Mr. COTTON (for himself, Mr. WICKER, Mr. BOOZMAN, Mr. COCHRAN, and Mr. SHELBY):

S. 3497. A bill to provide the force and effect of law for certain regulations relating to the taking of double-crested cormorants to reduce depredation at aquaculture facilities and protect public resources; to the Committee on Environment and Public Works.

By Mrs. BOXER:

S. 3498. A bill to ensure that the Secretary of the Army obtains consent from certain entities before granting certain permits, casements, or rights-of-way; to the Committee on Environment and Public Works.

By Mr. LEE (for himself, Mr. LEAHY, Mr. HOEVEN, and Mr. CRUZ):

S. 3499. A bill to establish the Daniel Webster Congressional Clerkship Program; to the Committee on Rules and Administration.

By Mr. WICKER (for himself and Mr. COCHRAN):

S. 3500. A bill to require the appropriate Federal banking agencies to treat certain non-significant investments in the capital of unconsolidated financial institutions as qualifying capital instruments, and for other purposes; to the Committee on Banking, Housing, and Urban Affairs.

By Mr. BLUMENTHAL (for himself and Mr. BOOKER):

S. 3501. A bill to require the Federal Communications Commission to submit to Congress a report on promoting broadband Internet access service for veterans; to the Committee on Commerce, Science, and Transportation.

By Mr. DAINES (for himself and Mr. BOOKER):

S. 3502. A bill to require the Federal Aviation Administration to establish annual performance objectives and to hold the Chief NextGen Officer accountable for meeting such objectives; to the Committee on Commerce, Science, and Transportation.

SUBMISSION OF CONCURRENT AND SENATE RESOLUTIONS

The following concurrent resolutions and Senate resolutions were read, and referred (or acted upon), as indicated:

By Mr. COONS (for himself and Mr. GRAHAM):

S. Res. 629. A resolution recognizing the 225th anniversary of Alexander Hamilton's seminal Report on the Subject of Manufactures; to the Committee on Commerce, Science, and Transportation.

By Mr. CORNYN (for himself, Mr. GRASSLEY, Mr. HATCH, Mr. LEE, Mr. SCOTT, and Mr. CRUZ):

S. Res. 630. A resolution recognizing the historical importance of Associate Justice Clarence Thomas; to the Committee on the Judiciary.

ADDITIONAL COSPONSORS

S. 298

At the request of Mr. GRASSLEY, the name of the Senator from North Dakota (Ms. HEITKAMP) was added as a cosponsor of S. 298, a bill to amend titles XIX and XXI of the Social Security Act to provide States with the option of providing services to children with medically complex conditions under the Medicaid program and Children's Health Insurance Program through a care coordination program focused on improving health outcomes for children with medically complex conditions and lowering costs, and for other purposes.

S. 313

At the request of Mr. GRASSLEY, the name of the Senator from Idaho (Mr. RISCH) was added as a cosponsor of S. 313, a bill to amend title XVIII of the Social Security Act to add physical therapists to the list of providers allowed to utilize locum tenens arrangements under Medicare.

S. 626

At the request of Mr. GRASSLEY, the name of the Senator from Idaho (Mr. RISCH) was added as a cosponsor of S. 626, a bill to amend title XIX of the Social Security Act to cover physician services delivered by podiatric physicians to ensure access by Medicaid beneficiaries to appropriate quality foot and ankle care, to amend title XVIII of such Act to modify the requirements for diabetic shoes to be included under Medicare, and for other purposes.

S. 1169

At the request of Mr. GRASSLEY, the name of the Senator from North Carolina (Mr. TILLIS) was added as a cosponsor of S. 1169, a bill to reauthorize and improve the Juvenile Justice and Delinquency Prevention Act of 1974, and for other purposes.

S. 2216

At the request of Ms. COLLINS, the name of the Senator from North Dakota (Mr. HOEVEN) was added as a cosponsor of S. 2216, a bill to provide immunity from suit for certain individuals who disclose potential examples of financial exploitation of senior citizens, and for other purposes.

S. 2268

At the request of Mr. CORNYN, the name of the Senator from Wisconsin (Ms. BALDWIN) was added as a cosponsor of S. 2268, a bill to award a Congressional Gold Medal to the United States Army Dust Off crews of the Vietnam War, collectively, in recognition of their extraordinary heroism and lifesaving actions in Vietnam.

S. 2800

At the request of Mr. COONS, the name of the Senator from Idaho (Mr. RISCH) was added as a cosponsor of S. 2800, a bill to amend the Internal Revenue Code of 1986 and the Higher Education Act of 1965 to provide an exclusion from income for student loan forgiveness for students who have died or become disabled.

S. 2817

At the request of Mr. PETERS, the name of the Senator from Minnesota (Ms. KLOBUCHAR) was added as a cosponsor of S. 2817, a bill to improve understanding and forecasting of space weather events, and for other purposes.

S. 2957

At the request of Mr. NELSON, the name of the Senator from Arkansas (Mr. COTTON) was added as a cosponsor of S. 2957, a bill to require the Secretary of the Treasury to mint commemorative coins in recognition of the 50th anniversary of the first manned landing on the Moon.

S. 2989

At the request of Ms. MURKOWSKI, the name of the Senator from Missouri (Mr. BLUNT) was added as a cosponsor of S. 2989, a bill to award a Congressional Gold Medal, collectively, to the United States merchant mariners of World War II, in recognition of their dedicated and vital service during World War II.

S. 3198

At the request of Mr. HATCH, the name of the Senator from South Dakota (Mr. ROUNDS) was added as a cosponsor of S. 3198, a bill to amend title 38, United States Code, to improve the provision of adult day health care services for veterans.

S. 3328

At the request of Mr. KAINE, his name was added as a cosponsor of S. 3328, a bill to amend title 38, United States Code, to reform the rights and processes relating to appeals of decisions regarding claims for benefits under the laws administered by the Secretary of Veterans Affairs, and for other purposes.

S. 3405

At the request of Mr. DAINES, the name of the Senator from Idaho (Mr. CRAPO) was added as a cosponsor of S. 3405, a bill to transfer certain items from the United States Munitions List to the Commerce Control List.

S. 3435

At the request of Mr. ROBERTS, the name of the Senator from West Virginia (Mrs. CAPITO) was added as a cosponsor of S. 3435, a bill to amend title XVIII of the Social Security Act to protect and preserve access of Medicare beneficiaries in rural areas to health care providers under the Medicare program, and for other purposes.

S. 3478

At the request of Mr. RUBIO, the name of the Senator from Arkansas (Mr. BOOZMAN) was added as a cosponsor of S. 3478, a bill to require continued and enhanced annual reporting to Congress in the Annual Report on International Religious Freedom on anti-Semitic incidents in Europe, the safety and security of European Jewish communities, and the efforts of the United States to partner with European governments, the European Union, and civil society groups, to combat anti-Semitism, and for other purposes.

S. RES. 616

At the request of Mrs. SHAHEEN, the name of the Senator from South Dakota (Mr. ROUNDS) was added as a cosponsor of S. Res. 616, a resolution supporting the goals and ideals of American Diabetes Month.

STATEMENTS ON INTRODUCED BILLS AND JOINT RESOLUTIONS

By Mr. CORNYN (for himself and Mr. CASEY):

S. 3496. A bill to amend the Internal Revenue Code of 1986 to allow members of the Ready Reserve of a reserve component of the Armed Forces to make elective deferrals on the basis of their service to the Ready Reserve and on the basis of their other employment; to the Committee on Finance.

Mr. CORNYN. Mr. President, I ask unanimous consent that the text of the bill be printed in the RECORD.

There being no objection, the text of the bill was ordered to be printed in the RECORD, as follows:

S. 3496

Be it enacted by the Senate and House of Representatives of the United States of America in Congress assembled,

SECTION 1. SHORT TITLE.

This Act may be cited as the "Servicemember Retirement Improvement Act".

SEC. 2. ELECTIVE DEFERRALS BY MEMBERS OF THE READY RESERVE OF A RESERVE COMPONENT OF THE ARMED FORCES.

(a) IN GENERAL.—Section 402(g) of the Internal Revenue Code of 1986 is amended by adding at the end the following new paragraph:

"(9) ELECTIVE DEFERRALS BY MEMBERS OF READY RESERVE.—

"(A) IN GENERAL.—In the case of a qualified ready reservist (other than a specified Federal employee ready reservist) for any taxable year, the limitations of subparagraphs (A) and (C) of paragraph (1) shall be applied separately with respect to—

"(i) elective deferrals of such qualified ready reservist with respect to the Thrift Savings Fund (as defined in section 7701(j)), and

"(ii) any other elective deferrals of such qualified ready reservist.

"(B) SPECIAL RULE FOR FEDERAL EMPLOYEES IN THE READY RESERVE NOT ELIGIBLE TO MAKE ELECTIVE DEFERRALS TO A PLAN OTHER THAN

THE THRIFT SAVINGS PLAN.—In the case of a specified Federal employee ready reservist for any taxable year—

"(i) the applicable dollar amount in effect under paragraph (1)(B) for such taxable year shall be twice such amount (as determined without regard to this subclause), and

"(ii) for purposes of paragraph (1)(C), the applicable dollar amount under section 414(v)(2)(B)(i) (as otherwise determined for purposes of paragraph (1)(C)) shall be twice such amount (as determined without regard to this subclause).

"(C) DEFINITIONS.—For purposes of this paragraph—

"(i) QUALIFIED READY RESERVIST.—The term 'qualified ready reservist' means any individual for any taxable year if such individual received compensation for service as a member of the Ready Reserve of a reserve component (as defined in section 101 of title 37, United States Code) during such taxable year.

"(ii) SPECIFIED FEDERAL EMPLOYEE READY RESERVIST.—The term 'specified Federal employee ready reservist' means any individual for any taxable year if such individual—

"(I) is a qualified ready reservist for such taxable year,

"(II) would be eligible to make elective deferrals with respect to the Thrift Savings Fund (as defined in section 7701(j)) during such taxable year determined without regard to the service of such individual described in clause (i), and

"(III) is not eligible to make elective deferrals with respect to any plan other than such Thrift Savings Fund during such taxable year.".

(b) EFFECTIVE DATE.—The amendment made by this section shall apply to taxable years beginning after the date of the enactment of this Act.

By Mr. DAINES (for himself and Mr. BOOKER):

S. 3502. A bill to require the Federal Aviation Administration to establish annual performance objectives and to hold the Chief NextGen Officer accountable for meeting such objectives; to the Committee on Commerce, Science, and Transportation.

Mr. DAINES. Mr. President, in 2003, Congress mandated the Next Generation Air Transportation System known as NextGen, transitioning our radar-based system with radio communication to a satellite-based one, to increase safety and efficiency. NextGen deployment has been bogged with delays and cost overruns, highlighted by Government Accountability Office reports. Final implementation is to be completed by 2025. This legislation would simply create measurable annual performance goals and hold federal officials accountable to meeting these goals through the remainder of implementation.

I want to thank Senator BOOKER for being original cosponsors of this bill and I ask my other Senate colleagues to join us in support of this legislation.

Mr. President, I ask unanimous consent that the text of the bill be printed in the RECORD.

There being no objection, the text of the bill was ordered to be printed in the RECORD, as follows:

S. 3502

Be it enacted by the Senate and House of Representatives of the United States of America in Congress assembled,

SECTION 1. SHORT TITLE.

This Act may be cited as the "NextGen Accountability Act".

SEC. 2. NEXTGEN ANNUAL PERFORMANCE GOALS.

Section 214 of the FAA Modernization and Reform Act of 2012 (Public Law 112–95; 49 U.S.C. 40101 note) is amended—

(1) by redesignating subsection (d) as subsection (e); and

(2) by inserting after subsection (c) the following:

"(d) ANNUAL PERFORMANCE GOALS.—The Administrator shall establish annual NextGen performance goals for each of the performance metrics set forth in subsection (a) to meet the performance metric baselines identified under subsection (b). Such goals shall be established in consultation with public and private NextGen stakeholders, including the NextGen Advisory Committee.".

SEC. 3. NEXTGEN METRICS REPORT.

Section 710(e)(2) of the Vision 100—Century of Aviation Reauthorization Act (Public Law 108–176; 49 U.S.C. 40101 note) is amended—

(1) in subparagraph (D), by striking "and" at the end;

(2) in subparagraph (E), by striking the period at the end and inserting "; and"; and

(3) by adding at the end the following:

"(F) a description of the progress made in meeting the annual NextGen performance goals relative to the performance metrics established under section 214 of the FAA Modernization and Reform Act of 2012 (Public Law 112–95; 49 U.S.C. 40101 note).".

SEC. 4. CHIEF NEXTGEN OFFICER.

Section 106(s) of title 49, United States Code, is amended—

(1) in paragraph (2)(B), by adding at the end the following: "In evaluating the performance of the Chief NextGen Officer for the purpose of awarding a bonus under this subparagraph, the Administrator shall consider the progress toward meeting the NextGen performance goals established pursuant to section 214(d) of the FAA Modernization and Reform Act of 2012 (Public Law 112–95; 49 U.S.C. 40101 note)"; and

(2) in paragraph (3), by adding at the end the following: "The annual performance goals set forth in the agreement shall include quantifiable NextGen airspace performance objectives regarding efficiency, productivity, capacity, and safety, which shall be established in consultation with public and private NextGen stakeholders, including the NextGen Advisory Committee.".

SUBMITTED RESOLUTIONS

SENATE RESOLUTION 629—RECOGNIZING THE 225TH ANNIVERSARY OF ALEXANDER HAMILTON'S SEMINAL REPORT ON THE SUBJECT OF MANUFACTURES

Mr. COONS (for himself and Mr. GRAHAM) submitted the following resolution; which was referred to the Committee on Commerce, Science, and Transportation:

S. RES. 629

Whereas December 5, 2016, is the 225th anniversary of Alexander Hamilton's landmark Report on the Subject of Manufactures (referred to in this preamble as the "Hamilton report"), which he delivered on December 5, 1791;

Whereas the groundbreaking Hamilton report stressed the importance of a diversified national economy in which manufacturing, alongside agriculture, contributes significantly to economic health;

Whereas Alexander Hamilton promoted a modern economic vision years ahead of his time based on investment, industry, internal improvements, and expanded commerce;

Whereas the Hamilton report had its roots in President George Washington's first annual message to Congress on January 8, 1790, when he argued that the people of the United States should promote manufacturing to make the United States independent of other nations for essential supplies, particularly military supplies;

Whereas the House of Representatives then requested the Secretary of the Treasury prepare a report describing plans to encourage "manufactories" that would promote that independence;

Whereas the Hamilton report recognized that the Federal Government could take steps to encourage innovation in the manufacturing sector, and recommended government promotion of manufacturing through incentives to encourage risk taking and innovation, as well as reasonable and flexible tariffs to counter Great Britain's mercantilist system;

Whereas Alexander Hamilton was one of the Founding Fathers, a delegate to the Constitutional Convention, a major author of the Federalist papers, a signatory to the Constitution of the United States, the first Secretary of the Treasury, and the founder of the First Bank of the United States and the Coast Guard;

Whereas Alexander Hamilton founded the Society for the Establishment of Useful Manufactures in Paterson, New Jersey, which became an important center for manufacturing production and innovation;

Whereas Alexander Hamilton used his influence to define the role of the Federal Government in promoting a sound financial foundation for the young nation;

Whereas manufacturing is critical to the United States economy, and contributes approximately $2,170,000,000,000 to the United States economy annually;

Whereas manufacturing makes an outsized contribution to the United States economy in terms of total output and employment, and supports more than 17,000,000 indirect jobs in the United States and approximately 12,000,000 individuals directly employed in manufacturing, more than 1/5 (21.3 percent) of total employment in the United States in 2013;

Whereas manufacturing represents more than 11 percent of the United States economy, and accounts for approximately 70 percent of industry-funded research and development;

Whereas manufacturing is entering a dynamic new phase, with new market opportunities in the developing world, game-changing innovations in materials and processes (including composites and nanomaterials, 3-D printing, and advanced robotics), and increased competition across the world;

Whereas manufacturing makes substantial contributions in the United States economy to research and development, exports, and productivity growth;

Whereas the number of manufacturing jobs coming into the United States, through reshoring and foreign direct investment, is now equal to or slightly higher than the number of jobs leaving the United States, which contributes to the manufacturing rebound;

Whereas manufacturing firms have a critical role in innovation, engaging new technologies that improve processes, support product innovation, and create well-paying jobs; and

Whereas the brand "Made in the USA" carries tremendous weight and appeal across the world: Now, therefore, be it

Resolved, That the Senate—

(1) recognizes the 225th anniversary of Alexander Hamilton's seminal Report on the Subject of Manufactures;

(2) recognizes the vision of Alexander Hamilton to make a case for a strong and diversified economy, which has withstood the test of time;

(3) expresses admiration and appreciation for the variety of ways in which Alexander Hamilton contributed to the success of the young United States;

(4) acknowledges the importance of the manufacturing industry's contributions to the United States in promoting innovation, job creation, and opportunity for the middle class; and

(5) supports efforts to grow and sustain United States manufacturing industries by creating a healthy business climate and establishing the level playing field vital to United States manufacturing success.

SENATE RESOLUTION 630—RECOGNIZING THE HISTORICAL IMPORTANCE OF ASSOCIATE JUSTICE CLARENCE THOMAS

Mr. CORNYN (for himself, Mr. GRASSLEY, Mr. HATCH, Mr. LEE, Mr. SCOTT, and Mr. CRUZ) submitted the following resolution; which was referred to the Committee on the Judiciary:

S. RES. 630

Whereas, in 1948, Clarence Thomas was born outside of Savannah, Georgia, in the small community of Pin Point, Georgia;

Whereas Clarence Thomas was born into poverty and under segregation;

Whereas, notwithstanding his humble beginnings and the many impediments he faced, Clarence Thomas demonstrated incredible intellect, discipline, and strength in attending and graduating from St. Benedict the Moor Catholic School, St. John Vianney Minor Seminar, the College of the Holy Cross, and Yale Law School;

Whereas Clarence Thomas had a distinguished legal career with service in State government and all branches of the Federal Government, including the Senate, the Department of Education, the Equal Employment Opportunity Commission, and the United States Court of Appeals for the District of Columbia Circuit;

Whereas, on July 1, 1991, President George Herbert Walker Bush nominated Clarence Thomas to be an Associate Justice of the Supreme Court of the United States (in this preamble referred to as the "Supreme Court");

Whereas Justice Thomas is the second African American to serve on the Supreme Court;

Whereas, during his quarter century on the Supreme Court, Justice Thomas has made a unique and indelible contribution to the jurisprudence of the United States;

Whereas Justice Thomas has propounded a jurisprudence that seeks to faithfully apply the original meaning of the text of the Constitution of the United States;

Whereas Justice Thomas has brought renewed focus to constitutional doctrines that the Framers intended to undergird our republican form of government, including federalism and the separation of powers;

Whereas, in fostering this philosophy of law, Justice Thomas reinvigorated not only the jurisprudence of the United States, but also the democracy of the United States;

Whereas Justice Thomas has been a remarkably prolific Associate Justice, writing influential opinions on topics including constitutional law, administrative law, and civil rights;

Whereas, on August 10, 1846, in the name of founding an establishment for the increase and diffusion of knowledge, Congress established the Smithsonian Institution as a trust to be administered by a Board of Regents and a Secretary of the Smithsonian Institution;

Whereas diversity, including intellectual diversity, is a core value of the Smithsonian Institution and the museums of the Smithsonian Institution should capitalize on the richness inherent in differences;

Whereas, upon opening, the National Museum of African American History and Culture (in this preamble referred to as the "Museum") is the only national museum devoted exclusively to the documentation of African American life, history, and culture;

Whereas the Museum omits the contribution made by Justice Thomas to the United States; and

Whereas the Senate is hopeful that the Museum will reflect that important contribution: Now, therefore, be it

Resolved, That it is the sense of the Senate that—

(1) Associate Justice Clarence Thomas is a historically significant African American who has—

(A) overcome great challenges;

(B) served his country honorably for more than 35 years; and

(C) made an important contribution to the United States, in particular the jurisprudence of the United States; and

(2) the life and work of Justice Thomas are an important part of the story of African Americans in the United States and should have a prominent place in the National Museum of African American History and Culture.

AMENDMENTS SUBMITTED AND PROPOSED

SA 5127. Mr. McCONNELL (for Mr. SHELBY (for himself and Mr. BROWN)) proposed an amendment to the bill H.R. 5602, to amend title 31, United States Code, to authorize the Secretary of the Treasury to include all funds when issuing certain geographic targeting orders, and for other purposes.

SA 5128. Mr. McCONNELL (for Mrs. ERNST) proposed an amendment to the bill S. 3336, to provide installation reutilization authority for arsenals, depots, and plants.

SA 5129. Mr. McCONNELL (for Mrs. ERNST) proposed an amendment to the bill S. 3336, supra.

SA 5130. Mr. MANCHIN (for himself and Mr. BROWN) submitted an amendment intended to be proposed by him to the bill H.R. 34, to authorize and strengthen the tsunami detection, forecast, warning, research, and mitigation program of the National Oceanic and Atmospheric Administration, and for other purposes; which was ordered to lie on the table.

SA 5131. Ms. WARREN (for herself and Mr. MERKLEY) submitted an amendment intended to be proposed by her to the bill H.R.

34, supra; which was ordered to lie on the table.

SA 5132. Ms. WARREN submitted an amendment intended to be proposed by her to the bill H.R. 34, supra; which was ordered to lie on the table.

SA 5133. Mr. FLAKE submitted an amendment intended to be proposed by him to the bill H.R. 34, supra; which was ordered to lie on the table.

SA 5134. Mr. MERKLEY (for himself and Ms. WARREN) submitted an amendment intended to be proposed by him to the bill H.R. 34, supra; which was ordered to lie on the table.

SA 5135. Mr. MERKLEY submitted an amendment intended to be proposed by him to the bill H.R. 34, supra; which was ordered to lie on the table.

SA 5136. Mr. LEAHY (for himself, Mr. GRASSLEY, Ms. KLOBUCHAR, and Mr. LEE) submitted an amendment intended to be proposed by him to the bill H.R. 34, supra; which was ordered to lie on the table.

SA 5137. Mr. McCONNELL (for himself and Mr. REID) proposed an amendment to the concurrent resolution H. Con. Res. 174, directing the Clerk of the House of Representatives to make a correction in the enrollment of H.R. 34.

TEXT OF AMENDMENTS

SA 5127. Mr. McCONNELL (for Mr. SHELBY (for himself and Mr. BROWN)) proposed an amendment to the bill H.R. 5602, to amend title 31, United States Code, to authorize the Secretary of the Treasury to include all funds when issuing certain geographic targeting orders, and for other purposes; as follows:

Strike all after the enacting clause and insert the following:

TITLE I—ENHANCING ANTITERRORISM TOOLS OF THE DEPARTMENT OF THE TREASURY

SEC. 101. INCLUSION OF ALL FUNDS.

(a) IN GENERAL.—Section 5326 of title 31, United States Code, is amended—

(1) in the heading of such section, by striking "coin and currency";

(2) in subsection (a)—

(A) by striking "subtitle and" and inserting "subtitle or to"; and

(B) in paragraph (1)(A), by striking "United States coins or currency (or such other monetary instruments as the Secretary may describe in such order)" and inserting "funds (as the Secretary may describe in such order),"; and

(3) in subsection (b)—

(A) in paragraph (1)(A), by striking "coins or currency (or monetary instruments)" and inserting "funds"; and

(B) in paragraph (2), by striking "coins or currency (or such other monetary instruments as the Secretary may describe in the regulation or order)" and inserting "funds (as the Secretary may describe in the regulation or order)".

(b) CLERICAL AMENDMENT.—The table of contents for chapter 53 of title 31, United States Code, is amended in the item relating to section 5326 by striking "coin and currency".

SEC. 102. IMPROVING ANTITERROR FINANCE MONITORING OF FUNDS TRANSFERS.

(a) STUDY.—

(1) IN GENERAL.—To improve the ability of the Department of the Treasury to better track cross-border fund transfers and identify potential financing of terrorist or other forms of illicit finance, the Secretary shall carry out a study to assess—

(A) the potential efficacy of requiring banking regulators to establish a pilot program to provide technical assistance to depository institutions and credit unions that wish to provide account services to money services businesses serving individuals in Somalia;

(B) whether such a pilot program could be a model for improving the ability of United States persons to make legitimate funds transfers through transparent and easily monitored channels while preserving strict compliance with the Bank Secrecy Act (Public Law 91–508; 84 Stat. 1114) and related controls aimed at stopping money laundering and the financing of terrorism; and

(C) consistent with current legal requirements regarding confidential supervisory information, the potential impact of allowing money services businesses to share certain State examination information with depository institutions and credit unions, or whether another appropriate mechanism could be identified to allow a similar exchange of information to give the depository institutions and credit unions a better understanding of whether an individual money services business is adequately meeting its anti-money laundering and counter-terror financing obligations to combat money laundering, the financing of terror, or related illicit finance.

(2) PUBLIC INPUT.—The Secretary should solicit and consider public input as appropriate in developing this study.

(b) REPORT.—Not later than 270 days after the date of the enactment of this Act, the Secretary shall submit to the Committee on Financial Services and the Committee on Foreign Affairs of the House of Representatives and the Committee on Banking, Housing, and Urban Affairs and the Committee on Foreign Relations of the Senate a report that contains all findings and determinations made in carrying out the study required under subsection (a).

SEC. 103. SENSE OF CONGRESS ON INTERNATIONAL COOPERATION REGARDING TERRORIST FINANCING INTELLIGENCE.

It is the sense of the Congress that the Secretary, acting through the Under Secretary for Terrorism and Financial Crimes, should intensify work with foreign partners to help the foreign partners develop intelligence analytic capacities, in a finance ministry or other appropriate agency, that are—

(1) commensurate to the threats faced by the foreign partner; and

(2) designed to better integrate intelligence efforts with the anti-money laundering and counter-terrorist financing regimes of the foreign partner.

SEC. 104. EXAMINING THE COUNTER-TERROR FINANCING ROLE OF THE DEPARTMENT OF THE TREASURY IN EMBASSIES.

Not later than 180 days after the enactment of this Act, the Secretary shall submit to the Committee on Financial Services and the Committee on Foreign Affairs of the House of Representatives and the Committee on Banking, Housing, and Urban Affairs and the Committee on Foreign Relations of the Senate a report that contains—

(1) a list of the United States embassies in which a full-time Department of the Treasury financial attaché is stationed and a description of how the interests of the Department of the Treasury relating to terrorist financing and money laundering are addressed (via regional attachés or otherwise) at US embassies where no such attachés are present;

(2) a list of the United States embassies at which the Department of the Treasury has assigned a technical assistance advisor from the Office of Technical Assistance of the Department of the Treasury;

(3) an overview of how Department of the Treasury financial attachés and technical assistance advisors assist in efforts to counter illicit finance, to include money laundering, terrorist financing, and proliferation financing; and

(4) an overview of patterns, trends, or other issues identified by Department of the Treasury attachés and whether resources are sufficient to address these issues.

TITLE II—NATIONAL STRATEGY FOR COMBATING TERRORIST AND OTHER ILLICIT FINANCING

SEC. 201. DEVELOPMENT OF NATIONAL STRATEGY.

(a) IN GENERAL.—The President, acting through the Secretary shall, in consultation with the Attorney General, the Secretary of State, the Secretary of Homeland Security, the Director of National Intelligence, and the appropriate Federal banking agencies, develop a national strategy for combating the financing of terrorism and related forms of illicit finance.

(b) TRANSMITTAL TO CONGRESS.—

(1) IN GENERAL.—Not later than January 31, 2018, the President shall submit to the appropriate congressional committees a comprehensive national strategy developed in accordance with subsection (a).

(2) UPDATES.—Not later than January 31, 2020, and January 31, 2022, the President shall submit to the appropriate congressional committees updated versions of the national strategy submitted under paragraph (1).

(c) SEPARATE PRESENTATION OF CLASSIFIED MATERIAL.—Any part of the national strategy that involves information that is properly classified under criteria established by the President shall be submitted to the Congress separately in a classified annex and, if requested by the chairman or ranking Member of one of the appropriate congressional committees, as a briefing at an appropriate level of security.

SEC. 202. CONTENTS.

(a) IN GENERAL.—The strategy described in section 201 shall contain the following:

(1) EVALUATION OF EXISTING EFFORTS.—An assessment of the effectiveness of and ways in which the United States is currently addressing the highest levels of risk of various forms of illicit finance, including those identified in the documents entitled "2015 National Money Laundering Risk Assessment" and "2015 National Terrorist Financing Risk Assessment", published by the Department of the Treasury and a description of how the strategy is integrated into, and supports, the broader counter terrorism strategy of the United States.

(2) GOALS, OBJECTIVES, AND PRIORITIES.—A comprehensive, research-based, long-range, quantifiable discussion of goals, objectives, and priorities for disrupting and preventing illicit finance activities within and transiting the financial system of the United States that outlines priorities to reduce the incidence, dollar value, and effects of illicit finance.

(3) THREATS.—An identification of the most significant illicit finance threats to the financial system of the United States.

(4) REVIEWS AND PROPOSED CHANGES.—Reviews of enforcement efforts, relevant regulations and relevant provisions of law and, if

appropriate, discussions of proposed changes determined to be appropriate to ensure that the United States pursues coordinated and effective efforts at all levels of government, and with international partners of the United States, in the fight against illicit finance.

(5) DETECTION AND PROSECUTION INITIATIVES.—A description of efforts to improve detection and prosecution of illicit finance, including efforts to ensure that—

(A) subject to legal restrictions, all appropriate data collected by the Federal Government that is relevant to the efforts described in this section be available in a timely fashion to—

(i) all appropriate Federal departments and agencies; and

(ii) as appropriate and consistent with section 314 of the International Money Laundering Abatement and Financial Anti-Terrorism Act of 2001 (31 U.S.C. 5311 note), to financial institutions to assist the financial institutions in efforts to comply with laws aimed at curbing illicit finance; and

(B) appropriate efforts are undertaken to ensure that Federal departments and agencies charged with reducing and preventing illicit finance make thorough use of publicly available data in furtherance of this effort.

(6) THE ROLE OF THE PRIVATE FINANCIAL SECTOR IN PREVENTION OF ILLICIT FINANCE.—A discussion of ways to enhance partnerships between the private financial sector and Federal departments and agencies with regard to the prevention and detection of illicit finance, including—

(A) efforts to facilitate compliance with laws aimed at stopping such illicit finance while maintaining the effectiveness of such efforts; and

(B) providing guidance to strengthen internal controls and to adopt on an industry-wide basis more effective policies.

(7) ENHANCEMENT OF INTERGOVERNMENTAL COOPERATION.—A discussion of ways to combat illicit finance by enhancing—

(A) cooperative efforts between and among Federal, State, and local officials, including State regulators, State and local prosecutors, and other law enforcement officials;

(B) cooperative efforts with and between governments of countries and with and between multinational institutions, including the Financial Action Task Force, with expertise in fighting illicit finance.

(8) TREND ANALYSIS OF EMERGING ILLICIT FINANCE THREATS.—A discussion of and data regarding trends in illicit finance, including evolving forms of value transfer such as so-called cryptocurrencies, other methods that are computer, telecommunications, or Internet-based, cyber crime, or any other threats that the Secretary may choose to identify.

(9) BUDGET PRIORITIES.—A multiyear budget plan that identifies sufficient resources needed to successfully execute the full range of missions called for in this section.

(10) TECHNOLOGY ENHANCEMENTS.—An analysis of current and developing ways to leverage technology to improve the effectiveness of efforts to stop the financing of terrorism and other forms of illicit finance, including better integration of open-source data.

TITLE III—DEFINITIONS

SEC. 301. DEFINITIONS.

In this Act—

(1) the term "appropriate congressional committees" means—

(A) the Committee on Financial Services, the Committee on Foreign Affairs, the Committee on Armed Services, the Committee on the Judiciary, Committee on Homeland Security, and the Permanent Select Committee

on Intelligence of the House of Representatives; and

(B) the Committee on Banking, Housing, and Urban Affairs, the Committee on Foreign Relations, Committee on Armed Services, Committee on the Judiciary, Committee on Homeland Security and Governmental Affairs, and the Select Committee on Intelligence of the Senate;

(2) the term "appropriate Federal banking agencies" has the meaning given the term in section 3 of the Federal Deposit Insurance Act (12 U.S.C. 1813);

(3) the term "Bank Secrecy Act" means—

(A) section 21 of the Federal Deposit Insurance Act (12 U.S.C. 1829b);

(B) chapter 2 of title I of Public Law 91–508 (12 U.S.C. 1951 et seq.); and

(C) subchapter II of chapter 53 of title 31, United States Code;

(4) the term "illicit finance" means the financing of terrorism, money laundering, or other forms of illicit financing domestically or internationally, as defined by the President;

(5) the term "money services business" has the meaning given the term under section 1010.100 of title 31, Code of Federal Regulations;

(6) the term "Secretary" means the Secretary of the Treasury; and

(7) the term "State" means each of the several States, the District of Columbia, and each territory or possession of the United States.

SA 5128. Mr. MCCONNELL (for Mrs. ERNST) proposed an amendment to the bill S. 3336, to provide installation reutilization authority for arsenals, depots, and plants; as follows:

On page 1, strike lines 3 and 4 and insert the following:

SECTION 1. INSTALLATION REUTILIZATION AUTHORITY FOR ARSENALS, DEPOTS, AND PLANTS.

On page 1, line 6, strike "arsenal, the Secretary concerned" and insert "arsenal, depot, or plant, the Secretary of the Army".

On page 2, line 4, insert ", depot, or plant" after "arsenal".

On page 2, line 8, insert ", depot, or plant" after "arsenal".

On page 2, line 12, insert ", depot, or plant" after "arsenal".

On page 2, line 17, strike "Secretary concerned" and insert "Secretary of the Army".

On page 2, line 21, insert ", depot, or plant" after "arsenal".

On page 4, line 3, insert ", DEPOT, OR PLANT" after "ARSENAL".

On page 4, line 5, insert ", depot, or plant" after "arsenal".

On page 4, line 6, strike "Department of the Defense" and insert "Army".

SA 5129. Mr. MCCONNELL (for Mrs. ERNST) proposed an amendment to the bill S. 3336, to provide installation reutilization authority for arsenals, depots, and plants; as follows:

Amend the title so as to read: "A bill to provide installation reutilization authority for arsenals, depots, and plants.".

SA 5130. Mr. MANCHIN (for himself and Mr. BROWN) submitted an amendment intended to be proposed by him to the bill H.R. 34, to authorize and strengthen the tsunami detection, forecast, warning, research, and mitigation program of the National Oceanic and

Atmospheric Administration, and for other purposes; which was ordered to lie on the table; as follows:

At the end, add the following:

TITLE XIX—MINERS PROTECTION

SEC. 19001. SHORT TITLE.

This title may be cited as the "Miners Protection Act of 2016".

SEC. 19002. INCLUSION OF CERTAIN RETIREES IN THE MULTIEMPLOYER HEALTH BENEFIT PLAN.

(a) IN GENERAL.—Section 402 of the Surface Mining Control and Reclamation Act of 1977 (30 U.S.C. 1232) is amended—

(1) in subsection (h)(2)(C)—

(A) by striking "A transfer" and inserting the following:

"(i) TRANSFER TO THE PLAN.—A transfer";

(B) by redesignating clauses (i) and (ii) as subclauses (I) and (II), respectively, and moving such subclauses 2 ems to the right; and

(C) by striking the matter following such subclause (II) (as so redesignated) and inserting the following:

"(ii) CALCULATION OF EXCESS.—The excess determined under clause (i) shall be calculated by taking into account only—

"(I) those beneficiaries actually enrolled in the Plan as of the date of the enactment of the Miners Protection Act of 2016 who are eligible to receive health benefits under the Plan on the first day of the calendar year for which the transfer is made, other than those beneficiaries enrolled in the Plan under the terms of a participation agreement with the current or former employer of such beneficiaries; and

"(II) those beneficiaries whose health benefits, defined as those benefits payable directly following death or retirement or upon a finding of disability by an employer in the bituminous coal industry under a coal wage agreement (as defined in section 9701(b)(1) of the Internal Revenue Code of 1986), would be denied or reduced as a result of a bankruptcy proceeding commenced in 2012 or 2015.

"(iii) ELIGIBILITY OF CERTAIN RETIREES.—Individuals referred to in clause (ii)(II) shall be treated as eligible to receive health benefits under the Plan.

"(iv) REQUIREMENTS FOR TRANSFER.—The amount of the transfer otherwise determined under this subparagraph for a fiscal year shall be reduced by any amount transferred for the fiscal year to the Plan, to pay benefits required under the Plan, from a voluntary employees' beneficiary association established as a result of a bankruptcy proceeding described in clause (ii).

"(v) VEBA TRANSFER.—The administrator of such voluntary employees' beneficiary association shall transfer to the Plan any amounts received as a result of such bankruptcy proceeding, reduced by an amount for administrative costs of such association."; and

(2) in subsection (i)—

(A) by redesignating paragraph (4) as paragraph (5); and

(B) by inserting after paragraph (3) the following:

"(4) ADDITIONAL AMOUNTS.—

"(A) CALCULATION.—If the dollar limitation specified in paragraph (3)(A) exceeds the aggregate amount required to be transferred under paragraphs (1) and (2) for a fiscal year, the Secretary of the Treasury shall transfer an additional amount equal to the difference between such dollar limitation and such aggregate amount to the trustees of the 1974 UMWA Pension Plan to pay benefits required under that plan.

"(B) CESSATION OF TRANSFERS.—The transfers described in subparagraph (A) shall cease as of the first fiscal year beginning after the first plan year for which the funded percentage (as defined in section 432(i)(2) of the Internal Revenue Code of 1986) of the 1974 UMWA Pension Plan is at least 100 percent.

"(C) PROHIBITION ON BENEFIT INCREASES, ETC.—During a fiscal year in which the 1974 UMWA Pension Plan is receiving transfers under subparagraph (A), no amendment of such plan which increases the liabilities of the plan by reason of any increase in benefits, any change in the accrual of benefits, or any change in the rate at which benefits become nonforfeitable under the plan may be adopted unless the amendment is required as a condition of qualification under part I of subchapter D of chapter 1 of the Internal Revenue Code of 1986.

"(D) TREATMENT OF TRANSFERS FOR PURPOSES OF WITHDRAWAL LIABILITY UNDER ERISA.—The amount of any transfer made under subparagraph (A) (and any earnings attributable thereto) shall be disregarded in determining the unfunded vested benefits of the 1974 UMWA Pension Plan and the allocation of such unfunded vested benefits to an employer for purposes of determining the employer's withdrawal liability under section 4201.

"(E) REQUIREMENT TO MAINTAIN CONTRIBUTION RATE.—A transfer under subparagraph (A) shall not be made for a fiscal year unless the persons that are obligated to contribute to the 1974 UMWA Pension Plan on the date of the transfer are obligated to make the contributions at rates that are no less than those in effect on the date which is 30 days before the date of enactment of the Miners Protection Act of 2016.

"(F) ENHANCED ANNUAL REPORTING.—

"(i) IN GENERAL.—Not later than the 90th day of each plan year beginning after the date of enactment of the Miners Protection Act of 2016, the trustees of the 1974 UMWA Pension Plan shall file with the Secretary of the Treasury or the Secretary's delegate and the Pension Benefit Guaranty Corporation a report (including appropriate documentation and actuarial certifications from the plan actuary, as required by the Secretary of the Treasury or the Secretary's delegate) that contains—

"(I) whether the plan is in endangered or critical status under section 305 of the Employee Retirement Income Security Act of 1974 and section 432 of the Internal Revenue Code of 1986 as of the first day of such plan year;

"(II) the funded percentage (as defined in section 432(i)(2) of such Code) as of the first day of such plan year, and the underlying actuarial value of assets and liabilities taken into account in determining such percentage;

"(III) the market value of the assets of the plan as of the last day of the plan year preceding such plan year;

"(IV) the total value of all contributions made during the plan year preceding such plan year;

"(V) the total value of all benefits paid during the plan year preceding such plan year;

"(VI) cash flow projections for such plan year and either the 6 or 10 succeeding plan years, at the election of the trustees, and the assumptions relied upon in making such projections;

"(VII) funding standard account projections for such plan year and the 9 succeeding plan years, and the assumptions relied upon in making such projections;

"(VIII) the total value of all investment gains or losses during the plan year preceding such plan year;

"(IX) any significant reduction in the number of active participants during the plan year preceding such plan year, and the reason for such reduction;

"(X) a list of employers that withdrew from the plan in the plan year preceding such plan year, and the resulting reduction in contributions;

"(XI) a list of employers that paid withdrawal liability to the plan during the plan year preceding such plan year and, for each employer, a total assessment of the withdrawal liability paid, the annual payment amount, and the number of years remaining in the payment schedule with respect to such withdrawal liability;

"(XII) any material changes to benefits, accrual rates, or contribution rates during the plan year preceding such plan year;

"(XIII) any scheduled benefit increase or decrease in the plan year preceding such plan year having a material effect on liabilities of the plan;

"(XIV) details regarding any funding improvement plan or rehabilitation plan and updates to such plan;

"(XV) the number of participants and beneficiaries during the plan year preceding such plan year who are active participants, the number of participants and beneficiaries in pay status, and the number of terminated vested participants and beneficiaries;

"(XVI) the information contained on the most recent annual funding notice submitted by the plan under section 101(f) of the Employee Retirement Income Security Act of 1974;

"(XVII) the information contained on the most recent Department of Labor Form 5500 of the plan; and

"(XVIII) copies of the plan document and amendments, other retirement benefit or ancillary benefit plans relating to the plan and contribution obligations under such plans, a breakdown of administrative expenses of the plan, participant census data and distribution of benefits, the most recent actuarial valuation report as of the plan year, copies of collective bargaining agreements, and financial reports, and such other information as the Secretary of the Treasury or the Secretary's delegate, in consultation with the Secretary of Labor and the Director of the Pension Benefit Guaranty Corporation, may require.

"(ii) ELECTRONIC SUBMISSION.—The report required under clause (i) shall be submitted electronically.

"(iii) INFORMATION SHARING.—The Secretary of the Treasury or the Secretary's delegate shall share the information in the report under clause (i) with the Secretary of Labor.

"(iv) PENALTY.—Any failure to file the report required under clause (i) on or before the date described in such clause shall be treated as a failure to file a report required to be filed under section 6058(a) of the Internal Revenue Code of 1986, except that section 6652(e) of such Code shall be applied with respect to any such failure by substituting '$100' for '$25'. The preceding sentence shall not apply if the Secretary of the Treasury or the Secretary's delegate determines that reasonable diligence has been exercised by the trustees of such plan in attempting to timely file such report.

"(G) 1974 UMWA PENSION PLAN DEFINED.—For purposes of this paragraph, the term '1974 UMWA Pension Plan' has the meaning given the term in section 9701(a)(3) of the Internal Revenue Code of 1986, but without regard to the limitation on participation to individuals who retired in 1976 and thereafter.".

(b) EFFECTIVE DATES.—

(1) IN GENERAL.—The amendments made by this section shall apply to fiscal years beginning after September 30, 2016.

(2) REPORTING REQUIREMENTS.—Section 402(i)(4)(F) of the Surface Mining Control and Reclamation Act of 1977 (30 U.S.C. 1232(i)(4)(F)), as added by this section, shall apply to plan years beginning after the date of the enactment of this Act.

SEC. 19003. CLARIFICATION OF FINANCING OBLIGATIONS.

(a) IN GENERAL.—Subsection (a) of section 9704 of the Internal Revenue Code of 1986 is amended—

(1) by striking paragraph (3),

(2) by striking "three premiums" and inserting "two premiums", and

(3) by striking ", plus" at the end of paragraph (2) and inserting a period.

(b) CONFORMING AMENDMENTS.—

(1) Section 9704 of the Internal Revenue Code of 1986 is amended—

(A) by striking subsection (d), and

(B) by redesignating subsections (e) through (j) as subsections (d) through (i), respectively.

(2) Subsection (d) of section 9704 of such Code, as so redesignated, is amended—

(A) by striking "3 separate accounts for each of the premiums described in subsections (b), (c), and (d)" in paragraph (1) and inserting "2 separate accounts for each of the premiums described in subsections (b) and (c)", and

(B) by striking "or the unassigned beneficiaries premium account" in paragraph (3)(B).

(3) Subclause (I) of section 9703(b)(2)(C)(ii) of such Code is amended by striking "9704(e)(3)(B)(i)" and inserting "9704(d)(3)(B)(i)".

(4) Paragraph (3) of section 9705(a) of such Code is amended—

(A) by striking "the unassigned beneficiary premium under section 9704(a)(3) and" in subparagraph (B), and

(B) by striking "9704(i)(1)(B)" and inserting "9704(h)(1)(B)".

(5) Paragraph (2) of section 9711(c) of such Code is amended—

(A) by striking "9704(j)(2)" in subparagraph (A)(i) and inserting "9704(i)(2)",

(B) by striking "9704(j)(2)(B)" in subparagraph (B) and inserting "9704(i)(2)(B)", and

(C) by striking "9704(j)" and inserting "9704(i)".

(6) Paragraph (4) of section 9712(d) of such Code is amended by striking "9704(j)" and inserting "9704(i)".

(c) ELIMINATION OF ADDITIONAL BACKSTOP PREMIUM.—

(1) IN GENERAL.—Paragraph (1) of section 9712(d) of the Internal Revenue Code of 1986 is amended by striking subparagraph (C).

(2) CONFORMING AMENDMENT.—Paragraph (2) of section 9712(d) of such Code is amended—

(A) by striking subparagraph (B),

(B) by striking ", and" at the end of subparagraph (A) and inserting a period, and

(C) by striking "shall provide for—" and all that follows through "annual adjustments" and inserting "shall provide for annual adjustments".

(d) EFFECTIVE DATE.—The amendments made by this section shall apply to plan years beginning after September 30, 2016.

SEC. 19004. CUSTOMS USER FEES.

(a) IN GENERAL.—Section 13031(j)(3)(A) of the Consolidated Omnibus Budget Reconciliation Act of 1985 (19 U.S.C. 58c(j)(3)(A)) is amended by striking "September 30, 2025" and inserting "May 6, 2026".

(b) RATE FOR MERCHANDISE PROCESSING FEES.—Section 503 of the United States-Korea Free Trade Agreement Implementation Act (Public Law 112–41; 19 U.S.C. 3805 note) is amended by striking "September 30, 2025" and inserting "May 6, 2026".

SA 5131. Ms. WARREN (for herself and Mr. MERKLEY) submitted an amendment intended to be proposed by her to the bill H.R. 34, to authorize and strengthen the tsunami detection, forecast, warning, research, and mitigation program of the National Oceanic and Atmospheric Administration, and for other purposes; which was ordered to lie on the table; as follows:

Strike section 3037.

SA 5132. Ms. WARREN submitted an amendment intended to be proposed by her to the bill H.R. 34, to authorize and strengthen the tsunami detection, forecast, warning, research, and mitigation program of the National Oceanic and Atmospheric Administration, and for other purposes; which was ordered to lie on the table; as follows:

Strike section 3033.

SA 5133. Mr. FLAKE submitted an amendment intended to be proposed by him to the bill H.R. 34, to authorize and strengthen the tsunami detection, forecast, warning, research, and mitigation program of the National Oceanic and Atmospheric Administration, and for other purposes; which was ordered to lie on the table; as follows:

At the end, add the following:

DIVISION C—FEDERAL RESEARCH TRANSPARENCY AND ACCOUNTABILITY

SEC. 20001. SHORT TITLE.

This division may be cited as the "Federal Research Transparency and Accountability Act of 2016".

SEC. 20002. DEFINITIONS.

In this division—

(1) the term "agency" has the meaning given the term in section 551 of title 5, United States Code; and

(2) the term "covered study" means any study that—

(A) is carried out in whole or in part with Federal funds; and

(B) is published, presented at a conference or meeting, or otherwise made publicly available.

SEC. 20003. FEDERALLY FUNDED RESEARCH DISCLOSURES AND DATABASE.

(a) PREVENTION OF DUPLICATIVE RESEARCH FUNDING.—The Director of the Office of Management and Budget shall coordinate with each agency that provides funding to entities to carry out research and development to establish a system to detect potential duplicative applications for funding in order to prevent duplicative funding.

(b) DATABASE OF FEDERALLY FUNDED RESEARCH AND DEVELOPMENT.—

(1) IN GENERAL.—Each agency shall include in a publicly accessible database a searchable listing of each unclassified research and development project that is funded by the agency, including a contract, grant, cooperative agreement, or task order.

(2) CONTENTS.—A database described in paragraph (1) shall, with respect to each unclassified research and development project of an agency, contain—

(A) the agency component that is carrying out or providing funding or other assistance for the project;

(B) the name of the project;

(C) an abstract or summary of the project;

(D) the funding level for the project;

(E) the duration of the project;

(F) the name of any contractor, subcontractor, or grantee;

(G) the title of any published study funded by or related to the project; and

(H) expected objectives and milestones for the project.

(3) EXISTING DATABASE.—An agency may satisfy the requirements under this subsection if the Director of the Office of Management and Budget determines that the agency maintains a publicly accessible database, including a database operated by or shared with another agency, that substantially meets the requirements of this subsection.

(c) REQUIREMENT FOR ACKNOWLEDGMENT IN COVERED STUDIES.—The acknowledgment section in each covered study shall include—

(1) the name of each agency that provided funding for the covered study;

(2) the project or award number associated with the covered study; and

(3) an estimate of the total cost of the covered study.

(d) STUDY.—Not later than 2 years after the date of enactment of this Act, the Comptroller General of the United States shall conduct a study and make publicly available a report, which shall—

(1) analyze the compliance of agencies, contractors, subcontractors, and grantees with the requirements of this division;

(2) identify any obstacles that remain to prevent the public from accessing the cost and findings of covered studies and other research and development projects funded by agencies; and

(3) analyze efforts by agencies to prevent duplicative spending.

SA 5134. Mr. MERKLEY (for himself and Ms. WARREN) submitted an amendment intended to be proposed by him to the bill H.R. 34, to authorize and strengthen the tsunami detection, forecast, warning, research, and mitigation program of the National Oceanic and Atmospheric Administration, and for other purposes; which was ordered to lie on the table; as follows:

Strike sections 5009 and 5011.

SA 5135. Mr. MERKLEY submitted an amendment intended to be proposed by him to the bill H.R. 34, to authorize and strengthen the tsunami detection, forecast, warning, research, and mitigation program of the National Oceanic and Atmospheric Administration, and for other purposes; which was ordered to lie on the table; as follows:

Strike sections 5002, 5003, 5004, and 5012 of division A.

SA 5136. Mr. LEAHY (for himself, Mr. GRASSLEY, Ms. KLOBUCHAR, and Mr. LEE) submitted an amendment intended to be proposed by him to the bill H.R. 34, to authorize and strengthen the tsunami detection, forecast, warning, research, and mitigation program of the National Oceanic and Atmospheric Administration, and for other purposes; which was ordered to lie on the table; as follows:

At the end of title III of division A, add the following:

Subtitle K—CREATES Act

SEC. 3201. SHORT TITLE.

This subtitle may be cited as the "Creating and Restoring Equal Access to Equivalent Samples Act of 2016" or the "CREATES Act of 2016".

SEC. 3202. FINDINGS.

Congress finds the following:

(1) It is the policy of the United States to promote competition in the market for drugs and biological products by facilitating the timely entry of low-cost generic and biosimilar versions of those drugs and biological products.

(2) Since their enactment in 1984 and 2010, respectively, the Drug Price Competition and Patent Term Restoration Act of 1984 (Public Law 98–417; 98 Stat. 1585) and the Biologics Price Competition and Innovation Act of 2009 (Subtitle A of title VII of Public Law 111–148; 124 Stat. 804), have provided pathways for making lower-cost versions of previously approved drugs and previously licensed biological products available to the people of the United States in a timely manner, thereby lowering overall prescription drug costs for patients and taxpayers by billions of dollars each year.

(3) In order for these pathways to function as intended, developers of generic drugs and biosimilar biological products (referred to in this section as "generic product developers") must be able to obtain quantities of the reference listed drug or biological product with which the generic drug or biosimilar biological product is intended to compete (referred to in this section as a "covered product") for purposes of supporting an application for approval by the Food and Drug Administration, including for testing to show that—

(A) a prospective generic drug is bioequivalent to the covered product in accordance with subsection (j) of section 505 of the Federal, Food, Drug, and Cosmetic Act (21 U.S.C. 355), or meets the requirements for approval of an application submitted under subsection (b)(2) of that section; or

(B) a prospective biosimilar biological product is biosimilar to or interchangeable with its reference biological product under section 351(k) of the Public Health Service Act (42 U.S.C. 262(k)), as applicable.

(4) For drugs and biological products that are subject to a risk evaluation and mitigation strategy, another essential component in the creation of low-cost generic and biosimilar versions of covered products is the ability of generic product developers to join the manufacturer of the covered product (referred to in this section as the "license holder") in a single, shared system of elements to assure safe use and supporting agreements, or secure a variance therefrom, as required by section 505–1 of the Federal Food, Drug, and Cosmetic Act (21 U.S.C. 355–1).

(5) Contrary to the policy of the United States to promote competition in the market for drugs and biological products by facilitating the timely entry of lower-cost generic and biosimilar versions of those drugs

and biological products, certain license holders are preventing generic product developers from obtaining quantities of the covered product necessary for the generic product developer to support an application for approval by the Food and Drug Administration, including testing to show bioequivalence, biosimilarity, or interchangeability to the covered product, in some instances based on the justification that the covered product is subject to a risk evaluation and mitigation strategy with elements to assure safe use under section 505–1 of the Federal Food, Drug, and Cosmetic Act (21 U.S.C. 355–1).

(6) The Director of the Center for Drug Evaluation and Research at the Food and Drug Administration has testified that some manufacturers of covered products have used REMS and distribution restrictions adopted by the manufacturer on their own behalf as reasons to not sell quantities of a covered product to generic product developers, causing barriers and delays in getting generic products on the market. The Food and Drug Administration has reported receiving significant numbers of inquiries from generic product developers who were unable to obtain samples of covered products to conduct necessary testing and otherwise meet requirements for approval of generic drugs.

(7) The Chairwoman of the Federal Trade Commission has testified that the Federal Trade Commission continues to be very concerned about potential abuses by manufacturers of brand drugs of REMS or other closed distribution systems to impede generic competition.

(8) Also contrary to the policy of the United States to promote competition in the market for drugs and biological products by facilitating the timely entry of lower-cost generic and biosimilar versions of those drugs and biological products, certain license holders are impeding the prompt negotiation and development on commercially reasonable terms of a single, shared system of elements to assure safe use, which may be necessary for the generic product developer to gain approval for its drug or licensing for its biological product.

(9) While the antitrust laws may address the refusal by some license holders to provide quantities of a covered product to a generic product developer, a more tailored legal pathway would help ensure that generic product developers can obtain necessary quantities of a covered product in a timely way for purposes of developing a generic drug or biosimilar biological product, facilitating competition in the marketplace for drugs and biological products.

(10) The antitrust laws may address actions by license holders who impede the prompt negotiation and development of a single, shared system of elements to assure safe use, and the Food and Drug Administration has some authority to waive the requirement of a single, shared system. Clearer regulatory authority to approve different systems that meet the statutory requirements to ensure patient safety, however, would limit the effectiveness of bad faith negotiations over single, shared systems to delay generic approval. At the same time, clearer regulatory authority would ensure all systems protect patient safety.

SEC. 3203. ACTIONS FOR DELAYS OF GENERIC DRUGS AND BIOSIMILAR BIOLOGICAL PRODUCTS.

(a) DEFINITIONS.—In this section—

(1) the term "covered product"—

(A) means—

(i) any drug approved under subsection (b) or (j) of section 505 of the Federal Food, Drug, and Cosmetic Act (21 U.S.C. 355) or biological product licensed under subsection (a) or (k) of section 351 of the Public Health Service Act (42 U.S.C. 262);

(ii) any combination of a drug or biological product described in clause (i); or

(iii) when reasonably necessary to demonstrate sameness, biosimilarity, or interchangeability for purposes of section 505 of the Federal Food, Drug, and Cosmetic Act (21 U.S.C. 355), or section 351 of the Public Health Service Act (42 U.S.C. 262), as applicable, any product, including any device, that is marketed or intended for use with such drug or biological product; and

(B) does not include any drug or biological product that the Secretary has determined to be currently in shortage and that appears on the drug shortage list in effect under section 506E of the Federal Food, Drug, and Cosmetic Act (21 U.S.C. 356e), unless the shortage will not be promptly resolved—

(i) as demonstrated by the fact that the drug or biological product has been in shortage for more than 6 months; or

(ii) as otherwise determined by the Secretary;

(2) the term "device" has the meaning given the term in section 201 of the Federal Food, Drug, and Cosmetic Act (21 U.S.C. 321);

(3) the term "eligible product developer" means a person that seeks to develop a product for approval pursuant to an application for approval under subsection (b)(2) or (j) of section 505 of the Federal Food, Drug, and Cosmetic Act (21 U.S.C. 355) or for licensing pursuant to an application under section 351(k) of the Public Health Service Act (42 U.S.C. 262(k));

(4) the term "license holder" means the holder of an application approved under subsection (c) or (j) of section 505 of the Federal Food, Drug, and Cosmetic Act (21 U.S.C. 355) or the holder of a license under subsection (a) or (k) of section 351 of the Public Health Service Act (42 U.S.C. 262) for a covered product;

(5) the term "REMS" means a risk evaluation and mitigation strategy under section 505–1 of the Federal Food, Drug, and Cosmetic Act (21 U.S.C. 355–1);

(6) the term "REMS with ETASU" means a REMS that contains elements to assure safe use under section 505–1 of the Federal Food, Drug, and Cosmetic Act (21 U.S.C. 355–1);

(7) the term "Secretary" means the Secretary of Health and Human Services;

(8) the term "single, shared system of elements to assure safe use" means a single, shared system of elements to assure safe use under section 505–1 of the Federal Food, Drug, and Cosmetic Act (21 U.S.C. 355–1); and

(9) the term "sufficient quantities" means an amount of a covered product that allows the eligible product developer to—

(A) conduct testing to support an application—

(i) for approval under subsection (b)(2) or (j) of section 505 of the Federal Food, and Cosmetic Act (21 U.S.C. 355); or

(ii) for licensing under section 351(k) of the Public Health Service Act (42 U.S.C. 262(k)); and

(B) fulfill any regulatory requirements relating to such an application for approval or licensing.

(b) CIVIL ACTION FOR FAILURE TO PROVIDE SUFFICIENT QUANTITIES OF A COVERED PRODUCT.—

(1) IN GENERAL.—An eligible product developer may bring a civil action against the license holder for a covered product seeking relief under this subsection in an appropriate district court of the United States alleging that the license holder has declined to provide sufficient quantities of the covered product to the eligible product developer on commercially reasonable, market-based terms.

(2) ELEMENTS.—

(A) IN GENERAL.—To prevail in a civil action brought under paragraph (1), an eligible product developer shall prove, by a preponderance of the evidence—

(i) that—

(I) the covered product is not subject to a REMS with ETASU; or

(II) if the covered product is subject to a REMS with ETASU—

(aa) the eligible product developer has obtained a covered product authorization from the Secretary in accordance with subparagraph (B); and

(bb) the eligible product developer has provided a copy of the covered product authorization to the license holder;

(ii) that, as of the date on which the civil action is filed, the product developer has not obtained sufficient quantities of the covered product on commercially reasonable, market-based terms;

(iii) that the eligible product developer has requested to purchase sufficient quantities of the covered product from the license holder; and

(iv) that the license holder has not delivered to the eligible product developer sufficient quantities of the covered product on commercially reasonable, market-based terms—

(I) for a covered product that is not subject to a REMS with ETASU, by the date that is 31 days after the date on which the license holder received the request for the covered product; and

(II) for a covered product that is subject to a REMS with ETASU, by 31 days after the later of—

(aa) the date on which the license holder received the request for the covered product; or

(bb) the date on which the license holder received a copy of the covered product authorization issued by the Secretary in accordance with subparagraph (B).

(B) AUTHORIZATION FOR COVERED PRODUCT SUBJECT TO A REMS WITH ETASU.—

(i) REQUEST.—An eligible product developer may submit to the Secretary a written request for the eligible product developer to be authorized to obtain sufficient quantities of an individual covered product subject to a REMS with ETASU.

(ii) AUTHORIZATION.—Not later than 90 days after the date on which a request under clause (i) is received, the Secretary shall, by written notice, authorize the eligible product developer to obtain sufficient quantities of an individual covered product subject to a REMS with ETASU for purposes of—

(I) development and testing that does not involve human clinical trials, if the eligible product developer has agreed to comply with any conditions the Secretary determines necessary; or

(II) development and testing that involves human clinical trials, if the eligible product developer has—

(aa)(AA) submitted protocols, informed consent documents, and informational materials for testing that include protections that provide safety protections comparable to those provided by the REMS for the covered product; or

(BB) otherwise satisfied the Secretary that such protections will be provided; and

(bb) met any other requirements the Secretary may establish.

(iii) NOTICE.—A covered product authorization issued under this subparagraph shall state that the provision of the covered product by the license holder under the terms of the authorization will not be a violation of the REMS for the covered product.

(3) AFFIRMATIVE DEFENSE.—In a civil action brought under paragraph (1), it shall be an affirmative defense, on which the defendant has the burden of persuasion by a preponderance of the evidence—

(A) that, on the date on which the eligible product developer requested to purchase sufficient quantities of the covered product from the license holder—

(i) neither the license holder nor any of its agents, wholesalers, or distributors was engaged in the manufacturing or commercial marketing of the covered product; and

(ii) neither the license holder nor any of its agents, wholesalers, or distributors otherwise had access to inventory of the covered product to supply to the eligible product developer on commercially reasonable, market-based terms; or

(B) that—

(i) the license holder sells the covered product through agents, distributors, or wholesalers;

(ii) the license holder has placed no restrictions, explicit or implicit, on its agents, distributors, or wholesalers to sell covered products to eligible product developers; and

(iii) the covered product can be purchased by the eligible product developer in sufficient quantities on commercially reasonable, market-based terms from the agents, distributors, or wholesalers of the license holder.

(4) REMEDIES.—

(A) IN GENERAL.—If an eligible product developer prevails in a civil action brought under paragraph (1), the court shall—

(i) order the license holder to provide to the eligible product developer without delay sufficient quantities of the covered product on commercially reasonable, market-based terms;

(ii) award to the eligible product developer reasonable attorney fees and costs of the civil action; and

(iii) award to the eligible product developer a monetary amount sufficient to deter the license holder from failing to provide other eligible product developers with sufficient quantities of a covered product on commercially reasonable, market-based terms, if the court finds, by a preponderance of the evidence—

(I) that the license holder delayed providing sufficient quantities of the covered product to the eligible product developer without a legitimate business justification; or

(II) that the license holder failed to comply with an order issued under clause (i).

(B) MAXIMUM MONETARY AMOUNT.—A monetary amount awarded under subparagraph (A)(iii) shall not be greater than the revenue that the license holder earned on the covered product during the period—

(i) beginning on—

(I) for a covered product that is not subject to a REMS with ETASU, the date that is 31 days after the date on which the license holder received the request; or

(II) for a covered product that is subject to a REMS with ETASU, the date that is 31 days after the later of—

(aa) the date on which the license holder received the request; or

(bb) the date on which the license holder received a copy of the covered product authorization issued by the Secretary in accordance with paragraph (2)(B); and

(ii) ending on the date on which the eligible product developer received sufficient quantities of the covered product.

(C) AVOIDANCE OF DELAY.—The court may issue an order under subparagraph (A)(i) before conducting further proceedings that may be necessary to determine whether the eligible product developer is entitled to an award under clause (ii) or (iii) of subparagraph (A), or the amount of any such award.

(c) LIMITATION OF LIABILITY.—A license holder for a covered product shall not be liable for any claim arising out of the failure of an eligible product developer to follow adequate safeguards to assure safe use of the covered product during development or testing activities described in this section, including transportation, handling, use, or disposal of the covered product by the eligible product developer.

(d) RULE OF CONSTRUCTION.—

(1) DEFINITION.—In this subsection, the term "antitrust laws"—

(A) has the meaning given the term in subsection (a) of the first section of the Clayton Act (15 U.S.C. 12); and

(B) includes section 5 of the Federal Trade Commission Act (15 U.S.C. 45) to the extent that such section applies to unfair methods of competition.

(2) ANTITRUST LAWS.—Nothing in this section shall be construed to limit the operation of any provision of the antitrust laws.

SEC. 3204. REMS APPROVAL PROCESS FOR SUBSEQUENT FILERS.

Section 505–1 of the Federal Food Drug and Cosmetic Act (21 U.S.C. 355–1) is amended—

(1) in subsection (g)(4)(B)—

(A) in clause (i) by striking "or" after the semicolon;

(B) in clause (ii) by striking the period at the end and inserting "; or"; and

(C) by adding at the end the following:

"(iii) accommodate different approved risk evaluation and mitigation strategies for a reference drug product and a drug that is the subject of an abbreviated new drug application."; and

(2) in subsection (i)(1), by striking subparagraph (B) and inserting the following:

"(B) Elements to assure safe use, if required under subsection (f) for the listed drug.

"(i) Subject to clause (ii), a drug that is the subject of an abbreviated new drug application may use—

"(I) a single, shared system with the listed drug under subsection (f); or

"(II) a different, comparable aspect of the elements to assure safe use under subsection (f).

"(ii) The Secretary may require a drug that is the subject of an abbreviated new drug application and the listed drug to use a single, shared system under subsection (f), if the Secretary determines that no different, comparable aspect of the elements to assure safe use could satisfy the requirements of subsection (f).".

SA 5137. Mr. McCONNELL (for himself and Mr. REID) proposed an amendment to the concurrent resolution H. Con. Res. 174, directing the Clerk of the House of Representatives to make a correction in the enrollment of H.R. 34; as follows:

Beginning on page 1, line 7, strike "following correction:" and all that follows and insert the following:

"following corrections:

"(1) Amend the long title so as to read: 'An Act to accelerate the discovery, development, and delivery of 21st century cures, and for other purposes.'.

"(2) Amend the section heading for section 1001 so as to read: '**BEAU BIDEN CANCER MOONSHOT AND NIH INNOVATION PROJECTS**'.

"(3) Amend the table of contents in section 1 so that the item relating to section 1001 reads as follows:

"'1001. Beau Biden Cancer Moonshot and NIH innovation projects.'.".

ACTION VITIATED—H.R. 5602, S. 3336, AND CALENDAR NOS. 675 THROUGH 683

Mr. MORAN. Mr. President, I ask unanimous consent to vitiate all action taken during today's session of the Senate on H.R. 5602, S. 3336, and Calendar Nos. 675 through 683.

The PRESIDING OFFICER. Without objection, it is so ordered.

ORDERS FOR TUESDAY, DECEMBER 6, 2016

Mr. MORAN. Mr. President, I ask unanimous consent that when the Senate completes its business today, it adjourn until 10 a.m., Tuesday, December 6; that following the prayer and pledge, the morning hour be deemed expired, the Journal of proceedings be approved to date, and the time for the two leaders be reserved for their use later in the day; further, that following leader remarks, the Senate resume consideration of the House message to accompany H.R. 34 postcloture; finally, that all time during adjournment and recess of the Senate count postcloture on the motion to concur.

The PRESIDING OFFICER. Without objection, it is so ordered.

ADJOURNMENT UNTIL 10 A.M. TOMORROW

Mr. MORAN. Mr. President, if there is no further business to come before the Senate, I ask unanimous consent that it stand adjourned under the previous order.

There being no objection, the Senate, at 6:52 p.m., adjourned until Tuesday, December 6, 2016, at 10 a.m.

HOUSE OF REPRESENTATIVES—*Monday, December 5, 2016*

The House met at noon and was called to order by the Speaker pro tempore (Mr. DENHAM).

DESIGNATION OF SPEAKER PRO TEMPORE

The SPEAKER pro tempore laid before the House the following communication from the Speaker:

WASHINGTON, DC,
December 5, 2016.

I hereby appoint the Honorable JEFF DENHAM to act as Speaker pro tempore on this day.

PAUL D. RYAN,
Speaker of the House of Representatives.

MORNING-HOUR DEBATE

The SPEAKER pro tempore. Pursuant to the order of the House of January 5, 2016, the Chair will now recognize Members from lists submitted by the majority and minority leaders for morning-hour debate.

The Chair will alternate recognition between the parties, with each party limited to 1 hour and each Member other than the majority and minority leaders and the minority whip limited to 5 minutes, but in no event shall debate continue beyond 1:50 p.m.

CELEBRATING CARTER HANSON, A GAGLIARDI RECIPIENT

The SPEAKER pro tempore. The Chair recognizes the gentleman from Minnesota (Mr. EMMER) for 5 minutes.

Mr. EMMER of Minnesota. Mr. Speaker, I rise today to celebrate one of Minnesota's most promising student athletes, St. John's linebacker Carter Hanson. Carter has been chosen as one of the semifinalists for the prestigious Gagliardi Trophy.

This trophy is named after the former St. John's University Hall of Fame, renowned football coach John Gagliardi and is given to the best Division III football player of the year. Carter Hanson has started every season for 4 years, was a preseason All-American, and this year led his team in tackles.

Carter doesn't just excel on the football field, but in the classroom and the community as well. He has maintained a 4.0 grade point average for 4 years, and this year, he has been selected as the only Division III finalist for the National Football Foundation's Campbell Trophy, which is given to the best student athlete in football.

Carter is a global business leadership major. He has already put his degree to good work by volunteering in Haiti and for organizations like Kids Against Hunger and St. Jude Children's Research Hospital.

I am proud that a young man like Carter hails from the great State of Minnesota, and I am positive that we are going to see great accomplishments from him in the future.

The winner of the Gagliardi Trophy will be announced shortly, and while there is great competition, I am convinced that no one is more deserving than Carter Hanson.

CELEBRATING MIKE GOHMAN OF W. GOHMAN CONSTRUCTION

Mr. EMMER of Minnesota. Mr. Speaker, I rise today to celebrate Mike Gohman of W. Gohman Construction for being named Builder of the Year by the Builders Association of Minnesota.

W. Gohman Construction was established in 1950 by Mike's grandfather, Willard Gohman, out of his shed. Like many of Minnesota's small businesses, this company has evolved and grown. Today Mike is the third generation to own and run this incredible company, and he continually works to uphold the integrity that his father and his grandfather started.

To Mike, it has never been just about the success of his company, but of the building industry as a whole. He has been an active member of the Builders Association of Minnesota and the Central Minnesota Builders Association, working to represent his and other companies throughout the St. Cloud community and our State.

Mike always goes above and beyond by hosting job site tours, advocating for the building industry at the State capitol, as well as educating elected officials on the issues and concerns of his field. He even recently represented his company and industry at a roundtable we hosted to explain their concerns about our Nation's failing healthcare system.

Mike is a true asset to our community and the building industry. He is well deserving of being named Builder of the Year.

Congratulations, Mike.

DODD-FRANK

Mr. EMMER of Minnesota. Mr. Speaker, the consequences of the Great Recession have been all too real: homes and jobs lost, retirement plans ruined, and fewer opportunities for Americans from all walks of life. Unfortunately, Dodd-Frank has further entrenched the too-big-to-fail bailout mentality, done little to reduce the likelihood of another severe recession, and hindered economic growth.

Thankfully, the Systemic Risk Designation Improvement Act amends the one-size-fits-all approach to regulation taken by Dodd-Frank for large banks, providing a more tailored assessment of these financial institutions when determining their level of risk. This law will require regulators to examine a range of indicators—not just the size of a bank—to understand whether or not a bank could threaten the financial integrity of the United States and whether it should be designated as systemically important. This reform will provide a more pragmatic approach to regulation, which will make the American economy stronger.

I want to thank Mr. LUETKEMEYER and Chairman HENSARLING for their leadership on this issue and those who supported it when it passed in the House last week.

RECESS

The SPEAKER pro tempore. Pursuant to clause 12(a) of rule I, the Chair declares the House in recess until 2 p.m. today.

Accordingly (at 12 o'clock and 5 minutes p.m.), the House stood in recess.

□ 1400

AFTER RECESS

The recess having expired, the House was called to order by the Speaker pro tempore (Mr. WOMACK) at 2 p.m.

PRAYER

The Chaplain, the Reverend Patrick J. Conroy, offered the following prayer:

Loving and gracious God, we give You thanks for giving us another day.

We ask today that You bless the Members of the people's House, to be the best and most faithful servants of the people they serve.

May they be filled with gratitude at the opportunity they have to serve in this place. We thank You for the abilities they have been given to do their work, to contribute to the common good.

As this second session of the 114th Congress draws near its end, and legislative business once again weighs heavily on this Hill, withhold not Your spirit of wisdom and truth from this assembly. Give each Member clarity of thought and purity of motive so that they may render their service as their best selves.

In this time of waiting, as people of faith prepare for holy celebrations,

---

bless our Nation with peace and good will. May all Americans of whatever faith or background work together to build a commonweal, something which can only be accomplished by Your grace.

May all that is done this day in the people's House, be for Your greater honor and glory.

Amen.

THE JOURNAL

The SPEAKER pro tempore. The Chair has examined the Journal of the last day's proceedings and announces to the House his approval thereof.

Pursuant to clause one, rule I, the Journal stands approved.

PLEDGE OF ALLEGIANCE

The SPEAKER pro tempore. Will the gentleman from South Carolina (Mr. WILSON) come forward and lead the House in the Pledge of Allegiance.

Mr. WILSON of South Carolina led the Pledge of Allegiance as follows:

I pledge allegiance to the Flag of the United States of America, and to the Republic for which it stands, one nation under God, indivisible, with liberty and justice for all.

HONORING AIR FORCE LIEUTENANT COLONEL ROCKO RODRIGUEZ

(Mr. WILSON of South Carolina asked and was given permission to address the House for 1 minute and to revise and extend his remarks.)

Mr. WILSON of South Carolina. Mr. Speaker, today, I am grateful to express my appreciation to Lieutenant Colonel Rocko Rodriguez, U.S. Air Force, of San Antonio, Texas.

For the past year, I have had the privilege of working alongside Rocko in the office as he served the people of South Carolina's Second Congressional District as a defense fellow on assignment from the Air Force.

Lieutenant Colonel Rodriguez was commissioned in 2001, through the Officer Training School at Maxwell Air Force Base, Alabama. He distinguished himself early as a leader, holding various positions in special operations and cyber operations. Rocko has served honorably in Operations Iraqi and Enduring Freedom, Southern Watch, and Deny Flight.

Rocko is a dedicated member of the Air Force with academic achievements. He will graduate from the Air Force Legislative Fellowship program this Thursday and will receive his masters of science degree from Georgetown University Government Affairs Institute. Lieutenant Colonel Rodriguez will soon be transitioning to work at the U.S. Cyber Command Legislative Affairs Branch.

I wish Rocko, his wife, Sarah, and his four children, Kaitlyn, Natalie, Troy,

and Timothy, all the best for continued success.

In conclusion, God bless our troops, and may the President, by his actions, never forget September the 11th in the global war on terrorism.

RECOGNIZING EL DORADO SPRINGS CHAMBER OF COMMERCE

(Mrs. HARTZLER asked and was given permission to address the House for 1 minute.)

Mrs. HARTZLER. Mr. Speaker, today, I rise to recognize the El Dorado Springs Chamber of Commerce, which was honored among the 200 local chambers as the 2016 Missouri Small Chamber of Commerce of the Year.

The title is much deserved as the El Dorado Springs Chamber of Commerce, under Executive Director Jackson Tough, has been a leader in promoting economic development, community service, and tourism in the area.

I am honored to represent this distinguished organization.

With around 125 members, the chamber has created a number of initiatives to better its community, including the "Clean-Up ElDo Mo" project to keep the city pristine, a youth scholarship fund to make sure tomorrow's leaders have the opportunities they need today, and a social media initiative "Be in the Know about ElDo Mo" to raise awareness about this wonderful city and its residents.

Communities like El Dorado Springs are the foundation of Missouri and our way of life. Thanks to the hard work and dedication of these chamber leaders, we continue to sustain and strengthen our communities.

I applaud the chamber's work to grow and sustain its community, recognizing its specific assets and opportunities, and I congratulate the chamber on all its accomplishments.

CONGRATULATING NEW DEMOCRAT COALITION LEADERSHIP

(Mr. PETERS asked and was given permission to address the House for 1 minute.)

Mr. PETERS. Mr. Speaker, I rise today to congratulate the newly elected leadership of the New Democrat Coalition.

Our new chair, JIM HIMES, and newly elected co-chairs, JARED POLIS, SUZAN DELBENE, TERRI SEWELL, and DEREK KILMER, are strong, bipartisan pro-growth leaders. They bring the vision and experience to guide the New Democrat Coalition in the 115th Congress.

New Dems are pragmatic leaders who stand up for working families and work across the aisle to expand economic opportunity. They are focused on creating jobs and building an economy that leaves no one behind, a mission that will not change under the next administration.

I am eager to work with our new leadership—and our 54 members—as we continue to make the New Democrat Coalition the home for strong civil rights and sensible, bipartisan, pro-growth policy in Congress.

COMMUNICATION FROM THE CLERK OF THE HOUSE

The SPEAKER pro tempore laid before the House the following communication from the Clerk of the House of Representatives:

OFFICE OF THE CLERK,
HOUSE OF REPRESENTATIVES,
Washington, DC, December 2, 2016.
Hon. PAUL D. RYAN,
The Speaker, House of Representatives,
Washington, DC.

DEAR MR. SPEAKER: Pursuant to the permission granted in Clause 2(h) of Rule II of the Rules of the U.S. House of Representatives, the Clerk received the following message from the Secretary of the Senate on December 2, 2016, at 1:35 p.m.:

That the Senate passed with an amendment H.R. 1561.

That the Senate agrees to the amendment of the House S. 2577.

With best wishes, I am,
Sincerely,
KAREN L. HAAS.

ANNOUNCEMENT BY THE SPEAKER PRO TEMPORE

The SPEAKER pro tempore. Under clause 5(d) of rule XX, the Chair announces to the House that, in light of the resignation of the gentlewoman from California (Ms. HAHN), the whole number of the House is 434.

RESIGNATION FROM THE HOUSE OF REPRESENTATIVES

The SPEAKER pro tempore laid before the House the following resignation from the House of Representatives:

CONGRESS OF THE UNITED STATES,
HOUSE OF REPRESENTATIVES,
Washington, DC, December 2, 2016.
Speaker PAUL D. RYAN,
Washington, DC.

DEAR SPEAKER RYAN: I hereby tender my resignation from the U.S. House of Representatives effective midnight on December 31, 2016. It has been my distinct honor to serve the people of Michigan's Tenth Congressional District for the past 14 years and I look forward to continuing my life in public service.

Sincerely,
CANDICE S. MILLER,
Member of Congress.

CONGRESS OF THE UNITED STATES,
HOUSE OF REPRESENTATIVES,
Washington, DC, December 2, 2016.
Governor RICK SNYDER,
Lansing, MI.

DEAR GOVERNOR SNYDER: I hereby tender my resignation from the U.S. House of Representatives effective midnight on December 31, 2016. It has been my distinct honor to serve the people of Michigan's Tenth Congressional District for the past 14 years and

I look forward to continuing my life in public service.

Sincerely,

CANDICE S. MILLER,
Member of Congress.

RECESS

The SPEAKER pro tempore. Pursuant to clause 12(a) of rule I, the Chair declares the House in recess until approximately 4:30 p.m. today.

Accordingly (at 2 o'clock and 7 minutes p.m.), the House stood in recess.

□ 1630

AFTER RECESS

The recess having expired, the House was called to order by the Speaker pro tempore (Mr. ROTHFUS) at 4 o'clock and 30 minutes p.m.

ANNOUNCEMENT BY THE SPEAKER PRO TEMPORE

The SPEAKER pro tempore. Pursuant to clause 8 of rule XX, the Chair will postpone further proceedings today on motions to suspend the rules on which a recorded vote or the yeas and nays are ordered, or on which the vote incurs objection under clause 6 of rule XX.

Record votes on postponed questions will be taken later.

ENHANCING WHISTLEBLOWER PROTECTION FOR CONTRACTOR AND GRANTEE EMPLOYEES

Mr. CHAFFETZ. Mr. Speaker, I move to suspend the rules and pass the bill (S. 795) to enhance whistleblower protection for contractor and grantee employees.

The Clerk read the title of the bill.

The text of the bill is as follows:

S. 795

Be it enacted by the Senate and House of Representatives of the United States of America in Congress assembled,

SECTION 1. ENHANCEMENT OF WHISTLEBLOWER PROTECTION FOR CONTRACTOR AND GRANTEE EMPLOYEES.

(a) PROTECTION FOR EMPLOYEES OF GRANTEES AND SUBGRANTEES.—

(1) DEFENSE GRANTS.—Section 2409(a)(1) of title 10, United States Code, is amended by inserting "or personal services contractor" after "subgrantee".

(2) CIVILIAN GRANTS.—Section 4712(a)(1) of title 41, United States Code, is amended by striking "or grantee" and inserting "grantee, or subgrantee or personal services contractor".

(3) PERMANENT EXTENSION OF PILOT PROGRAM FOR ENHANCEMENT OF CONTRACTOR PROTECTION FROM REPRISAL FOR DISCLOSURE OF CERTAIN INFORMATION.—

(A) IN GENERAL.—Section 4712 of title 41, United States Code, is amended—

(i) in the section heading by striking "**Pilot program for enhancement**" and inserting "**Enhancement**"; and

(ii) by striking subsection (i).

(B) CLERICAL AMENDMENT.—The table of sections at the beginning of chapter 47 of title 41, United States Code, is amended by striking the item relating to section 4712 and inserting the following new item:

"4712. Enhancement of contractor protection from reprisal for disclosure of certain information.".

(b) PROHIBITION ON REIMBURSEMENT FOR LEGAL FEES ACCRUED IN DEFENSE AGAINST REPRISAL CLAIMS.—

(1) DEFENSE CONTRACTS.—Section 2324(k) of title 10, United States Code, is amended—

(A) by inserting "or subcontractor, or personal services contractor" after "contractor" each place it appears;

(B) by inserting ", subcontract, or personal services contract" after "contract" each place it appears; and

(C) in paragraph (1), by inserting "or to any other activity described in subparagraphs (A) through (C) of section 2409(a)(1) of this title" after "statute or regulation".

(2) CIVILIAN CONTRACTS.—

(A) IN GENERAL.—Section 4310 of title 41, United States Code, is amended—

(i) by inserting ", subcontractor, or personal services contractor" after "contractor" each place it appears;

(ii) by inserting ", subcontract, or personal services contract" after "contract" each place it appears; and

(iii) in subsection (b)(1), by inserting "or to any other activity described in section 4712(a)(1) of this title" after "statute or regulation".

(B) CONFORMING AMENDMENT.—Section 4304(a)(15) of title 41, United States Code, is amended by inserting "or subcontractor, or personal service contractor" after "contractor".

(c) INCLUSION OF CONTRACT CLAUSE IN CONTRACTS AWARDED BEFORE EFFECTIVE DATE.—At the time of any major modification to a contract that was awarded before the date of the enactment of this Act, the head of the contracting agency shall make best efforts to include in the contract a contract clause providing for the applicability of the amendments made by this section and section 827 of the National Defense Authorization Act for Fiscal Year 2013 (Public Law 112–239; 126 Stat. 1833).

The SPEAKER pro tempore. Pursuant to the rule, the gentleman from Utah (Mr. CHAFFETZ) and the gentleman from Maryland (Mr. CUMMINGS) each will control 20 minutes.

The Chair recognizes the gentleman from Utah.

GENERAL LEAVE

Mr. CHAFFETZ. Mr. Speaker, I ask unanimous consent that all Members may have 5 legislative days in which to revise and extend their remarks and include extraneous materials on the bill under consideration.

The SPEAKER pro tempore. Is there objection to the request of the gentleman from Utah?

There was no objection.

Mr. CHAFFETZ. I yield myself such time as I may consume.

Mr. Speaker, I rise today in support of this bill, S. 795, a bill to enhance whistleblower protection for contractor and grantee employees. It is a bill with good bipartisan support in both Chambers of Congress.

I really do applaud and thank, in particular, the gentleman from Maryland (Mr. CUMMINGS), the ranking member on our committee, who has helped champion this and point this out and lead our efforts in the House on this.

In the House, the Committee on Oversight and Government Reform considered an identical bill, the Whistleblower Protections for Contractors Act, introduced by Ranking Member CUMMINGS and myself, and the committee reported this legislation by unanimous consent. In the Senate, it has been Senators MCCASKILL and RON JOHNSON who have worked arm in arm on this and are also very supportive of it. Today we bring up the Senate version of this bill to expedite its approval to get this bill to the President's desk.

As you know, Mr. Speaker, whistleblowers are invaluable to the oversight work of Congress. We rely on people who are on the front lines seeing things as they truly are to provide information and blow the whistle when they see something going awry. They are one of our best sources of information about waste, fraud, and abuse within the Federal Government.

As an institution, we should try to do everything we can to encourage them to come and speak with us, and when they do, to make sure that they have the proper and adequate protections. That is exactly what this bill does, by recognizing that not all whistleblowers are Federal employees. We have robust Federal recognition and whistleblower protection for Federal employees, and we believe that contractors and others should have that as well.

It makes permanent a successful pilot program that extended whistleblower protections to civilian contractor and grantee employees. It also ensures whistleblower protections are extended to subgrantees and personal services contractors for both defense and civilian contractors. It is important because the Federal Government spends half a trillion dollars a year on grants and contracts. Think about that; half a trillion dollars is going out the door. There is always somebody doing something stupid somewhere; so to have this protection for a whistleblower as a contractor, for instance, just seems wise and prudent.

In overseeing how these funds are spent, the best source for rooting out waste is from grantees, subgrantees, contractors, and subcontractors. One loophole this bill closes is that personal services contractors were not protected in the past. These contractors can be just as valuable in identifying the waste and fraud we are committed to preventing in the first place. It only makes sense to offer those personal services contractors the same protections we give other contractors.

With this bill, we are sending a strong message to both whistleblowers and their employers. We are serious about stopping waste, fraud, and abuse, and we are serious about protecting those who bring that information forward. Every dollar of wasted funds comes from the pocket of the same hardworking men and women who elected us to Congress. It is their money. It is not our money. It is not the Federal Government's money. It is the taxpayers' money.

As we work to protect these taxpayer dollars, we also have a duty and responsibility to protect these whistleblowers. They are the best allies we have. S. 795 accomplishes that goal. An identical bill was passed out of our committee. I would appreciate the support of our colleagues to further this.

Again, I thank Mr. CUMMINGS for his good work and passion on this.

Mr. Speaker, I reserve the balance of my time.

Mr. CUMMINGS. Mr. Speaker, I yield myself such time as I may consume.

Mr. Speaker, I rise in strong support of S. 795. I introduced the House companion of this legislation, the Whistleblower Protections for Contractors Act. We are taking up the Senate measure today to make sure this bill can be signed by the President before the end of this Congress.

I want to thank Senator MCCASKILL for all of her hard work and Senator JOHNSON for all that he did to make this bill come to this point.

I would also like to give special thanks to Chairman CHAFFETZ for being an original cosponsor and helping bring this bill to the floor. Our committee has always stood hand in hand with regard to protecting whistleblowers, and we have made it abundantly clear that we will do everything in our power to protect them from any type of retaliation or any type of harm.

Whistleblowers are the front line of defense against waste, fraud, and abuse. Employees who work on Federal contracts and grants see firsthand when taxpayer money is being wasted. They risk their careers to challenge abuses of power and mismanagement of government resources. They must be protected against retaliation when they blow the whistle on wrongdoing.

Just the other day, we had a witness come before our committee, and it was clear that she was very, very concerned about retaliation to the point of almost being shaken. You could actually see it. When we see these folks, we realize and we are reminded of the fact that they bring a very important resource to us as the Committee on Oversight and Government Reform, and that is they bring us information, information that allows us to be able to address problems that we wouldn't even know about if it were not for them.

I thank Chairman CHAFFETZ and our entire committee for taking the attitude of protecting whistleblowers to the greatest extent we possibly can.

This bill would ensure that more employees are protected by giving sub-grantees and personal services contractors the same whistleblower protections currently given to contractors, grant recipients, and subcontractors. This bill also would make protections for civilian contractors and grantees permanent. These are protections that contractors and grantees of the Department of Defense already enjoy.

I urge every Member of Congress to stand up for whistleblowers, to stand up for good government, and to pass this legislation.

Mr. Speaker, I urge all Members to vote in favor of this very important and meaningful legislation.

I yield back the balance of my time.

Mr. CHAFFETZ. Mr. Speaker, I urge adoption.

I yield back the balance of my time.

Ms. JACKSON LEE. Mr. Speaker, I rise in support of S. 795, a bill to enhance whistleblower protection for contractor and grantee employees.

The Government Accountability Project, a leading U.S. organization in support of Federal whistleblower laws, supports without qualifications S. 795, legislation to make permanent a pilot program that provides whistleblower rights for employees of government contractors.

The "Pilot program for enhancement of contractor protection from reprisal for disclosure of certain information" (pilot program) was established under 41 U.S.C. § 4712, as an amendment to the FY2012 National Defense Authorization Act (NDAA).

Federal whistleblower protection laws are not new; they provide a means for government employees to report waste, fraud, and abuse of taxpayer resources.

I support this bill because the bill extends federal contractor whistleblower protections to employees of:

(1) personal services contractors working on defense contracts (currently, the protections apply to employees of defense contractors, subcontractors, grantees, or sub-grantees); and

(2) personal services contractors or sub-grantees working on federal civilian contracts (currently, the protections apply to employees of civilian contractors, subcontractors, or grantees).

This bill would codify a pilot program that is already in place that allows employees of civilian contractors to report waste, fraud, and abuse and make permanent the civilian contractor protections.

S. 795 extends whistleblower protections to employees of subcontractors to report waste, fraud and abuse of federal taxpayer dollars.

Whistleblower disclosures by Federal contract employees can save lives as well as billions of taxpayer dollars.

For example, Section 1553 of the Obama Administration's American Recovery and Reinvestment Act of 2009 (ARRA) established whistleblower protections for all recipients of stimulus funds, including all state and local government employees and all contractors, including within the IC.

That provision was credited with the low rate of fraud reported around stimulus funds.

During the Congressional oversight hearings, the Chair of the Legislation Committee of the Council of Inspectors General on Integrity and Efficiency (CIGIE) testified that:

OIGs indicated that their investigations and reviews of the whistleblower complaints had resulted in recovery of approximately $1.85 million as of April of the first year it was in force.

One of the key provisions of ARRA is Section 1553 that gives the authority of OIGs to investigate reprisal complaints from non-Federal employee whistleblowers.

Federal whistleblower protection laws play a critical role in keeping our Government honest, efficient, and accountable by rooting out waste, fraud, and abuse as well as protecting public health and safety.

Whistleblowers can be some of the most powerful tools in the federal government arsenal to protect taxpayer dollars.

For example, the Securities and Exchange Commission finds of great assistance information from whistleblowers who know of possible securities law violations that could be among the most powerful weapons in the law enforcement arsenal of the Securities and Exchange Commission.

According to USASpending.gov, in Fiscal Year 2015, the Federal government spent over $1 trillion in contracts and grants—$438 billion in contracts and $614 billion in grants.

If this bill does not pass, contractors and grantees are in danger of losing hard-fought whistleblower protections if current protections are not extended.

This bill makes those protections permanent, ensuring that contractors and grantees continue to have the security they need to report waste, fraud and abuse of taxpayer dollars.

Much of this funding flows through the prime contractors and grantees to subcontractors and sub-grantees.

The bill applies to subcontractors' existing prohibitions on reimbursable costs for contractors, including in their defense against retaliation claims by whistleblowers.

Federal taxpayers should not foot the legal bills for contractors who retaliate against employees that report waste, fraud and abuse of taxpayer dollars.

The SPEAKER pro tempore. The question is on the motion offered by the gentleman from Utah (Mr. CHAFFETZ) that the House suspend the rules and pass the bill, S. 795.

The question was taken; and (two-thirds being in the affirmative) the rules were suspended and the bill was passed.

A motion to reconsider was laid on the table.

"APOLLO 11" 50TH ANNIVERSARY COMMEMORATIVE COIN ACT

Mr. POSEY. Mr. Speaker, I move to suspend the rules and pass the bill (H.R. 2726) to require the Secretary of the Treasury to mint commemorative coins in recognition of the 50th anniversary of the first manned landing on the Moon, as amended.

The Clerk read the title of the bill.

The text of the bill is as follows:

H.R. 2726

Be it enacted by the Senate and House of Representatives of the United States of America in Congress assembled,

SECTION 1. SHORT TITLE.

This Act may be cited as the "Apollo 11 50th Anniversary Commemorative Coin Act".

SEC. 2. FINDINGS.

The Congress finds the following:

(1) On July 16, 1969, the Apollo 11 spacecraft launched from Launch Complex 39A at the John F. Kennedy Space Center carrying Neil Armstrong, Buzz Aldrin, and Michael Collins, who would become the first of mankind to complete a crewed lunar landing.

(2) The United States is the only country ever to have attempted and succeeded in landing humans on a celestial body off the Earth and safely returning them home, completing an unprecedented engineering, scientific and political achievement.

(3) The Apollo 11 mission, culminating in man's first steps on the Moon on July 20, 1969, honored the fallen astronauts of the Apollo 1 crew, whose innovative work and bravery will be remembered forever.

(4) Apollo 11 accomplished the national goal set forth in 1961 by President John F. Kennedy, who stated at Rice University the following year, "We choose to go to the Moon. We choose to go to the Moon in this decade and do the other things, not because they are easy, but because they are hard, because that goal will serve to organize and measure the best of our energies and skills, because that challenge is one that we are willing to accept, one we are unwilling to postpone, and one which we intend to win".

(5) At the height of the Cold War, the Apollo space program provided the United States and the free world with a powerful symbolic win, demonstrating the strength, ambition, and determination of the United States in technological and economic advancement, and securing our Nation's leadership in space for generations to come.

(6) The National Aeronautics and Space Administration's (referred to in this Act as "NASA") Marshall Space Flight Center in Huntsville, Alabama, designed, assembled, and tested the most powerful launch vehicle in history, the Saturn V rocket, which was used for the Apollo missions in the 1960s and 1970s.

(7) The Saturn V weighed 6,200,000 pounds and generated 7,600,000 pounds of thrust, which NASA has equated to generating more power than 86 Hoover Dams.

(8) During the time period from 1969 through 1972, NASA completed eight Apollo missions and landed 12 men on the Moon. The six missions that landed on the Moon returned with a wealth of groundbreaking scientific data and over 800 pounds of lunar samples.

(9) An estimated 400,000 Americans contributed to the successful program that led to the lunar landing on July 20, 1969, including NASA scientists, engineers, astronauts, industry contractors and their engineering and manufacturing workforce, as well as the political leadership of Republicans and Democrats in Congress and the White House.

(10) The Apollo program, along with its predecessor Mercury and Gemini programs, inspired generations of American students to pursue careers in science, technology, engineering, and mathematics (STEM), which has fueled innovation and economic growth throughout a range of industries over the last four decades.

(11) July 20, 2019, will mark the 50th anniversary of the Apollo 11 landing of Neil Armstrong and Buzz Aldrin on the lunar surface.

SEC. 3. COIN SPECIFICATIONS.

(a) DENOMINATIONS.—In recognition and celebration of the 50th anniversary of the first manned Moon landing, the Secretary of the Treasury (hereafter in this Act referred to as the "Secretary") shall mint and issue the following coins:

(1) $5 GOLD COINS.—Not more than 50,000 $5 coins, which shall—

(A) weigh 8.359 grams;

(B) be struck on a planchet having a diameter of 0.850 inches; and

(C) contain not less than 90 percent gold.

(2) $1 SILVER COINS.—Not more than 400,000 $1 coins, which shall—

(A) weigh 26.73 grams;

(B) be struck on a planchet having a diameter of 1.500 inches; and

(C) contain not less than 90 percent silver.

(3) HALF-DOLLAR CLAD COINS.—Not more than 750,000 half-dollar coins which shall—

(A) weigh 11.34 grams;

(B) be struck on a planchet having a diameter of 1.205 inches; and

(C) be minted to the specifications for half-dollar coins contained in section 5112(b) of title 31, United States Code.

(4) PROOF SILVER $1 COINS.—Not more than 100,000 proof $1 silver coins which shall—

(A) weigh 5 ounces;

(B) be struck on a planchet having a diameter of 3 inches; and

(C) contain .999 fine silver.

(b) LEGAL TENDER.—The coins minted under this Act shall be legal tender, as provided in section 5103 of title 31, United States Code.

(c) NUMISMATIC ITEMS.—For purposes of sections 5134 and 5136 of title 31, United States Code, all coins minted under this Act shall be considered to be numismatic items.

(d) CONVEX SHAPE.—

(1) IN GENERAL.—The coins minted under this Act shall be produced in a fashion similar to the 2014 National Baseball Hall of Fame 75th Anniversary Commemorative Coin, so that the reverse of the coin is convex to more closely resemble the visor of the astronaut's helmet of the time and the obverse concave, providing a more dramatic display of the obverse design chosen pursuant to section 4(c).

(2) SENSE OF CONGRESS.—It is the sense of Congress that, to the extent possible without significantly adding to the purchase price of the coins, the coins minted under this Act should be produced with the design of the reverse of the coins continuing over what would otherwise be the edge of the coins, such that the reverse design extends all the way to the obverse design.

SEC. 4. DESIGN OF COINS.

(a) IN GENERAL.—The design for the coins minted under this Act shall be—

(1) selected by the Secretary after consultation with—

(A) the Commission of Fine Arts; and

(B) with respect to the design of the reverse of the coins, the Administrator of NASA; and

(2) reviewed by the Citizens Coinage Advisory Committee.

(b) DESIGNATIONS AND INSCRIPTIONS.—On each coin minted under this Act there shall be—

(1) a designation of the denomination of the coin;

(2) an inscription of the year "2019"; and

(3) inscriptions of the words "Liberty", "In God We Trust", "United States of America", and "E Pluribus Unum".

(c) SELECTION AND APPROVAL PROCESS FOR OBVERSE DESIGN.—

(1) IN GENERAL.—The Secretary shall hold a juried, compensated competition to determine the design of the common obverse of the coins minted under this Act, with such design being emblematic of the United States space program leading up to the first manned Moon landing.

(2) SELECTION PROCESS.—Proposals for the obverse design of coins minted under this Act may be submitted in accordance with the design selection and approval process developed by the Secretary in the sole discretion of the Secretary.

(3) PROPOSALS.—As part of the competition described in this subsection, the Secretary may accept proposals from artists, engravers of the United States Mint, and members of the general public, and any designs submitted for the design review process described herein shall be anonymized until a final selection is made.

(4) COMPENSATION.—The Secretary shall determine compensation for the winning design under this subsection, which shall be not less than $5,000.

(d) REVERSE DESIGN.—The design on the common reverse of the coins minted under this Act shall be a representation of a close-up of the famous "Buzz Aldrin on the Moon" photograph taken July 20, 1969, that shows just the visor and part of the helmet of astronaut Buzz Aldrin, in which the visor has a mirrored finish and reflects the image of the United States flag and the lunar lander and the remainder of the helmet has a frosted finish.

SEC. 5. ISSUANCE OF COINS.

(a) QUALITY OF COINS.—Except with respect to coins described under section 3(a)(4), coins minted under this Act shall be issued in uncirculated and proof qualities.

(b) PERIOD FOR ISSUANCE.—The Secretary may issue coins minted under this Act only during the 1-year period beginning on January 1, 2019.

SEC. 6. SALE OF COINS.

(a) SALE PRICE.—The coins issued under this Act shall be sold by the Secretary at a price equal to the sum of—

(1) the face value of the coins;

(2) the surcharge provided in section 7(a) with respect to such coins; and

(3) the cost of designing and issuing the coins (including labor, materials, dies, use of machinery, winning design compensation, overhead expenses, marketing, and shipping).

(b) BULK SALES.—The Secretary shall make bulk sales of the coins issued under this Act at a reasonable discount.

(c) PREPAID ORDERS.—

(1) IN GENERAL.—The Secretary shall accept prepaid orders for the coins minted under this Act before the issuance of such coins.

(2) DISCOUNT.—Sale prices with respect to prepaid orders under paragraph (1) shall be at a reasonable discount.

SEC. 7. SURCHARGES.

(a) IN GENERAL.—All sales of coins minted under this Act shall include a surcharge as follows:

(1) A surcharge of $35 per coin for the $5 coin.

(2) A surcharge of $10 per coin for the $1 coin described under section 3(a)(2).

(3) A surcharge of $5 per coin for the half-dollar coin.

(4) A surcharge of $50 per coin for the $1 coin described under section 3(a)(4).

(b) DISTRIBUTION.—Subject to section 5134(f) of title 31, United States Code, all surcharges received by the Secretary from the sale of coins issued under this Act shall be promptly paid by the Secretary as follows:

(1) one half to the Smithsonian Institution's National Air and Space Museum's "Destination Moon" exhibit, for design, education, and installation costs related to establishing and maintaining the exhibit, and for costs related to creating a traveling version of the exhibition;

(2) one quarter to the Astronauts Memorial Foundation, for costs related to the preservation, maintenance, and enhancement of the Astronauts Memorial and for promotion of space exploration through educational initiatives; and

(3) one quarter to the Astronaut Scholarship Foundation, to aid its missions of promoting the importance of science and technology to the general public and of aiding the United States in retaining its world leadership in science and technology by providing college scholarships for the very best and brightest students pursuing degrees in science, technology, engineering, or mathematics (STEM).

(c) AUDITS.—The recipients described under subsection (b) shall be subject to the audit requirements of section 5134(f)(2) of title 31, United States Code, with regard to the amounts received under subsection (b).

(d) LIMITATION.—Notwithstanding subsection (a), no surcharge may be included with respect to the issuance under this Act of any coin during a calendar year if, as of the time of such issuance, the issuance of such coin would result in the number of commemorative coin programs issued during such year to exceed the annual commemorative coin program issuance limitation under section 5112(m)(1) of title 31, United States Code (as in effect on the date of the enactment of this Act). The Secretary of the Treasury may issue guidance to carry out this subsection.

SEC. 8. FINANCIAL ASSURANCES.

The Secretary shall take such actions as may be necessary to ensure that—

(1) minting and issuing coins under this Act will not result in any net cost to the United States Government; and

(2) no funds, including applicable surcharges, are disbursed to any recipient designated in section 7 until the total cost of designing and issuing all of the coins authorized by this Act (including labor, materials, dies, use of machinery, winning design compensation, overhead expenses, marketing, and shipping) is recovered by the United States Treasury, consistent with sections 5112(m) and 5134(f) of title 31, United States Code.

The SPEAKER pro tempore. Pursuant to the rule, the gentleman from Florida (Mr. POSEY) and the gentlewoman from New York (Ms. VELÁZQUEZ) each will control 20 minutes.

The Chair recognizes the gentleman from Florida.

GENERAL LEAVE

Mr. POSEY. Mr. Speaker, I ask unanimous consent that all Members may have 5 legislative days in which to revise and extend their remarks and include extraneous material on this bill.

The SPEAKER pro tempore. Is there objection to the request of the gentleman from Florida?

There was no objection.

Mr. POSEY. Mr. Speaker, I yield myself such time as I may consume.

I rise in support of H.R. 2726, the Apollo 11 50th Anniversary Commemorative Coin Act, which I introduced, along with my colleague from Florida, Congresswoman FREDERICA WILSON. This has been a truly bipartisan endeavor, with 298 total cosponsors.

In 1961, President John F. Kennedy challenged the Nation with the following words:

"We choose to go to the Moon. We choose to go to the Moon in this decade and do the other things, not because they are easy, but because they are hard, because that goal will serve to organize and measure the best of our energies and skills, because that challenge is one that we are willing to accept, one we are unwilling to postpone, and one which we intend to win. . . ."

That famous speech launched the Apollo program but, more importantly, it galvanized our Nation and united us into accomplishing perhaps the greatest technological achievement in human history, and it was truly a national undertaking. An estimated 400,000 men and women from across the United States contributed to the effort. Components of the Saturn V rocket, command and service module, lunar landing module, and other critical parts were literally manufactured from every State in the Union—from Huntsville, Alabama, to Seal Beach, California; New Orleans, Louisiana, to Cedar Rapids, Iowa; and everywhere in between.

On July 16, 1969, a mere 8 years after the first American, Alan Shepard, traveled into space, a Saturn V rocket blasted off from Merritt Island, Florida, and raced to the Moon. Four days later, astronauts Neil Armstrong and Buzz Aldrin landed on the lunar surface as Michael Collins stood watch.

This legislation commemorates our Nation's commitment to space exploration, our pioneering spirit, and our unmatched ingenuity. The United States' leadership in space exploration has benefited our country's national security and economy, strengthened our international relationships, advanced scientific discovery and technology, and vastly improved life here on Earth for practically everyone.

American space exploration continues to inspire our next generation of pioneers and innovators. As such, we were deliberate in our efforts to ensure that the sale of these coins would support efforts to grow the next generation of space explorers while also honoring the courage and sacrifice of NASA astronauts lost in the line of duty.

This legislation would authorize the minting and sale in 2019 of a limited number of gold, silver, and clad coins in commemoration of the *Apollo 11* mission. The coins would be domed, with the reverse featuring a representation of a spacesuit visor similar to the famous Buzz Aldrin on the Moon photograph.

After all taxpayer costs are satisfied, surcharges on the sales price of the coins will fund college scholarships for our future scientists, engineers, and astronauts, support educational initiatives that promote space exploration, honor astronauts who have fallen in the line of duty, and memorialize this historical event through a stimulating new museum exhibit.

Mr. Speaker, July 20, 2019, will mark the 50th anniversary of the landing of the *Eagle* lunar module on the Moon's surface. We remain the only country that has ever landed humans on the Moon and returned them safely to Earth.

☐ 1645

This commemorative coin will celebrate what I feel is the most awe-inspiring engineering and technological deed of the 20th century. I urge its immediate support.

Mr. Speaker, I reserve the balance of my time.

COMMITTEE ON WAYS AND MEANS,
HOUSE OF REPRESENTATIVES,
Washington, DC, December 5, 2016.

Hon. JEB HENSARLING,
Chairman, Committee on Financial Services, Washington, DC.

DEAR CHAIRMAN HENSARLING: I am writing with respect to H.R. 2726, the "Apollo 11 50th Anniversary Commemorative Coin Act." This bill contains provisions within the Rule X jurisdiction of the Committee on Ways and Means.

The Committee on Ways and Means will not seek a sequential referral on H.R. 2726 so that it may proceed expeditiously to the House floor for consideration. This is done with the understanding that the jurisdictional interests of the Committee on Ways and Means over this and similar legislation are in no way diminished or altered. In addition, the Committee reserves the right to seek conferees on H.R. 2726 and requests your support when such a request is made.

I would appreciate your response confirming this understanding with respect to H.R. 2726 and ask that a copy of our exchange of letters on this matter be included in the Congressional Record during consideration of the bill on the House floor.

Sincerely,

KEVIN BRADY,
Chairman.

———

HOUSE OF REPRESENTATIVES,
COMMITTEE ON FINANCIAL SERVICES,
Washington, DC, December 5, 2016.

Hon. KEVIN BRADY,
Chairman, Committee on Ways and Means, Washington, DC.

DEAR CHAIRMAN BRADY: Thank you for your December 5th letter regarding H.R. 2726, the "Apollo 11 50th Anniversary Commemorative Coin Act."

I am most appreciative of your decision to forego action on H.R. 2726 so that it may move expeditiously to the House floor. I acknowledge that although you are waiving action on the bill, the Committee on Ways and Means is in no way waiving its jurisdictional interest in this or similar legislation. In addition, if a conference is necessary on this legislation, I will support any request that your committee be represented therein.

Finally, I shall be pleased to include your letter and this letter on H.R. 2726 in the Congressional Record during floor consideration of the same.

Sincerely,

JEB HENSARLING,
Chairman.

———

HOUSE OF REPRESENTATIVES,
COMMITTEE ON THE BUDGET,
Washington, DC, November 29, 2016.
Hon. JEB HENSARLING,
Chairman, Committee on Financial Services,
House of Representatives, Washington, DC.

DEAR CHAIRMAN HENSARLING: I am writing concerning H.R. 2726, the Apollo 11: 50th Anniversary Commemorative Coin Act, which the House is expected to consider the week of December 5th.

Section 9 of the bill includes budgetary compliance language, which falls under the jurisdiction of the Committee on the Budget. It is my understanding that this language will be removed from the bill prior to House consideration. In order to expedite House consideration of H.R. 2726, the Committee will forgo action on the bill. This is being done with the understanding that it does not in any way prejudice the Committee with respect its jurisdictional prerogatives on this or similar legislation.

I would appreciate your response to this letter, confirming this understanding with respect to H.R. 2726 and would ask that a copy of our exchange of letters on this matter be included in the Congressional Record during floor consideration.

Sincerely,

TOM PRICE, M.D.,
Chairman, Committee on the Budget.

———

HOUSE OF REPRESENTATIVES,
COMMITTEE FINANCIAL SERVICES,
Washington, DC, November 30, 2016.
Hon. TOM PRICE,
Chairman, Committee on the Budget,
Washington, DC.

DEAR CHAIRMAN PRICE: Thank you for your November 30th letter regarding H.R. 2726, the "Apollo 11 50th Anniversary Commemorative Coin Act,"

I am most appreciative of your decision to forego action on H.R. 2726 so that it may move expeditiously to the House floor. I acknowledge that although you are waiving action on the bill, the Committee on the Budget is in no way waiving its jurisdictional interest in this or similar legislation. In addition, if a conference is necessary on this legislation, I will support any request that your committee be represented therein.

Finally, I shall be pleased to include your letter and this letter on H.R. 2726 in the Congressional Record during floor consideration of the same.

Sincerely,

JEB HENSARLING,
Chairman.

———

Ms. VELÁZQUEZ. Mr. Speaker, I yield myself such time as I may consume.

Mr. Speaker, I rise to speak in favor of H.R. 2726, legislation that will authorize the issuance of gold, silver, and clad coins in commemoration of the 50th anniversary of the first time in history that mankind successfully completed a crewed lunar landing.

The *Apollo 11* mission was a momentous occasion in its own right, but it was also a bittersweet achievement, as it also served as a reminder of the first *Apollo* mission, whose courage we will never forget.

I am pleased that, in addition to honoring the *Apollo 11* crew, the legislation before us today also recognizes the estimated 400,000 Americans who contributed to make possible the Apollo 11 mission. By calling on the Treasury Department to mint and issue coins in honor of *Apollo 11*, I hope that we will continue to remind all Americans of the boundlessness of what can be achieved when we set our sights high and, quite literally, aim for the Moon.

I also hope the coin minted as part of this legislation will show our young people just how exciting the fields of science, mathematics, and engineering can be and how critical they are to building a brighter future for all.

By ensuring that a quarter of the proceeds raised will be made available to the Astronaut Scholarship Foundation to make college scholarships available for students pursuing degrees in science, technology, engineering, and mathematics, the legislation before us will make one step towards opening up these fields to our best and brightest.

The remaining surcharges associated with the sale of the coins will go towards the Smithsonian Institution's National Air and Space Museum's Destination Moon exhibit and be provided to the Astronauts Memorial Foundation for maintenance of the memorial and to further educational initiatives.

For these reasons, I hope all Members will support the legislation before us.

Mr. Speaker, I yield 3 minutes to the gentlewoman from Florida (Ms. WILSON), who has been a champion for this important legislation.

Ms. WILSON of Florida. Mr. Speaker, I rise today to express my full support for the passage of H.R. 2726, the *Apollo 11* 50th Anniversary Commemorative Coin Act.

I want to thank my longtime friend and Florida colleague, Representative POSEY, for his outstanding leadership as the sponsor of this bill. I am proud to have worked very closely with him to build bipartisan support for this legislation. I also want to thank Speaker RYAN, Chairman HENSARLING, Ranking Member WATERS, and the Financial Services Committee for their work to bring this bill to the floor.

Mr. Speaker, the bill before us today authorizes the minting and distribution of commemorative coins to celebrate the 50th anniversary of the first manned lunar landing mission, *Apollo 11*. These coins will honor *Apollo 11* crew members, Michael Collins, Buzz Aldrin, and Neil Armstrong; NASA scientists, engineers, and astronauts; and the other 400,000 Americans who made the mission possible.

Surcharges from the sale of these coins will further our commitment to promote STEM education, space explo-ration, and science discovery. It will honor astronauts who lost their lives in service of our country and support the Destination Moon exhibit, which will feature exciting *Apollo 11* artifacts.

As a former elementary school principal and leading advocate for STEM education, I am very happy that this bill supports college scholarships for future scientists, engineers, and astronauts.

Mr. Speaker, the *Apollo 11* mission is a testament to our values as Americans. The mission's success reminded the world of our commitment to hard work, determination, and patriotism.

When many questioned whether we could rise to the challenge of putting a man on the Moon within a decade, we came together, worked our hardest, and achieved this daunting task in just 8 years. We left the world in awe and wonder.

When our astronauts were 4 miles past the designated landing spot and mission control told them that they had just 60 seconds of fuel left before the landing would have to be aborted, they did not panic. With unrelenting resolve, they managed to land on the Moon with only 17 seconds to spare. When Buzz Aldrin and Neil Armstrong planted our flag on the Moon, millions of Americans felt a sense of pride that was exhilarating and inspiring.

The SPEAKER pro tempore. The time of the gentlewoman has expired.

Ms. VELÁZQUEZ. Mr. Speaker, I yield the gentlewoman an additional 30 seconds.

Ms. WILSON of Florida. As Members of Congress, we should look to *Apollo 11* as inspiration as we work to tackle challenges that seem unsurmountable. I urge all of my colleagues to join me in voting for this bipartisan legislation, which has 298 cosponsors and the support of Buzz Aldrin and Michael Collins, *Apollo 11*'s two surviving astronauts.

Ms. VELÁZQUEZ. Mr. Speaker, I yield myself the balance of my time.

Mr. Speaker, basically, I will say that it is an honor for me to support this bill and this legislation. I ask all my colleagues to support it.

Mr. Speaker, I yield back the balance of my time.

Mr. POSEY. Mr. Speaker, I yield myself the balance of my time.

Mr. Speaker, we owe a debt of gratitude to the brave astronauts of the *Apollo* program, some of whom made the ultimate sacrifice in the line of duty. We are beholden to the hundreds of thousands of men and women who, when challenged to go to the Moon in this decade, accepted the challenge with a passion and a resolve that accomplished that which was thought unachievable.

I want to thank the chairman and the ranking member for their leadership and support of this legislation. Of course, finally, I want to express my sincere gratitude to my longtime friend and colleague from Florida, (Ms. WILSON), for her staunch support and tireless efforts to ensure that this remarkable achievement is commemorated.

Mr. Speaker, we have one opportunity to celebrate this historical event with a commemorative coin. I urge my colleagues to join me in supporting this bill.

Mr. Speaker, I yield back the balance of my time.

The SPEAKER pro tempore. The question is on the motion offered by the gentleman from Florida (Mr. POSEY) that the House suspend the rules and pass the bill, H.R. 2726, as amended.

The question was taken; and (two-thirds being in the affirmative) the rules were suspended and the bill, as amended, was passed.

A motion to reconsider was laid on the table.

CREATING FINANCIAL PROSPERITY FOR BUSINESSES AND INVESTORS ACT

Mr. GARRETT. Mr. Speaker, I move to suspend the rules and pass the bill (H.R. 6427) to improve the operation of United States capital markets, and for other purposes.

The Clerk read the title of the bill.

The text of the bill is as follows:

H.R. 6427

Be it enacted by the Senate and House of Representatives of the United States of America in Congress assembled,

SECTION 1. SHORT TITLE; TABLE OF CONTENTS.

(a) SHORT TITLE.—This Act may be cited as the "Creating Financial Prosperity for Businesses and Investors Act".

(b) TABLE OF CONTENTS.—The table of contents for this Act is as follows:

Sec. 1. Short title; table of contents.

TITLE I—SMALL BUSINESS CAPITAL FORMATION ENHANCEMENT

Sec. 101. Annual review of government-business forum on capital formation.

TITLE II—SEC SMALL BUSINESS ADVOCATE

Sec. 201. Establishment of Office of the Advocate for Small Business Capital Formation and Small Business Capital Formation Advisory Committee.

TITLE III—SUPPORTING AMERICA'S INNOVATORS

Sec. 301. Investor limitation for qualifying venture capital funds.

TITLE IV—FIX CROWDFUNDING

Sec. 401. Crowdfunding vehicles.
Sec. 402. Crowdfunding exemption from registration.

TITLE V—FAIR INVESTMENT OPPORTUNITIES FOR PROFESSIONAL EXPERTS

Sec. 501. Definition of accredited investor.

TITLE VI—U.S. TERRITORIES INVESTOR PROTECTION

Sec. 601. Termination of exemption.

TITLE I—SMALL BUSINESS CAPITAL FORMATION ENHANCEMENT

SEC. 101. ANNUAL REVIEW OF GOVERNMENT-BUSINESS FORUM ON CAPITAL FORMATION.

Section 503 of the Small Business Investment Incentive Act of 1980 (15 U.S.C. 80c–1) is amended by adding at the end the following:

"(e) The Commission shall—

"(1) review the findings and recommendations of the forum; and

"(2) each time the forum submits a finding or recommendation to the Commission, promptly issue a public statement—

"(A) assessing the finding or recommendation of the forum; and

"(B) disclosing the action, if any, the Commission intends to take with respect to the finding or recommendation.".

TITLE II—SEC SMALL BUSINESS ADVOCATE

SEC. 201. ESTABLISHMENT OF OFFICE OF THE ADVOCATE FOR SMALL BUSINESS CAPITAL FORMATION AND SMALL BUSINESS CAPITAL FORMATION ADVISORY COMMITTEE.

(a) OFFICE OF THE ADVOCATE FOR SMALL BUSINESS CAPITAL FORMATION.—Section 4 of the Securities Exchange Act of 1934 (15 U.S.C. 78d) is amended by adding at the end the following:

"(j) OFFICE OF THE ADVOCATE FOR SMALL BUSINESS CAPITAL FORMATION.—

"(1) OFFICE ESTABLISHED.—There is established within the Commission the Office of the Advocate for Small Business Capital Formation (hereafter in this subsection referred to as the 'Office').

"(2) ADVOCATE FOR SMALL BUSINESS CAPITAL FORMATION.—

"(A) IN GENERAL.—The head of the Office shall be the Advocate for Small Business Capital Formation, who shall—

"(i) report directly to the Commission; and

"(ii) be appointed by the Commission, from among individuals having experience in advocating for the interests of small businesses and encouraging small business capital formation.

"(B) COMPENSATION.—The annual rate of pay for the Advocate for Small Business Capital Formation shall be equal to the highest rate of annual pay for other senior executives who report directly to the Commission.

"(C) NO CURRENT EMPLOYEE OF THE COMMISSION.—An individual may not be appointed as the Advocate for Small Business Capital Formation if the individual is currently employed by the Commission.

"(3) STAFF OF OFFICE.—The Advocate for Small Business Capital Formation, after consultation with the Commission, may retain or employ independent counsel, research staff, and service staff, as the Advocate for Small Business Capital Formation determines to be necessary to carry out the functions of the Office.

"(4) FUNCTIONS OF THE ADVOCATE FOR SMALL BUSINESS CAPITAL FORMATION.—The Advocate for Small Business Capital Formation shall—

"(A) assist small businesses and small business investors in resolving significant problems such businesses and investors may have with the Commission or with self-regulatory organizations;

"(B) identify areas in which small businesses and small business investors would benefit from changes in the regulations of the Commission or the rules of self-regulatory organizations;

"(C) identify problems that small businesses have with securing access to capital, including any unique challenges to minority-owned and women-owned small businesses;

"(D) analyze the potential impact on small businesses and small business investors of—

"(i) proposed regulations of the Commission that are likely to have a significant economic impact on small businesses and small business capital formation; and

"(ii) proposed rules that are likely to have a significant economic impact on small businesses and small business capital formation of self-regulatory organizations registered under this title;

"(E) conduct outreach to small businesses and small business investors, including through regional roundtables, in order to solicit views on relevant capital formation issues;

"(F) to the extent practicable, propose to the Commission changes in the regulations or orders of the Commission and to Congress any legislative, administrative, or personnel changes that may be appropriate to mitigate problems identified under this paragraph and to promote the interests of small businesses and small business investors;

"(G) consult with the Investor Advocate on proposed recommendations made under subparagraph (F); and

"(H) advise the Investor Advocate on issues related to small businesses and small business investors.

"(5) ACCESS TO DOCUMENTS.—The Commission shall ensure that the Advocate for Small Business Capital Formation has full access to the documents and information of the Commission and any self-regulatory organization, as necessary to carry out the functions of the Office.

"(6) ANNUAL REPORT ON ACTIVITIES.—

"(A) IN GENERAL.—Not later than December 31 of each year after 2016, the Advocate for Small Business Capital Formation shall submit to the Committee on Banking, Housing, and Urban Affairs of the Senate and the Committee on Financial Services of the House of Representatives a report on the activities of the Advocate for Small Business Capital Formation during the immediately preceding fiscal year.

"(B) CONTENTS.—Each report required under subparagraph (A) shall include—

"(i) appropriate statistical information and full and substantive analysis;

"(ii) information on steps that the Advocate for Small Business Capital Formation has taken during the reporting period to improve small business services and the responsiveness of the Commission and self-regulatory organizations to small business and small business investor concerns;

"(iii) a summary of the most serious issues encountered by small businesses and small business investors, including any unique issues encountered by minority-owned and women-owned small businesses and their investors, during the reporting period;

"(iv) an inventory of the items summarized under clause (iii) (including items summarized under such clause for any prior reporting period on which no action has been taken or that have not been resolved to the satisfaction of the Advocate for Small Business Capital Formation as of the beginning of the reporting period covered by the report) that includes—

"(I) identification of any action taken by the Commission or the self-regulatory organization and the result of such action;

"(II) the length of time that each item has remained on such inventory; and

"(III) for items on which no action has been taken, the reasons for inaction, and an identification of any official who is responsible for such action;

"(v) recommendations for such changes to the regulations, guidance and orders of the

Commission and such legislative actions as may be appropriate to resolve problems with the Commission and self-regulatory organizations encountered by small businesses and small business investors and to encourage small business capital formation; and

"(vi) any other information, as determined appropriate by the Advocate for Small Business Capital Formation.

"(C) CONFIDENTIALITY.—No report required by subparagraph (A) may contain confidential information.

"(D) INDEPENDENCE.—Each report required under subparagraph (A) shall be provided directly to the committees of Congress listed in such subparagraph without any prior review or comment from the Commission, any commissioner, any other officer or employee of the Commission, or the Office of Management and Budget.

"(7) REGULATIONS.—The Commission shall establish procedures requiring a formal response to all recommendations submitted to the Commission by the Advocate for Small Business Capital Formation, not later than 3 months after the date of such submission.

"(8) GOVERNMENT-BUSINESS FORUM ON SMALL BUSINESS CAPITAL FORMATION.—The Advocate for Small Business Capital Formation shall be responsible for planning, organizing, and executing the annual Government-Business Forum on Small Business Capital Formation described in section 503 of the Small Business Investment Incentive Act of 1980 (15 U.S.C. 80c–1).

"(9) RULE OF CONSTRUCTION.—Nothing in this subsection may be construed as replacing or reducing the responsibilities of the Investor Advocate with respect to small business investors.".

(b) SMALL BUSINESS CAPITAL FORMATION ADVISORY COMMITTEE.—Title I of the Securities Exchange Act of 1934 (15 U.S.C. 78a et seq.) is amended by adding at the end the following:

"SEC. 40. SMALL BUSINESS CAPITAL FORMATION ADVISORY COMMITTEE.

"(a) ESTABLISHMENT AND PURPOSE.—

"(1) ESTABLISHMENT.—There is established within the Commission the Small Business Capital Formation Advisory Committee (hereafter in this section referred to as the 'Committee').

"(2) FUNCTIONS.—

"(A) IN GENERAL.—The Committee shall provide the Commission with advice on the Commission's rules, regulations, and policies with regard to the Commission's mission of protecting investors, maintaining fair, orderly, and efficient markets, and facilitating capital formation, as such rules, regulations, and policies relate to—

"(i) capital raising by emerging, privately held small businesses ('emerging companies') and publicly traded companies with less than $250,000,000 in public market capitalization ('smaller public companies') through securities offerings, including private and limited offerings and initial and other public offerings;

"(ii) trading in the securities of emerging companies and smaller public companies; and

"(iii) public reporting and corporate governance requirements of emerging companies and smaller public companies.

"(B) LIMITATION.—The Committee shall not provide any advice with respect to any policies, practices, actions, or decisions concerning the Commission's enforcement program.

"(b) MEMBERSHIP.—

"(1) IN GENERAL.—The members of the Committee shall be—

"(A) the Advocate for Small Business Capital Formation;

"(B) not fewer than 10, and not more than 20, members appointed by the Commission, from among individuals—

"(i) who represent—

"(I) emerging companies engaging in private and limited securities offerings or considering initial public offerings ('IPO') (including the companies' officers and directors);

"(II) the professional advisors of such companies (including attorneys, accountants, investment bankers, and financial advisors); and

"(III) the investors in such companies (including angel investors, venture capital funds, and family offices);

"(ii) who are officers or directors of minority-owned small businesses or women-owned small businesses;

"(iii) who represent—

"(I) smaller public companies (including the companies' officers and directors);

"(II) the professional advisors of such companies (including attorneys, auditors, underwriters, and financial advisors); and

"(III) the pre-IPO and post-IPO investors in such companies (both institutional, such as venture capital funds, and individual, such as angel investors); and

"(iv) who represent participants in the marketplace for the securities of emerging companies and smaller public companies, such as securities exchanges, alternative trading systems, analysts, information processors, and transfer agents; and

"(C) three non-voting members—

"(i) one of whom shall be appointed by the Investor Advocate;

"(ii) one of whom shall be appointed by the North American Securities Administrators Association; and

"(iii) one of whom shall be appointed by the Administrator of the Small Business Administration.

"(2) TERM.—Each member of the Committee appointed under subparagraph (B), (C)(ii), or (C)(iii) of paragraph (1) shall serve for a term of 4 years.

"(3) MEMBERS NOT COMMISSION EMPLOYEES.—Members appointed under subparagraph (B), (C)(ii), or (C)(iii) of paragraph (1) shall not be treated as employees or agents of the Commission solely because of membership on the Committee.

"(c) CHAIRMAN; VICE CHAIRMAN; SECRETARY; ASSISTANT SECRETARY.—

"(1) IN GENERAL.—The members of the Committee shall elect, from among the members of the Committee—

"(A) a chairman;

"(B) a vice chairman;

"(C) a secretary; and

"(D) an assistant secretary.

"(2) TERM.—Each member elected under paragraph (1) shall serve for a term of 3 years in the capacity for which the member was elected under paragraph (1).

"(d) MEETINGS.—

"(1) FREQUENCY OF MEETINGS.—The Committee shall meet—

"(A) not less frequently than four times annually, at the call of the chairman of the Committee; and

"(B) from time to time, at the call of the Commission.

"(2) NOTICE.—The chairman of the Committee shall give the members of the Committee written notice of each meeting, not later than 2 weeks before the date of the meeting.

"(e) COMPENSATION AND TRAVEL EXPENSES.—Each member of the Committee who is not a full-time employee of the United States shall—

"(1) be entitled to receive compensation at a rate not to exceed the daily equivalent of the annual rate of basic pay in effect for a position at level V of the Executive Schedule under section 5316 of title 5, United States Code, for each day during which the member is engaged in the actual performance of the duties of the Committee; and

"(2) while away from the home or regular place of business of the member in the performance of services for the Committee, be allowed travel expenses, including per diem in lieu of subsistence, in the same manner as persons employed intermittently in the Government service are allowed expenses under section 5703 of title 5, United States Code.

"(f) STAFF.—The Commission shall make available to the Committee such staff as the chairman of the Committee determines are necessary to carry out this section.

"(g) REVIEW BY COMMISSION.—The Commission shall—

"(1) review the findings and recommendations of the Committee; and

"(2) each time the Committee submits a finding or recommendation to the Commission, promptly issue a public statement—

"(A) assessing the finding or recommendation of the Committee; and

"(B) disclosing the action, if any, the Commission intends to take with respect to the finding or recommendation.

"(h) FEDERAL ADVISORY COMMITTEE ACT.— The Federal Advisory Committee Act (5 U.S.C. App.) shall not apply with respect to the Committee and its activities.".

(c) ANNUAL GOVERNMENT-BUSINESS FORUM ON SMALL BUSINESS CAPITAL FORMATION.— Section 503(a) of the Small Business Investment Incentive Act of 1980 (15 U.S.C. 80c–1(a)) is amended by inserting "(acting through the Office of the Advocate for Small Business Capital Formation and in consultation with the Small Business Capital Formation Advisory Committee)" after "Securities and Exchange Commission".

TITLE III—SUPPORTING AMERICA'S INNOVATORS

SEC. 301. INVESTOR LIMITATION FOR QUALIFYING VENTURE CAPITAL FUNDS.

Section 3(c)(1) of the Investment Company Act of 1940 (15 U.S.C. 80a–3(c)(1)) is amended—

(1) by inserting after "one hundred persons" the following: "(or, with respect to a qualifying venture capital fund, 250 persons)"; and

(2) by adding at the end the following:

"(C) The term 'qualifying venture capital fund' means any venture capital fund (as defined pursuant to section 203(l)(1) of the Investment Advisers Act of 1940 (15 U.S.C. 80b–3(l)(1)) with no more than $10,000,000 in invested capital, as such dollar amount is annually adjusted by the Commission to reflect the change in the Consumer Price Index for All Urban Consumers published by the Bureau of Labor Statistics of the Department of Labor.".

TITLE IV—FIX CROWDFUNDING

SEC. 401. CROWDFUNDING VEHICLES.

(a) AMENDMENTS TO THE SECURITIES ACT OF 1933.—The Securities Act of 1933 (15 U.S.C. 77a et seq.) is amended—

(1) in section 4A(f)(3), by inserting "by any of paragraphs (1) through (14) of" before "section 3(c)"; and

(2) in section 4(a)(6)(B), by inserting after "any investor" the following: ", other than a crowdfunding vehicle (as defined in section 2(a) of the Investment Company Act of 1940),".

(b) AMENDMENTS TO THE INVESTMENT COMPANY ACT OF 1940.—The Investment Company Act of 1940 (15 U.S.C. 80a–1 et seq.) is amended—

(1) in section 2(a), by adding at the end the following:

"(55) The term 'crowdfunding vehicle' means a company—

"(A) whose purpose (as set forth in its organizational documents) is limited to acquiring, holding, and disposing securities issued by a single company in one or more transactions and made pursuant to section 4(a)(6) of the Securities Act of 1933;

"(B) which issues only one class of securities;

"(C) which receives no compensation in connection with such acquisition, holding, or disposition of securities;

"(D) no associated person of which receives any compensation in connection with such acquisition, holding or disposition of securities unless such person is acting as or on behalf of an investment adviser registered under the Investment Advisers Act of 1940 or registered as an investment adviser in the State in which the investment adviser maintains its principal office and place of business;

"(E) the securities of which have been issued in a transaction made pursuant to section 4(a)(6) of the Securities Act of 1933, where both the crowdfunding vehicle and the company whose securities it holds are co-issuers;

"(F) which is current in its ongoing disclosure obligations under Rule 202 of Regulation Crowdfunding (17 C.F.R. 227.202);

"(G) the company whose securities it holds is current in its ongoing disclosure obligations under Rule 202 of Regulation Crowdfunding (17 C.F.R. 227.202); and

"(H) is advised by an investment adviser registered under the Investment Advisers Act of 1940 or registered as an investment adviser in the State in which the investment adviser maintains its principal office and place of business."; and

(2) in section 3(c), by adding at the end the following:

"(15) Any crowdfunding vehicle.".

SEC. 402. CROWDFUNDING EXEMPTION FROM REGISTRATION.

Section 12(g)(6) of the Securities Exchange Act of 1934 (15 U.S.C. 78l(g)(6)) is amended—

(1) by striking "The Commission" and inserting the following:

"(A) IN GENERAL.—The Commission";

(2) by striking "section 4(6)" and inserting "section 4(a)(6)"; and

(3) by adding at the end the following:

"(B) TREATMENT OF SECURITIES ISSUED BY CERTAIN ISSUERS.—An exemption under subparagraph (A) shall be unconditional for securities offered by an issuer that had a public float of less than $75,000,000 as of the last business day of the issuer's most recently completed semiannual period, computed by multiplying the aggregate worldwide number of shares of the issuer's common equity securities held by non-affiliates by the price at which such securities were last sold (or the average bid and asked prices of such securities) in the principal market for such securities or, in the event the result of such public float calculation is zero, had annual revenues of less than $50,000,000 as of the issuer's most recently completed fiscal year.".

TITLE V—FAIR INVESTMENT OPPORTUNITIES FOR PROFESSIONAL EXPERTS

SEC. 501. DEFINITION OF ACCREDITED INVESTOR.

Section 2(a)(15) of the Securities Act of 1933 (15 U.S.C. 77b(a)(15)) is amended—

(1) by redesignating clauses (i) and (ii) as subparagraphs (A) and (F), respectively; and

(2) in subparagraph (A) (as so redesignated), by striking "; or" and inserting a semicolon, and inserting after such subparagraph the following:

"(B) any natural person whose individual net worth, or joint net worth with that person's spouse, exceeds $1,000,000 (which amount, along with the amounts set forth in subparagraph (C), shall be adjusted for inflation by the Commission every 5 years to the nearest $10,000 to reflect the change in the Consumer Price Index for All Urban Consumers published by the Bureau of Labor Statistics) where, for purposes of calculating net worth under this subparagraph—

"(i) the person's primary residence shall not be included as an asset;

"(ii) indebtedness that is secured by the person's primary residence, up to the estimated fair market value of the primary residence at the time of the sale of securities, shall not be included as a liability (except that if the amount of such indebtedness outstanding at the time of sale of securities exceeds the amount outstanding 60 days before such time, other than as a result of the acquisition of the primary residence, the amount of such excess shall be included as a liability); and

"(iii) indebtedness that is secured by the person's primary residence in excess of the estimated fair market value of the primary residence at the time of the sale of securities shall be included as a liability;

"(C) any natural person who had an individual income in excess of $200,000 in each of the two most recent years or joint income with that person's spouse in excess of $300,000 in each of those years and has a reasonable expectation of reaching the same income level in the current year;

"(D) any natural person who is currently licensed or registered as a broker or investment adviser by the Commission, the Financial Industry Regulatory Authority, or an equivalent self-regulatory organization (as defined in section 3(a)(26) of the Securities Exchange Act of 1934), or the securities division of a State or the equivalent State division responsible for licensing or registration of individuals in connection with securities activities;

"(E) any natural person the Commission determines, by regulation, to have demonstrable education or job experience to qualify such person as having professional knowledge of a subject related to a particular investment, and whose education or job experience is verified by the Financial Industry Regulatory Authority or an equivalent self-regulatory organization (as defined in section 3(a)(26) of the Securities Exchange Act of 1934); or".

TITLE VI—U.S. TERRITORIES INVESTOR PROTECTION

SEC. 601. TERMINATION OF EXEMPTION.

(a) IN GENERAL.—Section 6(a) of the Investment Company Act of 1940 (15 U.S.C. 80a–6(a)) is amended by striking paragraph (1).

(b) EFFECTIVE DATE AND SAFE HARBOR.—

(1) EFFECTIVE DATE.—Except as provided in paragraph (2), the amendment made by subsection (a) shall take effect on the date of the enactment of this Act.

(2) SAFE HARBOR.—With respect to a company that is exempt under section 6(a)(1) of the Investment Company Act of 1940 (15 U.S.C. 80a–6(a)(1)) on the day before the date of the enactment of this Act, the amendment made by subsection (a) shall take effect on the date that is 3 years after the date of the enactment of this Act.

(3) EXTENSION OF SAFE HARBOR.—The Securities and Exchange Commission, by rule and regulation upon its own motion, or by order upon application, may conditionally or unconditionally, under section 6(c) of the Investment Company Act of 1940 (15 U.S.C. 80a–6(c)), further delay the effective date for a company described in paragraph (2) for a maximum of 3 years following the initial 3-year period if, before the end of the initial 3-year period, the Commission determines that such a rule, regulation, motion, or order is necessary or appropriate in the public interest and for the protection of investors.

The SPEAKER pro tempore. Pursuant to the rule, the gentleman from New Jersey (Mr. GARRETT) and the gentlewoman from New York (Ms. VELÁZQUEZ) each will control 20 minutes.

The Chair recognizes the gentleman from New Jersey.

GENERAL LEAVE

Mr. GARRETT. Mr. Speaker, I ask unanimous consent that all Members may have 5 legislative days in which to revise and extend their remarks and include extraneous materials on this bill.

The SPEAKER pro tempore. Is there objection to the request of the gentleman from New Jersey?

There was no objection.

Mr. GARRETT. Mr. Speaker, I yield myself such time as I may consume.

Mr. Speaker, I rise today in support of H.R. 6427, the Creating Financial Prosperity for Businesses and Investors Act. It is a compilation of legislative initiatives that the Financial Services Committee has worked on in a very constructive and bipartisan manner during the 114th Congress.

For 6 years, our committee, and, in particular, the Subcommittee on Capital Markets and Government Sponsored Enterprises, has sought to break through the bipartisan gridlock in Washington and to ensure that the SEC, or the Securities and Exchange Commission, fulfills an important part of its mission to facilitate capital formation.

For example, the JOBS Act of 2012, much of which originated in our committee, has already been a measurable success, as hundreds of companies have used its provisions to file for an initial public offering, and other businesses have been able to raise well over $50 billion worth of capital through private channels.

Altogether, this translates to more growth, more innovation, and, most importantly, more jobs here for Americans who have been struggling in an economy that is producing only 1–2 percent growth, at best.

We didn't stop at the JOBS Act, and both Republicans and Democrats on our committee came together and continued to generate good ideas that modernize our Nation's security laws for the benefit of the small- and medium-sized enterprises, which often pay a disproportionate share of the costs that come along with regulation.

For example, during this Congress, our subcommittee has put forward nearly 40 bills to do just that, the vast majority of which gained, again, bipartisan support in both committee and here on the House floor. A year ago this month, a number of these measures were signed into law at the White House by the President.

Today, we bring together a package of another six bills on the House floor with the hopes that we, once again, can improve the environment in which entrepreneurs and small businesses can operate.

The provisions under H.R. 6427 include the following:

First, a bill from Mr. CARNEY and Mr. DUFFY that would create an Office of the Advocate for Small Business Capital Formation at the SEC. For too long, Mr. Speaker, the SEC has operated in a bureaucratic silo and ignored the needs of small and growing businesses and entrepreneurs. So we have Mr. DUFFY's bill, which gives small businesses a permanent voice at the SEC, and it passed out of committee unanimously by a vote of 56–0. It also passed in the House overwhelmingly.

Secondly, Mr. Speaker, is a bill from Mr. POLIQUIN that would require the SEC to respond to recommendations made at its annual government small business forum, ensuring that the SEC no longer simply ignores the ideas generated by small businesses at this event. This bill, again, passed our committee by a vote of 55–1 and passed the House by a vote of 390–1 earlier this year.

It also includes two bills from Mr. MCHENRY, who is on the floor and will be speaking later, one which would fix some of the more unworkable provisions of the crowd funding title of the JOBS Act, and a second bill that would modernize the threshold for when venture capital funds would have to register with the SEC. Again, there was huge bipartisan support, both passing out of committee 57–2 and garnering near-unanimous support here on the House floor.

There are two more.

Another title includes a bill from DAVE SCHWEIKERT that would reform the definition of an accredited investor for certain securities offerings so that it is not just the wealthy or the well-connected who are able to invest in these companies. This bill passed the House earlier, again, with near-unanimous support.

Finally, we have a bill from our Democratic colleague, Ms. VELÁZQUEZ, that would make a technical correction to an outdated law that exempts investment companies from having to register in U.S. territories.

In conclusion, Mr. Speaker, H.R. 6427 contains innovation and much-needed legislation to help get our economy off the slow growth track that it has been on for too long, and it continues the good bipartisanship that our committee is known for.

I want to take this moment to thank all my colleagues over the years for their hard work and willingness to work with us in a bipartisan manner to move legislation like this.

□ 1700

In particular, I thank our chairman, JEB HENSARLING, for his tremendous leadership of our full Financial Services Committee and for all the work that he has done to improve our capital markets in this country and to create a financial system that works for the benefit of all Americans.

Mr. Speaker, I reserve the balance of my time.

Ms. VELÁZQUEZ. Mr. Speaker, I yield myself such time as I may consume.

I rise in support of H.R. 6427, a bipartisan package of commonsense measures that will help small businesses raise capital and better protect investors and retirees of the U.S. territories.

Today's bill contains numerous bipartisan solutions to ensure the SEC is more responsive to small business regulatory concerns. For example, it creates a new Office of the Advocate for Small Business Capital Formation and a new Small Business Advisory Committee. Taken together, these efforts will ensure the agency is more responsive to entrepreneurs' needs.

Furthermore, we have all heard that demand for small business capital outstrips supply. H.R. 6427 makes targeted changes to attract more investors to the small business market. By expanding definition of accredited investor, raising the investor cap on small venture capital funds, and making improvements to the equity crowdfunding rules implemented under the JOBS Act, this bill will help more startups and fast-growing businesses secure financing.

Beyond the small business provisions, today's bill will provide investors and retirees in Puerto Rico and other U.S. territories the same protections as their mainland counterparts. For 7 decades, the Investment Company Act of 1940 provided U.S. investors with basic safeguards, regulating everything from leverage limits to capitalization levels, to preventing conflicts of interest.

Due to a historical artifact, however, all funds located in and sold only to residents of U.S. territories are exempted from the act. The reason is U.S. territories were deemed to be too geographically distant from Washington, D.C. Obviously, the cost of air travel today is no longer an issue. Regulators routinely travel to Hawaii and Alaska to conduct oversight. In fact, SEC Chair White testified earlier this year that the exemption should be removed.

To close the loophole and provide territorial residents with the protections they deserve, I introduced the U.S. Territories Investor Protection Act. Over the past year, we met with stakeholders, heard their concerns and further fine-tuned the bill.

Investment companies will have an initial 3-year compliance period, with an option at the approval of the SEC, for an additional 3 years. This balances investor protections while granting more than reasonable time for financial institutions to comply. It is important to note that if investment companies need further relief, they are able to request such a reprieve under existing law.

I thank Chairman HENSARLING, Ranking Member WATERS, and Congressman GARRETT for working with me on this provision. Their cooperation was critical to developing an approach that would apply the act in a manner sensitive to investors and investment companies alike.

In sum, I will argue that this is a strong bill. It will reduce compliance costs, facilitate access to capital for thousands of small businesses, and better protect investors and retirees in territories like Puerto Rico.

I urge Members to support this legislation, and I reserve the balance of my time.

Mr. GARRETT. Mr. Speaker, I yield such time as he may consume to the gentleman from North Carolina (Mr. MCHENRY). I appreciate all of his hard work for the JOBS Act and all the rest of his work as vice chair of the committee and the time together that we had.

Mr. MCHENRY. Mr. Speaker, I thank my colleague for his kind words and for his leadership on important issues in the capital markets.

Today I rise to support the Creating Financial Prosperity for Businesses and Investors Act.

Mr. Speaker, the title doesn't do the act justice. This is about helping families, communities, small businesses, entrepreneurs, those that are risk-takers in our society trying to make our society better, more prosperous, and helping families and communities like the one I represent in western North Carolina be better off. We need a growing economy to help families, to help small businesses, to help make us more prosperous as Americans.

So this act deals with a couple of those areas in particular for families, small businesses, and entrepreneurs so they can gain greater access to lending, to loans, to capital that they need to help businesses grow and create jobs.

Two of those bills, to that end, I authored earlier this year, which we passed with over 400 votes, as individual stand-alone items through the House of Representatives. Those two bills, Supporting America's Innovators Act, and the Fix Crowdfunding Act, in particular, amend existing securities laws to make it easier for small businesses and entrepreneurs to use innovative forms of capital formation. Investment crowdfunding and angel investing are two of those areas, in particular, to support those ideas that enable us to create jobs.

Those two bills were a part of the larger package, that are a part of the innovation initiative that Leader McCarthy and I launched at the beginning of this year. A number of bills have moved through the House with wide bipartisan support that update outdated laws.

So, today, this package is an important step in the right direction; but our work is not done. We have to continue to work with our Federal regulators and Members on both sides of the aisle to ensure that we update and ensure investment crowdfunding, angel investing, and other areas of innovation can actually be better deployed across our society and to more people.

I urge my colleagues to vote "yes" and ensure this bipartisan bill has wide approval here in the House today.

Ms. VELÁZQUEZ. Mr. Speaker, I continue to reserve the balance of my time.

Mr. GARRETT. Mr. Speaker, I yield such time as he may consume to the gentleman from Arizona (Mr. SCHWEIKERT).

Mr. SCHWEIKERT. Mr. Speaker, I am here to speak about one of the ideas in this package that I have, shall we say, 5 or 6 years in; and the interesting thing, it was a conversation back and forth with a number of Democrats on the other side. It was one of those—it started as sort of a philosophical debate.

Often you hear us fussing at each other here on the floor, and we will get into these debates of, well, the concentration of wealth in the country; you know, the number of folks who now hold so much wealth.

Yet, if you take a step backwards and look at the way we have our laws set up in this country, we don't decide that you get to invest in certain types of activities because of your talent. We don't decide you get to invest in certain activities because you are an expert in the technology or the business model.

We actually have a series of rules that, if you have $1 million, you and your wife have a certain income, then you are allowed to invest. You think about that. So if I came to you right now and said, I am going to judge you by the size of your bank account and not by your competence, that would be pretty outrageous.

I guess for years and years, none of us had really sort of talked about it, thought about it in that way, that the arbitrary rules that the SEC and we had allowed to continue were a world where we judged people by their wealth and then gave them additional oppor-

tunities instead of handing those same opportunities to people because of their expertise in investing or the technology, their expertise in understanding the risk profile of such technology. I am hoping that is where we are heading.

There was a number of compromises to make both sides feel comfortable, and that is actually one of the reasons we had such a bipartisan vote; and to that, I also thank my friend, Chairman GARRETT. I am going to miss you because you have worked hard to shepherd many of these concepts through for years now.

I think this is a great start because we are going to start judging our brothers and sisters by their talents and not necessarily their bank account size, and that is why I am so happy on this one.

Ms. VELÁZQUEZ. Mr. Speaker, I am prepared to close. I yield myself such time as I may consume.

Mr. Speaker, access to capital is the lifeblood of every business. By expanding the pool of accredited investors and venture capital firms, improving the equity crowdfunding rules, and giving small business a bigger voice in SEC decisionmaking, H.R. 6427 provides the tools necessary to inject much-needed equity capital into our Main Street businesses.

Finally, closing the U.S. territories loophole in the Investment Company Act of 1940 will harmonize regulatory oversight and give millions of investors and retirees, mostly in Puerto Rico, the peace of mind that their hard-earned money will receive the same level of protection afforded to those on the mainland.

I thank the chairman, ranking member, and all of the cosponsors for their hard work in bringing this bipartisan package to the floor. I urge Members to support this bill, and I yield back the balance of my time.

Mr. GARRETT. Mr. Speaker, I yield myself such time as I may consume.

I rise again to support the legislation. It dawns on me also that, as I rise today, this may be the last time that I rise on the floor. So let me just say what an honor it has been to stand at this podium to bring forth legislation like this, as I have done over the last 14 years, and to end where I began, to do so in a bipartisan manner, that they tell me we should be able to pass through today in a pretty overwhelmingly bipartisan manner as well.

The gentleman from Arizona ended his remarks with the statement: Every day is a new beginning.

So I look at that as my days ahead. This legislation is a new beginning for capital formation and is a new beginning for bipartisanship in future legislation as well.

I thank my colleagues from the other side of the aisle that I have had the honor and privilege to work with on

this legislation and other legislation as well. I thank my colleagues from my side of the aisle that I have had similar opportunity to do so as well. We have gone through challenging times, from good economic times and bad—maybe more bad than good—but, through it all, I think we have done so with the American public's interest in mind.

Behind me also are some of our members of our committee who I also wish to recognize for their work as well. They have left a profound impact on myself during the time that I have known them, and I thank them humbly for their being willing to put up with me and to deal with me throughout the years, but be able to work together for the benefit of the American public as well.

I think that, together, we have done great things. I look forward to watching what other great things will be done in a bipartisan manner as well.

I think my time may be just about out, but let me also just say this as well. I want to end where I began, which was thanking the chairman of this committee, Mr. JEB HENSARLING, for his leadership and, most importantly, for his friendship in the years I have known him in this capacity.

I urge every Member to support the underlying legislation, and I yield back the balance of my time.

The SPEAKER pro tempore. The question is on the motion offered by the gentleman from New Jersey (Mr. GARRETT) that the House suspend the rules and pass the bill, H.R. 6427.

The question was taken.

The SPEAKER pro tempore. In the opinion of the Chair, two-thirds being in the affirmative, the ayes have it.

Mr. GARRETT. Mr. Speaker, on that I demand the yeas and nays.

The yeas and nays were ordered.

The SPEAKER pro tempore. Pursuant to clause 8 of rule XX, further proceedings on this motion will be postponed.

☐ 1715

COMBAT-INJURED VETERANS TAX FAIRNESS ACT OF 2016

Mr. BRADY of Texas. Mr. Speaker, I move to suspend the rules and pass the bill (H.R. 5015) to restore amounts improperly withheld for tax purposes from severance payments to individuals who retired or separated from service in the Armed Forces for combat-related injuries, and for other purposes, as amended.

The Clerk read the title of the bill.

The text of the bill is as follows:

H.R. 5015

Be it enacted by the Senate and House of Representatives of the United States of America in Congress assembled,

SECTION 1. SHORT TITLE.

This Act may be cited as the "Combat-Injured Veterans Tax Fairness Act of 2016".

SEC. 2. FINDINGS.

Congress makes the following findings:

(1) Approximately 10,000 to 11,000 individuals are retired from service in the Armed Forces for medical reasons each year.

(2) Some of such individuals are separated from service in the Armed Forces for combat-related injuries (as defined in section 104(b)(3) of the Internal Revenue Code of 1986).

(3) Congress has recognized the tremendous personal sacrifice of veterans with combat-related injuries by, among other things, specifically excluding from taxable income severance pay received for combat-related injuries.

(4) Since 1991, the Secretary of Defense has improperly withheld taxes from severance pay for wounded veterans, thus denying them their due compensation and a significant benefit intended by Congress.

(5) Many veterans owed redress are beyond the statutory period to file an amended tax return because they were not or are not aware that taxes were improperly withheld.

SEC. 3. RESTORATION OF AMOUNTS IMPROPERLY WITHHELD FOR TAX PURPOSES FROM SEVERANCE PAYMENTS TO VETERANS WITH COMBAT-RELATED INJURIES.

(a) IN GENERAL.—Not later than one year after the date of the enactment of this Act, the Secretary of Defense shall—

(1) identify—

(A) the severance payments—

(i) that the Secretary paid after January 17, 1991;

(ii) that the Secretary computed under section 1212 of title 10, United States Code;

(iii) that were not considered gross income pursuant to section 104(a)(4) of the Internal Revenue Code of 1986; and

(iv) from which the Secretary withheld amounts for tax purposes; and

(B) the individuals to whom such severance payments were made; and

(2) with respect to each person identified under paragraph (1)(B), provide—

(A) notice of—

(i) the amount of severance payments in paragraph (1)(A) which were improperly withheld for tax purposes; and

(ii) such other information determined to be necessary by the Secretary of the Treasury to carry out the purposes of this section; and

(B) instructions for filing amended tax returns to recover the amounts improperly withheld for tax purposes.

(b) EXTENSION OF LIMITATION ON TIME FOR CREDIT OR REFUND.—

(1) PERIOD FOR FILING CLAIM.—If a claim for credit or refund under section 6511(a) of the Internal Revenue Code of 1986 relates to a specified overpayment, the 3-year period of limitation prescribed by such subsection shall not expire before the date which is 1 year after the date the information return described in subsection (a)(2) is provided. The allowable amount of credit or refund of a specified overpayment shall be determined without regard to the amount of tax paid within the period provided in section 6511(b)(2).

(2) SPECIFIED OVERPAYMENT.—For purposes of paragraph (1), the term "specified overpayment" means an overpayment attributable to a severance payment described in subsection (a)(1).

SEC. 4. REQUIREMENT THAT SECRETARY OF DEFENSE ENSURE AMOUNTS ARE NOT WITHHELD FOR TAX PURPOSES FROM SEVERANCE PAYMENTS NOT CONSIDERED GROSS INCOME.

The Secretary of Defense shall take such actions as may be necessary to ensure that amounts are not withheld for tax purposes from severance payments made by the Secretary to individuals when such payments are not considered gross income pursuant to section 104(a)(4) of the Internal Revenue Code of 1986.

SEC. 5. REPORT TO CONGRESS.

(a) IN GENERAL.—After completing the identification required by section 3(a) and not later than one year after the date of the enactment of this Act, the Secretary of Defense shall submit to the appropriate committees of Congress a report on the actions taken by the Secretary to carry out this Act.

(b) CONTENTS.—The report submitted under subsection (a) shall include the following:

(1) The number of individuals identified under section 3(a)(1)(B).

(2) Of all the severance payments described in section 3(a)(1)(A), the aggregate amount that the Secretary withheld for tax purposes from such payments.

(3) A description of the actions the Secretary plans to take to carry out section 4.

(c) APPROPRIATE COMMITTEES OF CONGRESS DEFINED.—In this section, the term "appropriate committees of Congress" means—

(1) the Committee on Armed Services, the Committee on Veterans' Affairs, and the Committee on Finance of the Senate; and

(2) the Committee on Armed Services, the Committee on Veterans' Affairs, and the Committee on Ways and Means of the House of Representatives.

The SPEAKER pro tempore. Pursuant to the rule, the gentleman from Texas (Mr. BRADY) and the gentleman from Massachusetts (Mr. NEAL) each will control 20 minutes.

The Chair recognizes the gentleman from Texas.

GENERAL LEAVE

Mr. BRADY of Texas. Mr. Speaker, I ask unanimous consent that all Members may have 5 legislative days within which to revise and extend their remarks and include extraneous material on H.R. 5015, currently under consideration.

The SPEAKER pro tempore. Is there objection to the request of the gentleman from Texas?

There was no objection.

Mr. BRADY of Texas. Mr. Speaker, I yield myself such time as I may consume.

Mr. Speaker, we have responsibilities for all the brave men and women who protect and defend our great Nation, especially those who are injured in the line of duty. The bill we are considering today by Representative ROUZER does just that.

Under our tax system, veterans who suffer from combat-related injuries are not required to pay taxes on the one-time lump-sum disability payment they receive when they leave the military. Unfortunately, errors in the Defense Department's automatic payment system have resulted in taxes being improperly withheld from these injured troops' payments—sometimes for years on end.

As a result, thousands of combat-injured veterans—men and women who have sacrificed greatly for our country—have not received the full compensation they are rightfully due. The Combat-Injured Veterans Tax Fairness Act provides an opportunity to right this wrong for veterans injured during their service. This legislation will allow veterans to recover income taxes that were improperly collected by the Department of Defense on certain disability severance payments.

Under this bill, the Defense Department will be required to identify all the veterans who have been impacted by this problem. They will inform these veterans of the full amount that has been improperly withheld from their disability payments, and they will provide detailed instructions on how veterans can recover the money through an amended tax return.

Our men and women in uniform and their families have sacrificed so much for our Nation. Errors like this are completely unacceptable and cannot be allowed to go unaddressed.

I thank Representative ROUZER for his leadership on the Combat-Injured Veterans Tax Fairness Act and his dedication. This legislation takes important action to ensure America's promises are kept to our combat-injured heroes and their families.

Mr. Speaker, I urge all of my colleagues to join me in supporting its passage.

I reserve the balance of my time.

COMMITTEE ON ARMED SERVICES,
HOUSE OF REPRESENTATIVES,
Washington, DC, November 30, 2016.
Hon. KEVIN BRADY,
Chairman, Committee on Ways and Means, House of Representatives, Washington, DC.

DEAR MR. CHAIRMAN: I write concerning H.R. 5015, the Combat-Injured Veterans Tax Fairness Act of 2016, which was referred to the Committee on Armed Services, and in addition to the Committee on Ways and Means, for a period to be subsequently determined by the Speaker.

In order to expedite this legislation for floor consideration, the Committee on Armed Services will forgo action on this bill. This decision is conditional on our mutual understanding that forgoing consideration in no way diminishes or alters the jurisdictional interests of the Committee on Armed Services in this bill, any subsequent amendments, or similar legislation.

Please place a copy of this letter and your response acknowledging our jurisdictional interest into the Congressional Record during consideration of the measure on the House floor.

Sincerely,
WILLIAM M. "MAC" THORNBERRY,
Chairman.

———

COMMITTEE ON WAYS AND MEANS,
HOUSE OF REPRESENTATIVES,
Washington, DC, December 1, 2016.
Hon. WILLIAM M. "MAC" THORNBERRY,
Chairman, Committee on Armed Services, House of Representatives, Washington, DC.

DEAR CHAIRMAN THORNBERRY: Thank you for your letter regarding H.R. 5015, the "Combat-Injured Veterans Tax Fairness Act of 2016." As you noted, the bill was referred to the Committee on Armed Services.

I am most appreciative of your decision to waive formal consideration of H.R. 5015 so that it may proceed expeditiously to the

House floor. I acknowledge that although you waived formal consideration of the bill, the Committee on Armed Services is in no way waiving its jurisdiction over the subject matter contained in those provisions of the bill that fall within your Rule X jurisdiction.

I will include a copy of our letters in the Congressional Record during consideration of this legislation on the House floor.

Sincerely,

KEVIN BRADY,
Chairman.

Mr. NEAL. Mr. Speaker, I yield myself such time as I may consume.

Mr. Speaker, I thank Chairman BRADY for his efforts on behalf of this legislation.

This is a pleasant responsibility that we have when you consider that its corrective action will alone help 175 former military members in the State of Massachusetts and 13,800 across the country.

Let me reiterate some of the points that were made by Chairman BRADY. The bill before us corrects an issue related to a provision that was designed to alleviate some of the tax burdens of our Nation's combat-injured veterans. Under Federal law, veterans who suffer combat-related injuries and who are separated from the military are not supposed to be taxed on the one-time lump-sum disability severance payment they receive from the Department of Defense.

Due to an accounting error at the Defense Finance and Accounting Service, approximately $78 million in tax payments were inadvertently taken from combat-disabled servicemembers. Some of this improper withholding has taken place outside the 3-year period in which taxpayers could file an amended tax return.

H.R. 5015 would right this wrong by instructing DOD to identify those who were wrongfully taxed so that they can be reimbursed. This bill would allow those veterans identified by the DOD to file amended returns to recoup those unintentionally withheld funds.

Mr. Speaker, I am curious with respect to two items in this bill, and I just would like to raise this ever so politely with the majority party. Veterans' issues in the Congress have long had a bipartisan flavor to them. We have been supportive across the board in the efforts that we make as it relates to our veterans, and the differences we have generally are very small; but in this case, it does not appear that a Democrat was asked to cosponsor the bill in its original introduction. So I would hope in the future that even though this bill was largely sponsored by Republican Members, that on this side you could have easily picked up 33 Members as well.

So I hope going forward there will be that effort that we would continue with here to ensure that matters of this magnitude are well met by both parties. I would say that I don't want to suggest for a moment that this was done in a partisan atmosphere as much as I would like to think that it was just overlooked. I hope in the future that we would be considered for sponsorship of this sort of legislation as well.

Also, I would like to highlight an issue that is akin to the matter that is before us, and it comes from our friends on the committee, SAM JOHNSON and JOHN LARSON. They worked together on legislation that would prevent exonerated felons from facing an undue tax burden with respect to payments they received due to their wrongful conviction—emphasis on "wrongful conviction."

Similar to the veterans in the situation before us, these wrongfully convicted individuals should not face an improper tax liability on amounts intended to compensate for the tremendous injustices they faced under our legal system. Legislation to that effect became law in 2015. However, due to the lengthy IRS process in providing guidance on the issue, the statute would only allow less than 5 months for these exonerated individuals to amend their prior year tax returns.

Mr. JOHNSON and Mr. LARSON of Connecticut have worked tirelessly to make sure that these individuals are not unfairly burdened further than they already have been and they have proposed extending the statutory deadline for these individuals to file amended returns.

So while I think the legislation before us is sound, I do hope that the committee and the Congress will find time to consider similar IRS filing-deadline legislation with respect to these exonerated individuals.

Mr. Speaker, I reserve the balance of my time.

Mr. BRADY of Texas. Mr. Speaker, I yield 3 minutes to the gentleman from North Carolina (Mr. ROUZER), who is the author of the bill in the House. Besides his advocacy for small businesses and job growth, he is also a champion for our military, especially those who have been injured in combat.

Mr. ROUZER. Mr. Speaker, first, I want to make mention to the fine ranking member of the committee that we did reach out, certainly, to as many staff on the Democrat side as we possibly could. Perhaps we could have done a little bit better job of that, but I do want to make mention that we did make that effort—a point duly noted, though—and we will follow up multiple times the next time I have a bill that I think the gentleman would be interested in.

Mr. Speaker, I filed H.R. 5015, the Combat-Injured Veterans Tax Fairness Act, after learning that nearly 14,000 veterans from all 50 States and the District of Columbia who suffered service-ending, combat-related injuries never received the full amount of their severance payment because taxes were wrongly withheld. Let me repeat that: nearly 14,000 veterans did not receive the money to which they were entitled because of a taxing error made by the Federal Government.

Now, in case you are wondering how this error occurred, here is some background: the Internal Revenue Code excludes recurring disability payments from taxable income for personal injuries or sickness resulting from active service in our Armed Forces. In 1991, a Federal district court case, St. Clair v. United States, determined that one-time lump-sum disability severance payments received for injuries resulting from active service should be excluded from taxable income as well.

Despite this court decision and the resulting regulatory guidance that stemmed from it, taxes on combat-related disability severance payments have been withheld for many years. As was mentioned earlier, the Defense Finance and Accounting System claimed this was due to the limitations of its automated computer payment system. Go figure. Regardless, this is an issue that needs to be addressed.

Many of the veterans affected are not even aware that their benefits were improperly reduced. In most cases, the 3-year period in which they could file an amended tax return to get their money back has long since passed.

This legislation directs the Department of Defense to identify instances of improper withholding and determine how much these combat-wounded veterans are owed. Those veterans who were adversely affected will then be able to apply to the IRS to receive the money they are rightfully due.

Our soldiers, sailors, airmen, and marines risk their lives every day to protect our freedoms, our values, and our Republic. The revelation that there are thousands of veterans who did not receive their full disability severance pay is unacceptable, and it must be corrected immediately.

Today we can make a great step towards rectifying this problem. I think we can all agree that these veterans deserve no less for their service and sacrifice to our Nation.

I want to make special mention of Senator BOOZMAN of Arkansas and Senator WARNER of Virginia who have sponsored an identical bill in the United States Senate. Their leadership on this issue has been absolutely critical. I commend this legislation to my colleagues and encourage its passage.

Mr. NEAL. Mr. Speaker, I want to acknowledge the gentleman for his good effort and his thoughtful response to the point that I raised.

Of course, thanks to Chairman BRADY, this is an example, again, in a small way of how we can do some good things around here in a bipartisan manner.

Mr. Speaker, I yield back the balance of my time.

Mr. BRADY of Texas. Mr. Speaker, I yield myself such time as I may consume.

First, I really do applaud the work of Representative ROUZER in this area and the bipartisan work of Senators BOOZMAN and WARNER.

This is an area that could have easily been just swept aside over the years and never really addressed. The gentleman continued to raise the issue, bring it to our attention, and work through the legislative process. Again, I thank the gentleman for his very important leadership.

I also thank the chairman of the Armed Services Committee, Chairman MAC THORNBERRY, and his team for their approval of this measure and willingness to work with the author to bring this forward.

I, too, thank the ranking member, Mr. NEAL, and congratulate him on his naming as ranking member for the Ways and Means Committee. I look forward to working with the gentleman on these and other issues moving forward.

On behalf of 14,000 veterans who deserve to get the dollars they earned from the Department of Defense, late is better than never. I applaud the efforts of Mr. ROUZER in doing that.

Mr. Speaker, I urge support for this bipartisan bill.

I yield back the balance of my time.

Ms. JACKSON LEE. Mr. Speaker, I rise in support of H.R. 5015, Combat-Injured Veterans Tax Fairness Act of 2016, because the legislation directs the Defense Department (DoD) to restore improperly withheld for taxes from severance payments to individuals who retired or separated from service in the Armed Forces for combat-related injuries.

The bill also requires the DoD to notify combat-injured veterans if it had improperly withheld tax on their severance pay any time after January 17, 1991 and provide the veterans with information on how to seek a refund from the Internal Revenue Service (IRS).

H.R. 5015 works to remedy the egregious action of withholding more than $78 million in taxes from almost 14,000 combat-injured veterans.

This legislation additionally ensures that further tax amounts will not be taken from combat-injured veterans in the future.

As a member of the House Committee on Homeland Security since its establishment, and current Ranking Member of the Judiciary Subcommittee on Crime, Terrorism and Homeland Security this bill is of importance to me.

The DoD held an average of over $5,500 from each of the veterans since 1991.

That amount of money could help combat-injured veterans with hospital bills and the difficult transition back into civilian life.

I am pleased that the DoD will also have to submit a report on the number of times it had withheld pay to combat-injured veterans, the amount of each severance payment it withheld, and its actions to prevent future improper withholding to Congress within one year of the bill's enactment for Congress to assess the situation.

Our veterans deserve to be treated with respect.

It is only through the efforts and sacrifice of our veterans that America has the freedoms and privileges we do today.

I urge my colleagues to join me in supporting H.R. 5015.

Mr. DANNY K. DAVIS of Illinois. Mr. Speaker, I rise in strong support of H.R. 5015, a bill that would improve the fairness of the tax code and treat our service members with the respect they are due.

Veterans who suffered combat-related injuries who separated from the military are not supposed to be taxed on any one-time disability payments. Unfortunately, an accounting error has cost about 14,000 veterans more than $78 million in taxes. Just under 500 of these veterans are from my home state of Illinois.

H.R. 5015 fixes this problem by instructing the DoD to identify those who were wrongfully taxed so that they can be reimbursed. The lion's share of the affected veterans are outside of the window for amending their tax returns to recoup the funds.

Consequently, this bill would allow those veterans identified by the DoD to file amended returns to recoup these unintentionally-withheld funds. This is a good bill that helps our service members as we should. I hope that this chamber can engage in similar bipartisan efforts to support other needy Americans as we move into the next Congress.

I am troubled that some stakeholders are advocating that a 15 to 20 percent corporate tax rate serve as the central metric by which we judge any tax reform effort. To achieve this rate, middle- and low-income families and small businesses will have to subsidize the wealthiest corporations, foregoing critical credits and deductions that provide much needed assistance.

I sincerely hope that we advance the intent of this bill to help Americans in need as we consider tax reform next year.

I strongly support H.R. 5015, and I urge my colleagues to support its passage.

The SPEAKER pro tempore. The question is on the motion offered by the gentleman from Texas (Mr. BRADY) that the House suspend the rules and pass the bill, H.R. 5015, as amended.

The question was taken.

The SPEAKER pro tempore. In the opinion of the Chair, two-thirds being in the affirmative, the ayes have it.

Mr. BRADY of Texas. Mr. Speaker, on that I demand the yeas and nays.

The yeas and nays were ordered.

The SPEAKER pro tempore. Pursuant to clause 8 of rule XX, further proceedings on this motion will be postponed.

PRESCRIBED BURN APPROVAL ACT OF 2016

Mr. LUCAS. Mr. Speaker, I move to suspend the rules and pass the bill (S. 3395) to require limitations on prescribed burns.

The Clerk read the title of the bill.

The text of the bill is as follows:

S. 3395

Be it enacted by the Senate and House of Representatives of the United States of America in Congress assembled,

SECTION 1. SHORT TITLE.

This Act may be cited as the "Prescribed Burn Approval Act of 2016".

SEC. 2. DEFINITIONS.

In this Act:

(1) NATIONAL FIRE DANGER RATING SYSTEM.—The term "national fire danger rating system" means the national system used to provide a measure of fire danger according to a range of low to moderate to high to very high to extreme.

(2) PRESCRIBED BURN.—The term "prescribed burn" means a planned fire intentionally ignited.

(3) SECRETARY.—The term "Secretary" means the Secretary of Agriculture, acting through the Chief of the Forest Service.

SEC. 3. LIMITATIONS ON PRESCRIBED BURNS.

(a) IN GENERAL.—Except as provided in subsection (b), the Secretary shall not authorize a prescribed burn on Forest Service land if, for the county or contiguous county in which the land is located, the national fire danger rating system indicates an extreme fire danger level.

(b) EXCEPTION.—The Secretary may authorize a prescribed burn under a condition described in subsection (a) if the Secretary coordinates with the applicable State government and local fire officials.

(c) REPORT.—At the end of each fiscal year, the Secretary shall submit to Congress a report describing—

(1) the number and locations of prescribed burns during that fiscal year; and

(2) each prescribed burn during that fiscal year that was authorized by the Secretary pursuant to subsection (b).

The SPEAKER pro tempore. Pursuant to the rule, the gentleman from Oklahoma (Mr. LUCAS) and the gentleman from Minnesota (Mr. PETERSON) each will control 20 minutes.

The Chair recognizes the gentleman from Oklahoma.

GENERAL LEAVE

Mr. LUCAS. Mr. Speaker, I ask unanimous consent that all Members have 5 legislative days within which to revise and extend their remarks and include extraneous material on the bill under consideration.

The SPEAKER pro tempore. Is there objection to the request of the gentleman from Oklahoma?

There was no objection.

□ 1730

Mr. LUCAS. Mr. Speaker, I yield myself such time as I may consume.

I rise today in support of S. 3395, the Prescribed Burn Approval Act of 2016.

Across much of the country, Forest Service land borders private lands that are essential to the livelihood of farmers, ranchers, and foresters. While the Forest Service is tasked with managing these lands, many techniques are effective but carry risk.

On April 3, 2013, the Forest Service conducted a controlled burn on the Dakota Prairie Grasslands intended for 130 acres. As weather conditions changed, the fire escaped its boundary and burned 16,000 acres of private land. The prescribed burn planned by Federal officials resulted in millions of dollars in damage to private lands in South Dakota, with ranchers losing valuable pasture, hay, fence, and structures.

In the aftermath of the fire, the Office of the General Counsel of USDA determined that the Forest Service had done nothing out of line and claimed no responsibility to those harmed by this carelessness. This commonsense piece of legislation that we are addressing today, simply put, would require the Forest Service to conduct prescribed burns only when the national fire rating system indicates that it is safe to do so in that county and contiguous counties.

Furthermore, this bill will encourage greater collaboration with local officials, helping to mitigate more of the risk to private lands.

We all strive to be good neighbors and hope our neighbors will do the same. With passage, this bill gives many neighbors to the Forest Service additional certainty, and I urge your support.

Mr. Speaker, I reserve the balance of my time.

HOUSE OF REPRESENTATIVES,
COMMITTEE ON NATURAL RESOURCES,
Washington, DC, December 1, 2016.
Hon. K. MICHAEL CONAWAY,
Chairman, Committee on Agriculture,
Washington, DC.

DEAR MR. CHAIRMAN: I write regarding S. 3395, the Prescribed Burn Approval Act of 2016. This bill contains provisions under the jurisdiction of the Committee on Natural Resources.

I recognize and appreciate your desire to bring this bill before the House of Representatives in an expeditious manner, and accordingly, I will agree that the Committee on Natural Resources be discharged from further consideration of the bill. I do so with the understanding that this action does not affect the jurisdiction of the Committee on Natural Resources.

I also ask that a copy of this letter and your response be included in the Congressional Record during consideration of S. 3395 on the House floor.

Thank you for your work on this important issue, and I look forward to its enactment soon.

Sincerely,
ROB BISHOP,
Chairman, Committee on Natural Resources.

HOUSE OF REPRESENTATIVES,
COMMITTEE ON AGRICULTURE,
Washington, DC, December 1, 2016.
Hon. ROB BISHOP,
Chairman, Committee on Natural Resources,
Washington, DC.

DEAR CHAIRMAN BISHOP: I am writing concerning S. 3395, the Prescribed Burn Approval Act of 2016. The bill was agreed to in the Senate on November 17, 2016, and was referred in the House primarily to the Committee on Agriculture, with an additional referral to the Committee on Natural Resources.

I ask that you allow the Committee on Natural Resources to be discharged from further consideration of the bill so that it may be scheduled by the Majority Leader. This discharge in no way affects your Committee's jurisdiction over the subject matter of the bill, and it will not serve as precedent for future referrals. In addition, should a conference on the bill be necessary, I would support your request to have the Committee on Natural Resources represented on the con-

ference committee. Finally, I would be pleased to include this letter and any response in Congressional Record to memorialize our mutual understanding.

Thank you for your consideration and for your continued cooperation between our committees.

Sincerely,
K. MICHAEL CONAWAY,
Chairman.

Mr. PETERSON. Mr. Speaker, I yield myself such time as I may consume.

Mr. Speaker, the Prescribed Burn Approval Act of 2016, S. 3395, will help alleviate unintentional disasters when prescribed burns don't go exactly as planned. This is commonsense legislation, and I urge my colleagues to vote in support of it.

Prescribed burns are an important tool used by the Forest Service to help manage our national forests and grasslands. However, there is the risk of damage to nearby private property when prescribed burns get out of control, which happened, as was described recently, in the upper Midwest.

This bill will allow the Forest Service to continue to use prescribed burns while taking practical steps to prevent disasters. S. 3395 prohibits the Forest Service from utilizing prescribed burns in areas of high fire risk, unless the Forest Service coordinates with State governments and local officials.

Having local officials and responders aware of activities can help them be prepared and equipped to assist, if necessary. Frankly, this is something I would hope the Forest Service is already doing, but this bill is a good step. It will make sure that it happens in the future.

Again, I urge my colleagues to support the bill.

I yield back the balance of my time.

Mr. LUCAS. Mr. Speaker, I yield 3 minutes to the gentlewoman from South Dakota (Mrs. NOEM), who not only understands these issues but lives these issues.

Mrs. NOEM. Mr. Speaker, I thank the chairman for yielding to me today.

Mr. Speaker, today, I rise in support of S. 3395, the Prescribed Burn Approval Act. This is a commonsense bill that will prohibit the U.S. Forest Service from authorizing prescribed burns in an area that is labeled an extreme fire danger except under circumstances that have local coordination. Unfortunately, we have seen instances where the Forest Service has acted recklessly by starting prescribed burns under extremely hazardous conditions.

The Pautre fire in South Dakota is one such example. Despite the hot and windy conditions and being warned repeatedly from local ranchers and local officials that it was too windy and too dry to be starting a controlled burn, the Forest Service still carried out a prescribed burn that was intended to cover just 130 acres of dead crested wheatgrass.

Within hours, the fire escalated out of control. More than 10,000 acres of

Forest Service land, grazing association controlled land, and private land was consumed by the wildfire. Millions of dollars of damage was done not only to the land but to fences and families. Families were devastated.

Multiple firefighting units and personnel were put in harm's way. This burn should not have occurred that day without the collaboration and additional precautions that such a burn will require. It should happen in consultation with local officials and those who know the land best, those who live on the land and work the land each and every day—local farmers and ranchers.

It only makes sense that the Forest Service has the responsibility to coordinate with local and State fire officials in circumstances where the threat of wildfire is high. This bill is a step in the right direction to make certain that necessary precautions are taken.

Furthermore, this bill would add transparency and a degree of accountability to the Forest Service's actions by ensuring that Congress is aware of the prescribed burns that are done under hazardous conditions.

I would like to thank Senator THUNE for his work on this bill and the chairman for bringing this bill forward.

I urge my colleagues to vote in favor.

Mr. PETERSON. Mr. Speaker, I have no further speakers, and I yield back the balance of my time.

Mr. LUCAS. Mr. Speaker, I yield myself such time as I may consume.

It is worth noting that before there were ever farmers and ranchers on the plains, before Coronado ever came up from the south, or Lewis and Clark crossed through the north, and even before our Native American friends first appeared in North America fire has been an important management tool in the ecosystem of the Great Plains—whether the northern plains where my colleague, Mrs. NOEM, lives or the southern plains where I live—an important tool. Maintaining the health of the grasslands, addressing the woody plants that are invasive, this is an important tool.

This is why today we rise together to ask for our colleagues to vote for this bill, to provide the ability for everyone who occupies the plains to comfortably work together to use this tool to maintain the health of the Great Plains.

Mr. Speaker, I urge all of my colleagues to join us in passing the bill.

I yield back the balance of my time.

The SPEAKER pro tempore. The question is on the motion offered by the gentleman from Oklahoma (Mr. LUCAS) that the House suspend the rules and pass the bill, S. 3395.

The question was taken; and (two-thirds being in the affirmative) the rules were suspended and the bill was passed.

A motion to reconsider was laid on the table.

DEPARTMENT OF STATE OPERATIONS AUTHORIZATION AND EMBASSY SECURITY ACT, FISCAL YEAR 2016

Mr. ROYCE. Mr. Speaker, I move to suspend the rules and pass the bill (S. 1635) to authorize the Department of State for fiscal year 2016, and for other purposes, as amended.

The Clerk read the title of the bill.

The text of the bill is as follows:

S. 1635

Be it enacted by the Senate and House of Representatives of the United States of America in Congress assembled,

SECTION 1. SHORT TITLE; TABLE OF CONTENTS.

(a) SHORT TITLE.—This Act may be cited as the "Department of State Authorities Act, Fiscal Year 2017".

(b) TABLE OF CONTENTS.—The table of contents for this Act is as follows:

Sec. 1. Short title; Table of contents.
Sec. 2. Definitions.

TITLE I—EMBASSY SECURITY AND PERSONNEL PROTECTION

Subtitle A—Review and Planning Requirements

Sec. 101. Designation of high risk, high threat posts.
Sec. 102. Contingency plans for high risk, high threat posts.
Sec. 103. Direct reporting.
Sec. 104. Accountability Review Board recommendations related to unsatisfactory leadership.

Subtitle B—Physical Security and Personnel Requirements

Sec. 111. Capital security cost sharing program.
Sec. 112. Local guard contracts abroad under diplomatic security program.
Sec. 113. Transfer authority.
Sec. 114. Security enhancements for soft targets.
Sec. 115. Exemption from certain procurement protest procedures for noncompetitive contracting in emergency circumstances.
Sec. 116. Sense of Congress regarding minimum security standards for temporary United States diplomatic and consular posts.
Sec. 117. Assignment of personnel at high risk, high threat posts.
Sec. 118. Annual report on embassy construction costs.
Sec. 119. Embassy security, construction, and maintenance.

Subtitle C—Security Training

Sec. 121. Security training for personnel assigned to high risk, high threat posts.
Sec. 122. Sense of Congress regarding language requirements for diplomatic security personnel assigned to high risk, high threat post.

Subtitle D—Expansion of the Marine Corps Security Guard Detachment Program

Sec. 131. Marine Corps Security Guard Program.

TITLE II—OFFICE OF INSPECTOR GENERAL OF THE DEPARTMENT OF STATE AND BROADCASTING BOARD OF GOVERNORS

Sec. 201. Competitive hiring status for former employees of the Office of the Special Inspector General for Iraq Reconstruction.
Sec. 202. Certification of independence of information technology systems of the Office of Inspector General of the Department of State and Broadcasting Board of Governors.
Sec. 203. Protecting the integrity of internal investigations.
Sec. 204. Report on Inspector General inspection and auditing of Foreign Service posts and bureaus and other offices of the Department.
Sec. 205. Implementing GAO and OIG recommendations.
Sec. 206. Inspector General salary limitations.

TITLE III—INTERNATIONAL ORGANIZATIONS

Sec. 301. Oversight of and accountability for peacekeeper abuses.
Sec. 302. Reimbursement of contributing countries.
Sec. 303. Withholding of assistance.
Sec. 304. United Nations peacekeeping assessment formula.
Sec. 305. Reimbursement or application of credits.
Sec. 306. Report on United States contributions to the United Nations relating to peacekeeping operations.
Sec. 307. Whistleblower protections for United Nations personnel.
Sec. 308. Encouraging employment of United States citizens at the United Nations.
Sec. 309. Statement of policy on Member State's voting practices at the United Nations.
Sec. 310. Qualifications of the United Nations Secretary General.
Sec. 311. Policy regarding the United Nations Human Rights Council.
Sec. 312. Additional report on other United States contributions to the United Nations.
Sec. 313. Comparative report on peacekeeping operations.

TITLE IV—PERSONNEL AND ORGANIZATIONAL ISSUES

Sec. 401. Locally-employed staff wages.
Sec. 402. Expansion of civil service opportunities.
Sec. 403. Promotion to the Senior Foreign Service.
Sec. 404. Lateral entry into the Foreign Service.
Sec. 405. Reemployment of annuitants and workforce rightsizing.
Sec. 406. Integration of foreign economic policy.
Sec. 407. Training support services.
Sec. 408. Special agents.
Sec. 409. Limited appointments in the Foreign Service.
Sec. 410. Report on diversity recruitment, employment, retention, and promotion.
Sec. 411. Market data for cost-of-living adjustments.
Sec. 412. Technical amendment to Federal Workforce Flexibility Act.
Sec. 413. Retention of mid- and senior-level professionals from traditionally under-represented minority groups.
Sec. 414. Employee assignment restrictions.
Sec. 415. Security clearance suspensions.
Sec. 416. Sense of Congress on the integration of policies related to the participation of women in preventing and resolving conflicts.
Sec. 417. Foreign Service families workforce study.
Sec. 418. Special envoys, representatives, advisors, and coordinators of the Department.
Sec. 419. Combating anti-Semitism.

TITLE V—CONSULAR AUTHORITIES

Sec. 501. Codification of enhanced consular immunities.
Sec. 502. Passports made in the United States.

TITLE VI—WESTERN HEMISPHERE DRUG POLICY COMMISSION

Sec. 601. Establishment.
Sec. 602. Duties.
Sec. 603. Membership.
Sec. 604. Powers.
Sec. 605. Staff.
Sec. 606. Sunset.

TITLE VII—MISCELLANEOUS PROVISIONS

Sec. 701. Foreign relations exchange programs.
Sec. 702. United States Advisory Commission on Public Diplomacy.
Sec. 703. Broadcasting Board of Governors.
Sec. 704. Rewards for Justice.
Sec. 705. Extension of period for reimbursement of seized commercial fishermen.
Sec. 706. Expansion of the Charles B. Rangel International Affairs Program, the Thomas R. Pickering Foreign Affairs Fellowship Program, and the Donald M. Payne International Development Fellowship Program.
Sec. 707. GAO report on Department critical telecommunications equipment or services obtained from suppliers closely linked to a leading cyber-threat actor.
Sec. 708. Implementation plan for information technology and knowledge management.
Sec. 709. Ransoms to foreign terrorist organizations.
Sec. 710. Strategy to combat terrorist use of social media.
Sec. 711. Report on Department information technology acquisition practices.
Sec. 712. Public availability of reports on nominees to be chiefs of mission.
Sec. 713. Recruitment and retention of individuals who have lived, worked, or studied in predominantly Muslim countries or communities.
Sec. 714. Sense of Congress regarding coverage of appropriate therapies for dependents with autism spectrum disorder (ASD).
Sec. 715. Repeal of obsolete reports.
Sec. 716. Prohibition on additional funding.

SEC. 2. DEFINITIONS.

In this Act:

(1) APPROPRIATE CONGRESSIONAL COMMITTEES.—The term "appropriate congressional committees" means—

(A) the Committee on Foreign Relations of the Senate; and

(B) the Committee on Foreign Affairs of the House of Representatives.

(2) DEPARTMENT.—Unless otherwise specified, the term "Department" means the Department of State.

(3) FOREIGN SERVICE.—The term "Foreign Service" has the meaning given such term in section 102 of the Foreign Service Act of 1980 (22 U.S.C. 3902).

(4) INSPECTOR GENERAL.—Unless otherwise specified, the term "Inspector General"

means the Office of Inspector General of the Department of State and the Broadcasting Board of Governors.

(5) PEACEKEEPING CREDITS.—The term "peacekeeping credits" means the amounts by which United States assessed peacekeeping contributions exceed actual expenditures, apportioned to the United States, of peacekeeping operations by the United Nations during a United Nations peacekeeping fiscal year.

(6) SECRETARY.—Unless otherwise specified, the term "Secretary" means the Secretary of State.

TITLE I—EMBASSY SECURITY AND PERSONNEL PROTECTION

Subtitle A—Review and Planning Requirements

SEC. 101. DESIGNATION OF HIGH RISK, HIGH THREAT POSTS.

(a) IN GENERAL.—Title I of the Omnibus Diplomatic Security and Antiterrorism Act of 1986 (22 U.S.C. 4801 et seq.; relating to diplomatic security) is amended by inserting after section 103 the following new sections:

"SEC. 104. DESIGNATION OF HIGH RISK, HIGH THREAT POSTS.

"(a) INITIAL DESIGNATION.—Not later than 30 days after the date of the enactment of this section, the Department of State shall submit to the appropriate congressional committees a report, in classified form, that contains a list of diplomatic and consular posts designated as high risk, high threat posts.

"(b) DESIGNATIONS BEFORE OPENING OR REOPENING POSTS.—Before opening or reopening a diplomatic or consular post, the Secretary shall determine if such post should be designated as a high risk, high threat post.

"(c) DESIGNATING EXISTING POSTS.—The Secretary shall regularly review existing diplomatic and consular posts to determine if any such post should be designated as a high risk, high threat post if conditions at such post or the surrounding security environment require such a designation.

"(d) DEFINITIONS.—In this section:

"(1) APPROPRIATE CONGRESSIONAL COMMITTEES.—The term 'appropriate congressional committees' means the Committee on Foreign Affairs of the House of Representatives and the Committee on Foreign Relations of the Senate.

"(2) HIGH RISK, HIGH THREAT POST.—The term 'high risk, high threat post' means a United States diplomatic or consular post or other United States mission abroad, as determined by the Secretary, that, among other factors—

"(A) is located in a country—

"(i) with high to critical levels of political violence and terrorism; and

"(ii) the government of which lacks the ability or willingness to provide adequate security; and

"(B) has mission physical security platforms that fall below the Department of State's established standards.

"SEC. 105. BRIEFINGS ON EMBASSY SECURITY.

"(a) BRIEFING.—The Secretary shall provide monthly briefings to the appropriate congressional committees on—

"(1) any plans to open or reopen a high risk, high threat post, including—

"(A) the importance and appropriateness of the objectives of the proposed post to the national security of the United States, and the type and level of security threats such post could encounter;

"(B) working plans to expedite the approval and funding for establishing and operating such post, implementing physical security measures, providing necessary security and management personnel, and the provision of necessary equipment;

"(C) security 'tripwires' that would determine specific action, including enhanced security measures or evacuation of such post, based on the improvement or deterioration of the local security environment; and

"(D) in coordination with the Secretary of Defense, an evaluation of available United States military assets and operational plans to respond to such posts in extremis;

"(2) personnel staffing and rotation cycles at high risk, high threat posts;

"(3) the current security posture at posts of particular concern as determined by such committees; and

"(4) the progress towards implementation of the provisions specified in title I of the Department of State Authorities Act, Fiscal Year 2017.

"(b) CONGRESSIONAL NOTIFICATION.—

"(1) IN GENERAL.—Except as provided in paragraph (2), not later than 30 days before opening or reopening a high risk, high threat post, the Secretary shall notify the appropriate congressional committees of the decision to open or reopen such post.

"(2) EMERGENCY CIRCUMSTANCES.—If the Secretary determines that the national security interests of the United States require the opening or reopening of a high risk, high threat post in fewer than 30 days, then as soon as possible, but not later than 48 hours before such opening or reopening, the Secretary shall transmit to the appropriate congressional committees a notification detailing the decision to open or reopen such post, the nature of the critical national security interests at stake, and the circumstances that prevented the normal 30-day notice under paragraph (1).

"(c) APPROPRIATE CONGRESSIONAL COMMITTEES.—In this section, the term 'appropriate congressional committees' means—

"(1) the Committee on Foreign Affairs, the Committee on Armed Services, the Permanent Select Committee on Intelligence, and the Committee on Appropriations of the House of Representatives; and

"(2) the Committee on Foreign Relations, the Committee on Armed Services, the Select Committee on Intelligence, and the Committee on Appropriations of the Senate.".

(b) CONFORMING AMENDMENT.—The table of contents of the Omnibus Diplomatic Security and Antiterrorism Act of 1986 is amended by inserting after the item relating to section 103 the following new items:

"Sec. 104. Designation of high risk, high threat posts.

"Sec. 105. Briefings on embassy security.".

SEC. 102. CONTINGENCY PLANS FOR HIGH RISK, HIGH THREAT POSTS.

Subsection (a) of section 606 of the Secure Embassy Construction and Counterterrorism Act of 1999 (22 U.S.C. 4865; relating to diplomatic security) is amended—

(1) in paragraph (1)(A), in the first sentence—

(A) by inserting "and from complex attacks (as such term is defined in section 416 of the Omnibus Diplomatic Security and Antiterrorism Act of 1986)," after "attacks from vehicles"; and

(B) by inserting "or such a complex attack" before the period at the end;

(2) in paragraph (7), by inserting before the period at the end the following: ", including at high risk, high threat posts (as such term is defined in section 104 of the Omnibus Diplomatic Security and Antiterrorism Act of 1986), including options for the deployment of additional military personnel or equipment to bolster security and rapid deployment of armed or surveillance assets in response to an attack".

SEC. 103. DIRECT REPORTING.

The Assistant Secretary for Diplomatic Security shall report directly to the Secretary, without being required to obtain the approval or concurrence of any other official of the Department, as threats and circumstances require.

SEC. 104. ACCOUNTABILITY REVIEW BOARD RECOMMENDATIONS RELATED TO UNSATISFACTORY LEADERSHIP.

(a) IN GENERAL.—Subsection (c) of section 304 of the Diplomatic Security Act (22 U.S.C. 4834) is amended—

(1) in the matter preceding paragraph (1)—

(A) by striking "Whenever" and inserting "If"; and

(B) by striking "has breached the duty of that individual" and inserting "has engaged in misconduct or unsatisfactorily performed the duties of employment of that individual, and such misconduct or unsatisfactory performance has significantly contributed to the serious injury, loss of life, or significant destruction of property, or the serious breach of security that is the subject of the Board's examination as described in subsection (a)";

(2) in paragraph (2), by striking "finding" each place it appears and inserting "findings"; and

(3) in the matter following paragraph (3)—

(A) by striking "has breached a duty of that individual" and inserting "has engaged in misconduct or unsatisfactorily performed the duties of employment of that individual as described in this subsection"; and

(B) by striking "to the performance of the duties of that individual".

(b) EFFECTIVE DATE.—The amendments made by subsection (a) shall apply with respect to any Accountability Review Board that is convened under section 301 of the Diplomatic Security Act (22 U.S.C. 4831) on or after the date of the enactment of this Act.

Subtitle B—Physical Security and Personnel Requirements

SEC. 111. CAPITAL SECURITY COST SHARING PROGRAM.

(a) SENSE OF CONGRESS ON THE CAPITAL SECURITY COST SHARING PROGRAM.—It is the sense of Congress that the Capital Security Cost Sharing Program should prioritize the construction of new facilities and the maintenance of existing facilities at high risk, high threat posts.

(b) RESTRICTION ON CONSTRUCTION OF OFFICE SPACE.—Paragraph (2) of section 604(e) of the Secure Embassy Construction and Counterterrorism Act of 1999 (title VI of division A of H.R. 3427, as enacted into law by section 1000(a)(7) of Public Law 106–113; 113 Stat. 1501A–453; 22 U.S.C. 4865 note) is amended by adding at the end the following new sentence: "A project to construct a diplomatic facility of the United States may not include office space or other accommodations for an employee of a Federal department or agency to the extent that the Secretary of State determines that such department or agency has not provided to the Department of State the full amount of funding required under paragraph (1), notwithstanding any authorization and appropriation of relevant funds by Congress.".

SEC. 112. LOCAL GUARD CONTRACTS ABROAD UNDER DIPLOMATIC SECURITY PROGRAM.

Section 136 of the Foreign Relations Authorization Act, Fiscal Years 1990 and 1991 (22 U.S.C. 4864) is amended by adding at the end the following new subsection:

"(h) AWARD OF LOCAL GUARD AND PROTECTIVE SERVICE CONTRACTS.—In evaluating proposals for local guard contracts under this section, the Secretary of State may award such contracts on the basis of best value as determined by a cost-technical tradeoff analysis (as described in Federal Acquisition Regulation part 15.101) and, with respect to such contracts for posts that are not high risk, high threat posts (as such term is defined in section 104 of the Omnibus Diplomatic Security and Antiterrorism Act of 1986 (22 U.S.C. 4801 et seq.; relating to diplomatic security)), subject to congressional notification 15-days prior to any such award.".

SEC. 113. TRANSFER AUTHORITY.

Section 4 of the Foreign Service Buildings Act, 1926 (22 U.S.C. 295) is amended by adding at the end the following new subsection:

"(j)(1) In addition to exercising any other transfer authority available to the Secretary of State, and subject to paragraphs (2) and (3), the Secretary may transfer to, and merge with, any appropriation for embassy security, construction, and maintenance such amounts appropriated for fiscal year 2018 for any other purpose related to the administration of foreign affairs on or after January 1, 2017, if the Secretary determines such transfer is necessary to provide for the security of sites and buildings in foreign countries under the jurisdiction and control of the Secretary.

"(2) Any funds transferred pursuant to paragraph (1)—

"(A) shall not exceed 20 percent of any appropriation made available for fiscal year 2018 for the Department of State under the heading 'Administration of Foreign Affairs', and no such appropriation shall be increased by more than 10 percent by any such transfer; and

"(B) shall be merged with funds in the heading to which transferred, and shall be available subject to the same terms and conditions as the funds with which merged.

"(3) Not later than 15 days before any transfer of funds pursuant to paragraph (1), the Secretary of State shall notify in writing the Committee on Foreign Relations and the Committee on Appropriations of the Senate and the Committee on Foreign Affairs and the Committee on Appropriations of the House of Representatives. Any such notification shall include a description of the particular security need necessitating the transfer at issue.".

SEC. 114. SECURITY ENHANCEMENTS FOR SOFT TARGETS.

Section 29 of the State Department Basic Authorities Act of 1956 (22 U.S.C. 2701) is amended, in the third sentence, by inserting "physical security enhancements and" after "may include".

SEC. 115. EXEMPTION FROM CERTAIN PROCUREMENT PROTEST PROCEDURES FOR NONCOMPETITIVE CONTRACTING IN EMERGENCY CIRCUMSTANCES.

A determination by the Department to use procedures other than competitive procedures under section 3304 of title 41, United States Code, in order to meet emergency security requirements, as determined by the Secretary or the Secretary's designee, including physical security upgrades, protective equipment, and other immediate threat mitigation projects, shall not be subject to challenge by protest under either subchapter V of chapter 35 of title 31, United States Code, or section 1491 of title 28, United States Code.

SEC. 116. SENSE OF CONGRESS REGARDING MINIMUM SECURITY STANDARDS FOR TEMPORARY UNITED STATES DIPLOMATIC AND CONSULAR POSTS.

It is the sense of Congress that—

(1) the Overseas Security Policy Board's security standards for facilities should apply to all facilities consistent with 12 FAM 311.2; and

(2) such facilities should comply with requirements for attaining a waiver or exception to applicable standards if it is in the national interest of the United States.

SEC. 117. ASSIGNMENT OF PERSONNEL AT HIGH RISK, HIGH THREAT POSTS.

The Secretary to the extent practicable shall station key personnel for sustained periods of time at high risk, high threat posts (as such term is defined in section 104 of the Omnibus Diplomatic Security and Antiterrorism Act of 1986, as added by section 401 of this Act) in order to—

(1) establish institutional knowledge and situational awareness that would allow for a fuller familiarization of the local political and security environment in which such posts are located; and

(2) ensure that necessary security procedures are implemented.

SEC. 118. ANNUAL REPORT ON EMBASSY CONSTRUCTION COSTS.

(a) IN GENERAL.—Not later than 180 days after the date of the enactment of this Act and annually thereafter, the Secretary shall submit to the appropriate congressional committees a comprehensive report regarding all ongoing embassy construction projects and major embassy security upgrade projects.

(b) CONTENTS.—Each report required under subsection (a) shall include the following with respect to each ongoing embassy construction projects and major embassy security upgrade projects:

(1) The initial cost estimate.

(2) The amount expended on the project to date.

(3) The projected timeline for completing the project.

(4) Any cost overruns incurred by the project.

(c) INITIAL REPORT.—The first report required under subsection (a) shall include an annex regarding all embassy construction projects and major embassy security upgrade projects completed during the 10-year period ending on the date of the enactment of this Act, including, for each such project, the following:

(1) The initial cost estimate.

(2) The amount actually expended on the project.

(3) Any additional time required to complete the project beyond the initial timeline.

(4) Any cost overruns incurred by the project.

SEC. 119. EMBASSY SECURITY, CONSTRUCTION, AND MAINTENANCE.

Section 1 of the Foreign Service Buildings Act, 1926 (22 U.S.C. 292), is amended by adding at the end the following new subsection:

"(c) AUTHORIZATION FOR IMPROVEMENTS AND CONSTRUCTION.—The Secretary of State may improve or construct facilities overseas for other Federal departments and agencies on an advance-of-funds or reimbursable basis if such advances or reimbursements are credited to the Embassy Security, Construction, and Maintenance account and remain available until expended.".

Subtitle C—Security Training

SEC. 121. SECURITY TRAINING FOR PERSONNEL ASSIGNED TO HIGH RISK, HIGH THREAT POSTS.

(a) IN GENERAL.—Title IV of the Omnibus Diplomatic Security and Antiterrorism Act of 1986 (22 U.S.C. 4851 et seq.; relating to diplomatic security) is amended by adding at the end the following new sections:

"SEC. 416. SECURITY TRAINING FOR PERSONNEL ASSIGNED TO A HIGH RISK, HIGH THREAT POST.

"(a) IN GENERAL.—Individuals assigned permanently to or who are in long-term temporary duty status as designated by the Secretary of State at a high risk, high threat post shall receive security training described in subsection (b) on a mandatory basis in order to prepare such individuals for living and working at such posts.

"(b) SECURITY TRAINING DESCRIBED.—Security training referred to in subsection (a)—

"(1) is training to improve basic knowledge and skills; and

"(2) may include—

"(A) an ability to recognize, avoid, and respond to potential terrorist situations, including a complex attack;

"(B) conducting surveillance detection;

"(C) providing emergency medical care;

"(D) ability to detect the presence of improvised explosive devices;

"(E) minimal firearms familiarization; and

"(F) defensive driving maneuvers.

"(c) EFFECTIVE DATE.—The requirements of this section shall take effect upon the date of the enactment of this section.

"(d) DEFINITIONS.—In this section and section 417:

"(1) COMPLEX ATTACK.—The term 'complex attack' has the meaning given such term by the North Atlantic Treaty Organization, as follows: 'An attack conducted by multiple hostile elements which employ at least two distinct classes of weapon systems (i.e., indirect fire and direct fire, improvised explosive devices, and surface to air fire).'.

"(2) HIGH RISK, HIGH THREAT POST.—The term 'high risk, high threat post' has the meaning given such term in section 104.

"SEC. 417. SECURITY MANAGEMENT TRAINING FOR OFFICIALS ASSIGNED TO A HIGH RISK, HIGH THREAT POST.

"(a) IN GENERAL.—Officials described in subsection (c) who are assigned to a high risk, high threat post shall receive security training described in subsection (b) on a mandatory basis in order to improve the ability of such officials to make security-related management decisions.

"(b) SECURITY TRAINING DESCRIBED.—Security training referred to in subsection (a) may include—

"(1) development of skills to better evaluate threats;

"(2) effective use of security resources to mitigate such threats; and

"(3) improved familiarity of available security resources.

"(c) OFFICIALS DESCRIBED.—Officials referred to in subsection (a) are the following:

"(1) Members of the Senior Foreign Service appointed under section 302(a)(1) or 303 of the Foreign Service Act of 1980 (22 U.S.C. 3942(a)(1) and 3943) or members of the Senior Executive Service (as such term is described in section 3132(a)(2) of title 5, United States Code).

"(2) Foreign Service officers appointed under section 302(a)(1) of the Foreign Service Act of 1980 (22 U.S.C. 3942(a)(1)) holding a position in classes FS-1 or FS-2.

"(3) Foreign Service Specialists appointed by the Secretary under section 303 of the Foreign Service Act of 1980 (22 U.S.C. 3943) holding a position in classes FS-1 or FS-2.

"(4) Individuals holding a position in grades GS-14 or GS-15.

"(5) Personal services contractors and other contractors serving in positions or capacities similar to the officials described in paragraphs (1) through (4).

"(d) EFFECTIVE DATE.—The requirements of this section shall take effect beginning on the date that is one year after the date of the enactment of this section.''.

(b) CONFORMING AMENDMENT.—The table of contents of the Omnibus Diplomatic Security and Antiterrorism Act of 1986 is amended by inserting after the item relating to section 415 the following new items:

"Sec. 416. Security training for personnel assigned to a high risk, high threat post.

"Sec. 417. Security management training for officials assigned to a high risk, high threat post.''.

SEC. 122. SENSE OF CONGRESS REGARDING LANGUAGE REQUIREMENTS FOR DIPLOMATIC SECURITY PERSONNEL ASSIGNED TO HIGH RISK, HIGH THREAT POST.

(a) IN GENERAL.—It is the sense of Congress that diplomatic security personnel assigned permanently to or who are in long-term temporary duty status as designated by the Secretary at a high risk, high threat post should receive language training described in subsection (b) in order to prepare such personnel for duty requirements at such post.

(b) LANGUAGE TRAINING DESCRIBED.—Language training referred to in subsection (a) should prepare personnel described in such subsection to—

(1) speak the language at issue with sufficient structural accuracy and vocabulary to participate effectively in most formal and informal conversations on subjects germane to security; and

(2) read within an adequate range of speed and with almost complete comprehension on subjects germane to security.

Subtitle D—Expansion of the Marine Corps Security Guard Detachment Program

SEC. 131. MARINE CORPS SECURITY GUARD PROGRAM.

(a) IN GENERAL.—Pursuant to the responsibility of the Secretary for diplomatic security under section 103 of the Diplomatic Security Act (22 U.S.C. 4802; enacted as part of the Omnibus Diplomatic Security and Antiterrorism Act of 1986 (Public Law 99-399)), the Secretary, in consultation with the Secretary of Defense, shall conduct an annual review of the Marine Corps Security Guard Program, including the following:

(1) An evaluation of whether the size and composition of the Marine Corps Security Guard Program is adequate to meet global diplomatic security requirements.

(2) An assessment of whether the Marine Corps security guards are appropriately deployed among United States embassies, consulates, and other diplomatic facilities to respond to evolving security developments and potential threats to United States interests abroad.

(3) An assessment of the mission objectives of the Marine Corps Security Guard Program and the procedural rules of engagement to protect diplomatic personnel under the Program.

(b) REPORTING REQUIREMENT.—Not later than 180 days after the date of the enactment of this Act and annually thereafter for three years, the Secretary, in consultation with the Secretary of Defense, shall submit to the Committee on Foreign Affairs, the Committee on Armed Services, and the Committee on Appropriations of the House of Representatives and the Committee on Foreign Relations, the Committee on Armed Services, and the Committee on Appropriations of the Senate an unclassified report, with a classified annex as necessary, that addresses the requirements specified in subsection (a).

TITLE II—OFFICE OF INSPECTOR GENERAL OF THE DEPARTMENT OF STATE AND BROADCASTING BOARD OF GOVERNORS

SEC. 201. COMPETITIVE HIRING STATUS FOR FORMER EMPLOYEES OF THE OFFICE OF THE SPECIAL INSPECTOR GENERAL FOR IRAQ RECONSTRUCTION.

Notwithstanding any other provision of law, any employee of the Office of the Special Inspector General for Iraq Reconstruction who completes at least 12 months of continuous employment within the Office at any time prior to October 5, 2013, and was not terminated for cause shall acquire competitive status for appointment to any position in the competitive service for which the employee possesses the required qualifications.

SEC. 202. CERTIFICATION OF INDEPENDENCE OF INFORMATION TECHNOLOGY SYSTEMS OF THE OFFICE OF INSPECTOR GENERAL OF THE DEPARTMENT OF STATE AND BROADCASTING BOARD OF GOVERNORS.

Not later than one year after the date of the enactment of this Act and annually thereafter for four years, the Secretary shall submit to the appropriate congressional committees, with respect to the network, information systems, and files of the Office of Inspector General of the Department and Broadcasting Board of Governors managed by the Department, a certification that the Department has ensured the integrity and independence of such network, information systems, and files, including the prevention of access to such network, information systems, and files other than as authorized by the Inspector General or the Attorney General, or, for purposes of ensuring information and systems security pursuant to applicable statute, the Chief Information Officer of the Department.

SEC. 203. PROTECTING THE INTEGRITY OF INTERNAL INVESTIGATIONS.

Subsection (c) of section 209 of the Foreign Service Act of 1980 (22 U.S.C. 3929) is amended by adding at the end the following new paragraph:

"(6) REQUIRED REPORTING OF ALLEGATIONS AND INVESTIGATIONS AND INSPECTOR GENERAL AUTHORITY.—

"(A) IN GENERAL.—The head of a bureau, post, or other office of the Department of State (in this paragraph referred to as a 'Department entity') shall submit to the Inspector General a report of any allegation of—

"(i) waste, fraud, or abuse in a Department program or operation;

"(ii) criminal or serious misconduct on the part of a Department employee at the FS-1, GS-15, or GM-15 level or higher;

"(iii) criminal misconduct on the part of a Department employee; and

"(iv) serious, noncriminal misconduct on the part of any Department employee who is authorized to carry a weapon, make arrests, or conduct searches, such as conduct that, if proved, would constitute perjury or material dishonesty, warrant suspension as discipline for a first offense, or result in loss of law enforcement authority.

"(B) DEADLINE.—The head of a Department entity shall submit to the Inspector General a report of an allegation described in subparagraph (A) not later than five business days after the date on which the head of such Department entity is made aware of such allegation.''.

SEC. 204. REPORT ON INSPECTOR GENERAL INSPECTION AND AUDITING OF FOREIGN SERVICE POSTS AND BUREAUS AND OTHER OFFICES OF THE DEPARTMENT.

(a) IN GENERAL.—Not later than 180 days after the date of the enactment of this Act, the Inspector General shall submit to the appropriate congressional committees a report on the requirement under section 209(a)(1) of the Foreign Service Act of 1980 (22 U.S.C. 3929(a)(1)) that the Inspector General inspect and audit, at least every five years, the administration of activities and operations of each Foreign Service post and each bureau or other office of the Department.

(b) CONSIDERATION OF MULTI-TIER SYSTEM.—The report required under subsection (a) shall assess the advisability and feasibility of implementing a multi-tier system for inspecting Foreign Service posts and bureaus and other offices of the Department under section 209(a)(1) of the Foreign Service Act of 1980 featuring more or less frequent inspections and audits based on risk, including security risk, as may be determined by the Inspector General.

SEC. 205. IMPLEMENTING GAO AND OIG RECOMMENDATIONS.

(a) SENSE OF CONGRESS.—It is the sense of Congress that the Department has not implemented all of the recommendations made by the Government Accountability Office (GAO) and the Office of the Inspector General (OIG) related to embassy security and that some recommendations may yield potentially significant cost savings to the Department.

(b) BRIEFING.—The Secretary shall provide a briefing to the appropriate congressional committees detailing the rationale for not implementing recommendations made by the GAO and OIG related to embassy security or those that may yield significant cost savings to the Department, if implemented.

SEC. 206. INSPECTOR GENERAL SALARY LIMITATIONS.

Section 412 of the Foreign Service Act of 1980 (22 U.S.C. 3972) is amended by inserting after subsection (a) the following new subsection:

"(b) The Inspector General of the United States Agency for International Development (USAID) shall limit the payment of special differentials to USAID Foreign Service criminal investigators to levels at which the aggregate of basic pay and special differential for any pay period would equal, for such criminal investigators, the bi-weekly pay limitations on premium pay regularly placed on other criminal investigators within the Federal law enforcement community. This provision shall be retroactive to January 1, 2013.''.

TITLE III—INTERNATIONAL ORGANIZATIONS

SEC. 301. OVERSIGHT OF AND ACCOUNTABILITY FOR PEACEKEEPER ABUSES.

(a) STRATEGY TO ENSURE REFORM AND ACCOUNTABILITY.—Not later than 180 days after the date of the enactment of this Act, the Secretary shall submit, in unclassified form, to the appropriate congressional committees—

(1) a United States strategy for combating sexual exploitation and abuse in United Nations peacekeeping operations; and

(2) an implementation plan for achieving the objectives set forth in the strategy described in paragraph (1).

(b) OBJECTIVES.—The objectives of the strategy required under subsection (a) shall be the following:

(1) To dramatically reduce the incidence of sexual exploitation and abuse committed by

civilian and military personnel assigned to United Nations peacekeeping operations.

(2) To ensure the introduction and implementation by the United Nations of improved training, oversight, and accountability mechanisms for United Nations peacekeeping operations and the personnel involved with such operations.

(3) To ensure swift justice for any such personnel who are found to have committed sexual exploitation or abuse.

(4) To assist the United Nations and troop- or police-contributing countries, as necessary and appropriate, to improve their ability to prevent, identify, and prosecute sexual exploitation or abuse by personnel involved in peacekeeping operations.

(c) ELEMENTS.—The strategy required under subsection (a) shall include the following elements and objectives:

(1) The amendment of the model memorandum of understanding and review of all current memorandums of understanding for troop- or police-contributing countries participating in United Nations peacekeeping operations to strengthen provisions relating to the investigation, repatriation, prosecution, and discipline of troops or police that are credibly alleged to have engaged in cases of misconduct.

(2) The establishment of onsite courts-martial, as appropriate, for the prosecution of crimes committed by military peacekeeping personnel, that is consistent with each peacekeeping operations' status of forces agreement with its host country.

(3) The exploration of appropriate arrangements to waive the immunity of civilian employees of the United Nations and its specialized agencies, funds, and programs to enable the prosecution of such employees who are credibly alleged to have engaged in sexual exploitation, abuse, or other crimes.

(4) The creation of a United Nations Security Council ombudsman office that—

(A) is authorized to conduct ongoing oversight of peacekeeping operations;

(B) reports directly to the Security Council on—

(i) offenses committed by peacekeeping personnel or United Nations civilian staff or volunteers; and

(ii) the actions taken in response to such offenses; and

(C) provides reports to the Security Council on the conduct of personnel in each peacekeeping operation not less frequently than annually and before the expiration or renewal of the mandate of any such peacekeeping operation.

(5) The provision of guidance from the United Nations on the establishment of a standing claims commission for each peacekeeping operation—

(A) to address any grievances by a host country's civilian population against United Nations personnel in cases of alleged abuses by peacekeeping personnel; and

(B) to provide means for the government of the country of which culpable United Nations peacekeeping or civilian personnel are nationals to compensate the victims of such crimes.

(6) The adoption of a United Nations policy and plan that increases the number of troop- or police-contributing countries that—

(A) obtain and maintain DNA samples from each national of such country who is a member of a United Nations military contingent or formed police unit, consistent with national laws, of such contingent or unit; and

(B) make such DNA samples available to investigators from the troop- or police contributing country (except that such should not be made available to the United Nations) if allegations of sexual exploitation or abuse arise.

(7) The adoption of a United Nations policy that bars troop- or police-contributing countries that fail to fulfill their obligation to ensure good order and discipline among their troops from providing any further troops for peace operations or restricts peacekeeper reimbursements to such countries until appropriate training, institutional reform, and oversight mechanisms to prevent such problems from recurring have been put in place.

(8) The implementation of appropriate risk reduction policies, including refusal by the United Nations to deploy uniformed personnel from any troop- or police-contributing country that does not adequately—

(A) investigate allegations of sexual exploitation or abuse involving nationals of such country; and

(B) ensure justice for those personnel determined to have been responsible for such sexual exploitation or abuse.

(d) IMPLEMENTATION.—The United States Permanent Representative to the United Nations shall use the voice, vote, and influence of the United States at the United Nations to advance the objectives of the strategy required by subsection (a).

(e) PEACEKEEPING TRAINING.—The United States should deny further United States peacekeeper training or related assistance, except for training specifically designed to reduce the incidence of sexual exploitation or abuse, or to assist in its identification or prosecution, to any troop- or police-contributing country that does not—

(1) implement and maintain effective measures to enhance the discovery of sexual exploitation and abuse offenses committed by peacekeeping personnel who are nationals of such country;

(2) adequately respond to complaints about such offenses by carrying out swift and effective disciplinary action against the personnel who are found to have committed such offenses; and

(3) provide detailed reporting to the ombudsman described in subsection (c)(4) (or other appropriate United Nations official) that describes the offenses committed by the nationals of such country and such country's responses to such offenses.

(f) ASSISTANCE.—The United States should develop support mechanisms to assist troop- or police-contributing countries, as necessary and appropriate—

(1) to improve their capacity to investigate allegations of sexual exploitation and abuse offenses committed by nationals of such countries while participating in a United Nations peacekeeping operation; and

(2) to appropriately hold accountable any individual who commits an act of sexual exploitation or abuse.

(g) HUMAN RIGHTS REPORTING.—In coordination with the ombudsman described in subsection (c)(4) (or other appropriate United Nations official), the Secretary shall identify, in the Department's annual country reports on human rights practices, the countries of origin of any peacekeeping personnel or units that—

(1) are characterized by noteworthy patterns of sexual exploitation or abuse; or

(2) have failed to institute appropriate institutional and procedural reforms after being made aware of any such patterns.

SEC. 302. REIMBURSEMENT OF CONTRIBUTING COUNTRIES.

It is the policy of the United States that—

(1) the present formula for determining the troop reimbursement rate paid to troop- and police-contributing countries for United Nations peacekeeping operations should be clearly explained and made available to the public on the United Nations Department of Peacekeeping Operations website;

(2) regular audits of the nationally-determined pay and benefits given to personnel from troop- and police-contributing countries participating in United Nations peacekeeping operations should be conducted to help inform the reimbursement rate referred to in paragraph (1); and

(3) the survey mechanism developed by the United Nations Secretary General's Senior Advisory Group on Peacekeeping Operations for collecting troop- and police-contributing country data on common and extraordinary expenses associated with deploying personnel to peacekeeping operations should be coordinated with the audits described in paragraph (2) to ensure proper oversight and accountability.

SEC. 303. WITHHOLDING OF ASSISTANCE.

It is the policy of the United States that security assistance should not be provided to any unit of the security forces of a foreign country if such unit has engaged in a gross violation of human rights or in acts of sexual exploitation or abuse, including while serving in a United Nations peacekeeping operation.

SEC. 304. UNITED NATIONS PEACEKEEPING ASSESSMENT FORMULA.

The Secretary shall direct the United States Permanent Representative to the United Nations to use the voice, vote, and influence of the United States at the United Nations to urge the United Nations to share the raw data used to calculate Member State peacekeeping assessment rates and to make available the formula for determining peacekeeping assessments.

SEC. 305. REIMBURSEMENT OR APPLICATION OF CREDITS.

Notwithstanding any other provision of law, the President shall direct the United States Permanent Representative to the United Nations to use the voice, vote, and influence of the United States at the United Nations to seek and timely obtain a commitment from the United Nations to make available to the United States any peacekeeping credits that are generated from a closed peacekeeping operation.

SEC. 306. REPORT ON UNITED STATES CONTRIBUTIONS TO THE UNITED NATIONS RELATING TO PEACEKEEPING OPERATIONS.

(a) IN GENERAL.—Paragraph (1) of section 4(c) of the United Nations Participation Act of 1945 (22 U.S.C. 287b(c)) is amended—

(1) by amending subparagraph (A) to read as follows:

"(A) A description of all assistance from the United States to the United Nations to support peacekeeping operations that—

"(i) was provided during the previous fiscal year;

"(ii) is expected to be provided during the fiscal year or

"(iii) is included in the annual budget request to Congress for the forthcoming fiscal year.";

(2) by amending subparagraph (D) to read as follows:

"(D) For assessed or voluntary contributions described in subparagraph (B)(iii) or (C)(iii) that exceed $100,000 in value, including in-kind contributions—

"(i) the total amount or estimated value of all such contributions to the United Nations and to each of its affiliated agencies and related bodies;

"(ii) the nature and estimated total value of all in-kind contributions in support of

United Nations peacekeeping operations and other international peacekeeping operations, including—

"(I) logistics;

"(II) airlift;

"(III) arms and materiel;

"(IV) nonmilitary technology and equipment;

"(V) personnel; and

"(VI) training;

"(iii) the approximate percentage of all such contributions to the United Nations and to each such agency or body when compared with all contributions to the United Nations and to each such agency or body from any source; and

"(iv) for each such United States Government contribution to the United Nations and to each such agency or body—

"(I) the amount or value of the contribution;

"(II) a description of the contribution, including whether it is an assessed or voluntary contribution;

"(III) the purpose of the contribution;

"(IV) the department or agency of the United States Government responsible for the contribution; and

"(V) the United Nations or United Nations affiliated agency or related body that received the contribution.''; and

(3) by adding at the end the following new subparagraph:

"(E) The report required under this subsection shall be submitted in unclassified form, but may include a classified annex.''.

(b) PUBLIC AVAILABILITY OF INFORMATION.— Not later than 14 days after submitting each report under section 4(c) of the United Nations Participation Act of 1945 (22 U.S.C. 287b(c)), the Director of the Office of Management and Budget shall post a text-based, searchable version of any unclassified information described in paragraph (1)(D) of such section (as amended by subsection (a) of this section) on a publicly available website.

SEC. 307. WHISTLEBLOWER PROTECTIONS FOR UNITED NATIONS PERSONNEL.

The President shall direct the United States Permanent Representative to the United Nations to use the voice, vote, and influence of the United States at the United Nations to—

(1) call for the removal of any official of the United Nations or of any United Nations agency, program, commission, or fund who the Secretary has determined has failed to uphold the highest standards of ethics and integrity established by the United Nations, including such standards specified in United Nations Codes of Conduct and Codes of Ethics, or whose conduct, with respect to preventing sexual exploitation and abuse by United Nations peacekeepers, has resulted in the erosion of public confidence in the United Nations;

(2) ensure that best practices with regard to whistleblower protections are extended to all personnel serving the United Nations or serving any United Nations agency, program, commission, or fund, especially personnel participating in United Nations peacekeeping operations, United Nations police officers, United Nations staff, contractors, and victims of misconduct, wrongdoing, or criminal behavior involving United Nations personnel;

(3) ensure that the United Nations implements protective measures for whistleblowers who report significant allegations of misconduct, wrongdoing, or criminal behavior by personnel serving the United Nations or serving any United Nations agency, program, commission, or fund, especially per-

sonnel participating in United Nations peacekeeping operations, United Nations staff, or contractors, specifically by implementing best practices for the protection of such whistleblowers from retaliation, including—

"(A) protection against retaliation for internal and lawful public disclosures;

"(B) legal burdens of proof;

"(C) statutes of limitation for reporting retaliation;

"(D) access to independent adjudicative bodies, including external arbitration; and

"(E) results that eliminate the effects of proven retaliation;

(4) insist that the United Nations provides adequate redress to any whistleblower who has suffered from retribution in violation of the protective measures specified in paragraph (3), including reinstatement to any position from which such whistleblower was wrongfully removed, or reassignment to a comparable position at the same level of pay, plus any compensation for any arrearage in salary to which such whistleblower would have otherwise been entitled but for the wrongful retribution;

(5) call for public disclosure of the number and general description of—

"(A) complaints submitted to the United Nations' Ethics Office, local Conduct and Discipline teams, or other entity designated to receive complaints from whistleblowers;

"(B) determinations that probable cause exists to conduct an investigation, and specification of the entity conducting such investigation, including the Office of Internal Oversight Services, the Office of Audit and Investigations (for UNDP), the Office of Internal Audit (for UNICEF), and the Inspector General's Office (for UNHCR);

"(C) dispositions of such investigations, including dismissal and referral for adjudication, specifying the adjudicating entity, such as the United Nations Dispute Tribunal; and

"(D) results of adjudication, including disciplinary measures proscribed and whether such measures were effected, including information with respect to complaints regarding allegations of sexual exploitation and abuse by United Nations peacekeepers, allegations of fraud in procurement and contracting, and all other allegations of misconduct, wrongdoing, or criminal behavior;

(6) insist that the full, unredacted text of any investigation or adjudication referred to in paragraph (5) are made available to Member States upon request; and

(7) call for an examination of the feasibility of establishing a stand-alone agency at the United Nations, independent of the Secretary General, to investigate all allegations of misconduct, wrongdoing, or criminal behavior, reporting to the Member States of the General Assembly, paid for from the United Nations regular budget, to replace existing investigative bodies, including the Office of Internal Oversight Services, the Office of Audit and Investigations, the Office of Internal Audit, and the Office of Inspector General of the Department of State and the Broadcasting Board of Governors.

SEC. 308. ENCOURAGING EMPLOYMENT OF UNITED STATES CITIZENS AT THE UNITED NATIONS.

Section 181 of the Foreign Relations Authorization Act, Fiscal Years 1992 and 1993 (22 U.S.C. 276c-4) is amended to read as follows:

"SEC. 181. EMPLOYMENT OF UNITED STATES CITIZENS BY CERTAIN INTERNATIONAL ORGANIZATIONS.

"Not later than 180 days after the date of the enactment of the Department of State

Authorization Act, Fiscal Year 2017, and annually thereafter for three years, the Secretary of State shall submit to Congress a report that provides—

"(1) for each international organization that had a geographic distribution formula in effect on January 1, 1991, an assessment of whether that organization—

"(A) is taking good faith steps to increase the staffing of United States citizens, including, as appropriate, as assessment of any additional steps the organization could be taking to increase such staffing; and

"(B) has met the requirements of its geographic distribution formula; and

"(2) an assessment of United States representation among professional and senior-level positions at the United Nations, including—

"(A) an assessment of the proportion of United States citizens employed at the United Nations Secretariat and at all United Nations specialized agencies, funds, and programs relative to the total employment at the United Nations Secretariat and at all such agencies, funds, and programs;

"(B) an assessment of compliance by the United Nations Secretariat and such agencies, funds, and programs with any applicable geographic distribution formula; and

"(C) a description of any steps taken or planned to be taken by the United States to increase the staffing of United States citizens at the United Nations Secretariat and such agencies, funds and programs.''.

SEC. 309. STATEMENT OF POLICY ON MEMBER STATE'S VOTING PRACTICES AT THE UNITED NATIONS.

It is the policy of the United States to strongly consider a Member State's voting practices at the United Nations before entering into any agreements with the Member State.

SEC. 310. QUALIFICATIONS OF THE UNITED NATIONS SECRETARY GENERAL.

(a) SENSE OF CONGRESS.—The Secretary shall direct the United States Permanent Representative to the United Nations to use the voice, vote, and influence of the United States at the United Nations to urge each future candidate for the position of the United Nations Secretary General to circulate to the Member States of the General Assembly a description of his or her priorities and objectives for leading the organization and ensuring that it upholds the principles outlined by the United Nations Charter, including specific recommendations to improve strategic planning and enact far-reaching management, performance, and accountability reforms.

(b) PROPOSAL FOR UNITED NATIONS REFORM.—The descriptions referred to in subsection (a) shall include the following elements:

(1) A process for determining the goals, objectives, and benchmarks for the timely withdrawal of peacekeeping forces prior to the approval by the United Nations Security Council of a new or expanded peacekeeping operation.

(2) A proposal for ensuring that the numbers and qualifications of staff are clearly aligned with the specific needs of each United Nations agency, mission, and program, including measures to ensure that such agencies, missions, and programs have the flexibility needed to hire and release employees as workforce needs change over time.

(c) STATEMENT OF POLICY.—It is the policy of the United States to withhold support for any candidate for the position of United Nations Secretary General unless such candidate has produced a clear vision for leading the United Nations, including a robust reform agenda as described in subsection (b), and circulated such 1 to the Member States of the General Assembly.

SEC. 311. POLICY REGARDING THE UNITED NATIONS HUMAN RIGHTS COUNCIL.

(a) SENSE OF CONGRESS.—It is the sense of Congress that the United States should use its voice, vote, and influence at the United Nations to work to ensure that—

(1) the United Nations Human Rights Council takes steps to remove permanent items on the United Nations Human Rights Council's agenda or program of work that target or single out a specific country or a specific territory or territories;

(2) the United Nations Human Rights Council does not include a Member State of the United Nations—

(A) subject to sanctions by the United Nations Security Council;

(B) under a United Nations Security Council-mandated investigation for human rights abuses;

(C) which the Secretary has determined, for purposes of section 6(j) of the Export Administration Act of 1979 (as continued in effect pursuant to the International Emergency Economic Powers Act), section 40 of the Arms Export Control Act, section 620A of the Foreign Assistance Act of 1961, or other provision of law, is a government that has repeatedly provided support for acts of international terrorism; or

(D) which the President has designated as a country of particular concern for religious freedom under section 402(b) of the International Religious Freedom Act of 1998; and

(3) the percentage of United States citizens employed at the senior level in each of the Research and Right to Development Division, the Human Rights Treaties Division, the Field Operations and Technical Cooperation Division, and the Human Rights Council and Special Procedures Division of the United Nations Human Rights Office of the High Commissioner during the most recently completed plenary session of the United Nations General Assembly is at least equivalent to the percentage of the total United States assessed contribution to the United Nations regular budget during such plenary session of the United Nations General Assembly.

(b) REPORT.—Not later than 90 days after the date of the enactment of this Act, and annually thereafter for each of the following five years, the Secretary shall submit to the appropriate congressional committees a report that describes—

(1) the resolutions that were considered in the United Nations Human Rights Council during the previous 12 months;

(2) the steps that have been taken during that 12-month period to remove permanent items on the United Nations Human Rights Council's agenda or program of work that target or single out a specific country or a specific territory or territories;

(3) a detailed list of any country currently on, or running for a seat on, the United Nations Human Rights Council that meets any of the criteria described in subparagraph (A), (B), (C), or (D) of subsection (a)(3); and

(4) the current employment breakdown by nationality at each of the four major divisions of the United Nations Human Rights Office of the High Commissioner as specified in subsection (a)(4).

SEC. 312. ADDITIONAL REPORT ON OTHER UNITED STATES CONTRIBUTIONS TO THE UNITED NATIONS.

(a) IN GENERAL.—Not later than 90 days after the date of the enactment of this Act and annually thereafter, the Director of the Office of Management and Budget shall submit to Congress a report on all assessed and voluntary contributions with a value greater than $100,000, including in-kind, of the United States Government to the United Nations and its affiliated agencies and related bodies during the previous fiscal year.

(b) CONTENT.—The report required under subsection (a) shall include the following elements:

(1) The total amount of all assessed and voluntary contributions, including in-kind, of the United States Government to the United Nations and its affiliated agencies and related bodies during the previous fiscal year.

(2) The approximate percentage of United States Government contributions to each United Nations affiliated agency or body in such fiscal year when compared with all contributions to each such agency or body from any source in such fiscal year.

(3) For each such United States Government contribution—

(A) the amount of each such contribution;

(B) a description of each such contribution (including whether assessed or voluntary);

(C) the department or agency of the United States Government responsible for each such contribution;

(D) the purpose of each such contribution; and

(E) the United Nations or its affiliated agency or related body receiving the contribution.

(c) SCOPE OF INITIAL REPORT.—The first report required under subsection (a) shall include the information required under this section for the previous three fiscal years.

(d) PUBLIC AVAILABILITY OF INFORMATION.—Not later than 14 days after submitting a report required under subsection (a), the Director of the Office of Management and Budget shall post a public version of such report on a text-based, searchable, and publicly available Internet Web site.

SEC. 313. COMPARATIVE REPORT ON PEACEKEEPING OPERATIONS.

Not later than one year after the date of the enactment of this Act, the Comptroller General of the United States shall submit to the appropriate congressional committees a report on the costs, strengths, and limitations of United States and United Nations peacekeeping operations, which shall include—

(1) a comparison of the costs of current United Nations peacekeeping operations and the estimated cost of comparable United States peacekeeping operations; and

(2) an analysis of the strengths and limitations of—

(A) a peacekeeping operation led by the United States; and

(B) a peacekeeping operation led by the United Nations.

TITLE IV—PERSONNEL AND ORGANIZATIONAL ISSUES

SEC. 401. LOCALLY-EMPLOYED STAFF WAGES.

(a) MARKET-RESPONSIVE STAFF WAGES.—Not later than 180 days after the date of enactment of this Act and periodically thereafter, the Secretary shall establish and implement a prevailing wage rates goal for positions in the local compensation plan, as described in section 408 of the Foreign Service Act of 1980 (22 U.S.C. 3968), at each diplomatic post that—

(1) is based on the specific recruiting and retention needs of each such post and local labor market conditions, as determined annually; and

(2) is not less than the 50th percentile of the prevailing wage for comparable employ-

ment in the labor market surrounding each such post.

(b) EXCEPTION.—The prevailing wage rate goal established under subsection (a) shall not apply if compliance with such subsection would be inconsistent with applicable United States law, the law in the locality of employment, or the public interest.

(c) RECORDKEEPING REQUIREMENT.—The analytical assumptions underlying the calculation of wage levels at each diplomatic post under subsection (a), and the data upon which such calculation is based—

(1) shall be filed electronically and retained for not less than five years; and

(2) shall be made available to the appropriate congressional committees upon request.

SEC. 402. EXPANSION OF CIVIL SERVICE OPPORTUNITIES.

It is the sense of Congress that the Department should—

(1) expand the Overseas Development Program from 20 positions to not fewer than 40 positions within one year of the date of the enactment of this Act;

(2) analyze the costs and benefits of further expansion of the Overseas Development Program; and

(3) expand the Overseas Development Program to more than 40 positions if the benefits identified in paragraph (2) outweigh the costs identified in such paragraph.

SEC. 403. PROMOTION TO THE SENIOR FOREIGN SERVICE.

Section 601(c) of the Foreign Service Act of 1980 (22 U.S.C. 4001(c)) is amended by adding at the end the following new paragraph:

"(6)(A) The promotion of any individual joining the Service on or after January 1, 2017, to the Senior Foreign Service shall be contingent upon such individual completing at least one tour in—

"(i) a global affairs bureau; or

"(ii) a global affairs position.

"(B) The requirements under subparagraph (A) shall not apply if the Secretary certifies that the individual proposed for promotion to the Senior Foreign Service—

"(i) has met all other requirements applicable to such promotion; and

"(ii) was unable to complete a tour in a global affairs bureau or global affairs position because there was not a reasonable opportunity for such individual to be assigned to such a position.

"(C) In this paragraph—

"(i) the term 'global affairs bureau' means any bureau of the Department that is under the responsibility of—

"(I) the Under Secretary for Economic Growth, Energy, and Environment;

"(II) the Under Secretary for Arms Control and International Security Affairs;

"(III) the Under Secretary for Management;

"(IV) the Assistant Secretary for International Organization Affairs;

"(V) the Under Secretary for Public Diplomacy and Public Affairs; or

"(VI) the Under Secretary for Civilian, Security, Democracy, and Human Rights; and

"(ii) the term 'global affairs position' means any position funded with amounts appropriated to the Department under the heading 'Diplomatic Policy and Support'.".

SEC. 404. LATERAL ENTRY INTO THE FOREIGN SERVICE.

(a) SENSE OF CONGRESS.—It is the sense of Congress that the Foreign Service should permit mid-career entry into the Foreign Service for qualified individuals who are willing to bring their outstanding talents and experiences to the work of the Foreign Service.

(b) PILOT PROGRAM.—Not later than 180 days after the date of the enactment of this Act, the Secretary shall establish a three-year pilot program for lateral entry into the Foreign Service that—

(1) targets mid-career individuals from the civil service and private sector who have skills and experience that would be extremely valuable to the Foreign Service;

(2) is in full comportment with current Foreign Service intake procedures, including the requirement to pass the Foreign Service exam;

(3) offers participants in such pilot program placement in the Foreign Service at a grade level higher than FS–4 if such placement is warranted by the education and qualifying experience of such individuals;

(4) requires only one directed assignment in a position appropriate to such pilot program participant's grade level;

(5) includes, as part of the required initial training, a class or module that specifically prepares participants in such pilot program for life in the Foreign Service, including conveying to such participants essential elements of the practical knowledge that is normally acquired during a Foreign Service officer's initial assignments; and

(6) includes an annual assessment of the progress of such pilot program by a review board consisting of Department officials with appropriate expertise, including employees of the Foreign Service, in order to evaluate such pilot program's success.

(c) ANNUAL REPORTING.—Not later than one year after the date of the enactment of this Act and annually thereafter for the duration of the pilot program described in subsection (b), the Secretary shall submit to the appropriate congressional committees a report that describes the following:

(1) The cumulative number of accepted and unaccepted applicants to such pilot program.

(2) The cumulative number of pilot program participants placed into each Foreign Service cone.

(3) The grade level at which each pilot program participant entered the Foreign Service.

(4) Information about the first assignment to which each pilot program participant was directed.

(5) The structure and operation of such pilot program, including—

(A) the operation of such pilot program to date; and

(B) any observations and lessons learned about such pilot program that the Secretary considers relevant.

(d) LONGITUDINAL DATA.—The Secretary shall—

(1) collect and maintain data on the career progression of each pilot program participant for the length of each participant's Foreign Service career; and

(2) make the data described in paragraph (1) available to the appropriate congressional committees upon request.

SEC. 405. REEMPLOYMENT OF ANNUITANTS AND WORKFORCE RIGHTSIZING.

(a) WAIVER OF ANNUITY LIMITATIONS.—Subsection (g) of section 824 of the Foreign Service Act of 1980 (22 U.S.C. 4064) is amended—

(1) in paragraph (1)(B), by striking "to facilitate the" and all that follows through "Afghanistan,";

(2) by striking paragraph (2); and

(3) by redesignating paragraph (3) as paragraph (2).

(b) REPEAL OF SUNSET PROVISION.—Subsection (a) of section 61 of the State Department Basic Authorities Act of 1956 (22 U.S.C. 2733) is amended to read as follows:

"(a) AUTHORITY.—The Secretary of State may waive the application of section 8344 or 8468 of title 5, United States Code, on a case-by-case basis, for employment of an annuitant in a position in the Department of State for which there is exceptional difficulty in recruiting or retaining a qualified employee, or when a temporary emergency hiring need exists.".

(c) RIGHTSIZING REPORT.—On the date on which the President's annual budget request is submitted to Congress each year through 2022, the Secretary shall submit to the appropriate congressional committees a report that describes the implementation status of all rightsizing recommendations made by the Office of Management, Policy, Rightsizing, and Innovation of the Department related to overseas staffing levels, including whether each such recommendation was accepted or rejected by the relevant chief of mission and regional bureau.

SEC. 406. INTEGRATION OF FOREIGN ECONOMIC POLICY.

(a) IN GENERAL.—The Secretary, in conjunction with the Under Secretary of Economic Growth, Energy, and the Environment, shall establish—

(1) foreign economic policy priorities for each regional bureau, including for individual countries, as appropriate; and

(2) policies and guidance for integrating such foreign economic policy priorities throughout the Department.

(b) DEPUTY ASSISTANT SECRETARY.—Within each regional bureau of the Department, the Secretary shall task an existing Deputy Assistant Secretary with appropriate training and background in economic and commercial affairs with the responsibility for economic matters and interests within the responsibilities of each such regional bureau, including the integration of the foreign economic policy priorities established pursuant to subsection (a).

(c) TRAINING.—The Secretary shall establish curriculum at the George P. Shultz National Foreign Affairs Training Center to develop the practical foreign economic policy expertise and skill sets of Foreign Service officers, including by making available distance-learning courses in commercial, economic, and business affairs, including in the following:

(1) The global business environment.

(2) The economics of development.

(3) Development and infrastructure finance.

(4) Current trade and investment agreements negotiations.

(5) Implementing existing multilateral and World Trade Organization agreements, and United States trade and investment agreements.

(6) Best practices for customs and export procedures.

(7) Market analysis and global supply chain management.

SEC. 407. TRAINING SUPPORT SERVICES.

Subparagraph (B) of section 704(a)(4) of the Foreign Service Act of 1980 (22 U.S.C. 4024(a)(4)) is amended by striking "language instructors, linguists, and other academic and training specialists" and inserting "education and training specialists, including language instructors and linguists, and other specialists who perform work directly relating to the design, delivery, oversight, or coordination of training delivered by the institution".

SEC. 408. SPECIAL AGENTS.

(a) IN GENERAL.—Paragraph (1) of section 37(a) of the State Department Basic Authorities Act of 1956 (22 U.S.C. 2709(a)) is amended to read as follows:

"(1) conduct investigations concerning—

"(A) illegal passport or visa issuance or use;

"(B) identity theft or document fraud affecting or relating to the programs, functions, or authorities of the Department of State; or

"(C) Federal offenses committed within the special maritime and territorial jurisdiction of the United States (as defined in section 7(9) of title 18, United States Code), except as such jurisdiction relates to the premises of United States military missions and related residences;".

(b) CONSTRUCTION.—Nothing in the amendment made by subsection (a) may be construed to limit the investigative authority of any Federal department or agency other than the Department.

SEC. 409. LIMITED APPOINTMENTS IN THE FOREIGN SERVICE.

Section 309 of the Foreign Service Act of 1980 (22 U.S.C. 3949), is amended—

(1) in subsection (a) by striking "subsection (b)" and inserting "subsections (b) and (c)";

(2) in subsection (b)—

(A) in paragraph (3)—

(i) by striking "if continued service" and inserting the following: "if—

"(A) continued service";

(ii) in such subparagraph (A) (as so inserted and designated by clause (i) of this subparagraph), by inserting "or" after the semicolon at the end; and

(iii) by adding at the end the following new subparagraph:

"(B) the individual is serving in the uniformed services (as defined in section 4303 of title 38, United States Code) and the limited appointment expires in the course of such service;";

(B) in paragraph (4), by striking "and" at the end;

(C) in paragraph (5), by striking the period at the end and inserting a semicolon; and

(D) by adding at the end the following new paragraph:

"(6) in exceptional circumstances if the Secretary determines the needs of the Service require the extension of—

"(A) a limited noncareer appointment for a period not to exceed one year; or

"(B) a limited appointment of a career candidate for the minimum time needed to resolve a grievance, claim, investigation, or complaint not otherwise provided for in this section."; and

(3) by adding at the end the following new subsection:

"(c)(1) Except as provided in paragraph (2) noncareer employees who have served for five consecutive years under a limited appointment under this section may be reappointed to a subsequent noncareer limited appointment if there is at least a one-year break in service before such new appointment.

"(2) The Secretary may waive the one-year break requirement under paragraph (1) in cases of special need.".

SEC. 410. REPORT ON DIVERSITY RECRUITMENT, EMPLOYMENT, RETENTION, AND PROMOTION.

(a) IN GENERAL.—The Secretary should provide oversight to the employment, retention, and promotion of traditionally under-represented minority groups.

(b) ADDITIONAL RECRUITMENT AND OUTREACH REQUIRED.—The Department should conduct recruitment activities that—

(1) develop and implement effective mechanisms to ensure that the Department is able effectively to recruit and retain highly

qualified candidates from a wide diversity of institutions; and

(2) improve and expand recruitment and outreach programs at minority-serving institutions.

(c) REPORT.—Not later than 180 days after the date of the enactment of this Act and quadrennially thereafter, the Secretary shall submit to Congress a comprehensive report that describes the efforts, consistent with existing law, including procedures, effects, and results of the Department since the period covered by the prior such report, to promote equal opportunity and inclusion for all American employees in direct hire and personal service contractors status, particularly employees of the Foreign Service, including equal opportunity for all traditionally under-represented minority groups.

SEC. 411. MARKET DATA FOR COST-OF-LIVING ADJUSTMENTS.

(a) REPORT.—Not later than 180 days after the date of the enactment of this Act, the Secretary shall submit to the appropriate congressional committees a report that examines the feasibility and cost effectiveness of using private sector market data to determine cost of living adjustments for Foreign Service officers and Federal Government civilians who are stationed abroad.

(b) CONTENT.—The report required under subsection (a) shall include—

(1) a list of at least four private sector providers of international cost-of-living data that the Secretary determines are qualified to provide such data;

(2) a list of cities in which the Department maintains diplomatic posts for which private sector cost-of-living data is not available;

(3) a comparison of—

(A) the cost of purchasing cost-of-living data from each provider listed in paragraph (1); and

(B) the cost (including Department labor costs) of producing such rates internally; and

(4) for countries in which the Department provides a cost-of-living allowance greater than zero and the World Bank estimates that the national price level of the country is less than the national price level of the United States, a comparison of cost-of-living allowances, excluding housing costs, of the private sector providers referred to in paragraph (1) to rates constructed by the Department's Office of Allowances.

(c) WAIVER.—If the Secretary determines that compliance with subsection (b)(4) at a particular location is cost-prohibitive, the Secretary may waive the requirement under such subsection for such location if the Secretary submits to the appropriate congressional committees written notice and an explanation of the reasons for such waiver.

SEC. 412. TECHNICAL AMENDMENT TO FEDERAL WORKFORCE FLEXIBILITY ACT.

Chapter 57 of title 5, United States Code, is amended—

(1) in subparagraph (A) of section 5753(a)(2), by inserting ", excluding members of the Foreign Service other than chiefs of mission and ambassadors at large" before the semicolon at the end; and

(2) in subparagraph (A) of section 5754(a)(2), by inserting ", excluding members of the Foreign Service other than chiefs of mission and ambassadors at large" before the semicolon at the end.

SEC. 413. RETENTION OF MID- AND SENIORLEVEL PROFESSIONALS FROM TRADITIONALLY UNDER-REPRESENTED MINORITY GROUPS.

The Secretary should provide attention and oversight to the employment, retention, and promotion of traditionally under-rep-

resented minority groups to promote a diverse representation among mid- and senior-level career professionals through programs such as—

(1) the International Career Advancement Program;

(2) Seminar XXI at the Massachusetts Institute of Technology's Center for International Studies; and

(3) other highly respected international leadership programs.

SEC. 414. EMPLOYEE ASSIGNMENT RESTRICTIONS.

(a) APPEAL OF ASSIGNMENT RESTRICTION.—The Secretary shall establish a right and process for employees to appeal any assignment restriction or preclusion.

(b) CERTIFICATION.—Upon full implementation of a right and process for employees to appeal an assignment restriction or preclusion under subsection (a), the Secretary shall submit to the appropriate congressional committee a report that—

(1) certifies that such process has been fully implemented;

(2) includes a detailed description of such process; and

(3) details the number and nature of assignment restrictions and preclusions for the previous three years.

(c) NOTICE.—The Secretary shall—

(1) publish in the Foreign Affairs Manual information relating to the right and process established pursuant to subsection (a); and

(2) include a reference to such publication in the report required under subsection (b).

(d) PROHIBITING DISCRIMINATION.—Paragraph (2) of section 502(a) of the Foreign Service Act of 1980 (22 U.S.C. 3982(a)) is amended—

(1) by inserting "or prohibited from being assigned to" after "assigned to"; and

(2) by striking "exclusively".

SEC. 415. SECURITY CLEARANCE SUSPENSIONS.

(a) IN GENERAL.—Section 610 of the Foreign Service Act of 1980 (22 U.S.C. 4010) is amended—

(1) by striking the section heading and inserting the following: "**SEPARATION FOR CAUSE; SUSPENSION**"; and

(2) by adding at the end the following new subsection:

"(c)(1) In order to promote the efficiency of the Service, the Secretary may suspend a member of the Service when—

"(A) the member's security clearance is suspended; or

"(B) there is reasonable cause to believe that the member has committed a crime for which a sentence of imprisonment may be imposed.

"(2) Any member of the Service for whom a suspension is proposed under this subsection shall be entitled to—

"(A) written notice stating the specific reasons for the proposed suspension;

"(B) a reasonable time to respond orally and in writing to the proposed suspension;

"(C) obtain at such member's own expense representation by an attorney or other representative; and

"(D) a final written decision, including the specific reasons for such decision, as soon as practicable.

"(3) Any member suspended under this subsection may file a grievance in accordance with the procedures applicable to grievances under chapter 11 of title I.

"(4) If a grievance is filed pursuant to paragraph (3)—

"(A) the review by the Foreign Service Grievance Board shall be limited to a determination of whether the provisions of paragraphs (1) and (2) have been fulfilled; and

"(B) the Board may not exercise the authority provided under section 1106(8).

"(5) In this subsection:

"(A) The term 'reasonable time' means—

"(i) with respect to a member of the Service assigned to duty in the United States, 15 days after receiving notice of the proposed suspension; and

"(ii) with respect to a member of the Service assigned to duty outside the United States, 30 days after receiving notice of the proposed suspension.

"(B) The terms 'suspend' and 'suspension' mean placing a member of the Foreign Service in a temporary status without duties.".

(b) CLERICAL AMENDMENT.—The table of contents in section 2 of the Foreign Service Act of 1980 is amended by striking the item relating to section 610 and inserting the following new item:

"Sec. 610. Separation for cause; Suspension.".

SEC. 416. SENSE OF CONGRESS ON THE INTEGRATION OF POLICIES RELATED TO THE PARTICIPATION OF WOMEN IN PREVENTING AND RESOLVING CONFLICTS.

It is the sense of Congress that—

(1) within each regional bureau of the Department, the Secretary should task an existing Deputy Assistant Secretary with the responsibility for overseeing the integration of policy priorities related to the importance of the participation of women in preventing and resolving conflicts; and

(2) the Director of the George P. Shultz National Foreign Affairs Training Center should incorporate at least one training session related to the importance of the participation of women in preventing and resolving conflicts into—

(A) the A-100 course attended by Foreign Service Officers; and

(B) with respect to Foreign Service Officers who have completed the A-100 course, at least one training course that will be completed not later than the date that is 1 year after the date of the enactment of this Act.

SEC. 417. FOREIGN SERVICE FAMILIES WORKFORCE STUDY.

Not later than 180 days after the date of the enactment of this Act, the Secretary shall submit to the appropriate congressional committees a report on workforce issues and challenges to career opportunities pertaining to tandem couples in the Foreign Service as well as couples with respect to which only one spouse is in the Foreign Service.

SEC. 418. SPECIAL ENVOYS, REPRESENTATIVES, ADVISORS, AND COORDINATORS OF THE DEPARTMENT.

Not later than 90 days after the date of the enactment of this Act, the Secretary shall submit to the appropriate congressional committees a report on special envoys, representatives, advisors, and coordinators of the Department, that includes—

(1) a tabulation of the current names, ranks, positions, and responsibilities of all special envoy, representative, advisor, and coordinator positions at the Department, with a separate accounting of all such positions at the level of Assistant Secretary (or equivalent) or above; and

(2) for each position identified pursuant to paragraph (1)—

(A) the date on which such position was created;

(B) the mechanism by which such position was created, including the authority under which such position was created;

(C) such positions authorized under section (d) of section 1 of the State Department

Basic Authorities Act of 1956 (22 U.S.C. 2651a);

(D) a description of whether, and the extent to which, the responsibilities assigned to such position duplicate the responsibilities of other current officials within the Department, including other special envoys, representatives, advisors, and coordinators;

(E) which current official of the Department would be assigned the responsibilities of such position in the absence of such position;

(F) to which current official of the Department such position directly reports;

(G) the total number of staff assigned to support such position; and

(H) with the exception of positions created by statute, a detailed explanation of the necessity of such position to the effective conduct of the foreign affairs of the United States.

SEC. 419. COMBATING ANTI-SEMITISM.

Not later than 180 days after the date of the enactment of this Act, the Special Envoy to Monitor and Combat Anti-Semitism of the Office to Monitor and Combat Anti-Semitism of the Department shall provide to the appropriate congressional committees a briefing on United States support to, and opportunities to coordinate with, American and European Jewish and other civil society organizations, focusing on youth, to combat anti-Semitism and other forms of religious, ethnic, or racial intolerance in Europe.

TITLE V—CONSULAR AUTHORITIES

SEC. 501. CODIFICATION OF ENHANCED CONSULAR IMMUNITIES.

Section 4 of the Diplomatic Relations Act (22 U.S.C. 254c) is amended—

(1) by striking "The President" and inserting the following:

"(a) IN GENERAL.—The President"; and

(2) by adding at the end the following new subsection:

"(b) CONSULAR IMMUNITY.—

"(1) IN GENERAL.—The Secretary of State, with the concurrence of the Attorney General, may, on the basis of reciprocity and under such terms and conditions as the Secretary may determine, specify privileges and immunities for a consular post, the members of a consular post, and their families which result in more favorable or less favorable treatment than is provided in the Vienna Convention on Consular Relations, of April 24, 1963 (T.I.A.S. 6820), entered into force for the United States on December 24, 1969.

"(2) CONSULTATION.—Before exercising the authority under paragraph (1), the Secretary of State shall consult with the Committee on Foreign Affairs of the House of Representatives and the Committee on Foreign Relations of the Senate regarding the circumstances that may warrant the need for privileges and immunities providing more favorable or less favorable treatment than is provided in the Vienna Convention.".

SEC. 502. PASSPORTS MADE IN THE UNITED STATES.

(a) SENSE OF CONGRESS.—It is the sense of Congress that all components of United States passports, including all passport security features, should be printed, manufactured, and assembled exclusively within the United States by United States companies and personnel, contractors, and subcontractors with appropriate security clearances.

(b) BRIEFINGS.—The Secretary, in coordination with the heads of other relevant Federal agencies, shall provide a briefing, which may be given in a classified environment if necessary, to the appropriate congressional committees that includes the following details:

(1) A list of all components of the United States passport made outside the United States.

(2) The costs of all components of the United States passports made outside the United States.

(3) Comparable costs to produce and procure in the United States the items identified in paragraphs (1) and (2).

TITLE VI—WESTERN HEMISPHERE DRUG POLICY COMMISSION

SEC. 601. ESTABLISHMENT.

There is established an independent commission to be known as the "Western Hemisphere Drug Policy Commission" (in this title referred to as the "Commission").

SEC. 602. DUTIES.

(a) REVIEW OF ILLICIT DRUG CONTROL POLICIES.—The Commission shall conduct a comprehensive review of United States foreign policy in the Western Hemisphere to reduce the illicit drug supply and drug abuse and reduce the damage associated with illicit drug markets and trafficking. The Commission shall also identify policy and program options to improve existing international counternarcotics policy. The review shall include the following topics:

(1) An evaluation of United States-funded international illicit drug control programs in the Western Hemisphere, including drug interdiction, crop eradication, alternative development, drug production surveys, police and justice sector training, demand reduction, and strategies to target drug kingpins.

(2) An evaluation of the impact of United States counternarcotics assistance programs in the Western Hemisphere, including the Colombia Strategic Development Initiative, the Merida Initiative, the Caribbean Basin Security Initiative and the Central America Regional Security Initiative, in curbing drug production, drug trafficking, and drug-related violence and improving citizen security.

(3) An evaluation of how the President's annual determination of major drug-transit and major illicit drug producing countries pursuant to section 706 of the Foreign Relations Authorization Act, Fiscal Year 2003 (22 U.S.C. 2291j-1) serves United States interests with respect to United States international illicit drug control policies.

(4) An evaluation of whether the proper indicators of success are being used to evaluate United States international illicit drug control policy.

(5) An evaluation of United States efforts to stop illicit proceeds from drug trafficking organizations from entering the United States financial system.

(6) An evaluation of the links between the illegal narcotics trade in the Western Hemisphere and terrorist activities around the world.

(7) An evaluation of United States efforts to combat narco-terrorism in the Western Hemisphere.

(8) An evaluation of the financing of foreign terrorist organizations by drug trafficking organizations and an evaluation of United States efforts to stop such activities.

(9) An evaluation of alternative drug policy models in the Western Hemisphere.

(10) An evaluation of the impact of local drug consumption in Latin America and the Caribbean in promoting violence and insecurity.

(11) Recommendations on how best to improve United States counternarcotics policies in the Western Hemisphere.

(b) COORDINATION WITH GOVERNMENTS, INTERNATIONAL ORGANIZATIONS, AND NON-GOVERNMENTAL ORGANIZATIONS IN THE WESTERN HEMISPHERE.—In conducting the review required under subsection (a), the Commission is encouraged to consult with—

(1) government, academic, and nongovernmental leaders, as well as leaders from international organizations, from throughout the United States, Latin America, and the Caribbean; and

(2) the Inter-American Drug Abuse Control Commission (CICAD).

(c) REPORT.—

(1) IN GENERAL.—Not later than 18 months after the first meeting of the Commission, the Commission shall submit to the Committee on Foreign Affairs of the House of Representatives, the Committee on Foreign Relations of the Senate, the Secretary, and the Director of the Office of National Drug Control Policy a report that contains—

(A) a detailed statement of the recommendations, findings, and conclusions of the Commission under subsection (a); and

(B) summaries of the input and recommendations of the leaders and organizations with which the Commission consulted under subsection (b).

(2) PUBLIC AVAILABILITY.—The report required under this subsection shall be made available to the public.

SEC. 603. MEMBERSHIP.

(a) NUMBER AND APPOINTMENT.—The Commission shall be composed of ten members to be appointed as follows:

(1) The majority leader and minority leader of the Senate shall each appoint two members.

(2) The Speaker and the minority leader of the House of Representatives shall each appoint two members.

(3) The President shall appoint two members.

(b) PROHIBITION.—

(1) IN GENERAL.—The Commission may not include—

(A) Members of Congress; or

(B) Federal, State, or local government officials.

(2) MEMBER OF CONGRESS.—In this subsection, the term "Member of Congress" includes a Delegate or Resident Commissioner to the Congress.

(c) APPOINTMENT OF INITIAL MEMBERS.—The initial members of the Commission shall be appointed not later than 30 days after the date of the enactment of this Act.

(d) VACANCIES.—Any vacancies shall not affect the power and duties of the Commission, but shall be filled in the same manner as the original appointment. An appointment required by subsection (a) should be made within 90 days of a vacancy on the Commission.

(e) PERIOD OF APPOINTMENT.—Each member shall be appointed for the life of the Commission.

(f) INITIAL MEETING AND SELECTION OF CHAIRPERSON.—

(1) IN GENERAL.—Not later than 60 days after the date of the enactment of this Act, the Commission shall hold an initial meeting to develop and implement a schedule for completion of the review and report required under section 362.

(2) CHAIRPERSON.—At the initial meeting, the Commission shall select a Chairperson from among its members.

(g) QUORUM.—Six members of the Commission shall constitute a quorum.

(h) COMPENSATION.—Members of the Commission—

(1) shall not be considered to be a Federal employee for any purpose by reason of service on the Commission; and

(2) shall serve without pay.

(i) TRAVEL EXPENSES.—Members shall receive travel expenses, including per diem in lieu of subsistence, in accordance with sections 5702 and 5703 of title 5, United States Code, while away from their homes or regular places of business in performance of services for the Commission.

SEC. 604. POWERS.

(a) MEETINGS.—The Commission shall meet at the call of the Chairperson or a majority of its members.

(b) HEARINGS.—The Commission may hold such hearings and undertake such other activities as the Commission determines necessary to carry out its duties.

(c) OTHER RESOURCES.—

(1) DOCUMENTS, STATISTICAL DATA, AND OTHER SUCH INFORMATION.—

(A) IN GENERAL.—The Library of Congress, the Office of National Drug Control Policy, the Department, and any other Federal department or agency shall, in accordance with the protection of classified information, provide reasonable access to documents, statistical data, and other such information the Commission determines necessary to carry out its duties.

(B) OBTAINING INFORMATION.—The Chairperson of the Commission shall request the head of an agency described in subparagraph (A) for access to documents, statistical data, or other such information described in such subparagraph that is under the control of such agency in writing when necessary.

(2) OFFICE SPACE AND ADMINISTRATIVE SUPPORT.—The Administrator of General Services shall make office space available for day-to-day activities of the Commission and for scheduled meetings of the Commission. Upon request, the Administrator shall provide, on a reimbursable basis, such administrative support as the Commission requests to fulfill its duties.

(d) AUTHORITY TO USE UNITED STATES MAILS.—The Commission may use the United States mails in the same manner and under the same conditions as other departments and agencies of the United States.

(e) AUTHORITY TO CONTRACT.—

(1) IN GENERAL.—Subject to the Federal Property and Administrative Services Act of 1949, the Commission is authorized to enter into contracts with Federal and State agencies, private firms, institutions, and individuals for the conduct of activities necessary to the discharge of its duties under section 602.

(2) TERMINATION.—A contract, lease, or other legal agreement entered into by the Commission may not extend beyond the date of termination of the Commission.

SEC. 605. STAFF.

(a) DIRECTOR.—The Commission shall have a Director who shall be appointed by a majority vote of the Commission. The Director shall be paid at a rate not to exceed the rate of basic pay for level IV of the Executive Schedule.

(b) STAFF.—

(1) IN GENERAL.—With the approval of the Commission, the Director may appoint such personnel as the Director determines to be appropriate. Such personnel shall be paid at a rate not to exceed the rate of basic pay for level IV of the Executive Schedule.

(2) ADDITIONAL STAFF.—The Commission may appoint and fix the compensation of such other personnel as may be necessary to enable the Commission to carry out its duties, without regard to the provisions of title 5, United States Code, governing appointments in the competitive service, and without regard to the provisions of chapter 51 and

subchapter III of chapter 53 of such title relating to classification and General Schedule pay rates, except that no rate of pay fixed under this subsection may exceed the equivalent of that payable to a person occupying a position at level V of the Executive Schedule.

(c) EXPERTS AND CONSULTANTS.—With the approval of the Commission, the Director may procure temporary and intermittent services under section 3109(b) of title 5, United States Code.

(d) DETAIL OF GOVERNMENT EMPLOYEES.—Upon the request of the Commission, the head of any Federal agency may detail, without reimbursement, any of the personnel of such agency to the Commission to assist in carrying out the duties of the Commission. Any such detail shall not interrupt or otherwise affect the civil service status or privileges of the personnel.

(e) VOLUNTEER SERVICES.—Notwithstanding section 1342 of title 31, United States Code, the Commission may accept and use voluntary and uncompensated services as the Commission determines necessary.

SEC. 606. SUNSET.

The Commission shall terminate on the date that is 60 days after the date on which the Commission submits its report to Congress pursuant to section 602(c).

TITLE VII—MISCELLANEOUS PROVISIONS

SEC. 701. FOREIGN RELATIONS EXCHANGE PROGRAMS.

(a) EXCHANGES AUTHORIZED.—Title I of the State Department Basic Authorities Act of 1956 (22 U.S.C. 2651a et seq.) is amended by adding at the end the following new section:

"SEC. 63. FOREIGN RELATIONS EXCHANGE PROGRAMS.

"(a) AUTHORITY.—The Secretary may establish exchange programs under which officers or employees of the Department of State, including individuals appointed under title 5, United States Code, and members of the Foreign Service (as defined in section 103 of the Foreign Service Act of 1980 (22 U.S.C. 3903)), may be assigned, for not more than one year, to a position with any foreign government or international entity that permits an employee to be assigned to a position with the Department of State.

"(b) SALARY AND BENEFITS.—

"(1) MEMBERS OF FOREIGN SERVICE.—During a period in which a member of the Foreign Service is participating in an exchange program authorized pursuant to subsection (a), such member shall be entitled to the salary and benefits to which such member would receive but for the assignment under this section.

"(2) NON-FOREIGN SERVICE EMPLOYEES OF DEPARTMENT.—An employee of the Department of State other than a member of the Foreign Service participating in an exchange program authorized pursuant to subsection (a) shall be treated in all respects as if detailed to an international organization pursuant to section 3343(c) of title 5, United States Code.

"(3) FOREIGN PARTICIPANTS.—The salary and benefits of an employee of a foreign government or international entity participating in an exchange program authorized pursuant to subsection (a) shall be paid by such government or entity during the period in which such employee is participating in such program, and shall not be reimbursed by the Department of State.

"(c) NON-RECIPROCAL ASSIGNMENT.—The Secretary may authorize a non-reciprocal assignment of personnel pursuant to this section, with or without reimbursement from the foreign government or international en-

tity for all or part of the salary and other expenses payable during such assignment, if such is in the interests of the United States.

"(d) RULE OF CONSTRUCTION.—Nothing in this section may be construed to authorize the appointment as an officer or employee of the United States of—

"(1) an individual whose allegiance is to any country, government, or foreign or international entity other than to the United States; or

"(2) an individual who has not met the requirements of sections 3331, 3332, 3333, and 7311 of title 5, United States Code, or any other provision of law concerning eligibility for appointment as, and continuation of employment as, an officer or employee of the United States.".

SEC. 702. UNITED STATES ADVISORY COMMISSION ON PUBLIC DIPLOMACY.

(a) IN GENERAL.—Section 1334 of the Foreign Affairs Reform and Restructuring Act of 1998 (22 U.S.C. 6553) is amended by striking "October 1, 2015" and inserting "October 1, 2020".

(b) RETROACTIVITY OF EFFECTIVE DATE.—The amendment made by subsection (a) shall take effect as of October 1, 2016. Any lapse in powers, authorities, or responsibilities of the United States Advisory Commission on Public Diplomacy from the period beginning on October 1, 2016, and ending on the date of the enactment of this Act, shall be deemed to have not so lapsed.

SEC. 703. BROADCASTING BOARD OF GOVERNORS.

(a) BROADCASTING TO ASIA.—Section 309 of the Foreign Relations Authorization Act, Fiscal Years 1994 and 1995 (22 U.S.C. 6208) is amended—

(1) in subsection (a)(1), by striking "the following countries" and all that follows through the period at the end and inserting "Asia."; and

(2) in subsection (b)(1), by striking "the respective countries of".

(b) PROHIBITIONS.—

(1) IN GENERAL.—Notwithstanding any other provision of law, any change to the Federal status of—

(A) the Cuba Service established pursuant to section 4 of the Radio Broadcasting to Cuba Act (22 U.S.C. 1465b; Public Law 98–111) is prohibited unless such section is explicitly repealed and such service is dissolved by an Act of Congress enacted on or after the date of the enactment of this Act; and

(B) the Television Marti Service established by section 244(a) of Television Broadcasting to Cuba Act (22 U.S.C. 1465cc; Public Law 101–246) is prohibited unless such section is explicitly repealed and such service is dissolved by an Act of Congress enacted on or after the date of the enactment of this Act.

(2) DEFINITION.—In this subsection, the term "change to the Federal status", with respect to a service referred to in subparagraph (A) or (B) of paragraph (1), includes any significant restructuring, privatization, subordination to a private or private-public entity, or merger with a private or public-private entity of such service.

(c) SENSE OF CONGRESS.—It is the sense of Congress that the Broadcasting Board of Governors should start broadcasting in the Sindhi language.

SEC. 704. REWARDS FOR JUSTICE.

(a) REWARDS AUTHORIZED.—

(1) IN GENERAL.—Section 36(b) of the State Department Basic Authorities Act of 1956 (22 U.S.C. 2708(b)) is amended in paragraphs (4) and (5) by striking "or (9)" each place it appears and inserting "(9), or (10)".

(2) REPORTS; DEFINITIONS.—Section 36 of the State Department Basic Authorities Act of 1956 (22 U.S.C. 2708) is amended—

(A) in subsection (g), by adding at the end the following new paragraph:

"(4) REPORTS ON REWARDS AUTHORIZED.— Not less than 15 days after a reward is authorized under this section, the Secretary of State shall submit to the appropriate congressional committees a report, which may be submitted in classified form if necessary to protect intelligence sources and methods, detailing information about the reward, including the identity of the individual for whom the reward is being made, the amount of the reward, the acts with respect to which the reward is being made, and how the reward is being publicized."; and

(B) in subsection (k)(2), by striking "International Relations" and inserting "Foreign Affairs".

(3) EFFECTIVE DATE.—The amendments made by paragraphs (1) and (2) take effect on the date of the enactment of this Act and apply with respect to any reward authorized under section 36 of the State Department Basic Authorities Act of 1956 (as so amended) on or after such date.

(b) EXTRADITIONS.—

(1) SENSE OF CONGRESS.—It is the sense of Congress that the refusal by other countries to extradite or otherwise render to the United States fugitives who have been indicted or convicted within the United States for serious crimes, including murder, hijacking, and acts of domestic terrorism, is an impediment to justice, undermines international security, and deserves high level diplomatic efforts toward resolution.

(2) BRIEFING REQUIREMENT.—Not later than 90 days after the date of the enactment of this Act, the President shall provide to Congress a briefing related to the issues raised in paragraph (1), including—

(A) the number of fugitives and others for whom the United States Government is seeking extradition or rendition, both in total and listed by country;

(B) the average length of time such extradition or rendition requests have been outstanding, both in general and by country;

(C) discussion of diplomatic and other efforts the United States has undertaken to secure the return of such fugitives;

(D) discussion of factors that have been barriers to the resolution of such cases; and

(E) information on the number of United States citizens whose extradition has been sought by foreign governments during the past five years, both in total and listed by country, and a discussion of the outcome of such requests.

SEC. 705. EXTENSION OF PERIOD FOR REIMBURSEMENT OF SEIZED COMMERCIAL FISHERMEN.

Subsection (e) of section 7 of the Fishermen's Protective Act of 1967 (22 U.S.C. 1977) is amended by striking "2008" and inserting "2018".

SEC. 706. EXPANSION OF THE CHARLES B. RANGEL INTERNATIONAL AFFAIRS PROGRAM, THE THOMAS R. PICKERING FOREIGN AFFAIRS FELLOWSHIP PROGRAM, AND THE DONALD M. PAYNE INTERNATIONAL DEVELOPMENT FELLOWSHIP PROGRAM.

(a) ADDITIONAL FELLOWSHIPS AUTHORIZED.—Beginning in fiscal year 2017, the Secretary shall—

(1) increase by ten the number of fellows selected for the Charles B. Rangel International Affairs Program;

(2) increase by ten the number of fellows selected for the Thomas R. Pickering Foreign Affairs Fellowship Program; and

(3) increase by five the number of fellows selected for the Donald M. Payne International Development Fellowship Program.

(b) RULE OF CONSTRUCTION.—Nothing in this section may be construed as authorizing the hiring of additional personnel at the Department beyond existing, projected hiring patterns.

SEC. 707. GAO REPORT ON DEPARTMENT CRITICAL TELECOMMUNICATIONS EQUIPMENT OR SERVICES OBTAINED FROM SUPPLIERS CLOSELY LINKED TO A LEADING CYBER-THREAT ACTOR.

(a) REPORT REQUIRED.—Not later than 180 days after the date of the enactment of this Act, the Comptroller General of the United States shall submit to Congress a report on any critical telecommunications equipment, technologies, or services obtained or used by the Department or its contractors or subcontractors that is—

(1) manufactured by a foreign supplier, or a contractor or subcontractor of such supplier, that is closely linked to a leading cyber-threat actor; or

(2) from an entity that incorporates or utilizes information technology manufactured by a foreign supplier, or a contractor or subcontractor of such supplier, that is closely linked to a leading cyber-threat actor.

(b) FORM.—The report shall be submitted in unclassified form, but may include a classified annex.

(c) DEFINITIONS.—In this section:

(1) LEADING CYBER-THREAT ACTOR.—The term "leading cyber-threat actor" means a country identified as a leading threat actor in cyberspace in the report entitled "Worldwide Threat Assessment of the US Intelligence Community", dated February 9, 2016.

(2) CLOSELY LINKED.—The term "closely linked", with respect to a foreign supplier, contractor, or subcontrator and a leading cyber-threat actor, means the foreign supplier, contractor, or subcontractor—

(A) has ties to the military forces of such actor;

(B) has ties to the intelligence services of such actor;

(C) is the beneficiary of significant low interest or no-interest loans, loan forgiveness, or other support of such actor; or

(D) is incorporated or headquartered in the territory of such actor.

SEC. 708. IMPLEMENTATION PLAN FOR INFORMATION TECHNOLOGY AND KNOWLEDGE MANAGEMENT.

Not later than 90 days after the date of the enactment of this Act, the Secretary shall submit to the appropriate congressional committees an implementation plan, including timelines and resources, required to—

(1) establish a hub for analytics, data science, strategy, and knowledge management at the Department; and

(2) migrate suitable information technology (as such term is defined in section 11101(6) of title 40 United States Code) to a cloud computing service or a cloud-based solution.

SEC. 709. RANSOMS TO FOREIGN TERRORIST ORGANIZATIONS.

(a) IN GENERAL.—Not later than 90 days after the date of the enactment of this Act, the President, in consultation with the Secretary, shall transmit to the appropriate congressional committees a report covering the previous calendar providing the following details:

(1) Which foreign governments are believed to have facilitated, directly or indirectly, the payment of ransoms.

(2) Which foreign terrorist organizations received payments from foreign governments identified in paragraph (1).

(3) The amount of each such payment.

(4) The means of delivering such payments.

(5) A summary of the efforts of the United States to counter such payments.

(6) Recommendations for improving coordination among the foreign allies of the United States to not pay ransoms.

(b) FORM.—The report required by subsection (a) shall be submitted in unclassified form, may include a classified annex, shall be made available to the public by posting the unclassified form of such report on the website of the Department, and may be included in any other report that is required to be made public.

SEC. 710. STRATEGY TO COMBAT TERRORIST USE OF SOCIAL MEDIA.

(a) IN GENERAL.—Not later than 90 days after the date of the enactment of this Act, the President shall transmit to the appropriate congressional committees a report on United States strategy to combat terrorists' and terrorist organizations' use of social media consistent with the President's 2011 "Strategic Implementation Plan for Empowering Local Partners to Prevent Violent Extremism in the United States".

(b) ELEMENTS.—The report required by subsection (a) shall include the following:

(1) An evaluation of what role social media plays in radicalization in the United States and elsewhere.

(2) An analysis of how terrorists and terrorist organizations are using social media, including trends.

(3) A summary of the Federal Government's efforts to disrupt and counter the use of social media by terrorists and terrorist organizations, an evaluation of the success of such efforts, and recommendations for improvement.

(4) An analysis of how social media is being used for counter-radicalization and counter-propaganda purposes, irrespective of whether or not such efforts are made by the Federal Government.

(5) An assessment of the value to law enforcement of social media posts by terrorists and terrorist organizations.

(6) An overview of social media training available to law enforcement and intelligence personnel that enables such personnel to understand and combat the use of social media by terrorists and terrorist organizations, as well as recommendations for improving or expanding existing training opportunities.

(c) FORM.—The report required by subsection (a) shall be submitted in unclassified form, but may include a classified annex in accordance with the protection of intelligence sources and methods.

(d) APPROPRIATE CONGRESSIONAL COMMITTEES DEFINED.—In this section, the term "appropriate congressional committees" means—

(1) the Committee on Foreign Affairs, the Committee on the Armed Services, the Committee on Homeland Security, the Committee on the Judiciary, and the Permanent Select Committee on Intelligence of the House of Representatives; and

(2) the Committee on Foreign Relations, the Committee on Armed Services, the Committee on Homeland Security and Governmental Affairs, the Committee on the Judiciary, and the Select Committee on Intelligence of the Senate.

SEC. 711. REPORT ON DEPARTMENT INFORMATION TECHNOLOGY ACQUISITION PRACTICES.

(a) REPORT REQUIRED.—Not later than 90 days after the date of the enactment of this

Act, the Secretary shall submit to the appropriate congressional committees a report detailing the Department's information technology acquisition practices.

(b) ELEMENTS OF REPORT.—The report required under subsection (a) shall include the following elements:

(1) Agency chief investment officer authority enhancements, including reporting on incremental developments regarding whether information technology investments are delivering functionality every six months.

(2) Enhanced transparency and risk management, including the methodology for calculating risk.

(3) The frequency and status of agency-wide portfolio reviews to identify opportunities for information technology efficiency, effectiveness, duplication, and potential savings.

(4) Data center consolidation and optimization, including potential savings.

SEC. 712. PUBLIC AVAILABILITY OF REPORTS ON NOMINEES TO BE CHIEFS OF MISSION.

Not later than seven days after submitting the report required under section 304(a)(4) of the Foreign Service Act of 1980 (22 U.S.C. 3944(a)(4)) to the Committee on Foreign Relations of the Senate, the President shall make the report available to the public, including by posting the report on the website of the Department in a conspicuous manner and location.

SEC. 713. RECRUITMENT AND RETENTION OF INDIVIDUALS WHO HAVE LIVED, WORKED, OR STUDIED IN PREDOMINANTLY MUSLIM COUNTRIES OR COMMUNITIES.

(a) FINDINGS.—Congress finds that successful engagement, including robust public diplomacy, with predominantly Muslim countries and communities is critical for achieving United States foreign policy objectives.

(b) SENSE OF CONGRESS.—It is the sense of Congress that the Department should recruit more employees that have a personal background in, and thorough understating of, the cultures, languages, and history of the Middle East and wider Muslim world.

(c) RECRUITMENT AND RETENTION OF CERTAIN INDIVIDUALS.—The Secretary shall make every effort to recruit and retain individuals that have lived, worked, or studied in predominantly Muslim countries or communities, including individuals who have studied at an Islamic institution of higher learning.

SEC. 714. SENSE OF CONGRESS REGARDING COVERAGE OF APPROPRIATE THERAPIES FOR DEPENDENTS WITH AUTISM SPECTRUM DISORDER (ASD).

(a) FINDING.—Congress finds that physical, occupational, speech, and applied behavioral analysis (ABA) therapies are evidenced-based interventions proven to bring about positive change and assist in the long term development of children with autism spectrum disorder (ASD).

(b) SENSE OF CONGRESS.—It is the sense of Congress that the Secretary should endeavor to ensure coverage and access, for dependents with ASD of overseas employees, to the therapies described in subsection (a), including through telehealth, computer software programs, or alternative means if appropriate providers are not accessible due to such employees' placement overseas.

SEC. 715. REPEAL OF OBSOLETE REPORTS.

(a) REPEAL OF CERTAIN REPORTING REQUIREMENTS.—The following provisions of law are repealed:

(1) Section 12 of the Foreign Service Buildings Act, 1926 (Act of May 7, 1926, 22 U.S.C. 303).

(2) Section 404 of the Foreign Relations Authorization Act, Fiscal Years 1992 and 1993 (Public Law 102–138, 22 U.S.C. 2778 note).

(b) OTHER REPORTING REFORM.—

(1) Section 613 of the Foreign Relations Authorization Act, Fiscal Year 2003 (Public Law 107–228, 22 U.S.C. 6901 note) is amended—

(A) by striking subsection (b);

(B) by striking "(a) POLICY.—"; and

(C) by redesignating paragraphs (1) and (2) as subsections (a) and (b), respectively, and moving such subsections, as so redesignated, two ems to the left.

(2) Section 721 of Appendix G of the Consolidated Appropriations Act of 2000 (Public Law 106–113, 22 U.S.C. 287 note) is amended—

(A) by striking subsection (c); and

(B) by redesignating subsection (d) as subsection (c).

(3) Section 10 of the Palestinian Anti-Terrorism Act of 2006 (Public Law 109–446, 22 U.S.C. 2378b note) is amended—

(A) by striking subsection (b); and

(B) by redesignating subsection (c) as subsection (b).

(4) Section 1207 of the Bob Stump National Defense Authorization Act for Fiscal Year 2003 (Public Law 107–314, 22 U.S.C. 6901 note) is amended—

(A) by striking subsection (d); and

(B) by redesignating subsection (e) as subsection (d).

(5) Subsection (c) of section 601 of the Foreign Service Act of 1980 (22 U.S.C. 4001) is amended by striking paragraphs (4) and (5).

SEC. 716. PROHIBITION ON ADDITIONAL FUNDING.

No additional funds are authorized to be appropriated to carry out this Act and the amendments made by this Act.

The SPEAKER pro tempore. Pursuant to the rule, the gentleman from California (Mr. ROYCE) and the gentleman from New York (Mr. ENGEL) each will control 20 minutes.

The Chair recognizes the gentleman from California.

GENERAL LEAVE

Mr. ROYCE. Mr. Speaker, I ask unanimous consent that all Members may have 5 legislative days to revise and extend their remarks and to include extraneous material on this bill.

The SPEAKER pro tempore. Is there objection to the request of the gentleman from California?

There was no objection.

Mr. ROYCE. Mr. Speaker, I yield myself such time as I may consume.

Mr. Speaker, I would like to thank the ranking member of this committee, Mr. ELIOT ENGEL, for his work on this important piece of legislation to protect U.S. personnel overseas, to improve the oversight of the Department of State, and to modernize its workforce. And I would also like to thank the other members of the committee for their input as well on this legislation.

The world is not getting any easier for the men and women serving overseas who represent this country at the Department of State. These men and women work with many other agencies, including the Defense Department. They have got a wide range of very important responsibilities.

They try to broker peace agreements. And, of course, not everybody wants

peace in these agreements. They have to fight human trafficking. In other words, they have got to stand up to the criminal syndicates in some of these countries. They have got to help our fellow Americans in distress. That is just to name a few of the dangerous tasks that they undertake. They work hard, often in very challenging, even life-threatening circumstances, so they deserve our support, which includes reforming a department that sorely needs to modernize.

Mr. Speaker, the annual authorization of the Department of State is critical to maintaining congressional oversight and making these needed agency reforms. The House has passed an authorization bill in each of the last six Congresses, but, unfortunately, it has been 15 years since this legislation was signed into law. This year, we have an opportunity to break that unfortunate streak, which makes this legislation all the more important.

First and foremost, the bill includes a number of critical embassy security reforms and improvements. For example, the Department will be authorized to use so-called best value criteria when contracting for local guards at U.S. facilities overseas. This is an important change.

This authority has consistently been requested by the professionals overseeing the security at our embassies and has been a particular focus of two members of the committee. So I would like to thank LOIS FRANKEL and RANDY WEBER for their work.

The bill requires the State Department to designate a list of high-risk, high-threat posts, effectively prioritizing the resources and the security for these posts. Now, these are the posts most at risk. The State Department and Defense Department are directed to jointly develop enhanced contingency plans. Why? Because there are going to be surprises overseas. There are going to be emergency situations, including planning for the rapid deployment of military resources to keep our personnel safe in a time of crisis.

It includes provisions that improve security for the children and the families of U.S. diplomats abroad. And it makes sure that security failures, due to misconduct or due to unsatisfactory performance, are identified and those responsible are held accountable, something that did not happen when it came to the Islamist terrorist attack in Benghazi. No one lost a day of pay as a consequence of the mistakes made there.

The bill increases accountability also for sexual exploitation and abuse by U.N. peacekeepers, which the Foreign Affairs Committee has helped expose through the hearings by Chairman CHRIS SMITH.

It also increases transparency for how U.S. funds are spent at the United Nations and mandates that the Department work to increase the number of

American citizens employed by the United Nations. This has been a focus of Mr. MO BROOKS.

We have also included important provisions to bolster the State Department's inspector general, an office that the Foreign Affairs Committee successfully fought to have filled after it sat vacant for 5 years.

And lastly, the bill increases flexibility in the Department's workforce, allowing civil servants more opportunities to serve overseas and authorizing a pilot program to acquire skilled workers from the private sector.

The passage of this legislation, S. 1635, would strengthen the law. It is a bipartisan bill, it improves congressional oversight of the Department, and I think it deserves unanimous support.

I reserve the balance of my time.

Mr. ENGEL. Mr. Speaker, I yield myself such time as I may consume.

I rise in support of this bill.

Mr. Speaker, let me start by thanking my friend and the chairman of the Foreign Affairs Committee, ED ROYCE of California. He and I and our staffs have been working on this bill for most of the 114th Congress. This may be the last Foreign Affairs bill the House will deal with this year, and it is an appropriate capstone for the committee's work.

Authorizing and overseeing the State Department is one of our committee's most important responsibilities. As the Obama administration comes to an end and we deal with the uncertainties of a transition in power, it is important that Congress help to set the tone for the future of our foreign policy. We need to do all we can to ensure the future of America's leadership role in the world.

□ 1745

This bill is also long, long overdue as the chairman pointed out. The last time the President signed a State Department authorization was in the year 2002. So much has changed since then—from the invasion of Iraq and the subsequent rise of ISIS to the ascendance of the Asia-Pacific in our foreign policy to the growing threat of climate change.

Think about the way terrorist groups use social media to recruit fighters and spread propaganda. This has become a major foreign policy concern; yet the last time we passed the State Department authorization, Twitter and Facebook were still a few years from coming online. Imagine that. That is just one example. In nearly 15 years, countless issues have cropped up as new foreign policy concerns, and traditional areas of diplomacy and development have evolved. This bill will help the State Department keep pace with the changes.

I would like to underscore a few provisions in this bill that I think are es-

pecially important. The main thing I want to talk about is the heart and soul of American diplomacy: our diplomats. Our diplomats are at the core of this bill. We want them to have the tools and resources for success.

These men and women pursue a path of public service unlike any other, going to work—sometimes in dangerous places—as America's face to the world. Diplomats are our front line of international engagement, advancing our interests and building bridges of friendship and understanding. This is incredibly important work. It requires the right people for the job—people with the skill, training, and confidence to carry out their work.

We need to do all we can to enable our diplomats to carry out diplomacy. They need to be able to get out from behind a desk and engage directly with cultures and communities, from government officials to civil society groups to everyday people on the street; so we have included provisions in this bill that are focused on the security of our Embassies and on the proper training of our personnel.

We need the best possible security for our Embassies and diplomats abroad, and good security doesn't always come cheap. This bill says that, when the State Department hires local personnel to protect our diplomatic facilities and staff, they shouldn't be constrained only to take the lowest cost bid. After all, the rule is generally true that you get what you pay for, and when it comes to the safety of our diplomats, we should be focused on quality in addition to cost; so we have included a provision that calls for the best value security rather than the lowest cost. There is a lot of value in keeping our diplomats safe, and I want to thank representative LOIS FRANKEL for her work on this provision.

With this bill, we have also focused on improving the security of what we call "soft targets," not typical diplomatic facilities, but things like schools and schoolbuses for the children of diplomats abroad.

It is also important that the State Department reflect who we are as a country. America is made up of people from all different backgrounds and perspectives. Our diversity is one of our strengths. Our Foreign Service should benefit from that strength and reflect it back to the world.

We also need to incorporate that strength into our foreign policy. A diverse workforce means a diversity of views and experiences to aid our leaders when they face tough decisions. Old ways of thinking and worn-out approaches aren't well suited to the modern range of challenges our diplomats face. This bill will push the Department to recruit, train, and retain a diverse workforce. Reports tell us that the State Department has been slow to change in these areas, so we want to give those efforts a shot in the arm.

Additionally, I thank Chairman ROYCE for including my Western Hemisphere Drug Policy Commission legislation in this bill. The heroin epidemic in this country is getting worse and worse. We need to make sure that our drug policy is focused on saving lives. Here at home, that means doing more on prevention and treatment. Looking abroad, we need to take stock of what has worked and what hasn't when it comes to our drug policy in Latin America and the Caribbean. That is what this commission will do, and I am grateful this measure is moving forward.

That idea, taking stock of our successes and failures, brings me to a few final thoughts on this bill. Even though Congress has a role in foreign policy, we are outside the day-to-day decisionmaking structures. That outside perspective gives us a chance to step back and ask: What can we be doing better? Where can we cut away dead wood? What changes going on in the world require us to change our approach?

Our State Department personnel may have great new ideas about the way to advance our interests, but they are constrained by existing law or are bogged down in the constant hard work demanded of them. Let's be honest. By their nature, bureaucracies tend not to change on their own. That is when Congress needs to step in and say: "We can help to solve this problem. We can make it easier for our diplomats to do their jobs." The thing is that we have to actually do that. We should try to pass a bill like this every year. It should become the way we do business, just like the defense authorization, because when we don't, we are letting our diplomats down; we are also ceding their work to other jurisdictions, and we are missing opportunities to bolster American diplomacy and national security.

Last week, we voted on the Defense Authorization Act. It included 80 provisions that fell, at least in part, under the jurisdiction of the Foreign Affairs Committee when it landed on the President's desk. I respect our friends on the Armed Services Committee a great deal, but I hear their message loud and clear, that if we don't act in our own jurisdiction, someone else will.

I am encouraged that we have made it this far on this bill. I hope it becomes a regular part of our committee's work and that, a year from now, we are back here debating more good ideas about improving American diplomacy. For now, I again thank the chairman. I am glad to support this bill, and I urge all my colleagues to do the same.

I reserve the balance of my time.

Mr. ROYCE. Mr. Speaker, I yield 4 minutes to the gentleman from New Jersey (Mr. SMITH). He is the chairman of the Foreign Affairs Subcommittee on Africa, Global Health, Global Human Rights, and International Organizations.

Mr. SMITH of New Jersey. I thank my good friend, the distinguished chairman of the Foreign Affairs Committee, Mr. ROYCE, for his leadership on this important bill. I thank ELIOT ENGEL, the ranking member, and, of course, Senators CORKER and CARDIN. This is a true bipartisan piece of legislation. I thank my colleagues for their leadership on this.

Mr. Speaker, a highly skilled group of Foreign Service Officers—about 15,000 strong—are deployed worldwide to promote peace and human rights, to support prosperity, and to protect Americans while advancing the vital interests of the United States abroad. For most, posting overseas requires serious personal sacrifice. For some, deployment entails serious danger—from disease, crime, and terrorism.

Mr. Speaker, after the American Embassies in Dar es Salaam and Nairobi were attacked by terrorists in August of 1998, I chaired hearings on Embassy security in my subcommittee and authored the Admiral James W. Nance and Meg Donovan Foreign Relations Authorization Act of 2000 and 2001 to significantly boost Embassy security, including reconfigured Embassies, setbacks—a zone that puts the street farther away from the building—and additional diplomatic security personnel. The bill, dubbed the "Embassy Security Act," which passed the House in 1999, never even got a vote in the Senate; but after much lobbying, my bill was included in its entirety in the FY 2000 appropriations omnibus. In 2005, Congress enacted into law another bill I sponsored, the Department of State Authorities Act, which, among other things, boosted danger pay.

Today, the Royce-Corker-Engel-Cardin bill authorizes $4.8 billion for Embassy security. It continues the all-important work of ensuring the most effective security possible for our Foreign Service and Americans abroad by directing joint DOD-State contingency plans—including the rapid deployment of Armed Forces—the designation of high-risk, high-threat posts with adequate funding and training commensurate with the danger, and the utilization of "best value" contracting.

The bill provides numerous enhancements of personnel issues for our men and women in the Foreign Service—from promotion opportunities to updated cost-of-living adjustments to improved care of Foreign Service officers' children-dependents with autism spectrum disorders.

During markup—and I thank the chair for being so gracious for supporting it—I sponsored an amendment that was approved that recognizes applied behavior analysis, or ABA, as proven evidence-based intervention for autistic children and that the Sec-

retary of State should ensure that coverage of and access to ABA for dependents with ASD of overseas employees is provided.

I travel all over the world, and I often hear from Foreign Service Officers who cannot get ABA treatment for their children. They are anguished because, if they try to go to a deployment where that is provided, it may hinder their Foreign Service careers; and, of course, they put their children first. That shouldn't be the case. There should be no choice. The children need to be supported as well as the Foreign Service Officers.

The House Foreign Affairs Committee also adopted another amendment I offered during markup, which is whistleblower protections for U.N. personnel—we have had hearings on that in our subcommittee—the capacity to investigate allegations of sexual exploitation committed by peacekeepers and to hold those who commit such heinous crimes accountable.

Mr. Speaker, I have traveled to places like Goma, in the DRC, where peacekeepers were raping 13-year-olds—U.N. peacekeepers. The series of hearings that we held on it found that the zero tolerance policy of the U.N. was really zero compliance. That has to improve. There have been some improvements made but far fewer than what are required. This legislation helps to push that ball significantly down that lane. Hopefully, the peacekeepers will do just that—protect. It is a duty for us to make sure that that happens. There are many other good things in this bill.

Again, I thank Chairman ROYCE for his leadership.

Mr. ROYCE. Mr. Speaker, in reclaiming my time, I thank CHRIS SMITH for his years of oversight and for his combating that type of abuse. I also thank him for our efforts to have this included now in what will become a new law.

I reserve the balance of my time.

Mr. ENGEL. Mr. Speaker, I yield 3 minutes to the gentleman from Virginia (Mr. CONNOLLY), my good friend and colleague on the Foreign Affairs Committee.

Mr. CONNOLLY. I thank the gentleman from New York (Mr. ENGEL), my dear friend and the distinguished ranking member of the House Foreign Affairs Committee.

I rise today in support of S. 1635, the Department of State Authorities Act. There is an expression in Latin. I studied Latin for 6 years, but I rarely get to use it. It is mirabile dictu—wonderful to relate—that we are actually going to pass the State Department authorization bill.

The bill is not perfect, and it is not as comprehensive as one would hope; however, it is a product of compromise under the fine leadership of ED ROYCE and ELIOT ENGEL. It is a welcome step

toward the annual authorization of the State Department operations I know we will get to next year. The regular enactment of a State Department authorization is a long-neglected priority, and the clarity of our diplomacy and development missions have suffered absent one. Congress has not enacted a full State authorization bill since 2002.

In a similar vein, the Foreign Assistance Act has not undergone a comprehensive reauthorization since 1985, when I was a staff member on the Senate Foreign Relations Committee. I have introduced the Global Partnerships Act, which would do just that, and I have tried to streamline and modernize the Foreign Assistance Act of 1961.

The bill on the floor today codifies high standards for Embassy security practices and ensures that we are making smart investments in diplomatic security. It also fights discrimination and promotes diversity within the Foreign Service.

I thank the committee—and particularly our leaders, Chairman ROYCE and Ranking Member ENGEL—for including my amendment that requires the State Department to report on its compliance with the Federal Information Technology Acquisition Reform Act, FITARA, which is the Federal IT reform bill I introduced and wrote with Mr. ISSA.

I support this bill because it enables the kind of serious, credible, and ambitious diplomacy that can solve the world's most intractable challenges, and I urge my colleagues to give it their full support.

Again, I congratulate our staffs—and particularly our chairman and ranking member, Mr. ROYCE and Mr. ENGEL, respectively—for their leadership in bringing this bill before us today.

Mr. ROYCE. Mr. Speaker, I reserve the balance of my time.

Mr. ENGEL. Mr. Speaker, I yield myself such time as I may consume.

I am waiting for one other speaker; so, while we are waiting, let me at least partially close.

I, first of all, thank Chairman ROYCE's staff for their hard work on this very important bill. I thank Tom Sheehy, Ed Burrier, Tom Hill, and Doug Anderson, and on my staff, Jason Steinbaum, Doug Campbell, Eric Jacobstein, Janice Kaguyutan, Sajit Gandhi, Jennifer Hendrixson White, and Mark Iozzi. We can only do as well as the wonderful staff that we have, and it is really appreciated, I know, by Chairman ROYCE and by me.

As was said before, Mr. Speaker, every single year, Congress passes a defense authorization. It happens without fail, and it should. It is a vitally important piece of legislation, and we have an obligation to give our women and men in uniform the support and the resources they need.

☐ 1800

The work of our diplomats is very different, but it is also critical to our national security. These dedicated public servants help to project stability, enhance security, and diffuse crises before they start.

From a dollars-and-cents perspective, it makes a lot more sense to prevent crises than to try to stop them after they are burning out of control. We need diplomacy to succeed so that using our military remains the last resort in our foreign policy. This legislation will help ensure that our diplomacy does succeed.

I hope this bill gets across the finish line soon; I hope the Senate does its job; and I hope we make a State Department authorization a yearly priority for the Foreign Affairs Committee, for the Congress, and for the American people.

I urge a "yes" vote on this bill.

I yield back the balance of my time.

Mr. ROYCE. Mr. Speaker, I yield 2 minutes to the gentleman from Texas (Mr. GOHMERT).

Mr. GOHMERT. Mr. Speaker, I am a big fan of Chairman ROYCE's work, and I appreciate all the work of the committee in these difficult areas.

Sometimes in trying to bring together a big authorization bill like this, language gets inserted that can be problematic. On page 105, for example, section 713, "Recruitment and retention of individuals who have lived, worked, or studied in predominantly Muslim countries or communities," we know that one of our problems when we were trying to deal with radical Islam is, number one, our President doesn't recognize radical Islam, although some of the best experts who are radical Islamists say, yes, it exists, and Muslim friends like President el-Sisi acknowledge it is a problem.

For example, here in subsection C, it says: "The Secretary shall make every effort to recruit and retain individuals that have lived, worked, or studied in predominantly Muslim countries or communities, including individuals who have studied at Islamic institutions of higher learning."

I know this was not submitted by a Muslim—far from it—but although we desperately need people who have lived and studied in this area, to tell the Secretary of State that the Secretary shall make every effort to get people like this is the way our enemies take advantage of us. We should not be telling the Secretary to make every effort.

As a former chief justice, that is the kind of thing—you have to say, well, he didn't make every effort or she didn't make every effort. We should not be coercing the State Department to hire people who—if they are not appropriate or have Muslim ties, they should not be pushed into the State Department.

Mr. ROYCE. Mr. Speaker, let me say in response that we should hire, in the State Department, people who do have some experience. We should have some people there with some experience with Muslim culture and Muslim countries, with that kind of a background. But that said, we want to work with the gentleman from Texas (Mr. GOHMERT) on implementation of this bill to make certain that these concerns are handled.

Mr. Speaker, I yield 2 minutes to the gentlewoman from Florida (Ms. FRANKEL).

Ms. FRANKEL of Florida. Mr. Speaker, I thank Chairman ROYCE and Ranking Member ENGEL, first, for the great bipartisan work. I really appreciate being on this committee.

I want to tell you a story that one of our Ambassadors told me that I thought was amazing. I won't say her name or where she was, but she told me she was overseas. The security that they hired was so poor that they actually had to hire criminals; and her security guard not only robbed her and her family, but killed their dog. That is just an example of some of the quality of security that we had for our Ambassadors, who deserve absolutely our utmost protection.

So I just want to thank both the chairman and the ranking member for working with me to get this provision in this bill that now is going to let our State Department get well-qualified security for Embassies, which they deserve to have.

Mr. ROYCE. Mr. Speaker, I yield myself such time as I may consume.

I want to thank the gentlewoman from Florida for her contribution to this legislation.

Mr. Speaker, as chairman, I also want to thank our ranking member, Mr. ENGEL. I want to thank all my committee colleagues for their contributions to this bill. I think we should take the opportunity to thank our counterparts, Senator CORKER and Senator CARDIN, in the Senate for working with us to bring the first State authorization bill to the President's desk in over 15 years.

Today, the Department is considering how to deploy diplomats in high-threat, high-risk places like South Sudan, like the Central African Republic, Yemen, Libya. It is our responsibility to make sure that U.S. personnel at these posts have every available means of protection, and this bill authorizes the Department to make critical upgrades in Embassy security.

This bill also mandates that the Department uses leverage at the United Nations to make improvements that have been ignored for too long. In just the last year, we have heard horrific stories of peacekeepers sexually abusing and exploiting those they are sent to protect. Sadly, these are not the first instances of such predatory behavior, but the United Nations has failed to take steps to stop it.

Oversight is necessary at any agency. It took 5 years for the Department's inspector general position to be filled, and this bill makes sure that the Department's watchdog has all the tools it needs to perform its mandate.

This bill deserves our support. The other body should move quickly so that these critical reforms can be signed into law by the President.

I yield back the balance of my time.

The SPEAKER pro tempore. The question is on the motion offered by the gentleman from California (Mr. ROYCE) that the House suspend the rules and pass the bill, S. 1635, as amended.

The question was taken.

The SPEAKER pro tempore. In the opinion of the Chair, two-thirds being in the affirmative, the ayes have it.

Mr. GOHMERT. Mr. Speaker, on that I demand the yeas and nays.

The yeas and nays were ordered.

The SPEAKER pro tempore. Pursuant to clause 8 of rule XX, further proceedings on this motion will be postponed.

RECESS

The SPEAKER pro tempore. Pursuant to clause 12(a) of rule I, the Chair declares the House in recess until approximately 6:30 p.m. today.

Accordingly (at 6 o'clock and 8 minutes p.m.), the House stood in recess.

☐ 1830

AFTER RECESS

The recess having expired, the House was called to order by the Speaker pro tempore (Mr. HARDY) at 6 o'clock and 30 minutes p.m.

ANNOUNCEMENT BY THE SPEAKER PRO TEMPORE

The SPEAKER pro tempore. Pursuant to clause 8 of rule XX, proceedings will resume on motions to suspend the rules previously postponed.

Votes will be taken in the following order:

H.R. 5015, by the yeas and nays;

H.R. 6427, by the yeas and nays;

S. 1635, by the yeas and nays.

The first electronic vote will be conducted as a 15-minute vote. Remaining electronic votes will be conducted as 5-minute votes.

COMBAT-INJURED VETERANS TAX FAIRNESS ACT OF 2016

The SPEAKER pro tempore. The unfinished business is the vote on the motion to suspend the rules and pass the bill (H.R. 5015) to restore amounts improperly withheld for tax purposes from severance payments to individuals who retired or separated from service in the Armed Forces for combat-related injuries, and for other purposes, as amended, on which the yeas and nays were ordered.

The Clerk read the title of the bill.

The SPEAKER pro tempore. The question is on the motion offered by the gentleman from Texas (Mr. BRADY) that the House suspend the rules and pass the bill, as amended.

The vote was taken by electronic device, and there were—yeas 392, nays 0, not voting 41, as follows:

[Roll No. 601]

YEAS—392

Abraham
Adams
Aderholt
Aguilar
Allen
Amash
Amodei
Ashford
Babin
Barletta
Barr
Barton
Bass
Beatty
Benishek
Bera
Beyer
Bilirakis
Bishop (GA)
Bishop (MI)
Bishop (UT)
Black
Blackburn
Blum
Blumenauer
Bonamici
Bost
Boustany
Boyle, Brendan F.
Brady (PA)
Brady (TX)
Brat
Brooks (AL)
Brooks (IN)
Brownley (CA)
Buchanan
Buck
Bucshon
Burgess
Bustos
Butterfield
Byrne
Calvert
Capps
Capuano
Cárdenas
Carson (IN)
Carter (GA)
Carter (TX)
Cartwright
Castor (FL)
Castro (TX)
Chabot
Chaffetz
Cicilline
Clark (MA)
Clarke (NY)
Clay
Cleaver
Clyburn
Coffman
Cohen
Cole
Collins (GA)
Collins (NY)
Comer
Comstock
Conaway
Connolly
Conyers
Cook
Cooper
Costa
Costello (PA)
Courtney
Cramer
Crawford
Crenshaw
Crowley
Cuellar
Culberson
Cummings
Curbelo (FL)
Davidson
Davis (CA)
Davis, Danny
Davis, Rodney
DeFazio
DeGette
Delaney
DeLauro
Denham
Dent
DeSantis
DeSaulnier
DesJarlais
Deutch
Diaz-Balart
Dingell
Doggett
Dold
Donovan
Doyle, Michael F.
Duckworth
Duncan (SC)
Duncan (TN)
Ellison
Emmer (MN)
Engel
Eshoo
Esty
Evans
Farenthold
Fitzpatrick
Fleischmann
Fleming
Flores
Fortenberry
Foster
Foxx
Frankel (FL)
Franks (AZ)
Frelinghuysen
Fudge
Gabbard
Gallego
Garamendi
Garrett
Gibbs
Gibson
Gohmert
Goodlatte
Gosar
Gowdy
Graham
Granger
Graves (GA)
Graves (LA)
Graves (MO)
Grayson
Green, Al
Green, Gene
Griffith
Grijalva
Grothman
Guinta
Guthrie
Gutiérrez
Hanabusa
Hardy
Harper
Hartzler
Hastings
Heck (NV)
Heck (WA)
Hensarling
Herrera Beutler
Higgins
Hill
Himes
Hinojosa
Holding
Hoyer
Hudson
Huelskamp
Huffman
Huizenga (MI)
Hultgren
Hurd (TX)
Israel
Issa
Jackson Lee
Jeffries
Jenkins (KS)
Jenkins (WV)
Johnson (GA)
Johnson (OH)
Johnson, E. B.
Johnson, Sam
Jones
Jordan
Joyce
Kaptur
Katko
Keating
Kelly (IL)
Kelly (MS)
Kelly (PA)
Kennedy
Kind
King (IA)
King (NY)
Kinzinger (IL)
Kline
Knight
Kuster
Labrador
LaHood
Lamborn
Lance
Langevin
Larsen (WA)
Larson (CT)
Latta
Lawrence
Levin
Lewis
Lieu, Ted
Lipinski
LoBiondo
Loebsack
Lofgren
Long
Loudermilk
Love
Lowenthal
Lowey
Lucas
Luetkemeyer
Lujan Grisham (NM)
Luján, Ben Ray (NM)
Lummis
Lynch
MacArthur
Maloney, Carolyn
Maloney, Sean
Marino
Massie
Matsui
McCarthy
McCaul
McClintock
McCollum
McGovern
McHenry
McKinley
McMorris Rodgers

McNerney
McSally
Meadows
Meehan
Meeks
Meng
Messer
Mica
Miller (FL)
Moolenaar
Mooney (WV)
Moore
Moulton
Mullin
Murphy (FL)
Murphy (PA)
Nadler
Neal
Neugebauer
Noem
Nolan
Norcross
Nugent
Nunes
O'Rourke
Olson
Palazzo
Pallone
Palmer
Pascrell
Paulsen
Payne
Pearce
Pelosi
Perlmutter
Perry
Peters
Peterson
Pingree
Pittenger
Pitts
Pocan
Poliquin
Polis
Pompeo
Posey
Price (NC)
Price, Tom
Quigley
Rangel
Ratcliffe
Reed
Renacci
Ribble
Rice (NY)
Rice (SC)
Rigell
Roby
Roe (TN)
Rogers (AL)
Rogers (KY)
Rokita
Rooney (FL)
Ros-Lehtinen
Roskam
Ross
Rothfus
Rouzer
Roybal-Allard
Royce
Ruiz
Ruppersberger
Russell
Ryan (OH)
Salmon
Sánchez, Linda T.
Sanford
Sarbanes
Scalise
Schakowsky
Schiff
Schrader
Schweikert
Scott (VA)
Scott, Austin
Scott, David
Sensenbrenner
Serrano
Sessions
Sewell (AL)
Sherman
Shimkus
Shuster
Simpson
Sinema
Sires
Slaughter
Smith (MO)
Smith (NE)
Smith (NJ)
Smith (TX)
Smith (WA)
Speier
Stefanik
Stewart
Stivers
Swalwell (CA)
Takano
Thompson (CA)
Thompson (MS)
Thompson (PA)
Thornberry
Tiberi
Tipton
Titus
Tonko
Torres
Trott
Tsongas
Turner
Upton
Valadao
Van Hollen
Vargas
Veasey
Vela
Velázquez
Visclosky
Wagner
Walberg
Walden
Walker
Walorski
Walters, Mimi
Walz
Wasserman Schultz
Waters, Maxine
Watson Coleman
Weber (TX)
Webster (FL)
Welch
Wenstrup
Westerman
Williams
Wilson (FL)
Wilson (SC)
Womack
Woodall
Yoder
Yoho
Young (AK)
Young (IA)
Young (IN)
Zeldin
Zinke

NOT VOTING—41

Becerra
Bridenstine
Brown (FL)
Carney
Chu, Judy
Clawson (FL)
DelBene
Duffy
Edwards
Ellmers (NC)
Farr
Fincher
Forbes
Hanna
Harris
Hice, Jody B.
Honda
Hunter
Hurt (VA)
Jolly
Kildee
Kilmer
Kirkpatrick
LaMalfa
Lee
Marchant
McDermott
Miller (MI)
Mulvaney
Napolitano
Newhouse
Poe (TX)
Reichert
Richmond
Rohrabacher
Rush
Sanchez, Loretta
Stutzman
Westmoreland
Wittman
Yarmuth

□ 1852

So (two-thirds being in the affirmative) the rules were suspended and the bill, as amended, was passed.

The result of the vote was announced as above recorded.

A motion to reconsider was laid on the table.

CREATING FINANCIAL PROSPERITY FOR BUSINESSES AND INVESTORS ACT

The SPEAKER pro tempore. The unfinished business is the vote on the motion to suspend the rules and pass the bill (H.R. 6427) to improve the operation of United States capital markets, and for other purposes, on which the yeas and nays were ordered.

The Clerk read the title of the bill.

The SPEAKER pro tempore. The question is on the motion offered by the gentleman from New Jersey (Mr. GARRETT) that the House suspend the rules and pass the bill.

This is a 5-minute vote.

The vote was taken by electronic device, and there were—yeas 391, nays 2, not voting 40, as follows:

[Roll No. 602]

YEAS—391

Abraham
Adams
Aderholt
Aguilar
Allen
Amash
Amodei
Ashford
Babin
Barletta
Barr
Barton
Bass
Beatty
Benishek
Bera
Beyer
Bilirakis
Bishop (GA)
Bishop (MI)
Bishop (UT)
Black
Blackburn
Blum
Blumenauer
Bonamici
Bost
Boustany
Boyle, Brendan F.
Brady (PA)
Brady (TX)
Brat
Brooks (AL)
Brooks (IN)
Brownley (CA)
Buchanan
Buck
Bucshon
Burgess
Bustos
Butterfield
Byrne
Calvert
Capps
Cárdenas
Carson (IN)
Carter (GA)
Carter (TX)
Cartwright
Castor (FL)
Castro (TX)
Chabot
Chaffetz
Cicilline
Clark (MA)
Clarke (NY)
Clay
Cleaver
Clyburn
Coffman
Cohen
Cole
Collins (GA)
Collins (NY)
Comer
Comstock
Conaway
Connolly
Conyers
Cook
Cooper
Costa
Courtney
Cramer
Crawford
Crenshaw
Crowley
Cuellar
Culberson
Cummings
Curbelo (FL)
Davidson
Davis (CA)
Davis, Danny
Davis, Rodney
DeFazio
DeGette
Delaney
DeLauro
Denham
Dent
DeSantis
DeSaulnier
DesJarlais
Deutch
Diaz-Balart
Dingell
Doggett
Dold
Donovan
Doyle, Michael F.
Duckworth
Duncan (SC)
Duncan (TN)
Ellison
Emmer (MN)
Engel
Eshoo
Esty
Evans
Farenthold
Fitzpatrick
Fleischmann
Fleming
Flores
Fortenberry
Foster
Foxx
Frankel (FL)
Franks (AZ)
Frelinghuysen
Fudge
Gabbard
Gallego
Garamendi
Garrett
Gibbs
Gibson
Gohmert
Goodlatte
Gosar
Gowdy
Graham
Granger
Graves (GA)
Graves (LA)
Graves (MO)
Grayson
Green, Al
Green, Gene
Griffith
Grijalva
Grothman
Guinta
Guthrie
Gutiérrez
Hanabusa
Hardy
Harper
Harris
Hartzler
Hastings
Heck (NV)
Heck (WA)
Hensarling
Herrera Beutler
Higgins
Hill
Himes
Hinojosa
Holding
Hoyer
Hudson
Huelskamp
Huffman
Huizenga (MI)
Hultgren
Hurd (TX)
Israel
Issa
Jackson Lee
Jeffries
Jenkins (KS)
Jenkins (WV)
Johnson (GA)
Johnson (OH)
Johnson, E. B.
Johnson, Sam
Jones
Jordan
Joyce
Kaptur
Katko
Keating
Kelly (IL)
Kelly (MS)
Kelly (PA)
Kennedy
Kind
King (IA)
King (NY)
Kinzinger (IL)
Kline
Knight
Kuster
Labrador
LaHood
Lamborn
Lance
Langevin
Larsen (WA)
Larson (CT)
Latta
Lawrence
Levin
Lewis
Lieu, Ted
Lipinski
LoBiondo
Loebsack
Lofgren
Long
Loudermilk
Love
Lowenthal
Lowey
Lucas
Luetkemeyer
Lujan Grisham (NM)
Luján, Ben Ray (NM)
Lummis
MacArthur
Maloney, Carolyn
Maloney, Sean
Marino
Massie
Matsui
McCarthy
McCaul
McClintock
McCollum
McGovern

McHenry	Reed	Stefanik
McKinley	Renacci	Stewart
McMorris	Ribble	Stivers
Rodgers	Rice (NY)	Swalwell (CA)
McNerney	Rice (SC)	Takano
McSally	Richmond	Thompson (CA)
Meadows	Rigell	Thompson (MS)
Meehan	Roby	Thompson (PA)
Meeks	Roe (TN)	Thornberry
Meng	Rogers (AL)	Tiberi
Mica	Rogers (KY)	Tipton
Miller (FL)	Rokita	Titus
Moolenaar	Rooney (FL)	Tonko
Mooney (WV)	Ros-Lehtinen	Torres
Moore	Roskam	Trott
Moulton	Ross	Tsongas
Mullin	Rothfus	Turner
Murphy (FL)	Rouzer	Upton
Murphy (PA)	Roybal-Allard	Valadao
Nadler	Royce	Van Hollen
Neal	Ruiz	Vargas
Neugebauer	Ruppersberger	Veasey
Noem	Russell	Vela
Nolan	Ryan (OH)	Velázquez
Norcross	Salmon	Visclosky
Nugent	Sánchez, Linda	Wagner
Nunes	T.	Walberg
O'Rourke	Sanford	Walden
Olson	Sarbanes	Walker
Palazzo	Scalise	Walorski
Pallone	Schakowsky	Walters, Mimi
Palmer	Schiff	Walz
Pascrell	Schrader	Wasserman
Paulsen	Schweikert	Schultz
Payne	Scott (VA)	Waters, Maxine
Pearce	Scott, Austin	Watson Coleman
Pelosi	Scott, David	Weber (TX)
Perlmutter	Sensenbrenner	Webster (FL)
Perry	Serrano	Welch
Peters	Sessions	Wenstrup
Peterson	Sewell (AL)	Westerman
Pingree	Sherman	Williams
Pittenger	Shimkus	Wilson (FL)
Pitts	Shuster	Wilson (SC)
Pocan	Simpson	Womack
Poliquin	Sinema	Woodall
Polis	Sires	Yarmuth
Pompeo	Slaughter	Yoder
Posey	Smith (MO)	Yoho
Price (NC)	Smith (NE)	Young (AK)
Price, Tom	Smith (NJ)	Young (IA)
Quigley	Smith (TX)	Young (IN)
Rangel	Smith (WA)	Zeldin
Ratcliffe	Speier	Zinke

NAYS—2

Capuano	Lynch

NOT VOTING—40

Becerra	Hanna	Miller (MI)
Bridenstine	Hice, Jody B.	Mulvaney
Brown (FL)	Honda	Napolitano
Carney	Hunter	Newhouse
Chu, Judy	Hurt (VA)	Poe (TX)
Clawson (FL)	Jolly	Reichert
Costello (PA)	Kildee	Rohrabacher
DelBene	Kilmer	Rush
Duffy	Kirkpatrick	Sanchez, Loretta
Edwards	LaMalfa	Stutzman
Ellmers (NC)	Lee	Westmoreland
Farr	Marchant	Wittman
Fincher	McDermott	
Forbes	Messer	

ANNOUNCEMENT BY THE SPEAKER PRO TEMPORE

The SPEAKER pro tempore (during the vote). There are 2 minutes remaining.

□ 1902

So (two-thirds being in the affirmative) the rules were suspended and the bill was passed.

The result of the vote was announced as above recorded.

A motion to reconsider was laid on the table.

DEPARTMENT OF STATE OPERATIONS AUTHORIZATION AND EMBASSY SECURITY ACT, FISCAL YEAR 2016

The SPEAKER pro tempore. The unfinished business is the vote on the motion to suspend the rules and pass the bill (S. 1635) to authorize the Department of State for fiscal year 2016, and for other purposes, as amended, on which the yeas and nays were ordered.

The Clerk read the title of the bill.

The SPEAKER pro tempore. The question is on the motion offered by the gentleman from California (Mr. ROYCE) that the House suspend the rules and pass the bill, as amended.

This is a 5-minute vote.

The vote was taken by electronic device, and there were—yeas 374, nays 16, not voting 43, as follows:

[Roll No. 603]

YEAS—374

Abraham	Cook	Graves (LA)
Adams	Cooper	Graves (MO)
Aderholt	Costa	Grayson
Aguilar	Courtney	Green, Al
Allen	Cramer	Green, Gene
Amash	Crawford	Grijalva
Amodei	Crenshaw	Guinta
Ashford	Crowley	Guthrie
Barletta	Cuellar	Gutiérrez
Barr	Culberson	Hanabusa
Barton	Cummings	Hardy
Bass	Curbelo (FL)	Harper
Beatty	Davidson	Hartzler
Benishek	Davis (CA)	Hastings
Bera	Davis, Danny	Heck (NV)
Beyer	Davis, Rodney	Heck (WA)
Bilirakis	DeFazio	Hensarling
Bishop (GA)	DeGette	Herrera Beutler
Bishop (MI)	Delaney	Higgins
Bishop (UT)	DeLauro	Hill
Blum	Denham	Himes
Blumenauer	Dent	Hinojosa
Bonamici	DeSantis	Holding
Bost	DeSaulnier	Hoyer
Boustany	DesJarlais	Hudson
Boyle, Brendan	Deutch	Huelskamp
F.	Diaz-Balart	Huffman
Brady (PA)	Dingell	Huizenga (MI)
Brady (TX)	Doggett	Hultgren
Brooks (AL)	Dold	Hurd (TX)
Brooks (IN)	Donovan	Israel
Brownley (CA)	Doyle, Michael	Issa
Buchanan	F.	Jackson Lee
Bucshon	Duckworth	Jeffries
Burgess	Duncan (SC)	Jenkins (KS)
Bustos	Duncan (TN)	Jenkins (WV)
Butterfield	Ellison	Johnson (GA)
Byrne	Emmer (MN)	Johnson (OH)
Calvert	Engel	Johnson, E. B.
Capps	Eshoo	Johnson, Sam
Capuano	Esty	Jordan
Cárdenas	Evans	Joyce
Carson (IN)	Farenthold	Kaptur
Carter (GA)	Fitzpatrick	Katko
Carter (TX)	Fleischmann	Kelly (IL)
Cartwright	Fleming	Kelly (MS)
Castor (FL)	Flores	Kelly (PA)
Castro (TX)	Fortenberry	Kennedy
Chabot	Foster	Kind
Chaffetz	Foxx	King (NY)
Cicilline	Frankel (FL)	Kinzinger (IL)
Clark (MA)	Franks (AZ)	Knight
Clarke (NY)	Frelinghuysen	Kuster
Clay	Fudge	Labrador
Cleaver	Gabbard	LaHood
Clyburn	Gallego	Lamborn
Coffman	Garamendi	Lance
Cohen	Garrett	Langevin
Cole	Gibbs	Larsen (WA)
Collins (GA)	Gibson	Larson (CT)
Collins (NY)	Gosar	Latta
Comer	Gowdy	Lawrence
Comstock	Graham	Levin
Connolly	Granger	Lewis
Conyers	Graves (GA)	Lieu, Ted
Lipinski	Pelosi	Sires
LoBiondo	Perlmutter	Slaughter
Loebsack	Perry	Smith (MO)
Lofgren	Peters	Smith (NE)
Long	Peterson	Smith (NJ)
Loudermilk	Pingree	Smith (TX)
Love	Pittenger	Smith (WA)
Lowenthal	Pitts	Speier
Lowey	Pocan	Stefanik
Lucas	Poliquin	Stewart
Luetkemeyer	Polis	Stivers
Lujan Grisham	Pompeo	Swalwell (CA)
(NM)	Posey	Takano
Luján, Ben Ray	Price (NC)	Thompson (CA)
(NM)	Price, Tom	Thompson (MS)
Lummis	Quigley	Thompson (PA)
Lynch	Rangel	Thornberry
MacArthur	Ratcliffe	Tiberi
Maloney,	Reed	Tipton
Carolyn	Renacci	Titus
Maloney, Sean	Ribble	Tonko
Marino	Rice (NY)	Torres
Matsui	Rice (SC)	Trott
McCarthy	Richmond	Tsongas
McCaul	Rigell	Turner
McClintock	Roby	Upton
McCollum	Roe (TN)	Valadao
McGovern	Rogers (AL)	Van Hollen
McHenry	Rogers (KY)	Vargas
McKinley	Rokita	Veasey
McMorris	Rooney (FL)	Vela
Rodgers	Ros-Lehtinen	Velázquez
McNerney	Roskam	Visclosky
McSally	Ross	Wagner
Meadows	Rothfus	Walberg
Meehan	Rouzer	Walden
Meeks	Roybal-Allard	Walker
Meng	Royce	Walorski
Mica	Ruiz	Walters, Mimi
Miller (FL)	Ruppersberger	Walz
Moolenaar	Russell	Wasserman
Mooney (WV)	Ryan (OH)	Schultz
Moore	Salmon	Waters, Maxine
Moulton	Sánchez, Linda	Watson Coleman
Mullin	T.	Weber (TX)
Murphy (FL)	Sanford	Welch
Murphy (PA)	Sarbanes	Wenstrup
Nadler	Scalise	Westerman
Neugebauer	Schakowsky	Williams
Noem	Schiff	Wilson (FL)
Nolan	Schrader	Wilson (SC)
Norcross	Schweikert	Womack
Nugent	Scott (VA)	Woodall
Nunes	Scott, Austin	Yarmuth
O'Rourke	Scott, David	Yoder
Olson	Serrano	Yoho
Palazzo	Sessions	Young (AK)
Pallone	Sewell (AL)	Young (IA)
Palmer	Sherman	Young (IN)
Pascrell	Shimkus	Zeldin
Paulsen	Shuster	Zinke
Payne	Simpson	
Pearce	Sinema	

NAYS—16

Babin	Gohmert	King (IA)
Black	Goodlatte	Massie
Blackburn	Griffith	Sensenbrenner
Brat	Grothman	Webster (FL)
Buck	Harris	
Conaway	Jones	

NOT VOTING—43

Becerra	Hice, Jody B.	Miller (MI)
Bridenstine	Honda	Mulvaney
Brown (FL)	Hunter	Napolitano
Carney	Hurt (VA)	Neal
Chu, Judy	Jolly	Newhouse
Clawson (FL)	Keating	Poe (TX)
Costello (PA)	Kildee	Reichert
DelBene	Kilmer	Rohrabacher
Duffy	Kirkpatrick	Rush
Edwards	Kline	Sanchez, Loretta
Ellmers (NC)	LaMalfa	Stutzman
Farr	Lee	Westmoreland
Fincher	Marchant	Wittman
Forbes	McDermott	
Hanna	Messer	

□ 1910

Messrs. CONAWAY, GOODLATTE, and GRIFFITH changed their vote from "yea" to "nay."

So (two-thirds being in the affirmative) the rules were suspended and the bill, as amended, was passed.

The result of the vote was announced as above recorded.

A motion to reconsider was laid on the table.

PERSONAL EXPLANATION

Mrs. NAPOLITANO. Madam Speaker, I was absent on Monday, December 5, 2016. Had I been present, I would have voted "yea" on rollcall No. 601—H.R. 5015—Combat-Injured Veterans Tax Fairness Act of 2016, as amended, "yea" on rollcall No. 602—H.R. 6427—Creating Financial Prosperity for Businesses and Investors Act, and "yea" on rollcall No. 603—House Amendment to S. 1635—Department of State Authorities Act, Fiscal Year 2017, as amended.

PRESIDENTIAL ALLOWANCE MODERNIZATION ACT OF 2016—VETO MESSAGE FROM THE PRESIDENT OF THE UNITED STATES

Mr. CHAFFETZ. Madam Speaker, notwithstanding the order of the House of September 22, 2016, I ask unanimous consent that the veto message of the President on the bill, H.R. 1777, together with the accompanying bill, be referred to the Committee on Oversight and Government Reform.

The SPEAKER pro tempore (Ms. MCSALLY). Is there objection to the request of the gentleman from Utah?

There was no objection.

PROVIDING FOR APPOINTMENT OF MEMBERS OF BOARD OF DIRECTORS OF OFFICE OF COMPLIANCE

Mr. RODNEY DAVIS of Illinois. Madam Speaker, I ask unanimous consent that the Committee on House Administration be discharged from further consideration of the bill (H.R. 6415) to provide for the appointment of members of the Board of Directors of the Office of Compliance to replace members whose terms expire during 2017, and for other purposes, and ask for its immediate consideration in the House.

The Clerk read the title of the bill.

The SPEAKER pro tempore. Is there objection to the request of the gentleman from Illinois?

There was no objection.

The text of the bill is as follows:

H.R. 6415

Be it enacted by the Senate and House of Representatives of the United States of America in Congress assembled,

SECTION 1. APPOINTMENT OF MEMBERS OF BOARD OF DIRECTORS OF OFFICE OF COMPLIANCE.

(a) APPOINTMENT OF MEMBERS.—

(1) MEMBERS REPLACING MEMBERS WHOSE TERMS EXPIRE IN MARCH 2017.—Notwithstanding the first sentence of section 301(e) of the Congressional Accountability Act of 1995 (2 U.S.C. 1381(e)), of the members of the Board of Directors of the Office of Compliance who are appointed to replace the 3 members whose terms expire in March 2017—

(A) one shall have a term of office of 3 years; and

(B) two shall have a term of office of 4 years,

as designated at the time of appointment by the persons specified in section 301(b) of such Act (2 U.S.C. 1381(b)).

(2) MEMBERS REPLACING MEMBERS WHOSE TERMS EXPIRE IN MAY 2017.—In accordance with the first sentence of section 301(e) of the Congressional Accountability Act of 1995 (2 U.S.C. 1381(e)), the members of the Board of Directors of the Office of Compliance who are appointed to replace the 2 members whose terms expire in May 2017 shall each have a term of office of 5 years.

(b) SERVICE OF CURRENT MEMBERS.—Notwithstanding the second sentence of section 301(e) of the Congressional Accountability Act of 1995 (2 U.S.C. 1381(e)) or section 3 of the Office of Compliance Administrative and Technical Corrections Act of 2015 (Public Law 114–6; 2 U.S.C. 1381 note)—

(1) an individual serving as a member of the Board of Directors of the Office of Compliance whose term expires in March 2017 may be reappointed to serve one additional term at the length designated under paragraph (1) of subsection (a), but may not be reappointed to any additional terms after that additional term expires; and

(2) an individual serving as a member of the Board of Directors of the Office of Compliance whose term expires in May 2017 may be reappointed to serve one additional term at the length referred to in paragraph (2) of subsection (a), but may not be reappointed to any additional terms after that additional term expires.

(c) PERMITTING MEMBERS TO SERVE UNTIL APPOINTMENT OF SUCCESSORS.—Section 301(e) of the Congressional Accountability Act of 1995 (2 U.S.C. 1381(e)) is amended by adding at the end the following new paragraph:

"(3) PERMITTING SERVICE UNTIL APPOINTMENT OF SUCCESSOR.—A member of the Board may serve after the expiration of that member's term until a successor has taken office.".

The bill was ordered to be engrossed and read a third time, was read the third time, and passed, and a motion to reconsider was laid on the table.

DIRECTING THE SECRETARY OF THE SENATE TO MAKE TECHNICAL CORRECTIONS IN THE ENROLLMENT OF S. 2943

Mr. THORNBERRY. Madam Speaker, I send to the desk a concurrent resolution and ask unanimous consent for its immediate consideration in the House.

The Clerk read the title of the concurrent resolution.

The SPEAKER pro tempore. Is there objection to the request of the gentleman from Texas?

There was no objection.

The text of the concurrent resolution is as follows:

H. CON. RES. 179

Resolved by the House of Representatives (the Senate concurring), That in the enrollment of the bill S. 2943, the Secretary of the Senate shall make the following corrections:

(1) In section 212(a), strike "less two" and insert "less than two".

(2) In section 217(a)(1), strike "is amended" and insert "as amended by section 821(a), is

further amended" and strike "2338" and insert "2339".

(3) In section 217(a)(2), strike "is amended" and insert ", as amended by section 821(b), is further amended" and strike "2338" and insert "2339".

(4) In section 217(b)(1)(A), strike "section 2338" and insert "sections 2338 and 2339".

(5) In section 512(c), strike "Section 7511" and insert "Section 7511(b)".

(6) In section 707(b)(4), strike "pursuant to section 709" and insert "pursuant to section 708".

(7) In the tables in section 4701, relating to Department of Energy National Security Programs, Infrastructure and Operations, Construction, strike "04–D–125–04 RLUOB equipment installation" and insert "04–D–125 Chemistry and metallurgy research replacement project, LANL".

The concurrent resolution was agreed to.

A motion to reconsider was laid on the table.

UNITED NATIONS

(Ms. ROS-LEHTINEN asked and was given permission to address the House for 1 minute.)

Ms. ROS-LEHTINEN. Madam Speaker, last week, the United Nations General Assembly passed six anti-Israel resolutions, including yet another one that denies and distances Jewish and Christian ties to the Temple Mount.

In fact, Madam Speaker, the General Assembly will have taken up 20 anti-Israel resolutions by the end of this session and will have only brought up four—one, two, three, four—measures against some of the world's worst human rights violators like Iran, China, Russia, North Korea, Venezuela, and Cuba—combined.

This just underscores, Madam Speaker, the need for systemwide reforms at the United Nations.

With the new administration, Madam Speaker, we have an opportunity in the upcoming Congress to wield our considerable influence and leverage to promote and enact reforms by reassessing how we contribute taxpayer dollars to the corrupt U.N. system.

The U.S. must stop legitimizing this farce at the United Nations. It is time for us to take action and bring much-needed reforms.

□ 1915

PLEASE MEET DAISY ARVIZU

(Mr. O'ROURKE asked and was given permission to address the House for 1 minute.)

Mr. O'ROURKE. Madam Speaker, please meet Daisy Arvizu, who was one of over 300 El Pasoans to join us at a DREAMers town hall that we held in downtown El Paso at the Community Foundation Room with the Border Network for Human Rights and Las Americas Immigration Center last week. It was an opportunity for our community to come forward, both the DREAMers in our community and those who support the DREAMers, like Daisy who was brought here at the tender age of 1 year and 8 months, who works two jobs, a day job and a night job, and is also a student at the El Paso Community College.

Because the President-elect has vowed to terminate the executive action known as DACA, that means Daisy has uncertainty, at a minimum. In the worst case scenario, she will be deported back to a country she does not know, a language she does not speak, and she and this country will lose the benefit of her potential.

Madam Speaker, we need to do the right thing. We need to keep Daisy and the 700-plus other DREAMers in this country for the benefit of our country and the potential that they can bring to the United States. I ask for your help, the help of the Members here, and the President-elect in making sure that we do the right thing for this country and for young DREAMers like Daisy.

10TH ANNIVERSARY OF THE STATE THEATRE

(Mr. THOMPSON of Pennsylvania asked and was given permission to address the House for 1 minute and to revise and extend his remarks.)

Mr. THOMPSON of Pennsylvania. Madam Speaker, on Saturday evening, I had the privilege of attending the 10th anniversary celebration of The State Theatre in State College, Centre County.

The State Theatre first opened as a movie house for Warner Bros. Pictures on October 15, 1938, showing "The Sisters," starring Errol Flynn and Bette Davis.

Closing in 2001, the theatre building was extensively refurbished and reopened in December 2006, as a state-of-the-art venue for theatre, dance, music, film, concerts, and other regional and international performances. Today, The State Theatre is a community-owned theatre dedicated to serving the Centre County region.

The theatre is a hub of local culture, featuring artists both homegrown and nationally renowned. There is something for everyone at The State Theatre—rock 'n' roll, country, indie, and blues; drama, musical theatre, comedy, and opera; movies, dance, stand-up, and children's programming.

There is rarely a day at the theatre without a show to be seen, a concert to be heard, or a laugh to be had.

Congratulations and thank you to the leadership, employees, volunteers, and supporters of The State Theatre for being a great venue for artists and audiences.

TRIBUTE TO THREE-TIME SPRINT CUP SERIES CHAMPION TONY STEWART

(Mr. HUDSON asked and was given permission to address the House for 1 minute and to revise and extend his remarks.)

Mr. HUDSON. Madam Speaker, I rise today to pay tribute to the incredible career of three-time Sprint Cup Series champion Tony Stewart on his retirement.

Tony Stewart, known to his many fans as "Smoke," started his career as a kid go-kart racing. He climbed the ladder one step at a time throughout his 20-year driving career to become the legend he is today.

Every time Tony faced an obstacle, he overcame it with unmatched tenacity. He is a reminder to all of us that champions aren't born winners; they are built through hard work, grit, and determination.

Tony is driven by that same doggedness off the track, leading Stewart-Haas Racing in my congressional district in Kannapolis, North Carolina, and helping folks in need through the Tony Stewart Foundation. His role might be changing, but I know Smoke's presence at the racetrack and his impact on the sport we love will continue.

Renee and I applaud Tony for his outstanding career, and we wish him all the best as he begins this next chapter.

Madam Speaker, on behalf of North Carolina's Eighth District and racing fans everywhere, I am proud to say congratulations to Tony—always a racer, forever a champion.

LEAVE OF ABSENCE

By unanimous consent, leave of absence was granted to:

Mr. NEWHOUSE (at the request of Mr. MCCARTHY) for today on account of flight delays due to weather.

Mr. POE of Texas (at the request of Mr. MCCARTHY) for today and the balance of the week on account of personal reasons.

Mr. DUFFY (at the request of Mr. MCCARTHY) for today on account of flight delays due to weather.

Mrs. NAPOLITANO (at the request of Ms. PELOSI) for today.

ENROLLED BILLS SIGNED

Karen L. Haas, Clerk of the House, reported and found truly enrolled bills of the House of the following titles, which were thereupon signed by the Speaker:

H.R. 5509. An act to name the Department of Veterans Affairs temporary lodging facility in Indianapolis, Indiana, as the "Dr. Otis Bowen Veteran House".

H.R. 5995. An act to strike the sunset on certain provisions relating to the authorized protest of a task or delivery order under section 4106 of title 41, United States Code.

SENATE ENROLLED BILL SIGNED

The Speaker announced his signature to an enrolled bill of the Senate of the following title:

S. 1550. An act to amend title 31, United States Code, to establish entities tasked with improving program and project management in certain Federal agencies, and for other purposes.

BILLS PRESENTED TO THE PRESIDENT

Karen L. Haas, Clerk of the House, reported that on December 2, 2016, she presented to the President of the United States, for his approval, the following bills:

H.R. 4419. To update the financial disclosure requirements for judges of the District of Columbia courts and to make other improvements to the District of Columbia courts.

H.R. 5785. To amend title 5, United States Code, to provide for an annuity supplement for certain air traffic controllers.

H.R. 6297. To reauthorize the Iran Sanctions Act of 1996.

H.R. 5111. To prohibit the use of certain clauses in form contracts that restrict the ability of a consumer to communicate regarding the goods or services offered in interstate commerce that were the subject of the contract, and for other purposes.

H.R. 3471. To amend title 38, United States Code, to make certain improvements in the provision of automobiles and adaptive equipment by the Department of Veterans Affairs.

Karen L. Haas, Clerk of the House, further reported that on December 5, 2016, she presented to the President of the United States, for his approval, the following bills:

H.R. 5509. To name the Department of Veterans Affairs temporary lodging facility in Indianapolis, Indiana, as the "Dr. Otis Bowen Veteran House".

H.R. 5995. To strike the sunset on certain provisions relating to the authorized protest of a task or delivery order under section 4106 of title 41, United States Code.

ADJOURNMENT

Mr. THOMPSON of Pennsylvania. Madam Speaker, I move that the House now adjourn.

The motion was agreed to; accordingly (at 7 o'clock and 19 minutes p.m.), under its previous order, the House adjourned until tomorrow, Tuesday, December 6, 2016, at 10 a.m. for morning-hour debate.

EXECUTIVE COMMUNICATIONS, ETC.

Under clause 2 of rule XIV, executive communications were taken from the Speaker's table and referred as follows:

7724. A letter from the Deputy Secretary, Commodity Futures Trading Commission, transmitting the Commission's final rules — Commodity Pool Operator Financial Reports (RIN: 3038-AE47) received December 1, 2016, pursuant to 5 U.S.C. 801(a)(1)(A); Public Law 104-121, Sec. 251; (110 Stat. 868); to the Committee on Agriculture.

7725. A letter from the Honors Attorney, Legal Division, Consumer Financial Protection Bureau, transmitting the Bureau's final rules — Consumer Leasing (Regulation M) [Docket No.: CFPB-2016-0036] (RIN: 3170-AA66) received December 1, 2016, pursuant to 5 U.S.C. 801(a)(1)(A); Public Law 104-121, Sec. 251; (110 Stat. 868); to the Committee on Financial Services.

7726. A letter from the Honors Attorney, Legal Division, Consumer Financial Protection Bureau, transmitting the Bureau's final rules — Truth in Lending (Regulation Z) [Docket No.: CFPB-2016-0037] (RIN: 3170-AA67) received December 1, 2016, pursuant to 5 U.S.C. 801(a)(1)(A); Public Law 104-121, Sec. 251; (110 Stat. 868); to the Committee on Financial Services.

7727. A letter from the Senior Counsel, Legal Division, Consumer Financial Protection Bureau, transmitting the Bureau's Major final rule — Prepaid Accounts Under the Electronic Fund Transfer Act (Regulation E) and the Truth in Lending Act (Regulation Z) [Docket No.: CFPB-2014-0031] (RIN: 3170-AA22) received November 30, 2016, pursuant to 5 U.S.C. 801(a)(1)(A); Public Law 104-121, Sec. 251; (110 Stat. 868); to the Committee on Financial Services.

7728. A letter from the Director, Office of Legislative and Intergovernmental Affairs, Securities and Exchange Commission, transmitting a Report on Modernization and Simplification of Regulation S-K, pursuant to 15 U.S.C. 77s note; Public Law 114-94, Sec. 72003(c); (129 Stat. 1785); to the Committee on Financial Services.

7729. A letter from the Associate General Counsel for Legislation and Regulations, Office of the Public and Indian Housing, Department of Housing and Urban Development, transmitting the Department's final rule — Native American Housing Assistance and Self-Determination Act; Revisions to the Indian Housing Block Grant Program Formula [Docket No.: FR-5650-F-14] (RIN: 2577-AC90) received December 1, 2016, pursuant to 5 U.S.C. 801(a)(1)(A); Public Law 104-121, Sec. 251; (110 Stat. 868); to the Committee on Financial Services.

7730. A letter from the Director, Regulatory Management Division, Environmental Protection Agency, transmitting the Agency's Major final rule — Renewable Fuel Standard Program: Standards for 2017 and Biomass-Based Diesel Volume for 2018 [EPA-HQ-OAR-2016-0004; FRL-9955-84-OAR] (RIN: 2060-AS72) received December 1, 2016, pursuant to 5 U.S.C. 801(a)(1)(A); Public Law 104-121; Sec. 251; (110 Stat. 868); to the Committee on Energy and Commerce.

7731. A letter from the Director, Regulatory Management Division, Environmental Protection Agency, transmitting the Agency's final rule — Air Plan Approval; Kentucky; Revisions to Louisville Definitions and Ambient Air Quality Standards [EPA-R04-OAR-2015-0521;FRL-9955-90-Region 4] received December 1, 2016, pursuant to 5 U.S.C. 801(a)(1)(A); Public Law 104-121, Sec. 251; (110 Stat. 868); to the Committee on Energy and Commerce.

7732. A letter from the Director, Regulatory Management Division, Environmental Protection Agency, transmitting the Agency's final rule — Air Quality Plans; Kentucky; Infrastructure Requirements for the 2010 Sulfur Dioxide National Ambient Air Quality Standard [EPA-R04-OAR-2014-0426; FRL-9955-96-Region 4] received December 1, 2016, pursuant to 5 U.S.C. 801(a)(1)(A); Public Law 104-121, Sec. 251; (110 Stat. 868); to the Committee on Energy and Commerce.

7733. A letter from the Director, Regulatory Management Division, Environmental Protection Agency, transmitting the Agency's final rule — Bicyclopyrone; Pesticide Tolerances [EPA-HQ-OPP-2015-0560; FRL-9954-63] received December 1, 2016, pursuant to 5 U.S.C. 801(a)(1)(A); Public Law 104-121, Sec. 251; (110 Stat. 868); to the Committee on Energy and Commerce.

7734. A letter from the Director, Regulatory Management Division, Environmental Protection Agency, transmitting the Agency's final rule — Determination of Attainment by the Attainment Date for the 2008 Ozone National Ambient Air Quality Standards; Pennsylvania; Pittsburgh-Beaver Valley [EPA-R03-OAR-2016-0368; FRL-9955-91-Region 3] received December 1, 2016, pursuant to 5 U.S.C. 801(a)(1)(A); Public Law 104-121, Sec. 251; (110 Stat. 868); to the Committee on Energy and Commerce.

7735. A letter from the Director, Regulatory Management Division, Environmental Protection Agency, transmitting the Agency's final rule — Muscodor albus strain SA-13 and the volatiles produced on rehydration; Exemption from the Requirement of a Tolerance [EPA-HQ-OPP-2014-0919; FRL-9952-88] received December 1, 2016, pursuant to 5 U.S.C. 801(a)(1)(A); Public Law 104-121, Sec. 251; (110 Stat. 868); to the Committee on Energy and Commerce.

7736. A letter from the Director, Regulatory Management Division, Environmental Protection Agency, transmitting the Agency's final rule — Oxathiapiprolin; Pesticide Tolerances [EPA-HQ-OPP-2016-0049; FRL-9954-69] received December 1, 2016, pursuant to 5 U.S.C. 801(a)(1)(A); Public Law 104-121, Sec. 251; (110 Stat. 868); to the Committee on Energy and Commerce.

7737. A letter from the Director, Regulatory Management Division, Environmental Protection Agency, transmitting the Agency's final rule — Quizalofop ethyl; Pesticide Tolerances [EPA-HQ-OPP-2015-0412; FRL-9950-89] received December 1, 2016, pursuant to 5 U.S.C. 801(a)(1)(A); Public Law 104-121, Sec. 251; (110 Stat. 868); to the Committee on Energy and Commerce.

7738. A letter from the Director, Regulatory Management Division, Environmental Protection Agency, transmitting the Agency's final rule — Tau-Fluvalinate; Pesticide Tolerance [EPA-HQ-OPP-2015-0439; FRL-9954-33] received December 1, 2016, pursuant to 5 U.S.C. 801(a)(1)(A); Public Law 104-121, Sec. 251; (110 Stat. 868); to the Committee on Energy and Commerce.

7739. A letter from the Deputy Bureau Chief, Wireline Competition Bureau, Federal Communications Commission, transmitting the Commission's final rule — Connect America Fund [WC Docket No.: 10-90] received December 1, 2016, pursuant to 5 U.S.C. 801(a)(1)(A); Public Law 104-121, Sec. 251; (110 Stat. 868); to the Committee on Energy and Commerce.

7740. A letter from the Deputy Chief, Wireline Competition Bureau, Federal Communications Commission, transmitting the Commission's final rule — Protecting the Privacy of Customers of Broadband and Other Telecommunications Services [WC Docket No.: 16-106] received December 1, 2016, pursuant to 5 U.S.C. 801(a)(1)(A); Public Law 104-121, Sec. 251; (110 Stat. 868); to the Committee on Energy and Commerce.

7741. A letter from the Director, Defense Security Cooperation Agency, Department of Defense, transmitting a notice of Proposed Lease Pursuant to Section 62(a) of the Arms Export Control Act, Transmittal No. 08-16; to the Committee on Foreign Affairs.

7742. A letter from the Assistant Secretary, Legislative Affairs, Department of State, transmitting a report titled "Designations of Countries of Particular Concern, Imposition of Presidential Actions, and Exercise of Waiver Authority Under the International Religious Freedom Act of 1998"; to the Committee on Foreign Affairs.

7743. A letter from the Director, International Cooperation, Office of Acquisition, Technology, and Logistics, Department of Defense, transmitting a letter informing Congress of the Department's intent to sign a Memorandum of Understanding Between the Department of Defense of the United States of America and the Federal Ministry of Defence of the Federal Republic of Germany, Transmittal No. 30-16, pursuant to Sec. 27(f) of the Arms Export Control Act and Executive Order 13637; to the Committee on Foreign Affairs.

7744. A letter from the Senior Procurement Executive, Office of Acquisition Policy, General Services Administration, transmitting the Administration's small entity compliance guide — Federal Acquisition Regulation; Federal Acquisition Circular 2005-92 [Docket No.: FAR 2016-0051, Sequence No.: 6] received November 21, 2016, pursuant to 5 U.S.C. 801(a)(1)(A); Public Law 104-121, Sec. 251; (110 Stat. 868); to the Committee on Oversight and Government Reform.

7745. A letter from the Acting Director, Office of Sustainable Fisheries, NMFS, National Oceanic and Atmospheric Administration, transmitting the Administration's temporary rule — Fisheries of the Exclusive Economic Zone Off Alaska; Groundfish Fishery by Vessels Using Trawl Gear in the Gulf of Alaska [Docket No.: 150818742-6210-02] (RIN: 0648-XE990) received December 1, 2016, pursuant to 5 U.S.C. 801(a)(1)(A); Public Law 104-121, Sec. 251; (110 Stat. 868); to the Committee on Natural Resources.

7746. A letter from the Acting Director, Office of Sustainable Fisheries, NMFS, National Oceanic and Atmospheric Administration, transmitting the Administration's temporary rule — Fisheries of the Exclusive Economic Zone Off Alaska; Pacific Ocean Perch in the Bering Sea Subarea of the Bering Sea and Aleutian Islands Management Area [Docket No.: 150916863-6211-02] (RIN: 0648-XE950) received December 1, 2016, pursuant to 5 U.S.C. 801(a)(1)(A); Public Law 104-121, Sec. 251; (110 Stat. 868); to the Committee on Natural Resources.

7747. A letter from the Deputy Assistant Administrator For Regulatory Programs, NMFS, National Oceanic and Atmospheric Administration, transmitting the Administration's final rule — Fisheries of the Exclusive Economic Zone Off Alaska; Chinook Salmon Bycatch Management in the Gulf of Alaska Trawl Fisheries; Amendment 103 [160229157-6781-02] (RIN: 0648-BF84) received December 1, 2016, pursuant to 5 U.S.C. 801(a)(1)(A); Public Law 104-121, Sec. 251; (110 Stat. 868); to the Committee on Natural Resources.

7748. A letter from the Deputy Assistant Administrator for Regulatory Programs, NMFS, National Oceanic and Atmospheric Administration, transmitting the Administration's proposed rule — Fisheries of the Exclusive Economic Zone Off Alaska; Modifications to Recordkeeping and Reporting Requirements [Docket No.: 160225147-6147-01] (RIN: 0648-BF83) received December 1, 2016, pursuant to 5 U.S.C. 801(a)(1)(A); Public Law 104-121, Sec. 251; (110 Stat. 868); to the Committee on Natural Resources.

7749. A letter from the Deputy Assistant Administrator For Regulatory Programs, NMFS, National Oceanic and Atmospheric Administration, transmitting the Administration's final rule — Fisheries of the Caribbean, Gulf of Mexico, and South Atlantic;

Reef Fish Fishery of the Gulf of Mexico; Red Grouper Management Measures [Docket No.: 160613514-6908-02] (RIN: 0648-BG12) received December 1, 2016, pursuant to 5 U.S.C. 801(a)(1)(A); Public Law 104-121, Sec. 251; (110 Stat. 868); to the Committee on Natural Resources.

7750. A letter from the Acting Director, Office of Sustainable Fisheries, NMFS, National Oceanic and Atmospheric Administration, transmitting the Administration's temporary rule — Fisheries of the Exclusive Economic Zone Off Alaska; Reallocation of Pacific Cod in the Bering Sea and Aleutian Islands Management Area [Docket No.: 150916863-6211-02] (RIN: 0648-XF012) received December 1, 2016, pursuant to 5 U.S.C. 801(a)(1)(A); Public Law 104-121, Sec. 251; (110 Stat. 868); to the Committee on Natural Resources.

7751. A letter from the Acting Director, Office of Sustainable Fisheries, NMFS, National Oceanic and Atmospheric Administration, transmitting the Administration's temporary rule — Fisheries of the Exclusive Economic Zone Off Alaska; Exchange of Flatfish in the Bering Sea and Aleutian Islands Management Area [Docket No.: 150916863-6211-02] (RIN: 0648-XF010) received December 1, 2016, pursuant to 5 U.S.C. 801(a)(1)(A); Public Law 104-121, Sec. 251; (110 Stat. 868); to the Committee on Natural Resources.

7752. A letter from the Deputy Assistant Administrator For Regulatory Programs, NMFS, Office of Sustainable Fisheries, National Oceanic and Atmospheric Administration, transmitting the Administration's final rule — Fisheries Off West Coast States; Coastal Pelagic Species Fisheries; Multi-Year Specifications for Monitored and Prohibited Harvest Species Stock Categories [Docket No.: 130808697-6907-02] (RIN: 0648-XC808) received December 1, 2016, pursuant to 5 U.S.C. 801(a)(1)(A); Public Law 104-121, Sec. 251; (110 Stat. 868); to the Committee on Natural Resources.

7753. A letter from the Assistant Secretary for Legislation, Office of the Secretary, Department of Health and Human Services, transmitting the Fiscal Year 2012 Report to Congress on Administration of the Tribal Self-Governance Program, pursuant to Sec. 458aaa-13(a), 25 U.S.C. 450 et seq., as amended; to the Committee on Natural Resources.

7754. A letter from the Assistant Secretary for Legislation, Office of the Secretary, Department of Health and Human Services, transmitting the Fiscal Year 2013 Report to Congress on Administration of the Tribal Self-Governance Program, pursuant to Sec. 458aaa-13(a), 25 U.S.C. 450 et seq., as amended; to the Committee on Natural Resources.

REPORTS OF COMMITTEES ON PUBLIC BILLS AND RESOLUTIONS

Under clause 2 of rule XIII, reports of committees were delivered to the Clerk for printing and reference to the proper calendar, as follows:

Mr. BISHOP of Utah: Committee on Natural Resources. H.R. 3711. A bill to authorize the Secretary of the Interior to conduct a special resource study of Chicano Park, located in San Diego, California, and for other purposes; with an amendment (Rept. 114–845). Referred to the Committee of the Whole House on the state of the Union.

PUBLIC BILLS AND RESOLUTIONS

Under clause 2 of rule XII, public bills and resolutions of the following

titles were introduced and severally referred, as follows:

By Mr. PALLONE (for himself, Mr. PASCRELL, and Mr. PAYNE):
H.R. 6434. A bill to provide for more transparent and appropriate reimbursement of insurers participating in the Write Your Own program under the National Flood Insurance Program, and for other purposes; to the Committee on Financial Services.

By Mr. MULLIN:
H.R. 6435. A bill to authorize the Directors of Veterans Integrated Service Networks of the Department of Veterans Affairs to enter into contracts with appropriate civilian accreditation entities or appropriate health care evaluation entities to investigate medical centers of the Department of Veterans Affairs; to the Committee on Veterans' Affairs.

By Mr. HECK of Washington (for himself, Mr. SHERMAN, and Ms. KUSTER):
H.R. 6436. A bill to require that any international insurance standards agreed to by parties representing the United States reflect existing United States laws, regulations, and policies on regulation of insurance, and for other purposes; to the Committee on Financial Services.

By Mr. HIMES:
H.R. 6437. A bill to prohibit funds available for the United States Armed Forces to be obligated or expended for introduction of the Armed Forces into hostilities, and for other purposes; to the Committee on Foreign Affairs, and in addition to the Committees on Rules, and Armed Services, for a period to be subsequently determined by the Speaker, in each case for consideration of such provisions as fall within the jurisdiction of the committee concerned.

By Mr. SAM JOHNSON of Texas (for himself and Mr. LARSON of Connecticut):
H.R. 6438. A bill to extend the waiver of limitations with respect to excluding from gross income amounts received by wrongfully incarcerated individuals; to the Committee on Ways and Means.

By Mr. THORNBERRY:
H. Con. Res. 179. Concurrent resolution directing the Secretary of the Senate to make certain corrections in the enrollment of S. 2943; considered and agreed to.

By Mr. CÁRDENAS (for himself and Ms. LOFGREN):
H. Res. 941. A resolution expressing support for the designation of February 22, 2017, as "National Heart Valve Disease Awareness Day", coinciding with American Heart Month; to the Committee on Energy and Commerce.

By Mr. SESSIONS (for himself, Mr. CARTER of Georgia, Mr. GOHMERT, Mr. BYRNE, Mr. STIVERS, Mr. BRAT, Mr. AUSTIN SCOTT of Georgia, Mr. COLLINS of Georgia, Mr. BROOKS of Alabama, Mr. FARENTHOLD, Mr. ROE of Tennessee, Mr. LABRADOR, Mr. DESANTIS, and Mr. MEADOWS):
H. Res. 942. A resolution recognizing the historical importance of Associate Justice Clarence Thomas; to the Committee on the Judiciary, and in addition to the Committee on House Administration, for a period to be subsequently determined by the Speaker, in each case for consideration of such provisions as fall within the jurisdiction of the committee concerned.

By Ms. GABBARD:
H. Res. 943. A resolution recognizing the 100th anniversary of the establishment of Hawaii Volcanoes National Park and Haleakala National Park in the State of Ha-

waii, and expressing support for designation of August 1, 2016, as "Hawaii Volcanoes and Haleakala National Parks Day"; to the Committee on Natural Resources.

MEMORIALS

Under clause 3 of rule XII,

310. The SPEAKER presented a memorial of the General Assembly of the State of Indiana, relative to Senate Enrolled Joint Resolution 14, requesting the Congress of the United States call a convention of the states to propose amendments to the Constitution of the United States; which was referred to the Committee on the Judiciary.

CONSTITUTIONAL AUTHORITY STATEMENT

Pursuant to clause 7 of rule XII of the Rules of the House of Representatives, the following statements are submitted regarding the specific powers granted to Congress in the Constitution to enact the accompanying bill or joint resolution.

By Mr. PALLONE:
H.R. 6434.
Congress has the power to enact this legislation pursuant to the following:
Clause 7 of Section 9 of Article I of the Constitution
By Mr. MULLIN:
H.R. 6435.
Congress has the power to enact this legislation pursuant to the following:
Article I, Section 8, Clause 18 of the U.S. Constitution
By Mr. HECK of Washington:
H.R. 6436.
Congress has the power to enact this legislation pursuant to the following:
Article I, Section 8, Clause 3 of the Constitution of the United States
By Mr. HIMES:
H.R. 6437.
Congress has the power to enact this legislation pursuant to the following:
Article I, Section 8 of the United States Constitution, clauses 11, 12, 13, 14, 18
By Mr. SAM JOHNSON of Texas:
H.R. 6438.
Congress has the power to enact this legislation pursuant to the following:
Article I, Section 8, Clause 1 of the Constitution of the United States of America.

ADDITIONAL SPONSORS

Under clause 7 of rule XII, sponsors were added to public bills and resolutions, as follows:

H.R. 1098: Mr. CONYERS.
H.R. 1457: Mr. KNIGHT.
H.R. 1608: Mr. LUETKEMEYER and Mr. BEYER.
H.R. 2293: Mr. WALZ.
H.R. 2537: Mr. REED.
H.R. 3591: Ms. LEE, Mr. SWALWELL of California, Mr. COURTNEY, Ms. NORTON, Mr. DESAULNIER, Ms. KUSTER, Mr. GARAMENDI, Mr. ASHFORD, and Mr. MCGOVERN.
H.R. 4216: Mr. HIGGINS and Mr. CLAY.
H.R. 4220: Mr. POLIS.
H.R. 5131: Ms. BROWNLEY of California.
H.R. 5235: Mr. KNIGHT and Mr. COOK.
H.R. 5274: Mr. REED.
H.R. 5386: Ms. LOFGREN and Mr. GALLEGO.
H.R. 5440: Mr. KIND.

H.R. 5689: Ms. LOFGREN.

H.R. 5721: Mr. TONKO.

H.R. 6020: Ms. PLASKETT.

H.R. 6021: Ms. PLASKETT.

H.R. 6072: Mr. DEFAZIO.

H.R. 6117: Ms. ROYBAL-ALLARD.

H.R. 6275: Mrs. BEATTY.

H.R. 6340: Ms. MICHELLE LUJAN GRISHAM of New Mexico, Mr. CONNOLLY, Mr. TAKANO, and Mr. SARBANES.

H.R. 6382: Mr. McGOVERN, Mr. BERA, Mr. HUFFMAN, Mr. SCOTT of Virginia, Ms. SCHAKOWSKY, and Mr. KILMER.

H.R. 6421: Mr. SHERMAN and Ms. MENG.

H.R. 6426: Mr. SMITH of Nebraska and Mr. MASSIE.

H.R. 6428: Mr. ELLISON, Ms. LOFGREN, Mr. LOEBSACK, and Mr. DEFAZIO.

H.R. 6431: Ms. SLAUGHTER, Mr. HIGGINS, Mr. CRAMER, Mr. NOLAN, Mr. COLLINS of New York, Mr. KIND, Mr. WELCH, Mr. HUIZENGA of Michigan, Mr. ZINKE, Mr. RYAN of Ohio, Mr. GUINTA, Mr. DEFAZIO, Ms. DELBENE, Mr. MURPHY of Pennsylvania, Mr. MICHAEL F. DOYLE of Pennsylvania, Mr. HECK of Washington, and Ms. LOFGREN.

H.R. 6433: Mr. DOLD.

H. Con. Res. 159: Mr. PETERS.

H. Con. Res. 176: Mr. VAN HOLLEN.

H. Res. 591: Mr. YARMUTH.

H. Res. 899: Ms. LOFGREN, Mr. POLIQUIN, and Mr. ROE of Tennessee.

H. Res. 928: Mr. SWALWELL of California, Mr. KING of New York, and Ms. FRANKEL of Florida.

PETITIONS, ETC.

Under clause 3 of rule XII,

95. The SPEAKER presented a petition of the City of Miami Commission, relative to Resolution R-16-0525, urging President Barack H. Obama and the Members of the 114th United States Congress to grant temporary protective status to Haitians in the United States; which was referred to the Committee on the Judiciary.

EXTENSIONS OF REMARKS

PEARLIE EVANS DID MAKE A DIFFERENCE

HON. WM. LACY CLAY
OF MISSOURI
IN THE HOUSE OF REPRESENTATIVES

Monday, December 5, 2016

Mr. CLAY. Mr. Speaker, I delivered the following remarks on behalf of my father, former Congressman William (Bill) Clay, at the funeral of Pearlie Evans on Saturday, November 26, 2016, in St. Louis, Missouri.

My friendship with Pearlie spans more than 50 years. During that time we worked together, laughed together, cried together, and raised a lot of hell together.

I first met Pearlie Evans in the early 1960s when a close political associate, Arthur Kennedy, introduced us. He and I had just helped A.J. Cervantes get elected. The new mayor asked me to recommend someone to fill the position of Commissioner of Social Services.

I invited Pearlie to lunch and offered her the position. She was honored but turned down the offer—telling me of her deep devotion in helping residents at the Fellowship Center and Plymouth House. Without any success, I mentioned that her salary would have been twice that at Fellowship Center and help many more people like those at the Plymouth House. Then, I took her to lunch twice and once to dinner before she agreed.

Finally, a well-fed Pearlie Evans accepted the offer and performed exceptionally well in the position.

Her background in social work, dealing with grassroots, ghetto residents, allowed her to develop a realistic grasp of the problems faced by low-income, unemployed, poverty stricken individuals. She provided the compassion and know-how in closing the gap that kept many of them from resolving their woes.

Having disdain and contempt for all kinds of discrimination and segregation, her agenda was about identifying injustice and reshaping our society until it adjusted to accommodate the needs of its underprivileged.

When my first District Director left, I asked Pearlie to run my congressional district office. But this time I knew better than to invite her to lunch or dinner. She accepted and made an ideal District Director for the next 28 years.

Perhaps, more than anyone else other than my wife Carol, Pearlie was able to successfully put up with me and all my audaciousness, my insolence, my sarcasm and my bluster. Her simple response of "ohhhhhhh, Congressman" more often than not was the perfect tonic to calm a rough or chaotic situation. She was by my side through good times and bad. Her advice and counsel was usually sound.

Pearlie was also a pioneer in politics who developed a new strategy for advancing the cause of civil rights and enhancing opportunities. She ushered in the concept that it was time to stop begging for what was ours by citizenship and to start demanding rights that were ours by birth. She played a key role in our developing the political appa-

ratus capable of delivering lopsided margins in electing candidates. She had the unique ability to attract and surround us with people of wisdom, vision, integrity and commitment to racial equality.

She joined a cadre of other outstanding women like Gwen Giles, Ruth Porter, Deverne Calloway, Marian Oldham and many others that enabled our group to convince many to overcome their political apathy and to reject disgraceful absentee elected officials pretending to represent our interests.

I owe a great deal of my political success to committed and dedicated women like Pearlie. In my elections to Congress, women managed all of my campaigns: Doris Moore, Gwen Giles, Gwen Reed and Pearlie Evans each served as campaign managers in all 16 of them.

Pearlie, Virginia Cook, and Gwen Reed also played a key role in electing my son Lacy Clay to Congress.

Pearlie journeyed through a career that forced the political system to change the face of our politics and to provide us with people who truly voiced our legitimate concerns.

She was always on the picket lines, at the sit-ins, in the marches for school equality, wherever the protests against injustice were being waged. She was there to give active support in campaigns that changed the landscape of bigoted policies and replaced them with opportunities for minorities in St. Louis.

Very few lived their life with the enthusiasm, the commitment, the determination, the gusto of Pearlie. She lived every day with the intent of giving back to the community and enhancing the lives of those denied the benefits of humane treatment. In touching their lives, it was a testament to her endearing respect for each individual's humanity.

Carol and I join with you in acknowledging that she was an uncommon lady with a phenomenal effect on those of us who were graced by her presence. She was something special, something beautiful, something precious.

Although Pearlie would tell us not to shed tears for her but rather for a world that is suffering the ravages of war, disease, hunger and racism—still, without ignoring her request not to shed tears for her passing, we are obligated to shed tears for future generations that will never experience the sight of her doing battle with the giants of society who have profited from exploiting those unable to fight back. We mourn for those who will never bear witness to her unyielding fight against bureaucratic bigots in fighting for racial justice.

Yes, Pearlie, when remembering you, what you stood for, how much of your mission is yet unfulfilled, our tears are justified. We cry today because we will have no more tomorrows with you. But we thank God for all the yesterdays we spent with you.

We remember all of the good you have done, all of the people you have helped, all of the causes you have championed. We take comfort in the fact that our community, our state and our nation are better as a result of your having been here.

We have witnessed in you a towering, incredible, noble, dedicated defender of what's right—so we say in all sincerity—so long, our courageous sister in the struggle for equal justice—so long!

HONORING RICHARD COOPER

HON. JARED HUFFMAN
OF CALIFORNIA
IN THE HOUSE OF REPRESENTATIVES

Monday, December 5, 2016

Mr. HUFFMAN. Mr. Speaker, I rise today in recognition of Richard Cooper, Chief Executive Officer of Mendo Lake Credit Union, who is retiring after forty years of service to credit union members.

Richard Cooper was born in Bend, Oregon, and raised in Alaska where he began his long career at Credit Union One in Anchorage. He continued his work in southern California until 2008 when he moved to Mendocino County and became the President and Chief Executive Officer at Mendo Lake Credit Union.

Under Mr. Cooper's leadership, Mendo Lake Credit Union has thrived as a business and flourished as an award-winning community partner. Renowned for his civic service, Mr. Cooper was recognized as the Credit Union Times "Rock Star of the Year" in 2016. During his tenure at Mendo Lake Credit Union, it was recognized with "Desjardins Youth Financial Education Award" from the Credit Union National Association in 2014; a "Trailblazer Award for Serving the Underserved" by the Credit Union Times in 2015; and as a "California Small Business Volunteer Program of the Year" by the Governor's Office in 2012.

In addition to his many contributions to these credit unions, Mr. Cooper has dedicated countless hours as an active board member of the Economic Development and Finance Corporation of Mendocino County, the Mendocino Coast Botanical Gardens, the Mendocino College Foundation, the Ukiah Senior Center Endowment Fund, and the Ukiah Valley Medical Center Community Advisory Council.

Richard Cooper's career is one of dedicated service and the highest level of civic engagement. Please join me in congratulating him on his retirement and expressing our deep appreciation for his outstanding contributions to the residents of Mendocino County.

CELEBRATING THE RETIREMENT OF MR. STEPHEN MANSTER

HON. ROBERT J. WITTMAN
OF VIRGINIA
IN THE HOUSE OF REPRESENTATIVES

Monday, December 5, 2016

Mr. WITTMAN. Mr. Speaker, I rise today to recognize Bowling Green Town Manager Stephen Manster on the occasion of his retirement from public service. Throughout his forty-

---

● This "bullet" symbol identifies statements or insertions which are not spoken by a Member of the Senate on the floor.

Matter set in this typeface indicates words inserted or appended, rather than spoken, by a Member of the House on the floor.

year career, he worked in both local and regional levels of government.

Mr. Manster was hired by the Town Council as Town Manager on January 3, 2006. Before coming to Bowling Green, he served for nineteen years as the Executive Director of the Rappahannock Area Development Commission (RADCO). During this time he was able to work with the Town and Caroline County extensively, leading to a seamless transition into the Town Manager position.

Stephen holds a Bachelor of Arts Degree in Sociology from Pennsylvania State University and a Degree of Master of City and Regional Planning from Rutgers University. He has also completed extensive graduate work in the Master of Public Administration program at Virginia Commonwealth University.

Mr. Manster's commitment to public service demonstrates a rare sense of dedication to duty, and I am pleased to recognize this special occasion. Mr. Speaker, I ask you to join me in celebrating the career of Mr. Stephen Manster.

IN RECOGNITION OF CAMERON D. CLARKE, 2017 RHODES SCHOLAR

HON. ROBERT C. "BOBBY" SCOTT

OF VIRGINIA

IN THE HOUSE OF REPRESENTATIVES

Monday, December 5, 2016

Mr. SCOTT of Virginia. Mr. Speaker, I rise today with great pride to recognize Cameron D. Clarke, a Howard University senior majoring in biology and community health, who was awarded a prestigious Rhodes Scholarship for 2017. Mr. Clarke lives in Richmond, Virginia and is the fourth student from Howard University to have received this honor.

While attending Howard University, Mr. Clarke engaged in research at the University's W. Montague Cobb Research Laboratory, which maintains a national repository for African-American skeletal remains. Mr. Clarke also participated in research at Bahir Dar University in Ethiopia through a Howard University-National Science Foundation grant. As an Amgen Scholar, he conducted research at the National Institutes of Health's Center for Cancer Research. Mr. Clarke is a certified emergency medical technician (EMT) and is the lead author on five out of six publications. He is co-president of Howard University's chapter of the Peer Health Exchange and a news editor of The Hilltop, the Howard University student newspaper. Currently, Mr. Clarke is among our own here on Capitol Hill as he is an intern for the U.S. House Committee on Science, Space, and Technology.

Mr. Clarke is one of 32 men and women selected from U.S. postsecondary institutions who competed with over 800 applicants to receive this award to study at the University of Oxford in England. With his Rhodes scholarship, Mr. Clarke intends to further his studies by pursuing a Master of Science degree with an emphasis in primary health care. Ultimately, Mr. Clarke wants to attend medical school and work in public health policy and clinical research.

"We are extremely proud of Mr. Clarke's accomplishments," said Dr. Wayne Frederick, President of Howard University. "Mr. Clarke's academic pursuits will lead to solutions in the broader society that are needed ever more so today. Cameron is the epitome of Howard University's gift of solutions to the world." His achievements demonstrate what a person committed to excellence in truth and service can obtain when provided the opportunity. He exemplifies the best of Howard University and the Commonwealth of Virginia.

I ask my colleagues in the U.S. House of Representatives to join me in congratulating Mr. Cameron D. Clarke for his impressive academic achievements and being selected as one of America's Rhodes Scholarship winners. It is with honor that I call attention to this outstanding young man's achievements. May he continue to obtain the success for which he works hard and may he always find purpose and fulfillment in his efforts.

HONORING ESTHER LOUISE HILL ON THE OCCASION OF HER 100TH BIRTHDAY

HON. BLAINE LUETKEMEYER

OF MISSOURI

IN THE HOUSE OF REPRESENTATIVES

Monday, December 5, 2016

Mr. LUETKEMEYER. Mr. Speaker, I rise today to honor Esther Louise Hill. She celebrated her 100th birthday on Sunday, December 4th, 2016.

Esther Louise Hill was born in Montgomery City, Missouri on December 4, 1916 to Roy and Emma Patterson. She has lived in Jonesburg, Missouri most of her life. Esther married Richard Hill, who is now deceased. She graduated from a three-year program in 1938 from Missouri Baptist Hospital School of Nursing as a registered nurse.

Her work experiences were in various divisions of healthcare: hospitals, industry, and public health. Esther started her career as a private duty nurse and after a year decided to join the Barnes Hospital Nursing Staff. Before World War II started, Esther moved to Dallas, Texas. She utilized her nursing degree by working at a substation with North American Aviation during the war. After the end of the war, Esther moved back to Missouri and joined the staff at a local nursing home, Katy Jane, located in Warrenton, Missouri. Unfortunately, during her time at Katy Jane, there was a devastating fire which had a profound effect on Esther. Esther started working as a public health nurse through the state of Missouri, first in Warren County and then moving to Montgomery County. She was moved by the loss of life at Katy Jane and realized commonsense steps could have prevented that tragedy.

Eventually, Esther obtained the position of Institutional Advisory Nurse, covering fifteen counties along the Missouri River. In this position, Esther taught nursing home caregivers the details of Missouri state law and procedures that should be part of nursing home care. The Institutional Advisory Nurse position led to a role with the Missouri Department of Health Licensure Program for Nursing Homes. With this position, she taught, investigated and inspected nursing home facilities, and en- forced licensure laws. Esther worked for the Visiting Nurse Association for a few years but eventually returned to the Missouri Department of Health. She ended her nursing career with the Missouri Department of Health. Esther appreciates the opportunity she was given to have a career that came full circle; from her days at the Katy Jane Nursing Home where lack of structure allowed for a tragedy, to being involved with the adoption of solutions to protect the most vulnerable. In addition to her successful career in nursing, Esther also taught at Tulane University in New Orleans, Louisiana. Esther has been a lifelong member of the Jonesburg United Methodist Church and during her time there has enjoyed participating in the Methodist Women organization. In her spare time, she enjoys reading, collecting antiques, cooking, and canning produce from her garden. She also has a passion for hybridized lilies and has even won prizes for them. Esther enjoys a good card game and has been a member of the Canasta Card Club for 50 years.

Please join me in recognizing Esther Louise Hill on the occasion of her 100th birthday.

IN HONOR OF BULLOCK COUNTY, ALABAMA UPON THE 150TH ANNIVERSARY OF ITS FOUNDING

HON. MARTHA ROBY

OF ALABAMA

IN THE HOUSE OF REPRESENTATIVES

Monday, December 5, 2016

Mrs. ROBY. Mr. Speaker, I rise today to honor Bullock County, Alabama which today is celebrating 150 years as a county.

What is now Bullock County was first inhabited by Creek Indians who moved westward from Georgia and began cultivating the rich, spring-filled land. After the bitter Creek War, American settlers brought schools, churches, and mercantile life to complement the thriving agriculture, and the town of Union Springs was born.

After the Civil War, portions of Macon, Montgomery, Barbour and Pike Counties were brought together to form Bullock County, after Confederate Colonel E.C. Bullock. The late 1800s and early 1900s were prosperous for Bullock County, as railroad connections and industrialization made the county seat of Union Springs an important hub for Alabama and the South.

That history can still be seen in Bullock County today. The National Register of Historic Places, lists 47 homes and businesses that have been preserved as standing monuments to the past.

One hundred and fifty years after its founding, Bullock County is home to fine, hardworking people that I am proud to represent in Congress.

Mr. Speaker, it is my privilege to acknowledge Bullock County's sesquicentennial anniversary and celebrate this special date with all those who call Bullock County home.

HONORING SUPERINTENDENT JAY SPECK

HON. MIKE THOMPSON

OF CALIFORNIA

IN THE HOUSE OF REPRESENTATIVES

Monday, December 5, 2016

Mr. THOMPSON of California. Mr. Speaker, I rise, along with Congressman JOHN GARAMENDI, today to recognize and honor Jay Speck who is retiring after forty years of service to our community as an educator and administrator with the Solano County Office of Education.

Mr. Speck began his career in education as a special education teacher at the elementary and secondary levels and has since worked with Solano County as a program manager, principal, director of special education, and assistant superintendent of human resources. Mr. Speck has served as an outstanding educator and leader in our community and demonstrates a unique and experienced understanding of our community's needs. He was sworn in for his first term as County Superintendent on January 3, 2011 and was re-elected and sworn in for his second term on January 5, 2015. Mr. Speck is known for his fair-mindedness and his strong belief in the potential of each individual student to learn and develop academically.

During his career, Mr. Speck pursued training in interest-based problem solving and collective bargaining to enhance his skills as a trusted leader, highly skilled problem-solver, and ardent collaborator. Mr. Speck has a solid educational foundation with a Bachelor of Arts degree from the University of California, Davis and holds teaching credentials from both California State University, Los Angeles and California State University, Sacramento. Mr. Speck has represented Solano County public schools as a member of many organizations including the California County Superintendents Educational Services Association, the Association of California School Administrators and the Workforce Investment Board.

Mr. Speaker, Superintendent Jay Speck has served our community with admirable leadership and dedication for forty years. It is fitting and proper that we honor him here today and extend our best wishes for an enjoyable retirement.

HONORING JIM HARRIS OF WAUSAU, WI FOR HIS SERVICE TO OTHERS

HON. SEAN P. DUFFY

OF WISCONSIN

IN THE HOUSE OF REPRESENTATIVES

Monday, December 5, 2016

Mr. DUFFY. Mr. Speaker, I am honored to stand before you today to recognize Mr. Jim Harris of Wausau, Wisconsin for his exceptional service to others.

Mr. Harris worked for more than 30 years in education. First, as a teacher in the Wisconsin Indian Teacher Corps, where he taught children of the Ho Chunk Tribe, and later as one of the first male kindergarten teachers in Wisconsin. Along his journey in education, Mr. Harris also spent two decades as a school administrator and an activist for public health.

During his many years of service in education, Mr. Harris got to know the children of Hmong Refugees who fled war in their home country to seek a better life in Wisconsin. Our state has a vibrant Hmong community that Mr. Harris has grown close to. He founded We Help War Victims, a nonprofit organization, with his wife, Marty, also a public school educator. Founded over 30 years ago, We Help War Victims has been working with refugee families in the Wausau, Wisconsin area, providing dozens of Lao schools with their first libraries, and helping families receive access to medical care.

Since 2006, his organization has been working with villagers in Laos to destroy land mines, bombs, rockets, mortars, and other unexploded ordnance. Mr. Harris' example directly inspired me to fight for this cause in Congress and his advice has directly affected the focus of my efforts. Countless farmers and families across Laos live in safer communities because of Mr. Harris' work and my community in Wisconsin has been strengthened by the work he and his wife do through We Help War Victims.

Mr. Speaker, please join me today to congratulate Mr. Harris on his accomplishments and work on behalf of others. His selfless demeanor in which he answers the call to serve in our district is truly valued.

IN HONOR OF SERGEANT 1ST CLASS JOHN MIMS

HON. RICHARD HUDSON

OF NORTH CAROLINA

IN THE HOUSE OF REPRESENTATIVES

Monday, December 5, 2016

Mr. HUDSON. Mr. Speaker, I rise today to honor the life and legacy of Sergeant 1st Class John Mims of the 82nd Airborne Division, a World War II veteran and Bataan Death March survivor who passed away on Sunday, November 27, 2016. Sergeant Mims was a true American hero and our thoughts and prayers go out to his friends and family as they mourn the loss of this great man.

When his country needed him the most, it was John Mims who answered the call to serve our great nation. After losing his father when he was young, Mims lied about his age in order to join the Army. At the age of 15, Mims served for nearly a year before the Army discovered his true age and discharged him. However, a few short years later Mims re-enlisted in the Army and headed out to the Philippines to begin his training.

After a year in the Philippines, Mims fought alongside his brothers in arms in the Battle of Bataan which culminated in the surrender of 75,000 allied soldiers. The men were then forced to march 65 miles, without food or water, to a prisoner-of-war camp in the Tarlac Province in what became known as the Bataan Death March. One of the greatest atrocities of the entire war, the men suffered beatings, endured torture, and witnessed unimaginable horrors as he faced what can only be described as a living hell. In total more than 10,000 men died during the trek.

Following the war, Mims continued his service in the Army, returning to Japan from 1952 to 1954 as sergeant in charge of the Tokyo Quartermaster Depot. After he retired in 1963, he returned home where he worked in a rug factory and a curtain company. Living in Aberdeen, North Carolina, he became an advocate for other veterans and was a constant presence at ceremonies remembering his fallen comrades. His work in the community made certain that the memories of those lost were not forgotten, and it is that legacy which we celebrate today. While we may have lost this great man, his legacy will live on and we will never forget the sacrifices made by Sergeant Mims or any of those who fought to protect our freedoms against unimaginable dangers.

Mr. Speaker, please join me today in commemorating the life of Sergeant 1st Class John Mims for his service to God and country.

PERSONAL EXPLANATION

HON. KEITH ELLISON

OF MINNESOTA

IN THE HOUSE OF REPRESENTATIVES

Monday, December 5, 2016

Mr. ELLISON. Mr. Speaker, due to other commitments, I missed the following roll call votes; had I been present, I would have voted as follows:

Roll call no. 594. I would have voted no.
Roll call no. 595. I would have voted no.
Roll call no. 596. I would have voted no.
Roll call no. 597. I would have vote no.
Roll call no. 598. I would have voted yes.
Roll call no. 599. I would have voted no.
Roll call no. 600. I would have voted no.

HONORING MR. JOHN SUTTER

HON. BARBARA LEE

OF CALIFORNIA

IN THE HOUSE OF REPRESENTATIVES

Monday, December 5, 2016

Ms. LEE. Mr. Speaker, I rise today to celebrate the remarkable life and career of Mr. John Sutter, and to congratulate him on his retirement from the Board of Directors of the East Bay Regional Park District.

As an outdoor enthusiast and lifelong resident of Oakland, California, John's life has been dedicated to preserving and protecting the environment of California's Bay Area. Throughout his sixty years in public service, he has been involved in the conservation of over 35,000 acres of land.

John's career in public service began in 1954 when he became an Alameda County deputy district attorney. He stayed in this position until 1965, when he was appointed to the Bay Conservation and Development Commission (BCDC) by Governor Pat Brown.

John also served as a member of Oakland's City Council for over a decade from 1971–1982, twice holding the position of vice mayor.

In 1982, John was appointed by Governor Jerry Brown to serve as a judge on the Alameda County Superior Court. He remained a judge for 14 years until his election in 1996 to the East Bay Regional Park District Board of Directors.

Over John's illustrious career, he has been directly involved in a variety of community projects and organizations with special emphasis on preserving the natural environment of the Bay Area.

In the 1950s he was prominently involved in the protection of the San Pablo Reservoir and the foundation of the Martin Luther King, Jr. Regional Shoreline. In 1961, John was the leader in the campaign that preserved Oakland's Snow Park.

In addition to his elected and appointed positions, John was a founding board member of the Greenbelt Alliance; and he has served as a board member for the Alameda County Solid Waste Management Authority, Oakland Charter Revision Committee, Oakland Cultural Affairs Commission, Chabot Space and Science Center, Save the Bay, Alameda County Bar Association, California Democratic Council, Oakland Citizens Committee for Urban Renewal, and the Metropolitan YMCA.

On behalf of the residents of California's 13th Congressional District, I wish to congratulate Mr. John Sutter on a well-deserved retirement, and thank him for his many years of service to our community.

PERSONAL EXPLANATION

HON. ED PERLMUTTER
OF COLORADO

IN THE HOUSE OF REPRESENTATIVES

Monday, December 5, 2016

Mr. PERLMUTTER. Mr. Speaker, on November 30, 2016, I was incorrectly recorded as voting "Nay" on H.R. 5047, the Protecting Veterans' Educational Choice Act of 2016. I wish to reflect my intentions on roll call No. 591, as a "Yea" vote.

HONORING JOHN D. PRIDNIA

HON. CANDICE S. MILLER
OF MICHIGAN

IN THE HOUSE OF REPRESENTATIVES

Monday, December 5, 2016

Mrs. MILLER of Michigan. Mr. Speaker, I rise today to recognize John D. Pridnia, loving husband, proud father and grandfather, and pillar of our community.

In search of a better life for his family, John moved to Northeast Michigan becoming a small business owner. Over the next 10 years, he became a successful businessman, passionate about building, developing, and creating new ideas, businesses, and adventures.

After raising his three children, he looked to a life of public service. He served two terms as a State Representative and two terms as a State Senator where he served as the Chairman of the Senate Health Policy Committee. Passionate about promoting business, encouraging tourism, and promoting conservation, John was respected by his colleagues on both sides of the isle.

Upon retiring from the legislature, John married his wife of 19 years Lisa Dailey. Living in the small community of Port Austin, their family grew to include five beautiful grandchildren and three great-grandchildren.

In the close-knit community of Port Austin, John was passionate about beautifying and developing the harbor and waterfront, creating spaces the entire community could come together and enjoy, such as a thriving local farmer's market.

Mr. Speaker, we can all agree that the tradition of giving back to our communities is something that makes our nation unique, one that makes this country the greatest in the world and this was a spirit that John embodied throughout his entire career and life. More importantly, he has served as an example for future generations, instilling in them the importance of giving back to the communities and country who have given us all so much.

I ask that my colleagues join me today in honoring John for his lifelong contributions to the 10th District of the great State of Michigan, our children, and the future of this country.

IN HONOR OF SENATOR ANDREW MAYNARD UPON HIS RETIREMENT

HON. JOE COURTNEY
OF CONNECTICUT

IN THE HOUSE OF REPRESENTATIVES

Monday, December 5, 2016

Mr. COURTNEY. Mr. Speaker, I rise today to thank an outstanding public servant for his many years of service to my home state of Connecticut. For ten years, Mr. Andrew Maynard has served as State Senator for the state's 18th Senate district, which includes Griswold, Groton, Stonington, Plainfield, Preston, North Stonington, Sterling and Voluntown. His retirement at the end of his term will conclude a distinguished career of public service that began at the local level many years ago as a borough warden in the Town of Stonington. Andy has been a powerful voice for southeastern Connecticut, earning the respect of both Democratic and Republican colleagues and serving as the Deputy Majority Leader for the Senate Democrats since 2011.

Andy currently serves as chair of the Transportation Committee, and a member of the Internship and Program Review & Investigation Committees. He also served as chair of the Select Committee on Veterans' Affairs, and a member of the Environment Committee. Andy's unwavering advocacy for our region's natural resources and tourist attractions brought to life the long-delayed Thames River Heritage Park and secured millions of dollars for expansion at the Mystic Seaport, our nation's leading maritime museum. Andy understood the integral role of tourism, not only within the state, but within our region. It was this understanding that guided his leadership as he fought to secure the crucial funding need to dredge the Mystic River and spearhead the Connecticut Treasures program.

Our region will miss Andy's advocacy on the floor of the State Senate, but I am sure he will remain a strong and respected voice in his community. A true gentleman, Andy brought a thoughtful, civilized tone in his campaigns for office and his bipartisan camaraderie which characterized his style in office. I ask my colleagues to join me in thanking Andy for his tenure as an accomplished public servant, and wish him well in his future endeavors.

ALL IS BRIGHT

HON. PETE SESSIONS
OF TEXAS

IN THE HOUSE OF REPRESENTATIVES

Monday, December 5, 2016

Mr. SESSIONS. Mr. Speaker, I rise today in honor of The Armed Forces and Their Families on this Christmas and Holiday Season, with a poetic tribute by Albert Carey Caswell. Let us remember their selfless sacrifice, and give a prayer of thanks for those who are separated by death and distance this Christmas.

Silent Night
Holy Night
As a magnificent hero lays down their life all is Bright
As our Lord smiles at their light all is Calm
All is Bright
Way up in heaven where your soul took flight! Round Yon Virgin Mother and Child
While, all in her tears your Mother so remembers your smile Holy Infant so tender and mild
As once all in your Mother's arms the while
Now sleep in heavenly peace my child
As your war is over my Daughter, my Son
Silent Night
Holy Night
As your family and your loved ones so miss you this night Silent Night
But, your new battle has just begun
As an Angel in The Army of Our Lord, my Daughter my Son All is Calm
All is Bright
And we will hear you on the wind
And we will sleep in Heavenly Peace
As we awake knowing you are watching over us as where you've been Until, we meet you once again in heaven where all is bright
And your Brothers and Sisters in Arms will live a good life
For you their best friend by remembering your light Silent Night
Holy Night
All is Calm
All is Bright
All because of The Men and Women of The Armed Forces, and Their Families who fight the fight
All is Bright
Sleep in Heavenly Peace
Amen

RECOGNIZING ROB AUSTRIAN AND MONICA MOSIMANN

HON. KEN BUCK
OF COLORADO

IN THE HOUSE OF REPRESENTATIVES

Monday, December 5, 2016

Mr. BUCK. Mr. Speaker, I rise today to recognize Rob Austrian and Monica Mosimann for their hard work and dedication to the people of Colorado's Fourth District as interns in my Washington, D.C. office for the Fall of 2016.

The work of this young man and woman has been exemplary, and I know they will have bright futures. They served as tour guides, interacted with constituents, and both learned a great deal about our nation's legislative process. I was glad to be able to offer this educational opportunity, and look forward to seeing them build their careers in public service.

Rob plans to continue pursuing his degree at the end of his internship, and I have recently hired Monica as a Staff Assistant in my D.C. office. I wish them both the best as they pursue their respective career paths. Mr. Speaker, it is an honor to recognize Rob Austrian and Monica Mosimann for their service the last several months to the people of Colorado's 4th district.

HONORING CITY OF REFUGE UCC

HON. BARBARA LEE

OF CALIFORNIA

IN THE HOUSE OF REPRESENTATIVES

Monday, December 5, 2016

Ms. LEE. Mr. Speaker, I rise today to honor the City of Refuge UCC upon its 25th anniversary for its legacy of promoting community building, inclusion, and faith in the Bay Area.

First established in San Francisco, the City of Refuge was founded in 1991 by a group of primarily gay and lesbian Christians with the goal of establishing a church that did not adhere to the exclusion of people based on gender or sexual orientation. Three years later in 1994, the City of Refuge joined the United Church of Christ (UCC) and became incorporated with over 5,000 churches worldwide working to uphold the denomination's commitment to social justice.

Founder and Senior Pastor Reverend Dr. Yvette A. Flunder has been nationally recognized for her work to promote the inclusion of gay and lesbian parishioners and to minister to their specific needs. In response to the AIDS epidemic, Rev. Dr. Flunder established the Ark of Refuge, a non-profit organization that provided direct services to homeless and low-income individuals, and also created the Hazard-Ashley House and Walker House in Oakland as a means to provide housing services, education, and training for people affected by HIV/AIDS. In 2000, she created the Fellowship of Affirming Ministries, a network of more than 100 primarily African American churches around the world that work to promote "radical inclusivity", whereby the ministry is open to all without prejudice or discrimination.

In 2013 the City of Refuge UCC relocated to Oakland. Through the hard work and dedication of the ministry, staff, and congregation, community members and in particular women, immigrants, and those who identify as LGBTQ, have found a safe space for self-expression, belonging, and religious participation. Through the Church's various ministries, this community provides support for those needing help addressing substance abuse, homelessness, HIV/AIDS treatment, and environmental justice.

On behalf of California's 13th Congressional District, I would like to congratulate the City of Refuge UCC on this important milestone, and thank the community for the many valuable services that they provide to those in need. I wish the congregation continued success in upholding its commitment to social justice and expanding the radical inclusivity that has come to be the City of Refuge's hallmark.

RECOGNIZING ROMANIA'S GREAT UNION DAY

HON. MICHAEL R. TURNER

OF OHIO

IN THE HOUSE OF REPRESENTATIVES

Monday, December 5, 2016

Mr. TURNER. Mr. Speaker, as the co-Chairman of the Congressional Romania Caucus and as the former President of the North Atlantic Treaty Organization Parliamentary Assembly, I congratulate Romania on its Great Union Day. Romania is celebrating the anniversary of its unification on December 1, 1918.

Romania is a loyal U.S. and NATO ally. Romania and the United States work closely together to confront a host of global challenges, including through our joint efforts to bolster regional defense, halt nuclear proliferation, and increase energy security. With the signing of the U.S.-Romania Ballistic Missile Defense Agreement in September 2011, Romania established itself as a key strategic partner in NATO's emerging missile defense capabilities effort. The Missile Defense Interceptor site at Deveselu Air Base near the Bulgarian border, which became operational in May 2016, now provides missile defense protection to our allies in Europe and the Middle East.

Tragically, ongoing events in Ukraine are unsettling the region and testing the transatlantic alliance. As you know, Russia seeks to once again destabilize much of Eastern Europe and restore influence over territories lost following the collapse of the Soviet Union. That is why it is critically important for the United States, Romania, and other European allies to continue to work together to strengthen the transatlantic alliance and bolster regional security.

The strategic partnership between the United States and Romania has greatly advanced our common interests in promoting transatlantic and regional security and free market opportunities. Our partnership should continue to foster greater economic and cultural exchanges, trade and investment, and social contacts.

Mr. Speaker, I urge all of my colleagues to join me in celebrating Romania's Great Union Day.

PERSONAL EXPLANATION

HON. MIA B. LOVE

OF UTAH

IN THE HOUSE OF REPRESENTATIVES

Monday, December 5, 2016

Mrs. LOVE. Mr. Speaker, I submit the following remarks regarding my absence from votes which occurred on December 2, 2016. A member of my immediate family experienced a medical crisis out of state, and I traveled to support him. As a result, I missed votes for the day.

MR. ANTHONY XUEREB

HON. LEE M. ZELDIN

OF NEW YORK

IN THE HOUSE OF REPRESENTATIVES

Monday, December 5, 2016

Mr. ZELDIN. Mr. Speaker, I rise today to pay a special tribute to Mr. Anthony Xuereb.

Anthony was born in Malta, and he had always yearned to come to the United States to make a better life for himself. He came to this country in 1934 during the Great Depression and struggled mightily to survive the terrible economic and social conditions of the time. He sought employment in the Brooklyn Navy Yard and had the pleasure to work on the USS *Missouri*. As he continued working and living in the United States, Anthony applied for U.S. citizenship and became a naturalized citizen in 1943.

During World War II, he applied for military service, but unfortunately he lost most of his hearing in his left ear due to a diving accident he suffered from, and was unable to serve. Anthony still wanted to contribute to the country in whatever way possible, so he volunteered for civilian duty as an Air Raid Warden and served in this position until the end of the war. Air Raid Wardens were vital in ensuring the safety of everyone in the neighborhood and he did not take his role lightly. He returned to Malta in 1948, met the love of his life, and returned to the United States to start their new life together.

Anthony's exemplary life of service was motivated and fueled by his love of God, family, and country. He was a humble man who lived on a modest income and was very proud of his service as an Air Raid Warden. The service these dedicated civilians provided was vital in keeping civilians safe. It is important we acknowledge people like Anthony, who dedicated their services to a nation in need during a time of war. In honor and memory of Anthony Xuereb and all who served, and continue to serve, our great nation, I would like to take this opportunity to recognize his devotion to our country.

SUPPORT OF H.R. 4665, THE OUTDOOR RECREATION JOBS AND ECONOMIC IMPACT ACT

HON. SUZANNE BONAMICI

OF OREGON

IN THE HOUSE OF REPRESENTATIVES

Monday, December 5, 2016

Ms. BONAMICI. Mr. Speaker, I rise today in support of H.R. 4665, the Outdoor Recreation Jobs and Economic Impact Act, introduced by my friend from Virginia, Congressman BEYER. I am proud to be a cosponsor of this legislation to highlight the importance of the outdoor recreation economy.

In Oregon, we know how important the outdoor industry is to our economy. Northwest Oregon businesses like Keen, Columbia Sportswear, and Nike have thrived and brought thousands of jobs to our communities. Surveys conducted by the Outdoor Industry Association in 2012 show that, in my home state, the industry contributes 141,000 direct jobs, $4.0 billion in wages and salaries, and $12.8 billion in consumer spending annually. Nationwide, outdoor recreation generates $646 billion in consumer spending every year.

The climbers, hikers, hunters, and anglers who are passionate about the outdoors spend time and money in hotels, campgrounds, restaurants, and stores in nearby communities, providing an economic boost for local economies. They also purchase necessary attire, gear, and footwear from innovative businesses to help them reach the summit, catch fish, and enjoy our nation's natural treasures.

I am proud to support the Outdoor Recreation Jobs and Economic Impact Act.

PAYING TRIBUTE TO NATHANIEL JONES ON HIS RETIREMENT

HON. SUSAN W. BROOKS
OF INDIANA

IN THE HOUSE OF REPRESENTATIVES

Monday, December 5, 2016

Mrs. BROOKS of Indiana. Mr. Speaker, I rise today to honor an outstanding educator, Superintendent Nathaniel Jones of the Metropolitan School District of Pike Township. Superintendent Jones is retiring after 43 years of exceptional service to students and the community. The people of the Fifth Congressional District of Indiana are forever grateful for Superintendent Jones' contributions and commitment to the students of the Pike Township School District and to our Hoosier community.

Superintendent Jones is an Indianapolis native. He received his formal education from the Indianapolis Public School (IPS) system. After graduating high school Superintendent Jones went to Indiana University where he pursued his interest in education. Upon completion of his B.S. in Elementary Education, he returned to IPS where he taught elementary school as well as adult education classes for five years. He returned to IUPUI to earn his M.S. in Education as well as an Administrative Certificate. In 1978, Superintendent Jones was named Assistant Principal to John Strange Elementary School of the Metropolitan School District of Washington Township, and shortly thereafter in 1980 he was named Principal of Delaware Trail Elementary, at age 27, making him one of the youngest principals in the state of Indiana. He served the Washington Township School system in a variety of positions over 25 years; he served Washington Township as Principal, Director of Elementary Education, and as Assistant Superintendent of Curriculum and Instruction. His leadership proved truly transformational as every school he led as Principal attained state and national recognition for academic achievement. In 1982, he earned his Education Specialist Degree in School Administration from Indiana University, Bloomington and in 1994 his Superintendent Certification. In 2003, he became the first African American to accept the role of Superintendent for the Metropolitan School District of Pike Township and the first African American IPS graduate to be a Superintendent in the state of Indiana.

Superintendent Jones has been instrumental in creating positive change in each of the school systems he has served. Pike High

School in particular has made monumental strides under Superintendent Jones' leadership. Pike High School has one of the most successful pre-collegiate programs in Indiana with over 85 percent of students attending post-secondary institutions upon graduating from high school and has a graduation rate of over 91 percent. In 2005, the Standard & Poor's ratings recognized Pike High School for significantly narrowing the Black-white and Hispanic-white achievement gaps. During Superintendent Jones' tenure the number of scholarships and grants received by Pike students has grown tremendously. Pike High School boasts the highest number of Gates Scholars in Indiana. Superintendent Jones also implemented the STEM Center and spearheaded major construction and renovation of many facilities, and earned over $75 million in Federal Competitive Grants from 2005 through 2015. Superintendent Jones' tireless efforts to seek educational grants and funding opportunities helped in part to create the Youth CareerConnect program. This program offers work-based learning opportunities that teaches students marketable and useful STEM skills empowering students in future learning as well as career opportunities. Through the collaboration of Superintendent Jones' visionary leadership, the help of a supportive board, dedicated administrators, extraordinary teachers, and engaged parents, Pike Township schools have become a more positive learning environment where student achievement continues to soar.

Throughout his career Superintendent Jones has received numerous awards that recognize the accomplishments and contributions he has made to education in our community. From Indiana University he received two "Distinguished Alumni Awards". In 1996, he earned the Milken Award, which aims to grant funds to accomplished mid-career educators. He received the Achiever Award from the Center for Leadership, is a recipient of a Sagamore of the Wabash Award, has received a Congressional Salute, and he received two District of Distinction awards. He was selected as one of the 100 top administrators in North America by the "Executive Educator" and has received over 60 local, state, and national awards for his leadership and innovative approach to educating students, teachers, and the community. His award winning work is well regarded not only from these institutions but from his peers and fellow educators. He has been invited to conduct and participate in numerous conferences throughout the United States. In addition, he is a lifetime member of the NAACP and in 2011 he was featured in the "Education Executive Publication" as a Trendsetter, and in a Who's Who in "Black Indianapolis".

Superintendent Jones continues to serve the community through his roles on numerous boards. He currently sits on the Board of Directors for American Heart Association, he was the Chair for National Council on Educating Black Children Conference in 2015, and he was the Board Chairman for Conner Prairie in 2011. In 2008, he served on the Indianapolis Marion-County Public Library Board of Directors and the Teachers' Treasures Board of Directors. He was the coordinator for the Lilly Initiative supported by the Lilly Endowment in

2000 through 2003. He was on the State Advisory Committee on Textbook Adoption in 2001 through 2003.

I am proud to thank Superintendent Jones for his service in helping the students of Pike Township graduate from high school with the essential skills necessary to be confident, creative, productive, and prosperous in college, careers, and life. He has always put the needs of students first throughout his educational career and truly enriched the lives of so many. He takes great pride in addressing the individual needs of the children he serves. Superintendent Jones never overlooked the fact that his students come to him from a variety of backgrounds, possessing individual gifts, talents, challenges and dreams. On behalf of all Hoosiers and the nation, I'd like to congratulate Superintendent Nathaniel Jones on his success and wish him, his wife Cynthia, two children, and their families all the best as Superintendent Jones enjoys a well-deserved retirement

PERSONAL EXPLANATION

HON. JAMES B. RENACCI
OF OHIO

IN THE HOUSE OF REPRESENTATIVES

Monday, December 5, 2016

Mr. RENACCI. Mr. Speaker, had I been present, I would have voted: YEA on Roll Call No. 594, YEA on Roll Call No. 595, YEA on Roll Call No. 596, YEA on Roll Call No. 597, and NAY on Roll Call No. 598.

HONORING MR. DOUG SIDEN

HON. BARBARA LEE
OF CALIFORNIA

IN THE HOUSE OF REPRESENTATIVES

Monday, December 5, 2016

Ms. LEE. Mr. Speaker, today I rise to honor the invaluable service to our community from the leadership of Mr. Doug Siden, and to congratulate him on his retirement from the East Bay Park District Board of Directors.

Mr. Siden has served for the past 24 years on the East Bay Regional Park District (EBRPD) Board. During his tenure, Mr. Siden recognized the importance that the East Bay Parks play in the lives of so many local residents, and has worked tirelessly to provide access and an enjoyable experience for visitors to all of the District's 66 locations.

As an EBRPD Board member, he worked diligently to help EBRPD pass Measures CC and WW to support and expand the system. At $500 million, Measure WW was the largest bond measure ever awarded to a local district to acquire and develop new parks, and it helped the Park District meet the increasing demand to preserve open space for recreation and wildlife habitat.

Mr. Siden served for many years on the East Bay Economic Development Alliance's Executive Board, was a founding member and served as a chairperson of the Martin Luther King Freedom Center in Oakland, and led the fight to establish the Alameda County Creek and Watershed Symposium. Additionally, during his career he has served on the advisory committees of the Golden Gate National Recreation Area and Pt. Reyes National Seashore.

Mr. Siden is also a longtime Rotarian and has served as a Baptist minister for over six decades. He directed a youth camp for Baptist Churches of the West for 20 years, and led the effort to establish year-round camps in Santa Cruz and near Lake Tahoe. He holds an honorary Doctorate of Humane Letters from the American Baptist Seminary of the West for his leadership.

On a personal note, Doug has been a longtime friend and partner in the East Bay, and I greatly appreciate his leadership and counsel. I wish him well on this new chapter of his life.

On behalf of the residents of California's 13th Congressional District, I congratulate Mr. Doug Siden on a well-deserved retirement. We honor his tireless support of open space, parks, and healthy recreation, and also for his vision of a more ideal world in which all can enjoy and benefit from these natural treasures.

BEST OF LUCK TO TEXAS 02'S FOOTBALL TEAMS AT STATE SEMI-FINALS

HON. TED POE

OF TEXAS

IN THE HOUSE OF REPRESENTATIVES

Monday, December 5, 2016

Mr. POE of Texas. Mr. Speaker, sweet tea, BBQ, and football—these are just some of the things Texans love dearly. From high school football to college football, Texans will come out to every game no matter what the temperature and weather are. Our commitment to our football teams is so strong that preachers will find a way to mention the local team in their sermons and make sure you get home just in time to watch the game with friends and family.

Football is a very special part of the culture in Texas. From the stadiums to the food to the different student clubs that gather in the stadiums, football games unite Texans. The bands, the drill teams, the cheerleading teams, the students that form it all—they are an extraordinary group that make the culture and character of Texas so unique in the United States. More than just uniting families and friends, football allows our community to share in the joy of victory and the sadness of temporary defeat; it teaches our children to keep working hard for their goals both individually and with their teammates.

Although professional and college football receive the most national attention, high school football is just as important in Texas. I still remember going to my son's football games, from his start at pee-wee leagues to his career playing for my alma mater, Abilene Christian University. Those memories make me even more proud to say that two high schools in my district have met their goals and broken records this season.

Atascocita High School is fighting for a chance to compete in the state championship. Last year they had a record-setting playoff run, reaching the Region II–6A Division I final. This year, they raised the bar even higher.

With the outstanding sportsmanship of their players, the football team of Atascocita High School has exceeded expectations. I know how proud the players, their parents, and their school must be. Ranking at Number 18 in the state, the Eagles have some of the most promising players on their team.

Quarterback Daveon Boyd, now a senior, has received four awards throughout his high school football career. He has surpassed the national average in number of yards, yards per game, touchdown passes, completion percentage, attempts, and interceptions. This season alone, he's had a 63 percent pass rate for 4,139 yards and 46 touchdowns.

But Boyd is not the only outstanding player in Atascocita High School. Samuel Cosmi, the offensive tackle, is a University of Houston pledge. Defensive tackles De'Marius Brooks and Kendrix Burford, along with defensive backs Justin Campbell, Alerick Soularie, and Travian Blaylock give the Eagles an edge in size and speed.

Another high school in my district, Klein Collins, won its first regional semi-finals at Baylor's McLane Stadium in the Division II Region II–6A playoffs. While all the players have done outstanding work, senior running back D'Anthony Doyle rushed 167 yards and got a couple of touchdowns, making him the hardest working player that game. His teammate, Josh Powell, also earned the team two more scores. At the end of the game, the team's hard work left the team with a 54–16 victory over John Tyler. As a proud dad who beamed in the stands watching his son play, I know how thrilled their parents will be watching them play against Spring Westfield on December 2.

I am incredibly proud of the students of the Atascocita and Klein Collins High School football teams for their successes this season. It is great to see students in my district represent us so well with their hard work and talent. I look forward to their upcoming games and seeing them succeed and exceed expectations for years to come. Best of luck at State Semi-Finals.

And that's just the way it is.

GEORGIA DAY OF CODE

HON. BARRY LOUDERMILK

OF GEORGIA

IN THE HOUSE OF REPRESENTATIVES

Monday, December 5, 2016

Mr. LOUDERMILK. Mr. Speaker, computer technology dominates our ever-evolving world. As we continue moving towards a society dependent on communicating through our technical devices, the need for qualified people in the STEM fields is rapidly growing.

Offering the opportunity for Georgia students to delve into computer programming will enhance industries across Georgia, our country, and the globe. Harnessing these skills benefits future generations, and will help build strong twenty-first century economies.

Georgia's Day of Code, during Computer Science Education week, is a great way to place coding in the public eye. We must continue to promote this important vocation, and engage in our communities to advance technology development.

The need for those in the technology field is vast and, in Georgia alone, employers post hundreds of IT-related jobs every day, which shows how promising this field is. Georgia's Day of Code encourages educators, parents, and policy makers to promote STEM-focused careers to students across the state. We must continue to advance and innovate in the technology sector, and what better way to do that than to invest in our next generation.

COMMEMORATING THE LIFE OF RAMONA NEILL

HON. MICHAEL K. SIMPSON

OF IDAHO

IN THE HOUSE OF REPRESENTATIVES

Monday, December 5, 2016

Mr. SIMPSON. Mr. Speaker, Ramona (Johnnie) North Neill of Blackfoot, Idaho passed away at the age of 88 on December 4, 2016 at the Gables of Blackfoot Assisted Living and Memory Center. Mona was born September 6, 1928 and raised in Kirksville, Missouri to Oscar and Zelma Jewell North. She lived there until the age of six when the family moved to Blackfoot, and attended grade school, junior high, followed by graduating from high school in 1946.

In December 1949 she met the love of her life: James (Jimmy) K. Neill who was an Employee of Idaho Power Company and was part of the Mobile Line Crew that was upgrading the Electrical Power Grid in Blackfoot. Their relationship quickly blossomed and they were married on May 26, 1950 in Winnemucca, Nevada. From there, Jim and Mona lived primarily in Boise, Idaho until they moved permanently to Blackfoot, Idaho in the summer of 1956 where she lived at the family home on Riverton Road up to the time that her health forced her to move last year.

Mona enjoyed outdoors trips with her husband and children, attending every scout, school, sports activity of her sons and the grandchildren residing in Blackfoot as well as visiting or following the adventures of her two grandchildren in Washington state.

Mona is survived by her sons: David K. Neill (Marie Carter, deceased), Blackfoot, Kim O. Neill (Christi Ann), Bainbridge Island, Washington, and James Todd Neill (Melody Renee), Scottsdale, Arizona, her four grandchildren: Cassandra Lynnette Neill, San Diego, California, Thomas K. Neill (Laura), Boise, Idaho, James K. Neill (Emily), Washington, D.C. and Andrew Albert Neill, Washington, D.C.

She will be laid to rest at Dry Creek Cemetery in Boise, Idaho where she will be next to her late husband James K. Neill.

MASTER SERGEANT MICHAEL THOMAS DONOHUE

HON. LEE M. ZELDIN

OF NEW YORK

IN THE HOUSE OF REPRESENTATIVES

Monday, December 5, 2016

Mr. ZELDIN. Mr. Speaker, I rise today to pay special tribute to Master Sergeant Michael

Thomas Donohue, in appreciation of his 30 years of meritorious service in the United States Army, Navy, Navy Reserve, and New York Army National Guard.

Throughout his military career, Master Sergeant Donohue has served with honor and distinction in numerous positions, from Aircraft Handler and Tank Mechanic, to Intelligence Analyst and Operations NCOIC, culminating with his service as a Senior Maintenance Supervisor for the 42nd CAB. His unwavering dedication to duty and unparalleled professionalism has consistently earned the respect of subordinates, peers, and superiors alike.

An innovative and relentless troubleshooter, his vast technical knowledge greatly aided in his Brigade's success while deployed in support of Operation Iraqi Freedom 08–09. His experience, gained from serving in two combat deployments in support of Operation Iraqi Freedom and Operation Enduring Freedom, proved invaluable as he mentored junior noncommissioned officers and officers on a wide spectrum of operational and technical topics, increasing their readiness for deployment and ultimately, unit effectiveness. His long and illustrious career has been marked by humility and service, and reflects great credit upon himself, the New York Army National Guard, United States Army, and United States Navy.

MSG Donohue's deployments include Operation El Dorado Canyon (USN, 1986), Operation Ernest Will (USN, 1988), multiple natural disasters (1997–2012), Counter Drug operations (1998–2001), World Trade Center (2001), OIF (2008–2009), and OEF (2012–2013). He provided mentorship and leadership and skillfully groomed the next generation of leaders, which resulted in the Soldier and NCO Warrior of the Year competitions for the Aviation Brigade in 2009, 2010, and 2011 and New York State Soldier of the Year in 2011. His faithfulness through these times was and is a testimony for others to follow, and I would like to take this opportunity to recognize his devotion to our country.

THE THIN BLUE LINE: OFFICER REGINALD GUTIERREZ

HON. TED POE
OF TEXAS
IN THE HOUSE OF REPRESENTATIVES
Monday, December 5, 2016

Mr. POE of Texas. Mr. Speaker, our men and women in blue are the best we have. They are the thin blue line between good and evil. Each day these men and women head out into the field not knowing what they will face, not knowing if their day will be filled with routine traffic stops, or extreme dangers. Our peace officers face the unknown and stand up for the rest of us.

Reginald "Jake" Gutierrez was one of these men. Gutierrez was responding to a domestic violence call in Tacoma, Washington after a woman approached animal control officers claiming her husband had locked her out of the house and taken her cell phone. Gutierrez and his partner entered the home. Shots rang out as he proceeded up the stairs to speak with the suspect. Two young children were held hostage inside the house, being used as human shields. His partner returned fire, taking the wife to safety. Gutierrez was shot multiple times, his life taken away by a vicious criminal.

Gutierrez gave his life to protect the young and innocent. As a veteran of the Department since 1999, 45-year-old Gutierrez was a model police officer. Each day he got up, put on the uniform and badge and dedicated himself to his profession and community. He is now the 132nd officer to die in the line of duty this year alone. At least eight of these deaths occurred while responding to reports of domestic disturbance and violence.

Hundreds of individuals came to honor Gutierrez as he made his way from the hospital to the medical examiner's office. The hospital was surrounded by fellow officers standing in support of their fallen brother. The King County Sheriff's Department ordered all Deputies to wear mourning bands in honor of the fallen peace officer.

The needless murder of our officers is absolutely unacceptable. These men and women work tirelessly, day in and day out trying to make a difference. It is time to put an end to the needless murder of our peace officers. Congress must stand up for those who work to protect the rest of us. The men and women behind the badge are some of America's best.

Officer Reginald "Jake" Gutierrez's life may be gone, but his memory serves as a reminder of all those who gave their lives for the thin blue line.

And that's just the way it is.

COMMEMORATING WORLD AIDS DAY 2016

HON. SHEILA JACKSON LEE
OF TEXAS
IN THE HOUSE OF REPRESENTATIVES
Monday, December 5, 2016

Ms. JACKSON LEE. Mr. Speaker, World AIDS Day affords us an opportunity to reflect on our progress in the fight against the global AIDS pandemic and to rededicate ourselves to ending the disease once and for all.

We have come a long way since the first World AIDS Day in 1988 by dramatically expanding investments in HIV/AIDS prevention, care, treatment, and research.

Strong advocacy has paved the way for the Ryan White Act, the Housing Opportunities for People with AIDS Initiative, growing investments in NIH research, and an end to the ban on federal funds for syringe exchange.

Beyond our borders, our efforts have extended care to millions in the developing world, through increased resources for PEPFAR and the Global Fund.

Our investments have saved lives—preventing millions of new HIV cases, expanding access to improved treatments, and enabling medical advances that help HIV/AIDS patients live longer and healthier.

Here and across the globe, AIDS deaths are on the decline, and studies are pointing the way to new approaches to limit the spread of the disease, with treatment as prevention.

While our efforts have grown, we still only reach half of all people eligible for HIV treatment; and more must be done.

Working together, we must continue to strengthen—not weaken—our national and international efforts to combat AIDS and other infectious diseases.

We must work to achieve the Obama Administration's goal of an AIDS-free generation.

We must honor the memory of those we have lost and act on our hope, optimism, and determination to end the HIV/AIDS pandemic.

We must continue to work with programs and clinics, like the Harris County Hospital District (HCHD), who are treating and caring for patients with HIV/AIDS.

In 1989, HCHD opened Thomas Street Health Center, the first free-standing facility dedicated to outpatient HIV/AIDS care in the nation. The center has become the cornerstone of all HIV/AIDS care available to Harris County residents.

The Thomas Street Health Center has dedicated their services to about 25 percent of Harris County's HIV/AIDS.

Annually, the health center, along with HCHD, serves 4,463 unique patients for about 37,000 patients' visits.

We will continue to fight a tough fight against HIV and AIDS.

We will continue to strengthen and support centers like Thomas Street Health Center that work diligently with HIV/AIDS patients.

Our focus on HIV/AIDS prevention and awareness will be to ensure all of our friends, relatives and children live healthy and full lives.

There is a pressing need to raise awareness and engage in education within the African American community where HIV infections have been and continue to rise.

The incidence of HIV has decreased for the majority population, while it has grown nearly unchecked among African Americans.

This must change—decisions regarding funding for agencies charged with infectious disease education and minority health must be supported.

PERSONAL EXPLANATION

HON. JAMES B. RENACCI
OF OHIO
IN THE HOUSE OF REPRESENTATIVES
Monday, December 5, 2016

Mr. RENACCI. Mr. Speaker, had I been present, I would have voted: YEA on Roll Call No. 599.

IN HONOR OF BEAUREGARD WINNING AHSAA CLASS 5A HIGH SCHOOL FOOTBALL TITLE

HON. MIKE ROGERS
OF ALABAMA
IN THE HOUSE OF REPRESENTATIVES
Monday, December 5, 2016

Mr. ROGERS of Alabama. Mr. Speaker, I ask for the House's attention today to recognize Beauregard High School for winning their first ever Alabama High School Athletic Association (AHSAA) Class 5A football state title.

The Hornets sealed their victory by beating Wenonah 33–13 on December 1st at Jordan-Hare Stadium in Auburn.

Not only was this Beauregard's first state title, but also Lee County's first ever state champion!

Mr. Speaker, please join me in congratulating the students and faculty of Beauregard High School, Coach Braun, the players and all the Hornets fans on this exciting achievement. Go Hornets!

HONORING THE LIFE OF KATHLEEN O'DAY

HON. JAMES P. McGOVERN
OF MASSACHUSETTS
IN THE HOUSE OF REPRESENTATIVES

Monday, December 5, 2016

Mr. McGOVERN. Mr. Speaker, I rise today to honor the extraordinary life of Kathleen O'Day.

Kathleen passed away on November 28, leaving three brothers, nieces, nephews, cousins and many dear friends. She resided in Arlington, Virginia, but was born and raised in my hometown of Worcester, Massachusetts. Her loved ones gathered in Worcester today to honor her life and pay tribute to a truly remarkable woman.

Kathleen had a distinguished legal career. After graduating from Assumption College and Boston College School of Law with honors, Kathleen began working in the legal division of the Board of Governors of the Federal Reserve System in 1978. She served in the Board's legal division for decades and became a well-known expert in international banking and trade negotiations.

Those who knew her best will miss her warmth, wit, and generosity. Scott Alvarez, the Fed's General Counsel, remarked, "Kathleen was a dedicated employee, serving nearly 40 years in the Board's Legal Division. She was a kind, brilliant, generous, witty, and wonderfully warm friend to all of us, and we will all miss her tremendously."

Mr. Speaker, Kathleen touched the lives of so many around her, and had a profound impact on all of us through her work with the Federal Reserve.

I deeply admire Kathleen's life-long commitment to public service, and extend my deepest sympathies to the family and friends she leaves behind. We will all miss her.

Mr. Speaker, I ask my colleagues to join me today in honoring Kathleen O'Day, and recognizing the important contributions she has made to our country.

IN HONOR OF PIEDMONT WINNING AHSAA CLASS 3A HIGH SCHOOL FOOTBALL TITLE

HON. MIKE ROGERS
OF ALABAMA
IN THE HOUSE OF REPRESENTATIVES

Monday, December 5, 2016

Mr. ROGERS of Alabama. Mr. Speaker, I ask for the House's attention today to recognize Piedmont High School for winning the Alabama High School Athletic Association (AHSAA) Class 3A football state title for the 2nd year in a row.

The Bulldogs sealed their victory by beating Mobile Christian 22–12 on December 1st at Jordan-Hare Stadium in Auburn, Alabama.

Mr. Speaker, please join me in congratulating the students and faculty of Piedmont High School, Coach Steve Smith, the players and all the Bulldogs fans on this exciting achievement for the second year in a row. Go Bulldogs!

PERSONAL EXPLANATION

HON. BILL FLORES
OF TEXAS
IN THE HOUSE OF REPRESENTATIVES

Monday, December 5, 2016

Mr. FLORES. Mr. Speaker, I rise to state that I was not able to be on the House floor for roll call vote 600—Adoption of the Conference Report to Accompany S. 2943—National Defense Authorization Act for Fiscal Year 2017 taken on December 2, 2016. Had I been present for this vote, I would have voted aye.

Congress has a duty to ensure our military has every resource necessary to fight and defeat the threats that exist in the world today. The National Defense Authorization Act provides America's uniformed men and women with the tools and support they need and deserve. It gives our troops a much needed pay raise and ensures that promises made to them are kept. This strong defense bill will strengthen our national security and help bring our military into the 21st century.

As I close, I ask everyone to continue praying for our country, and for our military and first responders who selflessly serve and sacrifice to protect us.

IN HONOR OF THE ORIGINAL CALDWELL GOSPEL SINGERS OF SEALE, ALABAMA

HON. MIKE ROGERS
OF ALABAMA
IN THE HOUSE OF REPRESENTATIVES

Monday, December 5, 2016

Mr. ROGERS of Alabama. Mr. Speaker, I ask for the House's attention today to recognize the Original Gospel Singers of Seale, Alabama.

For over 40 years, this family has been spreading the gospel through their musical talents. What started as a duet in 1965, grew to be on television for their first debut on the "Home with Rozell Show" on WRBL in 1969.

The group has traveled to several states and participated in many benefit programs to give back to their community. In 2014, the Russell County Commission dedicated a portion of roadway from Highway 169 South to Uchee Road as the "Original Caldwell Gospel Singers" Road.

Mr. Speaker, please join me in recognizing four decades of music by this special group.

RECOGNIZING MARS, INCORPORATED AND THE 40TH ANNIVERSARY OF ITS WACO, TEXAS PRODUCTION FACILITY

HON. BILL FLORES
OF TEXAS
IN THE HOUSE OF REPRESENTATIVES

Monday, December 5, 2016

Mr. FLORES. Mr. Speaker, I rise today to recognize Mars, Incorporated and the 40th Anniversary of its Waco, Texas production facility.

As a family-owned business since its founding in 1911, Mars has been a leading example of corporate responsibility practices that benefit the communities in which it operates. Guided by five core principles—Quality, Responsibility, Mutuality, Efficiency, and Freedom—Mars has had a positive social and economic impact on many communities within the Seventeenth Congressional District of Texas.

Since 1976, when Mars opened the doors of its facility in Waco the company has provided sustainable economic growth for our community. As such, the Waco facility currently employs over 550 full time associates, providing reliable jobs for many citizens in the District. The facility is responsible for producing both Mars Chocolate and Wrigley products, including Snickers, Skittles Candies, and Starburst Fruit Chews. In October, Mars announced its intent to combine its Chocolate and Wrigley segments to create Mars Wrigley Confectionery, which will help the company continue to deliver value to customers around the world.

In addition to its commitment to producing high quality products for its consumers, the Waco facility has sought to create an environment that is mutually beneficial to the local community. For example, the Waco facility promotes sustainability and environmental efficiency through the use of a Wetlands Wastewater Treatment Facility, saving three to five million gallons of water each year. The facility also uses locally sourced peanuts in its Snickers bars, and it sponsors the annual Waco Wild West Century Bike Tour to raise money for the American Red Cross. In recognition of its outstanding commitment to diversity and unity in the workplace, the Waco facility recently received the Model of Unity Award from the Community Race Relations Coalition.

On behalf of the Seventeenth Congressional District and the State of Texas, I am pleased to celebrate this important milestone with Mars' Waco facility, and I thank Mars for its continued dedication to our community.

As I close, I ask everyone to continue praying for our country, and for our military and first responders who selflessly serve and sacrifice to protect us.

SENATE COMMITTEE MEETINGS

Title IV of Senate Resolution 4, agreed to by the Senate of February 4, 1977, calls for establishment of a system for a computerized schedule of all meetings and hearings of Senate committees, subcommittees, joint committees, and committees of conference. This title requires all such committees to notify the Office of the Senate Daily Digest—designated by the Rules Committee—of the time, place and purpose of the meetings, when scheduled and any cancellations or changes in the meetings as they occur.

As an additional procedure along with the computerization of this information, the Office of the Senate Daily Digest will prepare this information for printing in the Extensions of Remarks section of the CONGRESSIONAL RECORD on Monday and Wednesday of each week.

Meetings scheduled for Tuesday, December 6, 2016 may be found in the Daily Digest of today's RECORD.

MEETINGS SCHEDULED

DECEMBER 7

10 a.m.
Committee on the Judiciary
Subcommittee on Antitrust, Competition Policy and Consumer Rights
To hold hearings to examine the competitive impact of the AT&T-Time Warner transaction.

SD-226

2 p.m.
Commission on Security and Cooperation in Europe
To receive a briefing on Baltic security after the Warsaw NATO summit.

CHOB-340

2:15 p.m.
Committee on Indian Affairs
To hold an oversight hearing to examine the Department of the Interior's Land Buy-Back Program for Tribal Nations, four years later.

SD-628

2:30 p.m.
Committee on Commerce, Science, and Transportation
Subcommittee on Surface Transportation and Merchant Marine Infrastructure, Safety and Security
To hold hearings to examine assessing the security of our critical surface transportation infrastructure.

SR-253

3 p.m.
Select Committee on Intelligence
To receive a closed briefing on certain intelligence matters.

SH-219

DECEMBER 8

10 a.m.
Committee on Foreign Relations
Subcommittee on State Department and USAID Management, International Operations, and Bilateral International Development
To hold hearings to examine State Department and United States Agency for International Development management challenges and opportunities for the next administration.

SD-419